The Open Bible

Presented to

_____

on this____ day of_____

_____

_____

_____

By_____

_____

New American Standard Bible

CONTAINING THE OLD AND NEW TESTAMENTS

The Open Bible®

EXPANDED EDITION

with Read-along References™, Read-along Translations™
Biblical Cyclopedic Index
The Christian's Guide to the New Life
Book Introductions and Outlines
Visual Survey of the Bible
Special Study Aids

Words of Christ in Red

THOMAS NELSON PUBLISHERS
Nashville • Camden • New York

Printed in the United States of America
3 4 5 6 7 8 9 10/89 88 87

Welcome to . . .

The Open Bible®

EXPANDED EDITION

The intent of this Study Bible is to make the Scriptures an open and rewarding book for the serious and committed Bible student, while at the same time presenting a meaningful Bible for the general reader. In combining scholarly commentary with one of the most widely read modern translations of our day, the publisher is pleased to present the labors of learned and reverent men who have sought to clarify the meaning of the Scriptures and bring the treasures of God's Holy Word into the possession of the reader. To that end, the following special features are provided. The helps and educational features found in this Bible have been prepared by eminent scholars under the supervision of Thomas Nelson Publishers. They are strictly non-sectarian. The New American Standard text is used.

In this edition Read-along References™ and Read-along Translations™ are used to help you understand the text. The symbol "R" beside a word denotes a Read-along Reference™ which lists at the end of the verse other passages which have similar meanings or further bearing on the word or phrase indicated. This exciting cross-reference method of Bible study ties the magnificent truths of Scripture together.

The symbol "T" beside a word or phrase indicates a Read-along Translation™, an easy-to-understand equivalent, alternate, or literal translation at the end of the verse.

When the symbol "A" is used, an alternate translation is given at the end of the verse. Such word clarifications built right into the text eliminate the need for constant referral to a Bible dictionary or other volumes. When more than one reference or translation follows a verse, a center point "•" is used for division. When space does not allow the symbol letter (R, T, or A) to precede the word or phrase referenced, then the symbol follows immediately at the end of the word or first word of the phrase referenced.

Immediately before each book of the Bible there is an introduction and outline of that book. These introductions are extensive and scholarly, and the outlines are designed to give the reader an overview of the book.

The period between the Old and the New Testament is treated fully and concisely in the definitive *Between the Testaments* section. This feature is designed to give the Bible student an understanding of this important period so he or she can properly relate history and the Holy Word.

The *Biblical Cyclopedic Index* is one of the major student aids in this edition. A marvel in itself, this distinctive section combines the most useful features of a concordance, reference system, and index, but is better than any of them separately or all put together in some manner. With the *Biblical Cyclopedic Index*, the serious Bible student will find the riches of the Word unfolding in logical fashion. The busy pastor or speaker, searching the Scriptures for a message, will find the *Biblical Cyclopedic Index* one of the most helpful tools to the explication of the Scriptures available in published form today.

An extremely important study feature is *The Christian's Guide to the New Life*. These outlines cover the major teachings of the Bible and literally help you open the Bible to the point-by-point development of each doctrine. With the study notes at the bottom of the pages, you actually cover the material of an advanced course in systematic theology, but in a much easier and clearer manner.

For convenience in Bible study, the reader is referred to the major classifications of *Bible Study Helps* found in THE OPEN BIBLE Expanded Edition. These helps provide a wealth of information normally found only in a complete library of books. Now they are your in this new Study Bible.

The *Bible Study Helps* section includes articles *How to Study the Bible, Read Your Bible Through in a Year, Harmony of the Gospels*, and *Teachings of Christ by Subject*. Many other helps are included to make Bible study more meaningful.

The *Biblical Information* section features many items not commonly understood in the Scriptures plus countless bits of practical information in concise form. There is an extensive article, *The English Bible and Its Development*, and of special interest is the article, *The Greatest Archaeological Discoveries*, which includes scholarly discussion of the most recent archaeological finds.

Messianic Prophecies are indicated in THE OPEN BIBLE Expanded Edition, by stars placed with the references in the appropriate passages. A *solid star* is used to indicate a prophecy that has been fulfilled in Jesus Christ. An *outline star* is used to indicate a prophecy later fulfilled in Jesus Christ.

This study edition of the Holy Bible is intended to make it an open book to the reverent reader. It is hoped that this unique edition will truly make the Scriptures plain enough so all can have an *Open Bible*.

The Publisher

CONTRIBUTORS
to the Study Aids

KENNETH D. BOA, Ph.D.
Introductions and Outlines to the Books of the Bible and Visual Survey of the Bible, Author and Editor
Director of Publications, Search Ministries
Atlanta, Georgia

†WICK BROOMALL, A.M., Th.M.
Biblical Cyclopedic Index
Minister, Presbyterian Church
Augusta, Georgia

W. A. CRISWELL, D.D., Ph.D.
The Scarlet Thread of Redemption
Pastor, First Baptist Church
Dallas, Texas

ARTHUR L. FARSTAD, Th.D.
Consulting Editor
Bible Editor
Dallas, Texas

PAUL R. FINK, Ed.S., Th.D.
The Christian's Guide to the New Life, Contributing Editor
Professor of Pastoral Ministries,
Liberty Baptist College
Lynchburg, Virginia

BOB GREEN, Attorney
The Laws of the Bible

DONALD E. HOKE, D.D.
How to Study the Bible
Pastor, Cedar Springs Presbyterian Church
Knoxville, Tennessee

†R. G. LEE, D.D., LL.D., Ph.D.
A Guide to Christian Workers
Pastor-Evangelist
Memphis, Tennessee

MYLES LORENZEN, Th.M.
Visual Survey of the Bible, Contributor
Co-Pastor, Fellowship Bible Church
Roswell, Georgia

†Deceased

JIM BILL McINTEER, B.A.
Harmony of the Gospels
Minister, West End Church of Christ
Nashville, Tennessee

†CHARLES F. PFEIFFER, Ph.D.
Between the Testaments and Books of the Apocrypha
Professor, Central Michigan University
Mount Pleasant, Michigan

†WILBUR M. SMITH, D.D.
The English Bible and Its Development
Author and Lecturer

†MERRILL F. UNGER, Th.D., Ph.D.
The Greatest Archaeological Discoveries
Professor Emeritus, Dallas Theological
Seminary
Dallas, Texas

C. M. WARD, D.D.
A Guide to Christian Workers
Assemblies of God Radio Evangelist
Santa Cruz, California

WILLIAM WHITE, Ph.D.
The Greatest Archaeological Discoveries
Consulting Editor
Warrington, Pennsylvania

BRUCE H. WILKINSON, Th.M.
Introductions and Outlines to the Books of the Bible, Executive Editor
President, Walk Thru the Bible Ministries
Atlanta, Georgia

NEAL D. WILLIAMS, Th.D.
The Christian's Guide to the New Life, Contributing Editor
Assistant Professor of Biblical Studies,
Liberty Baptist College
Lynchburg, Virginia

HAROLD L. WILLMINGTON, D.Min.
The Christian's Guide to the New Life, Executive Editor
Vice President, Liberty Baptist College
Lynchburg, Virginia

Books of the Old and New Testaments

CONTENTS
of the Open Bible

I. Text

II. Bible Study Helps

III. Biblical Information

FOREWORD

The text is that of the New American Standard Bible. It has been produced with the conviction that the words of Scripture as originally penned in the Hebrew, Aramaic, and Greek were inspired by God. Since they are the eternal Word of God, the Holy Scriptures speak with fresh power to each generation, to give wisdom that leads to salvation, that men may serve Christ to the glory of God.

The Editorial Board of the Lockman Foundation had a twofold purpose in making this translation: to adhere as closely as possible to the original languages of the Holy Scriptures, and to make the translation in a fluent and readable style according to current English usage.

THE FOURFOLD AIM
OF
THE LOCKMAN FOUNDATION

1. These publications shall be true to the original Hebrew, Aramaic, and Greek.
2. They shall be grammatically correct.
3. They shall be understandable to the masses.

4. They shall give the Lord Jesus Christ His proper place, the place which the Word gives Him; therefore, no translation work will ever be personalized.

*The grass withers, the flower
fades, but the word of our God
stands forever.*
Isaiah 40:8

PREFACE TO THE NEW AMERICAN STANDARD BIBLE

In the history of English Bible translations, the King James Version is the most prestigious. This time-honored version of 1611, itself a revision of the Bishops' Bible of 1568, became the basis for the English Revised Version appearing in 1881 (New Testament) and 1885 (Old Testament). The American counterpart of this last work was published in 1901 as the American Standard Version. Recognizing the values of the American Standard Version, the Lockman Foundation felt an urgency to update it by incorporating recent discoveries of Hebrew and Greek textual sources and by rendering it into more current English. Therefore, in 1959 a new translation project was launched, based on the ASV. The result is the New American Standard Bible.

The American Standard Version (1901) has been highly regarded for its scholarship and accuracy. A product of both British and American scholarship, it has frequently been used as a standard for other translations. It is still recognized as a valuable tool for study of the Scriptures. The New American Standard Bible has sought to preserve these and other lasting values of the ASV.

Furthermore, in the preparation of this work numerous other translations have been consulted along with the linguistic tools and literature of biblical scholarship. Decisions about English renderings were made by consensus of a team composed of educators and pastors. Subsequently, review and evaluation by other Hebrew and Greek scholars outside the Editorial Board were sought and carefully considered.

The Editorial Board has continued to function since publication of the complete Bible in 1971. Minor revisions and refinements, recommended over the last five years, are presented in this edition.

ABBREVIATIONS AND SPECIAL MARKINGS

Aram. = Aramaic
Gr. = Greek translation of O.T. (Septuagint or LXX) or Greek text of N.T.
Heb. = Hebrew text, usually Masoretic
M.T. = Masoretic text
Syr. = Syriac
Lit. = A literal translation
Or = An alternate translation justified by the Hebrew, Aramaic, or Greek
[ ] = In text, brackets indicate words probably not in the original writings
cf. = compare
ms., mss. = manuscript, manuscripts
v., vv. = verse, verses

PRINCIPLES OF TRANSLATION

NEW AMERICAN STANDARD

Modern English Usage: The attempt has been made to render the grammar and terminology in contemporary English. When it was felt that the word-for-word literalness was unacceptable to the modern reader, a change was made in the direction of a more current English idiom. In the instances where this has been done, the more literal rendering has been indicated in the notes.

Alternative Readings: In addition to the more literal renderings, notations have been made to include alternate translations, readings of variant manuscripts and explanatory equivalents of the text. Only such notations have been used as have been felt justified in assisting the reader's comprehension of the terms used by the original author.

Hebrew Text: In the present translation the latest edition of Rudolf Kittel's BIBLIA HEBRAICA has been employed together with the most recent light from lexicography, cognate languages, and the Dead Sea Scrolls.

Hebrew Tenses: Consecution of tenses in Hebrew remains a puzzling factor in translation. The translators have been guided by the requirements of a literal translation, the sequence of tenses, and the immediate and broad contexts.

The Proper Name of God in the Old Testament: In the Scriptures, the name of God is most significant and understandably so. It is inconceivable to think of spiritual matters without a proper designation for the Supreme Deity. Thus the most common name for Deity is God, a translation of the original Elohim. The normal word for Master is Lord, a rendering of Adonai. There is yet another name which is particularly assigned to God as His special or proper name, that is, the four letters YHWH (Exodus 3:14 and Isaiah 42:8). This name has not been pronounced by the Jews because of reverence for the great sacredness of the divine name. Therefore, it was consistently pronounced and translated LORD. The only exception to this translation of YHWH is when it occurs in immediate proximity to the word Lord, that is, Adonai. In that case it is regularly translated GOD in order to avoid confusion.

It is known that for many years YHWH has been transliterated as Yahweh, however, no complete certainty attaches to this pronunciation.

Greek Text: Consideration was given to the latest available manuscripts with a view to determining the best Greek text. In most instances the 23rd edition of Eberhard Nestle's NOVUM TESTAMENTUM GRAECE was followed.

Greek Tenses: A careful distinction has been made in the treatment of the Greek aorist tense (usually translated as the English past, "He did") and the Greek imperfect tense (rendered either as English past progressive, "He was doing"; or, if inceptive, as "He *began* to do" or "He started to do"; or else if customary past, as "He used to do"). "Began" is italicized if it renders an imperfect tense, in order to distinguish it from the Greek verb for "begin."

On the other hand, not all aorists have been rendered as English pasts ("He did"), for some of them are clearly to be rendered as English perfects ("He has done"), or even as past perfects ("He had done"), judging from the context in which they occur. Such aorists have been rendered as perfects or past perfects in this translation.

As for the distinction between aorist and present imperatives, the translators have usually rendered these imperatives in the customary manner, rather than attempting any such fine distinction as "Begin to do!" (for the aorist imperative), or, "Continually do!" (for the present imperative).

As for sequence of tenses, the translators took care to follow English rules rather than Greek in translating Greek presents, imperfects and aorists. Thus, where English says, "We knew that he was doing," Greek puts it, "We knew that he does"; similarly, "We knew that he had done" is the Greek, "We knew that he did." Likewise, the English, "When he had come, they met him," is represented in Greek by: "When he came, they met him." In all cases a consistent transfer has been made from the Greek tense in the subordinate clause to the appropriate tense in English.

In the rendering of negative questions introduced by the particle me (which always expects the answer, "No") the wording has been altered from a mere, "Will he not do this?" to a more accurate, "He will not do this, will he?"

Editorial Board
THE LOCKMAN FOUNDATION

EXPLANATION OF GENERAL FORMAT

FOOTNOTES are used only where the text especially requires them for clarification. Marginal notes and cross references have been deleted from this edition.

PARAGRAPHS are designated by bold face numbers or letters.

QUOTATION MARKS are used in the text in accordance with modern English usage.

"THOU," "THEE," AND "THY" are not used in this translation except in the language of prayer when addressing Deity.

PERSONAL PRONOUNS are capitalized when pertaining to Deity.

ITALICS are used in the text to indicate words which are not found in the original Hebrew, Aramaic, or Greek but implied by it. Italics are used in the footnotes to signify alternate readings for the text.

SMALL CAPS in the New Testament are used in the text to indicate Old Testament quotations or obvious allusions to Old Testament texts. Variations of Old Testament wording are found in New Testament citations depending on whether the New Testament writer translated from a Hebrew text, used existing Greek or Aramaic translations, or paraphrased the material. It should be noted that modern rules for the indication of direct quotation were not used in biblical times thus allowing freedom for omissions or insertions without specific indication of these.

ASTERISKS are used to mark verbs that are historical presents in the Greek which have been translated with an English past tense in order to conform to modern usage. The translators recognized that in some contexts the present tense seems more unexpected and unjustified to the English reader than a past tense would have been. But Greek authors frequently used the present tense for the sake of heightened vividness, thereby transporting their readers in imagination to the actual scene at the time of occurrence. However, the translators felt that it would be wise to change these historical presents to English past tenses.

ITALICIZED CROSS REFERENCES at the end of the verse indicate a passage parallel to the verse or verses they follow.

CONCEPTUAL REFERENCES are cross-references in square brackets. They refer to passages similar in concept.

LANGUAGE TRANSLATION for a particular word or phrase in the text is denoted with a superior letter "T" and indicates the Hebrew, Greek, or Aramaic translation.

ITALIC TYPE in the text indicates words not found in the original languages of Hebrew, Aramaic, or Greek, but needed for clarity in English.

ALTERNATE TRANSLATIONS are indicated with a superior letter "A". These words are different from those in the text, but they are justified by the original languages.

CROSS-REFERENCES, marked with a superior letter "R" in the text, point out verses using similar words or phrases.

---

2 SAMUEL 22   316

My savior, Thou dost save me from
violence.   Gen. 15:1 • Ps. 9:9
4 "I call upon the LORD, who is worthy to
be praised;   Ps. 48:1; 96:4
And I am saved from my enemies.
5 "For the waves of death encompassed
me;   Ps. 93:4; Jon. 2:3
The torrents of destruction ^overwhelmed me;   Heb., Belial • terrified
6 The cords of Sheol surrounded me;
The snares of death confronted me.
7 "In my distress I called upon the LORD,
Yes, I cried to my God;
And from His temple He heard my
voice,
And my cry for help came into His
ears.   Ps. 116:4; 120:1 • called
8 "Then the earth shook and quaked,
The foundations of heaven were trembling
And were shaken, because He was
angry.   Judg. 5:4; Ps. 97:4 • Job 26:11
9 "Smoke went up out of His nostrils,
And fire from His mouth devoured;
Coals were kindled by it.   in His wrath
10 "He bowed the heavens also, and came
down
With thick darkness under His feet.
11 "And He rode on a cherub and flew;
And He appeared on the wings of the
wind.   2 Sam. 6:2 • Ps. 104:3
12 "And He made darkness ^canopies
around Him,   Job 36:29 • pavilions
A mass of waters, thick clouds of the
sky.
13 "From the brightness before Him
^Coals of fire were kindled.   2 Sam. 22:9
14 "The LORD thundered from heaven,
And the Most High uttered His voice.
15 "And He sent out arrows, and scattered them,   Deut. 32:23; Josh. 10:10
Lightning, and routed them.   confused
16 "Then the channels of the sea appeared,
The foundations of the world were
^laid bare,
By the rebuke of the LORD,
^At the blast of the breath of His nostrils.   uncovered • Ex. 15:8; Nah. 1:4
17 "He sent from on high, He took me;
He drew me out of many waters.
18 "He delivered me from my strong enemy,
From those who hated me, for they
were too strong for me.
19 "They confronted me in the day of my
calamity,
But the LORD was my support.
20 "He also brought me forth into a broad
place;
He rescued me, because He delighted
in me.   Ps. 31:8; 118:5 • 2 Sam. 15:26
21 "The LORD has rewarded me according
to my righteousness;   1 Sam. 26:23
According to the cleanness of my
hands He has recompensed me.
22 "For I have kept the ways of the LORD,

And have not acted wickedly against
my God.   Gen. 18:19; Ps. 128:1
23 "For all His ordinances were before
me;   [Deut. 6:6-9]; Ps. 119:30, 102
And as for His statutes, I did not depart from them.   it
24 "I was also blameless toward Him,
And I kept myself from my iniquity.
25 "Therefore the LORD has recompensed
me according to my righteousness,
According to my cleanness before His
eyes.   2 Sam. 22:21
26 "With the kind Thou dost show Thyself
^kind,   [Matt. 5:7] • loyal
With the blameless Thou dost show
Thyself blameless;
27 "With the pure Thou dost show Thyself pure,   [Matt. 5:8; 1 John 3:3]
And with the perverted Thou dost
show Thyself astute.   twisted
28 "And Thou dost save an afflicted people;   Ex. 3:7, 8; Ps. 72:12, 13
But Thine eyes are on the haughty
whom Thou dost abase.   Is. 5:15
29 "For Thou art my lamp, O LORD;
And the LORD illumines my darkness.
30 "For by Thee I can [18]run upon a troop;
By my God I can leap over a wall.
31 "As for God, His way is blameless;
The word of the LORD is tested;
He is a shield to all who take refuge in
Him.   complete; or, having integrity
32 "For who is God, besides the LORD?
And who is a rock, besides our God?
33 "God is my strong fortress;
And He sets the blameless in His way.
34 "He makes my feet like hinds' feet,
And sets me on my high places.
35 "He trains my hands for battle,
So that my arms can bend a bow of
bronze.   Ps. 144:1 • Job 20:24
36 "Thou hast also given me the shield of
Thy salvation,   Eph. 6:16, 17
And Thy help makes me great.
37 "Thou dost enlarge my steps under me,
And my feet have not slipped.   ankles
38 "I pursued my enemies and destroyed
them,   Ex. 15:9
And I did not turn back until they
were consumed.
39 "And I have devoured them and shattered them, so that they did not
rise;
And they fell under my feet.   Mal. 4:3
40 "For Thou hast girded me with
strength for battle;
Thou hast subdued under me those
who rose up against me.   [Ps. 44:5]
41 "Thou hast also made my enemies turn
their backs to me,   Ex. 23:27
And I destroyed those who hated me.
42 "They looked, but there was none to
save;   Is. 17:7, 8
Even to the LORD, but He did not answer them.   1 Sam. 28:6; Is. 1:15

18 Or, crush a troop

SUPERIOR NUMBERS indicate important textual information needed for clarification. The corresponding notes are found at the foot of the same page.

THE OPEN BIBLE

An **OUTLINE STAR** or a **SOLID STAR** indicates a messianic reference. The outline star indicates the making of a prophecy. The solid star indicates the fulfillment of a prophecy.

POETRY and **SMALL CAPITALS** set certain portions of Bible verse apart for clarification. Poetry is structured as contemporary verse to reflect the poetic form and beauty of the original Hebrew, Aramaic, or Greek language. Small capitals in the New Testament indicate quotations or obvious allusions to Old Testament texts. Variations of Old Testament wording are found in New Testament citations.

RED LETTER type is used in the New Testament to signify the words of Jesus Christ.

SUBJECT HEADS and **PARALLEL PASSAGES** help the reader identify main subjects of the following text and locate parallel passages in Scripture.

The superior letter "T" and italic type in the reference indicate an **EQUIVALENT TRANSLATION** which explains the text word.

CHAPTER 3

The Person of John the Baptist
Mark 1:2-6; Luke 3:3-6

Now *in those days John the Baptist *came, *preaching in the wilderness of Judea, saying, Matt. 3:1-12 · *proclaiming as a herald
2"Repent, for the kingdom of heaven is at hand." (Mal. 4:5, 6 ★) *the heavens · *has come near
3 For this is the one referred to by Isaiah the prophet, saying, Luke 1:17 · *through
"THE VOICE OF ONE CRYING IN THE WILDERNESS,
'MAKE READY THE WAY OF THE LORD,
MAKE HIS PATHS STRAIGHT!' " Is. 40:3 ★
4 Now John himself had a garment of camel's hair, and a leather belt about his waist; and his food was locusts and wild honey. *his garment · 2 Kin. 1:8; Zech. 13:4
5 Then Jerusalem was going out to him, and all Judea, and all the district around the Jordan; Mark 1:5 · Luke 3:3
6 and they were being baptized by him in the Jordan River, as they confessed their sins. Matt. 3:11, 13-16; Mark 1:5; John 1:25, 26; 3:23

The Preaching of John the Baptist
Mark 1:7-9; Luke 3:7-9, 16, 17

7 But when he saw many of the Pharisees and Sadducees coming for baptism, he said to them, "You brood of vipers, who warned you to flee from the wrath to come?
8"Therefore bring forth fruit *in keeping with repentance; Luke 3:8 · Acts 26:20
9 and do not suppose that you can say to yourselves, 'We have Abraham for our father'; for I say to you, that God is able from these stones to raise up children to Abraham. Luke 3:8; 16:24; John 8:33, 39, 53; Acts 13:26
10"And the axe is already laid at the root of the trees; every tree therefore that does not bear good fruit is cut down and thrown into the fire. Luke 3:9 · Ps. 92:12-14
11"As for me, I baptize you *with water for repentance, but He who is coming after

*The Gr. here can be translated in, with or by
*Lit., My Son, the Beloved *Lit., later, afterward

me is mightier than I, and I am not fit to remove His sandals; He will baptize you with the Holy Spirit and fire.   Acts 2:4, 33 ☆
12"And His winnowing fork is in His hand, and He will thoroughly clear His threshing floor; and He will gather His wheat into the barn, but He will burn up the chaff with unquenchable fire." Matt. 13:30

Baptism of Jesus
Mark 1:9-11; Luke 3:21-23

13 *Then Jesus *arrived from Galilee at the Jordan coming to John, to be baptized by him. Matt. 3:13-17; John 1:31-34 · Matt. 2:22
14 But John tried to prevent Him, saying, "I have need to be baptized by You, and do You come to me?"
15 But Jesus answering said to him, "Permit it at this time; for in this way it is fitting for us to fulfill all righteousness." Then he *permitted Him. Ps. 40:7, 8; John 4:34; 8:29
16 And after being baptized, Jesus went up immediately from the water; and behold, the heavens were opened, and he saw the Spirit of God descending as a dove, and coming upon Him, He · Is. 11:2; 42:1; 61:1 ★
17 and behold, a voice out of the heavens, saying, "This is *My beloved Son, in whom I am well-pleased." Ps. 2:7; Is. 42:1; Matt. 12:18

CHAPTER 4

First Temptation
Mark 1:12, 13; Luke 4:1-4

Then Jesus was led up by the Spirit into the wilderness to be tempted by the devil.
2 And after He had fasted forty days and forty nights, He *then became hungry.
3 And the tempter came and said to Him, "If You are the Son of God, command that these stones become bread." *loaves*
4 But He answered and said, "It is written, 'MAN SHALL NOT LIVE ON BREAD ALONE, BUT ON EVERY WORD THAT PROCEEDS OUT OF THE MOUTH OF GOD.' " Deut. 8:3

3:17 God the Father of Christ—Every new Christian eventually wonders in what sense God may be called the Father of Christ and Christ the Son of God. The answer to this question is not a simple one. First, one must recognize that the title Son of God does not speak of physical nature, for God is spirit (Page 1067—John 4:24), and Christ was the Son of God before He assumed a human body in Bethlehem (Page 1066—John 3:16; Page 1179—Gal. 4:4). Passages which use terms implying physical origin must be taken in a figurative sense (Page 1230—Heb. 1:5).

Second, the title expresses a unique relationship. Christ distinguished His sonship from that of His disciples (Page 1087—John 20:17). He was begotten of God in a sense that no one else is (Page 1064—John 1:14; 3:16). Some call it "eternal generation," signifying the timelessness of this "God from God" relationship.

Third, the title describes a relationship of equality. The Son of God is no less than God. When Jesus claimed to be "one" with the Father, He was speaking of a unity of "substance" with the Father and thus equality in all the attributes of God (Page 1077—John 10:30). The Jews certainly understood this claim, for they took up stones to stone Him, protesting that "You, . . . make Yourself out to be God" (Page 1077—John 10:33).

Fourth, the title especially emphasizes Christ's role as the revealer of God. He alone possesses the knowledge of the Father (Page 1081—John 14:6-9; Page 1274—1 John 1:2) and He is the sole mediator of that knowledge (Page 1217—1 Tim. 2:5). Therefore no one can know the Father except through the Son (Page 1081—John 14:6). The narrowness of this way to God should be a sober incentive to take to all the world the message that the Son of God has come to impart to every person the life of the Father.

Now turn to Page 1137—Rom. 8:15: God the Father of Believers.

THE CHRISTIAN'S GUIDE TO THE NEW LIFE is a point-by-point Bible study. The introduction leads you to the page of the first underlined verse. Detailed notes at the bottom of the page discuss the passage. Then they refer you to the next verses for study. You cover the material of an advanced course in systematic theology.

HOW TO STUDY THE BIBLE

The Bible is the greatest book ever written. In it God Himself speaks to men. It is a book of divine instruction. It offers comfort in sorrow, guidance in perplexity, advice for our problems, rebuke for our sins, and daily inspiration for our every need.

The Bible is not simply one book. It is an entire library of books covering the whole range of literature. It includes history, poetry, drama, biography, prophecy, philosophy, science, and inspirational reading. Little wonder, then, that all or part of the Bible has been translated into more than 1,200 languages, and every year more copies of the Bible are sold than any other single book.

The Bible alone truly answers the greatest questions that men of all ages have asked: **"Where have I come from?" "Where am I going?" "Why am I here?" "How can I know the truth?"** For the Bible reveals the truth about God, explains the origin of man, points out the only way to salvation and eternal life, and explains the age-old problem of sin and suffering.

The great theme of the Bible is the Lord Jesus Christ and His work of redemption for mankind. The person and work of Jesus Christ are promised, prophesied, and pictured in the types and symbols of the Old Testament. In all of His truth and beauty, the Lord Jesus Christ is revealed in the Gospels; and the full meanings of His life, His death, and His resurrection are explained in the Epistles. His glorious coming again to earth in the future is unmistakably foretold in the Book of Revelation. The great purpose of the written Word of God, the Bible, is to reveal the living Word of God, the Lord Jesus Christ (read John 1:1–18).

Dr. Wilbur M. Smith relates seven great things that the study of the Bible will do for us:

1. **The Bible discovers sin and convicts us.**
2. **The Bible helps cleanse us from the pollutions of sin.**
3. **The Bible imparts strength.**
4. **The Bible instructs us in what we are to do.**
5. **The Bible provides us with a sword for victory over sin.**
6. **The Bible makes our lives fruitful.**
7. **The Bible gives us power to pray.**

You do not need a whole library of books to study the Bible. The Bible is its own best commentator and interpreter. With all of the instructive helps that you have in this new Bible, you have a whole lifetime of Bible study.

I. Personal Bible Study

A. Devotional Bible Study

The Bible is not an end in itself, but is a means to the end of knowing God and doing His will. The apostle Paul said, "Be diligent to present yourself approved to God as a workman who does not need to be ashamed, handling accurately the word of truth" (**2 Tim. 2:15**). God has given us the Bible in order that we might know Him and that we might do His will here on earth.

Therefore, devotional Bible study is the most important kind of Bible study. Devotional Bible study means reading and studying the Word of God in order that we may hear God's voice and that we may know how to do His will and to live a better Christian life.

A great scientist and medical doctor, Dr. Howard A. Kelly (Professor of Gynecology at Johns Hopkins University from 1889 through 1940), was also an avid student of the Bible. He once said: "The very best way to study the Bible is simply to read it daily with close attention and with prayer to see the light that shines from its pages, to meditate upon it, and to continue to read it until somehow it works itself, its words, its expressions, its teachings, its habits of thought, and its presentation of God and His Christ into the very warp and woof of one's being."

For your devotional reading and study of the Bible, here are several important, practical suggestions:

1. Begin your Bible reading with prayer (**Ps. 119:18; John 16:13–15**).

2. Take brief notes on what you read. Keep a small notebook for your Bible study (see number 4 below).

3. Read slowly through one chapter, or perhaps two or three chapters, or perhaps just one paragraph at a time. After reading, ask yourself what this passage means. Then reread it.

4. It is often very helpful in finding out the true meaning of a chapter or passage to ask yourself the following questions, then write the answers in your notebook:

   a. What is the main subject of this passage?
   b. Who are the persons revealed in this passage: Who is speaking? About whom is he speaking? Who is acting?
   c. What is the key verse of this passage?
   d. What does this passage teach me about the Lord Jesus Christ?
   e. Does this passage portray any sin for me to confess and forsake?
   f. Does this passage contain any command for me to obey?
   g. Is there any promise for me to claim?
   h. Is there any instruction for me to follow?

Not all of these questions may be answered in every passage.

5. Keep a spiritual diary. Either in your Bible study notebook mentioned above (number 2), or in a separate notebook entitled, "My Spiritual Diary," write down daily what God says to you

through the Bible. Write down the sins that you confess or the commands you should obey.

6. Memorize passages of the Word of God. No one is ever too old to memorize the Word of God. Write verses on cards with the reference on one side and the verse on the other. Carry these cards with you and review them while you're waiting for a train, standing in lunch line, etc.

Other persons prefer to memorize whole passages or chapters of the Bible. A small pocket Bible will help you to review these passages when you have spare moments. One of the best ways is to spend a few minutes every night before going to sleep, in order that your subconscious mind may help you fix these passages of God's Word in your mind while you're asleep (**Ps. 119:11**).

To meditate means "to reflect, to ponder, to consider, to dwell in thought." Through meditation the Word of God will become meaningful and real to you, and the Holy Spirit will use this time to apply the Word of God to your own life and its problems.

7. Obey the Word of God. As Paul said to Timothy in Second Timothy 3:16: "All Scripture is inspired by God and profitable for teaching, for reproof, for correction, for training in righteousness." The Bible has been given to us that we may live a holy life, well-pleasing to God. Therefore God says, "prove yourselves doers of the word, and not merely hearers" (**James 1:22**).

8. The Navigators, a group of men banded together just before World War II to encourage Bible study among Christian servicemen, developed a splendid plan for a personal, devotional study.

a. After prayer, first read the Bible passage slowly and silently; then read it again aloud.

b. In a large notebook divide the paper into columns and head each column as follows: Chapter title, Key verse, Significant truth, Cross-references, Difficulties in this passage (personal or possible), Application to me, and Summary or outline of the passage. In each of these columns, write the information desired.

Do not try to adopt all of these methods at once, but start out slowly, selecting those methods and suggestions which appeal to you. You will find, as millions of others have before you, that the more you read and study the Word of God, the more you'll want to read it. Therefore, the following suggestions of Bible study are made for those who wish to make a more intensive study of the Bible truths.

B. Study for Bible Knowledge

There are many valuable methods of Bible study. One may study the Bible, as if with a telescope, to see the great truths which stand out in every book. Or one may study the Bible as if with a microscope to find all of the marvelous details which are in this mine of spiritual riches. In this section there are several proven methods with which a person may conduct more intensive Bible study. The most important thing is to follow faithfully some systematic method of Bible study.

Bible Study by Chapters. In the Bible there are 1,189 chapters in the Old and New Testaments. In a little over three years, a person could make an intensive study of the whole Bible, taking a chapter a day. It is usually a good practice to start your Bible study in the New Testament.

1. Read through the chapter carefully, seeking to find its main subject or subjects.

2. As you read each chapter, give it a title which suggests its main content. If you are reading the Gospel of John, for example, you might give each chapter titles like this:

ch. 1 "Jesus Christ, the Word of God"
ch. 2 "The Wedding at Cana"
ch. 3 "The New Birth"
ch. 4 "The Woman at the Well"
ch. 5 "The Healing of the Man at the Pool of Bethesda"

3. Reread the chapter again and make a simple outline which will include its main thoughts. For example in **John 1,** you might make an outline like this:

"Jesus Christ, the Word of God":

a. Jesus Christ was the eternal Word of God, 1–9.

b. Jesus Christ came into the world, 10–18.

c. John witnesses that Christ is to come, 19–28.

d. John says that Jesus is the Lamb of God, 29–37.

e. Jesus Christ calls His first disciples, 38–51.

4. Concerning each chapter, ask and answer the questions suggested in item number 4 of devotional Bible study hints above. Especially take note of any practical or theological problems in this chapter. Then, using your concordance, look up the key words in those verses and find out what other portions of the Bible say about this question or problem. Compare Scripture with Scripture to find its true meaning. Usually, to understand an important Bible chapter, you must study it together with the preceding or following chapters.

Bible Study by Paragraphs. A paragraph is several sentences of thought in writing. When an author changes the subject of emphasis in writing, he usually begins a new paragraph. The beginning of a paragraph in this Bible is indicated by a bold face verse number. Studying the Bible by paragraphs like this is often called analytic Bible study.

1. Read the paragraph carefully for its main thought or subject.

2. In order to find the relation of the important words and sentences in this paragraph, it is often helpful to rewrite the text. For example, if you were going to study the paragraph on prayer in

the Sermon on the Mount found in **Matthew 6:5–8**, you could rewrite this text:

"And when you pray, you are not to be as the hypocrites; for they love to stand and pray in the synagogues and on the street corners, in order to be seen by men. Truly I say to you, they have their reward in full."

"But you, when you pray, go into your inner room, and when you have shut your door, pray to your Father who is in secret, and your Father who sees in secret will repay you."

"And when you are praying, do not use meaningless repetition, as the Gentiles do, for they suppose that they will be heard for their many words."

"Therefore do not be like them; for your Father knows what you need, before you ask Him."

3. From the text which you've now rewritten so that you can see the relationship of the various parts of the paragraph, it is easy to make a simple outline. For example, using **Matthew 6:5–15**, your outline of this passage would be something like this:

"Jesus Teaches Us How to Pray"—**Matthew 6:5–15.**

  a. How not to pray: **Matthew 6:5, 7, 8.**
    (1) Hypocritically in public, **6:5.**
    (2) With useless repetition, **6:7, 8.**
  b. How to pray: **Matthew 6:6, 9–13.**
    (1) In private to your heavenly Father, **6:6.**
    (2) Following the pattern of Jesus' model prayer, **6:9–13.**

4. It is helpful also to look up in the concordance important words that occur in this paragraph, for example, the words "hypocrites," "heathen," etc. By comparing other passages of the Bible which teach about prayer, you'll be kept from making any mistakes concerning the true nature, conditions, and results of prayer according to the will of God.

Bible Study by Verses. In studying the historical passages of the Bible, such as most of the Old Testament or parts of the Gospels, each verse may have only one simple meaning.

But many verses in both the Old and New Testaments are rich with many great Bible truths which will demand more detailed study. There are many ways that you can study a single Bible verse.

1. Study it by the verbs in the verse. For example, if you were studying **John 3:16** you would find the following verbs: "loved . . . gave . . . should not perish . . . have . . . ."

You could make a comparative list like this:
God loved Man believes
God gave Man shall not perish
              Man has eternal life.

Or simply take the nouns in this wonderful verse: "God . . . world . . . only begotten Son . . . whoever . . . eternal life."

2. Study a verse through the personalities revealed. For example, once again taking **John 3:16,** these very simple but significant points are brought to light: "God . . . only begotten Son . . . whoever . . . Him."

3. Study a verse by looking for the great ideas revealed in it. Let us look again at **John 3:16** as our example. We might title this verse, "The greatest verse in the Bible." The following ideas are found in it:

"God"—the greatest person
"so loved"—the greatest devotion
"the world"—the greatest number
"He gave"—the greatest act
"His only begotten Son"—the greatest gift
"that whoever believes"—the greatest condition
"should not perish"—the greatest mercy
"have eternal life"—the greatest result

4. Sometimes a combination of these various ideas applied to a verse will bring the richest results. For example, take **Romans 5:1:**

"Therefore"—This verse depends on **4:25.** Our justification is based on and is guaranteed by Jesus' resurrection.
"justified"—made righteous.
"by faith"—method of our justification (see also **3:24; 4:9**).
"have"—not future, but present tense—we have this *now.*
"peace with God"—We were enemies, but now there is peace between us and God because of what Christ has done.
"through our Lord Jesus Christ"—the way to peace with God is only through Jesus Christ.

Bible Study by Books. After you have begun to study the Bible by chapters or paragraphs or verses, you will be ready to study the Bible by books.

1. There are several methods of Bible book study.

  a. One is called the inductive method. This is a method of studying in detail the contents of a Bible book and then drawing from these details general conclusions or principles concerning the contents and purpose of the book.

  b. Another method of book study is called the synthetic method. By this method, one reads the Bible book over several times to receive the general impressions of the main ideas and purpose of the book without attention to the details. (It is sometimes hard to distinguish these two methods.)

  c. In some cases the study of a Bible book becomes a historical study, if that book relates the history of a nation or a man in a particular period of time. For example, the Book of Exodus tells the history of the children of Israel from the death of Joseph in Egypt until the erection of the tabernacle in

the wilderness in the time of Moses. This covers approximately 400 years.

2. Here are some methods for Bible study by books:

a. Read the book through to get the perspective and the general emphasis of the book.

b. Reread the book many times, each time asking yourself a relevant question and jotting down the answers you find as you read. Here are the most important questions to ask:

First reading: What is the central theme or emphasis of this book? What is the key verse?

Second reading: Remembering the theme of the book, see how it is emphasized and developed. Look for any special problems or applications.

Third reading: What does it tell me about the author and his circumstances when he wrote this book?

Fourth reading: What does the book tell me about the people to whom the book was written and their circumstances, need, or problems?

Fifth reading: What are the main divisions of the book? Is there any outline apparent in the logical organization and development of the book? During this reading, divide the text into the paragraphs as you see them and then give a title to each paragraph. Draw a line down the right side of the outline and on the other side write any problems, questions, words, or ideas that require further study by comparison with other passages in the Bible.

Sixth and successive readings: Look for other facts and/or information that your earlier readings have suggested. By now certain words will stand out in the book. See how often they recur. (For example, as you read the Book of Philippians, you will soon find that the word "joy" occurs many times. This is one of the key words of the book, so note its occurrences and the circumstances surrounding it.)

As you read and reread a book, you'll find that you begin to see its structure and its outline very clearly. It is true, however, that there are other outlines for any given book. It depends on the principle of division that you select. For example, as you study the Book of Romans, you might adopt the outline that Dr. G. Allen Fleece, president of Columbia Bible College, has written:

The Book of Romans
Subject: "The Gospel," 1:16
I. The Gospel for the lost sinner, 1—5
II. The Gospel for the Christian, 6—8
III. The Gospel for the whole world, 9—11

IV. The Gospel applied to daily living, 12—16

Of course, each of these great sections of this remarkable book can be divided into smaller subjects with great profit.

This method, applied to a book which is mainly historical, will also enable you to find a clear outline. In the case of a historical book, the outline will be largely chronological. The Book of Acts lends itself to this kind of study and outline.

The Book of Acts
Subject: "The Gospel Witness in the First Century"
Key verse: 1:8
Outline:
I. Introduction: The apostles receive power, 1:1—2:4
II. The witness in Jerusalem, 2:5—7:60
III. The witness in Judea and Samaria, 8:1—11:18
IV. The beginning of the witness to the end of the earth, 11:19—28:31

Once again more careful study will give the details and further subdivisions of each of these great units of gospel history in this inspired record of the origin of the Christian church.

Bible Study by Words. There are two profitable and helpful ways of studying great words or subjects in the Word of God.

1. Word study by Bible books. Certain words have special significance in certain Bible books. For example, after studying the Gospel of John as a book and by chapters, you'll find it instructive and inspiring to trace the words "believe" and "belief." They occur almost 100 times. By reading the book hurriedly and underlining each passage where the words "believe" and "belief" occur, you'll understand why Bible scholars contend that the purpose of the Gospel of John is expressed by the author in John 20:31.

2. General word study. The fine index and concordance in this Bible will be a great help. Through the study of great Bible words, you can soon become familiar with the great doctrines of the Bible and understand the great theological principles which the Bible reveals.

With the concordance you might begin with the study of the word "grace." By tracing the occurrences of this word through the Old Testament and then into the New Testament, you will come to see that God has always dealt with His people in grace, and you will find in a concrete way the great truth of **Ephesians 2:8.**

Bible Study by Topics. Closely related to the method of study by words is the study according to great topics or subjects: Bible prayers, Bible promises, Bible sermons, Bible songs, Bible poems, etc.

Or one might study Bible geography by read-

ing rapidly through and looking for rivers, seas, and mountains highlighted in Scripture. For example, the mountain-top experiences in the life of Abraham are a thrilling study.

Another challenging study is to read rapidly through the Gospels and Epistles looking for the commands of the Lord to us. The list of Bible topics is unlimited.

First, for a topical study on prayer, look up the word "prayer" or "pray" in your concordance. Look up every form of these words and such related words as "ask," "intercession," etc. After you have looked up these verses, study them and bring together all the teaching on prayer that you find. You will find conditions of prayer, words to be used in prayer, results to expect from prayer, when to pray, and where to pray.

Bible Study Through Biography. The Bible is a record of God's revealing Himself to men and through men. The Old Testament as well as the New is rich in such biographical studies. Here are a few:

> **The life of Noah: Genesis 5:32—10:32**
> **The life of Abraham: Genesis 12—25**
> **The life of Joseph: Genesis 37—50**
> **The life of Deborah: Judges 4, 5**

Let us summarize various methods for studying the great Bible biographies:

1. Read the Bible book or passages in which this person's life is prominent, e.g., Abraham in **Genesis 12—25**, plus references to Abraham in **Hebrews 11** and **Romans 4**.

2. Trace character with your concordance.

3. Be careful to note indirect references to the person in other portions of Scripture.

Conclusion. There are many other methods of studying the Bible: the psychological method, the sociological method, the cultural method, the philosophical method, etc. Use all the Bible study methods suggested above. From time to time, change your method so that you'll not become too accustomed to any one method or tired from delving too deeply into one type of study.

II. Family Bible Study

Nothing is more important in a Christian home than the family altar. At a convenient time when all members of the family are home, father or mother should lead them in worship of God and in reading His Word. A simple program for family worship includes singing a hymn, an opening prayer by a family member, a brief Bible study, and a concluding period of prayer in which all members take part.

The family altar and Bible study will bind the family together, eliminate juvenile delinquency, foster deeper love, and enable each member to become a stronger, better Christian. Since family Bible study usually includes small children, it is wise to avoid deep, difficult topics and study something of interest and help to all. Such sub-jects might be Bible biographies as outlined above, stories of miracles and deeds of Jesus as revealed in the Gospels, miracles in the Old Testament, and other narrative portions of the Bible. It is wise to keep the study brief and concentrate on a short passage of Scripture. For example, if the family is going to study the life of Moses, it could be divided into units like this:

> **First day: The birth of Moses: Exodus 2:1–10**
> **Second day: Moses' great choice and great mistake: Hebrews 11:24–27; Exodus 2:11–15**
> **Third day: Moses' wilderness training: Exodus 2:16–25**
> **Fourth day: Moses' call to serve God: Exodus 3:1–22**
> **Fifth day: Moses' argument with God: Exodus 4:1–17**
> **Sixth day: Moses' return to Egypt: Exodus 4:18–31**

Here are several practical hints on how to make your family Bible study interesting and profitable to all:

1. Keep your family Bible study reasonably short: one brief chapter or several paragraphs a day.

2. Have each member read a verse.

3. Appoint one family member to lead in worship each day and select the passage to read. This one may appoint others to help in the family worship.

4. Read through a Bible book, a chapter or several paragraphs each day. As you read, together decide on a name or a title for each chapter and memorize this.

5. After reading the passage, have each member in the family explain one verse or one paragraph.

6. Let the leader (or the father or mother) prepare five or ten questions on the Bible passage and ask various members of the family to answer these questions after the passage has been read.

7. Study the beautiful maps in your Bible together and trace Paul's journeys or the wandering of the children of Israel in Egypt.

8. Study Bible topics together. Assign verses concerning a topic or great word to each member of the family. Let each read a verse and tell what the verse teaches about the topic or word.

9. After the Bible reading, have each member tell what this verse means or how it can be applied to personal life.

10. Make up Bible games by having each member make up questions to try to stump the others.

11. Study a Bible book together, using the hints given above. There are many wonderful ways to make the Bible the heart of your home.

III. Principles of Bible Interpretation

Since the Bible was written by many men over a period covering 1,500 years, and since the last

author of the Bible has been dead 1,900 years, there are definite problems in understanding the exact meaning of certain passages of the Bible.

There is a need to interpret clearly certain passages of the Bible because there is a gap between the way we think and the words we use today and the way of thinking and the words that these Bible writers used thousands of years ago. Bible scholars have pointed out that there are language gaps—differences in words that we use; there are cultural gaps—different customs were in vogue then. There are geographical gaps—certain rivers that are spoken of in the Bible have long since dried up. Some places that are spoken of frequently in the Bible are not on our modern maps. And then there are historical gaps—the Bible speaks of kings and empires which existed years ago.

Therefore, there is a need for Bible interpretation. This is a fascinating study in itself, but I want to give you just a few principles of interpretation of the Bible that will keep you from error and help you understand the difficult passages of the Word of God.

1. Always remember that the Bible is God's infallible, inerrantly inspired Word. There are no mistakes in the Bible. God has included everything in the Bible that He wants you to know and is necessary for you to know concerning salvation and your Christian life.

2. The second principle of interpretation is to interpret the Bible in the light of its historical background. There are three aspects of this:

  a. Study the personal circumstances of the writer. In studying the Book of Revelation, it is important to understand where John was and what he was doing when God gave him this marvelous revelation. See **Revelation 1:1–10.**

  b. The second aspect of this principle is to study the culture and customs of the country at the time that the writing or story was taking place. For example, to understand the Book of Ruth, it is important to study the customs concerning widows, redemptions of property, etc., as they are explained in **Leviticus 25** and **Deuteronomy 25.**

  c. A third aspect of this principle is to study and interpret the Bible in the light of the actual historical situation and events that were taking place at the time of the story. For example, in studying the Gospels it is important to realize that the entire land of

Palestine and all of the Jews were being governed and oppressed by the Roman Empire at that time.

3. Interpret the Bible according to the purpose and plan of each book.

Every Bible book has its specific purpose intended by the Holy Spirit to bring some special message to man. For example, it is important to remember that **First John** (see **1 John 5:13**) was written to Christians. Therefore the promise in **First John 1:9** is specifically applied to Christians.

4. One of the most important principles of interpretation is always to interpret according to the context of a verse.

The "context" includes the verses immediately preceding and immediately following the verse you are studying. If you do not take care to interpret the verse according to the context, you could make the Bible teach atheism. For the Bible itself says, "There is no God" (**Ps. 14:1**). But the context makes very clear what this verse means: The immediately preceding sentence says, "The fool has said in his heart, 'There is no God.'"

Always study the passage immediately preceding and immediately following any verse, word, or topic to make sure that you see this truth in the setting which God intended.

5. Always interpret according to the correct meaning of words. You can find the correct meaning of a word in several ways. First of all, look up the usage of the word in other parts of the Bible to find how it was used in that generation. Another way is to look up its background or its root. You could do this with the use of a dictionary. Still another way is to look up the synonyms—words that are similar in meaning but slightly different: for example, "prayer," "intercession," "supplication."

6. Also interpret the Bible according to all of the parallel passages which deal with the subject and according to the message of the entire Bible.

The more you read the Bible, the more you will understand that in it God is revealing His way of salvation to men from beginning to end. And when you come to a difficult passage, think of it in the light of the overall purpose of the Bible. For example, the animal sacrifices of the Old Testament are meant to be a picture of the perfect sacrifice of Jesus Christ on the cross.

If you will follow these simple rules, you will be kept from error and extremes, and you will be helped to understand correctly the teachings of even the more difficult passages in God's Word.

THE CHRISTIAN'S GUIDE TO THE NEW LIFE

The Christian's Guide to the New Life offers a complete doctrinal overview of the Bible to assist you in a practical, simplified way to study your Bible. The six main areas of study, described below, are further amplified; these systematically cover all the important areas of biblical theology. This unique study feature places before the Bible student an exegesis of Scripture with hundreds of Scriptural references.

For the student just beginning Bible study, *The Christian's Guide to the New Life* covers in a fundamental way how you become a Christian, then steps the believer through the Christian life. The easy-to-use references and cross-references lead the reader toward a comprehensive, practical knowledge of God's Word.

The general organization of *The Christian's Guide to the New Life* includes six main areas of study:

> Knowing God's Word
> Understanding God's Being
> Beginning the New Life
> Growing in the New Life
> Facing Problems in the New Life
> Recognizing God's Institutions

These areas of study are subdivided into twenty-eight individual **Christian's Guides** with appropriate Bible references. All the material is organized in a simple format to assist you in more easily understanding the Bible, the inspired Word of God. Each numbered Christian's Guide has several discussions of Bible texts appearing on the page where the text occurs. For example within the main area of study **Knowing God's Word** is Christian's Guide (1) **How God's Word Came to Us.** There are three discussions concerning how God's Word came to us: on page 196 is **Revelation of God's Word;** on page 707 is **Inspiration of God's Word;** and on page 613 is **Illumination of God's Word.**

This article, *The Christian's Guide to the New Life,* will serve as a general introduction, index, and guide to the various Christian's Guides. Each time you study one of the discussions in the Bible the last line will tell you where to turn for the next discussion. When you finish a main area of study, such as **Knowing God's Word,** the last line in the last discussion will tell you to turn to this article, *The Christian's Guide to the New Life.* Then, after reading the synopsis of the next main area of study, you will be ready to turn to the first discussion and follow the development of that area of study.

The Christian's Guide to the New Life can be used in three easy ways: for monthly study, daily study, and topical study.

- Monthly study—once a day for twenty-eight days study one of the numbered Christian's Guides. Read each of the discussions and look up the listed references.
- Daily study—once a day for 105 days study a single discussion in the Bible text. Read the complete discussion and look up the listed references.
- Topical study—using this article, *The Christian's Guide to the New Life,* as an index, study individual Christian's Guides and discussions as the need arises.

You are now ready to begin using *The Christian's Guide to the New Life.* For each of the six main areas of study a synopsis and an organization are provided. For each of the Christian's Guides page numbers and scripture references are provided to help you find the various discussions in the Bible.

Knowing God's Word

Synopsis

Christians should know the Bible for many reasons, but the primary one is because God is its author. All Bible students know that God is Creator (Gen. 1:1), Redeemer (Is. 60:16), and Judge (Gen. 18:25), but do we think of Him as the author of the Bible? Human writers feel it vital that we read their books; it is much more important that we read God's book, the Bible.

About fourteen centuries before Christ, our Bible had its beginnings in the Sinai desert. In this arid place God spoke to Moses, who had once been a prince in Egypt and was nearly 120 years old at the time. At the Lord's command, Moses picked up his pen and began writing Scripture's first five books, Genesis through Deuteronomy. More than 1,500 years later, the divine manuscript was completed on a lonely, windswept island in the Mediterranean Sea by a former fisherman, John the apostle. From Genesis through Revelation, the final biblical book, there are sixty-six divinely inspired books. Over the centuries, approximately forty men and women—representing varied backgrounds and writing styles—served as channels for God's Word. Yet, in spite of these variations in time and talent, the completed work displays a marvelous historical, theological, geographical, topical, and biographical unity.

The Bible's practical benefits for us may well be summarized under two headings: knowing and growing. The Bible proclaims the good news of the gospel that we might know God; it explains

the will of God that all of us may grow spiritually before Him.

Scripture also reveals our place within God's program and answers crucial questions pertaining to our origin, purpose, and destiny. Because God has revealed His unchanging truths, the Christian faith provides real answers and guidance to every generation. Although we cannot grasp how individual events fit into God's program (Eccl. 11:5), we can understand God's basic plan in order to come to know and serve Him. Few joys can compare with realizing our places in God's program and working to fulfill our destinies.

Organization

1. **How God's Word Came to Us**
   Revelation of God's Word
   Page 196—Deut. 29:29
   Inspiration of God's Word
   Page 707—Is. 59:21
   Illumination of God's Word
   Page 613—Prov. 6:23

2. **What God's Word Does**
   God's Word Convicts
   Page 474—Neh. 8:9
   God's Word Corrects
   Page 534—Ps. 17:4
   God's Word Cleanses
   Page 590—Ps. 119:9
   God's Word Confirms
   Page 1074—John 8:31
   God's Word Equips
   Page 626—Prov. 22:21

3. **How We Benefit from God's Word**
   We Know God Through God's Word
   Page 849—Dan. 11:32
   We Know God's Will Through God's Word
   Page 548—Ps. 40:8

4. **What God's Word Tells Us About God's Program**
   God's Work in the Past
   Page 199—Deut. 32:7
   God's Work in the Present
   Page 600—Ps. 139:14

5. **What God's Word Tells Us About God's Covenants**
   The Edenic Covenant
   Page 5—Gen. 2:15–17
   The Adamic Covenant
   Page 7—Gen. 3:14–21
   The Noahic Covenant
   Page 11—Gen. 9:1–19
   The Abrahamic Covenant
   Page 14—Gen. 12:1–3
   The Mosaic Covenant
   Page 70—Ex. 19:5–8
   The Palestinian Covenant
   Page 195—Deut. 29:10–15; 30:11–20
   The Davidic Covenant

Page 300—2 Sam. 7:4–17
The New Covenant
Page 749—Jer. 31:31–34

Understanding God's Being

Synopsis

The Bible reveals the nature of God as spirit, unity, and trinity. He is a spirit—a personal, infinite being (John 4:24); He is one—one in substance or nature and incapable of being divided into separate parts (Deut. 6:4); and He is three—eternally existing in three coequal persons (Matt. 28:19). While great mystery surrounds God's nature, it is reassuring to know that our God is above us.

God's attributes are merely words we use to describe how God is and how He acts toward us. Among these attributes are love, holiness, constancy, justice, truth, eternality, omniscience (all-knowing), omnipresence (all-present), and omnipotence (all-powerful). The fact that we can grasp and understand this much about God is evidence of God's desire that all peoples may know Him.

The word *Father* is variously applied in the Bible. When God is spoken of as the Father of all men, it is as Creator; as the Father of Christ, it expresses an eternal, unique relationship; as the Father of believers, it denotes a relationship established by grace; and as Father of Israel, it means a bond established by covenant. However Father is used, it is a deliberately chosen word to communicate to men one of the primary ways God wants us to conceive of Him.

The title *Son of God* is one which Jesus never directly applied to Himself, but when others applied it to Him Jesus willingly accepted it as a claim to His own deity (John 10:24–38). Jesus often referred to Himself as "the Son," which was certainly an abbreviation for the Son of God. How significant is this term to the Christian? It is very important, because it helps establish some major truths without which we would be left with little evidence that the words of Jesus Christ were actually true. It can be said that as our relationship with the Son of God determines whether we will become Christians, our relationship with the Spirit of God determines what kind of believers we will be.

Organization

6. **God the Father**
   God the Father of All
   Page 930—Mal. 2:10
   God the Father of Christ
   Page 965—Matt. 3:17
   God the Father of Believers
   Page 1137—Rom. 8:15

7. **The Son of God**
   The Person of the Son of God

Beginning the New Life

Synopsis

Mankind is by nature sinful and needs the righteousness of God. We must be separated from sin and set apart to righteousness. If we are to approach God, we must do so on God's terms— we must have new lives in which our sins have been forgiven and obliterated.

It is one thing to be convinced of the need for the new life, but it is an entirely different thing to acquire the new life. When we are "saved" we are said to be new creatures (2 Cor. 5:17); to have passed from death to life (John 5:24); to have been transferred from the rule of darkness to the kingdom of God's Son (Col. 1:13); to have been born again (John 3:3); and to have been adopted by God (Gal. 4:4, 5). These wonderful results of having new life in Christ are offered freely to all who trust in Christ for salvation.

One of the most thrilling benefits of finding new life in Christ is "eternal [everlasting] life." We enter a new, personal relationship with God that gives us a fullness of spiritual vitality, and this new life is a gift which will never die. God can accomplish a life-changing transformation for all who truly believe in Christ.

Organization

9. **Need for the New Life**
   Holiness of God
   Page 662—Is. 6:3
   Adam's Sin
   Page 6—Gen. 3:6, 7
   Individual Sin
   Page 642—Eccl. 7:20

10. **Way to the New Life**
    New Life: A Free Gift
    Page 1136—Rom. 6:23
    New Life: Based on Christ's Death
    Page 1200—Col. 1:22
    New Life: Received by Faith
    Page 1113—Acts 16:31

11. **Results of the New Life**
    Everlasting Life
    Page 1069—John 5:24

New Nature
Page 1168—2 Cor. 5:17
Christ's Righteousness
Page 709—Is. 61:10
Placed into God's Family
Page 1276—1 John 3:2
Empowered by God
Page 1094—Acts 1:8

12. **Assurance of the New Life**
    Promise of God
    Page 1229—Titus 1:2
    Witness of the Spirit
    Page 1277—1 John 3:24
    Changed Life
    Page 1152—1 Cor. 6:11

Growing in the New Life

Synopsis

Knowing how to grow in the new life is essential. The old adage is ever true: "Sin will keep you from God's Word, and God's Word will keep you from sin."

No factor in Christian growth is more important than prayer. Prayer may be defined as talking with and listening to God. We talk to Him with our lips and heart, and He talks to us through His will. It involves a two-way conversation. Spiritual maturity is impossible without systematic prayer.

Worship is essential also to spiritual growth. Worship involves honor and respect toward God, the ceremony of private and public worship, and the joyful service of Christians to their Lord. Christians who submit to the Lordship of Christ in reverence and service will grow in their spiritual lives.

The Bible describes Christian life as "[walking] by the Spirit" (Gal. 5:16). Walking best represents the step-by-step character of the spiritual life. Living by the Spirit's power is a moment-by-moment yielding to the Spirit's will and control. The evidence that we are walking in the Spirit is simply the display of the fruit of the Spirit (Gal. 5:22, 23). Walking in the Spirit involves confession of sin, yielding to God, and being filled with or controlled by the Spirit.

Organization

13. **Bible Study**
    Reading God's Word
    Page 473—Neh. 8:3
    Memorizing God's Word
    Page 510—Job 22:22
    Meditating upon God's Word
    Page 206—Josh. 1:8
    Obedience to God's Word
    Page 198—Deut. 31:12

14. **Prayer**
    Praise
    Page 605—Ps. 150:1

Facing Problems in the New Life

Synopsis

Just as we have problems in our physical lives, we also experience problems in our spiritual or new lives. Facing and conquering difficulties cause us to grow and be strengthened, whether those problems are physical or spiritual. As we grow in our new strength, we bring glory to God as He demonstrates His faithfulness and that His grace is sufficient for every need (2 Cor. 12:9).

Some of the problems that are common in the new life are sin, temptation, suffering, knowing the will of God, and doubt.

A believer must be especially wary of places, situations, and times in which he or she may be vulnerable to temptation. Certainly the best antidote to temptation is to be a growing Christian. The mind that is occupied with the things of the Lord cannot at the same time be susceptible to temptation.

Of all the possible sins against God, the most serious is that of self-will. This sin led to the fall of Satan (Is. 14:12–14), and it can be said to be the root of Adam's transgression (Gen. 3:1–7). It is, therefore, of utmost importance that the child of God find His will and perform it.

The dismissal of doubt and strengthening of faith are best accomplished by reading and understanding the Word of God (Rom. 10:17). The Holy Spirit will convict the willing heart of its power. Growing in the Word produces growth in faith; reading and understanding the Word are like planting seeds of faith in the heart. They will bear the mature fruit of faith.

Organization

Recognizing God's Institutions

Synopsis

God gave humanity four basic institutions: the family, human government, Israel, and the church. It may be observed that each of these institutions demonstrates a characteristic or attribute of God.

- The family illustrates the unity of God (Gen. 2:24; Deut. 6:4).
- Human government illustrates the judgment of God (Rom. 13:1, 2).
- Israel illustrates the election of God (Rom. 9:1–18; 11:1–5).
- The church illustrates the love of God (Eph. 5:22–27).

The family was the first human institution God created. Through the family God illustrates visibly the relationships which exist in the Godhead and the relationship which exists between Christ and His church. Through the family God sought to bring into proper relationship the world with Himself. He created all of the heavens and earth and the things in them that they might prepare the way for and sustain the crown of His creation—humanity.

God's purpose in human government is that it serve as both a custodian and an enforcer of His eternal law. It has been correctly noted that all the thousands of good and practical laws passed by hundreds of legislative bodies and rulers throughout history are in reality only amplifications of the Ten Commandments.

God's selection of Israel as a special nation may puzzle the Bible student, but His choice becomes obvious through study. When God promised Abraham that he would become the father of a great nation, He also promised that He would bless all peoples through that nation (Gen. 12:1–3). Israel was to be a channel of blessing as well as a recipient.

The church, illustrating God's love for us, is the fourth institution through which God works. The universal church—the Body of Christ (Col. 1:18)—comprises all believers since the institution of the church.

Organization

Read Your Bible Through In a Year

A systematic division of the books of the Bible, primarily for reading.

JANUARY

Date	MORNING MATT.	EVENING GEN.
1	1	1, 2, 3
2	2	4, 5, 6
3	3	7, 8, 9
4	4	10, 11, 12
5	5: 1-26	13, 14, 15
6	5:27-48	16, 17
7	6: 1-18	18, 19
8	6:19-34	20, 21, 22
9	7	23, 24
10	8: 1-17	25, 26
11	8:18-34	27, 28
12	9: 1-17	29, 30
13	9:18-38	31, 32
14	10: 1-20	33, 34, 35
15	10:21-42	36, 37, 38
16	11	39, 40
17	12: 1-23	41, 42
18	12:24-50	43, 44, 45
19	13: 1-30	46, 47, 48
20	13:31-58	49, 50
		EX.
21	14: 1-21	1, 2, 3
22	14:22-36	4, 5, 6
23	15: 1-20	7, 8
24	15:21-39	9, 10, 11
25	16	12, 13
26	17	14, 15
27	18: 1-20	16, 17, 18
28	18:21-35	19, 20
29	19	21, 22
30	20: 1-16	23, 24
31	20:17-34	25, 26

FEBRUARY

Date	MORNING MATT.	EVENING EX.
1	21: 1-22	27, 28
2	21:23-46	29, 30
3	22: 1-22	31, 32, 33
4	22:23-46	34, 35
5	23: 1-22	36, 37, 38
6	23:23-39	39, 40
		LEV.
7	24: 1-28	1, 2, 3
8	24:29-51	4, 5
9	25: 1-30	6, 7
10	25:31-46	8, 9, 10
11	26: 1-25	11, 12
12	26:26-50	13
13	26:51-75	14
14	27: 1-26	15, 16
15	27:27-50	17, 18
16	27:51-66	19, 20
17	28	21, 22
	MARK	
18	1: 1-22	23, 24
19	1:23-45	25
20	2	26, 27
		NUM.
21	3: 1-19	1, 2
22	3:20-35	3, 4
23	4: 1-20	5, 6
24	4:21-41	7, 8
25	5: 1-20	9, 10, 11
26	5:21-43	12, 13, 14
27	6: 1-29	15, 16
28	6:30-56	17, 18, 19
29	7: 1-13	20, 21, 22

MARCH

Date	MORNING MARK	EVENING NUM.
1	7:14-37	23, 24, 25
2	8: 1-21	26, 27
3	8:22-38	28, 29, 30
4	9: 1-29	31, 32, 33
5	9:30-50	34, 35, 36
		DEUT.
6	10: 1-31	1, 2
7	10:32-52	3, 4
8	11: 1-18	5, 6, 7
9	11:19-33	8, 9, 10
10	12: 1-27	11, 12, 13
11	12:28-44	14, 15, 16
12	13: 1-20	17, 18, 19
13	13:21-37	20, 21, 22
14	14: 1-26	23, 24, 25
15	14:27-53	26, 27
16	14:54-72	28, 29
17	15: 1-25	30, 31
18	15:26-47	32, 33, 34
		JOSH.
19	16	1, 2, 3
	LUKE	
20	1: 1-20	4, 5, 6
21	1:21-38	7, 8, 9
22	1:39-56	10, 11, 12
23	1:57-80	13, 14, 15
24	2: 1-24	16, 17, 18
25	2:25-52	19, 20, 21
26	3	22, 23, 24
		JUDG.
27	4: 1-30	1, 2, 3
28	4:31-44	4, 5, 6
29	5: 1-16	7, 8
30	5:17-39	9, 10
31	6: 1-26	11, 12

APRIL

Date	MORNING LUKE	EVENING JUDG.
1	6:27-49	13, 14, 15
2	7: 1-30	16, 17, 18
3	7:31-50	19, 20, 21
		RUTH
4	8: 1-25	1, 2, 3, 4
		1 SAM.
5	8:26-56	1, 2, 3
6	9: 1-17	4, 5, 6
7	9:18-36	7, 8, 9
8	9:37-62	10, 11, 12
9	10: 1-24	13, 14
10	10:25-42	15, 16
11	11: 1-28	17, 18
12	11:29-54	19, 20, 21
13	12: 1-31	22, 23, 24
14	12:32-59	25, 26
15	13: 1-22	27, 28, 29
16	13:23-35	30, 31
		2 SAM.
17	14: 1-24	1, 2
18	14:25-35	3, 4, 5
19	15: 1-10	6, 7, 8
20	15:11-32	9, 10, 11
21	16	12, 13
22	17: 1-19	14, 15
23	17:20-37	16, 17, 18
24	18: 1-23	19, 20
25	18:24-43	21, 22
26	19: 1-27	23, 24
		1 KIN.
27	19:28-48	1, 2
28	20: 1-26	3, 4, 5
29	20:27-47	6, 7
30	21: 1-19	8, 9

MAY

Date	MORNING LUKE	EVENING 1 KIN.
1	21:20-38	10, 11
2	22: 1-20	12, 13
3	22:21-46	14, 15
4	22:47-71	16, 17, 18
5	23: 1-25	19, 20
6	23:26-56	21, 22
		2 KIN.
7	24: 1-35	1, 2, 3
8	24:36-53	4, 5, 6
	JOHN	
9	1: 1-28	7, 8, 9
10	1:29-51	10, 11, 12
11	2	13, 14
12	3: 1-18	15, 16
13	3:19-38	17, 18
14	4: 1-30	19, 20, 21
15	4:31-54	22, 23
16	5: 1-24	24, 25
		1 CHR.
17	5:25-47	1, 2, 3
18	6: 1-21	4, 5, 6
19	6:22-44	7, 8, 9
20	6:45-71	10, 11, 12
21	7: 1-27	13, 14, 15
22	7:28-53	16, 17, 18
23	8: 1-27	19, 20, 21
24	8:28-59	22, 23, 24
25	9: 1-23	25, 26, 27
26	9:24-41	28, 29
		2 CHR.
27	10: 1-23	1, 2, 3
28	10:24-42	4, 5, 6
29	11: 1-29	7, 8, 9
30	11:30-57	10, 11, 12
31	12: 1-26	13, 14

JUNE

Date	MORNING JOHN	EVENING 2 CHR.
1	12:27-50	15, 16
2	13: 1-20	17, 18
3	13:21-38	19, 20
4	14	21, 22
5	15	23, 24
6	16	25, 26, 27
7	17	28, 29
8	18: 1-18	30, 31
9	18:19-40	32, 33
10	19: 1-22	34, 35, 36
		EZRA
11	19:23-42	1, 2
12	20	3, 4, 5
13	21	6, 7, 8
	ACTS	
14	1	9, 10
		NEH.
15	2: 1-21	1, 2, 3
16	2:22-47	4, 5, 6
17	3	7, 8, 9
18	4: 1-22	10, 11
19	4:23-37	12, 13
		ESTH.
20	5: 1-21	1, 2
21	5:22-42	3, 4, 5
22	6	6, 7, 8
23	7: 1-21	9, 10
		JOB
24	7:22-43	1, 2
25	7:44-60	3, 4
26	8: 1-25	5, 6, 7
27	8:26-40	8, 9, 10
28	9: 1-21	11, 12, 13
29	9:22-43	14, 15, 16
30	10: 1-23	17, 18, 19

JULY

Date	MORNING	EVENING
	ACTS	**JOB**
1	10:24–48	20, 21
2	11	22, 23, 24
3	12	25, 26, 27
4	13: 1–25	28, 29
5	13:26–52	30, 31
6	14	32, 33
7	15: 1–21	34, 35
8	15:22–41	36, 37
9	16: 1–21	38, 39, 40
10	16:22–40	41, 42
		PS.
11	17: 1–15	1, 2, 3
12	17:16–34	4, 5, 6
13	18	7, 8, 9
14	19: 1–20	10, 11, 12
15	19:21–41	13, 14, 15
16	20: 1–16	16, 17
17	20:17–38	18, 19
18	21: 1–17	20, 21, 22
19	21:18–40	23, 24, 25
20	22	26, 27, 28
21	23: 1–15	29, 30
22	23:16–35	31, 32
23	24	33, 34
24	25	35, 36
25	26	37, 38, 39
26	27: 1–26	40, 41, 42
27	27:27–44	43, 44, 45
28	28	46, 47, 48
	ROM.	
29	1	49, 50
30	2	51, 52, 53
31	3	54, 55, 56

AUGUST

Date	MORNING	EVENING
	ROM.	**PS.**
1	4	57, 58, 59
2	5	60, 61, 62
3	6	63, 64, 65
4	7	66, 67
5	8: 1–21	68, 69
6	8:22–39	70, 71
7	9: 1–15	72, 73
8	9:16–33	74, 75, 76
9	10	77, 78
10	11: 1–18	79, 80
11	11:19–36	81, 82, 83
12	12	84, 85, 86
13	13	87, 88
14	14	89, 90
15	15: 1–13	91, 92, 93
16	15:14–33	94, 95, 96
17	16	97, 98, 99
	1 COR.	
18	1	100, 101, 102
19	2	103, 104
20	3	105, 106
21	4	107, 108, 109
22	5	110, 111, 112
23	6	113, 114, 115
24	7: 1–19	116, 117, 118
25	7:20–40	119: 1–88
26	8	119: 89–176
27	9	120, 121, 122
28	10: 1–18	123, 124, 125
29	10:19–33	126, 127, 128
30	11: 1–16	129, 130, 131
31	11:17–34	132, 133, 134

SEPTEMBER

Date	MORNING	EVENING
	1 COR.	**PS.**
1	12	135, 136
2	13	137, 138, 139
3	14: 1–20	140, 141, 142
4	14:21–40	143, 144, 145
5	15: 1–28	146, 147
6	15:29–58	148, 149, 150
		PROV.
7	16	1, 2
	2 COR.	
8	1	3, 4, 5
9	2	6, 7
10	3	8, 9
11	4	10, 11, 12
12	5	13, 14, 15
13	6	16, 17, 18
14	7	19, 20, 21
15	8	22, 23, 24
16	9	25, 26
17	10	27, 28, 29
18	11: 1–15	30, 31
		ECCL.
19	11:16–33	1, 2, 3
20	12	4, 5, 6
21	13	7, 8, 9
	GAL.	
22	1	10, 11, 12
		SONG
23	2	1, 2, 3
24	3	4, 5
25	4	6, 7, 8
		IS.
26	5	1, 2
27	6	3, 4
	EPH.	
28	1	5, 6
29	2	7, 8
30	3	9, 10

OCTOBER

Date	MORNING	EVENING
	EPH.	**IS.**
1	4	11, 12, 13
2	5: 1–16	14, 15, 16
3	5:17–33	17, 18, 19
4	6	20, 21, 22
	PHIL.	
5	1	23, 24, 25
6	2	26, 27
7	3	28, 29
8	4	30, 31
	COL.	
9	1	32, 33
10	2	34, 35, 36
11	3	37, 38
12	4	39, 40
	1 THESS.	
13	1	41, 42
14	2	43, 44
15	3	45, 46
16	4	47, 48, 49
17	5	50, 51, 52
	2 THESS.	
18	1	53, 54, 55
19	2	56, 57, 58
20	3	59, 60, 61
	1 TIM.	
21	1	62, 63, 64
22	2	65, 66
		JER.
23	3	1, 2
24	4	3, 4, 5
25	5	6, 7, 8
26	6	9, 10, 11
	2 TIM.	
27	1	12, 13, 14
28	2	15, 16, 17
29	3	18, 19
30	4	20, 21
	TITUS	
31	1	22, 23

NOVEMBER

Date	MORNING	EVENING
	TITUS	**JER.**
1	2	24, 25, 26
2	3	27, 28, 29
3	**PHILEM.**	30, 31
	HEB.	
4	1	32, 33
5	2	34, 35, 36
6	3	37, 38, 39
7	4	40, 41, 42
8	5	43, 44, 45
9	6	46, 47
10	7	48, 49
11	8	50
12	9	51, 52
		LAM.
13	10: 1–18	1, 2
14	10:19–39	3, 4, 5
		EZEK.
15	11: 1–19	1, 2
16	11:20–40	3, 4
17	12	5, 6, 7
18	13	8, 9, 10
	JAMES	
19	1	11, 12, 13
20	2	14, 15
21	3	16, 17
22	4	18, 19
23	5	20, 21
	1 PET.	
24	1	22, 23
25	2	24, 25, 26
26	3	27, 28, 29
27	4	30, 31, 32
28	5	33, 34
	2 PET.	
29	1	35, 36
30	2	37, 38, 39

DECEMBER

Date	MORNING	EVENING
	2 PET.	**EZEK.**
1	3	40, 41
	1 JOHN	
2	1	42, 43, 44
3	2	45, 46
4	3	47, 48
		DAN.
5	4	1, 2
6	5	3, 4
	2 JOHN	
7		5, 6, 7
	3 JOHN	
8		8, 9, 10
	JUDE	
9		11, 12
	REV.	**HOS.**
10	1	1, 2, 3, 4
11	2	5, 6, 7, 8
12	3	9, 10, 11
13	4	12, 13, 14
		JOEL / AMOS
14	5	
15	6	1, 2, 3
16	7	4, 5, 6
17	8	7, 8, 9
		OBAD.
18	9	
		JON. / MIC.
19	10	
20	11	1, 2, 3
21	12	4, 5
22	13	6, 7
		NAH.
23	14	
		HAB.
24	15	
		ZEPH.
25	16	
		HAG. / ZECH.
26	17	
27	18	1, 2, 3, 4
28	19	5, 6, 7, 8
29	20	9, 10, 11, 12
30	21	13, 14
		MAL.
31	22	

Biblical
Cyclopedic
Index

How to Use
The Biblical Cyclopedic Index

The Biblical Cyclopedic Index is a special kind of subject index that combines the best features of a concordance, a topical index, the usable study features of a syllabus, and other related study aids into one unique, quick, easy-to-use form. The Index offers advantages for personal Bible study that not even a combination of the above study helps would provide.

With over 8,000 subjects, names, places, things, concepts, events, and doctrines of the Bible, the Biblical Cyclopedic Index truly "opens" the Bible. It not only includes the Scripture references for the individual subjects (by appropriate sub-headings), it goes one convenient step further: it gives the actual page numbers in THE OPEN BIBLE where each Scripture verse or verses may be found.

An example will illustrate. Suppose you need to prepare or study a lesson on "The Peace of Jesus." Follow four easy steps.

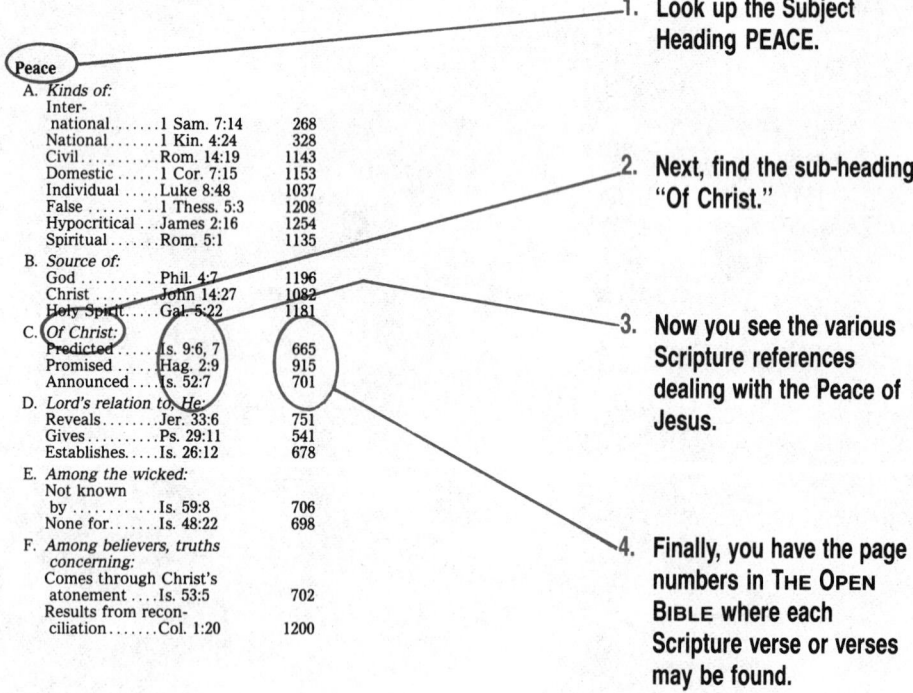

1. Look up the Subject Heading PEACE.

Peace
A. *Kinds of:*
Inter-
national.......1 Sam. 7:14   268
National.......1 Kin. 4:24   328
Civil..........Rom. 14:19   1143
Domestic......1 Cor. 7:15   1153
Individual ....Luke 8:48   1037
False ....1 Thess. 5:3   1208
Hypocritical ...James 2:16   1254
Spiritual ....Rom. 5:1   1135
B. *Source of:*
God ....Phil. 4:7   1196
Christ ....John 14:27   1082
Holy Spirit.....Gal. 5:22   1181
C. *Of Christ:*
Predicted......Is. 9:6, 7   665
Promised .....Hag. 2:9   915
Announced....Is. 52:7   701
D. *Lord's relation to, He:*
Reveals........Jer. 33:6   751
Gives..........Ps. 29:11   541
Establishes.....Is. 26:12   678
E. *Among the wicked:*
Not known
by ....Is. 59:8   706
None for.......Is. 48:22   698
F. *Among believers, truths concerning:*
Comes through Christ's
atonement ....Is. 53:5   702
Results from recon-
ciliation.......Col. 1:20   1200

2. Next, find the sub-heading "Of Christ."

3. Now you see the various Scripture references dealing with the Peace of Jesus.

4. Finally, you have the page numbers in THE OPEN BIBLE where each Scripture verse or verses may be found.

The Biblical Cyclopedic Index has provided two important sources of information for you. First, you have the scriptural material needed to prepare or study your lesson. Second, you have this material in order as it appears in the Bible, so you have a ready-made outline for your personal use.

Biblical Cyclopedic Index

FROM GENESIS TO REVELATION

ARRANGED ALPHABETICALLY GIVING THE BOOK, CHAPTER, VERSE AND PAGE
WHERE EVERY REFERENCE IN THIS INDEX IS FOUND

SUBJECT	REFERENCE	PAGE

5. Father of Queen
Esther ....Esth. 2:15   486

Abihu—*he is father*
Second of Aaron's four
sons..............Ex. 6:23   59
Ascends Mt.
Sinai ....Ex. 24:1, 9   75
Chosen as priest ..Ex. 28:1   78
Offers, with Nadab, strange
fire...............Lev. 10:1-7   103
Died in the presence of the
Lord ....Num. 3:4   130
Dies with heirs....1 Chr. 24:2   409

Abihud—*the father is majesty*
A Benjamite ......1 Chr. 8:3   395

Abijah—*Yahweh is Father*
1. Wife of
Hezron........1 Chr. 2:24   389
2. Son of
Becher........1 Chr. 7:8   394
3. Samuel's second son; follows
corrupt
ways..........1 Sam. 8:2   268
4. Descendant of Aaron; head of
an office of
priests ......1 Chr. 24:3, 10   409
Zechariah belongs
to.............Luke 1:5   1025
5. Son of
Jeroboam I....1 Kin. 14:1-18   340
6. Slays 500,000
Israelites......2 Chr. 13:13-20   429
7. Fathers 38 children by 14
wives ....2 Chr. 13:21   429
8. The mother of
Hezekiah......2 Chr. 29:1   441
Called Abi .....2 Kin. 18:2   374
9. A priest who signs the
document ......Neh. 10:7   477
10. A priest returning from Babylon
with Zerub-
babel.........Neh. 12:1, 4, 17   478

Abijam (another form of Abijah)
King of Judah.....1 Kin. 14:31   341
Son and successor of King
Rehoboam.......1 Kin. 15:1-7   341
Follows in his father's
sins ....1 Kin. 15:3, 4   341
Wars against King
Jeroboam ....1 Kin. 15:6, 7   341

Abilene—*grassy place*
A province or tetrarchy of
Syria.............Luke 3:1   1028

Ability—*power to perform*
A. Descriptive of:
Material
prosperity.....Deut. 16:17   184
Emotional
strength ......Num. 11:14   139
Military   ⎰Num. 13:31   142
power......... ⎱1 Kin. 9:21   335
Physical
strength .....Ex. 18:18, 23   70
Mental
power........Gen. 15:5   16
Moral power...1 Cor. 3:2   1150
Spiritual
power........James 3:2   1254
Divine power..Rom. 4:21   1134
B. Of God's power to:
Deliver ......1 Cor. 10:13   1156
Humble men...Dan. 4:37   841
Create life .....Matt. 3:9   965
Destroy......Matt. 10:28   973
Preserve
believers .....John 10:28   1077
Keep His
promise.......Rom. 4:21   1134
Make us
stand ......Rom. 16:25   1145
Supply grace..2 Cor. 9:8   1171
Exceed our
petitions ......Eph. 3:20   1186
Service ....1 Pet. 4:11   1264

Comfort
others.........2 Cor. 1:4   1166
Keep what we have
entrusted .....2 Tim. 1:12   1223
Save from
death ....Heb. 5:7   1241
Resurrect
men..........Heb. 11:19   1246
Keep from
falling........Jude 24, 25   1288
C. *Of Christ's power to:*
Heal..........Matt. 9:28   972
Subject all
things........Phil. 3:21   1195
Help His
own..........Heb. 2:18   1240
Have
compassion ...Heb. 4:15, 16   1241
Save
completely ....Heb. 7:25   1243
D. *Of the Christian's power to:*
Speak for the
Lord ....Luke 21:15   1053
Admonish .....Rom. 15:14   1144
Survive
testings ....1 Cor. 3:13   1150
Withstand
Satan ....Eph. 6:11, 13   1190
Convince
opposition.....Titus 1:9   1229
Bridle the whole
body.........James 3:2   1254

Abimael—*God is Father*
A son of Joktan...Gen. 10:28   13

Abimelech—*the father is king*
1. A Philistine king of
Gerar ....Gen. 20:1-18   20
Makes treaty with
Abraham......Gen. 21:22-34   21
2. A second king of
Gerar ....Gen. 26:1-12   26
Tells Isaac to go
home ....Gen. 26:13-16   26
Makes a treaty with Isaac
concerning certain
wells..........Gen. 26:17-33   26
3. A son of Gideon by a
concubine....Judg. 8:31   240
Conspires to become
king ....Judg. 9:1-4   240
Kills his 70
brothers.......Judg. 9:5   241
Made king of
Shechem......Judg. 9:6   241
Rebuked by Jotham, lone
survivor......Judg. 9:7-21   241
Conspired against by
Gaal ....Judg. 9:22-29   241
Captures Shechem and
Thebez.......Judg. 9:41-50   242
Death of .....Judg. 9:51-57   242
4. A son of Abiathar the
priest ....1 Chr. 18:16   405
Also called
Ahimelech ...1 Chr. 24:6   409

Abinadab—*the father is generous*
1. A man of Kiriath-jearim whose
house tabernacles
the ark of the
Lord ....1 Sam. 7:1, 2   268
2. The second of Jesse's eight
sons ....1 Sam. 16:8   276
A soldier in Saul's
army.........1 Sam. 17:13   277
3. A son of Saul slain at Mt.
Gilboa .....1 Sam. 31:1-8   290
Bones of, buried by men of
Jabesh ......1 Chr. 10:1-12   397

Abinoam—*the father is pleasantness*
Father of Barak ...Judg. 4:6   235

Abiram—*the father is exalted*
1. Reubenite who rebeled against
Moses........Num. 16:1-50   144

2. The first-born ⎰1 Kin. 16:34   343
son of Hiel...⎱Josh. 6:26   211

Abishag—*the father wanders*
A Shunammite employed as
David's nurse.....1 Kin. 1:1-4, 15   323
Witnessed David's choice of
Solomon as
successor........1 Kin. 1:15-31   323
Adonijah killed for desiring to
marry her ....1 Kin. 2:13-25   325

Abishai—*father of a gift*
A son of Zeruiah, David's
sister...........2 Sam. 2:18   296
Brother of Joab and
Asahel ....1 Chr. 2:16   389
Rebuked by
David ....1 Sam. 26:5-9   287
Serves under Joab in David's
army ....2 Sam. 2:17, 18   296
Joins Joab in blood-revenge
against Abner ...2 Sam. 2:18-24   296
Co-commander of David's
army ....2 Sam. 10:9, 10   303
Loyal to David during Absalom's
uprising ....2 Sam. 16:9-12   309
Sternly rebuked by
David ....2 Sam. 19:21-23   313
Loyal to David
during Sheba's   ⎰2 Sam. 20:1-6,
rebellion........⎱   10   314
Kills 300
Philistines.......2 Sam. 23:18   317
Kills 18,000
Edomites.........1 Chr. 18:12, 13   405
Saves David by killing a
giant..........2 Sam. 21:16, 17   315

Abishalom—*father of peace*
A variant form of
Absalom..........1 Kin. 15:2, 10   341

Abishua—*the father is salvation*
1. A Benjamite ...1 Chr. 8:3, 4   395
2. Phinehas'
son...........1 Chr. 6:4, 5, 50   392

Abishur—*the father is a wall*
A Jerahmeelite....1 Chr. 2:28, 29   389

Abital—*the father is dew*
Wife of David.....2 Sam. 3:2, 4   297

Abitub—*the father is goodness*
A Benjamite ......1 Chr. 8:8-11   395

Abiud (Greek form of Abihud)
Ancestor of
Jesus.............Matt. 1:13   963

Ablution—*ceremonial washing*
Of priests ......Ex. 30:18-21   82
Ex. 40:30, 31   92
Of ceremonially   ⎰Lev. 14:7-9   108
unclean ....⎱Lev. 15:5-10   109
Of a house.......Lev. 14:52   109
By Pharisees .....Mark 7:1-5   1006

Abner—*the father is a lamp*
Commands Saul's
army.............1 Sam. 14:50, 51   275
Introduces David to
Saul.............1 Sam. 17:55-58   279
Rebuked by   ⎰1 Sam. 26:5,
David ....⎱   14-16   287
Saul's cousin....1 Sam. 14:50, 51   275
Supports Ish-bosheth as Saul's
successor........2 Sam. 2:8-10   296
Defeated by David's
men.............2 Sam. 2:12-17   296
Kills Asahel in
self-defense.....2 Sam. 2:18-23   296
Pursued by Joab ..2 Sam. 2:24-32   296
Slain by Joab ....2 Sam. 3:8-27   297
Death of, condemned by
David ....2 Sam. 3:28-39   297

SUBJECT	REFERENCE	PAGE

Abuse—*continued*
Immoral acts .. 1 Cor. 6:9   1152
Torture .... Judg. 16:21   248
B. *Of spiritual things:*
Misuse of   ⎰Num. 20:10-13   149
authority.....⎱1 Cor. 9:18   1155
Using the world
wrongly.....1 Cor. 7:31   1154
Perverting the
truth.........2 Pet. 2:10-22   1269
Corrupting God's
ordinances .... 1 Sam. 2:12-17   264
     1 Cor. 11:17-22   1157
C. *Manifested by:*
Unbelieving.... Mark 15:29-32   1019

Abyss—*bottomless pit*
Demons commanded to
depart to......Luke 8:31   1036
"Bottomless   ⎰Rev. 9:1, 2, 11   1299
pit" ....⎱Rev. 17:8   1304

Acacia wood—*wood of the shittah tree*
Used in:
Making the ark ... Ex. 25:10, 13   76
Table ....Ex. 37:10   88
Altar of incense .. Ex. 30:1   81
Altar of burnt
offering ....Ex. 38:1, 6   89
Tabernacle
boards...........Ex. 26:15-37   77

Accad—*a city in the land of Shinar*
City in Shinar.....Gen. 10:10   12

Acceptance—*the reception of one's person or service*
A. *Objects of, before God:*
Righteousness and
justice ....Prov. 21:3   624
Our words and
meditations ... Ps. 19:14   537
Our
dedication.....Rom. 12:1, 2   1141
Service ....Rom. 14:18   1143
Giving........Rom. 15:16, 27   1144
Offerings .....Phil. 4:18   1196
Intercession ... 1 Tim. 2:1-3   1217
Helping
parents ....1 Tim. 5:4   1219
Spiritual
sacrifices......1 Pet. 2:5   1261
Suffering because of
Christ.........1 Pet. 2:20   1262
B. *Qualifications of, seen in:*
Coming at   ⎰Is. 49:8   698
God's time ...⎱2 Cor. 6:2   1169
Meeting God's require-
ments.........Job 42:8, 9   523
Receiving divine
sign...........Judg. 6:9-21   237
Noting God's   ⎰1 Sam. 7:8-10   268
response .....⎱John 12:28-30   1079
Responding to God's
renewal.......Ezek. 20:40-44   803
Manifesting spiritual
rectitude......Mic. 6:6-8   894
C. *Persons disqualified for, such as:*
The wicked....Ps. 82:2   572
Blemished
sacrifices......Mal. 1:8, 10, 13   929
Man's person .. Gal. 2:6   1178
Those who swear
deceitfully .... Ps. 24:3-6   539

Access to God
A. *By means of:*
Christ ....John 14:6   1081
Christ's
blood ....Eph. 2:13   1186
Holy Spirit....Eph. 2:18   1186
Faith ....Rom. 5:2   1135
Clean hands ... Ps. 24:3-5   539
God's grace....Eph. 1:6   1185
Prayer........Matt. 6:6   968
B. *Characteristics of:*
On God's
choosing......Ps. 64:4   559

Sinners
commanded   ⎰Is. 55:6   703
to seek......⎱James 4:8   1255
With
confidence .... Heb. 4:16   1241
Boldness.......Eph. 3:12   1186
Results from reconcili-
ation..........Col. 1:21, 22   1200
Open to
Gentiles.......Acts 14:27   1111
Experienced in Christ's
priesthood .... Heb. 7:19-25   1243
Sought by God's
people ....Ps. 27:4   540
Bold in
prayer ....Heb. 4:16   1241
A blessing to be
chosen........Ps. 65:4   560

Accident—*event not foreseen*
A. *Caused by:*
An animal ..... Num. 22:25   151
A fall...........2 Sam. 4:4   298
B. *Explanation of:*
Known to   ⎰Deut. 29:29   196
God..........⎱Prov. 16:9, 33   621
Misunderstood by
men...........Luke 13:4, 5   1044
Subject to God's
providence....Rom. 8:28   1138

Acco—*a seaport 8 miles north of Mt. Carmel (modern Acre)*
Assigned to
Asher ....Judg. 1:31   233
Called Ptolemais in the New
Testament.......Acts 21:7   1118

Accommodation—*adaptation caused by human limitations*
A. *Physically, caused by:*
Age and sex ... Gen. 33:13-15   34
Strength and
size...........1 Sam. 17:38-40   278
Inability to
repay..........Luke 7:41, 42   1035
B. *Spiritually, caused by:*
Man's
blindness......Matt. 13:10-14   976
Absence of the
Spirit ....John 16:12, 13   1083
Men of flesh ... 1 Cor. 3:1, 2   1150
Spiritual
immaturity....Rom. 14:1-23   1143
Man's present
limitations ... 1 Cor. 2:7-16   1150
Degrees of
light ....Heb. 9:7-15   1244

Accomplish—*to fulfill*
A. *Of God's Word concerning:*
Judah's
captivity ......2 Chr. 36:23   450
Judah's
return ....Dan. 9:2   846
God's sovereign
plan...........Is. 55:11   703
The Messiah's
advent.........Dan. 9:24-27   847
Christ's
suffering......Luke 18:31   1050
Christ's
death ....John 19:28-30   1086
Final events ... Dan. 12:7   850
B. *Of human things:*
Food ....1 Kin. 5:9   329
Beautification
rites ....Esth. 2:12   486
Priestly
service........Luke 1:23   1025
Time of
pregnancy ..... Luke 2:6   1027
Sufferings .....1 Pet. 5:9   1264

Accord—*united agreement*
Descriptive of:
A spontaneous
response.........Acts 12:10, 20   1108
Voluntary
action.............2 Cor. 8:17   1170
Single-
mindedness.....Josh. 9:2   213
Spiritual unity .... Acts 1:14   1094

Accountability—*responsibility for own acts*
A. *Kinds of:*
Universal......Rom. 14:12   1143
Personal.......2 Sam. 12:1-15   304
Personal and
family.........Josh. 7:1-26   211
Personal and
national.......2 Sam. 24:1-17   318
Delayed but
exacted ....2 Sam. 21:1-14   315
Final ....Rom. 2:1-12   1132
B. *Determined by:*
Federal   ⎰Gen. 3:1-24   6
headship .....⎱Rom. 5:12-21   1135
Personal responsi-
bility.........Ezek. 18:1-32   800
Faithfulness ... Matt. 25:14-30   989
Knowledge .... Luke 12:47, 48   1043
Conscience ....Rom. 2:12-16   1132
Greater light... Rom. 2:17-29   1133
Maturity of
judgment .....1 Cor. 8:1-13   1154

Accursed—*under a curse*
A. *Caused by:*
Hanging on a
tree...........Deut. 21:23   188
Sin among God's
people ....Josh. 7:12   211
Possessing a banned
thing..........Josh. 6:18   210
Preaching contrary to the
Gospel ....Gal. 1:8, 9   1177
Blaspheming
Christ..........1 Cor. 12:3   1157
B. *Objects of being:*
A city ....Josh. 6:17   210
A forbidden
thing..........Josh. 22:20   226
An old sinner .. Is. 65:20   712
Christ haters or non-
believers ......1 Cor. 16:22   1162
Paul (for the sake of
Israel)........Rom. 9:3   1138

Accusations—*charges*
A. *Kinds of:*
Pagan ....Dan. 3:8   838
Personal.......Dan. 6:24   843
Public ....John 18:29   1085
Perverted...... 1 Pet. 3:16   1263
B. *Sources of, in:*
The devil ......Job 1:6-12   495
     Rev. 12:9, 10   1301
Enemies ......Ezra 4:6   456
Man's
conscience ....John 8:9   1073
God's Word.... John 5:45   1070
Hypocritical ... John 8:6, 10, 11   1073
The last days ..2 Tim. 3:1, 3   1224
Apostates......2 Pet. 2:10, 11   1269
C. *Forbidden:*
Against
servants.......Prov. 30:10   633
Falsely.........Luke 3:14   1029
Among
women........Titus 2:3   1230
D. *False, examples of, against:*
Jacob..........Gen. 31:26-30   32
Joseph.........Gen. 39:10-21   39
Ahimelech ... 1 Sam. 22:11-16   283
David..........2 Sam. 10:3   302
Job............Job 2:4, 5   496
Jeremiah ......Jer. 26:8-11   744
Amos..........Amos 7:10, 11   876
Joshua.........Zech. 3:1-5   919

SUBJECT	REFERENCE	PAGE	SUBJECT	REFERENCE	PAGE	SUBJECT	REFERENCE	PAGE

D. Our duties prescribed by Him:

Our mission—world evange-
lization ......Matt. 28:16-20   995

Our means—the Holy
Spirit ....Acts 1:8   1094

Our might—the
Gospel ....Rom. 1:16   1132

Our motivation—the love of
Christ.........2 Cor. 5:14, 15   1168

Aeneas—*praise*

A paralytic healed by
Peter..........Acts 9:32-35   1105

Aenon—*springs*

A place near Salim where John the
Baptist baptized ..John 3:22, 23   1066

**Affability—*a personality overflowing
with benign sociability***

A. Manifested in:

Cordiality.....Gen. 18:1-8   18
Compassion ...Luke 10:33-37   1040
Generosity.....Phil. 4:10, 14-18   1196
Unantagonizing
speech ....1 Sam. 25:23-31   286

B. Examples of:

Jonathan ......1 Sam. 18:1-4   279
Titus ....2 Cor. 8:16-18   1170
Timothy.......Phil. 2:17-20   1194
Gaius ....3 John 1-6   1284
Demetrius .....3 John 12   1284

Affectation—*a studied pretense*

Parade of
egotism ....Esth. 6:6-9   489
Boast of the
power............Dan. 4:29, 30   840
Sign of
hypocrisy......Matt. 6:1, 2, 16   968
Outbreak of false
teachers.........2 Pet. 2:18, 19   1269
Sign of
antichrist.........2 Thess. 2:4, 9   1212
Proof of spiritual
decay ....1 Cor. 4:6-8   1151

Affection—*an inner feeling or emotion*

A. Kinds of:

Natural.......Rom. 1:31   1132
Paternal ......Luke 15:20   1046
Maternal ......1 Kin. 3:16-27   327
Fraternal ......Gen. 43:30-34   44
Filial..........Gen. 49:29, 30   49
National ......Ps. 137:1-6   599
Racial ....Rom. 9:1-3   1138
For wife ......Eph. 5:25-33   1189
For husband ..Titus 2:4   1230
Christian .....Rom. 12:10   1142
Heavenly ......Col. 3:1, 2   1201

B. Good, characteristics of:

Loyal,
intense......Ruth 1:14-18   256
Memorable ....2 Sam. 1:17-27   295
Natural,
normal.......2 Sam. 13:37-39   307
Tested, tried ...Gen. 22:1-19   22
Emotional ....John 11:33-36   1078
Grateful ......Luke 7:36-50   1035
Joyous........Ps. 126:1-6   596
Christ-
centered .....Matt. 10:37-42   973

C. Evil, characteristics of:

Unnatural.....Rom. 1:18-32   1132
Pretended ....Matt. 26:47-49   992
Abnormal .....2 Tim. 3:3   1225
Fleshly ....Rom. 13:13, 14   1142
Worldly.......2 Tim. 4:10   1225
Defiling,
degrading ....2 Pet. 2:10-12   1269
Agonizing, in
Hades........Luke 16:23-28   1047

Afflicted—*the unfortunate of the earth*

Characteristics of:
Gladness.........Is. 29:19   681
Supported........Ps. 147:6   604
Beautified........Ps. 149:4   604

See also Tribulation

Afflictions—*hardships and trials*

A. Visited upon:

Israel in
Egypt.........Gen. 15:13   16
Samson by
Philistines.....Judg. 16:5, 6, 19   247
David by
God..........Ps. 88:7   574
Judah by
God..........Lam. 3:33   779
Israel by the
world ....Ps. 129:1, 2   597
The just by   {Amos 5:12   875
the wicked...{Heb. 11:37   1247
Christians by the
world ....2 Cor. 1:6   1166

B. Design of, to:

Show God's
mercy.........Is. 63:9   710
Make us seek
God..........Hos. 5:15   856
Bring us back to
God..........Ps. 119:67   592
Humble us.....2 Chr. 33:12   446
Test us ....Is. 48:10   697

C. In the Christian's life:

A means of
testing........Mark 4:17   1003
A part of life...Matt. 24:9   988
To be
endured.......2 Tim. 4:5   1225
Part of
Gospel ....1 Thess. 1:6   1206
Must not be disturbed
by ....1 Thess. 3:3   1207
Commendable
examples of...2 Tim. 3:11   1225
Momentary....2 Cor. 4:17   1168
Sometimes
intense........2 Cor. 1:8-10   1166
Must be
shared ....Phil. 4:14   1196
Cannot separate from
God...........Rom. 8:35-39   1138
Deliverance from,
promised......Ps. 34:19   544
Need
prayer in.....James 5:13   1256
Terminated at Christ's
return.........2 Thess. 1:4-7   1212

See also Trials

Afraid—*overcome with fear*

A. Caused by:

Nakedness.....Gen. 3:10   6
Unusual
dream........Gen. 28:16, 17   29
God's
presence .....Ex. 3:6   56
Moses'
approach......Ex. 34:30   86
A burning
mountain ....Deut. 5:5   174
Giant's
raging ....1 Sam. 17:11, 24   277
A prophet's
words.........1 Sam. 28:20   289
Angel's
sword.........1 Chr. 21:30   407
God's
judgments ....Ps. 65:8   560
Gabriel's
presence ......Dan. 8:17   845
A terrifying
storm ....Jon. 1:5, 10   885
Peter's
sinking........Matt. 14:30   978
Changed
person ....Mark 5:15   1004
Heavenly
hosts..........Luke 2:9   1027

B. Overcome by:

The Lord's
presence ......Ps. 3:5, 6   529
Trusting God ..Ps. 27:1-3   540

God's
protection.....Ps. 91:4, 5   576
Stability of
heart..........Ps. 112:7, 8   588
God's coming
judgment .....Is. 10:24-26   667
The Messiah's
advent ....Is. 40:9-11   689
God's sovereign
power.........Is. 51:12, 13   700
Christ's comforting
words........Matt. 14:27   978

**Afterbirth—*membranes expelled after
childbirth***

Woman hostile
toward ....Deut. 28:56, 57   195

Aftergrowth

Shall not reap.....Lev. 25:5, 11   119

**Afternoon—*part of the day following
noon***

Called cool of the
day...............Gen. 3:8   6
End of daylight ...Judg. 19:14   250

Afterthought—*a later reflection*

Of Esau...........Heb. 12:16, 17   1248
Of the Israelites...Num. 14:40-45   143
Of one of two
sons..............Matt. 21:28-30   985
Of the prodigal
son..............Luke 15:17   1046
Of the unjust
steward ....Luke 16:1-8   1047
Of the rich man in
Hades..........Luke 16:23-31   1047
Of Judas ....Matt. 27:3-5   993

Afterward(s)

Your hands
will be.........Judg. 7:11   239
Those who are
invited ....1 Sam. 9:13   270
David's conscience
bothered him.....1 Sam. 24:5   285
His mouth will ....Prov. 20:17   624
Jesus found him...John 5:14   1069

Agabus—*he loved*

A Christian prophet who foretells a
famine and   {Acts 11:27, 28   1107
warns Paul ......{Acts 21:10, 11   1118

Agag—*flaming or violent*

1. A King of Amalek in Balaam's
prophecy........Num. 24:7   153
2. Amalekite king
spared by Saul,
but slain by   {1 Sam. 15:8, 9,
Samuel......{ 20-24, 32, 33   275

Agagite—*descendant of Agag*

A title applied to Haman, enemy of
the Jews ....Esth. 3:1, 10   486

**Agape—*Greek word rendered both as
"love and charity"***

Descriptive of
God.............1 John 4:8   1277
Demanded toward
God.............Matt. 22:37   986
Demanded toward
neighbors ....Matt. 22:39   986
Fulfills Law ......Matt. 22:40   986
Activity of
described.........1 Cor. 13:1-13   1158

Agate—*a stone of translucent quartz*

Worn by the high
priest.............Ex. 28:19   79

Age—*time counted by years*

A. Handicaps of, seen in:

Physical
infirmities.....Gen. 48:10   48
Unwillingness to
adventure.....2 Sam. 19:31-39   313

43

SUBJECT	REFERENCE	PAGE	SUBJECT	REFERENCE	PAGE	SUBJECT	REFERENCE	PAGE

Aliens—*citizens of a foreign country*

A. *Descriptive, naturally, of:*
Israel in the Egyptian
bondage ......Gen. 15:13   16
Abraham in
Canaan ......Gen. 23:4   22
Moses in
Egypt.........Ex. 18:3   69
Israel in
Babylon.......Ps. 137:4   599

B. *Descriptive, spiritually, of:*
Estrangement from
friends ....Job 19:15   507
Israel's   {Ezek. 23:17, 18,
apostasy .....{   22, 28   806
The condition of the
Gentiles.......Eph. 2:12   1186
Spiritual
deadness .....Eph. 4:18   1188

Alive—*the opposite of being dead*

A. *Descriptive of:*
Natural life ....Gen. 43:7, 27, 28   43
Spiritual life ...Luke 15:24, 32   1046
Restored physical
life...........Acts 9:41   1105
Christ's resurrected
life...........Acts 1:3   1094
The believer's glorified
life...........1 Cor. 15:22   1160
The unbeliever's life in
Sheol ....Num. 16:33   145

B. *The power of keeping:*
Belongs to
God...........Deut. 32:39   200
Not in man's
power.........Ps. 22:29   538
Promised to the
godly ....Ps. 33:19   544
Gratefully acknowl-
edged.........Josh. 14:10   218
Transformed by Christ's
return.........1 Thess. 4:15, 16   1208

Allammelech—*oath of a king*

Village of Asher...Josh. 19:26   222

Allegory—*an extended figure of speech using symbols*

A. *Of natural things:*
A king's
doom ....Judg. 9:8-15   241
Old age........Eccl. 12:3-7   645
Israel as a transplanted
vine...........Ps. 80:8-19   571

B. *Of spiritual things:*
Christian as
sheep ....John 10:1-16   1076
Two
covenants.....Gal. 4:21-31   1180
Israel and the
Gentiles.......Rom. 11:15-24   1140
Christ and His
Church ....Eph. 5:22-33   1189
The Christian's
armor.........Eph. 6:11-17   1190

Allemeth

A Levitical city....1 Chr. 6:60   393

Alliance with evil

A. *Forbidden to:*
Israel..........Ex. 34:11-16   85
Christians .....Rom. 13:12   1142
Christ ....Matt. 4:1-11   965

B. *Forbidden because:*
Leads to
idolatry ....Ex. 23:32, 33   75
Deceives.......Num. 25:1-3, 18   154
Enslaves.......2 Pet. 2:18, 19   1269
Defiles.........Ezra 9:1, 2   461
Brings God's
anger ....Ezra 9:13-15   461
Corrupts.......1 Cor. 15:33   1160
Incompatible with
Christ.........2 Cor. 6:14-16   1169
Pollutes.......Jude 23   1288

C. *The believer should:*
Avoid..........Prov. 1:10-15   609
Hate...........Ps. 26:4, 5   540
Confess.......Ezra 10:9-11   462
Separate
from ....2 Cor. 6:17   1169

D. *Examples of:*
Solomon.......1 Kin. 11:1-11   336
Jeroboam......1 Kin. 12:25-33   338
Jehoshaphat ...2 Chr. 20:35-37   435
Judas
Iscariot ......Matt. 26:14-16   991
Heretics ......Rev. 2:14-15, 20   1294

See Association

Alliances—*treaties between nations or individuals*

A. *In the time of the patriarchs:*
Abraham with Canaanite
chiefs ....Gen. 14:13   16
Abraham with
Abimelech ....Gen. 21:22-34   21
Isaac with
Abimelech ....Gen. 26:26-33   26
Jacob with
Laban.........Gen. 31:44-54   32

B. *In the time of the wilderness:*
Israel with
Moab ....Num. 25:1-3   154

C. *In the time of the conquest:*
Israel with
Gibeonites ....Judg. 9:3-27   240

D. *In the time of David:*
David with
Achish........1 Sam. 27:2-12   288

E. *In the time of Solomon:*
Solomon with
Hiram........1 Kin. 5:12-18   329
Solomon with
Egypt.........1 Kin. 3:1   326

F. *In the time of the divided kingdom:*
Asa with Ben-
hadad.........1 Kin. 15:18-20   342
Ahab with Ben-
hadad.........1 Kin. 20:31-34   348
Israel with
Aram ....2 Kin. 16:5-9   372
Hoshea with
Egypt.........2 Kin. 17:1-6   372

G. *In the time of Judah's sole kingdom:*
Hezekiah with
Egypt.........2 Kin. 18:19-24   375
Josiah with
Assyria ....2 Kin. 23:29   381
Jehoiakim with
Egypt.........2 Kin. 23:31-35   381

All in all—*complete*

Descriptive of:
God.............1 Cor. 15:28   1160
Christ...........Eph. 1:23   1185

Allon—*oak*

1. A Simeonite
prince.........1 Chr. 4:37   391
2. A town in south
Naphtali ......Josh. 19:33   223

Allon-bacuth—*oak of weeping*

A tree marking Deborah's
grave............Gen. 35:8   35

Allowance—*a stipulated amount*

Daily to
Jehoiachin.....2 Kin. 25:27-30   383
Also called daily
portion...........Jer. 52:34   773

Almighty—*a title of God*

Applied to   {Gen. 17:1   17
God ....{2 Cor. 6:18   1169
Applied to
Christ ....Rev.·1:8   1294

Almodad—*the beloved*

Eldest son of
Joktan ....Gen. 10:26   13

Almond—*a small tree bearing fruit*

Sent as a present to
Pharaoh.........Gen. 43:11   43
Used in the
tabernacle......Ex. 25:33, 34   76
Aaron's rod
produces ......Num. 17:2, 3, 8   146
Used figuratively of old
age.............Eccl. 12:5   645
Used by Jacob ...Gen. 30:37   31

Almon-diblathaim—*Almon of the double cake of figs*

An Israelite
encampment .....Num. 33:46, 47   163

Alms, almsgiving—*gifts prompted by love to help the needy*

A. *Design of, to:*
Help the
poor ....Lev. 25:35   120
Receive a
blessing.......Deut. 15:10, 11   183

B. *Manner of bestowing with:*
A willing
spirit..........Deut. 15:7-11   183
Simplicity.....Matt. 6:1-4   968
Cheerful-
ness..........2 Cor. 9:7   1171
True love.....1 Cor. 13:3   1158
Fairness to
all ....Acts 4:32-35   1098
Regularity .....Acts 11:29, 30   1107
Law of
reciprocity ....Rom. 15:25-27   1144

C. *Cautions concerning:*
Not for man's
honor.........Matt. 6:1-4   968
Not for lazy ...2 Thess. 3:10   1213
Needful for the
rich...........1 Tim. 6:17, 18   1220

D. *Rewarded:*
Now...........Deut. 14:28, 29   183
    2 Cor. 9:9, 10   1171
In heaven .....Matt. 19:21   983

E. *Examples of:*
Zaccheus .....Luke 19:8   1050
Dorcas.........Acts 9:36   1105
Cornelius......Acts 10:2   1105
The early
Christians.....Acts 4:34-37   1098

Almug—*a tree* (probably the red sandalwood)

Imported from Ophir by
Hiram's navy.....1 Kin. 10:11, 12   335
Used in constructing the
Temple...........2 Chr. 9:10, 11   426
Also imported from
Lebanon.........2 Chr. 2:8   420

Aloes—*a perfume-bearing tree*

A. *Used on:*
Beds...........Prov. 7:17   614
The dead ......John 19:39   1087

B. *Figurative of:*
Israel..........Num. 24:5, 6   153
The Church....Ps. 45:8   551

Alpha and Omega—*first and last letters of the Greek alphabet ("A to Z")*

Expressive of God
and Christ's   {Rev. 1:8, 17, 18   1294
eternity ....{Rev. 21:6, 7   1307

Alphabet—*the letters of a language*

The Hebrew, seen
in ....Ps. 119   590

Alphaeus—*leader, chief*

1. The father of Levi
(Matthew) ....Mark 2:14   1001
2. The father of
James.........Matt. 10:3   972

Special
honor.........1 Sam. 24:6, 10   285
Special
privilege ......Ps. 105:15   583
God's
blessing.......Ps. 23:5   539

Anointing of the Holy Spirit

A. *Of Christ:*
Predicted ......Is. 61:1   708
Fulfilled ....John 1:32-34   1065
Explained.....Luke 4:18   1030

B. *Of Christians:*
Predicted .....Ezek. 47:1-12   829
Foretold by
Christ.........John 7:38, 39   1073
Fulfilled at
Pentecost ....Acts 2:1-41   1095
Fulfilled at   (2 Cor. 1:21   1166
conversion...(1 John 2:20, 27   1275

Answer—*a reply*

A. *Good:*
Gentle........Prov. 15:1   620
Confident.....Dan. 3:16-18   838
Convicting....Dan. 5:17-28   841
Amazing......Luke 2:47   1028
Unan-
swerable .....Luke 20:3-8   1051
Spon-
taneous.......Luke 21:14, 15   1053
Spirit-
directed.......Luke 12:11, 12   1042
Ready ....1 Pet. 3:15   1263

B. *Evil:*
Unwise........1 Kin. 12:12-15   338
Incrim-
inating........2 Sam. 1:5-16   295
Insolent ......2 Kin. 18:27-36   375
Humiliating....Esth. 6:6-11   489
Satanic ......Job 1:8-11   495

Ant—*a small insect*

An example of   (Prov. 6:6-8   613
industry.........(Prov. 30:24   633

Antagonism—*unceasing opposition*

A. *Of men, against:*
God's   (Ex. 5:1-19   57
people ....(Deut. 2:26-33   171
The   (Amos 7:10-17   876
prophets .....(Zech. 1:2-6   918
The light .....John 3:19, 20   1066
The truth......John 8:12-47   1073
  Acts 7:54-60   1102
Christians ....Acts 16:16-24   1113

B. *Of Satan, against:*
Job ....Job 2:9-12   496
Christ ....Luke 4:1-13   1029
Peter ....Luke 22:31-34   1055
Paul ....1 Thess. 2:18   1207
Christians ....Eph. 6:11-18   1190

Antediluvians—*those who lived before the flood*

A. *Described as:*
Long-lived.....Gen. 5:3-32   8
Very wicked...Gen. 6:5   9
A mixed   (Gen. 6:1-4   9
race.........(Jude 6, 7   1287
Of great size...Gen. 6:4   9

B. *Warnings against, made by:*
Enoch ....Jude 14, 15   1287
Noah ....2 Pet. 2:5   1268
Christ ....1 Pet. 3:19, 20   1263

C. *Destruction of:*
Only Noah's family
escaped ....Gen. 7:21-23   10
Predicted .....Gen. 6:5-7   9
Comparable
to Christ's   (Matt. 24:37-39   989
return.......(Luke 17:26, 27   1048
Comparable to the world's
end ....2 Pet. 3:3-7   1269

Antelope—*ruminant mammal*

Approved for
food.............Deut. 14:5   182

Caught in nets....Is. 51:20   701

Anthothijah—*answers of Yahweh*

A Benjamite ......1 Chr. 8:24   395

Anthropomorphisms—*applying human attributes to God*

A. *Physical likenesses, such as:*
Feet ....Ex. 24:10   75
Hands ....Ex. 24:11   75
Mouth........Num. 12:8   141
Eyes...........Hab. 1:13   904
Arms ....Ex. 6:6   58

B. *Non-physical characteristics, such as:*
Memory ....Gen. 9:16   12
Anger ....Ex. 22:24   74
Jealousy.......Ps. 78:58   570
Repentance....Jon. 3:10   886

Antichrist—*Satan's final opponent of Christ and Christians*

A. *Called:*
Man of
lawlessness....2 Thess. 2:3   1212
Son of
destruction....2 Thess. 2:3   1212
Wicked one...2 Thess. 2:8   1212
Antichrist.....1 John 2:18, 22   1275
Beast..........Rev. 11:7   1300

B. *Described as:*
Lawless........2 Thess. 2:3-12   1212
Opposing
Christ.........2 Thess. 2:4   1212
Working
wonders ......2 Thess. 2:9   1212
Deceiving the   (2 John 7   1281
world ....(Rev. 19:20   1306
Persecuting
Christians.....Rev. 13:7   1301
Satan-
inspired.......2 Thess. 2:9   1212
Denying Christ's
incarnation ...1 John 4:3   1277
  2 John 7   1281
One and
many ....1 John 2:18-22   1275
A person and a
system ....2 Thess. 2:3, 7   1212
Seeking man's
worship.......2 Thess. 2:4   1212

C. *Coming of:*
Foretold ......2 Thess. 2:5   1212
In the last
time ....1 John 2:18   1275
Now
restrained.....2 Thess. 2:6   1212
Follows removal of
hindrance.....2 Thess. 2:7, 8   1212
Before Christ's
return.........2 Thess. 2:8   1212
By Satan's
deception.....2 Thess. 2:9, 10   1212

D. *Destruction of:*
At Christ's   (2 Thess. 2:8   1212
return.......(Rev. 19:20   1306
Eternal in lake of
fire...........Rev. 20:10   1306

Antidote—*a remedy given to counteract poison*

A. *Literal:*
A tree ....Ex. 15:23-25   68
Meal...........2 Kin. 4:38-41   359

B. *Figurative and spiritual, for:*
Sin, Christ.....Num. 21:8,9   150
  John 3:14, 15   1066
Christ's absence, the Holy
Spirit ....John 14:16-18   1081
Sorrow, joy....John 16:20-22   1083
Satan's lies, God's
truth..........1 John 4:1-6   1277
Earth's trials,
faith ....1 Pet. 1:6-8   1260
Testings,   (1 Cor. 10:13   1156
God's grace ..(2 Cor. 12:7-9   1173
Suffering, heaven's
glory..........Rom. 8:18   1138
  2 Cor. 5:1-10   1168

Antinomianism—*the idea that Christian liberty exempts one from the moral law*

A. *Prevalence of, among:*
Christians .....Rom. 6:1-23   1135
False   (2 Pet. 2:19   1269
Teachers.....(Jude 4   1287

B. *Based on error, that:*
Grace allows
sin............Rom. 6:1, 2   1135
Moral law is
abolished......Rom. 7:1-14   1136
Liberty has no
bounds........1 Cor. 10:23-33   1156

C. *Corrected by remembering, that liberty is:*
Not a license to
sin............Rom. 6:1-23   1135
Limited by moral
law ....Rom. 8:1-4   1137
Controlled by Holy
Spirit ....Rom. 8:5-14   1137
Not to be a
stumbling   (Rom. 14:1-23   1143
block ....(1 Cor. 8:1-13   1154
Motivated by
love...........Gal. 5:13-15   1180

Antioch—*a city of Syria*

Home of Nicolas ..Acts 6:5   1100
Haven of persecuted
Christians........Acts 11:19   1107
Home of first Gentile
church ....Acts 11:20, 21   1107
Name "Christian" originated
in ....Acts 11:26   1107
Barnabas ministered
here..............Acts 11:22-24   1107
Barnabas and Paul minister in
church of.........Acts 11:25-30   1107
Paul
commissioned by (Acts 13:1-4   1108
church of.......(Acts 15:35-41   1112
Paul reports to....Acts 14:26-28   1111
Church of,
troubled by   (Acts 15:1-4   1111
Judaizers........(Gal. 2:11-21   1178

Antioch—*a city of Pisidia*

Jewish
synagogue......Acts 13:14   1109
Paul visits........Acts 13:14, 42   1109
Jews of, reject the
Gospel.........Acts 13:45-51   1109
Paul revisits.......Acts 14:21   1110
Paul recalls
persecution at ....2 Tim. 3:11   1225

Antipas

A Christian martyr of
Pergamum ......Rev. 2:13   1294

Antipatris—*belonging to Antipater*

A city between Jerusalem and
Caesarea ....Acts 23:31   1121

Antonia, Tower of—*fortress built by Herod the Great, not mentioned by name in Scripture*

Called
"barracks" ......Acts 21:30-40   1119
Possible site of Jesus' trial, called
"the Pavement" ..John 19:13   1086

Anub—*strong*

A man of Judah...1 Chr. 4:8   390

Anvil—*a block for forging hot metals*

Used figuratively
in ....Is. 41:7   690

Anxiety—*A disturbed state of mind produced by real or imaginary fears*

A. *Caused by:*
Brother's
hatred ....Gen. 32:6-12   33
Son's
rebellion ......2 Sam. 18:24-33   312

SUBJECT	REFERENCE	PAGE	SUBJECT	REFERENCE	PAGE	SUBJECT	REFERENCE	PAGE

Anxiety—continued

King's decree . . Esth. 4:1-17 — 487

Child's

absence . . . . . . Luke 2:48 — 1028

Son's

sickness . . . . . . John 4:46-49 — 1068

Friend's

delay . . . . 2 Cor. 2:12, 13 — 1167

B. *Overcome by:*

Trust . . . . Ps. 37:1-5 — 546

Reliance upon the Holy

Spirit . . . . Mark 13:11 — 1015

God's

provision . . . . . Luke 12:22-30 — 1042

Upward look . . . Luke 21:25-28 — 1053

Assurance of God's

sovereignty . . . Rom. 8:28 — 1138

Angel's word . . Acts 27:21-25 — 1125

Prayer . . . . Phil. 4:6 — 1195

God's care . . . . . 1 Pet. 5:6, 7 — 1264

See Cares, worldly

Ape—*a monkey*

Article of trade . . . . 1 Kin. 10:22 — 336

Apelles

A Christian in

Rome . . . . Rom. 16:10 — 1145

Aphek—*strength, fortress*

1. A town in Plain of

Sharon . . . . Josh. 12:18 — 217

Site of

Philistine　　(1 Sam. 4:1 — 266

camp . . . . (1 Sam. 29:1 — 289

2. A city assigned to

Asher . . . . Josh. 19:30 — 223

3. Border city . . . . Josh. 13:4 — 217

4. A city in

Jezreel . . . . 1 Kin. 20:26-30 — 348

Aram's defeat prophesied

here . . . . 2 Kin. 13:14-19 — 368

Aphekah—*fortress*

A city of Judah . . . Josh. 15:53 — 220

Aphiah—*striving*

An ancestor of King

Saul . . . . 1 Sam. 9:1 — 269

Aphik—*strength, fortress*

Spared by Asher . . Judg. 1:31 — 233

See Aphek 2

Apocrypha—*hidden things*

Writings in Greek written during
the period between the
Testaments; rejected by
Protestants as uninspired

Apollonia—*pertaining to Apollo*

A town between Amphipolis and

Thessalonica . . . . Acts 17:1 — 1114

Apollos—*a short or pet name for
Apollonios*

An Alexandrian Jew mighty in the

Scriptures . . . . Acts 18:24, 25 — 1116

Receives further

instruction . . . . . . Acts 18:26 — 1116

Sent to preach in

Achaia . . . . Acts 18:27, 28 — 1116

A minister in　　(1 Cor. 1:12 — 1149

Corinth . . . . (1 Cor. 3:4, 22 — 1150

Cited by Paul . . . 1 Cor. 4:6 — 1151

Urged to revisit

Corinth . . . . 1 Cor. 16:12 — 1161

Journey of, noted by

Paul . . . . Titus 3:13 — 1231

Apollyon—*the destroyer*

Angel of the bottomless

pit . . . . Rev. 9:11 — 1299

Apostasy—*a falling away from God's
truth*

A. *Kinds of:*

National . . . . 1 Kin. 12:26-33 — 338

Individual . . . . . 2 Kin. 21:1-9 — 377

　　　　　　　　Heb. 3:12 — 1240

Satanic . . . . Rev. 12:7-9 — 1301

Angelic . . . . 2 Pet. 2:4 — 1268

General . . . . 2 Tim. 3:1-5 — 1224

Imputed . . . . . . Acts 21:21 — 1119

Final . . . . 2 Thess. 2:3 — 1212

Irremedial . . . . Heb. 6:1-8 — 1242

B. *Caused by:*

Satan . . . . Luke 22:31 — 1055

False

teachers . . . . . Acts 20:29, 30 — 1118

Perversion of

Scripture . . . . . . 2 Tim. 4:3, 4 — 1225

Persecution . . . Matt. 13:21 — 976

Unbelief . . . . . . Heb. 4:9-11 — 1241

Love of

world . . . . 2 Tim. 4:10 — 1225

Hardened

heart . . . . Acts 7:54, 57 — 1102

Spiritual

blindness . . . . Acts 28:25-27 — 1126

C. *Manifested in:*

Resisting

truth . . . . 2 Tim. 3:7, 8 — 1225

Resorting to

deception . . . . . 2 Cor. 11:13-15 — 1172

Reverting to　　(2 Pet. 2:14, 19-

immorality . . . (　　　 22 — 1269

D. *Safeguards against, found in:*

God's Word . . . 2 Tim. 3:13-17 — 1225

Spiritual

growth . . . . 2 Pet. 1:5-11 — 1268

Indoc-

trination . . . . . Acts 20:29-31 — 1118

Faithfulness . . . Matt. 24:42-51 — 989

Spiritual

perception . . . . 1 John 4:1-6 — 1277

Being grounded in the

truth . . . . Eph. 4:13-16 — 1187

Using God's

armor . . . . Eph. 6:10-20 — 1190

Preaching the

Word . . . . 2 Tim. 4:2, 5 — 1225

E. *Examples of, seen in:*

Israelites . . . . . . Ex. 32:1-35 — 83

Saul . . . . 1 Sam. 15:11 — 275

Solomon . . . . 1 Kin. 11:1-10 — 336

Amaziah . . . . . . 2 Chr. 25:14-16 — 438

Judas . . . . Matt. 26:14-16 — 991

Hymenaeus and

Philetus . . . . . 2 Tim. 2:17, 18 — 1224

Demas . . . . 2 Tim. 4:10 — 1225

Certain men . . . Jude 4 — 1287

Apostles—*men divinely commissioned
to represent Christ*

A. *Descriptive of:*

Christ . . . . Heb. 3:1 — 1240

The twelve . . . . Matt. 10:2 — 972

Others (Barnabas, James,

etc.) . . . . Acts 14:4 — 1110

　　　　　　　　Gal. 1:19 — 1178

Messengers . . . . 2 Cor. 8:23 — 1171

False

teachers . . . . . . 2 Cor. 11:13 — 1172

Simon Peter . . . Matt. 10:2 — 972

Andrew . . . . Matt. 10:2 — 972

James, son of

Zebedee . . . . . . Matt. 10:2 — 972

John . . . . Matt. 10:2 — 972

Philip . . . . Matt. 10:3 — 972

Bartholomew

(Na-　　　　(Matt. 10:3 — 972

thanael) . . . . . (John 1:45 — 1065

Thomas . . . . . . Matt. 10:3 — 972

Matthew　　　(Matt. 10:3 — 972

(Levi) . . . . (Luke 5:27 — 1032

James, son of

Alphaeus . . . . . Matt. 10:3 — 972

Thaddaeus　　(Matt. 10:3 — 972

(Judas) . . . . . . (John 14:22 — 1082

Simon the

Zealot . . . . Luke 6:15 — 1032

Judas

Iscariot . . . . . . Matt. 10:4 — 972

Matthias . . . . . . Acts 1:26 — 1095

Paul . . . . 2 Cor. 1:1 — 1166

Barnabas . . . . . Acts 14:14 — 1110

James, the Lord's

brother . . . . Gal. 1:19 — 1178

Silvanus and　(1 Thess. 1:1 — 1206

Timothy . . . . . (1 Thess. 2:9 — 1207

Andronicus and

Junias . . . . Rom. 16:7 — 1144

B. *Mission of, to:*

Perform

miracles . . . . . . Matt. 10:1, 8 — 972

Preach

Gospel . . . . Matt. 28:19, 20 — 995

Witness Christ's

resur-　　　　(Acts 1:22 — 1095

rection . . . . . . (Acts 10:40-42 — 1106

Write

Scripture . . . . . Eph. 3:5 — 1186

Establish the

Church . . . . Eph. 2:20 — 1186

C. *Limitations of, before
Pentecost:*

Lowly in

position . . . . . . Matt. 4:18 — 966

Unlearned . . . . . Acts 4:13 — 1098

Subject to

disputes . . . . . . Matt. 20:20-28 — 984

Faith often

obscure . . . . . . Matt. 16:21-23 — 980

Need of

instruction . . . . Matt. 17:4, 9-13 — 980

D. *Position of, after Pentecost:*

Interpreted

prophecy . . . . . Acts 2:14-36 — 1095

Defended

truth . . . . Phil. 1:7, 17 — 1193

Exposed

heretics . . . . . . Gal. 1:6-9 — 1177

Upheld

discipline . . . . . 2 Cor. 13:1-6 — 1174

Established

churches . . . . . Rom. 15:17-20 — 1144

Appaim—*nostrils*

A man of Judah . . . 1 Chr. 2:30, 31 — 389

Apparel—*clothing*

A. *Kinds of:*

Harlot's . . . . Gen. 38:14 — 38

Virgin's . . . . 2 Sam. 13:18 — 306

Mourner's . . . . . 2 Sam. 12:20 — 305

Splendid . . . . . . Luke 7:25 — 1034

Rich . . . . Ezek. 27:24 — 810

Worldly . . . . 1 Pet. 3:3 — 1262

Showy . . . . Luke 16:19 — 1047

Official . . . . 1 Kin. 10:5 — 335

Royal . . . . Esth. 6:8 — 489

Priestly . . . . Ezra 3:10 — 456

Angelic . . . . Acts 1:10 — 1094

Heavenly . . . . . Rev. 19:8 — 1305

B. *Attitude toward:*

Not to covet . . . Acts 20:33 — 1118

Without

show . . . . 1 Pet. 3:3 — 1262

Be modest in . . 1 Tim. 2:9 — 1218

C. *Figurative of:*

Christ's

blood . . . . Is. 63:1-3 — 710

Christ's righteous-

ness . . . . Zech. 3:1-5 — 919

The Church's

purity . . . . Ps. 45:13, 14 — 551

Apparition—*appearance of ghost or
disembodied spirit*

Samuel . . . . 1 Sam. 28:12-14 — 288

Christ mistaken　(Matt. 14:26 — 978

for . . . . (Luke 24:37, 39 — 1058

Appeal—*petition for higher judgment*

To Christ . . . . Luke 12:13, 14 — 1042

Of Paul,　　　　(Acts 25:11, 25-28 — 1123

to Caesar . . . . . . (Acts 26:32 — 1124

Appearance, outward

A. *Can conceal:*

Deception . . . . . Josh. 9:3-16 — 213

Hypocrisy . . . . . Matt. 23:25-28 — 987

Rottenness . . . . Acts 12:21-23 — 1108

SUBJECT	REFERENCE	PAGE	SUBJECT	REFERENCE	PAGE	SUBJECT	REFERENCE	PAGE

Reproved by a
prophet . . . . . . .2 Chr. 16:7-10 431
Diseased, seeks physicians
rather than the
Lord . . . . .2 Chr. 16:12 431
Buried in
Jerusalem . . . . .2 Chr. 16:13, 14 431
An ancestor of
Christ . . . . .Matt. 1:7 963
2. A Levite among
returnees . . . . .1 Chr. 9:16 396

Asahel—*God has made*

1. A son of Zeruiah, David's
sister . . . . .1 Chr. 2:16 389
Noted for ⎰2 Sam. 2:18 296
valor . . . . ⎱2 Sam. 23:24 318
Pursues
Abner . . . . .2 Sam. 2:19 296
Killed by
Abner . . . . .2 Sam. 2:23 296
Avenged by
Joab . . . . .2 Sam. 3:27, 30 297
Made a commander in David's
army . . . . .1 Chr. 27:7 412
2. A Levite
teacher . . . . . . .2 Chr. 17:8 431
3. A collector of
tithes . . . . .2 Chr. 31:13 444
4. A priest who opposes Ezra's
reforms . . . . . .Ezra 10:15 462

Asaiah—*Yahweh has made*

1. A Simeonite
chief . . . . .1 Chr. 4:36 391
2. A Levite during David's
reign . . . . .1 Chr. 6:30 392
Helps restore ark to
Jerusalem . . . . .1 Chr. 15:6, 11 401
3. An officer sent to
Huldah . . . . . . .2 Chr. 34:20-22 447
2 Kin. 22:12-14 379
4. The first-born of the
Shilonites . . . . .1 Chr. 9:5 396
Probably called
Maaseiah . . . . .Neh. 11:5 478

Asaph—*collector*

1. A Gershonite Levite choir
leader in the
time of David ⎰1 Chr. 15:16-19 401
and ⎱1 Chr. 16:4-7 402
Solomon . . . . .2 Chr. 5:12 422
Called a seer . . .2 Chr. 29:30 442
Sons of, made
musicians . . . . .1 Chr. 25:1-9 410
Twelve Psalms⎰Ps. 50—83 553
assigned to . . .⎱2 Chr. 29:30 442
Descendants of,
among ⎰Ezra 2:41 454
returnees . . . . .⎱Neh. 7:44 472
In dedication
ceremony . . . . .Ezra 3:10 456
2. The father of Hezekiah's
recorder . . . . . . .2 Kin. 18:18, 37 374
3. A chief forester whom
Artaxerxes commands to
supply timber to
Nehemiah . . . . .Neh. 2:8 468
4. A Korahite
Levite . . . . .1 Chr. 26:1 411
Also called
Ebiasaph . . . . . .1 Chr. 9:19 396

Asarel—*God has bound*

A son of
Jehallelel . . . . .1 Chr. 4:16 390

Ascension—*rising to a higher place*

A. *Descriptive of:*
Physical rising⎰Ex. 19:18 71
of smoke . . . . .⎱Josh. 8:20, 21 212
Going up hill . .Luke 19:28 1051
Rising to
heaven . . . . .Ps. 139:8 600
Christ's
ascension . . . . .John 6:62 1071
Sinful
ambition . . . . . .Is. 14:13, 14 670

B. *Of saints:*
Enoch, taken ⎰Gen. 5:24 9
up . . . .⎱Heb. 11:5 1246
Elijah,
translation ⎰2 Kin. 2:11 356
of . . . .⎱Matt. 17:1-9 980
Christians, at
Christ's ⎰1 Thess. 4:13-18 1208
return . . . .⎱1 Cor. 15:51, 52 1161

C. *Of Christ:*
Foretold in
the Old ⎰Ps. 68:18 561
Testament . . .⎱Eph. 4:8-10 1187
Announced ⎰Luke 9:51 1039
by Christ . . . . .⎱John 20:17 1087
Forty days after
His resur- ⎰Luke 24:48-51 1059
rection . . . .⎱Acts 1:1-12 1094
Necessary for the Spirit's
coming . . . . . . .John 16:7 1083
Enters heaven by
redemp- ⎰Heb. 6:19, 20 1242
tion . . . .⎱Heb. 9:12, 24 1244
Crowned with glory and
honor . . . . .Heb. 2:9 1240
Rules from David's
throne . . . . .Acts 2:29-36 1096
Sits at the
Father's ⎰Eph. 1:20 1185
side . . . .⎱Heb. 1:3 1239
Intercedes for the
saints . . . . .Rom. 8:34 1138
Preparing place for His
people . . . . . . .John 14:2 1081
Highly ⎰Acts 5:31 1099
exalted . . . .⎱Phil. 2:9 1194
Reigns tri- ⎰1 Cor. 15:24-28 1160
umphantly . .⎱Heb. 10:12, 13 1245
Exercises priestly
ministry . . . . . .Heb. 4:14-16 1241
Heb. 8:1, 2 1243

Asceticism—*stern restraint upon bodily appetites*

A. *Forms of, seen in:*
Nazarite,
vow . . . . .Num. 6:1-21 133
Manoah's
wife . . . . .Judg. 13:3-14 245
Samson . . . . . . .Judg. 16:16, 17 248
Elijah's life . . . .1 Kin. 19:4-9 346
The
Rechabites . . . .Jer. 35:1-19 753
John the ⎰Matt. 3:4 965
Baptist . . . .⎱Matt. 11:18 973
Jesus Christ . . .Matt. 4:2 965
Paul . . . . .1 Cor. 9:27 1155

B. *Teaching concerning:*
Extreme,
repudiated . . . .Luke 7:33-36 1035
False, ⎰Col. 2:20-23 1201
rejected . . . . . .⎱1 Tim. 4:3, 4 1219
Some, ⎰1 Cor. 9:26, 27 1155
necessary . . . .⎱2 Tim. 2:3, 4 1224
Temporary ⎰Ezra 8:21-23 460
helpful . . . .⎱1 Cor. 7:3-9 1153
Figurative of complete
consecra- ⎰Matt. 19:12 983
tion . . . .⎱Rev. 14:1-5 1302

Asenath—*belonging to the goddess Neith*

Daughter of Potiphera and wife of
Joseph . . . . .Gen. 41:45 41
Mother of Manasseh and
Ephraim . . . . .Gen. 41:50-52 42
Gen. 46:20 46

Ashamed—*shame instilled by evil doing*

A. *Caused by:*
Mistreat-
ment . . . . .2 Sam. 10:4, 5 303
Sad tidings . . . .2 Kin. 8:11-13 363
Trans-
gression . . . . . .Ps. 25:3 539
Inconsistent
action . . . . .Ezra 8:22 460
Idolatry . . . . . . .Is. 44:9-17 694

Rebellion against
God . . . . .Is. 45:24 696
Lewdness . . . . . .Ezek. 16:27 798
False
prophecy . . . . . .Zech. 13:3, 4 925
Rejecting God's
mercy . . . . .Is. 65:13 712
Unbelief . . . . . . .Mark 8:38 1009
Unpre-
paredness . . . . .2 Cor. 9:4 1171

B. *Avoidance of, by:*
Waiting for ⎰Ps. 34:5 544
the Lord . . . .⎱Is. 49:23 699
Regarding God's
commands . . . .Ps. 119:6 590
Blameless in
statutes . . . . . .Ps. 119:80 592
Trusting God . .Ps. 25:20 539
Believing in ⎰Rom. 9:33 1139
Christ . . . .⎱Rom. 10:11 1139
Christian
diligence . . . . . .2 Tim. 2:15 1224
Assurance of
faith . . . . .2 Tim. 1:12 1223
Abiding in
Christ . . . . .1 John 2:28 1276

C. *Possible objects of, in the Christian's life:*
Life's plans . . . .Phil. 1:20 1193
God's
message . . . . . . .2 Tim. 1:8 1223
The Gospel . . . .Rom. 1:16 1132
The old life . . . .Rom. 6:21 1136
One's faith . . . . .1 Pet. 4:16 1264

Ashan—*smoke*

A city of Judah . . .Josh. 15:42 219
Later allotted to
Judah . . . . .Josh. 19:7 222
Assigned to the
Levites . . . . .1 Chr. 6:59 393

Asharelah—*God has fulfilled with joy*

A son of Asaph in David's
time . . . . .1 Chr. 25:2 410
Called
Jesharelah . . . . . .1 Chr. 25:14 410

Ashbel—*having a long upper lip*

A son of ⎰Gen. 46:21 46
Benjamin . . . . .⎱1 Chr. 8:1 395
Progenitor of the
Ashbelites . . . . .Num. 26:38 155

Ashdod—*stronghold, fortress*

One of five Philistine
cities . . . . .Josh. 13:3 217
Anakim refuge . . . .Josh. 11:22 216
Assigned to
Judah . . . . .Josh. 15:46, 47 219
Seat of Dagon
worship . . . . .1 Sam. 5:1-8 266
Captured by
Assyria . . . . .Is. 20:1 673
Opposed
Nehemiah . . . . . .Neh. 4:7 469
Women of, marry
Jews . . . . .Neh. 13:23, 24 480
Called the
remnant . . . . .Jer. 25:20 743
Called Azotus . . . .Acts 8:40 1103

Ashdoth-pisgah—*springs of Pisgah*

The slopes of Mt. ⎰Deut. 3:17 172
Pisgah . . . .⎱Josh. 12:3 216
Translated
"slopes" in . . . . . .Deut. 4:49 174

Asher—*happy*

1. Jacob's second son by
Zilpah . . . . .Gen. 30:12, 13 30
Goes to Egypt with
Jacob . . . . .Gen. 46:17 46
Father of five
children . . . . . . .Gen. 46:17 46
Blessed by
Jacob . . . . .Gen. 49:20 49
2. The tribe fathered by Asher,
Jacob's son . . . .Deut. 33:24 202

SUBJECT	REFERENCE	PAGE	SUBJECT	REFERENCE	PAGE	SUBJECT	REFERENCE	PAGE

Jezebel by
Jehu . . . . .2 Kin. 9:30-37   365
Joash by
servants. . . . . . .2 Kin. 12:20, 21   368
Zechariah by
Shallum. . . . . . .2 Kin. 15:10   370
Shallum by
Menahem . . . . .2 Kin. 15:14   370
Pekahiah by
Pekah. . . . . .2 Kin. 15:25   371
Pekah by
Hoshea . . . . . . .2 Kin. 15:30   371
Amon by
servants. . . . . . .2 Kin. 21:23   378
Gedaliah by
Ishmael . . . . . . .2 Kin. 25:25   383
Sennacherib by his
sons . . . . .2 Kin. 19:37   376

B. *Attempted cases of:*
Jacob by
Esau. . . . . .Gen. 27:41-45   28
Joseph by his
brothers. . . . . . .Gen. 37:18-22   37
David by
Saul . . . . .1 Sam. 19:10-18   280
David by
Absalom . . . . . .2 Sam. 15:10-14   308
Joash by
Athaliah . . . . . .2 Kin. 11:1-3   366
Ahasuerus by
servants. . . . . . .Esth. 2:21-23   486
Jesus by the   {Luke 4:28-30   1030
Jews. . . . .{John 7:1   1072
Paul by the   {Acts 9:23-25   1104
Jews. . . . .{Acts 23:12-31   1121

C. *Crime of:*
Against God's image in
man . . . . .Gen. 9:6   11
Punishable by   {Ex. 21:12-15   72
death . . . . {Num. 35:33   165
Not to be
condoned . . . . .Deut. 19:11-13   186
Puts the guilty under a
curse. . . . . .Deut. 27:24   193
Abhorred by the
righteous . . . . .2 Sam. 4:4-12   298

Assembly—*a large gathering for official
business*

A. *Descriptive of:*
Israel as a
people . . . . . . .Num. 10:2-8   138
Israel as a   {Judg. 20:2   251
nation . . . .{2 Chr. 30:23   443
God's elect
people . . . . . . .Ps. 111:1   587
A civil court . . .Acts 19:32-41   1117
A church
gathering . . . . .James 2:2   1254

B. *Purposes of:*
Proclaim   {Judg. 10:17, 18   243
war . . . .{1 Sam. 14:20   274
Establish the ark in
Zion . . . . .1 Kin. 8:1-6   332
Institute   {Ezra 9:4-15   461
reforms . . . . . .{Neh. 9:1, 2   474
Celebrate
victory. . . . . . . .Esth. 9:17, 18   491
Condemn
Christ. . . . . . . .Matt. 26:3, 4, 57   990
Worship   {Acts 4:31   1098
God. . . . .{Heb. 10:25   1245

C. *Significant ones, at:*
Sinai. . . . . .Ex. 19:1-19   70
Joshua's   {Josh. 23:1-16   226
farewell . . . . . .{Josh. 24:1-28   227
David's
coronation . . . .2 Sam. 5:1-3   298
The Temple's
dedication. . . . .2 Chr. 5:1-14   422
Josiah's
reforma-   {2 Kin. 23:1-3, 21,
tion. . . . .{ 22   379
Ezra's reading the
Law. . . . . .Neh. 8:1-18   473
Jesus' trial . . . .Matt. 27:11-26   993
Pentecost. . . . . .Acts 2:1-21   1095

The Jerusalem
Council . . . . . . .Acts 15:5-21   1111

Assent—*agreeing to the truth of a
statement or fact*
A. *Concerning good things:*
Accepting God's
covenant. . . . . .Ex. 19:7, 8   71
Agreeing to   {1 Sam. 7:3, 4   268
reforms . . . . . .{Ezra 10:1-12, 19   461
Accepting a Scriptural
decision. . . . . . .Acts 15:13-22   1111
Receiving Christ as
Savior . . . . .Rom. 10:9, 10   1139
B. *Concerning evil things:*
Tolerating
idolatry . . . . . . .Jer. 44:15-19   761
Condemning Christ to
death . . . . .Matt. 27:17-25   993
Putting Stephen to
death . . . . .Acts 7:51-60   1102
Refusing to hear the
Gospel . . . . .Acts 13:44-51   1109

Asshur—*level plain*
1. One of the sons of Shem;
progenitor of
the   {Gen. 10:22   13
Assyrians . . . .{1 Chr. 1:17   387
2. The chief god of the Assyrians;
seen in names like
"Ashurbanipal"
(Osnapper). . . .Ezra 4:10   456
3. A city in   {Num. 24:22, 24   153
Assyria or   {Ps. 83:8   572
the nation of {Ezek. 27:23   810
Assyria. . . . . . .{Ezek. 32:22   815

Asshurim—*mighty ones*
Descendants of Abraham by
Keturah. . . . . . . .Gen. 25:3   25

Assir—*prisoner*
1. A son of   {Ex. 6:24   59
Korah. . . . .{1 Chr. 6:22   392
2. A son of
Ebiasaph . . . . . .1 Chr. 6:23, 37   392

Assistance, divine
A. *Offered, in:*
Battle. . . . . .2 Chr. 20:5-15   433
Trouble. . . . . . . .Ps. 50:15   553
Crises . . . . .Luke 21:14, 15   1053
Prayer . . . . .Rom. 8:16-27   1138
Testimony . . . . .2 Tim. 4:17   1226
Guidance . . . . .James 1:5-8   1253
B. *Given:*
Internally . . . . . .Phil. 2:13   1194
        Heb. 13:21   1249
By God . . . . .2 Cor. 8:9   1170
By Christ . . . . . .Phil. 4:13   1196
By the Spirit . . .Zech. 4:6   920
By God's
Word . . . . .1 Thess. 2:13   1207
By grace . . . . . .1 Cor. 15:10   1160
By prayer . . . . . .James 5:15-18   1256
By trusting
God. . . . . .Ps. 37:3-7   546
By God's
providence. . . . .Rom. 8:28   1138

Association—*joining together for
mutually beneficial purposes*
A. *Among believers, hindered by:*
Sin . . . . .Acts 5:1-11   1098
Friction. . . . . . . .Acts 6:1-6   1100
Inconsist-
ency . . . . .Gal. 2:11-14   1178
Disagree-
ment. . . . . .Acts 15:36-40   1112
Selfishness. . . . .3 John 9-11   1284
Ambition . . . . . .Matt. 20:20-24   984
Error . . . . .2 John 7-11   1281
Partiality . . . . . .James 2:1-5   1254
B. *Among believers, helped by:*
Common
faith . . . . .Acts 2:42-47   1096
Mutual
helpfulness. . . .Gal. 6:1-5   1181

United
prayer . . . . .Matt. 18:19, 20   982
Impending
dangers . . . . . . .Neh. 4:1-23   469
Grateful
praise . . . . .Acts 4:23-33   1098
See Alliance with evil; Fellowship

Assos—*a seaport of Mysia in Asia
Minor*
Paul walks to, from
Troas. . . . . .Acts 20:13, 14   1117

Assurance—*the security of knowing
that one's name is written in heaven*
A. *Objects of, one's:*
Election . . . . . . .1 Thess. 1:4   1206
Adoption . . . . . .Eph. 1:4, 5   1185
Union with
Christ. . . . . .1 Cor. 6:15   1152
Possession of   {John 5:24   1069
eternal life . . .{1 John 5:13   1278
Peace. . . . . .Rom. 5:1   1135
B. *Steps in:*
Believing God's
Word . . . . .1 Thess. 2:13   1207
Accepting Christ as
Savior . . . . .Rom. 10:9, 10   1139
Standing upon the
promises . . . . .John 10:28-30   1077
Desiring spiritual
things. . . . . .1 Pet. 2:2   1261
Growing in
grace . . . . .2 Pet. 1:5-11   1268
Knowing life   {2 Cor. 5:17   1168
is changed . . .{1 John 3:14-22   1276
Having inner
peace and   {Rom. 15:12, 13   1143
joy. . . . .{Phil. 4:7   1196
Victorious
living . . . . .1 John 5:4, 5   1278
The Spirit's
testimony . . . . .Rom. 8:15, 16   1137
Absolute   {Rom. 8:33-39   1138
assurance . . . .{2 Tim. 1:12   1223
C. *Compatible with:*
A nature still
subject to   {1 John 1:8-10   1274
sin . . . . {1 John 2:1   1274
Imperfection of
life. . . . . .Gal. 6:1   1181
Limited
knowledge . . . .1 Cor. 13:9-12   1158
Fatherly
discipline. . . . . .Heb. 12:5-11   1247

Assyria—*the nation ruled from Asshur
(first) and Nineveh (later)*
A. *Significant facts regarding:*
Of remote
antiquity . . . . .Gen. 2:14   5
Of Shem's
ancestry . . . . . .Gen. 10:22   13
Founded by   {Gen. 10:8-12   12
Nimrod . . . . . .{Mic. 5:6   893
Nineveh, chief city
of. . . . . .Gen. 10:11   12
Tigris river flows
through. . . . . . . .Gen. 2:14   5
Proud nation . .Is. 10:5-15   666
A cruel military
power. . . . . .Nah. 3:1-19   899
Agent of
God's   {Is. 7:17-20   663
purposes . . . . .{Is. 10:5, 6   666
B. *Contacts of, with Israel:*
Pul (Tiglath-pileser III, 745-727
B.C.) captures
Damascus. . . . .Is. 8:4   664
Puts Menahem under
tribute . . . . .2 Kin. 15:19, 20   371
Occasions Isaiah's
prophesy. . . . . .Is. 7, 8   663
Puts Pekah under
tribute . . . . .2 Kin. 15:29   371
Shalmaneser (727-722 B.C.)
besieges
Samaria. . . . . . .2 Kin. 17:3-5   372

SUBJECT	REFERENCE	PAGE	SUBJECT	REFERENCE	PAGE	SUBJECT	REFERENCE	PAGE

Awakening, spiritual—*continued*

Reading God's
Word ....Neh. 8:2-18   473
Confessing
sin............Ezra 10:1-17   461
Receiving the ⎰John 7:38, 39   1073
Spirit ....⎱Acts 2:1-47   1095

B. *Old Testament examples of,
under:*
Joshua........Josh. 24:1-31   227
Samuel........1 Sam. 7:3-6   268
Elijah........1 Kin. 18:21-40   345
Hezekiah .....2 Chr. 30:1-27   443
Josiah ....2 Kin. 23:1-3   379
Ezra..........Ezra 10:1-17   461

C. *New Testament examples of:*
John the
Baptist........Luke 3:2-14   1028
Jesus in
Samaria......John 4:28-42   1067
Philip in
Samaria......Acts 8:5-12   1103
Peter at
Lydda.........Acts 9:32-35   1105
Peter with
Cornelius .....Acts 10:34-48   1106
Paul at Antioch in
Pisidia ....Acts 13:14-52   1109
Paul at ⎰Acts 17:11, 12   1114
Berea ..⎱1 Thess. 1:1-10   1206
Paul at
Corinth .....2 Cor. 7:1-16   1169

Awe—*fear mingled with reverence*

A restraint on
sin ....Ps. 4:4   529
Proper attitude toward
God.............Ps. 33:8   543
Also toward God's
Word...........Ps. 119:161   594

Awl—*a sharp tool for piercing*

Used on the ear as a symbol of
perpetual ⎰Ex. 21:6   72
obedience ......⎱Deut. 15:17   184

Axe—*a sharp instrument for cutting
wood*

A. *Used in:*
Cutting
timber ....Judg. 9:48   242
War ....1 Chr. 20:3   406
Malicious
destruction....Ps. 74:5-7   566
A miracle; floated in
water ....2 Kin. 6:5, 6   360

B. *As a figure of:*
Judgment.......Matt. 3:10   965
Wrath ....Jer. 51:20-24   770
God's
sovereignty ...Is. 10:15   666

Ayin

Letter of the Hebrew
alphabet.........Ps. 119:121-136   593

Azaliah—*Yahweh has set aside*

Father of
Shaphan ....2 Kin. 22:3   378

Azaniah—*Yahweh has heard*

A Levite who signs the
document ....Neh. 10:9   477

Azarel—*God has helped*

1. A Levite in David's army at
Ziklag .....1 Chr. 12:6   399
2. A musician in David's
time ......1 Chr. 25:18   410
3. A prince of Dan under
David ....1 Chr. 27:22   412
4. A Jew who divorced his foreign
wife..........Ezra 10:41   463
5. A postexilic
priest ....Neh. 11:13   478
6. A musician in dedication
service.......Neh. 12:36   479

Azariah—*Yahweh has helped*

1. Man of
Judah.........1 Chr. 2:8   388
2. A Kohathite
Levite........1 Chr. 6:36   393
3. A son of Zadok the high
priest ....1 Kin. 4:2   327
4. A son of
Ahimaaz......1 Chr. 6:9   392
5. A great-grandson of
Ahimaaz.....1 Chr. 6:9, 10   392
6. Son of
Nathan ....1 Kin. 4:5   327
7. A son of Jehu, with Egyptian
ancestry .....1 Chr. 2:34-38   389
8. A prophet who encourages
King Asa......2 Chr. 15:1-8   430
9. Son of King Jehosh-
aphat ....2 Chr. 21:2   435
10. A captain under
Jehoiada .....2 Chr. 23:1   436
11. Another under
Jehoiada ......2 Chr. 23:1   436
12. A head of
Ephraim ......2 Chr. 28:12   441
13. A high priest who rebukes King
Uzziah........2 Chr. 26:16-20   439
14. Kohathite, father of
Joel..........2 Chr. 29:12   442
15. A reforming
Levite........2 Chr. 29:12   442
16. Chief priest in time of
Hezekiah......2 Chr. 31:9, 10   444
17. A high priest, son of
Hilkiah........1 Chr. 6:13, 14   392
18. Ancestor of
Ezra ....Ezra 7:1-3   458
19. An opponent of
Jeremiah......Jer. 43:2   760
20. The Hebrew name of Abed-
nego..........Dan. 1:7   835
21. Postexilic
Jew...........Neh. 7:6, 7   472
22. A workman under
Nehemiah.....Neh. 3:23, 24   469
23. A leader of
Judah........Neh. 12:32, 33   479
24. An expounder of the
law ....Neh. 8:7   474
25. A signer of the
document.....Neh. 10:1, 2   477
26. A descendant of
Hilkiah........1 Chr. 9:11   396

Azaz—*strong*

A Reubenite ......1 Chr. 5:8   391

Azaziah—*Yahweh is strong*

1. A musician ...1 Chr. 15:21   401
2. Father of
Hoshea ....1 Chr. 27:20   412
3. A temple
overseer .....2 Chr. 31:13   444

Azbuk—*pardon*

Father of a certain Nehemiah; but
not the celebrated
one..............Neh. 3:16   469

Azekah—*tilled*

Large stones
thrown on.......Josh. 10:11   214
Camp of ⎰1 Sam. 17:1, 4,
Goliath..........⎱ 17   277
Fortified by
Rehoboam........2 Chr. 11:9   428
Reoccupied after
exile...............Neh. 11:30   478
Captured by Nebuchad-
nezzar...........Jer. 34:7   752

Azel—*noble*

1. A descendant of
Jonathan....1 Chr. 8:37, 38   395
2. A place near
Jerusalem.....Zech. 14:5   925

Azgad—*fate is hard*

Head of exile ⎰Ezra 2:12   454
family...........⎱Ezra 8:12   460

Among document
signers ....Neh. 10:15   477

Aziel—*God strengthens*

A Levite
musician ....1 Chr. 15:20   401
Called Jaaziel .....1 Chr. 15:18   401

Aziza—*strong*

Divorced foreign
wife...............Ezra 10:27   462

Azmaveth—*death is strong*

1. One of David's mighty
men...........2 Sam. 23:31   318
2. A Benjamin ...2 Chr. 12:3   428
3. David's
treasurer......1 Chr. 27:25   412
4. A son of
Jehoaddah ....1 Chr. 8:36   395
5. A village near
Jerusalem.....Neh. 12:29   479
Also called Beth-
azmaveth .....Neh. 7:28   472

Azmon—*strong*

A place in south
Canaan..........Num. 34:4, 5   163

Aznoth-tabor—*peaks of Tabor*

Place in
Naphtali.........Josh. 19:34   223

Azor—*helper*

Ancestor of
Christ ....Matt. 1:13, 14   963

Azotus—*fortress*

Philip went
there.............Acts 8:40   1103
Same as Ashdod ..1 Sam. 6:17   268

Azriel—*God is a help*

1. A chief of
Manasseh.....1 Chr. 5:24   392
2. Father of
Jeremoth......1 Chr. 27:19   412
3. Father of
Seraiah ....Jer. 36:26   755

Azrikam—*my help has arisen*

1. Son of
Neariah........1 Chr. 3:23   390
2. A son of
Aziel..........1 Chr. 8:38   395
3. A Merarite
Levite.........1 Chr. 9:14   396
4. Governor under King
Ahaz..........2 Chr. 28:7   440

Azubah—*forsaken*

1. Wife of
Caleb.........1 Chr. 2:18, 19   389
2. Mother of Jehosh-
aphat ....1 Kin. 22:42   351

Azzan—*strong*

Father of Paltiel...Num. 34:26   164

Azzur—*helpful*

1. Father of
Hananiah .....Jer. 28:1   745
2. Father of
Jaazaniah.....Ezek. 11:1   793
3. A document
signer.........Neh. 10:17   477

B

Baal—*lord, possessor, husband*

A. *The nature of:*
The male god of the
Phoenicians and Canaanites;
the counterpart of
the female ⎰Judg. 10:6   242
Ashtaroth...⎱1 Sam. 7:4   268

Connected
with   ⌠Num. 25:3, 5   154
immorality...⌡Hos. 9:10   859
Incense
burned to.....Jer. 7:9   725
Kissing the   ⌠1 Kin. 19:18   347
image of.....⌡Hos. 13:1, 2   861
Dervish rites by
priests of......1 Kin. 18:26, 28   346
Children burned in
fire of.........Jer. 19:5   737
Eating
sacrifices....Ps. 106:28   584
B. *History of:*
Among Moabites in Moses'
time..........Num. 22:41   152
Altars built to, during
time of   ⌠Judg. 2:11-14   233
judges.......⌡Judg. 6:28-32   238
Jezebel introduces into
Israel.........1 Kin. 16:31, 32   343
Elijah's overthrow of, on Mt.
Carmel........1 Kin. 18:17-40   345
Athaliah
introduces it ⌠2 Kin. 11:17-20   367
into Judah...⌡2 Chr. 22:2-4   435
Revived again in
Israel and   ⌠Hos. 8:2   854
Judah........⌡Amos 5:26   875
Ahaz makes
images to....2 Chr. 28:2-4   440
Manasseh
worships......2 Kin. 21:3   377
Altars
everywhere...Jer. 11:13   729
Overthrown by
Josiah.........2 Kin. 23:4, 5   380
Denounced by ⌠Jer. 19:4, 5   737
prophets.....⌡Ezek. 16:20, 21   798
Historic
retrospect.....Rom. 11:4   1140

Baal—*master, possessor*

1. A Benjamite, son of
Jeiel..........1 Chr. 8:30   395
2. A descendant of
Reuben.......1 Chr. 5:5, 6   391
3. A village of
Simeon.......1 Chr. 4:33   391
Also called Baalath-
beer...........Josh. 19:8   222

Baalah—*mistress*

1. A town also known as Kirjath-
jearim........Josh. 15:9, 10   219
2. A hill in
Judah.........Josh. 15:11   219
3. A town in South
Judah.........Josh. 15:29   219
Probably the same as
Bilhah........1 Chr. 4:29   391
May be the same as
Balah ....Josh. 19:3   222

Baalath—*mistress*

A village of Dan ..Josh. 19:44   223
Fortified by
Solomon ....1 Kin. 9:18   335

Baalath-beer—*mistress of the well*

A border town of
Simeon..........Josh. 19:8   222
Called Ramath of the
Negev...........Josh. 19:8   222
Also called Baal ..1 Chr. 4:33   391

Baal-berith—*lord of covenant*

A god (Baal) of ⌠Judg. 8:33   240
Shechem........⌡Judg. 9:4   240
Also called
El-berith ....Judg. 9:46   242

Baale—*Judah*

A town of Judah ..2 Sam. 6:2   299
Also called Baalah and
Kiriath-jearim ....Josh. 15:9, 10   219

Baal-gad—*lord of good fortune*

A place in the valley of
Lebanon..........Josh. 11:17   216

Baal-hamon—*lord of a multitude*

Site of Solomon's
vineyard.........Song 8:11   653

Baal-hanan—*lord of grace*

1. Edomite king ..Gen. 36:38   37
2. David's
gardener......1 Chr. 27:28   412

Baal-hazor—*lord of a village*

A place near
Ephraim.........2 Sam. 13:23   306

Baal-hermon—*lord of Hermon*

A mountain east of
Jordan ....Judg. 3:3   234

Baali—*my master* (lord)

A title rejected by
Yahweh.........Hos. 2:16   854

Baalis

An Ammonite
king.............Jer. 40:14   758

Baal-meon—*lord of Menon* (habitation)

An Amorite city on the Moabite
boundary........Ezek. 25:9   808
Rebuilt by   ⌠Num. 32:38   162
Reubenites ......⌡Josh. 13:17   217

Baal-peor, Baal of Peor—*lord of Peor*

A Moabite god ...Num. 25:1-5   154
Infected Israel; 24,000
died..............Num. 25:1-9   154
Vengeance
taken on ....Num. 31:1-18   159
Sin   ⌠Deut. 4:3, 4   172
long   ⌡Josh. 22:17   225
remembered.....Ps. 106:28, 29   584
Historic
reminder ....1 Cor. 10:8   1156

Baal-perazim—*lord of breaking through*

Where David defeated the
Philistines........2 Sam. 5:18-20   299
Same as
Perazim ....Is. 28:21   679

Baal-shalishah—*lord of Shalisha*

A place from which Elisha received
food...........2 Kin. 4:42-44   359

Baal-tamar—*lord of the palm*

A place in
Benjamin.........Judg. 20:33   252

Baal-zebub—*lord of flies*

A Philistine god at
Ekron...........2 Kin. 1:2   355
Ahaziah
enquired of.......2 Kin. 1:2, 6, 16   355
Also called   ⌠Matt. 10:25   972
Beelzebub ....⌡Matt. 12:24   974

Baal-zephon—*lord of darkness*

Israelite camp ⌠Ex. 14:2, 9   66
site.............⌡Num. 33:7   162

Baana—*affliction*

1. Supply
officer..........1 Kin. 4:12   328
2. Zadok's
father..........Neh. 3:4   468
3. Supply officer in
Asher...........1 Kin. 4:16   328

Baanah—*affliction*

1. A murderer of Ish-
bosheth ....2 Sam. 4:1-12   298
2. Heled's
father..........1 Chr. 11:30   398
3. A returning ⌠Ezra 2:2   454
exile ....⌡Neh. 7:7   472
Signs
document ......Neh. 10:27   477

Baara—*foolish*

Shaharaim's
wife.............1 Chr. 8:8   395

Baaseiah—*work of Yahweh*

A Levite ancestor of
Asaph............1 Chr. 6:40   393

Baasha—*boldness*

Gains throne by
murder...........1 Kin. 15:27, 28   342
Kills Jeroboam's
household........1 Kin. 15:29, 30   342
Wars against
Asa..............1 Kin. 15:16, 32   342
Restricts access to
Judah............1 Kin. 15:17   342
Contravened by Asa's league with
Ben-hadad.......1 Kin. 15:18-22   342
Evil rule ....1 Kin. 15:33, 34   342

Babbler—*an inane talker*

The mumblings of
drunkards........Prov. 23:29-35   627
Like a serpent.....Eccl. 10:11   644
Paul called such...Acts 17:18   1114
Paul's warnings ⌠1 Tim. 6:20   1220
against..........⌡2 Tim. 2:16   1224

Babel—*confusion*

A city built by Nimrod in the plain
of Shinar.........Gen. 10:10   12

Babel, Tower of

A huge brick structure intended to
magnify man and preserve the
unity of the
race..............Gen. 11:1-4   13
Objectives thwarted by
God ....Gen. 11:5-9   13

Babylon, city of

A. *History of:*
Built by
Nimrod ....Gen. 10:9, 10   12
Tower built
there..........Gen. 11:1-9   13
Amraphel's
capital........Gen. 14:1   15
Once the capital of
Assyria ....2 Chr. 33:11   446
Greatest power under
Nebuchad-
nezzar ....Dan. 4:30   840
A magni-   ⌠Is. 13:19   669
ficent city....⌡Is. 14:4   669
Wide
walls of ......Jer. 51:44   771
Gates of ......Is. 45:1, 2   695
Bel, god of.....Is. 46:1   696
Jews carried ⌠2 Kin. 25:1-21   382
captive to....⌡2 Chr. 36:5-21   449
B. *Inhabitants, described as:*
Idolatrous .....Ps. 50:35, 38   769
   Dan. 3:18   838
Enslaved by
magic........Is. 47:1, 9-13   696
Sacrilegious....Dan. 5:1-3   841
C. *Prophecies concerning:*
Babylon,   ⌠Jer. 25:9   742
God's agent ..⌡Jer. 27:5-8   744
God fights
with ....Jer. 21:1-7   738
Jews, 70 years ⌠Jer. 25:12   742
in ....⌡Jer. 29:10   746
First of great ⌠Dan. 2:31-38   837
empires ......⌡Dan. 7:2-4   843
Downfall of....Is. 13:1-22   668
   Jer. 50:1-46   767
Cyrus, God's
agent ....Is. 45:1-4   695
Perpetual
desolation ⌠Is. 13:19-22   669
of............⌡Jer. 50:13, 39   768

SUBJECT	REFERENCE	PAGE	SUBJECT	REFERENCE	PAGE	SUBJECT	REFERENCE	PAGE

Ballad singers

Rendered "those who use
proverbs" ....Num. 21:27   150

Balm—*an aromatic resin or gum*

A product of
Gilead............Jer. 8:22   727
Sent to Joseph ....Gen. 43:11   43
Exported to
Tyre..............Ezek. 27:17   810
Healing   (Jer. 46:11   763
qualities of .....(Jer. 51:8   770

Balsam tree

Rustling of
leaves............2 Sam. 5:23, 24   299

Bamah—*high place*

A place of
idolatry ....Ezek. 20:29   802

Bamoth—*high places*

Encampment
site..............Num. 21:19, 20   150
Also called Bamoth-
baal..............Josh. 13:17   217

Bamoth-baal—*high places of Baal*

Assigned to
Reuben...........Josh. 13:17   217

Ban—*devote, consecrate to God*

Suffered by:
Jericho...........Josh. 6:17, 21   210
Sons of Israel .....Josh. 7:1   211
Achan ....Josh. 22:20   226

Ban (see Excommunication)

Bandage

Used as disguise...1 Kin. 20:37-41   348
In prophecy against
Egypt ....Ezek. 30:20-22   813

Bani—*built*

1. Gadite
warrior ......2 Sam. 23:36   318
2. A Judahite.....1 Chr. 9:4   396
3. A postexilic   (Ezra 2:10   454
family.........(Neh. 10:14   477
4. A Merarite
Levite........1 Chr. 6:46   393
5. A Levite; father of
Rehum........Neh. 3:17   469
Signed
document.....Neh. 10:13   477
6. Head of Levitical
family........Ezra 10:34   462
7. A postexilic
Levite.........Ezra 10:38   462
8. A descendant of
Asaph.........Neh. 11:22   478

Banishment—*forceful explusion from
one's place*

A. *Political, of:*
Absalom by
David......2 Sam. 14:13, 14   307
The Jews into
exile ....2 Chr. 36:20, 21   450
The Jews from
Rome.........Acts 18:2   1115

B. *Moral and spiritual, of:*
Adam from
Eden..........Gen. 3:22-24   7
Cain from
others.........Gen. 4:12, 14   8
Lawbreaker....Ezra 7:26   459
John to
Patmos ....Rev. 1:9   1294
Satan from
heaven........Rev. 12:7-9   1301
The wicked to (Rev. 20:15   1306
lake of fire ...(Rev. 21:8   1307

Bank

A. *A mound:*
Raised against
a besieged   (2 Sam. 20:15   314
city ....(Is. 37:33   687

B. *A place for money:*
Exchange
charges ....John 2:15   1066
Interest paid   (Matt. 25:27   990
on deposits...(Luke 19:23   1051

Bankruptcy—*inability to pay one's
debts*

A. *Literal:*
Condition of David's
men...........2 Sam. 22:2   315
Unjust
steward.......Matt. 18:25   982

B. *Moral and spiritual:*
Israel's
condition .....Hos. 4:1-5   855
Mankind's   (Rom. 1:20-32   1132
condition.....(Rom. 3:9-19   1133
Individual's   (Phil. 3:4-8   1195
condition.....(1 Tim. 1:13   1217

Banner—*a flag or standard*

A. *Literal:*
Used by
armies ....Num. 2:2, 3   129
Signal for blowing
trumpet.......Is. 18:3   672

B. *Figurative of:*
Yahweh's name ("The Lord is
My
Banner")......Ex. 17:15   69
God's   (Ps. 20:5   537
salvation.....(Ps. 60:4   558
God's
protection....Song 2:4   649
God's power...Song 6:4, 10   652

Banquet—*a sumptuous feast*

A. *Reasons for:*
Birthday.......Gen. 40:20   40
Marriage.......Gen. 29:22   29
Reunion ....Luke 15:22-25   1046
State affairs ...Esth. 1:3, 5   485
     Dan. 5:1   841

B. *Features of:*
Invitations   (Esth. 5:8, 9   488
sent...........(Luke 14:16, 17   1045
Non-acceptance merits
censure......Luke 14:18-24   1045
Courtesies to
guests.........Luke 7:40-46   1035
Special   (Matt. 22:11   986
garment.......(Rev. 3:4, 5   1295
A presiding
headwaiter....John 2:8   1065
Protocol of   (Gen. 43:33   44
seating.......(Prov. 25:6, 7   629
Anointing oil ..Ps. 45:7   551
Honor guest
noted ....1 Sam. 9:22-24   270

Baptism, Christian

A. *Commanded by:*
Christ ....Matt. 28:19, 20   995
     Mark 16:15, 16   1020
Peter ....Acts 10:46-48   1106
Christian
ministers......Acts 22:12-16   1120

B. *Administered by:*
The apostles ...Acts 2:1, 41   1095
Ananias ....Acts 9:17, 18   1104
Philip ....Acts 8:12   1103
     Acts 8:36-38   1103
Peter ....Acts 10:44-48   1106
Paul ....Acts 18:8   1115
     1 Cor. 1:14-17   1149

C. *Places:*
Jordan.........Matt. 3:13-16   965
     Mark 1:5-10   999
Jerusalem......Acts 2:5, 41   1095
Samaria ....Acts 8:12   1103
A house ....Acts 10:44-48   1106

A jail..........Acts 16:25-33   1113

D. *Subjects of:*
Believing
Jews..........Acts 2:41   1096
Believing   (Acts 10:44-48   1106
Gentiles.....(Acts 18:8   1115
Households ....Acts 16:15, 33   1113
     1 Cor. 1:16   1149

E. *Characteristics of:*
By water ......Acts 10:47   1106
Only one .....Eph. 4:5   1187
Necessary .....Acts 2:38, 41   1096
Source of
power.........Acts 1:5   1094
Follows faith ..Acts 2:41   1096
     Acts 18:8   1115

F. *Symbolism of:*
Forecast in   (Joel 2:28, 29   867
prophecy.....(Acts 2:16-21   1095
Prefigured in   (1 Cor. 10:2   1155
types.........(1 Pet. 3:20, 21   1263
Visualized by   (John 1:32, 33   1065
the Spirit's   (Acts 2:3, 4, 41   1095
descent .....(Acts 10:44-48   1106
Expressive of
spiritual   (1 Cor. 12:13   1158
unity.........(Gal. 3:27, 28   1179
Figurative of
regen-   (John 3:3, 5, 6   1066
eration.......(Rom. 6:3, 4, 11   1135
Illustrative of   (Acts 22:16   1120
cleansing.....(Titus 3:5   1230

Baptism, John's

Administrator—
John ....Matt. 3:7   965
Place—
at Jordan........Matt. 3:6, 13, 16   965
in Aenon........John 3:23   1066
Persons—people   (Mark 1:5, 9   999
and Jesus......(Acts 13:24   1109
Character—
repentance ......Luke 3:3   1028
Reception—rejected by
some.............Luke 7:29, 30   1034
Nature—
of God ....Matt. 21:25, 27   985
Insufficiency—
rebaptism ....Acts 19:1-7   1116
Intent—   (Matt. 3:11, 12   965
to   (Acts 11:16   1107
prepare..........(Acts 19:4   1116
Jesus' submission to—fulfilling all
righteousness.....Matt. 3:13-17   965

Barabbas—*son of Abba (father)*

A murderer released
in place of   (Matt. 27:16-26   993
Jesus ....(Acts 3:14, 15   1097

Barachel—*God has blessed*

Father of Elihu....Job 32:2, 6   515

Barak—*lightning*

Defeats Jabin .....Judg. 4:1-24   235
A man of faith ....Heb. 11:32   1247

Barbarian—*rude person*

Primitive people...Acts 28:2, 4   1126
Unintelligible
language ....1 Cor. 14:11   1159
Those included in   (Rom. 1:14   1131
the Gospel......(Col. 3:11   1201

Barber—*one who cuts hair*

Expressive of
divine   (Is. 7:20   663
judgment........(Ezek. 5:1   789

Bare—*uncovered, naked*

Figurative of:
Destitution......Ezek. 16:22, 39   798
Uncleanness .....Lev. 13:45   107
Undeveloped
state,   (Ezek. 16:7   797
immaturity......(1 Cor. 15:37   1161
Power revealed...Is. 52:10   701
Destruction ......Joel 1:7   865
Mourning ....Is. 32:9-11   683

SUBJECT   REFERENCE   PAGE | SUBJECT   REFERENCE   PAGE | SUBJECT   REFERENCE   PAGE

Barefoot—*bare feet*
Expression of great
distress..........2 Sam. 15:30   309
Forewarning of
judgement.......Is. 20:2-4   673
Indicative of
reverence ....Ex. 3:5   56

Bargain—*an agreement between persons*
A disastrous......Gen. 25:29-34   26
A blessed ......Gen. 28:20-22   29
Involving a wife..Gen. 29:15-20   29
Deception of .....Prov. 20:14   624
Resulting in
death..........Matt. 14:7-10   977
History's most
notorious........Matt. 26:14-16   991

Barhumite (another form of "Baharumite")
One of David's mighty
men.............2 Sam. 23:31   318

Bariah—*fugitive*
A decendant of
David ....1 Chr. 3:22   390

Bar-Jesus (Elymas)
A Jewish
imposter........Acts 13:6-12   1108

Barjona—*son of Jonah*
Surname of
Peter............Matt. 16:17   980

Barkos—*party-colored*
Postexilic family ..Ezra 2:53   455

Barley—*a bearded cereal grass*
A product of   ⎰Deut. 8:8   177
Palestine ....⎱Ruth 1:22   256
Food for
animals..........1 Kin. 4:28   328
Used by the
poor..............Ruth 2:17   257
Used in trade .....2 Chr. 2:10   420
In a miracle......John 6:9, 13   1070

Barn—*a storehouse*
A. *Literal:*
A place of   ⎰Deut. 28:8   193
storage.......⎱Joel 1:17   866
B. *Spiritual, of:*
God's   ⎰Prov. 3:10   611
blessings....⎱Mal. 3:10   931
Man's vanity...Luke 12:16-19   1042
Heaven itself ..Matt. 13:30, 43   976

Barnabas—*son of exhortation*
Gives property ....Acts 4:36, 37   1098
Supports Paul.....Acts 9:27   1104
Assists in
Antioch ....Acts 11:22-24   1107
Brings Paul from
Tarsus..........Acts 11:25, 26   1107
Carries contributions to
Jerusalem ....Acts 11:27-30   1107
Travels with
Paul.............Acts 13:2   1108
Called Zeus by the
multitudes.......Acts 14:12   1110
Speaks before Jerusalem
Council ....Acts 15:1, 2, 12   1111
With Paul, takes decree to
churches......Acts 15:22-31   1111
Breaks with Paul over John
Mark...........Acts 15:36-39   1112
Highly regarded   ⎰1 Cor. 9:6   1155
by Paul.........⎱Gal. 2:1, 9   1178
Not always
steady...........Gal. 2:13   1178

Barracks—*soldiers' quarters*
Paul ordered
into ....Acts 21:34, 37   1119
Examined by
scourging in......Acts 22:24   1120

Paul's nephew
enters...........Acts 23:16   1121

Barren—*unable to reproduce*
A. *Physically, of:*
Unproductive ⎰Joel 2:20   867
soil ....⎱Ps. 107:34   586
Trees..........Luke 13:6-9   1044
Females ......Prov. 30:16   633
B. *Significance of:*
A reproach ....Gen. 16:2   17
A judgment....2 Sam. 6:23   300
Absence of
God's   ⎰Ex. 23:26   75
blessing......⎱Deut. 7:14   176
Removal of, from the
Lord ....Ps. 113:9   588
C. *Spiritually:*
Removal of,
in new   ⎰Is. 54:1   702
Israel ....⎱Gal. 4:27   1180
Remedy
against........2 Pet. 1:8   1268
D. *Examples of:*
Sarah.........Gen. 21:2   21
Rebekah......Gen. 25:21   25
Rachel........Gen. 30:22   30
Manoah's
wife.........Judg. 13:2, 3, 24   245
Hannah.......1 Sam. 1:18-20   263
The Shunammite
woman.......2 Kin. 4:14-17   358
Elizabeth ....Luke 1:7, 13, 57   1025

Barsabbas—*son of Saba*
1. Nominated to replace
Judas ....Acts 1:23   1095
2. Sent to
Antioch......Acts 15:22   1111

Barter—*to exchange for something*
Between Joseph and the
Egyptians ......Gen. 47:17   47
Between Solomon and
Hiram..........1 Kin. 5:10, 11   329

Bartholomew—*son of Talmai*
One of Christ's ⎰Matt. 10:3   972
apostles ....⎱Acts 1:13   1094
Called
Nathanael.......John 1:45, 46   1065

Bartimaeus—*son of Timaeus*
Blind beggar healed by
Jesus............Mark 10:46-52   1012

Baruch—*blessed*
1. Son of
Neriah ....Jer. 32:12, 13   750
Jeremiah's faithful
friend ....Jer. 36:4-32   754
The Jewish remnant takes him
to Egypt ......Jer. 43:1-7   760
2. Son of
Zabbai........Neh. 3:20   469
Signs
document....Neh. 10:6   477
3. A Shilonite of
Judah.........Neh. 11:5   478

Barzillai—*of iron*
1. Helps David with
food ....2 Sam. 17:27-29   311
Age restrains him from
following
David.........2 Sam. 19:31-39   313
2. Father of
Adriel ....2 Sam. 21:8   315
3. A postexilic
priest ....Ezra 2:61   455

Base—*lowly*
Of evil character ..1 Cor. 1:28   1149

Basemath—*fragrance*
1. Wife of Esau...Gen. 26:34   27
Called Adah ...Gen. 36:2, 3   36
2. Wife of Esau...Gen. 36:3, 4, 13   36

Called
Mahalath .....Gen. 28:9   28
3. A daughter of
Solomon ......1 Kin. 4:15   328

Bashan—*smooth soil*
A vast highland east of
the Sea of Chinnereth
(Galilee).........Num. 21:33-35   150
Ruled by Og .....Deut. 29:7   195
Conquered by
Israel............Neh. 9:22   476
Assigned to
Manasseh ....Deut. 3:13   172
Defeated by
Hazael ....2 Kin. 10:32, 33   366
Fine cattle ....Ezek. 39:18   822
Typical of   ⎰Ps. 22:12   538
cruelty ....⎱Amos 4:1   873

Bashan Havvothjair
A district named after
Jair ....Deut. 3:14   172

Basin—*cup or bowl for containing liquids*
In the Temple.....Jer. 52:17-19   773
Moses used ......Ex. 24:6   75
Made for the
altar.............Ex. 27:3; 38:3   78
Brought for
David ....2 Sam. 17:28, 29   311
Hiram made.....1 Kin. 7:40   331
Made of gold and
silver.............2 Kin. 25:15   382

Baskets—*something made to hold objects*
A. *Used for carrying:*
Produce ......Deut. 26:2   191
Food ....Matt. 14:20   978
Ceremonial
offerings ....Ex. 29:3, 23   80
Paul...........Acts 9:24, 25   1104
Other objects
(heads).......2 Kin. 10:7   365
B. *Symbolic of:*
Approaching
death ....Gen. 40:16-19   40
Israel's
judgment .....Amos 8:1-3   877
Judah's
judgment .....Jer. 24:1-3   742

Bat—*a flying mammal*
Listed among   ⎰Lev. 11:19   104
unclean birds....⎱Deut. 14:18   183
Lives in dark
places ....Is. 2:19, 20   659

Bath—*a liquid measure (about 9 gallons)*
A tenth of a
homer............Ezek. 45:10   828
For measuring oil ⎰2 Chr. 2:10   420
and wine........⎱Is. 5:10   661

Bathing
A. *For pleasure:*
Pharaoh's
daughter......Ex. 2:5   55
Bathsheba .....2 Sam. 11:2, 3   303
B. *For purification:*
Cleansing the ⎰Gen. 24:32   24
feet ....⎱John 13:10   1080
Ceremonial ⎰Lev. 14:8   108
cleansing.....⎱2 Kin. 5:10-14   360
Before performing priestly
duties.........Ex. 30:19-21   82
Lev. 16:4, 24   110
Jewish
rituals........Mark 7:2   1006

Bath-rabbim—*daughter of multitides*
Gate of
Heshbon ....Song 7:4   652

Bathsheba—*daughter of an oath*
Wife of Uriah .....2 Sam. 11:2, 3   303

SUBJECT	REFERENCE	PAGE
Commits adultery with David	2 Sam. 11:4, 5	303
Husband's death contrived by David	2 Sam. 11:6-25	303
Mourns husband's death	2 Sam. 11:26	304
Becomes David's wife	2 Sam. 11:27	304
Her first child dies	2 Sam. 12:14-19	305
Solomon's mother	2 Sam. 12:24	305
Secures throne for Solomon	1 Kin. 1:15-31	323
Deceived by Adonijah	1 Kin. 2:13-25	325

Bath-shua—*daughter of prosperity*

SUBJECT	REFERENCE	PAGE
Same as Bathsheba	1 Chr. 3:5	390

Battering ram (see Armor)

SUBJECT	REFERENCE	PAGE
Used in destroying walls	{Ezek. 4:2 / Ezek. 21:22	788 / 804

Battle (see War)

Bavvai—*wisher*

SUBJECT	REFERENCE	PAGE
Postexilic worker	Neh. 3:18	469

Bay—*inlet*

SUBJECT	REFERENCE	PAGE
1. Dead Sea's cove at Jordan's mouth	Josh. 15:5	219
Used also of the Nile	Is. 11:15	668
2. Color of a horse	Zech. 6:2	920
3. Name of a tree; figurative of pride	Ps. 37:35	546

Bazaar—*marketplace or street of shops*

SUBJECT	REFERENCE	PAGE
Allowed by Ben-hadad	1 Kin. 20:34	348

Bazluth—*stripping*

SUBJECT	REFERENCE	PAGE
Head of a family	Ezra 2:52	455
Called Bazlith	Neh. 7:54	472

Bdellium—*an oily gum, or a white pearl*

SUBJECT	REFERENCE	PAGE
A valuable mineral of Havilah	Gen. 2:12	5
Manna appeared like	Num. 11:7	139

Beach—*coast*

Place of:

SUBJECT	REFERENCE	PAGE
Jesus' preaching	Matt. 13:2	975
Fisherman's task	Matt. 13:48	977
Jesus' meal with disciples	John 21:9	1088
A prayer meeting	Acts 21:5	1118
A notable shipwreck	Acts 27:39-44	1125
A miracle	Acts 28:1-6	1126

Beads—*ornaments*

SUBJECT	REFERENCE	PAGE
Of silver	Song 1:11	649

Bealiah—*Yahweh is Lord*

SUBJECT	REFERENCE	PAGE
A warrior	1 Chr. 12:5	399

Bealoth—*mistresses*

SUBJECT	REFERENCE	PAGE
Village of Judah	Josh. 15:24	219

Beam

A. *Physical:*

SUBJECT	REFERENCE	PAGE
Wood undergirding floors	1 Kin. 7:2	330
Part of weaver's frame	1 Sam. 17:7	277

B. *Figurative of:*

SUBJECT	REFERENCE	PAGE
The cry for vengeance	Hab. 2:11	904
God's power	Ps. 104:3	581

SUBJECT	REFERENCE	PAGE
Notorious faults	Matt. 7:3-5	969

Bean—*a food*

SUBJECT	REFERENCE	PAGE
Brought to David by friends	2 Sam. 17:27, 28	311
Mixed with grain for bread	Ezek. 4:9	789

Bear—*a wild animal*

A. *Natural:*

SUBJECT	REFERENCE	PAGE
Killed by David	1 Sam. 17:34, 35	278
Two tore up forty-two lads	2 Kin. 2:23, 24	357

B. *Figurative of:*

SUBJECT	REFERENCE	PAGE
Fierce revenge	2 Sam. 17:8	310
Fool's folly	Prov. 17:12	622
Wicked rulers	Prov. 28:15	631
World empire	Dan. 7:5	843
Final antichrist	Rev. 13:2	1301
Messianic times	Is. 11:7	668

Bear—*to carry, yield*

A. *Used literally of:*

SUBJECT	REFERENCE	PAGE
Giving birth	Gen. 17:19	18
Cross	Matt. 27:32	993

B. *Used figuratively of:*

SUBJECT	REFERENCE	PAGE
Excessive punishment	Gen. 4:13	8
Divine deliverance	Ex. 19:4	70
Respon-sibility for sin	{Lev. 5:17 / Lev. 24:15	99 / 119
Burden of leadership	Deut. 1:9, 12	169
Personal shame	Ezek. 16:54	799
Evangelism	Acts 9:15	1104
Spiritual help	Gal. 6:1, 2	1181
Spiritual produc-tivity	John 15:2, 4, 8	1082

Beard—*hair grown on the face*

A. *Long, worn by:*

SUBJECT	REFERENCE	PAGE
Aaron	Ps. 133:2	598
Samson	Judg. 16:17	248
David	1 Sam. 21:13	283

B. *In mourning:*

SUBJECT	REFERENCE	PAGE
Left untrimmed	2 Sam. 19:24	313
Plucked	Ezra 9:3	461
Cut	Jer. 48:37, 38	765

C. *Features regarding:*

SUBJECT	REFERENCE	PAGE
Leper's must be shaven	Lev. 13:29-33	107
Half-shaven, an indignity	2 Sam. 10:4, 5	303
Harming of,	{Lev. 19:27 / Lev. 21:5	114 / 115
Shaven, by Egyptians	Gen. 41:14	41
Saliva on, sign of lunacy	1 Sam. 21:13	283
Holding to, a token of respect	2 Sam. 20:9	314

Beasts—*four-footed animals; mammals*

A. *Characteristics of:*

SUBJECT	REFERENCE	PAGE
God-created	Gen. 1:21	4
Of their own order	1 Cor. 15:39	1161
Named by Adam	Gen. 2:20	6
Suffer in man's sin	Rom. 8:20-22	1138
Perish at death	Ps. 49:12-15	553
Follow instincts	{Is. 1:3 / Jude 10	657 / 1287
Under God's control	1 Sam. 6:7-14	267

SUBJECT	REFERENCE	PAGE
Wild	Mark 1:13	999
For man's food	{Gen. 9:3 / Acts 10:12, 13	11 / 1105
Eat people	1 Sam. 17:46 / 1 Cor. 15:32	278 / 1160
Used in sacrifices	Lev. 27:26-29	123
Spiritual lessons from	{1 Kin. 4:33 / Job 12:7	328 / 503

B. *Treatment of:*

SUBJECT	REFERENCE	PAGE
No sexual relation with	Lev. 20:15, 16	115
Proper care of, sign of righteous man	{Gen. 33:13, 14 / Prov. 12:10	34 / 618
Abuse of, rebuked	Num. 22:28-32	151
Extra food for, while working	{Deut. 25:4 / 1 Tim. 5:18	191 / 1219

C. *Typical of:*

SUBJECT	REFERENCE	PAGE
Man's folly	Ps. 73:22	565
Unregenerate men	Titus 1:12	1229
False prophets	2 Pet. 2:12	1269
Antichrist	Rev. 13:1-4	1301

See Animals

Beaten gold—*gold shaped by hammering*

SUBJECT	REFERENCE	PAGE
Ornamental shields	{1 Kin. 10:16, 17 / 2 Chr. 9:15, 16	336 / 426

Beaten oil—*highest quality of olive oil*

SUBJECT	REFERENCE	PAGE
In sacrifices	Ex. 29:39, 40	81
In tent of meeting lamp	Lev. 24:2	118
In trade	1 Kin. 5:10, 11	329

Beaten silver—*silver shaped by hammering*

SUBJECT	REFERENCE	PAGE
Overlaid idols	{Is. 30:22 / Hab. 2:19	682 / 905
In trade	Jer. 10:9	728

Beatings—*striking the body with blows; floggings*

A. *Inflicted on:*

SUBJECT	REFERENCE	PAGE
The wicked	Deut. 25:3	191
The guilty	Lev. 19:20	114
Children	Prov. 22:15	626
The disobe-dient	{Prov. 26:3 / Luke 12:47, 48	630 / 1043

B. *Victims of unjust beatings:*

SUBJECT	REFERENCE	PAGE
A servant	Luke 20:10, 11	1052
Christ	{Is. 50:6 / Mark 15:19	699 / 1019
The apostles	Acts 5:40	1100
Paul	Acts 16:19-24	1113

Beatitudes—*pronouncements of blessings*

SUBJECT	REFERENCE	PAGE
Jesus begins His sermon with	{Matt. 5:3-12 / Luke 6:20-22	966 / 1033

Beautiful gate—*gate at East of Temple area*

SUBJECT	REFERENCE	PAGE
Lame man healed there	Acts 3:1-10	1096

Beauty, physical

A. *Temporal:*

SUBJECT	REFERENCE	PAGE
Seen in nature	{Hos. 14:6 / Matt. 6:28, 29	861 / 969
Consumed in dissipation	Is. 28:1	679
Contest Abishag, winner of	1 Kin. 1:1-4	323
Esther, winner of	Esth. 2:1-17	485
Destroyed by sin	Ps. 39:11	548
Ends in grave	Ps. 49:14	553

SUBJECT	REFERENCE	PAGE

Beheading—*a form of capital punishment*

Ish-bosheth	2 Sam. 4:5-7	298
John the Baptist	Matt. 14:10	977
James	Acts 12:2	1107
Martyrs	Rev. 20:4	1306

Behemoth—*a colossal beast*

Described	Job 40:15-24	522

Beka (see Jewish measures)

Half a shekel	Ex. 38:26	90

Bel—*lord*

Patron god of	⎰Is. 46:1	696
Babylon	⎱Jer. 51:44	771
Marduk title	Jer. 50:2	767

Bela—*destruction*

1. King of
Edom	Gen. 36:32	37
2. Reubenite
chief	1 Chr. 5:8	391
3. Benjamin's
son	Gen. 46:21	46
4. A city | Gen. 14:2, 8 | 15 |

Belial—*worthless, wicked*

A. *Applied properly to:*
Seducers	Deut. 13:13	182
The profligate	Judg. 19:22	251
Eli's sons	1 Sam. 2:12	264
Rebels	1 Sam. 10:27	271
A fool	1 Sam. 25:25	286
The wicked	1 Sam. 30:22	290
Liars	1 Kin. 21:10, 13	349
Satan	2 Cor. 6:15	1169

B. *Applied improperly to:*
Hannah	1 Sam. 1:16	263
David	2 Sam. 16:7	309

Believers—*those who have received Christ; Christians*

Applied to	⎰Acts 5:14	1099
converts	⎱1 Tim. 4:12	1219

Bellows—*an instrument used in forcing air at fire*

A figure of affliction	Jer. 6:29	725
Descriptive of God's judgment	Jer. 6:27-30	725

Bells

On Aaron's	⎰Ex. 28:33, 34	79
garment	⎱Ex. 39:25, 26	91
Attention-getters	Is. 3:16, 18	660
Symbols of consecration	Zech. 14:20	926

Beloved—*a title of endearment*

A. *Applied naturally to:*
A wife	Deut. 21:15, 16	188
A husband	Song 6:1-3	651

B. *Applied spiritually to:*
Christ	Matt. 3:17	965
Spiritual Israel	Rom. 9:25	1139
Believers	Col. 3:12	1201
Christian friends	Rom. 16:8, 9	1145
New Jerusalem	Rev. 21:9, 10	1307

Belshazzar—*Bel protect the king*

Son of Nebuchadnezzar	Dan. 5:2	841
Gives feast	Dan. 5:1, 4	841
Disturbed by handwriting	Dan. 5:5-12	841
Seeks Daniel's aid	Dan. 5:13-16	841
Daniel interprets for him	Dan. 5:17-29	841
Last Chaldean king	Dan. 5:30, 31	842

SUBJECT	REFERENCE	PAGE

Belt

Used for:
Holding sword	1 Sam. 18:4	279

Belteshazzar—*protect his life*

Daniel's Babylonian name	Dan. 1:7	835

Ben—*son*

Levite gatekeeper	1 Chr. 15:18	401

Ben-abinadab

The father of one of Solomon's deputies	1 Kin. 4:11	328

Benaiah—*Yahweh has built*

1. Jehoiada's
son	2 Sam. 23:20	318
A mighty man	2 Sam. 23:20, 21	318
David's bodyguard	2 Sam. 8:18	302
Faithful to	⎰2 Sam. 15:18	308
David	⎱2 Sam. 20:23	314
Escorts Solomon to the throne	1 Kin. 1:38-40	324
Executes Adonijah, Joab and	⎰1 Kin. 2:25, 29-	
Shimei	⎱ 34, 46	326
Commander-in-chief	1 Kin. 2:35	326
2. One of David's mighty
men	2 Sam. 23:30	318
Divisional commander	1 Chr. 27:14	412
3. Levite
musician	1 Chr. 15:18-20	401
4. Priestly	⎰1 Chr. 15:24	401
trumpeter	⎱1 Chr. 16:6	402
5. Levite of Asaph's
family	2 Chr. 20:14	434
6. Simeonite | 1 Chr. 4:36 | 391 |
7. Levite
overseer	2 Chr. 31:13	444
8. Father of leader
Pelatiah	Ezek. 11:1, 13	793
9-12. Four postexilic Jews who divorced their foreign
wives	Ezra 10:25-43	462

Ben-ammi—*son of my kinsman*

Son of Lot; father of the Ammonites	Gen. 19:38	20

Ben-deker—*piercing; mattock*

Father of one of Solomon's officers	1 Kin. 4:9	328

Bene-berak—*sons of Berak* (lightning)

A town of Dan	Josh. 19:45	251

Benediction—*an act of blessing*

A. *Characteristics of:*
Instituted by God	Gen. 1:22, 28	4
Divinely approved	Deut. 10:8	179
Aaronic form	Num. 6:23-26	134
Apostolic form	2 Cor. 13:14	1174
Jesus' last words	Luke 24:50, 51	1059

B. *Pronounced upon:*
Creation	Gen. 1:22, 28	4
New world	Gen. 9:1, 2	11
Abraham	Gen. 14:19, 20	16
Marriage	Gen. 24:60	25
Son (Jacob)	Gen. 27:28, 29	27
Monarch (Pharaoh)	Gen. 47:7, 10	47
Sons (Joseph's)	⎰Gen. 48:15, 16,	
	⎱ 20	48
Tribes (Israel's)	Deut. 33:1-29	201
Foreigner	Ruth 1:8, 9	256
People	2 Sam. 6:18	300

SUBJECT	REFERENCE	PAGE

Jesus	Luke 2:34	1028
Song of Zacharias	Luke 1:68-79	1026
Children's blessing	Mark 10:16	1010

Benefactor—*one who bestows benefits*

A. *Materially, God as:*
Israel's	Deut. 7:6-26	176
Unbeliever's	Acts 14:15-18	1110
Christian's	Phil. 4:19	1196

B. *Spiritually:*
By God	Eph. 1:3-6	1185
Through Christ	Eph. 2:13-22	1186
For enrichment	Eph. 1:16-19	1185

C. *Attitudes toward:*
Murmuring	Num. 11:1-10	139
Forgetfulness	Ps. 106:13	584
Rejection	Acts 13:44-47	1109
Remembrance	Luke 7:1-5	1033
Gratefulness	Acts 13:48	1110

Benefice—*an enriching act or gift*

Manifested by a church	Phil. 4:15-17	1196
Encouraged in a friend	Philem. 17-22	1234
Justified in works	James 2:14-17	1254
Remembered in heaven	1 Tim. 6:18, 19	1220

Bene-jaakan—*sons of Jaakan*

A wilderness station	Num. 33:31	162

Benevolence—*generosity toward others*

A. *Exercised toward:*
The poor	Gal. 2:10	1178
The needy	Eph. 4:28	1188
Enemies	Prov. 25:21	629
God's servant	Phil. 4:14-17	1196

B. *Measured by:*
Ability	Acts 11:29	1107
Love	1 Cor. 13:3	1158
Sacrifice	Mark 12:41-44	1014
Bountifulness	2 Cor. 9:6-15	1171

C. *Blessings of:*
Fulfills a grace	Rom. 12:6, 13	1141
Performs a spiritual sacrifice	Heb. 13:16	1249
Makes us "more blessed"	Acts 20:35	1118
Enriches the	⎰Prov. 11:25	617
giver	⎱Is. 58:10, 11	705
Reward	1 Tim. 6:18, 19	1220

Ben-geber—*son of Geber*

Officer of Solomon	1 Kin. 4:13	328

Ben-hadad—*son of the god Hadad*

1. Ben-hadad I, king of Damascus. Hired by Asa, king of Judah, to attack Baasha, king of
Israel	1 Kin. 15:18-21	342
2. Ben-hadad II, king of Damascus. Makes war on Ahab, king of
Israel	1 Kin. 20:1-21	347
Defeated by Israel	1 Kin. 20:26-34	348
Fails in siege against	⎰2 Kin. 6:24-33	361
Samaria	⎱2 Kin. 7:6-20	362
Killed by Hazael	2 Kin. 8:7-15	363
3. Ben-hadad III, king of Damascus. Loses all Israelite conquests made by Hazael, his
father	2 Kin. 13:3-25	368

SUBJECT	REFERENCE	PAGE

SUBJECT	REFERENCE	PAGE

Binding—continued

B. *Used figuratively of:*
A fixed
agreement ....Num. 30:2 — 159
God's Word....Prov. 3:3 — 610
The broken-
hearted ....Is. 61:1 — 708
Satan.........Luke 13:16 — 1044
The wicked....Matt. 13:30 — 976
Ceremo-
nialism.......Matt. 23:4 — 987
The keys......Matt. 16:19 — 980
A determined
plan..........Acts 20:22 — 1118
Marriage......Rom. 7:2 — 1136

Binea
A son of Moza ....1 Chr. 8:37 — 395

Binnui—*built*
1. Head of postexilic
family........Neh. 7:15 — 472
Called Bani ...Ezra 2:10 — 454
2. Son of Pahath-
moab ....Ezra 10:30 — 462
3. Son of Bani ...Ezra 10:38 — 462
4. Postexilic
Levite.........Neh. 12:8 — 478
Henadad's
son ....Neh. 10:9 — 477
Family of, builds
wall..........Neh. 3:24 — 469

Bird cage
Used
figuratively......Jer. 5:27 — 723

Birds—*vertebrates with feathers and wings*
A. *List of:*
Buzzard ....Lev. 11:13 — 104
Carrion
vulture........Lev. 11:18 — 104
Cock ....Matt. 26:34, 74 — 991
Mark 14:30 — 1017
Luke 22:61 — 1055
John 18:27 — 1085
Cormorant.....Lev. 11:17 — 104
Dove ....Gen. 8:8 — 10
Eagle.........Job 39:27 — 521
Hawk.........Job 39:26 — 521
Hen ....Matt. 23:37 — 988
Heron ....Lev. 11:19 — 104
Hoopoe.......Lev. 11:19 — 104
Ostrich ....Lev. 11:16 — 104
Owls.........Job 30:29 — 514
Desert ....Ps. 102:6 — 580
Great........Lev. 11:17 — 104
Little ....Lev. 11:17 — 104
White ....Lev. 11:18 — 104
Peacock ......1 Kin. 10:22 — 336
Pelican ....Ps. 102:6 — 580
Pigeon........Lev. 12:6 — 105
Quail ....Num. 11:31, 32 — 140
Raven ....Job 38:41 — 521
Sea gull.......Lev. 11:16 — 104
Sparrow ......Matt. 10:29-31 — 973
Stork ....Ps. 104:17 — 582
Swallow ......Ps. 84:3 — 572
Swift ....Jer. 8:7 — 726
Vulture.......Lev. 11:13 — 104
Red kite ....Deut. 14:13 — 183
Partridge .....1 Sam. 26:20 — 287
Turtledove.....Song 2:12 — 649
B. *Features regarding:*
Created by
God..........Gen. 1:20, 21 — 4
Named by
Adam.........Gen. 2:19, 20 — 5
Clean,
unclean ......Gen. 8:20 — 11
Differ from
animals ......1 Cor. 15:39 — 1161
Under man's
dominion .....Ps. 8:8 — 531
For food......Gen. 9:2, 3 — 11
Belong to
God...........Ps. 50:11 — 553
God provides / Ps. 104:10-12 — 582
for........... \ Luke 12:23, 24 — 1042
Can be
tamed........James 3:7 — 1255

Differ in
singing........Song 2:12 — 649
Some
migratory.....Jer. 8:7 — 726
Solomon
writes of ......1 Kin. 4:33 — 328
Clean,
used in / Lev. 1:14 — 96
sacrifices.... \ Luke 2:24 — 1027
Worshiped by
man ....Rom. 1:23 — 1132
C. *Figurative of:*
Escape from
evil ....Ps. 124:7 — 596
A wanderer....Prov. 27:8 — 630
Snares of
death ....Eccl. 9:12 — 644
Cruel kings ...Is. 46:11 — 696
Hostile
nations.......Jer. 12:9 — 730
Wicked rich ..Jer. 17:11 — 735
Kingdom of
heaven.......Matt. 13:32 — 976
Maternal
love..........Matt. 23:37 — 988

Birsha—*with wickedness*
A king of
Gomorrah ....Gen. 14:2, 8, 10 — 15

Birth—*the act of coming into life*
A. *Kinds of:*
Natural........Eccl. 7:1 — 642
Figurative .....Is. 37:3 — 686
Super-
natural.......Matt. 1:18-25 — 963
The new......John 3:5 — 1066
See New birth
B. *Natural, features regarding:*
Pain of, results from
sin...........Gen. 3:16 — 7
Produces a sinful
being ....Ps. 51:5 — 554
Makes
ceremonially / Lev. 12:2, 5 — 105
unclean ...... \ Luke 2:22 — 1027
Affliction
from ....John 9:1 — 1075
Twins of,
differ.........Gen. 25:21-23 — 25
Sometimes brings
death ....Gen. 35:16-20 — 35
Pain of,
forgotten.....John 16:21 — 1083

Birthday—*date of one's birth*
Job and Jeremiah / Job 3:1-11 — 497
curse theirs...... \ Jer. 20:14, 15 — 738
Celebration:
Pharaoh's.........Gen. 40:20 — 40
Herod's ....Mark 6:21 — 1005

Birthright—*legal rights inherited by birth*
A. *Blessings of:*
Seniority ......Gen. 43:33 — 44
Double
portion........Deut. 21:15-17 — 188
Royal
succession ....2 Chr. 21:3 — 435
B. *Loss of:*
Esau's— / Gen. 25:29-34 — 26
by sale....... \ Rom. 9:12 — 1139
Reuben's—
as a pun- / Gen. 49:3, 4 — 48
ishment...... \ 1 Chr. 5:1, 2 — 391
Manasseh's—
by Jacob's / Gen. 48:15-20 — 48
will .... \ 1 Chr. 5:1, 2 — 391
David's brother—by divine
will ....1 Sam. 16:2-22 — 276
Adonijah's—by the
Lord ....1 Kin. 2:15 — 325
Hosah's son's—by his father's
will ....1 Chr. 26:10 — 411
C. *Transferred to:*
Jacob...........Gen. 27:6-46 — 27

Judah..........Gen. 49:8-10 — 49
Solomon.......1 Chr. 28:5-7 — 413
See First-born

Births, foretold
A. *Over a short period:*
Ishmael's ......Gen. 16:11 — 17
Isaac's........Gen. 18:10 — 18
Samson's .....Judg. 13:3, 24 — 245
Samuel's......1 Sam. 1:11, 20 — 263
Shunammite's
son's.........2 Kin. 4:16, 17 — 358
John the
Baptist's .....Luke 1:13 — 1025
B. *Over a longer period:*
Josiah's........1 Kin. 13:2 — 339
Cyrus' ....Is. 45:1-4 — 695
Christ's........Gen. 3:15 — 7
Mic. 5:1-3 — 893

Birthstool
Hebrew women
used..............Ex. 1:16 — 54

Birzaith—*olive well*
An Asherite ....1 Chr. 7:31 — 395

Bishlam—*in peace*
A Persian officer ..Ezra 4:7 — 456

Bishop—*an overseer; elder*
A. *Qualifications of, given by:*
Paul, called
"overseer" ....1 Tim. 3:1-7 — 1218
Peter, called
"elder"........1 Pet. 5:1-4 — 1264
B. *Duties of:*
Oversee the / Acts 20:17, —
church....... \ 28-31 — 1118
Shepherd God's
flock..........1 Pet. 5:2 — 1264
Watch over / 1 Thess. 5:14 — 1208
men's souls ..\ Heb. 13:17 — 1249
Teach ....1 Tim. 5:17 — 1219
C. *Office of:*
Same as
elder.........Acts 20:17, 28 — 1118
Several in a / Acts 20:17, 28 — 1118
church....... \ Phil. 1:1 — 1193
Follows
ordination....Titus 1:5, 7 — 1229
Held by
Christ.........1 Pet. 2:25 — 1262

Bit—*a part of a horse's bridle*
Figurative, of man's stubborn
nature...........Ps. 32:9 — 543
James 3:3 — 1254

Bithia—*daughter of Yahweh*
Pharaoh's daughter; wife of
Mered...........1 Chr. 4:18 — 390

Bithynia—*a province of Asia Minor*
The Spirit keeps Paul
from ....Acts 16:7 — 1112
Peter writes to
Christians of ...1 Pet. 1:1 — 1260

Bitter herbs
Part of Passover / Ex. 12:8 — 63
meal .... \ Num. 9:11 — 138
Descriptive of
sorrow ....Lam. 3:15 — 779

"Bitter is sweet"
Descriptive of man's
hunger..........Prov. 27:7 — 630

Bitterness—*extreme enmity; sour temper*
A. *Kinds of:*
The soul......Job 3:20 — 497
The heart.....Prov. 14:10 — 619
Words.......Ps. 64:3 — 559
Death ....1 Sam. 15:32 — 276
"Water of" ....Num. 5:24 — 133

77

SUBJECT	REFERENCE	PAGE	SUBJECT	REFERENCE	PAGE	SUBJECT	REFERENCE	PAGE

SUBJECT	REFERENCE	PAGE	SUBJECT	REFERENCE	PAGE	SUBJECT	REFERENCE	PAGE

Buried alive

Two rebellious
families..........Num. 16:27-34 — 145
Desire of some....Rev. 6:15, 16 — 1297

Burning bush

God speaks
from ....Ex. 3:2 — 56

Business—*one's work*

A. *Attitudes toward:*
See God's
hand..........James 4:13 — 1255
Be diligent.....Prov. 22:29 — 626
Be
industrious....Rom. 12:8, 11 — 1142
Be honest....2 Cor. 8:20-22 — 1170
Put God's
first.........Matt. 6:33, 34 — 969
Keep heaven in
mind.........Matt. 6:19-21 — 968
Give portion...Mal. 3:8-12 — 931
Avoid
anxiety ......Luke 12:22-30 — 1042
Remember the
fool..........Luke 12:15-21 — 1042

B. *Those diligent in:*
Joseph.........Gen. 39:11 — 39
Moses........Heb. 3:5 — 1240
Officers in
Israel........2 Chr. 34:11, 12 — 447
Daniel........Dan. 6:4 — 842
Mordecai .....Esth. 10:2, 3 — 491
Paul..........Acts 20:17-35 — 1118

Busybodies—*meddlers*

Women
guilty of.........1 Tim. 5:13 — 1219
Some   (2 Thess. 3:11,
Christians......(12 — 1213
Admonitions
against..........1 Pet. 4:15 — 1264

See Slander; Whisperer

Butler—*an officer*

Imprisonment of
Pharaoh's ....Gen. 40:1-13 — 40
Same as
"cupbearer" ......1 Kin. 10:5 — 335

Butter—*curdled milk*

Article of diet.....2 Sam. 17:29 — 311
Set before
visitors...........Gen. 18:8 — 18
Got by churning ..Prov. 30:33 — 633
Fed to infants....Is. 7:15, 22 — 663
Illustrative of
prosperity ....Deut. 32:14 — 199
Figurative of smooth
words ....Ps. 55:21 — 556

Buz—*contempt*

1. A Gadite.......1 Chr. 5:14 — 391
2. An Aramean tribe descending
from Nahor ...Gen. 22:20, 21 — 22

Buzi—*descendant of Buz*

Father of
Ezekiel...........Ezek. 1:3 — 786

Buzite—*belonging to Buz*

Of the tribe of
Buz.............Job 32:2 — 515

Byword—*saying; remark*

Predicted as a
taunt............Deut. 28:37 — 194
Job describes
himself..........Job 17:6 — 506

C

Cabbon—*surround*

Village of Judah...Josh. 15:40 — 219

Cabul—*unproductive*

1. Town of
Asher.........Josh. 19:27 — 222
2. A district of Galilee offered to
Hiram.........1 Kin. 9:12, 13 — 335
Solomon placed people
in.............2 Chr. 8:2 — 425

Caesar—*a title of Roman emperors*

A. *Used in reference to:*
1. Augustus Caesar (31B.C.–A.D.14)
Decree of brings Joseph and
Mary to
Bethlehem ....Luke 2:1 — 1027
    Mic. 5:2 — 893
2. Tiberius Caesar (A.D. 14–37)
Christ's ministry dated
by ....Luke 3:1-23 — 1028
Tribute paid
to............Matt. 22:17-21 — 986
Jews side
with ....John 19:12 — 1086
3. Claudius Caesar (A.D. 41–54)
Famine in time
of............Acts 11:28 — 1107
Banished Jews from
Rome.......Acts 18:2 — 1115
4. Nero Caesar (A.D. 54–68) Paul
appealed to ...Acts 25:8-12 — 1123
Converts in household
of............Phil. 4:22 — 1196
Paul before ...2 Tim. 4:16-18 — 1226
Paul to be sent
before.......Acts 25:21 — 1123

B. *Represented Roman authority:*
Image   (Matt. 22:19-21 — 986
on   {Mark 12:15-16 — 1014
coins........(Luke 20:24 — 1052
  (Matt. 22:19, 21 — 986
Received   {Mark 12:14, 17 — 1014
tax...........(Luke 20:25 — 1052
Jesus called (Luke 23:2 — 1056
threat to .....(John 19:12 — 1086
Pilate's loyalty to
questioned ....John 19:12 — 1086
Chosen over
Jesus........John 19:12 — 1086

Caesar's household—*the imperial staff*

Greeted the
Philippians ....Phil. 4:22 — 1196

Caesarea—*pertaining to Caesar*

Roman capital of (Acts 12:19 — 1108
Palestine........(Acts 23:33 — 1121
Home of Philip....Acts 8:40 — 1103
Home of
Cornelius.........Acts 10:1 — 1105
Peter
preached at ......Acts 10:34-43 — 1106
Paul preached here 3
times.............Acts 9:30 — 1104
Paul
escorted to ....Acts 23:23, 33 — 1121
Paul
imprisoned at.....Acts 25:4 — 1123
Paul appealed to
Caesar at........Acts 25:8-13 — 1123

Caesarea Philippi

A city in north Palestine; scene of
Peter's great
confession........Matt. 16:13-20 — 980
Probable place of the
transfiguration ...Matt. 17:1-13 — 980

Cage—*an enclosure*

Judah
compared to......Jer. 5:27 — 723
Figurative of
captivity ....Ezek. 19:9 — 801

Caiaphas—*depression*

Son-in-law of Annas; high
priest.............John 18:13 — 1085
Makes prophecy ..John 11:49-52 — 1078
Jesus before......John 18:23, 24 — 1085
Apostles before ...Acts 4:1-22 — 1097

Cain—*smith; spear*

Adam's son .....Gen. 4:1 — 7
Offering   (Gen. 4:2-7 — 7
rejected ....(Heb. 11:4 — 1246
Was of the evil
one..............1 John 3:12 — 1276
Murders Abel .....Gen. 4:8 — 7
Becomes a
wanderer ....Gen. 4:9-15 — 8
Builds city ....Gen. 4:16, 17 — 8
A type of evil .....Jude 11 — 1287

Cainan—*fixed*

A son of
Arphaxad ....Luke 3:36, 37 — 1029

Cake—*a bread*

A. *Kinds of:*
Bread..........Ex. 29:23 — 80
Unleavened....Num. 6:19 — 134
Fig ....1 Sam. 30:12 — 290
Raisin ....1 Chr. 16:3 — 402
Barley ....Ezek. 4:12 — 789
Of fine flour ...Lev. 2:4 — 96
Leavened ......Lev. 7:13 — 100
Baked with
oil ....Num. 11:8 — 139

B. *Used literally of:*
Food ....2 Sam. 13:6 — 306
Idolatry........Jer. 44:19 — 761
Food prepared for
Elijah ....1 Kin. 17:13 — 344

C. *Used figuratively of:*
Defeat.........Judg. 7:13 — 239
Weak
religion ....Hos. 7:8 — 857

Calah

A great city of Assyria built by
Nimrod..........Gen. 10:11, 12 — 12

Calamities—*disasters*

A. *Kinds of:*
Personal.......Job 6:2 — 499
Tribal.........Judg. 20:34-48 — 252
National......Lam. 1:1-22 — 776
Punitive ......Num. 16:12-35 — 145
Judicial.......Deut. 32:35 — 200
World-wide....Luke 21:25-28 — 1053
Sudden ....Prov. 6:15 — 613
    1 Thess. 5:3 — 1208

B. *Attitudes toward:*
Unrepent-
ance ....Prov. 1:24-26 — 610
Repentance....Jer. 18:8 — 736
Hardness of
heart..........Ex. 14:8, 17 — 66
Bitterness.....Ruth 1:20, 21 — 256
Defeat.........1 Sam. 4:15-18 — 266
Submission ....Job 2:9, 10 — 496
Prayer-
fulness........Ps. 141:5 — 601
Hopefulness ...Ps. 27:1-3 — 540

Calamus—*the sweet cane*

Figurative of
love..............Song 4:14 — 651
Rendered "fragrant
cane"...........Ex. 30:23 — 82
Rendered "sweet
cane" ....Jer. 6:20 — 724

Calcol

A son of Zerah....1 Chr. 2:6 — 388

Caleb—*dog; also bold*

1. Son of
Jephunneh....Josh. 15:13 — 219
Sent as spy ....Num. 13:2, 6 — 141
Gave good
report........Num. 13:27, 30 — 142

SUBJECT	REFERENCE	PAGE

Carmel—continued
"Fruitful
field"..........Is. 16:10 — 671
"Fruitful
country".....Jer. 2:7 — 718
2. City of
Judah........Josh. 15:55 — 220
Site of Saul's
victory....1 Sam. 15:12 — 275
Home of David's
wife..........1 Sam. 27:3 — 288
3. A mountain of
Palestine.....Josh. 19:26 — 222
Joshua defeated king
there.........Josh. 12:22 — 217
Scene of Elijah's
triumph....1 Kin. 18:19-45 — 345
Elisha visits....2 Kin. 2:25 — 357
Place of
beauty.......Song 7:5 — 652
Figurative of
strength .....Jer. 46:18 — 763
Barrenness
foretold.......Amos 1:2 — 871

Carmelite, Carmelitess
Nabal............1 Sam. 30:5 — 290
           2 Sam. 2:2 — 295
Hezro...........2 Sam. 23:35 — 318
Abigail...........1 Sam. 27:3 — 288

Carmi—vinedresser
1. Son of
Reuben.......Gen. 46:9 — 46
2. Father of
Achan........Josh. 7:1 — 211

Carnal—fleshly, worldly
Used literally of:
Sexual relations...Lev. 19:20 — 114

Carob pod—seedcase of the carob, or locust tree
Rendered "pod";
fed to swine.......Luke 15:16 — 1046

Carpenter—a skilled woodworker
David's house
built by.....2 Sam. 5:11 — 299
Temple
repaired by.......2 Chr. 24:12 — 437
Idols made by.....Is. 44:13 — 694
Temple
restored by.......Ezra 3:7 — 455
Joseph
works as.........Matt. 13:55 — 977

Carpenter tools—implements for the carpenter trade
Axe...............Deut. 19:5 — 186
Hammer..........Jer. 23:29 — 741
Line ....Zech. 2:1 — 919
Nail..............Jer. 10:4 — 728
Saw..............1 Kin. 7:9 — 330

Carpet—a woven cloth or mat
Described as:
Rich ....Judg. 5:10 — 236
Of many colors....Ezek. 27:24 — 810

Carpus—fruit
Paul's friend at
Troas............2 Tim. 4:13 — 1226

Carrion vulture
Unclean bird......Lev. 11:18 — 104

Carshena—plowman
Prince of Persia ...Esth. 1:14 — 485

Cart—a wagon
Made of wood.....1 Sam. 6:14 — 267
Sometimes
covered ....Num. 7:3 — 134
Drawn by cows ...1 Sam. 6:7 — 267
Used in
threshing.........Is. 28:28 — 680
Used for hauling ..Amos 2:13 — 873
Ark carried by ....2 Sam. 6:3 — 299
Figurative of sin ..Is. 5:18 — 661

Carving—cutting figures in wood or stone
Used in worship...Ex. 31:1-7 — 82
Found in homes...1 Kin. 6:18 — 329
Employed by
idolators.........Judg. 18:18 — 249
Used in the
Temple..........1 Kin. 6:35 — 330

Casement—lattice, criss-crossed strips of wood or metal
Looked through...Judg. 5:28 — 237
           Prov. 7:6 — 614
Fallen through ....2 Kin. 1:2 — 355

Casiphia—silvery
Home of exiled
Levites...........Ezra 8:17 — 460

Casluh
Descendant of
Ham ....1 Chr. 1:8, 12 — 387

Casluhim
A tribe descended from
Mizraim..........Gen. 10:14 — 13

Cassia—amber
An ingredient of holy
oil...............Ex. 30:24, 25 — 82
An article of
commerce........Ezek. 27:19 — 810
Noted for
fragrance.........Ps. 45:8 — 551

Castaway—worthless; reprobated
The   (Matt. 25:30 — 990
rejected ....\2 Pet. 2:4 — 1268
Warning
concerning.......1 Cor. 9:27 — 1155

Caste—divisions of society
Some leaders of
low..............Judg. 11:1-11 — 243
David aware of....1 Sam. 18:18, 23 — 279
Jews and Samaritans
observe..........John 4:9 — 1067
Abolished........Acts 10:28-35 — 1106

Castle—fortress, tower
A. *Used literally of:*
King's
residence......2 Kin. 15:25 — 371
B. *Used figuratively of:*
Offended
brother ....Prov. 18:19 — 623

Castration—removal of male testicles
Disqualified for
congregation .....Deut. 23:1 — 189
Rights restored in new
covenant.........Is. 56:3-5 — 704
Figurative of absolute
devotion.........Matt. 19:12 — 983

Caterpillar—an insect living on vegetation
Works with
locust ....Is. 33:4 — 684
Devours land......Amos 4:9 — 874

Cattle—animals (collectively)
Created by God ...Gen. 1:24 — 4
Adam named......Gen. 2:20 — 6
Entered the ark ...Gen. 7:13, 14 — 10
Struck by God ....Ex. 12:29 — 64
Firstborn of, belong to
God ....Ex. 34:19 — 86
Can be unclean ...Lev. 5:2 — 98
Taken as
plunder..........Josh. 8:2, 27 — 212
Belong to God ....Ps. 50:10 — 553
Nebuchadnezzar eats
like.............Dan. 4:33 — 840
Pastureless.......Joel 1:18 — 866
East of Jordan good
for ....Num. 32:1, 4 — 161
Given as ransom ..Num. 3:45 — 131

Cattle merchants
From Arabia .....Ezek. 27:21 — 810

Cattle thieves
Must return
double...........Ex. 22:4 — 73

Caution—provident care; alertness
For safety........Acts 23:10,
           16-24 — 1121
For defense ......Neh. 4:12-23 — 470
For attack ....1 Sam. 20:1-17 — 281
A principle.......Prov. 14:15, 16 — 619
Neglect of........1 Sam. 26:4-16 — 287

Cavalry—mounted soldiers
Captured by
David ....2 Sam. 8:3, 4 — 301
Employed by
Solomon ....1 Kin. 10:26 — 336
Nebuchad-
nezzar's ....Ezek. 26:7, 10 — 808

Cave—a cavern
A. *Used for:*
Habitation .....Gen. 19:30 — 20
Refuge ....1 Kin. 18:4 — 344
Burial.........John 11:38 — 1078
Conceal-
ment..........1 Sam. 22:1 — 283
Protection .....Is. 2:19 — 659
           Rev. 6:15 — 1297
B. *Mentioned in Scripture:*
Machpelah.....Gen. 23:9 — 22
Makkedah.....Josh. 10:16, 17 — 214
Adullam.......1 Sam. 22:1 — 283
Engedi.........1 Sam. 24:1, 3 — 284

Cedar—an evergreen tree
A. *Used in:*
Ceremonial
cleansing.....Lev. 14:4-7 — 108
Building
Temple........1 Kin. 5:5, 6 — 328
Building
palaces........2 Sam. 5:11 — 299
Gifts...........1 Chr. 22:4 — 407
Making idols...Is. 44:14, 17 — 694
B. *Figurative of:*
Israel's glory...Num. 24:6 — 153
Christ's glory ..Ezek. 17:22, 23 — 800
Growth of
saints ....Ps. 92:12 — 577
Mighty
nations........Amos 2:9 — 872
Arrogant
rulers ....Is. 2:13 — 659

Ceiling—upper surface of a room
Temple's ....1 Kin. 6:15 — 329

Celebrate—to commemorate
Feast of Weeks ...Ex. 34:22 — 86
Feast of
Ingathering .....Ex. 34:22 — 86
The Sabbath .....Lev. 23:32, 41 — 118
Passover ....2 Kin. 23:21 — 380
Feast of Unleavened
Bread ....2 Chr. 30:13 — 443
Feast of Booths ...Zech. 14:16 — 926

Celibacy—the unmarried state
Useful
sometimes........Matt. 19:10, 12 — 982
Not for overseer ..1 Tim. 3:2 — 1218
Requiring, a sign of
apostasy.........1 Tim. 4:1-3 — 1218
Figurative of absolute
devotion.........Rev. 14:4 — 1302

Cell—a place of imprisonment
Jeremiah in ....Jer. 37:16 — 755
Peter in...........Acts 12:7 — 1107

Cellars—depositories
Figurative of a hiding
place ....Luke 11:33 — 1041
Wines stored in ...1 Chr. 27:27 — 412

SUBJECT	REFERENCE	PAGE	SUBJECT	REFERENCE	PAGE	SUBJECT	REFERENCE	PAGE

Go to, to die...1 Kin. 2:26 — 326
Wretched
place..........Is. 10:30 — 667
Reproved Jeremiah
of............Jer. 29:27 — 747

Anathothite—*a native of Anathoth*
Abiezer thus
called............2 Sam. 23:27 — 318

Anchor—*a weight used to hold a ship in place*
Literally, of ⎰Acts 27:29-30,
Paul's ship......⎱ 40 — 1125
Figuratively of the believer's
hope............Heb. 6:19 — 1242

Ancient—*that which is old*
Applied to the beginning
(eternity).........Is. 45:21 — 696
Applied to
something very ⎰1 Sam. 24:13 — 285
old.............⎱Prov. 22:28 — 626

Ancient of Days
Title applied to
God...........Dan. 7:9, 13, 22 — 844

Andrew—*manly*
A fisherman......Matt. 4:18 — 966
A disciple of John the
Baptist..........John 1:40 — 1065
Brought Peter to
Christ...........John 1:40-42 — 1065
Called to Christ's
discipleship....Matt. 4:18, 19 — 966
Enrolled among the
Twelve..........Matt. 10:2 — 972
Told Jesus about a lad's
lunch............John 6:8, 9 — 1070
Carried a request to
Jesus.............John 12:20-22 — 1079
Sought further light on Jesus'
words ....Mark 13:3, 4 — 1015
Met in the upper
room............Acts 1:13 — 1094

Andronicus—*conqueror of men*
A notable Christian at
Rome ....Rom. 16:7 — 1144

Anem—*double fountain*
Levitical city.....1 Chr. 6:73 — 393

Aner—*waterfall*
1. Amorite
chief.........Gen. 14:13, 24 — 16
2. A Levitical
city...........1 Chr. 6:70 — 393

Angels—*heavenly beings created by God*
A. *Described as:*
Created.......Ps. 148:2, 5 — 604
Col. 1:16 — 1200
Spiritual
beings ....Heb. 1:14 — 1239
Immortal.....Luke 20:36 — 1052
Holy..........Matt. 25:31 — 990
Innumerable..Heb. 12:22 — 1248
Wise......2 Sam. 14:17, 20 — 307
Powerful......Ps. 103:20 — 581
Elect ....1 Tim. 5:21 — 1220
Meek.........Jude 9 — 1287
Sexless ....Matt. 22:30 — 986
Invisible......Num. 22:22-31 — 151
Obedient......Ps. 103:20 — 581
Possessing
emotions.....Luke 15:10 — 1046
Concerned in human
things.........1 Pet. 1:12 — 1261
Incarnate in human form at
times ....Gen. 18:2-8 — 18
Not perfect...Job 4:18 — 498
Organized in
ranks or ⎰Is. 6:2 — 662
orders........⎱1 Thess. 4:16 — 1208
B. *Ministry of, toward believers:*
Guide.........Gen. 24:7, 40 — 23
Provide for ...1 Kin. 19:5-8 — 346

Protect ....Ps. 34:7 — 544
Deliver ....Dan. 6:22 — 843
Acts 12:7-10 — 1107
Gather.........Matt. 24:31 — 989
Direct
activities......Acts 8:26 — 1103
Comfort ......Acts 27:23, 24 — 1125
Minister to.....Heb. 1:14 — 1239
C. *Ministry of, toward unbelievers:*
A destruc-
tion.........Gen. 19:13 — 19
A curse........Judg. 5:23 — 236
A pestilence ...2 Sam. 24:15-17 — 318
Sudden
death ....Acts 12:23 — 1108
Persecution....Ps. 35:5, 6 — 544
D. *Ministry of, in Christ's life, to:*
Announce His
conception....Matt. 1:20, 21 — 964
Herald His
birth ....Luke 2:10-12 — 1027
Sustain Him ...Matt. 4:11 — 966
Witness His
resurrection...1 Tim. 3:16 — 1218
Proclaim His
resurrection...Matt. 28:5-7 — 995
Accompany Him to
heaven........Acts 1:9-11 — 1094
E. *Ministry of, on special occasions, at:*
The world's
creation......Job 38:7 — 520
Sinai..........Acts 7:38, 53 — 1101
Satan's
binding ....Rev. 20:1-3 — 1306
Christ's ⎰Matt. 13:41, 49 — 977
return......⎱1 Thess. 4:16 — 1208
F. *Appearance of, during the Old Testament, to:*
Abraham ......Gen. 18:2-15 — 18
Hagar ....Gen. 16:7-14 — 17
Lot ....Gen. 19:1-22 — 19
Jacob..........Gen. 28:12 — 28
Moses ....Ex. 3:2 — 56
Balaam ....Num. 22:31-35 — 151
Joshua........Josh. 5:13-15 — 210
All Israel ......Judg. 2:1-4 — 233
Gideon ....Judg. 6:11-24 — 237
Manoah ....Judg. 13:6-21 — 245
David..........2 Sam. 24:16, 17 — 318
Elijah..........1 Kin. 19:5-7 — 346
Daniel ....Dan. 6:22 — 843
Zechariah .....Zech. 2:3 — 919
G. *Appearances of, during the New Testament, to:*
Zachariah .....Luke 1:11-20 — 1025
The virgin
Mary.........Luke 1:26-38 — 1025
Joseph........Matt. 1:20-25 — 964
Shepherds ....Luke 2:9-14 — 1027
Certain
women.......Matt. 28:1-7 — 994
Mary
Magdalene...John 20:12, 13 — 1087
The apostles ...Acts 1:10, 11 — 1094
Peter ....Acts 5:19, 20 — 1099
Philip.........Acts 8:26 — 1103
Cornelius .....Acts 10:3-32 — 1105
Paul ....Acts 27:23, 24 — 1125
John ....Rev. 1:1 — 1293
Seven
churches......Rev. 1:20 — 1294

Angels, fallen
Fall of, by pride ...Is. 14:12-15 — 670
Jude 6 — 1287
Seen by Christ ....Luke 10:18 — 1039
Make war on
saints ....Rev. 12:7-17 — 1301
Imprisoned.......2 Pet. 2:4 — 1268
Eternal fire prepared
for ....Matt. 25:41 — 990

Angel of God, the—*distinct manifestation of God*
A. *Names of:*
Angel of God ..Gen. 21:17 — 21

Angel of the
Lord...........Gen. 22:11 — 22
Captain of host of the
Lord ....Josh. 5:14 — 210
B. *Appearances of, to:*
Hagar ....Gen. 16:7, 8 — 17
Gen. 21:17 — 21
Abraham .....Gen. 22:11, 15 — 22
Gen. 18:1-33 — 18
Eliezer.........Gen. 24:7, 40 — 23
Jacob.........Gen. 31:11-13 — 31
Gen. 32:24-30 — 33
Moses ....Ex. 3:2 — 56
Children of ⎰Ex. 13:21, 22 — 66
Israel ....⎱Ex. 14:19 — 66
Balaam ....Num. 22:22-35 — 151
Joshua.........Judg. 2:1 — 233
David.........1 Chr. 21:16-18 — 407
C. *Divine characteristics:*
Deliver Israel ..Judg. 2:1-3 — 233
Extend
blessings ......Gen. 16:7-12 — 17
Pardon sin .....Ex. 23:20-22 — 75

Angels' food
Eaten by men ...Ps. 78:25 — 569
Eaten by Elijah ..1 Kin. 19:5-8 — 346

Anger of God
A. *Caused by man's:*
Sin ....Num. 32:10-15 — 161
Unbelief ......Ps. 78:21, 22 — 569
Error ....2 Sam. 6:7 — 299
Disobedi-
ence ....Josh. 7:1, 11, 12 — 211
Idolatry........Judg. 2:11-14 — 233
B. *Described as:*
Sometimes
delayed ....2 Kin. 23:25-27 — 381
Slow...........Neh. 9:17 — 475
Brief...........Ps. 30:5 — 541
Restrained.....Ps. 78:38 — 569
Burning ....Ps. 78:49, 50 — 569
Consuming ....Ps. 90:7 — 576
Powerful.......Ps. 90:11 — 576
Not forever....Mic. 7:18 — 895
To be feared...Ps. 76:7 — 567
C. *Visitation of, upon:*
Miriam and
Aaron........Num. 12:9-15 — 141
Israelites ......Num. 11:4-10 — 139
Balaam ....Num. 22:21, 22 — 151
Moses ....Deut. 4:21, 22 — 173
Israel..........Deut. 9:8 — 178
Aaron ....Deut. 9:20 — 178
Wicked cities ..Deut. 29:23 — 196
A land ....Deut. 29:24-28 — 196
A king........2 Chr. 25:15, 16 — 438
D. *Deliverance from, by:*
Intercessory ⎰Num. 11:1, 2 — 139
prayer ......⎱Deut. 9:19, 20 — 178
Decisive
action.........Num. 25:3-12 — 154
Obedience .....Deut. 13:16-18 — 182
Executing the
guilty ....Josh. 7:1, 10-26 — 211
Atonement ....Is. 63:1-6 — 710
See Wrath of God

Anger of Jesus
Provoked by
unbelievers....Mark 3:5 — 1001
In the Temple.....Matt. 21:12 — 984
Mark 11:15 — 1012

Anger of man
A. *Caused by:*
A brother's
deception .....Gen. 27:45 — 28
A wife's
complaint.....Gen. 30:1,2 — 30
Rape ....Gen. 34:1, 7 — 34
Inhuman
crimes ....Gen. 49:6, 7 — 48
A leader's
indignation....Ex. 11:8 — 63

SUBJECT	REFERENCE	PAGE	SUBJECT	REFERENCE	PAGE	SUBJECT	REFERENCE	PAGE

Choice, choose—continued

B. *Of God's choice:*
Moses as
leader.........Num. 16:28   145
Levites to
priesthood ....1 Sam. 2:28   265
Kings.........1 Sam. 10:24   271
Jerusalem......Deut. 12:5   180
Israel as His
people ....Deut. 7:6-8   176
Cyrus as
deliverer ......Is. 45:1-4   695
The Servant (the
Messiah)......Is. 42:1-7   691
The new Israel (the
Church).......1 Pet. 2:9   1261
The weak as God's
own.......1 Cor. 1:27, 28   1149
The elect .....Matt. 20:16   983

C. *Kind of:*
God and the
Devil........Gen. 3:1-11   6
Life and
death ....Deut. 30:19, 20   197
God and
idols ....Josh. 24:15-28   227
Obedience and disobedi-
ence ....1 Sam. 15:1-35   275
God and
Baal ....1 Kin. 18:21-40   345
Wisdom and
folly ....Prov. 8:1-21   614
Obedience and
sin............2 Pet. 2:4   1268
Christ and
antichrist .....1 John 2:18, 19   1275

D. *Factors determining choice,
man's:*
First choice....Rom. 5:12   1135
Depraved
nature ....John 3:19-21   1066
Spiritual
deadness......Eph. 4:17-19   1187
Blindness......John 9:39-41   1076
Inability ....Rom. 8:7, 8   1137

E. *Bad choice made by:*
Disobeying
God..........Num. 14:1-45   142
Putting the flesh
first..........Gen. 25:29-34   26
Following a false
prophet.......Matt. 24:11, 24   988
Letting the world
overcome.....Matt. 19:16-22   983
Rejecting God's
promises......Acts 13:44-48   1109

F. *Good choice made by:*
Using God's
Word ....Ps. 119:9-11   590
Believing
God..........Heb. 11:24-27   1247
Obedience .....Acts 26:19-23   1124
Prayer........Eph. 1:16-19   1185
Faith ....Heb. 11:8-10   1246

Choir—musicians trained to sing
together

Appointed by
Nehemiah.......Neh. 12:31   479
In house of God..Neh. 12:40   479
Under instructor ..1 Chr. 15:22, 27   401

Chor-ashan (see Ashan)

Chorazin

A city denounced for its
unbelief ....Matt. 11:21   973

Christ—the Anointed One

A. *Pre-existence of:*
Affirmed in Old
Testament ....Ps. 2:7   529
Confirmed by
Christ.........John 8:58   1075
Proclaimed by
apostles.......Col. 1:15-19   1200

B. *Birth of:*
Predicted ......Is. 7:14   663
Fulfilled ....Matt. 1:18-25   963

In the fullness of
time ....Gal. 4:4   1179

C. *Deity of:*
Prophecy ......Is. 9:6   665
Acknowledged by
Christ........John 20:28, 29   1088
Acclaimed by
witnesses .....John 1:14, 18   1064
Affirmed by   (Rom. 9:5   1138
apostles......(Heb. 1:8   1239

D. *Attributes of:*
All-powerful ...Matt. 28:18   995
All-knowing ...Col. 2:3   1200
Ever-present...Matt. 18:20   982
Eternal ....John 1:1, 2, 15   1064

E. *Humanity of:*
Foretold ....Gen. 3:15   7
         1 Cor. 15:45-47   1161
Took man's   (John 1:14   1064
nature ....(Heb. 2:9-18   1240
Seed of
woman........Gal. 4:4   1179
A son of
man ....Luke 3:38   1029
Of David's
line ....Matt. 22:45   987
A man.........1 Tim. 2:5   1217
Four
brothers......Mark 6:3   1005

F. *Mission of:*
Do God's will...John 6:38   1071
Save sinners...Luke 19:10   1050
Bring in everlasting right-
eousness......Dan. 9:24   847
Destroy
Satan's   (Heb. 2:14   1240
works........(1 John 3:8   1276
Fulfill the Old
Testament ....Matt. 5:17   967
Give life ......John 10:10, 28   1076
Abolish ceremo-
nialism........Dan. 9:27   847
Complete
revelation.....Heb. 1:1   1239

G. *Worship of, by:*
Old Testament
saints........Josh. 5:13-15   210
Demons ......Mark 5:6   1004
Men ....John 9:38   1076
Angels........Heb. 1:6   1239
Disciples......Luke 24:52   1059
Saints in
glory........Rev. 7:9, 10   1298
All............Phil. 2:10, 11   1194

H. *Character of:*
Holy..........Luke 1:35   1026
Righteous .....Is. 53:11   702
Just ....Zech. 9:9   922
Guileless......1 Pet. 2:22   1262
Sinless........2 Cor. 5:21   1169
Spotless ......1 Pet. 1:19   1261
Innocent .....Matt. 27:4   993
Gentle........Matt. 11:29   974
Merciful.......Heb. 2:17   1240
Humble.......Phil. 2:8   1194
Forgiving.....Luke 23:34   1057

I. *Types of:*
Adam..........Rom. 5:14   1135
Abel..........Heb. 12:24   1248
Moses ....Deut. 18:15   186
Passover......1 Cor. 5:7   1151
Manna........John 6:32   1071
Bronze
serpent.......John 3:14   1066

J. *Other names for:*
Adam, the
second........1 Cor. 15:45-47   1161
Advocate......1 John 2:1   1274
Almighty ......Rev. 19:15   1306
Alpha and
Omega......Rev. 21:6   1307
Amen.........Rev. 3:14   1295
Ancient of
Days.........Dan. 7:9   844
Angel of His
presence .....Is. 63:9   710

Anointed above His
fellows........Ps. 45:7   551
Anointed of the
Lord..........Ps. 2:2   528
Apostle of our
confession ....Heb. 3:1   1240
Arm of the
Lord..........Is. 51:9, 10   700
Author and perfecter of
our faith ......Heb. 12:2   1247
Author of
salvation.....Heb. 2:10   1240
Baby ....Luke 2:16   1027
Beginning and
end ....Rev. 21:6   1307
Beloved.......Eph. 1:6   1185
Beloved of
God..........Matt. 12:18   974
Beloved Son ...Mark 1:11   999
Blessed and only
Sovereign .....1 Tim. 6:15   1220
Born of God ...1 John 5:18   1278
Branch ....Zech. 3:8   919
Branch, a
righteous .....Jer. 23:5   740
Branch of righteous-
ness..........Jer. 33:15   752
Bread.........John 6:41   1071
Bread of Life...John 6:35   1071
Bridegroom....John 3:29   1067
Bright morning
star ....Rev. 22:16   1308
Carpenter......Mark 6:3   1005
Carpenter's
son ....Matt. 13:55   977
Chief corner   (Ps. 118:22   590
stone........(Mark 12:10   1013
Chief
Shepherd .....1 Pet. 5:4   1264
Child ....Is. 9:6   665
Child Jesus ....Luke 2:27   1027
Choice of
God...........1 Pet. 2:4   1261
Christ, the .....John 1:41   1065
         Acts 9:22   1104
Christ a King ..Luke 23:2   1056
Christ, Jesus ...Rom. 8:2   1137
Christ Jesus our
Lord..........Rom. 8:39   1138
Christ of God,
the............Luke 9:20   1038
Christ, of God, His Chosen
One..........Luke 23:35   1057
Christ, the
Lord ....Luke 2:11   1027
Christ, the power of
God...........1 Cor. 1:24   1149
Christ, the Son of the
Blessed........Mark 14:61   1018
Commander ...Is. 55:4   703
Consolation of
Israel ....Luke 2:25   1027
Costly
cornerstone...Is. 28:16   679
Counselor .....Is. 9:6   665
Covenant of the
people ....Is. 42:6   691
Deity ....Col. 2:9   1201
Deliverer ......Rom. 11:26   1141
Diadem........Is. 28:5   679
Door ....John 10:2   1076
Door into the
sheep ....John 10:1   1076
Eternal
Father ....Is. 9:6   665
Eternal life ....1 John 5:20   1278
Faithful and
True ....Rev. 19:11   1305
Faithful
witness ....Rev. 1:5   1293
Firmly placed
foundation ....Is. 28:16   679
First-born.....Heb. 1:6   1239
First-born from the
dead ....Col. 1:18   1200
First-born of the
dead ....Rev. 1:5   1293
First-born of all
creation.......Col. 1:15   1200

Christian attributes

SUBJECT	REFERENCE	PAGE

Christian attributes—continued

D. *Manifested in the world:*

Filled with....Eph. 5:18 — 1188
Guided by....John 16:13 — 1083
Praying in....Jude 20 — 1288
Quench not....1 Thess. 5:19 — 1209
Taught by....John 14:26 — 1082
Living in......Gal. 5:25 — 1181
Grieve not....Eph. 4:30 — 1188

D. *Manifested in the world:*
Chastity.......1 Tim. 5:22 — 1220
Content-
  ment..........Heb. 13:5 — 1248
Diligence......1 Thess. 3:7 — 1207
Forbearance...Eph. 4:2 — 1187
Honesty......Rom. 12:17 — 1142
Industry.......1 Thess. 4:11, 12 — 1208
Love toward
  enemies......Matt. 5:44 — 968
Peacefulness..Rom. 14:17-19 — 1143
Self-control....1 Cor. 9:25 — 1155
Tolerance......Rom. 14:1-23 — 1143
Zealous for good
  deeds.........Titus 2:14 — 1230

E. *Manifested toward other*
  Christians:
Bearing
  burdens.......Gal. 6:2 — 1181
Helping the
  needy.........Acts 11:14, 30 — 1107
Fellowship.....Acts 2:42 — 1096
Brotherly
  kindness......1 Pet. 4:7-11 — 1264
Mutual
  edification....1 Thess. 5:11 — 1208

F. *Manifested as signs of faith:*
Spiritual
  growth........2 Pet. 3:18 — 1270
Fruitfulness....John 15:1-6 — 1082
Perse-
  verance.......1 Cor. 15:58 — 1161
Persecution...2 Tim. 3:9-12 — 1225
Obedience....Phil. 2:12 — 1194
Good works...James 2:14-26 — 1254

G. *Manifested as internal graces:*
Kindness......Col. 3:12, 13 — 1201
Humility......1 Pet. 5:5, 6 — 1264
Gentleness....James 3:17, 18 — 1255
Love..........1 Cor. 13:1-13 — 1158
Self-control....Gal. 5:23 — 1181
Peace........Phil. 4:7 — 1196

Christianity, a way of life

Founded on
  Christ.........1 Cor. 3:10, 12 — 1150
Based on
  doctrines.......1 Cor. 15:1-4 — 1159
Designed for all...Matt. 28:18-20 — 995
Centers in
  salvation........Acts 4:12 — 1098
Produces
  change.........1 Cor. 6:11 — 1152

Christians—*Believers in Jesus Christ*

First applied at
  Antioch.........Acts 11:26 — 1107
Agrippa almost
  becomes......Acts 26:28 — 1124
Proof of, by
  suffering........1 Pet. 4:16 — 1264

Sometimes referred to as:
Aliens..........1 Pet. 2:11 — 1261
Believers......Acts 5:14 — 1099
Beloved children..Eph. 5:1 — 1188
Brethren.......Rom. 7:1 — 1136
Brethren,
  beloved......1 Thess. 1:4 — 1206
Brethren, holy....Heb. 3:1 — 1240
Children......2 Cor. 6:13 — 1169
Children of God...Rom. 8:16 — 1138
Children of
  Light........Eph. 5:8 — 1188
Disciples........Acts 9:25 — 1104
Elect, the.........Rom. 8:33 — 1138
Friends........John 15:14 — 1082
Heirs of God and fellow heirs
  with.........Rom. 8:17 — 1138
Light of the
  Lord.........Eph. 5:8 — 1188
Light of the
  world..........Matt. 5:14 — 967

Little children.....1 John 2:1 — 1274
Members..........1 Cor. 12:18, 25 — 1158
Priests...........Rev. 1:6 — 1293
Saints............Rom. 8:27 — 1138
Salt of the earth..Matt. 5:13 — 967
Servants of God...Acts 16:17 — 1113
Sheep...........John 10:27 — 1077
Soldier...........2 Tim. 2:4 — 1224
Sons of God......Rom. 8:14 — 1137
Vessels of honor..2 Tim. 2:21 — 1224
Witnesses........Acts 1:8 — 1094

Christlikeness

Model............2 Cor. 3:18 — 1167
Motivation.......2 Cor. 5:14-17 — 1168
Manifestation....Gal. 5:22, 23 — 1181
Means..........Rom. 8:1-17 — 1137
Mystery..........1 John 3:2 — 1276

Chronicles—(*two books of Old
Testament from Heb. meaning "the
words of the days"*)

Chrysolite—*gold stone*

In New
  Jerusalem.......Rev. 21:20 — 1307

Chrysoprase—*golden-green stone*

In New
  Jerusalem.......Rev. 21:20 — 1307

Church—*the called out ones*

A. *Descriptive of:*
Local church..Acts 8:1 — 1102
Churches
  generally.....Rom. 16:4 — 1144
Believers
  gathered.....Rom. 16:5 — 1144
The body of
  believers......1 Cor. 12:28 — 1158
Body of
  Christ.........Eph. 1:22, 23 — 1185

B. *Title applied to:*
The Bride of
  Christ.........Eph. 5:22-32 — 1189
The body......Col. 1:18 — 1200
One body......1 Cor. 12:18-24 — 1158
Body of
  Christ.........Eph. 4:12 — 1187
The Church....Eph. 3:21 — 1186
Church of the first-
  born.........Heb. 12:23 — 1248
Church of
  God..........1 Cor. 1:2 — 1149
Church of the Living
  God..........1 Tim. 3:15 — 1218
Churches of
  Christ.........Rom. 16:16 — 1145
Church of the
  Gentiles......Rom. 16:4 — 1144
City of God....Heb. 12:22 — 1248
Flock..........Acts 20:28 — 1118
Flock of God..1 Pet. 5:2 — 1264
Dwelling of
  God..........Eph. 2:22 — 1186
God's
  building......1 Cor. 3:9 — 1150
God's field.....1 Cor. 3:9 — 1150
Household of
  God..........Eph. 2:19 — 1186
Israel of God..Gal. 6:16 — 1181
Jerusalem......Gal. 4:26 — 1180
Kingdom......Heb. 12:28 — 1248
Kingdom of God's beloved
  Son..........Col. 1:13 — 1200
Lamb's bride...Rev. 19:7 — 1305
People of
  God..........1 Pet. 2:10 — 1261
Spiritual
  house.........1 Pet. 2:5 — 1261
Temple of
  God..........1 Cor. 3:16 — 1150
Mount Zion....Heb. 12:22 — 1248

C. *Relation to Christ:*
Saved by.....Eph. 5:25-29 — 1189
Purchased by..Acts 20:28 — 1118
Sanctified by..Eph. 5:26, 27 — 1189
Founded on...Eph. 2:19, 20 — 1186
Built by.......Matt. 16:18 — 980
Loved by......Eph. 5:25 — 1189
Subject to.....Rom. 7:4 — 1136

D. *Members of:*
Added by
  faith.........Acts 2:41 — 1096
Added by the
  Lord.........Acts 2:47 — 1096
Baptized into one
  Spirit.........1 Cor. 12:13 — 1158
Edified by the
  Word........Eph. 4:15, 16 — 1187
Persecuted....Acts 8:1-3 — 1102
Disciplined....Matt. 18:15-17 — 982
Worship.......Acts 20:7 — 1117
Fellowship
  together......Acts 2:42-46 — 1096
Urged to
  attend........Heb. 10:25 — 1245
Subject to pastoral
  oversight......1 Pet. 5:1-3 — 1264
Unified in
  Christ.........Gal. 3:28 — 1179

E. *Organization of:*
Under
  overseers......1 Tim. 3:1-7 — 1218
Function of
  deacons......Acts 6:3-6 — 1100
Place of
  evangelists....Eph. 4:11 — 1187
Official
  assemblies...Acts 15:1-31 — 1111
Function of the
  presbytery....1 Tim. 4:14 — 1219

F. *Mission of:*
Evangelize the
  world.........Matt. 28:18-20 — 995
Guard the
  truth..........2 Tim. 2:1, 2 — 1224
Edify the
  saints........Eph. 4:11-15 — 1187
Discipline the
  unruly........2 Cor. 13:1-10 — 1174

G. *Local, examples of:*
Antioch.......Acts 11:26 — 1107
Asia...........1 Cor. 16:19 — 1162
  ....Rev. 1:11 — 1294
Babylon.......1 Pet. 5:13 — 1264
Caesarea.....Acts 18:22 — 1115
Cenchrea.....Rom. 16:1 — 1144
Colossae......Col. 1:2 — 1199
Corinth........1 Cor. 1:2 — 1149
Ephesus......Acts 20:17 — 1118
Galatia........Gal. 1:2 — 1177
Jerusalem......Acts 8:1 — 1102
Judea........Gal. 1:22 — 1178
Laodicea......Col. 4:15 — 1203
Macedonia....2 Cor. 8:1 — 1170
Pergamum....Rev. 2:12 — 1294
Philadelphia...Rev. 3:7 — 1295
Philippi.......Phil. 1:1 — 1193
Rome.........Rom. 1:7 — 1131
Sardis........Rev. 3:1 — 1295
Smyrna.......Rev. 2:8 — 1294
Thyatira......Rev. 2:18 — 1295
Thessa-
  lonica.........1 Thess. 1:1 — 1206

Church sleeper

Falls from window during Paul's
  sermon...........Acts 20:7-12 — 1117

Chuza

Herod's steward...Luke 8:3 — 1035

Cilicia—*a province of Asia Minor*

Paul's country....Acts 21:39 — 1119
Students from, argued with
  Stephen......Acts 6:9 — 1100
Paul labors in.....Gal. 1:21 — 1178

Cinnamon—*a laurel-like spicy plant*

Used in holy oil...Ex. 30:23 — 82
A perfume.......Prov. 7:17 — 614
In Babylon's
  trade.........Rev. 18:13 — 1305
Figurative of a
  lover.........Song 4:12, 14 — 651

Circuit—*circle, regular course*

Judge's itinerary..1 Sam. 7:16 — 268
Sun's orbit.......Ps. 19:6 — 536

SUBJECT	REFERENCE	PAGE	SUBJECT	REFERENCE	PAGE	SUBJECT	REFERENCE	PAGE

SUBJECT	REFERENCE	PAGE	SUBJECT	REFERENCE	PAGE	SUBJECT	REFERENCE	PAGE

Consecration—continued

Sacred
anointing . . . . . 1 John 2:20, 27   1275
New
priesthood . . . 1 Pet. 2:5, 9   1261

Conservation—*preserving worthwhile things*

Material things. . . . John 6:12, 13   1070
Spiritual things. . . . Rev. 3:2, 3   1295
Good . . . . Acts 26:22, 23   1124
Unwise . . . . Luke 5:36, 37   1032

Consolation—*comfort fortified with encouragement*

God, source of . . . . Rom. 15:5   1143
Simeon waits
for . . . . Luke 2:25   1027
Source of joy . . . . . Acts 15:31   1112
To be shared . . . . 2 Cor. 1:4-11   1166

Conspiracy—*a plot to overthrow lawful authority*

Against:
Joseph . . . . Gen. 37:18-20   37
Moses. . . . . Num. 16:1-35   144
Samson. . . . . Judg. 16:4-21   247
Daniel . . . . Dan. 6:4-17   842
Jesus. . . . . Matt. 12:14   974
Paul . . . . Acts 23:12-15   1121

Constancy—*firmness of purpose*

Ruth's, to
Naomi. . . . . Ruth 1:16   256
Jonathan's, to
David . . . . 1 Sam. 20:17   281
Virgins', to
Christ . . . . Rev. 14:4, 5   1302

Constellation—*a group of stars*

The   { Job 9:9   501
Bear. . . . . { Job 38:32   520
The Serpent. . . . . . . Job 26:13   512
Orion . . . . Job 38:31   520
    Amos 5:8   874
Pleiades (seven   { Job 9:9   501
stars). . . . . { Job 38:31   520
Twin Brothers. . . . . Acts 28:11   1126
Judgment on. . . . . . Is. 13:10, 11   669
Incense burned
to . . . . 2 Kin. 23:5   380

Consultation—*seeking advice from others*

Demonical . . . . 1 Sam. 28:7-25   288
Divided . . . . 1 Kin. 12:6, 8   338
Determined . . . . Dan. 6:7   842
Devilish. . . . . John 12:10, 11   1079
    Matt. 26:4   990

Contempt—*scorn compounded with disrespect*

A. *Forbidden toward:*
Parents . . . . Prov. 23:22   627
Weak   { Matt. 18:10   981
Christians. . . . { Rom. 14:3   1143
Believing
masters . . . . . . 1 Tim. 6:2   1220
The poor . . . . . . James 2:1-3   1254

B. *Objects of:*
The
righteous . . . . . Ps. 80:6   571
Spiritual
things. . . . . Matt. 22:2-6   986
Christ . . . . John 9:28, 29   1076

C. *Examples of:*
Nabal. . . . . 1 Sam. 25:10, 11   285
Michal. . . . . 2 Sam. 6:16   300
Sanballat . . . . . Neh. 2:19   468
Jews. . . . . Matt. 26:67, 68   992
False
teachers . . . . . 2 Cor. 10:10   1172
The wicked . . . . Prov. 18:3   622

Contention—*a quarrelsome spirit*

A. *Caused by:*
Pride . . . . Prov. 13:10   618
Disagree-
ment. . . . . Acts 15:36-41   1112
Divisions . . . . . . 1 Cor. 1:11-13   1149

A quarrelsome
spirit. . . . . Gal. 5:15   1181

B. *Antidotes:*
Avoid the
contentious . . . Prov. 21:19   625
Avoid contro-
versies . . . . Titus 3:9   1230
Abandon the
quarrel. . . . . . . Prov. 17:14   622
Follow peace . . . Rom. 12:18-21   1142

Contentment—*an uncomplaining acceptance of one's share*

A. *Opposed to:*
Anxiety. . . . . Matt. 6:25, 34   968
Grumbling. . . . . 1 Cor. 10:10   1156
Greed. . . . . Heb. 13:5   1248
Jealousy . . . . . . James 3:16   1255

B. *Shown by our recognition of:*
Our unworthi-
ness. . . . . Gen. 32:10   33
Our trust . . . . . . Hab. 3:17-19   905
God's care . . . . . Ps. 145:7-21   603
God's
provisions. . . . . 1 Tim. 6:6-8   1220
God's
promises . . . . . Heb. 13:5   1248

Contracts—*covenants legally binding*

A. *Ratified by:*
Giving
presents. . . . . . Gen. 21:25-30   21
Public
witness . . . . . . Ruth 4:1-11   258
Oaths. . . . . Josh. 9:15, 20   213
Joining
hands . . . . Prov. 17:18   622
Pierced ear . . . . Ex. 21:2-6   72

B. *Examples of:*
Abraham and
Abimelech . . . . Gen. 21:25-32   21
Solomon and
Hiram. . . . . 1 Kin. 5:8-12   329

Contrition—*a profound sense of one's sinfulness*

Of the heart. . . . . . Ps. 51:17   554
The
tax-gatherer . . . . . Luke 18:13   1049
Peter's example . . Matt. 26:75   992

Controversy—*dispute between people*

Between men . . . . Deut. 25:1   191
Between God and
men. . . . . Hos. 4:1   855
A public . . . . Acts 15:1-35   1111
A private. . . . . Gal. 2:11-15   1178

Conversion—*turning to God from sin*

A. *Produced by:*
God . . . . Acts 21:19   1119
Christ . . . . Acts 3:26   1097
Holy Spirit. . . . . 1 Cor. 2:13   1150
The
Scriptures . . . . Ps. 19:7   536
Preaching. . . . . . Rom. 10:14   1140

B. *Of Gentiles:*
Foretold . . . . Is. 60:1-5   707
Explained. . . . . . Rom. 15:8-18   1143
    Acts 15:3   1111
Illustrated . . . . . Acts 10:1-48   1105
    Acts 16:25-34   1113
Confirmed . . . . . Acts 15:1-31   1111
Defended . . . . . . Gal. 3:1-29   1178

C. *Results in:*
Repentance. . . . . Acts 26:20   1124
New creation . . . 2 Cor. 5:17   1168
Transfor-
mation . . . . 1 Thess. 1:9, 10   1206

D. *Fruits of:*
Faithfulness . . . . Matt. 24:45-47   989
Gentleness . . . . . 1 Thess. 2:7   1207
Patience . . . . Col. 1:10-12   1200
Love. . . . . 1 John 3:14   1276
Obedience . . . . . Rom. 15:18   1144
Peacefulness . . . James 3:17, 18   1255
Self-control . . . . 2 Pet. 1:6   1268
Self-denial . . . . . John 12:25   1079

Conviction—*making one conscious of his guilt*

A. *Produced by:*
Holy Spirit. . . . . John 16:7-11   1083
The Gospel . . . . Acts 2:37   1096
Conscience . . . . Rom. 2:15   1133
The Law. . . . . . . James 2:9   1254

B. *Instances of:*
Adam. . . . . Gen. 3:8-10   6
Joseph's
brothers. . . . . . Gen. 42:21, 22   42
Israel . . . . Ex. 33:4   84
David. . . . . Ps. 51:1-17   554
Isaiah . . . . Is. 6:5   662
Men of
Nineveh. . . . . . . Matt. 12:41   975
Peter . . . . Luke 5:8   1031
Saul of
Tarsus . . . . Acts 9:4-18   1104
Philippian
jailer. . . . . Acts 16:29, 30   1113

Convocation—*a gathering for worship*

A. *Applied to:*
Sabbaths . . . . . . Lev. 23:2, 3   117
Passover. . . . . . . Ex. 12:16   64
Pentecost . . . . . . Lev. 23:21   117
Feast of
Trumpets . . . . . Num. 29:1   158
Feast of
Weeks . . . . Num. 28:26   157
Feast of
Booths. . . . . Lev. 23:34-36   118
Day of
Atonement. . . . Lev. 23:27   118

B. *Designed to:*
Gather the
people . . . . Josh. 23:1-16   226
Worship God . . 2 Kin. 23:21, 22   380

Cooking—*making food palatable*

Done by women . . Gen. 18:2-6   18
Carefully
performed. . . . . . . Gen. 27:3-10   27
Savory dish . . . . . . Gen. 27:4   27
Vegetables . . . . . . Gen. 25:29   26
Forbidden on the
Sabbath . . . . Ex. 35:3   86
Fish. . . . . Luke 24:42   1059

Cooperation—*working together*

A. *Kinds of:*
Man with
man . . . . Ex. 17:12   69
God with
man . . . . Phil. 2:12, 13   1194

B. *Needed to:*
Complete job . . Neh. 4:16, 17   470
Secure
results . . . . Matt. 18:19   982
Win converts . . John 1:40-51   1065
Maintain
peace . . . . Mark 9:50   1010

C. *Basis:*
Obedience to
God. . . . . Ps. 119:63   592
Faith . . . . Rom. 14:1   1143

Copper—*a metal*

From rock . . . . Job 28:2   512
Not to be
acquired. . . . . Matt. 10:9   972
Pots made of . . . . . Mark 7:4   1007
Coins made of . . . . Mark 12:42   1014
    Luke 21:10   1053

Coppersmith—*a metalworker*

Alexander—withstood
Paul. . . . . 2 Tim. 4:14   1226

Coral—*a rocklike substance formed from skeletons of sea creatures*

Wisdom more valuable
than. . . . . Job 28:18   513
Bought by
traders . . . . Ezek. 27:16   810

SUBJECT	REFERENCE	PAGE	SUBJECT	REFERENCE	PAGE	SUBJECT	REFERENCE	PAGE

Corban—*an offering*

Money
dedicated........Mark 7:11 — 1007

Cord—*a cord or heavy thread used for fastening*

Of priest's ⎰Ex. 28:28 — 79
garments.......⎱Ex. 39:21 — 91

Cordiality—*sincere affection and kindness*

Abraham's.......Gen. 18:1-8 — 18
Seen in
Jonathan.........1 Sam. 20:11-23 — 281
Lacking in
Nabal...........1 Sam. 25:9-13 — 285

Coriander

A plant whose seed is compared to
manna...........Ex. 16:31 — 69

Corinth—*a city of Greece*

Paul labors at.....Acts 18:1-18 — 1115
Site of church.....1 Cor. 1:2 — 1149
Visited by
Apollos...........Acts 19:1 — 1116
Abode of
Erastus...........2 Tim. 4:20 — 1226

Corinthians, the Epistles to the—*two books of the New Testament*

Written by Paul...1 Cor. 1:1 — 1149
2 Cor. 1:1 — 1166

Cormorant

An unclean bird...Lev. 11:17 — 104

Cornelius—*a horn*

A religious
Gentile...........Acts 10:1-48 — 1105

Cornerstone, corner stone—*a stone placed to bind two walls together*

Laid in Zion......Is. 28:16 — 679
Rejected..........Ps. 118:22 — 590
Christ is..........1 Pet. 2:6, 8 — 1261
Christ
promised as......Zech. 4:7 — 920
Christ fulfills.....Acts 4:11 — 1097
1 Pet. 2:7 — 1261

Corpse—*a dead body*

A. *Used literally of:*
Sons of
Israel.........Num. 14:29-33 — 143
Men...........Deut. 28:26 — 194
B. *Laws regarding:*
Dwelling made unclean
by...........Num. 19:11-22 — 148
Contact with, makes
unclean.......Lev. 11:39 — 105
Food made
unclean.......Lev. 11:40 — 105
C. *Used figuratively of:*
Those in hell...Is. 66:24 — 713
Idolatrous
kings.........Ezek. 43:7, 9 — 826
Attraction.....Matt. 24:28 — 988

Correction—*punishment designed to restore*

A. *Means of:*
God's
judgments....Jer. 46:28 — 763
The rod.......Prov. 22:15 — 626
Wickedness....Jer. 2:19 — 719
Prayer........Jer. 10:24 — 729
Scriptures.....2 Tim. 3:16 — 1225
B. *Benefits of:*
Needed for
children.......Prov. 23:13 — 627
Sign of
sonship.......Prov. 3:12 — 611
Brings rest.....Prov. 29:17 — 632
Makes happy..Job 5:17 — 498

Corruption—*rottenness; depravity*

A. *Descriptive of:*
Physical
blemishes.....Mal. 1:14 — 930
Physical
decay........Matt. 6:19, 20 — 968
Moral decay...Gen. 6:12 — 9
Eternal ruin...Gal. 6:8 — 1181
B. *Characteristics of:*
Unregenerate
men..........Luke 6:43, 44 — 1033
Apostates......2 Cor. 2:7 — 1166
2 Pet. 2:12, 19 — 1269
C. *Deliverance from:*
By Christ...Acts 2:27, 31 — 1096
Promised.....Rom. 8:21 — 1138
Through
conversion....1 Pet. 1:18, 23 — 1261
Perfected in
heaven.......1 Cor. 15:42, 50 — 1161

Corruption of body

Results from Adam's
sin..............Rom. 8:21 — 1138
Begins in this
life.............2 Cor. 5:4 — 1168
Consummated by
death..........John 11:39 — 1078
Freedom from,
promised.......Rom. 8:21 — 1138
Freedom from,
accomplished.....1 Cor. 15:42 — 1161

Cos

An island between Rhodes and
Meletus.........Acts 21:1 — 1118

Cosam—*a diviner*

Father of Addi....Luke 3:28 — 1029

Cosmetics

Used by Jezebel..2 Kin. 9:30 — 365
Futility of........Jer. 4:30 — 722

Cosmic conflagration—*to destroy by fire*

Day of
judgment........2 Pet. 3:7-10 — 1269

Council—*Jewish Sanhedrin*

A judicial court...Matt. 5:22 — 967
Christ's trial......Matt. 26:57-59 — 992
Powers of,
limited..........John 18:31 — 1085
Apostles before...Acts 4:5-30 — 1097
Stephen before....Acts 6:12-15 — 1100
Paul before......Acts 23:1-5 — 1120

Counsel, God's

A. *Called:*
Unchange-
able..........Heb. 6:17 — 1242
Faithful........Is. 25:1 — 677
Wonderful....Is. 28:29 — 680
Great..........Jer. 32:19 — 750
Sovereign.....Dan. 4:35 — 841
Eternal........Eph. 3:11 — 1186
B. *Events determined by:*
History........Is. 46:10, 11 — 696
Christ's
death.........Acts 2:23 — 1095
Christ's
Salvation......Rom. 8:28-30 — 1138
Union in
Christ.........Eph. 1:9, 10 — 1185
C. *Attitudes toward:*
Christians
declare........Acts 20:27 — 1118
Proper
reserve........Acts 1:7 — 1094
Wicked
despise........Is. 5:19 — 661
They reject....Luke 7:30 — 1034

Counsel, man's

Jethro's,
accepted.........Ex. 18:13-27 — 70
Hushai's
followed.........2 Sam. 17:14 — 310

Of a woman, brings
peace............2 Sam. 20:16-20 — 314
David's dying.....1 Kin. 2:1-10 — 325
Of old men,
rejected..........1 Kin. 12:8, 13 — 338
Of friends,
avenged.........Esth. 5:14 — 488

Counselor—*an advisor*

Christ is..........Is. 9:6 — 665
Thy testimonies
are...............Ps. 119:24 — 591
Safety in many...Prov. 11:14 — 617
Brings security...Prov. 15:22 — 620
Jonathan, a.......1 Chr. 27:32 — 412
Gamaliel.........Acts 5:33-40 — 1099

Count—*to number*

Things counted:
Stars.............Gen. 15:5 — 16
Days.............Lev. 15:13 — 110
Years............Lev. 25:8 — 119
Booty............Num. 31:26 — 160
Weeks...........Deut. 16:9 — 184
Money...........2 Kin. 22:4 — 378
People...........1 Chr. 21:17 — 407
Bones...........Ps. 22:17 — 538
Towers..........Ps. 48:12 — 552
Houses..........Is. 22:10 — 675

Countenance—*facial expression*

A. *Kinds of:*
Unfriendly.....Gen. 31:1, 2 — 31
Fierce ....Deut. 28:50 — 194
Awesome......Judg. 13:6 — 245
Sad............Neh. 2:2, 3 — 467
Beautiful ......1 Sam. 16:12 — 277
Cheerful.......Prov. 15:13 — 620
Angry.........Prov. 25:23 — 629
Hatred.........Prov. 10:18 — 616
B. *Transfigured:*
Moses'.........2 Cor. 3:7 — 1167
Christ's........Matt. 17:2 — 980
The
believer's......2 Cor. 3:18 — 1167

Counterfeit—*a spurious imitation of the real thing*

A. *Applied to persons:*
Christ ....Matt. 24:4, 5, 24 — 988
Apostles.......2 Cor. 11:13 — 1172
Ministers......2 Cor. 11:14, 15 — 1172
Christians .....Gal. 2:3, 4 — 1178
Teachers......2 Pet. 2:1 — 1268
Prophets.......John 4:1 — 1067
The
antichrist .....Rev. 19:20 — 1306
B. *Applied to things:*
Worship......Matt. 15:8, 9 — 978
Gospel........Gal. 1:6-12 — 1177
Miracles......2 Thess. 2:7-12 — 1212
Science........1 Tim. 6:20 — 1220
Command-
ments.......Titus 1:13, 14 — 1229
Doctrines.....Heb. 13:9 — 1248
Religion......James 1:26 — 1254
Prayers.......James 4:3 — 1255

Country—*the land of a nation*

Commanded to
leave............Gen. 12:1-4 — 14
Love of native ....Gen. 30:25 — 30
Exiled from ......Ps. 137:1-6 — 599
A prophet in his
own.............Luke 4:24 — 1030
A heavenly.......Heb. 11:16 — 1246

Courage—*fearlessness in the face of danger*

A. *Manifested:*
Among
enemies......Ezra 5:11 — 457
In battle.......1 Sam. 17:46 — 278
Against great
foes..........Judg. 7:7-23 — 238
Against great
odds..........1 Sam. 17:32, 50 — 278
When
threatened ....Dan. 3:16-18 — 838

SUBJECT	REFERENCE	PAGE

Craft
1. Ships of
   Tarshish ......Is. 2:16 — 659
2. A trade ......Rev. 18:22 — 1305

Craftiness—*cunning deception*
Man's, known by
   God ....1 Cor. 3:19 — 1151
Enemies', perceived by
   Christ ....Luke 20:23 — 1052
Use of, rejected ...2 Cor. 4:2 — 1167
Warning against ..Eph. 4:14 — 1187

Craftsmen—*men who work at a trade*
Makers of idols....Deut. 27:15 — 193
Destroyed in
   Babylon ......Rev. 18:21, 22 — 1305

Crane—*a migratory bird*
Twitters...........Is. 38:14 — 688

Creation—*causing what did not exist to exist*
A. *Author of:*
   God ....Heb. 11:3 — 1246
   Jesus Christ ...Col. 1:16, 17 — 1200
   Holy Spirit.....Ps. 104:30 — 582
B. *Objects of:*
   Heaven,
      earth.........Gen. 1:1-13 — 4
   Vegetation.....Gen. 1:11, 12 — 4
   Animals ......Gen. 1:21 — 4
   Man ....Gen. 1:26-28 — 4
   Stars ....Is. 40:26 — 690
C. *Expressive of God's:*
   Deity ....Rom. 1:20 — 1132
   Power ......Is. 40:26, 28 — 690
   Glory.........Ps. 19:1 — 536
   Goodness......Ps. 33:5-6 — 543
   Wisdom .....Ps. 104:24 — 582
   Sovereignty....Rev. 4:11 — 1296
D. *Illustrative of:*
   The new
      birth ....2 Cor. 5:17 — 1168
   Renewal of
      believers .....Ps. 51:10 — 554
   The eternal   {Is. 65:17 — 712
      world ......{2 Pet. 3:11, 13 — 1269

Creator—*the Supreme Being*
A title of God .....Is. 40:28 — 690
Man's disrespect
   of ....Rom. 1:25 — 1132
To be
   remembered......Eccl. 12:1 — 645

Creature—*a being with life*
Subject to
   vanity...........Rom. 8:19, 20 — 1138
Will be delivered ..Rom. 8:21 — 1138
Believer, a new...2 Cor. 5:17 — 1168

Creditor—*one to whom a debt is payable*
Interest,
   forbidden.........Ex. 22:25 — 74
Debts remitted ...Neh. 5:10-12 — 470
Some very cruel...Matt. 18:28-30 — 982
Christian
   principle.........Rom. 13:8 — 1142

Cremation—*burning a body*
Two hundred fifty were
   consumed ....Num. 16:35 — 145
Zimri's end.....1 Kin. 16:15-19 — 343

Crescens—*growing*
Paul's assistant....2 Tim. 4:10 — 1225

Crete—*an island in the Mediterranean Sea*
Some from, at
   Pentecost ....Acts 2:11 — 1095
Paul visits........Acts 27:7-21 — 1125
Titus
   dispatched to.....Titus 1:5 — 1229
Inhabitants of, evil and
   lazy ....Titus 1:12 — 1229

Criminal—*a law-breaker*
Paul
   considered a......Acts 25:16, 27 — 1123
Christ
   accused of........John 18:30 — 1085
Christ crucified
   between..........Luke 23:32, 33 — 1057
One unrepentant; one
   repentant.......Luke 23:39-43 — 1057

Cripple—*one physically impaired*
Mephibosheth, by a
   fall................2 Sam. 4:4 — 298
Paul's
   healing of ....Acts 14:8-10 — 1110
Jesus healed ......Matt. 15:30, 31 — 979

Crisis—*the crest of human endurance*
Bad advice in .....Job 2:9, 10 — 496
God's advice in....Luke 21:25-28 — 1053

Crispus—*curled*
Leader of synagogue at
   Corinth ....Acts 18:8 — 1115
Baptized by Paul ..1 Cor. 1:14 — 1149

Crop—*the craw of a bird*
Removed by
   priest...........Lev. 1:16 — 96

Cross—*a method of execution*
A. *Used literally of:*
   Christ's
      death ....Matt. 27:32 — 993
B. *Used figuratively of:*
   Duty ....Matt. 10:38 — 973
   Christ's
      sufferings .....1 Cor. 1:17 — 1149
   The Christian
      faith ....1 Cor. 1:18 — 1149
   Reconcili-
      ation...........Eph. 2:16 — 1186

Crown—*an emblem of glory*
A. *Worn by:*
   High priest ....Lev. 8:9 — 101
   Kings..........2 Sam. 12:30 — 305
   Queens ....Esth. 2:17 — 486
   Ministers of
      state ....Esth. 8:15 — 490
B. *Applied figuratively to:*
   A good wife ...Prov. 12:4 — 617
   Old age ....Prov. 16:31 — 621
   Grand-
      children......Prov. 17:6 — 622
   Honor ....Prov. 27:24 — 631
   Material
      blessings ......Ps. 65:11 — 560
C. *Applied spiritually to:*
   Christ ....Ps. 132:18 — 598
   Christ at His
      return........Rev. 19:12 — 1306
   Christ
      glorified.......Heb. 2:7-9 — 1239
   The church .....Is. 62:3 — 709
   The Christian's
      reward........2 Tim. 2:5 — 1224
   The minister's
      reward.......Phil. 4:1 — 1195
   Soul winners..1 Thess. 2:19 — 1207
   The Christian's imperishable
      prize..........1 Cor. 9:25 — 1155

Crown of thorns
Placed on   {Matt. 27:29 — 993
   Christ ....{John 19:2 — 1086

Crowns of Christians
Joy ....1 Thess. 2:19 — 1207
Righteousness....2 Tim. 4:8 — 1225
Life ....James 1:12 — 1253
Glory ....1 Pet. 5:4 — 1264
Imperishable ......1 Cor. 9:25 — 1155

Crucifixion—*death on a cross*
A. *Jesus' death by:*
   Predicted ......Matt. 20:19 — 984
   Demanded ....Mark 15:13, 14 — 1018

Gentiles ......Matt. 20:19 — 984
Jews...........Acts 2:23, 36 — 1095
Between
   thieves.......Matt. 27:38 — 994
Nature of, unrecog-
   nized..........1 Cor. 2:8 — 1150
B. *Figurative of:*
   Utter
      rejection ......Heb. 6:6 — 1242
   Apostasy ......Rev. 11:8 — 1300
   Union with
      Christ........Gal. 2:20 — 1178
   Separation.....Gal. 6:14 — 1181
   Sanctifi-
      cation........Rom. 6:6 — 1135
   Dedication.....1 Cor. 2:2 — 1150

Cruelty—*violence*
Descriptive of the
   wicked ....Ps. 74:20 — 566
To animals,
   forbidden........Num. 22:27-35 — 151

Crumbled—*Musty or stale*
Applied to bread ..Josh. 9:5, 12 — 213

Crumbs—*fragments of bread*
Dogs eat of ......Matt. 15:27 — 979
Lazarus begs for ..Luke 16:20, 21 — 1047

Crying—*an emotional upheaval*
Accusation........Gen. 4:10 — 8
Remorse ....Heb. 12:17 — 1248
Pretense ....Judg. 14:15-18 — 246
Sorrow...........2 Sam. 18:33 — 312
Others' sins ......Ps. 119:136 — 594
Pain ....Heb. 5:7 — 1241
None in heaven ...Rev. 21:4 — 1307

Crystal—*rock crystal*
Wisdom
   surpasses.......Job 28:17-20 — 513
Gates of Zion .....Is. 54:12 — 703
Descriptive of
   heaven...........Rev. 4:6 — 1296

Cubs—*offspring of beasts*
Figurative of:
   Babylonians......Jer. 51:38 — 771
   Assyrians ....Nah. 2:11, 12 — 899
   Princes of Israel...Ezek. 19:2-9 — 801

Cucumber—*an edible fruit grown on a vine*
Lusted after.......Num. 11:5 — 139
Grown in
   gardens ....Is. 1:8 — 658

Cud—*partly digested food*
Animals chew
   again..............Lev. 11:3-8 — 104

Cummin—*an annual of the parsley family*
Seeds threshed by a
   club..............Is. 28:25, 27 — 680
A trifle of
   tithing.........Matt. 23:23 — 987

Cun—*founding*
A town of Aram ..1 Chr. 18:8 — 404
Called Berothah...Ezek. 47:16 — 830

Cunning—*sly, clever*
A. *Used in a good sense:*
   David.........1 Sam. 23:19-22 — 284
   Jehu ....2 Kin. 10:19 — 366
B. *Used in a bad sense:*
   Thwarted by
      God..........Job 5:13 — 498
   Of harlot's
      heart.........Prov. 7:10 — 614

Cup
A. *Literal use of:*
   For drinking ...2 Sam. 12:3 — 304
B. *Figurative uses of:*
   One's portion ..Ps. 11:6 — 532

SUBJECT	REFERENCE	PAGE

Cup—continued

Blessings ......Ps. 23:5		539
Suffering .....Matt. 20:23		984
Hypocrisy .....Matt. 23:25, 26		987
New covenant......1 Cor. 10:16		1156

Cupbearer—*a high court official*

Many under Solomon ....1 Kin. 10:5		335
Nehemiah, a faithful..........Neh. 1:11		467

Cure—*to restore to health*

Of the body.......Matt. 17:16		981
Of the mind.......Mark 5:15		1004
Of the demonized ....Matt. 12:22		974
With means.......Is. 38:21		688
By faith..........Num. 21:8, 9		150
By prayer........James 5:14, 15		1256
By God's mercy ...Phil. 2:27		1194
Hindered..........2 Kin. 8:7-15		363

Curiosity—*seeking to know things forbidden or private*

Into God's secrets, forbidden......John 21:21, 22		1089
Leads 50,070 to death............1 Sam. 6:19		268

Curiosity seekers

Eve ....Gen. 3:6		6
Israelites..........Ex. 19:21, 24		71
Babylonians......2 Kin. 20:13		377
Herod........Matt. 2:4-8		964
Zaccheus ....Luke 19:1-6		1050
Certain Greeks...John 12:20, 21		1079
Lazarus' visitors...John 12:9		1079
Peter.............Matt. 26:58		992
At the crucifixion.......Matt. 27:46-49		994
Athenians........Acts 17:21		1114

Curse, cursing—*a violent expression of evil upon others*

A. *Pronounced upon:*

The earth......Gen. 3:17		7
Cain.........Gen. 4:11		8
Canaan.......Gen. 9:25		12
Two sons......Gen. 49:7		49
Disobedient....Deut. 28:15-45		193
Meroz ....Judg. 5:23		236
Jericho's rebuilders .....Josh. 6:26		211

B. *Forbidden upon:*

Parents.........Ex. 21:17		73
Ruler.........Ex. 22:28		74
Deaf..........Lev. 19:14		113
Enemies ......Luke 6:28		1033
God ....Job 2:9		496
God's people...Gen. 12:3		14

C. *Instances of:*

Goliath's.......1 Sam. 17:43		278
Balaam's attempted.....Num. 22:1-12		151
The fig tree...Mark 11:21		1013
Peter's........Matt. 26:74		992
The crucified ..Gal. 3:10, 13		1179

D. *Manifested by:*

Rebellious .....2 Sam. 16:5-8		309

Curtains—*an awning-like screen*

Ten, in tabernacle........Ex. 26:1-13		77
Figurative of the heavens..........Ps. 104:2		581

Cush—*black*

1. Ham's oldest son ....1 Chr. 1:8-10		387
2. Means Ethiopia.......Is. 18:1		672
3. A Benjamite ...Ps. 7 (Title)		530

Cushan—*blackness*

Probably same as Cush............Hab. 3:7		905

SUBJECT	REFERENCE	PAGE

Cushan-rishathaim—*extra wicked*

Mesopotamian king:

Oppressed Israel ..Judg. 3:8		234
Othniel delivers Israel from ....Judg. 3:9, 10		234

Cushi—*an Ethiopian*

1. Ancestor of Jehudi ....Jer. 36:14		754
2. Father of Zephaniah ....Zeph. 1:1		908

Cushite—*an Ethiopian*

1. David's servant ....2 Sam. 18:21-32		312
2. Moses' wife....Num. 12:1		140

Custom—*tax; usage*

A. *As a tax:*

Matthew collected .....Matt. 9:9		971
Kings require ..Matt. 17:25		981
Christians give..........Rom. 13:6, 7		1142

B. *As a common practice:*

Abominable....Lev. 18:30		113
Vain..........Jer. 10:3		728
Worthy.......Luke 4:16		1030
Traditional....Acts 21:21		1119

Cuth, Cuthah—*burning*

People from, brought to Samaria ....2 Kin. 17:24, 30		373

Cymbal—*hollow of a vessel*

A musical instrument ....1 Chr. 13:8		400
Figurative of pretense ....1 Cor. 13:1		1158

Cypress—*a hardwood tree*

Used by idol-makers...........Is. 44:14-17		694

Cypress—*evergreen tree of the pine family*

Tree of Lebanon ..1 Kin. 5:8, 10		329
Used in Solomon's Temple ......1 Kin. 6:15, 34		329
Made into spears ......Neh. 2:3		467

Cyprus—*fairness*

A large Mediterranean island; home of

Barnabas.........Acts 4:36		1098
Christians reach...Acts 11:19, 20		1107
Paul visits.......Acts 13:4-13		1108
Barnabas visits...Acts 15:39		1112
Paul twice sails past............Acts 21:3		1118

Cyrene—*wall*

A Greek colonial city in north Africa; home of

Simon ....Matt. 27:32		993
People from, at Pentecost ....Acts 2:10		1095
Synagogue of .....Acts 6:9		1100
Some from, become missionaries......Acts 11:20		1107

Cyrus—*sun, throne*

Prophecies concerning, God's:

"Anointed"........Is. 45:1		695
Liberator........Is. 45:1		695
Rebuilder ....Is. 44:28		695

D

Dabbesheth—*hump*

Town of Zebulun ....Josh. 19:10, 11		222

SUBJECT	REFERENCE	PAGE

Daberath—*pasture*

Correct rendering of Dabareh.........Josh. 21:28		224
Assigned to Gershomites......1 Chr. 6:71, 72		393

Dagon—*fish*

The national god of the Philistines........Judg. 16:23		248
Falls before ark ...1 Sam. 5:1-5		266

Daleth

The fourth letter in the Hebrew alphabet.........Ps. 119:25-32		591

Dalmanutha

A place near the Sea of Galilee ....Mark 8:10		1008

Dalmatia—*deceitful*

A region east of the Adriatic Sea; Titus departs to ....2 Tim. 4:10		1225

Dalphon—*crafty*

A son of Haman ..Esth. 9:7-10		490

Damages and Remuneration

A. *In law for:*

Personal injury........Ex. 21:18, 19		73
Causing miscarriage ...Ex. 21:22		73
Injuries by animals......Ex. 21:28-32		73
Injuries to animals ....Ex. 21:33-35		73
Losses ....Ex. 22:1-15		73
Stealing ......Lev. 6:1-7		99
Defaming a wife..........Deut. 22:13-19		189
Rape ....Deut. 22:28, 29		189

B. *In practice:*

Jacob's ....Gen. 31:38-42		32
Samson's ......Judg. 16:28-30		248
Tamar's.......2 Sam. 13:22-32		306
Zaccheus'.......Luke 19:8		1050
Paul's.........Acts 16:35-39		1113
Philemon's.....Philem. 10-18		1234

Damaris—*gentle*

An Athenian woman converted by Paul..........Acts 17:33, 34		1115

Damascus—*chief city of Aram*

A. *In the Old Testament:*

Abram passed through......Gen. 14:15		16
Abram heir from ....Gen. 15:2		16
Captured by David........2 Sam. 8:5, 6		301
Rezon, king of.......1 Kin. 11:23, 24		337
Ben-hadad, king of........1 Kin. 15:18		342
Rivers of, mentioned ....2 Kin. 5:12		360
Elisha's prophecy in ...2 Kin. 8:7-15		363
Taken by Assyrians ....2 Kin. 16:9		372
Prophecies concerning....Is. 8:4		664

B. *In the New Testament, Paul:*

Journeys to....Acts 9:1-9		1104
Is converted near ....Acts 9:3-19		1104
First preaches at ...Acts 9:20-22		1104
Escapes from ..2 Cor. 11:32, 33		1173
Revisits........Gal. 1:17		1177

Dan—*judge*

1. Jacob's son by Bilhah ....Gen. 30:6		30
Prophecy concerning....Gen. 49:16, 17		49
2. Tribe of: Census of.....Num. 1:38, 39		128

SUBJECT	REFERENCE	PAGE	SUBJECT	REFERENCE	PAGE	SUBJECT	REFERENCE	PAGE
All to be raised from	Acts 24:15	1122	Debts to be honored	Rom. 13:6	1142	**Decision**—*determination to follow a course of action*		
Illustrates regeneration	Rom. 6:2	1135	Interest (usury) forbidden	Ezek. 18:8-17	800	A. *Sources of:* Loyalty	Ruth 1:16	256
B. *Described as:* Return to			Love, the unpayable	Rom. 13:8	1142	Prayer	1 Sam. 23:1-13	283
dust	Gen. 3:19	7	Parable concerning	Matt. 18:23-35	982	The Lord	1 Kin. 12:15	338
Removal of breath	Gen. 25:8	25	B. *Evils of:*			Satan	1 Chr. 21:1	406
Removal from our house	2 Cor. 5:1	1168	Brings slavery	Lev. 25:39, 47	120	The world	Luke 14:16-24	1045
Naked	2 Cor. 5:3, 4	1168	Causes complaint	2 Kin. 4:1-7	358	Human need	Acts 11:27-30	1107
Sleep	John 11:11-14	1077	Produces strife	Jer. 15:10	733	Faith	Heb. 11:24-28	1247
Departure	Phil. 1:23	1193	Makes outlaws	1 Sam. 22:2	283	B. *Wrong, leading to:* Spiritual decline	Gen. 13:7-11	15
Last breath	Acts 5:10	1099	Endangers property	Prov. 6:1-5	612	Repentance	Heb. 12:16, 17	1248
C. *Recognition after:* Departed saints recognized by the living	Matt. 17:1-8	980	C. *Figurative of:* Sins	Matt. 6:12	968	Defeat	Num. 14:40-45	143
Greater knowledge in future world	1 Cor. 13:12	1158	Works	Rom. 4:4	1134	Rejection	1 Sam. 15:6-26	275
The truth illustrated	Luke 16:19-24	1047	Moral obligation	Rom. 1:14	1131	Apostasy	1 Kin. 11:1-13	336
Death of saints			God's mercy	Ps. 37:26	546	Division	1 Kin. 12:12-20	338
A. *Described as:* Sleep in Jesus	1 Thess. 4:14	1208	**Decalogue** (see Ten Commandments)			Death	Acts 1:16-20	1094
Blessed	Rev. 14:13	1302	**Decapolis**—*league of ten cities*			C. *Good, manifested in:* Siding with the Lord	Ex. 32:26	84
A gain	Phil. 1:21	1193	Multitudes from, follow Jesus	Matt. 4:25	966	Following God	{ Num. 14:24	142
Peace	Is. 57:1, 2	704	Healed demon-possessed, preaches in	Mark 5:20	1004		{ Josh. 14:8	218
Crown of righteousness	2 Tim. 4:8	1225	**Deceit, deceivers, deception**			Loving God	Deut. 6:5	175
B. *Exemplified in:* Abraham	Gen. 25:8	25	A. *The wicked:* Devise	Ps. 35:20	545	Seeking God	2 Chr. 15:12	430
Isaac	Gen. 35:28, 29	36	Speaks	Jer. 9:8	727	Obeying God	Neh. 10:28-30	477
Jacob	Gen. 49:33	49	Are full of	Rom. 1:29	1132	**Decision, valley of**—*location unknown*		
Elisha	2 Kin. 13:14, 20	368	Increase in	2 Tim. 3:13	1225	Called "Valley of Jehoshaphat"	Joel 3:2, 12, 14	867
The criminal	Luke 23:39-43	1057	B. *Agents of:* Satan	2 Cor. 11:14	1172	Refers to final judgment	Joel 3:1-21	867
Death of wicked			Sin	Rom. 7:11	1136	**Decisiveness**—*showing firmness of decision*		
Result of sin	Rom. 5:12	1135	Self	1 Cor. 3:18	1151	In serving God	Heb. 11:24, 25	1247
Often punishment	{ Ex. 23:25-29	75		James 1:22	1253		Josh. 24:15, 16	227
	{ Is. 65:11, 12	711	Others	2 Thess. 2:3	1212	Toward family	Ruth 1:15-18	256
Unpleasant for God	Ezek. 33:11	816	C. *Warnings against:* Among religious workers	2 Cor. 11:3-15	1172	Toward a leader	2 Kin. 2:1-6	356
Without hope	1 Thess. 4:13	1208	As a sign of apostasy	2 Thess. 2:10	1212	To complete a task	Neh. 4:14-23	470
	Rev. 20:10, 14, 15	1306	As a sign of the antichrist	1 John 4:1-6	1277	In morality	Gen. 39:10-12	39
Death penalty—*legal execution*			D. *Examples of:* Eve	1 Tim. 2:14	1218		Dan. 1:8	835
By stoning	Deut. 13:6-10	182	Abram	Gen. 12:11-13	14	In prayer	Dan. 6:1-16	842
	Deut. 17:5	185	Isaac	Gen. 26:6, 7	26	**Deck**—*floor of a ship*		
Debir—*oracle*			Jacob	Gen. 27:18-27	27	Made of ivory	Ezek. 27:6	809
1. King of Eglon	Josh. 10:3-26	214	Joseph's brothers	Gen. 37:31, 32	38	**Decree**—*a course of action authoritatively determined*		
2. City of Judah	Josh. 15:15	219	Pharaoh	Ex. 8:29	61	A. *As a human edict:* Published widely	Esth. 3:13-15	487
Also called Kiriath-sepher	Josh. 15:15	219	David	1 Sam. 21:12, 13	283	Providentially nullified	Esth. 8:3-17	489
Captured by Joshua	Josh. 10:38, 39	215	Amnon	2 Sam. 13:6-14	306	Sometimes beneficial	Dan. 4:25-28	840
Recaptured by Othniel	{ Josh. 15:15-17	219	Gehazi	2 Kin. 5:20-27	360	B. *As a divine edict, to:* Govern nature	Jer. 5:22	723
	{ Judg. 1:11-13	232	Elisha	2 Kin. 6:19-23	361	**Dedan**—*low*		
Assigned to priests	Josh. 21:13, 15	224	Herod	Matt. 2:7, 8	964	1. Raamah's son	Gen. 10:7	12
3. A place east of the Jordan	Josh. 13:26	218	Pharisees	Matt. 22:15, 16	986	2. Jokshan's son	Gen. 25:3	25
4. Town of Judah	Josh. 15:7	219	Peter	Mark 14:70, 71	1018	3. Descendants of Raamah; a commercial people	{ Ezek. 27:15, 20	809
Deborah—*a bee*			Ananias	Acts 5:1-11	1098		{ Ezek. 38:13	821
1. Rebekah's nurse	Gen. 35:8	35	The earth	Rev. 13:14	1301	**Dedication**—*setting apart for a sacred use*		
2. A prophetess and judge	Judg. 4:4-14	235	**Deceive**—*to delude or mislead*			A. *Of things:* Tabernacle	Ex. 40:34-38	92
Composed song of triumph	Judg. 5:1-31	236	A. *In Old Testament:* Eve, by Satan	Gen. 3:13	6	Solomon's Temple	1 Kin. 8:12-66	332
Debt, debtor			Israel, by the Midianites	Num. 25:18	154	Second temple	Ezra 6:1-22	458
A. *Safeguards regarding:* No oppression allowed	Deut. 23:19, 20	190	Joshua, by the Gibeonites	Josh. 9:22	214	B. *Offerings in, must be:* Voluntary	Lev. 22:18-25	116
Collateral protected	Ex. 22:25-27	74	B. *Of Christians:* By flattering words	Rom. 16:18	1145	Without defect	Lev. 1:3	96
Time limitation of	Deut. 15:1-18	183	By false report	2 Thess. 2:3	1212	Unredeemable	Lev. 27:28, 29	123
Non-payment forbidden	Neh. 5:5	470	By false reasoning	Col. 2:4	1200			

SUBJECT	REFERENCE	PAGE

Dedication—continued

C. *Examples of:*
- Samuel . . . . 1 Sam. 1:11, 22 — 263
- The believer . . . Rom. 12:1, 2 — 1141

Dedication, Feast of
- Jesus attended . . . . John 10:22, 23 — 1077

Deeds—*things done*

A. *Descriptive of one's:*
- Past record . . . . Luke 11:48 — 1042
- Present achieve-ments . . . . Acts 7:22 — 1101
- Future action . . . . 2 Cor. 10:11 — 1172

B. *Expressive of one's:*
- Evil nature . . . . 2 Pet. 2:8 — 1268
- Parentage . . . . . John 8:41 — 1074
- Record . . . . Luke 24:19 — 1058
- Profession . . . . 3 John 10 — 1284
- Love . . . . 1 John 3:18 — 1277
- Judgment . . . . . . Rom. 2:6 — 1132

C. *Toward God:*
- Weighed . . . . 1 Sam. 2:3 — 264
- Wrong punished . . . . . Luke 23:41 — 1057

D. *Lord's are:*
- Righteous . . . . . Judg. 5:11 — 236
-      1 Sam. 12:7 — 272
- Mighty . . . . Ps. 106:2 — 583
- Beyond description . . . . Ps. 106:2 — 583

E. *Considered positively:*
- Example of . . . . Titus 2:7 — 1230
- Zealous for . . . . Titus 2:14 — 1230
- Careful to engage in . . . . . Titus 3:8, 14 — 1230
- Stimulate to . . . Heb. 10:24 — 1245
- In heaven . . . . . Rev. 14:13 — 1302

Deeds, the unbeliever's

A. *Described as:*
- Evil . . . . Col. 1:21 — 1200
- Done in dark place . . . . Is. 29:15 — 680
- Abominable . . . Ps. 14:1 — 533
- Unfruitful . . . . . Eph. 5:11 — 1188

B. *God's attitude toward, will:*
- Never forget . . . Amos 8:7 — 877
- Render according to . . . . Prov. 24:12 — 628
- Bring to judgment . . . . . Rev. 20:12, 13 — 1306

C. *Believer's relation to:*
- Lay aside . . . . . . Rom. 13:12 — 1142
- Not partici-pate in . . . . Eph. 5:11 — 1188
- Be delivered from . . . . 2 Tim. 4:18 — 1226

Deer

A. *Described as:*
- Clean animal . . . . . . { Deut. 12:15 — 181
-      { Deut. 14:5 — 182

B. *Figurative of:*
- Troubled saints . . . . Ps. 42:1-3 — 549
- Converted sinners . . . . Is. 35:6 — 685

Defense—*protection during attack*
- Of a city . . . . . . 2 Kin. 19:34 — 376
- Of Israel . . . . Judg. 10:1 — 242
- Of a plot . . . . 2 Sam. 23:11, 12 — 317
- Of the upright . . Ps. 7:10 — 530
- Of one accused . . . . Acts 22:1 — 1119
- Of the Gospel . . . . . Phil. 1:7, 16 — 1193

Deference—*respectful yielding to another*
- To a woman's request . . . . Ruth 1:15-18 — 256
- To an old man's wish . . . . 2 Sam. 19:31-40 — 313
- Results in exaltation . . . . . . Matt. 23:12 — 987
- Commanded . . . . . . Heb. 13:17 — 1249

SUBJECT	REFERENCE	PAGE

Defilement—*making the pure impure*

A. *Ceremonial causes of:*
- Childbirth . . . . . Lev. 12:2-8 — 105
- Leprosy . . . . Lev. 13:3, 44-46 — 106
- Bodily discharge . . . . Lev. 15:1-15 — 109
- Copulation . . . . Lev. 15:17 — 110
- Menstrua-tion . . . . Lev. 15:19-33 — 110
- Touching the dead . . . . Lev. 21:1-4, 11 — 115

B. *Spiritual manifestations of:*
- Abomina-tions . . . . Jer. 32:34 — 751

C. *Objects of:*
- Conscience . . . . 1 Cor. 8:7 — 1154
- Fellowship . . . . . Heb. 12:15 — 1248
- Flesh . . . . Jude 8 — 1287

Defrauding—*depriving others through deceit*
- Forbidden . . . . Mark 10:19 — 1011
- To be accepted . . . 1 Cor. 6:5-8 — 1152
- In marriage . . . . . . 1 Cor. 7:3-5 — 1153
- Paul, not guilty of . . . . 2 Cor. 7:2 — 1169
- Product of sexual immorality . . . . . 1 Thess. 4:3-6 — 1208

Degrees, Songs of
- "Songs of Ascent" . . . . Ps. 120—134 — 595

Dehavites—*people who settled in Samaria during exile*
- Opposed rebuilding of Jerusalem . . . . Ezra 4:9-16 — 456

Deity of Christ (see Christ)

Delaiah—*Yahweh has delivered*
1. Descendant of Aaron . . . . 1 Chr. 24:18 — 409
2. Son of Shemaiah; urges Jehoiakim not to burn Jeremiah's scroll . . . . Jer. 36:12, 25 — 754
3. Founder of a family . . . . Ezra 2:60 — 455
4. A son of Elioenai . . . . 1 Chr. 3:24 — 390

Delegation—*an official commission*
- Coming to seek peace . . . . Luke 14:32 — 1046

Deliberation—*careful consideration of elements involved in a decision*
- Necessary in life . . Luke 14:28-32 — 1046
- Illustrated in Jacob . . . . Gen. 32:1-23 — 33

Delight—*great pleasure in something*

A. *Wrong kind of:*
- Showy display . . . . Esth. 6:6-11 — 489
- Physical strength . . . . . . Ps. 147:10 — 604
- Sacrifices . . . . . . Ps. 51:16 — 554
-      Is. 1:11 — 658
- Abomi-nations . . . . Is. 66:3 — 712

B. *Right kind of:*
- God's will . . . . Ps. 40:8 — 548
- God's command-ments . . . . Ps. 112:1 — 588
- God's goodness . . . . . . Neh. 9:25 — 476
- Lord Himself . . . Is. 58:14 — 706

Delilah—*lustful*
- Deceives Samson . . . . Judg. 16:4-22 — 247

Deliver—*to rescue or save from evil*

A. *By Christ, from:*
- Trials . . . . 2 Tim. 3:11 — 1225
- Evil . . . . 2 Tim. 4:18 — 1226
-      2 Pet. 2:9 — 1269

SUBJECT	REFERENCE	PAGE

- Death . . . . 2 Cor. 1:10 — 1166
- Domain of darkness . . . . . . Col. 1:13 — 1200
- God's wrath . . . 1 Thess. 1:10 — 1207

B. *Examples of, by God:*
- Noah . . . . Gen. 8:1-22 — 10
- Lot . . . . Gen. 19:29, 30 — 20
- Jacob . . . . Gen. 33:1-16 — 33
- Israel . . . . Ex. 12:29-51 — 64
- David . . . . 1 Sam. 23:1-29 — 283
- Jews . . . . Esth. 9:1-19 — 490
- Daniel . . . . Dan. 6:13-27 — 843
- Jesus . . . . Matt. 2:13-23 — 964
- Apostles . . . . . . Acts 5:17-26 — 1099
- Paul . . . . 2 Cor. 1:10 — 1166

Deluge, the—*the Flood*

A. *Warnings of:*
- Believed by Noah . . . . Heb. 11:7 — 1246
- Disbelieved by the world . . . . 2 Pet. 2:5 — 1268

B. *Coming of:*
- Announced . . . . Gen. 6:5-7 — 9
- Dated . . . . Gen. 7:11 — 10
- Sudden . . . . Matt. 24:38, 39 — 989

C. *Purpose of:*
- Punish sin . . . . . Gen. 6:1-7 — 9
- Manifest God's patience . . . . . 1 Pet. 3:20 — 1263
- Destroy the world . . . . 2 Pet. 3:5, 6 — 1269

D. *Its non-repetition based on God's:*
- Promise . . . . Gen. 8:21, 22 — 11
- Covenant . . . . . . Gen. 9:9-11 — 12
- Sign (the rainbow) . . . . . Gen. 9:12-17 — 12
- Pledge . . . . Is. 54:9, 10 — 702

E. *Type of:*
- Baptism . . . . 1 Pet. 3:20, 21 — 1263
- Christ's coming . . . . Matt. 24:36-39 — 989
- Destruction . . . . Is. 28:2, 18 — 679
- The end . . . . 2 Pet. 3:5-15 — 1269

Delusions, common—*self-deception*
- Rejecting God's existence . . . . Ps. 14:1 — 533
- Supposing God does not see . . . . Ps. 10:1-11 — 532
- Trusting in one's heritage . . . . Matt. 3:9 — 965
- Living for time alone . . . . Luke 12:17-19 — 1042
- Presuming on time . . . . Luke 13:23-30 — 1044
- Believing antichrist . . . . 2 Thess. 2:1-12 — 1212
- Denying facts . . . . 2 Pet. 3:5, 16, 17 — 1269

Demagogue—*one who becomes a leader by mass prejudice*
- Absalom . . . . 2 Sam. 15:2-6 — 308
- Haman . . . . Esth. 3:1-11 — 486
- Judas of Galilee . . . Acts 5:37 — 1100

Demas—*popular*
- Follows Paul . . . . . Col. 4:14 — 1203
- Deserts Paul . . . . . 2 Tim. 4:10 — 1225

Demetrius
1. A silversmith at Ephesus . . . . . . Acts 19:24-31 — 1116
2. A good Christian . . . . . . 3 John 12 — 1284

Demon—*an evil spirit*

A. *Nature of:*
- Evil . . . . Luke 10:17, 18 — 1039
- Powerful . . . . . . Luke 8:29 — 1036
- Numerous . . . . . Mark 5:8, 9 — 1004
- Unclean . . . . . . Matt. 10:1 — 972
- Under Satan . . . Matt. 12:24-30 — 974

B. *Ability of:*
- Recognize Christ . . . . Mark 1:23, 24 — 1000

SUBJECT	REFERENCE	PAGE	SUBJECT	REFERENCE	PAGE	SUBJECT	REFERENCE	PAGE

Dreams—continued
Solomon.......1 Kin. 3:5 — 327
Job............Job 7:14 — 500
Nebuchad-
nezzar........Dan. 2:1-13 — 836
Joseph........Matt. 1:19, 20 — 964
Pilate's wife ...Matt. 27:13, 19 — 993

Dregs—*the sediments of liquids; grounds*
Wicked shall drink
down............Ps. 75:8 — 567
Contains God's
anger............Is. 51:17, 22 — 701

Drink—*to swallow liquids*
A. *Used literally of:*
Water ....Gen. 24:14 — 23
Milk..........Judg. 5:25 — 236
Wine ....Gen. 9:21 — 12
B. *Used figuratively of:*
Famine ....2 Kin. 18:27 — 375
Misery........Is. 51:22, 23 — 701
Married
pleasure.......Prov. 5:15-19 — 612
Unholy
alliances .....Jer. 2:18 — 719
God's
blessings .....Zech. 9:15-17 — 923
Spiritual
communion ...John 6:53, 54 — 1071
Holy Spirit.....John 7:37-39 — 1073

Drink offerings
Of wine..........Hos. 9:4 — 858
Of water.........1 Sam. 7:6 — 268

Dropsy—*an unnatural accumulation of fluid in parts of the body*
Healing of........Luke 14:2-4 — 1045

Dross—*impurities separated from metals*
Result of
refinement ....Prov. 25:4 — 629
Figurative of
Israel............Is. 1:22, 25 — 658

Drought—*an extended dry season*
Unbearable
in the day ....Gen. 31:40 — 32
Seen in the
wilderness........Deut. 8:15 — 177
Comes in
summer ....Ps. 32:4 — 543
Sent as a
judgment........Hag. 1:11 — 914
Only God can
stop............Jer. 14:22 — 733
Descriptive of spiritual
barrenness ......Jer. 14:1-7 — 732
The wicked
dwell in ....Jer. 17:5, 6 — 735
The righteous
endure ....Jer. 17:8 — 735
Longest...........1 Kin. 18:1 — 344
Luke 4:25 — 1030

Drown
Of the
Egyptians ....Ex. 14:27-30 — 67
Jonah saved
from ....Jon. 1:15-17 — 886
Of severe
judgment........Matt. 18:6 — 981
The woman saved
from ....Rev. 12:15, 16 — 1301

Drowsiness—*the mental state preceding sleep*
Prelude to
poverty..........Prov. 23:21 — 627
Disciples
guilty of.........Matt. 26:43 — 992

Drunkenness—*state of intoxication*
A. *Evils of:*
Debases....Gen. 9:21, 22 — 12
Provokes
anger ....Prov. 20:1 — 624
Poverty......Prov. 23:21 — 627

Perverts
justice ....Is. 5:22, 23 — 661
Confuses the
mind.........Is. 28:7 — 679
Licentious-
ness..........Rom. 13:13 — 1142
Disorderli-
ness..........Matt. 24:48-51 — 989
Hinders watchful-
ness...........1 Thess. 5:6, 7 — 1208
B. *Actual instances of the evil of:*
Defeat in
battle ....1 Kin. 20:16-21 — 348
Degradation ...Esth. 1:10, 11 — 485
Debauchery...Dan. 5:1-4 — 841
Weakness .....Amos 4:1 — 873
Disorder.......1 Cor. 11:21, 22 — 1157
C. *Penalties of:*
Death ....Deut. 21:20, 21 — 188
Exclusion from
fellowship.....1 Cor. 5:11 — 1152
Exclusion from
heaven.....1 Cor. 6:9, 10 — 1152
D. *Figurative of:*
Destruction....Is. 49:26 — 699
Roaring
waves.........Ps. 107:27 — 585
Giddiness......Is. 19:14 — 673
Error ....Is. 28:7 — 679
Spiritual
blindness......Is. 29:9-11 — 680
International
chaos ....Jer. 25:15-29 — 743
Persecution....Rev. 17:6 — 1304

Dulcimer—*a bagpipe; musical instrument*
Used in Babylon ..Dan. 3:5-15 — 838

Dumah—*silence*
1. Descendants (a tribe) of
Ishmael.......Gen. 25:14 — 25
2. Town in
Judah.........Josh. 15:52 — 220

Dumb—*inability to speak*
A. *Used literally of dumbness:*
Natural........Ex. 4:11 — 57
Imposed ......Ezek. 3:26, 27 — 788
Demonized ....Mark 9:17, 25 — 1009
B. *Used figuratively of:*
External
calamity ......Ps. 38:13 — 547
Submis-
siveness.......Is. 53:7 — 702
Inefficient
leaders........Is. 56:10 — 704
Helplessness ...1 Cor. 12:2 — 1157
Lamb before
shearer is .....Acts 8:32 — 1103
With silence ...Ps. 39:2 — 547

Dung—*excrement*
A. *Used for:*
Fuel ....Ezek. 4:12, 15 — 789
Food in
famine........2 Kin. 6:25 — 361
B. *Figurative of:*
Something
worthless .....2 Kin. 9:37 — 365

Dungeon—*an underground prison*
Joseph's   {Gen. 40:8, 15 — 40
imprisonment   {Jer. 37:16 — 755

Dura—*circuit, wall*
Site of Nebuchadnezzar's golden
image ....Dan. 3:1 — 838

Dust—*powdery earth*
A. *Used literally of:*
Man's body ....Gen. 2:7 — 5
Dust of
Egypt.........Ex. 8:16, 17 — 60
Particles of
soil...........Num. 5:17 — 133

B. *Used figuratively of:*
Man's
mortality......Gen. 3:19 — 7
Descendants ...Gen. 13:16 — 15
Judgment.....Deut. 28:24 — 194
Act of
cursing........2 Sam. 16:13 — 309
Dejection......Job 2:12 — 497
Subjection....Is. 49:23 — 699
The grave .....Is. 26:19 — 678
Rejection......Matt. 10:14 — 972

Duty—*an obligation*
A. *Toward men:*
Husband to
wife..........Eph. 5:25-33 — 1189
Wife to
husband ......Eph. 5:22-24 — 1189
Parents to
children.......Eph. 6:4 — 1190
Children to
parents ....Eph. 6:1-3 — 1189
Subjects to
rulers ....1 Pet. 2:12-20 — 1261
Rulers to
subjects.......Rom. 13:1-7 — 1142
Men to men ...1 Pet. 3:8-16 — 1263
The weak......1 Cor. 8:1-13 — 1154
B. *Toward God:*
Love..........Deut. 11:1 — 179
Obey ....Matt. 12:50 — 975
Serve ....1 Thess. 1:9 — 1206
Worship.......John 4:23 — 1067

Dwarf—*a diminutive person*
Excluded from
priesthood......Lev. 21:20 — 116

Dyeing—*coloring*
Leather ....Ex. 25:5 — 76

Dysentery
Cured by Paul.....Acts 28:8 — 1126

E

Eagle—*a bird of prey of the falcon species*
A. *Described as:*
Unclean ....Lev. 11:13 — 104
A bird of
prey ....Job 9:26 — 501
Large.........Ezek. 17:3, 7 — 799
Swift ....2 Sam. 1:23 — 295
Keen in
vision.........Job 39:27-29 — 521
Nesting high...Jer. 49:16 — 766
B. *Figurative of:*
God's care....Ex. 19:4 — 70
Swift armies....Jer. 4:13 — 721
Spiritual
renewal ......Is. 40:31 — 690
Flight of
wealth ....Prov. 23:5 — 627
False
security......Jer. 49:16 — 766

Ear—*the organ of hearing*
A. *Ceremonies respecting:*
Priest's,
anointed .....Ex. 29:20 — 80
Leper's,
anointed .....Lev. 14:14, 25 — 108
Slave's,
pierced.......Ex. 21:5, 6 — 72
B. *The hearing of the unregenerate:*
Deafened ......Deut. 29:4 — 195
Stopped ......Ps. 58:4 — 557
Dulled........Matt. 13:15 — 976
Disobedient...Jer. 7:23, 24 — 725
Uncir-
cumcised......Acts 7:51 — 1102
Tickled ....2 Tim. 4:3, 4 — 1225
C. *Promises concerning, in:*
Prophecy .....Is. 64:4 — 711

SUBJECT	REFERENCE	PAGE
Ark sent to ....1 Sam. 5:10		267
Denounced by the		
prophets.........Jer. 25:9, 20		742

El (ancient word for God, often used as prefix to Hebrew names)

El-berith ....Judg. 9:46		242
El-bethel ....Gen. 35:6, 7		35

Ela

Father of
Shemei...........1 Kin. 4:18   328

Elah—*an oak*

1. Chief of
   Edom ....Gen. 36:41   37
2. Son of Caleb...1 Chr. 4:15   390
3. Benjamite .....1 Chr. 9:8   396
4. King of
   Israel ....1 Kin. 16:6, 8-10   343
5. Father of
   Hoshea ....2 Kin. 15:30   371
6. Valley of.......1 Sam. 17:2, 19   277

Elam—*hidden*

1. Son of Shem...Gen. 10:22   13
2. Benjamite .....1 Chr. 8:24   395
3. Korahite
   Levite.........1 Chr. 26:1, 3   411
4. Head of postexilic
   families ......Ezra 2:7   454
5. Another family
   head ....Ezra 2:31   454
6. One who signs
   document .....Neh. 10:1, 14   477
7. Priest.........Neh. 12:42   479

Elamites—*descendants of Elam*

A Semite (Shem)
people............Gen. 10:22   13
An ancient
nation............Gen. 14:1   15
Connected with
Media ....Is. 21:2   674
Destruction of ....Jer. 49:34-39   767
In Persian
empire ....Ezra 4:9   456
Jews from, at
Pentecost ....Acts 2:9   1095

Elasah—*God has made*

1. Shaphan's
   son ....Jer. 29:3   746
2. Son of
   Pashhur.......Ezra 10:22   462

El-berith—*god of the covenant*

Worshiped at
Shechem ....Judg. 9:46   242

El-bethel—*God of Bethel*

Site of Jacob's
altar..............Gen. 35:6, 7   35

Eldaah—*God has called*

Son of Midian.....Gen. 25:4   25

Eldad—*God has loved*

Elder of Moses ....Num. 11:26-29   140

Elderly

A. *Contributions of:*
   Counsel ....1 Kin. 12:6-16   338
            Job 12:12   503
   Spiritual
   service.......Luke 2:36-38   1028
   Fruitfulness....Ps. 92:13, 14   577
   Leadership.....Josh. 24:2, 14,
            15, 29   227
B. *Attitude toward:*
   Minister to
   needs ....1 Kin. 1:15   323
   Respect........Ps. 71:18, 19   564
   As cared for by
   God...........Is. 46:4   696
   Honor ....Lev. 19:32   114
            Prov. 16:31   621

Elders of Israel

A. *Functions of, in Mosaic period:*
   Rule the
   people ....Judg. 2:7   233
   Represent the
   nation ....Ex. 3:16, 18   56
   Share in national
   guilt ....Josh. 7:6   211
   Assist in
   government...Num. 11:16-25   140
   Perform religious
   acts.........Ex. 12:21, 22   64
B. *Functions of, in later periods:*
   Choose a
   king ....2 Sam. 3:17-21   297
   Ratify a
   covenant......2 Sam. 5:3   298
   Assist at a
   dedication....1 Kin. 8:1-3   332
   Counsel
   kings ....1 Kin. 12:6-8, 13   338
   Legislate
   reforms .....Ezra 10:8-14   462
   Try civil
   cases.........Matt. 26:3-68   990

Elders in the church

A. *Qualifications of, stated by:*
   Paul ....Titus 1:5-14   1229
   Peter ....1 Pet. 5:1-4   1264
B. *Duties of:*
   Administer
   relief.........Acts 11:29, 30   1107
   Correct error ..Acts 15:4, 6, 23   1111
   Hold fast the faithful
   Word ....Titus 1:5, 9   1229
   Rule well .....1 Tim. 5:17   1219
   Minister to the
   sick ....James 5:14, 15   1256
C. *Honors bestowed on:*
   Ordination.....Acts 14:19, 23   1110
   Obedience .....Heb. 13:7, 17   1248
   Due respect...1 Tim. 5:1, 19   1219
   See Bishop

Elead—*God has testified*

Ephraimite........1 Chr. 7:21   394

Eleadah—*God has adorned*

A descendant of
Ephraim..........1 Chr. 7:20   394

Elealeh—*God has ascended*

Moabite town .....Is. 15:1, 4   670
Rebuilt by
Reubenites ....Num. 32:37   162

Eleasah—*God has made*

1. Descendant of
   Judah.........1 Chr. 2:2-39   388
2. Descendant of
   Saul ....1 Chr. 8:33-37   395

Eleazar—*God has helped*

1. Son of Aaron ..Ex. 6:23   59
   Father of
   Phinehas......Ex. 6:25   59
   Consecrated a
   priest ....Ex. 28:1   78
   Ministers in priest's
   position......Lev. 10:6, 7   103
   Made chief
   Levite.........Num. 3:32   130
   Succeeds
   Aaron ....Num. 20:25-28   149
   Aids Joshua ...Josh. 14:1   218
   Buried at
   Ephraim ......Josh. 24:33   228
2. Merarite
   Levite.........1 Chr. 23:21, 22   409
3. Son of Abinadab; custodian of
   the ark........1 Sam. 7:1   268
4. One of David's mighty
   men...........2 Sam. 23:9   317
5. Priest.........Ezra 8:33   460
6. Son of
   Parosh........Ezra 10:25   462

7. Musician
   priest ....Neh. 12:27-42   479
8. Ancestor of
   Jesus.........Matt. 1:15   963

Elect

A. *Characteristics of:*
   Eternal ....Eph. 1:4   1185
   Personal......Acts 9:15   1104
   Sovereign......Rom. 9:11-16   1139
   Unmerited.....Rom. 9:11   1139
   God's fore-
   knowledge ....2 Pet. 1:3, 4   1268
   Of grace.......Rom. 11:5, 6   1140
   Through
   faith ....2 Thess. 2:13   1212
   Recorded in
   heaven........Luke 10:20   1039
   Knowable .....1 Thess. 1:4   1206
   Of high
   esteem........2 Tim. 2:4   1224
B. *Results in:*
   Adoption ......Eph. 1:5   1185
   Salvation ......2 Thess. 2:13   1212
   Conformity to
   Christ.........Rom. 8:29   1138
   Good works ...Eph. 2:10   1186
   Eternal glory ...Rom. 9:23   1139
   Inheritance....1 Pet. 1:2, 4, 5   1260
C. *Proof of:*
   Faith ....2 Pet. 1:10   1268
   Holiness.......Eph. 1:4, 5   1185
   Divine
   protection.....Mark 13:20   1015
   Manifest it in
   life............Col. 3:12   1201

El-Elohe-Israel—*God, the God of Israel*

Name of Jacob's
altar.............Gen. 33:20   34

Elements—*basic parts of anything*

A. *Used literally of:*
   Basic forces of
   nature ....2 Pet. 3:10, 12   1269
B. *Used figuratively of:*
   "Rudiments" of
   religion ....Gal. 4:3, 9   1179
   "Rudiments" of
   tradition ......Col. 2:8, 20   1201
   "First principles" of
   religion ....Heb. 5:12   1241

Eleven, the—*the disciples without Judas*

Were told of
resurrection ......Luke 24:9, 33   1058
Met Jesus........Matt. 28:16   995
At Pentecost .....Acts 2:1, 14   1095

Elhanan—*God has been gracious*

1. Son of Dodo ...2 Sam. 23:24   318
   Brave man.....1 Chr. 11:26   398
2. Son of Jair.....1 Chr. 20:5   406
   Slays a giant...2 Sam. 21:19   315

Eli—*my God*

Jesus' cry on the
cross.............Matt. 27:46   994
Same as "Eloi"....Mark 15:34   1019

Eli—*high (that is, God is high)*

1. Officiates in
   Shiloh.........1 Sam. 1:3   263
   Blesses
   Hannah.......1 Sam. 1:12-19   263
   Becomes Samuel's
   guardian.....1 Sam. 1:20-28   263
   Samuel ministers
   before.........1 Sam. 2:11   264
   Sons of ....1 Sam. 2:12-17   264
   Rebukes
   sons ....1 Sam. 2:22-25   264
   Rebuked by a man of
   God...........1 Sam. 2:27-36   265
   Instructs
   Samuel ......1 Sam. 3:1-18   265
   Death of ......1 Sam. 4:15-18   266
2. Father of Joseph, husband of
   Mary.........Luke 3:23   1029

119

SUBJECT	REFERENCE	PAGE

Fox—*a dog-like animal*

A. *Described as:*
Plentiful......Judg. 15:4 — 246
Destructive...Neh. 4:3 — 469
Crafty........Luke 13:32 — 1045
Carnivorous...Ps. 63:10 — 559
Living in
holes.........Matt. 8:20 — 970
Loves grapes...Song 2:15 — 649

B. *Figurative of:*
False
prophets.....Ezek. 13:4 — 795
Enemies......Song 2:15 — 649
Deceivers....Luke 13:32 — 1045

Fragrance—*a sweet odor*

Of perfume.......John 12:3 — 1079
Figurative of
restoration......Hos. 14:6 — 861

Fraud—*something designed to deceive*

A. *Examples of:*
Rebekah's, on
Isaac.........Gen. 27:5-36 — 27
Laban's, on
Jacob.......Gen. 29:21-25 — 29
Gibeonites', on
Israelites...Josh. 9:3-9 — 213
Jonathan's, on
Saul.........1 Sam. 20:11-17 — 281

B. *Discovery of, by:*
A miracle......Ex. 7:9-12 — 59
Events.........Matt. 28:11-15 — 995
Character......Matt. 26:47-50 — 992

Free moral agency of man—*ability to choose*

Resulted in sin....Gen. 2:16, 17 — 5
Recognized by ⎰Gen. 4:6-10 — 7
God...........⎱John 7:17 — 1072
Appealed to......Is. 1:18-20 — 658
Jer. 36:3, 7 — 754

Freedmen, Synagogue of

Cyrenians and Alexandrians
opposed
Stephen.........Acts 6:9 — 1100

Freedom—*unrestricted action*

A. *Of the unregenerate, limited by:*
Sin...........John 8:34 — 1074
Inability......John 8:43 — 1074
Satan.........John 8:41, 44 — 1074
Bondage.......Rom. 6:20 — 1136
Deadness.....Eph. 2:1 — 1185

B. *Of the regenerate:*
Made free by
Christ.......John 8:36 — 1074
Freed from
bondage......Rom. 6:18, 22 — 1136
Not of
license.......1 Pet. 2:16 — 1262
Not of bondage
again........Gal. 5:1 — 1180
Not of the
flesh.........Gal. 5:13 — 1180

Freewill offerings

Obligatory.......Deut. 12:6 — 180
Must be perfect...Lev. 22:17-25 — 116
Eaten in tabernacle by the
priests...........Lev. 7:16, 17 — 100
First of all
produce.......Prov. 3:9 — 611
According to one's
ability..........Deut. 16:17 — 184
Willing mind.....2 Cor. 8:10-12 — 1170
Cheerful heart....2 Cor. 9:6, 7 — 1171

Fretting—*a peevish state of mind*

Of the saints,
forbidden.........Ps. 37:1, 7, 8 — 546

Friend

A. *Nature of, common:*
Interest........1 Sam. 18:1 — 279
Love...........1 Sam. 20:17 — 281
Sympathy.....Job 2:11 — 496
Sacrifice......John 15:13 — 1082

B. *Value of:*
Contructive
criticism......Prov. 27:6 — 630
Helpful
advice........Prov. 27:7 — 630
Valuable in time of
need.........Prov. 27:10 — 630
Always
faithful........Prov. 17:17 — 622

C. *Dangers of:*
May entice to
sin............Deut. 13:6 — 182
Some are
necessary.....Prov. 14:20 — 619
Some are untrust-
worthy......Ps. 41:9 — 549

D. *Examples of:*
God and
Abraham......Is. 41:8 — 690
David and
Jonathan......1 Sam. 18:1 — 279
David and
Hushai........2 Sam. 15:37 — 309
Elijah and
Elisha........2 Kin. 2:1-14 — 356
Christ and His
disciples.....John 15:13-15 — 1082
Paul and
Timothy......2 Tim. 1:2 — 1223

Friendless—*lacking friends*

David's plight...Ps. 142:4 — 601
Prodigal son.....Luke 15:16 — 1046

Friendship

A. *Kinds of:*
True...........1 Sam. 18:1-3 — 279
Close.........Prov. 18:24 — 623
Ardent........2 Cor. 2:12, 13 — 1167
Treacherous...Matt. 26:48-50 — 992
Dangerous....Deut. 13:6-9 — 182
Unfaithful....Job 19:14-19 — 507
False.........2 Sam. 16:16-23 — 310
Worldly.......James 4:4 — 1255

B. *Tests of:*
Continued
loyalty.......2 Sam. 1:23 — 295
Willingness to
sacrifice.....John 15:13 — 1082
Obedient
spirit.........John 15:14, 15 — 1082
Likeminded-
ness..........Phil. 2:19-23 — 1194

Frog—*a small, leaping creature*

Plague on Egypt..Ps. 78:45 — 569
Of unclean
spirits...........Rev. 16:13 — 1303

Frontals—*ornaments worn on the forehead*

Of God's Word....Deut. 6:6-9 — 175

Frost

Figurative of God's
power.............Job 37:10 — 519
Figurative of God's creative
ability............Job 38:29 — 520

Frugality—*thrift*

Manifested by
Jesus.............John 6:11-13 — 1070
Wrong kind......Prov. 11:24, 25 — 617

Fruit—*product of life*

A. *Used literally of:*
Produce of
trees..........Gen. 1:29 — 5
Produce of the
earth..........Gen. 4:3 — 7
Progeny of
livestock......Deut. 28:51 — 194

B. *Factors destructive of:*
Blight.........Joel 1:12 — 865
Locusts........Joel 1:4 — 865
Enemies......Ezek. 25:4 — 808
Drought.......Hag. 1:10 — 914
God's anger....Jer. 7:20 — 725

C. *Used figuratively of:*
Repentance....Matt. 3:8 — 965
Industry.......Prov. 31:16, 31 — 634
Christian
graces........Gal. 5:22, 23 — 1181
Holy life.......Prov. 11:30 — 617
Christian
converts......John 4:36 — 1068
Christ.........Ps. 132:11 — 597
Sinful life.....Matt. 7:16 — 969
Reward of righ-
teousness.....Phil. 1:11 — 1193

Fruit-bearing—*productiveness of*

Old age.........Ps. 92:14 — 577
Good hearers.....Matt. 13:23 — 976
Christian
converts........Col. 1:6, 10 — 1199
Abiding...........John 15:2-8 — 1082

Fruitfulness

A. *Literally, dependent upon:*
Right soil......Matt. 13:8 — 976
Rain...........James 5:18 — 1256
Sunshine......Deut. 33:14 — 201
Seasons.......Matt. 21:34 — 985
Cultivation....Luke 13:8 — 1044
God's
blessing.......Acts 14:17 — 1110

B. *Spiritually, dependent upon:*
Death..........John 12:24 — 1079
New life.......Rom. 7:4 — 1136
Abiding in
Christ........John 15:2-8 — 1082
Yielding to
God..........Rom. 6:13-23 — 1135
Christian
effort.........2 Pet. 1:5-11 — 1268
Absence of,
reprobated....Matt. 21:19 — 985

Fruitless discussion—*self-conceited talk against God*

Characteristic of false
teachers.........1 Tim. 1:6, 7 — 1217

Fruit trees

Protected by
Law..............Lev. 19:23-25 — 114

Fulfill—*to bring to its designed end*

A. *Spoken of God's:*
Word..........Ps. 148:8 — 604
Prophecy......1 Kin. 2:27 — 326
Threat........2 Chr. 36:20, 21 — 450
Promise.......Acts 13:32, 33 — 1109
Righteous-
ness..........Matt. 3:15 — 965
Good
pleasure......2 Thess. 1:11 — 1212
Will..........Acts 13:22 — 1109

B. *Spoken of the believer's:*
Love..........Rom. 13:8 — 1142
Righ-
teousness.....Rom. 8:4 — 1137
Burden-
bearing.......Gal. 6:2 — 1181
Mission.......Col. 1:25 — 1200
Ministry.......Col. 4:17 — 1203

Full—*complete*

A. *Of natural things:*
Years.........Gen. 25:8 — 25
Breasts........Job 21:24 — 509
Children.......Ps. 127:5 — 596
Wagon........Amos 2:13 — 873
Leprosy.......Luke 5:12 — 1031

B. *Of miraculous things:*
Guidance......Judg. 6:38 — 238
Supply........2 Kin. 4:4, 6 — 358
Protection.....2 Kin. 6:17 — 361

C. *Of evil emotions:*
Evil...........Eccl. 9:3 — 643
Wrath.........Dan. 3:19 — 839
Rage.........Acts 19:28 — 1117
Envy.........Rom. 1:29 — 1132
Cursing.......Rom. 3:14 — 1133

SUBJECT	REFERENCE	PAGE

Galilee, Sea of—continued
Later called
Gennesaret......Luke 5:1 — 1031

Gall—bile
A. *Used literally of:*
Liver
secretion......Job 16:13 — 506
Poisonous
herb ....Matt. 27:34 — 994
B. *Used figuratively of:*
State of sin ....Acts 8:23 — 1103

Gallantry—a chivalrous act of bravery
Example of.......Ex. 2:16-21 — 55

Gallim—heaps
Village north of
Jerusalem ....Is. 10:29, 30 — 667
Home of Palti.....1 Sam. 25:44 — 287

Gallio—who lives on milk
Roman proconsul of Achaia;
dismisses charges against
Paul.............Acts 18:12-17 — 1115

Gallows—a structure used for hanging
Haman had
made............Esth. 5:14 — 488
Haman
hanged on........Esth. 7:9, 10 — 489
Haman's sons
hanged on........Esth. 9:13, 25 — 491

Gamaliel—God has rewarded
1. Leader of
Manasseh ....Num. 2:20 — 129
2. Famous Jewish
teacher ....Acts 22:3 — 1120
Respected by
people ......Acts 5:34-39 — 1099

Game—the flesh of wild animals
Isaac's favorite
dish ....Gen. 27:1-33 — 27

Games—various kinds of contests
Figurative examples of, (as of a race):
Requiring
discipline.........1 Cor. 9:25-27 — 1155
Requiring obedience to
rules ....2 Tim. 2:5 — 1224
Testing the
course...........Gal. 2:2 — 1178
Press on to the
goal.............Phil. 3:13, 14 — 1195

Gammadim—warriors
Manned Tyre's
towers ....Ezek. 27:11 — 809

Gamul—rewarded
Descendant of
Aaron............1 Chr. 24:17 — 409

Garden—a protected and cultivated place
A. *Notable examples of:*
In Eden........Gen. 2:15 — 5
In Egypt.......Deut. 11:10 — 180
In Susa........Esth. 1:5 — 485
In Geth-
semane ......Mark 14:32 — 1017
A royal ......2 Kin. 25:4 — 382
B. *Used for:*
Festivities .....Esth. 1:5 — 485
Idolatry........Is. 65:3 — 711
Meditations....Matt. 26:36 — 991
Burial.........John 19:41 — 1087
C. *Figurative of:*
Desolation.....Amos 4:9 — 874
Fruitfulness...Is. 51:3 — 700
Prosperity .....Is. 58:11 — 705
Righ-
teousness .....Is. 61:11 — 709

Gardener—one whose work is gardening
Adam, the first....Gen. 2:15 — 5
Christ,
mistaken for......John 20:15, 16 — 1087

Gareb—scab
1. One of David's
warriors........2 Sam. 23:38 — 318
2. Hill near
Jerusalem.....Jer. 31:39 — 750

Garland—ceremonial headdress or wreath
Brought by priests of
Zeus ....Acts 14:13 — 1110
Of grace ....Prov. 4:9 — 611
Granted to those who
mourn............Is. 61:3 — 708
Worn by
bridegrooms......Is. 61:10 — 709

Garlic—an onion-like plant
Egyptian food.....Num. 11:5 — 139

Garments (see Clothing)

Garmite—bony
Gentile name applied to
Keilah............1 Chr. 4:19 — 390

Garner—a place for storing grain
Full, prayed for ...Ps. 144:13 — 602

Garrison—a military post
Smitten by
Jonathan.........1 Sam. 13:3, 4 — 273
Attacked by
Jonathan.........1 Sam. 14:1-15 — 273

Gashmu—shower
Opposes
Nehemiah ......Neh. 6:6 — 471

Gatam—puny
Esau's grandson; chief of Edomite
clan..............Gen. 36:11-16 — 36

Gate—an entrance
A. *Made of:*
Wood..........Neh. 2:3, 17 — 467
Iron ....Acts 12:10 — 1108
Brass ....Ps. 107:16 — 585
Stones.........Rev. 21:12 — 1307
B. *Opening for:*
Camps.........Ex. 32:26, 27 — 84
Cities.........Judg. 16:3 — 247
Fortress ....Neh. 2:8 — 468
Sanctuary .....Ezek. 44:1, 2 — 826
Tombs.........Matt. 27:60 — 994
Prisons........Acts 12:5, 10 — 1107
C. *Used for:*
Business trans-
actions........1 Kin. 22:10 — 350
Legal
business......Ruth 4:1-11 — 258
Criminal
cases.........Deut. 25:7-9 — 191
Procla-
mations.......Jer. 17:19, 20 — 735
Festivities .....Ps. 24:7 — 539
Protection.....2 Sam. 18:24, 33 — 312
D. *Figurative of:*
Satanic
power........Matt. 16:18 — 980
Death ....Is. 38:10 — 688
Righteous-
ness........Ps. 118:19, 20 — 590
Salvation ......Matt. 7:13 — 969
Heaven........Rev. 21:25 — 1307

Gates of Jerusalem
1. Corner Gate ...2 Chr. 26:9 — 439
2. Refuse Gate ...Neh. 12:31 — 479
3. Of Ephraim ...Neh. 8:16 — 474
4. Fish Gate......Zeph. 1:10 — 908
5. Fountain
Gate ....Neh. 12:37 — 479
6. Horse Gate ....Jer. 31:40 — 750

7. Benjamin's
Gate ....Zech. 14:10 — 925
8. Gate of the
Guard........Neh. 12:39 — 479
9. Sheep Gate....Neh. 3:1 — 468
10. Upper Benjamin
Gate ....Jer. 20:2 — 737
11. Valley Gate....Neh. 2:13 — 468
12. Water Gate....Neh. 8:16 — 474

Gatekeeper
Duty of:
Zechariah.........1 Chr. 9:21 — 396
Shallum..........1 Chr. 9:17 — 396
Akkub ....1 Chr. 9:17 — 396
Talmon ....1 Chr. 9:17 — 396
Ahiman ....1 Chr. 9:17 — 396
Ben ....1 Chr. 15:18 — 401
Jaaziel ....1 Chr. 15:18 — 401
Shemiramoth .....1 Chr. 15:18 — 401
Jehiel ....1 Chr. 15:18 — 401
Unni ....1 Chr. 15:18 — 401
Eliab............1 Chr. 15:18 — 401
Benaiah ....1 Chr. 15:18 — 401
Maaseiah ....1 Chr. 15:18 — 401
Mattithiah ....1 Chr. 15:18 — 401
Eliphelehu ....1 Chr. 15:18 — 401
Mikneiah ....1 Chr. 15:18 — 401
Obed-edom.......1 Chr. 15:18 — 401
Jeiel ....1 Chr. 15:18 — 401
Heman...........1 Chr. 15:17 — 401
Asaph............1 Chr. 15:17 — 401
Ethan ....1 Chr. 15:17 — 401
Berechiah ....1 Chr. 15:23 — 401
Elkanah..........1 Chr. 15:23 — 401
Jehiah ....1 Chr. 15:24 — 401
Jeduthun ....1 Chr. 16:38 — 403
Hosah............1 Chr. 16:38 — 403

Gath—wine press
Philistine city .....1 Sam. 6:17 — 268
Last of Anakim
here...........Josh. 11:22 — 216
Ark carried to.....1 Sam. 5:8 — 267
Home of Goliath ..1 Sam. 17:4 — 277
David takes
refuge in ....1 Sam. 21:10-15 — 282
David's second
flight to ....1 Sam. 27:3-12 — 288
Captured by
David ....1 Chr. 18:1 — 404
Captured by
Hazael ....2 Kin. 12:17 — 368
Rebuilt by
Rehoboam.......2 Chr. 11:5, 8 — 428
Uzziah broke down
walls of ....2 Chr. 26:6 — 439
Destruction of,
prophetic........Amos 6:1-3 — 875
Name becomes
proverbial ....Mic. 1:10 — 891

Gath-hepher—wine press of the pit
Birthplace of
Jonah ....2 Kin. 14:25 — 370
Boundary of
Zebulun.........Josh. 19:13 — 222

Gath-rimmon—pomegranate press
1. City of Dan....Josh. 19:40-45 — 223
Assigned to
Levites.........Josh. 21:24 — 224
2. Town in
Manasseh .....Josh. 21:25 — 224

Gaza, Ayyah—strong place
1. Philistine
city ....Josh. 13:3 — 217
Conquered by
Joshua.........Josh. 10:41 — 215
Refuge of
Anakim........Josh. 11:22 — 216
Assigned to
Judah..........Josh. 15:47 — 219
Gates of, removed by
Samson.........Judg. 16:1-3 — 247
Samson deceived by Delilah
here ....Judg. 16:4-20 — 247
Samson blinded
here ....Judg. 16:21 — 248

SUBJECT	REFERENCE	PAGE	SUBJECT	REFERENCE	PAGE	SUBJECT	REFERENCE	PAGE

SUBJECT	REFERENCE	PAGE	SUBJECT	REFERENCE	PAGE	SUBJECT	REFERENCE	PAGE
E. *Moral attributes of:*			Chemosh			Makers of idols	Num. 33:52	163
Goodness (see Goodness of God)			(Moab)	1 Kin. 11:7	336	Guilds	Neh. 3:8, 32	468
Hatred	Ps. 5:5, 6	529	Dagon			**Golgotha**—*place of a skull*		
Holiness	Rev. 4:8	1296	(Philistine)	1 Sam. 5:1-7	266	Where Jesus		
Impartiality	1 Pet. 1:17	1261	Milcom			died	Matt. 27:33-35	993
Justice	Ps. 89:14	575	(Ammon)	1 Kin. 11:5	336	**Goliath**—*exile*		
Long-			Molech			1. Giant of		
suffering	Ex. 34:6, 7	85	(Ammon)	1 Kin. 11:7	336	Gath	1 Sam. 17:4	277
Love	1 John 4:8, 16	1277	Nebo			Killed by		
Mercy	Lam. 3:22, 23	779	(Babylon)	Is. 46:1	696	David	1 Sam. 17:50	279
Truth	Ps. 117:2	589	Nisroch			2. Another giant; killed by		
Vengeance	Deut. 32:34-41	200	(Assyria)	2 Kin. 19:37	376	Elhanan	2 Sam. 21:19	315
Wrath	Deut. 32:22	200	Rimmon			See Giants		
F. *Human expressions applied to:*			(Aram)	2 Kin. 5:18	360	**Gomer**—*completion*		
Fear	Deut. 32:26, 27	200	Tammuz			1. Son of	Gen. 10:2, 3	12
Grief	Gen. 6:6	9	(Babylon)	Ezek. 8:14	792	Japheth	1 Chr. 1:5, 6	387
Repentance	Gen. 6:7	9	Zeus			Northern		
Jealousy	Ex. 34:14	85	(Roman)	Acts 14:12, 13	1110	nation	Ezek. 38:6	820
Swearing	Jer. 44:26	762	B. *Evils connected with:*			2. Wife of		
Laughing	Ps. 2:4	528	Immorality	Num. 25:1-9	154	Hosea	Hos. 1:2, 3	853
Sleeping	Ps. 78:65	570	Prostitution	2 Kin. 23:7	380	**Gomorrah**—*submersion*		
Human parts	Ex. 33:21-23	85	Divination	Lev. 20:1-6	114	In a fruitful		
G. *Titles given to:*			Sacrilege	Dan. 5:4	841	valley	Gen. 13:10	15
Creator	Is. 40:12, 22, 26	689	Pride	2 Kin. 18:28-35	375	Defeated by		
Judge	Ps. 96:10, 13	578	Persecution	1 Kin. 19:1-3	346	Chedorlaomer	Gen. 14:8-11	15
King	Ps. 47:2, 7, 8	552	Child			Destroyed by		
Defender	Ps. 18:35	536	sacrifice	Jer. 7:29-34	726	God	Gen. 19:23-29	20
Preserver	Ps. 121:3-8	595	**Gog**—*mountain*			Symbol of evil	Is. 1:10	658
Shepherd	Gen. 49:24	49	1. Reubenite	1 Chr. 5:4	391	Symbol of		
H. *Works of, described as:*			2. Prince of Rosh, Meshech			destruction	Amos 4:11	874
Awesome	Ps. 66:3	560	and Tubal	Ezek. 38:2, 3	820	Punishment of	Matt. 10:15	972
Incompar-			3. Leader of the final			**Good for evil**		
able	Ps. 86:8	573	battle	Rev. 20:8-15	1306	Illustrated by		
Great	Ps. 92:5	577	**Goiim**—*nation*			Joseph	Gen. 45:5-15	45
Manifold	Ps. 104:24	582	Ruled by Tidal	Gen. 14:1	15	Christian duty	Luke 6:27, 35	1033
Marvelous	Ps. 139:14	600	Among conquests of			**Goodness of God**		
I. *Ways of, described as:*			Joshua	Josh. 12:7, 23	216	A. *Described as:*		
Perfect	Ps. 18:30	536	Possibly same as Harosheth-			Abundant	Ex. 34:6	85
Knowl-			hagoyim	Judg. 4:2, 13	235	Great	Ps. 31:19	542
edgeable	Ps. 86:11	573	**Golan**—*circuit*			Enduring	Ps. 52:1	554
Made known	Ps. 103:7	581	City of Bashan	Deut. 4:43	174	Satisfying	Ps. 65:4	560
Righteous	Ps. 145:17	603	Assigned to			Universal	Ps. 145:9	603
Not like			Levites	Josh. 21:27	224	B. *Manifested in:*		
man's	Is. 55:8, 9	703	City of refuge	Josh. 20:8	223	Material	Matt. 5:45	968
Everlasting	Hab. 3:6	905	**Gold**			blessings	Acts 14:17	1110
Inscrutable	Rom. 11:33	1141	A. *Found in:*			Spiritual		
Righteous and			Havilah	Gen. 2:11, 12	5	blessings	Ps. 31:19	542
true	Rev. 15:3	1303	Ophir	1 Kin. 9:28	335	Forgiving sin	Ps. 86:5	573
See Goodness of God; Love of God; Power of God			Sheba	1 Kin. 10:2, 10	335	C. *Saints' attitude toward:*		
			Arabia	2 Chr. 9:14	426	Rejoice in	Ex. 18:9	70
Godhead—*the Deity*			B. *Used for:*			Remember	Ps. 145:7	603
Revealed to			Money	Matt. 10:9	972	Be satisfied		
mankind	Rom. 1:20	1132	Offerings	Ex. 35:22	87	with	Jer. 31:14	748
Corrupted by			Presents	Matt. 2:11	964	**Gopher wood**		
mankind	Acts 17:29	1115	Holy			Used in Noah's		
Incarnated in Jesus			adornment	Ex. 28:4-6	78	ark	Gen. 6:14	9
Christ	Col. 2:9	1201	Jewelry	Gen. 24:22	23	**Gore**—*to push or thrust*		
			Physical			By an ox	Ex. 21:28-32	73
Godliness—*holy living*			adornment	Ex. 36:34, 38	88	Rendered		
Profitable	1 Tim. 4:7, 8	1219	Idols	Ex. 32:31	84	"push"	Deut. 33:17	201
Perverted	1 Tim. 6:5	1220	C. *Figurative of:*			Rendered		
Pursuit	1 Tim. 6:11	1220	Saints			"thrust"	Ezek. 34:21	817
Duty	Titus 2:12	1230	refined	Job 23:10	510	**Goshen**		
See Holiness of Christians			Babylonian			1. District of Egypt where Israel		
Gods, false			empire	Dan. 2:38	837	lived	Gen. 45:10	45
A. *Names of:*			Redeemed	2 Tim. 2:20	1224	Land of		
Adrammelech			Faith			pastures	Gen. 47:1-6	47
(Aram)	2 Kin. 17:31	373	purified	1 Pet. 1:7	1260	Called the land of		
Anammelech			Christ's			Rameses	Gen. 47:6-11	47
(Babylon)	2 Kin. 17:31	373	doctrine	Rev. 3:18	1296	2. Region in south		
Artemis			**Golden apples**			Judah	Josh. 10:41	215
(Greek)	Acts 19:35	1117	Appropriate			3. City of		
Ashtoreth			word	Prov. 25:11	629	Judah	Josh. 15:51	220
(Canaan)	1 Kin. 11:5	336	**Golden rule**			**Gospel**—*good news*		
Baal			For Christian	Matt. 7:12	969	A. *Described as, of:*		
(Canaan)	1 Kin. 18:19	345	conduct	Luke 6:31	1033	God	Rom. 1:1	1131
Baal of Peor			**Goldsmiths**			Christ	2 Cor. 2:12	1167
(Moab)	Num. 25:1-9	154	In the			The kingdom	Matt. 24:14	988
Baalzebub			tabernacle	Ex. 31:1-4	82	Grace of God	Acts 20:24	1118
(Philistine)	Luke 11:19-23	1041	Refiners	Mal. 3:3	931			
Bel			Shapers of					
(Babylon)	Jer. 51:44	771	objects	Ex. 25:11, 18	76			
Calf worship								
(Egypt)	Ex. 32:1-6	83						

SUBJECT	REFERENCE	PAGE

Guni—*colored*
1. One of Naphtali's
sons ....Gen. 46:24 — 46
     1 Chr. 7:13 — 394
Descendants called
Gunites ....Num. 26:48 — 155
2. Gadite........1 Chr. 5:15 — 391

Gur—*lion's cub*
Site of Ahaziah's
death............2 Kin. 9:27 — 364

Gur-baal—*sojourn of Baal*
Place in Arabia....2 Chr. 26:7 — 439

H

Haahashtari—*runner*
Son of Ashur......1 Chr. 4:5, 6 — 390

Habaiah—*Yahweh has hidden*
Father of excommunicated Jewish
priests...........Ezra 2:61, 62 — 455
Also spelled
Hobaiah.......Neh. 7:63, 64 — 473

Habakkuk—*embrace*
A. *Complaints of:*
God's silence ..Hab. 1:2-4 — 903
God's
response .....Hab. 1:5-11 — 903
Chaldean
cruelty.......Hab. 1:12-17 — 904
God's
response .....Hab. 2:1-20 — 904
B. *Prayer of:*
Praise of
God..........Hab. 3:1-19 — 905

Habakkuk, the Book of—*a book of the Old Testament*
Author...........Hab. 1:1 — 903
Setting..........Hab. 1:2-4 — 903
Historical
reference.......Hab. 1:6 — 903
The life of the
righteous........Hab. 2:4 — 904

Habazziniah
Grandfather of
Jaazaniah ....Jer. 35:3 — 753

Habit—*a custom*
Kinds of:
Doing evil........Jer. 13:23 — 732
Doing good ......Acts 10:38 — 1106
Of animals,
instinctive........2 Pet. 2:22 — 1269

Habitation—*a place of residence*
A. *Used literally of:*
Canaan.......Num. 15:2 — 143
A tree ......Dan. 4:20, 21 — 840
Nation........Acts 17:26 — 1114
B. *Used figuratively of:*
Eternity ....Is. 57:15 — 705
God's throne...Is. 63:15 — 710
Sky...........Hab. 3:11 — 905
Heaven........Luke 16:9 — 1047
New
Jerusalem...Is. 33:20 — 684

Habor—*joined together*
On the river of
Gozan...........2 Kin. 17:6 — 372

Hacaliah—*darkness of Yahweh*
Father of
Nehemiah ....Neh. 1:1 — 467

Hachilah—*dark, gloomy*
Hill in the wilderness of Ziph
where David
hid ....1 Sam. 23:19-26 — 284

Hachmoni
Tutor to king's
son..............1 Chr. 27:32 — 412

Hadad—*fierceness*
1. Ishmael's
son ....{Gen. 25:13, 15 — 25
{1 Chr. 1:30 — 388
2. King of
Edom........Gen. 36:35, 36 — 37
3. Another king of
Edom.........1 Chr. 1:50 — 388
Called Hadar ..Gen. 36:39 — 37
4. Edomite
leader.........1 Kin. 11:14-25 — 337

Hadadezer—*Hadad is a help*
King of Zobah ....2 Sam. 8:3-13 — 301
Defeated by
David ....2 Sam. 10:6-19 — 303

Hadadrimmon—*Hadad and Rimmon*
Name of the two Aramean deities;
a place in
Jezreel ....Zech. 12:11 — 924

Hadashah—*new*
Village of Judah...Josh. 15:37 — 219

Hadassah—*myrtle*
Esther's Jewish
name.............Esth. 2:7 — 486

Hades
Capernaum brought
down to..........Luke 10:15 — 1039
Rich man in
torment..........Luke 16:23 — 1047
Christ's soul not
abandoned to.....Acts 2:27, 31 — 1096
Gave up the dead
from ....Rev. 20:13, 14 — 1306

Hadid—*sharp*
Town of
Benjamin.........Neh. 11:31, 34 — 478

Hadlai—*restful*
Ephraimite .....2 Chr. 28:12 — 441

Hadoram—*Hadar is exalted*
1. Son of
Joktan........Gen. 10:26, 27 — 13
2. Son of Tou ....1 Chr. 18:9, 10 — 404
3. Rehoboam's tribute
officer.........2 Chr. 10:18 — 428
Called
Adoram.......1 Kin. 12:18 — 338
Probably same as
Adoniram ....1 Kin. 4:6 — 328

Hadrach—*periodical return*
Place in Aram.....Zech. 9:1 — 922

Haeleph—*ox*
Town of
Benjamin.........Josh. 18:28 — 222

Hagab—*locust*
Head of a family of Temple
servants..........Ezra 2:46 — 455

Hagaba—*locust*
Head of a family of Temple
servants.........Neh. 7:46, 48 — 472

Hagabah—*locust*
Head of a family of Temple
servants.........Ezra 2:43, 45 — 455

Hagar, Agar—*flight*
Sarah's Egyptian
handmaid ....Gen. 16:1 — 17
Flees from
Sarah ....Gen. 16:5-8 — 17
Returns; becomes mother of
Ishmael ....Gen. 16:3-16 — 17
Abraham sends her
away ....Gen. 21:14 — 21
Paul's
allegory of......Gal. 4:22-26 — 1180

Haggai—*festive*
Postexilic
prophet ....Ezra 5:1, 2 — 457
Contemporary of
Zechariah ....Ezra 6:14 — 458
Prophecies of, dated in reign of
Darius
Hystaspes {Hag. 1:1, 15 — 914
(520 B.C.) ....{Hag. 2:1, 10, 20 — 915

Haggai, the Book of—*a book of the Old Testament*
Purpose..........Hag. 1:1-15 — 914
The coming
glory............Hag. 2:4-9 — 915
On Levitical
cleanliness ......Hag. 2:10-14 — 915

Haggedolim
Father of
Zabdiel...........Neh. 11:14 — 478

Haggi—*festal*
Son of Gad.......Gen. 46:16 — 46
Head of tribal
family...........Num. 26:15 — 155

Haggiah—*festival of Yahweh*
Merarite Levite ...1 Chr. 6:30 — 392

Haggith—*festal*
One of David's
wives.............2 Sam. 3:4 — 297
Mother of
Adonijah.........1 Kin. 1:5 — 323

Hagri—*a Hagerite*
A mighty man of David's
guard ....1 Chr. 11:38 — 398
Called "Bani the
Gadite" in.......2 Sam. 23:36 — 318

Hagrites
Nomad people east of
Gilead............1 Chr. 5:10-22 — 391
Conspiring against
Israel............Ps. 83:2-6 — 572
Jaziz, keeper of David's
flocks ....1 Chr. 27:31 — 412

Hail—*frozen rain*
Illustrative of God's:
Wonders..........Job 38:22 — 520
Glory ....Ps. 18:12 — 535
Chastening.......Is. 28:2, 17 — 679
Wrath ....Rev. 8:7 — 1298

Hail—*a salutation ("Hale be thou")*
Gabriel to Mary...Luke 1:26-28 — 1025
Judas to Christ...Matt. 26:47-49 — 992
Soldiers to
Christ............Matt. 27:27-29 — 993

Hair
A. *Of women:*
Covering ......1 Cor. 11:15 — 1157
Uses of ....Luke 7:38 — 1035
Prohibitions {1 Tim. 2:9 — 1218
concerning...{1 Pet. 3:3 — 1262
B. *Of men:*
Not to be worn
long ....1 Cor. 11:14 — 1157
Rules for
cutting.......Lev. 19:27 — 114
Long, during Nazirite
vow...........Num. 6:5 — 134
Gray, sign
of age........1 Sam. 12:2 — 272
Absalom's {2 Sam. 14:25, —
beautiful.....{ 26 — 307
Numbered ....Matt. 10:30 — 973
C. *Figurative of:*
Minuteness....Judg. 20:16 — 251
Complete
safety........1 Sam. 14:45 — 275
Fear..........Job 4:14, 15 — 498
Great
numbers ......Ps. 40:12 — 548

SUBJECT	REFERENCE	PAGE	SUBJECT	REFERENCE	PAGE	SUBJECT	REFERENCE	PAGE

Hananiah—continued

14. Priest of Joiakim's
time .... Neh. 12:12 — 479

Hand

Mysterious .... Dan. 5:1-6 — 841
Healing
withered .... Mark 3:1-3 — 1001
Offending, to be cut
off. .... Matt. 18:8 — 981

Handbreadth—*a linear measurement*

Border of .... Ex. 37:12 — 88
Figurative of human
life .... Ps. 39:5 — 547

Handful

Of fine flour ...... Lev. 2:2—5:12 — 96
Of grain offering .. Num. 5:26 — 133
Of barley .... Ezek. 13:19 — 796

Handkerchief

Touch of, brings
healing .... Acts 19:12 — 1116
Rendered cloth .... John 11:44 — 1078
     John 20:7 — 1087

Handle—*to manage with the hands*

Used literally for:
Hold .... 2 Chr. 25:5 — 438
Touch .... Luke 24:39 — 1058
Feel .... Ps. 115:7 — 589

Used figuratively for:
Give attention .... Prov. 16:20 — 621
Treat .... Mark 12:4 — 1013

Handmaid—*female servant*

Examples of:
Hagar .... Gen. 16:1 — 17
Zilpah .... Gen. 29:24 — 29
Bilhah .... Gen. 30:4 — 30

Expressive of humility:
Ruth .... Ruth 2:13 — 257
Woman of   (1 Sam. 28:7, 21,
Endor .... (22 — 288
Mary .... Luke 1:38 — 1026

Hand of God

Expressive of:
Judgment .... Ex. 9:3 — 61
Chastening .... Job 19:21 — 507
Security .... John 10:29 — 1077
Miracles .... Ex. 3:20 — 56
Providence .... Ps. 31:15 — 542
Provision .... Ps. 145:16 — 603
Protection .... Ps. 139:10 — 600
Punishment ...... Ps. 75:8 — 567
Pleading .... Is. 65:2 — 711

Hands

Clapping—
in joy .... 2 Kin. 11:12 — 367
Washing—
in innocency ..... Matt. 27:24 — 993
Joining—
in agreement ...... 2 Kin. 10:15 — 365
Striking—
in suretyship ...... Prov. 17:16-18 — 622
Striking—
in anger .... Num. 24:10 — 153
Under thigh—
in oaths .... Gen. 47:29, 31 — 47
Right hand, expressive of:
Honor .... Ps. 45:9 — 551
Power .... Ps. 110:1 — 587
Love .... Song 2:6 — 649
Oath .... Is. 62:8 — 709
Accusation .... Zech. 3:1 — 919
Self-denial .... Matt. 5:30 — 967
Fellowship .... Gal. 2:9 — 1178

Hands, laying on of

A. *In the Old Testament:*
Blessing a
person .... Gen. 48:14, 20 — 48
Transferring one's
guilt .... Lev. 4:14, 15 — 98
Setting apart for
service .... Num. 8:10, 11 — 137

Inaugurating a
successor ..... Num. 27:18-23 — 156
B. *In the New Testament:*
Blessing .... Matt. 19:13-15 — 983
Healing .... Matt. 9:18 — 971
Ordaining
deacons .... Acts 6:6 — 1100
Sending out mission-
aries .... Acts 13:2, 3 — 1108
Ordaining
officers .... 1 Tim. 4:14 — 1219
In bestowing the Holy
Spirit .... Acts 8:17, 18 — 1103

Handwriting

Of a king,
changeable ...... Dan. 6:8-27 — 842
Of God,
unchangeable .... Dan. 5:5-31 — 841

Hanes—*mercury*

Probably an Egyptian
city .... Is. 30:4 — 681

Hanging—*a form of punishment*

Absalom .... 2 Sam. 18:9-17 — 311
Ahithophel .... 2 Sam. 17:23 — 311
Judas .... Matt. 27:5 — 993
Chief baker ...... Gen. 40:19, 22 — 40
King of Ai .... Josh. 8:29 — 213
Five Canaanite
kings .... Josh. 10:26, 27 — 215
Ish-bosheth's
murderers ..... 2 Sam. 4:12 — 298
Bodies of Saul and
Jonathan .... 2 Sam. 21:12 — 315
Law of .... Ezra 6:11 — 458
Haman .... Esth. 7:10 — 489
Haman's sons ..... Esth. 9:14 — 491
Curse of .... Gal. 3:13 — 1179
Saul's
descendants ..... 2 Sam. 21:9 — 315
Jesus Christ ...... John 19:31 — 1087

Hannah—*graciousness*

Favored wife of
Elkanah .... 1 Sam. 1:5 — 263
Childless .... 1 Sam. 1:5, 6 — 263
Provoked by
Peninnah .... 1 Sam. 1:6, 7 — 263
Wrongly accused by
Eli .... 1 Sam. 1:14 — 263
Prayerful .... 1 Sam. 1:10 — 263
Attentive to her
child .... 1 Sam. 1:22 — 263
Fulfills her vows .. 1 Sam. 1:11-28 — 263
Magnifies God ... 1 Sam. 2:1-10 — 264
Recognizes the Messiah ("His
Anointed") .... 1 Sam. 2:10 — 264
Model of Mary's
song .... Luke 1:46-54 — 1026

Hannathon—*regarded with favor*

Town of
Zebulun .... Josh. 19:14 — 222

Hanniel—*God has been gracious*

1. Manassite
leader .... Num. 34:23 — 164
2. Asherite .... 1 Chr. 7:30, 39 — 394

Hanoch—*dedicated*

1. Descendant of (Gen. 25:4 — 25
Abraham ..... (1 Chr. 1:33 — 388
2. Son of
Reuben .... Gen. 46:9 — 46
3. Head of tribal
family .... Num. 26:5 — 154

Hanun—*favored*

1. King of
Ammon .... 2 Sam. 10:1 — 302
Disgraces David's ambas-
sadors .... 2 Sam. 10:2-5 — 302
Is defeated by
David .... 2 Sam. 10:6-14 — 303
2, 3. Postexilic
workmen ..... Neh. 3:13, 30 — 468

Hapharaim—*double pit*

Town of
Issachar .... Josh. 19:19 — 222

Happiness of the saints

A. *Is derived from:*
Fear of God .... Ps. 128:1, 2 — 596
Trust in God .. Prov. 16:20 — 621
Obedience to
God .... John 13:15, 17 — 1080
Wisdom's
ways .... Prov. 3:13-18 — 611

B. *Examples of:*
Israel .... Deut. 33:29 — 202
Job .... James 5:11 — 1256
Mary .... Luke 1:46-55 — 1026
Paul .... Acts 26:2 — 1123

C. *In spite of:*
Discipline ...... Job 5:17 — 498
Suffering ...... 1 Pet. 4:12-14 — 1264
Persecution .... Matt. 5:10-12 — 966
Lack .... Phil. 4:6, 7 — 1195
Trouble .... 2 Cor. 4:7-18 — 1167

D. *Described as:*
Blessed .... Matt. 5:3-12 — 966
Filled .... Ps. 36:8 — 545
In God alone .. Ps. 73:25, 26 — 565

See Gladness; Joy

Happiness of the wicked

A. *Described as:*
Short .... Job 20:5 — 508
Uncertain ...... Luke 12:20 — 1042
Vain .... Eccl. 2:1, 2 — 638
Limited to this
life .... Luke 16:24, 25 — 1047
Under God's (Job 15:21 — 505
judgment ..... (Ps. 73:18-20 — 565

B. *Derived from:*
Prominence ... Job 21:7 — 508
     Ps. 37:35 — 546
Prosperity ..... Ps. 17:14 — 535
     Ps. 37:7 — 546
Sensuality ..... Is. 22:13 — 675

C. *Saints:*
Sometimes
stumble at .... Ps. 73:2, 3 — 565
Should not
envy .... Ps. 37:1, 7 — 546
Will see end ... Ps. 73:17-20 — 565

Happizzez—*shattering*

Chief of a priestly
course .... 1 Chr. 24:15 — 409

Hara—*hill*

Place in Assyria where captive
Israelites
settled .... 1 Chr. 5:26 — 392

Haradah—*fear*

Israelite
encampment ..... Num. 33:24 — 162

Haran—*mountainous*

1. Abraham's younger
brother .... Gen. 11:26-31 — 14
2. Gershonite
Levite .... 1 Chr. 23:9 — 408
3. Son of Caleb ... 1 Chr. 2:46 — 389
4. City of Mesopo-
tamia .... Gen. 11:31 — 14
Abraham
lives in .... Acts 7:2, 4 — 1100
Abraham
leaves .... Gen. 12:4, 5 — 14
Jacob
flees to .... Gen. 27:43 — 28
Jacob
dwells at ...... Gen. 29:4-35 — 29
Center of (Gen. 35:2 — 35
idolatry ...... (2 Kin. 19:12 — 376

Hararite—*mountaineer*

Applied to (2 Sam. 23:11,
David's mighty {   33 — 317
men .... (1 Chr. 11:34, 35 — 398

SUBJECT	REFERENCE	PAGE

Heartlessness—*without moral feeling; cruelty*

A. *Among unbelievers:*
Philistines, toward
Samson........Judg. 16:21   248
Saul, toward
David........1 Sam. 18:25   280
Nabal, toward
David........1 Sam. 25:4-12   285
Haman, toward
Jews.........Esth. 3:8, 9   487
Priest, toward a certain
man ....Luke 10:30-32   1040

B. *Among professing believers:*
Laban, toward
Jacob........Gen. 31:7, 36-42   31
Jacob's sons, toward
Joseph......Gen. 37:18-35   37
David, toward
Uriah........2 Sam. 11:9-27   303

Heat, hot

Figurative of:
God's wrath.......Deut. 9:19   178
Man's anger.......Deut. 19:6   186
Determination ....Gen. 31:36   32
Zeal ....Ps. 39:3   547
Persecution ......Matt. 13:6, 21   975
Heavy toil........Matt. 20:12   983
Real faith........Rev. 3:15   1296

Heathen (see Gentiles)

Heaven—*the place of everlasting bliss*

A. *Inhabitants of:*
God ....1 Kin. 8:30   333
Christ ....Heb. 9:12, 24   1244
Holy Spirit.....Ps. 139:7, 8   600
Angels........Matt. 18:10   981
Righteous
men.........Heb. 12:22, 23   1248

B. *Things lacking in:*
Marriage......Matt. 22:30   986
Death ....Luke 20:36   1052
Flesh and
blood ....1 Cor. 15:50   1161
Imper-
ishable........1 Cor. 15:42, 50   1161
Sorrow ....Rev. 7:17   1298
Pain ....Rev. 21:4   1307
Curse.........Rev. 22:3   1308
Night.........Rev. 22:5   1308
Wicked
people ....Rev. 22:15   1308
End...........Matt. 25:46   990
Rev. 22:5   1308

C. *Positive characteristics of:*
Joy ....Luke 15:7, 10   1046
Rest ....Rev. 14:13   1302
Peace.........Luke 16:25   1047
Righ-
teousness ....2 Pet. 3:13   1269
Service ....Rev. 7:15   1298
Reward.......Matt. 5:11, 12   966
Inheritance....1 Pet. 1:4   1260
Glory.........Rom. 8:17, 18   1138

D. *Entrance into, for:*
Righteous ....Matt. 23:34, 37   988
Changed.......1 Cor. 15:51   1161
Saved........John 3:5, 18, 21   1066
Called ....2 Pet. 1:10, 11   1268
Overcomers....Rev. 2:7, 10, 11   1294
Those
recorded .....Luke 10:20   1039
Obedient.......Rev. 22:14   1308
Holy ....Rev. 19:8   1305

E. *Believer's present attitude toward:*
Given
foretaste of ..Acts 7:55, 56   1102
Earnestly
desires........2 Cor. 5:2, 8   1168
Looks for......2 Pet. 3:12   1269
Considers "very much better"
than now .....Phil. 1:23   1193
Puts treasure
there.........Luke 12:33   1043

F. *Described as:*
House ....John 14:2   1081
Kingdom ......Matt. 25:34   990
Abraham's
bosom ......Luke 16:22, 23   1047
Paradise ....2 Cor. 12:2, 4   1173
Better
country.......Heb. 11:10, 16   1246
Holy city .....Rev. 21:2, 10-27   1307
Rev. 22:1-5   1307

Heavens, natural

A. *Facts regarding:*
Created by
God...........Gen. 1:1   4
Stretched   {Is. 42:5   691
out..........{Jer. 10:12   728
Will be   {Heb. 1:10-12   1239
destroyed ....{2 Pet. 3:10   1269
New heavens {Is. 65:17   712
to follow.....{2 Pet. 3:13   1269

B. *Purposes of:*
To declare God's
glory..........Ps. 19:1   536
To declare God's righ-
teousness ....Ps. 50:6   553
To manifest God's
wisdom ....Prov. 8:27   615

Heaviness—*a spirit of grief or anxiety*

Unrelieved by
joy ....Prov. 14:13   619
God's children
experience.......Phil. 2:26   1194
Needed
exchange......James 4:9   1255
Experienced by
Christ...........Ps. 69:20, 21   563
Remedy for ....Prov. 12:25   618

Heavy—*oppressive*

A. *Used literally of:*
Eli's weight....1 Sam. 4:18   266
Absalom's
hair........2 Sam. 14:26   308
Stone........Prov. 27:3   630

B. *Used figuratively of:*
Fatigue.......Matt. 26:43   992
Burdens ....2 Chr. 10:11, 14   427
Sins ....Is. 24:20   676
Sullenness.....1 Kin. 21:4   349
God's
judgments ....1 Sam. 5:6, 11   267

Heber, Eber—*associate*

1. Son of
Beriah ....Gen. 46:17   46
Descendants called
Heberites .....Num. 26:45   155
2. Husband of Jael, the slayer of
Sisera ......Judg. 4:11-24   235
3. Descendant of
Ezrah ....1 Chr. 4:17, 18   390
4. Gadite chief ...1 Chr. 5:11, 13   391
5. Benjamite ....1 Chr. 8:17   395
6. Benjamite
chief..........1 Chr. 8:22   395
7. In Christ's
genealogy....Luke 3:35   1029
Same as   {Gen. 10:24   13
Eber in.....{1 Chr. 1:25   388

Hebrew—*one from the other side*

Applied to:
Abram............Gen. 14:13   16
Israelites.........1 Sam. 4:6, 9   266
Jews..............Acts 6:1   1100
Paul, a sincere ....Phil. 3:5   1195

Hebrew language

Called Judean....2 Kin. 18:26, 28   375
Alphabet of, in
divisions.........Ps. 119   590
Language of   {John 19:13, 20   1086
Christ's time....{Acts 21:40   1119

See Aramaic

Hebrews, the Epistle to the—*a book of the New Testament*

Christ greater than the
angels............Heb. 1:3, 4   1239
Christ of the order of
Melchizedek......Heb. 4:14—5:10   1241
The new
covenant........Heb. 8:1—10:18   1243
The life of faith ...Heb. 10:19—
13:17   1245

Hebron, Ebron—*alliance*

1. Ancient town in
Judah........Num. 13:22   141
Originally called Kiriath-
arba ....Gen. 23:2   22
Abram dwells
here ....Gen. 13:18   15
Abraham buys cave
here ....Gen. 23:2-20   22
Isaac and Jacob sojourn
here ....Gen. 35:27   36
Visited by
spies ....Num. 13:22   141
Defeated by
Joshua........Josh. 10:1-37   214
Caleb expels Anakim
from ....Josh. 14:12-15   218
Assigned to
Levites........Josh. 21:10-13   224
City of
refuge.........Josh. 20:7   223
David's original
capital ....2 Sam. 2:1-3, 11   295
Birthplace of David's
sons ....2 Sam. 3:2   297
Abner's death
here ....2 Sam. 4:1   298
Absalom's rebellion
here ....2 Sam. 15:7-10   308
Fortified by
Rehoboam ....2 Chr. 11:10   428
2. Town of
Asher.........Josh. 19:28   222
3. Son of
Kohath ....Ex. 6:18   59
Descendants called
Hebronites....Num. 3:19, 27   130
4. Descendant of
Caleb ....1 Chr. 2:42, 43   389

Hebronites (see Hebron 3)

Hedge—*a fence or barrier*

Illustrative of:
God's protection ..Job 1:10   495
Afflictions........Job 19:8   507
Sluggishness......Prov. 15:19   620
Removal of
protection........Ps. 80:12   571

Hedgehog—*porcupine*

Figurative of   {Is. 14:23   670
desolation.....{Zeph. 2:14   910

Heedfulness—*giving proper attention to something important*

A. *Objects of:*
God's command-
ments.........Josh. 22:5   225
Our ways.....Ps. 39:1   547
False
teachers ......Matt. 16:6   979
God's Word....2 Pet. 1:19   1268

B. *Admonitions to Christians, concerning:*
Deception .....Matt. 24:4   988
Outward
display.......Matt. 6:1   968
Worldliness....Luke 21:34   1054
Duty ....Acts 20:28-31   1118
Foundation ...1 Cor. 3:10   1150
Liberty ....1 Cor. 8:9   1154
Security ....1 Cor. 10:12   1156
Effec-
tiveness.......Gal. 5:15   1181
Ministry ....Col. 4:17   1203
Myths ....1 Tim. 1:4   1217
Unbelief.......Heb. 3:12   1240

See Caution

SUBJECT	REFERENCE	PAGE

SUBJECT	REFERENCE	PAGE	SUBJECT	REFERENCE	PAGE	SUBJECT	REFERENCE	PAGE

Rebuilt by
Reuben..........Num. 32:37   162
On Gad's southern
boundary........Josh. 13:26   218
Levitical city....Josh. 21:39   225
Later held by
Moabites........Is. 15:1-4   670
Judgment of,
announced.......Is. 16:8-14   671
Fall of, predicted ..Jer. 48:2, 34, 35   764
Pools in..........Song 7:4   652

Heshmon—*fatness*

Town of Judah....Josh. 15:21, 27   219

Hesitation—*delay prompted by indecision*

Causes of:
Uncertain about God's
will...............1 Sam. 23:1-13   283
Fear of man......John 9:18-23   1075
Selfish
unconcern.......2 Cor. 8:10-14   1170
Unbelief ....John 20:24-28   1088

Hesli—*reserved*

Ancestor of
Christ...........Luke 3:25   1029

Heth

Letter of the Hebrew
alphabet.........Ps. 119:57-64   592

Heth—*terror*

Son of Canaan ....Gen. 10:15   13
Ancestor of the
Hittites...........Gen. 23:10   22
Abraham buys field from
sons of ....Gen. 23:3-20   22
Esau marries
daughters of.....Gen. 27:46   28
See Hittites

Hethlon—*hiding place*

Place indicating Israel's ideal
northern
boundary........Ezek. 47:15   830

Hewers of wood

A slave classification:
Gibeonites ....Josh. 9:17-27   213
Classed with "drawers of
water" ....Josh. 9:21, 23   214

Hezekiah—*Yahweh strengthens*

1. King of
Judah.........2 Chr. 29:1-3   441
Reforms Temple
services.......2 Chr. 29:3-36   441
Restores pure
worship.......2 Chr. 31:1-19   444
Military
exploits of ....2 Kin. 18:7-12   374
Defeated by Senna-
cherib.........2 Kin. 18:13   374
Sends messengers to
Isaiah.........2 Kin. 19:1-5   375
Rabshakeh's further
taunts.........2 Kin. 19:8-13   375
Prays
earnestly....2 Kin. 19:14-19   376
Encouraged by
Isaiah........2 Kin. 19:20-37   376
Healed; his life prolonged
15 years......2 Kin. 20:1-11   377
His thanks....Is. 38:9-22   688
Rebuked for his
pride.......2 Kin. 20:12-19   377
Death of.......2 Kin. 20:20, 21   377
Ancestor of
Christ........Matt. 1:9   963
2. Ancestor of
returning   { Ezra 2:1, 16   454
exiles ....{ Neh. 10:17   477
3. Ancestor of
Zephaniah ....Zeph. 1:1   908

Hezion—*vision*

Grandfather of
Ben-hadad........1 Kin. 15:18   342

Hezir—*swine*

1. Descendant of
Aaron.........1 Chr. 24:1, 15   409
2. One who signs
document.....Neh. 10:1, 20   477

Hezro

Carmelite ....2 Sam. 23:35   318
One of David's mighty
men...........1 Chr. 11:37   398

Hezron—*enclosure*

1. Place in south
Judah.........Josh. 15:1, 3   218
Same as
Hazaraddar ...Num. 34:4   163
2. Son of
Reuben ....Gen. 46:9   46
Founder of the
Hezronites ....Num. 26:6   154
3. Son of Perez...Gen. 46:12   46
Head of tribal
family........Num. 26:21   155
Ancestor of
David........Ruth 4:18-22   259
Ancestor of
Christ........Matt. 1:3   963

Hiddai—*joyful*

One of David's
warriors..........2 Sam. 23:30   318
Same as Hurai ....1 Chr. 11:32   398

Hiddekel—*rapid*

Hebrew name of   { Gen. 2:14   5
the river Tigris ..{ Dan. 10:4   847

Hide—*to conceal*

A. *Used literally of:*
Man in Eden...Gen. 3:10   6
Baby Moses....Ex. 2:2, 3   55
Spies ....Josh. 6:17, 25   210
B. *Used figuratively of:*
God's face ....Deut. 31:17, 18   198
Protection .....Is. 49:2   698
Darkness .....Ps. 139:12   600
The Gospel ....2 Cor. 4:3   1167
Believer's life ..Col. 3:3   1201

Hiel—*God lives*

Native of Bethel; rebuilds
Jericho..........1 Kin. 16:34   343
Fulfills Joshua's
curse..........Josh. 6:26   211

Hierapolis—*sacred city*

City of Asia Minor; center of
Christian
activity...........Col. 4:13   1202

Higgaion—*a deep sound*

Used as a musical
term ....Ps. 9:16   531
Translated
"redeemer" in ....Ps. 19:14   537
Translated
"resounding" in ..Ps. 92:3   577

High—*exalted, lofty*

Descriptive of:
Rich ....Ps. 49:2   552
Eminent people ...1 Chr. 17:17   404
God's mercy .....Ps. 103:11   581

High places—*places of idolatrous worship*

A. *Evils of:*
Contrary to one
sanctuary.....Deut. 12:1-14   180
Source of
idolatry ....2 Kin. 12:3   367
Place of child
sacrifices......Jer. 7:31   726

Cause of
God's   { 1 Kin. 14:22, 23   341
wrath........{ Ps. 78:58   570
Denounced by
the   { Ezek. 6:1-6   790
prophets .....{ Hos. 4:11-14   855
Cause of
exile..........Lev. 26:29-34   121
B. *Built by:*
Solomon.......1 Kin. 11:7-11   336
Jeroboam......1 Kin. 12:26-31   338
Jehoram......2 Chr. 21:9, 11   435
Ahaz ....2 Chr. 28:24, 25   441
Manasseh......2 Kin. 21:1, 3   377
People of
Judah.........1 Kin. 14:22, 23   341
People of
Israel ....2 Kin. 17:9   373
Sepharvites....2 Kin. 17:32   373
C. *Destroyed by:*
Asa...........2 Chr. 14:3, 5   430
Jehoshaphat ..2 Chr. 17:6   431
Hezekiah ......2 Kin. 18:4, 22   374
Josiah ....2 Kin. 23:5, 8, 13   380

High priest

A. *Duties of:*
Offer gifts and
sacrifices......Heb. 5:1   1241
Make
atonement ....Lev. 16:1-34   110
Inquire of
God...........1 Sam. 23:9-12   284
Consecrate
Levites........Num. 8:11-21   137
Anoint kings...1 Kin. 1:34   324
Bless the
people ....Num. 6:22-27   134
Preside over   { Matt. 26:3, 57-
courts.........{ 62   990
B. *Typical of Christ's priesthood:*
Called of
God...........Heb. 5:4, 5   1241
Making
atonement ....Lev. 16:33   112
Subject to
temptation....Heb. 2:18   1240
Exercise of
compassion ...Heb. 4:15, 16   1241
Holiness of
position.......Lev. 21:15   115
Marrying a
virgin.........2 Cor. 11:2   1172
Alone entering Holy of
Holies........Heb. 9:7, 12, 24   1244
Ministry of
inter-   { Num. 16:43-48   146
cession.......{ Heb. 7:25   1243
Blessing
people ....Acts 3:26   1097

Highway—*a main thoroughfare*

A. *Characteristics of:*
Roads for public
use ....Num. 20:19   149
Straight and
broad ....Is. 40:3   689
Made to cities of
refuge.........Deut. 19:2, 3   186
Robbers use ...Luke 10:30-33   1040
Animals
infest ....Is. 35:8, 9   685
Beggars sit
by ....Matt. 20:30   984
Highways sometimes
better........Judg. 5:6   236
Steps leading into the
Temple........1 Chr. 26:16, 18   411
B. *Figurative of:*
Holy way......Prov. 16:17   621
Israel's
restoration.....Is. 11:16   668
Gospel's call ...Is. 40:3   689
Way of
salvation......Is. 35:8-10   685
Two
destinies ......Matt. 7:13, 14   969
Christ ....John 14:6   1081

SUBJECT	REFERENCE	PAGE	SUBJECT	REFERENCE	PAGE	SUBJECT	REFERENCE	PAGE

Hilen—*strong place*

Town of Judah....1 Chr. 6:57, 58   393
Also called
Holon............Josh. 15:51   220

Hilkiah—*Yahweh is my portion*

1. Levite, son of
   Amzi.........1 Chr. 6:45, 46   393
2. Levite, son of
   Hosah.......1 Chr. 26:11   411
3. Father of
   Eliakim.......Is. 22:20   675
4. Priest, father of
   Jeremiah......Jer. 1:1   718
5. Father of
   Gemariah....Jer. 29:3   746
6. Shallum's
   son..........1 Chr. 6:13   392
   High priest in Josiah's
   reign..........2 Chr. 34:9-22   447
   Oversees Temple
   work........2 Kin. 22:4-7   378
   Finds the book of the
   Law..........2 Kin. 22:8-14   379
   Aids in
   reformation...2 Kin. 23:4   380
7. Chief of postexilic
   priest........Neh. 12:1, 7   478
   Later descendants
   of............Neh. 12:12, 21   479
8. One of Ezra's
   assistants.....Neh. 8:4   474

Hill, hill country—*an elevation of the earth's surface*

Rendered
"Gibeah".........1 Sam. 11:4   271
Rendered "hills" ..Luke 23:30   1057

Hillel—*he has praised*

Father of Abdon the
judge............Judg. 12:13, 15   245

Hind—*a doe (female deer)*

Figurative of:
Spiritual
vivacity..........2 Sam. 22:34   316
Buoyancy of
faith.............Hab. 3:19   905
Peaceful
quietude.........Song 2:7   649

Hindrances—*things which obstruct one's way*

A. *Physical:*
   Heavy   {1 Sam. 17:38,
   armor........{   39   278
   Ship's cargo ...Acts 27:18-38   1125
B. *Spiritual:*
   Satanic
   temptations...Matt. 4:8-10   966
   Riches........Matt. 19:24   983
   Unbelief.......Matt. 11:21-24   973
   Ceremo-
   nialism........Matt. 15:1-9   978
   Love of
   world.........2 Tim. 4:10   1225
   Sin ....Heb. 12:1   1247
C. *Removal of, by:*
   Faith.........Matt. 17:20, 21   981
   God's armor ...Eph. 6:11-18   1190
   Walking in the
   Spirit ....Gal. 5:16, 17   1181
   Self-control....1 Cor. 9:25-27   1155

Hinge—*a pivot of a door*

Of gold ....1 Kin. 7:50   332

Hinnom, valley of (Ben-Hinnom)

A. *Location of:*
   Near
   Jerusalem.....Jer. 19:2   737
   Boundary
   line ....Josh. 15:8   219
   Topheth ....Jer. 19:6, 11-14   737

B. *Uses of:*
   For idol
   worship.......1 Kin. 11:7   336
   For sacrificing
   children........2 Chr. 28:3   440
   Defiled by
   Josiah.........2 Kin. 23:10-14   380
   Jeremiah addresses people
   here ....Jer. 19:1-5   737
   Will become "valley of the
   Slaughter" ....Jer. 7:31, 32   726
   Make holy....Jer. 31:40   750

Hirah—*nobility*

Adullamite, a friend of
Judah ....Gen. 38:1, 12   38

Hiram—*highborn*

1. King of Tyre...2 Sam. 5:11   299
   Provides men and material
   for David's
   palace.........1 Chr. 14:1   400
   David's
   friend.........1 Kin. 5:1   328
   Provides men and material
   for Solomon's
   Temple.......1 Kin. 5:1-12   328
   Refuses gifts of cities from
   Solomon .....1 Kin. 9:10-13   334
   Helps Solomon {1 Kin. 9:14, 26-
   with money   {   28   335
   and seamen ..{1 Kin. 10:11   335
2. Craftsman; a son of a Tyrian
   and a widow of
   Naphtali...1 Kin. 7:13, 14   330
   Sent by King Solomon
   to work on   {1 Kin. 7:14-40,
   Temple.......{   45   330
   Called
   Huram.....2 Chr. 2:11   420

Hire—*wages*

A. *Used literally of payments to:*
   Prostitute.....Deut. 23:18   190
   Priests........Judg. 18:4   249
   Pay the poor...James 5:4   1255
   Mercenary
   soldiers ....2 Sam. 10:6   303
   Mercenary
   prophets .....Deut. 23:4   189
   Gospel
   messengers ...Luke 10:7   1039
B. *Used figuratively of:*
   Spiritual
   adultery.......Ezek. 16:33   798
   Sexual
   relations ......Gen. 30:16   30
   Reward
   ("wages").....John 4:36   1068

See Wages, hire

Hireling—*a common laborer*

Anxious for the day to
close ....Job 7:1, 2   500
Figurative of man's
life ....Job 14:6   504
Subject to
oppression........Mal. 3:5   931
Guilty of neglect ..John 10:12, 13   1076

History, Biblical

A. *Characteristics of:*
   Dated with
   human   {Hag. 1:1, 15   914
   events ......{Luke 3:1   1028
   Inspired ....2 Tim. 3:16   1225
   Free of
   myths.........2 Pet. 1:16   1268
B. *Valuable for:*
   Outline of ancient
   history.......Acts 7:1-53   1100
   Spiritual
   lessons........1 Cor. 10:1-11   1155
   Prophecy and
   fulfillment.....Acts 4:24-28   1098

Hittites—*an ancient nation*

A. *Facts concerning:*
   Descendants of
   Canaan ....Gen. 10:15   13
   One of seven Canaanite
   nations........Deut. 7:1   176
   Original inhabitants of
   Palestine......Ezek. 16:3, 45   797
   Ruled by
   kings ....1 Kin. 10:29   336
   Great nation...2 Kin. 7:6   362
   Their land promised to
   Israel ....Gen. 15:18, 20   16
   Destruction of, com-
   manded......Deut. 7:1, 2, 24   176
   Destruction of,
   incomplete....Judg. 3:5   234
B. *Intermarriage with:*
   By Esau ....Gen. 36:2   36
   By Israelites after the
   conquest......Judg. 3:5, 6   234
   By Solomon ...1 Kin. 11:1   336
   By Israelites after the
   exile ....Ezra 9:1, 2   461
C. *Notable persons of:*
   Ephron ....Gen. 49:30   49
   Ahimelech....1 Sam. 26:6   287
   Uriah ....2 Sam. 11:6, 21   303

Hivites

Descendants of
Canaan........Gen. 10:15, 17   13
One of seven Canaanite
nations...........Deut. 7:1   176
Esau intermarries
with..............Gen. 36:2   36
Gibeonites
belong to........Josh. 9:3, 7   213
Land of,
promised to   {Ex. 3:8   56
Israel...........{Ex. 23:23   75
Destruction of:
Commanded .....Deut. 7:1, 2, 24   176
Incomplete.......Judg. 3:3   234

Hizki—*my strength*

Benjamite.........1 Chr. 8:17   395

Hizkiah—*Yahweh strengthens*

Son of Neariah....1 Chr. 3:23   390

Hobah—*hiding place*

Town north of
Damascus........Gen. 14:15   16

Hod—*majesty*

Asherite ....1 Chr. 7:30, 37   394

Hodaviah—*praise ye Yahweh*

1. Son of
   Elioenai.......1 Chr. 3:24   390
2. Chief of
   Manasseh.....1 Chr. 5:23, 24   392
3. Benjamite .....1 Chr. 9:7   396
4. Levite, founder of a
   family.........Ezra 2:40   454
   Called Judah...Ezra 3:9   456

Hodesh—*new moon*

Wife of
Shaharaim......1 Chr. 8:8, 9   395

Hodiah—*splendor of Yahweh*

1. Judahite.......1 Chr. 4:1, 19   390
2. Levite
   interpreter ....Neh. 8:7   474
   Leads in
   prayer ....Neh. 9:5   475
   Probably the same as one of the
   signers of the
   document.....Neh. 10:10, 13   477
3. Signer of the
   document.....Neh. 10:18   477

Hoglah—*partridge*

Daughter of
Zelophehad......Num. 26:33   155

SUBJECT	REFERENCE	PAGE	SUBJECT	REFERENCE	PAGE	SUBJECT	REFERENCE	PAGE

Solomon
yields to ......1 Kin. 11:1-8 — 336
Jeroboam establishes
in (1 Kin. 12:26-33 — 338
Jerusalem.. (2 Chr. 11:15 — 428
Rehoboam tolerates in
Judah.........1 Kin. 14:22-24 — 341
Conflict—Elijah and
Ahab.........1 Kin. 18:1-46 — 344
Wicked kings (1 Kin. 21:25, 26 — 349
of Israel.....(2 Kin. 16:3 — 371
Prophet denounces in
Israel.........Hos. 4:12-19 — 855
Cause of Israel's
exile ....2 Kin. 17:5-23 — 372
Judah follows Israel's
example........2 Chr. 28:1-4 — 440
Manasseh climaxes Judah's
apostasy (2 Kin. 21:1-18 — 377
in............(2 Chr. 33:1-11 — 446
Reformation against, under
Asa ....2 Chr. 14:3-5 — 430
Under
Hezekiah......2 Chr. 29:15-19 — 442
Under Josiah ..2 Kin. 23:1-20 — 379
Prophets denounce in
Judah.........Jer. 16:11-21 — 734
Cause of Judah's
exile ....2 Kin. 23:26, 27 — 381
C. *Christians warned against:*
No company
with ....1 Cor. 5:11 — 1152
Flee from.....1 Cor. 10:14 — 1156
No fellowship
with ....1 Cor. 10:19, 20 — 1156
Guard from...1 John 5:21 — 1278
Testify
against.......Acts 14:15 — 1110
Turn from ....1 Thess. 1:9 — 1206
D. *Enticements to, due to:*
Heathen
back- (Josh. 24:2 — 227
ground.....(Ezek. 16:44, 45 — 798
Contact with
idolaters .....Num. 25:1-6 — 154
Inter-
marriage.....1 Kin. 11:1-13 — 336
Imagined
good.........Jer. 44:15-19 — 761
Corrupt
heart.........Rom. 1:21-23 — 1132
E. *Removed through:*
Punishment....Deut. 17:2-5 — 185
Display of
power- (1 Sam. 5:1-5 — 266
lessness......(1 Kin. 18:25-29 — 345
Logic ....Is. 44:6-20 — 694
Display of God's
power........2 Kin. 19:10-37 — 375
Denuncia-
tion..........Mic. 1:5-7 — 890
Exile.........Hos. 8:5-14 — 858
  Zeph. 1:4-6 — 908
New (Hos. 14:1-9 — 861
birth........(Amos 5:26, 27 — 875

Idumea—*pertaining to Edom*
Name used by Greeks and Romans
to designate
Edom ....Mark 3:8 — 1001
See Edom

Iezer—*father is help*
Descendant of
Manasseh.....Num. 26:30, 31 — 155

Igal—*He (God) redeems*
1. Issachar's
spy ....Num. 13:2, 7 — 141
2. One of David's mighty
men...........2 Sam. 23:36 — 318
3. Shemaiah's
son ....1 Chr. 3:22 — 390

Igdaliah—*great is Yahweh*
Father of Hanan the
prophet ....Jer. 35:4 — 753

Ignorance—*lack of knowledge*
A. *Kinds of:*
Pardonable ....Luke 23:34 — 1057
Pretended .....Luke 22:57-60 — 1055
Innocent ......Acts 19:2-5 — 1116
Excusable .....Acts 17:30 — 1115
Judicial.......Rom. 1:28 — 1132
Guilty ....Rom. 1:19-25 — 1132
Partial........1 Cor. 13:12 — 1158
Confident......Heb. 11:8 — 1246
B. *Causes of:*
Unregen-
eracy ....Eph. 4:18 — 1188
Unbelief.......1 Tim. 1:13 — 1217
Spiritual:
Darkness ....1 John 2:11 — 1275
Immaturity ..1 Cor. 8:7-13 — 1154
C. *Productive of:*
Unbelief ......John 8:19-43 — 1074
Error ....Matt. 22:29 — 986
D. *Objects of:*
God ....John 8:55 — 1075
Scriptures ....Matt. 22:29 — 986
Christ's (1 Thess. 4:13,
return........(14 — 1208

Iim—*ruins*
Town of Judah....Josh. 15:29 — 219

Ijon—*heap*
Town of Naphtali; captured by
Ben-hadad........1 Kin. 15:20 — 342
Captured by Tiglath-
pileser............2 Kin. 15:29 — 371

Ikkesh—*crooked*
Father of Ira......2 Sam. 23:26 — 318
Commander of
24,000 ....1 Chr. 27:9 — 412

Ilai—*supreme*
One of David's mighty
men ....1 Chr. 11:26, 29 — 398
Called Zalmon ..2 Sam. 23:28 — 318

Illumination—*enlightenment,
understanding*
Of Daniel ....Dan. 5:11, 14 — 841

Illumination, spiritual
By the Gospel.....John 1:9 — 1064
At conversion.....Heb. 6:4 — 1242
In Christian
truth.............Eph. 1:18 — 1185
By Holy Spirit....John 16:13-16 — 1083
By God ....1 Cor. 4:5 — 1151

Illustration—*something used to explain
something else*
From:
Ancient history ...1 Cor. 10:1-14 — 1155
Current history ...Mark 12:1-11 — 1013
Nature..........Prov. 6:6-11 — 613

Illyricum—*a province of Europe*
Paul preaches.....Rom. 15:19 — 1144

Image (see Idols, idolatry)

Image of God
A. *In man:*
Created in ....Gen. 1:26, 27 — 4
Reason for sanctity of
life............Gen. 9:6 — 11
Reason for man's
headship ....1 Cor. 11:7 — 1156
Restored by
grace ....Col. 3:10 — 1201
Transformed
of............2 Cor. 3:18 — 1167
B. *In Christ:*
In essential
nature ....Col. 1:15 — 1200
Manifested on
earth.........John 1:14, 18 — 1064
Believers
conformed ....Rom. 8:29 — 1138

Imitation—*attempting to duplicate*
Of the good:
God.............Eph. 5:1 — 1188
Paul's conduct ....2 Thess. 3:7, 9 — 1213
Apostles ....1 Thess. 1:6 — 1206
Heroes of the
faith.............Heb. 6:12 — 1242
Good ....3 John 11 — 1284
Other churches ...1 Thess. 2:14 — 1207
See Example of Christ, the

Imla—*fullness*
Father of Micaiah the
prophet ....2 Chr. 18:7, 8 — 432
As Imlah..........1 Kin. 22:8, 9 — 350

Immanuel—*God (is) with us*
Name given to
the child born of (Is. 7:14 — 663
the virgin ......(Matt. 1:23 — 964

Immer—*eloquent*
1. Descendant of
Aaron.........1 Chr. 24:1-14 — 409
2. Ancestor of
Pashur........Jer. 20:1 — 737
3. Founder of a postexilic
family........Ezra 2:37 — 454
The same as the father of
Meshille-
mith.........1 Chr. 9:12 — 396
Also the ancestor of priests
marrying
foreigners.....Ezra 10:19, 20 — 462
4. Person or place in
Babylon.....Neh. 7:61 — 473
5. Zadok's
father.........Neh. 3:29 — 469

Immorality—*state of a wrongful act or
relationship*
Attitude toward:
Consider sanctity of the
body ....1 Cor. 6:13-20 — 1152
Flee from it ....1 Cor. 6:18 — 1153
Get married ......1 Cor. 7:2 — 1153
Abstain from it....1 Thess. 4:3 — 1208
Mention it not ....Eph. 5:3 — 1188
Corrupts the
earth.............Rev. 19:2 — 1305

Immortality—*eternal existence*
A. *Proof of, based upon:*
God's image in
man ....Gen. 1:26, 27 — 4
Translation of
Enoch and (Gen. 5:24 — 9
Elijah........(2 Kin. 2:11, 12 — 356
Promises of (John 11:25, 26 — 1078
Christ.......(John 14:2, 3 — 1081
Appearance of Moses and
Elijah........Matt. 17:2-9 — 980
Eternal
rewards and
punish- (Matt. 25:31-46 — 990
ments.......(Luke 16:19-31 — 1047
Resurrection (Rom. 8:11 — 1137
of Christ .....(1 Cor. 15:12-58 — 1160
Resurrection (Dan. 12:2, 3 — 850
of men.......(John 5:28, 29 — 1069
B. *Expression indicative of:*
"I AM" ....Matt. 22:32 — 986
"Today".......Luke 23:43 — 1057
"Shall never
die".........John 11:25, 26 — 1078
"The redemption of our
body".........Rom. 8:22, 23 — 1138
"Neither
death" ....Rom. 8:38, 39 — 1138
"We know"....2 Cor. 5:1-10 — 1168
"A living
hope".........1 Pet. 1:3-8 — 1260
"We shall be like
Him"..........1 John 3:2 — 1276
See Eternal, everlasting; Life, eternal

SUBJECT	REFERENCE	PAGE	SUBJECT	REFERENCE	PAGE	SUBJECT	REFERENCE	PAGE

Izhar—*shining*

Son of Kohath ....Ex. 6:18, 21 — 59

Ancestor of the   (Num. 3:19 — 130
           (Num. 3:27 — 130
Izharites ....(1 Chr. 6:38 — 393

Izliah—*Yahweh delivers*

Son of Elpaal .....1 Chr. 8:18 — 395

Izrahiah—*Yahweh will shine*

Chief of
  Issachar.........1 Chr. 7:1, 3 — 394

Izrahite—*descendant of Zerah*

Applied to
  Shamhuth.......1 Chr. 27:8 — 412

Izri—*fashioner*

Leader of Levitical
  choir ....1 Chr. 25:11 — 410
Also called Zeri ...1 Chr. 25:3 — 410

Izziah—*Yahweh sprinkles*

One who divorced his foreign
  wife.............Ezra 10:25 — 462

J

Jaakan, Akan

Son of Ezer ....1 Chr. 1:42 — 388
Also called
  Akan............Gen. 36:27 — 36
Of Horite origin ...Gen. 36:20-27 — 36
Tribe of, at
  Beeroth ....Deut. 10:6 — 179
Dispossessed by
  Edomites.........Deut. 2:12 — 170
Same as
  Benejaakan .....Num. 33:31, 32 — 162

Jaakobah—*heel catcher*

Simeonite.........1 Chr. 4:36 — 391

Jaala, Jaalah—*wild she-goat*

Family head of exile
  returnees.......Ezra 2:56 — 455
Descendants of Solomon's
  servants.........Neh. 7:57, 58 — 472

Jaar—*wood, forest*

Possibly a place
  name.............Ps. 132:6 — 597

Jaare-oregim—*forests of weavers*

Father of
  Elhanan.........2 Sam. 21:19 — 315
Also called Jair ...1 Chr. 20:5 — 406

Jaareshiah—*Yahweh nourishes*

Benjamite head ...1 Chr. 8:27 — 395

Jaasiel—*God makes*

1. One of David's mighty
  men..........1 Chr. 11:47 — 398
2. Son of Abner ..1 Chr. 27:21 — 412

Jaasu—*Yahweh makes*

Son of Bani; divorced foreign
  wife.............Ezra 10:37 — 462

Jaazaniah—*Yahweh hearkens*

1. Military commander supporting
  Gedaliah ......2 Kin. 25:23 — 383
2. Rechabite
  leader........Jer. 35:3 — 753
3. Idolatrous Israelite
  elder.........Ezek. 8:11 — 792
4. Son of Azzur; seen in Ezekiel's
  vision.........Ezek. 11:1 — 793

Jaaziah—*Yahweh strengthens*

Merarite Levite ...1 Chr. 24:26, 27 — 410

Jaaziel—*God strengthens*

Levite musician ...1 Chr. 15:18, 20 — 401

Jabal—*moving*

Son of Lamech; father of
  herdsmen ....Gen. 4:20 — 8

Jabbok—*luxuriant river*

River entering the Jordan
  about 20 miles north of the
  Dead Sea.....Num. 21:24 — 150
Scene of Jacob's
  conflict..........Gen. 32:22-32 — 33
Boundary
  marker..........Deut. 3:16 — 172

Jabesh—*dry*

1. Father of   (2 Kin. 15:10, 13,
  Shallum......(14 — 370
2. Abbreviated name of Jabesh-
  gilead.........1 Sam. 11:1-10 — 271

Jabesh-gilead—*Jabesh of Gilead*

Consigned to
  destruction......Judg. 21:8-15 — 253
Saul struck the Ammonites
  here..............1 Sam. 11:1-11 — 271
Citizens of, rescue
  Saul's body....1 Sam. 31:11-13 — 291
David thanks
  citizens of.......2 Sam. 2:4-7 — 296

Jabez—*he makes sorrowful*

1. City of
  Judah.........1 Chr. 2:55 — 389
2. Man of Judah noted for his
  prayer........1 Chr. 4:9, 10 — 390

Jabin—*He (God) perceives*

1. Canaanite king of Hazor; leads
  confederacy against
  Joshua.......Josh. 11:1-14 — 215
2. Another king of Hazor;
  oppresses
  Israelites......Judg. 4:2 — 235
Defeated by Deborah and
  Barak........Judg. 4:3-24 — 235
Immortalized in
  poetry ....Judg. 5:1-31 — 236

Jabneel—*built of God*

1. Town in north
  Judah.........Josh. 15:11 — 219
Probably same as
  Jabneh.......2 Chr. 26:6 — 439
2. Town of
  Naphtali ......Josh. 19:33 — 223

Jacan—*troubled*

Gadite chief.......1 Chr. 5:13 — 391

Jachin—*He (God) establishes*

1. Son of
  Simeon ....Gen. 46:10 — 46
Family head ...Num. 26:12 — 155
Called Jarib...1 Chr. 4:24 — 391
2. Descendant of
  Aaron.........1 Chr. 24:1, 17 — 409
Representatives
  of.............Neh. 11:10 — 478
3. One of two pillars in front of
  Solomon's
  Temple........1 Kin. 7:21, 22 — 331

Jacinth—*a sapphire stone*

In high priest's
  breastpiece......Ex. 28:19 — 79
Foundation
  stone............Rev. 21:20 — 1307

Jackal—*a wild dog*

Referred to as:
Howling ....Is. 13:22 — 669
Haunting Edom ...Is. 34:5, 13 — 685
"Desert
  creatures".......Is. 13:21 — 669
Dwelling in
  ruins ....Is. 35:7 — 685

Jacob—*supplanter*

Son of Isaac and (Gen. 25:20-26 — 25
Rebekah........(Hos. 12:3 — 860

Born in answer to
  prayer............Gen. 25:21 — 25
Rebekah's
  favorite ....Gen. 25:27, 28 — 25
Obtains Esau's   (Gen. 25:29-34 — 26
  birthright.......(Heb. 12:16 — 1248
Obtains Isaac's
  blessing........Gen. 27:1-38 — 27
Hated by Esau ....Gen. 27:41-46 — 28
Departs for
  Haran...........Gen. 28:1-5 — 28
Sees heavenly
  ladder..........Gen. 28:10-19 — 28
Makes a vow.....Gen. 28:20-22 — 29
Meets Rachel and
  Laban..........Gen. 29:1-14 — 29
Serves for Laban's
  daughters .....Gen. 29:15-30 — 29
His children.......Gen. 29:31-35 — 30
Requests departure from
  Laban...........Gen. 30:25-43 — 30
Flees from
  Laban..........Gen. 31:1-21 — 31
Overtaken by
  Laban..........Gen. 31:22-43 — 31
Covenant with
  Laban..........Gen. 31:44-55 — 32
Meets angels......Gen. 32:1, 2 — 33
Sends message to
  Esau ....Gen. 32:3-8 — 33
Prays earnestly....Gen. 32:9-12 — 33
Sends gifts to
  Esau ....Gen. 32:13-21 — 33
Wrestles with an (Gen. 32:22-32 — 33
  angel..........(Hos. 12:3, 4 — 860
Name becomes
  Israel..........Gen. 32:32 — 33
Reconciled to
  Esau ....Gen. 33:1-16 — 33
Erects altar at
  Shechem ....Gen. 33:17-20 — 34
Trouble over
  Dinah ....Gen. 34:1-31 — 34
Renewal at
  Bethel.........Gen. 35:1-15 — 35
Buries Rachel .....Gen. 35:16-20 — 35
List of 12 sons ...Gen. 35:22-26 — 36
Buries Isaac......Gen. 35:27-29 — 36
His favoritism toward
  Joseph ....Gen. 37:1-31 — 37
Mourns over
  Joseph ....Gen. 37:32-35 — 38
Sends sons to Egypt for
  food............Gen. 42:1-5 — 42
Allows Benjamin
  to go...........Gen. 43:1-15 — 43
Revived by good
  news ....Gen. 45:25-28 — 46
Goes with family to
  Egypt..........Gen. 46:1-27 — 46
Meets Joseph .....Gen. 46:28-34 — 46
Meets Pharaoh....Gen. 47:7-12 — 47
Makes Joseph
  swear..........Gen. 47:28-31 — 47
Blesses Joseph's
  sons...........Gen. 48:1-22 — 48
Blesses his own
  sons...........Gen. 49:1-28 — 48
Dies in Egypt .....Gen. 49:29-33 — 49
Burial in
  Canaan.........Gen. 50:1-14 — 49

Jacob

Father of Joseph, Mary's
  husband.........Matt. 1:15, 16 — 963

Jacob's oracles—*blessing and curses on twelve tribes*

Recorded ....Gen. 49:1-27 — 48

Jacob's well

Christ teaches a Samaritan
  woman..........John 4:5-26 — 1067

Jada—*knowing*

Grandson of   (1 Chr. 2:26, 28,
  Jerahmeel.....(32 — 389

Jaddai—*praised*

Son of Nebo ......Ezra 10:43 — 463

SUBJECT   REFERENCE   PAGE | SUBJECT   REFERENCE   PAGE | SUBJECT   REFERENCE   PAGE

Jaddua—*known*
1. Chief layman who signs the document.....Neh. 10:21   477
2. Levite who returns with Zerubbabel....Neh. 12:8, 11   478

Jadon—*he judges*
Meronothite worker..........Neh. 3:7   468

Jael—*mountain goat*
Wife of Heber the Kenite...........Judg. 4:17   235
Slays Sisera......Judg. 4:17-22   235
Praised by Deborah.........Judg. 5:24-27   236

Jagur—*lodging place*
Town in south Judah...........Josh. 15:21   219

Jahath—*comfort, revival*
1. Grandson of Judah..........1 Chr. 4:2   390
2. Great-grandson of Levi..........1 Chr. 6:20, 43   392
3. Son of Shimei........1 Chr. 23:10   408
4. Son of Shelemoth....1 Chr. 24:22   410
5. Merarite Levite.........2 Chr. 34:12   447

Jahaz—*a place trodden under foot*
Town in Moab at which Sihon was defeated.........Num. 21:23   150
Assigned to Reubenites......Josh. 13:18   217
Levitical city......Josh. 21:36   225
Regained by Moabites.........Is. 15:4   670
Same as Jahzah..1 Chr. 6:78   394

Jahaziel—*God sees*
1. Kohathite Levite.........1 Chr. 23:19   409
2. Benjamite warrior.......1 Chr. 12:4   399
3. Priest..........1 Chr. 16:6   402
4. Inspired Levite.........2 Chr. 20:14   434

Jahdai—*Yahweh leads*
Judahite..........1 Chr. 2:47   389

Jahdiel—*God makes glad*
Manassite chief...1 Chr. 5:24   392

Jahdo—*union*
Gadite............1 Chr. 5:14   391

Jahleel—*wait for God*
Son of Zebulun...Gen. 46:14   46
Family head.......Num. 26:26   155

Jahleelites
Descendants of Jahleel..........Num. 26:26   155

Jahmai—*may God protect*
Descendant of Issachar...........1 Chr. 7:1, 2   394

Jahzeah—*Yahweh sees*
Postexilic returnee.........Ezra 10:15   462

Jahzeel—*God divides*
Son of Naphtali...Gen. 46:24   46
Same as Jahziel...1 Chr. 7:13   394

Jahzeelites
Descendants of Jahzeel..........Num. 26:48   155

Jahzerah—*prudent*
Priest..........1 Chr. 9:12   396
Called Ahzai......Neh. 11:13   478

Jahziel—*God divides*
Son of Naphtali...1 Chr. 7:13   394

Jailer—*one who guards a prison*
At Philippi, converted by Paul..............Acts 16:19-34   1113

Jair—*he enlightens*
1. Manassite warrior.......{ Num. 32:41   162 / Deut. 3:14   172
Conquers towns in Gilead........Num. 32:41   162
2. Eighth judge of Israel.........Judg. 10:3-5   242
3. Father of Mordecai, Esther's uncle..........Esth. 2:5   486
4. Father of Elhanan........1 Chr. 20:5   406
Called Jaare-oregim........2 Sam. 21:19   315

Jairite
Descendant of Jair, the Manassite........2 Sam. 20:26   314

Jairus—(Greek form of "Jair")
Ruler of the synagogue; Jesus raises his daughter........{ Mark 5:22-24, 35-43   1004

Jakeh—*pious*
Father of Agur....Prov. 30:1   632

Jakim—*He (God) raises up*
1. Descendant of Aaron.........1 Chr. 24:1, 12   409
2. Benjamite......1 Chr. 8:19   395

Jalam—*young man*
Son of Esau.......Gen. 36:5, 18   36

Jalon—*passing the night*
Calebite, son of Ezra..............1 Chr. 4:17   390

Jambres—*opposer*
Egyptian magician.........2 Tim. 3:8   1225
See Jannes and Jambres

James—*a form of Jacob*
1. Son of Zebedee.......Matt. 4:21   966
Fisherman.....Matt. 4:21   966
One of the Twelve........Matt. 10:2   972
In business with Peter..........Luke 5:10   1031
Called Boanerges.....Mark 3:17   1002
Of fiery disposition....Luke 9:52-55   1039
Makes a contention...Mark 10:35-45   1011
One of inner circle........Matt. 17:1   980
Sees the risen Lord.......John 21:1, 2   1088
Awaits the Holy Spirit.......Acts 1:13   1094
Slain by Herod Agrippa.......Acts 12:2   1107
2. Son of Alphaeus; one of the Twelve......Matt. 10:3, 4   972
Identified usually as "the less".......Mark 15:40   1019
Brother of Joses........Matt. 27:56   994
3. Son of Joseph and Mary........Matt. 13:55, 56   977
Lord's brother........Gal. 1:19   1178
Rejects Christ's claim........Mark 3:21   1002
Becomes a believer......Acts 1:13, 14   1094
Sees the risen Lord..........1 Cor. 15:7   1160
Becomes moderator of Jerusalem Council......Acts 15:13-23   1111
Paul confers with him...........Gal. 2:9, 12   1178
Wrote an epistle.......James 1:1   1253
Brother of Jude.........Jude 1   1287

James, the Epistle of—*a book of the New Testament*
Trials.............James 1:2-8   1253
Temptation......James 1:12-18   1253
Doing the word...James 1:19-25   1253
Faith and works..James 2:14-26   1254
Patience.........James 5:7-11   1255
Converting the sinner..........James 5:19, 20   1256

Jamin—*the right hand*
1. Son of Simeon.......Gen. 46:10   46
Family head...Ex. 6:14, 15   59
2. Man of Judah..........1 Chr. 2:27   389
3. Postexilic Levite; interprets the law..........Neh. 8:7, 8   474

Jaminites
Descendants of Jamin...........Num. 26:12   155

Jamlech—*whom He (God) makes king*
Simeonite chief...1 Chr. 4:34   391

Janai—*answerer*
Gadite chief.......1 Chr. 5:12   391

Jannai—*a form of John*
Ancestor of Christ...........Luke 3:23, 24   1029

Jannes and Jambres
Two Egyptian magicians; oppose Moses............2 Tim. 3:8   1225
Compare account.........Ex. 7:11-22   59

Janoah—*rest, quiet*
1. Town of Naphtali.......2 Kin. 15:29   371
2. Border town of Ephraim......Josh. 16:6,7   220

Janum—*sleep*
Town near Hebron...........Josh. 15:53   220

Japheth—*widespreading*
One of Noah's three sons.............Gen. 5:32   9
Saved in the ark..1 Pet. 3:20   1263
Receives Messianic blessing.........Gen. 9:20-27   12
His descendants occupy Asia Minor and Europe......Gen. 10:2-5   12

Japhia—*may He (God) cause to shine forth*
1. King of Lachish; slain by Joshua........Josh. 10:3-27   214
2. One of David's sons......2 Sam. 5:13-15   299
3. Border town of Zebulun.......Josh. 19:10, 12   222

Japhlet—*He (God) will deliver*
Asherite family....1 Chr. 7:32, 33   395

Japhletites
Unidentified tribe on Joseph's boundary.........Josh. 16:1, 3   220

Jar—*flask*
Small vessels for liquids...........{ Is. 22:24   675 / Jer. 48:12   764

SUBJECT	REFERENCE	PAGE	SUBJECT	REFERENCE	PAGE	SUBJECT	REFERENCE	PAGE

Jarah—*honeycomb*

Descendant of King
Saul..............1 Chr. 9:42   397
Called
Jehoaddah.......1 Chr. 8:36   395

Jareb—*he will contend*

Figurative description of Assyrian
king..............Hos. 5:13   856

Jared—*descent*

Father of Enoch...Gen. 5:15-20   8
Ancestor of
Noah..........1 Chr. 1:2   387
Ancestor of
Christ..........Luke 3:37   1029

Jarha

Egyptian slave; marries master's
daughter ....1 Chr. 2:34-41   389

Jarib—*he contends*

1. Head of a Simeonite
   family..........1 Chr. 4:24   391
   Called Jachin . . Gen. 46:10   46
2. Man sent to search for
   Levites........Ezra 8:16, 17   460
3. Priest who divorced his foreign
   wife..........Ezra 10:18   462

Jarmuth—*height*

1. Royal city of
   Canaan ......Josh. 10:3   214
   King of, slain by
   Joshua.....Josh. 10:3-27   214
   Assigned to
   Judah......Josh. 15:20, 35   219
   Inhabited after
   exile........Neh. 11:29   478
2. Town in Issachar assigned to
   the Levites....Josh. 21:28, 29   224
   Called
   Ramoth.......1 Chr. 6:73   393
   Called
   Remeth ......Josh. 19:21   222

Jaroah—*new moon*

Gadite chief.......1 Chr. 5:14   391

Jashar—*upright*

Book of, quoted...Josh. 10:13   214

Jashen—*sleeping*

Sons of, in David's
bodyguard........2 Sam. 23:32   318
Called Hashem....1 Chr. 11:34   398

Jashobeam—*let the people return*

1. Chief of David's mighty
   men..........1 Chr. 11:11   398
   Becomes military
   captain........1 Chr. 27:2, 3   412
2. Benjamite
   warrior ....1 Chr. 12:1, 2, 6   398

Jashub—*he returns*

1. Issachar's
   son ....1 Chr. 7:1   394
   Head of
   family......Num. 26:24   155
   Called Iob....Gen. 46:13   46
2. Son of Bani; divorced his
   foreign wife...Ezra 10:29   462

Jashubi-lehem—*bread returns*

A man of Judah...1 Chr. 4:22   391

Jashubites

Descendants of
Jashub ....Num. 26:24   155

Jason—(Greek equivalent for *"Joshua"* or *"Jesus"*)

Welcomes Paul at
Thessalonica .....Acts 17:5-9   1114
Described as Paul's
kinsman..........Rom. 16:21   1145

Jasper—*a precious stone* (quartz)

Set in high priest's
breastpiece.......Ex. 28:20   79
Descriptive of:
Tyre's
adornments ......Ezek. 28:12, 13   811
Heavenly vision...Rev. 4:3   1296

Jathniel—*God bestows*

Korahite
gatekeeper ....1 Chr. 26:1, 2   411

Jattir—*preeminence*

Town of Judah....Josh. 15:48   220
Assigned to Aaron's
children ....Josh. 21:13, 14   224
David sends   ⌠ 1 Sam. 30:26,
spoil to.......... ⌡   27   290

Javan—*Greece* (Ionia)

Son of Japheth....Gen. 10:2, 4   12
Descendants of, to receive
good news........Is. 66:19, 20   713
Trade with Tyre...Ezek. 27:13, 19   809
King of, in Daniel's
visions ....Dan. 8:21   845
Conflict with......Zech. 9:13   923

Javelin—*a light, short spear*

Used in war......Jer. 50:42   769

Jaw—*jawbone*

Used figuratively of:
Power over the   ⌠ Job 29:17   513
wicked............ ⌡ Prov. 30:14   633
God's
sovereignty......Is. 30:28   682
Human trial......Hos. 11:4   860

Jawbone—*cheek bone*

Weapon used by
Samson ....Judg. 15:15-19   247

Jazer—*helpful*

Town east of Jordan near
Gilead..........2 Sam. 24:5   318
Amorites driven
from ....Num. 21:32   150
Assigned to Gad ..Josh. 13:24, 25   218
Becomes Levitical
city ....Josh. 21:34, 39   224
Taken by
Moabites........Is. 16:8, 9   671
Desired by sons of Reuben and
Gad ....Num. 32:1-5   161

Jaziz—*shining*

Shepherd over David's
flocks ....1 Chr. 27:31   412

Jealous, jealousy

A. *Kinds of:*
Divine.........Ex. 20:5   71
Marital.......Num. 5:12-31   133
Motherly ......Gen. 30:1   30
Brotherly......Gen. 37:4-28   37
Sectional .....2 Sam. 19:41-43   313
National......Judg. 8:1-3   239

B. *Good causes of:*
Zeal for the
Lord ....Num. 25:11   154
Concern over
Christians.....2 Cor. 11:2   1172

C. *Evil causes of:*
Favoritism.....Gen. 37:3-11   37
Regard for
names ....1 Cor. 3:3-5   1150
Carnality ......2 Cor. 12:20   1174
             Amos 3:14-16   873

D. *Described as:*
Implacable....Prov. 6:34, 35   614
Cruel..........Song 8:6   653
Burning ....Deut. 29:20   196
Godly.........2 Cor. 11:2   1172

Jearim—*forests*

Mountain 10 miles west of
Jerusalem ....Josh. 15:10   219

Jeatherai—*steadfast*

Descendant of
Levi..............1 Chr. 6:21   392
Also called
Ethni............1 Chr. 6:41   393

Jeberechiah—*Yahweh blesses*

Father of Zechariah (not the
prophet)..........Is. 8:2   664

Jebus—*trodden under foot*

Same as
Jerusalem ....1 Chr. 11:4   397
Entry denied to
David..........1 Chr. 11:5   397
Levite came
near............Judg. 19:1, 11   250
See Zion; Sion

Jebusite—*trodden under foot*

Assigned to
Benjamin.........Josh. 18:28   222
Same as
Jerusalem ....Josh. 18:28   222
On the border of
Judah ....Josh. 15:8   219

Jebusites

Descendants of
Canaan..........Gen. 10:15, 16   13
Mountain tribe....Num. 13:29   142
Land of, promised to
Israel............Gen. 15:18-21   16
Adoni-zedec, their king, raises
confederacy .....Josh. 10:1-5   214
Their king killed by
Joshua ....Josh. 10:23-26   215
Join fight against
Joshua ....Josh. 11:1-5   215
Assigned to
Benjamin.........Josh. 18:28   222
Royal city not
taken ....Judg. 1:21   232
Taken by David...2 Sam. 5:6-8   298
Old inhabitants
remain ....2 Sam. 24:16-25   318
Become slaves ....1 Kin. 9:20, 21   335

Jechiliah—*Yahweh will enable*

Mother of
Uzziah ....2 Chr. 26:3   439
Called Jecoliah....2 Kin. 15:2   370

Jecoliah—*Yahweh is able*

Mother of King
Azariah ....2 Kin. 15:2   370
Called Jechiliah ...2 Chr. 26:3   439

Jeconiah—*Yahweh establishes*

Variant form of
Jehoiachin........1 Chr. 3:16, 17   390
Abbreviated to
Coniah..........Jer. 22:24, 28   740
Son of Josiah .....Matt. 1:11   963
See Jehoiachim

Jedaiah—*Yahweh has been kind*

1. Priestly
   family.........1 Chr. 24:7   409
2. Head of the
   priests ....Neh. 12:6   478
3. Another head
   priest ....Neh. 12:7, 21   478
4. Simeonite......1 Chr. 4:37   391
5. Postexilic
   worker........Neh. 3:10   468
6. One who brings gifts for the
   Temple........Zech. 6:10, 14   921

Jediael—*known of God*

1. Son of Benjamin and family
   head..........1 Chr. 7:6, 10, 11   394
2. Manassite; joins
   David.........1 Chr. 12:20   399

178

SUBJECT	REFERENCE	PAGE	SUBJECT	REFERENCE	PAGE	SUBJECT	REFERENCE	PAGE

Joshua, the Book of—continued

The divine
captain.........Josh. 5:13—6:5 210
Capture of
Jericho..........Josh. 6:6-27 210
Capture of Ai ....Josh. 8:1-29 212
Apportionment of ⌠Josh. 13:1—
the land........⌡ 22:34 217
Covenant at
Shechem........Josh. 24:1-28 227
Death of Joshua ..Josh. 24:29-33 228

Josiah—*Yahweh heals*

1. Son and successor of Amon,
king of
Judah........2 Kin. 21:25, 26 378
Crowned at 8; reigns
righteously 31
years..........2 Kin. 22:1 378
Named before
birth..........1 Kin. 13:1, 2 339
Repairs the
Temple........2 Kin. 22:3-9 378
Receives the Book of
Law........2 Kin. 22:10-17 379
Saved from predicted
doom ....2 Kin. 22:18-20 379
Reads the
Law..........2 Kin. 23:1, 2 379
Makes a
covenant......2 Kin. 23:3 379
Destroys ⌠2 Kin. 23:4, 20,
idolatry .....⌡ 24 380
Observes the
Passover ......2 Kin. 23:21-23 380
Exceptional
king ....2 Kin. 23:25 381
Slain in
battle.........2 Chr. 35:20-24 449
Lamented by
Jeremiah.......2 Chr. 35:25-27 449
Commended by
Jeremiah......Jer. 22:15-18 739
Ancestor (Josias) of
Christ........Matt. 1:10, 11 963
2. Son of
Zephaniah ....Zech. 6:10 921

Josiphiah—*Yahweh will increase*

Father of a postexilic
Jew ....Ezra 8:10 460

Jotbah—*pleasantness*

City of Haruz, the father of
Meshullemeth ....2 Kin. 21:19 378

Jotbathah—*pleasantness*

Israelite
encampment .....Num. 33:33 162
Called "land of brooks of
water" ....Deut. 10:7 179

Jotham—*Yahweh is perfect*

1. Gideon's youngest
son ....Judg. 9:5 241
Escapes Abimelech's
massacre.....Judg. 9:5, 21 241
Utters a prophetic
parable.......Judg. 9:7-21 241
Sees his prophecy
fulfilled ......Judg. 9:22-57 241
2. Son and successor of Azariah
(Uzziah), king of
Judah........2 Kin. 15:5, 7 370
Reign of, partly
good..........2 Kin. 15:32-38 371
Conquers
Ammonites ...2 Chr. 27:5-9 440
Contemporary of Isaiah and
Hosea........Is. 1:1 657
Ancestor (Joatham) of
Christ........Matt. 1:9 963
3. Son of
Jahdai ....1 Chr. 2:47 389

Journey—*an extended trip*

Preparation for, by:
Prayer ....Rom. 1:10 1131
God's providence
acknowledged ....James 4:13-17 1255

Joy—*gladness of heart*

A. *Kinds of:*
Foolish ....Prov. 15:21 620
Temporary....Matt. 13:20 976
Motherly ......Ps. 113:9 588
Figurative .....Is. 52:9 701
Future........Matt. 25:21, 23 990

B. *Described as:*
Everlasting ....Is. 51:11 700
Much..........Acts 8:8 1103
Complete ......1 John 1:4 1274
Abundant......2 Cor. 8:2 1170
Inexpress-
ible...........1 Pet. 1:8 1260

C. *Causes of:*
Victory ....1 Sam. 18:6 279
Christ's birth ..Luke 2:10, 11 1027
Christ's
resurrection...Matt. 28:7, 8 995
Sinner's
repentance...Luke 15:5, 10 1046
Miracles among the
Gentiles.......Acts 8:7, 8 1103
Forgiveness...Ps. 51:8, 12 554
God's Word...Jer. 15:16 734
Spiritual
discovery .....Matt. 13:44 977
Names written in
heaven........Luke 10:17, 20 1039
True faith .....1 Pet. 1:8 1260

D. *Place of, in:*
Prayer.........Is. 56:7 704
Christian:
Fellowship...Phil. 1:25 1193
Affliction .....2 Cor. 7:4-7 1169
Giving........2 Cor. 8:2 1170

E. *Contrasted with:*
Weeping......Ezra 3:12, 13 456
           Ps. 30:5 541
Tears..........Ps. 126:5 596
Sorrow ....Is. 35:10 686
Mourning.....Jer. 31:13 748
Pain...........John 16:20, 21 1083
Loss ....Heb. 10:34;
           13:17 1246
Adversity......Eccl. 7:14 642
Discipline.....Ps. 51:8 554
           Heb. 12:11 1247
Persecution....Luke 6:22, 23 1033

F. *Of angels:*
At creation ...Job 38:4, 7 520
At Christ's ⌠Luke 2:10, 13,
birth........⌡ 14 1027
At sinner's
conversion....Luke 15:10 1046

G. *Expressed by:*
Songs.........Gen. 31:27 32
Musical
instruments ..1 Sam. 18:6 279
Sounds ....1 Chr. 15:16 401
Praises........2 Chr. 29:30 442
Shouting .....Ezra 3:12, 13 456
Heart..........1 Kin. 21:7 349

See Gladness; Happiness of the Saints

Jozabad—*Yahweh has bestowed*

1, 2, 3. Three of David's mighty
men...........1 Chr. 12:4, 20 399
4. Levite overseer in Hezekiah's
reign..........2 Chr. 31:13 444
5. Levite officer in Josiah's
reign..........2 Chr. 35:9 448
6. Levite, son of
Jeshua ....Ezra 8:33 460
Probably the
same as in ....Ezra 10:23 462
7. Expounder of the
Law...........Neh. 8:7 474
8. Levitical
chief..........Neh. 11:16 478
Some consider 6, 7, 8 the same
person
9. Priest who divorced his foreign
wife..........Ezra 10:22 462

Jozacar—*Yahweh has remembered*

Assassin of
Joash............2 Kin. 12:19-21 368
Called Zabad......2 Chr. 24:26 438

Jozadak—*Yahweh is righteous*

Postexilic priest ...Ezra 3:2 455

Jubal—*playing*

Son of Lamech....Gen. 4:21 8

Jubilee, Year of

A. *Regulations concerning:*
Introduced by
trumpet.......Lev. 25:9 119
After 49
years.........Lev. 25:8 119
Rules for
fixing ⌠Lev. 25:15, 16,
prices........⌡ 25-28 119

B. *Purposes of:*
Restore liberty (to the
enslaved) .....Lev. 25:38-43 120
Restore property (to the
original
owner)........Lev. 25:23-28 119
Remit debt (to the
indebted) .....Lev. 25:47-55 120
Restore rest
(to the ⌠Lev. 25:11, 12,
land).........⌡ 18-22 119

C. *Figurative of:*
Christ's
mission ....Is. 61:1-3 708
Earth's
jubilee ....Rom. 8:19-24 1138

Judah—*let Him (God) be praised*

1. Son of Jacob and
Leah..........Gen. 29:15-35 29
Intercedes for
Joseph ....Gen. 37:26, 27 38
Marries a
Canaanite.....Gen. 38:1-10 38
Fathers Perez and Zerah by
Tamar ....Gen. 38:11-30 38
Through Tamar, an ancestor of
David ....Ruth 4:18-22 259
Ancestor of
Christ.........Matt. 1:3-16 963
Offers himself as Benjamin's
ransom ....Gen. 44:33, 34 45
Leads Jacob to
Goshen ......Gen. 46:28 46
Jacob gives birthright
on ....Gen. 49:3-10 48
Messiah promised
through.......Gen. 49:10 49
2. Judah, Tribe of
See separate article
3. Postexilic
Levite........Ezra 3:9 456
4. Levite returning with
Zerubbabel....Neh. 12:8 478
5. Levite divorced his foreign
wife..........Ezra 10:23 462
6. Postexilic
overseer ......Neh. 11:9 478
7. Priest and
musician......Neh. 12:36 479
Probably same as 4 and 5
8. Postexilic
leader........Neh. 12:32-34 479

Judah, Tribe of

Descendants of
Judah ....Gen. 29:35 30
Prophecy
concerning ......Gen. 49:8-12 49
Five families of....Num. 26:19-22 155
Leads in wilderness
journey ....Num. 2:3, 9 129
Registration of, at
Sinai ....Num. 1:26, 27 128
Numbering of, in
Moab..........Num. 26:22 155
Leads in conquest of
Canaan.........Judg. 1:1-19 232

SUBJECT	REFERENCE	PAGE	SUBJECT	REFERENCE	PAGE	SUBJECT	REFERENCE	PAGE

SUBJECT	REFERENCE	PAGE	SUBJECT	REFERENCE	PAGE	SUBJECT	REFERENCE	PAGE
Athaliah (Queen) (usurper, 6 yrs.)	2 Kin. 11:1-3	366	2. Town in Naphtali	1 Chr. 6:76	393	B. *Figurative of:* Complete: Submission to evil	Hos. 13:2	861
Joash (Jehoash) (40 yrs.)	2 Kin. 12:1, 21	367	Same as Kartan	Josh. 21:32	224	Submission to God	Ps. 2:12	529
Amaziah (29 yrs.)	2 Kin. 14:1-20	369	**Kiriath-arba**—*city of Arba, or four-fold city*			Recon- ciliation	Ps. 85:10	573
Azariah (Uzziah) (52 yrs.)	2 Kin. 15:1, 2	370	Ancient name of Hebron	Gen. 23:2	22	Utmost affection	Song 1:2	648
Jotham (16 yrs.)	2 Kin. 15:32-38	371	Named after Arba the Anakite	Josh. 14:15	218	C. *Kinds of:* Deceitful	2 Sam. 20:9, 10	314
Ahaz (16 yrs.)	2 Kin. 16:1-20	371	City of refuge	Josh. 20:7	223		Luke 22:48	1055
Hezekiah (29 yrs.)	2 Kin. 18:1— 20:21	374	Possessed by Judah	Judg. 1:10	232	Insincere	2 Sam. 15:5	308
Manasseh (55 yrs.)	2 Kin. 21:1-18	377	**Kiriath-huzoth**—*city of streets*			Fatherly	Gen. 27:26, 27	27
Amon (2 yrs.)	2 Kin. 21:19-26	378	Moabite city	Num. 22:39	152	Friendship	Ex. 18:7	70
Josiah (31 yrs.)	2 Kin. 22:1— 23:30	378	**Kiriath-jearim**—*city of forests*				1 Sam. 20:41	282
Jehoahaz (Shallum) (3 mos.)	2 Kin. 23:31-33	381	Gibeonite town	Josh. 9:17	213	Esteem	2 Sam. 19:32, 39	313
Jehoiakim (11 yrs.)	2 Kin. 23:34— 24:6	381	Assigned to Judah	Josh. 15:60	220	Sexual love	Gen. 29:11	29
Jehoiachin (Jeconiah) (3 mos.)	2 Kin. 24:8-16	381	Reassigned to Benjamin	Josh. 18:14	221		Song 1:2	648
Zedekiah (Mattaniah) (11 yrs.)	2 Kin. 24:17— 25:7	382	Ark of God taken from	1 Chr. 13:5	400	Illicit love	Prov. 7:13	614
			Home of Uriah	Jer. 26:20	744	False religion	1 Kin. 19:18 Hos. 13:2	347 861
Kings, the Books of—*books of the Old Testament*			Called: Baalah	Josh. 15:9, 10	219	Christian love	Rom. 16:16 1 Cor. 16:20	1145 1162
A. *First Kings:* Solomon ascends to the throne	1 Kin. 1:1—2:46	323	Kiriath-baal	Josh. 15:60	220	**Kite**—*a bird of the falcon family*		
The kingdom of Solomon	1 Kin. 3:1— 10:13	326	Baale-judah	2 Sam. 6:2	299	Ceremonially unclean	Lev. 11:14	104
The fall of Solomon	1 Kin. 11:1-40	336	Shortened to Kiriath- arim	Ezra 2:25	454	**Kitron**—*shortened, little*		
Rehoboam against Jeroboam	1 Kin. 12:1-33	338	**Kiriath-sannah**—*city of destruction*			Town in Zebulun	Judg. 1:30	232
Ahab and Jezebel	1 Kin. 16:29-34	343	City of Judah; also called Debir	Josh. 15:49	220	**Kittim**		
Ministry of Elijah	1 Kin. 17:1— 19:21	344	**Kirjath-sepher**—*city of books*			Sons of Javan	Gen. 10:4	12
Aram against Samaria	1 Kin. 20:1-34	347	Same as Debir	Judg. 1:11-13	232	Ships of, in Balaam's prophecy	Num. 24:24	154
Ahab and Naboth	1 Kin. 21:1-29	349	Taken by Othniel	Josh. 15:15-17	219	Mentioned in the prophets	Jer. 2:10	719
B. *Second Kings:* Ministry of Elijah and Elisha	2 Kin. 1:1—9:1	355	**Kish**—*bow*			**Kiyyun**—*detestable thing*		
Reign of Jehu	2 Kin. 9:11— 10:36	364	1. Benjamite of Gibeah; father of King Saul	1 Sam. 9:1-3 Acts 13:21	269 1109	Astral images made by Israel	Amos 5:26	875
Fall of Israel	2 Kin. 17:1-41	372	2. Benjamite of Jerusalem	1 Chr. 8:30	395	**Kneading**—*mixing elements together*		
Reign of Hezekiah	2 Kin. 18:1— 20:21	374	3. Merarite Levite in David's time	1 Chr. 23:21, 22	409	Part of food process	Gen. 18:6	18
Reform of Judah	2 Kin. 22:1— 23:4-30	378	4. Another Merarite Levite in Hezekiah's time	2 Chr. 29:12	442	Done by women	Jer. 7:18	725
Fall of Jerusalem	2 Kin. 25:1-21	382	5. Benjamite and great- grandfather of Mordecai	Esth. 2:5	486	**Kneading bowls**—*a bowl for kneading dough*		
Kingship of God—*the position of God as sovereign ruler of the universe*			**Kishi**—*snarer*			Overcome by frogs	Ex. 8:3	60
Over Jerusalem	Matt. 5:35	967	One of David's singers	1 Chr. 6:31, 44	392	Carried out of Egypt	Ex. 12:33-34	64
Kir—*wall*			Called Kushaiah	1 Chr. 15:17	401	**Knee**		
1. Place mentioned by Amos to which Arameans were taken	Amos 1:5	871	**Kishion**—*hardness*			A. *Place of weakness, due to:* Terror	Dan. 5:6	841
Tiglath-pileser carries people of Damascus here	2 Kin. 16:9	372	Border town of Issachar	Josh. 19:17, 20	222	Fasting	Ps. 109:24	587
Inhabitants of, against Judah	Is. 22:6	674	Given to Levites	Josh. 21:28	224	Disease	Deut. 28:35	194
2. Fortified city of Moab	Is. 15:1	670	See Kedesh 2			Lack of faith	Is. 35:3	685
Same as Kir- haraseth	Is. 16:7, 11	671	**Kishon**—*bending*			B. *Lying upon:* Sign of true parentage or adoption	Gen. 30:3	30
Strong place	2 Kin. 3:25	358	River of north Palestine; Sisera's army swept away by	Judg. 4:7, 13	235	Place of fondling	Is. 66:12	713
Kiriath—*city*			Elijah slew Baal prophets here	1 Kin. 18:40 Ps. 83:9	346 572	Place of sleep	Judg. 16:19	248
Town of Benjamin	Josh. 18:21, 28	222	**Kiss**—*a physical sign of affection*			C. *Bowing of:* Act of Respect	2 Kin. 1:13	356
Kiriathaim—*twin cities*			A. *Times employed, at:* Departure	Gen. 31:28, 55	32	False worship	1 Kin. 19:18	347
1. Assigned to Reuben	Num. 32:37	162	Separation	Acts 20:37	1118	True worship	Rom. 14:11	1143
Repossessed by Moabites	Jer. 48:1-23	764	Reunions	Luke 15:20	1046	D. *Bowing of, in prayer:* Solomon	2 Chr. 6:13, 14	423
			Great joy	Luke 7:38, 45	1035	Daniel	Dan. 6:10	842
			Blessing	Gen. 48:10-16	48	Christ	Luke 22:41	1055
			Anointings	1 Sam. 10:1	270	Stephen	Acts 7:59, 60	1102
			Reconcilia- tion	Gen. 33:4	34	Peter	Acts 9:40	1105
			Death	Gen. 50:1	49	Paul	Acts 20:36	1118
						Christians	Acts 21:5	1118

Knife—*a sharp instrument for cutting*

A. *Used for:*
Slaying
animals ......Gen. 22:6-10   22
Circum-
cision ....Josh. 5:2, 3   209
Dismembering a
body.........Judg. 19:29   251
Sharpening
pens ....Jer. 36:23   754

B. *Figurative of:*
Inordinate
appetite.......Prov. 23:2   627
Cruel
oppressors ....Prov. 30:14   633

Knock—*to rap on a door*

Rewarded.........Luke 11:9, 10   1040
Expectant.........Luke 12:36   1043
Disappointed......Luke 13:25-27   1044
Unexpected......Acts 12:13, 16   1108
Invitation........Rev. 3:20   1296

Knowledge

A. *Kinds of:*
Natural........Matt. 24:32   989
Deceptive......Gen. 3:5   6
Sinful..........Gen. 3:7   6
Personal.......Josh. 24:31   228
Practical.......Ex. 36:1   87
Experi-
mental........Ex. 14:4, 18   66
Friendly.......Ex. 1:8   54
Intuitive.......1 Sam. 22:22   283
Intellectual ...John 7:15, 28   1072
Saving.........John 17:3   1084
Spiritual ......1 Cor. 2:14   1150
Revealed ......Luke 10:22   1039

B. *Sources of:*
God ....Ps. 94:10   577
Nature.........Ps. 19:2   536
Scriptures .....2 Tim. 3:15   1225
Doing God's
will ....John 7:17   1072

C. *Believer's attitude toward:*
Not to be
arrogant ......1 Cor. 8:1   1154
Should grow
in ....2 Pet. 3:18   1270
Should add
to............2 Pet. 1:5   1268
Not to be forgetful
of.............2 Pet. 3:17   1270
Accept our limitations
of.............1 Cor. 13:8-12   1158
Be filled with ..Phil. 1:9   1193

D. *Christ's, of:*
God ....Luke 10:22   1039
Man's nature ..John 2:24, 25   1066
Man's
thoughts......Matt. 9:4   971
Believers.......John 10:14, 27   1077
Things
future........2 Pet. 1:14   1268
All things......Col. 2:3   1200

E. *Attitude of sinful men toward:*
Turn from .....Rom. 1:21   1132
Ignorant of ....1 Cor. 1:21   1149
Raised up
against........2 Cor. 10:5   1172
Did not acknowledge
God...........Rom. 1:28   1132
Never able to come
to............2 Tim. 3:7   1225

F. *Value of:*
Superior to
gold..........Prov. 8:10   615
Increases
power.........Prov. 24:5   627
Keeps from
destruction....Is. 5:13   661
Insures
stability.......Is. 33:6   684

Koa

People described as enemies of
Jerusalem ......Ezek. 23:23   806

Kohath—*assembly*

Second son of
Levi..............Gen. 46:8, 11   46
Goes with Levi to
Egypt ....Gen. 46:11   46
Brother of Jochebed,
mother of Aaron
and Moses........Ex. 6:16-20   59
Dies at age 133....Ex. 6:18   59

Kohathites—*descendants of Kohath*

A. *History of:*
Originate in Levi's son
(Kohath)......Gen. 46:11   46
Divided into 4 groups (Amram,
Izhar, Hebron,
Uzziel).......Num. 3:19, 27   130
Numbering
of.............Num. 3:27, 28   130
Duties assigned
to.............Num. 4:15-20   131
Cities assigned
to.............Josh. 21:4-11   224

B. *Privileges of:*
Aaron and
Moses..........Ex. 6:20   59
Special charge of sacred
instruments.....Num. 4:15-20   131
Temple music by Heman the
Kohathite.....1 Chr. 6:31-38   392
Under Jehoshaphat, lead in
praise........2 Chr. 20:19   434
Under Hezekiah,
help to cleanse
Temple........2 Chr. 29:12, 15   442

C. *Sins of:*
Korah (of
Izhar) leads   {Num. 16:1-35   144
rebellion .....{Jude 11   1287

Kolaiah—*voice of Yahweh*

1. Father of the false prophet
Ahab..........Jer. 29:21-23   746
2. Postexilic Benjamite
family.........Neh. 11:7   478

Korah—*baldness*

1. Son of Esau ...Gen. 36:5, 14, 18   36
2. Son of Eliphaz and grandson of
Esau..........Gen. 36:16   36
3. Calebite ....1 Chr. 2:42, 43   389
4. Son of Izhar the
Kohathite.....Ex. 6:21, 24   59
Leads a rebellion against Moses
and Aaron ....Num. 16:1-3   144
Warned by
Moses........Num. 16:4-27   145
Descend alive into
Sheol ....Num. 16:28-35   145
Sons of, not
destroyed .....Num. 26:9-11   154
Sons of,
gatekeepers ...1 Chr. 26:19   411

Korahites

Descendants of
Korah...........Ex. 6:24   59
Some become:
David's
warriors.........1 Chr. 12:6   399
Servants ....1 Chr. 9:19-31   396
Musicians........1 Chr. 6:22-32   392
A maskil for ......Ps. 42 (Title)   549

Kore—*a partridge*

1. Korahite
Levite...........1 Chr. 9:19   396
2. Keeper of the eastern
gate...........2 Chr. 31:14   444

Koz—*thorn*

Father of Anub ...1 Chr. 4:8   390

Kushaiah—*bow of Yahweh (that is, rainbow)*

Merarite Levite
musician........1 Chr. 15:17   401
Called Kishi.......1 Chr. 6:44   393

L

Laadah—*festival*

Judahite ....1 Chr. 4:21   391

Laban—*white*

1. Son of
Bethuel ......Gen. 24:24, 29   24
Brother of
Rebekah ......Gen. 24:15, 29   23
Father of Leah and
Rachel ....Gen. 29:16   29
Chooses Rebekah for
Isaac..........Gen. 24:29-60   24
Entertains
Jacob.........Gen. 29:1-14   29
Deceives Jacob in
marriage arrange-
ment..........Gen. 29:15-30   29
Agrees to Jacob's
business arrange-
ment..........Gen. 30:25-43   30
Changes attitude toward
Jacob.........Gen. 31:1-9   31
Pursues after fleeing
Jacob ....Gen. 31:21-25   31
Rebukes
Jacob ....Gen. 31:26-30   32
Rebuked by
Jacob ....Gen. 31:31-42   32
Makes covenant with
Jacob ....Gen. 31:43-55   32
2. City in the
Arabah........Deut. 1:1   169

Labor—*physical or mental effort*

A. *Physical:*
Nature of:
As old as
creation........Gen. 2:5, 15   5
Ordained by
God............Gen. 3:17-19   7
One of the command-
ments..........Ex. 20:9   72
From morning until
night.........Ps. 104:23   582
With the
hands.........1 Thess. 4:11   1208
To life's end ...Ps. 90:10   576
Without God,
vanity.........Eccl. 2:11   639
Shrinking from,
denounced ....2 Thess. 3:10   1213
Benefits of:
Profit.........Prov. 14:23   619
Happiness .....Ps. 128:2   596
Proclaim
gospel........1 Thess. 2:9   1207
Supply of
other's   {Acts 20:35   1118
needs ....{Eph. 4:28   1188
Restful sleep..Eccl. 5:12   641
Double
honor.........1 Tim. 5:17   1219
Eternal life ....John 6:27   1071
Not in vain ....1 Cor. 15:58   1161
Phil. 2:16   1194

B. *Spiritual:*
Characteristics of:
Commissioned by
Christ.........John 4:38   1068
Accepted by
few ....Matt. 9:37, 38   972
Working with
God...........1 Cor. 3:9   1150
By God's
grace ....1 Cor. 15:10   1160
Result of
faith ....1 Tim. 4:10   1219
Characterized by
love...........1 Thess. 1:3   1206
Done in
prayer ....Col. 4:12   1202
Subject to
discourage-   {Is. 49:4   698
ment..........{Gal. 4:11   1179
Interrupted by
Satan ....1 Thess. 3:5   1207

SUBJECT	REFERENCE	PAGE

Lamp—continued

Prosperity	Job 29:3	513
Industry	Prov. 31:18	634
Death	Job 18:6	507
Churches	Rev. 1:20	1294
Christ	Dan. 10:6	847
	Rev. 1:14	1294

Lampstand, The Golden

A. *Specifications regarding:*

Made of gold	Ex. 25:31	76
After a divine model	Ex. 25:31-40	76
Set in holy place	Heb. 9:2	1244
Continual burning of	Ex. 27:20, 21	78
Carried by Kohathites	Num. 4:4-15	131
Ten, in the Temple	1 Kin. 7:49, 50	332
Taken to Babylon	Jer. 52:19	773

B. *Used figuratively of:*

Christ	Zech. 4:2, 14	920
The church	Rev. 1:13, 20	1294

Lance—*a javelin or light spear*

Used by Baal's priests	1 Kin. 18:28	346

Landmark—*a boundary marker*

Removal of, forbidden	Deut. 19:14	187

Land of promise (Canaan)

A. *Described as:*

The land of promise	Heb. 11:9	1246
The land of Canaan	Ezek. 16:3, 29	797
The land of the Jews	Acts 10:39	1106
The holy land	Zech. 2:12	919
"Married"	Is. 62:4	709

B. *Conquest of, by:*

Divine command	Ex. 23:24	75
God's angel	Ex. 23:20, 23	75
Hornets	Ex. 23:28	75
Degrees	Ex. 23:29, 30	75

C. *Inheritance of:*

Promised to Abraham's descendants	Gen. 12:1-7	14
Awaits God's time	Gen. 15:7-16	16
Boundaries of, specified	Gen. 15:18-21	16
Some kept from	Deut. 1:34-40	170
For the obedient	Deut. 5:16	174
Sin separates from	Deut. 28:49-68	194

D. *Laws concerning:*

Land allotted to 12 tribes	Num. 26:52-55	155
None for priests	Num. 18:20, 24	147
Sale and redemption of	Lev. 25:15-33	119
Transfer of title	Ruth 4:3-8	258
Witness of sale	Ruth 4:9-11	258
Relieved of debt on	Neh. 5:3-13	470
Leased to others	Matt. 21:33-41	985
Widow's right in	Ruth 4:3-9	258
Rights of unmarried women in	Num. 27:1-11	156
Rest of, on the seventh year	Ex. 23:11	74

E. *Original inhabitants of:*

Seven Gentile nations	Deut. 7:1	176
	Josh. 24:11	227
Mighty	Deut. 4:38	173
Tall	Deut. 9:1, 2	177
Idolatrous	Ex. 23:23, 24	75
	Deut. 12:29-31	181
Corrupt	Lev. 18:1-30	112
	Ezek. 16:47	798
Mingled with Israel	Ps. 106:34-38	584

Language—*man's means of communication*

A. *Kinds of:*

Judean (Hebrew)	2 Kin. 18:28	375
Chaldee	Dan. 1:4	835
Aramaic	2 Kin. 18:26	375
Egyptian	Ps. 114:1	588
Arabic	Acts 2:11	1095
Greek	Acts 21:37	1119
Latin	John 19:19, 20	1086
Lycaonian	Acts 14:11	1110
Medes and Persians	Esth. 3:12	487

B. *Varieties of:*

Result of confusion (Babel)	Gen. 11:1-9	13
Result of division of Noah's three sons	Gen. 10:5, 20, 31	12
Seen in one empire	Esth. 1:22	485
	Dan. 3:4, 7, 29	838
Seen in Christ's inscription	John 19:19, 20	1086
Witnessed at Pentecost	Acts 2:6-12	1095
Evident in heaven	Rev. 5:9	1296

See Tongue

Lantern—*an enclosed lamp*

Used by soldiers arresting Jesus	John 18:3	1084

Laodicea—*a chief city of Asia Minor*

Church of, sharply rebuked	Rev. 1:11	1294
Epaphras labors here	Col. 4:12, 13	1202
Paul writes letter to	Col. 4:16	1203
Not visited by Paul	Col. 2:1	1200
	Col. 4:15	1203

Lap

A. *As a loose skirt of a garment:*

For carrying objects	2 Kin. 4:39	359
Lots cast into	Prov. 16:33	621

B. *As an act of dogs:*

For selecting Gideon's army	Judg. 7:5, 6, 7	238

Lappidoth—*torches*

Husband of Deborah the prophetess	Judg. 4:4	235

Lasea

Seaport of Crete	Acts 27:8	1125

Lash—*a punishment imposed with a whip or scourge*

Rendered "stripes"	Deut. 25:3	191
Imposed on Paul	2 Cor. 11:24	1173

Lasha—*bursting forth*

Boundary town of southeast Palestine	Gen. 10:19	13

Lasharon—*to Sharon*

Town possessed by Joshua	Josh. 12:1, 18	216

Last—*the terminal point*

A. *Senses of:*

Final consequence	Prov. 23:32	627
God	Is. 44:6	694

B. *Of events, last:*

Day (resurrection)	John 6:39, 40	1071
Day (judgment)	John 12:48	1080
Days (present age)	Acts 2:17	1095
Hour (present age)	1 John 2:18	1275
Times (present age)	1 Pet. 1:20	1261
Days (time before Christ's return)	2 Tim. 3:1	1224
	2 Pet. 3:3	1269
Enemy (death)	1 Cor. 15:26	1160
Time (Christ's return)	1 Pet. 1:5	1260
Trumpet (Christ's return)	1 Cor. 15:52	1161

Last Supper

At Feast of Unleavened Bread	Matt. 26:17	991
	Mark 14:12	1016
Fulfills Passover	Luke 22:15-18	1054

Latin—*the Roman language*

Used in writing Christ's inscription	John 19:19, 20	1086

Lattice—*a framework of crossed wood or metal strips*

Window of Sisera's mother	Judg. 5:28	237
Ahaziah fell through	2 Kin. 1:2	355

Laughter—*an emotion expressive of joy, mirth or ridicule*

A. *Kinds of:*

Divine	Ps. 59:8	557
Natural	Job 8:21	501
Derisive	Neh. 2:19	468
Fake	Prov. 14:13	619
Scornful	2 Chr. 30:10	443
Confident	Job 5:22	499
Joyful	Ps. 126:2	596

B. *Causes of:*

Man's futility	Ps. 2:4	528
Something unusual	Gen. 18:12-15	18
Something untrue	Matt. 9:24	971
Ridicule	2 Chr. 30:10	443
Highly contradictory	Ps. 22:7, 8	538

Laver—*a basin for washing*

Made for the tent of meeting	Ex. 30:18	82

Law—*an authoritative rule of conduct*

Law of man	Luke 20:22	1052
Natural Law written upon the heart	Rom. 2:14, 15	1132
Law of Moses	Gal. 3:17-21	1179
Entire Old Testament	John 10:34	1077
Expression of God's will	Rom. 7:2-9	1136
Operating principle	Rom. 3:27	1134

Law of Moses

A. *History of:*

Given at Sinai	Ex. 20:1-26	71
Called a covenant	Deut. 4:13, 23	173
Inaugurated with blood	Heb. 9:18-22	1244
Called the Law of Moses	Josh. 8:30-35	213

SUBJECT　　REFERENCE　PAGE | SUBJECT　　REFERENCE　PAGE | SUBJECT　　REFERENCE　PAGE

Lebanon—continued

B. *Significant as:*
A sight desired by
Moses........Deut. 3:25　172
Israel's northern
boundary.....Deut. 1:7　169
Captured by ⌠Josh. 11:16, 17　216
Joshua........⌡Josh. 12:7　216
Assigned to
Israelites......Josh. 13:5-7　217
Not completely
conquered....Judg. 3:1-3　234
Possessed by
Assyria.......Is. 37:24　687

C. *Figurative of:*
Great
kingdoms.....Is. 10:24, 34　667
Spiritual transfor-
mation........Is. 29:17　681
Jerusalem and the
Temple......Ezek. 17:3　799
Spiritual
growth........Hos. 14:5-7　861
Messiah's
glory..........Is. 35:2　685

D. *Noted for:*
Blossoms......Nah. 1:4　898
Wine........Hos. 14:6, 7　861
Wild beast.....2 Kin. 14:9　369
Snow........Jer. 5:15　723
Cedars........Song 5:15　651
Is. 14:8　669

Lebaoth—*lionesses*
Town of south
Judah........Josh. 15:32　219
Also called Beth-
labaoth..........Josh. 19:6　222

Leb-kamai
Another name for
Chaldea.........Jer. 51:1　769

Lebo-hamath—*entrance to Hamath*
Hittite city north of
Damascus.....Josh. 13:5　217
Spies visit........Num. 13:21　141
Israel's northern
boundary........Num. 34:8　163

Labonah—*incense*
Town north of
Shiloh........Judg. 21:19　253

Lecah—*journey*
Descendant of
Judah............1 Chr. 4:21　391

Ledge—*a protrusion around an altar*
Part of altars......Ex. 27:5　78

Leech
Figurative of insatiable
appetite.........Prov. 30:15, 16　633

Leek—*an onion-like plant*
Desired by
Israelites........Num. 11:5　139

Lees—*sediment in wine jars*
Figurative of:
Negligence and
ease..............Jer. 48:11　764

Left—*opposite of right*

A. *Of direction:*
North.........Gen. 14:15　16
Making a
choice.......Gen. 13:9　15
Locating a
place..........Matt. 20:21-23　984

B. *Of the hand:*
Unusual capacity of 700
men........Judg. 20:15, 16　251
Lesser importance
of............Gen. 48:13-20　48

C. *Figurative of:*
Weakness.....Eccl. 10:2　644
Shame........Matt. 25:33, 41　990

Bride's
choice........Song 2:6　649
Singleness of
purpose.......Matt. 6:3　968
Riches.........Prov. 3:16　611
Ministry of
God........2 Cor. 6:7　1169

Left—*that which remains over*

A. *Descriptive of:*
Aloneness.....Gen. 32:24　33
Entire
destruction....Josh. 11:11, 12　216
Entire
separation.....Ex. 10:26　63
Survival......Num. 26:65　156
Remnant......Is. 11:11, 16　668
Heir..........2 Sam. 14:7　307

B. *Blessings upon:*
Equal booty...1 Sam. 30:9-25　290
Greater
heritage......Is. 49:21-23　699
Greater
Holiness.....Is. 4:3　660
Lord's
protection.....Rom. 11:3-5　1140
Not wasted....Matt. 15:37　979

Legacy—*that which is bequeathed to heirs*
Left by:
Abraham.........Gen. 25:5, 6　25
David...........1 Kin. 2:1-7　325
Christ...........John 14:15-27　1081

Legion—*a great number or multitude*
Demons..........Mark 5:9, 15　1004
Christ's angels....Matt. 26:53　992

Legs—*lower parts of human or animal body*

A. *Used literally of:*
Animal's......Ex. 12:9　63
Man's......1 Sam. 17:6　277
Christ's.......John 19:31, 33　1087

B. *Used figuratively of:*
Fool..........Prov. 26:7　630
Man's
weakness.....Ps. 147:10　604
Sons of
Israel.........Amos 3:12　873
Strength......Dan. 2:33, 40　837
Christ's
appearance....Song 5:15　651

Lehabim—*flaming*
Nation (probably the Libyans)
related to the
Egyptians.......Gen. 10:13　12

Lehi—*cheek, jawbone*
Place in Judah; Samson kills
Philistines.......Judg. 15:9-19　247

Lemuel—*devoted to God*
King taught by his
mother...........Prov. 31:1-31　633

Lending—*to give to another for temporary use*

A. *As a gift to:*
Expecting no
return........Luke 6:34, 35　1033
To the LORD...1 Sam. 1:28　264
1 Sam. 2:20　264

B. *As a blessing:*
Recognized by
God..........Deut. 28:12, 44　193
Remembered by
God..........Ps. 112:5, 6　588
Rewarded by
God..........Ps. 37:25, 26　546

See Borrow

Length of life

A. *Factors prolonging:*
Keeping command-
ments........1 Kin. 3:14　327
Wisdom......Prov. 3:13, 16　611

Prayer.........2 Kin. 20:1-11　377
Honor to
parents.......Eph. 6:3　1189
Fear of the
LORD........Prov. 10:27　616

B. *Factors decreasing:*
Killing..........2 Sam. 3:27　297
God's
judgment.....Job 22:15, 16　509
Suicide........Matt. 27:5　993

Lentil—*plant of the legume family*
Prepared as Esau's
stew..............Gen. 25:29-34　26
Bread made of....Ezek. 4:9　789

Leopard—*a wild, spotted animal*

A. *Characteristics of:*
Swift..........Hab. 1:8　903
Watches......Jer. 5:6　722
Lies in wait....Hos. 13:7　861
Lives in
mountains....Song 4:8　650

B. *Figurative of:*
Man's inability to
change.......Jer. 13:23　718
Transfor-
mation........Is. 11:6　667
Greek
empire.......Dan. 7:6　843
Antichrist.....Rev. 13:2　1301

Leprosy—*scourge; a cancer-like disease*

A. *Characteristics of:*
Many diseased
with..........Luke 4:27　1030
Unclean.......Lev. 13:44, 45　107
Outcast......2 Kin. 15:5　370
Considered
incurable......2 Kin. 5:7　359
Often
hereditary....2 Sam. 3:29　297
Excluded from the
priesthood....Lev. 22:2-4　116

B. *Kinds of, in:*
Man..........Luke 17:12　1048
House........Lev. 14:33-57　109
Clothing......Lev. 13:47-59　107

C. *Treatment of:*
Symptoms
described.....Lev. 13:1-46　106
Cleansing
prescribed.....Lev. 14:1-32　108
Healing by a
miracle........Ex. 4:6, 7　56

D. *Used as a sign:*
Miriam........Num. 12:1-10　140
Gehazi........2 Kin. 5:25, 27　360
Uzziah........2 Chr. 26:16-21　439
Moses.........Ex. 4:6, 7　56

Letters—*written communications*

A. *Kinds of:*
Forged.........1 Kin. 21:7, 8　349
Rebellious....Jer. 29:24-32　746
Authori-
tative.........Acts 22:5　1120
Instructive...Acts 15:23-29　1111
Weighty.......2 Cor. 10:10　1172
Causing
sorrow........2 Cor. 7:8　1169

B. *Descriptive of:*
One's writing..Gal. 6:11　1181
Learning......John 7:15　1072
External......Rom. 2:27, 29　1133
Legalism.....Rom. 7:6　1136
Christians....2 Cor. 3:1, 2　1167

"Let us"
"Arise, go from
here"........John 14:31　1082
"Therefore lay aside the deeds of
darkness".......Rom. 13:12　1142
"Behave
properly"........Rom. 13:13　1142
"Be sober".......1 Thess. 5:8　1208
"Fear"...........Heb. 4:1　1241

SUBJECT	REFERENCE	PAGE

"Therefore be diligent to enter that
rest" ....Heb. 4:11 — 1241
"Therefore draw
near"............Heb. 4:16 — 1241
"Press on to
maturity" ....Heb. 6:1 — 1242
"Draw near with a sincere
heart"............Heb. 10:22 — 1245
"Hold fast".......Heb. 10:23 — 1245
"Consider how to
stimulate".......Heb. 10:24 — 1245
"Also lay aside"...Heb. 12:1 — 1247
"Go out to him" ..Heb. 13:13 — 1248
"Continually offer
up"..............Heb. 13:15 — 1248

Letushim—*sharpened*

Tribe descending from
Dedan............Gen. 25:3 — 25

Leummim—*peoples*

Tribe descending from
Dedan............Gen. 25:3 — 25

Levi—*joined*

1. Third son of Jacob and
Leah..........Gen. 29:34 — 30
Brings trouble to
Jacob.........Gen. 34:25-31 — 35
Father of Gershon, Kohath,
Merari ....Gen. 46:11 — 46
Descendants of, to be
scattered.....Gen. 49:5-7 — 48
Dies in Egypt at age
137............Ex. 6:16 — 59
2. Ancestor of
Christ.........Luke 3:24 — 1029
3. Another ancestor of
Christ.........Luke 3:29 — 1029
4. Apostle called
Matthew......Luke 5:27, 29 — 1032
5. Tribe descending from
Levi...........Ex. 32:26, 28 — 84

Leviathan—*twisted, coiled*

Sea monster created by
God...........Ps. 104:26 — 582
Habit of, graphically described
(crocodile).......Job 41:1-34 — 522
God's power
over............Ps. 74:14 — 566

Levites—*descendants of Levi*

A. *History of:*
Descendants of Levi, Jacob's
son ....Gen. 29:34 — 30
Jacob's prophecy
concerning....Gen. 49:5-7 — 48
Divided into three
families ....Ex. 6:16-24 — 59
Aaron, great-grandson of Levi,
chosen for
priesthood ....Ex. 28:1 — 78
Tribe of Levi rewarded for
dedication....Ex. 32:26-29 — 84
Chosen by God for holy
service........Deut. 10:8 — 179
Not numbered among
Israel ....Num. 1:47-49 — 128
Substituted for Israel's first-
born ....Num. 3:12-45 — 130
Given as gifts to Aaron's
sons ....Num. 8:6-21 — 137
Rebellion among, led by
Korah.........Num. 16:1-50 — 144
Choice of, confirmed by the
Lord ....Num. 17:1-13 — 146
Bear ark of the covenant across
the Jordan ...Josh. 3:2-17 — 208
Hear Law
read ....Josh. 8:31-35 — 213
Cities (48) ⎧Num. 35:2-8 — 164
assigned to..⎨Josh. 14:3, 4 — 218
One of, becomes Micah's
idolatrous ⎧Judg. 17:5-13 — 248
priest ......⎨Judg. 18:18-31 — 249
Perform priestly
functions.....1 Sam. 6:15 — 267
Appointed over service of
song ....1 Chr. 6:31-48 — 392

SUBJECT	REFERENCE	PAGE

Service of heads of
households....1 Chr. 9:26-34 — 396
Excluded by
Jeroboam .....2 Chr. 11:13-17 — 428
Help repair the
Temple........1 Chr. 23:2-4 — 408
Carried to
Babylon.......2 Chr. 36:19, 20 — 450
Return from
exile ....Ezra 2:40-63 — 454
Tithes withheld
from ....Neh. 13:10-13 — 480
Intermarry with
foreigners.....Ezra 10:2-24 — 461
Sign the
document.....Neh. 10:1, 9-28 — 477
Present defiled
offerings will ⎧Mal. 1:6-14 — 929
be purified ...⎨Mal. 3:1-4 — 930
B. *Duties of:*
Serve the
LORD.........Deut. 10:8 — 179
Serve the
priesthood ....Num. 3:5-9 — 130
Attend to sanctuary
duties........Num. 18:3 — 146
Distribute the
tithe ....2 Chr. 31:11-19 — 444
Prepare sacrifices for
priests ....2 Chr. 35:10-14 — 448
Teach the
people ....2 Chr. 17:9-11 — 431
Declare verdicts of
Law...........Deut. 17:9-11 — 185
Protect the
king ....2 Chr. 23:2-10 — 436
Perform
music ....1 Chr. 25:1-7 — 410
Precede the ⎧2 Chr. 20:20, 21,
army.........⎨ 28 — 434
C. *Spiritual truths illustrated by:*
Representation—duties of the
congre-
gation.........Num. 3:6-9 — 130
Substitution—
place of the ⎧Num. 3:12, 13,
first-born....⎨ 41, 45 — 130
Subordination—serve to the
priests ....Num. 3:5-10 — 130
Consecration—separated
as a wave
offering ....Num. 8:9-14 — 137
Holiness—
cleansed ......Num. 8:6, 7, 21 — 137
Election—God's
choice ....Num. 17:7-13 — 146
Inheritance—in the
Lord ....Num. 18:20 — 147

See Priest

Leviticus, the Book of—*a book of the
Old Testament*

Laws of
offerings.........⎧Lev. 1:1—
 ⎨ 7:38 — 96
Laws of purity ...Lev. 11:1—15:33 — 104
Day of
atonement.......Lev. 16:1-34 — 110
Laws of ⎧Lev. 17:1—
holiness ....⎨ 25:55 — 112
Blessings and
curses............Lev. 26:1-46 — 120

Levy—*forced labor imposed upon a
people*

Israelites..........1 Kin. 5:13-15 — 329
Canaanites........1 Kin. 9:15, 21 — 335

Lewd, lewdness—*wickedness*

A. *Characteristics of:*
Shameful .....Ezek. 16:27 — 798
Sexual.........Ezek. 22:11 — 805
Youthful......Ezek. 23:21 — 806
Adulterous....Jer. 13:27 — 732
Filthiness.....Ezek. 24:13 — 807
Disgraceful ...Judg. 20:6 — 251

SUBJECT	REFERENCE	PAGE

B. *Committed by:*
Men of
Gibeah........Judg. 20:6 — 251
Israel.........Hos. 2:10 — 854
Jerusalem......Ezek. 16:27, 43 — 798

Liars, lies, lying—*manifestation of
untruth*

A. *Defined as:*
Nature of the
devil...........John 8:44 — 1074
Denial that Jesus is
Christ.........1 John 2:22 — 1275
Not keeping Christ's command-
ments.........1 John 2:4 — 1275
Hating one's
brother........1 John 4:20 — 1277
All that is not of the
truth..........1 John 2:21, 27 — 1275
B. *Those who speak:*
Wicked........Ps. 58:3 — 557
False
witnesses .....Prov. 14:5, 25 — 619
Astrologers ....Dan. 2:9 — 836
Israel.........Hos. 7:3, 13 — 857
Judah.........Jer. 9:1-5 — 727
C. *Attitude of the wicked toward:*
Are always ....Titus 1:12 — 1229
Forge against the
righteous .....Ps. 119:69 — 592
Exchange God's truth
for............Rom. 1:25 — 1132
D. *Attitude of the righteous
toward:*
Keep far
from ....Prov. 30:8 — 633
"Tell no" ......Zeph. 3:13 — 910
Pray for deliverance
from ....Ps. 120:2 — 595
"Lay aside"....Eph. 4:25 — 1188
F. *Attitude of God toward:*
Will not ......Num. 23:19 — 152
Is an abomina-
tion...........Prov. 6:16-19 — 613
Will sweep away
refuge of.....Is. 28:15, 17 — 679
Is against.....Ezek. 13:8 — 795
G. *Punishment of, shall:*
Not escape....Prov. 19:5 — 623
Be stopped.....Ps. 63:11 — 559
Be silenced ....Ps. 31:18 — 542
Be short-
lived ....Prov. 12:19 — 618
End in lake of
fire............Rev. 21:8, 27 — 1307
H. *The evils of:*
Leads astray ...Amos 2:4 — 872
Increases
wickedness....Prov. 29:12 — 632
Destruction...Hos. 10:13-15 — 859
Death ....Prov. 21:6 — 624
 Zech. 13:3 — 925

Liberty, civil

Obtained by:
Purchase..........Acts 22:28 — 1120
Birth.............Acts 22:28 — 1120
Release ....Deut. 15:12-15 — 183
Victory...........Ex. 14:30, 31 — 67

Liberty, spiritual

A. *Described as:*
Predicted ......Is. 61:1 — 708
Where the
spirit is........2 Cor. 3:17 — 1167
B. *Relation of Christians toward,
they:*
Are called to...Gal. 5:13 — 1180
Abide by.......James 1:25 — 1254
Should
walk at ....Ps. 119:45 — 591
Have in Jesus
Christ.........Gal. 2:4, 5 — 1178

See Freedom

Libnah—*whiteness*

1. Israelite
camp ....Num. 33:20, 21 — 162

SUBJECT	REFERENCE	PAGE	SUBJECT	REFERENCE	PAGE	SUBJECT	REFERENCE	PAGE

Locust—continued

B. *Used literally of insects:*
Miraculously brought
forth..........Ex. 10:12-19 — 62
Sent as a {Deut. 28:38 — 194
judgment ....{1 Kin. 8:37 — 333
Used for
food ....Matt. 3:4 — 965

C. *Used figuratively of:*
Weakness .....Ps. 109:23, 24 — 587
Rushing men ..Is. 33:4 — 684
Nineveh's departing
glory..........Nah. 3:15, 17 — 900
Final plagues ..Rev. 9:3, 7 — 1299
See Grasshopper

Lod

Benjamite town...1 Chr. 8:1, 12 — 395
Mentioned in postexilic
books ....Ezra 2:33 — 454
Aeneas healed here, called
Lydda...........Acts 9:32-35 — 1105

Lo-debar

City in Manasseh
(in Gilead) ....2 Sam. 9:4, 5 — 302
David flees to ...2 Sam. 17:27 — 311

Lodge—*to pass the night*

Travelers—in a
house...........Judg. 19:4-20 — 250
Spies—in a
house ....Josh. 2:1 — 207
Animals—in
ruins ....Zeph. 2:14 — 910
Birds—in trees ....Matt. 13:32 — 976
Righteousness—in a
city ....Is. 1:21 — 658
Thoughts—in
Jerusalem ....Jer. 4:14 — 721

Loins

A. *Used literally of:*
Hips ....Gen. 37:34 — 38
   Ex. 28:42 — 80
Waist..........2 Sam. 20:8 — 314

B. *Used figuratively of:*
Physical
strength ......Ps. 66:11 — 560
Source of
knowledge ....Eph. 6:14 — 1190
Source of
hope..........1 Pet. 1:13 — 1261

Lois

Timothy's
grandmother .....2 Tim. 1:5 — 1223

Loneliness

Jacob—in
prayer...........Gen. 32:23-30 — 33
Joseph—in
weeping..........Gen. 43:30, 31 — 44
Elijah—in discourage-
ment ....1 Kin. 19:3-14 — 346
Jeremiah—in
witnessing........Jer. 15:17 — 734
Nehemiah—in a night
vigil..............Neh. 2:12-16 — 468
Christ—in
agony ....Matt. 26:36-45 — 991
Paul—in prison....2 Tim. 4:16 — 1226

Longevity—*a great span of life*

Allotted years,
70...............Ps. 90:10 — 576
See Length of life

Long live the king

First said of
Saul............1 Sam. 10:24 — 271

Look—*focusing the eyes toward
something*

Promise...........Gen. 15:5 — 16
Warning ....Gen. 19:17, 26 — 19
Astonishment.....Ex. 3:2-6 — 56
Disdain ....1 Sam. 17:42 — 278
Lust ....2 Sam. 11:2-4 — 303
Encouragement ...Ps. 34:5 — 544

Disappointment ...Is. 5:2, 4 — 661
Salvation ....Is. 45:22 — 696
Glory ....Acts 7:55 — 1102

Loom—*a machine for making cloth*

Samson's hair in ..Judg. 16:13, 14 — 247
Figurative of life ..Is. 38:12 — 688

Lord—*title of majesty and kingship*

A. *Applied to:*
God ....Gen. 3:1-23 — 6
Christ ....Luke 6:46 — 1033
Masters........Gen. 24:14, 27 — 23
Men ("sir") ...Matt. 21:29 — 985
Husbands......Gen. 18:12 — 18
   1 Pet. 3:6 — 1263

B. *As applied to Christ, "kyrios"
indicates:*
Identity with
Yahweh.......Joel 2:32 — 867
Confession of Christ's Lordship
("Jesus as
Lord") ....Rom. 10:9 — 1139
Absolute
Lordship ......Phil. 2:11 — 1194

Lord's Day (see First day of week)

Lord's Prayer

Taught by Jesus to His
disciples..........Matt. 6:9-13 — 968

Lord's Supper

A. *Described as:*
Sharing of
communion ...1 Cor. 10:16 — 1156
Breaking of
bread ....Acts 2:42, 46 — 1096
Lord's supper ..1 Cor. 11:20 — 1157
Eucharist "Giving of
thanks".......Luke 22:17, 19 — 1054

B. *Features concerning:*
Instituted by
Christ........Matt. 26:26-29 — 991
Commemorative of Christ's
death ....Luke 22:19, 20 — 1054
Introductory to the new
covenant.....Matt. 26:28 — 991
Means of Christian
fellowship.....Acts 2:42, 46 — 1096
Memorial
feast ....1 Cor. 11:23-26 — 1157
Inconsistent with demon
fellowship.....1 Cor. 10:19-22 — 1156
Preparation in,
required.......1 Cor. 11:27-34 — 1157
Spiritually
explained .....John 6:26-58 — 1070

Lordship—*supreme authority*

Human kings .....Mark 10:42 — 1011
Divine King.......Phil. 2:9-11 — 1194

Lo-ruhamah—*not pitied*

Symbolic name of Hosea's
daughter ....Hos. 1:6 — 853

Loss, spiritual

A. *Kinds of:*
One's soul ....Luke 9:24, 25 — 1038
Reward........1 Cor. 3:13-15 — 1150
Heaven........Luke 16:19-31 — 1047

B. *Causes of:*
Love of this
life............Luke 17:33 — 1049
Sin ....Ps. 107:17, 34 — 585

Lost—*not found*

Descriptive of men as:
Separated from
God ....Luke 15:24, 32 — 1046
Unregenerated....Matt. 15:24 — 979
Objects of Christ's
mission........Luke 15:4-6 — 1046
Blinded by
Satan ....2 Cor. 4:3, 4 — 1167
Defiled...........Titus 1:15, 16 — 1230

Lot—*covering*

A. *Life of:*
Abraham's
nephew.......Gen. 11:27-31 — 14
Goes with Abraham to
Canaan.......Gen. 12:5 — 14
Accompanies Abraham to
Egypt.........Gen. 13:1 — 15
Settles in
Sodom........Gen. 13:5-13 — 15
Rescued by
Abraham......Gen. 14:12-16 — 16
Befriends
angels.........Gen. 19:1-14 — 19
Saved from Sodom's
destruction.....Gen. 19:15, 26 — 19
His wife, disobedient, becomes
pillar of salt ...Gen. 19:15, 26 — 19
His daughters commit incest
with ....Gen. 19:30-38 — 20
Unwilling father of
Moabites and
Ammonites ...Gen. 19:37, 38 — 20

B. *Character of:*
Makes selfish
choice.........Gen. 13:5-13 — 15
Lacks mental
stability.......Gen. 19:6-10 — 19
Loses moral
influence......Gen. 19:14, 20 — 19
Still "oppressed" by
Sodomites.....2 Pet. 2:7, 8 — 1268

Lotan—*a covering*

Tribe of Horites {Gen. 36:20, 29 — 36
in Mt. Seir.......{1 Chr. 1:38, 39 — 388

Lot(s)—*a means of deciding doubtful
matters*

A. *Characteristic of:*
Preceded by
prayer........Acts 1:23-26 — 1095
With divine
sanction ......Num. 26:55 — 156
Considered
final ....Num. 26:56 — 156
Used also by the
ungodly.......Matt. 27:35 — 994

B. *Used for:*
Selection of
scapegoat.....Lev. 16:8 — 111
Detection of a
criminal.......Josh. 7:14-18 — 211
Selection of
warriors.......Judg. 20:9, 10 — 251
Choice of a
king...........1 Sam. 10:19-21 — 271
Deciding priestly
rotation.......Luke 1:9 — 1025

Lot's wife

Disobedient, becomes pillar of
salt................Gen. 19:26 — 20
Event to be
remembered......Luke 17:32 — 1049

Love, Christian

A. *Toward God:*
First command-
ment.........Matt. 22:37, 38 — 986
With all the
heart.........Matt. 22:37 — 986
More important than
ritual ....Mark 12:31-33 — 1014
Gives
boldness ......1 John 4:17-19 — 1277

B. *Toward Christ:*
Sign of true
faith ....John 8:42 — 1074
Manifested in {John 14:15, 21,
obedience....{ 23 — 1081
Leads to
service........2 Cor. 5:14 — 1168

C. *Toward others:*
Second
command .....Matt. 22:37-39 — 986
Commanded by
Christ.........John 13:34 — 1081

SUBJECT	REFERENCE	PAGE	SUBJECT	REFERENCE	PAGE	SUBJECT	REFERENCE	PAGE

Maacah, Maacath—continued

4. One of Caleb's
   concubines....1 Chr. 2:48   389
5. Father of
   Shephatiah....1 Chr. 27:16   412
6. Ancestress of {1 Chr. 8:29   395
   King Saul....1 Chr. 9:35   396
7. One of David's
   warriors......1 Chr. 11:43   398
8. Father of Achish, king of
   Gath..........1 Kin. 2:39   326
9. David's wife and mother of
   Absalom....2 Sam. 3:3   297
10. Wife of Rehoboam; mother of
    King Abijah...2 Chr. 11:18-21   428
    Makes idol, is deposed as
    queen-
    mother........1 Kin. 15:13   342

Maacathites—inhabitants of Maachah

Not conquered by
   Israel............Josh. 13:13   217
Among Israel's
   warriors..........2 Sam. 23:34   318
See Maacah

Maadai—ornament of Yahweh

Postexilic Jew; divorced his foreign
   wife.............Ezra 10:34   462

Maadiah

Priest who returns from Babylon
with
   Zerubbabel.......Neh. 12:5, 7   478
Same as Moadiah
in ....Neh. 12:17   479

Maai—compassionate

Postexilic
   trumpeter........Neh. 12:35, 36   479

Maarath—barren place

Town of Judah....Josh. 15:1, 59   218

Maasai—work of Yahweh

Priest of Immer's
   family...........1 Chr. 9:12   396

Maaseiah, Mahseiah—work of Yahweh

1. Levite musician during David's
   reign..........1 Chr. 15:16, 18   401
2. Levite captain under
   Jehoiada......2 Chr. 23:1   436
3. Official during King Uzziah's
   reign..........2 Chr. 26:11   439
4. Son of Ahaz, slain by
   Zichri.......2 Chr. 28:7   440
5. Official of Jerusalem during
   King Josiah's
   reign.........2 Chr. 34:1, 8   447
6. Ancestor of
   Baruch........Jer. 32:12   750
7. Father of the false prophet
   Zedekiah.....Jer. 29:21   746
8. Father of Zephaniah the
   priest.........Jer. 21:1   738
9. Temple
   doorkeeper....Jer. 35:4   753
10. Judahite postexilic
    Jew..........Neh. 11:5   478
11. Benjamin ancestor of a
    postexilic
    Jew..........Neh. 11:7   478
12, 13, 14. Three priests who
    divorced
    their foreign {Ezra 10:18, 21,
    wives 22   462
15. Layman who divorced his
    foreign wife...Ezra 10:30   462
16. Representative who signs the
    document.....Neh. 10:1, 25   477
17. One who stood by
    Ezra ....Neh. 8:4   474
18. Levite who explains the
    Law...........Neh. 8:7   474
19. Priest who takes part in
    dedication
    services.......Neh. 12:41   479
20. Another participating
    leader........Neh. 12:42   479
21. Father or ancestor of
    Azariah ....Neh. 3:23   469

Maath—to be small

Ancestor of
   Christ...........Luke 3:26   1029

Maaz—anger

Judahite.........1 Chr. 2:27   389

Maaziah—Yahweh is a refuge

1. Descendant of Aaron; heads a
   course of
   priests ....1 Chr. 24:1-18   409
2. One who signs the
   document.....Neh. 10:1, 8   477

Macedonia—Greece (northern)

A. In Old Testament prophecy:
   Called the kingdom of
   Greece........Dan. 11:2   848
   Bronze part of
   Nebuchadnezzar's
   image.........Dan. 2:32, 39   837
   Described as a leopard with
   four heads ....Dan. 7:6, 17   843
   Described as a {Dan. 8:5, 21   845
   male goat....Dan. 11:4   848

B. In New Testament missions:
   Man of, appeals
   to.............Acts 16:9, 10   1112
   Paul preaches in,
   at Philippi, {Acts 16:10—
   etc..........17:14   1112
   Paul's troubles
   in.............2 Cor. 7:5   1169
   Churches of,
   very {Rom. 15:26   1144
   generous.....2 Cor. 8:1-5   1170

Machbannai—clad with a cloak

One of David's mighty
   men.............1 Chr. 12:13   399

Machbena—lump

Son of Sheva......1 Chr. 2:49   389

Machi

Father of the Gadite
   spy............Num. 13:15   141

Machir—sold

1. Manasseh's only
   son ....Gen. 50:23   50
   Founder of the family of
   Machirites ....Num. 26:29   155
   Conqueror of
   Gilead ....Num. 32:39, 40   162
   Name used of Manasseh
   tribe ....Judg. 5:14   236
2. Son of
   Ammiel ...2 Sam. 9:4, 5   302
   Provides food for
   David ....2 Sam. 17:27-29   311

Machnadebai—gift of the noble one

Son of Bani; divorced foreign
   wife.............Ezra 10:34, 40   462

Machpelah—double

Field containing a cave; bought by
   Abraham.........Gen. 23:9-18   22
   Sarah and Abraham buried
   here.............Gen. 23:19   23
   Isaac, Rebekah, Leah, and Jacob
   buried here.......Gen. 49:29-31   49

Madai—middle

Third son of Japheth; ancestor of
   the Medes........Gen. 10:2   12

Made—something brought into being

A. Why Christ was made for us:
   Sin ....2 Cor. 5:21   1169
   In our
   likeness.......Phil. 2:7   1194
   High priest ....Heb. 6:20   1242

B. What Christians are made by
   Him:
   Righteous .....2 Cor. 5:21   1169
   Heirs ....Titus 3:7   1230

Madmannah—dunghill

Town in south
   Judah ....Josh. 15:20, 31   219
   Son of Shaaph ....1 Chr. 2:49   389

Madmen—dunghill

Moabite town.....Jer. 48:2   764

Madmenah—dunghill or dungheap

Town near
   Jerusalem ....Is. 10:31   667

Madness—emotional or mental derangement

A. Kinds of:
   Extreme
   jealousy.......1 Sam. 18:8-10   279
   Extreme rage ..Luke 6:11   1032

B. Causes of:
   Disobedience to God's
   Laws..........Deut. 28:28   194
   Judgment sent by
   God..........Dan. 4:31-33   840

C. Manifestations of:
   Irrational
   behavior ......1 Sam. 21:12-15   283
   Uncontrollable
   emotions......Mark 5:1-5   1003
   Moral decay ...Jer. 50:38   769
   See Insanity; Lunatic

Madon—contention

Canaanite town...Josh. 12:19   217
Joins confederacy against
   Joshua ....Josh. 11:1-12   215

Magadan—tower

City of Galilee ....Matt. 15:39   979

Magbish—strong

Town of Judah....Ezra 2:30   454

Magdalene—of Magdala

Descriptive of one of the
   Mary's ....Matt. 27:56   994
   See Mary 3

Magdiel—God is glory

Edomite chief.....Gen. 36:43   37

Magi—a priestly sect in Persia

Brings gifts to the infant
   Jesus............Matt. 2:1, 2   964

Magic, magician—the art of doing superhuman things by "supernatural" means

A. Special manifestations of:
   At the
   exodus........Ex. 7:11   59
   During apostolic
   Christianity ...Acts 8:9, 18-24   1103

B. Modified power of:
   Acknowledged in
   history........Ex. 7:11, 22   59
   Recognized in
   prophecy......2 Thess. 2:9-12   1212
   Fulfilled in
   antichrist .....Rev. 13:13-18   1301

C. Failure of, to:
   Perform
   miracles.......Ex. 8:18, 19   60
   Overcome
   demons ....Acts 19:13-19   1116

D. Condemnation of, by:
   Explicit Law ...Lev. 20:27   115
   Their
   inability.......Ex. 8:18   60
   Final
   judgment .....Rev. 21:8   1307
   See Divination

SUBJECT	REFERENCE	PAGE	SUBJECT	REFERENCE	PAGE	SUBJECT	REFERENCE	PAGE

Malformation—*irregular features*

Of a giant........2 Sam. 21:20   315

Malice—*active intent to harm others*

A. *Causes of:*
Unregenerate (Prov. 6:14-16, 18,
heart........(19   613
Satanic
hatred ....1 John 3:12   1276
Jealousy.......1 Sam. 18:8-29   279
Racial
prejudice......Esth. 3:5-15   487

B. *Christian's attitude toward:*
Pray for those guilty
of............Matt. 5:44   968
Clean out....1 Cor. 5:7, 8   1151
Put away......Eph. 4:31   1188
Put aside ......Col. 3:8   1201
Putting aside ..1 Pet. 2:1   1261
Avoid manifes-
tations......1 Pet. 2:16   1262

C. *Characteristics:*
Unregen-   (Rom. 1:29   1132
erate.......(Titus 3:3   1230
God's wrath ...Rom. 1:18, 29   1132
Brings own
punishment ...Ps. 7:15, 16   530

Mallothi—*I have talked*

Son of Heman ....1 Chr. 25:4, 26   410

Mallows—*saltiness*

Perennial shrub that grows in salty
marshes..........Job 30:4   514

Malluch—*reigning*

1. Merarite
Levite........1 Chr. 6:44   393
2. Head of postexilic
priests ....Neh. 12:2, 7   478
3. Son of Bani; divorced his
foreign wife...Ezra 10:29   462
4. Son of Harim; divorced his
foreign wife...Ezra 10:32   462
5, 6. Two who sign the
document.....Neh. 10:4, 27   477

Malluchi—*reigning*

Head of a
household........Neh. 12:14   479

Malta—*an island in the Mediterranean
Sea*

Paul's shipwreck ..Acts 28:1-8   1126

Mammon—*wealth*

Served as a master other than
God..............Matt. 6:24   968

Mamre—*firmness*

1. Town or district near
Hebron ....Gen. 23:19   23
West of
Machpelah ....Gen. 23:17, 19   23
Abraham dwelt by the oaks
of............Gen. 13:18   15
2. Amorite, brother of
Eschol ....Gen. 14:13   16

Man—*human being, male or female*

A. *Original state of:*
Created for God's
pleasure and (Is. 43:7   693
glory.........(Rev. 4:11   1296
Created by
God..........Gen. 1:26, 27   4
Made in God's
image........Gen. 9:6   11
Formed of
dust..........Gen. 2:7   5
Made upright ..Eccl. 7:29   643
Endowed with
intelli-   (Gen. 2:19, 20   5
gence.....(Col. 3:10   1201
Wonderfully
made ....Ps. 139:14-16   600
Given wide
dominion .....Gen. 1:28   5

From one......Acts 17:26-28   1114
Male and
female ....Gen. 1:27   4
Superior to
animals ......Matt. 10:31   973
Living being
(soul) ....Gen. 2:7   5

B. *Sinful state of:*
Result of Adam's
disobe-   (Gen. 2:16-17   5
dience ......(Gen. 3:1-6   6
Makes all
sinners........Rom. 5:12   1135
Brings   (Gen. 2:16, 17,
physical   (19   5
death ....(Rom. 5:12-14   1135
Makes spiritually
dead ....Eph. 2:1   1185

C. *Redeemed state of:*
Originates in God's
love..........John 3:16   1066
Provides salvation
for............Titus 2:11   1230
Accomplished by Christ's
death ....1 Pet. 1:18-21   1261
Fulfills the new
covenant......Heb. 8:8-13   1243
Entered by new
birth..........John 3:1-12   1066

D. *Final state of:*
Continues
eternally......Matt. 25:46   990
Cannot be
changed ......Luke 16:26   1047
Determined
by faith or by (John 3:36   1067
unbelief......(2 Thess. 1:6-10   1212

E. *Christ's relation to:*
Gives light
to............John 1:9   1064
Knows nature
of............John 2:25   1066
Took nature
of............Heb. 2:14-16   1240
In the
likeness.......Rom. 8:3   1137
Only Mediator
for............1 Tim. 2:5   1217
Died for ....1 Pet. 1:18-21   1261
Heb. 9:26, 28   1244

F. *Certain aspects of:*
First—Adam ..1 Cor. 15:45, 47   1161
Last—Christ ...1 Cor. 15:45   1161
Natural—unregen-
erate..........1 Cor. 2:14   1150
Outer—
physical.......2 Cor. 4:16   1168
Inner—
spiritual......Rom. 7:22   1137
New—
regenerate ....Eph. 2:15   1186

Man of sin (see Antichrist)

Manaen—*comforter*

Prophet and teacher in church at
Antioch ....Acts 13:1   1108

Manahath—*resting place*

1. Son of
Shobal........Gen. 36:23   36
2. City of exile for sons of
Ehud..........1 Chr. 8:6   395
Citizens of, called Manahath-
ites ....1 Chr. 2:54   389

Manasseh—*making to forget*

1. Joseph's first-born
son ....Gen. 41:50, 51   42
Adopted by
Jacob ....Gen. 48:5, 6   48
Loses his birthright to
Ephraim ......Gen. 48:13-20   48
Ancestor of a
tribe ....Num. 1:34, 35   128
2. Sons of ....Num. 26:28-34   155
Census of......Num. 1:34, 35   128

One half of, desire region in
east Jordan ...Num. 32:33-42   161
Help Joshua against
Canaanites....Josh. 1:12-18   206
Division of, into eastern and
western......Josh. 22:7   225
Region assigned to eastern
half ....Deut. 3:12-15   172
Land assigned to western
half ....Josh. 17:1-13   220
Zelophehad's daughters
included in....Josh. 17:3, 4   220
Question concerning
altar ....Josh. 22:9-34   225
Joshua's challenge
to.............Josh. 17:14-18   221
City (Golan) of refuge
in.............Josh. 20:8   223
Did not drive out
Canaanites....Judg. 1:27, 28   232
Gideon, a member
of.............Judg. 6:15   237
Some of, help
David.........1 Chr. 12:19-31   399
Many defect to
Asa...........2 Chr. 15:9   430
Attend
Passovers .....2 Chr. 30:1-18   443
Idols destroyed
in.............2 Chr. 31:1   444
3. Son and successor of Hezekiah,
king of
Judah.........2 Kin. 21:1   377
Reigns wickedly;
restores   (2 Kin. 21:1-16   377
idolatry ......(2 Chr. 33:1-9   446
Captured and taken to
Babylon.......2 Chr. 33:10, 11   446
Repents and is
restored......2 Chr. 33:12, 13   446
Removes idols and
altars ....2 Chr. 33:14-20   446
5, 6. Two men who put away their
foreign
wives ....Ezra 10:30, 33   462

Mandrake—*a rhubarb-like herb, having
narcotic qualities*

Supposed to
induce human (Gen. 30:14-16   30
fertility..........(Song 7:13   652

Manger—*a feeding place for cattle*

Place of Jesus'
birth ....Luke 2:7, 12   1027
Animals feed
from ....Is. 1:3   657
Figurative of the fruit of the
foolish...........Prov. 14:4   619
Same as "stall"
in ....Luke 13:15   1044

Manliness—*masculine characteristics at
their best*

A. *Qualities of:*
Self-control....1 Cor. 9:25-27   1155
Mature
thinking ......1 Cor. 14:20   1159
Courage in   (2 Sam. 10:11,
danger.......(12   303
Suffer
hardship ......2 Tim. 2:3-5   1224

B. *Examples of:*
Caleb..........Num. 13:30   142
Joshua........Josh. 1:1-11   206
Jonathan ......1 Sam. 14:1, 6-14   273
Daniel.........Dan. 6:1-28   842

Manna—*what is it?*

A. *Features regarding:*
Description
of............Num. 11:7-9   139
Bread given   (Ex. 16:4, 15   68
by God......(John 6:30-32   1071
Previously
unknown .....Deut. 8:3, 16   177
Fell at
evening......Num. 11:9   139
Despised by
people ....Num. 11:4-6   139

SUBJECT   REFERENCE   PAGE | SUBJECT   REFERENCE   PAGE | SUBJECT   REFERENCE   PAGE

Woman with
hemorrhage ⎰Matt. 9:20-22   971
healed   ⎱Mark 5:25-34   1004
(Capernaum).....Luke 8:43-48   1037
Blind men cured
(Capernaum).....Matt. 9:27-31   971
Dumb spirit cast out
(Capernaum).....Matt. 9:32, 33   972
Five   ⎰Matt. 14:15-21   978
thousand   ⎱Mark 6:35-44   1006
fed (Lower   Luke 9:10-17   1037
Galilee).........John 6:1-14   1070
Walking on the ⎰Matt. 14:25-33   978
sea (Lower   ⎱Mark 6:48-52   1006
Galilee).........John 6:15-21   1070
Syrophoenician's daughter
healed (District ⎰Matt. 15:21-28   979
of Tyre)....... ⎱Mark 7:24-30   1007
Four thousand
fed (Lower   ⎰Matt. 15:32-39   979
Galilee)....... ⎱Mark 8:1-9   1007
Deaf and dumb man cured
(Lower Galilee)..Mark 7:31-37   1007
Blind man healed
(Bethsaida).......Mark 8:22-26   1008
Demon cast out ⎰Matt. 17:14-18   981
of boy (near   ⎱Mark 9:14-29   1009
Caesarea) ....Luke 9:37-43   1038
Tribute money provided
(Capernaum)....Matt. 17:24-27   981
Passed unseen through crowd (in
Temple).........John 8:59   1075
Ten lepers cleansed
(Samaria) ....Luke 17:11-19   1048
Man born blind, healed
(Jerusalem)......John 9:1-7   1075
Lazarus raised from dead
(Bethany) ....John 11:38-44   1078
Woman with sickness cured
(Peraea).....Luke 13:11-17   1044
Man with dropsy cured
(Peraea).........Luke 14:1-6   1045
Two blind   ⎰Matt. 20:29-34   984
men cured   ⎱Mark 10:46-52   1012
(Jericho) ....Luke 18:35-43   1050
Fig tree withered ⎰Matt. 21:18-22   985
(Mt. Olivet)..... ⎱Mark 11:12-14   1012
Malchus' ear healed
(Gethsemane)...Luke 22:50, 51   1055
Second net full of fishes
(Lower Galilee)...John 21:1-14   1088
Resurrection of ⎰Luke 24:6   1057
Christ .... ⎱John 10:18   1077

*Appearances of Christ after His
resurrection, to:*
Mary Magdalene
(Jerusalem)......Mark 16:9   1020
Other women
(Jerusalem)......Matt. 28:9   995
Two disciples
(Emmaus).......Luke 24:15-31   1058
Peter
(Jerusalem)......1 Cor. 15:5   1160
Ten apostles, Thomas absent
(Jerusalem)......John 20:19, 24   1087
Eleven apostles, Thomas present
(Jerusalem)......John 20:26-28   1088
Seven disciples fishing
(Lower Galilee)...John 21:1-24   1088
Eleven apostles
(Galilee).........Matt. 28:16, 17   995
Five hundred
brethren.........1 Cor. 15:6   1160
James............1 Cor. 15:7   1160
Eleven apostles on day of His
ascension
(Bethany) ....Acts 1:2-9   1094
Paul at his   ⎰Acts 9:1-5   1104
conversion .....⎱1 Cor. 15:8   1160

Those associated with Peter:
Lame man cured..Acts 3:6   1097
Death of Ananias and
Sapphira ....Acts 5:5, 10   1099
Sick healed .....Acts 5:15   1099
Aeneas healed of
paralysis ....Acts 9:34   1105
Dorcas restored to
life ....Acts 9:40   1105

His release from
prison.........Acts 12:7-11   1107
Those associated with Paul:
His sight   ⎰Acts 9:17, 18   1104
restored   ⎱Acts 22:12, 13   1120
Elymas blinded....Acts 13:11   1108
Lame man cured..Acts 14:10   1110
Slave-girl freed of ⎰Acts 16:18   1113
evil spirits...... ⎱Acts 19:11, 12   1116
Earthquake at
Philippi.........Acts 16:25, 26   1113
Evil spirits overcame Sceva's seven
sons.............Acts 19:13-16   1116
Eutychus restored to
life ....Acts 20:10   1117
Unharmed by viper's
bite ....Acts 28:5   1126
Publius' father
healed...........Acts 28:8   1126

*Other miracles of the New
Testament:*
Outpouring of the Holy
Spirit............Acts 2:1-14   1095
Gift of tongues...Acts 2:3, 4, 11   1095
                  Acts 10:46   1106
                  Acts 19:6   1116
Apostles freed ⎰Acts 5:19   1099
from prison.....⎱Acts 12:7-11   1107
Agabus'   ⎰Acts 11:28   1107
prophesies.....⎱Acts 21:11   1118
Visions: ⎰Matt. 17:2   980
Three apostles' ...⎱Luke 9:32   1038

Of Christ, by dying:
Stephen........Acts 7:55, 56   1102
Ananias' ....Acts 9:10   1104
Peter's ....Acts 10:1-48   1105
                  Acts 11:1-30   1106
Cornelius'.........Acts 10:3, 4,
                  30-32   1105
Paul's.............Acts 16:9   1112
                  2 Cor. 12:1-5   1173
John's on   ⎰Rev. 1:10   1294
Patmos.......... ⎱Rev. 4—22   1296
Miracles by the
seventy..........Luke 10:17   1039
Stephen performed great
miracles.........Acts 6:8   1100
Philip cast out unclean
spirits ....Acts 8:6-13   1103

Miracles pretended, or false

Egyptian   ⎰Ex. 7:11-22   59
magicians ......⎱Ex. 8:18, 19   60
In support of false
religions.........Deut. 13:1-3   181
Spirit medium of
En-dor ....1 Sam. 28:9-12   288
False prophets ....Matt. 7:22, 23   969
                  Matt. 24:24   988
False christs ......Matt. 24:24   988
Deceive the   ⎰Rev. 13:13   1301
ungodly .... ⎱Rev. 19:20   1306
Sign of   ⎰2 Thess. 2:3, 9   1212
apostasy........⎱Rev. 13:13   1301

Mire—*deep mud*

A. *Places of:*
Cistern ....Jer. 38:22   757
Streets.........Is. 10:6   666
B. *Figurative of:*
Affliction ......Job 30:19   514
External
prosperity....Job 8:11   500
Insecurity .....Is. 57:20   705
Subjection.....2 Sam. 22:43   317
Plentifulness...Zech. 9:3   922

Miriam—*obstinacy (stubbornness)*

1. Sister of Aaron and
Moses.........Num. 26:59   156
Chosen by God; called a
prophetess.....Ex. 15:20   67
Leads in victory
song.........Ex. 15:20, 21   67
Punished for
rebellion ......Num. 12:1-16   140

Buried at
Kadesh ......Num. 20:1   148
2. Judahite.......1 Chr. 4:17   390

Mirmah—*deceit*

Benjamite.........1 Chr. 8:10   395

Mirror

In the
tabernacle........Ex. 38:8   89
Of molten
bronze ....Job 37:18   519
Used   ⎰2 Cor. 3:18   1167
figura-   ⎱James 1:23, 25   1253
tively..........⎱1 Cor. 13:12   1158
See Glass

Miscarriage—*premature ejection of a
fetus from the mother's womb,
resulting in the death of the fetus*

Wished for........Job 3:16   497
                  Eccl. 6:3   641
Against the
wicked ....Ps. 58:8   557

Miscegenation—*intermarriage of
different races*

A. *Restrictions in Law
of Moses........Ex. 34:12-16   85
B. Notable examples:*
Moses ....Num. 12:1-10   140
Ruth ....Matt. 1:5   963
C. *Unity of all races:*
Descended   ⎰Gen. 3:20   7
from Adam...⎱Rom. 5:12   1135
From one.......Acts 17:26   1114
D. *Christian marriage:*
Spiritual
basis..........Matt. 19:6   982
In the Lord ....2 Cor. 6:14   1169
                  1 Cor. 7:39   1154

Miser—*a covetous man*

A. *Characteristics of:*
Selfish ....Eccl. 4:8   640
Greed...........Luke 12:15   1042
Divided
loyalty ....Matt. 6:24   968
B. *Punishment of:*
Dissatis-
faction ....Eccl. 5:10   641
Loss ....Matt. 6:19   968
Pang ....1 Tim. 6:10   1220
Destruction...Ps. 52:5, 7   555
C. *Examples of:*
Rich fool .....Luke 12:16-21   1042
Rich ruler ....Luke 18:18-23   1049
Ananias and
Sapphira......Acts 5:1-11   1098

Miserable—*the wretched*

A. *State of:*
Wicked........Rom. 3:12-16   1133
Trapped ....Rom. 7:24   1137
Lost ....Luke 13:25-28   1044
B. *Caused by:*
Forgetfulness of
God...........Is. 22:12-14   675
Ignorance .....Luke 19:42-44   1051

Misfortune—*an unexpected adversity*

Explained by the
nations..........Deut. 29:24-28   196
Misunderstood by
Gideon ....Judg. 6:13   237
Understood by
David ....2 Sam. 16:5-13   309
Caused by sin.....Is. 59:1, 2   706

Mishael—*who is like God?*

1. Kohathite
Levite.........Ex. 6:22   59
Removes dead
bodies.........Lev. 10:4, 5   103
2. Hebrew name of
Meshach.....Dan. 1:6-19   835
3. One of Ezra's
assistants .....Neh. 8:4   474

SUBJECT	REFERENCE	PAGE	SUBJECT	REFERENCE	PAGE	SUBJECT	REFERENCE	PAGE

Mishal

Town in Asher .... Josh. 19:24, 26   222
Assigned to
Levites .... Josh. 21:30   224
Called Mashal ..... 1 Chr. 6:74   393

Misham—*swift*

Son of Elpaal ..... 1 Chr. 8:12   395

Mishma—*hearing*

1. Son of   {Gen. 25:13, 14   25
   Ishmael .. {1 Chr. 1:30   388
2. Descendant of
   Simeon .... 1 Chr. 4:25   391

Mishmannah—*fatness*

One of David's Gadite
warriors .... 1 Chr. 12:10   399

Mishraites

Family living in Kiriath-
jearim .... 1 Chr. 2:53   389

Mispar—*writing*

Exile returnee ..... Ezra 2:2   454
Called
Mispereth .... Neh. 7:7   472

Misrephoth-maim—*burning of waters*

Haven of fleeing
Canaanites .... Josh. 11:8   216
Near the
Sidonians .... Josh. 13:6   217

Missionaries—*those sent out to spread
the Gospel*

Jonah .... Jon. 3:2, 3   886
The early
church .... Acts 8:4   1103
Philip .... Acts 8:5   1103
Some from Cyrene become
missionaries ...... Acts 11:20   1107
Paul and
Barnabas .... Acts 13:1-4   1108
Peter .... Acts 15:7   1111
Apollos .... Acts 18:24   1116
Noah .... 2 Pet. 2:5   1268

Mission of Christ

Do God's will ..... John 6:38   1071
Save sinners ...... Luke 19:10   1050
Bring in everlasting
righteousness .... Dan. 9:24   847
Destroy Satan's   {Heb. 2:14   1240
works .... {1 John 3:8   1276
Fulfill the Old
Testament .... Matt. 5:17   967
Give life .... John 10:10, 28   1076
Stop sacrifices ..... Dan. 9:27   847
Complete
revelation .... Heb. 1:3   1239

Missions

A. *Commands concerning:*
  "Shall be" .... Matt. 24:14   988
  "Go" .... Matt. 28:18-20   995
  "Stay" .... Luke 24:49   1059
  "Come" .... Acts 16:9   1112
B. *Motives prompting:*
  God's love ..... John 3:16   1066
  Christ's love .. 2 Cor. 5:14, 15   1168
  Mankind's
  need .... Rom. 3:9-31   1133
C. *Equipment for:*
  Word .... Rom. 10:14, 15   1140
  Spirit .... Acts 1:8   1094
  Prayer .... Acts 13:1-4   1108

Mist—*a vapor (physical and spiritual)*

Physical (vapor)... Gen. 2:6   5
Spiritual
(blindness) ...... Acts 13:11   1108
Eternal
(darkness) .... 2 Pet. 2:17   1269

Mistake—*an error arising from human
weakness*

Causes of:
Motives
misunderstood .... Josh. 22:9-29   225
Appearance
misjudged .... 1 Sam. 1:13-15   263
Trust misplaced ... Josh. 9:3-27   213

Mistress—*a married woman*

Over a maid ...... Gen. 16:4, 8, 9   17
Figurative of
Nineveh .... Nah. 3:4   899

Misunderstandings—*disagreements
among*

Israelites .... Josh. 22:9-29   225
Christ's disciples .. Matt. 20:20-27   984
Apostles .... Gal. 2:11-15   1178
Christians .... Acts 6:1   1100

Mithkah—*sweetness*

Israelite
encampment ..... Num. 33:28, 29   162

Mithnite

Descriptive of Joshaphat, David's
officer .... 1 Chr. 11:43   398

Mithredath—*consecrated to Mithra*

1. Treasurer of
  Cyrus .... Ezra 1:8   454
2. Persian
  official .... Ezra 4:7   456

Mitylene—*a city on the island of Lesbos*

Visited by Paul.... Acts 20:13-15   1117

Mix (see Mingle; Miscegenation)

Mizar—*small*

Hill east of
Jordan .... Ps. 42:6   549

Mizpah, Mizpeh—*watchtower*

1. Site of covenant between Jacob
  and Laban .... Gen. 31:44-53   32
2. Town in Gilead; probably same
  as 1 .... Judg. 10:17   243
  Jephthah's   {Judg. 11:11, 29,
  home .... {   34   243
  Probably same as Ramath-
  mizpeh .... Josh. 13:26   218
3. Region near Mt.
  Hermon .... Josh. 11:3, 8   215
4. Town in
  Judah .... Josh. 15:1, 38   218
5. Place in Moab; David brings his
  parents to..... 1 Sam. 22:3, 4   283
6. Town of
  Benjamin ..... Josh. 18:21, 26   222
  Outraged Israelites gather
  here .... Judg. 20:1, 3   251
  Samuel
  gathers   {1 Sam. 7:5-16   268
  Israel .... {1 Sam. 10:17-25   271
  Built by Asa ... 1 Sam. 15:22   276
  Residence of
  Gedaliah ...... 2 Kin. 25:23, 25   383
  Home of exile
  returnees ..... Neh. 3:7, 15, 19   468

Mizraim— *Egypt*

1. Son of Ham; ancestor of Ludim,
  Anamim,
  etc. .... 1 Chr. 1:8, 11   387
2. Hebrew name for
  Egypt .... Gen. 50:11   50
  Called the land of
  Ham .... Ps. 105:23, 27   583

Mizzah—*fear*

Grandson of Esau; a chief of
Edom .... Gen. 36:13, 17   36

Mnason

Christian of Cyprus and Paul's
host .... Acts 21:16   1119

Moab—*seed*

1. Son of Lot ..... Gen. 19:33-37   20
2. Country of the
  Moabites ...... Deut. 1:5   169

Moabites—*inhabitants of Moab*

A. *History of:*
  Descendants of
  Lot .... Gen. 19:36, 37   20
  Became a great
  nation .... Num. 21:28, 30   150
  Governed by   {Num. 23:7   152
  kings .... {Josh. 24:9   227
  Driven out of their territory by
  Amorites ...... Num. 21:26   150
  Refused to let Israel
  pass .... Judg. 11:17, 18   243
  Joined Midian to curse
  Israel .... Num. 22:4   151
  Excluded from
  Israel .... Deut. 23:3-6   189
  Friendly relation with
  Israel .... Ruth 1:1, 4, 16   256
  Defeated by
  Saul .... 1 Sam. 14:47   275
  Refuge for David's
  parents .... 1 Sam. 22:3, 4   283
  Defeated by
  David .... 2 Sam. 8:2, 12   301
  Solomon married
  women of .... 1 Kin. 11:1, 3   336
  Paid tribute to
  Israel .... 2 Kin. 3:4   357
  Fought Israel and
  Judah .... 2 Kin. 3:5-7   357
  Conquered by Israel and
  Judah .... 2 Kin. 3:8-27   357
  Intermarried   {Ezra 9:1, 2   461
  with Jews.... {Neh. 13:23   480
B. *Characteristics of:*
  Idolatrous .... 1 Kin. 11:7   336
  Wealthy ...... Jer. 48:1, 7   764
  Super-
  stitious .... Jer. 27:3, 9   744
  Satisfied ...... Jer. 48:11   764
  Proud .... Jer. 48:29   765
C. *Prophecies concerning their:*
  Desolation .... Is. 15:1-9   670
  Ruin and
  destruction.... Jer. 27:3, 8   744
  Punishment... Amos 2:1-3   872
  Subjection .... Is. 11:14   668

Mob—*a lawless crowd*

Caused Pilate to pervert
justice .... Matt. 27:20-25   993
Made unjust
charges .... Acts 17:5-9   1114
Paul saved from... Acts 21:27-40   1119

Mocking—*imitating in fun or derision*

A. *Evil agents of:*
  Young lads ... 2 Kin. 2:23   357
  Men of Israel . 2 Chr. 30:10   443
  Men of
  Judah .... 2 Chr. 36:16   450
  Fools .... Prov. 14:9   619
  Wine .... Prov. 20:1   624
  Jews .... Matt. 20:19   984
  Roman
  soldiers ...... Luke 23:36   1057
  False
  teachers ..... Jude 18   1288
B. *Good agents of:*
  Donkey....... Num. 22:29   151
  Samson....... Judg. 16:10-15   247
  Elijah......... 1 Kin. 18:27   346
  Wisdom
  (God) .... Prov. 1:20, 26   610
  God .... Ps. 2:4   528
C. *Reasons for, to:*
  Show
  unbelief....... 2 Chr. 36:16   450
  Portray
  scorn .... 2 Chr. 30:10   443
  Ridicule ...... Acts 2:13   1095
  Insult........ Gen. 39:14, 17   39

SUBJECT	REFERENCE	PAGE	SUBJECT	REFERENCE	PAGE	SUBJECT	REFERENCE	PAGE

Officers—*men appointed to rule over others*

A. *Descriptive of:*
Magistrate.....Luke 12:58   1043
Deputy.........1 Kin. 4:5, 7   327
Policeman .....John 7:32   1072

B. *Functions of:*
Administer
justice ....Num. 11:16   140

Offices of Christ

As Prophet.......Deut. 18:18, 19   186
Is. 61:1-3   708
As Priest.........Ps. 110:4   587
Is. 53:1-12   701
As King..........2 Sam. 7:12-17   301
Luke 1:32, 33   1025

Offscouring—*something vile or worthless*

Jews thus
described........Lam. 3:45   780

Offset—*a supporting ledge*

For the beams of the
Temple...........1 Kin. 6:6   329

Offspring—*issue (physical or spiritual)*

A. *Used literally of:*
Set apart   (Ex. 13:12   65
every ....(Ex. 34:19   86
Of a donkey
you shall   (Ex. 13:13   65
redeem.......(Ex. 34:20   86
Man's issue
(children) .....Job 5:25   499
Man as created by
God...........Acts 17:28, 29   1115
Christ as a descendant of
David.........Rev. 22:16   1308

B. *Used figuratively of:*
True believer . .Is. 22:24   675
New Israel....Is. 44:3-5   693
Gentile
church........Is. 61:9   709
True Church..Is. 65:23   712

Og—*giant*

Amorite king of
Bashan....Deut. 3:1, 8   171
Extent of rule.....Deut. 3:8, 10   171
Residences at Ashtaroth and
Edrei.............Josh. 12:4   216
Man of great
size ....Deut. 3:11   171
Defeated and killed by
Israel............Num. 21:32-35   150
Territory of, assigned to
Manasseh ....Deut. 3:13   172
Memory of, long
remembered......Ps. 135:11   598

Ohad—*powerful*

Son of Simeon ....Gen. 46:10   46

Ohel—*family*

Son of
Zerubbabel.......1 Chr. 3:19, 20   390

Oholah—*her tent*

Symbolic name   (Ezek. 23:4, 5, 36,
of Samaria ......(44   805

Oholiab—*father's tent*

Danite who built the
tabernacle........Ex. 31:6   82

Oholibah—*my tent is in her*

Symbolic name of
Jerusalem and   (Ezek. 23:4, 11,
Judah ....(22, 36   805

Oholibamah—*tent of the high place*

1. A wife of   (Gen. 36:2, 18,
Esau.........(25   36
Called
Judith........Gen. 26:34   27
2. Edomite
chief.........Gen. 36:41   37

Oil—*a liquid extracted from olives*

A. *Features concerning:*
Given by
God..........Ps. 104:14, 15   582
Subject to
tithing ....Deut. 12:17   181

B. *Uses of:*
Food ....Num. 11:8   139
Anointing......1 Sam. 10:1   270
Illumination ..Ex. 30:26-32   82
Ex. 25:6   76
Matt. 25:3-8   989
Beautifi-
cation.........Ruth 3:3   257
Perfume........Eccl. 10:1   644

C. *Types of oil:*
Anointing......Ex. 25:6   76
Clear ....Ex. 27:20   78
Baking.........Ex. 29:23   80
Beaten.........Ex. 29:40   81
Olive ....Ex. 30:24   82
Fresh..........Num. 18:12   147
Precious ....2 Kin. 20:13   377
Perfumer's.....Eccl. 10:1   644
Purified.......Song 1:3   648
Golden ....Zech. 4:12   920

D. *Figurative of:*
Prosperity .....Deut. 32:13   199
Joy and
gladness ......Is. 61:3   708
Waste-
fulness ....Prov. 21:17   625
Brotherly
love..........Ps. 133:2   598
Real grace....Matt. 25:4   989
Holy Spirit....1 John 2:20, 27   1275

Old—*mature; ancient*

A. *Descriptive of:*
Age............Gen. 25:8   25
Mature
person ....1 Kin. 12:6-13   338
Experienced ...Ezek. 23:43   806
Ancient
times ....Mal. 3:4   931
Old Testament
age ....Matt. 5:21-33   967
Old covenant ..2 Cor. 3:14   1167
Unregenerate
nature ....Rom. 6:6   1135

B. *Of man's age, infirmities of:*
Waning sexual
desire.........Luke 1:18   1025
Physical
handicaps.....1 Kin. 1:1, 15   323
Failing
strength ......Ps. 71:9   564

C. *Of man's age, dangers of:*
Spiritual
decline........1 Kin. 11:4   336
Not receiving
instruction....Eccl. 4:13   640
Disrespect
toward........Deut. 28:50   194

D. *Of man's age, blessing of:*
God's care.....Is. 46:4   696
Continued
fruitfulness....Ps. 92:14   577
Security of
faith ....Prov. 22:6   625
Fulfillment of life's
goals..........Is. 65:20   712
Honor ....Lev. 19:32   114
Grand-
children......Prov. 17:6   622
Men dream
dreams.......Acts 2:17   1095
See Length of life

Old Testament

A. *Characteristics of:*
Inspired ......2 Tim. 3:16   1225
Authorita-
tive ....John 10:34, 35   1077
Written by the Holy
Spirit ....Heb. 3:7   1240

Uses many figurative
expressions ...Is. 55:1, 12, 13   703
Written for our
instruction....1 Cor. 10:1-11   1155
Israel now blinded
to.............2 Cor. 3:14-16   1167
Foreshadows the
New ....Heb. 9:1-28   1244

B. *With the New Testament, unified in:*
Authorship ....Heb. 1:1   1239
Plan of
salvation......1 Pet. 1:9-12   1260
Presenting Christ (see Messiah,
the)..........Luke 24:25-44   1058

Olive grove

Freely given .....Josh. 24:13   227
Taken in greed....2 Kin. 5:20, 26   360

Olive tree

A. *Used for:*
Oil of, many uses
(see Oil)......Ex. 27:20   78
Temple
furniture......1 Kin. 6:23   330
Temple construc-
tion...........1 Kin. 6:31-33   330
Booths.........Neh. 8:15   474

B. *Cultivation of:*
By grafting ....Rom. 11:24   1141
Hindered by
disease........Deut. 28:40   194
Failure of, a great
calamity ......Hab. 3:17, 18   905
Poor provided
for............Deut. 24:20   191
Palestine suitable
for............Deut. 6:11   175

C. *Figuratively of:*
Peace..........Gen. 8:11   10
Kingship.......Judg. 9:8, 9   241
Israel.........Jer. 11:16   730
The
righteous .....Ps. 52:8   555
Fruitful
people ....Is. 17:6   672
Gentile
believers......Rom. 11:17, 14   1140
True Church...Rom. 11:17, 24   1140
Prophetic   (Zech. 4:3, 11,
symbols   (12   920

Olives, Mount of

A. *Described as:*
"The Mount of
Olives".........Zech. 14:4   925
"The mountain which
is east of
Jerusalem"....1 Kin. 11:7   336
"The mount of destruc-
tion" ....2 Kin. 23:13   380
"The hills"....Neh. 8:15   474

B. *Scene of:*
David's flight ..2 Sam. 15:30   309
Solomon's
idolatry ....2 Kin. 23:13   380
Ezekiel's
vision.........Ezek. 11:23   794
Postexilic
festivities .....Neh. 8:15   474
Zechariah's
prophecy......Zech. 14:4   925
Triumphal
entry..........Matt. 21:1   984
Weeping.......Luke 19:37, 41   1051
Great prophetic
discourse......Matt. 24:3   988
Ascension .....Acts 1:12   1094

Olympas

Christian in
Rome ....Rom. 16:15   1145

Omar—*eloquent*

Grandson of   (Gen. 36:11, 15   36
Esau ....(1 Chr. 1:36   388

SUBJECT	REFERENCE	PAGE

Sanctuary—with
gold..............1 Kin. 6:21 — 330
Cherubim—with
gold..............1 Kin. 6:28 — 330
Earthen vessel—with
silver dross......Prov. 26:23 — 630
Images—with
silver............Is. 30:22 — 682

Overseer—*a leader or supervisor*
Kinds of:
Prime minister....Gen. 39:4, 5 — 39
Managers.........Gen. 41:34 — 41
Elders............Acts 20:17, 28 — 1118

Overwork—*too much work*
Complaint of
Israelites........Ex. 5:6-21 — 58
Solution of, for
Moses...........Ex. 18:14-26 — 70

Owe—*an obligation of*
Financial debt.....Matt. 18:24, 28 — 982
Moral debt.......Philem. 18, 19 — 1234
Spiritual debt.....Rom. 13:8 — 1142

Owl—*a large-eyed bird of prey*
Varieties of, all
unclean..........Lev. 11:13-17 — 104
Solitary in habit...Ps. 102:6 — 580

Ownership—*title of possession*
A. *By men, acquired by:*
Purchase......Gen. 23:16-18 — 23
Inheritance....Luke 15:12 — 1046
Covenant......Gen. 26:25-33 — 26
B. *By God, of:*
World.........Ps. 24:1 — 539
Souls of men..Ezek. 18:4 — 800
Redeemed.....1 Cor. 6:19, 20 — 1153

Ox
A. *Uses of:*
Pulling covered
carts...........Num. 7:3 — 134
Plowing.......1 Kin. 19:19 — 347
Food..........Deut. 14:4 — 182
Sacrifice......Ex. 20:24 — 72
Means of
existence......Job 24:3 — 511
Designs in
Temple........1 Kin. 7:25 — 331
B. *Laws concerning:*
To rest on
Sabbath.......Ex. 23:12 — 74
Not to be:
Worked with a
donkey.......Deut. 22:10 — 189
Muzzled while
threshing....Deut. 25:4 — 191
To be
restored......Ex. 22:4, 9-13 — 73
C. *Figurative of:*
Easy victory...Num. 22:4 — 151
Youthful
rashness......Prov. 7:22 — 614
Sumptuous
living.......Prov. 15:17 — 620
Preach the
Gospel......Is. 32:20 — 683
Minister's
support.......1 Cor. 9:9, 10 — 1155
D. *Descriptive of:*
Of great
strength.....Num. 23:22 — 152
Very wild and
ferocious.....Job 39:9-12 — 521
Frisky in
youth........Ps. 29:6 — 541

Oxgoad—*spike used to drive oxen*
As a weapon.....Judg. 3:31 — 235

Ozem—*anger*
1. Son of Jesse...1 Chr. 2:13, 15 — 389
2. Descendant of
Judah........1 Chr. 2:25 — 389

Ozni—*gives ear*
Son of Gad and head of a
family..........Num. 26:15, 16 — 155
Called Ezbon......Gen. 46:16 — 46

P

Paarai—*devotee of Peor*
One of David's mighty
men..............2 Sam. 23:35 — 318
Called Naarai.....1 Chr. 11:37 — 398

Pacification—*causing anger to rest*
A. *Means of:*
Gift............Prov. 21:14 — 625
Wise man.....Prov. 16:14 — 621
Yielding.......Eccl. 10:4 — 644
B. *Examples of:*
Esau, by
Jacob.........Gen. 32:11-19 — 33
Lord, toward His
people........Ezek. 16:63 — 799
Ahasuerus, by Haman's
death........Esth. 7:10 — 489

Pack animals
Used by
Israelites.........1 Chr. 12:40 — 400

Paddan-aram—*the plain of Aram*
(Mesopotamia)
Home of Isaac's
wife.............Gen. 25:20 — 25
Jacob flees to.....Gen. 28:2-7 — 28
Jacob returns
from.............Gen. 31:17, 18 — 31
Same as
Mesopotamia.....Gen. 24:10 — 23
People of, called
Arameans......Gen. 31:24 — 32
Language of, called
Aramaic.........2 Kin. 18:26 — 375
See Aramaic

Padon—*ransom*
Head of Temple   ⎰Ezra 2:44 — 455
servants........⎱Neh. 7:47 — 472

Pagan gods
A. *Mentioned:*
Molech........Lev. 18:21 — 113
Chemosh.....Judg. 11:24 — 244
Dagon.........Judg. 16:23 — 248
Baal...........2 Kin. 17:16 — 373
Nergal.........2 Kin. 17:30 — 373
Succoth-
benoth........2 Kin. 17:30 — 373
Ashima........2 Kin. 17:30 — 373
Nibhaz........2 Kin. 17:31 — 373
Tartak........2 Kin. 17:31 — 373
Adram-
melech........2 Kin. 17:31 — 373
Anam-
melech........2 Kin. 17:31 — 373
Nisroch.......Is. 37:38 — 688
Zeus...........Acts 14:12 — 1110
Hermes.......Acts 14:12 — 1110
Greek
Pantheon.....Acts 17:16-23 — 1114
Artemis......Acts 19:23-37 — 1116
B. *Worship of condemned:*
By Law........Ex. 20:3, 4 — 71
Deut. 5:7 — 174
By apostolic
command.....1 Cor. 10:14 — 1156

Pagans—*an irreligious people*
Slaves from.......Lev. 25:44 — 120
Non-Israelite
nations..........Deut. 4:26-28 — 173
Zion prevails
over..............Mic. 4:11-13 — 893
Greeks and
barbarians.......Rom. 1:14 — 1131

Wrath of God
against...........Rom. 1:17-32 — 1132
Descriptive of
unbelievers.......1 Cor. 12:2 — 1157
Called the "uncircum-
cision"..........Eph. 2:11, 12 — 1186
Reconciled to
God..............Eph. 2:11, 16 — 1186

Pagiel—*God meets*
Son of Ochran, chief of Asher's
tribe..............Num. 1:13 — 127

Pahath-moab—*governor of Moab*
Family of postexilic
returnees........Ezra 2:6 — 454
Members of, divorced foreign
wives...........Ezra 10:19, 30 — 462
One of, signs
document........Neh. 10:1, 14 — 477
Hasshub, one of, helps
Nehemiah........Neh. 3:11 — 468

Pain—*physical or mental suffering*
A. *Kinds of:*
Childbirth.....Rev. 12:2 — 1300
Physical
fatigue........2 Cor. 11:27 — 1173
Physical
afflictions.....Job 33:19 — 516
Mental
disturbance...Ps. 55:4 — 555
B. *Characteristics of:*
Affects face....Joel 2:6 — 866
Means of
chastening....Job 15:20 — 505
Affects the whole
person........Jer. 4:19 — 722
Common to all
men...........Rom. 8:22 — 1138
C. *Remedies for:*
Balm..........Jer. 51:8 — 770
Prayer........Ps. 25:17, 18 — 539
God's
deliverance....Acts 2:24 — 1095
Heaven.......Rev. 21:4 — 1307
D. *Figurative of:*
Mental
anguish.......Ps. 48:6 — 552
Impending
trouble........Jer. 22:23 — 740
Distressing
news..........Is. 21:2, 3 — 674
Israel's
captivity......Is. 26:17, 18 — 678

Paint—*to apply liquid colors*
Applied to a roomy
house...........Jer. 22:14 — 739
Used by women...2 Kin. 9:30 — 365
Used especially   ⎰Jer. 4:30 — 722
by prostitutes...⎱Ezek. 23:40 — 806

Paintings
Of Chaldeans (bas-
reliefs)..........Ezek. 23:14 — 806
Of animals and idols (on a
secret wall).....Ezek. 8:7-12 — 791

Pair—*two*
Branches.........Ex. 25:35 — 76
Donkeys.........Judg. 19:3 — 250
Oxen.............1 Kin. 19:21 — 347
Sheep............Is. 7:21 — 664
Scales............Is. 40:12 — 689
Sandals..........Amos 2:6 — 872
Turtledoves.....Luke 2:24 — 1027
Horsemen.......Is. 21:7, 9 — 674

Palace—*a royal building*
A. *Descriptive of:*
King's
residence......2 Chr. 9:11 — 426
Foreign city...Is. 25:2 — 677
Dwellings in
Zion..........Ps. 48:3 — 552

SUBJECT	REFERENCE	PAGE	SUBJECT	REFERENCE	PAGE	SUBJECT	REFERENCE	PAGE

Partiality—continued

B. *Inconsistent with:*
Household
harmony......Gen. 37:4-35   37
Justice in
law..........Lev. 19:15   113
Favoritism in:
Ministry.......1 Tim. 5:21   1220
Spiritual
things........2 Cor. 5:16   1168
Restriction of
salvation......Acts 10:28-35   1106

C. *Consistent with:*
Choice of
workers......Acts 15:36-40   1112
Estimate of
friends.......Phil. 2:19-22   1194
God's predes-
tination.......Rom. 9:6-24   1138
See Favoritism

Partner—*an associate in*

Crime............Prov. 29:24   632
Business.........Luke 5:7, 10   1031
Christian work....2 Cor. 8:23   1171
Philem. 17   1234

Partridge—*a wild bird meaning "the caller" (in Heb.)*

Hunted in
mountains........1 Sam. 26:20   287
Figurative of ill-gotten
fortune...........Jer. 17:11   735

Paruah—*sprouting*

Father of Jehoshaphat, an officer of
Solomon.........1 Kin. 4:17   328

Parvaim

Unidentified place providing gold
for Solomon's
Temple............2 Chr. 3:6   421

Pasach—*divider*

Asherite..........1 Chr. 7:33   395

Pasdammim—*boundary of bloodshed*

Philistines gathered
here...............1 Chr. 11:13   398

Paseah—*lame*

1. Judahite.......1 Chr. 4:12   390
2. Head of a family of Temple
servants.......Ezra 2:43, 49   455
One of, repairs
walls..........Neh. 3:6   468
3. A family of Temple
servants.......Neh. 7:46, 51   472

Pashhur—*free*

1. Official
opposing   {Jer. 21:1   738
Jeremiah.....{Jer. 38:1-13   756
Descendants of,
returnees.....Neh. 11:12   478
2. Priest who put Jeremiah in
jail...........Jer. 20:1-6   737
3. Father of Gedaliah, Jeremiah's
opponent.....Jer. 38:1   756
4. Priestly family of
returnees.....Ezra 2:38   454
Members of, divorced foreign
wives.........Ezra 10:22   462
5. Priest who signs the
document....Neh. 10:3   477
Blocked by burial
ground.......Ezek. 39:11   821
Stripped.......Mic. 2:8   891
Simon of
Cyrene.......Mark 15:21   1019

Passing away—*ceasing to exist*

A. *Things subject to:*
Our days.....Ps. 90:9   576
Old things.....2 Cor. 5:17   1168
World's from ..1 Cor. 7:31   1154
World's lust...1 John 2:17   1275
Heaven and
earth.........2 Pet. 3:10   1269

B. *Things not subject to:*
Christ's
words........Luke 21:33   1053
Christ's
dominion.....Dan. 7:14   844

Passion—*suffering*

A. *Descriptive of:*
Christ's
sufferings.....Acts 1:3   1094
Man's nature ..James 5:17   1256
Lusts.........Rom. 1:26   1132

B. *As applied (theologically) to*
Christ's sufferings:
Predicted......Is. 53:1-12   701
Portrayed
visibly........Mark 14:3-8   1016
Preached.....Acts 3:12-18   1097
1 Pet. 1:10-12   1260

Passover—*a Jewish festival*
commemorative of the exodus from
Egypt

A. *Features concerning:*
Commemorative of the tenth
plague........Ex. 12:3-28   63
Necessity of blood
applied........Ex. 12:7   63
To be repeated
annually.....Ex. 12:24-27   64

B. *Observances of:*
At Sinai.......Num. 9:1-14   137
At the
conquest.....Josh. 5:10-12   209
By Christ.....Matt. 26:18, 19   991

C. *Typical of the Lord's death (the*
Lord's Supper):
Lamb unblem-
ished.........1 Pet. 1:19   1261
One of their   {Ex. 12:5   63
own...........{Heb. 2:14, 17   1240
Lamb   {Ex. 12:3   63
chosen........{1 Pet. 2:4   1261
Slain at God's
appointed   {Ex. 12:6   63
time..........{Acts 2:23   1095
Christ is.......1 Cor. 5:7   1151
See Lamb of God, the

Password—*a secret word used to*
identify friends

Used by
Gileadites.......Judg. 12:5, 6   244

Pastor—*shepherd*

To equip the
saints...........Eph. 4:11, 12   1187
See Shepherd

Pasture—*a place for grazing animals*

A. *Used literally of:*
Places for:
Cattle to
feed..........Gen. 47:4   47
Wild animals to
feed..........Is. 32:14   683
God's material
blessings.....Ps. 65:11-13   560

B. *Used figuratively of:*
Restoration and
peace........Ezek. 34:13-15   817
True Israel....Ps. 95:7   578
Kingdom of
God..........Is. 49:9, 10   698
Kingdom of
Israel........Jer. 25:36   743
Gospel........Is. 30:23   682
Abundant provision for
salvation.....Ezek. 45:15   828

C. *Of the true Israel (the Church),*
described as:
God's people...Ps. 100:3   580
Provided for ...John 10:9   1076
Purchased.....Ps. 74:1, 2   566
Thankful......Ps. 79:13   570
Scattered by false
shepherds.....Jer. 23:1   740
See Shepherd

Patara—*a port of Lycia in Asia Minor*

Paul changes ships
here..............Acts 21:1, 2   1118

Pate—*the top of the head*

Figurative of
retribution.......Ps. 7:16   530

Path—*a walk; manner of life*

A. *Of the wicked:*
Brought to
nothing.......Job 6:18   499
Becomes
dark..........Job 24:13   511
Is crooked.....Is. 59:8   706
Leads to
death.........Prov. 2:18   610
Filled with
wickedness....Prov. 1:15, 16   609
Is destruc-
tive...........Is. 59:7   706
Followed by wicked
rulers.........Is. 3:12   660
Made difficult by
God...........Hos. 2:6   854

B. *Of believers:*
Beset with
difficulties......Job 19:8   507
Under God's
control........Job 13:27   504
Hindered by the
wicked........Job 30:13   514
Enriched by the
LORD..........Ps. 23:3   538
Upheld by
God...........Ps. 17:5   534
Provided with
light..........Ps. 119:105   593
Known by
God...........Ps. 139:3   600
Like a shining
light..........Prov. 4:18   612
Directed by
God...........Is. 26:7   677
To be
watched......Prov. 4:26   612
No death at the
end...........Prov. 12:28   618
Sometimes
unknown.....Is. 42:16   692
Sometimes seems
crooked......Lam. 3:9   779
To be made
straight.......Heb. 12:13   1248

C. *Of righteousness:*
Taught by
father........Prov. 4:1, 11   611
Kept..........Prov. 2:20   610
Shown to   {Ps. 16:11   534
Messiah.....{Acts 2:28   1096
Taught to
believers.....Ps. 25:4, 5   539
Sought by   {Ps. 119:35   591
believers.....{Is. 2:3   659
Rejected by
unbe-   {Jer. 6:16   724
lieving.......{Jer. 18:15   736

D. *Of the Lord:*
True...........Ps. 25:10   539
Level..........Ps. 27:11   540
Rich...........Ps. 65:11   560
Guarded......Prov. 2:8   610
Upright.......Prov. 2:13   610
Living........Prov. 2:19   610
Peaceful......Prov. 3:17   611

Pathros—*the Southland*

Name applied to South (Upper)
Egypt............Ezek. 29:10-14   812
Described as a lowly
kingdom.......Ezek. 29:14-16   812
Refuge for dispersed
Jews...........Jer. 44:1-15   761
Jews to be regathered
from............Is. 11:11   668
Called Pathrus ....1 Chr. 1:12   387

SUBJECT	REFERENCE	PAGE	SUBJECT	REFERENCE	PAGE	SUBJECT	REFERENCE	PAGE
Paul—continued			Reunited with			Wrote *Second Timothy* from		
Preached in Antioch			Titus in Acts 20:1		1117	Roman 2 Tim. 1:8		1223
(in Pisidia);			Macedonia ...2 Cor. 7:5-16		1169	prison........2 Tim. 4:6-8		1225
rejected by Acts 13:14-51		1109	Wrote *Second Corinthians*; sent			Sent final news and		
Jews.........2 Tim. 3:11		1225	Titus to Corinth with this			greetings......2 Tim. 4:9-22		1225
Rejected in Acts 13:51, 52		1110	letter..........2 Cor. 8:6-18		1170	B. *Missionary methods of:*		
Iconium......Acts 14:1-5		1110	Traveled			Pay his Acts 18:3		1115
Stoned at Acts 14:6-20		1110	exten- Acts 20:2		1117	own Acts 20:33-35		1118
Lystra........2 Tim. 3:11		1225	sively ....Rom. 15:19		1144	way..........2 Cor. 11:7, 9		1172
Went to			Visited Greece and			Preach to the Acts 13:46		1109
Derbe........Acts 14:20, 21		1110	Corinth ......Acts 20:2, 3		1117	Jews first ....Acts 17:1-5		1114
Returned to Antioch (in			Wrote *Romans* in			Establish churches		
Syria)........Acts 14:21-26		1110	Corinth ......Rom. 1:1		1131	in large Acts 19:1-10		1116
Told Christians about his			Returned through			cities........Rom. 1:7-15		1131
work.........Acts 14:27, 28		1111	Macedonia ....Acts 20:3		1117	Travel Acts 15:40		1112
Participated in			Preached long sermon in			with com- Acts 20:4		1117
Jerusalem Acts 15:2-22		1111	Troas ....Acts 20:5-13		1117	panions .....Col. 4:14		1203
Council ......Gal. 2:1-10		1178	Gave farewell talk to Ephesian			Report work to		
Rebuked Peter in Antioch for			elders at			sending Acts 14:26-28		1111
inconsis-			Miletus....Acts 20:14-38		1117	church ......Acts 21:17-20		1119
tency ....Gal. 2:11-21		1178	Arrived in			Use his Roman		
			Caesarea......Acts 21:1-8		1118	citizenship Acts 16:36-39		1113
Second Missionary Journey:			Warned by			when Acts 22:24-29		1120
Rejected John Mark as			Agabus ......Acts 21:9-14		1118	necessary ....Acts 25:10-12		1123
companion; took						Seek to		
Silas ....Acts 15:36-40		1112	*In Jerusalem and Caesarea:*			evangelize Col. 1:23-29		1200
Strengthened churches in Syria			Arrived in Jerusalem; welcomed			the world ....2 Tim. 4:17		1226
and Cilicia ....Acts 15:41		1112	by church.....Acts 21:15-19		1119	C. *Writings of:*		
Revisited Derbe and			Falsely charged; riot			Inspired 2 Cor. 13:3		1174
Lystra ....Acts 16:1		1112	follows.......Acts 21:20-40		1119	by 1 Thess. 2:13		1207
Took Timothy as			Defended his action; removed			God..........2 Tim. 3:15, 16		1225
worker.......Acts 16:1-5		1112	by Roman			Contain difficult		
Directed by the Spirit where to			police........Acts 22:1-30		1119	things.......2 Pet. 3:15, 16		1269
preach ....Acts 16:6, 7		1112	Defended his action before			Written by Gal. 6:11		1181
Responded to Macedonian			Jewish			himself......2 Thess. 3:17		1213
vision.......Acts 16:8, 9		1112	council.......Acts 23:1-10		1120	Sometimes dictated to a		
Joined by Luke			Saved from Jewish plot; taken			scribe ....Rom. 16:22		1145
("we") ....Acts 16:10		1112	to Caesarea...Acts 23:11-35		1121	Considered weighty by		
Entered			Defended himself before			some..........2 Cor. 10:10		1172
Macedonia ....Acts 16:10, 11		1112	Felix.........Acts 24:1-23		1122	His name sometimes		
Converted Lydia at			Preached to Felix and			forged ....2 Thess. 2:2		1212
Philippi ......Acts 16:12-15		1112	Drusilla ......Acts 24:24-26		1122	Reveal personal		
Thrown into prison; jailer			Imprisoned for two			infor- 2 Cor. 11:1-33		1172
converted.....Acts 16:16-34		1113	years.........Acts 24:27		1122	mation.......2 Cor. 12:1-11		1173
Used Roman			Accused before Festus by			Convey		
citizenship ....Acts 16:35-39		1113	Jews ....Acts 25:1-9		1122	personal Phil. 2:19-30		1194
Preached Acts 17:1-9		1114	Appealed to			messages.....Heb. 13:23, 24		1249
at Thessa- 1 Thess. 1:7		1206	Caesar........Acts 25:10-12		1123	Contain salutation and		
lonica........1 Thess. 2:2-18		1207	Defended himself			closing 2 Cor. 1:2, 3		1166
Received by the			before Acts 25:13-27		1123	doxology.....2 Cor. 13:14		1174
Bereans......Acts 17:10-13		1114	Agrippa ...Acts 26:1-32		1123	Disclose		
Left Silas and Timothy; went to						personal Phil. 2:19-24		1194
Athens.......Acts 17:14-17		1114	*Voyage to Rome:*			plans.........Philem. 22		1234
Preached on Mars' Hill (the			Sailed from Caesarea to			Some complimen-		
Areopagus) ...Acts 17:18-34		1114	Crete ....Acts 27:1-13		1124	tary.........Phil. 4:10-19		1196
Arrived in Corinth; stayed with			Ship tossed by			Some filled		
Aquila and			storm ....Acts 27:14-20		1125	with Gal. 1:6-8		1177
Priscilla ......Acts 18:1-5		1115	Assured by the			rebuke.......Gal. 5:1-10		1180
Reunited with			Lord ....Acts 27:21-25		1125	D. *Characteristics of:*		
Silas and Acts 18:5		1115	Ship wrecked; all			Consecrated ...1 Cor. 4:1-15		1151
Timothy .....1 Thess. 3:6		1207	saved ....Acts 27:26-44		1125	Phil. 3:7-14		1195
Wrote letters			On island of			Cheerful......Acts 16:25		1113
to Thessa- 1 Thess. 3:1-6		1207	Malta ....Acts 28:1-10		1126	2 Cor. 4:8-10		1167
lonians......2 Thess. 2:2		1212	Continued journey to			Courageous...Acts 9:29		1104
Established a church at			Rome ....Acts 28:11-16		1126	Acts 20:22-24		1118
Corinth ......Acts 18:5-18		1115	Rejected by Jews in			Considerate of Phil. 2:25-30		1194
Stopped briefly at			Rome ....Acts 28:17-29		1126	others........Philem. 7-24		1234
Ephesus......Acts 18:19-21		1115	Stayed in Rome two			Consci- 2 Cor. 1:12-17		1166
Saluted Jerusalem church;			years..........Acts 28:30, 31		1127	entious.......2 Cor. 6:3, 4		1169
returned to Antioch (in			Wrote *Ephesians*,			Christ- 2 Cor. 4:10, 11		1168
Syria).........Acts 18:22		1115	*Colossians*, Eph. 3:1		1186	centered .....Phil. 1:20-23		1193
			Philippians, Eph. 6:20		1190	Conciliatory ..2 Cor. 2:1-11		1166
Third Missionary Journey:			and Phil. 1:7, 13		1193	Gal. 2:1-15		1178
Strengthened churches of			*Philemon* Col. 4:7-18		1202	Composed .....2 Cor. 12:8-10		1173
Galatia and			here..........Philem. 10, 22		1234	2 Tim. 4:7, 8		1225
Phrygia ....Acts 18:23		1115						
Gave direction for relief			*Final ministry and death:*			**Pauline theology**		
collection .....1 Cor. 16:1		1161	Released from			Given by		
Ministered three			first Roman Phil. 1:25		1193	revelation......Gal. 1:11, 12		1177
years in Acts 19:1-12		1116	imprison- Phil. 2:17, 24		1194	Salvation by		
Ephesus......Acts 20:31		1118	ment.........2 Tim. 4:16, 17		1226	grace............Eph. 2:1-10		1185
Saved from angry			Wrote *First*			To Gentiles ....Eph. 3:1-12		1186
mob ....Acts 19:13-41		1116	*Timothy* and 1 Tim. 1:1-3		1217	**Paulus, Sergius**		
Probably wrote *Galatians*			*Titus*........Titus 1:1-5		1229	Roman proconsul of		
here ....Gal. 1:1		1177	Visited Macedonia and other			Cyprus......Acts 13:4, 7		1108
Wrote *First Corinthians*			places........2 Tim. 4:20		1226	**Pavement**—*a terrace made of bricks or*		
here ....1 Cor. 5:9		1152				*stones*		
Went to Troas; failed to meet						God's, made of		
Titus.........2 Cor. 2:12, 13		1167				sapphire..........Ex. 24:10		75

SUBJECT	REFERENCE	PAGE	SUBJECT	REFERENCE	PAGE	SUBJECT	REFERENCE	PAGE
Ahasuerus', made of precious stones	Esth. 1:5, 6	485	**Pearl**—*a precious gem found in oyster shells*			2. Leader dying while Ezekiel prophesies	Ezek. 11:1-13	793
Of stone	2 Kin. 16:17	372	A. *Used literally of:*			3. Descendant of Solomon	1 Chr. 3:21	390
Ezekiel's Temple, surrounded by	Ezek. 40:17, 18	823	Valuable gems	Rev. 18:12, 16	1305	4. One who signs the document	Neh. 10:1, 22	477
Judgment place of Pilate	John 19:13	1086	Woman's attire	1 Tim. 2:9	1218	**Peleg**—*division*		
See Gabbatha			B. *Used figuratively of:*			Brother of Joktan	Gen. 10:25	13
Pavilion—*a covered place, tent, booth*			Spiritual truths	Matt. 7:6	969	Son of Eber	Luke 3:35	1029
Canopy of God's abode	Job 36:29	519	Kingdom	Matt. 13:45, 46	977	**Pelet**—(God) *has freed*		
Protective covering ("tabernacle")	Is. 4:6	661	Worldly adornment	Rev. 17:4	1304	1. Judahite	1 Chr. 2:47	389
			Wonders of heaven's glories	Rev. 21:21	1307	2. Benjamite warrior under David	1 Chr. 12:3	399
Paws—*the feet of animals having claws*								
Descriptive of certain animals	Lev. 11:27	105	**Pedahel**—*God saves*			**Peleth**—*swiftness*		
Of bears and lions	1 Sam. 17:37	278	Leader of Naphtali	Num. 34:28	164	1. Reubenite, father of On	Num. 16:1	144
Pay—*to give something for something*			**Pedahzur**—*the Rock* (God) *has redeemed*			2. Judahite	1 Chr. 2:33	389
Lord's blessing	Prov. 19:17	623	Father of Gamaliel	Num. 1:10	127	**Pelethites**—*perhaps a contraction of Philistines*		
Punishment	Matt. 5:26	967						
Servitude and forgiveness	Matt. 18:23-35	982	**Pedaiah**—*Yahweh redeems*			David's faithful soliders during Absalom's and Sheba's rebellions	2 Sam. 15:18-22	308
Sign of righteousness	Ps. 37:21	546	1. Father of Joel, ruler in David's reign	1 Chr. 27:20	412	See Cherethites		
See Vow			2. Grandfather of Jehoiakim	2 Kin. 23:36	381	**Pelican**—*the vomiter*		
Pe			3. Son of Jeconiah	1 Chr. 3:18, 19	390	Ceremonially unclean bird	Lev. 11:18	104
Letter in the Hebrew alphabet	Ps. 119:129-136	593	4. Postexilic workman	Neh. 3:25	469	Dwells in wilderness	Ps. 102:6	580
Peace			5. Ezra's Levite attendant	Neh. 8:4	474	Lives in ruins	Is. 34:11	685
A. *Kinds of:*			6. Man appointed as treasurer	Neh. 13:13	480		Zeph. 2:14	910
International	1 Sam. 7:14	268	7. Postexilic Benjamite	Neh. 11:7	478	**Pelonite**		
National	1 Kin. 4:24	328				Descriptive of two of David's mighty men	1 Chr. 11:27, 36	398
Civil	Rom. 14:19	1143	**Peg**—*a stake used to fasten things down or hang things on*					
Domestic	1 Cor. 7:15	1153	*Used literally of:*			**Pen**		
Individual	Luke 8:48	1037	Tabernacle's, of bronze	Ex. 27:19	78	Figurative of tongue	Ps. 45:1	551
False	1 Thess. 5:3	1208	Jael's weapon	Judg. 4:21, 22	235	Lying	Jer. 8:8	726
Hypocritical	James 2:16	1254	*Used figuratively of:*			Not preferred	3 John 13	1284
Spiritual	Rom. 5:1	1135	God's grace	Ezra 9:8	461	**Penalties**—*punishment inflicted for wrong-doing*		
B. *Source of:*			Eliakim	Is. 22:23, 25	675	A. *For sexual sins:*		
God	Phil. 4:7	1196	Security	Zech. 10:4	923	Adultery— death	Lev. 20:10	114
Christ	John 14:27	1082	See Nail			Incest— death	Lev. 20:11-14	114
Holy Spirit	Gal. 5:22	1181	**Pekah**—*opening* (of the eye)			Sodomy— destruction	{ Gen. 19:13, 17, 24	19
C. *Of Christ:*			Son of Remaliah; usurps Israel's throne	2 Kin. 15:25-28	371			
Predicted	Is. 9:6, 7	665	Forms alliance with Rezin of Aram against Ahaz	Is. 7:1-9	663	B. *For bodily sins:*		
Promised	Hag. 2:9	915	Alliance defeated; captives returned	2 Kin. 16:5-9	372	Drunken- ness— exclusion	{ 1 Cor. 5:11	1152
Announced	Is. 52:7	701					{ 1 Cor. 6:9, 10	1152
D. *Lord's relation to, He:*			Territory of, overrun by Tiglath-pileser	2 Kin. 15:29	371	Murder— death	Ex. 21:12-15	72
Reveals	Jer. 33:6	751	Assassinated by Hoshea	2 Kin. 15:30	371	Persecution—God's judgment	Matt. 23:34-36	988
Gives	Ps. 29:11	541	**Pekahiah**—*Yahweh hath opened* (the eyes)			C. *For following heathen ways:*		
Establishes	Is. 26:12	678	Son of Menahem; king of Israel	2 Kin. 15:22-26	371	Human sacrifice— death	Lev. 20:2-5	114
E. *Among the wicked:*			Assassinated by Pekah	2 Kin. 15:23-25	371	Witchcraft— death	Ex. 22:18	74
Not known by	Is. 59:8	706	**Pekod**—*visitation*			Idolatry— death	Ex. 22:20	74
None for	Is. 48:22	698	Aramean tribe during Nebuchadnezzar's reign	Jer. 50:21	768	D. *For internal sins:*		
F. *Among believers, truths concerning:*						Ingratitude— punished	Prov. 17:13	622
Comes through Christ's atonement	Is. 53:5	702	**Pelaiah**—*Yahweh is wonderful*			Pride—abomination	Prov. 16:5	621
Results from reconciliation	Col. 1:20	1200	1. Judahite	1 Chr. 3:24	390	Unbelief— exclusion	Num. 20:12	149
Product of justification	Rom. 5:1	1135	2. Ezra's Levite attendant; reads document	Neh. 8:7	474	Swearing— curse	Jer. 23:10	740
Obtained by faith	Is. 26:3	677	**Pelaliah**—*Yahweh has judged*				Zech. 5:3	920
G. *Among believers, exhortations regarding:*			Postexilic priest	Neh. 11:12	478	Blasphemy— death	{ Lev. 24:14-16, 23	119
Should live in	2 Cor. 13:11	1174	**Pelatiah**—*Yahweh has freed*					
Should pursue	2 Tim. 2:22	1224	1. Simeonite leader in war with Amalekites	1 Chr. 4:42, 43	391	**Peniel**—*the face of God*		
Peacemakers—*those who work for peace*						Place east of Jordan; site of Jacob's wrestling with angel	Gen. 32:24-31	33
Christ the great	2 Cor. 5:18-21	1169				See Penuel 1		
Christians become	{ Matt. 5:9	966						
	{ Rom. 14:19	1143						
Rules regarding	1 Pet. 3:8-13	1263						
Peacock—*peafowl*								
Imported by Solomon from Tarshish	1 Kin. 10:22	336						
Trade item	2 Chr. 9:21	427						

SUBJECT	REFERENCE	PAGE	SUBJECT	REFERENCE	PAGE	SUBJECT	REFERENCE	PAGE

Peninnah—*coral, pearl*

Elkanah's second
wife............1 Sam. 1:2, 4   263

Penitence—*state of being sorry for one's sins*

A. *Results of:*
- Forgiveness....Ps. 32:5, 6   543
- Restoration....Job 22:23-29   510
- Renewed
  fellowship.....Ps. 51:12, 13   554

B. *Examples of:*
- Job............Job 42:1-6   523
- David.........Ps. 51:1-19   554
- Josiah......2 Kin. 22:1, 19   378
- Tax-gatherer...Luke 18:13   1049
- Thief on the
  cross.........Luke 23:39-42   1057

C. *Elements:*
- Acknowledg- (Job 33:27, 28   517
  ment of sin..(Luke 15:18, 21   1046
- Broken (Ps. 34:18   544
  heart........(Ps. 51:17   554
- Plea for
  mercy........Luke 18:13   1049
- Confession...1 John 1:9   1274

See Repentance

Pentecost—*fiftieth* (day)

A. *In the Old Testament:*
- Called "the Feast of
  Weeks".......Ex. 34:22, 23   86
- Marks completion of barley
  harvest.....Lev. 23:15, 16   117
- Called "Feast of
  Harvest".....Ex. 23:16   74
- Work during,
  prohibited....Lev. 23:21   117
- Two loaves
  presented....Lev. 23:17, 20   117
- Other sacrifices
  prescribed....Lev. 23:18   117
- Offerings given by
  Levites........Deut. 16:10-14   184
- Time of conse-
  cration.......Deut. 16:12, 13   184
- Observed during Solomon's
  time ....2 Chr. 8:12, 13   426

See Feasts, Hebrew

B. *In the New Testament:*
- Day of the Spirit's coming; the
  formation of the Christian
  Church ......Acts 2:1-47   1095
- Paul desires to
  attend ....Acts 20:16   1118
- Paul plans to stay in Ephesus
  until ....1 Cor. 16:8   1161

Penuel—*the face of God*

1. Inhabitants of, slain by
   Gideon.......Judg. 8:8, 9, 17   239
   Later refortified by
   Jeroboam .....1 Kin. 12:25   338
2. Judahite.......1 Chr. 4:4   390
3. Benjamite .....1 Chr. 8:25   395

People

Found among
Israel............Deut. 7:6   176
Not limited to
Israel.............Rom. 2:28, 29   1133
Called the
remnant..........Is. 11:10, 11, 16   668
Gentiles (Is. 19:25   673
included (Is. 65:1   711
in ....(Rom. 15:10, 11   1143
Became such by
covenant........Jer. 31:31-34   749
Secured through the
Messiah ....Ezek. 34:22-31   817
Accomplished by (Matt. 1:21   964
Christ's death ...(Luke 1:68, 77   1026
Separated from (2 Cor. 6:16-18   1169
others...........(Rev. 18:4   1304
God's true
Church..........1 Pet. 2:9, 10   1261

All nations (Rev. 5:9   1296
included in ......(Rev. 7:9   1298
God's eternal
people...........Rev. 21:3   1307

People of the land—*the conservative element of the population consisting mainly of landholders*

The influence of..2 Kin. 11:13-15   367
Taxed............2 Kin. 23:35   381

Peor—*opening*

1. Mountain of Moab opposite
   Jericho........Num. 23:28   153
   Israel's camp seen
   from ....Num. 24:2   153
2. Moabite god
   called Baal of (Num. 25:3, 5,
   Peor ....(18   154
   Israelites punished for worhsip
   of.............Num. 31:16   160

Perceive, perception—*knowledge derived through one of the senses*

Outward (2 Sam. 12:19   305
circumstances ...(Acts 27:10   1125
Outward (John 6:15   1070
intentions ....(Acts 23:29   1121
Intuition ....1 Sam. 3:8   265
        John 4:19   1067
Unusual (1 Sam. 12:17,
manifes- (18   272
tations ....Acts 10:34   1106
Spiritual (Neh. 6:12   471
insight ....(Acts 14:9   1110
God's blessings...2 Sam. 5:12   299
        Neh. 6:16   471
Bitter (Eccl. 1:17   638
experience.......(Eccl. 3:22   640
Obvious (Matt. 21:45   985
implication ......(Luke 20:19   1052
God's (Gal. 2:9   1178
revelation ....(1 John 3:16   1276
Internal (Luke 8:46   1037
consciousness ...(Acts 8:23   1103

Peres—*to split into pieces*

Sentence of
doom............Dan. 5:28   842

Peresh—*dung*

Man of
Manasseh ....1 Chr. 7:16   394

Perez—*a breach*

One of Judah's twin sons by
Tamar............Gen. 38:24-30   39
Numbered among Judah's
sons.............Gen. 46:12   46
Founder of a tribal
family............Num. 26:20, 21   155
Descendants of, notable in later
times............1 Chr. 27:3   412
Ancestor of David and
Christ............Ruth 4:12-18   258

Perezites

Descendants of
Perez............Num. 26:20   155

Perez-uzzah—*the breech of Uzzah*

Calamity with the
ark..............2 Sam. 6:6-8   299

Perfection—*the extreme degree of excellence*

A. *Applied to natural things:*
- Day ....Prov. 4:18   612
- Gold...........2 Chr. 4:21   422
- Weights ....Deut. 25:15   191
- Beauty.........Ezek. 28:12   811
- Offering ....Lev. 22:21   116

B. *Applied to spiritual graces:*
- Endurance.....James 1:4   1253
- Love...........Col. 3:14   1201
- Holiness ....2 Cor. 7:1   1169
- Praise.........Matt. 21:16   985
- Faith ....1 Thess. 3:10   1207
- Good works ...Heb. 13:21   1249
- Unity.........John 17:23   1084
- Power ....2 Cor. 12:9   1173

C. *Means of:*
- God ....1 Pet. 5:10   1264
- Christ ....Heb. 10:14   1245
- Holy Spirit.....Gal. 3:3   1178
- God's Word....2 Tim. 3:16, 17   1225
- Ministry ....Eph. 4:11, 12   1187
- Sufferings .....Heb. 2:10   1240

D. *Stages of:*
- Eternally accom-
  plished........Heb. 10:14   1245
- Objective
  goal...........Matt. 5:48   968
- Subjective
  process ....2 Cor. 7:1   1169
- Daily activity ..2 Cor. 13:9   1174
- Present
  possession ....1 Cor. 2:6   1150
- Experience not yet
  reached ....Phil. 3:12   1195
- Descriptive of the completed
  Church ....Heb. 11:40   1247
- Heaven's eternal
  standard ......1 Cor. 13:10-12   1158

Perfume—*a substance producing pleasant scents*

A. *Made by:*
- Perfumer ......Ex. 30:25, 35   82
- Combining:
  Various
  ingredients....Job 41:31   523
- Olive oil with imported
  aromatics ....1 Kin. 10:10   335

B. *Uses of:*
- Incense and ointment for
  tabernacle ....Ex. 30:22-28   82
- Personal
  adornment ....Prov. 27:9   630
- Seduction ....Prov. 7:17   614

C. *Figurative of:*
- Christ's:
  - Glories ....Ps. 45:8   551
  - Righteousness and
    intercession ...Song 3:6   650
- Spiritual
  prostitution ...Is. 57:9   704

Perfumer—*to mix, compound*

Great art.........Ex. 30:25   82
        Eccl. 10:1   644
Used in
tabernacle........Ex. 30:25, 35   82
Used in
embalming ....2 Chr. 16:14   431
A maker of
ointment ....Eccl. 10:1   644
Among
returnees........Neh. 3:8   468

Perga—*the capital of Pamphylia*

Visited by Paul....Acts 13:13, 14   1109
        Acts 14:25   1111

Pergamum—*a leading city in Mysia in Asia Minor*

One of the seven churches
here.............Rev. 1:11   1294
Antipas martyred
here.............Rev. 2:12, 13   1294
Special message
to ....Rev. 2:12-17   1294

Perida

Head of a family of Temple
servants.........Neh. 7:46, 57   472

Perils—*physical or spiritual dangers*

Escape from, by:
- Prayer ....Gen. 32:6-12   33
- Pacifying gifts.....Gen. 32:13-20   33
- Quick action ......1 Sam. 18:10, 11   279
- Flight ....Matt. 2:12-15   964
- Love of Christ ....Rom. 8:35   1138
- God..............2 Cor. 1:10   1166

SUBJECT	REFERENCE	PAGE

Perish—*to be destroyed violently*

A. *Applied to:*
Universe......Heb. 1:11 — 1239
Old world......2 Pet. 3:6 — 1269
Animals......Ps. 49:12, 20 — 553
Vegetation....Jon. 4:10 — 887
Food ....John 6:27 — 1071
Gold..........1 Pet. 1:7 — 1260
Human body...2 Cor. 4:16 — 1168
Soul..........Matt. 10:28 — 973

B. *Safeguards against:*
God's:
Power........John 10:28 — 1077
Will..........Matt. 18:14 — 982
Providence ....Luke 21:18 — 1053
Christ's
resurrection...1 Cor. 15:18, 19 — 1160
Repentance....Luke 13:3, 5 — 1044
See Lost

Perizzites—*dwellers in the open country*

One of seven Canaanite
nations.........Deut. 7:1 — 176
Possessed Palestine in Abraham's
time.........Gen. 13:7 — 15
Land of, promised to Abraham's
descendants....Gen. 15:18, 20 — 16
Jacob's fear of ....Gen. 34:30 — 35
Israel commanded to utterly
destroy.........Deut. 20:17 — 187
Israel forbidden to intermingle
with.........Ex. 23:23-25 — 75
Defeated by
Joshua ....Josh. 3:10 — 208
Many of, slain by
Judah ....Judg. 1:4, 5 — 232
Israel intermarries
with.........Judg. 3:5-7 — 234
Made slaves by
Solomon ....1 Kin. 9:20, 21 — 335
See Canaanites

Perjury—*swearing falsely*

Condemned by the
Law..............Lev. 19:12 — 113
Hated by God.....Zech. 8:17 — 922
Requires
atonement.......Lev. 6:2-7 — 99
Brings   {Zech. 5:3, 4 — 920
punishment .....{Mal. 3:5 — 931
See False Witnesses

Permission—*authority to do something*

Granted to Paul...Acts 21:40 — 1119
Demanded by
Satan ....Luke 22:31 — 1055

Perpetual—*lasting forever*

Statute..........Ex. 27:21 — 78
Incense..........Ex. 30:8 — 81
Covenant ....Ex. 31:16 — 83
Priesthood ......Ex. 40:15 — 92
Possession ......Lev. 25:34 — 120
Allotment......Num. 18:8 — 147
Ruins ....Ps. 9:6 — 531
Ps. 74:3 — 566
Pain ....Jer. 15:18 — 734
Hissing..........Jer. 18:16 — 736
Sleep............Jer. 51:39 — 771
Desolation ......Jer. 51:62 — 772
Mountains ....Hab. 3:6 — 905

Perplexity—*a state wherein no way out is seen*

Predicted by
Christ...........Luke 21:25 — 1053

Persecution—*to afflict, oppress, torment*

A. *Caused by:*
Man's sinful
nature ....Gal. 4:29 — 1180
Hatred of
God..........John 15:20-23 — 1082
Ignorance of
God..........John 16:1-3 — 1083
Hatred of   {1 Thess. 2:15 — 1207
Christ........{Rev. 12:13 — 1301

Preaching the   {Gal. 5:11 — 1180
cross........{Gal. 6:12 — 1181
Godly living ...Matt. 13:21 — 976
2 Tim. 3:12 — 1225
Mistaken   {Acts 13:50 — 1110
zeal..........{Acts 26:9-11 — 1124

B. *Christian's attitude under:*
Flee from.....Matt. 10:23 — 972
Rejoice in ....Matt. 5:12 — 966
Be patient
under........1 Cor. 4:12 — 1151
Glorify God
in............1 Pet. 4:16 — 1264
Pray during...Matt. 5:44 — 968

Persecution psalm

Of David.......Ps. 69 — 562

Perseverance—*steadfastness, persistence*

Elements involved in:
Spiritual growth...Eph. 4:15 — 1187
Fruitfulness......John 15:4-8 — 1082
God's armor......Eph. 6:11-18 — 1190
Discipline ......Heb. 12:5-13 — 1247
Assurance........2 Tim. 1:12 — 1223
Salvation ....Matt. 10:22 — 972
Reward ....Gal. 6:9 — 1181

Persis—*Persian*

Christian woman in
Rome ....Rom. 16:12 — 1145

Personal devotions

A. *Prayer:*
In morning...Ps. 5:3 — 529
Ps. 119:147 — 594
Three times   {Ps. 55:17 — 556
daily ....{Dan. 6:10 — 842
Continually....1 Thess. 3:10 — 1207
1 Tim. 5:5 — 1219

B. *Study:*
Daily ....Deut. 17:19 — 185
For learning ...Acts 17:11 — 1114
Rom. 15:4 — 1143

Personal work—*seeking to win persons to Christ*

Need of ....John 4:35-38 — 1068
Model of ....John 4:4-30 — 1067
Means of ....1 Thess. 1:5, 6 — 1206
Power of ....John 16:7-11 — 1083
Methods of.......1 Cor. 9:19-22 — 1155

Persuasion—*inclining another's will toward something*

A. *Good, to:*
Worship......Acts 18:13 — 1115
Steadfast-
ness..........Acts 13:43 — 1109
Belief.........Acts 18:4 — 1115
Acts 19:8 — 1116
Turn from
idolatry......Acts 19:26 — 1117
Trust Jesus ....Acts 28:23 — 1126

B. *Evil, to:*
Unbelief ....2 Chr. 32:10-19 — 445
Unholy
alliance ....2 Chr. 18:2 — 432
Fatal conflict ..1 Kin. 22:20-22 — 350
Turmoil........Acts 14:19 — 1110
Error ....Gal. 5:8 — 1180

C. *Objects of:*
Hereafter......Luke 16:31 — 1048
One's faith in
God..........Rom. 4:21 — 1134
Personal
assurance....Rom. 8:38 — 1138
Personal
liberty ....2 Tim. 1:12 — 1223
Spiritual
stability......Rom. 15:14 — 1144
Another's
faith ....2 Tim. 1:5 — 1223
God's
promises .....Heb. 11:13 — 1246

Peruda—*separated*

One of Solomon's servants whose
descendants
return from   {Ezra 2:55 — 455
exile............{Neh. 7:57 — 472

Perverseness—*willfully continuing in sinful ways*

A. *Applied to:*
Mind ....Prov. 12:8 — 618
Generation ....Phil. 2:15 — 1194

B. *Source of:*
False
doctrine......Acts 20:30 — 1118

C. *Results of:*
Comes from the
heart.........Prov. 6:14 — 613
Issues from the
mouth ....Prov. 2:12 — 610
Causes strife...Prov. 16:28 — 621
Abomination to
God..........Prov. 11:20 — 617
Hard way.....Prov. 22:5 — 625
Shall be cut
off ....Prov. 10:31 — 616

Pervert—*to change something from its right use*

A. *Evil of, in dealing with:*
Man's
judgment ....Deut. 24:17 — 191
God's:
Judgment.....Job 8:3 — 500
Word........Jer. 23:36 — 741
Ways........Acts 13:10 — 1108
Gospel........Gal. 1:7 — 1177

B. *Caused by:*
Drink.........Prov. 31:5 — 634
Worldly
wisdom ....Is. 47:10 — 697
Spiritual
blindness......Luke 23:2, 14 — 1056

Pestilence

Fifth Egyptian
plague...........Ex. 9:1-6 — 61
Threatened by
God ....Deut. 28:21 — 193
Sent because of   {2 Sam. 24:13, —
David's sin ......{ 15 — 318
Used for man's
corrections ....Ezek. 38:22 — 821
Precedes the Lord's
coming........Hab. 3:5 — 905

Pestle—*instrument used for pulverizing material*

Figurative of severe
discipline........Prov. 27:22 — 631

Peter

A. *Life of:*
Before his call:
Simon   {Matt. 16:17 — 980
Barjona......{John 21:15 — 1088
Brother of
Andrew......Matt. 4:18 — 966
Married   {Mark 1:30 — 1000
man..........{1 Cor. 9:5 — 1155
Not highly
educated.....Acts 4:13 — 1098
Fisherman....Matt. 4:18 — 966

From his call to Pentecost:
Brought to Jesus by
Andrew.......John 1:40-42 — 1065
Named Cephas by
Christ.........John 1:42 — 1065
Called to discipleship by
Christ.........Matt. 4:18-22 — 966
Mother-in-law
healed ....Matt. 8:14, 15 — 970
Called as
apostle........Matt. 10:2-4 — 972
Walks on
water ....Matt. 14:28-33 — 978
Confessed Christ's
deity.........Matt. 16:13-19 — 980

239

SUBJECT	REFERENCE	PAGE

Pilate, Pontius—continued
Destroyed
Galileans.........Luke 13:1 — 1044
Jesus brought
before...........Matt. 27:2 — 993
Washed hands in mock
innocency.......Matt. 27:24 — 993
Notorious in 〔Acts 3:13 — 1097
history.........〔Acts 4:27 — 1098

Pildash—*steely*
Son of Nahor and
Milcah..........Gen. 22:20-22 — 22

Pilfering—*stealing*
Forbidden........Titus 2:10 — 1230

Pilgrims—*God's people as*
A. *Elements involved in:*
Forsaking all 〔Luke 14:26, 27,
for Christ ....〔 33 — 1045
Traveling by
faith.........Heb. 11:9 — 1246
Faces set toward
Zion ....Jer. 50:5 — 767
Encouraged by God's
promises......Heb. 11:13 — 1246
Sustained by
God...........Is. 35:1-10 — 685
B. *Their journey in this world as:*
Aliens and
strangers......1 Pet. 2:11, 12 — 1261
Lights.........Phil. 2:15 — 1194
Salt...........Matt. 5:13 — 967
God's own......1 Pet. 2:9, 10 — 1261
Chosen out of 〔John 17:6 — 1084
the world ....〔1 Pet. 1:1, 2 — 1260
See Strangers

Pilha—*plowman*
Signer of the
document ....Neh. 10:24 — 477

Pillar—*a column or support*
A. *Descriptive of:*
Memorial
sites ....Gen. 28:18, 22 — 29
Woman turned to
salt ....Gen. 19:26 — 20
Altars of
idolatry ......Deut. 12:3 — 180
Supports for a 〔Judg. 16:25, 26,
building......〔 29 — 248
Covenant
site ....Ex. 24:4-8 — 75
Miracles ......Joel 2:30 — 867
B. *Figurative of:*
God's
presence ......Ex. 33:9, 10 — 84
Earth's
supports .....Job 9:6 — 501
God's sovereignty over
nations.......Is. 19:19 — 673
Man's legs.....Song 5:15 — 651
Important
persons ....Gal. 2:9 — 1178
Church........1 Tim. 3:15 — 1218
True
believers .....Rev. 3:12 — 1295
Angel's feet....Rev. 10:1 — 1299

Pillar of cloud and fire
A. *As means of:*
Guiding
Israel ....Ex. 13:21, 22 — 66
Protecting
Israel ....Ex. 14:19, 24 — 66
Regulating Israel's
journeys .....Num. 9:15-23 — 138
Manifesting His glory to
Israel ....Ex. 24:16-18 — 75
Manifesting His
presence .....Ex. 34:5-8 — 85
Communicating with
Israel ....Ex. 33:9, 10 — 84
B. *Effect of:*
Cause of fear ..Ex. 19:9, 16 — 71
Repeated in the
Temple........1 Kin. 8:10, 11 — 332

Long remem-
bered ....Ps. 99:7 — 579
Recalled with
gratitude......Neh. 9:12, 19 — 475
Repeated in Christ's transfigur-
ation..........Matt. 17:5 — 980
C. *Figurative of God's:*
Wonders......Joel 2:30 — 867
Departure from
Jerusalem.....Ezek. 9:3 — 792
Presence among
believers ......Matt. 18:20 — 982

Pillow—*a cushion*
Stone used as .....Gen. 28:11, 18 — 28
Quilt of goat's 〔1 Sam. 19:13,
hair ....〔 16 — 280
Cushion..........Mark 4:38 — 1003

Pilot—*one who guides*
Of Tyre's ships ..Ezek. 27:8-29 — 809
Captain ....Jon. 1:6 — 885
Used
figuratively.......James 3:4 — 1254

Piltai—*Yahweh delivers*
Priest of Joiakim's
time.............Neh. 12:12, 17 — 479

Pin—*a wooden or metal peg*
Used in a weaver's
loom ....Judg. 16:13, 14 — 247
See Nail

Pine away—*to waste away*
From
disobedience......Lev. 26:14, 16 — 121
Egypt.............Is. 19:8 — 673
Judah.............Is. 33:9 — 684
Jer. 15:9 — 733
Jerusalem.........Lam. 4:9 — 780

Pine trees—*evergreen trees*
Used in Solomon's
Temple...........2 Chr. 3:5 — 421
Product of
Lebanon..........Is. 60:13 — 708
Used
figuratively......Is. 41:19 — 691

Pinnacle—*a summit; highest ledge*
Of the Temple ....Matt. 4:5 — 966

Pinon—*darkness*
Edomite chief.....Gen. 36:41 — 37
1 Chr. 1:52 — 388

Pipe, piper—*a flute*
A. *Descriptive of:*
Flute ....1 Sam. 10:5 — 270
Player of a
flute ....Rev. 18:22 — 1305
Hollow tube ...Zech. 4:2, 12 — 920
B. *Figurative of:*
Joyful
deliverance....Is. 30:29 — 682
Mournful
lamentation...Jer. 48:36 — 765
Inconsistent
reactions...Matt. 11:17 — 973
Spiritual discern-
ment.........1 Cor. 14:7 — 1159

Piram—*indomitable*
Amorite king of
Jarmuth.......Josh. 10:3 — 214

Pirathon—*height*
Town in
Ephraim.........Judg. 12:15 — 245

Pirathonite—*inhabitant of Pirathon*
Descriptive of:
Abdon ....Judg. 12:13-15 — 245
Benaiah..........2 Sam. 23:30 — 318

Pisgah—*a mountain peak in the Abarim range in Moab*
Balaam offers sacrifice
upon ....Num. 23:14 — 152
Moses views promised land
from ....Deut. 3:27 — 172
Site of Moses'
death............Deut. 34:1-7 — 202
Summit of, called
Nebo............Deut. 32:49-52 — 201
See Nebo

Pishon—*freely flowing*
One of Eden's four
rivers.............Gen. 2:10, 11 — 5

Pisidia—*a mountainous district in Asia Minor*
Twice visited by 〔Acts 13:13, 14 — 1109
Paul.............〔Acts 14:24 — 1110

Pispa—*dispersion*
Asherite ....1 Chr. 7:38 — 395

Pistachio nuts
Sent by Israel.....Gen. 43:11 — 43

Pit—*a hole*
Figurative of:
Grave............Ps. 30:9 — 542
Snare ....Ps. 35:7 — 545
Harlot ....Prov. 23:27 — 627
Mouth of
Adulteress......Prov. 22:14 — 626
Destruction ....Ps. 55:23 — 556
Self-destruction ...Prov. 28:10 — 631
Hell.............Ps. 28:1 — 540
Devil's abode......Rev. 9:1, 2, 11 — 1299
See Abyss

Pitch
Ark covered
with.............Gen. 6:14 — 9
In Babel's tower...Gen. 11:3 — 13
In Moses' ark ....Ex. 2:3 — 55
Kings fall in......Gen. 14:10 — 15

Pitcher—*an earthenware vessel with handles*
A. *Used for:*
Water ....1 Kin. 18:33 — 346
Protection of a
torch..........Judg. 7:16, 19 — 239
B. *Figurative of:*
Heart..........Eccl. 12:6 — 645

Pithom—*mansion of the god Atum*
Egyptian city built by Hebrew
slaves ....Ex. 1:11 — 54

Pithon—*harmless*
Son of Micah .....1 Chr. 8:35 — 395

Pitilessness—*showing no mercy*
Examples of:
Rich man ....2 Sam. 12:1-6 — 304
Nebuchad-
nezzar...........2 Kin. 25:6-21 — 382
Medes ....Is. 13:18 — 669
Edom ....Amos 1:11 — 872
Heartless
creditor ....Matt. 18:29, 30 — 982
Strict
religionists ....Luke 10:30-32 — 1040
Merciless
murderers.......Acts 7:54-58 — 1102

Pity—*to show compassion*
A. *Of God, upon:*
Heathen........Jon. 4:10, 11 — 887
Israel..........Is. 63:9 — 710
Faithful
remnant ......Is. 54:8-10 — 702
Believer.......James 5:11 — 1256
B. *Of men:*
Pleaded........Job 19:21 — 507
Upon the
poor ....Prov. 19:17 — 623

SUBJECT	REFERENCE	PAGE	SUBJECT	REFERENCE	PAGE	SUBJECT	REFERENCE	PAGE

Poor in spirit—*humble, self-effacing*

Promised
blessing ....Matt. 5:3   966

Poplar tree

Used in deception of
Laban ....Gen. 30:37   31
Pagan rites
among ....Hos. 4:13   856
Probably same as
"willows" in .....Lev. 23:40   118

Popularity—*one's esteem in the world*

Obtained by:
Heroic exploits....Judg. 8:21, 22   240
Unusual wisdom ..1 Kin. 4:29-34   328
Trickery ....2 Sam. 15:1-6   308
Outward display ..Matt. 6:2, 5, 16   968

Popularity of Jesus

A. *Factors producing His:*
Teaching ......Mark 1:22, 27   1000
Healing........Mark 5:20   1004
Miracles ......John 12:9-19   1079
Feeding the
people ......John 6:15-27   1070
B. *Factors causing decline of His:*
High ethical
standards ....Mark 8:34-38   1008
Foretells His
death ....Matt. 16:21-28   980

Population—*the total inhabitants of a place*

Israel's, increased in
Egypt ....Ex. 1:7, 8   54
Nineveh's, great...Jon. 4:11   887
Heaven's, vast ....Rev. 7:9   1298

Poratha

One of Haman's
sons............Esth. 9:8   490

Porcius Festus—*successor to Felix*

Paul stands trial
before ....Acts 25:1-22   1122

Pork—*swine's flesh*

Classified as
unclean ....Lev. 11:7, 8   104

Porpoise—*a species of dolphin*

Skins of used in
tabernacle   (Ex. 26:14   77
coverings........(Ex. 35:7   86
Used for sandals ..Ezek. 16:10   797

Port—*a harbor*

At Joppa..........Jon. 1:3   885
Fair Havens......Acts 27:8   1125
Phoenix..........Acts 27:12   1125
Syracuse.........Acts 28:12   1126
Rhegium.........Acts 28:13   1126
Puteoli...........Acts 28:13   1126

Portico—*porch*

Solomon's........John 10:23   1077
Of Bethesda.......John 5:2   1068

Portion—*a stipulated part*

A. *Of things material:*
Inheritance ....Gen. 48:22   48
B. *Of good things:*
Spirit ....2 Kin. 2:9   356
Lord...........Ps. 119:57   592
Spiritual
riches.........Is. 61:7   708
C. *Of evil things:*
Things of the
world ....Ps. 17:14   535
Fellowship with the
wicked........Neh. 2:20   468
D. *Of things eternal:*
Punishment of the
wicked........Ps. 11:6   532

See Inheritance

Position—*place of influence*

Sought after by
Pharisees.........Matt. 23:5-7   987
James and John
request...........Mark 10:37   1011
Seeking after,
denounced ......Luke 14:7-11   1045
Diotrephes, a seeker
after ....3 John 9   1284

Possess—*to acquire*

A. *Objects of:*
Promised
land...........Deut. 4:1, 5   172
Ruins..........Is. 14:21   670
Spiritual
riches.........Is. 57:13   705
Christ ....Prov. 8:22   615
One's:
Life...........Luke 21:19   1053
Body of
wife........1 Thess. 4:4   1208
Sins.........Job 13:26   504
B. *Of Canaan:*
Promised ......Gen. 17:8   17
Under oath ....Neh. 9:15   475
Israel challenged
to.............Num. 13:20   141

Possible—*that which can exist*

A. *Things possible:*
All, with God ..Matt. 19:26   983
All, to the
believer ....Mark 9:23   1009
Peaceful
living ....Gal. 4:15   1180
B. *Things impossible:*
Deception of the
saints ....Matt. 24:24   988
Removal of the
Cross ....Matt. 26:39   991
Christ's remaining in the
grave ....Acts 2:24   1095
Removal of sins by animal
sacrifice......Heb. 10:4   1245

Posthumous—*after death*

Mary of
Bethany.........Matt. 26:13   991
Abel ....Heb. 11:4   1246
All believers.......Rev. 14:13   1302

Pot—*a rounded, open-mouthed vessel*

A. *Use of:*
Cooking ....Zech. 14:21   926
Refining ....Prov. 17:3   622
B. *Figurative of:*
Sudden
destruction....Ps. 58:9   557
Impending national
destruction....Jer. 1:13   718
Merciless
punishment ...Mic. 3:2, 3   891
Complete sanctifi-
cation........Zech. 14:20, 21   926

Potiphar—*whom Re (the sun god) has given*

High Egyptian
officer...........Gen. 39:1   39
Puts Joseph in
jail ....Gen. 39:20   39

Potiphera

Egyptian priest of On
(Heliopolis)......Gen. 41:45-50   41
Father of Asenath, Joseph's
wife.............Gen. 46:20   46

Potsherd—*a fragment of broken pottery*

Figurative of:
Weakness.........Ps. 22:15   538
Leviathan's
underparts ......Job 41:30   523
Uses of:
Scraping ....Job 2:8   496
Scooping water ..Is. 30:14   681

Potsherd gate—*a gate of Jerusalem*

By valley of Ben-
hinnom..........Jer. 19:2   737

Potter—*one who makes earthenware vessels*

A. *Art of, involves:*
Reducing clay to
paste..........Is. 41:25   691
Shaping by revolving
wheel.........Jer. 18:1-4   736
Molding by
hands........Jer. 18:6   736
B. *Figurative of:*
Complete
destruction....Is. 30:14   681
God's sovereignty over
men...........Is. 64:8   711
Israel's lack of under-
standing ....Is. 29:16   680

Potter's Field—*burial place for poor people*

Judas' money used for
purchase of.......Matt. 27:7, 8   993

Pour—*to flow freely from something*

A. *Applied to:*
Rain from
clouds ....Amos 9:6   877
Oil from
vessels ....Gen. 35:14   35
Blood from
animals ......Lev. 8:15   102
Water from
pitchers.......1 Kin. 18:33   346
B. *Used figuratively of:*
Christ's
death ....Ps. 22:14   538
Spirit's
coming.......Joel 2:28, 29   867
Holy Spirit....Ezek. 39:29   822
God's:
Wrath ....2 Chr. 34:21, 25   448
Blessings .....Mal. 3:10   931
Sover-
eignty.......Job 10:9, 10   502
Prayer and
repentance....Lam. 2:19   778
Extreme
emotions......1 Sam. 1:15   263

Poverty, spiritual

A. *In a bad sense, of spiritual:*
Decay ....Rev. 2:9   1294
Immaturity ....1 Cor. 3:1-3   1150
B. *Used in a good sense, of:*
The humble....Is. 66:2   712
God's people...Is. 14:32   670
C. *Caused by:*
Hastiness ......Prov. 21:5   624
Greed..........Prov. 22:16   626
Laziness ......Prov. 24:30-34   629

Power of Christ

A. *Described as:*
Given by
God...........John 17:2   1084
Derived from the
Spirit ....Luke 4:14   1030
Delegated to
others.........Luke 9:1   1037
Determined by
Himself ....John 10:18   1077
B. *Manifested as power in:*
Creation.......John 1:3, 10   1064
Upholds all
things.........Heb. 1:3   1239
Miracles ......Luke 4:36   1030
Regen-
eration........John 5:21-26   1069
Salvation .....Heb. 7:25   1243
Resurrecting
believers .....John 5:28, 29   1069
His return ....Matt. 24:30   989
C. *Manifested as authority to:*
Forgive sins ...Matt. 9:6, 8   971

SUBJECT	REFERENCE	PAGE

Rachel—continued

Prophecy

concerning, ⎰Jer. 31:15   748

quoted ....⎱Matt. 2:18   964

Rachel, tomb of

At Bethlehem—first mention

of in Bible........Gen. 35:19   35

Racial relations

Salvation is ⎰Eph. 2:11-22   1186

for all ....⎱Eph. 3:7-9   1186

All are same in

Christ............Col. 3:9-11   1201

Raddai—*Yahweh has subdued*

One of David's

brothers......1 Chr. 2:14   389

Radiance in life

Caused by:

Wisdom..........Prov. 4:7-9   611

Soul winning....Dan. 12:3   850

Transfiguration ...Matt. 17:2   980

Beholding the ⎰Ps. 34:5   544

Lord............⎱2 Cor. 3:7-18   1167

Rafters—*timbers used to support a roof*

Made of cypress...Song 1:17   649

Ragau (see Reu)

Rage—*raving and violent madness*

A. *Descriptive of:*

Anger ....Dan. 3:13   838

B. *Caused by:*

Insane

madness ......2 Chr. 16:7-10   431

Supposed

insult ....2 Kin. 5:11, 12   360

Jealousy.......Prov. 6:34   614

Insolence against

God..........2 Kin. 19:27, 28   376

Rags—*tattered and spoiled clothing*

Used as

cushions ....Jer. 38:11-13   756

Reward of

drowsiness ....Prov. 23:21   627

Man's righteousness

like............Is. 64:6   711

Rahab (I)—*violence*

Prostitute living in

Jericho..........Josh. 2:1   207

Concealed Joshua's

spies ....Josh. 2:1-24   207

Spared by invading

Israelites ....Josh. 6:17-25   210

Included among the

faithful..........Heb. 11:31   1247

Cited as an

example........James 2:25   1254

Ancestress of

Christ............Matt. 1:5   963

Rahab (II)—*pride, arrogance*

Used figuratively of

Egypt ....Ps. 87:4   574

Translated helpers of

Rahab............Job 9:13   501

Raham—*pity*

Descendant of

Caleb............1 Chr. 2:44   389

Rain—*water falling from clouds*

A. *Features concerning:*

Sent by God....Jer. 14:22   733

Sent on all

mankind......Matt. 5:45   968

Sign of God's

goodness......Deut. 28:12   193

Controlled by

God's ⎰Job 28:26   513

decrees ......⎱Job 37:6   519

Withheld because of

sin............Deut. 11:17   180

Sent as a result of

judgment .....Gen. 7:4   10

SUBJECT	REFERENCE	PAGE

Autumn and

spring........Jer. 5:24   723

To be prayed

for............1 Kin. 8:35, 36   333

B. *Figurative of:*

God's Word....Is. 55:10, 11   703

Spiritual

blessing......Ps. 72:6   564

Righteous-

ness..........Hos. 10:12   859

Final

judgment .....Matt. 7:24-27   969

Hell ....Ps. 11:6   532

Earth's

ingathering ...James 5:7   1255

Rainbow

Appears after the

flood ....Gen. 9:12, 13   12

Sign of God's

covenant......Gen. 9:16, 17   12

Around angel's

head..........Rev. 10:1   1299

Over God's

throne..........Rev. 4:3   1296

Raisin cake—*a dried food substance*

As an offering....1 Chr. 16:1-3   402

Mourned for ......Is. 16:7   671

Raisins—*dried grapes*

Nourishing food...1 Sam. 25:18   286

Provided for

David ....2 Sam. 16:1   309

Rakem—*variegated*

Manassite........1 Chr. 7:16   394

Rakkath—*bank, shore*

Fortified city of

Naphtali........Josh. 19:32, 35   223

Rakkon—*shore*

Danite village ....Josh. 19:40, 46   223

Ram (I)—*high, exalted*

1. Ancestor of

David ....Ruth 4:19   259

Ancestor of

Christ........Matt. 1:3, 4   963

2. Man of

Judah........1 Chr. 2:25, 27   389

Ram (II)—*a male sheep*

Used as food ......Gen. 31:38   32

Used in

offerings.........Gen. 22:13   22

Appointed for certain

offerings.........Lev. 5:15   99

Skin of, used as

coverings........Ex. 26:14   77

Horns of, used as

trumpets........Josh. 6:4-13   210

Ram (III)—*an instrument of war*

Used to destroy gates and

walls ....Ezek. 4:2   788

Ramah

1. Town of

Asher.........Josh. 19:24, 29   222

2. City of

Naphtali .....Josh. 19:32, 36   223

3. Benjamite city near

Jerusalem ....Josh. 18:21, 25   222

Deborah's palm near

here ....Judg. 4:5   235

Fortress built ..1 Kin. 15:17-22   342

Gathering of

captives......Jer. 40:1   758

Reinhabited after

exile ....Ezra 2:26   454

Probable site of Rachel's

tomb..........1 Sam. 10:2   270

Samuel's head-

quarters.......1 Sam. 7:15, 17   268

David flees

to............1 Sam. 19:18-23   280

4. Town called Ramoth-

gilead.........2 Kin. 8:28, 29   363

SUBJECT	REFERENCE	PAGE

Ramathaim-zophim

Home of

Elkanah..........1 Sam. 1:1   263

Also called

"Ramah".......1 Sam. 1:19   263

See Ramah 4

Ramathite—*an inhabitant of Ramah*

Shimei called......1 Chr. 27:27   412

Ramath-mizpeh—*a town in Palestine*

An inheritance of

Gad..............Josh. 13:24-26   218

Rameses

Treasure city built by Hebrew

slaves ....Ex. 1:11   54

See Raamses

Ramoth—*high places*

1. Town of Issachar; possibly

same as Remeth and

Jarmuth ......Josh. 19:21   222

2. Town of the south; see Ramah

3. Town of

Gilead ....Deut. 4:43   174

Ramoth-gilead

City of ⎰Deut. 4:43   174

refuge east ⎱Josh. 20:8   223

of Jordan........⎱1 Chr. 6:80   394

Site of Ahab's fatal conflict with

Arameans ....1 Kin. 22:1-39   350

Rampart—*a city's outer fortification*

Around:

Certain cities......2 Sam. 20:15   314

Jerusalem.........Ps. 48:13   552

Ransom—*to redeem by a payment*

A. *Of man, for:*

Israelites ......Ex. 30:12-16   81

Murderer,

forbidden .....Num. 35:31, 32   165

Some,

unpayable.....Prov. 6:34, 35   614

Brother,

impossible.....Ps. 49:7, 8   553

B. *Of Christ:*

For all ....Matt. 20:28   984

From grave....Hos. 13:14   861

From Satan....Jer. 31:11   748

Cause of joy...Is. 35:10   686

Rapacity—*seizing others' goods; covetous*

Descriptive of

Satan ....1 Pet. 5:8   1264

Characteristic of false

teachers.........Luke 11:39   1041

Rape—*forced sexual relations*

A. *Features concerning:*

Death penalty

for............Deut. 22:25-27   189

Captives subjected

to.............Is. 13:16   669

B. *Example of:*

Tamar ⎰2 Sam. 13:6-29,

Amnon......⎱ 32, 33   306

Rapha, Raphah—*he (God) has healed*

1. Benjamin's fifth

son ....1 Chr. 8:1, 2   395

But not

listed.........Gen. 46:21   46

2. Descendant of

Jonathan......1 Chr. 8:37   395

Called Rephaiah

in.............1 Chr. 9:43   397

3. Same word translated

"giant".......2 Sam. 21:16-20   315

Raphu—*cured*

Benjamite.........Num. 13:9   141

SUBJECT	REFERENCE	PAGE

Retribution—*merited punishment for evil done*

A. *Expressed by:*
God's wrath ...Rom. 1:18 — 1132
Lamb's wrath........Rev. 6:16, 17 — 1297
Vengeance.....Jude 7 — 1287
Punishment....2 Thess. 1:6-9 — 1212
Corruption.....2 Pet. 2:9-22 — 1269

B. *Due to the sinner's:*
Sin ....Rom. 2:1-9 — 1132
Evil works....Ex. 32:34 — 84
Persecution of the righteous......2 Thess. 1:6 — 1212
Rejection of Christ........Heb. 10:29, 30 — 1245

C. *Deliverance from, by:*
Christ ....1 Thess. 1:10 — 1207
God's appointment........1 Thess. 5:9 — 1208

Return

Descriptive of:
Going back home.............Gen. 31:3, 13 — 31
Repentance ....2 Chr. 6:24, 38 — 423
Vengeance or retribution ....1 Kin. 2:33, 44 — 326
Divine visitation ..Joel 2:14 — 866
Christ's advent....Acts 15:16 — 1111
Death.............Gen. 3:19 — 7

Reu—*friend*

Descendant of Shem.............Gen. 11:10-21 — 13
In the genealogy of Jesus.............Luke 3:35 — 1029

Reuben—*behold a son*

Jacob's eldest son..............Gen. 29:31, 32 — 30
Guilty of misconduct; loses preeminence........Gen. 35:22 — 36
Proposes plan to save Joseph's life ....Gen. 37:21-29 — 37
Offers sons as pledge.............Gen. 42:37 — 43
Father of four sons.............Gen. 46:8, 9 — 46
Pronounced unstable.........Gen. 49:3, 4 — 48
Descendants of....Num. 26:5-11 — 154

Reubenites—*descendants of Reuben*

Divided into four tribal families.........Num. 26:5-11 — 154
Elizur, warrior ....Num. 1:5 — 127
Census of, at Sinai ....Num. 1:18-21 — 127
Census of, at conquest ....Num. 26:7 — 154
Place of, in march.............Num. 2:10 — 129
Seek inheritance east of Jordan ....Num. 32:1-42 — 161
Join in war against Canaanites .....Josh. 1:12-18 — 206
Altar erected by, misunderstood....Josh. 22:10-34 — 225
Criticized by Deborah.........Judg. 5:15, 16 — 236
Enslaved by Assyria...........2 Kin. 15:29 — 371

Reuel—*friend of God*

1. Son of Esau ...Gen. 36:2-4 — 36
2. Moses' father-in-law ....Ex. 2:18 — 55
3. Benjamite .....1 Chr. 9:8 — 396
4. Gadite leader ..Num. 2:14 — 129
Called Deuel..Num. 7:42, 47 — 135

Reumah—*exalted*

Nahor's concubine........Gen. 22:24 — 22

Revelation—*an uncovering of something hidden*

A. *Source of:*
God ....Dan. 2:28-47 — 837
Christ ....John 1:18 — 1064
The Spirit.....1 Cor. 2:10 — 1150
Not in man ....Matt. 16:17 — 980

B. *Objects of:*
God ....Matt. 11:25, 27 — 974
Christ ....2 Thess. 1:7 — 1212
Man of sin ....2 Thess. 2:3, 6, 8 — 1212

C. *Instruments of:*
Prophets.......1 Pet. 1:12 — 1261
Daniel ....Dan. 10:1 — 847
Christ ....Heb. 1:1, 2 — 1239
Apostles.......1 Cor. 2:10 — 1150
Paul ....Gal. 1:16 — 1177

D. *Of the first advent:*
Predicted .....Is. 40:5 — 689
Revealed ......Is. 53:1 — 701
Rejected.......John 12:38-41 — 1080
Of God's righteousness......Is. 56:1 — 704
Of peace and truth.......{Jer. 33:6-8 / Eph. 2:11-17} — 751 / 1186

E. *Time of the second advent:*
Uncovering....Matt. 10:26 — 972
Judgment......Luke 17:26-30 — 1048
Victory ....2 Thess. 2:3, 6, 8 — 1212
Glory ....1 Pet. 5:1 — 1264
Resurrection..Rom. 8:18, 19 — 1138
Reward.......1 Cor. 3:13 — 1150
Glorification ..1 John 3:2 — 1276
Grace.........1 Pet. 1:5, 13 — 1260
Exultation ....1 Pet. 4:13 — 1264

F. *Of divine truth, characteristics of:*
God-originated...Dan. 2:47 — 838
Verbal........Heb. 1:1 — 1239
In the created world .....Ps. 19:1, 2 — 536
Illuminative ..Eph. 1:17 — 1185
Now revealed.......Rom. 16:26 — 1145
Truth communicating.....Eph. 3:3, 4 — 1186

Revelation, the—*a book of the New Testament*

Vision of the Son of Man.............Rev. 1:9-20 — 1294
Message to the seven churches ....Rev. 2:1—3:22 — 1294
The book of seven seals ....Rev. 4:1—6:17 — 1296
The judgment.....Rev. 7:1—9:21 — 1297
The two beasts...Rev. 13 — 1301
Babylon doomed ....{Rev. 17:1— / 18:24} — 1304
The marriage supper............Rev. 19:6-10 — 1305
The judgment of the wicked............Rev. 20:11-15 — 1306
New heaven and new earth............Rev. 21:1-8 — 1307
The new Jerusalem ......Rev. 21:9—22:5 — 1307
Christ's coming ...Rev. 22:6-21 — 1308

Revenge—*to take vengeance*

A. *Manifestation of:*
Belongs to God............Rev. 18:20 — 1305
Performed by rulers.........Rom. 13:4 — 1142
Righteously allowed ....1 Kin. 20:42 — 349
Pleaded for ....Jer. 11:20 — 730
Disallowed among men.........Prov. 20:22 — 624
Forbidden to disciples......Luke 9:54, 55 — 1039

B. *Antidotes of:*
Overcome by kindness .....1 Sam. 25:30-34 — 286
Exhibit love...Luke 6:35 — 1033

Bless ....Rom. 12:14 — 1142
Forbear wrath.........Rom. 12:19 — 1142
Manifest forbearance...Matt. 5:38-41 — 967
Flee from......Gen. 27:41-45 — 28

C. *Examples of:*
Simeon and Levi...........Gen. 34:25 — 35
Joseph........Gen. 42:9-24 — 42
Samson........Judg. 16:28-30 — 248
Joab...........2 Sam. 3:27, 30 — 297
Jezebel ....1 Kin. 19:2 — 346
Ahab ....1 Kin. 22:26, 27 — 350
Haman ....Esth. 3:8-15 — 487
Philistines ....Ezek. 25:15-17 — 808
Herodias......Mark 6:19-24 — 1005
Jews..........Acts 7:54, 59 — 1102

Reverence—*a feeling of deep respect, love, awe, and esteem*

Manifested toward:
God................Ps. 89:7 — 574
God's house.....Lev. 19:30 — 114
Christ...........Matt. 21:37 — 985
Kings............1 Kin. 1:31 — 324
Parents ....Heb. 12:9 — 1247
Husbands ......Eph. 5:33 — 1189

Reverend—*worthy of reverence*

Applies only to God in the Scriptures........Ps. 111:9 — 588

Revile—*to speak of another abusively*

Christ, object of ....Matt. 27:39 — 994
Christ, submissive under ....1 Pet. 2:23 — 1262
Christians, objects of ....Matt. 5:11 — 966
Right attitude toward ....1 Cor. 4:12 — 1151
Excludes from Christian fellowship ......1 Cor. 5:11 — 1152
Punishment of ....1 Cor. 6:10 — 1152
False teachers.....2 Pet. 2:10-12 — 1269

Revival—*renewed zeal to obey God*

Conditions for:
Humility..........2 Chr. 7:14 — 425
Prayer ....2 Chr. 7:14 — 425
James 5:16 — 1256
Broken heart....Ps. 34:18 — 544
Confession .....Ps. 66:18 — 560
Repentance ....2 Cor. 7:10 — 1170
Turning from sin {2 Chr. 7:14 / 2 Tim. 2:19} — 425 / 1224
Complete surrender.......{Acts 9:5, 6 / Rom. 12:1, 2} — 1104 / 1141

Revive—*to live again more vigorously*

A. *Descriptive of:*
Renewed strength ......Gen. 45:27 — 46
Refreshment...Judg. 15:19 — 247
Restoration....Neh. 4:2 — 469
Resurrection...1 Kin. 17:22 — 344

B. *Of the Spirit:*
Given to the humble ....Is. 57:15 — 705
Source of joy ..Ps. 85:6 — 573
Possible even in trouble........Ps. 138:7 — 599
Source of fruitfulness.......{Hos. 6:2, 3 / Hos. 14:7} — 856 / 861

Reward of the righteous

A. *Described as:*
Sure...........Prov. 11:18 — 617
Full...........Ruth 2:12 — 257
Remembered ....2 Chr. 15:7 — 430
Great.........Matt. 5:12 — 966
Open ....Matt. 6:4, 6, 18 — 968

B. *Obtained by:*
Keeping God's commandments........Ps. 19:11 — 537

258

SUBJECT	REFERENCE	PAGE	SUBJECT	REFERENCE	PAGE	SUBJECT	REFERENCE	PAGE
Ring—continued			**Rizia**—_delight_			Wild..........2 Sam. 2:18		296
Gifts...........Ex. 35:22		87	Asherite ....1 Chr. 7:39		395	Hunted by		
Feminine						men..........Prov. 6:5		613
adornment....Is. 3:16, 21		660	**Rizpah**—_glowing coal_			In Solomon's		
Expressive of			Saul's concubine taken			provisions.....1 Kin. 4:23		328
position.......Luke 15:22		1046	by Abner.........2 Sam. 3:6-8		297	B. _Figurative of:_		
Sign of social			Sons of, killed.....2 Sam. 21:8, 9		315	Timidity.......Is. 13:14		669
status.........James 2:2		1254	Grief-stricken, cares			Swiftness.....2 Sam. 2:18		296
Ringleader—_the leader of a mob_			for corpses ....2 Sam. 21:10-14		315	Good wife....Prov. 5:19		612
Paul contemptuously			**Rob, robbery**			Church........Song 4:5		650
called ....Acts 24:5		1122	A. _Used literally of:_			Christ........Song 2:9, 17		649
Rinnah—_ringing cry_			Plundering.....1 Sam. 23:1		283	_See Hart; Hind_		
Son of Shimon....1 Chr. 4:20		390	Taking from the			**Rogelim**—_spies_		
Riot—_an unruly mob_			poor ....Prov. 22:22		626	Town in Gilead ...2 Sam. 17:27		311
Pacified by town			Robbers ....Judg. 9:25		241	**Rogue**—_a mischievous individual_		
craftsman........Acts 19:20-41		1116	B. _Used figuratively of:_			Descriptive of the		
Riotous—_living without restraint_			Dishonest			fraudulent.....Is. 32:5, 7		683
Loose living.......Luke 15:13		1046	riches........Ps. 62:10		559	**Rohgah**—_tumult_		
Gluttonous			Holding back from			Asherite ....1 Chr. 7:34		395
eaters ....Prov. 23:20, 21		627	God..........Mal. 3:8, 9		931	**Romamti-ezer**—_I have raised up help_		
Sexual			False			Son of Heman ....1 Chr. 25:4, 31		410
promiscuity ......Rom. 13:13		1142	teachers ......John 10:1, 8		1076	**Roman**		
Riphath—_descendants of Gomer_			Taking			1. Inhabitant of		
Son of Gomer....Gen. 10:3		12	wages........2 Cor. 11:8		1172	Rome..........Acts 2:10		1095
Called Diphath....1 Chr. 1:6		387	**Rock**			2. Official agent of the Roman		
Rise, risen, rising, raised			A. _Used for:_			government...John 11:46		1078
A. _Of resurrection:_			Altars ....Judg. 6:20, 26		237	3. Person possessing Roman		
Christ's........Mark 8:31		1008	Idol worship...Is. 57:5		704	citizenship ....Acts 16:21-38		1113
Believers'			Protection .....1 Sam. 13:6		273	**Romans, the Epistle to the**—_a book of_		
(spiritually) ...Col. 2:12		1201	Shade ....Is. 32:2		683	_the New Testament_		
Believers'			Inscriptions...Job 19:24		507	The power of the		
(physically) ...John 11:23, 24		1078	Executions.....2 Chr. 25:12		438	Gospel ....Rom. 1:16		1132
B. _Of Christ's resurrection:_			Foundations ...Matt. 7:24, 25		969	The pagans		
Predicted ......Mark 14:28		1017	Shelter ....Job 24:8		511	condemned......Rom. 1:17-32		1132
Fulfilled ....Matt. 28:6, 7		995	Tomb.........Matt. 27:60		994	The Jews		
Remem-			B. _Miracles connected with:_			condemned......Rom. 2:1-9		1132
bered ....John 2:22		1066	Water from....Ex. 17:6		69	The advantages of		
Evidenced .....John 21:14		1088	Fire from ......Judg. 6:21		237	the Jews ....Rom. 3:1-8		1133
Preached ......1 Cor. 15:11-15		1160	Broken by			None righteous....Rom. 3:9-20		1133
Misunder-			wind..........1 Kin. 19:11		347	Righteousness through		
stood ....Mark 9:9, 10		1009	Torn at Christ's			faith.............Rom. 3:21-31		1133
Rissah—_ruin; rain_			death........Matt. 27:51		994	Abraham		
Israelite camp.....Num. 33:21, 22		162	C. _Figurative of Christ, as:_			justified.........Rom. 4		1134
Rithmah—_broom plant_			Refuge ....Is. 32:2		683	The second		
Israelite camp.....Num. 33:18, 19		162	Foundation of the			Adam ....Rom. 5:12-21		1135
Rivalry—_competition_			Church ....Matt. 16:18		980	On baptism ....Rom. 6		1135
Between man and			Source of			The pull of sin ....Rom. 7		1136
neighbor ....Eccl. 4:4		640	blessings.......1 Cor. 10:4		1156	The spiritual life ..Rom. 8		1137
River—_a large stream of water_			Stone of			The destiny of the		
A. _Uses of:_			stumbling....Is. 8:14		664	Jews ....Rom. 9—11		1138
Water ....Jer. 2:18		719	Foundation of			Life as worship....Rom. 12:1, 2		1141
Irrigation......Gen. 2:10		5	faith ....Matt. 7:24, 25		969	Serving the		
Bathing........Ex. 2:5		55	**Rock badger**—_the Aramean rock hyrax_			body ....Rom. 12:3-21		1141
Baptisms....Matt. 3:6		965	Listed as			Bearing with one		
Healing.......2 Kin. 5:10		360	unclean ....Lev. 11:5		104	another ....Rom. 14—15		1143
B. _List of:_			Lives among			Greetings.......Rom. 16:1-24		1144
Abanah ......2 Kin. 5:12		360	rocks............Ps. 104:18		582	**Rome**—_the chief city of Italy_		
Arnon ....Josh. 12:1		216	Likened to			Jews expelled		
Chebar .....Ezek. 10:15, 20		793	people............Prov. 30:26		633	from ....Acts 18:2		1115
Euphrates .....Gen. 2:14		5	**Rod**—_a staff or stick_			Paul:		
Gihon ....Gen. 2:13		5	A. _Used for:_			Writes to Christians		
Gozan ....2 Kin. 17:6		372	Sign of			of ....Rom. 1:7		1131
Jabbok ....Deut. 2:37		171	authority......Ex. 4:17, 20		57	Desires to go		
Jordan........Josh. 3:8		208	Egyptians'			to ....Acts 19:21		1116
Kanah........Josh. 16:8		220	staffs........Ex. 7:12		59	Comes to ....Acts 28:14		1126
Kishon ....Judg. 5:21		236	Punishment....Ex. 21:20		73	Imprisoned in ....Acts 28:16		1126
Nile (Shihor)...Jer. 2:18		719	Club...........1 Sam. 14:27		274	**Rompha**—_a name for Kiyyun (the_		
Pharpar........2 Kin. 5:12		360	Correction of			_planet Saturn)_		
Pison ....Gen. 2:11		5	children.......Prov. 13:24		619	Worshiped by (Amos 5:26		875
Tigris.........Gen. 2:14		5	B. _Figurative of:_			Israelites ....(Acts 7:41-43		1102
Ulai ....Dan. 8:2, 16		844	Christ ....Is. 11:1		667	**Root**—_the part of a plant underground_		
C. _Figurative of:_			Christ's rule ...Ps. 2:9		529	_Used figuratively of:_		
Prosperity of			Authority.....Is. 14:5, 29		669	Material		
saints ....Ps. 1:3		528	The Gospel ...Ps. 110:2		587	foundation ....Jer. 12:2		730
Affliction ......Ps. 124:4		596	**Rodanim**			Remnant..........Judg. 5:14		236
Christ ....Is. 32:1, 2		683	Descendants of			National		
God's			Javan...........1 Chr. 1:7		387	existence.........Is. 14:30		670
presence ......Is. 33:21		684	**Roe, roebuck**—_the deer, gazelle_			National source ...Rom. 11:16-18		1140
Peace.........Is. 66:12		713	A. _Described as:_			Source of evil .....1 Tim. 6:10		1220
Holy Spirit....John 7:38, 39		1073	Fit for food ....Deut. 12:15, 24		181			
			Cheerful.......Prov. 5:19		612			
			Swift ....1 Chr. 12:8		399			

SUBJECT   REFERENCE   PAGE | SUBJECT   REFERENCE   PAGE | SUBJECT   REFERENCE   PAGE

Judgment and
destruction........1 Kin. 14:15   341
Restoration ......2 Kin. 19:30   376
Spiritual life......Hos. 14:5   861
Spiritual
foundation ......Eph. 3:17   1186
Messiah..........Is. 11:1, 10   667

Rose—a beautiful flower
Of Sharon........Song 2:1   649

Rosh—head, chief
1. Benjamin's
son ....Gen. 46:21   46
2. Northern people connected with
Meshech and
Tubal ....Ezek. 38:2   820

Rot—to decay
A. *Used literally of:*
Sickness......Num. 5:21-27   133
Hardwood
trees..........Is. 40:20   689
B. *Used figuratively of:*
Wicked......Prov. 10:7   616
Foolish wife ..Prov. 12:4   617

Rowing—to navigate a boat with oars
Against odds.....Jon. 1:13   886
With much
labor ....Mark 6:48   1006

Royal—belonging to a king
A. *Used literally of:*
King's
children......2 Kin. 11:1   366
Robes of
royalty.......Esth. 6:8   489
City of a
king ....2 Sam. 12:26   305
B. *Used spiritually of:*
True Israel....Is. 62:3   709
True Church...1 Pet. 2:9   1261

Ruby—a precious stone
Used in the "breastpiece of
judgment".......Ex. 28:15-17   79
In the garden of
Eden........Ezek. 28:13   811
Worn by high
priest.............Ex. 28:17   79

Rudder—a steering apparatus
Literally..........Acts 27:40   1126
Figuratively......James 3:4   1254

Rudeness—discourtesy
Shown toward:
Christ.........Matt. 26:67, 68   992
Paul ....Acts 23:2   1120

Rue—a pungent perennial shrub
Tithed by
Pharisees.........Luke 11:42   1041

Rufus—red-haired
1. Son of Simeon of
Cyrene.......Mark 15:21   1019
2. Christian of
Rome ....Rom. 16:13   1145
Probably the same as 1.

Ruhamah—pitied
Symbolic name for
Israel.............Hos. 2:1   854

Rule—to govern
A. *Of natural things:*
Sun and
moon ....Gen. 1:16, 18   4
Sea ....Ps. 89:9   574
B. *Among men:*
Man over
woman.......Gen. 3:16   7
King over
people ....Ezra 4:20   457
Diligent over the
lazy...........Prov. 12:24   618

Servant over a
son ....Prov. 17:2   621
Rich over
poor ....Prov. 22:7   625
Servants over a
people ....Neh. 5:15   471
C. *Of the Messiah:*
Predicted ......Is. 40:9, 10   689
Promised .....Zech. 6:13   921
Victorious .....Ps. 110:2   587
Announced ....Matt. 2:6   964
Established ....Rev. 12:5   1301
Described......Rev. 2:27   1295

Ruler—one who governs
A. *Good characteristics of:*
Upholding the
good......Rom. 13:3   1142
Believing .....Matt. 9:18, 23   971
Chosen by
God..........2 Sam. 7:8   300
B. *Bad characteristics of:*
Men-pleasers ..John 12:42, 43   1080
Ignorant.......Acts 3:17   1097
Hostile.........Acts 4:26   1098
Loving
bribes........Hos. 4:18   856
C. *Respect toward:*
Commanded ....Ex. 22:28   74
Illustrated .....Acts 23:5   1121

Rumah—high place
Residence of
Pedaiah ....2 Kin. 23:36   381

Run—to move swiftly
A. *Used literally of:*
Man..........Num. 11:27   140
Water ....Ps. 105:41   583
Fire............Ex. 9:23   62
Race..........1 Cor. 9:24   1155
B. *Used figuratively of:*
Eagerness in:
Evil.........Prov. 1:16   609
Good ....Ps. 119:32   591
Joy of
salvation ....Ps. 23:5   539
Christian life..1 Cor. 9:26   1155

Running sore
Makes an animal
unacceptable .....Lev. 22:22   116

Rush—a cylindrical, often hollow marsh
plant
Cut off from Israel; rendered
"bulrush" ....Is. 9:14   665
Concerning
growth of ....Job 8:11   500
Signifying
restoration ......Is. 35:7   685

Rust—corrosion of metals
Destruction of earthly
treasures........Matt. 6:19, 20   968
Of gold and
silver............James 5:3   1255
Used
figuratively......Ezek. 24:6-12   807

Ruth—female companion
Moabitess........Ruth 1:4   256
Follows Naomi...Ruth 1:6-18   256
Marries Boaz.....Ruth 4:9-13   258
Ancestress of   { Ruth 4:13, 21,
Christ..........   {   22   258

Ruth, the Book of—a book of the Old
Testament
Naomi's
misfortunes ......Ruth 1:1-14   256
Ruth's loyalty.....Ruth 1:14-22   256
The favor of
Boaz ....Ruth 2:1-23   256
Boaz redeems .....Ruth 3:8—4:12   258
The generations of
Ruth ....Ruth 4:13-22   258

S

Sabachthani—hast thou forsaken me?
Christ's cry on the
cross.............Matt. 27:46   994

Sabaoth—hosts
God as Lord of....Rom. 9:29   1139
               James 5:4   1255
See Hosts, Lord of

Sabbath—rest
A. *History of:*
Instituted at
creation.......Gen. 2:2, 3   5
Observed before
Sinai..........Ex. 16:22-30   68
Commanded at
Sinai..........Ex. 20:8-11   72
Repeated at Canaan's
entry.........Deut. 5:12-15   174
References
to............2 Kin. 4:23   358
Proper observance of,
described......Is. 56:2-7   704
Postexilic Jews encouraged to
keep..........Neh. 10:31   477
Perversion of, condemned by
Christ.........Luke 13:14-17   1044
Christ teaches
on ....Mark 6:2   1005
Paul preached
on ....Acts 13:14   1109
B. *Features concerning:*
Commemorative of
creation......Ex. 20:8-11   72
Seventh day during the Old
Testament ....Deut. 5:14   174
Observance of, a perpetual
covenant......Ex. 31:16, 17   83
Made for man's
good.........Mark 2:27   1001
Christ's Lordship
over ....Luke 6:5   1032
C. *Regulations concerning:*
Work prohibited
on ....Lev. 23:3   117
Cattle must rest
on ....Ex. 20:10   72
Business forbidden
on ....Jer. 17:21, 22   736
To last from evening until
evening.......Lev. 23:32   118
Worship on ...Ezek. 46:3   828
Works of mercy
on ....Matt. 12:12   974
Necessities lawful
on ....Luke 13:15, 16   1044
See First day of the week

Sabbath day's journey—about 3,100 feet
Between Mt. Olivet and
Jerusalem ....Acts 1:12   1094

Sabbatical year—a rest every seventh
year
A. *Purpose of:*
Rest the land ..Ex. 23:10, 11   74
Emancipate
slaves.......Ex. 21:2-6   72
Remit debts....Deut. 15:1-6   183
B. *Allusions to, in history, in:*
Time of the
judges ....Ruth 4:1-10   258
Pre-exilic
times ....Jer. 32:6-16   750
Postexilic
times ....Neh. 10:31   477
C. *Spiritual significance of:*
Punishment for non-
observance....Lev. 26:33-35   121
Illustrative of
spiritual   { Is. 61:1-3   708
release ....{ Luke 4:18-21   1030

SUBJECT	REFERENCE	PAGE

Scribes—continued

Questioning His
authority......Luke 20:1, 2 — 1051

D. *Christ's attitude toward:*
Exposes
them.........Matt. 23:13-36 — 987
Condemns
them.........Luke 20:46, 47 — 1052
Calls them
hypocrites.....Matt. 15:1-9 — 978

Scriptures—*God's revelation*

A. *Called:*
Word of God ..Heb. 4:12 — 1241
Word of
truth.........James 1:18 — 1253
Oracles of
God.........Rom. 3:2 — 1133
Word.........James 1:21-23 — 1253
Holy
Scriptures.....Rom. 1:2 — 1131
Sword of the
Spirit ....Eph. 6:17 — 1190
Scriptures of the
prophets ......Rom. 16:26 — 1145

B. *Described as:*
Author-
itative.........1 Pet. 4:11 — 1264
Inspired ....2 Tim. 3:16 — 1225
Effectual in
life...........1 Thess. 2:13 — 1207
True...........Ps. 119:160 — 594
Sharp.........Heb. 4:12 — 1241

C. *Inspiration of, proved by:*
External
evidence ......Heb. 2:1-4 — 1239
Internal
nature ......2 Tim. 3:16, 17 — 1225
Infallibility.....John 10:35 — 1077
Fulfillment of (John 5:39,
prophecy.....(45-47 — 1070

D. *Understanding of, by:*
Spirit's
illumination...1 Cor. 2:10-14 — 1150
Searching.....John 5:39 — 1070
Reasoning .....Acts 17:2 — 1114
Comparing ...2 Pet. 1:20, 21 — 1268
Human help ...Acts 17:10-12 — 1114

E. *Proper uses of:*
Regener-
ation..........1 Pet. 1:23 — 1261
Salvation ......2 Tim. 3:15 — 1225
Producing
life............John 20:31 — 1088
Searching our
hearts........Heb. 4:12 — 1241
Spiritual
growth........Acts 20:32 — 1118
Sanctifi-
cation........John 17:17 — 1084
Illumination ...Ps. 119:105 — 593
Keeping from
sin............Ps. 119:9, 11 — 590
Defeating
Satan.........Eph. 6:16, 17 — 1190
Proving
truth.........Acts 18:28 — 1116

F. *Misuses of, by:*
Satan.........Matt. 4:6 — 966
Hypocrites.....Matt. 22:23-29 — 986
False
teachers ......2 Cor. 2:17 — 1167
Untaught ......2 Pet. 3:16 — 1269

G. *Positive attitudes toward:*
Let dwell in
richly ....Col. 3:16 — 1202
Search daily ...Acts 17:11 — 1114
Hide in the
heart.........Ps. 119:11 — 591
Delight in......Ps. 1:2 — 528
Love.........Ps. 119:97, 113,
167 — 593
Receive with
humility .....James 1:21 — 1253
Teach to
children.......Deut. 11:19 — 180
Obey ....James 1:22 — 1253

H. *Negative attitudes toward, not to:*
Add to or subtract
from ....Deut. 4:2 — 172
Adulterate.....2 Cor. 4:2 — 1167
Distort.........2 Pet. 3:16 — 1269
Invalidating by
traditions .....Mark 7:9-13 — 1007

I. *Fulfillment of, cited to show:*
Christ's:
Mission.......Luke 4:16-21 — 1030
Death ....Luke 24:27, 45-
47 — 1058
Rejection.....Acts 28:25-29 — 1126
Resurrec-
tion.........Acts 2:24-31 — 1095
Spirit's
descent ....John 14:16-21 — 1081
Faith ....Rom. 4:3 — 1134

J. *Distortion of:*
Condemned....Prov. 30:5, 6 — 633
Rev. 22:18-20 — 1308
Predicted ......2 Tim. 4:3, 4 — 1225

K. *Memorization of:*
Keeps from
sin............Ps. 119:11 — 591
Gives under-
standing ......Ps. 119:130 — 593
Facilitates
prayer ....John 15:7 — 1082

Scriptures, devotional readings

A. *For personal needs:*
Comfort ....Ps. 43:1-5 — 550
Rom. 8:26-28 — 1138
Courage ....Ps. 46:1-11 — 551
2 Cor. 4:7-18 — 1167
Direction ......Heb. 4:16 — 1241
James 1:5, 6 — 1253
Peace..........Ps. 4:1-8 — 529
Phil. 4:4-7 — 1195
Relief..........Ps. 91:1-16 — 576
2 Cor. 12:8-10 — 1173
Rest ....Matt. 11:28-30 — 974
Rom. 8:31-39 — 1138
Temptation ....Ps. 1:1-6 — 528
1 Cor. 10:6-13 — 1156
James 1:12-16 — 1253

B. *For Instruction:*
Sermon on the
mount ....Matt. 5:1—7:29 — 966
Prayer........Matt. 6:5-15 — 968
Phil. 4:6, 7 — 1195
Golden rule....Matt. 7:12 — 969
Great com-
mandment ...Matt. 22:36-40 — 986
Salvation .....John 3:1-36 — 1066
Good
shepherd......John 10:1-18 — 1076
Spiritual (John 15:1-17 — 1082
fruit..........(Gal. 5:22, 23 — 1181
Guilt ....Rom. 8:1 — 1137
Righ-
teousness .....Rom. 3:19-28 — 1133
Justification ...Rom. 5:1-21 — 1135
Christian (Rom. 12:1-21 — 1141
service ......(Rom. 13:1-14 — 1142
Love...........1 Cor. 13:1-13 — 1158
Stewardship ...2 Cor. 8:1-24 — 1170
2 Cor. 9:1-15 — 1171
Regenera-
tion...........Eph. 2:1-10 — 1185
Christ's
exaltation.....Phil. 2:5-11 — 1194
Resurrection...1 Thess. 4:13-18 — 1208
Judgment......Rev. 20:10-15 — 1306
New heaven (Rev. 21:1-27 — 1307
and earth ....(Rev. 22:1-5 — 1307

Scroll—*a papyrus or leather roll (book)*

Applied to the
sky...............Is. 34:4 — 685
Prophesy of the Messiah
written in ....Ps. 40:7 — 548
State documents
written on.......Ezra 6:1, 2 — 458
Sky split apart
like a............Rev. 6:14 — 1297

Scythians—*natives of Scythia*

In the Christian
church.........Col. 3:11 — 1201

Sea—*a large body of water*

A. *Described as:*
Created by
God.........Acts 4:24 — 1098
Deep ....Ps. 68:22 — 562
Turbulent and
dangerous.....Ps. 89:9 — 574
All rivers flow
into...........Eccl. 1:7 — 638
Bound by God's
decree ......Jer. 5:22 — 723
Manifesting God's
works........Ps. 104:24, 25 — 582

B. *List of, in the Bible:*
Great Sea (Mediter-
ranean) ......Ezek. 47:10 — 830
Salt or Dead
Sea ....Gen. 14:3 — 15
Red Sea ....Ex. 10:19 — 63
Sea of Galilee
(Chinnereth).. Num. 34:11 — 163
Adriatic......Acts 27:27 — 1125

C. *Figurative of:*
Extension of the
Gospel........Is. 11:9 — 668
Righ-
teousness .....Is. 48:18 — 698
False
teachers ......Jude 13 — 1287

Sea, cast metal

Bowl in the
Temple........1 Kin. 7:23 — 331

Sea monster

Jonah............Matt. 12:40 — 975
Created by God ...Gen. 1:21 — 4

Sea of glass

Before the throne of
God ....Rev. 4:6 — 1296

Seal—*instrument used to authenticate ownership*

A. *Used literally to:*
Guarantee business
deals.........Jer. 32:11-14 — 750
Ratify
documents....Neh. 10:1 — 477
Ensure a
prophecy......Dan. 9:24 — 847
Protect
books ....Rev. 5:2, 5, 9 — 1296
Lock doors ....Matt. 27:66 — 994

B. *Used figuratively of:*
Ownership of
married (Song 4:12 — 651
love...........(Song 8:6 — 653
God's witness to
Christ........John 6:27 — 1071
Believer's
security........2 Cor. 1:22 — 1166
Assurance .....Eph. 4:30 — 1188
God's ownership of His
people ....Rev. 7:3-8 — 1298

Seamstress—*a dressmaker*

Dorcas known
as.................Acts 9:36-42 — 1105

Search—*to make intensive investigation*

A. *Applied literally to:*
Records........Ezra 4:15, 19 — 456
Child ....Matt. 2:8 — 964
Scriptures ....John 5:39 — 1070

B. *Applied figuratively to:*
Man's heart....Ps. 139:1, 23 — 600
Under-
standing ......Prov. 2:4 — 610
Conscience ....Prov. 20:27 — 624
Self-examin-
ation..........Judg. 5:16 — 236

SUBJECT	REFERENCE	PAGE	SUBJECT	REFERENCE	PAGE	SUBJECT	REFERENCE	PAGE

SUBJECT	REFERENCE	PAGE	SUBJECT	REFERENCE	PAGE	SUBJECT	REFERENCE	PAGE

Shamble—*meat market*

Question concerning meat
bought in ....1 Cor. 10:25 — 1156

Shame—*a feeling of guilt*

A. *Caused by:*
Rape ....2 Sam. 13:13 — 306
Defeat.........2 Chr. 32:21 — 445
Folly ....Prov. 3:35 — 611
Idleness ......Prov. 10:5 — 616
Pride ....Prov. 11:2 — 616
A wicked
wife..........Prov. 12:4 — 617
Lying.........Prov. 13:5 — 618
Stub-
bornness.....Prov. 13:18 — 619
Haste in
speech ....Prov. 18:13 — 622
Mistreatment of
parents ....Prov. 19:26 — 623
Evil
companions ...Prov. 28:7 — 631
Juvenile
delinquency...Prov. 29:15 — 632
Nakedness.....Is. 47:3 — 696
Idolatry.......Jer. 2:26, 27 — 719
Impropriety....1 Cor. 11:6 — 1156
Lust ....Phil. 3:19 — 1195

B. *Of the unregenerate:*
Hardened in ...Jer. 8:12 — 726
Pleasure ⎰Rom. 1:26, 27,
in............⎱　　　32 — 1132
Vessels of.....Rom. 9:21 — 1139
Glory in ......Phil. 3:19 — 1195
Like foam ....Jude 13 — 1287

C. *In the Christian life, of:*
Unregenerate's
life..........Rom. 6:21 — 1136
Sinful things...Eph. 5:12 — 1188
Improper
behavior ......1 Cor. 11:14, 22 — 1157
Christ ....Rom. 1:16 — 1132

Shamgar—*cupbearer*

Judge of Israel; struck down 600
Philistines ....Judg. 3:31 — 235

Shamhuth—*desolation*

Commander in David's
army............1 Chr. 27:8 — 412

Shamir—*a sharp point*

1. Town in
Judah.........Josh. 15:1, 48 — 218
2. Town in
Ephraim .....Judg. 10:1 — 242
3. Levite ....1 Chr. 24:24 — 410

Shamma—*astonishment*

Asherite ....1 Chr. 7:36, 37 — 395

Shammah—*waste*

1. Son of Reuel...Gen. 36:13, 17 — 36
2. Son of Jesse ...1 Sam. 16:9 — 277
Called
Shimea ......1 Chr. 2:13 — 389
3. One of David's mighty
men..........2 Sam. 23:11 — 317
Also called Shammoth the
Harorite....1 Chr. 11:27 — 398

Shammai—*celebrated*

1. Grandson of
Jerahmeel...1 Chr. 2:28, 32 — 389
2. Descendant of
Caleb ....1 Chr. 2:44, 45 — 389
3. Descendant of
Judah.........1 Chr. 4:17 — 390

Shammoth—*waste*

One of David's mighty
men............1 Chr. 11:27 — 398

Shammua—*renowned*

1. Reubenite
spy ....Num. 13:2-4 — 141
2. Son of David ..2 Sam. 5:13, 14 — 299
3. Levite ....Neh. 11:17 — 478
4. Postexilic
priest ....Neh. 12:1, 18 — 478

Shamsherai—*sunlike*

Son of Jeroham ...1 Chr. 8:26 — 395

Shapham—*youthful*

Gadite ....1 Chr. 5:12 — 391

Shaphan—*prudent, shy*

Scribe under
Josiah............2 Kin. 22:3 — 378
Takes book of the Law to
Josiah............2 Kin. 22:8-10 — 379
Is sent to Huldah for
interpretation ....2 Kin. 22:14 — 379
Assists in repairs of
Temple...........2 Chr. 34:8 — 447
Father of notable ⎰Jer. 36:10-12,
son..............⎱　　25 — 754

Shaphat—*he has judged*

1. Simeonite
spy ....Num. 13:2-5 — 141
2. Son of
Shemaiah.....1 Chr. 3:22 — 390
3. Gadite chief ...1 Chr. 5:11, 12 — 391
4. One of David's
herdsmen .....1 Chr. 27:29 — 412
5. Father of the prophet
Elisha.........1 Kin. 19:16, 19 — 347

Shaphir—*glittering*

Town of Judah....Mic. 1:11 — 891

Sharai—*Yahweh is deliverer*

Divorced his foreign
wife..............Ezra 10:34, 40 — 462

Sharar—*firm*

Father of Ahiam ..2 Sam. 23:33 — 318

Sharers

A. *Of physical things:*
Sacrifices ......1 Cor. 10:18 — 1156
Suffering ......2 Cor. 1:7 — 1166
1 Pet. 4:13 — 1264

B. *Of evil things:*
Sins ....1 Tim. 5:22 — 1220

C. *Of spiritual things:*
Holiness ....Heb. 12:10 — 1247
Communion ...1 Cor. 10:16, 17 — 1156
Spiritual
things........Rom. 15:27 — 1144
Inheritance ....Col. 1:12 — 1200

Sharezer, Sherezer—*protect the king*

1. Son of Sennach-
erib..........Is. 37:38 — 688
2. Sent to Zechariah concerning
fasting........Zech. 7:1-3 — 921

Sharon—*plain*

1. Coastal plain between Joppa
and Mt.
Carmel........1 Chr. 27:29 — 412
Famed for
roses..........Song 2:1 — 649
2. Pasture east of the
Jordan ....1 Chr. 5:16 — 391

Sharonite—*an inhabitant of Sharon*

Shitrai ....1 Chr. 27:29 — 412

Sharp—*having a keen edge; biting*

A. *Descriptive of:*
Flints.........Ex. 4:25 — 57
Knives.........Josh. 5:2, 3 — 209
Plowshare ....1 Sam. 13:20, 21 — 273
Crag...........1 Sam. 14:4 — 273
Arrows ....Is. 5:28 — 662

B. *Used to compare a sword with:*
Tongue........Ps. 57:4 — 557
Adulteress....Prov. 5:4 — 612
Mouth........Is. 49:2 — 698
God's Word....Heb. 4:12 — 1241

C. *Figurative of:*
Deceit-
fulness.......Ps. 52:2 — 554

Falsehood .....Prov. 25:18 — 629
Disagree-
ment.........Acts 15:39 — 1112
Severe
rebuke........2 Cor. 13:10 — 1174
Christ's
conquest......Rev. 14:14-18 — 1302

Sharuhen—*abode of pleasure*

Town of Judah assigned to
Simeon..........Josh. 19:1, 6 — 222
Called ⎰Josh. 15:36 — 219
Shaaraim........⎱1 Chr. 4:31 — 391

Shashai—*whitish*

Divorced his foreign
wife ....Ezra 10:34, 40 — 462

Shashak—*assaulter*

Benjamite.........1 Chr. 8:14, 25 — 395

Shaul—*asked (of God)*

1. King of
Edom ....Gen. 36:37 — 37
2. Son of
Simeon ....Gen. 46:10 — 46
Founder of a tribal
family.........Num. 26:13 — 155
3. Kohathite
Levite.........1 Chr. 6:24 — 392

Shave—*to cut off the hair*

A. *Used worthily to express:*
Accommo-
dation........Gen. 41:14 — 41
Cleansing......Lev. 14:8, 9 — 108
Commit-
ment.........Deut. 21:12 — 188
Mourning......Job 1:18-20 — 496
Sorrow ....Jer. 41:5 — 759

B. *Used unworthily to express:*
Defeat of a
Nazirite.......Judg. 16:19 — 248
Contempt......2 Sam. 10:4 — 303
Unnatural-
ness...........1 Cor. 11:5, 6 — 1156

Shaveh—*plain*

Valley near Salem; Abram meets
king of Sodom
here..............Gen. 14:17, 18 — 16

Shaveh-kiriathaim—*plain of Kiriathaim*

Plain near Kiriathaim inhabited by
Emim ....Gen. 14:5 — 15

Shavsha, Shisha—*nobility*

David's
secretary ......1 Chr. 18:14, 16 — 405
Serves under Solomon
also ....1 Kin. 4:3 — 327

Sheal—*asking*

Divorced his foreign
wife..............Ezra 10:29 — 462

Shealtiel—*I have asked God*

Son of King Jeconiah and father of
Zerubbabel.......1 Chr. 3:17 — 390

Sheariah—*Yahweh has esteemed*

Descendant of
Saul..............1 Chr. 9:44 — 397

Shear-jashub—*a remnant shall return*

Symbolic name given to Isaiah's
son...............Is. 7:3 — 663

Sheath—*casing*

For God's sword ..Jer. 47:6 — 764

Sheba—*seven; an oath*

1. City in territory assigned to
Simeon........Josh. 19:1, 2 — 222
2. Benjamite insur-
rectionist ....2 Sam. 20:1-22 — 314
3. Descendant of Cush through
Raamah.......Gen. 10:7 — 12
4. Descendant of
Shem ....Gen. 10:28 — 13

SUBJECT	REFERENCE	PAGE	SUBJECT	REFERENCE	PAGE	SUBJECT	REFERENCE	PAGE

Shut—continued

Christ's
sovereignty ...Rev. 3:7, 8   1295

Shuthelah

1. Son of Ephraim; head of a
family........Num. 26:35, 36   155
2. Ephraimite.....1 Chr. 7:20, 21   394

Shuttle—*a weaving tool*

Our days swifter
than.............Job 7:6   500

Sia, Siaha—*assembly*

Family of
returning
Temple   ⌠Ezra 2:43, 44   455
servants.........⌡Neh. 7:47   472

Sibbecai

One of David's mighty
men.............1 Chr. 11:29   398
Kills a Philistine
giant...........2 Sam. 21:18   315
Commander of a
division ....1 Chr. 27:11   412

Sibmah—*balsam*

Town of Reuben ..Num. 32:3, 38   161
Famous for
wines ....Is. 16:8, 9   671

Sibraim—*double hope*

Place in north
Palestine ....Ezek. 47:16   830

Sick, Sickness—*the state of being unwell*

A. *Caused by:*
Age...........Gen. 48:1, 10   48
Ill ....2 Kin. 1:2   355
Wine ....Hos. 7:5   857
Sins ....Mic. 6:13   894
Despon-
dency........Prov. 13:12   618
Prophetic
visions ....Dan. 8:27   846
Love..........Song 2:5   649
God's
judgment .....2 Chr. 21:14-19   435
God's
sovereignty ...John 11:4   1077

B. *Healing of, by:*
Fig cake.......2 Kin. 20:7   377
Miracle ....1 Kin. 17:17-23   344
Prayer........James 5:14, 15   1256
God's mercy ...Phil. 2:25-30   1194

See Diseases; Healing

Sickle—*an instrument for cutting grain*

Literally..........Deut. 16:9   184
Figuratively......Mark 4:29   1003
               Rev. 14:14-19   1302

Siddim, Valley of

Valley of bitumen pits near the
Dead Sea........Gen. 14:3, 8, 10   15

Sidon—*fishery*

Canaanite city 20 miles north of
Tyre.............Gen. 10:15, 19   13
Israel's northern
boundary........Josh. 19:28   222
Canaanites not expelled
from ....Judg. 1:31   233
Israelites oppressed
by..............Judg. 10:12   243
Gods of, entice
Israelites ....1 Kin. 11:5, 33   336
Judgments pronounced
on..............Is. 23:12   676
Israelites sold as slaves
by..............Joel 3:4-6   867
People from, hear
Jesus.............Luke 6:17   1032
Visited by Jesus...Matt. 15:21   979
Paul visits at......Acts 27:3   1124

Siege of a city—*a military blockade*

A. *Methods employed in:*
Supplies cut
off ....2 Kin. 19:24   376
Ambushes
laid ....Judg. 9:34   241
Battering rams
used ....Ezek. 4:2   788
Arrows shot ...2 Kin. 19:32   376

B. *Suffering of:*
Famine........2 Kin. 6:26-29   361
Pestilence......Jer. 21:6   738

C. *Examples of:*
Jericho ....Josh. 6:2-20   210
Jerusalem......2 Kin. 24:10, 11   381

See War

Sieve, sift—*screen*

Used figuratively of:
God's judgment ...Amos 9:9   878
Satan's
temptation ......Luke 22:31   1055

Sign—*an outward token having spiritual significance*

A. *Descriptive of:*
Heavenly
bodies.........Gen. 1:14   4
Rainbow........Gen. 9:12-17   12
Circum-
cision ....Gen. 17:11   17
Bloodshed .....Ex. 12:13   64
God's
wonders ......Ps. 65:8   560
Covenant......Rom. 4:11   1134
Miracles ....Deut. 26:8   192
Memorial......Num. 16:38   146
Symbolic act...Is. 8:18   664
Witness........Is. 19:19, 20   673
Outward
display........John 4:48   1068

B. *Purposes of, to:*
Authenticate   ⌠Deut. 13:1   181
a prophecy...⌡1 Sam. 2:31, 34   265
Strengthen   ⌠Judg. 6:17   237
faith ....⌡Is. 7:11   663
Recall God's
blessings......Josh. 24:15-17   227
Confirm God's⌠2 Kin. 19:28, 29   376
Word ....⌡Heb. 2:4   1239
Insure a   ⌠2 Kin. 20:5,
promise ......⌡   9-11   377
Confirm a
prophecy......1 Kin. 13:3-5   339

C. *Concerning Christ in His:*
Nativity ....Luke 2:12   1027
Ministry ....John 20:30   1088
             Acts 2:22   1095
Resurrection...Matt. 12:38-40   975

D. *Value of:*
Discounted as
such ....Matt. 16:1-4   979
Demanded unneces-
sarily ....John 6:30   1071
Demonstrated by
apostles.......Acts 5:12   1099
Displayed by
Paul ....Rom. 15:19   1144

E. *In prophecy, concerning:*
Christ's first   ⌠Is. 7:11, 14   663
advent ....⌡Matt. 1:21-23   964
Second
advent ....Matt. 24:3, 30   988
Man of
lawlessness....2 Thess. 2:9   1212
End...........Rev. 15:1   1302

F. *As assurance of:*
Presence......Ex. 3:12   56
Judgment upon
sin............Num. 17:10   146
Goodness......Ps. 86:17   573

Signal—*a beacon*

Figurative of a warning to
others...........Is. 30:17   682

Sihon—*bold*

Amorite king residing at
Heshbon ....Num. 21:26-30   150
Victorious over
Moabites........Num. 21:26-30   150
Ruler of five Midianite
princes...........Josh. 13:21   217
Refused Israel's request for
passage ....Deut. 2:26-28   171
Defeated by
Israel...........Num. 21:21-32   150
Territory of, assigned to Reuben
and Gad.........Num. 32:1-38   161
Victory over, long
celebrated.......Deut. 31:4   197

Silas, Silvanus—*wooded*

Leader in the Jerusalem
church ....Acts 15:22   1111
Christian
prophet ....Acts 15:32   1112
Sent on a
mission..........Acts 15:22-35   1111
Became Paul's
companion ....Acts 15:36-41   1112
Roman citizen ....Acts 16:25-39   1113
Paul commended his work at
Corinth ....2 Cor. 1:19   1166
Called Silvanus...1 Thess. 1:1   1206
Associated in Paul's
writings.........2 Thess. 1:1   1212
Peter's helper .....1 Pet. 5:12   1264

Silence—*the lack of noise*

A. *Kinds of:*
Will of   ⌠Rev. 8:1   1298
God...........⌡1 Pet. 2:15   1262
Troubled.......Jer. 20:9   738

B. *Virtue of:*
Suitable time
for............Eccl. 3:7   639
Commanded...1 Cor. 14:34   1159
Sign of
prudence......Prov. 21:23   625
Sign of
wisdom ....Prov. 17:28   622

C. *Forbidden to God's:*
Watchmen.....Is. 62:6   709
Messengers....Acts 5:27-42   1099
Praisers........Ps. 30:12   542

D. *Considered as:*
Blessing ....Zech. 2:13   919
Curse..........1 Sam. 2:9   264

E. *Of God:*
Broken in
judgment .....Ps. 50:3   553
Misunderstood by
men..........Ps. 50:21, 23   553

F. *Of Christ:*
Predicted .....Is. 53:7   702
Before:
Sinners ....John 8:6   1073
High priest ...Matt. 26:62, 63   992
Pilate.........Matt. 27:14   993
Herod ....Luke 23:9   1056

Silk—*a clothing material derived from the silkworm*

Sign of:
Luxury............Ezek. 16:10, 13   797
Wantonness.......Rev. 18:12   1305

Silla—*twig; basket*

Quarter of suburb of
Jerusalem ....2 Kin. 12:20   368

Siloam, Shelah—*sent*

Pool at
Jerusalem ....Neh. 3:15   469
Tower of, kills 18
people...........Luke 13:4   1044
Blind man washes
in...............John 9:1-11   1075

SUBJECT	REFERENCE	PAGE	SUBJECT	REFERENCE	PAGE	SUBJECT	REFERENCE	PAGE

Silver—*a precious metal*

A. *Features concerning:*
Mined from the
earth..........Job 28:1   512
Melted by
fire..........Ezek. 22:22   805
Sign of
wealth........Gen. 13:2   15
Used as
money........Gen. 23:15, 16   23
Article of
commerce.....Ezek. 27:12   809
Given as
gifts......1 Kin. 10:25   336
Used in:
Tabernacle....Ex. 38:19   90
Temple.......2 Kin. 12:13   368
Christ sold for { Zech. 11:12   924
30 pieces of . { Matt. 26:15   991
Peter devoid
of............Acts 3:6   1097

B. *Figurative of:*
God's Word....Ps. 12:6   533
God's people..Zech. 13:9   925
Under-
standing......Prov. 3:13, 14   611
Degen-
eration........Is. 1:22   658
Rejection......Jer. 6:30   725

Silversmith—*a worker in silver*

Demetrius, an
Ephesian.........Acts 19:24-41   1116

Simeon—*hearing*

1. Son of Jacob by
Leah..........Gen. 29:33   30
Joined Levi in massacre of
Shechem-
ites..........Gen. 34:25-31   35
Held as hostage by
Joseph........Gen. 42:24, 36   42
Denounced by
Jacob........Gen. 34:30   35
Sons of.......Gen. 46:10   46
2. Tribe of, descendants of Jacob's
son...........Gen. 46:10   46
Number of, at first
census.......Num. 1:23   128
Number of, at second
census.......Num. 26:12-14   155
Position of, on Mt.
Gerizim......Deut. 27:12   192
Inheritance of, within
Judah's......Josh. 19:1-9   222
With Judah, fought
Canaanites....Judg. 1:1, 3, 17   232
Victory over Ham and
Amalekites...1 Chr. 4:24-43   391
Recognized in Ezekiel's
vision........Ezek. 48:24-33   831
3. Ancestor of
Christ........Luke 3:30   1029
4. Righteous man; blessed the
child Jesus....Luke 2:25-35   1027
5. Christian prophet at
Antioch.....Acts 13:1   1108

Similitude—*likeness of two things*

A. *Expressive of:*
Physical.......2 Chr. 4:3   421
Typical........Rom. 5:14   1135
Literary
(simile).......Ps. 144:12   602
Spiritual......James 3:9   1255

B. *Expressed by:*
"Like"........James 1:6   1253
"As"..........1 Pet. 2:5   1261
"Likeness".....Rom. 6:5   1135

Simon—*hearing*

1. Simon Peter...Matt. 4:18   966
See Peter
2. One of the Twelve; called "the
Zealot"......Matt. 10:4   972
3. One of Jesus'
brothers......Matt. 13:55   977
4. The leper.....Matt. 26:6   990

5. Pharisee......Luke 7:36-40   1035
6. Man of
Cyrene........Matt. 27:32   993
7. Father of Judas
Iscariot......John 6:71   1072
8. Magician.....Acts 8:9-24   1103
9. Tanner in
Joppa.........Acts 9:43   1105

Simple, the

Enlightened by { Ps. 119:105   593
God's Word.....{ Ps. 19:7   536
The LORD
preserves.........Ps. 116:6   589

Sin—*disobedience of God's Law*

A. *Defined as:*
Lawlessness...1 John 3:4   1276
Unrighteous-
ness...........1 John 5:17   1278
Omission of known
duty..........James 4:17   1255
Not from
faith..........Rom. 14:23   1143
Devising of
folly..........Prov. 24:9   628

B. *Sources of, in:*
Satan.........John 8:44   1074
Man's heart....Matt. 15:19, 20   979
Lust..........James 1:15   1253
Adam's transgres-
sion..........Rom. 5:12, 16   1135
Natural birth..Ps. 51:5   554

C. *Kinds of:*
National.......Prov. 14:34   620
Personal......Josh. 7:20   211
Secret........Ps. 90:8   576
Presump-
tuous........Ps. 19:13   536
Evident........1 Tim. 5:24   1220
Shameless.....Is. 3:9   660
Youthful......Ps. 25:7   539
Public........2 Sam. 24:10, 17   318
Unforgive- { Matt. 12:21, 32   974
able.......... { John 8:24   1074
Uninten-
tional.......Lev. 4:2   97
Willful........Heb. 10:26   1245

D. *Consequences of, among the
unregenerate:*
Blindness......John 9:41   1076
2 Cor. 4:3, 4   1167
Slavery........John 8:34   1074
Irreconcil-
able..........1 Tim. 3:1-7   1218
Death.........Rom. 6:23   1136

E. *God's attitude toward:*
Keeps men
from..........Gen. 20:6   20
Punishes for...Ex. 32:34   84
Provides a fountain
for............Zech. 13:1   925
Wipes out.....Is. 44:22   694
Casts away....Mic. 7:19   895
Forgives.......Ex. 34:7   85
Remembers no
more..........Jer. 31:34   749

F. *Christ's relationship to:*
Free of........1 John 3:5   1276
Knew no......2 Cor. 5:21   1169
Makes men conscious
of.............John 15:22, 24   1083
Died for our..1 Cor. 15:3   1160
As an offering { Is. 53:10   702
for............ { Heb. 9:28   1245
Substitu- { Is. 53:5, 6   702
tionary...... { Matt. 26:28   991
Takes it
away..........John 1:29   1064
Saves His people
from..........Matt. 1:21   964
Has authority to
forgive.......Matt. 9:6   971
Makes propitiation
for............Heb. 2:17   1240
Purifies our...Heb. 1:3   1239
Cleanses us
from..........1 John 1:7, 9   1274

Releases us
from..........Rev. 1:5   1293

G. *Regenerate must:*
Acknowl-
edge.........Ps. 32:5   543
Confess.......Ps. 51:3, 4   554
Be full of anxiety
because of ...Ps. 38:18   547
Not serve......Rom. 6:6   1135
Not obey.....Rom. 6:6, 12   1135
Subdue.......Rom. 6:14-22   1136
Lay aside.....Heb. 12:1   1247
Resist.........Heb. 12:4   1247
Keep from....Ps. 19:13   537

H. *Helps against:*
Use God's
Word........Ps. 119:11   591
Guard the
tongue.......Ps. 39:1   547
Walk in the
Spirit........Rom. 8:1-14   1137
Avoid evil
companions...1 Tim. 5:22   1220
Confess to the
Lord.........1 John 1:8, 9   1274
Exercise love ..1 Pet. 4:8   1264
Go to the
Advocate.....1 John 2:1   1274

Sin—*wrongdoing; transgression*

1. Wilderness between the Red
Sea and
Sinai..........Ex. 16:1   68
2. City of Egypt..Ezek. 30:15, 16   813

Sinai, Sina

Mountain (same as Horeb) where
the Law was
given...........Ex. 19:1-25   70
Used allegorically by
Paul............Gal. 4:24, 25   1180
See Horeb

Sincerity—*freedom from deceit;
genuineness*

A. *Descriptive of:*
Faith..........1 Tim. 1:5   1217
Believer's
love..........2 Cor. 8:8, 24   1170

B. *Should characterize:*
Worship.......John 4:23, 24   1067
Preaching......2 Cor. 2:17   1167
Believer's life ..2 Cor. 1:12   1166

C. *Examples of:*
Nathanael.....John 1:47   1065
Christ.........1 Pet. 2:22   1262
Paul..........1 Thess. 2:3-5   1207

Singed—*burnt hair*

Miraculously saved from
being............Dan. 3:27   839

Singers—*those who make music with
voice*

Leaders of........1 Chr. 25:2-6   410
Under teachers....1 Chr. 15:22, 27   401
Mixed.........2 Chr. 35:15, 25   449

Singing—*uttering words in musical
tones*

A. *Descriptive of:*
Birds.........Ps. 104:12   582
Trees.........1 Chr. 16:33   403
Believers......Eph. 5:19   1188
Redeemed.....Rev. 5:9   1296
Morning
stars.........Job 38:7   520

B. *Occasions of:*
Times of:
Victory.......Ex. 15:1, 21   67
Revelry......Ex. 32:18   83
Imprison-
ment........Acts 16:25   1113
Joy..........James 5:13   1256
Lord's
Supper......Matt. 26:30   991

SUBJECT	REFERENCE	PAGE	SUBJECT	REFERENCE	PAGE	SUBJECT	REFERENCE	PAGE
Unworthy of			Produced by			Spirit's		
Christians........2 Cor. 12:20		1174	insomnia......Esth. 6:1		488	advent........Joel 2:29, 30		867
			Brought on by					
Slave, slavery—*a state of bondage*			overwork.....Gen. 31:40		32	**Smyrna**—*a city of Iona in Asia Minor*		
A. *Acquired by:*			**Sling**—*an instrument for throwing*			One of the seven		
Purchase......Gen. 17:12		17	*stones*			churches........Rev. 1:11		1294
Voluntary			A. *Used by:*			**Snail**		
service........Ex. 21:5-6		72	Warriors......Judg. 20:16		251	Creature with a spiral		
Birth..........Ex. 21:2-4		72	David.........1 Sam. 17:40-50		278	tail...............Ps. 58:8		557
Capture.......Deut. 20:11-14		187	B. *Figurative of:*			**Snake**		
Debt............2 Kin. 4:1		358	God's			Produced from		
Arrest.........Ex. 22:2, 3		73	punishment...1 Sam. 25:29		286	eggs.............Is. 59:5		706
Inheritance....Lev. 25:46		120	Captivity......Jer. 10:18		729	"Bites the horses'		
Gift...........Gen. 29:24, 29		29	Foolishness....Prov. 26:8		630	heels"...........Gen. 49:17		49
B. *Rights of:*			**Slothfulness, sluggard**—*laziness*			**Snake charmer**		
Sabbath rest...Ex. 20:10		72	A. *Sources of, in:*			Alluded to.....Ps. 58:4, 5		557
Share in religious			Excessive					
feasts.........Deut. 12:12, 18		181	sleep.........Prov. 6:9-11		613	**Snares**—*traps*		
Membership in			Laziness......Prov. 19:15, 24		623	A. *Uses of:*		
covenant......Gen. 17:10-14		17	Indifference....Judg. 18:9		249	Catch birds....Prov. 7:23		614
Refuge for			Desires.......Prov. 21:25		625	B. *Figurative of:*		
fugitive......Deut. 23:15, 16		190	Fearful imagina-			Pagan		
Murder of,			tions..........Prov. 22:13		626	nations.......Josh. 23:12, 13		227
punishable....Ex. 21:12		72	B. *Way of:*			Idols..........Judg. 2:3		233
Freedom of, if			Brings			God's represen-		
maimed......Ex. 21:26, 27		73	hunger.......Prov. 19:15		623	tative.........Ex. 10:7		62
Entitled to			Leads to			Words.........Prov. 6:2		612
justice........Job 31:13-15		515	poverty......Prov. 20:4		624	Wicked		
C. *Privileges of:*			Leads to			works..........Ps. 9:16		531
Entrusted with			destruction....Prov. 18:9		622	Fear of man...Prov. 29:25		632
missions.....Gen. 24:1-14		23	Causes decay..Eccl. 10:18		644	Immoral		
Advice of,			Results in forced			woman.......Eccl. 7:26		642
heeded........1 Sam. 9:5-10		269	labor..........Prov. 12:24		618	Christ.........Is. 8:14, 15		664
Marriage in master's			C. *Antidotes of, in:*			Sudden		
house.........1 Chr. 2:34, 35		389	Faithfulness...Matt. 25:26-30		990	destruction....Luke 21:34, 35		1054
Rule over			Fervent spirit..Rom. 12:11		1142	Riches.........1 Tim. 6:9, 10		1220
sons..........Prov. 17:2		621	Imitating the			Devil's trap....2 Tim. 2:26		1224
May become			faithful........Heb. 6:12		1242	**Sneezed**		
heir...........Gen. 15:1-4		16	**Small**—*little in size; few in number*			Seven times.......2 Kin. 4:35		359
May secure			A. *Applied to God's:*			**Snow**—*frozen crystallized flakes of*		
freedom.......Ex. 21:2-6		72	Choice.........Num. 16:5, 9		145	*water*		
D. *State of, under Christianity:*			Faithful			A. *Characteristics of:*		
Union "in			remnant......Is. 1:9		658	Comes in		
Christ".......Gal. 3:28		1179	B. *Applied to man's:*			winter........Prov. 26:1		630
Treatment of, with			Sin...........Ezek. 16:20		798	Sent by God...Job 37:6		519
justice.......Eph. 6:9		1190	Unconcern.....Zech. 4:10		920	Waters the		
Duties of, as pleasing			**Smite, smitten**—*to clobber; plague*			earth..........Is. 55:10		703
God..........Eph. 6:5-8		1190	A. *Descriptive of:*			Melts with		
			God's punish-			heat..........Job 6:16, 17		499
Sleep—*a state of complete or partial*			ments.........Deut. 28:22-28		193	Notable event		
unconsciousness			B. *Expressive of God's judgment*			during........2 Sam. 23:20		318
A. *Descriptive of:*			*on:*			B. *Whiteness illustrative of:*		
Slumber.......Prov. 6:4, 10		613	Philistines.....1 Sam. 5:6, 9		267	Leprosy.......Ex. 4:6		56
Desolation.....Jer. 51:39, 57		771	King's house...2 Chr. 21:5-19		435	Converted (Ps. 51:7		554
Unregen-			C. *Used Messianically of Christ's:*			sinner.......\Is. 1:18		658
eracy.........1 Thess. 5:6, 7		1208	Bearing our			Consecrated		
Death.........John 11:11-14		1077	sins...........Is. 53:4		702	ones..........Lam. 4:7		780
Spiritual						Angel........Matt. 28:3		995
indifference...Matt. 25:5		989	**Smith**—*a metal worker*			Risen Christ...Rev. 1:14		1294
Prophetic			Blacksmith........1 Sam. 13:19, 20		273	**Snuffers, snuff dishes**		
vision........Dan. 8:18		845	Worker in iron....Is. 44:12		694	Used for trimming wicks in		
B. *Beneficial:*			Tubal-cain, first...Gen. 4:22		8	lamps..........Ex. 37:23		89
When given (Ps. 3:5		529	Demetrius,			Dishes used to catch snuff of		
by God......\Ps. 127:2		596	silversmith......Acts 19:24-27		1116	lamps............Ex. 25:38		76
While trusting			Alexander,			**So**		
God..........Ps. 4:8		529	coppersmith......2 Tim. 4:14		1226	Egyptian king.....2 Kin. 17:4		372
While obeying			**Smoke**			**Soap**		
parents.......Prov. 6:20-22		613	A. *Resulting from:*			Figuratively in....Mal. 3:2		930
When following			Destruction....Gen. 19:28		20	**Sober, sobriety**		
wisdom.......Prov. 3:21-24		611	God's			A. *Described as:*		
To the working			presence......Is. 6:4		662	Self- (Gal. 5:23		1181
man..........Eccl. 5:12		641	God's			control.......\1 Cor. 7:9		1153
After duty is			vengeance....Is. 34:8-10		685	B. *Incentives to, found in:*		
done.........Ps. 132:1-5		597	Babylon's			Lord's return..1 Thess. 5:1-7		1208
During a pleasant			end..........Rev. 14:8-11		1302	Nearness of the		
dream........Jer. 31:23-26		749	World's end....Is. 51:6		700	end...........1 Pet. 4:7		1264
C. *Condemned·*			B. *Figurative of:*			Satan's		
When			Spiritual			attacks........1 Cor. 7:5		1153
excessive......Prov. 6:9-11		613	distress.......Ps. 119:83		592			
During			Something					
harvest.......Prov. 10:5		616	offensive......Is. 65:5		711			
In times of								
danger........Matt. 26:45-47		992						
D. *Inability to:*								
Caused by								
worry.........Dan. 2:1		836						

SUBJECT	REFERENCE	PAGE	SUBJECT	REFERENCE	PAGE	SUBJECT	REFERENCE	PAGE

Sober, sobriety—continued

C. *Required of:*
Christians .....1 Thess. 5:6, 8   1208
Evangelists ....2 Tim. 4:5   1225
See Temperance

Sociability—*friendly relations in social gatherings*

A. *Manifested in:*
Family life.....John 12:1-9   1079
National life ...Neh. 8:9-18   474
Church life ....Acts 2:46   1096

B. *Christian's kind, governed by:*
No fellowship with
evil ....2 Cor. 6:14-18   1169
Righteous
living ....Titus 2:12   1230
Love..........Col. 3:9-14   1201

Socialism (see Communism, Christian)

Socoh—*thorn*

1. Town in south
Judah.........Josh. 15:1, 35   218
Where David killed
Goliath ....1 Sam. 17:1, 49   277
Spelled   {2 Chr. 11:7   428
Soco.........{2 Chr. 28:18   441
2. Town in Judah's hill
country ....Josh. 15:1, 48   218

Sodi—*an acquaintance*

Father of the Zebulunite
spy...........Num. 13:10   141

Sodom—*burnt*

A. *History of:*
Located in Jordan
valley........Gen. 13:10   15
Became Lot's
residence....Gen. 13:11-13   15
Wickedness of,
notorious .....Gen. 13:13   15
Plundered by Chedor-
laomer.......Gen. 14:9-24   15
Abraham interceded
for...........Gen. 18:16-33   18
Destroyed by
God...........Gen. 19:1-28   19
Lot sent out
of.............Gen. 19:29, 30   20

B. *Destruction of, illustrative of:*
God's wrath ...Deut. 29:23   196
Sudden
destruction....Lam. 4:6   780
Total
destruction....Jer. 49:18   766
Future
judgment....Matt. 11:23, 24   974
Example to the
ungodly.......2 Pet. 2:6   1268

C. *Sin of, illustrative of:*
Shame-
lessness.......Is. 3:9   660
Obduracy.....Jer. 23:14   741
Unnatural-
ness..........Jude 7   1287

D. *Figurative of:*
Wickedness....Deut. 32:32   200
Jerusalem.....Is. 1:9, 10   658
Judah.........Ezek. 16:46-63   798

Sodomite—*a male cult prostitute*

Prohibition of .....Deut. 23:17, 18   190
Prevalence of, under
Rehoboam.......1 Kin. 14:24   341
Asa's removal of ..1 Kin. 15:11, 12   341
Jehoshaphat's riddance
of ....1 Kin. 22:46   351
Josiah's reforms
against..........2 Kin. 23:7   380
Result of
unbelief ....Rom. 1:27   1132

Soil—*dirt*

It was planted in
good ....Ezek. 17:8   799
Uzziah loved it....2 Chr. 26:10   439

Sojourn, sojourner

A. *Descriptive of:*
Abram in
Egypt.........Gen. 12:10   14
Jacob with
Laban.........Gen. 32:4   33
Israel in
Egypt.........Gen. 47:4   47
Stranger.......Ex. 12:48, 49   65
Naomi in
Moab ....Ruth 1:1   256

B. *Characterized by:*
Being among
enemies.......2 Kin. 8:1, 2   362
LORD's
blessing.......Gen. 26:2, 3   26

C. *Figurative of:*
Righteous in the
world ....1 Chr. 29:15   415
See Foreigners; Strangers

Sold

Descriptive of:
Purchase.........Matt. 26:9   991
Slavery ....Ps. 105:17   583
Bondage to sin....Rom. 7:14   1136

Soldiers—*military agents of a nation*

A. *Good characteristics of:*
Obedience .....Matt. 8:9   970
Devotion ......Acts 10:7   1105
Subduing
riots ....Acts 21:31-35   1119
Guarding
prisoners......Acts 12:4-6   1107

B. *Bad charcteristics of:*
Cowardice....Deut. 20:8   187
Discontent and
violence......Luke 3:14   1029
Rashness ....Acts 27:42   1126
Bribery ....Matt. 28:12   995
Irreligion....John 19:2, 3, 23   1086

C. *Figurative of:*
Christians .....2 Tim. 2:4   1224
Christian
workers.......Phil. 2:25   1194
Spiritual
armor.........Eph. 6:10-18   1190

Solitude—*aloneness*

For:
Adam, not good...Gen. 2:18   5
Prayer, good .....Matt. 6:6   968
                Matt. 14:23   978
Rest, necessary....Mark 6:30, 31   1006

Solomon—*peace*

A. *Life of:*
David's son by
Bathsheba ....2 Sam. 12:24   305
Name of,
significant.....1 Chr. 22:9   408
Anointed over
opposition.....1 Kin. 1:5-48   323
Spared
Adonijah......1 Kin. 1:49-53   324
Received dying instruction from
David ....1 Kin. 2:1-10   325
Purged his kingdom of corrupt
leaders........1 Kin. 2:11-46   325
Prayer of, for
wisdom.......1 Kin. 3:1-15   326
Organized his
kingdom ....1 Kin. 4:1-28   327
Fame of, world
wide ....1 Kin. 4:29-34   328
Built the
Temple.......1 Kin. 5—6   328
Dedicated the
Temple.......1 Kin. 8:22-66   332
Built personal
palace.........1 Kin. 7:1-12   330
LORD reappeared
to.............1 Kin. 9:1-9   334
Strengthened his
kingdom ......1 Kin. 9:10-28   334

Received queen of
Sheba.........1 Kin. 10:1-13   335
Encouraged
commerce.....1 Kin. 10:14-29   336
Falls into polygamy and
idolatry ....1 Kin. 11:1-8   336
God warned
him...........1 Kin. 11:9-13   336
Adversaries arise against
him...........1 Kin. 11:14-40   337
Reign and
death ....1 Kin. 11:41-43   337

B. *Good features of:*
Chooses an understanding
heart..........1 Kin. 3:5-9   327
Exhibited sound
judgment .....1 Kin. 3:16-28   327
Excels in
wisdom ....1 Kin. 4:29-34   328
Great writer ...1 Kin. 4:32   328
Writer of
Psalms........Ps. 72 (Title)   564

C. *Bad features of:*
Loves luxury ..Eccl. 2:1-11   638
Marries
pagans........1 Kin. 11:1-3   336
Turns to
idolatry ....1 Kin. 11:4-8   336
Enslaves
Israel ....1 Kin. 12:1-4   338

Son

A. *Descriptive of:*
Half-brothers ..Gen. 25:9   25
Grandson.....Gen. 29:5   29
Disciple.......Prov. 7:1   614
One possessing a certain
character .....1 Sam. 2:12   264
One destined to a certain
end ....John 17:12   1084
Messiah ......Is. 7:14   663
Angels.........Job 1:6   495

B. *Characteristics of, sometimes:*
Jealous ....Judg. 9:2, 18   240
Quite
different ......Gen. 9:18-27   12
Disloyal ......Luke 15:25-30   1046
Unlike their
father.........2 Sam. 13:30-39   306
Spiritually
different ......Gen. 25:22-34   25

C. *Admonitions addressed to, concerning:*
Instruction ....Prov. 1:8   609
Sinners........Prov. 1:10-19   609
Wisdom ....Prov. 3:13-35   611
Discipline.....Prov. 3:11, 12   611
Immorality ...Prov. 5:1-23   612
Life's
dangers ......Prov. 6:1-35   612

Son-in-law—*a daughter's husband*

Sinful..............Gen. 19:14   19
Believing..........Mark 1:29, 30   1000

Son of God—*a title indicating Christ's deity*

A. *Descriptive of Christ as:*
Eternally   {Ps. 2:7   529
begotten .....{Heb. 1:5   1239
Messianic
King ....Ps. 89:26, 27   575
Virgin-born ....Luke 1:31-35   1025
Trinity-
member.......Matt. 28:19   995
Priest-king....Heb. 1:8   1239
              Heb. 5:5, 6   1241

B. *Witnesses of, by:*
Father.........Matt. 17:5   980
Angels........John 1:51   1065
Demons ....Mark 5:7   1004
Satan.........Matt. 4:3, 6   965
Men ....Matt. 16:16   980
Christ
Himself ....John 9:35-37   1076
His
resurrection...Rom. 1:1-4   1131
Christians .....Acts 2:36   1096

SUBJECT	REFERENCE	PAGE	SUBJECT	REFERENCE	PAGE	SUBJECT	REFERENCE	PAGE
Scriptures	John 20:31	1088	**Song of Solomon, the**—*a book of the*			Practiced by		
Inner			*Old Testament*			Manasseh	2 Chr. 33:6	446
witness	1 John 5:10-13	1278	The bride and the			Work of the		
C. *Significance of, as indicating:*			bridegroom	Song 1	648	flesh	Gal. 5:20	1181
Cost of man's reconcilia-			Song of the			**Sorek**—*a choice vine*		
tion	Rom. 5:6-11	1135	bride	Song 2:8—3:5	649	Valley, home of		
Greatness of God's			Song of the			Delilah	Judg. 16:4	247
love	John 3:16	1066	bridegroom	Song 4:1-15	650	**Sorrow**—*grief*		
Sin of			The bride			A. *Kinds of:*		
unbelief	Heb. 10:28, 29	1245	meditates	Song 4:16—6:3	651	Hypocritical	Matt. 14:9	977
Worship due			The bridegroom			Unfruitful	Matt. 19:22	983
Christ	Rev. 4:11	1296	appeals	Song 6:4—7:9	652	Temporary	John 16:6, 20-22	1083
Dignity of			Lovers united	Song 7:10—8:14	652	Unceasing	Rom. 9:2	1138
human	Rom. 8:3	1137	**Songs**			Fruitful	2 Cor. 7:8-11	1169
nature	Heb. 2:14	1240	A. *Described as:*			Christian	1 Thess. 4:13	1208
Humanity of			New	Rev. 5:9	1296	B. *Caused by:*		
Christ	Gal. 4:4	1179	Spiritual	Eph. 5:19	1188	Sin	Gen. 3:16, 17	7
Pattern of			B. *Uses of, as:*			Death	John 11:33-35	1078
glorifi-	Rom. 8:29	1138	Witness	Deut. 31:19-22	198	Drunken-		
cation	Phil. 3:21	1195	Torment	Ps. 137:3	599	ness	Prov. 23:29-35	627
Destruction of			March	Num. 21:17, 18	150	Love of		
Satan	1 John 3:8	1276	Processional	1 Chr. 13:7, 8	400	money	1 Tim. 6:10	1220
Uniqueness of			C. *Expressive of:*			Apostasy	Ps. 16:4	534
Christ	Heb. 1:5-9	1239	Triumph	Judg. 5:12	236	Persecution	Esth. 9:22	491
D. *Belief in Christ as:*			Physical joy	Gen. 31:27	32	Hardship of		
Derived from the			Spiritual joy	Ps. 119:54	592	life	Ps. 90:10	576
Scriptures	John 20:31	1088	Deliverance	Ps. 32:7	543	Wisdom	Eccl. 1:18	638
Necessary for eternal			Hypocrisy	Amos 5:23	875	Distressing		
life	John 3:18, 36	1066	Derision	Ps. 69:12	562	news	Acts 20:37, 38	1118
Source of eternal			D. *Figurative of:*			C. *Of the righteous:*		
life	John 6:40	1071	Passover			Not like the		
Foundation of the			(the Lord's	Is. 30:29	682	world's	1 Thess. 4:13	1208
faith	Acts 9:20	1104	Supper)	Matt. 26:26-30	991	Sometimes		
Affirmation of			Messiah's			intense	Ps. 18:4, 5	535
deity	1 John 2:23, 24	1275	advent	Is. 42:10	692	Seen in the		
Illustrated	John 11:14-44	1078	Gospel age	Is. 26:1, 2	677	face	Neh. 2:2-4	467
E. *Powers of Christ as, to:*			**Song writer**			None in God's		
Have life in			Solomon, famous			blessings	Prov. 10:22	616
Himself	John 5:26	1069	as	1 Kin. 4:32	328	Shown in		
Reveal the			**Sonship of believers**			repentance	2 Cor. 7:10	1170
Father	Matt. 11:27	974	A. *Evidences of, seen in:*			To be		
Glorify the			New nature	1 John 3:9-12	1276	removed	Is. 25:8	677
Father	John 17:1	1084	Possession of the			None in		
Do the Father's			Spirit	Rom. 8:15-17	1137	heaven	Rev. 21:4	1307
works	John 5:19, 20	1069	Discipline	Heb. 12:5-8	1247	Shall flee		
Redeem men	Gal. 4:4, 5	1179	B. *Blessedness of, manifested in:*			away	Is. 51:11	700
Give freedom	John 8:36	1074	Regener-			See Grief		
Raise the			ation	John 1:12	1064	**Sosipater**—*saving a father*		
dead	John 5:21, 25	1069	Adoption	Gal. 4:5, 6	1179	Kinsman of Paul	Rom. 16:21	1145
Judge men	John 5:22	1069	Glorification	Rom. 8:19-21	1138	**Sosthenes**—*of sound strength*		
Son of Man—*a self-designation of*			**Soothsayer**—*a diviner, fortune teller*			1. Leader of the synagogue at		
Christ			Among			Corinth	Acts 18:17	1115
A. *Title of, applied to:*			Philistines	Is. 2:6	659	2. Paul's Christian		
Ezekiel	Ezek. 2:1, 3, 6	787	See Divination			brother	1 Cor. 1:1	1149
Daniel	Dan. 8:17	845				**Sotai**—*Yahweh is turning aside*		
Messiah	Dan. 7:13	844	**Sopater**—*of sound parentage*			Head of a family of		
Christ:			One of Paul's			servants	Ezra 2:55	455
By Himself	Matt. 8:20	970	companions	Acts 20:4	1117	**Soul**—*the immaterial part of man*		
By only Stephen			**Sophereth**—*writer, scribe*			A. *Descriptive of:*		
elsewhere	Acts 7:56	1102	Descendants of Solomon's			Man's life	1 Sam. 24:11	285
In John's			servants	Neh. 7:57	472	People	Acts 2:41, 43	1096
vision	Rev. 1:13	1294	**Sorcerers**—*supposed possessors of*			Sinner	James 5:20	1256
B. *As indicative of Christ's:*			*supernatural powers*			Emotional		
Self-			A. *Prevalence of, in:*			life	1 Sam. 18:1, 3	279
designation	Matt. 16:13	980	Assyria	Nah. 3:4, 5	899	Spiritual life	Ps. 42:1, 2, 4	549
Humanity	Matt. 11:19	973	Egypt	Ex. 7:11	59	Disembodied	Rev. 6:9	1297
Messiahship	Luke 18:31	1050	Babylon	Is. 47:9-13	697	state	Rev. 20:4	1306
Lordship	Matt. 12:8	974	Palestine	Acts 8:9-24	1103	B. *Characteristics of:*		
Sovereignty	Matt. 13:41	977	Last days	Rev. 9:21	1299	Belongs to		
Obedience	Phil. 2:8	1194	B. *Punishment of, described:*			God	Ezek. 18:3, 4	800
Suffering	Mark 9:12	1009	Legally	Deut. 18:10-12	186	Possesses		
Death	Matt. 12:40	975	Prophet-			immortality	Matt. 10:28	973
Resurrection	Matt. 17:9-23	981	ically	Mal. 3:5	931	Most vital		
Regal power	Matt. 16:28	980	Symbolically	Rev. 21:8	1307	asset	Matt. 16:26	980
Return	Matt. 24:27-37	988	See Divination; Magic, magician			Leaves body at		
Glorification	Heb. 2:6-10	1239	**Sorcery**—*the practice of magic*			death	Gen. 35:18	35
C. *Christ's powers as, to:*			Forbidden in			C. *Abilities of, able to:*		
Forgive sins	Matt. 9:6	971	Israel	Deut. 18:10	186	Have faith	Heb. 10:39	1246
Save men	Luke 19:10	1050	Condemned by the			Love God	Luke 10:27	1040
Redeem men	Matt. 20:28	984	prophets	Mic. 5:12	893	Sin	Mic. 6:7	894
Recompense						Prosper	3 John 2	1284
men	Matt. 16:27	980						
Reward men	Matt. 19:28	983						
Rule His								
Church	Col. 1:17, 18	1200						

SUBJECT	REFERENCE	PAGE	SUBJECT	REFERENCE	PAGE	SUBJECT	REFERENCE	PAGE

Stephanas—*crowned*

Corinthian
Christian........1 Cor. 1:16   1149
First convert of
Achaia..........1 Cor. 16:15   1161
Visits Paul......1 Cor. 16:17   1162

Stephen—*wreath or crown*

One of the seven
deacons.........Acts 6:1-8   1100
Accused falsely by
Jews.............Acts 6:9-15   1100
Spoke before the Jewish
Sanhedrin.......Acts 7:2-53   1100
Became first Christian
martyr.......Acts 7:54-60   1102
Saul (Paul) instigated in death
of...............Acts 7:58   1102

Stew

Price of Esau's
birthright........Gen. 25:29-34   26
Eaten by Elisha's
disciples....2 Kin. 4:38-41   359

Steward, stewardship—*a trust granted for profitable use*

A. *Descriptive of:*
One over Joseph's
household.....Gen. 43:19   43
Curator or
guardian......Matt. 20:8   983
Manager.......Luke 16:2, 3   1047
Management of entrusted
duties........1 Cor. 9:17   1155

B. *Duties of, to:*
Expend
monies........Rom. 16:23   1145
Serve wisely...Luke 12:42   1043

C. *Of spiritual things, based on:*
Lord's   (Ps. 24:1, 2   539
ownership....(Rom. 14:8   1143
Our
redemption....1 Cor. 6:20   1153
Gifts
bestowed   (Matt. 25:14, 15   989
upon us......(1 Pet. 4:10   1264
Offices given   (Eph. 3:2-10   1188
to us.........(Titus 1:7   1229
Faithful in responsi-
bilities.......Luke 16:1-3   1047

Stewardship, personal financial

Basic principles:
Setting accounts ..Rom. 14:12   1143
God's   (Ps. 24:1   539
ownership.......(Rom. 14:7, 8   1143
Finances   (1 Cor. 6:20   1153
and   Matt. 19:16-22   983
spirituality   Luke 16:10-13   1047
inseparable ... 2 Cor. 8:3-8   1170
Needs will be   (Matt. 6:24-34   968
provided........(Phil. 4:19   1196
Content with   (Ps. 37:25   546
what God   1 Tim. 6:6-10   1220
provides.........(Heb. 13:5   1248
Righteousness.....Prov. 16:8   621
Rom. 12:17   1142
Avoid debt......Prov. 22:7   625
Rom. 13:8   1142
Do not   (Prov. 6:1-5   612
co-sign ....(Prov. 22:26   626
Inheritance   (Prov. 17:2   621
uncertain........(Prov. 20:21   624
Proper priority ....Matt. 6:19-21, 33   968
Prosperity   (Deut. 29:9   195
is from   (Ps. 1:1-3   528
God ....(3 John 2   1284
Saving ....Prov. 21:20   625
Laziness   (Prov. 24:30, 31   629
condemned......(Heb. 6:12   1242
Giving   (Prov. 3:9, 10   611
is   (Mal. 3:10-12   931
encouraged......(2 Cor. 9:6-8   1171

Sticks—*pieces of wood*

Gathering on Sabbath
condemned......Num. 15:32-35   144

Necessary........1 Kin. 17:10-12   344
Miracle
producing ....2 Kin. 6:6   360
Two become
one...............Ezek. 37:16-22   820
Viper in bundle
of...............Acts 28:3   1126

Stiff-necked—*rebellious; unteachable*

A. *Indicative of Israel's rebelliousness at:*
Captivity ......2 Chr. 36:13   450
Christ's first
advent........Acts 7:51   1102

B. *Remedies of, seen in:*
Circumcision (regen-
eration)......Deut. 10:16   179
Yield to God...2 Chr. 30:8   443

Stink—*a foul smell*

A. *Caused by:*
Dead fish ......Ex. 7:18, 21   60
Corpse...........John 11:39   1078

B. *Figurative of:*
Hostility toward
one ....Gen. 34:30   35
Hell ....Is. 34:3, 4   684

Stinkweed

Obnoxious among
barley.............Job 31:40   515

Stocks—*blocks of wood*

Instrument of
punishment ......Acts 16:19, 24   1113
Punishment.......Job 33:11   516

Stoics—*pertaining to a colonnade or porch*

Sect of philosophers
founded by Zeno around
308 B.C..........Acts 17:18   1114

Stomach—*the fourth stomach of ruminants (split-hoof animals)*

Given to the
priests...........Deut. 18:3   186

Stones—*rocks*

A. *Natural uses of:*
Weighing......Lev. 19:36   114
Knives......Ex. 4:25   57
Weapons ......1 Sam. 17:40-50   278
Holding
water........Ex. 7:19   60
Covering
wells.........Gen. 29:2   29
Covering
tombs.........Matt. 27:60   994
Landmarks ....Deut. 19:14   187
Writing
inscriptions ...Ex. 24:12   75
Buildings ......Matt. 24:1, 2   988
Missiles.......Ex. 21:18   73

B. *Religious uses of:*
Altars ....Ex. 20:25   72
Grave ......Josh. 7:26   212
Memorial ......Josh. 4:20   209
Witness......Josh. 24:26, 27   228
Inscriptions ...Deut. 27:4, 8   192
Idolatry.......Lev. 26:1   120

C. *Figurative of:*
Reprobation ...1 Sam. 25:37   286
Contempt......2 Sam. 16:6, 13   309
Christ's
rejection ......Ps. 118:22   590
Christ as
foundation ...Is. 28:16   679
Desolation.....Jer. 51:26   770
Unregen-
eracy ....Ezek. 11:19   794
Christ's
advent........Dan. 2:34, 35   837
Conscience ...Hab. 2:11   904
Insensibility ...Zech. 7:12   921
Gentiles ......Matt. 3:9   965
Christ as
Head ....Matt. 21:42-44   985

Good works ...1 Cor. 3:12   1150
Christians .....1 Pet. 2:5   1261
Spirit's
witness ......Rev. 2:17   1295

See Rock

Stones, precious

Emery ....Ezek. 3:9   788
Agate..........Is. 54:12   703
Amethyst ....Rev. 21:20   1307
Beryl.............Dan. 10:6   847
Chalcedony......Rev. 21:19   1307
Chrysolite........Rev. 21:20   1307
Crystal...........Rev. 22:1   1307
Diamond.........Jer. 17:1   735
Emerald........Ex. 28:17   79
Hyacinth.........Rev. 9:17   1299
Jasper...........Rev. 4:3   1296
Jacinth........Ex. 28:19   79
Lapis lazuli.....Ezek. 28:13   811
Onyx ....Gen. 2:12   5
Ruby...........Ex. 28:17   79
Sapphire ....Job 28:6, 16   512
Sardius ....Rev. 4:3   1296
Sardonyx ....Rev. 21:20   1307
Topaz...........Job 28:19   513
Turquoise.......Ex. 28:18   79

Stoning—*a means of executing criminals*

A. *Punishment inflicted for:*
Sacrificing
children......Lev. 20:2-5   114
Divination ....Lev. 20:27   115
Blasphemy ...Lev. 24:15-23   119
Sabbath-
breaking .....Num. 15:32-36   144
Apostasy .....Deut. 13:1-10   181
Idolatry......Deut. 17:2-7   185
Juvenile
rebellion .....Deut. 21:18-21   188
Adultery......Deut. 22:22   189

B. *Examples of:*
Achan.........Josh. 7:20-26   211
Adoram......1 Kin. 12:18   338
Naboth ....1 Kin. 21:13   349
Zechariah ...2 Chr. 24:20, 21   437
Stephen .....Acts 7:59   1102
Paul...........Acts 14:19   1110
Prophets......Heb. 11:37   1247

Stool

Birthstool........Ex. 1:16   54

Storage cities

Built by:
Israelites..........Ex. 1:11   54
Solomon ....1 Kin. 9:19   335
Jehoshaphat ...2 Chr. 17:12   432
Hezekiah.........2 Chr. 32:27-29   445

Stork—*a large, long-legged, migratory bird*

Nesting of........Ps. 104:17   582
Migration of.....Jer. 8:7   726
Ceremonially
unclean ....Lev. 11:19   104

Storm—*a violent upheaval of nature*

A. *Described as:*
Severe.........Ex. 9:23-25   62
Sent by God...Josh. 10:11   214
Destructive....Matt. 7:27   970

B. *Effects of, upon:*
Israelites ......Ex. 19:16, 19   71
Philistines ....1 Sam. 7:10   268
Sailors.........Jon. 1:4-14   885
Animals ....Ps. 29:3-9   541
Disciples ......Mark 4:37-41   1003
Soldiers and
sailors.......Acts 27:14-44   1125
Nature.........Ps. 29:3, 5, 8   541

Strange woman—*adulteress*

Uses flattery .....Prov. 2:16   610

Strangers   BIBLICAL CYCLOPEDIC INDEX   *Suffering for Christ*

SUBJECT	REFERENCE	PAGE	SUBJECT	REFERENCE	PAGE	SUBJECT	REFERENCE	PAGE

Strangers—*foreigners living among the Jews*

A. *Descriptive of:*
Non-Jews......Ex. 12:48   65
Natives.......Matt. 17:25   981
Transients....Luke 24:18   1058
Visitors.......Acts 2:10   1095
Christians ....1 Pet. 1:1   1260

B. *Positive laws, to:*
Love them.....Lev. 19:34   114
Sustain them ..Lev. 25:35   120
Provide for
them.........Deut. 10:18   179
Share in left-
overs.......Deut. 24:19-22   191
Treat fairly ...Deut. 24:14, 17   190
Share in religious
festivals......Deut. 16:11, 14   184
Observe the
Law..........Deut. 31:12   198

See Foreigners; Sojourn, sojourners

Stratagem—*a plan designed to deceive an enemy*

Joshua's famous ..Josh. 8:1-22   212
Gibeonites'
trickery ....Josh. 9:2-27   213
Hushai's
successful ....2 Sam. 17:6-14   310

Straw—*the stalk of wheat or barley*

Used for animals ..Gen. 24:25, 32   24
Used in making
bricks...........Ex. 5:7-18   58
Eaten by a lion....Is. 11:7   668
Something
worthless.........Job 41:27-29   523

Stray animals

Must be
returned.........Ex. 23:4   74
Saul's pursuit of...1 Sam. 9:3-5   269

Strength, strengthen—*resident power*

A. *Kinds of:*
Physical ....Prov. 20:29   624
Constitu-
tional.........Ps. 90:10   576
Hereditary.....Gen. 49:3   48
Angelic.......Ps. 103:20   581
Military.......Dan. 2:37   837
Spiritual.......Ps. 138:3   599
Superhuman...Judg. 16:5, 6, 19   247
Divine.........Is. 63:1   710

B. *Dissipation of, by:*
Iniquity.......Ps. 31:10   542
Hunger........1 Sam. 28:20, 22   289
Sexual
looseness......Prov. 31:3   634
Age...........Ps. 71:9   564
Visions ....Dan. 10:8, 16, 17   847

C. *Increase of:*
From:
God ....Is. 41:10   690
Christ ....2 Tim. 4:17   1226
Holy Spirit....Eph. 3:16   1186
Brothers.....Luke 22:32   1055
By:
Wisdom .....Eccl. 7:19   642
Waiting on the
Lord.........Is. 40:31   690
Lord's grace ..2 Cor. 12:9   1173

Strife—*conflicts between people*

A. *Sources of, in:*
Hatred.......Prov. 10:12   616
Perverse-
ness.........Prov. 16:28   621
Transgres-
sion..........Prov. 17:19   622
Scoffer.........Prov. 22:10   626
Anger ....Prov. 29:22   632
Flesh ....Gal. 5:19, 20   1181

B. *Actual causes of, seen in:*
Self-seeking ...Luke 22:24   1054
Dispute between
men...........Gen. 13:7-11   15

Contentious
man........Prov. 26:21   630
Being fleshly...1 Cor. 3:3   1150
Disputes.......1 Tim. 6:4   1220

C. *Avoidance of, by:*
Being slow to
anger ....Prov. 15:18   620
Simplicity of
life............Prov. 17:1   621

See Contention; Quarrel

Strike—*afflict; attack*

A. *Descriptive of:*
Plagues........Ex. 3:20   56
Miracle........Ex. 17:5, 6   69
Death ....2 Sam. 4:6, 7   298

B. *Of divine punishment, upon:*
Fool...........1 Sam. 25:38   286
Jews..........Jer. 14:19   733

C. *Used Messianically of Christ's:*
Scourging .....Is. 50:6   699
Judgment.....Is. 11:4   667
Death ....Zech. 13:7   925

Stripes—*used in scourging*

Limit of..........Deut. 25:1-4   191
Because of sin.....Ps. 89:32   575

Striving, spiritual

To enter the narrow
door.............Luke 13:24   1044
Against sin........Heb. 12:4   1247
With divine help ..Col. 1:29   1200
In prayer ....Rom. 15:30   1144
For the faith of the
Gospel ....Phil. 1:27   1194

Stroke—*a mark distinguishing similar letters*

Figurative of minute
requirements .....Matt. 5:18   967

Strong drink (see Drunkenness)

Stronghold—*fortress*

David captured....2 Sam. 5:7   299
David lived in .....2 Sam. 5:9   299
Way of the
Lord..........Prov. 10:29   616
The Lord is......Nah. 1:7   898

Study—*intensive intellectual effort*

Of the   { Acts 17:10, 11   1114
Scriptures ....{ 2 Tim. 3:16, 17   1225

Stumble—*to trip on some obstacle*

A. *Occasions of, found in:*
God's Word....1 Pet. 2:8   1261
Christ ....Rom. 9:32, 33   1139
Christ
crucified ......1 Cor. 1:23   1149
Christian
liberty ....1 Cor. 8:9   1154

B. *Avoidance of, by:*
Following
wisdom ....Prov. 3:21, 23   611

See Offend, offense

Stupid—*thick-headed*

Judah called ......Jer. 4:22   722

Suah—*sweepings*

Asherite ....1 Chr. 7:36   395

Subjection—*the state of being under another's control*

A. *Of domestic and civil relationships:*
Citizens to
government...Rom. 13:1-6   1142
Wives to
husbands .....Eph. 5:24   1189
Younger to
elder..........1 Pet. 5:5   1264

B. *Of spiritual relationships:*
Creation to
sin............Rom. 8:20, 21   1138

Demons to the
disciples.......Luke 10:17, 20   1039
Christians to
God..........Heb. 12:9   1247
Creation to
Christ.........Heb. 2:5, 8   1239
Church to
Christ.........Eph. 5:24   1189
Christ to
God...........1 Cor. 15:28   1160

Subjugation—*the state of being subdued by force*

Physical
force..........1 Sam. 13:19-23   273
Spiritual
power.........Mark 5:1-15   1003

Submission—*humble obedience to another's will*

Rulers ....1 Pet. 2:13   1262
Christian
leaders........Heb. 13:17   1249
God ....James 4:7   1255

Substitution—*replacing one person or thing for another*

Ram for the
man.............Gen. 22:13   22
Offering for the
offerer...........Lev. 16:21, 22   111
Levites for the first-
born............Num. 3:12-45   130
Christ for the   { Is. 53:4-6   702
sinner..........{ 1 Pet. 2:24   1262

Sucathites

Decendants of
Caleb.............1 Chr. 2:42, 55   389

Success—*accomplishment of goals in life*

A. *Rules of:*
Put God first...Matt. 6:32-34   969
Follow the
Book..........Josh. 1:7-9   206
Seek the
goal...........Phil. 3:13, 14   1195
Never give
up ....Gal. 6:9   1181
Do all for
Christ.........Phil. 1:20, 21   1193

B. *Hindrances of, seen in:*
Unbelief ....Heb. 4:6, 11   1241
Enemies ....Neh. 4:1-23   469
Sluggishness...Prov. 24:30-34   629
Love of the
world.........Matt. 16:26   980

Succoth—*booths*

1. Place east of the
Jordan........Judg. 8:4, 5   239
Jacob's residence
here ....Gen. 33:17   34
2. Israel's first
camp ....Ex. 12:37   64

Succoth-benoth—*tabernacles of girls*

Idol set up in Samaria by
Babylonians ......2 Kin. 17:30   373

Suck—*to give milk to offspring*

Characteristics of:
True among
animals..........1 Sam. 7:9   268
Normal for human
mothers.........Job 3:12   497
Figurative of Israel's
restoration ....Is. 60:16   708
Figurative of
wicked ....Job 20:16   508

Suffering for Christ

Necessary in
Christian   { 1 Cor. 12:26   1158
living............{ Phil. 1:29   1194
Blessed privilege ..Acts 5:41   1100
Never in vain .....Gal. 3:4   1178
After Christ's   { Phil. 3:10   1195
example.........{ 1 Pet. 2:20, 21   1262

SUBJECT	REFERENCE	PAGE	SUBJECT	REFERENCE	PAGE	SUBJECT	REFERENCE	PAGE

Suffering for Christ—continued

Of short
duration..........1 Pet. 5:10 — 1264

Not comparable
to heaven's ⎰Rom. 8:18 — 1138
glory............⎱1 Pet. 4:13 — 1264

Sufferings of Christ

A. *Features concerning:*
Predicted......1 Pet. 1:11 — 1260
Announced....Mark 9:12 — 1009
Explained.....Luke 24:26, 46 — 1058
Fulfilled.......Acts 3:18 — 1097
Witnessed.....1 Pet. 5:1 — 1264
Proclaimed....Acts 17:2, 3 — 1114

B. *Benefits of, to Christ:*
Preparation for
priesthood....Heb. 2:17, 18 — 1240
Learned
obedience.....Heb. 5:8 — 1241
Way to glory..Heb. 2:9, 10 — 1240

C. *Benefits of, to Christians:*
Brought to
God...........1 Pet. 3:18 — 1263
Our:
Sins atoned...Heb. 9:26-28 — 1244
Example......1 Pet. 2:21-23 — 1262
Fellowship....Phil. 3:10 — 1195
Comfort.....2 Cor. 1:5-7 — 1166

Suicide—*self-murder*

A. *Thought of, induced by:*
Life's
weariness.....Job 3:20-23 — 497
Life's futility...Eccl. 2:17 — 639
Anger.........Jon. 4:3, 8, 9 — 887

B. *Brought on by:*
Hopeless-
ness..........Judg. 16:29, 30 — 248
Sin............1 Kin. 16:18, 19 — 343
Disappoint-
ment.........2 Sam. 17:23 — 311
Betrayal of
Christ........Matt. 27:3-5 — 993

C. *Other features concerning:*
Desired by
some.........Rev. 9:6 — 1299
Attempted but
prevented.....Acts 16:27, 28 — 1113
Imputed to
Christ........John 8:22 — 1074
Satan tempts
Christ to......Luke 4:9 — 1030

D. *Principles prohibiting, found in:*
Body's
sacredness....1 Cor. 6:19 — 1153
Prohibition against
murder........Ex. 20:13 — 72
Faith's
expectancy....2 Tim. 4:6-8, 18 — 1225

Sakkiim

African people in Shishak's
army............2 Chr. 12:3 — 428

Summer

Made by God.....Ps. 74:17 — 566
Sign of God's
covenant........Gen. 8:22 — 11
Time of:
Fruit harvest.....2 Sam. 16:1, 2 — 309
Sowing and
harvest..........Prov. 6:6-8 — 613
Figurative of:
Industry.........Prov. 10:5 — 616
Opportunity......Jer. 8:20 — 727
Preceded by
spring..........Matt. 24:32 — 989

Sun

A. *Characteristics of:*
Created by
God...........Gen. 1:14, 16 — 4
Under God's ⎰Ps. 104:19 — 582
control.......⎱Matt. 5:45 — 968
Made to rule...Gen. 1:16 — 4
Necessary for
fruit..........Deut. 33:14 — 201

Given for
light...........Jer. 31:35 — 749
Made for God's
glory..........Ps. 148:3 — 604
Causes:
Scorching.....Jon. 4:8 — 887
Sunstroke.....2 Kin. 4:18, 19 — 358

B. *Miracles connected with:*
Stands still.....Josh. 10:12, 13 — 214
Shadows of, turned
back..........2 Kin. 20:9-11 — 377
Darkening of, at
crucifixion....Luke 23:44-49 — 1057
Going down at
noon..........Amos 8:9 — 877

C. *Worship of:*
Forbidden.....Deut. 4:19 — 173
By Manasseh..2 Kin. 21:3, 5 — 377
By Jews.......Jer. 8:2 — 726

D. *Figurative of:*
God's
presence......Ps. 84:11 — 572
Earth's sphere of
action........Eccl. 1:3, 9, 14 — 638
God's Law.....Ps. 19:4-7 — 536
Future glory...Matt. 13:43 — 977
Christ's glory..Matt. 17:2 — 980

Sunday (see First day of week)

Sunstroke—*stricken by sun's heat*

Child dies of......2 Kin. 4:18-20 — 358

Superstition—*gullible ideas based on fancy or fear*

A. *Causes of, in wrong views of:*
God...........1 Kin. 20:23 — 348
Holy objects...1 Sam. 4:3 — 266
God's
providence....Jer. 44:15-19 — 761

B. *Manifestations of, in:*
Seeking illogical
causes........Acts 28:4 — 1126
Ignorance of the true
God...........Acts 17:22 — 1114
Perverting true
religion.......Mark 7:1-16 — 1006

Suphah—*a region in Moab east of the Dead Sea*

Near Arnon......Num. 21:14 — 150

Supper (see Lord's Supper)

Supports

Placed under the
basin...........1 Kin. 7:30, 34 — 331

Sur—*turning aside, entrance*

Name given to a
gate..............2 Kin. 11:6 — 366
Called "Gate of the
Foundation"......2 Chr. 23:5 — 436

Surety—*one who guarantees another's debt*

A. *Descriptive of:*
Guarantee.....Gen. 43:9 — 43

B. *Features concerning:*
Risks involved
in............Prov. 11:15 — 617
Warning
against........Prov. 6:1-5 — 612

Susa—*a city of Elam*

Residence of Persian
monarchs.......Esth. 1:2 — 485
Located on Ulai
Canal..........Dan. 8:2 — 844
Court of Ahasuerus
here.............Esth. 1:2, 5 — 485

Susanna—*lily*

Believing woman contributing to
Christ..........Luke 8:2, 3 — 1035

Susi—*horseman*

Manassite spy...Num. 13:11 — 141

Suspicion—*doubt of another's intent*

A. *Kinds of:*
Unjustified.....Josh. 22:9-31 — 225
Pretended.....Gen. 42:7-12 — 42
Unsuspected...John 13:21-28 — 1081

B. *Objects of:*
Esau by
Jacob.........Gen. 32:3-12 — 33
Jeremiah by
officials.......Jer. 37:12-15 — 755
Jews by
Haman........Esth. 3:8, 9 — 487
Mary by
Joseph........Matt. 1:18-25 — 963
Peter by a servant-
girl...........Matt. 26:69-74 — 992

Sustenance—*means of sustaining life*

Israel by the
Lord.............Neh. 9:21 — 475
Elijah by ravens and a
widow...........1 Kin. 17:1-9 — 344
Believer by the
LORD............Ps. 3:5 — 529

Swallow—*a long-winged, migratory bird*

Nesting in the
sanctuary........Ps. 84:3 — 572
Noted for
twittering........Is. 38:14 — 688

Swallow—*to engulf; to overwhelm*

A. *Applied miraculously to:*
Aaron's rod...Ex. 7:12 — 59
Red Sea......Ex. 15:12 — 67
Ground.......Num. 16:30-34 — 145
Great fish....Jon. 1:17 — 886

B. *Applied figuratively to:*
God's
judgments....Ps. 21:9 — 537
Conquest......Jer. 51:34, 44 — 771
Captivity......Hos. 8:7, 8 — 858
Resurrection...Is. 25:8 — 677

Swearing—*taking an oath*

A. *Kinds of:*
Proclama-
tory..........Ex. 17:16 — 69
Protective.....Gen. 21:23 — 21
Purificatory...Neh. 13:25-30 — 480
Promissory....Luke 1:73 — 1026
Prohibited....James 5:12 — 1256

B. *Of God, objects of:*
God's
purpose.......Is. 14:24, 25 — 670
God's
covenant......Is. 54:9, 10 — 702
Messianic
priesthood....Heb. 7:21 — 1243

See Oaths

Sweat—*perspiration*

Penalty of man's
sin...............Gen. 3:18, 19 — 7
Cause of,
avoided........Ezek. 44:18 — 827
Of Jesus, in
prayer..........Luke 22:44 — 1055

Sweet—*that which is pleasing to the taste*

A. *Descriptive, literally, of:*
Water.........Ex. 15:25 — 68
Honey.........Judg. 14:18 — 246

B. *Descriptive, figuratively, of:*
God's Law....Ps. 19:10 — 537
God's Word...Ps. 119:103 — 593
Spiritual
fellowship.....Ps. 55:14 — 556
Pleasant
words.......Prov. 16:24 — 621
Sleep.........Prov. 3:24 — 611

Swim—*to propel oneself in water by natural means*

Naturally, of
people...........Acts 27:42, 43 — 1126

SUBJECT	REFERENCE	PAGE

B. *Of the believer:*
Compre-
hended by ⎰1 Chr. 28:9 — 413
God......... ⎱Ps. 139:2 — 600
Captivated by
Christ........2 Cor. 10:5 — 1172
Criticized by God's
Word ....Heb. 4:12 — 1241
In need of examin-
ation..........Ps. 139:23 — 600

C. *Of God:*
Not like
man's.........Is. 55:8, 9 — 703
To believer,
good..........Ps. 139:17 — 600

Thousand years
As one day........2 Pet. 3:8 — 1269
Millennial reign ...Rev. 20:1-7 — 1306

Thread
Refused by
Abram ....Gen. 14:23 — 16
Tied to hand .....Gen. 38:28 — 39
Tied in window ...Judg. 2:18 — 233
Lips like scarlet ...Song 4:3 — 650

Threatenings—*menacing actions or
words against another*
A. *Purposes of, to:*
Silence a
prophet ....1 Kin. 19:1, 2 — 346
Hinder a
work..........Neh. 6:1-14 — 471
Hinder the
Gospel........Acts 4:17, 21 — 1098
B. *Exemplified by:*
Jehoram against
Elisha.........2 Kin. 6:31 — 361
Jews against
Christians....Acts 4:29 — 1098
Saul against
Christians....Acts 9:1 — 1104

Threshing—*separating kernels of grain
by force*
A. *Characteristics of:*
Done by a
stick ....Is. 28:27 — 680
By cart wheels
also...........Is. 28:27, 28 — 680
By the feet of
oxen ....Hos. 10:11 — 859
Large and roomy
place..........Gen. 50:10 — 50
B. *Figurative of:*
God's
judgments ....Jer. 51:33 — 771
Minister's
labor..........1 Cor. 9:9, 10 — 1155

Throat—*the front part of the neck*
Glutton's
warning..........Prov. 23:2 — 627
Thirsty one ....Ps. 69:3 — 562
Source of evil ....Ps. 5:9 — 530

Throne—*the seat and symbol of regal
authority*
A. *Of men:*
Under God's
sovereignty ...Dan. 5:18-21 — 842
Established on righ-
teousness .....Prov. 16:12 — 621
Upheld by right-
eousness .....Prov. 20:28 — 624
Subject to:
Succession....2 Chr. 6:10, 16 — 423
Termin-
ation..........Jer. 22:4-30 — 739
B. *Of God:*
Resplendent in
glory..........Is. 6:1-3 — 662
Relentless in
power..........Dan. 2:44 — 837
Ruling over ⎰Dan. 4:25, 34,
all ....⎱ 35 — 840
Righteous in
execution .....Ps. 9:4, 7, 8 — 531

Regal throughout
eternity ......Rev. 22:1, 3 — 1307
C. *Of Christ:*
Based upon the Davidic
covenant......2 Sam. 7:12-16 — 301
Of eternal ⎰Ps. 89:4, 29, 36 — 574
duration .....⎱Dan. 7:13, 14 — 844
Explained in its
nature ....Is. 9:6, 7 — 665
Symbolized in its
functions.....Zech. 6:12, 13 — 921
Promised to
Christ........Luke 1:31-33 — 1025
Christ rises to
possess........Heb. 8:1 — 1243
Christ now ⎰Eph. 1:20-22 — 1185
rules from....⎱1 Pet. 3:20-22 — 1263
Shares with the
Godhead ......Rev. 5:12-14 — 1297
Shares with ⎰Luke 22:30 — 1055
believers .....⎱Rev. 3:21 — 1296
Judges men
from..........Matt. 25:31 — 990

Thumb—*first of man's fingers*
Anointing of, as an act of
consecration.....Lev. 8:23, 24 — 102
As an act of ⎰Lev. 14:14, 17,
purification......⎱ 25, 28 — 108
Cutting off of, an act of
subjugation .....Judg. 1:6, 7 — 232

Thunder—*the sound produced by
lightning*
A. *Supernaturally brought:*
Upon the
Egyptians.....Ex. 9:22-34 — 61
At Sinai ....Ex. 19:16 — 71
Against the
Philistines....1 Sam. 7:10 — 268
At David's
deliver- ⎰2 Sam. 22:14,
ance ....⎱ 15 — 316
B. *Figurative of:*
God's:
Power ....Job 26:14 — 512
Control.......Ps. 104:7 — 582
Majesty.......Rev. 4:5 — 1296
Visitations of
judgment .....Rev. 11:19 — 1300

Thyatira—*an important town in the
Roman province of Asia*
Residence of
Lydia............Acts 16:14 — 1112
One of the seven
churches ....Rev. 2:18-24 — 1295

Tiberias—*an important town on the Sea
of Galilee*
Sea of Galilee
called ....John 6:1, 23 — 1070

Tibhath—*slaughter*
Town in the kingdom of
Zobah............1 Chr. 18:8 — 404

Tibni—*intelligent*
Son of Ginath.....1 Kin. 16:21, 22 — 343

Tickle—*to arouse excitement or desire*
Of the ears, figurative of false
doctrine..........2 Tim. 4:2, 3 — 1225

Tidal—*splendor*
King allied with
Chedorlaomer ....Gen. 14:1, 9 — 15

Tiglath-pileser—*my trust is in the god
Ninib*
Powerful Assyrian king who
invades
Samaria ......2 Kin. 15:29 — 371

Tikvah—*hope*
1. Father-in-law of
Huldah........2 Kin. 22:14 — 379
Called
Tokhath ......2 Chr. 34:22 — 448

2. Father-in-law of
Jahzeiah ......Ezra 10:15 — 462

Tile
Earthen roof .....Luke 5:19 — 1031

Tiller—*a farmer*
Industry in,
commended ......Prov. 12:11 — 618

Tilon—*scorn*
Son of Shimon ....1 Chr. 4:20 — 390

Timaeus—*highly prized*
Father of
Bartimaeus......Mark 10:46 — 1012

Timbrel—*a small hand drum*
Used in:
Entertainment ....Gen. 31:27 — 32
Worship ....Ps. 81:1-4 — 571

Time—*the period between two
eternities*
A. *Computation of, by:*
Years...........Gen. 15:13 — 16
Months........1 Chr. 27:1 — 412
Weeks.........Dan. 10:2 — 847
Days ....Gen. 8:3 — 10
Moments ......Ex. 33:5 — 84
Stairway ......2 Kin. 20:9-11 — 377

B. *Events of, dated by:*
Succession of
families ......Gen. 5:1-32 — 8
Lives of great
men..........Gen. 7:6, 11 — 10
Succession of
kings ....1 Kin. 11:42, 43 — 337
Earthquakes...Amos 1:1 — 871
Important events (the
exodus) ....1 Kin. 6:1 — 329
Important
emperors......Luke 3:1 — 1028

C. *Periods of, stated in years:*
Bondage in
Egypt.........Acts 7:6 — 1100
Wilderness
wanderings ...Deut. 1:3 — 169
Judges.........Judg. 11:26 — 244
Captivity .....Dan. 9:2 — 846
Seventy weeks (490
years).........Dan. 9:24-27 — 847

D. *Sequence of prophetic events
in, indicated by:*
"The time is fulfilled" (Christ's
advent) ......Mark 1:15 — 999
"The fulness of the time"
(Christ's
advent) ....Gal. 4:4 — 1179
"The times of the Gentiles" (the
Gospel age) ...Luke 21:24 — 1053
"The day of salvation" (the
Gospel age) ...2 Cor. 6:2 — 1169
"In the last days" (the Gospel
age)..........Acts 2:17 — 1095
"In the last days"
(the time before
Christ's ⎰2 Tim. 3:1 — 1224
return).......⎱2 Pet. 3:3 — 1269
"The last day"
(Christ's ⎰John 6:39, 54 — 1071
return) ....⎱John 12:48 — 1080
"New heavens"
(eternity) .....2 Pet. 3:13 — 1269

E. *Importance of, indicated by:*
Shortness of
life.............Ps. 89:47 — 575
Making the most of
it ....Eph. 5:16 — 1188
Purpose of, for
salvation.....2 Pet. 3:9, 15 — 1269
Uncertainty
of.............Luke 12:16-23 — 1042
Our goal, ⎰Heb. 11:10, 13-
eternity.....⎱ 16 — 1246
God's plan in ..Acts 14:15-17 — 1110

SUBJECT	REFERENCE	PAGE	SUBJECT	REFERENCE	PAGE	SUBJECT	REFERENCE	PAGE

Tolad—*begetter*

Simeonite town ... 1 Chr. 4:29 — 391
Called Eltolad ..... Josh. 19:4 — 222

Tolerance—*an attitude of patience toward opposing views*

A. *Approved in dealing with:*
Disputes among
brothers ...... Mark 9:38-40 — 1010
Weaker
brother ...... Rom. 14:1-23 — 1143
Repentant
brother ...... 2 Cor. 2:4-11 — 1166

B. *Condemned in dealing with:*
Sin .... 1 Cor. 5:1-13 — 1151
Evil .... 2 Cor. 6:14-18 — 1169
Sin in
ourselves ...... Mark 9:43-48 — 1010
Error .... 2 John 10, 11 — 1281

Toll—*taxes*

Imposed by
Jews .... Ezra 4:20 — 457
Imposed upon
Jews .... Ezra 4:13 — 456
Levites excluded
from .... Ezra 7:24 — 459

Tomb—*a place of burial*

Non-burial, an
indignity .... Rev. 11:9 — 1300
John's body placed
in .... Mark 6:25-29 — 1005
Resurrection from,
announced ...... John 5:28 — 1069
Christ's body placed in that of
Joseph's .... Matt. 25:57-60 — 990
Place of
weeping .... John 11:31 — 1078
Resurrection from,
realized .... John 11:32-44 — 1078

Tongue—*the organ of speech*

A. *Descriptive of:*
Confusion of ... Gen. 11:1-9 — 13
Speech .... Ex. 4:10 — 57
The physical
organ .... Judg. 7:5 — 238
Externalism .... 1 John 3:18 — 1277
People or
race .... Is. 66:18 — 713
Spiritual gift ... 1 Cor. 12:10-30 — 1157
Submission .... Is. 45:23 — 696

B. *Kinds of:*
Backbiting ..... Prov. 25:23 — 629
As of fire ...... Acts 2:3 — 1095
Deceitful ...... Mic. 6:12 — 894
Double .... 1 Tim. 3:8 — 1218
Flattering ..... Prov. 6:24 — 613
Just .... Prov. 10:20 — 616
Lying .... Prov. 21:6 — 624
Muttering .... Is. 59:3 — 706
New .... Mark 16:17 — 1020
Sharpened .... Ps. 140:3 — 601
Slow .... Ex. 4:10 — 57
Soft .... Prov. 25:15 — 629
Stammering ... Is. 33:19 — 684
Soothing ...... Prov. 15:4 — 620
Wise .... Prov. 15:2 — 620

C. *Characteristics of:*
Small but
important ..... James 3:5 — 1254
Untameable .... James 3:6 — 1254
Source of
trouble .... Prov. 21:23 — 625
Means of sin .. Ps. 39:1 — 547
Known by
God .... Ps. 139:4 — 600

D. *Proper employment of, in:*
Speaking:
God's righteous-
ness .... Ps. 35:28 — 545
Wisdom ...... Ps. 37:30 — 546
God's Word .. Ps. 119:172 — 594
Singing
praises .... Ps. 126:2 — 596
Kindness ...... Prov. 31:26 — 634

Confessing
Christ .... Phil. 2:11 — 1194

See Slander

Tongues, speaking in

A. *At Pentecost:*
Opposite of
Babel .... Gen. 11:6-9 — 13
Sign of the Spirit's
coming ...... Acts 2:3, 4 — 1095
External manifesta-
tion .... Acts 2:4, 5 — 1095
Meaning of, interpreted by
Peter .... Acts 2:14-40 — 1095

B. *At Corinth:*
Spiritual gift   ⎰1 Cor. 12:8-10,
(last rank) ... ⎱ 28-30 — 1157
Interpreter of,
required .... 1 Cor. 14:27, 28 — 1159
Love superior
to .... 1 Cor. 13:1-13 — 1158
Subject to
abuse .... 1 Cor. 14:22-26 — 1159

Tools of the Bible

Anvil .... Is. 41:7 — 690
Awl .... Deut. 15:17 — 184
Axe .... 1 Chr. 20:3 — 406
Bellows .... Jer. 6:29 — 725
Brickkiln .... 2 Sam. 12:31 — 305
Cartwheel .... Is. 28:27 — 680
Compass .... Is. 44:13 — 694
Firepan .... Ex. 27:3 — 78
Furnace .... Prov. 17:3 — 622
Graving tool ..... Ex. 32:4 — 83
Hammer .... Ps. 74:6 — 566
Hoe .... 1 Sam. 13:21 — 273
Knife .... Gen. 22:6 — 22
Mattock .... 1 Sam. 13:21 — 273
Ox-goad .... Judg. 3:31 — 235
Pail .... Ex. 27:3 — 78
Plane .... Is. 44:13 — 694
Plowshare .... Is. 2:4 — 659
Plumb line ...... Amos 7:8 — 876
Pruning hook .... Is. 2:4 — 659
Razor .... Num. 6:5 — 134
Refining pot ..... Prov. 17:3 — 622
Saw .... 2 Sam. 12:31 — 305
Shovel .... Ex. 27:3 — 78
Sickle .... Deut. 16:9 — 184
Wheel .... Eccl. 12:6 — 645
Writing case .... Ezek. 9:2 — 792

Topaz—*a precious stone*

Used in
breastplate ...... Ex. 39:10 — 90
Of great value .... Job 28:19 — 513
In Eden .... Ezek. 28:13 — 811
In New
Jerusalem ...... Rev. 21:2, 20 — 1307

Tophel—*lime; cement*

Israelite camp ..... Deut. 1:1 — 169

Topheth—*altar*

Place of human sacrifice
in the valley of
Hinnom .... Jer. 7:31, 32 — 726

Torment—*to suffer unbearable pain*

A. *Kinds of:*
Physical .... Matt. 8:6 — 970
Eternal .... Rev. 20:10 — 1306

B. *Means of:*
Official .... Matt. 18:34 — 982
Persecutors .... Heb. 11:35 — 1247
Fear .... 1 John 4:18 — 1277
Flame .... Luke 16:23-25 — 1047
God .... Rev. 14:9-11 — 1302

Touch—*contact between two things*

A. *Kinds of:*
Unclean .... Lev. 5:2, 3 — 98
Angelic .... 1 Kin. 19:5, 7 — 346
Queenly .... Esth. 5:2 — 488
Cleansing ..... Is. 6:7 — 662
Healing .... Matt. 8:3 — 970

Sexual .... 1 Cor. 7:1 — 1153
Satanic .... 1 John 5:18 — 1278

B. *Purposes of, to:*
Purify .... Is. 6:7 — 662
Strengthen ... Dan. 10:10-18 — 847
Harm .... Zech. 2:8 — 919
Heal .... Mark 5:27-31 — 1004
Receive a
blessing ..... Mark 10:13 — 1010
Restore to
life .... Luke 7:14 — 1034
Manifest
faith .... Luke 7:39-50 — 1035

Towel—*a cloth used in drying*

Used by Christ .... John 13:4, 5 — 1080

Tower of Furnaces—*a tower of Jerusalem*

Rebuilt by
Nehemiah .... Neh. 3:11 — 468

Towers

A. *Purposes of, for:*
Protection ..... Matt. 21:33 — 985
Watchmen ..... 2 Kin. 9:17 — 364
Safeguarding
people .... 2 Chr. 26:10, 15 — 439

B. *Partial list of:*
Babel .... Gen. 11:4, 9 — 13
David .... Song 4:4 — 650
Lebanon ..... Song 7:4 — 652
Penuel .... Judg. 8:17 — 240
Shechem ...... Judg. 9:40, 47,
49 — 242
Siloam .... Luke 13:4 — 1044

Town clerk—*a keeper of court records*

Appeases the
people .... Acts 19:35 — 1117

Trachonitis—*hilly land*

Volcanic region southeast of
Damascus .... Luke 3:1 — 1028

Trade and transportation

A. *Objects of, such as:*
Gold .... 1 Kin. 9:28 — 335
Timber .... 1 Kin. 5:6, 8, 9 — 328
Hardwood .... 1 Kin. 10:11, 12 — 335
Spices .... 1 Kin. 10:10, 15 — 335
Property ...... Ruth 4:3, 4 — 258
Slaves .... Joel 3:6 — 868

B. *Means of, by:*
Wagons .... Gen. 46:5, 6 — 46
Cows .... 1 Sam. 6:7, 8 — 267
Rafts .... 1 Kin. 5:7-9 — 329
Camels .... 1 Kin. 10:1, 2 — 335
Donkey .... Num. 22:21-33 — 151
Horses .... 1 Kin. 20:20 — 348
Caravans ..... Gen. 37:25-36 — 38

C. *Centers of, in:*
Tyre .... Ezek. 27:1-36 — 809
Jerusalem ..... Neh. 13:15-21 — 480

Traders—*those who sell or trade goods*

They trouble
Nehemiah .... Neh. 13:20 — 480

Trades and crafts

Baker .... Gen. 40:1 — 40
Brick makers ..... Ex. 5:7 — 58
Engineers .... Gen. 11:3, 4 — 13
Farmers .... Ps. 104:13-15 — 582
Fishermen .... Matt. 4:18-22 — 966
Lawyers .... Luke 5:17 — 1031
Millers .... Ex. 11:5 — 63
Physician .... Col. 4:14 — 1203
Smiths .... Is. 44:12 — 694

Traditions—*precepts passed down from past generations*

A. *Jewish, described as:*
Commandments of
men .... Matt. 15:9 — 978
Rejection of God's
Word .... Mark 7:8, 9 — 1007

SUBJECT	REFERENCE	PAGE	SUBJECT	REFERENCE	PAGE	SUBJECT	REFERENCE	PAGE

SUBJECT	REFERENCE	PAGE	SUBJECT	REFERENCE	PAGE	SUBJECT	REFERENCE	PAGE

Visitors

Moses and
Elijah ....Matt. 17:3   980

Voice of God, the

A. *Importance of:*
Must be
obeyed........Gen. 3:1-19   6
Disobedience to,
judged........Jer. 42:5-22   759
Obedience to, the essence of
true religion...1 Sam. 15:19-24   276
Obedience to,
rewarded......Gen. 22:6-18   22
Sign of the
covenant......Josh. 24:24, 25   228

B. *Heard by:*
Adam..........Gen. 3:9, 10   6
Moses ....Ex. 19:19   71
Israel.........Deut. 5:22-26   174
Samuel ....1 Sam. 3:1-14   265
Elijah.........1 Kin. 19:12, 13   347
Isaiah ....Is. 6:8-10   662
Ezekiel ....Ezek. 1:24, 25   787
Christ ....Mark 1:11   999
Peter, James and
John........Matt. 17:1, 5   980
Paul..........Acts 9:4, 7   1104
John..........Rev. 1:10-15   1294

Vomit—*to throw up*

A. *Used literally of:*
Dog ....Prov. 26:11   630
One who eats in
excess ....Prov. 25:16   629
Drunken
man ....Is. 19:14   673
Great fish....Jon. 2:10   886

B. *Used figuratively of:*
False
teaching ......2 Pet. 2:22   1269
Judgment....Jer. 48:25, 26   765
Riches.........Job 20:15   508

Vophsi—*rich*

Naphtalite spy ....Num. 13:14   141

Vow—*a voluntary pledge to fulfill an agreement*

A. *Objects of one's:*
Life............Num. 6:1-21   133
Children ....1 Sam. 1:11-28   263
Possessions ....Gen. 28:22   29
Gifts...........Ps. 76:11   567

B. *Features concerning:*
Must be
voluntary .....Deut. 23:21, 22   190
Must be
uttered........Deut. 23:23   190
Once made,
binding ....Eccl. 5:4, 5   641
Benefits of, sometimes
included ......Gen. 28:20-22   29
Invalidity of,
specified .....Num. 30:1-16   159
Abuse of,
condemned ...Matt. 15:4-6   978
Rashness in,
condemned ...Prov. 20:25   624
Perfection in,
required......Lev. 22:18-25   116
Wickedness of
some.........Jer. 44:25   762

Voyage—*an extended trip*

Paul's to Rome....Acts 27:10   1125

Vulture—*a carrion-eating bird of prey*

Classed as
unclean ....Lev. 11:13, 14   104

W

Wadi—*dried up river bed*
Figurative of
deceit ....Job 6:15   499
Israelites camped
out...............Num. 21:12   150

Wafers—*thin cakes of flour*
Often made with
honey ....Ex. 16:31   69
Used in various (Ex. 29:2   80
offerings.........(Lev. 2:4   96

Wages, hire—*payments for work performed*

A. *Principles governing payment of:*
Must be paid
promptly......Deut. 24:14, 15   190
Withholding of,
forbidden .....James 5:4   1255
Laborer worthy
of............Matt. 10:10   972

B. *Paid to such classes as:*
Soldiers........2 Sam. 10:6   303
Fishermen .....Mark 1:20   999
Shepherds .....John 10:12, 13   1076
Masons and
carpenters ....2 Chr. 24:12   437
Farm
laborers......Matt. 20:1-16   983
Male
prostitutes ....Deut. 23:18   190
Wet nurses ....Ex. 2:9   55
Ministers ......1 Cor. 9:4-14   1155
Teachers......Gal. 6:6, 7   1181

C. *Figurative of:*
Spiritual
death ....Rom. 6:23   1136
Unrighteous-
ness..........2 Pet. 2:15   1269

Wagon, cart—*a vehicle with wheels*
Used to move Jacob to
Egypt ....Gen. 45:19, 21   45
Used in moving
objects ....Num. 7:3-9   134

Wailing, weeping—*crying out in constant mourning*

A. *Caused by:*
King's decree ..Esth. 4:3   487
City's
destruction....Ezek. 27:31, 32   810
God's
judgment .....Amos 5:16, 17   875
Girl's death ....Mark 5:38-42   1004
Christ's
return.........Rev. 1:7   1293
Hell's
torments.....Matt. 13:42, 50   977

B. *Performed by:*
Women........Jer. 9:17-20   728
Prophets.......Mic. 1:8   890
Merchants....Rev. 18:15, 19   1305

See Mourning

Waiting on the Lord

A. *Agents of:*
Creatures......Ps. 145:15   603
Creation.......Rom. 8:19, 23   1138
Gentiles ....Is. 51:5   700
Christians .....1 Cor. 1:7   1149

B. *Manner of:*
With the
soul..........Ps. 62:1, 5   558
With
quietness....Lam. 3:25, 26   779
With
patience ......Ps. 40:1   548
With
courage.......Ps. 27:14   540
All the day ....Ps. 25:5   539
Continually....Hos. 12:6   860
With great
hope..........Ps. 130:5, 6   597
With crying....Ps. 69:3   562

C. *Objects of God's:*
Salvation ......Is. 25:9   677
Law...........Is. 42:4   691
Protection .....Ps. 33:20   544
Pardon ....Ps. 39:7, 8   548
Food ....Ps. 104:27   582
Kingdom ......Mark 15:43   1019
Holy Spirit.....Acts 1:4   1094
Son............1 Thess. 1:10   1207

D. *Blessings attending, described as:*
Spiritual
renewal......Is. 40:31   690
Not be
ashamed......Ps. 69:6   562
Inherit the
land..........Ps. 37:9, 34   546
Something
unusual.......Is. 64:4   711
Unusual
blessing......Luke 12:36, 37   1043

Walk of believers

A. *Stated negatively, not:*
In darkness....John 8:12   1073
According to the
flesh ....Rom. 8:1, 4   1137
As Gentiles....Eph. 4:17   1187
In craftiness...2 Cor. 4:2   1167
In sin.........Col. 3:5-7   1201
In unruliness ..2 Thess. 3:6, 11   1213

B. *Stated positively:*
In the light....1 John 1:7   1274
In the truth....3 John 3, 4   1284
In Christ ......Col. 2:6   1201
In the Spirit ...Gal. 5:16, 25   1181
In love ....Eph. 5:2   1188
As children of
light ....Eph. 5:8   1188
As Christ
walked........1 John 2:6   1275
After His command-
ments.........2 John 6   1281
By faith.......2 Cor. 5:7   1168
In good
works........Eph. 2:10   1186
Worthy........Eph. 4:1   1187
Worthy of the
Lord..........Col. 1:10   1200
Worthy of
God..........1 Thess. 2:12   1207
With care......Eph. 5:15   1188
In wisdom.....Col. 4:5   1202
As instructed ..1 Thess. 4:1   1208

Wall—*a rampart or partition*

A. *Used for:*
Shooting arrows
from ....2 Sam. 11:24   304
Observation ...2 Sam. 18:24   312

B. *Unusual events connected with:*
Woman lives
on ....Josh. 2:15   207
Jericho's, falls by
faith ....Josh. 6:5, 20   210
Saul's body (1 Sam. 31:10,
fastened to...(11   291
Woman
throws stone (2 Sam. 11:20,
from ....(21   304
27,000 killed
by ....1 Kin. 20:30   348
Son sacrificed
on ....2 Kin. 3:27   358
Warning inscribed
on ....Dan. 5:5, 25-28   841
Paul escapes
through.......Acts 9:25   1104

C. *Figurative of:*
Defense........1 Sam. 25:16   286
Protection .....Ezra 9:9   461
Great power...Ps. 18:29   536
Peacefulness...Ps. 122:7   595
Self-
sufficiency ....Prov. 18:11   622
Powerless.....Prov. 25:28   629
Salvation .....Is. 26:1   677

SUBJECT	REFERENCE	PAGE	SUBJECT	REFERENCE	PAGE	SUBJECT	REFERENCE	PAGE
Woman—continued			(2) daughter of			Jecoliah, wife of		
Cunning	Prov. 7:10	614	Shilhi	1 Kin. 22:42	351	Amaziah	2 Kin. 15:1, 2	370
Fond of			Baara, wife of			Jedidah, mother of		
adornments	Is. 3:16-24	660	Shaharaim	1 Chr. 8:8	395	Josiah	2 Kin. 22:1	378
Self-			Basemath			Jehoaddin, wife of		
indulgent	Is. 32:9, 11	683	(1) daughter of			Joash	2 Kin. 14:1, 2	369
Easily led into			Elon	Gen. 26:34	27	Jehosheba, daughter of		
idolatry	Jer. 7:18	725	(2) a third wife of			Joram	2 Kin. 11:2	366
Led by			Esau	Gen. 36:2-3	36	Jemimah, Job's		
impulses	2 Tim. 3:6	1225	Bathsheba, wife of			daughter	Job 42:12, 14	523
H. *Prohibitions concerning, not to:*			David	2 Sam. 11:3, 27	303	Jerioth, wife of		
Wear man's			Bernice, sister of			Caleb	1 Chr. 2:18	389
clothing	Deut. 22:5	188	Agrippa	Acts 25:13	1123	Jerusha, daughter of		
Have head			Bilhah, Rachel's			Zadok	2 Kin. 15:33	371
shaved	1 Cor. 11:5-15	1156	maid	Gen. 29:29	30	Jezebel, wife of		
Usurp			Bithia, daughter of			Ahab	1 Kin. 16:30, 31	343
authority	1 Tim. 2:11-15	1218	Pharaoh	1 Chr. 4:17	390	Joanna, wife of		
Be unchaste	1 Pet. 3:1-7	1262	Candace, a			Chuza	Luke 8:3	1035
			queen	Acts 8:27	1103	Jochebed, mother of		
Womb—*the uterus*			Chloe, woman of			Moses	Ex. 6:20	59
A. *God's control over, to:*			Corinth	1 Cor. 1:11	1149	Judith, daughter of		
Close	Gen. 20:18	21	Claudia, Christian of			Beeri	Gen. 26:34	27
Open	Gen. 29:31	30	Rome	2 Tim. 4:21	1226	Julia, Christian woman of		
Fashion us in	Job 31:15	515	Cozbi, Midianite			Rome	Rom. 16:15	1145
Set apart and			killed	Num. 25:15-18	154	Keren-happuch, Job's		
call	Gal. 1:15	1177	Damaris, woman of			daughter	Job 42:14	523
Cause to			Athens	Acts 17:34	1115	Keturah, second wife of		
conceive	Luke 1:31	1025	Deborah			Abraham	Gen. 25:1	25
Make alive	Rom. 4:19-21	1134	(1) Rebekah's			Keziah, daughter of		
B. *Babe inside:*			nurse	Gen. 35:8	35	Job	Job 42:14	523
Grows mysteri-			(2) judge	Judg. 4:4	235	Leah, wife of		
ously	Eccl. 11:5	644	Delilah, Philistine			Jacob	Gen. 29:21-25	29
Known by			woman	Judg. 16:4, 5	247	Lois, grandmother of		
God	Ps. 139:13-16	600	Dinah, daughter of			Timothy	2 Tim. 1:5	1223
Deformed	Acts 3:2	1096	Jacob	Gen. 30:19, 21	30	Lo-ruhamah, daughter of		
Leaps	Luke 1:41, 44	1026	Dorcas, called			Gomer	Hos. 1:3-6	853
			Tabitha	Acts 9:36	1105	Lydia, first Christian convert in		
C. *Man coming from:*			Drusilla, wife of			Europe	Acts 16:14	1112
Different	Gen. 25:23, 24	25	Felix	Acts 24:24	1122	Maacah		
Consecrated	Judg. 13:5, 7	245	Eglah, one of David's			(1) daughter of		
Naked	Job 1:21	496	wives	2 Sam. 3:5	297	Nahor	Gen. 22:23, 24	22
Helpless	Ps. 22:9, 10	538	Elisheba, wife of			(2) daughter of		
Sustained	Ps. 71:6	563	Aaron	Ex. 6:23	59	Talmai	2 Sam. 3:3	297
Estranged	Ps. 58:3	557	Elizabeth, mother of John the			(3) daughter of		
			Baptist	Luke 1:5, 13	1025	Abishalom	1 Kin. 15:2	341
Women of the Bible, named			Ephah, concubine of			(4) mother of		
Abi, wife of			Caleb	1 Chr. 2:46	389	Asa	1 Kin. 15:9, 10	341
Ahaz	2 Kin. 18:1, 2	374	Ephrath, mother of			(5) concubine of		
Abijah, wife of			Hur	1 Chr. 2:19	389	Caleb	1 Chr. 2:48	389
Hezron	1 Chr. 2:24	389	Esther, a Jewess who became			(6) wife of		
Abigail			queen of Persia	Esth. 2:16, 17	486	Machir	1 Chr. 7:16	394
(1) wife of			Eunice, mother of			(7) wife of Jeiel	1 Chr. 8:29	395
Nabal	1 Sam. 25:3	285	Timothy	2 Tim. 1:5	1223	Mahalath		
(2) sister of			Euodia, a			(1) wife of		
David	1 Chr. 2:15, 16	389	deaconess	Phil. 4:2	1195	Esau	Gen. 28:9	28
Abihail, wife of			Eve, first			(2) granddaughter of		
Abishur	1 Chr. 2:29	389	woman	Gen. 3:20	7	David	2 Chr. 11:18	428
Abishag, nurse of			Gomer, wife of			Mahlah, daughter of		
David	1 Kin. 1:1-3	323	Hosea	Hos. 1:2, 3	853	Zelophehad	Num. 26:33	155
Abital, David's			Hagar, Sarai's			Mara, another name for		
wife	2 Sam. 3:1, 4	296	maid	Gen. 16:1	17	Naomi	Ruth 1:20	256
Achsah, daughter of			Haggith, wife of			Martha, friend of		
Caleb	Josh. 15:16	219	David	2 Sam. 3:2, 4	297	Christ	Luke 10:38-41	1040
Adah			Hammolecheth, mother of			Mary		
(1) a wife of			Ishhod	1 Chr. 7:18	394	(1) mother of		
Lamech	Gen. 4:19	8	Hamutal, daughter of			Jesus	Matt. 1:16	963
(2) Canaanite wife of			Jeremiah	2 Kin. 23:31	381	(2) Mary		
Esau	Gen. 36:2	36	Hannah, mother of			Magdalene	Matt. 27:56-61	994
Ahinoam			Samuel	1 Sam. 1:20	263	(3) Mary, sister of		
(1) wife of Saul	1 Sam. 14:50	275	Hazzelelponi, in genealogies of			Martha	Luke 10:38, 39	1040
(2) a			Judah	1 Chr. 4:1-3	390	(4) Mary, wife of		
Jezreelitess	1 Sam. 25:43	287	Helah, one of the wives of			Clopas	John 19:25	1086
Anah, daughter of			Ashhur	1 Chr. 4:5	390	(5) Mary, mother of		
Zibeon	Gen. 36:2	36	Hephzibah, mother of			Mark	Acts 12:12	1108
Anna, an aged			Manasseh	2 Kin. 21:1	377	(6) a Christian at		
widow	Luke 2:36, 37	1028	Herodias, sister-in-law of			Rome	Rom. 16:6	1144
Apphia, a Christian of			Herod	Matt. 14:3-6	977	Matred, mother-in-law of		
Colossae	Philem. 2	1234	Hodesh, wife of			Hadar	Gen. 36:39	37
Asenath, wife of			Shaharaim	1 Chr. 8:8, 9	395	Mehetabel, daughter of		
Joseph	Gen. 41:45	41	Hoglah, a daughter of			Matred	Gen. 36:39	37
Atarah, wife of			Zelophehad	Num. 26:33	155	Merab, King Saul's eldest		
Jerahmeel	1 Chr. 2:26	389	Huldah, a			daughter	1 Sam. 14:49	275
Athaliah, mother of			prophetess	2 Kin. 22:14	379	Meshullemeth, wife of		
Ahaziah	2 Kin. 8:26	363	Hushim, a			Manasseh	2 Kin. 21:18, 19	378
Azubah			Moabitess	1 Chr. 8:8-11	395	Michal, daughter of King		
(1) first wife of			Iscah, daughter of			Saul	1 Sam. 14:49	275
Caleb	1 Chr. 2:18	389	Haran	Gen. 11:29	14	Milcah		
			Jael, wife of			(1) daughter of		
			Heber	Judg. 4:17	235	Haran	Gen. 11:29	14

SUBJECT	REFERENCE	PAGE

Word of God—continued

E. Agency of, to:
Heal............Ps. 107:20 — 585
Make free.....John 8:32 — 1074
Illuminate.....Ps. 119:130 — 593
Bear witness..John 20:31 — 1088
Produce faith..Rom. 10:17 — 1140
Make wise....2 Tim. 3:15-17 — 1225
Exhort.........2 Tim. 4:2 — 1225
Delight the
  heart..........Jer. 15:16 — 734
Create the
  world.........Heb. 11:3 — 1246
Regenerate...James 1:18 — 1253
Destroy the
  world.........2 Pet. 3:5-7 — 1269

F. Proper attitude toward, to:
Stand in awe
  of.............Ps. 119:161 — 594
Tremble at.....Is. 66:2, 5 — 712
Speak
  faithfully....Jer. 23:28 — 741
Examine......Acts 17:11 — 1114
Speak boldly..Acts 4:29, 31 — 1098
Preach.......Acts 8:25 — 1103
Receive.......Acts 11:1 — 1106
Glorify.......Acts 13:48 — 1110
Teach........Acts 18:11 — 1115
Obey ....1 Pet. 3:1 — 1262
Handle
  accurately ....2 Tim. 2:15 — 1224
Do............James 1:22, 23 — 1253
Suffer for.....Rev. 1:9 — 1294

G. In the believer's life, as:
Restraint......Ps. 119:9, 11 — 590
Guide.........Ps. 119:133 — 594
Source of   (Ps. 119:47, 97,
  joy...........{ 162 — 592
Standard of
  conduct......Titus 2:5 — 1230
Source of new
  life...........1 Pet. 1:23 — 1261
Spiritual
  food ....1 Pet. 2:2 — 1261

H. Prohibitions concerning, not to be:
Preached in man's
  wisdom ....1 Cor. 2:4, 13 — 1150
Used
  deceitfully ...2 Cor. 4:2 — 1167
Altered ....Rev. 22:18, 19 — 1308

Words—*intelligible sounds or signs*

A. Described as:
Delightful......Eccl. 12:10 — 645
Lying and
  corrupt ....Dan. 2:9 — 836
Persuasive....1 Cor. 2:4 — 1150
Clear ....1 Cor. 14:9, 19 — 1159
Inexpres-
  sible.........2 Cor. 12:4 — 1173
Empty........Eph. 5:6 — 1188
Flattering.....1 Thess. 2:5 — 1207
Sound ....1 Tim. 6:3 — 1220

B. Power of, to:
Stir up anger ..Prov. 15:1 — 620
Wound ....Prov. 26:22 — 630
Sustain.......Is. 50:4 — 699
Determine
  destiny.......Matt. 12:36, 37 — 975

Work, Christ's

A. Defined as:
Doing God's
  will..........John 4:34 — 1068
Limited in
  time.........John 9:4 — 1075
Incompar-
  able..........John 15:24 — 1083
Initiated by
  God..........John 14:10 — 1081
Accomplished in the
  cross.........John 17:4 — 1084

B. Design of, to:
Attest His
  mission ......John 5:36 — 1069
Encourage
  faith.........John 14:11, 12 — 1081
Judge men....John 15:24 — 1083

Work, the Christian's

A. Agency of, by:
God...........Phil. 2:13 — 1194
Spirit ....1 Cor. 12:11 — 1157
God's Word....1 Thess. 2:13 — 1207
Faith ....Gal. 5:6 — 1180

B. Characteristics of:
Designed for God's
  glory.........Matt. 5:16 — 967
Divinely
  called ....Acts 13:2 — 1108
Produces eventual
  glory.........2 Cor. 4:17 — 1168
Subject to examin-
  ation.........Gal. 6:4 — 1181
Final perfection
  in............Heb. 13:21 — 1249

C. God's regard for, will:
Reward.......Jer. 31:16 — 748
Perfect ....Phil. 1:6 — 1193
Not forget.....Heb. 6:10 — 1242
See Labor, spiritual

Work, physical

Part of the curse..Gen. 3:19 — 7
Required of
  Christians........2 Thess. 3:7-14 — 1213
Nehemiah's zeal...Neh. 6:1-4 — 471
Paul's example....Acts 18:1-3 — 1115
See Labor, physical

Works, God's

A. Described as:
Perfect ....Deut. 32:4 — 199
Awesome.....Ps. 66:3 — 560
Incompar-
  able..........Ps. 86:8 — 573
Splendid and
  majestic ......Ps. 111:3 — 587
Wonderful....Ps. 139:14 — 600
Kind..........Ps. 145:17 — 603
Extra-
  ordinary .....Is. 28:21 — 679
Great and
  marvelous ....Rev. 15:3 — 1303

B. Manifested in:
Creation.......Gen. 1:1-3 — 4
Heavens......Ps. 8:3 — 531
Deeps ....Ps. 107:24 — 585
Regenerate
  people ....Is. 19:25 — 673

C. God's attitude toward:
Glad.........Ps. 104:31 — 582
Made known to His
  people ....Ps. 111:6 — 588
His mercies
  over ....Ps. 145:9 — 603
Glorified in ...Is. 60:21 — 708

D. Believer's attitude toward, to:
Consider......Ps. 8:3 — 531
Behold.......Ps. 46:8 — 552
Meditate.....Ps. 77:12 — 567
Muse on......Ps. 143:5 — 602
Sing for joy
  at............Ps. 92:4 — 577
Tell..........Ps. 107:22 — 585
Praise God
  for...........Ps. 145:4, 10 — 603
Pray for revival
  of............Hab. 3:2 — 905

E. Unbeliever's attitude toward:
Not
  regarding ....Ps. 28:5 — 541
Forgetting ....Ps. 78:11 — 568
Not believed ..Acts 13:41 — 1109

Works, good

A. Considered negatively, they cannot:
Justify........Rom. 4:2-6 — 1134
Determine God's
  choice ....Rom. 9:11 — 1139
Secure righteous-
  ness.........Rom. 9:31, 32 — 1139
Substitute for
  grace ....Rom. 11:6 — 1140

B. Considered positively:
Reward for ....1 Cor. 3:13-15 — 1150
Created for ....Eph. 2:10 — 1186
Prepared for ...2 Tim. 2:21 — 1224
Equipped for...2 Tim. 3:17 — 1225

Works, Satan's (see Satan)

World

A. God's relation to, as:
He who
  established....Jer. 10:12 — 728
Possessor......Ps. 24:1 — 539
Redeemer.....John 3:16 — 1066
Judge.........Ps. 96:13 — 579

B. Christ's relation to, as:
Maker........John 1:10 — 1064
Sin-bearer ....John 1:29 — 1064
Savior ....John 12:47 — 1080
Life...........John 6:33, 51 — 1071
Light ....John 8:12 — 1073
Judge.........Acts 17:31 — 1115
Overcomer....John 16:33 — 1084
Reconciler.....2 Cor. 5:19 — 1169

C. Christian's relation to:
Light of.......Matt. 5:14 — 967
Not of.........John 17:14, 16 — 1084
Chosen out
  of.............John 15:19 — 1082
Tribulation
  in............John 16:33 — 1084
Sent into by
  Christ........John 17:18 — 1084
Not conformed
  to............Rom. 12:2 — 1141
Crucified to....Gal. 6:14 — 1181
To live
  sensibly......Titus 2:12 — 1230
Unstained by ..James 1:27 — 1254
Overcomers
  of.............1 John 5:4, 5 — 1278
Denying desires
  of.............Titus 2:12 — 1230

D. Dangers of, arising from:
Wisdom ....1 Cor. 3:19 — 1151
Love of........2 Tim. 4:10 — 1225
Friendship ....James 4:4 — 1255
Corruptions...2 Pet. 1:4 — 1268
Lusts.........1 John 2:15-17 — 1275
False
  prophets .....1 John 4:1 — 1277
Deceivers......2 John 7 — 1281

E. In the plan of redemption:
Elect chosen
  before........Eph. 1:4 — 1185
Revelation made
  before........Matt. 13:35 — 976
Sin's entrance
  into..........Rom. 5:12 — 1135
Its guilt before
  God..........Rom. 3:19 — 1133
Original revelation
  to............Rom. 1:20 — 1132
God's love
  for...........John 3:16 — 1066
Christ's mission
  to............John 12:47 — 1080
Spirit's conviction
  of............John 16:8 — 1083
Gospel preached
  in............Matt. 24:14 — 988
Reconciliation
  of............2 Cor. 5:19 — 1169
Destruction
  of............2 Pet. 3:7 — 1269
Final judgment
  of............Acts 17:31 — 1115
Satan
  deceives......Rev. 12:9 — 1301

Worm—*a soft-bodied, slender, creeping animal*

A. Ravages of:
On bread ......Ex. 16:15, 20 — 68
On plants......Jon. 4:7 — 887
On the body ...Acts 12:23 — 1108
In Sheol......Job 24:19, 20 — 511
In hell........Mark 9:44-48 — 1010

Young men—continued

B. *Special needs of:*
God's Word....Ps. 119:9 590
Knowledge and
discretion .....Prov. 1:4 609
Encourage-
ment.........Is. 40:30, 31 690
Full
surrender .....Matt. 19:20-22 983
Sensibleness ...Titus 2:6 1230
Counsel ....1 John 2:13, 14 1275

Youth—*the early age of life*

A. *Evils of, seen in:*
Sin ....Ps. 25:7 539
Lusts ....2 Tim. 2:22 1224
Enticements ...Prov. 1:10-16 609
Self-will ......Luke 15:12, 13 1046

B. *Good of, seen in:*
Enthusiasm....1 Sam. 17:26-51 278
Children ......Ps. 127:3, 4 596
Hardships.....Lam. 3:27 779
Godly
example.......1 Tim. 4:12 1219

Z

Zaanan—*rich in flocks*

Town in west
Judah ....Mic. 1:11 891

Zaanannim

Border point of
Naphtali.........Josh. 19:32, 33 223

Zaavan—*unquiet*

Son of Ezer ....Gen. 36:27 36

Zabad—*gift*

1. Descendant of
Judah.........1 Chr. 2:3, 36 388
2. Ephraimite.....1 Chr. 7:20, 21 394
3. One of Joash's
murderers.....2 Chr. 24:26 438
Called
Jozacar ....2 Kin. 12:21 368
4. Son of Zattu...Ezra 10:27 462
5. Son of
Hashum......Ezra 10:33 462
6. Son of Nebo ...Ezra 10:43 463

Zabbai—*(God) has given*

1. Man who divorced his foreign
wife..........Ezra 10:28 462
2. Father of
Baruch........Neh. 3:20 469

Zabbud—*given (by God)*

Postexilic
returnee.........Ezra 8:14 460

Zabdi—*(God) has given*

1. Achan's
grandfather ...Josh. 7:1, 17, 18 211
2. Benjamite .....1 Chr. 8:1, 19 395
3. One of David's
officers........1 Chr. 27:27 412

Zabdiel—*God has given*

1. Father of
Jashobeam ....1 Chr. 27:2 412
2. Postexilic
overseer ......Neh. 11:14 478

Zabud—*bestowed*

Son of Nathan ....1 Kin. 4:5 327

Zaccai—*probably a contraction of Zechariah*

Head of a postexilic
family...........Ezra 2:9 454

Zaccheus—*pure*

Wealthy tax-gatherer converted to
Christ............Luke 19:1-10 1050

Zaccur—*remembered*

1. Father of the Reubenite
spy ....Num. 13:2, 4 141
2. Simeonite......1 Chr. 4:24, 26 391
3. Merarite
Levite.........1 Chr. 24:27 410
4. Asaphite
Levite.........1 Chr. 25:2, 10 410
5. Signer of the
document....Neh. 10:1, 12 477
6. Father of a storehouse
official ....Neh. 13:13 480

Zacharias

Father of John the
Baptist ....Luke 1:5-17 1025

Zadok—*righteous*

1. Descendant of
Aaron........1 Chr. 24:1-3 409
Co-priest with
Abiathar ......2 Sam. 20:25 314
Loyal to
David ....2 Sam. 15:24-29 309
Gently rebuked by
David ....2 Sam. 19:11-14 312
Remained aloof from Adonijah's
usurpation ...1 Kin. 1:8-26 323
Commanded by David to anoint
Solomon ......1 Kin. 1:32-45 324
Replaces
Abiathar ......1 Kin. 2:35 326
Sons of,
faithful.......Ezek. 48:11 830
2. Priest, the son or grandson of
Ahitub........1 Chr. 6:12 392
3. Jotham's maternal
grandfather ...2 Kin. 15:33 371
4. Postexilic workman, son of
Baana.........Neh. 3:4 468
5. Postexilic workman, son of
Immer........Neh. 3:29 469
6. Ancestor of
Christ........Matt. 1:14 963

Zaham—*foul*

Son of
Rehoboam.......2 Chr. 11:18, 19 428

Zair—*little*

Battle camp in
Edom ....2 Kin. 8:21 363

Zalaph—*caper-plant*

Father of
Hanum ....Neh. 3:30 469

Zalmon—*dark*

1. One of David's mighty
men..........2 Sam. 23:28 318
2. Mount near
Shechem ......Judg. 9:48 242

Zalmonah—*shady*

Israelite camp.....Num. 33:41, 42 163

Zalmunna—*deprived of shade*

Midianite king ....Judg. 8:4-21 239

Zamzummin—*murmurers*

Race of giants.....Deut. 2:20, 21 171
Same as the
Zuzim...........Gen. 14:5 15

Zanoah—*rejected*

1. Town in south
Judah.........Josh. 15:1, 34 218
2. Town of
Judah.........Josh. 15:56 220

Zaphenath-paneah—*revealer of secrets*

Name given to Joseph by
Pharaoh.........Gen. 41:45 41

Zaphon—*concealed*

Town of Gad east of the
Jordan ....Josh. 13:24, 27 218

Zarephath

Town of Sidon where Elijah
restores
widow's {1 Kin. 17:8-24 344
son ....{Luke 4:26 1030

Zarethan—*cooling*

Town near {Josh. 3:16 208
Jezreel ....{1 Kin. 4:12 328
Hiram worked
near...........1 Kin. 7:46 331

Zattu—*lovely*

Founder of a postexilic
family..........Ezra 2:2, 8 454
Members of,
divorced foreign {Ezra 10:18, 19,
wives..........{ 27 462
Signs document...Neh. 10:1, 14 477

Zayin

Letter of the Hebrew
alphabet..........Ps. 119:49-56 592

Zaza—*projection*

Jerahmeelite ......1 Chr. 2:33 389

Zeal—*intense enthusiasm for something*

A. *Kinds of:*
Divine ....Is. 9:7 665
Glorious ......Is. 63:15 710
Wrathful .....Ezek. 5:13 789
Stirring.......2 Cor. 9:2 1171
Intense ....2 Cor. 7:11 1170
Boastful ......Phil. 3:4, 6 1195
Ignorant......Rom. 10:2, 3 1139
Righteous .....John 2:15-17 1066
Sinful.........2 Sam. 21:1, 2 315

B. *Manifested in concern for:*
Lord's house...Num. 25:11, 13 154
Others'
salvation......Rom. 10:1 1139
Missionary
work..........Rom. 15:18-25 1144
Reformation of
character .....2 Cor. 7:11 1170
Desire for spiritual
gifts ....1 Cor. 14:12 1159
Doing good
deeds ....Titus 2:14 1230

C. *Illustrated in Paul's life by his:*
Desire to
reach the {Rom. 9:1-3 1138
Jews........{Rom. 10:1 1139
Determination to evangelize
all ....1 Cor. 9:19-23 1155
Willingness to lose all things for
Christ.........Phil. 3:4-16 1195
Plan to minister to unreached
places.........Rom. 1:14, 15 1131
Support of
himself........2 Cor. 11:7-12 1172

D. *Examples of:*
Moses ....Ex. 32:19-32 84
Phinehas ......Num. 25:7-13 154
Joshua........Josh. 24:14-16 227
Gideon ....Judg. 6:11-32 237
David..........1 Sam. 17:26-51 278
Elijah.........1 Kin. 19:10 347
Jehu...........2 Kin. 9:1-37 364
Josiah ....2 Kin. 22:1-20 378
Ezra...........Ezra 7:10 459
Nehemiah .....Neh. 4:1-23 469
Peter and
John..........Acts 4:8-20 1097
Timothy.......Phil. 2:19-22 1194
Epaphro-
ditus..........Phil. 2:25-30 1194
Epaphras ......Col. 4:12, 13 1202

Zealot—*zealous one*

Applied to Simon, the Canaanite; a
party of fanatical
Jews..........Luke 6:15 1032

Zebadiah—*Yahweh has bestowed*

1, 2. Two {1 Chr. 8:1, 15,
Benjamites...{ 17 395

SUBJECT	REFERENCE	PAGE	SUBJECT	REFERENCE	PAGE	SUBJECT	REFERENCE	PAGE

Zizah

Gershomite   ⌈1 Chr. 23:7, 10,
Levite..........⌊   11   408

See Zina

Zoan

City in Lower
Egypt............Num. 13:22   141
Places of God's
miracles..........Ps. 78:12, 43   568
Princes resided
at................Is. 30:2, 4   681
Object of God's
wrath............Ezek. 30:14   813

Zoar—*little*

Ancient city of Canaan originally
named Bela.......Gen. 14:2, 8   15
Spared destruction at Lot's
request..........Gen. 19:20-23   20
Seen by Moses from Mt.
Pisgah............Deut. 34:1-3   202
Object of prophetic
doom.............Is. 15:5   670

Zobah

Aramean kingdom; wars against
Saul..............1 Sam. 14:47   275

Zobebah—*the affable*

Judahite..........1 Chr. 4:1, 8   390

Zohar—*gray*

1. Father of Ephron the
Hittite........Gen. 23:8   22

2. Son of
Simeon.......Gen. 46:10   46

Zoheleth—*serpent*

Stone near
En-rogel..........1 Kin. 1:9   323

Zoheth—*proud*

Descendant of
Judah............1 Chr. 4:1, 20   390

Zophah—*pot-bellied jug*

Asherite ....1 Chr. 7:30, 35,
36   394

Zophar—*chirper*

Naamathite and friend of
Job...............Job 2:11   496

Zophim—*watchers*

Field on the top of Mt.
Pisgah............Num. 23:14   152

Zorah—*hornet*

Town of Judah....Josh. 15:1, 33   218
Inhabited by
Danites..........Josh. 19:40, 41   223
Place of Samson's
birth and   ⌈Judg. 13:24, 25   245
burial ....⌊Judg. 16:30, 31   248
Inhabited by
returnees........Neh. 11:25, 29   478

Zorathite

Native of Zorah...1 Chr. 4:2   390
Descendants of
Caleb.............1 Chr. 2:50, 53   389

Zorite

Same as
Zorathite.........1 Chr. 2:54   389

Zuar—*small, little*

Father of
Nethanel.........Num. 1:8   127

Zuph—*honeycomb*

1. Ancestor of
Samuel ....1 Chr. 6:33, 35   392
2. Region in
Judah.........1 Sam. 9:4-6   269

Zur—*rock*

1. A Midianite
leader........Num. 25:15, 18   154
2. Son of Jeiel....1 Chr. 8:30   395

Zuriel—*God is a rock*

Merarite Levite ...Num. 3:35   130

Zurishaddai—*the Almighty is a rock*

Father of
Shelumiel ....Num. 7:36, 41   135

Zuzim—*prominent; giant*

Tribe east of the
Jordan ....Gen. 14:5   15
Probably same as
Zamzummin......Deut. 2:20   171

MONIES, WEIGHTS, AND MEASURES

The Hebrews probably first used coins in the Persian period (500–350 B.C.). However, minting began around 700 B.C. in other nations. Prior to this, precious metals were weighed, not counted as money.

Some units appear as both measures of money and measures of weights. This comes from naming the coins after their weight. For example, the shekel was a weight long before it became the name of a coin.

It is helpful to relate biblical monies to current values. But we cannot make exact equivalents. The fluctuating value of money's purchasing power is difficult to determine in our own day. It is even harder to evaluate currencies used two- to three-thousand years ago.

Therefore, it is best to choose a value meaningful over time, such as a common laborer's daily wage. One day's wage corresponds to the ancient Jewish system (a silver shekel is four days' wages) as well as to the Greek and Roman systems (the drachma and the denarius were each coins representing a day's wage).

The monies chart below takes a current day's wage as thirty-two dollars. Though there are differences of economies and standards of living, this measure will help us apply meaningful value to the monetary units in the chart and in the biblical text.

Monies

Unit	Monetary Value	Equivalents	Translations
Jewish Weights Talent	gold—$5,760,000[1] silver—$384,000	3,000 shekels; 6,000 bekas	talent, one hundred pounds
Shekel	gold—$1,920 silver—$128	4 days' wages; 2 bekas; 20 gerahs	shekel
Beka	gold—$960 silver—$64	½ shekel; 10 gerahs	beka
Gerah	gold—$96 silver—$6.40	1/20 shekel	gerahs
Persian Coins Daric	gold—$1,280[2] silver—$64	2 days' wages; ½ Jewish silver shekel	daric, drachma
Greek Coins Tetradrachma (Stater)	$128	4 drachmas	stater
Didrachma	$64	2 drachmas	two-drachma tax
Drachma	$32	1 day's wage	coin, silver coins
Lepton	$.25	½ of a Roman kodrantes	cents, small copper coin
Roman Coins Aureus	$800	25 denarii	gold
Denarius	$32	1 day's wage	denarii
Assarius	$2	1/16 of a denarius	cent
Kodrantes	$.50	¼ of an assarius	cent

[1]Value of gold is fifteen times the value of silver.
[2]Value of gold is twenty times the value of silver.

Weights

Unit	Weight	Equivalents	Translations
Jewish Weights			
Talent	c. 75 pounds for common talent, c. 150 pounds for royal talent	60 minas; 3,000 shekels	talent, one hundred pounds
Mina	1.25 pounds	50 shekels	maneh, mina
Shekel	c. .4 ounce (11.4 grams) for common shekel c. .8 ounce for royal shekel	2 bekas; 20 gerahs	shekel
Beka	c. .2 ounce (5.7 grams)	½ shekel; 10 gerahs	half-shekel
Gerah	c. .02 ounce (.57 grams)	½₀ shekel	gerah
Roman Weight			
Litra	12 ounces		pound, pint

Measures of Length

Unit	Length	Equivalents	Translations
Day's journey	c. 20 miles		day's journey, day's walk
Roman mile	4,854 feet	8 stadia	mile
Sabbath day's journey	3,637 feet	6 stadia	a sabbath day's journey
Stadion	606 feet	⅛ Roman mile	mile, stadion
Rod	9 feet (10.5 feet in Ezekiel)	3 paces; 6 cubits	measuring rod
Fathom	6 feet	4 cubits	fathom
Pace	3 feet	⅓ rod; 2 cubits	pace
Cubit	18 inches	½ pace; 2 spans	cubit, yards
Span	9 inches	½ cubit; 3 handbreadths	span
Handbreadth	3 inches	⅓ span; 4 fingers	handbreadth
Finger	.75 inches	¼ handbreadth	finger

Dry Measures

Unit	Measure	Equivalents	Translations
Homer	6.52 bushels	10 ephahs	homer
Kor	6.52 bushels	1 homer; 10 ephahs	kor, measure
Lethech	3.26 bushels	½ kor	a homer and a half
Ephah	.65 bushel, 20.8 quarts	½₀ homer	ephah

Dry Measures—Continued

Unit	Measure	Equivalents	Translations
Modius	7.68 quarts		peck-measure
Seah	7 quarts	⅓ ephah	measure, pecks
Omer	2.08 quarts	⅒ ephah; 1⅘ kab	omer
Kab	1.16 quarts	4 logs	kab
Choenix	1 quart		quart
Xestes	1⅙ pints		pitcher
Log	.58 pint	¼ kab	log

Liquid Measures

Unit	Measure	Equivalents	Translations
Kor	60 gallons	10 baths	kor
Metretes	10.2 gallons		gallon
Bath	6 gallons	6 hins	measure, bath
Hin	1 gallon	2 kabs	hin
Kab	2 quarts	4 logs	kab
Log	1 pint	¼ kab	log

The

Old Testament

of

The Open Bible®

EXPANDED EDITION

New American Standard Bible

THE FIRST BOOK OF MOSES COMMONLY CALLED

GENESIS

THE BOOK OF GENESIS
The first part of Genesis focuses on the beginning and spread of sin in the world and culminates in the devastating flood in the days of Noah. The second part of the book focuses on God's dealings with one man, Abraham, through whom God promises to bring salvation and blessing to the world. Abraham and his descendants learn firsthand that it is always safe to trust the Lord in times of famine and feasting, blessing and bondage. From Abraham . . . to Isaac . . . to Jacob . . . to Joseph . . . God's promises begin to come to fruition in a great nation possessing a great land.

Genesis is a Greek word meaning "origin," "source," "generation," or "beginning." The original Hebrew title *Bereshith* means "In the Beginning."

The literary structure of Genesis is clear and is built around eleven separate units, each headed with the word *generations* in the phrase "These are *the records of* the generations" or "The book of the generations": (1) Introduction to the Generations (1:1—2:3); (2) Heaven and Earth (2:4—4:26); (3) Adam (5:1—6:8); (4) Noah (6:9—9:29); (5) Sons of Noah (10:1—11:9); (6) Shem (11:10—26); (7) Terah (11:27—25:11); (8) Ishmael (25:12—18); (9) Isaac (25:19—35:29); (10) Esau (36:1—37:1); (11) Jacob (37:2—50:26).

THE AUTHOR OF GENESIS
Although Genesis does not directly name its author, and although Genesis ends some three centuries before Moses was born, the whole of Scripture and church history are unified in their adherence to the Mosaic authorship of Genesis.

The Old Testament is replete with both direct and indirect testimonies to the Mosaic authorship of the entire Pentateuch (Ex. 17:14; Lev. 1:1, 2; Num. 33:2; Deut. 1:1; Josh. 1:7; 1 Kin. 2:3; 2 Kin. 14:6; Ezra 6:18; Neh. 13:1; Dan. 9:11–13; Mal. 4:4). The New Testament also contains numerous testimonies (Matt. 8:4; Mark 12:26; Luke 16:29; John 7:19; Acts 26:22; Rom. 10:19; 1 Cor. 9:9; 2 Cor. 3:15).

The Early Church openly held to the Mosaic authorship, as does the first-century Jewish historian Josephus. As would be expected the Jerusalem Talmud supports Moses as author.

It would be difficult to find a man in all the range of Israel's life who was better prepared

or qualifed to write this history. Trained in the "learning of the Egyptians" (Acts 7:22), Moses had been providentially prepared to understand and integrate, under the inspiration of God, all the available records, manuscripts, and oral narratives.

THE TIME OF GENESIS
Genesis divides neatly into three geographical settings: (1) the Fertile Crescent (1—11); (2) Israel (12—36); (3) Egypt (37—50).

The setting of the first eleven chapters changes rapidly as it spans more than two thousand years and fifteen hundred miles, and paints the majestic acts of the Creation, the garden of Eden, the Noahic Flood, and the towering citadel of Babel.

The middle section of Genesis rapidly funnels down from the broad brim of the two millenia spent in the Fertile Crescent to less than two hundred years in the little country of Canaan. Surrounded by the rampant immorality and idolatry of the Canaanites, the godliness of Abraham rapidly degenerates into gross immorality in some of his descendants.

In the last fourteen chapters, God dramatically saves the small Israelite nation from extinction by transferring the "seventy souls" to Egypt so that they may grow and multiply. Egypt is an unexpected womb for the growth of God's chosen nation Israel, to be sure, but one in which they are isolated from the maiming influence of Canaan.

Genesis spans more time than any other book in the Bible; in fact, it covers more than all sixty-five other books of the Bible put together.

Utilizing the same threefold division noted above, the following dates can be assigned:

A. 2,000 or more years 4000–2090 B.C. (Gen. 1—11)
   1. Creation, 4000 B.C. or earlier (Gen. 1:1)
   2. Death of Terah, 2090 B.C. (Gen. 11:32)

B. 193 years, 2090–1897 B.C. (Gen. 12—36)
   1. Death of Terah, 2090 B.C. (Gen. 11:32)
   2. Joseph to Egypt, c. 1897 B.C. (Gen. 37:2)

C. 93 years, 1897–1804 B.C. (Gen. 37—50)
   1. Joseph to Egypt, c. 1897 B.C. (Gen. 37:2)

2. Death of Joseph, 1804 B.C. (Gen. 50:26)

✝ THE CHRIST OF GENESIS

Genesis moves from the general to the specific in its messianic predictions: Christ is the seed of the woman (3:15), from the line of Seth (4:25), the son of Shem (9:27), the descendant of Abraham (12:3), of Isaac (21:12), of Jacob (25:23), and of the tribe of Judah (49:10).

Christ is also seen in people and events that serve as types. (A "type" is a historical fact that illustrates a spiritual truth.) Adam is "a type of Him who was to come" (Rom. 5:14). Both entered the world through a special act of God as sinless men. Adam is the head of the old creation; Christ is the Head of the new creation. Abel's acceptable offering of a blood sacrifice points to Christ, and there is a parallel in his murder by Cain. Melchizedek ("righteous king") is "made like the Son of God" (Heb. 7:3). He is the king of Salem ("peace") who brings forth bread and wine and is the priest of the Most High God. Joseph is also a type of Christ. Joseph and Christ are both objects of special love by their fathers, both are hated by their brothers, both are rejected as rulers over their brothers, both are conspired against and sold for silver, both are condemned though innocent, and both are raised from humiliation to glory by the power of God.

🔑 KEYS TO GENESIS

Key Word: Beginnings—Genesis gives the beginning of almost everything, including the beginning of the universe, life, man, sabbath, death, marriage, sin, redemption, family, literature, cities, art, language, and sacrifice.

Key Verses: Genesis 3:15; 12:3—"And I will put enmity between you and the woman, and between your seed and her seed; He shall bruise you on the head, and you shall bruise him on the heel" (3:15).

"And I will bless those who bless you, and the one who curses you I will curse. And in you all the families of the earth shall be blessed" (12:3).

Key Chapter: Genesis 15—Central to all of Scripture is the Abrahamic Covenant, which is given in 12:1-3 and ratified in 15:1-21. Israel receives three specific promises: (1) the promise of a great land—"From the river of Egypt as far as the great river, the river Euphrates" (15:18); (2) the promise of a great nation—"And I will make your descendants as the dust of the earth" (13:16); and (3) the promise of a great blessing—"And I will bless you, and make your name great; and so you shall be a blessing" (12:2).

🔎 SURVEY OF GENESIS

Genesis is not so much a history of man as it is the first chapter in the history of the redemption of man. As such, Genesis is a highly selective spiritual interpretation of history. Genesis is divided into four great events (1—11) and four great people (12—50).

The Four Great Events: Chapters 1—11 lay the foundation upon which the whole Bible is built and centers on four key events. (1) Creation: God is the sovereign Creator of matter, energy, space, and time. Man is the pinnacle of the Creation. (2) Fall: Creation is followed by corruption. In the first sin man is separated from God (Adam from God), and in the second sin, man is separated from man (Cain from Abel). In spite of the devastating curse of the Fall, God promises hope of redemption through the seed of the woman (3:15). (3) Flood: As man multiplies, sin also multiplies until God is compelled to destroy humanity

FOCUS	FOUR EVENTS				FOUR PEOPLE			
REFERENCE	1:1——3:1	6:1	10:1	12:1	25:19	27:1	37:1—50:26	
DIVISION	CREATION	FALL	FLOOD	NATIONS	ABRAHAM	ISAAC	JACOB	JOSEPH
TOPIC	HUMAN RACE				HEBREW RACE			
	HISTORICAL				BIOGRAPHICAL			
LOCATION	FERTILE CRESCENT (Eden-Haran)				CANAAN (Haran-Canaan)			EGYPT (Canaan-Egypt)
TIME	c. 2000 YEARS (c. 4004-2090 B.C.)				193 YEARS (2090-1897 B.C.)			93 YEARS (1897-1804 B.C.)

with the exception of Noah and his family. (4) *Nations:* Genesis teaches the unity of the human race: we are all children of Adam through Noah, but because of rebellion at the Tower of Babel, God fragments the single culture and language of the post-flood world and scatters people over the face of the earth.

The Four Great People: Once the nations are scattered, God focuses on one man and his descendants through whom He will bless all nations (12—50). (1) *Abraham:* The calling of Abraham (12) is the pivotal point of the book. The three covenant promises God makes to Abraham (land, descendants, and blessing) are foundational to His program of bringing

salvation upon the earth. (2) *Isaac:* God establishes His covenant with Isaac as the spiritual link with Abraham. (3) *Jacob:* God transforms this man from selfishness to servanthood and changes his name to Israel, the father of the twelve tribes. (4) *Joseph:* Jacob's favorite son suffers at the hands of his brothers and becomes a slave in Egypt. After his dramatic rise to the rulership of Egypt, Joseph delivers his family from famine and brings them out of Canaan to Goshen.

Genesis ends on a note of impending bondage with the death of Joseph. There is great need for the redemption that is to follow in the Book of Exodus.

CHAPTER 1

Creation of the World

IN^R the beginning ^{R}God ^{R}created the heavens and the earth.   [John 1:1] • Acts 17:24 • Job 38:4

2 And the earth was ¹formless and void, and darkness was over the ^{T}surface of the deep; and the Spirit of God was ²moving over the ^{T}surface of the waters.   *face of*

3 Then ^{R}God said, "Let there be light"; and there was light.   Ps. 33:6, 9; 2 Cor. 4:6

4 And God saw that the light was ^{R}good; and God ^{R}separated the light from the darkness.   [Ps. 145:9, 10] • Is. 45:7

5 And God called the light day, and the darkness He called night. And there was evening and there was morning, one day.

6 Then God said, "Let there be an expanse in the midst of the waters, and let it separate the waters from the waters."

7 And God made the ³expanse, and separated ^{R}the waters which were below the expanse from the waters which were above the expanse; and it was so.   Job 38:8-11

8 And God called the ^{A}expanse heaven. And there was evening and there was morning, a second day.   *firmament*

9 Then God said, "Let the waters below the heavens be gathered into one place, and let the dry land appear"; and it was so.

10 And God called the dry land earth, and the ^{R}gathering of the waters He called seas; and God saw that it was good. Ps. 33:7; 95:5

11 Then God said, "Let the earth sprout vegetation, plants yielding seed, *and* fruit trees bearing fruit after ^{T}their kind, with seed in them, on the earth"; and it was so.   *its*

12 And the earth brought forth ^{A}vegetation, ^{A}plants yielding ^{T}seed after ^{T}their kind, and trees bearing fruit, with seed in them, after their kind; and God saw that it was good.   *grass • herbs • its • in which is its seed*

13 And there was evening and there was morning, a third day.

14 Then God said, "Let there be ^{A}lights in the ^{A}expanse of the heavens to separate the day from the night, and let them be for signs, and for seasons, and for days and years;   *luminaries, light-bearers • firmament*

15 and let them be for ^{A}lights in the expanse of the heavens to give light on the earth"; and it was so.   *luminaries, light-bearers*

16 And God made the two great lights, the ^{R}greater light ^{T}to govern the day, and the lesser light ^{T}to govern the night; *He made the* stars also.   Ps. 136:8, 9 • *for the dominion of*

17 And God placed them in the expanse of the heavens to give light on the earth,

18 and to ^{R}govern the day and the night, and to separate the light from the darkness; and God saw that it was good.   Jer. 31:35

19 And there was evening and there was morning, a fourth day.

20 Then God said, "Let the waters ^{A}teem with swarms of living creatures, and let birds fly above the earth ^{T}in the open expanse of the heavens."   *swarm • on the face*

21 And God created ^{R}the great sea monsters, and every living creature that moves, with which the waters swarmed after their kind, and every winged bird after its kind; and God saw that it was good. Ps. 104:25-28

22 And God blessed them, saying, "Be fruitful and multiply, and fill the waters in the seas, and let birds multiply on the earth."

23 And there was evening and there was morning, a fifth day.

24 Then God said, "Let the earth bring forth living creatures after ^{T}their kind: cattle and creeping things and beasts of the earth after ^{T}their kind"; and it was so.   *its*

25 And God made the ^{R}beasts of the earth after ^{T}their kind, and the cattle after ^{T}their kind, and everything that creeps on the ground after its kind; and God saw that it was good.   Gen. 7:21, 22; Jer. 27:5 • *its*

26 Then God said, "Let Us make man in Our image, according to Our likeness; and let them rule over the fish of the sea and over the birds of the ^{T}sky and over the cattle and over all the earth, and over every creeping thing that creeps on the earth."   *heavens*

27 And God created man in His own image, in the image of God He created him; male and female He created them.

¹ Or, *a waste and emptiness*   ² Or, *hovering*
³ Or, *firmament*

28 And God blessed them; and God said to them, "Be[R]fruitful and multiply, and fill the earth, and subdue it; and rule over the fish of the sea and over the birds of the[T]sky, and over every living thing that[A]moves on the earth."   Gen. 9:1, 7 • *heavens* • *creeps*

29 Then God said, "Behold,[R]I have given you every plant yielding seed that is on the [T]surface of all the earth, and every tree which has fruit yielding seed; it shall be food for you;   Ps. 104:14; 136:25 • *face of*

30 and to every beast of the earth and to every bird of the[T]sky and to every thing that [A]moves on the earth [T]which has life, *I have given* every green plant for food"; and it was so.   *heavens* • *creeps* • *in which is a living soul*

31 And God saw all that He had made, and behold, it was very[R]good. And there was evening and there was morning, the sixth day.   [Ps. 104:24, 28; 119:68; 1 Tim. 4:4]

CHAPTER 2

THUS the heavens and the earth were completed, and all[R]their hosts.   Deut. 4:19

2 And by[R]the seventh day God completed His work which He had done; and[R]He rested on the seventh day from all His work which He had done.   Ex. 20:8-11; 31:17 • Heb. 4:4, 10

3 Then God blessed the seventh day and sanctified it, because in it He rested from all His work which God had created and made.

Creation of Man

4 [T]This is the account of the heavens and the earth when they were created, in [R]the day that the LORD God made earth and heaven.   *These are the generations* • [Gen. 1:3–31]

5 [R]Now no shrub of the field was yet in the earth, and no plant of the field had yet sprouted, for the LORD God had not sent rain upon the earth; and there was no man to [T]cultivate the ground.   Gen. 1:11 • *work, serve*

6 But a mist used to rise from the earth and water the whole surface of the ground.

7 Then the LORD God formed man of [R]dust from the ground, and breathed into his nostrils the breath of life; and[R]man became a living[T]being.   Gen. 3:19 • 1 Cor. 15:45 • *soul*

8 And the LORD God planted a garden toward the east, in Eden; and there He placed the man whom He had formed.

9 And out of the ground the LORD God caused to grow every tree that is pleasing to the sight and good for food;[R]the tree of life also in the midst of the garden, and the tree of the knowledge of good and evil. [Rev. 2:7]

10 Now a river[T]flowed out of Eden to water the garden; and from there it divided and became four[T]rivers.   *was going out* • *heads*

11 The name of the first is Pishon; it [T]flows around the whole land of [R]Havilah, where there is gold.   *surrounds* • Gen. 25:18

12 And the gold of that land is good; the bdellium and the onyx stone are there.

13 And the name of the second river is Gihon; it flows around the whole land of Cush.

14 And the name of the third river is Tigris; it [T]flows east of Assyria. And the fourth river is the Euphrates.   *is the one going*

15 Then the LORD God took the man and put him into the garden of Eden to cultivate it and keep it.

16 And the LORD God [R]commanded the man, saying, "From any tree of the garden you may eat freely;   Gen. 3:2, 3

17 but from the tree of the knowledge of good and evil you shall not [T]eat, for in the day that you eat from it [R]you shall surely die."   *eat from it* • Deut. 30:15, 19, 20; [Rom. 6:23]

18 Then the LORD God said, "It is not good for the man to be alone; I will make him a helper [4]suitable for him."

19 And[R]out of the ground the LORD God formed every beast of the field and every bird of the[T]sky, and brought *them* to the man

[4] Lit., *corresponding to*

2:15–17   The Edenic Covenant—The covenant in Eden is the first of the general or universal covenants. In it, Adam is charged to: (1) populate the earth (Gen. 1:28); (2) subdue the earth (Gen. 1:28); (3) exercise dominion over the animal creation (Gen. 1:28); (4) care for the garden of Eden and enjoy its fruit (Gen. 1:29; 2:15); and (5) refrain from eating the fruit of the tree of the knowledge of good and evil, under penalty of death (Gen. 2:16, 17). The Edenic Covenant was terminated by man's disobedience, when Adam and Eve ate of the fruit of the tree of the knowledge of good and evil, resulting in their spiritual and physical deaths. This failure necessitated the establishment of the covenant with Adam (Page 7—Gen. 3:14–21).

Now turn to Page 7—Gen. 3:14–21: The Adamic Covenant.

2:18–25   How the Family Began—Genesis 2:18–25 fills in the details of the simple statement in Genesis 1:27: "Male and female He created them." This account particularly amplifies the "and female" part of the statement and shows how woman was created. Three observations can be made on the passage that will help us to understand how the family began:

a. The need for woman (vv. 18–20). Woman is absolutely essential in God's plan. It was God who observed, "It is not good for the man to be alone" (v. 18), and determined to make a "helper" for Adam. Woman's role in the will of God was to be a "helper" who was suitable to man in every particular mental, spiritual, emotional, social, and physical need. God undertook an orientation program to show man the need that He alone had observed. He brought to man the birds and beasts He had created, so that man should exercise his dominion over them (v. 28) and name them (v. 19). However, in verse 20 it is noted that for Adam there was no "helper" similar to himself.

b. The provision of woman for man (vv. 21–24). God caused Adam to go to sleep, and God removed one of his "ribs." Exactly what God removed is not known, but it was adequate for His purpose. He "fashioned" (lit.,

(continued on next page)

to see what he would call them; and whatever the man called a living creature, that was its name.　　　　　　Gen. 1:24 • *heavens*

20 And the man gave names to all the cattle, and to the birds of the ᵀsky, and to every beast of the field, but for ⁵Adam there was not found a helper suitable for him.　*heavens*

21 So the LORD God caused aᴿdeep sleep to fall upon the man, and he slept; then He took one of his ribs, and closed up the flesh at that place.　　　　　　　　　Gen. 15:12

22 And the LORD God ⁶fashioned into a woman the rib which He had taken from the man, and brought her to the man.

23 And the man said,
"Thisᴿis now bone of my bones,
And flesh of my flesh;　　Gen. 29:14
ᵀShe shall be called Woman,　*This one*
Because she was taken out of Man."

24 For this cause a man shall leave his father and his mother, and shall cleave to his wife; and they shall become one flesh.

25 ᴿAnd the man and his wife were both naked and were not ashamed.　Gen. 3:7, 10, 11

CHAPTER 3

Temptation of Man

NOW ᴿthe serpent was more crafty than any beast of the field which the LORD God had made. And he said to the woman, "Indeed, has God said, 'You shall not eat from ᴬany tree of the garden'?"　[Rev. 12:9] • *every*

2 And the woman said to the serpent, "Fromᴿthe fruit of the trees of the garden we may eat;　　　　　　　　Gen. 2:16, 17

3 but from the fruit of the tree which is in the middle of the garden, God has said, 'You shall not eat from it or touch it, lest you die.'"

4 ᴿAnd the serpent said to the woman, "You surely shall not die!　　[2 Cor. 11:3]

5 "For God knows that in the day you eat from it your eyes will be opened, and you will be like God, knowing good and evil."

Fall of Man

6 ᴿWhen the woman saw that the tree was good for food, and that it was a delight to the eyes, and that the tree was desirable to make *one* wise, she took from its fruit and ate; and she gave also to her husband with her, and he ate.　　　[Rom. 5:12–19]; 1 Tim. 2:14

7 Then the eyes of both of them were opened, and they knew that they were naked; and they sewed fig leaves together and made themselvesᴬloin coverings.　*girdles*

Judgment on Man

8 And they heard the sound of the LORD God walking in the garden in the ᵀcool of the day, and the man and his wife hid themselves from the presence of the LORD God among the trees of the garden.　*wind, breeze*

9 Then the LORD God called to the man, and said to him, "Whereᴿare you?"　Gen. 4:9

10 And he said, "Iᴿheard the sound of Thee in the garden, and I was afraid because I was naked; so I hid myself."　Ex. 20:18, 19

11 And He said, "Who told you that you were naked? Have you eaten from the tree of which I commanded you not to eat?"

12 ᴿAnd the man said, "The woman whom Thou gavest *to be* with me, she gave me from the tree, and I ate."　　[Prov. 28:13]

13 Then the LORD God said to the woman, "What is this you have done?" And the woman said, "Theᴿserpent deceived me, and I ate."　　　2 Cor. 11:3; 1 Tim. 2:14

⁵ Or, *man*　⁶ Lit., *built*

(continued from previous page)

built) a woman (v. 22) whom Adam recognized as being his equal, "bone of my bones, and flesh of my flesh." This resulted in what has become known as the universal law of marriage (v. 24), in which it can be seen that: (1) the responsibility for marriage is on the man's shoulders—he is to "leave his father and his mother"; (2) the responsibility for keeping the union together is on the man's shoulders—he is to "cleave" his wife; and (3) the union is indissoluble—"they shall become one flesh."

c. The state of the first man and woman (v. 25). From the beginning the man and woman were "naked" in each other's presence and "were not ashamed." There is no shame in nudity when it occurs within the right context—the marital union. This passage clearly teaches that (1) sex was God's idea and is not sinful; (2) sex came before the Fall, and if the Fall had never taken place there still would be sexual relations between a man and his wife; and (3) propagation of the species is one, but not the exclusive, purpose for sex. The Bible gives two other reasons for sex: (1) to promote love between the husband and wife (Page 1248—Heb. 13:4), and (2) to prevent prevent fornication—the unlawful satisfaction of the God-given sexual desire (Page 1153— 1 Cor. 7:2).

Now turn to Page 175—Deut. 6:4–9: Three Essentials for a Christian Home.

3:6, 7　Adam's Sin—Adam's sin does not seem to be a very great sin from man's perspective. All he did was take a bite of some fruit. Adam's sin is serious in that the fruit was of the tree of the knowledge of good and evil, of which God said that he was not to eat under penalty of death (Page 5—Gen. 2:17). Up to this time Adam was morally innocent. When he sinned, he by nature became a sinner. As such he died. He died spiritually immediately and began to die physically. Adam was the first man ever to live upon the face of the earth. From Adam and Eve come every other human being who ever has lived upon the face of the earth. Thus Adam is the "federal head" from whom every other man came. Like begets like. Apples beget apples. Dogs beget dogs. Human beings beget human beings. Since Adam became a sinner before Eve conceived a child, every human being descended from him is a sinner just like him except Christ. Because of Adam's sin, death entered into the human race (Page 1135—Rom. 5:12–14); every human being needs to have the new life.

Now turn to Page 642—Eccl. 7:20: Individual Sin.

14 And the LORD God said to the serpent,
"Because you have done this,
Cursed are you more than all cattle,
And more than every beast of the
field;
On your belly shall you go,
And[R]dust shall you eat
All the days of your life;   Is. 65:25
15 And I will put[R]enmity   [Rev. 12:17]☆
Between you and the woman,
And between your seed and her seed;
He shall^bruise you on the head, crush
And you shall bruise him on the heel."
16 To the woman He said,
"I will greatly multiply
Your pain in childbirth,
In pain you shall bring forth children;
Yet your desire shall be for your hus-
band,
And[R]he shall rule over you."1 Cor. 14:34
17 Then to Adam He said, "Because you
have listened to the voice of your wife, and
have eaten from the tree about which I com-
manded you, saying, 'You shall not eat from
it';
Cursed is the ground because of you;
In^toil you shall eat of it   sorrow
All the days of your life.
18 "Both thorns and thistles it shall grow
for you;
And you shall eat the[T]plants of the
field;   plant
19 By the sweat of your face
You shall eat bread,
Till you[R]return to the ground, Ps. 90:3
Because[R]from it you were taken;
For you are dust,   Gen. 2:7
And to dust you shall return."
20 Now the man called his wife's name
[7]Eve,[R]because she was the mother of all the
living.   2 Cor. 11:3; 1 Tim. 2:13
21 And the LORD God made garments of
skin for Adam and his wife, and clothed
them.

22 Then the LORD God said, "Behold, the

man has become like one of [R]Us, knowing
good and evil; and now, lest he stretch out
his hand, and take also from the tree of life,
and eat, and live forever"—   Gen. 1:26
23 therefore the LORD God sent him out
from the garden of Eden, to cultivate the
ground from which he was taken.
24 So[R]He drove the man out; and at the
[R]east of the garden of Eden He stationed the
cherubim, and the flaming sword which
turned every direction, to guard the way to
the tree of life.   Ezek. 31:11 • Gen. 2:8

CHAPTER 4

The Initial Conflict

NOW the man[T]had relations with his wife
Eve, and she conceived and gave birth to
Cain, and she said, "I have gotten a man-
child with the help of the LORD."   knew
2 And again, she gave birth to his
brother Abel. And Abel was a keeper of
flocks, but Cain was a tiller of the ground.
3 So it came about[T]in the course of time
that Cain brought an offering to the LORD of
the fruit of the ground.   at the end of days
4 And [R]Abel, on his part also brought of
the firstlings of his flock and of their fat portions. And[R]the LORD had regard for Abel and
for his offering;   Heb. 11:4 • [1 Sam. 15:22]
5 but[R]for Cain and for his offering He had
no regard. So[R]Cain became very angry and
his countenance fell.   [1 Sam. 16:7] • [Is. 3:9]
6 Then the LORD said to Cain, "Why[R]are
you angry? And why has your countenance
fallen?   Jon. 4:4
7 "If you do well, will not your countenance be lifted up? And if you do not do
well, sin is crouching at the door; and its
desire is for you, but you must master it."
8 And Cain[T]told Abel his brother. And it
came about when they were in the field, that
Cain rose up against Abel his brother and
[R]killed him.   said to • Matt. 23:35; Luke 11:51

[7] I.e., living or life

3:14-21 The Adamic Covenant—The covenant with Adam is the second general or universal covenant. It could be called the covenant with mankind, for it sets forth the conditions which will hold sway until the curse of sin is lifted (cf. Page 667—Is. 11:6–10; Page 1138—Rom. 8:18–23). According to the covenant, the conditions which will prevail are:
a. The serpent, the tool used by Satan to effect the fall of man, is cursed. The curse affects not only the instrument, the serpent, but also the indwelling energizer, Satan. Great physical changes took place in the serpent. Apparently it was upright; now it will go on its belly (v. 14). It was the most desirable animal of the animal creation; now it is the most loathsome. The sight or thought of a snake should be an effective reminder of the devastating effects of sin.
b. Satan is judged—he will enjoy limited success ("you shall bruise him on the heel," v. 15), but ultimately he will be judged ("He shall bruise you on the head," v. 15).
c. The first prophecy of the coming of Messiah is given (v. 15).
d. There will be a multiplication of conception, necessitated by the introduction of death into the human race (v. 16).
e. There will be pain in childbirth (v. 16).
f. The woman is made subject to her husband (v. 16).
g. The ground is cursed and will bring forth weeds among the food which man must eat for his existence (vv. 17–19).
h. Physical change takes place in man; he will perspire when he works. He will have to work all his life long (v. 19).
i. In sinning, man dies spiritually, and ultimately will die physically. His flesh will decay until it returns to dust from which it was originally taken (v. 19).
   Now turn to Page 11—Gen. 9:1–19: The Noahic Covenant.

9 Then the LORD said to Cain, "Where[R] is Abel your brother?" And he said, "I do not know. Am I my brother's keeper?"   Gen. 3:9

10 And He said, "What have you done? [R] The voice of your brother's blood is crying to Me from the ground. Heb. 12:24; Rev. 6:9, 10

11 "And now you are cursed from the ground, which has opened its mouth to receive your brother's blood from your hand.

12 "When you cultivate the ground, it shall no longer yield its strength to you; you shall be a vagrant and a wanderer on the earth."

13 And Cain said to the LORD, "My punishment is too great to bear!

14 "Behold, Thou hast [R] driven me this day from the face of the ground; and from Thy face I shall be hidden, and I shall be a vagrant and a wanderer on the earth, and it will come about that [R] whoever finds me will kill me."   Jer. 52:3 • Num. 35:19

15 So the LORD said to him, "Therefore whoever kills Cain, vengeance will be taken on him [R] sevenfold." And the LORD [A] appointed a sign for Cain, lest anyone finding him should slay him.   Gen. 4:24 • *set a mark on*

The Ungodly Line of Cain

16 Then Cain went out from the presence [R] of the LORD, and [t] settled in the land of [t] Nod, east of Eden.   Jer. 23:39; 52:3 • *dwelt* • wandering

17 And Cain had relations with his wife and she conceived, and gave birth to Enoch; and he built a city, and called the name of the city Enoch, after the name of his son.

18 Now to Enoch was born Irad; and Irad became the father of Mehujael; and Mehujael became the father of Methushael; and Methushael became the father of Lamech.

19 And Lamech took to himself [R] two wives: the name of the one was Adah, and the name of the other, Zillah.   Gen. 2:24

20 And Adah gave birth to Jabal; he was the father of those who dwell in tents and *have* livestock.

21 And his brother's name was Jubal; he was the father of all those who play the lyre and pipe.

22 As for Zillah, she also gave birth to Tubal-cain, the forger of all implements of bronze and iron; and the sister of Tubal-cain was Naamah.

23 And Lamech said to his wives,
"Adah and Zillah,
Listen to my voice,
You wives of Lamech,
Give heed to my speech,
[R] For I [a] have killed a man for wounding me;   [Ex. 20:13; Lev. 19:18] • *kill*
And a boy for striking me;
24   If Cain is avenged sevenfold,
Then Lamech seventy-sevenfold."

The Godly Line of Seth
1 Chr. 1:1–4; Luke 3:36–38

25 And Adam [t] had relations with his wife

again; and she gave birth to a son, and named him [t] Seth, for, *she said,* "God has appointed me another offspring in place of Abel; for Cain killed him."   *knew* • Heb., *Sheth*

26 And to Seth, to him also [R] a son was born; and he called his name Enosh. Then *men* began [R] to call [A] upon the name of the LORD.   Luke 3:38 • Gen. 12:8; 26:25 • *by*

CHAPTER 5

THIS is the book of the generations of Adam. In the day when God created man, He made him in the likeness of God.

2 He created them [R] male and female, and He blessed them and named them [8] Man in the day when they were created.   Matt. 19:4

3 When Adam had lived one hundred and thirty years, he [9] became the father of *a son* in his own likeness, according to his image, and named him Seth.

4 Then the days of Adam after he became the father of Seth were eight hundred years, and he had *other* sons and daughters.

5 So all the days that Adam lived were nine hundred and thirty years, and he died.

6 And Seth lived one hundred and five years, and became the father of Enosh.

7 Then Seth lived eight hundred and seven years after he became the father of Enosh, and he had *other* sons and daughters.

8 So all the days of Seth were nine hundred and twelve years, and he died.

9 And Enosh lived ninety years, and became the father of Kenan.

10 Then Enosh lived eight hundred and fifteen years after he became the father of Kenan, and he had *other* sons and daughters.

11 So all the days of Enosh were nine hundred and five years, and he died.

12 And Kenan lived seventy years, and became the father of Mahalalel.

13 Then Kenan lived eight hundred and forty years after he became the father of Mahalalel, and he had *other* sons and daughters.

14 So all the days of Kenan were nine hundred and ten years, and he died.

15 And Mahalalel lived sixty-five years, and became the father of Jared.

16 Then Mahalalel lived eight hundred and thirty years after he became the father of Jared, and he had *other* sons and daughters.

17 So all the days of Mahalalel were eight hundred and ninety-five years, and he died.

18 And Jared lived one hundred and sixty-two years, and became the father of Enoch.

19 Then Jared lived eight hundred years after he became the father of Enoch, and he had *other* sons and daughters.

---

[8] Lit., *Adam*   [9] Lit., *begot,* and so throughout this context

20 So all the days of Jared were nine hundred and sixty-two years, and he died.
21 And Enoch lived sixty-five years, and became the father of Methuselah.
22 Then Enoch [R]walked with God three hundred years after he became the father of Methuselah, and he had *other* sons and daughters.   Gen. 6:9; 17:1; 24:40; 48:15; [Mic. 6:8]
23 So all the days of Enoch were three hundred and sixty-five years.
24 And [R]Enoch walked with God; and he was not, for God took him. 2 Kin. 2:11; Jude 14
25 And Methuselah lived one hundred and eighty-seven years, and became the father of Lamech.
26 Then Methuselah lived seven hundred and eighty-two years after he became the father of Lamech, and he had *other* sons and daughters.
27 So all the days of Methuselah were nine hundred and sixty-nine years, and he died.
28 And Lamech lived one hundred and eighty-two years, and became the father of a son.
29 Now he called his name Noah, saying, "This one shall give us rest from our work and from the toil of our hands *arising* from the ground which the LORD has cursed."
30 Then Lamech lived five hundred and ninety-five years after he became the father of Noah, and he had *other* sons and daughters.
31 So all the days of Lamech were seven hundred and seventy-seven years, and he died.
32 And Noah was [R]five hundred years old, and Noah became the father of Shem, Ham, and Japheth.   Gen. 7:6

CHAPTER 6

The Ungodly Multiply

NOW it came about, when men began to multiply on the face of the land, and daughters were born to them,
2 that the sons of God saw that the daughters of men were [T]beautiful; and they took wives for themselves, whomever they chose.   *good*
3 Then the LORD said, "My Spirit shall not strive with man forever, because he also is flesh; [A]nevertheless his days shall be one hundred and twenty years."   *therefore*
4 The [10]Nephilim[R] were on the earth in those days, and also afterward, when the sons of God came in to the daughters of men, and they bore *children* to them. Those were the mighty men who *were* of old, men of renown.   Num. 13:33

The Ungodly Sin Continually

5 Then the LORD saw that the wickedness of man was great on the earth, and that [R]every intent of the thoughts of his heart was only evil continually.   Matt. 15:19; Rom. 1:28-32

The Ungodly to Be Destroyed

6 And [R]the LORD was sorry that He had made man on the earth, and He was [R]grieved [T]in His heart.   Gen. 6:7 • Eph. 4:30 • *to*
7 And the LORD said, "I[R]will blot out man whom I have created from the face of the land, from man to animals to creeping things and to birds of the [T]sky; for I am sorry that I have made them."   Deut. 28:63 • *heavens*

The Godly to Be Saved

8 But[R]Noah[R]found favor in the eyes of the LORD.   Matt. 24:37; Luke 17:26 • Luke 1:30
9 These are *the records of* the generations of Noah. Noah was a righteous man, [T]blameless in his time; Noah walked with God.   *complete, perfect; or, having integrity*
10 And Noah[T]became the father of three sons: Shem, Ham, and Japheth.   *begot*
11 Now the earth was[R]corrupt in the sight of God, and the earth was[R]filled with violence.   Deut. 31:29; Judg. 2:19 • Ezek. 8:17
12 And God looked on the earth, and behold, it was corrupt; for [R]all flesh had corrupted their way upon the earth.   Ps. 14:1-3
13 Then God said to Noah, "The[R]end of all flesh has come before Me; for the earth is filled with violence because of them; and behold, I am about to destroy them with the earth.   Is. 34:1-4; Ezek. 7:2, 3; Amos 8:2; 1 Pet. 4:7
14 "Make for yourself an ark of gopher wood; you shall make the ark with rooms, and shall cover it inside and out with pitch.
15 "And this is how you shall make it: the length of the ark[T]three hundred [11]cubits, its breadth[T]fifty cubits, and its height[T]thirty cubits.   450 ft. • 75 ft. • 45 ft.
16 "You shall make a window for the ark, and finish it to a cubit from the top; and set the door of the ark in the side of it; you shall make it with lower, second, and third decks.
17 "And behold,[R]I, even I am bringing the flood of water upon the earth, to destroy all flesh in which is the breath of life, from under heaven; everything that is on the earth shall perish.   2 Pet. 2:5
18 "But I will establish[R]My covenant with you; and [R]you shall enter the ark—you and your sons and your wife, and your sons' wives with you.   Gen. 9:9-16; 17:7 • Gen. 7:7
19 "And[R]of every living thing of all flesh, you shall bring two of every *kind* into the ark, to keep *them* alive with you; they shall be male and female.   Gen. 7:2, 14, 15
20 "Of[R]the birds after their kind, and of the animals after their kind, of every creeping thing of the ground after its kind, two of every *kind* shall come to you to keep *them* alive.   Gen. 7:3
21 "And as for you, take for yourself some of all[R]food which is edible, and gather *it* to yourself; and it shall be for food for you and for them."   Gen. 1:29, 30
22 Thus Noah did; according to all that God had commanded him, so he did.

[10] Or, *giants*   [11] I.e., One cubit equals approx. 18 in.

CHAPTER 7

The Ark Is Entered

Then the Lord said to Noah, "Enter the ark, you and all your household; for you *alone* I have seen *to be* ^Rrighteous before Me in this ^Ttime.   Gen. 6:9 · *generation*

2 "You shall take ^Twith you of every clean animal ^Tby sevens, a male and his female; and of the animals that are not clean two, a male and his female;   *to · seven seven*

3 also of the birds of the ^Tsky, by sevens, male and female, to keep ^Toffspring alive on the face of all the earth.   *heavens · seed*

4 "For after seven more days, I will send rain on the earth forty days and forty nights; and I will blot out from the face of the land every living thing that I have made."

5 ^RAnd Noah did according to all that the Lord had commanded him.   Gen. 6:22

6 Now Noah was ^Rsix hundred years old when the flood of water ^Tcame upon the earth.   Gen. 5:32 · *was*

7 Then ^RNoah and his sons and his wife and his sons' wives with him entered the ark because of the water of the flood.   Luke 17:27

8 ^ROf clean animals and animals that are not clean and birds and everything that creeps on the ground,   Gen. 6:19, 20; 7:2, 3

9 there went into the ark to Noah ^Tby twos, male and female, as God had commanded Noah.   *two two*

10 And it came about after ^Rthe seven days, that the water of the flood ^Tcame upon the earth.   Gen. 7:4 · *were*

The Earth Is Flooded

11 In the six hundredth year of Noah's life, in the second month, on the seventeenth day of the month, on the same day all the fountains of the great deep burst open, and the floodgates of the sky were opened.

12 And ^Tthe rain ^Tfell upon the earth for forty days and forty nights.   Gen. 7:4, 17 · *was*

13 On the very same day ^RNoah and Shem and Ham and Japheth, the sons of Noah, and Noah's wife and the three wives of his sons with them, entered the ark,   Gen. 6:18

14 they and every beast after its kind, and all the cattle after ^Ttheir kind, and every creeping thing that creeps on the earth after its kind, and every bird after its kind, ^Tall sorts of birds.   *its · every bird, every wing*

15 So they went into the ark to Noah, ^Rby twos of all flesh in which was the breath of life.   Gen. 6:19; 7:9

16 And those that entered, male and female of all flesh, entered as God had commanded him; and the Lord closed *it* behind him.

17 Then the flood ^Tcame upon the earth for ^Rforty days; and the water increased and lifted up the ark, so that it rose above the earth.   *was* · Gen. 7:4

18 And the water prevailed and increased greatly upon the earth; and the ark ^Tfloated on the ^Tsurface of the water.   *went · face*

19 And the water prevailed more and more upon the earth, so that all the high mountains ^Teverywhere under the heavens were covered.   *which were under all the heavens*

20 The water prevailed fifteen cubits higher, and the mountains were covered.

21 ^RAnd all flesh that ^Tmoved on the earth perished, birds and cattle and beasts and every swarming thing that swarms upon the earth, and all mankind;   Gen. 6:7, 13, 17 · *crept*

22 of all that was on the dry land, all ^Rin whose nostrils was the breath of the spirit of life, died.   Gen. 2:7

23 Thus He blotted out ^Tevery living thing that was upon the face of the land, from man to animals to creeping things and to birds of the ^Tsky, and they were blotted out from the earth; and only ^RNoah was left, together with those that were with him in the ark.   *all existence · heavens* · Heb. 11:7; 1 Pet. 3:20

24 ^RAnd the water prevailed upon the earth one hundred and fifty days.   Gen. 8:3

CHAPTER 8

The Flood Recedes

But God remembered Noah and all the beasts and all the cattle that were with him in the ark; and God caused a wind to pass over the earth, and the water subsided.

2 Also ^Rthe fountains of the deep and the floodgates of the sky were closed, and the rain from the sky was restrained;   Gen. 7:11

3 and the water receded steadily from the earth, and at the end ^Rof one hundred and fifty days the water decreased.   Gen. 7:24

4 And in the seventh month, on the seventeenth day of the month, ^Rthe ark rested upon the mountains of Ararat.   Gen. 7:20

5 And the water decreased steadily until the tenth month; in the tenth month, on the first day of the month, the tops of the mountains became visible.

6 Then it came about at the end of forty days, that Noah opened the ^Rwindow of the ark which he had made;   Gen. 6:16

7 and he sent out a raven, and it ^Tflew here and there until the water was dried up from the earth.   *went out, going and returning*

8 Then he sent out a dove from him, to see if the water was abated from the face of the land;

9 but the dove found no resting place for the sole of her foot, so she returned to him into the ark; for the water was on the ^Tsurface of all the earth. Then he put out his hand and took her, and brought her into the ark to himself.   *face*

10 So he waited yet another seven days; and again he sent out the dove from the ark.

11 And the dove came to him toward evening; and behold, in her ^Tbeak was a freshly picked olive leaf. So Noah knew that the water was abated from the earth.   *mouth*

12 Then he waited yet another seven days, and sent out ^Rthe dove; but she did not return to him again.   Jer. 48:28

13 Now it came about in the six hundred and first year, in the first *month,* on the first of the month, the water was dried up ᵀfrom the earth. Then Noah removed the covering of the ark, and looked, and behold, the surface of the ground was dried up.   *from upon*
14 And in the second month, on the twenty-seventh day of the month, the earth was dry.
15 Then God spoke to Noah, saying,
16"Go out of the ark, you and your wife and your sons and your sons' wives with you.
17"Bring out with you every living thing of all flesh that is with you, birds and animals and every creeping thing that creeps on the earth, that they may ᴬbreedᴿabundantly on the earth, and be fruitful and multiply on the earth."   *swarm* • Gen. 1:22, 28
18 So Noah went out, and his sons and his wife and his sons' wives with him.
19 Every beast, every creeping thing, and every bird, everything that moves on the earth, went out ᴬby their families from the ark.   *according to their kind*

Noah Worships God

20 Then Noah built ᴿan altar to the LORD, and took of every ᶜclean animal and of every clean bird and offeredᴰburnt offerings on the altar.   Gen. 12:7, 8 • Lev. 11:1-47 • Ex. 10:25
21 And the LORD smelled the soothing aroma; and the LORD said to Himself, "I will never again curse the ground on account of man, for the intent of man's heart is evil

from his youth; and I will never again destroy every living thing, as I have done.
22 "While the earth remains,
Seedtime and harvest,
And cold and heat,
And ᴿsummer and winter,
And ᴿday and night
Shall not cease." Ps. 74:17 • Jer. 33:20, 25

CHAPTER 9

God's Covenant with Noah

AND God blessed Noah and his sons and said to them, "Beᴿfruitful and multiply, and fill the earth.   Gen. 1:28; 9:7
2"And the fear of you and the terror of you shall be on every beast of the earth and on every bird of the sky; with everything that creeps on the ground, and all the fish of the sea, into your hand they are given.
3"Every moving thing that is alive shall be food for you; I give all to you,ᴿas *I gave* the green plant.   Gen. 1:29
4"Only you shall not eat flesh with its life, *that is,*ᴿits blood.   Lev. 7:26f.; 17:10-16; 19:26

5"And surely I will require your lifeblood; ᵀfrom every beast I will require it. Andᵀfrom *every* man,ᵀfrom every man's brother I will require the life of man.   *from the hand of*

6 "Whoeverᴿsheds man's blood,
By man his blood shall be shed,
Forᴿin the image of God
He made man.   Lev. 24:17 • Gen. 1:26, 27

9:1–19   The Noahic Covenant—The covenant with Noah is the third general or universal covenant. Noah has just passed through the universal flood in which all the world's population had been wiped out. Only Noah, his wife, his three sons, and their wives—eight people—constitute the world's population. Noah might have thought that the things provided by the covenant with Adam had now been changed. However, God gives the Noahic Covenant so that Noah and all the human race to follow might know that the provisions made in the Adamic Covenant remain in effect with one notable addition: the principle of human government which includes the responsibility of suppressing the outbreak of sin and violence, so that it will not be necessary to destroy the earth again by a flood. The provisions of the covenant are:
a. The responsibility to populate the earth is reaffirmed (v. 1).
b. The subjection of the animal kingdom to man is reaffirmed (v. 2).
c. Man is permitted to eat the flesh of animals. However, he is to refrain from eating blood (vv. 3, 4).
d. The sacredness of human life is established. Whatever sheds man's blood, whether man or beast, must be put to death (vv. 5, 6).
e. This covenant is confirmed to Noah, all mankind, and every living creature on the face of the earth (vv. 9, 10).
f. The promise is given never to destroy the earth again by a universal flood (v. 11). The next time God destroys the earth, the means will be fire (Page 1269—2 Pet. 3:10).
g. The rainbow is designated as a testimony of the existence of this covenant and the promise never to destroy the earth by flood. As long as we can see the rainbow we will know that the Noahic Covenant is in existence (vv. 12–17).
    Now turn to Page 14—Gen. 12:1–3: The Abrahamic Covenant.

9:5   The Origin of Human Government—It has been assumed that human government was officially instituted after the great Flood in Genesis 9. However, some form of law and order undoubtedly existed prior to this period. This is strongly suggested by both Jesus and Jude. Jesus in Luke 17:26, 27 says that prior to the Flood in Noah's day people conducted their affairs in much the same manner as we do today. Jude gives us the text of a message Enoch preached to sinners prior to the Flood (Page 1287—Jude 14, 15). We learn that one of the main factors which brought about the Flood was man's disobedience to the revealed law of God.
    At any rate, there is certainly no doubt concerning the source of human government. God Himself is its divine author. Two individuals give testimony to this fact. Daniel reminds King Nebuchadnezzar that "the Most High is ruler over the realm of mankind, and bestows it on whomever He wishes" (Page 840—Dan. 4:25). The apostle Paul exhorts Christians to be subject to the laws of human government because all earthly powers exist through God's divine permission (Page 1142—Rom. 13).
    If one rightly understands the origin of human government, then the conclusion is reached that lawless anarchy is not only rebellion against human authority, but actual blasphemy against the divine Creator Himself.
    Now turn to Page 1142—Rom. 13:1–4: The Function of Human Government.

7 "And as for you,ᴿbe fruitful and multiply;   Gen. 9:1
ᵀPopulate the earth abundantly and
multiply in it."   *Swarm in the earth*
8 Then God spoke to Noah and to his
sons with him, saying,
9"Now behold,ᴿI Myself do establish My
covenant with you, and with yourᵀdescend-
ants after you;   Gen. 6:18 • *seed*
10 and with every living creature that is
with you, the birds, the cattle, and every
beast of the earth with you; of all that comes
out of the ark, even every beast of the earth.
11"And I establish My covenant with you;
and all flesh shall never again be cut off by
the water of the flood, neither shall there
again be a flood to destroy the earth."
12 And God said, "This is the sign of the
covenant which I am making between Me
and you and every living creature that is
with you, for all successive generations;
13 I set Myᴿbow in the cloud, and it shall
be for a sign of a covenant between Me and
the earth.   Ezek. 1:28
14"And it shall come about, when I bring a
cloud over the earth, that the bow shall be
seen in the cloud,
15 and ᴿI will remember My covenant,
which is between Me and you and every living creature of all flesh; and ᴿnever again
shall the water become a flood to destroy all
flesh.   Lev. 26:42, 45; Deut. 7:9 • Gen. 9:11
16"When the bow is in the cloud, then I
will look upon it, to remember the ᴿever-
lasting covenant between God and every
living creature of all flesh that is on the
earth."   Gen. 17:13, 19; 2 Sam. 23:5
17 And God said to Noah, "This is the sign
of the covenant which I have established between Me and all flesh that is on the earth."

The Sons of Noah

18 Now the sons of Noah who came out of
the ark were Shem and Ham and Japheth;
and Ham was the father of Canaan.
19 These three *were* the sons of Noah; and
from these the whole earth was populated.

Ham's Sin

20 Then Noah began ᵀfarming and planted
a vineyard.   *to be a farmer*
21 And he drank of the wine andᴿbecame
drunk, and uncovered himself inside his
tent.   Prov. 20:1
22 And Ham, the father of Canaan, ᴿsaw
the nakedness of his father, and told his two
brothers outside.   Hab. 2:15
23 But Shem and Japheth took a garment
and laid it upon both their shoulders and
walked backward and covered the nakedness of their father; and their faces were
ᵀturned away, so that they did not see their
father's nakedness.   *backward*
24 When Noah awoke from his wine, he
knew what his youngest son had done to
him.

The Curse on Canaan

25 So he said,
"Cursedᴿbe Canaan;   Deut. 27:16
¹²Aᴿservant of servants   Josh. 9:23
He shall be to his brothers."
26 He also said,
"Blessedᴿbe the Lᴏʀᴅ,   Gen. 14:20; 24:27
The God of Shem;
And let Canaan beᴬhis servant.   *their*
27 "MayᴿGod enlarge Japheth,   Is. 66:19
And let him dwell in the tents of
Shem;
And let Canaan beᴬhis servant."   *their*

Noah's Death

28 And Noah lived three hundred and fifty
years after the flood.
29 So all the days of Noah were nine hundred and fifty years, and he died.

CHAPTER 10

The Family of Japheth
1 Chr. 1:5–7

Nᴏᴡ these are *the records of* the generations of Shem, Ham, and Japheth, the sons
of Noah; and sons were born to them after
the flood.
2 ᴿThe sons of Japheth *were* ᴿGomer and
Magog and Madai and Javan and Tubal and
Meshech and Tiras.   1 Chr. 1:5-7 • Ezek. 38:2, 6
3 And the sons of Gomer *were* ᴿAshkenaz
and Riphath and Togarmah.   Jer. 51:27
4 And the sons of Javan *were* Elishah
and Tarshish, Kittim and Dodanim.
5 From these the coastlands of the nations were separated into their lands, every
one according to his language, according to
their families, into their nations.

The Family of Ham
1 Chr. 1:8–12

6 ᴿAnd the sons of Ham *were* Cush and
Mizraim and Put and Canaan.   1 Chr. 1:8-10
7 And the sons of Cush *were* ᴿSeba and
Havilah and Sabtah and ᴿRaamah and Sabteca; and the sons of Raamah *were* Sheba
and Dedan.   Is. 43:3 • Ezek. 27:22
8 Now Cush became the father of Nimrod; he became a mighty one on the earth.
9 He was a mighty hunter before the
Lᴏʀᴅ; therefore it is said, "Like Nimrod a
mighty hunter before the Lᴏʀᴅ."
10 And the beginning of his kingdom was
¹³Babelᴿand Erech and Accad and Calneh, in
the land ofᴿShinar.   Gen. 11:9 • Gen. 11:2; 14:1
11 From that land he went forthᴿinto Assyria, and built Nineveh and Rehoboth-Ir
and Calah,   Mic. 5:6
12 and Resen between Nineveh and Calah; that is the great city.
13 And Mizraimᵀbecame the father ofᵀLu-
dim and Anamim and Lehabim and Naphtu-
him   *begot* • Jer. 46:9

---

¹² I.e., The lowest of servants   ¹³ Or, *Babylon*

14 and Pathrusim and Casluhim (from which came the Philistines) and Caphtorim.

The Family of Canaan
1 Chr. 1:13–16

15 And Canaan ^Tbecame the father of ^RSidon, his first-born, and Heth   *begot* • Jer. 47:4

16 and ^Rthe Jebusite and the Amorite and the Girgashite   Gen. 15:19-21

17 and the Hivite and the Arkite and the Sinite

18 and the Arvadite and the Zemarite and the Hamathite; and afterward the families of the Canaanite were spread abroad.

19 And ^Rthe territory of the Canaanite ^Textended from Sidon as you go toward Gerar, as far as Gaza; as you go toward Sodom and Gomorrah and Admah and Zeboiim, as far as Lasha.   Num. 34:2-12 • *was*

20 These are the sons of Ham, according to their families, according to their languages, by their lands, by their nations.

The Family of Shem
1 Chr. 1:17–23

21 And also to Shem, the father of all the children of Eber, *and* the older brother of Japheth, children were born.

22 The sons of Shem *were* Elam and Asshur and Arpachshad and Lud and Aram.

23 And the sons of Aram *were* ^RUz and Hul and Gether and Mash.   Job 1:1; Jer. 25:20

24 And Arpachshad ^Tbecame the father of ^RShelah; and Shelah ^Tbecame the father of Eber.   *begot* • Gen. 11:12; Luke 3:35

25 And ^Rtwo sons were born to Eber; the name of the one *was* ^TPeleg, for in his days the earth was divided; and his brother's name *was* Joktan.   1 Chr. 1:19 • *division*

26 And Joktan ^Tbecame the father of Almodad and Sheleph and Hazarmaveth and Jerah   *begot*

27 and Hadoram and Uzal and Diklah

28 and Obal and Abimael and Sheba

29 and Ophir and Havilah and Jobab; all these were the sons of Joktan.

30 Now their ^Tsettlement ^Textended from Mesha as you go toward Sephar, the hill country of the east.   *dwelling* • *was*

31 These are the sons of Shem, according to their families, according to their languages, by their lands, according to their nations.

32 These are the families of the sons of Noah, according to their genealogies, by their nations; and out of these the nations were separated on the earth after the flood.

CHAPTER 11

Construction of the Tower

Now the whole earth ^Tused the same language and the same words.   *was one lip*

2 And it came about as they journeyed east, that they found a plain in the land ^Rof Shinar and ^Tsettled there.   Gen. 10:10 • *dwelt*

3 And they said to one another, "Come, let us make bricks and burn *them* thoroughly." And they used brick for stone, and they used ^Rtar for mortar.   Gen. 14:10

Rebellion at the Tower

4 And they said, "Come, let us build for ourselves a city, and a tower whose top ^R*will reach* into heaven, and let us make for ourselves a name; lest we be scattered abroad over the face of the whole earth."   Ps. 107:26

Judgment on All the Family Lines

5 ^RAnd the Lord came down to see the city and the tower which the sons of men had built.   Gen. 18:21; Ex. 3:8; 19:11, 18, 20

6 And the Lord said, "Behold, they are one people, and they all have the same language. And this is what they began to do, and now nothing which they purpose to do will be ^Timpossible for them.   *withheld from*

7 "Come, let Us go down and there confuse their language, that they may not understand one another's ^Tspeech."   *lip*

8 So the Lord ^Rscattered them abroad from there over the face of the whole earth; and they stopped building the city. Luke 1:51

9 Therefore its name was called ¹⁴Babel, ^R because there the Lord confused the ^Tlanguage of the whole earth; and from there the Lord scattered them abroad over the face of the whole earth.   Gen. 10:10 • *lip*

Abram's Family Line
1 Chr. 1:24–27; Luke 3:34–36

10 ^RThese are *the records of* the generations of Shem. Shem was one hundred years old, and became the father of Arpachshad two years after the flood;   Gen. 10:22-25

11 and Shem lived five hundred years after he became the father of Arpachshad, and he had *other* sons and daughters.

12 And Arpachshad lived thirty-five years, and became the father of Shelah;

13 and Arpachshad lived four hundred and three years after he became the father of Shelah, and he had *other* sons and daughters.

14 And Shelah lived thirty years, and became the father of Eber;

15 and Shelah lived four hundred and three years after he became the father of Eber, and he had *other* sons and daughters.

16 And Eber lived thirty-four years, and became the father of Peleg;

17 and Eber lived four hundred and thirty years after he became the father of Peleg, and he had *other* sons and daughters.

18 And Peleg lived thirty years, and became the father of Reu;

19 and Peleg lived two hundred and nine years after he became the father of Reu, and he had *other* sons and daughters.

20 And Reu lived thirty-two years, and became the father of Serug;

¹⁴ Or, *Babylon*

21 and Reu lived two hundred and seven years after he became the father of Serug, and he had *other* sons and daughters.
22 And Serug lived thirty years, and became the father of Nahor;
23 and Serug lived two hundred years after he became the father of Nahor, and he had *other* sons and daughters.
24 And Nahor lived twenty-nine years, and became the father of ᴿTerah;   Josh. 24:2
25 and Nahor lived one hundred and nineteen years after he became the father of Terah, and he had *other* sons and daughters.
26 And Terah lived seventy years, and became ᴿthe father of Abram, Nahor and Haran.   Josh. 24:2

Abram's Past

27 Now these are *the records of* the generations of Terah. Terah became the father of Abram, Nahor and Haran; and ᴿHaran became the father of Lot.   Gen. 11:31; 12:4
28 And Haran died ᴬin the presence of his father Terah in the land of his birth, in ᴿUr of the Chaldeans. *during the lifetime of* · Gen. 11:31
29 And Abram and ᴿNahor took wives for themselves. The name of Abram's wife was Sarai; and the name of Nahor's wife was Milcah, the daughter of Haran, the father of Milcah ᵀand Iscah. Gen. 24:10 · *and the father of*
30 And ᴿSarai was barren; she had no child.   Gen. 16:1
31 And Terah took Abram his son, and Lot the son of Haran, his grandson, and Sarai his daughter-in-law, his son Abram's wife; and they went out ᵀtogether from ᴿUr of the Chaldeans in order to enter the land of Canaan; and they went as far as Haran, and ᵀsettled there.   *with them* · Acts 7:4 · *dwelt*
32 And the days of Terah were two hundred and five years; and Terah died in Haran.

CHAPTER 12

Initiation of the Covenant

NᴼWᴿthe Lᴏʀᴅ said to Abram,   [Heb. 11:8]
"Goᵀforth from your country,
And from your relatives *Go for yourself*
And from your father's house,
To the land which I will show you;

2 And I will make you a great nation,
And ᴿI will bless you,   Gen. 22:17
And make your name great;
And so you shall be a blessing;
3 And I will bless those who bless you,
And the one who ᴬcurses you I will ᴬcurse.   *reviles · bind under a curse*
ᴿAnd in you all the families of the earth shall be blessed."   [Gal. 3:8]☆

4 So Abram went forth as the Lᴏʀᴅ had spoken to him; and ᴿLot went with him. Now Abram was seventy-five years old when he departed from Haran.   Gen. 11:27, 31
5 And Abram took Sarai his wife and Lot his nephew, and all their ᴿpossessions which they had accumulated, and the ᵀpersons which they had acquired in Haran, and they set out for the land of Canaan; and they came to the land of Canaan. Gen. 13:6 · *souls*
6 And Abram passed through the land as far as the site of ᴿShechem, to the °oak of Moreh. Now the Canaanite *was* then in the land.   Gen. 35:4; Deut. 11:30 · *terebinth*
7 And the Lᴏʀᴅ appeared to Abram and said, "Toᴿ your ᵀdescendants I will give this land." So he built an altar there to the Lᴏʀᴅ who had appeared to him.   Gen. 13:15 · *seed*
8 Then he proceeded from there to the mountain on the east of Bethel, and pitched his tent, with Bethel on the west and Ai on the east; and there he built an altar to the Lᴏʀᴅ and called upon the name of the Lᴏʀᴅ.
9 And Abram journeyed on, continuing toward ᴿthe ¹⁵Negev.   Gen. 13:1, 3; 20:1; 24:62
10 Now there was a famine in the land; so Abram went down to Egypt to sojourn there, for the famine was severe in the land.
11 And it came about when he ᵀcame near to Egypt, that he said to Sarai his wife, "See now, I know that you are a ᴿbeautiful woman;   *drew near to enter* · Gen. 26:7; 29:17
12 ᴿand it will come about when the Egyptians see you, that they will say, 'This is his wife'; and they will kill me, but they will let you live.   Gen. 20:11
13 "Please say that you are my sister so that it may go well with me because of you, and that I may live on account of you."

¹⁵ I.e., South country

12:1-3 The Abrahamic Covenant—The covenant with Abraham is the first of the theocratic covenants (pertaining to the rule of God). It is unconditional, depending solely upon God who obligates Himself in grace, indicated by the unconditional declaration, "I will," to bring to pass the promised blessings. The Abrahamic Covenant is the basis of all the other theocratic covenants and provides for blessings in three areas: (1) national—"I will make you a great nation," (2) personal—"I will bless you and make your name great; and so you shall be a blessing," and (3) universal—"in you all the families of the earth shall be blessed." This covenant was first given in broad outline and was later confirmed to Abraham in greater detail (cf. Page 15—Gen. 13:14–17; 15:1–7, 18–21; 17:1–8). The Abrahamic Covenant constitutes an important link in all that God began to do, has done throughout history, and will continue to do until the consummation of history. It is the one purpose of God for humans into which all of God's programs and works fit. The personal aspects of the Abrahamic Covenant are fourfold: (1) to be the father of a great nation, (2) to receive personal blessing, (3) to receive personal honor and reputation, and (4) to be the source of blessing to others. The universal aspects of the covenant are threefold: (1) blessings for those people and nations which bless Abraham and the nation which comes from him; (2) cursings upon those people and nations which curse Abraham and Israel; and (3) blessings upon all the families of the earth through the Messiah, who, according to the flesh, is Abraham's son and provides salvation for the entire world.
Now turn to Page 70—Ex. 19:5-8: The Mosaic Covenant.

14 And it came about when Abram came into Egypt, the Egyptians saw that the woman was very beautiful.

15 And Pharaoh's officials saw her and praised her to Pharaoh; and ^Rthe woman was taken into Pharaoh's house.   Gen. 20:2

16 Therefore he treated Abram well for her sake; and ^Tgave him sheep and oxen and donkeys and male and female servants and female donkeys and camels.   *he had*

17 But the LORD ^Rstruck Pharaoh and his house with great plagues because of Sarai, Abram's wife.   Gen. 20:18; 1 Chr. 16:21

18 Then Pharaoh called Abram and said, "What is this you have done to me? Why did you not tell me that she was your wife?

19 "Why did you say, 'She is my sister,' so that I took her for my wife? Now then, ^Ahere is your wife, take her and go."   *behold*

20 And Pharaoh commanded *his* men concerning him; and they escorted him away, with his wife and all that belonged to him.

CHAPTER 13

Abram's Separation from Lot

SO Abram went up from Egypt to ^Rthe ¹⁶Negev, he and his wife and all that belonged to him; and Lot with him.   Gen. 12:9

2 Now Abram was ^Rvery rich in livestock, in silver and in gold.   Gen. 24:35

3 And he went ^Ton his journeys from the ¹⁶Negev as far as Bethel, to the place where his tent had been at the beginning, ^Rbetween Bethel and Ai,   *by his stages* • Gen. 12:8

4 to the place of the ^Raltar, which he had made there formerly; and there Abram called on the name of the LORD.   Gen. 12:7, 8

5 Now ^RLot, who went with Abram, also had flocks and herds and tents.   Gen. 12:5

6 And ^Rthe land could not ^Tsustain them ^Twhile dwelling together; for their possessions were so great that they were not able to remain together.   Gen. 36:7 • *bear* • *to dwell*

7 ^RAnd there was strife between the herdsmen of Abram's livestock and the herdsmen of Lot's livestock. Now ^Rthe Canaanite and the Perizzite were dwelling then in the land.   Gen. 26:20 • Gen. 12:6

8 ^RThen Abram said to Lot, "Please let there be no strife between you and me, nor between my herdsmen and your herdsmen, for we are brothers.   [Prov. 15:18; 20:3]

9 "Is not the whole land before you? Please separate from me: if *to* the left, then I will go to the right; or if *to* the right, then I will go to the left."

10 And Lot lifted up his eyes and saw all the ^Tvalley ^Rof the Jordan, that it was well watered everywhere—*this was* before the LORD destroyed Sodom and Gomorrah— like the garden of the LORD, like the land of Egypt as you go to Zoar.   *circle* • Gen. 19:17-29

11 So Lot chose for himself all the ^Tvalley of the Jordan; and Lot journeyed eastward. Thus they separated from each other.   *circle*

12 Abram ^Tsettled in the land of Canaan, while Lot settled in the cities of the valley, and moved his tents as far as Sodom.   *dwelt*

13 Now the men of Sodom were wicked exceedingly and sinners against the LORD.

God's Promise to Abram

14 And the LORD said to Abram, after Lot had separated from him, "Now ^Rlift up your eyes and look from the place where you are, ^Rnorthward and southward and eastward and westward;   Deut. 3:27 • Gen. 28:14

15 ^Rfor all the land which you see, ^RI will give it to you and to your ^Tdescendants forever.   Gen. 12:7 • Gen. 13:17; 15:7; 17:8 • *seed*

16 "And I will make your ^Tdescendants as the dust of the earth; so that if anyone can number the dust of the earth, then your ^Tdescendants can also be numbered.   *seed*

17 "Arise, walk about the land through its length and breadth; for I will give it to you."

18 Then Abram moved his tent and came and dwelt by the ^Aoaks ^Rof Mamre, which are in Hebron, and there he built ^Ran altar to the LORD.   *terebinths* • Gen. 14:13 • Gen. 8:20

CHAPTER 14

Abram Rescues Lot

AND it came about in the days of Amraphel king of ^RShinar, Arioch king of Ellasar, Chedorlaomer king of ^RElam, and Tidal king of ^AGoiim,   Gen. 10:10 • Dan. 8:2 • *nations*

2 *that* they made war with Bera king of Sodom, and with Birsha king of Gomorrah, Shinab king of ^AAdmah, and Shemeber king of ^RZeboiim, and the king of Bela (that is, ^RZoar).   Gen. 10:19 • Deut. 29:23 • Gen. 13:10

3 All these ^Tcame as allies to the valley of Siddim (that is, the Salt Sea).   *joined together*

4 Twelve years they had served Chedorlaomer, but the thirteenth year they rebelled.

5 And in the fourteenth year Chedorlaomer and the kings that were with him, came and ^Tdefeated the ^RRephaim in Ashteroth-karnaim and the Zuzim in Ham and the Emim in Shaveh-kiriathaim,   *smote* • Deut. 3:11

6 and the Horites in their Mount Seir, as far as El-paran, which is by the wilderness.

7 Then they turned back and came to En-mishpat (that is, Kadesh), and conquered all the country of the Amalekites, and also the Amorites, who lived in Hazazon-tamar.

8 And the king of Sodom and the king of Gomorrah and the king of Admah and the king of Zeboiim and the king of Bela (that is, Zoar) came out; and they arrayed for battle against them in the valley of Siddim,

9 against Chedorlaomer king of Elam and Tidal king of ^AGoiim and Amraphel king of Shinar and Arioch king of Ellasar—four kings against five.   *nations*

10 Now the valley of Siddim was full of

¹⁶ I.e., South country

tar pits; and the kings of Sodom and Gomorrah fled, and they fell ᵀinto them. But those who survived fled to the hill country.   *there*

11 Then they took all the goods of Sodom and Gomorrah and all their food supply, and departed.

12 And they also took Lot, ᴿAbram's nephew, and his possessions and departed, for he was living in Sodom.   Gen. 11:27

13 Then ᵀa fugitive came and told Abram the Hebrew. Now he was ᵀliving by the ᴬoaks of Mamre the Amorite, brother of Eshcol and brother of Aner, and these were allies with Abram.   *the · abiding · terebinths*

14 And when Abram heard that ᴿhis ᵀrelative had been taken captive, he ᴬled out his trained men, born in his house, three hundred and eighteen, and went in pursuit as far as Dan.   Gen. 14:12 · *brother · mustered*

15 And he divided ᵀhis forces against them by night, he and his servants, and ᵀdefeated them, and pursued them as far as Hobah, which is north of Damascus.   *himself · smote*

16 And he ᴿbrought back all the goods, and also brought back his ᵀrelative Lot with his possessions, and also the women, and the people.   1 Sam. 30:8, 18, 19 · *brother*

Abram Refuses Reward

17 Then after his return from the ᵀdefeat of Chedorlaomer and the kings who were with him, ᴿthe king of Sodom went out to meet him at the valley of Shaveh (that is, the King's Valley).   *smiting* · Gen. 14:10

18 And Melchizedek king of Salem brought out bread and wine; now he was a priest of ᵀGod Most High.   Heb., *El Elyon*

19 And he blessed him and said,

"Blessed be Abram of God Most High,
   ᴬPossessor of heaven and earth; *Creator*

20   And blessed be ᵀGod Most High,
   Who has delivered your enemies into
     your hand."   Heb., *El Elyon*
ᴿAnd he gave him a tenth of all. [Heb. 7:4–10]

21 And the king of Sodom said to Abram, "Give the ᵀpeople to me and take the goods for yourself."   *soul*

22 And Abram said to the king of Sodom, "I have sworn to the LORD God Most High, ᴬpossessor of heaven and earth,   *Creator*

23 that I will not take a thread or a sandal thong or anything that is yours, lest you should say, 'I have made Abram rich.'

24 "I will take nothing except what the young men have eaten, and the share of the men who went with me, Aner, Eshcol, and Mamre; let them take their share."

CHAPTER 15

God's Promise of Children

Aᶠᵗᵉʳ these things ᴿthe word of the LORD came to Abram in a vision, saying, Gen. 15:4
"Do ᴿnot fear, Abram,   Is. 41:10
I am ᴿa shield to you;   Deut. 33:29
Your reward shall be very great."

2 And Abram said, "O Lord GOD, what wilt Thou give me, since I am childless, and the heir of my house is Eliezer of Damascus?"

3 And Abram said, "Since ᵀThou hast given no ᵀoffspring to me, ᵀone born in my house is my heir."   *Behold · seed · and behold, a son of*

4 Then behold, the word of the LORD came to him, saying, "This man will not be your heir; but one who shall come forth from your own body, he shall be your heir."

5 And He took him outside and said, "Now look toward the heavens, and ᴿcount the stars, if you are able to count them." And He said to him, "So ᴿshall your ᵀdescendants be."   Deut. 1:10 · Rom. 4:18 · *seed*

6 ᴿThen he believed in the LORD; and He reckoned it to him as righteousness. Gal. 3:6

7 And He said to him, "I am the LORD who brought you out of Ur of the Chaldeans, to give you this land to possess it."

8 And he said, "O Lord GOD, how may I know that I shall ᴬpossess it?"   *inherit*

9 So He said to him, "Bring ᵀMe a three year old heifer, and a three year old female goat, and a three year old ram, and a turtledove, and a young pigeon."   *Take*

10 Then he ᵀbrought all these to Him and cut them in two, and laid each half opposite the other; but he did not cut the birds. *took*

11 And the birds of prey came down upon the carcasses, and Abram drove them away.

12 Now when the sun was going down, a deep sleep fell upon Abram; and behold, terror *and* great darkness fell upon him.

13 And *God* said to Abram, "Know for certain that ᴿyour ᵀdescendants will be strangers in a land that is not theirs, where ᴿthey will be enslaved and oppressed four hundred years.   Acts 7:6, 17 · *seed* · Ex. 1:11

14 "But I will also judge the nation whom they will serve; and afterward they will come out with ᵀmany possessions.   *great*

15 "And as for you, ᴿyou shall go to your fathers in peace; you shall be buried at a good old age.   Gen. 25:8; 47:30

16 "Then in ᴿthe fourth generation they shall return here, for the iniquity of the Amorite is not yet complete."   Gen. 15:13

17 And it came about when the sun had set, that it was very dark, and behold, *there* appeared a smoking oven and a flaming torch which passed between these pieces.

18 On that day the LORD made a covenant with Abram, saying,
"To ᴿyour ᵀdescendants I have given this
     land,   Josh. 21:43; Acts 7:5 · *seed*
From the river of Egypt as far as the
     great river, the river Euphrates:

19 ᴿthe Kenite and the Kenizzite and the Kadmonite   Ex. 3:17; 23:28; Josh. 24:11; Neh. 9:8

20 and the Hittite and the Perizzite and the Rephaim

21 and the Amorite and the Canaanite and the Girgashite and the Jebusite."

CHAPTER 16

A Carnal Plan for Children

Now [R]Sarai, Abram's wife had borne him no *children*, and she had an Egyptian maid whose name was Hagar.   Gen. 11:30

2 So Sarai said to Abram, "Now behold, the LORD has prevented me from bearing *children.* Please go in to my maid; perhaps I shall obtain children through her." And Abram listened to the voice of Sarai.

3 And after Abram had [T]lived ten years in the land of Canaan, Abram's wife Sarai took Hagar the Egyptian, her maid, and gave her to her husband Abram as his wife.   *dwelt*

4 And he went in to Hagar, and she conceived; and when she saw that she had conceived, her mistress was despised in her sight.

5 And Sarai said to Abram, "May [R]the wrong done me be upon you. I gave my maid into your [T]arms; but when she saw that she had conceived, I was despised in her [T]sight. May the LORD judge between [T]you and me."   Jer. 51:35 · *bosom · eyes · me and you*

6 But Abram said to Sarai, "Behold, your maid is in your power; do to her what is good in your sight." So Sarai treated her harshly, and she fled from her presence.

7 Now [R]the angel of the LORD found her by a spring of water in the wilderness, by the spring on the way to Shur. Gen. 21:17, 18

8 And he said, "Hagar, Sarai's maid, where have you come from and where are you going?" And she said, "I am fleeing from the presence of my mistress Sarai."

9 Then the angel of the LORD said to her, "Return to your mistress, and submit yourself [T]to her authority."   *under her hands*

10 Moreover, the angel of the LORD said to her, "I will greatly multiply your [T]descendants so that [A]they shall be too many to count."   *seed · it shall not be counted for multitude*

11 The angel of the LORD said to her further,

"Behold, you are with child,
And you shall bear a son;
And you shall call his name [17]Ishmael,
Because [R]the LORD [T]has given heed to your affliction.   Ex. 2:23, 24 · *has heard*

12 "And he will be a [R]wild donkey of a man,   Job 24:5; 39:5-8
His hand *will be* against everyone,
And everyone's hand *will be* against him;
And he will [T]live [R]to the east of all his brothers."   *dwell · Gen. 25:18*

13 Then she called the name of the LORD who spoke to her, "Thou art [T]a God who sees"; for she said, "Have I even remained alive here after seeing Him?"   Heb., *Elroi*

14 Therefore the well was called [18]Beer-lahai-roi; behold, it is between [R]Kadesh and Bered.   Gen. 14:7

15 So Hagar bore Abram a son; and

Abram called the name of his son, whom Hagar bore, Ishmael.

16 And Abram was eighty-six years old when Hagar bore Ishmael to [T]him.   *Abram*

CHAPTER 17

Institution of the Covenant: Circumcision

Now when Abram was ninety-nine years old, [R]the LORD appeared to Abram and said to him,   Gen. 12:7; 18:1

"I am [T]God Almighty;   Heb., *El Shaddai*
Walk before Me, and be blameless.

2 "And I will [T]establish My [R]covenant between Me and you,   *give · Gen. 15:18*
And I will multiply you exceedingly."

3 And Abram [R]fell on his face, and God talked with him, saying,   Gen. 17:17; 18:2

4 "As for Me, behold, My covenant is with you,
And you shall be the father of a [R]multitude of nations.   Gen. 35:11; 48:19

5 "No longer shall your name be called [19]Abram,
But your name shall be [20]Abraham;
For [R]I will make you the father of a multitude of nations.   Rom. 4:17

6 "And I will make you exceedingly fruitful, and I will make nations of you, and [R]kings shall come forth from you. Gen. 17:16

7 "And I will [R]establish My covenant between Me and you and your descendants after you throughout their generations for an everlasting covenant, to be God to you and to your descendants after you.   [Gal. 3:17]☆

8 "And [R]I will give to you and to your [T]descendants after you, the land of your sojournings, all the land of Canaan, for an everlasting possession; and [R]I will be their God."   Acts 7:5 · *seed* · Deut. 29:13; Rev. 21:7

9 God said further to Abraham, "Now as for you, [R]you shall keep My covenant, you and your [T]descendants after you throughout their generations.   Ex. 19:5 · *seed*

10 "This [R]is My covenant, which you shall keep, between Me and you and your [T]descendants after you: every male among you shall be circumcised. Acts 7:8; Rom. 4:11 · *seed*

11 "And you shall be circumcised in the flesh of your foreskin; and it shall be the sign of the covenant between Me and you.

12 "And every male among you who is [R]eight days old shall be circumcised throughout your generations, a *servant* who is born in the house or who is bought with money from any foreigner, who is not of your [T]descendants.   Lev. 12:3 · *seed*

13 "A *servant* who is born in your house or who is bought with your money shall surely be circumcised; thus shall My covenant be in your flesh for an everlasting covenant.

14 "But an uncircumcised male who is not circumcised in the flesh of his foreskin, that

[17] I.e., God hears
[18] I.e., the well of the living one who sees me
[19] I.e., exalted father   [20] I.e., father of a multitude

person shall be ᴿcut off from his people; he has broken My covenant." Ex. 4:24-26

15 Then God said to Abraham, "As for Sarai your wife, you shall not call her name Sarai, but ²¹Sarah *shall* be her name.

16"And I will bless her, and indeed I will give you a son by her. Then I will bless her, and she shall be *a mother of* nations; kings of peoples shall ᵗcome from her."   *be*

17 Then Abraham ᴿfell on his face and laughed, and said in his heart, "Will a child be born to a man one hundred years old? And ᴿwill Sarah, who is ninety years old, bear *a child?*"   Gen. 17:3; 18:12 • Gen. 21:7

18 And Abraham said to God, "Oh that Ishmael might live before Thee!"

19 But God said, "No, butᴿSarah your wife shall bear you a son, and you shall call his name ²²Isaac; and I will establish My covenant with him for an everlasting covenant for his descendants after him.   [Gal. 4:28]☆

20"And as for Ishmael, I have heard you; behold, I will bless him, and will make him fruitful, and will multiply him exceedingly. He shall become the father of twelve princes, and I will make him a great nation.

21"But My ᵢcovenant I will establish with ᴿIsaac, whom ᴿSarah will bear to you at this season next year."   Gen. 17:19 • Gen. 21:2

22 And when He finished talking with him,ᴿGod went up from Abraham. Gen. 18:33

23 Then Abraham took Ishmael his son, and all *the servants* who wereᴿborn in his house and all who were bought with his money, every male among the men of Abraham's household, and circumcised the flesh of their foreskin in the very same day, as God had said to him.   Gen. 14:14

24 Now Abraham was ninety-nine years old whenᴿhe was circumcised in the flesh of his foreskin.   [Rom. 4:11]

25 AndᴿIshmael his son was thirteen years old when he was circumcised in the flesh of his foreskin.   Gen. 16:16

26 In the very same day Abraham was circumcised, and Ishmael his son.

27 And all the men of his household, who wereᴿborn in the house or bought with money from a foreigner, were circumcised with him.   Gen. 14:14

CHAPTER 18

Sarah's Faith Is Tested

NOW the LORD appeared to him by the ᵃoaks of Mamre, while he was sitting at the tent door in the heat of the day.   *terebinths*

2 And when he lifted up his eyes and looked, behold, threeᴿmen were standing opposite him; and when he saw *them,* he ran from the tent door to meet them, and bowed himself to the earth,   Judg. 13:6-11; Heb. 13:2

3 and said, "Myᵈlord, if now I have found favor in your sight, please do not ᵗpass your servant by.   *O Lord • pass away from your servant*

4"Please let a little water be brought and

ᴿwash your feet, andᵀrest yourselves under the tree;   Gen. 19:2; 24:32; 43:24 • *support*

5 and I willᵗbring a piece of bread, that you may ᵗrefresh yourselves; after that you may go on, since you have ᵗvisited your servant." And they said, "So do, as you have said."   *take • sustain your heart • come to*

6 So Abraham hurried into the tent to Sarah, and said, "Quickly, prepare three measures of fine flour, knead *it,* and make bread cakes."   *Hasten three measures*

7 Abraham also ran to the herd, and took a tender and ᵗchoice calf, and gave *it* to the servant; and he hurried to prepare it.   *good*

8 And he took curds and milk and the calf which he had prepared, and placed *it* before them; and he was standing by them under the tree ᵃas they ate.   *and*

9 Then they said to him, "Where is Sarah your wife?" And he said, "Behold, in the tent."

10 And he said, "Iᴿ will surely return to you ᵗat this time next year; and behold, Sarah your wife shall have a son." And Sarah was listening at the tent door, which was behind him.   Rom. 9:9 • *when the time revives*

11 Now Abraham and Sarah were old, advanced in age; Sarah was past childbearing.

12 And Sarah laughed ᵗto herself, saying, "After I have become old, shall I have pleasure, my lord being old also?"   *within*

13 And the LORD said to Abraham, "Why did Sarah laugh, saying, 'Shall I indeedᵀbear *a child,* when I am *so* old?'   *surely bear*

14"Isᴿ anything too ᵈdifficult for the LORD? At the appointed time I will return to you,ᵀat this time next year, and Sarah shall have a son."   Zech. 8:6 • *wonderful • when the time revives*

15 Sarah denied *it* however, saying, "I did not laugh"; for she was afraid. And He said, "No, but you did laugh."

Abraham's Faith Is Tested

16 Then the men rose up from there, and looked down toward Sodom; and Abraham was walking with them to send them off.

17 Andᵗthe LORD said, "Shall I hide from Abraham what I am about to do,   Amos 3:7

18 since Abraham will surely become a great and mighty nation, and in him all the nations of the earth will be blessed?

19"For I haveᵀchosen him, in order that he may command his children and his household after him to keep the way of the LORD by doing righteousness and justice; in order that the LORD may bring upon Abraham what He has spoken about him."   *known*

20 And the LORD said, "Theᴿ outcry of Sodom and Gomorrah is indeed great, and their sin is exceedingly grave.   Ezek. 16:49, 50

21"I will ᴿgo down now, and see if they have done entirely according to its outcry, which has come to Me; and if not, I will know."   Gen. 11:5; Ex. 3:8; Ps. 14:2

---

²¹ I.e., princess   ²² I.e., he laughs

22 Then the men turned away from there and went toward Sodom, while Abraham was still standing before the LORD.

23 And Abraham came near and said, "Wilt[R] Thou indeed sweep away the righteous with the wicked?   Ex. 23:7; Num. 16:22

24"Suppose there are fifty righteous within the city; wilt Thou indeed sweep *it* away and not[A]spare the place for the sake of the fifty righteous who are in it?   *forgive*

25"Far be it from Thee to do such a thing, to slay the righteous with the wicked, so that the righteous and the wicked are *treated* alike. Far be it from Thee! Shall not the Judge of all the earth deal justly?"

26 So the LORD said, "If I find in Sodom fifty righteous within the city, then I will spare the whole place on their account."

27 And Abraham answered and said, "Now behold, I have ventured to speak to the Lord, although I am *but* dust and ashes.

28"Suppose the fifty righteous are lacking five, wilt Thou destroy the whole city because of five?" And He said, "I will not destroy *it* if I find forty-five there."

29 And he spoke to Him yet again and said, "Suppose forty are found there?" And He said, "I will not do *it* on account of the forty."

30 Then he said, "Oh may the Lord not be angry, and I shall speak; suppose thirty are found there?" And He said, "I will not do *it* if I find thirty there."

31 And he said, "Now behold, I have ventured to speak to the Lord; suppose twenty are found there?" And He said, "I will not destroy *it* on account of the twenty."

32 Then he said, "Oh may the Lord not be angry, and I shall speak only this once; suppose ten are found there?" And He said, "I will not destroy *it* on account of the ten."

33 And as soon as He had finished speaking to Abraham [R]the LORD departed; and Abraham returned to his place.   Gen. 17:22

CHAPTER 19

Destruction of Sodom and Gomorrah

NOW the[R]two angels came to Sodom in the evening as Lot was sitting in the gate of Sodom. When Lot saw *them,* he rose to meet them and[T]bowed down *with his* face to the ground.   Gen. 18:2, 22 · *bowed himself*

2 And he said, "Now behold, my lords, please turn aside into your servant's house, and spend the night, and wash your feet; then you may rise early and go on your way." They said however, "No, but we shall spend the night in the square."

3 Yet he urged them strongly, so they turned aside to him and entered his house; [R]and he prepared a feast for them, and baked unleavened bread, and they ate.   Gen. 18:6-8

4 Before they lay down, the men of the city, the men of Sodom, surrounded the house, both young and old, all the people [T]from every quarter;   *from every end*

5 and they called to Lot and said to him, "Where[R] are the men who came to you to-night? Bring them out to us that we may have relations with them."   Judg. 19:22

6 But Lot went out to them at the door-way, and shut the door behind him,

7 and said, "Please, my brothers, do not act wickedly.

8"Now behold, I have two daughters who have not[T]had relations with man; please let me bring them out to you, and do to them whatever you like; only do nothing to these men, inasmuch as they have come under the [T]shelter of my roof."   had intercourse · *shadow*

9 But they said, "Stand aside." Furthermore, they said, "This one came in as an alien, and already he is acting like a judge; now we will treat you worse than them." So they pressed hard against [T]Lot and came near to break the door.   *the man, against Lot*

10 But [R]the men reached out their [T]hands and brought Lot into the house [T]with them, and shut the door.   Gen. 19:1 · *hand · to*

11 And they [T]struck the men who were at the doorway of the house with blindness, both small and great, so that they wearied *themselves trying* to find the doorway. *smote*

12 Then the men said to Lot, "Whom else have you here? A son-in-law, and your sons, and your daughters, and whomever you have in the city, bring *them* out of the place;

13 for we are about to destroy this place, because [R]their outcry has become so great before the LORD that[T]the LORD has sent us to destroy it."   Gen. 18:20 · Lev. 26:30-33

14 And Lot went out and spoke to his sons-in-law, who were to marry his daughters, and said, "Up, get out of this place, for the LORD will destroy the city." But he appeared to his sons-in-law to be jesting.

15 And when morning dawned, the angels urged Lot, saying, "Up, take your wife and your two daughters, who are here, lest you be swept away in the [A]punishment of the city."   *iniquity*

16 But he hesitated. So the men seized his hand and the hand of his wife and the[T]hands of his two daughters, for the compassion of the LORD *was* upon him; and they brought him out, and put him outside the city.   *hand*

17 And it came about when they had brought them outside, that [T]one said, "Escape[R]for your life! Do not look behind you, and do not stay[T]anywhere in the valley; escape to the [T]mountains, lest you be swept away."   *he · Jer. 48:6 · in all the circle · mountain*

18 But Lot said to them, "Oh no, my lords!

19"Now behold, your servant has found favor in your sight, and you have magnified your lovingkindness, which you have shown me by saving my life; but I cannot escape to the [T]mountains, lest the disaster overtake me and I die;   *mountain*

20 now behold, this town is near *enough* to flee to, and it is small. Please, let me escape there (is it not small?)ᵀthat my life may be saved." *and my soul will live*

21 And he said to him, "Behold, I grant you thisᵀrequest also, not to overthrow the town of which you have spoken. *thing*

22"Hurry, escape there, for I cannot do anything until you arrive there." Therefore the name of the town was called ²³Zoar.

23 The sun had risen over the earth when Lot came to Zoar.

24 Then the LORDᴿrained on Sodom and Gomorrah brimstone and fire from the LORD out of heaven. Deut. 29:23; Ps. 11:6; Is. 13:19

25 and He overthrew those cities, and all theᵀvalley, and all the inhabitants of the cities, and what grew on the ground. *circle*

26 But his wife, from behind him, looked *back;* and she became a pillar of salt.

27 Now Abraham arose early in the morning *and went* toᴿthe place where he had stood before the LORD; Gen. 18:22

28 and he looked down toward Sodom and Gomorrah, and toward all the land of theᵀvalley, and he saw, and behold, ᴿthe smoke of the land ascended like the smoke of aᵀfurnace. *circle* • Rev. 9:2; 18:9 • *kiln*

29 Thus it came about, when God destroyed the cities of theᵀvalley, that God remembered Abraham, and sent Lot out of the midst of the overthrow, when He overthrew the cities in which Lot lived. *circle*

The Sin of Lot

30 And Lot went up from Zoar, and ᵀstayed in theᵀmountains, and his two daughters with him; for he was afraid toᵀstay in Zoar; and he stayed in a cave, he and his two daughters. *dwelt • mountain • dwell*

31 Then the first-born said to the younger, "Our father is old, and there is not a manˆon earth toᴿcome in to us after the manner of the earth. *in the land* • Gen. 16:2, 4; 38:8

32"Come, let us make our father drink wine, and let us lie with him, that we may preserve our family through our father."

33 So they made their father drink wine that night, and the first-born went in and lay with her father; and he did not know when she lay down or when she arose.

34 And it came about on the morrow, that the first-born said to the younger, "Behold, I lay last night with my father; let us make him drink wine tonight also; then you go in and lie with him, that we may preserveᵀour family through our father." *seed from our father*

35 So they made their father drink wine that night also, and the younger arose and lay with him; and he did not know when she lay down or when she arose.

36 Thus both the daughters of Lot were with child by their father.

37 And the first-born bore a son, and called his nameᴿMoab; he is the father of the Moabites to this day. Deut. 2:9

38 And as for the younger, she also bore a son, and called his name Ben-ammi; he is the father of the sons of Ammon to this day.

CHAPTER 20

The Test of Abimelech

Now Abraham journeyed from ᴿthere toward the land of the ²⁴Negev, and ᵀsettled between Kadesh and Shur; then he sojourned in Gerar. Gen. 18:1 • *dwelt*

2 And Abraham said of Sarah his wife, "Sheᴿis my sister." So Abimelech king of Gerar sent and took Sarah. Gen. 12:11-13

3 But God came to Abimelech in a dream of the night, and said to him, "Behold, you are a dead man because of the woman whom you have taken, for she is married."

4 Now Abimelech had not come near her; and he said, "Lord, wilt Thou slay a nation, even *though*ᵀblameless? *righteous*

5"Did he not himself say to me, 'She is my sister'? And she herself said, 'He is my brother.' In the integrity of my heart and the innocence of my hands I have done this."

6 Then God said to him in the dream, "Yes, I know that in the integrity of your heart you have done this, and I alsoᵀkept you from sinning against Me; therefore I did not let you touch her. *restrained*

7"Now therefore, restore the man's wife, forᴿhe is a prophet, and he will pray for you, and you will live. But if you do not restore *her,* know that you shall surely die, you and all who are yours." 1 Sam. 7:5; 2 Kin. 5:11

8 So Abimelech arose early in the morning and called all his servants and told all these things in their hearing; and the men were greatly frightened.

9ᴿThen Abimelech called Abraham and said to him, "What have you done to us? Andᵀhow have I sinned against you, that you have brought on me and on my kingdom a great sin? You have done to meᵀthings that ought not to be done." Gen. 12:18 • *what* • *deeds*

10 And Abimelech said to Abraham, "What have youᵀencountered, that you have done this thing?" *seen*

11 And Abraham said, "Because I thought, surely there is noᴿfear of God in this place; andᴿthey will kill me because of my wife. Neh. 5:15; Prov. 16:6 • Gen. 12:12; 26:7

12"Besides, she actually is my sister, the daughter of my father, but not the daughter of my mother, and she became my wife;

13 and it came about, when God caused me to wander from my father's house, that I said to her, 'This is the kindness which you will show to me: ᵀeverywhere we go, say of me, "He is my brother." ' " *at every place where*

14 ᴿAbimelech then took sheep and oxen and male and female servants, and gave

²³ I.e., small   ²⁴ I.e., South country

them to Abraham, and restored his wife Sarah to him.					Gen. 12:16

15 And Abimelech said, "Behold, my land is before you; settle wherever you please."

16 And to Sarah he said, "Behold, I have given your brother a thousand pieces of silver; behold, it is 'your vindication before all who are with you, and before all men you are cleared."			*for you a covering of the eyes*

17 And Abraham prayed to God; and God healed Abimelech and his wife and his maids, so that they bore *children.*

18 ᴿFor the Lᴏʀᴅ had closed fast all the wombs of the household of Abimelech because of Sarah, Abraham's wife.	Gen. 12:17

CHAPTER 21

Birth of Isaac

THENᴿthe Lᴏʀᴅ took note of Sarah as He had said, and the Lᴏʀᴅ did for Sarah as He had 'promised.	Gen. 17:16, 21; 18:10, 14 • *spoken*

2 So Sarah conceived and bore a son to Abraham in his old age, at the appointed time of which God had spoken to him.

3 And Abraham called the name of his son who was born to him, whom Sarah bore to him,ᴿIsaac.			Gen. 17:19, 21

4 Then Abraham circumcised his son Isaac when he was ᴿeight days old, as God had commanded him.		Gen. 17:12; Acts 7:8

5 Now Abraham was one hundred years old when his son Isaac was born to him.

6 And Sarah said, "God has madeᴿlaughter for me; everyone who hears will laugh 'with me."		Gen. 18:13; Ps. 126:2; Is. 54:1 • *for*

7 And she said, "Who would have said to Abraham that Sarah would nurse children? Yet I have borne him a son in his old age."

8 And the child grew and was weaned, and Abraham made a great feast on the day that Isaac was weaned.

9 Now Sarah sawᴿthe son of Hagar the Egyptian, whom she had borne to Abraham, 'mocking.		Gen. 16:1, 4, 15 • *playing*

10 Therefore she said to Abraham, "Driveᴿ out this maid and her son, for the son of this maid shall not be an heir 'with my son Isaac."			Gal. 4:30 • *with Isaac*

11 ᴿAnd the matter distressed Abraham greatly because of his son.		Gen. 17:18

12 But God said to Abraham, "Do not be distressed because of the lad and your maid; whatever Sarah tells you, listen to her, for ᴿthrough Isaac your descendants shall be named.			Matt. 1:2☆

13"And of ᵗthe son of the maid I will make a nation also, because he is your 'descendant."		Gen. 16:10; 21:18; 25:12-18 • *seed*

14 So Abraham rose early in the morning, and took bread and a skin of water, and gave *them* to Hagar, putting *them* on her shoulder, and *gave her* the boy, and sent her away. And she departed, and wandered about in the wilderness of Beersheba.

15 And the water in the skin was used up,

and she 'left the boy under one of the bushes.					*cast*

16 Then she went and sat down opposite him, about a bowshot away, for she said, "Do not let me 'see the boy die." And she sat opposite him, and 'lifted up her voice and wept.		*look upon the death of the child* • Jer. 6:26

17 And Godᴿheard the lad crying; and the angel of God called to Hagar from heaven, and said to her, "What is the matter with you, Hagar? Do not fear, for God has heard the voice of the lad where he is.		Ex. 3:7

18"Arise, lift up the lad, and hold him by 'the hand;ᴿfor I will make a great nation of him."			*your* • Gen. 16:10; 21:13; 25:12-16

19 Then God opened her eyes and she saw a well of water; and she went and filled the skin with water, and gave the lad a drink.

20 And ᴿGod was with the lad, and he grew; and he 'lived in the wilderness, and became an archer.		Gen. 28:15; 39:2, 3, 21 • *dwelt*

21 Andᴿhe 'lived in the wilderness of Paran; and his mother took a wife for him from the land of Egypt.		Gen. 25:18 • *dwelt*

22 Now it came about at that time, that ᴿAbimelech and Phicol, the commander of his army, spoke to Abraham, saying, "God is with you in all that you do;	Gen. 20:2, 14

23 now therefore, swear to me here by God that you will not deal falsely with me, or with my offspring, or with my posterity; but according to the kindness that I have shown to you, you shall show to me, and to the land in which you have sojourned."

24 And Abraham said, "I swear it."

25 But Abraham 'complained to Abimelech because of the well of water which the servants of Abimelech had seized.	*reproved*

26 And Abimelech said, "I do not know who has done this thing; neither did you tell me, nor did I hear of it 'until today."	*except*

27 And Abraham took sheep and oxen, and gave them to Abimelech; andᴿthe two of them made a covenant.		Gen. 26:31

28 Then Abraham set seven ewe lambs of the flock by themselves.

29 And Abimelech said to Abraham, "What do these seven ewe lambs mean, which you have set by themselves?"

30 And he said, "You shall take these seven ewe lambs from my hand in order that it may be aᴿwitness to me, that I dug this well."			Gen. 31:48

31 Therefore he called that place ᴿBeersheba; because there the two of them took an oath.			Gen. 21:14; 26:33

32 So they made a covenant at Beersheba; and Abimelech and Phicol, the commander of his army, arose and returned to the land of the Philistines.

33 And *Abraham* planted a tamarisk tree at Beersheba, and there he called on the name of the Lᴏʀᴅ, the Everlasting God.

34 And Abraham sojournedᴿin the land of the Philistines for many days.	Gen. 22:19

CHAPTER 22

Offering of Isaac

Now it came about after these things, that God tested Abraham, and said to him, "Abraham!" And he said, "Here I am."

2 And He said, "Take now [R]your son, your only son, whom you love, Isaac, and go to the land of Moriah; and offer him there as a burnt offering on one of the mountains of which I will tell you."   John 3:16; 1 John 4:9

3 So Abraham rose early in the morning and saddled his donkey, and took two of his young men with him and Isaac his son; and he split wood for the burnt offering, and arose and went to the place of which God had told him.

4 On the third day Abraham raised his eyes and saw the place from a distance.

5 And Abraham said to his young men, "Stay here with the donkey, and I and the lad will go yonder; and we will worship and return to you."

6 And Abraham took the wood of the burnt offering and [R]laid it on Isaac his son, and he took in his hand the fire and the knife. So the two of them walked on together.   John 19:17

7 And Isaac spoke to Abraham his father and said, "My father!" And he said, "Here I am, my son." And he said, "Behold, the fire and the wood, but where is the [T]lamb for the burnt offering?"   Ex. 29:38-42; John 1:29, 36

8 And Abraham said, "God will [T]provide for Himself the lamb for the burnt offering, my son." So the two of them walked on together.   *see*

9 Then they came to [R]the place of which God had told him; and Abraham built the altar there, and arranged the wood, and bound his son Isaac, and laid him on the altar on top of the wood.   Gen. 22:2

10 And Abraham stretched out his hand, and took the knife to slay his son.

11 But the angel of the LORD called to him from heaven, and said, "Abraham, Abraham!" And he said, "Here I am."

12 And he said, "Do not stretch out your hand against the lad, and do nothing to him; for now I know that you [T]fear God, since you have not withheld your son, your only son, from Me."   *are a fearer of God*

13 Then Abraham raised his eyes and looked, and behold, behind *him* a ram caught in the thicket by his horns; and Abraham went and took the ram, and offered him up for a burnt offering in the place of his son.

14 And Abraham called the name of that place [T]The LORD Will Provide, as it is said to this day, "In the mount of the LORD it will [T]be provided."   Heb., *YHWH-jireh • be seen*

15 Then the angel of the LORD called to Abraham a second time from heaven,

16 and said, "By [R]Myself I have sworn, de-

clares the LORD, because you have done this thing, and have not withheld your son, your only son,   Ps. 105:9; Luke 1:73; Heb. 6:13, 14

17 indeed I will greatly bless you, and I will greatly multiply your [A]seed as the stars of the heavens, and as the sand which is on the seashore; and your [A]seed shall possess the gate of [T]their enemies.   *descendants • his*

18 "And in your seed [R]all the nations of the earth shall [A]be blessed, because you have obeyed My voice."   Gal. 3:16☆ • *bless themselves*

19 [R]So Abraham returned to his young men, and they arose and went together to Beersheba; and Abraham lived at Beersheba.   Gen. 22:5

20 Now it came about after these things, that it was told Abraham, saying, "Behold, [R]Milcah [T]also has borne children to your brother Nahor: Gen. 11:29 • *she also*

21 Uz his first-born and Buz his brother and Kemuel the father of Aram

22 and Chesed and Hazo and Pildash and Jidlaph and Bethuel."

23 And Bethuel [T]became the father of [R]Rebekah: these eight Milcah bore to Nahor, Abraham's brother.   *begot • Gen. 24:15*

24 And his concubine, whose name was Reumah, [T]also bore Tebah and Gaham and Tahash and Maacah.   *she also*

CHAPTER 23

Death of Sarah

Now [T]Sarah lived one hundred and twenty-seven years; *these were* the years of the life of Sarah.   *the life of Sarah was*

2 And Sarah died in [R]Kiriath-arba (that is, Hebron) in the land of Canaan; and Abraham [A]went in to mourn for Sarah and to weep for her.   Josh. 14:15; 15:13 • *proceeded*

3 Then Abraham rose from before his dead, and spoke to the sons of Heth, saying,

4 "I am a stranger and a sojourner among you; give me a burial site among you, that I may bury my dead out of my sight."

5 And the sons of Heth answered Abraham, saying to him,

6 "Hear us, my lord, you are a mighty prince among us; bury your dead in the choicest of our graves; none of us will refuse you his grave for burying your dead."

7 So Abraham rose and bowed to the people of the land, the sons of Heth.

8 And he spoke with them, saying, "If it is your wish *for me* to bury my dead out of my sight, hear me, and approach [R]Ephron the son of Zohar for me,   Gen. 25:9

9 that he may give me the cave of Machpelah which he owns, which is at the end of his field; for the full price let him give it to me in your presence for a burial site."

10 Now Ephron was sitting among the sons of Heth; and Ephron the Hittite answered Abraham in the hearing of the sons of Heth; *even* [R]of all who went in at the gate of his city, saying,   Gen. 23:18; 34:20, 24

11"No, my lord, hear me; [R]I give you the field, and I give you the cave that is in it. In the presence of the sons of my people I give it to you; bury your dead."   2 Sam. 24:21-24

12 And Abraham bowed before the people of the land.

13 And he spoke to Ephron in the hearing of the people of the land, saying, "If you will only please listen to me; I will give the price of the field, accept *it* from me, that I may bury my dead there."

14 Then Ephron answered Abraham, saying to him,

15"My lord, listen to me; a piece of land worth [T]four hundred [R]shekels of silver, what is that between me and you? So bury your dead." $51,200 • Ex. 30:13; Ezek. 45:12

16 And Abraham listened to Ephron; and Abraham [R]weighed out for Ephron the silver which he had named in the [T]hearing of the sons of Heth, four hundred shekels of silver, commercial standard.   2 Sam. 14:26 • *ears*

17 So Ephron's field, which was in Machpelah, which faced Mamre, the field and cave which was in it, and all the trees which were in the field, that were within all the confines of its border, were deeded over

18 to Abraham for a possession [R]in the presence of the sons of Heth, before all who went in at the gate of his city.   Gen. 23:10

19 And after this, Abraham buried Sarah his wife in the cave of the field at Machpelah facing Mamre (that is, Hebron) in the land of Canaan.

20 So the field, and the cave that is in it, [A]were deeded over to Abraham for a burial site by the sons of Heth.   *were ratified*

CHAPTER 24

Isaac's Marriage

NOW [R]Abraham was old, advanced in age; and the LORD had [R]blessed Abraham in every way.   Gen. 18:11 • Gen. 12:2; 13:2; 24:35

2 And Abraham said to his servant, the oldest of his household, who had [R]charge of all that he owned, "Please [R]place your hand under my thigh,   Gen. 39:4-6 • Gen. 24:9; 47:29

3 and I will make you swear by the LORD, [R]the God of heaven and the God of earth, that you [R]shall not take a wife for my son from the daughters of the Canaanites, among whom I live,   Gen. 14:19, 22 • Deut. 7:3

4 but you shall go to [R]my country and to my relatives, and take a wife for my son Isaac."   Gen. 12:1; Heb. 11:15

5 And the servant said to him, "Suppose the woman will not be willing to follow me to this land; should I take your son back to the land from where you came?"

6 Then Abraham said to him, "Beware [R] lest you take my son back there!   Gen. 24:8

7"The [R] LORD, the God of heaven, who took me from my father's house and from the land of my birth, and who spoke to me, and

who swore to me, saying, 'To your [T]descendants I will give this land,' He will send His angel before you, and you will take a wife for my son from there.   Gen. 24:3 • *seed*

8"But if the woman is not willing to follow you, then you will be free from this my oath; only do not take my son back there."

9 So the servant [R]placed his hand under the thigh of Abraham his master, and swore to him concerning this matter.   Gen. 24:2

10 Then the servant took ten camels from the camels of his master, and set out with a variety of [R]good things of his master's in his hand; and he arose, and went to Mesopotamia, to the city of Nahor.   Gen. 24:22, 53

11 And he made the camels kneel down outside the city by [T]the well of water at evening time, [T]the time when women go out to draw water.   Gen. 24:42 • Ex. 2:16; 1 Sam. 9:11

12 And he said, "O LORD, the God of my master Abraham, please [T]grant [R]me success today, and show lovingkindness to my master Abraham.   *cause to occur for me* • Gen. 27:20

13"Behold, I am standing by the [T]spring, and the daughters of the men of the city are coming out to draw water;   *fountain of water*

14 now may it be that the girl to whom I say, 'Please let down your jar so that I may drink,' and [T]who answers, 'Drink, and I will water your camels also';—*may* she *be the one* whom Thou hast appointed for Thy servant Isaac; and by this I shall know that Thou hast shown lovingkindness to my master."   *she will say*

15 And it came about [R]before he had finished speaking, that behold, Rebekah who was born to Bethuel the son of Milcah, the wife of Abraham's brother Nahor, came out with her jar on her shoulder.   Gen. 24:45

16 And the girl was [R]very beautiful, a virgin, and no man had [T]had relations with her; and she went down to the spring and filled her jar, and came up.   Gen. 12:11 • *known*

17 Then the servant ran to meet her, and said, "Please [R]let me drink a little water from your jar."   John 4:7

18 And [R]she said, "Drink, my lord"; and she quickly lowered her jar to her hand, and gave him a drink.   Gen. 24:14, 46

19 Now when she had finished giving him a drink, she said, "I will draw also for your camels until they have finished drinking."

20 So she quickly emptied her jar into the trough, and ran back to the well to draw, and she drew for all his camels.

21 Meanwhile, the man was gazing at her in silence, to know whether the LORD had made his journey successful or not.

22 Then it came about, when the camels had finished drinking, that the man took a [R]gold ring weighing a half-shekel and two bracelets for her [T]wrists weighing ten shekels in gold,   Gen. 24:47; Ex. 32:2, 3 • *hands*

23 and said, "Whose daughter are you? Please tell me, is there room for us to lodge in your father's house?"

24 And she said to him, "I^Ram the daughter of Bethuel, the son of Milcah, whom she bore to Nahor." Gen. 24:15

25 Again she said to him, "We have plenty of both straw and feed, and room to lodge in."

26 Then the man ^Rbowed low and worshiped the Lord. Gen. 24:48, 52; Ex. 4:31

27 And he said, "Blessed^Rbe the Lord, the God of my master Abraham, who has not forsaken His lovingkindness and His truth toward my master; as for me, the Lord has guided me in the way to the house of my master's brothers." Ruth 4:14; 1 Sam. 25:32

28 Then^Rthe girl ran and told her mother's household about these things. Gen. 29:12

29 Now _RRebekah had a brother whose name was^RLaban; and Laban ran outside to the man at the spring. Gen. 29:5, 13

30 And it came about that when he saw the ring, and the bracelets on his sister's wrists, and when he heard the words of Rebekah his sister, saying, "This^T is what the man said to me," he went to the man; and behold, he was standing by the camels at the spring. hands • Thus the man

31 And he said, "Come^R in,^Rblessed of the Lord! Why do you stand outside since I have prepared the house, and a place for the camels?" Gen. 29:13 • Gen. 26:29; Ruth 3:10

32 So the man entered the house. Then ^TLaban^R unloaded the camels, and he gave straw and feed to the camels, and water to wash his feet and the feet of the men who were with him. he • Gen. 43:24; Judg. 19:21

33 But when food was set before him to eat, he said, "I will not eat until I have told my business." And he said, "Speak on."

34 So he said, "I am Abraham's servant.

35"And the Lord has greatly^Rblessed my master, so that he has become^Trich; and He has given him ^Rflocks and herds, and silver and gold, and servants and maids, and camels and donkeys. Gen. 24:1 • great • Gen. 13:2

36"Now Sarah my master's wife bore a son to my master^Tin her old age; and he has given him all that he has. after she was old

37"And^R my master made me swear, saying, 'You shall not take a wife for my son from the daughters of the Canaanites, in whose land I^Tlive; Gen. 24:2-4 • dwell

38 but you shall go to my father's house, and to my relatives, and take a wife for my son.'

39"And^RI said to my master, 'Suppose the woman does not follow me.' Gen. 24:5

40"And he said to me, 'The Lord, before whom I have walked, will send His angel with you to make your journey successful, and you will take a wife for my son from my relatives, and from my father's house;

41 ^Rthen you will be free from my oath, when you come to my relatives; and if they do not give her to you, you will be free from my oath.' Gen. 24:8

42"So^RI came today to the spring, and said, 'O Lord, the God of my master Abraham, if now Thou wilt make my journey on which I go^Rsuccessful; Gen. 24:11, 12 • Neh. 1:11

43 behold, I am standing by the spring, and may it be that the maiden who comes out to draw, and to whom I say, "Please let me drink a little water from your jar";

44 and she will say to me, "You drink, and I will draw for your camels also"; let her be the woman whom the Lord has appointed for my master's son.'

45"Before I had finished ^Rspeaking in my heart, behold,^RRebekah came out with her jar on her shoulder, and went down to the spring and drew; and I said to her, 'Please let me drink.' 1 Sam. 1:13 • Gen. 24:15

46"And she quickly lowered her jar from her shoulder, and said, 'Drink,^R and I will water your camels also'; so I drank, and she watered the camels also. Gen. 24:18, 19

47"Then I asked her, and said, 'Whose daughter are you?' And she said, 'The daughter of Bethuel, Nahor's son, whom Milcah bore to him'; and I put the ring on her nose, and the bracelets on her wrists.

48"And I bowed low and worshiped the Lord, and blessed the Lord, the God of my master Abraham, who had guided me in the right way to take the daughter of my master's^Tkinsman for his son. brother

49"So now if you are going to ²⁵deal^R kindly and truly with my master, tell me; and if not, let me know, that I may turn to the right hand or the left." Josh. 2:14

50 Then Laban and Bethuel answered and said, "The matter comes from the Lord; so we cannot speak to you bad or good.

51"Behold, Rebekah is before you, take her and go, and let her be the wife of your master's son, as the Lord has spoken."

52 And it came about when Abraham's servant heard their words, that he bowed himself to the ground^Tbefore the Lord. to

53 And the servant brought out^Rarticles of silver and articles of gold, and garments, and gave them to Rebekah; he also gave precious things to her brother and to her mother. Gen. 24:10, 22; Ex. 3:22; 11:2; 12:35

54 Then he and the men who were with him ate and drank and spent the night. When they arose in the morning, he said, "Send me away to my master."

55 But her brother and her mother said, "Let^R the girl stay with us a few days, say ten; afterward she may go." Judg. 19:4

56 And he said to them, "Do not delay me, since the Lord has prospered my way. Send me away that I may go to my master."

57 And they said, "We will call the girl and^Tconsult her wishes." ask her mouth

58 Then they called Rebekah and said to her, "Will you go with this man?" And she said, "I will go."

59 Thus they sent away their sister Rebekah and^Rher nurse with Abraham's servant and his men. Gen. 35:8

²⁵ Lit., show lovingkindness and truth

60 And they blessed Rebekah and said to her,

"May you, our sister,
Become thousands of ten thousands,
And may your descendants possess
The gate of those who hate them."

61 Then Rebekah arose with her maids, and they mounted the camels and followed the man. So the servant took Rebekah and departed.

62 Now Isaac had come from going to Beer-lahai-roi; for he ^Twas living in^Rthe ^TNeg-ev.   *was dwelling* • Gen. 20:1 • South country

63 And Isaac went out^Rto ^Ameditate in the field toward evening; and he lifted up his eyes and looked, and behold, camels were coming.   Josh. 1:8 • *stroll:* meaning uncertain

64 And Rebekah lifted up her eyes, and when she saw Isaac she dismounted from the camel.

65 And she said to the servant, "Who is that man walking in the field to meet us?" And the servant said, "He is my master." Then she took her veil and covered herself.

66 And the servant told Isaac all the things that he had done.

67 Then Isaac brought her into his mother Sarah's tent, and^Rhe took Rebekah, and she became his wife; and ^Rhe loved her; thus Isaac was comforted after ^Rhis mother's death.   Gen. 25:20 • Gen. 29:18 • Gen. 23:1, 2

CHAPTER 25

Abraham Dies—1 Chr. 1:28–33

NOW Abraham took another wife, ^Twhose name was Keturah.   *and her name*

2 And ^Rshe bore to him Zimran and Jokshan and Medan and Midian and Ishbak and Shuah.   1 Chr. 1:32, 33

3 And Jokshan became the father of Sheba and Dedan. And the sons of Dedan were Asshurim and Letushim and Leummim.

4 And the sons of Midian *were* Ephah and Epher and Hanoch and Abida and Eldaah. All these *were* the sons of Keturah.

5 ^RNow Abraham gave all that he had to Isaac;   Gen. 24:35, 36

6 but to the sons of his concubines, Abraham gave gifts while he was still living, and^Rsent them away from his son Isaac eastward, to the land of the east.   Gen. 21:14

7 And these are ^Tall the years of Abraham's life that he lived, ^Rone hundred and seventy-five years.   *the days of* • Gen. 12:4

8 And Abraham breathed his last and died^Rin a ^Tripe old age, an old man and satisfied *with life;* and he was ^Rgathered to his people.   Gen. 15:15; 47:8, 9 • *good* • Gen. 25:17

9 Then his sons Isaac and Ishmael buried him in^Tthe cave of Machpelah, in the field of Ephron the son of Zohar the Hittite, facing Mamre,   Gen. 23:17, 18; 49:29, 30; 50:13

10 ^Rthe field which Abraham purchased from the sons of Heth; there Abraham was buried with Sarah his wife.   Gen. 23:3-16

11 And it came about after the death of Abraham, that God blessed his son Isaac; and Isaac^Tlived by Beer-lahai-roi.   *dwelt*

12 Now these are *the records of* the generations of^RIshmael, Abraham's son, whom Hagar the Egyptian, Sarah's maid, bore to Abraham;   Gen. 16:15

13 and these are the names of the sons of Ishmael, by their names, in the order of their birth: Nebaioth, the first-born of Ishmael, and Kedar and Adbeel and Mibsam

14 and Mishma and Dumah and Massa,

15 Hadad and Tema, Jetur, Naphish and Kedemah.

16 These are the sons of Ishmael and these are their names, by their villages, and by their camps;^Rtwelve princes according to their^Atribes.   Gen. 17:20 • *peoples*

17 And these are the years of the life of Ishmael, ^Rone hundred and thirty-seven years; and he breathed his last and died, and was gathered to his people.   Gen. 16:16

18 And they ^Tsettled from Havilah to Shur which is ^Teast of Egypt ^Tas one goes toward Assyria; he ^Tsettled in defiance of all his relatives.   *dwelt* • *before* • *as you go* • *fell over against*

The Family of Isaac

19 Now these are *the records of*^Rthe generations of Isaac, Abraham's son: Abraham ^Tbecame the father of Isaac;   Matt. 1:2 • *begot*

20 and Isaac was forty years old when he took Rebekah, the daughter of Bethuel the ^TAramean of Paddan-aram, the sister of Laban the ^TAramean, to be his wife.   Syrian

21 And Isaac prayed to the LORD on behalf of his wife, because she was barren; and the LORD ^Tanswered him and Rebekah his wife conceived.   *was entreated of him*

22 But the children struggled together within her; and she said, "If it is so, why then am I *this way?*" So she went to^Rinquire of the LORD.   1 Sam. 9:9; 10:22

23 And the LORD said to her,

"Two nations are in your womb;
^RAnd two peoples shall be separated
  from your body;   Gen. 27:29
And one people shall be stronger than
  the other;
And^Rthe older shall serve the younger."   Gen. 27:40; Mal. 1:2, 3; Rom. 9:12

24 When her days to be delivered were fulfilled, behold, there were twins in her womb.

25 Now the first came forth red, ^Rall over like a hairy garment; and they named him Esau.   Gen. 27:11

26 And afterward his brother came forth with his hand holding on to Esau's heel, so his name was called ²⁶Jacob; and Isaac was sixty years old when she gave birth to them.

27 When the boys grew up, Esau became a skillful hunter, a man of the field; but Jacob was a peaceful man, living in tents.

28 Now Isaac loved Esau, because he had a taste for game; but Rebekah loved Jacob.

²⁶ I.e., one who takes by the heel, or supplants

29 And when Jacob had cooked ᴿstew, Esau came in from the field and he was ᵀfamished;　　　2 Kin. 4:38 • *weary*

30 and Esau said to Jacob, "Please let me have a swallow of ᵀthat red stuff there, for I am ᵀfamished." Therefore his name was called ²⁷Edom.　　　*the red, this red • weary*

31 But Jacob said, "Firstᵀ sell me your ᴿbirthright."　　　*Today • Deut. 21:16, 17; 1 Chr. 5:1, 2*

32 And Esau said, "Behold, I am about to die; so of what *use* then is the birthright to me?"

33 And Jacob said, "Firstᵀ swear to me"; so he swore to him, and ᴿsold his birthright to Jacob.　　　*Today • Heb. 12:16*

34 Then Jacob gave Esau bread and lentil stew; and he ate and drank, and rose and went on his way. Thus Esau despised his birthright.

CHAPTER 26

The Failure of Isaac

Now there was a famine in the land, besides the previous famine that had occurred in the days of Abraham. So Isaac went to Gerar, to Abimelech king of the Philistines.

2 And the Lᴏʀᴅ appeared to him and said, "Do not go down to Egypt; ᵀstay in the land of which I shall tell you.　　　*dwell*

3 "Sojourn in this land andᴿI will be with you and bless you, for to you and to your ᵀdescendants I will give all these lands, and I will establish the oath which I swore to your father Abraham.　　*Gen. 26:24; 28:15; 31:3 • seed*

4 "Andᴿ I will multiply your descendants as the stars of heaven, and will give your ᵀdescendants all these lands; and by your descendants all the nations of the earth ᴬshall be blessed;　　*Gal. 3:8☆ • seed • bless themselves*

5 because Abraham ᵀobeyed Me and kept My charge, My commandments, My statutes and My laws."　　*hearkened to My voice*

6 So Isaac ᵀlived in Gerar.　　　*dwell*

7 When the men of the place asked about his wife, he said, "She is my sister," for he was afraid to say, "my wife," *thinking*, "the men of the place might kill me on account of Rebekah, for she is beautiful."

8 And it came about, when he had been there a long time, that Abimelech king of the Philistines looked out through a window, and saw, and behold, Isaac was caressing his wife Rebekah.

9 Then Abimelech called Isaac and said, "Behold, certainly she is your wife! How then did you say, 'She is my sister'?" And Isaac said to him, "Because I said, 'Lest I die on account of her.' "

10 And Abimelech said, "What is this you have done to us? One of the people might easily have lain with your wife, and you would have brought guilt upon us."

11 So Abimelech charged all the people, saying, "He who ᴿtouches this man or his wife shall surely be put to death."　*Ps. 105:15*

12 Now Isaac sowed in that land, and ᵀreaped in the same year a hundredfold. And ᴿthe Lᴏʀᴅ blessed him,　　*found • Job 42:12*

13 and the man ᴿbecame rich, and continued to grow ᵀricher until he became very ᵀwealthy;　　　*[Prov. 10:22] • great*

14 for he had possessions of flocks ᵀand herds and a great household, so that the Philistines envied him.　　*and possessions of herds*

15 Now all the wells which his father's servants had dug in the days of Abraham his father, the Philistines stopped up ᵀby filling them with earth.　　　*and filled them*

16 Then Abimelech said to Isaac, "Go away from us, for you are ᵀtooᴿpowerful for us."　　*much mightier than we • Ex. 1:9*

17 And Isaac departed from there and camped in the valley of Gerar, and ᵀsettled there.　　　*dwelt*

18 Then Isaac dug again the wells of water which had been dug in the days of his father Abraham, for the Philistines had stopped them up after the death of Abraham; and he gave them the same names which his father had ᵀgiven them.　　*called*

19 But when Isaac's servants dug in the valley and found there a well of ᵀflowing water,　　　*living*

20 the herdsmen of Gerar quarreled with the herdsmen of Isaac, saying, "The water is ours!" So he named the well ᴱEsek, because they contended with him.　　　*contention*

21 Then they dug another well, and they quarreled over it too, so he named it Sitnah.

22 And he moved away from there and dug another well, and they did not quarrel over it; so he named it Rehoboth, for he said, "At last the Lᴏʀᴅ has made room for us, and we shall be fruitful in the land."

23 Then he went up from there to ᴿBeersheba.　　　Gen. 22:19

24 And the Lᴏʀᴅ ᴿappeared to him the same night and said,　　　Gen. 26:2

　"I am the God of your father Abraham;
　Do not fear, for I am with you.
　Iᴿwill bless you, and multiply your ᵀdescendants,
　For the sake of My servant Abraham."　　Gen. 22:17; 26:3, 4 • *seed*

25 So he built an ᴿaltar there, and called upon the name of the Lᴏʀᴅ, and pitched his tent there; and there Isaac's servants dug a well.　　Gen. 12:7, 8; 13:4, 18; Ps. 116:17

26 Then ᴿAbimelech came to him from Gerar with his adviser Ahuzzath, and Phicol the commander of his army.　　　Gen. 21:22

27 And Isaac said to them, "Whyᴿhave you come to me, since you hate me, and have sent me away from you?"　　Judg. 11:7

28 And they said, "We see plainlyᵀthat the Lᴏʀᴅ has been with you; so we said, 'Let there now be an oath between us, *even* between ᵀyou and us, and let us make a covenant with you,　　Gen. 21:22, 23 • *us and you*

29 that you will do us no harm, just as we

²⁷ I.e., red

have not touched you [and have done to you nothing but good, and have sent you away in peace. You are now the [R]blessed of the LORD.' " *and just as we* • Gen. 24:31; Ps. 115:15

30 Then [R]he made them a feast, and they ate and drank. Gen. 19:3

31 And in the morning they arose early and exchanged oaths; then Isaac sent them away and they departed from him in peace.

32 Now it came about on the same day, that Isaac's servants came in and told him about the well which they had dug, and said to him, "We have found water."

33 So he called it Shibah; therefore the name of the city is Beersheba to this day.

The Failure of Esau

34 And when Esau was forty years old [R]he [T]married Judith the daughter of Beeri the Hittite, and Basemath the daughter of Elon the Hittite; Gen. 28:8; 36:2 • *took as wife*

35 and [R]they [28]brought grief to Isaac and Rebekah. Gen. 27:46

CHAPTER 27

Jacob Gains Esau's Blessing

NOW it came about, when Isaac was old, and his eyes were too dim to see, that he called his older son Esau and said to him, "My son." And he said to him, "Here I am."

2 And [T]Isaac said, "Behold now, I am old *and* I do not know the day of my death. *he*

3 "Now then, please take your gear, your quiver and your bow, and go out to the field and [R]hunt game for me; Gen. 25:28

4 and prepare a savory dish for me such as I love, and bring it to me that I may eat, so that my soul may bless you before I die."

5 And Rebekah was listening while Isaac spoke to his son Esau. So when Esau went to the field to hunt for game to bring *home,*

6 [R]Rebekah said to her son Jacob, "Behold, I heard your father speak to your brother Esau, saying, Gen. 25:28

7 'Bring me *some* game and prepare a savory dish for me, that I may eat, and bless you in the presence of the LORD before my death.'

8 "Now therefore, my son, listen to [T]me [T]as I command you. *my voice* • *according to what*

9 "Go now to the flock and [T]bring me two choice [T]kids from there, that I may prepare them *as* a savory dish for your father, such as he loves. *take* • *kids of goats*

10 "Then you shall bring *it* to your father, that he may eat, so that he may bless you before his death."

11 And Jacob [T]answered his mother Rebekah, "Behold, Esau my brother is a hairy man and I am a smooth man. *said to*

12 "Perhaps [R]my father will feel me, then I shall be as a [T]deceiver in his sight; and I shall bring upon myself a curse and not a blessing." Gen. 27:21, 22 • *mocker*

13 But his mother said to him, "Your

curse be on me, my son; only [R]obey my voice, and go, get *them* for me." Gen. 27:8

14 So he went and got *them,* and brought *them* to his mother; and his mother made savory food such as his father loved.

15 Then Rebekah took the [T]best [R]garments of Esau her elder son, which were with her in the house, and put them on Jacob her younger son. *desirable;* or, *choice* • Gen. 27:27

16 And she put the skins of the kids on his hands and on the smooth part of his neck.

17 She also gave the savory food and the bread, which she had made, [T]to her son Jacob. *into the hand of*

18 Then he came to his father and said, "My father." And he said, "Here I am. Who are you, my son?"

19 And Jacob said to his father, "I am Esau your first-born; I have done as you told me. Get up, please, sit and eat of my game, that [T]you may bless me." *your soul* • Gen. 27:4

20 And Isaac said to his son, "How is it that you have *it* so quickly, my son?" And he said, "Because [R]the LORD your God caused *it* to happen to me." Gen. 24:12

21 Then Isaac said to Jacob, "Please come close, that I may feel you, my son, whether you are really my son Esau or not."

22 So Jacob came close to Isaac his father, and he felt him and said, "The voice is the voice of Jacob, but the hands are the hands of Esau."

23 And he did not recognize him, because his hands were [R]hairy like his brother Esau's hands; so he blessed him. Gen. 27:16

24 And he said, "Are you really my son Esau?" And he said, "I am."

25 So he said, "Bring *it* to me, and I will eat of my son's game, that [T]I may bless you." And he brought *it* to him, and he ate; he also brought him wine and he drank. *my soul*

26 Then his father Isaac said to him, "Please come close and kiss me, my son."

27 So he came close and kissed him; and when he smelled the smell of his garments, he [R]blessed him and said, Heb. 11:20

"See, [R]the smell of my son Song 4:11
Is like the smell of a field [R]which the
  LORD has blessed; Ps. 65:10
28 Now may [R]God give you of the dew of
  heaven, Gen. 27:39; Deut. 33:13, 28
And of the [R]fatness of the earth,
And an abundance of grain and new
  wine; Num. 18:12
29 [R]May peoples serve you, Gen. 25:23
And nations bow down to you;
Be master of your brothers,
[R]And may your mother's sons bow
  down to you. Gen. 37:7, 10
Cursed be those who curse you,
And blessed be those who bless you."

30 Now it came about, as soon as Isaac had finished blessing Jacob, and Jacob had hardly gone out from the presence of Isaac

[28] Lit., *were a bitterness of spirit to*

his father, that Esau his brother came in from his hunting.

31 Then he also made savory food, and brought it to his father; and he said to his father, "Let my father arise, and eat of his son's game, that you may bless me."

32 And Isaac his father said to him, "Who[R] are you?" And he said, "I am your son,[R]your first-born, Esau."   Gen. 27:18 • Gen. 25:33, 34

33 Then Isaac trembled violently, and said, "Who[R] was he then that hunted game and brought it to me, so that I ate of all of it before you came, and blessed him?[R]Yes, and he shall be blessed."   Gen. 27:35 • Num. 23:20

34 When Esau heard the words of his father,[R]he cried out with an exceedingly great and bitter cry, and said to his father, "Bless me, even me also, O my father!" [Heb. 12:17]

35 And he said, "Your[R]brother came deceitfully, and has taken away your blessing."   Gen. 27:19

36 Then he said, "Is he not rightly named [R]Jacob, for he has supplanted me these two times? He took away my birthright, and behold, now he has taken away my blessing." And he said, "Have you not reserved a blessing for me?"   Gen. 25:26, 32-34

37 But Isaac answered and said to Esau, "Behold, I have made him your master, and all his [T]relatives I have given to him [T]as servants; and with grain and new wine I have sustained him. Now as for you then, what can I do, my son?"   brothers • for

38 And Esau said to his father, "Do you have only one blessing, my father? Bless me, even me also, O my father." So Esau lifted his voice and[R]wept.   Heb. 12:17

39 Then [R]Isaac his father answered and said to him,   Heb. 11:20

"Behold,[A]away from the fertility of the
   earth shall be your dwelling,
And [A]away from the dew of heaven
   from above.   of • fatness

40 "And by your sword you shall live,
And your brother you shall serve;
But it shall come about [R]when you become restless,
That you shall [T]break his yoke from
   your neck."   2 Kin. 8:20-22 • tear off

41 So Esau bore a grudge against Jacob because of the blessing with which his father had blessed him; and Esau said to himself, "The days of mourning for my father are near; then I will kill my brother Jacob."

42 Now when the words of her elder son Esau were reported to Rebekah, she sent and called her younger son Jacob, and said to him, "Behold your brother Esau is consoling himself concerning you, by planning to kill you.

43"Now therefore, my son,[R]obey my voice, and arise, [T]flee to Haran, to my brother Laban!   Gen. 27:8, 13 • flee for yourself

44"And stay with him a few days, until your brother's fury [T]subsides,   turns away

45 until your brother's anger [T]against you

subsides, and he forgets what you did to him. Then I shall send and get you from there. Why should I be bereaved of you both in one day?"   turns away from you

46 And Rebekah said to Isaac, "I am tired of living because of the daughters of Heth; if Jacob takes a wife from the daughters of Heth, like these, from the daughters of the land, what good will my life be to me?"

CHAPTER 28

So Isaac called Jacob and[R]blessed him and charged him, and said to him, "You[R] shall not take a wife from the daughters of Canaan.   Gen. 27:33 • Gen. 24:3, 4

2"Arise, go to Paddan-aram, to the house of Bethuel your mother's father; and from there take to yourself a wife from the daughters of Laban your mother's brother.

3"And may God Almighty bless you and make you fruitful and multiply you, that you may become a company of peoples.

4"May He also give you the[R]blessing of Abraham, to you and to your [T]descendants with you; that you may possess the land of your[R]sojournings, which God gave to Abraham."   Gen. 12:2; 22:17 • seed • Ps. 39:12

5 Then Isaac sent Jacob away, and he went to Paddan-aram to Laban, son of Bethuel the Aramean, the brother of Rebekah, the mother of Jacob and Esau.

6 Now Esau saw that Isaac had blessed Jacob and sent him away to Paddan-aram, to take to himself a wife from there, and that when he blessed him he charged him, saying, "You[R] shall not take a wife from the daughters of Canaan,"   Gen. 28:1

7 and that Jacob had obeyed his father and his mother and had gone to Paddan-aram.

8 So Esau saw that[R]the daughters of Canaan displeased his father Isaac;   Gen. 24:3

9 and Esau went to Ishmael, and [T]married, besides the wives that he had, Mahalath the daughter of Ishmael, Abraham's son, the sister of Nebaioth.   took for his wife

Jacob's Dream

10 Then Jacob departed from Beersheba and went toward[R]Haran.   Gen. 12:4, 5; 27:43

11 And he [T]came to [T]a certain place and spent the night there, because the sun had set; and he took one of the stones of the place and put it under his head, and lay down in that place.   lighted on • the place

12 And he had a dream, and behold, a ladder was set on the earth with its top reaching to heaven; and behold, the angels of God were ascending and descending on it.

13 And behold, the LORD stood [A]above it and said, "I am the LORD, the God of your father Abraham and the God of Isaac; the land on which you lie, I will give it to you and to your [T]descendants.   beside him • seed

14"Your [T]descendants shall also be like the

dust of the earth, and you shall ^Tspread out to the west and to the east and to the north and to the south; and in you and in your descendants shall all the families of the earth be^Rblessed.   *seed • break through • Gal. 3:8☆*

15 "And behold, I am with you, and ^Rwill keep you wherever you go, and will bring you back to this land; for ^TI will not leave you until I have done what I have ^Tpromised you."   Ps. 121:5, 7, 8 • Num. 23:19 • *spoken to*

16 Then Jacob ^Rawoke from his sleep and said, "Surely the LORD is in this place, and I did not know it."   1 Kin. 3:15; Jer. 31:26

17 And he was afraid and said, "How^R awesome is this place! This is none other than the house of God, and this is the gate of heaven."   [Ps. 68:35]

18 So Jacob rose early in the morning, and took^Rthe stone that he had put ^Tunder his head and set it up as a pillar, and poured oil on its top.   Gen. 28:11; 35:14 • *at his head-place*

19 And he called the name of that place ²⁹Bethel,^R however, ^Tpreviously the name of the city had been Luz.   Judg. 1:23 • *at the first*

20 Then Jacob made a vow, saying, "If God will be with me and will keep me on this journey that I ^Ttake, and will give me ^Tfood to eat and garments to wear,   *go • bread*

21 and I return to my father's house in ^Tsafety, then the LORD will be my God.   *peace*

22 "And this stone, which I have set up as a pillar, ^Rwill be God's house; and ^Rof all that Thou dost give me I will surely give a tenth to Thee."   Gen. 35:7 • [Lev. 27:30]; Deut. 14:22

CHAPTER 29

Jacob's Labors

THEN Jacob ³⁰went on his journey, and came to the land of the sons of the east.

2 And he looked, and ^Tsaw a well in the field, and behold, three flocks of sheep were lying there beside it, for from that well they watered the flocks. Now the stone on the mouth of the well was large.   *behold*

3 When all the flocks were gathered there, they would then roll the stone from the mouth of the well, and water the sheep, and put the stone back in its place on the mouth of the well.

4 And Jacob said to them, "My brothers, where are you from?" And they said, "We are from^RHaran."   Gen. 28:10

5 And he said to them, "Do you know Laban the ^Rson of Nahor?" And they said, "We know *him*."   Gen. 24:24, 29

6 And he said to them, "Is it well with him?" And they said, "It is well, and behold, ^RRachel his daughter is coming with the sheep."   Ex. 2:16

7 And he said, "Behold, it is still high day; it is not time for the livestock to be gathered. Water the sheep, and go, pasture them."

8 But they said, "We cannot, until all the

flocks are gathered, and they roll the stone from the mouth of the well; then we water the sheep."

9 While he was still speaking with them, Rachel came with her father's sheep, for she was a shepherdess.

10 And it came about, when Jacob saw Rachel the daughter of Laban his mother's brother, and the sheep of Laban his mother's brother, that Jacob went up, and rolled the stone from the mouth of the well, and watered the flock of Laban his mother's brother.

11 Then Jacob ^Rkissed Rachel, and lifted his voice and wept.   Gen. 33:4

12 And Jacob told Rachel that he was a relative of her father and that he was Rebekah's son, and she ran and told her father.

13 So it came about, when Laban heard the news of Jacob his sister's son, that he ran to meet him, and embraced him and kissed him, and brought him to his house. Then he related to Laban all these things.

14 And Laban said to him, "Surely you are ^Rmy bone and my flesh." And he stayed with him a month.   Gen. 2:23; Judg. 9:2

15 Then Laban said to Jacob, "Because you are my ^Trelative, should you therefore serve me for nothing? Tell me, what shall your^Rwages be?"   *brother* • Gen. 31:41

16 Now Laban had two daughters; the name of the older was Leah, and the name of the younger was Rachel.

17 And Leah's eyes were weak, but Rachel was beautiful of form and face.

18 Now Jacob^Rloved Rachel, so he said, "I^R will serve you seven years for your younger daughter Rachel."   Gen. 24:67 • Hos. 12:12

19 And Laban said, "It is better that I give her to you than that I should give her to another man; stay with me."

20 So Jacob served seven years for Rachel and they seemed to him but a few days^Rbecause of his love for her.   Song 8:7

21 Then Jacob said to Laban, "Give *me* my wife, for my ^Ttime is completed, that I may ^Rgo in to her."   *days are* • Judg. 15:1

22 And Laban gathered all the men of the place, and made a feast.

23 Now it came about in the evening that he took his daughter Leah, and brought her to him; and *Jacob* went in to her.

24 Laban also gave his maid Zilpah to his daughter Leah as a maid.

25 So it came about in the morning that, behold, it was Leah! And he said to Laban, "What is this you have done to me? Was it not for Rachel that I served with you? Why then have you^Rdeceived me?"   1 Sam. 28:12

26 But Laban said, "It is not ^Tthe practice in our place, to ^Tmarry off the younger before the first-born.   *done thus in • give*

27 "Complete the week of this one, and we will give you the other also for the service

---

²⁹ I.e., the house of God   ³⁰ Lit., *lifted up his feet*

which ^Ryou shall serve with me for another seven years."   Gen. 31:41

28 And Jacob did so and completed his week, and he gave him his daughter Rachel as his wife.

29 Laban also gave his maid Bilhah to his daughter Rachel as her maid.

30 So *Jacob* went in to Rachel also, and indeed^Rhe loved Rachel more than Leah, and he served with ^TLaban for ^Ranother seven years.   Gen. 29:17, 18 • *him* • Gen. 31:41

31 Now the LORD saw that Leah was^Tunloved, and He opened her womb, but Rachel was barren.   *hated*

32 And Leah conceived and bore a son and named him Reuben, for she said, "Because the LORD has seen my affliction; surely now my husband will love me."

33 Then she conceived again and bore a son and said, "Because the LORD has ^Theard that I am ^Tunloved, He has therefore given me this *son* also." So she named him Simeon.   Heb., *shama*, related to Simeon • *hated*

34 And she conceived again and bore a son and said, "Now this time my husband will become ^Tattached to me, because I have borne him three sons." Therefore he was named Levi.   Heb., *lavah*, related to Levi

35 And she conceived again and bore a son and said, "This time I will praise the LORD." Therefore she named him Judah. Then she stopped bearing.   Heb., *Jehudah*

CHAPTER 30

NOW when Rachel saw that she bore Jacob no children, ^Tshe became jealous of her sister; and she said to Jacob, "Give^R me children, or else I die."   *Rachel* • 1 Sam. 1:5, 6

2 Then Jacob's anger burned against Rachel, and he said, "Am I in the place of God, who has^Rwithheld from you the fruit of the womb?"   Gen. 20:18; 29:31

3 And she said, "Here is my maid Bilhah, go in to her, that she may bear on my knees, that through her I too may have children."

4 So^Rshe gave him her maid Bilhah as a wife, and Jacob went in to her.   Gen. 16:3, 4

5 And Bilhah conceived and bore Jacob a son.

6 Then Rachel said, "God has^Tvindicated^R me, and has indeed heard my voice and has given me a son." Therefore she named him ^TDan.   *judged* • Ps. 24; 35; 43:1 • He judged

7 And Rachel's maid Bilhah conceived again and bore Jacob a second son.

8 So Rachel said, "With ^Tmighty wrestlings I have wrestled with my sister, *and* I have indeed prevailed." And she named him Naphtali.   *wrestlings of God*

9 When Leah saw that she had stopped bearing, she took her maid Zilpah and gave her to Jacob as a wife.

10 And Leah's maid Zilpah bore Jacob a son.

11 Then Leah said, "How fortunate!" So she named him^TGad.   *Fortune*

12 And Leah's maid Zilpah bore Jacob a second son.

13 Then Leah said, "Happy^T am I! For women will call me happy." So she named him ^TAsher.   *With my happiness!* • Happy

14 Now in the days of wheat harvest Reuben went and found^Rmandrakes in the field, and brought them to his mother Leah. Then Rachel said to Leah, "Please give me some of your son's mandrakes."   Song 7:13

15 But she said to her, "Is it a small matter for you to take my husband? And would you take my son's mandrakes also?" So Rachel said, "Therefore he may lie with you tonight in return for your son's mandrakes."

16 When Jacob came in from the field in the evening, then Leah went out to meet him and said, "You must come in to me, for I have surely hired you with my son's mandrakes." So he lay with her that night.

17 And God gave heed to Leah, and she conceived and bore Jacob a fifth son.

18 Then Leah said, "God has given me my wages, because I gave my maid to my husband." So she named him Issachar.

19 And Leah conceived again and bore a sixth son to Jacob.

20 Then Leah said, "God has endowed me with a good gift; now my husband will dwell with me, because I have borne him six sons." So she named him Zebulun.

21 And afterward she bore a daughter and named her Dinah.

22 Then ^RGod remembered Rachel, and God gave heed to her and ^Ropened her womb.   1 Sam. 1:19, 20 • Gen. 29:31

23 So she conceived and bore a son and said, "God has taken away my reproach."

24 And she named him Joseph, saying, "May the LORD give me another son."

25 Now it came about when Rachel had borne Joseph, that Jacob said to Laban, "Send^R me away, that I may go to my own place and to my own country.   Gen. 24:54, 56

26 "Give *me* my wives and my children^Rfor whom I have served you, and let me depart; for you yourself know my service which I have ^Trendered you."   Hos. 12:12 • *served*

27 But Laban said to him, "If now ³¹it pleases you, *stay with me;* I have divined ^Rthat the LORD has blessed me on your account."   Gen. 26:24; 39:3, 5; Is. 61:9

28 And he ^Tcontinued, "Name^R me your wages, and I will give it."   *said* • Gen. 29:15

29 But he said to him, "You^T yourself know how I have served you and how your cattle have ^Tfared with me.   Gen. 31:6 • *been*

30 "For you had little before^TI came, and it has ^Tincreased to a multitude; and the LORD has blessed you^Twherever I turned. But now, when shall I provide for my own household also?"   *me* • *broken forth* • *at my foot*

31 So he said, "What shall I give you?"

---

³¹ Lit., *I have found favor in your eyes*

And Jacob said, "You shall not give me anything. If you will do this *one* thing for me, I will again pasture *and* keep your flock:

32 let me pass through your entire flock today, removing from there every ᴿspeckled and spotted sheep, and every black one among the lambs, and the spotted and speckled among the goats; and *such* shall be my wages.   Gen. 31:8

33"So my ᵀhonesty will answer for me later, when you come concerning my ᵀwages. Every one that is not speckled and spotted among the goats and black among the lambs, *if found* with me, will be considered stolen."   *righteousness • wages which are before you*

34 And Laban said, "Good, let it be according to your word."

35 So he removed on that day the striped and spotted male goats and all the speckled and spotted female goats, every one with white in it, and all the black ones among the sheep, and gave them into the ᵀcare of his sons.   /hand

36 And he put *a distance of* ᵀthree days' journey between himself and Jacob, and Jacob fed the rest of Laban's flocks.   60 mi.

37 Then Jacob ᵀtook fresh rods of poplar and almond and plane trees, and peeled white stripes in them, exposing the white which *was* ᵀin the rods.   *took to himself • on*

38 And he set the rods which he had peeled in front of the flocks in the gutters, *even* in the watering troughs, where the flocks came to drink; and they ᵀmated when they came to drink.   *conceived*

39 So the flocks ᵀmated by the rods, and the flocks brought forth striped, speckled, and spotted.   *conceived*

40 And Jacob separated the lambs, and ᵀmade the flocks face toward the striped and all the black in the flock of Laban; and he put his own herds apart, and did not put them with Laban's flock.   *set the faces*

41 Moreover, it came about whenever the ᵀstronger of the flock were mating, that Jacob would place the rods in the sight of the flock in the gutters, so that they might mate by the rods;   *bound one, i.e., firm and compact*

42 but when the flock was feeble, he did not put *them* in; so the feebler were Laban's and the stronger Jacob's.

43 So the man became exceedingly prosperous, and had large flocks and female and male servants and camels and donkeys.

CHAPTER 31

Jacob's Flight

Nᴼᵂ ᵀJacob heard the words of Laban's sons, saying, "Jacob has taken away all that was our father's, and from what belonged to our father he has made all this wealth."   *he*

2 And Jacob saw the ³²attitude of Laban, and behold, it was not *friendly* toward him as formerly.

3 Then the LᴼᴿD said to Jacob, "Returnᴿ to the land of your fathers and to your relatives, and I will be with you."   Gen. 32:9

4 So Jacob sent and called Rachel and Leah to his flock in the field,

5 and said to them, "Iᴿ see your father's ᵀattitude, that it is not *friendly* toward me as formerly, butᴿthe God of my father has been with me.   Gen. 31:2 • *face* • Is. 41:10; Heb. 13:5

6"Andᴿyou know that I have served your father with all my strength.   Gen. 30:29

7"Yet your father has ᴿcheated me and changed my wages ten times; however, God did not allow him to hurt me.   Gen. 29:25

8"Ifᶜʰhe spoke thus, 'The speckled shall be your wages,' then all the flock brought forth speckled; and if he spoke thus, 'The striped shall be your wages,' then all the flock brought forth striped.   Gen. 30:32

9"Thus God has taken away your father's livestock and given *them* to me.

10"And it came about at the time when the flock were mating that I lifted up my eyes and saw in a dream, and behold, the male goats which were ᵀmating *were* striped, speckled, and mottled.   *leaping upon the flock*

11"Then the angel of God said to me in the dream, 'Jacob,' and I said, 'Here I am.'

12"And he said, 'Lift up, now, your eyes and see *that* all the male goats which are ᵀmating are striped, speckled, and mottled; for ᴿI have seen all that Laban has been doing to you.   *leaping upon the flock* • Ex. 3:7

13 'I am the God *of* Bethel, where you anointed a pillar, where you made a vow to Me; now arise,ᵀleave this land, and return to the land of your birth.'"   *go out from*

14 And Rachel and Leah answered and said to him, "Do we still have any portion or inheritance in our father's house?

15"Are we not reckoned by him as foreigners? For he has sold us, and has also entirely consumed our purchase price.

16"Surely all the wealth which God has taken away from our father belongs to us and our children; now then, do whatever God has said to you."

17 Then Jacob arose and put his children and his wives upon camels;

18 and he drove away all his livestock and all his property which he had gathered, his acquired livestock which he had gathered in Paddan-aram,ᴿto go to the land of Canaan to his father Isaac.   Gen. 35:27

19 When Laban had gone to shear his flock, then Rachel stole the ᵀhouseholdᴿidols that were her father's.   Heb., *teraphim* • Hos. 3:4

20 And Jacob deceived Laban the Aramean, by not telling him that he was fleeing.

21 So he fled with all that he had; and he arose and crossed the *Euphrates* River, and set his face toward the hill country of ᴿGilead.   Gen. 37:25

22 When it was told Laban on the third day that Jacob had fled,

³²Lit., *face*

23 then he took his᾽kinsmen with him, and pursued him *a distance of*᾽seven days' journey; and he overtook him in the hill country of Gilead. *brothers* • 140 mi.

24 And God came to Laban the Aramean in a dream of the night, and said to him, "Be᾽ careful that you do not speak to Jacob either good or bad." *Take heed to yourself*

25 And Laban caught up with Jacob. Now Jacob had pitched his tent in the hill country, and Laban with his᾽kinsmen camped in the hill country of Gilead. *brothers*

26 Then Laban said to Jacob, "What have you done by deceiving me and carrying away my daughters like captives of the sword?

27"Why did you flee secretly and deceive me, and did not tell me, so that I might have sent you away with joy and with songs, with ᴿtimbrel and with lyre; *steal me* • Ex. 15:20

28 and did not allow me᾽to kiss my sons and my daughters? Now you have done foolishly. *Gen. 31:55*

29"It is in ᵀmy power to do you harm, but the God of your father spoke to me last night, saying, 'Be careful not to speak either good or bad to Jacob.' *the power of my hand*

30"And now you have indeed gone away because you longed greatly for your father's house; *but* why did you steal my gods?"

31 Then Jacob answered and said to Laban, "Because I was afraid, for I said, 'Lest you would take your daughters from me by force.'

32"The one with whom you find your gods shall not live; in the presence of our kinsmen point out what is yours among my belongings and take *it* for yourself." For Jacob did not know that Rachel had stolen them.

33 So Laban went into Jacob's tent, and into Leah's tent, and into the tent of the two maids, but he did not find *them.* Then he went out of Leah's tent and entered Rachel's tent.

34 Now Rachel had taken the household idols and put them in the camel's saddle, and she sat on them. And Laban felt through all the tent, but did not find *them.*

35 And she said to her father, "Let not my lord be angry that I cannot᾽rise before you, for the manner of women is upon me." So he searched, but did not find the᾽household idols. *Lev. 19:32* • Heb., *teraphim* • Gen. 31:19

36 Then Jacob became angry and contended with Laban; and Jacob answered and said to Laban, "What is my transgression? What is my sin, that you have hotly pursued me?

37"Though you have felt through all my goods, what have you found of all your household goods? Set *it* here before my ᵀkinsmen and your ᵀkinsmen, that they may decide between us two. *brothers*

38"These twenty years I *have been* with you; your ewes and your female goats have not miscarried, nor have I eaten the rams of your flocks.

39"That which was torn *of beasts* I did not bring to you; I bore the loss of it myself. You required it of my hand *whether* stolen by day or stolen by night.

40"*Thus* I was: by day the᾽heat consumed me, and the frost by night, and my sleep fled from my eyes. *drought*

41"These twenty years I have been in your house; I served you fourteen years for your two daughters, and six years for your flock, and you changed my wages ten times.

42"If the God of my father, the God of Abraham, and the fear of Isaac, had not been for me, surely now you would have sent me away empty-handed.ᴿGod has seen my affliction and the toil of my hands, so He rendered judgment last night." *Ex. 3:7*

43 Then Laban answered and said to Jacob, "The daughters are my daughters, and the children are my children, andᴿthe flocks are my flocks, and all that you see is mine. But what can I do this day to these my daughters or to their children whom they have borne? *Gen. 31:1*

44"So now come, let us make a covenant, ᵀyou and I, and let it be a witness between ᵀyou and me." *I and you* • *me and you*

45 Then Jacob tookᴿa stone and set it up *as* a pillar. *Gen. 28:18; Josh. 24:26, 27*

46 And Jacob said to his ᵀkinsmen, "Gather stones." So they took stones and made a heap, and they ate there by the heap. *brothers*

47 Now Laban ᴿcalled it ³³Jegar-sahadutha, but Jacob called it ³⁴Galeed. *Josh. 22:34*

48 And Laban said, "This heap is a witness between ᵀyou and me this day." Therefore it was named Galeed; *me and you*

49 and ³⁵Mizpah, for he said, "May the LORD watch between you and me when we are ᵀabsent one from the other. *hidden*

50"If you mistreat my daughters, or if you take wives besides my daughters, *although* no man is with us, see,ᴿGod is witness between᾽you and me." *Jer. 29:23* • *me and you*

51 And Laban said to Jacob, "Behold this heap and behold the pillar which I have set between᾽you and me. *me and you*

52"This heap is a witness, and the pillar is a witness, that I will not pass by this heap to you for harm, and you will not pass by this heap and this pillar to me, for harm.

53"Theᴿ God of Abraham and the God of Nahor, the God of their father, ᴿjudge between us." So Jacob swore by the fear of his father Isaac. *Gen. 28:13* • *Gen. 16:5*

54 Then Jacob offered a sacrifice on the mountain, and called his ᵀkinsmen to᾽the meal; and they ate the meal and spent the night on the mountain. *brothers* • *eat bread*

55 ᵀAnd early in the morning Laban arose, and kissed his sons and his daughters and blessed them. Then Laban departed and returned to his place. *Ch. 32:1 in Heb.*

³³ I.e., the heap of witness, in Aramaic
³⁴ I.e., the heap of witness, in Hebrew
³⁵ I.e., the watchtower

CHAPTER 32

Jacob Fights with the Angel

Now as Jacob went on his way, ^Rthe angels of God met him.   2 Kin. 6:16, 17; [Ps. 34:7]

2 And Jacob said when he saw them, "This is God's ³⁶camp." So he named that place ³⁷Mahanaim.   Josh. 21:38; 2 Sam. 2:8

3 Then Jacob sent messengers before him to his brother Esau in the land of ^RSeir, the ^Tcountry of Edom.   Gen. 14:6; 33:14 · *field*

4 He also commanded them saying, "Thus you shall say to my lord Esau: 'Thus says your servant Jacob, "I have sojourned with Laban, and ^Rstayed until now;   Gen. 31:41

5 and ^RI have oxen and donkeys *and* flocks and male and female servants; and I have sent to tell my lord, ^Rthat I may find favor in your sight." ' "   Gen. 30:43 · Gen. 33:8

6 And the messengers returned to Jacob, saying, "We came to your brother Esau, and furthermore ^Rhe is coming to meet you, and four hundred men are with him."   Gen. 33:1

7 Then Jacob was greatly afraid and distressed; and he divided the people who were with him, and the flocks and the herds and the camels, into two companies.   Gen. 32:11

8 for he said, "If Esau comes to the one company and attacks it, then the company which is left will escape."   *smites*

9 And Jacob said, "O ^RGod of my father Abraham and God of my father Isaac, O Lord, who didst say to me, 'Return to your country and to your relatives, and I will ^Tprosper you,'   Gen. 28:13 · *do good with you*

10 ^TI am unworthy of all the lovingkindness and of all the faithfulness which Thou hast shown to Thy servant; for with my staff *only* I crossed this Jordan, and now I have become two companies.   *I am less than all*

11 "Deliver^R me, I pray, from the hand of my brother, from the hand of Esau; for I fear him, lest he come and ^Tattack me, the mothers with the children.   Ps. 59:1, 2 · *smite*

12 "For Thou didst say, 'I will surely prosper you, and make your descendants as the sand of the sea, which cannot be numbered for multitude.' "   *do good with · seed*

13 So he spent the night there. Then he ^Tselected from what he had with him a ^Rpresent for his brother Esau: *took* · Gen. 43:11

14 two hundred female goats and twenty male goats, two hundred ewes and twenty rams,

15 thirty milking camels and their colts, forty cows and ten bulls, twenty female donkeys and ten male donkeys.

16 And he delivered *them* into the hand of his servants, every drove by itself, and said to his servants, "Pass on before me, and put a space between droves."

17 And he commanded the one in front, saying, "When my brother Esau meets you and asks you, saying, 'To whom do you belong, and where are you going, and to whom do these *animals* in front of you belong?'

18 then you shall say, '*These* belong to your servant Jacob; it is a present sent to my lord Esau. And behold, he also is behind us.' "

19 Then he commanded also the second and the third, and all those who followed the droves, saying, "After this manner you shall speak to Esau when you find him;

20 and you shall say, 'Behold, your servant Jacob also is behind us.' " For he said, "I will appease him with the present that goes before me. Then afterward I will see his face; perhaps he will accept me."

21 So the present passed on before him, while he himself spent that night in the camp.

22 Now he arose that same night and took his two wives and his two maids and his eleven children, and crossed the ford of the ^RJabbok.   Deut. 3:16; Josh. 12:2

23 And he took them and sent them across the stream. And he sent across whatever he had.

24 Then Jacob was left alone, and a man wrestled with him until daybreak.

25 And when he saw that he had not prevailed against him, he touched the socket of his thigh; so the socket of Jacob's thigh was dislocated while he wrestled with him.

26 Then he said, "Let me go, for the dawn is breaking." But he said, "I^R will not let you go unless you bless me."   Hos. 12:4

27 So he said to him, "What is your name?" And he said, "Jacob."

28 And ^Rhe said, "Your name shall no longer be Jacob, but ³⁸Israel; for you have striven with God and with men and have prevailed."   Gen. 35:10; 1 Kin. 18:31

29 Then ^RJacob asked him and said, "Please tell me your name." But he said, "Why is it that you ask my name?" And he blessed him there.   Judg. 13:17, 18

30 So Jacob named the place ³⁹Peniel, for *he said*, "I have seen God face to face, yet my ^Tlife has been preserved."   *soul*

31 Now the sun rose upon him just as he crossed over ^RPenuel, and he was limping on his thigh.   Judg. 8:8

32 Therefore, to this day the sons of Israel do not eat the sinew of the hip which is on the socket of the thigh, because he touched the socket of Jacob's thigh in the sinew of the hip.

CHAPTER 33

Jacob Makes Peace with Esau

Then Jacob lifted his eyes and looked, and behold, ^REsau was coming, and four hundred men with him. So he divided the children ^Tamong Leah and Rachel and the two maids.   Gen. 32:6 · *to*

³⁶ Or, *company*
³⁷ I.e., Two Camps, or, Two Companies
³⁸ I.e., he who strives with God, or, God strives
³⁹ I.e., the face of God

2 And he put the maids and their children [T]in front, and Leah and her children next, and Rachel and Joseph last.   *first*

3 But he himself passed on ahead of them and bowed down to the ground seven times, until he came near to his brother.

4 Then Esau ran to meet him and embraced him, and[R]fell on his neck and kissed him, and they wept.   Gen. 45:14, 15

5 And he lifted his eyes and saw the women and the children, and said, "Who[A] are these with you?" So he said, "The[R] children whom God has graciously given your servant."   *What relation are these to you?* • Is. 8:18

6 Then the maids came near [T]with their children, and they bowed down.   *they and*

7 And Leah likewise came near with her children, and they bowed down; and afterward Joseph came near with Rachel, and they bowed down.

8 And he said, "What do you mean by all this company which I have met?" And he said, "To find favor in the sight of my lord."

9 But Esau said, "I have plenty, my brother; let what you have be your own."

10 And Jacob said, "No, please, if now I have found favor in your sight, then take my present from my hand, for I see your face as one sees the face of God, and you have received me favorably.

11 "Please take my gift which has been brought to you, because God has dealt graciously with me, and because I have plenty." Thus he urged him and he took *it.*

12 Then [T]Esau said, "Let us take our journey and go, and I will go before you."   *he*

13 But he said to him, "My lord knows that the children are frail and that the flocks and herds which are nursing are [A]a care to me. And if they are driven hard one day, all the flocks will die.   *upon me*

14 "Please let my lord pass on before his servant; and I will proceed at my leisure, according to the pace of the cattle that are before me and according to the pace of the children, until I come to my lord at Seir."

15 And Esau said, "Please let me leave with you some of the people who are with me." But he said, "[40]What need is there? Let me find favor in the sight of my lord."

16 So Esau returned that day on his way to Seir.

17 And Jacob journeyed to [41]Succoth[R], and built for himself a house, and made booths for his livestock, therefore the place is named Succoth.   Josh. 13:27; Judg. 8:5, 14

[R]**18** Now Jacob came safely to the city of Shechem, which is in the land of Canaan, when he came from Paddan-aram, and camped before the city.   Josh. 24:1; Judg. 9:1

19 And he bought the piece of land where he had pitched his tent from the hand of the sons of Hamor, Shechem's father, for one hundred [T]pieces of money.   Heb., *qesitah*

20 Then he erected there an altar, and called it [42]El-Elohe-Israel.

CHAPTER 34

The Defilement of Dinah

N OW [R]Dinah the daughter of Leah, whom she had borne to Jacob, went out to [T]visit the daughters of the land.   Gen. 30:21 • *see*

2 And when Shechem the son of Hamor the Hivite, the prince of the land, saw her, he took her and lay with her by force.

3 And [T]he was deeply attracted to Dinah the daughter of Jacob, and he loved the girl and spoke tenderly to her.   *his soul clung*

4 So Shechem [R]spoke to his father Hamor, saying, "Get me this young girl for a wife."   Judg. 14:2

5 Now Jacob heard that he had defiled Dinah his daughter; but his sons were with his livestock in the field, so Jacob kept silent until they came in.

6 Then Hamor the father of Shechem went out to Jacob to speak with him.

7 Now the sons of Jacob came in from the field when they heard *it;* and the men were grieved, and they were very angry because he had done a [T]disgraceful thing in Israel [T]by lying with Jacob's daughter, for such a thing ought not to be done.   *senseless* • *to lie*

8 But Hamor spoke with them, saying, "The soul of my son Shechem longs for your daughter; please give her to him [T]in marriage.   *for a wife*

9 "And intermarry with us; give your daughters to us, and take our daughters for yourselves.

10 "Thus you shall [T]live with us, and the land shall be *open* before you; live and trade in it, and acquire property in it."   *dwell*

11 Shechem also said to her father and to her brothers, "If I find favor in your sight, then I will give whatever you say to me.

12 "Ask me ever so much bridal payment and gift, and I will give according as you say to me; but give me the girl in marriage."

13 But Jacob's sons answered Shechem and his father Hamor, with deceit, and spoke to them, because he had defiled Dinah their sister.

14 And they said to them, "We cannot do this thing, to give our sister to [R]one who is uncircumcised, for that would be a disgrace to us.   Gen. 17:14

15 "Only on this *condition* will we consent to you: if you will become like us, in that every male of you be circumcised,

16 then we will give our daughters to you, and we will take your daughters for ourselves, and we will [T]live with you and become one people.   *dwell*

17 "But if you will not listen to us to be circumcised, then we will take our daughter and go."

18 Now their words seemed [T]reasonable to Hamor and Shechem, Hamor's son.   *good*

[40] Lit., *"Why this?"*   [41] I.e., booths
[42] I.e., God, the God of Israel

19 And the young man did not delay to do the thing, because he was delighted with Jacob's daughter. Now he was more respected than all the household of his father.

20 So Hamor and his son Shechem came to the ᴿgate of their city, and spoke to the men of their city, saying, Ruth 4:1; 2 Sam. 15:2

21 "These men are friendly with us; therefore let them ᵀlive in the land and trade in it, for behold, the land is large enough for them. Let us take their daughters in marriage, and give our daughters to them. *dwell*

22 "Only on this *condition* will the men consent to us to ᵀlive with us, to become one people: that every male among us be circumcised as they are circumcised. *dwell*

23 "Will not their livestock and their property and all their animals be ours? Only let us consent to them, and they will ᵀlive with us." *dwell*

24 And all who went out of the gate of his city listened to Hamor and to his son Shechem, and every male was circumcised, all who went out of the gate of his city.

25 Now it came about on the third day, when they were in pain, that two of Jacob's sons, ᴿSimeon and Levi, Dinah's brothers, each took his sword and came upon the city unawares, and killed every male. Gen. 49:5-7

26 And they killed Hamor and his son Shechem with the edge of the sword, and took Dinah from Shechem's house, and went forth.

27 Jacob's sons came upon the slain and looted the city, because they had defiled their sister.

28 They took their flocks and their herds and their donkeys, and that which was in the city and that which was in the field;

29 and they captured and looted all their wealth and all their little ones and their wives, even all that *was* in the houses.

30 Then Jacob said to Simeon and Levi, "You have brought trouble on me, by ᴿmaking me odious among the inhabitants of the land, among the Canaanites and the Perizzites; and ᴵmy men being few in number, they will gather together against me and ᵀattack me and I shall be destroyed, I and my household." Ex. 5:21 • *I, few in number* • *smite*

31 But they said, "Should he ᴬtreat our sister as a harlot?" *make*

CHAPTER 35

The Devotion at Bethel

THEN God said to Jacob, "Arise, go up to Bethel, and ᵀlive there; and make an altar there to God, who appeared to you when you fled from your brother Esau." *dwell*

2 So Jacob said to his household and to all who were with him, "Put away the foreign gods which are among you, and purify yourselves, and change your garments;

3 and let us arise and go up to Bethel; and I will make an altar there to God, who answered me in the day of my distress, and has been with me wherever I have gone."

4 So they gave to Jacob all the foreign gods which they had, and the rings which were in their ears; and Jacob hid them under the oak which was near Shechem.

5 As they journeyed, there was ᴬa ᴿgreat terror upon the cities which were around them, and they did not pursue the sons of Jacob. *a terror of God* • Ex. 15:16; 23:27

6 So Jacob came to ᴿLuz (that is, Bethel), which is in the land of Canaan, he and all the people who were with him. Gen. 28:19

7 And he built an altar there, and called the place ᵀEl-bethel, because there God had revealed Himself to him, when he fled ᵀfrom his brother. the God of Bethel • *from the face of*

8 Now Deborah, Rebekah's nurse, died, and she was buried below Bethel under the oak; it was named ⁴³Allon-bacuth.

9 Then God appeared to Jacob again when he came from Paddan-aram, and He ᴿblessed him. Gen. 32:29

10 And ᴿGod said to him, Gen. 17:5; 32:28
"Your name is Jacob;
You shall no longer be called Jacob,
But Israel shall be your name."
Thus He called ᵀhim Israel. *his name*

11 God also said to him,
"I am ᵀGod Almighty; Heb., *El Shaddai*
ᴿBe fruitful and multiply; Gen. 17:1; 28:3
A nation and a company of nations
shall ᴬcome from you, *come into being*
And kings shall come forth from you.

12 "And ᴿthe land which I gave to Abraham and Isaac,
I will give it to you,
And I will give the land to your ᵀdescendants after you." Ex. 32:13 • *seed*

13 Then God went up from him in the place where He had spoken with him.

14 And Jacob set up a pillar in the place where He had spoken with him, a pillar of stone, and he poured out a ᴬlibation on it; he also poured oil on it. *drink offering*

15 So Jacob named the place where God had spoken with him, ⁴⁴Bethel. Gen. 28:19

The Deaths of Rachel and Isaac

16 Then they journeyed from Bethel; and when there was still some distance to go to ᴿEphrath, Rachel began to give birth and she suffered severe labor. Ruth 4:11; Mic. 5:2

17 And it came about when she was in severe labor that the midwife said to her, "Do not fear, for now you have *another* son."

18 And it came about as her soul was departing (for she died), that she named him ⁴⁵Ben-oni; but his father called him ⁴⁶Benjamin.

19 So Rachel died and was buried on the way to Ephrath (that is, Bethlehem).

20 And Jacob set up a pillar over her

---

⁴³ I.e., oak of weeping   ⁴⁴ I.e., the house of God
⁴⁵ I.e., the son of my sorrow
⁴⁶ I.e., the son of the right hand

grave; that is the ^Rpillar of Rachel's grave to this day.   1 Sam. 10:2

21 Then Israel journeyed on and pitched his tent beyond the tower of ^cEder.   *flock*

22 And it came about while Israel was dwelling in that land, that ^RReuben went and lay with Bilhah his father's concubine; and Israel heard *of it.*   Gen. 49:4; 1 Chr. 5:1

Now there were twelve sons of Jacob—

23 ^Rthe sons of Leah: Reuben, Jacob's firstborn, then Simeon and Levi and Judah and Issachar and Zebulun;   Gen. 29:31-35; 30:18-20

24 ^Rthe sons of Rachel: Joseph and Benjamin;   Gen. 30:22-24; 35:18

25 and ^Rthe sons of Bilhah, Rachel's maid: Dan and Naphtali;   Gen. 30:5-8

26 and the sons of Zilpah, Leah's maid: Gad and Asher. These are the sons of Jacob who were born to him in Paddan-aram.

27 And Jacob came to his father Isaac at Mamre of Kiriath-arba (that is, Hebron), where Abraham and Isaac had sojourned.

28 Now the days of Isaac were ^Rone hundred and eighty years.   Gen. 25:26

29 And Isaac breathed his last and died, and was gathered to his people, an ^Rold man ^Tof ripe age; and his sons Esau and Jacob buried him.   Gen. 15:15 • *and satisfied with days*

CHAPTER 36

The History of Esau—1 Chr. 1:35–42

Now these are *the records of* the generations of ^REsau (that is, Edom).   Gen. 25:30

2 Esau ^Rtook his wives from the daughters of Canaan: Adah the daughter of Elon the Hittite, and ^ROholibamah the daughter of Anah and the ^Rgranddaughter of Zibeon the Hivite;   Gen. 28:9 • Gen. 36:25 • Gen. 36:24

3 also Basemath, Ishmael's daughter, the sister of Nebaioth.

4 And Adah bore ^REliphaz to Esau, and Basemath bore Reuel,   1 Chr. 1:35

5 and Oholibamah bore Jeush and Jalam and Korah. These are the sons of Esau who were born to him in the land of Canaan.

6 Then Esau took his wives and his sons and his daughters and all ^This household, and his livestock and all his cattle and all his goods which he had acquired in the land of Canaan, and went to *another* land away from his brother Jacob.   *the souls of his house*

7 For their property had become too great for them to ^Tlive together, and the land where they sojourned could not sustain them because of their livestock.   *dwell*

8 So Esau lived in the hill country of ^RSeir; Esau is ^REdom.   Gen. 32:3 • Gen. 36:1, 19

9 These then are *the records of* the generations of Esau the father of ^Tthe Edomites in the hill country of Seir.   *Edom*

10 These are the names of Esau's sons: Eliphaz the son of Esau's wife Adah, Reuel the son of Esau's wife Basemath.

11 And the sons of Eliphaz were Teman, Omar, Zepho and Gatam and Kenaz.

12 And Timna was a concubine of Esau's son Eliphaz and she bore ^RAmalek to Eliphaz. These are the sons of Esau's wife Adah.   Ex. 17:8-16; Num. 24:20; Deut. 25:17-19

13 And these are the sons of Reuel: Nahath and Zerah, Shammah and Mizzah. These were the sons of Esau's wife Basemath.

14 And these were the sons of Esau's wife Oholibamah, the daughter of Anah and the granddaughter of Zibeon: she bore to Esau, Jeush and Jalam and Korah.   Gr., *son*

15 These are the chiefs of the sons of Esau. The sons of Eliphaz, the first-born of Esau, are chief Teman, chief Omar, chief Zepho, chief Kenaz,

16 chief Korah, chief Gatam, chief Amalek. These are the chiefs ^Tdescended from Eliphaz in the land of Edom; these are the sons of Adah.   *of Eliphaz*

17 And these are the sons of Reuel, Esau's son: chief Nahath, chief Zerah, chief Shammah, chief Mizzah. These are the chiefs descended from Reuel in the land of Edom; these are the sons of Esau's wife Basemath.

18 And these are the sons of Esau's wife Oholibamah: chief Jeush, chief Jalam, chief Korah. These are the chiefs ^Tdescended from Esau's wife Oholibamah, the daughter of Anah.   *of Oholibamah, Esau's wife*

19 These are the sons of Esau (that is, Edom), and these are their chiefs.

20 These are the sons of Seir ^Rthe Horite, the inhabitants of the land: Lotan and Shobal and Zibeon and Anah,   1 Chr. 1:38-42

21 and Dishon and Ezer and Dishan. These are the chiefs descended from the Horites, the sons of Seir in the land of Edom.

22 And the sons of Lotan were Hori and Hemam; and Lotan's sister was Timna.

23 And these are the sons of Shobal: ^TAlvan and Manahath and Ebal, ^TShepho and Onam.   In 1 Chr. 1:40, *Alian* • In 1 Chr. 1:40, *Shephi*

24 And these are the sons of Zibeon: Aiah and Anah—he is the Anah who found the hot springs in the wilderness when he was pasturing the donkeys of his father Zibeon.

25 And these are the children of Anah: Dishon, and Oholibamah, the daughter of Anah.

26 And these are the sons of ^TDishon: ^THemdan and Eshban and Ithran and Cheran.   Heb., *Dishan* • In 1 Chr. 1:41, *Hamran*

27 These are the sons of Ezer: Bilhan and Zaavan and ^TAkan.   In 1 Chr. 1:42, *Jaakan*

28 These are the sons of Dishan: Uz and Aran.

29 These are the chiefs ^Tdescended from the Horites: chief Lotan, chief Shobal, chief Zibeon, chief Anah,   *of the Horites*

30 chief Dishon, chief Ezer, chief Dishan. These are the chiefs descended from the Ho-

rites, according to their *various* chiefs in the land of Seir.   *of the Horites*

31 Now these are the kings who reigned in the land of Edom before any^Rking reigned over the sons of Israel.   Gen. 17:6, 16; 35:11

32 Bela the son of Beor reigned in Edom, and the name of his city was Dinhabah.

33 Then Bela died, and Jobab the son of Zerah of Bozrah became king in his place.

34 Then Jobab died, and Husham of the land of the Temanites became king in his place.

35 Then Husham died, and Hadad the son of Bedad, who 'defeated Midian in the field of Moab, became king in his place; and the name of his city was Avith.   *smote*

36 Then Hadad died, and Samlah of Masrekah became king in his place.

37 Then Samlah died, and Shaul of Rehoboth on the *Euphrates* River became king in his place.

38 Then Shaul died, and Baal-hanan the son of Achbor became king in his place.

39 Then Baal-hanan the son of Achbor died, and Hadar became king in his place; and the name of his city was Pau; and his wife's name was Mehetabel, the daughter of Matred, daughter of Mezahab.

40 Now these are the names of the chiefs descended from Esau, according to their families *and* their localities, by their names: chief Timna, chief Alvah, chief Jetheth,

41 chief Oholibamah, chief Elah, chief Pinon,

42 chief Kenaz, chief Teman, chief Mibzar,

43 chief Magdiel, chief Iram. These are the chiefs of Edom (that is, Esau, the father of the Edomites), according to their habitations in the land of their possession.

CHAPTER 37

Joseph's Family Sins Against Him

Now Jacob lived in the land where his father had sojourned, in the land of Canaan.

2 These are *the records of* the generations of Jacob.

Joseph, when^Rseventeen years of age, was pasturing the flock with his brothers while he was *still* a youth, along with the sons of Bilhah and the sons of Zilpah, his father's wives. And Joseph brought back a bad report about them to their father.   Gen. 41:46

3 Now Israel loved Joseph more than all his sons, because he was the son of his old age; and he made him a ⁴⁷varicolored tunic.

4 And his brothers saw that their father loved him more than all his brothers; and so they^Rhated him and could not speak to him ⁴⁸on friendly terms.   Gen. 27:41; 1 Sam. 17:28

5 Then Joseph^Thad^Ra dream, and when he told it to his brothers, they hated him even more.   *dreamed* • Gen. 28:12; 31:10, 11, 24

6 And he said to them, "Please listen to this dream which I have^Thad;   *dreamed*

7 for behold, we were binding sheaves in the field, and lo, my sheaf rose up and also stood erect; and behold, your sheaves gathered around and bowed down to my sheaf."

8 Then his brothers said to him, "Are^R you actually going to reign over us? Or are you really going to rule over us?" So they hated him even more for his dreams and for his words.   Gen. 49:26; Deut. 33:16

9 Now he^Thad still another dream, and related it to his brothers, and said, "Lo, I have^Thad still another dream; and behold, the sun and the moon and eleven stars were bowing down to me."   *dreamed*

10 And he related *it* to his father and to his brothers; and his father rebuked him and said to him, "What is this dream that you have^Thad? Shall I and your mother and your brothers actually come to bow ourselves down before you to the ground?"   *dreamed*

11 And his brothers were jealous of him, but his father kept the saying *in mind*.

12 Then his brothers went to pasture their father's flock in Shechem.

13 And Israel said to Joseph, "Are not your brothers pasturing *the flock* in Shechem? Come, and I will send you to them." And he said to him, "I^Twill go."   *Behold me*

14 Then he said to him, "Go now and see about the welfare of your brothers and the welfare of the flock; and bring word back to me." So he sent him from the valley of^RHebron, and he came to Shechem.   Judg. 1:10

15 And a man found him, and behold, he was wandering in the field; and the man asked him, "What are you looking for?"

16 And he said, "I am looking for my brothers; please tell me where they are pasturing *the flock*."

17 Then the man said, "They have moved from here; for I heard *them* say, 'Let us go to Dothan.'" So Joseph went after his brothers and found them at Dothan.

18 ^AWhen they saw him from a distance and before he came close to them, they plotted against him to put him to death.   *And*

19 And they said to one another, "Here comes this dreamer!

20 "Now then, come and let us kill him and throw him into one of the pits; and we will say, 'A wild beast devoured him.' Then let us see what will become of his dreams!"

21 But^RReuben heard *this* and rescued him out of their hands and said, "Let us not^Ttake his life."   Gen. 42:22 • *smite his soul*

22 Reuben further said to them, "Shed no blood. Throw him into this pit that is in the wilderness, but do not lay hands on him"— that he might rescue him out of their hands, to restore him to his father.

23 So it came about, when Joseph^Treached

⁴⁷ Or, *full-length robe*   ⁴⁸ Lit., *in peace*

his brothers, that they stripped Joseph of his tunic, the varicolored tunic that was on him;   *came to · full-length robe*

24 and they took him and threw him into the pit. Now the pit was empty, without any water in it.

25 Then they sat down to eat a meal. And as they raised their eyes and looked, behold, a caravan of Ishmaelites was coming from Gilead, with their camels bearing aromatic gum and balm and myrrh, on their way to bring *them* down to Egypt.   *bread · going*

26 And Judah said to his brothers, "What profit is it for us to kill our brother and cover up his blood?   Gen. 37:20

27 "Come and let us sell him to the Ishmaelites and not lay our hands on him; for he is our brother, our *own* flesh." And his brothers listened *to him*.   Gen. 42:21

28 Then some Midianite traders passed by, so they pulled *him* up and lifted Joseph out of the pit, and sold him to the Ishmaelites for twenty *shekels* of silver. Thus they brought Joseph into Egypt.   Acts 7:9 · *Joseph*

29 Now Reuben returned to the pit, and behold, Joseph was not in the pit; so he tore his garments.   Gen. 37:34; 44:13

30 And he returned to his brothers and said, "The boy is not *there*; as for me, where am I to go?"   Gen. 42:13, 36

31 So they took Joseph's tunic, and slaughtered a male goat, and dipped the tunic in the blood;   Gen. 37:3, 23

32 and they sent the varicolored tunic and brought it to their father and said, "We found this; please examine *it* to *see* whether it is your son's tunic or not."   *recognize*

33 Then he examined it and said, "It is my son's tunic. A wild beast has devoured him; Joseph has surely been torn to pieces!"

34 So Jacob tore his clothes, and put sackcloth on his loins, and mourned for his son many days.   Gen. 37:29

35 Then all his sons and all his daughters arose to comfort him, but he refused to be comforted. And he said, "Surely I will go down to Sheol in mourning for my son." So his father wept for him. Gen. 25:8; 35:29; 42:38

36 Meanwhile, the Midianites sold him in Egypt to Potiphar, Pharaoh's officer, the captain of the bodyguard.   *Medanites*

CHAPTER 38
Joseph's Family Sins with the Canaanites

AND it came about at that time, that Judah departed from his brothers, and visited a certain Adullamite, whose name was Hirah.   *went down · turned aside to ·* Josh. 15:35

2 And Judah saw there a daughter of a certain Canaanite whose name was Shua; and he took her and went in to her.

3 So she conceived and bore a son and he named him Er.   Gen. 46:12; Num. 26:19

4 Then she conceived again and bore a son and named him Onan.   Gen. 46:12

5 And she bore still another son and named him Shelah; and it was at Chezib that she bore him.   Num. 26:20 · *when*

6 Now Judah took a wife for Er his first-born, and her name *was* Tamar.

7 But Er, Judah's first-born, was evil in the sight of the LORD, so the LORD took his life.   Gen. 46:12; Num. 26:19; 1 Chr. 2:3

8 Then Judah said to Onan, "Go in to your brother's wife, and perform your duty as a brother-in-law to her, and raise up offspring for your brother."   Matt. 22:24 · *seed*

9 And Onan knew that the offspring would not be his; so it came about that when he went in to his brother's wife, he wasted his seed on the ground, in order not to give offspring to his brother.   *seed*

10 But what he did was displeasing in the sight of the LORD; so He took his life also.

11 Then Judah said to his daughter-in-law Tamar, "Remain a widow in your father's house until my son Shelah grows up"; for he thought, "I *am afraid* that he too may die like his brothers." So Tamar went and lived in her father's house.   *said · Lest he also die*

12 Now after a considerable time Shua's daughter, the wife of Judah, died; and when the time of mourning was ended, Judah went up to his sheepshearers at Timnah, he and his friend Hirah the Adullamite.

13 And it was told to Tamar, "Behold, your father-in-law is going up to Timnah to shear his sheep."   *saying, Behold ·* Judg. 14:1

14 So she removed her widow's garments and covered *herself* with a [49]veil, and wrapped herself, and sat in the gateway of Enaim, which is on the road to Timnah; for she saw that Shelah had grown up, and she had not been given to him as a wife.

15 When Judah saw her, he thought she *was* a harlot, for she had covered her face.

16 So he turned aside to her by the road, and said, "Here now, let me come in to you"; for he did not know that she was his daughter-in-law. And she said, "What will you give me, that you may come in to me?"

17 He said, therefore, "I will send you a kid from the flock." She said, moreover, "Will you give a pledge until you send *it*?"

18 And he said, "What pledge shall I give you?" And she said, "Your seal and your cord, and your staff that is in your hand." So he gave *them* to her, and went in to her, and she conceived by him.   Gen. 38:25; 41:42

19 Then she arose and departed, and removed her veil and put on her widow's garments.   *removed from herself · shawl*

20 When Judah sent the kid by his friend the Adullamite, to receive the pledge from the woman's hand, he did not find her.

21 And he asked the men of her place, saying, "Where is the temple prostitute who was by the road at Enaim?" But they said,

[49] Or, *shawl*

"There has been no temple prostitute here."

22 So he returned to Judah, and said, "I did not find her; and furthermore, the men of the place said, 'There has been no temple prostitute here.' "

23 Then Judah said, "Let her keep them, lest we become a laughingstock. After all, I sent this kid, but you did not find her."

24 Now it was about three months later that Judah was informed, "Your[T] daughter-in-law Tamar has played the harlot, and behold, she is also with child by harlotry." Then Judah said, "Bring her out and[R]let her be burned!"   *saying, Your · Lev. 21:9*

25 It was while she was being brought out that she sent to her father-in-law, saying, "I am with child by the man to whom these things belong." And she said, "Please[R]examine and see, whose signet ring and cords and staff are these?"   Gen. 37:32

26 And Judah recognized *them*, and said, "She is more righteous than I, inasmuch as I did not give her to my son Shelah." And he did not have relations with her again.

27 And it came about at the time she was giving birth, that behold, there were[R]twins in her womb.   Gen. 25:24-26

28 Moreover, it took place while she was giving birth, one put out a hand, and the midwife took and tied a scarlet *thread* on his hand, saying, "This one came out first."

29 But it came about as he drew back his hand, that behold, his brother came out. Then she said, "What a breach you have made for yourself!" So he was named [50]Perez.[R]   Gen. 46:12; Ruth 4:12

30 And afterward his brother came out who had the scarlet *thread* on his hand; and he was named [51]Zerah.[R]   1 Chr. 2:4

CHAPTER 39

Joseph's Test with the Egyptian Woman

NOW Joseph had been taken down to Egypt; and Potiphar, an Egyptian officer of Pharaoh, the captain of the bodyguard, bought him[T]from the Ishmaelites, who had taken him down there.   *from the hand of*

2 And the LORD was with Joseph, so he became a[A]successful man. And he was in the house of his master, the Egyptian.   *prosperous*

3 Now his master saw that the LORD was with him and *how* the LORD[R]caused all that he did to prosper in his hand.   Ps. 1:3

4 So Joseph found favor in his sight, and became his personal servant; and he made him overseer over his house, and[R]all that he owned he put in his[T]charge.   Gen. 24:2 · *hand*

5 And it came about that from the time he made him overseer in his house, and over all that he owned, the LORD blessed the Egyptian's house on account of Joseph; thus the LORD's blessing was upon all that he owned, in the house and in the field.

6 So he left everything he owned in Jo-

seph's[T]charge; and with him *there* he did not[T]concern himself with anything except the food which he ate. Now Joseph was handsome in form and appearance.   *hand · know*

7 And it came about after these events that his master's wife looked with desire at Joseph, and she said, "Lie with me."

8 But he refused and said to his master's wife, "Behold, with me *here*, my master[T]does not concern himself with anything in the house, and he has put all that he owns in my charge.   *does not know what is in the house*

9"There[A] is no one greater in this house than I, and he has withheld nothing from me except you, because you are his wife. How then could I do this great evil, and [R]sin against God?"   *He is not greater · Ps. 51:4*

10 And it came about as she spoke to Joseph day after day, that he did not listen to her to lie beside her, *or* be with her.

11 Now it happened one day that he went into the house to do his work, and none of the men of the household was there inside.

12 And she caught him by his garment, saying, "Lie with me!" And he left his garment in her hand and fled, and went outside.

13 When she saw that he had left his garment in her hand, and had fled outside,

14 she called to the men of her household, and said to them, "See, he has brought in a Hebrew to us to make sport of us; he came in to me to lie with me, and I screamed.

15"And it came about when he heard that I raised my voice and [52]screamed, that he left his garment beside me and fled, and went outside."

16 So she[T]left his garment beside her until his master came home.   *let . . . lie beside*

17 Then she [R]spoke to him [T]with these words, "The[T] Hebrew slave, whom you brought to us, came in to me to make sport of me;   Ex. 23:1 · *according to · saying, "The*

18 and it happened as I raised my voice and [T]screamed, that he left his garment beside me and fled outside."   *called out*

19 Now it came about when his master heard the words of his wife, which she spoke to him, saying, "This is what your slave did to me," that his anger burned.

20 So Joseph's master took him and [R]put him into the jail, the place where the king's prisoners were confined; and he was there in the jail.   Gen. 40:3; Ps. 105:18

21 But[T]the LORD was with Joseph and extended kindness to him, and gave him favor in the sight of the chief jailer.   Ps. 105:19

22 And the chief jailer committed to Joseph's[T]charge all the prisoners who were in the jail; so that whatever was done there, he was[T]responsible *for it*.   *hand · the doer*

23 The chief jailer did not supervise anything under [T]Joseph's charge because the LORD was with him; and whatever he did, the LORD made to prosper.   *his hand*

---

[50] I.e., a breach   [51] I.e., a dawning or brightness
[52] Lit., *called out*

CHAPTER 40

Joseph's Test with the Egyptian Society

THEN it came about after these things the cupbearer and the baker for the king of Egypt offended their lord, the king of Egypt.

2 And Pharaoh was ^Rfurious with his two officials, the chief cupbearer and the chief baker.   Prov. 16:14

3 So he put them in confinement in the house of the ^Rcaptain of the bodyguard, in the jail, the *same* place where Joseph was imprisoned.   Gen. 39:1, 20

4 And the captain of the bodyguard put Joseph in charge of them, and he ^Ttook care of them; and they were in confinement for ^Tsome time.   *ministered to • days*

5 Then the cupbearer and the baker for the king of Egypt, who were confined in jail, both had a dream the same night, each man with his *own* dream *and* each dream with its *own* interpretation.

6 ^AWhen Joseph came to them in the morning and observed them, ^Tbehold, they were dejected.   *And • and behold*

7 And he asked Pharaoh's officials who were with him in confinement in his master's house, "Why ^Tare your faces so sad today?"   *saying, Why*

8 Then they said to him, "We have had a dream and there is no one to interpret it." Then Joseph said to them, "Do not interpretations belong to God? Tell *it* to me, please."

9 So the chief cupbearer told his dream to Joseph, and said to him, "In my dream, behold, *there was* a vine in front of me;

10 and on the vine *were* three branches. And as it was budding, its blossoms came out, *and* its clusters produced ripe grapes.

11 "Now Pharaoh's cup was in my hand; so I took the grapes and squeezed them into Pharaoh's cup, and I put the cup into Pharaoh's ^Thand."   *palm*

12 Then Joseph said to him, "This is the ^Rinterpretation of it: the three branches are three days;   Dan. 2:36; 4:18, 19

13 within three more days Pharaoh will ⁵³lift up your head and restore you to your ^Toffice; and you will put Pharaoh's cup into his hand according to your former custom when you were his cupbearer.   *place*

14 "Only ^Tkeep me in mind when it goes well with you, and please do me a kindness by mentioning me to Pharaoh, and get me out of this house.   *remember me with yourself*

15 "For ^RI was in fact kidnapped from the land of the Hebrews, and even here I have done nothing that they should have put me into the ^Adungeon."   Gen. 37:26-28 • *pit*

16 When the chief baker saw that he had interpreted favorably, he said to Joseph, "I also *saw* in my dream, and behold, *there were* three baskets of white bread on my head;

17 and in the top basket *there were* some of all ^Tsorts of baked food for Pharaoh, and the birds were eating them out of the basket on my head."   *food for Pharaoh made by a baker*

18 Then Joseph answered and said, "This is its interpretation: the three baskets are three days;

19 within three more days Pharaoh will lift up your head from you and will hang you on a tree; and the birds will eat your flesh off you."

20 Thus it came about on the third day, *which was* ^RPharaoh's birthday, that he made a feast for all his servants; ^Rand he lifted up the head of the chief cupbearer and the head of the chief baker among his servants.   Matt. 14:6 • 2 Kin. 25:27; Jer. 52:31

21 And he restored the chief cupbearer to his office, and ^Rhe put the cup into Pharaoh's ^Thand;   *wine-pouring* • Gen. 40:13 • *palm*

22 but ^Rhe hanged the chief baker, just as Joseph had interpreted to them.   Esth. 7:10

23 Yet the chief cupbearer did not remember Joseph, but ^Rforgot him.   Job 19:14

CHAPTER 41

Joseph's Test with Pharaoh's Dreams

NOW it happened at the end of two full years that Pharaoh had a dream, and behold, he was standing by the Nile.

2 And lo, from the Nile there came up seven ^Rcows, sleek and ^Tfat; and they grazed in the ^Rmarsh grass.   *fat of flesh* • Job 8:11

3 Then behold, seven other cows came up after them from the Nile, ugly and ^Tgaunt, and they stood by the *other* cows on the bank of the Nile.   *lean of flesh*

4 And the ugly and ^Tgaunt cows ate up the seven sleek and fat cows. Then Pharaoh awoke.   *lean of flesh*

5 And he fell asleep and dreamed a second time; and behold, seven ears of grain came up on a single stalk, plump and good.

6 Then behold, seven ears, thin and scorched by the east wind, sprouted up after them.

7 And the thin ears swallowed up the seven plump and full ears. Then Pharaoh awoke, and behold, *it was* a dream.

8 Now it came about in the morning that ^Rhis spirit was troubled, so he sent and called for all the magicians of Egypt, and all its wise men. And Pharaoh told them his ^Tdreams, but there was no one who could interpret them to Pharaoh.   Dan. 2:1 • *dream*

9 Then the chief cupbearer spoke to Pharaoh, saying, "I would make mention today of ^Tmy *own* ^Roffenses.   Gen. 40:14, 23 • *sins*

10 "Pharaoh was furious with his servants, and ^Rhe put me in confinement in the house of the captain of the bodyguard, *both* me and the chief baker.   Gen. 39:20

11 "And we had a dream on the same night, he and I; each of us dreamed according to the interpretation of his *own* dream.

12 "Now a Hebrew youth *was* with us

⁵³ Or possibly, *forgive you*

41

there, a servant of the captain of the bodyguard, and we related *them* to him, and he interpreted our dreams for us. To each one he interpreted according to his *own* dream.

13 "And it came about that just as he interpreted for us, so it happened; he restored me in my office, but he hanged him." *place*

14 Then Pharaoh sent and called for Joseph, and they hurriedly brought him out of the dungeon; and when he had shaved himself and changed his clothes, he came to Pharaoh. Ps. 105:20 • Dan. 2:25

15 And Pharaoh said to Joseph, "I have had a dream, but no one can interpret it; and I have heard it said about you, that when you hear a dream you can interpret it."

16 Joseph then answered Pharaoh, saying, "It is not in me; God will give Pharaoh a favorable answer." *Apart from me* • Gen. 40:8

17 So Pharaoh spoke to Joseph, "In my dream, behold, I was standing on the bank of the Nile;

18 and behold, seven cows, fat and sleek came up out of the Nile; and they grazed in the marsh grass. *fat of flesh*

19 "And lo, seven other cows came up after them, poor and very ugly and gaunt, such as I had never seen for ugliness in all the land of Egypt; *lean of flesh • badness*

20 and the lean and ugly cows ate up the first seven fat cows. *bad*

21 "Yet when they had devoured them, it could not be detected that they had devoured them; for they were just as ugly as before. Then I awoke. *entered their inward parts*

22 "I saw also in my dream, and behold, seven ears, full and good, came up on a single stalk;

23 and lo, seven ears, withered, thin, *and* scorched by the east wind, sprouted up after them;

24 and the thin ears swallowed the seven good ears. Then I told it to the magicians, but there was no one who could explain it to me." Is. 8:19; Dan. 4:7 • *soothsayer priests*

25 Now Joseph said to Pharaoh, "Pharaoh's dreams are one *and the same*; God has told to Pharaoh what He is about to do.

26 "The seven good cows are seven years; and the seven good ears are seven years; the dreams are one *and the same*. *dream is*

27 "And the seven lean and ugly cows that came up after them are seven years, and the seven thin ears scorched by the east wind shall be seven years of famine.

28 "It is as I have spoken to Pharaoh: God has shown to Pharaoh what He is about to do. *That is the thing which I spoke* • Gen. 41:25, 32

29 "Behold, seven years of great abundance are coming in all the land of Egypt;

30 and after them seven years of famine will come, and all the abundance will be forgotten in the land of Egypt; and the famine will ravage the land. Ps. 105:16 • *arise • destroy*

31 "So the abundance will be unknown in the land because of that subsequent famine; for it *will be* very severe.

32 "Now as for the repeating of the dream to Pharaoh twice, *it means* that the matter is determined by God, and God will quickly bring it about. Gen. 41:25, 28

33 "And now let Pharaoh look for a man discerning and wise, and set him over the land of Egypt. Gen. 41:39

34 "Let Pharaoh take action to appoint overseers in charge of the land, and let him exact a fifth *of the produce* of the land of Egypt in the seven years of abundance.

35 "Then let them gather all the food of these good years that are coming, and store up the grain for food in the cities under Pharaoh's authority, and let them guard *it*.

36 "And let the food become as a reserve for the land for the seven years of famine which will occur in the land of Egypt, so that the land may not perish during the famine."

Joseph's Exaltation over Egypt

37 Now the proposal seemed good to Pharaoh and to all his servants. *word*

38 Then Pharaoh said to his servants, "Can we find a man like this, in whom is a divine spirit?" [Job 32:8]; Dan. 4:8, 9, 18; 5:11, 14

39 So Pharaoh said to Joseph, "Since God has informed you of all this, there is no one so discerning and wise as you are. Gen. 41:33

40 "You shall be over my house, and according to your command all my people shall do homage; only in the throne I will be greater than you." Acts 7:10 • *mouth • kiss*

41 And Pharaoh said to Joseph, "See I have set you over all the land of Egypt."

42 Then Pharaoh took off his signet ring from his hand, and put it on Joseph's hand, and clothed him in garments of fine linen, and put the gold necklace around his neck.

43 And he had him ride in his second chariot; and they proclaimed before him, "Bow the knee!" And he set him over all the land of Egypt. *the second ... which was his*

44 Moreover, Pharaoh said to Joseph, "Though I am Pharaoh, yet without your permission no one shall raise his hand or foot in all the land of Egypt." *you no one*

45 Then Pharaoh named Joseph [54]Zaphenath-paneah; and he gave him Asenath, the daughter of Potiphera priest of On, as his wife. And Joseph went forth over the land of Egypt. *Heliopolis* • Jer. 43:13; Ezek. 30:17

46 Now Joseph was thirty years old when he [55]stood before Pharaoh, king of Egypt. And Joseph went out from the presence of Pharaoh, and went through all the land of Egypt. Gen. 37:2

47 And during the seven years of plenty the land brought forth abundantly.

48 So he gathered all the food of *these* seven years which occurred in the land of Egypt, and placed the food in the cities; he

[54] Probably Egyptian for "God speaks; he lives"
[55] Or, *entered the service of*

placed in every city the food from its own surrounding fields.

49 Thus Joseph stored up grain[T]in great abundance like the sand of the sea, until he stopped [T]measuring *it,* for it was [A]beyond measure.   *very much · numbering · without number*

50 Now before the year of famine came, [R]two sons were born to Joseph, whom Asenath, the daughter of Potiphera priest of [56]On, bore to him.   Gen. 48:5

51 And Joseph named the first-born [57]Manasseh, "For," *he said,* "God has made me forget all my trouble and all my father's household."

52 And he named the second [58]Ephraim, "For," *he said,* "God[R]has made me fruitful in the land of my affliction."   Gen. 17:6; 28:3

53 When the seven years of plenty which had been in the land of Egypt came to an end,

54 and[R]the seven years of famine began to come, just as Joseph had said, then there was famine in all the lands; but in all the land of Egypt there was bread.   Acts 7:11

55 So when all the land of Egypt was famished, the people cried out to Pharaoh for bread; and Pharaoh said to all the Egyptians, "Go to Joseph;[R]whatever he says to you, you shall do."   John 2:5

56 When the famine was *spread* over all the face of the earth, then Joseph opened all [T]the storehouses, and sold to the Egyptians; and the famine was severe in the land of Egypt.   *that which was in them*

57 And *the people of* all the earth came to Egypt to buy grain from Joseph, because the famine was severe in all the earth.

CHAPTER 42

Joseph's Brothers Visit Egypt

NOW [R]Jacob saw that there was grain in Egypt, and Jacob said to his sons, "Why are you staring at one another?"   Acts 7:12

2 And he said, "Behold,[R]I have heard that there is grain in Egypt; go down there and buy *some* for us[T]from that place, so that we may live and not die."   Acts 7:12 · *from there*

3 Then ten brothers of Joseph went down to buy grain from Egypt.

4 But Jacob did not send Joseph's brother[R]Benjamin with his brothers, for he said, "I[T]am[R]afraid that harm may befall him."   Gen. 35:24 · *Lest harm* · Gen. 42:38

5 So the sons of Israel came to buy grain among those who were coming,[R]for the famine was in the land of Canaan *also.* Acts 7:11

6 Now [R]Joseph was the ruler over the land; he was the one who sold to all the people of the land. And Joseph's brothers came and[R]bowed down to him with *their* faces to the ground.   Gen. 41:41, 55 · Is. 60:14

7 When Joseph saw his brothers he recognized them, but he disguised himself to them and [R]spoke to them harshly. And he said to them, "Where have you come

from?" And they said, "From the land of Canaan, to buy food."   Gen. 42:30

8 But Joseph had recognized his brothers, although they did not recognize him.

9 And Joseph remembered the dreams which he had about them, and said to them, "You are spies; you have come to look at the undefended parts of our land."

10 Then they said to him, "No, my lord, but your servants have come to buy food.

11 "We are all sons of one man; we are honest men, your servants are not spies."

12 Yet he said to them, "No, but you have come to look at the[T]undefended parts of our land!"   *nakedness of the land*

13 But they said, "Your servants are twelve brothers *in all,* the sons of one man in the land of Canaan; and behold, the youngest is with[R]our father today, and[R]one is no more."   Gen. 43:7 · Gen. 37:30; 42:32; 44:20

14 And Joseph said to them, "It is as I said [T]to you, you are spies;   *to you, saying*

15 by this you will be tested: by the life of Pharaoh, you shall not go from this place unless your youngest brother comes here!

16 "Send one of you that he may get your brother, while you remain confined, that your words may be tested, whether there is [R]truth in you. But if not, by the life of Pharaoh, surely you are spies."   Gen. 42:11

17 So he put them all together in[R]prison for three days.   Gen. 40:4, 7

18 Now Joseph said to them on the third day, "Do this and live, for I fear God:

19 if you are honest men, let one of your brothers be confined in your prison; but as for *the rest of* you, go, carry grain for the famine of your households,

20 and[R]bring your youngest brother to me, so your words may be verified, and you will not die." And they did so.   Gen. 42:34; 43:5

21 Then they said to one another, "Truly we are guilty concerning our brother, because we saw the distress of his soul when he pleaded with us, yet we would not listen; therefore this distress has come upon us."

22 And Reuben answered them, saying, "Did I not tell[T]you, 'Do not sin against the boy'; and you would not listen? Now comes the reckoning for his blood."   *you saying*

23 They did not know, however, that Joseph understood, for there was an interpreter between them.

24 And he turned away from them and [R]wept. But when he returned to them and spoke to them, he took Simeon from them and bound him before their eyes. Gen. 43:30

25 [R]Then Joseph gave orders to fill their bags with grain and to restore every man's money in his sack, and to give them provisions for the journey. And thus it was done for them.   [Rom. 12:17, 20, 21; 1 Pet. 3:9]

26 So they loaded their donkeys with their grain, and departed from there.

[56] Or, *Heliopolis*   [57] I.e., making to forget
[58] I.e., fruitfulness

27 And as one *of them* opened his sack to give his donkey fodder at the lodging place, he saw his [R]money; and behold, it was in the mouth of his sack.   Gen. 43:21, 22

28 Then he said to his brothers, "My money has been returned, and behold, it is even in my sack." And their hearts sank, and they *turned* trembling to one another, saying, "What is this that God has done to us?"

29 When they came to their father Jacob in the land of Canaan, they told him all that had happened to them, saying,

30 "The man, the lord of the land, [R]spoke harshly with us, and took us for spies of the country.   Gen. 42:7

31 "But we said to him, 'We are [R]honest men; we are not spies.   Gen. 42:11

32 'We are twelve brothers, sons of our father; one is no more, and the youngest is with our father today in the land of Canaan.'

33 "And the man, the lord of the land, said to us, 'By [R]this I shall know that you are honest men: leave one of your brothers with me and take *grain for* the famine of your households, and go.   Gen. 42:19, 20

34 'But bring your youngest brother to me that I may know that you are not spies, but honest men. I will give your brother to you, and you may [T]trade in the land.' "   Gen. 34:10

35 Now it came about as they were emptying their sacks, that behold, [R]every man's bundle of money *was* in his sack; and when they and their father saw their bundles of money, they were dismayed.   Gen. 43:12, 15, 21

36 And their father Jacob said to them, "You have [R]bereaved me of my children: Joseph is no more, and Simeon is no more, and you would take Benjamin; all these things are against me."   Gen. 43:14

37 Then Reuben spoke to his father, saying, "You may put my two sons to death if I do not bring him *back* to you; put him in my [T]care, and I will return him to you."   *hand*

38 But [J]Jacob said, "My son shall not go down with you; for his brother is dead, and he alone is left. [R]If harm should befall him on the journey [T]you are taking, then you will bring my gray hair down to Sheol in sorrow."   *he · Gen. 42:4 · on which you are going*

CHAPTER 43

Joseph's Brothers' Second Journey to Egypt

NOW the famine was severe in the land.

2 So it came about when they had finished eating the grain which they had brought from Egypt, that their father said to them, "Go back, buy us a little food."

3 Judah spoke to him, however, saying, "The [R]man solemnly warned [T]us, 'You shall not see my face unless your brother is with you.'   Gen. 43:5; 44:23 · *us, saying*

4 "If you send our brother with us, we will go down and buy you food.

5 "But if you do not send *him*, we will not go down; for the man said to us, 'You shall

not see my face unless your brother is with you.' "

6 Then Israel said, "Why did you treat me so badly [T]by telling the man whether you still had *another* brother?"   *to tell*

7 But they said, "The man questioned particularly about us and our relatives, saying, 'Is your father still alive? Have you *another* brother?' So we answered his questions. Could we possibly know that he would say, 'Bring your brother down'?"

8 And Judah said to his father Israel, "Send the lad with me, and we will arise and go, [R]that we may live and not die, we as well as you and our little ones.   Gen. 42:2

9 "I myself will be surety for him; [T]you may hold me responsible for him. If I do not bring him *back* to you and set him before you, then let me bear the blame before you forever.   *from my hand you may require him*

10 "For if we had not delayed, surely by now we could have returned twice."

11 Then their father Israel said to them, "If *it must be* so, then do this: take some of the best products of the land in your bags, and carry down to the man as a present, a little balm and a little honey, aromatic gum and myrrh, pistachio nuts and almonds.

12 "And take double *the* money in your hand, and take back in your hand the money that was returned in the mouth of your sacks; perhaps it was a mistake.

13 "Take your brother also, and arise, return to the man;

14 and may [T]God Almighty grant you compassion in the sight of the man, that he may release to you your other brother and Benjamin. And as for me, if I am bereaved of my children, I am bereaved."   *Heb., El Shaddai*

15 So the men took [R]this present, and they took double *the* money in their hand, and Benjamin; then they arose and went down to Egypt and stood before Joseph.   Gen. 43:11

16 When Joseph saw Benjamin with them, he said to his [R]house steward, "Bring the men into the house, and slay *an animal* and make ready; for the men are to dine with me at noon."   Gen. 44:1

17 So the man did as Joseph said, and brought the men to Joseph's house.

18 Now the men were afraid, because they were brought to Joseph's house; and they said, "It *is* because of the money that was returned in our sacks the first time that we are being brought in, that he may seek occasion against us and fall upon us, and take us for slaves with our donkeys."

19 So they came near to Joseph's house steward, and spoke to him at the entrance of the house,

20 and said, "Oh, my lord, we indeed came down the first time to buy food,

21 and it came about when we came to the lodging place, that we opened our sacks, and behold, each man's money was in the mouth of his sack, our money in [T]full. So we have brought it back in our hand.   *its weight*

22"We have also brought down other money in our hand to buy food; we do not know who put our money in our sacks."

23 And he said, "[59]Be at ease, do not be afraid.[R]Your God and the God of your father has given you treasure in your sacks; [I] had your money." Then he brought Simeon out to them.　　　Gen. 42:28 · *your money had come to me*

24 Then the man brought the men into Joseph's house and [R]gave them water, and they [R]washed their feet; and he gave their donkeys fodder.　　　Gen. 18:4; 19:2; 24:32 · Luke 7:44

25 So they prepared the present [T]for Joseph's coming at noon; for they had heard that they were to eat a meal there.　　*until*

26 When Joseph came home, they brought into the house to him the present which was in their hand and [R]bowed to the ground before him.　　　Gen. 37:7, 10

27 Then he asked them about their welfare, and said, "Is your old father well, of whom you spoke? Is he still alive?"

28 And they said, "Your servant our father is well; he is still alive." [R]And they bowed down in homage.　　　Gen. 37:7, 10

29 As he lifted his eyes and saw his brother Benjamin, his mother's son, he said, "Is this[R]your youngest brother, of whom you spoke to me?" And he said, "May God be gracious to you, my son."　　　Gen. 42:13

30 And Joseph hurried *out* for [R]he was deeply stirred over his brother, and he sought a *place* to weep; and he entered his chamber and wept there.　　　1 Kin. 3:26

31 Then he washed his face, and came out; and he [R]controlled himself and said, "Serve[T]the meal."　　　Gen. 45:1 · *Set on bread.*

32 So they served him by himself, and them by themselves, and the Egyptians, who ate with him, by themselves; because the Egyptians could not eat bread with the Hebrews, for that is [T]loathsome[R] to the Egyptians.　　　*an abomination* · Gen. 46:34; Ex. 8:26

33 Now they were seated before him, the first-born according to his birthright and the youngest according to his youth, and the men looked at one another in astonishment.

34 And he took portions to them from[T]his own table; but Benjamin's portion was five times as much as any of theirs. So they feasted and drank freely with him.　　*his face*

CHAPTER 44

THEN[R]he commanded his house steward, saying, "Fill the men's sacks with food, as much as they can carry, and put each man's money in the mouth of his sack.　　Gen. 42:25

2"And put my cup, the silver cup, in the mouth of the sack of the youngest, and his money for the grain." And he did [T]as Joseph had told *him*.　　　*according to the word*

3 As soon as it was light, the men were sent away, they with their donkeys.

4 They had *just* gone out of[R]the city, *and* were not far off, when Joseph said to his

house steward, "Up, follow the men; and when you overtake them, say to them, 'Why have you repaid evil for good?　　Gen. 44:13

5 'Is not this the one from which my lord drinks, and which he indeed uses for divination? You have done wrong in doing this.'"

6 So he overtook them and spoke these words to them.

7 And they said to him, "Why does my lord speak such words as these? Far be it from your servants to do such a thing.

8"Behold, [T]the money which we found in the mouth of our sacks we have brought back to you from the land of Canaan. How then could we steal silver or gold from your lord's house?　　　Gen. 43:21

9"With[R] whomever of your servants it is found, let him die, and we also will be my lord's slaves."　　　Gen. 31:32 · Gen. 44:16

10 So he said, "Now let it also be according to your words; he with whom it is found shall be my slave, and *the rest of* you shall be innocent."

11 Then they hurried, each man lowered his sack to the ground, and each man opened his sack.

12 And he searched, beginning with the oldest and ending with the youngest, and the cup was found in Benjamin's sack.

13 Then they[R]tore their clothes, and when each man loaded his donkey, they returned to[R]the city.　　　Num. 14:6; 2 Sam. 1:11 · Gen. 44:4

14 When Judah and his brothers came to Joseph's house, he was still there, and[T]they fell to the ground before him.　　Gen. 37:7, 10

15 And Joseph said to them, "What is this deed that you have done? Do you not know that such a man as I can indeed practice [T]divination?"　　　Gen. 44:5

16 So Judah said, "What can we say to my lord? What can we speak? And how can we justify ourselves? God has found out the iniquity of your servants; behold, we are my lord's slaves, both we and the one in whose [T]possession the cup has been found."　　*hand*

17 But he said, "Far be it from me to do this. The man in whose possession the cup has been found, he shall be my slave; but as for you, go up in peace to your father."

18 Then Judah approached him, and said, "Oh my lord, may your servant please speak a word in my lord's ears, and [T]do not be angry with your servant; for you are equal to Pharaoh.　　　*let not your anger burn against*

19"My[R] lord asked his servants, saying, 'Have you a father or a brother?'　　Gen. 43:7

20"And we said to my lord, 'We have an old father and a little child of *his* old age. Now his brother is dead, so he alone is left of his mother, and his father loves him.'

21"Then you said to your servants, 'Bring[R] him down to me, that I may set my eyes on him.'　　　Gen. 42:15, 20

22"But we said to my lord, 'The lad cannot

[59] Lit., *Peace be to you*

leave his father, for if he should leave his father, his father would die.'

23"You said to your servants, however, 'Unless your youngest brother comes down with you, you shall not see my face again.'

24"Thus it came about when we went up to your servant my father, we told him the words of my lord.

25"And our father said, 'Go back, buy us a little food.' Gen. 43:2

26"But we said, 'We cannot go down. If our youngest brother is with us, then we will go down; for we cannot see the man's face unless our youngest brother is with us.'

27"And your servant my father said to us, 'You know that my wife bore me two sons;

28 and the one went out from me, and I said, "Surely he is torn in pieces," and I have not seen him since. Gen. 37:31-35

29 'And if you take this one also from me, and harm befalls him, you will bring my gray hair down to Sheol in sorrow.' my face

30"Now, therefore, when I come to your servant my father, and the lad is not with us, since his life is bound up in the lad's life,

31 it will come about when he sees that the lad is not with us, that he will die. Thus your servants will bring the gray hair of your servant our father down to Sheol in sorrow. Gen. 44:29

32"For your servant became surety for the lad to my father, saying, 'If I do not bring him back to you, then let me bear the blame before my father forever.' Gen. 43:9

33"Now, therefore, please let your servant remain instead of the lad a slave to my lord, and let the lad go up with his brothers.

34"For how shall I go up to my father if the lad is not with me, lest I see the evil that would overtake my father?" find

CHAPTER 45

THEN Joseph could not control himself before all those who stood by him, and he cried, "Have everyone go out from me." So there was no man with him when Joseph made himself known to his brothers. stood

2 And he wept so loudly that the Egyptians heard it, and the household of Pharaoh heard of it. gave forth his voice in weeping

3 Then Joseph said to his brothers, "I am Joseph! Is my father still alive?" But his brothers could not answer him, for they were dismayed at his presence. Acts 7:13

4 Then Joseph said to his brothers, "Please come closer to me." And they came closer. And he said, "I am your brother Joseph, whom you sold into Egypt. near

5"And now do not be grieved or angry with yourselves, because you sold me here; for God sent me before you to preserve life.

6"For the famine has been in the land these two years, and there are still five years in which there will be neither plowing nor harvesting. Gen. 37:2; 41:46, 53

7"And God sent me before you to preserve for you a remnant in the earth, and to keep you alive by a great deliverance.

8"Now, therefore, it was not you who sent me here, but God; and He has made me a father to Pharaoh and lord of all his household and ruler over all the land of Egypt.

9"Hurry and go up to my father, and say to him, 'Thus says your son Joseph, "God has made me lord of all Egypt; come down to me, do not delay. Acts 7:14

10"And you shall live in the land of Goshen, and you shall be near me, you and your children and your children's children and your flocks and your herds and all that you have. dwell • Gen. 46:28, 34; 47:1

11"There I will also provide for you, for there are still five years of famine to come, lest you and your household and all that you have be impoverished." ' Gen. 47:12

12"And behold, your eyes see, and the eyes of my brother Benjamin see, that it is my mouth which is speaking to you.

13"Now you must tell my father of all my splendor in Egypt, and all that you have seen; and you must hurry and bring my father down here." Acts 7:14

14 Then he fell on his brother Benjamin's neck and wept; and Benjamin wept on his neck. Gen. 45:2

15 And he kissed all his brothers and wept on them, and afterward his brothers talked with him.

16 Now when the news was heard in Pharaoh's house that Joseph's brothers had come, it pleased Pharaoh and his servants.

17 Then Pharaoh said to Joseph, "Say to your brothers, 'Do this: load your beasts and go to the land of Canaan, come, go

18 and take your father and your households and come to me, and I will give you the best of the land of Egypt and you shall eat the fat of the land.' Gen. 27:28 • good

19"Now you are ordered, 'Do this: take wagons from the land of Egypt for your little ones and for your wives, and bring your father and come. take for yourselves • Num. 7:3-8

20 'And do not concern yourselves with your goods, for the best of all the land of Egypt is yours.' " good

21 Then the sons of Israel did so; and Joseph gave them wagons according to the command of Pharaoh, and gave them provisions for the journey. Gen. 45:19 • mouth

22 To each of them he gave changes of garments, but to Benjamin he gave three hundred pieces of silver and five changes of garments. $38,400 • all of them he gave each man

23 And to his father he sent as follows: ten donkeys loaded with the best things of Egypt, and ten female donkeys loaded with grain and bread and sustenance for his father on the journey. like this • good • for

24 So he sent his brothers away, and as they departed, he said to them, "Do not quarrel on the journey." be agitated

25 Then they went up from Egypt, and came to the land of Canaan to their father Jacob.

26 And they told him, saying, "Joseph is still alive, and indeed he is ruler over all the land of Egypt." But [T]he was stunned, for he did not believe them.   *his heart grew numb*

27 When they told him all the words of Joseph that he had spoken to them, and when he saw the [R]wagons that Joseph had sent to carry him, the spirit of their father Jacob revived.   Gen. 45:19

28 Then Israel said, "It is enough; my son Joseph is still alive. I will go and see him before I die."

CHAPTER 46

Jacob's Family Safe in Egypt

So Israel set out with all that he had, and came to [R]Beersheba, and offered sacrifices to the God of his father Isaac.   Gen. 21:31; 28:10

2 And [R]God spoke to Israel [T]in visions of the night and said, "Jacob, Jacob." And he said, "Here I am."   Num. 12:6 • *in the visions*

3 And He said, "I[R] am God, the God of your father; do not be afraid to go down to Egypt, for I will [R]make you a great nation there.   Gen. 17:1; 28:13 • Gen. 12:2; Ex. 1:9

4 "I will go down with you to Egypt, and I will also surely bring you up again; and Joseph will [close your eyes."   *put his hand on*

5 Then Jacob arose from Beersheba; and the sons of Israel carried their father Jacob and their little ones and their wives, in the [R]wagons which Pharaoh had sent to carry him.   Gen. 45:21

6 And they took their livestock and their property, which they had acquired in the land of Canaan, and came to Egypt, Jacob and all his [descendants with him: *seed*

7 his sons and his grandsons with him, his daughters and his granddaughters, and all his [descendants he brought with him to Egypt.   *seed*

8 Now these are the [R]names of the sons of Israel, Jacob and his sons, who went to Egypt: Reuben, Jacob's first-born.   Ex. 1:1-4

9 And the sons of Reuben: Hanoch and Pallu and Hezron and Carmi.

10 And the sons of Simeon: Jemuel and Jamin and Ohad and Jachin and Zohar and Shaul the son of a Canaanite woman.

11 And the sons of Levi: [T]Gershon, Kohath, and Merari.   In 1 Chr. 6:16, *Gershom*

12 And the sons of Judah: Er and Onan and Shelah and Perez and Zerah (but Er and Onan died in the land of Canaan). And the sons of Perez were Hezron and Hamul.

13 And the sons of Issachar: Tola and Puvvah and Iob and Shimron.

14 And the sons of Zebulun: Sered and Elon and Jahleel.

15 These are the sons of Leah, whom she bore to Jacob in Paddan-aram, with his daughter Dinah; [all his sons and his daughters *numbered* thirty-three.   *all the souls of*

16 And the [R]sons of Gad: [T]Ziphion and Haggi, Shuni and Ezbon, Eri and Arodi and Areli.   Num. 26:15-18 • In Num. 26:15, *Zephon*

17 And the [R]sons of Asher: Imnah and Ishvah and Ishvi and Beriah and their sister Serah. And the [sons of Beriah: Heber and Malchiel.   1 Chr. 7:30 • 1 Chr. 7:31

18 These are the sons of Zilpah, whom Laban gave to his daughter Leah; and she bore to Jacob these sixteen persons.

19 The sons of Jacob's wife Rachel: Joseph and Benjamin.

20 [R]Now to Joseph in the land of Egypt were born Manasseh and Ephraim, whom Asenath, the daughter of Potiphera, priest of On, bore to him.   Gen. 41:50-52

21 And the sons of Benjamin: Bela and Becher and Ashbel, Gera and Naaman, Ehi and Rosh, Muppim and Huppim and Ard.

22 These are the sons of Rachel, who were born to Jacob; *there were* fourteen persons in all.

23 And the sons of Dan: Hushim.

24 And the sons of Naphtali: Jahzeel and Guni and Jezer and Shillem.

25 These are the [R]sons of Bilhah, whom [R]Laban gave to his daughter Rachel, and she bore these to Jacob; *there were* seven persons in all.   Gen. 30:5, 7 • Gen. 29:29

26 [R]All the persons belonging to Jacob, who came to Egypt, his direct descendants, not including the wives of Jacob's sons, *were* sixty-six persons in all,   Ex. 1:5

27 and the sons of Joseph, who were born to him in Egypt were [two; [R]all the persons of the house of Jacob, who came to Egypt, *were* seventy.   *two souls* • Deut. 10:22; Acts 7:14

28 Now he sent Judah before him to Joseph, to point out *the way* before him to [R]Goshen; and they came into the land of Goshen.   Gen. 45:10

29 And Joseph [prepared his chariot and went up to Goshen to meet his father Israel; as soon as he appeared [before him, he fell on his neck and [R]wept on his neck a long time.   *tied, harnessed* • *to* • Gen. 45:14, 15

30 Then Israel said to Joseph, "Now let me die, since I have seen your face, that you are still alive."

31 And Joseph said to his brothers and to his father's household, "I[R] will go up and tell Pharaoh, and will say to him, 'My brothers and my father's household, who *were* in the land of Canaan, have come to me;   Gen. 47:1

32 and the men are shepherds, for they have been [keepers of livestock; and they have brought their flocks and their herds and all that they have.'   *men*

33 "And it shall come about when Pharaoh calls you and says, 'What[R] is your occupation?'   Gen. 47:2, 3

34 that you shall say, 'Your servants have been [keepers of livestock from our youth even until now, both we and our fathers,' that you may [live in the land of Goshen; for

every shepherd is ᵀloathsome ᴿ to the Egyptians."   *men • dwell • an abomination* • Ex. 8:26

CHAPTER 47

THEN Joseph went in and told Pharaoh, and said, "My father and my brothers and their flocks and their herds and all that they have, have come out of the land of Canaan; and behold, they are in the land of Goshen."

2 And he took five men from among his brothers, and presented them to Pharaoh.

3 Then Pharaoh said to his brothers, "Whatᴿ is your occupation?" So they said to Pharaoh, "Your servants are shepherds, both we and our fathers."   Gen. 46:33

4 And they said to Pharaoh, "Weᴿ have come to sojourn in the land, for there is no pasture for your servants' flocks, for the famine is severe in the land of Canaan. Now, therefore, please let your servantsᵀlive in the land of Goshen."   Deut. 26:5 • *dwell*

5 Then Pharaoh said to Joseph, "Your father and your brothers have come to you.

6"The land of Egypt is ⁶⁰at your disposal; ᵀsettle your father and your brothers in the best of the land, let them live in the land of Goshen; and if you know any capable men among them, then put them in charge of my livestock."   *cause them to dwell*

7 Then Joseph brought his father Jacob and ᵀpresented him to Pharaoh; and Jacob ᴿblessed Pharaoh.   *set him before* • 1 Kin. 8:66

8 And Pharaoh said to Jacob, "How many years have you lived?"

9 So Jacob said to Pharaoh, "The ᵀyears of my sojourning are one hundred and thirty; few and ᵀunpleasant have been the years of my life, nor have they attained the years that my fathers lived during the days of their sojourning."   *days of the years • evil*

10 And Jacobᴿblessed Pharaoh, and went out fromᵀhis presence.   Gen. 47:7 • *Pharaoh's*

11 So Joseph settled his father and his brothers, and gave them a possession in the land of Egypt, in the best of the land, in the land of Rameses, as Pharaoh had ordered.

12 And Joseph provided his father and his brothers and all his father's household with ᴬfood, according to their little ones.   *bread*

13 Now there was noᵀfood in all the land, because the famine was very severe, so that the land of Egypt and the land of Canaan languished because of the famine.   *bread*

14 And ᴿJoseph gathered all the money that was found in the land of Egypt and in the land of Canaan for the grain which they bought, and Joseph brought the money into Pharaoh's house.   Gen. 41:56

15 And when the money was all spent in the land of Egypt and in the land of Canaan, all the Egyptians came to Joseph and said, "Give us food, for why should we die in your presence? For *our* money is gone."

16 Then Joseph said, "Give up your livestock, and I will give you *food* for your livestock, since *your* money ᵀis gone."   *ceases*

17 So they brought their livestock to Joseph, and Joseph gave them food in exchange for the horses and the flocks and the herds and the donkeys; and he ᵀfed them with food in exchange for all their livestock ᵀthat year.   *led them as a shepherd • in that year*

18 And when that year was ended, they came to him the ᵀnext year and said to him, "We will not hide from my lord that our money is all spent, and the cattle are my lord's. There is nothing left for my lord except our bodies and our lands.   *second*

19"Why should we die before your eyes, both we and our land? Buy us and our land for ᴬfood, and we and our land will be slaves to Pharaoh. So give us seed, that we may live and not die, and that the land may not be desolate."   *bread*

20 So Joseph bought all the land of Egypt for Pharaoh, for every Egyptian sold his field, because the famine was severe upon them. Thus the land became Pharaoh's.

21 And as for the people, he removed them to the cities from one end of Egypt's border to the other.

22 Only the land of the priests he did not buy, for the priests had an allotment from Pharaoh, and they ᵀlived off the allotment which Pharaoh gave them. Therefore, they did not sell their land.   *ate their allotment*

23 Then Joseph said to the people, "Behold, I have today bought you and your land for Pharaoh; now, *here* is seed for you, and you may sow the land.

24"And at the harvest you shall give aᴿfifth to Pharaoh, and ᵀfour-fifths shall be your own for seed of the field and for your food and for those of your households and as food for your little ones." Gen. 41:34 • *four parts*

25 So they said, "You have saved our lives! Let us find favor in the sight of my lord, and we will be Pharaoh's slaves."

26 And Joseph made it a statute concerning the land of Egypt *valid* to this day, that Pharaoh should have the fifth; only the land of the priests did not become Pharaoh's.

Jacob Blesses the Family in Egypt

27 Now Israel ᵀlived in the land of Egypt, inᵀGoshen, and they ᴿacquired property in it and were fruitful and became very numerous.   *dwelt • in the land of Goshen* • Gen. 47:11

28 And Jacob lived in the land of Egypt seventeen years; so the length of Jacob's life was one hundred and forty-seven years.

29 When the time for Israel to die drew near, he called his son Joseph and said to him, "Please, if I have found favor in your sight, place now your hand under my thigh and deal with me in kindness and ⁶¹faithfulness. Please do not bury me in Egypt,

30 but when I lie down with my fathers, you shall carry me out of Egypt and bury

⁶⁰ Lit., *before you*   ⁶¹ Lit., *truth*

me in ᴿtheir burial place." And he said, "I will do as you have said."   Acts 7:15, 16

31 And he said, "Swearᴿ to me." So he swore to him. Then Israel bowed *in worship* at the head of the bed.   Gen. 21:23, 24; 24:3

CHAPTER 48

Now it came about after these things that ᵀJoseph was told, "Behold, your father is sick." So he took his two sons Manasseh and Ephraim with him.   *one said to Joseph*

2 When it was told to Jacob, "Behold, your son Joseph has come to you," Israel collected his strength and sat up in the bed.

3 Then Jacob said to Joseph, "Godᵀ Almighty appeared to me at Luz in the land of Canaan and blessed me,   Heb., *El Shaddai*

4 and He said to me, 'Behold, I will make you fruitful and numerous, and I will make you a company of peoples, and will give this land to your ᵀdescendants after you for ᴿan everlasting possession.'   *seed* • Gen. 17:8

5 "And now your two sons, who were born to you in the land of Egypt before I came to you in Egypt, are mine; ᴿEphraim and Manasseh shall be mine, asᴿReuben and Simeon are.   Josh. 14:4 • 1 Chr. 5:1, 2

6 "But your offspring that ᵀhave been born after them shall be yours; they shall be called by the ᵀnames of their brothers in their inheritance.   *you have begotten* • *name*

7 "Now as for me, when I came fromᴿPaddan, Rachel died, ᵀto my sorrow, in the land of Canaan on the journey, when there was still some distance to go to Ephrath; and I buried her there on the way to Ephrath (that is, Bethlehem)."   Gen. 33:18 • *upon me*

8 When Israel ᴿsaw Joseph's sons, he said, "Who are these?"   Gen. 48:10

9 And Joseph said to his father, "Theyᴿ are my sons, whom God has given me here." So he said, "Bring them to me, please, that I may bless them."   Gen. 33:5

10 Now the eyes of Israel were *so* dim from age *that* he could not see. Then ᵀJoseph brought them close to him, and he ᴿkissed them and embraced them.   *he* • Gen. 27:27

11 And Israel said to Joseph, "I never expected to see your face, and behold, God has let me see your ᵀchildren as well."   *seed*

12 Then Joseph took them from his knees, and bowed with his face to the ground.

13 And Joseph took them both, Ephraim with his right hand toward Israel's left, and Manasseh with his left hand toward Israel's right, and brought them close to him.

14 But Israel stretched out his right hand and laid it on the head of Ephraim, who was the younger, and his left hand on Manasseh's head, crossing his hands, ᵀalthough Manasseh was the first-born.   *when*

15 And he blessed Joseph, and said,
"The God before whom my fathers
    Abraham and Isaac walked,
ᴿThe God who has been my shepherd
    all my life to this day,   Gen. 49:24

16 ᴿThe angel who has redeemed me from
    all evil,   Gen. 22:11, 15-18; 28:13-15; 31:11
ᴿBless the lads;   [Heb. 11:21]
And may my name live on in them,
And the ᵀnames of my fathers Abra-
    ham and Isaac;   *name*
And may they grow into a multitude
    in the midst of the earth."

17 When Joseph saw that his fatherᴿlaid his right hand on Ephraim's head, it displeased him; and he grasped his father's hand to remove it from Ephraim's head to Manasseh's head.   Gen. 48:14

18 And Joseph said to his father, "Not so, my father, for this one is the first-born. Place your right hand on his head."

19 But his father refused and said, "I know, my son, I know; he also shall become a people and he also shall be great. However, his younger brother shall be greater than he, and his ᵀdescendants shall become a ᵀmultitude of nations."   *seed* • *fulness*

20 Andᴿhe blessed them that day, saying,
"By you Israel shall pronounce bless-
    ing, saying,
'May God make you like Ephraim and
    Manasseh!' "   [Heb. 11:21]
Thus he put Ephraim before Manasseh.

21 Then Israel said to Joseph, "Behold, I am about to die, butᴿGod will be with you, andᴿbring you back to the land of your fathers.   Gen. 26:3 • Gen. 28:15; 46:4; 50:24

22 "And I give you one ᴧportion more than your brothers, ᴿwhich I took from the hand of the Amorite with my sword and my bow."   *ridge*; lit., *shoulder*; Heb., *Shechem* • John 4:5

CHAPTER 49

Then Jacob summoned his sons and said, "Assemble yourselves that I may tell you what shall befall you in the days to come.
2 "Gather together and hear, O sons of
    Jacob;
And listen to Israel your father.

3 "Reuben, you are my first-born;
My might and ᴿthe beginning of my
    strength,   Deut. 21:17; Ps. 78:51; 105:36
ᵀPreeminent in dignity andᵀpreeminent
    in power.   *preeminence*

4 "Uncontrolledᴧ as water, you shall not
    have preeminence,   *Boiling over*
ᴿBecause you went up to your father's
    bed;   Gen. 35:22; Deut. 27:20; 1 Chr. 5:1
Then you defiled *it*—he went up to
    my couch.

5 "Simeonᴿ and Levi are brothers;
Their swords are implements of vio-
    lence.   Gen. 34:25-30

6 "Letᴿmy soul not enter into their coun-
    cil;   Ps. 64:2
Let not my glory be united with their
    assembly;
Because in their anger they slewᵀmen,

And in their self-will they lamed ^Toxen.   *a man • an ox*

7 "Cursed be their anger, for it is fierce;
And their wrath, for it is cruel.
I will ^Tdisperse them in Jacob,   *divide*
And scatter them in Israel.

8 "Judah, your brothers shall praise you;
Your hand shall be on the neck of
_Ryour enemies;
Your father's sons shall bow down to
you.   Gen. 27:29; 1 Chr. 5:2

9 "Judah is a^Rlion's whelp;   Ezek. 19:5-7
From the prey, my son, you have gone
up.
He couches, he lies down as a lion,
And as a ^Alion, who ^Tdares rouse him
up?   *lioness • shall*

10 "The^Rscepter shall not depart from Judah,   Ps. 60:7; 108:8; Rev. 5:5 ☆
Nor the ruler's staff from between his
feet,
⁶²Until Shiloh comes,
And^Rto him *shall be* the obedience of
the peoples.   Ps. 2:6-9; 72:8-11

11 "He^Tties *his* foal to the vine, *Binding of*
And his donkey's colt to the choice
vine;
He washes his garments in wine,
And his robes in the blood of grapes.

12 "His eyes are ⁶³dull from wine,
And his teeth ⁶⁴white from milk.

13 "Zebulun shall dwell at the seashore;
And he *shall be* a haven for ships,
And his flank *shall be* toward Sidon.

14 "Issachar is a strong donkey,
Lying down between the sheepfolds.

15 "When he saw that a resting place was
good
And that the land was pleasant,
He bowed his shoulder to bear *bur-
dens,*
And became a slave at forced labor.

16 "Dan shall^Rjudge his people,   Gen. 30:6
As one of the tribes of Israel.

17 "Dan shall be a serpent in the way,
A horned snake in the path,
That bites the horse's heels,
So that his rider falls backward.

18 "For Thy salvation I wait, O LORD.

19 "As for Gad, raiders shall raid him,
But he shall raid *at* their heels.

20 "As for Asher, his food shall be rich,
And he shall yield royal dainties.

21 "Naphtali^Ris a doe let loose,   Deut. 33:23
He gives beautiful words.

22 "Joseph is a fruitful ⁶⁵bough,
A fruitful bough by a spring;
Its ⁶⁶branches run over a wall.

23 "The archers bitterly attacked him,
And shot *at him* and harassed him;

24 But his^Rbow remained firm,   Job 29:20
And^Rhis arms were agile,   Is. 41:10

From the hands of the^RMighty One of
Jacob   Ps. 132:2, 5; Is. 1:24; 49:26
(From there is the Shepherd, ^Rthe
Stone of Israel), Is. 28:16; [1 Pet. 2:6–8]

25 From ^Rthe God of your father who
helps you,   Gen. 28:13; 32:9
And by the Almighty who blesses you
With blessings of heaven above,
Blessings of the deep that lies be-
neath,
Blessings of the breasts and of the
womb.

26 "The blessings of your father
Have surpassed the blessings of my
ancestors
Up to the ^Tutmost bound of the everlasting hills;   *limit; or, desire*
May they be on the head of Joseph,
And on the crown of the head of the
one distinguished among his brothers.

27 "Benjamin is a ^Travenous wolf;
In the morning he devours the prey,
And in the evening he divides the
spoil."   *a wolf that tears*

28 All these are the twelve tribes of Israel,
and this is what their father said to them
^Twhen he blessed them. He blessed them, ev-
ery one ^Twith the blessing appropriate to
him.   *and • according to his blessing*

29 Then he charged them and said to
them, "I am about to be gathered to my people; bury me with my fathers in the cave
that is in the field of Ephron the Hittite,

30 in the ^Tcave that is in the field of Machpelah, which is before Mamre, in the land of
Canaan, which Abraham bought along with
the field from Ephron the Hittite for a^Tburial
site.   Gen. 23:3-20 • *possession of a burial place*

31 "There they buried Abraham and his
wife Sarah, there they buried Isaac and his
wife Rebekah, and there I buried Leah—

32 the field and the cave that is in it, purchased from the sons of Heth."

Jacob Dies in Egypt

33 When Jacob finished charging his sons,
he drew his feet into the bed and breathed
his last, and was gathered to his people.

CHAPTER 50

THEN Joseph fell on his father's face, and
wept over him and kissed him.

2 And Joseph commanded his servants
the physicians to embalm his father. So the
physicians ^Rembalmed Israel.   Matt. 26:12

3 Now forty days ^Twere required for ^Ait,
for such is the period required for embalm-
ing. And the Egyptians ^Rwept for him seventy days. *fulfilled • him •* Num. 20:29; Deut. 34:8

⁶² Or, *Until he comes to Shiloh*   ⁶³ Or, *darker than*
⁶⁴ Or, *whiter than*   ⁶⁵ Lit., *son*   ⁶⁶ Lit., *daughters*

4 And when the days of [T]mourning for him were past, Joseph spoke to the household of Pharaoh, saying, "If now I have found favor in your sight, please speak[T]to Pharaoh, saying,   *weeping • In the ears of*

5 'My father made me swear, saying, "Behold, I am about to die; in my grave [R]which I dug for myself in the land of Canaan, there you shall bury me." Now therefore, please let me go up and bury my father; then I will return.' "   Is. 22:16; Matt. 27:60

6 And Pharaoh said, "Go up and bury your father, as he made you swear."

7 So Joseph went up to bury his father, and with him went up all the servants of Pharaoh, the elders of his household and all the elders of the land of Egypt,

8 and all the household of Joseph and his brothers and his father's household; they left only their little ones and their flocks and their herds in the land of Goshen.

9 There also went up with him both chariots and horsemen; and it was a very great company.

10 When they came to the threshing floor of Atad, which is beyond the Jordan, they lamented there with a very great and [T]sorrowful lamentation; and he observed seven days mourning for his father.   *heavy*

11 Now when the inhabitants of the land, the Canaanites, saw the mourning at the threshing floor of Atad, they said, "This is a [T]grievous mourning for the Egyptians." Therefore it was named Abel-mizraim, which is beyond the Jordan.   *heavy*

12 And thus his sons did for him as he had charged them;

13 for his sons carried him to the land of Canaan, and buried him in the cave of the field of Machpelah before Mamre, which Abraham had bought along with the field for a burial site from Ephron the Hittite.

14 And after he had buried his father, Joseph returned to Egypt, he and his brothers, and all who had gone up with him to bury his father.

Joseph Dies in Egypt

15 When Joseph's brothers saw that their father was dead, they said, "What[R] if Joseph should bear a grudge against us and pay us back in full for all the wrong which we did to him!"   Gen. 37:28; 42:21, 22

16 So they [T]sent *a message* to Joseph, saying, "Your father charged before he died, saying,   *commanded*

17 'Thus you shall say to Joseph, "Please forgive, I beg you, the transgression of your brothers and their sin, for they did you wrong." ' And now, please forgive the transgression of the servants of the God of your father." And Joseph wept when they spoke to him.

18 Then his brothers also came and [R]fell down before him and said, "Behold, we are your servants."   Gen. 37:8-10; 41:43

19 But Joseph said to them, "Do not be afraid, for am I in God's place?

20 "And as for you, you meant evil against me, *but* God meant it for good in order to bring about [T]this present result, to preserve many people alive.   *as it is this day*

21 "So therefore, do not be afraid; I will provide for you and your little ones." So he comforted them and spoke kindly to them.

22 Now Joseph stayed in Egypt, he and his father's household, and Joseph lived one hundred and ten years.

23 And Joseph saw the third generation of Ephraim's sons; also the sons of Machir, the son of Manasseh, were [R]born on Joseph's knees.   Gen. 30:3

24 And Joseph said to his brothers, "I am about to die, but God will surely[T]take care of you, and bring you up from this land to the land which He [T]promised on oath to Abraham, to Isaac and to Jacob."   *visit • swore*

25 Then Joseph made the sons of Israel swear, saying, "God will surely[T]take care of you, and[R]you shall carry my bones up from here."   *visit •* Ex. 13:19; Josh. 24:32; Heb. 11:22

26 So Joseph died at the age of one hundred and ten years; and he was [R]embalmed and placed in a coffin in Egypt.   Gen. 50:2

EXODUS

THE BOOK OF EXODUS

Exodus is the record of Israel's birth as a nation. Within the protective "womb" of Egypt, the Jewish family of seventy rapidly multiplies. At the right time, accompanied with severe "birth pains," an infant nation, numbering between two and three million people, is brought into the world where it is divinely protected, fed, and nurtured.

The Hebrew title, *We'elleh Shemoth,* "Now These *Are* the Names," comes from the first phrase in 1:1. Exodus begins with "Now" to show it as a continuation of Genesis. The Greek title is *Exodus,* a word meaning exit, departure, or going out. The Septuagint uses this word to describe the book by its key event (see 19:1, "gone out"). In Luke 9:31 and in Second Peter 1:15, the word *exodus* speaks of physical death (Jesus and Peter). This embodies Exodus's theme of redemption, because redemption is accomplished only through death. The Latin title is *Liber Exodus,* "Book of Departure," taken from the Greek title.

THE AUTHOR OF EXODUS

Critics have challenged the Mosaic authorship of Exodus in favor of a series of oral and written documents that were woven together by editors late in Israel's history. Their arguments are generally weak and far from conclusive, especially in view of the strong external and internal evidence that points to Moses as the author.

External Evidence: Exodus has been attributed to Moses since the time of Joshua (cf. Ex. 20:25 with Josh. 8:30–32). Other biblical writers attribute Exodus to Moses: Malachi (Mal. 4:4), the disciples (John 1:45), and Paul (Rom. 10:5). This is also the testimony of Jesus (Mark 7:10; 12:26; Luke 20:37; John 5:46, 47; 7:19, 22, 23). Jewish and Samaritan traditions consistently hold to the Mosaic authorship of Exodus.

Internal Evidence: Portions of Exodus are directly attributed to Moses (Ex. 15; 17:8–14; 20:1–17; 24:4, 7, 12; 31:18; 34:1–27). Moses' usual procedure was to record events soon after they occurred in the form of historical annals. It is clear from Exodus that the author must have been an eyewitness of the Exodus and an educated man. He was acquainted with details about the customs and climate of Egypt and the plants, animals, and terrain of the wilderness. A consistency of style and development also points to a single author. Its antiquity is supported by the frequent use of ancient literary constructions, words, and expressions.

THE TIME OF EXODUS

If the early date for the Exodus (c. 1445 B.C.) is assumed, this book was composed during the forty-year wilderness journey, between 1445 B.C. and 1405 B.C. Moses probably kept an account of God's work, which he then edited in the plains of Moab shortly before his death. Exodus covers the period from the arrival of Jacob in Egypt (c. 1875 B.C.) to the erection of the tabernacle 431 years later in the wilderness (c. 1445 B.C.).

THE CHRIST OF EXODUS

Exodus contains no direct messianic prophecies, but it is full of types and portraits of Christ. Here are seven: (1) *Moses:* In dozens of ways Moses is a type of Christ (Deut. 18:15). Both Moses and Christ are prophets, priests, and kings (although Moses was never made king, he functioned as the ruler of Israel); both are kinsman-redeemers; both are endangered in infancy; both voluntarily renounce power and wealth; both are deliverers, lawgivers, and mediators. (2) *The Passover:* John 1:29, 36 and First Corinthians 5:7 make it clear that Christ is our slain God and the Passover Lamb. (3) *The seven feasts:* Each of these feasts portrays some aspect of the ministry of Christ. (4) *The Exodus:* Paul relates baptism to the exodus event because baptism symbolizes death to the old and identification with the new (Rom. 6:2, 3; 1 Cor. 10:1, 2). (5) *The manna and water:* The New Testament applies both to Christ (John 6:31–35, 48–63; 1 Cor. 10:3, 4). (6) *The tabernacle:* In its materials, colors, furniture, and arrangement, the tabernacle clearly speaks of the person of Christ and the way of redemption. The development is progressive from suffering, blood, and death, to beauty, holiness, and the glory of God. The tabernacle is theology in a physical form. (7) *The High Priest:* In several ways the high priest foreshadows the ministry of Christ, our great High Priest (Heb. 4:14–16; 9:11, 12, 24–28).

KEYS TO EXODUS

Key Word: Redemption—Central to the Book of Exodus is the concept of redemption. Israel was redeemed *from* bond-

age in Egypt and *into* a covenant relationship with God. From the redemption of Moses in the Nile to the redeeming presence of God in the tabernacle, Exodus records God's overwhelming acts of deliverance, by which He demonstrates His right to be Israel's King.

Key Verses: Exodus 6:6; 19:5, 6—"Say, therefore, to the sons of Israel, 'I am the LORD, and I will bring you out from under the burdens of the Egyptians, and I will deliver you from their bondage. I will also redeem you with an outstretched arm and with great judgments'" (6:6).

"Now then, if you will indeed obey My voice and keep My covenant, then you shall be My own possession among all the peoples, for all the earth is Mine; and you shall be to Me a kingdom of priests and a holy nation" (19:5, 6).

Key Chapters: Exodus 12—14—The climax of the entire Old Testament is recorded in chapters 12—14: the salvation of Israel through blood (the Passover) and through power (the Red Sea). The exodus is the central event of the Old Testament as the cross is of the New Testament.

SURVEY OF EXODUS

Exodus abounds with God's powerful redemptive acts on behalf of His oppressed people. It begins in pain and ends in liberation; it moves from the groaning of the people to the glory of God. It is the continuation of the story that begins in Genesis with the seventy descendants of Jacob who move from Canaan to Egypt. They have multiplied under adverse conditions to a multitude of over two million people. When the Israelites finally turn to God for deliverance from their bondage, God quickly responds by redeeming them

"with an outstretched arm and with great judgments" (6:6). God faithfully fulfills His promise made to Abraham centuries before (Gen. 15:13, 14).

The book falls into two parts: (1) redemption from Egypt (1—18); and (2) revelation from God (19—40).

Redemption from Egypt (1—18): After four centuries of slavery, the people of Israel cry to the God of Abraham, Isaac, and Jacob for deliverance. God has already prepared Moses for this purpose, and has commissioned him at the burning bush to stand before Pharaoh as the advocate for Israel. However, Pharaoh hardens his heart: "Who is the LORD that I should obey His voice to let Israel go?" (5:2).

God soon reveals Himself to Pharaoh through a series of object lessons, the ten plagues. These plagues grow in severity until the tenth brings death to the first-born of every household of Egypt. Israel is redeemed through this plague by means of the Passover lamb. The Israelites' faith in God at this point becomes the basis for their national redemption. As they leave Egypt, God guides them by a pillar of fire and smoke, and saves them from Egypt's pursuing army through the miraculous crossing of the sea. In the wilderness He protects and sustains them throughout their journeys.

Revelation from God (19—40): Now that the people have experienced God's deliverance, guidance, and protection, they are ready to be taught what God expects of them. The redeemed people must now be set apart to walk with God. This is why the emphasis moves from narration in chapters 1—18 to legislation in chapters 19—40. On Mount Sinai, Moses receives God's moral, civil, and ceremonial laws, as well as the pattern for the tabernacle

FOCUS	REDEMPTION FROM EGYPT				REVELATION FROM GOD	
REFERENCE	1:1——2:1	——5:1	——15:22	——19:1	——32:1	——40:38
DIVISION	THE NEED FOR REDEMPTION	THE PREPARATION FOR REDEMPTION	THE REDEMPTION OF ISRAEL	THE PRESERVATION OF ISRAEL	THE REVELATION OF THE COVENANT	THE RESPONSE OF ISRAEL TO THE COVENANT
TOPIC	NARRATION				LEGISLATION	
	SUBJECTION		REDEMPTION		INSTRUCTION	
LOCATION	EGYPT			WILDERNESS	MOUNT SINAI	
TIME	430 YEARS			2 MONTHS	10 MONTHS	

to be built in the wilderness. After God judges the people for their worship of the golden calf, the tabernacle is constructed and consecrated.

It is a building of beauty in a barren land and reveals much about the person of God and the way of redemption.

OUTLINE OF EXODUS

Part One: Redemption from Egypt (1:1—18:27)

Part Two: Revelation from God (19:1—40:38)

CHAPTER 1

Israel's Rapid Multiplication

NOW these are the names of the sons of Israel who came to Egypt with Jacob; they came each one ᵀwith his household: *and*

2 Reuben, Simeon, Levi and Judah;
3 Issachar, Zebulun and Benjamin;
4 Dan and Naphtali, Gad and Asher.
5 And all the ᵇpersons who came from the loins of Jacob were seventy in number, but Joseph was *already* in Egypt.   *souls*
6 And ᴿJoseph died, and all his brothers and all that generation.   Gen. 50:26
7 But the sons of Israel were fruitful and ᵀincreased greatly, and multiplied, and became exceedingly ᴬmighty, so that the land was filled with them.   *swarmed • numerous*

Israel's Severe Affliction

8 Now a newᴿking arose over Egypt, who did not know Joseph.   Acts 7:18, 19
9 And he said to his people, "Behold, the people of the sons of Israel are ᴬmore and mightier than we. *too many and too mighty for us*
10"Come, let us deal wisely with them,

lest they multiply and ᴵin the event of war, they also join themselves to those who hate us, and fight against us, and depart from the land."   *it came about when war befalls that*
11 So they appointed ᴿtaskmasters over them to afflict them with ᵀhard labor. And they built for Pharaoh storage cities, Pithom and Raamses.   Ex. 3:7; 5:6 • *their burdens*
12 But the more they afflicted them, ᴮthe more they multiplied and the more they ᵇspread out, so that they were in dread of the sons of Israel.   Ex. 1:7 • *broke forth*
13 And the Egyptians compelled the sons of Israelᴿto labor rigorously;   Deut. 4:20
14 and they made their lives bitter with hard labor in mortar and bricks and at all *kinds* of labor in the field, all their labors which they rigorously imposed on them.

Israel's Planned Extinction

15 Then the king of Egypt spoke to the Hebrew midwives, one of whom was named Shiphrah, and the other was named Puah;
16 and he said, "When you are helping the Hebrew women to give birth and see *them* upon the birthstool,ᴵif it is a son, then you

shall put him to death; but if it is a daughter, then she shall live." Acts 7:19

17 But the midwives ^Afeared God, and did not do as the king of Egypt had ^Tcommanded them, but let the boys live.   *revered • spoken to*

18 So the king of Egypt called for the midwives, and said to them, "Why have you done this thing, and let the boys live?"

19 And the midwives said to Pharaoh, "Because the Hebrew women are not as the Egyptian women; for they are vigorous, and they give birth before the midwife ^Tcan get to them."   *comes to*

20 So ^RGod was good to the midwives, and the people multiplied, and became very ^Amighty.   [Prov. 11:18]; Eccl. 8:12 • *numerous*

21 And it came about because the midwives ^Afeared God, that He ^Testablished ^Ahouseholds for them.   *revered • made • families*

22 Then Pharaoh commanded all his people, saying, "Every ^Rson who is born ^1you are to cast into ^Rthe Nile, and every daughter you are to keep alive."   Acts 7:19 • Gen. 41:1

CHAPTER 2

Moses Is Redeemed from Murder

NOW a man from the house of Levi went and ^Tmarried a daughter of Levi.   *took*

2 And the woman conceived and bore a son; and when she saw ^Tthat he was beautiful, she hid him for three months.   *him that*

3 But when she could hide him no longer, she got him a ^2wicker ^Rbasket ^Aand covered it over with tar and pitch. Then she put the child into it, and set *it* among the ^Rreeds by the bank of the Nile.   Is. 18:2 • *chest* • Is. 19:6

4 And his sister stood at a distance to ^Tfind out what would happen to him.   *know*

5 Then the daughter of Pharaoh came down to bathe at the Nile, with her maidens walking alongside the Nile; and she saw the ^Abasket among the reeds and sent her maid, and she brought it *to her.*   *chest*

6 When she opened *it,* she ^Tsaw the child, and behold, *the* boy was crying. And she had pity on him and said, "This is one of the Hebrews' children."   *Heb., saw it, the child*

7 Then his sister said to Pharaoh's daughter, "Shall I go and call ^Ta nurse for you from the Hebrew women, that she may nurse the child for you?"   *a woman giving suck*

8 And Pharaoh's daughter said to her, "Go *ahead.*" So the girl went and called the child's mother.

9 Then Pharaoh's daughter said to her, "Take this child away and nurse him for me and I shall give *you* your wages." So the woman took the child and nursed him.

10 And the child grew, and she brought him to Pharaoh's daughter, and he became her son. And she named him Moses, and said, "Because I drew him out of the water."

Moses Tries to Redeem by Murder

11 Now it came about in those days, ^Rwhen

Moses had grown up, that he went out to his brethren and looked on their ^Thard labors; and he saw an Egyptian beating a Hebrew, one of his brethren.   Acts 7:23 • *burdens*

12 So he ^Tlooked this way and that, and when he saw there was no one *around,* he ^Rstruck down the Egyptian and hid him in the sand.   *turned* • Acts 7:24, 25

13 And he went out the next day, and behold, two Hebrews were ^Afighting with each other; and he said to the offender, "Why are you striking your companion?"   *quarreling*

14 But he said, "Who made you a ^Tprince or a judge over us? Are you intending to kill me, as you killed the Egyptian?" Then Moses was afraid, and said, "Surely the matter has become known."   *man, a prince*

15 When Pharaoh heard of this matter, he tried to kill Moses. But Moses fled from the presence of Pharaoh and ^Tsettled in the land of Midian; and he sat down by a well.   *dwelt*

16 Now ^Rthe priest of Midian had seven daughters; and ^Athey came to draw water, and filled the troughs to water their father's flock.   Ex. 3:1; 18:12 • 1 Sam. 9:11

17 Then the shepherds came and drove them away, but ^RMoses stood up and helped them, and watered their flock.   Gen. 29:3, 10

18 When they came to ^RReuel their father, he said, "Why have you come *back* so soon today?"   Ex. 3:1; Num. 10:29

19 So they said, "An Egyptian delivered us from the hand of the shepherds; and what is more, he even drew the water for us and watered the flock."

20 And he said to his daughters, "Where is he then? Why is it that you have left the man behind? Invite him ^Tto have something to eat."   *that he may eat bread*

21 ^RAnd Moses was willing to dwell with the man, and he gave his daughter ^RZipporah to Moses.   Acts 7:29 • Ex. 4:25; 18:2

22 Then she gave birth to a son, and he named him Gershom, for he said, "I have been a sojourner in a foreign land."

Israel Calls upon God

23 Now it came about in *the course of* those many days that the king of Egypt died. And the sons of Israel sighed because of the bondage, and they cried out; and their cry for help because of *their* bondage rose up to God.

24 So ^RGod heard their groaning; and God remembered His covenant with Abraham, Isaac, and Jacob.   Ex. 6:5; Acts 7:34

25 And God saw the sons of Israel, and God ^Ttook notice *of them.*   *knew* them

CHAPTER 3

God Miraculously Appears

NOW Moses was pasturing the flock of ^RJethro his father-in-law, the priest of Mid-

---

[1] Some versions insert, *to the Hebrews*
[2] I.e., papyrus reeds

ian; and he led the flock to the 'west side of the wilderness, and came to Horeb, the mountain of God.   Num. 10:29 • *rear part*

2 And 'the angel of the LORD appeared to him in a blazing fire from the midst of 'a bush; and he looked, and behold, the bush was burning with fire, yet the bush was not consumed.   Ex. 3:4-11, 16; Judg. 13:13-21 • *the*

3 So Moses said, "I 'must turn aside now, and see this 'marvelous sight, why the bush is not burned up."   *Let me turn* • *great*

4 When the LORD saw that he turned aside to look, 'God called to him from the midst of the bush, and said, "Moses, Moses!" And he said, "Here I am."   Ex. 4:5

5 Then He said, "Do not come near here; 'remove your sandals from your feet, for the place on which you are standing is holy ground."   Josh. 5:15; Acts 7:33

6 He said also, "I am the God of your father, the God of Abraham, the God of Isaac, and the God of Jacob." Then Moses hid his face, for he was afraid to look at God.

God Calls Moses to Leadership

7 And the LORD said, "I have surely 'seen the affliction of My people who are in Egypt, and have given heed to their cry because of their taskmasters, for I am aware of their sufferings.   Ps. 106:44; [Is. 63:9]; Acts 7:34

8 "So I have come down to deliver them from the 'power of the Egyptians, and to bring them up from that land to a good and spacious land, to a land flowing with milk and honey, to the place of the Canaanite and the Hittite and the Amorite and the Perizzite and the Hivite and the Jebusite.   *hand*

9 "And now, behold, 'the cry of the sons of Israel has come to Me; furthermore, I have seen the oppression with which the Egyptians are oppressing them.   Ex. 2:23

10 "Therefore, come now, and I will send you to Pharaoh, so that you may bring My people, the sons of Israel, out of Egypt."

"Who Am I?"

11 But Moses said to God, "Who 'am I, that I should go to Pharaoh, and that I should bring the sons of Israel out of Egypt?"   Ex. 4:10; 6:12; 1 Sam. 18:18

12 And He said, "Certainly I will be with you, and this shall be the sign to you that it is I who have sent you: when you have brought the people out of Egypt, you shall 'worship God at this mountain."   *serve*

"What Is His Name?"

13 Then Moses said to God, "Behold, I am going to the sons of Israel, and I shall say to them, 'The God of your fathers has sent me to you.' Now they may say to me, 'What is His name?' What shall I say to them?"

14 And God said to Moses, "[3]I 'AM WHO [3]I AM"; and He said, "Thus you shall say to the sons of Israel, '[3]I AM has sent me to you.' "   [Ex. 6:3; John 8:24, 28, 58; Heb. 13:8]

15 And God, furthermore, said to Moses,

"Thus you shall say to the sons of Israel, 'The 'LORD, the God of your fathers, the God of Abraham, the God of Isaac, and the God of Jacob, has sent me to you.' This is My name forever, and this is My memorial-name to all generations.   Ex. 3:6, 13

16 "Go and gather the elders of Israel together, and say to them, 'The LORD, the God of your fathers, the God of Abraham, Isaac and Jacob, has appeared to me, saying, "I 'am indeed concerned about you and what has been done to you in Egypt.   Ps. 33:18f.

17 "So I said, I will bring you up out of the affliction of Egypt to the land of the Canaanite and the Hittite and the Amorite and the Perizzite and the Hivite and the Jebusite, to a land flowing with milk and honey." '

18 "And they will pay heed to what you say; and you with the elders of Israel will come to the king of Egypt, and you will say to him, 'The LORD, the God of the Hebrews, has met with us. So now, please, let us go a three days' journey into the wilderness, that we may sacrifice to the LORD our God.'

19 "But I know that the king of Egypt 'will not permit you to go, 'except 'under compulsion.   Ex. 5:2 • Ex. 6:1 • *by a strong hand*

20 "So I will stretch out My hand, and strike Egypt with all My 'miracles which I shall do in the midst of it; and after that he will let you go.   Jer. 32:20; Acts 7:36

21 "And I will grant this people favor in the sight of the Egyptians; and it shall be that when you go, you will not go empty-handed.

22 "But every woman shall ask of her neighbor and the woman who lives in her house, articles of silver and articles of gold, and clothing; and you will put them on your sons and daughters. Thus you will 'plunder the Egyptians."   [Ezek. 39:10]

CHAPTER 4

"They Will Not Believe Me"

THEN Moses answered and said, "What if they will not believe me, or listen 'to what I say? For they may say, 'The 'LORD has not appeared to you.' "   *to my voice* • Ex. 3:15, 16

2 And the LORD said to him, "What is that in your hand?" And he said, "A staff."

3 Then He said, "Throw it on the ground." So he threw it on the ground, and it became a serpent; and Moses fled from it.

4 But the LORD said to Moses, "Stretch out your hand and grasp *it* by its tail"—so he stretched out his hand and caught it, and it became a staff in his 'hand—   *palm*

5 "that they may believe that 'the LORD, the God of their fathers, the God of Abraham, the God of Isaac, and the God of Jacob, has appeared to you."   Gen. 28:13; 48:15

6 And the LORD furthermore said to him, "Now put your hand into your bosom." So he put his hand into his bosom, and when he

[3] Related to the name of God, YHWH, rendered LORD, which is derived from the verb HAYAH, to be

took it out, behold, his hand was ^Rleprous like snow.   Num. 12:10; 2 Kin. 5:27

7 Then He said, "Put your hand into your bosom again." So he put his hand into his bosom again; and when he took it out of his bosom, behold, ^Rit was restored like *the rest of* his flesh.   [Matt. 8:3]; Luke 17:12–14

8"And it shall come about that if they will not believe you or ^Theed the ^Twitness of the first sign, they may believe the^Twitness of the last sign.   *listen to • voice*

9"But it shall be that if they will not believe even these two signs or heed what you say, then you shall take some water from the Nile and pour it on the dry ground; and the water which you take from the Nile will become blood on the dry ground."

"I Am Slow of Speech"

10 Then Moses said to the LORD, "Please, Lord, I have never been eloquent, neither recently nor in time past, nor since Thou hast spoken to Thy servant; for I am slow of speech and slow of tongue."   *a man of words*

11 And the LORD said to him, "Who has made man's mouth? Or ^Rwho makes *him* dumb or deaf, or seeing or blind? Is it not I, the LORD?   Ps. 94:9; 146:8; Matt. 11:5

12"Now then go, and^RI, even I, will be with your mouth, and teach you what you are to say."   Ex. 4:15, 16; Deut. 18:18; Is. 50:4; Jer. 1:9

13 But he said, "Please, Lord, now send *the message* by whomever Thou wilt."

14 Then the anger of the LORD burned against Moses, and He said, "Is there not your brother Aaron the Levite? I know that he speaks fluently. And moreover, behold, ^Rhe is coming out to meet you; when he sees you, he will be glad in his heart.   Ex. 4:27

15"And you are to speak to him and ^Rput the words in his mouth; and I, even I, will be with your mouth and his mouth, and I will teach you what you are to do.   Deut. 18:18

16"Moreover,^Rhe shall speak for you to the people; and it shall come about that he shall be as a mouth for you, and you shall be as God to him.   Ex. 7:1, 2

17"And you shall take in your hand ^Rthis staff, ^Rwith which you shall perform the signs."   Ex. 4:2, 20; 17:9 • Ex. 7:9-20; 14:16

Moses Returns to Egypt

18 Then Moses departed and returned to ^TJethro ^Rhis father-in-law, and said to him, "Please, let me go, that I may return to my brethren who are in Egypt, and see if they are still alive." And Jethro said to Moses, "Go in peace."   Heb., *Jether* • Ex. 2:21; 3:1

19 Now the LORD said to Moses in Midian, "Go ^Tback to Egypt, for all the men who were seeking your life are dead."   *return*

20 So Moses took his wife and his ^Rsons and mounted them on a donkey, and he returned to the land of Egypt. Moses also took the staff of God in his hand.   Acts 7:29

21 And the LORD said to Moses, "When you go back to Egypt see that you perform before Pharaoh all the wonders which I have put in your power; but I will harden his heart so that he will not let the people go.

22"Then you shall say to Pharaoh, 'Thus says the LORD, "Israel^Ris My son, My first-born.   Is. 63:16; 64:8; Jer. 31:9; Hos. 11:1; [Rom. 9:4]

23"So I said to you, 'Let^RMy son go, that he may serve Me'; but you have refused to let him go. Behold, ^RI will kill your son, your first-born." ' "   Ex. 5:1; 6:11; 7:16 • Ps. 105:36

Moses Reinstitutes Circumcision

24 Now it came about at the lodging place on the way that the LORD met him and ^Rsought to put him to death.   Num. 22:22

25 Then Zipporah took a flint and cut off her son's foreskin and ^Tthrew *it* at Moses' feet, and she said, "You are indeed a bridegroom of blood to me." *made it touch at his feet*

26 So He let him alone. At that time she said, "*You are* a bridegroom of blood"—^Tbecause of the circumcision. *with reference to*

Israel Accepts the Call of Moses as Deliverer

27 ^RNow the LORD said to Aaron, "Go to meet Moses in the wilderness." So he went and met him at the^Rmountain of God, and he kissed him.   Ex. 4:14 • Ex. 3:1; 18:5; 24:13

28 And^RMoses told Aaron all the words of the LORD with which He had sent him, and ^Rall the signs that He had commanded him *to do.*   Ex. 4:15f. • Ex. 4:8f.

29 Then Moses and Aaron went and assembled all the elders of the sons of Israel;

30 and Aaron spoke all the words which the LORD had spoken to Moses. He then performed the signs in the sight of the people.

31 So the people believed; and when they heard that the LORD ^Twas^Rconcerned about the sons of Israel and that He had seen their affliction, then ^Rthey bowed low and worshiped.   *had visited* • Gen. 50:24 • 1 Chr. 29:20

CHAPTER 5

Pharaoh Rejects Moses

AND afterward Moses and Aaron came and said to Pharaoh, "Thus^R says the LORD, the God of Israel, 'Let^R My people go that they may celebrate a feast to Me in the wilderness.' "   Ex. 3:18 • Ex. 4:23; 6:11; 7:16

2 But Pharaoh said, "Who^R is the LORD that I should obey His voice to let Israel go? I do not know the LORD, and besides, I will not let Israel go."   2 Kin. 18:35; 2 Chr. 32:14

3 Then they said, "The^R God of the Hebrews has met with us. Please, let us go a ^Tthree days' journey into the wilderness that we may sacrifice to the LORD our God, lest He fall upon us with pestilence or with the sword."   Ex. 3:18 • 60 mi.

4 But the king of Egypt said to them, "Moses and Aaron, why do you ^Tdraw the people away from their ^Twork? Get *back* to your^Tlabors!"   *loose • works • burdens*

5 Again Pharaoh said, "Look, the people of the land are now many, and you would have them cease from their labors!"

6 So the same day Pharaoh commanded [R]the taskmasters over the people and their foremen, saying,   Ex. 1:11; 3:7; 5:10, 13, 14

7"You are no longer to give the people straw to make brick as previously; let them go and gather straw for themselves.

8"But the quota of bricks which they were making previously, you shall impose on them; you are not to reduce any of it. Because they are lazy, therefore they cry out, 'Let us go and sacrifice to our God.'

9"Let the labor be heavier on the men, and let them work at it that they may pay no attention to false words."

10 So[R]the taskmasters of the people and their foremen went out and spoke to the people, saying, "Thus says Pharaoh, 'I am not going to give you any straw.   Ex. 1:11

11 'You go and get straw for yourselves wherever you can find it; but none of your labor will be reduced.' "

12 So the people scattered through all the land of Egypt to gather stubble for straw.

13 And the taskmasters pressed them, saying, "Complete your work quota, your daily amount, just as when you had straw."

14 Moreover, the foremen of the sons of Israel, whom Pharaoh's taskmasters had set over them, were beaten [t]and were asked, "Why have you not completed your required amount either yesterday or today in making brick as previously?"   saying

Israel Rejects Moses

15 Then the foremen of the sons of Israel came and cried out to Pharaoh, saying, "Why do you deal this way with your servants?

16"There is no straw given to your servants, yet they keep saying to us, 'Make bricks!' And behold, your servants are being beaten; but it is the fault of your own people."

17 But he said, "You are[R]lazy, very lazy; therefore you say, 'Let us go and sacrifice to the LORD.'   Ex. 5:8

18"So go now and work; for you shall be given no straw, yet you must deliver the quota of bricks."

19 And the foremen of the sons of Israel saw that they were in trouble [t]because they were told, "You must not reduce your daily amount of bricks."   saying

20 When they left Pharaoh's presence, they met Moses and Aaron as they were [t]waiting for them.   standing to meet

21 And they said to them, "May the LORD look upon you and judge you, for you have [R]made [4]us odious in Pharaoh's sight and in the sight of his servants, to put a sword in their hand to kill us."   2 Sam. 10:6; 1 Chr. 19:6

Moses Questions God's Plan

22 Then Moses returned to the LORD and said, "O[R]Lord, why hast Thou brought harm to this people? Why didst Thou ever send me?   Num. 11:11; Jer. 4:10

23"Ever since I came to Pharaoh to speak in Thy name, he has done harm to this people;[R]and Thou hast not delivered Thy people at all."   Ex. 3:8

CHAPTER 6

God Reassures Moses

THEN the LORD said to Moses, "Now you shall see what I will do to Pharaoh; for[t]under[R]compulsion he shall let them go, and[t]under compulsion he shall drive them out of his land."   by a strong hand · Ex. 3:19, 20; 7:4, 5

2 God spoke further to Moses and said to him, "I am[R]the LORD;   Ex. 3:14, 15

3 and I appeared to Abraham, Isaac, and Jacob, as [t]God[R]Almighty, but by My name, [5]LORD, I did not make Myself known to them.   Heb., El Shaddai · Gen. 17:1; 35:11; 48:3

4"And I also established [R]My covenant with them, to give them the land of Canaan, the land in which they sojourned.   Gen. 12:7

5"And furthermore I have [R]heard the groaning of the sons of Israel, because the Egyptians are holding them in bondage; and I have remembered My covenant.   Ex. 2:24

6"Say, therefore, to the sons of Israel, 'I am the LORD, and I will bring you out from under the burdens of the Egyptians, and I will deliver you from their bondage. I will also redeem you with [R]an outstretched arm and with great judgments.   Deut. 4:34; 5:15

7 'Then I will take you [t]for My people, and I will be [t]your God; and you shall know that I am the LORD your God, who brought you out from under the burdens of the Egyptians.   to Me for a people · to you for a God

8 'And I will bring you to the land which[R]I [t]swore to give to Abraham, Isaac, and Jacob, and I will give it to you for a possession; I am the LORD.' "   Neh. 9:15 · lifted up My hand

Moses Reassures Israel

9 So Moses spoke thus to the sons of Israel, but they did not listen to Moses on[R]account of their[t]despondency and cruel bondage.   Ex. 2:23 · shortness of spirit

God Recommissions Moses

10 Now the LORD spoke to Moses, saying,

11"Go, tell Pharaoh king of Egypt to let the sons of Israel go out of his land."

12 But Moses spoke before the LORD, saying, "Behold, the sons of Israel have not listened to me; how then will Pharaoh listen to me, for I am[R]unskilled in speech?"   Jer. 1:6

13 Then the LORD spoke to Moses and to Aaron, and gave them a charge to the sons of Israel and to Pharaoh king of Egypt, to bring the sons of Israel out of the land of Egypt.

[4] Lit., our savor to stink
[5] Heb., YHWH, usually rendered LORD

14 These are the heads of their fathers' households. The sons of Reuben, Israel's first-born: Hanoch and Pallu, Hezron and Carmi; these are the families of Reuben.

15 And the [R]sons of Simeon: Jemuel and Jamin and Ohad and Jachin and Zohar and Shaul the son of a Canaanite woman; these are the families of Simeon.   1 Chr. 4:24

16 And these are the names of [t]the sons of Levi according to their generations: Gershon and Kohath and Merari; and the [t]length of Levi's life was one hundred and thirty-seven years.   Gen. 46:11; Num. 3:17 • years

17 [R]The sons of Gershon: Libni and Shimei, according to their families.   Num. 3:18-20

18 And [t]the sons of Kohath: Amram and Izhar and Hebron and Uzziel; and the [t]length of Kohath's life was one hundred and thirty-three years.   Num. 3:19; 1 Chr. 6:2, 18 • years

19 And [t]the sons of Merari: Mahli and Mushi. These are the families of the Levites according to their generations.   Num. 3:20

20 And Amram married his father's sister Jochebed, and she bore him Aaron and Moses; and the [t]length of Amram's life was one hundred and thirty-seven years.   years

21 And [t]the sons of Izhar: Korah and Nepheg and Zichri.   Num. 16:1; 1 Chr. 6:37, 38

22 And the sons of Uzziel: Mishael and [t]Elzaphan and Sithri.   In Num. 3:30, Elizaphan

23 And Aaron [t]married Elisheba, the daughter of Amminadab, the sister of Nahshon, and she bore him Nadab and Abihu, Eleazar and Ithamar.   took to him to wife

24 And the sons of Korah: Assir and Elkanah and [T]Abiasaph; these are the families of the Korahites.   In 1 Chr. 6:23 and 9:19, Ebiasaph

25 And Aaron's son Eleazar [T]married one of the daughters of Putiel, and she bore him [R]Phinehas. These are the heads of the fathers' households of the Levites according to their families.   took to him to wife • Ps. 106:30

26 It was the same Aaron and Moses to whom the LORD said, "Bring [R]out the sons of Israel from the land of Egypt according to their [R]hosts."   Ex. 3:10; 6:13 • Ex. 7:4; 12:17, 51

27 They were the ones [R]who spoke to Pharaoh king of Egypt [T]about bringing out the sons of Israel from Egypt; it was the same Moses and Aaron.   Ex. 5:1 • to bring out

Moses Objects

28 Now it came about on the day when the LORD spoke to Moses in the land of Egypt,

29 that the LORD spoke to Moses, saying, "I [t]am the LORD; speak to Pharaoh king of Egypt all that I speak to you."   Ex. 6:2, 6, 8

30 But Moses said before the LORD, "Behold, I am [t]unskilled in speech; how then will Pharaoh listen to me?"   uncircumcised of lips

CHAPTER 7

God Reassures Moses

THEN the LORD said to Moses, "See, I make you as God to Pharaoh, and your brother Aaron shall be your prophet.

2 "You shall speak all that I command you, and your brother [R]Aaron shall speak to Pharaoh that he let the sons of Israel go out of his land.   Ex. 4:15

3 "But [R]I will harden Pharaoh's heart that I may [h]multiply My signs and My wonders in the land of Egypt.   Ex. 4:21 • Acts 7:36

4 "When Pharaoh will not listen to you, then I will lay My hand on Egypt, and bring out My hosts, My people the sons of Israel, from the land of Egypt by great judgments.

5 "And [R]the Egyptians shall know that I am the LORD, when I stretch out My hand on Egypt and bring out the sons of Israel from their midst."   Ex. 7:17; 8:19, 22; 10:7; 14:4, 18, 25

6 So Moses and Aaron did it; [t]as the LORD commanded them, thus they did.   Gen. 6:22

7 And Moses was [R]eighty years old and Aaron [T]eighty-three, when they spoke to Pharaoh.   Deut. 29:5; 31:2; 34:7 • 83 years old

Aaron's Rod Swallows
Pharaoh's Rods

8 Now the LORD spoke to Moses and Aaron, saying,

9 "When Pharaoh speaks to you, saying, 'Work [T]a miracle,' then you shall say to Aaron, 'Take your staff and throw it down before Pharaoh, that it may become a serpent.' "   Show a wonder for yourselves

10 So Moses and Aaron came to Pharaoh, and thus they did just as the LORD had commanded; and Aaron threw his staff down before Pharaoh and [T]his servants, and it [T]became a serpent.   before his • Ex. 4:3; 7:9

11 Then Pharaoh also [R]called for the wise men and the sorcerers, and they also, the [A]magicians of Egypt, did [t]the same with their secret arts.   Dan. 2:2 • soothsayer priests • thus

12 For each one threw down his staff and they turned into serpents. But Aaron's staff swallowed up their staffs.

13 Yet [R]Pharaoh's heart was [T]hardened, and he did not listen to them, as the LORD had said.   Ex. 4:21; 7:3, 22; 8:15, 19, 32 • strong

First Plague: Blood

14 Then the LORD said to Moses, "Pharaoh's heart is [s]stubborn; he refuses to let the people go.   hard; lit., heavy

15 "Go to Pharaoh in the morning [T]as [R]he is going out to the water, and station yourself to meet him on the bank of the Nile; and you shall take in your hand the staff that was turned into a serpent.   behold • Ex. 2:5; 8:20

16 "And [t]you will say to him, 'The LORD, the God of the Hebrews, sent me to you, saying, "Let My people go, that they may serve Me in the wilderness. But behold, you have not listened until now."   Ex. 3:13, 18; 4:22; 5:1

17 'Thus says the LORD, "By [t]this you shall know that I am the LORD: behold, I will strike [t]the water that is in the Nile with the staff that is in my hand, and it shall be turned into blood.   Ezek. 25:17 • upon the waters

18"And the fish that are in the Nile will die, and the Nile will ᵀbecome foul; and the Egyptians will find difficulty in drinking water from the Nile." ' "   *have a bad smell*
19 Then the LORD said to Moses, "Say to Aaron, 'Take your staff and ᴿstretch out your hand over the waters of Egypt, over their rivers, over their ^streams, and over their pools, and over all their reservoirs of water, that they may become blood; and there shall be blood throughout all the land of Egypt, both in *vessels of* wood and in *vessels of* stone.' "   Ex. 8:5, 6, 16; 9:22; 10:12, 21 • *canals*
20 So Moses and Aaron did even as the LORD had commanded. And he lifted up ᵀthe staff and struck the water that *was* in the Nile, in the sight of Pharaoh and in the sight of his servants, and all the water that *was* in the Nile was turned to blood.   *with the staff*
21 And the fish that *were* in the Nile died, and the Nile ᵀbecame foul, so that the Egyptians could not drink water from the Nile. And the blood was through all the land of Egypt.   *had a bad smell*
22 But the magicians of Egypt did ᵀthe same with their secret arts; and Pharaoh's heart was ᵀhardened, and he did not listen to them, as the LORD had said.   *thus • strong*
23 Then Pharaoh turned and went into his house with no concern even for this.
24 So all the Egyptians dug around the Nile for water to drink, for they could not drink of the water of the Nile.
25 And seven days ᵇpassed after the LORD had struck the Nile.   *were fulfilled*

CHAPTER 8

Second Plague: Frogs

Tᴴᴱᴺ the LORD said to Moses, "Go to Pharaoh and say to him, 'Thus says the LORD, "Let ᴿ My people go, that they may serve Me."   Ex. 3:18; 4:23
2"But if you refuse to let *them* go, behold, I will smite your whole territory with frogs.
3"And the Nile will ᴿswarm with frogs, which will come up and go into your house and into your bedroom and on your bed, and into the houses of your servants and on your people, and into your ovens and into your kneading bowls.   Ps. 105:30
4"So the frogs will come up on you and your people and all your servants." ' "
5 Then the LORD said to Moses, "Say to Aaron, 'Stretch out your hand with your staff over the rivers, over the ^streams and over the pools, and make frogs come up on the land of Egypt.' "   *canals*
6 So Aaron stretched out his hand over the waters of Egypt, and the ᵀfrogs came up and covered the land of Egypt.   *frog*
7 And the magicians did ᵀthe same with their secret arts, ᵀmaking frogs come up on the land of Egypt.   *thus • and made*
8 Then Pharaoh called for Moses and Aaron and said, "Entreat ᴿ the LORD that He remove the frogs from me and from my peo-

ple; and I will let the people go, that they may sacrifice to the LORD."   Num. 21:7
9 And Moses said to Pharaoh, "The ᵀhonor is yours to tell me: when shall I entreat for you and your servants and your people, that the frogs be ᵀdestroyed from you and your houses, *that* they may be left only in the Nile?"   *Glory over me • cut off*
10 Then he said, "Tomorrow." So he said, "*May it be* according to your word, that you may know that there is ʰno one like the LORD our God.   Ex. 9:14; Deut. 4:35, 39; 33:26
11"And the frogs will depart from you and your houses and your servants and your people; they will be left only in the Nile."
12 Then Moses and Aaron went out from Pharaoh, and ᴿMoses cried to the LORD concerning the frogs which He had ᶦinflicted upon Pharaoh.   Ex. 8:30; 9:33; 10:18 • *placed*
13 And the LORD did according to the word of Moses, and the frogs died out of the houses, the courts, and the fields.
14 So they piled them in heaps, and the land ᵀbecame foul.   *had a bad smell*
15 But when Pharaoh saw that there was relief, he hardened his heart and did not listen to them, as the LORD had said.

Third Plague: Gnats

16 Then the LORD said to Moses, "Say to Aaron, 'Stretch out your staff and strike the dust of the earth, that it may become ⁶gnats through all the land of Egypt.' "
17 And they did so; and Aaron stretched out his hand with his staff, and struck the dust of the earth, and there were gnats on man and beast. All the dust of the earth became gnats through all the land of Egypt.
18 And the magicians tried with their secret arts to bring forth gnats, but they could not; so there were gnats on man and beast.
19 Then the magicians said to Pharaoh, "This ᴿ is the finger of God." But Pharaoh's heart was ᵀhardened, and he did not listen to them, as the LORD had said.   Ps. 8:3 • *strong*

Fourth Plague: Flies

20 Now the LORD said to Moses, "Rise early in the morning and present yourself before Pharaoh, as he comes out to the water, and say to him, 'Thus says the LORD, "Let My people go, that they may serve Me.
21"For if you will not let My people go, behold, I will send swarms of insects on you and on your servants and on your people and into your houses; and the houses of the Egyptians shall be full of swarms of insects, and also the ground on which they *dwell*.
22"But on that day I will set apart the land of Goshen, where My people are ᶦliving, so that no swarms of insects will be there, in order that you may know that I, the LORD, am in the midst of the land.   *standing*
23"And I will ⁷put a division between My

---

⁶ Or, *lice*   ⁷ Lit., *set a ransom*

people and your people. Tomorrow this sign shall occur.'''"

24 Then the LORD did so. And there came great swarms of insects into the house of Pharaoh and the houses of his servants and the land was laid waste because of the swarms of insects in all the land of Egypt.

25 And Pharaoh [R]called for Moses and Aaron and said, "Go, sacrifice to your God within the land."   Ex. 8:8; 9:27; 10:16

26 But Moses said, "It is not right to do so, for we shall sacrifice to the LORD our God [T]what is an abomination to the Egyptians. If we sacrifice [T]what is an abomination to the Egyptians before their eyes, will they not then stone us?   *the abomination of Egypt*

27"We must go a [T]three days' journey into the wilderness and sacrifice to the LORD our God as He [T]commands us."   60 mi. • *says to us*

28 And Pharaoh said, "I will let you go, that you may sacrifice to the LORD your God in the wilderness; only you shall not go very far away. Make supplication for me."

29 Then Moses said, "Behold, I am going out from you, and I shall make supplication to the LORD that the swarms of insects may depart from Pharaoh, from his servants, and from his people tomorrow; only do not let Pharaoh deal deceitfully again in not letting the people go to sacrifice to the LORD."

30 So [R]Moses went out from Pharaoh and made supplication to the LORD.   Ex. 8:12

31 And the LORD did [T]as Moses asked, and removed the swarms of insects from Pharaoh, from his servants and from his people; not one remained. *according to the word of Moses*

32 But Pharaoh hardened his heart this time also, and he did not let the people go.

CHAPTER 9

Fifth Plague:
Disease on Beasts

THEN the LORD said to Moses, "Go to Pharaoh and speak to him, 'Thus says the LORD, the God of the Hebrews, "Let[R] My people go, that they may serve Me.   Ex. 4:23

2 "For[R]if you refuse to let *them* go, and [T]continue to hold them,   Ex. 8:2 • *still hold*

3 behold,[R]the hand of the LORD [T]will come *with* a very severe pestilence on your livestock which are in the field, on the horses, on the donkeys, on the camels, on the herds, and on the flocks.   Ps. 39:10 • *will be*

4 "But the LORD will make a distinction between the livestock of Israel and the livestock of Egypt, so that nothing will die of all that belongs to the sons of Israel."'"

5 And the LORD set a definite time, saying, "Tomorrow the LORD will do this thing in the land."

6 So the LORD did this thing on the morrow, and [a]all the livestock of Egypt died;[b]but of the livestock of the sons of Israel, not one died.   Ex. 9:19, 20, 25; Ps. 78:48 • Ex. 9:4

7 And Pharaoh sent, and behold, there

was not even one of the livestock of Israel dead. But the heart of Pharaoh was [T]hardened, and he did not let the people go. *heavy*

Sixth Plague:
Boils on Man and Beast

8 Then the LORD said to Moses and Aaron, "Take for yourselves handfuls of soot from a kiln, and let Moses throw it toward the sky in the sight of Pharaoh.

9"And it will become fine dust over all the land of Egypt, and will become [R]boils breaking out with sores on man and beast through all the land of Egypt."   Deut. 28:27

10 So they took soot from a kiln, and stood before Pharaoh; and Moses threw it toward the sky, and it became boils breaking out with sores on man and beast.

11 And the [A]magicians could not stand before Moses because of the boils, for the boils were on the magicians [T]as well as on all the Egyptians.   *soothsayer priests • and on all*

12 And the LORD [T]hardened Pharaoh's heart, and he did not listen to them, just as the LORD had spoken to Moses.   *made strong*

Seventh Plague: Hail

13 Then the LORD said to Moses, "Rise[R] up early in the morning and stand before Pharaoh and say to him, 'Thus says the LORD, the God of the Hebrews, "Let[R] My people go, that they may serve Me.   Ex. 8:20 • Ex. 4:23

14"For this time I will send all My plagues [T]on you and your servants and your people, so that you may know that there is no one like Me in all the earth.   *to your heart*

15"For *if by* now I had put forth My hand and struck you and your people with pestilence, you would then have been cut off from the earth.

16"But, indeed, for this cause I have allowed you to [T]remain, in order to show you My power, and in order to proclaim My name through all the earth.   *stand*

17"Still you exalt yourself against My people [T]by not letting them go.   *so as not to let*

18"Behold, about this time tomorrow, I will [T]send a very heavy hail, such as has not been *seen* in Egypt from the day it was founded [T]until now.   *cause to rain • and until now*

19"Now therefore send, bring your livestock and whatever you have in the field to safety. Every man and beast that is found in the field and is not brought home, when the hail comes down on them, will die."'"

20 [R]The one among the servants of Pharaoh who[A]feared the word of the LORD made his servants and his livestock flee into the houses;   [Prov. 13:13] • *revered*

21 but he who [T]paid no regard to the word of the LORD left his servants and his livestock in the field.   *did not set his heart to*

22 Now the LORD said to Moses, "Stretch out your hand toward the sky, that [T]hail may fall on all the land of Egypt, on man and beast and on every plant of the field, throughout the land of Egypt."   Rev. 16:21

23 And Moses stretched out his staff toward the sky, and the LORD sent thunder and hail, and fire ran down to the earth. And the LORD rained hail on the land of Egypt.

24 So there was hail, and fire ᵀflashing continually in the midst of the hail, very severe, such as had not been in all the land of Egypt since it became a nation.   *taking hold of itself*

25 And ᵀthe hail struck all that was in the field through all the land of Egypt, both man and beast; the hail also struck every plant of the field and shattered every tree of the field.   Ex. 9:19; Ps. 78:47, 48; 105:32, 33

26 Only in the land of Goshen, where the sons of Israel *were*, there was no hail.

27 Then Pharaoh ᴿsent for Moses and Aaron, and said to them, "I have sinned this time; the LORD is the righteous one, and I and my people are the wicked ones.   Ex. 8:8

28 "Make ᴿ supplication to the LORD, for there has been enough of God's ᵀthunder and hail; and I will let you go, and you shall stay no longer."   Ex. 8:8, 28; 10:17 • *sounds*

29 And Moses said to him, "As soon as I go out of the city, I will spread out my hands to the LORD; the thunder will cease, and there will be hail no longer, that you may know that the earth is the LORD's.

30 "But as for you and your servants, I know that ᴿyou do not yet ᵀfear ᵀthe LORD God."   [Is. 26:10] • *reverence* • *before the LORD*

31 (Now the flax and the ᴿbarley were ᵀruined, for the barley was in the ear and the flax was in bud.   Ruth 1:22; 2:23 • *smitten*

32 But the wheat and the spelt were not ᵀruined, for they *ripen* late.)   *smitten*

33 So Moses went out of the city from Pharaoh, and spread out his hands to the LORD; and the thunder and the hail ceased, and rain no longer poured on the earth.

34 But when Pharaoh saw that the rain and the hail and the ᵀthunder had ceased, he sinned again and ᵀhardened his heart, he and his servants.   *sounds* • *made heavy*

35 And Pharaoh's heart was hardened, and he did not let the sons of Israel go, just as the LORD had spoken through Moses.

CHAPTER 10

Eighth Plague: Locusts

THEN the LORD said to Moses, "Go to Pharaoh, for I have ⁸hardened his heart and the heart of his servants, that I may perform these signs of Mine ᵀamong them,   *in his midst*

2 and that you may tell in the ᵀhearing of your son, and of your grandson, how I made a mockery of the Egyptians, and how I ᵀperformed My signs among them; that you may know that I am the LORD."   *ears* • *put*

3 And Moses and Aaron went to Pharaoh and said to him, "Thus says the LORD, the God of the Hebrews, 'How long will you refuse to humble yourself before Me?ᴿLet My people go, that they may serve Me.   Ex. 4:23

4 'For if you refuse to let My people go,

behold, tomorrow I will bring locusts into your territory.

5 'And they shall cover the surface of the land, so that no one shall be able to see the land.ᴿThey shall also eat the rest of what has escaped—what is left to you from the hail—and they shall eat every tree which sprouts for you out of the field.   Joel 1:4; 2:25

6 'Then your houses shall be filled, and the houses of all your servants and the houses of all the Egyptians, *something* which neither your fathers nor your grandfathers have seen, from the day that they ᵀcame upon the earth until this day.' " And he turned and went out from Pharaoh. *were*

7 And Pharaoh's servants said to him, "How long will this man be ᴿa snare to us? Let the men go, that they may serve the LORD their God. Do you not ᵀrealize that Egypt is destroyed?"   Josh. 23:13 • *know*

8 So Moses and Aaron were brought back to Pharaoh, and he said to them, "Go, serve the LORD your God!ᵀWho are the ones that are going?"   *Who and who are*

9 And Moses said, "Weᴿ shall go with our young and our old; with our sons and our daughters, ᴿwith our flocks and our herds we will go, for we ᵀmust hold a feast to the LORD."   Ex. 12:37, 38 • Ex. 10:26 • *have a feast*

10 Then he said to them, "Thus may the LORD be with you, ᵀif ever I let you and your little ones go! Take heed, for evil is ᵀin your mind.   *when I* • *before your face*

11 "Not so! Go now, the men *among you*, and serve the LORD, for ᵀthat is what you desire." So ᴿthey were driven out from Pharaoh's presence.   *you desire it* • Ex. 10:28

12 Then the LORD said to Moses, "Stretch ᴿ out your hand over the land of Egypt for the locusts, that they may come up on the land of Egypt, and eat every plant of the land, *even* all that the hail has left."   Ex. 7:19

13 So Moses stretched out his staff over the land of Egypt, and the LORD directed an east wind on the land all that day and all that night; and when it was morning, the east wind ᵀbrought the locusts.   *carried*

14 And the locusts came up over all the land of Egypt and settled in all the territory of Egypt; *they were* very ᵀnumerous. There had never been so *many* locusts, nor would there be so *many* ᵀagain.   *heavy* • *after them*

15 For they covered the surface of the whole land, so that the land was darkened; and they ate every plant of the land and all the fruit of the trees that the hail had left. Thus nothing green was left on tree or plant of the field through all the land of Egypt.

16 Then Pharaoh hurriedly ᴿcalled for Moses and Aaron, and he said, "Iᴿ have sinned against the LORD your God and against you.   Ex. 8:8 • Ex. 9:27

17 "Now therefore, please forgive my sin only this once, and ᴿmake supplication to the LORD your God, that He would only remove this death from me."   1 Kin. 13:6

⁸ Lit., *made heavy*

18 And [H]he went out from Pharaoh and made supplication to the LORD.   Ex. 8:30
19 So the LORD shifted *the wind* to a very strong west wind which took up the locusts and drove them into the [9]Red Sea; not one locust was left in all the territory of Egypt.
20 But the LORD hardened Pharaoh's heart, and he did not let the sons of Israel go.

Ninth Plague: Darkness

21 Then the LORD said to Moses, "Stretch out your hand toward the sky, that there may be darkness over the land of Egypt, even a darkness which may be felt."
22 So Moses stretched out his hand toward the sky, and there was thick darkness in all the land of Egypt for three days.
23 They did not see one another, nor did anyone rise from his place for three days, [R]but all the sons of Israel had light in their dwellings.   Ex. 8:22
24 Then Pharaoh [R]called to Moses, and said, "Go, serve the LORD; only let your flocks and your herds be detained. Even your little ones may go with you."   Ex. 10:10
25 But Moses said, "You must also let us have sacrifices and burnt offerings, that we may sacrifice *them* to the LORD our God.
26 "Therefore, [R] our livestock, too, will go with us; not a hoof will be left behind, for we shall take some of them to serve the LORD our God. And until we arrive there, we ourselves do not know with what we shall serve the LORD."   Ex. 10:9
27 But the LORD hardened Pharaoh's heart, and he was not willing to let them go.
28 Then Pharaoh said to him, "Get [R] away from me! [T]Beware, do not see my face again, for in the day you see my face you shall die!"   Ex. 10:11 · *Take heed to yourself*
29 And Moses said, "You are right; [R]I shall never see your face again!"   Heb. 11:27

CHAPTER 11

Tenth Plague: Death Announced

NOW the LORD said to Moses, "One more plague I will bring on Pharaoh and on Egypt; after that he will let you go from here. When he lets you go, he will surely drive you out from here completely.
2 "Speak now in the [T]hearing of the people that each man ask from his neighbor and each woman from her neighbor for articles of silver and articles of gold."   *ears*
3 [R]And the LORD gave the people favor in the sight of the Egyptians. [R]Furthermore, the man Moses *himself* was [T]greatly esteemed in the land of Egypt, *both* in the sight of Pharaoh's servants and in the sight of the people.   Ps. 106:46 · Deut. 34:10-12 · *very great*
4 And Moses said, "Thus says the LORD, 'About [R]midnight I am going out into the midst of Egypt,   Ex. 12:29
5 and [R]all the first-born in the land of Egypt shall die, from the first-born of the

Pharaoh who sits on his throne, even to the first-born of the slave girl who is behind the millstones; all the first-born of the cattle as well.   Ex. 12:12, 29; Ps. 78:51; 105:36
6 'Moreover, there shall be [R]a great cry in all the land of Egypt, such as there has not been *before* and such as shall never be again.   Ex. 12:30
7 'But against any of the sons of Israel a dog shall not *even* [T]bark, whether against man or beast, that you may [T]understand how the LORD makes a distinction between Egypt and Israel.'   *sharpen his tongue · know*
8 "And all these your servants will come down to me and bow themselves before me, saying, 'Go out, you and all the people who follow you,' and after that I will go out." And he went out from Pharaoh in hot anger.
9 Then the LORD said to Moses, "Pharaoh will not listen to you, so that My wonders will be multiplied in the land of Egypt."
10 And [R]Moses and Aaron performed all these wonders before Pharaoh; yet the LORD hardened Pharaoh's heart, and he did not let the sons of Israel go out of his land.   Ex. 4:21

CHAPTER 12

Instructions for the Passover

NOW the LORD said to Moses and Aaron in the land of [T]Egypt,   *Egypt, saying*
2 "This [R] month shall be the beginning of months for you; it is to be the first month of the year to you. Ex. 13:4; 23:15; 34:18; Deut. 16:1
3 "Speak to all the congregation of Israel, saying, 'On the tenth of this month they are each one to take a [A]lamb for themselves, according to their fathers' households, a [A]lamb for each household.   *kid · the*
4 'Now if the household is too small for a [A]lamb, then he and his neighbor nearest to his house are to take one according to the number of persons *in them;* according to [T]what each man should eat, you are to [T]divide the lamb.   *kid · each man's eating · compute for*
5 'Your [A]lamb shall be [R]an unblemished male a year old; you may take it from the sheep or from the goats.   *kid* · 1 Pet. 1:19
6 'And you shall keep it until the fourteenth day of the same month, then the whole assembly of the congregation of Israel is to kill it [R]at twilight.   Deut. 16:4, 6
7 'Moreover, [R] they shall take some of the blood and put it on the two doorposts and on the lintel [T]of the houses in which they eat it.   Ex. 12:22 · *upon*
8 'And they shall eat the flesh that *same* night, roasted with fire, and they shall eat it with unleavened bread and bitter herbs.
9 'Do not eat any of it raw or boiled at all with water, but rather [R]roasted with fire, *both* its head and its legs along with [R]its entrails.   Ex. 12:8 · Ex. 29:13, 17, 22
10 'And [R]you shall not leave any of it over

[9] *Lit., Sea of Reeds*

until morning, but whatever is left of it until morning, you shall burn with fire.   Ex. 16:19

11 'Now you shall eat it in this manner: *with* your loins girded, your sandals on your feet, and your staff in your hand; and you shall eat it in haste—it is [R]the LORD's Passover.   Ex. 12:13, 21, 27, 43

12 'For I will go through the land of Egypt on that night, and will strike down all the first-born in the land of Egypt, both man and beast; and against all the gods of Egypt I will execute judgments—I am the LORD.

13 'And the blood shall be a sign for you on the houses where you [T]live; and when I see the blood I will pass over you, and no plague will befall you [T]to destroy *you* when I strike the land of Egypt.   *are* • *for destruction*

14 'Now [R]this day will be a memorial to you, and you shall celebrate it *as* a feast to the LORD; throughout your generations you are to celebrate it *as* [A]a permanent ordinance.   Ex. 12:6; Lev. 23:4, 5 • *an eternal*

15 'Seven[R] days you shall eat unleavened bread, but on the first day you shall [T]remove leaven from your houses; for whoever eats anything leavened from the first day until the seventh day, that [T]person shall be cut off from Israel.   Num. 28:17 • *cause to cease* • *soul*

16 'And [R]on the first day you shall have a holy assembly, and *another* holy assembly on the seventh day; no work at all shall be done on them, except what must be eaten [T]by every person, that alone may be [T]prepared by you.   Lev. 23:7, 8 • *pertaining to* • *done*

17 'You shall also observe [R]the *Feast of* Unleavened Bread, for on this very day I brought your hosts out of the land of Egypt; therefore you shall observe this day throughout your generations as a [A]permanent ordinance.   Deut. 16:3-8 • *eternal*

18 'In[R] the first *month,* on the fourteenth day of the month at evening, you shall eat unleavened bread, until the twenty-first day of the month at evening.   Ex. 12:2; Lev. 23:5-8

19 'Seven days there shall be no leaven found in your houses; for whoever eats what is leavened, that [T]person shall be cut off from the congregation of Israel, whether *he is* an alien or a native of the land.   *soul*

20 'You shall not eat anything leavened; in all your dwellings you shall eat unleavened bread.' "

Participation in the Passover

21 Then Moses called for all the elders of Israel, and said to them, "Go[T] and take for yourselves lambs according to your families, and slay the Passover *lamb.*   *Draw out*

22 "And you shall take a bunch of hyssop and dip it in the blood which is in the basin, and [T]apply some of the blood that is in the basin to the lintel and the two doorposts; and none of you shall go outside the door of his house until morning.   *cause to touch*

23 "For the LORD will pass through to smite the Egyptians; and when He sees the blood on the lintel and on the two doorposts, the LORD will pass over the door and will [R]not allow the destroyer to come in to your houses to smite *you.*   Rev. 7:3; 9:4

24 "And you shall observe this event as an ordinance for you and your children forever.

25 "And it will come about when you enter the land which the LORD will give you, as He has [T]promised, that you shall observe this [T]rite.   *spoken* • *service*

26 "And it will come about when your children will say to you, 'What[T] does this rite mean to you?'   *What is this service to you?*

27 that you shall say, 'It is a Passover sacrifice to [R]the LORD [T]who passed over the houses of the sons of Israel in Egypt when He smote the Egyptians, but [T]spared our homes.' " And the people bowed low and worshiped.   Ex. 12:11 • *because He* • *delivered*

28 Then the sons of Israel went and did *so;* just as the LORD had commanded Moses and Aaron, so they did.

Redemption Through the Passover

29 Now it came about at [R]midnight that[R]the LORD struck all the first-born in the land of Egypt, from the first-born of Pharaoh who sat on his throne to the first-born of the captive who was in the dungeon, and all the first-born of cattle.   Ex. 11:4, 5 • Ps. 135:8

30 And Pharaoh arose in the night, he and all his servants and all the Egyptians; and there was [A]a great cry in Egypt, for there was no home where there was not someone dead.   Ex. 11:6

31 Then [R]he called for Moses and Aaron at night and said, "Rise up, [R]get out from among my people, both you and the sons of Israel; and go, [A]worship the LORD, as you have said.   Ex. 8:8 • Ex. 8:25 • *serve*

32 "Take[R]both your flocks and your herds, as you have said, and go, and bless me also."   Ex. 10:9, 26

33 And[R]the Egyptians urged the people, to send them out of the land in haste, for they said, "We shall all be dead."   Ps. 105:38

34 So the people took their dough before it was leavened, *with* their kneading bowls bound up in the clothes on their shoulders.

35 Now the sons of Israel had done according to the word of Moses, for they had requested from the Egyptians articles of silver and articles of gold, and clothing;

36 and the LORD had given the people favor in the sight of the Egyptians, so that they let them have their request. Thus they [R]plundered the Egyptians.   Ex. 3:22

Freedom Because of the Passover

37 Now the sons of Israel journeyed from Rameses to Succoth, about six hundred thousand men on foot, aside from children.

38 And a mixed multitude also went up with them, [T]along with flocks and herds, a very large number of livestock.   *and*

39 And they baked the dough which they had brought out of Egypt into cakes of unleavened bread. For it had not become leavened, since they were driven out of Egypt and could not delay, nor had they prepared any provisions for themselves.   *made*

40 Now the time^that the sons of Israel lived in Egypt was^four hundred and thirty years.   *of the sons of Israel who dwelt* • Acts 7:6

41 And it came about at the end of four hundred and thirty years, to the very day, that all the hosts of the LORD went out from the land of Egypt.

42 It is a night^to be observed for the LORD for having brought them out from the land of Egypt; this night is for the LORD,^to be observed^by all the sons of Israel throughout their generations.   *of vigil* • *to the sons*

43 And the LORD said to Moses and Aaron, "This is the ordinance of^the Passover: no ^10foreigner is to eat of it;   Num. 9:14

44 but every man's ^slave purchased with money, after you have circumcised him, then he may eat of it. Gen. 17:12, 13; Lev. 22:11

45 "A^sojourner or a hired servant shall not eat of it.   Lev. 22:10

46 "It is to be eaten in a single house; you are not to bring forth any of the flesh outside of the house,^nor are you to break any bone of it. Num. 9:12; Ps. 34:20; [John 19:33, 36]☆

47 "All^ the congregation of Israel are to ^celebrate this.   Ex. 12:6; Num. 9:13, 14 • *do*

48 "But if a ^stranger sojourns with you, and celebrates the Passover to the LORD, let all his males be circumcised, and then let him come near to celebrate it; and he shall be like a native of the land. But no uncircumcised person may eat of it.   *sojourner*

49 "The^ same law shall ^apply to the native as to the ^stranger who sojourns among you."   *One law • be • sojourner*

50 Then all the sons of Israel did *so;* they did just as the LORD had commanded Moses and Aaron.

51 And it came about on that same day that the LORD brought the sons of Israel out of the land of Egypt^by their hosts. Ex. 6:26

CHAPTER 13

Sanctification as a Result
of the Passover

THEN the LORD spoke to Moses, saying,

2 "Sanctify^ to Me every first-born, the first ^offspring of every womb among the sons of Israel, both of man and beast; it belongs to Me."   Deut. 15:19; Luke 2:23 • *opening*

3 And Moses said to the people, "Remember this day in which you went out from Egypt, from the house of ^slavery; for by ^a powerful hand the LORD brought you out from this place. And nothing leavened shall be eaten.   *slaves • strength of hand*

4 "On this day in the ^month of Abib, you are about to go forth.   Deut. 16:1

5 "And it shall be when the LORD brings you to the land of the Canaanite, the Hittite, the Amorite, the Hivite and the Jebusite, which He swore to your fathers to give you, a land flowing with milk and honey, that you shall observe this rite in this month.

6 "For ^seven days you shall eat unleavened bread, and on the seventh day there shall be a feast to the LORD.   Ex. 12:15-20

7 "Unleavened bread shall be eaten throughout the seven days; and ^nothing leavened shall be seen^among you, nor shall any leaven be seen^among you in all your borders.   Ex. 12:19 • *to*

8 "And^you shall tell your son on that day, saying, 'It is because of what the LORD did for me when I came out of Egypt.' Ps. 44:1

9 "And it shall ^serve as a sign to you on your hand, and as a reminder on your forehead, that the law of the LORD may be in your mouth; for with a powerful hand the LORD brought you out of Egypt.   *be for*

10 "Therefore, you shall ^keep this ordinance at its appointed time from ^year to year.   Ex. 12:24, 25; 13:5 • *days to days*

11 "Now it shall come about when ^the LORD brings you to the land of the Canaanite, as^He swore to you and to your fathers, and gives it to you,   Ex. 13:5 • Ps. 105:42-45

12 that you shall ^devote to the LORD the first offspring of every womb, and the first offspring of every beast that you own; the males belong to the LORD.   *cause to pass over*

13 "But ^every first ^offspring of a donkey you shall redeem with a lamb, but if you do not redeem *it,* then you shall break its neck; and every first-born of man among your sons you shall redeem.   Num. 18:15 • *opening*

14 "And it shall be when your son asks you in time to come, saying, 'What is this?' then you shall say to him, 'With a^powerful hand the LORD brought us out of Egypt, from the house of ^slavery.   *strength of hand • slaves*

15 'And it came about, when Pharaoh was stubborn about letting us go, that the LORD killed every first-born in the land of Egypt, both the first-born of man and the first-born of beast. Therefore, I sacrifice to the LORD the males, the first offspring of every womb, but every first-born of my sons I redeem.'

16 "So it shall ^serve as a sign on your hand, and as phylacteries ^on your forehead, for with a powerful hand the LORD brought us out of Egypt."   *be for • between your eyes*

God Leads Israel

17 Now it came about when Pharaoh had let the people go, that God did not lead them by the way of the land of the Philistines, even though it was near; for God said, "Lest the people change their minds when they see war, and they return to Egypt."

18 Hence God led the people around by the way of the wilderness to the ^Red Sea;

---

^10 Lit., *son of a stranger*

and the sons of Israel went up in martial array from the land of Egypt.   *Sea of Reeds*

19 And Moses took[R]the bones of Joseph with him, for he had made the sons of Israel solemnly swear, saying, "God shall surely [T]take care of you; and you shall carry my bones from here with you."   Josh. 24:32 • *visit*

20 Then they set out from [R]Succoth and camped in Etham on the edge of the wilderness.   Ex. 12:37; Num. 33:6

21 And [R]the LORD was going before them in a pillar of cloud by day to lead them on the way, and in a pillar of fire by night to give them light, that they might [T]travel by day and by night.   Ps. 78:14; 99:7; 105:39 • *go*

22 He[R]did not take away the pillar of cloud by day, nor the pillar of fire by night, from before the people.   Neh. 9:19

CHAPTER 14

NOW the LORD spoke to Moses, saying,
2"Tell the sons of Israel to turn back and camp before [R]Pi-hahiroth, between Migdol and the sea; you shall camp in front of Baalzephon, opposite it, by the sea.   Num. 33:7

Pharaoh Follows Israel

3"For Pharaoh will say of the sons of Israel, 'They are wandering aimlessly in the land; the wilderness has shut them in.'
4"Thus I will[T]harden Pharaoh's heart, and he will chase after them; and I will be honored through Pharaoh and all his army, and the Egyptians will know that I am the LORD." And they did so.   *make strong*
5 When the king of Egypt was told that the people had fled, [T]Pharaoh and his servants had a change of heart toward the people, and they said, "What is this we have done, that we have let Israel go from serving us?"   *the heart of Pharaoh . . . was changed*
6 So he made his chariot ready and took his people with him;
7 and he took six hundred select chariots, and all the *other* chariots of Egypt with officers over all of them.
8 And the LORD [T]hardened the heart of Pharaoh, king of Egypt, and he chased after the sons of Israel as the sons of Israel were going out[T]boldly.   *made strong • with a high hand*
9 Then[R]the Egyptians chased after them *with* all the horses *and* chariots of Pharaoh, his horsemen and his army, and they overtook them camping by the sea, beside Pi-hahiroth, in front of Baal-zephon.   Josh. 24:6

Israel Rebels Against God

10 And as Pharaoh drew near, the sons of Israel [T]looked, and behold, the Egyptians were marching after them, and they became very frightened; [R]so the sons of Israel cried out to the LORD.   *lifted up their eyes •* Josh. 24:7
11 Then[R]they said to Moses, "Is it because there were no graves in Egypt that you have

taken us away to die in the wilderness? Why have you dealt with us in this way,[T]bringing us out of Egypt?   Ps. 106:7, 8 • *so as to bring*
12"Is[R] this not the word that we spoke to you in Egypt, saying, 'Leave us alone that we may serve the Egyptians'? For it would have been better for us to serve the Egyptians than to die in the wilderness."   Ex. 6:9

God Opens the Red Sea

13 But Moses said to the people, "Do[R] not fear![A]Stand by and see the salvation of the LORD which He will accomplish for you today; for the Egyptians whom you have seen today, you will never see them again forever.   Gen. 15:1; 46:3; Ex. 20:20 • *Take your stand*
14"The[R] LORD will fight for you while[R]you keep silent."   Ex. 14:25; Deut. 1:30 • [Is. 30:15]
15 Then the LORD said to Moses, "Why are you crying out to Me? Tell the sons of Israel to go forward.
16"And as for you, lift up your staff and stretch out your hand over the sea and divide it, and the sons of Israel shall go through the midst of the sea on dry land.
17"And as for Me, behold, I will [T]harden the hearts of the Egyptians so that they will go in after them; and I will be honored through Pharaoh and all his army, through his chariots and his horsemen.   *make strong*
18"Then[R] the Egyptians will know that I am the LORD, when I am honored through Pharaoh, through his chariots and his horsemen."   Ex. 14:25
19 And [R]the angel of God, who had been going before the camp of Israel, moved and went behind them; and the pillar of cloud moved from before them and stood behind them.   Ex. 13:21, 22
20 So it came between the camp of Egypt and the camp of Israel; and there was the cloud [A]along with the darkness, yet it gave light at night. Thus the one did not come near the other all night.   *and the darkness*
21 Then[R] Moses stretched out his hand over the sea; and the LORD [T]swept the sea *back* by a strong east wind all night, and turned the sea into dry land, so the waters were divided.   Ex. 7:19; 14:16 • *caused to go*
22 And the sons of Israel [T]went through the midst of the sea on the dry land, and the waters *were like* a wall to them on their right hand and on their left.   *entered the*
23 Then [R]the Egyptians took up the pursuit, and all Pharaoh's horses, his chariots and his horsemen went in after them into the midst of the sea.   Ex. 14:4, 17
24 And it came about at the morning watch, that the LORD looked down on the [T]army of the Egyptians[A]through the pillar of fire and cloud and brought the[T]army of the Egyptians into confusion.   *camp • in*
25 And He [A]caused their chariot wheels to swerve, and He made them drive with difficulty; so the Egyptians said, "Let [T]us flee from Israel, for the LORD is fighting for them against the Egyptians."   *removed • me*

26 Then the LORD said to Moses, "Stretch out your hand over the sea so that the waters may come back over the Egyptians, over their chariots and their horsemen."

27 So Moses stretched out his hand over the sea, and the sea returned to its normal state at daybreak, while the Egyptians were fleeing right into it; then the LORD overthrew the Egyptians in the midst of the sea.

28 And the waters returned and covered the chariots and the horsemen, ᵀeven Pharaoh's entire army that had gone into the sea after them; ᴿnot even one of them remained.   *in respect to* · Ps. 78:53; 106:11

29 But the sons of Israel walked on ᴿdry land through the midst of the sea, and the waters *were like* a wall to them on their right hand and on their left. Ps. 66:6; Is. 11:15

30 Thus the LORD saved Israel that day from the hand of the Egyptians, and Israel saw the Egyptians dead on the seashore.

31 And when Israel saw the great ᵀpower which the LORD had ᵘused against the Egyptians, the people ᴬfeared the LORD, and ᴿthey believed in the LORD and in His servant Moses. *hand · done · revered* · John 2:11; 11:45

CHAPTER 15

Israel Praises God

THEN Moses and the sons of Israel sang this song to the LORD, and said,
"Iᴬ will sing to the LORD, for He is highly exalted;   *Let me sing*
ᴿThe horse and its rider He has hurled into the sea.   Jer. 51:21

2 "The LORD is my strength and song,
And He has become my salvation;
This is my God, and I will praise Him;
My father's God, and I will extol Him.

3 "The ᴿLORD is a warrior;   Rev. 19:11
ᴿThe LORD is His name.   Ps. 24:8; 83:18

4 "Pharaoh's chariots and his army He has cast into the sea;
And the choicest of his officers are ᵀdrowned in the ¹¹Red Sea. *sunk*

5 "The deeps cover them;
ᴿThey went down into the depths like a stone.   Ex. 15:10; Neh. 9:11

6 "Thyᴿright hand, O LORD, is majestic in power,   Ex. 3:20; 6:1
ᴿThy right hand, O LORD, shatters the enemy.   Ps. 118:15, 16

7 "And in the greatness of Thine ᵉxcellence Thou dost overthrow those who rise up against Thee;   *exaltation*
Thou dost send forth Thy burning anger, *and* it consumes them as chaff.

8 "Andᴿat the blast of Thy nostrils the waters were piled up,   Job 4:9
ᴿThe flowing waters stood up like a heap;   Ps. 78:13
The deeps were congealed in the heart of the sea.

9 "The enemy said, 'I will pursue, I will overtake, I will divide the spoil;

My ᵀdesire shall be ᵍratified against them;   *soul · be filled with them*
I will draw out my sword, my hand shall destroy them.'

10 "Thouᴿ didst blow with Thy wind, the sea covered them;   Ex. 14:27, 28
ᴿThey sank like lead in the ᴬmighty waters.   Ex. 15:5 · *majestic*

11 "Whoᴿis like Thee among the gods, O LORD?   2 Sam. 7:22; 1 Kin. 8:23
Who is like Thee, majestic in holiness,
ᴿAwesome in praises, ᴿworking wonders?   Ps. 22:23 · Ps. 72:18; 136:4

12 "Thouᵀdidst stretch out Thy right hand,
The earth swallowed them.   Ex. 15:6

13 "In Thy lovingkindness Thou hastᴿled the people whom Thou hast redeemed;   Neh. 9:12; [Ps. 77:20]
In Thy strength Thou hast guided *them* to Thy holy habitation.

14 "Theᴿ peoples have heard, they tremble;
Anguish has gripped the inhabitants of Philistia.   Deut. 2:25; Hab. 3:7

15 "Then the ᴿchiefs of Edom were dismayed;   Gen. 36:15, 40
ᴿThe leaders of Moab, trembling grips them;   Num. 22:3, 4
ᴿAll the inhabitants of Canaan have melted away.   Josh. 2:9, 11, 24; 5:1

16 "Terror and dread fall upon them;
ᴿBy the greatness of Thine arm they are motionless as stone;   Ex. 15:5, 6
Until Thy people pass over, O LORD,
Until the people pass over whom Thouᴿhast purchased.   2 Pet. 2:1

17 "Thou wilt bring them and ᴿplant them in ᴿthe mountain of Thine inheritance,   Ps. 44:2; 80:8, 15 · Ps. 2:6
ᴿThe place, O LORD, which Thou hast made for Thy dwelling,   Ps. 68:16
ᴿThe sanctuary, O Lord, which Thy hands have established.   Ps. 78:69

18 "Theᴿ LORD shall reign forever and ever."   Ps. 10:16; 29:10; Is. 57:15

19 ᴿFor the horses of Pharaoh with his chariots and his horsemen went into the sea, and the LORD brought back the waters of the sea on them; but the sons of Israel walked on ᴿdry land through the midst of the sea.   Ex. 14:23, 28 · Ex. 14:22, 29

20 And ᴿMiriam the prophetess, Aaron's sister, took the timbrel in her hand, and all the women went out after her with timbrels and with ᵈancing.   Ex. 2:4; Num. 26:59 · *dances*

21 And Miriam answered them,
"Singᴿto the LORD, for Heᴬis highly exalted;   Ex. 15:1 · *has triumphed gloriously*
The horse and his rider He has hurled into the sea."

Preserved from Thirst

22 Then Moses led Israel from the ᵀRed Sea, and they went out into the wilderness

¹¹ Lit., *Sea of Reeds*

of Shur; and they went three days in the wilderness and found no water.   *Sea of Reeds*

23 And when they came to [R]Marah, they could not drink the waters of Marah, for they were [T]bitter; therefore it was named [12]Marah.   Num. 33:8 • *from* • Heb., *Marim*

24 So the people [R]grumbled at Moses, saying, "What shall we drink?"   Ps. 106:13

25 Then he cried out to the LORD, and the LORD showed him a tree; and he threw *it* into the waters, and the waters became sweet. There He made for them a statute and regulation, and there He tested them.

26 And He said, "If [R]you will give earnest heed to the voice of the LORD your God, and do what is right in His sight, and give ear to His commandments, and keep all His statutes, I will put none of the diseases on you which I have put on the Egyptians; for I, the LORD, am your healer."   Ex. 19:5, 6; Deut. 7:12

27 Then they came to [R]Elim where there *were* twelve springs of water and seventy date palms, and they camped there beside the waters.   Num. 33:9

CHAPTER 16

Preserved from Hunger

THEN they set out from Elim, and all the congregation of the sons of Israel came to the wilderness of [R]Sin, which is between Elim and Sinai, on the fifteenth day of the second month after their departure from the land of Egypt.   Num. 33:10, 11; Ezek. 30:15

2 And the whole congregation of the sons of Israel [R]grumbled against Moses and Aaron in the wilderness.   1 Cor. 10:10

3 And the sons of Israel said to them, "Would [R]that we had died by the LORD's hand in the land of Egypt, when we sat by the pots of [A]meat, when we ate bread to the full; for you have brought us out into this wilderness to kill this whole assembly with hunger."   Num. 14:2, 3; 20:3; Lam. 4:9 • *flesh*

4 Then the LORD said to Moses, "Behold, [R]I will rain bread from heaven for you; and the people shall go out and gather a day's portion every day, that I may test them, whether or not they will walk in My [13]instruction.   Ps. 78:23–25; 105:40; [John 6:31]

5"And it will come about [R]on the sixth day, when they prepare what they bring in, it will be twice as much as they gather daily."   Ex. 16:22

6 So Moses and Aaron said to all the sons of Israel, "At evening [T]you [R]will know that the LORD has brought you out of the land of Egypt;   *and you* • Ex. 6:7

7 and in the morning [T]you will see the glory of the LORD, for He hears your grumblings against the LORD; and what are we, that you grumble against us?"   *and you*

8 And Moses said, "*This will happen* when the LORD gives you [A]meat to eat in the evening, and bread to the full in the morning; for the LORD hears your grumblings which you grumble against Him. And what are we? Your grumblings are [A]not against us but against the LORD."   *flesh* • 1 Sam. 8:7

9 Then Moses said to Aaron, "Say to all the congregation of the sons of Israel, 'Come [R]near before the LORD, for He has heard your grumblings.' "   Num. 16:16

10 And it came about as Aaron spoke to the whole congregation of the sons of Israel, that they [T]looked toward the wilderness, and behold, [R]the glory of the LORD appeared in the cloud.   *turned* • Ex. 13:21; 16:7; Num. 16:19

11 And the LORD spoke to Moses, saying,

12"I have heard the grumblings of the sons of Israel; speak to them, saying, 'At twilight you shall eat meat, and in the morning you shall be filled with bread; and you shall know that I am the LORD your God.' "

13 So it came about at evening that [A]the quails came up and covered the camp, and in the morning there was a layer of dew around the camp.   Ps. 78:27–29; 105:40

14 When the layer of dew [T]evaporated, behold, on the surface of the wilderness there was a fine flake-like thing, fine as the frost on the ground.   *had gone up* • *face of*

15 When the sons of Israel saw *it*, they said to one another, "What is it?" For they did not know what it was. And Moses said to them, "It is the bread which the LORD has given you to eat.   Heb., *Man hu*, cf. v. 31

16"This is what the LORD has commanded, 'Gather of it every man [T]as much as he should eat; you shall take an omer apiece according to the number of persons each of you has in his tent.' "   *according to his eating*

17 And the sons of Israel did so, and *some* gathered much and *some* little.

18 When they measured it with an [T]omer, [R]he who had gathered much had no excess, and he who had gathered little had no lack; every man gathered [T]as much as he should eat.   2 qt. • 2 Cor. 8:15 • *according to his eating*

19 And Moses said to them, "Let [R]no man leave any of it until morning." Ex. 12:10; 16:23

20 But they did not listen to Moses, and some left part of it until morning, and it bred worms and became foul; and Moses was angry with them.

21 And they gathered it morning by morning, every man as much as he should eat; but when the sun grew hot, it would melt.

22 Now it came about on the sixth day they gathered twice as much bread, two omers for each one. When all the leaders of the congregation came and told Moses,

23 then he said to them, "This is what the LORD [T]meant:[R]Tomorrow is a sabbath observance, a holy sabbath to the LORD. Bake what you will bake and boil what you will boil, and all that is left over [T]put aside to be kept until morning."   *spoke* • Gen. 2:3 • *lay up for you*

24 So they [A]put it aside until morning, as

Moses had ordered, and it did not become foul, nor was there any worm in it. *laid it up*

25 And Moses said, "Eat it today, for today is a sabbath to the LORD; today you will not find it in the field.

26 "Six[R] days you shall gather it, but on the seventh day, *the* sabbath, there will be [T]none." Ex. 20:9, 10 • *none on it*

27 And it came about on the seventh day that some of the people went out to gather, but they found none.

28 Then the LORD said to Moses, "How[R] long do you refuse to keep My commandments and My [14]instructions? 2 Kin. 17:14

29 "See, [T]the LORD has given you the sabbath; therefore He gives you bread for two days on the sixth day. Remain every man in his place; let no man go out of his place on the seventh day." *for the LORD*

30 So the people rested on the seventh day.

31 And the house of Israel named it manna, and it was like coriander seed, white; and its taste was like wafers with honey.

32 Then Moses said, "This is [T]what the LORD has commanded, 'Let an[T]omerful of it be kept throughout your generations, that they may see the bread that I fed you in the wilderness, when I brought you out of the land of Egypt.'" *the thing which* • 2 qt.

33 And Moses said to Aaron, "Take[R]a jar and put an omerful of manna in it, and place it before the LORD, to be kept throughout your generations." Heb. 9:4; Rev. 2:17

34 As the LORD commanded Moses, so Aaron placed it before[R]the Testimony, to be kept. Ex. 25:16, 21; 27:21; 40:20; Num. 17:10

35 [R]And the sons of Israel ate the manna forty years, until they came to an inhabited land; they ate the manna until they came to the border of the land of Canaan. Deut. 8:2f.

36 (Now an omer is a tenth of an ephah.)

CHAPTER 17

Preserved from Thirst Again

THEN all the congregation of the sons of Israel journeyed by stages from the wilderness of Sin, according to the command of the LORD, and camped at Rephidim, and there was no water for the people to drink.

2 Therefore the people [R]quarreled with Moses and said, "Give us water that we may drink." And Moses said to them, "Why do you quarrel with me?[R]Why do you test the LORD?" Ex. 14:11; Num. 20:2, 3, 13 • [Deut. 6:16]

3 But the people thirsted there for water; and [T]they grumbled against Moses and said, "Why, now, have you brought us up from Egypt, to kill [T]us and [T]our children and [T]our livestock with thirst?" *the people • me • my*

4 So Moses cried out to the LORD, saying, "What shall I do to this people? A [R]little more and they will stone me." Num. 14:10

5 Then the LORD said to Moses, "Pass be-

fore the people and take with you some of [R]the elders of Israel; and take in your hand your staff with which [R]you struck the Nile, and go. Ex. 3:16, 18 • Ex. 7:20

6 "Behold, I will stand before you there on the rock at[R]Horeb; and you shall strike the rock, and water will come out of it, that the people may drink." And Moses did so in the sight of the elders of Israel. Ex. 3:1

7 And he named the place [15]Massah and [16]Meribah because of the quarrel of the sons of Israel, and because they tested the LORD, saying, "Is the LORD among us, or not?"

Preserved from Defeat

8 Then [R]Amalek came and fought against Israel at Rephidim. Deut. 25:17-19; 1 Sam. 15:2

9 So Moses said to Joshua, "Choose men for us, and go out, fight against Amalek. Tomorrow I will station myself on the top of the hill with the staff of God in my hand."

10 And Joshua did as Moses told him, and fought against Amalek; and Moses, Aaron, and Hur went up to the top of the hill.

11 So it came about when Moses held his hand up, that Israel prevailed, and when he let his hand [T]down, Amalek prevailed. *rest*

12 But Moses' hands were heavy. Then they took a stone and put it under him, and he sat on it; and Aaron and Hur [R]supported his hands, one on one side and one on the other. Thus his hands were steady until the sun set. Is. 35:3

13 So Joshua overwhelmed Amalek and his people with the edge of the sword.

14 Then the LORD said to Moses, "Write this in [T]a book as a memorial, and recite it to Joshua, that I will utterly blot out the memory of Amalek from under heaven." *the book*

15 And Moses built an altar, and named it [R]The LORD is My Banner; Gen. 22:14; Judg. 6:24

16 and he said, "The[R] LORD has sworn; the LORD will have war against Amalek from generation to generation." Gen. 22:16

CHAPTER 18

Preserved from Chaos—Deut. 1:12-17

NOW[R]Jethro, the priest of Midian, Moses' father-in-law, heard of all that God had done for Moses and for Israel His people, how the LORD had brought Israel out of Egypt. Ex. 2:16, 18; 3:1

2 And Jethro, Moses' father-in-law, took Moses' wife[R]Zipporah, after he had sent her away, Ex. 2:21; 4:25

3 and her two sons, of whom one was named Gershom, for he said, "I have been a [T]sojourner in a foreign land." Heb., *ger*

4 And [T]the other was named Eliezer, for he said, "The[R] God of my father was my help, and delivered me from the sword of Pharaoh." *the name of the other was* • Gen. 49:25

[14] Or, *laws*   [15] I.e., *test*   [16] I.e., *quarrel*

5 Then Jethro, Moses' father-in-law, came with his sons and his wife to Moses^{T}in the wilderness where he was camped, at^{R}the mount of God.   *unto* • Ex. 3:1, 12; 4:27; 24:13

6 And he ^{T}sent word to Moses, "I, your father-in-law Jethro, am coming to you with your wife and her two sons with her."   *said*

7 Then Moses went out to meet his father-in-law, and^{R}he bowed down and kissed him; and they asked each other of their welfare, and went into the tent.   Gen. 43:26, 28

8 And Moses told his father-in-law all that the LORD had done to Pharaoh and to the Egyptians for Israel's sake, all the hardship that had befallen them on the journey, and *how* the LORD had delivered them.

9 And Jethro rejoiced over all^{T}the goodness which the LORD had done to Israel, ^{T}in delivering^{T}them from the hand of the Egyptians.   [Is. 63:7–14] • *in that He had delivered* • *him*

10 So Jethro said, "Blessed^R be the LORD who delivered you from the hand of the Egyptians and from the hand of Pharaoh, *and* who delivered the people from under the hand of the Egyptians.   Gen. 14:20

11 "Now I know that the LORD is greater than all the gods; ^{T}indeed, it was proven when they dealt proudly against ^{T}the people."   *indeed, in the thing in which they* • *them*

12 ^{R}Then Jethro, Moses' father-in-law, took a burnt offering and sacrifices for God, and Aaron came with all the elders of Israel to eat ^{T}a meal with Moses' father-in-law before God.   Gen. 31:54; Ex. 24:5 • *bread*

13 And it came about the next day that Moses sat to judge the people, and the people stood about Moses from the morning until the evening.

14 Now when Moses' father-in-law saw all that he was doing for the people, he said, "What is this thing that you are doing for the people? Why do you alone sit *as judge* and all the people stand about you from morning until evening?"

15 And Moses said to his father-in-law, "Because the people come to me ^{R}to inquire of God.   Num. 9:6, 8; 27:5; Deut. 17:8-13

16 "When they have a ^{T}dispute,^{R} it comes to me, and I judge between a man and his neighbor, and make known the statutes of God and His laws."   *matter* • Ex. 24:14

17 And Moses' father-in-law said to him, "The thing that you are doing is not good.

18 "You^{R}will surely wear out, both yourself and ^{T}these people who are with you, for the ^{T}task is too heavy for you; you cannot do it alone.   Num. 11:14, 17; Deut. 1:12 • *this* • *matter*

19 "Now listen to^{T}me: I shall give you counsel, and God be with you. You be the peo-

ple's representative before God, and you bring the ^{T}disputes to God,   *my voice* • *matters*

20 ^{R}then teach them the statutes and the laws, and make known to them^{R}the way in which they are to walk, and the work they are to do.   Deut. 1:18; 4:1, 5; 5:1 • Ps. 143:8

21 "Furthermore, you shall ^{T}select out of all the people ^{R}able men who fear God, men of truth, those who hate dishonest gain; and you shall place *these* over them, *as* leaders of thousands, ^{T}of hundreds, ^{T}of fifties and ^{T}of tens.   see • 2 Chr. 19:5-10; Ps. 15:1-5 • *leaders of*

22 "And let them judge the people at all times; and let it be^{R}that every major ^{T}dispute they will bring to you, but every minor^{T}dispute they themselves will judge. So it will be easier for you, and they will bear *the burden* with you.   Deut. 1:17, 18 • *matter*

23 "If you do this thing and God so commands you, then you will be able to ^{T}endure, and all ^{T}these people also will go to ^{T}their place in peace."   *stand* • *this* • *his*

24 So Moses listened ^{T}to his father-in-law, and did all that he had said.   *to the voice of*

25 And Moses chose able men out of all Israel, and made them heads over the people, leaders of thousands, of hundreds, of fifties and of tens.

26 And they judged the people at all times; the difficult ^{T}dispute they would bring to Moses, but every minor ^{T}dispute they themselves would judge.$_R$ *matter*

27 Then Moses ^{T}bade^R his father-in-law farewell, and he went his way into his own land.   *sent off his father-in-law* • Num. 10:29, 30

CHAPTER 19

Location of the Giving of the Covenant

IN the third month after the sons of Israel had gone out of the land of Egypt, ^{T}on that very day they came into the wilderness of $_R$Sinai.   *on this day* • Deut. 1:6; 4:10, 15; 5:2

2 When they set out from ^{R}Rephidim, they came to the wilderness of Sinai, and camped in the wilderness; and there Israel camped in front of the mountain.   Num. 33:15

Purpose of the Covenant

3 And Moses went up to God, and ^{R}the LORD called to him from the mountain, saying, "Thus you shall say to the house of Jacob and tell the sons of Israel: Ex. 3:4

4 'You yourselves have seen what I did to the Egyptians, and *how* I bore you on eagles' wings, and brought you to Myself.

5 'Now then,^{R} if you will indeed obey My

19:5–8   The Mosaic Covenant—The covenant with Moses is the second of the theocratic covenants (pertaining to the rule of God) and is conditional. It is introduced by the conditional formula,"if you will indeed obey My voice . . . then you shall be My own possession." This covenant was given to the nation Israel so that those who believed God's promise given to Abraham in the Abrahamic Covenant (Page14—Gen. 12:1–3) would know how they should conduct themselves. The Mosaic Covenant in its entirety governs three areas of their lives: (1) the commandments governed their personal lives particularly as they related to God (Page71—Ex. 20:1–26); (2) the judgments governed their social lives particularly as they related to one another (Page72—Ex. 21:1—24:11); and

voice and keep My covenant, then you shall be My [17]own possession among all the peoples, for all the earth is Mine;   Deut. 5:2f.

6 and you shall be to Me[R]a kingdom of priests and[R]a holy nation.' These are the words that you shall speak to the sons of Israel."   [1 Pet. 2:5, 9; Rev. 1:6; 5:10] • Is. 62:12

Israel Accepts the Covenant

7[R]So Moses came and called the elders of the people, and set before them all these words which the LORD had commanded him.   Ex. 4:29, 30

8 [R]And all the people answered together and said, "All that the LORD has spoken we will do!" And Moses brought back the words of the people to the LORD.   Ex. 4:31

Israelites Sanctify Themselves

9 And the LORD said to Moses, "Behold, I shall come to you in[R]a thick cloud, in order that the[R]people may hear when I speak with you, and may also believe in you forever." Then Moses told the words of the people to the LORD.   Deut. 4:11; Ps. 99:7 • Deut. 4:12, 36

10 The LORD also said to Moses, "Go to the people and [R]consecrate them today and tomorrow, and let them [R]wash their garments;   Lev. 11:44, 45 • Gen. 35:2; Lev. 15:5

11 and let them be ready for the third day, for on [R]the third day the LORD will come down on Mount Sinai in the sight of all the people.   Ex. 19:16

12"And you shall set bounds for the people all around, saying, 'Beware that you do not go up on the mountain or touch the border of it; [R]whoever touches the mountain shall surely be put to death.   Heb. 12:20

13 'No hand shall touch him, but[R]he shall surely be stoned or [18]shot through; whether beast or man, he shall not live.' When the ram's horn sounds a long blast, they shall come up to the mountain."   Heb. 12:20

14 So Moses went down from the mountain to the people and consecrated the people, and they washed their garments.

15 And he said to the people, "Be ready for the third day; do not go near a woman."

16 [R]So it came about on the third day, when it was morning, that there were[T]thunder and lightning flashes and a thick cloud upon the mountain and a very loud trumpet sound, so that all the people who were in the camp trembled.   Heb. 12:18, 19, 21 • sounds

17 And Moses brought the people out of the camp to meet God, and they stood at the [T]foot of the mountain.   lower part

18 [R]Now Mount Sinai was all in smoke because the LORD descended upon it in fire; and its smoke ascended like the smoke of a furnace, and the whole mountain [A]quaked violently.   Deut. 4:11; Ps. 104:32; 144:5 • trembled

19 When the sound of the trumpet grew louder and louder, Moses spoke and God answered him with[T]thunder.   a voice; lit., a sound

20 [R]And the LORD came down on Mount Sinai, to the top of the mountain; and the LORD called Moses to the top of the mountain, and Moses went up.   Neh. 9:13

21 Then the LORD spoke to Moses, "Go down, [T]warn the people, lest [R]they break through to the LORD to gaze, and many of them [T]perish.   testify to • 1 Sam. 6:19 • fall

22"And also let the[R]priests who come near to the LORD consecrate themselves, lest the LORD break out against them."   Lev. 10:3

23 And Moses said to the LORD, "The people cannot come up to Mount Sinai, for Thou didst warn us, saying, 'Set bounds about the mountain and consecrate it.'"

24 Then the LORD said to him, "Go[T] down and come up again, you and Aaron with you; but do not let the priests and the people break through to come up to the LORD, lest He break forth upon them."   Go, descend

25 So Moses went down to the people and told them.

CHAPTER 20

Commandments Relating to God

THEN God spoke all these words, saying,

2"I[R] am the LORD your God, who brought you out of the land of Egypt, out of the house of [T]slavery.   Lev. 26:1; Deut. 5:6 • slaves

3"You[R] shall have no other gods [19]before Me.   Deut. 6:14; 2 Kin. 17:35; Jer. 25:6; 35:15

4"You[R] shall not make for yourself [20]an idol, or any likeness of what is in heaven above or on the earth beneath or in the water under the earth.   Lev. 19:4; 26:1

5"You[T] shall not worship them or serve them; for I, the LORD your God, am a jealous God, visiting the iniquity of the fathers on

17 Or, special treasure   18 I.e., with arrows
19 Or, besides Me   20 Or, a graven image

---

(3) the ordinances governed their religious lives so that the people would know how to approach God on the terms that He dictates (Page75—Ex. 24:12—31:18). The Mosaic Covenant in no way replaced or set aside the Abrahamic Covenant. Its function is clearly set forth by Paul (Page1179—Gal. 3:17–19), who points out that the law, the Mosaic Covenant, came 430 years after the Abrahamic Covenant. The Mosaic Covenant was added alongside the Abrahamic Covenant so that the people of Israel would know how to conduct their lives until "the seed," the Christ, comes and makes the complete and perfect sacrifice, toward which the sacrifices of the Mosaic Covenant only point. The Mosaic Covenant was never given so that by keeping it people could be saved, but so that they might realize that they cannot do what God wants them to do even when God writes it down on tablets of stone. The law was given that man might realize that he is helpless and hopeless when left to himself, and realize that his only hope is to receive the righteousness of God by faith in Jesus (Page1179—Gal. 3:22–24).

Now turn to Page195—Deut. 29:10–15; 30:11–20: The Palestinian Covenant.

the children, on the third and the fourth generations of those who hate Me, Josh. 23:7

6 but showing lovingkindness to ʳthousands, to those who love Me and keep My commandments.   Deut. 7:9

7"You^ʳ shall not take the name of the LORD your God in vain, for the LORD will not ᴬleave him unpunished who takes His name in vain.   Lev. 19:12; Deut. 6:13 · *hold him guiltless*

8"Remember^ʳthe sabbath day, to keep it holy.   Ex. 23:12; 31:13-16; Lev. 26:2; Deut. 5:12

9"Six^ʳdays you shall labor and do all your work,   Lev. 23:3; Deut. 5:13; Luke 13:14

10 but the seventh day is a sabbath of the LORD your God; *in it* you shall not do any work, you or your son or your daughter, your male or your female servant or your cattle or your sojourner who stays with you.

11"For^ʳ in six days the LORD made the heavens and the earth, the sea and all that is in them, and rested on the seventh day; therefore the LORD blessed the sabbath day and made it holy.   Gen. 2:2, 3; Ex. 31:17

Commandments Relating to Man

12"Honor your father and your mother, that your days may be prolonged in the land which the LORD your God gives you.

13"You^ʳ shall not murder.   [Matt. 5:21]; 19:18

14"You^ʳ shall not commit adultery.

15"You^ʳ shall not steal.   Matt. 19:18; Rom. 13:9

16"You^ʳ shall not bear false witness against your neighbor.   Ex. 23:1, 7; Deut. 5:20

17"You^ʳ shall not covet your neighbor's house; you shall not covet your neighbor's wife or his male servant or his female servant or his ox or his donkey or anything that belongs to your neighbor."   Rom. 7:7; 13:9

The Response of Israel

18 And all the people perceived the ᵀthunder and the lightning flashes and the sound of the trumpet and the mountain smoking; and when the people saw *it*, they trembled and stood at a distance.   *sounds*

19 ᴿThen they said to Moses, "Speak^ᵀto us yourself and we will listen; but let not God speak^ᵀto us, lest we die."   Heb. 12:19 · *with*

20 And Moses said to the people, "Do not be afraid; for God has come in order to test you, and in order that the fear of Him may remain with you, so that you may not sin."

21 So the people stood at a distance, while Moses approached ^ʳthe thick cloud where God *was*.   Ex. 19:16; Deut. 5:22

Provision for Approaching God

22 Then the LORD said to Moses, "Thus you shall say to the sons of Israel, 'You yourselves have seen that^ʳI have spoken ^ᵀto you from heaven.   Deut. 4:36; 5:24, 26 · *with*

23 'You^ʳ shall not make *other gods* besides Me; gods of silver or gods of gold, you shall not make for yourselves.   Ex. 20:3

24 'You shall make ^ᵃan altar of earth for Me, and you shall sacrifice on it your burnt offerings and your peace offerings, your sheep and your oxen; in every place where I cause My name to be remembered, I will come to you and bless you.   Ex. 20:25; 27:1-8

25 'And if you make an altar of stone for Me, you shall not build it of cut stones, for if you wield your tool on it, you will profane it.

26 'And you shall not go up by steps to My altar, that ^ʳyour nakedness may not be exposed on it.'   Ex. 28:42, 43

CHAPTER 21

Rights of Persons

"Now these are the ^ᵇordinances which you are to set before them.   Deut. 4:14; 6:1

2"If you buy a Hebrew slave, he shall serve for six years; but on the seventh he shall go out as a free man without payment.

3"If he comes ᵃalone, he shall go out ^ᵀalone; if he is the husband of a wife, then his wife shall go out with him.   *by himself*

4"If his master gives him a wife, and she bears him sons or daughters, the wife and her children shall belong to her master, and he shall go out ᵃalone.   *by himself*

5"But^ᵇif the slave plainly says, 'I love my master, my wife and my children; I will not go out as a free man,'   Deut. 15:16, 17

6 then his master shall bring him to ²¹God, then he shall bring him to the door or the doorpost. And his master shall pierce his ear with an awl; and he shall serve him permanently.

7"And^ᵇ if a man sells his daughter as a female slave, she is not to ^ᵀgo free ^ʳas the male slaves do.   Neh. 5:5 · *go out* · Ex. 21:2, 3

8"If she is ᵇdispleasing in the eyes of her master who designated her for himself, then he shall let her be redeemed. He does not have authority to sell her to a foreign people because of his unfairness to her.   *bad*

9"And if he designates her for his son, he shall deal with her according to the custom of daughters.

10"If he takes to himself another woman, he may not reduce her ᵀfood, her clothing, or ^ʳher conjugal rights.   *flesh* · [1 Cor. 7:3, 5]

11"And if he will not do these three *things* for her, then she shall go out for nothing, without *payment* of money.

12"He^ʳ who strikes a man so that he dies shall surely be put to death.   Gen. 9:6

13"But if he did not lie in wait *for him*, but God let *him* fall into his hand, then I will appoint you a place to which he may flee.

14"If,^ʳ however, a man acts presumptuously toward his neighbor, so as to kill him craftily, you are to take him *even* from My altar, that he may die.   Deut. 19:11, 12

15"And he who strikes his father or his mother shall surely be put to death.

²¹ Or, *the judges who acted in God's name*

16"And he who ᵀkidnaps a man, whether he sells him or he is found in his ᵀpossession, shall surely be put to death.   *steals · hand*

17"And he who curses his father or his mother shall surely be put to death.

18"And if men have a quarrel and one strikes the other with a stone or with *his* fist, and he does not die but remains in bed;

19 if he gets up and walks around outside on his staff, then he who struck him shall go unpunished; he shall only pay for his ᵀloss of time, and shall take care of him until he is completely healed.   *his sitting*

20"And if a man strikes his male or female slave with a rod and he dies ᵃat his hand, he shall ᵀbe punished.   *under · suffer vengeance*

21"If, however, he ᵀsurvives a day or two, no vengeance shall be taken; ᴿfor he is his ᵀproperty.   *stands · Lev. 25:44-46 · money*

22"And *if* men struggle with each other and strike a woman with child so that she has a miscarriage, yet there is no *further* injury, he shall surely be fined as the woman's husband may demand of him; and he shall pay ᵀas the judges *decide.*   *by arbitration*

23"But if there is *any further* injury, then you shall appoint *as a penalty* life for life,

24 ᴿeye for eye, tooth for tooth, hand for hand, foot for foot,   Lev. 24:20; Deut. 19:21

25 burn for burn, wound for wound, ᵀbruise for bruise.   *welt*

26"And if a man strikes the eye of his male or female slave, and destroys it, he shall let him go free on account of his eye.

27"And if he ᵀknocks out a tooth of his male or female slave, he shall let him go free on account of his tooth.   *causes to fall*

28"And if an ox gores a man or a woman ᵀto death, the ox shall surely be stoned and its flesh shall not be eaten; but the owner of the ox shall go unpunished.   *so that he dies*

29"If, however, an ox was previously in the habit of goring, and its owner has been warned, yet he does not confine it, and it kills a man or a woman, the ox shall be stoned and its owner also shall be put to death.

30"If a ransom is ᵈdemanded of him, then he shall give for the redemption of his life whatever is ᵀdemanded of him.   *laid on him*

31"Whether it gores a son or ᵃa daughter, it shall be done to him according to ᵗthe same rule.   *gores a daughter · this judgment*

32"If the ox gores a male or female slave, the owner shall give his *or her* master thirty shekels of silver, and the ox shall be stoned.

Rights of Property

33"And if a man opens a pit, or ᵇdigs a pit and does not cover it over, and an ox or a donkey falls into it,   *if a man digs*

34 the owner of the pit shall make restitution; he shall ᵀgive money to its owner, and the dead *animal* shall become his.   *give back*

35"And if one man's ox hurts another's so that it dies, then they shall sell the live ox and divide its price equally; and also they shall divide the dead ox.

36"Or *if* it is known that the ox was previously in the habit of goring, yet its owner has not confined it, he shall surely pay ox for ox, and the dead *animal* shall become his.

CHAPTER 22

"**I**F a man steals an ox or a sheep, and slaughters it or sells it, he shall pay five oxen for the ox and ᴿfour sheep for the sheep.   2 Sam. 12:6; Luke 19:8

2"If the thief is ᵀcaught while breaking in, and is struck so that he dies, there will be no bloodguiltiness on his account.   *found*

3"*But* if the sun has risen on him, there will be bloodguiltiness on his account. He shall surely make restitution; if he owns nothing, then he shall be sold for his theft.

4"If what he stole is actually found alive in his ᵀpossession, whether an ox or a donkey or a sheep, he shall pay double.   *hand*

5"If a man lets a field or vineyard be grazed *bare* and lets his animal loose so that it grazes in another man's field, he shall make restitution from the best of his own field and the best of his own vineyard.

6"If a fire breaks out and spreads to thorn bushes, so that stacked grain or the standing grain or the field *itself* is consumed, he who started the fire shall surely make restitution.

7"If ᴿa man gives his neighbor money or goods to keep *for him*, and it is stolen from the man's house, if the thief is ᵀcaught, he shall pay double.   Lev. 6:1-7 · *found*

8"If the thief is not ᵀcaught, then the owner of the house shall appear before the judges, *to* determine whether he laid his hands on his neighbor's property.   *found*

9"For every ᴬbreach of trust, *whether it is* for ox, for donkey, for sheep, for clothing, or for any lost thing about which one says, 'This is it,' the ᵀcase of both parties shall come before ᵃthe judges; he whom the judges condemn shall pay double to his neighbor.   *matter of transgression · matter · God*

10"If a man gives his neighbor a donkey, an ox, a sheep, or any animal to keep *for him*, and it dies or is hurt or is driven away while no one is looking,

11 an oath before the LORD shall be made by the two of them, ᵀthat he has not ᵀlaid hands on his neighbor's property; and its owner shall accept *it*, and he shall not make restitution.   *whether · stretched his hand*

12"But if it is actually stolen from him, he shall make restitution to its owner.

13"If it is all torn to pieces, let him bring it as evidence; he shall not make restitution for what has been torn to pieces.

14"And if a man ᵀborrows *anything* from his neighbor, and it is injured or dies while

its owner is not with it, he shall make full restitution. *asks*

15"If its owner is with it, he shall not make restitution; if it is hired, it came for its hire.

Proper Conduct

16"And[R] if a man seduces a virgin who is not engaged, and lies with her, he must pay a dowry for her *to be* his wife. Deut. 22:28, 29

17"If her father absolutely refuses to give her to him, he shall [T]pay money equal to the [R]dowry for virgins. *weigh out silver* · Gen. 34:12

18"You shall not allow a sorceress to live.

19"Whoever[R] lies with an animal shall surely be put to death. Lev. 18:23; 20:15, 16

20"He[R] who sacrifices to [T]any god, other than to the LORD alone, shall be [T]utterly destroyed. Lev. 17:7 · *the gods* · *put under the ban*

21"And [T]you shall not wrong a stranger or oppress him, for you were strangers in the land of Egypt. Ex. 23:9; Lev. 19:33, 34; 25:35

22"You[R] shall not afflict any widow or orphan. Deut. 24:17, 18; Prov. 23:10, 11; Jer. 7:6, 7

23"If you afflict him at all, *and* if he does cry out to Me, I will surely hear his cry;

24 and My anger will be kindled, and I will kill you with the sword; [b]and your wives shall become widows and your children fatherless. Ps. 109:2, 9

25"If[R] you lend money to My people, to the poor [T]among you, you are not to [T]act as a creditor to him; you shall not [T]charge him interest. Lev. 25:35-37 · *with* · *be* · *lay upon*

26"If you ever take your neighbor's cloak [R]as a pledge, you are to return it to him before the sun sets, Deut. 24:6, 10-13; Job 24:3

27 for that is his only covering; it is his cloak for his [T]body. What else shall he sleep in? And it shall come about that [R]when he cries out to Me, I will hear *him*, for [R]I am gracious. *skin* · Ex. 22:23 · Ex. 34:6

28"You shall not [A]curse[R] God, nor curse a ruler of your people. *revile* · Lev. 24:15, 16

29"You shall not delay *the offering from* your harvest and your vintage. The firstborn of your sons you shall give to Me.

30"You[T] shall do the same with your oxen *and* with your sheep. It shall be with its mother seven days; on the eighth day you shall give it to Me. Deut. 15:19; Lev. 22:27

31"And [R]you shall be holy men to Me, therefore [T]you shall not eat *any* flesh torn to pieces in the field; you shall throw it to the dogs. Lev. 7:24; 17:15; Ezek. 4:14

CHAPTER 23

Proper Justice

"Y OU[R] shall not bear a false report; do not join your hand with a wicked man to be a malicious witness. Lev. 19:11f.; Deut. 5:20

2"You shall not follow [T]a multitude in doing evil, nor shall you [T]testify in a dispute so as to turn aside after a multitude in order to pervert *justice*; *many men* · *answer*

3 [R]nor shall you [T]be partial to a poor man in his dispute. Ex. 23:6; Lev. 19:15 · *honor*

4"If[R] you meet your enemy's ox or his donkey wandering away, you shall surely return it to him. Deut. 22:1-4

5"If[R] you see the donkey of one who hates you lying *helpless* under its load, you shall refrain from leaving it to him, you shall surely release *it* with him. Deut. 22:4

6"You[R] shall not pervert the justice *due* to your needy *brother* in his dispute. Lev. 19:15

7"Keep[R] far from a false charge, and do not kill the innocent or the righteous, for I will not acquit the guilty. Ps. 119:29; Eph. 4:25

8"And you shall not take a bribe, for a bribe blinds the clear-sighted and [A]subverts the cause of the just. *distorts the words*

9"And[R] you shall not oppress a [A]stranger, since you yourselves know the [T]feelings of a [A]stranger, for you *also* were [A]strangers in the land of Egypt. Ex. 22:21 · *sojourner(s)* · *soul*

Sabbatical Year

10"And[R] you shall sow your land for six years and gather in its yield, Lev. 25:1-7

11 but *on* the seventh year you shall let it [T]rest and lie fallow, so that the needy of your people may eat; and whatever they leave the beast of the field may eat. You are to do the same with your vineyard *and* your olive grove. *drop*

12"Six[R] days you are to do your work, but on the seventh day you shall cease *from labor* in order that your ox and your donkey may rest, and the son of your female slave, as well as [T]your stranger, may refresh themselves. Lev. 23:3; Deut. 5:13f. · *the sojourner*

13"Now concerning everything which I have said to you, be on your guard; and do not mention the name of other gods, nor let *them* be heard [T]from your mouth. *on*

Three National Feasts

14"Three[R] times a year you shall celebrate a feast to Me. Ex. 23:17; 34:22-24; Deut. 16:16

15"You shall observe the Feast of Unleavened Bread; for seven days you are to eat unleavened bread, as I commanded you, at the appointed time in the month Abib, for in it you came out of Egypt. And [T]none shall appear before Me empty-handed. *they . . . not*

16"Also *you shall observe*[R] the Feast of the Harvest *of* the first fruits of your labors *from* what you sow in the field; also the Feast of the Ingathering at the end of the year when you gather in *the fruit of* your labors from the field. Ex. 34:22; Lev. 23:10

17"Three[t] times a year all your males shall appear before the Lord GOD. Deut. 16:16

18"You shall not offer the blood of My sacrifice with leavened bread; nor is the fat of My feast to remain overnight until morning.

19"You shall bring[R] the choice first fruits of your soil into the house of the LORD your God. You are not to boil a kid in the milk of its mother. Deut. 26:2, 10; Neh. 10:35; Prov. 3:9

Conquest Regulations

20"Behold, I am going to send [R]an angel before you to guard you along the way, and to bring you into the place which I have prepared. Ex. 3:2; 14:19; 23:23; 32:34; 33:2

21"Be on your guard before him and obey his voice; [R]do not be rebellious toward him, for he will not pardon your transgression, since My name is in him. Ps. 78:40, 56

22"But if you will truly obey his voice and do all that I say, then[R]I will be an enemy to your enemies and an adversary to your adversaries. Gen. 12:3; Num. 24:9; Deut. 30:7

23"For[R] My angel will go before you and bring you in to *the land of* the Amorites, the Hittites, the Perizzites, the Canaanites, the Hivites and the Jebusites; and I will completely destroy them. Ex. 23:20; Josh. 24:8, 11

24"You[R] shall not worship their gods, nor serve them, nor do according to their deeds; but you shall utterly overthrow them, and break their *sacred* pillars in pieces. Ex. 20:5

25"But[R]you shall serve the Lord your God, [A]and He will bless your bread and your water; and I will remove sickness from your midst. Lev. 26:3-13 • *that He may bless*

26"There shall be no one miscarrying or [R]barren in your land;[R]I will fulfill the number of your days. Deut. 7:14 • Deut. 4:40; Job 5:26

27"I will send My terror ahead of you, and [R]throw into confusion all the people among whom you come, and I will make all your enemies turn *their* backs to you. Deut. 7:23

28"And I will send hornets ahead of you, that they may drive out the Hivites, the Canaanites, and the Hittites before you.

29"I[R]will not drive them out before you in a single year, that the land may not become desolate, and the beasts of the field become too numerous for you. Deut. 7:22

30"I will drive them out before you[R]little by little, until you become fruitful and take possession of the land. Deut. 7:22

31"And I will fix your boundary from the [T]Red Sea to the sea of the Philistines, and from the wilderness to the River *Euphrates;* [R]for I will deliver the inhabitants of the land into your hand, and you will drive them out before you. Sea of Reeds • Deut. 2:36; Josh. 21:44

32"You shall[T]make no covenant with them or with their gods. Ex. 34:12; Deut. 7:2 • *cut*

33"They[R] shall not live in your land, lest they make you sin against Me; for *if* you serve their gods,[R]it will surely be a snare to you." Deut. 7:1-5, 16 • Deut. 12:30; Josh. 23:13

CHAPTER 24

The Covenant Is Ratified Through Blood

THEN He said to Moses, "Come up to the Lord, you and Aaron,[R]Nadab and Abihu and seventy of the elders of Israel, and you shall worship at a distance. Lev. 10:1, 2

2"Moses alone, however, shall come near to the Lord, but they shall not come near, nor shall the people come up with him."

3 Then Moses came and recounted to the people all the words of the Lord and all the ordinances; and all the people answered with one voice, and said, "All the words which the Lord has spoken we will do!"

4 And[R]Moses wrote down all the words of the Lord. Then he arose early in the morning, and built an altar [T]at the foot of the mountain with twelve pillars for the twelve tribes of Israel. Ex. 17:14; 34:27 • *under*

5 And he sent young men of the sons of Israel, [R]and they offered burnt offerings and sacrificed young bulls as peace offerings to the Lord. Ex. 18:12

6 And[R]Moses took half of the blood and put *it* in basins, and the *other* half of the blood he sprinkled on the altar. Heb. 9:18

7 Then he took[R]the book of the covenant and read *it* in the hearing of the people; and they said, "All that the Lord has spoken we will do, and we will be obedient!" Heb. 9:19

8 So[R]Moses took the blood and sprinkled *it* on the people, and said, "Behold the blood of the covenant, which the Lord has [T]made with you [T]in accordance with all these words." [Heb. 9:19, 20] • *cut* • *on all*

The God of the Covenant
Is Revealed

9 Then Moses went up[T]with Aaron, [R]Nadab and Abihu, and seventy of the elders of Israel, *and* • Ex. 24:1

10 and they saw the God of Israel; and under His feet there appeared to be a pavement of sapphire, as clear as the sky itself.

11 Yet He did not stretch out His hand against the nobles of the sons of Israel; and they beheld God, and they ate and drank.

The Revelation Is Given
on Mount Sinai

12 Now the Lord said to Moses, "Come up to Me on the mountain and[T]remain there, and I will give you the stone tablets[T]with the law and the commandment which I have written for their instruction." *be* • *and*

13 So Moses arose[T]with [R]Joshua his [A]servant, and Moses went up to the mountain of God. *and* • Ex. 17:9-14; 33:11 • *minister*

14 But to the elders he said, "Wait here for us until we return to you. And behold, Aaron and Hur are with you; whoever has a legal matter, let him approach them."

15 Then Moses went up to the mountain, and the cloud covered the mountain.

16 And the glory of the Lord [T]rested on Mount Sinai, and the cloud covered it for six days; and on the seventh day He called to Moses from the midst of the cloud. *dwelt*

17 And to the eyes of the sons of Israel the appearance of the glory of the Lord was like a consuming fire on the mountain top.

18 And Moses entered the midst of the cloud as he went up to the mountain; and Moses was on the mountain[R]forty days and forty nights. *and* • Ex. 34:28; Deut. 9:9; 10:10

CHAPTER 25

The Offering for the Tabernacle

THEN the LORD spoke to Moses, saying,
2 "Tell the sons of Israel to raise a contribution for Me; from every man whose heart moves him you shall raise My contribution.
3 "And this is the ^contribution which you are to ^raise from them: gold, silver and bronze,   *heave offering · take*
4 ^A blue,^R purple and scarlet *material,* fine linen, goat ^hair,   *violet · Ex. 28:5, 6, 8*
5 rams' skins dyed red, porpoise skins, acacia wood,
6 ^oil for lighting, spices for the anointing oil and for the fragrant incense,   Ex. 27:20
7 onyx stones and setting stones, for the ephod and for the ^breastpiece.   *pouch*

The Purpose of the Tabernacle

8 "And let them construct a sanctuary for Me, ^that I may dwell among them. Num. 5:3
9 "According^R to all that I am going to show you, *as* the pattern of the tabernacle and the pattern of all its furniture, just so you shall construct *it.*   Acts 7:44; Heb. 8:2, 5

The Ark of the Covenant

10 "And they shall construct an ark of acacia wood two and a half ^cubits long, and one and a half cubits wide, and one and a half cubits high.   One cubit equals approx. 18 in.
11 "And you shall overlay it with pure gold, inside and out you shall overlay it, and you shall make a gold molding around it.
12 "And you shall cast four gold rings for it, and ^fasten them on its four feet, and two rings shall be on one side of it and two rings on the other side of it.   *put*
13 "And you shall make poles of acacia wood and overlay them with gold.
14 "And you shall put the poles into the rings on the sides of the ark, to carry the ark with them.
15 "The poles shall remain in the rings of the ark; they shall not be removed from it.
16 "And you shall ^put into the ark the testimony which I shall give you.   Deut. 10:2
17 "And you shall make a ²²mercy seat of pure gold, two and a half cubits long and one and a half cubits ^wide.   *its width*
18 "And you shall make two cherubim of gold, make them of hammered work ^at the two ends of the mercy seat.   *from*
19 "And make one cherub ^at one end and one cherub^T at the other end; you shall make the cherubim *of one piece* with the mercy seat at its two ends.   *from*
20 "And the cherubim shall have *their* wings spread upward, covering the mercy seat with their wings and ^facing one another; the faces of the cherubim are to be turned toward the mercy seat.   *their faces to*
21 "And you shall put the mercy seat on top of the ark, and in the ark you shall put the testimony which I shall give to you.

22 "And there I will meet with you; and from above the mercy seat, from ^between the two cherubim which are upon the ark of the testimony, I will speak to you about all that I will give you in commandment for the sons of Israel.   Num. 7:89; 1 Sam. 4:4; 2 Sam. 6:2

The Table of Showbread

23 "And you shall make a table of acacia wood, two cubits ^long and one cubit wide and one and a half cubits high.   *its length*
24 "And you shall overlay it with pure gold and make a gold ^border around it.   Ex. 25:11
25 "And you shall make for it a rim of a handbreadth around *it;* and you shall make a gold border for the rim around it.
26 "And you shall make four gold rings for it and put rings on the four corners which are on its four feet.
27 "The rings shall be close to the rim as holders for the poles to carry the table.
28 "And you shall make the poles of acacia wood and overlay them with gold, so that with them the table may be carried.
29 "And you shall make its ^dishes^and its pans and its jars and its ^bowls, with which to pour libations; you shall make them of pure gold.   *platters · Num. 4:7 · libation bowls*
30 "And you shall set the bread of the Presence on the table before Me at all times.

The Golden Lampstand

31 "Then^R you shall make a lampstand of pure gold. The lampstand *and* its base and its shaft are to be made of hammered work; its cups, its ^bulbs and its flowers shall be *of one piece* with it.   1 Kin. 7:49; Zech. 4:2 · *calyx*
32 "And ^six branches shall go out from its sides; three branches of the lampstand from its one side, and three branches of the lampstand from its ^other side.   Ex. 37:18 · *second*
33 "Three^cups *shall be* shaped like almond *blossoms* in the one branch, a ²³bulb and a flower, and three cups shaped like almond *blossoms* in the ^other branch, a bulb and a flower—so for six branches going out from the lampstand;   Ex. 37:19 · *one branch*
34 and ^in the lampstand four cups shaped like almond *blossoms,* its ^bulbs and its flowers.   Ex. 37:20 · *calyxes*
35 "And a bulb shall be under the *first* pair of branches *coming* out of it, and a bulb under the *second* pair of branches *coming* out of it, and a bulb under the *third* pair of branches *coming* out of it, for the six branches coming out of the lampstand.
36 "Their bulbs and their branches *shall be* of one piece with it; all of it shall be one piece of hammered work of pure gold.
37 "Then you shall make its lamps seven *in number;* and they shall mount its lamps so as to shed light on the space in front of it.
38 "And its snuffers and ^their trays *shall be* of pure gold.   *its snuff dishes*

²² Lit., *propitiatory;* and so through v. 22   ²³ Or, *calyx*

39"It shall be made from a[T]talent of pure gold, with all these utensils. $5,760,000

40"And [R]see that you make *them* [A]after the pattern for them, which was shown to you on the mountain.   [Heb. 8:5] • Acts 7:44

CHAPTER 26

The Curtains of Linen

"M[R]OREOVER you shall make the tabernacle with ten curtains of fine twisted linen and [24]blue and purple and scarlet *material;* you shall make them with cherubim, the work of a skillful workman.   Ex. 36:8-19

2"The length of each curtain shall be twenty-eight cubits, and the width of each curtain four cubits; all the curtains shall have [T]the same measurements.   *one measure*

3"Five curtains shall be[A]joined to one another; and *the other* five curtains *shall be* [A]joined to one another.   *coupled*

4"And you shall make loops of [A]blue on the edge of the outermost curtain in the *first* set, and likewise you shall make *them* on the edge of the curtain that is outermost in the second [T]set.   *violet • coupling*

5"You shall make fifty loops in the one curtain, and you shall make fifty loops on the edge of the curtain that is in the second set; the loops shall be opposite each other.

6"And you shall make fifty clasps of gold, and join the curtains to one another with the clasps, that the [25]tabernacle may be a unit.

7"Then [A]you shall make curtains of goats' *hair* for a tent over the tabernacle; you shall make eleven curtains in all.   Ex. 36:14

8"The length of each curtain *shall be* [T]thirty cubits, and the width of each curtain four cubits; the eleven curtains shall have [T]the same measurements.   45 ft. • *one measure*

9"And you shall [A]join five curtains by themselves, and the *other* six curtains by themselves, and you shall double over the sixth curtain at the front of the tent. *couple*

10"And you shall make fifty loops on the edge of the curtain that is outermost in the *first* set, and fifty loops on the edge of the curtain *that is outermost in* the second set.

11"And you shall make fifty clasps of [26]bronze, and you shall put the clasps into the loops and [A]join the tent together, that it may be [A]a unit.   *couple • one*

12"And the [b]overlapping part that is left over in the curtains of the tent, the half curtain that is left over, shall lap over the back of the tabernacle.   *excess*

13"And the[T]cubit on one side and the cubit on the other, of what is left over in the length of the curtains of the tent, shall lap over the sides of the tabernacle on one side and on the other, to cover it.   1.5 ft.

14"And [A]you shall make a covering for the tent of rams' skins [d]dyed red, and a covering of porpoise skins above.   Ex. 36:19 • *tanned*

The Boards and Sockets

15"Then you shall make[R]the boards for the tabernacle of acacia wood, standing upright.   Ex. 36:20-34

16"Ten[T]cubits *shall be* the length of [e]each board, and[T]one and a half cubits the width of each board.   15 ft. • *the* • 27 in.

17"There *shall be* two tenons for each board, fitted to one another; thus you shall do for all the boards of the tabernacle.

18"And you shall make the boards for the tabernacle: twenty boards [f]for the south side.   *toward the side of the Negev to the south*

19"And you shall make forty [27]sockets[R] of silver under the twenty boards, two sockets under one board for its two tenons and two sockets under another board for its two tenons;   Ex. 38:27

20 and for the second side of the tabernacle, on the north side, twenty boards,

21 and their forty [A]sockets of silver; two [A]sockets under one board and two [A]sockets under another board.   *bases*

22"And for the rear of the tabernacle, to the west, you shall make six boards.

23"And you shall make two boards for the corners of the tabernacle at the rear.

24"And they shall be double beneath, and together they shall be complete to its top to the first ring; thus it shall be with both of them: they shall form the two corners.

25"And there shall be eight boards with their [a]sockets of silver, sixteen [A]sockets; two [A]sockets under one board and two [a]sockets under another board.   *bases*

26"Then you shall make [R]bars of acacia wood, five for the boards of one side of the tabernacle,   Ex. 36:31

27 and five bars for the boards of the [T]other side of the tabernacle, and five bars for the boards of the side of the tabernacle for the rear *side* to the west.   *second*

28"And the middle bar in the center of the boards shall pass through from end to end.

29"And you shall overlay the boards with gold and make their rings of gold *as* holders for the bars; and you shall overlay the bars with gold.

30"Then you shall erect the tabernacle [R]according to its plan which you have been shown in the mountain.   Acts 7:44; [Heb. 8:5]

The Inner Veil

31"And you shall make [R]a veil of[A]blue and purple and scarlet *material* and fine twisted linen; it shall be made with cherubim, the work of a skillful workman.   Heb. 9:3 • *violet*

32"And you shall[T]hang it on four pillars of acacia overlaid with gold, their hooks *also being of* gold, on four sockets of silver. *put*

33"And you shall [t]hang up the veil under the clasps, and shall bring in the ark of the testimony there within the veil; and the veil

---

[24] Or, *violet,* and so throughout this context
[25] Or, *dwelling place,* and so throughout the ch.
[26] Or, *copper*   [27] Or, *bases,* and so throughout this context

shall serve for you as a partition between the holy place and the holy of holies.   *put*

34"And [R]you shall put the mercy seat on the ark of the testimony in the holy of holies.   Ex. 25:21; 40:20; Lev. 16:2

35"And [R]you shall set the table outside the veil, and the [R]lampstand opposite the table on the side of the tabernacle toward the south; and you shall put the table on the north side.   Ex. 40:22 • Ex. 40:24

The Outer Veil

36"And [R]you shall make a screen for the doorway of the tent of [t]blue and purple and scarlet *material* and fine twisted linen, the work of a weaver.   Ex. 36:37 • *violet*

37"And you shall make five pillars of acacia for the screen, and overlay them with gold, their hooks *also being of* gold; and you shall cast five sockets of bronze for them.

CHAPTER 27

The Bronze Altar

"**A**ND you shall make the altar of acacia wood, five [t]cubits long and five cubits wide; the altar shall be square, and its height shall be three cubits.   One cubit equals approx. 18 in.

2"And you shall make its horns on its four corners; its horns shall be of one piece with it, and you shall overlay it with bronze.

3"And you shall make its pails for removing its ashes, and its shovels and its basins and its forks and its firepans; you shall make all its utensils of bronze.

4"And you shall make for it a grating of network of bronze, and on the net you shall make four bronze rings at its four corners.

5"And you shall put it beneath, under the ledge of the altar, that the net may reach halfway up the altar.

6"And you shall make poles for the altar, poles of acacia wood, and overlay them with bronze.

7"And its poles shall be inserted into the rings, so that the poles shall be on the two sides of the altar when it is carried.

8"You shall make it hollow with planks; [R]as it was shown to you in the mountain, so they shall make *it*.   Ex. 25:40; 26:30; Acts 7:44

The Court of the Tabernacle

9"And you shall make the court of the tabernacle. On the south side *there shall be* hangings for the court of fine twisted linen one hundred cubits long for one side;

10 and its pillars *shall be* twenty, with their twenty sockets of bronze; the hooks of the pillars and their bands *shall be* of silver.

11"And likewise for the north side in length *there shall be* hangings one hundred *cubits* long, and its twenty pillars with their twenty sockets of bronze; the hooks of the pillars and their bands *shall be* of silver.

12"And *for* the width of the court on the west side *shall be* hangings of fifty cubits *with* their ten pillars and their ten sockets.

13"And the width of the court on the [t]east side *shall be* fifty cubits.   *east side eastward*

14"The hangings for the *one* [t]side *of the gate shall be* fifteen cubits *with* their three pillars and their three sockets.   *shoulder*

15"And for the [t]other [t]side *shall be* hangings of fifteen cubits *with* their three pillars and their three sockets.   *second • shoulder*

16"And for the gate of the court there *shall be* a screen of twenty cubits, of blue and purple and scarlet *material* and fine twisted linen, the work of a weaver, *with* their four pillars and their four sockets.

17"All the pillars around the court shall be furnished with silver bands *with* their hooks of silver and their [A]sockets of bronze.   *bases*

18"The length of the court *shall be* one hundred cubits, and the width fifty throughout, and the height five cubits of fine twisted linen, and their [A]sockets of bronze.   *bases*

19"All the utensils of the tabernacle *used* in all its service, and all its pegs, and all the pegs of the court, *shall be* of bronze.

The Oil for the Lamp

20"And you shall charge the sons of Israel, that they bring you [R]clear oil of beaten olives for the [A]light, to make a lamp [t]burn continually.   Ex. 35:8, 28; Lev. 24:1-4 • *luminary • ascend*

21"In the tent of meeting, outside the veil which is before [R]the testimony, Aaron and his sons shall keep it in order from evening to morning before the LORD; *it shall be* a perpetual statute throughout their generations [t]for the sons of Israel.   [Ex. 25:22] • *from*

CHAPTER 28

The Command to Make
the Priests' Garments

"**T**HEN[R]bring near to yourself Aaron your brother, and his sons with him, from among the sons of Israel, to minister as priest to Me—Aaron, Nadab and Abihu, Eleazar and Ithamar, Aaron's sons.   Num. 18:7; Ps. 99:6

2"And you shall make [R]holy garments for Aaron your brother, for glory and for beauty.   Ex. 29:5, 29; 31:10; 39:1-31; Lev. 8:7-9, 30

3"And you shall speak to all the [t]skillful persons whom I have endowed with the spirit of wisdom, that they make Aaron's garments to consecrate him, that he may minister as priest to Me.   *wise of heart*

4"And these are the garments which they shall make: a [28]breastpiece and an ephod and a robe and a tunic of checkered work, a turban and a sash, and they shall make holy garments for Aaron your brother and his sons, that he may minister as priest to Me.

5"And they shall take [R]the gold and the

---

[28] Or, *pouch*

^Ablue and the purple and the scarlet *material* and the fine linen.   Ex. 25:3 • *violet*

The Ephod

6"They shall also make^Rthe ephod of gold, of^Ablue and purple *and* scarlet *material* and fine twisted linen, the work of the skillful workman.   Ex. 39:2-7; Lev. 8:7 • *violet*
7"It shall have two shoulder pieces joined to its two ends, that it may be joined.
8"And the skillfully woven band, which is on it, shall be like its workmanship, of the same material: of gold, of blue and purple and scarlet *material* and fine twisted linen.
9"And you shall take two onyx stones and engrave on them the names of the sons of Israel,
10 six of their names on the one stone, and the names of the remaining six on the ^Tother stone, according to their birth.   *second*
11"As a jeweler engraves a signet, you shall engrave the two stones according to the names of the sons of Israel; you shall set them in filigree *settings* of gold.
12"And you shall put the two stones on the shoulder pieces of the ephod, *as* stones of memorial for the sons of Israel, and Aaron shall bear their names before the LORD on his two shoulders for a memorial.
13"And^Ryou shall make filigree *settings* of gold,   Ex. 39:16-18
14 and two chains of pure gold; you shall make them of twisted cordage work, and you shall put the corded chains on the filigree *settings*.

The Breastpiece

15"And you shall make a breastpiece of judgment, the work of a skillful workman; like the work of the ephod you shall make it: of gold, of blue and purple and scarlet *material* and fine twisted linen you shall make it.
16"It shall be square *and* folded double, a span^Tin length and a span^Tin width.   *its*
17"And you shall mount on it four rows of stones; the first row *shall be* a row of ruby, topaz and emerald;
18 and the second row a turquoise, a sapphire and a diamond;
19 and the third row a jacinth, an agate and an amethyst;
20 and the fourth row a beryl and an onyx and a jasper; they shall be ^Tset in gold filigree.   *interwoven with gold in their settings*
21"And the stones shall be according to the names of the sons of Israel: twelve, according to their names; they shall be *like* the engravings of a seal, each ^Raccording to his name for the twelve tribes.   Rev. 7:4-8; 21:12
22"And you shall make on the breastpiece chains of twisted cordage work in pure gold.
23"And you shall make on the breastpiece two rings of gold, and shall put the two rings on the two ends of the breastpiece.
24"And you shall put the two cords of gold on the two rings at the ends of the breastpiece.

25"And you shall put the *other* two ends of the two cords on the two filigree *settings*, and put them on the shoulder pieces of the ephod, at the front of it.
26"And you shall make two rings of gold and shall place them on the two ends of the breastpiece, on the edge of it, which is toward the inner side of the ephod.
27"And you shall make two rings of gold and put them on the bottom of the two shoulder pieces of the ephod, on the front of it close to the place where it is joined, above the skillfully woven band of the ephod.
28"And they shall bind the breastpiece by its rings to the rings of the ephod with a ^Ablue cord, that it may be on the skillfully woven band of the ephod, and that the breastpiece may not come loose from the ephod.   *violet*
29"And Aaron shall carry the names of the sons of Israel in the breastpiece of judgment over his heart when he enters the holy place, for a memorial before the LORD continually.

The Urim and Thummim

30"And you shall put in the breastpiece of judgment the [29]Urim and the Thummim, and they shall be over Aaron's heart when he goes in before the LORD; and Aaron shall carry the judgment of the sons of Israel over his heart before the LORD continually.

The Robe of the Ephod

31"And ^Ryou shall make the robe of the ephod all of^Ablue.   Ex. 39:22-26 • *violet*
32"And there shall be an opening^Aat its top in the middle of it; around its opening there shall be a binding of woven work, as *it were* the opening of a coat of mail, that it may not be torn.   *for his head*
33"And you shall make on its hem pomegranates of blue and purple and scarlet *material,* all around on its hem, and bells of gold between them all around:
34 a golden bell and a pomegranate, a golden bell and a pomegranate, all around on the hem of the robe.
35"And it shall be on Aaron^Twhen he ministers; and its tinkling may be heard when he enters and leaves the holy place before the LORD, that he may not die. *for ministering*

The Holy Crown

36"You shall also make ^Ra plate of pure gold and shall engrave on it, like the engravings of a seal, 'Holy to the LORD.'   Lev. 8:9
37"And you shall ^Tfasten it on a^Ablue cord, and it shall be on the turban; it shall be at the front of the turban.   *place • violet*
38"And it shall be on Aaron's forehead, and Aaron shall ^Atake away the iniquity of the holy things which the sons of Israel consecrate, with regard to all their holy gifts;

[29] I.e., lights and perfections

and it shall always be on his forehead, that they may be accepted before the LORD. *bear*

The Priest's Tunic

39"And you shall weave the tunic of checkered work of fine linen, and shall make a turban of fine linen, and you shall make a sash, the work of a weaver.

40"And for Aaron's sons you shall make tunics; you shall also make sashes for them, and you shall make caps^T for them, for glory and for beauty.   *headgear* • Ezek. 44:18

41"And you shall put them on Aaron your brother and on his sons with him; and you shall ^Ranoint them and ordain them and consecrate them, that they may serve Me as priests.   Ex. 29:7, 9; 30:30; 40:15 • *fill their hand*

42"And you shall make for them linen breeches to cover *their* bare flesh; they shall ^Treach from the loins even to the thighs. *be*

43"And they shall be on Aaron and on his sons when they enter the tent of meeting, or when they approach the altar to minister in the holy place, so that they do not incur guilt and die. It *shall be* a statute forever to him and to his descendants after him. *seed*

CHAPTER 29

The Consecration of the Priests

"NOW^R this is^T what you shall do to them to consecrate them to minister as priests to Me: take one young bull and two rams without blemish,   Lev. 8:1-34 • *the thing which*

2 and unleavened bread and unleavened cakes mixed with oil, and unleavened wafers spread with oil; you shall make them of fine wheat flour.   Lev. 2:4; 6:19-23 • *anointed*

3"And you shall put them in one basket, and present them in the basket along with the bull and the two rams.

4"Then ^Ryou shall bring Aaron and his sons to the doorway of the tent of meeting, and wash them with water.   Lev. 8:6

5"And you shall take the garments, and put on Aaron the ^Rtunic and the robe of the ephod and the ephod and the ^breastpiece, and gird him with the skillfully woven band of the ephod;   Ex. 28:39; Lev. 8:7 • *pouch*

6 and you shall set the turban on his head, and put the holy crown on the turban.

7"Then you shall take the anointing oil, and pour it on his head and anoint him.

8"And you shall bring his sons and put ^Rtunics on them.   Ex. 28:39, 40; Lev. 8:13

9"And you shall gird them with sashes, Aaron and his sons, and bind ^Tcaps on them, and they shall have the priesthood by a perpetual statute. So you shall ordain Aaron and his sons.   *headgear* • *fill the hand of*

10"Then you shall bring the bull before the tent of meeting, and Aaron and his sons shall lay their hands on the head of the bull.

11"And you shall slaughter the bull before the LORD at the doorway of the tent of meeting.

12"And you shall take some of the blood of the bull and put *it* on the horns of the altar with your finger; and you shall pour out all the blood at the base of the altar.

13"And you shall take all the fat that covers the entrails and the lobe of the liver, and the two kidneys and the fat that is on them, and offer them up in smoke on the altar.

14"But ^Rthe flesh of the bull and its hide and its refuse, you shall burn with fire outside the camp; it is a sin offering. Heb. 13:11

15"You^R shall also take the one ram, and Aaron and his sons shall lay their hands on the head of the ram;   Lev. 8:18

16 and you shall slaughter the ram and shall take its blood and sprinkle it around on the altar.

17"Then you shall cut the ram into its pieces, and wash its entrails and its legs, and put *them* with its pieces and its head.

18"And you shall offer up in smoke the whole ram on the altar; it is a burnt offering to the LORD: ^Rit is a soothing aroma, an offering by fire to the LORD.   Gen. 8:21; Ex. 29:25

19"Then ^Ryou shall take the other ram, and Aaron and his sons shall lay their hands on the head of the ram.   Lev. 8:22f. • *second*

20"And you shall slaughter the ram, and take some of its blood and put *it* on the lobe of Aaron's right ear and on the lobes of his sons' right ears and on the thumbs of their right hands and on the big toes of their right feet, and sprinkle the *rest of the* blood around on the altar.

21"Then you shall take some of the blood that is on the altar and some of the ^Ranointing oil, and sprinkle *it* on Aaron and on his garments, and on his sons and on his sons' garments with him; so he and his garments shall be consecrated, as well as his sons and his sons' garments with him.   Lev. 8:30

22"You shall also take the fat from the ram and the fat tail, and the fat that covers the entrails and the lobe of the liver, and the two kidneys and the fat that is on them and the right thigh (for it is a ram of ordination),

23 and one cake of bread and ^Rone cake of bread *mixed with* oil and one wafer from the basket of unleavened bread which is *set* before the LORD;   Lev. 8:26

24 and you shall put ^Tall these^T in the^T hands of Aaron and^T in the^T hands of his sons, and shall wave them as a wave offering before the LORD.   *the whole* • *on* • *palms*

25"And ^Ryou shall take them from their hands, and offer them up in smoke on the altar on the burnt offering for a soothing aroma before the LORD; it is an offering by fire to the LORD.   Lev. 8:28

26"Then you shall take^R the breast of Aaron's ram of ^Tordination, and wave it as a wave offering before the LORD; and it shall be your portion.   Lev. 7:31, 34; 8:29 • *filling*

27"And you shall consecrate the breast of

the wave offering and the thigh of the heave offering which was waved and which was Toffered from the ram of ordination, from the one which was for Aaron and from the one which was for his sons.   *heaved; or, lifted up*

28"And it shall be for Aaron and his sons as *their* portion forever from the sons of Israel, for it is a heave offering; and it shall be a heave offering from the sons of Israel from the sacrifices of their peace offerings, *even* their heave offering to the LORD.

29"And the holy garments of Aaron shall be for his sons after him, that in them they may be anointed and ordained.

30"For seven days the one of his sons who is priest in his stead shall put them on when he enters the tent of meeting to minister in the holy place.

31"And you shall take the ram of Tordination and boil its flesh in a holy place. *filling*

32"And Aaron and his sons shall eat the flesh of the ram, and the bread that is in the basket, at the doorway of the tent of meeting.

33"Thus they shall eat Tthose things by which atonement was made at their ordination *and* consecration; but a layman shall not eat *them*, because they are holy. *them*

34"And if any of the flesh of ordination or any of the bread remains until morning, then you shall burn the remainder with fire; it shall not be eaten, because it is holy.

35"And thus you shall do to Aaron and to his sons, according to all that I have commanded you; you shall Tordain them through Rseven days.   *fill their hand* • Lev. 8:33

36"And each day you shall offer a bull as a sin offering for atonement, and you shall purify the altar when you make atonement for it; and you shall anoint it to consecrate it.

37"For seven days you shall make atonement Tfor the altar and consecrate it; then the altar shall be most holy, *and* whatever touches the altar shall be holy.   *upon*

The Continual Offerings of the Priests

38"Now Rthis is what you shall offer on the altar: two one year old lambs each day, continuously.   Num. 28:3-31; 29:6-38

39"The one lamb you shall offer in the morning, and the Tother lamb you shall offer at Ttwilight;   *second • between the two evenings*

40 and there *shall be* Tone-tenth *of an ephah* of fine flour mixed with Tone-fourth of a hin of beaten oil, and one-fourth of a hin of wine for a libation with one lamb. 2 qt. • 1 qt.

41"And the Tother lamb you shall offer at twilight, and shall offer with it the same grain offering as the morning and Tthe same libation, for a soothing aroma, an offering by fire to the LORD.   *second • according to its*

42"It shall be a continual burnt offering throughout your generations at the doorway Rof the tent of meeting before the LORD, Twhere I will meet with you, to speak to you there.   Ex. 25:22; Num. 17:4

43"And I will meet there with the sons of Israel, and it shall be consecrated by My glory.

44"And I will consecrate the tent of meeting and the altar; I will also consecrate Aaron and his sons to minister as priests to Me.

45"And RI will dwell among the sons of Israel and will be their God.   Lev. 26:12

46"And they shall know that RI am the LORD their God who brought them out of the land of Egypt, that I might dwell among them; I am the LORD their God.   Ex. 20:2

CHAPTER 30

The Altar of Incense

"MOREOVER, you shall make Ran altar as a place for burning incense; you shall make it of acacia wood.   Ex. 37:25-29

2"Its length *shall be* a Tcubit, and its width a cubit, it shall be square, and its height *shall be* two cubits; its horns *shall be* of one piece with it.   One cubit equals approx. 18 in.

3"And you shall overlay it with pure gold, its top and its Tsides all around, and its horns; and you shall make a gold molding all around for it.   *walls*

4"And you shall make two gold rings for it under its molding; you shall make *them* on its two side walls—on Topposite sides— and Tthey shall be holders for poles with which to carry it.   *its two • it*

5"And you shall make the poles of acacia wood and overlay them Twith gold.

6"And you shall put Tthis altar in front of the veil that is Tnear the ark of the testimony, in front of the Tmercy seat that is over *the ark of* the testimony, where I will meet with you.   *it • upon*, or *over • propitiatory*

7"And Aaron shall burn fragrant incense on it; he shall burn it every morning when he trims the lamps.

8"And when Aaron Ttrims the lamps at twilight, he shall burn incense. *There shall be* perpetual incense before the LORD throughout your generations. *causes to ascend*

9"You shall not offer any strange incense on Tthis altar, or burnt offering or meal offering; and you shall not pour out a libation on it.   *it*

10"And Aaron shall make atonement on its horns once a year; he shall make atonement on it with the blood of the sin offering of atonement once a year throughout your generations. It is most holy to the LORD."

The Ransom Money

11 The LORD also spoke to Moses, saying,

12"When you take a Tcensus of the sons of Israel Tto number them, then each one of them shall give a ransom for himself to the LORD, when you number them, that there may be no plague among them when you number them.   *sum • for their being mustered*

13"This is what everyone who is num-

bered shall give: half a shekel according to the shekel of the sanctuary (the^R shekel is twenty gerahs),^Thalf a shekel as a contribution to the LORD. Num. 3:47 • $64 • *heave offering*

14"Everyone who is numbered, from twenty years old and over, shall give the contribution to the LORD.

15"The rich shall not pay more, and the poor shall not pay less than the half shekel, when you give the contribution to the LORD to make atonement for yourselves. *your souls*

16"And you shall take the atonement money from the sons of Israel, and shall give it for the service of the tent of meeting, that it may be a memorial for the sons of Israel before the LORD, to make atonement for yourselves." *your souls*

The Laver of Bronze

17 And the LORD spoke to Moses, saying,
18"You shall also make a laver of bronze, with its base of bronze, for washing; and you shall put it between the tent of meeting and the altar, and you shall put water in it.
19"And Aaron and his sons shall wash their hands and their feet from it; Is. 52:11
20 when they enter the tent of meeting, they shall wash with water, that they may not die; or when they approach the altar to minister, by offering up in smoke a fire *sacrifice* to the LORD.
21"So they shall wash their hands and their feet, that they may not die; and it shall be a perpetual statute for them, for Aaron and his descendants throughout their generations." Ex. 28:43 • *him* • *seed*

The Anointing Oil

22 Moreover, the LORD spoke to Moses, saying,
23"Take also for yourself the finest of spices: of flowing myrrh five hundred *shekels,* and of fragrant cinnamon half as much, two hundred and fifty, and of fragrant cane two hundred and fifty, 12.5 lb.
24 and of cassia five hundred, according to the shekel of the sanctuary, and of olive oil a hin.
25"And you shall make of these a holy anointing oil, a perfume mixture, the work of a perfumer; it shall be a holy anointing oil. *it* • Ex. 37:29; 40:9; Lev. 8:10
26"And with it you shall anoint the tent of meeting and the ark of the testimony,
27 and the table and all its utensils, and the lampstand and its utensils, and the altar of incense,
28 and the altar of burnt offering and all its utensils, and the laver and its stand.
29"You shall also consecrate them, that they may be most holy; whatever touches them shall be holy.
30"And^R you shall anoint Aaron and his sons, and consecrate them, that they may minister as priests to Me. Ex. 29:7; Lev. 8:12

31"And you shall speak to the sons of Israel, saying, 'This shall be a holy anointing oil to Me throughout your generations.
32 'It shall not be poured on anyone's body, nor shall you make *any* like it, in the same proportions; it is holy, *and* it shall be holy to you. *the flesh of man* • *its proportion*
33 'Whoever shall mix *any* like it, or whoever puts any of it on a layman, shall be cut off from his people.' " *stranger* • *even he shall*

The Incense

34 Then the LORD said to Moses, "Take for yourself spices, stacte and onycha and galbanum, spices with pure frankincense; there shall be an equal part of each.
35"And with it you shall make incense, a perfume, the work of a perfumer, salted, pure, *and* holy.
36"And you shall beat some of it very fine, and put part of it before the testimony in the tent of meeting, where I shall meet with you; it shall be most holy to you. Ex. 29:42
37"And the incense which you shall make, you shall not make in the same proportions for yourselves; it shall be holy to you for the LORD. Ex. 30:32 • *its proportion*
38"Whoever shall make *any* like it, to use as perfume, shall be cut off from his people." Ex. 30:33 • *smell of it* • *even he shall*

CHAPTER 31

Instructions for Building the Tabernacle

NOW the LORD spoke to Moses, saying,
2"See, I have called by name Bezalel, the son of Uri, the son of Hur, of the tribe of Judah. 1 Chr. 2:20
3"And I have filled him with the Spirit of God in wisdom, in understanding, in knowledge, and in all *kinds of* craftsmanship,
4 to make artistic designs for work in gold, in silver, and in bronze, *devise devices*
5 and in the cutting of stones for settings, and in the carving of wood, that he may work in all *kinds of* craftsmanship.
6"And behold, I Myself have appointed with him Oholiab, the son of Ahisamach, of the tribe of Dan; and in the hearts of all who are skillful I have put skill, that they may make all that I have commanded you: *given*
7 the tent of meeting, and the ark of testimony, and the mercy seat upon it, and all the furniture of the tent, *propitiatory*
8 the table also and its utensils, and the pure *gold* lampstand with all its utensils, and the altar of incense, *vessels* • Lev. 24:4
9 the altar of burnt offering also with all its utensils, and the laver and its stand,
10 the woven garments as well, and the holy garments for Aaron the priest, and the garments of his sons, *with which* to carry on their priesthood; *minister as priests*

11 ^{R}the anointing oil also, and the^{Rc}fragrant incense for the holy place, they are to make *them* according to all that I have commanded you." Ex. 30:23-32 • Ex. 30:34-38

Sign of the Covenant:
the Sabbath

12 And the LORD spoke to Moses, saying, 13"But as for you, speak to the sons of Israel, saying, 'You^R shall surely observe My sabbaths; for *this* is ^{R}a sign between Me and you throughout your generations, that you may know that I am the LORD who sanctifies you. Ex. 20:8 • Ex. 31:17; Ezek. 20:12, 20

14 'Therefore you are to observe the sabbath, for it is holy to you. Everyone who profanes it shall surely be put to death; for whoever does any work on it, that person shall be cut off from among his people.

15 'For six days work may be done, but on the seventh day there is a ^{s}sabbath of complete rest, holy to the LORD; whoever does any work on the sabbath day shall surely be put to death. Gen. 2:2f.; Ex. 16:23; 20:8; 35:2, 3

16 'So the sons of Israel shall observe the sabbath, to celebrate the sabbath throughout their generations as a perpetual covenant.' *do*

17"It is a sign between Me and the sons of Israel forever; for in six days the LORD made heaven and earth, but on the seventh day He ceased *from labor,* and was refreshed."

The Two Tablets Are Presented

18 And when He had finished speaking with him upon Mount Sinai, He gave Moses the two tablets of the testimony, tablets of stone, written by the finger of God.

CHAPTER 32

Israel Willfully Breaks the Covenant

Now when the people saw that Moses delayed to come down from the mountain, the people assembled about Aaron, and said to him, "Come, make us ^{a}a god who will go before us; as for this Moses, the man who brought us up from the land of Egypt, we do not know what has become of him." *gods*

2 And Aaron said to them, "Tear^R off the gold rings which are in the ears of your wives, your sons, and your daughters, and bring *them* to me." Ex. 35:22

3 Then all the people tore off the gold rings which were in their ears, and brought *them* to Aaron.

4 And he took *this* from their hand, and fashioned it with a graving tool, and made it into a molten calf; and they said, "This^a is your god, O Israel, who brought you up from the land of Egypt." *These are your gods*

5 Now when Aaron saw *this,* he built an altar before it; and Aaron made a proclamation and said, "Tomorrow *shall be* a feast to the LORD."

6 So the next day they rose early and ^{b}offered burnt offerings, and brought peace offerings; and the people sat down to eat and to drink, and rose up to play. Acts 7:41

God to Destroy Israel

7 Then the LORD spoke to Moses, "Go ^{T}down at once, for your people, whom ^{R}you brought up from the land of Egypt, have corrupted *themselves.* *go down* • Deut. 9:12

8"They have quickly turned aside from the way which I commanded them. They have made for themselves a molten calf, and have worshiped it, and have sacrificed to it, and said, 'This^A is your god, O Israel, who brought you up from the land of Egypt!' " *These are your gods*

9 ^{R}And the LORD said to Moses, "I have seen this people, and behold, they are an obstinate people. Num. 14:11-20 • *a stiff-necked*

10"Now then^{R}let Me alone, that My anger may burn against them, and that I may destroy them; and^{R}I will make of you a great nation." Deut. 9:14 • Num. 14:12

Moses Intercedes for Israel

11 Then Moses entreated the LORD his God, and said, "O LORD, why doth Thine anger burn against Thy people whom Thou hast brought out from the land of Egypt with great power and with a mighty hand?

12"Why should^{R}the Egyptians speak, saying, 'With evil *intent* He brought them out to kill them in the mountains and to destroy them from the face of the earth'? Turn from Thy burning anger and change Thy mind about *doing* harm to Thy people. Josh. 7:9

13"Remember Abraham, Isaac, and Israel, Thy servants to whom Thou didst swear by Thyself, and didst say to them, 'I will multiply your descendants as the stars of the heavens, and all this land of which I have spoken I will give to your^{T}descendants, and they shall inherit *it* forever.' " *seed*

14 ^{R}So the LORD changed His mind about the harm which He said He would do to His people. Ps. 106:45

Moses Disciplines Israel

15 Then Moses turned and went down from the mountain with the two tablets of the testimony in his hand, tablets which were written on both ^{T}sides; they were written on one *side* and the other. *their sides*

16 And the tablets were God's work, and the writing was God's writing engraved on the tablets.

17 Now when Joshua heard the sound of the people ^{a}as they shouted, he said to Moses, "There is a sound of war in the camp." *in its shouting*

18 But he said,

"It is not the sound of the cry of triumph,

Nor is it the sound of the cry of defeat;
But the sound of singing I hear."
19 And it came about, as soon as Moses came near the camp, that he saw the calf and *the* dancing; and Moses' anger burned, and he threw the tablets from his hands and shattered them at the foot of the mountain.
20 ^RAnd he took the calf which they had made and burned *it* with fire, and ground it to powder, and scattered it over the surface of the water, and made the sons of Israel drink *it*.   Deut. 9:21
21 Then Moses said to Aaron, "What did this people do to you, that you have brought *such* great sin upon them?"
22 And Aaron said, "Do not let the anger of my lord burn; you know the people yourself, that they are prone to evil.   *in evil*
23 "For they said to me, 'Make a god for us who will go before us; for this Moses, the man who brought us up from the land of Egypt, we do not know what has become of him.'   Ex. 32:1-4 • *gods*
24 "And I said to them, 'Whoever has any gold, let them tear it off.' So they gave *it* to me, and I threw it into the fire, and out came this calf."   Ex. 32:4
25 Now when Moses saw that the people were out of control—for Aaron had let them get out of control to be a derision among their enemies—   *those who rise against them*
26 then Moses stood in the gate of the camp, and said, "Whoever is for the LORD, *come* to me!" And all the sons of Levi gathered together to him.
27 And he said to them, "Thus says the LORD, the God of Israel, 'Every man *of you* put his sword upon his thigh, and go back and forth from gate to gate in the camp, and kill every man his brother, and every man his friend, and every man his neighbor.'"
28 So the sons of Levi did as Moses instructed, and about three thousand men of the people fell that day.   Num. 25:7-13
29 Then Moses said, "Dedicate yourselves today to the LORD—for every man has been against his son and against his brother—in order that He may bestow a blessing upon you today."   *Fill your hand*

Moses Atones for Israel

30 And it came about on the next day that Moses said to the people, "You yourselves have committed a great sin; and now I am going up to the LORD, perhaps I can make atonement for your sin."   *sinned* • Num. 25:13
31 Then Moses returned to the LORD, and said, "Alas, this people has committed a great sin, and they have made a god of gold for themselves.   *sinned* • *gods* • Ex. 20:23
32 "But now, if Thou wilt, forgive their sin—and if not, please blot me out from Thy book which Thou hast written!"   Ps. 69:28
33 And the LORD said to Moses, "Whoever has sinned against Me, I will blot him out of My book.   Deut. 29:20; Ps. 9:5; Rev. 3:5

God Sends His Angel

34 "But go now, lead the people where I told you. Behold, My angel shall go before you; nevertheless in the day when I punish, I will punish them for their sin."   *visit*
35 Then the LORD smote the people, because of what they did with the calf which Aaron had made.   Ex. 32:28 • Ex. 32:4, 24

CHAPTER 33

The Tabernacle Is Moved
Outside the Camp

THEN the LORD spoke to Moses, "Depart, go up from here, you and the people whom you have brought up from the land of Egypt, to the land of which I swore to Abraham, Isaac, and Jacob, saying, 'To your descendants I will give it.'   Gen. 26:1-3 • *seed*
2 "And I will send an angel before you and I will drive out the Canaanite, the Amorite, the Hittite, the Perizzite, the Hivite and the Jebusite.   Ex. 23:27-31; Josh. 24:11
3 "*Go up* to a land flowing with milk and honey; for I will not go up in your midst, because you are an obstinate people, lest I destroy you on the way."   *a stiff-necked*
4 When the people heard this sad word, they went into mourning, and none of them put on his ornaments.   *evil* • Num. 14:1, 39
5 For the LORD had said to Moses, "Say to the sons of Israel, 'You are an obstinate people; should I go up in your midst for one moment, I would destroy you. Now therefore, put off your ornaments from you, that I may know what I will do with you.'"
6 So the sons of Israel stripped themselves of their ornaments from Mount Horeb *onward*.
7 Now Moses used to take the tent and pitch it outside the camp, a good distance from the camp, and he called it the tent of meeting. And it came about, that everyone who sought the LORD would go out to the tent of meeting which was outside the camp.   Ex. 18:7, 12-16 • Ex. 29:42f.

Moses Talks to God

8 And it came about, whenever Moses went out to the tent, that all the people would arise and stand, each at the entrance of his tent, and gaze after Moses until he entered the tent.
9 And it came about, whenever Moses entered the tent, the pillar of cloud would descend and stand at the entrance of the tent; and the LORD would speak with Moses.
10 When all the people saw the pillar of cloud standing at the entrance of the tent, all the people would arise and worship, each at the entrance of his tent.
11 Thus the LORD used to speak to Moses face to face, just as a man speaks to his friend. When Moses returned to the camp, his servant Joshua, the son of Nun, a young man, would not depart from the tent.   *he*

God Will Show Moses the Way

12 Then Moses said to the LORD, "See, Thou dost say to me, 'Bring up this people!' But Thou Thyself hast not let me know whom Thou wilt send with me. Moreover, Thou hast said, 'I have known you by name, and you have also found favor in My sight.' **13** "Now therefore, I pray Thee, if I have found favor in Thy sight, ᴿlet me know Thy ways, that I may know Thee, so that I may find favor in Thy sight. Consider too, that this nation is Thy people." Ps. 25:4; 27:11 **14** And He said, "Myᴿ presence shall go *with you,* and I will give you rest." Is. 63:9 **15** Then he said to Him, "IfᴿThy presence does not go *with us,* do not lead us up from here. Ps. 80:3, 7, 19 **16** "For how then can it be known that I have found favor in Thy sight, I and Thy people? Is it not by Thy going with us, so that we, I and Thy people, may be distinguished from all the *other* people who are upon the face of the ᵀearth?" *ground* **17** And the LORD said to Moses, "I will also do this thing of which you have spoken; ᴿfor you have found favor in My sight, and I have known you by name." Ex. 33:12

God Shows Moses His Glory

18 ᴿThen ᵀMoses said, "I pray Thee, show me Thy glory!" Ex. 33:20-23 · *he* **19** And He said, "I Myself will make all My goodness pass before you, and will proclaim the name of the LORD before you; and ᴿI will be gracious to whom I will be gracious, and will show compassion on whom I will show compassion." [Rom. 9:15] **20** But He said, "You cannot see My face, for no man can see Me and live!" **21** Then the LORD said, "Behold, there is a place by Me, and you shall stand *there* on the rock; **22** and it will come about, while My glory is passing by, that I will put you in the cleft of the rock and ᴿcover you with My hand until I have passed by. Ps. 91:1, 4; Is. 49:2; 51:16 **23** "Then I will take My hand away and you shall see My back, butᴿMy face shall not be seen." Ex. 33:20; [John 1:18]

CHAPTER 34

Hewing of the Two Tablets

NOW the LORD said to Moses, "Cut out for yourself two stone tablets like the former ones, andᴿI will write on the tablets the words that were on the former tablets which you shattered. Deut. 10:2, 4 **2** "So be ready by morning, and come up in the morning toᴿMount Sinai, and ᵖpresent yourself there to Me on the top of the mountain. Ex. 19:11, 18, 20 · *place yourself before* **3** "And no man is to come up with you, nor let any man be seen anywhere on the mountain; even the flocks and the herds may not graze in front of that mountain." **4** So he cut outᵗtwo stone tablets like the former ones, and Moses rose up early in the morning and went up to Mount Sinai, as the LORD had commanded him, and he took two stone tablets in his hand. Ex. 34:1

The Nature of God Is Revealed

5 And ᴿthe LORD descended in the cloud and stood there with him as he called upon the name of the LORD. Ex. 19:9; 33:9 **6** Then the LORD passed by in front of him and proclaimed, "The LORD, the LORD God, ᴿcompassionate and gracious, slow to anger, and abounding in lovingkindness and ᴬtruth; Joel 2:13; Rom. 2:4 · *faithfulness* **7** who ᴿkeeps lovingkindness for thousands, who forgives iniquity, transgression and sin; yet He will by no means leave *the guilty* unpunished, visiting the iniquity of fathers on the children and on the grandchildren to the third and fourth generations." Ex. 20:5, 6; Deut. 5:10; 7:9; Ps. 103:3 **8** And Moses made haste ᴿto bow low toward the earth and worship. Ex. 4:31 **9** And he said, "If now I have found favor in Thy sight, O Lord, I pray, let the Lord go along in our midst, even though ᵗthe people are so obstinate; and do Thou pardon our iniquity and our sin, and take us as Thine own possession." *it is a people stiff-necked*

Renewal of the Covenant

10 Then ᵀGod said, "Behold, I am going to make a covenant. Before all your people I will perform miracles which have not been produced in all the earth, nor among any of the nations; and all the people ᵀamong whom you live will see the working of the LORD, for it is a fearful thing that I am going to perform with you. *He · in whose midst you are* **11** "Beᵀ sure to observe what I am commanding you this day: behold, I am going to drive out the Amorite before you, and the Canaanite, the Hittite, the Perizzite, the Hivite and the Jebusite. *Observe for yourself* **12** "Watchᴿ yourself that you make no covenant with the inhabitants of the land into which you are going, lest it become a snare in your midst. Ex. 23:32, 33 **13** "But *rather,* you are to tear down their altars and smash their *sacred* pillars and cut down their ³⁰Asherim Ex. 23:24; Deut. 12:3 **14** —for ᵛyou shall not worship any other god, for the LORD, whose name is Jealous, is a jealous God— [Ex. 20:3, 5; Deut. 4:24] **15** lest you make a covenant with the inhabitants of the land and they play the harlot with their gods, and sacrifice to their gods, and someoneᴿinvite you ᵗto eat of his sacrifice; Num. 25:1, 2 · *and you eat* **16** and ᵛyou take some of his daughters for your sons, and his daughters play the harlot

---

³⁰ I.e., wooden symbols of a female deity

with their gods, and cause your sons *also* to play the harlot with their gods.   Deut. 7:3

17 "You[R]shall make for yourself no molten gods.   Ex. 20:4, 23; Lev. 19:4; Deut. 5:8

18 "You shall observe the Feast of Unleavened Bread. For seven days you are to eat unleavened bread, as I commanded you, at the appointed time in the month of Abib, for in the month of Abib you came out of Egypt.

19 "The first offspring from every womb belongs to Me, and all your male livestock, the first offspring from cattle and sheep.

20 "And you shall redeem with a lamb the [T]first offspring from a donkey; and if you do not redeem *it*, then you shall break its neck. You shall redeem all the first-born of your sons. And [T]none shall appear before Me empty-handed.   *first opening of • they shall not*

21 "You shall work six days, but on the seventh day you shall rest; *even* during plowing time and harvest you shall rest.

22 "And you shall celebrate [R]the Feast of Weeks, *that is,* the first fruits of the wheat harvest, and the Feast of Ingathering at the turn of the year.   Ex. 23:16; Num. 28:26

23 "Three times a year all your males are to appear before the Lord[T]GOD, the God of Israel.   Heb., *YHWH,* usually rendered *LORD*

24 "For I will drive out nations before you and enlarge your borders, and no man shall covet your land when you go up three times a year to appear before the LORD your God.

25 "You shall not [T]offer the blood of My sacrifice with leavened bread, nor is the sacrifice of the Feast of the Passover to [T]be left over until morning.   *slaughter • remain overnight*

26 "You shall bring [R]the very first of the first fruits of your soil into the house of the LORD your God. You shall not boil a kid in its mother's milk."   Ex. 23:19; Deut. 26:2

27 Then the LORD said to Moses, "Write [T]down these words, for in accordance with these words I have made [R]a covenant with you and with Israel."   *for yourself • Ex. 34:10*

28 So he was there with the LORD forty days and forty nights; he did not eat bread or drink water. And he wrote on the tablets the words of the covenant, [R]the Ten [T]Commandments.   Deut. 4:13; 10:4 • *Words*

Moses Returns from God

29 And it came about when Moses was coming down from Mount Sinai (and the two tablets of the testimony *were* in Moses' hand as he was coming down from the mountain), that Moses did not know that [R]the skin of his face shone because of his speaking with Him.   Matt. 17:2; 2 Cor. 3:7

30 So when Aaron and all the sons of Israel saw Moses, behold, the skin of his face shone, and [R]they were afraid to come near him.   2 Cor. 3:7

31 Then Moses called to them, and Aaron and all the rulers in the congregation returned to him; and Moses spoke to them.

32 And afterward all the sons of Israel came near, and he commanded them *to do*

everything that the LORD had spoken[T]to him on Mount Sinai.   *with*

33 When Moses had finished speaking with them, he put a veil over his face.

34 But whenever Moses went in before the LORD to speak with Him,[R]he would take off the veil until he came out; and whenever he came out and spoke to the sons of Israel what he had been commanded,   [2 Cor. 3:16]

35 the sons of Israel would see the face of Moses, that the skin of Moses' face shone. So Moses would replace the veil over his face until he went in to speak with Him.

CHAPTER 35

*Israel Brings Offerings
in Abundance*

THEN Moses assembled all the congregation of the sons of Israel, and said to them, "These[R] are the things that the LORD has commanded *you* to [T]do.   Ex. 34:32 • *do them.*

2 "For[R]six days work may be done, but on the seventh day you shall have a holy *day,* a sabbath of complete rest to the LORD; [T]whoever does any work on it shall be put to death.   Lev. 23:3; Deut. 5:13f. • Num. 15:32-36

3 "You shall not kindle a fire in any of your dwellings on the sabbath day."

4 And Moses spoke to all the congregation of the sons of Israel, saying, "This is the thing which the LORD has commanded, saying,

5 'Take from among you a contribution to the LORD; whoever is of a willing heart, let him bring it as the LORD's [A]contribution: gold, silver, and bronze,   *heave offering*

6 and[A]blue, purple and scarlet *material,* fine linen, goats' *hair,*   *violet*

7 and rams' skins[A]dyed red, and porpoise skins, and acacia wood,   *tanned*

8 and oil for lighting, and spices for the anointing oil, and for the fragrant incense,

9 and onyx stones and setting stones, for the ephod and for the[A]breastpiece.   *pouch*

10 'And[R]let every skillful man among you come, and make all that the LORD has commanded: Ex. 31:6

11 the [T]tabernacle, its tent and its covering, its hooks and its boards, its bars, its pillars, and its[A]sockets;   *dwelling place • bases*

12 the ark and its poles, the [T]mercy seat, and the curtain of the screen;   *propitiatory*

13 the table and its poles, and all its[A]utensils, and the bread of the [31]Presence; *vessels*

14 the[R]lampstand also for the light and its utensils and its lamps and the oil for the light;   Ex. 25:31 ff.

15 and the altar of incense and its poles, and the anointing oil and the fragrant incense, and the screen for the doorway at the [A]entrance of the tabernacle;   *doorway*

[31] Lit., *Face*

16 the altar of burnt offering with its
^Abronze grating, its poles, and all its ^Butensils,
the ^Bbasin and its stand;   *copper • vessels • laver*
17 ^Rthe hangings of the court, its pillars
and its ^Bsockets, and the screen for the gate
of the court;   Ex. 27:9-18 • *bases*
18 the pegs of the tabernacle and the pegs
of the court and their cords;
19 the ^Bwoven garments, for ministering in
the holy place, the holy garments for Aaron
the priest, and the garments of his sons, to
minister as priests.' "   *service garments*
20 Then all the congregation of the sons of
Israel departed from Moses' presence.
21 And everyone whose heart ^Bstirred him
and everyone whose spirit moved him came
and brought the Lord's contribution for the
work of the tent of meeting and for all its
service and for the holy garments.   *lifted up*
22 Then all whose hearts moved them,
both men and women, came *and* brought
brooches and ^Bearrings and signet rings and
bracelets, all articles of gold; so *did* every
man who ^Bpresented an offering of gold to
the Lord.   *nose rings • waved a wave offering*
23 And every man, ^Bwho had in his possession ^Bblue and purple and scarlet *material*
and fine linen and goats' *hair* and rams'
skins ^Bdyed red and porpoise skins, brought
them.   *with whom was found • violet • tanned*
24 Everyone who could make a contribu-
tion of silver and ^Bbronze brought the Lord's
contribution; and every man, ^Bwho had in his
possession acacia wood for any work of the
service, brought it. *copper • with whom was found*
25 And all the ^Bskilled women spun with
their hands, and brought what they had
spun, *in* blue and purple *and* scarlet material and *in* fine linen.   *women wise of heart*
26 And all the women whose heart stirred
with a skill spun the goats' *hair.*
27 And the rulers brought the onyx stones
and the stones for setting for the ephod and
for the ^Bbreastpiece;   *pouch*
28 and ^Rthe spice and the oil for the light
and for the anointing oil and for the fragrant
incense.   Ex. 30:23ff.
29 The ^BIsraelites, all the men and women,
whose heart moved them to bring *material*
for all the work, which the Lord had commanded through Moses to be done, brought
a freewill offering to the Lord.   *sons of Israel*
30 ^RThen Moses said to the sons of Israel,
"See, the Lord has called by name Bezalel
the son of Uri, the son of Hur, of the tribe of
Judah.   Ex. 31:1-6
31 "And He has filled him with the Spirit of
God, in wisdom, in understanding and in
knowledge and in all ^Bcraftsmanship;   *work*
32 ^Bto make designs for working in gold
and in silver and in bronze,   *devise devices*
33 and in the cutting of stones for settings, and in the carving of wood, so as to
perform in every inventive work.
34 "He also has put in his heart to teach,
both he and ^ROholiab, the son of Ahisamach,
of the tribe of Dan.   Ex. 31:6

35 "He has filled them with ^Bskill to perform
every work of an engraver and of a designer
and of an embroiderer, in blue and in purple
and in scarlet *material,* and in fine linen,
and of a weaver, as performers of every
work and makers of designs.   *wisdom of heart*

CHAPTER 36

"**N**OW Bezalel and Oholiab, and every
^Bskillful person in whom the Lord has put
skill and understanding to know how to perform all the work in the construction of the
sanctuary, shall perform in accordance with
all that the Lord has commanded."   *wisdom*
2 Then Moses called Bezalel and Oholiab
and every skillful person in whom the Lord
had put skill, everyone whose heart stirred
him, to come to the work to perform it.
3 And they received from Moses all the
^Bcontributions which the sons of Israel had
brought to perform the work ^Bin the construction of the sanctuary. And they still
continued bringing to him freewill offerings
every morning.   *lifted offering • of the service of*
4 And all the ^Bskillful men who were performing all the work of the sanctuary came,
each from ^Bthe work which ^Bhe was performing,   *wise • his • they were*
5 and they said to Moses, "The people
are bringing much more than enough for the
^Bconstruction work which the Lord commanded *us* to perform."   *service for the work*
6 So Moses issued a command, and a
proclamation was circulated throughout the
camp, saying, "Let neither man nor woman
any longer perform work for the contributions of the sanctuary." Thus the people
were restrained from bringing *any* more.
7 ^RFor the ^Bmaterial they had was sufficient and more than enough for all the
work, to perform it.   1 Kin. 8:64 • *work*

The Curtains

8 And all the ^Bskillful men among those
who were performing the work made the
tabernacle with ten curtains; of fine twisted
linen and blue and purple and scarlet *material,* with cherubim, the work of a skillful
workman, Bezalel made them.   *wise of heart*
9 The length of each curtain was twenty-
eight cubits, and the width of each curtain
four ^Bcubits; all the curtains had the same
measurements.   One cubit equals approx. 18 in.
10 And he ^Bjoined five curtains to one another, and *the other* five curtains he ^Bjoined
to one another.   *coupled*
11 And he made loops of blue on the edge
of the outermost curtain in the first ^Bset; he
did likewise on the edge of the curtain that
was outermost in the second ^Bset.   *coupling*
12 He made fifty loops in the one curtain
and he made fifty loops on the ^Bedge of the
curtain that was in the second ^Bset; the loops
were opposite each other.   *end • coupling*

13 And he made fifty clasps of gold, and joined the curtains to one another with the clasps, so the tabernacle was a unit.   *one*

14 Then ʳhe made curtains of goats' *hair* for a tent over the tabernacle; he made eleven curtains ᵀin all.   Ex. 26:7-14 • *in number*

15 The length of each curtain was ᵀthirty cubits, and ᵀfour cubits the width of each curtain; the eleven curtains had ᵗthe same measurements.   45 ft. • 6 ft. • *one measure*

16 And he ᴬjoined five curtains by themselves, and *the other* six curtains by themselves.   *coupled*

17 Moreover, he made fifty loops on the edge of the curtain that was outermost in the *first* ᵀset, and he made fifty loops on the edge of the curtain *that was outermost in* the second ᵗset.   *coupling*

18 And he made fifty clasps of ᴬbronze to ᴬjoin the tent together, that it might be ᵀa unit.   *copper • couple • one*

19 And he made a covering for the tent of rams' skins ᴬdyed red, and a covering of porpoise skins above.   *tanned*

The Boards

20 Then he made the boards for the tabernacle of acacia wood, standing upright.

21 ᵀTen cubits was the length of ᵀeach board, and ᵀone and a half cubits the width of each board.   15 ft. • *the* • 27 in.

22 There were two tenons for each board, ᵗfitted to one another; thus he did for all the boards of the tabernacle.   *bound*

23 And he made the boards for the tabernacle: twenty boards for the south side;

24 and he made forty sockets of silver under the twenty boards; two sockets under one board for its two tenons and two sockets under another board for its two tenons.

25 Then for the second side of the tabernacle, on the north side, he made twenty boards,

26 and their forty ᴬsockets of silver; two ᴬsockets under one board and two ᴬsockets under another board.   *bases*

27 And for the ᵗrear of the tabernacle, to the west, he made six boards.   *extreme parts*

28 And he made two boards for the corners of the tabernacle at the rear.

29 And they were double beneath, and together they were complete to its ᴬtop ᴬto the first ring; thus he did with both of them for the two corners.   *head • with reference to*

30 And there were eight boards with their ᴬsockets of silver, sixteen ᴬsockets, ᵗtwo under every board.   *bases • two sockets*

31 Then he made bars of acacia wood, five for the boards of one side of the tabernacle,

32 and five bars for the boards of the ᴬother side of the tabernacle, and five bars for the boards of the tabernacle for the ᵀrear *side* to the west.   *second • extreme parts*

33 And he made the middle bar to pass through in the ᵗcenter of the boards from end to end.   *midst*

34 And he overlaid the boards with gold and made their rings of gold *as* holders for the bars, and overlaid the bars with gold.

The Veils

35 ʳMoreover, he made the veil of ᴬblue and purple and scarlet *material*, and fine twisted linen; he made it with cherubim, the work of a skillful workman.   Ex. 26:31-37 • *violet*

36 And he made four pillars of acacia for it, and overlaid them with gold, with their hooks of gold; and he cast four ᴬsockets of silver for them.   *bases*

37 And he made a screen for the doorway of the tent, of blue and purple and scarlet *material*, and fine twisted linen, the work of a ᵗweaver;   *variegator;* i.e., a weaver in colors

38 and *he made* its five pillars with their hooks, and he overlaid their tops and their ᴬbands with gold; but their five ᴬsockets were of ᴬbronze.   *fillets, rings • bases • copper*

CHAPTER 37

The Ark of the Covenant

Nowʳ Bezalel made the ark of acacia wood; its length was two and a half cubits, and its width one and a half cubits, and its height one and a half cubits;   Ex. 25:10-20

2 and he overlaid it with pure gold inside and out, and made a gold molding for it all around.

3 And he cast four rings of gold for it on its four feet; even two rings on one side of it, and two rings on the ᵗother side of it.   *second*

4 And he made poles of acacia wood and overlaid them with gold.

5 And he put the poles into the rings on the sides of the ark, to carry ᵗit.   *the ark*

6 And he made a ᵗmercy seat of pure gold, two and a half cubits ᵗlong, and one and a half cubits wide.   *propitiatory • its length*

7 And he made two cherubim of gold; he made them of hammered work, ᵀat the two ends of the mercy seat;   *from*

8 one cherub ᵀat the one end, and one cherub ᵀat the other end; he made the cherubim *of one piece* with the mercy seat ᵀat the two ends.   *from*

9 And the cherubim had *their* wings spread upward, covering the ᵗmercy seat with their wings, with their faces toward each other; the faces of the cherubim were toward the mercy seat.   *propitiatory*

The Table of Showbread

10 Then he made the table of acacia wood, two cubits ᵀlong and a cubit ᵀwide and one and a half cubits high.   *its length • its width*

11 And he overlaid it with pure gold, and made a gold molding for it all around.

12 And he made a rim for it of a handbreadth all around, and made a gold molding for its rim all around.

13 And he cast four gold rings for it and put the rings on the four corners that were on its four feet.

14 Close by the rim were the rings, the holders for the poles to carry the table.

15 And he made the poles of acacia wood and overlaid them with gold, to carry the table.

16 And he made the utensils which were on the table, its ᵃdishes and its pans and its ᵀbowls and its jars, with which to pour out libations, of pure gold.　　*platters • libation bowls*

The Gold Lampstand

17 ᴿThen he made the lampstand of pure gold. He made the lampstand of hammered work, its base and its shaft; its cups, its ᴬbulbs and its flowers were *of one piece* with it.　　Ex. 25:31-39 • *calyxes*

18 And there were six branches going out of its sides; three branches of the lampstand from the one side of it, and three branches of the lampstand from the other side of it;

19 three cups shaped like almond *blossoms,* aᴬbulb and a flower in one branch, and three cups shaped like almond *blossoms,* a ᴬbulb and a flower in the other branch—so for the six branches going out of the lampstand.　　*calyx*

20 And in the lampstand *there were* four cups shaped like almond *blossoms,* itsᴬbulbs and its flowers;　　*calyxes*

21 and aᴬbulb was under the *first* pair of branches *coming* out of it, and aᴬbulb under the *second* pair of branches *coming* out of it, and aᴬbulb under the *third* pair of branches *coming* out of it, for the six branches coming out of the lampstand.　　*calyx*

22 Theirᴬbulbs and their branches were *of one piece* with it; the whole of it *was* a single hammered work of pure gold.　　*calyxes*

23 And he made its seven lamps with its snuffers and its trays of pure gold.

24 He made it and all its utensils from a ᵀtalent of pure gold.　　$5,760,000

The Altar of Incense

25 Then he made the altar of incense of acacia wood: aᵀcubit ᵀlong and a cubit ᵀwide, square, and two cubits high; its horns were *of one piece* with it.　　18 in. • *its length • its width*

26 And he overlaid it with pure gold, its top and its ᶠsides all around, and its horns; and he made a gold molding for it all around.　　*walls*

27 And he made two golden rings for it under its molding, on its two sides—on opposite sides—as holders for poles with which to carry it.

28 And he made the poles of acacia wood and overlaid them with gold.

29 ᴿAnd he made the holy anointing oil and the pure, fragrant incense of spices, the work of a perfumer.　　Ex. 30:23-25, 34, 35

CHAPTER 38
The Altar of Burnt Offerings

THEN he made the altar of burnt offering of acacia wood, five cubits long, and five cubits wide, square, and three cubits high.

2 And he made its horns on its four corners, its horns ᵀbeing *of one piece* with it, and he overlaid it with bronze.　　*were*

3 And he made all the utensils of the altar, the pails and the shovels and the basins, the flesh hooks and the firepans; he made all its utensils of bronze.

4 And he made for the altar a grating of bronze network beneath, under its ledge, reaching halfway up.

5 And he cast four rings on the four ends of the bronze grating *as* holders for the poles.

6 And he made the poles of acacia wood and overlaid them with bronze.

7 And he inserted the poles into the rings on the sides of the altar, with which to carry it. He made it hollow with planks.

The Bronze Laver

8 ᴿMoreover, he made the laver of bronze with its base of bronze, ᵀfrom the mirrors of the serving women who served at the doorway of the tent of meeting.　　Ex. 30:18 • *with*

The Court

9 Then he made the court: for the south side the hangings of the court were of fine twisted linen,ᵀone hundred cubits;　　150 ft.

10 their twenty pillars, and their twenty ᴬsockets, *made* of bronze; the hooks of the pillars and their bands *were* of silver.　　*bases*

11 And for the north side *there were*ᵀone hundred cubits; their twenty pillars and their twenty ᴬsockets *were* of bronze, the hooks of the pillars and theirᴬbands *were* of silver.　　150 ft. • *bases • fillets, rings*

12 And for the west side *there were* hangings of fifty cubits *with* their ten pillars and their ten sockets; the hooks of the pillars and theirᴬbands *were* of silver.　　*fillets, rings*

13 And for the east side fifty cubits.

14 The hangings for the one ᵀside *of the gate were* fifteen cubits, *with* their three pillars and their three ᴬsockets,　　*shoulder • bases*

15 and so for the ᵇother side. On both sides of the gate of the court *were* hangings of fifteen cubits, *with* their three pillars and their three ᴬsockets.　　*second • shoulder • bases*

16 All the hangings of the court all around *were* of fine twisted linen.

17 And the sockets for the pillars *were* of ᴬbronze, the hooks of the pillars and their bands, of silver; and the overlaying of their tops, of silver, and all the pillars of the court were furnished with silver bands.　　*copper*

18 And the screen of the gate of the court was the work of the weaver, of blue and

purple and scarlet *material*, and fine twisted linen. And the length was twenty cubits and the height was five cubits, corresponding to the hangings of the court.   *height in width*

19 And their four pillars and their four sockets *were* of bronze; their hooks *were* of silver, and the overlaying of their tops and their bands *were* of silver.   *bases · fillets, rings*

20 And all the pegs of the tabernacle and of the court all around *were* of bronze.

The Sum of the Materials

21 This is the number of *the things for* the tabernacle, the tabernacle of the testimony, as they were numbered according to the command of Moses, for the service of the Levites, by the hand of Ithamar, the son of Aaron the priest.   *dwelling place · appointed*

22 Now Bezalel, the son of Uri the son of Hur, of the tribe of Judah, made all that the LORD had commanded Moses.   Ex. 31:2

23 And with him was Oholiab, the son of Ahisamach, of the tribe of Dan, an engraver and a skillful workman and a weaver in blue and in purple and in scarlet *material*, and fine linen.   *variegator;* i.e., a weaver in colors

24 All the gold that was used for the work, in all the work of the sanctuary, even the gold of the wave offering, was 29 talents and 730 shekels, according to the shekel of the sanctuary.   Lev. 27:25; Num. 3:47; 18:16

25 And the silver of those of the congregation who were numbered was 100 talents and 1,775 shekels, according to the shekel of the sanctuary;   Ex. 30:11-16 · *mustered*

26 a beka a head (*that is,* half a shekel according to the shekel of the sanctuary), for each one who passed over to those who were numbered, from twenty years old and upward, for 603,550 men.   *mustered*

27 And the hundred talents of silver were for casting the sockets of the sanctuary and the sockets of the veil; one hundred sockets for the hundred talents, a talent for a socket.

28 And of the 1,775 *shekels,* he made hooks for the pillars and overlaid their tops and made bands for them.   *fillets, rings*

29 And the bronze of the wave offering was 70 talents, and 2,400 shekels.   5,323 lb.

30 And with it he made the sockets to the doorway of the tent of meeting, and the bronze altar and its bronze grating, and all the utensils of the altar,   *bases*

31 and the sockets of the court all around and the sockets of the gate of the court, and all the pegs of the tabernacle and all the pegs of the court all around.   *dwelling place*

CHAPTER 39

The Clothes for the Priests

M OREOVER, from the blue and purple and scarlet *material*, they made finely woven garments for ministering in the holy place, as well as the holy garments which were for Aaron, just as the LORD had commanded Moses.   *violet · and they made*

2 And he made the ephod of gold, *and* of blue and purple and scarlet *material*, and fine twisted linen.   Ex. 28:6-12 · *violet*

3 Then they hammered out gold sheets and cut *them* into threads to be woven in with the blue and the purple and the scarlet *material*, and the fine linen, the work of a skillful workman.   *to work · violet*

4 They made attaching shoulder pieces for the ephod; it was attached at its two upper ends.   *it*

5 And the skillfully woven band which was on it was like its workmanship, of the same material: of gold *and* of blue and purple and scarlet *material*, and fine twisted linen, just as the LORD had commanded Moses.   *from it · violet*

6 And they made the onyx stones, set in gold filigree *settings;* they were engraved *like* the engravings of a signet, according to the names of the sons of Israel.   Ex. 28:9-11

7 And he placed them on the shoulder pieces of the ephod, *as* memorial stones for the sons of Israel, just as the LORD had commanded Moses.   Ex. 28:12

8 And he made the breastpiece, the work of a skillful workman, like the workmanship of the ephod: of gold *and* of blue and purple and scarlet *material* and fine twisted linen.

9 It was square; they made the breastpiece folded double, a span long and a span wide when folded double.   *its length · its width*

10 And they mounted four rows of stones on it. The first row *was* a row of ruby, topaz, and emerald;   *filled*

11 and the second row, a turquoise, a sapphire and a diamond;

12 and the third row, a jacinth, an agate, and an amethyst;

13 and the fourth row, a beryl, an onyx, and a jasper. They were set in gold filigree *settings* when they were mounted.   *filled*

14 And the stones were corresponding to the names of the sons of Israel; they were twelve, corresponding to their names, *engraved with* the engravings of a signet, each with its name for the twelve tribes.

15 And they made on the breastpiece chains like cords, of twisted cordage work in pure gold.

16 And they made two gold filigree *settings* and two gold rings, and put the two rings on the two ends of the breastpiece.

17 Then they put the two gold cords in the two rings at the ends of the breastpiece.

18 And they put the *other* two ends of the two cords on the two filigree *settings*, and put them on the shoulder pieces of the ephod at the front of it.

19 And they made two gold rings and placed *them* on the two ends of the breastpiece, on its inner edge which was next to the ephod.

20 Furthermore, they made two gold rings and placed them on the bottom of the two shoulder pieces of the ephod, on the front of it, close to the place where it joined, above the woven band of the ephod.

21 And they bound the breastpiece by its rings to the rings of the ephod with a ^{A}blue cord, that it might be on the woven band of the ephod, and that the breastpiece might not come loose from the ephod, just as the LORD had commanded Moses.   *violet*

22 ^{R}Then he made the robe of the ephod of woven work, all of ^{A}blue;   Ex. 28:31, 34 • *violet*

23 ^{R}and the opening of the robe was *at the top* in the center, as the opening of a coat of mail, with a binding all around its opening, that it might not be torn.   Ex. 28:32

24 And they made pomegranates of ^{A}blue and purple and scarlet *material and* twisted *linen* on the hem of the robe.   *violet*

25 They also made bells of pure gold, and put the bells between the pomegranates all around on the hem of the robe,

26 ^{t}alternating a bell and a pomegranate all around on the hem of the robe, for the service, just as the LORD had commanded Moses.   *a bell and a pomegranate, a bell...*

27 And they made the tunics of finely woven linen for Aaron and his sons,

28 and the turban of fine linen, and the decorated ^{t}caps of fine linen, and the linen breeches of fine twisted linen,   *headgear*

29 and the sash of fine twisted linen, and ^{A}blue and purple and scarlet *material,* the work of the weaver, just as the LORD had commanded Moses.   *violet*

30 And they made the plate of the holy crown of pure gold, and inscribed it like the engravings of a signet, "Holy to the LORD."

31 And they ^{t}fastened a ^{A}blue cord to it, to ^{t}fasten it on the turban above, just as the LORD had commanded Moses.   *put • violet*

The Tabernacle Is Inspected by Moses

32 Thus all the work of the tabernacle of the tent of meeting was completed; and the sons of Israel did according to all that the LORD had commanded Moses; so they did.

33 And they brought the tabernacle to Moses, the tent and all its ^{32}furnishings: its clasps, its boards, its bars, and its pillars and its ^{A}sockets;   *bases*

34 and the covering of rams' skins ^{A}dyed red, and the covering of porpoise skins, and the screening veil;   *tanned*

35 the ark of the testimony and its poles and the ^{t}mercy seat;   *propitiatory*

36 the table, all its utensils, and the bread of the ^{t}Presence;   *Face*

37 the pure *gold* lampstand, with its arrangement of lamps and all its utensils, and the oil for the light;

38 and the gold altar, and the anointing oil and the fragrant incense, and the veil for the doorway of the tent;

39 the ^{A}bronze altar and its ^{A}bronze grating, its poles and all its utensils, the laver and its stand;   *copper*

40 the hangings for the court, its pillars and its ^{A}sockets, and the screen for the gate of the court, its cords and its pegs and all the ^{t}equipment for the service of the tabernacle, for the tent of meeting;   *bases • utensils*

41 the woven garments for ministering in the holy place and the holy garments for Aaron the priest and the garments of his sons, to minister as priests.

42 So the sons of Israel did all the work according to all that the LORD had commanded Moses.

43 And Moses ^{t}examined all the work and behold, they had done it; just as the LORD had commanded, this they had done. So Moses ^{R}blessed them.   *saw • Lev. 9:22, 23*

CHAPTER 40

The Tabernacle Is Erected

THEN the LORD spoke to Moses, saying,

2 "On the first day of the first month you shall set up the ^{t}tabernacle of the tent of meeting.   *dwelling place*

3 "And ^{R}you shall place the ark of the testimony there, and you shall screen the ark with the veil.   Ex. 26:33; 40:21; Num. 4:5

4 "And you shall bring in the table and arrange what belongs on it; and you shall bring in the lampstand and mount its lamps.

5 "Moreover, you shall ^{R}set the gold altar of incense before the ark of the testimony, and set up the veil for the doorway to the tabernacle.   Ex. 40:26

6 "And you shall set the altar of burnt offering in front of the doorway of the tabernacle of the tent of meeting.

7 "And you shall ^{R}set the laver between the tent of meeting and the altar, and put water ^{t}in it.   Ex. 30:18; 40:30 • *there*

8 "And you shall set up the court all around and ^{t}hang up the veil for the gateway of the court.   *put the screen*

9 "Then you shall take the anointing oil and ^{a}anoint the tabernacle and all that is in it, and shall consecrate it and all its ^{A}furnishings; and it shall be holy.   Lev. 8:10 • *utensils*

10 "And you shall anoint the altar of burnt offering and all its utensils, and consecrate the altar; and the altar shall be most holy.

11 "And you shall anoint the laver and its stand, and consecrate it.

12 "Then you shall ^{R}bring Aaron and his sons to the doorway of the tent of meeting and wash them with water.   Lev. 8:1-6

13 "And you shall put the holy garments on Aaron and anoint him and consecrate him, that he may minister as a priest to Me.

---

^{32} Or, *utensils,* and so throughout this context

14"And you shall bring his sons and put tunics on them;

15 and you shall anoint them even as you have anointed their father, that they may minister as priests to Me; and their anointing shall qualify them for a perpetual priesthood throughout their generations."

16 Thus Moses did; according to all that the LORD had commanded him, so he did.

17 Now it came about in the first month of the second year, on the first day of the month, that the tabernacle was erected.   *in*

18 And Moses erected the tabernacle and ᵗlaid its sockets, and set up its boards, and inserted its bars and erected its pillars.   *put*

19 And he spread the tent over the tabernacle and put the covering of the tent ᵀon top of it, just as the LORD had commanded Moses.   *over it above*

20 Then he took the testimony and put *it* into the ark, and ᵀattached the poles to the ark, and put the ᵀmercy seat ᵀon top of the ark.   *set • propitiatory • over the ark above*

21 And he brought the ark into the tabernacle, and ᵇset up a veil for the screen, and screened off the ark of the testimony, just as the LORD had commanded Moses.   Ex. 26:33

22 Then he ᴿput the table in the tent of meeting, on the north side of the tabernacle, outside the veil.   Ex. 26:35

23 And he set the arrangement of ᴿbread in order on it before the LORD, just as the LORD had commanded Moses.   Ex. 25:30; Lev. 24:5, 6

24 Then he placed the lampstand in the tent of meeting, opposite the table, on the south side of the tabernacle.

25 And he ᴿlighted the lamps before the LORD, just as the LORD had commanded Moses.   Ex. 25:37; 40:4

26 Then he ᴿplaced the gold altar in the tent of meeting in front of the veil;   Ex. 30:6

27 and he burned fragrant incense on it, just as the LORD had commanded Moses.

28 Then he set up the ᴬveil for the doorway of the tabernacle.   *screen*

29 And he ᴿset the altar of burnt offering *before* the doorway of the tabernacle of the tent of meeting, and offered on it the burnt offering and the meal offering, just as the LORD had commanded Moses.   Ex. 40:6

30 And he placed the laver between the tent of meeting and the altar, and put water in it for washing.

31 And from it Moses and Aaron and his sons washed their hands and their feet.

32 When they entered the tent of meeting, and when they approached the altar, they washed, just as the LORD had commanded Moses.

33 And he erected the court all around the tabernacle and the altar, and ᵗhung up the veil for the gateway of the court. Thus Moses finished the work.   *put the screen*

God Fills the Tabernacle with His Glory

34 ᴿThen the cloud covered the tent of meeting, and the ᴿglory of the LORD filled the tabernacle.   Num. 9:15-23 • 1 Kin. 8:11

35 And Moses ᴿwas not able to enter the tent of meeting because the cloud had settled on it, and the glory of the LORD filled the tabernacle.   1 Kin. 8:11; 2 Chr. 5:13, 14

36 And throughout all their journeys ᴿwhenever the cloud was taken up from over the tabernacle, the sons of Israel would set out;   Num. 9:17; Neh. 9:19

37 but ᴿif the cloud was not taken up, then they did not set out until the day when it was taken up.   Num. 9:19-22

38 For throughout all their journeys, ᴿthe cloud of the LORD was on the tabernacle by day, and there was fire in it by night, in the sight of all the house of Israel.   Num. 9:12, 15

Weights

Unit	Weight	Equivalents	Translations
Jewish Weights			
Talent	c. 75 pounds for common talent, c. 150 pounds for royal talent	60 minas; 3,000 shekels	talent, one hundred pounds
Mina	1.25 pounds	50 shekels	maneh, mina
Shekel	c. .4 ounce (11.4 grams) for common shekel c. .8 ounce for royal shekel	2 bekas; 20 gerahs	shekel
Beka	c. .2 ounce (5.7 grams)	½ shekel; 10 gerahs	half-shekel
Gerah	c. .02 ounce (.57 grams)	¹⁄₂₀ shekel	gerah
Roman Weight			
Litra	12 ounces		pound, pint

LEVITICUS

THE BOOK OF LEVITICUS

Leviticus is God's guidebook for His newly redeemed people, showing them how to worship, serve, and obey a holy God. Fellowship with God through sacrifice and obedience shows the awesome holiness of the God of Israel. Indeed, "You shall be holy, for I the LORD your God am holy" (19:2).

Leviticus focuses on the worship and walk of the nation of God. In Exodus, Israel was redeemed and established as a kingdom of priests and a holy nation. Leviticus shows how God's people are to fulfill their priestly calling.

The Hebrew title is *Wayyiqra,* "And He Called." The Talmud refers to Leviticus as the "Law of the Priests," and the "Law of the Offerings." The Greek title appearing in the Septuagint is *Leuitikon,* "That Which Pertains to the Levites." From this word, the Latin Vulgate derived its name *Leviticus* which was adopted as the English title. This title is slightly misleading because the book does not deal with the Levites as a whole but more with the priests, a segment of the Levites.

THE AUTHOR OF LEVITICUS

The kind of arguments used to confirm the Mosaic authorship of Genesis and Exodus also apply to Leviticus because the Pentateuch is a literary unit. In addition to these arguments, others include the following:

External Evidence: (1) A uniform ancient testimony supports the Mosaic authorship of Leviticus. (2) Ancient parallels to the Levitical system of trespass offerings have been found in the Ras Shamra Tablets dating from about 1400 B.C. and discovered on the coast of northern Syria. (3) Christ ascribes the Pentateuch (which includes Leviticus) to Moses (cf. Matt. 8:2–4 and Lev. 14:1–4; Matt. 12:4 and Lev. 24:9; see also Luke 2:22).

Internal Evidence: (1) Fifty-six times in the twenty-seven chapters of Leviticus it is stated that God imparted these laws to Moses (see 1:1; 4:1; 6:1, 24; 8:1). (2) The Levitical Code fits the time of Moses. Economic, civil, moral, and religious considerations show it to be ancient. Many of the laws are also related to a migratory life-style.

THE TIME OF LEVITICUS

No geographical movement takes place in Leviticus: the children of Israel remain camped at the foot of Mount Sinai (25:1, 2; 26:46; 27:34). The new calendar of Israel begins with the first Passover (Ex. 12:2); and, according to Exodus 40:17, the tabernacle is completed exactly one year later.

Leviticus picks up the story at this point and takes place in the first month of the second year. Numbers 1:1 opens at the beginning of the second month. Moses probably wrote much of Leviticus during that first month and may have put it in its final form shortly before his death in Moab, about 1405 B.C.

THE CHRIST OF LEVITICUS

The Book of Leviticus is replete with types and allusions to the person and work of Jesus Christ. Some of the more important include:

(1) *The five offerings:* The burnt offering typifies Christ's total offering in submission to His Father's will. The meal offering typifies Christ's sinless service. The peace offering is a type of the fellowship believers have with God through the work of the cross. The sin offering typifies Christ as our guilt-bearer. The trespass offering typifies Christ's payment for the damage of sin. (2) *The high priest:* There are several comparisons and contrasts between Aaron, the first high priest, and Christ, our eternal high priest. (3) *The seven feasts:* Passover speaks of the substitutionary death of the Lamb of God. Christ died on the day of Passover. Unleavened Bread speaks of the holy walk of the believer (1 Cor. 5:6–8). First Fruits speaks of Christ's resurrection as the first fruit of the resurrection of all believers (1 Cor. 15:20–23). Christ rose on the day of the First Fruits. Pentecost speaks of the descent of the Holy Spirit after Christ's ascension. Trumpets, the Day of Atonement, and Tabernacles speak of events associated with the second advent of Christ. This may be why these three are separated by a long gap from the first four in Israel's annual cycle.

KEYS TO LEVITICUS

Key Word: Holiness—Leviticus centers around the concept of the holiness of God, and how an unholy people can acceptably approach Him and then remain in continued fellowship. The way to God is only through blood sacrifice, and the walk with God is only through obedience to His laws.

Key Verses: Leviticus 17:11; 20:7, 8—"For the life of the flesh is in the blood" and I have given it to you on the altar to make atonement

for your souls; for it is the blood by reason of the life that makes atonement" (17:11).

"You shall consecrate yourselves therefore and be holy, for I am the LORD your God. And you shall keep My statutes and practice them; I am the LORD who sanctifies you" (20:7, 8).

Key Chapter: Leviticus 16—The Day of Atonement ("*Yom Kippur*") was the most important single day in the Hebrew calendar as it was the only day the high priest entered into the Holy of Holies "that atonement shall be made for you to cleanse you; you shall be clean from all your sins before the LORD" (16:30).

SURVEY OF LEVITICUS

It has been said that it took God only one night to get Israel out of Egypt, but it took forty years to get Egypt out of Israel. In Exodus, Israel is redeemed and established as a kingdom of priests and a holy nation; and in Leviticus, Israel is taught how to fulfill their priestly call. They have been led out from the land of bondage in Exodus and into the sanctuary of God in Leviticus. They move from redemption to service, from deliverance to dedication. This book serves as a handbook for the Levitical priesthood, giving instructions and regulations for worship. Used to guide a newly redeemed people into worship, service, and obedience to God, Leviticus

falls into two major sections: (1) sacrifice (1—17), and (2) sanctification (18—27).

Sacrifice (1—17): This section teaches that God must be approached by the sacrificial offerings (1—7), by the mediation of the priesthood (8—10), by the purification of the nation from uncleanness (11—15), and by the provision for national cleansing and fellowship (16 and 17). The blood sacrifices remind the worshipers that because of sin the holy God requires the costly gift of life (17:11). The blood of the innocent sacrificial animal becomes the substitute for the life of the guilty offerer: "without shedding of blood there is no forgiveness" (Heb. 9:22).

Sanctification (18—27): The Israelites serve a holy God who requires them to be holy as well. To be holy means to be "set apart" or "separated." They are to be separated *from* other nations *unto* God. In Leviticus the idea of holiness appears eighty-seven times, sometimes indicating ceremonial holiness (ritual requirements), and at other times moral holiness (purity of life). This sanctification extends to the people of Israel (18—20), the priesthood (21 and 22), their worship (23 and 24), their life in Canaan (25 and 26), and their special vows (27). It is necessary to remove the defilement that separates the people from God so that they can have a walk of fellowship with their Redeemer.

FOCUS	SACRIFICE				SANCTIFICATION				
REFERENCE	1:1——8:1———		11:1———	16:1——	18:1—21:1—		23:1———	25:1——	27:1——27:34
DIVISION	THE LAWS OF				THE LAWS OF SANCTIFICATION				
	THE OFFERINGS	CONSECRATION OF THE PRIESTS	CONSECRATION OF THE PEOPLE	NATIONAL ATONEMENT	FOR THE PEOPLE	FOR THE PRIESTS	IN WORSHIP	IN THE LAND OF CANAAN	THROUGH VOWS
TOPIC	THE WAY TO GOD				THE WALK WITH GOD				
	THE LAWS OF ACCEPTABLE APPROACH TO GOD				THE LAWS OF CONTINUED FELLOWSHIP WITH GOD				
LOCATION	MOUNT SINAI								
TIME	c. 1 MONTH								

OUTLINE OF LEVITICUS

Part One: The Laws of Acceptable Approach to God: Sacrifice (1:1—17:16)

Part Two: The Laws of Acceptable Walk with God: Sanctification (18:1—27:34)

CHAPTER 1

The Burnt Offering

THEN the LORD called to Moses and spoke to him from the tent of meeting, saying,

2 "Speak to the sons of Israel and say to them, 'When any man of you brings an offering to the LORD, you shall bring your offering of animals from the herd or the flock.

3 'If his offering is a [R]burnt offering from the herd, he shall offer it, a male [R]without defect; he shall offer it at the doorway of the tent of meeting, that he may be accepted before the LORD.   Lev. 6:8-13 · Ex. 12:5; Deut. 15:21

4 'And [R]he shall lay his hand on the head of the burnt offering, that it may be accepted for him to make [R]atonement on his behalf.   Ex. 29:10, 15, 19; Lev. 3:2, 8 · Ex. 29:33

5 'And he shall slay the [A]young bull before the LORD; and Aaron's sons, the priests, shall offer up the blood and sprinkle the blood around on the altar that is at the doorway of the tent of meeting.   *one of the herd*

6 'He [R]shall then skin the burnt offering and cut it into its pieces.   Lev. 7:8

7 'And [R]the sons of Aaron the priest shall put fire on the altar and arrange wood on the fire.   Lev. 6:8-13

8 'Then Aaron's sons, the priests, shall arrange the pieces, the head, and the [R]suet over the wood which is on the fire that is on the altar.   Lev. 1:12; 3:3, 4; 8:20

9 'Its [R]entrails, however, and its legs he shall wash with water. And the priest shall offer up in smoke all of it on the altar for a burnt offering, an offering by fire of [R]a soothing aroma to the LORD.   Ex. 12:9 · Gen. 8:21

10 'But if his offering is from the flock, of the sheep or of the goats, for a burnt offering, he shall offer it a male without defect.

11 'And [R]he shall slay it on the side of the altar northward before the LORD, and Aaron's sons, the priests, shall sprinkle its blood around on the altar.   Lev. 1:5; 8:19

12 'He shall then cut it into its pieces with its head and its [R]suet, and the priest shall arrange them on the wood which is on the fire that is on the altar.   Lev. 3:3, 4

13 'The entrails, however, and the legs he shall wash with water. And the priest shall offer all of it, and offer it up in smoke on the altar; it is a burnt offering, an offering by fire of a soothing aroma to the LORD.

14 'But if his offering to the LORD is a burnt offering of birds, then he shall bring his offering from the [R]turtledoves or from young pigeons.   Gen. 15:9; Lev. 5:7, 11; 12:8

15 'And the priest shall bring it to the altar and wring off its head, and offer it up in smoke on the altar; and its blood is to be drained out [R]on the side of the altar.   Lev. 5:9

16 'He shall also take away its crop with its feathers, and cast it beside the altar eastward, to the place of the [A]ashes.   *fat ashes*

17 'Then he shall tear it by its wings, but

shall not sever *it*. And the priest shall offer it up in smoke on the altar on the wood which is on the fire; it is a burnt offering, an offering by fire of a soothing aroma to the LORD.

CHAPTER 2

The Meal Offering

'NOW when anyone presents a grain offering as an offering to the LORD, his offering shall be of fine flour, and he shall pour oil on it and put frankincense on it.

2 'He shall then bring it to Aaron's sons, the priests; and shall take from it [R]his handful of its fine flour and of its oil with all of its frankincense. And the priest shall offer *it* up in smoke *as* its [R]memorial portion on the altar, an offering by fire of a soothing aroma to the LORD.   Lev. 5:12; 6:15 · Lev. 2:9, 16; 5:12

3 'And the remainder of the grain offering belongs to Aaron and his sons: a thing most holy, of the offerings to the LORD by fire.

4 'Now when you bring an offering of a grain offering baked in an oven, *it shall be* unleavened cakes of fine flour mixed with oil, or unleavened wafers spread with oil.

5 'And if your offering is a grain offering made [R]on the griddle, *it shall be* of fine flour, unleavened, mixed with oil;   Lev. 6:21; 7:9

6 you shall break it into bits, and pour oil on it; it is a grain offering.

7 'Now if your offering is a grain offering made [R]in a [T]pan, it shall be made of fine flour with oil.   Lev. 7:9 · *lidded cooking pan*

8 'When you bring in the grain offering which is made of these things to the LORD, it shall be presented to the priest and he shall bring it to the altar.

9 'The priest then shall take up from the grain offering [R]its memorial portion, and shall offer *it* up in smoke on the altar *as* an offering by fire of a soothing aroma to the LORD.   Lev. 2:2, 16; 5:12

10 'And the remainder of the grain offering belongs to Aaron and his sons: a thing most holy, of the offerings to the LORD by fire.

11 'No grain offering, which you bring to the LORD, shall be made with leaven, for you shall not offer up in smoke any leaven or any honey as an offering by fire to the LORD.

12 'As an offering of first fruits, you shall bring them to the LORD, but they shall not ascend for a soothing aroma on the altar.

13 'Every grain offering of yours, moreover, you shall season with salt, so that [R]the salt of the covenant of your God shall not be lacking from your grain offering; with all your offerings you shall offer salt. Num. 18:19

14 'Also if you bring a grain offering of early ripened things to the LORD, you shall bring [R]fresh heads of grain roasted in the fire, grits of new growth, for the grain offering of your early ripened things.   Lev. 23:14

15 'You shall then put oil on it and lay incense on it; it is a grain offering.

16 'And the priest shall offer up in smoke
[R]its memorial portion, part of its grits and its
oil with all its incense as an offering by fire
to the LORD.   Lev. 2:2

CHAPTER 3

The Peace Offering

'NOW if his offering is a sacrifice of peace
offerings, if he is going to offer out of the
herd, whether male or female, he shall offer
it [R]without defect before the LORD.   Lev. 1:3
2 'And[R]he shall lay his hand on the head
of his offering and [t]slay it at the doorway of
the tent of meeting, and Aaron's sons, the
priests, shall sprinkle the blood around on
the altar.   Lev. 1:4 • Ex. 29:11, 16, 20
3 'And from the sacrifice of the peace offerings, he shall present an offering by fire
to the LORD, the fat that covers the entrails
and all the fat that is on the entrails,
4 and the two kidneys with the fat that is
on them, which is on the loins, and the[L]lobe
of the liver, which he shall remove with the
kidneys.   appendage on
5 'Then [R]Aaron's sons shall offer it up in
smoke on the altar [R]on the burnt offering,
which is on the wood that is on the fire; it is
an offering by fire of a soothing aroma to
the LORD.   Lev. 7:28-34 • Ex. 29:38-42
6 'But if his offering for a sacrifice of
peace offerings to the LORD is from the
flock, he shall offer it, male or female, [R]with-
out defect.   Lev. 3:1; 22:20-24
7 'If he is going to offer a lamb for his
offering, then he shall offer it before the
LORD,
8 and [R]he shall lay his hand on the head of
his offering, and [R]slay it before the tent of
meeting; and Aaron's sons shall sprinkle its
blood around on the altar.   Lev. 1:4 • Lev. 3:2
9 'And from the sacrifice of peace offerings he shall bring as an offering by fire to
the LORD, its fat,[t]the entire fat tail which he
shall remove close to the backbone, and the
fat that covers the entrails and all the fat
that is on the entrails,   the fat tail, entire
10 and the two kidneys with the fat that is
on them, which is on the loins, and the[L]lobe
of the liver, which he shall remove[R]with the
kidneys.   appendage on • Lev. 3:4, 15
11 'Then the priest shall offer it up in
smoke [R]on the altar, as [t]food, an offering by
fire to the LORD.   Lev. 3:5 • Lev. 3:16; 21:6, 8, 17
12 'Moreover, if his offering is[R]a goat, then
he shall offer it before the LORD, Num. 15:6-11
13 and he shall lay his hand on its head
and slay it before the tent of meeting; and
the sons of Aaron shall sprinkle its blood
around on the altar.
14 'And from it he shall present his offering as an offering by fire to the LORD, the fat
that covers the entrails and all the fat that is
on the entrails,

15 and the two kidneys with the fat that is
on them, which is on the loins, and the[L]lobe
of the liver, which he shall remove[R]with the
kidneys.   appendage on • Lev. 3:4; 7:4
16 'And the priest shall offer them up in
smoke on the altar as food, an offering by
fire for a soothing aroma; [R]all fat is the
LORD's.   Lev. 7:23-25
17 'It is a perpetual statute throughout
your generations in all your dwellings: you
shall not eat any fat or any blood.' "

CHAPTER 4

The Sin Offering

THEN the LORD spoke to Moses, saying,
2 "Speak to the sons of Israel, saying, 'If a
person sins unintentionally in any of the
things which the LORD has commanded not
to be done, and commits any of them,
3 if the anointed priest sins so as to bring
guilt on the people, then let him offer to the
LORD a bull without defect as a sin offering
for the sin he has[t]committed.   sinned
4 'And he shall bring the bull to the doorway of the tent of meeting before the LORD,
and he shall lay his hand on the head of the
bull, and slay the bull before the LORD.
5 'Then the [R]anointed priest is to take
some of the blood of the bull and bring it to
the tent of meeting,   Lev. 4:3, 17
6 and the priest shall dip his finger in the
blood, and sprinkle some of the blood seven
times before the LORD, in front of[R]the veil of
the sanctuary.   Ex. 40:21, 26
7 'The priest shall also put some of the
blood on the horns of[R]the altar of fragrant
incense which is before the LORD in the tent
of meeting; and all the blood of the bull he
shall pour out at the base of the altar of
burnt offering which is at the doorway of
the tent of meeting.   Lev. 4:18, 25, 30, 34; 8:15
8 'And[R]he shall remove from it all the fat
of the bull of the sin offering: the fat that
covers the entrails, and all the fat which is
on the entrails,   Lev. 3:3, 4
9 and the two kidneys with the fat that is
on them, which is on the loins, and the[L]lobe
of the liver, which he shall remove[R]with the
kidneys   appendage on • Lev. 3:4
10 (just as it is removed from the ox of the
sacrifice of peace offerings), and the priest
is to offer them up in smoke on the altar of
burnt offering.
11 'But[R]the hide of the bull and all its flesh
with its head and its legs and its entrails and
its refuse,   Lev. 9:11; Num. 19:5
12 [t]that is, all the rest of the bull, he is to
bring out to a clean place outside the camp
where the ashes are poured out, and burn it
on wood with fire; where the ashes are
poured out it shall be burned.   and
13 'Now[R]if the whole congregation of Israel commits error, and the matter[t]escapes
the notice of the assembly, and they commit
any of the things which the LORD has com-

manded not to be done, and they become guilty; Num. 15:24-26 • *is hidden from the eyes of*

14 when the sin which they have committed becomes known, then the assembly shall offer a bull of the herd for a sin offering, and bring it before the tent of meeting.

15 'Then ᴿthe elders of the congregation shall lay their hands on the head of the bull before the LORD, and the bull shall be slain before the LORD.   Lev. 8:14, 18, 22

16 'Then the anointed priest is to bring some of the blood of the bull to the tent of meeting;ᴿ

17 and the priest shall dip his finger in the blood, and sprinkle *it* seven times before the LORD, in front of the veil.   Lev. 4:6

18 'And he shall put some of the blood on the horns of the altar which is before LORD ᵀin the tent of meeting; and all the blood he shall pour out at the base of the altar of burnt offering which is at the doorway of the tent of meeting.   *which is in*

19 'Andᴿhe shall remove all its fat from it and offer it up in smoke on the altar. Lev. 4:8

20 'He shall also do with the bull just as he did withᴿthe bull of the sin offering; thus he shall do with it. Soᴿthe priest shall make atonement for them, and they shall be forgiven.   Lev. 4:8, 21 • Num. 15:25, 28

21 'Then he is to bring out the bull to *a place* outside the camp, and burn it as he burned the first bull; it isᴿthe sin offering for the assembly. Lev. 4:13f.; 16:15-17; Num. 15:24-26

22 'Whenᴿa leader sins and unintentionally does any one of all the things which the LORD God has commanded not to be done, and he becomes guilty,   Num. 31:13; 32:2

23 ᵀif his sin which he has committed is made known to him, he shall bring for his offering a goat, a male without defect.   *or*

24 'And he shall lay his hand on the head of the male goat, and slay it in the place where ᵀthey slay the burnt offering before the LORD; it is a sin offering.   *one slays*

25 'Then the priest is to take some of the blood of the sin offering with his finger, and put it on the horns of the altar of burnt offering; and *the rest of* its blood he shall pour out at the base of the altar of burnt offering.

26 'And all its fat he shall offer up in smoke on the altar as *in the case of* the fat of the sacrifice of peace offerings. Thus the priest shall make atonement for him in regard to his sin, and he shall be forgiven.

27 'Now if ᵀanyone of the common people sins unintentionally in doing any of the things which the LORD has commanded not to be done, and becomes guilty,   *one soul*

28 if his sin, which he has ᵀcommitted is made known to him, he shall bring for his offering a goat, a female without defect, for his sin which he has ᵀcommitted. *sinned*

29 'Andᴿhe shall lay his hand on the head of the sin offering, and slay the sin offering at the place of the burnt offering.   Lev. 1:4

30 'And the priest shall take some of its blood with his finger and put it on the horns

ofᴿthe altar of burnt offering; andᴿall *the rest of* its blood he shall pour out at the base of the altar.   Lev. 4:7, 18, 25, 34 • Lev. 4:7

31 'Then he shall remove all its fat, just as the fat was removed from the sacrifice of peace offerings; and the priest shall offer it up in smoke on the altar for a soothing aroma to the LORD. Thus the priest shall make atonement for him, and he shall be forgiven.

32 'But if he bringsᴿa lamb as his offering for a sin offering, he shall bring it, a female without defect.   Lev. 4:28

33 'Andᴿhe shall lay his hand on the head of the sin offering, and slay it for a sin offeringᴿin the place whereᵀthey slay the burnt offering.   Lev. 1:4, 5 • Lev. 4:29 • *one slays*

34 'And the priest is to take some of the blood of the sin offering with his finger and put it on the horns of the altar of burnt offering; andᴿall *the rest of* its blood he shall pour out at the base of the altar.   Lev. 4:7

35 'Then he shall removeᴿall its fat, just as the fat of the lamb is removed from the sacrifice of the peace offerings, and the priest shall offer them up in smoke on the altar, on the offerings by fire to the LORD. Thus the priest shall make atonement for him in regard to his sin which he has ᵀcommitted, and he shall be forgiven.   Lev. 4:26, 31 • *sinned*

CHAPTER 5

¹Nᴏᴡ if a person sins, after he hears a ᵀpublic adjuration *to testify*, when he is a witness, whether he has seen or *otherwise* known, if he does not tell *it*, then he will bear his ᴬguilt.   *voice of an oath* • *iniquity*

2 'Or if a person touches ᴿany unclean thing, whether a carcass of an unclean beast, or the carcass of unclean cattle, or a carcass of unclean swarming things, though it is hidden from him, and he is unclean, then he will be guilty.   Lev. 11:8, 11, 24-40

3 'Or if he touches human uncleanness, of whatever *sort* his uncleanness *may* be with which he becomes unclean, and it is hidden from him, and then he comes to know *it*, he will be guilty.

4 'Or if a person ᴿswears thoughtlessly with his lips to do evil or to do good, in whatever matter a man may speak thoughtlessly with an oath, and it is hidden from him, and then he comes to know *it*, he will be guilty in one of these.   Num. 30:6, 8

5 'So it shall be when he becomes guilty in one of these, that he shall ᴿconfess that in which he has sinned.   Lev. 16:21; 26:40

6 'He shall also bring his guilt offering to the LORD for his sin which he has committed, a female from the flock, a lamb or a goat as a sin offering. So the priest shall make atonement on his behalf for his sin.

7 'But if he cannot afford a lamb, then he shall bring to the LORD his guilt offering for that in which he has sinned, two turtledoves

or two young pigeons,^Rone for a sin offering and the other for a burnt offering.   Lev. 12:6

8 'And he shall bring them to the priest, who shall offer first that which is for the sin offering and shall nip its head at the front of its neck, but he^Rshall not sever *it*.   Lev. 1:17

9 'He shall also sprinkle some of the blood of the sin offering^Ron the side of the altar, while the rest of the blood shall be drained out^Rat the base of the altar: it is a sin offering.   Lev. 1:15 • Lev. 4:7, 18

10 'The second he shall then prepare as a burnt offering according to the ordinance. So the priest shall make atonement on his behalf for his sin which he has ^Tcommitted, and it shall be forgiven him.   *sinned*

11 'But^Rif his^Tmeans are insufficient for two turtledoves or two young pigeons, then for his offering for that which he has sinned, he shall bring the tenth of an ¹ephah of fine flour for a sin offering; he shall not put oil on it or place incense on it, for it is a sin offering.   Lev. 14:21-32; 27:8 • *hand does not reach*

12 'And he shall bring it to the priest, and the priest shall take his handful of it as its memorial portion and offer *it* up in smoke on the altar, ^Twith the offerings of the LORD by fire: it is a sin offering.   *upon*

13 'So the priest shall make atonement for him concerning his sin which he has ^Tcommitted from one of these, and it shall be forgiven him; then *the rest* shall become the priest's, like the grain offering.' "   *sinned*

The Guilt Offering

14 Then the LORD spoke to Moses, saying, 15 "If a person acts unfaithfully and sins ^Runintentionally against the LORD'S holy things, then he shall bring his guilt offering to the LORD: a ram without defect from the flock, according to your valuation in silver by shekels, in *terms of* the shekel of the sanctuary, for a guilt offering.   Lev. 4:2; 22:14

16 "And he shall make restitution for that which he has sinned against the holy thing, and shall add to it a fifth part of it, and give it to the priest. The priest shall then make atonement for him with the ram of the guilt offering, and it shall be forgiven him.

17 "Now if a person sins and does any of the things which the LORD has commanded not to be done, though he was unaware, still he is guilty, and shall bear his punishment.

18 "He is then to bring to the priest^Ra ram without defect from the flock, according to your valuation, for a guilt offering. So the priest shall make atonement for him concerning his error in which he sinned^Runintentionally and did not know *it*, and it shall be forgiven him.   Lev. 5:15 • Lev. 5:17

19 "It is a guilt offering; he was certainly guilty before the LORD."

CHAPTER 6

THEN the LORD spoke to Moses, saying, 2 "When a person sins and acts unfaith-

fully against the LORD, and deceives his companion in regard to a deposit or a security entrusted *to him*, or through robbery, or *if* he has extorted from his companion,

3 or^Rhas found what was lost and lied about it and sworn falsely, so that he sins in regard to any one of the things a man may do;   Ex. 23:4; Deut. 22:1-4

4 then it shall be, when he sins and becomes guilty, that he shall restore what he took by robbery, or what he got by extortion, or the deposit which was entrusted to him, or the lost thing which he found,

5 or anything about which he swore falsely; he shall make restitution for it^Tin full, and add to it one-fifth more. He shall give it to the one to whom it belongs on the day *he presents* his guilt offering.   *in its sum*

6 "Then he shall bring to the priest his guilt offering to the LORD,^Ra ram without defect from the flock, according to your valuation, for a guilt offering,   Lev. 5:15

7 and^Rthe priest shall make atonement for him before the LORD; and he shall be forgiven for any one of the things which he may have done to incur guilt."   Lev. 7:2-5

The Burnt Offering

8 Then the LORD spoke to Moses, saying, 9 "Command Aaron and his sons, saying, 'This is^Rthe law for the burnt offering: the burnt offering itself *shall remain* on the hearth on the altar all night until the morning, and the fire on the altar is to be kept burning on it.   Ex. 29:38-42; Num. 28:3-10

10 'And the priest is to put on^Rhis linen robe, and he shall put on undergarments next to his flesh; and he shall take up the ^Aashes *to* which the fire^Treduces the burnt offering on the altar, and place them beside the altar.   Ex. 28:39, 42 • *fat ashes • consumes*

11 'Then he shall take off his garments and put on other garments, and carry the ^Aashes outside the camp to a clean place.   *fat ashes*

12 'And the fire on the altar shall be kept burning on it. It shall not go out, but the priest shall burn wood on it every morning; and he shall lay out the burnt offering on it, and offer up in smoke the fat portions of the peace offerings^Ron it.   Lev. 3:5

13 'Fire shall be kept burning continually on the altar; it is not to go out.

The Meal Offering

14 'Now this is the law of the grain offering: the sons of Aaron shall present it before the LORD in front of the altar.

15 'Then one *of them* shall lift up from it a handful of the fine flour of the grain offering,^Twith its oil and all the incense that is on the grain offering, and he shall offer *it* up in smoke on the altar, a soothing aroma, as its memorial offering to the LORD.   *and some of*

16 'And^Rwhat is left of it Aaron and his

¹ I.e., Approx. one bushel

sons are to eat. It shall be eaten as unleavened cakes in a holy place; they are to eat it in the court of the tent of meeting. Lev. 2:3

17 'It[R] shall not be baked with leaven. I have given it as their share from My offerings by fire;[R] it is most holy, like the sin offering and the guilt offering. Lev. 2:11 • Ex. 40:10

18 'Every male among the sons of Aaron may eat it; it is a permanent ordinance throughout your generations, from the offerings by fire to the LORD. Whoever touches them shall become consecrated.' "

19 Then the LORD spoke to Moses, saying,

20 "This is the offering which Aaron and his sons are to present to the LORD on the day when he is anointed; the tenth of an [R]ephah of fine flour as a [T]regular grain offering, half of it in the morning and half of it in the evening. Lev. 5:11 • grain offering continually

21 "It shall be prepared with oil on a [R]griddle. When it is well stirred, you shall bring it. You shall present the grain offering in baked pieces as a soothing aroma to the LORD. Lev. 2:5

22 "And the anointed priest who will be in his place [T]among his sons shall offer it. By a permanent ordinance it shall be entirely offered up in smoke to the LORD. from among

23 "So every grain offering of the priest shall be burned entirely. It shall not be eaten."

The Sin Offering

24 Then the LORD spoke to Moses, saying,

25 "Speak to Aaron and to his sons, saying, 'This is the law of the sin offering:[R] in the place where the burnt offering is slain the sin offering shall be slain before the LORD; it is most holy. Lev. 1:11

26 'The[R] priest who offers it for sin shall eat it. It shall be eaten in a holy place, in the court of the tent of meeting. Lev. 6:29

27 'Anyone who touches its flesh shall become consecrated; and when any of its blood splashes on a garment, in a holy place you shall wash what was splashed on.

28 'Also[R] the earthenware vessel in which it was boiled shall be broken; and if it was boiled in a bronze vessel, then it shall be scoured and rinsed in water. Lev. 11:33; 15:12

29 'Every[R] male among the priests may eat of it;[R] it is most holy. Lev. 6:18 • Lev. 6:17, 25

30 'But no sin offering of which any of the blood is brought into the tent of meeting to make atonement[R] in the holy place shall be eaten; it shall be burned with fire. Lev. 4:7, 18

CHAPTER 7

The Guilt Offering

'NOW this is the law of the[R] guilt offering; it is most holy. Lev. 5:14-6:7

2 'In[R] the place where they slay the burnt offering they are to slay the guilt offering,

and he shall sprinkle its blood around on the altar. Lev. 1:11

3 'Then he shall offer from it all its fat: the[R] fat tail and the fat that covers the entrails, Lev. 3:9

4 and the two kidneys with the fat that is on them, which is on the loins, and the lobe on the liver he shall remove[R] with the kidneys. Lev. 3:4

5 'And the priest shall offer them up in smoke on the altar as an offering by fire to the LORD; it is a guilt offering.

6 'Every[R] male among the priests may eat of it. It shall be eaten in a holy place; it is most holy. Lev. 6:18, 29; Num. 18:9

7 'The guilt offering is like the sin offering, there is one law for them; the priest who makes atonement with it shall have it.

8 'Also the priest who presents any man's burnt offering, [T]that priest shall have for himself the skin of the burnt offering which he has presented. for the priest, it shall be for him

9 'Likewise, every grain offering that is baked in the oven, and everything prepared in a [T]pan or on a griddle, shall belong to the priest who presents it. lidded cooking pan

10 'And every grain offering mixed with oil, or dry, shall [T]belong to all the sons of Aaron, [T]to all alike. be • a man as his brother

The Peace Offering

11 'Now this is the law of the [R]sacrifice of peace offerings which shall be presented to the LORD. Lev. 3:1

12 'If he offers it by way of [R]thanksgiving, then along with the sacrifice of thanksgiving he shall offer[R] unleavened cakes mixed with oil, and unleavened wafers[A] spread with oil, and cakes of well stirred fine flour mixed with oil. Lev. 7:15 • Lev. 2:4; Num. 6:15 • anointed

13 'With the sacrifice of his peace offerings for thanksgiving, he shall present his offering with cakes of leavened bread.

14 'And of [T]this he shall present one of every offering as a contribution to the LORD; it shall [T]belong to the priest who sprinkles the blood of the peace offerings. it • be for

15 'Now as for the flesh of the sacrifice of his thanksgiving peace offerings, it shall be eaten on the day of his offering; he shall not leave any of it over until morning.

16 'But if the sacrifice of his offering is a [R]votive or a freewill offering, it shall be eaten on the day that he offers his sacrifice; and on the [T]next day what is left of it may be eaten; Lev. 19:5-8 • morrow and what

17 [R]but what is left over from the flesh of the sacrifice on the third day shall be burned with fire. Ex. 12:10

18 'So if any of the flesh of the sacrifice of his peace offerings should ever be eaten on the third day, he who offers it shall not be accepted, and it shall not be reckoned to his benefit. It shall be an [R]offensive thing, and the person who eats of it shall bear his own iniquity. Lev. 19:7; [Prov. 15:8]

19 'Also the flesh that touches anything unclean shall not be eaten; it shall be burned with fire. ᵀAs for *other* flesh, anyone who is clean may eat *such* flesh.   *And the flesh*

20 'But ᴿthe person who eats the flesh of the sacrifice of peace offerings which belong to the LORD, in his uncleanness, that person shall be cut off from his people.   Lev. 22:3-7

21 'And ᴿ when anyone touches anything unclean, whether human uncleanness, or an unclean animal, or any unclean ²detestable thing, and eats of the flesh of the sacrifice of peace offerings which belong to the LORD, that person shall be cut off from his people.' "   Lev. 5:2, 3

22 Then the LORD spoke to Moses, saying, 23"Speak to the sons of Israel, saying, 'You shall not eat ᴿany fat *from* an ox, a sheep, or a goat.   Lev. 3:17

24 'Also the fat of *an animal* which dies, and the fat of an animal ᴿtorn *by beasts*, may be put to any other use, but you must certainly not eat it.   Ex. 22:31; Lev. 17:15; 22:8

25 'For whoever eats the fat of the animal from which an offering by fire is offered to the LORD, even the person who eats shall be cut off from his people.

26 'And ᴿyou are not to eat any blood, either of bird or animal, in any of your dwellings.   Gen. 9:4; Lev. 17:10-16; 19:26; Deut. 12:23

27 'Any person who eats any blood, even that person shall be cut off from his people.' "

28 Then the LORD spoke to Moses, saying, 29"Speak to the sons of Israel, saying, 'He who offers ᴿthe sacrifice of his peace offerings to the LORD shall bring his offering to the LORD from the sacrifice of his peace offerings.   Lev. 3:1

30 'His own hands are to bring offerings by fire to the LORD. He shall bring the fat with the breast, that the breast may be ᵀpresented as a wave offering before the LORD.   *waved*

31 'And the priest shall offer up the fat in smoke on the altar; but ᴿthe breast shall belong to Aaron and his sons.   Num. 18:11

32 'And you shall give the right thigh to the priest as a ᴬcontribution from the sacrifices of your peace offerings.   *heave offering*

33 'The one among the sons of Aaron who offers the blood of the peace offerings and the fat, the right thigh shall be his as *his* portion.

34 'For I have taken ᴿthe breast of the wave offering and the thigh of the contribution from the sons of Israel from the sacrifices of their peace offerings, and have given them to Aaron the priest and to his sons as *their* due forever from the sons of Israel. Ex. 29:27

35 'This is ᵀthat which is consecrated to Aaron and ᵀthat which is consecrated to his sons from the offerings by fire to the LORD, in that day when he presented them to serve as priests to the LORD.   *the anointed portion of*

36 'These the LORD had commanded to be given them from the sons of Israel in the day that He anointed them. It is *their* due forever throughout their generations.' "

The Summary of the Offerings

37 This is the law of the burnt offering, the grain offering and the sin offering and the guilt offering and the ordination offering and the sacrifice of peace offerings,

38 which the LORD commanded Moses at Mount Sinai in the day that He commanded the sons of Israel to ᴬpresent their offerings to the LORD in the wilderness of Sinai.   *offer*

CHAPTER 8

Consecration Commanded by God

THEN the LORD spoke to Moses, saying, 2"Take ᴿAaron and his sons with him, and the garments and the anointing oil and the bull of the sin offering, and the two rams and the basket of unleavened bread; Ex. 28:1

3 and assemble all the congregation at the doorway of the tent of meeting."

4 So Moses did just as the LORD commanded him. When the congregation was assembled at the doorway of the tent of meeting,

5 Moses said to the congregation, "This is the thing which the LORD has commanded to do."

Cleansing the Priests with Water

6 Then Moses had Aaron and his sons come near, and washed them with water.

Special Garments

7 And he ᴿput the tunic on him and girded him with the sash, and clothed him with the robe, and put the ephod on him; and he girded him with the artistic band of the ephod, with which he tied *it* to him. Ex. 28:4

8 He then placed the ᵀbreastpiece on him, and in the ᵀbreastpiece he put ³the Urim and the Thummim.   *pouch*

9 He also placed the turban on his head, and on the turban, at its front, he placed ᴿthe golden plate, the holy crown, just as the LORD had commanded Moses.   Ex. 28:36

Anointing with Oil

10 Moses then took the anointing oil and anointed the ᴬtabernacle and all that was in it, and consecrated them.   *dwelling place*

11 And he sprinkled some of it on the altar seven times and anointed the altar and all its utensils, and the basin and its stand, to ᴿconsecrate them.   Ex. 29:36, 37; 30:29

12 Then he poured some of the ᴿanointing oil on Aaron's head and anointed him, to consecrate him.   Ex. 29:7; 30:30; Lev. 21:10, 12

---

² Some mss. read *swarming thing*
³ I.e., the lights and perfections

13 ᴿNext Moses had Aaron's sons come near and clothed them with tunics, and girded them with sashes, and bound ᵀcaps on them, just as the LORD had commanded Moses.   Ex. 29:8, 9 · *headgear*

Consecrating with Blood

14 Then he brought ᴿthe bull of the sin offering, and Aaron and his sons laid their hands on the head of the bull of the sin offering.   Ex. 29:10; Lev. 4:4; Ps. 66:15; Ezek. 43:19

15 Next Moses slaughtered *it* and took the blood and with his finger ᴿput *some of it* around on the horns of the altar, and purified the altar. Then he poured out *the rest of* the blood at the base of the altar and consecrated it, to make atonement for it.   Lev. 4:7

16 He also ᴬtook all the fat that was on the entrails and the lobe of the liver, and the two kidneys and their fat; and Moses offered it up in smoke on the altar.   Ex. 29:13

17 ᴿBut the bull and its hide and its flesh and its refuse, he burned in the fire outside the camp, just as the LORD had commanded Moses.   Ex. 29:14; Lev. 4:11, 12

18 Then he presented ᴿthe ram of the burnt offering, and Aaron and his sons laid their hands on the head of the ram.   Ex. 29:15

19 And Moses slaughtered *it* and sprinkled the blood around on the altar.

20 When he had cut the ram into its pieces, Moses ᴿoffered up the head and the pieces and the suet in smoke.   Lev. 1:8

21 After he had washed the entrails and the legs with water, Moses ᴿoffered up the whole ram in smoke on the altar. It was a burnt offering for a soothing aroma; it was an offering by fire to the LORD, just as the LORD had commanded Moses.   Ex. 29:18

22 Then he presented the second ram, the ram of ⁴ordination; and Aaron and his sons laid their hands on the head of the ram.

23 And ᵀMoses slaughtered *it* and took some of its blood and ᴿput it on the lobe of Aaron's right ear, and on the thumb of his right hand, and on the big toe of his right foot.   *he slaughtered it and Moses took* · Ex. 29:20, 21

24 He also had Aaron's sons come near; and Moses put some of the blood on the lobe of their right ear, and on the thumb of their right hand, and on the big toe of their right foot. Moses then ᴿsprinkled *the rest of* the blood around on the altar.   [Heb. 9:18–22]

25 And he took the fat, and the fat tail, and all the fat that was on the entrails, and the ᴬlobe of the liver and the two kidneys and their fat and the right thigh.   *appendage on*

26 And ᴿfrom the basket of unleavened bread that was before the LORD, he took one unleavened cake and one cake of bread *mixed with* oil and one wafer, and placed *them* on the portions of fat and on the right thigh.   Ex. 29:23

27 He then ᴿput all *these* on the hands of Aaron and on the hands of his sons, and presented them as a wave offering before the LORD.   Ex. 29:24

28 Then Moses took them from their hands and offered them up in smoke on the altar with the burnt offering. They were an ordination offering for ᴿa soothing aroma; it was an offering by fire to the LORD. Gen. 8:21

29 Moses also took ᴿthe breast and presented it for a wave offering before the LORD; it was ᴿMoses' portion of the ram of ordination, just as the LORD had commanded Moses.   Lev. 7:31-34 · Ex. 29:26; Ps. 99:6

30 So Moses ᴿtook some of the anointing oil and some of the blood which was on the altar, and sprinkled it on Aaron, on his garments, on his sons, and on the garments of his sons with him; and he consecrated Aaron, his garments, and his sons, and the garments of his sons with him.   Ex. 29:21

The Priests Are to Remain
in the Tabernacle

31 Then Moses said to Aaron and to his sons, "Boil the flesh at the doorway of the tent of meeting, and eat it there together with the bread which is in the basket of the ordination offering, just as I commanded, saying, 'Aaron and his sons shall eat it.'

32"And ᴿthe remainder of the flesh and of the bread you shall burn in the fire. Ex. 29:34

33"And ᴿyou shall not go outside the doorway of the tent of meeting for seven days, until the day that the period of your ordination is fulfilled; for he will ᵀordain you through seven days.   Ex. 29:35 · *fill your hands*

34"The LORD has commanded to do as has been done this day, to make atonement on your behalf.

35"At the doorway of the tent of meeting, moreover, you shall remain day and night for seven days, and ᴿkeep the charge of the LORD, that you may not die, for so I have been commanded."   Num. 3:7; 9:19; Deut. 11:1

36 Thus Aaron and his sons did all the things which the LORD had commanded through Moses.

CHAPTER 9

Offerings for the Priest

Now it came about ᴿon the eighth day that Moses called Aaron and his sons and the elders of Israel;   Ezek. 43:27

2 and he said to Aaron, "Take ᴿfor yourself a calf, a bull, for a sin offering and a ram for a burnt offering, *both* without defect, and offer *them* before the LORD.   Ezek. 29:1

3"Then to the sons of Israel you shall speak, saying, 'Take a male goat for a sin offering, and a calf and a lamb, both one year old, without defect, for a burnt offering,

4 and an ox and a ram for peace offerings, to sacrifice before the LORD, and a

---

⁴ Lit., *filling,* and so throughout this context

grain offering mixed with oil; for today[R]the LORD shall appear to you.' "   Ex. 29:43

5 So they took what Moses had commanded to the front of the tent of meeting, and the whole congregation came near and stood before the LORD.

6 And Moses said, "This is the thing which the LORD has commanded you to do, that[R]the glory of the LORD may appear to you."   Ex. 24:16; Lev. 9:23

7 Moses then said to Aaron, "Come near to the altar and[T]offer your sin offering and your burnt offering, that you may make atonement for yourself and for the people; then make the offering[T]for the people, that you may make atonement for them, just as the LORD has commanded."   make • of

8 [R]So Aaron came near to the altar and slaughtered the calf of the sin offering which was for himself.   Lev. 4:1-12

9 [R]And Aaron's sons presented the blood to him; and he dipped his finger in the blood, and[R]put some on the horns of the altar, and poured out the rest of the blood at the base of the altar.   Lev. 9:12, 18 • Lev. 4:7

10 The fat and the kidneys and the[T]lobe of the liver of the sin offering, he then offered up in smoke on the altar just as the LORD had commanded Moses.   appendage on

11 The flesh and the skin, however, he burned with fire outside the camp.

12 Then he slaughtered the burnt offering; and Aaron's sons handed the blood to him and he sprinkled it around on the altar.

13 And they handed the burnt offering to him in[T]pieces with the head, and he offered them up in smoke on the altar.   its pieces

14 He also washed the entrails and the legs, and offered them up in smoke with the burnt offering on the altar.

Offerings for the People

15 Then he presented the people's offering, and took the goat of the sin offering which was for the people, and slaughtered it and offered it for sin, like the first.

16 He also presented the burnt offering, and offered it according to the ordinance.

17 Next he presented the grain offering, and filled his[T]hand with some of it and offered it up in smoke on the altar,[R]besides the burnt offering of the morning.   palm • Lev. 3:5

18 Then[R]he slaughtered the ox and the ram, the sacrifice of peace offerings which was for the people; and Aaron's sons handed the blood to him and he sprinkled it around on the altar.   Lev. 3:1-11

19 As for the portions of fat from the ox and from the ram, the fat tail, and the fat [R]covering, and the kidneys and the[T]lobe of the liver,   Lev. 3:9 • appendage on

20 they now placed the portions of fat on the breasts; and he offered[T]them up in smoke on the altar.   the portions of fat

21 But the breasts and the right thigh Aaron[T]presented as a wave offering before the LORD, just as Moses had commanded. waved

The Lord Accepts the Offerings

22 Then Aaron lifted up his hands toward the people and [R]blessed them, and he stepped down after making the sin offering and the burnt offering and the peace offerings.   Num. 6:22-26; Deut. 21:5; Luke 24:50

23 And Moses and Aaron went into the tent of meeting. When they came out and blessed the people,[R]the glory of the LORD appeared to all the people.   Lev. 9:6; Num. 16:19

24 [R]Then fire came out from before the LORD and consumed the burnt offering and the portions of fat on the altar; and when all the people saw it, they shouted and fell on their faces.   1 Kin. 18:38, 39; 2 Chr. 7:1

CHAPTER 10

The Sin of Nadab and Abihu

NOW[R]Nadab and Abihu, the sons of Aaron, took their respective firepans, and after putting fire in them, placed incense on it and offered strange fire before the LORD, which He had not commanded them.   Ex. 24:1, 9

2 [R]And fire came out from the presence of the LORD and consumed them, and they died before the LORD.   Num. 3:4; 16:35; 26:61

3 Then Moses said to Aaron, "It is what the LORD spoke, saying,

'By those who come near Me I[^]will be
        treated as holy,   will show Myself holy
And before all the people I will[R]be honored.' "   Ex. 14:4, 17; Is. 49:3

So Aaron, therefore, kept silent.

4 Moses called also to Mishael and Elzaphan, the sons of Aaron's uncle Uzziel, and said to them, "Come forward, carry your[T]relatives away from the front of the sanctuary to the outside of the camp."   brothers

5 So they came forward and carried them still in their[R]tunics to the outside of the camp, as Moses had said.   Ex. 29:5; Lev. 8:13

6 Then Moses said to Aaron and to his sons Eleazar and Ithamar, "Do not [5]uncover your heads nor tear your clothes, so that you may not die, and that He may not become wrathful against all the congregation. But your[T]kinsmen, the whole house of Israel, shall bewail the burning which the LORD has[T]brought about.   brothers • burned

7 "You shall not even go out from the doorway of the tent of meeting, lest you die; for the LORD's anointing oil is upon you." So they did according to the word of Moses.

8 The LORD then spoke to Aaron, saying,

9 "Do[R]not drink wine or strong drink, neither you nor your sons with you, when you come into the tent of meeting, so that you may not die—it is a perpetual statute throughout your generations—   [Prov. 20:1]

10 and [R]so as to make a distinction between the holy and the profane, and between the unclean and the clean,   Lev. 11:47

---

[5] Lit., unbind

11 and[R]so as to teach the sons of Israel all the statutes which the LORD has spoken to them through Moses."   Deut. 17:10, 11; 33:10

The Sin of Eleazar and Ithamar

12 Then Moses spoke to Aaron, and to his surviving sons, Eleazar and Ithamar, "Take the grain offering that is left over from the LORD's offerings by fire and eat it unleavened beside the altar, for it is most holy.
13 "You shall eat it, moreover, in a holy place, because it is your due and your sons' due out of the LORD's offerings by fire; for thus I have been commanded.
14 "The[R]breast of the wave offering, however, and the thigh of the offering you may eat in a clean place, you and your sons and your daughters with you; for they have been given as your due and your sons' due out of the sacrifices of the peace offerings of the sons of Israel.   Lev. 7:30-34; Num. 18:11
15 "The[R]thigh offered by lifting up and the breast offered by waving, they shall bring along with the offerings by fire of the portions of fat, to present as a wave offering before the LORD; so it shall be a thing perpetually due you and your sons with you, just as the LORD has commanded."   Lev. 7:34
16 But Moses searched carefully for the [R]goat of the sin offering, and behold, it had been burned up! So he was angry with Aaron's surviving sons Eleazar and Ithamar, saying,   Lev. 9:3, 15
17 "Why[R]did you not eat the sin offering at the holy place? For it is most holy, and[A]He gave it to you to bear away the guilt of the congregation, to make atonement for them before the LORD.   Lev. 6:24-30 • was given
18 "Behold,[R]since its blood had not been brought inside, into the sanctuary, you should certainly have[R]eaten it in the sanctuary, just as I commanded."Lev. 6:30 • Lev. 6:26
19 But Aaron spoke to Moses, "Behold, this very day they presented their sin offering and their burnt offering before the LORD. When things like these happened to me, if I had eaten a sin offering today, would it have been good in the sight of the LORD?"
20 And when Moses heard that, it seemed good in his sight.

CHAPTER 11

Animals of the Earth

THE LORD spoke again to Moses and to Aaron, saying to them,
2 "Speak to the sons of Israel, saying, 'These are the creatures which you may eat from all the animals that are on the earth.
3 'Whatever divides a hoof, thus making split hoofs, and chews the cud, among the animals, that you may eat.
4 'Nevertheless, you are not to eat of these, among those which chew the cud, or among those which divide the hoof: the camel, for though it chews cud, it does not divide the hoof, it is unclean to you.
5 'Likewise, the rock badger, for though it chews cud, it does not divide the hoof, it is unclean to you;
6 the [A]rabbit also, for though it chews cud, it does not divide the hoof, it is unclean to you;   hare
7 and the pig, for though it divides the hoof, thus making a split hoof, it does not chew cud, it is unclean to you.
8 'You shall not eat of their flesh nor touch their carcasses; they are unclean to you.

Living Things in the Waters

9 'These[R]you may eat, whatever is in the water: all that have fins and scales, those in the water, in the seas or in the rivers, you may eat.   Deut. 14:9
10 'But whatever is in the seas and in the rivers, that do not have fins and scales among all the teeming life of the water, and among all the living creatures that are in the water, they are detestable things to you,
11 and they shall be [6]abhorrent to you; you may not eat of their flesh, and their carcasses you shall detest.
12 'Whatever in the water does not have fins and scales is abhorrent to you.

Birds of the Air

13 'These, moreover, you shall detest among the birds; they are[T]abhorrent, not to be eaten: the [A]eagle and the vulture and the [A]buzzard,   a detestable thing • vulture • black vulture
14 and the kite and the falcon in its kind,
15 every raven in its kind,
16 and the ostrich and the owl and the sea gull and the hawk in its kind,
17 and the little owl and the cormorant and the great owl,
18 and the white owl and the [A]pelican and the carrion vulture,   owl or jackdaw
19 and the stork, the heron in its kinds, and the hoopoe, and the bat.

Winged Insects

20 'All the winged insects that walk on all fours are detestable to you.
21 'Yet these you may eat among all the winged insects which walk on all fours: those which have above their feet jointed legs with which to jump on the earth.
22 'These of them you may eat: the locust in its kinds, and the devastating locust in its kinds, and the cricket in its kinds, and the grasshopper in its kinds.
23 'But all other winged insects which are four-footed are detestable to you.

The Carcasses of the Unclean Animals

24 'By these, moreover, you will be made

[6] Lit., detestable things

unclean: whoever touches their carcasses becomes unclean until evening,

25 and^Rwhoever picks up any of their carcasses shall wash his clothes and be unclean until evening. Lev. 11:40

26 'Concerning all the animals which divide the hoof, but do not make a split *hoof*, or which do not chew cud, they are unclean to you: whoever touches them becomes unclean.

27 'Also whatever walks on its paws, among all the creatures that walk on *all* fours, are unclean to you; whoever touches their carcasses becomes unclean until evening,

28 and the one who picks up their carcasses shall wash his clothes and be unclean until evening; they are unclean to you.

Swarming Things

29 'Now these are to you the unclean among the swarming things which swarm on the earth: the mole, and the mouse, and the^Agreat lizard in its kinds,   *thorn-tailed lizard*

30 and the gecko, and the ^Acrocodile, and the lizard, and the sand reptile, and the chameleon.   *lizard*

31 'These are to you the unclean among all the swarming things; whoever touches them when they are dead becomes unclean until evening.

32 'Also anything on which one of them may fall when they are dead, becomes unclean, including any wooden article, or clothing, or a skin, or a sack—any article of which use is made—^Eit shall be put in the water and be unclean until evening, then it becomes clean. Lev. 15:12

33 'As for any ^Rearthenware vessel into which one of them may fall, whatever is in it becomes unclean and you shall break^Tthe vessel. Lev. 6:28; 15:12 • *it*

34 'Any of the food which may be eaten, on which water comes, shall become unclean; and any liquid which may be drunk in every vessel shall become unclean.

35 'Everything, moreover, on which part of their carcass may fall becomes unclean; an oven or a ⁷stove shall be smashed; they are unclean and shall continue as unclean to you.

36 'Nevertheless a spring or a cistern collecting water shall be clean, though the one who touches their carcass shall be unclean.

37 'And if a part of their carcass falls on any seed for sowing which is to be sown, it is clean.

38 'Though if water is put on the seed, and a part of their carcass falls on it, it is unclean to you.

The Carcasses
of the Clean Animals

39 'Also if one of the animals dies which you have for food, the one who touches its carcass becomes unclean until evening.

40 'He^R too, who eats some of its carcass shall wash his clothes and be unclean until evening; and the one who picks up its carcass shall wash his clothes and be unclean until evening. Lev. 17:15; 22:8; Deut. 14:21

The Purpose of Dietary Laws

41 'Now^R every swarming thing that swarms on the earth is detestable, not to be eaten. Lev. 11:29

42 'Whatever crawls on its belly, and whatever walks on *all* fours, whatever has many feet, in respect to every swarming thing that swarms on the earth, you shall not eat them, for they are detestable.

43 'Do^R not render ^Tyourselves detestable through any of the swarming things that swarm; and you shall not make yourselves unclean with them so that you become unclean. Lev. 20:25 • *your souls*

44 'For^RI am the LORD your God. Consecrate yourselves therefore, and be holy; for I am holy. And you shall not make yourselves unclean with any of the swarming things that swarm on the earth.   Ex. 6:7; 16:12; 23:25

45 'For I am the LORD, who brought you up from the land of Egypt, to be your God; thus ^Ryou shall be holy for I am holy.' " Lev. 19:2

46 This is the law regarding the animal, and the bird, and every living thing that moves in the waters, and everything that swarms on the earth,

47 ^Rto make a distinction between the unclean and the clean, and between the edible creature and the creature which is not to be eaten. Lev. 10:10

CHAPTER 12

Laws Concerning Childbirth

THEN the LORD spoke to Moses, saying,

2"Speak to the sons of Israel, saying, 'When a woman ^Tgives birth and bears a male *child*, then she shall be unclean for seven days, as in the days of her menstruation she shall be unclean.   *produces seed*

3 'And on^Rthe eighth day the flesh of his foreskin shall be circumcised.   Gen. 17:12

4 'Then she shall remain in the blood of *her* purification for thirty-three days; she shall not touch any consecrated thing, nor enter the sanctuary, until the days of her purification are completed.

5 'But if she bears a female *child*, then she shall be unclean for two weeks, as in her menstruation; and she shall remain in the blood of *her* purification for sixty-six days.

6 'And^Rwhen the days of her purification are completed, for a son or for a daughter, she shall bring to the priest at the doorway of the tent of meeting, a one year old lamb for a burnt offering, and a young pigeon or a turtledove for a sin offering. Luke 2:22

⁷ Lit., *hearth for supporting (two) pots*

7 'Then he shall offer it before the LORD and make atonement for her; and she shall be cleansed from the flow of her blood. This is the law for her who bears *a child, whether* a male or a female. *fountain*

8 'But if she cannot afford a lamb, then she shall take two turtledoves or two young pigeons, the one for a burnt offering and the other for a sin offering; and the priest shall make atonement for her, and she shall be clean.' " Luke 2:22-24 · Lev. 5:7 · Lev. 4:26

CHAPTER 13

Examination of People

THEN the LORD spoke to Moses and to Aaron, saying,

2"When a man has on the skin of his body a swelling or a scab or a bright spot, and it becomes ⁸an infection of leprosy on the skin of his body, then he shall be brought to Aaron the priest, or to one of his sons the priests. *flesh* · Deut. 24:8

3"And the priest shall look at the mark on the skin of the body, and if the hair in the infection has turned white and the infection appears to be deeper than the skin of his body, it is an infection of leprosy; when the priest has looked at him, he shall pronounce him unclean. *flesh*

4"But if the bright spot is white on the skin of his body, and it does not appear to be deeper than the skin, and the hair on it has not turned white, then the priest shall isolate *him who has* the infection for seven days. *the appearance of it is not deeper* · *shut up*

5"And the priest shall look at him on the seventh day, and if in his eyes the infection has not changed, *and* the infection has not spread on the skin, then the priest shall isolate him for seven more days. *has stood*

6"And the priest shall look at him again on the seventh day; and if the infection has faded, and the mark has not spread on the skin, then the priest shall pronounce him clean; it is *only* a scab. And he shall wash his clothes and be clean. Lev. 11:25; 14:8

7"But if the scab spreads farther on the skin, after he has shown himself to the priest for his cleansing, he shall appear again to the priest.

8"And the priest shall look, and if the scab has spread on the skin, then the priest shall pronounce him unclean; it is leprosy.

9"When the infection of leprosy is on a man, then he shall be brought to the priest.

10"The priest shall then look, and if there is a white swelling in the skin, and it has turned the hair white, and there is quick raw flesh in the swelling, Num. 12:10; 2 Kin. 5:27

11 it is a chronic leprosy on the skin of his body, and the priest shall pronounce him unclean; he shall not isolate him, for he is unclean. *an old* · *flesh* · *shut up*

12"And if the leprosy breaks out farther on the skin, and the leprosy covers all the skin of *him who has* the infection from his head even to his feet, as far as the priest can see, *with regard to the whole sight of the priest's eyes*

13 then the priest shall look, and behold, *if* the leprosy has covered all his body, he shall pronounce clean *him who has* the infection; it has all turned white *and* he is clean. *flesh*

14"But whenever raw flesh appears on him, he shall be unclean.

15"And the priest shall look at the raw flesh, and he shall pronounce him unclean; the raw flesh is unclean, it is leprosy.

16"Or if the raw flesh turns again and is changed to white, then he shall come to the priest, Luke 5:12-14

17 and the priest shall look at him, and behold, *if* the infection has turned to white, then the priest shall pronounce clean *him who has* the infection; he is clean.

18"And when the body has a boil on its skin, and it is healed, *flesh*

19 and in the place of the boil there is a white swelling or a reddish-white, bright spot, then it shall be shown to the priest;

20 and the priest shall look, and behold, *if* it appears to be lower than the skin, and the hair on it has turned white, then the priest shall pronounce him unclean; it is the infection of leprosy, it has broken out in the boil.

21"But if the priest looks at it, and behold, there are no white hairs in it and it is not lower than the skin and is faded, then the priest shall isolate him for seven days;

22 and if it spreads farther on the skin, then the priest shall pronounce him unclean; it is an infection.

23"But if the bright spot remains in its place, and does not spread, it is *only* the scar of the boil; and the priest shall pronounce him clean.

24"Or if the body sustains in its skin a burn by fire, and the raw *flesh* of the burn becomes a bright spot, reddish-white, or white, *flesh*

25 then the priest shall look at it. And if the hair in the bright spot has turned white, and it appears to be deeper than the skin, it is leprosy; it has broken out in the burn. Therefore, the priest shall pronounce him unclean; it is an infection of leprosy. Ex. 4:6

26"But if the priest looks at it, and indeed, there is no white hair in the bright spot, and it is no deeper than the skin, but is dim, then the priest shall isolate him for seven days;

27 and the priest shall look at him on the seventh day. If it spreads farther in the skin, then the priest shall pronounce him unclean; it is an infection of leprosy.

28"But if the bright spot remains in its place, and has not spread in the skin, but is dim, it is the swelling from the burn; and the

⁸ Lit., *a mark, stroke,* and so throughout this context

priest shall pronounce him clean, for it is
only the scar of the burn.

29"Now if a man or woman has an infection on the head or on the beard,

30 then the priest shall look at the infection, and if it appears to be deeper than the skin, and there is thin yellowish hair in it, then the priest shall pronounce him unclean; it is a scale, it is leprosy of the head or of the beard.

31"But if the priest looks at the infection of the scale, and indeed, it appears to be no deeper than the skin, and there is no black hair in it, then the priest shall ^Tisolate *the person* with the scaly infection for seven days.   *shut up*

32"And on the seventh day the priest shall look at the infection, and if the scale has not spread, and no yellowish hair has ^Tgrown in it, and the appearance of the scale is no deeper than the skin,   *been*

33 then he shall shave himself, but he shall not shave the scale; and the priest shall ^Tisolate *the person* with the scale seven more days.   *shut up*

34"Then on the seventh day the priest shall look at the scale, and if the scale has not spread in the skin, and it appears to be no deeper than the skin, the priest shall pronounce him clean; and he shall wash his clothes and be clean.

35"But if the scale spreads farther in the skin after his cleansing,

36 then the priest shall look at him, and if the scale has spread in the skin, the priest need not seek for the yellowish hair; he is unclean.

37"If in his sight the scale has remained, however, and black hair has grown in it, the scale has healed, he is clean; and the priest shall pronounce him clean.

38"And when a man or a woman has bright spots on the skin of the ^Tbody, *even* white bright spots,   *flesh*

39 then the priest shall look, and if the bright spots on the skin of their ^Tbodies are a faint white, it is ^Teczema that has broken out on the skin; he is clean.   *flesh · tetter*

40"Now if a ^Tman loses the hair of his head, he is bald; he is clean.   *man's head becomes bald*

_T41"And if his head becomes bald at the front and sides, he is bald on the forehead; he is clean.   *border of his face*

42"But if on the bald head or the bald forehead, there occurs a reddish-white infection, it is leprosy breaking out on his bald head or on his bald forehead.

43"Then ^Rthe priest shall look at him; and if the swelling of the infection is reddish-white on his bald head or on his bald forehead, like the appearance of leprosy in the skin of the ^Tbody,   Lev. 10:10; Ezek. 22:26 · *flesh*

44 he is a leprous man, he is unclean. The priest shall surely pronounce him unclean; his infection is on his head.

45"As for the leper who has the infection, his clothes shall be torn, and the hair of his head shall be uncovered, and he shall cover his mustache and cry, 'Unclean! Unclean!'

46"He shall remain unclean all the days during which he has the infection; he is unclean. He shall live alone; his dwelling shall be ^Routside the camp.   Num. 5:1-4; 12:14

Examination of Garments

47"When a garment has a ^Tmark of leprosy in it, whether it is a wool garment or a linen garment,   *infection*

48 whether in ^Awarp or woof, of linen or of wool, whether in leather or in any article made of leather,   *weaving or texture*

49 if the mark is greenish or reddish in the garment or in the leather, or in the ^Awarp or in the woof, or in any article of leather, it is a leprous mark and shall be shown to the priest.   *weaving or texture*

50"Then ^Rthe priest shall look at the mark, and shall ^Tquarantine the article with the mark for seven days.   Ezek. 44:23 · *shut up*

51"He shall then look at the mark on the seventh day; if the mark has spread in the garment, whether in the warp or in the woof, or in the leather, whatever the purpose for which the leather is used, the mark is a leprous malignancy, it is unclean.

52"So he shall burn the garment, whether the warp or the woof, in wool or in linen, or any article of leather in which the mark occurs, for it is a ^Tleprous malignancy; it shall be burned in the fire.   *malignant leprosy*

53"But if the priest shall look, and indeed, the mark has not spread in the garment, either in the warp or in the woof, or in any article of leather,

54 then the priest shall order them to wash the thing in which the mark occurs, and he shall ^Tquarantine it for seven more days.   *shut up*

55"After the article with the mark has been washed, the priest shall again look, and if the mark has not changed its appearance, even though the mark has not spread, it is unclean; you shall burn it in the fire, whether an eating away has produced bareness on the top or on the front of it.

56"Then if the priest shall look, and if the mark has faded after it has been washed, then he shall tear it out of the garment or out of the leather, whether from the warp or from the woof;

57 and if it appears again in the garment, whether in the warp or in the woof, or in any article of leather, it is an outbreak; the article with the mark shall be burned in the fire.

58"And the garment, whether the warp or the woof, or any article of leather from which the mark has departed when you washed it, it shall then be washed a second time and shall be clean."

59 This is the law for the mark of leprosy in a garment of wool or linen, whether in the warp or in the woof, or in any article of leather, for pronouncing it clean or unclean.

CHAPTER 14

Cleansing of People

THEN the LORD spoke to Moses, saying, 2 "This shall be the law of the leper in the day of his cleansing.[R]Now he shall be brought to the priest,   Matt. 8:4; Mark 1:44

3 and the priest shall go [R]out to the outside of the camp. Thus the priest shall look, and if the [T]infection of leprosy has been healed in the leper,   Lev. 13:46 • mark, stroke

4 then the priest shall give orders to take two live clean birds and [R]cedar wood and a [T]scarlet string and hyssop for the one who is to be cleansed.   Num. 19:6 • scarlet color and

5 "The priest shall also give orders to slay the one bird in an earthenware vessel over [T]running water.   living

6 "As for the live bird, he shall take it, together with the cedar wood and the scarlet string and the hyssop, and shall dip them and the live bird in the blood of the bird that was slain over the [T]running water.   living

7 "He shall then sprinkle seven times the one who is to be cleansed from the leprosy, and shall pronounce him clean, and shall let the live bird go free over the open field.

8 "The one to be cleansed shall then wash his clothes and shave off all his hair, and bathe in water and be clean. Now afterward, he may enter the camp, but he shall stay outside his tent for seven days.

9 "And it will be on the seventh day that he shall shave off all his hair: he shall shave his head and his beard and his eyebrows, even all his hair. He shall then wash his clothes and bathe his [T]body in water and [R]be clean.   flesh • Lev. 14:8, 20

10 "Now on the eighth day he is to take two male lambs without defect, and a yearling ewe lamb without defect, and three-tenths of an ephah of fine flour mixed with oil for a grain offering, and one [9]log of oil;

11 and the priest who pronounces him clean shall present the man to be cleansed and the [T]aforesaid before the LORD at the doorway of the tent of meeting.   them

12 "Then the priest shall take the one male lamb and bring it for a guilt offering, with the [T]log of oil, and present them as a wave offering before the LORD.   Approx. one pt.

13 "Next he shall slaughter the male lamb in [R]the place where they slaughter the sin offering and the burnt offering, at the place of the sanctuary—for the guilt offering, [R]like the sin offering, belongs to the priest; it is most holy. Ex. 29:11; Lev. 1:11; 4:24 • Lev. 6:24-30

14 "The priest shall then take some of the blood of the [R]guilt offering, and the priest shall put it on [R]the lobe of the right ear of the one to be cleansed, and on the thumb of his right hand, and on the big toe of his right foot.   Lev. 14:19 • Ex. 29:20; Lev. 8:23, 24

15 "The priest shall also take some of the log of oil, and pour it into his left palm;

16 the priest shall then dip his right-hand finger into the oil that is in his left palm, and

with his finger sprinkle some of the oil seven times before the LORD.

17 "And of the remaining oil which is in his palm, the priest shall put some on the right ear lobe of the one to be cleansed, and on the thumb of his right hand, and on the big toe of his right foot, on the blood of the guilt offering;

18 while the rest of the oil that is in the priest's palm, he shall put on the head of the one to be cleansed. So the priest shall make atonement on his behalf before the LORD.

19 "The priest shall next offer the sin offering and make atonement for the one to be cleansed from his uncleanness. Then afterward, he shall slaughter the burnt offering.

20 "And the priest shall offer up the burnt offering and the grain offering on the altar. Thus the priest shall make atonement for him, and [R]he shall be clean.   Lev. 14:8, 9

21 "But if he is poor, and his means are insufficient, then he is to take one male lamb for a guilt offering as a wave offering to make atonement for him, and one-tenth of an [T]ephah of fine flour mixed with oil for a grain offering, and a log of oil, Approx. one bu.

22 and two turtledoves or two young pigeons which [a]are within his means,[R]the one shall be a sin offering and the other a burnt offering.   his hand reaches • Lev. 5:7

23 "Then[R] the eighth day he shall bring them for his cleansing to the priest, at the doorway of the tent of meeting, before the LORD.   Lev. 14:10, 11

24 "And the priest shall take the lamb of the guilt offering, and [R]the log of oil, and the priest shall offer them for a wave offering before the LORD.   Lev. 14:10

25 "Next he shall slaughter the lamb of the guilt offering; and the priest is to take some of the blood of the guilt offering and put it on the lobe of the right ear of the one to be cleansed and on the thumb of his right hand, and on the big toe of his right foot.

26 "The priest shall also pour some of the oil into his left palm;

27 and with his right-hand finger the priest shall sprinkle some of the oil that is in his left palm seven times before the LORD.

28 "The priest shall then put some of the oil that is in his palm on the lobe of the right ear of the one to be cleansed, and on the thumb of his right hand, and on the big toe of his right foot, on the place of the blood of the guilt offering.

29 "Moreover, the rest of the oil that is in the priest's palm he shall put on the head of the one to be cleansed, to make atonement on his behalf before the LORD.

30 "He shall then offer one of the turtledoves or young pigeons, [T]which are within his means.   from those which his hand can reach

31 "He shall offer what [T]he can afford,[R]the one for a sin offering, and the other for a burnt offering, together with the grain offer-

9 I.e., Approx. one pint, and so through v. 24

ing. So the priest shall make atonement before the Lord on behalf of the one to be cleansed. ^{his hand can reach} · Lev. 5:7

32"This is the law *for him* in whom there is an infection of leprosy, whose^Tmeans are limited for his cleansing." ^{hand does not reach}

Cleansing of Houses

33 The Lord further spoke to Moses and to Aaron, saying,

34"When^R you enter the land of Canaan, which I give you for a possession, and I put a mark of leprosy on a house in the land of your possession, ^{Gen. 17:8; Num. 32:22}

35 then the one who owns the house shall come and tell the priest, saying, 'Something like^Ra mark *of leprosy* has become visible to me in the house.' ^[Ps. 91:10]

36"The priest shall then order that they empty the house before the priest goes in to look at the mark, so that everything in the house need not become unclean; and afterward the priest shall go in to look at the house.

37"So he shall look at the mark, and if the mark on the walls of the house has greenish or reddish depressions, and appears deeper than the^Tsurface; ^{wall}

38 then the priest shall come out of the house, to the^Tdoorway, and quarantine the house for seven days. ^{doorway of the house}

39"And the priest shall return on the seventh day and ^Tmake an inspection. If the mark has indeed spread in the walls of the house, ^{look}

40 then the priest shall order them to tear out the stones with the mark in them and throw them away^Tat an unclean place outside the city. ^{to}

41"And he shall have the house scraped all around^Tinside, and they shall dump the plaster that they scrape off at an unclean place outside the city. ^{from the house around}

42"Then they shall take other stones and replace *those* stones; and he shall take other plaster and replaster the house.

43"If, however, the mark breaks out again in the house, after he has torn out the stones and scraped the house, and after it has been replastered,

44 then the priest shall come in and^Tmake an inspection. If he sees that the mark has indeed spread in the house, it is a malignant mark in the house; it is unclean. ^{look}

45"He shall therefore tear down the house, its stones, and its timbers, and all the plaster of the house, and he shall take *them* outside the city to an^Runclean place. ^{Lev. 14:41}

46"Moreover, whoever goes into the house during the time that he has^Tquarantined it, becomes unclean until evening. ^{shut up}

47"Likewise, whoever lies down in the house shall wash his clothes, and whoever eats in the house shall wash his clothes.

48"If, on the other hand, the priest comes in and^Tmakes an inspection, and the mark

has not indeed spread in the house after the house has been replastered, then the priest shall pronounce the house clean because the mark has^Tnot reappeared. ^{looks · healed}

49"To cleanse the house then, he shall take^Rtwo birds and cedar wood and a^Tscarlet string and hyssop, ^{Lev. 14:4} · ^{scarlet color}

50 and he shall slaughter the one bird in an earthenware vessel over running water.

51"Then he shall take the cedar wood and the hyssop and the scarlet string, with the live bird, and dip them in the blood of the slain bird, as well as in the^Trunning water, and sprinkle the house seven times. ^{living}

52"He shall thus cleanse the house with the blood of the bird and with the^Trunning water, along with the live bird and with the cedar wood and with the hyssop and with the^Tscarlet string. ^{living · scarlet color}

53"However, he shall let the live bird go free outside the city into the open field. So he shall make atonement for the house, and it shall be clean."

The Purpose of the Laws
of Leprosy

54 This is the law for any mark of leprosy—even for a^Rscale, ^{Lev. 13:30}

55 and for the leprous garment or house,

56 and^Rfor a swelling, and for a scab, and for a bright spot— ^{Lev. 13:2}

57 to teach^Twhen they are unclean, and when they are clean. This is the law of leprosy. ^{in the day of uncleanness}

CHAPTER 15

Discharges of the Man

THE Lord also spoke to Moses and to Aaron, saying,

2"Speak to the sons of Israel, and say to them, 'When any man has a discharge from his^Tbody, his discharge is unclean. ^{flesh}

3 'This, moreover, shall be his uncleanness in his discharge: it is his uncleanness whether his body allows its discharge to flow, or whether his body obstructs its discharge.

4 'Every bed on which the person with the discharge lies becomes unclean, and everything on which he sits becomes unclean.

5 'Anyone, moreover, who touches his bed shall wash his clothes and bathe in water and be unclean until evening;

6 and whoever sits on the thing on which the man with the discharge has been sitting, shall wash his clothes and bathe in water and be unclean until evening.

7 'Also whoever touches the person with the discharge shall wash his clothes and bathe in water and be unclean until evening.

8 'Or if the man with the discharge spits on one who is clean, he too shall wash his clothes and bathe in water and be unclean until evening.

9 'And every saddle on which the person with the discharge rides becomes unclean.

10 'Whoever then touches any of the things which were under him shall be unclean until evening, and he who carries them shall wash his clothes and bathe in water and be unclean until evening.

11 'Likewise, whomever the one with the discharge touches without having rinsed his hands in water shall wash his clothes and bathe in water and be unclean until evening.

12 'However, an^Rearthenware vessel which the person with the discharge touches shall be broken, and every wooden vessel shall be rinsed in water.   Lev. 6:28; 11:33

13 'Now when the man with the discharge becomes cleansed from his discharge, then he^Rshall count off for himself seven days for his cleansing; he shall then wash his clothes and bathe his body in ^Trunning water and shall become clean.   Lev. 8:33; 14:8 · *living*

14 'Then on the eighth day he shall take for himself^Rtwo turtledoves or two young pigeons, and come before the LORD to the doorway of the tent of meeting, and give them to the priest;   Lev. 14:22, 23

15 and the priest shall offer them,^Rone for a sin offering, and the other for a burnt offering. So^Rthe priest shall make atonement on his behalf before the LORD because of his discharge.   Lev. 5:7; 14:31 · Lev. 14:19, 31

16 'Now^Rif a man has a seminal emission, he shall bathe all his body in water and be unclean until evening. Lev. 22:4; Deut. 23:10, 11

17 'As for any garment or any leather on which there is seminal emission, it shall be washed with water and be unclean until evening.

18 'If a man lies with a woman *so that* there is a seminal emission, they shall both bathe in water and be unclean until evening.

Discharges of the Woman

19 'When^Ra woman has a discharge, *if* her discharge in her body is blood, she shall continue in her menstrual impurity for seven days; and whoever touches her shall be unclean until evening.   Lev. 12:2

20 'Everything also on which she lies during her menstrual impurity shall be unclean, and everything on which she sits shall be unclean.

21 'And anyone who touches her bed shall wash his clothes and bathe in water and be unclean until evening.

22 'And whoever touches any thing on which she sits shall wash his clothes and bathe in water and be unclean until evening.

23 'Whether it be on the bed or on the thing on which she is sitting, when he touches it, he shall be unclean until evening.

24 'And^Rif a man actually lies with her, so that her menstrual impurity is on him, he shall be unclean seven days, and every bed on which he lies shall be unclean. Lev. 18:19

25 'Now if a woman has a discharge of her blood many days, not at the period of her menstrual impurity, or if she has a discharge beyond^Tthat period, all the days of her impure discharge she shall continue as though^Tin her menstrual impurity; she is unclean.   *her menstrual impurity · in the days of*

26 'Any bed on which she lies all the days of her discharge shall be to her like her bed at menstruation; and every thing on which she sits shall be unclean, like her uncleanness at that time.

27 'Likewise, whoever touches them shall be unclean and shall wash his clothes and bathe in water and be unclean until evening.

28 'When she becomes clean from her discharge, she shall count off for herself seven days; and afterward she shall be clean.

29 'Then on the eighth day she shall take for herself two turtledoves or two young pigeons, and bring them in to the priest, to the doorway of the tent of meeting.

30 'And the priest shall offer the^Rone for a sin offering and the other for a burnt offering. So the priest shall make atonement on her behalf before the LORD because of her impure discharge.'   Lev. 5:7

The Purpose of the Laws of Discharges

31 "Thus you shall keep the sons of Israel separated from their uncleanness, lest they die in their uncleanness by their^Rdefiling My tabernacle that is among them."   Lev. 20:3

32 This is the law for the one with a discharge, and for the man who has a seminal emission so that he is unclean by it,

33 and for the woman who is ill because of menstrual impurity, and for the one who has a discharge, whether a male or a female, or a man who lies with an unclean woman.

CHAPTER 16

Preparation of the High Priest

NOW the LORD spoke to Moses after^Rthe death of the two sons of Aaron, when they had approached the presence of the LORD and died.   Lev. 10:1, 2

2 And the LORD said to Moses, "Tell your brother Aaron that he shall not enter^Rat any time into the holy place inside the veil, before the ¹⁰mercy seat which is on the ark, lest he die; for I will appear in the cloud over the mercy seat.   Ex. 30:10; Heb. 6:19; 9:7, 25

3 "Aaron shall enter the holy place with this: with a^Rbull for a sin offering and a ram for a burnt offering.   *bull of the herd*

4 "He shall put on the holy linen tunic, and the linen undergarments shall be next to his body, and he shall be girded with the linen sash, and attired with the linen turban (these are holy garments). Then he shall bathe his body in water and put them on.

5 "And he shall take from the congrega-

¹⁰ Lit., *propitiatory*

tion of the sons of Israel^Rtwo male goats for a sin offering and one ram for a burnt offering.   Lev. 4:13-21; 2 Chr. 29:21; Ezek. 45:22

Identification of the Sacrifices

6"Then ^RAaron shall offer the bull for the sin offering which is for himself, that he may make atonement for himself and for his household.   [Heb. 5:3]
7"And he shall take the two goats and present them before the LORD at the doorway of the tent of meeting.
8"And Aaron shall cast lots for the two goats, one lot for the LORD and the other lot for the ^11scapegoat.
9"Then Aaron shall offer the goat on which the lot for the LORD fell, and make it a sin offering.
10"But the goat on which the lot for the ^Tscapegoat fell, shall be presented alive before the LORD, to make atonement upon it, to send it into the wilderness as the ^Tscapegoat.   *goat of removal*

Atonement for the Priest

11"Then Aaron shall offer the bull of the sin offering which is for himself, and make atonement for himself and ^Rfor his household, and he shall slaughter the bull of the sin offering which is for himself.   Lev. 16:33
12"And he shall take a^Rfirepan full of coals of fire from upon the altar before the LORD, and two handfuls of finely ground sweet incense, and bring *it* inside the veil.   Lev. 10:1
13"And he shall put the incense on the fire before the LORD, that the cloud of incense may cover the^Tmercy seat that is on *the ark of* the testimony, lest he die.   *propitiatory*
14"Moreover, ^Rhe shall take some of the blood of the bull and sprinkle *it*^Rwith his finger on the mercy seat on the east *side*; also in front of the^Tmercy seat he shall sprinkle some of the blood with his finger seven times.   [Heb. 9:25] • Lev. 4:6, 17 • *propitiatory*

Atonement for the Tabernacle

15"Then he shall slaughter the goat of the sin offering ^Rwhich is for the people, and bring its blood inside the veil, and do with its blood as he did with the blood of the bull, and sprinkle it on the mercy seat and in front of the mercy seat.   [Heb. 7:27]
16"And^Rhe shall make atonement for the holy place, because of the impurities of the sons of Israel, and because of their transgressions, in regard to all their sins; and thus he shall do for the tent of meeting which abides with them in the midst of their impurities.   Ex. 29:36, 37; 30:10; [Heb. 2:17]
17"When he goes in to make atonement in the holy place, no one shall be in the tent of meeting until he comes out, that he may make atonement for himself and for his household and for all the assembly of Israel.

18"Then he shall go out to the altar that is before the LORD and make atonement for it, and shall take some of the blood of the bull and of the blood of the goat, and^Rput it on the horns of the altar on all sides.   Lev. 4:25
19"And ^Rwith his finger he shall sprinkle some of the blood on it seven times, and cleanse it, and from the impurities of the sons of Israel consecrate it.   Lev. 16:14

Atonement for the People

20"When he finishes atoning for the holy place, and the tent of meeting and the altar, he shall offer the live goat.
21"Then Aaron shall lay both of his hands on the head of the live goat, and ^Rconfess over it all the iniquities of the sons of Israel, and all their transgressions^Tin regard to all their sins; and he shall lay them on the head of the goat and send *it* away into the wilderness by the hand of a man who *stands in* readiness.   Lev. 5:5 • *in addition to*
22"And the goat shall bear on itself all their iniquities to a solitary land; and he shall release the goat in the wilderness.
23"Then Aaron shall come into the tent of meeting, and take off ^Rthe linen garments which he put on when he went into the holy place, and shall leave them there.   Lev. 16:4
24"And he shall bathe his body with water in a holy place and put on his clothes, and come forth and offer his burnt offering and the burnt offering of the people, and make atonement for himself and for the people.
25"Then he shall offer up in smoke the fat of the sin offering on the altar.
26"And the one who released the goat as the scapegoat shall wash his clothes and bathe his^Tbody with water; then afterward he shall come into the camp.   *flesh*
27"But the bull of the sin offering and the goat of the sin offering, ^Rwhose blood was brought in to make atonement in the holy place, shall be taken outside the camp, and they shall burn their hides, their flesh, and their refuse in the fire.   Lev. 6:30; Heb. 13:11
28"Then the ^Rone who burns them shall wash his clothes and bathe his body with water, then afterward he shall come into the camp.   Num. 19:8

Purpose of the Day of Atonement

29"And *this* shall be a permanent statute for you: in the seventh month, on the tenth day of the month, you shall humble your souls, and not do any work, whether the native, or the alien who sojourns among you;
30 for it is on this day that ^Tatonement shall be made for you to^Rcleanse you; you shall be clean from all your sins before the LORD.   *he shall make atonement* • Ps. 51:2
31"It is to be a sabbath of solemn rest for

---

^11 Lit., *goat of removal*, or else a name: *Azazel*

you, that you may[R]humble your souls; it is a permanent statute. Lev. 23:32; Ezra 8:21

32"So the priest who is anointed and ordained to serve as priest in his father's place shall make atonement: he shall thus put on the linen garments, the holy garments,

33 and make atonement for the holy sanctuary; and he shall make atonement for the tent of meeting and for the altar. He shall also make atonement for the[R]priests and for all the people of the assembly. Lev. 16:11

34"Now you shall have this as a[R]permanent statute, to[R]make atonement for the sons of Israel for all their sins once every year." And just as the LORD had commanded Moses, so he did. Lev. 23:31·[Heb. 9:7]

CHAPTER 17

Laws Concerning the Location of Sacrifices

THEN the LORD spoke to Moses, saying,
2"Speak to Aaron and to his sons, and to all the sons of Israel, and say to them, 'This is what the LORD has commanded, saying,

3"Any man from the house of Israel who slaughters an ox, or a lamb, or a goat in the camp, or who slaughters it outside the camp,

4 and has not brought it to the doorway of the tent of meeting to present *it* as an offering to the LORD before the tabernacle of the LORD, bloodguiltiness is to be reckoned to that man. He has shed blood and that man shall be cut off from among his people.

5"The[T]reason is so that the sons of Israel may bring their sacrifices which they were sacrificing in the open field, that they may bring them in to the LORD, at the doorway of the tent of meeting to the priest, and sacrifice them as sacrifices of peace offerings to the LORD. *In order that*

6"And the priest shall sprinkle the blood on the altar of the LORD at the doorway of the tent of meeting, and offer up the fat in smoke as a soothing aroma to the LORD.

7"And[R]they shall no longer sacrifice their sacrifices to the[A]goat demons with which they play the harlot. This shall be a permanent statute to them throughout their generations." ' Ex. 22:20; 32:8; 34:15 · *goat-idols*

8"Then you shall say to them, 'Any man from the house of Israel, or from the aliens who sojourn among them, who offers a burnt offering or sacrifice,

9 and[R]does not bring it to the doorway of the tent of meeting to[T]offer it to the LORD, that man also shall be cut off from his people. Ex. 20:24; Lev. 17:4 · *do*

Laws Concerning the Use of Blood

10 'And[R]any man from the house of Israel, or from the aliens who sojourn among them, who eats any blood, I will set My face against that person who eats blood, and will cut him off from among his people. Gen. 9:4

11 'For[R]the[T]life of the flesh is in the blood, and I have given it to you on the altar to make atonement for your souls; for it is the blood by reason of the[T]life that makes atonement.' Gen. 9:4; Lev. 17:14 · *soul*

12"Therefore I said to the sons of Israel, 'No person among you may eat blood, nor may any alien who sojourns among you eat blood.'

13"So when any man from the sons of Israel, or from the aliens who sojourn among them, [T]in hunting catches a beast or a bird which may be eaten, he shall pour out its blood and cover it with earth. *who in hunting*

14"For *as for the* life of all flesh, its blood is *identified* with its life. Therefore I said to the sons of Israel, 'You are not to eat the blood of any flesh, for the life of all flesh is its blood; whoever eats it shall be cut off.'

15"And[R]when any person eats *an animal* which dies, or is torn *by beasts*, whether he is a native or an alien, he shall wash his clothes and bathe in water, and remain unclean until evening; then he will become clean. Ex. 22:31; Lev. 7:24; 22:8; Deut. 14:21

16"But if he does not wash *them* or bathe his body, then he shall bear his guilt."

CHAPTER 18

Laws of Sexual Sin

THEN the LORD spoke to Moses, saying,
2"Speak to the sons of Israel and say to them, 'I[R]am the LORD your God. Ex. 6:7

3 'You shall not do[T]what is done in the land of Egypt where you lived, nor are you to do[T]what is done in the land of Canaan where I am bringing you; you shall not walk in their statutes. *according to the deed of*

4 'You are to perform My judgments and keep My statutes, to live in accord with them;[R]I am the LORD your God. Lev. 18:2

5 'So you shall keep My statutes and My judgments,[R]by which a man may live if he does them; I am the LORD. Neh. 9:29

6 'None of you shall approach any blood relative[T]of his to uncover nakedness; I am the LORD. *of his flesh*

7 'You[R]shall not uncover the nakedness of your father, that is, the nakedness of your mother. She is your mother; you are not to uncover her nakedness. Lev. 20:11; Deut. 27:20

8 'You[R]shall not uncover the nakedness of your father's wife; it is your father's nakedness. Lev. 20:11; Deut. 22:30; 27:20; 1 Cor. 5:1

9 'The[R] nakedness of your sister, *either* your father's daughter or your mother's daughter, whether born at home or born outside, their nakedness you shall not uncover. Lev. 18:11; 20:17; Deut. 27:22

10 'The nakedness of your son's daughter or your daughter's daughter, their naked-

ness you shall not uncover; for ᵀtheir nakedness is yours.   *they are your nakedness*

11 'The nakedness of your father's wife's daughter, born to your father, she is your sister, you shall not uncover her nakedness.

12 'You ᴿshall not uncover the nakedness of your father's sister; she is your father's blood relative.   Lev. 20:19

13 'You shall not uncover the nakedness of your mother's sister, for she is your mother's blood relative.

14 'You ᴿshall not uncover the nakedness of your father's brother; you shall not approach his wife, she is your aunt.   Lev. 20:20

15 'You shall not uncover the nakedness of your daughter-in-law; she is your son's wife, you shall not uncover her nakedness.

16 'You ᴿshall not uncover the nakedness of your brother's wife; it is your brother's nakedness.   Lev. 20:21

17 'You shall not uncover the nakedness of a woman and of her daughter, nor shall you take her son's daughter or her daughter's daughter, to uncover her nakedness; they are blood relatives. It is lewdness.

18 'And you shall not ᵀmarry a woman in addition to her sister as a rival while she is alive, to uncover her nakedness.   *take a wife*

19 'Also ᴿyou shall not approach a woman to uncover her nakedness during her ᴿmenstrual impurity.   Lev. 15:24; 20:18 • Lev. 12:2

20 'And ᴿ you shall not have intercourse with your neighbor's wife, to be defiled with her.   Lev. 20:10; [Prov. 6:29; Matt. 5:27, 28]

21 'Neither shall you give any of your offspring ᴿto ᵀoffer them to Molech, nor shall you profane the name of your God; I am the LORD.   Lev. 20:2-5; Deut. 12:31 • *cause to pass over*

22 'You shall not lie with a male as one lies with a female; it is an abomination.

23 'Also ᴿ you shall not have intercourse with any animal to be defiled with it, nor shall any woman stand before an animal to ᴬmate with it; it is a perversion.   Ex. 22:19 • *lie*

24 'Do not defile yourselves by any of these things; for by all these ᴿthe nations which I am casting out before you have become defiled.   Lev. 18:3; Deut. 18:12

25 'For the land has become defiled, therefore I have visited its punishment upon it, so the land has spewed out its inhabitants.

26 'But as for you, you are to keep My statutes and My judgments, and shall not do any of these abominations, *neither* the native, nor the alien who sojourns among you

27 (for the men of the land who have been before you have done all these abominations, and the land has become defiled);

28 so that the land may not spew you out, should you defile it, as it has spewed out the nation which has been before you.

29 'For whoever does any of these abominations, ᴬthose persons who do *so* shall be cut off from among their people.   *and the*

30 'Thus you are to keep ᴿMy charge, that you do not practice any of the abominable customs which have been practiced before

you, so as not to defile yourselves with them; I am the LORD your God.' "   Lev. 22:9

CHAPTER 19

Laws of Social Order

THEN the LORD spoke to Moses, saying, 2"Speak to all the congregation of the sons of Israel and say to them, 'You shall be holy, for I the LORD your God am holy.

3 'Every one of you shall reverence his mother and his father, and you shall keep My sabbaths; I am the LORD your God.

4 'Do not turn to ᴿidols or make for yourselves molten ᴿgods; I am the LORD your God.   Lev. 26:1; Ps. 96:5; 115:4-7 • Ex. 20:23

5 'Now when you offer a sacrifice of peace offerings to the LORD, you shall offer it so that you may be accepted.

6 'It shall be eaten the same day you offer *it*, and the next day; but what remains until the third day shall be burned with fire.

7 'So if it is eaten at all on the third day, it is an offense; it will not be accepted.

8 'And everyone who eats it will bear his iniquity, for he has profaned the holy thing of the LORD; and that person shall be cut off from his people.

9 'Now ᴿ when you reap the harvest of your land, you shall not reap to the very corners of your field, neither shall you gather the gleanings of your harvest.   Lev. 23:22

10 'Nor shall you glean your vineyard, nor shall you gather the fallen fruit of your vineyard; you shall leave them for the needy and for the stranger. I am the LORD your God.

11 'You ᴿ shall not steal, nor deal falsely, ᴿnor lie to one another.   Ex. 20:15, 16 • Jer. 9:3-5

12 'And ᴿyou shall not swear falsely by My name, so as to profane the name of your God; I am the LORD.   Ex. 20:7; Deut. 5:11

13 'You ᴿ shall not oppress your neighbor, nor rob *him*.ᴿThe wages of a hired man are not to remain with you all night until morning.   Ex. 22:7-15, 21-27 • Deut. 24:15; James 5:4

14 'You shall not curse a deaf man, nor ᴿplace a stumbling block before the blind, but you shall revere your God; I am the LORD.   Deut. 27:18

15 'You ᴿ shall do no injustice in judgment; you shall not be partial to the poor nor defer to the great, but you are to judge your neighbor fairly.   Ex. 23:3, 6; Deut. 1:17

16 'You shall not go about as ᴿa slanderer among your people, and you are not to ᵀact against the ᵀlife of your neighbor; I am the LORD.   Ps. 15:3; Jer. 6:28; 9:4 • *stand* • *blood*

17 'You ᴿshall not hate your ᵀfellow countryman in your heart; you may surely reprove your neighbor, but shall not incur sin because of him.   [1 John 2:9, 11; 3:15] • *brother*

18 'You ᴿshall not take vengeance, nor bear any grudge against the sons of your people, but you shall love your neighbor as yourself; I am the LORD.   [Deut. 32:35; Rom. 12:19]

19 'You are to keep My statutes. You shall not breed together two kinds of your cattle; you shall not sow your field with two kinds of seed, nor wear a garment upon you of two kinds of material mixed together.

20 'Now if a man lies carnally with a woman who is a slave acquired for *another* man, but who has in no way been redeemed, nor given her freedom, there shall be punishment; they shall not, *however,* be put to death, because she was not free.

21 'And he shall bring his guilt offering to the LORD to the doorway of the tent of meeting, ^Ra ram for a guilt offering.   Lev. 6:1-7

22 'The priest shall also make atonement for him with the ram of the guilt offering before the LORD for his sin which he has committed, and the sin which he has committed shall be forgiven him.

23 'And when you enter the land and plant all kinds of trees for food, then you shall count their fruit as ^Tforbidden. Three years it shall be ^Tforbidden to you; *it* shall not be eaten.   *uncircumcised*

24 'But in the fourth year all its fruit shall be holy, an offering of praise to the LORD.

25 'And in the fifth year you are to eat of its fruit, that its yield may increase for you; I am the LORD your God.

26 'You shall not eat *anything* ^Rwith the blood, nor practice ^Rdivination or soothsaying.   Gen. 9:4 • Deut. 18:10; 2 Kin. 17:17

27 'You ^Rshall not round off the side-growth of your heads, nor harm the edges of your beard.   Lev. 21:5; Deut. 14:1

28 'You shall not make any cuts in your ^Tbody for the dead, nor make any tattoo marks on yourselves: I am the LORD.   *flesh*

29 'Do ^Rnot ^Aprofane your daughter by making her a harlot, so that the land may not fall to harlotry, and the land become full of lewdness.   Lev. 21:9; Deut. 22:21 • *degrade*

30 'You shall ^Rkeep My sabbaths and revere My sanctuary; I am the LORD.   Lev. 19:3

31 'Do not turn to ^Amediums or spiritists; do not seek them out to be defiled by them. I am the LORD your God.   *ghosts or spirits*

32 'You shall rise up before the grayheaded, and honor the ^Taged, and you shall revere your God; I am the LORD.   *face of the aged*

33 'When a stranger resides with you in your land, you shall not do him wrong.

34 'The stranger who resides with you shall be to you as the native among you, and ^Ryou shall love him as yourself; for you were aliens in the land of Egypt: I am the LORD your God.   Lev. 19:18

35 'You shall do no wrong in judgment, in measurement of weight, or capacity.

36 'You shall have ^Rjust balances, just weights, a just ¹²ephah, and a just ¹³hin: I am the LORD your God, who brought you out from the land of Egypt.   Deut. 25:13-15

37 'You shall thus observe all My statutes, and all My ordinances, and do them: I am the LORD.' "

CHAPTER 20

The Penalty for Worshiping Molech

THEN the LORD spoke to Moses, saying,

2 "You shall also say to the sons of Israel, 'Any man from the sons of Israel or from the aliens sojourning in Israel, ^Rwho gives any of his ^Toffspring to Molech, shall surely be put to death; the people of the land shall stone him with stones.   Lev. 18:21 • *seed*

3 'I will also set My face against that man and will cut him off from among his people, because he has given some of his ^Toffspring to Molech, ^Rso as to defile My sanctuary and to profane My holy name.   *seed* • Lev. 15:31

4 'If the people of the land, however, should ever disregard that man when he gives any of his ^Toffspring to Molech, so as not to put him to death,   *seed*

5 then I Myself will set My face against that man and against his family; and I will cut him off from among their people both him and all those who play the harlot after him, by playing the harlot after Molech.

The Penalty for Consulting Spirits

6 'As for the person who turns to ^Amediums ^Rand to spiritists, to play the harlot after them, I will also set My face against that person and will cut him off from among his people.   *ghosts and spirits* • Lev. 19:31

7 'You shall consecrate yourselves therefore and ^Rbe holy, for I am the LORD your God.   [Eph. 1:4]; 1 Pet. 1:16

8 'And ^Ryou shall keep My statutes and practice them; I am the LORD who sanctifies you.   Ex. 31:13

The Penalty for Cursing Parents

9 'If *there is* anyone who curses his father or his mother, he shall surely be put to death; he has cursed his father or his mother, his bloodguiltiness is upon him.

The Penalty for Committing Sexual Sins

10 'If ^R*there is* a man who commits adultery with another man's wife, one who commits adultery with his friend's wife, the adulterer and the adulteress shall surely be put to death.   Ex. 20:14; Lev. 18:20; Deut. 5:18

11 'If *there is* a man who lies with his father's wife, he has uncovered his father's nakedness; both of them shall surely be put to death, their bloodguiltiness is upon them.

12 'If *there is* a man who lies with his daughter-in-law, both of them shall surely be put to death; they have committed incest, their bloodguiltiness is upon them.

13 'If ^R*there is* a man who lies with a male as those who lie with a woman, both of them have committed a detestable act; they shall surely be put to death. Their bloodguiltiness is upon them.   Lev. 18:22

¹² I.e., Approx. one bushel   ¹³ I.e., Approx. one gallon

14 'If *there is* a man who᷒marries a woman and her mother, it is immorality; both he and they shall be burned with fire, that there may be no immorality in your midst.   *takes*

15 'If᷒*there is* a man who lies with an animal, he shall surely be put to death; you shall also kill the animal.   Lev. 18:23

16 'If *there is* a woman who approaches any animal to᷒mate with it, you shall kill the woman and the animal; they shall surely be put to death. Their bloodguiltiness is upon them.   *lie*

17 'If᷒*there is* a man who takes his sister, his father's daughter or his mother's daughter, so that he sees her nakedness and she sees his nakedness, it is a disgrace; and they shall be cut off in the sight of the sons of their people. He has uncovered his sister's nakedness; he bears his guilt.   Lev. 18:9

18 'If᷒*there is* a man who lies with a᷒menstruous woman and uncovers her nakedness, he has laid bare her flow, and she has ᷄exposed the flow of her blood; thus both of them shall be cut off from among their people.   Lev. 15:24; 18:19 · *sick* · *uncovered*

19 'You shall also not uncover the nakedness of your mother's sister or of your father's sister, for such a one has made naked his blood relative; they shall bear their guilt.

20 'If᷄*there is* a man who lies with his uncle's wife he has uncovered his uncle's nakedness; they shall bear their sin. They shall die childless.   Lev. 18:14

21 'If᷄*there is* a man who takes his brother's wife, it is ᷄abhorrent; he has uncovered his brother's nakedness. They shall be childless.   Lev. 18:16 · *an impure deed*

The Purpose of the Laws
of Sanctification of the People

22 'You are therefore to keep all My statutes and all My ordinances and do them, so that the land to which I am bringing you to ᷆live will not spew you out.   *dwell in it*

23 'Moreover, you shall not follow᷄the customs of the nation which I shall drive out before you, for they did all these things, and therefore I have abhorred them.   Lev. 18:3

24 'Hence I have said to you, "You᷄are to possess their land, and I Myself will give it to you to possess it, a land flowing with milk and honey." I am the LORD your God, who has separated you from the peoples.   Ex. 13:5

25 'You are therefore to make a distinction between the clean animal and the unclean, and between the unclean bird and the clean; and you shall not make᷄yourselves detestable by animal or by bird or by anything that creeps on the ground, which I have separated for you as unclean.   *your souls*

26 'Thus you are to be holy to Me, for I the LORD am holy; and I᷄have set you apart from the peoples to be Mine.   Lev. 20:24

27 'Now a man or a woman who is a medium or a spiritist shall surely be put to death. They shall be stoned with stones, their bloodguiltiness is upon them.' "

CHAPTER 21
Laws Concerning Priests

THEN the LORD said to Moses, "Speak to the priests, the sons of Aaron, and say to them, 'No᷄one shall defile himself for a *dead* person among his people,   Lev. 19:28

2 ᷄except for his relatives who are nearest to him, his mother and his father and his son and his daughter and his brother,   Lev. 21:11

3 also for his virgin sister, who is near to him because she has had no husband; for her he may defile himself.

4 'He shall not defile himself as a᷄relative by marriage among his people, and so profane himself.   *husband among*

5 'They shall not make any baldness on their heads, nor shave off the edges of their beards, nor make any cuts in their flesh.

6 'They shall be holy to their God and not profane the name of their God, for they present the offerings by fire to the LORD, the bread of their God; so they shall be holy.

7 'They᷄shall not take a woman who is profaned by harlotry, nor shall they take a woman divorced from her husband; for he is holy to his God.   Lev. 21:13, 14

8 'You shall consecrate him, therefore, for he offers᷄the bread of your God; he shall be holy to you; for I the LORD, who sanctifies you, am holy.   Lev. 21:6

9 'Also the daughter of any priest, if she profanes herself by harlotry, she profanes her father; she shall be burned with fire.

Laws Concerning the High Priest

10 'And the priest who is the highest among his brothers, on whose head the anointing oil has been poured, and ᷆who has been consecrated to wear the garments, shall not ᷆uncover his head, nor tear his clothes;   *whose hand has been filled · unbind*

11 ᷄nor shall he approach any dead person, nor defile himself *even* for his father or his mother;   Lev. 19:28; Num. 19:14

12 nor shall he go out of the sanctuary, nor profane the sanctuary of his God; for ᷄the consecration of the anointing oil of his God is on him: I am the LORD.   Ex. 29:6, 7

13 'And he shall take a wife in her virginity.

14 'A᷄ widow, or a divorced woman, or one who is profaned by harlotry, these he may not take; but rather he is to᷆marry a virgin of his own people;   Lev. 21:7 · *take as wife*

15 that he may not profane his ᷆offspring among his people: for I am the LORD who sanctifies him.' "   *seed*

People Prohibited
from the Priesthood

16 Then the LORD spoke to Moses, saying,

17 "Speak to Aaron, saying, 'No man of your ᷆offspring throughout their generations who has a defect shall approach to offer the ᷄bread of his God.   *seed* · Lev. 21:6

18 'For[R]no one who has a defect shall approach: a blind man, or a lame man, or he who has a [T]disfigured *face*, or any deformed *limb*,   Lev. 22:19-25 • *slit*

19 or a man who has a broken foot or broken hand,

20 or a hunchback or a dwarf, or *one who has a* [R]defect in his eye or eczema or scabs or [R]crushed testicles.   *obscurity* • Deut. 23:1

21 'No man among the [T]descendants of Aaron the priest, who has a defect, is to come near to offer the LORD's offerings by fire; *since* he has a defect, he shall not come near to offer the bread of his God.   *seed*

22 'He may eat[R]the bread of his God, *both* of the most holy and of the holy, 1 Cor. 9:13

23 only he shall not go in to the veil or come near the altar because he has a defect, that he may not profane My sanctuaries. For I am the LORD who sanctifies them.' "

24 So Moses spoke to Aaron and to his sons and to all the sons of Israel.

CHAPTER 22

Things Prohibited of the Priesthood

T HEN the LORD spoke to Moses, saying,
2"Tell Aaron and his sons to be careful with the holy *gifts* of the sons of Israel, which they dedicate to Me, so as not to profane My holy name; I am the LORD.

3"Say to them, 'If any man among all your [T]descendants throughout your generations approaches the holy *gifts* which the sons of Israel dedicate to the LORD, while he has an uncleanness, that person shall be cut off from before Me. I am the LORD.   *seed*

4 'No man, of the descendants of Aaron, who is a leper or who has a discharge, may eat of the holy *gifts* until he is clean. And if one touches anything made unclean by a corpse or if a man has a seminal emission,

5 or[R]if a man touches any teeming things, by which he is made unclean, or any man by whom he is made unclean, whatever his uncleanness;   Lev. 11:23-28

6 a[T]person who touches any such shall be unclean until evening, and shall not eat of the holy *gifts*, unless he has bathed his[T]body in water.   *soul* • *flesh*

7 'But when the sun sets, he shall be clean, and afterward he shall eat of the holy *gifts*, for[R]it is his[T]food.   Num. 18:11 • *bread*

8 'He shall not eat[R]*an animal* which dies or is torn *by beasts*, becoming unclean by it; I am the LORD.   Lev. 7:24; 11:39, 40; 17:15

9 'They shall therefore keep My charge, so that[R]they may not bear sin because of it, and die thereby because they profane it; I am the LORD who sanctifies them. Ex. 28:43

10 'No [14]layman, however, is to eat the holy *gift*; a sojourner with the priest or a hired man shall not eat of the holy *gift*.

11 'But if a priest buys a[T]slave as *his* property with his money,[T]that one may eat of it,

and those who are born in his house may eat of his[T]food.   *soul* • *he may* • *bread*

12 'And if a priest's daughter is married to a[T]layman, she shall not eat of the [T]offering of the *gifts*.   *stranger* • *heave offering*

13 'But if a priest's daughter becomes a widow or divorced, and has no child and returns to her father's house as in her youth, she shall eat of her father's[T]food; but no[T]layman shall eat of it.   *bread* • *stranger*

14 'But if a man eats a holy *gift* unintentionally, then he shall add to it a fifth of it and shall give the holy *gift* to the priest.

15 'And [R]they shall not profane the holy *gifts* of the sons of Israel which they offer to the LORD,   Num. 18:32

16 and *so* cause them[R]to bear punishment for guilt by eating their holy *gifts*; for I am the LORD who sanctifies them.' "   Lev. 22:9

Sacrifices Prohibited of the Priesthood

17 Then the LORD spoke to Moses, saying,
18"Speak to Aaron and to his sons and to all the sons of Israel, and say to them, 'Any[R] man of the house of Israel or of the aliens in Israel who presents his offering, whether it is any of their[T]votive or any of their freewill offerings, which they present to the LORD for a burnt offering—   Num. 15:14 • *vows*

19[R]for you to be accepted—*it must be* a male without defect from the cattle, the sheep, or the goats.   Lev. 21:18-21; Deut. 15:21

20 'Whatever has a defect, you shall not offer, for it will not be accepted for you.

21 'And when a man offers a sacrifice of peace offerings to the LORD to fulfill a special vow, or for a freewill offering, of the herd or of the flock, it must be perfect to be accepted; there shall be no defect in it.

22 'Those *that are* blind or fractured or maimed or having a running sore or eczema or scabs, you shall not offer to the LORD, nor make of them an offering by fire on the altar to the LORD.

23 'In respect to an ox or a lamb which has an [T]overgrown or stunted *member*, you may present it for a freewill offering, but for a vow it shall not be accepted.   *a deformed*

24 'Also anything *with its testicles* bruised or crushed or torn or cut, you shall not offer to the LORD, or[T]sacrifice in your land,   *do*

25 nor shall you accept any such from the hand of a foreigner for offering[R]as the[T]food of your God; for their corruption is in them, they have a defect, they shall not be accepted for you.' "   Lev. 21:22 • *bread*

26 Then the LORD spoke to Moses, saying,
27"When an ox or a sheep or a goat is born, it shall [T]remain [R]seven days [T]with its mother, and from the eighth day on it shall be accepted as a sacrifice of an offering by fire to the LORD.   *be* • Ex. 22:30 • *under*

28"But,[R] *whether* it is an ox or a sheep, you

[14] Lit., *stranger*

shall not kill *both* it and its young in one day.   Deut. 22:6, 7

29"And when you sacrifice ^Ra sacrifice of thanksgiving to the LORD, you shall sacrifice it so that you may be accepted.   Lev. 7:12

30"It shall be eaten on the same day, you shall leave none of it until morning: I am the LORD.

The Purpose of the Laws of the Priesthood

31"So^Ryou shall keep My commandments, and do them: I am the LORD.   Lev. 19:37

32"And you shall not profane My holy name, but I will be sanctified among the sons of Israel: I am the LORD who sanctifies you,

33 who brought you out from the land of Egypt, to be your God: I am the LORD."

CHAPTER 23

The Weekly Sabbath

THE LORD spoke again to Moses, saying,

2"Speak to the sons of Israel, and say to them, 'The LORD's appointed times which you shall ^Rproclaim as holy convocations— My appointed times are these: Lev. 23:21

3 'For^Rsix days work may be done; but on the seventh day there is a sabbath of complete rest, a holy convocation. You shall not do any work; it is a sabbath to the LORD in all your dwellings.   Ex. 20:9, 10; 23:12

Passover

4 'These are the appointed times of the LORD, holy convocations which you shall proclaim at the times appointed for them.

5 'In the first month, on the fourteenth day of the month ^Tat twilight is the LORD's Passover.   *between the two evenings*

Unleavened Bread

6 'Then on the fifteenth day of the same month there is the ^RFeast of Unleavened Bread to the LORD; for seven days you shall eat unleavened bread.   Ex. 12:14-20; 23:15

7 'On the first day you shall have a holy convocation; you shall^Rnot do any laborious work.   Lev. 23:8, 21, 25, 35, 36

8 'But for seven days you shall present an offering by fire to the LORD. On the seventh day is a holy convocation; you shall not do any laborious work.'"

First Fruits

9 Then the LORD spoke to Moses, saying,

10"Speak to the sons of Israel, and say to them, 'When you enter the land which I am going to give to you and^Rreap its harvest, then you shall bring in the sheaf of the first fruits of your harvest to the priest. Ex. 23:19

11 'And he shall wave the sheaf before the LORD for you to be accepted; on the day after the sabbath the priest shall wave it.

12 'Now on the day when you wave the sheaf, you shall offer a male lamb one year old without defect for a burnt offering to the LORD.

13 'Its ^Rgrain offering shall then be ^Ttwo-tenths *of an ephah* of fine flour mixed with oil, an offering by fire to the LORD *for* a soothing aroma, with its libation, a^Tfourth of a ¹⁵hin of wine.   Lev. 6:20 • 2 qt. • 1 qt.

14 'Until this same day, until you have brought in the offering of your God,^Ryou shall eat neither bread nor roasted grain nor new growth. It is to be a perpetual statute throughout your generations in all your dwelling places.   Ex. 34:26; Num. 15:20, 21

Pentecost

15 'You^R shall also count for yourselves from the day after the sabbath, from the day when you brought in the sheaf of the wave offering; there shall be seven complete sabbaths.   Num. 28:26-31; Deut. 16:9-12

16 'You shall count fifty days to the day after the seventh sabbath; then you shall present a new grain offering to the LORD.

17 'You shall bring in from your dwelling places two *loaves* of bread for a wave offering, made of two-tenths *of an* ^T*ephah*; they shall be of a fine flour, baked with leaven as first fruits to the LORD.   Approx. one bu.

18 'Along with the bread, you shall present seven one year old male lambs without defect, and a bull of the herd, and two rams; they are to be a burnt offering to the LORD, with their grain offering and their libations, an offering by fire of a soothing aroma to the LORD.

19 'You shall also offer one male goat for a sin offering and two male lambs one year old for a sacrifice of peace offerings.

20 'The priest shall then wave them with the bread of the first fruits for a wave offering with two lambs before the LORD; they are to be holy to the LORD for the priest.

21 'On this same day you shall ^Rmake a proclamation as well; you are to have a holy convocation. You shall do no laborious ^Rwork. It is to be a perpetual statute in all your dwelling places throughout your generations.   Lev. 23:2, 4 • Lev. 23:7

22 'When^R you reap the harvest of your land, moreover, you shall not reap to the very corners of your field, nor gather the gleaning of your harvest; you are to leave them for the needy and the alien. I am the LORD your God.'"   Lev. 19:9, 10; Deut. 24:19

Trumpets

23 Again the LORD spoke to Moses, saying,

24"Speak to the sons of Israel, saying, 'In the seventh month on the first of the month,

¹⁵ I.e., Approx. one gallon

you shall have a¹rest, a reminder by blowing *of trumpets*, a holy convocation.   *sabbath rest*
25 'You shall^R not do any laborious work, but you shall present an offering by fire to the LORD.' "   Lev. 23:21

Day of Atonement

26 And the LORD spoke to Moses, saying, 27"On exactly the tenth day of this seventh month is^R the day of atonement; it shall be a holy convocation for you, and you shall humble your souls and present an offering by fire to the LORD.   Ex. 30:10; Lev. 16:30
28"Neither shall you do any work on this same day, for it is a ^R day of atonement,^R to make atonement on your behalf before the LORD your God.   Lev. 23:27 • Lev. 16:34
29"If there is any ^T person who will not humble himself on this same day,^R he shall be cut off from his people.   *soul* • Gen. 17:14
30"As for any person who does any work on this same day, that person I will destroy from among his people.
31"You shall do no work at all. It is to be a perpetual statute throughout your generations in all your dwelling places.
32"It is to be a sabbath of complete rest to you, and you shall humble your souls; on the ninth of the month at evening, from evening until evening you shall keep your sabbath."

Tabernacles

33 Again the LORD spoke to Moses, saying,
34"Speak to the sons of Israel, saying, 'On the fifteenth of this seventh month is the Feast of Booths for seven days to the LORD.
35 'On the first day is a holy convocation; you shall do no laborious work of any kind.
36 'For seven days you shall present an offering by fire to the LORD. On the eighth day you shall have a holy convocation and present an offering by fire to the LORD; it is an assembly. You shall do no laborious work.
37 'These are ^T the appointed times of the LORD which you shall proclaim as holy convocations, to present offerings by fire to the LORD—burnt offerings and grain offerings, sacrifices and libations, ^R each day's matter on its own day—   Lev. 23:2 • Num. 28:1—29:38
38 besides *those of* the sabbaths of the LORD, and besides your gifts, and besides all your ^T votive and freewill offerings, which you give to the LORD.   *vows, and besides all your*
39 'On exactly the fifteenth day of the seventh month, when you have gathered in the crops of the land, you shall celebrate the feast of the LORD for seven days, with a rest on the first day and a rest on the eighth day.
40 'Now on the first day you shall take for yourselves the ^T foliage of beautiful trees, palm branches and boughs of leafy trees and willows of the brook; and you shall rejoice before the LORD your God for seven days.   *products, fruit*
41 'You shall thus celebrate it *as* a feast to

the LORD for seven days in the year. It *shall be* a perpetual statute throughout your generations; you shall celebrate it in the seventh month.
42 'You shall ^T live^R in booths for seven days; all the native-born in Israel shall ^T live in booths,   *dwell* • Lev. 23:34
43 so that your generations may know that I had the sons of Israel live in booths when I brought them out from the land of Egypt. I am the LORD your God.' "
44 So Moses declared to the sons of Israel ^R the appointed times of the LORD.   Lev. 23:37

CHAPTER 24

Oil for the Lamps

THEN the LORD spoke to Moses, saying, 2"Command the sons of Israel that they bring to you clear oil from beaten olives for the light, to make a lamp burn continually.
3"Outside the veil of testimony in the tent of meeting, Aaron shall keep it in order from evening to morning before the LORD continually; *it shall be* a perpetual statute throughout your generations.
4"He shall keep the lamps in order on the ^R pure *gold* lampstand before the LORD continually.   Ex. 25:31; 31:8; 37:17

The Showbread

5"Then^R you shall take fine flour and bake twelve cakes with it; two-tenths *of an ephah* shall be *in* each cake.   Ex. 25:30; 39:36; 40:23
6"And you shall set them *in* two rows, six to a row, on the ^R pure *gold* table before the LORD.   Ex. 25:24; 1 Kin. 7:48
7"And you shall put pure frankincense on each row, that it may be^R a memorial portion for the bread, *even* an offering by fire to the LORD.   Lev. 2:2, 9, 16
8"Every sabbath day he shall set it in order before the LORD continually; it is an everlasting covenant for the sons of Israel.
9"And^R it shall be for Aaron and his sons, and they shall eat it in a holy place; for it is most holy to him from the LORD's offerings by fire, *his* portion forever."   Matt. 12:4

Law of the Sanctified Name of God

10 Now the son of an Israelite woman, whose father was an Egyptian, went out among the sons of Israel; and the Israelite woman's son and a man of Israel struggled with each other in the camp.
11 And the son of the Israelite woman blasphemed the^R Name and cursed. So they brought him to Moses. (Now his mother's name was Shelomith, the daughter of Dibri, of the tribe of Dan.)   Ex. 3:15; 22:28; Job 2:5, 9
12 And they put him in^R custody so that the command of the LORD might be made clear to them.   *prison* • Ex. 18:15
13 Then the LORD spoke to Moses, saying,

14"Bring the one who has cursed outside the camp, and let all who heard him ^Rlay their hands on his head; then let all the congregation stone him.   Deut. 13:9; 17:7

15"And you shall speak to the sons of Israel, saying, 'If^Ranyone curses his God, then he shall bear his sin.   Ex. 22:28

16 'Moreover, the one who^Rblasphemes the name of the LORD shall surely be put to death; all the congregation shall certainly stone him. The alien as well as the native, when he blasphemes the Name, shall be put to death.   1 Kin. 21:10; [Matt. 12:31; Mark 3:28f.]

17 'And if a man takes the life of any human being, he shall surely be put to death.

18 'And the one who^Ttakes the life of an animal shall make it good, life for life. smites

19 'And if a man injures his neighbor, just as he has done, so it shall be done to him:

20 fracture for fracture, eye for eye, tooth for tooth; just as he has^Tinjured a man, so it shall be^Tinflicted on him. given a blemish · given

21 'Thus the one who^Tkills an animal shall make it good, but^Rthe one who^Tkills a man shall be put to death.   smites · Lev. 24:17

22 'There shall be one^Tstandard for you; it shall be for the stranger as well as the native, for I am the LORD your God.' " judgment

23 Then Moses spoke to the sons of Israel, and they brought the one who had cursed outside the camp and stoned him with stones. Thus the sons of Israel did, just as the LORD had commanded Moses.

CHAPTER 25

Law of the Sabbath Year

THE LORD then spoke to Moses ^Aat Mount Sinai, saying,   on

2"Speak to the sons of Israel, and say to them, 'When you come into the land which I shall give you, then the land shall have a sabbath to the LORD.

3 'Six^Ryears you shall sow your field, and six years you shall prune your vineyard and gather in its crop,   Ex. 23:10, 11

4 but during^Rthe seventh year the land shall have a sabbath rest, a sabbath to the LORD; you shall not sow your field nor prune your vineyard.   Lev. 25:20

5 'Your harvest's [16]aftergrowth you shall not reap, and your grapes of untrimmed vines you shall not gather; the land shall have a sabbatical year.

6 'And^Rall of you shall have the sabbath *products* of the land for food; yourself, and your male and female slaves, and your hired man and your foreign resident, those who live as aliens with you.   Lev. 25:20, 21

7 'Even your cattle and the animals that are in your land shall have all its crops to eat.

Law of the Year of Jubilee

8 'You are also to count off seven sabbaths of years for yourself, seven times

seven years, so that you have the time of the seven sabbaths of years, *namely,* forty-nine years.

9 'You shall then sound a ram's horn abroad on the tenth day of the seventh month; on the day of atonement you shall sound a horn all through your land.

10 'You shall thus consecrate the fiftieth year and ^Rproclaim [17]a release through the land to all its inhabitants. It shall be a jubilee for you, ^Aand each of you shall return to his own property, ^Aand each of you shall return to his family.   Jer. 34:8, 15, 17 · when

11 'You shall have the fiftieth year as a jubilee; you shall not sow, nor reap its aftergrowth, nor gather in *from* its untrimmed vines.

12 'For it is a jubilee; it shall be holy to you. You shall eat its crops out of the field.

13 'On^Rthis year of jubilee each of you shall return to his own property.   Lev. 25:10; 27:24

14 'If you make a sale, moreover, to your friend, or buy from your friend's hand,^Ryou shall not wrong one another.   Lev. 25:17

15 'Corresponding to the number of years after the jubilee, you shall buy from your ^{Tc}friend; he is to sell to you according to the number of years of crops.   *friend's hands*

16 'In proportion to the ^Textent of the years you shall increase its price, and in proportion to the fewness of the years, you shall diminish its price; for *it is* a number of crops he is selling to you.   *multitude*

17 'So^Ryou shall not wrong one another, but you shall^Afear your God; for I am the LORD your God.   Lev. 25:14 · *reverence*

18 'You shall thus observe My statutes, and keep My judgments, so as to carry them out, that you may live securely on the land.

19 'Then the land will yield its produce, so that you can eat your fill and live securely on it.

20 'But if you say, "What^Rare we going to eat on the seventh year^Aif we do not sow or gather in our crops?"   Lev. 25:4 · *behold*

21 then^RI will so order My blessing for you in the sixth year that it will bring forth the crop for three years.   Deut. 28:8

22 'When you are sowing the eighth year, you can still eat ^Rold things from the crop, eating *the old* until the ninth year when its crop comes in.   Lev. 26:10

23 'The land, moreover, shall not be sold permanently, for the land is Mine; for you are *but* aliens and sojourners with Me.

24 'Thus for every^Tpiece of your property, you are to provide for the redemption of the land.   *land*

25 'If^Ra fellow countryman of yours becomes so poor he has to sell part of his property, then his nearest kinsman is to come and buy back what his ^Trelative has sold.   Ruth 2:20; 4:4, 6 · *brother*

26 'Or in case a man has no kinsman, but

---

[16] Lit., *growth from spilled kernels*   [17] Or, *liberty*

so ^{T}recovers his means as to find sufficient for its redemption,   *his hand reaches*
27 ^{R}then he shall calculate the years since its sale and refund the balance to the man to whom he sold it, and so return to his property.   Lev. 25:16
28 'But if he has not found sufficient means to get it back for himself, then what he has sold shall remain in the hands of its purchaser until the year of jubilee; but at the jubilee it shall ^{T}revert, that ^{R}he may return to his property.   *go out* · Lev. 25:10, 13
29 'Likewise, if a man sells a dwelling house in a walled city, then his redemption right remains valid until a full year from its sale; his right of redemption lasts a full year.
30 'But if it is not bought back for him within the space of a full year, then the house that is in the walled city passes permanently to its purchaser throughout his generations; it does not revert in the jubilee.
31 'The houses of the villages, however, which have no surrounding wall shall be considered as open fields; they have redemption rights and revert in the jubilee.
32 'As for ^{R}cities of the Levites, the Levites have a permanent right of redemption for the houses of the cities which are their possession.   Num. 35:1-8; Josh. 21:2
33 'What, therefore, belongs to the Levites may be redeemed and a house sale in the city of this possession reverts in the jubilee, for the houses of the cities of the Levites are their possession among the sons of Israel.
34 'But ^{R}pasture fields of their cities shall not be sold, for that is their perpetual possession.   Num. 35:2-5
35 'Now ^{R}in case a ^{T}countryman of yours becomes poor and his ^{T}means with regard to you falter, then you are to sustain him, like a stranger or a sojourner, that he may live with you.   Deut. 15:7-11 · *brother* · *hand*
36 'Do not take ^{T}usurious interest from him, but revere your God, that your countryman may live with you.   *interest and usury*
37 'You shall not give him your silver at interest, nor your food for gain.
38 'I am the LORD your God, who brought you out of the land of Egypt to give you the land of Canaan *and* to be your God.
39 'And ^{R}if a ^{T}countryman of yours becomes so poor with regard to you that he sells himself to you, you shall not subject him to a slave's service.   Ex. 21:2-6 · *brother*
40 'He shall be with you as a hired man, as ^{R}if he were a sojourner; he shall serve with you until the year of jubilee.   Ex. 21:2
41 'He shall then go out from you, he and his sons with him, and shall go back to his family, that he may return to the property of his forefathers.
42 'For they are My servants whom I brought out from the land of Egypt; they are not to be sold *in* a slave sale.
43 'You ^{R}shall not rule over him with severity, but are to revere your God.   Ex. 1:13, 14
44 'As for your male and female slaves whom you may have—you may acquire male and female slaves from the pagan nations that are around you.
45 'Then, too, *it is* out of the sons of the sojourners who live as aliens among you that you may gain acquisition, and out of their families who are with you, whom they will have ^{T}produced in your land; they also may become your possession.   *begotten*
46 'You may even bequeath them to your sons after you, to receive as a possession; you can use them as permanent slaves. ^{R}But in respect to your ^{T}countrymen, the sons of Israel, you shall not rule with severity over one another.   Lev. 25:43 · *brothers*
47 'Now if the means of a stranger or of a sojourner with you becomes sufficient, and a countryman of yours becomes so poor with regard to him as to sell himself to a stranger who is sojourning with you, or to the descendants of a stranger's family,
48 then he shall have redemption right after he has been sold. One of his brothers may redeem him,
49 or his uncle, or his uncle's son, may redeem him, or one of his blood relatives from his family may redeem him; or ^{R}if he prospers, he may redeem himself.   Lev. 25:26, 27
50 'He then with his purchaser shall calculate from the year when he sold himself to him up to the year of jubilee; and the price of his sale shall correspond to the number of years. *It is* like the days of a hired man *that* he shall be with him.
51 'If there are still many years, he shall refund part of his purchase price in proportion to them for his own redemption;
52 and if few years remain until the year of jubilee, he shall so calculate with him. In proportion to his years he is to refund *the amount for* his redemption.
53 'Like a man hired year by year he shall be with him; ^{R}he shall not rule over him with severity in your sight.   Lev. 25:43
54 'Even if he is not redeemed by ^{A}these *means*, he shall still go out in the year of jubilee, he and his sons with him.   *these years*
55 'For the sons of Israel are My servants; they are My servants whom I brought out from the land of Egypt. I am the LORD your God.

CHAPTER 26

Basic Requirements of Obedience

'Y OU shall not make for yourselves ^{A}idols, nor shall you set up for yourselves an image or a *sacred* pillar, nor shall you place a figured stone in your land to bow down to it; for I am the LORD your God.   *graven images*
2 'You shall keep My sabbaths and reverence My sanctuary; I am the LORD.

*Conditions and Results
of Obedience*

3 'If you walk in My statutes and keep

My commandments so as to carry them out,
4 then I shall give you rains in their season, so that the land will yield its produce and the trees[R] of the field will bear their fruit.
5 'Indeed, your threshing will last for you until grape gathering, and grape gathering will last until sowing time. You will thus eat your [T]food to the full and live securely in your land.   Deut. 11:15; Joel 2:19, 26 • *bread*
6 'I[R] shall also grant peace in the land, so that you may lie down with no one making *you* tremble. I shall also eliminate harmful beasts from the land, and no sword will pass through your land.   Ps. 29:11; 85:8; 147:14
7 'But you will chase your enemies, and they[R] will fall before you by the sword;
8 'five of you will chase a hundred, and a hundred of you will chase ten thousand, and your enemies will fall before you by the sword.   Deut. 32:30
9 'So I will turn toward you and [R]make you fruitful and multiply you, and I will confirm My covenant with you.   Gen. 17:6; 22:17
10 'And you will eat the old supply and clear out the old because of the new.
11 'Moreover, I will make My dwelling among you, and My soul will not reject you.
12 'I[R] will also walk among you and be your God, and you shall be My people.   Gen. 3:8
13 'I am the LORD your God, who brought you out of the land of Egypt so that *you* should not be their slaves, and I broke the bars of your yoke and made you walk erect.

Conditions and Results
of Disobedience

14 'But if you do not obey Me and do not carry out all these commandments,
15 if, instead, you[R] reject My statutes, and if your soul abhors My ordinances so as not to carry out all My commandments, *and* so break My covenant,   Lev. 26:11; 2 Kin. 17:15
16 I, in turn, will do this to you: I will appoint over you a [R]sudden terror, consumption and fever that shall waste away the eyes and cause the soul to pine away; also, you shall sow your seed uselessly, for your enemies shall eat it up.   Deut. 28:22; Ps. 78:33
17 'And I will set My face against you so that you shall be struck down before your enemies; and[R] those who hate you shall rule over you, and[R] you shall flee when no one is pursuing you.   Ps. 106:41 • Lev. 26:36, 37
18 'If also after these things, you do not obey Me, then I will punish you[R] seven times more for your sins.   Lev. 26:21, 24, 28
19 'And I will also[R] break down your pride of power; I will also make your sky like iron and your earth like bronze.   Is. 28:1-3
20 'And[R] your strength shall be spent uselessly, for your land shall not yield its produce and the trees of the land shall not yield their fruit.   Ps. 127:1; Is. 17:10, 11; 49:4
21 'If then, you [T]act with hostility against Me and are unwilling to obey Me, I will in-

crease the plague on you [R]seven times according to your sins.   *walk* • Lev. 26:18
22 'And [R]I will let loose among you the beasts of the field, which shall bereave you of your children and destroy your cattle and reduce your number so that[R] your roads lie deserted.   2 Kin. 17:25 • Judg. 5:6
23 'And[R] if by these things you are not turned to Me, but act with hostility against Me,   Lev. 26:21; Jer. 5:3
24 then I will [R]act with hostility against you; and I, even I, will strike you [R]seven times for your sins.   Lev. 26:28, 41 • Lev. 26:21
25 'I will also bring upon you a sword which will execute[R] vengeance for the covenant; and when you gather together into your cities, I will send [R]pestilence among you, so that you shall be delivered into enemy hands.   Jer. 50:28; 51:11 • Num. 14:12
26 'When[R] I break your staff of bread, ten women will bake your bread in one oven, and they will bring back your bread [18]in rationed amounts, so that you will eat and not be satisfied.   Is. 3:1; Ezek. 4:16, 17; 5:16
27 'Yet if in spite of this, you do not obey Me, but act with hostility against Me,
28 then [R]I will act with wrathful hostility against you; and I, even I, will punish you seven times for your sins.   Lev. 26:24, 41
29 'Further,[R] you shall eat the flesh of your sons and the flesh of your daughters you shall eat.   2 Kin. 6:29
30 'I then will destroy your high places, and cut down your incense altars, and heap your[T] remains on the [T]remains of your idols; for My soul shall abhor you.   *corpses*
31 'I will lay waste your cities as well, and will make your sanctuaries desolate; and I will not smell your soothing aromas.
32 'And I will make[R] the land desolate so that your enemies who settle in it shall be appalled over it.   Jer. 9:11; 12:11; 25:11; 33:10
33 'You, however, I[R] will scatter among the nations and will draw out a sword after you, as your land becomes desolate and your cities become waste.   Deut. 4:27; 28:64
34 'Then[R] the land will [T]enjoy its sabbaths all the days of the desolation, while you are in your enemies' land; then the land will rest and [T]enjoy its sabbaths.   Lev. 26:43 • *satisfy*
35 'All the days of *its* desolation it will observe the rest which it did not observe on your sabbaths, while you were living on it.
36 'As for those of you who may be left, I will also bring[R] weakness into their hearts in the lands of their enemies. And the sound of a driven leaf will chase them and even when no one is pursuing, they will flee as though from the sword, and they will fall.   Is. 30:17
37 'They[R] will therefore stumble over each other as if *running* from the sword, although no one is pursuing; and you will have *no strength* to stand up before your enemies.   Jer. 6:21; Nah. 3:3 • *you will stand*

---

[18] Lit., *by weight*

38 'But you will perish among the nations, and your enemies' land will consume you.
39 'Soᴿthose of you who may be left will rot away because of their iniquity in the lands of your enemies; and also because of the iniquities of their forefathers they will rot away with them.   Ezek. 4:17; 33:10

The Promise of Restoration

40 'Ifᵗthey confess their iniquity and the iniquity of their forefathers, in their unfaithfulness which they committed against Me, and also in their acting with hostility against Me—   Jer. 3:12-15; 14:20; Hos. 5:15
41 I also was acting with hostility against them, to bring them into the land of their enemies—ᴿor if their uncircumcised heart becomes humbled so that they then make amends for their iniquity,   Jer. 4:4; 9:25, 26
42 then I will remember ᴿMy covenant with Jacob, and I will remember alsoᴿMy covenant with Isaac, and My covenant with Abraham as well, and I will remember the land.   Gen. 28:13-15; 35:11, 12 • Gen. 26:2-5
43 'Forᴿthe land shall be abandoned by them, and shall make up for its sabbaths while it is made desolate without them. They, meanwhile, shall be making amends for their iniquity,ᵗbecause they rejected My ordinances and their soul abhorred My statutes.   Lev. 26:34 • because and by the cause
44 'Yet in spite of this, when they are in the land of their enemies, I will not reject them, nor will I soᴿabhor them as to destroy them, breaking My covenant with them; for I am the LORD their God.   Lev. 26:11
45 'But I will remember for them theᴿcovenant with their ancestors, whom I brought out of the land of Egypt in the sight of the nations, thatᴿI might be their God. I am the LORD.' "   Ex. 6:6-8 • Gen. 17:7
46 These are the statutes and ordinances and laws which the LORD established between Himself and the sons of Israel ᵗthrough Moses at Mount Sinai. by the hand of

CHAPTER 27

Consecration of Persons

AGAIN, the LORD spoke to Moses, saying,
2"Speak to the sons of Israel, and say to them, 'When a man makes a difficult vow, he shall be valued according to your valuation of persons belonging to the LORD.
3 'If your valuation is of the male from twenty years even to sixty years old, then your valuation shall be fifty shekels of silver, after the shekel of the sanctuary.
4 'Or if it is a female, then your valuation shall beᵗthirty shekels. $3,840
5 'And if it be from five years even to twenty years old then your valuation for the male shall beᵗtwenty shekels, and for the femaleᵗten shekels. $2,560 • $1,280

6 'But if they are from a month even up to five years old, then your valuation shall be ᴿfive shekels of silver for the male, and for the female your valuation shall beᵗthree shekels of silver.   Num. 18:16 • $384
7 'And if they are from sixty years old and upward, if it is a male, then your valuation shall be fifteen shekels, and for the female ten shekels.
8 'But if he is poorer than your valuation, then he shall be placed before the priest, and the priest shall value him;ᴿaccording to ᵗthe means of the one who vowed, the priest shall value him. Lev. 5:11 • what the hand reaches

Consecration of Animals

9 'Now if it is an animal of the kind which ᵗmen can present as an offering to the LORD, any such that one gives to the LORD shall be holy.   they
10 'He shall not replace it or exchange it, a good for a bad, or a bad for a good; or if he does exchange animal for animal, then both it and its substitute shall become holy.
11 'If, however, it is any unclean animal of the kind whichᵗmen do not present as an offering to the LORD, then he shall place the animal before the priest.   they
12 'And the priest shall value itᵗas either good or bad; as you, the priest, value it, so it shall be.   between
13 'But if he should ever wish to redeem it, then he shall add one-fifth of it to your valuation.

Consecration of Houses

14 'Now if a man consecrates his house as holy to the LORD, then the priest shall value itᵗas either good or bad; as the priest values it, so it shall stand.   between good
15 'Yet if the one who consecrates it should wish to redeem his house, then he shall add one-fifth of your valuation price to it, so that it may be his.

Consecration of Fields

16 'Again, if a man consecrates to the LORD part of the fields of his own property, then your valuation shall be proportionate to the seed needed for it: a homer of barley seed atᵗfifty shekels of silver. $6,400
17 'If he consecrates his field as of the year of jubilee, according to your valuation it shall stand.
18 'If he consecrates his field after the jubilee, however, then the priest shall calculate the price forᴬhimᵗproportionate to the years that are left until the year of jubilee; and it shall be deducted from your valuation.   it • according to the years
19 'And if the one who consecrates it should ever wish to redeem the field, then he shall add one-fifth of your valuation price to it, so that it may pass to him.
20 'Yet if he will not redeem the field,ᴬbut

has sold the field to another man, it may no longer be redeemed;   *if he*

21 and when it^Treverts in the jubilee, the field shall be holy to the LORD, like a field set apart; it shall be for the priest as his^Tproperty.   *goes out · devoted, banned · possession*

22 'Or if he consecrates to the LORD a field which he has bought, which is not a part of the field of his own^Tproperty,   *possession*

23 then the priest shall calculate for ^him the amount of your valuation up to the year of jubilee; and he shall on that day give your valuation as holy to the LORD.   *it*

24 'In the year of jubilee the field shall return to the one from whom he bought it, to whom the possession of the land belongs.

25 'Every valuation of yours, moreover, shall be after ^Rthe shekel of the sanctuary. The shekel shall be twenty gerahs. Ex. 30:13

First-born Clean Animals

26 'However,^R a first-born among animals, which as a first-born belongs to the LORD, no man may consecrate it; whether ox or sheep, it is the LORD's.   Ex. 13:2

27 'But if *it is* among the unclean animals, then he shall redeem it according to your valuation, and add to it one-fifth of it; and if it is not redeemed, then it shall be sold according to your valuation.   *ransom*

¹⁹ Or, *puts under the ban*

Devoted Things

28 'Nevertheless, ^Ranything which a man ¹⁹sets apart to the LORD out of all that he has, of man or animal or of the fields of his own property, shall not be sold or redeemed. Anything devoted to destruction is most holy to the LORD.   Num. 18:14

29 'No ^Tone who may have been set apart among men shall be ransomed; he shall surely be put to death.   *one devoted; or banned*

Tithes

30 'Thus ^Rall the tithe of the land, of the seed of the land or of the fruit of the tree, is the LORD's; it is holy to the LORD. Gen. 28:22

31 'If, therefore, a man wishes to redeem part of his tithe, he shall add to it one-fifth of it.

32 'And for every tenth part of herd or flock, whatever passes under the rod, the tenth one shall be holy to the LORD.

33 'He^R is not to be concerned whether *it is* good or bad, nor shall he exchange it; or if he does exchange it, then both it and its substitute shall become holy. It shall not be redeemed.' "   Lev. 27:10

The Conclusion of Leviticus

34 ^RThese are the commandments which the LORD commanded Moses for the sons of Israel at Mount Sinai.   Lev. 26:46; Deut. 4:5

Measures of Length

Unit	Length	Equivalents	Translations
Day's journey	c. 20 miles		day's journey, day's walk
Roman mile	4,854 feet	8 stadia	mile
Sabbath day's journey	3,637 feet	6 stadia	a sabbath day's journey
Stadion	606 feet	⅛ Roman mile	mile, stadion
Rod	9 feet (10.5 feet in Ezekiel)	3 paces; 6 cubits	measuring rod
Fathom	6 feet	4 cubits	fathom
Pace	3 feet	⅓ rod; 2 cubits	pace
Cubit	18 inches	½ pace; 2 spans	cubit, yards
Span	9 inches	½ cubit; 3 handbreadths	span
Handbreadth	3 inches	⅓ span; 4 fingers	handbreadth
Finger	.75 inches	¼ handbreadth	finger

NUMBERS

THE BOOK OF NUMBERS

Numbers is the book of wanderings. It takes its name from the two numberings of the Israelites—the first at Mount Sinai and the second on the plains of Moab. Most of the book, however, describes Israel's experiences as they wander in the wilderness. The lesson of Numbers is clear. While it may be necessary to pass through wilderness experiences, one does not have to live there. For Israel, an eleven-day journey became a forty-year agony.

The title of Numbers comes from the first word in the Hebrew text, *Wayyedabber*, "And He Said." Jewish writings, however, usually refer to it by the fifth Hebrew word in 1:1, *Bemidbar*, "In the Wilderness," which more nearly indicates the content of the book. The Greek title in the Septuagint is *Arithmoi*, "Numbers." The Latin Vulgate followed this title and translated it *Liber Numeri*, "Book of Numbers." These titles are based on the two numberings: the generation of Exodus (Num. 1) and the generation that grew up in the wilderness and conquered Canaan (Num. 26). Numbers has also been called the "Book of the Journeyings," the "Book of the Murmurings," and the "Fourth Book of Moses."

THE AUTHOR OF NUMBERS

The evidence that points to Moses as the author of Numbers is similar to that for the previous books of the Pentateuch. These five books form such a literary unit that they rise or fall together on the matter of authorship.

External Evidence: The Jews, the Samaritans, and the early church give testimony to the Mosaic authorship of Numbers. Also a number of New Testament passages cite events from Numbers and associate them with Moses. These include John 3:14; Acts 7 and 13; First Corinthians 10:1–11; Hebrews 3 and 4; and Jude 11.

Internal Evidence: There are more than eighty claims that "the LORD spoke to Moses" (the first is 1:1). In addition, Numbers 33:2 makes this clear statement: "And Moses recorded their starting places according to their journeys by the command of the LORD." Moses kept detailed records as an eyewitness of the events in this book. As the central character in Exodus through Deuteronomy, he was better

qualified than any other man to write these books.

Some scholars have claimed that the third-person references to Moses point to a different author. However, use of the third person was a common practice in the ancient world. Caesar, for example, did the same in his writings.

THE TIME OF NUMBERS

Leviticus covers only one month, but Numbers stretches over almost thirty-nine years (c. 1444–1405 B.C.). It records Israel's movement from the last twenty days at Mount Sinai (1:1; 10:11), the wandering around Kadesh-barnea, and finally the arrival in the plains of Moab in the fortieth year (22:1; 26:3; 33:50; Deut. 1:3). Their tents occupy several square miles whenever they camp since there are probably over two-and-a-half million people (based on the census figures in Numbers 1 and 26). God miraculously feeds and sustains them in the desert—He preserves their clothing and gives them manna, meat, water, leaders, and a promise (14:34).

THE CHRIST OF NUMBERS

Perhaps the clearest portrait of Christ in Numbers is the bronze serpent on the stake, a picture of the Crucifixion (21:4–9): "And as Moses lifted up the serpent in the wilderness, even so must the Son of Man be lifted up" (John 3:14). The rock that quenches the thirst of the multitudes is also a type of Christ: "they were drinking from a spiritual rock which followed them; and the rock was Christ" (1 Cor. 10:4). The daily manna pictures the Bread of Life who later comes down from heaven (John 6:31–33).

Balaam foresees the rulership of Christ: "I see him, but not now; I behold him, but not near; a star shall come forth from Jacob, and a scepter shall rise from Israel" (24:17). The guidance and presence of Christ is seen in the pillar of cloud and fire, and the sinner's refuge in Christ may be seen in the six cities of refuge. The red heifer sacrifice (Num. 19) is also considered a type of Christ.

KEYS TO NUMBERS

Key Word: Wanderings—Numbers records the failure of Israel to believe in the promise of God and the resulting judgment of wandering in the wilderness for forty years.

Key Verses: Numbers 14:22, 23; 20:12— "Surely all the men who have seen My glory and My signs, which I performed in Egypt and in the wilderness, yet have put Me to the test these ten times and have not listened to My voice, shall by no means see the land which I swore to their fathers, nor shall any of those who spurned Me see it" (14:22, 23).

"But the LORD said to Moses and Aaron, 'Because you have not believed Me, to treat Me as holy in the sight of the sons of Israel, therefore you shall not bring this assembly into the land which I have given them' " (20:12).

Key Chapter: Numbers 14—The critical turning point of Numbers may be seen in Numbers 14 when Israel rejects God by refusing to go up and conquer the Promised Land. God judges Israel "According to the number of days which you spied out the land, forty days, for every day you shall bear your guilt a year, *even* forty years, and you shall know My opposition" (14:34).

SURVEY OF NUMBERS

Israel as a nation is in its infancy at the outset of this book, only thirteen months after the exodus from Egypt. In Numbers, the book of divine discipline, it becomes necessary for the nation to go through the painful process of testing and maturation. God must teach His people the consequences of irresponsible decisions. The forty years of wilderness experience transforms them from a rabble of ex-slaves into a nation ready to take the Promised Land. Numbers begins with the old generation (1:1—10:10), moves through a tragic transitional period (10:11—25:18), and ends with the new generation (26—36) at the doorway to the land of Canaan.

The Old Generation (1:1—10:10): The generation that witnessed God's miraculous acts of deliverance and preservation receives further direction from God while they are still at the foot of Mount Sinai (1:1—10:10). God's instructions are very explicit, reaching every aspect of their lives. He is the Author of order, not confusion; and this is seen in the way He organizes the people around the tabernacle. Turning from the outward conditions of the camp (1—4) to the inward conditions (5—10), Numbers describes the spiritual preparation of the people.

The Tragic Transition (10:11—25:18): Israel follows God step by step until Canaan is in sight. Then in the crucial moment at Kadesh they draw back in unbelief. Their murmurings had already become incessant, "Now the people became like those who complain of adversity in the hearing of the LORD" (11:1). But their unbelief after sending out the twelve spies at Kadesh-barnea is something God will not tolerate. Their rebellion at Kadesh marks the pivotal point of the book. The generation of the Exodus will not be the generation of the conquest.

Unbelief brings discipline and hinders God's blessing. The old generation is doomed to literally kill time for forty years of wilderness wanderings—one year for every day spent by the twelve spies in inspecting the land. They are judged by disinheritance and death as their journey changes from one of anticipation to one of aimlessness. Only Joshua and Caleb, the two spies who believed God, enter Canaan. Almost nothing is recorded about these transitional years.

The New Generation (26—36): When the transition to the new generation is complete, the people move to the plains of Moab, directly east of the Promised Land (22:1). Before they can enter the land they must wait until all is ready. Here they receive new instructions, a new census is taken, Joshua is appointed as

FOCUS	THE OLD GENERATION		THE TRAGIC TRANSITION				THE NEW GENERATION		
REFERENCE	1:1———5:1—		—10:11—13:1—	—15:1—	—20:1—26:1—		—28:1—31:1—36:13		
DIVISION	ORGANIZATION OF ISRAEL	SANCTIFICATION OF ISRAEL	TO KADESH	AT KADESH	IN WILDERNESS	TO MOAB	REORGANIZA-TION OF ISRAEL	REGULATIONS OF OFFERINGS AND VOWS	CONQUEST AND DIVISION OF ISRAEL
TOPIC	ORDER		DISORDER				REORDER		
	PREPARATION		POSTPONEMENT				PREPARATION		
LOCATION	MOUNT SINAI		WILDERNESS				PLAINS OF MOAB		
TIME	20 DAYS		38 YEARS 3 MONTHS AND 10 DAYS				c. 5 MONTHS		

Moses' successor, and some of the people settle in the Transjordan.

Numbers records two generations (1—14 and 26—36), two numberings (1 and 26), two journeyings (10—14 and 21—27), and two sets of instructions (5—9 and 28—36). It illustrates both the kindness and severity of God (Rom. 11:22) and teaches that God's people can move forward only as they trust and depend on Him.

OUTLINE OF NUMBERS

CHAPTER 1

The First Census of Israel

THEN the LORD spoke to Moses in the wilderness of Sinai, in the tent of meeting, on [R]the first of the second month, in the second year after they had come out of the land of Egypt, saying,   Ex. 40:2, 17

2 "Take a [1]census of all the congregation of the sons of Israel, by their families, by their fathers' households, according to the number of names, every male, head by head,

3 from [R]twenty years old and upward, whoever *is able to* go out to war in Israel, you and Aaron shall [2]number them by their armies.   Ex. 30:14; 38:26

4 "With you, moreover, there shall be a man of each tribe, [R]each one head of his father's household.   Ex. 18:21, 25; Num. 1:16

5 "These then are the names of the men who shall stand with you: [R]of Reuben, Elizur the son of Shedeur;   Gen. 24:32; Ex. 1:2

6 of Simeon, Shelumiel the son of Zurishaddai;

7 of Judah, [R]Nahshon the son of Amminadab;   Ruth 4:20; 1 Chr. 2:10; Luke 3:32

[1] Lit., *sum*   [2] Lit., *muster*, and so throughout this context
[3] Lit., *thousands*, or, *clans*

8 of Issachar, Nethanel the son of Zuar;

9 of Zebulun, Eliab the son of Helon;

10 of the sons of Joseph: of Ephraim, Elishama the son of Ammihud; of Manasseh, Gamaliel the son of Pedahzur;

11 of Benjamin, Abidan the son of Gideoni;

12 of Dan, Ahiezer the son of Ammishaddai;

13 of Asher, Pagiel the son of Ochran;

14 of Gad, Eliasaph the son of Deuel;

15 of Naphtali, Ahira the son of Enan.

16 "These are they who were [R]called of the congregation, the leaders of their fathers' tribes; they were the heads of [3]divisions of Israel."   Ex. 18:21; Num. 7:2; 16:2; 26:9

17 So Moses and Aaron took these men who had been designated by name,

18 and they assembled all the congregation together on the first of the second month. Then they registered by ancestry in their families, by their fathers' households, according to the number of names, from twenty years old and upward, head by head,

19 just as [R]the LORD had commanded Moses. So he numbered them in the wilderness of Sinai.   2 Sam. 24:1

20 Now the sons of Reuben, Israel's firstborn, their genealogical registration by their families, by their fathers' households, ac-

cording to the number of names, head by head, every male from twenty years old and upward, whoever *was able to* go out to war, 21 their numbered men, of the tribe of Reuben, *were* 46,500.

22 Of the sons of Simeon, their genealogical registration by their families, by their fathers' households, their numbered men, according to the number of names, head by head, every male from twenty years old and upward, whoever *was able to* go out to war, 23 their numbered men, of the tribe of Simeon, *were* 59,300.

24 Of the sons of Gad, their genealogical registration by their families, by their fathers' households, according to the number of names, from twenty years old and upward, whoever *was able to* go out to war, 25 their numbered men, of the tribe of Gad, *were* 45,650.

26 Of the sons of Judah, their genealogical registration by their families, by their fathers' households, according to the number of names, from twenty years old and upward, whoever *was able to* go out to war, 27 their numbered men, of the tribe of Judah, *were* 74,600.

28 [R]Of the sons of Issachar, their genealogical registration by their families, by their fathers' households, according to the number of names, from twenty years old and upward, whoever *was able to* go out to war,   Num. 26:23-25
29 their numbered men, of the tribe of Issachar, *were* 54,400.

30 [R]Of the sons of Zebulun, their genealogical registration by their families, by their fathers' households, according to the number of names, from twenty years old and upward, whoever *was able to* go out to war,   Num. 26:26, 27
31 their numbered men, of the tribe of Zebulun, *were* 57,400.

32 Of the sons of Joseph, *namely,* of the sons of Ephraim, their genealogical registration by their families, by their fathers' households, according to the number of names, from twenty years old and upward, whoever *was able to* go out to war, 33 their numbered men, of the tribe of Ephraim, *were* 40,500.

34 [R]Of the sons of Manasseh, their genealogical registration by their families, by their fathers' households, according to the number of names, from twenty years old and upward, whoever *was able to* go out to war,   Num. 26:28-34
35 their numbered men, of the tribe of Manasseh, *were* 32,200.

36 [R]Of the sons of Benjamin, their genealogical registration by their families, by their fathers' households, according to the number of names, from twenty years old and upward, whoever *was able to* go out to war,   Gen. 49:27; Num. 26:38-41; 2 Chr. 17:17

37 their numbered men, of the tribe of Benjamin, *were* 35,400.

38 Of the sons of Dan, their genealogical registration by their families, by their fathers' households, according to the number of names, from twenty years old and upward, whoever *was able to* go out to war, 39 their numbered men, of the tribe of Dan, *were* 62,700.

40 Of the sons of Asher, their genealogical registration by their families, by their fathers' households, according to the number of names, from twenty years old and upward, whoever *was able to* go out to war, 41 their numbered men, of the tribe of Asher, *were* 41,500.

42 [R]Of the sons of Naphtali, their genealogical registration by their families, by their fathers' households, according to the number of names, from twenty years old and upward, whoever *was able to* go out to war,   Num. 26:48-50
43 their numbered men, of the tribe of Naphtali, *were* 53,400.

44 These are the ones who were numbered, whom Moses and Aaron numbered, with the leaders of Israel, twelve men, each of whom was of his father's household.

45 So all the numbered men of the sons of Israel by their fathers' households, from twenty years old and upward, whoever *was able to* go out to war in Israel, 46 even all the numbered men were [R]603,550.   Ex. 12:37; 38:26; Num. 2:32; 26:51

47 The Levites, however, were not numbered among them by their fathers' tribe.

48 For the LORD had spoken to Moses, saying,

49"Only the tribe of Levi [R]you shall not number, nor shall you take their [T]census among the sons of Israel.   Num. 26:62 • *sum*

50"But you shall appoint the Levites over the [4]tabernacle of the testimony, and over all its furnishings and over all that belongs to it. They shall carry the tabernacle and all its furnishings, and they shall take care of it; they shall also camp around the tabernacle.

51"So[R] when the tabernacle is to set out, the Levites shall take it down; and when the tabernacle encamps, the Levites shall set it up. But[R]the [5]layman who comes near shall be put to death.   Num. 4:1-33 • Num. 3:10, 38

52"And the sons of Israel shall camp, each man by his own camp, and each man by his own standard, according to their armies.

53"But the Levites shall camp around the tabernacle of the testimony, that there may be[R]no wrath on the congregation of the sons of Israel. So the Levites shall keep charge of the tabernacle of the testimony."   Lev. 10:6

54 Thus the sons of Israel did; according to all which the LORD had commanded Moses, so they did.

---

[4] Lit., *dwelling place,* and so throughout this context
[5] Lit., *stranger*

CHAPTER 2

On the East

Now the Lord spoke to Moses and to Aaron, saying,

2 "The sons of Israel shall camp, each by his own standard, with the ᵀbanners of their fathers' households; they shall camp around the tent of meeting at a distance.   *signs*

3 "Now those who camp on the east side toward the sunrise *shall be* of the standard of the camp of Judah, by their armies, and the leader of the sons of Judah:ᴿNahshon the son of Amminadab,   Num. 1:7; 10:14; Ruth 4:20

4 and his army, even their ᵀnumbered men, 74,600.   *mustered*

5 "And those who camp next to him *shall be* the tribe of Issachar, and the leader of the sons of Issachar:ᴿNethanel the son of Zuar,   Num. 1:8; 7:18, 23

6 and his army, even their numbered men, 54,400.

7 "Then *comes* the tribe of Zebulun, and the leader of the sons of Zebulun:ᴿEliab the son of Helon,   Num. 1:9

8 and his army, even his numbered men, 57,400.

9 "The total of the numbered men of the camp of Judah: 186,400, by their armies. ᴿThey shall set out first.   Num. 10:14

On the South

10 "On the south side *shall be* the standard of the camp of Reuben by their armies, and the leader of the sons of Reuben:ᴿElizur the son of Shedeur,   Num. 1:5

11 and his army, even their numbered men, 46,500.

12 "And those who camp next to him *shall be* the tribe of Simeon, and the leader of the sons of Simeon:ˢShelumiel the son of Zurishaddai,   Num. 1:6

13 and his army, even their numbered men, 59,300.

14 "Then *comes* the tribe of Gad, and the leader of the sons of Gad:ᴿEliasaph the son of Deuel,   Num. 1:14; 7:42

15 and his army, even their numbered men, 45,650.

16 "The total of the numbered men of the camp of Reuben: 151,450 by their armies. Andᴿthey shall set out second.   Num. 10:18

On the Middle

17 "Thenᴿ the tent of meeting shall set out *with* the camp of the Levites in the midst of the camps; just as they camp, so they shall set out, every man in his place, by their standards.   Num. 1:53

On the West

18 "On the west side *shall be* the standard of the camp of Ephraim by their armies, and the leader of the sons of Ephraim *shall be* ᴿElishama the son of Ammihud,   Num. 1:10

19 and his army, even their numbered men, 40,500.

20 "And next to him *shall be* the tribe of Manasseh, and the leader of the sons of Manasseh: Gamaliel the son of Pedahzur,

21 and his army, even their numbered men, 32,200.

22 "Then *comes* the tribe ofᴿBenjamin, and the leader of the sons of Benjamin: ᴬAbidan the son of Gideoni,   Ps. 68:27 · Num. 1:11

23 and his army, even their numbered men, 35,400.

24 "The total of the numbered men of the camp of Ephraim: 108,100, by their armies. Andᴿthey shall set out third.   Num. 10:22

On the North

25 "On the north side *shall be* the standard of the camp of Dan by their armies, and the leader of the sons of Dan: ᴬAhiezer the son of Ammishaddai,   Num. 1:12

26 and his army, even their numbered men, 62,700.

27 "And those who camp next to him *shall be* the tribe of Asher, and the leader of the sons of Asher: Pagiel the son of Ochran,

28 and his army, even their numbered men, 41,500.

29 "Then *comes* the tribe ofᴿNaphtali, and the leader of the sons of Naphtali: ᴿAhira the son of Enan,   Gen. 30:8 · Num. 1:15

30 and his army, even their numbered men, 53,400.

31 "The total of the numbered men of the camp of Dan, *was* 157,600. ᴿThey shall set out last by their standards."   Num. 10:25

The Camp Is Arranged

32 These are the numbered men of the sons of Israel by their fathers' households; the total of the numbered men of the camps by their armies,ᴿ603,550.   Ex. 38:26; Num. 1:46

33 ᴿThe Levites, however, were not numbered among the sons of Israel, just as the Lord had commanded Moses.   Num. 1:47

34 Thus the sons of Israel did; according to all that the Lord commanded Moses, so they camped by their standards, and so they set out, every one by his family, according to his father's household.

CHAPTER 3

The Family of Aaron

Now these are *the records of* the generations of Aaron and Moses at the time when the Lord spoke with Moses on Mount Sinai.

2 ᴿThese then are the names of the sons of Aaron: Nadab the first-born, and Abihu, Eleazar and Ithamar.   Ex. 6:23; Num. 26:60

3 These are the names of the sons of Aaron, theᴿanointed priests, whom he ᵀordained to serve as priests.   Ex. 28:41 · *filled their hand*

4 ᴿBut Nadab and Abihu died before the LORD when they offered strange fire before the LORD in the wilderness of Sinai; and they had no children. So Eleazar and Ithamar served as priestsᵀin the lifetime of their father Aaron.   Lev. 10:1, 2 • *before the face*

5 Then the LORD spoke to Moses, saying,

The Ministry of the Levites

6"Bringᴿthe tribe of Levi near and set them before Aaron the priest, that they may serve him.   Num. 8:6-22; 18:1-7; Deut. 10:8

7"And they shall perform the duties for him and for the whole congregation before the tent of meeting, to do theᴿservice of the tabernacle.   Num. 1:50

8"They shall also keep all the furnishings of the tent of meeting, along with the duties of the sons of Israel, to do the service of the tabernacle.

9"You shall thus give the Levites to Aaron and to his sons; they are wholly given to him from among the sons of Israel.

10"So you shall appoint Aaron and his sons thatᴿthey may keep their priesthood, butᴿtheᵀlayman who comes near shall be put to death."   Ex. 29:9 • Num. 1:51 • *stranger*

11 Again the LORD spoke to Moses, saying,

12"Now, behold, Iᴿhave taken the Levites from among the sons of Israel instead of everyᴿfirst-born, the first issue of the womb among the sons of Israel. So the Levites shall be Mine.   Num. 3:45; 8:14 • Ex. 13:2

13"Forᴿall the first-born are Mine; on the day that I struck down all the first-born in the land of Egypt, I sanctified to Myself all the first-born in Israel, from man to beast. They shall be Mine; I am the LORD." Ex. 13:2

The Census Is Commanded

14 Then the LORD spoke to Mosesᴿin the wilderness of Sinai, saying,   Ex. 19:1

15"Numberᵀthe sons of Levi by their fathers' households, by their families; every male from a month old and upward you shall number."   *muster*

16 So Moses numbered them according to theᵀword of the LORD, just as he had been commanded.   *mouth*

17 These then are the sons of Levi by their names: Gershon and Kohath and Merari.

18 And these are the names of the sons of Gershon by their families: Libni and Shimei;

19 and the sons of Kohath by their families: Amram and Izhar, Hebron and Uzziel;

20 and the sons of Merari by their families: Mahli and Mushi. These are the families of the Levites according to their fathers' households.

The Census of Gershon

21 Of Gershon *was* the family of the Libnites and the family of the Shimeites; these *were* the families of the Gershonites.

22 Their numbered men, in the numbering

of every male from a month old and upward, *even* their numbered men *were* 7,500.

23 The families of the Gershonites were to camp behind the tabernacle westward,

24 and the leader of the fathers' households of the Gershonites *was* Eliasaph the son of Lael.

25 Now the duties of the sons of Gershon in the tent of meeting *involved* the tabernacle and the tent, its covering, and the screen for the doorway of the tent of meeting,

26 andᴿthe hangings of the court, and the screen for the doorway of the court, which is around the tabernacle and the altar, and its cords, according to all the service ᵀconcerning them.   Ex. 27:9, 12, 14, 15 • *of it*

The Census of Kohath

27 And of Kohath *was* the family of the Amramites and the family of the Izharites and the family of the Hebronites and the family of the Uzzielites; these were the families of the Kohathites.

28 In the numbering of every male from a month old and upward, *there were* 8,600, performing the duties of the sanctuary.

29 The families of the sons of Kohath were to camp on the southward side of the tabernacle,

30 and the leader of the fathers' households of the Kohathite families was Elizaphan the son of Uzziel.

31 Nowᴿtheir duties *involved*ᴿthe ark, the table, the lampstand, the altars, and the utensils of the sanctuary with which they minister, and the screen, and all the service ᵀconcerning them;   Num. 4:15 • Ex. 25:10-22 • *of it*

32 and Eleazar the son of Aaron the priest *was* the chief of the leaders of Levi, *and had* the oversight of those who perform the duties of the sanctuary.

The Census of Merari

33 Of Merari *was* the family of the Mahlites and the family of the Mushites; these *were* the families of Merari.

34 Their numbered men in the numbering of every male from a month old and upward, *were* 6,200.

35 And the leader of the fathers' households of the families of Merari *was* Zuriel the son of Abihail. They *were* to camp on the northward side of the tabernacle.

36 Now the appointed duties of the sons of Merari *involved* the frames of the tabernacle, its bars, its pillars, its sockets, all its equipment, and the service concerning them,

37 and the pillars around the court with their sockets and their pegs and their cords.

The Summary of the Census

38 Now those who were to camp before the tabernacle eastward, before the tent of meeting toward the sunrise, are Moses and

Aaron and his sons, performing the duties of the sanctuary for the obligation of the sons of Israel; but^Rthe^Tlayman coming near was to be put to death.   Num. 1:51 • *stranger*

39 All the numbered men of the Levites, whom Moses and Aaron numbered at the ^Tcommand of the LORD by their families, every male from a month old and upward, were^R22,000.   *word* • Num. 3:43; 4:48; 26:62

The Substitution of the Levites
for the First-born

40 Then the LORD said to Moses, "Number^R every first-born male of the sons of Israel from a month old and upward, and^Tmake a list of their names.   Num. 3:15 • *take the number*
41"And you shall take the Levites for Me, I am the LORD, instead of all the first-born among the sons of Israel, and the cattle of the Levites instead of all the first-born among the cattle of the sons of Israel."
42 So Moses numbered all the first-born among the sons of Israel, just as the LORD had commanded him;
43 and all the first-born males by the number of names from a month old and upward, for their numbered men were 22,273.
44 Then the LORD spoke to Moses, saying,
45"Take^Rthe Levites instead of all the first-born among the sons of Israel and the cattle of the Levites. And the Levites shall be Mine; I am the LORD.   Num. 3:12
46"And^Rfor the ransom of the 273 of the first-born of the sons of Israel who are in excess beyond the Levites,   Ex. 13:13, 15
47 you shall take^Rfive shekels apiece, per head; you shall take *them* in terms of the shekel of the sanctuary (the shekel is twenty ⁶gerahs),   Lev. 27:6; Num. 18:16
48 and give the money, the ransom of those who are in excess among them, to Aaron and to his sons."
49 So Moses took the ransom money from those who were in excess, beyond those ransomed by the Levites;
50 from the first-born of the sons of Israel he took the money in terms of the shekel of the sanctuary, 1,365.
51 Then Moses gave the ransom money to Aaron and to his sons, at the ^Tcommand of the LORD, just as the LORD had commanded Moses.   *mouth*

CHAPTER 4

The Ministry of Kohath

THEN the LORD spoke to Moses and to Aaron, saying,
2"Take a census of the descendants of Kohath from among the sons of Levi, by their families, by their fathers' households,
3 from^Rthirty years and upward, even to fifty years old, all who enter the service to do the work in the tent of meeting.   Ezra 3:8

⁶ I.e., A gerah equals approx. one-fortieth ounce

4"This is the work of the^Tdescendants of Kohath in the tent of meeting, *concerning* the most holy things.   *sons*
5"When the camp sets out, Aaron and his sons shall go in and they shall take down ^Rthe veil of the screen and cover the ark of the testimony with it;   Ex. 40:5; Lev. 16:2
6 and they shall lay a covering of porpoise skin on it, and shall spread over *it* a cloth of pure blue, and shall insert its poles.
7"Over the table of the bread of the Presence they shall also spread a cloth of^Ablue and put on it the dishes and the pans and the sacrificial bowls and the jars for the libation, and^Rthe continual bread shall be on it.   *violet* • Ex. 25:30; Lev. 24:5-9
8"And they shall spread over them a cloth of scarlet *material*, and cover the same with a covering of porpoise skin, and they shall insert its poles.
9"Then they shall take a blue cloth and cover the lampstand for the light, along with its lamps and its snuffers, and its trays and all its oil vessels, by which they serve it;
10 and they shall put it and all its utensils in a covering of porpoise skin, and shall put it on the carrying bars.
11"And over the golden altar they shall spread a^Ablue cloth and cover it with a covering of porpoise skin, and shall insert its poles;   *violet*
12 and they shall take all the utensils of service, with which they serve in the sanctuary, and put them in a^Ablue cloth and cover them with a covering of porpoise skin, and put them on the carrying bars.   *violet*
13"Then they shall take away the ^Aashes from the ^Raltar, and spread a purple cloth over it.   *fat ashes* • Ex. 27:1-8
14"They shall also put on it all its utensils by which they serve in connection with it: the firepans, the forks and shovels and the basins, all the utensils of the altar; and they shall spread a cover of porpoise skin over it and insert its poles.
15"And when Aaron and his sons have finished covering the holy *objects* and all the furnishings of the sanctuary, when the camp is to set out, after that the sons of Kohath shall come to carry *them*, so that they may not touch the holy *objects* and die. These are the things in the tent of meeting which the sons of Kohath are to carry.
16"And the responsibility of Eleazar the son of Aaron the priest is^Rthe oil for the light and the fragrant incense and the continual grain offering and the anointing oil—the responsibility of all the ^Atabernacle and of all that is in it, with the sanctuary and its furnishings."   Lev. 24:1-3 • *dwelling place*
17 Then the LORD spoke to Moses and to Aaron, saying,
18"Do not let the tribe of the families of the Kohathites be cut off from among the Levites.
19"But do this to them that they may live and^Rnot die when they approach the most

holy *objects:* Aaron and his sons shall go in and assign each of them to his work and to his load;   Num. 4:15

20 but they shall not go in to see the holy *objects* even for a moment, lest they die."

The Ministry of Gershon

21 Then the LORD spoke to Moses, saying,

22 "Take [T]a census of the sons of Gershon [T]also, by their fathers' households, by their families;   *the sum • also them*

23 from [R]thirty years and upward to fifty years old, you shall [T]number them; all who enter to perform the service to do the work in the tent of meeting.   Num. 4:3 • *muster*

24 "This is the service of the families of the Gershonites, in serving and in carrying:

25 they shall carry [R]the curtains of the tabernacle and the tent of meeting *with* its covering and the covering of porpoise skin that is on top of it, and the screen for the doorway of the tent of meeting,   Ex. 40:19

26 and the hangings of the court, and the screen for the doorway of the gate of the court which is around the tabernacle and the altar, and their cords and all the equipment for their service; and all that is to be done,[T]they shall perform.   *so they shall serve*

27 "All the service of the sons of the Gershonites, in all their loads and in all their work, shall be *performed* at the [T]command of Aaron and his sons; and you shall assign to them as a duty all their loads.   *mouth*

28 "This is the service of the families of the sons of the Gershonites in the tent of meeting, and their duties *shall be* [T]under the direction of Ithamar the son of Aaron the priest.   *in the hand*

The Ministry of Merari

29 "As *for* the sons of Merari, you shall number them by their families, by their fathers' households;

30 from [R]thirty years and upward even to fifty years old, you shall number them, everyone who enters the service to do the work of the tent of meeting.   Num. 4:3

31 "Now this is the duty of their loads, for all their service in the tent of meeting: the boards of the tabernacle and its bars and its pillars and its [A]sockets,   *bases*

32 and the pillars around the court and their sockets and their pegs and their cords, with all their equipment and with all their service; and you shall assign *each man* by name the items he is to carry.   *bases*

33 "This is the service of the families of the sons of Merari, according to all their service in the tent of meeting, under the direction of Ithamar the son of Aaron the priest."

The Census of the Working Levites

34 So Moses and Aaron and the leaders of the congregation numbered the sons of the Kohathites by their families, and by their fathers' households,

35 from thirty years and upward even to fifty years old, everyone who entered the service for work in the tent of meeting.

36 And their numbered men by their families were 2,750.

37 These are the numbered men of the Kohathite families, everyone who was serving in the tent of meeting, whom Moses and Aaron numbered according to the commandment of the LORD through Moses.

38 And the numbered men of the sons of Gershon by their families, and by their fathers' households,

39 from thirty years and upward even to fifty years old, everyone who entered the service for work in the tent of meeting.

40 And their numbered men by their families, by their fathers' households, were 2,630.

41 These are the numbered men of the families of the sons of Gershon, everyone who was serving in the tent of meeting, whom Moses and Aaron numbered according to the commandment of the LORD.

42 And the numbered men of the families of the sons of Merari by their families, by their fathers' households,

43 from thirty years and upward even to fifty years old, everyone who entered the service for work in the tent of meeting.

44 And their numbered men by their families were 3,200.

45 These are the numbered men of the families of the sons of Merari, whom Moses and Aaron numbered according to the commandment of the LORD through Moses.

46 All the numbered men of the Levites, whom Moses and Aaron and the leaders of Israel numbered, by their families and by their fathers' households,

47 from thirty years and upward even to fifty years old, everyone who could enter to do the work of service and the work of carrying in the tent of meeting.

48 And their numbered men were 8,580.

49 According to the commandment of the LORD [T]through Moses, they were numbered, everyone by his serving or carrying; thus these were his numbered men, just as the LORD had commanded Moses.   *by the hand of*

CHAPTER 5

Separation of Unclean Persons

THEN the LORD spoke to Moses, saying,

2 "Command the sons of Israel that they send away from the camp every leper and everyone having a discharge and everyone who is unclean because of a *dead* person.

3 "You shall send away both male and female; you shall send them outside the camp so that they will not defile their camp where I dwell [R]in their midst."   Lev. 26:12; Num. 35:34

4 And the sons of Israel did so and sent them outside the camp; just as the LORD had spoken to Moses, thus the sons of Israel did.

Separation in Restitution for Sin

5 Then the LORD spoke to Moses, saying,
6 "Speak to the sons of Israel, 'When[R] a man or woman commits any of the sins of mankind, acting unfaithfully against the LORD, and that person is guilty,   Lev. 5:14–6:7
7 then[T] he shall[R] confess[T] his sins which[T] he has committed, and he shall make restitution in full for his wrong, and add to it one-fifth of it, and give it to him whom he has wronged.   they • Lev. 5:5; 26:40 • their • they have
8 'But if the man has no [7]relative to whom restitution may be made for the wrong, the restitution which is made for the wrong must go to the LORD for the priest, besides the ram of atonement, by which atonement is made for him.
9 'Also every contribution pertaining to all the holy gifts of the sons of Israel, which they offer to the priest, shall be his.
10 'So every man's holy gifts shall be his; whatever any man gives to the priest, it[R] becomes his.' "   Lev. 10:13

Separation from Suspected Infidelity

11 Then the LORD spoke to Moses, saying,
12 "Speak to the sons of Israel, and say to them, 'If any man's wife[R] goes astray and is unfaithful to him,   Num. 5:19-21, 29
13 and a man has[R] intercourse with her and it is hidden from the eyes of her husband and she is [T]undetected, although she has defiled herself, and there is no witness against her and she has not been caught in the act,   Lev. 18:20; 20:10 • concealed
14 [T]if a spirit of jealousy comes over him and he is jealous of his wife when she has defiled herself, or if a spirit of jealousy comes over him and he is jealous of his wife when she has not defiled herself,   and
15 the man shall then bring his wife to the priest, and shall bring as[T] an offering for her one-tenth of an [T]ephah of barley meal; he shall not pour oil on it, nor put frankincense on it, for it is a grain offering of jealousy, a grain offering of memorial,[R] a reminder of iniquity.   her • Approx. one bu. • 1 Kin. 17:18
16 'Then the priest shall bring her near and have her stand before the LORD,
17 and the priest shall take holy water in an earthenware vessel; and he shall take some of the dust that is on the floor of the tabernacle and put it into the water.
18 'The priest shall then have the woman stand before the LORD and let the hair of the woman's head go loose, and place the grain offering of memorial[T] in her hands, which is the grain offering of jealousy, and in the hand of the priest is to be the water of bitterness that brings a curse.   on her palms

[7] Lit., redeemer

19 'And the priest shall have her take an oath and shall say to the woman, "If no man has lain with you and if you have not gone astray into uncleanness, being under the authority of your husband, be immune to this water of bitterness that brings a curse;
20 if you, however, have [R]gone astray, being under the authority of your husband, and if you have defiled yourself and a man other than your husband has had intercourse with you"   Num. 5:12
21 (then the priest shall have the woman swear with the oath of the curse, and the priest shall say to the woman), "the LORD make you a curse and an oath among your people by the LORD's making your thigh [T]waste away and your abdomen swell;   fall
22 and this water that brings a curse shall go into your stomach, and make your abdomen swell and your thigh[T] waste away." And the woman shall say, "Amen. Amen."   fall
23 'The priest shall then write these curses on a scroll, and he shall[T] wash them off into the water of bitterness.   wipe
24 'Then he shall make the woman drink the water of bitterness that brings a curse, so that the water which brings a curse will go into her [T]and cause bitterness.   to
25 'And the priest shall take the grain offering of jealousy from the woman's hand, and he shall wave the grain offering before the LORD and bring it to the altar;
26 and[R] the priest shall take a handful of the grain offering as its memorial offering and offer it up in smoke on the altar, and afterward he shall make the woman drink the water.   Lev. 2:2, 9
27 'When he has made her drink the water, then it shall come about, if she has defiled herself and has been unfaithful to her husband, that the water which brings a curse shall go into her [T]and cause bitterness, and her abdomen will swell and her thigh will [T]waste away, and the woman will become[R] a curse among her people.   to • fall • Jer. 29:18
28 'But if the woman has not defiled herself and is clean, she will then be free and conceive[T] children.   seed
29 'This is the law of jealousy: when a wife, being under the authority of her husband, goes astray and defiles herself,
30 or when a spirit of jealousy comes over a man and he is jealous of his wife, he shall then make the woman stand before the LORD, and the priest shall apply all this law to her.
31 'Moreover, the man shall be free from guilt, but that woman shall bear her guilt.' "

CHAPTER 6

Sanctification
Through the Nazirite Vow

AGAIN the LORD spoke to Moses, saying,
2 "Speak to the sons of Israel, and say to

them, 'When a man or woman makes a^special vow, the vow of a [8]Nazirite, to^dedicate himself to the LORD,   *difficult • live as a Nazirite*

3 he shall^Rabstain from wine and strong drink; he shall drink no vinegar, whether made from wine or strong drink, neither shall he drink any grape juice, nor eat fresh or dried grapes.   Luke 1:15

4 'All the days of his [9]separation he shall not eat anything that is produced by the grape vine, from *the* seeds even to *the* skin.

5 'All the days of his vow of separation no razor shall pass over his head. He shall be holy until the days are fulfilled for which he separated himself to the LORD; he shall let the locks of hair on his head grow long.

6 'All the days of his separation to the LORD he shall not go near to a dead person.

7 'He^Rshall not make himself unclean for his father or for his mother, for his brother or for his sister, when they die, because his separation to God is on his head.   Num. 9:6

8 'All the days of his separation he is holy to the LORD.

9 'But if a man dies very suddenly beside him and he defiles his dedicated head *of hair,* then^Rhe shall shave his head on the day when he becomes clean;^Rhe shall shave it on the seventh day.   Lev. 14:8, 9 • Num. 6:18

10 'Then on the eighth day he shall bring ^Rtwo turtledoves or two young pigeons to the priest, to the doorway of the tent of meeting.   Lev. 5:7; 14:22

11 'And the priest shall offer one for a sin offering and *the* other for a burnt offering, and make atonement for him concerning his sin because of the *dead* person. And that same day he shall consecrate his head,

12 and shall dedicate to the LORD his days ^Aas a^TNazirite, and shall bring a male lamb a year old for a guilt offering; but the former days shall be void because his separation was defiled.   *of dedication • one separated*

13 'Now this is the law of the Nazirite ^Rwhen the days of his separation are fulfilled, he shall bring^Tthe offering to the doorway of the tent of meeting.   Acts 21:26 • *it*

14 'And he shall present his offering to the LORD: one male lamb a year old without defect for a burnt offering and one^Rewe-lamb a year old without defect for a sin offering and one ram without defect for a peace offering,   Lev. 14:10; Num. 15:27

15 and a basket of ^Runleavened cakes of fine flour mixed with oil and unleavened wafers spread with oil, along with their grain offering and their libations.   Ex. 29:2

16 'Then the priest shall present *them* before the LORD and shall offer his sin offering and his burnt offering.

17 'He shall also offer the ram for a sacrifice of peace offerings to the LORD, together with the basket of unleavened cakes; the priest shall likewise offer its grain offering and its libation.

18 'The Nazirite shall then shave his dedi-

cated head *of hair* at the doorway of the tent of meeting, and take the dedicated hair of his head and put *it* on the fire which is under the sacrifice of peace offerings.

19 'And^R the priest shall take the ram's shoulder *when it has been* boiled, and one unleavened cake out of the basket, and one unleavened wafer, and shall put *them* on the ^Thands of the Nazirite after he has shaved his ^Adedicated *hair.*   Lev. 7:28-34 • *palms • separated*

20 'Then the priest shall wave them for a wave offering before the LORD. It is holy for the priest, together with the breast offered by waving and the thigh offered by lifting up; and ^Rafterward the Nazirite may drink wine.'   Eccl. 9:7

21 "This is the law of the Nazirite who vows his offering to the LORD according to his separation, in addition to what *else*^The can afford; according to his vow which he takes, so he shall do according to the law of his separation."   *his hand can reach*

22 Then the LORD spoke to Moses, saying,

23 "Speak to Aaron and to his sons, saying, 'Thus^Ryou shall bless the sons of Israel. You shall say to them: 1 Chr. 23:13

24   The LORD bless you, and keep you;

25   The LORD^Rmake His face shine on you, And be gracious to you;   Ps. 80:3, 7, 19

26   The LORD^Rlift up His countenance on you,   Ps. 4:6; 44:3

     And^Rgive you peace.'   Ps. 29:11; 37:37

27 "So they shall invoke My name on the sons of Israel, and I then will bless them."

CHAPTER 7

Israel Gives Donations

NOW it came about on^Rthe day that Moses had finished setting up the tabernacle, he ^Ranointed it and consecrated it with all its furnishings and the altar and all its utensils; he anointed them and consecrated them also.   Ex. 40:17 • Ex. 40:9-11; Num. 7:10, 84, 88

2 Then^Rthe leaders of Israel, the heads of their fathers' households, made an offering (they were the leaders of the tribes; they were the ones who^Twere over the^Tnumbered men).   Num. 1:5-16 • *stood • mustered*

3 When they brought their offering before the LORD, six^Rcovered carts and twelve oxen, a cart for *every* two of the leaders and an ox for each one, then they presented them before the tabernacle.   Is. 66:20

4 Then the LORD spoke to Moses, saying,

5 "Accept *these things* from them, that they may be^Tused in the service of the tent of meeting, and you shall give them to the Levites, *to* each man according to his service."   *for serving*

6 So Moses took the carts and the oxen, and gave them to the Levites.

[8] I.e., one separated
[9] Or, *living as a Nazirite,* and so through v. 21

7 Two carts and four oxen he gave to the sons of Gershon, according to their service, 8 and four carts and eight oxen he gave to the sons of Merari, according to ^Rtheir service, under the ^Tdirection of Ithamar the son of Aaron the priest.   Num. 4:31, 32 · *hand*

9 But he did not give *any* to the sons of Kohath because theirs *was* ^Rthe service of the holy *objects, which* they carried on the shoulder.   Num. 4:5-15

10 And the leaders offered the dedication *offering*^Tfor the altar^Twhen^Rit was anointed, so the leaders offered their offering before the altar.   *of · in the day that* · Num. 7:1

11 Then the LORD said to Moses, "Let them present their offering, one leader each day, for the dedication of the altar."

12 Now the one who presented his offering on the first day *was* Nahshon the son of Amminadab, of the tribe of Judah;

13 and his offering *was* one silver ¹⁰dish whose weight *was*^Tone hundred and thirty *shekels,* one silver bowl of^Tseventy shekels, according to ¹¹the shekel of the sanctuary, both of them full of fine flour mixed with oil for a grain offering; $16,640 · $8,960

14 one gold pan of^Tten *shekels,* full of incense; $19,200

15 one^Abull, one ram, one male lamb one year old, for a burnt offering; *bull of the herd*

16 one male goat for a sin offering;

17 and for the sacrifice of peace offerings, two oxen, five rams, five male goats, five male lambs one year old. This *was* the offering of Nahshon the son of Amminadab.

18 On the second day Nethanel the son of Zuar, leader of Issachar, presented *an offering;*

19 he presented as his offering one silver dish whose weight *was* one hundred and thirty *shekels,* one silver bowl of seventy shekels, according to the shekel of the sanctuary, both of them full of fine flour mixed with oil for a grain offering;

20 one gold pan of ten *shekels,* full of incense;

21 one bull, one ram, one male lamb one year old, for a burnt offering;

22 one male goat for a sin offering;

23 and for the sacrifice of^Rpeace offerings, two oxen, five rams, five male goats, five male lambs one year old. This *was* the offering of Nethanel the son of Zuar. Lev. 7:11-13

24 On the third day *it was* Eliab the son of Helon, leader of the sons of Zebulun;

25 his offering *was* one silver dish whose weight *was* one hundred and thirty *shekels,* one silver bowl of seventy shekels, according to the shekel of the sanctuary, both of them full of fine flour mixed with oil for a grain offering;

26 one gold pan of ten *shekels,* full of incense;

27 one young bull, one ram, one male lamb one year old, for a burnt offering;

28 one male goat for a sin offering;

29 and for the sacrifice of peace offerings, two oxen, five rams, five male goats, five male lambs one year old. This *was* the offering of Eliab the son of Helon.

30 On the fourth day *it was* Elizur the son of Shedeur, leader of the sons of Reuben;

31 his offering *was* one silver dish whose weight *was* one hundred and thirty *shekels,* one silver bowl of seventy shekels, according to the shekel of the sanctuary, both of them full of fine flour mixed with oil for a grain offering;

32 one gold pan of ten *shekels,* full of incense;

33 one bull, one ram, one^Rmale lamb one year old, for a burnt offering; [Heb. 9:28]

34 one male goat for a sin offering;

35 and for the sacrifice of peace offerings, two oxen, five rams, five male goats, five male lambs one year old. This *was* the offering of Elizur the son of Shedeur.

36 On the fifth day *it was* Shelumiel the son of Zurishaddai, leader of the children of Simeon;

37 his offering *was* one silver dish whose weight *was* one hundred and thirty *shekels,* one silver bowl of seventy shekels, according to the shekel of the sanctuary, both of them full of fine flour mixed with oil for a grain offering;

38 one gold pan of ten *shekels,* full of incense;

39 one bull, one ram, one male lamb one year old, for a burnt offering;

40 one male goat for a sin offering;

41 and for the sacrifice of peace offerings, two oxen, five rams, five male goats, five male lambs one year old. This *was* the offering of Shelumiel the son of Zurishaddai.

42 On the sixth day *it was* Eliasaph the son of Deuel, leader of the sons of Gad;

43 his offering *was* one silver dish whose weight *was* one hundred and thirty *shekels,* one silver bowl of seventy shekels, according to the shekel of the sanctuary, both of them full of^Rfine flour mixed with oil for a grain offering;   Lev. 2:5; 14:10

44 one gold pan of ten *shekels,* full of incense;

45 ^Rone bull, one ram, one male lamb one year old, for a burnt offering; Ps. 50:8-14

46 one male goat for a sin offering;

47 and for the sacrifice of peace offerings, two oxen, five rams, five male goats, five male lambs one year old. This *was* the offering of Eliasaph the son of Deuel.^R

48 On the seventh day *it was*^RElishama the son of Ammihud, leader of the sons of Ephraim;   Num. 1:10; 2:18; 1 Chr. 7:26

49 his offering *was* one silver dish whose weight *was* one hundred and thirty *shekels,* one silver bowl of seventy shekels, according to the shekel of the sanctuary, both of

---

¹⁰ Or, *platter,* and so through v. 85
¹¹ I.e., Approx. one-half ounce, and so through v. 86

them full of fine flour mixed with oil for a grain offering;

50 one gold pan of ten *shekels,* full of [R]incense;   Deut. 33:10; Ezek. 8:11; Luke 1:10

51 [R]one bull, one ram, one male lamb one year old, for a burnt offering;   [Mic. 6:6-8]

52 one male goat for a sin offering;

53 and for the sacrifice of peace offerings, two oxen, five rams, five male goats, five male lambs one year old. This *was* the offering of Elishama the son of Ammihud.

54 On the eighth day *it was* [R]Gamaliel the son of Pedahzur, leader of the sons of Manasseh;   Num. 2:20

55 his offering *was* one silver dish whose weight *was* one hundred and thirty *shekels,* one silver bowl of seventy shekels, according to the shekel of the sanctuary, both of them full of fine flour mixed with oil for a grain offering;

56 one gold pan of ten *shekels,* full of [R]incense;   Ex. 30:7

57 one bull, one ram, one [R]male lamb one year old, for a burnt offering;   Ex. 12:5

58 one male goat for a sin offering;

59 and for the sacrifice of peace offerings, two oxen, five rams, five male goats, five male lambs one year old. This *was* the offering of Gamaliel the son of Pedahzur.

60 On the ninth day *it was* Abidan the son of Gideoni, leader of the sons of Benjamin;

61 his offering *was* one silver dish whose weight *was* one hundred and thirty *shekels,* one silver bowl of seventy shekels, according to the shekel of the sanctuary, both of them full of fine flour mixed with oil for a grain offering;

62 one gold pan of ten *shekels,* full of [R]incense;   [Rev. 5:8; 8:3, 4]

63 one bull, one ram, one male lamb one year old, for a burnt offering;

64 one male goat for a sin offering;

65 and for the sacrifice of [R]peace offerings, two oxen, five rams, five male goats, five male lambs one year old. This *was* the offering of Abidan the son of Gideoni.   Col. 1:20

66 On the tenth day *it was* [R]Ahiezer the son of Ammishaddai, leader of the sons of Dan;   Num. 1:12; 2:25

67 his offering *was* one silver dish whose weight *was* one hundred and thirty *shekels,* one silver bowl of seventy shekels, according to the [R]shekel of the sanctuary, both of them full of fine flour mixed with oil for a grain offering;   Ex. 30:13; Lev. 27:25

68 one gold pan of ten *shekels,* full of [R]incense;   Ps. 141:2

69 one bull, one ram, one male lamb one year old, for a burnt offering;

70 one male goat for a sin offering;

71 and for the sacrifice of peace offerings, two oxen, five rams, five male goats, five male lambs one year old. This *was* the offering of Ahiezer the son of Ammishaddai.

72 On the eleventh day *it was* Pagiel the son of Ochran, leader of the sons of Asher;

73 his offering *was* one silver dish whose weight *was* one hundred and thirty *shekels,* one silver bowl of seventy shekels, according to the shekel of the sanctuary, both of them full of fine flour mixed with oil for a grain offering;

74 one gold pan of ten *shekels,* full of [R]incense;   Mal. 1:11

75 one bull, one ram, one male lamb one year old, for a burnt offering;

76 one male goat for a sin offering;

77 and for the sacrifice of peace offerings, two oxen, five rams, five male goats, five male lambs one year old. This *was* the offering of Pagiel the son of Ochran.

78 On the twelfth day *it was* Ahira the son of Enan, leader of the sons of Naphtali;

79 his offering *was* one [R]silver dish whose weight *was* one hundred and thirty *shekels,* one silver bowl of seventy shekels, according to the shekel of the sanctuary, both of them full of fine flour mixed with oil for a grain offering;   Ezra 1:9, 10; Dan. 5:2

80 one gold pan of ten *shekels,* full of incense;

81 one bull, one ram, one male lamb one year old, for a burnt offering;

82 one male goat for a sin offering;

83 and for the sacrifice of peace offerings, two oxen, five rams, five male goats, five male lambs one year old. This *was* the offering of Ahira the son of Enan.

84 This *was* the dedication *offering*[T] for the altar from the leaders of Israel[T] when it was anointed: twelve silver dishes, twelve silver bowls, twelve gold pans,   *of · in the day that*

85 each silver dish *weighing* one hundred and thirty *shekels* and each bowl seventy; all the silver of the utensils *was* 2,400 *shekels,* according to the shekel of the sanctuary;

86 the twelve gold pans, full of incense, *weighing* ten *shekels* apiece, according to the [R]shekel of the sanctuary, all the gold of the pans[T] 120 *shekels;*   Ex. 30:13 · $230,400

87 all the oxen for the burnt offering twelve bulls, *all* the rams twelve, the male lambs one year old with their grain offering twelve, and the male goats for a sin offering twelve;

88 and all the oxen for the sacrifice of peace offerings 24 bulls, *all* the rams 60, the male goats 60, the male lambs one year old 60.[R] This *was* the dedication *offering* for the altar after it was anointed.   Num. 7:1, 10

89 Now when[R] Moses went into the tent of meeting to speak with Him, he heard the voice speaking to him from above the[T] mercy seat that was on the ark of the testimony, from between the two cherubim, so He spoke to him.   Ex. 40:34, 35 · *propitiatory*

CHAPTER 8

The Levites Are Consecrated

THEN the LORD spoke to Moses, saying, 2 "Speak to Aaron and say to him, 'When

you mount the lamps, the seven lamps will give light in the front of the lampstand.'"

3 Aaron therefore did so; he ᵀmounted its lamps at the front of the lampstand, just as the LORD had commanded Moses.   *raised up*

4 ᴿNow this was the workmanship of the lampstand, hammered work of gold; from its base to its flowers, it was hammered work; ᴿaccording to the pattern which the LORD had showed Moses, so he made the lampstand.   Ex. 25:31-40 • Ex. 25:9, 31-40; 26:30

5 Again the LORD spoke to Moses, saying,

6"Take the Levites from among the sons of Israel and ᵀcleanse them.   Is. 52:11

7"And thus you shall do to them, for their ᵀcleansing: *sprinkle*ᵀpurifying water on them, and let them use a razor over their whole ᵀbody, and wash their clothes, and they shall be clean.   *this their cleansing • water of sin • flesh*

8"Then let them take a bull with its grain offering, fine flour mixed with oil; and a second bull you shall take for a sin offering.

9"So you shall present the Levites before the tent of meeting. You shall also assemble the whole congregation of the sons of Israel,

10 and present the Levites before the LORD; and the sons of Israel ᴿshall lay their hands on the Levites.   Lev. 1:4

11"Aaron then shall ᵀpresent the Levites before the LORD as a wave offering from the sons of Israel, that they may ᵀqualify to perform the service of the LORD.   *wave • be able*

12"Now ᴿthe Levites shall lay their hands on the heads of the bulls; then offer the one for a sin offering and the other for a burnt offering to the LORD, to make atonement for the Levites.   Ex. 29:10

13"And you shall have the Levites stand before Aaron and before his sons so as to present them as a wave offering to the LORD.

14"Thus you shall separate the Levites from among the sons of Israel, and ᴿthe Levites shall be Mine.   Num. 3:12; 16:9

15"Then after that the Levites may go in to serve the tent of meeting. But you shall cleanse them and ᴿpresent them as a wave offering;   Ex. 29:24

16 for they are wholly given to Me from among the sons of Israel. I have taken them for Myself instead of every first issue of the womb, the first-born of all the sons of Israel.

17"For ᴿevery first-born among the sons of Israel is Mine, among the men and among the animals; on the day that I struck down all the first-born in the land of Egypt I sanctified them for Myself.   Ex. 13:2, 12, 13, 15

18"But I have taken the Levites instead of every first-born among the sons of Israel.

19"And I have given the Levites as ᵀa gift to Aaron and to his sons from among the sons of Israel, to perform the service of the sons of Israel at the tent of meeting, and to make atonement on behalf of the sons of Israel, that there may be no plague among the

sons of Israel by ᵀtheir coming near to the sanctuary."   *given ones • the sons of Israel's*

20 Thus did Moses and Aaron and all the congregation of the sons of Israel to the Levites; according to all that the LORD had commanded Moses concerning the Levites, so the sons of Israel did to them.

21 ᴿThe Levites, too, purified themselves from sin and washed their clothes; and Aaron presented them as a wave offering before the LORD. Aaron also made atonement for them to cleanse them.   Num. 8:7

22 Then after that the Levites went in to perform their service in the tent of meeting before Aaron and before his sons; just as the LORD had commanded Moses concerning the Levites, so they did to them.

23 Now the LORD spoke to Moses, saying,

24"This is what *applies* to the Levites: from ᴿtwenty-five years old and upward ᵀthey shall enter to perform service in the work of the tent of meeting.   Num. 4:3 • *he*

25"But at the age of fifty years they shall ᵀretire from service in the work and not work any more.   *return*

26"They may, however, ᵀassist their brothers in the tent of meeting,ᴿto keep an obligation; but they *themselves* shall do no work. Thus you shall deal with the Levites concerning their obligations."   *serve* • Num. 1:53

CHAPTER 9

The Passover Is Celebrated

THUS the LORD spoke to Moses in the wilderness of Sinai, in ᴿthe first month of the second year after they had come out of the land of Egypt, saying,   Ex. 40:2, 17; Num. 1:1

2"Now, let the sons of Israel observe the Passover at ᴿits appointed time.   Ex. 12:6

3"On the fourteenth day of this month, ᴵat twilight, you shall observe it at its appointed time; you shall observe it according to all its statutes and according to all its ordinances."   *between the two evenings*

4 So Moses ᵀtold the sons of Israel to observe the Passover.   *spoke to*

5 And they observed the Passover in the first *month,* on the fourteenth day of the month, at twilight, in the wilderness of Sinai; according to all that the LORD had commanded Moses, so the sons of Israel did.

6 But there were *some* men who were ᴿunclean because of the ᵀdead person, so that they could not observe Passover on that day; so they came before Moses and Aaron on that day.   Num. 5:2; 19:11-22 • *soul of man*

7 And those men said to him, "Though we are unclean because of the ᵀdead person, why are we restrained from presenting the offering of the LORD at its appointed time among the sons of Israel?"   *soul of man*

8 Moses therefore said to them, "Wait,ᵀ and I will listen to what the LORD will command concerning you."   *Stand*

9 Then the LORD spoke to Moses, saying,
10 "Speak to the sons of Israel, saying, 'If any one of you or of your generations becomes unclean because of a *dead*[T]person, or is on a distant journey, he may, however, observe the Passover to the LORD.   *soul*
11 'In the second month on the [R]fourteenth day at twilight, they shall observe it; they [R]shall eat it with unleavened bread and bitter herbs.   2 Chr. 30:2, 15 • Ex. 12:8
12 'They[R]shall leave none of it until morning, [R]nor break a bone of it; according to all the statute of the Passover they shall observe it.   Ex. 12:10 • Ex. 12:46; [John 19:36]☆
13 'But the man who is clean and is not on a journey, and yet [A]neglects to observe the Passover, that[T]person shall then be cut off from his people, for he did not present the offering of the LORD at its appointed time. That man shall bear his sin.   *ceases • soul*
14 'And if an alien sojourns among you and observes the Passover to the LORD, according to the statute of the Passover and according to its ordinance, so he shall do; you shall have one statute, both for the alien and for the native of the land.' "

Guidance of the Cloud

15 Now on [R]the day that the tabernacle was erected the cloud covered the tabernacle, the tent of the testimony, and in the evening it was like the appearance of fire over the tabernacle, until morning.   Ex. 40:2, 17
16 So it was continuously; [R]the cloud would cover it *by day*, and the appearance of fire by night.   Ex. 40:34; Neh. 9:12
17 [R]And whenever the cloud was lifted from over the tent, afterward the sons of Israel would then set out; and in the place where the cloud settled down, there the sons of Israel would camp.   Ex. 40:36-38
18 At the [T]command of the LORD the sons of Israel would set out, and at the[T]command of the LORD they would camp;[R]as long as the cloud settled over the tabernacle, they remained camped.   *mouth • 1 Cor. 10:1*
19 Even when the cloud lingered over the tabernacle for many days,[T]the sons of Israel would keep the LORD's charge and not set out.   *and the*
20 If[T]sometimes the cloud remained a few days over the tabernacle, according to the [T]command of the LORD they remained camped. Then according to the[T]command of the LORD they set out.   *it was that • mouth*
21 If[T]sometimes the cloud[T]remained from evening until morning, when the cloud was lifted in the morning, they would move out; or *if it remained* in the daytime and at night, whenever the cloud was lifted, they would set out.   *it was that • was*
22 Whether it was two days or a month or a year that the cloud lingered over the tabernacle, staying above it, the sons of Israel remained camped and did not set out; but when it was lifted, they did set out.
23 [R]At the [T]command of the LORD they

camped, and at the[T]command of the LORD they set out; they kept the LORD's charge, according to the [T]command of the LORD through Moses.   Ps. 73:24; 107:7 • *mouth*

CHAPTER 10

Guidance of the Silver Trumpets

THE LORD spoke further to Moses, saying,
2 "Make yourself two trumpets of silver, of hammered work you shall make them; and you shall use them for[R]summoning the congregation and for having the camps set out.   Is. 1:13
3 "And[R]when both are blown, all the congregation shall gather themselves to you at the doorway of the tent of meeting.   Jer. 4:5
4 "Yet if *only* one is blown, then the leaders, the heads of the[T]divisions of Israel, shall assemble before you.   *thousands;* or, *clans*
5 "But when you blow an alarm, the camps that are pitched[R]on the east side shall set out.   Num. 10:14
6 "And when you blow an alarm the second time, the camps that are pitched on[R]the south side shall set out; an alarm is to be blown for them to set out.   Num. 10:18
7 "When convening the assembly, however, you shall blow without[R]sounding an alarm.   Joel 2:1
8 "The[R] priestly sons of Aaron, moreover, shall blow the trumpets; and[T]this shall be for you a perpetual statute throughout your generations.   Num. 31:6; Josh. 6:4 • *it*
9 "And when you go to war in your land against the adversary who[R]attacks you, then you shall sound an alarm with the trumpets, that you may be remembered before the LORD your God, and be saved from your enemies.   Judg. 2:18; 1 Sam. 10:18; Ps. 106:42
10 "Also in the day of your gladness and in your appointed[A]feasts, and on the first *days* of your months, you shall blow the trumpets over your burnt offerings, and over the sacrifices of your peace offerings; and they shall be as a reminder of you before your God. I am the LORD your God."   *times*

Israel Departs Mount Sinai

11 Now it came about in the second year, in the second month, on the twentieth of the month, that the cloud was lifted from over the tabernacle of the testimony;
12 and the sons of Israel set out on[R]their journeys from the wilderness of Sinai. Then the cloud settled down in the[R]wilderness of Paran.   Ex. 40:36 • Gen. 21:21; Num. 12:16
13 [R]So they moved out for the first time according to the [T]commandment of the LORD through Moses.   Deut. 1:6 • *mouth*
14 And the standard of the camp of the sons of Judah, according to their armies,[R]set out first, with Nahshon the son of Amminadab, over its army,   Num. 2:3-9
15 and Nethanel the son of Zuar, over the tribal army of the sons of Issachar;

16 and Eliab the son of Helon over the tribal army of the sons of Zebulun.

17 [R]Then the tabernacle was taken down; and the sons of Gershon and the sons of Merari, who were carrying the tabernacle, set out.   Num. 4:21-32

18 Next the standard of the camp of Reuben, according to their armies, set out with Elizur the son of Shedeur, over its army,

19 and Shelumiel the son of Zurishaddai over the tribal army of the sons of Simeon,

20 and Eliasaph the son of Deuel was over the tribal army of the sons of Gad.

21 [R]Then the Kohathites set out, carrying the holy *objects;* and the tabernacle was set up before their arrival.   Num. 4:4-20

22 [R]Next the standard of the camp of the sons of Ephraim, according to their armies, was set out, with Elishama the son of Ammihud over its army,   Num. 2:18-24

23 and Gamaliel the son of Pedahzur over the tribal army of the sons of Manasseh;

24 and Abidan the son of Gideoni over the tribal army of the sons of Benjamin.

25 [R]Then the standard of the camp of the sons of Dan, according to their armies, *which formed* the rear guard for all the camps, set out, with Ahiezer the son of Ammishaddai over its army,   Num. 2:25-31

26 and Pagiel the son of Ochran over the tribal army of the sons of Asher;

27 and Ahira the son of Enan over the tribal army of the sons of Naphtali.

28 This was the order of march of the sons of Israel by their armies as they set out.

29 Then Moses said to Hobab the son of Reuel the Midianite, Moses' father-in-law, "We are setting out to the place of which the LORD said, 'I will give it to you'; come with us and we will do you good, for the LORD has promised good concerning Israel."

30 But he said to him, "I[R] will not come, but rather will go to my *own* land and relatives."   Judg. 1:16; Matt. 21:28, 29

31 Then he said, "Please do not leave us, inasmuch as you know where we should camp in the wilderness, and you[R] will be as eyes for us.   Job 29:15

32 "So it will be, if you go with us, it will come about that whatever good the LORD [T]does for us, we will do for you."   *does good*

33 Thus they set out from the mount of the LORD three days' journey, with the ark of the covenant of the LORD journeying in front of them for the [T]three days, to seek out a resting place for them.   *three days' journey*

34 [R]And the cloud of the LORD was over them by day, when they set out from the camp.   Num. 9:15-23

35 Then it came about when the ark set out that Moses said,

  "Rise[R] up, O LORD!   Ps. 68:1, 2; Is. 17:12-14
  And let Thine enemies be scattered,
  And let those[R] who hate Thee flee [12]before Thee."   Deut. 7:10; 32:41

36 And when it came to rest, he said,
  "Return[R] Thou, O LORD,   Is. 63:17
  To the myriad thousands of Israel."

CHAPTER 11

*Israel Complains
About Circumstances*

NOW the people became like [R]those who complain of adversity in the hearing of the LORD; and when the LORD heard *it*, His anger was kindled, and the fire of the LORD burned among them and consumed *some* of the outskirts of the camp.   Num. 14:2; 16:11

2 [R]The people therefore cried out to Moses, and Moses prayed to the LORD, and the fire [T]died out.   Num. 12:11, 13 · *sank down*

3 So the name of that place was called [13]Taberah,[R] because the fire of the LORD burned among them.   Deut. 9:22

Israel Complains About Food

4 And the[R] rabble who were among them [T]had greedy desires; and also the sons of Israel wept again and said, "Who will give us [T]meat to eat?   Ex. 12:38 · *desired a desire · flesh*

5 "We[R] remember the fish which we used to eat free in Egypt, the cucumbers and the melons and the leeks and the onions and the garlic,   Ex. 16:3

6 but now our [14]appetite is gone. There is nothing at all to look at except this manna."

7 [R]Now the manna was like coriander seed, and its appearance like that of[R] bdellium.   Ex. 16:31 · Gen. 2:12

8 The people would go about and gather *it* and grind *it* between two millstones or beat *it* in the mortar, and boil *it* in the pot and make cakes with it; and its taste was as the taste of [T]cakes baked with oil.   *juice of oil*

9 And when the dew fell on the camp at night, the manna would fall[T] with it.   *on*

Moses Complains About the People

10 Now Moses heard the people weeping throughout their families, each man at the doorway of his tent; and the anger of the LORD was kindled greatly, and [T]Moses was displeased.   it was *evil in Moses' sight*

11 [R]So Moses said to the LORD, "Why hast Thou [15]been so hard on Thy servant? And why have I not found favor in Thy sight, that Thou hast laid the burden of all this people on me?   Ex. 5:22; Deut. 1:12

12 "Was it I who conceived all this people? Was it I who brought them forth, that Thou shouldest say to me, 'Carry them in your bosom as a[T] nurse carries a nursing infant, to the land which[R] Thou didst swear to their fathers'?   *foster-father* · Gen. 24:7; Ex. 13:5, 11

13 "Where am I to get meat to give to all this people? For they weep before me, saying, 'Give us meat that we may eat!'

*Moses Complains
About His Own Life*

14 "I[R] alone am not able to carry all this

people, because it is too [T]burdensome for me.   Ex. 18:18; Deut. 1:12 • *heavy*

15 "So[R] if Thou art going to deal thus with me, please kill me at once, if I have found favor in Thy sight, and do not let me see my wretchedness."   Ex. 32:32

God Provides for Moses

16 The LORD therefore said to Moses, "Gather for Me[R]seventy men from the elders of Israel, whom you know to be the elders of the people and their officers and bring them to the tent of meeting, and let them take their stand there with you.   Ex. 24:1, 9

17 "Then[R] I will come down and speak with you there, and I will take of[T]the Spirit who is upon you, and will put *Him* upon them; and they shall bear the burden of the people with you, so that you shall not bear *it* all alone.   Num. 11:25 • 1 Sam. 10:6; [Joel 2:28]

18 "And say to the people, 'Consecrate[R] yourselves for tomorrow, and you shall eat meat; for you have wept in the ears of the LORD, saying, "Oh that someone would give us meat to eat! For we were well-off in Egypt." Therefore the LORD will give you meat and you shall eat.   Ex. 19:10, 22

19 'You shall eat, not one day, nor two days, nor five days, nor ten days, nor twenty days,

20 [T]but a whole month, until it comes out of your nostrils and becomes loathsome to you; because[R]you have rejected the LORD who is among you and have wept before Him, saying, "Why did we ever leave Egypt?" ' "   *until* • Josh. 24:27; 1 Sam. 10:19

21 But Moses said, "The people, among whom I am, are 600,000 on foot; yet Thou hast said, 'I will give them meat in order that they may eat for a whole month.'

22 "Should flocks and herds be slaughtered for them, to be sufficient for them? Or should all the fish of the sea be gathered together for them, to be sufficient for them?"

23 And the LORD said to Moses, "Is[T]the LORD's [T]power limited? Now you shall see whether My word will[T]come true for you or not."   Is. 50:2; 59:1 • *hand short* • *befall you*

24 So Moses went out and[R]told the people the words of the LORD. Also, he gathered seventy men of the elders of the people, and stationed them around the tent.   Num. 11:16

25 Then the LORD came down in the cloud and spoke to him; and He took of the Spirit who was upon him and placed *Him* upon the seventy elders. And it came about that when the Spirit rested upon them, they prophesied. But they did not do *it* again.

26 But two men had remained in the camp; the name of one was Eldad and the name of the [T]other Medad. And[R]the Spirit rested upon them (now they were among those who had been registered, but had not gone out to the tent), and they prophesied in the camp.   *second* • Num. 24:2; 1 Sam. 10:6

27 So a young man ran and told Moses

and said, "Eldad and Medad are prophesying in the camp."

28 Then Joshua the son of Nun, the attendant of Moses from his youth, answered and said, "Moses, my lord, restrain them."

29 But Moses said to him, "Are you jealous for my sake?[R]Would that all the LORD's people were prophets, that the LORD would put His Spirit upon them!"   1 Cor. 14:5

30 Then Moses[T]returned to the camp, *both* he and the elders of Israel.   *removed himself*

God Provides Quail

31 Now there went forth a wind from the LORD, and it brought quail from the sea, and let *them* fall beside the camp, about a day's journey on this side and a day's journey on the other side, all around the camp, and about two[T]cubits *deep* on the surface of the ground.   One cubit equals approx. 18 in.

32 And the people [T]spent all day and all night and all the next day, and gathered the quail (he who gathered least gathered ten [R]homers) and they spread *them* out for themselves all around the camp.   *rose* • Ezek. 45:11

God Sends Plagues

33 [R]While the meat was still between their teeth, before it was chewed, the anger of the LORD was kindled against the people, and the LORD struck the people with a very severe plague.   Ps. 78:29-31; 106:15

34 So the name of that place was called [16]Kibroth-hattaavah, because there they buried the people who had been greedy.

35 From Kibroth-hattaavah[R]the people set out for Hazeroth, and they[T]remained at Hazeroth.   Num. 33:17 • *were*

CHAPTER 12

Miriam and Aaron Rebel

THEN Miriam and Aaron spoke against Moses because of the Cushite woman whom he had married (for he had married a[R]Cushite woman);   Ex. 2:21

2 [R]and they said, "Has the LORD indeed spoken only through Moses? Has He not spoken through us as well?" And the LORD heard it.   Num. 16:3

3 (Now the man Moses was[R]very humble, more than any man who was on the face of the earth.)   [Matt. 11:29]

Miriam Is Punished

4 And suddenly the LORD said to Moses and Aaron and to Miriam, "You three come out to the tent of meeting." So the three of them came out.

5 [R]Then the LORD came down in a pillar of cloud and stood at the doorway of the tent,

[16] I.e., the graves of greediness

and He called Aaron and Miriam. When they had both come forward,   Ex. 19:9; 34:5

6 He said,
"Hear now My words:
If there is a prophet among you,
I, the Lord, shall make Myself known
  to him in a [R]vision.   Gen. 46:2
I shall speak with him in a dream.
7 "Not so, with My servant Moses,
He is faithful in all My household;
8 With him I speak mouth to mouth,
Even openly, and not in dark sayings,
And he beholds [R]the form of the Lord.
Why then were you not afraid
To speak against My servant, against
  Moses?"   Ex. 20:4; 24:10, 11

9 So the anger of the Lord burned against them and [R]He departed.   Gen. 17:22

10 But when the cloud had withdrawn from over the tent, behold, Miriam *was* leprous, as *white as* snow. As Aaron turned toward Miriam, behold, she *was* leprous.

Moses Intercedes

11 Then Aaron said to Moses, "Oh, my lord, I beg you, [R]do not account *this* sin to us, in which we have acted foolishly and in which we have sinned.   2 Sam. 19:19; 24:10

12 "Oh, do not let her be like one dead, whose flesh is half eaten away when he comes from his mother's womb!"

13 And Moses cried out to the Lord, saying, "O God, [R]heal her, I pray!"   Ps. 30:2; 41:4

Miriam Is Restored

14 But the Lord said to Moses, "If her father had but spit in her face, would she not bear her shame for seven days? Let her be shut up for seven days outside the camp, and afterward she may be received again."

15 So Miriam was shut up outside the camp for seven days, and the people did not move on until Miriam was received again.

16 Afterward, however, the people moved out from Hazeroth and camped in the wilderness of Paran.

CHAPTER 13

Investigation of the Promised Land
Deut. 1:22–40

THEN the Lord spoke to Moses saying,

2 "Send out for yourself men so that they may spy out the land of Canaan, which I am going to give to the sons of Israel; you shall send a man from each of their fathers' tribes, every one a leader among them."

3 So Moses sent them from the wilderness of Paran at the [r]command of the Lord, all of them men who were heads of the sons of Israel.   *mouth*

4 These then *were* their names: from the

tribe of Reuben, Shammua the son of Zaccur;

5 from the tribe of Simeon, Shaphat the son of Hori;

6 from the tribe of Judah, [R]Caleb the son of Jephunneh;   Num. 14:6, 30; Josh. 14:6

7 from the tribe of Issachar, Igal the son of Joseph;

8 from the tribe of Ephraim, [R]Hoshea the son of Nun;   Num. 13:16; Deut. 32:44

9 from the tribe of Benjamin, Palti the son of Raphu;

10 from the tribe of Zebulun, Gaddiel the son of Sodi;

11 from the tribe of Joseph, from the tribe of Manasseh, Gaddi the son of Susi;

12 from the tribe of Dan, Ammiel the son of Gemalli;

13 from the tribe of Asher, Sethur the son of Michael;

14 from the tribe of Naphtali, Nahbi the son of Vophsi;

15 from the tribe of Gad, Geuel the son of Machi.

16 These are the names of the men whom Moses sent to spy out the land; but Moses called Hoshea the son of Nun, Joshua.

17 When Moses sent them to spy out the land of Canaan, he said to them, "Go up [T]there into [R]the [17]Negev; then go up into the hill country.   *here* • Gen. 12:9; 13:1, 3

18 "And see what the land is like, and whether the people who live in it are strong or weak, whether they are few or many.

19 "And how is the land in which they live, is it good or bad? And how are the cities in which they live, are they [T]like *open* camps or with fortifications?   *in*

20 "And [R]how is the land, is it fat or lean? Are there trees in it or not? [T]Make an effort then to get some of the fruit of the land." Now the time was the time of the first ripe grapes.   Deut. 1:24, 25 • *Use your strength*

21 So they went up and spied out the land from the wilderness of Zin as far as Rehob, [A]at Lebo-hamath.   *to the entrance of Hamath*

22 When they had gone up into the Negev, they came to Hebron where Ahiman, Sheshai and Talmai, the [T]descendants of Anak were. (Now Hebron was built seven years before Zoan in Egypt.)   *children*

23 Then they came to the [A]valley of [18]Eshcol and from there cut down a branch with a single cluster of grapes; and they carried it on a pole between two *men*, with some of the pomegranates and the figs.   *wadi*

24 That place was called the valley of [r]Eshcol, because of the cluster which the sons of Israel cut down from there.   *cluster*

25 When they returned from spying out the land, at the end of forty days,

26 they proceeded to come to Moses and Aaron and to all the congregation of the sons of Israel [T]in the wilderness of Paran, at Kadesh; and they brought back word to them and to all the congregation and showed them the fruit of the land.   *to*

[17] I.e., South country, and so throughout this context
[18] I.e., cluster

27 Thus they told him, and said, "We went in to the land where you sent us; and[R]it certainly does flow with milk and honey, and this is its fruit.   Ex. 3:8, 17; 13:5
28"Nevertheless, the people who live in the land are strong, and the cities are fortified *and* very large; and moreover, we saw the[T]descendants of Anak there.   *born ones*
29"Amalek is living in the land of[T]the Negev and the Hittites and the Jebusites and the Amorites are living in the hill country, and the Canaanites are living by the sea and by the side of the Jordan."   Num. 13:17; 14:25, 45
30 Then Caleb quieted the people[T]before Moses, and said, "We should by all means go up and take possession of it, for we shall surely overcome it."   *toward*
31 But the men who had gone up with him said, "We are not able to go up against the people, for they are too strong for us."
32 So they gave out to the sons of Israel a bad report of the land which they had spied out, saying, "The land through which we have gone, in spying it out, is a land that devours its inhabitants; and all the people whom we saw in it are men of *great* size.
33"There also we saw the Nephilim (the sons of Anak are part of the Nephilim); and we became like grasshoppers in our own sight, and so we were in their sight."

CHAPTER 14

Israel Rebels Against God

THEN all the congregation[T]lifted up their voices and cried, and the people wept[T]that night.   *lifted and gave their voice • in that*
2 And all the sons of Israel[R]grumbled against Moses and Aaron; and the whole congregation said to them, "Would that we had died in the land of Egypt! Or would that we had died in this wilderness!   Num. 11:1
3"And why is the LORD bringing us into this land,[R]to fall by the sword?[R]Our wives and our little ones will become plunder; would it not be better for us to return to Egypt?"   Ex. 5:21; 16:3 • Num. 14:31; Deut. 1:39
4 So they said to one another, "Let us appoint a leader and return to Egypt."
5 Then Moses and Aaron fell on their faces in the presence of all the assembly of the congregation of the sons of Israel.
6 And Joshua the son of Nun and Caleb the son of Jephunneh, of those who had spied out the land, tore their clothes;
7 and they spoke to all the congregation of the sons of Israel, saying, "The[R] land which we passed through to spy out is an exceedingly good land.   Num. 13:27; Deut. 1:25
8"If[T]the LORD is pleased with us, then He will bring us into this land, and give it to us—[R]a land which flows with milk and honey.   Deut. 10:15 • Ex. 3:8; Num. 13:27
9"Only do not rebel against the LORD; and do not fear the people of the land, for they shall be our[T]prey. Their[T]protection has

been removed from them, and the LORD is with us; do not fear them."   *food • shadow*
10[R]But all the congregation said to stone them with stones. Then[R]the glory of the LORD appeared in the tent of meeting to all the sons of Israel.   Ex. 17:4 • Ex. 16:10; Lev. 9:23

Moses Intercedes

11[R]And the LORD said to Moses, "How long will this people spurn Me? And how long will[R]they not believe in Me, despite all the signs which I have performed in their midst?   Ex. 32:9-13 • Ps. 106:24
12"I will smite them with pestilence and dispossess them, and I will make you into a nation greater and mightier than they."
13[R]But Moses said to the LORD, "Then the Egyptians will hear of it, for by Thy strength Thou didst bring up this people from their midst,   Ex. 32:11-14; Ps. 106:23
14 and they will tell *it* to the inhabitants of this land. They have heard that Thou, O LORD, art in the midst of this people, for[R]Thou, O LORD, art seen eye to eye, while Thy cloud stands over them; and Thou dost go before them in a pillar of cloud by day and in a pillar of fire by night.   Ex. 13:21; Deut. 5:4
15"Now if Thou dost slay this people as one man,[R]then the nations who have heard of Thy fame will[T]say,   Ex. 32:12 • *speak, saying*
16 'Because the LORD[R]could not bring this people into the land which He promised them by oath, therefore He slaughtered them in the wilderness.'   Josh. 7:7
17"But now, I pray, let the power of the Lord be great, just as Thou hast declared,
18 'The[R] LORD is slow to anger and abundant in lovingkindness, forgiving iniquity and transgression; but He will by no means clear *the guilty*, visiting the iniquity of the fathers on the children[T]to the third and the fourth *generations*.'   Ex. 20:6; 34:6, 7 • *on*
19"Pardon,[R] I pray, the iniquity of this people according to the greatness of Thy lovingkindness, just as Thou also hast forgiven this people, from Egypt even until now."   Ex. 32:32; 34:9

Israel to Wander and Die

20 So the LORD said, "I[R] have pardoned *them* according to your word;   Mic. 7:18-20
21 but indeed, as I live,[T]all the earth will be filled with the glory of the LORD.   *and all*
22"Surely[R]all the men who have seen My glory and My signs, which I performed in Egypt and in the wilderness, yet[R]have put Me to the test these ten times and have not listened to My voice,   1 Cor. 10:5 • Ex. 5:21
23[R]shall by no means see the land which I swore to their fathers, nor shall any of those who spurned Me see it.   Num. 26:65; 32:11
24"But My servant Caleb,[R]because he has had a different spirit and has followed Me fully,[T]I will bring into the land[T]which he entered, and his[T]descendants shall take possession of it.   Num. 14:6-9 • *him I • where • seed*

25"Now[R]the Amalekites and the Canaanites live in the valleys; turn tomorrow and set out to the wilderness by the way of the [T]Red Sea."   Num. 13:29 • *Sea of Reeds*
26 And the LORD spoke to Moses and Aaron, saying,
27"How long *shall I bear* with this evil congregation who are grumbling against Me? I have heard the complaints of the sons of Israel, which they are making against Me.
28"Say to them, 'As[R]I live,' says the LORD, 'just as[R]you have spoken in My hearing, so I will surely do to you;   Num. 14:21 • Num. 14:2
29 [R]your corpses shall fall in this wilderness, even all[R]your [T]numbered men, according to your complete number from twenty years old and upward, who have grumbled against Me.   Heb. 3:17 • Num. 1:45, 46 • *mustered*
30 'Surely you shall not come into the land in which I [T]swore to settle you,[R]except Caleb the son of Jephunneh and Joshua the son of Nun.   *raised My hand* • Num. 14:24
31 'Your[R] children, however, whom you said would become a prey—I will bring them in, and they shall know the land which you have rejected.   Num. 14:3
32 'But[R] as for you, your corpses shall fall in this wilderness.   Num. 26:64, 65; 32:13
33 'And your sons shall be shepherds for forty years in the wilderness, and they shall suffer *for* your [T]unfaithfulness, until your corpses lie in the wilderness.   *fornications*
34 'According to the [R]number of days which you spied out the land, forty days, for every day you shall bear your [T]guilt a year, *even* forty years, and you shall know My opposition.   Num. 13:25 • *iniquities*
35 'I,[R] the LORD, have spoken, surely this I will do to all this evil congregation who are gathered together against Me. In this wilderness they shall be destroyed, and there they shall die.' "   Num. 23:19

Spies Die Immediately

36 [R]As for the men whom Moses sent to spy out the land and who returned and made all the congregation grumble against him by bringing out a bad report concerning the land,   Num. 13:4-16, 32
37 even [R]those men who brought out the very bad report of the land died by a plague before the LORD.   [1 Cor. 10:10]; Heb. 3:17, 18
38 But Joshua the son of Nun and Caleb the son of Jephunneh remained alive out of those men who went to spy out the land.

Moses Warns Israel—Deut. 1:41-44

39 And when Moses spoke[R]these words to all the sons of Israel,[T]the people mourned greatly.   Num. 14:28-35 • Ex. 33:4
40 In the morning, however, they rose up early and went up to the ridge of the hill country, saying, "Here[R]we are; we have indeed sinned, but we will go up to the place which the LORD has promised."   Deut. 1:41-44
41 But Moses said, "Why then are you transgressing the [T]commandment of the LORD, when it will not succeed?   *mouth*
42"Do[R]not go up, lest you be struck down before your enemies, for the LORD is not among you.   Deut. 1:42
43"For the Amalekites and the Canaanites will be there in front of you, and you will fall by the sword, inasmuch as you have turned back from following the LORD. And the LORD will not be with you."
44 But they went up heedlessly to the [A]ridge of the hill country; neither[R]the ark of the covenant of the LORD nor Moses left the camp.   *top of the mountain* • Num. 31:6

Amalekites Defeat Israel

45 Then the Amalekites and the Canaanites who lived in that hill country came down, and struck them and beat them down as far as[R]Hormah.   Num. 21:3

CHAPTER 15

Offerings to Thank the Lord

Now the LORD spoke to Moses, saying,
2"Speak[R]to the sons of Israel, and say to them, 'When you enter the land where you are to live, which I am giving you, Lev. 23:10
3 then make an offering by fire to the LORD, a burnt offering or a sacrifice to[A]fulfill a special vow, or as a freewill offering or in your appointed times, to make a soothing aroma to the LORD, from the herd or from the flock.   *make a special votive offering*
4 'And the one who presents his offering shall present to the LORD a grain offering of [T]one-tenth *of an ephah* of fine flour mixed with[T]one-fourth of a [19]hin of oil,   2 qt. • 1 qt.
5 and you shall prepare wine for the libation, one-fourth of a hin, with the burnt offering or for the sacrifice, for each lamb.
6 'Or for a ram you shall prepare as a grain offering two-tenths *of an ephah* of fine flour mixed with one-third of a hin of oil;
7 and for the libation you shall offer one-third of a hin of wine as a soothing aroma to the LORD.
8 'And when you prepare a bull as a burnt offering or a sacrifice, to fulfill a special vow, or for peace offerings to the LORD,
9 then you shall offer with the bull a grain offering of three-tenths *of an ephah* of fine flour mixed with one-half a hin of oil;
10 and you shall offer as the libation one-half a hin of wine as an offering by fire, as a soothing aroma to the LORD.
11 'Thus it shall be done for each ox, or for each ram, or for each of the male lambs, or of the goats.
12 'According to the number that you prepare, so you shall do for everyone according to their number.

[19] I.e., Approx. one gallon, and so through v. 10

13 'All who are native shall do these things in this manner, in presenting an offering by fire, as a soothing aroma to the LORD.

14 'And if an alien sojourns with you, or one who may be among you throughout your generations, and he *wishes to* make an offering by fire, as a soothing aroma to the LORD, just as you do, so he shall do.

15 'As *for* the assembly, there shall be one statute for you and for the alien who sojourns *with you,* a perpetual statute throughout your generations; as you are, so shall the alien be before the LORD.

16 'There is to be ᴿone law and one ordinance for you and for the alien who sojourns with you.' "   Lev. 24:22

17 Then the LORD spoke to Moses, saying,

18 "Speak to the sons of Israel, and say to them, 'When you enter the land where I bring you,

19 then it shall be, that when you eat of the ᵀfood of the land, you shall lift up ᴬan offering to the LORD.   *bread · a heave offering*

20 'Of the first of your 20dough you shall lift up a cake as an offering; as the offering of the threshing floor, so you shall lift it up.

21 'From the first of your 20dough you shall give to the LORD an ᴮoffering throughout your generations.   *offering lifted up*

Offerings for Unintentional Sins

22 'But when you unwittingly fail and do not observe all these commandments, which the LORD has spoken to Moses,

23 *even* all that the LORD has commanded youᵀthrough Moses, from the day when the LORD gave commandment and onward throughout your generations, *by the hand of*

24 then it shall be, if it is done unintentionally,ᵀwithout the knowledge of the congregation, that all the congregation shall offer one bull for a burnt offering, as a soothing aroma to the LORD, with its grain offering, and its libation, according to the ordinance, and one male goat for a sin offering.   *from the eyes of the congregation*

25 'Then the priest shall make atonement for all the congregation of the sons of Israel, and they shall be forgiven; for it was an error, and they have brought their offering, an offering by fire to the LORD, and their sin offering before the LORD, for their error.

26 'So all the congregation of the sons of Israel will be forgiven, with the alien who sojourns among them, for *it happened* to all the people throughᴿerror.   Num. 15:24

27 'Also if one person sinsᴿunintentionally, then he shall offer a one year old female goat for a sin offering.   Lev. 4:27-31

28 'And the priest shall make atonement before the LORD for the person who goes astray when he sins unintentionally, making atonement for him that he may be forgiven.

29 'You shall have one law for him who does *anything* unintentionally, for him who

is native among the sons of Israel and for the alien who sojourns among them.

No Offering for Intentional Sins

30 'But the person who does *anything* defiantly, whether he is native or an alien, that one is blaspheming the LORD; and that person shall be cut off from among his people.

31 'Because he has despised the word of the LORD and has broken His commandment, that person shall be completely cut off; his ᴬguilt *shall be* on him.' "   *iniquity*

32 Now while the sons of Israel were in the wilderness, they found a manᴿgathering wood on the sabbath day.   Ex. 31:14, 15

33 And those who found him gathering wood brought him to Moses and Aaron, and to all the congregation;

34 and they put him in ᴬcustodyᴿbecause it had not been ᵀdeclared what should be done to him.   *prison · Num. 9:8 · declared distinctly*

35 Then the LORD said to Moses, "The man shall surely be put to death;ᴿall the congregation shall stone him with stones outside the camp."   Lev. 20:2, 27; 24:14-23

36 So all the congregation brought him outside the camp, and stoned himᵀto death with stones, just as the LORD had commanded Moses.   *with stones and he died*

The Tassel on the Garment

37 The LORD also spoke to Moses, saying,

38 "Speak to the sons of Israel, and tell ᴿthem that they shall make for themselves tassels on the corners of their garments throughout their generations, and that they shall put on the tassel of each corner a cord of blue.   Deut. 22:12; Matt. 23:5

39 "And it shall be a tassel for you to look at and remember all the commandments of the LORD, so as to do them and not ᵀfollow after your own heart and your own eyes, after which you played the harlot,   *seek*

40 in order that you may remember to do all My commandments, andᴿbe holy to your God.   Lev. 11:44, 45

41 "I am the LORD your God who brought you out from the land of Egypt to be your God; I am the LORD your God."

CHAPTER 16

Korah Rebels
Against Moses and Aaron

NOWᴿKorah the son of Izhar, the son of Kohath, the son of Levi, with Dathan and Abiram, the sons of Eliab, and On the son of Peleth, sons of Reuben, took *action,*   Jude 11

2 and they rose up before Moses, ᵀtogether with some of the sons of Israel, two hundred and fifty leaders of the congrega-

20 Or, *coarse meal*

tion, ^Tchosen^R in the assembly, men of renown.   *and men from • called ones of •* Num. 1:16

3 And they assembled together ^Ragainst Moses and Aaron, and said to them, "You^T have gone far enough, for all the congregation are holy, every one of them, and the LORD is in their midst; so why do you exalt yourselves above the assembly of the LORD?"   Num. 12:2 • *It is much for you*

4 When Moses heard *this*,^Rhe fell on his face;   Lev. 14:5

5 and he spoke to Korah and all his company, saying, "Tomorrow morning the LORD will show who is His, and^Rwho is holy, and will bring *him* near to Himself; even^Rthe one whom He will choose, He will bring near to Himself.   Lev. 10:3; Ps. 65:4 • Num. 17:5, 8

6"Do this: take censers for yourselves, Korah and all^Tyour company,   *his*

7 and put fire in them, and lay incense upon them in the presence of the LORD tomorrow; and the man whom the LORD chooses *shall be* the one who is holy. You have gone far enough, you sons of Levi!"

8 Then Moses said to Korah, "Hear now, you sons of Levi,

9 is it^Tnot enough for you that the God of Israel has separated you from the *rest of* the congregation of Israel, to bring you near to Himself, to do the service of the tabernacle of the LORD, and to stand before the congregation to minister to them;   *too little for you*

10 and that He has brought you near, *Korah*, and all your brothers, sons of Levi, with you? And are you^Rseeking for the priesthood also?   Num. 3:10; 18:1-7

11"Therefore you and all your company are gathered together^Ragainst the LORD; but as for Aaron, ^Twho is he that^Ryou grumble against him?"   Ex. 16:7 • *what* • 1 Cor. 10:10

12 Then Moses sent^Ta summons to Dathan and Abiram, the sons of Eliab; but they said, "We will not come up.   *to call*

13"Is it^Tnot enough that you have brought us up out of a land flowing with milk and honey to have us die in the wilderness, but you would also lord it over us?   *a little thing*

14"Indeed, you have not brought us into a land flowing with milk and honey, nor have you given us an inheritance of fields and vineyards. Would you^Tput out the eyes of these men? We will not come up!"   *bore out*

God Judges Korah

15 Then Moses became very angry and said to the LORD, "Do not regard their offering! I have not taken a single donkey from them, nor have I done harm to any of them."

16 And Moses said to Korah, "You and all your company be present before the LORD tomorrow, both you and they along with Aaron.

17"And each of you take his firepan and put incense on^Tit, and each of you bring his censer before the LORD, two hundred and fifty firepans; also you and Aaron *shall* each *bring* his firepan."   *them*

18 So they each took his *own* censer and put fire on^Tit, and laid incense on^Tit; and they stood at the doorway of the tent of meeting, with Moses and Aaron.   *them*

19 Thus Korah assembled all the congregation against them at the doorway of the tent of meeting. And^Rthe glory of the LORD appeared to all the congregation.   Num. 14:10

20 Then the LORD spoke to Moses and Aaron, saying,

21"Separate^R yourselves from among this congregation,^Rthat I may consume them instantly."   Num. 16:45 • Ex. 32:10, 12

22 But they fell on their faces, and said, "O God,^RThou God of the spirits of all flesh, when one man sins, wilt Thou be angry with the entire congregation?"   Num. 27:16

23 Then the LORD spoke to Moses, saying,

24"Speak to the congregation, saying, 'Get^R back from around the dwellings of Korah, Dathan and Abiram.' "   Num. 16:45

25 Then Moses arose and went to Dathan and Abiram, with the elders of Israel following him,

26 and he spoke to the congregation, saying, "Depart^R now from the tents of these wicked men, and touch nothing that belongs to them,^Rlest you be swept away in all their sin."   Is. 52:11 • Gen. 19:15, 17

27 So they got back from around the dwellings of Korah, Dathan and Abiram; and Dathan and Abiram came out *and* stood at the doorway of their tents, along with their wives and ^Rtheir sons and their little ones.   Num. 26:11

28 And Moses said, "By this you shall know that the LORD has sent me to do all these deeds; for this is not my doing.

29"If these men die^Tthe death of all men, or if they suffer the fate of all men, *then* the LORD has not sent me.   *like the death*

30"But if the LORD ^Tbrings about an entirely new thing and the ground opens its mouth and swallows them up with all that is theirs, and they descend alive into Sheol, then you will understand that these men have spurned the LORD."   *creates a new creation*

31 Then it came about as he finished speaking all these words, that the ground that was under them split open;

32 and ^Rthe earth opened its mouth and swallowed them up, and their households, and all the men who belonged to Korah, with *their* possessions.   Num. 26:10; Deut. 11:6

33 So they and all that belonged to them went down alive to ^TSheol; and the earth closed over them, and they perished from the midst of the assembly.   *the nether world*

34 And all Israel who *were* around them fled at their^Toutcry, for they said, "The^T earth may swallow us up!"   *voice • Lest the earth*

35 Fire also came forth from the LORD and consumed the ^Rtwo hundred and fifty men who were offering the incense.   Num. 16:2

36 Then the LORD spoke to Moses, saying,

37"Say to Eleazar, the son of Aaron the priest, that he shall take up the censers out

of the midst of the blaze, for they are holy; and you scatter the burning coals abroad.

38"As for the censers of these men who have sinned at the cost of their lives, let them be made into hammered sheets for a plating of the altar, since they did present them before the LORD and they are holy; and they shall be for a sign to the sons of Israel."

39 So Eleazar the priest took the bronze censers which the men who were burned had offered; and they hammered them out as a plating for the altar,

40 as a reminder to the sons of Israel that no layman who is not of the descendants of Aaron should come near to burn incense before the LORD; that he might not become like Korah and his company—just as the LORD had spoken to him through Moses.

Israel Rebels
Against Moses and Aaron

41 But on the next day all the congregation of the sons of Israel ᴿgrumbled against Moses and Aaron, saying, "You are the ones who have caused the death of the LORD's people."   Num. 16:3

God Judges Israel

42 It came about, however, when the congregation had assembled against Moses and Aaron, that they turned toward the tent of meeting, and behold, the cloud covered it and the glory of the LORD appeared.

43 Then Moses and Aaron came to the front of the tent of meeting,

44 and the LORD spoke to Moses, saying,

45"Getᴬaway from among this congregation, that I may consume them instantly." Then they fell on their faces.   Arise

46 And Moses said to Aaron, "Take your censer and put in it fire from the altar, and lay incense on it; then bring it quickly to the congregation and ᴿmake atonement for them, for wrath has gone forth from the LORD, the plague has begun!"   Num. 25:13

47 Then Aaron took it as Moses had spoken, and ran into the midst of the assembly, for behold, the plague had begun among the people.ᴿSo he put on the incense and made atonement for the people.   Num. 25:6-8, 13

48 And he took his stand between the dead and the living, so that the plague was checked.

49 ᴿBut those who died by the plague were 14,700, besides those whoᴮdied on account of Korah.   Num. 25:9 • Num. 16:32, 35

50 Then Aaron returned to Moses at the doorway of the tent of meeting, for the plague had been checked.

CHAPTER 17

Confirmation of the Divine Call

THEN the LORD spoke to Moses, saying, 2"Speak to the sons of Israel, and get from them a rod for each father's household: twelve rods, from all their leaders according to their fathers' households. You shall write each name on his rod,

3 and write Aaron's name on the rod of Levi; for there is one rod for the head of each of their fathers' households.

4"You shall then deposit them in the tent of meeting in front ofᴿthe testimony, where I meet with you.   Ex. 25:16, 21, 22; Num. 17:7

5"And it will come about that the rod of ᴿthe man whom I choose will sprout. Thus I shall lessen from upon Myself the grumblings of the sons of Israel, who are grumbling against you."   Num. 16:5

6 Moses therefore spoke to the sons of Israel, and all their leaders gave him a rod apiece, for each leader according to their fathers' households, twelve rods, with the rod of Aaron among their rods.

7 So Moses deposited the rods before the LORD inᴿthe tent of the testimony. Num. 9:15

8 Now it came about on the next day that Moses went into the tent of the testimony; and behold,ᴿthe rod of Aaron for the house of Levi had sprouted and put forth buds and produced blossoms, and it bore ripe almonds.   [Ezek. 17:24]; Heb. 9:4

9 Moses then brought out all the rods from the presence of the LORD to all the sons of Israel; and they looked, and each man took his rod.

10 But the LORD said to Moses, "Put back the rod of Aaronᴿbefore the testimony to be kept as a sign against the rebels, that you may put an end to their grumblings against Me, so that they should not die."   Num. 17:4

11 Thus Moses did; just as the LORD had commanded him, so he did.

12 Then the sons of Israel spoke to Moses, saying, "Beholdᴿ we perish, we are dying, we are all dying!   [Is. 6:5]

13"Everyoneᴿwho comes near, who comes near to the tabernacle of the LORD, must die. Are we to perish completely?"   Num. 1:51

CHAPTER 18

Remuneration of the Priesthood

SO the LORD said to Aaron, "You and your sons and your father's household with you shall bear the guilt ᵀin connection with the sanctuary; and you and your sons with you shall bear the guiltᵀin connection with the priesthood.   of the sanctuary • of your priesthood

2"But bring with you also your brothers, the tribe of Levi, the tribe of your father, that they may beᴿjoined with you and serve you, while you and your sons with you are before the tent of the testimony. Num. 3:5-10

3"And they shall thus attend to your obligation and the obligation of all the tent, but ᴿthey shall not come near to the furnishings of the sanctuary andᴿthe altar, lest both they and you die.   Num. 4:15-20 • Num. 1:51; 18:7

4"And they shall be joined with you and attend to the obligations of the tent of meeting, for all the service of the tent; but an ^Toutsider may not come near you.   *a stranger*

5"So you shall attend to the ^Robligations of the sanctuary and the obligations of the altar,^Rthat there may no longer be wrath on the sons of Israel.   Ex. 27:21 · Num. 16:46

6"And behold, I Myself^Rhave taken your ^Tfellow Levites from among the sons of Israel; they are a gift to you, ^Tdedicated to the LORD, to perform the service for the tent of meeting.   Num. 3:12, 45 · *brethren the · given*

7"But you and your sons with you shall attend to your priesthood for everything concerning the altar and inside the veil, and you are to perform service. I am giving you the priesthood as ^Ra ^Tbestowed service, but the ^Toutsider who comes near shall be put to death."   1 Pet. 5:2, 3 · *service of gift · stranger*

8 Then the LORD spoke to Aaron, "Now behold, I Myself have given you charge of My ^Tofferings, even all the holy gifts of the sons of Israel, I have given them to you as a portion, and to your sons as a perpetual allotment.   *heave offerings,* and so throughout the ch.

9"This shall be yours from the most holy *gifts,* reserved from the fire; every offering of theirs, even ^Revery grain offering and every sin offering and every guilt offering, which they shall render to Me, shall be most holy for you and for your sons.   Lev. 2:1-16

10"As the most holy *gifts* you shall eat it; every male shall eat it. It shall be holy to you.

11"This also is yours, the offering of their gift, even all the wave offerings of the sons of Israel; I have ^Rgiven them to you and to your sons and daughters with you, as a perpetual allotment. Everyone of your household who is clean may eat it.   Lev. 22:1-16

12"All the ^Tbest of the fresh oil and all the ^Tbest of the fresh wine and of the grain, the first fruits of those which they give to the LORD, I give them to you.   *fat*

13"The^Rfirst ripe fruits of all that is in their land, which they bring to the LORD, shall be yours; everyone of your household who is clean may eat it.   Ex. 22:29; 23:19; 34:26

14"Every^R devoted thing in Israel shall be yours.   Lev. 27:1-33

15"Every^T first issue of the womb of all flesh, whether man or animal, which they offer to the LORD, shall be yours; nevertheless the first-born of man you shall surely redeem, and the first-born of unclean animals you shall redeem.   *Everything that opens*

16"And as to their redemption price, from a month old you shall redeem them, by your valuation, five ²¹shekels in silver, according to the shekel of the sanctuary, which is twenty gerahs.

17"But ^Rthe first-born of an ox or the first-born of a sheep or the first-born of a goat, you shall not redeem; they are holy.^RYou

shall sprinkle their blood on the altar and shall offer up their fat in smoke *as* an offering by fire, for a soothing aroma to the LORD.   Deut. 15:19 · Lev. 3:2

18"And their ^Tmeat shall be yours; it shall be yours like the^Rbreast of a wave offering and like the right thigh.   *flesh ·* Lev. 7:31

19"All^R the offerings of the holy *gifts,* which the sons of Israel offer to the LORD, I have given to you and your sons and your daughters with you, as a perpetual allotment. It is ^Ran everlasting covenant of salt before the LORD to you and your ^Tdescendants with you."   Num. 18:11 · 2 Chr. 13:5 · *seed*

20 Then the LORD said to Aaron, "You^R shall have no inheritance in their land, nor own any portion among them; ^RI am your portion and your inheritance among the sons of Israel.   Deut. 10:9; 12:12 · Deut. 18:2

21"And to the sons of Levi, behold, I have given all the tithe in Israel for an inheritance, in return for their service which they perform, the service of the tent of meeting.

22"And^Rthe sons of Israel shall not come near the tent of meeting again, lest they bear sin and die.   Num. 1:51

23"Only the Levites shall perform the service of the tent of meeting, and they shall ^Rbear their iniquity; it shall be a perpetual statute throughout your generations, and among the sons of Israel^Rthey shall have no inheritance.   Num. 18:1 · Num. 18:20

24"For the tithe of the sons of Israel, which they offer as an offering to the LORD, I have given to the Levites for an inheritance; therefore I have said concerning them, 'They^R shall have no inheritance among the sons of Israel.' "   Deut. 10:9

25 Then the LORD spoke to Moses, saying,

26"Moreover, you shall speak to the Levites and say to them, 'When you take from the sons of Israel^Rthe tithe which I have given you from them for your inheritance, then you shall present an offering from it to the LORD, a tithe of the tithe.   Num. 18:21

27 'And your offering shall be reckoned to you as the grain from the threshing floor or the full produce from the wine vat.

28 'So you shall also present an offering to the LORD from your tithes, which you receive from the sons of Israel; and from it you shall give the LORD's offering to Aaron the priest.

29 'Out of all your gifts you shall present every offering due to the LORD, from all the best of them, the sacred part from them.'

30"And you shall say to them, 'When you have ^Toffered from it the best of it, then *the rest* shall be reckoned to the Levites as the product of the threshing floor, and as the product of the wine vat.   *lifted*

31 'And you may eat it anywhere, you and your households, for it is your compensation in return for your service in the tent of meeting.

---

²¹ I.e., A shekel equals approx. one-half ounce

32 'And you shall bear no sin by reason of it, when you have ᵀoffered the ᵀbest of it. But you shall not profane the sacred gifts of the sons of Israel, lest you die.' "   *lifted · fat*

CHAPTER 19

Purification of the Red Heifer

THEN the LORD spoke to Moses and Aaron, saying,

2 "This is the statute of the law which the LORD has commanded, saying, 'Speak to the sons of Israel that they bring you an unblemished red heifer in which is no defect, *and* on which a yoke has never been placed.

3 'And you shall give it to Eleazar the priest, and it shall be brought outside the camp and be slaughtered in his presence.

4 'Next Eleazar the priest shall take some of its blood with his finger, and ᴿsprinkle some of its blood toward the front of the tent of meeting seven times.   Lev. 4:6, 17

5 'Then the heifer shall be burned in his sight; ᴿits hide and its flesh and its blood, with its refuse, shall be burned.   Lev. 4:11, 12

6 'And the priest shall take cedar wood and hyssop and scarlet *material,* and cast it into the midst of the burning heifer.

7 'The priest ᴿshall then wash his clothes and bathe his ᵀbody in water, and afterward come into the camp, but the priest shall be unclean until evening.   Lev. 16:26, 28 · *flesh*

8 'The one who burns it shall also wash his clothes in water and bathe his body in water, and shall be unclean until evening.

9 'Now a man who is clean shall gather up the ashes of the heifer and deposit them outside the camp in a clean place, and the congregation of the sons of Israel shall keep it asᴿwater to remove impurity; it is ᴬpurification from sin.   Num. 8:7; 31:23 · *a sin offering*

10 'And the one who gathers the ashes of the heifer ᴿshall wash his clothes and be unclean until evening; and it shall be a perpetual statute to the sons of Israel and to the alien who sojourns among them.   Num. 19:7

11 'The one who touches the corpse of any person shall be unclean for seven days.

12 'That one shall ᴿpurify himself from uncleanness with ᵀthe water on the third day and on the seventh day, *and then* he shall be clean; but if he does not purify himself on the third day and on the seventh day, he shall not be clean.   Num. 19:19; 31:19 · *it*

13 'Anyone who touches a corpse, the ᵀbody of a man who has died, and does not purify himself, defiles the tabernacle of the LORD; and that person shall be cut off from Israel. Because the water for impurity was not ᴬsprinkled on him, he shall be unclean; his uncleanness is still on him.   *soul · thrown*

14 'This is the law when a man dies in a tent: everyone who comes into the tent and everyone who is in the tent shall be unclean for seven days.

15 'And every open vessel, which has no covering tied down on it, shall be unclean.

16 'Also,ᴿ anyone who in the open field touches one who has been slain with a sword or who has died *naturally,* or a human bone or a grave, shall be unclean for seven days.   Num. 31:19

17 'Then for the unclean *person* they shall take some of the ᵀashes of the burnt purification from sin and ᵀflowing water shall be ᵀadded to them in a vessel.   *dust · living · put*

18 'And a clean person shall take hyssop and dip *it* in the water, and sprinkle *it* on the tent and on all the furnishings and on the persons who were there, and on the one who touched the bone or the one slain or the one dying *naturally* or the grave.

19 'Then the clean *person*ᴿshall sprinkle on the unclean on the third day and on the seventh day; and on the seventh day he shall purify him from uncleanness, and he shall wash his clothes and bathe *himself* in water and shall be clean by evening.   Ezek. 36:25

20 'But the man who is unclean and does not purify himself from uncleanness, that person shall be cut off from the midst of the assembly, because he has ᴿdefiled the sanctuary of the LORD; the water for impurity has not been sprinkled on him, he is unclean.   Num. 19:13

21 'So it shall be a perpetual statute for them. And he ᴿwho sprinkles the water for impurity shall wash his clothes, and he who touches the water for impurity shall be unclean until evening.   Num. 19:7

22 'Furthermore,ᴿ anything that the unclean *person* touches shall be unclean; and the person who touches *it* shall be unclean until evening.' "   Lev. 5:2, 3; 7:21; 22:5, 6

CHAPTER 20

Miriam Dies

THEN the sons of Israel, the whole congregation, came to the ᴿwilderness of Zin in the first month; and the people stayed at Kadesh. Now Miriam died there and was buried there.   Num. 13:21; 27:14; 33:36

The Sin of Israel

2 And there was no water for the congregation; ᴿand they assembled themselves against Moses and Aaron.   Num. 16:19, 42

3 ᴿThe people thus contended with Moses and spoke, saying, "Ifᴿonly we had perished ᴿwhen our brothers perished before the LORD!   Ex. 17:2 · Num. 14:2, 3 · Num. 16:31-35

4 "Whyᴿthen have you brought the LORD's assembly into this wilderness, for us and our beasts to dieᵀhere?   Ex. 17:3 · *there*

5 "And why have you made us come up from Egypt, to bring us in to this wretched place? ᵀIt is not a place of ᵀgrain or figs or vines or pomegranates, nor is there water to drink."   Num. 16:14 · *seed*

6 Then Moses and Aaron came in from the presence of the assembly to the doorway of the tent of meeting, and [R]fell on their faces. Then the glory of the LORD appeared to them;   Num. 14:5

The Command of God

7 and the LORD spoke to Moses, saying, 8 "Take the rod; and you and your brother Aaron assemble the congregation and speak to the rock before their eyes, that it may yield its water. You shall thus bring forth water for them out of the rock and let the congregation and their beasts drink."

The Sin of Moses

9 So Moses took the rod from before the LORD, just as He had commanded him;
10 and Moses and Aaron gathered the assembly before the rock. And he said to them, "Listen now, you rebels; shall we bring forth water for you out of this rock?"
11 Then Moses lifted up his hand and struck the rock twice with his rod; and [R]water came forth abundantly, and the congregation and their beasts drank.   Ps. 78:16
12 But the LORD said to Moses and Aaron, "Because you have not believed Me, to treat Me as holy in the sight of the sons of Israel, therefore you shall not bring this assembly into the land which I have given them."
[A] 13 Those *were* the waters of [22]Meribah[R], because the sons of Israel contended with the LORD, and He proved Himself holy among them.   Ex. 17:7; Ps. 95:8 • *where*

Edom Refuses Passage

14 From Kadesh Moses then sent messengers to [R]the king of Edom: "Thus your brother Israel has said, 'You know all the hardship that has befallen us;   Gen. 36:31-39
15 that our fathers went down to Egypt, and we stayed in Egypt a long time, and the Egyptians treated us and our fathers badly.
16 'But [R]when we cried out to the LORD, He heard our voice and sent [R]an angel and brought us out from Egypt; now behold, we are at Kadesh, a town on the edge of your territory.   Ex. 2:23; 3:7 • Ex. 14:19
17 'Please let us pass through your land. We shall not pass through field or through vineyard; we shall not even drink water from a well. We shall go along the king's highway, not turning to the right or left, until we pass through your territory.' "
18 Edom, however, said to him, "You shall not pass through [T]us, lest I come out with the sword against you."   *me*
19 Again, the sons of Israel said to him, "We shall go up by the highway, and if I and

my livestock do drink any of your water, then I will [T]pay its price. Let me only pass through on my feet, nothing *else.*"   *give*
20 But he said, "You shall not pass through." And Edom came out against him with a heavy force, and with a strong hand.
21 [R]Thus Edom refused to allow Israel to pass through his territory; [R]so Israel turned away from him.   Judg. 11:17 • Deut. 2:8

Aaron Dies

22 Now when they set out from [R]Kadesh, the sons of Israel, the whole congregation, came to Mount Hor.   Num. 20:1, 14
23 Then the LORD spoke to Moses and Aaron at [R]Mount Hor by the border of the land of Edom, saying,   Num. 33:37
24 "Aaron shall be [R]gathered to his people; for he shall not enter the land which I have given to the sons of Israel, because [R]you rebelled against My [T]command at the waters of Meribah.   Gen. 25:8 • Num. 20:5, 10 • *mouth*
25 "Take Aaron and his son [R]Eleazar, and bring them up to Mount Hor;   Num. 3:4
26 and strip Aaron of his garments and put them on his son Eleazar. So Aaron will be [R]gathered *to his people,* and will die there."   Num. 20:24
27 So Moses did just as the LORD had commanded, and they went up to Mount Hor in the sight of all the congregation.
28 And after Moses had stripped Aaron of his garments and [R]put them on his son Eleazar, [R]Aaron died there on the mountain top. Then Moses and Eleazar came down from the mountain.   Ex. 29:29 • Num. 33:38
29 And when all the congregation saw that Aaron had died, all the house of Israel wept for Aaron thirty [R]days.   Gen. 1:5; 50:3, 10

CHAPTER 21

Israel's Victory over the Canaanites

W HEN the Canaanite, the king of [R]Arad, who lived in the [23]Negev, heard that Israel was coming by the way of [24]Atharim, then he fought against Israel, and took some of them captive.   Num. 33:40; Josh. 12:14; Judg. 1:16
2 So [R]Israel made a vow to the LORD, and said, "If Thou wilt indeed deliver this people into my hand, then I will [T]utterly destroy their cities."   Gen. 28:20 • *devote to destruction*
3 And the LORD heard the voice of Israel, and delivered up the Canaanites; then they utterly destroyed them and their cities. Thus the name of the place was called [25]Hormah.

Israel Complains—Deut. 2:1

4 Then they set out from Mount Hor by the way of the [R]Red Sea, to go around the land of Edom; and the people became impatient because of the journey.   *Sea of Reeds*
5 And the people spoke against God and

[22] I.e., contention   [23] I.e., South country   [24] Or, *the spies*
[25] I.e., a devoted thing; or, Destruction

Moses, "Why have you brought us up out of Egypt to die in the wilderness? For there is no 'food and no water, and 'we loathe this miserable food."   *bread • our soul loathes*

God Judges with Serpents

6 And the LORD sent fiery serpents among the people and ᴿthey bit the people, so that many people of Israel died.   Jer. 8:17

The Bronze Serpent

7 ᴿSo the people came to Moses and said, "We have sinned, because we have spoken against the LORD and you; ᴿintercede with the LORD, that He may remove the serpents from us." And Moses interceded for the people.   Num. 11:2; Ps. 78:34 • Ex. 8:8; Acts 8:24
8 Then the LORD said to Moses, "Make a fiery *serpent*, and set it on a standard; and it shall come about, that everyone who is bitten, when he looks at it, he shall live."
9 And Moses made a bronze serpent and set it on the standard; and it came about, that if a serpent bit any man, when he looked to the bronze serpent, he lived.

Journey to Moab

10 ᴿNow the sons of Israel moved out and camped in Oboth.   Num. 33:43, 44
11 And they journeyed from Oboth, and camped at Iyeabarim, in the wilderness which is opposite Moab, to the 'east.   *sunrise*
12 'From there they set out and camped in ²⁶Wadi Zered.   Num. 33:45
13 From there they journeyed and camped on the other side of the Arnon, which is in the wilderness that comes out of the border of the Amorites, ᴿfor the Arnon is the border of Moab, between Moab and the Amorites.   Num. 22:36; Judg. 11:18
14 Therefore it is said in the Book of the Wars of the LORD,
"Waheb in Suphah,
And the wadis of the Arnon,
15 And the slope of the wadis
That extends to the site of Ar,
And leans to the border of Moab."
16 ᴿAnd from there *they* continued to 'Beer, that is the well where the LORD said to Moses, "Assemble the people, that I may give them water."   Num. 33:46-49 • a well
17 ᴿThen Israel sang this song: Ex. 15:1
"Spring up, O well! Sing to it!
18 "The well, which the leaders sank,
Which the nobles of the people dug,
With the scepter *and* with their staffs."
And from the wilderness *they* continued to Mattanah,
19 and from Mattanah to Nahaliel, and from Nahaliel to Bamoth,
20 and from Bamoth to the valley that is in the land of Moab, at the top of Pisgah which overlooks the 'wasteland.   *Jeshimon*

Israel's Victory over the Amorites
Deut. 2:2–36

21 ᴿThen Israel sent messengers to Sihon, king of the Amorites, saying,   Deut. 2:26-37
22 "Let'me pass through your land. We will not turn off into field or vineyard; we will not drink water from wells. We will go by the king's highway until we have passed through your border."   Num. 20:16, 17
23 ᴿBut Sihon would not permit Israel to pass through his border. So Sihon gathered all his people and went out against Israel in the wilderness, and came to ᴿJahaz and fought against Israel.   Num. 20:21 • Deut. 2:32
24 Then ᴿIsrael struck him with the edge of the sword, and took possession of his land from the Arnon to the Jabbok, as far as the sons of Ammon; for the ᴿborder of the sons of Ammon *was* Jazer.   Amos 2:9 • Deut. 2:37
25 And Israel took all these cities and Israel lived in all the cities of the Amorites, in Heshbon, and in all her 'villages.   *daughters*
26 For Heshbon was the city of Sihon, king of the Amorites, who had fought against the former king of Moab and had taken all his land out of his hand, as far as the Arnon.
27 Therefore those who use proverbs say,
"Come to Heshbon! Let it be built!
So let the city of Sihon be established.
28 "For a fire went forth from Heshbon,
A flame from the town of Sihon;
It devoured ᴿAr of Moab,   Num. 21:15
The dominant heights of the Arnon.
29 "Woeᴿto you, O Moab!   Jer. 48:46
You are ruined, O people of Chemosh!
He has given his sons as fugitives,
ᴿAnd his daughters into captivity,
To an Amorite king, Sihon.   Is. 16:2
30 "But we have cast them down,
Heshbon is ruined as far asᴿDibon,
Then we have laid waste even to Nophah,   Num. 32:3, 34; Jer. 48:18, 22
Which *reaches* to Medeba."
31 Thus Israel lived in the land of the Amorites.
32 And Moses sent to spy out ᴿJazer, and they captured its villages and dispossessed the Amorites who *were* there.   Jer. 48:32

Israel's Victory over Bashan—Deut. 3:1-4

33 ᴿThen they turned and went up by the way of Bashan, and Og the king of Bashan went out 'with all his people, for battle at ᴿEdrei.   Deut. 3:1-7 • *he and* • Josh. 13:12
34 But the LORD said to Moses, "Do not fear him, for I have given him into your hand, and all his people and his land; and you shall do to him as you did to Sihon, king of the Amorites, who lived at Heshbon."
35 So they 'killed him and his sons and all his people, until there was no remnant left him; and they possessed his land.   *smote*

²⁶ I.e., a dry ravine except during rainy season

CHAPTER 22

Balaam Is Sought by Balak

THEN[R] the sons of Israel journeyed, and camped in the plains of Moab beyond the Jordan *opposite* Jericho.   Num. 33:48, 49

2 Now Balak the son of Zippor saw all that Israel had done to the Amorites.

3 So Moab was in great fear because of the people, for they were numerous; and Moab was in dread of the sons of Israel.

4 And Moab said to the elders of[R] Midian, "Now this [T]horde will lick up all that is around us, as the ox licks up the grass of the field." And Balak the son of Zippor was king of Moab at that time.   Num. 31:1-3 • *assembly*

5 So he sent messengers to Balaam the son of Beor, at Pethor, which is near the [27]River, *in* the land of the sons of his people, to call him, saying, "Behold, a people came out of Egypt; behold, they cover the surface of the land, and they are living opposite me.

6 "Now, therefore, please come, curse this people for me since they are too [^]mighty for me; perhaps I may be able to [T]defeat them and drive them out of the land. For I know that he whom you bless is blessed, and he whom you curse is cursed."   *numerous • smite*

7 So the elders of Moab and the elders of Midian departed with the *fees for* divination in their hand; and they came to Balaam and [T]repeated Balak's words to him.   *spoke*

8 And he said to them, "Spend the night here, and I will bring word back to you as the LORD may speak to me." And the leaders of Moab stayed with Balaam.

9 Then [R]God came to Balaam and said, "Who are these men with you?"   Gen. 20:3

10 And Balaam said to God, "Balak the son of Zippor, king of Moab, has sent *word* to me,

11 'Behold, there is a people who came out of Egypt and they cover the surface of the land; now come, curse them for me; perhaps I may be able to fight against them, and drive them out.' "

12 And God said to Balaam, "Do not go with them; [R]you shall not curse the people; for they [R]are blessed."   Num. 23:8 • Gen. 12:2

13 So Balaam arose in the morning and said to Balak's leaders, "Go back to your land, for the LORD has refused to let me go with you."

14 And the leaders of Moab arose and went to Balak, and said, "Balaam refused to come with us."

15 Then Balak again sent leaders, more numerous and more distinguished than [T]the former.   *these*

16 And they came to Balaam and said to him, "Thus says Balak the son of Zippor, 'Let nothing, I beg you, hinder you from coming to me;

17 for I will indeed honor you richly, and I will do whatever you say to me. Please come then, curse this people for me.' "

18 And Balaam answered and said to the servants of Balak, "Though[R] Balak were to give me his house full of silver and gold, I could not do anything, either small or great, contrary to the [T]command of the LORD my God.   Num. 22:38; 24:13; 1 Kin. 22:14 • *mouth*

19 "And now please, you also stay here tonight, and I will find out what else the LORD will speak to me."

20 And God came to Balaam at night and said to him, "If the men have come to call you, rise up *and* go with them; but only the word which I speak to you shall you do."

21 [R]So Balaam arose in the morning, and saddled his donkey, and went with the leaders of Moab.   2 Pet. 2:15

22 But God was angry because he was going, [R]and the angel of the LORD took his stand in the way as an adversary against him. Now he was riding on his donkey and his two servants were with him.   Ex. 23:20

23 When the donkey saw the angel of the LORD standing in the way with his drawn sword in his hand, the donkey turned off from the way and went into the field; but Balaam struck the donkey to turn her back into the way.

24 Then the angel of the LORD stood in a narrow path of the vineyards, *with* a wall on this side and a wall on that side.

25 When the donkey saw the angel of the LORD, she pressed herself to the wall and pressed Balaam's foot against the wall, so he struck her again.

26 And the angel of the LORD went further, and stood in a narrow place where there was no way to turn to the right hand or the left.

27 When the donkey saw the angel of the LORD, she lay down under Balaam; so [R]Balaam was angry and struck the donkey with his stick.   James 1:19

28 And [R]the LORD opened the mouth of the donkey, and she said to Balaam, "What have I done to you, that you have struck me these three times?"   2 Pet. 2:16

29 Then Balaam said to the donkey, "Because you have made a mockery of me! If there had been a sword in my hand,[R] I would have killed you by now."   [Prov. 12:10]

30 And the donkey said to Balaam, "Am I not your donkey on which you have ridden all your life to this day? Have I ever been accustomed to do so to you?" And he said, "No."

31 Then the LORD opened the eyes of Balaam, and he saw the angel of the LORD standing in the way with his drawn sword in his hand; and he bowed [T]all the way to the ground.   *and prostrated himself to his face*

32 And the angel of the LORD said to him, "Why have you struck your donkey these three times? Behold, I have come out as an[R] adversary, because your way was [T]contrary[R] to me.   *reckless* • [2 Pet. 2:15]

---

[27] I.e., Euphrates

33 "But the donkey saw me and turned aside from me these three times. If she had not turned aside from me, I would surely have killed you just now, and let her live."

34 And Balaam said to the angel of the LORD, "I^R have sinned, for I did not know that you were standing in the way against me. Now then, if it is displeasing to you, I will turn back."   Num. 14:40

35 But the angel of the LORD said to Balaam, "Go with the men, but you shall speak only the word which I shall tell you." So Balaam went along with the leaders of Balak.

36 When Balak heard that Balaam was coming, he went out to meet him at the city of Moab, which is on the Arnon border, ^Tat the extreme end of the border.   *which is at*

37 Then Balak said to Balaam, "Did I not urgently send to you to call you? Why did you not come to me? Am I really unable to honor you?"

38 So Balaam said to Balak, "Behold, I have come now to you! ^RAm I able to speak anything at all? The word that God puts in my mouth, that I shall speak."   Num. 22:18

39 And Balaam went with Balak, and they came to Kiriath-huzoth.

40 And Balak sacrificed oxen and sheep, and sent *some* to Balaam and the leaders who were with him.

The First Oracle of Balaam

41 Then it came about in the morning that Balak took Balaam, and brought him up to ^Tthe high places of Baal; and he saw from there a portion of the people.   *Bamoth-baal*

CHAPTER 23

T HEN Balaam said to Balak, "Build seven altars for me here, and prepare seven bulls and seven rams for me here."

2 And Balak did just as Balaam had spoken, and Balak and Balaam offered up a bull and a ram on each altar.

3 Then Balaam said to Balak, "Stand beside your burnt offering, and I will go; perhaps the LORD will come to meet me, and whatever He shows me I will tell you." So he went to a bare hill.

4 Now God met Balaam, and he said to Him, "I have set up the seven altars, and I have offered up a bull and a ram on each altar."

5 Then the LORD ^Rput a word in Balaam's mouth and said, "Return to Balak, and you shall speak thus."   Num. 22:20; Deut. 18:18

6 So he returned to him, and behold, he was standing beside his burnt offering, he and all the leaders of Moab.

7 And he took up his ²⁸discourse and said,

"From ^RAram Balak has brought me,
Moab's king from the mountains of the East,   Num. 22:5; Deut. 23:4

'Come^R curse Jacob for me,   Num. 22:6
And come, denounce Israel!'

8 "How^R shall I curse, whom God has not cursed?   Num. 22:12
And how can I denounce, whom the LORD has not denounced?

9 "As I see him from the top of the rocks, And I look at him from the hills,
^RBehold, a people *who* dwells apart, And shall not be reckoned among the nations.   Deut. 32:8; 33:28

10 "Who can count the dust of Jacob, Or number the fourth part of Israel?
Let ^Tme die the death of the upright, And let my end be like his!"   *my soul*

11 Then Balak said to Balaam, "What have you done to me? ^RI took you to curse my enemies, but behold, you have actually blessed them!"   Neh. 13:2

12 And he answered and said, "Must I not be careful to speak ^Rwhat the LORD puts in my mouth?"   Num. 22:20

The Second Oracle of Balaam

13 Then Balak said to him, "Please come with me to another place from where you may see them, although you will only see the extreme end of them, and will not see all of them; and curse them for me from there."

14 So he took him to the field of Zophim, to the top of Pisgah, and built seven altars and offered a bull and a ram on *each* altar.

15 And he said to Balak, "Stand here beside your burnt offering, while I myself meet *the* LORD yonder."

16 Then the LORD met Balaam and ^Rput a word in his mouth and said, "Return to Balak, and thus you shall speak."   Num. 22:20

17 And he came to him, and behold, he was standing beside his burnt offering, and the leaders of Moab with him. And Balak said to him, "What has the LORD spoken?"

18 Then he took up his ²⁸discourse and said,

"Arise, O Balak, and hear;
Give ear to me, O son of Zippor!

19 "God^R is not a man, that He should lie,
Nor a son of man, that He should repent;   1 Sam. 15:29
^RHas He said, and will He not do it?
Or has He spoken, and will He not make it good?   Is. 40:8; 55:11

20 "Behold, I have received *a command* to bless;
^RWhen He has blessed, then ^RI cannot revoke it.   Gen. 12:2; 22:17 • [Is. 43:13]

21 "He^R has not observed ^Tmisfortune in Jacob;   Num. 14:18, 19, 34 • *iniquity*
^RNor has He seen trouble in Israel;
The LORD his God is with him,
^RAnd the shout of a king is among them.   Deut. 9:24; 32:5 • Ps. 89:15-18

22 "God^R brings them out of Egypt,
He is for them like the ^Rhorns of the wild ox.   Num. 24:8 • Deut. 33:17

²⁸ Lit., *parable*, and so throughout this context

23 "For^R there is no omen against Jacob,
   Nor is there any divination against Israel;   Num. 22:7; 24:1; Josh. 13:22
   At the proper time it shall be said to
   Jacob
   And to Israel, what God has done.
24 "Behold,^R a people rises like a lioness,
   And as a lion it lifts itself;
   It shall not lie down until it devours
   the prey,   Gen. 49:9; Nah. 2:11, 12
   And drinks the blood of the slain."
25 Then Balak said to Balaam, "Do not
curse them at all nor bless them at all!"
26 But Balaam answered and said to Ba-
lak, "Did I not tell you, 'Whatever^T the LORD
speaks, that I must do'?"   *saying, 'Whatever*

The Third Oracle of Balaam

27 Then Balak said to Balaam, "Please
come, I will take you to another place; perhaps it will be agreeable with God that you
curse him for me from there."
28 So Balak took Balaam to the top of
Peor which overlooks the wasteland.
29 And Balaam said to Balak, "Build
seven altars for me here and prepare seven
bulls and seven rams for me here."
30 And Balak did just as Balaam had said,
and offered up a bull and a ram on *each* altar.

CHAPTER 24

WHEN Balaam saw that it ^Tpleased the
LORD to bless Israel, he did not go as at other times to seek omens but he set his face
toward the wilderness.   *was good in the eyes of*
2 And Balaam lifted up his eyes and saw
Israel ^Tcamping tribe by tribe; and^R the Spirit
of God came upon him.   *dwelling* • Num. 11:26
3 And he took up his discourse and said,
   "The^R oracle of Balaam the son of Beor,
   And the oracle of the man whose eye
   is opened;   Num. 24:15, 16
4 The oracle of him who ^Rhears the
   ^Twords of God,   Num. 22:20 • *sayings*
   Who sees the^R vision of ^Tthe Almighty,
   Falling down, yet having his eyes un-
   covered,   Gen. 15:1 • Heb., *Shaddai*
5 How fair are your tents, O Jacob,
   Your dwellings, O Israel!
6 "Like valleys that stretch out,
   Like gardens beside the river,
   Like aloes planted by the LORD,
   Like ^Tcedars beside the waters. Ps. 1:3
7 "Water shall flow from his buckets,
   And his seed *shall be* by many waters,
   And his king shall be higher than
   ^RAgag,   Num. 24:20; 1 Sam. 15:8
   And his kingdom shall be exalted.
8 "God^R brings him out of Egypt,
   He is for him like the horns of the
   wild ox.   Num. 23:22

²⁹ I.e., tumult

^RHe shall devour the nations *who are*
   his adversaries,   Num. 23:24; Ps. 2:9
   And shall crush their bones in pieces,
   And shatter *them* with his arrows.
9 "He ^Tcouches, he lies down as a lion,
   And as a ^Tlion, who ^Tdares rouse him?
   Blessed is everyone who blesses you,
   And cursed is everyone who curses
   you."   *bows down • lioness • shall*
10 Then Balak's anger burned against Ba-
laam, and he struck his ^Thands together; and
Balak said to Balaam, "I called you to curse
my enemies, but behold, you have persisted
in blessing them these three times!   *palms*
11 "Therefore, flee to your place now. I
said I would honor you greatly, but behold,
the LORD has held you back from honor."
12 And Balaam said to Balak, "Did^R I not
tell your messengers whom you had sent to
me, saying,   Num. 22:18
13 'Though Balak were to give me his
house full of silver and gold, I could not do
anything contrary to the command of the
LORD, either good or bad, of my own accord.
What the LORD speaks, that I will speak'?

The Fourth Oracle of Balaam

14 "And now behold,^R I am going to my people; come, *and* I will advise you what this
people will do to your people in the ^Tdays to
come."   Num. 31:8, 16; Josh. 13:22 • *end of the days*
15 And he took up his discourse and said,
   "The^R oracle of Balaam the son of Beor,
   And the oracle of the man whose eye
   is opened,   Num. 24:3, 4
16 The oracle of him who hears the
   ^Twords of God,   *sayings*
   And knows the knowledge of the
   ^TMost High,   Heb., *Elyon*
   Who sees the vision of ^Tthe Almighty,
   Falling down, yet having his eyes uncovered.   Heb., *Shaddai*
17 "I see him, but not now;
   I behold him, but not near;
   ^RA star shall come forth from Jacob,
   ^RAnd a scepter shall rise from Israel,
   And shall crush through the forehead
   of Moab,   Matt. 1:2☆ • Gen. 49:10
   And tear down all the sons of ²⁹Sheth.
18 "And^R Edom shall be a possession,
   ^RSeir, its enemies, also shall be a possession,   Gen. 27:29 • Gen. 32:3
   While Israel performs valiantly.
19 "One from Jacob shall have dominion,
   And shall destroy the remnant from
   the city."
20 And he looked at Amalek and took up
his discourse and said,
   "Amalek was the first of the nations,
   But his end *shall be* destruction."
21 And he looked at the^R Kenite, and took
up his discourse and said,   Gen. 15:19
   "Your dwelling place is enduring,
   And your nest is set in the cliff.
22 "Nevertheless Kain shall be consumed;

How long shall ᴿAsshurᵀkeep you captive?"   Gen. 10:21, 22 • take

23 And he took up his discourse and said, "Alas, who can live except God has ordained it?

24 "But ships *shall come* from the coast ofᴿKittim,   Gen. 10:4; Ezek. 27:6
And they shall afflict Asshur and shall afflictᴿEber;   Gen. 10:21
ᴿSo they also *shall come* to destruction."   Num. 24:20

25 Then Balaam arose and departed and returned toᴿhis place, and Balak also went his way.   Num. 24:14

CHAPTER 25

Israel Commits Harlotry

WHILE Israel remained at ᴿShittim, the people beganᴿto play the harlot with the daughters of Moab.   Num. 33:49 • Num. 31:16

2 Forᴿthey invited the people to the sacrifices of their gods, and the people ate and bowed down to their gods.   Ex. 34:15

Phinehas Stays the Plague

3 Soᴿlsrael joined themselves toᴬBaal of Peor, and the LORD was angry against Israel.   Ps. 106:28, 29; Hos. 9:10 • *Baal-peor*

4 And the LORD said to Moses, "Take all the leaders of the people and execute them ᵀin broad daylight before the LORD, ᴿso that the fierce anger of the LORD may turn away from Israel."   *in front of the sun* • Deut. 13:17

5 So Moses said to the judges of Israel, "Each of you slay his men who have joined themselves toᴬBaal of Peor."   *Baal-peor*

6 Then behold, one of the sons of Israel came and brought to hisᵀrelatives a Midianite woman, in the sight of Moses and in the sight of all the congregation of the sons of Israel, while they were weeping at the doorwayᵀof the tent of meeting.   *brothers*

7 ᴿWhen Phinehas the son of Eleazar, the son of Aaron the priest, saw it, he arose from the midst of the congregation, and took a spear in his hand;   Ps. 106:30

8 and he went after the man of Israel into theᴬtent, and pierced both of them through, theᵀman of Israel and the woman, through theᴬbody. So the plague on the sons of Israel was checked.   *inner rooms • belly*

9 ᴿAnd those who died by the plague were 24,000.   Num. 14:37; 16:48-50; 31:16

10 Then the LORD spoke to Moses, saying, 11"Phinehasᴿthe son of Eleazar, the son of Aaron the priest, has turned away My wrath from the sons of Israel, in that he was jealous with My jealousy among them, so that I did not destroy the sons of Israelᴿin My jealousy.   Ps. 106:30 • [Ex. 20:5]

12"Therefore say, 'Behold,ᴿ I give him My ᴿcovenant of peace;   Ps. 106:30, 31 • Is. 54:10

13 and it shall be for him and his ᵀdescendants after him, a covenant of a ᴿperpetual priesthood, because he was jealous for his God, andᴿmade atonement for the sons of Israel.' "   *seed* • Ex. 29:9 • Num. 16:46

14 Now the name of the ᵀslain man of Israel who was ᵀslain with the Midianite woman, was Zimri the son of Salu, a leader of a father's household among the Simeonites.   *smitten*

15 And the name of the Midianite woman who was ᵀslain was Cozbi the daughter of Zur, ᵀwho was head of the people of a father's household in Midian.   *smitten • he*

Israel to Destroy Moab

16 Then the LORD spoke to Moses, saying, 17"Beᴿ hostile to the Midianites and strike them;   Num. 25:1; 22:4; 31:1-3

18 for they have been hostile to you with their tricks, with which they have deceived you in the affair of Peor, and in the affair of Cozbi, the daughter of the leader of Midian, their sister who was slain on the day of the plague because of Peor."

CHAPTER 26

The Second Census

THEN it came about after theᴿplague, that the LORD spoke to Moses and to Eleazar the son of Aaron the priest, saying,   Num. 25:9

2"Take a census of all the congregation of the sons of Israel from twenty years old and upward, by their fathers' households, whoever is able to go out to war in Israel."

3 So Moses and Eleazar the priest spoke with themᴿin the plains of Moab by the Jordan at Jericho, saying,   Num. 22:1; 33:48; 35:1

4"*Take a census of the people* from twenty years old and upward, as the LORD has commanded Moses."

Now the sons of Israel who came out of the land of Egypt *were:*

5 Reuben, Israel's first-born, the sons of Reuben: *of* Hanoch, the family of the Hanochites; of Pallu, the family of the Palluites;

6 of Hezron, the family of the Hezronites; of Carmi, the family of the Carmites.

7 These are the families of the Reubenites, and those who were numbered of them wereᴿ43,730.   Num. 1:21

8 And the son of Pallu: Eliab.

9 And the sons of Eliab: Nemuel and Dathan and Abiram. These are the Dathan and Abiram who were called by the congregation, who contended against Moses and against Aaron in the company of Korah, when they contended against the LORD,

10 and the earth opened its mouth and swallowed them up along with Korah, when that company died, when the fire devoured 250 men, so that they became a warning.

11 ᴿThe sons of Korah, however, did not die.   Num. 16:27, 33; Deut. 24:16

12 The sons of Simeon according to their families: of Nemuel, the family of the Nemuelites; of Jamin, the family of the Jaminites; of Jachin, the family of the Jachinites;
13 of Zerah, the family of the Zerahites; of Shaul, the family of the Shaulites.
14 These are the families of the Simeonites,^R22,200.   Num. 1:23
15 The sons of Gad according to their families: of Zephon, the family of the Zephonites; of Haggi, the family of the Haggites; of Shuni, the family of the Shunites;
16 of Ozni, the family of the Oznites; of Eri, the family of the Erites;
17 of Arod, the family of the Arodites; of Areli, the family of the Arelites.
18 These are the families of the sons of Gad according to those who were numbered of them,^R40,500.   Num. 1:25
19 The sons of Judah *were* Er and Onan, but Er and Onan died in the land of Canaan.
20 And the sons of Judah according to their families were: of Shelah, the family of the Shelanites; of Perez, the family of the Perezites; of Zerah, the family of the Zerahites.   Gen. 49:8; 1 Chr. 2:3; Rev. 7:5
21 And the sons of Perez were: of Hezron, the family of the Hezronites; of Hamul, the family of the Hamulites.
22 These are the families of Judah according to those who were numbered of them, ^R76,500.   Num. 1:27
23 The sons of Issachar according to their families: *of* Tola, the family of the Tolaites; of Puvah, the family of the Punites;
24 of Jashub, the family of the Jashubites; of Shimron, the family of the Shimronites.
25 These are the families of Issachar according to those who were numbered of them,^R64,300.   Num. 1:29
26 The sons of Zebulun according to their families: of Sered, the family of the Seredites; of Elon, the family of the Elonites; of Jahleel, the family of the Jahleelites.
27 These are the families of the Zebulunites according to those who were numbered of them,^R60,500.   Num. 1:31
28 The^Rsons of Joseph according to their families: Manasseh and Ephraim. Gen. 46:20
29 The sons of Manasseh: of Machir, the family of the Machirites; and ^RMachir ^Tbecame the father of Gilead: of Gilead, the family of the Gileadites.   Josh. 17:1 • *begot*
30 These are the sons of Gilead: *of* Iezer, the family of the ^RIezerites; of Helek, the family of the Helekites;   Judg. 6:11, 24, 34
31 and *of* Asriel, the family of the Asrielites; and *of* Shechem, the family of the Shechemites;
32 and *of* Shemida, the family of the Shemidaites; and *of* Hepher, the family of the Hepherites.
33 Now Zelophehad the son of Hepher had no sons, but only daughters; and the names of the daughters of Zelophehad were Mahlah, Noah, Hoglah, Milcah and Tirzah.
34 These are the families of Manasseh;

and those who were numbered of them were^R52,700.   Num. 1:35
35 These are the sons of Ephraim according to their families: of Shuthelah, the family of the Shuthelahites; of Becher, the family of the Becherites; of Tahan, the family of the Tahanites.
36 And these are the sons of Shuthelah: of Eran, the family of the Eranites.
37 These are the families of the sons of Ephraim according to those who were numbered of them, 32,500. These are the sons of Joseph according to their families.
38 The sons of Benjamin according to their families: of Bela, the family of the Belaites; of Ashbel, the family of the Ashbelites; of Ahiram, the family of the Ahiramites;
39 of Shephupham, the family of the Shuphamites; of Hupham, the family of the Huphamites.
40 And the sons of Bela were Ard and Naaman: *of Ard*, the family of the Ardites; of Naaman, the family of the Naamites.
41 These are the sons of Benjamin according to their families; and those who were numbered of them were^R45,600.   Num. 1:37
42 These are the sons of Dan according to their families: of Shuham, the family of the Shuhamites. These are the families of Dan according to their families.
43 All the families of the Shuhamites, according to those who were numbered of them, were^R64,400.   Num. 1:39
44 The^Rsons of Asher according to their families: of Imnah, the family of the Imnites; of Ishvi, the family of the Ishvites; of Beriah, the family of the Beriites. Gen. 46:17
45 Of the sons of Beriah: of Heber, the family of the Heberites; of Malchiel, the family of the Malchielites.
46 And the name of the daughter of Asher *was* Serah.
47 These are the families of the sons of Asher according to those who were numbered of them,^R53,400.   Num. 1:41
48 The sons of Naphtali according to their families: of Jahzeel, the family of the Jahzeelites; of Guni, the family of the Gunites;
49 of Jezer, the family of the Jezerites; of Shillem, the family of the Shillemites.
50 These are the families of Naphtali according to their families; and those who were numbered of them were 45,400.
51 These are those who were numbered of the sons of Israel,^R601,730.   Ex. 12:37; 38:26

Method for Dividing the Land

52 Then the LORD spoke to Moses, saying,
53"Among^T these the land shall be divided for an inheritance according to the number of names.   *To*
54"To the larger *group* you shall increase their inheritance, and to the smaller *group* you shall diminish their inheritance; each shall be given their inheritance according to those who were numbered of them.

55"But the land shall be ^Rdivided by lot. They shall ^Treceive their inheritance according to the names of the tribes of their fathers.   Num. 33:54; 34:13 • *inherit according to*

56"According to the selection by lot, their inheritance shall be divided between the larger and the smaller *groups.*"

The Levites Have No Inheritance

57 And these are those who were numbered of the Levites according to their families: of Gershon, the family of the Gershonites; of Kohath, the family of the Kohathites; of Merari, the family of the Merarites.

58 These are the families of Levi: the family of the Libnites, the family of the Hebronites, the family of the Mahlites, the family of the Mushites, the family of the Korahites. And Kohath became the father of Amram.

59 And the name of Amram's wife ^rwas Jochebed, the daughter of Levi, who was born to Levi in Egypt; and she bore to Amram: Aaron and Moses and their sister Miriam.   Ex. 2:1, 2; 6:20

60 ^RAnd to Aaron were born Nadab and Abihu, Eleazar and Ithamar.   Num. 3:2

61 But Nadab and Abihu died when they offered strange fire before the LORD.

62 And those who were numbered of them were^R23,000, every male from a month old and upward, for ^rthey were not numbered among the sons of Israel ^ssince no inheritance was given to them among the sons of Israel.   Num. 3:39 • Num. 1:47 • Num. 18:23, 24

The Old Generation
Has No Inheritance

63 These are those who were numbered by Moses and Eleazar the priest, who numbered the sons of Israel in the plains of Moab by the Jordan at Jericho.

64 ^RBut among these there was not a man of those who were numbered by Moses and Aaron the priest, who numbered the sons of Israel in the wilderness of Sinai.   Heb. 3:17

65 For the LORD had said 'of them, "They^R shall surely die in the wilderness." And not a man was left of them, ^Rexcept Caleb the son of Jephunneh, and Joshua the son of Nun.   *to* • Num. 14:26-35; Ps. 90:3-10 • Deut. 1:36

CHAPTER 27

The Special Laws of Inheritance

THEN ^Rthe daughters of Zelophehad, the son of Hepher, the son of Gilead, the son of Machir, the son of Manasseh, of the families of Manasseh the son of Joseph, came near; and these are ^Rthe names of his daughters: Mahlah, Noah and Hoglah and Milcah and Tirzah.   Num. 26:33; 36:1 • Num. 26:33

2 And they stood before Moses and before Eleazar the priest and before the lead-ers and all the congregation, at the doorway of the tent of meeting, saying,

3"Our father died in the wilderness, yet he was not among the company of those who gathered themselves together against the LORD in the company of Korah; but he died in his own sin, and he had no sons.

4"Why should the name of our father be withdrawn from among his family because he had no son? Give us a possession among our father's brothers."

5 ^RAnd Moses brought their case before the LORD.   Num. 9:8; 27:21

6 Then the LORD spoke to Moses, saying,

7"The^R daughters of Zelophehad are right in *their* statements. You shall surely give them a hereditary possession among their father's brothers, and you shall transfer the inheritance of their father to them. Josh. 17:4

8"Further, you shall speak to the sons of Israel, saying, 'If a man dies and has no son, then you shall transfer his inheritance to his daughter.

9 'And if he has no daughter, then you shall give his inheritance to his brothers.

10 'And if he has no brothers, then you shall give his inheritance to his father's brothers.

11 'And if his father has no brothers, then you shall give his inheritance to his nearest relative in his own family, and he shall possess it; and it shall be a 'statutory ordinance to the sons of Israel, just as the LORD commanded Moses.'"   Num. 35:29

Moses Is Set Aside

12 Then the LORD said to Moses, "Go up to this mountain of Abarim, and see the land which I have given to the sons of Israel.

13"And when you have seen it, you too ^Rshall be gathered to your people, as Aaron your brother 'was;   Num. 31:2 • *was gathered*

14 for in the wilderness of Zin, during the strife of the congregation, you rebelled against My ^Tcommand ^Tto treat Me as holy before their eyes at the water." (These are the waters of Meribah of Kadesh in the wilderness of Zin.)   *mouth* • *for My sanctity*

Joshua Is Appointed

15 Then Moses spoke to the LORD, saying,

16"May^R the LORD, the God of the spirits of all flesh, appoint a man over the congregation,   Num. 16:22

17 who will go out ^Tand come in before them, and who will lead them out and^Tbring them in, that the congregation of the LORD may not be like sheep which have no shepherd."   *before them and who will • who will bring*

18 So the LORD said to Moses, "Take Joshua the son of Nun, a man in whom is the Spirit, and lay your hand on him;

19 and have him stand before Eleazar the priest and before all the congregation; and ^Rcommission him in their sight.   Deut. 3:28

20"And you shall put some of your [T]authority on him, in order that all the congregation of the sons of Israel may obey *him*.   *majesty*
21"Moreover, he shall stand before Eleazar the priest, who shall inquire for him[R]by the judgment of the Urim before the LORD. At his [T]command they shall go out and at his command they shall come in, *both* he and the sons of Israel with him, even all the congregation."   Ex. 28:30; 1 Sam. 28:6 • *mouth*
22 And Moses did just as the LORD commanded him; and he took Joshua and set him before Eleazar the priest, and before all the congregation.
23 Then he laid his hands on him and commissioned him, just as the LORD had spoken [T]through Moses.   *by the hand of*

CHAPTER 28

Daily Offering

THEN the LORD spoke to Moses, saying,
2"Command the sons of Israel and say to them, 'You shall [T]be careful to present My offering, My[R]food for My offerings by fire, of a soothing aroma to Me, at their appointed time.'   *watch* • Lev. 3:11
3"And[R]you shall say to them, 'This is the offering by fire which you shall offer to the LORD; two male lambs one year old without defect *as* a continual burnt offering every day.   Ex. 29:38-42
4 'You shall offer the one lamb in the morning, and the other lamb you shall offer [T]at twilight;   *between the two evenings*
5 also [R]a tenth of an ephah of fine flour for a [R]grain offering, mixed with a fourth of a hin of beaten oil.   Ex. 16:36; Num. 15:4 • Lev. 2:1
6 'It is a continual burnt offering which was ordained in Mount Sinai as a soothing aroma, an offering by fire to the LORD.
7 'Then the libation with it *shall be* a fourth of a hin for each lamb, [R]in the holy place you shall pour out a libation of strong drink to the LORD.   Ex. 29:42
8 'And the other lamb you shall offer at twilight; as the grain offering of the morning and as its libation, you shall offer it, an offering by fire, a soothing aroma to the LORD.

Weekly Offering

9 'Then on the sabbath day two male lambs one year old without defect, and two-tenths *of an ephah* of fine flour mixed with oil as a grain offering, and its libation:
10 'This is the burnt offering of every sabbath in addition to the [R]continual burnt offering and its libation.   Num. 28:3

Monthly Offering

11 'Then at the beginning of each of your months you shall present a burnt offering to the LORD; two bulls and one ram, seven male lambs one year old without defect,

12 [R]and three-tenths *of an* [T]ephah of fine flour for a grain offering, mixed with oil, for each bull; and two-tenths of fine flour for a grain offering, mixed with oil, for the one ram;   Num. 15:4-12 • Approx. one bu.
13 and a[T]tenth *of an ephah* of fine flour mixed with oil for a grain offering for each lamb, for a burnt offering of a soothing aroma, an offering by fire to the LORD.   2 qt.
14 'And their libations shall be half a hin of wine for a bull and a third of a hin for the ram and a fourth of a hin for a lamb; this is the burnt offering of each month throughout the months of the year.
15 'And one male goat for a sin offering to the LORD; it shall be offered with its libation in addition to the continual burnt offering.

Passover

16 'Then on the fourteenth day of the first month shall be the LORD's Passover.

Unleavened Bread

17 'And [R]on the fifteenth day of this month *shall be* a [R]feast, unleavened bread *shall be* eaten for seven days.   Lev. 23:6 • Ex. 23:15
18 'On the first day *shall be* a holy convocation; you shall do no laborious work.
19 'And you shall present an offering by fire, a burnt offering to the LORD: two bulls and one ram and seven male lambs one year old,[R]having them without defect.   Deut. 15:21
20 'And for their grain offering, you shall offer fine flour mixed with oil: three-tenths *of an* [T]ephah for a bull and two-tenths for the ram.   Approx. one bu.
21 'A tenth *of an ephah* you shall offer for [T]each of the seven lambs,   *each lamb*
22 and one male goat for a [R]sin offering, to make atonement for you.   Lev. 16:18; [Rom. 8:3]
23 'You shall present these besides [R]the burnt offering of the morning, which is for a continual burnt offering.   Num. 28:3
24 'After this manner you shall present daily, for seven days, the food of the offering by fire, of a soothing aroma to the LORD; it shall be presented with its libation in addition to the continual burnt offering.
25 'And on the seventh day you shall have a holy convocation;[R]you shall do no laborious work.   Num. 28:18

First Fruits

26 'Also on[R]the day of the first fruits, when you present a new grain offering to the LORD in your *Feast of* Weeks, you shall have a holy convocation;[R]you shall do no laborious work.   Ex. 23:16; 34:22 • Num. 28:18
27 'And you shall offer a burnt offering for a soothing aroma to the LORD, two young bulls, one ram, seven male lambs one year old,
28 and their grain offering, fine flour mixed with oil, three-tenths *of an ephah* for each bull, two-tenths for the one ram,

29 a tenth for each of the seven lambs,

30 one male goat to make atonement for you.

31 'Besides the continual burnt offering and its grain offering, you shall present *them* with their libations. They shall be ^Twithout defect.   *without defect to you*

CHAPTER 29

Trumpets

'N^ROW in the seventh month, on the first day of the month, you shall also have a holy convocation; ^Ryou shall do no laborious work. It will be to you a day for blowing trumpets.   Ex. 23:16; 34:22 • Num. 28:26

2 'And you shall offer a burnt offering as a soothing aroma to the LORD: one bull, one ram, *and* seven male lambs one year old without defect;

3 also their grain offering, fine flour mixed with oil,^Tthree-tenths *of an ephah* for the bull, two-tenths for the ram,   6 qt.

4 and ^Tone-tenth for ^Reach of the seven lambs.   2 qt. • each lamb, and so throughout the ch.

5 'And *offer* one male goat for a sin offering, to make atonement for you,

6 ^Rbesides the burnt offering of the new moon, and its grain offering, and the ^Rcontinual burnt offering and its grain offering, and their libations, according to their ordinance, for a soothing aroma, an offering by fire to the LORD.   Num. 28:27 • Num. 28:3

Atonement

7 'Then on ^Rthe tenth day of this seventh month you shall have a holy convocation, and you shall humble yourselves; you shall not do any work.   Lev. 16:29-34; 23:26-32

8 'And you shall present a burnt offering to the LORD *as* a soothing aroma: one bull, one ram, seven male lambs one year old, ^Rhaving them without defect;   Lev. 22:20

9 and their grain offering, fine flour mixed with oil, three-tenths *of an ephah* for the bull, two-tenths for the one ram,

10 a tenth for each of the seven lambs;

11 one male goat for a sin offering, be-sides ^Rthe sin offering of atonement and the continual burnt offering and its grain offering, and their libations.   Lev. 16:3, 5

Tabernacle

12 'Then on ^Rthe fifteenth day of the seventh month you shall have a holy convocation; you ^Rshall do no laborious work, and you shall observe a feast to the LORD for seven days.   Lev. 23:33-35 • Num. 29:1

13 'And you shall present a burnt offering, an offering by fire as a soothing aroma to the LORD: thirteen bulls, two rams, fourteen male lambs one year old, which are without defect,

14 and their grain offering, fine flour mixed with oil, three-tenths *of an ephah* for ^Teach of the thirteen bulls, two-tenths for ^Teach of the two rams,   *each bull • each ram*

15 and a tenth for each of the fourteen lambs;

16 and one male goat for a sin offering, ^Rbesides the continual burnt offering, its grain offering and its libation.   Num. 28:3

17 'Then on ^Rthe second day: twelve bulls, two rams, fourteen male lambs one year old without defect;   Lev. 23:36

18 and their grain offering and their libations for the bulls, for the rams and for the lambs, by their number ^Raccording to the or-dinance;   Lev. 2:1-16

19 and one male goat for a sin offering, ^Rbesides the continual burnt offering and its grain offering, and their libations. Num. 28:8

20 'Then on the third day: eleven bulls, two rams, fourteen male lambs one year old without defect;

21 and their grain offering and their libations for the bulls, for the rams and for the lambs, by their number according to the or-dinance;

22 and one male goat for a sin offering, besides the continual burnt offering and its grain offering and its libation.

23 'Then on the fourth day: ten bulls, two rams, fourteen male lambs one year old without defect;

24 their grain offering and their libations for the bulls, for the rams and for the lambs, by their number according to the ordinance;

25 and one male goat for a sin offering, besides the continual burnt offering, its grain offering and its libation.

26 'Then on the fifth day: nine bulls, two rams, fourteen male lambs one year old ^Rwithout defect;   [Heb. 7:26]

27 and their grain offering and their libations for the bulls, for the rams and for the lambs, by their number according to the or-dinance;

28 and one male goat for a sin offering, besides the continual burnt offering and its grain offering and its libation.

29 'Then on the sixth day: eight bulls, two rams, fourteen male lambs one year old without defect;

30 and their grain offering and their libations for the bulls, for the rams and for the lambs, by their number according to the or-dinance;

31 and one male goat for a sin offering, besides the continual burnt offering, its grain offering and its libations.

32 'Then on the seventh day: seven bulls, two rams, fourteen male lambs one year old without defect;

33 and their grain offering and their libations for the bulls, for the rams and for the lambs, by their number according to the or-dinance;

34 and one male goat for a sin offering, besides the continual burnt offering, its grain offering and its libation.

35 'On^R the eighth day you shall have a solemn assembly; you shall do no laborious work.   Lev. 23:36

36 'But you shall present a burnt offering, an offering by fire, as a soothing aroma to the LORD: one bull, one ram, seven male lambs one year old without defect;

37 their grain offering and their libations for the bull, for the ram and for the lambs, by their number according to the ordinance;

38 and one male goat for a sin offering, besides the continual burnt offering and its grain offering and its libation.

39 'You shall present these to the LORD at your ^R appointed times, besides your ^T votive offerings and your freewill offerings, for your burnt offerings and for your grain offerings and for your libations and for your peace offerings.' "   Lev. 23:2 · vows

40 And Moses spoke to the sons of Israel in accordance with all that the LORD had commanded Moses.

CHAPTER 30

The Regulations of Vows

THEN Moses spoke to the heads of the tribes of the sons of Israel, saying, "This is the word which the LORD has commanded.

2 "If ^R a man makes a vow to the LORD, or takes an oath to bind himself with a binding obligation, he shall not violate his word; he shall do according to all that proceeds out of his mouth.   Deut. 23:21-23; Matt. 5:33

3 "Also if a woman makes a vow to the LORD, and binds herself by an obligation in her father's house in her youth,

4 and her father hears her vow and her obligation by which she has bound herself, and her father says nothing to her, then all her vows shall stand, and every obligation by which she has bound herself shall stand.

5 "But if her father should forbid her on the day he hears of it, none of her vows or her obligations by which she has bound herself shall stand; and the LORD will forgive her because her father had forbidden her.

6 "However, if she should marry while under her vows or the rash statement of her lips by which she has bound herself,

7 and her husband hears of it and says nothing to her on the day he hears it, then her vows shall stand and her obligations by which she has bound herself shall stand.

8 "But if on the day her husband hears of it, he forbids her, then he shall annul her vow which she is under and the rash statement of her lips by which she has bound herself; and the LORD will forgive her.

9 "But the vow of a widow or of a divorced woman, everything by which she has bound herself, shall stand against her.

10 "However, if she vowed in her husband's house, or bound herself by an obligation with an oath,

11 and her husband heard it, but said nothing to her and did not forbid her, then all her vows shall stand, and every obligation by which she bound herself shall stand.

12 "But if her husband indeed annuls them on the day he hears them, then whatever proceeds out of her lips concerning her vows or concerning the obligation of herself, shall not stand; her husband has annulled them, and the LORD will forgive her.

13 "Every vow and every binding oath to humble herself, her husband may confirm it or her husband may annul it.

14 "But if her husband indeed says nothing to her from day to day, then he confirms all her vows or all her obligations which are on her; he has confirmed them, because he said nothing to her on the day he heard them.

15 "But if he indeed annuls them after he has heard them, then he shall bear her guilt."

16 These are the statutes which the LORD commanded Moses, as between a man and his wife, and as between a father and his daughter, while she is in her youth in her father's house.

CHAPTER 31

Destruction of the Midianites

THEN the LORD spoke to Moses, saying,

2 "Take ^R full vengeance for the sons of Israel on the Midianites; afterward you will be gathered to your people."   Num. 25:1, 16, 17

3 And Moses spoke to the people, saying, "Arm men from among you for the war, that they may ^T go against Midian, to execute the LORD's vengeance on Midian.   be

4 "A thousand from each tribe of all the tribes of Israel you shall send to the war."

5 So there were ^T furnished from the thousands of Israel, a thousand from each tribe, twelve thousand armed for war.   delivered

6 And Moses sent them, a thousand from each tribe, to the war, and Phinehas the son of Eleazar the priest, to the war with them, ^R and the holy vessels and the trumpets for the alarm in his hand.   Num. 14:44

7 So they made war against Midian, just as the LORD had commanded Moses, and ^R they killed every male. Deut. 20:13; Judg. 21:11

8 And they killed the kings of Midian along with the rest of their slain: ^R Evi and Rekem and Zur and Hur and Reba, the five kings of Midian; they also killed Balaam the son of Beor with the sword.   Josh. 13:21

9 And the sons of Israel captured the women of Midian and their little ones; and all their cattle and all their flocks and all their goods, they plundered.

10 Then they burned all their cities where they lived and all their camps with fire.

11 And ^R they took all the spoil and all the prey, both of man and of beast.   Deut. 20:14

12 And they brought the captives and the prey and the spoil to Moses, and to Eleazar the priest and to the congregation of the sons of Israel, to the camp at the plains of Moab, which are by the Jordan opposite Jericho.

13 And Moses and Eleazar the priest and all the leaders of the congregation went out to meet them outside the camp.

14 And Moses was angry with the officers of the army, the captains of thousands and the captains of hundreds, who had come from service in the war.

15 And Moses said to them, "Have you ^Tspared all the women?   *let ... live*

16"Behold, these ^bcaused the sons of Israel, through the ^ccounsel of ^RBalaam, to trespass against the LORD in the matter of Peor, so the plague was among the congregation of the LORD.   *were to • word • Num. 31:8*

17"Now therefore, kill every male among the little ones, and kill every woman who has known man ^fintimately. *by lying with a man*

18"But all the girls who have not known man intimately, spare for yourselves.

Purification of Israel

19"And ^Ryou, camp outside the camp seven days; whoever has killed any person, and whoever has touched any slain, purify yourselves, you and your captives, on the third day and on the seventh day.   Num. 19:11-22

20"And you shall purify for yourselves every garment and every article of ^dleather and all the work of goats' *hair*, and all articles of wood."   *skin*

21 Then Eleazar the priest said to the men of war who had gone to battle, "This is the statute of the law which the LORD has commanded Moses:

22 only the gold and the silver, the bronze, the iron, the tin and the lead,

23 everything that can stand the fire, you shall pass through the fire, and it shall be clean, but it shall be purified with water for impurity. But whatever cannot stand the fire you shall pass through the water.

24"And you shall wash your clothes on the seventh day and be clean, and afterward you may enter the camp."

Distribution of the Spoils

25 Then the LORD spoke to Moses, saying,

26"You and Eleazar the priest and the heads of the fathers' *households* of the congregation, take a count of the booty that was captured, both of man and of animal;

27 and ^bdivide the booty between the warriors who went out to battle and all the congregation.   Josh. 22:8

28"And levy a tax for the LORD from the men of war who went out to battle, one in five hundred of the persons and of the cattle and of the donkeys and of the sheep;

29 take it from their half and give it to Eleazar the priest, as an offering to the LORD.

30"And from the sons of Israel's half, you shall take one drawn out of every fifty of the persons, of the cattle, of the donkeys and of the sheep, from all the animals, and give them to the Levites who ^Rkeep charge of the tabernacle of the LORD."   Num. 18:3, 4

31 And Moses and Eleazar the priest did just as the LORD had commanded Moses.

32 Now the booty that remained from the spoil which the ^Tmen of war had plundered was 675,000 sheep,   *people*

33 and 72,000 cattle,

34 and 61,000 donkeys,

35 and of human beings, of the women who had not known man ^Tintimately, all the persons were 32,000.   *by lying with a man*

36 And the half, the portion of those who went out to war, was *as follows:* the number of sheep was 337,500,

37 and the LORD's levy of the sheep was 675,

38 and the cattle were 36,000, from which the LORD's levy was 72.

39 And the donkeys were 30,500, from which the LORD's levy was 61.

40 And the human beings were 16,000, from whom the LORD's levy was 32 persons.

41 And Moses gave the levy *which was* the LORD's offering to Eleazar the priest, just as the LORD had commanded Moses.

42 As for the sons of Israel's half, which Moses ^Aseparated from the men who had gone to war—   *divided*

43 now the congregation's half was 337,500 sheep,

44 and 36,000 cattle,

45 and 30,500 donkeys,

46 and the human beings were 16,000—

47 and from the sons of Israel's half, Moses took one drawn out of every fifty, both of man and of animals, and gave them to the Levites, who kept charge of the tabernacle of the LORD, just as the LORD had commanded Moses.

48 Then the officers who were over the thousands of the army, the captains of thousands and the captains of hundreds, approached Moses;

49 and they said to Moses, "Your servants have taken a census of men of war who are in our charge, and no man of us is missing.

50"So we have brought as an offering to the LORD what each man found, articles of gold, armlets and bracelets, signet rings, earrings and necklaces, ^Rto make atonement for ourselves before the LORD."   Ex. 30:12-16

51 And Moses and Eleazar the priest took the gold from them, all kinds of wrought articles.

52 And all the gold of the offering which they offered up to the LORD, from the captains of thousands and the captains of hundreds, was ^T16,750 shekels. $32,160,000

53 ^RThe men of war had taken booty, every man for himself.   Num. 31:32; Deut. 20:14

54 So Moses and Eleazar the priest took the gold from the captains of thousands and of hundreds, and brought it to the tent of meeting as [R]a memorial for the sons of Israel before the LORD.   Ex. 30:16

CHAPTER 32

Division of the Land
East of Jordan—Deut. 3:12–19

Now the sons of Reuben and the sons of Gad had an [R]exceedingly large number of livestock. So when they saw the land of Jazer and the land of Gilead, that it was indeed a place suitable for livestock, Ex. 12:38

2 the sons of Gad and the sons of Reuben came and spoke to Moses and to Eleazar the priest and to the leaders of the congregation, saying,

3 "Ataroth, Dibon, Jazer, Nimrah, Heshbon, Elealeh, Sebam, Nebo and Beon,

4 the land [R]which the LORD conquered before the congregation of Israel, is a land for livestock; and your servants have livestock."   Num. 21:34 • smote

5 And they said, "If we have found favor in your sight, let this land be given to your servants as a possession; do not take us across the Jordan."

6 But Moses said to the sons of Gad and to the sons of Reuben, "Shall your brothers go to war while you yourselves sit here?

7 "Now why are you discouraging the sons of Israel from crossing over into the land which the LORD has given them?

8 "This[T] is what your fathers did when I sent them from [R]Kadesh-barnea to see the land.   Thus your fathers • Deut. 1:19-25

9 "For when they went up to the valley of Eshcol and saw the land, they discouraged the sons of Israel so that they did not go into the land which the LORD had given them.

10 "So [R]the LORD's anger burned in that day, and He swore, saying,   Num. 14:11f.

11 'None[R] of the men who came up from Egypt, from twenty years old and upward, shall see the land which I swore to Abraham, to Isaac and to Jacob; for they did not follow Me fully,   Num. 14:28-30

12 except Caleb the son of Jephunneh the Kenizzite and Joshua the son of Nun, for they have followed the LORD fully.'

13 "So[R] the LORD's anger burned against Israel, and He made them wander in the wilderness forty years, until the entire generation of those who had done evil in the sight of the LORD was destroyed.   Num. 14:33-35

14 "Now behold, you have risen up in your fathers' place, a brood of sinful men, to add still more to the burning [R]anger of the LORD against Israel.   Deut. 1:34f.

15 "For if you [R]turn away from following Him, He will once more abandon them in the wilderness; and you will destroy all these people."   Deut. 30:17, 18; 2 Chr. 7:19, 20

16 Then they came near to him and said,

"We will build here sheepfolds for our livestock and cities for our little ones;

17 [R]but we ourselves will be armed ready to go before the sons of Israel, until we have brought them to their place, while our little ones live in the fortified cities because of the inhabitants of the land.   Josh. 4:12, 13

18 "We[R] will not return to our homes until every one of the sons of Israel has possessed his inheritance.   Josh. 22:1-4

19 "For we will not have an inheritance with them on the other side of the Jordan and beyond, because our inheritance has fallen to us[R] on this side of the Jordan toward the east."   Josh. 12:1; 13:8

20 [R]So Moses said to them, "If you will do this, if you will arm yourselves before the LORD for the war,   Deut. 3:18 • this thing

21 and all of you armed men cross over the Jordan before the LORD until He has driven His enemies out from before Him,

22 [R]and the land is subdued before the LORD, then afterward you shall return and be free of obligation toward the LORD and toward Israel, and this land shall be yours for a possession before the LORD. Deut. 3:20

23 "But if you will not do so, behold, you have sinned against the LORD, and be sure [R]your sin will find you out.   Gen. 4:7; 44:16

24 "Build yourselves cities for your little ones, and sheepfolds for your sheep; and [R]do what you have promised."   Num. 30:2

25 And the sons of Gad and the sons of Reuben spoke to Moses, saying, "Your servants will do just as my lord commands.

26 "Our[R] little ones, our wives, our livestock and all our cattle shall [T]remain there in the cities of Gilead;   Josh. 1:14 • be

27 while your servants, everyone who is armed for war, will[R] cross over in the presence of the LORD to battle, just as my lord says."   Josh. 4:12

28 So Moses gave command concerning them to Eleazar the priest, and to Joshua the son of Nun, and to the heads of the fathers' households of the tribes of the sons of Israel.

29 And Moses said to them, "If the sons of Gad and the sons of Reuben, everyone who is armed for battle, will cross with you over the Jordan in the presence of the LORD, and the land will be subdued before you, then you shall give them the land of Gilead for a possession;

30 but if they will not cross over with you armed, they shall have possessions among you in the land of Canaan."

31 And the sons of Gad and the sons of Reuben answered, saying, "As the LORD has said to your servants, so we will do.

32 "We ourselves will cross over armed in the presence of the LORD into the land of Canaan, and the possession of our inheritance shall remain with us across the Jordan."

33 So Moses gave to them, to the sons of

Gad and to the sons of Reuben and to the half-tribe of Joseph's son Manasseh, the kingdom of Sihon, king of the Amorites and the kingdom of Og, the king of Bashan, the land with its cities with *their* [t]territories, the cities of the surrounding land.   *borders*

34 And the sons of Gad built Dibon and Ataroth and [R]Aroer,   Deut. 2:36

35 and Atroth-shophan and Jazer and Jogbehah,

36 and Beth-nimrah and Beth-haran as fortified cities, and sheepfolds for sheep.

37 And the sons of Reuben built Heshbon and Elealeh and Kiriathaim,

38 and [R]Nebo and Baal-meon—*their* names being changed—and Sibmah, and they gave *other* names to the cities which they built.   Is. 46:1

39 And the sons of Machir the son of Manasseh went to Gilead and took it, and dispossessed the Amorites who were in it.

40 So Moses gave Gilead to Machir the son of Manasseh, and he lived in it.

41 And Jair the son of Manasseh went and took its [t]towns, and called them [t]Havvoth-jair.[R]   *tent villages • the towns of Jair •* Judg. 10:4

42 And Nobah went and took Kenath and its villages, and called it Nobah after [R]his own name.   2 Sam. 18:18; Ps. 49:11

CHAPTER 33

From Egypt to Sinai

THESE are the journeys of the sons of Israel, by which they came out from the land of Egypt by their armies, under [t]the [R]leadership of Moses and Aaron.   Ps. 77:20 • *hand*

2 And Moses recorded their starting places according to their journeys by the command of the LORD, and these are their journeys according to their starting places.

3 And they journeyed from Rameses in the first month, on the fifteenth day of the first month; on the [t]next day after the Passover the sons of Israel started out boldly in the sight of all the Egyptians,   *morrow*

4 while the Egyptians were burying all their first-born whom the LORD had struck down among them. The LORD had also executed judgments [t]on their gods.   Ex. 12:12

5 Then [t]the sons of Israel journeyed from Rameses, and camped in Succoth.   Ex. 12:37

6 [R]And they journeyed from Succoth, and camped in Etham, which is on the edge of the wilderness.   Ex. 13:20

7 [R]And they journeyed from Etham, and turned back to Pi-hahiroth, which faces Baal-zephon; and they camped before Migdol.   Ex. 14:1, 2

8 [R]And they journeyed from before Hahiroth, and passed through the midst of the sea into the wilderness; and they went three days' journey in the wilderness of Etham, and camped at Marah.   Ex. 14:22

9 [R]And they journeyed from Marah, and came to Elim; and in Elim there were twelve springs of water and seventy palm trees; and they camped there.   Ex. 15:27

10 And they [t]journeyed from Elim, and camped by the [R]Red Sea.   *Sea of Reeds*

11 And they journeyed from the Red Sea, and camped in the wilderness of Sin.

12 And they journeyed from the wilderness of Sin, and camped at Dophkah.

13 And they journeyed from Dophkah, and camped at Alush.

14 And they journeyed from Alush, and camped [R]at Rephidim; now it was there that the people had no water to drink.   Ex. 17:1

15 And they journeyed from Rephidim, and camped in the wilderness of Sinai.

From Sinai to Kadesh

16 And they journeyed from the wilderness of Sinai, and camped at [R]Kibroth-hattaavah.   Num. 11:34

17 And they journeyed from Kibroth-hattaavah, and camped at Hazeroth.

The Wilderness Wanderings

18 And they journeyed from Hazeroth, and camped at Rithmah.

19 And they journeyed from Rithmah, and camped at Rimmon-perez.

20 And they journeyed from Rimmon-perez, and camped at [R]Libnah.   Deut. 1:1

21 And they journeyed from Libnah, and camped at Rissah.

22 And they journeyed from Rissah, and camped in Kehelathah.

23 And they journeyed from Kehelathah, and camped at Mount Shepher.

24 And they journeyed from Mount Shepher, and camped at Haradah.

25 And they journeyed from Haradah, and camped at Makheloth.

26 And they journeyed from Makheloth, and camped at Tahath.

27 And they journeyed from Tahath, and camped at Terah.

28 And they journeyed from Terah, and camped at Mithkah.

29 And they journeyed from Mithkah, and camped at Hashmonah.

30 And they journeyed from Hashmonah, and camped at [R]Moseroth.   Deut. 10:6

31 And they journeyed from Moseroth, and camped at Bene-jaakan.

32 And they journeyed from [R]Bene-jaakan, and camped at Hor-haggidgad.   Gen. 36:27

33 And they journeyed from Hor-haggidgad, and camped at [R]Jotbathah.   Deut. 10:7

34 And they journeyed from Jotbathah, and camped at Abronah.

35 And they journeyed from Abronah, and camped at [R]Ezion-geber.   Deut. 2:8

36 And they journeyed from Ezion-geber, and camped in the wilderness of [R]Zin, that is, Kadesh.   Num. 20:1

From Kadesh to Moab

37 And they journeyed from Kadesh, and

camped at ᴿMount Hor, ᴿat the edge of the land of Edom.   Num. 20:22 • Num. 20:16

38 Then Aaron the priest went up to Mount Hor at the command of the LORD, and died there, in the fortieth year after the sons of Israel had come from the land of Egypt on the first *day* in the fifth month.

39 And Aaron was one hundred twenty-three years old when he died on Mount Hor.

40 Now the Canaanite, the king of ᴿArad ᵀwho lived in the ᵀNegev in the land of Canaan, heard of the coming of the sons of Israel.   Num. 21:1 • *and he* • South country

41 Then they journeyed from Mount Hor, and camped at Zalmonah.

42 And they journeyed from Zalmonah, and camped at Punon.

43 And they journeyed from Punon, and camped at ᴿOboth.   Num. 21:10, 11

44 And they journeyed from Oboth, and camped at Iye-abarim, at the border of Moab.

45 And they journeyed from Iyim, and camped at Dibon-gad.

46 And they journeyed from Dibon-gad, and camped at Almon-diblathaim.

47 And they journeyed from Almon-diblathaim, and camped in the mountains of ᴿAbarim, before Nebo.   Num. 27:12

48 And they journeyed from the mountains of Abarim, and camped in the plains of Moab by the Jordan *opposite* Jericho.

49 And they camped by the Jordan, from Beth-jeshimoth as far as ᴿAbel-shittim in the plains of Moab.   Num. 25:1

Instructions for Conquering Canaan

50 Then the LORD spoke to Moses in the plains of Moab by the Jordan *opposite* Jericho, saying,

51"Speak to the sons of Israel and say to them, 'Whenᴿ you cross over the Jordan into the land of Canaan,   Josh. 3:17

52 then you shall drive out all the inhabitants of the land from before you, and ᴿdestroy all their figured stones, and destroy all their molten images and demolish all their high places;   Ex. 23:24; Lev. 26:1; Deut. 7:5

53 ᴿand you shall take possession of the land and live in it, for I have given the land to you to possess it.   Deut. 11:31; 17:14

54 'Andᴿ you shall inherit the land by lot according to your families; to the larger you shall give more inheritance, and to the smaller you shall give less inheritance. Wherever the lot falls to anyone, that shall be his. You shall inherit according to the tribes of your fathers.   Num. 26:53-56

55 'But if you do not drive out the inhabitants of the land from before you, then it shall come about that those whom you let remain of them *will become* ᴿas pricks in your eyes and as thorns in your sides, and

they shall trouble you in the land in which you live.   Josh. 23:13

56 'And it shall come about that as I plan to do to them, so I will do to you.' "

CHAPTER 34

The South

Tʜᴇɴ the LORD spoke to Moses, saying,

2"Command the sons of Israel and say to them, 'When you enterᴿthe land of Canaan, this is the land that shall fall to you as an inheritance, *even the* land of Canaan according to its borders.   Gen. 17:8; Ps. 78:54, 55

3 'Your southern sector shall extend from the wilderness of Zin along the side of Edom, and your southern border shall extend from the end of the Salt Sea eastward.

4 'Then your border shall turn *direction* from the south to the ascent of Akrabbim, and ᵗcontinue to Zin, and its ³⁰termination shall be to the south ofᴿKadesh-barnea; and it shallᵀreach Hazaraddar, and continue to Azmon.   *pass along* • Num. 32:8 • *go forth to*

5 'And the border shall turn *direction* from Azmon to the brook of Egypt, and its termination shall be atᵗthe sea.   Josh. 15:4

The West

6 'As for the western border, you shall have the Great Sea, that is, *its* ᵗcoastline; this shall be your west border.   *border*

The North

7 'Andᴿ this shall be your north border: you shall draw your *border* line from the Great Sea to Mount Hor.   Ezek. 47:15-17

8 'You shall draw a line from Mount Hor toᵗthe Lebo-hamath, and the termination of the border shall be at Zedad;   Josh. 13:5

9 and the border shall proceed to Ziphron, and its termination shall be at Hazar-enan. This shall be your north border.

The East

10 'For your eastern border you shall also draw a line from Hazar-enan to Shepham,

11 and the border shall go down from Shepham toᴿRiblah on the east side of Ain; and the border shall go down and reach to the ³¹slope on the east side of the Sea of ᵗChinnereth.   2 Kin. 23:33 • Deut. 3:17

12 'And the border shall go down to the Jordan and its termination shall be at the Salt Sea. This shall be your land according to its borders all around.' "

13 So Moses commanded the sons of Israel, saying, "Thisᴿis the land that you are to apportion by lot among you as a possession, which the LORD has commanded to give to the nine and a half tribes.   Gen. 15:18

14"Forᴿ the tribe of the sons of Reuben have received *theirs* according to their fathers' households, and the tribe of the sons

---

³⁰ Lit., *goings out,* and so throughout this context
³¹ Lit., *shoulder*

of Gad according to their fathers' house-holds, and the half-tribe of Manasseh have received their possession.   Num. 32:33

15"The two and a half tribes have received their possession across the Jordan opposite Jericho, eastward toward the sunrising."

Officials for Dividing Canaan

16 Then the LORD spoke to Moses, saying,
17"These^R are the names of the men who shall apportion the land to you for inheri-tance: Eleazar the priest and Joshua the son of Nun.   Josh. 14:1, 2

18"And you shall take one leader of every tribe to apportion the land for inheritance.
19"And these are the names of the men: of the tribe of^RJudah,^RCaleb the son of Jephun-neh.   Gen. 29:35; Deut. 33:7 • Num. 13:6, 30; 26:65

20"And of the tribe of the sons of^RSimeon, Samuel the son of Ammihud.   Gen. 29:33; 49:5

21"Of the tribe of ^RBenjamin, Elidad the son of Chislon.   Gen. 49:27; Deut. 33:12

22"And of the tribe of the sons of Dan a leader, Bukki the son of Jogli.

23"Of the sons of Joseph: of the tribe of the sons of Manasseh a leader, Hanniel the son of Ephod.

24"And of the tribe of the sons of Ephraim a leader, Kemuel the son of Shiphtan.

25"And of the tribe of the sons of Zebulun a leader, Elizaphan the son of Parnach.

26"And of the tribe of the sons of Issachar a leader, Paltiel the son of Azzan.

27"And of the tribe of the sons of Asher a leader, Ahihud the son of Shelomi.

28"And of the tribe of the sons of Naphtali a leader, Pedahel the son of Ammihud."

29 These are those whom the LORD com-manded to apportion the inheritance to the sons of Israel in the land of Canaan.

CHAPTER 35

Cities for the Levites

NOW^R the LORD spoke to Moses in the plains of Moab by the Jordan opposite Jeri-cho, saying,   Lev. 25:32-34

2"Command the sons of Israel that they give to the Levites from the inheritance of their possession, cities to live in; and you shall give to the Levites pasture lands around the cities.

3"And the cities shall be theirs to live in; and their pasture lands shall be for their cat-tle and for their herds and for all their beasts.

4"And the pasture lands of the cities which you shall give to the Levites *shall ex-tend* from the wall of the city outward a ^Tthousand cubits around.   and outward • 1500 ft.

5"You shall also measure outside the city on the east side two thousand cubits, and on the south side two thousand cubits, and on the west side two thousand cubits, and on the north side two thousand cubits,

with the city in the center. This shall be-come theirs as pasture lands for the cities.

6"And the cities which you shall give to the Levites *shall be* the ^Rsix cities of refuge, which you shall give for the manslayer to flee to; and in addition to them you shall give forty-two cities.   Josh. 20:7-9

7"All the cities which you shall give to the Levites *shall be* forty-eight cities, ^Tto-gether with their pasture lands.   *them*

8"As for the cities which you shall give from the possession of the sons of Israel, you shall take more from the larger and you shall take less from the smaller; each shall give some of his cities to the Levites in pro-portion to his possession which he inherits."

Cities of Refuge

9 Then the LORD spoke to Moses, saying,
10"Speak^R to the sons of Israel and say to them, 'When you cross the Jordan into the land of Canaan,   Josh. 20:1-9

11 then you shall select for yourselves cities to be your cities of refuge, that the manslayer who has^Tkilled any person ^Runin-tentionally may flee there.   *smote* • Ex. 21:13

12 'And^Rthe cities shall be to you as a ref-uge from the avenger, so that the manslayer may not die until he stands before the con-gregation for^Ttrial.   Deut. 19:4-6 • *judgment*

13 'And the cities which you are to give shall be your six cities of refuge.

14 'You shall give three cities across the Jordan and three cities in the land of Ca-naan; they are to be cities of refuge.

15 'These six cities shall be for refuge for the sons of Israel, and for the alien and for the sojourner among them; that anyone who kills a person unintentionally may flee there.

16 'But if he struck him down with an iron object, so that he died, he is a murderer; the murderer shall surely be put to death.

17 'And if he struck him down with a stone in the hand, by which he may die, and *as a result* he died, he is a murderer; the mur-derer shall surely be put to death.

18 'Or if he struck him with a wooden ob-ject in the hand, by which he may die, and *as a result* he died, he is a murderer; the murderer shall surely be put to death.

19 'The blood avenger himself shall put the murderer to death; he shall put him to death when he meets him.

20 'And ^Rif he pushed him of hatred, or threw something at him^Rlying in wait and *as a result* he died,   Gen. 4:8 • Ex. 21:14

21 or if he struck him down with his hand in enmity, and *as a result* he died, the one who struck him shall surely be put to death, he is a murderer; the blood avenger shall put the murderer to death when he meets him.

22 'But^R if he pushed him suddenly without enmity, or threw something at him without lying in wait,   Num. 35:11

23 or with any 'deadly object of stone, and without seeing it dropped on him so that he died, while he was not his enemy nor seeking his injury,   *by which he may die*

24 then 'the congregation shall judge between the slayer and the blood avenger according to these ordinances.   Josh. 20:6

25 'And the congregation shall deliver the manslayer from the hand of the blood avenger, and the congregation shall restore him to his city of refuge to which he fled; and he shall live in it until the death of the high priest who was anointed with the holy oil.

26 'But if the manslayer shall at any time go beyond the border of his city of refuge to which he may flee,

27 and the blood avenger finds him outside the border of his city of refuge, and the blood avenger kills the manslayer, he shall not be guilty of blood

28 because he should have remained in his city of refuge until the death of the high priest. But after the death of the high priest the manslayer shall return to the land of his possession.

29 'And these things shall be for a ᴿstatutory ordinance to you throughout your generations in all your dwellings.   Num. 27:11

30 'If anyone kills a person, the murderer shall be put to death at the ᵀevidence of witnesses, but no person shall be put to death on the testimony of one witness.   *mouth*

31 'Moreover, you shall not take ransom for the life of a murderer who is guilty of death, but he shall surely be put to death.

32 'And you shall not take ransom for him who has fled to his city of refuge, that he may return to live in the land ᴬbefore the death of the priest.   *until*

33 'So you shall not pollute the land in which you are; for blood pollutes the land and no expiation can be made for the land for the blood that is shed on it, except ᴿby the blood of him who shed it.   Gen. 9:6

34 'And you shall not ᴿdefile the land in which you live, in the midst of which I dwell; for I the LORD am dwelling in the midst of the sons of Israel.' "   Lev. 18:24, 25

CHAPTER 36

*Special Problems of Inheritance
in Canaan*

Aᴺᴰᴿ the heads of the fathers' *households* of the family of the sons of Gilead, the son of Machir, the son of Manasseh, of the families of the sons of Joseph, came near and spoke before Moses and before the leaders, the heads of the fathers' *households* of the sons of Israel,   Num. 27:1

2 and they said, "The LORD commanded my lord to give the land by lot to the sons of Israel as an inheritance, and my lord ᴿwas commanded by the LORD to give the inheritance of Zelophehad our brother to his daughters.   Num. 27:5-7

3 "But if they ᵀmarry one of the sons of the *other* tribes of the sons of Israel, their inheritance will be withdrawn from the inheritance of our fathers and will be added to the inheritance of the tribe to which they belong; thus it will be withdrawn from our allotted inheritance.   *become wives to,* in this ch.

4 "And when the ᴿjubilee of the sons of Israel ᶜcomes, then their inheritance will be added to the inheritance of the tribe to which they belong; so their inheritance will be withdrawn from the inheritance of the tribe of our fathers."   Lev. 25:10 • *shall be*

5 Then Moses commanded the sons of Israel according to the ᵀword of the LORD, saying, "The tribe of the sons of Joseph are right in *their* statements.   *mouth*

6 "This is ᵂhat the LORD has commanded concerning the daughters of Zelophehad, saying, 'Let them marry whom they wish; only they must marry within the family of the tribe of their father.'   *the thing which*

7 "Thus no inheritance of the sons of Israel shall be transferred from tribe to tribe, for the sons of Israel shall each ᵀhold to the inheritance of the tribe of his fathers. *cleave*

8 "And ᴿ every daughter who comes into possession of an inheritance of any tribe of the sons of Israel, shall be wife to one of the family of the tribe of her father, so that the sons of Israel each may possess the inheritance of his fathers.   1 Chr. 23:22

9 "Thus no inheritance shall ᵀbe transferred from one tribe to another tribe, for the tribes of the sons of Israel shall each hold to his own inheritance."   *turn about*

10 Just as the LORD had commanded Moses, so the daughters of Zelophehad did:

11 ᴿMahlah, Tirzah, Hoglah, Milcah and Noah, the daughters of Zelophehad married their uncles' sons.   Num. 26:33

12 They married *those* from the families of the sons of Manasseh the son of Joseph, and their inheritance ᵀremained with the tribe of the family of their father.   *was*

13 ᴿThese are the commandments and the ordinances which the LORD commanded to the sons of Israel through Moses in the plains of Moab by the Jordan *opposite* Jericho.   Lev. 26:46; 27:34; Num. 22:1

DEUTERONOMY

THE BOOK OF DEUTERONOMY

Deuteronomy, Moses' "Upper Desert Discourse," consists of a series of farewell messages by Israel's 120-year-old leader. It is addressed to the new generation destined to possess the land of promise—those who survived the forty years of wilderness wandering.

Like Leviticus, Deuteronomy contains a vast amount of legal detail, but its emphasis is on the laymen rather than the priests. Moses reminds the new generation of the importance of obedience if they are to learn from the sad example of their parents.

The Hebrew title of Deuteronomy is *Haddebharim*, "The Words," taken from the opening phrase in 1:1, "These are the words." The parting words of Moses to the new generation are given in oral and written form so that they will endure to all generations. Deuteronomy has been called "five-fifths of the Law" since it completes the five books of Moses. The Jewish people have also called it *Mishneh Hattorah*, "repetition of the Law," which is translated in the Septuagint as *To Deuteronomion Touto*, "This Second Law." Deuteronomy, however, is not a second law but an adaptation and expansion of much of the original law given on Mount Sinai. The English title comes from the Greek title *Deuteronomion*, "Second Law." Deuteronomy has also been appropriately called the "Book of Remembrance."

THE AUTHOR OF DEUTERONOMY

The Mosaic authorship of Deuteronomy has been vigorously attacked by critics who claim that Moses is only the originator of the tradition on which these laws are based. Some critics grant that part of Deuteronomy may have come from Mosaic times through oral tradition. The usual argument is that it was anonymously written not long before 621 B.C. and used by King Josiah to bring about his reform in that year (2 Kin. 22 and 23). There are several reasons why these arguments are not valid.

External Evidence: (1) The Old Testament attributes Deuteronomy and the rest of the Pentateuch to Moses (see Josh. 1:7; Judg. 3:4; 1 Kin. 2:3; 2 Kin. 14:6; Ezra 3:2; Neh. 1:7; Ps. 103:7; Dan. 9:11; Mal. 4:4). (2) Evidence from Joshua and First Samuel indicates that these laws existed in the form of codified written statutes and exerted an influence on the Israelites in Canaan. (3) Christ quotes it as God's Word in turning back Satan's three temptations (Matt. 4:4, 7, 10) and attributes it directly to Moses (Matt. 19:7–9; Mark 7:10; Luke 20:28; John 5:45–47). (4) Deuteronomy is cited more than eighty times in seventeen of the twenty-seven New Testament books. These citations support the Mosaic authorship (see Acts 3:22; Rom. 10:19). (5) Jewish and Samaritan traditions point to Moses.

Internal Evidence: (1) Deuteronomy includes about forty claims that Moses wrote it. Read Deuteronomy 31: 24–26 (see also 1:1–5; 4:44–46; 29:1; 31:9). (2) Deuteronomy fits the time of Moses, not Josiah: Canaan is viewed from the outside; the Canaanite religion is seen as a future menace; it assumes the hearers remember Egypt and the wilderness; Israel is described as living in tents; and there is no evidence of a divided kingdom. (3) A serious problem of misrepresentation and literary forgery would arise if this book were written in the seventh century B.C. (4) Geographical and historical details indicate a firsthand knowledge. (5) Deuteronomy follows the treaty form used in the fifteenth and fourteenth centuries B.C. (6) Moses' obituary in Chapter 34 was probably written by Joshua.

THE TIME OF DEUTERONOMY

Like Leviticus, Deuteronomy does not progress historically. It takes place entirely on the plains of Moab due east of Jericho and the Jordan River (1:1; 29:1; Josh. 1:2). It covers about one month: combine Deuteronomy 1:3 and 34:8 with Joshua 5:6–12. The book was written at the end of the forty-year period in the wilderness (c. 1405 B.C.) when the new generation was on the verge of entering Canaan. Moses wrote it to encourage the people to believe and obey God in order to receive God's blessings.

THE CHRIST OF DEUTERONOMY

The most obvious portrait of Christ is found in 18:15: "The LORD your God will raise up for you a prophet like me from among you, from your countrymen, you shall listen to him" (see also 18:16–19; Acts 7:37). Moses is a type of Christ in many ways as he is the only biblical figure other than Christ to fill the three offices of prophet (34:10–12), priest (Ex. 32:31–35), and king (although Moses was not king, he functioned as ruler of Israel; 33:4, 5). Both are in danger of death during child-

hood; both are saviors, intercessors, and believers; and both are rejected by their brothers. Moses is one of the greatest men who ever lived, combining not just one or two memorable virtues but many.

KEYS TO DEUTERONOMY

Key Word: Covenant—The primary theme of the entire Book of Deuteronomy is the renewal of the covenant. Originally established at Mount Sinai, the covenant is enlarged and renewed on the plains of Moab.

Key Verses: Deuteronomy 10:12, 13; 30:19, 20—"And now, Israel, what does the LORD your God require from you, but to fear the LORD your God, to walk in all His ways and love Him, and to serve the LORD your God with all your heart and with all your soul, *and* to keep the LORD'S commandments and His statutes which I am commanding you today for your good?" (10:12, 13).

"I call heaven and earth to witness against you today, that I have set before you life and death, the blessing and the curse. So choose life in order that you may live, you and your descendants, by loving the LORD your God, by obeying His voice, and by holding fast to Him; for this is your life and the length of your days, that you may live in the land which the LORD swore to your fathers, to Abraham, Isaac, and Jacob, to give them" (30:19, 20).

Key Chapter: Deuteronomy 27—The formal ratification of the covenant occurs in Deuteronomy 27 as Moses, the priests, the Levites, and all of Israel "Be silent and listen, O Israel! This day you have become a people for the LORD your God" (27:9).

SURVEY OF DEUTERONOMY

Deuteronomy, in its broadest outline, is the record of the renewal of the Old Covenant given at Mount Sinai. This covenant is reviewed, expanded, enlarged, and finally ratified in the plains of Moab. Moses accomplishes this primarily through three sermons that move from a retrospective, to an introspective, and finally to a prospective look at God's dealings with Israel.

Moses' First Sermon (1:1—4:43): Moses reaches into the past to remind the people of two undeniable facts in their history: (1) the moral judgment of God upon Israel's unbelief, and (2) the deliverance and provision of God during times of obedience. The simple lesson is that obedience brings blessing and disobedience brings punishment.

Moses' Second Sermon (4:44—26:19): This moral and legal section is the longest in the book because Israel's future as a nation in Canaan will depend upon a right relationship with God. These chapters review the three categories of the Law: (1) *The testimonies (5—11)*. These are the moral duties—a restatement and expansion of the Ten Commandments plus an exhortation not to forget God's gracious deliverance. (2) *The statutes (12:1—16:17)*. These are the ceremonial duties—sacrifices, tithes, and feasts. (3) *The ordinances (16:18—26:19)*. These are the civil (16:18—20:20) and social (21—26) duties—the system of justice, criminal laws, laws of warfare, rules of property, personal and family morality, and social justice.

Moses' Third Sermon (27—34): In these chapters Moses writes history in advance. He predicts what will befall Israel in the near future (blessings and cursings) and in the distant future (dispersion among the nations and eventual return). Moses lists the terms of the covenant soon to be ratified by the people. Because Moses will not be allowed to enter the land, he appoints Joshua as his successor and delivers a farewell address to the multitude. God Himself buries Moses in an unknown

FOCUS	FIRST SERMON	SECOND SERMON				THIRD SERMON		
REFERENCE	1:1————4:44	————12:1————	16:18———21:1		———27:1	———29:1———31:1	———34:12	
DIVISION	REVIEW OF GOD'S ACTS FOR ISRAEL	EXPOSITION OF THE DECALOGUE	CEREMONIAL LAWS	CIVIL LAWS	SOCIAL LAWS	RATIFICATION OF COVENANT	PALESTINIAN COVENANT	TRANSITION OF COVENANT MEDIATOR
TOPIC	WHAT GOD HAS DONE	WHAT GOD EXPECTED OF ISRAEL				WHAT GOD WILL DO		
	HISTORICAL	LEGAL				PROPHETICAL		
LOCATION	PLAINS OF MOAB							
TIME	c. 1 MONTH							

place, perhaps to prevent idolatry. Moses finally enters the Promised Land when he appears with Christ on the Mount of Trans- figuration (Matt. 17:3). The last three verses of the Pentateuch (34:10–12) are an appropriate epitaph for this great man.

CHAPTER 1

The Preamble of the Covenant

THESE are the words which Moses spoke to all Israel[R]across the Jordan in the wilderness, in the[R]Arabah opposite Suph, between Paran and Tophel and Laban and Hazeroth and Dizahab.   Deut. 4:46 • Deut. 2:8

2 It is eleven days' *journey* from Horeb by the way of Mount Seir to Kadesh-barnea.

3 And it came about in the[R]fortieth year, on the first day of the eleventh month, that Moses spoke to the children of Israel, according to all that the LORD had commanded him *to give* to them,   Num. 33:38

4 after he had [T]defeated[R]Sihon the king of the Amorites, who lived in Heshbon, and Og the king of Bashan, who lived in [R]Ashtaroth and Edrei.   *smitten* • Deut. 2:26-35 • Josh. 12:4

5 Across the Jordan in the land of Moab, Moses undertook to expound this law, saying,

From Mount Sinai to Kadesh
Ex. 18:18–26

6"The LORD our God[R]spoke to us at Horeb, saying, 'You have [T]stayed long enough at this mountain.   Num. 10:11-13 • *dwelt*

7 'Turn and set your journey, and go to [R]the hill country of the Amorites, and to all their neighbors in the Arabah, in the hill country and in the lowland and in the [1]Negev and by the seacoast, the land of the Canaanites, and Lebanon, as far as the great river, the river Euphrates.   Gen. 15:18

8 'See, I have placed the land before you; go in and possess the land which the LORD [R]swore to give to your fathers, to Abraham, to Isaac, and to Jacob, to them and their [T]descendants after them.'   Gen. 12:7; 26:3 • *seed*

9"And I spoke to you at that time, saying, 'I[R] am not able to bear *the burden* of you alone.   Ex. 18:18, 24; Num. 11:14

10 'The LORD your God has[R]multiplied you, and behold, you are this day as the stars of heaven for multitude.   Deut. 7:7; 10:22; 26:5

11 'May the LORD, the God of your fathers, increase you a thousand-fold more than you are, and bless you, [R]just as He has[T]promised you!   Deut. 1:8, 10 • *spoken to*

12 'How can I alone bear the load and burden of you and your strife?

13 'Choose[T] wise and discerning and experienced men from your tribes, and I will appoint them as your heads.' *Give for yourselves*

14"And you answered me and said, 'The thing which you have said to do is good.'

15"So I took the heads of your tribes, wise and experienced men, and [T]appointed them heads over you, leaders of thousands, and[T]of hundreds,[T]of fifties and [T]of tens, and officers for your tribes.   *gave* • *leaders of*

16"Then I charged your judges at that time, saying, 'Hear *the cases* between your [T]fellow countrymen, and judge righteously between a man and his fellow countryman, or the alien who is with him.   *brothers*

17 'You[R]shall not show partiality in judgment; you shall hear the small and the great alike. You shall not fear [T]man, for the judgment is God's. And the case that is too hard for you, you shall bring to me, and I will hear it.'   Acts 10:34; James 2:1, 9 • *because of man*

18"And[R]I commanded you at that time all the things that you should do.   Ex. 18:20

At Kadesh—Num. 13:1—14:45

19"Then we set out from[R]Horeb, and went through all that [R]great and terrible wilderness which you saw, on the way to the hill country of the Amorites, just as the LORD our God had commanded us; and we came to Kadesh-barnea.   Deut. 1:2 • Deut. 2:7; 8:15

20"And I said to you, 'You have come to the hill country of the Amorites which the LORD our God is about to give us.

21 'See, the LORD your God has placed the land before you; go up, take possession, as the LORD, the God of your fathers, has spoken to you. Do not fear or be dismayed.'

22"Then[R] all of you approached me and said, 'Let us send men before us, that they may search out the land for us, and bring back to us word of the way by which we should go up, and the cities which we shall enter.'   Num. 13:1-3

23"And the thing pleased me and I took twelve of your men, one man for each tribe.

24"And[R]they turned and went up into the hill country, and came to the valley of Eshcol, and spied it out.   Num. 13:21-25

25"Then they took *some* of the fruit of the land in their hands and brought it down to us; and they brought us back a report and said, 'It is a good land which the LORD our God is about to give us.'

26"Yet[R]you were not willing to go up, but [R]rebelled against the[T]command of the LORD your God;   Num. 14:1-4 • Deut. 9:23 • *mouth*

27 and [R]you grumbled in your tents and said, 'Because the LORD hates us, He has brought us out of the land of Egypt to deliver us into the hand of the Amorites to destroy us.   Deut. 9:28; Ps. 106:25

28 'Where can we go up? Our brethren have made our hearts melt, saying, "The people are bigger and taller than we; the cities are large and fortified to heaven. And besides, we saw [R]the sons of the Anakim there." '   Num. 13:28, 33; Deut. 9:2

29"Then I said to you, 'Do not be shocked, nor fear them.

30 'The LORD your God who goes before you will Himself fight on your behalf, just as He did for you in Egypt before your eyes,

31 and in the wilderness where you saw how[R]the LORD your God carried you, just as a man carries his son, in all the way which you have walked, until you came to this place.'   Deut. 32:10-12; Is. 46:3, 4; 63:9; Hos. 11:3

[1] I.e., South country

32"But [T]for[R] all this, you did not trust the LORD your God,   *in this matter* · Num. 14:11

33 who goes before you on *your* way,[R] to seek out a place for you to encamp, in fire by night and cloud by day, to show you the way in which you should go.   Num. 10:33

34"Then the LORD heard the sound of your words, and He was angry and [R]took an oath, saying,   Num. 14:28-30; [Heb. 3:18]

35 'Not[R] one of these men, this evil generation, shall see the good land which I swore to give your fathers,   1 Cor. 10:5; [Heb. 3:14-19]

36 except Caleb the son of Jephunneh; he shall see it, and to him and to his sons I will give the land on which he has set foot, because he has followed the LORD fully.'

37"The[R] LORD was angry with me also on your account, saying, 'Not[R] even you shall enter there.   Num. 20:12 · Num. 27:13, 18

38 'Joshua the son of Nun, who stands before you, he shall enter there; encourage him, for he shall cause Israel to inherit it.

39 'Moreover, your little ones who you said would become a prey, and your sons, who this day have[R] no knowledge of good or evil, shall enter there, and I will give it to them, and they shall possess it.   Is. 7:15, 16

40 'But as for you, [T]turn around and set out for the wilderness by the way to the [T]Red Sea.'   Num. 14:25 · *Sea of Reeds*

41"Then you answered and said to me, 'We have sinned against the LORD; we will indeed go up and fight, just as the LORD our God commanded us.' And every man of you girded on his weapons of war, and regarded it as easy to go up into the hill country.

42"And[R] the LORD said to me, 'Say to them, "Do not go up, nor fight, for I am not among you; lest you be [T]defeated before your enemies." '   Num. 14:41-43 · *smitten*

43"So I spoke to you, but you would not listen. Instead you rebelled against the command of the LORD, and acted presumptuously and went up into the hill country.

44"And[R] the Amorites who [T]lived in that hill country came out against you, and chased you [T]as bees do, and crushed you from Seir to Hormah.   Num. 14:45 · *dwelt* · Ps. 118:12

45"Then you returned and wept before the LORD; but the[R] LORD did not listen to your voice, nor give ear to you.   [Job 27:8, 9]

46"So you remained in Kadesh many days, [T]the days that you spent *there*.   *as the days*

CHAPTER 2

"Do Not Meddle with Edom"
Num. 21:4

"THEN we turned and set out for the wilderness by the way to the [T]Red Sea, as the LORD spoke to me, and circled[R] Mount Seir for many days.   *Sea of Reeds* · Deut. 1:2

2"And the LORD spoke to me, saying,

3 'You have circled this mountain long enough. *Now* turn north,

4 and command the people, saying, "You will pass through the [R]territory of your brothers the sons of Esau who live in Seir; and [R]they will be afraid of you. So be very careful;   Gen. 36:8 · Ex. 15:15, 16

5 do not provoke them, for I will not give you any of their land, even *as little as* a [T]footstep because I have given Mount Seir to Esau as a possession.   *treading of a sole of a foot*

6"You shall buy food from them with money so that you may eat, and you shall also purchase water from them with money so that you may drink.

7"For the LORD your God has blessed you in all [T]that you have done; He has known your [T]wanderings through this great wilderness. These forty years the LORD your God has been with you; you have not lacked a thing." '   *the work of your hand* · *goings*

8"So we passed beyond our brothers the sons of Esau, who live in Seir, away from the [R]Arabah road, away from Elath and [R]from Ezion-geber. And we turned and passed through by the way of the wilderness of Moab.   Deut. 1:1 · Num. 33:35; 1 Kin. 9:26

"Do Not Harass Moab"

9"Then the LORD said to me, 'Do not harass Moab, nor provoke them to war, for I will not give you any of [T]their land as a possession, because I have given [R]Ar to the sons of Lot as a possession.   *his* · Num. 21:15, 28

10 (The[R] Emim lived there formerly, a people as great, numerous, and tall as the Anakim.   Gen. 14:5

11 Like the Anakim, they are also regarded as[R] Rephaim, but the Moabites call them Emim.   Gen. 14:5; Deut. 2:20

12 The[R] Horites formerly lived in Seir, but the sons of Esau dispossessed them and destroyed them from before them and settled in their place,[R] just as Israel did to the land of [T]their possession which the LORD gave to them.)   Gen. 36:20 · Num. 21:25, 35 · *his*

13 'Now arise and cross over the brook Zered yourselves.' So we crossed over the [A]brook Zered.   *wadi*

14"Now the time that it took for us to come from Kadesh-barnea, until we crossed over the brook Zered, was thirty-eight years; until all the generation of the men of war perished from within the camp, as the LORD had sworn to them.

15"Moreover[R] the hand of the LORD was against them, to destroy them from within the camp, until they all perished.   Jude 5

"Do Not Harass Ammon"

16"So it came about when [T]all the men of war had finally perished from among the people,   Deut. 2:14

17 that the LORD spoke to me, saying,

18 'You shall cross over [R]Ar, the border of Moab, today.   Deut. 2:9

19 'And when you come opposite the ᴿsons of Ammon, do not harass them nor provoke them, for I will not give you any of the land of the sons of Ammon as a possession, because I have given it to ᴿthe sons of Lot as a possession.'　　　　Gen. 19:38 · Deut. 2:9

20 (It is also regarded as the land of the Rephaim, *for* Rephaim formerly lived in it, but the Ammonites call them Zamzummin,

21 a people as great, numerous, and tall as the Anakim, but the Lᴏʀᴅ destroyed them before them. And they dispossessed them and settled in their place,

22 just as He did for the sons of Esau, who ᴿlive in Seir, when He destroyed ᵀthe Horites from before them; and they dispossessed them, and settled in their place even to this day.　　Gen. 36:8; Deut. 2:5 · Deut. 2:12

23 And the ᴿAvvim, who lived in villages as far as Gaza, the ²Caphtorimᴿ who came from ³Caphtor,ᴿ destroyed them and lived in their place.)　　Josh. 13:3 · Gen. 10:14 · Jer. 47:4

The Conquest of Sihon—Num. 21:21–25

24 'Arise, set out, and pass through the ᴬvalleyᴿof Arnon. Look! I have given Sihon the Amorite, king of Heshbon, and his land into your hand; begin to take possession and contend with him in battle.　*wadi* · Judg. 11:18

25 'This day I will begin to put the dread and fear of you ᵀupon the peoples everywhere under the heavens, who, when they hear the report of you, shall tremble and be in anguish because of you.'　　*in front of*

26 "Soᴿ I sent messengers from the wilderness of Kedemoth to Sihon king of Heshbon with words of peace, saying,　　Num. 21:21-32

27 'Let me pass through your land, I will ᵀtravel only on the highway; I will not turn aside to the right or to the left.　*go by the way*

28 'You will sell me food for money so that I may eat, and give me water for money so that I may drink, ᴿonly let me pass through on ᵀfoot,　　Num. 20:19 · *my feet*

29 just as the sons of Esau who live in Seir and the Moabites who live in Ar did for me, until I cross over the Jordan into the land which the Lᴏʀᴅ our God is giving to us.'

30 "But Sihon king of Heshbon was not willing for us to pass ᵀthrough his land; for the Lᴏʀᴅ your God hardened his spirit and made his heart obstinate, in order to deliver him into your hand, as *he is* today.　*by him*

31 "And the Lᴏʀᴅ said to me, 'See, I have begun to deliver Sihon and his land ᵀover to you. Begin to ᵀoccupy, that you may possess his land.'　　*before you · possess*

32 "Then Sihon ᵀwith all his people came out to meet us in battle at Jahaz.　*he and*

33 "And the Lᴏʀᴅ our God delivered him ᵀover to us; and we ᵀdefeated him with his sons and all his people.　*before us · smote*

34 "So we captured all his cities at that time, and ᵀutterly destroyed ᵀthe men, women and children of every city. We left no survivor.　　*put under the ban · every city of man . . .*

35 "We took ᴿonly the animals as our booty and the spoil of the cities which we had captured.　　Deut. 3:7

36 "From Aroer which is on the edge of the ᴬvalley of Arnon and *from* the city which is in the ᴬvalley, even to Gilead, there was no city that was too high for us; the Lᴏʀᴅ our God delivered all ᵀover to us.　*wadi · before us*

37 "Only ᴿyou did not go near to the land of the sons of Ammon, all along the ᴬriver ᴿJabbok and the cities of the hill country, and wherever the Lᴏʀᴅ our God had commanded us.　　Deut. 2:19 · *wadi* · Gen. 32:22

CHAPTER 3

The Conquest of Og—Num. 21:33–35

"**T**HENᴿ we turned and went up the road to Bashan, and Og, king of Bashan, ᵀwith all his people came out to meet us in battle at Edrei.　　Num. 21:33-35 · *he and*

2 "But the Lᴏʀᴅ said to me, 'Do not fear him, for I have delivered him and all his people and his land into your hand; and you shall do to him just as you did to Sihon king of the Amorites, who lived at Heshbon.'

3 "So the Lᴏʀᴅ our God delivered Og also, king of Bashan, with all his people into our hand, and we smote ᵀthem until no survivor was ᵀleft.　　*him · left to him*

4 "And we captured all his cities at that time; there was not a city which we did not take from them: sixty cities, all the region of Argob, the kingdom of Og in Bashan.

5 "All these were cities fortified with high walls, gates and bars, besides a great many ᴬunwalled towns.　　*rural*

6 "And we utterly destroyed them, as we did to Sihon king of Heshbon, ᴿutterly destroying ᵀthe men, women and children of every city.　　Deut. 2:34 · *every city of men . . .*

7 "But ᴿall the animals and the spoil of the cities we took as our booty.　　Deut. 2:35

8 "Thus we took the land at that time from the hand of the two kings of the Amorites who were beyond the Jordan, from the ᴬvalley of Arnon to Mount Hermon　*wadi*

9 (Sidonians call Hermonᴿ Sirion, and the Amorites call it ᴿSenir):　Ps. 29:6 · 1 Chr. 5:23

10 all the cities of the tableland and all Gilead and ᴿall Bashan, as far as Salecah and Edrei, cities of the kingdom of Og in Bashan.　　Josh. 13:11

11 (For only Og king of Bashan was left of the remnant of the Rephaim. Behold, his bedstead was an iron bedstead; it is in Rabbah of the sons of Ammon. Its length was ᵀnine cubits and its widthᵀfour cubitsᵀby ordinary cubit.)　13.5 ft. · 6 ft. · *by a man's forearm*

Land Is Granted to Two-and-a-Half Tribes
Num. 32:25–41

12"So we took possession of this land at that time. From Aroer, which is by the ᵛvalley of Arnon, and half the hill country of Gilead and its cities, I gave to the Reubenites and to the Gadites.   *wadi* • Num. 32:32-38

13"And the rest of Gilead, and all Bashan, the kingdom of Og, I gave to the half-tribe of Manasseh, all the region of Argob (concerning all Bashan, it is called the land of Rephaim.

14 Jair the son of Manasseh took all the region of Argob as far as the border of the Geshurites and the Maacathites, and called ᵀit, *that is*, Bashan, after his own name, Havvoth-jair, *as it is* to this day.)   *them*

15"And to Machir I gave Gilead.

16"And to the Reubenites and to the Gadites, I gave from Gilead even as far as the ᵛvalley of Arnon, the middle of theᴬvalleyᵀas a border and as far as the ᵀriver Jabbok, the border of the sons of Ammon;   *wadi • and*

17 the Arabah also, with the Jordan as *a* border, from ⁴Chinnereth even as far as the sea of the Arabah, the Salt Sea, ᵀat the foot of the slopes of Pisgah on the east.   *under*

18"Then I commanded you at that time, saying, 'Theᴿ LORD your God has given you this land to possess it; ᴿall you valiant men shall cross over armed before your brothers, the sons of Israel.   Josh. 1:13 • Num. 32:20

19 'Butᴿyour wives and your little ones and your livestock (I know that you haveᴿmuch livestock), shall remain in your cities which I have given you,   Josh. 1:14 • Ex. 12:38

20 ᴿuntil the LORD gives rest to your fellow countrymen as to you, and they also possess the land which the LORD your God will give them beyond the Jordan.ᴿThen you may return every man to his possession, which I have given you.'   Josh. 1:15 • Josh. 22:4

Transition of Leadership

21"And I commanded Joshua at that time, saying, 'Your eyes have seen all that the LORD your God has done to these two kings; so the LORD shall do to all the kingdoms into which you are about to cross.

22 'Do not fear them, for the LORD your Godᴿis the one fighting for you.'   Ex. 14:14

23"I also pleaded with the LORD at that time, saying,

24 'O Lord GOD, Thou hast begun to show Thy servantᴿThy greatness and Thy strong hand; for whatᴿgod is there in heaven or on earth who can do such works and mighty acts as Thine?   Deut. 11:2 • Ex. 8:10; 15:11

25 'Let me, I pray, cross over and see the fair land that is beyond the Jordan, ᵀthat good hill country and Lebanon.'   *this*

26"But the LORD was angry with me on your account, and would not listen to me; and the LORD said to me, 'Enough!ᵀSpeak to Me no more of this matter.   *Enough for you*

27 'Go up to the top ofᴿPisgah and lift up your eyes to the west and north and south and east, and see *it* with your eyes, for you shall not cross over this Jordan.   Num. 23:14

28 'But charge Joshua and encourage him and strengthen him;ᴿfor he shall go acrossᵀat the head of this people, and he shall give them as an inheritance the land which you will see.'   Deut. 1:38 • *before this people*

29"So we remained in the valley opposite ᴿBeth-peor.   Num. 25:1-3; Deut. 4:46; 34:6

CHAPTER 4

Summary of the Covenant

"AND now, O Israel, listen to the statutes and the judgments whichᴿI am teaching you to perform, in order thatᴿyou may live and go in and take possession of the land which the LORD, the God of your fathers, is giving you.   Deut. 1:3 • Lev. 18:5; Deut. 5:33; 8:1; 16:20

2"You shall not add to the word which I am commanding you, nor take away from it, that you may keep the commandments of the LORD your God which I command you.

3"Your eyes have seen what the LORD has done in the case of Baal-peor, for all the men who followed Baal-peor, the LORD your God has destroyed them from among you.

4"But you who held fast to the LORD your God are alive today, every one of you.

5"See, I have taught you statutes and judgments just as the LORD my God commanded me, that you should do thus in the land where you are entering to possess it.

6"So keep and do *them*, ᴿfor that is your wisdom and your understanding in the sight of the peoples who will hear all these statutes and say, 'Surely this great nation is a wise and understanding people.' [2 Tim. 3:15]

7"Forᴿwhat great nation is there that has a god so near to it as is the LORD our God whenever we call on Him?   Deut. 4:32-34

8"Or what great nation is there that has ᴿstatutes and judgments as righteous as this whole law which I am setting before you today?   [Ps. 89:14; 97:2; 119:144, 160, 172]

9"Only ᴿgive heed to yourself and keep your soul diligently, lest you forget the things which your eyes have seen, and lest they depart from your heart all the days of your life; but make them known to your sons and your grandsons.   Deut. 4:23; 6:12

10"*Remember* the day you stood before the LORD your God at Horeb, when the LORD said to me, 'Assemble the people to Me, that I may let them hear My wordsᴿso they may learn to ⁵fear Me all the days they live on the earth, and that they mayᴿteach their children.'   Deut. 14:23; 17:19 • Deut. 4:9

11"And you came near and stood at the foot of the mountain, and the mountain burned with fire to the *very* heart of the

⁴ I.e., the Sea of Galilee
⁵ Or, *reverence*

heavens: darkness, cloud and thick gloom.

12 "Then the LORD spoke to you from the midst of the fire; you heard the sound of words, but you saw no form—only a voice.

13 "So He declared to you His covenant which He commanded you to perform, *that is,* the ten [T]commandments; and He wrote them on two tablets of stone.   *words*

14 "And the LORD commanded me at that time to teach you statutes and judgments, that you might perform them in the land where you are going over to possess it.

15 "So [R]watch yourselves carefully, since you did not see any [T]form on the day the LORD spoke to you at Horeb from the midst of the fire,   Josh. 23:11 • Is. 40:18

16 lest you act corruptly and make a graven image for yourselves in the form of any figure, the likeness of male or female,

17 the likeness of any animal that is on the earth, the likeness of [R]any winged bird that flies in the sky,   Rom. 1:23

18 the likeness of anything that creeps on the ground, the likeness of any fish that is in the water below the earth.

19 "And *beware,* lest you lift up your eyes to heaven and see the sun and the moon and the stars, [R]all the host of heaven, [T]and be drawn away and worship them and serve them, those which the LORD your God has allotted to all the peoples under the whole heaven.   Gen. 2:1; Deut. 17:3 • Job 31:26-28

20 "But the LORD has taken you and brought you out of [R]the iron furnace, from Egypt, to [R]be a people for His own possession, as today.   1 Kin. 8:51; Jer. 11:4 • Deut. 7:6

21 "Now [R]the LORD was angry with me on your account, and swore that I should not cross the Jordan, and that I should not enter the good land which the LORD your God is giving you as an inheritance.   Num. 20:12

22 "For I shall die in this land, I shall not cross the Jordan, but you shall cross and take possession of this [R]good land.   Deut. 3:25

23 "So watch yourselves, [R]lest you forget the covenant of the LORD your God, which He made with you, and [R]make for yourselves a graven image in the form of anything *against* which the LORD your God has commanded you.   Deut. 4:9 • Deut. 4:16

24 "For the LORD your God is a [R]consuming fire, a [R]jealous God.   Ex. 24:17 • Deut. 5:9

25 "When you [T]become the father of children and children's children and have remained long in the land, and act corruptly, and [R]make an [A]idol in the form of anything, and do that which is evil in the sight of the LORD your God *so as* to provoke Him to anger,   *beget* • Deut. 4:23 • *a graven image*

26 I [R]call heaven and earth to witness against you today, that you shall surely perish quickly from the land where you are going over the Jordan to possess it. You shall not [T]live long on it, but shall be utterly destroyed.   Deut. 30:19; 31:28 • *prolong your days*

27 "And the LORD will [R]scatter you among the peoples, and you shall be left few in number among the nations, where the LORD shall drive you.   Lev. 26:33; Deut. 28:64; 29:28

28 "And [R]there you will serve gods, the work of man's hands, [R]wood and stone, [R]which neither see nor hear nor eat nor smell.   Jer. 16:13 • Deut. 29:17 • Ps. 115:4-8

29 "But [R]from there you will seek the LORD your God, and you will find *Him* if you search for Him [R]with all your heart and all your soul.   [Deut. 30:1–3, 10] • [Deut. 6:5; 10:12]

30 "When you are in distress and all these things have come upon you, [R]in the latter days, [R]you will return to the LORD your God and listen to His voice.   Heb. 1:2 • Jer. 4:1, 2

31 "For the LORD your God is a [R]compassionate God; He will not fail you nor destroy you nor forget the covenant with your fathers which He swore to them.   Ex. 34:6

32 "Indeed, [A]ask now concerning the former days which were before you, since the [R]day that God created [A]man on the earth, and *inquire* from one end of the heavens to the other. [R]Has *anything* been done like this great thing, or has *anything* been heard like it?   Deut. 32:7 • Gen. 1:27 • *Adam* • Deut. 4:7

33 "Has [R]any people heard the voice of God speaking from the midst of the fire, as you have heard *it,* and survived?   Ex. 20:22

34 "Or has a god tried to go to take for himself a nation from within *another* nation by trials, by signs and wonders and by war and [R]by a mighty hand and by an outstretched arm and by great terrors, [T]as the LORD your God did for you in Egypt before your eyes?   Deut. 5:15 • *according to all that*

35 "To you it was shown that you might know that the LORD, He is God; [R]there is no other besides Him.   Ex. 8:10; 9:14; [Deut. 4:39]

36 "Out of the heavens He let you hear His voice [R]to discipline you; and on earth He let you see His great fire, and you heard His words from the midst of the fire.   [Deut. 8:5]

37 "Because [T]He loved your fathers, therefore He chose their descendants after them. And He personally brought you from Egypt by His great power,   *And instead, because*

38 driving out from before you nations greater and mightier than you, to bring you in *and* [R]to give you their land for an inheritance, as it is today.   Num. 32:4; 34:14, 15

39 "Know therefore today, and take it to your heart, that [T]the LORD, He is God in heaven above and on the earth below; there is no other.   Deut. 4:35; Josh. 2:11

40 "So you shall keep His statutes and His commandments which I am [T]giving you today, that it may go well with you and with your children after you, and that you may live long on the land which the LORD your God is giving you for all time."   *commanding*

41 Then Moses set apart three cities across the Jordan to the [T]east,   *sunrise*

42 that a manslayer might flee there, who unintentionally slew his neighbor without having enmity toward him in time past; and by fleeing to one of these cities he might live:

43 ᴿBezer in the wilderness on the plateau for the Reubenites, and Ramoth in Gilead for the Gadites, and Golan in Bashan for the Manassites.   Josh. 20:8

The Introduction to the Law of God

44 Now this is the law which Moses set before the sons of Israel;

45 these are the testimonies and the statutes and the ordinances which Moses spoke to the sons of Israel, when they came out from Egypt,

46 across the Jordan, in the valley opposite Beth-peor, in the land of Sihon king of the Amorites who lived at Heshbon, whom Moses and the sons of Israel ᵀdefeated when they came out from Egypt.   smote

47 And they took possession of his land and the land of ᴬOg king of Bashan, the two kings of the Amorites, who were across the Jordan to the ᵀeast,   Deut. 1:4; 3:3, 4 • sunrise

48 from ᴬAroer, which is on the edge of the ᴬvalley of Arnon, even as far as Mount Sion (that is, Hermon),   Deut. 2:36; 3:12 • wadi

49 with all the Arabah across the Jordan to the east, even as far as the sea of the Arabah, at the foot of the slopes of Pisgah.

CHAPTER 5

Setting of the Covenant

THEN Moses summoned all Israel, and said to them, "Hear, O Israel, the statutes and the ordinances which I am speaking today in your ᵀhearing, that you may learn them and observe them carefully.   ears

2 "The LORD our God made ᴿa covenant with us at Horeb.   Ex. 19:5; Mal. 4:4

3 "The ᴿ LORD did not make this covenant with our fathers, but with us, with all those of ᵀus alive here today.   Heb. 8:9 • us ourselves

4 "The LORD spoke to you face to face at the mountain from the midst of the fire,

5 while I was standing between the LORD and you at that time, to declare to you the word of the LORD;ᴿfor you were afraid because of the fire and did not go up the mountain. ᵀHe said,   Heb. 12:18-21 • saying

Commandments of the Covenant

6 'Iᴿam the LORD your God, who brought you out of the land of Egypt, out of the house of ᵀslavery.   Ex. 20:2-17; Lev. 26:1 • slaves

7 'Youᴿshall have no other gods ᴬbefore Me.   Ex. 20:3 • besides

8 'You shall not make for yourself ᴬan idol, or any likeness of what is in heaven above ᵀor on the earth beneath ᵀor in the water under the earth.   a graven image • or what is

9 'You shall not worship them or serve them; for I, the LORD your God, am a jealous God,ᴿvisiting the iniquity of the fathers on the children, and on the third and the fourth generations of those who hate Me,   Ex. 34:7

10 but ᴿshowing lovingkindness to thousands, to those who love Me and keep My commandments.   Num. 14:18; Deut. 7:9

11 'Youᴿ shall not take the name of the LORD your God in vain, for the LORD will not ᴬleave him unpunished who takes His name in vain.   Ex. 20:7; Lev. 19:12 • hold him guiltless

12 'Observeᴿ the sabbath day to keep it holy, as the LORD your God commanded you.   Ex. 16:23-30; 20:8-11; 31:13f.; Mark 2:27f.

13 'Six days you shall labor and do all your work,

14 but the seventh day is a sabbath of the LORD your God; in it you shall not do any work, you or your son or your daughter or your male servant or your female servant or your ox or your donkey or any of your cattle or your sojourner who ᵀstays with you, so that your male servant and your female servant may rest as well as you.   is in your gates

15 'Andᴿyou shall remember that you were a slave in the land of Egypt, and the LORD your God brought you out of there by a mighty hand and by an outstretched arm; therefore the LORD your God commanded you to observe the sabbath day.   Ex. 20:11

16 'Honorᴿyour father and your mother, as the LORD your God has commanded you, that your days may be prolonged, and that it may go well with you on the land which the LORD your God gives you.   Ex. 20:12; Lev. 19:3

17 'Youᴿshall not murder.   Gen. 9:6; Ex. 20:13

18 'You shall not commit adultery.

19 'Youᴿshall not steal.   Ex. 20:15; Lev. 19:11

20 'Youᴿ shall not bear false witness against your neighbor.   Ex. 20:16; 23:1

21 'You shall not covet your neighbor's wife, and you shall not desire your neighbor's house, his field or his male servant or his female servant, his ox or his donkey or anything that belongs to your neighbor.'

Response of Israel

22 "These words the LORD spoke to all your assembly at the mountain from the midst of the fire, of the cloud and of the thick gloom, with a great voice, and He added no more. AndᴿHe wrote them on two tablets of stone and gave them to me.   Ex. 24:12; 31:18

23 "And it came about, when you heard the voice from the midst of the darkness, while the mountain was burning with fire, that you came near to me, all the heads of your tribes and your elders.

24 "And you said, 'Behold, the LORD our God has shown us His glory and His greatness, and we have heard His voice from the midst of the fire; we have seen today that God speaks with man, yet he lives.

25 'Nowᴿthen why should we die? For this great fire will consume us; if we hear the voice of the LORD our God any longer, then we shall die.   Ex. 20:18, 19; Deut. 18:16

26 'For ᴿwho is there of all flesh, who has heard the voice of the living God speaking

from the midst of the fire, as we *have*, and lived?   Deut. 4:33

27 'Go[T] near and hear all that the LORD our God says; then speak to us all that the LORD our God will speak to you, and we will hear and do *it.*'   *Go yourself*

Response of God

28"And the LORD heard the voice of your words when you spoke to me, [R]and the LORD said to me, 'I have heard the voice of the words of this people which they have spoken to you. They have done well in all that they have spoken.   Deut. 18:17

29 'Oh that they had such a heart in them, that they would fear Me, and keep all My commandments always, that it may be well with them and with their sons forever!

30 'Go, say to them, "Return to your tents."

31 'But[R] as for you, stand here by Me, that I may speak to you all the commandments and the statutes and the judgments which you shall teach them, that they may observe *them* in the land which I give them to possess.'   Ex. 24:12

32"So you shall observe to do just as the LORD your God has commanded you; you shall not turn aside to the right or to the left.

33"You[R] shall walk in all the way which the LORD your God has commanded you, that you may live, and that it may be well with you, and that you may prolong *your* days in the land which you shall possess.   Jer. 7:23

CHAPTER 6

The Command to Teach the Law

"NOW this is the commandment, the statutes and the judgments which the LORD your God has commanded *me* to teach you, that you might do *them* in the land where you are going over to possess it,

2 so that you and your son and your grandson might[R] fear the LORD your God, to keep all His statutes and His commandments, which I command you, [R]all the days of your life, and that your days may be prolonged.   Ex. 20:20; Deut. 10:12 • Deut. 4:9

3"O Israel, you should listen and be careful to do *it*, that it may be well with you and that you may multiply greatly, just as the LORD, the God of your fathers, has promised you, *in* a land flowing with milk and honey.

[R] 4"Hear,[R] O Israel! The LORD is our God, the LORD is one!   Matt. 22:37 • Deut. 4:35, 39

5"And you shall love the LORD your God with all your heart and with all your soul and with all your might.   Deut. 4:29; 10:12

6"And these words, which I am commanding you today, shall be on your heart;

7 and[R] you shall teach them diligently to your sons and shall talk of them when you sit in your house and when you walk by the way and when you lie down and when you rise up.   Deut. 4:9; 11:19; [Eph. 6:4]

8"And you shall bind them as a sign on your hand and they shall be as[A]frontals[T] on your forehead.   *frontlet bands • between your eyes*

9"And you shall write them on the doorposts of your house and on your gates.

10"Then it shall come about when the LORD your God brings you into the land which He swore to your fathers, Abraham, Isaac and Jacob, to give you, great and splendid cities which you did not build,

11 and houses full of all good things which you did not fill, and hewn cisterns which you did not dig, vineyards and olive trees which you did not plant, and[R] you shall eat and be satisfied,   Deut. 8:10; 11:15; 14:29

12 then watch yourself, lest you forget the LORD who brought you from the land of Egypt, out of the house of slavery.   *slaves*

13"You[R] shall [6]fear *only* the LORD your God; and you shall[A] worship Him, and[R] swear by His name.   Deut. 13:4 • *serve* • Matt. 5:33

[6] Or, *reverence*

6:4–9   Three Essentials for a Christian Home—A new generation of Israel is gathered on the plains of Moab to hear Moses review the law in preparation for their entrance to the Promised Land. The previous generation had died in unbelief in the wilderness. Moses begins his instruction by telling the people of Israel what a home is all about. He sets forth three components which must be true if the home is rightly related to God:

a. There must be a revelation of God (6:4). God revealed three things about Himself: (1) His eternality (Yahweh, Hebrew *YHWH*, the Eternal); (2) His plurality (*Elohim*, Hebrew plural of God, there are three Persons in the Godhead); and (3) His unity—"the LORD is one"—the three Persons of the Godhead constitute one God; each is essential.

b. There must be a response to God's revelation (6:5). The response is to be a total response of love with all one's being, heart, soul, and mind. This is the only fitting response to the eternal God who has revealed Himself.

c. There must be a threefold responsibility (6:6–9). This threefold responsibility acts as a check upon the proper response. If the earthly father responds to God with love he will be fulfilling his threefold responsibility. If he fails in any particular, confession of sin is necessary because he does not love God with all his heart, soul, and mind. The threefold responsibility is: (1) to have God's truth govern his heart (6:6)—there must be heart reality, not mere external conformity or ceremony; (2) to have God's truth govern his home—this is evidenced by the fact that the father teaches the truths of God's revelation to his children by both formal (teach them diligently) and informal (talk of them) instruction; and (3) to have God's truth govern his habits and conduct personally, privately, and publicly. In short, the home is to be a divine school in which the father is to be the teacher, under Christ.

Now turn to Page 1262—1 Pet. 3:1–6: The Role of the Wife.

14"You shall not follow other gods, any of the gods of the peoples who surround you,

15 for the LORD your God in the midst of you is a ᴿjealous God; otherwise the anger of the LORD your God will be kindled against you, and He will ᵀwipe you off the face of the earth.   Deut. 4:24; 5:9 • *destroy*

16"You shall not put the LORD your God to the test, as you tested *Him* at Massah.

17"Youᴿ should diligently keep the commandments of the LORD your God, and His testimonies and His statutes which He has commanded you.   Deut. 11:22; Ps. 119:4

18"And you shall do what is right and good in the sight of the LORD, thatᴿit may be well with you and that you may go in and possess the good land which the LORD swore to *give* your fathers,   Deut. 4:40

19 by driving out all your enemies from before you, as the LORD has spoken.

20"Whenᴿ your son asks you in time to come, saying, 'What *do* the testimonies and the statutes and the judgments *mean* which the LORD our God commanded you?' Ex. 13:8

21 then you shall say to your son, 'We were slaves to Pharaoh in Egypt; and the LORD brought us from Egypt with a mighty hand.

22 'Moreover, the LORD showed great and distressing signs and wonders before our eyes against Egypt, Pharaoh and all his household;

23 and He brought us out from there in order to bring us in, to give us the land which He had sworn to our fathers.'

24"So the LORD commanded us to observe all these statutes,ᴿto fear the LORD our God for our good always andᴿfor our survival, as *it is* today.   Deut. 10:12; Jer. 32:39 • [Luke 10:28]

25"And ᴿit will be righteousness for us if we ᵀare careful to observe all this commandment before the LORD our God, just as He commanded us.   Deut. 24:13; [Rom. 10:3] • *keep*

CHAPTER 7

The Command to Conquer Canaan

"WᴿHEN the LORD your God shall bring you into the land where you are entering to possess it, and shall clear away many nations before you, the Hittites and the Girgashites and the Amorites and the Canaanites and the Perizzites and the Hivites and the Jebusites, ᴿseven nations greater and stronger than you,   Deut. 20:16-18 • Acts 13:19

2 and when the LORD your God shall deliver them before you, and you shall defeat them, then you shall ᵀutterly destroy them. You shall make no covenant with them and show no favor to them. *surely devote to the ban*

3"Furthermore, you shall not intermarry with them; you shall not give your ᵀdaughters to ᵀtheir sons, nor shall you take their daughters for your sons.   *daughter • his son*

4"For ᵀthey will turn your sons away from

following Me to serve other gods; then the anger of the LORD will be kindled against you, and He will quickly destroy you.   *he*

5"But thus you shall do to them: you shall tear down their altars, and smash their *sacred* pillars, and hew down their ⁷Asherim, and burn their graven images with fire.

6"For you are ᴿa holy people to the LORD your God; the LORD your God has chosen you to be a people for His ᴬown possession out of all the peoples who are on the face of the ᵀearth.   Ex. 19:6 • *special treasure • ground*

7"The ᴿLORD did not set His love on you nor choose you because you were more in number than any of the peoples, for you were the fewest of all peoples,   Deut. 4:37

8 but because the LORD loved you and kept the ᴿoath which He swore to your forefathers, ᴿthe LORD brought you out by a mighty hand, and redeemed you from the house of ᵀslavery, from the hand of Pharaoh king of Egypt.   Ex. 32:13 • Ex. 13:3 • *slaves*

9"Know therefore that the LORD your God, He is God, the faithful God, who keeps ᵀHis covenant and ᵀHis lovingkindness to a thousandth generation with those who love Him and keep His commandments;   *the*

10 but ᴿrepays those who hate Him to ᵀtheir faces, to destroy ᵀthem; He will not delay ᵀwith him who hates Him, He will repay him to his face.   Is. 59:18 • *his face • him • to*

11"Therefore, you shall keep the commandment and the statutes and the judgments which I am commanding you today, to do them.

12"Then it shall come about, because you listen to these judgments and keep and do them, that the LORD your God will keep with you ᵀHis covenant and ᵀHis lovingkindness which He swore to your forefathers.   *the*

13"And He will love you and bless you and multiply you; He will also bless the fruit of your womb and the fruit of your ground, your grain and your new wine and your oil, the increase of your herd and the young of your flock, ᵀin the land which He swore to your forefathers to give you.   *on the ground*

14"You shall be blessed above all peoples; there shall be no male or female ᴿbarren among you or among your cattle.   Ex. 23:26

15"And ᴿthe LORD will remove from you all sickness; and He will not put on you any of the harmful diseases of Egypt which you have known, but He will lay them on all who hate you.   Ex. 15:26

16"And you shall consume all the peoples whom the LORD your God will deliver to you; ᴿyour eye shall not pity them, neither shall you serve their gods, for that *would be* ᴿa snare to you.   Deut. 7:2 • Ex. 23:33; Judg. 8:27

17"If you should say in your heart, 'These nations are greater than I; how can I ᴰdispossess them?'   Num. 33:53

18 you shall not be afraid of them; you

⁷ I.e., wooden symbols of a female deity

shall well remember what the LORD your God did to Pharaoh and to all Egypt:

19 [R]the great trials which your eyes saw and the signs and the wonders and the mighty hand and the outstretched arm by which the LORD your God brought you out. So shall the LORD your God do to all the peoples of whom you are afraid. Deut. 4:34

20"Moreover, the LORD your God will send the hornet against them, until those who are left and hide themselves from you perish.

21"You shall not dread them, for the LORD your God is in your midst,[A]a great and awesome God. from before them • Neh. 1:5; 9:32

22"And the LORD your God will clear away these nations before you little by little; you will not be able to put an end to them quickly, lest the [T]wild beasts grow too numerous for you. beasts of the field

23"But the LORD your God shall deliver them before you, and will throw them into great confusion until they are destroyed.

24"And[R] He will deliver their kings into your hand so that you shall make their name perish from under heaven; [R]no man will be able to stand before you until you have destroyed them. Josh. 6:2 • Josh. 1:5

25"The graven images of their gods you are to burn with fire; you shall not covet the silver or the gold that is on them, nor take it for yourselves, lest you be snared by it, for it is an abomination to the LORD your God.

26"And you shall not bring an abomination into your house, and like it come under the[R]ban; you shall utterly detest it and you shall utterly abhor it, for it is something banned. Lev. 27:28f.

CHAPTER 8

The Command to Remember the Lord

"ALL the commandments that I am commanding you today you shall be careful to do, that you[R]may live and multiply, and go in and possess the land which the LORD swore *to give* to your forefathers. Deut. 4:1

2"And you shall remember all the way which the LORD your God has[R]led you in the wilderness these forty years, that He might humble you,[R]testing you, to know what was in your heart, whether you would keep His commandments or not. Ps. 136:16 • Ex. 15:25

3"And He humbled you and let you be hungry, and fed you with manna which you did not know, nor did your fathers know, that He might make you[T]understand that [R]man does not live by bread alone, but man lives by everything that proceeds out of the mouth of the LORD. know • Matt. 4:4

4"Your clothing did not wear out on you, nor did your foot swell these forty years.

5"Thus you are to know in your heart that the LORD your God was disciplining you just as a man disciplines his son.

6"Therefore, you shall keep the commandments of the LORD your God, to walk in His ways and to[A]fear Him. reverence

7"For[T]the LORD your God is bringing you into a good land, a land of brooks of water, of fountains and springs, flowing forth in valleys and hills; Deut. 11:9-12; Jer. 2:7

8 a land of wheat and barley, of vines and fig trees and pomegranates, a land of olive oil and honey;

9 a land where you shall eat food without scarcity, in which you shall not lack anything; a land whose stones are iron, and out of whose hills you can dig copper.

10"When you have eaten and are satisfied, you shall bless the LORD your God for the good land which He has given you.

11"Beware lest you[R]forget the LORD your God by not keeping His commandments and His ordinances and His statutes which I am commanding you today; Deut. 4:9

12 lest,[R]when you have eaten and are satisfied, and have built good houses and lived *in them,* Prov. 30:9; Hos. 13:6

13 and when your herds and your flocks multiply, and your silver and gold multiply, and all that you have multiplies,

14 then your heart becomes [T]proud, and you[R]forget the LORD your God who brought you out from the land of Egypt, out of the house of [T]slavery. lifted up • Ps. 106:21 • slaves

15"He led you through[R]the great and terrible wilderness, *with its* fiery serpents and scorpions and thirsty ground where there was no water; He[R]brought water for you out of the rock of flint. Deut. 1:19 • Ex. 17:6

16"In the wilderness He fed you manna which your fathers did not know, that He might humble you and that He might test you, to do good for you in the end.

17"Otherwise,[R]you may say in your heart, 'My power and the strength of my hand made me this wealth.' Deut. 9:4

18"But you shall remember the LORD your God, for[R]it is He who is giving you power to make wealth, that He may confirm His covenant which He swore to your fathers, as *it is* this day. Prov. 10:22; Hos. 2:8

19"And it shall come about if you ever forget the LORD your God, and go after other gods and serve them and worship them,[R]I testify against you today that you shall surely perish. Deut. 4:26; 30:18

20"Like the nations that the LORD makes to perish before you, so[R]you shall perish; because you would not listen to the voice of the LORD your God. Ezek. 5:5-17

CHAPTER 9

Moses Rehearses Israel's Rebellion

"HEAR, O Israel! You are crossing over the Jordan today to go in to dispossess nations greater and mightier than you, great cities[T]fortified to heaven, *and fortified*

2 a people great and tall, the sons of the Anakim, whom you know and of whom you have heard *it said*, 'Who[R] can stand before the sons of Anak?' Num. 13:22, 28, 33

3"Know therefore today that [R]it is the LORD your God who is crossing over before you as [R]a consuming fire. He will destroy them and He will subdue them before you, so that[R]you may drive them out and destroy them quickly, just as the LORD has spoken to you. Deut. 31:3 • Deut. 4:24 • Deut. 7:24

4"Do[R] not say in your heart when the LORD your God has driven them out before [T]you, 'Because of my righteousness the LORD has brought me in to possess this land,' but *it is*[R]because of the wickedness of these nations *that* the LORD is dispossessing them before you. Deut. 8:17 • *you saying* • Deut. 12:31

5"It is[R]not for your righteousness or for the uprightness of your heart that you are going to possess their land, but *it is* because of the wickedness of these nations *that* the LORD your God is driving them out before you, in order to confirm[R]the [T]oath which the LORD swore to your fathers, to Abraham, Isaac and Jacob. [Titus 3:5] • Gen. 12:7 • *word*

6"Know, then, *it is* not because of your righteousness *that* the LORD your God is giving you this good land to possess, for you are a[T]stubborn people. *stiff-necked*

7"Remember, do not forget how you provoked the LORD your God to wrath in the wilderness; from the day that you left the land of Egypt until you arrived at this place, you have been rebellious against the LORD.

8"Even at Horeb you provoked the LORD to wrath, and the LORD was so angry with you that He would have destroyed you.

9"When I went up to the mountain to receive the tablets of stone, the tablets of the covenant which the LORD had made with you, then I remained on the mountain forty days and nights; [R]I neither ate bread nor drank water. Ex. 24:18; 34:28; Deut. 8:3; 9:18

10"And the LORD gave me the two tablets of stone written by the finger of God; and on them *were* all the words which the LORD had spoken with you at the mountain from the midst of the fire on the day of the assembly.

11"And it came about [R]at the end of forty days and nights that the LORD gave me the two tablets of stone, the tablets of the covenant. Deut. 9:9

12"Then[R] the LORD said to me, 'Arise, go down from here quickly, for your people whom you brought out of Egypt have acted corruptly. They have [R]quickly turned aside from the way which I commanded them; they have made a molten image for themselves.' Ex. 32:7, 8 • Judg. 2:17

13"The[R]LORD spoke further to me, saying, 'I have seen this people, and indeed, it is a [T]stubborn people. Ex. 32:9 • *stiff-necked*

14 'Let[R]Me alone, that I may destroy them and[R]blot out their name from under heaven; and I will make of you a nation mightier and greater than they.' Ex. 32:10 • Ps. 9:5; 109:13

15"So[R] I turned and came down from the mountain while the mountain was burning with fire, and the two tablets of the covenant were in my two hands. Ex. 32:15-19

16"And I saw that you had indeed sinned against the LORD your God. You had made for yourselves a molten calf; you had turned aside quickly from the way which the LORD had commanded you.

17"And I took hold of the two tablets and threw them from my hands, and smashed them before your eyes.

18"And I fell down before the LORD,[R]as at the first, forty days and nights; I neither ate bread nor drank water,[R]because of all your sin which you had committed in doing what was evil in the sight of the LORD to provoke Him to anger. Deut. 10:10 • Ex. 34:9

19"For[R]I was afraid of the anger and hot displeasure with which the LORD was wrathful against you in order to destroy you,[R]but the LORD listened to me that time also. Heb. 12:21 • Ex. 34:10; Deut. 10:10

20"And the LORD was angry enough with Aaron to destroy him; so I also prayed for Aaron at the same time.

21"And[R] I took your [T]sinful *thing*, the calf which you had made, and burned it with fire and crushed it, grinding it very small until it was as fine as dust; and I threw its dust into the brook that came down from the mountain. Ex. 32:20 • *sin*

22"Again at[R]Taberah and at[R]Massah and at [R]Kibroth-hattaavah you provoked the LORD to wrath. Num. 11:3 • Ex. 17:7 • Num. 11:34

23"And when the LORD sent you from Kadesh-barnea, saying, 'Go up and possess the land which I have given you,' then you rebelled against the [T]command of the LORD your God;[R]you neither believed Him nor listened to His voice. *mouth* • Ps. 106:24

24"You[R] have been rebellious against the LORD from the day I knew you. Deut. 9:7

25"So I fell down before the LORD the forty days and nights, which I did because the LORD had said He would destroy you.

26"And[R]I prayed to the LORD, and said, 'O Lord GOD, do not destroy Thy people, even Thine inheritance, whom Thou hast redeemed through Thy greatness, whom Thou hast brought out of Egypt with a mighty hand. Ex. 32:11-13; 1 Sam. 7:9; Jer. 15:1

27 'Remember Thy servants, Abraham, Isaac, and Jacob; do not look at the stubbornness of this people or at their wickedness or their sin.

28 'Otherwise the land from which Thou didst bring us may say, "Because the LORD was not able to bring them into the land which He had[T]promised them and because He hated them He has brought them out to slay them in the wilderness." *spoken to*

29 'Yet they are Thy people, even[T]Thine inheritance, whom Thou hast brought out by Thy [R]great power and Thine outstretched arm.' Deut. 4:20; 1 Kin. 8:51 • Deut. 4:34

CHAPTER 10

Moses Rehearses God's Mercy

"AT that time the LORD said to me, 'Cut[R] out for yourself two tablets of stone like the former ones, and come up to Me on the mountain, and [R]make an ark of wood for yourself. Ex. 34:1 • Ex. 25:10

2 'And [R]I will write on the tablets the words that were on the former tablets which you shattered, and[R]you shall put them in the ark.' Deut. 4:13 • Ex. 25:16

3 "So[R]I made an ark of acacia wood and [R]cut out two tablets of stone like the former ones, and went up on the mountain with the two tablets in my hand. Ex. 25:5 • Ex. 34:4

4 "And He wrote on the tablets, like the former writing, the Ten [T]Commandments [R]which the LORD had spoken to you on the mountain from the midst of the fire[R]on the day of the assembly; and the LORD gave them to me. Words • Ex. 20:1 • Deut. 9:10

5 "Then I turned and [R]came down from the mountain, and [R]put the tablets in the ark which I had made; and there they are, as the LORD commanded me." Ex. 34:29 • Ex. 40:20

6 (Now the sons of Israel set out from [A]Beeroth Bene-jaakan to Moserah. There Aaron died and there he was buried and Eleazar his son ministered as priest in his place. *the wells of the sons of Jaakan*

7 [R]From there they set out to Gudgodah; and from Gudgodah to Jotbathah, a land of brooks of water. Num. 33:33, 34

8 [R]At that time the LORD set apart the tribe of Levi to carry the ark of the covenant of the LORD, to stand before the LORD[R]to serve Him and to bless in His name until this day. Num. 3:6; 18:1-7 • Deut. 17:12; 18:5

9 [R]Therefore, Levi does not have a portion or inheritance with his brothers; the LORD is his inheritance, just as the LORD your God spoke to him.) Num. 18:20, 24; Deut. 18:1, 2

10 "I,[R] moreover, stayed on the mountain forty days and forty nights like the first time, and the LORD listened to me that time also; the LORD was not willing to destroy you. Ex. 34:28; Deut. 9:18

11 "Then the LORD said to me, 'Arise, proceed on your journey ahead of the people, that they may go in and possess the land which I swore to their fathers to give them.'

Love God

12 "And now, Israel, what does the LORD your God require from you, but to fear the LORD your God, to walk in all His ways and love Him, and to serve the LORD your God with all your heart and with all your soul,

13 *and* to keep the LORD's commandments and His statutes which I am commanding you today for your good?

14 "Behold, to the LORD your God belong

heaven and the [T]highest heavens,[R]the earth and all that is in it. *heaven of heavens* • Ps. 24:1

15 "Yet on your fathers did the LORD set His affection to love them, and He chose their [T]descendants after them, *even* you above all peoples, as *it is* this day. *seed*

16 "Circumcise then [T]your heart, and stiffen your neck no more. *the foreskin of your heart*

17 "For the LORD your God is the God of gods and the Lord of lords, the great, the mighty, and the awesome God who does not show partiality, nor[T]take a bribe. Deut. 16:19

18 "He executes justice for[R]the orphan and the widow, and shows His love for the alien by giving him food and clothing. Ps. 68:5

19 "So[R]show your love for the alien, for you were aliens in the land of Egypt. Lev. 19:34

20 "You shall fear the LORD your God; you shall serve Him and [E]cling to Him, and you shall swear by His name. Deut. 11:22; 13:4

21 "He is your praise and He is your God, who has done these great and awesome things for you which your eyes have seen.

22 "Your[R]fathers went down to Egypt seventy persons *in all,* [R]and now the LORD your God has made you as numerous as the stars of heaven. Gen. 46:27 • Deut. 1:10

CHAPTER 11

Study and Obey the Commands

"YOU shall therefore[R]love the LORD your God, and always[R]keep His charge, His statutes, His ordinances, and His commandments. Deut. 6:5; 10:12 • Lev. 18:30; 22:9

2 "And know this day that I *am* not *speaking* with your sons who have not known and who have not seen the [8]discipline of the LORD your God—His greatness, His mighty hand, and His outstretched arm,

3 and[R]His signs and His works which He did in the midst of Egypt to Pharaoh the king of Egypt and to all his land; Ex. 7:8-21

4 and what He did to Egypt's army, to its horses and its chariots, when He made the water of the [T]Red Sea to engulf them while they were pursuing you, and the LORD completely destroyed them; *Sea of Reeds*

5 and what He did to you in the wilderness until you came to this place;

6 and what He did to Dathan and Abiram, the sons of Eliab, the son of Reuben, when the earth opened its mouth and swallowed them, their households, their tents, and every living thing that [T]followed them, among all Israel— *was at their feet*

7 but your own eyes have seen all the great work of the LORD which He did.

8 "You shall therefore keep every commandment which I am commanding you today,[R]so that you may be strong and go in and possess the land into which you are about to cross to possess it; Deut. 31:6, 7, 23

9 so that you may prolong *your* days on

[8] Or, *instruction*

the land which the LORD swore to your fathers to give to them and to their descendants, a land flowing with milk and honey.

10"For the land, into which you are entering to possess it, is not like the land of Egypt from which you came, where you used to sow your seed and water it with your ⁹foot like a vegetable garden.

11"But the land into which you are about to cross to possess it, a land of hills and valleys, drinks water from the rain of heaven,

12 a land for which the LORD your God cares; the eyes of the LORD your God are always on it, from the ᵀbeginning even to the end of the year.   *beginning of the year*

13"And it shall come about, if you listen obediently to my commandments which I am commanding you today, to love the LORD your God and to serve Him ᴿwith all your heart and all your soul,   Deut. 4:29

14 that He ᴿwill give the rain for your land in its season, the ¹⁰early ᴿand late rain, that you may gather in your grain and your new wine and your oil.   Deut. 28:12 · James 5:7

15"And ᴿHe will give grass in your fields for your cattle, and ᴿyou shall eat and be satisfied.   Ps. 104:14 · Deut. 6:11

16"Beware, ᵀ lest your hearts be deceived and you turn away and serve other gods and worship them.   *Watch yourselves*

17"Or the anger of the LORD will be kindled against you, and He will ᴿshut up the heavens so that there will be no rain and the ground will not yield its fruit; and ᵀyou will perish quickly from the good land which the LORD is giving you.   2 Chr. 6:26 · Deut. 4:26

18"You shall therefore impress these words of mine on your heart and on your soul; and you shall bind them as a sign on your hand, and they shall be as ᵀfrontals on your forehead.   *frontlet bands · between your eyes*

19"And you shall teach them to your sons, talking of them when you sit in your house and when you walk along the road and when you lie down and when you rise up.

20"And you shall write them on the doorposts of your house and on your gates,

21 so that your days and the days of your sons may be multiplied on the land which the LORD swore to your fathers to give them, as ᵀlong ᴿas the heavens *remain* above the earth.   *the days of the heavens · Ps. 72:5*

Victory Depends upon Obedience

22"For if you are careful to keep all this commandment which I am commanding you, to do it, to love the LORD your God, to walk in all His ways and hold fast to Him;

23 then the LORD will ᴿdrive out all these nations from before you, and you will ᵀdispossess nations greater and mightier than you.   Deut. 4:38 · Deut. 9:1

24"Every ᴿplace on which the sole of your foot shall tread shall be yours; your border shall be from the wilderness to Lebanon,

and from the river, the river Euphrates, as far as ¹¹the western sea.   Josh. 1:3; 14:9

25"There ᴿshall no man be able to stand before you; the LORD your God shall lay the dread of you and the fear of you on all the land on which you set foot, as He has spoken to you.   Ex. 23:27; Deut. 7:24

26"See, ᴿ I am setting before you today a blessing and a curse: Deut. 30:1, 19

27 the ᴿblessing, if you listen to the commandments of the LORD your God, which I am commanding you today;   Deut. 28:1-14

28 and the curse, if you do not listen to the commandments of the LORD your God, but turn aside from the ᵀway which I am commanding you today, ᵀby following other gods which you have not known.   *to follow*

29"And it shall come about, when the LORD your God brings you into the land where you are entering to possess it, ᴿthat you shall place the blessing on Mount Gerizim and the curse on Mount Ebal.   Josh. 8:33

30"Are they not across the Jordan, west of the way toward the sunset, in the land of the Canaanites who live in the Arabah, opposite Gilgal, beside the ᵀoaks of Moreh?   *terebinths*

31"For you are about to cross the Jordan to go in to possess the land which the LORD your God is giving you, and ᴿyou shall possess it and live in it,   Deut. 17:14; Josh. 21:43

32 and you shall be careful to do all the statutes and the judgments which I am setting before you today.

CHAPTER 12

Law of the Central Sanctuary

"THESE are the statutes and the judgments which you shall carefully observe in the land which the LORD, the God of your fathers, has given you to possess ᵀas long as you live on the ᵀearth.   *all the days · ground*

2"You shall utterly destroy all the places where the nations whom you shall dispossess serve their gods, on the high mountains and on the hills and under every green tree.

3"And ᴿyou shall tear down their altars and smash their *sacred* pillars and burn their ¹²Asherim with fire, and you shall cut down the engraved images of their gods, and you shall ᴿobliterate their name from that place.   Num. 33:52 · Ex. 23:13; Ps. 16:4

4"You shall not act like this toward the LORD your God.

5"But ᴿyou shall seek *the* LORD at the place which the LORD your God shall choose from all your tribes, to establish His name there for His dwelling, and there you shall come.   Ex. 20:24; Deut. 12:11, 13; 2 Chr. 7:12

6"And there you shall bring your burnt offerings, your sacrifices, your tithes, the contribution of your hand, your votive offer-

---

⁹ I.e., probably a treadmill   ¹⁰ I.e., autumn and spring rain
¹¹ I.e., the Mediterranean
¹² I.e., wooden symbols of a female deity

ings, your freewill offerings, and the first-born of your herd and of your flock.

7"There also you and your households shall eat before the LORD your God, and[R]rejoice in all your undertakings in which the LORD your God has blessed you.   Lev. 23:40

8"You shall not do at all what we are doing here today, every man *doing* whatever is right in his own eyes;

9 for you have not as yet come to[R]the resting place and the inheritance which the LORD your God is giving you.   Deut. 3:20

10"When you cross the Jordan and live in the land which the LORD your God is giving you to inherit, and[R]He gives you rest from all your enemies around *you* so that you live in security,   Josh. 11:23

11 [R]then it shall come about that the place in which the LORD your God shall choose for His name to dwell, there you shall bring all that I command you: your burnt offerings and your sacrifices, your tithes and the[A]contribution of your hand, and all your choice votive offerings which you will vow to the LORD.   Deut. 12:5; 15:20; 16:2 • *heave offering*

12"And you shall rejoice before the LORD your God, you and your sons and daughters, your male and female servants, and the Levite who is within your gates, since he has no portion or inheritance with you.

13"Be careful that you do not offer your burnt offerings in every *cultic* place you see,

14 but in the place which the LORD chooses in one of your tribes, there you shall offer your burnt offerings, and there you shall do all that I command you.

15"However, you may slaughter and eat meat within any of your gates, [T]whatever you desire, according to the blessing of the LORD your God which He has given you; the unclean and the clean may eat of it, as of the gazelle and the deer.   *in every desire of your soul*

16"Only you shall not eat the blood; you are to pour it out on the ground like water.

17"You[R]are not allowed to eat within your gates the tithe of your grain, or new wine, or oil, or the first-born of your herd or flock, or any of your votive offerings which you vow, or your freewill offerings, or the [T]contribution of your hand.   Deut. 12:26 • *heave offering*

18"But you shall eat them before the LORD your God in the place which the LORD your God will choose, you and your son and daughter, and your male and female servants, and the Levite who is within your gates; and you shall rejoice before the LORD your God in all your undertakings.

19"Be careful that you do not forsake the Levite as long as you live in your land.

20"When the LORD your God extends your border [R]as He has promised you, and you say, 'I will eat meat,' because[T]you desire to eat meat, *then* you may eat meat, whatever you desire.   Deut. 11:24; 19:8 • *your soul desires*

21"If the place which the LORD your God chooses to put His name is too far from you, then you may slaughter of your herd and

flock which the LORD has given you, as I have commanded you; and you may eat within your gates whatever you desire.

22"Just as a gazelle or a deer is eaten, so you shall eat it; the unclean and the clean alike may eat of it.

23"Only be sure[R]not to eat the blood, for the blood is the[T]life, and you shall not eat the[T]life with the flesh.   Lev. 17:10-14 • *soul*

24"You shall not eat it; you shall pour it out on the ground like water.

25"You shall not eat it, in order that[R]it may be well with you and your sons after you, for [R]you will be doing what is right in the sight of the LORD.   Deut. 4:40 • 1 Kin. 11:38

26"Only[R]your holy things which you may have and your votive offerings, you shall take and go to the place which the LORD chooses.   Num. 5:9f.; 18:19; Deut. 12:17

27"And [R]you shall offer your burnt offerings, the flesh and the blood, on the altar of the LORD your God; and the blood of your sacrifices shall be poured out on the altar of the LORD your God, and [R]you shall eat the flesh.   Lev. 1:9, 13 • Lev. 3:1-17

28"Be careful to listen to all these words which I command you, in order that it may be well with you and your sons after you forever, for you will be doing what is good and right in the sight of the LORD your God.

Law of Idolatry

29"When[R]the LORD your God cuts off before you the nations which you are going in to dispossess, and you dispossess them and dwell in their land,   Josh. 23:4

30 beware that you are not ensnared to follow them, after they are destroyed before you, and that you do not inquire after their gods, saying, 'How do these nations serve their gods, that I also may do likewise?'

31"You[R] shall not behave thus toward the LORD your God, for every abominable act which the LORD hates they have done for their gods; for they even burn their sons and daughters in the fire to their gods.   Deut. 9:5

32"Whatever[T]I command you, you shall be careful to do;[R]you shall not add to nor take away from it.   *Everything that* • Rev. 22:18

CHAPTER 13

"IF[R] a prophet or a dreamer of dreams arises among you and gives you a sign or a wonder,   Matt. 24:24; Mark 13:22; 2 Thess. 2:9

2 and the sign or the wonder comes true, concerning which he spoke to you, saying, 'Let us go after other gods (whom you have not known) and let us serve them,'

3 you shall not listen to the words of that prophet or that dreamer of dreams; for the LORD your God is testing you to find out if you love the LORD your God with all your heart and with all your soul.

4"You[R] shall follow the LORD your God and fear Him; and you shall keep His com-

mandments, listen to His voice, serve Him, and ᴿcling to Him.   2 Kin. 23:3 • Deut. 10:20

5"But that prophet or that dreamer of dreams shall be put to death, because he has ᵀcounseled ᵀrebellion against the LORD your God who brought you from the land of Egypt and redeemed you from the house of ᵀslavery, to seduce you from the way in which the LORD your God commanded you to walk. So you shall purge the evil from among you.   spoken • turning aside • slaves

6"If your brother, your mother's son, or your son or daughter, or the wife ᵀyou cherish, or your friend who is as your own soul, entice you secretly, saying, 'Let us go and serve other gods' (whom neither you nor your fathers have known,   of your bosom

7 of the gods of the peoples who are around you, near you or far from you, from one end of the earth to the other end),

8 you shall not yield to him or listen to him; ᴿand your eye shall not pity him, nor shall you spare or conceal him.   Deut. 7:2

9"But ᴿyou shall surely kill him; ᴿyour hand shall be first against him to put him to death, and afterwards the hand of all the people.   Deut. 13:5 • Lev. 24:14; Deut. 17:7

10"So you shall stone him ᵀto death because he has sought to seduce you from the LORD your God who brought you out from the land of Egypt, out of the house of ᵀslavery.   with stones so that he dies • slaves

11"Then ᴿall Israel will hear and be afraid, and will never again do such a wicked thing among you.   Deut. 19:20

12"If you hear in one of your cities, which the LORD your God is giving you to live in, anyone saying that

13 some worthless men have gone out from among you and have seduced the inhabitants of their city, saying, 'Let ᴿus go and serve other gods' (whom you have not known),   Deut. 13:2

14 then you shall investigate and search out and inquire thoroughly. And if it is true and the matter established that this abomination has been done among you,

15 ᴿyou shall surely strike the inhabitants of that city with the edge of the sword, utterly destroying it and all that is in it and its cattle with the edge of the sword.   Deut. 13:5

16"Then ᴿyou shall gather all its booty into the middle of its open square and burn the city and all its booty with fire as a whole burnt offering to the LORD your God; and it shall be a ᵀruin ᴿforever. It shall never be rebuilt.   Deut. 7:25, 26 • mound • Josh. 8:28

17"And nothing from that which is put under the ban shall cling to your hand, in order that the LORD may turn from His burning anger and show mercy to you, and have compassion on you and make you increase, just as He has sworn to your fathers,

18 ᴬif you will listen to the voice of the LORD your God, ᵀkeeping all His commandments which I am commanding you today, ᵀand doing what is right in the sight of the LORD your God.   for • to keep • to do

CHAPTER 14

Law of Food

"Y OU are ᴿthe sons of the LORD your God; you shall not cut yourselves nor shave your forehead for the sake of the dead. [Gal. 3:26]

2"For you are a holy people to the LORD your God; and the LORD has chosen you to be a people for His own possession out of all the peoples who are on the face of the earth.

3"You shall not eat any detestable thing.

4"These ᴿare the animals which you may eat: the ox, the sheep, the goat,   Lev. 11:2-45

5 the deer, the gazelle, the roebuck, the wild goat, the ibex, the antelope and the mountain sheep.

6"And any animal that divides the hoof and has the hoof split in two and chews the cud, among the animals, that you may eat.

7"Nevertheless, you are not to eat of these among those which chew the cud, or among those that divide the hoof in two: the camel and the rabbit and the rock-badger, for though they chew the cud, they do not divide the hoof; they are unclean for you.

8"And the pig, because it divides the hoof but does not chew the cud, it is unclean for you. You shall not eat any of their flesh nor touch their carcasses.

14:2 Purpose of Israel—The modern-day student of the Bible may well ask why so much of Scripture is taken up with the history of a single nation. Certainly many Christians wonder why one nation should be called "God's chosen people." The answer to this question is bound up in God's purpose for Israel. When God promised Abraham that he would become the father of a great nation, He also promised that He would bless all peoples through that nation (Page 14—Gen. 12:1–3). Therefore Israel was to be a channel of blessing as well as a recipient. Even their deliverance from Egypt was partially designed to show other nations that Israel's God was the only true God (Page 59—Ex. 7:5; 14:18; Page 207—Josh. 2:9–11). It was further prophesied by Isaiah that the Messiah would bring salvation to the Gentiles (Page 698—Is. 49:6). Also in the Psalms there are many invitations to other nations to come and worship the Lord in Israel (Page 529—Ps. 2:10–12; Page 589—117:1). Ruth the Moabitess is an example of a foreigner who believed in Israel's God.

It is clear that God's promise to Abraham to bless the whole world through him is still being fulfilled. The life, ministry, and death of Jesus Christ, and the existence and influence of the church today, all came about through God's choice of Israel. All whom the church wins to Christ, whether Jew or Gentile, enter into those great blessings channeled through Israel.

Now turn to Page 413—1 Chr. 28:4–6: Government of Israel.

9"These you may eat of all that are in water: anything that has fins and scales you may eat,

10 but anything that does not have fins and scales you shall not eat; it is unclean for you.

11"You may eat any clean bird.

12"But ᴿthese are the ones which you shall not eat: the ᴬeagle and the vulture and the ᴬbuzzard,   Lev. 11:13 • *vulture • black vulture*

13 and the red kite, the falcon, and the kite in their kinds,

14 and every raven in its kind,

15 and the ostrich, the owl, the sea gull, and the hawk in their kinds,

16 the little owl, the ᴬgreat owl, the white owl,   *great horned owl*

17 the pelican, the carrion vulture, the cormorant,

18 the stork, and the heron in their kinds, and the hoopoe and the bat.

19"And all the teeming life with wings are unclean to you; they shall not be eaten.

20"You may eat any clean bird.

21"You shall not eat anything which dies *of itself.* You may give it to the alien who is in your ᵀtown, so that he may eat it, or you may sell it to a foreigner, for you are a holy people to the LORD your God. You shall not boil a kid in its mother's milk.   *gates*

Law of the Tithes

22"You ᴿshall surely tithe all the produce from ᵀwhat you sow, which comes out of the field every year.   Deut. 12:6, 17 • *your seed*

23"And you shall eat in the presence of the LORD your God, ᴿat the place where He chooses to establish His name, the tithe of your grain, your new wine, your oil, and the first-born of your herd and your flock, in order that you may ᴿlearn to fear the LORD your God always.   Deut. 12:5 • Deut. 4:10

24"And if the ᵀdistance is so great for you that you are not able to bring *the tithe,* since the place where the LORD your God chooses to set His name is too far away from you when the LORD your God blesses you,   *way*

25 then you shall exchange *it* for money, and bind the money in your hand and go to the place which the LORD your God chooses.

26"And you may spend the money for whatever your ᵀheart desires, for oxen, or sheep, or wine, or strong drink, or whatever your ᵀheart desires; and there you shall eat in the presence of the LORD your God and rejoice, you and your household.   *soul*

27"Also you shall not neglect the Levite who is in your ᵀtown, ᴿfor he has no portion or inheritance among you.   *gates* • Num. 18:20

28"At the end of every third year you shall bring out all the tithe of your produce in that year, and shall deposit *it* in your town.

29"And the Levite, because he has no portion or inheritance among you, and ᴿthe alien, the ᴬorphan and the widow who are in your ᵀtown, shall come and ᴿeat and be satisfied, in order that the LORD your God may bless you in all the work of your hand which you do.   Ps. 94:6 • *fatherless • gates* • Deut. 6:11

CHAPTER 15

Law of the Debts

"AT the end of *every* seven years you shall ¹³grant a remission *of debts.*

2"And this is the manner of remission: every creditor shall release what he has loaned to his neighbor; he shall not exact it of his neighbor and his brother, because the LORD's remission has been proclaimed.

3"From ᴿa foreigner you may exact *it,* but your hand shall release whatever of yours is with your brother.   Deut. 23:20

4"However, there shall be no poor among you, since ᴿthe LORD will surely bless you in the land which the LORD your God is giving you as an inheritance to possess,   Deut. 28:8

5 if only you listen obediently to the voice of the LORD your God, to observe carefully all this commandment which I am commanding you today.

6"For ᴿthe LORD your God shall bless you as He has promised you, and you will lend to many nations, but you will not borrow; and you will rule over many nations, but they will not rule over you.   Deut. 28:12, 13

7"If there is a poor man with you, one of your brothers, in any of your ᵀtowns in your land which the LORD your God is giving you, you shall not harden your heart, nor close your hand from your poor brother;   *gates*

8 but you shall freely open your hand to him, and shall generously lend him sufficient for his need *in* whatever he lacks.

9"Beware, lest there is a base thought in your heart, saying, 'The seventh year, the year of remission, is near,' and your eye is hostile toward your poor brother, and you give him nothing; then he may cry to the LORD against you, and it will be a sin in you.

10"You shall generously give to him, and your heart shall not be grieved when you give to him, because ᴿfor this thing the LORD your God will bless you in all your work and in all your undertakings.   Deut. 14:29; Ps. 41:1

11"For ᴿthe poor will never cease *to be*ᵀin the land; therefore I command you, saying, 'You shall freely open your hand to your brother, to your needy and poor in your land.'   Matt. 26:11; Mark 14:7 • *in the midst of*

Law of the Slaves

12"If your ᵀkinsman, a Hebrew man or woman, is sold to you, then he shall serve you six years, but in the seventh year you shall set him ᵀfree.   *brother • free from you*

13"And when you set him free, you shall not send him away empty-handed.

¹³ Lit., *make a release*

14"You shall furnish him liberally from your flock and from your threshing floor and from your wine vat; you shall give to him as the LORD your God has blessed you.

15"And you shall remember that you were a slave in the land of Egypt, and the LORD your God redeemed you; therefore I command you ᵗthis today.   *this thing*

16"And it shall come about ᴿif he says to you, 'I will not go out from you,' because he loves you and your household, since he fares well with you;   Ex. 21:5, 6

17 then you shall take an awl and pierce it through his ear into the door, and he shall be your servant forever. And also you shall do likewise to your maidservant.

18"It shall not seem hard to you when you set him ᵗfree, for he has given you six years *with* ᵈdouble the service of a hired man; so the LORD your God will bless you in whatever you do.   *free from you • double the amount*

Law of the First-born

19"You shall consecrate to the LORD your God all the first-born males that are born of your herd and of your flock; you shall not work with the first-born of your herd, nor shear the first-born of your flock.

20"You ᴿand your household shall eat it every year before the LORD your God in the place which the LORD chooses.   Lev. 7:15-18

21"But if it has any defect, *such as* lameness or blindness, *or* any serious defect, you shall not sacrifice it to the LORD your God.

22"You shall eat it within your gates; ᵗthe unclean and the clean alike *may eat it,* as a gazelle or a deer.   Deut. 12:15, 16, 22

23"Only you shall not eat its blood; you are to pour it out on the ground like water.

CHAPTER 16

Law of the Feasts

"**O**BSERVE the month of Abib and ᵗcelebrate the Passover to the LORD your God, for in the month of Abib the LORD your God brought you out of Egypt by night. *perform*

2"And you shall sacrifice the Passover to the LORD your God from the flock and the herd, in the place where the LORD chooses to establish His name.

3"You ᴿshall not eat leavened bread with it; seven days you shall eat with it unleavened bread, the bread of affliction (for you came out of the land of Egypt in haste), in order that you may remember ᴿall the days of your life the day when you came out of the land of Egypt.   Ex. 34:18 • Deut. 4:9

4"For seven days no leaven shall be seen with you in all your territory, and ᴿnone of the flesh which you sacrifice on the evening of the first day shall remain overnight until morning.   Ex. 12:8, 10; 34:25

5"You are not allowed to sacrifice the Passover in any of your ᵗtowns which the LORD your God is giving you;   *gates*

6 but ᴿat the place where the LORD your God chooses to establish His name, you shall sacrifice the Passover in the evening at sunset, at the time that you came out of Egypt.   Deut. 12:5

7"And you shall ᴿcook and eat *it* in the place which the LORD your God chooses. And in the morning you are to return to your tents.   Ex. 12:8; 2 Chr. 35:13

8"Six days you shall eat unleavened bread, and on the seventh day there shall be ᴿa solemn assembly to the LORD your God; you shall do no work *on it.*   Lev. 23:8, 36

9"You ᴿshall count seven weeks for yourself; you shall begin to count seven weeks from the time you begin to put the sickle to the standing grain.   Ex. 23:16; 34:22; Lev. 23:15

10"Then you shall ᵗcelebrate the Feast of Weeks to the LORD your God with a tribute of a freewill offering of your hand, which you shall give just as the LORD your God blesses you;   *perform*

11 and you shall ᴿrejoice before the LORD your God, you and your son and your daughter and your male and female servants and the Levite who is in your ᵗtown, and the stranger and the ᴬorphan and the widow who are in your midst, in the place where the LORD your God chooses to establish His name.   Deut. 12:7 • *gates • fatherless*

12"And ᴿyou shall remember that you were a slave in Egypt, and you shall be careful to observe these statutes.   Deut. 15:15

13"You shall celebrate the Feast of Booths seven days after you have gathered in from your threshing floor and your wine vat;

14 and you shall rejoice in your feast, you and your son and your daughter and your male and female servants and the Levite and the stranger and the orphan and the widow who are in your ᵗtowns.   *gates*

15"Seven days you shall celebrate a feast to the LORD your God in the place which the LORD chooses, because the LORD your God will bless you in all your produce and in all the work of your hands, so that you shall be altogether joyful.

16"Three ᴿtimes in a year all your males shall appear before the LORD your God in the place which He chooses, at the Feast of Unleavened Bread and at the Feast of Weeks and at the Feast of Booths, and ᴿthey shall not appear before the LORD empty-handed.   Ex. 23:14-17; 34:23, 24 • Ex. 34:20

17"Every man shall give as he is able, according to the blessing of the LORD your God which He has given you.

Law of the Administration of the Judges

18"You shall appoint for yourself judges and officers in all your ᵗtowns which the LORD your God is giving you, according to

your tribes, and they shall judge the people with righteous judgment.   *gates*

19"You shall not distort justice; you shall not be partial, and you shall not take a bribe, for a bribe blinds the eyes of the wise and perverts the words of the righteous.

20"Justice, *and only* justice, you shall pursue, that you may live and possess the land which the LORD your God is giving you.

21"You shall not plant for yourself an 'Asherah of any kind of tree beside the altar of the LORD your God, which you shall make for yourself.   *wooden symbol of a female deity*

22"Neither[R]shall you set up for yourself a *sacred* pillar which the LORD your God hates.   Lev. 26:1

CHAPTER 17

"YOU[R]shall not sacrifice to the LORD your God an ox or a sheep which has a blemish or any 'defect, for that is a detestable thing to the LORD your God.   Deut. 15:21 • *evil thing*

2"If there is found in your midst, in any of your 'towns, which the LORD your God is giving you, a man or a woman who does what is evil in the sight of the LORD your God, by transgressing His covenant,   *gates*

3 and has gone and [R]served other gods and worshiped them,[R]or the sun or the moon or any of the heavenly host, which I have not commanded,   Ex. 22:20 • Job 31:26-28

4 and if it is told you and you have heard of it, then you shall inquire thoroughly. And behold, if it is true and the thing certain that this detestable thing has been done in Israel,

5 then you shall bring out that man or that woman who has done this evil deed, to your gates, *that is,* the man or the woman, and[R]you shall stone them to death. Josh. 7:25

6"On[R] the 'evidence of two witnesses or three witnesses, he who is to die shall be put to death; he shall not be put to death on the 'evidence of one witness.   Num. 35:30 • *mouth*

7"The hand of the witnesses shall be first against him to put him to death, and afterward the hand of all the people.[R]So you shall purge the evil from your midst.   1 Cor. 5:13

8"If any case is too difficult for you to decide, between one kind of homicide or another, between one kind of lawsuit or another, and between one kind of assault or another, being cases of dispute in your courts, then you shall arise and go up to the place which the LORD your God chooses.

9"So you shall come to [R]the Levitical priest or the judge who is *in office* in those days, and you shall inquire *of them,* and they will declare to you the verdict in the case.   Deut. 19:17

10"And you shall do according to the 'terms of the verdict which they declare to you from that place which the LORD chooses; and you shall be careful to observe according to all that they teach you. *mouth*

11"According[R] to the 'terms of the law which they teach you, and according to the verdict which they tell you, you shall do; you shall not turn aside from the word which they declare to you, to the right or the left.   Deut. 25:1 • *mouth*

12"And the man who acts[R]presumptuously by not listening to the priest who stands there to serve the LORD your God, nor to the judge, that man shall die; thus you shall purge the evil from Israel.   Num. 15:30

13"Then all the people will hear and be afraid, and will not act [R]presumptuously again.   Deut. 17:12

Law of the Administration of the King

14"When you enter the land which the LORD your God gives you, and you[R]possess it and live in it, and you say, 'I[R]will set a king over me like all the nations who are around me,'   Deut. 11:31; Josh. 21:43 • 1 Sam. 8:5, 19, 20

15 you shall surely set a king over you whom the LORD your God chooses, one[R]from among your 'countrymen you shall set as king over yourselves; you may not put a foreigner over yourselves who is not your 'countryman.   Jer. 30:21 • *brother(s)*

16"Moreover,[R] he shall not multiply horses for himself, nor shall he[R]cause the people to return to Egypt to multiply horses, since the LORD has said to you, 'You shall never again return that way.'   1 Kin. 4:26 • Ezek. 17:15

17"Neither[R] shall he multiply wives for himself, 'lest his heart turn away; nor shall he greatly increase silver and gold for himself.   2 Sam. 5:13; 12:11; 1 Kin. 11:3, 4 • *nor*

18"Now it shall come about when he sits on the throne of his kingdom, he shall write for himself a copy of this law on a scroll in the presence of the Levitical priests.

19"And it shall be with him, and he shall read it [R]all the days of his life, that he may learn to fear the LORD his God,'by carefully observing all the words of this law and these statutes,   Deut. 4:9, 10 • *to keep to do them*

20[R]that his heart may not be lifted up above his 'countrymen [R]and that he may not turn aside from the commandment, to the right or the left; in order that he and his sons may continue long in his kingdom in the midst of Israel. John 1:45☆ • *brothers* • 1 Kin. 15:5

CHAPTER 18

Law of the Administration of the Priest and Prophet

"THE Levitical priests, the whole tribe of Levi, shall have no portion or inheritance with Israel; they shall eat the LORD's offerings by fire and His 'portion.   *inheritance*

2"And they shall have no inheritance among their countrymen; the LORD is their inheritance, as He promised them.   *spoke to*

3"Now^{R}this shall be the priests' due from the people, from those who offer a sacrifice, either an ox or a sheep, of which they shall give to the priest the shoulder and the two cheeks and the stomach.   Lev. 7:32-34

4"You shall give him the ^{R}first fruits of your grain, your new wine, and your oil, and the first shearing of your sheep.   Num. 18:12

5"For the LORD your God has chosen him and his sons from all your tribes, to stand and serve in the name of the LORD forever.

6"Now if a Levite comes from any of your ^{T}towns throughout Israel where he resides, and comes whenever he desires to the place which the LORD chooses,   gates

7 then he shall serve in the name of the LORD his God, like all his fellow Levites who stand there before the LORD.

8"They^R shall eat ^{T}equal portions, except *what they receive* from the sale of their fathers' *estates.*   Lev. 27:30-33 • *portion like portion*

9"When you enter the land which the LORD your God gives you, you shall not learn to ^{T}imitate^R the detestable things of those nations.   *do according to* • Deut. 9:5

10"There shall not be found among you anyone who makes his son or his daughter pass through the fire, one who uses divination, one who practices witchcraft, or one who interprets omens, or a sorcerer,

11 or one who casts a spell, or a medium, or a spiritist, or one who calls up the dead.

12"For whoever does these things is detestable to the LORD; and^{R}because of these detestable things the LORD your God will drive them out before you.   Lev. 18:24

13"You shall be^{T}blameless before the LORD your God.   *complete, perfect; or, having integrity*

14"For those nations, which you shall dispossess, listen to those who^{R}practice witchcraft and to diviners, but as for you, the LORD your God has not allowed you *to do* so.   2 Kin. 21:6

15"The^R LORD your God will raise up for you a prophet like me from among you, from your ^{T}countrymen, you shall listen to him.   Matt. 21:11; Luke 2:25-34; 7:16☆ • *brothers*

16"This is according to all that you asked of the LORD your God in Horeb on the day of the assembly, saying, 'Let me not hear again the voice of the LORD my God, let me not see this great fire anymore, lest I die.'

17"And the LORD said to me, 'They have ^{T}spoken well.   *done well what they have spoken*

18 'I will raise up a prophet from among their countrymen like you, and^{R}I will put My words in his mouth, and he shall speak to them all that I command him.   John 4:25☆

19 'And^R it shall come about that whoever will not listen to My words which he shall speak in My name, I Myself will require *it* of him.   Acts 3:23; Heb. 12:25☆

20 'But the prophet who shall speak a word presumptuously in My name which I have not commanded him to speak, or which$_T$he shall speak in the name of other gods, ^{T}that prophet shall die.'   *and that*

21"And^{T}you may say in your heart, 'How shall we know the word which the LORD has not spoken?'   *if you say*

22"When^{R}a prophet speaks in the name of the LORD, if the thing does not come about or come true, that is the thing which the LORD has not spoken. The prophet has spoken it ^{R}presumptuously; you shall not be afraid of him.   Jer. 28:9 • Deut. 18:20

CHAPTER 19

Cities of Refuge

"WHEN the LORD your God cuts off the nations, whose land the LORD your God gives you, and you dispossess them and settle in their cities and in their houses,

2 you shall set aside three cities for yourself in the midst of your land, which the LORD your God gives you to possess.

3"You shall prepare the ^{T}roads for yourself, and divide into three parts the territory of your land, which the LORD your God will give you as a possession, so that any manslayer may flee there.   road

4"Now this is the case of the manslayer who may flee there and live: when he ^{T}kills his friend ^{T}unintentionally, not hating him previously—   *smites* • *without knowledge*

5 as when *a man* goes into the forest with his friend to cut wood, and his hand ^{T}swings the axe to cut down the tree, and the iron *head* slips off the^{T}handle and strikes his friend so that he dies—he may flee to one of these cities and live;   *is thrust with* • *wood*

6 lest the avenger of blood pursue the manslayer^{T}in the heat of his anger, and overtake him, because the way is long, and^{T}take his life, though he was not deserving of death, since he had not hated him previously.   *while his heart is hot* • *smite him in the soul*

7"Therefore, I command you, saying, 'You shall set aside three cities for yourself.'

8"And if the LORD your God enlarges your territory, just as He has sworn to your fathers, and gives you all the land which He ^{T}promised to give your fathers—   spoke

9 if you carefully observe all this commandment, which I command you today, to love the LORD your God, and to walk in His ways always—then you shall add three more cities for yourself, besides these three.

10"So innocent blood will not be shed in the midst of your land which the LORD your God gives you as an inheritance, and^{R}bloodguiltiness be on you.   Num. 35:33; Deut. 21:1-9

11"But if there is a man who hates his neighbor and lies in wait for him and rises up against him and strikes him so that he dies, and he flees to one of these cities,

12 then the elders of his city shall send and take him from there and deliver him into the hand of the avenger of blood, that he may die.

13"You^T shall not pity him, but you shall purge the blood of the innocent from Israel, that it may go well with you.   *Your eye*

14"You[R] shall not move your neighbor's boundary mark, which the ancestors have set, in your inheritance which you shall inherit in the land that the LORD your God gives you to possess.   Deut. 27:17 • *possess it*

Law of Witnesses

15"A single witness shall not rise up against a man on account of any iniquity or any sin which he has committed; on the evidence of two or three witnesses a matter shall be confirmed.   *in any sin, which he sins*

16"If a malicious witness rises up against a man to accuse him of wrongdoing,

17 then both the men who have the dispute shall stand[R] before the LORD, before the priests and the judges who will be *in office* in those days.   Deut. 17:9

18"And the judges shall investigate thoroughly; and if the witness is a false witness *and* he has accused his brother falsely,

19 then[R] you shall do to him just as he had intended to do to his brother. Thus you shall purge the evil from among you.   Prov. 19:5

20"And[R] the rest will hear and be afraid, and will never again do such an evil thing among you.   Deut. 17:13; 21:21

21"Thus[T] you shall not show pity: life for life, eye for eye, tooth for tooth, hand for hand, foot for foot.   *your eye* • Matt. 5:38

CHAPTER 20

Law of Warfare

"WHEN you go out to battle against your enemies and see[R] horses and chariots *and* people more numerous than you, do not be afraid of them; for the LORD your God, who brought you up from the land of Egypt, is with you.   Deut. 3:22; 7:18 • 2 Chr. 32:7, 8

2"Now it shall come about that when you are approaching the battle, the priest shall come near and speak to the people.

3"And he shall say to them, 'Hear, O Israel, you are approaching the battle against your enemies today. Do not be fainthearted. Do not be afraid, or panic, or tremble before them,   Deut. 20:1; Josh. 23:10

4 for the LORD your God is the one who goes with you, to fight for you against your enemies, to save you.'   Deut. 1:30; 3:22

5"The officers also shall speak to the people, saying, 'Who is the man that has built a new house and has not dedicated it? Let him depart and return to his house, lest he die in the battle and another man dedicate it.

6 'And who is the man that has planted a vineyard and has not begun to use its fruit? Let him depart and return to his house, lest he die in the battle and another man begin to use its fruit.   *treat(ed) it as common*

7 'And who is the man that is engaged to a woman and has not married her? Let him depart and return to his house, lest he die in the battle and another man marry her.' *take*

8"Then the officers shall speak further to the people, and they shall say, 'Who is the man that is afraid and fainthearted? Let him depart and return to his house, so that he might not make his brothers' hearts melt like his heart.'   Judg. 7:3

9"And it shall come about that when the officers have finished speaking to the people, they shall appoint commanders of armies at the head of the people.

10"When you approach a city to fight against it, you shall offer it terms of peace.

11"And it shall come about, if it agrees to make peace with you and opens to you, then it shall be that all the people who are found in it shall become your forced labor and shall serve you.   *answers peace* • 1 Kin. 9:21

12"However, if it does not make peace with you, but makes war against you, then you shall besiege it.

13"When the LORD your God gives it into your hand, you shall strike all the men in it with the edge of the sword.   *males*

14"Only the women and the children and the animals and all that is in the city, all its spoil, you shall take as booty for yourself; and you shall use the spoil of your enemies which the LORD your God has given you.

15"Thus you shall do to all the cities that are very far from you, which are not of the cities of these nations nearby.   *here*

16"Only in the cities of these peoples that the LORD your God is giving you as an inheritance, you shall not leave alive anything that breathes.   Ex. 23:31-33; Num. 21:2, 3

17"But you shall utterly destroy them, the Hittite and the Amorite, the Canaanite and the Perizzite, the Hivite and the Jebusite, as the LORD your God has commanded you,

18 in order that they may not teach you to do according to all their detestable things which they have done for their gods, so that you would sin against the LORD your God.

19"When you besiege a city a long time, to make war against it in order to capture it, you shall not destroy its trees by swinging an axe against them; for you may eat from them, and you shall not cut them down. For is the tree of the field a man, that it should be besieged by you? *come before you in the siege*

20"Only the trees which you know are not fruit trees you shall destroy and cut down, that you may construct siegeworks against the city that is making war with you until it falls.   *they are not trees for food*

CHAPTER 21

Law of Unknown Murder

"IF a slain person is found lying in the open country in the land which the LORD your God gives you to possess, *and* it is not known who has struck him,   *possess it*

2 then your elders and your judges shall go out and measure *the distance* to the cities which are around the slain one.

3"And it shall be that the city which is nearest to the slain man, that is, the elders of that city, shall take a heifer of the herd, which has not been worked and which has not pulled in a yoke;

4 and the elders of that city shall bring the heifer down to a valley with running water, which has not been plowed or sown, and shall break the heifer's neck there in the valley.

5"Then the priests, the sons of Levi, shall come near, for the LORD your God has chosen them to serve Him and to bless in the name of the LORD; and every dispute and every assault shall be settled by them.

6"And all the elders of that city 'which is nearest to the slain man shall ᴿwash their hands over the heifer whose neck was broken in the valley;   who are · Matt. 27:24

7 and they shall answer and say, 'Our hands have not shed this blood, nor did our eyes see it.

8 'Forgive ¹⁴ Thy people Israel whom Thou hast redeemed, O LORD, and do not place the guilt of ᴿinnocent blood in the midst of Thy people Israel.' And the blood-guiltiness shall be forgiven them.   Jon. 1:14

9"So you shall remove the guilt of innocent blood from your midst, when you do what is right in the eyes of the LORD.

Law of Marriage

10"When you go out to battle against your enemies, and 'the LORD your God delivers them into your hands, and you take them away captive,   Josh. 21:44

11 and see among the captives a beautiful woman, and have a desire for her and would take her as a wife for yourself,

12 then you shall bring her home to your house, and she shall ᴿshave her head and 'trim her nails.   Lev. 14:8, 9; Num. 6:9 · do

13"She shall also ᵀremove the clothes of her captivity and shall remain in your house, and 'mourn her father and mother a full month; and after that you may go in to her and be her husband and she shall be your wife.   remove from her · Ps. 45:10

14"And it shall be, if you are not pleased with her, then you shall let her go wherever she wishes; but you shall certainly not sell her for money, you shall not 'mistreat her, because you have humbled her.   enslave

15"If a man has two wives, the one loved and the other ᵀunloved, and both the loved and the 'unloved have borne him sons, if the first-born son belongs to the 'unloved,   hated

16 then it shall be in the day he wills what he has to his sons, he cannot make the son of the loved the first-born before the son of the 'unloved, who is the first-born.   hated

17"But he shall acknowledge the first-born, the son of the 'unloved, by giving him a double portion of all that he has, for he is the beginning of his strength; to him belongs the right of the first-born.   hated

Law of the Rebellious Son

18"If any man has a stubborn and rebellious son who will 'not obey his father or his mother, and when they chastise him, he will not even listen to them,   Ex. 20:12; Lev. 19:3

19 then his father and mother shall seize him, and bring him out to the elders of his city at the gateway of his home town.

20"And they shall say to the elders of his city, 'This son of ours is stubborn and rebellious, he will not obey us, he is a glutton and a drunkard.'

21"Then ᴿall the men of his city shall stone him to death; so 'you shall remove the evil from your midst, and all Israel shall hear of it and fear.   Lev. 20:2, 27 · Deut. 19:19

22"And if a man has committed a sin ᴿworthy of death, and he is put to death, and you hang him on a tree,   Deut. 22:26; Matt. 26:66

23 his corpse shall not hang all night on the tree, but you shall surely bury him on the same day (for he who is hanged is 'accursed of God), so that you do not defile your land which the LORD your God gives you as an inheritance.   the curse of God

CHAPTER 22

Law of Your Countryman's Property

"Yᴼᵁᴿ shall not see your countryman's ox or his sheep straying away, and pay no attention to them; you shall certainly bring them back to your countryman.   Ex. 23:4, 5

2"And if your countryman is not near you, or if you do not know him, then you shall bring it home to your house, and it shall remain with you until your countryman looks for it; then you shall restore it to him.

3"And thus you shall do with his donkey, and you shall do the same with his garment, and you shall do likewise with anything lost by your countryman, which he has lost and you have found. You are not allowed to ᵀneglect them.   hide yourself

4"You shall not see your countryman's donkey or his ox fallen down on the way, and pay no attention to them; you shall certainly help him to raise them up.

Law of Separation

5"A woman shall not wear man's clothing, nor shall a man put on a woman's clothing; for whoever does these things is an abomination to the LORD your God.

6"If you happen to come upon a bird's nest along the way, in any tree or on the ground, with young ones or eggs, and the mother sitting on the young or on the eggs, 'you shall not take the mother with the young;   Lev. 22:28

7 you shall certainly let the mother go, but the young you may take for yourself, ᴿin

¹⁴ Lit., Cover over, atone for

order that it may be well with you, and that you may prolong your days.   Deut. 4:40

8 "When you build a new house, you shall make a parapet for your roof, that you may not bring bloodguilt on your house if anyone falls from it.

9 "You shall not sow your vineyard with two kinds of seed, lest all the produce of the seed which you have sown, and the increase of the vineyard become defiled.   *the fulness*

10 "You^R shall not plow with an ox and a donkey together.   [2 Cor. 6:14–16]

11 "You^R shall not wear a material mixed of wool and linen together.   Lev. 19:19

12 "You^R shall make yourself tassels on the four corners of your garment with which you cover yourself.   Num. 15:37-41; Matt. 23:5

Law of Marriage

13 "If any man takes a wife and goes in to her and then^T turns against her,   *hates her*

14 and charges her with shameful deeds and publicly defames her, and says, 'I took this woman, *but* when I came near her, I did not find her a virgin,'

15 then the girl's father and her mother shall take and bring out the *evidence* of the girl's virginity to the elders of the city at the gate.

16 "And the girl's father shall say to the elders, 'I gave my daughter to this man for a wife, but he^T turned against her;   *hated her*

17 and behold, he has charged her with shameful deeds, saying, "I did not find your daughter a virgin." But^T this is the *evidence* of my daughter's virginity.' And they shall spread the garment before the elders of the city.   *these are*

18 "So^R the elders of that city shall take the man and chastise him,   Ex. 18:21; Deut. 1:9-18

19 and they shall fine him a hundred *shekels* of silver and give it to the girl's father, because he publicly defamed a virgin of Israel. And she shall remain his wife; he cannot divorce her all his days.   *send her away*

20 "But if this^T charge is true, that the girl was not found a virgin,   *matter* • Deut. 17:4

21 then they shall bring out the girl to the doorway of her father's house, and the men of her city shall stone her^T to death because she has committed an act of folly in Israel, by playing the harlot in her father's house; thus^R you shall purge the evil from among you.   *with stones so that she dies* • Deut. 13:5

22 "If^R a man is found lying with a married woman, then both of them shall die, the man who lay with the woman, and the woman; thus you shall purge the evil from Israel.   Lev. 20:10; Ezek. 16:38; [Matt. 5:27, 28]

23 "If^R there is a girl who is a virgin engaged to a man, and *another* man finds her in the city and lies with her,   Lev. 19:20-22

24 then you shall bring them both out to the gate of that city and you shall stone them to death; the girl, because she did not cry out in the city, and the man, because he

has violated his neighbor's wife. Thus you shall purge the evil from among you.

25 "But if in the field the man finds the girl who is engaged, and the man forces her and lies with her, then only the man who lies with her shall die.

26 "But you shall do nothing to the girl; there is no sin in the girl worthy of death, for just as a man rises against his neighbor and murders him, so is this case.

27 "When he found her in the field, the engaged girl cried out, but there was no one to save her.

28 "If^R a man finds a girl who is a virgin, who is not engaged, and seizes her and lies with her and they are discovered,   Ex. 22:16

29 then the man who lay with her shall give to the girl's father fifty *shekels* of silver, and she shall become his wife because he has violated her; he cannot divorce her all his days.

30 "A^R man shall not take his father's wife so that he shall not uncover his father's skirt.   Lev. 18:8; 20:11; Deut. 27:20; 1 Cor. 5:1

CHAPTER 23

Law of Acceptance into the Assembly

"N O one who is^T emasculated, or has his male organ cut off, shall enter the assembly of the LORD.   *wounded by crushing of testicles*

2 "No one of illegitimate birth shall enter the assembly of the LORD; none of his *descendants*, even to the tenth generation, shall enter the assembly of the LORD.

3 "No Ammonite or Moabite shall enter the assembly of the LORD; none of their *descendants*, even to the tenth generation, shall ever enter the assembly of the LORD,

4 because they did not meet you with^T food and water on the way when you came out of Egypt, and because they hired against you^R Balaam the son of Beor from Pethor of Mesopotamia, to curse you.   *bread* • Jude 11

5 "Nevertheless, the LORD your God was not willing to listen to Balaam, but the LORD your God^T turned the curse into a blessing for you because the LORD your God^R loves you.   [Prov. 26:2] • Deut. 4:37

6 "You^R shall never seek their peace or their prosperity all your days.   Ezra 9:12

7 "You shall not detest an Edomite, for^R he is your brother; you shall not detest an Egyptian,^{R} because you were an alien in his land.   Gen. 25:24-26; Obad. 10 • Ex. 22:21; 23:9

8 "The sons of the third generation who are born to them may enter the assembly of the LORD.

9 "When you go out as^A an army against your enemies, then you shall keep yourself from every evil thing.   *a camp*

10 "If there is among you any man who is unclean because of a nocturnal emission, then he must go outside the camp; he may not^T reenter the camp.   *come to the midst of*

11"But it shall be when evening approaches, he shall bathe himself with water, and at sundown he may reenter the camp.

12"You shall also have a place outside the camp and go out there,

13 and you shall have a 'spade among your tools, and it shall be when you sit down outside, you shall dig with it and shall turn 'to cover up your excrement.   *peg • and*

14"Since the LORD your God walks in the midst of your camp to deliver you and to defeat your enemies before you, therefore your camp must be holy; and He must not see anything indecent among you lest He turn away from you.   *give • Ex. 3:5 • and*

15"You shall not hand over to his master a slave who has escaped from his master to you.   *1 Sam. 30:15 • delivered himself*

16"He shall live with you in your midst, in the place which he shall choose in one of your 'towns where it pleases him; you shall not mistreat him.   *gates • Ex. 22:21; Prov. 22:22*

17"None of the daughters of Israel shall be a cult prostitute, nor shall any of the sons of Israel be a cult prostitute.   *Lev. 19:29*

18"You shall not bring the hire of a harlot or the wages of a [15]dog into the house of the LORD your God for any votive offering, for both of these are an abomination to the LORD your God.   *Lev. 18:22; 20:13*

19"You shall not charge interest to your countrymen: interest on money, food, *or* anything that may be loaned at interest.

20"You may charge interest to a foreigner, but to your 'countryman you shall not charge interest, so that the LORD your God may bless you in all 'that you undertake in the land which you are about to enter to possess.   *brother • the putting forth of your hand*

21"When you make a vow to the LORD your God, you shall not delay to pay it, for it would be sin in you, 'and the LORD your God will surely require it of you.   *Job 22:27 • for*

22"However, if you refrain from vowing, it would not be sin in you.

23"You shall be careful to perform what goes out from your lips, just as you have voluntarily vowed to the LORD your God, what you have promised.

Laws for Harmony in the Nation

24"When you enter your neighbor's vineyard, then you may eat grapes until you are fully satisfied, but you shall not put any in your basket.   *vessel*

25"When you enter your neighbor's standing grain, then you may pluck the heads with your hand, but you shall not wield a sickle in your neighbor's standing grain.

CHAPTER 24

"WHEN a man takes a wife and marries her, and it happens 'that she finds no favor in his eyes because he has found some indecency in her, and he writes her a certificate of divorce and puts *it* in her hand and sends her out from his house,   *if • Deut. 22:13-21*

2 and she leaves his house and goes and becomes another man's *wife,*

3 and if the latter husband 'turns against her and writes her a certificate of divorce and puts *it* in her hand and sends her out of his house, or if the latter husband dies who took her to be his wife,   *hates her*

4 *then* her former husband who sent her away is not allowed to take her again to be his wife, since she has been defiled; for that is an abomination before the LORD, and you shall not bring sin on the land which the LORD your God gives you as an inheritance.

5"When a man takes a new wife, he shall not go out with the army, nor be charged with any duty; he shall be free at home one year and shall give happiness to his wife whom he has taken.   *Deut. 20:7 • Prov. 5:18*

6"No one shall take a handmill or an upper millstone in pledge, for he would be taking a life in pledge.

7"If a man is 'caught kidnapping any of his 'countrymen of the sons of Israel, and he deals with him violently, or sells him, then that thief shall die; so you shall purge the evil from among you.   *found stealing • brothers*

8"Be careful against 'an infection of leprosy, that you diligently observe and do according to all that the Levitical priests shall teach you; as I have commanded them, so you shall be careful to do.   *a mark or stroke*

9"Remember what the LORD your God did 'to Miriam on the way as you came out of Egypt.   *Num. 12:10*

10"When you make your neighbor a loan of any sort, you shall not enter his house to take his pledge.   *Ex. 22:26, 27*

11"You shall remain outside, and the man to whom you make the loan shall bring the pledge out to you.

12"And if he is a poor man, you shall not sleep with his pledge.

13"When the sun goes down you shall surely return the pledge to him, that he may sleep in his cloak and bless you; and it will be righteousness for you before the LORD your God.   *Ex. 22:26 • Deut. 6:25; Dan. 4:27*

14"You shall not oppress a hired servant *who is* poor and needy, whether *he is* one of your 'countrymen or one of your aliens who is in your land in your towns.   *brothers*

15"You shall give him his wages on his day 'before the sun sets, for he is poor and sets his 'heart on it; so that he may not cry against you to the LORD and it become sin in you.   *that the sun shall not go down on it • soul*

16"Fathers shall not be put to death 'for *their* sons, nor shall sons be put to death 'for *their* fathers; everyone shall be put to death for his own sin.   *2 Kin. 14:6; 2 Chr. 25:4 • with*

[15] I.e., male prostitute, sodomite

17"You[R] shall not pervert the justice due an alien *or* [16]an orphan, nor take a widow's garment in pledge.   Ex. 23:9; Lev. 19:33

18"But you shall remember that you were a slave in Egypt, and that the LORD your God redeemed you from there; therefore I am commanding you to do this thing.

19"When you reap your harvest in your field and have forgotten a sheaf in the field, you shall not go back to get it; it shall be for the alien, for the òrphan, and for the widow, in order that the LORD your God may bless you in all the work of your hands.   *fatherless*

20"When you beat your olive tree, you shall not go over the boughs [T]again; it shall be[R] for the alien, for the [A]orphan, and for the widow.   *after yourself* · Deut. 24:19 · *fatherless*

21"When you gather the grapes of your vineyard, you shall not [']go over it again; it shall be for the alien, for the òrphan, and for the widow.   *glean it after yourself* · *fatherless*

22"And you shall remember that you were a slave in the land of Egypt; therefore I am commanding you to do this thing.

CHAPTER 25

"I[F][R] there is a dispute between men and they go to [T]court, and the judges decide their case, and they justify the righteous and condemn the wicked,   Deut. 17:8-13 · *the judgment*

2 then it shall be if the wicked man deserves to be beaten, the judge shall then make him lie down and be beaten in his presence with the number of stripes according to his [']guilt.   *is a son of beating* · *wickedness*

3"He[R] may beat him forty times *but* no more, lest he beat him with many more stripes than these, and your brother be [D]degraded in your eyes.   2 Cor. 11:24 · Job 18:3

4"You[R] shall not muzzle the ox while he is threshing.   [Prov. 12:10; 1 Cor. 9:9; 1 Tim. 5:18]

5"When brothers live together and one of them dies and has no son, the wife of the deceased shall not be *married* outside *the family* to a strange man. [R]Her husband's brother shall go in to her and take her to himself as wife and perform the duty of a husband's brother to her.   Matt. 22:24

6"And it shall be [T]that the first-born whom she bears shall [']assume the name of his dead brother, that his name may not be blotted out from Israel.   *stand on*

7"But[R] if the man does not desire to take his brother's wife, then his brother's wife shall go up to the gate to the elders and say, 'My husband's brother refuses to establish a name for his brother in Israel; he is not willing to perform the duty of a husband's brother to me.'   Ruth 4:5, 6

8"Then the elders of his city shall summon him and speak to him. And *if* he per-

sists and says, 'I do not desire to take her,'
9 then his brother's wife shall come to him in the sight of the elders, and pull his sandal off his foot and spit in his face; and she shall declare, 'Thus it is done to the man who does not build up his brother's house.'

10"And in Israel his name shall be called, 'The house of him whose sandal is removed.'

11"If *two* men, a man and his countryman, are struggling together, and the wife of one comes near to deliver her husband from the hand of the one who is striking him, and puts out her hand and seizes his genitals,
12 then you shall cut off her [']hand; [']you shall not show pity.   *palm* · *your eye*

13"You[R] shall not have in your bag differing weights, a large and a small.   Ezek. 45:10

14"You shall not have in your house differing measures, a large and a small.

15"You shall have a full and just weight; you shall have a full and just [T]measure, that your days may be prolonged in the land which the LORD your God gives you.   *ephah*

16"For [R]everyone who does these things, everyone who acts unjustly is an abomination to the LORD your God.   Prov. 11:1

17"Remember[R] what Amalek did to you along the way when you came out from Egypt,   Ex. 17:8-16

18 how he met you along the way and attacked among you all the stragglers at your rear when you were faint and weary; and he [']did not [17]fear God.   [Ps. 36:1]; Rom. 3:18

19"Therefore it shall come about when the LORD your God has given you [']rest from all your surrounding enemies, in the land which the LORD your God gives you as an inheritance to[']possess, you shall blot out the memory of Amalek from under heaven; you must not forget.   Deut. 12:9 · *possess it*

CHAPTER 26

Law of the Tithe

"T HEN it shall be, when you enter the land which the LORD your God gives you as an inheritance, and you possess it and live in it,

2 that you shall take some of the first of all the produce of the ground which you shall bring in from your land that the LORD your God gives you, and you shall put *it* in a basket and go to the place where the LORD your God chooses to establish His name.

3"And you shall go to the priest who is in office at that time, and say to him, 'I declare this day to the LORD my God that I have entered the land which the LORD swore to our fathers to give us.'

4"Then the priest shall take the basket from your hand and set it down before the altar of the LORD your God.

5"And you shall answer and say before the LORD your God, 'My father was a [A]wan-

---

[16] Or, *the fatherless*, and so throughout this context
[17] Or, *reverence*

dering Aramean, and he went down to Egypt and sojourned there, few in number; but there he became a great, mighty and populous nation.   *perishing · lived as an alien*

6 'And the [R]Egyptians treated us harshly and afflicted us, and imposed hard labor on us.   Ex. 1:8-11

7 'Then [R]we cried to the LORD, the God of our fathers, and the LORD heard our voice and saw our affliction and our toil and our oppression;   Ex. 2:23-25; 3:9

8 [R]and the LORD brought us out of Egypt with a mighty hand and an outstretched arm and with great terror and with signs and wonders;   Deut. 4:34; 34:11, 12

9 and He has brought us to this place, and has given us this land, [R]a land flowing with milk and honey.   Ex. 3:8, 17

10 'And now behold, I have brought the first of the produce of the ground which Thou, O LORD hast given me.' And you shall set it down before the LORD your God, and worship before the LORD your God;

11 and you and [R]the Levite and the alien who is among you shall rejoice in all the good which the LORD your God has given you and your household.   Deut. 12:12

12 "When you have finished paying all the tithe of your increase in the third year, the year of tithing, then you shall give it to the Levite, to the stranger, to the [A]orphan and to the widow, that they may eat in your [T]towns, and be satisfied.   *fatherless · gates*

13 "And you shall say before the LORD your God, 'I have removed the sacred *portion* from *my* house, and also have given it to the Levite and the alien, the orphan and the widow, according to all Thy commandments which Thou hast commanded me; [R]I have not transgressed or forgotten any of Thy commandments.   Ps. 119:141, 153, 176

14 'I have not eaten of it [T]while mourning, nor have I removed any of it while I was unclean, nor offered any of it to the dead. I have listened to the voice of the LORD my God; I have done according to all that Thou hast commanded me.   *while in my*

15 'Look [R]down from Thy holy habitation, from heaven, and bless Thy people Israel, and the ground which Thou hast given us, a land flowing with milk and honey, as Thou didst swear to our fathers.'   Ps. 80:14; Is. 63:15

Vow of Israel and of God

16 "This day the LORD your God commands you to do these statutes and ordinances. You shall therefore be careful to do them [R]with all your heart and with all your soul.   Deut. 4:29

17 "You [R]have today declared the LORD to be your God, and [T]that you would walk in His ways and keep His statutes, His commandments and His ordinances, and listen to His voice.   Ps. 48:14 · *to walk in*

18 "And the LORD has today declared you to be [R]His people, a treasured possession, as He promised you, and [T]that you should keep all His commandments;   Ex. 6:7 · *to keep all*

19 and [T]that He shall [R]set you high above all nations which He has made, for praise, fame, and honor; and that you shall be a consecrated people to the LORD your God, as He has spoken."   *to set you* · Deut. 4:7, 8

CHAPTER 27

Erection of the Altar

THEN Moses and the elders of Israel charged the people, saying, "Keep all the commandments which I command you today.

2 "So [R]it shall be on the day when you shall cross the Jordan to the land which the LORD your God gives you, that you shall set up for yourself large stones, and coat them with lime   Josh. 8:30-32

3 and write on them all the words of this law, when you cross over, in order that you may enter the land which the LORD your God gives you, [R]a land flowing with milk and honey, as the LORD, the God of your fathers, [T]promised you.   Deut. 26:9 · *spoke to*

4 "So it shall be when you cross the Jordan, you shall set up on Mount Ebal, these stones, [T]as I am commanding you today, and you shall coat them with lime.   *which*

5 "Moreover, you shall build there an altar to the LORD your God, an altar of stones; you shall not wield an iron *tool* on them.

6 "You shall build the altar of the LORD your God of [T]uncut stones; and you shall offer on it burnt offerings to the LORD your God;   *whole*

7 and you shall sacrifice peace offerings and eat there, and you shall [R]rejoice before the LORD your God.   Deut. 26:11

8 "And you shall write on the stones all the words of this law very distinctly."

Admonition to Obey the Law

9 Then Moses and the Levitical priests spoke to all Israel, saying, "Be silent and listen, O Israel! This day you have become a people for the LORD your God.

10 "You shall therefore obey the LORD your God, and do His commandments and His statutes which I command you today."

Proclamation of the Curses

11 Moses also charged the people on that day, saying,

12 "When you cross the Jordan, these shall stand on [R]Mount Gerizim to bless the people: [R]Simeon, Levi, Judah, Issachar, Joseph, and Benjamin.   Deut. 11:29 · Josh. 8:33-35

13 "And for the curse, these shall stand on Mount Ebal: Reuben, Gad, Asher, Zebulun, Dan, and Naphtali.

14"The Levites shall then answer and say to all the men of Israel with a loud voice,

15 'Cursed is the man who makes an idol or a molten image, an abomination to the LORD, the work of the hands of the craftsman, and sets *it* up in secret.' And all the people shall answer and say, 'Amen.'

16 'Cursed[R] is he who dishonors his father or mother.' And all the people shall say, 'Amen.'   Ex. 20:12; 21:17; Lev. 19:3; Deut. 5:16

17 'Cursed[R] is he who moves his neighbor's boundary mark.' And all the people shall say, 'Amen.'   Deut. 19:14; Prov. 22:28

18 'Cursed[R] is he who misleads a blind *person* on the road.' And all the people shall say, 'Amen.'   Lev. 19:14

19 'Cursed is he who distorts the justice due an alien, orphan,[fatherless] and widow.' And all the people shall say, 'Amen.'

20 'Cursed is he who lies with his father's wife, because he has uncovered his father's skirt.' And all the people shall say, 'Amen.'

21 'Cursed is he who lies with any animal.' And all the people shall say, 'Amen.'

22 'Cursed is he who lies with his sister, the daughter of his father or of his mother.' And all the people shall say, 'Amen.'

23 'Cursed is he who lies with his mother-in-law.' And all the people shall say, 'Amen.'

24 'Cursed[R] is he who strikes his neighbor in secret.' And all the people shall say, 'Amen.'   Ex. 21:12; Lev. 24:17; Num. 35:30, 31

25 'Cursed[R] is he who accepts a bribe to strike down an innocent person.' And all the people shall say, 'Amen.'   Ex. 23:7; Deut. 10:17

26 'Cursed[R] is he who does not confirm the words of this law by doing them.' And all the people shall say, 'Amen.'   Ps. 119:21

CHAPTER 28

Promised Blessings for Obedience

"NOW it shall be, if you will diligently obey the LORD your God, being careful to do all His commandments which I command you today, the LORD your God will set you high above all the nations of the earth.

2"And all these blessings shall come upon you and overtake you, if you will obey the LORD your God.   *listen to the voice of*

3"Blessed *shall* you be in the city, and blessed *shall* you be in the country.[field]

4"Blessed *shall* be the offspring of your body and the produce of your ground and the offspring of your beasts, the increase of your herd and the young of your flock.

5"Blessed *shall* be your basket and your kneading bowl.

6"Blessed *shall* you be [R]when you come in, and blessed *shall* you be when you go out.   Ps. 121:8

7"The LORD will cause your enemies who

rise up against you to be defeated before you; they shall come out against you one way and shall flee before you seven ways.

8"The LORD will command the blessing upon you in your barns and in [R]all that you put your hand to, and He will bless you in the land which the LORD your God gives you.   Deut. 15:10

9"The LORD will establish you as a holy people to Himself, as He swore to you, if you will keep the commandments of the LORD your God, and walk in His ways.

10"So all the peoples of the earth shall see that[R] you are called by the name of the LORD; and they shall be afraid of you.   2 Chr. 7:14

11"And the LORD will make you abound in prosperity, in the offspring of your body and in the offspring of your beast and in the produce of your ground, in the land which the LORD swore to your fathers to give you.

12"The LORD will open for you His good storehouse, the heavens, to give rain to your land in its season and to bless all the work of your hand; and you shall lend to many nations, but you shall not borrow.

13"And the LORD shall make you the head and not the tail, and you only shall be above, and you shall not be underneath, if you will listen to the commandments of the LORD your God, which I charge you today, to observe *them* carefully,   *keep and do*

14 and do[R] not turn aside from any of the words which I command you today, to the right or to the left, to go after other gods to serve them.   Deut. 5:32; Josh. 1:7

Promised Curses for Disobedience

15"But[R] it shall come about, if you will not obey the LORD your God, to observe to do all His commandments and His statutes with which I charge you today, that all these curses shall come upon you and overtake you.   Lev. 26:14-43; Dan. 9:11 • *listen to the voice of*

16"Cursed *shall* you be in the city, and cursed *shall* you be in the country.   *field*

17"Cursed[R] *shall be* your basket and your kneading bowl.   Deut. 28:5

18"Cursed *shall be* the offspring of your body and the produce of your ground, the increase of your herd and the young of your flock.   Deut. 28:4 • *fruit • womb*

19"Cursed *shall* you be when you come in, and cursed *shall* you be when you go out.

20"The LORD will send upon you curses, confusion, and rebuke, in all you undertake to do, until you are destroyed and until you perish quickly, on account of the evil of your deeds, because you have forsaken Me.

21"The[R] LORD will make the pestilence cling to you until He has consumed you from the land, where you are entering to possess it.   Lev. 26:25; Num. 14:12; Jer. 24:10

22"The LORD will smite you with consumption and with fever and with inflammation and with fiery heat and with [18]the

18 Another reading is *drought*

sword and with blight and with mildew, and they shall pursue you until you perish.

23"And 'the heaven which is over your head shall be bronze, and the earth which is under you, iron.   *your*

24"The Lord will make the rain of your land powder and dust; from heaven it shall come down on you until you are destroyed.

25"The Lord will cause you to be defeated before your enemies; you shall go out one way against them, but you shall flee seven ways before them, and you shall be an example of terror to all the kingdoms of the earth.   Deut. 28:7; Is. 30:17 • *smitten* • Jer. 15:4

26"And your carcasses shall be food to all birds of the sky and to the beasts of the earth, and there shall be no one to frighten *them* away.   Jer. 7:33; 16:4; 19:7; 34:20

27"The Lord will smite you with the boils of Egypt and with tumors and with the scab and with the itch, from which you cannot be healed.   Ex. 9:9; Deut. 7:15 • 1 Sam. 5:6

28"The Lord will smite you with madness and with blindness and with bewilderment of heart;

29 and you shall 'grope at noon, as the blind man gropes in darkness, and you shall not prosper in your ways; but you shall only be oppressed and robbed continually, with none to save you.   *be groping* • Ex. 10:21

30"You shall betroth a wife, but another man shall violate her; you shall build a house, but you shall not live in it; you shall plant a vineyard, but you shall not 'use its fruit.   Job 31:10; Jer. 8:10 • Amos 5:11 • *begin it*

31"Your ox shall be slaughtered before your eyes, but you shall not eat of it; your donkey shall be torn away from you, and shall not be restored to you; your sheep shall be given to your enemies, and you shall have none to save you.

32"Your sons and your daughters shall be given to another people, while your eyes shall look on and yearn for them continually; but there shall be nothing you can do.

33"A people whom you do not know shall eat up the produce of your ground and all your labors, and you shall never be anything but oppressed and crushed continually.

34"And you shall be driven mad by the sight of 'what you see.   *your eyes which you*

35"The Lord will strike you on the knees and legs with sore boils, from which you cannot be healed, from the sole of your foot to the crown of your head.   Deut. 28:27

36"The Lord will bring you and your king, whom you shall set over you, to a nation which neither you nor your fathers have known, and there you shall serve other gods, wood and stone.   Deut. 4:28; Jer. 16:13

37"And you shall become a horror, a proverb, and a taunt among all the people where the Lord will drive you.   1 Kin. 9:7, 8; Jer. 19:8

38"You shall bring out much seed to the field but you shall gather in little, for the locust shall consume it.   Is. 5:10 • Ex. 10:4

39"You shall plant and cultivate vineyards, but you shall neither drink of the wine nor gather *the grapes,* for the worm shall devour them.   Is. 5:10; 17:10, 11

40"You shall have olive trees throughout your territory but you shall not anoint yourself with the oil, for your olives shall drop off.   Jer. 11:16; Mic. 6:15

41"You shall have sons and daughters but they shall not be yours, for they shall go into captivity.   Deut. 28:32 • *beget*

42"The cricket shall possess all your trees and the produce of your ground.   Deut. 28:38

43"The alien who is among you shall rise above you higher and higher, but you shall go down lower and lower.   Deut. 28:13

44"He shall lend to you, but you shall not lend to him; he shall be the head, and you shall be the tail.   Deut. 28:12 • Deut. 28:13

45"So all these curses shall come on you and pursue you and overtake you until you are destroyed, because you would not obey the Lord your God by keeping His commandments and His statutes which He commanded you.   *listen to the voice of*

46"And they shall become a sign and a wonder on you and your 'descendants forever.   Num. 26:10; Is. 8:18; Ezek. 5:15; 14:8 • *seed*

47"Because you did not serve the Lord your God with joy and a glad heart, for the abundance of all things;   Neh. 9:35-37

48 therefore you shall serve your enemies whom the Lord shall send against you, in hunger, in thirst, in nakedness, and in the lack of all things; and He will put an iron yoke on your neck until He has destroyed you.   Lam. 4:4-6 • Jer. 28:13, 14

49"The Lord will bring a nation against you from afar, from the end of the earth, as the eagle swoops down, a nation whose language you shall not understand,   Jer. 48:40

50 a nation of fierce countenance who shall have no respect for the old, nor show favor to the young.   Is. 47:6

51"Moreover, it shall eat the offspring of your herd and the produce of your ground until you are destroyed, who also leaves you no grain, new wine, or oil, nor the increase of your herd or the young of your flock until they have caused you to perish.   *fruit*

52"And it shall besiege you in all your 'towns until your high and fortified walls in which you trusted come down throughout your land, and it shall besiege you in all your 'towns throughout your land which the Lord your God has given you.   *gates*

53"Then you shall eat the offspring of your own body, the flesh of your sons and of your daughters whom the Lord your God has given you, during the siege and the distress by which your enemy shall oppress you.

54"The man who is 'refined and very delicate among you 'shall be hostile toward his brother and toward the wife he cherishes and toward the rest of his children who remain,   *tender* • *his eye shall be evil toward*

55 so that he will not give *even* one of them any of the flesh of his children which he shall eat, since he has nothing *else* left, during the siege and the distress by which your enemy shall ᶦoppress you in all your ᵀtowns. *distress • gates*

56"The refined and delicate woman among you, who would not venture to set the sole of her foot on the ground for delicateness and refinement, ᶦshall be hostile toward the husband she cherishes and toward her son and daughter, *her eye shall be evil toward*

57 and toward her afterbirth which issues from between her ᶦlegs and toward her children whom she bears; for she shall eat them secretly for lack of anything *else*, during the siege and the distress by which your enemy shall oppress you in your towns. *feet*

58"If you are not careful to observe all the words of this law which are written in this book, to fear this honored and awesome name,ᵀthe LORD your God, *Heb., YHWH*

59 then the LORD will bring extraordinary plagues on you andᵀyour descendants, even severe and lasting plagues, and miserable and chronic sicknesses. *plague on your seed*

60"AndᴿHe will bring back on you all the diseases of Egypt of which you were afraid, and they shall cling to you. *Deut. 28:27*

61"Also every sickness and every plague which, not written in the book of this law, the LORD will bring on youᴿuntil you are destroyed. *Deut. 4:25, 26*

ᴿ62"Then you shall be left few in number, ᴿwhereas you were as the stars of heaven for multitude, because you did not ᶦobey the LORD your God. *Neh. 9:23 • listen to the voice of*

63"And it shall come about that as the LORD delighted over you to prosper you, and multiply you, so the LORD will ᶦdelight over you to make you perish and destroy you; and you shall be torn from the land where you are entering to possess it. *Prov. 1:26*

64"Moreover, the LORD will scatter you among all peoples, from one end of the earth to the other end of the earth; and there you shall serve other gods, wood and stone, which you or your fathers have not known.

65"And among those nations you shall find no rest, and there shall be no resting place for the sole of your foot; but thereᴿthe LORD will give you a trembling heart, failing of eyes, and despair of soul. *Lev. 26:36*

66"So your life shall ᶦhang in doubt before you; and you shall be in dread night and day, and shall have no assurance of your life. *be hung for you in front*

67"Inᴿ the morning you shall say, 'Would that it were evening!' And at evening you shall say, 'Would that it were morning!' because of the dread of your heart which you dread, and for the sight of your eyes which you shall see. *Job 7:4*

68"And the LORD will bring you back to Egypt in ships, by the way about which I spoke to you, 'You will never see it again!' And there you shall offer yourselves for sale to your enemies as male and female slaves, but there will be no buyer."

CHAPTER 29

The Covenant Is Based on the Power of God

THESEᴿ are the words of the covenant which the LORD commanded Moses to make with the sons of Israel in the land of Moab, besides the ᴿcovenant which He had made with them at Horeb. *Lev. 26:46 • Deut. 5:2, 3*

2 And Moses summoned all Israel and said to them, "You have seen all that the LORD did before your eyes in the land of Egypt to Pharaoh and all his servants and all his land;

3 the great trials which your eyes have seen, those great signs and wonders.

4"Yet to this dayᴿthe LORD has not given you a heart to know, nor eyes to see, nor ears to hear. [Ezek. 12:2]; Matt. 13:14; Rom. 11:8

5"And I have led you forty years in the wilderness; ᶦyour clothes have not worn out on you, and your sandal has not worn out on your foot. *Deut. 8:4*

6"Youᴿ have not eaten bread, nor have you drunk wine or strong drink, in order that you might know that I am the LORD your God. *Deut. 8:3*

7"When you ᵀreached this place, Sihon the king of Heshbon and Og the king of Bashan came out to meet us for battle, but we ᶦdefeated them; *came to • smote*

8 and we took their land and gave it as an inheritance to the Reubenites, the Gadites, and the half-tribe of the Manassites.

9"Soᴿ keep the words of this covenant to do them, ᴿthat you may prosper in all that you do. *Deut. 4:6; 1 Kin. 2:3 • Josh. 1:7*

Parties of the Covenant

10"You stand today, all of you, before the LORD your God: your chiefs, your tribes, your elders and your officers, *even* all the men of Israel,

---

29:10–15; 30:11–20　The Palestine Covenant—The covenant concerning Palestine is the third of the theocratic covenants (pertaining to the rule of God). The Palestinian Covenant has two aspects: (1) the legal aspects which are immediate and conditional (Page 192—Deut. 27—29); and (2) the grace aspects which are future and unconditional (Page 197—Deut. 30:1–9). The enjoyment of the immediate blessings are introduced by the conditional formula: "if you will diligently obey the LORD your God . . . the LORD your God will set you high above all the nations of the earth" (Page 193—Deut. 28:1). Sadly, Israel did not meet the condition of obedience, and is still experiencing God's curses and punishment for their disobedience (Page 193—Deut. 28:15–68). The uncondi-

(continued on next page)

11 your little ones, your wives, and the alien who is within your camps, from*the one who chops your wood to the one who draws your water,   Josh. 9:21, 23, 27

12 that you may enter into the covenant with the LORD your God, and into His oath which the LORD your God is making with you today,

13 in order that He may establish you today as His people and that*He may be your God, just as He spoke to you and as He swore to your fathers, to Abraham, Isaac, and Jacob.   Gen. 17:7; Ex. 6:7

14"Now not with you alone am I*making this covenant and this oath,   [Jer. 31:31]

15*but both with those who stand here with us today in the presence of the LORD our God and with those who are not with us here today   Acts 2:39

Scattering of Israel

16 (for you know how we lived in the land of Egypt, and how we came through the midst of the nations through which you passed.

17"Moreover, you have seen their abominations and their idols *of* wood, stone, silver, and gold, which *they had* with them);

18 lest there shall be among you a man or woman, or family or tribe, whose heart turns away today from the LORD our God, to go and serve the gods of those nations; lest there shall be among you*a root bearing poisonous fruit and wormwood.   Deut. 32:32

19"And it shall be when he hears the words of this curse, that he will boast, saying, 'I have peace though I walk in the stubbornness of my heart in order to destroy the watered *land* with the dry.'

20"The LORD shall never be willing to forgive him, but rather the anger of the LORD and His jealousy will*burn against that man, and every curse which is written in this book will rest on him, and the LORD will blot out his name from under heaven.   *smoke*

21"Then the LORD will single him out for adversity from all the tribes of Israel, according to all the curses of the covenant which are written in this book of the law.

22"Now the generation to come, your sons who rise up after you and*the foreigner who comes from a distant land, when they see the plagues of the land and the diseases with which the LORD has *afflicted it, will say,   Jer. 19:8; 49:17; 50:13 • *made it sick*

23 'All its land is brimstone and salt, *a burning waste, unsown and unproductive, and no grass grows in it, like the overthrow of *Sodom and Gomorrah, Admah and Zeboiim, which the LORD overthrew in His anger and in His wrath.'   Is. 1:7; 64:11 • Jude 7

24"And all the nations shall say, 'Why*has the LORD done thus to this land? Why this great *outburst of anger?'   1 Kin. 9:8 • *heat*

25"Then *men* shall say, 'Because*they forsook the covenant of the LORD, the God of their fathers, which He made with them when He brought them out of the land of Egypt.   2 Kin. 17:9-23; 2 Chr. 36:13-21

26 'And they went and served other gods and worshiped them, gods whom*they have not known and whom He had not*allotted to them.   *portioned*

27 'Therefore, the anger of the LORD burned against that land, to bring upon it every curse which is written in this book;

28 and*the LORD uprooted them from their land in anger and in fury and in great wrath, and cast them into another land, as *it is* this day.'   2 Chr. 7:20; Ps. 52:5; Prov. 2:22

29"The secret things belong to the LORD our God, but*the things revealed belong to

(continued from previous page)

tional grace aspects of the Palestinian Covenant have yet to be realized. God will regather the scattered people of Israel and establish them in the land He has promised unconditionally to give them. Deuteronomy concludes the Palestinian Covenant with a final warning and challenge for obedience (Page 197—Deut. 30:1–20).
    Now turn to Page 300—2 Sam. 7:4-17: The Davidic Covenant.

    29:29 Revelation of God's Word—Revelation may be defined as that process by which God imparted to man truths which he otherwise could not know. The details of creation in Genesis 1 and 2 are an example of revelation. As man was not created until the sixth day, we could not have possibly known the events occurring prior to this until God gave the facts to Moses.
    We know God spoke to the human authors of our Bible; but just how did He speak? Was it in Hebrew? Greek? Angelic language? He spoke to them in their own language. God's call to young Samuel in the temple (Page 265—1 Sam. 3:1–10) proves this, for the boy at first mistook God's voice for that of the aged priest Eli. Sometimes God spoke through angels: Gabriel was sent from heaven to tell Mary she would give birth to the Messiah (Page 1025—Luke 1:26–37). On other occasions the Lord spoke directly to a man, as He did to Noah concerning the Great Flood (Page 9—Gen. 6:13–21).
    One of God's methods of communication in Scripture is to reveal His message through dreams and visions: The wise men (Page 964—Matt. 2:12) were warned in a dream not to return to Herod, while Peter was later instructed in a vision to minister to Cornelius (Page 1105—Acts 10:10–16). God has communicated in many different ways. He revealed Himself to Moses from a burning bush (Page 56—Ex. 3:4) and to Moses, Aaron, and Miriam out of a cloud (Page 140—Num. 12:4, 5).
    One of the most important ways that divine truths were given in the Old Testament was through the Angel of the Lord. Most Bible students perceive this heavenly messenger to be the pre-incarnate Christ Himself. For example, it is the Angel of the Lord who reassured Joshua on the eve of a battle (Page 210—Josh. 5:13–15).
    Now turn to Page 707—Is. 59:21: Inspiration of God's Word.

us and to our sons forever, that we may observe all the words of this law.   [2 Tim. 3:16]

CHAPTER 30

Restoration of Israel

"SO it shall be when all of these things have come upon you, the blessing and the curse which I have set before you, and you call *them* to mind ^Rin all nations where the LORD your God has banished you, 1 Kin. 8:47

2 and you return to the LORD your God and ^Tobey Him with all your heart and soul according to all that I command you today, you and your sons,   *listen to His voice*

3 then the LORD your God will restore ^Tyou from captivity, and have compassion on you, and ^Rwill gather you again from all the peoples where the LORD your God has scattered you.   *your captivity* • Ps. 147:2; Jer. 32:37

4 "If your outcasts are at the ends of the ^Tearth, ^Rfrom there the LORD your God will gather you, and from there He will ^Tbring you back.   *sky* • Neh. 1:9; Is. 43:6 • *take you*

5 "And ^Rthe LORD your God will bring you into the land which your fathers possessed, and you shall possess it; and He will prosper you and ^Rmultiply you more than your fathers.   Jer. 29:14; 30:3 • Deut. 7:13; 13:17

6 "Moreover the LORD your God will circumcise your heart and the heart of your descendants, ^Tto love the LORD your God with all your heart and with all your soul, in order that you may live.   *seed* • Deut. 6:5

7 "And the LORD your God will ^Tinflict all these curses on your enemies and on those who hate you, who persecuted you.   *put*

8 "And you shall again ^Tobey the LORD, and observe all His commandments which I command you today.   *listen to the voice of*

9 "Then the LORD your God will ^Tprosper you abundantly in all the work of your hand, in the offspring of your body and in the offspring of your cattle and in the produce of your ground, for the LORD will again rejoice over you for good, just as He rejoiced over your fathers;   *make you have excess for good*

10 if you ^Tobey the LORD your God to keep His commandments and His statutes which are written in this book of the law, if you turn to the LORD your God with all your heart and soul.   *listen to the voice of*

Ratification of the Palestinian Covenant

11 "For this commandment which I command you today is not too difficult for you, nor is it ^Tout of reach.   *far off*

12 "It is not in heaven, ^Tthat you should say, 'Who ^Rwill go up to heaven for us to get it for us and make us hear it, that we may observe it?'   *to say* • Rom. 10:6-8

13 "Nor is it beyond the sea, ^Tthat you should say, 'Who will cross the sea for us to get it for us and make us hear it, that we may observe it?'   *to say*

14 "But the word is very near you, in your mouth and in your heart, that you may observe it.

15 "See, I have set before you today life and prosperity, and death and adversity;

16 in that I command you today ^Rto love the LORD your God, to walk in His ways and to keep His commandments and His statutes and His judgments, that you ^Rmay live and multiply, and that the LORD your God may bless you in the land where you are entering to possess it.   Deut. 6:5 • Deut. 4:1

17 "But if your heart turns away and you will not obey, but are drawn away and worship other gods and serve them,

18 I declare to you today that you shall surely perish. You shall not prolong *your* days in the land where you are crossing the Jordan to enter ^Tand possess it.   *to*

19 "I call heaven and earth to witness against you today, that I have set before you life and death, ^Rthe blessing and the curse. So choose life in order that you may live, you and your ^Tdescendants,   Deut. 30:1 • *seed*

20 by loving the LORD your God, by obeying His voice, and by holding fast to Him; for ^Tthis is your life and the length of your days, that you may live in the land which the LORD swore to your fathers, to Abraham, Isaac, and Jacob, to give them."   *that*

CHAPTER 31

Moses Charges Joshua and Israel

SO Moses went and spoke these words to all Israel.

2 And he said to them, "I am a hundred and twenty years old today; I am no longer able to come and go, and the LORD has said to me, ^R'You shall not cross this Jordan.'

3 "It ^Ris the LORD your God who will cross ahead of you; He will destroy these nations before you, and you shall dispossess them. Joshua is the one who will cross ahead of you, just as the LORD has spoken.   Deut. 9:3

4 "And the LORD will do to them just as He did to Sihon and Og, the kings of the Amorites, and to their land, when He destroyed them.

5 "And ^Rthe LORD will deliver them up before you, and you shall do to them according to all the commandments which I have commanded you.   Deut. 7:2

6 "Be strong and courageous, ^Rdo not be afraid or tremble at them, for the LORD your God is the one who goes with you. He will not fail you or forsake you."   Deut. 1:29; 7:18

7 Then Moses called to Joshua and said to him in the sight of all Israel, "Be strong and courageous, for you shall go with this people into the land which the LORD has sworn to their fathers to give them, and you shall give it to them as an inheritance.

8 "And ^Rthe LORD is the one who goes ahead of you; He will be with you. ^RHe will

not fail you or forsake you. Do not fear, or be dismayed." Ex. 13:21 • Josh. 1:5; Heb. 13:5

9 So Moses wrote this law and gave it to the priests, the sons of Levi[R] who carried the ark of the covenant of the LORD, and to all the elders of Israel. Num. 4:5, 6, 15; Deut. 10:8

10 Then Moses commanded them, saying, "At the end of *every* seven years, at the time of [R]the year of remission of debts, at the [R]Feast of Booths, Deut. 15:1, 2 • Lev. 23:34

11 when all Israel comes[R] to appear before the LORD your God at the place which He will choose, you shall read this law in front of all Israel in their hearing. Deut. 16:16

12"Assemble the people, the men and the women and children and the alien who is in your town, in order that they may hear and learn and fear the LORD your God, and be careful to observe all the words of this law.

13"And their children, who have not known, will hear and learn to fear the LORD your God, as long as you live on the land [T]which you are about to cross the Jordan to [T]possess." *where • possess it*

God Charges Israel

14 Then the LORD said to Moses, "Behold, [T]the time for you to die is near; call Joshua, and present yourselves at the tent of meeting, that I may commission him." So Moses and Joshua went and presented themselves at the tent of meeting. *your days to die are*

15 [R]And the LORD appeared in the tent in a pillar of cloud, and the pillar of cloud stood at the doorway of the tent. Ex. 33:9

16 And the LORD said to Moses, "Behold, you are about to lie down with your fathers; and[R] this people will arise and play the harlot with the strange gods of the land, into the midst of which they are going, and[R] will forsake Me and break My covenant which I have made with them. Ex. 34:15 • Judg. 10:6

17"Then My anger will be kindled against them in that day, and[R] I will forsake them and[R] hide My face from them, and they shall be consumed, and many evils and troubles shall come upon them; so that they will say

in that day, 'Is[R] it not because our God is not among us that these evils have come upon us?' 2 Chr. 15:2 • Ps. 104:29 • Num. 14:42

18"But I will surely hide My face in that day because of all the evil which they will do, for they will turn to other gods.

19"Now therefore, [R]write this song for yourselves, and teach it to the sons of Israel; put it on their lips, in order that this song may be a witness for Me against the sons of Israel. Deut. 31:22 • *in their mouths*

20"For when I bring them into the land flowing with milk and honey, which I swore to their fathers, and they have eaten and are satisfied and become prosperous, then they will turn to other gods and serve them, and spurn Me and break My covenant. *fat*

21"Then it shall come about, when many evils and troubles have come upon them, that this song will testify before them as a witness (for it shall not be forgotten from the [T]lips of their descendants); for I know their intent which they are developing today, before I have brought them into the land which I swore." *mouth of its seed*

The Book of the Law Is Deposited

22 So Moses wrote this song the same day, and taught it to the sons of Israel.

23 Then He commissioned Joshua the son of Nun, and said, "Be[R] strong and courageous, for you shall bring the sons of Israel into the land which I swore to them, and[R] I will be with you." Josh. 1:6 • Ex. 3:12

24 And it came about, when Moses finished writing the words of this law in a book until they were complete,

25 that Moses commanded the Levites [R]who carried the ark of the covenant of the LORD, saying, Deut. 31:9

26"Take this book of the law and place it beside the ark of the covenant of the LORD your God, that it may[T] remain there as a witness against you. *be*

27"For I know your rebellion and [T]your [T]stubbornness; behold, while I am still alive with you today, you have been rebellious against the LORD; how much more, then, after my death? Ex. 32:9 • *stiff neck*

31:12 Obedience to God's Word—Reading, memorizing, and meditating upon the Word of God are of no value without obedience to the Word of God. To obey the Word of God, you do what the Word of God indicates should be done in any situation. Obedience to the Word of God is the only way that the child of God can be pleasing to God in the new life. Obedience to God's Word results in: being treasured by God (Page 70—Ex. 19:5); blessedness (happiness) in life (Page 590—Ps. 119:2); not being ashamed (Page 590—Ps. 119:4-6); understanding (Page 593—Ps. 119:100); avoidance of evil (Page 593—Ps. 119:101); guidance for life (Page 593—Ps. 119:105); safety and freedom from anxiety (Page 610—Prov. 1:33); life (Page 623—Prov. 19:16; Page 800—Ezek. 18:19; Page 1075—John 8:51); God's blessing (Page 658—Is. 1:19); greatness in the kingdom of heaven (Page 967—Matt. 5:19); bearing fruit for God (Page 976—Matt. 13:23); manifesting love for God (Page 1082—John 14:23; Page 1275—1 John 2:5); promise of God's presence (Page 1082—John 14:23; Page 1281—2 John 9); abiding in the love of God (Page 1082—John 15:10); evidence of the doctrine that has been taught (Page 1136—Rom. 6:17); assurance of salvation (Page 1275—1 John 2:3); eternal life (Page 1275—1 John 2:17); dwelling in God (Page 1277—1 John 3:24); love of God's children (Page 1278—1 John 5:2); and entrance into heaven (Page 1308—Rev. 22:7).
Now turn to Page 605—Ps. 150:1: Praise.

28"Assemble to me all the elders of your tribes and your officers, that I may speak these words in their hearing and ^Rcall the heavens and the earth to witness against them.   Deut. 4:26; 30:19; 32:1

29"For I know that after my death you will ^Ract corruptly and turn from the way which I have commanded you; and evil will befall you in the latter days, for you will do that which is evil in the sight of the LORD, provoking Him to anger with the work of your hands."   Judg. 2:19

30 Then Moses spoke in the hearing of all the assembly of Israel the words of this song, until they were complete:

CHAPTER 32

The Song of Moses

"GIVE^Rear, O heavens, and let me speak;
And let the earth hear the words of my
    mouth.   Deut. 4:26; Ps. 50:4; Is. 1:2
2"Let my teaching drop as the rain,
My speech distill as the dew,
As the droplets on the fresh grass
And as the showers on the herb.
3"For I proclaim the name of the LORD;
Ascribe greatness to our God!
4"The Rock! His work is perfect,
For all His ways are^Ajust;
^RA God of faithfulness and without in-
    justice,   *judgment* • Deut. 7:9
Righteous and upright is He.
5"They^T have acted corruptly toward
    Him,
They are not His children, because of
    their defect;
^R*But are* a perverse and crooked genera-
    tion.   *It has* • Matt. 17:17
6"Do you thus^Rrepay the LORD, Ps. 116:12
^RO foolish and unwise people?
^RIs not He your Father who has bought
    you?   Deut. 32:28 • Deut. 1:31; Ps. 74:2

19 I.e., Israel

He has made you and established you.

7"Remember the days of old,
Consider the years of all generations.
^RAsk your father, and he will inform
    you,   Ex. 12:26; Ps. 78:5-8
Your elders, and they will tell you.

8"When^R the Most High gave the nations
    their inheritance,   Acts 17:26
When He separated the sons of 'man,
He set the boundaries of the peoples
^RAccording to the number of the sons of
    Israel.   *Adam* • Num. 23:9; Deut. 33:28
9"For^R the LORD's portion is His people;
Jacob is the allotment of His inheri-
    tance.   1 Sam. 10:1; 1 Kin. 8:51, 53
10"He^R found him in a desert land,
And in the howling waste of a wilder-
    ness;   Deut. 1:19
He encircled him, He cared for him,
He guarded him as the pupil of His eye.
11"Like^R an eagle that stirs up its nest,
That hovers over its young,   Ex. 19:4
He spread His wings and caught them,
He carried them on His pinions.
12"The^R LORD alone guided him,
^RAnd there was no foreign god with
    him.   Deut. 4:35, 39 • Is. 43:12
13"He^Rmade him ride on the high places of
    the earth,   Is. 58:14
And he ate the produce of the field;
^RAnd He made him suck honey from the
    rock,   Deut. 8:8; Ps. 81:16
And 'oil from the flinty rock, Job 29:6
14 Curds of cows, and milk of the flock,
With fat of lambs,
And rams, the breed of Bashan, and
    goats,
^RWith the finest of the wheat—
And of the^Rblood of grapes you drank
    wine.   Ps. 81:16; 147:14 • Gen. 49:11

15"But ¹⁹Jeshurun grew fat and kicked—
You are grown fat, thick, and sleek—
Then he forsook God who made him,
And scorned the Rock of his salvation.

32:7 God's Work in the Past—The Bible's revelation of God's work in the past provides an informative and exciting panorama of centuries of divine activity toward man.

First, it gives man an *education* in truths unknowable apart from divine revelation. For example, the creation of man described in Genesis 1 and 2 answers man's most basic questions: "Who am I?" and "Where did I come from?" Only God Himself could disclose these facts.

Second, the Bible sets forth a mass of historical *evidence* for the truthfulness of the Christian faith. The most outstanding of these evidences are fulfilled prophecy, the miracles of Christ, and Christ's death and resurrection. The believer's faith is thus grounded in historical events and is far removed from what some have called "a leap into the dark."

Third, the Bible records *examples* to help present-day Christians. Various failures of Israel and the resulting judgments of God are often cited in the New Testament as things to avoid, for example, their idolatry and grumbling in the wilderness (Page 1156—1 Cor. 10:11), and their unbelief at Kadesh (Page 1241—Heb. 4:11). Paul is said to be a living example for believers to follow (Page 1151—1 Cor. 4:16; 11:1), as is Jesus' humility in the midst of suffering (Page 1262—1 Pet. 2:21).

Fourth, the Bible provides *encouragement* for Christians in their life and witness. If God could use an adulterer and murderer like David, then God can certainly use a struggling Christian today if he possesses David's devotion to the Lord. Likewise, if God saved Saul of Tarsus, the chief enemy of the early church (Page 1104—Acts 9:1–31), then surely He can save the people with whom Christians daily share their faith.

Now turn to Page 600—Ps. 139:14: God's Work in Our Lives.

16"They[R] made Him jealous with strange
    gods;
  [R]With abominations they provoked Him
    to anger.   Ps. 78:58 • Ps. 106:29
17"They[R] sacrificed to demons who were
    not God,   Lev. 17:7; 1 Cor. 10:20
  To gods whom they have not known,
  [R]New gods who came lately,   Judg. 5:8
  Whom your fathers did not dread.
18"You neglected [A]the Rock who begot
    you,
  [A]And forgot the God who gave you
    birth.   Deut. 32:4 • Ps. 106:21

19"And[R] the LORD saw this, and spurned
    them   Lev. 26:30; Ps. 106:40
  [R]Because of the provocation of His sons
    and daughters.   Jer. 44:21-23
20"Then He said, 'I will hide My face from
    them,
  I will see what their end shall be;
  For they are a perverse generation,
  Sons in whom is no faithfulness.
21 'They[R] have made Me jealous with what
    is not God;   Deut. 32:16; 1 Cor. 10:22
  They have provoked Me to anger with
    their [T]idols.[R]   vanities • 1 Kin. 16:13, 26
  [R]So I will make them jealous with those
    who are not a people;   Rom. 10:19
  I will provoke them to anger with a
    foolish nation,
22 For a fire is kindled in My anger,
  And burns to the lowest part of [T]Sheol,
  And consumes the earth with its yield,
  And sets on fire the foundations of the
    mountains.   the nether world

23 'I will heap misfortunes on them;
  [R]I will use My arrows on them. Ps. 18:14
24 'They shall be wasted by famine, and
    consumed by [T]plague   burning heat
  [R]And bitter destruction;   Ps. 91:6
  [R]And the teeth of beasts I will send
    upon them,   Lev. 26:22
  [R]With the venom of crawling things of
    the dust.   Amos 5:18, 19
25 'Outside[R] the sword shall bereave,
  And inside terror—   Lam. 1:20; Ezek. 7:15
  [R]Both young man and virgin,   Lam. 2:21
  The nursling with the man of gray hair.
26 'I would have said, "I[R] will cut them to
    pieces,   Deut. 4:27; 28:64
  [R]I will remove the memory of them
    from men,"   Deut. 9:14
27 Had I not feared the provocation by the
    enemy,
  Lest their adversaries should misjudge,
  Lest they should say, "Our[R] hand is [T]tri-
    umphant,   Num. 15:30 • high
  And the LORD has not done all this."'

28"For[R] they are a nation [T]lacking in coun-
    sel,   Deut. 32:6 • perishing
  And there is no understanding in them.
29"Would[R] that they were wise, that they
    understood this,   Deut. 5:29

  That they would discern their future!
30"How could one chase a thousand,
  And two put ten thousand to flight,
  Unless their Rock had sold them,
  And the LORD had given them up?
31"Indeed their rock is not like our Rock,
  [R]Even our enemies [T]themselves judge
    this.   Ex. 14:25 • are judges
32"For their vine is from the vine of Sod-
    om,
  And from the fields of Gomorrah;
  Their grapes are grapes of [R]poison,
  Their clusters, bitter.   Deut. 29:18
33"Their wine is the venom of serpents,
  And the [T]deadly poison of cobras.   cruel

34 'Is[R] it not laid up in store with Me,
  Sealed up in My treasuries?   Job 14:17
35 'Vengeance[R] is Mine, and retribution,
  In due time their foot will slip;   Ps. 94:1
  [R]For the day of their calamity is near,
  And the impending things are hasten-
    ing upon them.'   Ezek. 7:5-10
36"For[R] the LORD will vindicate His people,
  [R]And will have compassion on His ser-
    vants;   Ps. 135:14 • Deut. 30:1-3
  When He sees that their [T]strength is
    gone,   hand
  And there is none remaining, bond or
    free.
37"And He will say, 'Where are their gods,
  The rock in which they sought refuge?
38 'Who ate the fat of their sacrifices,
  And drank the wine of their libation?
  Let them rise up and help you,
  Let them be your hiding place!
39 'See[R] now that I, I am He,   Is. 41:4; 43:10
  And there is no god besides Me;
  It is I who put to death and give life.
  [R]I have wounded, and it is I who heal;
  [R]And there is no one who can deliver
    from My hand.   Ps. 51:8 • Ps. 50:22
40 'Indeed,[R] I lift up My hand to heaven,
  And say, as I live forever,   Ezek. 20:5, 6
41 If I sharpen My [T]flashing sword,
  And My hand takes hold on justice,
  [R]I will render vengeance on My adver-
    saries,   lightning • Jer. 50:28-32
  And I will repay those who hate Me.
42 'I[R] will make My arrows drunk with
    blood,   Deut. 32:23
  [R]And My sword shall devour flesh,
  With the blood of the slain and the cap-
    tives,   Jer. 12:12; 46:10, 14
  From the long-haired [T]leaders of the
    enemy.'   head
43"Rejoice,[R] O nations, with His people;
  [R]For He will avenge the blood of His
    servants,   Rom. 15:10 • Rev. 6:10; 19:2
  [R]And will render vengeance on His ad-
    versaries,   Is. 1:24, 25
  [R]And will atone for His land and His
    people."   Ps. 65:3; 79:9; 85:1
44 Then Moses came and spoke all the

words of this song in the hearing of the people, he, with 'Joshua the son of Nun. *Hoshea*

45 When Moses had finished speaking all these words to all Israel,

46 he said to them, "Take^R to your heart all the words with which I am warning you today, which you shall command^Tyour sons to observe^Tcarefully, *even* all the words of this law.   Ezek. 40:4; 44:5 • Deut. 4:9 • *to do*

47"For it is not an idle word for you; indeed^Rit is your life. And^Rby this word you shall prolong your days in the land,^Twhich you are about to cross the Jordan to^Tpossess."   Deut. 8:3 • Deut. 4:40 • *where • possess it*

Moses Is Ordered to Mount Nebo

48 And^Rthe LORD spoke to Moses that very same day, saying,   Num. 27:12

49"Go^d up to this mountain of the Abarim, Mount Nebo, which is in the land of Moab ^Topposite Jericho, and look at the land of Canaan, which I am giving to the sons of Israel for a possession.   Deut. 3:27 • *which is opposite*

50"Then die on the mountain where you ascend, and be ^Rgathered to your people, as Aaron your brother died on Mount Hor and was gathered to his people,   Gen. 25:8

51 because you broke faith with Me in the midst of the sons of Israel at the waters of Meribah-kadesh, in the ^Rwilderness of Zin, because you did not treat Me as holy in the midst of the sons of Israel.   Num. 27:14

52"For you shall see the land at a distance, but you shall not go there, into the land which I am giving the sons of Israel."

CHAPTER 33

Moses Blesses the Tribes

NOW this is the blessing with which Moses^Rthe man of God blessed the sons of Israel before his death.   Josh. 14:6

2 And he said,
    "The^RLORD came from Sinai, Ps. 68:8, 17
    And dawned on them from Seir;
    He shone forth from Mount Paran,
    And He came from the midst of ten
       thousand holy ones;
    At His right hand there was^Aflashing
       lightning for them.   *a fiery law*

3 "Indeed, He loves^Tthe people; *peoples*
    All^TThy holy ones are in Thy hand,
    And they followed in Thy steps; *His*
    Everyone receives of Thy words.

4 "Moses^Rcharged us with a law,
    ^RA possession for the assembly of Ja-
       cob.   Deut. 4:2; John 7:19 • Ps. 119:111

5 "And^RHe was king in Jeshurun,
    When the heads of the people were
       gathered,   Num. 23:21
    The tribes of Israel together.

6 "May^RReuben live and not die,
    Nor his men be few."   Gen. 49:3, 4

7 And^Rthis regarding Judah; so he said,
    "Hear, O LORD, the voice of Judah,
    And bring him to his people.
    With his hands he contended for
       'them;
    And mayest Thou be a help against
       his adversaries."   Gen. 49:8-12 • *him*

8 And of Levi he said,
    "Let Thy Thummim and^TThy Urim *be-*
       long to Thy godly man,   *him*
    ^RWhom Thou didst prove at Massah,
    With whom Thou didst contend at the
       waters of Meribah;   Ex. 17:7

9 ^RWho said of his father and his
       mother,   Ex. 32:27-29
    'I did not consider them';
    And he did not acknowledge his
       brothers,
    Nor did he regard his own sons,
    For^Rthey observed Thy word,
    And kept Thy covenant.   Mal. 2:5

10 "They^Rshall teach Thine ordinances to
       Jacob,   Lev. 10:11; Deut. 31:9-13
    And Thy law to Israel.
    They shall put incense^Tbefore Thee,
    And^Rwhole burnt offerings on Thine
       altar.   *in Thy nostrils* • Ps. 51:19

11 "O LORD, bless his substance,
    And accept the work of his hands;
    Shatter the loins of those who rise up
       against him,
    And those who hate him, so that they
       may not rise *again*."

12 Of Benjamin he said,
    "May^Rthe beloved of the LORD dwell in
       security by Him,   Deut. 4:37f.; 12:10
    ^RWho shields him all the day,
    ^RAnd he dwells between His shoul-
       ders."   Deut. 32:11 • Ex. 28:12

13 And of Joseph he said,
    "Blessed^Rof the LORD *be* his land,
    With the choice things of heaven,
       with the dew, Gen. 27:27, 28; 49:22-26
    And from the deep lying beneath,

14   And with the choice yield of the sun,
    And with the choice produce of the
       months.

15 "And with the^Abest things of ^Rthe an-
       cient mountains,
    And with the choice things of the
       everlasting hills,   *chief* • Hab. 3:6

16   And with the choice things of the
       earth and its fulness,
    And the favor ^Rof Him who dwelt in
       the bush.
    Let it come to the head of Joseph,
    And to the crown of the head of the
       one distinguished among his broth-
       ers.   Ex. 2:2-6; 3:2, 4

17 "As the first-born of his ox, majesty is
       his,
    And his horns are the horns of ^Rthe
       wild ox;   Num. 23:22

With them he shall [R]push the peoples,
All [A]at once, *to* the ends of the earth.
And those are the ten thousands of
Ephraim,   1 Kin. 22:11; Ps. 44:5
And those are the thousands of Ma-
nasseh."   *together*

18 [R]And of Zebulun he said,   Gen. 49:13-15
"Rejoice, Zebulun, in your going forth,
And, Issachar, in your tents.
19 "They[R] shall call peoples *to* the mountain;   Ex. 15:17; Ps. 2:6; Is. 2:3
There they shall offer [R]righteous sacrifices;   Ps. 4:5; 51:19
For they shall [T]draw out [R]the abundance of the seas,   *suck*
And the hidden treasures of the
sand."   Is. 60:5

20 [R]And of Gad he said,   Gen. 49:19
"Blessed is the one who enlarges Gad;
He lies down [R]as a [A]lion,
And tears the arm, also the crown of
the head.   Gen. 49:9 • *lioness*
21 "Then[R] he [T]provided the first *part* for
himself,   Num. 32:1-5 • *saw*
[R]For there the ruler's portion was [T]re-
served;   Num. 34:14 • *covered up*
[R]And he came *with* the leaders of the
people;   Josh. 4:12
He executed the justice of the LORD,
And His ordinances with Israel."

22 [R]And of Dan he said,   Gen. 49:16
"Dan is [A]a lion's whelp,   Ezek. 19:2, 3
That leaps forth from Bashan."

23 And of Naphtali he said,
"O[R] Naphtali, satisfied with favor,
And full of the blessing of the LORD,
Take possession of the sea and the
south."   Gen. 49:21

24 [R]And of Asher he said,   Gen. 49:20
"More blessed than sons is Asher;
May he be favored by his brothers,
And may he dip his foot in oil.
25 "Your locks shall be iron and bronze,
[R]And according to your days, so shall
your leisurely walk be.   Deut. 4:40

26 "There[R] is none like the God of [20]Jeshu-
run,   Ex. 15:11; Deut. 4:35; Ps. 86:8
Who rides the heavens to your help,
And through the skies in His majesty.
27 "The[R] eternal God is a [A]dwelling place,
[R]And underneath are the everlasting
arms;   Ps. 90:1, 2 • *refuge* • Gen. 49:24
[R]And He drove out the enemy from be-
fore you,   Ex. 34:11; Josh. 24:18
[R]And said, 'Destroy!'   Deut. 7:2
28 "So[R] Israel dwells in security,   Jer. 23:6
The fountain of Jacob secluded,
In a land of grain and new wine;

[20] I.e., Israel   [21] I.e., Mediterranean Sea

His heavens also drop down dew.
29 "Blessed[R] are you, O Israel;   Ps. 1:1
[R]Who is like you, a people saved by the
LORD,   Deut. 4:32; 2 Sam. 7:23
[R]Who is the shield of your help,
[R]And the sword of your majesty!
[R]So your enemies shall cringe before
you,   Gen. 15:1 • Ps. 68:34 • Ps. 66:3
[R]And you shall tread upon their high
places."   Num. 33:52

CHAPTER 34

Moses Views the Promised Land

NOW[R] Moses went up from the plains of
Moab to Mount Nebo, to the top of Pisgah,
which is opposite Jericho. And the LORD
[R]showed him all the land, Gilead as far as
Dan,   Deut. 32:49 • Deut. 32:52
2 and all Naphtali and the land of Ephraim and Manasseh, and all the land of Judah
as far as the [21]western[R] sea,   Deut. 11:24
3 and the [T]Negev and the plain in the valley of Jericho, [R]the city of palm trees, as far
as Zoar.   South country • Judg. 1:16; 3:13
4 Then the LORD said to him, "This is the
land which I swore to Abraham, Isaac, and
Jacob, saying, 'I will give it to your [R]descend-
ants'; I have let you see *it* with your eyes,
but you shall not go over there."   *seed*

Moses Dies and Is Mourned

5 So Moses[R] the servant of the LORD died
there in the land of Moab, according to the
[T]word of the LORD.   Num. 12:7 • *mouth*
6 And He buried him in the valley in the
land of Moab, opposite Beth-peor; but no
man knows his burial place to this day.
7 Although Moses was [R]one hundred and
twenty years old when he died, his eye was
not dim, nor his vigor abated.   Deut. 31:2
8 So the sons of Israel wept for Moses in
the plains of Moab thirty days; then the
days of weeping *and* mourning for Moses
came to an end.

Moses Is Replaced by Joshua

9 Now Joshua the son of Nun was [R]filled
with the spirit of wisdom, for Moses had
laid his hands on him; and the sons of Israel
listened to him and did as the LORD had
commanded Moses.   Num. 27:18, 23; Is. 11:2

Moses Is Extolled in Israel

10 Since then[R] no prophet has risen in Israel like Moses, whom[R] the LORD knew face
to face.   Deut. 18:15, 18 • Num. 12:8; Deut. 5:4
11 for all the signs and wonders which the
LORD sent him to perform in the land of
Egypt against Pharaoh, all his servants, and
all his land,
12 and for all the mighty[T] power and for all
the great terror which Moses performed in
the sight of all Israel.   *hand*

THE BOOK OF

JOSHUA

THE BOOK OF JOSHUA

Joshua, the first of the twelve historical books (Joshua–Esther), forges a link between the Pentateuch and the remainder of Israel's history. Through three major military campaigns involving more than thirty enemy armies, the people of Israel learn a crucial lesson under Joshua's capable leadership: victory comes through faith in God and obedience to His word, rather than through military might or numerical superiority.

The title of this book is appropriately named after its central figure, Joshua. His original name is *Hoshea*, "Salvation" (Num. 13:8); but Moses evidently changes it to *Yehoshua* (Num. 13:16), "Yahweh Is Salvation." He is also called *Yeshua*, a shortened form of *Yehoshua*. This is the Hebrew equivalent of the Greek name *Iesous* (Jesus). Thus, the Greek title given to the book in the Septuagint is *Iesous Naus*, "Joshua the Son of Nun." The Latin title is *Liber Josue*, the "Book of Joshua."

His name is symbolic of the fact that although he is the leader of the Israelite nation during the conquest, the Lord is the Conqueror.

THE AUTHOR OF JOSHUA

Although it cannot be proven, Jewish tradition seems correct in assigning the authorship of this book to Joshua himself. Joshua 24:26 makes this clear statement: "And Joshua wrote these words in the book of the law of God." This refers at least to Joshua's farewell charge, if not to the book as a whole (see also 18:9). Joshua, as Israel's leader and an eyewitness of most of the events, was the person best qualified to write the book. He even uses the first person in one place (5:6, "us"; "we" appears in some manuscripts of 5:1). The book was written soon after the events occurred: Rahab was still alive (6:25). Other evidences for early authorship are the detailed information about Israel's campaigns and use of the ancient names of Canaanite cities.

The unity of style and organization suggest a single authorship for the majority of the book. Three small portions, however, must have been added after Joshua's death. These are: (1) Othniel's capture of Kiriath-sepher (15:13-19; cf. Judg. 1:9-15), (2) Dan's migration to the north (19:47; cf. Judg. 18:27–29), and (3) Joshua's death and burial (24:29–33). These may have been inserted early in the time of the judges by Eleazer the priest and his son Phinehas (24:33).

Joshua, born a slave in Egypt, becomes a conqueror in Canaan. He serves as personal attendant to Moses, as one of the twelve spies (of whom only he and Caleb believed God), and as Moses' successor. His outstanding qualities are obedient faith, courage, and dedication to God and His Word.

THE TIME OF JOSHUA

Joshua divides neatly into three geographical settings: (1) the Jordan River (1—5); (2) Canaan (6—13:7); and (3) the twelve tribes situated on both sides of the Jordan (13:8—24:33).

The setting of the first five chapters begins east of the Jordan as Joshua replaces Moses, crosses the Jordan on dry land, and finally prepares for war west of the Jordan.

Like a wise general, Joshua utilizes the divide-and-conquer strategy; and his campaign leads him to central Canaan (6—8), southern Canaan (9 and 10), and finally to northern Canaan (11 and 12).

After listing those areas yet to be conquered (13:1-7), Joshua undertakes the long task of dividing the Promised Land to all the tribes. First, he settles those two-and-a-half tribes east of the Jordan (13:8-33) and then the nine-and-a-half tribes west of the Jordan (14:1-19, 51). Completing this, he is free to assign the six Cities of Refuge and the forty-eight Cities of Levites, which are scattered among all the tribes.

The Book of Joshua cannot be dated precisely, but utilizing the same threefold division noted above, the following dates can be assigned:

A. One month, March-April, 1405 B.C. (Josh. 1—5)
   1. Death of Moses, March 1405 B.C. (Deut. 34:5–9)
   2. Crossing the Jordan, April 10, 1405 B.C. (Josh. 4:19)
B. Seven years, April 1405–1398 B.C. (Josh. 6:1—13:7)
   1. Caleb forty years old at Kadesh (Josh. 14:7)
   2. Caleb eighty-five years old at that time (Josh. 14:10)
      Note: forty-five years less thirty-eight years of wandering leaves seven years.
C. Eight years, 1398/7–1390 B.C. (Josh. 13:8-24)
   1. Division begun, 1398/7 B.C. (Josh. 14:7-10)
   2. Joshua dies at 110, c. 1390 B.C. (Josh. 24:39)

THE CHRIST OF JOSHUA

Although there are no direct messianic prophecies in the book, Joshua is clearly a type of Christ. His name *Yeshua* ("Yahweh Is Salvation") is the Hebrew equivalent of the name Jesus. In his role of triumphantly leading his people into their possessions, he foreshadows the One who will bring "many sons to glory" (Heb. 2:10). "But thanks be to God, who always leads us in His triumph in Christ" (2 Cor. 2:14; see Rom. 8:37). Joshua succeeds Moses and wins the victory unreached by Moses. Christ will succeed the Mosaic law and win the victory unreachable by the Law (John 1:17; Rom. 8:2–4; Gal. 3:23–25; Heb. 7:18, 19).

The "captain of the host of the LORD" (5:13–15) met by Joshua is evidently a preincarnate appearance of Christ (cf. Josh. 5:15 with Ex. 3:2).

Rahab's scarlet cord portrays safety through the blood (Heb. 9:19–22); and amazingly, this gentile woman is found in Christ's genealogy (Matt. 1:5).

KEYS TO JOSHUA

Key Word: Conquest—The entire Book of Joshua describes the entering, conquering, and occupying of the land of Canaan. The book begins with a statement of the promise of conquest, "Moses My servant is dead; now therefore arise, cross this Jordan. . . . Every place on which the sole of your foot treads, I have given it to you" (1:2, 3) and ends with the completion of conquest "that not one word of all the good words which the LORD your God spoke concerning you has failed; all have been fulfilled for you, not one of them has failed" (23:14).

Key Verses: Joshua 1:8; 11:23—"This book of the law shall not depart from your mouth, but you shall meditate on it day and night, so that you may be careful to do according to all that is written in it; for then you will make your way prosperous, and then you will have success" (1:8).

"So Joshua took the whole land, according to all that the LORD had spoken to Moses, and Joshua gave it for an inheritance to Israel according to their divisions by their tribes. Thus the land had rest from war" (11:23).

Key Chapter: Joshua 24—Some of the most critical periods in Israel's history are the transitions of leadership: Moses to Joshua; Joshua to the judges; the judges to the kings, and so on. Before his death and in preparation for a major transition of leadership by one man (Joshua) to many (the judges), Joshua reviews for the people God's fulfillment of His promises and then challenges them to review their commitment to the covenant (24:24, 25), which is the foundation for all successful national life.

SURVEY OF JOSHUA

Joshua resumes the narrative where Deuteronomy left off, and takes Israel from the wilderness to the Promised Land. Israel has now reached its climactic point of fulfilling the centuries-old promise in Genesis of a homeland. The first half of Joshua (1:1—13:7) describes the seven-year conquest of the land, and the second half (13:8—24:33) gives the details of the division and settlement of the land.

Conquest (1:1—13:7): The first five chapters record the spiritual, moral, physical, and military preparation of Joshua and the people for the impending conquest of Canaan. Joshua is given a charge by God to complete the task begun by Moses (1:2). After being encouraged by God, Joshua sends out two spies who come back with a favorable report (in contrast to the spies of the previous generation). Obedience and faith are united in the miraculous crossing of the Jordan River (3:1—4:24).

Joshua's campaign in central Canaan (6:1—

FOCUS	CONQUEST OF CANAAN		SETTLEMENT IN CANAAN			
REFERENCE	1:1 ——— 6:1———	13:8———	14:1———	20:1———	22:1———	24:33
DIVISION	PREPARATION OF ISRAEL	CONQUEST OF CANAAN	SETTLEMENT OF EAST JORDAN	SETTLEMENT OF WEST JORDAN	SETTLEMENT OF RELIGIOUS COMMUNITY	CONDITIONS FOR CONTINUED SETTLEMENT
TOPIC	ENTERING CANAAN	CONQUERING CANAAN	DIVIDING CANAAN			
	PREPARATION	SUBJECTION	POSSESSION			
LOCATION	JORDAN RIVER	CANAAN	TWO AND A HALF TRIBES—EAST JORDAN NINE AND A HALF TRIBES—WEST JORDAN			
TIME	c. 1 MONTH	c. 7 YEARS	c. 8 YEARS			

8:35) places a strategic wedge between the northern and southern cities preventing a massive Canaanite alliance against Israel. This divide-and-conquer strategy proves effective, but God's directions for taking the first city (Jericho) sound like foolishness from a military point of view. The Lord uses this to test the people and to teach them that Israel's success in battle will always be by His power and not their own might or cleverness. Sin must be dealt with at once because it brings severe consequences and defeat at Ai (7:1–26).

The southern and northern campaigns (9:1–13:7) are also successful, but an unwise oath made to the deceptive Gibeonites forces Israel to protect them and to disobey God's command to eliminate the Canaanites.

Settlement (13:8—24:33): Joshua is growing old, and God tells him to divide the land among the twelve tribes. Much remains to be won, and the tribes are to continue the conquest by faith after Joshua's death. Chapters 13:8—21:45 describe the allocation of the land to the various tribes as well as the inheritances of Caleb (14 and 15) and the Levites (21).

The last chapters (22:1—24:33) record the conditions for continued successful settlement in Canaan. Access to God, as well as His forgiveness, come only through the divinely established sacrificial system; and civil war almost breaks out when the eastern tribes build an altar that is misinterpreted by the western tribes.

Realizing that blessing comes from God only as Israel obeys His covenant, Joshua preaches a moving sermon, climaxed by Israel's renewal of her allegiance to the covenant.

OUTLINE OF JOSHUA

Part One: The Conquest of Canaan (1:1—13:7)

Part Two: The Settlement in Canaan (13:8—24:33)

CHAPTER 1

Joshua Is Commissioned by God

Now it came about after the death of Moses the servant of the LORD that the LORD spoke to Joshua the son of Nun, Moses' [1]servant, saying,

2"Moses[R]My servant is dead; now therefore arise, cross this Jordan, you and all this people, to the land which I am giving to them, to the sons of Israel.   Num. 12:7

3"Every[R]place on which the sole of your foot treads, I have given it to you, just as I spoke to Moses.   Deut. 11:24

4"From[R]the wilderness and this Lebanon, even as far as the great river, the river Euphrates, all the land of the Hittites, and as far as the Great Sea toward the setting of the sun, will be your territory.   Gen. 15:18

5"No man will *be able to* stand before you all the days of your life. Just as I have been with Moses, I will be with you;[R]I will not fail you or forsake you.   Deut. 31:6, 7

6"Be strong and courageous, for you shall give this people possession of the land which I swore to their fathers to give them.

7"Only be strong and very courageous; [T]be[R] careful to do according to all the law which Moses My servant commanded you; do not turn from it to the right or to the left, so that you may[A]have success wherever you go.   *observe* • Deut. 5:32 • *act wisely*

8"This book of the law shall not depart from your mouth, but you shall meditate on it day and night, so that you may[T]be careful to do according to all that is written in it; for then you will make your way prosperous, and then you will have success.   *observe*

9"Have I not commanded you?[R]Be strong and courageous![R]Do not tremble or be dismayed, for the LORD your God is with you wherever you go."   Josh. 1:7 • [Deut. 31:8]

Joshua Commands the Tribes West of the Jordan

10 Then Joshua commanded the officers of the people, saying,

11"Pass through the midst of the camp and command the people, saying, 'Prepare provisions for yourselves, for within[R]three days you are to cross this Jordan, to go in to possess the land which the LORD your God is giving you, to possess it.' "   Josh. 3:2

Joshua Commands the Tribes East of the Jordan

12 [R]And to the Reubenites and to the Gadites and to the half-tribe of Manasseh, Joshua[T]said,   Num. 32:20-22 • *said, saying*

13"Remember the word which Moses the servant of the LORD commanded you, saying, 'The[R]LORD your God gives you rest, and will give you this land.'   Deut. 3:18-20

14"Your wives, your little ones, and your cattle shall remain in the land which Moses gave you beyond the Jordan, but you shall cross before your brothers in battle array, all your valiant warriors, and shall help them,

15 until the LORD gives your brothers rest, as *He gives* you, and they also possess the land which the LORD your God is giving them. Then you shall return to your own land, and possess[T]that which Moses[R]the servant of the LORD gave you beyond the Jordan toward the sunrise."   *it* • Josh. 1:1

[1] Or, *minister*

1:8 Meditating upon God's Word—Joshua had just succeeded Moses in the leadership of the nation Israel. Moses had led the nation for forty years and had the benefit that all the wisdom and culture of Egypt and the king's household could provide. Moses was a seasoned, multi-talented man who had walked closely with God. Joshua, by contrast, was relatively untried. He was assuming an awesome responsibility in taking command of two-and-a-half million people. If anyone needed a formula for success, Joshua did. Likely there were many well-meaning people with all kinds of advice and formulas to help Joshua in the seemingly impossible task that lay ahead. What comfort and assurance it must have been as the LORD (Yahweh) spoke directly to Joshua, assuring him of His presence with him as He had been with Moses (Josh. 1:5), and giving him the key to success—meditating upon God's Word.

Joshua is to meditate upon the Word of God day and night (i.e., at all times), and is promised (1) prosperity and (2) good success in the God-given task that lies ahead. Reading and memorizing God's Word provide the basis for meditating upon God's Word. You meditate upon the Word of God by rehearsing its thoughts over and over in order to understand its implications for the situations of life. Meditating upon the Word of God will guarantee prosperity and success in the new life.

Now turn to Page 198—Deut. 31:12: Obedience to God's Word.

Joshua Is Accepted by Israel

16 And they answered Joshua, saying, "All that you have commanded us we will do, and wherever you send us we will go.

17 "Just as we obeyed Moses in all things, so we will obey you; only ᴿmay the LORD your God be with you, as He was with Moses.   Josh. 1:5, 9

18 "Anyone who rebels against your command and does not obey your words in all that you command him, shall be put to death; only be strong and courageous."

CHAPTER 2

The Faith of Rahab

THEN Joshua the son of Nun sent two men as spies secretly from ᴿShittim, saying, "Go, view the land, especially Jericho." So they went and came into the house of ʰa harlot whose name was Rahab, and ᵀlodged there.   Num. 25:1 • James 2:25 • *lay down*

2 And it was told the king of Jericho, saying, "Behold, men from the sons of Israel have come here tonight to search out the land."

3 And the king of Jericho sent *word* to Rahab, saying, "Bring out the men who have come to you, who have entered your house, for they have come to search out all the land."

4 But theᴿwoman had taken the two men and hidden them, and she said, "Yes, the men came to me, but I did not know where they were from.   2 Sam. 17:19

5 "And it came about when *it was time* to shut the gate, at dark, that the men went out; I do not know where the men went. Pursue them quickly, for you will overtake them."

6 But she had brought them up to the roof and hidden them in the stalks of flax which she had laid in order on the roof.

7 So the men pursued them on the road to the Jordan to the fords; and as soon as those who were pursuing them had gone out, they shut the gate.

8 Now before they lay down, ᵀshe came up to them on the roof,   *then she*

9 and said to the men, "I know that the LORD has given you the land, and that the terror of you has fallen on us, and that all the inhabitants of the land have ˄melted away before you.   *become demoralized*

10 "For we have heard how the LORD dried up the water of the ᵀRed Sea before you when you came out of Egypt, and what you did to the two kings of the Amorites who were beyond the Jordan, to Sihon and Og, whom you utterly destroyed.   *Sea of Reeds*

11 "And when we heard *it*, ᴿour hearts melted and noᵀcourage remained in any man any longer because of you; for the LORD your God, He is God in heaven above and on earth beneath.   Josh. 5:1; 7:5 • *spirit arose*

12 "Now therefore, please swear to me by the LORD, since I have dealt kindly with you, that you also will deal kindly with my father's household, and give me a ᴿpledge of ˄truth,   Josh. 2:18, 19 • *faithfulness*

13 and ᵀspare my father and my mother and my brothers and my sisters, with all who belong to them, and deliver our ²lives from death."   *let live*

14 So the men said to her, "Our life ᵀfor yours if you do not tell this business of ours; and it shall come about when the LORD gives us the land that we will deal kindly and faithfully with you."   *instead of you to die*

15 Then she let them down by a rope through the window, for her house was on the city wall, so that she was living on the wall.

16 And she said to them, "Goᴿ to the hill country, lest the pursuers happen upon you, and hide yourselves there for three days, until the pursuers return. Then afterward you may go on your way."   James 2:25

17 And the men said to her, "Weᴿshall be free from this oath ᵀto you which you have made us swear,   Gen. 24:8 • *of yours*

18 ᵀunless, when we come into the land, you tie this cord of scarlet thread in the window through which you let us down, and ᴿgather to yourself into the house your father and your mother and your brothers and all your father's household.   *behold* • Josh. 2:12

19 "And it shall come about that anyone who goes out of the doors of your house into the street, his blood *shall be* on his own head, and we *shall be* free; but anyone who is with you in the house, his blood *shall be* on our head, if a hand is *laid* on him.

20 "But if you tell this business of ours, then we shall be free from the oath which you have made us swear."

21 And she said, "According to your words, so be it." So she sent them away, and they departed; and she tied the scarlet cord in the window.

The Faith of the Spies

22 And they departed and came to the hill country, and remained there for three days until the pursuers returned. Now the pursuers had sought *them* ᵀall along the road, but had not found *them*.   *through all the road*

23 Then the two men returned and came down from the hill country and crossed over and came to Joshua the son of Nun, and they related to him all that had happened to them.

24 And they said to Joshua, "Surely the LORD has given all the land into our hands, and ᴿall the inhabitants of the land, moreover, have melted away before us."   Josh. 2:9

²Lit., *souls*

CHAPTER 3

The Miraculous Crossing
of the Jordan

THEN Joshua rose early in the morning; and he and all the sons of Israel set out from ᴿShittim and came to the Jordan, and they lodged there before they crossed.   Josh. 2:1

2 And it came about ᴿat the end of three days the officers went through the midst of the camp;   Josh. 1:11

3 and they commanded the people, saying, "When you see the ᴿark of the covenant of the LORD your God with the Levitical priests carrying it, then you shall set out from your place and go after it.   Deut. 31:9

4 "However, there shall be between you and it a distance of about 2,000 cubits by measure. Do not come near it, that you may know the way by which you shall go, for you have not passed this way before."

5 Then Joshua said to the people, "Consecrate ᴿyourselves, for tomorrow the LORD will do wonders among you."   Ex. 19:10, 11

6 And Joshua spoke to the priests, saying, "Take up the ark of the covenant and cross over ahead of the people." So they took up the ark of the covenant and went ahead of the people.

7 Now the LORD said to Joshua, "This day I will begin to exalt you in the sight of all Israel, that they may know that just as I have been with Moses, I will be with you.

8 "You shall, moreover, command the priests who are carrying the ark of the covenant, saying, 'When you come to the edge of the waters of the Jordan, you shall stand still in the Jordan.' "

9 Then Joshua said to the sons of Israel, "Come here, and hear the words of the LORD your God."

10 And Joshua said, "By this you shall know that ᴿthe living God is among you, and that He will assuredly ᴿdispossess from before you the Canaanite, the Hittite, the Hivite, the Perizzite, the Girgashite, the Amorite, and the Jebusite.   Deut. 5:26 • Ex. 33:2

11 "Behold, the ark of the covenant of ᴿthe Lord of all the earth is crossing over ahead of you into the Jordan.   Job 41:11; Ps. 24:1

12 "Now then, ᴿtake for yourselves twelve men from the tribes of Israel, one man for each tribe.   Josh. 4:2

13 "And it shall come about when the soles of the feet of the priests who carry the ark of the LORD, the Lord of all the earth, shall rest in the waters of the Jordan, the waters of the Jordan shall be cut off, and the waters which are ʰflowing down from above ʰshall stand in one heap."   going • and they shall

14 So it came about when the people set out from their tents to cross the Jordan with the priests carrying ᴿthe ark of the covenant before the people,   Ps. 132:8; Acts 7:44f.

15 and when those who carried the ark came into the Jordan, and the feet of the priests carrying the ark were dipped in the edge of the water (for the Jordan overflows all its banks all the days of harvest),

16 ᴿthat the waters which were flowing down from above stood and rose up in ᴿone heap, a great distance away at Adam, the city that is beside Zarethan; and those which were ʰflowing down toward the sea of the ᴿArabah, the Salt Sea, were completely cut off. So the people crossed opposite Jericho.   Ps. 66:6 • Josh. 3:13 • going • Deut. 1:1

17 And the priests who carried the ark of the covenant of the LORD stood firm on dry ground in the middle of the Jordan while all Israel crossed on dry ground, until all the nation had finished crossing the Jordan.

CHAPTER 4

The Memorial of the Crossing

NOW it came about when all the nation had finished crossing the ᴿJordan, that the LORD spoke to Joshua, saying,   Deut. 27:2

2 "Take for yourselves twelve men from the people, one man from each tribe,

3 and command them, saying, 'Take up for yourselves twelve stones from here out of the middle of the Jordan, from the place where the priests' feet are standing firm, and carry them over with you, and lay them down in ᴿthe lodging place where you will lodge tonight.' "   Josh. 4:20

4 So Joshua called the twelve men whom he had appointed from the sons of Israel, one man from each tribe;

5 and Joshua said to them, "Cross again to the ark of the LORD your God into the middle of the Jordan, and each of you take up a stone on his shoulder, according to the number of the tribes of the sons of Israel.

6 "Let this be a sign among you, so that when your children ask ᵀlater, saying, 'What do these stones mean to you?'   tomorrow

7 then you shall say to them, 'Because the waters of the Jordan were cut off before the ark of the covenant of the LORD; when it crossed the Jordan, the waters of the Jordan were cut off.' So these stones shall become a memorial to the sons of Israel forever."

8 And thus the sons of Israel did, as Joshua commanded, and took up twelve stones from the middle of the Jordan, just as the LORD spoke to Joshua, according to the number of the tribes of the sons of Israel; and they carried them over with them to ᴿthe lodging place, and put them down there.   Josh. 4:20

9 Then Joshua set up twelve ᴿstones in the middle of the Jordan at the place where the feet of the priests who carried the ark of the covenant were standing, and they are there to this day.   Gen. 28:18; Josh. 24:26f.

10 For the priests who carried the ark were standing in the middle of the Jordan

until everything was completed that the
LORD had commanded Joshua to speak to
the people, according to all that Moses had
commanded Joshua. And the people hurried
and crossed;

11 and it came about when all the people
had finished crossing, that the ark of the
LORD and the priests crossed before the people.

12 And the sons of Reuben and the sons of
Gad and the half-tribe of Manasseh crossed
over in battle array before the sons of Israel,
just as Moses had spoken to them;

13 about 40,000, equipped for war,
crossed for battle before the LORD to the
desert plains of Jericho.

14 [R]On that day the LORD exalted Joshua in
the sight of all Israel; so that they [3]revered
him, just as they had revered Moses all the
days of his life.   Josh. 3:7

15 Now the LORD said to Joshua,

16"Command the priests who carry [R]the
ark of the testimony that they come up from
the Jordan."   Ex. 25:16

17 So Joshua commanded the priests, saying, "Come up from the Jordan."

18 And it came about when the priests
who carried the ark of the covenant of the
LORD had come up from the middle of the
Jordan, and the soles of the priests' feet
were lifted up to the dry ground, that the
waters of the Jordan returned to their place,
and went over all its banks as before.

19 Now the people came up from the Jordan on the [R]tenth of the first month and
camped at Gilgal on the eastern edge of
Jericho.   Deut. 1:3

20 [R]And [T]those twelve stones which they
had taken from the Jordan, Joshua set up [R]at
Gilgal.   Josh. 4:8 • these • Josh. 4:3, 8

21 And he said to the sons of [T]Israel,
"When your children ask their fathers in
time to come, saying, 'What are these
stones?'   Israel, saying

22 then you shall inform your children,
saying, 'Israel crossed this Jordan on [R]dry
ground.'   Josh. 3:17

23"For the LORD your God dried up the
waters of the Jordan before you until you
had crossed, just as the LORD your God had
done to the [T]Red Sea, which He dried up before us until we had crossed;   Sea of Reeds

24 that all the peoples of the earth may
know that the [R]hand of the LORD is mighty,
so that you may [A]fear the LORD your God [T]for-
ever."   1 Chr. 29:12 • reverence • all the days

CHAPTER 5

The Canaanites Fear Israel

Now it came about when all the kings of
the Amorites who were beyond the Jordan

to the west, and all the kings of the [R]Canaan-
ites who were by the sea, [R]heard how the
LORD had dried up the waters of the Jordan
before the sons of Israel until they had
crossed, that their hearts melted, and there
was no spirit in them any longer, because of
the sons of Israel.   Num. 13:29 • Josh. 2:10, 11

Circumcision Is Practiced

2 At that time the LORD said to Joshua,
"Make for yourself [R]flint knives and circumcise again the sons of Israel the second
time."   Ex. 4:25

3 So Joshua made himself flint knives
and circumcised the sons of Israel at [4]Gib-
eath-haaraloth.

4 And this is the reason why Joshua circumcised them: [R]all the people who came out
of Egypt who were males, all the men of
war, died in the wilderness along the way,
after they came out of Egypt.   Deut. 2:14

5 For all the people who came out were
circumcised, but all the people who were
born in the wilderness along the way as they
came out of Egypt had not been circumcised.

6 For the sons of Israel walked forty
years in the wilderness, until all the nation,
that is, the men of war who came out of
Egypt, [T]perished because they did not listen
to the voice of the LORD, [R]to whom the LORD
had sworn that He would not let them see
the land which the LORD had sworn to their
fathers to give us, a land flowing with milk
and honey.   were finished • Num. 14:29-35

7 And their children whom He raised up
in their place, Joshua circumcised; for they
were uncircumcised, because they had not
circumcised them along the way.

8 Now it came about when they had finished circumcising all the nation, that they
remained in their places in the camp until
they were [T]healed.   revived

9 Then the LORD said to Joshua, "Today I
have rolled away [R]the reproach of Egypt
from you." So the name of that place is
called [5]Gilgal to this day.   Zeph. 2:8

Passover Is Celebrated

10 While the sons of Israel camped at Gilgal, [R]they observed the Passover on the evening of the fourteenth day of the month on
the desert plains of Jericho.   Ex. 12:18

11 And on the [T]day after the Passover, on
[T]that very day, they ate some of the produce
of the land, unleavened cakes and parched
grain.   morrow • this

From Manna to Produce

12 And the manna ceased on the [T]day after
they had eaten some of the produce of the
land, so that the sons of Israel no longer had
manna, but they ate some of the yield of the
land of Canaan during that year.   morrow

[3] Or, feared   [4] I.e., the hill of the foreskins   [5] I.e., rolling

The Captain of the Lord Appears

13 Now it came about when Joshua was by Jericho, that he lifted up his eyes and looked, and behold, [R]a man was standing opposite him with his sword drawn in his hand, and Joshua went to him and said to him, "Are you for us or for our adversaries?"   Gen. 18:1, 2; 32:24, 30; Num. 22:31

14 And he said, "No, rather I indeed come now *as* captain of the host of the LORD." And Joshua[R]fell on his face to the earth, and bowed down, and said to him, "What has my lord to say to his servant?"   Gen. 17:3

15 And the captain of the LORD's host said to Joshua, "Remove[R]your sandals from your feet, for the place where you are standing is holy." And Joshua did so.   Ex. 3:5

CHAPTER 6

Victory at Jericho

Now Jericho was tightly shut because of the sons of Israel; no one went out and no one came in.

2 And the LORD said to Joshua, "See, I have given Jericho into your hand, with[R]its king *and* the valiant warriors.   Deut. 7:24

3 "And you shall march around the city, all the men of war circling the city once. You shall do so for six days.

4 "Also seven priests shall carry seven [R]trumpets of rams' horns before the ark; then on the seventh day you shall march around the city seven times, and the priests shall blow the trumpets.   Lev. 25:9

5 "And it shall be that when they make a long blast with the ram's horn, and when you hear the sound of the trumpet, all the people shall shout with a great shout; and the wall of the city will fall down[T]flat, and the people will go up every man straight [T]ahead."   *in its place • before himself*

6 So Joshua the son of Nun called the priests and said to them, "Take up the ark of the covenant, and let seven priests carry seven trumpets of rams' horns before the ark of the LORD."

7 Then [A]he said to the people, "Go forward, and march around the city, and let the armed men go on before the ark of the LORD."   *they*

8 And it was *so*, that when Joshua had spoken to the people, the seven priests carrying the seven trumpets of rams' horns before the LORD went forward and blew the trumpets; and the ark of the covenant of the LORD followed them.

9 And the armed men went before the priests who blew the trumpets, and[R]the rear guard came after the ark, while they continued to blow the trumpets.   Josh. 6:13; Is. 52:12

10 But Joshua commanded the people, saying, "You shall not shout nor let your voice be heard, nor let a word proceed out of your mouth, until the day I tell you, 'Shout!' Then you shall shout!"

11 So he had the ark of the LORD [T]taken around the city, circling *it* once; then they came into the camp and spent the night in the camp.   *to go around*

12 Now Joshua rose early in the morning, and the priests took up the ark of the LORD.

13 And [R]the seven priests carrying the seven trumpets of rams' horns before the ark of the LORD went on continually, and blew the trumpets; and the armed men went before them, and[R]the rear guard came after the ark of the LORD, while they continued to blow the trumpets.   Josh. 6:4 • Josh. 6:9

14 Thus the second day they marched around the city once and returned to the camp; they did so for six days.

15 Then it came about on the seventh day that they rose early at the dawning of the day and marched around the city in the same manner seven times; only on that day they marched around the city seven times.

16 And it came about at the seventh time, when the priests blew the trumpets, Joshua said to the people, "Shout![R]For the LORD has given you the city.   2 Chr. 13:14f.

17 "And the city shall be under the ban, it and all that is in it belongs to the LORD; only Rahab the harlot[T]and all who are with her in the house shall live, because she hid the messengers whom we sent.   *she and all*

18 "But as for you, only keep yourselves from the things under the ban, lest you covet *them* and take some of the things under the ban, so you would make the camp of Israel accursed and bring trouble on it.

19 "But all the silver and gold and articles of bronze and iron are holy to the LORD; they shall go into the treasury of the LORD."

20 So the people shouted, and *priests* blew the trumpets; and it came about, when the people heard the sound of the trumpet, that the people shouted with a great shout and the wall fell down[T]flat, so that the people went up into the city, every man straight ahead, and they took the city.   *in its place*

21 And they[A]utterly destroyed everything in the city, both man and woman, young and old, and ox and sheep and donkey, with the edge of the sword.   *put under the ban*

22 And Joshua said to the two men who had spied out the land, "Go into the harlot's house and bring the woman and all she has out of there, as you have sworn to her."

23 So the young men who were spies went in and[R]brought out Rahab and her father and her mother and her brothers and all she had; they also brought out all her relatives, and placed them outside the camp of Israel.   Heb. 11:31

24 And they burned the city with fire, and all that was in it. Only the silver and gold

and articles of bronze and iron, they put into the treasury of the [6]house of the LORD.

25 However, Rahab the harlot and her father's household and all she had, Joshua spared; and she has lived in the midst of Israel to this day, for she hid the messengers whom Joshua sent to spy out Jericho.

26 Then Joshua made them take an oath at that time, saying, "Cursed[R] before the LORD is the man who rises up and builds this city Jericho; with *the loss of* his firstborn he shall lay its foundation, and with *the loss of* his youngest son he shall set up its gates."   1 Kin. 16:34

27 So[R] the LORD was with Joshua, and his fame was in all the land.   Gen. 39:2; Judg. 1:19

CHAPTER 7

Defeat at Ai

B UT[R] the sons of Israel acted unfaithfully in regard to the things under the ban, for Achan, the son of Carmi, the son of Zabdi, the son of Zerah, from the tribe of Judah, took some of the things under the ban, therefore the anger of the LORD burned against the sons of Israel.   Josh. 6:17-19

2 Now Joshua sent men from Jericho to Ai, which is near Beth-aven, east of Bethel, and said to them, "Go up and spy out the land." So the men went up and spied out Ai.

3 And they returned to Joshua and said to him, "Do not let all the people go up; *only* about two or three thousand men need go up[T] to Ai; do not make all the people toil up there, for they are few."   *and smite*

4 So about three thousand men from the people went up there, but[R] they fled[T] from the men of Ai.   Lev. 26:17; Deut. 28:25 • *before*

5 And the men of Ai struck down about thirty-six of their men, and pursued them from the gate as far as Shebarim, and struck them down on the descent, so the hearts of the people melted and became as water.

6 Then Joshua[R] tore his clothes and fell to the earth on his face before the ark of the LORD until the evening, *both* he and the elders of Israel; and[R] they put dust on their heads.   Job 2:12 • Job 42:6; Lam. 2:10

7 And Joshua said, "Alas, O Lord[T] GOD, why didst Thou ever bring this people over the Jordan, *only* to deliver us into the hand of the Amorites, to destroy us? If only we had been willing to dwell beyond the Jordan!   Heb., *YHWH*, usually rendered LORD

8 "O Lord, what can I say since Israel has turned *their* back before their enemies?

9 "For[R] the Canaanites and all the inhabitants of the land will hear of it, and they will surround us and cut off our name from the earth. And what wilt Thou do for Thy great name?"   Ex. 32:12; Deut. 9:28

10 So the LORD said to Joshua, "Rise up! Why is it that you have fallen on your face?

11 "Israel has sinned, and they have also transgressed My covenant which I commanded them. And they have even taken some of the things under the ban and have both stolen and deceived. Moreover, they have also put *them* among their own things.

12 "Therefore the sons of Israel cannot stand before their enemies; they turn *their* [T] backs before their enemies, for they have become accursed. I will not be with you anymore unless you destroy the things under the ban from your midst.   *necks*

13 "Rise up! Consecrate the people and say, 'Consecrate yourselves for tomorrow, for thus the LORD, the God of Israel, has said, "There are things under the ban in your midst, O Israel. You cannot stand before your enemies until you have removed the things under the ban from your midst."

14 'In the morning then you shall come near by your tribes. And it shall be that the tribe which[R] the LORD takes *by lot* shall come near by families, and the family which the LORD takes shall come near by households, and the household which the LORD takes shall come near man by man.   [Prov. 16:33]

15 'And it shall be that the one who is taken with the things under the ban shall be burned with fire, he and all that belongs to him, because he has transgressed the covenant of the LORD, and because he has committed a disgraceful thing in Israel.' "

16 So Joshua arose early in the morning and brought Israel near by [T] tribes, and the tribe of Judah was taken.   *its tribes*

17 And he brought the family of Judah near, and he took the family of the Zerahites; and he brought the family of the Zerahites near man by man, and Zabdi was taken.

18 And he brought his household near man by man; and[R] Achan, son of Carmi, son of Zabdi, son of Zerah, from the tribe of Judah, was taken.   Num. 32:23; Acts 5:1-10

19 Then Joshua said to Achan, "My son, I implore you,[R] give glory to the LORD, the God of Israel, and give praise to Him; and tell me now what you have done. Do not hide it from me."   1 Sam. 6:5; 2 Chr. 30:22; Jer. 13:16

20 So Achan answered Joshua and said, "Truly, I have sinned against the LORD, the God of Israel, and this is what I did:

21 when I saw among the spoil a beautiful mantle from Shinar and[T] two hundred shekels of silver and a bar of gold[T] fifty shekels in weight, then I[R] coveted them and took them; and behold, they are concealed in the earth inside my tent with the silver underneath it." $24,000 • $96,000 • [Eph. 5:5; 1 Tim. 6:10]

22 So Joshua sent messengers, and they ran to the tent; and behold, it was concealed in his tent with the silver underneath it.

23 And they took them from inside the tent and brought them to Joshua and to all the sons of Israel, and they poured them out before the LORD.

24 Then Joshua and all Israel with him,

took Achan the son of Zerah, the silver, the mantle, the bar of gold, his sons, his daughters, his oxen, his donkeys, his sheep, his tent and all that belonged to him; and they brought them up to the valley of [7]Achor.

25 And Joshua said, "Why have you troubled us? The LORD will trouble you this day." And all Israel stoned [T]them with stones; and they burned them with fire after they had stoned them with stones.   *him*

26 And they raised over him a great heap of stones that stands to this day, and the LORD turned from the fierceness of His anger. Therefore the name of that place has been called the valley of [7]Achor to this day.

CHAPTER 8

Victory at Ai

NOW the LORD said to Joshua, "Do[R] not fear or be dismayed. Take all the people of war with you and arise, go up to Ai; see, I have given into your hand the king of Ai, his people, his city, and his land.   Josh. 1:9; 10:8

2 "And you shall do to Ai and its king just as you did to Jericho and its king; you shall [R]take only its spoil and its cattle as plunder for yourselves. [T]Set an ambush for the city behind it."   Deut. 20:14 • *Set for yourself*

3 So Joshua rose with all the people of war to go up to Ai; and Joshua chose 30,000 men, valiant warriors, and sent them out at night.

4 And he commanded them, saying, "See, you are[R]going to ambush the city from behind[T]it. Do not go very far from the city, but all of you be ready.   Judg. 20:29 • *the city*

5 "Then I and all the people who are with me will approach the city. And it will come about when they come out to meet us as at the first, that we will flee before them.

6 "And they will come out after us until we have drawn them away from the city, for they will say, 'They are fleeing before us as at the first.' So we will flee before them.

7 "And you shall rise from *your* ambush and take possession of the city, for the LORD your God will deliver it into your hand.

8 "Then it will be when you have seized the city, that you shall set the city on fire. You shall do *it* according to the word of the LORD. See, I have commanded you."

9 So Joshua sent them away, and they went to the place of ambush and remained between Bethel and Ai, on the west side of Ai; but Joshua spent that night among the people.

10 Now Joshua[R]rose early in the morning and mustered the people, and he went up with the elders of Israel before the people to Ai.   Gen. 22:3

11 Then all the people of war who *were* with him went up and drew near and arrived in front of the city, and camped on the north side of Ai. Now *there was* a valley between him and Ai.

12 And he took about 5,000 men and set them in ambush between[R]Bethel and Ai, on the west side of the[T]city.   Gen. 12:8 • Ai

13 So they stationed the people, all the army that was on the north side of the city, and its rear guard on the west side of the city, and Joshua spent that night in the midst of the valley.

14 And it came about when the king of Ai saw *it,* that the men of the city hurried and rose up early and went out to meet Israel in battle, he and all his people at the appointed place before the desert plain. But he did not know that *there was* an ambush against him behind the city.

15 And Joshua and all Israel pretended to be beaten before them, and fled[R]by the way of the wilderness.   Josh. 15:61; 16:1; 18:12

16 And all the people who were in the city were called together to pursue them, and they pursued Joshua, and[R]were drawn away from the city.   Judg. 20:31

17 So not a man was left in Ai or Bethel who had not gone out after Israel, and they left the city unguarded and pursued Israel.

18 Then the LORD said to Joshua, "Stretch[R] out the javelin that is in your hand toward Ai, for I will give it into your hand." So Joshua stretched out the javelin that was in his hand toward the city.   Ex. 14:16; 17:9-13

19 And the *men in* ambush rose quickly from their place, and when he had stretched out his hand, they ran and entered the city and captured it; and they quickly set the city on fire.

20 When the men of Ai turned[T]back and looked, behold, the smoke of the city ascended to the sky, and they had no place to flee this way or that, for the people who had been fleeing to the wilderness turned against the pursuers.   *behind them*

21 When Joshua and all Israel saw that the *men in* ambush had captured the city and that the smoke of the city ascended, they turned back and slew the men of Ai.

22 And[T]the others came out from the city to encounter them, so that they were *trapped* in the midst of Israel, [T]some on this side and some on that side; and they slew them until no one was left of those who survived or escaped.   *these came • these ... those*

23 But they took alive the king of Ai and brought him to Joshua.

24 Now it came about when Israel had finished killing all the inhabitants of Ai in the field in the wilderness where they pursued them, and all of them were fallen by the edge of the sword until they were destroyed, then all Israel returned to Ai and struck it with the edge of the sword.

25 [R]And all who fell that day, both men

[7] I.e., trouble

and women, were 12,000—all the [T]people
of Ai.   Deut. 20:16-18 • *men*
26 For Joshua[R]did not withdraw his hand
with which he stretched out the javelin until
he had[A]utterly destroyed all the inhabitants
of Ai.   Ex. 17:11, 12 • *put under the ban*
27 [R]Israel took only the cattle and the spoil
of that city as plunder for themselves, according to the word of the LORD which He
had commanded Joshua.   Josh. 8:2
28 So Joshua burned Ai and made it a
heap forever, a desolation until this day.
29 And he hanged the king of Ai on a tree
until evening; and at sunset Joshua gave
command and they took his body down
from the tree, and threw it at the entrance
of the city gate, and raised over it a great
heap of stones *that stands* to this day.

Israel Worships the Lord

30 Then Joshua built an altar to the LORD,
the God of Israel, in Mount Ebal,
31 just as Moses the servant of the LORD
had commanded the sons of Israel, as it is
written in the book of the law of Moses, [R]an
altar of uncut stones, on which no man had
wielded an iron *tool;* and they offered burnt
offerings on it to the LORD, and sacrificed
peace offerings.   Ex. 20:25

Israel Renews the Covenant

32 And he wrote there on the stones a
copy of the law of Moses, which he had
written, in the presence of the sons of Israel.
33 [R]And all Israel with their elders and officers and their judges were standing on both
sides of the ark before the Levitical priests
who carried the ark of the covenant of the
LORD, the stranger as well as the native.
Half of them *stood* in front of[R]Mount Gerizim and half of them in front of Mount Ebal,
just as Moses the servant of the LORD had
given command at first to bless the people
of Israel.   Deut. 27:11-14 • Deut. 11:29
34 Then afterward he read all the words
of the law, the blessing and the curse, according to all that is written in[R]the book of
the law.   Josh. 1:8
35 There was not a word of all that Moses
had commanded which Joshua did not read
before all the assembly of Israel with the
women and the little ones and the strangers
who were[T]living among them.   *walking*

CHAPTER 9

Failure with the Gibeonites

NOW it came about when[R]all the kings
who were beyond the Jordan, in the hill
country and in the lowland and on all the
[R]coast of the Great Sea toward Lebanon,
[R]the Hittite and the Amorite, the Canaanite,

the Perizzite, the Hivite and the Jebusite,
heard of it,   Num. 13:29 • Num. 34:6 • Ex. 3:17
2 that they gathered themselves together
with [T]one[R] accord to fight with Joshua and
with Israel.   *one mouth* • Ps. 83:3, 5
3 When the inhabitants of Gibeon heard
what Joshua had done to Jericho and to Ai,
4 they also acted craftily and [T]set out as
envoys, and took worn-out sacks on their
donkeys, and wineskins, worn-out and torn
and[T]mended,   *went and traveled as envoys* • *tied up*
5 and worn-out and patched sandals on
their feet, and worn-out clothes on themselves; and all the bread of their provision
was dry *and* had become crumbled.
6 And they went to Joshua to the camp
at Gilgal, and said to him and to the men of
Israel, "We have come from a far country;
now therefore, make a covenant with us."
7 And the men of Israel said to the[R]Hi-
vites, "Perhaps you are living[T]within our
land;[R]how then shall we make a covenant
with you?"   Josh. 9:1 • *among us* • Ex. 23:32
8 But they said to Joshua, "We are your
servants." Then Joshua said to them, "Who
are you, and where do you come from?"
9 And they said to him, "Your servants
have come from a very far country because
of the[A]fame of the LORD your God; for[R]we
have heard the report of Him and all that He
did in Egypt,   *name* • Josh. 2:9; 9:24
10 and all that He did to the two kings of
the Amorites who were beyond the Jordan,
to Sihon king of Heshbon and to Og king of
Bashan who was at Ashtaroth.
11 "So our elders and all the inhabitants of
our country spoke to us, saying, 'Take provisions in your hand for the journey, and go
to meet them and say to them, "We[R]are your
servants; now then, make a covenant with
us." '   Josh. 9:8
12 "This our bread *was* warm *when* we
took it for our provisions out of our houses
on the day that we left to come to you; but
now behold, it is dry and has become crumbled.
13 "And these wineskins which we filled
were new, and behold, they are torn; and
these our clothes and our sandals are worn
out because of the very long journey."
14 So the men *of Israel* took some of their
provisions, and[R]did not ask for the [T]counsel
of the LORD.   Num. 27:21 • *mouth*
15 [R]And Joshua made peace with them and
made a covenant with them, to let them live;
and the leaders of the congregation swore
an oath to them.   Ex. 23:32
16 And it came about at the end of three
days after they had made a covenant with
them, that they heard that they were neighbors and that they were living[T]within their
land.   *among them*
17 Then the sons of Israel set out and
came to their cities on the third day. Now
their cities *were*[R]Gibeon and Chephirah and
Beeroth and Kiriath-jearim.   Josh. 18:25

18 And the sons of Israel did not strike them because the leaders of the congregation had sworn to them by the LORD the God of Israel. And the whole congregation grumbled against the leaders.

19 But all the leaders said to the whole congregation, "We have sworn to them by the LORD, the God of Israel, and now we cannot touch them.

20 "This we will do to them, even let them live, lest wrath be upon us for the oath which we swore to them."

21 And the leaders said to them, "Let them live." So they became ᴿhewers of wood and drawers of water for the whole congregation, just as the leaders had spoken to them.   Deut. 29:11

22 Then Joshua called for them and spoke to them, saying, "Why have you deceived us, saying, 'We are very far from you,' when you are living ᵀwithin our land?   among us

23 "Now therefore, you are ᴿcursed, and you shall never cease being slaves, both hewers of wood and drawers of water for the house of my God."   Gen. 9:25

24 So they answered Joshua and said, "Because ᴿit was certainly told your servants that the LORD your God had commanded His servant Moses to give you all the land, and to destroy all the inhabitants of the land before you; therefore we feared greatly for our lives because of you, and have done this thing.   Josh. 9:9

25 "And now behold, ᴿwe are in your hands; do as it seems good and right in your sight to do to us."   Gen. 16:6

26 Thus he did to them, and delivered them from the hands of the sons of Israel, and they did not kill them.

27 But Joshua made them that day hewers of wood and drawers of water for the congregation and for the altar of the LORD, to this day, ᴿin the place which He would choose.   Deut. 12:5

CHAPTER 10

Victory over the Amorites

NOW it came about when Adoni-zedek king of Jerusalem heard that Joshua had captured Ai, and had utterly destroyed it (just as he had done to Jericho and its king, so he had done to Ai and its king), and that the inhabitants of Gibeon had made peace with Israel and were within their land,

2 that ᴿhe ᴿfeared greatly, because Gibeon *was* a great city, like one of the royal cities, and because it was greater than Ai, and all its men *were* mighty.   they · Ex. 15:14-16

3 Therefore Adoni-zedek king of Jerusalem sent *word* to Hoham king of Hebron and to Piram king of Jarmuth and to Japhia king of Lachish and to Debir king of Eglon, saying,

4 "Come up to me and help me, and let us ᵀattack Gibeon, for it has made peace with Joshua and with the sons of Israel."   smite

5 So the five kings of the Amorites, the king of Jerusalem, the king of Hebron, the king of Jarmuth, the king of Lachish, *and* the king of Eglon, gathered together and went up, they with all their armies, and camped by Gibeon and fought against it.

6 Then the men of Gibeon sent *word* to Joshua to the camp at Gilgal, saying, "Do not abandon your servants; come up to us quickly and save us and help us, for all the kings of the Amorites that live in the hill country have assembled against us."

7 So Joshua went up from Gilgal, he and ᴿall the people of war with him and all the valiant warriors.   Josh. 8:1

8 And the LORD said to Joshua, "Do ᴿnot fear them, for I have given them into your hands; not ᵀone of them shall stand before you."   Josh. 1:5, 9 · *a man*

9 So Joshua came upon them suddenly by marching all night from Gilgal.

10 ᴿAnd the LORD confounded them before Israel, and He ᵀslew them with a great slaughter at Gibeon, and pursued them by the way of the ascent of Beth-horon, and struck them as far as Azekah and Makkedah.   Deut. 7:23 · *struck*

11 And it came about as they fled from before Israel, *while* they were at the descent of Beth-horon, that the LORD threw large stones from heaven on them as far as Azekah, and they died; *there were* more who died from the hailstones than those whom the sons of Israel killed with the sword.

12 Then Joshua spoke to the LORD in the day when the LORD delivered up the Amorites before the sons of Israel, and he said in the sight of Israel,

"O ᴿsun, stand still at Gibeon,   Hab. 3:11
And O moon in the valley of Aijalon."

13 ᴿSo the sun stood still, and the moon stopped,   Hab. 3:11
Until the nation avenged themselves of their enemies.

Is it not written in ᴿthe book of Jashar? And ᴿthe sun stopped in the middle of the sky, and did not hasten to go *down* for about a whole day.   2 Sam. 1:18 · Is. 38:8

14 And there was no day like that before it or after it, when the LORD listened to the voice of a man; for ᴿthe LORD fought for Israel.   Ex. 14:14; Deut. 1:30; Josh. 10:42

15 Then Joshua and all Israel with him returned to the camp to Gilgal.

16 Now these five kings had fled and hidden themselves in the cave at Makkedah.

17 And it was told Joshua, saying, "The five kings have been found hidden in the cave at Makkedah."

18 And Joshua said, "Roll large stones against the mouth of the cave, and assign men by it to guard them,

19 but do not stay *there* yourselves; pursue your enemies and ᵀattack them in the

rear. Do not allow them to enter their cities, for the LORD your God has delivered them into your hand."   *smite their tail*

20 And it came about when Joshua and the sons of Israel had finished slaying them with a very great slaughter, until they were destroyed, and the survivors *who* remained of them had entered the fortified cities,

21 that all the people returned to the camp to Joshua at Makkedah in peace. No one [T]uttered a word against any of the sons of Israel.   *sharpened his tongue*

22 Then Joshua said, "Open the mouth of the cave and bring these five kings out to me from the cave."

23 And they did so, and[R]brought these five kings out to him from the cave: the king of Jerusalem, the king of Hebron, the king of Jarmuth, the king of Lachish, *and* the king of Eglon.   Deut. 7:24

24 And it came about when they brought these kings out to Joshua, that Joshua called for all the men of Israel, and said to the chiefs of the men of war who had gone with him, "Come near,[R]put your feet on the necks of these kings." So they came near and put their feet on their necks.   Mal. 4:3

25 Joshua then said to them, "Do[R]not fear or be dismayed! Be strong and courageous, for thus the LORD will do to all your enemies with whom you fight."   Josh. 10:8

26 So afterward Joshua struck them and put them to death, and he[R]hanged them on five trees; and they hung on the trees until evening.   Josh. 8:29

27 And it came about at sunset that Joshua commanded, and [R]they took them down from the trees and threw them into the cave where they had hidden themselves, and put large stones over the mouth of the cave, to this very day.   Deut. 21:22, 23

28 Now Joshua captured Makkedah on that day, and struck it and its king with the edge of the sword;[R]he [A]utterly destroyed it and every [8]person who was in it. He left no survivor. Thus he did to the king of Makkedah [R]just as he had done to the king of Jericho.   Deut. 20:16 • *put under the ban* • Josh. 6:21

29 Then Joshua and all Israel with him passed on from Makkedah to[R]Libnah, and fought against Libnah.   Josh. 15:42; 21:13

30 And the LORD gave it also with its king into the hands of Israel, and he struck it and every person who *was* in it with the edge of the sword. He left no survivor in it. Thus he did to its king just as he had done to the king of Jericho.

31 And Joshua and all Israel with him passed on from Libnah to Lachish, and they camped by it and fought against it.

32 And the LORD gave Lachish into the hands of Israel; and he captured it on the second day, and struck it and every person who *was* in it with the edge of the sword,

according to all that he had done to Libnah.

33 Then Horam king of Gezer came up to help Lachish, and Joshua defeated him and his people until he had left him no survivor.

34 And Joshua and all Israel with him passed on from Lachish to Eglon, and they camped by it and fought against it.

35 And they captured it on that day and struck it with the edge of the sword; and he [A]utterly destroyed that day every person who *was* in it, according to all that he had done to Lachish.   *put under the ban*

36 Then Joshua and all Israel with him went up from Eglon to [R]Hebron, and they fought against it.   Num. 13:22; Judg. 1:10, 20

37 And they captured it and struck it and its king and all its cities and all the persons who *were* in it with the edge of the sword. He left no survivor, according to all that he had done to Eglon. And he utterly destroyed it and every person who *was* in it.

38 Then Joshua and all Israel with him returned to Debir, and they fought against it.

39 And he captured it and its king and all its cities, and they struck them with the edge of the sword, and utterly destroyed every person *who was* in it. He left no survivor. Just as he had done to Hebron, so he did to Debir and its king, as he had also done to Libnah and its king.

40 Thus Joshua struck all the land, the hill country and the [9]Negev and the lowland and the slopes and all their kings. He left no survivor, but he [A]utterly destroyed all who breathed, just as the LORD, the God of Israel, had commanded.   *put it under the ban*

41 And Joshua struck them from Kadesh-barnea even as far as Gaza, and all the country of Goshen even as far as Gibeon.

42 And Joshua captured all these kings and their lands at one time, because the LORD, the God of Israel, fought for Israel.

43 So Joshua and all Israel with him returned to the camp at Gilgal.

CHAPTER 11

Conquest of Northern Canaan

THEN it came about, when Jabin king of [R]Hazor heard *of it*, that he sent to Jobab king of Madon and to the king of Shimron and to the king of Achshaph,   Josh. 11:10

2 and to the kings who were of the north in the hill country, and in the Arabah—south of [10]Chinneroth and in the lowland and on the heights of Dor on the west—

3 to the Canaanite on the east and on the west, and the Amorite and the Hittite and the Perizzite and the Jebusite in the hill country, and [R]the Hivite [T]at the foot of Hermon in the land of Mizpeh.   Deut. 7:1 • *under*

4 And they came out, they and all their armies with them, [R]as many people *as* the sand that is on the seashore, with very many horses and chariots.   Judg. 7:12

5 So all of these kings having agreed to meet, came and encamped together at the waters of Merom, to fight against Israel.

6 Then the LORD said to Joshua, "Do^Rnot be afraid because of them, for tomorrow at this time I will deliver all of them slain before Israel; you shall hamstring their horses and burn their chariots with fire." Josh. 10:8

7 So Joshua and all the people of war with him came upon them suddenly by the waters of Merom, and attacked them.

8 And the LORD delivered them into the hand of Israel, so that they ^Tdefeated them, and pursued them as far as Great Sidon and ^RMisrephoth-maim and the valley of Mizpeh to the east; and they struck them until no survivor was left to them.   smote · Josh. 13:6

9 And Joshua did to them as the LORD had told him; he hamstrung their horses, and burned their chariots with fire.

10 Then Joshua turned back at that time, and captured^RHazor and struck its king with the sword; for Hazor formerly was the head of all these kingdoms.   Josh. 11:1

11 And they struck every person who was in it with the edge of the sword, utterly destroying *them;* there was no one left who breathed. And he burned Hazor with fire.

12 And Joshua captured all the cities of these kings, and all their kings, and he struck them with the edge of the sword, *and* utterly destroyed them; just as Moses the servant of the LORD had commanded.

13 However, Israel did not burn any cities that stood on their mounds, except Hazor alone, *which* Joshua burned.

14 And all the spoil of these cities and the cattle, the sons of Israel took as their plunder; but they struck every man with the edge of the sword, until they had destroyed them. They left no one who breathed.

15 Just as the LORD had commanded Moses his servant, so Moses commanded Joshua, and so Joshua did; he left nothing undone of all that the LORD had commanded Moses.

The Summary of Conquered Territory

16 Thus Joshua took all that land: the hill country and all the Negev, all that land of Goshen, the lowland, ^Rthe Arabah, the hill country of Israel and its lowland   Josh. 11:2

17 from Mount Halak, that rises toward Seir, even as far as Baal-gad in the valley of Lebanon^Tat the foot of Mount Hermon. And he captured all their kings and struck them down and put them to death.   *under*

18 Joshua waged war a long time with all these kings.

19 There was not a city which made peace with the sons of Israel except ^Rthe Hivites living in Gibeon; they took them all in battle.   Josh. 9:3, 7

20 ^RFor it was of the LORD to^Tharden their hearts, to meet Israel in battle in order that he might utterly destroy them, that they

might ^Treceive no mercy, but that he might destroy them, just as the LORD had commanded Moses.   Ex. 14:17 · *make strong · have*

21 Then Joshua came at that time and cut off^Rthe Anakim from the hill country, from Hebron, from Debir, from Anab and from all the hill country of Judah and from all the hill country of Israel. Joshua utterly destroyed them with their cities.   Num. 13:33

22 There were no Anakim left in the land of the sons of Israel; only in Gaza, in ^RGath, and in Ashdod some remained.   1 Sam. 17:4

23 So Joshua took the whole land, according to all that the LORD had spoken to Moses, and Joshua gave it for an inheritance to Israel according to their divisions by their tribes. Thus the land had rest from war.

CHAPTER 12

Kings Are Conquered by Moses

Now these are the ^Rkings of the land whom the sons of Israel ^Tdefeated, and whose land they possessed beyond the Jordan toward the sunrise, from the valley of the Arnon as far as Mount Hermon, and all the Arabah to the east: Num. 32:33 · *smote*

2 Sihon king of the Amorites, who lived in Heshbon, *and* ruled^Rfrom Aroer, which is on the edge of the valley of the Arnon, both the middle of the valley and half of Gilead, even as far as the brook Jabbok, the border of the sons of Ammon;   Deut. 2:36

3 and the Arabah as far as the Sea of ¹¹Chinneroth toward the east, and as far as the sea of the Arabah, *even* the Salt Sea, eastward toward Beth-jeshimoth, and on the south, at the foot of the slopes of Pisgah;

4 and the territory of Og king of Bashan, one of^Rthe remnant of Rephaim, who lived at Ashtaroth and at Edrei,   Deut. 3:11

5 and ruled over Mount Hermon and^RSalecah and all Bashan, as far as^Rthe border of the Geshurites and the Maacathites, and half of Gilead, *as far as* the border of Sihon king of Heshbon.   Deut. 3:10 · Deut. 3:14

6 Moses the servant of the LORD and the sons of Israel ^Tdefeated them; and^RMoses the servant of the LORD gave it to the Reubenites and the Gadites, and the half-tribe of Manasseh as a possession.   *smote* · Deut. 3:12

Kings Are Conquered by Joshua

7 Now these are the kings of the land whom Joshua and the sons of Israel ^Tdefeated beyond the Jordan toward the west, from Baal-gad in the valley of Lebanon even as far as ^RMount Halak, which rises toward Seir; and Joshua gave it to the tribes of Israel as a possession according to their divisions,   *smote* · Josh. 11:17

---

¹¹ I.e., Galilee

8 in the hill country, in the lowland, in the Arabah, on the slopes, and in the wilderness, and in the ᵀNegev; the Hittite, the Amorite and the Canaanite, the Perizzite, the Hivite and the Jebusite: South country

9 theᴿking of Jericho, one; the king of Ai, which is beside Bethel, one;   Josh. 6:2

10 theᴿking of Jerusalem, one; the king of Hebron, one;   Josh. 10:23

11 the king of Jarmuth, one; the king of Lachish, one;

12 the king of Eglon, one; the king of Gezer, one;

13 the king of Debir, one; the king of Geder, one;

14 the king of Hormah, one; the king of ᴿArad, one;   Num. 21:1

15 the king of Libnah, one; the king of Adullam, one;

16 the king of Makkedah, one; the king of Bethel, one;

17 the king of Tappuah, one; theᴿking of Hepher, one;   1 Kin. 4:10

18 the king of ᴿAphek, one; the king of Lasharon, one;   Josh. 13:4; 2 Kin. 13:17

19 the king of Madon, one; the king of Hazor, one;

20 the king of Shimron-meron, one; the king of Achshaph, one;

21 the king of Taanach, one; the king of Megiddo, one;

22 the king of ᴿKedesh, one; the king of Jokneam in Carmel, one;   Josh. 19:37; 20:7

23 the king of Dor in the heights of Dor, one; the king of Goiim in Gilgal, one;

24 the king of Tirzah, one; ᴿin all, thirty-one kings.   Deut. 7:24

CHAPTER 13

Unconquered Parts of Canaan

NOW Joshua was old *and* advanced in years when the LORD said to him, "You are old *and* advanced in years, and very much of the land remains to be possessed.

2 "This is the land that remains: all the regions *of* the Philistines and all *those of* the ᴿGeshurites;   Josh. 13:11; 1 Sam. 27:8

3 from the Shihor which is ᵀeast of Egypt, even as far as the border of Ekron to the north (it is counted as Canaanite); the five lords of the Philistines: the Gazite, the Ashdodite, the Ashkelonite, the Gittite, the Ekronite; and the Avvite   on the face of

4 ᴬto the south, all the land of the Canaanite, and Mearah that belongs to the Sidonians, as far as ᴿAphek, to the border of the Amorite;   from the Teman • 1 Kin. 20:26, 30

5 and the land of the Gebalite, and all of Lebanon, toward the ᵀeast, from Baal-gad below Mount Hermon as far as ᴬLebo-hamath.   sunrise • the entrance of Hamath

6 "All the inhabitants of the hill country from Lebanon as far as Misrephoth-maim, all the Sidonians, I will ᴬdrive them out from before the sons of Israel; ᴿonly allot it to Israel for an inheritance as I have commanded you.   dispossess • Num. 33:54

7 "Now therefore, apportion this land for an inheritance to the nine tribes, and the half-tribe of Manasseh."

Geographical Boundaries

8 With ᵀthe other half-tribe, the Reubenites and the Gadites received their inheritance which Moses gave them beyond the Jordan to the east, just as Moses the servant of the LORD gave to them;   it, the

9 from Aroer, which is on the edge of the valley of the Arnon, with the city which is in the middle of the valley, and all the plain of Medeba, as far as Dibon;

10 and all the cities of Sihon king of the Amorites, who reigned in Heshbon, as far as the border of the sons of Ammon;

11 and Gilead, and the territory of the Geshurites and Maacathites, and all Mount Hermon, and all Bashan as far as Salecah;

12 all the kingdom of Og in Bashan, who reigned in Ashtaroth and in Edrei (he alone was left of the remnant of the Rephaim); for Moses struck them and dispossessed them.

13 But the sons of Israel did not dispossess the Geshurites or the Maacathites; for Geshur and Maacath live among Israel until this day.

Boundaries of Levi

14 ᴿOnly to the tribe of Levi he did not give an inheritance; the offerings by fire to the LORD, the God of Israel, are ᵀtheir inheritance, as He spoke to him.   Deut. 18:1, 2 • his

Boundaries of Reuben

15 So Moses gave *an inheritance* to the tribe of the sons of Reuben according to their families.

16 And their territory was from Aroer, which is on the edge of the valley of the Arnon, with the city which is in the middle of the valley and all the plain by Medeba;

17 Heshbon, and all its cities which are on the plain: Dibon and Bamoth-baal and Beth-baal-meon,

18 and ᴿJahaz and Kedemoth and Mephaath,   Num. 21:23; Judg. 11:20; Is. 15:4; Jer. 48:34

19 and Kiriathaim and Sibmah and Zereth-shahar on the hill of the valley,

20 and Beth-peor and the slopes of Pisgah and Beth-jeshimoth,

21 even all the cities of the plain and all the kingdom of Sihon king of the Amorites who reigned in Heshbon, whom Moses struck with the chiefs of Midian, Evi and Rekem and Zur and Hur and Reba, the princes of Sihon, who lived in the land.

22 The sons of Israel also killed ᴿBalaam the son of Beor, the diviner, with the sword among *the rest of* their slain.   Num. 31:8

23 And the border of the sons of Reuben was the Jordan. This was the inheritance of the sons of Reuben according to their families, the cities and their villages.

Boundaries of Gad

24 Moses also gave *an inheritance* to the tribe of Gad, to the sons of Gad, according to their families.

25 And their territory was ᴿJazer, and all the cities of Gilead, and half the land of the sons of Ammon, as far as Aroer which is before Rabbah;   2 Sam. 24:5; 1 Chr. 6:81; 26:31

26 and from Heshbon as far as Ramath-mizpeh and Betonim, and from Mahanaim as far as the border of ᵀDebir;   *Lidebir*

27 and in the valley, Beth-haram and Beth-nimrah and Succoth and Zaphon, the rest of the kingdom of Sihon king of Heshbon, with the Jordan ᵀas a border, as far as the *lower* end of the Sea of Chinnereth beyond the Jordan to the east.   *and border*

28 This is the inheritance of the sons of Gad according to their families, the cities and their villages.

Boundaries of the Half-tribe of Manasseh

29 Moses also gave *an inheritance* to the half-tribe of Manasseh; and it was for the half-tribe of the sons of Manasseh according to their families.

30 And their territory was from Mahanaim, all Bashan, all the kingdom of Og king of Bashan, and all the ᵀtowns of Jair, which are in Bashan, sixty cities;   *tent villages*

31 also half of Gilead, with ᴿAshtaroth and Edrei, the cities of the kingdom of Og in Bashan, *were* for the sons of Machir the son of Manasseh, for half of the sons of Machir according to their families.   Josh. 9:10; 12:4

32 These are *the territories* which Moses apportioned for an inheritance in the plains of Moab, beyond the Jordan at Jericho to the east.

33 But ᴿto the tribe of Levi, Moses did not give an inheritance; the Lord, the God of Israel, is their inheritance, as He had ᵀprom-ised to them.   Deut. 18:1f. • *spoken to*

CHAPTER 14

Method of Setting Tribal Boundaries

Now these are *the territories* which the sons of Israel inherited in the land of Canaan, which Eleazar the priest, and Joshua the son of Nun, and the heads of the households of the tribes of the sons of Israel apportioned to them for an inheritance,

2 by the lot of their inheritance, as the Lord commanded ᵀthrough Moses, for the nine tribes and the half-tribe.   *by the hand of*

3 For ᴿMoses had given the inheritance of the two tribes and the half-tribe beyond the Jordan; but he did not give an inheritance to the Levites among them.   Num. 32:33

4 For the sons of Joseph were two tribes, Manasseh and Ephraim, and they did not give a portion to the Levites in the land, except cities to live in, with their pasture lands for their livestock and for their property.

5 Thus the sons of Israel did just ᴿas the Lord had commanded Moses, and they divided the land.   Num. 35:1f.; Josh. 21:2

Boundaries of Caleb

6 Then the sons of Judah drew near to Joshua in Gilgal, and Caleb the son of Jephunneh the Kenizzite said to him, "You know the word which the Lord spoke to Moses the man of God concerning ᵀyou and me in Kadesh-barnea.   *me and concerning you*

7 "I was forty years old when Moses the servant of the Lord sent me from Kadesh-barnea to spy out the land, and I brought word back to him as *it was* in my heart.

8 "Nevertheless my brethren who went up with me made the heart of the people ᵀmelt with fear; but ᴿI followed the Lord my God fully.   *become demoralized* • Num. 14:24

9 "So Moses swore on that day, saying, 'Surely ᴿthe land on which your foot has trodden shall be an inheritance to you and to your children forever, because you have followed the Lord my God fully.'   Deut. 1:36

10 "And now behold, the Lord has let me live, just as He spoke, these forty-five years, from the time that the Lord spoke this word to Moses, when Israel walked in the wilderness; and now behold, I am eighty-five years old today.

11 "I am still as strong today as I was in the day Moses sent me; as my strength was then, so my strength is now, for war and for ᴿgoing out and coming in.   Deut. 31:2

12 "Now then, give me this hill country about which the Lord spoke on that day, for you heard on that day that Anakim *were* there, with great fortified cities; perhaps the Lord will be with me, and I shall ᴬdrive them out as the Lord has spoken."   *dispossess*

13 So Joshua ᴿblessed him, and ᴿgave Hebron to Caleb the son of Jephunneh for an inheritance.   Josh. 22:6 • Judg. 1:20; 1 Chr. 6:55f.

14 Therefore, Hebron became the inheritance of Caleb the son of Jephunneh the Kenizzite until this day, because he followed the Lord God of Israel fully.

15 Now the name of Hebron was formerly ᵀKiriath-arba; *for Arba* was the greatest man among the Anakim. ᴿThen the land had rest from war.   *the city of Arba* • Josh. 11:23

CHAPTER 15

Boundaries of the Remainder of Judah

Now the lot for the tribe of the sons of Judah according to their families ᵀreached

the border of Edom, southward to the wilderness of Zin at the extreme south. *was to*

2 And their south border was from the lower end of the Salt Sea, from the bay that turns to the south.

3 Then it proceeded southward to the ascent of Akrabbim and continued to Zin, then went up by the south of Kadesh-barnea and continued to Hezron, and went up to Addar and turned about to Karka.

4 And it continued to Azmon and proceeded to the ᴬbrook of Egypt; and the ᵀborder ended at the sea. This shall be your south border. *wadi • goings out of the border were*

5 And the east border *was* the Salt Sea, as far as the ᵀmouth of the Jordan. And the border of the north side was from the bay of the sea at the ᵀmouth of the Jordan. *end*

6 Then the border went up to Beth-hoglah, and continued on the north of Beth-arabah, and the border went up to the stone of Bohan the son of Reuben.

7 And the border went up to Debir from ᴿthe valley of Achor, and turned northward toward Gilgal which is opposite the ascent of Adummim, which is on the south of the valley; and the border continued to the waters of En-shemesh, and ᵀit ended at En-rogel. Josh. 7:24 • *the goings out of it were*

8 Then the border went up the valley of Ben-hinnom to the slope of the ᴿJebusite on the south (that is, Jerusalem); and the border went up to the top of the mountain which is before the valley of Hinnom to the west, which is at the end of the valley of Rephaim toward the north. Josh. 15:63

9 And from the top of the mountain the border curved to the spring of the waters of Nephtoah and proceeded to the cities of Mount Ephron, then the border curved to ᴿBaalah (that is, Kiriath-jearim). 1 Chr. 13:6

10 And the border turned about from Baalah westward to Mount Seir, and continued to the slope of Mount Jearim on the north (that is, Chesalon), and went down to Beth-shemesh and continued through Timnah.

11 And the border proceeded to the side of Ekron northward. Then the border curved to Shikkeron and continued to Mount Baalah and proceeded to Jabneel, and the border ended at the sea.

12 And the west border *was* ᴿat the Great Sea, even *its* ᵀcoastline. This is the border around the sons of Judah according to their families. Num. 34:6 • *border*

13 Now he gave to Caleb the son of Jephunneh a portion among the sons of Judah, according to the ᶜcommand of the Lᴏʀᴅ to Joshua, *namely,* Kiriath-arba, *Arba being* the father of Anak (that is, Hebron). *mouth*

14 And Caleb drove out from there the three ᴿsons of Anak: Sheshai and Ahiman and Talmai, the children of Anak. Deut. 9:2

15 Then ᴿhe went up from there against the inhabitants of Debir; now the name of Debir formerly was Kiriath-sepher. Josh. 10:38

16 And Caleb said, "The one who ᵀattacks Kiriath-sepher and captures it, I will give him Achsah my daughter as a wife." *smites*

17 And ᴿOthniel the son of Kenaz, the brother of Caleb, captured it; so he gave him Achsah his daughter as a wife. Judg. 1:13

18 And it came about that when she came *to him,* she persuaded him to ask her father for a field. So she alighted from the donkey, and Caleb said to her, "What do you want?"

19 Then she said, "Give me a blessing; since you have given me the land of the ᵀNegev, give me also springs of water." So he gave her the upper springs and the lower springs. South country

20 This is the inheritance of the tribe of the sons of Judah according to their families.

21 Now the cities at the extremity of the tribe of the sons of Judah toward the border of Edom in the south were Kabzeel and ᴿEder and Jagur, Gen. 35:21

22 and Kinah and Dimonah and Adadah,

23 and Kedesh and Hazor and Ithnan,

24 Ziph and Telem and Bealoth,

25 and Hazor-hadattah and Kerioth-hezron (that is, Hazor),

26 Amam and Shema and Moladah,

27 and Hazar-gaddah and Heshmon and Beth-pelet,

28 and Hazar-shual and ᴿBeersheba and Biziothiah, Gen. 21:31

29 Baalah and Iim and Ezem,

30 and Eltolad and Chesil and Hormah,

31 and ᴿZiklag and Madmannah and Sansannah, 1 Sam. 27:6; 30:1

32 and Lebaoth and Shilhim and Ain and Rimmon; in all, twenty-nine cities with their villages.

33 In the lowland: ᴿEshtaol and Zorah and Ashnah, Judg. 13:25; 16:31

34 and Zanoah and En-gannim, Tappuah and Enam,

35 Jarmuth and ᴿAdullam, Socoh and Azekah, 1 Sam. 22:1

36 and Shaaraim and Adithaim and Gederah and Gederothaim; fourteen cities with their villages.

37 Zenan and Hadashah and Migdal-gad,

38 and Dilean and Mizpeh and Joktheel,

39 Lachish and Bozkath and Eglon,

40 and Cabbon and Lahmas and Chitlish,

41 and Gederoth, Beth-dagon and Naamah and Makkedah; sixteen cities with their villages.

42 Libnah and Ether and Ashan,

43 and Iphtah and Ashnah and Nezib,

44 and Keilah and Achzib and Mareshah; nine cities with their villages.

45 Ekron, with its towns and its villages;

46 from Ekron even to the sea, all that were by the ᵀside of Ashdod, with their villages. *hand*

47 Ashdod, its towns and its villages; Gaza, its towns and its villages; as far as ᴿthe ᴬbrook of Egypt and the Great Sea, even *its* ᵀcoastline. Josh. 15:4 • *wadi • border*

48 And in the hill country: Shamir and Jattir and Socoh,

49 and Dannah and Kiriath-sannah (that is, Debir),

50 and Anab and Eshtemoh and Anim,

51 and Goshen and Holon and Giloh; eleven cities with their villages.

52 Arab and Dumah and Eshan,

53 and Janum and Beth-tappuah and Aphekah,

54 and Humtah and Kiriath-arba (that is, Hebron), and Zior; nine cities with their villages.

55 Maon, Carmel and Ziph and Juttah,

56 and Jezreel and Jokdeam and Zanoah,

57 Kain, Gibeah and Timnah; ten cities with their villages.

58 Halhul, Beth-zur and Gedor,

59 and Maarath and Beth-anoth and Eltekon; six cities with their villages.

60 Kiriath-baal (that is, Kiriath-jearim), and Rabbah; two cities with their villages.

61 In the wilderness: Beth-arabah, Middin and Secacah,

62 and Nibshan and the City of Salt and Engedi; six cities with their villages.

63 Now as for the ^RJebusites, the inhabitants of Jerusalem, the sons of Judah could not ^fdrive them out; so the Jebusites live with the sons of Judah at Jerusalem until this day.   Judg. 1:21; 2 Sam. 5:6 · *dispossess them*

CHAPTER 16

Boundaries of Joseph

THEN the lot for the sons of Joseph went from the Jordan at Jericho to the waters of Jericho on the east into ^Rthe wilderness, going up from Jericho through the hill country to Bethel.   Josh. 8:15; 18:12

2 And it went from Bethel to Luz, and ^Rcontinued to the border of the Archites at Ataroth.   Josh. 18:13

3 And it went down westward to the territory of the Japhletites, as far as the territory of lower Beth-horon even to Gezer, and ^fit ended at the sea.   *the goings out of it were*

4 And the sons of Joseph, Manasseh and Ephraim, received their inheritance.

Boundaries of Ephraim

5 Now *this* was the territory of the sons of Ephraim according to their families: the border of their inheritance eastward was Ataroth-addar, as far as upper Beth-horon.

6 Then the border went westward at ^RMichmethath on the north, and the border turned about eastward to Taanath-shiloh, and continued *beyond* it to the east of Janoah.   Josh. 17:7

7 And it went down from Janoah to Ataroth and to ^RNaarah, then reached Jericho and came out at the Jordan.   1 Chr. 7:28

8 From Tappuah the border continued westward to the [^]brook of Kanah, and ^fit ended at the sea. This is the inheritance of the tribe of the sons of Ephraim according to their families,   *wadi · the goings out of it were*

9 *together* with the cities which were set apart for the sons of Ephraim in the midst of the inheritance of the sons of Manasseh, all the cities with their villages.

10 But they did not ^fdrive out the Canaanites who lived in Gezer, so the Canaanites live in the midst of Ephraim to this day, and they became forced laborers.   *dispossess*

CHAPTER 17

Boundaries of the Half-tribe of Manasseh

NOW *this* was the lot for the tribe of Manasseh, for he was the first-born of Joseph. To Machir the first-born of Manasseh, the father of Gilead, was allotted Gilead and Bashan, because he was a man of war.

2 So *the lot* was *made* for the rest of the sons of Manasseh according to their families: for the sons of Abiezer and for the sons of Helek and for the sons of Asriel and for the sons of Shechem and for the sons of Hepher and for the sons of Shemida; these *were* the male *descendants* of Manasseh the son of Joseph according to their families.

3 However, ^RZelophehad, the son of Hepher, the son of Gilead, the son of Machir, the son of Manasseh, had no sons, only daughters; and these are the names of his daughters: Mahlah and Noah, Hoglah, Milcah and Tirzah.   Num. 26:33; 27:1-7

4 And they came near before Eleazar the priest and before Joshua the son of Nun and before the leaders, saying, "The LORD commanded Moses to give us an inheritance among our brothers." So according to the command of the LORD he gave them an inheritance among their father's brothers.

5 Thus there fell ten portions to Manasseh, besides the land of Gilead and Bashan, which is beyond the Jordan,

6 because the daughters of Manasseh received an inheritance among his sons. And the ^Rland of Gilead belonged to the rest of the sons of Manasseh.   Josh. 13:30, 31

7 And the border of Manasseh ^fran from Asher to Michmethath which was east of Shechem; then the border went southward to the inhabitants of En-tappuah.   *was*

8 The land of Tappuah belonged to Manasseh, but Tappuah on the border of Manasseh *belonged* to the sons of Ephraim.

9 And the border went down to the brook of Kanah, southward of the brook (these cities *belonged* to Ephraim among the cities of Manasseh), and the border of Manasseh *was* on the north side of the brook, and ^fit ended at the sea.   *goings out of it were*

10 The south side *belonged* to Ephraim

and the north side to Manasseh, and the sea was their border; and they reached to Asher on the north and to Issachar on the east.

11 And in Issachar and in Asher, [R]Manasseh had Beth-shean and its towns and Ibleam and its towns, and the inhabitants of Dor and its towns, and the inhabitants of En-dor and its towns, and the inhabitants of Taanach and its towns, and the inhabitants of Megiddo and its towns, the third is [R]Napheth.   1 Chr. 7:29 · Josh. 11:2; 12:23

12 But the sons of Manasseh could not take possession of these cities, because the Canaanites persisted in living in that land.

13 And it came about when the sons of Israel became strong, [R]they put the Canaanites to forced labor, but they did not 'drive them out completely.   Josh. 16:10 · *dispossess*

14 Then the [R]sons of Joseph spoke to Joshua, saying, "Why have you given me only one lot and one portion for an inheritance, since I am a numerous people whom the LORD has thus far blessed?"   Num. 13:7

15 And Joshua said to them, "If you are a numerous people, go [T]up to the forest and [T]clear a place for yourself there in the land of the Perizzites and of the Rephaim, since the hill country of Ephraim is too narrow for you."   *up for yourself · cut down*

16 And the sons of Joseph said, "The hill country is not enough for us, and all the Canaanites who live in the valley land have [R]chariots of iron, both those who are in Beth-shean and its towns, and those who are in the valley of Jezreel."   Josh. 17:18; Judg. 1:19

17 And Joshua spoke to the house of Joseph, to Ephraim and Manasseh, saying, "You are a numerous people and have great power; you shall not have one lot *only,*

18 but the hill country shall be yours. For though it is a forest, you shall 'clear it, and to its 'farthest borders it shall be yours; for you shall 'drive out the Canaanites, even though they have chariots of iron *and* though they are strong."   *cut it down · goings out · dispossess*

CHAPTER 18

The Remaining Tribes Move to Shiloh

THEN the whole congregation of the sons of Israel assembled themselves at [R]Shiloh, and set up the tent of meeting there; and the land was subdued before them.   Judg. 21:19

New Method of Setting Tribal Boundaries

2 And there remained among the sons of Israel seven tribes who had not divided their inheritance.

3 So Joshua said to the sons of Israel, "How long will you put off entering to take possession of the land which the LORD, the God of your fathers, has given you?

4 "Provide for yourselves three men from [T]each tribe that I may send them, and that they may arise and walk through the land and write a description of it according to their inheritance; then they shall 'return to me.   *the · come*

5 "And they shall divide it into seven portions; [R]Judah shall stay in its territory on the south, and the house of Joseph shall stay in their territory on the north.   Josh. 15:1

6 "And you shall describe the land in seven divisions, and bring *the description* here to me. [R]And I will cast lots for you here before the LORD our God.   Josh. 14:2

7 "For [R]the Levites have no portion among you, because the priesthood of the LORD is [T]their inheritance. Gad and Reuben and the half-tribe of Manasseh also have received their inheritance eastward beyond the Jordan, which Moses the servant of the LORD gave them."   Num. 18:7, 20; Josh. 13:33 · *his*

8 Then the men arose and went, and Joshua commanded those who went to describe the land, saying, "Go and walk through the land and describe it, and return to me; then I will cast lots for you here before the LORD in [R]Shiloh."   Josh. 18:1

9 So the men went and passed through the land, and described it by cities in seven divisions in a book; and they came to Joshua to the camp at Shiloh.

10 And [R]Joshua cast lots for them in Shiloh before the LORD, and there Joshua divided the land to the sons of Israel according to their divisions.   Num. 34:16-29; Josh. 19:51

Boundaries of Benjamin

11 Now the lot of the tribe of the sons of Benjamin came up according to their families, and the territory of their lot [T]lay between the sons of Judah and the sons of Joseph.   *went out*

12 And their border on the north side was from the Jordan, then the border went up to the side of Jericho on the north, and went up through the hill country westward; and [12]it ended at the wilderness of Beth-aven.

13 And from there the border continued to [R]Luz, to the side of Luz (that is, Bethel) southward; and the border went down to Ataroth-addar, near the hill which *lies* on the south of lower Beth-horon.   Gen. 28:19

14 And the border extended *from there,* and turned round on the west side southward, from the hill which *lies* before Beth-horon southward; and [12]it ended at Kiriath-baal (that is, Kiriath-jearim), a city of the sons of Judah. This *was* the west side.

15 Then the [R]south side *was* from the edge of Kiriath-jearim, and the border went westward and went to the fountain of the waters of Nephtoah.   Josh. 15:5-9

16 And the border went down to the edge of the hill which is in the valley of Ben-hinnom, which is in the valley of Rephaim northward; and it went down to the valley

12 Lit., *goings out of it were*

of Hinnom, to the slope of the Jebusite southward, and went down to En-rogel.

17 And it extended northward and went to En-shemesh and went to Geliloth, which is opposite the ascent of Adummim, and it went down to the^Rstone of Bohan the son of Reuben.   Josh. 15:6

18 And it continued to the side in front of the Arabah northward, and went down to the Arabah.

19 And the border continued to the side of Beth-hoglah northward; and the border ended at the north bay of the Salt Sea, at the south end of the Jordan. This *was* the south border.

20 Moreover, the Jordan was its border on the east side. This *was* the inheritance of the sons of Benjamin, according to their families *and* according to its borders all around.

21 Now the cities of the tribe of the sons of Benjamin according to their families were Jericho and Beth-hoglah and Emek-keziz,

22 and Beth-arabah and Zemaraim and Bethel,

23 and Avvim and Parah and Ophrah,

24 and Chephar-ammoni and Ophni and Geba; twelve cities with their villages.

25 Gibeon and Ramah and Beeroth,

26 and Mizpeh and Chephirah and Mozah,

27 and Rekem and Irpeel and Taralah,

28 and ^RZelah, Haeleph and the Jebusite (that is, Jerusalem), Gibeah, Kiriath; fourteen cities with their villages. This is the inheritance of the^Rsons of Benjamin according to their families.   2 Sam. 21:14 • Num. 26:38

CHAPTER 19

Boundaries of Simeon

THEN the second lot^Tfell to Simeon, to the tribe of the sons of Simeon according to their families, and their inheritance was in the midst of the inheritance of the sons of Judah.   *came out*

2 So they had as their inheritance Beer-sheba or Sheba and Moladah,

3 and Hazar-shual and Balah and Ezem,

4 and Eltolad and Bethul and Hormah,

5 and Ziklag and Beth-marcaboth and Hazar-susah,

6 and Beth-lebaoth and Sharuhen, thirteen cities with their villages;

7 Ain, Rimmon and Ether and Ashan, four cities with their villages;

8 and all the villages which *were* around these cities as far as Baalath-beer, Ramah of the ^TNegev. This *was* the inheritance of the tribe of the sons of Simeon according to their families.   *South country*

9 The inheritance of the sons of Simeon *was taken* from the portion of the sons of Judah, for the share of the sons of Judah was too large for them; so the sons of Simeon received *an* inheritance in the midst of ^TJudah's inheritance.   *their*

Boundaries of Zebulun

10 Now the third lot came up for the sons of Zebulun according to their families. And the territory of their inheritance was as far as Sarid.

11 Then their border went up to the west and to Maralah, it then ^Atouched Dabbe-sheth, and reached to the^Abrook that is before Jokneam.   *reached to • wadi*

12 Then it turned from Sarid to the east toward the sunrise as far as the border of Chisloth-tabor, and it proceeded to Daberath and^Tup to Japhia.   *went up*

13 And from there it continued eastward toward the sunrise to Gath-hepher, to Eth-kazin, and it proceeded to Rimmon^Awhich stretches to Neah.   *and is marked off*

14 And the border circled around it on the north to Hannathon, and^Tit ended at the valley of Iphtahel.   *the goings out of it were*

15 *Included* also *were* Kattah and Nahalal and Shimron and Idalah and Bethlehem; twelve cities with their villages.

16 This *was* the inheritance of the sons of Zebulun according to their families, these cities with their villages.

Boundaries of Issachar

17 The fourth lot fell to Issachar, to the sons of Issachar according to their families.

18 And their territory was to Jezreel and *included* Chesulloth and^RShunem,   2 Kin. 4:8

19 and Hapharaim and Shion and Anaharath,

20 and Rabbith and Kishion and Ebez,

21 and Remeth and En-gannim and En-haddah and Beth-pazzez.

22 And the border reached to^RTabor and Shahazumah and Beth-shemesh, and their border ended at the Jordan; sixteen cities with their villages.   Judg. 4:6; Ps. 89:12

23 This *was* the inheritance of the tribe of the sons of Issachar according to their families, the cities with their villages.

Boundaries of Asher

24 Now the fifth lot fell to the tribe of the sons of Asher according to their families.

25 And their territory was Helkath and Hali and Beten and Achshaph,

26 and Allammelech and Amad and Mishal; and it reached to Carmel on the west and to Shihor-libnath.

27 And it turned toward the ^Teast to Beth-dagon, and reached to Zebulun, and to the valley of Iphtahel northward to Beth-emek and Neiel; then it proceeded on^Tnorth to^RCa-bul,   *sunrise • from the left hand •* 1 Kin. 9:13

28 and Ebron and Rehob and Hammon and Kanah, as far as Great^RSidon.   Acts 27:3

29 And the border turned to Ramah, and to the fortified city of Tyre; then the border turned to Hosah, and^Tit ended at the sea by the region of Achzib.   *the goings out of it were*

30 *Included* also *were* Ummah, and Aphek and Rehob; twenty-two cities with their villages.

31 This *was* the inheritance of the tribe of the sons of Asher according to their families, these cities with their villages.

Boundaries of Naphtali

32 The sixth lot ᵀfell to the sons of Naphtali; to the sons of Naphtali according to their families.   *came out*

33 And their border was from Heleph, from the oak in Zaanannim and Adami-nekeb and Jabneel, as far as Lakkum; and ᵀit ended at the Jordan.   *the goings out of it were*

34 Then the border turned westward to Aznoth-tabor, and proceeded from there to Hukkok; and it reached to Zebulun on the south and touched Asher on the west, and to Judah at the Jordan toward the east.

35 And the fortified cities *were* Ziddim, Zer and ᴿHammath, Rakkath and ᴿChinnereth,   Gen. 10:18; 1 Kin. 8:65 • Deut. 3:17

36 and Adamah and Ramah and Hazor,

37 and Kedesh and Edrei and En-hazor,

38 and Yiron and Migdal-el, Horem and Beth-anath and Beth-shemesh; nineteen cities with their villages.

39 This *was* the inheritance of the tribe of the sons of Naphtali according to their families, the cities with their villages.

Boundaries of Dan

40 The seventh lot fell to the tribe of the sons of Dan according to their families.

41 And the territory of their inheritance was Zorah and Eshtaol and Ir-shemesh,

42 and Shaalabbin and Aijalon and Ithlah,

43 and Elon and Timnah and Ekron,

44 and Eltekeh and Gibbethon and Baalath,

45 and Jehud and Bene-berak and Gath-rimmon,

46 and Me-jarkon and Rakkon, with the territory over against ᵀJoppa.   *Heb., Japho*

47 And the territory of the sons of Dan proceededᵀbeyond them; for the sons of Dan went up and fought with Leshem and captured it. Then they struck it with the edge of the sword and possessed it and ᵀsettled in it; and they calledᵀLeshem Dan after the name of Dan their father.   *from* • *dwelt* • Laish

48 This *was* the inheritance of the tribe of the sons of Dan according to their families, these cities with their villages.

Boundaries of Joshua

49 When they finished apportioning the land for inheritance by its borders, the sons of Israel gave an inheritance in their midst to Joshua the son of Nun.

50 In accordance with the ᵀcommand of the LORD they gave him the city for which he asked,ᴿTimnath-serah in the hill country of Ephraim. So he built the city and ᵀsettled in it.   *mouth* • Num. 13:8; Josh. 24:30 • *dwelt*

51 ᴿThese are the inheritances which Eleazar the priest and Joshua the son of Nun and the heads of the ᵀhouseholds of the tribes of the sons of Israel distributed by lot in Shiloh before the LORD, at the doorway of the tent of meeting. So they finished dividing the land.   Josh. 18:10 • *fathers*

CHAPTER 20

Six Cities of Refuge

THEN the LORD spoke to Joshua, saying,

2 "Speak to the sons of Israel, saying, 'Designate the cities of refuge, of which I spoke to you through Moses,

3 that the manslayer who ᵀkills any person unintentionally, without premeditation, may flee there, and they shall become your refuge from the avenger of blood.   *smites*

4 'And he shall flee to one of these cities, and shall stand at the entrance of the gate of the city and state his case in the hearing of the elders of that city; and they shall take him into the city to them and give him a place, so that he may dwell among them.

5 'Now ᴿif the avenger of blood pursues him, then they shall not deliver the manslayer into his hand, because he struck his neighbor without premeditation and did not hate him beforehand.   Num. 35:12

6 'And he shall dwell in that city until he stands before the congregation for judgment, until the death of the one who is high priest in those days. Then the manslayer shall return to his own city and to his own house, to the city from which he fled.' "

7 So they ᵀset apart Kedesh in ᵀGalilee in the hill country of Naphtali and Shechem in the hill country of Ephraim, and Kiriath-arba (that is, Hebron) in ᴿthe hill country of Judah.   *sanctified* • Heb., *Galil* • Luke 1:39

8 And beyond the Jordan east of Jericho, they ᵀdesignated Bezer in the wilderness on the plain from the tribe of Reuben, and Ramoth in Gilead from the tribe of Gad, and Golan in Bashan from the tribe of Manasseh.   *set*

9 ᴿThese were the appointed cities for all the sons of Israel and for the stranger who sojourns among them, that whoever ᵀkills any person unintentionally may flee there, and not die by the hand of the avenger of blood until he stands before the congregation.   Num. 35:13ff. • *smites*

CHAPTER 21

The Families to Be Assigned Cities
1 Chr. 6:54–81

THEN the heads of ᵀhouseholds of ᴿthe Levites approached Eleazar the priest and

Joshua the son of Nun and the heads of [T]households of the tribes of the sons of Israel.   *fathers* • Num. 35:1-8

2 And they spoke to them at Shiloh in the land of Canaan, saying, "The[R] LORD commanded [T]through Moses to give us cities to live in, with their pasture lands for our cattle."   Num. 35:2 • *by the hand of*

3 So the sons of Israel gave the Levites from their inheritance these cities with their pasture lands, according to the [T]command of the LORD.   *mouth*

4 Then the lot came out for the families of the Kohathites. And the sons of Aaron the priest, who were of the Levites,[T] received thirteen cities by lot from the tribe of Judah and from the tribe of the Simeonites and from the tribe of Benjamin.   *had*

5 And the rest of the sons of Kohath received ten cities by lot from the families of the tribe of Ephraim and from the tribe of Dan and from the half-tribe of Manasseh.

6 And the sons of Gershon[T] received thirteen cities by lot from the families of the tribe of Issachar and from the tribe of Asher and from the tribe of Naphtali and from the half-tribe of Manasseh in Bashan.   *had*

7 The sons of Merari according to their families [T]received twelve cities from the tribe of Reuben and from the tribe of Gad and from the tribe of Zebulun.   *had*

Cities for the Kohathites

8 Now the [R]sons of Israel gave by lot to the Levites these cities with their pasture lands, as the LORD had commanded [T]through Moses.   Gen. 49:5ff. • *by the hand of*

9 And they gave these cities which are *here* mentioned by name from the tribe of the sons of Judah and from the tribe of the sons of Simeon;

10 and they were for the sons of Aaron, one of the families of the Kohathites, of the sons of Levi, for the lot was theirs first.

11 Thus they gave them Kiriath-arba, *Arba being* the [R]father of Anak (that is, Hebron), in the hill country of Judah, with its surrounding pasture lands.   Josh. 14:15; 15:13

12 But the fields of the city and its villages, they gave to Caleb the son of Jephunneh as his possession.

13 So[R] to the sons of Aaron the priest they gave Hebron, the city of refuge for the manslayer, with its pasture lands, and Libnah with its pasture lands,   1 Chr. 6:57

14 and [R]Jattir with its pasture lands and Eshtemoa with its pasture lands,   Josh. 15:48

15 and Holon with its pasture lands and [R]Debir with its pasture lands,   Josh. 15:49

16 and Ain with its pasture lands and [R]Juttah with its pasture lands *and* [R]Bethshemesh with its pasture lands; nine cities from these two tribes.   Josh. 15:55 • Josh. 15:10

17 And from the tribe of Benjamin,[R] Gibeon with its pasture lands, [R]Geba with its pasture lands,   Josh. 18:25 • Josh. 18:24

18 Anathoth with its pasture lands and Almon with its pasture lands; four cities.

19 All the cities of the sons of Aaron, the priests, were thirteen cities with their pasture lands.

20 Then the cities from the tribe of Ephraim were allotted to the [R]families of the sons of Kohath, the Levites, *even to* the rest of the sons of Kohath.   1 Chr. 6:66

21 And they gave them [R]Shechem, the city of refuge for the manslayer, with its pasture lands, in the hill country of Ephraim, and Gezer with its pasture lands,   Josh. 20:7

22 and Kibzaim with its pasture lands and Beth-horon with its pasture lands; four cities.

23 And from the tribe of Dan, Elteke with its pasture lands, Gibbethon with its pasture lands,

24 Aijalon with its pasture lands, Gathrimmon with its pasture lands; four cities.

25 And from the half-tribe of Manasseh, *they allotted* Taanach with its pasture lands and Gath-rimmon with its pasture lands; two cities.

26 All the cities with their pasture lands for the families of the rest of the sons of Kohath were ten.

Cities for the Gershonites

27 And[R] to the sons of Gershon, one of the families of the Levites, from the half-tribe of Manasseh, *they gave* Golan in Bashan, the city of refuge for the manslayer, with its pasture lands, and Be-eshterah with its pasture lands; two cities.   1 Chr. 6:71

28 And from the tribe of Issachar, *they gave* Kishion with its pasture lands, Daberath with its pasture lands,

29 Jarmuth with its pasture lands, Engannim with its pasture lands; four cities.

30 And from the tribe of Asher, *they gave* Mishal with its pasture lands, Abdon with its pasture lands,

31 Helkath with its pasture lands and Rehob with its pasture lands; four cities.

32 And from the tribe of Naphtali, *they gave* Kedesh in Galilee, the city of refuge for the manslayer, with its pasture lands and Hammoth-dor with its pasture lands and Kartan with its pasture lands; three cities.

33 All the cities of the Gershonites according to their families were thirteen cities with their pasture lands.

Cities for the Merarites

34 And to the families of [R]the sons of Merari, the rest of the Levites, *they gave* from the tribe of Zebulun, Jokneam with its pasture lands and Kartah with its pasture lands,   1 Chr. 6:77

35 Dimnah with its pasture lands, Nahalal with its pasture lands; four cities.

36 And from the tribe of Reuben, *they gave*^RBezer with its pasture lands and Jahaz with its pasture lands,   Deut. 4:43; Josh. 20:8
37 Kedemoth with its pasture lands and Mephaath with its pasture lands; four cities.
38 And from the tribe of Gad, *they gave* ^RRamoth in Gilead, the city of refuge for the manslayer, with its pasture lands and Mahanaim with its pasture lands,   1 Kin. 4:13
39 Heshbon with its pasture lands, Jazer with its pasture lands; four cities in all.
40 All *these were* the cities of the sons of Merari according to their families, the rest of the families of the Levites; and their lot was twelve cities.
41 All the cities of the Levites in the midst of the possession of the sons of Israel were forty-eight cities with their pasture lands.
42 These cities each had its surrounding pasture lands; thus *it was* with all these cities.

The Settlement of Israel Is Completed

43 So the LORD gave Israel all the land which He had sworn to give to their fathers, and they possessed it and lived in it.
44 And the LORD^Rgave them rest on every side, according to all that He had sworn to their fathers, and no one of all their enemies stood before them; the LORD gave all their enemies into their hand.   Josh. 1:13; 23:1
45 Not ^Tone of the good ^Tpromises which the LORD had made to the house of Israel failed; all came to pass.   *a word · words*

CHAPTER 22

Joshua Challenges the Eastern Tribes

THEN^RJoshua summoned the Reubenites and the Gadites and the half-tribe of Manasseh,   Num. 32:20-22
2 and said to them, "You have kept all that Moses the servant of the LORD commanded you,^Rand have listened to my voice in all that I commanded you.   Josh. 1:12-18
3"You have not forsaken your brothers these many days to this day, but have kept the charge of the commandment of the LORD your God.
4"And now^Rthe LORD your God has given rest to your brothers, as He spoke to them; therefore turn now and go to your tents, to the land of your possession, which Moses the servant of the LORD gave you beyond the Jordan.   Num. 32:18; Deut. 3:20
5"Only be very careful to observe the commandment and the law which Moses the servant of the LORD commanded you, to love the LORD your God and walk in all His ways and keep His commandments and hold fast to Him and serve Him with all your heart and with all your soul."
6 So Joshua blessed them and sent them away, and they went to their tents.

7 Now^Rto the one half-tribe of Manasseh Moses had given *a possession* in Bashan, but to the other half Joshua gave *a possession* among their brothers westward beyond the Jordan. So when Joshua sent them away to their tents, he blessed them,   Num. 32:33
8 and said to them, "Return to your tents with great riches and with very much livestock, with silver, gold, bronze, iron, and with very many clothes; divide the spoil of your enemies with your brothers."
9 And the sons of Reuben and the sons of Gad and the half-tribe of Manasseh returned *home* and departed from the sons of Israel at Shiloh which is in the land of Canaan, to go to the land of Gilead, to the land of their possession which they had possessed, according to the ^Tcommand of the LORD^Tthrough Moses.   *mouth · by the hand of*

Construction of the Altar

10 And when they came to the region of the Jordan which is in the land of Canaan, the sons of Reuben and the sons of Gad and the half-tribe of Manasseh built an altar there by the Jordan, a large altar in appearance.

Misunderstanding of the Altar

11 And the sons of Israel heard *it* said, "Behold, the sons of Reuben and the sons of Gad and the half-tribe of Manasseh have built an altar at the ^Tfrontier of the land of Canaan, in the region of the Jordan, on the side *belonging to* the sons of Israel."   *front*
12 And when the sons of Israel heard *of it*, the whole congregation of the sons of Israel gathered themselves at ^RShiloh, to go up against them in war.   Josh. 18:1
13 Then the sons of Israel sent to the sons of Reuben and to the sons of Gad and to the half-tribe of Manasseh, into the land of Gilead, Phinehas the son of Eleazar the priest,
14 and with him ten chiefs, one chief for each father's household from each of the tribes of Israel; and^Reach one of them *was* the head of his father's household among the^Athousands of Israel.   Num. 1:4 · *families*
15 And they came to the sons of Reuben and to the sons of Gad and to the half-tribe of Manasseh, to the land of Gilead, and they spoke with them saying,
16"Thus says the whole congregation of the LORD, 'What is this unfaithful act which you have committed against the God of Israel, turning away from following the LORD this day, by^Rbuilding yourselves an altar, to rebel against the LORD this day?   Josh. 22:11
17 'Is not the iniquity of Peor ^Tenough for us, from which we have not cleansed ourselves to this day, although a plague came on the congregation of the LORD,   *little for us*
18 that you must turn away this day from

following the LORD? And it will come about if you rebel against the LORD today, that[R]He will be angry with the whole congregation of Israel tomorrow.   Num. 16:22

19 'If, however, the land of your possession is unclean, then [T]cross into the land of the possession of the LORD, where the LORD's tabernacle [T]stands, and take possession among us. Only do not rebel against the LORD, or rebel against us by building an altar for yourselves, besides the altar of the LORD our God.   cross for yourselves · abides

20 'Did not [R]Achan the son of Zerah act unfaithfully in the things under the ban, and wrath fall on all the congregation of Israel? And that man did not perish alone in his iniquity.' "   Josh. 7:1-26

Explanation of the Altar

21 Then the sons of Reuben and the sons of Gad and the half-tribe of Manasseh answered, and spoke to the heads of the [T]families of Israel.   thousands

22 "The Mighty One, God, the LORD, the Mighty One, God, the LORD![R]He knows, and may Israel itself know. If it was in rebellion, or if in an unfaithful act against the LORD do not Thou save us this day! [Job 10:7; Ps. 44:21]

23 "If we have built us an altar to turn away from following the LORD, or if to[R]offer a burnt offering or grain offering on it, or if to offer sacrifices of peace offerings on it, may the LORD Himself require it. Deut. 12:11

24 "But truly we have done this out of concern, for a reason, saying, 'In time to come your sons may say to our sons, "What have you to do with the LORD, the God of Israel?

25 "For the LORD has made the Jordan a border between us and you, you sons of Reuben and sons of Gad; you have no portion in the LORD." So your sons may make our sons stop fearing the LORD.'

26 "Therefore we said, 'Let us build an altar, not for burnt offering or for sacrifice;

27 rather it shall be[R]a witness between us and you and between our generations after us, that we are to[R]perform the service of the LORD before Him with our burnt offerings, and with our sacrifices and with our peace offerings, that your sons may not say to our sons in time to come, "You have no portion in the LORD." '   Gen. 31:48 · Deut. 12:6, 11, 26f.

28 "Therefore we said, 'It shall also come about if they say this to us or to our generations in time to come, then we shall say, "See the copy of the altar of the LORD which our fathers made, not for burnt offering or for sacrifice; rather it is a witness between us and you." "

29 "Far be it from us that we should rebel against the LORD and turn away from following the LORD this day, by building an altar for burnt offering, for grain offering or for sacrifice, besides the altar of the LORD our God which is before His [13]tabernacle."

Celebration by the Western Tribes

30 So when Phinehas the priest and the leaders of the congregation, even the heads of the [T]families of Israel who were with him, heard the words which the sons of Reuben and the sons of Gad and the sons of Manasseh spoke, it pleased them.   thousands

31 And Phinehas the son of Eleazar the priest said to the sons of Reuben and to the sons of Gad and to the sons of Manasseh, "Today we know that the [R]LORD is in our midst, because you have not committed this unfaithful act against the LORD; now you have delivered the sons of Israel from the hand of the LORD."   Ex. 25:8; Lev. 26:11f.

32 Then Phinehas the son of Eleazar the priest and the leaders returned from the sons of Reuben and from the sons of Gad, from the land of Gilead, to the land of Canaan, to the sons of Israel, and brought back word to them.

33 And the word pleased the sons of Israel, and the sons of Israel blessed God; and they did not speak of going up against them in war, to destroy the land in which the sons of Reuben and the sons of Gad were living.

34 And the sons of Reuben and the sons of Gad [R]called the altar Witness; "For," they said, "it is a witness between us that the LORD is God."   Gen. 31:47-49

CHAPTER 23

A Reminder from History

NOW it came about after many days, when the LORD had given rest to Israel from all their enemies [T]on every side, and Joshua was old, advanced in years,   from round about

2 that [R]Joshua called for all Israel, for their elders and their heads and their judges and their officers, and said to them, "I am old, advanced in years.   Josh. 24:1

3 "And you have seen all that the LORD your God has done to all these nations because of you, for[R]the LORD your God is He who has been fighting for you.   Deut. 1:30

4 "See, I have apportioned to you these nations which remain as an inheritance for your tribes, with all the nations which I have cut off, from the Jordan even to the Great Sea toward the setting of the sun.

5 "And the LORD your God, He shall thrust them out from before you and [A]drive them from before you; and[R]you shall possess their land, just as the LORD your God[T]promised you.   dispossess · Num. 33:53 · spoke to

6 "Be[R] very firm, then, to keep and do all that is written in the book of the law of Moses, so that you may not turn aside from it to the right hand or to the left,   Deut. 5:32

7 in order that you may not [T]associate

---

13 Lit., dwelling place

with these nations, these which remain among you, or mention the name of their gods, or make *anyone* swear *by them*, or serve them, or bow down to them. go among

8"But you are to cling to the LORD your God, as you have done to this day.

9"For[R]the LORD has driven out great and strong nations from before you; and as for you,[R]no man has stood before you to this day. Ex. 23:23, 30 · *dispossessed* · Deut. 7:24

10"One of your men puts to flight a thousand, for the LORD your God is He who fights for you, just as He promised you.

11"So take diligent heed to yourselves to love the LORD your God.

12"For if you ever go back and[R]cling to the rest of these nations, these which remain among you, and[R]intermarry with them, so that you associate with them and they with you, Ex. 34:15, 16 · Deut. 7:3, 4 · *go among*

13 know with certainty that the LORD your God will not continue to drive these nations out from before you; but they shall be a snare and a trap to you, and a whip on your sides and thorns in your eyes, until you perish from off this good land which the LORD your God has given you. *dispossess*

14"Now behold, today I am going the way of all the earth, and you know in all your hearts and in all your souls that [R]not one word of all the good words which the LORD your God spoke concerning you has failed; all have [T]been fulfilled for you, not [T]one of them has failed. Josh. 21:45 · *come* · *one word*

15"And it shall come about that just as all the good words which the LORD your God spoke to you have come upon you, so [R]the LORD will bring upon you all the threats, until He has destroyed you from off this good land which the LORD your God has given you. Lev. 26:14-33; Deut. 28:15

16"When[R] you transgress the covenant of the LORD your God, which He commanded you, and go and serve other gods, and bow down to them, then the anger of the LORD will burn against you, and you shall perish quickly from off the good land which He has given you." Deut. 4:25, 26

CHAPTER 24

Renewal of the Covenant

THEN[R]Joshua gathered all the tribes of Israel to Shechem, and called for the elders of Israel and for their heads and their judges and their officers; and they presented themselves before God. Josh. 23:2

2 And Joshua said to all the people, "Thus says the LORD, the God of Israel, 'From ancient times your fathers lived beyond the [14]River, namely,[R]Terah, the father of Abraham and the father of Nahor, and they served other gods. Gen. 11:27-32

3 'Then I took your father Abraham from beyond the [14]River, and led him through all the land of Canaan, and multiplied his [T]descendants and gave him Isaac. *seed*

4 'And to Isaac I gave Jacob and Esau, and to Esau I gave Mount Seir, to possess it; but Jacob and his sons went down to Egypt.

5 'Then I sent Moses and Aaron, and I plagued Egypt [T]by what I did in its midst; and afterward I brought you out. *according to*

6 'And I brought your fathers out of Egypt, and you came to the sea; and Egypt pursued your fathers with chariots and horsemen to the[T]Red Sea. *Sea of Reeds*

7 'But when they cried out to the LORD, He put darkness between you and the Egyptians, and brought the sea upon them and covered them; and your own eyes saw what I did in Egypt. And[R]you lived in the wilderness for a long time. Deut. 1:46; 2:14

8 'Then I brought you into the land of the Amorites who lived beyond the Jordan, and they fought with you; and I gave them into your hand, and you took possession of their land when I destroyed them before you.

9 'Then[R]Balak the son of Zippor, king of Moab, arose and fought against Israel, and he sent and summoned Balaam the son of Beor to curse you. Num. 22:2-6

10 'But I[R]was not willing to listen to Balaam. So he had to bless you, and I delivered you from his hand. Deut. 23:5

11 'And you crossed the Jordan and came to Jericho; and the citizens of Jericho fought against you, *and* the Amorite and the Perizzite and the Canaanite and the Hittite and the Girgashite, the Hivite and the Jebusite. Thus[R]I gave them into your hand. Ex. 23:31

12 'Then I[T]sent the hornet before you and it [T]drove out the two kings of the Amorites from before you, *but*[R]not by your sword or your bow. Ex. 23:28 · *drove them out* · Ps. 44:3

13 'And[R]I gave you a land on which you had not labored, and cities which you had not built, and you have lived in them; you are eating of vineyards and olive groves which you did not plant.' Deut. 6:10, 11

14"Now, therefore, [A]fear the LORD and serve Him in sincerity and [A]truth; and put away the gods which your fathers served beyond the [T]River and in Egypt, and serve the LORD. *reverence* · *faithfulness* · Euphrates

15"And if it is disagreeable in your sight to serve the LORD, choose for yourselves today whom you will serve: whether the gods which your fathers served which were beyond the River, or the gods of the Amorites in whose land you are living; but as for me and my house, we will serve the LORD."

16 And the people answered and said, "Far be it from us that we should forsake the LORD to serve other gods;

17 for the LORD our God is He who brought us and our fathers up out of the land of Egypt, from the house of[T]bondage, and who did these great signs in our sight

and preserved us through all the way in which we went and among all the peoples through whose midst we passed.   *bondmen*

18"And the LORD drove out from before us all the peoples, even the Amorites who lived in the land. We also will serve the LORD, for He is our God."

19 Then Joshua said to the people, "You will not be able to serve the LORD, for He is a holy God. He is a jealous God; He will not forgive your transgression or your sins.

20"If[R]you forsake the LORD and serve foreign gods, then He will turn and do you harm and consume you after He has done good to you."   Deut. 4:25, 26

21 And the people said to Joshua, "No, but we will serve the LORD."

22 And Joshua said to the people, "You are witnesses against yourselves that[R]you have chosen for yourselves the LORD, to serve Him." And they said, "We are witnesses."   Ps. 119:173

23"Now therefore, put away the foreign gods which are in your midst, and incline your hearts to the LORD, the God of Israel."

24 [R]And the people said to Joshua, "We will serve the LORD our God and we will [T]obey His voice."   Ex. 19:8; 24:3, 7 · *listen to*

25 [R]So Joshua made a covenant with the people that day, and made for them a statute and an ordinance in Shechem.   Ex. 24:8

26 And Joshua wrote these words in the book of the law of God; and he took a large stone and set it up there under the oak that was by the sanctuary of the LORD.

27 And Joshua said to all the people, "Be-hold, [R]this stone shall be for a witness against us, for it has heard all the words of the LORD which He spoke[T]to us; thus it shall be for a witness against you, lest you deny your God."   Josh. 22:27, 34 · *with*

28 Then Joshua dismissed the people, each to his inheritance.

Joshua and Eleazar Die

29 And it came about after these things that Joshua the son of Nun, the servant of the LORD, died, being one hundred and ten years old.

30 And they buried him in the territory of his inheritance in[R]Timnath-serah, which is in the hill country of Ephraim, on the north of Mount Gaash.   Josh. 19:50

31 And[R]Israel served the LORD all the days of Joshua and all the days of the elders who [T]survived Joshua, and had known all the deeds of the LORD which He had done for Israel.   Judg. 2:6f. · *prolonged days after*

32 Now they buried the bones of Joseph, which the sons of Israel brought up from Egypt, at Shechem, in the piece of ground which Jacob had bought from the sons of Hamor the father of Shechem for one hundred[T]pieces of money; and they became the inheritance of Joseph's sons.   Heb., *qesitalr*

33 And Eleazar the son of Aaron died; and they buried him [A]at Gibeah of[R]Phinehas his son, which was given him in the hill country of Ephraim.   *on the hill* · Josh. 22:13

Jewish Feasts

Feast of	Month on Jewish Calendar	Day	Corresponding Month	References
*Passover (Unleavened Bread)	Nisan	14–21	Mar.–Apr.	Ex. 12:43—13:10; Matt. 26:17–20
*Pentecost (First Fruits or Weeks)	Sivan	6 (50 days after Passover)	May–June	Deut. 16:9–12; Acts 2:1
Trumpets, *Rosh Hashanah*	Tishri	1, 2	Sept.–Oct.	Num. 29:1–6
Day of Atonement, *Yom Kippur*	Tishri	10	Sept.–Oct.	Lev. 23:26–32; Heb. 9:7
*Tabernacles (Booths or Ingathering)	Tishri	15–22	Sept.–Oct.	Neh. 8:13–18; John 7:2
Dedication (Lights), *Hanukkah*	Chislev	25 (8 days)	Nov.–Dec.	John 10:22
Purim (Lots)	Adar	14, 15	Feb.–Mar.	Esth. 9:18–32

*The three major feasts for which all males of Israel were required to travel to the Temple in Jerusalem (Ex. 23:14–19).

THE BOOK OF

JUDGES

THE BOOK OF JUDGES

The Book of Judges stands in stark contrast to Joshua. In Joshua an obedient people conquered the land through trust in the power of God. In Judges, however, a disobedient and idolatrous people are defeated time and time again because of their rebellion against God.

In seven distinct cycles of sin to salvation, Judges shows how Israel had set aside God's law and in its place substituted "what was right in his own eyes" (21:25). The recurring result of abandonment from God's law is corruption from within and oppression from without. During the nearly four centuries spanned by this book, God raises up military champions to throw off the yoke of bondage and to restore the nation to pure worship. But all too soon the "sin cycle" begins again as the nation's spiritual temperature grows steadily colder.

The Hebrew title is *Shophetim*, meaning "judges," "rulers," "deliverers," or "saviors." *Shophet* not only carries the idea of maintaining justice and settling disputes, but it is also used to mean "liberating" and "delivering." First the judges deliver the people; then they rule and administer justice. The Septuagint used the Greek equivalent of this word, *Kritai* ("Judges"). The Latin Vulgate called it *Liber Judicum*, the "Book of Judges." This book could also appropriately be titled "The Book of Failure."

THE AUTHOR OF JUDGES

The author of Judges is anonymous, but Samuel or one of his prophetic students may have written it. Jewish tradition contained in the Talmud attributes Judges to Samuel, and certainly he was the crucial link between the period of the judges and the period of the kings.

It is clear from 18:31 and 20:27 that the book was written after the ark was removed from Shiloh (1 Sam. 4:3–11). The repeated phrase "In those days there was no king in Israel" (17:6; 18:1; 19:1; 21:25) shows that Judges was also written after the commencement of Saul's reign but before the divided kingdom. The fact that the Jebusites were dwelling in Jerusalem "to this day" (1:21) means that it was written before 1004 B.C. when David dispossessed the Jebusites (2 Sam. 5:5–9). Thus, the book was written during the

time of Samuel; and it is likely that Samuel compiled this book from oral and written source material. His prophetic ministry clearly fits the moral commentary of Judges, and the consistent style and orderly scheme of Judges point to a single compiler.

Judges 18:30 contains a phrase that poses a problem to this early date of composition: "until the day of the captivity of the land." If this refers to the 722 B.C. Assyrian captivity of Israel it could have been inserted by a later editor. It is more likely a reference to the Philistine captivity of the land during the time of the judges. This event is described as "captivity" in Psalm 78:61.

THE TIME OF JUDGES

If Judges was not written by Samuel it was at least written by one of his contemporaries between 1043 B.C. (the beginning of Saul's reign) and 1004 B.C. (David's capture of Jerusalem).

Joshua's seven-year conquest is general in nature; much of the land remains to be possessed (Josh. 13:1). There are still important Canaanite strongholds to be taken by the individual tribes. Some of the nations have been left "to test Israel" (Judg. 3:1, 4). During this time, the Egyptians maintain strong control along the coastal routes, but they are not interested in the hill country where Israel is primarily established.

The events covered in Judges range from about 1380 B.C.–1045 B.C. (c. 335 years), but the period of the judges extends another thirty years since it includes the life of Samuel (1 Sam. 1:1—25:1). Evidently, the rulerships of some of the judges overlap because not all of them ruled over the entire land. Judges describes the cycles of apostasy, oppression, and deliverance in the southern region (3:7–31), the northern region (4:1—5:31), the central region (6:1—10:5), the eastern region (10:6—12:15), and the western region (13:1—16:31). The spread of apostasy covers the whole land.

THE CHRIST OF JUDGES

Each judge is a savior and a ruler, a spiritual and political deliverer. Thus, the judges portray the role of Christ as the Savior-King of His people. The Book of Judges also illustrates the need for a righteous king.

Including First Samuel, seventeen judges

are mentioned altogether. Some are warrior-rulers (e.g., Othniel and Gideon), one is a priest (Eli), and one is a prophet (Samuel). This gives a cumulative picture of the three offices of Christ, who excelled all His predecessors in that He was the ultimate Prophet, Priest, and King.

KEYS TO JUDGES

Key Word: Cycles—The Book of Judges is written primarily on a thematic rather than a chronological basis (chs. 16—21 actually precede chs. 3—15). The author uses the accounts of the various judges to prove the utter failure of living out the closing verse of Judges: "everyone did what was right in his own eyes." To accomplish this, the author uses a five-point cycle to recount the repeated spiral of disobedience, destruction, and defeat. The five parts are: (1) sin, (2) servitude, (3) supplication, (4) salvation, and (5) silence.

Key Verses: Judges 2:20, 21; 21:25—"So the anger of the LORD burned against Israel, and He said, 'Because this nation has transgressed My covenant which I commanded their fathers, and has not listened to My voice, I also will no longer drive out before them any of the nations which Joshua left when he died' " (2:20, 21).

"In those days there was no king in Israel; everyone did what was right in his own eyes" (21:25).

Key Chapter: Judges 2—The second chapter of Judges is a miniature of the whole book as it records the transition of the godly to the ungodly generation, the format of the cycles, and the purpose of God in not destroying the Canaanites.

SURVEY OF JUDGES

Following the death of Joshua, Israel plunges into a 350-year Dark Age. After Joshua and the generation of the conquest pass on, "there arose another generation after them who did not know the LORD, nor yet the work which He had done for Israel" (2:10; see also 2:7-10; Josh. 24:31). Judges opens with a description of Israel's deterioration, continues with seven cycles of oppression and deliverance, and concludes with two illustrations of Israel's depravity.

Deterioration (1:1—3:4): Judges begins with short-lived military successes after Joshua's death, but quickly turns to the repeated failure of all the tribes to drive out their enemies. The people feel the lack of a unified central leader, but the primary reasons for their failure are a lack of faith in God and a lack of obedience to Him (2:1-3). Compromise leads to conflict and chaos. Israel does not drive out the inhabitants (1:21, 27, 29, 30); instead of removing the moral cancer spread by the inhabitants of Canaan, they contract the disease. The Canaanite gods literally become a snare to them (2:3). Judges 2:11-23 is a microcosm of the pattern found in Chapters 3—16 of Judges.

Deliverances (3:5—16:31): This section describes seven apostasies (fallings away from God), seven servitudes, and seven deliverances. Each of the seven cycles has five steps: sin, servitude, supplication, salvation, and silence. These also can be described by the words rebellion, retribution, repentance, restoration, and rest. The seven cycles connect together as a descending spiral of sin (2:19). Israel vacillates between obedience and apostasy as the people continually fail to learn from their mistakes. Apostasy grows, but the

FOCUS	DETERIORATION		DELIVERANCE							DEPRAVITY		
REFERENCE	1:1———2:1—		—3:5——4:1—	—6:1—	—10:6—	—12:8—	—13:1—	—17:1—		—19:1—	—20:1–21:25		
DIVISION	ISRAEL FAILS TO COMPLETE THE CONQUEST	GOD JUDGES ISRAEL	SOUTHERN CAMPAIGN	NORTHERN CAMPAIGN (1st)	CENTRAL CAMPAIGN	EASTERN CAMPAIGN	NORTHERN CAMPAIGN (2nd)	WESTERN CAMPAIGN	SIN OF IDOLATRY	SIN OF IMMORALITY	SIN OF CIVIL WAR	
TOPIC	CAUSES OF THE CYCLES		CURSE OF THE CYCLES						CONDITIONS DURING THE CYCLES			
	LIVING WITH THE CANAANITES		WAR WITH THE CANAANITES						LIVING LIKE THE CANAANITES			
LOCATION	CANAAN											
TIME	c. 350 YEARS											

rebellion is not continual. The times of rest and peace are longer than the times of bondage. The monotony of Israel's sins can be contrasted with the creativity of God's methods of deliverance.

The judges are military and civil leaders during this period of loose confederacy. Thirteen are mentioned in this book, and four more are found in First Samuel (Eli, Samuel, Joel, and Abijah).

Depravity (17:1—21:25): These chapters illustrate (1) religious apostasy (17 and 18) and (2) social and moral depravity (19—21) during the period of the judges. Chapters 19—21 contain one of the worst tales of degradation in the Bible. Judges closes with a key to understanding the period: "everyone did what was right in his own eyes" (21:25). The people are not doing what is wrong in their own eyes, but what is "evil in the sight of the LORD."

OUTLINE OF JUDGES

Part One: The Deterioration of Israel and Failure to Complete the Conquest of Canaan (1:1—3:4)

Part Two: The Deliverance of Israel During the Seven Cycles (3:5—16:31)

Part Three: The Depravity of Israel in Sinning Like the Canaanites (17:1—21:25)

CHAPTER 1

Failure of Judah

NOW it came about after the death of Joshua that the sons of Israel[R]inquired of the LORD, saying, "Who shall go up first for us [R]against the Canaanites, to fight against them?"   Num. 27:21 • Judg. 1:27; 2:21-23; 3:1-6

2 And the LORD said, "Judah shall go up; behold, I have given the land into his hand."

3 Then Judah said to Simeon his brother, "Come up with me into the[T]territory allotted me, that we may fight against the Canaanites; and [I]I in turn will go with you into the territory allotted you." So Simeon went with him.   *my lot • I, even I*

4 And Judah went up, and[the LORD gave the Canaanites and the Perizzites into their hands; and they [T]defeated ten thousand men at Bezek.   [Ps. 44:2; 78:55] • *smote them*

5 And they found Adoni-bezek in Bezek and fought against him and they [T]defeated the Canaanites and the Perizzites.   *smote*

6 But Adoni-bezek fled; and they pursued him and caught him and cut off his thumbs and big toes.

7 And Adoni-bezek said, "Seventy kings with their thumbs and their big toes cut off used to gather up *scraps* under my table; as I have done, so God has repaid me." So they brought him to Jerusalem and he died there.

8 Then the sons of Judah fought against [R]Jerusalem and captured it and struck it with the edge of the sword and set the city on fire.   Josh. 15:63; Judg. 1:21

9 And afterward the sons of Judah went down to fight against the Canaanites living in the hill country and in the [1]Negev and in the lowland.

10 So Judah went against the Canaanites who lived in Hebron (now the name of Hebron formerly *was* Kiriath-arba); and they struck Sheshai and Ahiman and Talmai.

11 Then [R]from there he went against the inhabitants of Debir (now the name of Debir formerly *was* Kiriath-sepher).   Josh. 15:15

12 And Caleb said, "The one who attacks Kiriath-sepher and captures it, I will even give him my daughter Achsah for a wife."

13 And[R]Othniel the son of Kenaz, Caleb's younger brother, captured it; so he gave him his daughter Achsah for a wife.   Judg. 3:9

14 Then[R]it came about when she came *to him*, that she persuaded him to ask her father for a field. Then she alighted from[T]her donkey, and Caleb said to her, "What [T]do you want?"   Josh. 15:18 • *the • for yourself*

15 And she said to him, "Give me a blessing, since you have given me the land of the [1]Negev, give me also springs of water." So Caleb gave her the upper springs and the lower springs.

16 And the [T]descendants of [R]the Kenite, Moses' father-in-law, went up from the[R]city of palms with the sons of Judah, to the wilderness of Judah which is in the south of

[R]Arad; and they went and lived with the people.   sons • Judg. 4:11 • Deut. 34:3 • Num. 21:1

17 Then Judah went with Simeon his brother, and they struck the Canaanites living in Zephath, and utterly destroyed it. So the name of the city was called Hormah.

18 And Judah took[R]Gaza with its territory and Ashkelon with its territory and Ekron with its territory.   Josh. 11:22

19 Now the LORD was with Judah, and they took possession of the hill country; but they could not drive out the inhabitants of the valley because they had iron chariots.

20 Then they gave Hebron to Caleb, as Moses had[T]promised; and he drove out from there the three sons of Anak.   *spoken*

Failure of Benjamin

21 [R]But the sons of Benjamin did not drive out the Jebusites who lived in Jerusalem; so the Jebusites have lived with the sons of Benjamin in Jerusalem to this day. Judg. 1:8

Failure of Tribes of Joseph

22 Likewise the house of Joseph went up against Bethel, and the LORD was with them.

23 And the house of Joseph spied out Bethel (now[R]the name of the city was formerly Luz).   Gen. 28:19

24 And the spies saw a man coming out of the city, and they said to him, "Please show us the entrance to the city and[R]we will treat you kindly."   Josh. 2:12

25 So he showed them the entrance to the city, and they struck the city with the edge of the sword,[R]but they let the man and all his family go free.   Josh. 6:25

26 And the man went into the land of the Hittites and built a city and named it Luz [T]which is its name to this day.   *it*

27 But Manasseh did not take possession of Beth-shean and its villages, or Taanach and its villages, or the inhabitants of Dor and its villages, or the inhabitants of Ibleam and its villages, or the inhabitants of Megiddo and its villages; so [R]the Canaanites persisted in living in that land.   Judg. 1:1

28 And it came about when Israel became strong, that they put the Canaanites to forced labor, but they did not drive them out completely.

29 Neither did Ephraim drive out the Canaanites who were living in Gezer; so the Canaanites lived in Gezer among them.

Failure of Zebulun

30 Zebulun did not drive out the inhabitants of Kitron, or the inhabitants of Nahalol; so the Canaanites lived among them and became subject to forced labor.

---

[1] I.e., South country

Failure of Asher

31 Asher did not drive out the inhabitants of Acco, or the inhabitants of Sidon, or of Ahlab, or of Achzib, or of Helbah, or of Aphik, or of Rehob.

32 So the Asherites lived among the Canaanites, the inhabitants of the land; for they did not drive them out.

Failure of Naphtali

33 Naphtali did not drive out the inhabitants of Beth-shemesh, or the inhabitants of Beth-anath, but lived among the Canaanites, the inhabitants of the land; and the inhabitants of Beth-shemesh and Beth-anath became forced labor for them.

Failure of Dan

34 Then the Amorites forced the sons of Dan into the hill country, for they did not allow them to come down to the valley;

35 yet the Amorites persisted in living in Mount Heres, in Aijalon and in Shaalbim; but when the power of the house of Joseph grew strong, they became forced labor.

36 And the border of the Amorites ran from the^Rascent of Akrabbim, from Sela and upward.   Josh. 15:3

CHAPTER 2

Angel Announces Judgment

Now^Rthe angel of the Lord came up from Gilgal to Bochim. And he said, "I^Rbrought you up out of Egypt and led you into the land which I have sworn to your fathers; and I said, 'I^Rwill never break My covenant with you,   Judg. 6:11 · Ex. 20:2 · Deut. 7:9

2 and as for you, you shall make no covenant with the inhabitants of this land; you shall tear down their altars.' But you have not obeyed Me; what is this you have done?

3"Therefore I also said, 'I^Rwill not drive them out before you; but they shall ²become ^R*as thorns* in your sides, and their gods shall be a snare to you.' "   Josh. 23:13 · Num. 33:55

4 And it came about when the angel of the Lord spoke these words to all the sons of Israel, that the people lifted up their voices and wept.

5 So they named that place ³Bochim; and there they sacrificed to the Lord.

Godly Generation Dies

6^RWhen Joshua had dismissed the people, the sons of Israel went each to his inheritance to possess the land.   Josh. 24:28-31

7 And the people served the Lord all the days of Joshua, and all the days of the elders who^Tsurvived Joshua, who had seen all the great work of the Lord which He had done for Israel.   *prolonged days after*

8 Then Joshua the son of Nun, the servant of the Lord, died at the age of one hundred and ten.

9 And they buried him in the territory of his inheritance in Timnath-heres, in the hill country of Ephraim, north of Mount Gaash.

10 And all that generation also were gathered to their fathers; and there arose another generation after them who ^Rdid not know the Lord, nor yet the work which He had done for Israel.   Ex. 5:2; 1 Sam. 2:12

Judgment of God Is Described

11 Then the sons of Israel did evil in the sight of the Lord, and ⁴served the Baals,

12 and^Rthey forsook the Lord, the God of their fathers, who had brought them out of the land of Egypt, and followed other gods from *among* the gods of the peoples who were around them, and bowed themselves down to them; thus they provoked the Lord to anger.   Deut. 31:16

13 So they forsook the Lord and ^Rserved Baal and the Ashtaroth.   Judg. 10:6

14 And the anger of the Lord burned against Israel, and He gave them into the hands of plunderers who plundered them; and He sold them into the hands of their enemies around *them,* so that they could no longer stand before their enemies.

15 Wherever they went, the hand of the Lord was against them for evil, as the Lord had spoken and as the Lord had sworn to them, so that they were severely distressed.

16^RThen the Lord raised up judges^Twho delivered them from the hands of those who plundered them.   Ps. 106:43-45 · *and they*

17 And yet they did not listen to their judges, for they played the harlot after other gods and bowed themselves down to them. They turned aside quickly from the way^Rin which their fathers had walked in obeying the commandments of the Lord; they did not do as *their fathers.*   Judg. 2:7

18 And when the Lord raised up judges for them,^Rthe Lord was with the judge and delivered them from the hand of their enemies all the days of the judge; for the Lord was ^Rmoved to pity by their groaning because of those who oppressed and afflicted them.   Josh. 1:5 · Deut. 32:36; Ps. 106:44

19 But it came about when the judge died, that they would turn back and act more corruptly than their fathers, in following other gods to serve them and bow down to them; they did not abandon their practices or their stubborn ways.

Enemy Is Left as a Test

20^RSo the anger of the Lord burned

---

² Some ancient mss. read *be adversaries, and*
³ I.e., *weepers*   ⁴ Or, *worshiped*

against Israel, and He said, "Because this nation has transgressed My covenant which I commanded their fathers, and has not listened to My voice,   Judg. 2:14
21 ᴿI also will no longer drive out before them any of the nations which Joshua left when he died,   Josh. 23:4, 5, 13
22 in order to test Israel by them, whether they will keep the way of the LORD to walk in it as their fathersᵀdid, or not."   kept
23 So the LORD allowed those nations to remain, not driving them out quickly; and He did not give them into the hand of Joshua.

CHAPTER 3

Now ᴿ these are the nations which the LORD left, to test Israel by them (that is, all who had notᵀexperienced any of the wars of Canaan;   Judg. 1:1; 2:21, 22 • known
2 only in order that the generations of the sons of Israel might be taught war,ᵀthose who had not experienced it formerly).   only
3 These nations are: the five lords of the Philistines and all the Canaanites and the Sidonians and the Hivites who lived in Mount Lebanon, from Mount Baal-hermon as far asᴬLebo-hamath.   the entrance of Hamath
4 And they were forᵀtesting Israel, to find out if they would obey the commandments of the LORD, which He had commanded their fathers through Moses.   testing by them

The Judge Othniel

5 And the sons of Israel lived among the Canaanites, the Hittites, the Amorites, the Perizzites, the Hivites, and the Jebusites;
6 and ᴿthey took their daughters for themselves as wives, and gave their own daughters to their sons, and served their gods.   Ex. 34:15, 16; Deut. 7:3, 4; Josh. 23:12
7 And the sons of Israel didᴿwhat was evil in the sight of the LORD, andᴿforgot the LORD their God, and served the Baals and the ⁵Asheroth.   Judg. 2:11 • Deut. 4:9
8 Then the anger of the LORD was kindled against Israel, so that He sold them into the hands of Cushan-rishathaim king of Mesopotamia; and the sons of Israel served Cushan-rishathaim eight years.
9 And when the sons of Israel cried to the LORD, the LORD raised up a deliverer for the sons of Israel to deliver them, Othniel the son of Kenaz, Caleb's younger brother.
10 And the Spirit of the LORD came upon him, and he judged Israel. When he went out to war, the LORD gave Cushan-rishathaim king of Mesopotamia into his hand, so that he prevailed over Cushan-rishathaim.
11 Then the land had rest forty years. And Othniel the son of Kenaz died.

The Judge Ehud

12 Now the sons of Israel againᴿdid evil in the sight of the LORD. So ᴿthe LORD strengthened Eglon the king of Moab against Israel, because they had done evil in the sight of the LORD.   Judg. 2:11 • Judg. 2:14
13 And he gathered to himself the sons of Ammon and Amalek; and he went and ᵀdefeated Israel, and they possessedᴿthe city of the palm trees.   smote • Deut. 34:3; Judg. 1:16
14 And the sons of Israel served Eglon the king of Moab eighteen years.
15 But when the sons of Israelᴿcried to the LORD, the LORD raised up a deliverer for them, Ehud the son of Gera, the Benjamite, a left-handed man. And the sons of Israel sent tribute by ᵀhim to Eglon the king of Moab.   Ps. 78:34 • his hand
16 And Ehud made himself a sword which had two edges, a cubit in length; and he bound it on his right thigh under his cloak.
17 And he presented the tribute to Eglon king of Moab. Now Eglon was a very fat man.
18 And it came about when he had finished presenting the tribute, that he sent away the people who had carried the tribute.
19 But he himself turned back from the idols which were at Gilgal, and said, "I have a secret message for you, O king." And he said, "Keep silence." And all who attended him left him.
20 And Ehud came to him while he was sitting alone in his cool roof chamber. And Ehud said, "I have a message from God for you." And he arose from his seat.
21 And Ehud stretched out his left hand, took the sword from his right thigh and thrust it into his belly.
22 The handle also went in after the blade, and the fat closed over the blade, for he did not draw the sword out of his belly; and the refuse came out.
23 Then Ehud went out into the vestibule and shut the doors of the roof chamber behind him, and locked them.
24 When he had gone out, his servants came and looked, and behold, the doors of the roof chamber were locked; and they said, "Heᴿ is only ᵀrelieving himself in the cool room."   1 Sam. 24:3 • covering his feet
25 And they waited until they became anxious; but behold, he did not open the doors of the roof chamber. Therefore they took the key and opened them, and behold, their master had fallen to the floor dead.
26 Now Ehud escaped while they were delaying, and he passed by the idols and escaped to Seirah.
27 And it came about when he had arrived, thatᴿhe blew the trumpet in the hill country of Ephraim; and the sons of Israel

⁵ I.e., wooden symbol of a female deity

went down with him from the hill country, and he *was* in front of them. Judg. 6:34

28 And he said to them, "Pursue *them,* for the LORD has given your enemies the Moabites into your hands." So they went down after him and seized[R]the fords of the Jordan opposite Moab, and did not allow anyone to cross. Judg. 7:24; 12:5

29 And they struck down at that time about ten thousand Moabites, all robust and valiant men; and no one escaped.

30 So Moab was subdued that day under the hand of Israel. And the land was undisturbed for eighty years.

The Judge Shamgar

31 And after him came[R]Shamgar the son of Anath, who struck down six hundred Philistines with an oxgoad; and he also saved Israel. Judg. 5:6

CHAPTER 4

Deborah and Barak Are Called

THEN the sons of Israel again did evil in the sight of the LORD, after Ehud died.

2 And the LORD sold them into the hand of Jabin king of Canaan, who reigned in Hazor; and the commander of his army was Sisera, who lived in Harosheth-hagoyim.

3 And the sons of Israel cried to the LORD; for he had nine hundred[R]iron chariots, and he oppressed the sons of Israel severely for twenty years. Judg. 1:19

4 Now Deborah, a prophetess, the wife of Lappidoth, was judging Israel at that time.

5 And she used to[A]sit under the palm tree of Deborah between Ramah and Bethel in the hill country of Ephraim; and the sons of Israel came up to her for judgment. *live*

6 Now she sent and summoned [R]Barak the son of Abinoam from Kedesh-naphtali, and said to him, "Behold, the LORD, the God of Israel, has commanded, 'Go and march to Mount Tabor, and take with you ten thousand men from the sons of Naphtali and from the sons of Zebulun. Heb. 11:32

7 'And I will draw out to you Sisera, the commander of Jabin's army, with his chariots and his many *troops* to the river Kishon; and I will give him into your hand.' "

8 Then Barak said to her, "If you will go with me, then I will go; but if you will not go with me, I will not go."

9 And she said, "I will surely go with you; nevertheless, the honor shall not be yours on the journey that you are about to take,[R]for the LORD will sell Sisera into the hands of a woman." Then Deborah arose and went with Barak to Kedesh. Judg. 4:21

10 And Barak called Zebulun and Naphtali together to Kedesh, and ten thousand men went up[T]with[R]him; Deborah also went up with him. *at his feet* · Judg. 4:14; 5:15

11 Now Heber the Kenite had separated himself from the Kenites, from the sons of Hobab the father-in-law of Moses, and had pitched his tent as far away as the [A]oak in Zaanannim, which is near Kedesh. *terebinth*

Canaanites Are Defeated

12 Then they told Sisera that Barak the son of Abinoam had gone up to Mount Tabor.

13 And Sisera called together all his chariots,[R]nine hundred iron chariots, and all the people who *were* with him, from Harosheth-hagoyim to the river Kishon. Judg. 4:3

14 And Deborah said to Barak, "Arise! For this is the day in which the LORD has given Sisera into your hands; [6]behold,[R]the LORD has gone out before you." So Barak went down from Mount Tabor with ten thousand men following him. 2 Sam. 5:24

15 And the LORD routed Sisera and all *his* chariots and all *his* army, with the edge of the sword before Barak; and Sisera alighted from *his* chariot and fled away on foot.

16 But Barak pursued the chariots and the army as far as Harosheth-hagoyim, and all the army of Sisera fell by the edge of the sword;[R]not even one was left. Ex. 14:28

17 Now Sisera fled away on foot to the tent of Jael the wife of Heber the Kenite, for *there was* peace between Jabin the king of Hazor and the house of Heber the Kenite.

18 And Jael went out to meet Sisera, and said to him, "Turn aside, my master, turn aside to me! Do not be afraid." And he turned aside to her into the tent, and she covered him with a[A]rug. *blanket*

19 [R]And he said to her, "Please give me a little water to drink, for I am thirsty." So she opened a [7]bottle of milk and gave him a drink; then she covered him. Judg. 5:24-27

20 And he said to her, "Stand in the doorway of the tent, and it shall be if anyone comes and inquires of you, and says, 'Is there anyone here?' that you shall say, 'No.' "

21 But Jael, Heber's wife,[R]took a tent peg and[T]seized a hammer in her hand, and went secretly to him and drove the peg into his temple, and it went through into the ground; for he was sound asleep and exhausted. So he died. Judg. 5:26 · *placed*

22 And behold, as Barak pursued Sisera, Jael came out to meet him and said to him, "Come, and I will show you the man whom you are seeking." And he entered[T]with her, and behold Sisera was lying dead with the tent peg in his temple. *to*

23 So God subdued on that day Jabin the king of Canaan before the sons of Israel.

24 And the hand of the sons of Israel

[6] Or, *has not the LORD gone . . . ?* [7] I.e., skin container

pressed heavier and heavier upon Jabin the king of Canaan, until they had 'destroyed Jabin the king of Canaan.   *cut off*

CHAPTER 5

The Song of Deborah and Barak

T HEN^R Deborah and Barak the son of Abinoam sang on that day, saying,   Ex. 15:1

2 "That 'the leaders led in Israel,
That the people volunteered,
Bless the LORD!   *locks hung loose in*

3 "Hear, O kings; give ear, O rulers!
^R I—to the LORD, I will sing,
I will sing praise to the LORD, the God
of Israel.   Ps. 27:6

4 "LORD^R when Thou didst go out from
Seir,   Deut. 33:2; Ps. 68:7
When Thou didst march from the
field of Edom,
^R The earth quaked, the heavens also
dripped,   Ps. 68:8, 9
Even the clouds dripped water.

5 "The^R mountains 'quaked at the presence of the LORD,   Ex. 19:18 · *flowed*
^R This Sinai, at the presence of the
LORD, the God of Israel.   Ps. 68:8

6 "In the days of ^R Shamgar the son of
Anath,   Judg. 3:31
In the days of 'Jael, the highways 'were
deserted,   Judg. 4:17 · *had ceased*
And travelers 'went by 'roundabout
ways.   *walked · twisted*

7 "The peasantry ceased, they ceased in
Israel,
Until I, Deborah, arose,
Until I arose, a mother in Israel.

8 "New^R gods were chosen;   Deut. 32:17
Then war *was* in the gates.
Not a shield or a spear was seen
Among forty thousand in Israel.

9 "My heart *goes out* to ^R the commanders
of Israel,
The volunteers among the people;
Bless the LORD!   Judg. 5:2

10 "You^R who ride on ^A white donkeys,
You who sit on *rich* carpets,
And you who travel on the road—
^A sing!   Judg. 10:4 · *tawny · declare it*

11 "At the sound of those who divide
flocks among ^R the watering places,
There they shall recount the righteous
deeds of the LORD,   Gen. 24:11; 29:2, 3
The righteous deeds for His ^A peasantry
in Israel.   *rural dwellers*
Then the people of the LORD went
down ^R to the gates.   Judg. 5:8

12 "Awake, awake, Deborah;   Ps. 57:8
Awake, awake, ^A sing a song!   *utter*
Arise, Barak, and 'take away your captives, O son of Abinoam.   Eph. 4:8

13 "Then survivors came down to the
nobles;

The people of the LORD came down to
me as warriors.

14 "From Ephraim those whose root is ^R in
Amalek *came down*,   Judg. 12:15
Following you, Benjamin, with your
peoples;
From Machir commanders came
down,
And from Zebulun those who wield
the staff of 'office.   *the scribe*

15 "And the princes of Issachar *were* with
Deborah;
As *was* Issachar, so *was* Barak;
Into the valley they rushed ^R at his
'heels;   Judg. 4:10 · *feet*
Among the divisions of Reuben
There were great resolves of heart.

16 "Why did you sit among ^R the ^8 sheepfolds,   Num. 32:1, 2, 24, 36
To hear the piping for the flocks?
Among the divisions of Reuben
There were great searchings of heart.

17 "Gilead 'remained across the Jordan;
And why did Dan stay in ships?
Asher sat at the seashore,
And ^A remained by its landings.   *dwelt*

18 "Zebulun^R *was* a people who despised
their lives *even* to death,
And Naphtali also, on the high places
of the field.   Judg. 4:6, 10

19 "The^R kings came *and* fought;
Then fought the kings of Canaan
^R At Taanach near the waters of Megiddo;   Josh. 11:1-5 · Judg. 1:27
They took no plunder in silver.

20 "The^R stars fought from heaven,
From their courses they fought
against Sisera.   Josh. 10:12-14

21 "The torrent of Kishon swept them
away,
The ancient torrent, the torrent Kishon.
O my soul, march on with strength.

22 "Then the horses' hoofs beat
From the dashing, the dashing of his
'valiant steeds.   *mighty ones*

23 'Curse Meroz,' said the angel of the
LORD,
'Utterly curse its inhabitants;
^R Because they did not come to the help
of the LORD,
To the help of the LORD against the
warriors.'   Judg. 5:13

24 "Most^R blessed of women is Jael,
The wife of Heber the Kenite;
Most blessed is she of women in the
tent.   Judg. 4:19-21

25 "He asked for water *and* she gave him
milk;
In a magnificent bowl she brought
him curds.

26 "She reached out her hand for the tent
peg,

^8 Or, *saddlebags*

And her right hand for the workmen's
hammer.
Then she struck Sisera, she smashed
his head;
And she shattered and pierced his
temple.

27 "Between her feet he bowed, he fell, he
lay;
Between her feet he bowed, he fell;
Where he bowed, there he fell dead.

28 "Out of the window she looked and lamented,
The mother of Sisera through the^Alat-
tice,
'Why does his chariot delay in coming?
Why do the^Thoofbeats of his chariots
tarry?'   *window • steps*

29 "Her wise princesses would answer
her,
Indeed she repeats her words to herself,

30 'Are^R they not finding, are they not di-
viding the spoil?   Ex. 15:9
A maiden, two maidens for every
warrior;
To Sisera a spoil of dyed work,
A spoil of dyed work embroidered,
Dyed work of double embroidery on
the neck of the spoiler?'

31 "Thus^R let all Thine enemies perish, O
LORD;
^RBut let those who love Him be like the
rising of the sun in its might."

And the land was undisturbed for forty
years.   Ps. 68:2; 92:9 • Ps. 19:4-6; 89:36, 37

CHAPTER 6
Israel Sins

THEN the sons of Israel did what was evil
in the sight of the LORD; and the LORD gave
them into the hands of Midian seven years.

2 And the ^Tpower of Midian prevailed
against Israel. Because of Midian the sons of
Israel made for themselves^Rthe dens which
were in the mountains and the caves and
the strongholds.   *hand* • 1 Sam. 13:6; Heb. 11:38

3 For it was when Israel had sown, that
the Midianites would come up with the
Amalekites and the sons of the east and ^Tgo
against them.   *go up*

4 So they would camp against them and
^Rdestroy the produce of the earth as far as
Gaza, and leave no sustenance in Israel as
well as no sheep, ox, or donkey.   Lev. 26:16

5 For they would come up with their
livestock and their tents, they would come
in like locusts for number, both they and
their camels were innumerable; and they
came into the land to devastate it.

6 So Israel was brought ^Rvery low because of Midian, and the sons of Israel cried
to the LORD.   Deut. 28:43

9 I.e., Approx. one bushel

7 Now it came about when the sons of
Israel cried to the LORD on account of Midian,

8 that the LORD sent a prophet to the
sons of Israel, and he said to them, "Thus
says the LORD, the God of Israel, 'It was I
who brought you up from Egypt, and
brought you out from the house of slavery.

9 'And I delivered you from the hands of
the Egyptians and from the hands of all
your oppressors, and dispossessed them before you and gave you their land,

10 and I said to you, "I am the LORD your
God; you shall not fear the gods of the Amorites in whose land you live. But you have
not^Tobeyed Me."'"   *listened to My voice*

Gideon Called

11 Then the angel of the LORD came and
sat under the oak that was in Ophrah, which
belonged to Joash the Abiezrite as his son
Gideon was beating out wheat in the wine
press in order to save *it* from the Midianites.

12 And the angel of the LORD appeared to
him and said to him, "The LORD is with you,
O valiant warrior."

13 Then Gideon said to him, "O my lord, if
the LORD is with us, why then has all this
happened to us? And where are all His miracles which our fathers told us about, saying, 'Did not the LORD bring us up from
Egypt?' But now the LORD has abandoned us
and given us into the hand of Midian."

14 And the LORD^Alooked at him and said,
"Go^R in this your strength and deliver Israel
from the hand of Midian. Have I not sent
you?"   *turned toward* • Heb. 11:32-34

15 And he said to Him, "O Lord,^Thow shall
I deliver Israel? Behold, my family is the
least in^RManasseh, and I am the youngest in
my father's house."   *with what* • Judg. 6:11

16 ^RBut the LORD said to him, "Surely I will
be with you, and you shall ^Tdefeat Midian as
one man."   Ex. 3:12; Josh. 1:5 • *smite*

17 So Gideon said to Him, "If now I have
found favor in Thy sight, then show me a
sign that it is Thou who speakest with me.

18 "Please do not depart from here, until I
come *back* to Thee, and bring out my offering and lay it before Thee." And He said, "I
will remain until you return."

19 Then Gideon went in and prepared a
kid and unleavened bread from an 9ephah of
flour; he put the meat in a basket and the
broth in a pot, and brought *them* out to him
under the^Aoak, and presented *them*. *terebinth*

20 And the angel of God said to him,
"Take the meat and the unleavened bread
and lay them on this rock, and pour out the
broth." And he did so.

21 Then the angel of the LORD put out the
end of the staff that was in his hand and
touched the meat and the unleavened bread;
and^Rfire sprang up from the rock and consumed the meat and the unleavened bread.

Then the angel of the Lord[A]vanished from his sight.   Lev. 9:24 • *departed*

22 [R]When Gideon saw that he was the angel of the Lord,[T]he said, "Alas, O Lord God! For now I have seen the angel of the Lord face to face."   Gen. 32:30; Ex. 33:20 • *Gideon*

23 And the Lord said to him, "Peace to you, do not fear; you shall not die."

24 Then Gideon built an altar there to the Lord and named it[T]The Lord is Peace. To this day it is still[R]in Ophrah of the Abiezrites.   Heb., *Yahweh-shalom* • Judg. 8:32

25 Now the same night it came about that the Lord said to him, "Take your father's bull[A]and a second bull seven years old, and pull down the altar of Baal which belongs to your father, and cut down the [10]Asherah[R] that is beside it;   *even* • Ex. 34:13

26 and build an altar to the Lord your God on the top of this stronghold in an orderly manner, and take a second bull and offer a burnt offering with the wood of the Asherah which you shall cut down."

27 Then Gideon took ten men of his servants and did as the Lord had spoken to him; and it came about, because he was too afraid of his father's household and the men of the city to do it by day, that he did it by night.

28 When the men of the city arose early in the morning, behold, the altar of Baal was torn down, and the Asherah which was beside it was cut down, and the second bull was offered on the altar which had been built.

29 And they said to one another, "Who did this thing?" And when they searched about and inquired, they said, "Gideon the son of Joash did this thing."

30 Then the men of the city said to Joash, "Bring out your son, that he may die, for he has torn down the altar of Baal, and indeed, he has cut down the Asherah which was beside it."

31 But Joash said to all who stood against him, "Will you contend for Baal, or will you deliver him? Whoever will [A]plead for him shall be put to death by morning. If he is a god, let him contend for himself, because someone has torn down his altar."   *contend*

32 Therefore on that day he named him [R]Jerubbaal, that is to say, "Let Baal contend against him," because he had torn down his altar.   Judg. 7:1

33 Then all the Midianites and the Amalekites and the sons of the east assembled themselves; and they crossed over and camped in[R]the valley of Jezreel.   Josh. 17:16

34 So the Spirit of the Lord came upon Gideon; and he blew a trumpet, and the Abiezrites were called together to follow him.

35 And he sent messengers throughout Manasseh, and they also were called together to follow him; and he sent messengers to Asher,[R]Zebulun, and Naphtali, and they came up to meet them.   Judg. 4:6; 5:18

36 Then Gideon said to God, "If[R]Thou wilt deliver Israel[T]through me, as Thou hast spoken,   Judg. 6:14, 16, 17 • *by my hand*

37 behold, I will put a fleece of wool on the threshing floor. If there is dew on the fleece only, and it is dry on all the ground, then I will know that Thou wilt deliver Israel through me, as Thou hast spoken."

38 And it was so. When he arose early the next morning and squeezed the fleece, he drained the dew from the fleece, a bowl full of water.

39 Then Gideon said to God, "Do[R] not let Thine anger burn against me that I may speak once more; please let me make a test once more with the fleece, let it now be dry only on the fleece, and let there be dew on all the ground."   Gen. 18:32

40 And God did so that night; for it was dry only on the fleece, and dew was on all the ground.

CHAPTER 7

Midianites Defeated

THEN Jerubbaal (that is, Gideon) and all the people who were with him, rose early and camped beside the spring of Harod; and the camp of Midian was on the north side of [T]them by the hill of Moreh in the valley.   *him*

2 And the Lord said to Gideon, "The people who are with you are too many for Me to give Midian into their hands, lest Israel become boastful, saying, 'My own power has delivered me.'

3 "Now therefore [A]come, proclaim in the hearing of the people, saying, 'Whoever is afraid and trembling, let him return and depart from Mount Gilead.' " So 22,000 people returned, but 10,000 remained.   *please*

4 [R]Then the Lord said to Gideon, "The people are still too many; bring them down to the water and I will test them for you there. Therefore it shall be that he of whom I say to you, 'This one shall go with you,' he shall go with you; but everyone of whom I say to you, 'This one shall not go with you,' he shall not go."   1 Sam. 14:6

5 So he brought the people down to the water. And the Lord said to Gideon, "You shall separate everyone who laps the water with his tongue, as a dog laps, as well as everyone who kneels to drink."

6 Now the number of those who lapped, putting their hand to their mouth, was 300 men; but all the rest of the people kneeled to drink water.

7 And the Lord said to Gideon, "I will deliver you[R]with the 300 men who lapped and will give the Midianites into your hands; so let all the *other* people go, each man to his[T]home."   1 Sam. 14:6 • *place*

8 So[T]the 300 men took the people's provi-

---

[10] I.e., wooden symbol of a female deity

sions and their trumpets into their hands. And [T]Gideon sent all the *other* men of Israel, each to his tent, but retained the 300 men; and the camp of Midian was below him in the valley.   *they • he*

9 Now the same night it came about that the LORD said to him, "Arise, go down against the camp, [R]for I have given it into your hands.   Josh. 2:24; 10:8; 11:6

10 "But if you are afraid to go down, go with Purah your servant down to the camp,

11 and you will hear what they say; and [R]afterward your hands will be strengthened that you may go down against the camp." So he went with Purah his servant down to the [T]outposts of the army that was in the camp.   Judg. 7:15 • *extremity of the battle array*

12 Now the Midianites and the Amalekites and all the sons of the east were lying in the valley [R]as numerous as locusts; and their camels were without number, as numerous as the sand on the seashore.   Judg. 6:5; 8:10

13 When Gideon came, behold, a man was relating a dream to his friend. And he said, "Behold, I [T]had a dream; [T]a loaf of barley bread was tumbling into the camp of Midian, and it came to the tent and struck it so that it fell, and turned it upside down so that the tent lay flat."   *dreamed • and behold, a loaf*

14 And his friend answered and said, "This is nothing less than the sword of Gideon the son of Joash, a man of Israel; God has given Midian and all the camp [R]into his hand."   Josh. 2:9

15 And it came about when Gideon heard the account of the dream and its interpretation, that he bowed in worship. He returned to the camp of Israel and said, "Arise, for the LORD has given the camp of Midian into your hands."

16 [T]And he divided the 300 men into three [T]companies, and he put trumpets and empty pitchers into the hands of all of them, with torches inside the pitchers.   *heads*

17 And he said to them, "Look at me, and do likewise. And behold, when I come to the outskirts of the camp, do as I do.

18 "When I and all who are with me blow the trumpet, then you also blow the trumpets all around the camp, and say, 'For the LORD and for Gideon.' "

19 So Gideon and the hundred men who were with him came to the outskirts of the camp at the beginning of the middle watch, when they had just posted the watch; and they blew the trumpets and smashed the pitchers that were in their hands.

20 When the three [T]companies blew the trumpets and broke the pitchers, they held the torches in their left hands and the trumpets in their right hands for blowing, and cried, "A sword for the LORD and for Gideon!"   *heads*

21 And each stood in his place around the camp; and [R]all the [11]army ran, crying out as they fled.   2 Kin. 7:7

22 And when they blew 300 trumpets, the [R]LORD set the sword of one against another even throughout the whole [A]army; and the [A]army fled as far as Beth-shittah toward Zererah, as far as the edge of [A]Abel-meholah, by Tabbath.   1 Sam. 14:20 • *camp* • 1 Kin. 4:12

23 And the men of Israel were summoned from [R]Naphtali and Asher and all Manasseh, and they pursued Midian.   Judg. 6:35

24 And Gideon sent messengers throughout all the hill country of Ephraim, saying, "Come down [T]against Midian and take the waters before them, as far as Beth-barah and the Jordan." So all the men of Ephraim were summoned, and they took the waters as far as Beth-barah and the Jordan. *to meet*

25 And they captured the two leaders of Midian, [R]Oreb and Zeeb, and they killed Oreb at the rock of Oreb, and they killed Zeeb at the wine press of Zeeb, while they pursued Midian; and they brought the heads of Oreb and Zeeb to Gideon [R]from across the Jordan.   Ps. 83:11; Is. 10:26 • Judg. 8:4

CHAPTER 8

THEN the men of Ephraim said to him, "What [A]is this thing you have done to us, not calling us when you went to fight against Midian?" And they contended with him vigorously.   Judg. 12:1

2 But he said to them, "What have I done now in comparison with you? Is not the gleaning *of the grapes* of Ephraim better than the vintage of Abiezer?

3 "God has given the leaders of Midian, Oreb and Zeeb into your hands; and what was I able to do in comparison with you?" Then their [A]anger toward him subsided when he said [T]that.   *spirit • this thing*

4 Then Gideon and the 300 men who were with him came [R]to the Jordan *and* crossed over, weary yet pursuing. Judg. 7:25

5 And he said to the men of [R]Succoth, "Please give loaves of bread to the people who are following me, for they are weary, and I am pursuing Zebah and Zalmunna, the kings of Midian."   Gen. 33:17

6 And the leaders of Succoth said, "Are [T] the hands of Zebah and Zalmunna already in your hands, that we should give bread to your army?"   *Is the palm*

7 And Gideon said, "All [T]right, [R]when the LORD has given Zebah and Zalmunna into my hand, then I will [A]thrash your [T]bodies with the thorns of the wilderness and with briers."   *For thus* • Judg. 7:15 • *trample • flesh*

8 And he went up from there to [R]Penuel, and spoke similarly to them; and the men of Penuel answered him just as the men of Succoth had answered.   Gen. 32:31

9 So he spoke also to the men of Penuel, saying, "When I return safely, [R]I will tear down this tower."   Judg. 8:17

10 Now Zebah and Zalmunna were in Karkor, and their armies with them, about 15,000 men, all who were left of the entire army of the sons of the east; for the fallen were 120,000 ᵀswordsmen.   *men who drew sword*

11 And Gideon went up by the way of those who lived in tents on the east of Nobah and Jogbehah, and ᵀattacked the camp, when the camp was unsuspecting.   *smote*

12 When Zebah and Zalmunna fled, he pursued them and captured the two kings of Midian, Zebah and Zalmunna, and routed the whole^army.   *camp*

13 Then Gideon the son of Joash returned from the battle by the ascent of Heres.

14 And he captured a youthᵀfrom Succoth and questioned him. Then *the youth* wrote down for him the princes of Succoth and its elders, seventy-seven men.   *of the men of*

15 And he came to the men of Succoth and said, "Behold Zebah and Zalmunna, concerning whom you taunted me, saying, 'Are the hands of Zebah and Zalmunna already in your hand, that we should give bread to your men who are weary?' "

16 And he took the elders of the city, and thorns of the wilderness and briers, and he disciplined the men of Succoth with them.

17 ᴿAnd he tore down the tower of Penuel and killed the men of the city.   Judg. 8:9

18 Then he said to Zebah and Zalmunna, "What kind of men *were* they whom you killed at Tabor?" And they said, "They were like you, each one ᵀresembling the son of a king."   *like the form of the sons*

19 And he said, "They *were* my brothers, the sons of my mother. *As* the LORD lives, if only you had let them live, I would not kill you."

20 So he said to Jether his first-born, "Rise, kill them." But the youth did not draw his sword, for he was afraid, because he was still a youth.

21 Then Zebah and Zalmunna said, "Rise up yourself, and fall on us; for as the man, so is his strength." ᴿSo Gideon arose and killed Zebah and Zalmunna, and ᴿtook the crescent ornaments which were on their camels' necks.   Ps. 83:11 · Judg. 8:26

Gideon Judges

22 Then the men of Israel said to Gideon, "Rule over us, both you and your son, also your son's son, for you have delivered us from the hand of Midian."

23 But Gideon said to them, "I will not rule over you, nor shall my son rule over you; ᴿthe LORD shall rule over you." Ps. 10:16

24 Yet Gideon said to them, "I would request of you, that each of you give me an earring from his spoil." (For they had gold earrings, because they were Ishmaelites.)

25 And they said, "We will surely give *them*." So they spread out a garment, and every one of them threw an earring there from his spoil.

26 And the weight of the gold earrings that he requested was 1,700 *shekels* of gold, besides the crescent ornaments and the pendants and the purple robes which *were* on the kings of Midian, and besides the neck bands that *were* on their camels' necks.

27 And Gideon made it into an ephod, and placed it in his city, Ophrah, and all Israel played the harlot with it there, so that it became a snare to Gideon and his household.

28 So Midian was subdued before the sons of Israel, and they did not lift up their heads anymore. And the land was undisturbed for forty years in the days of Gideon.

29 Then ᴿJerubbaal the son of Joash went and lived in his own house.   Judg. 7:1

30 Now Gideon had ᴿseventy sons who ᵀwere his direct descendants, for he had many wives.   Judg. 9:2, 5 · *came from his loins*

31 And his concubine who was in Shechem also bore him a son, and he ᵀnamed him Abimelech.   *appointed his name*

32 And Gideon the son of Joash died at a ripe old age and was buried in the tomb of his father Joash, in Ophrah of the Abiezrites.

Confusion After Gideon Dies

33 Then it came about, as soon as Gideon was dead, ᴿthat the sons of Israel again played the harlot with the Baals, and made Baal-berith their god.   Judg. 2:11, 12

34 Thus the sons of Israelᴿdid not remember the LORD their God, who had delivered them from the hands of all their enemies on every side;   Deut. 4:9; Judg. 3:7

35 ᴿnor did they show kindness to the household of Jerubbaal (*that is*, Gideon), in accord with all the good that he had done to Israel.   Judg. 9:16-18

CHAPTER 9

Deception of Abimelech

AND Abimelech the son of Jerubbaal went to Shechem to his mother's relatives, and spoke to them and to the whole clan of the household of his mother's father, saying,

2"Speak, now, in the hearing of all the leaders of Shechem, 'Which is better for you, thatᴿseventy men, all the sons of Jerubbaal, rule over you, or that one man rule over you?' Also, remember that I amᴿyour bone and your flesh."   Judg. 8:30 · Gen. 29:14

3 And his mother's relatives spoke all these words on his behalf in the hearing of all the leaders of Shechem; and ᵀthey were inclined to follow Abimelech, for they said, "He is our relative."   *their hearts inclined after*

4 And they gave him seventy *pieces* of silver from the house of Baal-berith with which Abimelech hired worthless and reckless fellows, and they followed him.

5 Then he went to his father's house at Ophrah, and[R]killed his brothers the sons of Jerubbaal, seventy men, on one stone. But Jotham the youngest son of Jerubbaal was left, for he hid himself.   Judg. 8:30; 9:2, 18

6 And all the men of Shechem and all [12]Beth-millo assembled together, and they went and made Abimelech king, by the oak of the pillar which was in Shechem.

Revelation of Jotham

7 Now when they told Jotham, he went and stood on the top of[R]Mount Gerizim, and lifted his voice and called out. Thus he said to them, "Listen to me, O men of Shechem, that God may listen to you.   Deut. 11:29, 30

8"Once the trees went forth to anoint a king over them, and they said to the olive tree, 'Reign over us!'

9"But the olive tree said to them, 'Shall I leave my fatness with which God and men are honored, and go to wave over the trees?'

10"Then the trees said to the fig tree, 'You come, reign over us!'

11"But the fig tree said to them, 'Shall I leave my sweetness and my good[A]fruit, and go to wave over the trees?'   produce

12"Then the trees said to the vine, 'You come, reign over us!'

13"But the vine said to them, 'Shall I leave my new wine, which cheers God and men, and go to wave over the trees?'

14"Finally all the trees said to the bramble, 'You come, reign over us!'

15"And the bramble said to the trees, 'If in truth you are anointing me as king over you, come and take refuge in my shade; but if not, may fire come out from the bramble and consume the cedars of Lebanon.'

16"Now therefore, if you have dealt in [A]truth and integrity in making Abimelech king, and if you have dealt well with Jerubbaal and his house, and[T]have dealt with him as he deserved—   sincerity • if you have

17 for my father fought for you and[T]risked his life and delivered you from the hand of Midian;   cast his soul in front

18 but you have risen against my father's house today and have killed[R]his sons, seventy men, on one stone, and have made Abimelech, the son of his maidservant, king over the men of Shechem, because he is your[T]relative—   Judg. 8:30; 9:2, 5 • brother

19 if then you have dealt in[T]truth and integrity with Jerubbaal and his house this day, rejoice in Abimelech, and let him also rejoice in you.   sincerity

20"But if not, let fire come out from Abimelech and consume the men of Shechem and [A]Beth-millo; and let fire come out from the men of Shechem and from[A]Beth-millo, and consume Abimelech."   the house of Millo

21 Then Jotham escaped and fled, and

went to Beer and remained there because of Abimelech his brother.

Destruction of Shechem

22 Now Abimelech ruled over Israel three years.

23[R]Then God sent an evil spirit between Abimelech and the men of Shechem; and the men of Shechem [R]dealt treacherously with Abimelech,   1 Sam. 16:14 • [Is. 33:1]

24 in order that the violence[T]done to the seventy sons of Jerubbaal might come, and [R]their blood might be laid on Abimelech their brother, who killed them, and on the men of Shechem, who strengthened his hands to kill his brothers.   of the seventy • Num. 35:33

25 And the men of Shechem set[T]men in ambush against him on the tops of the mountains, and they robbed all who might pass by them along the road; and it was told to Abimelech.   liers-in-wait for

26 Now Gaal the son of Ebed came with his[T]relatives, and crossed over into Shechem; and the men of Shechem put their trust in him.   brothers

27 And they went out into the field and gathered the grapes of their vineyards and trod them, and held a[T]festival; and they went into the house of their god, and ate and drank and cursed Abimelech.   rejoicing

28 Then Gaal the son of Ebed said, "Who is Abimelech, and who is Shechem, that we should serve him? Is he not the son of Jerubbaal, and is Zebul not his[T]lieutenant? Serve the men of Hamor the father of Shechem; but why should we serve him?   overseer

29"Would, therefore, that this people were under my authority! Then I would remove Abimelech." And he said to Abimelech, "Increase your army, and come out."

30 And when Zebul the ruler of the city heard the words of Gaal the son of Ebed, his anger burned.

31 And he sent messengers to Abimelech deceitfully, saying, "Behold, Gaal the son of Ebed and his[T]relatives have come to Shechem; and behold, they are[T]stirring up the city against you.   brothers • besieging

32"Now therefore, arise by night, you and the people who are with you, and lie in wait in the field.

33"And it shall come about in the morning, as soon as the sun is up, that you shall rise early and rush upon the city; and behold, when he and the people who are with him come out against you, you shall do to them[T]whatever you can."   as your hand can find

34 So Abimelech and all the people who were with him arose by night and lay in wait against Shechem in four[T]companies.   heads

35 Now Gaal the son of Ebed went out and stood in the entrance of the city gate; and Abimelech and the people who were with him arose from the ambush.

36 And when Gaal saw the people, he said to Zebul, "Look,[T] people are coming down

[12] Or, the house of Millo

from the tops of the mountains." But Zebul said to him, "You are seeing the shadow of the mountains as *if they were* men." *Behold*

37 And Gaal spoke again and said, "Behold, people are coming down from the highest part of the land, and one company comes by the way of the diviners' oak."

38 Then Zebul said to him, "Where is your ᵀboasting now with which you said, 'Who is Abimelech that we should serve him?' Is this not the people whom you despised? Go out now and fight with them!"   *mouth*

39 So Gaal went out before the leaders of Shechem and fought with Abimelech.

40 And Abimelech chased him, and he fled before him; and many fell wounded up to the entrance of the gate.

41 Then Abimelech remained at Arumah, but Zebul drove out Gaal and his relatives so that they could not remain in Shechem.

42 Now it came about the next day, that the people went out to the field, and it was told to Abimelech.

43 So he tookᵀhis people and divided them into three ᵀcompanies, and lay in wait in the field; when he looked and ᵀsaw the people coming out from the city, he arose against them and slew them.   *the • heads • behold*

44 Then Abimelech and the company who was with him dashed forward and stood in the entrance of the city gate; the other two ᵀcompanies then dashed against all who *were* in the field and slew them.   *heads*

45 And Abimelech fought against the city all that day, and he captured the city and killed the people who *were* in it; then he razed the city and sowed it with salt.

46 When all the leaders of the tower of Shechem heard of it, they entered the inner chamber of theᵀtemple of El-berith.   *house*

47 And it was told Abimelech that all the leaders of the tower of Shechem were gathered together.

48 So Abimelech went up to Mount ᴿZalmon, he and all the people who *were* with him; and Abimelech tookᵀan axe in his hand and cut down a branch from the trees, and lifted it and laid *it* on his shoulder. Then he said to the people who *were* with him, "What you have seen me do, hurry *and* do ᵀlikewise."   *Ps. 68:14 • the axes • like me*

49 And all the people also cut down each one his branch and followed Abimelech, and put *them* on the inner chamber and set the inner chamber on fire over those *inside,* so that all the men of the tower of Shechem also died, about a thousand men and women.

Death of Abimelech

50 Then Abimelech went to Thebez, and he camped against Thebez and captured it.

51 But there was a strong tower in the center of the city, and all the men and women with all the leaders of the city fled there and shut themselves in; and they went up on the roof of the tower.

52 So Abimelech came to the tower and fought against it, and approached the entrance of the tower to burn it with fire.

53 But ᴿa certain woman threw an upper millstone on Abimelech's head, crushing his skull.   *2 Sam. 11:21*

54 Then ᴿhe called quickly to the young man, his armor bearer, and said to him, "Draw your sword and kill me, lest it be said of me, 'A woman slew him.' " So ᵀthe young man pierced him through, and he died.   *1 Sam. 31:4 • his*

55 And when the men of Israel saw that Abimelech was dead, each departed to his ᵀhome.   *place*

56 Thus ᴿGod repaid the wickedness of Abimelech, which he had done to his father, in killing his seventy brothers.   *Gen. 9:5, 6*

57 Also God returned all the wickedness of the men of Shechem on their heads, and the curse of Jotham the son of Jerubbaal cameᵀupon them.   *to*

CHAPTER 10

The Judge Tola

Now after Abimelech died, Tola the son of Puah, the son of Dodo, a man of Issachar, ᴿarose to save Israel; and he lived in Shamir in the hill country of Ephraim.   *Judg. 2:16*

2 And he judged Israel twenty-three years. Then he died and was buried in Shamir.

The Judge Jair

3 And after him, Jair the Gileadite arose, and judged Israel twenty-two years.

4 And he had thirty sons who rode on thirty donkeys, and they had thirty citiesᵀin the land of Gilead that are calledᵀHavvothjair to this day.   *which are in • the towns of Jair*

5 And Jair died and was buried in Kamon.

Israel Sins

6 Then the sons of Israel again did evil in the sight of the LORD,ᴿserved the Baals and the Ashtaroth, the gods of Aram, the gods of Sidon, the gods of Moab, the gods of the sons of Ammon, and the gods of the Philistines; thus ᴿthey forsook the LORD and did not serve Him.   *Judg. 2:13 • Deut. 31:16, 17*

7 And the anger of the LORD burned against Israel, and He ᴿsold them into the hands of the Philistines, and into the hands of the sons of Ammon.   *1 Sam. 12:9*

8 And theyᵀafflicted and crushed the sons of Israel ᵀthat year; for eighteen years they *afflicted* all the sons of Israel who were beyond the Jordanᵀin Gilead in the land of the Amorites.   *shattered • in that • which is in*

9 And the sons of Ammon crossed the Jordan to fight also against Judah, Benja-

min, and the house of Ephraim, so that Israel was greatly distressed.

10 Then the[R]sons of Israel cried out to the
LORD, saying, "We have sinned against
Thee, for indeed, we have forsaken our God
and served the Baals."   1 Sam. 12:10

11 And the LORD said to the sons of Israel,
"*Did I not deliver you*[R]from the Egyptians,
[R]the Amorites, the sons of Ammon, and the
Philistines?   Judg. 2:12 • Num. 21:21-25

12"Also when the Sidonians, the Amalekites and the Maonites [R]oppressed you, you
cried out to Me, and I delivered you from
their hands.   Ps. 106:42

13"Yet[R]you have forsaken Me and served
other gods; therefore I will deliver you no
more.   Jer. 2:13

14"Go[R] and cry out to the gods which you
have chosen; let them deliver you in the
time of your distress."   Deut. 32:37

15 And the sons of Israel said to the LORD,
"We have sinned,[R]do to us whatever seems
good to Thee; only please deliver us this
day."   1 Sam. 3:18

16 So they put away the foreign gods
from among them, and served the LORD; and
He could bear the misery of Israel no longer.

17 Then the sons of Ammon were summoned, and they camped in Gilead. And the
sons of Israel gathered together, and
camped in[R]Mizpah.   Judg. 11:29

18 And the people, the leaders of Gilead,
said to one another, "Who is the man who
will begin to fight against the sons of Ammon? He shall become head over all the inhabitants of Gilead."

CHAPTER 11

Jephthah Is Called

NOW Jephthah the Gileadite was a valiant warrior, but he was the son of a harlot.
And Gilead was the father of Jephthah.

2 And Gilead's wife bore him sons; and
when his wife's sons grew up, they drove
Jephthah out and said to him, "You shall
not have an inheritance in our father's
house, for you are the son of another
woman."

3 So Jephthah fled from his brothers and
lived in the land of Tob; and worthless fellows gathered themselves [T]about Jephthah,
and they went out with him.   *to*

4 And it came about after a while that
the sons of Ammon fought against Israel.

5 And it happened when the sons of Ammon fought against Israel that the elders of
Gilead went to get Jephthah from the land
of Tob;

6 and they said to Jephthah, "Come and
be our chief that we may fight against the
sons of Ammon."

7 Then Jephthah said to the elders of Gilead, "Did you not hate me and drive me
from my father's house? So why have you

come to me now when you are in trouble?"

8 And the elders of Gilead said to Jephthah, "For this reason we have now returned to you, that you may go with us and
fight with the sons of Ammon and become
head over all the inhabitants of Gilead."

9 So Jephthah said to the elders of Gilead, "If you take me back to fight against
the sons of Ammon and the LORD gives
them up to me, will I become your head?"

10 And the elders of Gilead said to Jephthah, "The LORD is [T]witness between us;
surely we will do as you have said."   *hearer*

11 Then Jephthah went with the elders of
Gilead, and the people made him head and
chief over them; and Jephthah spoke all his
words before the LORD at[R]Mizpah. Judg. 20:1

Jephthah Judges

12 Now Jephthah sent messengers to the
king of the sons of Ammon, saying, "What
is between you and me, that you have come
to me to fight against my land?"

13 And the king of the sons of Ammon
said to the messengers of Jephthah, "Because Israel[R]took away my land when they
came up from Egypt, from the Arnon as far
as the Jabbok and the Jordan; therefore, return them peaceably now."   Num. 21:24

14 But Jephthah sent messengers again to
the king of the sons of Ammon,

15 and they said to him, "Thus says Jephthah, 'Israel did not take away the land of
Moab, nor the land of the sons of Ammon.

16 'For when they came up from Egypt,
and Israel[R]went through the wilderness to
the Red Sea and came to Kadesh, Deut. 1:40

17 then Israel[R]sent messengers to the king
of Edom, saying, "Please let us pass through
your land," but the king of Edom would not
listen. And they also sent to the king of
Moab, but he would not consent. So Israel
remained at Kadesh.   Num. 20:14-21

18 'Then they went through the wilderness
and[R]around the land of Edom and the land
of Moab, and came to the east side of the
land of Moab, and they camped beyond the
Arnon; but they[R]did not enter the territory
of Moab, for the Arnon was the border of
Moab.   Num. 21:4; Deut. 2:8 • Deut. 2:9, 18, 19

19 'And Israel sent messengers to Sihon
king of the Amorites, the king of Heshbon,
and Israel said to him, "Please let us pass
through your land to our place."

20 'But Sihon did not trust Israel to pass
through his territory; so Sihon gathered all
his people and camped in Jahaz, and fought
with Israel.

21 'And the LORD, the God of Israel, gave
Sihon and all his people into the hand of Israel, and they[T]defeated[R]them; so Israel possessed all the land of the Amorites, the inhabitants of that country.   *smote* • Num. 21:24

22 'So[R] they possessed all the territory of
the Amorites, from the Arnon as far as the

Jabbok, and from the wilderness as far as the Jordan.   Deut. 2:36, 37

23 'Since now the LORD, the God of Israel, drove out the Amorites from before His people Israel, are you then to possess it?

24 'Do you not possess what ᴿChemosh your god gives you to possess? So whatever the LORD our God has driven out before us, we will possess it.   Num. 21:29; 1 Kin. 11:7

25 'And now are you any better than ᴿBalak the son of Zippor, king of Moab? Did he ever strive with Israel, or did he ever fight against them?   Num. 22:2; Josh. 24:9; Mic. 6:5

26 'While Israel lived in Heshbon and its villages, and in Aroer and its villages, and in all the cities that are on the banks of the Arnon, three hundred years, why did you not recover them within that time?

27 'I therefore have not sinned against you, but you are doing me wrong by making war against me; ᴿmay the LORD, the Judge, judge today between the sons of Israel and the sons of Ammon.' "   Gen. 16:5; 18:25; 31:53

28 But the king of the sons of Ammon ᵀdisregarded the message which Jephthah sent him.   *did not listen to the words*

Jephthah Vows

29 Now ᴿthe Spirit of the LORD came upon Jephthah, so that he passed through Gilead and Manasseh; then he passed through Mizpah of Gilead, and from Mizpah of Gilead he went on to the sons of Ammon.   Judg. 3:10

30 And Jephthah made a vow to the LORD and said, "If Thou wilt indeed give the sons of Ammon into my hand,

31 then it shall be that whatever comes out of the doors of my house to meet me when I return in peace from the sons of Ammon, it shall be the LORD's, and I will offer it up as a burnt offering."

32 So Jephthah crossed over to the sons of Ammon to fight against them; and the LORD gave them into his hand.

33 And he struck them with a very great slaughter from Aroer to the entrance of ᴿMinnith, twenty cities, and as far as Abel-keramim. So the sons of Ammon were subdued before the sons of Israel.   Ezek. 27:17

34 When Jephthah came to his house at ᴿMizpah, behold, his daughter was coming out to meet him ᴿwith tambourines and with dancing. Now she was his one *and* only child; besides her he had neither son nor daughter.   Judg. 10:17; 11:11 • Ex. 15:20

35 And it came about when he saw her, that he tore his clothes and said, "Alas, my daughter! You have brought me very low, and you are among those who trouble me; for I have ᵀgiven my word to the LORD, and I cannot take *it* back."   *opened my mouth*

36 So she said to him, "My father, you have ᵀgiven your word to the LORD; ᴿdo to me as you have said, since the LORD has avenged you of your enemies, the sons of Ammon."   *opened your mouth* • Num. 30:2

37 And she said to her father, "Let this thing be done for me; let me alone two months, that I may ᵀgo to the mountains and weep because of ᴿmy virginity, I and my companions."   *go and go down on* • Gen. 30:23

38 Then he said, "Go." So he sent her away for two months; and she left with her companions, and wept on the mountains because of her virginity.

39 And it came about at the end of two months that she returned to her father, who did to her according to the vow which he had made; and she had no relations with a man. Thus it became a custom in Israel,

40 that the daughters of Israel went yearly to commemorate the daughter of Jephthah the Gileadite four days in the year.

CHAPTER 12

Ephraim Is Conquered

Tʜᴇɴ the men of Ephraim were summoned, and they crossed ᴬto Zaphon and ᴿsaid to Jephthah, "Why did you cross over to fight against the sons of Ammon without calling us to go with you? We will burn your house down on you."   *northward* • Judg. 8:1

2 And Jephthah said to them, "I and my people were at great strife with the sons of Ammon; when I called you, you did not deliver me from their hand.

3"And when I saw that you would not deliver *me*, I ᵀtook my life in my hands and crossed over against the sons of Ammon, and the LORD gave them into my hand. Why then have you come up to me this day, to fight against me?"   *put my soul in my palm*

4 Then Jephthah gathered all the men of Gilead and fought Ephraim; and the men of Gilead ᵀdefeated Ephraim, because they said, "You are fugitives of Ephraim, O Gileadites, in the midst of Ephraim *and* in the midst of Manasseh."   *smote*

5 And the Gileadites ᴿcaptured the fords of the Jordan opposite Ephraim. And it happened when *any of* the fugitives of Ephraim said, "Let me cross over," the men of Gilead would say to him, "Are you an Ephraimite?" If he said, "No,"   Judg. 3:28

6 then they would say to him, "Say now, 'Shibboleth.' " But he said, "Sibboleth," for he could not ᵀpronounce it correctly. Then they seized him and slew him at the fords of the Jordan. Thus there fell at that time 42,000 of Ephraim.   *speak so*

7 And Jephthah judged Israel six years. Then Jephthah the Gileadite died and was buried in *one of* the cities of Gilead.

The Judge Ibzan

8 Now Ibzan of Bethlehem judged Israel after him.

9 And he had thirty sons, and thirty

daughters *whom* he ^Tgave in marriage outside *the family*, and he brought in thirty daughters from outside for his sons. And he judged Israel seven years.   *sent outside*

10 Then Ibzan died and was buried in Bethlehem.

The Judge Elon

11 Now Elon the Zebulunite judged Israel after him; and he judged Israel ten years.

12 Then Elon the Zebulunite died and was buried at Aijalon in the land of Zebulun.

The Judge Abdon

13 Now Abdon the son of Hillel the Pirathonite judged Israel after him.

14 And he had forty sons and thirty grandsons who rode on seventy donkeys; and he judged Israel eight years.

15 Then Abdon the son of Hillel the Pirathonite died and was buried at Pirathon in the land of Ephraim, in the hill country of the Amalekites.

CHAPTER 13

Miraculous Birth of Samson

Now the sons of Israel ^Ragain did evil in the sight of the LORD, so that the LORD gave them into the hands of the Philistines forty years.   Judg. 2:11

2 And there was a certain man of ^{cR}Zorah, of the family of the Danites, whose name was Manoah; and his wife was barren and had borne no *children.*   Josh. 19:41

3 ^RThen the angel of the LORD appeared to the woman, and said to her, "Behold now, you are barren and have borne no *children,* but you shall conceive and give birth to a son.   Judg. 6:11, 14; 13:6, 8, 10, 11; Luke 1:11-13

4 "Now therefore, be careful ^Rnot to drink wine or strong drink, nor eat any unclean thing.   Num. 6:2, 3; Luke 1:15

5 "For ^Rbehold, you shall conceive and give birth to a son, and no razor shall come upon his head, for the boy shall be a ^RNazirite to God from the womb; and he shall begin to deliver Israel from the hands of the Philistines."   Luke 1:15 • Num. 6:2-5

6 Then the woman came and told her husband, saying, "A ^Rman of God came to me and his appearance was like the appearance of the angel of God, very awesome. And I did not ask him where he *came* from, nor did he tell me his name.   Judg. 6:11

7 "But he said to me, 'Behold, you shall conceive and give birth to a son, and now you shall not drink wine or strong drink nor eat any unclean thing, for the boy shall be a Nazirite to God from the womb to the day of his death.' "

8 Then Manoah entreated the LORD and said, "O Lord, please let ^Rthe man of God whom Thou hast sent come to us again that he may teach us what to do for the boy who is to be born."   Judg. 13:3, 7

9 And God listened to the voice of Manoah; and the angel of God came again to the woman as she was sitting in the field, but Manoah her husband was not with her.

10 So the woman ran quickly and told her husband, "Behold, the man who ^Tcame the *other* day has appeared to me."   *came to me*

11 Then Manoah arose and followed his wife, and when he came to the man he said to him, "Are you ^Rthe man who spoke to the woman?" And he said, "I am."   Judg. 13:8

12 And Manoah said, "Now when your words come *to pass,* what shall be the boy's mode of life and his vocation?"

13 So ^Rthe angel of the LORD said to Manoah, "Let ^Rthe woman pay attention ^Tto all that I said.   Judg. 13:11 • Judg. 13:4 • *from*

14 "She should not eat anything that comes from the vine nor drink wine or strong drink, nor eat any unclean thing; let her observe all that I commanded."

15 Then Manoah said to ^Rthe angel of the LORD, "Please let us detain you so that we may prepare a kid for you."   Judg. 13:3

16 And the angel of the LORD said to Manoah, "Though you detain me, ^RI will not eat your ^Tfood, but if you prepare a burnt offering, *then* offer it to the LORD." For Manoah did not know that he was the angel of the LORD.   Judg. 6:20 • *bread*

17 And Manoah said to the angel of the LORD, "What ^Ris your name, so that when your words come *to pass,* we may honor you?"   Gen. 32:29

18 But the angel of the LORD said to him, "Why do you ask my name, seeing it is [13]wonderful?"

19 So ^RManoah took the kid with the grain offering and offered it on the rock to the LORD, and He performed wonders while Manoah and his wife looked on.   Judg. 6:20, 21

20 For it came about when the flame went up from the altar toward heaven, that the angel of the LORD ascended in the flame of the altar. When Manoah and his wife saw *this,* they fell on their faces to the ground.

21 Now the angel of the LORD appeared no more to Manoah or his wife. ^RThen Manoah knew that he was the angel of the LORD.   Judg. 13:16

22 So Manoah said to his wife, "We shall surely die, for we have seen God."

23 But his wife said to him, "If the LORD had desired to kill us, He would not have accepted a burnt offering and a grain offering from our hands, nor would He have ^Rshown us all these things, nor would He have let us hear *things* like this at this time."   Ps. 25:14

24 Then the woman gave birth to a son and named him Samson; and the ^Rchild grew up and the LORD blessed him.   1 Sam. 3:19

[13] I.e., incomprehensible

25 And[R]the Spirit of the LORD began to stir him in [14]Mahaneh-dan[R] between Zorah and Eshtaol.   Judg. 3:10 • Judg. 18:11, 12

CHAPTER 14

Sinful Marriage of Samson

THEN Samson went down to Timnah and saw a woman in Timnah, *one* of the daughters of the Philistines.

2 So he came[T]back and told his father and mother, "I saw a woman in Timnah, *one* of the daughters of the Philistines; now therefore, get her for me as a wife."   *up*

3 Then his father and his mother said to him, "Is there no woman among the daughters of your[T]relatives, or among all[T]our people, that you go to take a wife from the uncircumcised Philistines?" But Samson said to his father, "Get her for me, for she[T]looks good to me."   *brothers • my • is right in my eyes*

4 However, his father and mother did not know that[R]it was of the LORD, for He was seeking an occasion against the Philistines. Now at that time the Philistines were ruling over Israel.   Josh. 11:20

5 Then Samson went down to Timnah with his father and mother, and came as far as the vineyards of Timnah; and behold, a young lion *came* roaring toward him.

6 And[R]the Spirit of the LORD[T]came upon him mightily, so that he tore him as one tears a kid though he had nothing in his hand; but he did not tell his father or mother what he had done.   Judg. 3:10 • *rushed upon*

7 So he went down and talked to the woman; and she looked good to Samson.

8 When he returned later to take her, he turned aside to look at the carcass of the lion; and behold, a swarm of bees and honey were in the body of the lion.

9 So he scraped[T]the honey into his[T]hands and went on, eating as he went. When he came to his father and mother, he gave *some* to them and they ate *it;* but he did not tell them that he had scraped the honey out of the body of the lion.   *it • palms*

10 Then his father went down to the woman; and Samson made a feast there, for the young men customarily did this.

11 And it came about when they saw him that they brought thirty companions to be with him.

12 Then Samson said to them, "Let me now[R]propound a riddle to you; if you will indeed tell it to me within the seven days of the feast, and find it out, then I will give you thirty linen wraps and thirty [R]changes of clothes.   Ezek. 17:2 • Gen. 45:22; 2 Kin. 5:22

13"But if you are unable to tell me, then you shall give me thirty linen wraps and thirty changes of clothes." And they said to him, "Propound your riddle, that we may hear it."

14 So he said to them,

"Out of the eater came something to eat,
And out of the strong came something sweet."

But they could not tell the riddle in three days.

15 Then it came about on the fourth day that they said to Samson's wife, "Entice[R] your husband, that he may tell us the riddle, lest we burn you and your father's house with fire. Have you invited us to impoverish us? Is this not *so?*"   Judg. 16:5

16 And Samson's wife wept before him and said, "You[R]only hate me, and you do not love me; you have propounded a riddle to the sons of my people, and have not told *it* to me." And he said to her, "Behold, I have not told *it* to my father or mother; so should I tell you?"   Judg. 16:15

17 However she wept before him seven days while their feast lasted. And it came about on the seventh day that he told her because she pressed him so hard. She then told the riddle to the sons of her people.

18 So the men of the city said to him on the seventh day before the sun went down,

"What is sweeter than honey?
And what is stronger than a lion?"

And he said to them,

"If you had not plowed with my heifer,
You would not have found out my riddle."

19 Then[R]the Spirit of the LORD[T]came upon him mightily, and he went down to Ashkelon and killed thirty of them and took their spoil, and gave the changes *of clothes* to those who told the riddle. And his anger burned, and he went up to his father's house.   Judg. 3:10; 13:25 • *rushed upon*

20 But Samson's wife was *given* to his companion who had been his friend.

CHAPTER 15

Judgeship of Samson

BUT after a while, in the time of wheat harvest, it came about that Samson visited his wife[R]with a young goat, and said, "I will go in to my wife in *her* room." But her father did not let him enter.   Gen. 38:17

2 And her father said, "I really thought that you hated her intensely; so I gave her to your companion. Is not her younger sister [T]more beautiful than she? Please let her be yours[T]instead."   *better • instead of her*

3 Samson then said to them, "This time I shall be blameless in regard to the Philistines when I do them harm."

4 And Samson went and caught three hundred foxes, and took torches, and turned *the foxes'* tail to tail, and put one torch in the middle between two tails.

[14] I.e., the camp of Dan

5 When he had set fire to the torches, he released[T]the foxes into the standing grain of the Philistines, thus burning up both the shocks and the standing grain, along with the vineyards *and* groves.   *them*

6 Then the Philistines said, "Who did this?" And they said, "Samson, the son-in-law of the Timnite, because[T]he took his wife and gave her to his companion." So the Philistines came up and[R]burned her and her father with fire.   the Timnite • Judg. 14:15

7 And Samson said to them, "Since you act like this, I will surely take revenge on you, but after that I will quit."

8 And he struck them[T]ruthlessly with a great slaughter; and he went down and lived in the cleft of the rock of Etam.   *leg on thigh*

9 Then the Philistines went up and camped in Judah, and spread out in Lehi.

10 And the men of Judah said, "Why have you come up against us?" And they said, "We have come up to bind Samson in order to do to him as he did to us."

11 Then 3,000 men of Judah went down to the cleft of the rock of Etam and said to Samson, "Do you not know[R]that the Philistines are rulers over us? What then is this that you have done to us?" And he said to them, "As they did to me, so I have done to them."   Lev. 26:25; Deut. 28:43f.; Judg. 13:1; 14:4

12 And they said to him, "We have come down to bind you so that we may give you into the hands of the Philistines." And Samson said to them, "Swear to me that you will not[T]kill me."   *fall upon me yourselves*

13 So they said to[T]him, "No, but we will bind you fast and give you into their hands; yet surely we will not kill you." Then they bound him with two new ropes and brought him up from the rock.   *him, saying*

14 When he came to Lehi, the Philistines shouted as they met him. And the Spirit of the LORD [T]came upon him mightily so that the ropes that were on his arms were as flax that is burned with fire, and his bonds dropped from his hands.   *rushed upon*

15 And he found a fresh jawbone of a donkey, so he[T]reached out and took it and killed a thousand men with it.   *stretched out his hand*

16 Then Samson said,

"With the jawbone of a donkey,
Heaps upon heaps,
With the jawbone of a donkey
I have[T]killed a thousand men."   *smitten*

17 And it came about when he had finished speaking, that he threw the jawbone from his hand; and he named that place [15]Ramath-lehi.

18 Then he became very thirsty, and he called to the LORD and said, "Thou hast given this great deliverance by the hand of Thy servant, and now shall I die of thirst[T]and fall into the hands of the uncircumcised?"   *or*

19 But God split the hollow place that is in Lehi so that water came out of it. When he drank, his strength returned and he revived. Therefore, he named it[T]En-hakkore, which is in Lehi to this day.   the spring of him who called

20 So[R]he judged Israel twenty years in[R]the days of the Philistines.   Heb. 11:32 • Judg. 13:1

CHAPTER 16

Failure of Samson

NOW Samson went to [R]Gaza and saw a harlot there, and went in to her.   Josh. 15:47

2 *When it was told* to the Gazites, saying, "Samson has come here," they surrounded *the place* and lay in wait for him all night at the gate of the city. And they kept silent all night, saying, "*Let us wait* until the morning light, then we will kill him."

3 Now Samson lay until midnight, and at midnight he arose and took hold of the doors of the city gate and the two posts and pulled them up along with the bars; then he put them on his shoulders and carried them up to the top of the mountain which is opposite Hebron.

4 After this it came about that he loved a woman in the valley of Sorek, whose name was Delilah.

5 And the lords of the Philistines came up to her, and said to her, "Entice him, and see where his great strength *lies* and how we may overpower him that we may bind him to afflict him. Then we will each give you eleven hundred *pieces* of silver."

6 So Delilah said to Samson, "Please tell me where your great strength is and [T]how you may be bound to afflict you."   *by what*

7 And Samson said to her, "If they bind me with seven fresh cords that have not been dried, then I shall become weak and be like any *other* man."

8 Then the lords of the Philistines brought up to her seven fresh cords that had not been dried, and she bound him with them.

9 Now she had *men* lying in wait in an inner room. And she said to him, "The Philistines are upon you, Samson!" But he snapped the cords as a string of tow snaps when it[T]touches fire. So his strength was not discovered.   *smells*

10 Then Delilah said to Samson, "Behold, you have deceived me and told me lies; now please tell me, how you may be bound."

11 And he said to her, "If they bind me tightly with new ropes which have not been used, then I shall become weak and be like any *other* man."

12 So Delilah took new ropes and bound him with them and said to him, "The Philistines are upon you, Samson!" For the *men* were lying in wait in the inner room. But he snapped [T]the ropes from his arms like a thread.   *them*

13 Then Delilah said to Samson, "Up to

---

[15] I.e., the high place of the jawbone

now you have deceived me and told me lies; tell me [T]how you may be bound." And he said to her, "If you weave the seven locks of my[T]hair with the web [16][and fasten it with a pin, then I shall become weak and be like any other man."   *by what • head*

14 So while he slept, Delilah took the seven locks of his[T]hair and wove them into the web]. And she fastened *it* with the pin, and said to him, "The Philistines are upon you, Samson!" But he awoke from his sleep and pulled out the pin of the loom and the web.   *head*

15 Then she said to him, "How[R] can you say, 'I love you,' when your heart is not with me? You have deceived me these three times and have not told me where your great strength is."   Judg. 14:16

16 And it came about when she pressed him daily with her words and urged him, that his soul was annoyed to death.

17 So he told her all *that was* in his heart and said to her, "A razor has never come on my head, for I have been a Nazirite to God from my mother's womb. If I am shaved, then my strength will leave me and I shall become weak and be like any *other* man."

18 When Delilah saw that he had told her all *that was* in his heart, she sent and called the lords of the Philistines, saying, "Come up once more, for he has told me all *that is* in his heart." Then the lords of the Philistines came up to her, and brought the money in their hands.

19 And she made him sleep on her knees, and called for a man and had him shave off the seven locks of his hair. Then she began to afflict him, and his strength left him.

20 And she said, "The Philistines are upon you, Samson!" And he awoke from his sleep and said, "I will go out as at other times and shake myself free." But he did not know that the LORD had departed from him.

21 Then the Philistines seized him and gouged out his eyes; and they brought him down to Gaza and bound him with bronze chains, and he was a grinder in the prison.

22 However, the hair of his head began to grow again after it was shaved off.

23 Now the lords of the Philistines assembled to offer a great sacrifice to[R]Dagon their god, and to rejoice, for they said,

"Our god has given Samson our enemy into our hands."   1 Sam. 5:2

24 When the people saw him,[R]they praised their god, for they said,

"Our god has given our enemy into our hands,   1 Sam. 31:9; 1 Chr. 10:9; Ps. 97:7
Even the destroyer of our country,
Who has slain many of us."

25 It so happened when[T]they were in high spirits, that they said, "Call for Samson, that he may amuse us." So they called for Samson from the prison, and he entertained them. And they made him stand between the pillars.   *their heart was pleasant*

26 Then Samson said to the boy who was holding his hand, "Let me feel the pillars on which the house rests, that I may lean against them."

27 Now the house was full of men and women, and all the lords of the Philistines were there. And about 3,000 men and women were on the roof looking on while Samson was amusing *them*.

28 [R]Then Samson called to the LORD and said, "O Lord GOD, please remember me and please strengthen me just this time, O God, that I may at once be avenged of the Philistines for my two eyes."   Judg. 15:18

29 And Samson grasped the two middle pillars on which the house rested, and braced himself against them, the one with his right hand and the other with his left.

30 And Samson said, "Let me die with the Philistines!" And he bent with[T]all his might so that the house fell on the lords and all the people who were in it. So the dead whom he killed at his death were more than those whom he killed in his life.   *strength*

31 Then his brothers and all his father's household came down, took him, brought him up, and buried him between Zorah and Eshtaol in the tomb of Manoah his father. Thus he had judged Israel twenty years.

CHAPTER 17

Example of Personal Idolatry

NOW there was a man of the hill country of Ephraim whose name was Micah.

2 And he said to his mother, "The eleven hundred *pieces* of silver which were taken from you, about which you uttered a curse in my hearing, behold, the silver is with me; I took it." And his mother said, "Blessed be my son by the LORD."

3 He then returned the eleven hundred *pieces* of silver to his mother, and his mother said, "I wholly dedicate the silver from my hand to the LORD for my son to make a graven image and a molten image; now therefore, I will return them to you."

4 So when he returned the silver to his mother, his mother took two hundred *pieces* of silver and gave them to the silversmith who made[T]them into a graven image and a molten image, and[T]they were in the house of Micah.   *it • it was*

5 And the man Micah had a [17]shrine and he made an ephod and[T]household idols and consecrated one of his sons,[R]that he might become his priest.   Heb., *teraphim* • Num. 3:10

6 In those days[R]there was no king in Israel; [R]every man did what was right in his own eyes.   Judg. 18:1; 19:1 • Deut. 12:8

7 Now there was a young man from Bethlehem in Judah, of the family of Judah,

---

[16] The passage in brackets is found in Gr. but not in any Heb. mss.
[17] Lit., *house of gods*

who was a Levite; and he was staying there.

8 Then the man departed from the city, from Bethlehem in Judah, to 'stay wherever he might find *a place;* and as he made his journey, he came to the hill country of Ephraim to the house of Micah.   *sojourn*

9 And Micah said to him, "Where do you come from?" And he said to him, "I am a Levite from Bethlehem in Judah, and I am going to stay wherever I may find *a place.*"

10 Micah then said to him, "Dwell with me and be^Ra father and a priest to me, and I will give you ten *pieces* of silver a year, a suit of clothes, and your maintenance." So the Levite went *in.*   Judg. 18:19

11 And the Levite agreed to live with the man; and the young man became to him like one of his sons.

12 So Micah 'consecrated the Levite, and the young man became his priest and 'lived in the house of Micah.   *filled the hand of • was*

13 Then Micah said, "Now I know that the LORD will prosper me, seeing I have a Levite as priest."

CHAPTER 18

Example of Tribal Idolatry

IN those days there was no king of Israel; and in those days the tribe of the Danites was seeking an inheritance for themselves to live in, for until that day 'an inheritance had not 'been allotted to them as a possession among the tribes of Israel.   *it • fallen*

2 So the sons of Dan sent from their family five men out of their whole number, 'valiant men from Zorah and Eshtaol, to spy out the land and to search it; and they said to them, "Go, search the land." And they came to the hill country of Ephraim, to the house of Micah, and lodged there.   *men, sons of valor*

3 When they were near the house of Micah, they recognized the voice of the young man, the Levite; and they turned aside there, and said to him, "Who brought you here? And what are you doing in this *place?* And what do you have here?"

4 And he said to them, "Thus and so has Micah done to me, and he has hired me, and ^RI have become his priest."   Judg. 17:12

5 And they said to him, "Inquire of God, please, that we may know whether our way on which we are going will be prosperous."

6 And the priest said to them, "Go in peace; your way in which you are going 'has the LORD'S approval."   *is before the LORD*

7 Then the five men departed and came to Laish and saw the people who were in it living in security, after the manner of the Sidonians, quiet and secure; for there was no ruler humiliating *them* for anything in the land, and they were far from the Sidonians and had no dealings with anyone.

8 When they came back to their brothers at Zorah and Eshtaol, their brothers said to them, "What do you *report?*"

9 And they said, "Arise, and let us go up against them; for we have seen the land, and behold, it is very good. And will you 'sit still? Do not delay to go, to enter, to possess the land.   *be*

10 "When you enter, you shall come to a secure people with a spacious land; for God has given it into your hand, ^Ra place where there is no lack of anything that is on the earth."   Deut. 8:9

11 Then from the family of the Danites, from Zorah and from Eshtaol, six hundred men armed with weapons of war set out.

12 And they went up and camped at Kiriath-jearim in Judah. Therefore they called that place ¹⁸Mahaneh-dan to this day; behold, it is 'west of Kiriath-jearim.   *behind*

13 And they passed from there to the hill country of Ephraim and came to the house of Micah.

14 Then the five men who went to spy out the country of Laish answered and said to their kinsmen, "Do you know that there are in these houses ^Ran ephod and ¹⁹household idols and a graven image and a molten image? Now therefore, consider what you should do."   Judg. 17:5

15 And they turned aside there and came to the house of the young man, the Levite, to the house of Micah, and asked him of his welfare.

16 And the six hundred men armed with their weapons of war, who were of the sons of Dan, stood by the entrance of the gate.

17 Now the five men who went to spy out the land went up *and* entered there, *and* took ^Rthe graven image and the ephod and 'household idols and the molten image, while the priest stood by the entrance of the gate with the six hundred men armed with weapons of war.   Is. 41:29 • Heb., *teraphim*

18 And when these went into Micah's house and took the graven image, the ephod and 'household idols and the molten image, the priest said to them, "What are you doing?"   Heb., *teraphim*

19 And they said to him, "Be silent, ^Rput your hand over your mouth and come with us, and be to us ^Ra father and a priest. Is it better for you to be a priest to the house of one man, or to be priest to a tribe and a family in Israel?"   Job. 21:5; 29:9; 40:4 • Judg. 17:10

20 And the priest's heart was glad, and he took the ephod and household idols and the graven image, and went among the people.

21 Then they turned and departed, and put the little ones and the livestock and the valuables in front of them.

22 When they had gone some distance from the house of Micah, the men who *were* in the houses near Micah's house assembled and overtook the sons of Dan.

23 And they cried to the sons of Dan, who

¹⁸ I.e., the camp of Dan
¹⁹ Heb., *teraphim,* and so throughout this context

turned [T]around and said to Micah, "What is *the matter* with you, that you have assembled together?"   *their faces*

24 And he said, "You have taken away my gods which I made, and the priest, and have gone away, and what do I have besides? So how can you say to me, 'What is *the matter* with you?'"

25 And the sons of Dan said to him, "Do not let your voice be heard among us, lest fierce men fall upon you and you lose your life, with the lives of your household."

26 So the sons of Dan went on their way; and when Micah saw that they were too strong for him, he turned and went back to his house.

27 Then they took what Micah had made and the priest who had belonged to him, and came to [R]Laish, to a people quiet and secure, and struck them with the edge of the sword; and they burned the city with fire. Judg. 18:7

28 And there was no one to deliver *them,* because it was far from Sidon and they had no dealings with anyone, and it was in the valley which is near [R]Beth-rehob. And they rebuilt the city and lived in it.   2 Sam. 10:6

29 And [R]they called the name of the city Dan, after the name of Dan their father who was born in Israel; however, the name of the city formerly was Laish.   Josh. 19:47

30 And the sons of Dan set up for themselves [R]the graven image; and Jonathan, the son of [R]Gershom, the son of [20]Manasseh, [R]he and his sons were priests to the tribe of the Danites until the day of the captivity of the land.   Judg. 17:3, 5 • Ex. 2:22 • Judg. 17:3, 5

31 So they set up for themselves Micah's graven image which he had made, all the time that the house of God was at Shiloh.

CHAPTER 19

Example of Personal Immorality

Now it came about in those days, when [R]there was no king in Israel, that there was a certain Levite 'staying in the remote part of the hill country of Ephraim, who took a concubine for himself from Bethlehem in Judah.   Judg. 18:1 • *sojourning*

2 But his concubine played the harlot against him, and she went away from him to her father's house in Bethlehem in Judah, and was there for a period of four months.

3 Then her husband arose and went after her to speak tenderly to her in order to bring her back, [T]taking with him his servant and a pair of donkeys. So she brought him into her father's house, and when the girl's father saw him, he was glad to meet him.   *and*

4 And his father-in-law, the girl's father, detained him; and he remained with him three days. So they ate and drank and lodged there.

5 Now it came about on the fourth day that they got up early in the morning, and he prepared to go; and the girl's father said to his son-in-law, "Sustain yourself with a piece of bread, and afterward you may go."

6 So both of them sat down and ate and drank together; and the girl's father said to the man, "Please be willing to spend the night, and let your heart be merry."

7 Then the man arose to go, but his father-in-law urged him so that he spent the night there again.

8 And on the fifth day he arose to go early in the morning, and the girl's father said, "Please sustain [T]yourself, and wait until afternoon"; so both of them ate.   *your heart*

9 When the man arose to go along with his concubine and servant, his father-in-law, the girl's father, said to him, "Behold now, the day has drawn to a close; please spend the night. Lo, the day is coming to an end; spend the night here that your heart may be merry. Then tomorrow you may arise early for your journey so that you may go home."

10 But the man was not willing to spend the night, so he arose and departed and came to *a place* opposite [R]Jebus (that is, Jerusalem). And there were with him a pair of saddled donkeys; his concubine also was with him.   1 Chr. 11:4, 5

Example of Tribal Immorality

11 When they *were* near Jebus, the day was almost gone; and [R]the servant said to his master, "Please come, and let us turn aside into this city of the Jebusites and spend the night in it."   Judg. 19:19

12 However, his master said to him, "We will not turn aside into the city of foreigners who are not of the sons of Israel; but we will go on as far as Gibeah."

13 And he said to his servant, "Come and let us approach one of these places; and we will spend the night in Gibeah or Ramah."

14 So they passed along and went their way, and the sun set on them near Gibeah which belongs to Benjamin.

15 And they turned aside there in order to enter *and* lodge in Gibeah. When they entered, they sat down in the open square of the city, for no one took them into *his* house to spend the night.

16 Then behold, an old man was coming out of the field from his work at evening. Now the man was from the hill country of Ephraim, and he was staying in Gibeah, but the men of the place were Benjamites.

17 And he lifted up his eyes and saw the traveler in the open square of the city; and the old man said, "Where are you going, and where do you come from?"

18 And he said to him, "We are passing from Bethlehem in Judah to the remote part of the hill country of Ephraim, *for* I am from there, and I went to Bethlehem in Judah. But I am *now* going to my house, and no man will take me into his house.

[20] Some ancient versions read *Moses*

19"Yet there is both straw and fodder for our donkeys, and also bread and wine for me, [T]your maidservant, and [R]the young man who is with your servants; there is no lack of anything."   my concubine • Judg. 19:11

20 And the old man said, "Peace[R] to you. Only let me *take care of* all your needs; however, do not spend the night in the open square."   Gen. 43:23; Judg. 6:23

21 [R]So he took him into his house and gave the donkeys fodder, and they washed their feet and ate and drank.   Gen. 24:32, 33

22 While they were making merry, behold, the men of the city, certain [T]worthless fellows, surrounded the house, pounding the door; and they spoke to the owner of the house, the old man, saying, "Bring out the man who came into your house that we may have relations with him."   *sons of Belial*

23 Then the man, the owner of the house, went out to them and said to them, "No, my fellows, please do not act so wickedly; since this man has come into my house, [R]do not commit this act of folly.   Gen. 34:7; Deut. 22:21

24"Here[R] is my virgin daughter and his concubine. Please let me bring them out that you may ravish them and do to them whatever you wish. But do not commit such an act of folly against this man."   Gen. 19:8

25 But the men would not listen to him, so the man seized his concubine and brought *her* out to them. And they raped her and abused her all night until morning, then let her go at the approach of dawn.

26 [T]As the day began to dawn, the woman came and fell down at the doorway of the man's house where her master was, until *full* daylight.   *At the turning of the morning*

27 When her master arose in the morning and opened the doors of the house and went out to go on his way, then behold, his concubine was lying at the doorway of the house, with her hands on the threshold.

28 And he said to her, "Get up and let us go," but there was no answer. Then he placed her on the donkey; and the man arose and went to his [T]home.   *place*

29 When he entered his house, he took a knife and laid hold of his concubine and cut her in twelve pieces, limb by limb, and sent her throughout the territory of Israel.

30 And it came about that all who saw *it* said, "Nothing like this has *ever* happened or been seen from the day when the sons of Israel came up from the land of Egypt to this day. Consider it, [R]take counsel and speak up!"   Judg. 20:7; Prov. 13:10

CHAPTER 20

War Between Israel and Benjamin

THEN all the sons of Israel from Dan to Beersheba, including the land of Gilead,

came out, and the congregation assembled as one man to the LORD at Mizpah.

2 And the [T]chiefs of all the people, *even* of all the tribes of Israel, took their stand in the assembly of the people of God, 400,000 foot soldiers who drew the sword.   *cornerstones*

3 (Now the sons of Benjamin heard that the sons of Israel had gone up to Mizpah.) And the sons of Israel said, "Tell *us*, how did this wickedness take place?"

4 So the Levite, the husband of the woman who was murdered, answered and said, "I came with my concubine to spend the night at Gibeah which belongs to Benjamin.

5"But the [R]men of Gibeah rose up against me and surrounded the house at night because of me. They intended to kill me; instead, they [R]ravished my concubine so that she died.   Judg. 19:22 • Judg. 19:25f.

6"And I [R]took hold of my concubine and cut her in pieces and sent her throughout the land of Israel's inheritance; for [R]they have committed a lewd and disgraceful act in Israel.   Judg. 19:29 • Gen. 34:7; Josh. 7:15

7"Behold, all you sons of Israel, [R]give your advice and counsel here."   Judg. 19:30

8 Then all the people arose as one man, saying, "Not one of us will go to his tent, nor will any of us return to his house.

9"But now this is the thing which we will do to Gibeah; *we will go up* against it by lot.

10"And we will take 10 men out of 100 throughout the tribes of Israel, and 100 out of 1,000, and 1,000 out of 10,000 to [T]supply food for the people, that when they come to [T]Gibeah of Benjamin, they may [T]punish *them* for all the disgraceful acts that they have committed in Israel."   *take* • Heb., *Geba* • *do*

11 Thus all the men of Israel were gathered against the city, united as one man.

12 Then the tribes of Israel sent men through the entire [T]tribe of Benjamin, saying, "What is this wickedness that has taken place among you?   *tribes*

13"Now then, deliver up the men, the [2][1]worthless [R]fellows in Gibeah, that we may put them to death and [R]remove *this* wickedness from Israel." But the sons of Benjamin would not listen to the voice of their brothers, the sons of Israel.   [2 Cor. 6:15] • Deut. 13:5

14 And the sons of Benjamin gathered from the cities to Gibeah, to go out to battle against the sons of Israel.

15 And from the cities on that day the [R]sons of Benjamin were [A]numbered, 26,000 men who draw the sword, besides the inhabitants of Gibeah who were [A]numbered, 700 choice men.   Num. 1:36, 37; 2:23 • *mustered*

16 Out of all these people 700 [R]choice men were left-handed; each one could sling a stone at a hair and not miss.   Judg. 3:15

17 Then the men of Israel besides Benjamin were numbered, 400,000 men who draw the sword; all these were men of war.

18 Now the sons of Israel arose, went up to Bethel, and inquired of God, and said,

[1] Lit., *sons of Belial*

"Who shall go up first for us to battle against the sons of Benjamin?" Then the LORD said, "Judah *shall go up* first."

19 So the sons of Israel arose in the morning and camped against Gibeah.

20 And the men of Israel went out to battle against Benjamin, and the men of Israel arrayed for battle against them at Gibeah.

21 Then the sons of Benjamin came out of Gibeah and ᵀfelledᴿto the ground on that day 22,000 men of Israel.   *destroyed* · Judg. 20:25

22 But the people, the men of Israel, encouraged themselves and arrayed for battle again in the place where they had arrayed themselves the first day.

23 ᴿAnd the sons of Israel went up and wept before the LORD until evening, andᴿinquired of the LORD, saying, "Shall we again draw near for battle against the sons of my brother Benjamin?" And the LORD said, "Go up against him."   Josh. 7:6, 7 · Judg. 20:18

24 Then the sons of Israel came against the sons of Benjamin the second day.

25 And Benjamin went out ᵀagainst them from Gibeah the second day and felled to the ground again 18,000 men of the sons of Israel; all these drew the sword.   *to meet*

26 Then ᴿall the sons of Israel and all the people went up and came to Bethel and wept; thus they remained there before the LORD and fasted that day until evening. And they offered burnt offerings and peace offerings before the LORD.   Judg. 20:23; 21:2

27 And the sons of Israelᴿinquired of the LORD (for the ark of the covenant of God *was* there in those days,   Judg. 20:18

28 and Phinehas the son of Eleazar, Aaron's son, stood before it to *minister* in those days), saying, "Shall I yet again go out to battle against the sons of my brother Benjamin, or shall I cease?" And the LORD said, "Go up, ᴿfor tomorrow I will deliver them into your hand."   Judg. 7:9

29 ᴿSo Israel set men in ambush around Gibeah.   Josh. 8:4

30 And the sons of Israel went up against the sons of Benjamin on the third day and arrayed themselves against Gibeah, as at other times.

31 And the sons of Benjamin went out ᵀagainst the people and were drawn away from the city, and they began to strike and kill some of the people, as at other times, on the highways, one of which goes up to Bethel and the other to Gibeah, *and* in the field, about thirty men of Israel.   *to meet*

32 And the sons of Benjamin said, "They are struck down before us, as at the first." But the sons of Israel said, "Let us flee that we may draw them away from the city to the highways."

33 Then all the men of Israel arose from their place and arrayed themselves at Baaltamar; ᴿand the men of Israel in ambush broke out of their place, even out of Maareh-geba.   Josh. 8:19

34 When ten thousand choice men from all Israel came against Gibeah, the battle became ᵀfierce; but ᵀBenjamin did not know that disaster was close to them.   *heavy* · *they*

35 And the LORD struck Benjamin before Israel, so that the sons of Israel destroyed 25,100 men of Benjamin that day, all ᵀwho draw the sword.   *these*

36 So the sons of Benjamin saw that they were ᵀdefeated.ᴿWhen the men of Israel gave ᵀground to Benjamin because they relied on the men in ambush whom they had set against Gibeah,   *smitten* · Josh. 8:15 · *place*

37 ᴿthe men in ambush hurried and rushed against Gibeah; the men in ambush also deployed and struck all the city with the edge of the sword.   Josh. 8:19

38 Now the appointed sign between the men of Israel and the men in ambush was ᴿthat they should make a great cloud of smoke rise from the city.   Josh. 8:20

39 Then the men of Israel turned in the battle, and Benjamin began to strikeᵀand kill about thirty men of Israel, for they said, "Surely they are ᵀdefeated before us, as in the first battle."   *slain ones* · *smitten*

40 But when the cloud began to rise from the city in a column of smoke, Benjamin looked behind them; and behold, the whole city was going up *in smoke* to heaven.

41 Then the men of Israel turned, and the men of Benjamin were terrified; for they saw that ᵀdisaster was close to them.   *evil*

42 Therefore, they turned their backs before the men of Israel toward the direction of the wilderness, but the battle overtook them while those who came out of the cities destroyed them in the midst of them.

43 They surrounded Benjamin, pursued them without rest *and* trod them down opposite Gibeah toward the ᵀeast.   *sunrise*

44 Thus 18,000 men of Benjamin fell; all these were valiant warriors.

45 The rest turned and fled toward the wilderness to the rock ofᴿRimmon, but they ᵀcaught 5,000 of them on the highways and overtook them ᵀat Gidom andᵀkilled 2,000 of them.   Judg. 21:13 · *gleaned* · *as far as* · *smote*

46 So all of Benjamin who fell that day were 25,000 men who draw the sword; all these were valiant warriors.

47 But 600 men turned and fled toward the wilderness to the rock of Rimmon, and they remained at the rock of Rimmon four months.

48 The men of Israel then turned back against the sons of Benjamin and struck them with the edge of the sword, both the entire city with the cattle and all that they found; they also set on fire all the cities which they found.

CHAPTER 21

Israel's Foolish Vow

NOW the men of Israel had sworn in Mizpah, saying, "None of us shall give his daughter to Benjamin in marriage."

2 [R]So the people came to Bethel and sat there before God until evening, and lifted up their voices and wept bitterly.   Judg. 20:26

3 And they said, "Why, O LORD, God of Israel, has this come about in Israel, so that one tribe should be *missing* today in Israel?"

4 And it came about the next day that the people arose early and built [R]an altar there, and offered burnt offerings and peace offerings.   Deut. 12:5; 2 Sam. 24:25

5 Then the sons of Israel said, "Who is there among all the tribes of Israel who did not come up in the assembly to the LORD?" For [T]they had taken a great oath concerning him [R]who did not come up to the LORD at Mizpah, saying, "He shall surely be put to death."   *there was a great oath* · Judg. 5:23

6 And the sons of Israel were sorry for their brother Benjamin and said, "One tribe is cut off from Israel today.

7"What shall we do for wives for those who are left, since we have [R]sworn by the LORD not to give them any of our daughters in marriage?"   Judg. 21:1

Men at Jabesh-gilead Murdered

8 And they said, "What one is there of the tribes of Israel who did not come up to the LORD at Mizpah?" And behold, no one had come to the camp from Jabesh-gilead to the assembly.

9 For when the people were [ʼ]numbered, behold, not one of the inhabitants of Jabesh-gilead was there.   *mustered*

10 And the congregation sent 12,000 of the valiant warriors there, and commanded them, saying, "Go and strike the inhabitants of Jabesh-gilead with the edge of the sword, with the women and the little ones.

11"And this is the thing that you shall do: you shall utterly destroy every man and every woman who has lain with a man."

12 And they found among the inhabitants of Jabesh-gilead 400 young virgins who had not known a man by lying with [T]him; and they brought them to the camp at Shiloh, which is in the land of Canaan.   *a male*

13 Then the whole congregation sent *word* and spoke to the sons of Benjamin who were [R]at the rock of Rimmon, and proclaimed peace to them.   Judg. 20:47

14 And Benjamin returned at that time, and they gave them the women whom they had kept alive from the women of Jabesh-

gilead; yet they were not enough for them.

15 And the people were sorry for Benjamin because the LORD had made a breach in the tribes of Israel.

Women of Shiloh Kidnapped

16 Then the elders of the congregation said, "What shall we do for wives for those who are left, since the women are destroyed out of Benjamin?"

17 And they said, "*There must be* an inheritance for the survivors of Benjamin, that a tribe may not be blotted out from Israel.

18"But we cannot give them wives of our daughters." For the sons of Israel [R]had sworn, saying, "Cursed is he who gives a wife to Benjamin."   Judg. 21:1

19 So they said, "Behold, there is a feast of the LORD from year to year in [R]Shiloh, which is on the north side of Bethel, on the east side of the highway that goes up from Bethel to Shechem, and on the south side of Lebonah."   Josh. 18:1; Judg. 18:31; 1 Sam. 1:3

20 And they commanded the sons of Benjamin, saying, "Go and lie in wait in the vineyards,

21 and watch; and behold, if the daughters of Shiloh come out to [T]take[R] part in the dances, then you shall come out of the vineyards and each of you shall catch his wife from the daughters of Shiloh, and go to the land of Benjamin.   *dance* · Ex. 15:20

22"And it shall come about, when their fathers or their brothers come to complain to us, that we shall say to them, 'Give them to us voluntarily, because we did not take for each man *of Benjamin* [T]a wife in battle, [T]nor[R] did you give *them* to them, *else* you would now be guilty.' "   *his* · *because* · Judg. 21:1, 18

23 And the sons of Benjamin did so, and took wives according to their number from those who danced, whom they carried away. And they went and returned to their inheritance, and [R]rebuilt the cities and lived in them.   Judg. 20:48

24 And the sons of Israel departed from there at that time, every man to his tribe and family, and each one of them went out from there to his inheritance.

25 [R]In those days there was no king in Israel; everyone did what was right in his own eyes.   Judg. 17:6; 18:1; 19:1

THE BOOK OF

RUTH

THE BOOK OF RUTH

Ruth is a cameo story of love, devotion, and redemption set in the black context of the days of the judges. It is the story of a Moabite woman who forsakes her pagan heritage in order to cling to the people of Israel and to the God of Israel. Because of her *faithfulness* in a time of national *faithlessness*, God rewards her by giving her a new husband (Boaz), a son (Obed), and a privileged position in the lineage of David and Christ (she is the great-grandmother of David).

Ruth is the Hebrew title of this book. This name may be a Moabite modification of the Hebrew word *reuit*, meaning friendship or association. The Septuagint entitles the book *Routh*, the Greek equivalent of the Hebrew name. The Latin title is *Ruth*, a transliteration of *Routh*.

THE AUTHOR OF RUTH

The author of Ruth is not given anywhere in the book, nor is he known from any other biblical passage. Talmudic tradition attributes it to Samuel but this is unlikely since David appears in Ruth 4:17, 22, and Samuel died before David's coronation (1 Sam. 25:1). Ruth was probably written during David's reign since Solomon's name is not included in the genealogy. The anonymity of the book, however, should not detract from its spiritual value or literary beauty.

THE TIME OF RUTH

Ruth divides neatly into four distinct settings: (1) the country of Moab (1:1–18); (2) a field in Bethlehem (1:19—2:23); (3) a threshing floor in Bethlehem (3:1–18); and (4) the city of Bethlehem (4:1–22).

The setting of the first eighteen verses is Moab, a region northeast of the Dead Sea. The Moabites, descendants of Lot, worshiped Chemosh and other pagan gods. Scripture records two times when they fight against Israel (Judg. 3:12–30 and 1 Sam. 14:47). Ruth takes place about two centuries after the first war and about eighty years before the second.

Ruth 1:1 gives the setting of the remainder of the book: "Now it came about in the days when the judges governed." This is a time of apostasy, warfare, decline, violence, moral decay, and anarchy. Ruth provides a cameo of the other side of the story—the godly remnant who remain true to the laws of God.

Because Ruth is written more to tell a beautiful story than to give all the historical facts of that period, the assignment of time is somewhat difficult. Utilizing the same fourfold division noted above, the following can be assigned:

A. Ruth 1:1–18 (note 1:4): The country of Moab (c. ten years)

B. Ruth 1:19—2:23 (note 1:22; 2:23): A field in Bethlehem (months)

C. Ruth 3:1–18 (note 3:2, 8, 14, 18): A threshing floor in Bethlehem (one day)

D. Ruth 4:1–22 (note 4:13–16): The city of Bethlehem (c. one year)

THE CHRIST OF RUTH

The concept of the kinsman-redeemer or *goel* (3:9, "close relative") is an important portrayal of the work of Christ. The *goel* must (1) be related by blood to those he redeems (Deut. 25:5, 7–10; John 1:14; Rom. 1:3; Phil. 2:5–8; Heb. 2:14, 15); (2) be able to pay the price of redemption (2:1; 1 Pet. 1:18, 19); (3) be willing to redeem (3:11; Matt. 20:28; John 10:15, 18; Heb. 10:7); (4) be free himself (Christ was free from the curse of sin). The word *goel*, used thirteen times in this short book, presents a clear picture of the mediating work of Christ.

KEYS TO RUTH

Key Word: Kinsman-Redeemer—The Hebrew word for kinsman (*goel*) appears thirteen times in Ruth and basically means "one who redeems." By buying back the land of Naomi, as well as marrying Ruth and fathering a son to keep the family line alive, Boaz acts as a redeemer.

Key Verses: Ruth 1:16; 3:11—"But Ruth said, 'Do not urge me to leave you *or* turn back from following you; for where you go, I will go, and where you lodge, I will lodge. Your people *shall be* my people, and your God, my God' " (1:16).

"And now, my daughter, do not fear. I will do for you whatever you ask, for all my people in the city know that you are a woman of excellence" (3:11).

Key Chapter: Ruth 4—In twenty-two short verses, Ruth moves from widowhood and poverty to marriage and wealth (2:1). In exercising the law regulating the redemption of property (Lev. 25:25–34) and the law concern-

ing a brother's duty to raise up seed (children) in the name of the deceased (Deut. 25:5–10), Boaz brings a Moabite woman into the family line of David and eventually of Jesus Christ.

SURVEY OF RUTH

Ruth is the story of a virtuous woman who lives above the norm of her day. Although it was probably written during the time of David, the events take place during the time of the judges. This period in Israel's history was generally a desert of rebellion and immorality, but the story of Ruth stands in contrast as an oasis of integrity and righteousness.

Ruth is "a woman of excellence" (3:11) who shows loyal love to her mother-in-law Naomi and her near-kinsman Boaz. In both relationships, goodness and love are clearly manifested. Her love is demonstrated in chapters 1 and 2 and rewarded in chapters 3 and 4.

Ruth's Love Is Demonstrated (1 and 2): The story begins with a famine in Israel, a sign of disobedience and apostasy (Deut. 28—30). An Israelite named Elimelech ("My God Is King") in a desperate act moves from Bethlehem ("House of Bread"—note the irony) to Moab. Although he seeks life in that land, he and his two sons Mahlon ("Sick") and Chilion ("Pining") find only death. The deceased sons leave two Moabite widows, Orpah ("Stubbornness") and Ruth ("Friendship"). Elimelech's widow, Naomi, hears that the famine in Israel is over and decides to return, no longer as Naomi ("Pleasant") but as Mara ("Bitter"). She tells her daughters-in-law to remain in Moab and remarry since there was no security for an unmarried woman in those days. Orpah chooses to leave Naomi and is never mentioned again. Ruth, on the other hand, resolves to cling to Naomi and follow Yahweh, the God of Israel. She therefore gives up her culture, people, and language because of her love.

Naomi's misfortune leads her to think that God is her enemy, but He has plans she does not yet realize. In her plight, she must let Ruth glean at the edge of a field. This is a humiliating and dangerous task because of the character of many of the reapers. However, God's providential care brings her to the field of Boaz, Naomi's kinsman. Boaz ("In Him Is Strength") begins to love, protect, and provide for her.

Ruth's Love Is Rewarded (3 and 4): Boaz takes no further steps toward marriage, so Naomi follows the accepted customs of the day and requests that Boaz exercise his right as kinsman-redeemer. In 3:10–13, Boaz reveals why he has taken no action: he is older than Ruth (perhaps twenty years her senior), and he is not the nearest kinsman. Nevertheless, God rewards Ruth's devotion by giving her Boaz as a husband and by providing her with a son, Obed, the grandfather of David.

FOCUS	RUTH'S LOVE DEMONSTRATED		RUTH'S LOVE REWARDED	
REFERENCE	1:1 ——————— 1:19 ———————		3:1 ——————— 4:1 ——————— 4:22	
DIVISION	RUTH'S DECISION TO STAY WITH NAOMI	RUTH'S DEVOTION TO CARE FOR NAOMI	RUTH'S REQUEST FOR REDEMPTION BY BOAZ	RUTH'S REWARD OF REDEMPTION BY BOAZ
TOPIC	RUTH AND NAOMI		RUTH AND BOAZ	
	DEATH OF FAMILY	RUTH CARES FOR NAOMI	BOAZ CARES FOR RUTH	BIRTH OF FAMILY
LOCATION	MOAB	FIELDS OF BETHLEHEM	THRESHING FLOOR OF BETHLEHEM	BETHLEHEM
TIME	c. 12 YEARS			

OUTLINE OF RUTH

Part One: Ruth's Love Is Demonstrated (1:1—2:23)

I. Ruth's Decision to Remain with Naomi....1:1–18
    A. Ruth's Need to Remain with Naomi.....1:1–5
    B. Ruth's Opportunity to Leave Naomi....1:6–15
    C. Ruth's Choice to Remain
       with Naomi......................1:16–18

II. Ruth's Devotion to Care for Naomi....1:19—2:23
    A. Ruth and Naomi Return
       to Bethlehem......................1:19–22
    B. Ruth Gleans for Food................2:1–23
       1. Boaz Meets Ruth................2:1–7
       2. Boaz Protects Ruth 2:8–16
       3. Boaz Provides for Ruth 2:17–23

Part Two: Ruth's Love Is Rewarded (3:1—4:22)

CHAPTER 1

Ruth's Need to Remain with Naomi

Now it came about in the days when the judges governed, that there was a famine in the land. And a certain man of Bethlehem in Judah went to sojourn in the land of Moab ᵀwith his wife and his two sons.   *he, and*

2 And the name of the man *was* Elimelech, and the name of his wife, Naomi; and the names of his two sons *were* Mahlon and Chilion, Ephrathites of Bethlehem in Judah. Now they ᴿentered the land of Moab and remained there.   Judg. 3:30

3 Then Elimelech, Naomi's husband, died; and she was left with her two sons.

4 And they took for themselves Moabite women *as* wives; the name of the one was Orpah and the name of the other Ruth. And they lived there about ten years.

5 Then ᵀboth Mahlon and Chilion also died; and the woman was bereft of her two children and her husband.   *both of them*

Ruth's Opportunity to Leave Naomi

6 Then she arose with her daughters-in-law that she might return from the land of Moab, for she had heard in the land of Moab that the LORD had ᴿvisited His people in ᴿgiving them food.   Ex. 4:31; Jer. 29:10 • Matt. 6:11

7 So she departed from the place where she was, and her two daughters-in-law with her; and they went on the way to return to the land of Judah.

8 And Naomi said to her two daughters-in-law, "Go, return each of you to her mother's house. ᴿMay the LORD deal kindly with you as you have dealt with the dead and with me.   2 Tim. 1:16

9 "May the LORD grant that you may find rest, each in the house of her husband." Then she kissed them, and they lifted up their voices and wept.

10 And they said to her, "*No*, but we will surely return with you to your people."

11 But Naomi said, "Return, my daughters. Why should you go with me? Have I yet sons in my womb, that ᴿthey may be your husbands?   Gen. 38:11; Deut. 25:5

12 "Return, my daughters! Go, for I am too old to have a husband. If I said I have hope, if I should even have a husband tonight and also bear sons,

13 would you therefore wait until they were grown? Would you therefore refrain from marrying? No, my daughters; for it is harder for me than for you, for the hand of the LORD has gone forth against me."

14 And they lifted up their voices and wept again; and Orpah kissed her mother-in-law, but Ruth clung to her.

15 Then she said, "Behold, your sister-in-law has gone back to her people and her gods; return after your sister-in-law."

Ruth's Choice to Remain with Naomi

16 But Ruth said, "Do not urge me to leave you *or* turn back from following you; for where you go, I will go, and where you lodge, I will lodge. Your people *shall be* my people, and your God, my God.

17 "Where you die, I will die, and there I will be buried. Thus may ᴿthe LORD do to me, and worse, if *anything but* death parts you and me."   1 Sam. 3:17; 2 Kin. 6:31

18 When ᴿshe saw that she was determined to go with her, she ᵀsaid no more to her.   Acts 21:14 • *ceased to speak*

Ruth and Naomi Return to Bethlehem

19 So they both went until they came to Bethlehem. And it came about when they had come to Bethlehem, that ᴿall the city was stirred because of them, and ᵀthe women said, "Is this Naomi?"   Matt. 21:10 • *they*

20 And she said to them, "Do not call me ¹Naomi; call me ²Mara, for ᵀthe Almighty has dealt very bitterly with me.   Heb., *Shaddai*

21 "I went out full, but ᴿthe LORD has brought me back empty. Why do you call me Naomi, since the LORD has witnessed against me and ᵀthe Almighty has afflicted me?"   Job 1:21 • Heb., *Shaddai*

22 So Naomi returned, and with her Ruth the Moabitess, her daughter-in-law, who returned from the land of Moab. And they came to Bethlehem at ᴿthe beginning of barley harvest.   Ex. 9:31; Lev. 23:10, 11

CHAPTER 2

Boaz Meets Ruth

Now Naomi had a kinsman of her husband, a man of great wealth, of the family of ᴿElimelech, whose name was Boaz.   Ruth 1:2

¹ I.e., pleasant   ² I.e., bitter

2 And Ruth the Moabitess said to Naomi, "Please let me go to the field and [R]glean among the ears of grain after one in whose sight I may find favor." And she said to her, "Go, my daughter."   Lev. 19:9, 10; 23:22

3 So she departed and went and gleaned in the field after the reapers; and [T]she happened to come to the portion of the field belonging to Boaz, who was of the family of Elimelech.   *her chance chanced upon*

4 Now behold, Boaz came from Bethlehem and said to the reapers, "May[R]the LORD be with you." And they said to him, "May the LORD bless you."   Judg. 6:12; Ps. 129:8

5 Then Boaz said to his servant who was [T]in charge of the reapers, "Whose young woman is this?"   *appointed over*

6 And the servant[T]in charge of the reapers answered and said, "She is the young Moabite woman who returned with Naomi from the land of Moab. *who was appointed over*

7"And she said, 'Please let me glean and gather after the reapers among the sheaves.' Thus she came and has remained from the morning until now; she has been sitting in the house for a little while."

Boaz Protects Ruth

8 Then Boaz said to Ruth, "Listen carefully, my daughter. Do not go to glean in another field; furthermore, do not go on from this one, but stay here with my maids.

9"Let your eyes be on the field which they reap, and go after them. Indeed, I have commanded the servants not to touch you. When you are thirsty, go to the water jars and drink from what the servants draw."

10 Then she fell on her face, bowing to the ground and said to him, "Why have I found favor in your sight that you should take notice of me, since I am a foreigner?"

11 And Boaz answered and said to her, "All that you have done for your mother-in-law after the death of your husband has been fully reported to me, and how you left your father and your mother and the land of your birth, and came to a people that you did not previously know.

12"May[R]the LORD reward your work, and your wages be full from the LORD, the God of Israel,[R]under whose wings you have come to seek refuge."   1 Sam. 24:19 • Ruth 1:16

13 Then she said, "I have found favor in your sight, my lord, for you have comforted me and indeed have spoken[T]kindly to your maidservant, though I am not like one of your maidservants."   *to the heart of your*

14 And at mealtime Boaz said to her, "Come[T]here, that you may eat of the bread and dip your piece of bread in the vinegar." So she sat beside the reapers; and he[T]served her roasted grain, and she ate and was satisfied and had some left. *Draw near • held out to*

15 When she rose to glean, Boaz commanded his servants, saying, "Let her glean even among the sheaves, and do not insult her.

16"And also you shall purposely pull out for her *some grain* from the bundles and leave *it* that she may glean, and do not rebuke her."

Boaz Provides for Ruth

17 So she gleaned in the field until evening. Then she beat out what she had gleaned, and it was about an[T]ephah of barley.   .65 bushels

18 And she took *it* up and went into the city, and her mother-in-law saw what she had gleaned. She also took *it* out and [R]gave [T]Naomi what she had left after[T]she was satisfied.   Ruth 2:14 • *her • her satiety*

19 Her mother-in-law then said to her, "Where did you glean today and where did you work? May he who[R]took notice of you be blessed." So she told her mother-in-law with whom she had worked and said, "The name of the man with whom I worked today is Boaz."   [Ps. 41:1]

20 And Naomi said to her daughter-in-law, "May he be blessed of the LORD who has not withdrawn his kindness to the living and to the dead." Again Naomi said to her, "The man is [T]our relative, he is one of our [T]closest relatives."   *near to us • redeemers*

21 Then Ruth the Moabitess said, "Furthermore,[T] he said to me, 'You should stay close to my servants until they have finished all my harvest.'"   *Also that*

22 And Naomi said to Ruth her daughter-in-law, "It is good, my daughter, that you go out with his maids, lest *others* fall upon you in another field."

23 So she stayed close by the maids of Boaz in order to glean until[R]the end of the barley harvest and the wheat harvest. And she lived with her mother-in-law. Deut. 16:9

CHAPTER 3

Naomi Seeks Redemption for Ruth

THEN Naomi her mother-in-law said to her, "My daughter, shall I not seek[T]security for you, that it may be well with you?   *rest*

2"And now is not Boaz our kinsman, with whose maids you were? Behold, he winnows barley at the threshing floor tonight.

3"Wash yourself therefore, and anoint yourself and put on your *best* clothes, and go down to the threshing floor; *but* do not make yourself known to the man until he has finished eating and drinking.

4"And it shall be when he lies down, that you shall[T]notice the place where he lies, and you shall go and uncover his feet and lie down; then he will tell you what you shall do."   *know*

5 And she said to her, "All^{R}that you say I will do."   [Eph. 6:1; Col. 3:20]

Ruth Obeys Naomi

6 So she went down to the threshing floor and did according to all that her mother-in-law had commanded her.

7 When Boaz had eaten and drunk and ^{R}his heart was merry, he went to lie down at the end of the heap of grain; and she came secretly, and uncovered his feet and lay down.   Judg. 19:6, 9; 2 Sam. 13:28; 1 Kin. 21:7

8 And it happened in the middle of the night that the man was startled and ^{T}bent forward; and behold, a woman was lying at his feet.   *twisted himself*

9 And he said, "Who are you?" And she answered, "I am Ruth your maid. So spread your covering over your maid, for you are a ^{3}close relative."

Boaz Desires to Redeem Ruth

10 Then he said, "May^R you be blessed of the LORD, my daughter. You have shown your last kindness to be better than the first by not going after young men, whether poor or rich.   Ruth 2:20

11"And now, my daughter, do not fear. I will do for you whatever you^{T}ask, for all my people in the ^{T}city know that you are ^{R}a woman of excellence.   *say · gate* · Prov. 12:4

12"And now it is true I am a close relative; however, there is a relative closer than I.

13"Remain this night, and when morning comes, if he will redeem you, good; let him redeem you. But if he does not wish to redeem you, then I will redeem you, as the LORD lives. Lie down until morning."

14 So she lay at his feet until morning and rose before one could recognize another; and he said, "Let it not be known that the woman came to the threshing floor."

15 Again he said, "Give me the cloak that is on you and hold it." So she held it, and he measured six *measures* of barley and laid *it* on her. Then she went into the city.

16 And when she came to her mother-in-law, she said, "How^T did it go, my daughter?" And she told her all that the man had done for her.   *Who are you?*

17 And she said, "These six *measures* of barley he gave to me, for he said, 'Do not go to your mother-in-law empty-handed.'"

18 Then she said, "Wait, my daughter, until you know how the matter^{T}turns out; for the man will not rest until he has^{T}settled it today."   *falls · finished the matter*

CHAPTER 4

Boaz Marries Ruth

NOW Boaz went up to the gate and sat down there, and behold, the^{c}close relative of whom Boaz spoke was passing by, so he said, "Turn aside, friend, sit down here." And he turned aside and sat down. *redeemer*

2 And he took ten men of the^{R}elders of the city and said, "Sit down here." So they sat down.   1 Kin. 21:8; Prov. 31:23

3 Then he said to the ^{c}closest relative, "Naomi, who has come back from the land of Moab, has to sell the piece of land which belonged to our brother Elimelech. *redeemer*

4"So I thought to ^{T}inform you, saying, 'Buy *it* before those who are sitting *here,* and before the elders of my people. If you will redeem *it,* redeem *it;* but if not, tell me that I may know; for there is no one but you to redeem *it,* and I am after you.'" And he said, "I will redeem *it.*"   *uncover your ear*

5 Then Boaz said, "On the day you buy the field from the hand of Naomi, you must also acquire Ruth the Moabitess, the widow of the deceased, in order to raise up the name of the deceased on his inheritance."

6 And the^{c}closest relative said, "I cannot redeem *it* for myself, lest I ^{T}jeopardize my own inheritance. Redeem *it* for yourself; you *may have* my right of redemption, for I cannot redeem *it.*"   *redeemer · ruin*

7 Now this was ^{R}*the custom* in former times in Israel concerning the redemption and the exchange *of land* to confirm any matter: a man removed his sandal and gave it to another; and this was the *manner* of attestation in Israel.   Deut. 25:8-10

8 So the ^{c}closest relative said to Boaz, "Buy *it* for yourself." And he removed his sandal.   *redeemer*

9 Then Boaz said to the elders and all the people, "You are witnesses today that I have bought from the hand of Naomi all that belonged to Elimelech and all that belonged to Chilion and Mahlon.

10"Moreover, I have acquired Ruth the Moabitess, the widow of Mahlon, to be my wife in order to raise up the name of the deceased on his inheritance, so that the name of the deceased may not be cut off from his brothers or from the ^{c}court of his *birth* place; you are witnesses today." *gate*

11 And all the people who were in the court, and the elders, said, "*We are* witnesses. May the LORD make the woman who is coming into your home like Rachel and Leah, both of whom built the house of Israel; and may you achieve wealth in Ephrathah and become famous in Bethlehem.

12"Moreover, may your house be like the house of Perez whom Tamar bore to Judah, through the ^{T}offspring which the LORD shall give you by this young woman."   *seed*

Ruth Bears a Son, Obed

13 So Boaz took Ruth, and she became his wife, and he went in to her. And^{R}the LORD

---

^{3} Or, *redeemer,* and so throughout this context

ᵀenabled her to conceive, and she gave birth to a son. Gen. 29:31; 33:5 • *gave her conception*

14 Then the women said to Naomi, "Blessed is the LORD who has not left you without a redeemer today, and may his nameᵀbecome famous in Israel. *be called in*

15 "May he also be to you a restorer of life and a sustainer of your old age; for your daughter-in-law, who loves you ᵀand ᴿis better to you than seven sons, has given birth to him." *who* • Ruth 1:16, 17; 2:11, 12

Naomi Receives a New Family

16 Then Naomi took the child and laid him in her lap, and became his nurse.

Ruth Is the Great-Grandmother of David
Matt. 1:3-6

17 And the neighbor women gave him a name, saying, "A son has been born to Naomi!" So they named him Obed. He is the father of Jesse, the father of David.

18 Now these are the generations of Perez: ᴿto Perez was born Hezron, Matt. 1:3-6

19 and to Hezron was born Ram, and to Ram, Amminadab,

20 and to Amminadab was born Nahshon, and to Nahshon, Salmon,

21 and to Salmon was born Boaz, and to Boaz, Obed,

22 and to Obed was born Jesse, and to Jesse, David.

Monies

Unit	Monetary Value	Equivalents	Translations
Jewish Weights			
Talent	gold—$5,760,000[1] silver—$384,000	3,000 shekels; 6,000 bekas	talent, one hundred pounds
Shekel	gold—$1,920 silver—$128	4 days' wages; 2 bekas; 20 gerahs	shekel
Beka	gold—$960 silver—$64	½ shekel; 10 gerahs	beka
Gerah	gold—$96 silver—$6.40	¹⁄₂₀ shekel	gerahs
Persian Coins			
Daric	gold—$1,280[2] silver—$64	2 days' wages; ½ Jewish silver shekel	daric, drachma
Greek Coins			
Tetradrachma (Stater)	$128	4 drachmas	stater
Didrachma	$64	2 drachmas	two-drachma tax
Drachma	$32	1 day's wage	coin, silver coins
Lepton	$.25	½ of a Roman kodrantes	cents, small copper coin
Roman Coins			
Aureus	$800	25 denarii	gold
Denarius	$32	1 day's wage	denarii
Assarius	$2	¹⁄₁₆ of a denarius	cent
Kodrantes	$.50	¼ of an assarius	cent

[1]Value of gold is fifteen times the value of silver.
[2]Value of gold is twenty times the value of silver.

SAMUEL

THE BOOK OF FIRST SAMUEL

The Book of First Samuel describes the transition of leadership in Israel from judges to kings. Three characters are prominent in the book: Samuel, the last judge and first prophet; Saul, the first king of Israel; and David, the king-elect, anointed but not yet recognized as Saul's successor.

The books of First and Second Samuel were originally one book in the Hebrew Bible, known as the "Book of Samuel" or simply "Samuel." This name has been variously translated "The Name of God," "His Name Is God," "Heard of God," and "Asked of God." The Septuagint divides Samuel into two books even though it is one continuous account. This division artificially breaks up the history of David. The Greek (Septuagint) title is *Bibloi Basileion*, "Books of Kingdoms," referring to the later kingdoms of Israel and Judah. First Samuel is called *Basileion Alpha*, "First Kingdoms." Second Samuel and First and Second Kings are called "Second, Third, and Fourth Kingdoms." The Latin Vulgate originally called the books of Samuel and Kings *Libri Regum*, "Books of the Kings." Later the Latin Bible combined the Hebrew and Greek titles for the first of these books, calling it *Liber I Samuelis*, the "First Book of Samuel," or simply "First Samuel."

THE AUTHOR OF FIRST SAMUEL

The author of First and Second Samuel is anonymous, but Jewish talmudic tradition says that it was written by Samuel. Samuel may have written the first portion of the book, but his death recorded in First Samuel 25:1 makes it clear that he did not write all of First and Second Samuel. Samuel did write a book (10:25), and written records were available. As the head of a company of prophets (10:5; 19:20), Samuel would be a logical candidate for biblical authorship.

First Chronicles 29:29 refers to "the chronicles of Samuel the seer," "the chronicles of Nathan the prophet," and "the chronicles of Gad the seer." All three men evidently contributed to these two books; and it is very possible that a single compiler, perhaps a member of the prophetic school, used these chronicles to put together the Book of Samuel. This is also suggested by the unity of plan and purpose and by the smooth transitions between sections.

THE TIME OF FIRST SAMUEL

If Samuel wrote the material in the first twenty-four chapters, he did so soon before his death (c. 1015 B.C.). He was born around 1105 B.C., and ministered as a judge and prophet in Israel between about 1067 and 1015 B.C. The books of Samuel end in the last days of David; so they must have been compiled after 971 B.C. The reference in First Samuel 27:6 to the divided monarchy in which Judah is separate from Israel indicates a compilation date after Solomon's death in 931 B.C. However, the silence regarding the Assyrian captivity of Israel in 722 B.C. probably means that First Samuel was written before this key event.

First Samuel covers the ninety-four-year period from the birth of Samuel to the death of Saul (c. 1105–1011 B.C.). The Philistines strongly oppress Israel from 1087 B.C. until the battle of Ebenezer in 1047 B.C. (7:10–14). However, even after this time the Philistines exercise military and economic control. They live in the coastal plains; and the hill country in which the Israelites dwell protects them from total conquest by the Philistines.

THE CHRIST OF FIRST SAMUEL

Samuel is a type of Christ in that he is a prophet, priest, and judge. Highly revered by the people, he brings in a new age.

David is one of the primary Old Testament portrayals of the person of Christ. He is born in Bethlehem, works as a shepherd, and rules as king of Israel. He is the anointed king who becomes the forerunner of the messianic King. His typical messianic psalms are born of his years of rejection and danger (see Ps. 22). God enables David, a man "after His own heart" (13:14), to become Israel's greatest king. The New Testament specifically calls Christ the "descendant of David according to the flesh" (Rom. 1:3) and "the root and the offspring of David" (Rev. 22:16).

KEYS TO FIRST SAMUEL

Key Word: Transition—First Samuel records the critical transition in Israel from the rule of God through the judges to His rule through the kings.

This transition goes through three stages: Eli to Samuel, Samuel to Saul, and Saul to David.
Key Verses: First Samuel 13:14; 15:22—"But

now your kingdom shall not endure. The LORD has sought out for Himself a man after His own heart, and the LORD has appointed him as ruler over His people, because you have not kept what the LORD commanded you" (13:14).

"And Samuel said, 'Has the LORD as much delight in burnt offerings and sacrifices, as in obeying the voice of the LORD? Behold, to obey is better than sacrifice, *and* to heed than the fat of rams' " (15:22).

Key Chapter: First Samuel 15—First Samuel 15 records the tragic transition of kingship from Saul to David. As in all three changes recorded in First Samuel, God removes His blessing from one and gives it to another because of sin. "Because you have rejected the word of the LORD, He has also rejected you from *being* king" (15:23).

SURVEY OF FIRST SAMUEL

First Samuel records the crucial transition from the theocracy under the judges to the monarchy under the kings. The book is built around three key men: Samuel (1—7), Saul (8—31) and David (16—31).

Samuel (1—7): Samuel's story begins late in the turbulent time of the judges when Eli is the judge-priest of Israel. The birth of Samuel and his early call by Yahweh are found in chapters 1—3. Because of his responsiveness to God (3:19), he is confirmed as a prophet (3:20, 21) at a time when the "word from the LORD was rare in those days, visions were infrequent" (3:1).

Corruption at Shiloh by Eli's notoriously wicked sons leads to Israel's defeat in the crucial battle with the Philistines (4:1–11). The ark of the covenant, God's "throne" among the people, is lost to the Philistines; the priesthood is disrupted by the deaths of Eli and his sons;

and the glory of God departs from the tabernacle (Ichabod, "no glory," 4:21). Samuel begins to function as the last of the judges and the first in the order of the prophets (Acts 3:24). His prophetic ministry (7:3–17) leads to a revival in Israel, the return of the ark, and the defeat of the Philistines. When Samuel is old and his sons prove to be unjust judges, the people wrongly cry out for a king. They want a visible military and judicial ruler so they can be "like all the nations" (8:5–20).

Saul (8—15): In their impatient demand for a king, Israel chooses less than God's best. Their motive (8:5) and criteria (9:2) are wrong. Saul begins well (9—11), but his good characteristics soon degenerate. In spite of Samuel's solemn prophetic warning (12), Saul and the people begin to act wickedly. Saul presumptuously assumes the role of a priest (cf. 2 Chr. 26:18) and offers up sacrifices (13). He makes a foolish vow (14) and disobeys God's command to destroy the Amalekites (15). Samuel's powerful words in 15:22, 23 evoke a pathetic response in 15:24–31.

Saul and David (16—31): When God rejects Saul, He commissions Samuel to anoint David as Israel's next king. God's king-elect serves in Saul's court (16:14—23:29) and defeats the Philistine Goliath (17). Jonathan's devotion to David leads him to sacrifice the throne (20:30, 31) in acknowledgment of David's divine right to it (18). David becomes a growing threat to the insanely jealous Saul; but he is protected from Saul's wrath by Jonathan, Michal, and Samuel (19).

Saul's open rebellion against God is manifested in his refusal to give up what God has said cannot be his. David is protected again by Jonathan from Saul's murderous intent (20), but Saul becomes more active in his pursuit of David. The future king flees to a Philistine city

FOCUS	SAMUEL		SAUL		
REFERENCE	1:1————————4:1—————	8:1————————————	13:1————	15:10————	31:13
DIVISION	FIRST TRANSITION OF LEADERSHIP: ELI—SAMUEL	JUDGESHIP OF SAMUEL	SECOND TRANSITION OF LEADERSHIP: SAMUEL—SAUL	REIGN OF SAUL	THIRD TRANSITION OF LEADERSHIP: SAUL—DAVID
TOPIC	DECLINE OF JUDGES		RISE OF KINGS		
	ELI	SAMUEL	SAUL		DAVID
LOCATION	CANAAN				
TIME	c. 94 YEARS				

where he feigns insanity (21), and flees again to Adullam where a band of men forms around him (22).

David continues to escape from the hand of Saul, and on two occasions spares Saul's life when he has the opportunity to take it (24—26). David again seeks refuge among the Phil-istines, but is not allowed to fight on their side against Israel. Saul, afraid of impending bat-tle against the Philistines, foolishly consults a medium at En-dor to hear the deceased Sam-uel's advice (28). The Lord rebukes Saul and pronounces his doom; he and his sons are killed by the Philistines on Mount Gilboa (31).

OUTLINE OF FIRST SAMUEL

Part One: Samuel, the Last Judge (1:1—7:17)

Part Two: Saul, the First King (8:1—31:13)

CHAPTER 1

Hannah's Barrenness

NOW there was a certain man from Ramathaim-zophim from the hill country of Ephraim, and his name was Elkanah the son of Jeroham, the son of Elihu, the son of Tohu, the son of Zuph, an Ephraimite.

2 And he had[R]two wives: the name of one was Hannah and the name of the other Peninnah; and Peninnah had children, but Hannah had no children.   Deut. 21:15-17

3 Now this man would go up from his city[R]yearly[R]to worship and to sacrifice to the LORD of hosts in[R]Shiloh. And the two sons of Eli, Hophni and Phinehas were priests to the LORD there.   Ex. 34:23 • Ex. 23:14 • Josh. 18:1

4 And when the day came that Elkanah sacrificed, he[R]would give portions to Peninnah his wife and to all her sons and her daughters;   Deut. 12:17, 18

5 but to Hannah he would give a double portion, for he loved Hannah,[R]but the LORD had closed her womb.   Gen. 16:1; 30:1

6 Her rival, however,[R]would provoke her bitterly to irritate her, because the LORD had closed her womb.   Job 24:21

7 And it happened year after year, as often as she went up to the house of the LORD, she would provoke her, so she wept and would not eat.

8 Then Elkanah her husband said to her, "Hannah, why do you weep and why do you not eat and why is your heart sad?[R]Am I not better to you than ten sons?"   Ruth 4:15

9 Then Hannah rose after eating and drinking in Shiloh. Now Eli the priest was sitting on the seat by the doorpost of[R]the temple of the LORD.   1 Sam. 3:3

10 And she,[T]greatly distressed, prayed to the LORD and wept bitterly.   *bitter of soul*

11 And she made a vow and said, "O LORD of hosts, if Thou wilt indeed[R]look on the affliction of Thy maidservant and remember me, and not forget Thy maidservant, but wilt give Thy maidservant a[T]son, then I will give him to the LORD all the days of his life, and[R]a razor shall never come on his head."   Gen. 29:32 • *seed of men* • Num. 6:5

12 Now it came about, as she[T]continued praying before the LORD, that Eli was watching her mouth.   *multiplied*

13 As for Hannah, [R]she was speaking in her heart, only her lips were moving, but her voice was not heard. So Eli thought she was drunk.   Gen. 24:42-45

14 Then Eli said to her, "How[R]long will you make yourself drunk? Put away your wine from you."   Acts 2:4, 13

15 But Hannah answered and said, "No, my lord, I am a woman[T]oppressed in spirit; I have drunk neither wine nor strong drink, but I[R]have poured out my soul before the LORD.   *severe* • Job 30:16; Ps. 42:4; 62:8

16 "Do not[T]consider your maidservant as a worthless woman; for I have spoken until now out of my great concern and[T]provocation."   *give* • *my provocation*

17 Then Eli answered and said, "Go in peace; and may the God of Israel grant your petition that you have asked of Him."

18 And she said, "Let[R]your maidservant find favor in your sight." So the woman went her way and ate, and[R]her face was no longer *sad*.   Gen. 33:15; Ruth 2:13 • [Rom. 15:13]

Samuel's Birth

19 Then they arose early in the morning and worshiped before the LORD, and returned again to their house in Ramah. And Elkanah[T]had relations with Hannah his wife, and the LORD remembered her.   *knew*

20 And it came about[T]in due time, after Hannah had conceived, that she gave birth to a son; and she named him Samuel, *saying*, "Because[R] I have asked him of the LORD."   *at the circuit of the days* • Gen. 41:51, 52

21 Then the man Elkanah[R]went up with all his household to offer to the LORD the yearly sacrifice and *pay* his vow.   Deut. 12:11

22 But Hannah did not go up, for she said to her husband, "*I will not go up* until the child is weaned; then I will[R]bring him, that he may appear before the LORD and[R]stay there forever."   Luke 2:22 • 1 Sam. 1:11, 28

1:17 **Petition**—One great difference between Christianity and all other religions is that the believer has a prayer-hearing and prayer-answering God. In the Old Testament during a contest with Elijah, the priests of Baal make desperate efforts to speak with their god by crying out and cutting themselves, but to no avail. "But there was no voice and no one answered" (Page 346—1 Kin. 18:26). How different from these words are those of the Psalmist: "But certainly God has heard; He has given heed to the voice of my prayer" (Page 561—Ps. 66:19).

  a. The nature of our petitions. First of all, God has commanded us to pray (Page 969—Matt. 7:7, 8; Page 1218—1 Tim. 2:8). When we pray, our petitions should be made by faith (Page 1253—James 1:6) in the name of Jesus (Page 1081—John 14:13). If these simple rules are followed, we can rest assured our prayers are being heard (Page 1277—1 John 3:22; 5:14, 15).

  b. The objects of our prayers. For whom or what should we pray? First of all, we need to pray for ourselves, because unless we are in God's will, He cannot hear our petitions about other things. Thus we should begin by asking for cleansing (Page 1274—1 John 1:9) and wisdom (Page 1253—James 1:5). Other areas of our petitons concern spiritual leaders (Page 1202—Col. 4:3), sick believers (Page 1256—James 5:14, 15), rulers (Page 1217—1 Tim. 2:1–3), and even for our enemies (Page 968—Matt. 5:44).

    Now turn to Page 1195—Phil. 4:6: Thanksgiving.

23 And Elkanah her husband said to her, "Do what seems best to you. Remain until you have weaned him; only may the LORD confirm His word." So the woman remained and nursed her son until she weaned him.

24 Now when she had weaned him, ^Rshe took him up with her, with a three-year-old bull and one ephah of flour and a jug of wine, and brought him to^Rthe house of the LORD in Shiloh, although the child was young.   Num. 15:9, 10; Deut. 12:5, 6 • Josh. 18:1

25 Then ^Rthey slaughtered the bull, and ^Rbrought the boy to Eli.   Lev. 1:5 • Luke 2:22

26 And she said, "Oh, my lord! As your soul lives, my lord, I am the woman who stood here beside you, praying to the LORD.

27 "For this boy I prayed, and the LORD has given me my petition which I asked of Him.

28 "So^R I have also ¹dedicated him to the LORD; as long as he lives he is ¹dedicated to the LORD." And ^Rhe worshiped the LORD there.   1 Sam. 1:11, 22 • Gen. 24:26, 52

CHAPTER 2

Hannah's Prophetic Prayer

THEN Hannah prayed and said,
  "My heart exults in the LORD;
  My^Thorn is exalted in the LORD,
  My mouth^Tspeaks boldly against my
    enemies,   strength • is enlarged
  Because I rejoice in Thy salvation.
2 "There is no one holy like the LORD,
  Indeed, there is no one besides Thee,
  Nor is there any rock like our God.
3 "Boast^Tno more so very proudly,
  ^RDo not let arrogance come out of your
    mouth;   Talk much • Prov. 8:13
  For the LORD is a God of knowledge,
  And with Him actions are weighed.
4 "The bows of the mighty are shattered,
  But the feeble gird on strength.
5 "Those who were full hire themselves
    out for bread,
  But those who were hungry cease to
    hunger.
  ^REven the barren gives birth to seven,
  But^Rshe who has many children lan-
    guishes.   Ruth 4:15; Ps. 113:9 • Jer. 15:9
6 "The^RLORD kills and makes alive;
  He brings down to^TSheol and raises
    up.   Deut. 32:39 • the nether world
7 "The LORD makes poor and rich;
  ^RHe brings low, He also exalts. Ps. 75:7
8 "He raises the poor from the dust,
  He lifts the needy from the ash heap
  ^RTo make them sit with nobles,
  And inherit a seat of honor;
  ^RFor the pillars of the earth are the
    LORD's,   Job 36:7 • Job 38:4-6; Ps. 75:3
  And He set the world on them.
9 "He^R keeps the feet of His godly ones,
  ^RBut the wicked ones are silenced in
    darkness;   Ps. 91:11, 12 • [Matt. 8:12]
  For not by might shall a man prevail.

10 "Those^R who contend with the LORD
    will be shattered;   Ex. 15:6; Ps. 2:9
  ^RAgainst them He will thunder in the
    heavens,   2 Sam. 22:14; Ps. 18:13, 14
  ^RThe LORD will judge the ends of the
    earth;   [Ps. 96:13; 98:9; Matt. 25:31, 32]
  ^RAnd He will give strength to His king,
  And will exalt the ^Thorn of His
    anointed."   Ps. 21:1, 7 • strength
11 Then Elkanah went to his home at^RRa-
mah.^RBut the boy ministered to the LORD before Eli the priest.   1 Sam. 1:1, 19 • 1 Sam. 1:28

Sinfulness of Eli's Sons

12 Now the sons of Eli were ²worthless^R men; they did not know the LORD   Jer. 2:8

13 ^Rand the custom of the priests with the people. When any man was offering a sacri-fice, the priest's servant would come while the meat was boiling, with a three-pronged fork in his hand.   Lev. 7:29-34

14 Then he would thrust it into the pan, or kettle, or caldron, or pot; all that the fork brought up the priest would take for him-self. Thus they did in Shiloh to all the Israel-ites who came there.

15 Also, before ^Rthey burned the fat, the priest's servant would come and say to the man who was sacrificing, "Give the priest meat for roasting, as he will not take boiled meat from you, only raw."   Lev. 3:3-5, 16

16 And if the man said to him, "They must surely^Tburn the fat first, and then take as much as you desire," then he would say, "No, but you shall give it to me now; and if not, I will take it by force."   offer up in smoke

17 Thus the sin of the young men was very great before the LORD, for the men^Rde-spised the offering of the LORD.   [Mal. 2:7-9]

18 Now Samuel was ministering before the LORD, as a boy wearing a linen ephod.

19 And his mother would make him a lit-tle ^Rrobe and bring it to him from year to year when she would come up with her hus-band to offer the yearly sacrifice.   Ex. 28:31

20 Then Eli would^Rbless Elkanah and his wife and say, "May the LORD give you^Tchil-dren from this woman in place of the one she dedicated to the LORD." And they went to their own^Thome.   Luke 2:34 • seed • place

21 And^Rthe LORD visited Hannah; and she conceived and gave birth to three sons and two daughters. And^Rthe boy Samuel grew before the LORD.   Gen. 21:1 • Judg. 13:24

Compromise of Eli as Father

22 Now Eli was very old; and he heard all that his sons were doing to all Israel, and how they lay with^Rthe women who served at the doorway of the tent of meeting. Ex. 38:8

¹ Lit., lent   ² Lit., sons of Belial

23 And he said to them, "Why do you do such things, the evil things that I hear from all these people?

24"No, my sons; for the report is not good which I hear the LORD's people circulating.

25"If one man sins against another,^RGod will mediate for him; but if a man sins against the LORD, who can intercede for him?" But they would not listen to the voice of their father, for the^RLORD desired to put them to death.   Deut. 1:17 • Josh. 11:20

26 Now the boy Samuel^Twas growing in stature and in favor both with the LORD and with men.   *was going on both great and good*

27 Then^Ra man of God came to Eli and said to him, "Thus says the LORD, 'Did^RI *not* indeed reveal Myself to the house of your father when they were in Egypt *in bondage* to Pharaoh's house?   Deut. 33:1 • Ex. 4:14-16

28 'And^Rdid I *not* choose them from all the tribes of Israel to be My priests, to go up to My altar, to carry an ephod before Me; and did I *not*^Rgive to the house of your father all the fire *offerings* of the sons of Israel?   Ex. 28:1-4; 30:7, 8 • Lev. 7:35, 36

29 'Why do you kick at My sacrifice and at My offering which I have commanded *in My* dwelling, and honor your sons above Me, by making yourselves fat with the^choicest of every offering of My people Israel?'   *first*

30"Therefore the LORD God of Israel declares, 'I^Rdid indeed say that your house and the house of your father should walk before Me forever'; but now the LORD declares, 'Far be it from Me—for^Rthose who honor Me I will honor, and those who despise Me will be lightly esteemed.   Ex. 29:9 • Ps. 50:23

31 'Behold, the days are coming when I will break your^strength and the^strength of your father's house so that there will not be an old man in your house.   *arm*

32 'And you will see^Rthe distress of *My* dwelling, in *spite of* all that^TI do good for Israel; and an old man will not be in your house forever.   1 Kin. 2:26, 27 • *He does*

33 'Yet I will not cut off every man of yours from My altar that your eyes may fail *from weeping* and your soul grieve, and all the increase of your house will die^Tin the prime of life.   *as men*

34 'And this will be^Rthe sign to you which shall come concerning your two sons, Hophni and Phinehas:^Ron the same day both of them shall die.   1 Kin. 13:3 • 1 Sam. 4:11, 17

35 'But I will raise up for Myself a faithful priest who will do according to what is in My heart and in My soul; and I will build him an enduring house, and he will walk before^RMy anointed always.   1 Sam. 10:9, 10

36 'And it shall come about that everyone who is left in your house shall come and bow down to him for a^piece of silver or a loaf of bread, and say, "Please^Tassign me to one of the priest's offices so that I may eat a piece of bread." ' "   *payment • attach*

CHAPTER 3

The Word of the Lord
Does Not Come to Eli

N OW the boy Samuel was ministering to the LORD before Eli. And^Rword from the LORD was rare in those days,^Tvisions were infrequent.   Ps. 74:9 • *no vision spread abroad*

The Word of the Lord
Comes to Samuel

2 And it happened at that time as Eli was lying down in his place (now^Rhis eyesight had begun to grow dim *and* he could not see well),   Gen. 27:1; 48:10; 1 Sam. 4:15

3 and the lamp of God had not yet gone out, and Samuel was lying down in the temple of the LORD where the ark of God *was*,

4 that the LORD called Samuel; and he said, "Here^RI am."   [Is. 6:8]

5 Then he ran to Eli and said, "Here I am, for you called me." But he said, "I did not call, lie down again." So he went and lay down.

6 And the LORD called yet again, "Samuel!" So Samuel arose and went to Eli, and said, "Here I am, for you called me." But he ^Tanswered, "I did not call, my son, lie down again."   *said*

7 ^RNow Samuel did not yet know the LORD, nor had the word of the LORD yet been revealed to him.   Acts 19:2; 1 Cor. 13:11

8 So the LORD called Samuel again for the third time. And he arose and went to Eli, and said, "Here I am, for you called me." Then Eli discerned that the LORD was calling the boy.

9 And Eli said to Samuel, "Go lie down, and it shall be if He calls you, that you shall say, 'Speak, LORD, for Thy servant is listening.' " So Samuel went and lay down in his place.

10 Then the LORD came and stood and called as at other times, "Samuel! Samuel!" And Samuel said, "Speak, for Thy servant is listening."

11 And the LORD said to Samuel, "Behold, ^RI am about to do a thing in Israel at which both ears of everyone who hears it will tingle.   2 Kin. 21:12; Jer. 19:3

12"In that day^RI will carry out against Eli all that I have spoken concerning his house, from beginning to end.   1 Sam. 2:27-36

13"For^RI have told him that I am about to judge his house forever for ^Rthe iniquity which he knew, because his sons brought a curse on themselves and^Rhe did not rebuke them.   1 Sam. 2:29-31 • 1 Sam. 2:22 • Deut. 17:12

14"And therefore I have sworn to the house of Eli that^Rthe iniquity of Eli's house shall not be atoned for by sacrifice or offering forever."   Lev. 15:31; Is. 22:14

15 So Samuel lay down until morning. Then he^Ropened the doors of the house of the LORD. But Samuel was afraid to tell^Rthe vision to Eli.   1 Chr. 15:23 • 1 Sam. 3:10

16 Then Eli called Samuel and said, "Samuel, my son." And he said, "Here I am."

17 And he said, "What is the word that He spoke to you? Please do not hide it from me. ^RMay God do so to you, and more also, if you hide anything from me of all the words that He spoke to you." 2 Sam. 3:35

18 So Samuel told him everything and hid nothing from him. And he said, "It is the LORD; let Him do what seems good to Him."

Samuel Is Recognized
as the New Leader of Israel

19 Thus Samuel grew and the LORD was with him and let none of his words fail.

20 And all Israel^Rfrom Dan even to Beersheba knew that Samuel was confirmed as a prophet of the LORD.   Judg. 20:1

21 And the LORD appeared again at Shiloh, because the LORD revealed Himself to Samuel at Shiloh by the word of the LORD.

CHAPTER 4
Conquest of Israel by Philistia

THUS the word of Samuel came to all Israel. Now Israel went out to meet the Philistines in battle and camped beside Ebenezer while the Philistines camped in Aphek.

2 And the Philistines drew up in battle array to meet Israel. When the battle spread, Israel was ^Tdefeated before the Philistines who killed about four thousand men on the battlefield.   smitten

3 When the people came into the camp, the elders of Israel said, "Why^Rhas the LORD defeated us today before the Philistines?^RLet us take to ourselves from Shiloh the ark of the covenant of the LORD, that^Ait may come among us and deliver us from the power of our enemies."   Josh. 7:7, 8 • Num. 10:35 • he

4 So the people sent to Shiloh, and from there they carried the ark of the covenant of the LORD of hosts^Rwho sits above the cherubim; and the two sons of Eli, Hophni and Phinehas, were there with the ark of the covenant of God.   Ex. 25:22; 2 Sam. 6:2; Ps. 80:1

5 And it happened as the ark of the covenant of the LORD came into the camp, that ^Rall Israel shouted with a great shout, so that the earth resounded.   Josh. 6:5, 20

6 And when the Philistines heard the noise of the shout, they said, "What does the noise of this great shout in the camp of the Hebrews mean?" Then they understood that the ark of the LORD had come into the camp.

7 And the Philistines were afraid, for they said, "God has come into the camp." And they said, "Woe^Rto us! For nothing like this has happened before.   Ex. 15:14

8"Woe to us! Who shall deliver us from the hand of these mighty gods? These are the gods who smote the Egyptians with all kinds of plagues in the wilderness.

9"Take^R courage and be men, O Philis-

tines, lest you become slaves to the Hebrews, as they have been slaves to you; therefore, be men and fight."   1 Cor. 16:13

10 So the Philistines fought and Israel was defeated, and every man fled to his tent, and the slaughter was very great; for there fell of Israel thirty thousand foot soldiers.

Eli and His Sons Die

11 And the ark of God was taken; and the two sons of Eli, Hophni and Phinehas, died.

12 Now a man of Benjamin ran from the battle line and came to Shiloh the same day with his clothes torn and dust on his head.

13 When he came, behold,^REli was sitting on his seat by the road eagerly watching, because his heart was trembling for the ark of God. So the man came to tell it in the city, and all the city cried out. 1 Sam. 1:9; 4:18

14 When Eli heard the noise of the outcry, he said, "What does the noise of this commotion mean?" Then the man came hurriedly and told Eli.

15 Now Eli was ninety-eight years old, and^Rhis eyes were set so that he could not see.   1 Sam. 3:2; 1 Kin. 14:4

16 And the man said to Eli, "I am the one who came from the battle line. Indeed, I escaped from the battle line today." And he said, "How did things go, my son?"

17 Then the one who brought the news answered and said, "Israel has fled before the Philistines and there has also been a great slaughter among the people, and your two sons also, Hophni and Phinehas, are dead, and the ark of God has been taken."

18 And it came about when he mentioned the ark of God that^TEli fell off the seat backward beside the gate, and his neck was broken and he died, for he was old and heavy. Thus he judged Israel forty years.   he

19 Now his daughter-in-law, Phinehas' wife, was pregnant and about to give birth; and when she heard the news that the ark of God was taken and that her father-in-law and her husband had died, she kneeled down and gave birth, for her pains came upon her.

20 And about the time of her death the women who stood by her said to her, "Do^R not be afraid, for you have given birth to a son." But she did not answer or pay attention.   Gen. 35:16-19

21 And she called the boy ³Ichabod, saying, "The glory has departed from Israel," because the ark of God was taken and because of her father-in-law and her husband.

22 And she said, "The glory has departed from Israel, for the ark of God was taken."

CHAPTER 5
The Philistines' Sin with the Ark

NOW the Philistines took the ark of God and brought it from Ebenezer to Ashdod.

___
³ I.e., no glory

2 Then the Philistines took the ark of God and brought it to ^Rthe house of Dagon, and set it by Dagon.   Judg. 16:23-30

3 When the Ashdodites arose early the next morning, behold, ^RDagon had fallen on his face to the ground before the ark of the LORD. So they took Dagon and^Rset him in his place again.   Is. 19:1; 46:1, 2 • Is. 46:7

4 But when they arose early the next morning, behold, ^RDagon had fallen on his face to the ground before the ark of the LORD. And the head of Dagon and both the palms of his hands were cut off on the threshold; only the trunk of Dagon was left to him.   Ezek. 6:4, 6; Mic. 1:7

5 Therefore neither the priests of Dagon nor all who enter Dagon's house^Rtread on the threshold of Dagon in Ashdod to this day.   Zeph. 1:9

6 Now^Rthe hand of the LORD was heavy on the Ashdodites, and ^RHe ravaged them and smote them with tumors, both Ashdod and its territories.   Ex. 9:3 • 1 Sam. 6:5

7 When the men of Ashdod saw that it was so, they said, "The ark of the God of Israel must not remain with us, for His hand is severe on us and on Dagon our god."

8 So they sent and^Rgathered all the lords of the Philistines to them and said, "What shall we do with the ark of the God of Israel?" And they said, "Let the ark of the God of Israel be brought around to Gath." And they brought the ark of the God of Israel around.   1 Sam. 5:11; 29:6-11

9 And it came about that after they had brought it around,^Rthe hand of the LORD was against the city with very great confusion; and He smote the men of the city, both young and old, so that^Rtumors broke out on them.   Deut. 2:15; 1 Sam. 5:11; 7:13 • 1 Sam. 5:6

10 So they sent the ark of God to Ekron. And it happened as the ark of God came to Ekron that the Ekronites cried out, saying, "They have brought the ark of the God of Israel around to ^Tus, to kill ^Tus and^Tour people."   me • my

11 They sent therefore and gathered all the lords of the Philistines and said, "Send away the ark of the God of Israel, and let it return to its own place, that it may not kill ^Tus and^Tour people." For there was a deadly confusion throughout the city; the hand of God was very heavy there.   me • my

12 And the men who did not die were smitten with tumors and^Rthe cry of the city went up to heaven.   Ex. 12:30; Is. 15:3

CHAPTER 6

NOW the ark of the LORD had been in the country of the Philistines seven months.

2 And the Philistines called for the priests and the diviners, saying, "What shall we do with the ark of the LORD? Tell us^Thow we shall send it to its place."   with what

3 And they said, "If you send away the ark of the God of Israel,^Rdo not send it empty; but you shall surely^Rreturn to Him a guilt offering. Then you shall be healed and it shall be known to you why His hand is not removed from you."   Ex. 23:15 • Lev. 5:15, 16

4 Then they said, "What shall be the guilt offering which we shall return to Him?" And they said, "Five golden tumors and five golden mice according to the number of the lords of the Philistines, for one plague was on all of you and on your lords.

5 "So you shall make likenesses of your tumors and likenesses of your mice that ravage the land, and you shall give glory to the God of Israel; perhaps He will ease His hand from you, your gods, and your land.

6 "Why then do you harden your hearts^Ras the Egyptians and Pharaoh hardened their hearts? When He had severely dealt with them, did they not allow ^Tthe people to go, and they departed?   Ex. 7:13; 8:15, 32 • them

7 "Now therefore take and^Rprepare a new cart and two milch cows on which there^Rhas never been a yoke; and hitch the cows to the cart and take their calves home, away from them.   2 Sam. 6:3 • Num. 19:2; Deut. 21:3, 4

8 "And take the ark of the LORD and place it on the cart; and put^Rthe articles of gold which you return to Him as^Ra guilt offering in a box by its side. Then send it away that it may go.   1 Sam. 6:4, 5 • 1 Sam. 6:3

9 "And watch, if it goes up by the way of its own territory to Beth-shemesh, then He has done us this great evil. But if not, then we shall know that it was not His hand that struck us; it happened to us by chance."

The Israelites' Sin with the Ark

10 Then the men did so, and took two milch cows and hitched them to the cart, and shut up their calves at home.

11 And they put the ark of the LORD on the cart, and the box with the golden mice and the likenesses of their tumors.

12 And the cows took the straight way in the ^Tdirection of Beth-shemesh; they went along the highway, lowing as they went, and did not turn aside to the right or to the left. And the lords of the Philistines followed them to the border of Beth-shemesh.   way

13 Now the people of Beth-shemesh were reaping their wheat harvest in the valley, and they raised their eyes and saw the ark and were glad to see it.

14 And the cart came into the field of Joshua the Beth-shemite and stood there where was a large stone; and they split the wood of the cart and offered the cows as a burnt offering to the LORD.

15 And the Levites took down the ark of the LORD and the box that was with it, in which were the articles of gold, and put them on the large stone; and the men of Beth-shemesh offered burnt offerings and sacrificed sacrifices that day to the LORD.

16 And when the[R]five lords of the Philistines saw it, they returned to Ekron that day.   Josh. 13:3; Judg. 3:3

17 And[R]these are the golden tumors which the Philistines returned for a guilt offering to the LORD: one for Ashdod, one for Gaza, one for Ashkelon, one for Gath, one for Ekron;   1 Sam. 6:4

18 and the golden mice, *according* to the number of all the cities of the Philistines belonging to the five lords, [R]both of fortified cities and of country villages. [R]The large stone on which they set the ark of the LORD *is a witness* to this day in the field of Joshua the Beth-shemite.   Deut. 3:5 • 1 Sam. 6:14, 15

19 And[R]He struck down some of the men of Beth-shemesh because they had looked into the ark of the LORD. He struck down of all the people, 50,070 men, and the people mourned because the LORD had struck the people with a great slaughter.   Ex. 19:21

20 And the men of Beth-shemesh said, "Who[R]is able to stand before the LORD, this holy God? And to whom shall He go up from us?"   Lev. 11:44, 45; 2 Sam. 6:9; Mal. 3:2

21 So they sent messengers to the inhabitants of Kiriath-jearim, saying, "The Philistines have brought back the ark of the LORD; come down and take it up to you."

CHAPTER 7

The Acceptable Return of the Ark

A[ND] the men of Kiriath-jearim came and took the ark of the LORD and[R]brought it into the house of Abinadab on the hill, and consecrated Eleazar his son to keep the ark of the LORD.   2 Sam. 6:3, 4

2 And it came about from the day that the ark remained at Kiriath-jearim that the time was long, for it was twenty years; and all the house of Israel lamented after the LORD.

Israel Returns to the Lord

3 Then Samuel spoke to all the house of Israel, saying, "If[R]you return to the LORD with all your heart,[R]remove the foreign gods and the Ashtaroth from among you and direct your hearts to the LORD and serve Him alone; and He will deliver you from the hand of the Philistines."   1 Kin. 8:48 • Gen. 35:2

4 So the sons of Israel removed the Baals and the Ashtaroth and served the LORD alone.

5 Then Samuel said, "Gather all Israel to [R]Mizpah, and [R]I will pray to the LORD for you."   Judg. 10:17; 20:1 • 1 Sam. 8:6; 12:17-19

6 And they gathered to Mizpah, and drew water and[R]poured it out before the LORD, and[R]fasted on that day, and said

there, "We[R]have sinned against the LORD." And Samuel judged the sons of Israel at Mizpah.   1 Sam. 1:15 • Lev. 16:29 • Judg. 10:10

Israel's Victory over Philistia

7 Now when the Philistines heard that the sons of Israel had gathered to Mizpah, the lords of the Philistines went up against Israel. And when the sons of Israel heard it, they were afraid of the Philistines.

8 Then the sons of Israel said to Samuel, "Do[R]not cease to cry to the LORD our God for us, that He may save us from the hand of the Philistines."   1 Sam. 12:19-24; Is. 37:4

9 And Samuel took[R]a suckling lamb and offered it for a whole burnt offering to the LORD; and Samuel cried to the LORD for Israel and the LORD answered him.   Lev. 22:27

10 Now Samuel was offering up the burnt offering, and the Philistines drew near to battle against Israel. But the LORD thundered with a great [T]thunder on that day against the Philistines and confused them, so that they were routed before Israel. *voice*

11 And the men of Israel went out of Mizpah and pursued the Philistines, and struck them down as far as below Beth-car.

12 Then Samuel[R]took a stone and set it between Mizpah and Shen, and named it [4]Ebenezer, saying, "Thus far the LORD has helped us."   Gen. 35:14; Josh. 4:9; 24:26

13 [R]So the Philistines were subdued and [R]they did not come anymore within the border of Israel. And the hand of the LORD was against the Philistines all the days of Samuel.   Judg. 13:1-15 • 1 Sam. 13:5

14 And the cities which the Philistines had taken from Israel were restored to Israel, from Ekron even to Gath; and Israel delivered their territory from the hand of the Philistines. So there was peace between Israel and[R]the Amorites.   Num. 13:29

15 Now Samuel[R]judged Israel all the days of his life.   1 Sam. 7:6

16 And he used to go annually on circuit to [R]Bethel and Gilgal and Mizpah, and he judged Israel in all these places.   Gen. 28:19

17 Then his return *was* to Ramah, for his house *was* there, and there he judged Israel; and he built there an altar to the LORD.

CHAPTER 8

*Israel Rejects Samuel's Sons
as Leaders*

A[ND] it came about when Samuel was old that[R]he appointed his sons judges over Israel.   Deut. 16:18, 19

2 Now the name of his first-born was

---

[4] I.e., the stone of help

Joel, and the name of his second, Abijah; *they* were judging in [R]Beersheba.   Gen. 22:19

3 His sons, however, did not walk in his ways, but turned aside after dishonest gain and took bribes and perverted justice.

4 Then all the elders of Israel gathered together and came to Samuel at Ramah;

5 and they said to him, "Behold, you have grown old, and your sons do not walk in your ways. Now [R]appoint a king for us to judge us like all the nations."   Deut. 17:14, 15

Israel Rejects God as King

6 But the thing was ^displeasing [R] in the sight of Samuel when they said, "Give us a king to judge us." And [R]Samuel prayed to the LORD.   *evil* • 1 Sam. 12:17 • 1 Sam. 15:11

7 And the LORD said to Samuel, "Listen to the voice of the people in regard to all that they say to you, for [R]they have not rejected you, but they have rejected Me from being king over them.   Ex. 16:8; 1 Sam. 10:19

8 "Like all the deeds which they have done since the day that I brought them up from Egypt even to this day—in that they have forsaken Me and served other gods— so they are doing to you also.

9 "Now then, listen to their voice; [R]however, you shall solemnly [T]warn them and tell them of the [5]procedure of the king who will reign over them."   Ezek. 3:18 • *testify to*

Samuel Warns Israel

10 So Samuel spoke all the words of the LORD to [R]the people who had asked of him a king.   1 Sam. 8:4

11 And he said, "This will be the [T]procedure of the king who will reign over you: he will take your sons and place *them* for himself in his chariots and among his horsemen and they will run before his chariots.   *custom*

12 "And he will appoint for himself commanders of thousands and of fifties, and *some* to [T]do his plowing and to reap his harvest and to make his weapons of war and equipment for his chariots.   *plow his plowing*

13 "He will also take your daughters for perfumers and cooks and bakers.

14 "And [R]he will take the best of your fields and your vineyards and your olive groves, and give *them* to his servants.   1 Kin. 21:7

15 "And he will take a tenth of your seed and of your vineyards, and give to his officers and to his servants.

16 "He will also take your male servants and your female servants and your best young men and your donkeys, and [T]use *them* for his work.   *make*

17 "He will take a tenth of your flocks, and you yourselves will become his servants.

18 "Then [R]you will cry out in that day because of your king whom you have chosen for yourselves, but [R]the LORD will not answer you in that day."   Is. 8:21 • Is. 1:15; Mic. 3:4

19 Nevertheless, the people refused to listen to the voice of Samuel, and they said, "No, but there shall be a king over us,

20 [R]that we also may be like all the nations, that our king may judge us and go out before us and fight our battles."   1 Sam. 8:5

21 Now after Samuel had heard all the words of the people, [R]he repeated them in the LORD's hearing.   Judg. 11:11

22 And the LORD said to Samuel, "Listen to their voice, and [T]appoint them a king." So Samuel said to the men of Israel, "Go every man to his city."   *cause a king to reign for them*

CHAPTER 9

God Chooses Saul

NOW there was a man of Benjamin whose name was [R]Kish the son of Abiel, the son of Zeror, the son of Becorath, the son of Aphiah, the son of a Benjamite, a mighty man of ^valor.   1 Chr. 8:33; 9:36-39 • *wealth* or *influence*

2 And he had a son whose name was Saul, a [R]choice and handsome *man,* and there was not a more handsome person than he among the sons of Israel; [R]from his shoulders and up he was taller than any of the people.   1 Sam. 10:24 • 1 Sam. 10:23

3 Now the donkeys of Kish, Saul's father, were lost. So Kish said to his son Saul, "Take now with you one of the servants, and arise, go search for the donkeys."

4 And he passed through [R]the hill country of Ephraim and passed through the land of [R]Shalishah, but they did not find *them.* Then they passed through the land of Shaalim, but *they were* not *there.* Then he passed through the land of the Benjamites, but did not find *them.*   Josh. 24:33 • 2 Kin. 4:42

5 When they came to the land of Zuph, Saul said to his servant who was with him, "Come, and let us return, [R]lest my father cease *to be concerned* about the donkeys and become anxious for us."   1 Sam. 10:2

6 And he said to him, "Behold now, there is [R]a man of God in this city, and the man is held in honor; [R]all that he says surely comes true. Now let us go there, [R]perhaps he can tell us about our journey on which we have set out."   Deut. 33:1 • 1 Sam. 3:19 • Gen. 24:42

7 Then Saul said to his servant, "But behold, if we go, what shall we bring the man? For the bread is gone from our sack and there is [R]no present to bring to the man of God. What do we have?"   1 Kin. 14:3

8 And the servant answered Saul again and said, "Behold, I have in my hand a fourth of a shekel of silver; I will give it to the man of God and he will tell us our way."

9 (Formerly in Israel, when a man went to inquire of God, he used to say, "Come, and let us go to the seer": for *he who is*

called a prophet now was formerly called[R]a seer.)   2 Sam. 24:11; 2 Kin. 17:13; 1 Chr. 9:22

10 Then Saul said to his servant, "Well said; come, let us go." So they went to the city where the man of God was.

11 As they went up the slope to the city, they found young women going out to draw water, and said to them, "Is the seer here?"

12 And they answered them and said, "He is; see, *he is* ahead of you. Hurry now, for he has come into the city today, for the people have a sacrifice on the high place today.

13"As soon as you enter the city you will find him before he goes up to the high place to eat, for the people will not eat until he comes, because[R]he must bless the sacrifice; afterward those who are invited will eat. Now therefore, go up for you will find him at once."   Luke 9:16; John 6:11

14 So they went up to the city. As they came into the city, behold, Samuel was coming out toward them to go up to the high place.

15 Now a day before Saul's coming, the LORD had revealed *this* to Samuel saying,

16"About this time tomorrow I will send you a man from the land of Benjamin, and [R]you shall anoint him to be prince over My people Israel; and he shall deliver My people from the hand of the Philistines. For[R]I have regarded My people, because their cry has come to Me."   1 Sam. 10:1 • Ex. 3:7, 9

17 When Samuel saw Saul, the LORD said to him, "Behold, the man of whom I spoke to you! This one shall rule over My people."

18 Then Saul approached Samuel in the gate, and said, "Please tell me where the seer's house is."

19 And Samuel answered Saul and said, "I am the seer. Go up before me to the high place, for you shall eat with me today; and in the morning I will let you go, and will tell you all that is on your mind.

20"And[R]as for your donkeys which were lost three days ago, do not set your mind on them, for they have been found. And[R]for whom is all that is desirable in Israel? Is it not for you and for all your father's household?"   1 Sam. 9:3 • 1 Sam. 8:5; 12:13

21 And Saul answered and said, "Am I not a Benjamite, of the smallest of the tribes of Israel, and my family the least of all the families of the tribe of Benjamin? Why then do you speak to me in this way?"

22 Then Samuel took Saul and his servant and brought them into the hall, and gave them a place at the head of those who were invited, who were about thirty men.

23 And Samuel said to the cook, "Bring[T] the portion that I gave you, concerning which I said to you, 'Set it aside.'"   *Give*

24 Then the cook took up the leg with what was on it and set *it* before Saul. And *Samuel* said, "Here is what has been reserved! Set *it* before you *and* eat, because it has been kept for you until the appointed

time,[T]since I said I have invited the people." So Saul ate with Samuel that day.   *saying*

25 When they came down from the high place into the city, *Samuel* spoke with Saul [R]on the roof.[6]   Deut. 22:8; Luke 5:19; Acts 10:9

26 And they arose early; and it came about at daybreak that Samuel called to Saul on the roof, saying, "Get up, that I may send you away." So Saul arose, and both he and Samuel went out into the street.

27 As they were going down to the edge of the city, Samuel said to Saul, "Say to the servant that he might go ahead of us and pass on, but you remain standing now, that I may proclaim the word of God to you."

CHAPTER 10

THEN Samuel took the flask of oil, poured it on his head,[R]kissed him and said, "Has not [R]the LORD anointed you a ruler over[R]His inheritance?   Ps. 2:12 • 1 Sam. 16:13 • Deut. 32:9

2"When you go from me today, then you will find two men close to[R]Rachel's tomb in the territory of Benjamin at Zelzah; and they will say to you, 'The donkeys which you went to look for have been found. Now behold, your father has[T]ceased to be concerned about the donkeys and is anxious for you, saying, "What shall I do about my son?"'   Gen. 35:16-20 • *abandoned the matter of*

3"Then you will go on further from there, and you will come as far as the[^]oak of Tabor, and there three men going up to God at Bethel will meet you, one carrying three kids, another carrying three loaves of bread, and another carrying a jug of wine;   *terebinth*

4 and they will greet you and give you two *loaves* of bread, which you will accept from their hand.

5"Afterward you will come to the hill of God where the Philistine garrison is; and it shall be as soon as you have come there to the city, that you will meet a group of prophets coming down from the high place with harp, tambourine, flute, and a lyre before them, and they will be prophesying.

6"Then[R]the Spirit of the LORD will come upon you mightily, and[R]you shall prophesy with them and be changed into another man.   Num. 11:25, 29 • 1 Sam. 10:10; 19:23, 24

7"And it shall be when these signs come to you, do for yourself what[T]the occasion requires; for God is with you.   *your hand finds*

8"And[R]you shall go down before me to Gilgal; and behold, I will come down to you to offer burnt offerings and[R]sacrifice peace offerings.[R]You shall wait seven days until I come to you and show you what you should do."   1 Sam. 11:14 • 1 Sam. 11:15 • 1 Sam. 13:8

9 Then it happened when he turned his back to leave Samuel, God [R]changed[T]his heart; and all those signs came about on that day.   1 Sam. 10:6 • *for him another heart*

---

[6] Gr. adds *and they spread a bed for Saul on the roof and he slept.*

10 When they came to^Athe hill there, behold, a group of prophets met him; and the Spirit of God came upon him mightily, so that he prophesied among them.   *Gibeath*

11 And it came about, when all who knew him previously saw that he prophesied now with the prophets, that the people said to one another, "What has happened to the son of Kish?^RIs Saul also among the prophets?"   1 Sam. 19:24; Amos 7:14, 15; Matt. 13:54-57

12 And a man there answered and said, "Now, who is their father?" Therefore it became a proverb: "Is^R Saul also among the prophets?"   1 Sam. 19:23, 24

13 When he had finished prophesying, he came to the high place.

14 Now^RSaul's uncle said to him and his servant, "Where did you go?" And he said, "To^R look for the donkeys. When we saw that they could not be found, we went to Samuel."   1 Sam. 14:50 • 1 Sam. 9:3-6

15 And Saul's uncle said, "Please tell me what Samuel said to you."

16 So Saul said to his uncle, "He told us plainly that the donkeys had been found." But he did not tell him about the matter of the kingdom which Samuel had mentioned.

Samuel Anoints Saul

17 Thereafter Samuel called the^Rpeople together to the Lord at Mizpah;   Judg. 20:1

18 and he said to the sons of Israel, "Thus^R says the Lord, the God of Israel, 'I brought Israel up from Egypt, and I delivered you from the hand of the Egyptians, and from the^Tpower of all the kingdoms that were oppressing you.'   Judg. 6:8, 9 • *hand*

19"But you^Rtoday rejected your God, who delivers you from all your calamities and your distresses; yet you have said, 'No, but set a king over us!' Now therefore,^Rpresent yourselves before the Lord by your tribes and by your clans."   1 Sam. 8:6, 7 • Prov. 16:33

20 Thus Samuel brought all the tribes of Israel near, and the tribe of Benjamin was taken by lot.

21 Then he brought the tribe of Benjamin near by its families, and the Matrite family was taken. And Saul the son of Kish was taken; but when they looked for him, he could not be found.

22 Therefore^Rthey inquired further of the Lord, "Has the man come here yet?" So the Lord said, "Behold, he is hiding himself by the baggage."   1 Sam. 23:2, 4

23 So they ran and took him from there, and when he stood among the people, ^Rhe was taller than any of the people from his shoulders upward.   1 Sam. 9:2

24 And Samuel said to all the people, "Do you see him whom the Lord has chosen? Surely there is no one like him among all the people." So all the people shouted and said, "Long^Tlive the king!"   *May the king live*

25 Then Samuel told the people^Rthe ordinances of the kingdom, and wrote *them* in the book and^Rplaced *it* before the Lord. And Samuel sent all the people away, each one to his house.   Deut. 17:14-20 • Deut. 31:26

26 And Saul also went^Rto his house at Gibeah; and the valiant *men* whose hearts God had touched went with him.   1 Sam. 11:4; 15:34

27 But certain^Tworthless men said, "How can this one deliver us?"^: And they despised him and did not bring him any present. But he kept silent.   *sons of Belial*, cf. 2 Cor. 6:15

CHAPTER 11

Israel Makes Saul King

NOW^RNahash the Ammonite came up and besieged Jabesh-gilead; and all the men of Jabesh said to Nahash, "Make a covenant with us and we will serve you."   1 Sam. 12:12

2 But Nahash the Ammonite said to them, "I will make *it* with you on this condition,^Rthat I will gouge out the right eye of every one of you, thus I will make it^Ra reproach on all Israel."   Num. 16:14 • Ps. 44:13

3 And^Rthe elders of Jabesh said to him, "Let us alone for seven days, that we may send messengers throughout the territory of Israel. Then, if there is no one to deliver us, we will come out to you."   1 Sam. 8:4

4 Then the messengers came^Rto Gibeah of Saul and spoke these words in the hearing of the people, and all the people^Rlifted up their voices and wept.   1 Sam. 10:26 • Gen. 27:38

5 Now behold, Saul was coming from the field^Rbehind the oxen; and^The said, "What is *the matter* with the people that they weep?" So they related to him the words of the men of Jabesh.   1 Kin. 19:19 • *Saul*

6 Then the Spirit of God came upon Saul mightily when he heard these words, and^The became very angry.   *his anger burned exceedingly*

7 And he took a yoke of oxen and^Rcut them in pieces, and sent *them* throughout the territory of Israel by the hand of messengers, saying, "Whoever^R does not come out after Saul and after Samuel, so shall it be done to his oxen." Then the dread of the Lord fell on the people, and they came out as one man.   Judg. 19:29 • Judg. 21:5, 8

8 And he^Tnumbered them in^RBezek; and the sons of Israel were 300,000, and the men of Judah 30,000.   *mustered* • Judg. 1:5

9 And they said to the messengers who had come, "Thus you shall say to the men of Jabesh-gilead, 'Tomorrow, by the time the sun is hot, you shall have deliverance.' " So the messengers went and told the men of Jabesh; and they were glad.

10 Then the men of Jabesh said, "Tomorrow we will come out to you, and you may do to us whatever seems good to you."

11 And it happened the next morning that Saul put the people^Rin three companies; and they came into the midst of the camp at the

morning watch, and struck down the Ammonites until the heat of the day. And it came about that those who survived were scattered, so that no two of them were left together.   Judg. 7:16, 20

12 Then the people said to Samuel, "Who[R] is he that said, 'Shall Saul reign over us?' [T]Bring[R] the men, that we may put them to death."   1 Sam. 10:27 • *Give* • Luke 19:27

13 But Saul said, "Not a man shall be put to death this day, for today the LORD has accomplished deliverance in Israel."

14 Then Samuel said to the people, "Come and let us go to[R]Gilgal and[R]renew the kingdom there."   1 Sam. 7:16 • 1 Sam. 10:25

15 So all the people went to Gilgal, and there they made Saul king[R]before the LORD in Gilgal. There they also[R]offered sacrifices of peace offerings before the LORD; and there Saul and all the men of Israel rejoiced greatly.   1 Sam. 10:17 • 1 Sam. 10:8

CHAPTER 12

Samuel Confirms Saul

THEN Samuel said to all Israel, "Behold,[R]I have listened to your voice in all that you said to me, and I[R]have[T]appointed a king over you.   1 Sam. 8:7, 9, 22 • 1 Sam. 10:24 • *made*

2"And now, here is the king walking before you, but I am old and gray, and behold my sons are with you. And I have walked before you from my youth even to this day.

3"Here I am; bear witness against me before the LORD and[R]His anointed.[R]Whose ox have I taken, or whose donkey have I taken, or whom have I defrauded? Whom have I oppressed, or from whose hand have I taken a bribe to blind my eyes with it? I will restore *it* to you."   1 Sam. 10:1 • Ex. 20:17

4 And they said, "You have not defrauded us, or oppressed us, or taken anything from any man's hand."

5 And he said to them, "The LORD is witness against you, and His anointed is witness this day that you have found nothing in my hand." And they said, *"He is* witness."

6 Then Samuel said to the people, "It is the LORD who[T]appointed[R]Moses and Aaron and who brought your fathers up from the land of Egypt.   *made* • Ex. 6:26; Mic. 6:4

7"So now, take your stand,[R]that I may plead with you before the LORD concerning all the righteous acts of the LORD which He did for you and your fathers.   Ezek. 20:35

8"When[R]Jacob went into Egypt and your fathers cried out to the LORD, then[R]the LORD sent Moses and Aaron[T]who brought your fathers out of Egypt and settled them in this place.   Gen. 46:5, 6 • Ex. 3:10 • *and they brought*

9"But they forgot the LORD their God, so He sold them into the hand of Sisera, captain of the army of Hazor, and into the hand of the Philistines and into the hand of the king of Moab, and they fought against them.

10"And [R]they cried out to the LORD and said, 'We have sinned because we have forsaken the LORD and have served[R]the Baals and the Ashtaroth; but[R]now deliver us from the hands of our enemies, and we will serve Thee.'   Judg. 10:10 • Judg. 2:13 • Judg. 10:15, 16

11"Then the LORD sent Jerubbaal and [T]Bedan and Jephthah and Samuel, and delivered you from the hands of your enemies all around, so that you lived in security.

12"When you saw[R]that Nahash the king of the sons of Ammon came against you, you said to me, 'No[R] but a king shall reign over us,'[R]although the LORD your God *was* your king.   1 Sam. 11:1, 2 • 1 Sam. 8:6, 19 • Judg. 8:23

13"Now therefore,[R]here is the king whom you have chosen,[R]whom you have asked for, and behold, the LORD has set a king over you.   1 Sam. 10:24 • 1 Sam. 8:5; 12:17, 19

14"If you will fear the LORD and serve Him, and listen to His voice and not rebel against the[T]command of the LORD, then both you and also the king who reigns over you will follow the LORD your God.   *mouth*

15"And if you will not listen to the voice of the LORD, but rebel against the command of the LORD, then the hand of the LORD will be against you, *as it was* against your fathers.

16"Even now,[R]take your stand and see this great thing which the LORD will do before your eyes.   Ex. 14:13, 31

17"Is it not the wheat harvest today? I will call to the LORD, that He may send[T]thunder and rain. Then you will know and see that [R]your wickedness is great which you have done in the sight of the LORD by asking for yourselves a king."   *sounds* • 1 Sam. 8:7

18 So Samuel called to the LORD, and the LORD sent[T]thunder and rain that day; and[R]all the people greatly feared the LORD and Samuel.   *sounds* • Ex. 14:31

19 Then all the people said to Samuel, "Pray[R]for your servants to the LORD your God, so that we may not die, for we have added to all our sins[R]this evil by asking for ourselves a king."   Ex. 9:28 • 1 Sam. 12:17, 20

20 And Samuel said to the people, "Do not fear. You have committed all this evil, yet [R]do not turn aside from following the LORD, but serve the LORD with all your heart.   Deut. 11:16

21"And you must not turn aside, for *then* you *would go* after futile things which can not profit or deliver, because they are futile.

22"For[R]the LORD will not abandon His people[R]on account of His great name, because the LORD has been pleased to make you a people for Himself.   Deut. 31:6 • Ex. 32:12

23"Moreover, as for me,[R]far be it from me that I should sin against the LORD by ceasing to pray for you; but[R]I will instruct you in the good and right way.   Rom. 1:9 • Prov. 4:11

24"Only[R] [S]fear the LORD and serve Him in truth with all your heart; for consider what great things He has done for you. Eccl. 12:13

---

[7] Gr. and Syr. read *Barak*   [8] Or, *reverence*

25 "But[R] if you still do wickedly, both you and your king shall be swept away." Is. 1:20

CHAPTER 13

The Early Success of King Saul

SAUL was *forty* years old when he began to reign, and he reigned *thirty*-two years over Israel.

2 Now Saul chose for himself 3,000 men of Israel, of which 2,000 were with Saul in [R]Michmash and in the hill country of Bethel, while 1,000 were with Jonathan at Gibeah of Benjamin. But he sent away the rest of the people, each to his tent.   1 Sam. 13:5; 14:31

3 And Jonathan smote [R]the garrison of the Philistines that was in Geba, and the Philistines heard of *it*. Then Saul[R]blew the trumpet throughout the land, saying, "Let the Hebrews hear."   1 Sam. 10:5 • Judg. 3:27

4 And all Israel heard[T]the news that Saul had smitten the garrison of the Philistines, and also that Israel had become odious to the Philistines. The people were then summoned[T]to Saul at Gilgal.   *saying • after*

Saul's Sinful Sacrifices

5 Now the Philistines assembled to fight with Israel, 30,000 chariots and 6,000 horsemen, and[R]people like the sand which is on the seashore in abundance; and they came up and camped in Michmash, east of[R]Beth-aven.   Josh. 11:4 • Josh. 18:12; 1 Sam. 14:23

6 When the men of Israel saw that they were in a strait (for the people were hardpressed), then[R]the people hid themselves in caves, in thickets, in cliffs, in cellars, and in pits.   Judg. 6:2

7 Also *some of* the Hebrews crossed the Jordan into the land of[R]Gad and Gilead. But as for Saul, he *was* still in Gilgal, and all the people followed him trembling.   Num. 32:33

8 Now[R]he waited seven days, according to the appointed time set by Samuel, but Samuel did not come to Gilgal; and the people were scattering from him.   1 Sam. 10:8

9 So Saul said, "Bring to me the burnt offering and the peace offerings." And[R]he offered the burnt offering.   Deut. 12:5-14

10 And it came about as soon as he finished offering the burnt offering, that behold, Samuel came; and Saul went out to meet him *and* to[T]greet him.   *bless*

11 But Samuel said, "What have you done?" And Saul said, "Because I saw that the people were scattering from me, and that you did not come within the appointed days, and that[R]the Philistines were assembling at Michmash,   1 Sam. 13:2, 5, 16, 23

12 therefore I said, 'Now the Philistines will come down against me at Gilgal, and I have not asked the favor of the LORD.' So I forced myself and offered the burnt offering."

13 And Samuel said to Saul, "You[R] have acted foolishly;[R]you have not kept the commandment of the LORD your God, which He commanded you, for now the LORD would have established your kingdom[T]over Israel forever.   2 Chr. 16:9 • 1 Sam. 15:11, 22, 28 • *to*

14 "But [R]now your kingdom shall not endure.[R]The LORD has sought for Himself a man after His own heart, and the LORD has appointed him as ruler over His people, because you have not kept what the LORD commanded you."   1 Sam. 15:28 • Acts 7:46

15 Then Samuel arose and went up from Gilgal to Gibeah of Benjamin. And Saul [T]numbered the people who were present with him, about six hundred men.   *mustered*

16 Now Saul and his son Jonathan and the people who were present with them were staying in[R]Geba of Benjamin while the Philistines camped at Michmash.   1 Sam. 13:2, 3

17 And the[T]raiders came from the camp of the Philistines in three[T]companies: one[T]company turned toward[R]Ophrah, to the land of Shual,   *destroyers • heads • head* • Josh 18:23

18 and another [T]company turned toward Beth-horon, and another [T]company turned toward the border which overlooks the valley of Zeboim toward the wilderness.   *head*

19 Now no blacksmith could be found in all the land of Israel, for the Philistines said, "Lest the Hebrews make swords or spears."

20 So all Israel went down to the Philistines, each to sharpen his plowshare, his mattock, his axe, and his hoe.

21 And the charge was two-thirds of a shekel for the plowshares, the mattocks, the forks, and the axes, and to fix the hoes.

22 So it came about on the day of battle that neither sword nor spear was found in the hands of any of the people who *were* with Saul and Jonathan, but they were found with Saul and his son Jonathan.

23 And the garrison of the Philistines went out to[R]the pass of Michmash.   Is. 10:28

CHAPTER 14

Saul's Selfish Curse

NOW the day came that Jonathan, the son of Saul, said to the young man who was carrying his armor, "Come and let us cross over to the Philistines' garrison that is on yonder side." But he did not tell his father.

2 And Saul was staying in the outskirts of Gibeah under the pomegranate tree which is in Migron. And the people who *were* with him *were* about six hundred men,

3 and Ahijah, the son of Ahitub, Ichabod's brother, the son of Phinehas, the son of Eli, the priest of the LORD at Shiloh, was [T]wearing an ephod. And the people did not know that Jonathan had gone.   *carrying*

4 And between the passes by which Jonathan sought to cross over to the Philistines' garrison, there was a sharp crag on

the one side, and a sharp crag on the other side, and the name of the one was Bozez, and the name of the other Seneh.

5 The one crag rose on the north opposite Michmash, and the other on the south opposite Geba.

6 Then Jonathan said to the young man who was carrying his armor, "Come and let us cross over to the garrison of ^Rthese uncircumcised; perhaps the LORD will work for us, for ^Rthe LORD is not restrained to save by many or by few."   Jer. 9:25, 26 • Judg. 7:4, 7

7 And his armor bearer said to him, "Do all that is in your heart; turn yourself, *and* here I am with you according to your ^Tdesire."   *heart*

8 Then Jonathan said, "Behold, ^R we will cross over to the men and reveal ourselves to them.   Judg. 7:9-14

9 "If they ^Tsay to us, 'Wait until we come to you'; then we will stand in our place and not go up to them.   *say thus*

10 "But if they ^Tsay, 'Come up to us,' then we will go up, for the LORD has given them into our hands; and ^Rthis shall be the sign to us."   *say thus* • Gen. 24:14; Judg. 6:36

11 And when both of them revealed themselves to the garrison of the Philistines, the Philistines said, "Behold, ^RHebrews are coming out of the holes where they have hidden themselves."   1 Sam. 13:6; 14:22

12 So the men of the garrison ^Thailed Jonathan and his armor bearer and said, "Come up to us and we will tell you something." And Jonathan said to his armor bearer, "Come up after me, for the LORD has given them into the hands of Israel."   *answered*

13 Then Jonathan climbed up on his hands and feet, with his armor bearer behind him; and they fell before Jonathan, and his armor bearer put some to death after him.

14 And that first slaughter which Jonathan and his armor bearer made was about twenty men within about half a furrow in an acre of land.

15 And there was a trembling in the camp, in the field, and among all the people. Even the garrison and the raiders trembled, and ^Rthe earth quaked so ^Rthat it became a ⁹great trembling.   1 Sam. 7:10 • Gen. 35:5

16 Now Saul's watchmen in Gibeah of Benjamin looked, and behold, the multitude melted away; and they went here and *there.*

17 And Saul said to the people who *were* with him, "Number ^Tnow and see who has gone from us." And when they had ^Tnumbered, behold, Jonathan and his armor bearer were not *there.*   *muster(ed)*

18 Then Saul said to Ahijah, "Bring ^R the ark of God here." For the ark of God was at that time with the sons of Israel.   1 Sam. 23:9

19 And it happened ^Rwhile Saul talked to the priest, that the commotion in the camp of the Philistines continued and increased; so Saul said to the priest, "Withdraw your hand."   Num. 27:21

20 Then Saul and all the people who *were*

with him rallied and came to the battle; and behold, every man's sword was against his fellow, *and there was* very great confusion.

21 Now the Hebrews *who* were with the Philistines previously, who went up with them all around in the camp, even ^Rthey also *turned* to be with the Israelites who *were* with Saul and Jonathan.   1 Sam. 29:4

22 When all the ^Rmen of Israel who had hidden themselves in the hill country of Ephraim heard that the Philistines had fled, even they also pursued them closely in the battle.   1 Sam. 13:6

23 So the LORD delivered Israel that day, and the battle spread beyond Beth-aven.

24 Now the men of Israel were hardpressed on that day, for Saul had put the people under oath, saying, "Cursed be the man who eats food before evening, and until I have avenged myself on my enemies." So none of the people tasted food.

25 And all *the people of* the land entered the forest, and there was honey on the ground.

26 When the people entered the forest, behold, ^R*there was* a flow of honey; but no man put his hand to his mouth, for the people feared the oath.   Matt. 3:4

27 But Jonathan had not heard when his father put the people under oath; therefore, ^Rhe put out the end of the staff that *was* in his hand and dipped it in the honeycomb, and put his hand to his mouth, and ^Rhis eyes brightened.   1 Sam. 14:43 • 1 Sam. 30:12

28 Then one of the people answered and said, "Your father strictly put the people under oath, saying, 'Cursed be the man who eats food today.' " And the people were weary.

29 Then Jonathan said, "My ^R father has troubled the land. See now, how my eyes have brightened because I tasted a little of this honey.   Josh. 7:25; 1 Kin. 18:18

30 "How much more, if only the people had eaten freely today of the spoil of their enemies which they found! For now the slaughter among the Philistines has not been great."

31 And they struck among the Philistines that day from ^RMichmash to Aijalon. And the people were very weary.   1 Sam. 14:5

32 And the people rushed greedily upon the spoil, and took sheep and oxen and calves, and slew *them* on the ground; and the people ate *them* ^Rwith the blood.   Gen. 9:4

33 Then they told Saul, saying, "Behold, the people are ^Rsinning against the LORD by eating with the blood." And he said, "You have acted treacherously; roll a great stone to me today."   Lev. 7:26, 27; 19:26

34 And Saul said, "Disperse yourselves among the people and say to them, 'Each one of you bring me his ox or his sheep, and slaughter *it* here and eat; and do not sin against the LORD by eating with the

⁹ Lit., *trembling of God*

blood.' " So all the people that night brought each one his ox^Twith him, and slaughtered *it* there.   *in his hand*

35 And Saul built an altar to the LORD; it was the first altar that he built to the LORD.

36 Then Saul said, "Let us go down after the Philistines by night and take spoil among them until the morning light, and let us not leave a man of them." And they said, "Do whatever seems good to you." So the priest said, "Let us draw near to God here."

37 And Saul^Rinquired of God, "Shall I go down after the Philistines? Wilt Thou give them into the hand of Israel?" But He did not answer him on that day.   1 Sam. 10:22

38 And Saul said, "Draw near here, all you chiefs of the people, and investigate and see how this sin has happened today.

39 "For^Ras the LORD lives, who delivers Israel, though it is in Jonathan my son, he shall surely die." But not one of all the people answered him.   1 Sam. 14:24, 44; 2 Sam. 12:5

40 Then he said to all Israel, "You shall be on one side and I and Jonathan my son will be on the other side." And the people said to Saul, "Do what seems good to you."

41 Therefore, Saul said to the LORD, the God of Israel, "Give^R a perfect *lot*." And Jonathan and Saul were taken, but the people escaped.   Acts 1:24

42 And Saul said, "Cast *lots* between me and Jonathan my son." And Jonathan was taken.

43 Then Saul said to Jonathan, "Tell^R me what you have done." So Jonathan told him and said, "I indeed tasted a little honey with the end of the staff that was in my hand. Here I am, I must die!"   Josh. 7:19

44 And Saul said, "May^RGod do^Tthis *to me* and more also, for ^Ryou shall surely die, Jonathan."   Ruth 1:17 • *thus* • 1 Sam. 14:39

45 But the people said to Saul, "Must Jonathan die, who has^Tbrought about this great deliverance in Israel? Far from it! As the LORD lives, there shall not one hair of his head fall to the ground, for he has worked with God this day." So the people rescued Jonathan and he did not die.   *worked*

46 Then Saul went up from^Tpursuing the Philistines, and the Philistines went to their own place.   *after*

47 Now when Saul had taken the kingdom over Israel, he fought against all his enemies on every side, against Moab, the sons of Ammon, Edom, the kings of Zobah, and^Rthe Philistines; and wherever he turned, he^Ainflicted punishment.   1 Sam. 14:52 • *condemned*

48 And he acted valiantly and defeated the Amalekites, and delivered Israel from the hands of those who plundered them.

49 Now ^Rthe sons of Saul were Jonathan and Ishvi and Malchi-shua; and the names of his two daughters *were these:* the name of the first-born^RMerab and the name of the younger Michal.   1 Sam. 31:2 • 1 Sam. 18:17-19

50 And the name of Saul's wife was Ahinoam the daughter of Ahimaaz. And^Rthe name of the captain of his army was Abner the son of Ner, Saul's uncle.   2 Sam. 2:8

51 ^RAnd Kish *was* the father of Saul, and Ner the father of Abner *was* the son of Abiel.   1 Sam. 9:1, 21

52 Now the war against the Philistines was severe all the days of Saul; and when Saul saw any mighty man or any valiant man, he^Tattached him to his staff.   *gathered*

CHAPTER 15

Saul's Incomplete Obedience

THEN Samuel said to Saul, "The LORD sent me to anoint you as king over His people, over Israel; now therefore, listen to the ^Twords of the LORD.   *sound of the words*

2 "Thus says the LORD of hosts, 'I will ^Apunish Amalek *for* what he did to Israel, how he set himself against him on the way while he was coming up from Egypt.   *visit*

3 'Now go and strike Amalek and^Rutterly destroy all that he has, and do not spare him; but^Rput to death both man and woman, child and infant, ox and sheep, camel and donkey.' "   Num. 24:20 • 1 Sam. 22:19

4 Then Saul summoned the people and ^Tnumbered them in Telaim, 200,000 foot soldiers and 10,000 men of Judah.   *mustered*

5 And Saul came to the city of Amalek, and set an ambush in the valley.

6 And Saul said to the Kenites, "Go, depart, go down from among the Amalekites, lest I destroy you with them; for you showed kindness to all the sons of Israel when they came up from Egypt." So the Kenites departed from among the Amalekites.

7 So^RSaul^Tdefeated the Amalekites, from Havilah as you go to^RShur, which is^Teast of Egypt.   1 Sam. 14:48 • *smote* • Ex. 15:22 • *before*

8 And he captured Agag the king of the Amalekites alive, and utterly destroyed all the people with the edge of the sword.

9 But Saul and the people^Rspared Agag and the best of the sheep, the oxen, the fatlings, the lambs, and all that was good, and were not willing to destroy them utterly; but everything despised and worthless, that they utterly destroyed.   1 Sam. 15:3, 15, 19

God Rejects Saul as King

10 Then the word of the LORD came to Samuel, saying,

11 "I^Rregret that I have made Saul king, for he has turned back from^Tfollowing Me, and has not carried out My commands." And Samuel was distressed and^Rcried out to the LORD all night.   Ex. 32:14 • *after* • Ex. 32:11-13

12 And Samuel rose early in the morning to meet Saul; and it was told Samuel, saying, "Saul came to Carmel, and behold, he

set up a monument for himself, then turned and proceeded on down to Gilgal."

13 And Samuel came to Saul, and Saul said to him, "Blessed are you of the LORD! I have carried out the command of the LORD."

14 But Samuel said, "What then is this bleating of the sheep in my ears, and the ᵀlowing of the oxen which I hear?"   *sound*

15 And Saul said, "They have brought them from the Amalekites, forᴿthe people spared the best of the sheep and oxen, to sacrifice to the LORD your God; but the rest we have utterly destroyed."   [Gen. 3:12, 13]

16 Then Samuel said to Saul, "Wait, and let me tell you what the LORD said to me last night." And he said to him, "Speak!"

17 And Samuel said, "Is it not true, though you were little in your own eyes, you were *made* the head of the tribes of Israel? And the LORD anointed you king over Israel,

18 and the LORD sent you on a ᵀmission, and said, 'Go and utterly destroy the sinners, the Amalekites, and fight against them until they are exterminated.'   *way*

19"Why then did you not obey the voice of the LORD, but rushed upon the spoil and did what was evil in the sight of the LORD?"

20 Then Saul said to Samuel, "I did obey the voice of the LORD, and went on the ᵀmission on which the LORD sent me, and have brought back Agag the king of Amalek, and have utterly destroyed the Amalekites. *way*

21"Butᴿthe people took *some* of the spoil, sheep and oxen, the choicest of the things devoted to destruction, to sacrifice to the LORD your God at Gilgal."   Ex. 32:22, 23

22 And Samuel said,
"Hasᴿ the LORD as much delight in burnt offerings and sacrifices
As in obeying the voice of the LORD?
Behold,ᴿto obey is better than sacrifice,   [Ps. 40:6–8 • Jer. 7:22, 23; Hos. 6:6]
And to heed than the fat of rams.

23 "For rebellion is as the sin of ᴿdivination,   Deut. 18:10
And insubordination is asᴿiniquity and idolatry.   Gen. 31:19, 34
Because you have rejected the word of the LORD,
ᴿHe has also rejected you from *being* king."   1 Sam. 13:14

24 Then Saul said to Samuel, "Iᴿ have sinned;ᴿI have indeed transgressed the ᵀcommand of the LORD and your words, because I feared the people and listened to their voice.   Num. 22:34 • [Prov. 29:25] • *mouth*

25"Now therefore, ᴿplease pardon my sin and return with me, that I may worship the LORD."   Ex. 10:17

26 But Samuel said to Saul, "I will not return with you; for you have rejected the word of the LORD, and the LORD has rejected you from being king over Israel."

27 And as Samuel turned to go, *Saul* seized the edge of his robe, and it tore.

28 So Samuel said to him, "TheᴿLORD has torn the kingdom of Israel from you today, and has given it to your neighbor who is better than you.   1 Sam. 28:17, 18; 1 Kin. 11:31

29"And also theᴿGlory of Israel will not lie or change His mind; for He is not a man that He should change His mind."   *Eminence*

30 Then he said, "I have sinned; ᴿ*but* please honor me now before the elders of my people and before Israel, and go back with me,ᴿthat I may worship the LORD your God."   [John 5:44; 12:43] • [Is. 29:13]

31 So Samuel went back following Saul, and Saul worshiped the LORD.

32 Then Samuel said, "Bring me Agag, the king of the Amalekites." And Agag came to himᴬcheerfully. And Agag said, "Surely the bitterness of death is past."   *in bonds*

33 But Samuel said, "Asᴿyour sword has made women childless, so shall your mother be childless among women." And Samuel hewed Agag to pieces before the LORD at Gilgal.   [Gen. 9:6]; Judg. 1:7; [Matt. 7:2]

34 Then Samuel went to Ramah, but Saul went up to his house at Gibeah of Saul.

35 AndᴿSamuel did not see Saul again until the day of his death; for Samuel grieved over Saul. And the LORD regretted that He had made Saul king over Israel.   1 Sam. 19:24

CHAPTER 16

God Anoints David as King

Now the LORD said to Samuel, "How long will you grieve over Saul, since I have rejected him from being king over Israel? Fill your horn with oil, and go; I will send you to Jesse the Bethlehemite, for I have selected a king for Myself among his sons."

2 But Samuel said, "How can I go? When Saul hears *of it*, he will kill me." And the LORD said, "Take a heifer with you, and say, 'I have come to sacrifice to the LORD.'

3"And you shall invite Jesse to the sacrifice, andᴿI will show you what you shall do; and you shall anoint for Me the one whom I ᵀdesignate to you."   Ex. 4:15 • *say to you*

4 So Samuel did what the LORD said, and came toᴿBethlehem. And the elders of the city came trembling to meet him and said, "Do you come in peace?"   Gen. 48:7; Luke 2:4

5 And he said, "In peace; I have come to sacrifice to the LORD.ᴿConsecrate yourselves and come with me to the sacrifice." He also consecrated Jesse and his sons, and invited them to the sacrifice.   Gen. 35:2; Ex. 19:10

6 Then it came about when they entered, that he looked at Eliab and thought, "Surely the LORD's anointed is before Him."

7 But the LORD said to Samuel, "Do not look at his appearance or at the height of his stature, because I have rejected him; for God *sees* not as man sees, for man looks at the outward appearance,ᴿbut the LORD looks at the heart."   1 Sam. 2:3; 1 Kin. 8:39; 1 Chr. 28:9

8 Then Jesse called Abinadab, and made

him pass before Samuel. And he said, "Neither has the LORD chosen this one."

9 Next Jesse made ʀShammah pass by. And he said, "Neither has the LORD chosen this one."   1 Sam. 17:13

10 Thus Jesse made seven of his sons pass before Samuel. But Samuel said to Jesse, "The LORD has not chosen these."

11 And Samuel said to Jesse, "Are these all the children?" And he said, "There remains yet the youngest, and behold, he is tending the sheep." Then Samuel said to Jesse, "Send andᵀbring him; for we will not sit down until he comes here."   *take*

12 So he sent and brought him in. Now he was ruddy, withʀbeautiful eyes and a handsome appearance. And the LORD said, "Arise, anoint him; for this is he." Gen. 39:6

13 Then Samuel took the horn of oil and anointed him in the midst of his brothers; and the Spirit of the LORD came mightily upon David from that day forward. And Samuel arose and went to Ramah.

God Takes His Spirit from Saul

14 ʀNow the Spirit of the LORD departed from Saul, andʀan evil spirit from the LORD terrorized him.   Judg. 16:20 • Judg. 9:23

15 Saul's servants then said to him, "Behold now, an evil spirit from God is terrorizing you.

16"Let our lord now command your servants who are before you. Let them seek a man who is a skillful player on the harp; and it shall come about when the evil spirit from God is on you, that he shall play *the harp* with his hand, and you will be well."

17 So Saul said to his servants, "Provide for me now a man who can play well, and bring *him* to me."

18 Then one of the young men answered and said, "Behold, I have seen a son of Jesse the Bethlehemite who is a skillful musician, ʀa mighty man of valor, a warrior, one prudent in speech, and a handsome man; and the LORD is with him."   1 Sam. 17:32-36

19 So Saul sent messengers to Jesse, and said, "Send me your son David who is with the flock."

20 And Jesse took a donkey *loaded with* bread and a jug of wine and a young goat, and sent *them* to Saul by David his son.

21 Then David came to Saul andᵀattended him, andᵀSaul loved him greatly; and he became his armor bearer.   *stood before him* • *he*

22 And Saul sent to Jesse, saying, "Let David now stand before me; for he has found favor in my sight."

23 So it came about whenever the *evil* spirit from God came to Saul, David would take the harp and play *it* with his hand; and Saul would be refreshed and be well, and the evil spirit would depart from him.

CHAPTER 17

David Defeats Goliath

NOW ʀthe Philistines gathered their armies for battle; and they were gathered at Socoh which belongs to Judah, and they camped between ʀSocoh and Azekah, in Ephes-dammim.   1 Sam. 13:5 • Josh. 15:35

2 And Saul and the men of Israel were gathered, and camped inᵀthe valley of Elah, and drew up in battle array to encounter the Philistines.   1 Sam. 21:9

3 And the Philistines stood on the mountain on one side while Israel stood on the mountain on the other side, with the valley between them.

4 Then a champion came out from the armies of the Philistines named ʀGoliath, from ʀGath, whose height was ᵀsix ¹⁰cubits and a span. 2 Sam. 12:19 • Josh. 11:22 • 9 ft., 9 in.

5 And *he had* a bronze helmet on his head, and he was clothed with scale-armor ᵀwhich weighed ᵀfive thousand shekels of bronze.   *and the weight of the armor was* • 125 lbs.

6 *He* also *had* bronze ¹¹greaves on his legs and aʀbronze javelin *slung* between his shoulders.   1 Sam. 17:45

7 And the shaft of his spear was like a weaver's beam, and the head of his spear *weighed* six hundred shekels of iron; his shield-carrier also walked before him.

8 And he stood and shouted to the ranks of Israel, and said to them, "Why do you come out to draw up in battle array? Am I not the Philistine and youʀservants of Saul? Choose a man for yourselves and let him come down to me.   1 Sam. 8:17

9"Ifʀhe is able to fight with me and ᵀkill me, then we will become your servants; but if I prevail against him and ᵀkill him, then you shall become our servants and serve us."   2 Sam. 2:12-16 • *smite*

10 Again the Philistine said, "Iʀdefy the ranks of Israel this day; give me a man that we may fight together."   1 Sam. 17:26, 36, 45

11 When Saul and all Israel heard these words of the Philistine, they were dismayed and greatly afraid.

12 Now David wasʀthe son ofᵀthe Ephrathite of Bethlehem in Judah, whose name was Jesse, and he had eight sons. And ᵀJesse was old in the days of Saul, advanced *in years* among men.   Ruth 4:22 • *this* • *the man*

13 And the three older sons of Jesse had gone after Saul to the battle. And the names of his three sons who went to the battle were Eliab the first-born, and the second to him Abinadab, and the third Shammah.

14 AndʀDavid was the youngest. Now the three oldest followed Saul,   1 Sam. 16:11

15 but David went back and forth from Saul to tend his father's flock at Bethlehem.

16 And the Philistine cameᵀforward morning and evening for forty days, and took his stand.   *near*

17 Then Jesse said to David his son, "Takeʀ

---

¹⁰ I.e., One cubit equals approx. 18 in.   ¹¹ Or, *shin guards*

now for your brothers an ephah of this roasted grain and these ten loaves, and run to the camp to your brothers.   1 Sam. 25:18

18 "Bring^R also these ten cuts of cheese to the commander of *their* thousand, and look into the welfare of your brothers, and bring back^T news of them.   1 Sam. 16:20 • *their pledge*

19 "For Saul and they and all the men of Israel are in the valley of Elah, fighting with the Philistines."

20 So David arose early in the morning and left the flock with a keeper and took *the supplies* and went as Jesse had commanded him. And he came to the^R circle of the camp while the army was going out in battle array shouting the war cry.   1 Sam. 26:5, 7

21 And Israel and the Philistines drew up in battle array, army against army.

22 Then David left his^R baggage in the^T care of the baggage keeper, and ran to the battle line and entered in order to greet his brothers.   Judg. 18:21; Is. 10:28 • *hand*

23 As he was talking with them, behold, the champion, the Philistine from Gath named Goliath, was coming up from the army of the Philistines, and he spoke these same words; and David heard *them*.

24 When all the men of Israel saw the man, they fled from him and were greatly afraid.

25 And the men of Israel said, "Have you seen this man who is coming up? Surely he is coming up to defy Israel. And it will be that the king will enrich the man who kills him with great riches and^R will give him his daughter and make his father's house ¹²free in Israel."   Josh. 15:16

26 Then David spoke to the men who were standing by him, saying, "What will be done for the man who kills this Philistine, and takes away ^Rthe reproach from Israel? For who is this ^Runcircumcised Philistine, that he should taunt the armies of^R the living God?"   1 Sam. 11:2 • 1 Sam. 14:6 • Deut. 5:26

27 And the people ^Tanswered him in accord with this word, saying, "Thus it will be done for the man who kills him."   *said to*

28 Now Eliab his oldest brother heard when he spoke to the men; and^R Eliab's anger burned against David and he said, "Why have you come down? And with whom have you left those few sheep in the wilderness? I know your insolence and the wickedness of your heart; for you have come down in order to see the battle."   Gen. 37:4, 8-36

29 But David said, "What have I done now? Was it not just a^T question?"   *word*

30 Then he turned away from him to another and said the same thing; and the people answered the same thing as before.

31 When the words which David spoke were heard, they told *them*^T to Saul, and he sent for him.   *before*

32 And David said to Saul, "Let no man's heart fail on account of him; your servant will go and fight with this Philistine."

33 Then Saul said to David, "You are not able to go against this Philistine to fight with him; for you are *but* a youth while he has been a warrior from his youth."

34 But David said to Saul, "Your servant was tending his father's sheep. When a lion or a bear came and took a lamb from the flock,

35 I went out after him and attacked him, and rescued *it* from his mouth; and when he rose up against me, I seized *him* by his beard and^T struck him and killed him.   *smote*

36 "Your servant has killed both the lion and the bear; and this uncircumcised Philistine will be like one of them, since he has taunted the armies of the living God."

37 And David said, "The^R LORD who delivered me from the paw of the lion and from the paw of the bear, He will deliver me from the hand of this Philistine." And Saul said to David, "Go,^R and may the LORD be with you."   [2 Cor. 1:10; 2 Tim. 4:17, 18] • 1 Sam. 20:13

38 Then Saul clothed David with his garments and put a bronze helmet on his head, and he clothed him with armor.

39 And David girded his sword over his armor and tried to walk, for he had not tested *them*. So David said to Saul, "I cannot go with these, for I have not tested *them*." And David took them off.

40 And he took his stick in his hand and chose for himself five smooth stones from the brook, and put them in the shepherd's bag which he had, even in *his* pouch, and^R his sling was in his hand; and he approached the Philistine.   Judg. 20:16

41 Then the Philistine came on and approached David, with the shield-bearer in front of him.

42 When the Philistine looked and saw David,^R he disdained him; for he was *but* a youth, and^R ruddy, with a handsome appearance.   [Ps. 123:4; Prov. 16:18] • 1 Sam. 16:12

43 And the Philistine said to David, "Am I a dog, that you come to me with sticks?" And the Philistine cursed David by his gods.

44 The Philistine also said to David, "Come to me, and I will give your flesh^R to the birds of the sky and the beasts of the field."   1 Sam. 17:46

45 Then David said to the Philistine, "You come to me with a sword, a spear, and a javelin,^R but I come to you in the name of the LORD of hosts, the God of the armies of Israel, whom you have taunted.   2 Sam. 22:35

46 "This day the LORD will deliver you up into my hands, and I will strike you down and remove your head from you. And I will give the^R dead bodies of the army of the Philistines this day to the birds of the sky and the wild beasts of the earth, ^Rthat all the earth may know that there is a God in Israel,   Deut. 28:26 • Josh. 4:24; 1 Kin. 8:43; 18:36

47 and that all this assembly may know that^R the LORD does not deliver by sword or

¹² I.e., free from taxes and public service

by spear; for the battle is the LORD's and He will give you into our hands." *1 Sam. 14:6*

48 Then it happened when the Philistine rose and came and drew near to meet David, that^RDavid ran quickly toward the battle line to meet the Philistine. *Ps. 27:3*

49 And David put his hand into his bag and took from it a stone and slung *it*, and struck the Philistine on his forehead. And the stone sank into his forehead, so that he fell on his face to the ground.

50 Thus David prevailed over the Philistine with a sling and a stone, and he struck the Philistine and killed him; but there was no sword in David's hand.

51 Then David ran and stood over the Philistine and took his sword and drew it out of its sheath and killed him, and cut off his head with it. When the Philistines saw that their champion was dead, they fled.

52 And the men of Israel and Judah arose and shouted and pursued the Philistines as far as the valley, and to the gates of Ekron. And the slain Philistines^Tlay along the way to Shaaraim, even to Gath and Ekron. *fell*

53 And the sons of Israel returned from chasing the Philistines and plundered their camps.

54 Then David took the Philistine's head and brought it to Jerusalem, but he put his weapons in his tent.

55 Now when Saul saw David going out against the Philistine, he said to Abner the commander of the army, "Abner, whose son is this young man?" And Abner said, "By your life, O king, I do not know."

56 And the king said, "You inquire whose son the youth is."

57 So when David returned from killing the Philistine, Abner took him and^Rbrought him before Saul with the Philistine's head in his hand. *1 Sam. 17:54*

58 And Saul said to him, "Whose son are you, young man?" And David answered, "*I*^R *am* the son of your servant Jesse the Bethlehemite." *1 Sam. 17:12*

CHAPTER 18

Jonathan Loves David

NOW it came about when he had finished speaking to Saul, that^Rthe soul of Jonathan was knit to the soul of David, and^RJonathan loved him as himself. *Gen. 44:30 • Deut. 13:6*

2 And Saul took him that day and did not let him return to his father's house.

3 Then Jonathan made a covenant with David because he loved him as himself.

4 And^RJonathan stripped himself of the robe that was on him and gave it to David, with his armor, including his sword and his bow and his belt. *Gen. 41:42; 1 Sam. 17:38*

Israel Elevates David over Saul

5 So David went out wherever Saul sent

him, *and*^Aprospered; and Saul set him over the men of war. And it was pleasing in the sight of all the people and also in the sight of Saul's servants. *acted wisely*

6 And it happened as they were coming, when David returned from killing the Philistine, that^Rthe women came out of all the cities of Israel, singing and dancing, to meet King Saul, with tambourines, with joy and with ¹³musical instruments. *Ps. 68:25; 149:3*

7 And the women^Rsang as they^Aplayed, and said, *Ex. 15:21; 1 Sam. 21:11; 29:5 • danced*
"Saul has slain his thousands,
And David his ten thousands."

8 Then Saul became very angry, for this saying displeased him; and he said, "They have ascribed to David ten thousands, but to me they have ascribed thousands. Now what more can he have but the kingdom?"

9 And Saul looked at David with suspicion from that day on.

The Attempts of Saul to Slay David:
By Throwing a Spear at David

10 Now it came about on the next day that^Ran evil spirit from God came mightily upon Saul, and he raved in the midst of the house, while David was playing *the harp* with his hand,^Tas usual; and^Ta spear *was* in Saul's hand. *1 Sam. 16:14 • day by day • the*

11 And Saul hurled the spear for he thought, "I will pin David to the wall." But David escaped from his presence twice.

12 Now^RSaul was afraid of David,^Rfor the LORD was with him but had departed from Saul. *1 Sam. 18:15, 29 • 1 Sam. 16:13, 18*

13 Therefore Saul removed him from^This presence, and appointed him as his commander of a thousand; and he went out and came in before the people. *with him*

14 And David was prospering in all his ways for^Rthe LORD *was* with him. *Josh. 6:27*

15 When Saul saw that he was^Aprospering greatly, he dreaded him. *acting very wisely*

16 But all Israel and Judah loved David, and he went out and came in before them.

By Tricking David to Fight
the Philistines

17 Then Saul said to David, "Here is my older daughter Merab; I will give her to you as a wife, only be a valiant man for me and fight the LORD's battles." For Saul thought, "My hand shall not be against him, but let the hand of the Philistines be against him."

18 But David said to Saul, "Who am I, and what is my life *or* my father's family in Israel, that I should be the king's son-in-law?"

19 So it came about at the time when Merab, Saul's daughter, should have been given to David, that she was given to^RAdriel the Meholathite for a wife. *2 Sam. 21:8*

20 Now ^RMichal, Saul's daughter, loved David. When they told Saul, the thing was agreeable^Tto him. *1 Sam. 18:28 • in his sight*

21 And Saul thought, "I will give her to

13 I.e., triangles, or three-stringed instruments

him that she may become a snare to him, and[R]that the hand of the Philistines may be against him." Therefore Saul said to David, "For[R]a second time you may be my son-in-law today."   1 Sam. 18:17 • 1 Sam. 18:26

22 Then Saul commanded his servants, "Speak to David secretly, saying, 'Behold, the king delights in you, and all his servants love you; now therefore, become the king's son-in-law.' "

23 So Saul's servants spoke these words [T]to David. But David said, "Is it trivial in your sight to become the king's son-in-law, [R]since I am a poor man and lightly esteemed?"   in the ears of • Gen. 29:20; 34:12

24 And the servants of Saul reported to him[T]according to these words which David spoke.   by saying according

25 Saul then said, "Thus you shall say to David, 'The king does not desire any[R]dowry except a hundred foreskins of the Philistines, to take vengeance on the king's enemies.' " Now Saul planned to make David fall by the hand of the Philistines.   Ex. 22:17

26 When his servants told David these words, [T]it pleased David to become the king's son-in-law. Before the days had expired   it was agreeable in the sight of

27 David rose up and went, [R]he and his men, and struck down two hundred men among the Philistines. Then David brought their foreskins, and they gave them in full number to the king, that he might become the king's son-in-law. So Saul gave him Michal his daughter for a wife.   1 Sam. 18:17

28 When Saul saw and knew that the LORD was with David, and that Michal, Saul's daughter, loved him,

29 then Saul was even more afraid of David. Thus Saul was David's enemy continually.

30 Then the commanders of the Philistines went out to battle, and it happened as often as they went out, that David behaved himself more wisely than all the servants of Saul. So his name was highly esteemed.

CHAPTER 19

By Commanding His Servants to Kill David

NOW Saul told Jonathan his son and all his servants to put David to death. But Jonathan, Saul's son, greatly delighted in David.

2 So Jonathan told David saying, "Saul my father is seeking to put you to death. Now therefore, please be on guard in the morning, and stay in a secret place and hide yourself.

3 "And I will go out and stand beside my father in the field where you are, and I will speak with my father about you; if I[T]find out anything, then I shall tell you."   see

4 Then Jonathan spoke well of David to Saul his father, and said to him, "Do not let the king sin against his servant David, since he has not sinned against you, and since his deeds have been very beneficial to you.

5 "For he took his life in his hand and struck the Philistine, and the LORD brought about a great deliverance for all Israel; you saw it and rejoiced.[R]Why then will you sin against innocent blood, by putting David to death without a cause?"   Ps. 94:21; Matt. 27:4

6 And Saul listened to the voice of Jonathan, and Saul vowed, "As the LORD lives, he shall not be put to death."

7 Then Jonathan called David, and Jonathan told him all these words. And Jonathan brought David to Saul, and he was in his presence as[R]formerly.   1 Sam. 16:21; 18:2, 10, 13

By Throwing a Spear at David Again

8 When there was war again, David went out and fought with the Philistines, and[T]defeated them with great slaughter, so that they fled before him.   smote

9 Now there was[R]an evil spirit from the LORD on Saul as he was sitting in his house with his spear in his hand, and David was playing the harp with his hand.   1 Sam. 16:14

10 [I]And Saul tried to[T]pin David to the wall with the spear, but he slipped away out of Saul's presence, so that he stuck the spear into the wall. And David fled and escaped that night.   Prov. 1:16 • strike David and the wall

By Sending Messengers to Kill David

11 Then[R]Saul sent messengers to David's house to watch him, in order to put him to death in the morning. But Michal, David's wife, told him, saying, "If you do not save your life tonight, tomorrow you will be put to death."   Judg. 16:2; Ps. 59:title

12 [R]So Michal let David down through a window, and he went out and fled and escaped.   Josh. 2:15; Acts 9:25; 2 Cor. 11:33

13 And Michal took[R]the [T]household idol and laid it on the bed, and put a quilt of goats' hair at its head, and covered it with clothes.   Gen. 31:19 • Heb., teraphim

14 When Saul sent messengers to take David, she said, "He[R]is sick."   Josh. 2:5

15 Then Saul sent messengers to see David, saying, "Bring him up to me on[T]his bed, that I may put him to death."   the

16 When the messengers entered, behold, the[T]household idol was on the bed with the quilt of goats' hair at its head.   Heb., teraphim

17 So Saul said to Michal, "Why have you deceived me like this and let my enemy go, so that he has escaped?" And Michal said to Saul, "He said to me, 'Let me go! [R]Why should I put you to death?' "   2 Sam. 2:22

By Coming to Kill David at Samuel's House

18 Now David fled and escaped and came [R]to Samuel at Ramah, and told him all that Saul had done to him. And he and Samuel went and stayed in Naioth.   1 Sam. 7:17

19 And it was told Saul, saying, "Behold, David is at Naioth in Ramah."

20 Then ᴿSaul sent messengers to take David, but when they saw the company of the prophets prophesying, with Samuel standing *and* presiding over them, the Spirit of God came upon the messengers of Saul; and ᴿthey also prophesied.   John 7:32 • Num. 11:25

21 And when it was told Saul, he sent other messengers, and they also prophesied. So Saul sent messengers again the third time, and they also prophesied.

22 Then he himself went to Ramah, and came as far as the large well that is in Secu; and he asked and said, "Where are Samuel and David?" And *someone* said, "Behold, they are at Naioth in Ramah."

23 And he ᵀproceeded there to Naioth in Ramah; and ᴿthe Spirit of God came upon him also, so that he went along prophesying continually until he came to Naioth in Ramah.   *went* • 1 Sam. 10:10

24 And he also stripped off his clothes, and he too prophesied before Samuel and ᵀlay down ᴿnaked all that day and all that night. Therefore they say, "Is Saul also among the prophets?"   *fell* • 2 Sam. 6:20

CHAPTER 20

By Commanding Jonathan to Bring David to be Killed

THEN David fled from Naioth in Ramah, and came and ᴿsaid ᵀto Jonathan, "What have I done? What is my iniquity? And what is my sin before your father, that he is seeking my life?"   1 Sam. 24:9 • *before*

2 And he said to him, "Far from it, you shall not die. Behold, my father does nothing either great or small without disclosing it to me. So why should my father hide this thing from me? It is not so!"

3 Yet David ᴿvowed again, ᵀsaying, "Your father knows well that I have found favor in your sight, and he has said, 'Do not let Jonathan know this, lest he be grieved.' But truly as the LORD lives and as your soul lives, there is ᵀhardly a step between me and death."   Deut. 6:13 • *and said* • *about*

4 Then Jonathan said to David, "Whatever you say, I will do for you."

5 So David said to Jonathan, "Behold, tomorrow is the new moon, and I ought ᴿto sit down to eat with the king. But let me go, ᴿthat I may hide myself in the field until the third evening.   1 Sam. 20:24, 27 • 1 Sam. 19:2

6 "If your father misses me at all, then say, 'David earnestly asked *leave* of me to run to Bethlehem his city, because it is the yearly sacrifice there for the whole family.'

7 "If he ᵀsays, 'It is good,' your servant *shall* be safe; but if he is very angry, know that he has decided on evil.   *says thus*

8 "Therefore deal kindly with your servant, for ᴿyou have brought your servant into a covenant of the LORD with you. But ᴿif there is iniquity in me, put me to death

yourself; for why then should you bring me to your father?"   1 Sam. 18:3 • 2 Sam. 14:32

9 And Jonathan said, "Far be it from you! For if I should indeed learn that evil has been decided by my father to come upon you, then would I not tell you about it?"

10 Then David said to Jonathan, "Who will tell me ᵀif your father answers you harshly?"   *or what*

11 And Jonathan said to David, "Come, and let us go out into the field." So both of them went out to the field.

12 Then Jonathan said to David, "The LORD, the God of Israel, *be witness*! When I have sounded out my father about this time tomorrow, *or* the third day, behold, if there is good *feeling* toward David, shall I not then send to you and make it known to you?

13 "If it please my father *to do* you harm, may the LORD do so to Jonathan and more also, if I do not ᵀmake it known to you and send you away, that you may go in safety. And may the LORD be with you as He has been with my father.   *uncover your ear*

14 "And if I am still alive, will you not show me the lovingkindness of the LORD, that I may not die?

15 "And you shall not cut off your lovingkindness from my house forever, not even when the LORD cuts off every one of the enemies of David from the face of the earth."

16 So Jonathan made a *covenant* with the house of David, *saying*, "May the LORD require *it* at the hands of David's enemies."

17 And Jonathan made David vow again because of his love for him, because he loved him as he loved his own life.

18 Then Jonathan said to him, "Tomorrow is the new moon, and you will be missed because your seat will be empty.

19 "When you have stayed for three days, you shall go down quickly and come to the place where you hid yourself on that eventful day, and you shall remain by the stone Ezel.

20 "And I will shoot three arrows to the side, as though I shot at a target.

21 "And behold, I will send the lad, *saying*, 'Go, find the arrows.' If I specifically say to the lad, 'Behold, the arrows are on this side of you, get them,' then come; for there is safety for you and ᵀno harm, as the LORD lives.   *there is nothing*

22 "But if I ᵀsay to the youth, 'Behold,ᴿ the arrows are beyond you,' go, for the LORD has sent you away.   *say thus* • 1 Sam. 20:37

23 "As for the ᵀagreement of which you and I have spoken, behold,ᴿ the LORD is between you and me forever."   *word* • Gen. 31:49, 53

24 So David hid in the field; and when the new moon came, the king sat down to eat food.

25 And the king sat on his seat as usual, the seat by the wall; then Jonathan rose up and Abner sat down by Saul's side, but ᴿDavid's place was empty.   1 Sam. 20:18

26 Nevertheless Saul did not speak anything that day, for he thought, "It is an accident, he is not clean, surely *he is* not clean."

27 And it came about the next day, the second *day* of the new moon, that David's place was empty; so Saul said to Jonathan his son, "Why has the son of Jesse not come to the meal, either yesterday or today?"

28 Jonathan then answered Saul, "David^R earnestly asked leave of me *to go* to Bethlehem,   1 Sam. 20:6

29 for he said, 'Please^{T}let me go, since our family has a sacrifice in the city, and my brother has commanded me to attend. And now, if I have found favor in your sight, please let me get away that I may see my brothers.' For this reason he has not come to the king's table."   *send me away*

30 Then Saul's anger burned against Jonathan and he said to him, "You son of a perverse, rebellious woman! Do I not know that you are choosing the son of Jesse to your own shame and to the shame of your mother's nakedness?

31 "For as long as the son of Jesse lives on the earth, neither you nor your kingdom will be established. Therefore now, send and bring him to me, for he must surely die."

32 But Jonathan answered Saul his father and said to him, "Why^{R}should he be put to death? What has he done?"   Gen. 31:36

33 Then Saul hurled his spear at him to strike him down; so Jonathan knew that his father had decided to put David to death.

34 Then Jonathan arose from the table in fierce anger, and did not eat food on the second day of the new moon, for he was grieved over David because his father had dishonored him.

35 Now it came about in the morning that Jonathan went out into the field for the appointment with David, and a little lad *was* with him.

36 And he said to his lad, "Run,^{R} find now the arrows which I am about to shoot." As the lad was running, he shot^{T}an arrow past him.   1 Sam. 20:20, 21 • *the*

37 When the lad reached the place of the arrow which Jonathan had shot, Jonathan called after the lad, and said, "Is^{R}not the arrow beyond you?"   1 Sam. 20:22

38 And Jonathan called after the lad, "Hurry, be quick, do not stay!" And Jonathan's lad picked up the arrow and came to his master.

39 But the lad was not aware of anything; only Jonathan and David knew about the matter.

40 Then Jonathan gave his weapons to his lad and said to him, "Go, bring *them* to the city."

41 When the lad was gone, David rose from the south side and fell on his face to the ground, and^{R}bowed three times. And they kissed each other and wept together, but^{R}David more.   Gen. 42:6 • 1 Sam. 18:3

42 And Jonathan said to David, "Go in safety, inasmuch as we have sworn to each other in the name of the LORD, saying, 'The LORD will be between me and you, and between my^{T}descendants and your^{T}descendants forever.'" Then he rose and departed, while Jonathan went into the city.   *seed*

CHAPTER 21

David Is Protected by the Priest

THEN David came to^{R}Nob to Ahimelech the priest; and Ahimelech came trembling to meet David, and said to him, "Why are you alone and no one with you?"   Neh. 11:32

2 And David said to Ahimelech the priest, "The king has commissioned me with a matter, and has said to me, 'Let^{R}no one know anything about the matter on which I am sending you and with which I have commissioned you; and I have directed the young men to a certain place.'   Ps. 141:3

3 "Now therefore, what^{T}do you have on hand? Give me five loaves of bread, or whatever can be found."   *is under your hand?*

4 And the priest answered David and said, "There is no ordinary bread^{T}on hand, but there is^{R}consecrated bread; if only the young men have ^{R}kept themselves from women."   *under my hand* • Ex. 25:30 • Ex. 19:15

5 And David answered the priest and said to him, "Surely women have been kept from us as previously when I set out and the vessels of the young men were holy, though it was an ordinary journey; how much more then today will their vessels *be holy*?"

6 So the priest gave him consecrated *bread*; for there was no bread there but the bread of the Presence which was removed from before the LORD, in order to put hot bread *in its place* when it was taken away.

7 Now one of the servants of Saul was there that day, detained before the LORD; and his name was^{R}Doeg the Edomite, the chief of Saul's shepherds.   1 Sam. 14:47; 22:9

8 And David said to Ahimelech, "Now is there not a spear or a sword^{T}on hand? For I brought neither my sword nor my weapons ^{T}with me, because the king's matter was urgent."   *under your hand* • *in my hand*

9 Then the priest said, "The sword of Goliath the Philistine, whom you^{T}killed in the valley of Elah, behold, it is wrapped in a cloth behind the ephod; if you would take it for yourself, take *it*. For there is no other except it here." And David said, "There is none like it; give it to me."   *smote*

David Pretends to be Mad

10 Then David arose and fled that day from Saul, and went to Achish king of Gath.

11 But the^{R}servants of Achish said to him, "Is this not David the king of the land?^{R}Did they not sing of this one as they danced, saying,   Ps. 56:title • 1 Sam. 18:7; 29:5
'Saul has slain his thousands,
And David his ten thousands'?"

12 And David took these words to heart, and greatly feared Achish king of Gath.

13 So he[R]disguised his sanity before them, and acted insanely in their hands, and scribbled on the doors of the gate, and let his saliva run down into his beard.   Ps. 34:title

14 Then Achish said to his servants, "Behold, you see the man behaving as a madman. Why do you bring him to me?

15"Do I lack madmen, that you have brought this one to act the madman in my presence? Shall this one come into my house?"

CHAPTER 22

David Flees to Adullam—1 Chr. 12:16–18

SO David departed from there and[R]escaped to the cave of Adullam; and when his brothers and all his father's household heard *of it*, they went down there to him.   Ps. 57:title

2 And everyone who was in distress, and everyone who was in debt, and everyone who was discontented, gathered to him; and he became captain over them. Now there were about four hundred men with him.

3 And David went from there to Mizpah of Moab; and he said to the king of Moab, "Please let my father and my mother come *and stay* with you until I know what God will do for me."

4 Then he left them with the king of Moab; and they stayed with him all the time that David was in the stronghold.

5 And the prophet Gad said to David, "Do not stay in the stronghold; depart, and go into the land of Judah." So David departed and went into the forest of Hereth.

Saul Slays the Priests of God

6 Then Saul heard that David and the men who were with him had been discovered. Now[R]Saul was sitting in Gibeah, under the tamarisk tree on the height with his spear in his hand, and all his servants were standing around him.   Judg. 4:5; 1 Sam. 14:2

7 And Saul said to his servants who stood around him, "Hear now, O Benjamites! Will the son of Jesse also give to all of you fields and vineyards?[R]Will he make you all commanders of thousands and commanders of hundreds?   1 Sam. 8:12

8"For all of you have conspired against me so that there is no one who[T]discloses to me when my son makes *a covenant* with the son of Jesse, and there is none of you who is sorry for me or discloses to me that my son has stirred up my servant against me to lie in ambush, as *it is* this day."   *uncovers my ear*

9 Then Doeg the Edomite, who was standing by the servants of Saul, answered and said, "I saw the son of Jesse coming to Nob, to Ahimelech the son of Ahitub.

10"And[R]he inquired of the LORD for him, gave him provisions, and gave him the sword of Goliath the Philistine."   Num. 27:21

11 Then the king sent someone to summon Ahimelech the priest, the son of Ahitub, and all his father's household, the priests who were in Nob; and all of them came to the king.

12 And Saul said, "Listen now, son of Ahitub." And he [T]answered, "Here I am, my lord."   *said*

13 Saul then said to him, "Why have you and the son of Jesse conspired against me, in that you have given him bread and a sword and have inquired of God for him, that he should rise up against me[R]by lying in ambush as *it is* this day?"   1 Sam. 22:8

14 [R]Then Ahimelech answered the king and said, "And who among all your servants is as faithful as David, even the king's son-in-law, who is captain over your guard, and is honored in your house? 1 Sam. 19:4, 5; 20:32

15"Did I *just* begin[R]to inquire of God for him today? Far be it from me! Do not let the king impute anything to his servant *or* to any of the household of my father, for your servant knows nothing [T]at all of this whole affair."   2 Sam. 5:19, 23 • *small* or *great*

16 But the king said, "You shall surely die, Ahimelech, you and all your father's household!"

17 And the king said to the [T]guards who were attending him, "Turn around and put the priests of the LORD to death, because their hand also is with David and because they knew that he was fleeing and did not reveal it to me." But the servants of the king were not willing to put forth their hands to attack the priests of the LORD.   *runners*

18 Then the king said to Doeg, "You turn around and[T]attack the priests." And Doeg the Edomite turned around and attacked the priests, who wore the linen ephod.   *smite*

19 And [R]he struck Nob the city of the priests with the edge of the sword, both men and women, children and infants; also oxen, donkeys, and sheep, *he struck* with the edge of the sword.   1 Sam. 15:3

20 But[R]one son of Ahimelech the son of Ahitub, named Abiathar,[R]escaped and fled after David.   1 Sam. 23:6, 9; 30:7 • 1 Sam. 23:6

21 And Abiathar told David that Saul had killed the priests of the LORD.

22 Then David said to Abiathar, "I knew on that day, when [R]Doeg the Edomite was there, that he would surely tell Saul. I have brought about *the death* of every person in your father's household.   1 Sam. 21:7

23"Stay with me, do not be afraid, for[R]he who seeks my life seeks your life; for you are[T]safe with me."   1 Kin. 2:26 • *a charge*

CHAPTER 23

David Attacks the Philistines

THEN they told David, saying, "Behold, the Philistines are fighting against Keilah, and are plundering the threshing floors."

2 So David inquired of the LORD, saying,

"Shall I go and [T]attack these Philistines?" And the LORD said to David, "Go and[T]attack the Philistines, and deliver Keilah."   *smite*

3 But David's men said to him, "Behold, we are afraid here in Judah. How much more then if we go to Keilah against the ranks of the Philistines?"

4 Then David inquired of the LORD once more. And the LORD answered him and said, "Arise, go down to Keilah, for[T]I will give the Philistines into your hand." Josh. 8:7; Judg. 7:7

5 So David and his men went to Keilah and fought with the Philistines; and he led away their livestock and struck them with a great slaughter. Thus David delivered the inhabitants of Keilah.

6 Now it came about, when Abiathar the son of Ahimelech[R]fled to David at Keilah, *that* he came down *with* an ephod in his hand.   1 Sam. 22:20

7 When it was told Saul that David had come to Keilah, Saul said, "God has [T]delivered him into my hand, for he shut himself in by entering a city with double gates and bars."   *alienated*

8 So Saul summoned all the people for war, to go down to Keilah to besiege David and his men.

9 Now David knew that Saul was plotting evil against him; so he said to Abiathar the priest, "Bring the ephod here."

10 Then David said, "O LORD God of Israel, Thy servant has heard for certain that Saul is seeking to come to Keilah to destroy the city on my account.

11 "Will the men of Keilah surrender me into his hand? Will Saul come down just as Thy servant has heard? O LORD God of Israel, I pray, tell Thy servant." And the LORD said, "He will come down."

12 Then David said, "Will the men of Keilah surrender me and my men into the hand of Saul?" And the LORD said, "They[R]will surrender you."   Judg. 15:10-13; 1 Sam. 23:20

Saul Chases David

13 Then David and his men, about six hundred, arose and departed from Keilah, and they went wherever they could go. When it was told Saul that David had escaped from Keilah, he gave up the pursuit.

14 And David stayed in the wilderness in the strongholds, and remained in the hill country in the wilderness of[R]Ziph. And Saul sought him every day, but[R]God did not deliver him into his hand.   Josh. 15:55 • Ps. 32:7

15 Now David became aware that Saul had come out to seek his life while David was in the wilderness of Ziph at Horesh.

16 And Jonathan, Saul's son, arose and went to David at Horesh, and [14]encouraged[R] him in God.   1 Sam. 30:6; Neh. 2:18

17 Thus he said to him, "Do[R]not be afraid, because the hand of Saul my father shall not find you, and you will be king over Israel

and I will be next to you; and[R]Saul my father knows that also."   [Ps. 27:1, 3] • 1 Sam. 20:31

18 So the two of them made a covenant before the LORD; and David stayed at Horesh while Jonathan went to his house.

19 Then[R]Ziphites came up to Saul at Gibeah, saying, "Is David not hiding with us in the strongholds at Horesh, on [R]the hill of Hachilah, which is on the[T]south of [15]Jeshimon?   1 Sam. 26:1 • 1 Sam. 26:3 • *right side*

20 "Now then, O king, come down according to all the desire of your soul to[T]do so; and[R]our part *shall be* to surrender him into the king's hand."   *come down* • 1 Sam. 23:12

21 And Saul said, "May you be blessed of the LORD;[R]for you have had compassion on me.   1 Sam. 22:8

22 "Go now, make more sure, and investigate and see his place where his[T]haunt is, *and* who has seen him there; for I am told that he is very cunning.   *foot*

23 "So look, and learn about all the hiding places where he hides himself, and return to me with certainty, and I will go with you; and it shall come about if he is in the land that I will search him out among all the thousands of Judah."

24 Then they arose and went to Ziph before Saul. Now David and his men were in the wilderness of Maon, in the Arabah to the[T]south of [A]Jeshimon.   *right side* • *the desert*

25 When Saul and his men went to seek *him,* they told David, and he came down to the rock and stayed in the wilderness of Maon. And when Saul heard *it,* he pursued David in the wilderness of Maon.

26 And Saul went on one side of the mountain, and David and his men on the other side of the mountain; and David was hurrying to get away from Saul, for Saul and his men[R]were surrounding David and his men to seize them.   Ps. 17:9

27 But a messenger came to Saul, saying, "Hurry and come, for the Philistines have made a raid on the land."

28 So Saul returned from pursuing David, and went to meet the Philistines; therefore they called that place the Rock of Escape.

29 And David went up from there and stayed in the strongholds of Engedi.

CHAPTER 24

David Saves Saul's Life

NOW it came about[R]when Saul returned from pursuing the Philistines, [B]he was told, saying, "Behold, David is in the wilderness of Engedi."   1 Sam. 23:28, 29 • 1 Sam. 23:19

2 Then[R]Saul took three thousand chosen men from all Israel, and went to seek David and his men in front of the Rocks of the Wild Goats.   1 Sam. 26:2

3 And he came to the sheepfolds on the way, where there *was* a cave; and Saul[R]went in to [T]relieve himself. Now[R]David and his

[14] Lit., *strengthened his hand*   [15] Or, *the desert*

men were sitting in the inner recesses of the cave. ᴶᵘᵈᵍ. 3:24 • *cover his feet* • Ps. 57:title

4 And the men of David said to him, "Behold, *this is* the day of which the Lᴏʀᴅ said to you, 'Behold; I am about to give your enemy into your hand, and you shall do to him as it seems good to you.' " Then David arose and cut off the edge of Saul's robe secretly.

5 And it came about afterward that David's conscience bothered him because he had cut off the edge of Saul's *robe.*

6 So he said to his men, "Farᴿbe it from me because of the Lᴏʀᴅ that I should do this thing to my lord, the Lᴏʀᴅ's anointed, to stretch out my hand against him, since he is the Lᴏʀᴅ's anointed." 1 Sam. 26:11

7 And David ᵀpersuaded his men with *these* words and did not allow them to rise up against Saul. And Saul arose, ᵀleft the cave, and went on *his* way. *tore apart • from*

8 Now afterward David arose and went out of the cave and called after Saul, saying, "My lord the king!" And when Saul looked behind him, David bowed with his face to the ground and prostrated himself.

9 And David said to Saul, "Why do you listen to the words of men, saying, 'Behold, David seeksᵀto harm you'? *your hurt*

10"Behold, this day your eyes have seen that the Lᴏʀᴅ had given you today into my hand in the cave, and some said to kill you, but *my eye* had pity on you; and I said, 'I will not stretch out my hand against my lord, for he is the Lᴏʀᴅ's anointed.'

11"Now, my father, see! Indeed, see the edge of your robe in my hand! For in that I cut off the edge of your robe and did not kill you, know and perceive that there is no evil or ᵀrebellion in my hands, and I have not sinned against you, though you are lying in wait for my life to take it. *transgression*

12"May the Lᴏʀᴅ judge between you and me, and may the Lᴏʀᴅ avenge me on you; but my hand shall not be against you.

13"As the proverb of the ancients says, 'Out of the wicked comes forth wickedness'; but my hand shall not be against you.

14"After whom has the king of Israel come out? Whom are you pursuing? ᴿA dead dog,ᴿa single flea? 2 Sam. 9:8 • 1 Sam. 26:20

15 "The Lᴏʀᴅ therefore be judge and decide betweenᵀyou and me; and may He see andᴿplead my cause, and ᵀdeliver me from your hand." *me and you* • Ps. 35:1 • *vindicate*

16 Now it came about when David had finished speaking these words to Saul, that Saul said, "Isᴿthis your voice, my son David?" Then Saul lifted up his voice and wept. 1 Sam. 26:17

17 ᴿAnd he said to David, "You are more righteous than I; for ᴿyou have dealt well with me, while I have dealt wickedly with you. 1 Sam. 26:21 • [Matt. 5:44]

18"And you have declared today that you have done good to me, thatᴿthe Lᴏʀᴅ delivered me into your hand and *yet* you did not kill me. 1 Sam. 26:23

19"For if a man finds his enemy, will he let him go away safely? May the Lᴏʀᴅ therefore reward you with good in return for what you have done to me this day.

20"And now, behold, I know that you shall surely be king, and that the kingdom of Israel shall be established in your hand.

21"So now swear to me by the Lᴏʀᴅ that you will not cut off my ᵀdescendants after me, and that you will not destroy my name from my father's household." *seed*

22 And David swore to Saul. And Saul went to his home, but David and his men went up toᴿthe stronghold. 1 Sam. 23:29

CHAPTER 25

Samuel the Judge Dies

THEN Samuel died; and all Israel gathered together and mourned for him, and buried him at his house in Ramah. And David arose and went down to the wilderness of Paran.

David Marries Abigail

2 Now *there was* a man in Maon whose business was in Carmel; and the man was very rich, and he had three thousand sheep and a thousand goats. And it came about while he was shearing his sheep in Carmel

3 (now the man's name was Nabal, and his wife's name was Abigail. And the woman was intelligent and beautiful in appearance, but the man was harsh and evil in *his* dealings, and he was a Calebite),

4 that David heard in the wilderness that Nabal was shearing his sheep.

5 So David sent ten young men, and David said to the young men, "Go up to Carmel, visit Nabal and greet him in my name;

6 and thus you shall say, 'Have a long life, peace be to you, and peace be to your house, and peace be to all that you have.

7 'And now I have heardᴿthat you have shearers; now your shepherds have been with us and we have not insulted them, nor have they missed anything all the days they were in Carmel. 2 Sam. 13:23, 24

8 'Ask your young men and they will tell you. Therefore let *my* young men find favor in your eyes, for we have come on a festive day. Please give whatever you find at hand to your servants and to your son David.' "

9 When David's young men came, they spoke to Nabal according to all these words in David's name; then they waited.

10 But Nabal answered David's servants, and said, "Whoᴿis David? And who is the son of Jesse? There are many servants today who are each breaking away from his master. Judg. 9:28

11"Shall I then take my bread and my water and my meat that I have slaughtered for my shearers, and give it to menᵀwhose origin I do not know?" *from where they are*

12 So David's young men retraced their way and went back; and they came and told him according to all these words.

13 And David said to his men, "Each *of you* gird on his sword." So each man girded on his sword. And David also girded on his sword, and about ᴿfour hundred men went up behind David while two hundredᴿstayed with the baggage.   1 Sam. 23:13 • 1 Sam. 30:24

14 But one of the young men told Abigail, Nabal's wife, saying, "Behold, David sent messengers from the wilderness to ᵀgreet our master, and he scorned them.   *bless*

15 "Yet the men were very good to us, and we were not insulted, nor did we miss anythingᵀas long as we went about with them, while we were in the fields.   *all the days*

16 "Theyᴿwere a wall to us both by night and by day, all the time we were with them tending the sheep.   Ex. 14:22; Job 1:10

17 "Now therefore, know and ᵀconsider what you should do, for evil is plotted against our master and against all his household; and he is such a worthless man that no one can speak to him."   *see*

18 Then Abigail hurried and took two hundred *loaves* of bread and two jugs of wine and five sheep already prepared and five measures of roasted grain and a hundred clusters of raisins and two hundred cakes of figs, and loaded *them* on donkeys.

19 And she said to her young men, "Go on before me; behold, I am coming after you." But she did not tell her husband Nabal.

20 And it came about as she was riding on her donkey and coming down by the hidden part of the mountain, that behold, David and his men were coming down toward her; so she met them.

21 Now David had said, "Surely in vain I have guarded all that this *man* has in the wilderness, so that nothing was missed of all that belonged to him; and he has ᴿreturned me evil for good.   Ps. 109:5; [Prov. 17:13]

22 "MayᴿGod do so to the enemies of David, and more also, if by morning I leave *as much as* one ᵀmale of any who belong to him."   1 Sam. 3:17 • *who urinates against the wall*

23 When Abigail saw David, she hurried and dismounted from her donkey, and fell on her face before David,ᴿand bowed herself to the ground.   1 Sam. 20:41

24 And she fell at his feet and said, "On me alone, my lord, be the blame. And please let your maidservant speak to you, and listen to the words of your maidservant.

25 "Please do not let my lordᵀpay attention to this ᵀworthless man, Nabal, for as his name is, so is he.ᵀNabal is his name and folly is with him; but I your maidservant did not see the young men of my lord whom you sent.   *set his heart to • man of Belial •* Fool

26 "Now therefore, my lord, as the LORD lives, and as your soul lives, since the LORD has restrained you from shedding blood, and from avenging yourself by your own hand, now then let your enemies, and those who seek evil against my lord, be as Nabal.

27 "And now let this gift which your maidservant has brought to my lord be given to the young men who accompany my lord.

28 "Please forgive ᴿthe transgression of your maidservant; for ᴿthe LORD will certainly make for my lord an enduring house, because my lord is fighting the battles of the LORD, andᴿevil shall not be found in you all your days.   1 Sam. 25:24 • 1 Sam. 22:14 • Ps. 7:3

29 "And should anyone rise up to pursue you and to seek yourᵀlife, then theᵀlife of my lord shall be bound in the bundle of the living with the LORD your God; but theᵀlives of your enemies He will sling outᵀas from the hollow of a sling.   *soul • in the midst*

30 "And it shall come about when the LORD shall do for my lord according to all the good that He has spoken concerning you, and shall appoint you ruler over Israel,

31 that this will not cause grief or a troubled heart to my lord, both by having shed blood without cause and by my lord having ᵀavenged himself.ᴿWhen the LORD shall deal well with my lord, then remember your maidservant."   *saved •* Gen. 40:14; 1 Sam. 25:30

32 Then David said to Abigail, "Blessedᴿ be the LORD God of Israel, who sent you this day to meet me,   Ex. 18:10; 1 Kin. 1:48; Ps. 41:13

33 and blessed be your discernment, and blessed be you, who have kept me this day fromᵀbloodshed, and fromᵀavenging myself by my own hand.   *coming in with blood • saving*

34 "Nevertheless, as the LORD God of Israel lives, who has restrained me from harming you, unless you had come quickly to meet me, surely there would not have been left to Nabal until the morning light *as much as* oneᵀmale."   *who urinates against the wall*

35 So David received from her hand what she had brought him, and he said to her, "Go up to your house in peace. See, I have listened to you and granted your request."

36 Then Abigail came to Nabal, and behold, he was holding a feast in his house, like the feast of a king. And Nabal's heart was merry within him, for he was very drunk; so she did not tell him anythingᵀat all until the morning light.   *small or large*

37 But it came about in the morning, when the wine had gone out of Nabal, that his wife told him these things, and his heart died within him so that he became *as a* stone.

38 And about ten days later, it happened that the LORD struck Nabal, and he died.

39 When David heard that Nabal was dead, he said, "Blessed be the LORD, who has pleaded the cause of my reproach from the hand of Nabal, and has kept back His servant from evil. The LORD has also returned the evildoing of Nabal on his own head." Then David sentᵀa proposal to Abigail, to take her as his wife.   *and spoke*

40 When the servants of David came to Abigail at Carmel, they spoke to her, saying,

"David has sent us to you, to take you as his wife."

41 And she arose[R]and bowed with her face to the ground and said, "Behold, your maidservant is a maid[R]to wash the feet of my lord's servants."   1 Sam. 25:23 • Mark 1:7

42 Then Abigail quickly arose, and rode on a donkey, with her five maidens who attended her; and she followed the messengers of David, and became his wife.

43 David had also taken Ahinoam of Jezreel, and they both became his wives.

44 Now Saul had given[R]Michal his daughter, David's wife, to Palti the son of Laish, who was from[R]Gallim.   2 Sam. 3:14 • Is. 10:30

CHAPTER 26

David Saves Saul's Life Again

THEN the Ziphites came to Saul at Gibeah, saying, "Is not David hiding on the hill of Hachilah, which is before [16]Jeshimon?"

2 So Saul arose and went down to the wilderness of Ziph, having with him[R]three thousand chosen men of Israel, to search for David in the wilderness of Ziph.   1 Sam. 13:2

3 And Saul camped in the hill of Hachilah, which is before [16]Jeshimon,[R]beside the road, and David was staying in the wilderness. When[R]he saw that Saul came after him into the wilderness,   1 Sam. 24:3 • 1 Sam. 23:15

4 David sent out spies, and he knew that Saul was definitely coming.

5 David then arose and came to the place where Saul had camped. And David saw the place where Saul lay, and Abner the son of Ner, the commander of his army; and Saul was lying in the circle of the camp, and the people were camped around him.

6 Then David answered and said to Ahimelech[R]the Hittite and to [R]Abishai the son of Zeruiah, Joab's brother, saying, "Who will go down with me to Saul in the camp?" And Abishai said, "I will go down with you."   Gen. 23:3; 26:34 • 1 Chr. 2:16

7 So David and Abishai came to the people by night, and behold, Saul lay sleeping inside the circle of the camp, with his spear stuck in the ground at his head; and Abner and the people were lying around him.

8 Then Abishai said to David, "Today God has delivered your enemy into your hand; now therefore, please let me strike him with the spear[T]to the ground with one stroke, and I will not[T]strike him the second time."   even into • repeat with respect to him

9 But David said to Abishai, "Do not destroy him, for[R]who can stretch out his hand against the LORD's anointed and be without guilt?"   1 Sam. 24:6, 7; 2 Sam. 1:14, 16

10 David also said, "As the LORD lives, [R]surely the LORD will strike him, or[R]his day will come that he dies, or he will go down into battle and perish.   [Heb. 10:30] • Ps. 37:13

11 "The LORD forbid that I should stretch

[16] Or, the desert

out my hand against the LORD's anointed; but now please take the spear that is at his head and the jug of water, and let us go."

12 So David took the spear and the jug of water from beside Saul's head, and they went away, but no one saw or knew it, nor did any awake, for they were all asleep, because [R]a sound sleep from the LORD had fallen on them.   Gen. 2:21; 15:12; Is. 29:10

13 Then David crossed over to the other side, and stood on top of the mountain at a distance with a large area between them.

14 And David called to the people and to Abner the son of Ner, saying, "Will you not answer, Abner?" Then Abner answered and said, "Who are you who calls to the king?"

15 So David said to Abner, "Are you not a man? And who is like you in Israel? Why then have you not guarded your lord the king? For one of the people came to destroy the king your lord.

16 "This thing that you have done is not good. As the LORD lives, all of you[R]must surely die, because you did not guard your lord, the LORD's anointed. And now, see where the king's spear is, and the jug of water that was at his head."   1 Sam. 20:31

17 Then Saul recognized David's voice and said, "Is[R]this your voice, my son David?" And David said, "It is my voice, my lord the king."   1 Sam. 24:16

18 He also said, "Why[R]then is my lord pursuing his servant? For what have I done? Or what evil is in my hand? 1 Sam. 24:9, 11-14

19 "Now therefore, please let my lord the king listen to the words of his servant. If the LORD has stirred you up against me, let Him [T]accept an offering; but if it is men, cursed are they before the LORD, for they have driven me out today that I should have no attachment with the inheritance of the LORD, saying, 'Go, serve other gods.'   smell

20 "Now then, do not let my blood fall to the ground away from the presence of the LORD; for the king of Israel has come out to search for[R]a single flea, just as one hunts a partridge in the mountains."   1 Sam. 24:14

Saul Admits His Guilt

21 Then Saul said, "I[R]have sinned. Return, my son David, for I will not harm you again because my life was precious in your sight this day. Behold, I have played the fool and have committed a serious error."   Ex. 9:27

22 And David answered and said, "Behold the spear of the king! Now let one of the young men come over and take it.

23 "And[R]the LORD will repay each man for his righteousness and his faithfulness; for the LORD delivered you into my hand today, but[R]I refused to stretch out my hand against the LORD's anointed.   Ps. 7:8 • 1 Sam. 24:12

24 "Now behold, as your life was highly valued in my sight this day, so may my life be highly valued in the sight of the LORD, and may He deliver me from all distress."

25 Then Saul said to David, "Blessed[R]are you, my son David; you will both accomplish much and surely prevail." So [R]David went on his way, and Saul returned to his place.   1 Sam. 24:19 • 1 Sam. 24:22

CHAPTER 27

David Joins with the Philistines

THEN David said[T]to himself, "Now I will perish one day by the hand of Saul. There is nothing better for me than[T]to escape into the land of the Philistines. Saul then will despair of searching for me anymore in all the territory of Israel, and I will escape from his hand."   in his heart • that I should surely escape

2 So David arose and crossed over, he and[R]the six hundred men who were with him, to [R]Achish the son of Maoch, king of Gath.   1 Sam. 25:13 • 1 Sam. 21:10; 1 Kin. 2:39

3 And David lived with Achish at Gath, he and his men, each with his household, even David with[R]his two wives, Ahinoam the Jezreelitess, and Abigail the Carmelitess, Nabal's[T]widow.   1 Sam. 25:42, 43 • wife

4 Now it was told Saul that David had fled to Gath, so he no longer searched for him.

5 Then David said to Achish, "If now I have found favor in your sight, let them give me a place in one of the cities in the country, that I may live there; for why should your servant live in the royal city with you?"

6 So Achish gave him Ziklag that day; therefore[R]Ziklag has belonged to the kings of Judah to this day.   Josh. 15:31; 19:5

7 And the number of days that David lived in the country of the Philistines was[R]a year and four months.   1 Sam. 29:3

8 Now David and his men went up and raided[R]the Geshurites and the Girzites and [R]the Amalekites; for they were the inhabitants of the land from ancient times, as you come to [R]Shur even as far as the land of Egypt.   Josh. 13:2, 13 • Ex. 17:8 • Ex. 15:22

9 And David[T]attacked the land and did not leave a man or a woman alive, and he took away the sheep, the cattle, the donkeys, the camels, and the clothing. Then he returned and came to Achish.   smote

10 Now Achish said, "Where have you [R]made a raid today?" And David said, "Against the [17]Negev of Judah and against the Negev of the Jerahmeelites and against the Negev of the Kenites."   1 Sam. 23:27

11 And David did not leave a man or a woman alive, to bring to Gath, saying, "Lest they should tell about us, saying, 'So has David done and so has been his practice all the time he has lived in the country of the Philistines.' "

12 So Achish believed David, saying, "He has surely made himself odious among his people Israel; therefore he will become my servant forever."

CHAPTER 28

NOW it came about in those days that[R]the Philistines gathered their armed camps for war, to fight against Israel. And Achish said to David, "Know assuredly that you will go out with me in the camp, you and your men."   1 Sam. 29:1

2 And David said to Achish, "Very well, you shall know what your servant can do." So Achish said to David, "Very well, I will make you my bodyguard for life."

God Does Not Answer Saul

3 Now [R]Samuel was dead, and all Israel had lamented him and buried him[R]in Ramah his own city. And Saul had removed from the land those who[R]were mediums and spiritists.   1 Sam. 25:1 • 1 Sam. 7:17 • Lev. 19:31

4 So the Philistines gathered together and came and camped[R]in Shunem; and Saul gathered all Israel together and they camped in[R]Gilboa.   Josh. 19:18 • 1 Sam. 31:1

5 When Saul saw the camp of the Philistines, he was afraid and his heart trembled greatly.

6 [R]When Saul inquired of the LORD, the LORD did not answer him, either by dreams or by Urim or by prophets.   1 Chr. 10:13, 14

Saul Visits the Witch

7 Then Saul said to his servants, "Seek for me a woman who is a medium, that I may go to her and inquire of her." And his servants said to him, "Behold, there is a woman who is a medium at En-dor."

8 Then Saul[R]disguised himself by putting on other clothes, and went, he and two men with him, and they came to the woman by night; and he said, "Conjure[R] up for me, please, and bring up for me whom I shall [T]name to you."   2 Chr. 18:29 • Is. 8:19 • say

9 But the woman said to him, "Behold, you know what Saul has done, how he has cut off those who are mediums and spiritists from the land. Why are you then laying a snare for my life to bring about my death?"

10 And Saul vowed to her by the LORD, saying, "As the LORD lives, there shall no punishment come upon you for this thing."

11 Then the woman said, "Whom shall I bring up for you?" And he said, "Bring up Samuel for me."

12 When the woman saw Samuel, she cried out with a loud voice; and the woman spoke to Saul, saying, "Why have you deceived me? For you are Saul."

13 And the king said to her, "Do not be afraid; but what do you see?" And the woman said to Saul, "I see a[A]divine being coming up out of the earth."   god

14 And he said to her, "What is his form?" And she said, "An old man is coming up,

[17] I.e., South country

and he is wrapped with a robe." And Saul knew that it was Samuel, and he bowed with his face to the ground and did homage.

15 Then Samuel said to Saul, "Why have you disturbed me by bringing me up?" And Saul answered, "I am greatly distressed; for the Philistines are waging war against me, and[R]God has departed from me and[R]answers me no more, either through prophets or by dreams; therefore I have called you, that you may make known to me what I should do."   1 Sam. 16:14; 18:12 • 1 Sam. 28:6

16 And Samuel said, "Why then do you ask me, since the LORD has departed from you and has become your adversary?

17"And the LORD has done[T]accordingly as He spoke through me; for the LORD has torn the kingdom out of your hand and given it to your neighbor, to David.   for himself

18"As you did not obey the LORD and did not execute His fierce wrath on Amalek, so the LORD has done this thing to you this day.

19"Moreover the LORD will also give over Israel along with you into the hands of the Philistines, therefore tomorrow [R]you and your sons will be with me. Indeed the LORD will give over the army of Israel into the hands of the Philistines!"   1 Sam. 31:2

20 Then Saul immediately fell full length upon the ground and was very afraid because of the words of Samuel; also there was no strength in him, for he had eaten no [T]food all day and all night.   bread

21 And the woman came to Saul and saw that he was terrified, and said to him, "Behold, your maidservant has[T]obeyed you, and [R]I have[T]taken my life in my hand, and have listened to your words which you spoke to me.   listened to your voice • Judg. 12:3 • put

22"So now also, please listen to the voice of your maidservant, and let me set a piece of bread before you that you may eat and have strength when you go on your way."

23 But he refused and said, "I[R] will not eat." However, his servants together with the woman urged him, and he listened to [T]them. So he arose from the ground and sat on[R]the bed.   1 Kin. 21:4 • their voices • Esth. 1:6

24 And the woman had a[R]fattened calf in the house, and she quickly slaughtered it; and she took flour, kneaded it, and baked unleavened bread from it.   Gen. 18:7

25 And she brought it before Saul and his servants, and they ate. Then they arose and went away that night.

CHAPTER 29

David Is Spared from Fighting Saul

NOW[R]the Philistines gathered together all their armies to [R]Aphek, while the Israelites were camping by the spring which is in[R]Jezreel.   1 Sam. 28:1 • Josh. 12:18 • 1 Kin. 21:1

2 And the lords of the Philistines were proceeding on by hundreds and by thousands, and David and his men were proceeding on in the rear with Achish.

3 Then the commanders of the Philistines said, "What are these Hebrews doing here?" And Achish said to the commanders of the Philistines, "Is this not David, the servant of Saul the king of Israel, who has been with me these days, or rather these years, and I have found no fault in him from the day he[T]deserted to me to this day?"   fell

4 But the commanders of the Philistines were angry with him, and the commanders of the Philistines said to him, "Make the man go back, that he may return[R]to his place where you have assigned him, and do not let him go down to battle with us, lest in the battle he become an adversary to us. For with what could this man make himself acceptable to his lord? Would it not be with the heads of[T]these men?   1 Sam. 27:6 • those

5"Is this not David,[R]of whom they sing in the dances, saying,   1 Sam. 18:7; 21:11

'Saul has slain his thousands,
And David his ten thousands'?"

6 Then Achish called David and said to him, "As the LORD lives, you have been upright, and[R]your going out and your coming in with me in the army are pleasing in my sight;[R]for I have not found evil in you from the day of your coming to me to this day. Nevertheless, you are not pleasing in the sight of the lords.   2 Sam. 3:25 • 1 Sam. 27:8-12

7"Now therefore return, and go in peace, that you may not displease the lords of the Philistines."

8 And David said to Achish, "But[R]what have I done? And what have you found in your servant from the day when I came before you to this day, that I may not go and fight against the enemies of my lord the king?"   1 Sam. 27:10-12

9 But Achish answered and said to David, "I know that you are pleasing in my sight, like an angel of God; nevertheless the commanders of the Philistines have said, 'He must not go up with us to the battle.'

10"Now then arise early in the morning [R]with the servants of your lord who have come with you, and as soon as you have arisen early in the morning and have light, depart."   1 Chr. 12:19, 22

11 So David arose early, he and his men, to depart in the morning, to return to the land of the Philistines. And the Philistines went up to Jezreel.

CHAPTER 30

God Answers David

THEN it happened when David and his men came to Ziklag on the third day, that the Amalekites had made a raid on the[T]Negev and on Ziklag, and had overthrown Ziklag and burned it with fire;   South country

2 and they took captive the women and all who were in it, both small and great,

ᵀwithout killing anyone, and carried *them* off and went their way.   *they did not kill*

3 And when David and his men came to the city, behold, it was burned with fire, and their wives and their sons and their daughters had been taken captive.

4 Then David and the people who were with him lifted their voices and wept until there was no strength in them to weep.

5 Now David's two wives had been taken captive, Ahinoam the Jezreelitess and Abigail theᵀwidow of Nabal the Carmelite. *wife*

6 Moreover David was greatly distressed becauseᴿthe people spoke of stoning him, for all the people wereᵀembittered, each one because of his sons and his daughters. But ᴿDavid strengthened himself in the LORD his God.   Ex. 17:4 • *bitter in soul* • 1 Sam. 23:16

7 ThenᴿDavid said toᴿAbiathar the priest, the son of Ahimelech, "Please bring me the ephod." So Abiathar brought the ephod to David.   1 Sam. 23:6, 9 • 1 Sam. 22:20-23

8 AndᴿDavid inquired of the LORD, saying, "ShallᴵI pursue this band? Shall I overtake them?" And He said to him, "Pursue, for you shall surely overtake them, and you shall surely rescue *all*."   Ps. 50:15 • Ex. 15:9

David Kills the Enemy

9 So David went,ᴴhe and the six hundred men who were with him, and came to the brook Besor, *where* those left behind remained.   1 Sam. 27:2

10 But David pursued, he and four hundred men, forᴿtwo hundred who were too exhausted to cross the brook Besor, remained *behind*.   1 Sam. 30:9, 21

11 Now they found an Egyptian in the field and brought him to David, and gave him bread and he ate, and they provided him water to drink.

12 And they gave him a piece of fig cake and two clusters of raisins, and he ate;ᴿthen his spirit ᵀrevived. For he had not eaten bread or drunk water for three days and three nights.   Judg. 15:19 • *returned to him*

13 And David said to him, "To whom do you belong? And where are you from?" And he said, "I am a young man of Egypt, a servant of an Amalekite; and my master left me behind when I fell sick three days ago.

14"We made a raid on theᵀNegev of the Cherethites, and on that which belongs to Judah, and on theᵀNegev of Caleb, and we burned Ziklag with fire."   South country

15 Then David said to him, "Will you bring me down to this band?" And he said, "Swear to me by God that you will not kill me or deliver me into the hands of my master, and I will bring you down to this band."

16 And when he had brought him down, behold, they wereᵀspread over all the land, eating and drinking andᵀdancing because of all the great spoil that they had taken from the land of the Philistines and from the land of Judah.   *left* • *keeping a pilgrim-feast*

17 And DavidᵀAslaughtered them from the twilightᵀuntil the evening ofᵀthe next day; and not a man of them escaped, except four hundred young men who rode on camels and fled.   *smote* • *even until* • *their*

18 So DavidᴿRrecovered all that the Amalekites had taken, and ᵀrescued his two wives.   Gen. 14:16 • *David rescued*

19 But nothing of theirs was missing, whether small or great, sons or daughters, spoil or anything that they had taken for themselves; David brought *it* all back.

20 So David had ᵀcaptured all the sheep and the cattle *which the people* drove ahead ofᵀthe *other* livestock, and they said, "This is David's spoil."   *taken* • *those livestock*

21 WhenᴿDavid came to the two hundred men who were too exhausted to follow David, who had also been left at the brook Besor, and they went out to meet David and to meet the people who were with him, then David approached the people and greeted them.   1 Sam. 30:10

22 Then all the wicked and worthless men among those who went with David answered and said, "Because they did not go withᵀus, we will not give them any of the spoil that we have recovered, except to every man his wife and his children, that they may lead *them* away and depart."   *me*

23 Then David said, "You must not do so, my brothers, with what the LORD has given us, who has kept us safe and delivered into our hand the band that came against us.

24"And who will listen to you in this matter? For as his share is who goes down to the battle, so shall his share be who stays by the baggage; they shall share alike."

25 And so it has been from that day forward, that he made it a statute and an ordinance for Israel to this day.

26 Now when David came to Ziklag, he sent *some* of the spoil to the elders of Judah, to his friends, saying, "Behold, a gift for you from the spoil of the enemies of the LORD:

27 to those who were inᴿBethel, and to those who were in Ramoth of the Negev, and to those who were in Jattir,   Gen. 12:8

28 and to those who were inᴿAroer, and to those who were in Siphmoth, and to those who were in Eshtemoa,   Josh. 13:16

29 and to those who were in Racal, and to those who were in the cities ofᴿthe Jerahmeelites, and to those who were in the cities ofᴿthe Kenites,   1 Sam. 27:10 • Judg. 1:16

30 and to those who were inᴿHormah, and to those who were in Bor-ashan, and to those who were in Athach,   Num. 14:45; 21:3

31 and to those who were inᴿHebron, and to all the places where David himself and his men were accustomed to go."   2 Sam. 2:1

CHAPTER 31

The Enemy Kills Saul—1 Chr. 10:1-14

NOWᴿthe Philistines were fighting against Israel, and the men of Israel fled from be-

fore the Philistines and fell slain[R]on Mount Gilboa. 1 Chr. 10:1-12 • 1 Sam. 28:4

2 And the Philistines overtook Saul and his sons; and the Philistines[T]killed[R]Jonathan and Abinadab and Malchi-shua the sons of Saul. smote • 1 Chr. 8:33f.

3 And the battle went heavily against Saul, and the archers[T]hit him; and he was badly wounded by the archers. found

4 [R]Then Saul said to his armor bearer, "Draw your sword and pierce me through with it, lest[R]these uncircumcised come and pierce me through and make sport of me." But his armor bearer would not, for he was greatly afraid. So Saul took his sword and fell on it. Judg. 9:54; 1 Chr. 10:4 • Judg. 14:3

5 And when his armor bearer saw that Saul was dead, he also fell on his sword and died with him.

6 Thus Saul died with his three sons, his armor bearer, and all his men on that day together.

7 And when the men of Israel who were on the other side of the valley, with those who were beyond the Jordan, saw that the men of Israel had fled and that Saul and his sons were dead, they abandoned the cities

and fled; then the Philistines came and lived in them.

8 And it came about on the [T]next day when the Philistines came to strip the slain, that they found Saul and his three sons fallen on Mount Gilboa. morrow

9 And they cut off his head, and stripped off his weapons, and sent them[T]throughout the land of the Philistines,[R]to carry the good news to the house of their idols and to the people. into . . . around • 2 Sam. 1:20

10 And they put his weapons in the[T]temple of Ashtaroth, and they fastened his body to the wall of[R]Beth-shan. house • Josh. 17:11

11 Now when[R]the inhabitants of Jabesh-gilead heard[T]what the Philistines had done to Saul, 1 Sam. 11:1-13 • about him what

12 [R]all the valiant men rose and walked all night, and took the body of Saul and the bodies of his sons from the wall of Beth-shan, and they came to Jabesh, and[R]burned them there. 2 Sam. 2:4-7 • 2 Chr. 16:14

13 And they took their bones and buried them under[R]the tamarisk tree at Jabesh, and [R]fasted seven days. 1 Sam. 22:6 • 2 Sam. 1:12

Weights

Unit	Weight	Equivalents	Translations
Jewish Weights Talent	c. 75 pounds for common talent, c. 150 pounds for royal talent	60 minas; 3,000 shekels	talent, one hundred pounds
Mina	1.25 pounds	50 shekels	maneh, mina
Shekel	c. .4 ounce (11.4 grams) for common shekel c. .8 ounce for royal shekel	2 bekas; 20 gerahs	shekel
Beka	c. .2 ounce (5.7 grams)	½ shekel; 10 gerahs	half-shekel
Gerah	c. .02 ounce (.57 grams)	1/20 shekel	gerah
Roman Weight Litra	12 ounces		pound, pint

Liquid Measures

Unit	Measure	Equivalents	Translations
Kor	60 gallons	10 baths	kor
Metretes	10.2 gallons		gallon
Bath	6 gallons	6 hins	measure, bath
Hin	1 gallon	2 kabs	hin
Kab	2 quarts	4 logs	kab
Log	1 pint	¼ kab	log

THE SECOND BOOK OF

SAMUEL

THE BOOK OF SECOND SAMUEL

The Book of Second Samuel records the highlights of David's reign, first over the territory of Judah, and finally over the entire nation of Israel. It traces the ascension of David to the throne, his climactic sins of adultery and murder, and the shattering consequences of those sins upon his family and the nation.

See First Samuel for details on the titles of the books of Samuel. The Hebrew title for both books (originally one) is Samuel. The Greek title for Second Samuel is *Basileion Beta*, "Second Kingdoms." The Latin title is *Liber II Samuelis*, the "Second Book of Samuel," or simply "Second Samuel."

THE AUTHOR OF SECOND SAMUEL

Second Samuel was probably compiled by one man who combined the written chronicles of Nathan the prophet and Gad the seer (1 Chr. 29:29). In addition to these written sources, the compiler evidently used another source called "the book of Jashar" (1:18). See comments under First Samuel.

THE TIME OF SECOND SAMUEL

The date of the composition for First and Second Samuel was sometime after the death of Solomon (931 B.C.) but before the Assyrian captivity of the northern kingdom (722 B.C.). It is likely that Samuel was composed early in the divided kingdom, perhaps around 900 B.C.

The story of David begins in First Samuel 16 and ends in First Kings 2. Second Samuel records the major events of David's forty-year rule. His reign in Hebron begins in 1011 B.C. and ends in 1004 B.C. (5:5). His thirty-three-year reign over the united Judah and Israel lasts from 1004 B.C. to 971 B.C.

THE CHRIST OF SECOND SAMUEL

As seen in the introduction to First Samuel, David is one of the most important types of Christ in the Old Testament. In spite of his sins, he remains a man after God's own heart because of his responsive and faithful attitude toward God. He sometimes fails in his personal life, but he never flags in his relationship to the Lord. Unlike most of the kings who succeed him, he never allows idolatry to become a problem during his reign. He is a true servant of Yahweh, obedient to His law, and an ideal king. His rule is usually characterized by justice, wisdom, integrity, courage, and compassion. Having conquered Jerusalem, he sits upon the throne of Melchizedek, the "king of righteousness" (Heb. 7:2). David is the standard by which all subsequent kings are measured.

Of course, David's life as recorded in chapters 1—10 is a far better portrayal of the future Messiah than is his life as it is seen in 11—24. Sin mars potential. The closest way in which he foreshadows the coming King can be seen in the important covenant God makes with him (7:4–17). David wants to build a house for God; but instead, God makes a house for David. The same three promises of an eternal kingdom, throne, and seed are later given to Christ (Luke 1:32, 33). There are nine different dynasties in the northern kingdom of Israel, but there is only one dynasty in Judah. The promise of a permanent dynasty is fulfilled in Christ, the "Son of David" (Matt. 21:9; 22:45), who will sit upon the throne of David (Is. 9:7; Luke 1:32).

KEYS TO SECOND SAMUEL

Key Word: David—The central character of Second Samuel is David, around whom the entire book is written. The key truth illustrated is the same as the theme of Deuteronomy: obedience brings blessing and disobedience brings judgment.

Key Verses: Second Samuel 7:12, 13; 22:21—"When your days are complete and you lie down with your fathers, I will raise up your descendant after you, who will come forth from you, and I will establish his kingdom. He shall build a house for My name, and I will establish the throne of his kingdom forever" (7:12, 13).

"The LORD has rewarded me according to my righteousness; According to the cleanness of my hands He has recompensed me" (22:21).

Key Chapter: Second Samuel 11—The eleventh chapter of Second Samuel is pivotal for the entire book. This chapter records the tragic sins of David regarding Bathsheba and her husband Uriah. All of the widespread blessings on David's family and his kingdom are quickly removed as God chastises His anointed one.

SURVEY OF SECOND SAMUEL

Second Samuel continues the account of the life of David at the point where First Samuel concludes. Soon after the death of Saul, the king-elect becomes the king enthroned, first over Judah when he reigns in Hebron for seven-and-a-half years and finally over all Israel when he reigns in Jerusalem for thirty-three years. This book reviews the key events in the forty-year reign of the man who is the halfway point between Abraham and Christ. It can be surveyed in the three divisions: the triumphs of David (1—10), the transgressions of David (11), and the troubles of David (12—24).

The Triumphs of David (1—10): Chapters 1—4 record the seven-year reign of David over the territory of Judah. Even though Saul is David's murderous pursuer, David does not rejoice in his death because he recognizes that Saul has been divinely anointed as king. Saul's son Ish-bosheth is installed by Abner as a puppet king over the northern tribes of Israel. David's allies led by Joab defeat Abner and Israel (2:17; 3:1). Abner defects and arranges to unite Israel and Judah under David, but Joab kills Abner in revenge. The powerless Ish-bosheth is murdered by his own men, and David is made king of Israel (5:3). David soon captures and fortifies Jerusalem and makes it the civil and religious center of the now united kingdom. Under David's rule the nation prospers politically, spiritually, and militarily. David brings the ark to Jerusalem and seeks to build a house for God (7). His obedience in placing the Lord at the center of his rule leads to great national blessing (8—10). "And the LORD helped David wherever he went" (8:14).

The Transgressions of David (11): David's crimes of adultery and murder mark the pivotal point of the book. Because of these transgressions, David's victories and successes are changed to the personal, family, and national troubles which are recorded throughout the rest of Second Samuel.

The Troubles of David (12—24): The disobedience of the king produces chastisement and confusion at every level. David's glory and fame fade, never to be the same again. Nevertheless, David confesses his guilt when confronted by Nathan the prophet and is restored by God. A sword remains in David's house as a consequence of the sin: the baby born to David and Bathsheba dies, his son Amnon commits incest, and his son Absalom murders Amnon.

The consequences continue with Absalom's rebellion against his father. He shrewdly "stole away the hearts of the men of Israel" (15:6). David is forced to flee from Jerusalem, and Absalom sets himself up as king. David would have been ruined, but God keeps Absalom from pursuing him until David has time to regroup his forces. Absalom's army is defeated by David's, and Joab kills Absalom in disobedience of David's orders to have him spared.

David seeks to amalgamate the kingdom, but conflict breaks out between the ten northern tribes of Israel and the two southern tribes of Judah and Benjamin. Israel decides to follow a man named Sheba in a revolt against David, but Judah remains faithful to him. This leads to war, and Joab defeats the rebels.

The closing chapters are actually an appendix to the book because they summarize David's words and deeds. They show how intimately the affairs of the people as a whole are tied to the spiritual and moral condition of the king. The nation enjoys God's blessing when David is obedient to the Lord, and suffers hardship when David disobeys God.

FOCUS	DAVID'S TRIUMPHS			DAVID'S TRANSGRESSIONS	DAVID'S TROUBLES	
REFERENCE	1:1————— 6:1—————		8:1—————————	11:1——————————	12:1————————	13:37——— 24:25
DIVISION	POLITICAL TRIUMPHS	SPIRITUAL TRIUMPHS	MILITARY TRIUMPHS	SINS OF ADULTERY AND MURDER	TROUBLES IN DAVID'S HOUSE	TROUBLES IN THE KINGDOM
TOPIC	SUCCESS			SIN	FAILURE	
	OBEDIENCE			DISOBEDIENCE	JUDGMENT	
LOCATION	DAVID IN HEBRON	DAVID IN JERUSALEM				
TIME	7½ YEARS	33 YEARS				

OUTLINE OF SECOND SAMUEL

Part One: The Triumphs of David (1:1—10:19)

Part Two: The Transgressions of David (11:1–27)

Part Three: The Troubles of David (12:1—24:25)

CHAPTER 1

King Saul Dies

Now it came about after [R]the death of Saul, when David had returned from the slaughter of the Amalekites, that David remained two days in Ziklag.   1 Sam. 31:6

2 And it happened on the third day, that behold, a man came out of the camp from Saul, with his clothes torn and [T]dust on his head. And it came about when he came to David that [R]he fell to the ground and prostrated himself.   *ground* • 1 Sam. 25:23

3 Then David said to him, "From where do you come?" And he said to him, "I have escaped from the camp of Israel."

4 And David said to him, "How [R] did things go? Please tell me." And he said, "The people have fled from the battle, and also many of the people have fallen and are dead; and Saul and Jonathan his son are dead also."   1 Sam. 4:16

5 So David said to the young man who told him, "How do you know that Saul and his son Jonathan are dead?"

6 And the young man who told him said, "By chance I happened to be on [R]Mount Gilboa, and behold, Saul was leaning on his spear. And behold, the chariots and the horsemen pursued him closely.   1 Sam. 28:4

7 "And when he looked behind him, he saw me and called to me. And I said, 'Here I am.'

8 "And he said to me, 'Who are you?' And I [T]answered him, 'I am an Amalekite.'   *said to*

9 "Then he said to me, 'Please stand beside me and kill me; for agony has seized me because my life still lingers in me.'

10 "So I stood beside him [R]and killed him, because I knew that he could not live after he had fallen. And [R]I took the crown which *was* on his head and the bracelet which *was* on his arm, and I have brought them here to my lord."   Judg. 9:54 • 2 Kin. 11:12

11 Then [R]David took hold of his clothes and tore them, and *so* also *did* all the men who *were* with him.   Gen. 37:29, 34; Josh. 7:6

12 And they mourned and wept and [R]fasted until evening for Saul and his son Jonathan and for the people of the LORD and the house of Israel, because they had fallen by the sword.   2 Sam. 3:35

13 And David said to the young man who told him, "Where are you from?" And he [T]answered, "I [R]am the son of an alien, an Amalekite."   *said* • 2 Sam. 1:8

14 Then David said to him, "How is it you were not afraid [R]to stretch out your hand to destroy the LORD's anointed?"   1 Sam. 24:6

15 And David called one of the young men and said, "Go, [T]cut him down." So he struck him and he died.   *fall upon him*

16 And David said to him, "Your [R]blood is on your head, for [R]your mouth has testified against you, saying, 'I have killed the LORD's anointed.' "   1 Sam. 26:9 • 2 Sam. 1:10; Luke 19:22

17 Then David [R]chanted with this lament over Saul and Jonathan his son,   2 Chr. 35:25

18 and he told *them* to teach the sons of Judah *the song of* the bow; behold, it is written in [R]the book of Jashar.   Josh. 10:13

19 "Your [R]beauty, O Israel, is slain on your high places!   *The* How have the mighty fallen!

20 "Tell [R]*it* not in Gath, Proclaim it not in the streets of Ashkelon;   1 Sam. 31:8-13; Mic. 1:10 Lest [R]the daughters of the Philistines rejoice,   Ex. 15:20, 21; 1 Sam. 18:6 Lest the daughters of [R]the uncircumcised exult.   1 Sam. 14:6

21 "O [R]mountains of Gilboa, [R]Let not dew or rain be on you, nor fields of offerings; For there the shield of the mighty was defiled, The shield of Saul, not [R]anointed with oil.   1 Sam. 31:1 • Ezek. 31:15 • Is. 21:5

22 "From [R]the blood of the slain, from the fat of the mighty,   Deut. 32:42; Is. 34:6 [R]The bow of Jonathan did not turn back,   1 Sam. 18:4 And the sword of Saul did not return empty.

23 "Saul and Jonathan, beloved and pleasant in their life, And in their death they were not parted; They were swifter than eagles, They were stronger than lions.

24 "O daughters of Israel, weep over Saul, Who clothed you luxuriously in scarlet, Who put ornaments of gold on your apparel.

25 "How [R] have the mighty fallen in the midst of the battle!   2 Sam. 1:19, 27 Jonathan is slain on your high places.

26 "I am distressed for you, my brother Jonathan; You have been very pleasant to me. [R]Your love to me was more wonderful Than the love of women.   1 Sam. 18:1-4

27 "How have the mighty fallen, And the weapons of war perished!"

CHAPTER 2

David Is Anointed as King over Judah

Then it came about afterwards that [R]David inquired of the LORD, saying, "Shall I go up to one of the cities of Judah?" And the LORD said to him, "Go up." So David said, "Where shall I go up?" And He said, "To [R] Hebron."   1 Sam. 23:2, 4, 9-12 • Josh. 14:13

2 So David went up there, and his two wives also, Ahinoam the Jezreelitess and Abigail the widow of Nabal the Carmelite.

3 And [R]David brought up his men who *were* with him, each with his household; and they lived in the cities of Hebron.   1 Chr. 12:1

4 Then the men of Judah came and there [R]anointed David king over the house of Judah.   1 Sam. 16:13; 2 Sam. 5:3, 5

And they told David, saying, "It was the men of Jabesh-gilead who buried Saul."

5 And David sent messengers to the men of Jabesh-gilead, and said to them, "May[R] you be blessed of the LORD because you have[T]shown this kindness to Saul your lord, and have buried him.   1 Sam. 23:21 • *done*

6"And now[R]may the LORD [T]show lovingkindness and truth to you; and I also will [T]show this goodness to you, because you have done this thing.   Ex. 34:6; 2 Tim. 1:16 • *do*

7"Now therefore, let your hands be strong, and be[T]valiant; for Saul your lord is dead, and also the house of Judah has anointed me king over them."   *sons of valor*

Ish-bosheth Is Made King over Israel

8 But[R]Abner the son of Ner, commander of Saul's army, had taken [1]Ish-bosheth the son of Saul, and brought him over to[R]Mahanaim.   1 Sam. 14:50 • Gen. 32:2; 2 Sam. 17:24

9 And he made him king over [R]Gilead, over the [R]Ashurites, over [R]Jezreel, over Ephraim, and over Benjamin, even over all Israel.   Josh. 22:9 • Judg. 1:32 • 1 Sam. 29:1

10 Ish-bosheth, Saul's son, was forty years old when he became king over Israel, and he was king for two years. The house of Judah, however, followed David.

11 And the[T]time that David was king in Hebron over the house of Judah was seven years and six months.   *number of days*

David's Victory over Ish-bosheth

12 Now Abner the son of Ner, went out from Mahanaim to[R]Gibeon with the servants of Ish-bosheth the son of Saul.   Josh. 10:12

13 And Joab the son of Zeruiah and the servants of David went out and met[T]them by the pool of Gibeon; and they sat down, one on the one side of the pool and the other on the other side of the pool.   *them together*

14 Then Abner said to Joab, "Now let the young men arise and [2]hold a contest before us." And Joab said, "Let them arise."

15 So they arose and went over by count, twelve for Benjamin and Ish-bosheth the son of Saul, and twelve of the servants of David.

16 And each one of them seized his[T]opponent by the head, and *thrust* his sword in his opponent's side; so they fell down together. Therefore that place was called [3]Helkathhazzurim, which is in Gibeon.   *fellow*

17 And that day the battle was very severe, and Abner and the men of Israel were beaten before the servants of David.

18 Now the three sons of Zeruiah were there, Joab and Abishai and Asahel; and Asahel *was as*[T]swift-footed as one of the gazelles which is in the field.   *light in his feet*

19 And Asahel pursued Abner and did not [T]turn to the right or to the left from following Abner.   *turn to go to*

20 Then Abner looked behind him and said, "Is that you, Asahel?" And he answered, "It is I."

21 So Abner said to him, "Turn to your right or to your left, and take hold of one of the young men for yourself, and take for yourself his spoil." But Asahel was not willing to turn aside from following him.

22 And Abner repeated again to Asahel, "Turn aside from following me. Why should I strike you to the ground? How then could I lift up my face to your brother Joab?"

23 However, he refused to turn aside; therefore Abner struck him in the belly with the butt end of the spear, so that the spear came out at his back. And he fell there and died on the spot. And it came about that all who came to the place where [R]Asahel had fallen and died, stood still.   2 Sam. 20:12

24 But Joab and Abishai pursued Abner, and when the sun was going down, they came to the hill of Ammah, which is in front of Giah by the way of the wilderness of Gibeon.

25 And the sons of Benjamin gathered together behind Abner and became one band, and they stood on the top of a certain hill.

26 Then Abner called to Joab and said, "Shall the sword devour forever? Do you not know that it will be bitter in the end? How long will you [T]refrain from telling the people to turn back from following their brothers?"   *not tell the people*

27 And Joab said, "As God lives, if you had not spoken, surely then the people would have gone away in the morning, each from following his brother."

28 So Joab blew the trumpet; and all the people halted and pursued Israel no longer, nor did they continue to fight anymore.

29 And Abner and his men then went through the Arabah all that night; so they crossed the Jordan, walked all morning, and came to [R]Mahanaim.   2 Sam. 2:8

30 Then Joab returned from following Abner; when he had gathered all the people together,[T]nineteen of David's servants besides Asahel were missing.   *nineteen men*

31 But the servants of David had struck down many of Benjamin and Abner's men, so *that* three hundred and sixty men died.

32 And they took up Asahel and buried him in his father's tomb which was in Bethlehem. Then Joab and his men went all night until the day dawned at Hebron.

CHAPTER 3

David's Growth over Ish-bosheth

N[OW][R]there was a long war between the house of Saul and the house of David; and

[1] I.e., man of shame   [2] Lit., *make sport*
[3] I.e., the field of sword-edges

David grew steadily stronger, but the house of Saul grew weaker continually.   [Ps. 46:9]

2 [R]Sons were born to David at Hebron: his first-born was Amnon, by [R]Ahinoam the Jezreelitess;   1 Chr. 3:1-3 · 1 Sam. 25:42, 43

3 and his second, Chileab, by Abigail the[T]widow of Nabal the Carmelite; and the third, Absalom the son of Maacah, the daughter of Talmai, king of Geshur;   *wife*

4 and the fourth, [E]Adonijah the son of Haggith; and the fifth, Shephatiah the son of Abital;   1 Kin. 1:5

5 and the sixth, Ithream, by David's wife Eglah. These were born to David at Hebron.

Abner's Murder

6 And it came about while there was war between the house of Saul and the house of David that [F]Abner was making himself strong in the house of Saul.   2 Sam. 2:8, 9

7 Now Saul had a concubine whose name was Rizpah, the daughter of Aiah; and Ish-bosheth said to Abner, "Why have you gone in to my father's concubine?"

8 Then Abner was very angry over the words of Ish-bosheth and said, "Am[R] I a dog's head that belongs to Judah? Today I show kindness to the house of Saul your father, to his brothers and to his friends, and have not delivered you into the hands of David; and yet today you charge me with a guilt concerning the woman.   1 Sam. 24:14

9 "May[R] God do so to Abner, and more also, if as the LORD has sworn to David, I do not accomplish this for him,   1 Kin. 19:2

10 [R]to transfer the kingdom from the house of Saul, and to establish the throne of David over Israel and over Judah,[R]from Dan even to Beersheba."   1 Sam. 15:28 · 1 Sam. 3:20

11 And he could no longer answer Abner a word, because he was afraid of him.

12 Then Abner sent messengers to David in his place, saying, "Whose is the land? Make your covenant with me, and behold, my hand shall be with you to bring all Israel over to you."

13 And he said, "Good! I will make a covenant with you, but I demand one thing of you,[T]namely, you shall not see my face unless you first bring Michal, Saul's daughter, when you come to see[T]me."   *saying · my face*

14 So David sent messengers to Ish-bosheth, Saul's son, saying, "Give me my wife Michal, to whom I was betrothed for a hundred foreskins of the Philistines."

15 And Ish-bosheth sent and took her from *her* husband, from Paltiel the son of Laish.

16 But her husband went with her, weeping as he went, and followed her as far as [R]Bahurim. Then Abner said to him, "Go, return." So he returned.   2 Sam. 16:5; 19:16

17 Now Abner had consultation with the elders of Israel, saying, "In times past you were seeking for David to be king over you.

18 "Now then, do *it*! For the LORD has spo-

ken of David, saying, 'By[R]the hand of My servant David I will save My people Israel from the hand of the Philistines and from the hand of all their enemies.' "   1 Sam. 9:16

19 And Abner also spoke in the hearing of Benjamin; and in addition Abner went to speak in the hearing of David in Hebron all that seemed good to Israel and to[R]the whole house of Benjamin.   1 Sam. 10:20, 21

20 Then Abner and twenty men with him came to David at Hebron. And David made a feast for Abner and the men who were with him.

21 And Abner said to David, "Let me arise and go, and[R]gather all Israel to my lord the king that they may make a covenant with you, and that you may be king over all that your soul desires." So David sent Abner away, and he went in peace.   2 Sam. 3:10, 12

22 And behold,[R]the servants of David and Joab came from a raid and brought much spoil with them; but Abner was not with David in Hebron, for he had sent him away, and he had gone in peace.   1 Sam. 27:8

23 When Joab and all the army that was with him arrived, they told Joab, saying, "Abner the son of Ner came to the king, and he has sent him away, and he has gone in peace."

24 Then Joab came to the king and said, "What have you done? Behold, Abner came to you; why then have you sent him away and he is already gone?

25 "You know Abner the son of Ner, that he came to deceive you and to learn of[R]your going out and coming in, and to find out all that you are doing."   Deut. 28:6; 1 Sam. 29:6

26 When Joab came out from David, he sent messengers after Abner, and they brought him back from the well of Sirah; but David did not know *it*.

27 So when Abner returned to Hebron, Joab took him aside into the middle of the gate to speak with him privately, and there he struck him in the belly so that he died on account of the blood of Asahel his brother.

28 And afterward when David heard it, he said, "I and my kingdom are innocent before the LORD forever of the blood of Abner the son of Ner.

29 "May it fall on the head of Joab and on all his father's house; and may there not fail from the house of Joab one who has a discharge, or who is a leper, or who takes hold of a distaff, or who falls by the sword, or who lacks bread."

30 So Joab and Abishai his brother killed Abner because he had put their brother Asahel to death in the battle at Gibeon.

31 Then David said to Joab and to all the people who were with him, "Tear[R] your clothes and gird on sackcloth and lament before Abner." And King David walked behind the bier.   Gen. 37:34; Judg. 11:35

32 Thus they buried Abner in Hebron; and

the king lifted up his voice and wept at the grave of Abner, and all the people wept.

33 And [R] the king chanted a *lament* for Abner and said,   2 Sam. 1:17; 2 Chr. 35:25

"Should Abner die as a fool dies?

34 "Your hands were not bound, nor your feet put in fetters;

As one falls before the [T] wicked, you have fallen."   *sons of wickedness*

And all the people wept again over him.

35 Then all the people came to [T] persuade David to eat bread while it was still day; but David vowed, saying, "May God do so to me, and more also, if I taste bread or anything else before the sun goes down."   *cause*

36 Now all the people took note *of it,* and it pleased them, just as everything the king did pleased all the people.

37 So all the people and all Israel understood that day that it had not been *the will* of the king to put Abner the son of Ner to death.

38 Then the king said to his servants, "Do you not know that a prince and a great man has fallen this day in Israel?

39 "And I am [R] weak today, though anointed king; and these men the sons of Zeruiah are too difficult for me. May the LORD repay the evildoer according to his evil."   1 Chr. 29:1

CHAPTER 4

Ish-bosheth's Murder

NOW when Ish-bosheth, Saul's son, heard that Abner had died in Hebron, [R] he lost courage, and all Israel was disturbed.   Ezra 4:4

2 And Saul's son *had* two men who were commanders of bands: the name of the one was Baanah and the name of the other Rechab, sons of Rimmon the Beerothite, of the sons of Benjamin (for [R] Beeroth is also considered *part* of Benjamin,   Josh. 9:17

3 and the Beerothites fled to Gittaim, and have been aliens there until this day).

4 Now [R] Jonathan, Saul's son, had a son crippled in his feet. He was five years old when the report of Saul and Jonathan came from Jezreel, and his nurse took him up and fled. And it happened that in her hurry to flee, he fell and became lame. And his name was [T] Mephibosheth.   2 Sam. 9:3, 6 • *Merib-baal*

5 So the sons of Rimmon the Beerothite, Rechab and Baanah, departed and came to the house of Ish-bosheth in the heat of the day while he was taking his midday rest.

6 [T] And they came to the middle of the house as [T] if to get wheat, and they struck him in the belly; and Rechab and Baanah his brother escaped.   *And here • takers of wheat*

7 Now when they came into the house, as he was lying on his bed in his bedroom, they struck him and killed him and beheaded him. And they took his head and [T] traveled by way of the Arabah all night.   *went*

8 Then they brought the head of Ish-bosheth to David at Hebron, and said to the king, "Behold, the head of Ish-bosheth, [R] the son of Saul, your enemy, who sought your life; thus the LORD has given my lord the king vengeance this day on Saul and his [T] descendants."   1 Sam. 24:4; 25:29 • *seed*

Judgment on the Murder of Ish-bosheth

9 And David answered Rechab and Baanah his brother, sons of Rimmon the Beerothite, and said to them, "As the LORD lives, who has redeemed my life from all distress,

10 [R] when one told me, saying, 'Behold, Saul is dead,' and thought he was bringing good news, I seized him and killed him in Ziklag, which was the reward I gave him for *his* news.   2 Sam. 1:2, 4, 15

11 "How much more, when wicked men have killed a righteous man in his own house on his bed, shall I not now [R] require his blood from your hand, and [T] destroy you from the earth?"   [Gen. 9:5; Ps. 9:12] • *burn*

12 Then [R] David commanded the young men, and they killed them and cut off their hands and feet, and hung them up beside the pool in Hebron. But they took the head of Ish-bosheth [R] and buried it in the grave of Abner in Hebron.   2 Sam. 1:15 • 2 Sam. 3:32

CHAPTER 5

David Is Anointed to Reign over Israel—1 Chr. 11:1–3

THEN all the tribes of Israel came to David at Hebron and [T] said, "Behold, we are your bone and your flesh.   *said, saying*

2 "Previously, when Saul was king over us, you were the one who led Israel out and in. And the LORD said to you, 'You [R] will shepherd My people Israel, and you will be [R] a ruler over Israel.' "   Gen. 49:24 • 1 Sam. 25:30

3 So all the elders of Israel came to the king at Hebron, and King David made a covenant with them before the LORD at Hebron; then they anointed David king over Israel.

4 David was thirty years old when he became king, *and* he reigned forty years.

5 At Hebron [R] he reigned over Judah seven years and six months, and in Jerusalem he reigned thirty-three years over all Israel and Judah.   2 Sam. 2:11; 1 Chr. 3:4; 29:27

Conquest of Jerusalem—1 Chr. 11:4–9

6 Now the king and his men went to Jerusalem against the Jebusites, the inhabitants of the land, and they said to [T] David, "You shall not come in here, but the blind and lame shall turn you away"; thinking, "David cannot enter here."   *David, saying*

7 Nevertheless, David captured the stronghold of Zion, that is the city of David.

8 And David said on that day, "Whoever would strike the Jebusites, let him reach the lame and the blind, who are hated by David's soul, through the water tunnel." Therefore they say, "The blind or the lame shall not come into the house."

9 So David lived in the stronghold, and called it the city of David. And David built all around from the ⁴Millo and inward.

10 And ᴿDavid became greater and greater, for the LORD God of hosts was with him.   2 Sam. 3:1

Alliance with Tyre—1 Chr. 14:1, 2

11 ᴿThen Hiram king of Tyre sent messengers to David with cedar trees and carpenters and stonemasons; and ᴿthey built a house for David.   1 Kin. 5:1, 10, 18 · Ps. 30:title

12 And David realized that the LORD had established him as king over Israel, and that He had exalted his kingdom for the sake of His people Israel.

David's Family

13 Meanwhile ᴿDavid took more concubines and wives from Jerusalem, after he came from Hebron; and more sons and daughters were born to David.   [Deut. 17:17]

14 Now ᴿthese are the names of those who were born to him in Jerusalem: Shammua, Shobab, Nathan, Solomon,   1 Chr. 3:5-8

15 Ibhar, Elishua, Nepheg, Japhia,

16 Elishama, Eliada and Eliphelet.

Conquest of Philistia—1 Chr. 14:9–17

17 When the Philistines heard that they had anointed David king over Israel, ᴿall the Philistines went up to seek out David; and when David heard of it, he went down to the ᴿstronghold.   1 Sam. 29:1 · 2 Sam. 23:14

18 Now the Philistines came and spread themselves out in the valley of Rephaim.

19 Then ᴿDavid inquired of the LORD, saying, "Shall I go up against the Philistines? Wilt Thou give them into my hand?" And ᴿthe LORD said to David, "Go up, for I will certainly give the Philistines into your hand."   1 Sam. 23:2 · 2 Sam. 2:1

20 So David came to ᴿBaal-perazim, and defeated them there; and he said, "The LORD has broken through my enemies before me like the breakthrough of waters." Therefore he named that place ⁵Baal-perazim. Is. 28:21

21 And they abandoned their idols there, so David and his men carried them away.

22 Now ᴿthe Philistines came up once again and spread themselves out in the valley of Rephaim.   2 Sam. 5:18

23 And when ᴿDavid inquired of the LORD, He said, "You shall not go directly up; circle around behind them and come at them in front of the ⁶balsam trees.   2 Sam. 5:19

24 "And it shall be, when you hear the sound of marching in the tops of the ⁶balsam trees, then you shall act promptly, for then the LORD will have gone out before you to strike the army of the Philistines."

25 Then David did so, just as the LORD had commanded him, and struck down the Philistines from Geba as far as Gezer.

CHAPTER 6

Incorrect Transportation of the Ark
1 Chr. 13:1-14

N OW ᴿDavid again gathered all the chosen men of Israel, thirty thousand.   1 Chr. 13:5-14

2 And David arose and went with all the people who were with him to ᵀBaale-judah, to bring up from there the ark of God which is called by the ᴿName, the very name of the LORD of hosts who is ᵀenthroned above the cherubim.   Kiriath-jearim · Lev. 24:16 · sitting

3 And they ᵀplaced the ark of God on a new cart that they might bring it from the house of Abinadab which was on the hill; and Uzzah and Ahio, the sons of Abinadab, were leading the new cart.   caused to ride

4 So ᴿthey brought it with the ark of God from the house of Abinadab, which was on the hill; and Ahio was walking ahead of the ark.   1 Sam. 7:1; 1 Chr. 13:7

5 Meanwhile, David and all the house of Israel were celebrating before the LORD ᴿwith all kinds of instruments made of ᴬfir wood, and with lyres, harps, tambourines, castanets and cymbals.   1 Chr. 13:8 · cypress

6 But when they came to the ᴿthreshing floor of Nacon, Uzzah reached out toward the ark of God and took hold of it, for the oxen nearly upset it.   1 Chr. 13:9

7 And the anger of the LORD burned against Uzzah, and ᴿGod struck him down there for ᵀhis irreverence; and he died there by the ark of God.   1 Sam. 6:19 · the

8 And David became angry because of the LORD's outburst against Uzzah, and that place is called ⁷Perez-uzzah to this day.

9 So ᴿDavid was afraid of the LORD that day; and he said, "How can the ark of the LORD come to me?"   Ps. 119:120; Luke 5:8

10 And David was unwilling to move the ark of the LORD into the city of David with him; but David took it aside to the house of ᴿObed-edom the Gittite.   1 Chr. 26:4-8

11 Thus the ark of the LORD remained in the house of Obed-edom the Gittite three months, and the LORD ᴿblessed Obed-edom and all his household.   Gen. 30:27; 39:5

Correct Transportation of the Ark—1 Chr. 15:25

12 Now it was told King David, saying,

---

4 I.e., citadel   5 I.e., the master of breakthrough
6 Or, baka-shrubs   7 I.e., the breakthrough of Uzzah

"The LORD has blessed the house of Obed-edom and all that belongs to him, on account of the ark of God." [B]And David went and brought up the ark of God from the house of Obed-edom into[R]the city of David with gladness.   1 Chr. 15:25-16:3 • 1 Kin. 8:1

David Rejoices over the Ark—1 Chr. 15:26–28

13 And so it was, that when the[R]bearers of the ark of the LORD had gone six paces, he sacrificed an ox and a fatling.   1 Chr. 15:2, 15
14 And David was dancing before the LORD with all *his* might, and David was [T]wearing[R]a linen ephod.   *girded with* • Ex. 19:6
15 So David and all the house of Israel were bringing up the ark of the LORD with shouting and the sound of the trumpet.

Michal Despises David—1 Chr. 15:29—16:3

16 Then it happened *as* the ark of the LORD came into the city of David that[R]Michal the daughter of Saul looked out of the window and saw King David leaping and dancing before the LORD; and she despised him in her heart.   2 Sam. 3:14
17 So they brought in the ark of the LORD and set it[R]in its place inside the tent which David had pitched for it; and[R]David offered burnt offerings and peace offerings before the LORD.   1 Chr. 15:1 • 1 Kin. 8:62-65
18 And when David had finished offering the burnt offering and the peace offering,[R]he blessed the people in the name of the LORD of hosts.   1 Kin. 8:14, 15
19 Further, he distributed to all the people, to all the multitude of Israel, both to men and women, a cake of bread and one of dates and one of raisins to each one. Then all the people departed each to his house.
20 But when David returned to bless his household, Michal the daughter of Saul came out to meet David and said, "How the king of Israel distinguished himself today! He uncovered himself today in the eyes of his servants' maids as one of the foolish ones shamelessly uncovers himself!"

21 So David said to Michal, "*It was* before the LORD, who chose me above your father and above all his house, to appoint me ruler over the people of the LORD, over Israel; therefore I will celebrate before the LORD.
22 "And I will be more lightly esteemed than this and will be humble in my own eyes, but with the maids of whom you have spoken, with them I will be distinguished."
23 And Michal the daughter of Saul had no child to the day of her death.

CHAPTER 7

*David Is Forbidden to Build
God a House—1 Chr. 17:1, 2*

NOW it came about when the king lived in his house, and the LORD had given him rest on every side from all his enemies,
2 that the king said to [R]Nathan the prophet, "See now, I dwell in[R]a house of cedar, but the ark of God[R]dwells within tent curtains."   2 Sam. 7:17 • 2 Sam. 5:11 • Ex. 26:1
3 And Nathan said to the king, "Go,[R] do all that is in your mind, for the LORD is with you."   1 Kin. 8:17, 18; 1 Chr. 22:7

*God Promises David an Eternal House
1 Chr. 17:3–15*

4 But it came about in the same night that the word of the LORD came to Nathan, saying,
5 "Go and say to My servant David, 'Thus says the LORD, "Are[R]you the one who should build Me a house to dwell in?   1 Kin. 5: 3, 4
6 "For I have not dwelt in a house since the day I brought up the sons of Israel from Egypt, even to this day; but I have been moving about in a tent, even in a tabernacle.
7 "Wherever I have gone with all the sons of Israel, did I speak a word with one of the tribes of Israel, which I commanded to shepherd My people Israel, saying, 'Why have you not built Me a house of cedar?' "'
8 "Now therefore, thus you shall say to My servant David, 'Thus says the LORD of hosts,

---

7:4–17 The Davidic Covenant—The covenant with David is the fourth of the theocratic covenants (pertaining to the rule of God). In this covenant David is promised three things: (1) a land forever (v. 10); (2) an unending dynasty (vv. 11, 16); and (3) an everlasting kingdom (vv. 13, 16). The birth of Solomon, David's son who is to succeed him, is predicted (v. 12). His particular role is to establish the throne of the Davidic Kingdom forever (v. 13). His throne continues, though his seed is cursed in the person of Jeconiah (Coniah), who was the king under whom the nation was carried captive to Babylon. Jeremiah prophesies that no one whose genealogical descent could be traced back to David through Jeconiah and Solomon would ever sit on David's throne (Page 740—Jer. 22:24–30). Joseph, the legal, but not physical, father of Jesus traces his lineage to David through Jeconiah (Page 963—Matt. 1:1–17). David, however, had another son, Nathan. His line was not cursed. Mary, the physical mother of Jesus, traces her lineage back to David through Nathan (Page 1029—Luke 3:23–38). Notice the care and the extent to which God goes to keep His word and to preserve its truthfulness. The virgin birth was absolutely essential not only to assure the sinless character of Jesus but also to fulfill the Davidic Covenant. Jesus receives His "blood right" to David's throne through His earthly mother, Mary, and His "legal right" to David's throne through His adoptive earthly father, Joseph. The virgin birth guarantees that one of David's line will sit on David's throne and rule forever, while at the same time preserving intact the curse and restriction on the line of descent through Jeconiah.

Now turn to Page 749—Jer. 31:31–34: The New Covenant.

"I took you from the pasture, from following the sheep, that you should be ruler over My people Israel.

9"And[R]I have been with you wherever you have gone and have cut off all your enemies from before you; and I will make you a great name, like the names of the great men who are on the earth.   1 Sam. 5:10

10"I will also appoint a place for My people Israel and will plant them, that they may live in their own place and not be disturbed again,[R]nor will the[T]wicked afflict them any more as formerly,   Is. 60:18 · sons of wickedness

11 even[R]from the day that I commanded judges to be over My people Israel; and I will give you rest from all your enemies. The LORD also declares to you that the LORD will make a house for you.   Judg. 2:14-16

12"When[R]your days are complete and you lie down with your fathers,[R]I will raise up your[T]descendant after you, who will come forth from[T]you, and I will establish his kingdom.   1 Kin. 2:1 · Ps. 132:11☆ · seed · your bowels

13"He[R]shall build a house for My name, and [R]I will establish the throne of his kingdom forever.   1 Kin. 6:12; 8:19 · [Is. 9:7; 49:8]☆

14"I[T]will be a father to him and he will be a son to Me; when he commits iniquity, I will correct him with the rod of men and the strokes of the sons of men,   [Ps. 89:26, 27]

15 but My lovingkindness shall not depart from him, as I took it away from Saul, whom I removed from before you.

16"And[R]your house and your kingdom shall endure before Me forever; your throne shall be established forever." ' "   Matt. 25:31 ☆

17 In accordance with all these words and all this vision, so Nathan spoke to David.

David Praises God—1 Chr. 17:16-27

18 Then David the king went in and sat before the LORD, and he said, "Who[R]am I, O Lord GOD, and what is my house, that Thou hast brought me this far?   Ex. 3:11

19"And yet this was insignificant in Thine eyes, O Lord GOD,[R]for Thou hast spoken also of the house of Thy servant concerning the distant future. And this is the ^custom of man, O Lord GOD.   2 Sam. 7:11-16 · law

20"And again what more can David say to Thee? For[R]Thou knowest Thy servant, O Lord GOD!   [1 Sam. 16:7]; John 21:17

21"For the sake of Thy word, and according to Thine own heart, Thou hast done all this greatness to let Thy servant know.

22"For this reason[R]Thou art great, O Lord GOD; for there is none like Thee, and there is no God besides Thee, according to all that we have heard with our ears.   Ps. 48:1; 86:10

23"And what one nation on the earth is like Thy people Israel, whom God went to redeem for Himself as a people and to make a name for Himself, and to do a great thing

for Thee and awesome things for Thy land, before [R]Thy people whom [R]Thou hast redeemed for Thyself from Egypt, from nations and their gods?   Deut. 15:15 · Deut. 9:26

24"For[R]Thou hast established for Thyself Thy people Israel as Thine own people forever, and[R]Thou, O LORD, hast become their God.   [Deut. 32:6] · Gen. 17:7, 8; Ex. 6:7

25"Now[R]therefore, O LORD God, the word that Thou hast spoken concerning Thy servant and his house, confirm it forever, and do as Thou hast spoken,   Matt. 19:28☆

26 that Thy name may be magnified forever, by saying, 'The LORD of hosts is God over Israel'; and may the house of Thy servant David be established before Thee.

27"For Thou, O LORD of hosts, the God of Israel, hast[T]made a revelation to Thy servant, saying, 'I will build you a house'; therefore Thy servant has found courage to pray this prayer to Thee.   uncovered the ear of

28"And now, O Lord GOD, Thou art God, and Thy words are truth, and Thou hast promised this good thing to Thy servant.

29"Now therefore, may it please Thee to bless the house of Thy servant, that it may continue forever before Thee. For Thou, O Lord GOD, hast spoken; and[R]with Thy blessing may the house of Thy servant be blessed forever."   Num. 6:24-26

CHAPTER 8

David Defeats Philistia—1 Chr. 18:1

NOW after this it came about that David [T]defeated the Philistines and subdued them; and David took control of the chief city from the hand of the Philistines.   smote

David Defeats Moab—1 Chr. 18:2

2 And he[T]defeated[B]Moab, and measured them with the line, making them lie down on the ground; and he measured two lines to put to death and one full line to keep alive. And the Moabites became servants to David, bringing tribute.   smote · 1 Sam. 22:3, 4

David Defeats Zobah and Aram—1 Chr. 18:3-8

3 Then David[T]defeated Hadadezer, the son of Rehob king of Zobah, as he went to restore his[T]rule at the [8]River.   smote · hand

4 And David captured from him 1,700 horsemen and 20,000 foot soldiers; and David hamstrung the chariot horses, but reserved enough of them for 100 chariots.

5 And when the Arameans of Damascus came to help Hadadezer, king of Zobah, David[T]killed 22,000 Arameans.   smote

6 Then David put garrisons among the Arameans of Damascus, and[R]the Arameans became servants to David, bringing tribute. And[R]the LORD helped David wherever he went.   2 Sam. 8:2 · 2 Sam. 3:18

[8] I.e., Euphrates

7 And David took the shields of gold which were ᵀcarried by the servants of Hadadezer, and brought them to Jerusalem.   on

8 And from Betah and from ᴿBerothai, cities of Hadadezer, King David took a very large amount of bronze.   Ezek. 47:16

David Receives Spoil
from His Enemies—1 Chr. 18:9–12

9 Now when Toi king of ᴿHamath heard that David had ᵀdefeated all the army of Hadadezer,   1 Kin. 8:65; 2 Chr. 8:4 • smitten

10 Toi sent Joram his son to King David to greet him and bless him, because he had fought against Hadadezer and defeated him; for Hadadezer ᵀhad been at war with Toi. And Joram brought with him articles of silver, of gold and of bronze.   was a man of wars

11 King David also ᴿdedicated these to the LORD, with the silver and gold that he had dedicated from all the nations which he had subdued: 1 Kin. 7:51

12 from ⁹Aram and ᴿMoab and ᴿthe sons of Ammon and the Philistines and Amalek, and from the spoil of Hadadezer, son of Rehob, king of Zobah.   2 Sam. 8:2 • 2 Sam. 10:14

David's Righteous Rule over Israel
1 Chr. 18:13–17

13 So David made a name for himself when he returned from ᵀkilling 18,000 ⁹Arameans in the Valley of Salt.   smiting

14 And he put garrisons in Edom. In all Edom he put garrisons, and all the Edomites became servants to David. And ᴿthe LORD helped David wherever he went.   2 Sam. 8:6

15 So David reigned over all Israel; and David ᵀadministered justice and righteousness for all his people.   was doing

16 And ᴿJoab the son of Zeruiah was over the army, and ᴿJehoshaphat the son of Ahilud was recorder.   1 Chr. 11:6 • 1 Kin. 4:3

17 And ᴿZadok the son of Ahitub and Ahimelech the son of Abiathar were priests, and Seraiah was secretary.   1 Chr. 6:4-8

18 And Benaiah the son of Jehoiada was over the Cherethites and the Pelethites; and David's sons were ᵀchief ministers.   priests

CHAPTER 9

David's Righteous Rule
over Mephibosheth

THEN David said, "Is there yet ᵀanyone left of the house of Saul, that I may show him kindness for Jonathan's sake?"   he who is

2 Now there was a servant of the house of Saul whose name was Ziba, and they called him to David; and the king said to him, "Are you ᴿZiba?" And he said, "I am your servant."   2 Sam. 16:1-4; 19:17, 29

3 And the king said, "Is there not yet anyone of the house of Saul to whom I may show the ᴿkindness of God?" And Ziba said to the king, "There is still a son of Jonathan who is crippled in both feet."   1 Sam. 20:14

4 So the king said to him, "Where is he?" And Ziba said to the king, "Behold, he is ᴿin the house of Machir the son of Ammiel in Lo-debar."   2 Sam. 17:27-29

5 Then King David sent and brought him from the house of Machir the son of Ammiel, from Lo-debar.

6 And ᴿMephibosheth, the son of Jonathan the son of Saul, came to David and fell on his face and prostrated himself. And David said, "Mephibosheth." And he said, "Here is your servant!"   2 Sam. 16:4; 19:24-30

7 And David said to him, "Do not fear, for I will surely show kindness to you for the sake of your father Jonathan, and will restore to you all the ᵀland of your ᵀgrandfather Saul; and you shall ᵀeat at my table regularly."   field • father • eat bread

8 Again he prostrated himself and said, "What is your servant, that you should regard ᴿa dead dog like me?"   2 Sam. 16:9; 24:14

9 Then the king called Saul's servant Ziba, and said to him, "All ᴿthat belonged to Saul and to all his house I have given to your master's ᵀgrandson.   2 Sam. 16:4 • son

10 "And you and your sons and your servants shall cultivate the land for him, and you shall bring in the produce so that your master's grandson may have food; nevertheless Mephibosheth your master's grandson shall eat at my table regularly." Now Ziba had fifteen sons and twenty servants.

11 Then Ziba said to the king, "According ᴿto all that my lord the king commands his servant so your servant will do." So Mephibosheth ate at ᵀDavid's table as one of the king's sons.   2 Sam. 16:1-4; 19:24-30 • my

12 And Mephibosheth had a young son whose name was Mica. And all who lived in the house of Ziba were servants to Mephibosheth.

13 So Mephibosheth lived in Jerusalem, for ᴿhe ate at the king's table regularly. Now he was lame in both feet.   2 Sam. 9:7, 11

CHAPTER 10

Insult of Ammon—1 Chr. 19:1–5

NOW it happened afterwards that ᴿthe king of the Ammonites died, and Hanun his son became king in his place.   1 Sam. 11:1

2 Then David said, "I will show kindness to Hanun the son of Nahash, just as his father showed kindness to me." So David sent some of his servants to console him concerning his father. But when David's servants came to the land of the Ammonites,

3 the princes of the Ammonites said to Hanun their lord, "Do you think that David

⁹ Some mss. read Edom(ites)

is honoring your father because he has sent consolers to you? [R]Has David not sent his servants to you in order to search the city, to spy it out and overthrow it?" Gen. 42:9, 16

4 So Hanun took David's servants and [R]shaved off half of their beards, and[R]cut off their garments in the middle as far as their hips, and sent them away.　Is. 15:2 • Is. 20:4

5 When they told *it* to David, he sent to meet them, for the men were greatly humiliated. And the king said, "Stay at Jericho until your beards grow, and *then* return.

Ammon Is Defeated—1 Chr. 19:6–15

6 Now when the sons of Ammon saw that they had become odious to David, the sons of Ammon sent and hired the Arameans of[R]Beth-rehob and the Arameans of Zobah, 20,000 foot soldiers, and the king of [R]Maacah with 1,000 men, and the men of Tob with 12,000 men.　Judg. 18:28 • Deut. 3:14

7 When David heard *of it,* he sent Joab and all the army, the mighty men.

8 And the sons of Ammon came out and drew up in battle array at the entrance of the[T]city, while the Arameans of Zobah and of Rehob and the men of Tob and Maacah *were* by themselves in the field.　gate

9 Now when Joab saw that [T]the battle was set against him in front and in the rear, he selected from all the choice men of Israel, and arrayed *them* against the Arameans.　*the faces of the battle were against*

10 But the remainder of the people he placed in the hand of Abishai his brother, and he arrayed *them* against the sons of Ammon.

11 And he said, "If the Arameans are too strong for me, then you shall help me, but if the sons of Ammon are too strong for you, then I will come to help you.

12"Be strong, and let us show ourselves courageous for the sake of our people and for the cities of our God; and[R]may the Lord do what is good in His sight."　1 Sam. 3:18

13 So Joab and the people who were with him drew near to the battle against the Arameans, and they fled before him.

14 When the sons of Ammon saw that the Arameans fled, they *also* fled before Abishai and entered the city. [R]Then Joab returned from *fighting* against the sons of Ammon and came to Jerusalem.　2 Sam. 11:1

Aram Is Defeated—1 Chr. 19:16–19

15 When the Arameans saw that they had been [T]defeated by Israel, they gathered themselves together.　*smitten before*

16 And Hadadezer sent and brought out the Arameans who were beyond the [10]River, and they came to Helam; and[R]Shobach the commander of the army of Hadadezer[T]led them.　1 Chr. 19:16 • *before*

[10] I.e., Euphrates

17 Now when it was told David, he gathered all Israel together and crossed the Jordan, and came to Helam. And the Arameans arrayed themselves to meet David and fought against him.

18 But the Arameans fled before Israel, and David killed[R]700 charioteers of the Arameans and 40,000 horsemen and struck down Shobach the commander of their army, and he died there.　1 Chr. 19:18

19 When all the kings, servants of Hadadezer, saw that they were defeated by Israel, they made peace with Israel and served them. So the Arameans feared to help the sons of Ammon anymore.

CHAPTER 11

The Sin of Adultery

THEN it happened [T]in the spring, at the time when kings go out *to battle,* that David sent Joab and his servants with him and all Israel, and they destroyed the sons of Ammon and besieged Rabbah. But David stayed at Jerusalem.　*at the return of the year*

2 Now when evening came David arose from his bed and walked around on[R]the roof of the king's house, and from the roof he saw a woman bathing; and the woman was very beautiful in appearance.　Deut. 22:8

3 So David sent and inquired about the woman. And one said, "Is this not [R]Bathsheba, the daughter of Eliam, the wife of [R]Uriah the Hittite?"　1 Chr. 3:5 • 2 Sam. 23:39

4 And David sent messengers and took her, and when she came to him, he lay with her; and when she had purified herself from her uncleanness, she returned to her house.

5 And the woman conceived; and she sent and told David, and said, "I[R]am pregnant."　Lev. 20:10; Deut. 22:22

Uriah Does Not Sleep with Bathsheba

6 Then David sent to Joab, *saying,* "Send me Uriah the Hittite." So Joab sent Uriah to David.

7 When Uriah came to him, David asked concerning the welfare of Joab and[T]the people and the state of the war.　*welfare of*

8 Then David said to Uriah, "Go down to your house, and wash your feet." And Uriah went out of the king's house, and a present from the king was sent out after him.

9 But Uriah slept[R]at the door of the king's house with all the servants of his lord, and did not go down to his house. 1 Kin. 14:27, 28

10 Now when they told David, saying, "Uriah did not go down to his house," David said to Uriah, "Have you not come from a journey? Why did you not go down to your house?"

11 And Uriah said to David, "The[R]ark and Israel and Judah are staying in^temporary

shelters, and my lord Joab and[R]the servants of my lord are camping in the open field. Shall I then go to my house to eat and to drink and to lie with my wife? By your life and the life of your soul, I will not do this thing."   2 Sam. 7:2, 6 • *booths* • 2 Sam. 20:6

12 Then David said to Uriah, "Stay[R]here today also, and tomorrow I will let you go." So Uriah remained in Jerusalem that day and the[T]next.   Job 20:12-14 • *morrow*

13 Now David called him, and he ate and drank before him, and he[R]made him drunk; and in the evening he went out to lie on his bed with his lord's servants, but he did not go down to his house.   [Prov. 20:1; 23:29–35]

David Commands Uriah's Murder

14 Now it came about in the morning that David[R]wrote a letter to Joab, and sent *it* by the hand of Uriah.   1 Kin. 21:8-10

15 And he had written in the letter, saying, "Place[T] Uriah in the front line of the fiercest battle and withdraw from him, so that he may be struck down and die."   *Give*

16 So it was as Joab kept watch on the city, that he put Uriah at the place where he knew there *were* valiant men.

17 And the men of the city went out and fought against Joab, and some of the people among David's servants fell; and[R]Uriah the Hittite also died.   2 Sam. 11:21

18 Then Joab sent and reported to David all the events of the war.

19 And he charged the messenger, saying, "When you have finished telling all the events of the war to the king,

20 and if it happens that the king's wrath rises and he says to you, 'Why did you go so near to the city to fight? Did you not know that they would shoot from the wall?

21 'Who struck down Abimelech the son of Jerubbesheth? Did not a woman throw an upper millstone on him from the wall so that he died at Thebez? Why did you go so near the wall?'—then you shall say, 'Your servant Uriah the Hittite is dead also.' "

22 So the messenger departed and came and reported to David all that Joab had sent him *to tell.*

23 And the messenger said to David, "The men prevailed against us and came out against us in the field, but we[T]pressed them as far as the entrance of the gate.   *were upon*

24"Moreover, the archers shot at your servants from the wall; so some of the king's servants are dead, and your servant Uriah the Hittite is also dead."

25 Then David said to the messenger, "Thus you shall say to Joab, 'Do not let this thing [T]displease you, for the sword devours one as well as another; make your battle against the city stronger and overthrow it'; and *so* encourage him."   *be evil in your sight*

David and Bathsheba Marry

26 Now when the wife of Uriah heard that

Uriah her husband was dead,[R]she mourned for her husband.   Gen. 50:10; Deut. 34:8

27 When the *time of* mourning was over, David sent and brought her to his house and she became his wife; then she bore him a son. But the thing that David had done was evil in the sight of the LORD.

CHAPTER 12

Prophecy of the Sword

THEN the LORD sent Nathan to David. And he came to him, and[T]said,   *said to him*
          "There were two men in one city, the
               one rich and the other poor.
2 "The rich man had a great many flocks
               and herds.
3 "But the poor man had nothing except
          [R]one little ewe lamb   2 Sam. 11:3
          Which he bought and nourished;
          And it grew up together with him and
               his children.
          It would eat of his[T]bread and drink of
               his cup and lie in his bosom,   *morsel*
          And was like a daughter to him.
4 "Now a traveler came to the rich man,
          And he[T]was unwilling to take from his
               own flock or his own herd,
          To prepare for the wayfarer who had
               come to him;
          Rather he took the poor man's ewe
               lamb and prepared it for the man
               who had come to him."   *spared*

5 Then David's anger burned greatly against the man, and he said to Nathan, "As the LORD lives, surely the man who has done this[T]deserves to die.   *is a son of death*

6"And he must make restitution for the lamb[R]fourfold, because he did this thing and had no compassion."   [Ex. 22:1]; Luke 19:8

7 Nathan then said to David, "You[R] are the man! Thus says the LORD God of Israel, 'It[R] is I who anointed you king over Israel and it is I who delivered you from the hand of Saul.   1 Kin. 20:42 • 1 Sam. 16:13

8 'I also gave you your master's house and your master's wives into your care, and I gave you the house of Israel and Judah; and if *that had been* too little, I would have added to you many more things like these!

9 'Why have you despised the word of the LORD by doing evil in His sight? [R]You have struck down Uriah the Hittite with the sword,[R]have taken his wife to be your wife, and have killed him with the sword of the sons of Ammon.   2 Sam. 11:14-17 • 2 Sam. 11:27

10 'Now therefore,[R]the sword shall never depart from your house, because you have despised Me and have taken the wife of Uriah the Hittite to be your wife.' 1 Kin. 2:25

11"Thus says the LORD, 'Behold, I will raise up evil against you from your own household; I will even take your wives before your eyes, and give *them* to your com-

panion, and he shall lie with your wives in ^Tbroad daylight. *the sight of this sun*

12 'Indeed^Ryou did it secretly, but^RI will do this thing before all Israel, and ^Tunder the sun.' "   2 Sam. 11:4-15 • 2 Sam. 16:22 • *before*

David Repents for His Sin

13 Then David said to Nathan, "I^R have sinned against the LORD." And Nathan said to David, "The LORD also has taken away your sin; you shall not die.   1 Sam. 15:24, 30

14"However, because by this deed you have^Rgiven occasion to the enemies of the LORD to blaspheme, the child also that is born to you shall surely die."   Is. 52:5

God Takes Away the Son of Adultery

15 So Nathan went to his house.
Then the LORD struck the child that Uriah's ^Twidow bore to David, so that he was *very* sick.   *wife*

16 David therefore inquired of God for the child; and David^Rfasted and went and^Rlay all night on the ground.   Neh. 1:4 • 2 Sam. 13:31

17 And^Rthe elders of his household stood beside him in order to raise him up from the ground, but he was unwilling and would not eat food with them.   Gen. 24:2

18 Then it happened on the seventh day that the child died. And the servants of David were afraid to tell him that the child was dead, for they said, "Behold, while the child was *still* alive, we spoke to him and he did not listen to our voice. How then can we tell him that the child is dead, since he might do *himself* harm!"

19 But when David saw that his servants were whispering together, David perceived that the child was dead; so David said to his servants, "Is the child dead?" And they said, "He is dead."

20 So David arose from the ground, ^Rwashed, anointed *himself,* and changed his clothes; and he came into the house of the LORD and worshiped. Then he came to his own house, and when he requested, they set food before him and he ate.   Ruth 3:3

21 Then his servants said to him, "What is this thing that you have done? ^TWhile the child was alive, you fasted and wept; but when the child died, you arose and ate food."   *On account of*

22 And he said, "While the child was *still* alive, ^RI fasted and wept; for I said, 'Who^R knows, the LORD may be gracious to me, that the child may live.'   Is. 38:1-3 • Jon. 3:9

23"But now he has died; why should I fast? Can I bring him back again? I shall go to him, but he will not return to me."

God Gives Another Son

24 Then David comforted his wife Bathsheba, and went in to her and lay with her; and she gave birth to a son, and he named him Solomon. Now the LORD loved him

25 and sent *word* through Nathan the prophet, and he named him ¹¹Jedidiah for the LORD's sake.

Joab's Loyalty to David—1 Chr. 20:1–3

26 ^RNow Joab fought against ^RRabbah of the sons of Ammon, and captured the royal city.   1 Chr. 20:1-3 • Deut. 3:11

27 And Joab sent messengers to David and said, "I have fought against Rabbah, I have even captured the city of waters.

28"Now therefore, gather the rest of the people together and camp against the city and capture it, lest I capture the city myself and it be named after me."

29 So David gathered all the people and went to Rabbah, fought against it, and captured it.

30 Then^Rhe took the crown of their king from his head; and its weight *was* a talent of gold, and *in it*^A*was* a precious stone; and it was *placed* on David's head. And he brought out the spoil of the city in great amounts.   1 Chr. 20:2 • *were precious stones*

31 He also brought out the people who were in it, and^Rset *them* under saws, sharp iron instruments, and iron axes, and made them pass through the brickkiln. And thus he did to all the cities of the sons of Ammon. Then David and all the people returned *to* Jerusalem.   1 Chr. 20:3; Heb. 11:37

CHAPTER 13

Incest in David's House

Now it was after this that Absalom the son of David had a beautiful sister whose name was ^RTamar, and ^RAmnon the son of David loved her.   1 Chr. 3:9 • 2 Sam. 3:2

2 And Amnon was so frustrated because of his sister Tamar that he made himself ill, for she was a virgin, and it seemed hard to Amnon to do anything to her.

3 But Amnon had a friend whose name was Jonadab, the son of^RShimeah, David's brother; and Jonadab was a very shrewd man.   1 Sam. 16:9

4 And he said to him, "O son of the king, why are you so depressed morning after morning? Will you not tell me?" Then Amnon said to him, "I am in love with Tamar, the sister of my brother Absalom."

5 Jonadab then said to him, "Lie down on your bed and pretend to be ill; when your father comes to see you, say to him, 'Please let my sister Tamar come and give me *some* food to eat, and let her prepare the food in

¹¹ I.e., beloved of the LORD

my sight, that I may see *it* and eat from her hand.' "

6 So Amnon lay down and pretended to be ill; when the king came to see him, Amnon said to the king, "Please let my sister Tamar come and make me a couple of cakes in my sight, that I may eat from her hand."

7 Then David sent to the house for Tamar, saying, "Go now to your brother Amnon's house, and prepare food for him."

8 So Tamar went to her brother Amnon's house, and he was lying down. And she took dough, kneaded *it,* made cakes in his sight, and baked the cakes.

9 And she took the pan and dished *them* out before him, but he refused to eat. And Amnon said, "Have everyone go out from me." So everyone went out from him.

10 Then Amnon said to Tamar, "Bring the food into theᴬbedroom, that I may eat from your hand." So Tamar took the cakes which she had made and brought them into the bedroom to her brother Amnon.   *inner room*

11 When she brought *them* to him to eat, heᴿtook hold of her and said to her, "Come, lie with me, my sister."   Gen. 39:12

12 But she answered him, "No, my brother, do not violate me, forᴿsuch a thing is not done in Israel; do not do thisᴿdisgraceful thing!   [Lev. 20:17] • Judg. 19:23; 20:6

13"As for me, where could Iᵀget rid of my reproach? And as for you, you will be like one of the fools in Israel. Now therefore, please speak to the king, for he will not withhold me from you."   *cause to go*

14 However, he would not listen toᵀher; since he was stronger than she, heᴿviolated her and lay with her.   *her voice* • Lev. 18:9

15 Then Amnon hated her with a very great hatred; for the hatred with which he hated her was greater than the love with which he had loved her. And Amnon said to her, "Get up, go away!"

16 But she said to him, "No, because this wrong in sending me away is greater than the other that you have done to me!" Yet he would not listen to her.

17 Then he called his young man who attended him and said, "Now throw this woman out of my *presence,* and lock the door behind her."

18 Now she had on aᵀlong-sleeved garment; for in this manner the virgin daughters of the king dressed themselves in robes. Then his attendant took her out and locked the door behind her.   *a varicolored tunic*

19 And Tamar putᴬashes on her head, and tore her long-sleeved garment which *was* on her; and she put her hand on her head and went away, crying aloud as she went.   *dust*

20 Then Absalom her brother said to her, "Has Amnon your brother been with you? But now keep silent, my sister, he is your brother; do not take this matter to heart." So Tamar remained and was desolate in her brother Absalom's house.

Amnon Is Murdered

21 Now when King David heard of all these matters, he was very angry.

22 But Absalom did not speak to Amnon ᴿeither good or bad; forᴿAbsalom hated Amnon because he had violated his sister Tamar.   Gen. 31:24 • [Lev. 19:17; 1 John 2:9, 11]

23 Now it came about after two full years that Absalom ᴿhad sheepshearers in Baalhazor, which is near Ephraim, and Absalom invited all the king's sons.   1 Sam. 25:7

24 And Absalom came to the king and said, "Behold now, your servant has sheepshearers; please let the king and his servants go with your servant."

25 But the king said to Absalom, "No, my son, we should not all go, lest we be burdensome to you." Although heᵀurged him, he would not go, but blessed him.   *broke through*

26 Then ᴿAbsalom said, "If not, please let my brother Amnon go with us." And the king said to him, "Why should he go with you?"   2 Sam. 3:27; 11:13-15

27 But when Absalom urged him, he let Amnon and all the king's sons go with him.

28 And Absalom commanded his servants, saying, "See now, when Amnon's heart is merry with wine, and when I say to you, 'Strike Amnon,' then put him to death. Do not fear; have not I myself commanded you? Be courageous and be valiant."

29 And the servants of Absalom did to Amnon just as Absalom had commanded. Then all the king's sons arose and each mountedᴿhis mule and fled.   2 Sam. 18:9

30 Now it was while they were on the way that the report came to David, saying, "Absalom has struck down all the king's sons, and not one of them is left."

31 Then the king arose, tore his clothes and lay on the ground; and all his servants were standing by with clothes torn.

32 And Jonadab, the son of Shimeah, David's brother, responded, "Do not let my lord suppose they have put to death all the young men, the king's sons, for Amnon alone is dead; because by theᵀintent of Absalom this has been determined since the day that he violated his sister Tamar.   *mouth*

33"Now therefore, do not let my lord the king ᴿtake the report toᵀheart, namely, 'all the king's sons are dead,' for only Amnon is dead."   2 Sam. 19:19 • *his heart*

34 Now ᴿAbsalom had fled. And the young man who was the watchman raised his eyes and looked, and behold, many people were coming from the road behind him by the side of the mountain.   2 Sam. 13:37, 38

35 And Jonadab said to the king, "Behold, the king's sons have come; according to your servant's word, so it happened."

36 And it came about as soon as he had finished speaking, that behold, the king's sons came and lifted their voices and wept; and also the king and all his servants wept ᵀvery bitterly.   *with a very great weeping*

Flight of Absalom

37 Now Absalom fled and went to Talmai the son of Ammihud, the king of Geshur. And *David* mourned for his son every day.
38 ^RSo Absalom had fled and gone to Geshur, and was there three years. 2 Sam. 13:34
39 And *the heart of* King David longed to go out to Absalom; for he was comforted concerning Amnon, since he was dead.

CHAPTER 14

Return of Absalom

NOW Joab the son of Zeruiah perceived that ^Rthe king's heart *was inclined* toward Absalom.   2 Sam. 13:39
2 So Joab sent to Tekoa and brought a wise woman from there and said to her, "Please pretend to be a mourner, and put on mourning garments now, and do not anoint yourself with oil, but be like a woman who has been mourning for the dead many days;
3 then go to the king and speak to him in this manner." So Joab put ^Rthe words in her mouth.   2 Sam. 14:19
4 Now when the woman of Tekoa ¹²spoke to the king, she fell on her face to the ground and ^Rprostrated herself and said, "Help,^R O king."   1 Sam. 25:23 · 2 Kin. 6:26-28
5 And the king said to her, "What is your trouble?" And she ^Tanswered, "Truly I am a widow, for my husband is dead.   *said*
6 "And your maidservant had two sons, but the two of them struggled together in the field, and there was no ¹³one to separate them, so one struck the other and killed him.
7 "Now behold,^Rthe whole family has risen against your maidservant, and they say, 'Hand over the one who struck his brother, that we may put him to death for the life of his brother whom he killed,^Rand destroy the heir also.' Thus they will extinguish my coal which is left, so as to ^Tleave my husband neither name nor remnant on the face of the earth."   Num. 35:19 · Matt. 21:38 · *set*
8 Then the king said to the woman, "Go to your house, and I will give orders concerning you."
9 And the woman of Tekoa said to the king, "O my lord, the king,^Rthe iniquity is on me and my father's house, but the king and his throne are guiltless."   Gen. 43:9
10 So the king said, "Whoever speaks to you, bring him to me, and he will not touch you anymore."
11 Then she said, "Please let the king remember the LORD your God, *so that* the avenger of blood may not continue to destroy, lest they destroy my son." And he said, "As the LORD lives, not one hair of your son shall fall to the ground."

12 Then the woman said, "Please let your maidservant speak a word to my lord the king." And he said, "Speak."
13 And the woman said, "Why^Rthen have you planned such a thing against the people of God? For in speaking this word the king is as one who is guilty, *in that* the king does not bring back his banished one.   2 Sam. 12:7
14 "For we shall surely die and are like water spilled on the ground which cannot be gathered up again. Yet God does not take away life, but plans ways so that the banished one may not be cast out from him.
15 "Now^Tthe reason I have come to speak this word to my lord the king is because the people have made me afraid; so your maidservant said, 'Let me now speak to the king, perhaps the king will perform the^Trequest of his maidservant.   *that · word*
16 'For the king will hear ^Tand deliver his maidservant from the^Thand of the man who would destroy^Tboth me and my son from the inheritance of God.'   *to · palm · together*
17 "Then your maidservant said, 'Please let the word of my lord the king be^Tcomforting, for as the angel of God, so is my lord the king to discern good and evil. And may the LORD your God be with you.'"   *for rest*
18 Then the king answered and said to the woman, "Please do not hide anything from me that I am about to ask you." And the woman said, "Let my lord the king please speak."
19 So the king said, "Is the hand of Joab with you in all this?" And the woman answered and said, "As your soul lives, my lord the king, no one can turn to the right or to the left from anything that my lord the king has spoken. Indeed, it was^Ryour servant Joab who commanded me, and it was he who put all these words in the mouth of your maidservant;   2 Sam. 14:3
20 in order to change the appearance of things your servant Joab has done this thing. But my lord is wise,^Rlike the wisdom of the angel of God, to know all that is in the earth."   2 Sam. 14:17; 19:27
21 Then the king said to Joab, "Behold now, I will surely do this thing; go therefore, bring back the young man Absalom."
22 And Joab fell on his face to the ground, prostrated himself and blessed the king; then Joab said, "Today your servant knows that I have found favor in your sight, O my lord, the king, in that the king has performed the^Trequest of his servant."   *word*
23 So Joab arose and went to^RGeshur, and brought Absalom to Jerusalem.   Deut. 3:14
24 However the king said, "Let him turn to^Rhis own house, and let him not see my face." So Absalom turned to his own house and did not see the king's face. 2 Sam. 13:20

Deceit of Absalom

25 Now in all Israel was no one as hand-

¹² Many mss. and ancient versions read *came*
¹³ Lit., *deliverer between*

some as Absalom, so highly praised; ^Rfrom the sole of his foot to the crown of his head there was no defect in him.   Job 2:7; Is. 1:6

26 And when he^Rcut the hair of his head (and it was at the end of every year that he cut *it*, for it was heavy on him so he cut it), he weighed the hair of his head at^T200 shekels by the king's weight.   5 lb. • Ezek. 44:20

27 And^Rto Absalom there were born three sons, and one daughter whose name was ^RTamar; she was a woman of beautiful appearance.   2 Sam. 18:18 • 2 Sam. 13:1

28 Now Absalom lived two full years in Jerusalem, and did not see the king's face.

29 Then Absalom sent for Joab, to send him to the king, but he would not come to him. So he sent again a second time, but he would not come.

30 Therefore he said to his servants, "See, Joab's ¹⁴field is next to mine, and he has barley there; go and set it on fire." So Absalom's servants set the field on fire.

31 Then Joab arose, came to Absalom at his house and said to him, "Why have your servants set my ¹⁴field on fire?"

32 And Absalom answered Joab, "Behold, I sent for you, saying, 'Come here, that I may send you to the king, to say, "Why have I come from Geshur? It would be better for me still to be there." ' Now therefore, let me see the king's face; and if there is iniquity in me, let him put me to death."

33 So when Joab came to the king and told him, he called for Absalom. Thus he came to the king and prostrated himself on his face to the ground before the king, and ^Rthe king kissed Absalom.   Gen. 33:4

CHAPTER 15

Now it came about after this that Absalom provided for himself a chariot and horses, and fifty men as runners before him.

2 And Absalom used to rise early and ^Rstand beside the way to the gate; and it happened that when any man had a suit to come to the king for judgment, Absalom would call to him and say, "From what city are you?" And he would say, "Your servant is from one of the tribes of Israel."   Ruth 4:1

3 Then Absalom would say to him, "See, your^Tclaims are good and right, but no man listens to you on the part of the king." *words*

4 Moreover, Absalom would say, "Oh^R that one would appoint me judge in the land, then every man who has any suit or cause could come to me, and I would give him justice."   Judg. 9:29

5 And it happened that when a man came near to prostrate himself before him, he would put out his hand and take hold of him and^Rkiss him.   2 Sam. 14:33; 20:9

6 And in this manner Absalom dealt with all Israel who came to the king for judgment;^Rso Absalom stole away the hearts of the men of Israel.   [Rom. 16:18]

Rebellion of Absalom

7 Now it came about at the end of ¹⁵forty years that Absalom said to the king, "Please let me go and pay my vow which I have vowed to the LORD, in^RHebron.   2 Sam. 3:2, 3

8"For your servant vowed a vow while I was living at Geshur in Aram, saying, 'If the LORD shall indeed bring me back to Jerusalem, then I will serve the LORD.' "

9 And the king said to him, "Go in peace." So he arose and went to Hebron.

10 But Absalom sent spies throughout all the tribes of Israel, saying, "As soon as you hear the sound of the trumpet, then you shall say, 'Absalom is king in Hebron.' "

11 Then two hundred men went with Absalom from Jerusalem, ^Rwho were invited and went^Tinnocently, and they did not know anything.   1 Sam. 9:13 • *in their integrity*

12 And Absalom sent for Ahithophel the Gilonite, David's counselor, from his city Giloh, while he was offering the sacrifices. And the conspiracy was strong, for the people increased continually with Absalom.

Flight of David

13 Then a messenger came to David, saying, "The^R hearts of the men of Israel are ^Twith Absalom."   Judg. 9:3; 2 Sam. 15:6 • *after*

14 And David said to all his servants who were with him at Jerusalem, "Arise^Rand let us flee, for *otherwise* none of us shall escape from Absalom. Go in haste, lest he overtake us quickly and bring down calamity on us and strike the city with the edge of the sword."   2 Sam. 12:11; Ps. 3:title

15 Then the king's servants said to the king, "Behold, your servants *are ready to do* whatever my lord the king chooses."

16 So the king went out and all his household^Twith him. But the king left ten concubines to keep the house.   *at his feet*

17 And the king went out and all the people^Twith him, and they stopped at the last house.   *at his feet*

18 Now all his servants passed on beside him,^Rall the Cherethites, all the Pelethites, and all the Gittites, six hundred men who had come^Twith him from Gath, passed on before the king.   2 Sam. 8:18 • *at his feet*

19 Then the king said to Ittai the Gittite, "Why will you also go with us? Return and remain with the king, for you are a foreigner and also an exile; *return* to your own place.

20"You came *only* yesterday, and shall I today make you wander with us, while I go where I will? Return and take back your brothers; mercy and truth be with you."

21 But Ittai answered the king and said, "As the LORD lives, and as my lord the king lives, surely^Rwherever my lord the king may

¹⁴ Lit., *portion*   ¹⁵ Some ancient versions render *four*

be, whether for death or for life, there also your servant will be."   Ruth 1:16, 17

22 Therefore David said to Ittai, "Go and pass over." So Ittai the Gittite passed over with all his men and all the little ones who *were* with him.

23 While all the country was weeping with a loud voice, all the people passed over. The king also passed over the brook Kidron, and all the people passed over toward the way of the wilderness.

24 Now behold, Zadok also *came,* and all the Levites with him carrying the ark of the covenant of God. And they set down the ark of God, and Abiathar came up until all the people had finished passing from the city.

25 And the king said to Zadok, "Return the ark of God to the city. If I find favor in the sight of the LORD, then^RHe will bring me back again, and show me both it and ^RHis habitation.   [Ps. 43:3] • Ex. 15:13; Jer. 25:30

26"But if He should say thus, 'I have no delight in you,' behold, here I am, let Him do to me as seems good^Tto Him."   *in His sight*

27 The king said also to Zadok the priest, "Are you *not* a seer? Return to the city in peace and your two sons with you, your son Ahimaaz and Jonathan the son of Abiathar.

28"See, I am going to wait^Rat the fords of the wilderness until word comes from you to inform me."   Josh. 5:10; 2 Sam. 17:16

29 Therefore Zadok and Abiathar returned the ark of God to Jerusalem and remained there.

30 And David went up the ascent of the *Mount of* Olives, and wept as he went, and ^Rhis head was covered and he walked^Rbarefoot. Then all the people who were with him each covered his head and went up weeping as they went.   Esth. 6:12 • Is. 20:2-4

31 Now someone told David, saying, "Ahithophel^Ris among the conspirators with Absalom." And David said, "O LORD, I pray, ^Rmake the counsel of Ahithophel foolishness."   2 Sam. 15:12 • 2 Sam. 16:23; 17:14, 23

32 It happened as David was coming to the summit, where God was worshiped, that behold, Hushai the Archite met him with his coat torn, and^Tdust on his head.   *ground*

33 And David said to him, "If you pass over with me, then you will be^Ra burden to me.   2 Sam. 19:35

34"But if you return to the city, and say to Absalom, 'I will be your servant, O king; as I have been your father's servant in time past, so I will now be your servant,' then you can thwart the counsel of Ahithophel for me.

35"And are not Zadok and Abiathar the priests with you there? So it shall be that ^Rwhatever you hear from the king's house, you shall report to Zadok and Abiathar the priests.   2 Sam. 17:15, 16

36"Behold^Rtheir two sons are with them there, Ahimaaz, Zadok's son and Jonathan, Abiathar's son; and by them you shall send me everything that you hear."   2 Sam. 15:27

37 So Hushai, David's friend, came into the city, and Absalom came into Jerusalem.

CHAPTER 16

NOW when David had passed^Ra little beyond the summit, behold, ^RZiba the servant of Mephibosheth met him with a couple of saddled donkeys, and on them *were* two hundred loaves of bread, a hundred clusters of raisins, a hundred summer fruits, and a jug of wine.   2 Sam. 15:32 • 2 Sam. 9:2-13

2 And the king said to Ziba, "Why do you have these?" And Ziba said, "The donkeys are for the king's household to ride, and the bread and summer fruit for the young men to eat, and the wine, for whoever is faint in the wilderness to drink."

3 Then the king said, "And where is your master's son?" And Ziba said to the king, "Behold, he is staying in Jerusalem, for he said, 'Today the house of Israel will restore the kingdom of my father to me.' "

4 So the king said to Ziba, "Behold, all that belongs to Mephibosheth is yours." And Ziba said, "I prostrate myself; let me find favor in your sight, O my lord, the king!"

5 When King David came to ^RBahurim, behold, there came out from there a man of the family of the house of Saul whose name was Shimei, the son of Gera; he came out cursing continually as he came.   2 Sam. 3:16

6 And he threw stones at David and at all the servants of King David; and all the people and all the mighty men were at his right hand and at his left.

7 And thus Shimei said when he cursed, "Get out, get out,^Ryou man of bloodshed, and worthless fellow!   2 Sam. 12:9

8"The LORD has returned upon you all the bloodshed of the house of Saul, in whose place you have reigned; and the LORD has given the kingdom into the hand of your son Absalom. And behold, you are *taken* in your own evil, for you are a man of bloodshed!"

9 Then Abishai the son of Zeruiah said to the king, "Why should this dead dog^Rcurse my lord the king? Let me go over now, and ^Tcut off his head."   Ex. 22:28 • *take off*

10 But the king said, "What^Rhave I to do with you, O sons of Zeruiah?^RIf he curses, and if the LORD has told him, 'Curse David,' ^Rthen who shall say, 'Why have you done so?' "   2 Sam. 3:39 • John 18:11 • [Rom. 9:20]

11 Then David said to Abishai and to all his servants, "Behold, my son who came out from^Tme seeks my life; how much more now this Benjamite? Let him alone and let him curse, for the LORD has told him.   *my body*

12"Perhaps the LORD will look on my affliction and^Treturn good to me instead of his cursing this day."   *the LORD will return*

13 So David and his men went on the way; and Shimei went along on the hillside paral-

lel with him and as he went he cursed, and cast stones and threw dust at him.

14 And the king and all the people who were with him arrived weary and he refreshed himself there.

Reign of Absalom

15 [R]Then Absalom and all the people, the men of Israel, entered Jerusalem, and Ahithophel with him.   2 Sam. 15:12, 37

16 Now it came about when [R]Hushai the Archite, David's friend, came to Absalom, that Hushai said to Absalom, "Long live the king! Long live the king!"   2 Sam. 15:37

17 And Absalom said to Hushai, "Is this your [A]loyalty to your friend? Why did you not go with your friend?"   kindness

18 Then Hushai said to Absalom, "No! For whom the LORD, this people, and all the men of Israel have chosen, his will I be, and with him I will remain.

19 "And besides, whom should I serve? Should I not serve in the presence of his son? As I have served in your father's presence, so I will be in your presence."

20 Then Absalom said to Ahithophel, "Give your advice. What shall we do?"

21 And Ahithophel said to Absalom, "Go[R] in to your father's concubines, whom he has left to keep the house; then all Israel will hear that you have made yourself odious to your father. The hands of all who are with you will also be strengthened."   2 Sam. 15:16

22 So they pitched a tent for Absalom on the roof, and Absalom went in to his father's concubines in the sight of all Israel.

23 And [R]the advice of Ahithophel, which he [T]gave in those days, was as if one inquired of the word of God; [R]so was all the advice of Ahithophel regarded by both David and Absalom.   2 Sam. 17:14, 23 • advised • 2 Sam. 15:12

CHAPTER 17

FURTHERMORE, Ahithophel said to Absalom, "Please let me choose 12,000 men that I may arise and pursue David tonight.

2 "And I will come upon him while he is weary and exhausted and will terrify him so that all the people who are with him will flee. Then I will strike down the king alone,

3 and I will bring back all the people to you. The return of everyone depends on the man you seek; then all the people shall be at [R]peace."   Jer. 6:14

4 So the plan pleased Absalom and all the elders of Israel.

5 Then Absalom said, "Now call [R]Hushai the Archite also, and let us hear what [T]he has to say."   2 Sam. 15:32-34 • is in his mouth—even he

6 When Hushai had come to Absalom, Absalom said to [T]him, "Ahithophel has spoken [T]thus. Shall we carry out his plan? If not, you speak."   him, saying • according to this word

7 So Hushai said to Absalom, "This [R]time

the advice that Ahithophel has [T]given is not good."   2 Sam. 16:21 • advised

8 Moreover, Hushai said, "You know your father and his men, that they are mighty men and they are [T]fierce, like a bear robbed of her cubs in the field. And your father is an expert in warfare, and will not spend the night with the people.   bitter of soul

9 "Behold, he has now hidden himself in one of the [T]caves or in another place; and it will be when he falls on them at the first attack, that whoever hears it will say, 'There has been a slaughter among the people who follow Absalom.'   pits

10 "And even the one who is valiant, whose heart is like the heart of a lion, will completely [T]lose heart; for all Israel knows that your father is a mighty man and those who are with him are valiant men.   melt

11 "But I counsel that all Israel be surely gathered to you, [R]from Dan even to Beersheba, [R]as the sand that is by the sea in abundance, and that [T]you personally go into battle.   1 Sam. 3:20 • Gen. 22:17 • your face go

12 "So we shall come to him in one of the places where he can be found, and we will [T]fall on him as the dew falls on the ground; and of him and of all the men who are with him, not even one will be left.   settle down

13 "And if he withdraws into a city, then all Israel shall bring ropes to that city, and we will drag it into the [A]valley until not even a small stone is found there."   wadi

14 Then Absalom and all the men of Israel said, "The counsel of Hushai the Archite is better than the counsel of Ahithophel." For the LORD had ordained to thwart the good counsel of Ahithophel, in order that the LORD might bring calamity on Absalom.

15 Then Hushai said to Zadok and to Abiathar the priests, "This is what Ahithophel counseled Absalom and the elders of Israel, and this is what I have counseled.

16 "Now therefore, send quickly and tell David, saying, 'Do not spend the night at the fords of the wilderness, but by all means cross over, lest the king and all the people who are with him be destroyed.'"

17 [R]Now Jonathan and Ahimaaz were staying at [R]En-rogel, and a maidservant would go and tell them, and they would go and tell King David, for they could not be seen entering the city.   2 Sam. 15:27, 36 • Josh. 15:7

18 But a lad did see them, and told Absalom; so the two of them departed quickly and came to the house of a man [R]in Bahurim, who had a well in his courtyard, and they went down [T]into it.   2 Sam. 3:16; 16:5 • there

19 And [R]the woman [T]took a covering and spread it over the well's mouth and scattered grain on it, so that nothing was known.   Josh. 2:4-6 • took and spread the covering

20 Then Absalom's servants came to the woman at the house and said, "Where are Ahimaaz and Jonathan?" And [R]the woman said to them, "They have crossed the brook of water." And when they searched and

could not find *them*, they returned to Jerusalem.   [Lev. 19:11]; Josh. 2:3–5; 1 Sam. 19:12–17

21 And it came about after they had departed that they came up out of the well and went and told King David; and they said to David, "Arise[R] and cross over the water quickly for thus Ahithophel has counseled against you."   2 Sam. 17:15, 16

22 Then David and all the people who *were* with him arose and crossed the Jordan; and by dawn not even one remained who had not crossed the Jordan.

23 Now when Ahithophel saw that his counsel was not [T]followed, he [T]saddled *his* donkey and arose and went to his home, to his city, and set his house in order, and strangled himself; thus he died and was buried in the grave of his father.   *done • bound*

24 Then David came to [R]Mahanaim. And Absalom crossed the Jordan, he and all the men of Israel with him.   Gen. 32:2, 10

25 And Absalom set Amasa over the army in place of Joab. Now Amasa was the son of a man whose name was Ithra the Israelite, who went in to Abigail the daughter of Nahash, sister of Zeruiah, Joab's mother.

26 And Israel and Absalom camped in the land of Gilead.

27 Now when David had come to Mahanaim, Shobi[it]the son of Nahash from Rabbah of the sons of Ammon, Machir the son of Ammiel from Lo-debar, and Barzillai the Gileadite from Rogelim,   1 Sam. 11:1

28 brought [R]beds, basins, pottery, wheat, barley, flour, parched *grain*, beans, lentils, parched *seeds*,   [Prov. 11:25; Matt. 5:7]

29 honey, curds, sheep, and cheese of the herd, for David and for the people who *were* with him,[R]to eat; for they said, "The people are hungry and weary and thirsty in the wilderness."   2 Sam. 16:2, 14; Prov. 21:26; Eccl. 11:1

CHAPTER 18

Absalom's Murder

THEN David [T]numbered the people who were with him and[R]set over them commanders of thousands and commanders of hundreds.   *mustered* • Ex. 18:25; Num. 31:14

2 And David sent the people out, [R]one third under the[T]command of Joab, one third under the[T]command of Abishai the son of Zeruiah, Joab's brother, and one third under the[T]command of Ittai the Gittite. And the king said to the people, "I myself will surely go out with you also."   Judg. 7:16 • *hand*

3 But the people said, "You should not go out; for if we indeed flee, they will not care about us, even if half of us die, they will not care about us. But you are worth ten thousand of us; therefore now it is better that you *be ready* to help us from the city."

4 Then the king said to them, "Whatever seems best to you I will do." So the king stood beside the gate, and all the people went out by hundreds and thousands.

5 And the king charged Joab and Abishai and Ittai, saying, "*Deal* gently for my sake with the young man Absalom." And all the people heard when the king charged all the commanders concerning Absalom.

6 Then the people went out into the field against Israel, and the battle took place in [R]the forest of Ephraim.   Josh. 17:15, 18

7 And the people of Israel were[T]defeated there before the servants of David, and the slaughter there that day was great, 20,000 men.   *smitten*

8 For the battle there was spread over the whole countryside, and the forest devoured more people that day than the sword devoured.

9 Now Absalom happened to meet the servants of David. For Absalom was riding on *his* mule, and the mule went under the thick branches of a great oak. And his head caught fast in the oak, so he was[T]left hanging between heaven and earth, while the mule that was under him kept going.   *placed*

10 When a certain man saw *it*, he told Joab and said, "Behold, I saw Absalom hanging in an oak."

11 Then Joab said to the man who had told him, "Now behold, you saw *him!* Why then did you not strike him there to the ground? And I would have given you ten *pieces* of silver and a belt."

12 And the man said to Joab, "Even if I should receive a thousand *pieces of* silver in my hand, I would not put out my hand against the king's son; for[R]in our hearing the king charged you and Abishai and Ittai, saying, 'Protect for me the young man Absalom!'   2 Sam. 18:5

13 "Otherwise, if I had dealt treacherously against his life (and[R]there is nothing hidden from the king), then you yourself would have stood aloof."   2 Sam. 14:19, 20

14 Then Joab said, "I will not[T]waste time here with you." So he took three spears in his hand and thrust them through the heart of Absalom while he was yet alive in the [T]midst of the oak.   *tarry thus • heart*

15 And ten young men who carried Joab's armor gathered around and struck Absalom and killed him.

16 Then [R]Joab blew the trumpet, and the people returned from pursuing Israel, for Joab restrained the people.   2 Sam. 2:28; 20:22

17 And they took Absalom and cast him into[T]a deep pit in the forest and erected over him a very great heap of stones. And all Israel fled, each to his tent.   *the great*

18 Now Absalom in his lifetime had taken and[R]set up for himself a pillar which is in the King's Valley, for he said, "I have no son to preserve my name." So he named the pillar after his own name, and it is called Absalom's monument to this day.   1 Sam. 15:12

19 Then [R]Ahimaaz the son of Zadok said, "Please let me run and bring the king news

that the LORD has 'freed him from the hand of his enemies."   2 Sam. 15:36 • *vindicated*

20 But Joab said to him, "You are not the man to carry news this day, but you shall carry news another day; however, you shall carry no news today because the king's son is dead."

21 Then Joab said to the Cushite, "Go, tell the king what you have seen." So the Cushite bowed to Joab and ran.

22 Now Ahimaaz the son of Zadok said once more to Joab, "But whatever happens, please let me also run after the Cushite." And Joab said, "Why would you run, my son, since ᴿyou will have no reward for going?"   2 Sam. 18:29

23 "But whatever happens," *he said,* "I will run." So he said to him, "Run." Then Ahimaaz ran by way of the plain and passed up the Cushite.

24 Now ᴿDavid was sitting between the two gates; andᴿthe watchman went up to the roof of the gate by the wall, and raised his eyes and looked, and behold, a man running by himself.   2 Sam. 19:8 • 2 Sam. 13:34

25 And the watchman called and told the king. And the king said, "If he is by himself there is good news in his mouth." And he came nearer and nearer.

26 Then the watchman saw another man running; and the watchman called to the gatekeeper and said, "Behold, *another* man running by himself." And the king said, "This one also is bringing good news."

27 And the watchman said, "Iᵀthink the running of the first oneᴿis like the running of Ahimaaz the son of Zadok." And the king said, "Thisᴿis a good man and comes with good news."   *see* • 2 Kin. 9:20 • 1 Kin. 1:42

28 And Ahimaaz called and said to the king, "¹⁶All is well." Andᴿhe prostrated himself before the king with his face to the ground. And he said, "Blessedᴿis the LORD your God, who has delivered up the men who lifted their hands against my lord the king."   1 Sam. 25:23; 2 Sam. 14:4 • 1 Sam. 17:46

29 And the king said, "Isᴿit well with the young man Absalom?" And Ahimaaz answered, "When Joab sent the king's servant, and your servant, I saw a great tumult, but I did not know what *it was.*"   2 Kin. 4:26

30 Then the king said, "Turn aside and stand here." So he turned aside and stood still.

31 And behold, the Cushite arrived, and the Cushite said, "Let my lord the king receive good news, for the LORD hasᵀfreed you this day from the hand of all those who rose up against you."   *vindicated*

32 Then the king said to the Cushite, "Is it well with the young man Absalom?" And the Cushite answered, "Let the enemies of my lord the king, and all who rise up against you for evil, be as that young man!"

33 And the king was deeply moved and went up to the chamber over the gate and wept. And thus he said as he walked, "Oᴿmy son Absalom, my son, my son Absalom! Would I had died instead of you, O Absalom, my son, my son!"   2 Sam. 19:4

CHAPTER 19

Reproof of Joab

THEN it was told Joab, "Behold, the king is weeping and mourns for Absalom."

2 And theᵀvictory that day was turned to mourning for all the people, for the people heard *it* said that day, "The king is grieved for his son."   *salvation*

3 So the people went by stealth into the city that day, as people who are humiliated steal away when they flee in battle.

4 And the king covered his face and cried out with a loud voice, "O my son Absalom, O Absalom, my son, my son!"

5 Then Joab came into the house to the king and said, "Today you have covered with shame the faces of all your servants, who today have saved your life and the lives of your sons and daughters, the lives of your wives, and the lives of your concubines,

6 by loving those who hate you, and by hating those who love you. For you have shown today that princes and servants are nothing to you; for I know this day that if Absalom were alive and all of us were dead today, then you would be pleased.

7 "Now therefore arise, go out and speak kindly to your servants, for I swear by the LORD, if you do not go out, surely not a man will pass the night with you, and this will be worse for you than all the evil that has come upon you from your youth until now."

Restoration of David

8 So the king arose and sat in the gate. When they told all the people, saying, "Behold, the king isᴿsitting in the gate," then all the people came before the king.   2 Sam. 15:2

Now Israel had fled, each to his tent.

9 And all the people were quarreling throughout all the tribes of Israel, saying, "The king delivered us from theᵀhand of our enemies and saved us from theᵀhand of the Philistines, but nowᴿhe has fled out of the land from Absalom.   *palm* • 2 Sam. 15:14

10 "However, Absalom, whom we anointed over us, has died in battle. Now then, why are you silent about bringing the king back?"

11 Then King David sent to ᴿZadok and Abiathar the priests, saying, "Speak to the elders of Judah, saying, 'Why are you the last to bring the king back to his house, since the word of all Israel has come to the king, *even* to his house?   2 Sam. 15:29

12 'You are my brothers;ᴿyou are my bone

16 Lit., *Peace.*

and my flesh. Why then should you be the last to bring back the king?'   2 Sam. 5:1

13 "And say to ᴿAmasa, 'Are you not my bone and my flesh?ᴿMay God do so to me, and more also, if you will not be commander of the army before me continually in place of Joab.' "   2 Sam. 17:25 • 1 Kin. 19:2

14 Thus he turned the hearts of all the men of Judahᴿas one man, so that they sent *word* to the king, *saying*, "Return, you and all your servants."   Judg. 20:1

15 The king then returned and came as far as the Jordan. And Judah came toᴿGilgal in order to go to meet the king, to bring the king across the Jordan.   Josh. 5:9

16 ThenᴿShimei the son of Gera, the Benjamite who was from Bahurim, hurried and came down with the men of Judah to meet King David.   2 Sam. 16:5-13; 1 Kin. 2:8

17 And there were a thousand men of Benjamin with him, with Ziba the servant of the house of Saul, and his fifteen sons and his twenty servants with him; and they rushed to the Jordan before the king.

18 Then they kept crossing the ford to bring over the king's household, and to do what was good in his sight. And Shimei the son of Gera fell down before the king as he was about to cross the Jordan.

19 So he said to the king, "Let not my lord consider me guilty, nor remember what your servant did wrong on the day when my lord the king came out from Jerusalem, so that the king shouldᵀtake *it* to heart.   set

20 "For your servant knows that I have sinned; therefore behold, I have come today, ᴿthe first of all the house of Joseph to go down to meet my lord the king."   2 Sam. 16:5

21 But Abishai the son of Zeruiah answered and said, "Shouldᴿnot Shimei be put to death for this, ᴿbecause he cursed the LORD's anointed?"   [2 Sam. 16:7, 8 • Ex. 22:28]

22 David then said, "What have I to do with you, O sons of Zeruiah, that you should this day be an adversary to me? Should any man be put to death in Israel today? For do I not know that I am king over Israel today?"

23 And the king said to Shimei, "You shall not die." Thus the king swore to him.

24 Then Mephibosheth the ¹⁷son of Saul came down to meet the king; andᴿhe had neither ᵀcared for his feet, norᵀtrimmed his mustache, norᴿwashed his clothes, from the day the king departed until the day he came *home* in peace.   2 Sam. 12:20 • done • Ex. 19:10

25 And it was when he came from Jerusalem to meet the king, that the king said to him, "Whyᴿdid you not go with me, Mephibosheth?"   2 Sam. 16:17

26 So he answered, "O my lord, the king, my servant deceived me; for your servant said, 'I will saddle a donkey for myself that I may ride on it and go with the king,'ᴿbecause your servant is lame.   2 Sam. 9:3

27 "Moreover,ᴿhe has slandered your servant to my lord the king; but my lord the king is like the angel of God, therefore do what is good in your sight.   2 Sam. 16:3, 4

28 "For ᴿall my father's household was nothing but dead men before my lord the king; yet you set your servant among those who ate at your own table. What right do I have yet that I shouldᵀcomplain anymore to the king?"   2 Sam. 21:6-9 • cry out

29 So the king said to him, "Why do you still speak of your affairs? I have ᵀdecided, 'You and Ziba shall divide the land.' "   said

30 And Mephibosheth said to the king, "Let him even take it all, since my lord the king has come safely to his own house."

31 NowᴿBarzillai the Gileadite had come down from Rogelim; and he went on to the Jordan with the king toᵀescort him over the Jordan.   2 Sam. 17:27-29; 1 Kin. 2:7 • send

32 Now Barzillai was very old, being eighty years old; and he had^sustained the king while he stayed at Mahanaim, for he was a very great man.   provided food for

33 And the king said to Barzillai, "You cross over with me and I will^sustain you in Jerusalem with me."   provide food for

34 But Barzillai said to the king, "Howᴿ long have I yet to live, that I should go up with the king to Jerusalem?   Gen. 47:8

35 "I am now eighty years old. Can I distinguish between good and bad? Or can your servant taste what I eat or what I drink? Or can I hear anymore the voice of singing men and women? Why then should your servant be an added burden to my lord the king?

36 "Your servant would merely cross over the Jordan with the king. Why should the king compensate me *with* this reward?

37 "Please let your servant return, that I may die in my own city near the grave of my father and my mother. However, here is your servantᴿChimham, let him cross over with my lord the king, and do for him what is good in your sight."   2 Sam. 19:40; 1 Kin. 2:7

38 And the king answered, "Chimham shall cross over with me, and I will do for him what is good in your sight; and whatever you require of me, I will do for you."

39 All the people crossed over the Jordan and the king crossed too. The king then ᴿkissed Barzillai and blessed him, and he returned to his place.   Gen. 31:55; Ruth 1:14

40 Now the king went on to Gilgal, and Chimham went on with him; and all the people of Judah and also half the people of Israelᵀaccompanied the king.   crossed over with

41 And behold, all the men of Israel came to the king and said to the king, "Whyᴿhad our brothersᴿthe men of Judah stolen you away, and brought the king and his household and all David's men with him over the Jordan?"   Judg. 8:1; 12:1 • 2 Sam. 19:11, 12

42 Then all the men of Judah answered the men of Israel, "Because the king is a close relative toᵀus. Why thenᵀare you angry about this matter? Have we eaten at all at

---

¹⁷ I.e., grandson

the king's *expense*, or has ᴬanything been taken for us?"   *me • is it hot to you • a gift*

43 But the men of Israel answered the men of Judah and said, "We have ten parts in the king, therefore we also have more *claim* on David than you. Why then did you treat us with contempt? Was it not our advice first to bring back our king?" Yet the words of the men of Judah were harsher than the words of the men of Israel.

CHAPTER 20

Nᴏᴡᴿa worthless fellow happened to be there whose name was Sheba, the son of ᴿBichri, a Benjamite; and he blew the trumpet and said,   2 Sam. 16:7 • Gen. 46:21

"Weᴿhave no portion in David,
Nor do we have inheritance inᴿthe son
   of Jesse;   2 Sam. 19:43 • 1 Sam. 22:7-9
Every man to his tents, O Israel!"

2 So all the men of Israelᵀwithdrew from following David, *and* followed Sheba the son of Bichri; but the men of Judah ᵀremained steadfast to their king, from the Jordan even to Jerusalem.   *went up • clung to*

3 Then David came to his house at Jerusalem, and the king took the ten women, the concubines whom he had left to keep the house, and placed them under guard and provided them with sustenance, but did not go in to them. So they were shut up until the day of their death, living as widows.

4 Then the king said toᴿAmasa, "Call out the men of Judah for me within three days, and be present here yourself."   2 Sam. 17:25

5 So Amasa went to call out *the men of* Judah, but he delayed longer than the set time which he had appointed him.

6 And David said to Abishai, "Now Sheba the son of Bichri will do us more harm than Absalom; take your lord's servants and pursue him, lest he find for himself fortified cities and escape from our sight."

7 So Joab's men went out after him, ᴿalong with the Cherethites and the Pelethites and all the mighty men; and they went out from Jerusalem to pursue Sheba the son of Bichri.   2 Sam. 8:18; 1 Kin. 1:38

8 When they were at the large stone which is inᴿGibeon, Amasa cameᵀto meet them. Now Joab was dressed in his military attire, and over it was a belt with a sword in its sheath fastened at his waist; and as he went forward, it fell out.   2 Sam. 2:13 • *before*

9 And Joab said to Amasa, "Is it well with you, my brother?" And ᴿJoab took Amasa by the beard with his right hand to kiss him.   Matt. 26:49

10 But Amasa was not on guard against the sword which was in Joab's hand soᴿhe struck him in the belly with it and poured out his inward parts on the ground, and did not *strike* him again; and he died. Then Joab and Abishai his brother pursued Sheba the son of Bichri.   2 Sam. 2:23; 3:27; 1 Kin. 2:5

11 Now there stood by him one of Joab's young men, and said, "Whoever favors Joab and whoever is for David, ᴿlet *him* follow Joab."   2 Sam. 20:13

12 But Amasa lay wallowing in *his* blood in the middle of the highway. And when the man saw that all the people stood still, he ᵀremoved Amasa from the highway into the field and threw a garment over him when he saw that everyone who came by him stood still.   *caused to turn*

13 As soon as he was removed from the highway, all the men passed on after Joab to pursue Sheba the son of Bichri.

14 Now he went through all the tribes of Israel to Abel even to Beth-maacah and all the Berites; and they were gathered together and also went after him.

15 And they came and besieged him in Abel Beth-maacah, and ᴿthey ᵀcast up a mound against the city, and it stood by the rampart; and all the people who were with Joab were wreaking destruction in order to topple the wall.   2 Kin. 19:32 • *poured out*

16 Then a wise woman called from the city, "Hear, hear! Please tell Joab, 'Come here that I may speak with you.' "

17 So he approached her, and the woman said, "Are you Joab?" And he answered, "I am." Then she said to him, "Listen to the words of your maidservant." And he answered, "I am listening."

18 Then she spoke, saying, "Formerly they used to say, 'They will surely ask *advice* at Abel,' and thus they ended *the dispute.*

19"I am of those who are peaceable *and* faithful in Israel.ᴿYou are seeking to destroy a city even a mother in Israel. Why would you swallow up ᴿthe inheritance of the Lᴏʀᴅ?"   Deut. 20:10 • 2 Sam. 14:16; 21:3

20 And Joab answered and said, "Far be it, far be it from me that I should swallow up or destroy!

21"Such is not the case. But a man from ᴿthe hill country of Ephraim, Sheba the son of Bichri by name, has lifted up his hand against King David. Only hand him over, and I will depart from the city." And the woman said to Joab, "Behold, his head will be thrown to you over the wall."   Josh. 24:33

22 Then the woman wisely came to all the people. And they cut off the head of Sheba the son of Bichri and threw it to Joab. Soᴿhe blew the trumpet, and they were dispersed from the city, each to his tent. Joab also returned to the king at Jerusalem.   2 Sam. 20:1

23 Now Joab was over the whole army of Israel, and Benaiah the son of Jehoiada was over the Cherethites and the Pelethites;

24 and Adoram was over the forced labor, and ᴿJehoshaphat the son of Ahilud was the recorder;   1 Kin. 4:3

25 and Sheva was scribe, and Zadok and ᴿAbiathar were priests;   1 Kin. 4:4

26 and Ira the Jairite was also a priest to David.

CHAPTER 21

Famine

NOW there was [R]a famine in the days of David for three years, year after year; and [R]David sought the presence of the LORD. And the LORD said, "It is for Saul and his bloody house, because he put the Gibeonites to death." Gen. 12:10; 26:1; 42:5 • Num. 27:21

2 So the king called the Gibeonites and spoke to them (now the Gibeonites were not of the sons of Israel but of the remnant of the Amorites, and the sons of Israel [T]made a covenant with them, but Saul had sought to [T]kill them in his zeal for the sons of Israel and Judah). *had sworn to • smite*

3 Thus David said to the Gibeonites, "What should I do for you? And how can I make atonement that you may bless[R]the inheritance of the LORD?" 1 Sam. 26:19

4 Then the Gibeonites said to him, "We[R] have no *concern* of silver or gold with Saul or his house, nor is it for us to put any man to death in Israel." And he said, "I will do for you whatever you say." Num. 35:31, 32

5 So they said to the king, "The man who consumed us, and who planned[T]to exterminate us from remaining within any border of Israel, *against us that we should be exterminated*

6 let seven men from his sons be given to us, and we will hang them before the LORD in Gibeah of Saul, the chosen of the LORD." And the king said, "I will give *them*."

7 But the king spared[R]Mephibosheth, the son of Jonathan the son of Saul,[R]because of the oath of the LORD which was between them, between David and Saul's son Jonathan. 2 Sam. 4:4; 9:10 • 1 Sam. 18:3; 20:12-17

8 So the king took the two sons of Rizpah the daughter of Aiah, Armoni and Mephibosheth whom she had born to Saul, and the five sons of Merab the daughter of Saul, whom she had born to Adriel the son of Barzillai the[R]Meholathite. 1 Kin. 19:16

9 Then he gave them into the hands of the Gibeonites, and they[T]hanged them in the mountain before the LORD, so that the seven of them fell together; and they were put to death in the first days of harvest at the beginning of barley harvest. *exposed them*

10 [R]And Rizpah the daughter of Aiah took sackcloth and spread it for herself on the rock, from the beginning of harvest until[T]it rained on them from the sky; and she [T]allowed neither the birds of the sky to rest on them by day nor the beasts of the field by night. Deut. 21:23 • *water was poured* • *gave*

11 When it was told David what Rizpah the daughter of Aiah, the concubine of Saul, had done,

12 then David went and took[R]the bones of Saul and the bones of Jonathan his son from the men of Jabesh-gilead, who had stolen them from the open square of Beth-shan, where the Philistines had hanged them on the day[R]the Philistines struck down Saul in Gilboa. 1 Sam. 31:11-13 • 1 Sam. 31:3, 4

13 And he brought up the bones of Saul and the bones of Jonathan his son from there, and they gathered the bones of those who had been[T]hanged. *exposed*

14 And they buried the bones of Saul and Jonathan his son in the country of Benjamin in[R]Zela, in the grave of Kish his father; thus they did all that the king commanded, and after that[R]God was moved by entreaty for the land. Josh. 18:28 • Josh. 7:26; 2 Sam. 24:25

War with Philistia—1 Chr. 20:4-8

15 Now when[R]the Philistines were at war again with Israel, David went down and his servants with him; and as they fought against the Philistines, David became weary. 2 Sam. 5:17-25

16 Then Ishbi-benob, who was among the descendants of the giant, the weight of whose spear was three hundred *shekels* of bronze in weight, was girded with a new *sword*, and he[T]intended to kill David. *said*

17 But [R]Abishai the son of Zeruiah helped him, and struck the Philistine and killed him. Then the men of David swore to him, saying, "You shall not go out again with us to battle, that you may not extinguish[R]the lamp of Israel." 2 Sam. 20:6-10 • 1 Kin. 11:36

18 [R]Now it came about after this that there was war again with the Philistines at Gob; then Sibbecai the Hushathite struck down Saph, who was among the descendants of the[T]giant. 1 Chr. 20:4-8 • Heb., *Raphah*

19 And there was war with the Philistines again at Gob, and Elhanan the son of Jaareoregim the Bethlehemite[T]killed Goliath the Gittite,[R]the shaft of whose spear was like a weaver's beam. *smote* • 1 Sam. 17:7

20 And there was war at Gath again, where there was a man of *great* stature who had six fingers on each hand and six toes on each foot, twenty-four in number; and he also had been born to the[T]giant. Heb., *Raphah*

21 And when he defied Israel, Jonathan the son of Shimei, David's brother, struck him down.

22 These four were born to the [T]giant in Gath, and they fell by the hand of David and by the hand of his servants. Heb., *Raphah*

CHAPTER 22

Psalms of Thanksgiving

AND David spoke[R]the words of this song to the LORD in the day that the LORD delivered him from the[T]hand of all his enemies and from the[T]hand of Saul. Ex. 15:1 • *palm*

2 And he said,

"The[R]LORD is my[T]rock and my fortress and my deliverer; 1 Sam. 23:25 • *crag*

3 [T]My[R]God, my rock, in whom I take refuge; *God of my rock* • Deut. 32:4, 37
My[R]shield and the horn of my salvation, my stronghold and[R]my refuge;

My savior, Thou dost save me from violence. Gen. 15:1 • Ps. 9:9

4 "I call upon the LORD,[R]who is worthy to be praised; Ps. 48:1; 96:4
And I am saved from my enemies.

5 "For[R]the waves of death encompassed me; Ps. 93:4; Jon. 2:3
The torrents of [T]destruction [A]overwhelmed me; Heb., *Belial* • *terrified*

6 The cords of Sheol surrounded me;
The snares of death confronted me.

7 "In[R]my distress I called upon the LORD,
Yes, I[A]cried to my God;
And from His temple He heard my voice,
And my cry for help *came* into His ears. Ps. 116:4; 120:1 • *called*

8 "Then[R]the earth shook and quaked,
[R]The foundations of heaven were trembling
And were shaken, because He was angry. Judg. 5:4; Ps. 97:4 • Job 26:11

9 "Smoke went up[^]out of His nostrils,
And fire from His mouth devoured;
Coals were kindled by it. *in His wrath*

10 "He bowed the heavens also, and came down
With thick darkness under His feet.

11 "And[R] He rode on a cherub and flew;
And He appeared on[R]the wings of the wind. 2 Sam. 6:2 • Ps. 104:3

12 "And[R] He made darkness [A]canopies around Him, Job 36:29 • *pavilions*
A mass of waters, thick clouds of the sky.

13 "From the brightness before Him
[R]Coals of fire were kindled. 2 Sam. 22:9

14 "The LORD thundered from heaven,
And the Most High uttered His voice.

15 "And[R] He sent out arrows, and scattered them, Deut. 32:23; Josh. 10:10
Lightning, and[T]routed them. *confused*

16 "Then the channels of the sea appeared,
The foundations of the world were [A]laid bare,
By the rebuke of the LORD,
[R]At the blast of the breath of His nostrils. *uncovered* • Ex. 15:8; Nah. 1:4

17 "He sent from on high, He took me;
He drew me out of many waters.

18 "He delivered me from my strong enemy,
From those who hated me, for they were too strong for me.

19 "They confronted me in the day of my calamity,
But the LORD was my support.

20 "He[R]also brought me forth into a broad place;
He rescued me,[R]because He delighted in me. Ps. 31:8; 118:5 • 2 Sam. 15:26

21 "The[R]LORD has rewarded me according to my righteousness; 1 Sam. 26:23
According to the cleanness of my hands He has recompensed me.

22 "For[R]I have kept the ways of the LORD,

And have not acted wickedly against my God. Gen. 18:19; Ps. 128:1

23 "For[R] all His ordinances *were* before me; [Deut. 6:6–9]; Ps. 119:30, 102
And *as for* His statutes, I did not depart from[T]them. *it*

24 "I was also blameless toward Him,
And I kept myself from my iniquity.

25 "Therefore[R]the LORD has recompensed me according to my righteousness,
According to my cleanness before His eyes. 2 Sam. 22:21

26 "With[R]the[A]kind Thou dost show Thyself [A]kind, [Matt. 5:7] • *loyal*
With the blameless Thou dost show Thyself blameless;

27 [R]With the pure Thou dost show Thyself pure, [Matt. 5:8; 1 John 3:3]
And with the perverted Thou dost show Thyself[T]astute. *twisted*

28 "And[R]Thou dost save an afflicted people; Ex. 3:7, 8; Ps. 72:12, 13
[R]But Thine eyes are on the haughty *whom* Thou dost abase. Is. 5:15

29 "For Thou art my lamp, O LORD;
And the LORD illumines my darkness.

30 "For by Thee I can [18]run upon a troop;
By my God I can leap over a wall.

31 "As for God, His way is[T]blameless;
The word of the LORD is tested;
He is a shield to all who take refuge in Him. *complete: or, having integrity*

32 "For who is God, besides the LORD?
And who is a rock, besides our God?

33 "God is my strong fortress;
And He sets the blameless in His way.

34 "He makes my feet like hinds' *feet*,
And sets me on my high places.

35 "He[R]trains my hands for battle,
[R]So that my arms can bend a bow of bronze. Ps. 144:1 • Job 20:24

36 "Thou hast also given me[R]the shield of Thy salvation, Eph. 6:16, 17
And Thy help makes me great.

37 "Thou dost enlarge my steps under me,
And my[T]feet have not slipped. *ankles*

38 "I pursued my enemies and[R]destroyed them, Ex. 15:9
And I did not turn back until they were consumed.

39 "And I have devoured them and shattered them, so that they did not rise;
And[R]they fell under my feet. Mal. 4:3

40 "For Thou hast girded me with strength for battle;
Thou hast subdued under me[R]those who rose up against me. [Ps. 44:5]

41 "Thou hast also[R]made my enemies turn *their* backs to me, Ex. 23:27
And I destroyed those who hated me.

42 "They[R] looked, but there was none to save; Is. 17:7, 8
[R]*Even* to the LORD, but He did not answer them. 1 Sam. 28:6; Is. 1:15

[18] Or, *crush a troop*

43 "Then[R]I pulverized them as the dust of
the earth,   2 Kin. 13:7
[R]I crushed *and* stamped them as the
mire of the streets.   Is. 10:6; Mic. 7:10
44 "Thou[R]hast also delivered me from the
contentions of my people;
[R]Thou hast kept me as head of the nations;   2 Sam. 3:1 • 2 Sam. 8:1-14
[R]A people whom I have not known
serve me.   Is. 55:5
45 "Foreigners pretend obedience to me;
As soon as they hear, they obey me.
46 "Foreigners[T]lose heart,   *languish*
And[T]come trembling out of their[T]for-
tresses.   *gird themselves • fastnesses*
47 "The LORD lives, and blessed be my
rock;
And exalted be[T]God, the rock of my
salvation,   *the God of the rock*
48 [R]The God who executes vengeance for
me,   1 Sam. 24:12; 25:39; 2 Sam. 4:8
And brings down peoples under me,
49 Who also brings me out from my enemies;
Thou dost even lift me above[R]those
who rise up against me;
[R]Thou dost rescue me from the violent
man.   Ps. 44:5 • Ps. 140:1, 4, 11
50 "Therefore I will give thanks to Thee,
O LORD, among the nations,
And I will sing praises to Thy name.
51 "He[R]is a tower of [19]deliverance to His
king,   Ps. 144:10
And [R]shows lovingkindness to His
anointed,   Ps. 89:24
[R]To David and his [T]descendants forever."   2 Sam. 7:12-16 • *seed*

CHAPTER 23

Now these are the last words of David.
David the son of Jesse declares,
[R]And the man who was raised on high
declares,   2 Sam. 7:8, 9; Ps. 78:70, 71
The anointed of the God of Jacob,
And the sweet psalmist of Israel,
2 "The Spirit of the LORD spoke by me,
And His word was on my tongue.
3 "The God of Israel said,
The Rock of Israel spoke to me,
'He who rules over men righteously,
Who rules in the fear of God,
4 [R]Is as the light of the morning *when*
the sun rises,   Judg. 5:31; Ps. 72:6
A morning without clouds,
When the tender grass *springs* out of
the earth,
Through sunshine after rain.'
5 "Truly is not my house so with God?
For[R]He has made an everlasting cov-
enant with me,   Ps. 89:29; Is. 55:3
Ordered in all things, and secured;
For all my salvation and all *my* desire,
Will He not indeed make *it* grow?

[19] I.e., victories

6 "But[R]the worthless, every one of them
will be thrust away like thorns,
Because they cannot be taken in
hand;   [Matt. 13:41]
7 But the man who touches them
Must be [T]armed with iron and the
shaft of a spear,   *filled*
And they will be completely burned
with fire in *their*[T]place."   *sitting*

Deeds of David's Mighty Men—1 Chr. 11:10-41

8 These are the names of the mighty men
whom David had: Josheb-basshebeth a Tah-
chemonite, chief of the [^]captains, he was
called Adino the Eznite, because of eight
hundred slain *by him* at one time;   *three*
9 and after him was Eleazar the son of
Dodo the Ahohite, one of the three mighty
men with David when they[T]defied the Philistines who were gathered there to battle and
the men of Israel had withdrawn. *reproached*
10 He arose and struck the Philistines until his hand was weary and [T]clung to the
sword, and the LORD brought about a great
victory that day; and the people returned after him only to strip *the slain.* *his hand clung*
11 Now after him was Shammah the son
of Agee a[R]Hararite. And the Philistines were
gathered into a troop, where there was a
plot of ground full of lentils, and the people
fled from the Philistines.   2 Sam. 23:33
12 But he took his stand in the midst of
the plot, defended it and struck the Philistines; and[R]the LORD brought about a great
[T]victory.   2 Sam. 23:10 • *salvation*
13 Then three of the thirty chief men went
down and came to David in the harvest time
to the[R]cave of Adullam, while the troop of
the Philistines was camping in[R]the valley of
Rephaim.   1 Sam. 22:1 • 2 Sam. 5:18
14 And David was then[R]in the stronghold,
while the garrison of the Philistines was
then in Bethlehem.   1 Sam. 22:4, 5
15 [R]And David had a craving and said, "Oh
that someone would give me water to drink
from the well of Bethlehem which is by the
gate!"   1 Chr. 11:17
16 So the three mighty men broke
through the camp of the Philistines, and
drew water from the well of Bethlehem
which was by the gate, and took *it* and
brought *it* to David. Nevertheless he would
not drink it, but poured it out to the LORD;
17 and he said, "Be it far from me, O
LORD, that I should do this. *Shall I drink* the
blood of the men who went in *jeopardy* of
their lives?" Therefore he would not drink it.
These things the three mighty men did.
18 And [R]Abishai, the brother of Joab, the
son of Zeruiah, was chief of the thirty. And
he swung his spear against three hundred
[T]and killed *them,* and had a name as well as
the three.   2 Sam. 10:10, 14; 18:2 • *slain ones*
19 He was most honored of the thirty,
therefore he became their commander;
however, he did not attain to the three.

20 Then Benaiah the son of Jehoiada, the son of a valiant man of Kabzeel, who had done mighty deeds,[T]killed the[A]two *sons of* Ariel of Moab. He also went down and killed a lion in the middle of a pit on a snowy day.   *smote • two lion-like heroes*

21 And he[T]killed an Egyptian,[T]an impressive man. Now the Egyptian *had* a spear in his hand, but he went down to him with a club and snatched the spear from the Egyptian's hand, and killed him with his own spear.   *smote • a man of appearance*

22 These *things* [R]Benaiah the son of Jehoiada did, and had a name as well as the three mighty men.   2 Sam. 23:20

23 He was honored among the thirty, but he did not attain to the three. And David appointed him over his guard.

24 [R]Asahel the brother of Joab was among the thirty; Elhanan the son of Dodo of Bethlehem,   2 Sam. 2:18; 1 Chr. 27:7

25 [R]Shammah the[R]Harodite, Elika the Harodite,   1 Chr. 11:27 • Judg. 7:1

26 Helez the Paltite, Ira the son of Ikkesh the[R]Tekoite,   2 Sam. 14:2

27 Abiezer the[R]Anathothite, Mebunnai the Hushathite,   Josh. 21:18

28 Zalmon the Ahohite, Maharai the [R]Netophathite,   2 Kin. 25:23

29 [R]Heleb the son of Baanah the Netophathite, Ittai the son of Ribai of[R]Gibeah of the sons of Benjamin,   1 Chr. 11:30 • Josh. 18:28

30 Benaiah a [R]Pirathonite, Hiddai of the brooks of[R]Gaash,   Judg. 12:13, 15 • Josh. 24:30

31 Abi-albon the Arbathite, Azmaveth the [R]Barhumite,   2 Sam. 3:16

32 Eliahba the [R]Shaalbonite, the sons of Jashen, Jonathan,   Josh. 19:42

33 Shammah the Hararite, Ahiam the son of Sharar the Ararite,

34 Eliphelet the son of Ahasbai, the son of the Maacathite, Eliam the son of Ahithophel the Gilonite,

35 Hezro the Carmelite, Paarai the Arbite,

36 Igal the son of Nathan of[R]Zobah, Bani the Gadite,   2 Sam. 8:3

37 Zelek the Ammonite, Naharai the[R]Beerothite, armor bearers of Joab the son of Zeruiah,   2 Sam. 4:2

38 Ira the Ithrite, Gareb the Ithrite,

39 Uriah the Hittite; thirty-seven in all.

CHAPTER 24

The Census and the Plague—1 Chr. 29:26–30

NOW[R]again the anger of the LORD burned against Israel, and it incited David against them to say, "Go[,] number Israel and Judah."   2 Sam. 21:1, 2 • 1 Chr. 27:23, 24

2 And the king said to Joab the commander of the army who was with him, "Go about now through all the tribes of Israel, [R]from Dan to Beersheba, and [T]register the people, that I may know the number of the people."   Judg. 20:1; 2 Sam. 3:10 • *muster*

3 But Joab said to the king, "Now may the LORD your God add to the people a hundred times as many as they are, while the eyes of my lord the king *still* see; but why does my lord the king delight in this thing?"

4 Nevertheless, the king's word prevailed against Joab and against the commanders of the army. So Joab and the commanders of the army went out from the presence of the king, to[T]register the people of Israel.   *muster*

5 And they crossed the Jordan and camped in Aroer, on the right side of the city that is in the middle of the valley of Gad, and toward[R]Jazer.   Num. 21:32; 32:35

6 Then they came to Gilead and to [20]the land of Tahtim-hodshi, and they came to Dan-jaan and around to[R]Sidon,   Judg. 1:31

7 and came to the[R]fortress of Tyre and to all the cities of the[R]Hivites and of the Canaanites, and they went out to the south of Judah, *to* Beersheba.   Josh. 19:29 • Josh. 11:3

8 So when they had gone about through the whole land, they came to Jerusalem at the end of nine months and twenty days.

9 And Joab gave the number of the registration of the people to the king; and there were in Israel eight hundred thousand valiant men who drew the sword, and the men of Judah were five hundred thousand men.

10 Now David's heart troubled him after he had numbered the people. So David said to the LORD, "I have sinned greatly in what I have done. But now, O LORD, please [T]take away the iniquity of Thy servant, for I have acted very foolishly."   *cause to pass away*

11 When David arose in the morning, the word of the LORD came to[R]the prophet Gad, David's[R]seer, saying,   1 Sam. 22:5 • 1 Sam. 9:9

12 "Go and speak to David, 'Thus the LORD says, "I am offering you three things; choose for yourself one of them, which I may do to you." ' "

13 So Gad came to David and told him, and said to him, "Shall[R]seven years of famine come to you in your land? Or will you flee three months before your foes while they pursue you? Or shall there be three days' pestilence in your land? Now consider and see what answer I shall return to Him who sent me."   1 Chr. 21:12; Ezek. 14:21

14 Then David said to Gad, "I am in great distress. Let us now fall into the hand of the LORD[R]for His mercies are great, but do not let me fall into the hand of man."   [Ps. 51:1]

15 So the LORD[T]sent a pestilence upon Israel from the morning until the appointed time; and seventy thousand men of the people from Dan to Beersheba died.   *gave*

16 [R]When the angel stretched out his hand toward Jerusalem to destroy it,[R]the LORD relented from the calamity, and said to the angel who destroyed the people, "It is enough! Now relax your hand!" And the angel of the

[20] Or, *Kadesh in the land of the Hittite*

LORD was by the threshing floor of Araunah the Jebusite.   Ex. 12:23; 2 Kin. 19:35 • Ex. 32:14

17 Then David spoke to the LORD when he saw the angel who was striking down the people, and said, "Behold,ᴿit is I who have sinned, and it is I who have done wrong; but ᴿthese sheep, what have they done? Please let Thy hand be against me and against my father's house."   2 Sam. 24:10 • 2 Sam. 7:8

18 So Gad came to David that day and said to him, "Goᴿup, erect an altar to the LORD on the threshing floor of Araunah the Jebusite."   1 Chr. 21:18

19 And David went up according to the word of Gad, just as the LORD had commanded.

20 And Araunah looked down and saw the king and his servants crossing over toward him; and Araunah went out and bowed his face to the ground before the king.

21 Then Araunah said, "Why has my lord the king come to his servant?" And David said, "To buy the threshing floor from you, in order to build an altar to the LORD,ᴿthat the plague may be held back from the people."   Num. 16:44-50

22 And Araunah said to David, "Let my lord the king take and offer up what is good in his sight. Look,ᴿthe oxen for the burnt offering, the threshing sledges and the yokes of the oxen for the wood.   1 Sam. 6:14

23"Everything, O king, Araunah gives to the king." And Araunah said to the king, "May the LORD your God accept you."

24 However, the king said to Araunah, "No, but I will surely buy you for a price, for I will not offer burnt offerings to the LORD my Godᵀwhich cost me nothing." So David bought the threshing floor and the oxen for fifty shekels of silver.   gratuitously

25 And David built there an altar to the LORD, and offered burnt offerings and peace offerings.ᴿThus the LORD was moved by entreaty for the land, and the plague was held back from Israel.   2 Sam. 21:14

The Jewish Calendar

The Jews used two kinds of calendars:
Civil Calendar—official calendar of kings, childbirth, and contracts.
Sacred Calendar—from which festivals were computed.

NAMES OF MONTHS	CORRESPONDS WITH	NO. OF DAYS	MONTH OF CIVIL YEAR	MONTH OF SACRED YEAR	
TISHRI	Sept.–Oct.	30 days	1st	7th	The Jewish day was from sunset to sunset, in 8 equal parts:
HESHVAN	Oct.–Nov.	29 or 30	2nd	8th	
CHISLEV	Nov.–Dec.	29 or 30	3rd	9th	
TEBETH	Dec.–Jan.	29	4th	10th	FIRST WATCH ..... SUNSET TO 9 P.M.
SHEBAT	Jan.–Feb.	30	5th	11th	SECOND WATCH ... 9 P.M. TO MIDNIGHT
ADAR	Feb.–Mar.	29 or 30	6th	12th	THIRD WATCH ..... MIDNIGHT TO 3 A.M.
NISAN	Mar.–Apr.	30	7th	1st	FOURTH WATCH ... 3 A.M. TO SUNRISE
IYAR	Apr.–May	29	8th	2nd	
SIVAN	May–June	30	9th	3rd	FIRST WATCH ..... SUNRISE TO 9 A.M.
TAMMUZ	June–July	29	10th	4th	SECOND WATCH ... 9 A.M. TO NOON
AB	July–Aug.	30	11th	5th	THIRD WATCH ..... NOON TO 3 P.M.
*ELUL	Aug.–Sept.	29	12th	6th	FOURTH WATCH ... 3 P.M. TO SUNSET

*Hebrew months were alternately 30 and 29 days long. Their year, shorter than ours, had 354 days. Therefore, about every 3 years (7 times in 19 years) an extra 29-day-month, VEADAR, was added between ADAR and NISAN.

KINGS

📖 THE BOOK OF FIRST KINGS

The first half of First Kings traces the life of Solomon. Under his leadership Israel rises to the peak of her size and glory. Solomon's great accomplishments, including the unsurpassed splendor of the temple which he constructs in Jerusalem, bring him worldwide fame and respect. However, Solomon's zeal for God diminishes in his later years, as pagan wives turn his heart away from worship in the temple of God. As a result, the king with the divided heart leaves behind a divided kingdom. For the next century, the Book of First Kings traces the twin histories of two sets of kings and two nations of disobedient people who are growing indifferent to God's prophets and precepts.

Like the two books of Samuel, the two books of Kings were originally one in the Hebrew Bible. The original title was *Melechim*, "Kings," taken from the first word in 1:1, *Vehamelech*, "Now King." The Septuagint artificially divided the book of Kings in the middle of the story of Ahaziah into two books. It called the books of Samuel "First and Second Kingdoms" and the books of Kings "Third and Fourth Kingdoms." The Septuagint may have divided Samuel, Kings, and Chronicles into two books each because the Greek required a greater amount of scroll space than did the Hebrew. The Latin title for these books is *Liber Regum Tertius et Quartus*, "Third and Fourth Book of Kings."

✒️ THE AUTHOR OF FIRST KINGS

The author of First and Second Kings is unknown, but evidence supports the talmudic tradition that Kings was written by the prophet Jeremiah. The author was clearly a prophet/historian as seen in the prophetic exposé of apostasy. Both First and Second Kings emphasize God's righteous judgment on idolatry and immorality. The style of these books is also similar to that found in Jeremiah. The phrase "to this day" in First Kings 8:8 and 12:19 indicates a time of authorship prior to the Babylonian captivity (586 B.C.). However, the last two chapters of Second Kings were written after the captivity, probably by a Jewish captive in Babylon.

Evidently, the majority of First and Second Kings was written before 586 B.C. by a compiler who had access to several historical documents. Some of these are mentioned: "the

book of the acts of Solomon" (11:41), "the Book of the Chronicles of the Kings of Israel" (14:19), and "the Book of the Chronicles of the Kings of Judah" (14:29; 15:7). These books may have been a part of the official court records (see 2 Kin. 18:18). In addition, Isaiah 36—39 was probably used as a source (cf. 2 Kin. 18—20).

⏳ THE TIME OF FIRST KINGS

The Book of Kings was written to the remaining kingdom of Judah before and after its Babylonian exile. The majority was compiled by a contemporary of Jeremiah, if not by Jeremiah himself (c. 646–570 B.C.). It is a record of disobedience, idolatry, and ungodliness which serves as an explanation for the Assyrian captivity of Israel (722 B.C.) and the Babylonian captivity of Judah (586 B.C.). First Kings covers the 120 years from the beginning of Solomon's reign in 971 B.C. through Ahaziah's reign ending in 851 B.C. The key date is 931 B.C., the year the kingdom was divided into the northern nation of Israel and the southern nation of Judah.

✝️ THE CHRIST OF FIRST KINGS

Solomon typifies Christ in a number of ways. His fabled wisdom points ahead to "Christ Jesus, who became to us wisdom from God," (1 Cor. 1:30). Solomon's fame, glory, wealth, and honor foreshadow Christ in His kingdom. Solomon's rulership brings knowledge, peace, and worship. However, despite Solomon's splendor, the Son of Man later says of His coming, "Behold, something greater than Solomon is here" (Matt. 12:42).

The prophet Elijah is more typical of John the Baptist than of Christ, but his prophetic ministry and miraculous works illustrate aspects of the life of Christ.

🗝️ THE KEYS TO FIRST KINGS

Key Word: Division of the Kingdom— The theme of First Kings centers around the fact that the welfare of Israel and Judah depends upon the faithfulness of the people and their king to the covenant. Historically, it was written to give an account of the reigns of the kings from Solomon to Jehoshaphat (Judah) and Ahaziah (Israel). The two books of Kings as a whole trace the monarchy from the point of its greatest prosperity

under Solomon to its demise and destruction in the Assyrian and Babylonian captivities.

Theologically, First Kings provides a prophetically oriented evaluation of the spiritual and moral causes that led to the political and economic demise of the two kingdoms. The material is too selective to be considered a biography of the kings. For example, Omri was one of Israel's most important rulers from a political point of view, but because of his moral corruption, his achievements are dismissed in a mere eight verses. The lives of these kings are used to teach that observance of God's law produces blessing, but apostasy is rewarded by judgment.

Key Verses: First Kings 9:4, 5; 11:11—"And as for you, if you will walk before Me as your father David walked, in integrity of heart and uprightness, doing according to all that I have commanded you *and* will keep My statutes and My ordinances, then I will establish the throne of your kingdom over Israel forever, just as I promised to your father David, saying, 'You shall not lack a man on the throne of Israel' " (9:4, 5).

"So the LORD said to Solomon, 'Because you have done this, and you have not kept My covenant and My statutes, which I have commanded you, I will surely tear the kingdom from you, and will give it to your servant' " (11:11).

Key Chapter: First Kings 12—The critical turning point in First Kings occurs in chapter 12 when the united kingdom becomes the divided kingdom. Solomon dies, and his son Rehoboam becomes king and unwisely leads the nation into a civil war which tragically rips the nation into two separate, and at times conflicting, nations. Instead of unity, First Kings records the history of the two kings, two capitals, and two religions.

SURVEY OF FIRST KINGS

The first half of First Kings concerns the life of one of the most amazing men who ever lived. More than any man before or since, he knew how to amass and creatively use great wealth. With the sole exception of Jesus Christ, Solomon is the wisest man in human history. He brings Israel to the peak of its size and glory, and yet, the kingdom is disrupted soon after his death, torn in two by civil strife. This book divides clearly into two sections: the united kingdom (1—11) and the divided kingdom (12—22).

United Kingdom (1—11): These chapters give an account of Solomon's attainment of the throne, wisdom, architectural achievements, fame, wealth, and tragic unfaithfulness. Solomon's half-brother Adonijah attempts to take the throne as David's death is nearing, but Nathan the prophet alerts David who quickly directs the coronation of Solomon as coregent (ch. 1). Solomon still has to consolidate his power and deal with those who oppose his rule. Only when this is done is the kingdom "established in the hands of Solomon" (2:46). Solomon's ungodly marriages (cf. 3:1) eventually turn his heart from the Lord, but he begins well with a genuine love for Yahweh and a desire for wisdom. This wisdom leads to the expansion of Israel to the zenith of her power. Solomon's empire stretches from the border of Egypt to the border of Babylon, and peace prevails.

From a theocratic perspective, Solomon's greatest achievement is the building of the temple. The ark is placed in this exquisite building, which is filled with the glory of God. Solomon offers a magnificent prayer of dedication and binds the people with an oath to remain faithful to Yahweh.

FOCUS	UNITED KINGDOM			DIVIDED KINGDOM		
REFERENCE	1:1———	3:1———	9:1———	12:1———	15:1———	16:29———22:53
DIVISION	ESTABLISHMENT OF SOLOMON	RISE OF SOLOMON	DECLINE OF SOLOMON	DIVISION OF THE KINGDOM	REIGNS OF VARIOUS KINGS	REIGN OF AHAB WITH ELIJAH
TOPIC	SOLOMON			MANY KINGS		
	KINGDOM IN TRANQUILLITY			KINGDOMS IN TURMOIL		
LOCATION	JERUSALEM: CAPITAL OF UNITED KINGDOM			SAMARIA: CAPITAL OF ISRAEL JERUSALEM: CAPITAL OF JUDAH		
TIME	c. 40 YEARS			c. 90 YEARS		

Because the Lord is with him, Solomon continues to grow in fame, power, and wealth. However, his wealth later becomes a source of trouble when he begins to purchase forbidden items. He acquires many foreign wives who lead him into idolatry. It is an irony of history that this wisest of men acts as a fool in his old age. God pronounces judgment and foretells that Solomon's son will rule only a fraction of the kingdom (Judah).

Divided Kingdom (12—22): Upon Solomon's death, God's words come to pass. Solomon's son Rehoboam chooses the foolish course of promising more severe taxation. Jeroboam, an officer in Solomon's army, leads the ten northern tribes in revolt. They make him their king, leaving only Judah and Benjamin in the south under Rehoboam. This is the beginning of a chaotic period with two nations and two sets of kings. Continual enmity and strife exist between the northern and southern kingdoms. The north is plagued by apostasy (Jeroboam

sets up a false system of worship) and the south by idolatry. Of all the northern and southern kings listed in this book, only Asa (15:9–24) and Jehoshaphat (22:41–50) "did what was right in the sight of the LORD" (15:11; 22:43). All the others are idolaters, usurpers, and murderers.

Ahab brings a measure of cooperation between the northern and southern kingdoms, but he reaches new depths of wickedness as a king. He is the man who introduces Jezebel's Baal worship to Israel. The prophet Elijah ministers during this low period in Israel's history, providing a ray of light and witness of the word and power of God. But Ahab's encounter with Elijah never brings him to turn from his false gods to God. Ahab's treachery in the matter of Naboth's vineyard causes a prophetic rebuke from Elijah (21). Ahab repents (21:27–29), but later dies in battle because of his refusal to heed the words of Micaiah, another prophet of God.

OUTLINE OF FIRST KINGS

Part One: The United Kingdom (1:1—11:43)

Part Two: The Divided Kingdom (12:1—22:53)

CHAPTER 1

Decline of David

Now KING David was old, advanced in age; and they covered him with clothes, but he could not keep warm.

2 So his servants said to him, "Let them seek a young virgin for my lord the king, and let her [T]attend the king and become his nurse; and let her lie in your bosom, that my lord the king may keep warm."   *stand before*

3 So they searched for a beautiful girl throughout all the territory of Israel, and found Abishag the [R]Shunammite, and brought her to the king. Josh. 19:18; 1 Sam. 28:4

4 And the girl was very beautiful; and she became the king's nurse and served him, but the king did not cohabit with her.

Plot of Adonijah to Be King

5 Now [R]Adonijah the son of Haggith exalted himself, saying, "I will be king." So he prepared for himself chariots and horsemen with fifty men to run before him.   2 Sam. 3:4

6 And his father had never [T]crossed him at any time by asking, "Why have you done so?" And he was also a very handsome man; and he was born after Absalom.   *pained him*

7 And he had conferred with Joab the son of Zeruiah and with Abiathar the priest; and following Adonijah they helped him.

8 But [R]Zadok the priest, Benaiah the son of Jehoiada, Nathan the prophet, Shimei, Rei, and the mighty men who belonged to David, were not with Adonijah.   2 Sam. 20:25

9 And Adonijah sacrificed sheep and oxen and fatlings by the [1]stone of Zoheleth,

[1] Or, *Gliding* or *Serpent Stone*

which is beside [R]En-rogel; and he invited all his brothers, the king's sons, and all the men of Judah, the king's servants.   Josh. 15:7

Anointing of Solomon

10 But he did not invite Nathan the prophet, Benaiah, the mighty men, and [R]Solomon his brother.   2 Sam. 12:24

11 Then Nathan spoke to [R]Bathsheba the mother of Solomon, saying, "Have you not heard that Adonijah the son of Haggith has become king, and David our lord does not know *it*?   2 Sam. 12:24

12 "So now come, please let me [R]give you counsel and save your life and the life of your son Solomon.   [Prov. 15:22]

13 "Go [T]at once to King David and say to him, 'Have you not, my lord, O king, sworn to your maidservant, saying, "Surely [R]Solomon your son shall be king after me, and he shall sit on my throne"? Why then has Adonijah become king?'   *and enter* • 1 Kin. 1:30

14 "Behold, while you are still there speaking with the king, I will come in after you and confirm your words."

15 So Bathsheba went in to the king in the bedroom. Now the king was very old, and Abishag the Shunammite was ministering to the king.

16 Then Bathsheba bowed and prostrated herself [T]before the king. And the king said, "What [T]do you wish?"   *to • to you*

17 And she said to him, "My lord, you swore to your maidservant by the LORD your God, *saying,* 'Surely [R]your son Solomon shall be king after me and he shall sit on my throne.'   1 Kin. 1:13

18 "And now, behold, Adonijah is king; and now, my lord the king, you do not know *it*.

19"And he has sacrificed oxen and fatlings and sheep in abundance, and has invited all the sons of the king and Abiathar the priest and Joab the commander of the army; but he has not invited Solomon your servant.

20"And as for you now, my lord the king, the eyes of all Israel are on you, to tell them who shall sit on the throne of my lord the king after him.

21"Otherwise it will come about, ^Ras soon as my lord the king sleeps with his fathers, that I and my son Solomon will be considered ^Toffenders."   Deut. 31:16 • *sinners*

22 And behold, while she was still speaking with the king, Nathan the prophet came in.

23 And they told the king, saying, "Here is Nathan the prophet." And when he came in before the king, he prostrated himself before the king with his face to the ground.

24 Then Nathan said, "My lord the king, have you said, 'Adonijah shall be king after me, and he shall sit on my throne'?

25"For^R he has gone down today and has sacrificed oxen and fatlings and sheep in abundance, and has invited all the king's sons and the commanders of the army and Abiathar the priest, and behold, they are eating and drinking before him; and they say, 'Long live King Adonijah!'   1 Kin. 1:9

26"But^Rme, *even* me your servant, and Zadok the priest and Benaiah the son of Jehoiada and your servant Solomon, he has not invited.   1 Kin. 1:8, 10

27"Has this thing been done by my lord the king, and you have not shown to your servants who should sit on the throne of my lord the king after him?"

28 Then King David answered and said, "Call Bathsheba to me." And she came into the king's presence and stood before the king.

29 And the king vowed and said, "As^Rthe LORD lives, who has redeemed my life from all distress,   2 Sam. 4:9

30 surely as^RI vowed to you by the LORD the God of Israel, saying, 'Your son Solomon shall be king after me, and he shall sit on my throne in my place'; I will indeed do so this day."   1 Kin. 1:13, 17

31 Then Bathsheba bowed with her face to the ground, and prostrated herself^Tbefore the king and said, "May^Rmy lord King David live forever."   *to* • Dan. 2:4; 3:9

32 Then King David said, "Call to me^RZadok the priest, Nathan the prophet, and Benaiah the son of Jehoiada." And they came into the king's presence.   1 Kin. 1:8

33 And the king said to them, "Take with you^Rthe servants of your lord, and have my son Solomon ride on my own mule, and bring him down to Gihon.   2 Sam. 20:6, 7

34"And let Zadok the priest and Nathan the prophet ^Ranoint him there as king over Israel, and blow the trumpet and say, 'Long live King Solomon!'   1 Sam. 10:1; 16:3, 12

35"Then you shall come up after him, and he shall come and sit on my throne and be king in my place; for I have appointed him to be ruler over Israel and Judah."

36 And Benaiah the son of Jehoiada answered the king and said, "Amen! Thus may the LORD, the God of my lord the king, say.

37"As^Rthe LORD has been with my lord the king, so may He be with Solomon, and make his throne greater than the throne of my lord King David!"   1 Sam. 20:13

38 So ^RZadok the priest, Nathan the prophet, Benaiah the son of Jehoiada, the Cherethites, and the Pelethites went down and had Solomon ride on King David's mule, and brought him to Gihon.   I Kin. 1:8

39 Zadok the priest then ^Rtook the horn of oil from the tent and anointed Solomon. Then they blew the trumpet, and all the people said, "*Long live King Solomon!*"   Ps. 89:20

40 And all the people went up after him, and the people ^Twere playing on flutes and rejoicing with great joy, so that the earth ^Tshook at their noise.   *fluting* • *was split*

Submission of Adonijah

41 Now Adonijah and all the guests who were with him heard *it,* as they finished eating. When Joab heard the sound of the trumpet, he said, "Why ^Tis the city making such an uproar?"   *is the sound of the city an uproar*

42 While he was still speaking, behold, ^RJonathan the son of Abiathar the priest came. Then Adonijah said, "Come in, for ^Ryou are a valiant man and bring good news."   2 Sam. 15:27 • 2 Sam. 18:27

43 But Jonathan answered and said to Adonijah, "No! Our lord King David has made Solomon king.

44"The king has also sent with him Zadok the priest, Nathan the prophet, Benaiah the son of Jehoiada, the Cherethites, and the Pelethites; and they have made him ride on the king's mule.

45"And Zadok the priest and Nathan the prophet have anointed him king in Gihon, and they have come up from there rejoicing, ^Rso that the city is in an uproar. This is the noise which you have heard.   1 Kin. 1:40

46"Besides, Solomon has even taken his seat on the throne of the kingdom.

47"And moreover, the king's servants came to bless our lord King David, saying, 'May^Ryour God make the name of Solomon better than your name and his throne greater than your throne!' And the king bowed himself on the bed.   1 Kin. 1:37

48"The king has also said thus, 'Blessed be the LORD, the God of Israel, who ^Rhas granted one to sit on my throne today while my own eyes see *it.*'"   2 Sam. 7:12; 1 Kin. 3:6

49 Then all the guests of Adonijah were terrified; and they arose and each went on his way.

50 And Adonijah was afraid of Solomon,

and he arose, went and [R]took hold of the horns of the altar. Ex. 27:2; 30:10; 1 Kin. 2:28

51 Now it was told Solomon, saying, "Behold, Adonijah is afraid of King Solomon, for behold, he has taken hold of the horns of the altar, saying, 'Let King Solomon swear to me today that he will not put his servant to death with the sword.' "

52 And Solomon said, "If he will be a worthy man, [R]not one of his hairs will fall to the ground; but if wickedness is found in him, he will die." 1 Sam. 14:45; 2 Sam. 14:11

53 So King Solomon sent, and they brought him down from the altar. And he came and prostrated himself [T]before King Solomon, and Solomon said to him, "Go to your house." *to*

CHAPTER 2

David's Charge to Solomon

As David's [T]time to die drew near, he charged Solomon his son, saying, *days*

2 "I am going the way of all the earth. Be strong, therefore, and show yourself a man.

3 "And keep the charge of the LORD your God, to walk in His ways, to keep His statutes, His commandments, His ordinances, and His testimonies, [R]according to what is written in the law of Moses, that [R]you may succeed in all that you do and wherever you turn, Deut. 17:18-20 · 1 Chr. 22:12, 13

4 so that the LORD may carry out His promise which He spoke concerning me, saying, 'If your sons are careful of their way, to walk before Me in [2]truth with all their heart and with all their soul, you shall not lack a man on the throne of Israel.'

5 "Now you also know what Joab the son of Zeruiah did to me, what he did to the two commanders of the armies of Israel, to Abner the son of Ner, and to Amasa the son of Jether, whom he killed; he also [T]shed the blood of war in peace. And he put the blood of war on his belt [T]about his waist, and on his sandals on his feet. *made · that was about*

6 "So [R]act according to your wisdom, and do not let his gray hair go down to [T]Sheol in peace. 1 Kin. 2:9 · the nether world

7 "But [R]show kindness to the sons of Barzillai the Gileadite, and let them be among those who eat at your table; for they [T]assisted me when I fled from Absalom your brother. 2 Sam. 19:31-38 · came near to

8 "And behold, there is with you Shimei the son of Gera the Benjamite, of Bahurim; now it was he who cursed me with a [A]violent curse on the day I went to Mahanaim. But when he came down to me at the Jordan, I swore to him by the LORD, saying, 'I will not put you to death with the sword.' *grievous*

9 "Now therefore, do not let him go unpunished, [R]for you are a wise man; and you will know what you ought to do to him, and you will bring his gray hair down to [T]Sheol with blood." 1 Kin. 2:6 · the nether world

David Dies—1 Chr. 3:4; 29:26–28

10 Then [R]David slept with his fathers and was buried in the city of David. Acts 2:29

11 And [T]the days that David reigned over Israel *were* forty years: seven years he reigned in Hebron, and thirty-three years he reigned in Jerusalem. 2 Sam. 5:4, 5; 1 Chr. 3:4

Solomon Is Established as King
1 Chr. 29:23

12 And [R]Solomon sat on the throne of David his father, and his kingdom was firmly established. 1 Chr. 29:23; 2 Chr. 1:1

Adonijah Is Executed

13 Now Adonijah the son of Haggith came to Bathsheba the mother of Solomon. And she said, "Do you [R]come peacefully?" And he said, "Peacefully." 1 Sam. 16:4

14 Then he said, "I have something *to say* to you." And she said, "Speak."

15 So he said, "You know that the kingdom was mine and that all Israel [T]expected me to be king; however, the kingdom has turned about and become my brother's, for it was his from the LORD. *set their faces on me*

16 "And now I am making one request of you; do not [3]refuse me." And she said to him, "Speak."

17 Then he said, "Please speak to Solomon the king, for he will not [T]refuse you, that he may give me [R]Abishag the Shunammite as a wife." *turn away your face · 1 Kin. 1:3, 4*

18 And Bathsheba said, "Very well; I will speak to the king for you."

19 So Bathsheba went to King Solomon to speak to him for Adonijah. And the king arose to meet her, bowed before her, and sat on his throne; then he had a throne set for the king's mother, and she sat on his right.

20 Then she said, "I am making one small request of you; do not [T]refuse me." And the king said to her, "Ask, my mother, for I will not refuse you." *turn away my face*

21 So she said, "Let [R]Abishag the Shunammite be given to Adonijah your brother as a wife." 1 Kin. 1:3, 4

22 And King Solomon answered and said to his mother, "And why are you asking Abishag the Shunammite for Adonijah? Ask for him also the kingdom—for he is my older brother—even for him, for Abiathar the priest, and for Joab the son of Zeruiah!"

23 Then King Solomon swore by the LORD, saying, "May God do so to me and more also, if Adonijah has not spoken this word against his own [T]life. *soul*

24 "Now therefore, as the LORD lives, who

---

[2] Or, *faithfulness*
[3] Lit., *turn away my (your) face,* and so in vv. 17, 20

has established me and set me on the throne of David my father, and^Rwho has made me a house as He promised, surely Adonijah will be put to death today." 2 Sam. 7:11, 13

25 So King Solomon^Rsent Benaiah the son of Jehoiada; and he fell upon him so that he died. 2 Sam. 8:18

Abiathar Is Removed

26 Then to Abiathar the priest the king said, "Go to Anathoth to your own field, for you deserve to die; but I will not put you to death at this time, because you carried the ark of the Lord GOD before my father David, and because you were afflicted in everything with which my father was afflicted."

27 So Solomon dismissed Abiathar from being priest to the LORD, in order to fulfill the word of the LORD, which He had spoken concerning the house of Eli in Shiloh.

Joab Is Executed

28 Now the news came to Joab,^Rfor Joab had followed Adonijah,^Ralthough he had not followed Absalom. And Joab fled to the tent of the LORD and took hold of the horns of the altar. 1 Kin. 1:7 • 2 Sam. 17:25

29 And it was told King Solomon that Joab had fled to the tent of the LORD, and behold, he is beside the altar. Then Solomon ^Rsent Benaiah the son of Jehoiada, saying, "Go, fall upon him." 1 Kin. 2:25

30 So Benaiah came to the tent of the LORD, and said to him, "Thus the king has said, 'Come out.' " But he said, "No, for I will die here." And Benaiah brought the king word again, saying, "Thus spoke Joab, and thus he answered me."

31 And the king said to him, "Do^Ras he has spoken and fall upon him and bury him, that you may remove from me and from my father's house the blood which Joab shed without cause. [Ex. 21:14]

32 "And^Rthe LORD will return his blood on his own head,^Rbecause he fell upon two men more righteous and better than he and killed them with the sword, while my father David did not know it: Abner the son of Ner, commander of the army of Israel, and Amasa the son of Jether, commander of the army of Judah. [Gen. 9:6] • 2 Chr. 21:13, 14

33 "So shall their blood return on the head of Joab and on the head of his ^Tdescendants forever; but to David and his ^Tdescendants and his house and his throne, may there be peace from the LORD forever." seed

34 Then^RBenaiah the son of Jehoiada went up and fell upon him and put him to death, and he was buried at his own house^Rin the wilderness. 1 Kin. 2:25 • Matt. 3:1

35 And ^Rthe king appointed Benaiah the son of Jehoiada over the army in his place, and the king appointed Zadok the priest in the place of Abiathar. 1 Kin. 4:4

Shimei Is Executed

36 Now the king sent and called for ^RShimei and said to him, "Build for yourself a house in Jerusalem and live there, and do not go out from there to any place. 1 Kin. 2:8

37 "For it will happen on the day you go out and cross over the brook Kidron, you will know for certain that you shall surely die; your blood shall be on your own head."

38 Shimei then said to the king, "The word is good. As my lord the king has said, so your servant will do." So Shimei lived in Jerusalem many days.

39 But it came about at the end of three years, that two of the servants of Shimei ran away ^Rto Achish son of Maacah, king of Gath. And they told Shimei, saying, "Behold, your servants are in Gath." 1 Sam. 27:2

40 Then Shimei arose and saddled his donkey, and went to Gath to Achish to look for his servants. And Shimei went and brought his servants from Gath.

41 And it was told Solomon that Shimei had gone from Jerusalem to Gath, and had returned.

42 So the king sent and called for Shimei and said to him, "Did I not make you swear by the LORD and solemnly warn you, saying, 'You will know for certain that on the day you depart and go anywhere, you shall surely die'? And you said to me, 'The word which I have heard is good.'

43 "Why then have you not kept the oath of the LORD, and the command which I^Thave laid on you?" commanded

44 The king also said to Shimei, "You know all the evil which^Tyou acknowledge in your heart, which you did to my father David; therefore the LORD shall return your evil on your own head. your heart acknowledges

45 "But King Solomon shall be blessed, and^Rthe throne of David shall be established before the LORD forever." [Prov. 25:5]

46 So the king commanded Benaiah the son of Jehoiada, and he went out and fell upon him so that he died. Thus the kingdom was established in the hands of Solomon.

CHAPTER 3

Unwise Marriage of Solomon

THEN ^RSolomon formed a marriage alliance with Pharaoh king of Egypt, and took Pharaoh's daughter and brought her to the city of David, until he had finished building his own house and the house of the LORD and the wall around Jerusalem. 1 Kin. 7:8

2 ^RThe people were still sacrificing on the high places, because there was no house built for the name of the LORD until those days. Lev. 17:3-5; Deut. 12:2, 13, 14; 1 Kin. 22:43

Request For Wisdom—2 Chr. 1:2-13

3 Now^RSolomon loved the LORD,^Rwalking in the statutes of his father David, except he

sacrificed and burned incense on the high places.   [Deut. 6:5] • 1 Kin. 2:3; 9:4; 11:4, 6, 38

4 [R]And the king went to[R]Gibeon to sacrifice there, for that was the great high place; Solomon offered a thousand burnt offerings on that altar.   2 Chr. 1:3 • Josh. 18:21-25

5 [R]In Gibeon the LORD appeared to Solomon in a dream at night; and God said, "Ask what *you wish* me to give you."   1 Kin. 9:2

6 Then Solomon said, "Thou hast shown great lovingkindness to Thy servant David my father, according as he walked before Thee in [4]truth and righteousness and uprightness of heart toward Thee; and Thou hast[T]reserved for him this great lovingkindness, that Thou hast given him a son to sit on his throne, as *it is* this day.   kept

7"And now, O LORD my God,[R]Thou hast made Thy servant king in place of my father David, yet I am but a little child; I do not know how to go out or come in.   1 Chr. 22:9

8"And[R]Thy servant is in the midst of Thy people which Thou hast chosen,[a]a great people who cannot be numbered or counted for multitude.   [Ex. 19:6] • Gen. 15:5; 22:17

9"So give Thy servant[T]an understanding heart to judge Thy people to discern between good and evil. For who is able to judge this great people of Thine?"   a hearing

10 And it was pleasing in the sight of the Lord that Solomon had asked this thing.

11 And God said to him, "Because you have asked this thing and have not asked for yourself long life, nor have asked riches for yourself, nor have you asked for the life of your enemies, but have asked for yourself discernment to understand justice,

12 behold,[R]I have done according to your words. Behold, I have given you a wise and discerning heart, so that there has been no one like you before you, nor shall one like you arise after you.   [1 John 5:14, 15]

13"And[R]I have also given you what you have not asked, both riches and honor, so that there will not be any among the kings like you all your days.   1 Kin. 4:21-24; 10:23, 27

14"And[R]if you walk in My ways, keeping My statutes and commandments, as your father David walked, then I will [R]prolong your days."   1 Kin. 3:6 • Ps. 91:16; Prov. 3:2

15 Then[R]Solomon awoke, and behold, it was a dream. And he came to Jerusalem and stood before the ark of the covenant of the Lord, and offered burnt offerings and made peace offerings, and[R]made a feast for all his servants.   Gen. 41:7 • 1 Kin. 8:65

Display of Solomon's Wisdom

16 Then two women who were harlots came to the king and stood before him.

17 And the one woman said, "Oh, my lord,[T]this woman and I live in the same house; and I gave birth to a child while *was* in the house.   I and this woman

18"And it happened on the third day after I gave birth, that this woman also gave birth to a child, and we were together. There was no stranger with us in the house, only the two of us in the house.

19"And this woman's son died in the night, because she lay on it.

20"So she arose in the middle of the night and took my son from beside me while your maidservant slept, and laid him in her bosom, and laid her dead son in my bosom.

21"And when I rose in the morning to nurse my son, behold, he was dead; but when I looked at him carefully in the morning, behold, he was not my son, whom I had borne."

22 Then the other woman said, "No! For the living one is my son, and the dead one is your son." But [T]the first woman said, "No! For the dead one is your son, and the living one is my son." Thus they spoke before the king.   this one was saying

23 Then the king said, "The[T] one says, 'This is my son who is living, and your son is the dead one'; and[T]the other says, 'No! For your son is the dead one, and my son is the living one.' "   this one

24 And the king said, "Get me a sword." So they brought a sword before the king.

25 And the king said, "Divide the living child in two, and give half to the one and half to the other."

26 Then the woman whose child *was* the living one spoke to the king, for [T]she[R] was deeply stirred over her son and said, "Oh, my lord, give her the living child, and by no means kill him." But the other said, "He shall be neither mine nor yours; divide *him!*"   her compassion grew warm • Is. 49:15

27 Then the king answered and said, "Give the first woman the living child, and by no means kill him. She is his mother."

National Recognition of Solomon's Wisdom

28 When all Israel heard of the judgment which the king had [T]handed down, they feared the king; for[T]they saw that the wisdom of God was in him to[T]administer justice.   judged • 1 Kin. 3:9 • do

CHAPTER 4

Eleven Princes

NOW King Solomon was king over all Israel.

2 And these were his officials: Azariah the son of Zadok *was*[R]the priest;   1 Chr. 6:10

3 Elihoreph and Ahijah, the sons of Shisha *were* secretaries;[R]Jehoshaphat the son of Ahilud *was* the recorder;   2 Sam. 8:16

4 and[R]Benaiah the son of Jehoiada *was* over the army; and Zadok and [R]Abiathar *were* priests;   1 Kin. 2:35 • 1 Kin. 2:27

5 and Azariah the son of Nathan *was*

[4] Or, *faithfulness*

over the deputies; and Zabud the son of Nathan, a priest, *was* the king's friend;

6 and Ahishar was over the household; and Adoniram the son of Abda *was* over the men subject to forced labor.

Twelve Deputies

7 And Solomon had twelve deputies over all Israel, who[T]provided for the king and his household; each man had to[T]provide for a month in the year.   *nourished • nourish*

8 And these are their names: Ben-hur, in the[R]hill country of Ephraim;   Josh. 24:33

9 Ben-deker in Makaz and Shaalbim and Beth-shemesh and Elonbeth-hanan;

10 Ben-hesed, in Arubboth (Socoh[R]*was* his and all the land of Hepher);   Josh. 15:35

11 Ben-abinadab, *in* all[A]the[R]height of Dor (Taphath the daughter of Solomon was his wife);   *Naphoth-dor • Josh. 11:1, 2*

12 Baana the son of Ahilud, *in*[R]Taanach and Megiddo, and all[R]Beth-shean which is beside Zarethan below Jezreel, from Beth-shean to Abel-meholah as far as the other side of Jokmeam;   Judg. 5:19 • Josh. 17:11

13 Ben-geber, in [R]Ramoth-gilead (the towns of Jair, the son of Manasseh, which are in Gilead were his: the region of Argob, which is in Bashan, sixty great cities with walls and bronze bars *were* his); 1 Kin. 22:3f.

14 Ahinadab the son of Iddo, *in*[R]Mahanaim;   Josh. 13:26

15 Ahimaaz, in Naphtali (he also married Basemath the daughter of Solomon);

16 Baana the son of[R]Hushai, in Asher and [A]Bealoth;   2 Sam. 15:32 • *in Aloth*

17 Jehoshaphat the son of Paruah, in Issachar;

18 Shimei the son of Ela, in Benjamin;

19 Geber the son of Uri, in the land of Gilead, the country of Sihon king of the Amorites and of Og king of Bashan; and *he was* the only deputy who *was* in the land.

Solomon Reigns in Wisdom

20 [R]Judah and Israel *were* as numerous as the sand that is on the[T]seashore in abundance; *they* were eating and drinking and rejoicing.   Gen. 22:17; 32:12; 1 Kin. 3:8 • *sea*

21 [R]Now Solomon ruled over all the kingdoms[R]from the [5]River *to* the land of the Philistines and to the border of Egypt; *they* brought tribute and served Solomon all the days of his life.   2 Chr. 9:26 • Gen. 15:18

22 And Solomon's[T]provision for one day was[T]thirty [6]kors of fine flour and[T]sixty kors of meal,   *bread • 195.72 bushels • 391.44 bushels*

23 ten fat oxen, twenty[T]pasture-fed oxen, a hundred sheep besides deer, gazelles, roebucks, and fattened fowl.   *oxen of the pasture*

24 For he had dominion over everything[T]west of the River, from Tiphsah even to [R]Gaza,[R]over all the kings[T]west of the River; and he had peace on all sides around about him.   *beyond • Judg. 1:18 • Ps. 72:11*

25 [R]So Judah and Israel lived in safety, every man under his vine and his fig tree,[R]from Dan even to Beersheba, all the days of Solomon.   [Jer. 23:6; Mic. 4:4; Zech. 3:10] • 1 Sam. 3:20

26 [R]And Solomon had [7]40,000 stalls of horses for his chariots, and 12,000 horsemen.   1 Kin. 10:26; 2 Chr. 1:14

27 And those deputies[A]provided for King Solomon and all who came to King Solomon's table, each in his month; they left nothing lacking.   *nourished*

28 They also brought barley and straw for the horses and[R]swift steeds to the place where it should be, each according to his charge.   Esth. 8:10, 14; Mic. 1:13

29 Now God gave Solomon wisdom and very great discernment and breadth of mind, like the sand that is on the seashore.

30 And Solomon's wisdom surpassed the wisdom of all[R]the sons of the east and[R]all the wisdom of Egypt.   Gen. 29:1 • Is. 19:11

31 For he was wiser than all men, than Ethan the Ezrahite, Heman, Calcol and Darda, the sons of Mahol; and his[T]fame was *known* in all the surrounding nations.   *name*

32 [R]He also spoke 3,000 proverbs, and his songs were 1,005.   Prov. 1:1; 10:1; Eccl. 12:9

33 And he spoke of trees, from the cedar that is in Lebanon even to the hyssop that grows on the wall; he spoke also of animals and birds and creeping things and fish.

34 And men came from all peoples to hear the wisdom of Solomon, from all the kings of the earth who had heard of his wisdom.

CHAPTER 5

Temple Materials—2 Chr. 2:3–12

NOW Hiram king of Tyre sent his servants to Solomon, when he heard that they had anointed him king in place of his father, for Hiram had[T]always been a friend of David.   *all the day*

2 Then [R]Solomon sent *word* to Hiram, saying,   2 Chr. 2:3

3 "You know that[R]David my father was unable to build a house for the name of the LORD his God because of the wars which surrounded him, until the LORD put them under the soles of his feet.   1 Chr. 28:2, 3

4 "But now the LORD my God has given me rest on every side; there is neither adversary nor[T]misfortune.   *evil occurrence*

5 "And behold,[R]I[T]intend to build a house for the name of the LORD my God, as the LORD spoke to David my father, saying, 'Your son, whom I will set on your throne in your place, he will build the house for My name.'   2 Sam. 7:12, 13; 1 Chr. 17:12 • *say*

6 "Now therefore, command that they cut for me[R]cedars from Lebanon, and my servants will be with your servants; and I will give you wages for your servants according

[5] I.e., Euphrates, and so through v. 24
[6] I.e., One kor equals approx. 10 bushels
[7] One ms. reads 4,000, cf. 2 Chr. 9:25

to all that you say, for you know that there is no one among us who knows how to cut timber like the Sidonians."   2 Chr. 2:8

7 And it came about when Hiram heard the words of Solomon, that he rejoiced greatly and said, "Blessed be the LORD today, who has given to David a wise son over this great people."

8 So Hiram sent *word* to Solomon, saying, "I have heard *the message* which you have sent me; I will do what you desire concerning the cedar and cypress timber.

9 "My servants will bring *them* down from Lebanon to the sea; and I will make them into rafts *to go* by sea to the place where you 'direct me, and I will have them broken up there, and you shall carry *them* away. Then you shall accomplish my desire by giving food to my household."   *send*

10 So Hiram gave Solomon as much as he desired of the cedar and cypress timber.

11 "Solomon then gave Hiram 20,000 kors of wheat as food for his household, and twenty kors of beaten oil; thus Solomon would give Hiram year by year.   2 Chr. 2:10

12 And the LORD gave wisdom to Solomon, just as He promised him; and there was peace between Hiram and Solomon, and the two of them made a covenant.

Temple Laborers—2 Chr. 2:2, 17, 18

13 Now King Solomon 'levied forced laborers from all Israel; and the forced laborers numbered 30,000 men.   *raised up*

14 And he sent them to Lebanon, 10,000 a month in relays; they were in Lebanon a month *and* two months at home. And Adoniram *was* over the forced laborers.

15 Now 'Solomon had 70,000 'transporters, and 80,000 hewers *of stone* in the mountains, 1 Kin. 9:20-22; 2 Chr. 2:17, 18 · *burden bearers*

16 besides Solomon's 3,300 chief deputies who *were* over the project *and* who ruled over the people who were doing the work.

17 Then the king commanded, and they quarried great stones, costly stones, to lay the foundation of the house with cut stones.

18 So Solomon's builders and 'Hiram's builders and the Gebalites 'cut them, and prepared the timbers and the stones to build the house.   Heb., *Hirom's* · *chiseled*

CHAPTER 6

The Temple Is Completed
2 Chr. 3:1–14

Now 'it came about in the four hundred and eightieth year after the sons of Israel came out of the land of Egypt, in the fourth year of Solomon's reign over Israel, in the month of Ziv which is the second month, that he 'began to build the house of the LORD.   2 Chr. 3:1, 2 · *built*

2 As for the house which King Solomon built for the LORD, its length *was* sixty [8]cubits and its width 'twenty *cubits* and its height 'thirty cubits.   90 ft. · 30 ft. · 45 ft.

3 And the porch in front of the nave of the house *was* twenty cubits 'in length, 'corresponding to the width of the house, *and* its depth along the front of the house *was* 'ten cubits.   *in its length · on the face of* · 15 ft.

4 Also for the house 'he made windows with *artistic* frames.   Ezek. 40:16; 41:16

5 And 'against the wall of the house he built stories encompassing the walls of the house around both the nave and the 'inner sanctuary; thus he made side chambers all around.   Ezek. 41:6 · 1 Kin. 6:16, 19, 20

6 The lowest story *was* five cubits wide, and the middle *was* six cubits wide, and the third *was* seven cubits wide; for on the outside he made offsets *in the wall* of the house all around in order that *the beams* should not be inserted in the walls of the house.

7 And 'the house, while it was being built, was built of stone 'prepared at the quarry, and there was neither hammer nor axe nor any iron tool heard in the house while it was being built.   Ex. 20:25; Deut. 27:5, 6 · *finished*

8 The doorway for the [9]lowest side chamber *was* on the right side of the house; and they would go up by winding stairs to the middle *story*, and from the middle to the third.

9 So 'he built the house and finished it; and he covered the house with beams and 'planks of cedar.   1 Kin. 6:14, 38 · *rows*

10 He also built the stories against the whole house, each 'five cubits high; and they 'were fastened to the house with timbers of cedar.   7.5 ft. · *took hold*

11 Now the word of the LORD came to Solomon saying,

12 "Concerning this house which you are building,'if you will walk in My statutes and execute My ordinances and keep all My commandments by walking in them, then I will carry out My word with you which I spoke to David your father.   2 Sam. 7:5-16

13 "And I will dwell among the sons of Israel, and will not forsake My people Israel."

14 "So Solomon built the house and finished it.   1 Kin. 6:9, 38

15 Then he 'built the walls of the house on the inside with boards of cedar; from the floor of the house to the 'ceiling he overlaid *the walls* on the inside with wood, and he overlaid the floor of the house with boards of cypress.   1 Kin. 7:7 · *walls of ceiling*

16 "And he built 'twenty cubits 'on the rear part of the house with boards of cedar from the floor to the 'ceiling; he built *them* for it on the inside as an inner sanctuary, *even as* the most holy place.   2 Chr. 3:8 · 30 ft. · *walls*

17 And the house, that is, the nave in front of the inner sanctuary, was 'forty 'cubits long.   60 ft. · One cubit equals approx. 18 in.

18 And there was cedar on the house

---

[8] I.e., One cubit equals approx. 18 in.
[9] So with Gr. and versions; M.T., *middle*

within, carved *in the shape* of ^{R}gourds and open flowers; all was cedar, there was no stone seen.   1 Kin. 7:24

19 Then he prepared an inner sanctuary within the house in order to place there the ark of the covenant of the LORD.

20 And ^{T}the inner sanctuary *was* twenty cubits in length, ^{T}twenty cubits in width, and twenty cubits in height, and he overlaid it with pure gold. He also overlaid the altar with cedar.   *before* • 30 ft.

21 So Solomon overlaid the inside of the house with pure gold. And he drew chains of gold across the front of the inner sanctuary; and he overlaid it with gold.

22 And he overlaid the whole house with gold, until all the house was finished. Also ^{R}the whole altar which was by the inner sanctuary he overlaid with gold. Ex. 30:1, 3, 6

23 ^{R}Also in the inner sanctuary he made two cherubim of olive wood, each ^{T}ten cubits high.   Ex. 37:7–9; 2 Chr. 3:10–12 • 15 ft.

24 And ^{T}five cubits *was* the one wing of the cherub and five cubits the other wing of the cherub; from the end of one wing to the end of the other wing *were* ten cubits.   7.5 ft.

25 And the other cherub *was* ^{T}ten cubits; both the cherubim were of the same measure and the same form.   15 ft.

26 The height of the one cherub *was* ^{T}ten cubits, and so *was* the other cherub.   15 ft.

27 And he placed the cherubim in the midst of the inner house, and ^{R}the wings of the cherubim were spread out, so that the wing of the one was touching the *one* wall, and the wing of the other cherub was touching the other wall. So their wings were touching each other in the center of the house.   Ex. 25:20; 37:9; 1 Kin. 8:7

28 He also overlaid the cherubim with gold.

29 Then he carved all the walls of the house round about with carved engravings of cherubim, palm trees, and open flowers, inner and outer *sanctuaries*.

30 And he overlaid the floor of the house with gold, inner and outer *sanctuaries*.

31 And for the entrance of the inner sanctuary he made doors of olive wood, the lintel *and* five-sided doorposts.

32 So *he made* two doors of olive wood, and he carved on them carvings of cherubim, palm trees, and open flowers, and overlaid them with gold; and he spread the gold on the cherubim and on the palm trees.

33 So also he made for the entrance of the nave four-sided doorposts of olive wood

34 And ^{R}two doors of cypress wood; the two leaves of the one door turned on pivots, and the two leaves of the other door turned on pivots.   Ezek. 41:23-25

35 And he carved *on it* cherubim, palm trees, and open flowers; and he overlaid *them* with gold evenly applied on the engraved work.

36 And he built the inner court with three rows of cut stone and a row of cedar beams.

37 ^{R}In the fourth year the foundation of the house of the LORD was laid, in the month of Ziv.   1 Kin. 6:1

38 And in the eleventh year, in the month of Bul, which is the eighth month, the house was finished throughout all its parts and according to all its plans. So he was seven years in building it.

CHAPTER 7

Construction of Solomon's House

NOW ^{R}Solomon was building his own house thirteen years, and he finished all his house.   1 Kin. 3:1; 9:10; 2 Chr. 8:1

2 And ^{R}he built the house of the forest of Lebanon; its length was ^{T}100 ^{10}cubits and its width 50 cubits and its height 30 cubits, on four rows of cedar pillars with cedar beams on the pillars. 1 Kin. 10:17, 21; 2 Chr. 9:16 • 150 ft.

3 And it was paneled with cedar above the side chambers which were on the 45 pillars, 15 in each row.

4 And *there were artistic window* frames in three rows, and window was opposite window in three ranks.

5 And all the doorways and doorposts *had* squared *artistic* frames, and window was opposite window in three ranks.

6 Then he made ^{R}the hall of pillars; its length was 50 cubits and its width 30 cubits, and a porch *was* in front of them and pillars and a threshold in front of them.   1 Kin. 7:12

7 And he made the hall of the ^{R}throne where he was to judge, the hall of judgment, and ^{R}it was paneled with cedar from floor to floor.   Ps. 122:5; [Prov. 20:8] • 1 Kin. 6:15, 16

8 And his house where he was to live, the other court inward from the hall, was of the same workmanship. ^{R}He also made a house like this hall for Pharaoh's daughter, whom Solomon had married.   1 Kin. 9:24; 2 Chr. 8:11

9 All these were of costly stones, of stone cut according to measure, sawed with saws, inside and outside; even from the foundation to the coping, and so on the outside to the great court.

10 And the foundation was of costly stones, *even* large stones, stones of ^{T}ten cubits and stones of ^{T}eight cubits.   15 ft. • 12 ft.

11 And above were costly stones, stone cut according to measure, and cedar.

12 ^{R}So the great court all around *had* three rows of cut stone and a row of cedar beams even as the inner court of the house of the LORD, and the porch of the house. 1 Kin. 6:36

Furnishings of the Temple
2 Chr. 3:15—5:1

13 Now ^{R}King Solomon sent and brought Hiram from Tyre.   2 Chr. 2:13, 14; 4:11

14 He was a widow's son from the tribe of Naphtali, and his father was a man of Tyre, a worker in bronze; and he was filled with

^{10} I.e., One cubit equals approx. 18 in.

wisdom and understanding and skill for doing any work in bronze. So he came to King Solomon and performed all his work.

15 And he fashioned [R]the two pillars of bronze; eighteen cubits was the height of one pillar, and a line of twelve cubits measured the circumference of both. 2 Kin. 25:17

16 He also made two capitals of molten bronze to set on the tops of the pillars; the height of the one capital was [T]five cubits and the height of the other capital was five cubits. 7.5 ft.

17 *There were* nets of network and twisted threads of chainwork for the capitals which were on the top of the pillars; seven for the one capital and seven for the other capital.

18 So he made the pillars, and two rows around on the one network to cover the capitals which were on the top of the pomegranates; and so he did for the other capital.

19 And the capitals which *were* on the top of the pillars in the porch were of lily design, [T]four cubits.   6 ft.

20 And *there were* capitals on the two pillars, even above *and* close to the [T]rounded projection which was beside the network; and the pomegranates *numbered* two hundred in rows around both capitals.   *belly*

21 [R]Thus he set up the pillars at the porch of the nave; and he set up the right pillar and named it [11]Jachin, and he set up the left pillar and named it [12]Boaz.   2 Chr. 3:17

22 And on the top of the pillars was lily design. So the work of the pillars was finished.

23 [R]Now he made the sea of cast *metal* [T]ten cubits from brim to brim, circular in form, and its height was five cubits, and thirty cubits in circumference.   2 Chr. 4:2 • 15 ft.

24 And under its brim gourds went around encircling it ten to [T]a cubit, completely surrounding the sea; the gourds were in two rows, cast with the rest.   18 in.

25 [R]It stood on twelve oxen, three facing north, three facing west, three facing south, and three facing east; and the sea *was set* on top of them, and all their rear parts *turned* inward.   2 Chr. 4:4, 5; Jer. 52:20

26 And it was a handbreadth thick, and its brim was made like the brim [T]of a cup, *as* a lily blossom; it could hold [T]two thousand baths.   12,000 gal.

27 Then [R]he made the ten stands of bronze; the length of each stand was [T]four cubits and its width four cubits and its height three cubits.   1 Kin. 7:38; 2 Kin. 25:13; 2 Chr. 4:14 • 6 ft.

28 And this was the design of the stands: they had borders, even borders between the [13]frames,

29 and on the borders which were between the [13]frames *were* lions, oxen and cherubim; and on the [13]frames there *was* a pedestal above, and beneath the lions and oxen *were* wreaths of hanging work.

30 Now each stand had four bronze wheels with bronze axles, and its four feet had supports; beneath the basin *were* cast supports with wreaths at each side.

31 And its opening inside the crown at the top *was* [T]a cubit, and its opening *was* round like the design of a pedestal, [T]a cubit and a half; and also on its opening *there were* engravings, and their borders were square, not round.   18 in. • 27 in.

32 And the four wheels *were* underneath the borders, and the axles of the wheels *were* on the stand. And the height of a wheel *was* a [T]cubit and a half.   27 in.

33 And the workmanship of the wheels *was* like the workmanship of a chariot wheel. Their axles, their rims, their spokes, and their hubs *were* all cast.

34 Now *there were* four supports at the four corners of each stand; its supports *were* part of the stand itself.

35 And on the top of the stand *there was* a circular form half a [T]cubit high, and on the top of the stand its stays and its borders *were* part of it.   One cubit equals approx. 18 in.

36 And he engraved on the plates of its stays and on its borders, cherubim, lions and palm trees, according to the clear space on each, with wreaths *all* around.

37 [R]He made the ten stands like this: all of them had one casting, one measure and one form.   2 Chr. 4:14

38 [R]And he made ten basins of bronze, one basin held [T]forty baths; each basin *was* [T]four cubits, *and* on each of the ten stands *was* one basin.   Ex. 30:18; 2 Chr. 4:6 • 240 gal. • 6 ft.

39 Then he set the stands, five on the right side of the house and five on the left side of the house; and he set the sea *of cast metal* on the right side of the house eastward toward the south.

40 Now Hiram made the basins and the shovels and the bowls. So Hiram finished doing all the work which he performed for King Solomon *in* the house of the LORD:

41 the two pillars and the *two* bowls of the capitals which *were* on the top of the two pillars, and the two networks to cover the two bowls of the capitals which *were* on the top of the pillars;

42 and the four hundred pomegranates for the two networks, two rows of pomegranates for each network to cover the two bowls of the capitals which *were* on the tops of the pillars;

43 and the ten stands with the ten basins on the stands;

44 and [R]the one sea and the twelve oxen under the sea;   1 Kin. 7:23, 25

45 and [R]the pails and the shovels and the bowls; even all these utensils which Hiram made for King Solomon *in* the house of the LORD *were* of polished bronze.   2 Chr. 4:16

46 [R]In the plain of the Jordan the king cast them, in the clay ground between [R]Succoth and Zarethan.   2 Chr. 4:17 • Gen. 33:17

[11] I.e., he shall establish
[12] I.e., in it is strength   [13] Or, *crossbars*

47 And Solomon left all the utensils *un-weighed*, because *they were* too many;[R]the weight of the bronze could not be ascertained.   1 Chr. 22:3, 14

48 And Solomon made all the furniture which *was in* the house of the LORD:[R]the golden altar and the golden table on which *was* the bread of the Presence;   2 Chr. 4:8

49 and the lampstands, five on the right side and five on the left, in front of the inner sanctuary, of pure gold; and[R]the flowers and the lamps and the tongs, of gold; Ex. 25:31-38

50 and the cups and the snuffers and the bowls and the spoons and the[R]firepans, of pure gold; and the hinges both for the doors of the inner house, the most holy place, *and* for the doors of the house, *that is,* of the nave, of gold.   Ex. 27:3; 2 Kin. 25:15

51 Thus all the work that King Solomon performed in the house of the LORD was finished. And Solomon brought in the things dedicated by his father David, the silver and the gold and the utensils, *and* he put them in the treasuries of the house of the LORD.

CHAPTER 8

The Ark Returns—2 Chr. 5:2-12

THEN[R] Solomon assembled the elders of Israel and all[R]the heads of the tribes, the leaders of the fathers' *households* of the sons of Israel, to King Solomon in Jerusalem, to bring up the ark of the covenant of the LORD from the city of David, which is Zion.   2 Chr. 5:2-10 • Num. 1:4; 7:2

2 And all the men of Israel assembled themselves to King Solomon at[R]the feast, in the month Ethanim, which is the seventh month.   Lev. 23:34; 1 Kin. 8:65; 2 Chr. 7:8-10

3 Then all the elders of Israel came, and [R]the priests took up the ark.   Num. 7:9

4 And they brought up the ark of the LORD and the tent of meeting and all the holy utensils, which were in the tent, and the priests and the Levites brought them up.

5 And King Solomon and all the congregation of Israel, who were assembled to him,[R]were with him before the ark, sacrificing so many sheep and oxen they could not be counted or numbered.   2 Chr. 1:6

6 Then the priests brought the ark of the covenant of the LORD to its place, into the inner sanctuary of the house, to the most holy place, under the wings of the cherubim.

7 For the cherubim spread *their* wings over the place of the ark, and the cherubim made a covering over the ark and its poles from above.

8 But[R]the poles were so long that the ends of the poles could be seen from the holy place before the inner sanctuary, but they could not be seen outside; they are there to this day.   Ex. 25:13-15; 37:4, 5

9 [R]There was nothing in the ark except the two tablets of stone which Moses put there at Horeb, where the LORD made a cov-

enant with the sons of Israel, when they came out of the land of Egypt.   Ex. 25:16, 21

The Shekinah Returns—2 Chr. 5:13, 14

10 And it came about when the priests came from the holy place, that[R]the cloud filled the house of the LORD,   Ex. 40:34, 35

11 so that the priests could not stand to minister because of the cloud, for the glory of the LORD filled the house of the LORD.

Solomon's Sermon—2 Chr. 6:1-11

12 [R]Then Solomon said,   2 Chr. 6:1
    "The LORD has said that [R]He would
        dwell in the thick cloud.   Lev. 16:2

13 "I have surely built Thee a lofty house,
    A place for Thy dwelling forever."

14 Then the king faced about and[R]blessed all the assembly of Israel, while all the assembly of Israel was standing.   1 Kin. 8:55

15 And he said, "Blessed[R]be the LORD, the God of Israel,[R]who spoke with His mouth to my father David and has fulfilled *it* with His hand, saying,   1 Chr. 29:10, 20 • 2 Sam. 7:12

16 'Since the day that I brought My people Israel from Egypt, I did not choose a city out of all the tribes of Israel *in which* to build a house that My name might be there, but I chose David to be over My people Israel.'

17 "Now it was[T]in the heart of my father David to build a house for the name of the LORD, the God of Israel.   *with*

18 "But the LORD said to my father David, 'Because it was[T]in your heart to build a house for My name, you did well that it was [T]in your heart.   *with*

19 'Nevertheless you shall not build the house, but your son who shall be born to you, he shall build the house for My name.'

20 "Now the LORD has fulfilled His word which He spoke; for[R]I have risen in place of my father David and sit on the throne of Israel, as the LORD[T]promised, and have built the house for the name of the LORD, the God of Israel.   1 Chr. 28:5, 6 • *spoke*

21 "And there I have set a place for the ark, [R]in which is the covenant of the LORD, which He made with our fathers when He brought them from the land of Egypt."   Deut. 31:26

Solomon's Prayer—2 Chr. 6:12-39

22 Then[R]Solomon stood before the altar of the LORD in the presence of all the assembly of Israel and[R]spread out his hands toward heaven.   1 Kin. 8:54 • Ex. 9:33; Ezra 9:5

23 And he said, "O LORD, the God of Israel, [R]there is no God like Thee in heaven above or on earth beneath,[R]who art keeping covenant and *showing* lovingkindness to Thy servants who walk before Thee with all their heart,   1 Sam. 2:2 • [Deut. 7:9; Neh. 1:5]

24 who hast kept with Thy servant, my father David, that which Thou hast[T]promised him; indeed, Thou hast spoken with Thy

mouth and hast fulfilled it with Thy hand as it is this day.   *spoken to*

25"Now therefore, O LORD, the God of Israel, keep with Thy servant David my father that which Thou hast[T]promised him, saying, 'You[R] shall not lack a man to sit on the throne of Israel, if only your sons take heed to their way to walk before Me as you have walked.'   *spoken to* • 1 Kin. 2:4

26"Now therefore, O God of Israel, let Thy word, I pray Thee, be confirmed[R]which Thou hast spoken to Thy servant, my father David.   2 Sam. 7:25

27"But will God indeed dwell on the earth? Behold, heaven and the[T]highest heaven cannot contain Thee, how much less this house which I have built!   *heaven of heavens*

28"Yet have regard to the prayer of Thy servant and to his supplication, O LORD my God, to listen to the cry and to the prayer which Thy servant prays before Thee today;

29[R]that Thine eyes may be open toward this house night and day, toward the place of which Thou hast said, 'My name shall be there,' to listen to the prayer which Thy servant shall pray toward this place.   Neh. 1:6

30"And listen to the supplication of Thy servant and of Thy people Israel, when they pray toward this place; hear Thou in heaven Thy dwelling place; hear and forgive.

31"If[R]a man sins against his neighbor and is made to take an oath, and he comes *and* takes an oath before Thine altar in this house,   Ex. 22:8-11

32 then hear Thou in heaven and act and judge Thy servants,[R]condemning the wicked by bringing his way on his own head and justifying the righteous by giving him according to his righteousness.   Deut. 25:1

33"When Thy people Israel are [T]defeated before an enemy, because they have sinned against Thee, if they turn to Thee again and confess Thy name and pray and make supplication to Thee in this house,   *smitten*

34 then hear Thou in heaven, and forgive the sin of Thy people Israel, and bring them back to the land which Thou didst give to their fathers.

35"When the heavens are shut up and there is no rain, because they have sinned against Thee, and they pray toward this place and confess Thy name and turn from their sin when Thou dost afflict them,

36 then hear Thou in heaven and forgive the sin of Thy servants and of Thy people Israel,[R]indeed, teach them the good way in which they should walk. And send rain on Thy land, which Thou hast given Thy people for an inheritance.   1 Sam. 12:23; Ps. 5:8; 25:4

37"If there is famine in the land, if there is pestilence, if there is blight *or* mildew, locust *or* grasshopper, if their enemy besieges them in the land of their [T]cities, whatever plague, whatever sickness there is,   *gates*

38 whatever prayer or supplication is made by any man *or* by all Thy people Israel,[T]each knowing the[T]affliction of his own heart, and spreading his hands toward this house;   *who shall know each • plague*

39 then hear Thou in heaven Thy dwelling place, and forgive and act and render to each according to all his ways,[R]whose heart Thou knowest, for Thou alone dost know the hearts of all the sons of men, [1 Sam. 2:3]

40 that they may [14]fear Thee all the days that they live[T]in the land which Thou hast given to our fathers.   *on the face of the land*

41"Also concerning the foreigner who is not of Thy people Israel, when he comes from a far country for Thy name's sake

42 (for they will hear of Thy great name [R]and Thy mighty hand, and of Thine outstretched arm); when he comes and prays toward this house,   Ex. 13:3; Deut. 3:24

43 hear Thou in heaven Thy dwelling place, and do according to all for which the foreigner calls to Thee, in order that all the peoples of the earth may know Thy name, to [14]fear Thee, as *do* Thy people Israel, and that they may know that this house which I have built is called by Thy name.

44"When Thy people go out to battle against their enemy, by whatever way Thou shalt send them, and they pray to the LORD toward the city which Thou hast chosen and the house which I have built for Thy name,

45 then hear in heaven their prayer and their supplication, and maintain their cause.

46"When they sin against Thee (for there is no man who does not sin) and Thou art angry with them and dost deliver them to an enemy, so that they take them away captive to the land of the enemy, far off or near;

47 [R]if they take thought in the land where they have been taken captive, and repent and make supplication to Thee in the land of those who have taken them captive, saying, 'We have sinned and have committed iniquity, we have acted wickedly';   Neh. 9:2

48 [R]if they return to Thee with all their heart and with all their soul in the land of their enemies who have taken them captive, and pray to Thee toward their land which Thou hast given to their fathers, the city which Thou hast chosen, and the house which I have built for Thy name;   Deut. 4:29

49 then hear their prayer and their supplication in heaven Thy dwelling place, and maintain their [T]cause,   *judgment*

50 and forgive Thy people who have sinned against Thee and all their transgressions which they have transgressed against Thee, and make them *objects of* compassion before those who have taken them captive, that they may have compassion on them

51 (for[R]they are Thy people and Thine inheritance which Thou hast brought forth from Egypt,[R]from the midst of the iron furnace),   Ex. 32:11, 12 • Deut. 4:20; Jer. 11:4

[14] Or, *revere*

52 ^Rthat Thine eyes may be open to the supplication of Thy servant and to the supplication of Thy people Israel, to listen to them whenever they call to Thee.   1 Kin. 8:29

53"For Thou hast separated them from all the peoples of the earth as Thine inheritance, as Thou didst speak through Moses Thy servant, when Thou didst bring our fathers forth from Egypt, O Lord GOD."

54 ^RAnd it came about that when Solomon had finished praying this entire prayer and supplication to the LORD,^Rhe arose from before the altar of the LORD, from kneeling on his knees with his ^Thands spread toward heaven.   2 Chr. 7:1 • 2 Chr. 6:13 • *palms*

55 And he stood and blessed all the assembly of Israel with a loud voice, saying,

56"Blessed be the LORD, who has given rest to His people Israel, according to all that He^Tpromised; not one word has failed of all His good promise, which He^Tpromised through Moses His servant.   *spoke*

57"May the LORD our God be with us, as He was with our fathers;^Rmay He not leave us or forsake us,   Deut. 31:6, 17; Josh. 1:5

58 that^RHe may incline our hearts to Himself, to walk in all His ways and to keep His commandments and His statutes and His ordinances, which He commanded our fathers.   Ps. 119:36; Jer. 31:33

59"And may these words of mine, with which I have made supplication before the LORD, be near to the LORD our God day and night, that He may maintain the ^Tcause of His servant and the cause of His people Israel, as each day requires,   *judgment*

60 so^Rthat all the peoples of the earth may know that^Rthe LORD is God; there is no one else.   Josh. 4:24 • Deut. 4:35; 1 Kin. 18:39

61"Let^Ryour heart therefore be^Twholly devoted to the LORD our God, to walk in His statutes and to keep His commandments, as at this day."   Deut. 18:13 • *complete with*

Israel Rejoices—2 Chr. 7:4-10

62 ^RNow the king and all Israel with him offered sacrifice before the LORD.   2 Chr. 7:4

63 And Solomon offered for the sacrifice of peace offerings, which he offered to the LORD, 22,000 oxen and 120,000 sheep.^RSo the king and all the sons of Israel dedicated the house of the LORD.   Ezra 6:15-18; Neh. 12:27

64 On the same day the king consecrated the middle of the court that *was* before the house of the LORD, because there he offered the burnt offering and the grain offering and the fat of the peace offerings; for the bronze altar that *was* before the LORD *was* too small to hold the burnt offering and the grain offering and the fat of the peace offerings.

65 So Solomon observed the feast at that time, and all Israel with him, a great assembly from the entrance of Hamath to the brook of Egypt, before the LORD our God,

for seven days and seven *more* days, *even* fourteen days.

66 On the eighth day he sent the people away and they blessed the king. Then they went to their tents joyful and glad of heart for all the goodness that the LORD had ^Tshown to David His servant and to Israel His people.   *done*

CHAPTER 9

Reiteration of the Davidic Covenant
2 Chr. 7:11-22

NOW^Rit came about when Solomon had finished building the house of the LORD, and ^Rthe king's house, and all that Solomon desired to do,   2 Chr. 7:11 • 1 Kin. 7:1, 2

2 that^Rthe LORD appeared to Solomon a second time, as He had appeared to him at Gibeon.   1 Kin. 3:5; 11:9; 2 Chr. 1:7

3 And the LORD said to him, "I have heard your prayer and your supplication, which you have made before Me; I have consecrated this house which you have built by putting My name there forever, and My eyes and My heart will be there perpetually.

4"And as for you, if you will walk before Me as your father David walked, in integrity of heart and uprightness, doing according to all that I have commanded you *and* will keep My statutes and My ordinances,

5 then I will establish the throne of your kingdom over Israel forever, just as I promised to your father David, saying, 'You shall not lack a man on the throne of Israel.'

6"But if you or your sons shall indeed turn away from following Me, and shall not keep My commandments and My statutes which I have set before you and shall go and serve other gods and worship them,

7 ^Rthen I will cut off Israel from the land which I have given them, and^Rthe house which I have consecrated for My name, I will^Tcast out of My sight. So Israel will become a proverb and a byword among all peoples.   Deut. 4:26 • [Jer. 7:4-14] • *send*

8"And this house will become a heap of ruins; everyone who passes by will be astonished and hiss and say, 'Why has the LORD done thus to this land and to this house?'

9"And they will say, 'Because they forsook the LORD their God, who brought their fathers out of the land of Egypt, and adopted other gods and worshiped them and served them, therefore the LORD has brought all this adversity on them.'"

Sale of Cities in Israel—2 Chr. 8:1, 2

10 ^RAnd it came about^Rat the end of twenty years in which Solomon had built the two houses, the house of the LORD and the king's house   2 Chr. 8:1 • 1 Kin. 6:37, 38; 7:1; 9:1

11 (Hiram king of Tyre had supplied Solomon with cedar and cypress timber and gold according to all his desire), then King

Solomon gave Hiram twenty cities in the land of Galilee.

12 So Hiram came out from Tyre to see the cities which Solomon had given him, and they did not please him.

13 And he said, "What are these cities which you have given me, my brother?" So [T]they were called the land of [15]Cabul[R]to this day.   *he called them* • Josh. 19:27

14 [R]And Hiram sent to the king[T]120 talents of gold.   1 Kin. 9:11 • $691,200,000

Enslavement of the Canaanites
2 Chr. 8:4–18

15 Now this is the account of the forced labor which King Solomon[R]levied to build the house of the LORD, his own house, the [16]Millo[R], the wall of Jerusalem, Hazor, Megiddo, and Gezer.   1 Kin. 5:13 • 2 Sam. 5:9

16 *For* Pharaoh king of Egypt had gone up and captured Gezer, and burned it with fire, and killed the[R]Canaanites who lived in the city, and had given it *as* a dowry to his daughter, Solomon's wife.   Josh. 16:10

17 So Solomon rebuilt Gezer and the lower[R]Beth-horon   Josh. 10:10; 16:3; 21:22; 2 Chr. 8:5

18 and[R]Baalath and Tamar in the wilderness, in the land *of Judah,*   Josh. 19:44

19 and all the storage cities which Solomon had, even the cities for his chariots and the cities for his horsemen, and all that it pleased Solomon to build in Jerusalem, in Lebanon, and in all the land under his rule.

20 *As for* all the people who were left of the Amorites, the Hittites, the Perizzites, the Hivites and the Jebusites, who were not of the sons of Israel,

21 [R]their descendants who were left after them in the land[R]whom the sons of Israel were unable to destroy utterly, from them Solomon levied forced laborers, even to this day.   Judg. 1:21-29 • Josh. 15:63; 17:12

22 But Solomon did not make slaves of the sons of Israel; for they were men of war, his servants, his princes, his captains, his chariot commanders, and his horsemen.

23 These *were* the[c]chief[R]officers who were over Solomon's work, five hundred and fifty, who ruled over the people doing the work.   *officers of the deputies* • 2 Chr. 8:10

24 As soon as[R]Pharaoh's daughter came up from the city of David to her house which *Solomon* had built for her,[R]then he built the Millo.   1 Kin. 3:1 • 2 Sam. 5:9

25 Now three times in a year Solomon offered burnt offerings and peace offerings on the altar which he built to the LORD, burning incense with them *on the altar* which *was* before the LORD. So he finished the house.

26 King Solomon also built a fleet of ships in Ezion-geber, which is near Eloth on the shore of the Red Sea, in the land of Edom.

27 [R]And Hiram sent his servants with the fleet, sailors who knew the sea, along with the servants of Solomon.   1 Kin. 5:6, 9; 10:11

28 And they went to Ophir, and took four hundred and twenty talents of gold from there, and brought *it* to King Solomon.

CHAPTER 10

Multiplication of Wealth—2 Chr. 9:1-24

NOW when the [R]queen of [R]Sheba heard about the fame of Solomon concerning the name of the LORD, she came to test him with difficult questions.   2 Chr. 9:1 • Gen. 10:7

2 So she came to Jerusalem with a very large retinue, with camels carrying spices and very much gold and precious stones. When she came to Solomon, she spoke with him about all that was in her heart.

3 And Solomon answered all her questions; nothing was hidden from the king which he did not[T]explain to her.   *tell her*

4 When the queen of Sheba perceived all the wisdom of Solomon, the house that he had built,

5 the food of his table, the seating of his servants, the attendance of his waiters and their attire, his cupbearers, and his stairway by which he went up to the house of the LORD, there was no more spirit in her.

6 Then she said to the king, "It was a true report which I heard in my own land about your words and your wisdom.

7 "Nevertheless I did not believe the[T]reports, until I came and my eyes had seen it. And behold, the half was not told me. You exceed *in* wisdom and prosperity the report which I heard.   *words*

8 "How [R]blessed are your men, how blessed are these your servants who stand before you continually *and* hear your wisdom.   Prov. 8:34

9 "Blessed[R]be the LORD your God who delighted in you to set you on the throne of Israel; because the LORD loved Israel forever, therefore He made you king, to do justice and righteousness."   1 Kin. 5:7

10 And[R]she gave the king[T]a hundred and twenty talents of gold, and a very great *amount* of spices and precious stones. Never again did such abundance of spices come in as that which the queen of Sheba gave King Solomon.   1 Kin. 10:2 • $691,200,000

11 [R]And also the ships of Hiram, which brought gold from Ophir, brought in from Ophir a very great *number of* almug trees and precious stones.   1 Kin. 9:27, 28; Job 22:24

12 And the king made of the almug trees supports for the house of the LORD and for the king's house, also lyres and harps for the singers; such almug trees have not come in *again,* nor have they been seen to this day.

13 And King Solomon gave to the queen of Sheba all her desire which she requested, besides what he gave her according to his

---

[15] I.e., as good as nothing   [16] I.e., citadel

royal bounty. Then she turned and went to her own land together with her servants.

14 [R]Now the weight of gold which came in to Solomon in one year *was* [t]666 talents of gold,   2 Chr. 9:13-28 · $3,836,160,000

15 besides *that* from the traders and the [17]wares of the merchants and all the kings of the[R]Arabs and the governors of the country.   2 Chr. 9:14

16 And King Solomon made 200 large shields of beaten gold,[T]using 600 *shekels of* gold on each large shield.   *he brought up*

17 And *he* made 300 shields of beaten gold, [t]using [T]three minas of gold on each shield, and the king put them in the house of the forest of Lebanon. *he brought up* · $288,000

18 Moreover, the king made a great throne of[R]ivory and overlaid it with refined gold.   1 Kin. 10:22; 2 Chr. 9:17; Ps. 45:8

19 There *were* six steps to the throne and a round top to the throne at its rear, and [T]arms on each side of the seat, and two lions standing beside the[T]arms.   *hands*

20 And twelve lions were standing there on the six steps on the one side and on the other; nothing like *it* was made for any other kingdom.

21 And all King Solomon's drinking vessels *were* of gold, and all the vessels of the house of the forest of Lebanon *were* of pure gold. None was of silver; it was not considered [18]valuable in the days of Solomon.

22 For[R]the king had at sea the ships of Tarshish with the ships of Hiram; once every three years the ships of Tarshish came bringing gold and silver, ivory and apes and peacocks.   1 Kin. 9:26-28; 22:48; 2 Chr. 20:36

23 [R]So King Solomon became greater than all the kings of the earth in riches and in wisdom.   1 Kin. 3:12, 13; 4:30

24 And all the earth was seeking the presence of Solomon,[R]to hear his wisdom which God had put in his heart.   1 Kin. 3:9, 12, 28

25 And[R]they brought every man his gift, articles of silver and gold, garments, weapons, spices, horses, and mules, so much year by year.   Ps. 68:29

Multiplication of Horses
2 Chr. 1:14-17; 9:25-28

26 [R]Now Solomon gathered chariots and horsemen; and he had 1,400 chariots and 12,000 horsemen, and he[T]stationed them in the[R]chariot cities and with the king in Jerusalem.   1 Kin. 4:26 · Heb., *led* · 1 Kin. 9:19

27 [R]And the king made silver *as common* as stones in Jerusalem, and he made cedars as plentiful as sycamore trees that are in the [19]lowland.   [Deut. 17:17]; 2 Chr. 1:15

28 Also Solomon's import of horses was from Egypt and Kue, and the king's merchants procured *them* from Kue for a price.

29 And a chariot was imported from Egypt for 600 *shekels* of silver, and a horse for 150; and by the same means they exported them[R]to all the kings of the Hittites and to the kings of the Arameans.   2 Kin. 7:6

CHAPTER 11

Intermarriage with Foreign Women

NOW[R]King Solomon loved many foreign women along with the daughter of Pharaoh: Moabite, Ammonite, Edomite, Sidonian, and Hittite women, [Deut. 17:17; Neh. 13:23-27]

2 from the nations concerning which the LORD had said to the sons of Israel, "You shall not[T]associate with them, neither shall they[T]associate with you, *for* they will surely turn your heart away after their gods." Solomon held fast to these in love.   *go among*

3 [R]And he had seven hundred wives, princesses, and three hundred concubines, and his wives turned his heart away. 2 Sam. 5:13f.

Worship of Idols

4 For it came about when Solomon was old, his wives turned his heart away after other gods; and[R]his heart was not [20]wholly devoted to the LORD his God, as the heart of David his father *had been*.   1 Kin. 9:4

5 For Solomon went after Ashtoreth the goddess of the Sidonians and after Milcom the detestable idol of the Ammonites.

6 And Solomon did what was evil in the sight of the LORD, and did not follow the LORD fully, as David his father *had done*.

7 Then Solomon built a high place for [R]Chemosh the detestable idol of Moab, on the mountain which is [T]east of Jerusalem, and for Molech the detestable idol of the sons of Ammon.   Judg. 11:24 · *before*

8 Thus also he did for all his foreign wives, who burned incense and sacrificed to their gods.

The Rebuke of God

9 Now[R]the LORD was angry with Solomon[R]because his heart was turned away from the LORD, the God of Israel, who had appeared to him twice, Ps. 90:7 · 1 Kin. 11:2, 4

10 and[R]had commanded him concerning this thing, that he should not go after other gods; but he did not observe what the LORD had commanded.   1 Kin. 6:12; 9:6, 7

11 So the LORD said to Solomon, "Because [T]you have done this, and you have not kept My covenant and My statutes, which I have commanded you,[R]I will surely tear the kingdom from you, and will give it to your servant.   *this is with you* · 1 Sam. 2:30

12 "Nevertheless I will not do it in your days for the sake of your father David, *but* I will tear it out of the hand of your son.

13 "However,[R] I will not tear away all the kingdom, *but*[R]I will give one tribe to your

[17] Or, *traffic*   [18] Lit., *anything*
[19] Or, *Shephelah*   [20] Lit., *complete with*

son for the sake of My servant David and for the sake of Jerusalem which I have chosen."   2 Sam. 7:15 • 1 Kin. 11:32, 36; 12:20

The Chastisement of God

14 Then the LORD raised up an adversary to Solomon, Hadad the Edomite; he was of the ᵀroyal line in Edom.   *king's seed*
15 For it came about,ᴿwhen David was in Edom, and Joab the commander of the army had gone up to bury the slain, and had struck down every male in Edom 2 Sam. 8:14
16 (for Joab and all Israel stayed there six months, until he had cut off every male in Edom),
17 that Hadad fled to Egypt, he and certain Edomites of his father's servants with him, while Hadad *was* a young boy.
18 And they arose from Midian and came to Paran; and they took men with them from Paran and came to Egypt, to Pharaoh king of Egypt, who gave him a house and assigned him food and gave him land.
19 Now Hadad found great favor ᵀbefore Pharaoh, so that he gave him in marriage the sister of his own wife, the sister of Tahpenes the queen.   *in the sight of*
20 And the sister of Tahpenes bore his son Genubath, whom Tahpenes weaned in Pharaoh's house; and Genubath was in Pharaoh's house among the sons of Pharaoh.
21 Butᴿwhen Hadad heard in Egypt that David slept with his fathers, and that Joab the commander of the army was dead, Hadad said to Pharaoh, "Send me away, that I may go to my own country."   1 Kin. 2:10
22 Then Pharaoh said to him, "But what have you lacked with me, that behold, you are seeking to go to your own country?" And he answered, "Nothing; nevertheless you must surelyᵀlet me go."   *send me away*
23 God also raised up *another* adversary to him, Rezon the son of Eliada, who had fled from his lord Hadadezer king of Zobah.
24 And he gathered men to himself and became leader of a marauding band,ᴿafter David slew them of *Zobah;* and they went to Damascus and stayedᵀthere, and reigned in Damascus.   2 Sam. 10:8, 18 • *in it*
25 So he was an adversary to Israel all the days of Solomon, along with the evil that Hadad *did;* and he abhorred Israel and reigned over Aram.
26 Then Jeroboam the son of Nebat, an Ephraimite of Zeredah, Solomon's servant, whose mother's name was Zeruah, a widow, alsoᵀrebelled against the king. *lifted up a hand*
27 Now this was the reason why heᵀrebelled against the king: Solomon built the Millo, *and* closed up the breach of the city of his father David.   *lifted up a hand*
28 Now the man Jeroboam was a valiant warrior, and when Solomon saw that the young man was ᵀindustrious, he appointed him over all theᵀforced labor of the house of Joseph.   *a doer of work • burden*

29 And it came about at that time, when Jeroboam went out of Jerusalem, thatᴿthe prophet Ahijah the Shilonite found him on the road. Now ᵀAhijah had clothed himself with a new cloak; and both of them were alone in the field.   1 Kin. 12:15; 14:2 • *he*
30 ThenᴿAhijah took hold of the new cloak which was on him, and tore it into twelve pieces.   1 Sam. 15:27, 28
31 And he said to Jeroboam, "Take for yourself ten pieces; for thus says the LORD, the God of Israel, 'Behold, ᴿI will tear the kingdom out of the hand of Solomon and give you ten tribes   1 Kin. 11:11, 12
32 (butᴿhe will have one tribe, for the sake of My servant David and for the sake of Jerusalem, the city which I have chosen from all the tribes of Israel),   1 Kin. 11:13; 12:21
33 because they have forsaken Me, and ᴿhave worshiped Ashtoreth the goddess of the Sidonians,ᴿChemosh the god of Moab, and Milcom the god of the sons of Ammon; and they have not walked in My ways, doing what is right in My sight and *observing* My statutes and My ordinances, as his father David *did*.   1 Sam. 7:3 • Num. 21:29
34 'Nevertheless I will not take the whole kingdom out of his hand, but I will make him ruler all the days of his life, for the sake of My servant David whom I chose, who observed My commandments and My statutes;
35 but ᴿI will take the kingdom from his son's hand and give it to you, *even* ten tribes.   1 Kin. 11:12; 12:16, 17
36 'But to his son I will give one tribe, that My servant David may have a lamp always before Me in Jerusalem, the city where I have chosen for Myself to put My name.
37 'And I will take you, and you shall reign over whateverᵀyou desire, and you shall be king over Israel.   *your soul desires*
38 'Then it will be, that if you listen to all that I command you and walk in My ways, and do what is right in My sight by observing My statutes and My commandments, as My servant David did, then I will be with you and build you an enduring house as I built for David, and I will give Israel to you.
39 'Thus I will afflict the ᵀdescendants of David for this, but not always.' "   *seed*
40 Solomon sought therefore to put Jeroboam to death; but Jeroboam arose and fled to Egypt to Shishak king of Egypt, and he was in Egypt until the death of Solomon.

Death of Solomon—2 Chr. 9:29–31

41 ᴿNow the rest of the acts of Solomon and whatever he did, and his wisdom, are they not written in the book of the acts of Solomon?   2 Chr. 9:29
42 Thus the time that Solomon reigned in Jerusalem over all Israel was forty years.
43 And Solomon ᴿslept with his fathers

and was buried in the city of his father David, and his son[R]Rehoboam reigned in his place.   1 Kin. 2:10 • 1 Kin. 14:21; Matt. 1:7

CHAPTER 12

Request of Israel to Rehoboam
2 Chr. 10:1-5

THEN[R]Rehoboam went to Shechem, for all Israel had come to[R]Shechem to make him king.   2 Chr. 10:1 • Judg. 9:6

2 Now it came about[R]when Jeroboam the son of Nebat heard *of it*, that[T]he was living in Egypt (for he was yet in Egypt, where he had fled from the presence of King Solomon).   1 Kin. 11:26, 40 • *Jeroboam*

3 Then they sent and called him, and Jeroboam and all the assembly of Israel came and spoke to Rehoboam, saying,

4 "Your[R] father made our yoke hard; now therefore lighten the hard service of your father and his heavy yoke which he put on us, and we will serve you."   1 Sam. 8:11-18

5 Then he said to them, "Depart[T]for[T]three days, then return to me." So the people departed.   1 Kin. 12:12 • *yet three*

Foolish Response of Rehoboam
2 Chr. 10:6-15

6 And King Rehoboam consulted with the elders who had served his father Solomon while he was still alive, saying, "How do you counsel *me* to answer this people?"

7 Then they spoke to him, saying, "If you will be a servant to this people today, will serve them, grant them their petition, and speak good words to them, then they will be your servants forever."   *answer them*

8 But he forsook the counsel of the elders which they had given him, and consulted with the young men who grew up with him and served him.   *who stood before*

9 So he said to them, "What counsel do you give that we may answer this people who have spoken to me, saying, 'Lighten the yoke which your father put on us'?"

10 And the young men who grew up with him spoke to him, saying, "Thus you shall say to this people who spoke to you, saying, 'Your father made our yoke heavy, now you make it lighter for us!' But you shall speak to them, 'My little finger is thicker than my father's loins!

11 'Whereas my father loaded you with a heavy yoke, I will add to your yoke; my father disciplined you with whips, but I will discipline you with scorpions.'"

12 Then Jeroboam and all the people came to Rehoboam on the third day as the king had[T]directed, saying, "Return[R]to me on the third day."   *spoken* • 1 Kin. 12:5

13 And the king answered the people harshly, for he forsook the advice of the elders which they had given him,   *advised*

14 and he spoke to them according to the advice of the young men, saying, "My[T]father made your yoke heavy, but I will add to your yoke; my father disciplined you with whips, but I will discipline you with scorpions."   Ex. 1:13, 14; 5:5-9, 16-18

15 So the king did not listen to the people; for it was a turn *of events* from the LORD, that He might establish His word, which the LORD spoke through Ahijah the Shilonite to Jeroboam the son of Nebat.   Deut. 2:30

Revolt of the Northern Tribes
2 Chr. 10:16-19; 11:1-4

16 When all Israel *saw* that the king did not listen to them, the people answered the king, saying,

"What portion do we have in David?
We have no inheritance in the son of
        Jesse;
[R]To your tents, O Israel!   2 Sam. 20:1
Now look after your own house, David!"
So Israel departed to their tents.

17 But[R]as for the sons of Israel who lived in the cities of Judah, Rehoboam reigned over them.   1 Kin. 11:13, 36

18 Then King Rehoboam sent Adoram, who was over the forced labor, and all Israel stoned him[T]to death. And King Rehoboam made haste to mount his chariot to flee to Jerusalem.   *with stones that he died*

19 [R]So Israel has been in rebellion against the house of David to this day.   2 Kin. 17:21

20 And it came about when all Israel heard that Jeroboam had returned, that they sent and called him to the assembly and made him king over all Israel. None but the tribe of Judah followed the house of David.

21 [R]Now when Rehoboam had come to Jerusalem, he assembled all the house of Judah and the tribe of Benjamin, 180,000 chosen men who were warriors, to fight against the house of Israel to restore the kingdom to Rehoboam the son of Solomon.   2 Chr. 11:1

22 But the word of God came to[R]Shemaiah the man of God, saying,   2 Chr. 11:2; 12:5-7

23 "Speak to Rehoboam the son of Solomon, king of Judah, and to all the house of Judah and Benjamin and to the[R]rest of the people, saying,   1 Kin. 12:17

24 'Thus says the LORD, "You must not go up and fight against your[T]relatives the sons of Israel; return every man to his house,[R]for this thing has come from Me." ' " So they listened to the word of the LORD, and returned and went *their way* according to the word of the LORD.   *brothers* • 1 Kin. 12:15

Sin of Jeroboam

25 Then[R]Jeroboam built Shechem in the hill country of Ephraim, and lived[T]there. And he went out from there and built[R]Penuel.   Gen. 12:6 • *in it* • Gen. 32:30

26 And Jeroboam said in his heart, "Now the kingdom will return to the house of David.

27"If^Rthis people go up to offer sacrifices in the house of the LORD at Jerusalem, then the heart of this people will return to their lord, *even* to Rehoboam king of Judah; and they will kill me and return to Rehoboam king of Judah." [Deut. 12:5–7, 14]

28 So the king ^Tconsulted, and made two golden calves, and he said to them, "It is too much for you to go up to Jerusalem; behold your gods, O Israel, that brought you up from the land of Egypt." *took counsel*

29 And he set^Rone in^RBethel, and the other he put in Dan. Hos. 10:5 • Gen. 28:19

30 Now^Rthis thing became a sin, for the people went *to worship* before the one as far as Dan. 1 Kin. 13:34; 2 Kin. 17:21

31 And he made houses on high places, and made priests from among all the people who were not of the sons of Levi.

32 And Jeroboam^Tinstituted a feast in the eighth month on the fifteenth day of the month, like the feast which is in Judah, and he ^Awent up to the altar; thus he did in Bethel, sacrificing to the calves which he had made. And he stationed in Bethel the priests of the high places which he had made. *made • offered upon*

33 Then he went up to the altar which he had made in Bethel on the fifteenth day in the eighth month, even in the month which he had ^Tdevised in his own heart; and he^Tinstituted a feast for the sons of Israel, and went up to the altar to burn incense. *made*

CHAPTER 13

Warning of the Prophet

NOW behold, there came ^Ra man of God from Judah to Bethel by the word of the LORD, while Jeroboam was standing by the altar to burn incense. 2 Kin. 23:17

2 And he cried against the altar by the word of the LORD, and said, "O altar, altar, thus says the LORD, 'Behold, a son shall be born to the house of David, Josiah by name; and on you he shall sacrifice the priests of the high places who burn incense on you, and human bones shall be burned on you.'"

3 Then he gave a^Tsign the same day, saying, "This is the ^Tsign which the LORD has spoken, 'Behold, the altar shall be split apart and the ^Tashes which are on it shall be poured out.'" *wonder • ashes of fat*

4 Now it came about when the king heard the saying of the man of God, which he cried against the altar in Bethel, that Jeroboam stretched out his hand from the altar, saying, "Seize him." But his hand which he stretched out against him dried up, so that he could not draw it back to himself.

5 The altar also was split apart and the ashes were poured out from the altar, according to the ^Tsign which the man of God had given by the word of the LORD. *wonder*

21 Lit., *soften(ed) the face of*

6 And the king answered and said to the man of God, "Please ²¹entreat^R the LORD your God, and pray for me, that my hand may be restored to me." So^Rthe man of God ²¹entreated the LORD, and the king's hand was restored to him, and it became as it was before. Ex. 8:8, 28; 9:28 • [Luke 6:27, 28]

Sin of the Prophet

7 Then the king said to the man of God, "Come home with me and refresh yourself, and^RI will give you a reward." 2 Kin. 5:15

8 But the man of God said to the king, "If^R you were to give me half your house I would not go with you, nor would I eat bread or drink water in this place. Num. 22:18; 24:13

9"For so ^Tit was commanded me by the word of the LORD, saying, 'You shall eat no bread, nor drink water, nor return by the way which you came.'" *he commanded me*

10 So he went another way, and did not return by the way which he came to Bethel.

11 Now ^Ran old prophet was living in Bethel; and his ^Tsons came and told him all the deeds which the man of God had done that day in Bethel; the words which he had spoken to the king, these also they related to their father. 2 Kin. 23:18 • *son*

12 And their father said to them, "Which^T way did he go?" Now his sons had seen the way which the man of God who came from Judah had gone. *Where is the way he went*

13 Then he said to his sons, "Saddle the donkey for me." So they saddled the donkey for him and he rode away on it.

14 So he went after the man of God and found him sitting under ^Aan oak; and he said to him, "Are you the man of God who came from Judah?" And he said, "I am." a *terebinth*

15 Then he said to him, "Come home with me and eat bread."

16 And he said, "I cannot return with you, nor go with you, nor will I eat bread or drink water with you in this place.

17"For a command *came* to me by the word of the LORD, 'You shall eat no bread, nor drink water there; do not return by going the way which you came.'"

18 And he said to him, "I^R also am a prophet like you, and an angel spoke to me by the word of the LORD, saying, 'Bring him back with you to your house, that he may eat bread and drink water.'" *But* he lied to him. Matt. 7:15; [1 John 4:1]

19 So he went back with him, and ate bread in his house and drank water.

Judgment on the Prophet

20 Now it came about, as they were sitting down at the table, that the word of the LORD came to the prophet who had brought him back;

21 and he cried to the man of God who

came from Judah, saying, "Thus says the LORD, 'Because you have ^Tdisobeyed the command of the LORD, and have not observed the commandment which the LORD your God commanded you,   *rebelled against*

22 but have returned and eaten bread and drunk water in the place of which He said to you, "Eat no bread and drink no water"; your body shall not come to the grave of your fathers.' "

23 And it came about after he had eaten bread and after he had drunk, that he saddled the donkey for him, for the prophet whom he had brought back.

24 Now when he had gone,^Ra lion met him on the way and killed him, and his body was thrown on the road, with the donkey standing beside it; the lion also was standing beside the body.   1 Kin. 20:36

25 And behold, men passed by and saw the body thrown on the road, and the lion standing beside the body; so they came and told *it* in the city where ^Rthe old prophet lived.   1 Kin. 13:11

26 Now when the prophet who brought him back from the way heard *it*, he said, "It is the man of God, who disobeyed the command of the LORD; therefore the LORD has given him to the lion, which has torn him and killed him, according to the word of the LORD which He spoke to him."

27 Then he spoke to his sons, saying, "Saddle the donkey for me." And they saddled *it*.

28 And he went and found his body thrown on the road with the donkey and the lion standing beside the body; the lion had not eaten the body nor torn the donkey.

29 So the prophet took up the body of the man of God and laid it on the donkey, and brought it back and he came to the city of the old prophet to mourn and to bury him.

30 And he laid his body in his own grave, and they mourned over him, *saying*, "Alas,^R my brother!"   Jer. 22:18

31 And it came about after he had buried him, that he spoke to his sons, saying, "When I die, bury me in the grave in which the man of God is buried;^Rlay my bones beside his bones.   Ruth 1:17; 2 Kin. 23:17, 18

32"For^Rthe thing shall surely come to pass which he cried by the word of the LORD against the altar in Bethel and against all the houses of the high places which are in the cities of Samaria."   1 Kin. 13:2

Continued Sin of Jeroboam

33 After this event Jeroboam did not return from his evil way, but again he made priests of the high places from among 'all the people; any who would, he ordained, to be priests of the high places.   *extremities of*

34 ^RAnd this event became sin to the house of Jeroboam, even to blot *it* out and destroy *it* from off the face of the earth.   1 Kin. 12:30

CHAPTER 14

Judgment on Jeroboam

AT that time Abijah the son of Jeroboam became sick.

2 And Jeroboam said to his wife, "Arise now, and^Rdisguise yourself so that they may not know that you are the wife of Jeroboam, and go to Shiloh; behold, Ahijah the prophet is there, who spoke concerning me *that I would be* king over this people.   1 Sam. 28:8

3"And take ten loaves with you, *some* cakes and a jar of honey, and go to him. He will tell you what will happen to the boy."

4 And Jeroboam's wife did so, and arose and went to Shiloh, and came to the house of Ahijah. Now Ahijah could not see, for his eyes were 'dim because of his age.   *set*

5 Now the LORD had said to Ahijah, "Behold, the wife of Jeroboam is coming to 'inquire of you concerning her son, for he is sick. You shall say thus and thus to her, for it will be when she arrives that she will pretend to be another woman."   *seek a word from*

6 And it came about when Ahijah heard the sound of her feet coming in the doorway, that he said, "Come in, wife of Jeroboam, why do you pretend to be another woman? For I am sent to you *with* a harsh message.

7"Go, say to Jeroboam, 'Thus says the LORD God of Israel, "Because^RI exalted you from among the people and made you leader over My people Israel,   2 Sam. 12:7

8 and^Rtore the kingdom away from the house of David and gave it to you—yet you have not been like My servant David, who kept My commandments and who followed Me with all his heart, to do only that which was right in My sight;   1 Kin. 11:31

9 you also have done more evil than all who were before you, and^Rhave gone and made for yourself other gods and molten images to provoke Me to anger, and have cast Me behind your back—   1 Kin. 12:28

10 therefore behold, I am bringing calamity on the house of Jeroboam, and will cut off from Jeroboam every male person, both bond and free in Israel, and I will make a clean sweep of the house of Jeroboam, as one sweeps away dung until it is all gone.

11"Anyone belonging to Jeroboam who dies in the city the dogs will eat. And he who dies in the field the birds of the heavens will eat; for the LORD has spoken *it*.' "

12"Now you arise, go to your house. When your feet enter the city the child will die.

13"And all Israel shall mourn for him and bury him, for he alone of Jeroboam's *family* shall come to the grave, because in him something good was found toward the LORD God of Israel in the house of Jeroboam.

14"Moreover, the LORD will raise up for Himself a king over Israel who shall cut off the house of Jeroboam this day 'and from now on.   *and what even now?*

15"For the LORD will strike Israel, as a reed is shaken in the water; and[R]He will uproot Israel from this good land which He gave to their fathers, and will scatter them beyond the *Euphrates* River, because they have made their [22]Asherim, provoking the LORD to anger.   Deut. 29:28; 2 Kin. 17:6; Ps. 52:5

16"And He will give up Israel on account of the sins of Jeroboam, which he committed and with which he made Israel to sin."

17 Then Jeroboam's wife arose and departed and came to[R]Tirzah. [R]As she was entering the threshold of the house, the child died.   1 Kin. 15:21 • 1 Kin. 14:12

18 [R]And all Israel buried him and mourned for him, according to the word of the LORD which He spoke through His servant Ahijah the prophet.   1 Kin. 14:13

19 Now the rest of the acts of Jeroboam, [R]how he made war and how he reigned, behold, they are written in the Book of the Chronicles of the Kings of Israel. 1 Kin. 14:30

20 And the time that Jeroboam reigned *was* twenty-two years; and he slept with his fathers, and Nadab his son reigned in his place.

Sin of Rehoboam

21 [R]Now Rehoboam the son of Solomon reigned in Judah. Rehoboam was forty-one years old when he became king, and he reigned seventeen years in Jerusalem, [R]the city which the LORD had chosen from all the tribes of Israel to put His name there. And his mother's name was Naamah the Ammonitess.   2 Chr. 12:13 • 1 Kin. 11:32, 36

22 And Judah did evil in the sight of the LORD, and they provoked Him to jealousy more than all that their fathers had done, with the sins which they committed.

23 For they also built for themselves high places and *sacred* pillars and [T]Asherim on every high hill and beneath every luxuriant tree.   wooden symbols of a female deity

24 And there were also male cult prostitutes in the land. They did according to all the abominations of the nations which the LORD dispossessed before the sons of Israel.

Judgment on Rehoboam—2 Chr. 12:2–16

25 Now it came about in the fifth year of King Rehoboam, that Shishak the king of Egypt came up against Jerusalem.

26 And he took away the treasures of the house of the LORD and the treasures of the king's house, and[R]he took everything, [T]even taking all the shields of gold which Solomon had made.   1 Kin. 15:18 • *and he took away*

27 So King Rehoboam made shields of bronze in their place, and [R]committed them to the [T]care of the commanders of the

[22] I.e., wooden symbols of a female deity. Also v. 23
[23] Lit., *runner(s)*

[23]guard who guarded the doorway of the king's house.   1 Sam. 8:11; 22:17 • *hand*

28 Then it happened as often as the king entered the house of the LORD, that the [23]guards would carry them and would bring them back into the guards' room.

29 [R]Now the rest of the acts of Rehoboam and all that he did, are they not written in the Book of the Chronicles of the Kings of Judah?   2 Chr. 12:15, 16

30 [R]And there was war between Rehoboam and Jeroboam continually.   1 Kin. 12:21; 15:6

31 And Rehoboam slept with his fathers, and was buried with his fathers in the city of David; and[R]his mother's name was Naamah the Ammonitess. And Abijam his son became king in his place.   1 Kin. 14:21

CHAPTER 15

Reign of Abijam in Judah
2 Chr. 13:1, 2; 14:1

N OW[R]in the eighteenth year of King Jeroboam, the son of Nebat, Abijam became king over Judah.   2 Chr. 13:1

2 He reigned three years in Jerusalem; and his mother's name was [R]Maacah the daughter of Abishalom.   2 Chr. 13:2

3 And he walked in all the sins of his father, which he had committed before him; and[R]his heart was not[T]wholly devoted to the LORD his God, like the heart of his father David.   1 Kin. 11:4; Ps. 119:80 • *complete with*

4 But for David's sake the LORD his God gave him a lamp in Jerusalem, to raise up his son after him and to establish Jerusalem;

5 [R]because David did what was right in the sight of the LORD, and had not turned aside from anything that He commanded him all the days of his life, except in the case of Uriah the Hittite.   1 Kin. 9:4; 14:8

6 And there was war between Rehoboam and Jeroboam all the days of his life.

7 Now[R]the rest of the acts of Abijam and all that he did, are they not written in the Book of the Chronicles of the Kings of Judah? [R]And there was war between Abijam and Jeroboam.   2 Chr. 13:2 • 2 Chr. 13:3-20

8 And Abijam slept with his fathers and they buried him in the city of David; and Asa his son became king in his place.

Obedience of Asa—2 Chr. 14:2; 15:16–18

9 So in the twentieth year of Jeroboam the king of Israel, Asa began to reign as king of Judah.

10 And he reigned forty-one years in Jerusalem; and[R]his mother's name was Maacah the daughter of Abishalom.   1 Kin. 15:2

11 And Asa did what was right in the sight of the LORD, like David his father.

12 He also put away the male cult prostitutes from the land, and removed all the idols which his fathers had made.

13 And he also removed Maacah his mother from *being* queen mother, because she had made a horrid image ᴬas an Asherah; and Asa cut down her horrid image and burned *it* at the brook Kidron.   *for Asherah*
14 But the high places were not taken away; nevertheless the heart of Asa was wholly devoted to the LORD all his days.
15 And ᴿhe brought into the house of the LORD the dedicated things of his father and his own dedicated things: silver and gold and utensils.   1 Kin. 7:51

Disobedience of Asa—2 Chr. 16:1–6

16 Now there was war between Asa and Baasha king of Israel all their days.
17 And Baasha king of Israel went up against Judah and ᵀfortified Ramah in order to prevent *anyone* from going out or coming in to Asa king of Judah.   *built*
18 Then ᴿAsa took all the silver and the gold which were left in the treasuries of the house of the LORD and the treasuries of the king's house, and delivered them into the hand of his servants. And King Asa sent them to Ben-hadad the son of Tabrimmon, the son of Hezion, king of Aram, who lived in Damascus, saying,   1 Kin. 14:26; 15:15
19"*Let there be* aᴿtreaty between ᵀyou and me, *as* between my father and your father. Behold, I have sent you a present of silver and gold; go, break your treaty with Baasha king of Israel so that he will withdraw from me."   2 Chr. 16:7 • *me and you*
20 So Ben-hadad listened to King Asa and sent the commanders of his armies against the cities of Israel, and ᵀconquered Ijon, Dan, Abel-beth-maacah and all Chinneroth, besides all the land of Naphtali.   *smote*
21 And it came about when Baasha heard of *it* that ᴿhe ceased ᵀfortifying Ramah, and remained in Tirzah.   1 Kin. 15:17 • *building*
22 Then King Asa made a proclamation to all Judah—none was exempt—and they carried away the stones of Ramah and its timber with which Baasha had built. And King Asa built with them ᴿGeba of Benjamin and Mizpah.   Josh. 18:24; 21:17

Death of Asa—2 Chr. 16:12—17:1

23 ᴿNow the rest of all the acts of Asa and all his might and all that he did and the cities which he built, are they not written in the Book of the Chronicles of the Kings of Judah? But in the time of his old age he was diseased in his feet.   2 Chr. 16:11-14
24 And Asa slept with his fathers and was buried with his fathers in the city of David his father; and ᴿJehoshaphat his son reigned in his place.   1 Kin. 22:41-44; 2 Chr. 17:1

Reign of Nadab in Israel

25 Now ᴿNadab the son of Jeroboam be-

came king over Israel in the second year of Asa king of Judah, and he reigned over Israel two years.   1 Kin. 14:20
26 And he did evil in the sight of the LORD, and walked in the way of his father and in his sin which he made Israel sin.
27 Then ᴿBaasha the son of Ahijah of the house of Issachar conspired against him, and Baasha struck him down at ᵀGibbethon, which belonged to the Philistines, while Nadab and all Israel were laying siege to Gibbethon.   1 Kin. 14:14 • Josh. 19:44; 21:23
28 So Baasha killed him in the third year of Asa king of Judah, and reigned in his place.
29 And it came about, as soon as he was king, he struck down all the household of Jeroboam. He did not leave to Jeroboam ᵀany persons alive, until he had destroyed them, ᴿaccording to the word of the LORD, which He spoke by His servant Ahijah the Shilonite,   *any breath* • 1 Kin. 14:9-16
30 *and* because of the sins of Jeroboam which he sinned, and ᴿwhich he made Israel sin, because of his provocation with which he provoked the LORD God of Israel to anger.   1 Kin. 15:26
31 ᴿNow the rest of the acts of Nadab and all that he did, are they not written in the Book of the Chronicles of the Kings of Israel?   1 Kin. 14:19

Reign of Baasha in Israel

32 And there was war between Asa and Baasha king of Israel all their days.
33 In the third year of Asa king of Judah, Baasha the son of Ahijah became king over all Israel at Tirzah, *and reigned* twenty-four years.
34 And he did evil in the sight of the LORD, and ᴿwalked in the way of Jeroboam and in his sin which he made Israel sin. 1 Kin. 15:26

CHAPTER 16

Nᴏw the word of the LORD came to Jehu the son of Hanani against Baasha, saying,
2"Inasmuch as I exalted you from the dust and made you leader over My people Israel, and you have walked in the way of Jeroboam and have made My people Israel sin, provoking Me to anger with their sins,
3 behold, I will consume Baasha and his house, and I will make your house like the house of Jeroboam the son of Nebat.
4"Anyone ᴿof Baasha who dies in the city the dogs shall eat, and anyone of his who dies in the field the birds of the heavens will eat."   1 Kin. 14:11; 21:24
5 ᴿNow the rest of the acts of Baasha and what he did and his might, are they not written in the Book of the Chronicles of the Kings of Israel?   1 Kin. 14:19; 15:31

6 And Baasha slept with his fathers and was buried in[R]Tirzah, and Elah his son became king in his place. 1 Kin. 14:17; 15:21

7 Moreover, the word of the LORD through[R]the prophet Jehu the son of Hanani also came against Baasha and his household, both because of all the evil which he did in the sight of the LORD, provoking Him to anger with the work of his hands, in being like the house of Jeroboam, and because he struck[A]it. 1 Kin. 16:1 • *him*

Reign of Elah in Israel

8 In the twenty-sixth year of Asa king of Judah, Elah the son of Baasha became king over Israel at Tirzah, *and reigned* two years.

9 And his servant[R]Zimri, commander of half his chariots, conspired against him. Now he *was* at Tirzah drinking himself drunk in the house of Arza, who *was* over the household at Tirzah. 2 Kin. 9:30-33

10 Then Zimri went in and struck him and put him to death, in the twenty-seventh year of Asa king of Judah, and became king in his place.

11 And it came about, when he became king, as soon as he sat on his throne, that he [T]killed all the household of Baasha; he did not leave a single male, neither of his[T]relatives nor of his friends. *smote • redeemers*

12 Thus Zimri destroyed all the household of Baasha, [R]according to the word of the LORD, which He spoke against Baasha through Jehu the prophet, 1 Kin. 16:3

13 for all the sins of Baasha and the sins of Elah his son, which they sinned and which they made Israel sin, provoking the LORD God of Israel to anger with their idols.

14 Now the rest of the acts of Elah and all that he did, are they not written in the Book of the Chronicles of the Kings of Israel?

Reign of Zimri in Israel

15 In the twenty-seventh year of Asa king of Judah, Zimri reigned seven days at Tirzah. Now the people were camped against [R]Gibbethon, which belonged to the Philistines. 1 Kin. 15:27

16 And the people who were camped heard it said, "Zimri has conspired and has also struck down the king." Therefore all Israel made Omri, the commander of the army, king over Israel that day in the camp.

17 Then Omri and all Israel with him went up from Gibbethon, and they besieged Tirzah.

18 And it came about, when Zimri saw that the city was taken, that he went into the citadel of the king's house and burned the king's house over him with fire, and [R]died, 1 Sam. 31:4, 5; 2 Sam. 17:23

19 because of his sins which he sinned, doing evil in the sight of the LORD,[R] walking

24 I.e., wooden symbol of a female deity

in the way of Jeroboam, and in his sin which he did, making Israel sin. 1 Kin. 12:28; 14:16

20 Now the rest of the acts of Zimri and his conspiracy which he [T]carried out, are they not written in the Book of the Chronicles of the Kings of Israel? *conspired*

Reign of Omri in Israel

21 Then the people of Israel were divided into two parts: half of the people followed Tibni the son of Ginath, to make him king; the *other* half followed Omri.

22 But the people who followed Omri prevailed over the people who followed Tibni the son of Ginath. And Tibni died and Omri became king.

23 In the thirty-first year of Asa king of Judah, Omri became king over Israel, *and reigned* twelve years; he reigned six years at [R]Tirzah. 1 Kin. 15:21

24 And he bought the hill [T]Samaria from Shemer for two talents of silver; and he built on the hill, and named the city which he built Samaria, after the name of Shemer, the owner of the hill. *Heb., Shomeron*

25 And[R]Omri did evil in the sight of the LORD, and[R]acted more wickedly than all who *were* before him. Mic. 6:16 • 1 Kin. 14:9

26 For he walked in all the way of Jeroboam the son of Nebat and in his sins which he made Israel sin, provoking the LORD God of Israel with their[T]idols. *vanities*

27 Now the rest of the acts of Omri which he did and his might which he [T]showed, are they not written in the Book of the Chronicles of the Kings of Israel? *did*

28 So Omri slept with his fathers, and was buried in Samaria; and Ahab his son became king in his place.

Sin of Ahab

29 Now Ahab the son of Omri became king over Israel in the thirty-eighth year of Asa king of Judah, and Ahab the son of Omri reigned over Israel in Samaria twenty-two years.

30 And Ahab the son of Omri did evil in the sight of the LORD[R]more than all who were before him. 1 Kin. 14:9; 16:25

31 And it came about, as though it had been a trivial thing for him to walk in the sins of Jeroboam the son of Nebat, that[R]he married Jezebel the daughter of Ethbaal king of the Sidonians, and went to serve Baal and worshiped him. Deut. 7:1-5

32 So he erected an altar for Baal in the house of Baal, which he built in Samaria.

33 And Ahab also made[R]the [24]Asherah. Thus [R]Ahab did more to provoke the LORD God of Israel than all the kings of Israel who were before him. 2 Kin. 13:6 • 1 Kin. 14:9

34 [R]In his days Hiel the Bethelite built Jericho; he laid its foundations with the *loss of*

Abiram his first-born, and set up its gates with the *loss of* his youngest son Segub, according to the word of the LORD, which He spoke by Joshua the son of Nun.   Josh. 6:26

CHAPTER 17

Prophecy of the Drought

N OW Elijah the Tishbite, who was of the settlers of Gilead, said to Ahab, "As the LORD, the God of Israel lives, before whom I stand, surely there shall be neither dew nor rain these years, except by my word."

Miracle of Food

2 And the word of the LORD came to him, saying,

3 "Go away from here and turn eastward, and hide yourself by the brook Cherith, which is east of the Jordan.   *before*

4 "And it shall be that you shall drink of the brook, and ᴿI have commanded the ravens to provide for you there."   1 Kin. 17:9

5 So he went and did according to the word of the LORD, for he went and lived by the brook Cherith, which is east of the Jordan.   *before*

6 And the ravens brought him bread and meat in the morning and bread and meat in the evening, and he would drink from the brook.

7 And it happened after a while, that the brook dried up, because there was no rain in the land.

8 Then the word of the LORD came to him, saying,

9 "Arise, go to ᴿZarephath, which belongs to Sidon, and stay there; behold, ᴿI have commanded a widow there to provide for you."   Obad. 20; Luke 4:26 • 1 Kin. 17:4

10 So he arose and went to Zarephath, and when he came to the gate of the city, behold, a widow was there gathering sticks; and he called to her and said, "Please get me a little water in a jar, that I may drink."

11 And as she was going to get *it*, he called to her and said, "Please bring me a piece of bread in your hand."

12 But she said, "As the LORD your God lives, I have no bread, only a handful of flour in the bowl and a little oil in the jar; and behold, I am gathering a few sticks that I may go in and prepare for me and my son, that we may eat it and die."   *cake*

13 Then Elijah said to her, "Do not fear; go, do as you have said, but make me a little bread cake from it first, and bring *it* out to me, and afterward you may make *one* for yourself and your son.   *there*

14 "For thus says the LORD God of Israel, 'The bowl of flour shall not be exhausted, nor shall the jar of oil be empty, until the

day that the LORD sends rain on the face of the earth.' "   *pitcher • lack*

15 So she went and did according to the word of Elijah, and she and he and her household ate for *many* days.

16 The bowl of flour was not exhausted nor did the jar of oil become empty, according to the word of the LORD which He spoke through Elijah.   *pitcher • lack*

Miracle of the Resurrection of the Gentile Son

17 Now it came about after these things, that the son of the woman, the mistress of the house, became sick; and his sickness was so severe, that there was no breath left in him.

18 So she said to Elijah, "What do I have to do with you, O man of God? You have come to me to bring my iniquity to remembrance, and to put my son to death!"

19 And he said to her, "Give me your son." Then he took him from her bosom and carried him up to the upper room where he was living, and laid him on his own bed.

20 And he called to the LORD and said, "O LORD my God, hast Thou also brought calamity to the widow with whom I am staying, by causing her son to die?"   *sojourning*

21 Then he stretched himself upon the child three times, and called to the LORD, and said, "O LORD my God, I pray Thee, let this child's life return to him."   Acts 20:10

22 And the LORD heard the voice of Elijah, ᴿand the life of the child returned to him and he revived.   Luke 7:14 • *upon his inward part*

23 And Elijah took the child, and brought him down from the upper room into the house and gave him to his mother; and Elijah said, "See, your son is alive."

24 Then the woman said to Elijah, "Now ᴿI know that you are a man of God, and that the word of the LORD in your mouth is truth."   John 2:11; 3:2; 16:30

CHAPTER 18

Challenge to Ahab

N OW it came about ᴿafter many days, that the word of the LORD came to Elijah in the third year, saying, "Go, show yourself to Ahab, and ᴿI will send rain on the face of the earth."   1 Kin. 17:1 • Deut. 28:12

2 So Elijah went to show himself to Ahab. Now the famine *was* severe in Samaria.

3 And Ahab called Obadiah ᴿwho *was* over the household. (Now Obadiah ²⁵feared ᴿthe LORD greatly;   1 Kin. 16:9 • Neh. 7:2

4 for it came about, ᴿwhen Jezebel ᵀdestroyed the prophets of the LORD, that Obadiah took a hundred prophets and hid them

²⁵ Or, *revered*

by fifties in a cave, and provided them with bread and water.) 1 Kin. 18:13 · *cut off*

5 Then Ahab said to Obadiah, "Go through the land to all the springs of water and to all the valleys; perhaps we will find grass and keep the horses and mules alive, and not have to kill some of the cattle."

6 So they divided the land between them to survey it; Ahab went one way by himself and Obadiah went another way by himself.

7 Now as Obadiah was on the way, behold, Elijah[T]met him,[R]and he recognized him and fell on his face and said, "Is this you, Elijah my master?"   *to meet* · 2 Kin. 1:6-8

8 And he said to him, "It is I. Go, say to your master, 'Behold, Elijah *is here.*'"

9 And he said, "What sin have I committed, that you are giving your servant into the hand of Ahab, to put me to death?

10"As the LORD your God lives, there is no nation or kingdom where my master has not sent to search for you; and when they said, 'He is not *here,*' he made the kingdom or nation swear that they could not find you.

11"And now you are saying, 'Go, say to your master, "Behold, Elijah *is here."*'

12"And it will come about when I leave you that the Spirit of the LORD will carry you where I do not know; so when I come and tell Ahab and he cannot find you, he will kill me, although *I* your servant have [A]feared the LORD from my youth.   *revered*

13"Has[R]it not been told to my master what I did when Jezebel killed the prophets of the LORD, that I hid a hundred prophets of the LORD by fifties in a cave, and provided them with bread and water?   1 Kin. 18:4

14"And now you are saying, 'Go, say to your master, "Behold, Elijah *is here"*'; he will then kill me."

15 And Elijah said, "As[R]the LORD of hosts lives, before whom I stand, I will surely show myself to him today."   1 Kin. 17:1

26 Lit., *The matter is good*

16 So Obadiah went to meet Ahab, and told him; and Ahab went to meet Elijah.

17 And it came about, when Ahab saw Elijah that [R]Ahab said to him, "Is this you, you troubler of Israel?" Josh. 7:25; 1 Kin. 21:20

18 And he said, "I have not troubled Israel, but you and your father's house *have,* because[R]you have forsaken the commandments of the LORD, and[R]you have followed the Baals.   [1 Kin. 9:9] · 1 Kin. 16:31; 21:25

19"Now then send *and* gather to me all Israel at Mount Carmel, *together* with 450 prophets of Baal and 400 prophets of the Asherah, who eat at Jezebel's table."

Victory on Carmel

20 So Ahab sent *a message* among all the sons of Israel, and brought the prophets together at Mount Carmel.

21 And Elijah came near to all the people and said, "How[R]long *will* you hesitate between two opinions? If the LORD is God, follow Him; but if Baal, follow him." But the people did not answer him a word. Matt. 6:24

22 Then Elijah said to the people, "I[R]alone am left a prophet of the LORD, but Baal's prophets are 450 men.   1 Kin. 19:10, 14

23"Now let them give us two oxen; and let them choose one ox for themselves and cut it up, and place it on the wood, but put no fire *under it*; and I will prepare the other ox, and lay it on the wood, and I will not put a fire *under it.*

24"Then you call on the name of your god, and I will call on the name of the LORD, and [R]the God who answers by fire, He is God." And all the people answered and said, "[26]That is a good idea."   1 Kin. 18:38

25 So Elijah said to the prophets of Baal, "Choose one ox for yourselves and prepare it first for you are many, and call on the

---

18:21 Cure for Doubt—The cure for doubt depends to some extent on the thing doubted. However, the real problem is not in the object doubted but in the subject who doubts. Therefore, the following steps should be taken by the doubting Christian:

a. Confess the doubt to God as sin. Doubt is basically unbelief in God and His Word and is therefore sin (Page 1143—Rom. 14:23; Page 1246—Heb. 11:6). God has promised to hear our confession of even the darkest unbelief.

b. Study the evidence for the Christian faith. Christians have nothing to fear by looking into the facts from any source of knowledge. The greatest evidence for the validity of Christianity, the resurrection of Christ, is attested by many proofs. Among these are the empty tomb, post-resurrection appearances, and transformed disciples. Since the resurrection is true, it verifies everything the Bible says.

c. Make certain of your salvation. Paul exhorts Christians to examine themselves to make sure they are Christians (Page 1174—2 Cor. 13:5). So did the author of Hebrews (Page 1242—Heb. 6:1–9). Salvation from sin is by simple trust in Jesus Christ. Until you are assured of your salvation you will be troubled by enormous doubts.

d. Faithfully study the Word of God. "So faith *comes* from hearing, and hearing by the word of Christ" (Page 1140—Rom. 10:17). Through study and application of the Bible, our faith is strengthened and matured. Most especially, we must master the doctrines or basic teachings of the Bible if we are to be stable, mature Christians (Page 1219—1 Tim. 4:13, 16; Page 1225—2 Tim. 3:16; Page 1230—Titus 2:1, 10).

e. Pray. The surest way to face doubts when they come is to have an extensive past history of answered prayer. The more a Christian prays with faith, the more that Christian sees God answer prayer; the more a person sees God answer prayer, the stronger that person's faith becomes while the doubt becomes less.

Now turn to Page 25—THE CHRISTIAN'S GUIDE: Recognizing God's Institutions.

name of your god, but put no fire *under it.*"

26 Then they took the ox which was given them and they prepared it and called on the name of Baal from morning until noon saying, "O Baal, answer us." But there was no voice and no one answered. And they leaped about the altar which they made.

27 And it came about at noon, that Elijah mocked them and said, "Call out with a loud voice, for he is a god; either he is occupied or gone aside, or is on a journey, or perhaps he is asleep and needs to be awakened."

28 So they cried with a loud voice and ᴿcut themselves according to their custom with swords and lances until the blood gushed out on them.   [Lev. 19:28; Deut. 14:1]

29 And it came about when midday was past, that they ᵀraved until the time of the offering of the *evening* sacrifice; but there was no voice, no one answered, and no ᵀone paid attention.   *prophesied • attentiveness*

30 Then Elijah said to all the people, "Come near to me." So all the people came near to him. Andᴿhe repaired the altar of the LORD which had been torn down. 1 Kin. 19:10

31 And Elijah took twelve stones according to the number of the tribes of the sons of Jacob, to whom the word of the LORD had come, saying, "Israel shall be your name."

32 So with the stones he built an altar in ᴿthe name of the LORD, and he made a trench around the altar, large enough to hold two ᵀmeasures of seed.   [Col. 3:17] • Heb., *seahs*

33 Then he arranged the wood and cut the ox in pieces and laid *it* on the wood. And he said, "Fill four pitchers with water and pour *it* on the burnt offering and on the wood."

34 And he said, "Do it a second time," and they did it a second time. And he said, "Do it a third time," and they did it a third time.

35 And the water flowed around the altar, and he also filled the trench with water.

36 Then it came about at the time of the offering of the *evening* sacrifice, that Elijah the prophet came near and said, "O LORD, the God of Abraham, Isaac and Israel, today let it be known that Thou art God in Israel, and that I am Thy servant, and that I have done all these things at Thy word.

37"Answer me, O LORD, answer me, that this people may know that Thou, O LORD, art God, and *that* Thou hast turned their heart back again."

38 Then theᴿfire of the LORD fell, and consumed the burnt offering and the wood and the stones and the dust, and licked up the water that was in the trench.   Gen. 15:17

39 And when all the people saw it, they fell on their faces; and they said, "TheᴿLORD, He is God; the LORD, He is God." 1 Kin. 18:21

40 Then Elijah said to them, "Seize the prophets of Baal; do not let one of them escape." So they seized them; and Elijah brought them down to ᴿthe brook Kishon, and slew them there.   Judg. 4:7; 5:21

Miracle of the Rain

41 Now Elijah said to Ahab, "Go up, eat and drink; for there is the sound of the roar of a *heavy* shower."

42 So Ahab went up to eat and drink. But Elijah went up to the top ofᴿCarmel; and he crouched down on the earth, and put his face between his knees.   1 Kin. 18:19, 20

43 And he said to his servant, "Go up now, look toward the sea." So he went up and looked and said, "There is nothing." And he said, "Go back" seven times.

44 And it came about at the seventh *time,* that he said, "Behold, a cloud as small as a man's hand is coming up from the sea." And he said, "Go up, say to Ahab, 'Prepareᵀyour *chariot* and go down, so that the *heavy* shower does not stop you.'"   *Tie, harness*

45 So it came about in a little while, that the sky grew black with clouds and wind, and there was a heavy shower. And Ahab rode and went toᴿJezreel.   Judg. 6:33

46 Then theᴿhand of the LORD was on Elijah, and he girded up his loins and ᵀoutran Ahab to Jezreel.   2 Kin. 3:15 • *ran before*

CHAPTER 19

Elijah Flees from Jezebel

NOW Ahab told Jezebel all that Elijah had done, andᵀhowᴿhe had killed all the prophets with the sword.   *all* about *how* • 1 Kin. 18:40

2 Then Jezebel sent a messenger to Elijah, saying, "Soᴿmay the gods do to me and even more, if I do not make your ²⁷life as the life of one of them by tomorrow about this time."   Ruth 1:17; 1 Kin. 20:10; 2 Kin. 6:31

3 And he was afraid and arose and ran for his ²⁷life and came to Beersheba, which belongs to Judah, and left his servant there.

Elijah Desires to Die

4 But he himself went a day's journey into the wilderness, and came and sat down under aˆjuniper tree; and he requested for himself that he might die, and said, "It is enough; now, O LORD, take my ²⁷life, for I am not better than my fathers."   *broom-tree*

5 And he lay down and slept under aˆjuniper tree; and behold, there was anᴿangel touching him, and he said to him, "Arise, eat."   *broom-tree* • Gen. 28:12

6 Then he looked and behold, there was at his head a bread cake *baked on* hot stones, and a jar of water. So he ate and drank and lay down again.

7 And the angel of the LORD came again a second time and touched him and said, "Arise, eat, because the journey is too great for you."

8 So he arose and ate and drank, and

²⁷ Lit., *soul*

went in the strength of that food[R]forty days and forty nights to[R]Horeb, the mountain of God.   Ex. 24:18; 34:28 • Ex. 3:1; 4:27

Elijah Has Self-pity

9 Then he came there to a cave, and lodged there; and behold,[R]the word of the LORD *came* to him, and He said to him, "What are you doing here, Elijah?" Ex. 33:21

10 And he said, "I have been very zealous for the LORD, the God of hosts; for the sons of Israel have forsaken Thy covenant, torn down Thine altars and killed Thy prophets with the sword. And I alone am left; and they seek my life, to take it away."

11 So He said, "Go[R]forth, and stand on the mountain before the LORD." And behold, the LORD was passing by! And a great and strong wind was rending the mountains and breaking in pieces the rocks before the LORD; *but* the LORD *was* not in the wind. And after the wind an earthquake, *but* the LORD *was* not in the earthquake.   Ex. 19:20

12 And after the earthquake a fire, *but* the LORD *was* not in the fire; and after the fire[R]a sound of a gentle blowing.   Job 4:16; Zech. 4:6

13 And it came about when Elijah heard *it,* that[R]he wrapped his face in his mantle, and went out and stood in the entrance of the cave. And behold,[R]a voice *came* to him and said, "What are you doing here, Elijah?"   Ex. 3:6 • 1 Kin. 19:9

14 Then he said, "I have been very zealous for the LORD, the God of hosts; for the sons of Israel have forsaken Thy covenant, torn down Thine altars and killed Thy prophets with the sword. And I alone am left; and they seek my life, to take it away."

15 And the LORD said to him, "Go, return on your way to the wilderness of Damascus, and when you have arrived, you shall anoint Hazael king over Aram;   2 Kin. 8:8-15

16 and[R]Jehu the son of Nimshi you shall anoint king over Israel; and Elisha the son of Shaphat of Abel-meholah you shall anoint as prophet in your place.   2 Kin. 9:1-10

17 "And it shall come about, the[R]one who escapes from the sword of Hazael, Jehu[R]shall put to death, and the one who escapes from the sword of Jehu, Elisha shall put to death.   2 Kin. 8:12 • 2 Kin. 9:14—10:25

18 "Yet I will leave 7,000 in Israel, all the knees that have not bowed to Baal and every mouth that has not kissed him."

Call of Elisha

19 So he departed from there and found Elisha the son of Shaphat, while he was plowing with twelve pairs of *oxen* before him, and he with the twelfth. And Elijah passed over to him and threw[R]his mantle on him.   1 Sam. 28:14; 2 Kin. 2:8, 13, 14

20 And he left the oxen and ran after Elijah and said, "Please[R]let me kiss my father and my mother, then I will follow you." And

he said to him, "Go back again, for what have I done to you?"   Matt. 8:21f.; Luke 9:61f.

21 So he returned from following him, and took the pair of oxen and sacrificed them and[R]boiled their flesh with the implements of the oxen, and gave *it* to the people and they ate. Then he arose and followed Elijah and ministered to him.   2 Sam. 24:22

CHAPTER 20

First Victory over Aram

NOW[R]Ben-hadad king of Aram gathered all his army,[R]and there *were* thirty-two kings with him, and horses and chariots. And he went up and besieged Samaria, and fought against it.   1 Kin. 15:18, 20 • 1 Kin. 22:31

2 Then he sent messengers to the city to Ahab king of Israel, and said to him, "Thus says Ben-hadad,

3 'Your silver and your gold are mine; your most beautiful wives and children are also mine.' "

4 And the king of Israel answered and said, "It is according to your word, my lord, O king; I am yours, and all that I have."

5 Then the messengers returned and said, "Thus says[T]Ben-hadad, 'Surely, I sent to you saying, "You shall give me your silver and your gold and your wives and your children,"   *Ben-hadad, saying*

6 but about this time tomorrow I will send my servants to you, and they will search your house and the houses of your servants; and it shall come about, whatever is desirable in your eyes, they will[T]take in their hand and carry away.' "   *put*

7 Then the king of Israel called all the elders of the land and said, "Please observe and[R]see how this man is looking for trouble; for he sent to me for my wives and my children and my silver and my gold, and I did not refuse him."   2 Kin. 5:7

8 And all the elders and all the people said to him, "Do not listen or consent."

9 So he said to the messengers of Ben-hadad, "Tell my lord the king, 'All that you sent for to your servant at the first I will do, but this thing I cannot do.' " And the messengers departed and brought him word again.

10 And Ben-hadad sent to him and said, "May the gods do so to me and more also, if the dust of Samaria shall suffice for handfuls for all the people who follow me."

11 Then the king of Israel answered and said, "Tell *him,* 'Let not him who girds on *his armor* boast like him who takes *it* off.' "

12 And it came about when Ben-hadad heard this message, as[R]he was drinking[T]with the kings in the[A]temporary shelters, that he said to his servants, "Station *yourselves.*" So they stationed *themselves* against the city.   1 Kin. 16:9 • *he and* • *booths*

13 Now behold, a prophet approached

Ahab king of Israel and said, "Thus says the LORD, 'Have you seen all this great multitude? Behold,[R]I will deliver them into your hand today, and[R]you shall know that I am the LORD.'"   1 Kin. 20:28 • 1 Kin. 18:36

14 And Ahab said, "By whom?" So he said, "Thus says the LORD, 'By the young men of the rulers of the provinces.'" Then he said, "Who shall[T]begin the battle?" And he[T]answered, "You."   bind • said

15 Then he mustered the young men of the rulers of the provinces, and there were 232; and after them he mustered all the people, even all the sons of Israel, 7,000.

16 And they went out at noon, while Ben-hadad was drinking himself drunk in the [A]temporary shelters with the thirty-two kings who helped him.   booths

17 And the young men of the rulers of the provinces went out first; and Ben-hadad sent out and they told him, saying, "Men have come out from Samaria."

18 Then he said, "If they have come out for peace, take them alive; or if they have come out for war, take them alive."

19 So these went out from the city, the young men of the rulers of the provinces, and the army which followed them.

20 And they[T]killed each his man; and the Arameans fled, and Israel pursued them, and Ben-hadad king of Aram escaped on a horse with horsemen.   smote

21 And the king of Israel went out and [T]struck the horses and chariots, and [T]killed the Arameans with a great slaughter.   smote

Second Victory over Aram

22 Then[R]the prophet came near to the king of Israel, and said to him, "Go, strengthen yourself and observe and see what you have to do; for at the turn of the year the king of Aram will come up against you." 1 Kin. 20:13

23 Now the servants of the king of Aram said to him, "Their[R]gods are gods of the mountains, therefore they were stronger than we; but rather let us fight against them in the plain, and surely we shall be stronger than they." 1 Kin. 14:23; Jer. 16:19-21; Rom. 1:21-23

24"And do this thing: remove the kings, each from his place, and put captains in their place,

25 and[T]muster an army like the army that you have lost, horse for horse, and chariot for chariot. Then we will fight against them in the plain, and surely we shall be stronger than they." And he listened to their voice and did so.   number

26 So it came about[R]at the turn of the year, that Ben-hadad mustered the Arameans and went up to[R]Aphek to fight against Israel.   1 Kin. 20:22 • 2 Kin. 13:17

27 And the sons of Israel were mustered and were provisioned and went to meet them; and the sons of Israel camped before them like two little flocks of goats,[R]but the Arameans filled the country.   1 Sam. 13:5-8

28 Then[R]a man of God came near and spoke to the king of Israel and said, "Thus says the LORD, 'Because the Arameans have said, "The[R]LORD is a god of the mountains, but He is not a god of the valleys"; therefore I will give all this great multitude into your hand, and you shall know that I am the LORD.'"   1 Kin. 17:18 • 1 Kin. 20:23

29 So they camped one over against the other seven days. And it came about that on the seventh day, the battle was joined, and the sons of Israel[T]killed of the Arameans 100,000 foot soldiers in one day.   smote

30 But the rest fled to[R]Aphek into the city, and the wall fell on 27,000 men who were left. And Ben-hadad fled and came into the city into an inner chamber.   1 Kin. 20:26

31 And his servants said to him, "Behold now, we have heard that the kings of the house of Israel are merciful kings, please let us put sackcloth on our loins and ropes on our heads, and go out to the king of Israel; perhaps he will save your[T]life."   soul

32 So they girded sackcloth on their loins and put ropes on their heads, and came to the king of Israel and said, "Your servant Ben-hadad says, 'Please let me live.'" And he said, "Is he still alive? He is my brother."

33 Now the men took this as an omen, and quickly catching his word said, "Your brother Ben-hadad." Then he said, "Go, bring him." Then Ben-hadad came out to him, and he took him up into the chariot.

34 And Ben-hadad said to him, "The[R]cities which my father took from your father I will restore, and you shall make streets for yourself in Damascus, as my father made in Samaria." Ahab said, "And I will let you go with this covenant." So he made a covenant with him and let him go.   1 Kin. 15:20

35 Now a certain man of the sons of the prophets said to[T]another by the word of the LORD, "Please strike me." But the man refused to strike him.   his neighbor

36 Then he said to him, "Because you have not listened to the voice of the LORD, behold, as soon as you have departed from me, a lion will[T]kill you." And as soon as he had departed from him a lion found him, and[T]killed him.   smite • smote

37 Then he found another man and said, "Please [T]strike me." And the man [T]struck him, wounding him.   smite • smote

38 So the prophet departed and waited for the king by the way, and[R]disguised himself with a bandage over his eyes.   1 Kin. 14:2

39 And as the king passed by, he cried to the king and said, "Your servant went out into the midst of the battle; and behold, a man turned aside and brought a man to me and said, 'Guard this man; if for any reason he is missing, then your life shall be for his life, or else you shall pay a talent of silver.'

40"And while your servant was busy here and there, he was gone." And the king of

Israel said to him, "So shall your judgment be; you yourself have decided *it*."

41 Then he hastily took the bandage away from his eyes, and the king of Israel recognized him that he was of the prophets.

42 And he said to him, "Thus says the LORD, 'Because you have let go out of *your* hand the man whom I had devoted to destruction, therefore your[T]life shall go for his life, and your people for his people.' "   *soul*

43 So the king of Israel went to his house sullen and vexed, and came to Samaria.

CHAPTER 21

Murder of Naboth

NOW it came about after these things, that Naboth the Jezreelite had a vineyard which *was* in [R]Jezreel beside the palace of Ahab king of Samaria.   1 Kin. 18:45, 46

2 And Ahab spoke to Naboth, saying, "Give me your vineyard, that I may have it for a vegetable garden because it is close beside my house, and I will give you a better vineyard than it in its place; if you like, I will give you the price of[T]it in money."   *this*

3 But Naboth said to Ahab, "The LORD forbid me[R]that I should give you the inheritance of my fathers."   [Lev. 25:23; Num. 36:7]

4 So Ahab came into his house sullen and vexed because of the word which Naboth the Jezreelite had spoken to him; for he said, "I will not give you the inheritance of my fathers." And he lay down on his bed and turned away his face and ate no food.

5 But Jezebel his wife came to him and said to him, "How is it that your spirit is so sullen that you are not eating[T]food?"   *bread*

6 So he said to her, "Because I spoke to Naboth the Jezreelite, and said to him, 'Give me your vineyard for money; or else, if it pleases you, I will give you a vineyard in its place.' But he said, 'I will not give you my vineyard.' "

7 And Jezebel his wife said to him, "Do you now reign over Israel? Arise, eat bread, and let your heart be joyful; I will give you the vineyard of Naboth the Jezreelite."

8 So she wrote letters in Ahab's name and sealed them with his seal, and sent letters to the elders and to the nobles who were living with Naboth in his city.

9 Now she wrote in the letters, saying, "Proclaim a fast, and seat Naboth at the head of the people;

10 and seat two worthless men before him, and let them testify against him, saying, 'You cursed God and the king.' Then take him out and stone him to death."

11 So the men of his city, the elders and the nobles who lived in his city, did as Jezebel had sent *word* to them, just as it was written in the letters which she had sent them.

12 They[R]proclaimed a fast and seated Naboth at the head of the people.   Is. 58:4

13 Then the two worthless men came in and sat before him; and the worthless men testified against him, even against Naboth, before the people, saying, "Naboth cursed God and the king."[R]So they took him outside the city and stoned him [T]to death with stones.   2 Kin. 9:26 • *with stones so that he died*

14 Then they sent *word* to Jezebel, saying, "Naboth has been stoned, and is dead."

15 And it came about when Jezebel heard that Naboth had been stoned and was dead, that Jezebel said to Ahab, "Arise, take possession of the vineyard of Naboth, the Jezreelite, which he refused to give you for money; for Naboth is not alive, but dead."

16 And it came about when Ahab heard that Naboth was dead, that Ahab arose to go down to the vineyard of Naboth the Jezreelite, to take possession of it.

Prediction of Ahab's Death

17 Then the word of the LORD came to Elijah the Tishbite, saying,

18"Arise, go down to meet Ahab king of Israel,[R]who is in Samaria; behold, he is in the vineyard of Naboth where he has gone down to take possession of it.   1 Kin. 16:29

19"And you shall speak to him, saying, 'Thus says the LORD, "Have[R]you murdered, and also taken possession?" ' And you shall speak to him, saying, 'Thus says the LORD, "In the place where the dogs licked up the blood of Naboth the dogs shall lick up your blood, even yours." ' "   2 Sam. 12:9

20 And Ahab said to Elijah, "Have you found me, O my enemy?" And he answered, "I have found *you*, because you have sold yourself to do evil in the sight of the LORD.

21"Behold, I will bring evil upon you, and [R]will utterly sweep you away, and will cut off from Ahab every male, both bond and free in Israel;   1 Kin. 14:10; 2 Kin. 9:8

22 and[R]I will make your house like the house of Jeroboam the son of Nebat, and like the house of Baasha the son of Ahijah, because of the provocation with which you have provoked *Me* to anger, and *because* you have made Israel sin.   1 Kin. 15:29

23"And of Jezebel also has the LORD spoken, saying, 'The[R]dogs shall eat Jezebel in the district of Jezreel.'   2 Kin. 9:10, 30-37

24"The[R]one belonging to Ahab, who dies in the city, the dogs shall eat, and the one who dies in the field the birds of heaven shall eat."   1 Kin. 14:11; 16:4

25 Surely there was no one like Ahab who sold himself to do evil in the sight of the LORD, because Jezebel his wife incited him.

26 And[R]he acted very abominably in following idols, according to all that the Amorites had done, whom the LORD cast out before the sons of Israel.   1 Kin. 15:12; 2 Kin. 17:12

27 And it came about when Ahab heard these words, that he tore his clothes and put

on sackcloth and fasted, and he lay in sackcloth and went about ᴬdespondently.   *softly*
28 Then the word of the LORD came to Elijah the Tishbite, saying,
29"Do you see how Ahab has humbled
himself before Me? Because he has humbled
himself before Me, I will not bring the evil in
his days, *but* I will bring the evil upon his
houseᴮin his son's days."   2 Kin. 9:25-37

CHAPTER 22

Promise of Victory by the False Prophets
2 Chr. 18:2-11

Aɴᴅᵀthree years passed without war between Aram and Israel.   *they sat for three years*
2 ᴿAnd it came about in the third year,
that Jehoshaphat the king of Judah came
down to the king of Israel.   2 Chr. 18:2
3 Now the king of Israel said to his servants, "Do you know that ᴿRamoth-gilead
belongs to us, and weᵀare still doing nothing
to take it out of the hand of the king of
Aram?"   Deut. 4:43 • *are silent so as not*
4 And he said to Jehoshaphat, "Will you
go with me to battle at Ramoth-gilead?"
And Jehoshaphat said to the king of Israel,
"Iᴿam as you are, my people as your people,
my horses as your horses."   2 Kin. 3:7
5 Moreover, Jehoshaphat said to the
king of Israel, "Please inquireᵀfirst for the
word of the LORD."   *as the day*
6 Then ᴿthe king of Israel gathered the
prophets together, about four hundred men,
and said to them, "Shall I go against Ramoth-gilead to battle or shall I refrain?"
And they said, "Go up, for the Lord will give
it into the hand of the king."   1 Kin. 18:19
7 Butᴿ Jehoshaphat said, "Is there not yet
a prophet of the LORD here, that we may inquire of him?"   2 Kin. 3:11
8 And the king of Israel said to Jehoshaphat, "There is yet one man by whom we
may inquire of the LORD, but I hate him, because he does not prophesy good concerning me, but evil. *He is* Micaiah son of Imlah." But Jehoshaphat said, "Let not the
king say so."
9 Then the king of Israel called an officer
and said, "Bringᵀquickly Micaiah son of Imlah."   *Hasten Micaiah*
10 Now the king of Israel and Jehoshaphat king of Judah were sitting each on his
throne, arrayed in *their* robes, at the threshing floor at the entrance of the gate of Samaria; andᴿall the prophets were prophesying before them.   1 Kin. 22:6
11 Then Zedekiah the son of Chenaanah
made ᴿhorns of iron for himself and said,
"Thus says the LORD, 'Withᴿthese you shall
gore the Arameans until they are consumed.' "   Zech. 1:18-21 • Deut. 33:17
12 And all the prophets were prophesying
thus, saying, "Go up to Ramoth-gilead and
prosper, for the LORD will give *it* into the
hand of the king."

Promise of Defeat by Micaiah
2 Chr. 18:12-27

13 Then the messenger who went to summon Micaiah spoke to him saying, "Behold
now, the words of the prophets are uniformly favorable to the king. Please let your
word be like the word of one of them, and
speak favorably."
14 But Micaiah said, "Asᴿthe LORD lives,
what ᵀthe LORD says to me, that I will
speak."   1 Kin. 18:10 • Num. 22:18; 24:13
15 When he came to the king, the king
said to him, "Micaiah, shall we go to Ramoth-gilead to battle, or shall we refrain?"
And heᵀanswered him, "Goᴿup and succeed,
and the LORD will give *it* into the hand of the
king."   *said to* • 1 Kin. 22:12
16 Then the king said to him, "How many
times must I adjure you to speak to me
nothing but the truth in the name of the
LORD?"
17 So he said,
"I saw all Israel
Scattered on the mountains,
Like sheep which have no shepherd.
And the LORD said, 'These have no
      master.
Let each of them return to his house
      in peace.' "
18 Then the king of Israel said to Jehoshaphat, "Did I not tell you that he would not
prophesy good concerning me, but evil?"
19 And Micaiah said, "Therefore, hear the
word of the LORD. I saw the LORD sitting on
His throne, and all the host of heaven standing by Him on His right and on His left.
20"And the LORD said, 'Who will entice
Ahab to go up and fall at Ramoth-gilead?'
And one said this while another said that.
21"Then a spirit came forward and stood
before the LORD and said, 'I will entice him.'
22"And the LORD said to him, 'How?' And
he said, 'I will go out and ᴿbe a deceiving
spirit in the mouth of all his prophets.' Then
He said, 'You are to entice *him* and also prevail. Go and do so.'   Judg. 9:23; 1 Sam. 16:14
23"Now therefore, behold,ᴿthe LORD has
put a deceiving spirit in the mouth of all
these your prophets; and the LORD has proclaimed disaster against you."   [Ezek. 14:9]
24 Thenᴿ Zedekiah the son of Chenaanah
came near and struck Micaiah on the cheek
and said, "How did the Spirit of the LORD
pass from me to speak to you?"   1 Kin. 22:11
25 And Micaiah said, "Behold, you shall
see on that day when youᴿenter an inner
room to hide yourself."   1 Kin. 20:30
26 Then the king of Israel said, "Take Micaiah and return him to Amon the governor
of the city and to Joash the king's son;
27 and say, 'Thus says the king, "Put this
man in prison, and feed him sparingly with
bread and water until I return safely." ' "
28 And Micaiah said, "If you indeed return safely the LORD has not spoken by me."
And he said, "Listen, all you people."

Defeat of Israel—2 Chr. 18:28–34

29 So[R]the king of Israel and Jehoshaphat king of Judah went up against Ramoth-gilead.   1 Kin. 22:3, 4

30 And the king of Israel said to Jehoshaphat, "I[R]will disguise myself and go into the battle, but you put on your robes." So the king of Israel disguised himself and went into the battle.   2 Chr. 35:22

31 Now the king of Aram had commanded the thirty-two captains of his chariots, saying, "Do not fight with small or great, but with the king of Israel alone."

32 So it came about, when the captains of the chariots saw Jehoshaphat, that they said, "Surely it is the king of Israel," and they turned aside to fight against him, and Jehoshaphat cried out.

33 Then it happened, when the captains of the chariots saw that it was not the king of Israel, that they turned back from pursuing him.

34 Now a certain man drew his bow at random and struck the king of Israel in a joint of the armor. So he said to the driver of his chariot, "Turn around, and take me out of the fight; for I am severely wounded."

35 And the battle[T]raged that day, and the king was propped up in his chariot in front of the Arameans, and died at evening, and the blood from the wound ran into the bottom of the chariot.   *went up*

36 Then a cry passed throughout the army close to sunset, saying, "Every man to his city and every man to his[T]country."   *land*

Death of Ahab

37 So the king died and was brought to Samaria, and they buried the king in Samaria.

38 And they washed the chariot by the pool of Samaria, and the dogs licked up his blood (now the harlots bathed themselves *there*),[R]according to the word of the LORD which He spoke.   1 Kin. 21:19

39 Now the rest of the acts of Ahab and all that he did and[R]the ivory house which he built and all the cities which he built, are they not written in the Book of the Chronicles of the Kings of Israel?   Amos 3:15

40 So Ahab slept with his fathers, and Ahaziah his son became king in his place.

The Reign of Jehoshaphat in Judah
2 Chr. 20:31—21:1

41 [R]Now Jehoshaphat the son of Asa became king over Judah in the fourth year of Ahab king of Israel.   2 Chr. 20:31

42 Jehoshaphat was thirty-five years old when he became king, and he reigned twenty-five years in Jerusalem. And his mother's name was Azubah the daughter of Shilhi.

43 [R]And he walked in all the way of Asa his father; he did not turn aside from it, doing right in the sight of the LORD.[R]However, the high places were not taken away; the people still sacrificed and burnt incense on the high places.   2 Chr. 17:3 · 1 Kin. 15:14; 2 Kin. 12:3

44 [R]Jehoshaphat also made peace with the king of Israel.   1 Kin. 22:2; 2 Kin. 8:16, 18

45 Now the rest of the acts of Jehoshaphat, and his might which he showed and how he warred, are they not written[R]in the Book of the Chronicles of the Kings of Judah?   2 Chr. 20:34

46 And the remnant of the sodomites who remained in the days of his father Asa, he [T]expelled from the land.   *consumed*

47 Now[R]there was no king in Edom; a deputy was king.   2 Sam. 8:14; 2 Kin. 3:9

48 Jehoshaphat made ships of Tarshish to go to Ophir for gold, but they did not go for the ships were broken at Ezion-geber.

49 Then Ahaziah the son of Ahab said to Jehoshaphat, "Let my servants go with your servants in the ships." But Jehoshaphat was not willing.

50 [R]And Jehoshaphat slept with his fathers and was buried with his fathers in the city of his father David, and Jehoram his son became king in his place.   2 Chr. 21:1

The Reign of Ahaziah in Israel

51 Ahaziah the son of Ahab[R]became king over Israel in Samaria in the seventeenth year of Jehoshaphat king of Judah, and he reigned two years over Israel.   1 Kin. 22:40

52 And he did evil in the sight of the LORD and[R]walked in the way of his father and in the way of his mother and in the way of Jeroboam the son of Nebat, who caused Israel to sin.   1 Kin. 15:26; 21:25

53 So he served Baal and worshiped him and provoked the LORD God of Israel to anger according to all that his father had done.

KINGS

THE BOOK OF SECOND KINGS

The Book of Second Kings continues the drama begun in First Kings—the tragic history of two nations on a collision course with captivity. The author systematically traces the reigning monarchs of Israel and Judah, first by carrying one nation's history forward, then retracing the same period for the other nation.

Nineteen consecutive evil kings rule in Israel, leading to the captivity by Assyria. The picture is somewhat brighter in Judah, where godly kings occasionally emerge to reform the evils of their predecessors. In the end, however, sin outweighs righteousness and Judah is marched off to Babylon. See "The Book of First Kings" for more details concerning the title.

THE AUTHOR OF SECOND KINGS

See "The Author of First Kings" for a discussion of authorship. If this now divided book was not written by Jeremiah, it probably was written by a prophetic contemporary. The majority of Second Kings was written before the Babylonian captivity (see "to this day" in 17:34, 41).

The literary style of Second Kings is similar to that of the Book of Jeremiah, and it has been observed that the omission of Jeremiah's ministry in the account of King Josiah and his successors may indicate that Jeremiah himself was the recorder of the events. However, the last two chapters were evidently added to the book after the Babylonian captivity and written by someone other than Jeremiah. The prophet Jeremiah was forced to flee to Egypt (Jer. 43:1–8), not to Babylon. It is interesting that Second Kings 24:18—25:30 is almost the same as Jeremiah 52.

THE TIME OF SECOND KINGS

The last recorded event in Second Kings is the release of Jehoiachin (25:27–30), which takes place in 560 B.C. Most of First and Second Kings probably was written just prior to 586 B.C., but chapters 24 and 25 were written after Jehoiachin's release, perhaps about 550 B.C.

Chapters 1—17 cover the 131 years from 853 B.C. (King Ahaziah of Israel) to 722 B.C. (the Assyrian captivity of Israel). Chapters 18—25

cover the 155 years from the beginning of Hezekiah's reign in 715 B.C. to the release of Jehoiachin in Babylon in 560 B.C. The united kingdom lasts for 112 years (1043–931 B.C.), the northern kingdom of Israel exists for another 209 years (931–722 B.C.), and the southern kingdom of Judah continues for an additional 136 years (722–586 B.C.). During this 457-year kingdom period, there are great shifts of world power. Egyptian and Assyrian control over Palestine fluctuates; Assyria rises to preeminence, declines, and is finally conquered by Babylon.

The books of Kings show that judgment comes to the kingdoms of Israel and Judah because of their idolatry, immorality, and disunity. Judah lasts 136 years longer than Israel because of the relative goodness of eight of its twenty kings. Israel never breaks away from Jeroboam's idolatrous calf worship, but Judah experiences some periods of revival in the worship of Yahweh. During these years, God sends many of His prophets. Elijah, Elisha, Amos, and Hosea are in the northern kingdom, while in the southern kingdom Obadiah, Joel, Isaiah, Micah, Nahum, Zephaniah, Jeremiah, and Habakkuk are prophesying.

THE CHRIST OF SECOND KINGS

Unlike the nine different dynasties in the northern kingdom, the kings of Judah reign as one continuous dynasty. In spite of Queen Athaliah's attempt to destroy the house of David, God remains faithful to His covenant with David (2 Sam. 7) by preserving his lineage. Jesus the Messiah is his direct descendant.

While Elijah is a type of John the Baptist (Matt. 11:14; 17:10–12; Luke 1:17), Elisha reminds us of Christ. Elijah generally lives apart from the people and stresses law, judgment, and repentance. Elisha lives among the people and emphasizes grace, life, and hope.

KEYS TO SECOND KINGS

Key Word: Captivities of the Kingdom—Second Kings records both the destruction and captivity of Israel by the Assyrians (2 Kin. 17), as well as the destruction and captivity of Judah by the Babylonians (2 Kin. 25).

The book was written selectively, not exhaustively, from a prophetic viewpoint to

teach that the decline and collapse of the two kingdoms occurred because of failure on the part of the rulers and people to heed the warnings of God's messengers. The spiritual climate of the nation determined its political and economic conditions.

The prophets of Yahweh play a prominent role in First and Second Kings as God uses them to remind the kings of their covenant responsibilities as His theocratic administrators. When the king keeps the covenant, he and the nation are richly blessed. But judgment consistently falls upon those who refuse to obey God's law. God is seen in Kings as the controller of history who reveals His plan and purpose to His people. Unhappily, the people are concerned more with their own plans, and their rejection of God's rule leads to exile at the hands of the Assyrians and Babylonians.

Key Verses: Second Kings 17:22, 23; 23:27— "And the sons of Israel walked in all the sins of Jeroboam which he did; they did not depart from them, until the LORD removed Israel from His sight, as He spoke through all His servants the prophets. So Israel was carried away into exile from their own land to Assyria until this day" (17:22, 23).

"And the LORD said, 'I will remove Judah also from My sight, as I have removed Israel. And I will cast off Jerusalem, this city which I have chosen, and the temple of which I said, "My name shall be there" ' " (23:27).

Key Chapter: Second Kings 25—The last chapter of Second Kings records the utter destruction of the city of Jerusalem and its glorious temple. Only the poor of Israel are left, and even some of them flee for their lives to Egypt. Hope is still alive, however, with the remnant in the Babylonian captivity as Evilmerodach frees Jehoiachin from prison and treats him kindly.

SURVEY OF SECOND KINGS

Without interruption Second Kings continues the narrative of First Kings. The twin kingdoms of Israel and Judah pursue a collision course with captivity as the glory of the once united kingdom becomes increasingly diminished. Division has led to decline and now ends in double deportation with Israel captured by Assyria and Judah by Babylon. This book traces the history of the divided kingdom in chapters 1—17 and the history of the surviving kingdom in chapters 18—25.

Divided Kingdom (1—17): These chapters record the story of Israel's corruption in a relentless succession of bad kings from Ahaziah to Hoshea. The situation in Judah during this time (Jehoram to Ahaz) is somewhat better, but far from ideal. This dark period in the northern kingdom of Israel is interrupted only by the ministries of such godly prophets as Elijah and Elisha. At the end of Elijah's miraculous ministry, Elisha is installed and authenticated as his successor. He is a force for righteousness in a nation that never served the true God or worshiped at the temple in Jerusalem. Elisha's ministry is characterized by miraculous provisions of sustenance and life. Through him God demonstrates His gracious care for the nation and His concern for any person who desires to come to Him. However, like his forerunner Elijah, Elisha is basically rejected by Israel's leadership.

Elisha instructs one of his prophetic assistants to anoint Jehu king over Israel. Jehu fulfills the prophecies concerning Ahab's descendants by putting them to death. He kills Ahab's wife Jezebel, his sons, and also the priests of Baal. But he does not depart from the calf worship originally set up by Jeroboam. The loss of the house of Ahab means the alienation of Israel and Judah and the weak-

FOCUS	DIVIDED KINGDOM			SURVIVING KINGDOM		
REFERENCE	1:1————9:1————		17:1————	18:1————	22:1————	25:1————25:30
DIVISION	MINISTRY OF ELISHA UNDER AHAZIAH AND JEHORAM	REIGNS OF TEN KINGS OF ISRAEL AND EIGHT KINGS OF JUDAH	FALL OF ISRAEL	REIGNS OF HEZEKIAH AND TWO EVIL KINGS	REIGNS OF JOSIAH AND FOUR EVIL KINGS	FALL OF JUDAH
TOPIC	ISRAEL AND JUDAH			JUDAH		
	AHAZIAH TO HOSHEA			HEZEKIAH TO ZEDEKIAH		
LOCATION	ISRAEL DEPORTED TO ASSYRIA			JUDAH DEPORTED TO BABYLONIA		
TIME	131 YEARS (853—722 B.C.)			155 YEARS (715—560 B.C.)		

ening of both. Israel's enemies begin to get the upper hand. Meanwhile, in Judah, Jezebel's daughter Athaliah kills all the descendants of David, except for Joash, and usurps the throne. However, Jehoiada the priest eventually removes her from the throne and places Joash in power. Joash restores the temple and serves God.

Aram gains virtual control over Israel, but there is no response to God's chastisement: the kings and people refuse to repent. Nevertheless, there is a period of restoration under Jeroboam II, but the continuing series of wicked kings in Israel leads to its overthrow by Assyria.

Surviving Kingdom (18—25): Of Israel's nineteen kings, not one is righteous in God's sight. All but one of its nine dynasties are created by murdering the previous king. In Judah, where there is only one dynasty, eight of its twenty rulers do what is right before God.

Nevertheless, Judah's collapse finally comes, resulting in the Babylonian exile. Chapters 18—25 read more easily than chapters 1—17 because alternating the histories of the northern and southern kingdoms is no longer necessary. Only Judah remains.

Six years before the overthrow of Israel's capital of Samaria, Hezekiah becomes king of Judah. Because of his exemplary faith and reforms, God spares Jerusalem from Assyria and brings a measure of prosperity to Judah. However, Hezekiah's son Manasseh is so idolatrous that his long reign leads to the downfall of Judah. Even Josiah's later reforms cannot stem the tide of evil, and the four kings who succeed him are exceedingly wicked. Judgment comes with three deportations to Babylon. The third occurs in 586 B.C. when Nebuchadnezzar destroys Jerusalem and the temple. Still, the book ends on a note of hope with God preserving a remnant for Himself.

OUTLINE OF SECOND KINGS

Part One: The Divided Kingdom (1:1—17:41)

CHAPTER 1

Political Situation Under Ahaziah
2 Kin. 3:5

NOW [R]Moab rebelled against Israel after the death of Ahab.   2 Sam. 8:2; 2 Kin. 3:5

Death of Ahaziah

2 And Ahaziah fell through the lattice in his upper chamber which *was* in Samaria, and became ill. So he sent messengers and said to them, "Go, [R]inquire of Baal-zebub, the god of Ekron, [R]whether I shall recover from this sickness."   2 Kin. 1:3 • 2 Kin. 8:7-10

3 But the angel of the LORD said to [R]Elijah the Tishbite, "Arise, go up to meet the messengers of the king of Samaria and say to them, 'Is it because there is no God in Israel *that* you are going to inquire of [B]Baal-zebub, the god of Ekron?'   1 Kin. 17:1 • 2 Kin. 1:2

4 "Now therefore thus says the LORD,

'You shall not come down from the bed where you have gone up, but you shall surely die.' " Then Elijah departed.

5 When the messengers returned to him he said to them, "Why have you returned?"

6 And they said to him, "A man came up to meet us and said to us, 'Go, return to the king who sent you and say to him, "Thus says the LORD, 'Is it because there is no God in Israel *that* you are sending [R]to inquire of Baal-zebub, the god of Ekron? Therefore you shall not come down from the bed where you have gone up, but shall surely die.' " ' "   2 Kin. 1:2

7 And he said to them, "What kind of man was he who came up to meet you and spoke these words to you?"

8 And they [T]answered him, "[R]*He* was a hairy man with a leather girdle [A]bound about his loins." And he said, "It is Elijah the Tishbite."   *said* • Zech. 13:4 • *girt*

9 Then *the* king [R]sent to him a captain of

fifty with his fifty. And he went up to him, and behold, he was sitting on the top of the hill. And he said to him, "O man of God, the king says, 'Come down.'" 2 Kin. 6:13, 14

10 And Elijah answered and said to the captain of fifty, "If I am a man of God,[R]let fire come down from heaven and consume you and your fifty."[R]Then fire came down from heaven and consumed him and his fifty. Luke 9:54 • Job 1:16

11 So he again sent to him another captain of fifty with his fifty. And he answered and said to him, "O man of God, thus says the king, 'Come down quickly.'"

12 And Elijah answered and said to them, "If I am a man of God, let fire come down from heaven and consume you and your fifty." Then the fire of God came down from heaven and consumed him and his fifty.

13 So he again sent the captain of a third fifty with his fifty. When the third captain of fifty went up, he came and bowed down on his knees before Elijah, and begged him and said to him, "O man of God, please let my life and the lives of these fifty servants of yours be precious in your sight. Jer. 5:3

14 "Behold fire came down from heaven, and consumed the first two captains of fifty with their fifties; but now let my[T]life be precious in your sight." soul

15 And[R]the angel of the LORD said to Elijah, "Go down with him;[R]do not be afraid of him." So he arose and went down with him to the king. 2 Kin. 1:3 • Is. 51:12; Jer. 1:17

16 Then he said to him, "Thus says the LORD, 'Because you have sent messengers [R]to inquire of Baal-zebub, the god of Ekron—is it because there is no God in Israel to inquire of His word?—therefore you shall not come down from the bed where you have gone up, but shall surely die.'" 2 Kin. 1:3

17 So Ahaziah died according to the word of the LORD which Elijah had spoken. And because he had no son, Jehoram became king in his place in the second year of Jehoram the son of Jehoshaphat, king of Judah.

18 Now the rest of the acts of Ahaziah which he did, are they not written in the Book of the Chronicles of the Kings of Israel?

CHAPTER 2

Chariot of Fire Takes Elijah

AND it came about when the LORD was about to[R]take up Elijah by a[A]whirlwind to heaven, that Elijah went with Elisha from Gilgal. Gen. 5:24; [Heb. 11:5] • windstorm

2 And Elijah said to Elisha, "Stay here please, for the LORD has sent me as far as Bethel." But Elisha said, "As the LORD lives and as you yourself live, I will not leave you." So they went down to Bethel.

3 Then the sons of the prophets who were at Bethel came out to Elisha and said to him, "Do you know that the LORD will take away your master from over you today?" And he said, "Yes, I know; be still."

4 And Elijah said to him, "Elisha, please [R]stay here, for the LORD has sent me to[R]Jericho." But he said, "As the LORD lives, and as you yourself live, I will not leave you." So they came to Jericho. 2 Kin. 2:2 • Josh. 6:26

5 And the sons of the prophets who were at Jericho approached Elisha and said to him, "Do you know that the LORD will take away your master from over you today?" And he answered, "Yes, I know; be still."

6 Then Elijah said to him, "Please[R]stay here, for the LORD has sent me to the Jordan." And he said, "As the LORD lives, and as you yourself live, I will not leave you." So the two of them went on. 2 Kin. 2:2

7 Now[R]fifty men of the sons of the prophets went and stood opposite them at a distance, while the two of them stood by the Jordan. 2 Kin. 2:15, 16

8 And Elijah took his mantle and folded it together and struck the waters, and they were divided here and there, so that the two of them crossed over on dry ground.

9 Now it came about when they had crossed over, that Elijah said to Elisha, "Ask what I shall do for you before I am taken from you." And Elisha said, "Please, let a[R]double portion of your spirit be upon me." Num. 11:17-25; Deut. 21:17

10 And he said, "You have asked a hard thing. Nevertheless, if you[R]see me when I am taken from you, it shall be so for you; but if not, it shall not be so." Acts 1:10

11 Then it came about as they were going along and talking, that behold, there appeared a chariot of fire and horses of fire which separated the two of them. And Elijah went up by a whirlwind to heaven.

Authority of Elijah
Is Taken by Elisha

12 And Elisha saw it and cried out, "My father, my father, the[R]chariots of Israel and its horsemen!" And he saw him no more. Then he took hold of his own clothes and tore them in two pieces. chariot

13 He also took up the mantle of Elijah that fell from him, and returned and stood by the bank of the Jordan.

14 And he took the mantle of Elijah that fell from him, and struck the waters and said, "Where is the LORD, the God of Elijah?" And when he also had[R]struck the waters, they were divided here and there; and Elisha crossed over. 2 Kin. 2:8

15 Now when[R]the sons of the prophets who were at Jericho opposite him saw him, they said, "The spirit of Elijah rests on Elisha." And they came to meet him and

bowed themselves to the ground before him. 2 Kin. 2:7

16 And they said to him, "Behold now, there are with your servants fifty strong men, please let them go and search for your master; perhaps the Spirit of the LORD has taken him up and cast him on some mountain or into some valley." And he said, "You shall not send." *lest* • 1 Kin. 18:12; Acts 8:39

17 But when they urged him until he was ashamed, he said, "Send." They sent therefore fifty men; and they searched three days, but did not find him. 2 Kin. 8:11

18 And they returned to him while he was staying at Jericho; and he said to them, "Did I not say to you, 'Do not go'?"

19 Then the men of the city said to Elisha, "Behold now, the situation of this city is pleasant, as my lord sees; but the water is bad, and the land is unfruitful."

20 And he said, "Bring me a new jar, and put salt in it." So they brought *it* to him.

21 And he went out to the spring of water, and threw salt in it and said, "Thus says the LORD, 'I have purified these waters; there shall not be from there death or unfruitfulness any longer.' " *there* • *healed*

22 So the waters have been purified to this day, according to the word of Elisha which he spoke. *healed*

23 Then he went up from there to Bethel; and as he was going up by the way, young lads came out from the city and mocked him and said to him, "Go up, you baldhead; go up, you baldhead!" 2 Chr. 36:16; Ps. 31:17, 18

24 When he looked behind him and saw them, he cursed them in the name of the LORD. Then two female bears came out of the woods and tore up forty-two lads of their number. Neh. 13:25-27 • *them*

25 And he went from there to Mount Carmel, and from there he returned to Samaria.

CHAPTER 3

Spiritual Evaluation of Jehoram

Now Jehoram the son of Ahab became king over Israel at Samaria in the eighteenth year of Jehoshaphat king of Judah, and reigned twelve years. 2 Kin. 1:17

2 And he did evil in the sight of the LORD, though not like his father and his mother; for he put away the *sacred* pillar of Baal which his father had made. Ex. 23:24

3 Nevertheless, he clung to the sins of Jeroboam the son of Nebat, which he made Israel sin; he did not depart from them.

Political Situation Under Jehoram

4 Now Mesha king of Moab was a sheep breeder, and used to pay the king of Israel 100,000 lambs and the wool of 100,000 rams. 2 Sam. 8:2; Is. 16:1, 2

5 But it came about, when Ahab died, the king of Moab rebelled against the king of Israel. 2 Kin. 1:1

6 And King Jehoram went out of Samaria at that time and mustered all Israel.

7 Then he went and sent *word* to Jehoshaphat the king of Judah, saying, "The king of Moab has rebelled against me. Will you go with me to fight against Moab?" And he said, "I will go up; I am as you are, my people as your people, my horses as your horses." 1 Kin. 22:4

8 And he said, "Which way shall we go up?" And he answered, "The way of the wilderness of Edom." *said*

9 So the king of Israel went with the king of Judah and the king of Edom; and they made a circuit of seven days' journey, and there was no water for the army or for the cattle that followed them. 2 Kin. 3:1 • 140 mi.

10 Then the king of Israel said, "Alas! For the LORD has called these three kings to give them into the hand of Moab."

11 But Jehoshaphat said, "Is there not a prophet of the LORD here, that we may inquire of the LORD by him?" And one of the king of Israel's servants answered and said, "Elisha the son of Shaphat is here, who used to pour water on the hands of Elijah."

12 And Jehoshaphat said, "The word of the LORD is with him." So the king of Israel and Jehoshaphat and the king of Edom went down to him.

13 Now Elisha said to the king of Israel, "What do I have to do with you? Go to the prophets of your father and to the prophets of your mother." And the king of Israel said to him, "No, for the LORD has called these three kings *together* to give them into the hand of Moab." 1 Kin. 18:19; 22:6-11, 22-25

14 And Elisha said, "As the LORD of hosts lives, before whom I stand, were it not that I regard the presence of Jehoshaphat the king of Judah, I would not look at you nor see you. 1 Kin. 17:1; 2 Kin. 5:16

15 "But now bring me a minstrel." And it came about, when the minstrel played, that the hand of the LORD came upon him.

16 And he said, "Thus says the LORD, 'Make this valley full of trenches.'

17 "For thus says the LORD, 'You shall not see wind nor shall you see rain; yet that valley shall be filled with water, so that you shall drink, both you and your cattle and your beasts. Ps. 107:35

18 'And this is but a slight thing in the sight of the LORD; He shall also give the Moabites into your hand. Jer. 32:17, 27; Mark 10:27

19 'Then you shall strike every fortified city and every choice city, and fell every good tree and stop all springs of water, and mar every good piece of land with stones.' "

20 And it happened in the morning about the time of offering the sacrifice, that behold, water came by the way of Edom, and the country was filled with water. Ex. 29:39

21 Now all the Moabites heard that the

kings had come up to fight against them. And all who were able to^Tput on armor and older were summoned, and stood on the border.   *gird themselves with a belt*

22 And they rose early in the morning, and the sun shone on the water, and the Moabites saw the water opposite *them* as red as blood.

23 Then they said, "This is blood; the kings have surely fought together, and they have slain one another. Now therefore, Moab, to the spoil!"

24 But when they came to the camp of Israel, the Israelites arose and struck the Moabites, so that they fled before them; and they went forward^Tinto the land, ^Tslaughtering the Moabites.   *into it · smiting*

25 ^RThus they destroyed the cities; and each one threw a stone on every piece of good land and filled it. So they stopped all the springs of water and felled all the good trees, until in^RKir-haraseth *only* they left its stones; however, the slingers went about *it* and struck it.   2 Kin. 3:19 · Jer. 48:31, 36

26 When the king of Moab saw that the battle was too fierce for him, he took with him 700 men who drew swords, to break through to the king of Edom; but they could not.

27 Then he took his oldest son who was to reign in his place, and offered him as a burnt offering on the wall. And there came great wrath against Israel, and they departed from him and returned to their own land.

CHAPTER 4

Miracle of the Increase of the Widow's Oil

Now a certain woman of the wives of the sons of the prophets cried out to^TElisha, "Your servant my husband is dead, and you know that your servant feared the LORD; and the creditor has come to take my two children to be his slaves."   *Elisha, saying*

2 And Elisha said to her, "What shall I do for you? Tell me, what do you have in the house?" And she said, "Your maidservant has nothing in the house except a jar of oil."

3 Then he said, "Go, borrow vessels at large for yourself from all your neighbors, *even* empty vessels; do not get a few.

4 "And you shall go in and shut the door behind you and your sons, and pour out into all these vessels; and you shall set aside what is full."

5 So she went from him and shut the door behind her and her sons; they were bringing *the vessels* to her and she poured.

6 And it came about when^Rthe vessels were full, that she said to her son, "Bring me another vessel." And he said to her, "There is not one vessel more." And the oil stopped.   Matt. 14:20

7 Then she came and told^Rthe man of God. And he said, "Go, sell the oil and pay your debt, and you *and* your sons can live on the rest."   1 Kin. 12:22

Miracle of the Shunammite's Son

8 Now there came a day when Elisha passed over to Shunem, where there was a prominent woman, and she persuaded him to eat food. And so it was, as often as he passed by, he turned in there to eat food.

9 And she said to her husband, "Behold now, I perceive that this is a holy^Rman of God passing by us continually.   2 Kin. 4:7

10 "Please, let us^Rmake a little walled upper chamber and let us set a bed for him there, and a table and a chair and a lampstand; and it shall be, when he comes to us, *that* he can turn in there."   Matt. 10:41; 25:40

11 One day he came there and turned in to the upper chamber and^Trested.   *lay there*

12 Then he said to^RGehazi his servant, "Call this Shunammite." And when he had called her, she stood before him.   2 Kin. 4:29

13 And he said to him, "Say now to her, 'Behold, you have been^Tcareful for us with all this care; what can I do for you? Would you be spoken for to the king or to the captain of the army?'" And she answered, "I live among my own people."   *fearful*

14 So he said, "What then is to be done for her?" And Gehazi^Tanswered, "Truly she has no son and her husband is old."   *said*

15 And he said, "Call her." When he had called her, she stood in the doorway.

16 Then he said, "At this season^Tnext year you shall embrace a son." And she said, "No, my lord, O man of God, do not lie to your maidservant."   *when the time revives*

17 And the woman conceived and bore a son at that season^Tthe next year, as Elisha had said to her.   *when the time revived*

18 When the child was grown, the day came that he went out to his father to the reapers.

19 And he said to his father, "My head, my head." And he said to his servant, "Carry him to his mother."

20 When he had taken him and brought him to his mother, he sat on her^Tlap until noon, and *then* died.   *knees*

21 And she went up and^Rlaid him on the bed of the man of God, and shut *the door* behind him, and went out.   2 Kin. 4:32

22 Then she called to her husband and said, "Please send me one of the servants and one of the donkeys, that I may run to the man of God and return."

23 And he said, "Why will you go to him today? It is neither^Rnew moon nor sabbath." And she said, "*It will be* well."   Num. 10:10

24 Then she saddled a donkey and said to her servant, "Drive and go forward; do not slow down^Tthe pace for me unless I tell you."   *riding*

25 So she went and came to the man of

God to Mount Carmel. And it came about when the man of God saw her at a distance, that he said to Gehazi his servant, "Behold, ^Tyonder is the Shunammite.   *this Shunammite*

26 "Please run now to meet her and say to her, 'Is it well with you? Is it well with your husband? Is it well with the child?' " And she ^Tanswered, "It is well."   *said*

27 When she came to the man of God to the hill, she caught hold of his feet. And Gehazi came near to push her away; but the man of God said, "Let her alone, for her soul is ^Ttroubled within her; and the LORD has hidden it from me and has not told me."   *bitter*

28 Then she said, "Did I ask for a son from my lord? Did I not say, 'Do^R not deceive me'?"   2 Kin. 4:16

29 Then he said to Gehazi, "Gird^R up your loins and ^Ttake my staff in your hand, and go your way; if you meet any man, do not ^Rsalute him, and if anyone salutes you, do not answer him; and lay my staff on the lad's face."   1 Kin. 18:46 • Ex. 4:17 • Luke 10:4

30 And the mother of the lad said, "As ^Tthe LORD lives and as you yourself live, I will not leave you." And he arose and followed her.   2 Kin. 2:2, 4

31 Then Gehazi passed on before them and laid the staff on the ^Tlad's face, but there was neither sound nor ^Tresponse. So he returned to meet him and told him, "The lad ^Rhas not awakened."   *attentiveness* • John 11:11

32 When Elisha came into the house, behold the lad was dead and laid on his bed.

33 So he entered and shut the door behind them both, and prayed to the LORD.

34 And ^Rhe went up and lay on the child, and put his mouth on his mouth and his eyes on his eyes and his hands on his hands, and he stretched himself on him; and the flesh of the child became warm.   1 Kin. 17:21

35 Then he returned and walked in the house once back and forth, and went up and ^Rstretched himself on him; and the lad sneezed seven times and the lad opened his eyes.   1 Kin. 17:21

36 And he called Gehazi and said, "Call this Shunammite." So he called her. And when she came in to him, he said, "Take up your son."

37 Then she went in and fell at his feet and bowed herself to the ground, and ^Rshe took up her son and went out.   [Heb. 11:35]

Miracle of the Deadly Stew

38 When Elisha returned to Gilgal, *there was* a famine in the land. ^TAs the sons of the prophets were sitting before him, he said to his servant, "Put on the large pot and boil stew for the sons of the prophets."   *And*

39 Then one went out into the field to gather herbs, and found a wild vine and gathered from it his lap full of wild gourds, and came and sliced them into the pot of stew, for they did not know *what they were.*

40 So they poured *it* out for the men to eat. And it came about as they were eating of the stew, that they cried out and said, "O man of God, there is ^Rdeath in the pot." And they were unable to eat.   Ex. 10:17

41 But he said, "Now bring meal." ^RAnd he threw it into the pot, and he said, "Pour *it* out for the people that they may eat." Then there was no harm in the pot.   Ex. 15:25

Miracle of the Multiplication of the Loaves

42 Now a man came from Baal-shalishah, and brought the man of God bread of the first fruits, twenty loaves of barley and fresh ears of grain in his sack. And he said, "Give *them* to the people that they may eat."

43 And his attendant said, "What, ^Rshall I set this before a hundred men?" But he said, "Give *them* to the people that they may eat, for thus says the LORD, 'They shall eat and have *some* left over.' "   Luke 9:13; John 6:9

44 ^RSo he set *it* before them, and they ate and ^Rhad *some* left over, according to the word of the LORD.   Matt. 14:20; 15:37; John 6:13

CHAPTER 5

Miracle of the Healing of Naaman

NOW ^RNaaman, captain of the army of the king of Aram, was a great man ^Twith his master, and highly respected, because by him the LORD had given victory to Aram. The man was also a valiant warrior, *but he was* a leper.   Luke 4:27 • *before*

2 Now the Arameans had gone out ^Rin bands, and had taken captive a little girl from the land of Israel; and she ^Twaited on Naaman's wife.   2 Kin. 6:23 • *was before*

3 And she said to her mistress, "I wish that my master were ^Twith the prophet who is in Samaria! Then he would cure him of his leprosy."   *before*

4 And ^TNaaman went in and told his master, saying, "Thus and thus spoke the girl who is from the land of Israel."   *he*

5 Then the king of Aram said, "Go ^Tnow, and I will send a letter to the king of Israel." And he departed and took with him ten talents of silver and six thousand *shekels* of gold and ten changes of clothes.   *enter*

6 And he brought the letter to the king of Israel, saying, "And now as this letter comes to you, behold, I have sent Naaman my servant to you, that you may cure him of his leprosy."

7 And it came about when the king of Israel read the letter, that ^Rhe tore his clothes and said, "Am I God, to kill and to make alive, that this man is sending *word* to me to cure a man of his leprosy? But ^Tconsider now, and see how he is seeking ^Ta quarrel against me."   Gen. 37:29 • *an occasion*

8 And it happened when Elisha ^Rthe man

of God heard that the king of Israel had torn his clothes, that he sent *word* to the king, saying, "Why have you torn your clothes? Now let him come to me, and he shall know that there is a prophet in Israel." 1 Kin. 12:22

9 So Naaman came with his horses and his chariots, and stood at the doorway of the house of Elisha.

10 And Elisha sent a messenger to him, saying, "Go^R and wash in the Jordan seven times, and your flesh shall be restored to you and *you shall* be clean."   John 9:7

11 But Naaman was furious and went away and said, "Behold, I thought, 'He will surely come out to me, and stand and call on the name of the LORD his God, and wave his hand over the place, and cure the leper.'

12 "Are not Abanah and Pharpar, the rivers of Damascus, better than all the waters of Israel? Could I not wash in them and be clean?" So he turned and^Rwent away in a rage.   [Prov. 14:17]

13 ^RThen his servants came near and spoke to him and said, "My^R father, had the prophet told you *to do some* great thing, would you not have done *it*? How much more *then*, when he says to you, 'Wash, and be clean'?"   1 Sam. 28:23 • 2 Kin. 2:12

14 So he went down and dipped *himself* seven times in the Jordan, according to the word of the man of God; and^Rhis flesh was restored like the flesh of a little child, and^Rhe was clean.   2 Kin. 5:10; Job 33:25 • Luke 4:27

15 When he returned to the man of God ^Twith all his company, and came and stood before him, he said, "Behold now, I know that there is no God in all the earth, but in Israel; so please take a ^Tpresent from your servant now."   *he and* • *blessing*

16 But he said, "As the LORD lives, before whom I stand, I will take nothing." And he urged him to take *it*, but he refused.

17 And Naaman said, "If not, please let your servant at least be given two mules' load of ^Rearth; for your servant will no more offer burnt offering nor will he sacrifice to other gods, but to the LORD.   Ex. 20:24

18 "In this matter may the LORD pardon your servant: when my master goes into the house of Rimmon to worship there, and^Rhe leans on my hand and I bow myself in the house of Rimmon, when I bow myself in the house of Rimmon, the LORD pardon your servant in this matter."   2 Kin. 7:2, 17

19 And he said to him, "Go in peace." So he departed from him some distance.

20 But Gehazi, the servant of Elisha the man of God, ^Tthought, "Behold, my master has spared this Naaman the Aramean, by not receiving from his hands what he brought. As the LORD lives, I will run after him and take something from him."   *said*

21 So Gehazi pursued Naaman. When Naaman saw one running after him, he came down from the chariot to meet him and said, "Is all well?"

22 And he said, "All^R is well. My master has sent me, saying, 'Behold, just now two young men of the sons of the prophets have come to me from the hill country of Ephraim. Please give them a talent of silver and two changes of clothes.' "   2 Kin. 4:26

23 And Naaman said, "Be^Rpleased to take ^Ttwo talents." And he urged him, and bound two talents of silver in two bags with two changes of clothes, and gave them to two of his servants; and they carried *them* before him.   2 Kin. 6:3 • $768,000

24 When he came to the^Thill, he took them from their hand and^Rdeposited them in the house, and he sent the men away, and they departed.   *Ophel* • [Josh. 7:1, 11, 12, 21]

25 But he went in and stood before his master. And Elisha said to him, "Where have you been, Gehazi?" And he said, "Your^R servant went nowhere."   2 Kin. 5:22

26 Then he said to him, "Did not my heart go *with you*, when the man turned from his chariot to meet you?^RIs it a time to receive money and to receive clothes and olive groves and vineyards and sheep and oxen and male and female servants?   2 Kin. 5:16

27 "Therefore, the leprosy of Naaman shall cleave to you and to your ^Tdescendants forever." So he went out from his presence a leper *as white* as snow.   *seed*

CHAPTER 6

Miracle of the Floating Axe Head

NOW the sons of the prophets said to Elisha, "Behold now, the place before you where we are living is too limited for us.

2 "Please let us go to the Jordan, and each of us take from there a beam, and let us make a place there for ourselves where we may live." So he said, "Go."

3 Then one said, "Please be willing to go with your servants." And he ^Tanswered, "I shall go."   *said*

4 So he went with them; and when they came to the Jordan, they cut down trees.

5 But as one was felling a beam,^Tthe axe head fell into the water; and he cried out and said, "Alas, my master! For it was borrowed."   *as for the iron, it fell*

6 Then the man of God said, "Where did it fall?" And when he showed him the place, ^Rhe cut off a stick, and threw *it* in there, and made the iron float.   Ex. 15:25; 2 Kin. 2:21; 4:41

7 And he said, "Take it up for yourself." So he put out his hand and took it.

Aram's War Plan

8 Now the king of Aram was warring against Israel; and he ^Tcounseled with his servants saying, "In such and such a place shall be my camp."   *took counsel*

9 And^Rthe man of God sent *word* to the

king of Israel saying, "Beware that you do not pass this place, for the Arameans are coming down there." 2 Kin. 4:1, 7; 6:12

10 And the king of Israel sent to the place about which the man of God had told him; thus he warned him, so that he guarded himself there, more than once or twice.

11 Now the heart of the king of Aram was enraged over this thing; and he called his servants and said to them, "Will you tell me which of us is for the king of Israel?"

12 And one of his servants said, "No, my lord, O king; but Elisha, the prophet who is in Israel, tells the king of Israel the words that you speak in your bedroom."

God's Chariots and Horses

13 So he said, "Go and see where he is, that I may send and take him." And it was told him, saying, "Behold, he is in Dothan."

14 And he sent horses and chariots and a great army there, and they came by night and surrounded the city.

15 Now when the attendant of the man of God had risen early and gone out, behold, an army with horses and chariots was circling the city. And his servant said to him, "Alas, my master!^TWhat shall we do?" How

16 So he^Tanswered, "Do^Rnot fear, for those who are with us are more than those who are with them." said • Ex. 14:13

17 Then Elisha prayed and said, "O LORD, I pray, open his eyes that he may see." And the LORD opened the servant's eyes, and he saw; and behold, the mountain was full of horses and chariots of fire all around Elisha.

Aram's Army Is Blinded

18 And when they came down to him, Elisha prayed to the LORD and said, "Strike this^Tpeople with blindness, I pray." So He ^Rstruck them with blindness according to the word of Elisha. nation • Gen. 19:11

19 Then Elisha said to them, "This is not the way, nor is this the city; follow me and I will bring you to the man whom you seek." And he brought them to Samaria.

20 And it came about when they had come into Samaria, that Elisha said, "O ^RLORD, open the eyes of these *men,* that they may see." So the LORD opened their eyes, and they saw; and behold, they were in the midst of Samaria. 2 Kin. 6:17

21 Then the king of Israel when he saw them, said to Elisha, "My^Rfather, shall I^Tkill them? Shall I^Tkill them?" 2 Kin. 2:12 • smite

22 And he^Tanswered, "You shall not kill *them.* Would you^Tkill^Rthose you have taken captive with your sword and with your bow? Set bread and water before them, that they may eat and drink and go to their master." said • smite • Deut. 20:11-16

¹ I.e., One kab equals approx. 2 quarts

23 So he prepared a great feast for them; and when they had eaten and drunk he sent them away, and they went to their master. And the marauding bands of Arameans did not come again into the land of Israel.

Siege of Samaria Causes Famine

24 Now it came about after this, that Benhadad king of Aram gathered all his army and went up and besieged Samaria.

25 And there was a great^Rfamine in Samaria; and behold, they besieged it, until a donkey's head was sold for^Teighty *shekels* of silver, and a fourth of a ¹kab of dove's dung for five *shekels* of silver. Lev. 26:26 • $10,240

26 And as the king of Israel was passing by on the wall a woman cried out to him, saying, "Help, my lord, O king!"

27 And he said, "If the LORD does not help you, from where shall I help you? From the threshing floor, or from the wine press?"

28 And the king said to her, "What^Ris^Tthe matter with you?" And she^Tanswered, "This woman said to me, 'Give your son that we may eat him today, and we will eat my son tomorrow.' Judg. 18:23 • to you • said

29"So^Rwe boiled my son and ate him; and I said to her on the next day, 'Give your son, that we may eat him'; but she has hidden her son." Lev. 26:27-29; Deut. 28:52, 53, 57

Elisha's Prophecies

30 And it came about when the king heard the words of the woman, that he tore his clothes—now he was passing by on the wall—and the people looked, and behold, he had sackcloth^Tbeneath on his body. within

31 Then he said, "May God do so to me and more also, if the head of Elisha the son of Shaphat^Tremains on him today." stands

32 Now Elisha was sitting in his house, and^Rthe elders were sitting with him. And *the king* sent a man from his presence; but before the messenger came to him, he said to the elders, "Do you see how this son of a murderer has sent to take away my head? Look, when the messenger comes, shut the door and^Thold the door shut against him. Is not the sound of his master's feet behind him?" Ezek. 8:1 • press him with the door

33 And while he was still talking with them, behold, the messenger came down to him, and he said, "Behold,^R this evil is from the LORD; why should I wait for the LORD any longer?" Is. 8:21

CHAPTER 7

THEN Elisha said, "Listen to the word of the LORD; thus says the LORD, 'Tomorrow^R about this time a^Tmeasure of fine flour shall be *sold* for a^Tshekel, and^Ttwo measures of

barley for a shekel, in the gate of Samaria.'"   2 Kin. 7:18 • Heb. *seah* • $128 • 4.349 bu.

2 And [R]the royal officer on whose hand the king was leaning answered the man of God and said, "Behold, [R]if the LORD should make windows in heaven, could this thing be?" Then he said, "Behold you shall see it with your own eyes, but you shall not eat [T]of it."   2 Kin. 5:18 • Gen. 7:11 • *from there*

3 Now there were four [R]leprous men at the entrance of the gate; and they said to one another, "Why do we sit here until we die?   Lev. 13:45, 46; Num. 5:2-4; 12:10-14

4 "If we say, 'We will enter the city,' then the famine is in the city and we shall die there; and if we sit here, we die also. Now therefore come, and let us [T]go over to [R]the camp of the Arameans. If they spare us, we shall live; and if they kill us, we shall but die."   *fall* • 2 Kin. 6:24

5 And they arose at twilight to go to the camp of the Arameans; when they came to the outskirts of the camp of the Arameans, behold, there was no one there.

6 For [R]the Lord had caused the army of the Arameans to hear a sound of chariots and a sound of horses, *even* the sound of a great army, so that they said to one another, "Behold, the king of Israel has hired against us the kings of the Hittites and the kings of the Egyptians, to come upon us."   2 Sam. 5:24

7 Therefore they [R]arose and fled in the twilight, and left their tents and their horses and their donkeys, even the camp just as it was, and fled for their life.   Ps. 48:4; Prov. 28:1

8 When these lepers came to the outskirts of the camp, they entered one tent and ate and drank, and [R]carried from there silver and gold and clothes, and went and hid *them*; and they returned and entered another tent and carried from there *also,* and went and hid *them*.   Josh. 7:21

9 Then they said to one another, "We are not doing right. This day is a day of good news, but we are keeping silent; if we wait until morning light, punishment will [T]overtake us. Now therefore come, let us go and tell the king's household."   *find*

10 So they came and called to the gatekeepers of the city, and they told them, saying, "We came to the camp of the Arameans, and behold, there was no one there, nor the voice of man, only the horses tied and the donkeys tied, and the tents just as they were."

11 And the gatekeepers called, and told *it* within the king's household.

12 Then the king arose in the night and said to his servants, "I will now tell you what the Arameans have done to us. They know that [R]we are hungry; therefore they have gone from the camp to hide themselves in the field, saying, 'When they come out of the city, we shall capture them alive and get into the city.' "   2 Kin. 6:25-29

13 And one of his servants answered and said, "Please, let some *men* take five of the

horses which remain, which are left [T]in the city. Behold, they *will be in any case* like all the multitude of Israel who are left in it; behold, they *will be in any case* like all the multitude of Israel who have already perished, so let us send and see."   *in it*

14 They took therefore two chariots with horses, and the king sent after the army of the Arameans, saying, "Go and see."

15 And they went after them to the Jordan, and behold, all the way was full of clothes and equipment, which the Arameans had thrown away in their haste. Then the messengers returned and told the king.

16 So the people went out and plundered the camp of the Arameans. Then a [T]measure of fine flour *was sold* for [T]a shekel and two [T]measures of barley for a shekel, according to the word of the LORD.   Heb., *seah* • $128

17 Now the king appointed [T]the royal officer on whose hand he leaned [T]to have charge of the gate; but the people trampled on him at the gate, and he died just as the man of God had said, who spoke when the king came down to him.   2 Kin. 7:2 • *over the gate*

18 And it came about just as the man of God had spoken to the king, saying, "Two [R]measures of barley for a shekel and [T]a measure of fine flour for a shekel, shall be *sold* tomorrow about this time at the gate of Samaria."   2 Kin. 7:1 • 2.175 bushels

19 Then the royal officer answered the man of God and said, "Now behold, if the LORD should make windows in heaven, could such a thing be?" And he said, "Behold, you shall see it with your own eyes, but you shall not eat [T]of it."   *from there*

20 And so it happened to him, for the people trampled on him at the gate, and he died.

CHAPTER 8

Elisha's Ministry
with the Shunammite Woman

NOW Elisha spoke to the woman whose son he had restored to life, saying, "Arise and go [T]with your household, and sojourn wherever you can sojourn; for the LORD has called for a famine, and it shall even come on the land for seven years."   *you and your*

2 So the woman arose and did according to the word of the man of God, and she went with her household and sojourned in the land of the Philistines seven years.

3 And it came about at the end of seven years, that the woman returned from the land of the Philistines; and she went out to [T]appeal to the king for her house and for her field.   *cry out*

4 Now the king was talking with [R]Gehazi, the servant of the man of God, saying, "Please relate to me all the great things that Elisha has done."   2 Kin. 4:12; 5:20-27

5 And it came about, as he was relating

to the king^Rhow he had restored to life the one who was dead, that behold, the woman whose son he had restored to life,^Tappealed to the king for her house and for her field. And Gehazi said, "My lord, O king, this is the woman and this is her son, whom Elisha restored to life."   2 Kin. 4:35 • *cried out*

6 When the king asked the woman, she related *it* to him. So the king appointed for her a certain officer, saying, "Restore all that was hers and all the produce of the field from the day that she left the land even until now."

Elisha's Ministry with the King of Aram

7 Then Elisha came to^RDamascus. Now ^RBen-hadad king of Aram was sick, and it was told him, saying, "The man of God has come here."   1 Kin. 11:24 • 2 Kin. 6:24

8 And the king said to Hazael, "Take a gift in your hand and go to meet the man of God, and inquire of the LORD by him, saying, 'Will I recover from this sickness?' "

9 So Hazael went to meet him and took a gift in his hand, even every kind of good thing of Damascus, forty camels' loads; and he came and stood before him and said, "Your^Rson Ben-hadad king of Aram has sent me to you, saying, 'Will I recover from this sickness?' "   2 Kin. 5:13

10 Then Elisha said to him, "Go,^R say to him, 'You shall surely recover,' but the ^RLORD has shown me that he will certainly die."   2 Kin. 8:14 • 2 Kin. 8:15

11 And he^Tfixed his gaze steadily *on him* until he was ashamed, and the man of God wept.   *made his face stand fast and he set*

12 And Hazael said, "Why does my lord weep?" Then he^Tanswered, "Because^RI know the evil that you will do to the sons of Israel: their strongholds you will set on fire, and their young men you will kill with the sword, and their little ones you^Rwill dash in pieces, and their women with child you will rip up."   *said* • 2 Kin. 10:32 • 2 Kin. 15:16

13 Then Hazael said, "But what is your servant,^R*who is but* a dog, that he should do this great thing?" And Elisha ^Tanswered, "The LORD has shown me that you will be king over Aram."   1 Sam. 17:43 • *said*

14 So he departed from Elisha and returned to his master, who said to him, "What did Elisha say to you?" And he ^Tanswered, "He told me that^Ryou would surely recover."   *said* • 2 Kin. 8:10

15 And it came about on the morrow, that he took the cover and dipped it in water and spread it on his face,^Rso that he died. And Hazael became king in his place.   2 Kin. 8:10

The Reign of Jehoram in Judah 2 Chr. 21:5–10, 20

16 Now in the fifth year of Joram the son of Ahab king of Israel, Jehoshaphat being then the king of Judah, Jehoram the son of Jehoshaphat king of Judah became king.

17 He was^Rthirty-two years old when he became king, and he reigned eight years in Jerusalem.   2 Chr. 21:5-10

18 And he walked in the way of the kings of Israel, just as the house of Ahab had done, for the daughter of Ahab became his wife; and he did evil in the sight of the LORD.

19 However, the LORD was not willing to destroy Judah, for the sake of David His servant, since He had^Tpromised him to give a lamp to him through his sons always.   *said*

20 In his days^REdom revolted from under the hand of Judah, and made a king over themselves.   1 Kin. 22:47; 2 Kin. 3:9, 26, 27; 8:22

21 Then Joram crossed over to Zair, and all his chariots with him. And it came about that he arose by night and struck the Edomites who had surrounded him and the captains of the chariots;^Rbut *his* ^Tarmy fled to their tents.   2 Sam. 18:17; 19:8 • *the people*

22 So Edom revolted against Judah to this day. Then Libnah revolted at the same time.

23 And the rest of the acts of Joram and all that he did, are they not written in the Book of the Chronicles of the Kings of Judah?

^R24 So Joram slept with his fathers, and ^Twas buried with his fathers in the city of David; and ^RAhaziah his son became king in his place.   2 Chr. 21:20 • 2 Chr. 21:1, 7

Spiritual Evaluation of Ahaziah 2 Kin. 9:29; 2 Chr. 22:1–4

25 In the twelfth year of Joram the son of Ahab king of Israel, Ahaziah the son of Jehoram king of Judah began to reign.

26 ^RAhaziah *was* twenty-two years old when he became king, and he reigned one year in Jerusalem. And his mother's name *was* Athaliah the granddaughter of Omri king of Israel.   2 Chr. 22:2

27 And^Rhe walked in the way of the house of Ahab, and did evil in the sight of the LORD, like the house of Ahab *had done*, because he was a son-in-law of the house of Ahab.   2 Chr. 22:3

Battle Against Aram 2 Kin. 9:15, 16; 2 Chr. 22:5, 6

28 Then he went with Joram the son of Ahab to war against^RHazael king of Aram at ^RRamoth-gilead, and the Arameans^Twounded Joram.   2 Kin. 8:15 • 1 Kin. 22:3 • *smote*

29 So King Joram returned to be healed in Jezreel of the wounds which the Arameans had ^Tinflicted on him at Ramah, when he fought against Hazael king of Aram. Then Ahaziah the son of Jehoram king of Judah went down to see Joram the son of Ahab in Jezreel because he was sick.   *struck*

CHAPTER 9

Anointing of Jehu King over Israel

NOW Elisha the prophet called one of the sons of the prophets, and said to him, "Gird up your loins, and take this flask of oil in your hand, and go to Ramoth-gilead.
2 "When you arrive there, search out Jehu the son of Jehoshaphat the son of Nimshi, and go in and bid him arise from among his brothers, and bring him to an inner room.
3 "Then take the flask of oil and pour it on his head and say, 'Thus says the LORD, "I have anointed you king over Israel." ' Then open the door and flee and do not wait."
4 So^Rthe young man, the servant of the prophet, went to Ramoth-gilead.   2 Kin. 9:1
5 When he came, behold, the captains of the army were sitting, and he said, "I have a word for you, O captain." And Jehu said, "For^T which *one* of us?" And he said, "For you, O captain."   *To whom of us all?*
6 And he arose and went into the house, and he poured the oil on his head and said to him, "Thus says the LORD, the God of Israel, 'I^Thave anointed you king over the people of the LORD, *even* over Israel.   1 Sam. 2:7, 8
7 'And you shall strike the house of Ahab your master,^Rthat I may avenge^Rthe blood of My servants the prophets, and the blood of all the servants of the LORD, at the hand of Jezebel.   [Deut. 32:35] • 1 Kin. 18:4
8 'For the whole house of Ahab shall perish, and I will cut off from Ahab every male person both bond and free in Israel.
9 'And^RI will make the house of Ahab like the house of Jeroboam the son of Nebat, and^Rlike the house of Baasha the son of Ahijah.   1 Kin. 14:10 • 1 Kin. 16:3-5, 11, 12
10 'And the dogs shall eat Jezebel in the territory of Jezreel, and none shall bury her.' " Then he opened the door and fled.
11 Now Jehu came out to the servants of his master, and one said to him, "Is^Rall well? Why did this mad fellow come to you?" And he said to them, "You know *very well* the man and his talk."   2 Kin. 9:17, 19, 22
12 And they said, "It is a lie, tell us now." And he said, "Thus and thus he said to me, 'Thus says the LORD, "I have anointed you king over Israel." ' "
13 Then^Rthey hurried and each man took his garment and placed it under him on the bare steps, and^Rblew the trumpet, saying, "Jehu is king!"   Matt. 21:7 • 2 Sam. 15:10

Execution of Joram

14 So Jehu the son of Jehoshaphat the son of Nimshi conspired against Joram. Now Joram^Twith all Israel was defending Ramoth-gilead against Hazael king of Aram,   *he and*
15 but King ²Joram had returned to Jezreel to be healed of the wounds which the Ar-

ameans had^Tinflicted on him when he fought with Hazael king of Aram. So Jehu said, "If this is your mind, *then* let no one escape *or* leave the city to go tell *it* in Jezreel."   *struck*
16 Then Jehu rode in a chariot and went to Jezreel, for Joram was lying there. ^RAnd Ahaziah king of Judah had come down to see Joram.   2 Kin. 8:29
17 Now the watchman was standing on the tower in Jezreel and he saw the ^Tcompany of Jehu as he came, and said, "I see a ^Tcompany." And Joram said, "Take a horseman and send him to meet them and let him say, 'Is it peace?' "   *multitude*
18 So a horseman went to meet him and said, "Thus says the king, 'Is it peace?' " And Jehu said, "What have you to do with peace? Turn behind me." And the watchman ^Treported, "The messenger came to them, but he did not return."   *told, saying*
19 Then he sent out a second horseman, who came to them and said, "Thus says the king, 'Is it peace?' " And Jehu ^Tanswered, "What have you to do with peace? Turn behind me."   *said*
20 And the watchman^Treported, "He came even to them, and he did not return; and the driving is like the driving of Jehu the son of Nimshi, for he drives furiously." *told, saying*
21 Then Joram said, "Get ready." And they made his chariot ready. And Joram king of Israel and Ahaziah king of Judah went out, each in his chariot, and they went out to meet Jehu and found him in the^Tproperty of Naboth the Jezreelite.   *portion*
22 And it came about, when ^TJoram saw Jehu, that he said, "Is it peace, Jehu?" And he answered, "What peace, so long as the harlotries of your mother Jezebel and her witchcrafts are so many?"   *Heb., Jehoram*
23 So ^TJoram ^Treined about and fled and said to Ahaziah, "*There is* treachery, O Ahaziah!"   *Heb., Jehoram • turned his hands*
24 And Jehu drew his bow with his full strength and shot Joram between his arms; and the arrow went through his heart, and he sank in his chariot.
25 Then *Jehu* said to Bidkar his officer, "Take *him* up and cast him into the ³property of the field of Naboth the Jezreelite, for I remember when you and I were riding together after Ahab his father, that the LORD laid this oracle against him:
26 'Surely^RI have seen yesterday the blood of Naboth and the blood of his sons,' says the LORD, 'and I will repay you in this ³property,' says the LORD. Now then, take and cast him into the property, according to the word of the LORD."   1 Kin. 21:13

Death of Ahaziah
2 Kin. 8:25; 2 Chr. 22:9

27 When Ahaziah the king of Judah saw

---

² Heb., *Jehoram,* and so throughout this context
³ Lit., *portion,* and so throughout this context

this, he fled by the way of the garden house. And Jehu pursued him and said, "Shoot[T] him too, in the chariot." *So they shot him* at the ascent of Gur, which is at Ibleam. But he fled to Megiddo and died there.   *smite*

28 Then his servants carried him in a chariot to Jerusalem, and buried him in his grave with his fathers in the city of David.

29 Now in[R]the eleventh year of Joram, the son of Ahab, Ahaziah became king over Judah.   2 Kin. 8:25

Fulfillment of Elisha's Prophecy

30 When Jehu came to Jezreel, Jezebel heard *of it*, and [R]she painted her eyes and adorned her head, and looked out the window.   [Jer. 4:30]; Ezek. 23:40

31 And as Jehu entered the gate, she said, "Is it well, Zimri, your master's murderer?"

32 Then he lifted up his face to the window and said, "Who is on my side? Who?" And two or three officials looked down at him.

33 And he said, "Throw her down." So they threw her down, and some of her blood was sprinkled on the wall and on the horses, and he trampled her under foot.

34 When he came in, he ate and drank; and he said, "See now to this cursed woman and bury her, for she is a king's daughter."

35 And they went to bury her, but they found no more of her than the skull and the feet and the palms of her hands.

36 Therefore they returned and told him. And he said, "This is the word of the LORD, which He spoke by His servant Elijah the Tishbite, saying, 'In the property of Jezreel the dogs shall eat the flesh of Jezebel;

37 and [R]the corpse of Jezebel shall be as dung on the face of the field in the[T]property of Jezreel, so they cannot say, "This is Jezebel." ' "   Jer. 8:1-3 • *portion*

CHAPTER 10

NOW Ahab had seventy sons in[R]Samaria. And Jehu wrote letters and sent *them* to Samaria, to the rulers of Jezreel, the elders, and to the guardians of *the children of Ahab*, saying,   1 Kin. 16:24-29

2 "And now, when this letter comes to you, since your master's sons are with you, as well as the chariots and horses and a fortified city and the weapons,

3 select the best and [4]fittest of your master's sons, and set *him* on his father's throne, and fight for your master's house."

4 But they feared greatly and said, "Behold, [R]the two kings did not stand before him; how then can we stand?"   2 Kin. 9:24

5 And the one who *was* over the house-

hold, and he who *was* over the city, the elders, and the guardians of *the children*, sent *word* to Jehu, saying, "We[R] are your servants, all that you say to us we will do, we will not make any man king; do what is good in your sight."   Josh. 9:8, 11; 1 Kin. 20:4

6 Then he wrote a letter to them a second time saying, "If you are on my side, and you will listen to my voice, take the heads of the men, your master's sons, and come to me at Jezreel tomorrow about this time." Now the king's sons, seventy persons, *were* with the great men of the city, *who* were rearing them.

7 And it came about when the letter came to them, that they took the king's sons, and [R]slaughtered *them*, seventy persons, and put their heads in baskets, and sent *them* to him at Jezreel.   Judg. 9:5

8 When the messenger came and told him, saying, "They have brought the heads of the king's sons," he said, "Put them in two heaps at the entrance of the gate until morning."

9 Now it came about in the morning, that he went out and stood, and said to all the people, "You are[T]innocent; behold, I conspired against my master and killed him, but who[T]killed all these?   *just • smote*

10 "Know then that there shall fall to the earth nothing of the word of the LORD, which the LORD spoke concerning the house of Ahab, for the LORD has done what He spoke through His servant Elijah."

11 So Jehu[T]killed all who remained of the house of Ahab in Jezreel, and all his great men and his acquaintances and his priests, until he left him without a survivor.   *smote*

12 Then he arose and departed, and went to Samaria. On the way while he was at [5]Beth-eked of the shepherds,

13 Jehu[T]met the[T]relatives of Ahaziah king of Judah and said, "Who are you?" And they answered, "We are the[T]relatives of Ahaziah; and we have come down to greet the sons of the king and the sons of the queen mother."   *found • brothers*

14 And he said, "Take them alive." So they took them alive, and killed them at the pit of Beth-eked, forty-two men; and he left none of them.

15 Now when he had departed from there, he met Jehonadab the son of Rechab *coming* to meet him; and he greeted him and said to him, "Is your heart right, as my heart is with your heart?" And Jehonadab [T]answered, "It is." *Jehu said*, "If it is, give *me* your hand." And he gave him his hand, and he took him up to him into the chariot.   *said*

16 And he said, "Come with me and[R]see my zeal for the LORD." So[T]he made him ride in his chariot.   1 Kin. 19:10 • *they*

17 And when he came to Samaria, he killed all who remained to Ahab in Samaria, until he had destroyed him, according to the word of the LORD, which He spoke to Elijah.

---

[4] Lit., *most upright*   [5] I.e., house of binding

18 Then Jehu gathered all the people and said to them, "Ahab[R] served Baal a little; Jehu will serve him much.   1 Kin. 16·31, 32

19 "And now,[R] summon all the prophets of Baal, all his worshipers and all his priests; let no one be missing, for I have a great sacrifice for Baal; whoever is missing shall not live." But Jehu did it in [T]cunning, in order that he might destroy the worshipers of Baal.   1 Kin. 18:19; 22:6 · *insidiousness*

20 And Jehu said, "Sanctify a solemn assembly for Baal." And they proclaimed *it*.

21 Then Jehu sent [T]throughout Israel and all the worshipers of Baal came, so that there was not a man left who did not come. And when they went into[R]the house of Baal, the house of Baal was filled from one end to the other.   *in all* · 1 Kin. 16·32

22 And he said to the one who *was* [T]in charge of the wardrobe, "Bring out garments for all the worshipers of Baal." So he brought out garments for them.   *over the*

23 And Jehu went into the house of Baal with Jehonadab the son of Rechab; and he said to the worshipers of Baal, "Search and see that there may be here with you none of the servants of the LORD, but only the worshipers of Baal."

24 Then they went in to offer sacrifices and burnt offerings. Now Jehu had stationed for himself eighty men outside, and he had said, "The one who permits any of the men whom I bring into your hands to escape, shall give up his life in exchange."

25 Then it came about, as soon as he had finished offering the burnt offering, that Jehu said to the [T]guard and to the royal officers, "Go in, [T]kill them; let none come out." And they killed them with the edge of the sword; and the [T]guard and the royal officers threw *them* out, and went to the inner room of the house of Baal.   *runners · smite*

26 And they brought out the *sacred* pillars of the house of Baal, and burned them.

27 They also broke down the *sacred* pillar of Baal and broke down the house of Baal, and[R]made it a latrine to this day.   [Ezra 6:11]

28 Thus Jehu eradicated Baal out of Israel.

Spiritual Evaluation of Jehu

29 However,[R] *as for* the sins of Jeroboam the son of Nebat, which he made Israel sin, from these Jehu did not depart, *even* the [R]golden calves that *were* at Bethel and that *were* at Dan.   1 Kin. 12:28-30 · 1 Kin. 12:29

30 And the LORD said to Jehu, "Because you have done well in executing what is right in My eyes, *and* have done to the house of Ahab according to all that *was* in My heart,[R] your sons of the fourth generation shall sit on the throne of Israel."   2 Kin. 15:12

31 But Jehu was not careful to walk in the law of the LORD, the God of Israel, with all his heart; he did not depart from the sins of Jeroboam, which he made Israel sin.

Political Situation Under Jehu

32 In those days the LORD began to cut off *portions* from Israel; and Hazael defeated them throughout the territory of Israel:

33 from the Jordan eastward, all the land of Gilead, the Gadites and the Reubenites and the Manassites, from [R]Aroer, which is by the valley of the Arnon, even[R]Gilead and Bashan.   Deut. 2:36 · Amos 1:3-5

Death of Jehu

34 Now the rest of the acts of Jehu and all that he did and all his might, are they not written in the Book of the Chronicles of the Kings of Israel?

35 And Jehu slept with his fathers, and they buried him in Samaria. And Jehoahaz his son became king in his place.

36 Now the time which Jehu reigned over Israel in Samaria *was* twenty-eight years.

CHAPTER 11

Salvation of Joash

WHEN Athaliah the mother of Ahaziah saw that her son was dead, she rose and destroyed all the royal [T]offspring.   *seed*

2 But Jehosheba, the daughter of King Joram, sister of Ahaziah,[R]took Joash the son of Ahaziah and stole him from among the king's sons who were being put to death, and placed him and his nurse in the bedroom. So they hid him from Athaliah, and he was not put to death.   2 Kin. 11:21; 12:1

3 So he was hidden with her in the house of the LORD six years, while Athaliah was reigning over the land.

Overthrow of Athaliah by Jehoiada
2 Chr. 23:1–11

4 Now in the seventh year Jehoiada sent and brought the captains of hundreds of the Carites and of the [6]guard, and brought them to him in the house of the LORD. Then he made a covenant with them and put them under oath in the house of the LORD, and showed them the king's son.

5 And he commanded them, saying, "This is the thing that you shall do: one third of you, who come in on the sabbath and keep watch over the king's house

6 (one third also *shall be* at the gate Sur, and one third at the gate behind the [6]guards), [T]shall keep watch over the house for defense.   *and shall*

[6] Lit., *runners*

7"And two parts of you, *even* all who go out on the sabbath, shall also keep watch over the house of the LORD for the king.

8"Then you shall surround the king, each with his weapons in his hand; and whoever comes within the ranks shall be put to death. And ᴿbe with the king when he goes out and when he comes in."	Num. 27:16, 17

9 So the captains of hundreds did according to all that Jehoiada the priest commanded. And each one of them took his men who were to come in on the sabbath, with those who were to go out on the sabbath, and came to Jehoiada the priest.

10 And ᴿthe priest gave to the captains of hundreds the spears and shields that had been King David's, which *were* in the house of the LORD.	2 Sam. 8:7; 1 Chr. 18:7

11 And the guards stood each with his weapons in his hand, from the right side of the house to the left side of the house, by the altar and by the house, around the king.

ᴿ**12** Then he brought the king's son out and put the crown on him, and *gave him* the testimony; and they made him king and anointed him, and they clapped their hands and said, "*Long* live the king!"	2 Sam. 1:10

Death of Athaliah—2 Chr. 23:12–15

13 ᴿWhen Athaliah heard the noise of the guard *and* of the people, she came to the people in the house of the LORD.	2 Chr. 23:12

14 And she looked and behold, the king was standingᴿby the pillar, according to the custom, with the captains and the ᵀtrumpeters beside the king; and all the people of the land rejoiced and blew trumpets. Then Athaliah tore her clothes and cried, "Treason! Treason!"	2 Kin. 23:3 • *trumpets*

15 And Jehoiada the priest commanded the captains of hundreds who were appointed over the army, and said to them, "Bring her out between the ranks, and whoever follows her put to death with the sword." For the priest said, "Let her not be put to death in the house of the LORD."

16 So they seized her, and when she arrived at the horses' entrance of the king's house, she wasᴿput to death there.	Gen. 9:6

Renewal of the Covenant
2 Chr. 23:16—24:1

17 Then ᴿJehoiada made a covenant between the LORD and the king and the people, that they should be the LORD's people, also between the king and the people.	Josh. 24:25

18 And all the people of the land went to the house of Baal, and tore it down; his altars and his images they broke in pieces thoroughly, and killed Mattan the priest of Baal before the altars. And the priest appointed officers over the house of the LORD.

---

⁷ Lit., *breaches,* and so through v. 12

19 And he took the captains of hundreds and the ᴿCarites and the ᵀguards and all the people of the land; and they brought the king down from the house of the LORD, and came by the way of the gate of theᵀguards to the king's house. And he sat on the throne of the kings.	2 Kin. 11:4 • *runners*

20 So ᴿall the people of the land rejoiced and the city was quiet. For they had put Athaliah to death with the sword at the king's house.	[Prov. 11:10]

21 ᴿJehoash was seven years old when he became king.	2 Chr. 24:1-14

CHAPTER 12

Spiritual Evaluation of Joash (Jehoash)
2 Chr. 24:1, 2

Iɴ the seventh year of Jehu, ᴿJehoash became king, and he reigned forty years in Jerusalem; and his mother's name was Zibiah of Beersheba.	2 Chr. 24:1

2 And Jehoash did right in the sight of the LORD all his days in which Jehoiada the priest instructed him.

3 Only ᴿthe high places were not taken away; the people still sacrificed and burned incense on the high places.	2 Kin. 14:4; 15:35

Spiritual Situation Under Joash (Jehoash)
2 Chr. 24:5–14

4 Then Jehoash said to the priests, "All the money of the sacred things which is brought into the house of the LORD, in current money, *both* the money of each man's assessment *and* all the money which any man's heart prompts him to bring into the house of the LORD,

5 let the priests take it for themselves, each from his acquaintance; and they shall repair the ⁷damages of the house wherever any damage may be found.

6 But it came about that in the twenty-third year of King Jehoash the priests had not repaired the damages of the house.

7 Then King Jehoash called for Jehoiada the priest, and for the *other* priests and said to them, "Why do you not repair the damages of the house? Now therefore take no *more* money from your acquaintances, but pay it for the damages of the house."

8 So the priests agreed that they should take no *more* money from the people, nor repair the damages of the house.

9 But ᴿJehoiada the priest took a chest and bored a hole in its lid, and put it beside the altar, on the right side as one comes into the house of the LORD; and the priests who guarded the threshold put in it all the money which was brought into the house of the LORD.	Mark 12:41; Luke 21:1

10 And when they saw ᴿthat there was much money in the chest,ᴿthe king's scribe and the high priest came up and tied *it* in

bags and counted the money which was found in the house of the LORD.   2 Sam. 8:17

11 And they gave the money which was weighed out into the hands of those who did the work, who had the oversight[T] of the house of the LORD; and they paid it out to the carpenters and the builders, who worked on the house of the LORD;   *brought*

12 and[R] to the masons and the stonecutters, and for buying timber and hewn stone to repair the damages to the house of the LORD, and for all that was[T] laid out for the house to repair it.   2 Kin. 22:5, 6 • *went out*

13 But[R] there were not made for the house of the LORD silver cups, snuffers, bowls, trumpets, any vessels of gold, or vessels of silver from the money which was brought into the house of the LORD;   2 Chr. 24:14

14 for they gave that to those who did the work, and with it they repaired the house of the LORD.

15 Moreover, they did not require an accounting from the men into whose hand they gave the money to pay to those who did the work, for they dealt faithfully.

16 The[R] money from the guilt offerings and the[R] money from the sin offerings, was not brought into the house of the LORD; it was for the priests.   [Lev. 5:15–18] • Lev. 4:24, 29

Political Situation Under Joash (Jehoash)

17 Then Hazael king of Aram went up and fought against Gath and captured it, and Hazael set his face to go up to Jerusalem.

18 And[R] Jehoash king of Judah took all the sacred things that Jehoshaphat and Jehoram and Ahaziah, his fathers, kings of Judah, had dedicated, and[R] his own sacred things and all the gold that was found among the treasuries of the house of the LORD and of the king's house, and sent *them* to Hazael king of Aram. Then he went away from Jerusalem.   1 Kin. 14:26 • 2 Kin. 12:4

Death of Joash—2 Chr. 24:25–27

19 Now the rest of the acts of Joash and all that he did, are they not written in the Book of the Chronicles of the Kings of Judah?

20 And[R] his servants arose and made a conspiracy, and[R] struck down Joash at the house of Millo *as he was* going down to Silla.   2 Chr. 24:25-27 • 2 Kin. 14:5

21 For Jozacar the son of Shimeath, and Jehozabad the son of[R] Shomer, his servants, struck *him*, and he died; and they buried him with his fathers in the city of David, and[R] Amaziah his son became king in his place.   2 Chr. 24:26 • 2 Kin. 14:1

CHAPTER 13

The Reign of Jehoahaz in Israel

IN the twenty-third year of Joash the son of Ahaziah, king of Judah, Jehoahaz the son

of Jehu became king over Israel at Samaria, *and he reigned* seventeen years.

2 And he did evil in the sight of the LORD, and followed the sins of Jeroboam the son of Nebat,[R] with which he made Israel sin; he did not turn from them.   1 Kin. 12:26-33

3 [R] So the anger of the LORD was kindled against Israel, and He gave them continually into the hand of[R] Hazael king of Aram, and into the hand of Ben-hadad the son of Hazael.   Judg. 2:14 • 2 Kin. 12:17

4 Then[R] Jehoahaz entreated the favor of the LORD, and the LORD listened to him; for He saw the oppression of Israel, how the king of Aram oppressed them.   Num. 21:7-9

5 And the LORD gave Israel a [8]deliverer,[R] so that they escaped from under the hand of the Arameans; and the sons of Israel lived in their tents as formerly.   Neh. 9:27 • *went out*

6 Nevertheless they did not turn away from the sins of the house of Jeroboam,[R] with which he made Israel sin, but walked in[T] them; and the Asherah also remained standing in Samaria.   2 Kin. 13:2 • *it*

7 For he left to Jehoahaz of the[T] army not more than fifty horsemen and ten chariots and 10,000 footmen, for the king of Aram had destroyed them and[R] made them like the dust at threshing.   *people* • [Amos 1:3]

8 Now the rest of the acts of Jehoahaz, and all that he did, and his might, are they not written in the Book of the Chronicles of the Kings of Israel?

9 And Jehoahaz slept with his fathers, and they buried him in Samaria; and Joash his son became king in his place.

Rule of Jehoash—2 Kin. 14:15, 16

10 In the thirty-seventh year of Joash king of Judah, Jehoash the son of Jehoahaz, became king over Israel in Samaria, *and reigned* sixteen years.

11 And he did evil in the sight of the LORD; he did not turn away from all the sins of Jeroboam the son of Nebat, with which he made Israel sin, but he walked in[T] them.   *it*

12 Now[R] the rest of the acts of Joash and all that he did and his might with which he fought against Amaziah king of Judah, are they not written in the Book of the Chronicles of the Kings of Israel?   2 Kin. 13:14-19

13 So Joash slept with his fathers, and Jeroboam sat on his throne; and Joash was buried in Samaria with the kings of Israel.

Prophecy of Israel's Victory

14 When Elisha became sick with the illness of which he was to die, Joash the king of Israel came down to him and wept over[T] him and said, "My father, my father, the chariots of Israel and its horsemen!" *his face*

[8] Or, *savior*

15 And Elisha said to him, "Take a bow and arrows." So he took a bow and arrows.
16 Then he said to the king of Israel, "Put your hand on the bow." And he put his hand *on it*, then Elisha laid his hands on the king's hands.
17 And he said, "Open the window toward the east," and he opened *it*. Then Elisha said, "Shoot!" And he shot. And he said, "The LORD's arrow of victory, even the arrow of victory over Aram; for you shall [T]defeat the Arameans at [R]Aphek until you have destroyed *them*."   smite • 1 Kin. 20:26
18 Then he said, "Take the arrows," and he took them. And he said to the king of Israel, "Strike the ground," and he struck *it* three times and stopped.   stood
19 So the man of God was angry with him and said, "You should have struck five or six times, then you would have struck Aram until you would have destroyed *it*. But now you shall strike Aram *only* three times."

Death of Elisha

20 And Elisha died, and they buried him. Now the bands of the Moabites would invade the land in the spring of the year.

Miracle of Resurrection
at Elisha's Tomb

21 And as they were burying a man, behold, they saw a marauding band; and they cast the man into the grave of Elisha. And when the man touched the bones of Elisha he revived and stood up on his feet.

Israel's Victory over Aram

22 Now Hazael king of Aram had oppressed Israel all the days of Jehoahaz.
23 But the [R]LORD was gracious to them and [R]had compassion on them and turned to them because of His covenant with Abraham, Isaac, and Jacob, and would not destroy them or cast them from His presence until now.   2 Kin. 14:27 • 1 Kin. 8:28
24 When Hazael king of Aram died, Benhadad his son became king in his place.
25 Then [R]Jehoash the son of Jehoahaz took again from the hand of Ben-hadad the son of Hazael the cities which he had taken in war from the hand of Jehoahaz his father. Three times Joash [T]defeated him and recovered the cities of Israel.   2 Kin. 10:32, 33; 14:25 • smote

CHAPTER 14

Spiritual Evaluation of Amaziah
2 Chr. 25:1-4

I[N]N the second year of Joash son of Joahaz king of Israel, Amaziah the son of Joash king of Judah became king.   2 Chr. 25:1

2 He was twenty-five years old when he became king, and he reigned twenty-nine years in Jerusalem. And his mother's name was Jehoaddin of Jerusalem.
3 And he did right in the sight of the LORD, yet not like David his father; he did according to all that Joash his father had done.
4 Only [R]the high places were not taken away; the people still sacrificed and burned incense on the high places.   2 Kin. 12:3
5 Now it came about, as soon as the kingdom was firmly in his hand, that he [T]killed [R]his servants who had slain the king his father.   smote • 2 Kin. 12:20
6 But the sons of the [T]slayers he did not put to death, according to what is written in the book of the law of Moses, as the LORD commanded, saying, "The fathers shall not be put to death for the sons, nor the sons be put to death for the fathers; but each shall be put to death for his own sin."   smiters

Political Situation Under Amaziah
2 Chr. 25:11, 17-24

7 He [T]killed *of* Edom in [R]the Valley of Salt 10,000 and took Sela by war, and named it Joktheel to this day.   smote • 2 Sam. 8:13
8 [R]Then Amaziah sent messengers to Jehoash, the son of Jehoahaz son of Jehu, king of Israel, saying, "Come, [R]let us face each other."   2 Chr. 25:17-24 • 2 Sam. 2:14-17
9 And Jehoash king of Israel sent to Amaziah king of Judah, saying, "The thorn bush which was in Lebanon sent to the cedar which was in Lebanon, saying, 'Give your daughter to my son in marriage.' But there passed by a wild beast that was in Lebanon, and trampled the thorn bush.
10 "You have indeed [T]defeated Edom, and your heart has become proud. Enjoy your glory and stay at home; for why should you provoke trouble so that you, even you, should fall, and Judah with you?"   smitten
11 But Amaziah would not listen. So Jehoash king of Israel went up; and he and Amaziah king of Judah faced each other at Beth-shemesh, which belongs to Judah.
12 And Judah was defeated [T]by Israel, and they fled each to his tent.   before
13 Then Jehoash king of Israel captured Amaziah king of Judah, the son of Jehoash the son of Ahaziah, at Beth-shemesh, and came to Jerusalem and tore down the wall of Jerusalem from [R]the Gate of Ephraim to the Corner Gate, 400 cubits.   Neh. 8:16; 12:39
14 And [R]he took all the gold and silver and all the utensils which were found in the house of the LORD, and in the treasuries of the king's house, the hostages also, and returned to Samaria.   1 Kin. 14:26; 2 Kin. 12:18

Death of Jehoash—2 Kin. 13:12, 13

15 [R]Now the rest of the acts of Jehoash

which he did, and his might and how he fought with Amaziah king of Judah, are they not written in the Book of the Chronicles of the Kings of Israel?   2 Kin. 13:12, 13

16 So Jehoash slept with his fathers and was buried in Samaria with the kings of Israel; and Jeroboam his son became king in his place.

Death of Amaziah—2 Chr. 25:25—26:2

17 And Amaziah the son of Joash king of Judah lived fifteen years after the death of Jehoash son of Jehoahaz king of Israel.

18 Now the rest of the acts of Amaziah, are they not written in the Book of the Chronicles of the Kings of Judah?

19 And they conspired against him in Jerusalem, and he fled to [R]Lachish; but they sent after him to Lachish and killed him there.   Josh. 10:31; 2 Kin. 18:14, 17

20 Then they brought him on horses and he was buried at Jerusalem with his fathers in the city of David.

21 And all the people of Judah took Azariah, who *was* sixteen years old, and made him king in the place of his father Amaziah.

22 He built Elath and restored it to Judah, after the king slept with his fathers.

The Reign of Jeroboam II in Israel

23 In the fifteenth year of Amaziah the son of Joash king of Judah, Jeroboam the son of Joash king of Israel became king in Samaria, *and reigned* forty-one years.

24 And he did evil in the sight of the LORD; he did not depart from all the sins of Jeroboam the son of Nebat, which he made Israel sin.

25 He restored the border of Israel from the entrance of Hamath as far as the Sea of the Arabah, according to the word of the LORD, the God of Israel, which He spoke through His servant Jonah the son of Amittai, the prophet, who was of Gath-hepher.

26 For the [R]LORD saw the affliction of Israel, *which was* very bitter; for [R]there was neither bond nor free, nor was there any helper for Israel.   2 Kin. 13:4 · Deut. 32:36

27 And the [R]LORD did not say that He would blot out the name of Israel from under heaven, but He saved them by the hand of Jeroboam the son of Joash.   [2 Kin. 13:23]

28 Now the rest of the acts of Jeroboam and all that he did and his might, how he fought and how he recovered for Israel, Damascus and Hamath, *which had belonged* to Judah, are they not written in the Book of the Chronicles of the Kings of Israel?

29 And Jeroboam slept with his fathers, even with the kings of Israel, and Zechariah his son became king in his place.

CHAPTER 15

The Reign of Azariah in Judah
2 Chr. 26:3–23

IN[R] the twenty-seventh year of Jeroboam king of Israel, Azariah son of Amaziah king of Judah became king.   2 Kin. 14:17

2 He was sixteen years old when he became king, and he reigned fifty-two years in Jerusalem; and his mother's name was Jecoliah of Jerusalem.

3 And he did right in the sight of the LORD, according to all that his father Amaziah had done.

4 Only [R]the high places were not taken away; the people still sacrificed and burned incense on the high places.   2 Kin. 12:3

5 And the LORD struck the king, so that he was a leper to the day of his death. And he[R]lived in a separate house,[T]while Jotham the king's son was over the household, judging the people of the land.   [Lev. 13:46] · *and*

6 Now the rest of the acts of Azariah and all that he did, are they not written in the Book of the Chronicles of the Kings of Judah?

7 And Azariah slept with his fathers, and they buried him with his fathers in the city of David, and Jotham his son became king in his place.

The Reign of Zechariah in Israel

8 [R]In the thirty-eighth year of Azariah king of Judah, Zechariah the son of Jeroboam became king over Israel in Samaria *for* six months.   2 Kin. 15:1

9 And he did evil in the sight of the LORD, as his fathers had done; he did not depart from the sins of Jeroboam the son of Nebat, which he made Israel sin.

10 Then Shallum the son of Jabesh conspired against him and [R]struck him before the people and[T]killed him, and reigned in his place.   Amos 7:9 · *smote*

11 Now the rest of the acts of Zechariah, behold they are written in the Book of the Chronicles of the Kings of Israel.

12 This is[R]the word of the LORD which He spoke to Jehu, saying, "Your sons to the fourth generation shall sit on the throne of Israel." And so it was.   2 Kin. 10:30

The Reign of Shallum in Israel

13 Shallum son of Jabesh became king in the thirty-ninth year of Uzziah king of Judah, and he reigned one month in Samaria.

14 Then Menahem son of Gadi went up from Tirzah and came to Samaria, and struck Shallum son of Jabesh in Samaria, and killed him and became king in his place.

15 Now the rest of the acts of Shallum and his conspiracy which he made, behold

they are written in the Book of the Chronicles of the Kings of Israel.

16 Then Menahem struck Tiphsah and all who were in it and its borders from Tirzah, because they did not open *to him,* therefore he struck *it;* and he ripped up [R]all its women who were with child.   2 Kin. 8:12; Hos. 13:16

17 In the[R]thirty-ninth year of Azariah king of Judah, Menahem son of Gadi became king over Israel *and reigned* ten years in Samaria.   2 Kin. 15:1, 8, 13

18 And he did evil in the sight of the Lord; he did not depart all his days from the sins of Jeroboam the son of Nebat, which he made Israel sin.

19 [R]Pul, king of Assyria, came against the land, and Menahem gave Pul[a]a thousand talents of silver so that his hand might be with him to strengthen the kingdom [T]under his rule.   1 Chr. 5:25, 26 · $384,000,000 · *in his hand*

20 Then Menahem exacted the money from Israel, even from all the mighty men of wealth, from each man[T]fifty shekels of silver to pay the king of Assyria. So the king of Assyria returned and did not remain there in the land. $6,400

21 Now the rest of the acts of Menahem and all that he did, are they not written in the Book of the Chronicles of the Kings of Israel?

22 And Menahem slept with his fathers, and Pekahiah his son became king in his place.

The Reign of Pekahiah in Israel

23 In[R]the fiftieth year of Azariah king of Judah, Pekahiah son of Menahem became king over Israel in Samaria, *and reigned* two years.   2 Kin. 15:1, 8, 13, 17

24 And he did evil in the sight of the Lord; he did not depart from the sins of Jeroboam son of Nebat, which he made Israel sin.

25 Then Pekah son of Remaliah, his officer, conspired against him and struck him in Samaria, in[R]the castle of the king's house with Argob and Arieh; and with him were fifty men of the Gileadites, and he killed him and became king in his place.   1 Kin. 16:18

26 Now the rest of the acts of Pekahiah and all that he did, behold they are written in the Book of the Chronicles of the Kings of Israel.

The Reign of Pekah in Israel

27 In[R]the fifty-second year of Azariah king of Judah, [R]Pekah son of Remaliah became king over Israel in Samaria, *and reigned* twenty years.   2 Kin. 15:23 · 2 Chr. 28:6

28 And he did evil in the sight of the Lord;

he did not depart from the sins of Jeroboam son of Nebat, which he made Israel sin.

29 In the days of Pekah king of Israel, Tiglath-pileser king of Assyria came and [T]captured Ijon and Abel-beth-maacah and Janoah and Kedesh and Hazor and Gilead and Galilee, all the land of Naphtali; and he carried them captive to Assyria.   *took*

30 And Hoshea the son of Elah made a conspiracy against Pekah the son of Remaliah, and struck him and put him to death and became king in his place, in the twentieth year of Jotham the son of Uzziah.

31 Now the rest of the acts of Pekah and all that he did, behold, they are written in the Book of the Chronicles of the Kings of Israel.

The Reign of Jotham in Judah
2 Chr. 27:1–9

32 In the second year of Pekah the son of Remaliah king of Israel, Jotham the son of [T]Uzziah king of Judah became king.   Azariah

33 [R]He was twenty-five years old when he became king, and he reigned sixteen years in Jerusalem; and his mother's name *was* Jerusha the daughter of Zadok.   2 Chr. 27:1

34 And[R]he did what was right in the sight of the Lord; he did according to all that his father Uzziah had done.   2 Kin. 15:3, 4

35 Only[R]the high places were not taken away; the people still sacrificed and burned incense on the high places. He built the upper gate of the house of the Lord. 2 Kin. 12:3

36 Now the rest of the acts of Jotham and all that he did, are they not written in the Book of the Chronicles of the Kings of Judah?

37 In those days[R]the Lord began to send Rezin king of Aram and Pekah the son of Remaliah against Judah.   2 Kin. 16:5; Is. 7:1

38 And Jotham slept with his fathers, and he was buried with his fathers in the city of David his father; and Ahaz his son became king in his place.

CHAPTER 16

Spiritual Evaluation of Ahaz
2 Chr. 28:1–4

IN the seventeenth year of Pekah the son of Remaliah, [R]Ahaz the son of Jotham, king of Judah, became king.   2 Chr. 28:1

2 [R]Ahaz *was* twenty years old when he became king, and he reigned sixteen years in Jerusalem; and he did not do what was right in the sight of the Lord his God, as his father David *had done.*   2 Chr. 28:1-4

3 But he walked in the way of the kings of Israel, and even made his son pass through the fire, according to the abominations of the nations whom the Lord had driven out from before the sons of Israel.

4 And he ^Rsacrificed and burned incense on the high places and on the hills and under every green tree.   [Deut. 12:2]; 2 Kin. 14:4

Political Situation Under Ahaz
2 Chr. 28:5, 16, 21; Is. 7:1

5 Then Rezin king of Aram and Pekah son of Remaliah, king of Israel, came up to Jerusalem to *wage* war; and they besieged Ahaz, but could not ^Tovercome him.   *fight*

6 At that time Rezin king of Aram recovered ^RElath for Aram, and cleared the Judeans out of ^TElath entirely; and the Arameans came to Elath, and have lived there to this day.   2 Kin. 14:22; 2 Chr. 26:2 • *Eloth*

7 ^RSo Ahaz sent messengers to Tiglath-pileser king of Assyria, saying, "I am your servant and your son; come up and deliver me from the hand of the king of Aram, and from the ^Thand of the king of Israel, who are rising up against me."   2 Chr. 28:16 • *palm*

8 And ^RAhaz took the silver and gold that was found in the house of the LORD and in the treasuries of the king's house, and sent a present to the king of Assyria.   2 Kin. 12:17

9 ^RSo the king of Assyria listened to him; and the king of Assyria went up against Damascus and ^Rcaptured it, and carried *the people of* it away into exile to Kir, and put Rezin to death.   2 Chr. 28:21 • Amos 1:3-5

10 Now King Ahaz went to Damascus to meet ^RTiglath-pileser king of Assyria, and saw the altar which *was* at Damascus; and King Ahaz sent to Urijah the priest the ^Tpattern of the altar and its model, according to all its workmanship.   2 Kin. 15:29 • *likeness*

11 So Urijah the priest built an altar; according to all that King Ahaz had sent from Damascus, thus Urijah the priest made *it,* ^Tbefore the coming of King Ahaz from Damascus.   *until*

12 And when the king came from Damascus, the king saw the altar; then the king approached the altar and went up to it,

13 and ^Tburned his burnt offering and his meal offering, and poured his libation and sprinkled the blood of his peace offerings on the altar.   *offered in smoke*

14 And ^Rthe bronze altar, which *was* before the LORD, ^The brought from the front of the house, from between *his* altar and the house of the LORD, and he put it on the north side of *his* altar.   Ex. 27:1, 2; 40:6, 29 • *he also*

15 Then King Ahaz ^Tcommanded Urijah the priest, saying, "Upon the great altar burn the morning burnt offering and the evening meal offering and the king's burnt offering and his meal offering, with the burnt offering of all the people of the land and their meal offering and their libations; and sprinkle on it all the blood of the burnt offering and all the blood of the sacrifice. But the bronze altar shall be for me to inquire by."   *commanded him, Urijah*

16 So Urijah the priest did according to all that King Ahaz commanded.

17 Then King Ahaz ^Rcut off the borders of the stands, and removed the laver from them; he also took down the sea from the bronze oxen which were under it, and put it on a pavement of stone.   1 Kin. 7:27, 28, 38

18 And the covered way for the sabbath which they had built in the house, and the outer entry of the king, he removed from the house of the LORD because of the king of Assyria.

Death of Ahaz—2 Chr. 28:26, 27

19 Now the rest of the acts of Ahaz which he did, are they not written in the Book of the Chronicles of the Kings of Judah?

20 So Ahaz slept with his fathers, and was buried with his fathers in the city of David; and his son Hezekiah reigned in his place.

CHAPTER 17

Spiritual Evaluation of Hoshea

IN the twelfth year of Ahaz king of Judah, Hoshea the son of Elah became king over Israel in Samaria, *and reigned* nine years.

2 And he did evil in the sight of the LORD, only not as the kings of Israel who were before him.

Imprisonment of Hoshea

3 ^RShalmaneser king of Assyria came up against him, and Hoshea became his servant and paid him tribute.   Hos. 10:14

4 But the king of Assyria found conspiracy in Hoshea, who had sent messengers to So king of Egypt and had offered no tribute to the king of Assyria, as *he had done* year by year; so the king of Assyria shut him up and bound him in prison.

Captivity of Samaria—2 Kin. 18:9–12

5 Then the king of Assyria invaded the whole land and went up to ^RSamaria and besieged it three years.   Hos. 13:16

6 In the ninth year of Hoshea, ^Rthe king of Assyria captured Samaria and carried Israel away into exile to Assyria, and settled them in Halah and Habor, *on* the river of Gozan, and in the cities of the Medes.   Hos. 13:16

Causes of the Captivity

7 Now ^Rthis came about, because the sons of Israel had sinned against the LORD their God, who had brought them up from the land of Egypt from under the hand of Pharaoh, king of Egypt, and they had ⁹feared other gods   Josh. 23:16

⁹ Lit., *revered,* and so throughout this context

8 and walked in the customs of the nations whom the LORD had driven out before the sons of Israel, and *in the customs* of the kings of Israel which they had introduced.

9 And the sons of Israel did things secretly which were not right, against the LORD their God. Moreover, they built for themselves high places in all their towns, from^Rwatchtower to fortified city.   2 Kin. 18:8

10 And^Tthey set for themselves *sacred* pillars and [10]Asherim on every high hill and under every green tree,   [Ex. 34:12–14]

11 and there they burned incense on all the high places as the nations *did* which the LORD had carried away to exile before them; and they did evil things provoking the LORD.

12 And they served idols, ^Rconcerning which the LORD had said to them, "You shall not do this thing."   [Ex. 20:4]

13 Yet the^RLORD warned Israel and Judah, through all His prophets *and* every seer, saying, "Turn from your evil ways and keep My commandments, My statutes according to all the law which I commanded your fathers, and which I sent to you through My servants the prophets."   Neh. 9:29, 30

14 However, they did not listen, but ^Rstiffened their neck like their fathers, who did not believe in the LORD their God.   [Acts 7:51]

15 And they rejected His statutes and His covenant which He made with their fathers, and His warnings with which He warned them. And they followed vanity and became vain, and *went* after the nations which surrounded them, concerning which the LORD had commanded them not to do like them.

16 And they forsook all the commandments of the LORD their God and made for themselves molten images, *even*^Rtwo calves, and made an Asherah and worshiped all the host of heaven and served Baal.   1 Kin. 12:28

17 Then ^Rthey made their sons and their daughters pass through the fire, and practiced divination and enchantments, and sold themselves to do evil in the sight of the LORD, provoking Him.   2 Kin. 16:3

18 So the LORD was very angry with Israel, and removed them from His sight; none was left except the tribe of Judah.

19 Also Judah did not keep the commandments of the LORD their God, but walked in the customs which Israel had introduced.

20 And the LORD rejected all the ^Tdescendants of Israel and afflicted them and gave them into the hand of plunderers, until He had cast them out of His sight.   *seed*

21 When He had torn Israel from the house of David, they made Jeroboam the son of Nebat king. Then Jeroboam drove Israel away from following the LORD, and made them ^Tcommit a great sin.   *sin*

22 And the sons of Israel walked in all the sins of Jeroboam which he did; they did not depart from them,

[10] I.e., wooden symbols of a female deity

23 ^Runtil the LORD removed Israel from His sight,^Ras He spoke through all His servants the prophets. So Israel was carried away into exile from their own land to Assyria until this day.   2 Kin. 17:6 • 2 Kin. 17:13

Sins of the Foreigners

24 And the king of Assyria brought *men* from Babylon and from Cuthah and from Avva and from Hamath and Sephar-vaim, and settled *them* in the cities of Samaria in place of the sons of Israel. So they possessed Samaria and lived in its cities.

25 And it came about at the beginning of their living there, that they did not fear the LORD; therefore the LORD sent lions among them which killed some of them.

26 So they spoke to the king of Assyria, saying, "The nations whom you have carried away into exile in the cities of Samaria do not know the custom of the god of the land; so he has sent lions among them, and behold, they kill them because they do not know the custom of the god of the land."

27 Then the king of Assyria commanded, saying, "Take there one of the priests whom you carried away into exile, and let^Thim go and live there; and let him teach them the custom of the god of the land."   *them*

28 So one of the priests whom they had carried away into exile from Samaria came and lived at Bethel, and taught them how they should fear the LORD.

29 But every nation still made gods of its own and put them^Rin the houses of the high places which the people of Samaria had made, every nation in their cities in which they lived.   1 Kin. 12:31; 13:32

30 And the men of Babylon made Succoth-benoth, the men of Cuth made Nergal, the men of Hamath made Ashima,

31 and the Avvites made Nibhaz and Tartak; and^Rthe Sepharvites burned their children in the fire to Adrammelech and Anammelech the gods of Sepharvaim.   2 Kin. 17:17

32 ^RThey also feared the LORD and appointed from among themselves priests of the high places, who acted for them in the houses of the high places.   Zeph. 1:5

33 They feared the LORD and served their own gods according to the custom of the nations from among whom they had been carried away into exile.

34 To this day they do according to the earlier customs: they do not fear the LORD, nor do they^Tfollow their statutes or their ordinances or the law, or the commandments which the LORD commanded the sons of Jacob, whom He named Israel;   *do according to*

35 with whom the LORD made a covenant and commanded them, saying, "You^R shall not fear other gods, nor bow down your-

selves to them nor serve them nor sacrifice
to them.   Judg. 6:10
36"But the LORD, who brought you up
from the land of Egypt with great power
and with an outstretched arm, Him you
shall fear, and to Him you shall bow yourselves down, and to Him you shall sacrifice.
37"And the statutes and the ordinances
and the law and the commandment, which
He wrote for you, you shall observe to do
forever; and you shall not fear other gods.
38"And the covenant that I have made
with you, you shall not forget, nor shall you
fear other gods.   Deut. 4:23; 6:12
39"But the LORD your God you shall fear;
and He will deliver you from the hand of all
your enemies."
40 However, they did not listen, but they
did according to their earlier custom.
41 So while these nations feared the
LORD, they also served their idols; their children likewise and their grandchildren, as
their fathers did, so they do to this day.

CHAPTER 18

Spiritual Evaluation of Hezekiah
2 Chr. 29:1, 2; 31:1

Now it came about in the third year of
Hoshea, the son of Elah king of Israel, that
Hezekiah the son of Ahaz king of Judah became king.   2 Kin. 16:2; 17:1 • 2 Chr. 28:27
2 He was twenty-five years old when he
became king, and he reigned twenty-nine
years in Jerusalem; and his mother's name
was Abi the daughter of Zechariah.
3 And he did right in the sight of the
LORD, according to all that his father David
had done.   2 Kin. 20:3; 2 Chr. 31:20
4 He removed the high places and broke
down the sacred pillars and cut down the
[11]Asherah. He also broke in pieces the
bronze serpent that Moses had made, for
until those days the sons of Israel burned
incense to it; and it was called [12]Nehushtan.
5 He trusted in the LORD, the God of Israel; so that after him there was none like
him among all the kings of Judah, nor
among those who were before him.
6 For he clung to the LORD; he did not
depart from following Him, but kept His
commandments, which the LORD had commanded Moses.   Deut. 10:20; Josh. 23:8
7 And the LORD was with him; wherever
he went he prospered. And he rebelled
against the king of Assyria and did not
serve him.   Gen. 39:2, 3 • 2 Kin. 16:7
8 He defeated the Philistines as far as
Gaza and its territory, from watchtower to
fortified city.   2 Chr. 28:18; Is. 14:29 • smote

Invasion of Israel by Assyria
2 Kin. 17:5-7

9 Now it came about in the fourth year
of King Hezekiah, which was the seventh
year of Hoshea son of Elah king of Israel,
that Shalmaneser king of Assyria came up
against Samaria and besieged it. 2 Kin. 17:3-7
10 And at the end of three years they captured it; in the sixth year of Hezekiah, which
was the ninth year of Hoshea king of Israel,
Samaria was captured.   2 Kin. 17:6
11 Then the king of Assyria carried Israel
away into exile to Assyria, and put them in
Halah and on the Habor, the river of Gozan,
and in the cities of the Medes,   1 Chr. 5:26
12 because they did not obey the voice of
the LORD their God, but transgressed His
covenant, even all that Moses the servant of
the LORD commanded; they would neither
listen, nor do it.   1 Kin. 9:6; Dan. 9:6, 10

First Invasion of Judah by Assyria
Is. 36:1

13 Now in the fourteenth year of King
Hezekiah, Sennacherib king of Assyria
came up against all the fortified cities of Judah and seized them. 2 Chr. 32:1; Is. 36:1—39:8
14 Then Hezekiah king of Judah sent to
the king of Assyria at Lachish, saying, "I
have done wrong. Withdraw from me;
whatever you impose on me I will bear." So
the king of Assyria required of Hezekiah
king of Judah three hundred talents of silver
and thirty talents of gold.   Return
15 And Hezekiah gave him all the silver
which was found in the house of the LORD,
and in the treasuries of the king's house.
16 At that time Hezekiah cut off the gold
from the doors of the temple of the LORD,
and from the doorposts which Hezekiah
king of Judah had overlaid, and gave it to
the king of Assyria.

Second Invasion of Judah by Assyria
2 Chr. 32:9-21; Is. 36:2—37:38

17 Then the king of Assyria sent Tartan
and Rab-saris and Rabshakeh from Lachish
to King Hezekiah with a large army to Jerusalem. So they went up and came to Jerusalem. And when they went up, they came and
stood by the conduit of the upper pool,
which is on the highway of the [13]fuller's
field.   Is. 20:1 • 2 Kin. 20:20; Is. 7:3
18 When they called to the king, Eliakim
the son of Hilkiah, who was over the household, and Shebnah the scribe and Joah the
son of Asaph the recorder, came out to
them.   2 Kin. 19:2; Is. 22:20 • Is. 22:15

[11] I.e., wooden symbol of a female deity
[12] I.e., a piece of bronze   [13] I.e., launderer's

19 Then Rabshakeh said to them, "Say now to Hezekiah, 'Thus says the great king, the king of Assyria, "What[R] is this confidence that you[T]have?   2 Chr. 32:10 • *trust*

20"You say (but *they are* [T]only empty words), 'I *have* counsel and strength for the war.' Now on whom do you rely, that you have rebelled against me?   *a word of the lips*

21"Now behold, you[T]rely on the staff of this crushed reed, *even* on Egypt; on which if a man leans, it will go into his[T]hand and pierce it. So is Pharaoh king of Egypt to all who rely on him.   *rely for yourself* • *palm*

22"But if you say to me, 'We trust in the LORD our God,' is it not He whose high places and[R]whose altars Hezekiah has taken away, and has said to Judah and to Jerusalem, 'You shall worship before this altar in Jerusalem'?   2 Kin. 18:4; 2 Chr. 31:1

23"Now therefore, come, make a bargain with my master the king of Assyria, and I will give you two thousand horses, if you are able on your part to set riders on them.

24"How then can you[T]repulse one [A]official of the least of my master's servants, and rely on Egypt for chariots and for horsemen?   *turn away the face of* • *governor*

25"Have I now come up without the LORD's approval against this place to destroy it? The LORD said to me, 'Go up against this land and destroy it.' "[R]"

26 Then Eliakim the son of Hilkiah, and Shebnah and Joah, said to Rabshakeh, "Speak now to your servants in Aramaic, for we[T]understand *it;* and do not speak with us in [R]Judean, in the hearing of the people who are on the wall."   *hear* • Ezra 4:7

27 But Rabshakeh said to them, "Has my master sent me only to your master and to you to speak these words, *and* not to the men who sit on the wall, *doomed* to eat their own dung and drink their own urine with you?"

28 Then Rabshakeh stood and cried with a loud voice in Judean, saying, "Hear the word of the great king, the king of Assyria.

29"Thus says the king, 'Do not let Hezekiah deceive you, for he will not be able to deliver you from[T]my hand;   Heb., *his*

30 nor let Hezekiah make you trust in the LORD, saying, "The LORD will surely deliver us, and this city shall not be given into the hand of the king of Assyria."

31 'Do not listen to Hezekiah, for thus says the king of Assyria, "Make your peace with me and come out to me, and eat[R]each of his vine and each of his fig tree and drink each of the waters of his own cistern,   1 Kin. 4:20

32 until I come and take you away[R]to a land like your own land, a land of grain and new wine, a land of bread and vineyards, a land of olive trees and honey, that you may live and not die." But do not listen to Hezekiah, when he misleads you, saying, "The LORD will deliver us."   Deut. 8:7-9; 11:12

33 'Has[R]any one of the gods of the nations delivered his land from the hand of the king of Assyria?   2 Kin. 19:12; Is. 10:10, 11

34 'Where[R]are the gods of Hamath and [R]Arpad? Where are the gods of Sepharvaim, Hena and Ivvah? Have they delivered Samaria from my hand?   2 Kin. 19:13 • Is. 10:9

35 'Who among all the gods of the lands [T]have delivered their land from my hand, [R]that the LORD should deliver Jerusalem from my hand?' "   *who have* • Ps. 2:1-3

36 But the people were silent and answered him not a word, for the king's commandment was, "Do not answer him."

37 Then Eliakim the son of Hilkiah, who was over the household, and Shebna the scribe and Joah the son of Asaph, the recorder, came to Hezekiah with their clothes torn and told him the words of Rabshakeh.

CHAPTER 19

AND when King Hezekiah heard *it*, he tore his clothes, covered himself with sackcloth and entered the house of the LORD.

2 Then he sent Eliakim who was over the household with Shebna the scribe and the elders of the priests, covered with sackcloth, to Isaiah the prophet the son of Amoz.

3 And they said to him, "Thus says Hezekiah, 'This day is a day of distress, rebuke, and rejection; for children have come to birth, and there is no strength to *deliver.*

4 'Perhaps[R]the LORD your God will hear all the words of Rabshakeh, whom his master the king of Assyria has sent[R]to reproach the living God, and will rebuke the words which the LORD your God has heard. Therefore, offer a prayer for[R]the remnant that is left.' "   Josh. 14:12 • 2 Kin. 18:35 • Is. 1:9

5 So the servants of King Hezekiah came to Isaiah.

6 And Isaiah said to them, "Thus you shall say to your master, 'Thus says the LORD, "Do not be afraid because of the words that you have heard, with which the [R]servants of the king of Assyria[R]have blasphemed Me.   2 Kin. 18:17 • 2 Kin. 18:22-25

7"Behold, I will put a spirit in him so that [R]he shall hear a rumor and return to his own land. And I will make him fall by the sword in his own land." ' "   2 Kin. 7:6

8 Then Rabshakeh returned and found the king of Assyria fighting against[R]Libnah, for he had heard that[T]the king had left[R]Lachish.   Josh. 10:29 • *he* • 2 Kin. 18:14

9 When he heard *them* say concerning Tirhakah king of [A]Cush, "Behold, he has come out to fight against you," he sent messengers again to Hezekiah saying,   *Ethiopia*

10"Thus you shall say to Hezekiah king of [T]Judah, 'Do not[R]let your God in whom you trust deceive you saying, "Jerusalem shall not be given into the hand of the king of Assyria."   *Judah, saying* • 2 Kin. 18:5

11 'Behold, you have heard what the kings of Assyria have done to all the lands, de-

stroying them completely. So will you be 'spared?   *delivered*

12 'Did the gods of 'those nations which my fathers destroyed deliver them, *even* Gozan and Haran and Rezeph and the sons of Eden who *were* in Telassar?   *the*

13 'Where'is the king of Hamath, the king of Arpad, the king of the city of Sepharvaim, and *of* Hena and Ivvah?' " 2 Kin. 18:34

14 Then Hezekiah took the letter from the hand of the messengers and read it, and he went up to the house of the LORD and spread it out before the LORD.

15 And Hezekiah prayed before the LORD and said, "O LORD, the God of Israel, who art 'enthroned *above* the cherubim, Thou art the God, Thou alone, of all the kingdoms of the earth. Thou hast made heaven and earth.   Ex. 25:22; Is. 37:14 • *seated*

16"Incline Thine ear, O LORD, and hear; open Thine eyes, O LORD, and see; and listen to the words of Sennacherib, which he has sent to reproach the living God.   Ps. 31:2

17"Truly, O LORD, the kings of Assyria have devastated the nations and their lands 18 and have cast their gods into the fire, for they were not gods but the work of men's hands, wood and stone. So they have destroyed them.   [Is. 44:9-20; Acts 17:29]

19"And now, O LORD our God, I pray, deliver us from his hand that all the kingdoms of the earth may know that Thou alone, O LORD, art God."   1 Kin. 8:42 • 2 Kin. 19:15

20 Then Isaiah the son of Amoz sent to Hezekiah saying, "Thus says the LORD, the God of Israel, 'Because you have prayed to Me about Sennacherib king of Assyria, I have heard *you*.'   2 Kin. 20:5

21"This is the word that the LORD has spoken against him:

'She has despised you and mocked you,
The virgin daughter of Zion;   Jer. 14:17
She has shaken *her* head behind you,
The daughter of Jerusalem!

22 'Whom have you reproached and blasphemed?   2 Kin. 19:4 • 2 Kin. 19:6
And against whom have you raised *your* voice,
And haughtily lifted up your eyes?
Against the Holy One of Israel!

23 'Through your messengers you have reproached the Lord,   2 Kin. 18:17
And you have said, "With my many chariots
I came up to the heights of the mountains,
To the remotest parts of Lebanon;
And I cut down its tall cedars *and* its choice cypresses.
And I entered its farthest lodging place, its thickest forest.

24 "I dug *wells* and drank foreign waters,
And with the sole of my feet I dried up   Is. 19:6
All the rivers of Egypt."

25 'Have you not heard?   [Is. 45:7]
Long ago I did it;
From ancient times I planned it.
Now I have brought it to pass, Is. 10:5
That you should turn fortified cities into ruinous heaps.

26 'Therefore their inhabitants were short of strength,
They were dismayed and put to shame;
They were as the vegetation of the field and as the green herb, Ps. 129:6
As grass on the housetops is scorched before it is grown up.

27 'But I know your sitting down,
And your going out and your coming in,   Ps. 139:1
And your raging against Me.

28 'Because of your raging against Me,
And because your 'arrogance has come up to My ears,   *complacency*
Therefore I will put My hook in your nose,   Ezek. 19:9; 29:4
And My bridle in your lips,
And I will turn you back by the way which you came.   2 Kin. 19:33, 36

29 'Then this shall be the sign for you: you shall eat this year what grows of itself, in the second year what springs from the same, and in the third year sow, reap, plant vineyards, and eat their fruit.   *eating*

30 'And the surviving remnant of the house of Judah shall again take root downward and bear fruit upward.   2 Kin. 19:4

31 'For out of Jerusalem shall go forth a remnant, and out of Mount Zion survivors. The zeal of [14]the LORD shall perform this.

32 'Therefore thus says the LORD concerning the king of Assyria, "He shall not come to this city or shoot an arrow there; neither shall he come before it with a shield, nor throw up a mound against it.   Is. 8:7-10

33"By the way that he came, by the same he shall return, and he shall not come to this city," ' declares the LORD.   2 Kin. 19:28

34 'For I will defend this city to save it for My own sake and for My servant David's sake.' "   2 Kin. 20:6 • 1 Kin. 11:12, 13

35 Then it happened that night that the angel of the LORD went out, and struck 185,000 in the camp of the Assyrians; and when 'men rose early in the morning, behold, all of them were dead.   *they*

36 So Sennacherib king of Assyria departed and returned *home*, and lived at Nineveh.   2 Kin. 19:7, 28, 33 • Jon. 1:2

37 And it came about as he was worshiping in the house of Nisroch his god, that Adrammelech and Sharezer killed him with the sword; and they escaped into the land of Ararat. And Esarhaddon his son became king in his place.   2 Kin. 19:17 • Gen. 8:4

[14] Some ancient mss. read *the LORD of hosts*

CHAPTER 20

Miraculous Recovery of Hezekiah
2 Chr. 32:24; Is. 38:1–8

IN those days Hezekiah became [T]mortally ill. And Isaiah the prophet the son of Amoz came to him and said to him, "Thus says the LORD, 'Set your house in order, for you shall die and not live.' "   *sick to the point of death*

2 Then he turned his face to the wall, and prayed to the LORD, saying,

3 "Remember[R] now, O LORD, I beseech Thee, how I have walked before Thee in truth and with a whole heart, and have done what [T]is good in Thy sight." And Hezekiah wept [T]bitterly.   Neh. 5:19 • *great weeping*

4 And it came about before Isaiah had gone out of the middle court, that the word of the LORD came to him, saying,

5 "Return and say to [R]Hezekiah the leader of My people, 'Thus says the LORD, the God of your father David, "I have heard your prayer, I have seen your tears; behold, I will heal you. On the third day you shall go up to the house of the LORD.   1 Sam. 9:16; 10:1

6 "And I will add fifteen years to your [T]life, and I will deliver you and this city from the hand of the king of Assyria; and [R]I will defend this city for My own sake and for My servant David's sake." ' "   *days* • 2 Kin. 19:34

7 Then Isaiah said, "Take a cake of figs." And they took and laid *it* on the boil, and he recovered.

8 Now Hezekiah said to Isaiah, "What will be the sign that the LORD will heal me, and that I shall go up to the house of the LORD the third day?"

9 And Isaiah said, "This [R]shall be the sign to you from the LORD, that the LORD will do the thing that He has spoken: shall the shadow go forward ten steps or go back ten steps?"   Is. 38:7

10 So Hezekiah [T]answered, "It is easy for the shadow to decline ten steps; no, but let the shadow turn backward ten steps."   *said*

11 And Isaiah the prophet cried to the LORD, and He brought the shadow on the [T]stairway back ten steps by which it had gone down on the [T]stairway of Ahaz.   *steps*

Judah's Wealth Is Exposed
to Babylon—Is. 39:1, 2

12 [R]At that time Berodach-baladan a son of Baladan, king of Babylon, sent letters and a present to Hezekiah, for he heard that Hezekiah had been sick.   2 Chr. 32:31; Is. 39:1-8

13 And Hezekiah listened to them, and showed them all his treasure house, the silver and the gold and the spices and the precious oil and the house of his armor and all that was found in his treasuries. There was nothing in his house, nor in all his dominion, that Hezekiah did not show them.

Babylonian Exile Is Prophesied
Is. 39:3–8

14 Then Isaiah the prophet came to King Hezekiah and said to him, "What did these men say, and from where have they come to you?" And Hezekiah said, "They have come from a far country, from Babylon."

15 And he said, "What have they seen in your house?" So Hezekiah [T]answered, "They have seen all that is in my house; there is nothing among my treasuries that I have not shown them."   *said*

16 Then Isaiah said to Hezekiah, "Hear the word of the LORD.

17 'Behold, the days are coming when [R]all that is in your house, and all that your fathers have laid up in store to this day shall be carried to Babylon; nothing shall be left,' says the LORD.   2 Kin. 24:13; 25:13; 2 Chr. 36:10

18 'And some of your sons who shall issue from you, whom you shall beget, shall be taken away; and they shall become officials in the palace of the king of Babylon.' "

19 Then Hezekiah said to Isaiah, "The word of the LORD which you have spoken is good." For he thought, "Is it not so, if there shall be peace and truth in my days?"

Death of Hezekiah—2 Chr. 32:32, 33

20 Now the rest of the acts of Hezekiah and all his might, and how he made the pool and the conduit, and brought water into the city, are they not written in the Book of the Chronicles of the Kings of Judah?

21 So Hezekiah slept with his fathers, and Manasseh his son became king in his place.

CHAPTER 21

Spiritual Evaluation of Manasseh
2 Chr. 32:1–9

MANASSEH[R]was twelve years old when he became king, and he reigned fifty-five years in Jerusalem; and his mother's name was Hephzibah.   2 Chr. 33:1-9

2 And [R]he did evil in the sight of the LORD, [R]according to the abominations of the nations whom the LORD dispossessed before the sons of Israel.   Jer. 15:4 • 2 Kin. 16:3

3 For he rebuilt the high places which Hezekiah his father had destroyed; and he erected altars for Baal and made an [T]Asherah, as Ahab king of Israel had done, and worshiped all the host of heaven and served them.   *a wooden symbol of a female deity*

4 And [R]he built altars in the house of the LORD, of which the LORD had said, "In Jerusalem I will put My name."   2 Kin. 16:10-16

5 For he built altars for [R]all the host of heaven in [T]the two courts of the house of the LORD.   2 Kin. 23:4, 5 • 1 Kin. 7:12

6 And[R]he made his son pass through the fire, practiced witchcraft and used divination, and dealt with mediums and spiritists. He did much evil in the sight of the LORD provoking Him to anger. Lev. 18:21; 2 Kin. 16:3

7 Then[R]he set the carved image of Asherah that he had made, in the house of which the LORD said to David and to his son Solomon, "In this house and in Jerusalem, which I have chosen from all the tribes of Israel, I will put My name forever. Deut. 16:21

8 "And I will not make the feet of Israel wander anymore from the land which I gave their fathers, if only they will observe to do according to all that I have commanded them, and according to all the law that My servant Moses commanded them."

[R]9 But they did not listen, and Manasseh seduced them to do evil more than the nations whom the LORD destroyed before the sons of Israel. [Prov. 29:12]

10 Now the LORD spoke through His servants the prophets, saying,

11 "Because[R]Manasseh king of Judah has done these abominations, having done wickedly more than all the Amorites did who were before him, and has also made Judah sin with his idols; 2 Kin. 21:2; 24:3, 4

12 therefore thus says the LORD, the God of Israel, 'Behold, I am bringing such calamity on Jerusalem and Judah, that whoever hears of it, both his ears shall tingle.

13 'And[R]I will stretch over Jerusalem the line of Samaria and the plummet of the house of Ahab, and I will wipe Jerusalem as one wipes a dish, wiping it and turning it upside down. Is. 34:11; Amos 7:7, 8

14 'And I will abandon the remnant of My inheritance and deliver them into the hand of their enemies, and they shall become as plunder and spoil to all their enemies;

15 because they have done evil in My sight, and have been provoking Me to anger, since the day their fathers came from Egypt, even to this day.' "

Political Situation Under Manasseh

16 [R]Moreover, Manasseh shed very much innocent blood until he had filled Jerusalem from one end to another; besides his sin with which he made Judah sin, in doing evil in the sight of the LORD. 2 Kin. 24:4

Death of Manasseh

17 Now the rest of the acts of Manasseh and all that he did and his sin which he committed, are they not written in the Book of the Chronicles of the Kings of Judah?

18 [R]And Manasseh slept with his fathers and was buried in the garden of his own house, in the garden of Uzza, and Amon his son became king in his place. 2 Chr. 33:20

The Reign of Amon in Judah
2 Chr. 33:21–25

19 Amon was twenty-two years old when he became king, and he reigned two years in Jerusalem; and his mother's name was Meshullemeth the daughter of Haruz of Jotbah.

[R]20 And he did evil in the sight of the LORD, as Manasseh his father had done. 2 Kin. 21:2

21 For he walked in all the way that his father had walked, and served the idols that his father had served and worshiped them.

22 So[R]he forsook the LORD, the God of his fathers, and did not walk in the way of the LORD. 2 Kin. 22:17; 1 Chr. 28:9

23 And[R]the servants of Amon conspired against him and killed the king in his own house. 2 Kin. 12:20; 14:19

24 Then the people of the land[T]killed all those who had conspired against King Amon, and the people of the land made Josiah his son king in his place. smote

25 Now the rest of the acts of Amon which he did, are they not written in the Book of the Chronicles of the Kings of Judah?

26 And he was buried in his grave[R]in the garden of Uzza, and Josiah his son became king in his place. 2 Kin. 21:18

CHAPTER 22

Spiritual Evaluation of Josiah
2 Chr. 34:1, 2

JOSIAH was eight years old when he became king, and he reigned thirty-one years in Jerusalem; and his mother's name was Jedidah the daughter of Adaiah of Bozkath.

2 And he did right in the sight of the LORD and walked in all the way of his father David, nor did he[R]turn aside to the right or to the left. Deut. 5:32; Josh. 1:7

The Temple Is Repaired
2 Chr. 34:8–13

3 Now[R]it came about in the eighteenth year of King Josiah that the king sent Shaphan, the son of Azaliah the son of Meshullam the scribe, to the house of the LORD saying, 2 Chr. 34:8

4 "Go up to Hilkiah the high priest that he may [A]count the money brought in to the house of the LORD which the doorkeepers have gathered from the people. total

5 "And let them deliver it into the hand of the workmen who have the oversight of the house of the LORD, and let them give it to the workmen who are in the house of the LORD to repair the damages of the house,

6 to the carpenters and the builders and the masons and for buying timber and hewn stone to repair the house.

7 "Only[R]no accounting shall be made with them for the money delivered into their hands, for they deal faithfully." [1 Cor. 4:2]

The Book of the Law Is Discovered
2 Chr. 34:15-18

8 Then Hilkiah the high priest said to Shaphan the scribe, "I[R]have found the book of the law in the house of the LORD." And Hilkiah gave the book to Shaphan who read it.   Deut. 31:24-26; 2 Chr. 34:14, 15

9 And Shaphan the scribe came to the king and brought back word to the king and said, "Your servants have emptied out the money that was found in the house, and have delivered it into the hand of the workmen who have the oversight of the house of the LORD."

10 Moreover, Shaphan the scribe told the king saying, "Hilkiah the priest has given me a book." And Shaphan read it in the presence of the king.

Repentance of Josiah—2 Chr. 34:19-22

11 And it came about when the king heard the words of the book of the law, that[R]he tore his clothes.   Gen. 37:34; Josh. 7:6

12 Then the king commanded Hilkiah the priest,[R]Ahikam the son of Shaphan, Achbor the son of Micaiah, Shaphan the scribe, and Asaiah the king's servant saying, 2 Kin. 25:22

13"Go, inquire of the LORD for me and the people and all Judah concerning the words of this book that has been found, for[R]great is the wrath of the LORD that burns against us, because our fathers have not listened to the words of this book, to do according to all that is written concerning us." Deut. 29:23-28

14 So Hilkiah the priest, Ahikam, Achbor, Shaphan, and Asaiah went to Huldah the prophetess, the wife of Shallum the son of Tikvah, the son of Harhas, keeper of the wardrobe (now she lived in Jerusalem in the Second Quarter); and they spoke to her.

Prophecy of Blessing—2 Chr. 34:23-28

15 And she said to them, "Thus says the LORD God of Israel, 'Tell the man who sent you to me,

16 thus says the LORD, "Behold, I[R]bring evil on this place and on its inhabitants, *even* all the words of the book which the king of Judah has read.   [Dan. 9:11-14]

17"Because[R]they have forsaken Me and have burned incense to other gods that they might provoke Me to anger with all the work of their hands, therefore My wrath burns against this place, and it shall not be quenched." '   Deut. 29:25, 26; 2 Kin. 21:22

18"But to the king of Judah who sent you to inquire of the LORD thus shall you say to him, 'Thus says the LORD God of Israel, "*Regarding* the words which you have heard,

19 because your heart was tender and you humbled yourself before the LORD when you heard what I spoke against this place and against its inhabitants that they should become a desolation and a curse, and you have torn your clothes and wept before Me, I truly have heard you," declares the LORD.

20"Therefore, behold, I will gather you to your fathers, and[R]you shall be gathered to your grave in peace, neither shall your eyes see all the evil which I will bring on this place." ' " So they brought back word to the king.   2 Kin. 23:30

CHAPTER 23

Institution of the Covenant
2 Chr. 34:29-32

THEN[R]the king sent, and they gathered to him all the elders of Judah and of Jerusalem.   2 Chr. 34:29-32

2 And the king went up to the house of the LORD and all the men of Judah and all the inhabitants of Jerusalem with him, and the priests and the prophets and all the people, both small and great; and[R]he read in their hearing all the words of the book of the covenant,[R]which was found in the house of the LORD.   Deut. 31:10-13 · 2 Kin. 22:8

3 And the king stood by the pillar and made a covenant before the LORD, to walk after the LORD, and to keep His commandments and His testimonies and His statutes with all *his* heart and all *his* soul, to carry out the words of this covenant that were written in this book. And all the people[T]entered into the covenant.   *took a stand in*

23:3 Knowing the Will of God Through the Scriptures—The best way to study a subject often begins with a definition of that subject. What do we mean by the will of God? It is that holy and stated purpose of the Father to make His dear children as much like Christ as possible.

Without doubt the most important factor in finding God's will is the Bible itself. God speaks to us not in some loud voice, but through the Scriptures. *First,* the Scriptures declare He does have a definite will for my life. "The steps of a man are established by the LORD" (Page 546—Ps. 37:23). "I will instruct you and teach you in the way which you should go" (Page 543—Ps. 32:8). See also Ephesians 2:10; Hebrews 12:1. *Second,* God desires us to know His will for our lives. "So then do not be foolish, but understand what the will of the Lord is" (Page 1188—Eph. 5:17). *Third,* this will is continuous. It does not begin when I am thirty years of age. God has a will for children, young people, adults, and senior citizens. See Isaiah 58:11. *Fourth,* God's will is specific. "And your ears will hear a word behind you, 'This is the way, walk in it' " (Page 682—Is. 30:21), "But the path of the upright is a highway" (Page 620—Prov. 15:19). *Fifth,* God's will is profitable (Page 206—Josh. 1:8; Page 528—Ps. 1:1-3).

(continued on next page)

Reforms Because of the Covenant
2 Chr. 34:33—35:19

4 Then the king commanded Hilkiah the high priest and [R] the priests of the second order and the doorkeepers, to bring out of the temple of the LORD all the vessels that were made for Baal, for [15]Asherah, and for all the host of heaven; and he burned them outside Jerusalem in the fields of the Kidron, and carried their ashes to Bethel.   2 Kin. 25:18

5 And he did away with the idolatrous priests whom the kings of Judah had appointed to burn incense in the high places in the cities of Judah and in the surrounding area of Jerusalem, also those who burned incense to Baal, to the sun and to the moon and to the constellations and to all the [R]host of heaven.   2 Kin. 21:3

6 And he brought out the Asherah from the house of the LORD outside Jerusalem to the brook Kidron, and burned it at the brook Kidron, and ground *it* to dust, and threw its dust on the graves of the common people.

7 He also broke down the houses of the *male* cult prostitutes which *were* in the house of the LORD, where the women were weaving [A]hangings for the Asherah.   *tents*

8 Then he brought all the priests from the cities of Judah, and defiled the high places where the priests had burned incense, from [R]Geba to Beersheba; and he broke down the high places of the gates which *were* at the entrance of the gate of Joshua the governor of the city, which *were* on one's left at the city gate.   1 Kin. 15:22

9 Nevertheless [R]the priests of the high places did not go up to the altar of the LORD in Jerusalem, but they ate unleavened bread among their brothers.   [Ezek. 44:10–14]

10 [R]He also defiled [16]Topheth, which is in the valley of the son of Hinnom, that no man might make his son or his daughter pass through the fire for Molech.   Is. 30:33

11 And he did away with the horses which the kings of Judah had given to the [R]sun, at the entrance of the house of the LORD, by the chamber of Nathan-melech the official, which *was* in the precincts; and he burned the chariots of the sun with fire.   Deut. 4:19

12 And [R]the altars which *were* on the roof, the upper chamber of Ahaz, which the kings of Judah had made, and the altars which Manasseh had made in the two courts of the house of the LORD, the king broke down; and he [17]smashed them there, and threw their dust into the brook Kidron.   Jer. 19:13

13 And the high places which *were* before Jerusalem, which *were* on the right of [R]the mount of destruction which Solomon the king of Israel had built for [R]Ashtoreth the abomination of the Sidonians, and for Chemosh the abomination of Moab, and for Milcom the abomination of the sons of Ammon, the king defiled.   1 Kin. 11:7 • 1 Kin. 11:5

14 And [R]he broke in pieces the *sacred* pillars and cut down the Asherim and filled their places with human bones.   Deut. 7:5, 25

15 Furthermore, the altar that *was* at Bethel *and* the high place which Jeroboam the son of Nebat, who made Israel sin, had made, even that altar and the high place he broke down. Then he [T]demolished its stones, ground them to dust, and burned the Asherah.   Heb., *burned the high place*

16 Now when Josiah turned, he saw the graves that *were* there on the mountain, and he sent and took the bones from the graves and burned *them* on the altar and defiled it [R]according to the word of the LORD which the man of God proclaimed, who proclaimed these things.   1 Kin. 13:2

17 Then he said, "What is this monument that I see?" And the men of the city told him, "It [T]is the grave of the man of God who came from Judah and proclaimed these things which you have done against the altar of Bethel."   1 Kin. 13:1, 30, 31

18 And he said, "Let him alone; let no one disturb his bones." So they left his bones undisturbed [R]with the bones of the prophet who came from Samaria.   1 Kin. 13:11, 31

19 And Josiah also removed all the houses of the high places which *were* in the cities of Samaria, which the kings of Israel had made provoking the LORD; and he did to them just as he had done in Bethel.

20 And all the priests of the high places who *were* there [R]he slaughtered on the altars and burned human bones on them; then he returned to Jerusalem.   2 Kin. 10:25; 11:18

21 Then the king commanded all the people saying, "Celebrate [R]the Passover to the LORD your God [R]as it is written in this book of the covenant."   2 Chr. 35:1-17 • Num. 9:2-4

22 Surely such a Passover had not been celebrated from the days of the judges who judged Israel, nor in all the days of the kings of Israel and of the kings of Judah.

23 But in the eighteenth year of King Josiah, this Passover was observed to the LORD in Jerusalem.

[15] I.e., wooden symbol of a female deity
[16] I.e., place of burning   [17] Or, *ran from there*

(continued from previous page)

What is the will of God for us? As we have already noted, it differs from believer to believer. But here are four aspects in the will of God which apply to every Christian:

a. It is His will that we learn more about God (Page 1200—Col. 1:9).
b. It is His will that we grow in grace (Page 1208—1 Thess. 4:3).
c. It is His will that we study His Word (Page 1225—2 Tim. 3:14–17).
d. It is His will that we share our faith (Page 1094—Acts 1:8; Page 1217—1 Tim. 2:4; Page 1269—2 Pet. 3:9).
    Now turn to Page 846—Dan. 9:3, 4: Knowing the Will of God Through Prayer and Fasting.

24 Moreover, Josiah removed the mediums and the spiritists and the teraphim and the idols and all the abominations that were seen in the land of Judah and in Jerusalem, that he might confirm the words of the law which were written in the book that Hilkiah the priest found in the house of the LORD.

25 And before him there was no king like him who turned to the LORD with all his heart and with all his soul and with all his might, according to all the law of Moses; nor did any like him arise after him.

26 However, the LORD did not turn from the fierceness of His great wrath with which His anger burned against Judah,ᴿbecause of all the provocations with which Manasseh had provoked Him.   2 Kin. 21:11-13; Jer. 15:4

27 And the LORD said, "I will remove Judah also from My sight, as I have removed Israel. And I will cast off Jerusalem, this city which I have chosen, and the temple of which I said, 'My name shall be there.' "

Political Situation Under Josiah
2 Chr. 35:20–23

28 Now the rest of the acts of Josiah and all that he did, are they not written in the Book of the Chronicles of the Kings of Judah?

29 ᴿIn his days Pharaoh Neco king of Egypt went up to the king of Assyria to the river Euphrates. And King Josiah went to meet him, and when *Pharaoh Neco* saw him he killed him at Megiddo.   2 Chr. 35:20-24

Death of Josiah—2 Chr. 35:24—36:1

30 And his servants drove his body in a chariot from Megiddo, and brought him to Jerusalem and buried him in his own tomb. Then the people of the land took Jehoahaz the son of Josiah and anointed him and made him king in place of his father.

The Reign of Jehoahaz in Judah
2 Chr. 36:2–4

31 ᴿJehoahaz was twenty-three years old when he became king, and he reigned three months in Jerusalem; and his mother's name was Hamutal the daughter of Jeremiah of Libnah.   1 Chr. 3:15; Jer. 22:11

32 And he did evil in the sight of the LORD, according to all that his fathers had done.

33 AndᴿPharaoh Neco imprisoned him at Riblah in the land of Hamath, that he might not reign in Jerusalem; and he imposed on the land a fine of one hundred talents of silver and a talent of gold.   2 Kin. 23:29

34 And Pharaoh Neco madeᴿEliakim the son of Josiah king in the place of Josiah his father, and changed his name to Jehoiakim. But he took Jehoahaz away and brought *him* to Egypt, and he died there.   1 Chr. 3:15

The Reign of Jehoiakim in Judah
2 Chr. 36:5–8

35 So Jehoiakim gave the silver and gold to Pharaoh, but he taxed the land in order to give the money at the ᵀcommand of Pharaoh. He exacted the silver and gold from the people of the land, each according to his valuation, to give it to Pharaoh Neco.   *mouth*

36 ᴿJehoiakim was twenty-five years old when he became king, and he reigned eleven years in Jerusalem; and his mother's name *was* Zebidah the daughter of Pedaiah of Rumah.   2 Chr. 36:5; Jer. 22:18, 19; 26:1

37 And he did evil in the sight of the LORD, according to all that his fathers had done.

CHAPTER 24

IN ᴿhis days Nebuchadnezzar king of Babylon came up, and Jehoiakim became his servant *for* three years; then he turned and rebelled against him.   2 Chr. 36:6; Jer. 25:1

2 And the LORD sent against himᴿbands of Chaldeans,ᴿbands of Arameans, bands of Moabites, and bands of Ammonites. So He sent them against Judah to destroy it, according to the word of the LORD, which He had spoken through His servants the prophets.   Jer. 35:11f. • 2 Kin. 6:23

3 Surely at the ᵀcommand of the LORD it came upon Judah, to remove *them* from His sight because of the sins of Manasseh, according to all that he had done,   *mouth*

4 and also for the innocent blood which he shed, for he filled Jerusalem with innocent blood; and the LORD would not forgive.

5 Now the rest of the acts of Jehoiakim and all that he did, are they not written in the Book of the Chronicles of the Kings of Judah?

6 So ᴿJehoiakim slept with his fathers, and Jehoiachin his son became king in his place.   Jer. 22:18, 19

7 Andᵀthe king of Egypt did not come out of his land again,ᴿfor the king of Babylon had taken all that belonged to the king of Egypt from the brook of Egypt to the river Euphrates.   Jer. 37:5-7 • Jer. 46:2

The Reign of Jehoiachin in Judah
2 Chr. 36:9, 10

8 ᴿJehoiachin was ᴿeighteen years old when he became king, and he reigned three months in Jerusalem; and his mother's name *was* Nehushta the daughter of Elnathan of Jerusalem.   1 Chr. 3:16 • 2 Chr. 36:9

9 And he did evil in the sight of the LORD, according to all that his father had done.

10 At that time the servants of Nebuchadnezzar king of Babylon went up to Jerusalem, and the city came under siege.

11 And Nebuchadnezzar the king of Babylon came to the city, while his servants were besieging it.

12 And Jehoiachin the king of Judah went out to the king of Babylon, he and his mother and his servants and his captains and his officials. So the king of Babylon took

him captive in the eighth year of his reign.

13 And[R]he carried out from there all the treasures of the house of the LORD, and the treasures of the king's house, and cut in pieces all the vessels of gold which Solomon king of Israel had made in the temple of the LORD, just as the LORD had said.   Is. 39:6

14 Then[R]he led away into exile all Jerusalem and all the captains and all the mighty men of valor,[R]ten thousand captives, and[R]all the craftsmen and the smiths. None remained except the poorest people of the land.   Jer. 24:1 • 2 Kin. 24:16 • Jer. 24:1

15 So[R]he led Jehoiachin away into exile to Babylon; also the king's mother and the king's wives and his officials and the leading men of the land, he led away into exile from Jerusalem to Babylon.   2 Chr. 36:10; Jer. 22:24

16 And all the men of valor,[R]seven thousand, and the craftsmen and the smiths, one thousand, all strong and fit for war, and these the king of Babylon brought into exile to Babylon.   2 Kin. 24:14

Spiritual Evaluation of Zedekiah
2 Chr. 36:10–16; Jer. 52:1, 2

17 Then the king of Babylon made his uncle Mattaniah, king in his place, and changed his name to Zedekiah.

18[R]Zedekiah was twenty-one years old when he became king, and he reigned eleven years in Jerusalem; and his mother's name was[R]Hamutal the daughter of Jeremiah of Libnah.   Jer. 27:1 • 2 Kin. 23:31

19 And he did evil in the sight of the LORD, according to all that Jehoiakim had done.

Political Situation Under Zedekiah
2 Chr. 36:17–20; Jer. 52:3–27

20 For through the anger of the LORD *this* came about in Jerusalem and Judah until He cast them out from His presence. And Zedekiah rebelled against the king of Babylon.

CHAPTER 25

Now[R]it came about in the ninth year of his reign, on the tenth day of the tenth month, that Nebuchadnezzar king of Babylon came, he and all his army, against Jerusalem, camped[T]against it, and built a siege wall all around[T]it.   Jer. 39:1-7 • *against it*

2 So the city was under siege until the eleventh year of King Zedekiah.

3 On the ninth day of the *fourth* month the famine was so severe in the city that there was no food for the people of the land.

4[R]Then the city was broken into, and all the men of war *fled* by night by way of the gate between the two walls beside[T]the king's garden, though the Chaldeans were all around the city. And they went by way of the Arabah.   Ezek. 33:21 • Neh. 3:15

5 But the army of the Chaldeans pursued the king and overtook him in the plains of Jericho and all his army was scattered from him.

6 Then they captured the king and brought him to the king of Babylon at Riblah, and he passed sentence on him.

7 And[T]they slaughtered the sons of Zedekiah before his eyes, then put out the eyes of Zedekiah and bound him with bronze fetters and brought him to Babylon.   Jer. 39:6, 7

8[R]Now on the seventh day of the [R]fifth month, which was the nineteenth year of King Nebuchadnezzar, king of Babylon, Nebuzaradan the captain of the guard, a servant of the king of Babylon, came to Jerusalem.   Jer. 52:12 • Jer. 39:8-12

9 And[R]he burned the house of the LORD, [R]the king's house, and all the houses of Jerusalem; even every great house he burned with fire.   1 Kin. 9:8; 2 Chr. 36:19 • Amos 2:5

10 So all the army of the Chaldeans who *were with* the captain of the guard[R]broke down the walls around Jerusalem.   Neh. 1:3

11 Then the rest of the people who were left in the city and the deserters who had deserted to the king of Babylon and the rest of the multitude, Nebuzaradan the captain of the guard carried away into exile.

12 But the captain of the guard left some of[R]the poorest of the land to be vinedressers and plowmen.   2 Kin. 24:14; Jer. 40:7

13 Now the bronze pillars which were in the house of the LORD, and the stands and the bronze sea which were in the house of the LORD, the Chaldeans broke in pieces and carried the[T]bronze to Babylon. *bronze of them*

14 [R]And they took away the pots, the shovels, the snuffers, the spoons, and all the bronze vessels which were used in *temple* service.   Ex. 27:3; 1 Kin. 7:47-50; 2 Chr. 4:16

15 The captain of the guard also took away the firepans and the basins, what was fine gold and what was fine silver.

16 The two pillars, the one sea, and the stands which Solomon had made for the house of the LORD—[R]the bronze of all these vessels was beyond weight.   1 Kin. 7:47

17 The height of the one pillar was eighteen cubits, and a bronze capital was on it; the height of the capital was three cubits, with a network and pomegranates on the capital all around, all of bronze. And the second pillar was like these with network.

18 Then the captain of the guard took [R]Seraiah the chief priest and Zephaniah the second priest, with the three[T]officers of the temple.   Ezra 7:1 • *keepers of the door*

19 And from the city he took one official who was overseer of the men of war, and [R]five of the king's advisers who were found in the city; and the scribe of the captain of the army, who mustered the people of the land; and sixty men of the people of the land who were found in the city.   Esth. 1:14

20 And Nebuzaradan the captain of the guard took them and brought them to the king of Babylon at[R]Riblah.   2 Kin. 23:33

21 Then the king of Babylon struck them down and put them to death at Riblah in the land of Hamath.^RSo Judah was led away into exile from its land.   Deut. 28:64; 2 Kin. 23:27

The Governorship of Gedaliah
Jer. 40:5—41:18

22 Now *as for* the people who were left in the land of Judah, whom Nebuchadnezzar king of Babylon had left, he appointed ^RGedaliah the son of Ahikam, the son of Sha-phan over them.   Jer. 39:14; 40:7-9
23 ^RWhen all the captains of the forces, they and *their* men, heard that the king of Babylon had appointed Gedaliah *governor*, they came to Gedaliah to^RMizpah, namely, Ishmael the son of Nethaniah, and Johanan the son of Kareah, and Seraiah the son of Tanhumeth the Netophathite, and Jaaza-niah the son of the Maacathite, they and their men.   Jer. 40:7-9 • Josh. 18:26
24 And Gedaliah swore to them and their men and said to them, "Do not be afraid of the servants of the Chaldeans; live in the land and serve the king of Babylon, and it will be well with you."
25 ^RBut it came about in the seventh month, that Ishmael the son of Nethaniah,

the son of Elishama, of the royal ^Tfamily, came with ten men and struck Gedaliah down so that he died along with the Jews and the Chaldeans who were with him at Mizpah.   Jer. 41:1, 2 • *seed*
26 ^RThen all the people, both small and great, and the captains of the forces arose and went to Egypt; for they were afraid of the Chaldeans.   Jer. 43:4-7

The Release of Jehoiachin
in Babylon—Jer. 52:31-34

27 Now it came about in the thirty-seventh year of the exile of Jehoiachin king of Judah, in the twelfth month, on the twenty-seventh *day* of the month, that Evil-merodach king of Babylon, in the year that he became king,^Treleased Jehoiachin king of Judah from prison;   *lifted up the head of*
28 and he^Rspoke kindly to him and set his throne above the throne of the kings who *were* with him in Babylon.   Dan. 2:37; 5:18, 19
29 And Jehoiachin changed his prison clothes, and had his meals in the king's presence regularly all the days of his life;
30 and for his allowance, a regular allow-ance was given him by the king, a portion for each day, all the days of his life.

THE FIRST BOOK OF THE
CHRONICLES

THE BOOK OF FIRST CHRONICLES

The books of First and Second Chronicles cover the same period of Jewish history described in Second Samuel through Second Kings, but the perspective is different. These books are no mere repetition of the same material, but rather form a divine editorial on the history of God's people. While Second Samuel and First and Second Kings give a political history of Israel and Judah, First and Second Chronicles present a religious history of the Davidic dynasty of Judah. The former are written from a prophetic and moral viewpoint, and the latter from a priestly and spiritual perspective. The Book of First Chronicles begins with the royal line of David and then traces the spiritual significance of David's righteous reign.

The books of First and Second Chronicles were originally one continuous work in Hebrew. The title was *Dibere Hayyamim*, meaning "The Words [accounts, events] of the Days." The equivalent meaning today would be "The Events of the Times." Chronicles was divided into two parts in the third century B.C. Greek translation of the Hebrew Bible (the Septuagint). At that time it was given the name *Paraleipomenon*, "Of Things Omitted," referring to the things omitted from Samuel and Kings. Some copies add the phrase, *Basileon Iouda*, "Concerning the Kings of Judah." The first book of Chronicles was called *Paraleipomenon Primus*, "The First Book of Things Omitted." The name "Chronicles" comes from Jerome in his Latin Vulgate Bible (A.D. 385–405): *Chronicorum Liber*. He meant his title in the sense of "The Chronicles of the Whole of Sacred History."

THE AUTHOR OF FIRST CHRONICLES

Although the text does not identify the author, several facts seem to support the tradition in the Jewish Talmud that Ezra the priest was the author. The content points to a priestly authorship because of the emphasis on the temple, the priesthood, and the theocratic line of David in the southern kingdom of Judah. The narrative also indicates that Chronicles was at least written by a contemporary of Ezra. Chronicles is quite similar in style to the Book of Ezra, and both share a priestly perspective: genealogies, temple worship, ministry of the priesthood, and obedience to the law of God. In addition, the closing verses of Second Chronicles (36:22, 23) are repeated with minor changes as the opening verses of Ezra (1:1–3). Thus, Chronicles and Ezra may have been one consecutive history as were Luke and Acts.

Ezra was an educated scribe (Ezra 7:6), and according to the apocryphal book of Second Maccabees 2:13–15, Nehemiah collected an extensive library which was available to Ezra for his use in compiling Chronicles. Many of these documents and sources are listed in the book (see "The Author of Second Chronicles"). Scholars of Israel accumulated and compared historical material, and the author of Chronicles was actually a compiler who drew from many sources under the guidance and inspiration of the Holy Spirit.

THE TIME OF FIRST CHRONICLES

The genealogies in chapters 1—9 cover the time from Adam to David, and chapters 10—29 focus on the thirty-three years of David's rule over the united kingdoms of Israel and Judah (1004–971 B.C.). However, the genealogies extend to about 500 B.C., as seen in the mention of Zerubbabel, grandson of King Jeconiah, who leads the first return of the Jews from exile in 538 B.C., and also Zerubbabel's two grandsons Pelatiah and Jesaiah (3:21).

Ezra probably completed Chronicles between 450 and 430 B.C. and addressed it to the returned remnant. Ezra leads some of the exiles to Jerusalem in 457 B.C. and ministers to the people as their spiritual leader. During Ezra's time, Nehemiah is the political leader and Malachi is the moral leader. Chronicles spends a disproportionate time on the reigns of David and Solomon because they bring the nation to its pinnacle. The book is written to the people of Israel's "Second Commonwealth" to encourage them and to remind them that they must remain the covenant people of God. This reminds the Jews of their spiritual heritage and identity during the difficult times they are facing.

THE CHRIST OF FIRST CHRONICLES

See the introductions to First and Second Samuel for descriptions of David as a type of Christ. The Davidic Covenant of Second

Samuel 7 is found again in First Chronicles 7:11–14. Solomon fulfilled part, but the promise of the eternality of David's throne can only point to the coming of the Messiah.

The tribe of Judah is placed first in the national genealogy in First Chronicles because the monarchy, temple, and Messiah (Gen. 49:10) will come from this tribe. Since the books of Chronicles are the last books of the Hebrew Bible, the genealogies in chapters 1— 9 are a preamble to the genealogy of Christ in the first book of the New Testament.

KEYS TO FIRST CHRONICLES

Key Verses: First Chronicles 17:11–14; 29:11—"And it shall come about when your days are fulfilled that you must go *to be* with your fathers, that I will set up *one of* your descendants after you, who shall be of your sons; and I will establish his kingdom. He shall build for Me a house, and I will establish his throne forever. I will be his father, and he shall be My son; and I will not take My loving-kindness away from him, as I took it from him who was before you. But I will settle him in My house and in My kingdom forever, and his throne shall be established forever" (17:11–14).

"Thine, O LORD, is the greatness and the power and the glory and the victory and the majesty, indeed everything that is in the heavens and the earth; Thine is the dominion, O LORD, and Thou dost exalt Thyself as head over all" (29:11).

Key Chapter: First Chronicles 17—Pivotal for the Book of First Chronicles as well as for the rest of the Scriptures is the Davidic Covenant recorded in Second Samuel 7 and First Chronicles 17. God promises David that He will "settle him [David's ultimate offspring, Jesus Christ] in My house and in My kingdom

forever, and his throne shall be established forever" (17:14).

SURVEY OF FIRST CHRONICLES

Chronicles retraces the whole story of Israel's history up to the return from captivity in order to give the returned remnant a divine perspective on the developments of their past. The whole Book of First Chronicles, like Second Samuel, is dedicated to the life of David. It begins with the royal line of David (1—9) before surveying key events of the reign of David (10—29).

Royal Line of David (1—9): These nine chapters are the most comprehensive genealogical tables in the Bible. They trace the family tree of David and Israel as a whole, but in a highly selective manner. The genealogies place a disproportionate emphasis on the tribes of Judah and Benjamin because Chronicles is not concerned with the northern kingdom but with the southern kingdom and the Davidic dynasty. They show God at work in selecting and preserving a people for Himself from the beginning of human history to the period after the Babylonian exile. The genealogies move from the patriarchal period (Adam to Jacob; 1:1—2:2) to the national period (Judah, Levi, and the other tribes of Israel; 2:3—9:44). They demonstrate God's keeping of His covenant promises in maintaining the Davidic line through the centuries. The priestly perspective of Chronicles is evident in the special attention given to the tribe of Levi.

Reign of David (10—29): Compared with Second Samuel, David's life in First Chronicles is seen in an entirely different light. This is clear from both the omissions and the additions. Chronicles completely omits David's struggles with Saul, his seven-year reign in Hebron, his various wives, and Absalom's rebel-

FOCUS	ROYAL LINE OF DAVID	REIGN OF DAVID				
REFERENCE	1:1————10:1————	13:1————	18:1————	21:1————	28:1——29:30	
DIVISION	GENEALOGIES OF DAVID AND ISRAEL	ACCESSION OF DAVID AS KING	ACQUISITION OF THE ARK	VICTORIES OF DAVID	PREPARATION FOR THE TEMPLE	LAST DAYS OF DAVID
TOPIC	GENEALOGY	HISTORY				
	ANCESTRY	ACTIVITY				
LOCATION	ISRAEL					
TIME	THOUSANDS OF YEARS	c. 33 YEARS				

lion. It also omits the event in Second Samuel that hurt the rest of his life—his sin with Bathsheba. Chronicles is written from a more positive perspective, emphasizing God's grace and forgiveness, in order to encourage the Jews who have just returned from captivity. Chronicles adds events not found in Second Samuel, such as David's preparations for the temple and its worship services.

Only one chapter is given to Saul's reign (10), because his heart was not right with God. David's story begins with his coronation over all Israel after he has already reigned for seven years as king over Judah. Chronicles stresses his deep spiritual commitment, courage, and integrity. It emphasizes his concern for the things of the Lord, including his return of the ark and his desire to build a temple for

God. God establishes His crucial covenant with David (17), and the kingdom is strengthened and expanded under his reign (18—20). His sin in numbering the people is recorded to teach the consequences of disobeying God's law. Most of the rest of the book (22—29) is concerned with David's preparations for the building of the temple and the worship associated with it. The priestly perspective of Chronicles can be seen in the disproportionate space given to the temple and the priests. David is not allowed to build the temple (28:3), but he designs the plans, gathers the materials, prepares the site, and arranges for the Levites, priests, choirs, porters, soldiers, and stewards. The book closes with his beautiful public prayer of praise and the accession of Solomon.

OUTLINE OF FIRST CHRONICLES

Part One: The Royal Line of David (1:1—9:44)

Part Two: The Reign of David (10:1—29:30)

CHAPTER 1

The Genealogy from Adam to Noah
Gen. 5:1–32; Luke 3:36–38

ADAM,[R] Seth, Enosh,　　　Gen. 4:25—5:32
2 Kenan, Mahalalel, Jared,
3 Enoch, Methuselah, Lamech,
4 Noah, Shem, Ham and Japheth.

Sons of Japheth—Gen. 10:2–5

5 [R] The sons of Japheth *were* Gomer, Magog, Madai, Javan, Tubal, Meshech, and Tiras.　　　Gen. 10:2-4
6 And the sons of Gomer *were* Ashkenaz, Diphath, and Togarmah.
7 And the sons of Javan *were* Elishah, Tarshish, Kittim, and Rodanim.

Sons of Ham—Gen. 10:6–18

8 The sons of Ham *were* Cush, Mizraim, Put, and Canaan.
9 And the sons of Cush *were* Seba, Havilah, Sabta, Raama, and Sabteca; and the sons of Raamah *were* Sheba and Dedan.

10 And Cush [T] became the father of Nimrod; he began to be a mighty one in the earth.　　　*begot,* and so throughout the ch.
11 And Mizraim became the father of the people of Lud, Anam, Lehab, Naphtuh,
12 Pathrus, Casluh, from which the [A] Philistines came, and Caphtor.　　*people of Pelisht*
13 And Canaan became the father of Sidon, his first-born, Heth,
14 and the Jebusites, the Amorites, the Girgashites,
15 the Hivites, the Arkites, the Sinites,
16 the Arvadites, the Zemarites, and the Hamathites.

Sons of Shem
Gen. 10:21–29; 11:10–26; Luke 3:34–36

17 The sons of Shem *were* Elam, Asshur, Arpachshad, Lud, Aram, Uz, Hul, Gether, and [T] Meshech.　　　In Gen. 10:23, *Mash*
18 And Arpachshad became the father of Shelah and Shelah became the father of Eber.
19 And two sons were born to Eber, the name of the one was Peleg, for in his days

the earth was divided, and his brother's name was Joktan.

20 And Joktan became the father of Almodad, Sheleph, Hazarmaveth, Jerah,

21 Hadoram, Uzal, Diklah,

22 ^Ebal, Abimael, Sheba,   In Gen. 10:28, *Obal*

23 Ophir, Havilah, and Jobab; all these *were* the sons of Joktan.

24 ^RShem, Arpachshad, Shelah,   Luke 3:34-36

25 Eber, Peleg, Reu,

26 Serug, Nahor, Terah,

27 Abram, that is Abraham.

The Genealogy from Abraham to Isaac
Gen. 25:1-4, 12-16

28 The sons of Abraham *were* Isaac and Ishmael.

29 ^RThese are their genealogies: the first-born of Ishmael *was* Nebaioth, then Kedar, Adbeel, Mibsam,   Gen. 25:13-16

30 Mishma, Dumah, Massa, Hadad, Tema,

31 Jetur, Naphish and Kedemah; these *were* the sons of Ishmael.

32 ^RAnd the sons of Keturah, Abraham's concubine, *whom* she bore, *were* Zimran, Jokshan, Medan, Midian, Ishbak, and Shuah. And the sons of Jokshan *were* Sheba and Dedan.   Gen. 25:1-4

33 And the sons of Midian *were* Ephah, Epher, Hanoch, Abida, and Eldaah. All these were the sons of Keturah.

34 And ^RAbraham became the father of Isaac. The sons of Isaac *were*^REsau and Israel.   1 Chr. 1:28 • Gen. 25:25, 26; 32:28

Sons of Esau—Gen. 36:1-30

35 ^RThe sons of Esau *were* Eliphaz, Reuel, Jeush, Jalam, and Korah.   Gen. 36:4-10

36 The sons of Eliphaz *were* Teman, Omar, ^AZephi, Gatam, Kenaz, Timna, and Amalek.   In Gen. 36:11, *Zepho*

37 The sons of Reuel *were* Nahath, Zerah, Shammah, and Mizzah.

38 ^RAnd the sons of Seir *were* Lotan, Shobal, Zibeon, Anah, Dishon, Ezer, and Dishan.   Gen. 36:20-28

39 And the sons of Lotan *were* Hori and Homam; and Lotan's sister *was* Timna.

40 The sons of Shobal *were* Alian, Manahath, Ebal, Shephi, and Onam. And the sons of Zibeon *were* Aiah and Anah.

41 The^Tson of Anah *was* Dishon. And the sons of Dishon^Awere Hamran, Eshban, Ithran, and Cheran.   *sons* • In Gen. 36:26, *Hemdan*

42 The sons of Ezer *were* Bilhan,^AZaavan and Jaakan. The sons of Dishan *were* Uz and Aran.   *Akan,* as in Gen. 36:27

Kings of Edom

43 ^RNow these are the kings who reigned in the land of Edom before any king of the sons of Israel reigned. Bela *was* the son of Beor, and the name of his city was Dinhabah.   Gen. 36:31-43

44 When Bela died, Jobab the son of Zerah of Bozrah became king in his place.

45 When Jobab died, Husham of the land of the Temanites became king in his place.

46 When Husham died, Hadad the son of Bedad, who ^Tdefeated Midian in the field of Moab, became king in his place; and the name of his city *was* Avith.   *smote*

47 When Hadad died, Samlah of Masrekah became king in his place.

48 When Samlah died, Shaul of Rehoboth by the River became king in his place.

49 When Shaul died, Baal-hanan the son of Achbor became king in his place.

50 When Baal-hanan died,^AHadad became king in his place; and the name of his city was Pai, and his wife's name was Mehetabel, the daughter of Matred, the daughter of Mezahab.   In Gen. 36:39, *Hadar*

Chiefs of Edom

51 Then Hadad died. Now the chiefs of Edom were: chief Timna, chief ^AAliah, chief Jetheth,   In Gen. 36:40, *Alvah*

52 chief Oholibamah, chief Elah, chief Pinon,

53 chief Kenaz, chief Teman, chief Mibzar,

54 chief Magdiel, chief Iram. These *were* the chiefs of Edom.

CHAPTER 2

The Genealogy of the Sons of Jacob
Gen. 29:31—30:24; 35:16-18

THESE are the sons of Israel: Reuben, Simeon, Levi, Judah, Issachar, Zebulun,

2 Dan, Joseph, Benjamin, Naphtali, Gad, and Asher.

The Genealogy of the Sons of Judah
Gen. 46:12; Ruth 4:18-22;
Matt. 1:3-6; Luke 3:31-33

3 ^RThe sons of Judah *were* Er, Onan, and Shelah; *these* three were born to him by Bath-shua the Canaanitess. And Er, Judah's first-born, was wicked in the sight of the LORD, so He put him to death.   Gen. 38:2-10

4 And ^RTamar his daughter-in-law bore him Perez and Zerah. Judah had five sons in all.   Gen. 38:13-30

5 The sons of Perez *were* Hezron and Hamul.

6 And the sons of Zerah *were* ^AZimri, Ethan, Heman, Calcol, and Dara; five of them in all.   In Josh. 7:1, *Zabdi*

7 And the son of Carmi *was* Achar, the troubler of Israel, who violated the ban.

8 And the son of Ethan *was* Azariah.

9 Now the sons of Hezron, who were born to him *were* Jerahmeel, Ram, and Chelubai.

10 And Ram became the father of Am-

minadab, and Amminadab [T]became the father of Nahshon, leader of the sons of Judah;   *begot,* and so throughout the ch.

11 Nahshon became the father of Salma, Salma became the father of Boaz,

12 Boaz became the father of Obed, and Obed became the father of Jesse;

13 and Jesse became the father of Eliab his first-born, then Abinadab the second, Shimea the third,

14 Nethanel the fourth, Raddai the fifth,

15 Ozem the sixth, David the seventh;

16 and their sisters *were* Zeruiah and Abigail. And the three sons of Zeruiah *were* [^]Abshai, Joab, and Asahel.   In 2 Sam. 2:18, *Abishai*

17 And Abigail bore Amasa, and the father of Amasa was Jether the Ishmaelite.

18 Now Caleb the son of Hezron had sons by Azubah *his* wife, and by Jerioth; and these were her sons: Jesher, Shobab, and Ardon.

19 When Azubah died, Caleb married Ephrath, who bore him Hur.

20 And Hur became the father of Uri, and Uri became the father of Bezalel.

21 Afterward Hezron went in to the daughter of Machir the father of Gilead, whom he married when he was sixty years old; and she bore him Segub.

22 And Segub became the father of Jair, who had twenty-three cities in the land of Gilead.

23 But Geshur and Aram took the towns of Jair from them, with Kenath and its villages, *even* sixty cities. All these were the sons of Machir, the father of Gilead.

24 And after the death of Hezron in Caleb-ephrathah, Abijah, Hezron's wife, bore him Ashhur the father of Tekoa.

25 Now the sons of Jerahmeel the first-born of Hezron *were* Ram the first-born, then Bunah, Oren, Ozem, *and* Ahijah.

26 And Jerahmeel had another wife, whose name was Atarah; she was the mother of Onam.

27 And the sons of Ram, the first-born of Jerahmeel, were Maaz, Jamin, and Eker.

28 And the sons of Onam were Shammai and Jada. And the sons of Shammai *were* Nadab and Abishur.

29 And the name of Abishur's wife *was* Abihail, and she bore him Ahban and Molid.

30 And the sons of Nadab *were* Seled and Appaim, and Seled died without sons.

31 And the [T]son of Appaim *was* Ishi. And the [T]son of Ishi *was* Sheshan. And the [T]son of Sheshan *was* Ahlai.   *sons*

32 And the sons of Jada the brother of Shammai *were* Jether and Jonathan, and Jether died without sons.

33 And the sons of Jonathan *were* Peleth and Zaza. These were the sons of Jerahmeel.

34 Now Sheshan had no sons, only daughters. And Sheshan had an Egyptian servant whose name was Jarha.

35 And Sheshan gave his daughter to Jarha his servant in marriage, and she bore him Attai.

36 And Attai became the father of Nathan, and Nathan became the father of Zabad,

37 and Zabad became the father of Ephlal, and Ephlal became the father of Obed,

38 and Obed became the father of Jehu, and Jehu became the father of Azariah,

39 and Azariah became the father of Helez, and Helez became the father of Eleasah,

40 and Eleasah became the father of Sismai, and Sismai became the father of Shallum,

41 and Shallum became the father of Jekamiah, and Jekamiah became the father of Elishama.

42 Now the sons of Caleb, the brother of Jerahmeel, *were* Mesha his first-born, who was the father of Ziph; and [T]his son was Mareshah, the father of Hebron.   *the sons of*

43 And the sons of Hebron *were* Korah and Tappuah and Rekem and Shema.

44 And Shema became the father of Raham, the father of Jorkeam; and Rekem became the father of Shammai.

45 And the son of Shammai was Maon, and Maon *was* the father of Bethzur.

46 And Ephah, Caleb's concubine, bore Haran, Moza, and Gazez; and Haran became the father of Gazez.

47 And the sons of Jahdai *were* Regem, Jotham, Geshan, Pelet, Ephah, and Shaaph.

48 Maacah, Caleb's concubine, bore Sheber and Tirhanah.

49 She also bore Shaaph the father of Madmannah, Sheva the father of Machbena and the father of Gibea; and the daughter of Caleb *was* Achsah.

50 These were the sons of Caleb.

The [T]sons of Hur, the first-born of Ephrathah, *were* Shobal the father of Kiriath-jearim,   *son*

51 Salma the father of Bethlehem *and* Hareph the father of Beth-gader.

52 And Shobal the father of Kiriath-jearim had sons: Haroeh, half of the Manahathites,

53 and the families of Kiriath-jearim: the Ithrites, the Puthites, the Shumathites, and the Mishraites; from these came the Zorathites and the Eshtaolites.

54 The sons of Salma *were* Bethlehem and the Netophathites, Atroth-beth-joab and half of the Manahathites, the Zorites.

55 And the families of scribes who lived at Jabez *were* the Tirathites, the Shimeathites, *and* the Sucathites. Those are the Kenites who came from Hammath, the father of the house of Rechab.

CHAPTER 3

The Genealogy of the Sons of David

N[R]OW these were the sons of David who were born to him in Hebron: the first-born *was* Amnon, by Ahinoam the Jezreelitess;

the second *was* Daniel, by Abigail the Carmelitess;   2 Sam. 3:2-5

2 the third *was* Absalom the son of Maacah, the daughter of Talmai king of Geshur; the fourth *was* Adonijah the son of Haggith;

3 the fifth *was* Shephatiah, by Abital; the sixth *was* Ithream, by his wife Eglah.

4 Six were born to him in Hebron, and ^{R}there he reigned seven years and six months. And in Jerusalem he reigned thirty-three years.   2 Sam. 2:11; 5:4, 5; 1 Kin. 2:11

5 ^{R}And these were born to him in Jerusalem: Shimea, Shobab, Nathan, and ^{R}Solomon, four, by Bath-shua the daughter of Ammiel;   2 Sam. 5:14-16 • 2 Sam. 12:24, 25

6 and Ibhar, Elishama, Eliphelet,

7 Nogah, Nepheg, and Japhia,

8 Elishama, Eliada, and Eliphelet, nine.

9 All *these were* the sons of David, besides the sons of the concubines; and ^{R}Tamar *was* their sister.   2 Sam. 13:1

The Genealogy of the Sons of Solomon
Matt. 1:7-12

10 Now Solomon's son *was* Rehoboam, Abijah *was* his son, Asa his son, Jehoshaphat his son,

11 Joram his son, Ahaziah his son, Joash his son,

12 Amaziah his son, Azariah his son, Jotham his son,

13 Ahaz his son, Hezekiah his son, Manasseh his son,

14 Amon his son, Josiah his son.

15 And the sons of Josiah *were* Johanan the first-born, and the second *was* Jehoiakim, the third Zedekiah, the fourth Shallum.

16 And the sons of Jehoiakim *were* Jeconiah his son, Zedekiah his son.

17 And the sons of Jeconiah, the prisoner, *were* Shealtiel his son,

18 and Malchiram, Pedaiah, Shenazzar, Jekamiah, Hoshama, and Nedabiah.

19 And the sons of Pedaiah *were* Zerubbabel and Shimei. And the ^{s}sons of Zerubbabel *were* Meshullam and Hananiah, and Shelomith *was* their sister;   son

20 and Hashubah, Ohel, Berechiah, Hasadiah, and Jushab-hesed, five.

21 And the ^{s}sons of Hananiah *were* Pelatiah and Jeshaiah, the sons of Rephaiah, the sons of Arnan, the sons of Obadiah, the sons of Shecaniah.   son

22 And the ^{1}son of Shecaniah *was* Shemaiah, and the sons of Shemaiah *were* Hattush, Igal, Bariah, Neariah, and Shaphat, six.

23 And the ^{s}sons of Neariah *were* Elioenai, Hizkiah, and Azrikam, three.   son

24 And the sons of Elioenai *were* Hodaviah, Eliashib, Pelaiah, Akkub, Johanan, Delaiah, and Anani, seven.

CHAPTER 4
The Genealogy of Judah

THE^R sons of Judah *were* Perez, Hezron, Carmi, Hur, and Shobal.   1 Chr. 2:3

2 And Reaiah the son of Shobal^{T}became the father of Jahath, and Jahath became the father of Ahumai and Lahad. These *were* the families of the Zorathites.   begot

3 And these *were* the ^{s}sons of Etam: Jezreel, Ishma, and Idbash; and the name of their sister *was* Hazzelelponi.   Heb., *father*

4 And Penuel *was* the father of Gedor, and Ezer the father of Hushah. These *were* the sons of Hur, the first-born of Ephrathah, the father of Bethlehem.

5 And Ashhur, the father of Tekoa, had two wives, Helah and Naarah.

6 And Naarah bore him Ahuzzam, Hepher, Temeni, and Haahashtari. These *were* the sons of Naarah.

7 And the sons of Helah *were* Zereth, ^{A}Izhar and Ethnan.   Another reading is *Zohar*

8 And Koz became the father of Anub and Zobebah, and the families of Aharhel the son of Harum.

9 And Jabez was more honorable than his brothers, and his mother named him Jabez saying, "Because I bore *him* with pain."

10 Now Jabez called on the God of Israel, saying, "Oh that Thou wouldst bless me indeed, and enlarge my border, and that Thy hand might be with me, and that Thou wouldst keep *me* from harm, that *it* may not pain me!" And God granted him what he requested.

11 And Chelub the brother of Shuhah became the father of Mehir, who was the father of Eshton.

12 And Eshton became the father of Bethrapha and Paseah, and Tehinnah the father of Ir-nahash. These are the men of Recah.

13 Now the sons of Kenaz *were* Othniel and Seraiah. And the ^{T}son of Othniel *was* Hathath.   sons

14 And Meonothai became the father of Ophrah, and Seraiah became the father of Joab the father of ^{A}Ge-harashim, for they were craftsmen.   valley of craftsmen

15 And the sons of Caleb the son of Jephunneh *were* Iru, Elah and Naam; and the ^{T}son of Elah *was*^{T}Kenaz.   sons • *and Kenaz*

16 And the sons of Jehallelel *were* Ziph and Ziphah, Tiria and Asarel.

17 And the ^{T}sons of Ezrah *were* Jether, Mered, Epher, and Jalon. (And these are the sons of Bithia the daughter of Pharaoh, whom Mered took) and she conceived *and* bore Miriam, Shammai, and Ishbah the father of Eshtemoa.   son

18 And his Jewish wife bore Jered the father of Gedor, and Heber the father of Soco, and Jekuthiel the father of Zanoah.

19 And the sons of the wife of Hodiah, the sister of Naham, *were* the fathers of Keilah the Garmite and Eshtemoa the Maacathite.

20 And the sons of Shimon *were* Amnon and Rinnah, Benhanan and Tilon. And the sons of Ishi *were* Zoheth and Ben-zoheth.

^{1} Lit., *sons*

21 The sons of Shelah the son of Judah *were* Er the father of Lecah and Laadah the father of Mareshah, and the families of the house of the linen workers at Beth-ashbea;
22 and Jokim, the men of Cozeba, Joash, Saraph, who ruled in Moab, and Jashubi-lehem. And the[T]records are ancient.   *words*
23 These were the potters and the inhabitants of Netaim and Gederah; they lived there with the king for his work.

The Genealogy of Simeon—Gen. 46:10

24 The sons of Simeon *were* Nemuel and Jamin, [A]Jarib, Zerah, Shaul; Num. 26:12, *Jachin*
25 Shallum his son, Mibsam his son, Mishma his son.
26 And the sons of Mishma *were* Hammuel his son, Zaccur his son, Shimei his son.
27 Now Shimei had sixteen sons and six daughters; but his brothers did not have many sons, nor did all their family multiply like the sons of Judah.
28 And they lived at Beersheba, Moladah, and Hazar-shual,
29 at Bilhah, Ezem, Tolad,
30 Bethuel, Hormah, Ziklag,
31 Beth-marcaboth, Hazar-susim, Bethbiri, and Shaaraim. These *were* their cities until the reign of David.
32 And their villages *were* Etam, Ain, Rimmon, Tochen, and Ashan, five cities;
33 and all their villages that *were* around the same cities as far as [A]Baal. These *were* their settlements, and they have their genealogy.   In Josh. 19:8, *Baalath*
34 And Meshobab and Jamlech and Joshah the son of Amaziah,
35 and Joel and Jehu the son of Joshibiah, the son of Seraiah, the son of Asiel,
36 and Elioenai, Jaakobah, Jeshohaiah, Asaiah, Adiel, Jesimiel, Benaiah,
37 Ziza the son of Shiphi, the son of Allon, the son of Jedaiah, the son of Shimri, the son of Shemaiah;
38 these mentioned by name *were* leaders in their families; and their fathers' houses increased greatly.
39 And they went to the entrance of Gedor, even to the east side of the valley, to seek pasture for their flocks.
40 And they found rich and good pasture, and [R]the land was broad and quiet and peaceful; for those who lived there formerly *were* Hamites.   Judg. 18:7-10
41 And these, recorded by name, came in the days of Hezekiah king of Judah, and attacked their tents, and the Meunites who were found there, and destroyed them utterly to this day, and lived in their place; because there was pasture there for their flocks.
42 And from them, from the sons of Simeon, five hundred men went to Mount Seir, with Pelatiah, Neariah, Rephaiah, and Uzziel, the sons of Ishi, as their leaders.

43 And[R]they[T]destroyed the remnant of the Amalekites who escaped, and have lived there to this day.   1 Sam. 15:7, 8 • *smote*

CHAPTER 5

The Genealogy of Reuben—Gen. 45:8, 9

NOW the sons of Reuben the first-born of Israel (for[R]he was the first-born, but because he defiled his father's bed, his birthright was given to the sons of Joseph the son of Israel; so that he is not enrolled in the genealogy according to the birthright.   Gen. 29:32
2 [R]Though Judah prevailed over his brothers, and from him *came* the leader, yet the birthright belonged to Joseph), Ps. 60:7; 108:8
3 [R]the sons of Reuben the first-born of Israel *were* Hanoch and Pallu, Hezron and Carmi.   Gen. 49:9; Ex. 6:14; Num. 26:5-9
4 The sons of Joel *were* Shemaiah his son, Gog his son,[R]Shimei his son, 1 Chr. 5:8
5 Micah his son, Reaiah his son, Baal his son,
6 Beerah his son, whom Tilgath-pilneser king of Assyria carried away into exile; he was leader of the Reubenites.
7 And his[T]kinsmen by their families, in the genealogy of their generations, *were* Jeiel the chief, then Zechariah   *brothers*
8 and Bela the son of Azaz, the son of Shema, the son of Joel, who lived in [R]Aroer, even to Nebo and Baal-meon.   Josh. 12:2
9 And to the east he settled as far as the entrance of the wilderness from the river Euphrates, [R]because their cattle had increased in the land of Gilead.   Josh. 22:8, 9
10 And in the days of Saul they made war with the Hagrites, who fell by their hand, so that they[T]occupied their tents throughout all the land east of Gilead.   *dwelt in*

The Genealogy of Gad

11 Now the sons of Gad lived opposite them in the land of[R]Bashan as far as[R]Salecah.   Josh. 13:11 • Deut. 3:10
12 Joel *was* the chief, and Shapham the second, then Janai and Shaphat in Bashan.
13 And their kinsmen of their fathers' households *were* Michael, Meshullam, Sheba, Jorai, Jacan, Zia, and Eber, seven.
14 These *were* the sons of Abihail, the son of Huri, the son of Jaroah, the son of Gilead, the son of Michael, the son of Jeshishai, the son of Jahdo, the son of Buz;
15 Ahi the son of Abdiel, the son of Guni, *was* head of their fathers' households.
16 And they lived in Gilead, in Bashan and in its towns, and in all the pasture lands of Sharon, as far as their[T]borders.   *goings out*
17 All of these were enrolled in the genealogies in the days of Jotham king of Judah and in the days of Jeroboam king of Israel.
18 The sons of Reuben and the Gadites and the half-tribe of Manasseh, *consisting* of valiant men, men who bore shield and sword and shot with bow, and *were* skillful in battle, *were* 44,760, who went to war.

19 And they made war against^Rthe Hagrites, Jetur, Naphish, and Nodab. 1 Chr. 5:10

20 And they were helped against them, and the Hagrites and all who were with them were given into their hand; for^Rthey cried out to God in the battle, and He was entreated for them, because^Rthey trusted in Him.   2 Chr. 14:11-13 • Ps. 9:10; 20:7

21 And they took away their cattle: their 50,000 camels, 250,000 sheep, 2,000 donkeys, and 100,000^Tmen.   *souls of men*

22 For many fell slain, because^Rthe war was of God. And^Rthey settled in their place until the exile.   [Josh. 23:10] • 1 Chr. 4:41

The Genealogy of Manasseh

23 Now the sons of the half-tribe of Manasseh lived in the land; from Bashan to Baal-hermon and^RSenir and Mount Hermon they were numerous.   Deut. 3:9

24 And these were the heads of their fathers' households, even Epher, Ishi, Eliel, Azriel, Jeremiah, Hodaviah, and Jahdiel, mighty men of valor, famous men, heads of their fathers' households.

25 But they acted treacherously against the God of their fathers, and played the harlot after the gods of the peoples of the land, whom God had destroyed before them.

26 So the God of Israel stirred up the spirit of Pul, king of Assyria, even the spirit of Tilgath-pilneser king of Assyria, and he carried them away into exile, namely the Reubenites, the Gadites, and the half-tribe of Manasseh, and brought them to Halah, Habor, Hara, and to the river of Gozan, to this day.

CHAPTER 6

The High Priestly Line
Gen. 46:11; 1 Chr. 6:50–53

T HE^Rsons of Levi were Gershon, Kohath and Merari.   Gen. 46:11

2 And the sons of Kohath were Amram, Izhar, Hebron, and Uzziel.

3 And the children of Amram were Aaron, Moses, and Miriam. And the sons of Aaron were Nadab, Abihu, Eleazar, and Ithamar.

4 Eleazar became the father of Phinehas, and Phinehas became the father of Abishua,

5 and Abishua became the father of Bukki, and Bukki became the father of Uzzi,

6 and Uzzi became the father of Zerahiah, and Zerahiah became the father of Meraioth,

7 Meraioth became the father of Amariah, and Amariah became the father of Ahitub,

8 and ^RAhitub became the father of Zadok, and Zadok^Rbecame the father of Ahimaaz,   2 Sam. 8:17 • 2 Sam. 15:27

9 and Ahimaaz became the father of Azariah, and Azariah became the father of Johanan,

10 and Johanan became the father of Azariah (it^Rwas he who served as the priest in the house^Rwhich Solomon built in Jerusalem),   2 Chr. 26:17 • 1 Kin. 6:1; 2 Chr. 3:1

11 and ^RAzariah became the father of Amariah, and Amariah became the father of Ahitub,   Ezra 7:3

12 and Ahitub became the father of Zadok, and Zadok became the father of Shallum,   In ch. 9:11, *Meshullam*

13 and Shallum became the father of Hilkiah, and Hilkiah became the father of Azariah,

14 and Azariah became the father of^RSeraiah, and Seraiah became the father of Jehozadak;   Neh. 11:11

15 and Jehozadak went along when the LORD carried Judah and Jerusalem away into exile^Tby Nebuchadnezzar. *by the hand of*

The Levitical Line

16 ^RThe sons of Levi were Gershom, Kohath, and Merari.   Ex. 6:16

17 And these are the names of the sons of Gershom: Libni and Shimei.

18 And the sons of Kohath were Amram, Izhar, Hebron, and Uzziel.

19 The sons of Merari were Mahli and Mushi. And these are the families of the Levites according to their fathers' *households*.

20 Of Gershom: Libni his son, Jahath his son, Zimmah his son,

21 Joah his son, Iddo his son, Zerah his son, Jeatherai his son.

22 The sons of Kohath were Amminadab his son, Korah his son, Assir his son,

23 Elkanah his son, Ebiasaph his son, and Assir his son,

24 Tahath his son, Uriel his son, Uzziah his son, and Shaul his son.

25 And the sons of Elkanah were Amasai and Ahimoth.

26 As for Elkanah, the sons of Elkanah were Zophai his son and Nahath his son,

27 Eliab his son, Jeroham his son, Elkanah his son.

28 And the sons of Samuel were^RJoel, the first-born and Abijah, the second. 1 Sam. 8:2

29 The sons of Merari were Mahli, Libni his son, Shimei his son, Uzzah his son,

30 Shimea his son, Haggiah his son, Asaiah his son.

The Musicians' Guild

31 ^RNow these are those whom David appointed over the service of song in the house of the LORD, ^Rafter the ark rested there.   1 Chr. 15:16-22 • 2 Sam. 6:17; 1 Kin. 8:4

32 And they ministered with song before the tabernacle of the tent of meeting, until Solomon had built the house of the LORD in Jerusalem; and they ^Tserved in their office according to their order.   *stood over*

33 And these are those who ^Tserved with their sons. From the sons of the Kohathites

were Heman the singer, the son of Joel, the son of Samuel,   *stood*

34 the son of Elkanah, the son of Jeroham, the son of Eliel, the son of Toah,

35 the son of Zuph, the son of Elkanah, the son of Mahath, the son of Amasai,

36 the son of Elkanah, the son of Joel, the son of Azariah, the son of Zephaniah,

37 the son of Tahath, the son of Assir, the son of Ebiasaph, the son of Korah,

38 the son of Izhar, the son of Kohath, the son of Levi, the son of Israel.

39 And *Heman's* brother Asaph stood at his right hand, even Asaph the son of Berechiah, the son of Shimea,

40 the son of Michael, the son of Baaseiah, the son of Malchijah,

41 the son of Ethni, the son of Zerah, the son of Adaiah,

42 the son of Ethan, the son of Zimmah, the son of Shimei,

43 the son of Jahath, the son of Gershom, the son of Levi.

44 And on the left hand *were* their kinsmen the sons of Merari: Ethan the son of Kishi, the son of Abdi, the son of Malluch,

45 the son of Hashabiah, the son of Amaziah, the son of Hilkiah,

46 the son of Amzi, the son of Bani, the son of Shemer,

47 the son of Mahli, the son of Mushi, the son of Merari, the son of Levi.

48 And their ᵀkinsmen the Levites were ᵀappointed for all the service of the tabernacle of the house of God.   *brothers • given*

The Generations of Aaron

49 But Aaron and his sons ᵀoffered on the altar of burnt offering and on the altar of incense, for all the work of the most holy place, and to make atonement for Israel, according to all that Moses the servant of God had commanded.   *offered up in smoke*

50 ᴿAnd these are the sons of Aaron: Eleazar his son, Phinehas his son, Abishua his son,   1 Chr. 6:4-8; Ezra 7:5

51 Bukki his son, Uzzi his son, Zerahiah his son,

52 Meraioth his son, Amariah his son, Ahitub his son,

53 Zadok his son, Ahimaaz his son.

Cities of the Priests and Levites
Josh. 21:1-42

54 Now these are their settlements according to their camps within their borders. To the sons of Aaron of the families of the Kohathites (for theirs was the *first* lot),

55 to them they gave Hebron in the land of Judah, and its pasture lands around it;

56 but the fields of the city and its villages, they gave to Caleb the son of Jephunneh.

57 And ᴿto the sons of Aaron they gave the *following* cities of refuge: Hebron, Libnah

also with its pasture lands, Jattir, Eshtemoa with its pasture lands,   Josh. 21:13, 19

58 ᴬHilen with its pasture lands, Debir with its pasture lands,   In Josh. 21:15, *Holon*

59 Ashan with its pasture lands, and Bethshemesh with its pasture lands;

60 and from the tribe of Benjamin: Geba with its pasture lands, Allemeth with its pasture lands, and Anathoth with its pasture lands. All their cities throughout their families were thirteen cities.

61 ᴿThen to the rest of the sons of Kohath *were given* by lot, from the family of the tribe, from the half-tribe, the half of Manasseh, ten cities.   Josh. 21:5; 1 Chr. 6:66-70

62 And to the sons of Gershom, according to their families, *were given* from the tribe of Issachar and from the tribe of Asher, the tribe of Naphtali, and the tribe of Manasseh, thirteen cities in Bashan.

63 ᴿTo the sons of Merari *were given* by lot, according to their families, from the tribe of Reuben, the tribe of Gad, and the tribe of Zebulun, twelve cities.   Josh. 21:7, 34-40

64 So the sons of Israel gave to the Levites the cities with their pasture lands.

65 And they gave by lot from the tribe of the sons of Judah, the tribe of the sons of Simeon, and the tribe of the sons of Benjamin, ᴿthese cities which are mentioned by name.   1 Chr. 6:57-60

66 ᴿNow some of the families of the sons of Kohath had cities of their territory from the tribe of Ephraim.   Josh. 21:20-26

67 And they gave to them the *following* cities of refuge: Shechem in the hill country of Ephraim with its pasture lands, Gezer also with its pasture lands,

68 Jokmeam with its pasture lands, Bethhoron with its pasture lands,

69 Aijalon with its pasture lands, and Gath-rimmon with its pasture lands;

70 and from the half-tribe of Manasseh: Aner with its pasture lands and Bileam with its pasture lands, for the rest of the family of the sons of Kohath.

71 To the sons of Gershom *were given,* from the family of the half-tribe of Manasseh: Golan in Bashan with its pasture lands and Ashtaroth with its pasture lands;

72 and from the tribe of Issachar: Kedesh with its pasture lands, Daberath with its pasture lands,

73 and Ramoth with its pasture lands, Anem with its pasture lands;

74 and from the tribe of Asher: Mashal with its pasture lands, Abdon with its pasture lands,

75 Hukok with its pasture lands, and Rehob with its pasture lands;

76 and from the tribe of Naphtali: Kedesh in Galilee with its pasture lands, Hammon with its pasture lands, and Kiriathaim with its pasture lands.

77 To the rest of *the Levites,* the sons of

Merari, *were given,* from the tribe of Zebulun: Rimmono with its pasture lands, Tabor with its pasture lands;

78 and beyond the Jordan at Jericho, on the east side of the Jordan, *were given them,* from the tribe of Reuben: Bezer in the wilderness with its pasture lands, Jahzah with its pasture lands,

79 Kedemoth with its pasture lands, and Mephaath with its pasture lands;

80 and from the tribe of Gad: Ramoth in Gilead with its pasture lands, Mahanaim with its pasture lands,

81 Heshbon with its pasture lands, and Jazer with its pasture lands.

CHAPTER 7

The Genealogy of Issachar—Gen. 46:13

Now the sons of Issachar *were* four: Tola, Puah, ^AJashub, and Shimron. In Gen. 46:13, *Job*

2 And the sons of Tola *were* Uzzi, Rephaiah, Jeriel, Jahmai, Ibsam, and Samuel, heads of their fathers' households. *The sons* of Tola *were* mighty men of valor in their generations; ^Etheir number in the days of David was 22,600.   2 Sam. 24:1-9

3 And the ^Tson of Uzzi *was* Izrahiah. And the sons of Izrahiah *were* Michael, Obadiah, Joel, Isshiah; all five of them *were* ^Rchief men.   sons • 1 Chr. 5:24

4 And with them by their generations according to their fathers' households were 36,000^Atroops of the army for war, for they had many wives and sons.   *bands*

5 And their^Trelatives among all the families of Issachar *were* mighty men of valor, enrolled by genealogy, in all 87,000. *brothers*

The Genealogy of Benjamin—Gen. 46:21

6 ^R*The sons of* Benjamin *were* three: Bela and Becher and Jediael.   1 Chr. 8:1-40

7 And the sons of Bela were five: Ezbon, Uzzi, Uzziel, Jerimoth, and Iri. They *were* heads of fathers' households, mighty men of valor, and were 22,034 enrolled by genealogy.

8 And the sons of Becher *were* Zemirah, Joash, Eliezer, Elioenai, Omri, Jeremoth, Abijah, Anathoth, and Alemeth. All these *were* the sons of Becher.

9 And they were enrolled by genealogy, according to their generations, heads of their fathers' households, 20,200 mighty men of valor.

10 And the ^Tson of Jediael *was* Bilhan. And the sons of Bilhan *were* Jeush, Benjamin, Ehud, Chenaanah, Zethan, Tarshish, and Ahishahar.   sons

11 All these *were* sons of Jediael, according to the heads of their fathers' households, 17,200 mighty men of valor, who were^Tready to go out with the army to war.   *going out*

12 And Shuppim and Huppim *were* the sons of Ir; Hushim *was* the son of Aher.

The Genealogy of Naphtali—Gen. 46:24

13 The sons of Naphtali *were* ^AJahziel, Guni, Jezer, and Shallum, the sons of Bilhah.   In Gen. 46:24, *Jahzeel*

The Genealogy of Manasseh

14 The sons of Manasseh *were* Asriel, whom his Aramean concubine bore; she bore Machir the father of Gilead.

15 And Machir took a wife for Huppim and Shuppim, ^Twhose sister's name was Maacah. And the name of the second was Zelophehad, and Zelophehad had daughters.   *and his*

16 And Maacah the wife of Machir bore a son, and she named him Peresh; and the name of his brother *was* Sheresh, and his sons *were* Ulam and Rakem.

17 And the ^Sson of Ulam *was* Bedan. These *were* the sons of Gilead the son of Machir, the son of Manasseh.   sons

18 And his sister Hammolecheth bore Ishhod and Abiezer and Mahlah.

19 And the sons of Shemida were Ahian and Shechem and Likhi and Aniam.

The Genealogy of Ephraim

20 And the ^Rsons of Ephraim *were* Shuthelah and Bered his son, Tahath his son, Eleadah his son, Tahath his son, Num. 26:35

21 Zabad his son, Shuthelah his son, and Ezer and Elead whom the men of Gath who were born in the land killed, because they came down to take their livestock.

22 And their father Ephraim ^Rmourned many days, and his relatives ^Scame to comfort him.   Gen. 37:34 • Job 2:11; John 11:19

23 Then he went in to his wife, and she conceived and bore a son, and he named him ^TBeriah, because misfortune had come upon his house.   *on misfortune*

24 And his daughter was Sheerah, ^Rwho built lower and upper Beth-horon, also Uzzen-sheerah.   Josh. 16:3, 5; 2 Chr. 8:5

25 And Rephah was his son *along* with Resheph, Telah his son, Tahan his son,

26 Ladan his son, Ammihud his son, Elishama his son,

27 Non his son, and Joshua his son.

28 And^Rtheir possessions and settlements *were* Bethel with its towns, and to the east Naaran, and to the west Gezer with its towns, and Shechem with its towns as far as Ayyah with its towns,   Josh. 16:2

29 and along the borders of the sons of Manasseh, Beth-shean with its towns, Taanach with its towns, Megiddo with its towns, Dor with its towns. In these lived the ^Ssons of Joseph the son of Israel. Judg. 1:22-29

The Genealogy of Asher—Gen. 46:17

30 The sons of Asher *were* Imnah, Ishvah, Ishvi and Beriah, and Serah their sister.

31 And the sons of Beriah *were* Heber and Malchiel, who was the father of Birzaith.

32 And Heber[T]became the father of Japhlet,[A]Shomer and Hotham, and Shua their sister. *begot* • In v. 34, *Shemer*

33 And the sons of Japhlet *were* Pasach, Bimhal, and Ashvath. These were the sons of Japhlet.

34 And the sons of[A]Shemer *were* Ahi and Rohgah, Jehubbah and Aram. In v. 32, *Shomer*

35 And the [T]sons of his brother Helem *were* Zophah, Imna, Shelesh, and Amal. *son*

36 The sons of Zophah *were* Suah, Harnepher, Shual, Beri, and Imrah,

37 Bezer, Hod, Shamma, Shilshah, Ithran, and Beera.

38 And the sons of Jether *were* Jephunneh, Pispa, and Ara.

39 And the sons of Ulla *were* Arah, Hanniel, and Rizia.

40 All these *were* the sons of Asher, heads of the fathers' houses, choice and mighty men of valor, heads of the princes. And the number of them enrolled by genealogy for service in war was 26,000 men.

CHAPTER 8

The Genealogy of Benjamin—Gen. 46:21

A ND[R]Benjamin[T]became the father of Bela his first-born, Ashbel the second, [R]Aharah the third, Gen. 46:21 • *begot* • 1 Chr. 7:12

2 Nohah the fourth, and Rapha the fifth.

3 And Bela had sons: [A]Addar, Gera, Abihud, In Gen. 46:21 and Num. 26:40, *Ard*

4 Abishua, Naaman, Ahoah,

5 Gera, Shephuphan, and Huram.

6 And these are the sons of Ehud: these are the heads of fathers' *households* of the inhabitants of Geba, and they carried them into exile to Manahath,

7 namely, Naaman, Ahijah, and Gera—he carried them into exile; and he became the father of Uzza and Ahihud.

8 And Shaharaim became the father of children in the country of Moab, after he had sent away Hushim and Baara his wives.

9 And by Hodesh his wife he became the father of Jobab, Zibia, Mesha, Malcam,

10 Jeuz, Sachia, Mirmah. These were his sons, heads of fathers' *households*.

11 And by Hushim he became the father of Abitub and Elpaal.

12 And the sons of Elpaal *were* Eber, Misham, and Shemed, who built Ono and Lod, with its towns;

13 and Beriah and Shema, who were heads of fathers' *households* of the inhabitants of Aijalon, who put to flight the inhabitants of Gath;

14 and Ahio, Shashak, and Jeremoth.

15 And Zebadiah, Arad, Eder,

16 Michael, Ishpah, and Joha *were* the sons of Beriah.

17 And Zebadiah, Meshullam, Hizki, Heber,

18 Ishmerai, Izliah, and Jobab *were* the sons of Elpaal.

19 And Jakim, Zichri, Zabdi,

20 Elienai, Zillethai, Eliel,

21 Adaiah, Beraiah, and Shimrath *were* the sons of[A]Shimei. In v. 13, *Shema*

22 And Ishpan, Eber, Eliel,

23 Abdon, Zichri, Hanan,

24 Hananiah, Elam, Anthothijah,

25 Iphdeiah, and Penuel *were* the sons of Shashak.

26 And Shamsherai, Shehariah, Athaliah,

27 Jaareshiah, Elijah, and Zichri *were* the sons of Jeroham.

28 These were heads of the fathers' *households* according to their generations, chief men,[T]who lived in Jerusalem. *these*

29 Now in Gibeon, *Jeiel,* the father of Gibeon lived, and his wife's name was Maacah;

30 and his first-born son *was* Abdon, then Zur, Kish, Baal, Nadab,

31 Gedor, Ahio, and Zecher.

32 And Mikloth[A]became the father of Shimeah. And they also lived with their [T]relatives in Jerusalem opposite their *other* [T]relatives. In ch. 9:38, *Shimeam* • *brothers*

33 [R]And Ner became the father of Kish, and Kish became the father of Saul, and Saul became the father of Jonathan, Malchishua, Abinadab, and Eshbaal. 1 Chr. 9:39-44

34 And the son of Jonathan *was* Meribbaal, and[A]Merib-baal became the father of Micah. In 2 Sam. 4:4, *Mephibosheth*

35 And the sons of Micah *were* Pithon, Melech,[A]Tarea, and Ahaz. In 9:41, *Tahrea*

36 And Ahaz became the father of[A]Jehoaddah, and Jehoaddah became the father of Alemeth, Azmaveth, and Zimri; and Zimri became the father of Moza. In 9:42, *Jarah*

37 And Moza became the father of Binea; [A]Raphah *was* his son, Eleasah his son, Azel his son. In 9:43, *Rephaiah*

38 And Azel had six sons, and these *were* their names: Azrikam, Bocheru, Ishmael, Sheariah, Obadiah and Hanan. All these *were* the sons of Azel.

39 And the sons of Eshek his brother *were* Ulam his first-born, Jeush the second, and Eliphelet the third.

40 And the sons of Ulam were mighty men of valor, archers, and had many sons and grandsons, 150 *of them.* All these *were* of the sons of Benjamin.

CHAPTER 9

The Genealogy of the Twelve Tribes Who Returned

S O all Israel was enrolled by genealogies; and behold, they are written in the Book of the Kings of Israel. And[R]Judah was carried away into exile to Babylon for their unfaithfulness. 1 Chr. 5:25, 26

2 Now the first who lived in their possessions in their cities *were* Israel, the priests, the Levites and the temple servants.

3 And some of the sons of Judah, of the sons of Benjamin, and of the sons of Ephraim and Manasseh lived in Jerusalem:

4 Uthai the son of Ammihud, the son of Omri, the son of Imri, the son of Bani, from the sons of Perez the son of Judah.

5 And from the Shilonites *were* Asaiah the first-born and his sons.

6 And from the sons of Zerah *were* Jeuel and their ᵀrelatives, 690 *of them.*   brothers

7 And from the sons of Benjamin *were* Sallu the son of Meshullam, the son of Hodaviah, the son of Hassenuah,

8 and Ibneiah the son of Jeroham, and Elah the son of Uzzi, the son of Michri, and Meshullam the son of Shephatiah, the son of Reuel, the son of Ibnijah;

9 and their relatives according to their generations, ᴿ956. All these *were* heads of fathers' *households* according to their fathers' houses.   Neh. 11:8

The Genealogy of the Priests
Who Returned

10 ᴿAnd from the priests *were* Jedaiah, Jehoiarib, Jachin,   Neh. 11:10-14

11 and Azariah the son of Hilkiah, the son of Meshullam, the son of Zadok, the son of Meraioth, the son of Ahitub, ᴿthe chief officer of the house of God;   Jer. 20:1

12 and Adaiah the son of Jeroham, the son of Pashhur, the son of Malchijah, and Maasai the son of Adiel, the son of Jahzerah, the son of Meshullam, the son of Meshillemith, the son of Immer;

13 and their relatives, heads of their fathers' households, 1,760 very able men for the work of the service of the house of God.

The Genealogy of the Levites
Who Returned

14 And of the Levites *were* Shemaiah the son of Hasshub, the son of Azrikam, the son of Hashabiah, of the sons of Merari;

15 and Bakbakkar, Heresh and Galal and Mattaniah the son of Mica, the son of ᴬZichri, the son of Asaph,   In Neh. 11:17, *Zabdi*

16 and ᴬObadiah the son of Shemaiah, the son of Galal, the son of Jeduthun, and Berechiah the son of Asa, the son of Elkanah, who lived in the villages of the Netophathites.   In Neh. 11:17, *Abda*

17 Now the gatekeepers *were* Shallum and Akkub and Talmon and Ahiman and their relatives (Shallum the chief

18 *being stationed* until now at the king's gate to the east). These *were* the gatekeepers for the camp of the sons of Levi.

19 And Shallum the son of Kore, the son of ᴬEbiasaph, the son of Korah, and his relatives, of his father's house, the Korahites, *were* over the work of the service, keepers of the thresholds of the tent; and their fathers had been over the camp of the LORD, keepers of the entrance.   In Ex. 6:24, *Abiasaph*

20 And ᴿPhinehas the son of Eleazar was ruler over them previously, *and* the LORD was with him.   Num. 25:7-13

21 ᴿZechariah the son of Meshelemiah was gatekeeper of the entrance of the tent of meeting.   1 Chr. 26:2, 14

22 All these who were chosen to be gatekeepers in the thresholds were 212. These were enrolled by genealogy in their villages, ᴿwhom David and Samuel the seer appointed ᴿin their office of trust.   1 Chr. 26:1 · 2 Chr. 31:15

23 So they and their sons had charge of the gates of the house of the LORD, *even* the house of the tent, as guards.

24 The gatekeepers were on the four sides, to the east, west, north, and south.

25 And their relatives in their villages ᴿwere to come in every seven days from time to time *to be* with ᵀthem;   2 Chr. 23:8 · *these*

26 for the four chief gatekeepers who were Levites, were in an office of trust, and were over the chambers and over the treasuries in the house of God.

27 And they spent the night around the house of God, because the watch was ᵀcommitted to them; and they *were* in charge of opening *it* morning by morning.   on them

28 Now some of them ᵀhad charge of the utensils of service, for they counted them when they brought them in and when they took them out.   *were over the*

29 Some of them also were appointed over the furniture and over all the utensils of the sanctuary and ᴿover the fine flour and the wine and the oil and the frankincense and the spices.   1 Chr. 23:29

30 And some of ᴿthe sons of the priests prepared the mixing of the spices. Ex. 30:23

31 And Mattithiah, one of the Levites, who was the first-born of Shallum the Korahite, had the ᵀresponsibility over the things which were baked in pans.   *office of trust*

32 And some of their relatives of the sons of the Kohathites ᴿwere over the showbread to prepare it every sabbath.   Lev. 24:5-8

33 Now these are the singers, heads of fathers' *households* of the Levites, *who lived* in the chambers *of the temple* free *from* other service; for they were ᵀengaged in their work day and night.   *over them in the work*

34 These were heads of fathers' households of the Levites according to their generations, chief men, who lived in Jerusalem.

The Genealogy of Saul

35 And in Gibeon Jeiel the father of Gibeon lived, and his wife's name was Maacah,

36 and his first-born son *was* Abdon, then Zur, Kish, Baal, Ner, Nadab,

37 Gedor, Ahio, Zechariah, and Mikloth.

38 And Mikloth became the father of Shimeam. And they also lived with their relatives in Jerusalem opposite their *other* relatives.

39 ᴿAnd Ner became the father of Kish,

and Kish became the father of Saul, and Saul became the father of Jonathan, Malchishua, Abinadab, and Eshbaal.   1 Chr. 8:33-38

40 And the son of Jonathan *was* Meribbaal; and Merib-baal became the father of Micah.

41 And the sons of Micah *were* Pithon, Melech, Tahrea, [R]*and Ahaz.*   1 Chr. 8:35-37

42 And Ahaz became the father of Jarah, and Jarah became the father of Alemeth, Azmaveth, and Zimri; and Zimri became the father of Moza,

43 and Moza became the father of Binea and Rephaiah his son, Eleasah his son, Azel his son.

44 And Azel had six sons whose names are these: Azrikam, Bocheru and Ishmael and Sheariah and Obadiah and Hanan. These were the sons of Azel.

CHAPTER 10

The House of Saul Dies in Battle
1 Sam. 31:1-7

NOW the Philistines fought against Israel; and the men of Israel fled before the Philistines, and fell slain on Mount Gilboa.

2 And the Philistines closely pursued Saul and his sons, and the Philistines struck down Jonathan, [R]Abinadab and Malchi-shua, the sons of Saul.   1 Sam. 31:4

3 And the battle became heavy against Saul, and the archers [T]overtook him; and he was wounded by the archers.   *found him*

4 Then Saul said to his armor bearer, "Draw your sword and thrust me through with it, lest these uncircumcised come and abuse me." But his armor bearer would not, for he was greatly afraid. [R]Therefore Saul took his sword and fell on it.   1 Sam. 31:4

5 And when his armor bearer saw that Saul was dead, he likewise fell on his sword and died.

6 Thus Saul died with his three sons, and all *those* of his house died together.

7 When all the men of Israel who were in the valley saw that they had fled, and that Saul and his sons were dead, they forsook their cities and fled; and the Philistines came and lived in them.

The Philistines Defile Saul
1 Sam. 31:8-13

8 And it came about the next day, when the Philistines came to strip the slain, that they found Saul and his sons fallen on Mount Gilboa.

9 So they stripped him and took his head and his armor and sent *messengers* around the land of the Philistines, to carry the good news to their idols and to the people.

[2] I.e., citadel

10 And they put his armor in the house of their gods and fastened his head in the house of Dagon.

11 When all Jabesh-gilead heard all that the Philistines had done to Saul,

12 [R]all the valiant men arose and took away the body of Saul and the bodies of his sons, and brought them to Jabesh and buried their bones under the oak in Jabesh, and fasted seven days.   1 Sam. 31:12f.

The Cause of Saul's Death

13 [R]So Saul died for his trespass which he committed against the LORD, because of the word of the LORD which he did not keep; and also because he asked counsel of a medium, making inquiry *of it*,   1 Sam. 13:13, 14

14 and did not inquire of the LORD. Therefore He killed him, and [R]turned the kingdom to David the son of Jesse.   1 Sam. 15:28

CHAPTER 11

Anointing of David as King
2 Sam. 5:1-3

THEN [R]all Israel gathered to David at Hebron [T]and said, "Behold, we are your bone and your flesh.   2 Sam. 5:1, 3 • *saying*

2 "In times past, even when Saul was king, you *were* the one who led out and brought in Israel; and the LORD your God said to you, 'You [R]shall shepherd My people Israel, and you shall be prince over My people Israel.' "   2 Sam. 5:2; 7:7

3 So all the elders of Israel came to the king at Hebron, and David made a covenant with them in Hebron before the LORD; and [R]they anointed David king over Israel, [R]according to the word of the LORD through Samuel.   2 Sam. 2:4 • 1 Sam. 16:1, 3, 12

Conquest of Jerusalem—2 Sam. 5:6-10

4 Then David and all Israel went to Jerusalem (that is, Jebus); and the Jebusites, the inhabitants of the land, *were* there.

5 And the inhabitants of Jebus said to David, "You shall not enter here." Nevertheless David captured the stronghold of Zion (that is, the city of David).

6 Now David had said, "Whoever strikes down a Jebusite first shall be chief and commander." [R]And Joab the son of Zeruiah went up first, so he became chief.   2 Sam. 8:16

7 Then David dwelt in the stronghold; therefore it was called the city of David.

8 And he [A]built the city all around, from the [2]Millo even to the surrounding area; and Joab repaired the rest of the city.   *fortified*

9 And David became greater and greater, for the LORD of hosts *was* with him.

The Chiefs—2 Sam. 23:8–12

10 Now these are the heads of the mighty men whom David had, who gave him strong support in his kingdom, together with all Israel, to make him king, according to the word of the LORD concerning Israel.

11 And these *constitute* the list of the mighty men whom David had: Jashobeam, the son of a Hachmonite, the chief of the thirty; he lifted up his spear against three hundred whom he killed at one time.

12 And after him was Eleazar the son of ^RDodo, the Ahohite, who *was* ^Tone of the three mighty men.   1 Chr. 27:4 • *among*

13 He was with David at Pasdammim ^Rwhen the Philistines were gathered together there to battle, and there was a plot of ground full of barley; and the people fled before the Philistines.   2 Sam. 23:11, 12

14 And they took their stand in the midst of the plot, and defended it, and struck down the Philistines; and the LORD saved them by a great ^Avictory.   *salvation*

The Thirty Chief Men
2 Sam. 23:13–23

15 Now three of the thirty chief men went down to the rock to David, into the cave of Adullam, while the army of the Philistines was camping in the valley of Rephaim.

16 And David was then in the stronghold, while ^Rthe garrison of the Philistines *was* then in Bethlehem.   1 Sam. 10:5

17 And David had a craving and said, "Oh that someone would give me water to drink from the well of Bethlehem, which is by the gate!"

18 So the three broke through the camp of the Philistines, and drew water from the well of Bethlehem which *was* by the gate, and took *it* and brought *it* to David; nevertheless David would not drink it, but poured it out to the LORD;

19 and he said, "Be it far from me before my God that I should do this. Shall I drink the blood of these men *who went*^Tat the risk of their lives? For at the risk of their lives they brought it." Therefore he would not drink it. These things the three mighty men did.   *with their souls*

20 As for ^AAbshai the brother of Joab, he was chief of the thirty, and he swung his spear against three hundred ^Tand killed them; and he had a name as well as the thirty.   In 2 Sam. 23:18, *Abishai • slain ones*

21 Of the three in the second *rank* he was the most honored, and became their commander; however, he did not attain to the *first* three.

22 Benaiah the son of Jehoiada, the son of a valiant man of Kabzeel, mighty in deeds, struck down the^Atwo *sons of* Ariel of Moab. He also went down and killed a lion inside a pit on a snowy day.   *two lion-like heroes* of

23 And he killed an Egyptian, a man of *great* stature five cubits tall. Now in the

Egyptian's hand *was* a spear like a weaver's beam, but he went down to him with a club and snatched the spear from the Egyptian's hand, and killed him with his own spear.

24 These *things* Benaiah the son of Jehoiada did, and had a name as well as the three mighty men.

25 Behold, he was honored among the thirty, but he did not attain to the three; and David appointed him over his guard.

The Mighty Men—2 Sam. 23:24–39

26 Now the mighty men of the armies *were* Asahel the brother of Joab, Elhanan the son of Dodo of Bethlehem,

27 ^AShammoth the Harorite, Helez the Pelonite,   In 2 Sam. 23:25, *Shammah the Harodite*

28 Ira the son of Ikkesh the Tekoite, Abiezer the Anathothite,

29 ^ASibbecai the Hushathite, Ilai the Ahohite,   In 2 Sam. 23:27, *Mebunnai*

30 Maharai the Netophathite, Heled the son of Baanah the Netophathite,

31 Ithai the son of Ribai of Gibeah of the sons of Benjamin, Benaiah the Pirathonite,

32 ^AHurai of the brooks of Gaash, Abiel the Arbathite,   In 2 Sam. 23:30, *Hiddai*

33 Azmaveth the Baharumite, Eliahba the Shaalbonite,

34 the sons of Hashem the Gizonite, Jonathan the son of Shagee the Hararite,

35 Ahiam the son of ^ASacar the Hararite, Eliphal the son of Ur,   In 2 Sam. 23:33, *Sharar*

36 Hepher the Mecherathite, Ahijah the Pelonite,

37 Hezro the Carmelite,^ANaarai the son of Ezbai,   In 2 Sam. 23:35, *Paarai the Arbite*

38 Joel the brother of Nathan, Mibhar the son of Hagri,

39 Zelek the Ammonite, Naharai the Berothite, the armor bearer of Joab the son of Zeruiah,

40 Ira the Ithrite, Gareb the Ithrite,

41 Uriah the Hittite, Zabad the son of Ahlai,

42 Adina the son of Shiza the Reubenite, a chief of the Reubenites, and thirty with him,

43 Hanan the son of Maacah and Joshaphat the Mithnite,

44 Uzzia the Ashterathite, Shama and Jeiel the sons of Hotham the Aroerite,

45 Jediael the son of Shimri and Joha his brother, the Tizite,

46 Eliel the Mahavite and Jeribai and Joshaviah, the sons of Elnaam, and Ithmah the Moabite,

47 Eliel and Obed and Jaasiel the Mezobaite.

CHAPTER 12

The Mighty Men at Ziklag

NOW^Rthese are the ones who came to David at Ziklag, while he was still restricted

because of Saul the son of Kish; and they were among the mighty men who helped *him* in war.   1 Sam. 27:2-6

2 They were equipped with bows, using both the right hand and the left *to sling* stones and *to shoot* arrows from the bow; *they were* Saul's kinsmen from Benjamin.

3 The chief was Ahiezer, then Joash, the sons of Shemaah the Gibeathite; and Jeziel and Pelet, the sons of Azmaveth, and Beracah and Jehu the Anathothite,

4 and Ishmaiah the Gibeonite, a mighty man among the thirty, and over the thirty. Then Jeremiah, Jahaziel, Johanan, Jozabad the Gederathite,

5 Eluzai, Jerimoth, Bealiah, Shemariah, Shephatiah the Haruphite,

6 Elkanah, Isshiah, Azarel, Joezer, Jashobeam, the Korahites,

7 and Joelah and Zebadiah, the sons of Jeroham of Gedor.

8 And from the Gadites there ᵀcame over to David in the stronghold in the wilderness, mighty men of valor, men trained for war, who could handle shield and spear, and ᵣwhose faces were like the faces of lions, and ᵗ*they were* as swift as the gazelles on the mountains.   *separated themselves* • 2 Sam. 2:18

9 Ezer *was* the first, Obadiah the second, Eliab the third,

10 Mishmannah the fourth, Jeremiah the fifth,

11 Attai the sixth, Eliel the seventh,

12 Johanan the eighth, Elzabad the ninth,

13 Jeremiah the tenth, Machbannai the eleventh.

14 These of the sons of Gad were captains of the army; he who was least was equal to a hundred and the greatest to a thousand.

15 ᴿThese are the ones who crossed the Jordan in the first month when it was overflowing all its banks and they put to flight all those in the valleys, both to the east and to the west.   Josh. 3:15; 4:18

16 Then some of the sons of Benjamin and Judah came to the stronghold to David.

17 And David went out to meet them, and answered and said to them, "If you come peacefully to me to help me, my heart shall be united with you; but if to betray me to my adversaries, since there is no ᵀwrong in my hands, may the God of our fathers look on *it* and decide."   *violence*

18 Then the Spirit came upon Amasai, who was the chief of the thirty, *and he said,*
    "*We* are yours, O David,
    And with you, O son of Jesse!
    ᴿPeace, peace to you,   1 Sam. 25:5, 6
    And peace to him who helps you;
    Indeed, your God helps you!"
Then David received them and made them ᴬcaptains of the band.   *chiefs*

19 ᴿFrom Manasseh also some defected to David, when he was about to go to battle with the Philistines against Saul. But they did not help them, for the lords of the Philis-

tines after consultation sent him away, saying, "At *the cost of* our heads he may defect to his master Saul."   1 Sam. 29:2-9

20 As he went to Ziklag, there defected to him from Manasseh: Adnah, Jozabad, Jediael, Michael, Jozabad, Elihu, and Zillethai, ᴬcaptains of thousands who belonged to Manasseh.   *chiefs*

21 And they helped David against ᴿthe band of raiders, for they were all mighty men of valor, and were captains in the army.   1 Sam. 30:1

22 For day by day *men* came to David to help him, until there was a great army ᴿlike the army of God.   Gen. 32:2; Josh. 5:13-15

The Mighty Men at Hebron

23 Now these are the numbers of the divisions equipped for war, who came to David at Hebron, to turn the kingdom of Saul to him, according to the word of the LORD.

24 The sons of Judah who bore shield and spear *were* 6,800, equipped for war.

25 Of the sons of Simeon, mighty men of valor for war, 7,100.

26 Of the sons of Levi 4,600.

27 Now Jehoiada was the leader of *the house of* Aaron, and with him were 3,700,

28 also ᴿZadok, a young man mighty of valor, and of his father's house twenty-two captains.   2 Sam. 8:17; 1 Chr. 6:8, 53

29 And of the sons of Benjamin, ᴿSaul's kinsmen, 3,000; for until now ᴿthe greatest part of them had kept their allegiance to the house of Saul.   1 Chr. 12:2 • 2 Sam. 2:8, 9

30 And of the sons of Ephraim 20,800, mighty men of valor, famous men in their fathers' households.

31 And of the half-tribe of Manasseh 18,000, who were designated by name to come and make David king.

32 And of the sons of Issachar, ᴿmen who understood the times, with knowledge of what Israel should do, their chiefs were two hundred; and all their kinsmen were at their command.   Esth. 1:13

33 Of Zebulun, there were 50,000 who went out in the army, who could draw up in battle formation with all kinds of weapons of war and helped *David* ᵀwith ᴿan undivided heart.   *not of double heart* • Ps. 12:2

34 And of Naphtali *there were* 1,000 captains, and with them 37,000 with shield and spear.

35 And of the Danites who could draw up in battle formation, *there were* 28,600.

36 And of Asher *there were* 40,000 who went out in the army to draw up in battle formation.

37 And from the other side of the Jordan, of the Reubenites and the Gadites and of the half-tribe of Manasseh, *there were* 120,000 with all *kinds* of weapons of war for the battle.

38 All these, being men of war, who could draw up in battle formation, came to Hebron with a perfect heart, to make David king over all Israel; and all the rest also of Israel were of one mind to make David king.

39 And they were there with David three days, eating and drinking; for their kinsmen had prepared for them.

40 Moreover those who were near to them, *even* as far as Issachar and Zebulun and Naphtali, ᴿbrought food on donkeys, camels, mules, and on oxen, great quantities of flour cakes, fig cakes and bunches of raisins, wine, oil, oxen and sheep. There was joy indeed in Israel.　　1 Sam. 25:18

CHAPTER 13

Preparation to Move the Ark

THEN David consulted with the captains of the thousands and the hundreds, even with every leader.

2 And David said to all the assembly of Israel, "If it seems good to you, and if it is from the LORD our God, let us send everywhere to our kinsmen who remain in all the land of Israel, also to the priests and Levites who are with them in their cities with pasture lands, that they may meet with us;

3 and let us bring back the ark of our God to us, ᴿfor we did not seek it in the days of Saul."　　1 Sam. 7:1, 2

4 Then all the assembly said that they would do so, for the thing was right in the eyes of all the people.

5 ᴿSo David assembled all Israel together, from the Shihor of Egypt even to the entrance of Hamath, to bring the ark of God from Kiriath-jearim.　　2 Sam. 6:1; 1 Kin. 8:65

Uzza Dies for Touching the Ark
2 Sam. 6:1–11

6 ᴿAnd David and all Israel went up toᴿBaalah, *that is,* to Kiriath-jearim, which belongs to Judah, to bring up from there the ark of God, the LORD ᴿwho is enthroned *above* the cherubim, where His name is called.　　2 Sam. 6:2-11 · Josh. 15:9 · Ex. 25:22

7 And they ᵀcarried the ark of God on a new cart from the house of Abinadab, and Uzza and Ahio drove the cart.　　*caused to ride*

8 And David and all Israel were celebrating before God with all *their* might, even with songs and with lyres, harps, tambourines, cymbals, and with trumpets.

9 When they came to the threshing floor of Chidon, Uzza put out his hand to hold the ark, because the oxen nearly upset *it.*

10 And the anger of the LORD burned against Uzza, so He struck him downᴿbecause he put out his hand to the ark; and he died there before God.　　1 Chr. 15:13, 15

11 Then David became angry because of the LORD's outburst against Uzza; and he called that place ³Perez-uzza to this day.

12 And David was afraid of God that day, saying, "How can I bring the ark of God *home* to me?"

13 So David did not take the ark with him to the city of David, but took it asideᴿto the house of Obed-edom the Gittite.　2 Chr. 15:25

14 Thus the ark of God remained with the family of Obed-edom in his house three months; andᴿthe LORD blessed the family of Obed-edom with all that he had.　1 Chr. 26:4

CHAPTER 14

David's House Is Constructed
2 Sam. 5:11, 12

NOWᴿHiram king of Tyre sent messengers to David with cedar trees, masons, and carpenters, to build a house for him.　2 Sam. 5:11

2 And David realized that the LORD had established him as king over Israel, *and* that his kingdom was highly exalted, for the sake of His people Israel.

David's Children in Jerusalem

3 Then David took more wives at Jerusalem, and Davidᵀbecame the father of more sons and daughters.　　　　　　*begot*

4 And these are the names of the childrenᵀborn *to him* in Jerusalem: Shammua, Shobab, Nathan, Solomon,　　*were to*

5 Ibhar, Elishua, Elpelet,

6 Nogah, Nepheg, Japhia,

7 Elishama, Beeliada and Eliphelet.

David's Victory over the Philistines
2 Sam. 5:17–25

8 When the Philistines heard that David had been anointed king over all Israel, all the Philistines went up in search of David; and David heard of it and went out against them.

9 Now the Philistines had come and made a raid in the valley of Rephaim.

10 And David inquired of God, saying, "Shall I go up against the Philistines? And wilt Thou give them into my hand?" Then the LORD said to him, "Go up, for I will give them into your hand."

11 So they came up to Baal-perazim, and David defeated them there; and David said, "God has broken through my enemies by my hand, like the breakthrough of waters." Therefore they named that place ⁴Baalperazim.

³ I.e., the breakthrough of Uzza
⁴ I.e., the master of breakthrough

12 And they abandoned their gods there; so David gave the order and they were burned with fire.

13 And the Philistines made[R] yet another raid in the valley.   1 Chr. 14:9

14 And David inquired again of God, and God said to him, "You shall not go up after them; circle around behind them, and come at them in front of the balsam trees.

15 "And it shall be when you hear the sound of marching in the tops of the balsam trees, then you shall go out to battle, for God will have gone out before you to strike the army of the Philistines."

16 And David did just as God had commanded him, and they struck down the army of the Philistines from[A] Gibeon even as far as Gezer.   In 2 Sam. 5:25, *Geba*

17 Then the fame of David went out into all the lands; and[R] the LORD brought the fear of him on all the nations.   [Ex. 15:14-16]

CHAPTER 15

Spiritual Preparation
to Move the Ark

NOW *David* built houses for himself in the city of David; and he prepared a place for the ark of God, and pitched a tent for it.

2 Then David said, "No[R] one is to carry the ark of God but the Levites; for the LORD chose them to carry the ark of God, and to minister to Him forever." Num. 4:15; Deut. 10:8

3 And David assembled all Israel at Jerusalem, to bring up the ark of the LORD to its place, which he had prepared for it.

4 And David gathered together the sons of Aaron, and[R] the Levites: 1 Chr. 6:16-30; 12:26

5 of the sons of Kohath, Uriel the chief, and 120 of his[T] relatives;   *brothers*

6 of the sons of Merari, Asaiah the chief, and 220 of his relatives;

7 of the sons of Gershom, Joel the chief, and 130 of his relatives;

8 of the sons of Elizaphan, Shemaiah the chief, and 200 of his relatives;

9 of the sons of Hebron, Eliel the chief, and 80 of his relatives;

10 of the sons of Uzziel, Amminadab the chief, and 112 of his relatives.

11 Then David called for[R] Zadok and [R]Abiathar the priests, and for the Levites, for Uriel, Asaiah, Joel, Shemaiah, Eliel, and Amminadab,   1 Chr. 12:28 · 1 Sam. 22:20-23

12 and said to them, "You are the heads of the fathers' *households* of the Levites; [R]consecrate yourselves both you and your relatives, that you may bring up the ark of the LORD God of Israel, to *the place* that I have prepared for it.   Ex. 19:14, 15; 2 Chr. 35:6

13 "Because[R] you did not *carry it* at the first, the LORD our God made an outburst on us, for we did not seek Him according to the ordinance."   2 Sam. 6:3; 1 Chr. 13:7

14 So the priests and the Levites consecrated themselves to bring up the ark of the LORD God of Israel.

15 And the sons of the Levites carried the ark of God on their shoulders, with the poles thereon as Moses had commanded according to the word of the LORD.

16 Then David spoke to the chiefs of the Levites[R] to appoint their relatives the singers, with instruments of music, harps, lyres, loud-sounding cymbals, to raise sounds of joy.   1 Chr. 13:8; 25:1

17 So[R] the Levites appointed Heman the son of Joel, and from his relatives, Asaph the son of Berechiah; and from the sons of Merari their relatives, Ethan the son of Kushaiah,   1 Chr. 25:1

18 and with them their relatives of the second rank, Zechariah, Ben, Jaaziel, Shemiramoth, Jehiel, Unni, Eliab, Benaiah, Maaseiah, Mattithiah, Eliphelehu, Mikneiah, Obed-edom, and Jeiel, the gatekeepers.

19 So the singers, Heman, Asaph, and Ethan *were appointed* to sound aloud cymbals of bronze;

20 and Zechariah, Aziel, Shemiramoth, Jehiel, Unni, Eliab, Maaseiah, and Benaiah, with harps tuned to[R]alamoth;   Ps. 46:title

21 and Mattithiah, Eliphelehu, Mikneiah, Obed-edom, Jeiel, and Azaziah, to lead with [A]lyres tuned to the sheminith.   *octave harps*

22 And Chenaniah, chief of the Levites, was *in charge* of the singing; he gave instruction in singing because he was skillful.

23 And Berechiah and Elkanah were gatekeepers for the ark.

24 And Shebaniah, Joshaphat, Nethanel, Amasai, Zechariah, Benaiah, and Eliezer, the priests, [R]blew the trumpets before the ark of God. Obed-edom and Jehiah also *were* gatekeepers for the ark.   1 Chr. 15:28

Joyful Transportation of the Ark
2 Sam. 6:12-16

25 [R]So *it was* David, with the elders of Israel and the captains over thousands, who went to bring up the ark of the covenant of the LORD from [R]the house of Obed-edom with joy.   2 Sam. 6:12, 15 · 1 Chr. 13:13

26 And it came about because God was helping the Levites who were carrying the ark of the covenant of the LORD, that they sacrificed seven bulls and seven rams.

27 Now David was clothed with a robe of fine linen with all the Levites who were carrying the ark, and the singers and Chenaniah the leader of the singing *with* the singers. David also wore an ephod of linen.

28 Thus all Israel brought up the ark of the covenant of the LORD with shouting, and with sound of the horn, with trumpets, with loud-sounding cymbals, with harps and lyres.

29 And it happened when the ark of the covenant of the LORD came to the city of

David, that [R]Michal the daughter of Saul looked out of the window, and saw King David leaping and making merry; and she despised him in her heart.   2 Sam. 3:13f.; 6:16

CHAPTER 16

Offering of Sacrifices—2 Sam. 6:17–19

AND they brought in the ark of God and placed it inside the tent which David had pitched for it, and they offered burnt offerings and peace offerings before God.

2 When David had finished offering the burnt offering and the peace offerings, he blessed the people in the name of the LORD.

3 And he distributed to everyone of Israel, both man and woman, to everyone a loaf of bread and a portion *of meat* and a raisin cake.

Appointing Musicians

4 And he appointed some of the Levites *as* ministers before the ark of the LORD, even to celebrate and to thank and praise the LORD God of Israel:

5 Asaph the chief, and second to him Zechariah, *then* [A]Jeiel, Shemiramoth, Jehiel, Mattithiah, Eliab, Benaiah, Obed-edom, and Jeiel, with musical instruments, harps, lyres; also Asaph *played* loud-sounding cymbals,   In 1 Chr. 15:18, *Jaaziel*

6 and Benaiah and Jahaziel the priests *blew* trumpets continually before the ark of the covenant of God.

Praise Psalm of David

7 Then on that day David first assigned [T]Asaph and his [T]relatives to give thanks to the LORD.   *by the hand of Asaph • brothers*

8 [R]Oh give thanks to the LORD, call upon His name;   1 Chr. 16:8-36; Ps. 105:1-15
[R]Make known His deeds among the peoples.   1 Kin. 8:43; 2 Kin. 19:19

9 Sing to Him, sing praises to Him;
[5]Speak of all His wonders.

10 [A]Glory in His holy name;   *Boast*
Let the heart of those who seek the LORD be glad.

11 Seek the LORD and His strength;
Seek His face continually.

12 [R]Remember His wonderful deeds which He has done,   Ps. 103:2
[R]His marvels and the judgments from His mouth,   Ps. 78:43-68

13 O seed of Israel His servant,
Sons of Jacob, His chosen ones!

14 He is the LORD our God;
His judgments are in all the earth.

15 Remember His covenant forever,
The word which He commanded to a thousand generations,

16 [R]The covenant which He made with Abraham,   Gen. 12:7; 17:2; 22:16-18; 26:3
And His oath to Isaac.

17 [R]He also confirmed it to Jacob for a statute,   Gen. 35:11, 12
To Israel as an everlasting covenant,

18 Saying, "To [R]you I will give the land of Canaan,   Gen. 13:15
As the portion of your inheritance."

19 [R]When they were only a few in number,   Deut. 7:7
Very few, and strangers in it,

20 And they wandered about from nation to nation,
And from *one* kingdom to another people,

21 He permitted no man to oppress them,
And [R]He reproved kings for their sakes, *saying,*   Gen. 12:17; 20:3

22 "Do not touch My anointed ones,
And do My prophets no harm."

23 Sing to the LORD, all the earth;
Proclaim good tidings of His salvation from day to day.

24 Tell of His glory among the nations,
His wonderful deeds among all the peoples.

25 For [R]great is the LORD, and greatly to be praised;   Ps. 144:3-6
He also is to be feared above all gods.

26 For all the gods of the peoples are [A]idols,   *non-existent things • Lev. 19:4*
But the LORD made the heavens.

27 Splendor and majesty are before Him,
Strength and joy are in His place.

28 Ascribe to the LORD, O families of the peoples,
Ascribe to the LORD glory and strength.

29 Ascribe to the LORD the glory due His name;
Bring an [A]offering, and come before Him;   *a grain offering*
Worship the LORD in holy array.

30 Tremble before Him, all the earth;
Indeed, the world is firmly established, it will not be moved.

[5] Or, *Meditate on*

16:29 The Meaning of Worship—Worship refers to the supreme honor or veneration given either in thought or deed to a person or thing. The Bible teaches that God alone is worthy of worship (Page 541—Ps. 29:2), but it also sadly records accounts of those who worshiped other objects. Among those were people (Page 838—Dan. 2:46), false gods (Page 366—2 Kin. 10:19), images and idols (Page 659—Is. 2:8; Page 838—Dan. 3:5), heavenly bodies (Page 377—2 Kin. 21:3), Satan (Page 1301—Rev. 13:4), and demons (Page 1299—Rev. 9:20). It is indeed tragic that many worshiped gods they could carry and not the God who could carry them. God Almighty alone is worthy of worship (Page 1296—Rev. 4:11).

31 [R]Let the heavens be glad, and let the earth rejoice;   Is. 44:23; 49:13
And let them say among the nations, "The[R]LORD reigns."   Ps. 93:1; 96:10

32 Let the sea roar, and all it contains; Let the field exult, and all that is in it.

33 Then the trees of the forest will sing for joy before the LORD;
For He is coming to judge the earth.

34 [R]O give thanks to the LORD, for *He is* good;   2 Chr. 5:13; 7:3; Ezra 3:11
For His lovingkindness is everlasting.

35 [R]Then say, "Save us, O God of our salvation,
And gather us and deliver us from the nations,   Ps. 106:47, 48
To give thanks to Thy holy name,
And [T]glory in Thy praise."   *boast*

36 Blessed be the LORD, the God of Israel,
From everlasting even to everlasting.
Then all the people [R]said, "Amen," and praised the LORD.   Deut. 27:15; Neh. 8:6

Constant Ministry at the Ark

37 So he left Asaph and his[T]relatives there before the ark of the covenant of the LORD, to minister before the ark continually, as every day's work required;   *brothers*

38 and Obed-edom with [T]his 68 relatives; Obed-edom, also the son of Jeduthun, and Hosah as gatekeepers.   *their brothers*

39 And *he left* Zadok the priest and his [T]relatives the priests before the [T]tabernacle of the LORD in the high place which *was* at Gibeon,   *brothers · dwelling place*

40 to offer burnt offerings to the LORD on the altar of burnt offering continually morning and evening, [R]even according to all that is written in the law of the LORD, which He commanded Israel. [Ex. 29:38–42; Num. 28:3, 4]

41 And with them *were*[R]Heman and Jeduthun, and [R]the rest who were chosen, who were designated by name, to give thanks to the LORD, because His lovingkindness is everlasting.   1 Chr. 6:33 · 1 Chr. 25:1-6

42 And with them *were* Heman and Jeduthun *with* trumpets and cymbals for those who should sound aloud, and *with* instruments for[R]the songs of God, and the sons of Jeduthun for the gate.   1 Chr. 25:7; 2 Chr. 7:6

43 [R]Then all the people departed each to his house, and David returned to bless his household.   2 Sam. 6:19

CHAPTER 17

Desire of David to Build God's House
2 Sam. 7:1–3

A[R]ND it came about, when David dwelt in his house, that David said to Nathan the prophet, "Behold, I am dwelling in a house of cedar, but the ark of the covenant of the LORD is under curtains."   2 Sam. 7:1-29

2 Then Nathan said to David, "Do all that is in your heart, for God is with you."

Covenant of God to Build David's House
2 Sam. 7:4–17

3 And it came about the same night, that the word of God came to Nathan, saying,

4 "Go and tell David My servant, 'Thus says the LORD, "You[R]shall not build a house for Me to dwell in;   1 Chr. 28:2, 3

5 for I have not dwelt in a house since the day that I brought up Israel to this day, but I have [T]gone from tent to tent and from one dwelling place *to another*.   *been*

6 "In all places where I have walked with all Israel, have I spoken a word with any of the judges of Israel, whom I commanded to shepherd My people, saying, 'Why have you not built for Me a house of cedar?' " '

7 "Now, therefore, thus shall you say to My servant David, 'Thus says the LORD of hosts, "I took you from the pasture, from following the sheep, that you should be leader over My people Israel.

8 "And I have been with you wherever you have gone, and have cut off all your enemies from before you; and I will make you a name like the name of the great ones who are in the earth.

True worship involves at least three important elements:

a. Worship requires reverence. This includes the honor and respect directed toward the Lord in thought and feeling. It is one thing to obey a superior unwillingly; it is quite another to commit one's thoughts and emotions in that obedience. Jesus said that those who worship God must do so "in spirit and truth" (Page 1067—John 4:24). The term *spirit* speaks of the personal nature of worship: It is from my person to God's person and involves the intellect, emotions, and will. The word *truth* speaks of the content of worship: God is pleased when we worship Him, understanding His true character.

b. Worship includes public expression. This was particularly prevalent in the Old Testament because of the sacrificial system. For example, when a believer received a particular blessing for which he wanted to thank God, it was not sufficient to say it privately; he expressed his thanks publicly with a thank-offering (Page 100—Lev. 7:12).

c. Worship means service. These two concepts are often linked together in Scripture (Page 177—Deut. 8:19). Furthermore, the words for worship in both Testaments originally referred to the labor of slaves for the master. Worship especially includes the joyful service which Christians render to Christ their Master. The concept of worship must not be restricted to church attendance, but should embrace an entire life of obedience to God.

Now turn to Page 1248—Heb. 13:15: The Expressions of Worship.

9"And I will appoint a place for My people Israel, and will plant them, that they may dwell in their own place and be moved no more; neither shall the [T]wicked waste them anymore as formerly, *sons of wickedness*

10 even from the day that I commanded judges *to be* over My people Israel. And I will subdue all your enemies. Moreover, I tell you that the LORD will build a house for you.

11"And it shall come about when your days are fulfilled that you must go *to be* with your fathers, that I will set up *one of* your descendants after you, who shall be of your sons; and I will establish his kingdom.

12"He[R] shall build for Me a house, and I will establish his throne forever. [Luke 1:33] ✫

13"I[R] will be his father, and he shall be My son; and I will not take My lovingkindness away from him, [R]as I took it from him who was before you.   2 Cor. 6:18 • 1 Chr. 10:14 ✫

14"But[R]I will settle him in My house and in My kingdom forever, and his throne shall be established forever." ' "   Acts 2:30 ✫

15 According to all these words and according to all this vision, so Nathan spoke to David.

Praise Prayer of David—2 Sam. 7:18–29

16 Then David the king went in and sat before the LORD and said, "Who[R] am I, O LORD God, and what is my house that Thou hast brought me this far?   2 Sam. 7:18

17"And this was a small thing in Thine eyes, O God; but Thou hast spoken of Thy servant's house for a great while to come, and hast regarded me according to the standard of a man of high degree, O LORD God.

18"What more can David still *say to* Thee concerning the honor *bestowed* on Thy servant? For Thou knowest Thy servant.

19"O LORD,[R]for Thy servant's sake, and according to Thine own heart, Thou hast wrought all this greatness, to make known all these great things.   2 Sam. 7:21; Is. 37:35

20"O LORD, there is none like Thee, neither is there any God besides Thee, according to all that we have heard with our ears.

21"And what one nation in the earth is like Thy people Israel, whom God went to redeem for Himself *as* a people, to make Thee a name by great and terrible things, in driving out nations from before Thy people, whom Thou didst redeem out of Egypt?

22"For[R]Thy people Israel Thou didst make Thine own people forever, and Thou, O LORD, didst become their God.   Ex. 19:5, 6

23"And now, O LORD, let the word that Thou hast spoken concerning Thy servant and concerning his house, be established forever, and do as Thou hast spoken.

24"And let Thy name be established and magnified forever, saying, 'The LORD of hosts is the God of Israel, *even* a God to Is-

rael; and the house of David Thy servant is established before Thee.'

25"For Thou, O my God, hast revealed to Thy servant that Thou wilt build for him a house; therefore Thy servant hath found *courage* to pray before Thee.

26"And now, O LORD, Thou art God, and hast [T]promised this good thing to Thy servant.   *said*

27"And now it hath pleased Thee to bless the house of Thy servant, that it may [T]continue forever before Thee; for Thou, O LORD, hast blessed, and it is blessed forever."   *be*

CHAPTER 18

Victory over Philistia—2 Sam. 8:1

N[OW] after this[R]it came about that David defeated the Philistines and subdued them and took Gath and its towns from the hand of the Philistines.   2 Sam. 8:1-18

Victory over Moab—2 Sam. 8:2

2 And he defeated Moab, and the Moabites became servants to David, bringing tribute.

Victory over Zobah—2 Sam. 8:3, 4

3 David also defeated Hadadezer king of Zobah *as far as* Hamath, as he went to establish his [T]rule to the Euphrates River. *hand*

4 And David took from him 1,000 chariots and 7,000 horsemen and 20,000 foot soldiers, and David hamstrung all the chariot horses, but reserved *enough* of them for 100 chariots.

Victory over Aram—2 Sam. 8:5–13

5 When the Arameans of Damascus came to help Hadadezer king of Zobah, David killed 22,000 men of the Arameans.

6 Then David put *garrisons* among the Arameans of [T]Damascus; and the Arameans became servants to David, bringing tribute. And the LORD helped David wherever he went.   Heb., *Darmeseq*

7 And David took the shields of gold which were [T]carried by the servants of Hadadezer, and brought them to Jerusalem. *on*

8 Also from[A]Tibhath and from Cun, cities of Hadadezer, David took a very large amount of bronze, with which Solomon made the bronze sea and the pillars and the bronze utensils.   In 2 Sam. 8:8, *Betah*

9 Now when[A]Tou king of Hamath heard that David had defeated all the army of Hadadezer king of Zobah,   In 2 Sam. 8:10, *Toi*

10 he sent[A]Hadoram his son to King David, to greet him and to bless him, because he had fought against Hadadezer and had

^Tdefeated him; for Hadadezer had been at war with Tou. And *Hadoram brought* all kinds of articles of gold and silver and bronze. *In 2 Sam. 8:10, Joram · smitten*

11 King David also dedicated these to the LORD with the silver and the gold which he had carried away from all the nations: from Edom, Moab, the sons of Ammon, the Philistines, and from Amalek.

Victory over Edom—2 Sam. 8:14–18

12 Moreover Abishai the son of Zeruiah ^Tdefeated 18,000 Edomites in the Valley of Salt. *smote*

13 Then he put garrisons in Edom, and all the Edomites became servants to David. And the LORD helped David wherever he went.

14 So David reigned over all Israel; and he ^Tadministered justice and righteousness for all his people. *was doing*

15 And ^RJoab the son of Zeruiah *was* over the army, and Jehoshaphat the son of Ahilud *was* recorder; *1 Chr. 11:6*

16 and Zadok the son of Ahitub and Abimelech the son of Abiathar *were* priests, and Shavsha *was* secretary;

17 and Benaiah the son of Jehoiada *was* over the Cherethites and the Pelethites, and the sons of David *were* chiefs at the king's side.

CHAPTER 19

Humiliation of David's Servants
2 Sam. 10:1–5

NOW it came about after this, that Nahash the king of the sons of Ammon died, and his son became king in his place.

2 Then David said, "I will show kindness to Hanun the son of Nahash, because his father showed kindness to me." So David sent messengers to console him concerning his father. And David's servants came into the land of the sons of Ammon to Hanun, to console him.

3 But the princes of the sons of Ammon said to Hanun, "Do you think that David is honoring your father, in that he has sent comforters to you? Have not his servants come to you to search and to overthrow and to spy out the land?"

4 So Hanun took David's servants and shaved them, and cut off their garments in the middle as far as their hips, and sent them away.

5 Then *certain persons* went and told David about the men. And he sent to meet them, for the men were greatly humiliated. And the king said, "Stay at Jericho until your beards grow, and *then* return."

Victory over the Ammonites
2 Sam. 10:6–14

6 When the sons of Ammon saw that they had made themselves odious to David, Hanun and the sons of Ammon sent 1,000 talents of silver to hire for themselves chariots and horsemen from Mesopotamia, from Aram-maacah, and ^Rfrom Zobah. *1 Chr. 18:5, 9*

7 So they hired for themselves 32,000 chariots, and the king of Maacah and his people, who came and camped before Medeba. And the sons of Ammon gathered together from their cities and came to battle.

8 When David heard *of it,* he sent Joab and all the army, the mighty men.

9 And the sons of Ammon came out and drew up in battle array at the entrance of the city, and the kings who had come were by themselves in the field.

10 Now when Joab saw that the ^Tbattle was set against him in front and in the rear, he selected from all the choice men of Israel and they arrayed themselves against the Arameans. *the face of the battle*

11 But the remainder of the people he placed in the hand of ^AAbshai his brother; and they arrayed themselves against the sons of Ammon. *In 2 Sam. 10:10, Abishai*

12 And he said, "If the Arameans are too strong for me, then you shall help me; but if the sons of Ammon are too strong for you, then I will help you.

13 "Be strong, and let us show ourselves courageous for the sake of our people and for the cities of our God; and may the LORD do what is good in His sight."

14 So Joab and the people who were with him drew near to the battle against the Arameans, and they fled before him.

15 When the sons of Ammon saw that the Arameans fled, they also fled before Abshai his brother, and entered the city. Then Joab came to Jerusalem.

Victory over the Arameans
2 Sam. 10:15–19

16 When the Arameans saw that they had been ^Tdefeated by Israel, they sent messengers, and brought out the Arameans who were beyond the ⁶River, with Shophach the commander of the army of Hadadezer leading them. *smitten before*

17 When it was told David, he gathered all Israel together and crossed the Jordan, and came upon them and drew up in formation against them. And when David drew up in battle array against the Arameans, they fought against him.

18 And the Arameans fled before Israel, and David killed of the Arameans 7,000 charioteers and 40,000 foot soldiers, and put to death Shophach the commander of the army.

19 So when the servants of Hadadezer saw that they were ^Tdefeated by Israel, they

⁶ I.e., Euphrates

made peace with David and served him. Thus the Arameans were not willing to help the sons of Ammon anymore.   *smitten before*

CHAPTER 20

Victory over the Ammonites
2 Sam. 11:1; 12:26–31

THEN it happened in the spring, at the time when kings go out *to battle,* that Joab led out the army and ravaged the land of the sons of Ammon, and came and besieged Rabbah. But David stayed at Jerusalem. And Joab struck Rabbah and overthrew it.

2 ^RAnd David took the crown of their king from his head, and he found it to weigh a talent of gold, and there was a precious stone in it; and it was placed on David's head. And he brought out the spoil of the city, a very great amount.   2 Sam. 12:30, 31

3 And he brought out the people who *were* in it, ^Rand cut *them* with saws and with sharp instruments and with axes. And thus David did to all the cities of the sons of Ammon. Then David and all the people returned *to* Jerusalem.   2 Sam. 12:31

Victory over the Philistine Giants
2 Sam. 21:18–22

4 Now it came about after this, that war ^Tbroke out at Gezer with the Philistines; then Sibbecai the Hushathite^Tkilled Sippai, one of the descendants of the^Tgiants, and they were subdued.   *stood up • smote •* Heb., *Raphah*

5 And there was war with the Philistines again, and Elhanan the son of ^RJair ^Tkilled Lahmi the brother of Goliath the Gittite, the ^Rshaft of whose spear *was* like a weaver's beam.   2 Sam. 21:19 • *smote* • 1 Sam. 17:7

6 And again there was war at Gath, where there was a man of *great* stature who had twenty-four fingers and toes, six *fingers on each hand* and six *toes on each foot;* and he also was descended from the giants.

7 And when he taunted Israel, Jonathan the son of Shimea, David's brother, ^Tkilled him.   *smote*

8 These were descended from the giants in Gath, and they fell by the hand of David and by the hand of his servants.

CHAPTER 21

Temptation of David by Satan

THEN^RSatan stood up against Israel and moved David to number Israel. 2 Sam. 24:1-25

2 So David said to Joab and to the princes of the people, "Go, number Israel from Beersheba even to Dan, and bring me *word* that I may know their number."

3 And Joab said, "May^Rthe LORD add to His people a hundred times as many as they are! But, my lord the king, are they not all my lord's servants? Why does my lord seek this thing? Why should he be a cause of guilt to Israel?"   Deut. 1:11

4 Nevertheless, the king's word prevailed against Joab. Therefore, Joab departed and went throughout all Israel, and came to Jerusalem.

Enumeration of Israel

5 And Joab gave the ^Tnumber of the^Tcensus of *all* the people to David. And^Rall Israel were 1,100,000 men who drew the sword; and Judah *was* 470,000 men who drew the sword.   *muster • numbering •* 2 Sam. 24:9

21:1 Temptation by Satan—The role of Satan against the Christian is well summed up by the meaning of the name Satan—"adversary." He is also called "the devil," meaning "accuser." He can appear as a hideous dragon (Page 1300—Rev. 12:3, 4, 9) or as a beautifully deceptive "angel of light" (Page 1172—2 Cor. 11:14). He stands hatefully opposed to all the work of God and resourcefully promotes defiance among men (Page 1003—Mark 4:15; Page 496—Job 2:4, 5).

When Satan sinned he was expelled from heaven (Page 1039—Luke 10:18), although apparently he still had some access to God (Page 495—Job 1:6). A multitude of angels cast in their lot with him in his fall and subsequently became the demons mentioned often in the Bible (Page 974—Matt. 12:24; Page 1301—Rev. 12:7). Although Satan's doom was secured by Jesus' death on the cross (Page 1083—John 16:11), he will continue to hinder God's program until he and his angels are cast into the lake of fire (Page 990—Matt. 25:41; Page 1306—Rev. 20:10).

The terrifying work of Satan in the unbeliever is described in Scripture as follows: he blinds their minds (Page 1167—2 Cor. 4:4); he takes the Word of God from their hearts (Page 1035—Luke 8:12); and he controls them (Page 1108—Acts 13:8). In regard to Christians, Satan may accuse them (Page 1301—Rev. 12:10), devour their testimony for Christ (Page 1264—1 Pet. 5:8), deceive them (Page 1172—2 Cor. 11:14), hinder their work (Page 1207—1 Thess. 2:18), tempt them to immorality (Page 1153—1 Cor. 7:5), and even be used by God to discipline Christians (Page 1151—1 Cor. 5:5; Page 1173—2 Cor. 12:7).

The Christian's response to Satan is to recognize his power and deception (Page 1167—2 Cor. 2:11; Page 1190—Eph. 6:11), to adhere steadfastly to the faith (Page 1264—1 Pet. 5:9), to resist him openly (Page 1255—James 4:7), and not to give him opportunities (Page 1188—Eph. 4:27). In practice, the best way to oppose him is to be a growing Christian. Also, in the light of his tremendous power to blind men to the gospel, Christians must always be aggressively and compassionately witnessing to the lost in order to snatch them from Satan's control (Page 1124—Acts 26:18). Believers can respond to temptation by Satan with confidence. We know that nothing can separate us from the love of God (Page 1138—Rom. 8:28–39).

Now turn to Page 1263—1 Pet. 3:17: Kinds of Suffering.

6 But he did not [T]number Levi and Benjamin among them, for the king's [T]command was abhorrent to Joab.   *muster • word*

Prayer of David

7 And God was displeased with this thing, so He struck Israel.

8 And David said to God, "I have sinned greatly, in that I have done this thing. But now, please take away the iniquity of Thy servant, for I have done very foolishly."

Three Choices of David

[R]9 And the Lord spoke to [R]Gad, David's seer, saying,   2 Sam. 24:11 • 1 Sam. 9:9

10 "Go and speak to David, saying, 'Thus says the Lord, "I [I]offer you three things; choose for yourself one of them, that I may do *it* to you."' "   *stretch out to*

11 So Gad came to David and said to him, "Thus says the Lord, 'Take for yourself

12 [R]either three years of famine, or three months to be swept away before your foes, while the sword of your enemies overtakes *you*, or else three days of the sword of the Lord, even pestilence in the land, and the angel of the Lord destroying throughout all the territory of Israel.' Now, therefore, consider what answer I shall return to Him who sent me."   2 Sam. 24:13

13 And David said to Gad, "I am in great distress; please let me fall into the hand of the Lord, for His mercies are very great. But do not let me fall into the hand of man."

Judgment of Pestilence

14 [R]So the Lord [T]sent a pestilence on Israel; 70,000 men of Israel fell.   1 Chr. 27:24 • *gave*

15 And God sent an angel to Jerusalem to destroy it; but as he was about to destroy *it*, the Lord saw and [R]was sorry over the calamity, and said to the destroying angel, "It is enough; now relax your hand." And the angel of the Lord was standing by the threshing floor of Ornan the Jebusite.   Ex. 32:14

16 Then David lifted up his eyes and saw the angel of the Lord standing between earth and heaven, with his drawn sword in his hand stretched out over Jerusalem. Then David and the elders, [R]covered with sackcloth, fell on their faces.   1 Kin. 21:27

17 And David said to God, "Is it not I who [T]commanded to count the people? Indeed, I am the one who has sinned and done very wickedly, [R]but these sheep, what have they done? O Lord my God, please let Thy hand be against me and my father's household, but not against Thy people that they should be plagued."   *said • 2 Sam. 7:8; Ps. 74:1*

Withholding of Judgment
by Sacrifices

18 Then the angel of the Lord commanded Gad to say to David, that David should go up and build an altar to the Lord on the threshing floor of Ornan the Jebusite.

19 So David went up at the word of Gad, which he spoke in the name of the Lord.

20 Now Ornan turned back and saw the angel, and his four sons *who were* with him hid themselves. And Ornan was threshing wheat.

21 And as David came to Ornan, Ornan looked and saw David, and went out from the threshing floor, and prostrated himself before David with his face to the ground.

22 Then David said to Ornan, "Give me the [T]site of *this* threshing floor, that I may build on it an altar to the Lord; for the full price you shall give it to me, that the plague may be restrained from the people."   *place*

23 And Ornan said to David, "Take *it* for yourself; and let my lord the king do what is good in his sight. See, I will give the oxen for burnt offerings and the threshing sledges for wood and the wheat for the grain offering; I will give *it* all."

24 But King David said to Ornan, "No, but I will surely buy *it* for the full price; for I will not take what is yours for the Lord, or offer a burnt offering which costs me nothing."

25 So David gave Ornan 600 shekels of gold by weight for the [T]site.   *place*

26 Then David built an altar to the Lord there, and offered burnt offerings and peace offerings. And he called to the Lord and [R]He answered him with fire from heaven on the altar of burnt offering.   Lev. 9:24; Judg. 6:21

27 And the Lord commanded the angel, and he put his sword back in its sheath.

28 At that time, when David saw that the Lord had answered him on the threshing floor of Ornan the Jebusite, he offered sacrifice there.

29 [R]For the tabernacle of the Lord, which Moses had made in the wilderness, and the altar of burnt offering *were* in the high place at Gibeon at that time.   1 Kin. 3:4; 1 Chr. 16:39

30 But David could not go before it to inquire of God, for he was terrified by the sword of the angel of the Lord.

CHAPTER 22

Material Provisions
for the Temple's Construction

THEN David said, "This [R]is the house of the Lord God, and this is the altar of burnt offering for Israel."   1 Chr. 21:18-28; 2 Chr. 3:1

2 So David [T]gave orders to gather [R]the foreigners who were in the land of Israel, and he set stonecutters to hew out stones to build the house of God.   *said to • 2 Chr. 2:17*

3 And David [R]prepared large quantities of iron [T]to make the nails for the doors of the gates and for the clamps, and more bronze than could be weighed;   1 Chr. 29:2, 7 • *for*

4 and timbers of cedar logs beyond num-

ber, for the Sidonians and Tyrians brought large quantities of cedar timber to David.

5 And David said, "My son ^RSolomon is young and inexperienced, and the house that is to be built for the LORD shall be exceedingly magnificent, famous and glorious throughout all lands. *Therefore* now I will make preparation for it." So David made ample preparations before his death. 1 Chr. 29:1

David's Charge to Solomon

6 Then ^Rhe called for his son Solomon, and charged him to build a house for the LORD God of Israel.   1 Kin. 2:1

7 And David said to Solomon, "My son, ^TI had intended to build a house to the name of the LORD my God.   *as for me, it was in my heart*

8"But the word of the LORD came to me, saying, 'You have shed much blood, and have waged great wars; you shall not build a house to My name, because you have shed *so* much blood on the earth before Me.

9 'Behold, a son shall be born to you, who shall be a man of rest; and I will give him rest from all his enemies on every side; for his name shall be ⁷Solomon, and I will give peace and quiet to Israel in his days.

10 'He shall build a house for My name, and ^Rhe shall be My son, and I will be his father; and I will establish the throne of his kingdom over Israel forever.'   Matt. 1:6☆

11"Now, my son, ^Rthe LORD be with you that you may be successful, and build the house of the LORD your God just as He has spoken concerning you.   1 Chr. 22:16

12"Only ^Tthe LORD give you discretion and understanding, and give you charge over Israel, so that you may ^Rkeep the law of the LORD your God.   1 Kin. 3:9-12 • 1 Kin. 2:3

13"Then you shall prosper, if you are careful to observe the statutes and the ordinances which the LORD commanded Moses concerning Israel. Be strong and courageous, do not fear nor be dismayed.

14"Now behold, ^Twith great pains I have prepared for the house of the LORD ^R100,000 talents of gold and 1,000,000 talents of silver, and bronze and iron beyond weight, for ^Tthey are in great quantity; also timber and stone I have prepared, and you may add to them.   *in my affliction* • 1 Chr. 29:4 • *it is*

15"Moreover, there are many workmen with you, stonecutters and masons of stone and carpenters, and all men who are skillful in every kind of work.

16"Of the gold, the silver and the bronze and the iron, there is no limit. Arise and work, and may the LORD be with you."

David's Charge to the Leaders

17 David also commanded all the leaders of Israel to help his son Solomon, *saying,*

18"Is not the LORD your God with you? And has He not given you rest on every

side? For He has given the inhabitants of the land into my hand, and the land is subdued before the LORD and before His people.

19"Now ^Rset your heart and your soul to seek the LORD your God; arise, therefore, and build the sanctuary of the LORD God, ^Rso that you may bring the ark of the covenant of the LORD, and the holy vessels of God into the house that is to be built for the name of the LORD."   1 Chr. 28:9 • 1 Kin. 8:6, 21

CHAPTER 23

Enumeration of the Levites

NOW when David reached old age, he made his son Solomon king over Israel.

2 And he gathered together all the leaders of Israel with the priests and the Levites.

3 And the Levites were numbered from thirty years old and upward, and their number by ^Tcensus of men was 38,000. *their heads*

4 Of these, 24,000 were ^Rto oversee the work of the house of the LORD; and 6,000 *were* officers and judges,   Ezra 3:8, 9

5 and 4,000 *were* gatekeepers, and 4,000 *were* praising the LORD with the instruments which ^TDavid made for giving praise. *I made*

6 And David divided them into divisions ^Raccording to the sons of Levi: Gershon, Kohath, and Merari.   1 Chr. 6:1

Organization of the Gershonites

7 Of the Gershonites *were* ^ALadan and Shimei.   In Ex. 6:17, *Libni*

8 The sons of Ladan *were* Jehiel the first and Zetham and Joel, three.

9 The sons of Shimei *were* Shelomoth and Haziel and Haran, three. These were the heads of the fathers' *households* of Ladan.

10 And the sons of Shimei *were* Jahath, ^AZina, Jeush, and Beriah. These four *were* the sons of Shimei.   In v. 11, *Zizah*

11 And Jahath was the first, and Zizah the second; but Jeush and Beriah did not have many sons, so they became a father's household, one ^Tclass.   *mustering*

Organization of the Kohathites

12 The sons of Kohath were four: Amram, Izhar, Hebron and Uzziel.

13 The sons of Amram were Aaron and Moses. And Aaron was set apart to sanctify him as most holy, he and his sons forever, to burn incense before the LORD, to minister to Him and to bless in His name forever.

14 But *as for* Moses the man of God, his sons were named among the tribe of Levi.

⁷ I.e., peaceful

15 The sons of Moses *were* Gershom and Eliezer.
16 The ᵀson of Gershom *was* ᴬShebuel the chief.   *sons* • In ch. 24:20, *Shubael*
17 And the son of Eliezer was Rehabiah the chief; and Eliezer had no other sons, but the sons of Rehabiah were very many.
18 The ᵀson of Izhar was ᴬShelomith the chief.   *sons* • In ch. 24:22, *Shelomoth*
19 The sons of Hebron *were* Jeriah the first, Amariah the second, Jahaziel the third and Jekameam the fourth.
20 The sons of Uzziel *were* Micah the first and Isshiah the second.

Organization of the Merarites

21 The sons of Merari were Mahli and Mushi. The sons of Mahli *were* Eleazar and Kish.
22 And Eleazar died and had no sons, but daughters only, so their brothers, the sons of Kish, took them *as wives.*
23 The sons of Mushi *were* three: Mahli, Eder, and Jeremoth.

Duties of the Levites

24 These were the sons of Levi according to their fathers' households, *even* the heads of the fathers' *households* of those of them who wereᵀcounted, in the number of names by their ᵀcensus, doing the work for the service of the house of the LORD, from twenty years old and upward.   *mustered* • *heads*
25 For David said, "The LORD God of Israel ᴿhas given rest to His people, and He dwells in Jerusalem forever.   1 Chr. 22:18
26 "And also, ᴿthe Levites will no longer need to carry the tabernacle and all its utensils for its service." Num. 4:5, 15; 7:9; Deut. 10:8
27 For by the last words of David the sons of Levi *were* numbered, from twenty years old and upward.
28 For their office is to assist the sons of Aaron with the service of the house of the LORD, in the courts and in the chambers and in the purifying of all holy things, even the work of the service of the house of God,
29 ᴿand with the showbread, and ᴿthe fine flour for a grain offering, and unleavened wafers, or *what is baked in* the pan, or what is well-mixed, and all measures of volume and size.   Lev. 24:5-9 • Lev. 6:20
30 And they are to stand every morning to thank and to praise the LORD, and likewise at evening,
31 and to offer all burnt offerings to the LORD, ᴿon the sabbaths, the new moons and ᴿthe fixed festivals in the number *set* by the ordinance concerning them, continually before the LORD.   Is. 1:13, 14 • Lev. 23:2-4
32 Thus ᴿthey are to keep charge of the tent of meeting, and ᴿcharge of the holy place, and ᴿcharge of the sons of Aaron their ᵀrelatives, for the service of the house of the LORD.   [Num. 1:53] • Num. 3:6-9 • *brothers*

CHAPTER 24

Divisions of the Sons of Aaron

NOW the divisions of the ᵀdescendants of Aaron *were these:* the sons of Aaron *were* Nadab, Abihu, Eleazar, and Ithamar.   *sons*
2 But Nadab and Abihu died before their father and had no ᴬsons. So Eleazar and Ithamar served as priests.   *children*
3 And David, with Zadok of the sons of Eleazar and Ahimelech of the sons of Ithamar, divided them according to their offices ᵀfor their ministry.   *in their service*
4 Since more chief men were found from the ᵀdescendants of Eleazar than the ᵀdescendants of Ithamar, they divided them thus: *there were* sixteen heads of fathers' households of the ᵀdescendants of Eleazar, and eight of the ᵀdescendants of Ithamar according to their fathers' households.   *sons*
5 ᴿThus they were divided by lot, the one as the other; for they were officers of the sanctuary and officers of God, both from the ᵀdescendants of Eleazar and the ᵀdescendants of Ithamar.   1 Chr. 24:31 • *sons*
6 And Shemaiah, the son of Nethanel the scribe, from the Levites, recorded them in the presence of the king, the princes, Zadok the priest, ᴿAhimelech the son of Abiathar, and the heads of the fathers' *households* of the priests and of the Levites; one father's household taken for Eleazar and one taken for Ithamar.   1 Chr. 18:16
7 Now the first lot came out for Jehoiarib, the second for Jedaiah,
8 the third for Harim, the fourth for Seorim,
9 the fifth for Malchijah, the sixth for Mijamin,
10 the seventh for Hakkoz, the eighth for ᴿAbijah,   Neh. 12:4; Luke 1:5
11 the ninth for Jeshua, the tenth for Shecaniah,
12 the eleventh for Eliashib, the twelfth for Jakim,
13 the thirteenth for Huppah, the fourteenth for Jeshebeab,
14 the fifteenth for Bilgah, the sixteenth for Immer,
15 the seventeenth for Hezir, the eighteenth for Happizzez,
16 the nineteenth for Pethahiah, the twentieth for Jehezkel,
17 the twenty-first for Jachin, the twenty-second for Gamul,
18 the twenty-third for Delaiah, the twenty-fourth for Maaziah.
19 These were their offices for their ministry, when *they* came in to the house of the LORD according to the ordinance *given* to

them through Aaron their father, just as the LORD God of Israel had commanded him.

Organization of the Kohathites

20 Now for the rest of the sons of Levi: of the sons of Amram, ^Shubael; of the sons of Shubael, Jehdeiah.   In 23:16, *Shebuel*
21 Of Rehabiah: of the sons of Rehabiah, Isshiah the first.
22 Of the Izharites, ^Shelomoth; of the sons of Shelomoth, Jahath. In 23:18, *Shelomith*
23 And the sons ^of *Hebron:* Jeriah *the first,* Amariah the second, Jahaziel the third, Jekameam the fourth.   1 Chr. 23:19
24 Of the sons of Uzziel, Micah; of the sons of Micah, Shamir.
25 The brother of Micah, Isshiah; of the sons of Isshiah, Zechariah.

Organization of the Merarites

26 The sons of Merari, Mahli and Mushi; the sons of Jaaziah, Beno.
27 The sons of Merari: by Jaaziah *were* Beno, Shoham, Zaccur, and Ibri.
28 By Mahli: Eleazar, who had no sons.
29 By Kish: the sons of Kish, Jerahmeel.
30 And the sons of Mushi: Mahli, Eder, and Jerimoth. These *were* the sons of the Levites according to their fathers' households.
31 ^These also cast lots just as their ^relatives the sons of Aaron in the presence of David the king, Zadok, Ahimelech, and the heads of the fathers' *households* of the priests and of the Levites—the head of fathers' *households* as well as those of his younger brother.   1 Chr. 24:5, 6 • *brothers*

CHAPTER 25

Organization of the Orders of the Musicians

MOREOVER, David and the commanders of the army set apart for the service *some* of the sons of Asaph and of Heman and of Jeduthun, who *were* to prophesy with lyres, harps, and cymbals; and the number of those who performed their service was:
2 Of the sons of Asaph: Zaccur, Joseph, Nethaniah, and ^Asharelah; the sons of Asaph *were* under the ^direction of Asaph, who prophesied under the ^direction of the king.   In v. 14, *Jesharelah • hand(s)*
3 ^Of Jeduthun, the sons of Jeduthun: Gedaliah, Zeri, Jeshaiah, Shimei, Hashabiah, and Mattithiah, six, under the ^direction of their father Jeduthun with the harp, who prophesied in giving thanks and praising the LORD.   1 Chr. 16:41, 42 • *hands*

4 Of Heman, the sons of Heman: Bukkiah, Mattaniah, ^Uzziel, Shebuel and Jerimoth, Hananiah, Hanani, Eliathah, Giddalti and Romamti-ezer, Joshbekashah, Mallothi, Hothir, Mahazioth.   In v. 18, *Azarel*
5 All these *were* the sons of Heman the king's seer to exalt him according to the words of God, for God gave fourteen sons and three daughters to Heman.
6 All these were under the ^direction of their father to sing in the house of the LORD, ^with cymbals, harps and lyres, for the service of the house of God. ^Asaph, Jeduthun and Heman *were* under the ^direction of the king.   *hands* • 1 Chr. 15:16 • 1 Chr. 15:19
7 And their number who were trained in singing to the LORD, with their [8]relatives, all who were skillful, *was* ^288.   1 Chr. 23:5
8 And ^they cast lots for their duties, all alike, the small as well as the great, the teacher *as well* as the pupil.   1 Chr. 26:13
9 Now the first lot came out for Asaph to Joseph, the second for Gedaliah, he with his relatives and sons *were* twelve;
10 the third to Zaccur, his sons and his relatives, twelve;
11 the fourth to ^Izri, his sons and his relatives, twelve;   In v. 3, *Zeri*
12 the fifth to Nethaniah, his sons and his relatives, twelve;
13 the sixth to Bukkiah, his sons and his relatives, twelve;
14 the seventh to ^Jesharelah, his sons and his relatives, twelve;   In v. 2, *Asherelah*
15 the eighth to Jeshaiah, his sons and his relatives, twelve;
16 the ninth to Mattaniah, his sons and his relatives, twelve;
17 the tenth to Shimei, his sons and his relatives, twelve;
18 the eleventh to Azarel, his sons and his relatives, twelve;
19 the twelfth to Hashabiah, his sons and his relatives, twelve;
20 for the thirteenth, Shubael, his sons and his relatives, twelve;
21 for the fourteenth, Mattithiah, his sons and his relatives, twelve;
22 for the fifteenth to Jeremoth, his sons and his relatives, twelve;
23 for the sixteenth to Hananiah, his sons and his relatives, twelve;
24 for the seventeenth to Joshbekashah, his sons and his relatives, twelve;
25 for the eighteenth to Hanani, his sons and his relatives, twelve;
26 for the nineteenth to Mallothi, his sons and his relatives, twelve;
27 for the twentieth to Eliathah, his sons and his relatives, twelve;
28 for the twenty-first to Hothir, his sons and his relatives, twelve;
29 for the twenty-second to Giddalti, his sons and his relatives, twelve;

[8] Lit., *brothers,* and so throughout this context

30 for the twenty-third to Mahazioth, his sons and his relatives, twelve;

31 for the twenty-fourth to Romamti-ezer, his sons and his relatives, twelve.

CHAPTER 26

Organization of the Gatekeepers

F OR the divisions of the gatekeepers *there were* of the Korahites, Meshelemiah the son of Kore, of the sons of Asaph.

2 And Meshelemiah had sons: Zechariah the first-born, Jediael the second, Zebadiah the third, Jathniel the fourth,

3 Elam the fifth, Johanan the sixth, Eliehoenai the seventh.

4 And ^RObed-edom had sons: Shemaiah the first-born, Jehozabad the second, Joah the third, Sacar the fourth, Nethanel the fifth,   2 Sam. 6:11; 1 Chr. 13:14

5 Ammiel the sixth, Issachar the seventh, *and* Peullethai the eighth; God had indeed blessed him.

6 Also to his son Shemaiah sons were born who ruled over the house of their father, for they were mighty men of valor.

7 The sons of Shemaiah *were* Othni, Rephael, Obed, and Elzabad, whose brothers, Elihu and Semachiah, were valiant men.

8 All these *were* of the sons of Obed-edom; they and their sons and their relatives *were* able men with strength for the service, 62 from Obed-edom.   *brothers*

9 And Meshelemiah had sons and relatives, 18 valiant men.

10 Also Hosah, *one* of the sons of Merari had sons: Shimri the first (although he was not the first-born, his father made him first),

11 Hilkiah the second, Tebaliah the third, Zechariah the fourth; all the sons and relatives of Hosah *were* 13.

12 To these divisions of the gatekeepers, the chief men, *were given* duties like their relatives to minister in the house of the LORD.

13 ^RAnd they cast lots, the small and the great alike, according to their fathers' households, for every gate. 1 Chr. 24:5, 31; 25:8

14 And the lot to the east fell to Shelemiah. Then they cast lots *for* his son Zechariah, a counselor with insight, and his lot came out to the north.   In 9:17, *Shallum*

15 For Obed-edom *it fell* to the south, and to his sons went the storehouse.

16 For Shuppim and Hosah *it was* to the west, by the gate of Shallecheth, on the ascending highway. Guard corresponded to guard.

17 On the east there were six Levites, on the north four daily, on the south four daily, and at the storehouse two by two.

18 At the ⁹Parbar on the west *there were*

four at the highway and two at the Parbar.

19 These were the divisions of the gatekeepers of the sons of Korah and of the sons of Merari.

Organization of the Treasurers of the Temple

20 ¹⁰And the Levites, their relatives, had charge of the treasures of the house of God, and of the treasures of the dedicated gifts.

21 The sons of Ladan, the sons of the Gershonites belonging to Ladan, *namely,* the Jehielites, *were* the heads of the fathers' *households,* belonging to Ladan the Gershonite.

22 The sons of Jehieli, Zetham and Joel his brother, had charge of the treasures of the house of the LORD.   *were over*

23 As for the Amramites, the Izharites, the Hebronites, and the Uzzielites,

24 Shebuel the son of Gershom, the son of Moses, was officer over the treasures.

25 And his relatives by Eliezer *were* Rehabiah his son, Jeshaiah his son, Joram his son, Zichri his son, and Shelomoth his son.

26 This Shelomoth and his relatives had charge of all the treasures of the dedicated gifts, which King David and the heads of the fathers' *households,* the commanders of thousands and hundreds, and commanders of the army, had dedicated.   *were over*

27 They dedicated part of the spoil won in battles to repair the house of the LORD.

28 And all that Samuel the seer had dedicated and Saul the son of Kish, Abner the son of Ner and Joab the son of Zeruiah, everyone who had dedicated *anything, all of this* was in the care of Shelomoth and his relatives.   *under the hand · Heb., Shelomith*

Organization of the Officers Outside of the Temple

29 As for the Izharites, Chenaniah and his sons were *assigned* to outside duties for Israel, as officers and judges.   Neh. 11:16

30 As for the Hebronites, Hashabiah and his relatives, 1,700 capable men, had charge of the affairs of Israel west of the Jordan, for all the work of the LORD and the service of the king.   *beyond the Jordan westward*

31 As for the Hebronites, Jerijah the chief (these Hebronites were investigated according to their genealogies and fathers' *households,* in the fortieth year of David's reign, and men of outstanding capability were found among them at Jazer of Gilead)

32 and his relatives, capable men, *were* 2,700 in number, heads of fathers' *households.* And King David made them overseers of the Reubenites, the Gadites and the half-tribe of the Manassites concerning all the affairs of God and of the king.

---

⁹ Possibly *court* or *colonnade*
¹⁰ So Gr.; Heb., *As for the Levites, Ahijah had*

CHAPTER 27

The Twelve Commanders of Israel

Now *this is* the enumeration of the sons of Israel, the heads of fathers' *households,* the commanders of thousands and of hundreds, and their officers who served the king in all the affairs of the divisions which came in and went out month by month throughout all the months of the year, each division *numbering* 24,000.

2 Jashobeam the son of Zabdiel [11]had charge of the first division for the first month; and in his division *were* 24,000.

3 *He was* from the sons of Perez, *and was* chief of all the commanders of the army for the first month.

4 Dodai the Ahohite and his division had charge of the division for the second month, Mikloth *being* the chief officer; and in his division *were* 24,000.

5 The third commander of the army for the third month *was* Benaiah, the son of Jehoiada the priest, *as* chief; and in his division *were* 24,000.

6 This Benaiah *was* the mighty man of the thirty, and had charge of thirty; and over his division was Ammizabad his son.

7 The fourth for the fourth month *was* Asahel the brother of Joab, and Zebadiah his son after him; and in his division *were* 24,000.

8 The fifth for the fifth month *was* the commander Shamhuth the Izrahite; and in his division *were* 24,000.

9 The sixth for the sixth month *was* Ira the son of Ikkesh the Tekoite; and in his division *were* 24,000.

10 The seventh for the seventh month *was* Helez the Pelonite of the sons of Ephraim; and in his division *were* 24,000.

11 The eighth for the eighth month *was* Sibbecai the Hushathite of the Zerahites; and in his division *were* 24,000.

12 The ninth for the ninth month *was* Abiezer the Anathothite of the Benjamites; and in his division *were* 24,000.

13 The tenth for the tenth month *was* Maharai the Netophathite of the Zerahites; and in his division *were* 24,000.

14 The eleventh for the eleventh month *was* Benaiah the Pirathonite of the sons of Ephraim; and in his division *were* 24,000.

15 The twelfth for the twelfth month *was* Heldai the Netophathite of Othniel; and in his division *were* 24,000.

The Princes of the Twelve Tribes

16 Now in charge of the tribes of Israel: chief officer for the Reubenites was Eliezer the son of Zichri; for the Simeonites, Shephatiah the son of Maacah;

17 for Levi, Hashabiah the son of Kemuel; for Aaron, Zadok;

18 for Judah, Elihu, *one* of David's brothers; for Issachar, Omri the son of Michael;

19 for Zebulun, Ishmaiah the son of Obadiah; for Naphtali, Jeremoth the son of Azriel;

20 for the sons of Ephraim, Hoshea the son of Azaziah; for the half-tribe of Manasseh, Joel the son of Pedaiah;

21 for the half-tribe of Manasseh in Gilead, Iddo the son of Zechariah; for Benjamin, Jaasiel the son of Abner;

22 for Dan, Azarel the son of Jeroham. [R]These *were* the princes of the tribes of Israel.   1 Chr. 28:1

23 But David did not [T]count those twenty years of age and under, because the LORD had said He would multiply Israel as the stars of heaven.   *take their number from*

24 Joab the son of Zeruiah had begun to count *them,* but did not finish; and because of [R]this, wrath came upon Israel, and the number was not included in the account of the chronicles of King David.   2 Sam. 24:12-15

The Royal Officers of David

25 Now Azmaveth the son of Adiel had charge of the king's storehouses. And Jonathan the son of Uzziah had charge of the storehouses in the country, in the cities, in the villages, and in the towers.

26 And Ezri the son of Chelub had charge of the [T]agricultural workers who tilled the soil.   *doers of the work of the field for the tilling of*

27 And Shimei the Ramathite had charge of the vineyards; and Zabdi the Shiphmite had charge of the produce of the vineyards *stored* in the wine cellars.

28 And Baal-hanan the Gederite had charge of the olive and sycamore trees in the [12]Shephelah; and Joash had charge of the stores of oil.

29 And Shitrai the Sharonite had charge of the cattle which were grazing in [R]Sharon; and Shaphat the son of Adlai had charge of the cattle in the valleys.   1 Chr. 5:16

30 And Obil the Ishmaelite had charge of the camels; and Jehdeiah the Meronothite had charge of the donkeys.

31 And Jaziz the Hagrite had charge of the flocks. All these were overseers of the property which belonged to King David.

The Counselors of David

32 Also Jonathan, David's uncle, *was* a counselor, a man of understanding, and a scribe; and Jehiel the son of Hachmoni [T]tutored the king's sons.   *was with*

33 And [R]Ahithophel was counselor to the king; and [R]Hushai the Archite was the king's friend.   2 Sam. 15:12 • 2 Sam. 15:32, 37

[11] Lit., *was over,* and so throughout the ch.
[12] Or, *lowlands*

34 And Jehoiada the son of Benaiah, and Abiathar succeeded Ahithophel; and Joab was the commander of the king's army.

CHAPTER 28

Charge to Israel

NOW ^RDavid assembled at Jerusalem all the officials of Israel, the princes of the tribes, and the commanders of the divisions that served the king, and the commanders of thousands, and the commanders of hundreds, and the overseers of all the property and livestock belonging to the king and his sons, with the officials and the mighty men, even all the valiant men.   1 Chr. 23:2; 27:1-31

2 Then King David rose to his feet and said, "Listen to me, my brethren and my people; I^R*had* ¹³intended to build a ¹⁴permanent home for the ark of the covenant of the LORD and for the footstool of our God. So I had made preparations to build *it.* 1 Chr. 17:1

3"But God said to me, 'You shall not build a house for My name because you are a man of war and have shed blood.'

4"Yet, the LORD, the God of Israel,^Rchose me from all the house of my father to be king over Israel forever. For He has chosen Judah to be a leader; and in the house of Judah, my father's house, and among the sons of my father He took pleasure in me to make *me* king over all Israel.   1 Sam. 16:6-13

5"And of all my sons (for the LORD has given me many sons),^RHe has chosen my son

---

¹³ Lit., *in my heart*   ¹⁴ Lit., *house of rest*

Solomon to sit on the throne of the kingdom of the LORD over Israel.   1 Chr. 22:9, 10

6"And He said to me, 'Your son^RSolomon is the one who shall build My house and My courts; for I have chosen him to be a son to Me, and I will be a father to him.   2 Sam. 7:13

7 'And^RI will establish his kingdom forever, ^Rif he resolutely performs My commandments and My ordinances, as^Tis done now.'   Mat. 1:6☆ • 1 Chr. 22:13 • *at this day*

8"So now, in the sight of all Israel, the assembly of the LORD, and in the hearing of our God, observe and seek after all the commandments of the LORD your God in order that you may possess the good land and bequeath *it* to your sons after you forever.

Charge to Solomon

9"As for you, my son Solomon, know the God of your father, and serve Him with a whole heart and a willing mind; for the LORD searches all hearts, and understands every intent of the thoughts. If you seek Him, He will let you find Him; but if you forsake Him, He will reject you forever.

10"Consider now, for the LORD has chosen you to build a house for the sanctuary;^Rbe courageous and act."   1 Chr. 22:13

Plan for the Temple

11 Then David gave to his son Solomon the plan of the porch *of the temple,* its buildings, its storehouses, its upper rooms, its inner rooms, and the room for the mercy seat;

28:4–6 Government of Israel—The government of Israel may be considered under two important headings: the laws, and the leaders.
The laws:
a. The "commandments," especially the Ten Commandments, revealed God's holiness and set up a divine standard of righteousness for the people to follow (Page 71—Ex. 20:1–17).
b. The judgments governed the social life of the people and concerned masters and servants (Page 72—Ex. 21:1–11), physical injuries (Page 72—Ex. 21:12–36), protection of property rights (Page 73—Ex. 22:1–15), etc.
c. The ordinances included the sacrifices that showed that blood must be shed for sinners to be forgiven (Page 96—Lev. 1—17).
The leaders: At first Moses was the sole leader; then he was replaced by Joshua. After Joshua's death the nation was governed for many years by judges, who were usually raised up by God to oppose a specific enemy. Finally, at the people's request, God granted them a king, thus establishing the monarchy (Page 269—1 Sam. 8:5, 22). Under the monarchy there were four key leaders:
a. The *king* was the Lord's representative who ruled the people, but only as the Lord's servant. He led in war (Page 269—1 Sam. 8:20) and made judicial decisions (Page 308—2 Sam. 15:2); but he could not make law, since he himself was under the law (Page 185—Deut. 17:19). His relationship was so close to the Lord that he was adopted by the Lord (Page 301—2 Sam. 7:14; Page 529—Ps. 2:7).
b. The *priest* taught the Lord's laws and officiated at the offering of the sacrifices (Page 96—Lev. 1:5; Page 736—Jer. 18:18).
c. The *prophet* was the man of God who spoke for God and gave divine pronouncements for the present (forthtelling) or for the future (foretelling).
d. The *wise man* produced literary works stressing practical wisdom (Page 609—Prov. 1:1), taught discipline of character to the young (Page 626—Prov. 22:17), and gave counsel to the king (Page 310—2 Sam. 16:20). The choice of these men indicates an important biblical principle: God uses people to reach other people, a principle that is also evident in the Great Commission given to Christians (Page 995—Matt. 28:19, 20).
Now turn to Page 541—Ps. 29:2: Worship by Israel.

12 and the plan of all that he had in mind, for the courts of the house of the LORD, and for all the surrounding rooms, for the storehouses of the house of God, and for the storehouses of the dedicated things;

13 also for the divisions of the priests and the Levites and for all the work of the service of the house of the LORD and for all the utensils of service in the house of the LORD;

14 for the golden *utensils*, the weight of gold for all utensils for every kind of service; for the silver utensils, the weight *of silver* for all utensils for every kind of service;

15 and the weight *of gold* for the ᴿgolden lampstands and their golden lamps, with the weight of each lampstand and its lamps; and *the weight of silver* for the silver lampstands, with the weight of each lampstand and its lamps according to the use of each lampstand;   Ex. 25:31-39

16 and the gold by weight for the tables of showbread, for each table; and silver for the silver tables;

17 and the forks, the basins, and the pitchers of pure gold; and for the golden bowls with the weight for each bowl; and for the silver bowls with the weight for each bowl;

18 and for ᴿthe altar of incense refined gold by weight; and gold for the model of the chariot, *even* the cherubim, that spread out *their wings*, and covered the ark of the covenant of the LORD.   Ex. 30:1-10

19 "All *this*," said David, "the LORD made me understand in writing by His hand upon me, all the ᵀdetails of this pattern."   *works*

20 Then David said to his son Solomon, "Be strong and courageous, and act; do not fear nor be dismayed, for the LORD God, my God, is with you. ᴿHe will not fail you nor forsake you until all the work for the service of the house of the LORD is finished. Josh. 1:5

21 "Now behold, ᴿthere *are* the divisions of the priests and the Levites for all the service of the house of God, and ᴿevery willing man of any skill will be with you in all the work for all kinds of service. The officials also and all the people will be entirely at your command."   1 Chr. 28:13 • Ex. 35:25-35; 36:1, 2

CHAPTER 29

Provisions of David
for the Temple

THEN King David said to the entire assembly, "My son Solomon, whom alone God has chosen, is still young and inexperienced and the work is great; for the ᵀtemple is not for man, but for the LORD God. *palace*

2 "Now ᴿwith all my ability I have provided for the house of my God the gold for the *things of* gold, and the silver for the *things of* silver, and the bronze for the *things of* bronze, the iron for the *things of* iron, and wood for the *things of* wood, onyx

stones and inlaid *stones,* stones of antimony, and stones of various colors, and all kinds of precious stones, and alabaster in abundance.   1 Chr. 22:3-5

3 "And moreover, in my delight in the house of my God, the treasure I have of gold and silver, I give to the house of my God, over and above all that I have already provided for the holy ¹⁵temple,

4 *namely,* 3,000 talents of gold, of the gold of Ophir, and 7,000 talents of refined silver, to overlay the walls of the buildings;

5 of gold for the *things of* gold, and of silver for the *things of* silver, that is, for all the work ᵀdone by the craftsmen. Who then is willing to consecrate himself this day to the LORD?"   *by the hand of the craftsmen*

Provisions of Israel
for the Temple

6 Then ᴿthe rulers of the fathers' *households,* and the princes of the tribes of Israel, and the commanders of thousands and of hundreds, with the overseers over the king's work, offered willingly;   1 Chr. 27:1; 28:1

7 and for the service for the house of God they gave 5,000 talents and 10,000 ᵈdarics of gold, and 10,000 talents of silver, and 18,000 talents of brass, and 100,000 talents of iron.   Ezra 2:69; Neh. 7:70

8 And ᵀwhoever possessed *precious* stones gave them to the treasury of the house of the LORD, in care of Jehiel the Gershonite.   *those with whom were found*

9 Then the people rejoiced because they had offered so willingly, for they made their offering to the LORD ᴿwith a whole heart, and King David also rejoiced greatly.   2 Cor. 9:7

David's Final Prayer of Thanksgiving

10 So David blessed the LORD in the sight of all the assembly; and David said, "Blessed art Thou, O LORD God of Israel our father, forever and ever.

11 "Thine, O LORD, is the greatness and the power and the glory and the victory and the majesty, indeed everything that is in the heavens and the earth; Thine is the dominion, O LORD, and Thou dost exalt Thyself as head over all.   Matt. 6:13; Rev. 5:13

12 "Both ᴿriches and honor *come* from Thee, and Thou dost rule over all, and ᴿin Thy hand is power and might; and it lies in Thy hand to make great, and to strengthen everyone.   2 Chr. 1:12 • 2 Chr. 20:6

13 "Now therefore, our God, we thank Thee, and praise Thy glorious name.

14 "But who am I and who are my people that we should ᵀbe able to offer as generously as this? For all things come from

¹⁵ Lit., *house*

Thee, and from Thy hand we have given Thee.   *retain strength*

15 "For[R] we are sojourners before Thee, and tenants, as all our fathers were; our days on the earth are like a shadow, and there is no hope.   Lev. 25:23 • Job 14:2, 10-12

16 "O LORD our God, all this abundance that we have provided to build Thee a house for Thy holy name, it is from Thy hand, and all is Thine.

17 "Since I know, O my God, that[R] Thou triest the heart and[R] delightest in uprightness, I, in the integrity of my heart, have willingly offered all these *things;* so now with joy I have seen Thy people, who are present here, make *their* offerings willingly to Thee.   1 Chr. 28:9 • Ps. 15:2

18 "O LORD, the God of Abraham, Isaac, and Israel, our fathers, preserve this forever in the intentions of the heart of Thy people, and direct their heart to Thee;

19 "and[R] give to my son Solomon a perfect heart to keep Thy commandments, Thy testimonies, and Thy statutes, and to do *them* all, and to build the[T] temple, for which I have made provision."   [1 Chr. 28:9]; Ps. 72:1 • *palace*

Coronation of Solomon
1 Kin. 1:38–40; 2:12

20 Then David said to all the assembly, "Now bless the LORD your God." And[R] all the assembly blessed the LORD, the God of their fathers, and bowed low and did homage to the LORD and to the king.   Josh. 22:33

21 And on the next day they[T] made sacrifices to the LORD and offered burnt offerings to the LORD, 1,000 bulls, 1,000 rams *and* 1,000 lambs, with their libations and sacrifices in abundance for all Israel.   *sacrificed*

22 So they ate and drank that day before the LORD with great gladness.

And they made Solomon the son of David king a second time, and they anointed *him* as ruler for the LORD and Zadok as priest.

23 Then Solomon sat on the throne of the LORD as king instead of David his father; and he prospered, and all Israel obeyed him.

24 And all the officials, the mighty men, and also all the sons of King David pledged allegiance to King Solomon.

25 And[R] the LORD highly exalted Solomon in the sight of all Israel, and bestowed on him royal majesty which had not been on any king before him in Israel.   2 Chr. 1:1

Death of King David

26 Now[R] David the son of Jesse reigned over all Israel.   1 Chr. 18:14

27 [R] And the period which he reigned over Israel *was* forty years; he reigned in Hebron seven years and[T] in Jerusalem thirty-three years.   2 Sam. 5:4, 5; 1 Kin. 2:11 • *he reigned in*

28 Then he died in[R] a[T] ripe old age, full of days, riches and honor; and his son Solomon reigned in his place.   Gen. 15:15 • *good*

29 Now the acts of King David, from first to last, are written in the chronicles of[R] Samuel the seer, in the chronicles of[R] Nathan the prophet, and in the chronicles of Gad the seer,   1 Sam. 9:9 • 2 Sam. 7:2-4; 12:1-7

30 with all his reign, his power, and the circumstances which came on him, on Israel, and on all the kingdoms of the lands.

CHRONICLES

THE BOOK OF SECOND CHRONICLES

The Book of Second Chronicles parallels First and Second Kings but virtually ignores the northern kingdom of Israel because of its false worship and refusal to acknowledge the temple in Jerusalem. Chronicles focuses on those kings who pattern their lives and reigns after the life and reign of godly King David. It gives extended treatment to such zealous reformers as Asa, Jehoshaphat, Joash, Hezekiah, and Josiah.

The temple and temple worship, central throughout the book, befit a nation whose worship of God is central to its very survival. The book begins with Solomon's glorious temple and concludes with Cyrus's edict to rebuild the temple more than four hundred years later.

See "The Book of First Chronicles" for more detail on the title.

THE AUTHOR OF SECOND CHRONICLES

For a discussion of the author of First and Second Chronicles, see "The Author of First Chronicles." The sources of First and Second Chronicles include official and prophetic records: (1) The Book of the Kings of Israel and Judah (or Judah and Israel) (1 Chr. 9:1; 2 Chr. 16:11; 20:34; 25:26; 27:7; 28:26; 32:32; 35:27; 36:8), (2) A Commentary on the Book of the Kings (2 Chr. 24:27), (3) Chronicles of Samuel the Seer (1 Chr. 29:29), (4) Chronicles of Nathan the Prophet (1 Chr. 29:29; 2 Chr. 9:29), (5) Chronicles of Gad the Seer (1 Chr. 29:29), (6) The Prophecy of Ahijah the Shilonite (2 Chr. 9:29), (7) The Visions of Iddo the Seer (2 Chr. 9:29; 12:15; 13:22), (8) Records of Shemaiah the Prophet (2 Chr. 12:15), (9) Records of Iddo the Prophet on Genealogies (2 Chr. 12:15), (10) Treatise of the Prophet Iddo (2 Chr. 13:22), (11) The Annals of Jehu the Son of Hanani (2 Chr. 20:34), (12) The Acts of Uzziah by Isaiah the Prophet (2 Chr. 26:22), (13) The Vision of Isaiah the Prophet (2 Chr. 32:32), (14) The Records of the Hozai (2 Chr. 33:19), (15) The Account of the Chronicles of King David (1 Chr. 27:24), (16) The Writing of David and His Son Solomon (2 Chr. 35:4). In addition to these, the author-compiler had access to genealogical lists and documents, such as the message and letters of Sennacherib (2 Chr. 32:10–17).

THE TIME OF SECOND CHRONICLES

See "The Time of First Chronicles" for the background of First and Second Chronicles. Chapters 1—9 cover the forty years from 971 B.C. to 931 B.C., and chapters 10—36 cover the 393 years from 931 B.C. to 538 B.C. Jeremiah's prediction of a seventy-year captivity in Babylon (36:21; Jer. 29:10) is fulfilled in two ways: (1) a political captivity in which Jerusalem is overcome from 605 B.C. to 536 B.C., and (2) a religious captivity involving the destruction of the temple in 586 B.C. and the completion of the new temple in 516 or 515 B.C.

THE CHRIST OF SECOND CHRONICLES

The throne of David has been destroyed, but the line of David remains. Murders, treachery, battles, and captivity all threaten the messianic line; but it remains clear and unbroken from Adam to Zerubbabel. The fulfillment in Christ can be seen in the genealogies of Matthew 1 and Luke 3.

The temple also prefigures Christ. Jesus says, "something greater than the temple is here" (Matt. 12:6). He also likens His body to the temple: "Destroy this temple, and in three days I will raise it up" (John 2:19). In Revelation 21:22 He replaces the temple: "And I saw no temple in it, for the Lord God, the Almighty, and the Lamb, are its temple."

KEYS TO SECOND CHRONICLES

Key Word: Priestly View of Judah—
The Book of Second Chronicles provides topical histories of the end of the united kingdom (Solomon) and the kingdom of Judah. More than historical annals, Chronicles is a divine editorial on the spiritual characteristics of the Davidic dynasty. This is why it focuses on the southern rather than the northern kingdom. Most of the kings fail to realize that apart from the true mission as a covenant nation called to bring others to Yahweh, Judah has no calling, no destiny, and no hope of becoming great on her own. Only what is done in accordance with God's will has any lasting value. Chronicles concentrates on the kings who are concerned with maintaining the proper service of God and the times of spiritual reform. However, growing apostasy inevitably leads to judgment.

The temple in Jerusalem is the major unify-

ing theme of First and Second Chronicles. Much of the material found in Second Samuel to Second Kings is omitted from Chronicles because it does not develop this theme. In First Chronicles 11—29, the central message is David's preparation for the construction and service of the temple. Most of Second Chronicles 1—9 is devoted to the building and consecration of the temple. Chapters 10—36 omit the kings of Israel in the north because they have no ties with the temple. Prominence is given to the reigns of Judah's temple restorers (Asa, Jehoshaphat, Joash, Hezekiah, and Josiah). The temple symbolizes God's presence among His people and reminds them of their high calling. It provides the spiritual link between their past and future. Thus, Ezra wrote this book to encourage the people to accept the new temple raised on the site of the old and to remind them of their true calling and God's faithfulness despite their low circumstances. The Davidic line, temple, and priesthood are still theirs.

Key Verses: Second Chronicles 7:14; 16:9— "And My people who are called by My name humble themselves and pray, and seek My face and turn from their wicked ways, then I will hear from heaven, will forgive their sin, and will heal their land" (7:14).

"For the eyes of the LORD move to and fro throughout the earth that He may strongly support those whose heart is completely His. You have acted foolishly in this. Indeed, from now on you will surely have wars" (16:9).

*Key Chapter: Second Chronicles 34—*Second Chronicles records the reforms and revivals under such kings as Asa, Jehoshaphat, Joash, Hezekiah, and Josiah. Chapter 34 traces the dramatic revival that takes place under Josiah when the "book of the law" is found, read, and obeyed.

SURVEY OF SECOND CHRONICLES

This book repeatedly teaches that whenever God's people forsake Him, He withdraws His blessings, but trust in and obedience to the Lord bring victory. Since everything in Chronicles is related to the temple, it is not surprising that this concludes with Cyrus's edict to rebuild it. Solomon's glory is seen in chapters 1—9, and Judah's decline and deportation in chapters 10—36.

Solomon's Reign (1—9): The reign of Solomon brings in Israel's golden age of peace, prosperity, and temple worship. The kingdom is united and its boundaries extend to their greatest point. Solomon's wealth, wisdom, palace, and temple become legendary. His mighty spiritual, political, and architectural feats raise Israel to her zenith. However, it is in keeping with the purpose of Chronicles that six of these nine chapters concern the construction and dedication of the temple.

The Reign of Judah's Kings (10—36): Unfortunately, Israel's glory is short-lived. Soon after Solomon's death the nation is divided, and both kingdoms begin a downward spiral that can only be delayed by the religious reforms. The nation generally forsakes the temple and the worship of Yahweh, and is soon torn by warfare and unrest. The reformation efforts on the part of some of Judah's kings are valiant, but never last beyond one generation. Nevertheless, about seventy percent of chapters 10—36 deals with the eight good kings, leaving only thirty percent to cover the twelve evil rulers. Each king is seen with respect to his relationship to the temple as the center of worship and spiritual strength. When the king serves Yahweh, Judah is blessed with political and economic prosperity.

Here is a brief survey of Judah's twenty

FOCUS	REIGN OF SOLOMON			REIGNS OF THE KINGS OF JUDAH		
REFERENCE	1:1————2:1————————8:1————			———10:1————14:1————————		36:1——36:23
DIVISION	INAUGURATION OF SOLOMON	COMPLETION OF THE TEMPLE	THE GLORY OF SOLOMON'S REIGN	THE DIVISION OF THE KINGDOM	THE REFORMS UNDER ASA, JEHOSHAPHAT, JOASH, HEZEKIAH, AND JOSIAH	THE FALL OF JUDAH
TOPIC	THE TEMPLE IS CONSTRUCTED			THE TEMPLE IS DESTROYED		
	SPLENDOR			DISASTER		
LOCATION	JUDAH					
TIME	c. 40 YEARS			c. 393 YEARS		

rulers: (1) *Rehoboam*—Although he is not righteous, he humbles himself before God and averts His wrath (12:12). (2) *Abijah*—He enjoys a short and evil reign, but he conquers Israel because "the sons of Judah . . . trusted in the LORD" (13:18). (3) *Asa*—Although he destroys foreign altars and idols, conquers Ethiopia against great odds through his trust in God, and restores the altar of the Lord, yet he fails to trust God when threatened by Israel. (4) *Jehoshaphat*—He brings in a great revival; "he took great pride in the ways of the LORD" (17:6). Jehoshaphat overthrows idols, teaches God's Word to the people, and trusts in God before battle. (5) *Jehoram*—A wicked king, he follows the ways of Ahab and marries his daughter. He leads Judah into idolatry and when he dies in pain, departs "with no one's regret" (21:20). (6 and 7) *Ahaziah* and *Athaliah*—Ahaziah is as wicked as his father, as is his mother Athaliah. Both are murdered. (8) *Joash*—Although he repairs the temple and restores the worship of God, when Jehoiada the priest dies, Joash allows the people to abandon the temple and return to idolatry. (9) *Amaziah*—Mixed in his relationship to God, he later forsakes the Lord for the gods of Edom. He is defeated by Israel and later murdered. (10) *Uzziah*—He begins well with the Lord and is blessed with military victories. However, when he becomes strong, he proudly and presumptuously plays the role of a priest by offering incense in the temple and therefore is struck with leprosy. (11) *Jotham*—Because

he rebuilds the gate of the temple and reveres God, the Lord blesses him with prosperity and victory. (12) *Ahaz*—A wicked king and an idolater, he is oppressed by his enemies and forced to give tribute to the Assyrians from the temple treasures. (13) *Hezekiah*—He repairs and reopens the temple and puts away the altars and idols set up by his father, Ahaz. Judah is spared destruction by Assyria because of his righteousness. His reforms are given only a few verses in Kings but three chapters in Chronicles. (14 and 15) *Manasseh* and *Amon*—Manasseh is Judah's most wicked king. He sets up idols and altars all over the land. However, he repents when he is carried away by Assyria. God brings him back to Judah and he makes a halfway reform, but it comes too late. Amon follows in his father's wickedness. Both kings are murdered. (16) *Josiah*—A leader in reforms and spiritual revival, he centers worship around the temple, finds the law and obeys it, and reinstitutes the Passover. (17, 18, and 19) *Jehoahaz, Jehoiakim, Jehoiachin*—Their relentless evil finally brings the downfall of Judah. The temple is ravaged in each of their reigns. (20) *Zedekiah*—Judah's last king is also wicked. Jerusalem and the temple are destroyed, and the captivity begins. Second Chronicles nevertheless ends on a note of hope at the end of the captivity, when Cyrus issues the decree for the restoration of Judah: "Whoever there is among you of all His people, may the LORD his God be with him, and let him go up!" (36:23).

OUTLINE OF SECOND CHRONICLES

Part One: The Reign of Solomon (1:1—9:31)

Part Two: The Reigns of the Kings of Judah (10:1—36:23)

CHAPTER 1

The Worship of Solomon—1 Kin. 3:4

NOW [R]Solomon the son of David established himself securely over his kingdom, and the LORD his God *was* with him and exalted him greatly.   1 Kin. 2:12, 46

2 And Solomon spoke to all Israel, to the commanders of thousands and of hundreds and to the judges and to every leader in all Israel, the heads of the fathers' *households.*

3 Then Solomon, and all the assembly with him, went to the [R]high place which was at Gibeon; for God's tent of meeting was there, which Moses the servant of the LORD had made in the wilderness.   1 Kin. 3:4

4 However, David had brought up [R]the ark of God from Kiriath-jearim to the place he had prepared for it; for he had pitched a tent for it in Jerusalem.   1 Chr. 15:25-28

5 Now [R]the bronze altar, which Bezalel the son of Uri, the son of Hur, had made, [R]was there before the tabernacle of the LORD, and Solomon and the assembly sought it out.   Ex. 31:9; 38:1-7 • *he put*

6 And Solomon went up there before the LORD to the bronze altar which *was* at the tent of meeting, and [R]offered a thousand burnt offerings on it.   1 Kin. 3:4

The Petition for Wisdom—1 Kin. 3:5-9

7 [R]In that night God appeared to Solomon and said to him, "Ask what I shall give you."   1 Kin. 3:5-14

8 And Solomon said to God, "Thou hast dealt with my father David with great lovingkindness, and^Rhast made me king in his place.   1 Chr. 28:5

9"Now, O LORD God,^RThy^Tpromise to my father David is fulfilled; for Thou hast made me king over a people as numerous as the dust of the earth.   2 Sam. 7:12-16 • word

10"Give^Rme now wisdom and knowledge, ^Tthat I may go out and come in before this people; for who can rule this great people of Thine?"   1 Kin. 3:9 • Num. 27:17; 2 Sam. 5:2

The Provision of Wisdom—1 Kin. 3:10-14

11 ^RAnd God said to Solomon, "Because ^Tyou had this in mind, and did not ask for riches, wealth, or honor, or the life of those who hate you, nor have you even asked for long life, but you have asked for yourself wisdom and knowledge, that you may rule My people, over whom I have made you king,   1 Kin. 3:11 • this was in your heart

12 wisdom and knowledge have been granted to you. And I will give you riches and wealth and honor, such as none of the kings who were before you has possessed, nor those who will come after you."

The Wealth of Solomon
1 Kin. 10:26-29; 2 Chr. 9:25-28

13 ^RSo Solomon went ^Tfrom the high place which was at Gibeon, from the tent of meeting, to Jerusalem, and he reigned over Israel.   2 Chr. 1:3 • to

14 ^RAnd Solomon amassed chariots and horsemen. ^RHe had 1,400 chariots, and 12,000 horsemen, and he stationed them in the chariot cities and with the king at Jerusalem.   1 Kin. 10:26-29 • 1 Kin. 4:26

15 And^Rthe king made silver and gold as plentiful in Jerusalem as stones, and he made cedars as plentiful as sycamores in the^Tlowland.   1 Kin. 10:27 • shephelah

16 And Solomon's horses were imported from Egypt and from Kue; the king's traders procured them from Kue for a price.

17 And they imported chariots from Egypt for 600 shekels of silver apiece, and horses for 150 apiece, and by the same means they exported them to all the kings of the Hittites and the kings of Aram.

CHAPTER 2

Selection of the Temple Builders
1 Kin. 5:15, 16

NOW Solomon ^Tdecided to build a house for the name of the LORD, and a royal palace for himself.   said

2 So ^RSolomon ^Tassigned 70,000 men to carry loads, and 80,000 men to quarry stone in the mountains, and 3,600 to supervise them.   1 Kin. 5:15, 16 • numbered

Selection of the Temple Materials

3 Then Solomon sent word to^THuram the king of Tyre, saying, "As you dealt with David my father, and sent him cedars to build him a house to dwell in, so do for me. Hiram

4"Behold, I am about to build a house for the name of the LORD my God, dedicating it to Him, ^Rto burn fragrant incense before Him, and to set out^Rthe showbread continually, and to offer burnt offerings morning and evening, on sabbaths and on new moons and on the appointed feasts of the LORD our God, this being required forever in Israel.   Ex. 30:7 • Ex. 25:30

5"And the house which I am about to build will be great; for ^Rgreater is our God than all the gods.   Ex. 15:11; 1 Chr. 16:25

6"But ^Rwho is able to build a house for Him, for the heavens and the highest heavens cannot contain Him? So who am I, that I should build a house for Him, except to ¹burn incense before Him?   1 Kin. 8:27

7"And now ^Rsend me a skilled man to work in gold, silver, brass and iron, and in purple, crimson and violet fabrics, and who knows how to make engravings, to work with the skilled men^Twhom I have in Judah and Jerusalem, whom David my father provided.   Ex. 31:3-5 • who are with me

8"Send^Rme also cedar, cypress and algum timber from Lebanon, for I know that your servants know how to cut timber of Lebanon; and indeed,^Rmy servants will work with your servants,   1 Kin. 5:6 • 2 Chr. 9:10, 11

9 to prepare timber in abundance for me, for the house which I am about to build will be great and wonderful.

10"Now behold, ^RI will give to your servants, the woodsmen who cut the timber, 20,000 ²kors of crushed wheat, and 20,000 kors of barley, and^T20,000 baths of wine, and 20,000 baths of oil."1 Kin. 5:11 • 120,000 gal.

11 Then Huram, king of Tyre, ^Tanswered in a letter sent to Solomon: "Because^Rthe LORD loves His people, He has made you king over them."   said . . . and he sent • 1 Kin. 10:9

12 Then Huram continued, "Blessed be the LORD, the God of Israel, who has made heaven and earth, who has given King David a wise son, endowed with discretion and understanding, who will build a house for the LORD and a royal palace for himself.

13"And now I am sending a skilled man, endowed with understanding, Huram-abi,

14 the son of a¹Danite woman and a Tyrian father, who knows how to work in gold,

---

¹ Lit., offer up in smoke
² I.e., A kor equals approx. 10 bushels

silver, bronze, iron, stone and wood, *and* in purple, violet, linen and crimson fabrics, and *who knows how* to make all kinds of engravings and to execute any design which may be assigned to him, *to work* with your skilled men, and with those of my lord David your father. *a woman of the daughters of Dan*

15 "Now then, let my lord send to his servants wheat and barley, oil and wine, of ^Rwhich he has spoken. 2 Chr. 2:10

16 "And ^Rwe will cut whatever timber you need from Lebanon, and bring it to you on rafts by sea to Joppa, so that you may carry it up to Jerusalem." 1 Kin. 5:8, 9

17 And Solomon numbered all the aliens who *were* in the land of Israel, following the ^Tcensus which his father David had taken; and 153,600 were found. *numbering*

18 ^RAnd he appointed 70,000 of them to carry loads, and 80,000 to quarry *stones* in the mountains, and 3,600 supervisors to make the people work. 2 Chr. 2:2

CHAPTER 3

Construction of the Temple
1 Kin. 6:1—7:51

THEN Solomon began to build the house of the LORD in Jerusalem on Mount Moriah, where *the LORD* had appeared to his father David, at the place that David had prepared, on the threshing floor of Ornan the Jebusite.

2 And he began to build on the second *day* in the second month ^Tof the fourth year of his reign. *in*

3 Now these are the foundations which Solomon laid for building the house of God. The length in ³cubits, according to the old standard *was* ^Tsixty cubits, and the width twenty cubits. 90 ft.

4 And the porch which was in front of the house was as long as the width of the house, twenty cubits, and the height 120; and inside he overlaid it with pure gold.

5 And he overlaid the ^Tmain room with cypress wood and overlaid it with fine gold, and ^Tornamented it with palm trees and chains. *great house • put on it palm trees*

6 Further, he ^Tadorned the house with precious stones; and the gold was gold from ^AParvaim. *overlaid . . . for beauty • country of gold*

7 ^RHe also overlaid the house with gold— the beams, the thresholds, and its walls, and its doors; and he ^Rcarved cherubim on the walls. 1 Kin. 6:20-22 • 1 Kin. 6:29-35

8 Now he made the ^Troom of the holy of holies: its length, across the width of the house, *was* ^Ttwenty cubits, and its width *was* twenty cubits; and he overlaid it with fine gold, *amounting* to 600 talents. *house • 30 ft.*

9 And the weight of the nails *was* ^Tfifty shekels of gold. He also overlaid ^Rthe upper rooms with gold. 18.2 oz. • 1 Chr. 28:11

10 Then he made two sculptured cherubim in the room of the holy of holies and overlaid them with gold.

11 And the wingspan of the cherubim *was* ^Ttwenty cubits; the wing of one, of ^Tfive cubits, touched the wall of the house, and *its* other wing, of five cubits, touched the wall of the other cherub. 30 ft. • 7.5 ft.

12 And the wing of the other cherub, of five cubits, touched the wall of the house; and *its* other wing of five cubits, was attached to the wing of the ^Tfirst cherub. *other*

13 The wings of these cherubim extended ^Ttwenty cubits, and they stood on their feet ^Tfacing the *main* room. 30 ft. • *and their faces to*

14 ^RAnd he made the veil of violet, purple, crimson and fine linen, and he worked cherubim on it. Ex. 26:31

15 He also made two pillars for the front of the house, thirty-five cubits high, and the capital on the top of each *was* five cubits.

16 And he made chains in the inner sanctuary, and placed *them* on the tops of the pillars; and he made one hundred pomegranates and placed *them* on the chains.

17 ^RAnd he erected the pillars in front of the temple, one on the right and the other on the left, and named the one on the right Jachin and the one on the left Boaz. 1 Kin. 7:21

CHAPTER 4

THEN ^Rhe made a bronze altar, twenty cubits in length and twenty cubits in width and ten cubits in height. Ex. 27:1; 2 Kin. 16:14

2 ^RAlso he made the cast *metal* sea, ^Tten cubits from brim to brim, circular in form, and its height *was* five cubits and its circumference thirty cubits. 1 Kin. 7:23-26 • 15 ft.

3 Now figures like oxen *were* under it *and* all around it, ^Tten cubits, entirely encircling the sea. The oxen *were* in two rows, cast ^Tin one piece. 15 ft. • *in its casting*

4 It stood on twelve oxen, three facing the north, three facing west, three facing south, and three facing east; and the sea *was set* on top of them, and all their hindquarters turned inwards.

5 And it was a handbreadth thick, and its brim was made like the brim of a cup, *like* a lily blossom; it could hold 3,000 baths.

6 ^RHe also made ten basins in which to wash, and he set five on the right side and five on the left, ^Tto rinse things for the burnt offering; but the sea *was* for the priests to wash in. Ex. 30:17-21 • *in which to*

7 Then ^Rhe made the ten golden lampstands in the way prescribed for them, and he set them in the temple, five on the right side and five on the left. Ex. 25:31; 1 Kin. 7:49

8 He also made ^Rten tables and placed them in the temple, five on the right side and five on the left. And he made one hundred golden bowls. 1 Kin. 7:48

9 Then he made the court of the priests

³ I.e., One cubit equals approx. 18 in.

and the great court and doors for the court, and overlaid their doors with bronze.

10 And he set the sea on the right side of the house toward the southeast.   shoulder

11 [R]Huram also made the pails, the shovels, and the bowls. So Huram finished doing the work which he performed for King Solomon in the house of God: 1 Kin. 7:40-51

12 the two pillars, the bowls and the two capitals on top of the pillars, and the two networks to cover the two bowls of the capitals which were on top of the pillars,

13 and the four hundred pomegranates for the two networks, two rows of pomegranates for each network to cover the two bowls of the capitals which were on the pillars.   1 Kin. 7:20

14 [R]He also made the stands and he made the basins on the stands,   1 Kin. 7:27-43

15 and the one sea with the twelve oxen under it.

16 And the pails, the shovels, the forks, and all its utensils, [R]Huram-abi made of polished bronze for King Solomon for the house of the LORD.   1 Kin. 7:14; 2 Chr. 2:13

17 On the plain of the Jordan the king cast them, in the clay ground between Succoth and Zeredah.

18 [R]Thus Solomon made all these utensils in great quantities, for the weight of the bronze could not be found out.   1 Kin. 7:47

19 Solomon also made all the things that were in the house of God: even the golden altar, the tables with the bread of the Presence on them,   2 Chr. 4:8

20 the lampstands with their lamps of pure gold, to burn in front of the inner sanctuary in the way prescribed;   Ex. 25:31-37

21 the flowers, the lamps, and the tongs of gold, of purest gold;

22 and the snuffers, the bowls, the spoons, and the firepans of pure gold; and the entrance of the house, its inner doors for the holy of holies, and the doors of the house, that is, of the nave, of gold.

CHAPTER 5

THUS[R] all the work that Solomon performed for the house of the LORD was finished. And Solomon brought in the things that David his father had dedicated, even the silver and the gold and all the utensils, and put them in the treasuries of the house of God.   1 Kin. 7:51 • dedicated things of David

The Installation of the Ark
1 Kin. 8:1-9

2 Then Solomon assembled to Jerusalem the elders of Israel and all the heads of the tribes, the leaders of the fathers' households of the sons of Israel, [R]to bring up the ark of the covenant of the LORD out of the city of David, which is Zion. 1 Chr. 15:25-28; 2 Chr. 1:4

3 And all the men of Israel assembled themselves to the king at the feast, that is in the seventh month.   1 Kin. 8:2

4 Then all the elders of Israel came, and the Levites took up the ark.   2 Chr. 5:7

5 And they brought up the ark and the tent of meeting and all the holy utensils which were in the tent; the Levitical priests brought them up.

6 And King Solomon and all the congregation of Israel who were assembled with him before the ark were sacrificing so many sheep and oxen, that they could not be counted or numbered.

7 Then the priests brought the ark of the covenant of the LORD to its place, into the inner sanctuary of the house, to the holy of holies, under the wings of the cherubim.

8 For the cherubim spread their wings over the place of the ark, so that the cherubim made a covering over the ark and its poles.   poles above

9 And the poles were so long that the ends of the poles of the ark could be seen in front of the inner sanctuary, but they could not be seen outside; and they are there to this day.   1 Kin. 8:8, 9 • it is

10 [R]There was nothing in the ark except the two tablets which Moses put there at Horeb, where the LORD made a covenant with the sons of Israel, when they came out of Egypt.   Deut. 10:2-5; Heb. 9:4

11 And when the priests came forth from the holy place (for all the priests who were present had sanctified themselves, without regard to divisions),   1 Chr. 24:1-5

12 and all the Levitical singers, [R]Asaph, Heman, Jeduthun, and their sons and kinsmen, clothed in fine linen, with cymbals, harps, and lyres, standing east of the altar, and with them one hundred and twenty priests blowing trumpets   1 Chr. 25:1-4

The Glory of the Lord
Fills the Temple—1 Kin. 8:10, 11

13 in unison when the trumpeters and the singers were to make themselves heard with one voice to praise and to glorify the LORD, and when they lifted up their voice accompanied by trumpets and cymbals and instruments of music, and when they praised the LORD saying, "He indeed is good for His lovingkindness is everlasting," then the house, the house of the LORD, was filled with a cloud,   1 Chr. 16:42 • 1 Chr. 16:34

14 so that the priests could not stand to minister because of the cloud, for the glory of the LORD filled the house of God.

CHAPTER 6

The Sermon of Solomon
1 Kin. 8:12-21

THEN[R] Solomon said,   1 Kin. 8:12-50
"The LORD has said that He would dwell in the thick cloud.

2 "I have built Thee a lofty house,
And a place for Thy dwelling forever."

3 Then the king faced about and blessed all the assembly of Israel, while all the assembly of Israel was standing.

4 And he said, "Blessed be the LORD, the God of Israel, who spoke with His mouth to my father David and has fulfilled *it* with His hands, saying,

5 'Since the day that I brought My people from the land of Egypt, I did not choose a city out of all the tribes of Israel *in which* to build a house that My name might be there, nor did I choose any man for a leader over My people Israel;

6 but [R]I have chosen Jerusalem that My name might be there, and I have chosen David to be over My people Israel.'   2 Chr. 12:13

7 "Now [T]it was [T]in the heart of my father David to build a house for the name of the LORD, the God of Israel.   1 Kin. 5:3 • *with*

8 "But the LORD said to my father David, 'Because it was [T]in your heart to build a house for My name, you did well that it was [T]in your heart.   *with*

9 'Nevertheless you shall not build the house, but your son who shall be born to you, he shall build the house for My name.'

10 "Now the LORD has fulfilled His word which He spoke; for I have risen in the place of my father David and sit on the throne of Israel, as the LORD [T]promised, and have built the house for the name of the LORD, the God of Israel.   *spoke*

11 "And there I have set the ark, [R]in which is the covenant of the LORD, which He made with the sons of Israel."   2 Chr. 5:7, 10

The Prayer of Solomon—1 Kin. 8:22–53

12 Then he stood before the altar of the LORD in the presence of all the assembly of Israel and spread out his hands.

13 [R]Now Solomon had made a bronze platform, [T]five cubits long, five cubits wide, and three cubits high, and had set it in the midst of the court; and he stood on it, [R]knelt on his knees in the presence of all the assembly of Israel, and spread out his hands toward heaven.   Neh. 8:4 • 7.5 ft. • 1 Kin. 8:54

14 And he said, "O LORD, the God of Israel, [R]there is no god like Thee in heaven or on earth, keeping covenant and *showing* lovingkindness to Thy servants who walk before Thee with all their heart;   [Ex. 15:11]

15 [R]who has kept with Thy servant David, my father, that which Thou hast [T]promised him; indeed, Thou hast spoken with Thy mouth, and hast fulfilled it with Thy hand, as it is this day.   1 Chr. 22:9, 10 • *spoken to*

16 "Now therefore, O LORD, the God of Israel, keep with Thy servant David, my father, that which Thou hast [T]promised him, saying, 'You shall not lack a man to sit on the throne of Israel, if only your sons take heed to their way, to walk in My law as you have walked before Me.'   *spoken to*

17 "Now therefore, O LORD, the God of Israel, let Thy word be confirmed which Thou hast spoken to Thy servant David.

18 "But will God indeed dwell with mankind on the earth? Behold, heaven and the highest heaven cannot contain Thee; how much less this house which I have built.

19 "Yet have regard to the prayer of Thy servant and to his supplication, O LORD my God, to listen to the cry and to the prayer which Thy servant prays before Thee;

20 that Thine [R]eyes may be open toward this house day and night, toward [R]the place of which Thou hast said that *Thou wouldst* put Thy name there, to listen to the prayer which Thy servant shall pray toward this place.   Ps. 33:18; 34:15 • Deut. 12:11

21 "And listen to the supplications of Thy servant and of Thy people Israel, when they pray toward this place; hear Thou from Thy dwelling place, from heaven; [R]hear Thou and forgive.   [Is. 43:25; 44:22; Mic. 7:18]

22 "If a man sins against his neighbor, and is made to take an oath, and he comes *and* takes an oath before Thine altar in this house,

23 then hear Thou from heaven and act and judge Thy servants, [T]punishing the wicked by bringing his way on his own head and justifying the righteous by giving him according to his righteousness.   *returning*

24 "And if Thy people Israel [T]are defeated before an enemy, because they have sinned against Thee, and they return *to Thee* and confess Thy name, and pray and make supplication before Thee in this house,   *smitten*

25 then hear Thou from heaven and forgive the sin of Thy people Israel, and bring them back to the land which Thou hast given to them and to their fathers.

26 "When the heavens are shut up and there is no rain because they have sinned against Thee, and they pray toward this place and confess Thy name, and turn from their sin when Thou dost afflict them;

27 then hear Thou in heaven and forgive the sin of Thy servants and Thy people Israel, indeed, [R]teach them the good way in which they should walk. And send rain on Thy land, which Thou hast given to Thy people for an inheritance.   Ps. 94:12

28 "If there is [R]famine in the land, if there is pestilence, if there is blight or mildew, if there is locust or grasshopper, if their enemies besiege them in the land of their [T]cities, whatever plague or whatever sickness *there is*,   2 Chr. 20:9 • *gates*

29 whatever prayer or supplication is made by any man or by all Thy people Israel, [T]each knowing his own affliction and his own pain, and spreading his hands toward this house,   *whoever shall know*

30 then hear Thou from heaven Thy dwelling place, and forgive, and render to each according to all his ways, whose heart Thou knowest for Thou alone dost know the hearts of the sons of men,   [1 Sam. 16:7]

31 that they may [4]fear Thee, to walk in Thy ways as long as they live in the land which Thou hast given to our fathers.

32 "Also concerning the foreigner who is not from Thy people Israel, when he comes from a far country for Thy great name's sake and Thy mighty hand and Thine outstretched arm, when they come and pray toward this house,   Is. 56:3-8

33 then hear Thou from heaven, from Thy dwelling place, and do according to all for which the foreigner calls to Thee, in order that all the peoples of the earth may know Thy name, and [4]fear Thee, as do Thy people Israel, and that they may know that this house which I have built is called by Thy name.   *Thy name is called upon this house*

34 "When Thy people go out to battle against their enemies, by whatever way Thou shalt send them, and they pray to Thee toward this city which Thou hast chosen, and the house which I have built for Thy name,

35 then hear Thou from heaven their prayer and their supplication, and maintain their cause.

36 "When they sin against Thee (for there is no man who does not sin) and Thou art angry with them and dost deliver them to an enemy, so that they take them away captive to a land far off or near,   Job 15:14; James 3:2

37 if they take thought in the land where they are taken captive, and repent and make supplication to Thee in the land of their captivity, saying, 'We have sinned, we have committed iniquity, and have acted wickedly';   *return to their heart*

38 if they return to Thee with all their heart and with all their soul in the land of their captivity, where they have been taken captive, and pray toward their land which Thou hast given to their fathers, and the city

which Thou hast chosen, and toward the house which I have built for Thy name,

39 then hear from heaven, from Thy dwelling place, their prayer and supplications, and maintain their cause, and forgive Thy people who have sinned against Thee.

40 "Now, O my God, I pray Thee, let Thine eyes be open, and Thine ears attentive to the prayer *offered* in this place.   2 Chr. 7:15

41 "Now therefore arise, O LORD God, to Thy resting place, Thou and the ark of Thy might; let Thy priests, O LORD God, be clothed with salvation, and let Thy godly ones rejoice in what is good.   Ps. 132:8, 9

42 "O LORD God, do not turn away the face of Thine anointed; remember *Thy* lovingkindness to Thy servant David."   Ps. 89:24, 28

CHAPTER 7

The Fire of the Lord Consumes the Sacrifices

Now when Solomon had finished praying, fire came down from heaven and consumed the burnt offering and the sacrifices; and the glory of the LORD filled the house.

2 And the priests could not enter into the house of the LORD, because the glory of the LORD filled the LORD's house.   2 Chr. 5:14

3 And all the sons of Israel, seeing the fire come down and the glory of the LORD upon the house, bowed down on the pavement with their faces to the ground, and they worshiped and gave praise to the LORD, *saying,* "Truly He is good, truly His lovingkindness is everlasting."   2 Chr. 5:13; 20:21

The Nation Offers Sacrifices
1 Kin. 8:62–64

4 Then the king and all the people offered sacrifice before the LORD.   1 Kin. 8:62, 63

[4] Or, *reverence*

5 And King Solomon offered a sacrifice of 22,000 oxen, and 120,000 sheep. Thus the king and all the people dedicated the house of God.

6 And the priests stood at their posts and the Levites, with the instruments of music to the LORD, which King David had made for giving praise to the LORD—"for His lovingkindness is everlasting"—whenever [T]he gave praise by their [T]means, while the priests on the other side blew trumpets; and all Israel was standing.   *David • hand*

7 Then Solomon consecrated the middle of the court that *was* before the house of the LORD, for there he offered the burnt offerings and the fat of the peace offerings, because the bronze altar which Solomon had made was not able to contain the burnt offering, the grain offering, and the fat.

The Nation Celebrates
the Feasts of Tabernacles
1 Kin. 8:65—9:1

8 So Solomon observed the feast at that time for seven days, and all Israel with him, a very great assembly, *who came* from the entrance of Hamath to the brook of Egypt.

9 And on the eighth day they held [R]a solemn assembly, for the dedication of the altar they observed seven days, and the feast seven days.   Lev. 23:36

10 Then on the twenty-third day of the seventh month he sent the people to their tents, rejoicing and happy of heart because of the goodness that the LORD had shown to David and to Solomon and to His people Israel.

11 Thus Solomon finished the house of the LORD and the king's palace, and successfully completed all that [T]he had planned on doing in the house of the LORD and in his palace.   *came upon the heart of Solomon to do*

The Lord Confirms the Covenant
1 Kin. 9:2-9

12 Then the LORD appeared to Solomon at night and said to him, "I have heard your prayer, and [R]have chosen this place for Myself as a house of sacrifice.   Deut. 12:5, 11

13"If [R]I shut up the heavens so that there is no rain, or if I command the locust to devour the land, or if I send pestilence among My people,   2 Chr. 6:26-28

14 and My people who are called by My name humble themselves and pray, and seek My face and turn from their wicked ways, then I will hear from heaven, will forgive their sin, and will heal their land.

15"Now [R]My eyes shall be open and My ears attentive to the [T]prayer *offered* in this place.   2 Chr. 6:20, 40 • *prayer of this place*

16"For [R]now I have chosen and consecrated this house that My name may be there forever, and My eyes and My heart will be there perpetually.   2 Chr. 7:12

17"And as for you, if you walk before Me as your father David walked even to do according to all that I have commanded you and will keep My statutes and My ordinances,

18 then I will establish your royal throne as I covenanted with your father David, saying, 'You [T]shall not lack a man *to be* ruler in Israel.'   *There shall not be cut off to you a man*

19"But [R]if you turn away and forsake My statutes and My commandments which I have set before you and shall go and serve other gods and worship them,   Lev. 26:14, 33

20 then I will uproot you from My land which I have given you, and this house which I have consecrated for My name I will cast out of My sight, and I will make it a proverb and a byword among all peoples.

21"As for this house, which was exalted, everyone who passes by it will be astonished and say, 'Why [R]has the LORD done thus to this land and to this house?'   Deut. 29:24f.

22"And they will say, 'Because they forsook the LORD, the God of their fathers, who brought them from the land of Egypt, and they adopted other gods and worshiped them and served them, therefore He has brought all this adversity on them.' "

CHAPTER 8

Enlargement of Solomon's Territory
1 Kin. 9:10-19

NOW it came about at the end of the twenty years in which Solomon had built the house of the LORD and his own house

2 that he built the cities which Huram had given to [T]him, and settled the sons of Israel there.   *Solomon*

3 Then Solomon went to Hamath-zobah and captured it.

4 And he built Tadmor in the wilderness and all the storage cities which he had built in Hamath.

5 He also built upper [R]Beth-horon and lower Beth-horon, [R]fortified cities *with* walls, gates, and bars;   1 Chr. 7:24 • 2 Chr. 14:7

6 and Baalath and all the storage cities that Solomon had, and all the cities for [T]his chariots and cities for [T]his horsemen, and all that it pleased Solomon to build in Jerusalem, in Lebanon, and in all the land [T]under his rule.   *the • of*

Subjugation of the Enemies
of Solomon—1 Kin. 9:20-23

7 [R]All of the people who were left of the Hittites, the Amorites, the Perizzites, the Hivites, and the Jebusites, who were not of Israel,   Gen. 15:18-21; 1 Kin. 9:20

8 namely, from their descendants who were left after them in the land whom the sons of Israel had not destroyed, them Solomon raised as forced laborers to this day.

9 But Solomon did not make slaves for his work from the sons of Israel; they were men of war, his chief captains, and com-

manders of his chariots and his horsemen.

10 And these were the chief [A]officers of King Solomon, two hundred and fifty who ruled over the people.   *deputies*

Religious Practices of Solomon
1 Kin. 9:24, 25

11 [R]Then Solomon brought Pharaoh's daughter up from the city of David to the house which he had built for her; for he said, "My wife shall not dwell in the house of David king of Israel, because [T]the places are holy where the ark of the LORD has entered."   1 Kin. 3:1; 7:8 • *they are*

12 Then Solomon offered burnt offerings to the LORD on [R]the altar of the LORD which he had built before the porch;   2 Chr. 4:1

13 and [R]did *so* according to the daily rule, offering *them* up according to the commandment of Moses, for the sabbaths, the new moons, and the three annual feasts—the Feast of Unleavened Bread, the Feast of Weeks, and the Feast of Booths.   Ex. 29:38-42

14 Now according to the ordinance of his father David, he appointed [R]the divisions of the priests for their service, and [R]the Levites for their duties of praise and ministering before the priests according to the daily rule, and the gatekeepers by their divisions at every gate; for David the man of God had so commanded.   1 Chr. 24:1 • 1 Chr. 25:1

15 And they did not depart from the commandment of the king to the priests and Levites in any manner or concerning the storehouses.

16 Thus all the work of Solomon was carried out from the day of the foundation of the house of the LORD, and until it was finished. So the house of the LORD was completed.

Economic Operations of Solomon
1 Kin. 9:26-28

17 Then Solomon went to Ezion-geber and to [R]Eloth on the seashore in the land of Edom.   1 Kin. 9:26; 2 Kin. 14:22

18 And Huram by his servants sent him ships and servants who knew the sea; and they went with Solomon's servants to Ophir, and [R]took from there four hundred and fifty talents of gold, and brought them to King Solomon.   2 Chr. 9:10, 13

CHAPTER 9
The Queen of Sheba Visits
1 Kin. 10:1-13

N[R]OW when the queen of Sheba heard of the fame of Solomon, she came to Jerusalem to test Solomon with difficult questions. She had a very large retinue, with camels carrying spices, and a large amount of gold and precious stones; and when she came to Solomon, she spoke with him about all that was on her heart.   1 Kin. 10:1-13; [Matt. 12:42]

2 And Solomon answered all her questions; nothing was hidden from Solomon which he did not [T]explain to her.   *tell*

3 And when the queen of Sheba had seen the wisdom of Solomon, the house which he had built,

4 the food at his table, the seating of his servants, the attendance of his ministers and their attire, his cupbearers and their attire, and [A]his stairway by which he went up to the house of the LORD, she was breathless.   *his burnt offering which he offered*

5 Then she said to the king, "It was a true report which I heard in my own land about your words and your wisdom.

6 "Nevertheless I did not believe their reports until I came and my eyes had seen it. And behold, the half of the greatness of your wisdom was not told me. You surpass the report that I heard.

7 "How [A]blessed are your men, how [A]blessed are these your servants who stand before you continually and hear your wisdom.   *happy*

8 "Blessed be the LORD your God who delighted in you, [R]setting you on His throne as king for the LORD your God; because your God loved Israel establishing them forever, therefore He made you king over them, to do justice and righteousness."   1 Chr. 28:5

9 Then she gave the king one hundred and twenty talents of gold, and a very great *amount of* spices and precious stones; there had never been spice like that which the queen of Sheba gave to King Solomon.

10 And the servants of Huram and the servants of Solomon [R]who brought gold from Ophir, also brought algum trees and precious stones.   1 Kin. 10:11; 2 Chr. 8:18

11 And from the algum the king made steps for the house of the LORD and for the king's palace, and lyres and harps for the singers; and none like that was seen before in the land of Judah.

12 And King Solomon gave to the queen of Sheba all her desire which she requested besides *a return for* what she had brought to the king. Then she turned and went to her own land with her servants.

Solomon's Wealth
1 Kin. 10:14-29; 2 Chr. 1:14-17

13 [R]Now the weight of gold which came to Solomon in one year was [T]666 talents of gold,   1 Kin. 10:14-28 • *$3,836,160,000*

14 besides that which the traders and merchants brought; and all the kings of Arabia and the governors of the country brought gold and silver to Solomon.

15 And King Solomon made 200 large shields of beaten gold, using 600 *shekels of* beaten gold on each large shield.

16 And *he made* 300 shields of beaten gold, [T]using three hundred shekels of gold on each shield, and the king put them in the house of the forest of Lebanon.   *he brought up*

17 Moreover, the king made a great

throne of ivory and overlaid it with pure gold.

18 And *there were* six steps to the throne and a footstool in gold attached to the throne, and arms on each side of the seat, and two lions standing beside the arms.

19 And twelve lions were standing there on the six steps on the one side and on the other; nothing like *it* was made for any *other* kingdom.

20 And all King Solomon's drinking vessels *were* of gold, and all the vessels of the house of the forest of Lebanon *were* of pure gold; silver was not considered[T]valuable in the days of Solomon.   *anything*

21 [R]For the king had ships which went to Tarshish with the servants of Huram; once every three years the ships of Tarshish came bringing gold and silver, ivory and apes and peacocks.   2 Chr. 20:36, 37

22 [R]So King Solomon became greater than all the kings of the earth in riches and wisdom.   1 Kin. 3:13; 2 Chr. 1:12

23 And all the kings of the earth were seeking the presence of Solomon, to hear his wisdom which God had put in his heart.

24 And[R]they brought every man his gift, articles of silver and gold, garments, weapons, spices, horses, and mules, so much year by year.   Ps. 72:10

25 Now Solomon had [R]4,000 stalls for horses and chariots and 12,000 horsemen, and he stationed them in the chariot cities and with the king in Jerusalem.   Deut. 17:16

26 [R]And he was the ruler over all the kings from the Euphrates River even to the land of the Philistines, and as far as the border of Egypt.   Gen. 15:18; 1 Kin. 4:21, 24

27 [R]And the king made silver *as common* as stones in Jerusalem, and he made cedars as plentiful as sycamore trees that are in the [T]lowland.   2 Chr. 1:15-17 • Heb., *shephelah*

28 And they were bringing horses for Solomon from Egypt and from all countries.

The Death of Solomon—1 Kin. 11:41–43

29 Now the rest of the acts of Solomon, from first to last, are they not written in the [T]records of Nathan the prophet, and in the prophecy of Ahijah the Shilonite, and in the visions of[T]Iddo the seer concerning Jeroboam the son of Nebat?   *words • Jedo*

30 And[R]Solomon reigned forty years in Jerusalem over all Israel.   1 Kin. 11:42, 43

31 And Solomon slept with his fathers and was buried in[R]the city of his father David; and his son Rehoboam reigned in his place.   1 Kin. 2:10

CHAPTER 10
Division of the Kingdom
1 Kin. 12:1–19

T HEN[R]Rehoboam went to Shechem, for all Israel had come to Shechem to make him king.   1 Kin. 12:1-20

2 And it came about when Jeroboam the son of Nebat heard *of it* (for[R]he was in Egypt

where he had fled from the presence of King Solomon), that Jeroboam returned from Egypt.   1 Kin. 11:40

3 So they sent and summoned him. When Jeroboam and all Israel came, they spoke to Rehoboam, saying,

4"Your father made our[R]yoke hard; now therefore lighten the hard service of your father and his heavy yoke which he put on us, and we will serve you."   1 Kin. 5:13-16

5 And he said to them, "Return to me again in three days." So the people departed.

6 Then King Rehoboam consulted with the elders who had served his father Solomon while he was still alive, saying, "How do you counsel *me* to answer this people?"

7 And they spoke to him, saying, "If you will be kind to this people and please them and [R]speak good words to them, then they will be your servants forever."   [Prov. 15:1]

8 But he forsook the counsel of the elders which they had given him, and consulted with the young men who grew up with him[T]and served him.   *who stood before*

9 So he said to them, "What counsel do you give that we may answer this people, who have spoken to me, saying, 'Lighten the yoke which your father put on us'?"

10 And the young men who grew up with him spoke to him, saying, "Thus you shall say to the people who spoke to you, saying, 'Your father made our yoke heavy, but you make it lighter for us.' Thus you shall say to them, 'My little finger is thicker than my father's loins!

11 'Whereas my father loaded you with a heavy yoke, I will add to your yoke; my father disciplined you with whips, but I *will discipline you* with scorpions.' "

12 So Jeroboam and all the people came to Rehoboam on the third day as the king had [T]directed, saying, "Return to me on the third day."   *spoken*

13 And the king answered them harshly, and King Rehoboam forsook the counsel of the elders.

14 And he spoke to them according to the advice of the young men, saying, "My father made your yoke heavy, but I will add to it; my father disciplined you with whips, but I *will discipline you* with scorpions."

15 So the king did not listen to the people, [R]for it was a turn *of events* from God that the LORD might establish His word, which He spoke through Ahijah the Shilonite to Jeroboam the son of Nebat.   2 Chr. 25:16-20

16 And when all Israel *saw* that the king did not listen to them the people answered the king, saying,

"What portion do we have in David?
    We have no inheritance in the son of
        Jesse.
Every man to your tents, O Israel;
    Now look after your own house,
        David."
So all Israel departed to their tents.

17 But as for the sons of Israel who lived in the cities of Judah, Rehoboam reigned over them.

18 Then King Rehoboam sent Hadoram, who was over the forced labor, and the sons of Israel stoned him*to death. And King Rehoboam made haste to mount his chariot to flee to Jerusalem.   *with stones that he died

19 So*Israel has been in rebellion against the house of David to this day.   1 Kin. 12:19

CHAPTER 11

Kingdom of Judah Is Strengthened
1 Kin. 12:21–24

N OW*when Rehoboam had come to Jerusalem, he assembled the house of Judah and Benjamin, 180,000 chosen men who were warriors, to fight against Israel to restore the kingdom to Rehoboam.   1 Kin. 12:21-24

2 But the word of the LORD came to Shemaiah the man of God, saying,

3 "Speak to Rehoboam the son of Solomon, king of Judah, and to all Israel in Judah and Benjamin, saying,

4 'Thus says the LORD, "You shall not go up or fight against*your*relatives; return every man to his house, for this thing is from Me." ' " So they listened to the words of the LORD and returned from going against Jeroboam.   2 Chr. 28:8-11 • *brothers*

5 Rehoboam lived in Jerusalem and*built cities for defense in Judah.   2 Chr. 8:2-6; 11:23

6 Thus he built Bethlehem, Etam, Tekoa,

7 Beth-zur, Soco, Adullam,

8 Gath, Mareshah, Ziph,

9 Adoraim, Lachish, Azekah,

10 Zorah, Aijalon, and Hebron, which are fortified cities in Judah and in Benjamin.

11 He also strengthened the fortresses and put officers in them and stores of food, oil and wine.

12 And *he put* shields and spears in every city and strengthened them greatly. So he held Judah and Benjamin.

13 Moreover, the priests and the Levites who were in all Israel stood with him from all their districts.

14 For*the Levites left their pasture lands and their property and came to Judah and Jerusalem, for*Jeroboam and his sons had excluded them from serving as priests to the LORD.   Num. 35:2-5 • 1 Kin. 12:28-33

15 And*he set up priests of his own for the high places, for the satyrs, and for the calves which he had made. 1 Kin. 12:31; 13:33

16 And those from all the tribes of Israel who set their hearts on seeking the LORD God of Israel, followed them to Jerusalem to sacrifice to the LORD God of their fathers.

17 *And they strengthened the kingdom of Judah and supported Rehoboam the son of Solomon for three years, for they walked in the way of David and Solomon for three years.   2 Chr. 12:1

18 Then Rehoboam took as a wife Mahalath the daughter of Jerimoth the son of Da-

vid *and of* Abihail the daughter of*Eliab the son of Jesse,   1 Sam. 16:6

19 and she bore him sons: Jeush, Shemariah, and Zaham.

20 And after her he took *Maacah the daughter of Absalom, and she bore him Abijah, Attai, Ziza, and Shelomith.   1 Kin. 15:2

21 And Rehoboam loved Maacah the daughter of Absalom more than all his *other* wives and concubines. For *he had taken eighteen wives and sixty concubines and fathered twenty-eight sons and sixty daughters.   Deut. 17:17

22 And*Rehoboam appointed Abijah the son of Maacah as head and leader among his brothers, for he *intended* to make him king.   Deut. 21:15-17

23 And he acted wisely and distributed some of his sons through all the territories of Judah and Benjamin to all the fortified cities, and he gave them food in abundance. And he sought many wives *for them.*

CHAPTER 12

Kingdom of Judah Is Weakened
1 Kin. 14:25–28

I T took place*when the kingdom of Rehoboam was established and strong that*he and all Israel with him forsook the law of the LORD.   2 Chr. 11:17 • 2 Chr. 26:13-16

2 *And it came about in King Rehoboam's fifth year, because they had been unfaithful to the LORD, that Shishak king of Egypt came up against Jerusalem   1 Kin. 14:25

3 with 1,200 chariots and 60,000 horsemen. And the people who came with him from Egypt were without number: the Lubim, the Sukkiim, and the Ethiopians.

4 And he captured the fortified cities of Judah and came as far as Jerusalem.

5 Then Shemaiah the prophet came to Rehoboam and the princes of Judah who had gathered at Jerusalem because of Shishak, and he said to them, "Thus says the LORD, 'You have forsaken Me, so I also have forsaken you*to Shishak.' "   *in the hand of*

6 So the princes of Israel and the king humbled themselves and said, "The*LORD is righteous."   Ex. 9:27; [Dan. 9:14]

7 And when the LORD saw that they humbled themselves, the word of the LORD came to Shemaiah, saying, "They* have humbled themselves so I will not destroy them, but I will grant them some *measure* of deliverance, and *My wrath shall not be poured out on Jerusalem by means of Shishak.   1 Kin. 21:29 • 2 Chr. 34:25-27; Ps. 78:38

8 "But they will become his slaves so*that they may learn *the difference between* My service and the service of the kingdoms of the countries."   [Deut. 28:47, 48]

9 *So Shishak king of Egypt came up against Jerusalem, and took the treasures of the house of the LORD and the treasures of the king's palace. He took everything; he

even took the golden shields which Solomon had made.   1 Kin. 14:26-28

10 Then King Rehoboam made shields of bronze in their place, and committed them to the care of the commanders of the guard who guarded the door of the king's house.

11 And it happened as often as the king entered the house of the LORD, the ᵀguards came and carried them and *then* brought them back into the ᵀguards' room.   *runners*

12 And ᴿwhen he humbled himself, the anger of the LORD turned away from him, so as not to destroy *him* completely; and also conditions were good in Judah.   2 Chr. 12:6, 7

Death of Rehoboam
1 Kin. 14:21, 22, 29–31

13 ᴿSo King Rehoboam strengthened himself in Jerusalem, and reigned. Now Rehoboam was forty-one years old when he began to reign, and he reigned seventeen years in Jerusalem, the city which the LORD had chosen from all the tribes of Israel, to put His name there. And his mother's name was Naamah the Ammonitess.   1 Kin. 14:21

14 And he did evilᴿbecause he did not set his heart to seek the LORD.   2 Chr. 19:3

15 ᴿNow the acts of Rehoboam, from first to last, are they not written in the ᵀrecords of Shemaiah the prophet and of Iddo the seer, according to genealogical enrollment? And *there were* wars between Rehoboam and Jeroboam continually.   1 Kin. 14:29 • *words*

16 And Rehoboam slept with his fathers, and was buried in the city of David; and his son Abijah became king in his place.

CHAPTER 13

War of Abijah and Jeroboam
1 Kin. 15:1, 2, 7

Iᴺᴿthe eighteenth year of King Jeroboam, Abijah became king over Judah.   1 Kin. 15:1, 2

2 He reigned three years in Jerusalem; and his mother's name was Micaiah the daughter of Uriel of Gibeah. And there was war between Abijah and Jeroboam.

3 And Abijah began the battle with an army of valiant warriors, 400,000 chosen men, while Jeroboam drew up in battle formation against him with 800,000 chosen men *who were* valiant warriors.

4 Then Abijah stood on Mount ᴿZemaraim, which is in the hill country of Ephraim, and said, "Listen to me, Jeroboam and all Israel: Josh. 18:22

5 "Do you not know that the LORD God of Israel gave the rule over Israel forever to David and his sons by a covenant of salt?

6 "Yet Jeroboam the son of Nebat, the servant of Solomon the son of David, rose up and rebelled against his ᴬmaster,   *lord*

7 and worthless men gathered about him, scoundrels, who proved too strong for Rehoboam, the son of Solomon, when ᵀheᴿ was young and timid and could not hold his own against them.   *Rehoboam* • 2 Chr. 12:13

8 "So now you intend to resist the kingdom of the LORD ᵀthrough the sons of David, ᵀbeing a great multitude and *having* with you the golden calves which Jeroboam made for gods for you.   *in the hands of* • *and you are a*

9 "Haveᴿ you not driven out the priests of the LORD, the sons of Aaron and the Levites, and made for yourselves priests like the peoples of *other* lands? Whoever comes to consecrate himself with a young bull and seven rams, even he may become a priest of *what are* ᴿno gods.   2 Chr. 11:14 • Jer. 2:11; 5:7

10 "But as for us, the LORD is our God, and we have not forsaken Him; and the sons of Aaron are ministering to the LORD as priests, and the Levites attend to their work.

11 "And every morning and evening ᴿthey burn to the LORD burnt offerings and fragrant incense, and the showbread is *set* on the clean table, and the golden lampstand with its lamps is *ready* to light every evening; for we keep the charge of the LORD our God, but you have forsaken Him.   Ex. 29:38

12 "Now behold, God is with us at *our* head and His priests with the signal trumpets to sound the alarm against you. O sons of Israel, do not fight against the LORD God of your fathers, for you will not succeed."

13 But Jeroboam ᴿhad set an ambush to come from the rear, so that *Israel* was in front of Judah, and the ambush was behind them.   Josh. 8:4-9

14 When Judah turned around, behold, they were attacked both front and rear; so they cried to the LORD, and the priests blew the trumpets.

15 Then the men of Judah raised a war cry, and when the men of Judah raised the war cry, then it was that God ᵀroutedᴿ Jeroboam and all Israel before Abijah and Judah.   *smote* • 2 Chr. 14:12

16 And when the sons of Israel fled before Judah, God gave them into their hand.

17 And Abijah and his people defeated them with a great slaughter, so that 500,000 chosen men of Israel fell slain.

18 Thus the sons of Israel were subdued at that time, and the sons of Judah ᵀconquered because they trusted in the LORD, the God of their fathers.   *were strong*

19 And Abijah pursued Jeroboam, and captured from him *several* cities, Bethel with its villages, Jeshanah with its villages, and Ephron with its villages.

20 And Jeroboam did not again recover strength in the days of Abijah; and the ᴿLORD struck him and he died.   1 Sam. 25:38

Death of Abijah

21 But Abijah became powerful, and took fourteen wives to himself; and became the father of twenty-two sons and sixteen daughters.

22 Now the rest of the acts of Abijah, and his ways and his words are written in the ᵀtreatise of the prophet Iddo.   Heb., *midrash*

CHAPTER 14

Evaluation of Asa—1 Kin. 15:8–12

So Abijah slept with his fathers, and they buried him in the city of David, and his son Asa became king in his place. The land was undisturbed for ten years during his days.

2 And Asa did good and right in the sight of the LORD his God,

3 for he removed[R]the foreign altars and high places, tore down the *sacred* pillars, cut down the [5]Asherim,   Deut. 7:5

4 and commanded Judah to seek the LORD God of their fathers and to observe the law and the commandment.

5 He also removed the high places and the[R]incense altars from all the cities of Judah. And the kingdom was undisturbed under him.   2 Chr. 34:4, 7

6 And he built fortified cities in Judah, since the land was undisturbed, and there was no one at war with him during those years, because the LORD had given him rest.

7 For he said to Judah, "Let[R] us build these cities and surround *them* with walls and towers, gates and bars. The land is still[T]ours, because we have sought the LORD our God; we have sought Him, and He has given us rest on every side." So they built and prospered.   2 Chr. 8:5 · *before us*

8 Now Asa had an army of 300,000 from Judah, bearing large shields and spears, and 280,000 from Benjamin, bearing shields and wielding bows; all of them were valiant warriors.   2 Chr. 13:3

Victory over the Ethiopians

9 Now Zerah the Ethiopian came out against them with an army of a million men and 300 chariots, and he came to Mareshah.

10 So Asa went out[T]to meet him, and they drew up in battle formation in the valley of Zephathah at Mareshah.   *before him*

11 Then Asa called to the LORD his God, and said, "LORD, there is no one besides Thee to help *in the battle* between the powerful and those who have no strength; so help us, O LORD our God, for we trust in Thee, and in Thy name have come against this multitude. O LORD, Thou art our God; let not man prevail against Thee."

12 So[R]the LORD[T]routed the Ethiopians before Asa and before Judah, and the Ethiopians fled.   2 Chr. 13:15 · *struck*

13 And Asa and the people who *were* with him pursued them as far as[R]Gerar; and so many Ethiopians fell that they could not recover, for they were shattered before the LORD, and before His army. And they carried away very much plunder.   Gen. 10:19

14 And they destroyed all the cities around Gerar, for the dread of the LORD had fallen on them; and they despoiled all the cities, for there was much plunder in them.

15 They also struck down [T]those who

owned livestock, and they carried away large numbers of sheep and camels. Then they returned to Jerusalem.   *tents of livestock*

CHAPTER 15

Exhortation of Azariah

Now[R]the Spirit of God came on Azariah the son of Oded,   2 Chr. 20:14; 24:20

2 and he went out[T]to meet Asa and said to him, "Listen to me, Asa, and all Judah and Benjamin: the LORD is with you when you are with Him. And if you seek Him, He will let you find Him; but if you forsake Him, He will forsake you.   *before Asa*

3 "And[R]for many days Israel was without the true God and without[R]a teaching priest and without law.   1 Kin. 12:28-33 · 2 Chr. 17:9

4 "But[R]in their distress they turned to the LORD God of Israel, and they sought Him, and He let them find Him.   [Deut. 4:29]

5 "And[R]in those times there was no peace to him who went out or to him who came in, for many disturbances [T]afflicted all the inhabitants of the lands.   Judg. 5:6 · *were on*

6 "And[R]nation was crushed by nation, and city by city, for God troubled them with every kind of distress.   Matt. 24:7

7 "But you, be strong and do not lose courage, for there is reward for your work."

Reforms of Asa—1 Kin. 15:13–15

8 Now when Asa heard these words and the prophecy which Azariah the son of Oded the prophet spoke, he took courage and removed the abominable idols from all the land of Judah and Benjamin and from the cities which he had captured in the hill country of Ephraim.[R]He then restored the altar of the LORD which was in front of the porch of the LORD.   2 Chr. 4:1; 8:12

9 And he gathered all Judah and Benjamin and those from Ephraim, Manasseh, and Simeon who resided with them, for many defected to him from Israel when they saw that the LORD his God was with him.

10 So they assembled at Jerusalem in the third month of the fifteenth year of Asa's reign.

11 And[R]they sacrificed to the LORD that day 700 oxen and 7,000 sheep from the spoil they had brought.   2 Chr. 14:13-15

12 And[R]they entered into the covenant to seek the LORD God of their fathers with all their heart and soul;   2 Chr. 23:16

13 and whoever would not seek the LORD God of Israel should be put to death, whether small or great, man or woman.

14 Moreover, they made an oath to the LORD with a loud voice, with shouting, with trumpets, and with horns.

15 And all Judah rejoiced concerning the

---

[5] I.e., wooden symbols of a female deity

oath, for they had sworn with their whole heart and had sought Him [T]earnestly, and He let them find Him. So the LORD gave them rest on every side. *with their whole desire*

16 And he also removed Maacah, the mother of King Asa, from the *position of* queen mother, because she had made a horrid image [A]as [R]an Asherah, and Asa cut down her horrid image, crushed *it* and burned *it* at the brook Kidron. *for Asherah* • Ex. 34:13

17 But the high places were not removed from Israel; nevertheless Asa's heart was blameless all his days.

18 And he brought into the house of God the dedicated things of his father and his own dedicated things: silver and gold and utensils.

19 And there was no more war until the thirty-fifth year of Asa's reign.

CHAPTER 16

Victory over the Arameans
1 Kin. 15:16–22

IN the thirty-sixth year of Asa's reign [R]Baasha king of Israel came up against Judah and [T]fortified Ramah in order to prevent *anyone* from going out or coming in to Asa king of Judah. *1 Kin. 15:17-22* • *built*

2 Then Asa brought out silver and gold from the treasuries of the house of the LORD and the king's house, and sent them to Benhadad king of Aram, who lived in Damascus, saying,

3 "*Let there be* a treaty between you and me, *as* between my father and your father. Behold, I have sent you silver and gold; go, break your treaty with Baasha king of Israel so that he will withdraw from me."

4 So Ben-hadad listened to King Asa and sent the commanders of his armies against the cities of Israel, and they [T]conquered Ijon, Dan, Abel-maim, and all the [T]store cities of Naphtali. *smote* • *storage places of the cities*

5 And it came about when Baasha heard *of it* that he ceased [T]fortifying Ramah and stopped his work. *building*

6 Then King Asa brought all Judah, and they carried away the stones of Ramah and its timber with which Baasha had been building, and with them he [T]fortified Geba and Mizpah. *built*

Rebuke of Hanani

7 At that time [R]Hanani the seer came to Asa king of Judah and said to him, "Because you have relied on the king of Aram and have not relied on the LORD your God, therefore the army of the king of Aram has escaped out of your hand. *1 Kin. 16:1*

8 "Were not the Ethiopians and the Lubim an immense army with very many chariots and horsemen? Yet, because you relied on the LORD, He delivered them into your hand.

9 "For [k]the eyes of the LORD move to and fro throughout the earth that He may

strongly support those [R]whose heart is completely His. You have acted foolishly in this. Indeed, from now on you will surely have wars." [Prov. 15:3; Jer. 16:17] • 2 Chr. 15:17

10 Then Asa was angry with the seer and put him in [T]prison, for he was enraged at him for this. And Asa oppressed some of the people at the same time. *the house of the stocks*

Death of Asa—1 Kin. 15:23, 24

11 [R]And now, the acts of Asa from first to last, behold, they are written in the Book of the Kings of Judah and Israel. 1 Kin. 15:23, 24

12 And in the thirty-ninth year of his reign Asa became diseased in his feet. His disease was severe, yet even in his disease he did not seek the LORD, but the physicians.

13 So Asa slept with his fathers, [T]having died in the forty-first year of his reign. *and*

14 And they buried him in his own tomb which he had cut out for himself in the city of David, and they laid him in the resting place which he had filled with spices of various kinds blended by the perfumers' art; and they made a very great fire for him.

CHAPTER 17

Evaluation of Jehoshaphat

JEHOSHAPHAT [R]his son then became king in his place, and made his position over Israel firm. 1Kin. 15:24

2 He placed troops in all [R]the fortified cities of Judah, and set garrisons in the land of Judah, and in the cities of Ephraim which Asa his father had captured. 2 Chr. 11:5

3 And the LORD was with Jehoshaphat because he [T]followed the example of his father David's earlier days and did not seek the Baals, *walked in the earlier ways of his father*

4 but sought the God of his father, [T]followed His commandments, [R]and did not act as Israel did. *walked in* • 1 Kin. 12:28

5 So the LORD established the kingdom in his [T]control, and all Judah brought tribute to Jehoshaphat, and [R]he had great riches and honor. *hand* • 2 Chr. 18:1

6 And he took great pride in the ways of the LORD and again removed the high places and the Asherim from Judah.

Instruction by the Priests and Levites

7 Then in the third year of his reign he sent his officials, Ben-hail, Obadiah, Zechariah, Nethanel, and Micaiah, [R]to teach in the cities of Judah; 2 Chr. 15:3; 35:3

8 and with them the Levites, Shemaiah, Nethaniah, Zebadiah, Asahel, Shemiramoth, Jehonathan, Adonijah, Tobijah, and Tobadonijah, the Levites; and with them Elishama and Jehoram, the priests.

9 And they taught in Judah, *having* the book of [R]the law of the LORD with them; and they went throughout all the cities of Judah and taught among the people. Deut. 6:4-9

Expansion of the Kingdom

10 Now^Rthe dread of the LORD was on all the kingdoms of the lands which *were* around Judah, so that they did not make war against Jehoshaphat.   2 Chr. 14:14

11 And some of the Philistines brought gifts and silver as tribute to Jehoshaphat; the Arabians also brought him flocks, 7,700 rams and 7,700 male goats.

12 So Jehoshaphat grew greater and greater, and he built fortresses and store cities in Judah.

13 And he had large supplies in the cities of Judah, and warriors, valiant men, in Jerusalem.

14 And this was their muster according to their fathers' households: of Judah, commanders of thousands, Adnah *was* the commander, and with him 300,000 valiant warriors;

15 and next to him *was* Johanan the commander, and with him 280,000;

16 and next to him Amasiah the son of Zichri, who volunteered for the LORD, and with him 200,000 valiant warriors;

17 and of Benjamin, Eliada a valiant warrior, and with him 200,000 armed with bow and shield;

18 and next to him Jehozabad, and with him 180,000 equipped for war.

19 These are they who served the king, apart from those whom the king put in the fortified cities through all Judah.   2 Chr. 17:2

CHAPTER 18

Alliance with Ahab—1 Kin. 22:2-35

NOW ^RJehoshaphat had great riches and honor; and he allied himself by marriage with Ahab.   2 Chr. 17:5

2 ^RAnd some years later he went down to *visit* Ahab at Samaria. And Ahab slaughtered many sheep and oxen for him and the people who were with him, and induced him to go up against Ramoth-gilead. 1 Kin. 22:2-35

3 And Ahab king of Israel said to Jehoshaphat king of Judah, "Will you go with me *against* Ramoth-gilead?" And he said to him, "I am as you are and my people as your people, and *we will be* with you in the battle."

4 Moreover, Jehoshaphat said to the king of Israel, "Please inquire ^Tfirst for the word of the LORD."   *as the day*

5 Then the king of Israel assembled the prophets, four hundred men, and said to them, "Shall we go against Ramoth-gilead to battle, or shall I refrain?" And they said, "Go up, for God will give *it* into the hand of the king."

6 But Jehoshaphat said, "Is there not yet a prophet of the LORD here that we may inquire of him?"

7 And the king of Israel said to Jehoshaphat, "There is yet one man by whom we may inquire of the LORD, but I hate him, for he never prophesies good concerning me but always evil. He is Micaiah, son of Imla." But Jehoshaphat said, "Let not the king say so."

8 Then the king of Israel called an officer and said, "Bring ^Tquickly Micaiah, Imla's son."   *Hasten*

9 Now the king of Israel and Jehoshaphat the king of Judah were sitting each on his throne, arrayed in *their* robes, and *they* were sitting at the threshing floor at the entrance of the gate of Samaria; and all the prophets were prophesying before them.

10 And Zedekiah the son of Chenaanah made horns of iron for himself and said, "Thus says the LORD, 'With these you shall gore the Arameans, until they are consumed.'"

11 And all the prophets were prophesying thus, saying, "Go up to Ramoth-gilead and succeed, for the LORD will give *it* into the hand of the king."

12 Then the messenger who went to summon Micaiah spoke to him saying, "Behold, the words of the prophets are uniformly favorable to the king. So please let your word be like one of them and speak favorably."

13 But Micaiah said, "As the LORD lives, what my God says, that I will speak."

14 And when he came to the king, the king said to him, "Micaiah, shall we go to Ramoth-gilead to battle, or shall I refrain?" He said, "Go up and succeed, for they will be given into your hand."

15 Then the king said to him, "How many times must I adjure you to speak to me nothing but the truth in the name of the LORD?"

16 So he said,
"I saw all Israel
Scattered on the mountains,
Like sheep which have no shepherd;
And the LORD said,
'These have no master.
Let each of them return to his house
    in peace.'"

17 Then the king of Israel said to Jehoshaphat, "Did I not tell you that he would not prophesy good concerning me, but evil?"

18 And Micaiah said, "Therefore, hear the word of the LORD.^RI saw the LORD sitting on His throne, and all the host of heaven standing on His right and on His left.   Is. 6:1-5

19 "And the LORD said, 'Who will entice Ahab king of Israel to go up and fall at Ramoth-gilead?' And one said this while another said that.

20 "Then a ^Rspirit came forward and stood before the LORD and said, 'I will entice him.' And the LORD said to him, 'How?'   Job 1:6

21 "And he said, 'I will go and be^Ra deceiving spirit in the mouth of all his prophets.' Then He said, 'You are to entice *him* and prevail also. Go and do so.'   John 8:44

22 "Now therefore, behold,^Rthe LORD has put a deceiving spirit in the mouth of these

your prophets; for the LORD has proclaimed disaster against you." Is. 19:14; Ezek. 14:9

23 Then Zedekiah the son of Chenaanah came near and struck Micaiah on the cheek and said, "How^Tdid the Spirit of the LORD pass from me to speak to you?" *Which way*

24 And Micaiah said, "Behold, you shall see on that day, when you enter an inner room to hide yourself."

25 Then the king of Israel said, "Take Micaiah and return him to Amon the governor of the city, and to Joash the king's son;

26 and say, 'Thus says the king, "Put this *man* in prison, and feed him sparingly with bread and water until I return safely." ' "

27 And Micaiah said, "If you indeed return safely, the LORD has not spoken by me." And he said, "Listen, all you people."

28 So the king of Israel and Jehoshaphat king of Judah went up against Ramoth-gilead.

29 And the king of Israel said to Jehoshaphat, "I will disguise myself and go into battle, but you put on your robes." So the king of Israel disguised himself, and they went into battle.

30 Now the king of Aram had commanded the captains of his chariots, saying, "Do not fight with small or great, but with the king of Israel alone."

31 So it came about when the captains of the chariots saw Jehoshaphat, that they said, "It is the king of Israel," and they turned aside to fight against him. But Jehoshaphat cried out, and the LORD helped him, and God diverted them from him.

32 Then it happened when the captains of the chariots saw that it was not the king of Israel, that they turned back from pursuing him.

33 And a certain man drew his bow at random and struck the king of Israel in a joint of the armor. So he said to the driver of the chariot, "Turn around, and take me out of the fight; for I am severely wounded."

34 And the battle raged that day, and the king of Israel propped himself up in his chariot in front of the Arameans until the evening; and at sunset he died.

CHAPTER 19

THEN Jehoshaphat the king of Judah returned in safety to his house in Jerusalem.

2 And Jehu the son of Hanani the seer went out to meet him and said to King Jehoshaphat, "Should you help the wicked and love those who hate the LORD and so *bring* wrath on yourself from the LORD?

3"But there is *some* good in you, for you have removed the Asheroth from the land and you have set your heart to seek God."

4 So Jehoshaphat lived in Jerusalem and went out again among the people from Beersheba to the hill country of Ephraim and^Rbrought them back to the LORD, the God of their fathers. 2 Chr. 15:8-13

Organization of the Kingdom

5 And he appointed judges in the land in all the fortified cities of Judah, city by city.

6 And he said to the judges, "Consider what you are doing, for you do not judge for man but for the LORD who is with you^Twhen you render judgment. *in the word of judgment*

7"Now then let the fear of the LORD be upon you; ^Tbe very careful what you do, for the LORD our God will^Rhave no part in unrighteousness, or partiality, or the taking of a bribe." *be careful and do* · Gen. 18:25

8 And in Jerusalem also Jehoshaphat appointed some^Rof the Levites and priests, and some of the heads of the fathers' *households* of Israel, for the judgment of the LORD and to judge disputes among the inhabitants of Jerusalem. 2 Chr. 17:8, 9

9 Then he charged them saying, "Thus you shall do in the fear of the LORD, faithfully and wholeheartedly.

10"And whenever any dispute comes to you from your brethren who live in their cities, between blood and blood, between law and commandment, statutes and ordinances, you shall warn them that they may not be guilty before the LORD, and wrath may *not* come on you and your brethren. Thus you shall do and you will not be guilty.

11"And behold, Amariah the chief priest will be over you in^Tall that pertains to the LORD; and Zebadiah the son of Ishmael, the ruler of the house of Judah, in ^Tall that pertains to the king. Also the Levites shall be officers before you. Act resolutely, and the LORD be with the upright." *every matter of*

CHAPTER 20

Victory over Moab and Ammon

NOW it came about after this that the sons of Moab and the sons of Ammon, together with some of the^RMeunites, came to make war against Jehoshaphat. 1 Chr. 4:41

2 Then some came and reported to Jehoshaphat, saying, "A great multitude is coming against you from beyond the sea, out of Aram and behold, they are in^RHazazon-tamar (that is Engedi)." Gen. 14:7

3 And Jehoshaphat was afraid and turned his attention to seek the LORD; and proclaimed a fast throughout all Judah.

4 So Judah gathered together to seek help from the LORD; they even came from all the cities of Judah to seek the LORD.

5 Then Jehoshaphat stood in the assembly of Judah and Jerusalem, in the house of the LORD before the new court,

6 and he said, "O LORD, the God of our fathers, ^Rart Thou not God in the heavens? And ^Rart Thou not ruler over all the kingdoms of the nations? Power and might are in Thy hand so that no one can stand against Thee. Deut. 4:39 · 1 Chr. 29:11

7"Didst Thou not, O our God, drive out

the inhabitants of this land before Thy people Israel, and ^Rgive it to the descendants of Abraham Thy friend forever?   Is. 41:8

8"And they lived in it, and have built Thee a sanctuary there for Thy name, saying,

9 'Should^R evil come upon us, the sword, or judgment, or pestilence, or famine, we will stand before this house and before Thee (for^RThy name is in this house) and cry to Thee in our distress, and Thou wilt hear and deliver us.'   2 Chr. 6:28-30 • 2 Chr. 6:20

10"And now behold, the sons of Ammon and Moab and ^TMount Seir, whom Thou didst not let Israel invade when they came out of the land of Egypt (they turned aside from them and did not destroy them),   Edom

11 behold how they are rewarding us, by coming to drive us out from Thy possession which Thou hast given us as an inheritance.

12"O our God, wilt Thou not judge them? For we are powerless before this great multitude who are coming against us; nor do we know what to do, but our eyes are on Thee."

13 And all Judah was standing before the LORD, with their infants, their wives, and their children.

14 Then in the midst of the assembly^Rthe Spirit of the LORD came upon Jahaziel the son of Zechariah, the son of Benaiah, the son of Jeiel, the son of Mattaniah, the Levite of the sons of Asaph;   2 Chr. 15:1; 24:20

15 and he said, "Listen, all Judah and the inhabitants of Jerusalem and King Jehoshaphat: thus says the LORD to you, 'Do not fear or be dismayed because of this great multitude, for the battle is not yours but God's.

16 'Tomorrow go down against them. Behold, they will come up by the ascent of Ziz, and you will find them at the end of the valley in front of the wilderness of Jeruel.

17 'You need not fight in this battle; station yourselves,^Rstand and see the salvation of the LORD on your behalf, O Judah and Jerusalem.' Do not fear or be dismayed; tomorrow go out to face them,^Rfor the LORD is with you."   Ex. 14:13 • [2 Chr. 15:2]

18 And Jehoshaphat^Rbowed his head with his face to the ground, and all Judah and the inhabitants of Jerusalem fell down before the LORD, worshiping the LORD.   Ex. 4:31

19 And the Levites, from the sons of the Kohathites and of the sons of the Korahites, stood up to praise the LORD God of Israel, with a very loud voice.

20 And they rose early in the morning and went out to the wilderness of Tekoa; and when they went out, Jehoshaphat stood and said, "Listen to me, O Judah and inhabitants of Jerusalem, put your trust in the LORD your God, and you will be established. Put your trust in His prophets and succeed."

21 And when he had consulted with the people, he appointed those who sang to the LORD and those who^Rpraised Him in holy attire, as they went out before the army and said, "Give thanks to the LORD, for His lovingkindness is everlasting."   1 Chr. 16:29

22 And when they began singing and praising, the LORD^Rset ambushes against the sons of Ammon, Moab, and Mount Seir, who had come against Judah; so they were ^Trouted.   2 Chr. 13:13 • struck down

23 For the sons of Ammon and Moab rose up against the inhabitants of Mount Seir destroying them completely, and when they had finished with the inhabitants of Seir, they helped to destroy one another.

24 When Judah came to the lookout of the wilderness, they looked toward the multitude; and behold, they were corpses lying on the ground, and no one had escaped.

25 And when Jehoshaphat and his people came to take their spoil, they found much among them, including goods, garments, and valuable things which they took for themselves, more than they could carry. And they were three days taking the spoil because there was so much.

26 Then on the fourth day they assembled in the valley of Beracah, for there they blessed the LORD. Therefore they have named that place "The Valley of ⁶Beracah" until today.

27 And every man of Judah and Jerusalem returned with Jehoshaphat at their head, returning to Jerusalem with joy,^Rfor the LORD had made them to rejoice over their enemies.   Neh. 12:43

28 And they came to Jerusalem with harps, lyres, and trumpets to the house of the LORD.

29 And^Rthe dread of God was on all the kingdoms of the lands when they heard that the LORD had fought against the enemies of Israel.   2 Chr. 14:14; 17:10

30 So the kingdom of Jehoshaphat was at peace, for his God gave him rest on all sides.

Summary of the Reign of Jehoshaphat
1 Kin. 22:41-45

31 Now Jehoshaphat reigned over Judah. He was thirty-five years old when he became king, and he reigned in Jerusalem twenty-five years. And his mother's name was Azubah the daughter of Shilhi.

32 And he walked in the way of his father Asa and did not depart from it, doing right in the sight of the LORD.

33 The high places, however, were not removed; the people had not yet directed their hearts to the God of their fathers.

34 Now the rest of the acts of Jehoshaphat, first^Tto last, behold, they are written in the annals of^RJehu the son of Hanani, which is^Trecorded in the Book of the Kings of Israel.   and • 2 Chr. 19:2 • taken up

⁶ I.e., blessing

The Sin and Death of Jehoshaphat
1 Kin. 22:48

35 And after this Jehoshaphat king of Judah allied himself with Ahaziah king of Israel. He acted wickedly[T]in so doing.   *to do*
36 So he allied himself with him to make ships to go[R]to Tarshish, and they made the ships in Ezion-geber.   2 Chr. 9:21
37 Then Eliezer the son of Dodavahu of Mareshah prophesied against Jehoshaphat saying, "Because you have allied yourself with Ahaziah, the LORD has destroyed your works." So the ships were broken and could not go to Tarshish.

CHAPTER 21

Evaluation of Jehoram
1 Kin. 22:50; 2 Kin. 8:17–19

THEN[R]Jehoshaphat slept with his fathers and was buried with his fathers in the city of David, and Jehoram his son became king in his place.   1 Kin. 22:50
2 And he had brothers, the sons of Jehoshaphat: Azariah, Jehiel, Zechariah, Azaryahu, Michael, and Shephatiah. All these *were* the sons of Jehoshaphat king of Israel.
3 And their father gave them many gifts of silver, gold and precious things, [t]with fortified cities in Judah, but he gave the kingdom to Jehoram because he was the first-born.   2 Chr. 11:5
4 Now when Jehoram had taken over the kingdom of his father and made himself secure, he killed all his brothers with the sword, and some of the rulers of Israel also.
5 [R]Jehoram *was* thirty-two years old when he became king, and he reigned eight years in Jerusalem.   2 Kin. 8:17-22
6 [R]And he walked in the way of the kings of Israel, just as the house of Ahab did (for Ahab's daughter was his wife), and he did evil in the sight of the LORD.   1 Kin. 12:28-30
7 Yet the LORD was not willing to destroy the house of David because of the covenant which He had made with David, [R]and since He had promised to give a lamp to him and his sons forever.   2 Sam. 7:12-17

Revolt by Edom and Libnah
2 Kin. 8:20–22

8 In his days[R]Edom revolted [7]against the rule of Judah, and set up a king over themselves.   2 Chr. 20:22, 23; 21:10
9 Then Jehoram crossed over with his commanders and all his chariots with him. And it came about that he arose by night and struck down the Edomites who were surrounding him and the commanders of the chariots.
10 So Edom revolted [7]against Judah to this day. Then Libnah revolted at the same time against his rule, because he had forsaken the LORD God of his fathers.

11 Moreover,[R]he made high places in the mountains of Judah, and caused the inhabitants of Jerusalem[R]to play the harlot and led Judah astray.   1 Kin. 11:7 • Lev. 20:5

Warning of Elijah

12 Then a letter came to him from Elijah the prophet saying, "Thus says the LORD God of your father David, 'Because [R]you have not walked in the ways of Jehoshaphat your father [a]and the ways of Asa king of Judah,   2 Chr. 17:3, 4 • 2 Chr. 14:2–5
13 but have walked in the way of the kings of Israel, and have caused Judah and the inhabitants of Jerusalem to play the harlot as the house of Ahab played the harlot, and you have also killed your brothers, your own family, who were better than you,
14 behold, the LORD is going to strike your people, your sons, your wives, and all your possessions with a great [t]calamity;   *blow*
15 and [t]you will suffer [t]severe sickness, a disease of your bowels, until your bowels come out because of the sickness, day by day.' "   2 Chr. 21:18 • *in many sicknesses*

Invasion by Philistia and Arabia

16 Then the LORD stirred up against Jehoram the spirit of the Philistines and the Arabs who bordered the Ethiopians;
17 and they came against Judah and invaded it, and carried away all the possessions found in the king's house together with his sons and his wives, so that no son was left to him except [a]Jehoahaz, the youngest of his sons.   In 2 Chr. 22:1, *Ahaziah*

Death of Jehoram

18 So after all this the LORD smote him in his bowels with an incurable sickness.
19 Now it came about in the course of time, at the end of two years, that his bowels came out because of his sickness and he died in great pain. And his people made no fire for him like the fire for his fathers.
20 He was thirty-two years old when he became king, and he reigned in Jerusalem eight years; and he departed with no one's regret, and they buried him in the city of David, but not in the tombs of the kings.

CHAPTER 22

The Reign of Ahaziah—2 Kin. 8:27–29;
9:15, 16, 27, 28; 10:12–14

THEN the inhabitants of Jerusalem made [a]Ahaziah, his youngest son, king in his place, for the band of men who came with the Arabs to the camp had slain all the older *sons.* So Ahaziah the son of Jehoram king of Judah began to reign. In 2 Chr. 21:17, *Jehoahaz*
2 Ahaziah *was* twenty-two years old when he became king, and he reigned one year in Jerusalem. And his mother's name was Athaliah, the granddaughter of Omri.

[7] Lit., *from under the hand of*

3 He also walked in the ways of the house of Ahab, for his mother was his counselor to do wickedly.

4 And he did evil in the sight of the LORD like the house of Ahab, for they were his counselors after the death of his father, to ^Rhis destruction.   Prov. 13:20

5 He also walked according to their counsel, and went with Jehoram the son of Ahab king of Israel to wage war against Hazael king of Aram at Ramoth-gilead. But the ^TArameans wounded Joram.   Heb., archers

6 So he returned to be healed in Jezreel of the wounds ^Twhich they had inflicted on him at Ramah, when he fought against Hazael king of Aram. And Ahaziah, the son of Jehoram king of Judah, went down to see Jehoram the son of Ahab in Jezreel, because he was sick.   with which ... smitten

7 Now ^Rthe destruction of Ahaziah was from God, in that ^The went to Joram. For when he came,^Rhe went out with Jehoram against Jehu the son of Nimshi, whom the LORD had anointed to cut off the house of Ahab.   2 Chr. 10:15 • to go • 2 Kin. 9:21

8 ^RAnd it came about when Jehu was executing judgment on the house of Ahab, he found the princes of Judah and the sons of Ahaziah's brothers, ministering to Ahaziah, and slew them.   2 Kin. 10:11-14

9 ^RHe also sought Ahaziah, and they caught him while he was hiding in Samaria; they brought him to Jehu, put him to death, and buried him. For they said, "He is the son of Jehoshaphat, ^Rwho sought the LORD with all his heart." So there was no one of the house of Ahaziah to retain the power of the kingdom. 2 Kin. 9:27 • 2 Kin. 9:28 • 2 Chr. 17:4

The Reign of Athaliah—2 Kin. 11:1-16

10 ^RNow when Athaliah the mother of Ahaziah saw that her son was dead, she rose and destroyed all the royal offspring of the house of Judah.   2 Kin. 11:1-3 • seed

11 But Jehoshabeath the king's daughter took Joash the son of Ahaziah, and stole him from among the king's sons who were being put to death, and placed him and his nurse in the bedroom. So Jehoshabeath, the daughter of King Jehoram, the wife of Jehoiada the priest (for she was the sister of Ahaziah), hid him from Athaliah so that she would not put him to death.

12 And he was hidden with them in the house of God six years while Athaliah reigned over the land.

CHAPTER 23

Now^R in the seventh year Jehoiada strengthened himself, and took captains of hundreds: Azariah the son of Jeroham, Ishmael the son of Johanan, Azariah the son of Obed, Maaseiah the son of Adaiah, and Elishaphat the son of Zichri, *and they entered* into a covenant with him. 2 Kin. 11:4-20

2 And they went throughout Judah and gathered the Levites from all the cities of Judah, and the heads of the fathers' *households* of Israel, and they came to Jerusalem.

3 Then all the assembly made a covenant with the king in the house of God. And ^TJehoiada said to them, "Behold, the king's son shall reign, ^Ras the LORD has spoken concerning the sons of David.   he • 2 Sam. 7:12

4"This is the thing which you shall do: one third of you, of the priests and Levites ^Rwho come in on the sabbath, *shall be* gatekeepers,   1 Chr. 9:25

5 and one third *shall be* at the king's house, and a third at the Gate of the Foundation; and all the people *shall be* in the courts of the house of the LORD.

6"But let no one enter the house of the LORD except the priests and ^Rthe ministering Levites; they may enter, for they are holy. And let all the people keep the charge of the LORD.   1 Chr. 23:28-32

7"And the Levites will surround the king, each man with his weapons in his hand; and whoever enters the house, let him be killed. Thus be with the king when he comes in and when he goes out."

8 So the Levites and all Judah did according to all that Jehoiada the priest commanded. And each one of them took his men who were to come in on the sabbath, with those who were to go out on the sabbath, for Jehoiada the priest did not dismiss *any of* the divisions.   1 Chr. 24:1

9 Then Jehoiada the priest gave to the captains of hundreds the spears and the large and small shields which had been King David's, which *were* in the house of God.

10 And he stationed all the people, each man with his weapon in his hand, from the right ^Tside of the house to the left ^Tside of house, by the altar and by the house, around the king.   shoulder

11 Then they brought out the king's son and put the crown on him, and *gave him*^Rthe testimony, and made him king. And Jehoiada and his sons anointed him and said, "^RLong live the king!"   Ex. 25:16 • 1 Sam. 10:24

12 When Athaliah heard the noise of the people running and praising the king, she came into the house of the LORD to the people.

13 And she looked, and behold, the king was standing by his pillar at the entrance, and the captains and the ^Ttrumpeters *were* beside the king. And all the people of the land rejoiced and blew trumpets, the singers with *their* musical instruments leading the praise. Then Athaliah tore her clothes and said, "Treason! Treason!"   trumpets

14 And Jehoiada the priest brought out the captains of hundreds who were appointed over the army, and said to them, "Bring her out between the ranks; and whoever follows her, put to death with the sword." For the priest said, "Let her not be put to death in the house of the LORD."

15 So they ᵀseized her,, and when she arrived at the entrance of ᴿthe Horse Gate of the king's house, they put her to death there.   *placed hands to her* • Neh. 3:28

Revival of Jehoiada—2 Kin. 11:17–20

16 Then Jehoiada made a covenant between himself and all the people and the king, that they should be the Lᴏʀᴅ's people.

17 And all the people went to the house of Baal, and tore it down, and they broke in pieces his altars and his images, and killed Mattan the priest of Baal before the altars.

18 Moreover, Jehoiada placed the offices of the house of the Lᴏʀᴅ under the authority of the Levitical priests, whom David had assigned over the house of the Lᴏʀᴅ, to offer the burnt offerings of the Lᴏʀᴅ, as it is written in the law of Moses—with rejoicing and singing according to the order of David.

19 And he stationed the gatekeepers of the house of the Lᴏʀᴅ, so that no one should enter who was in any way unclean.

20 And ᴷhe took the captains of hundreds, the nobles, the rulers of the people, and all the people of the land, and brought the king down from the house of the Lᴏʀᴅ, and came through the upper gate to the king's house. And they placed the king upon the royal throne.   2 Kin. 11:19

21 So all of the people of the land rejoiced and the city was quiet. For they had put Athaliah to death with the sword.

CHAPTER 24

Evaluation of Joash—2 Kin. 11:21—12:2

Jᴏᴀꜱʜᴿwas seven years old when he became king, and he reigned forty years in Jerusalem; and his mother's name was Zibiah from Beersheba.   2 Kin. 11:21; 12:1-15

2 And ᴿJoash did what was right in the sight of the Lᴏʀᴅ all the days of Jehoiada the priest.   2 Chr. 26:4, 5

3 And Jehoiada took two wives for him, and he became the father of sons and daughters.

Repair of the Temple—2 Kin. 12:4–16

4 Now it came about after this that Joash decided to restore the house of the Lᴏʀᴅ.

5 And he gathered the priests and Levites, and said to them, "Go out to the cities of Judah, and collect money from all Israel to ᵀrepair the house of your God annually, and you shall do the matter quickly." But the Levites did not act quickly.   *to strengthen*

6 So the king summoned Jehoiada the chief *priest* and said to him, "Why have you not required the Levites to bring in from Judah and from Jerusalem ᴿthe levy *fixed by* Moses the servant of the Lᴏʀᴅ on the congregation of Israel ᴿfor the tent of the testimony?"   Ex. 30:12-16 • Num. 1:50

7 For ᴿthe sons of the wicked Athaliah

⁸ I.e., wooden symbols of a female deity

had broken into the house of God and even ᵀused the holy things of the house of the Lᴏʀᴅ for the Baals.   2 Chr. 21:17 • *made*

8 So the king commanded, and ᴿthey made a chest and set it outside by the gate of the house of the Lᴏʀᴅ.   2 Kin. 12:9

9 And ᴿthey made a proclamation in Judah and Jerusalem to bring to the Lᴏʀᴅ the levy *fixed by* Moses the servant of God on Israel in the wilderness.   2 Chr. 36:22

10 And all the officers and all the people rejoiced and brought in their levies and ᵀdropped *them* into the chest until they had finished.   *threw*

11 And it came about whenever the chest was brought in to the king's officer by the Levites, and when they saw that there was much money, then the king's scribe and the chief priest's officer would come, empty the chest, take it, and return it to its place. Thus they did daily and collected much money.

12 And the king and Jehoiada gave it to those who did the work of the service of the house of the Lᴏʀᴅ; and they hired masons and carpenters to restore the house of the Lᴏʀᴅ, and also workers in iron and bronze to ᵀrepair the house of the Lᴏʀᴅ.   *to strengthen*

13 So the workmen labored, and the repair ᵀwork progressed in their hands, and they ᵀrestored the house of God according to its specifications, and strengthened it. *set up*

14 And when they had finished, they brought the rest of the money before the king and Jehoiada; and it was made into utensils for the house of the Lᴏʀᴅ, utensils for the service and the burnt offering, and pans and utensils of gold and silver. And they offered burnt offerings in the house of the Lᴏʀᴅ continually all the days of Jehoiada.

Death of Jehoiada

15 Now when Jehoiada reached a ripe old age he died; he was one hundred and thirty years old at his death.

16 And they buried him in the city of David among the kings, because he had done well in Israel and to God and His house.

Murder of Jehoiada's Son

17 But after the death of Jehoiada the officials of Judah came and bowed down to the king, and the king listened to them.

18 And they abandoned ᴿthe house of the Lᴏʀᴅ, the God of their fathers, and ᴿserved the ⁸Asherim and the idols; so ᴿwrath came upon Judah and Jerusalem for this their guilt.   2 Chr. 24:4 • Ex. 34:12-14 • Josh. 22:20

19 Yet ᴿHe sent prophets to them to bring them back to the Lᴏʀᴅ; though they testified against them, they would not listen. Jer. 7:25

20 Then the Spirit of God ᵀcame on Zechariah the son of Jehoiada the priest; and he stood above the people and said to them,

"Thus God has said, 'Why do you transgress the commandments of the LORD and do not prosper? Because you have forsaken the LORD, He has also forsaken you.' "   *clothed*

21 So they conspired against him and at the command of the king they stoned him to death in the court of the house of the LORD.

22 Thus Joash the king did not remember the kindness which his father Jehoiada had shown him, but he murdered his son. And as he died he said, "May ^Rthe LORD see and ^Tavenge!"   Gen. 9:5 • *seek*, or *require*

Destruction of Judah by Aram

23 Now it came about at the turn of the year that the army of the Arameans came up against him; and they came to Judah and Jerusalem, destroyed all the officials of the people from among the people, and sent all their spoil to the king of Damascus.

24 Indeed the army of the Arameans came with a small number of men; yet ^Rthe LORD delivered a very great army into their hands, ^Rbecause they had forsaken the LORD, the God of their fathers. Thus they executed judgment on Joash.   2 Chr. 16:7 • 2 Chr. 24:20

Death of Joash—2 Kin. 12:20, 21

25 And when they had departed from him (for they left him very sick), his own servants conspired against him because of the blood of the son of Jehoiada the priest, and murdered him on his bed. So he died, and they buried him in the city of David, but they did not bury him in the tombs of the kings.

26 Now these are those who conspired against him: Zabad the son of Shimeath the Ammonitess, and Jehozabad the son of Shimrith the Moabitess.

27 As to his sons and the many oracles against him and the rebuilding of the house of God, behold, they are written in the treatise of the Book of the Kings. Then Amaziah his son became king in his place.

CHAPTER 25

Evaluation of Amaziah—2 Kin. 14:1-6

AMAZIAH^R was twenty-five years old when he became king, and he reigned twenty-nine years in Jerusalem. And his mother's name was Jehoaddan of Jerusalem.   2 Kin. 14:1-6

2 And he did right in the sight of the LORD, yet not with a whole heart.

3 Now ^Rit came about as soon as the kingdom was firmly in his grasp, that he killed his servants who had slain his father the king.   2 Kin. 14:5 • *firm upon him*

4 However, he did not put their children to death, but *did* as it is written in the law in the book of Moses, which the LORD commanded, saying, "Fathers ^Rshall not be put to death for sons, nor sons be put to death for fathers, but each shall be put to death for his own sin."   Deut. 24:16

Victory over Edom

5 Moreover, Amaziah assembled Judah and appointed them according to *their* fathers' households under commanders of thousands and commanders of hundreds throughout Judah and Benjamin; and he ^Ttook a census of those from twenty years old and upward, and found them to be 300,000 choice men, *able* to go to war *and* handle spear and shield.   *mustered*

6 He hired also 100,000 valiant warriors out of Israel for ^Tone hundred talents of silver. $38,400,000

7 But ^Ra man of God came to him saying, "O king, do not let the army of Israel go with you, for the LORD is not with Israel *nor with* any of the sons of Ephraim.   2 Kin. 4:9

8 "But if you do go, do *it*, be strong for the battle; *yet* God will ^Tbring you down before the enemy, ^Rfor God has power to help and to bring down."   *cause to stumble* • 2 Chr. 14:11

9 And Amaziah said to the man of God, "But what *shall* we do for the hundred talents which I have given to the troops of Israel?" And the man of God answered, "The LORD has much more to give you than this."

10 Then Amaziah dismissed them, the troops which came to him from Ephraim, to go home; so their anger burned against Judah and they returned home in fierce anger.

11 Now Amaziah strengthened himself, and led his people forth, and went to ^Rthe Valley of Salt, and struck down 10,000 of the sons of Seir.   2 Kin. 14:7

12 The sons of Judah also captured 10,000 alive and brought them to the top of the cliff, and threw them down from the top of the cliff so that they were all dashed to pieces.

13 But the ^Ttroops whom Amaziah sent back from going with him to battle, raided the cities of Judah, from Samaria to Bethhoron, and struck down 3,000 of them, and plundered much spoil.   *sons of the troops*

Idolatry of Amaziah

14 Now it came about after Amaziah came from slaughtering the Edomites that he brought the gods of the sons of Seir, set them up as his gods, bowed down before them, and burned incense to them.

15 Then the anger of the LORD burned against Amaziah, and He sent him a prophet who said to him, "Why have you sought the gods of the people who have not delivered their own people from your hand?"

16 And it came about as he was talking with him that ^Tthe king said to him, "Have we appointed you a royal counselor? Stop! Why should you be struck down?" Then the prophet stopped and said, "I know that God has planned to destroy you, because you have done this, and have not listened to my counsel."   *he*

Defeat of Judah by Israel
2 Kin. 14:8–14

17 Then Amaziah king of Judah took counsel and sent to Joash the son of Jehoahaz the son of Jehu, the king of Israel, saying, "Come, let us face each other."
18 And Joash the king of Israel sent to Amaziah king of Judah, saying, "The thorn bush which was in Lebanon sent to the cedar which was in Lebanon, saying, 'Give your daughter to my son in marriage.' But there passed by a wild beast that was in Lebanon, and trampled the thorn bush.
19 "You said, 'Behold, you have 'defeated Edom.' And your heart has become proud in boasting. Now stay at home; for why should you provoke trouble that you, even you, should fall and Judah with you?"　*smitten*
20 But Amaziah would not listen, for it was from God, that He might deliver them into the hand *of Joash* because they had sought the gods of Edom.
21 So Joash king of Israel went up, and he and Amaziah king of Judah faced each other at Beth-shemesh, which belonged to Judah.
22 And Judah was defeated ᵀby Israel, and they fled each to his tent.　*before*
23 Then Joash king of Israel captured Amaziah king of Judah, the son of Joash the son of Jehoahaz, at Beth-shemesh, and brought him to Jerusalem, and tore down the wall of Jerusalem from the Gate of Ephraim to the Corner Gate, 400 cubits.
24 And *he took* all the gold and silver, and all the utensils which were found in the house of God with ᴿObed-edom, and the treasures of the king's house, the hostages also, and returned to Samaria.　1 Chr. 26:15

Death of Amaziah—2 Kin. 14:17–20

25 And Amaziah, the son of Joash king of Judah, lived fifteen years after the death of Joash, son of Jehoahaz, king of Israel.
26 Now the rest of the acts of Amaziah, from first to last, behold, are they not written in the Book of the Kings of Judah and Israel?
27 And from the time that Amaziah turned away from following the LORD they conspired against him in Jerusalem, and he fled to Lachish; but they sent after him to Lachish and killed him there.
28 Then they brought him on horses and buried him with his fathers in the city of Judah.

CHAPTER 26

Evaluation of Uzziah
2 Kin. 14:21, 22; 15:1–3

Aᴺᴰ all the people of Judah took Uzziah, who *was* sixteen years old, and made him king in the place of his father Amaziah.

2 He built Eloth and restored it to Judah after the king slept with his fathers.
3 Uzziah was sixteen years old when he became king, and he reigned fifty-two years in Jerusalem; and his mother's name was ᴬJechiliah of Jerusalem.　In 2 Kin. 15:2, *Jecoliah*
4 And he did right in the sight of the LORD according to all that his father Amaziah had done.
5 And he continued to seek God in the days of Zechariah, who had understanding through the vision of God; and as long as he sought the LORD, God prospered him.

Victories of Uzziah

6 Now he went out and ᴿwarred against the Philistines, and broke down the wall of Gath and the wall of Jabneh and the wall of Ashdod; and he built cities in *the area of* Ashdod and among the Philistines.　Is. 14:29
7 And ᴿGod helped him against the Philistines, and against the Arabians who lived in Gur-baal, and the Meunites.　2 Chr. 21:16
8 The Ammonites also gave tribute to Uzziah, and his fame extended to the border of Egypt, for he became very strong.
9 Moreover, Uzziah built towers in Jerusalem at ᴿthe Corner Gate and at the ᴿValley Gate and at the corner buttress and fortified them.　2 Chr. 25:23 • Neh. 2:13, 15; 3:13
10 And he built towers in the wilderness and hewed many cisterns, for he had much livestock, both in the ᵀlowland and in the plain. *He also had* plowmen and vinedressers in the hill country and the fertile fields, for he loved the soil.　Heb., *shephelah*
11 Moreover, Uzziah had an army ready for battle, which entered combat by divisions, according to the number of their muster, prepared by Jeiel the scribe and Maaseiah the official, under the direction of Hananiah, one of the king's officers.
12 The total number of the heads of the households, of valiant warriors, was 2,600.
13 And under their direction was an ᵀelite army of ᴿ307,500, who could wage war with great power, to help the king against the enemy.　*powerful* • 2 Chr. 25:5
14 Moreover, Uzziah prepared 'for all the army shields, spears, helmets, body armor, bows and sling stones.　*for them, for all*
15 And in Jerusalem he made engines *of war* invented by skillful men to be on the towers and on the corners, for the purpose of shooting arrows and great stones. Hence his ᵀfame spread afar, for he was marvelously helped until he *was* strong.　*name*

Sinful Offering of Uzziah

16 But when he became strong, his heart was so 'proud that he acted corruptly, and he was unfaithful to the LORD his God, for he entered the temple of the LORD to burn incense on the altar of incense.　*lifted up*

17 Then [R]Azariah the priest entered after him and with him eighty priests of the LORD, valiant men.　　　　　1 Chr. 6:10

18 And they opposed Uzziah the king and said to him, "It is not for you, Uzziah, to burn incense to the LORD, [R]but for the priests, the sons of Aaron who are consecrated to burn incense. Get out of the sanctuary, for you have been unfaithful, and will have no honor from the LORD God." Ex. 30:7

19 But Uzziah, with a censer in his hand for burning incense, was enraged; and while he was enraged with the priests,[R]the leprosy broke out on his forehead before the priests in the house of the LORD, beside the altar of incense.　　　　　2 Kin. 5:25-27

20 And Azariah the chief priest and all the priests looked at him, and behold, he *was* leprous on his forehead; and they hurried him out of there, and he himself also hastened to get out because the LORD had smitten him.

21 [R]And King Uzziah was a leper to the day of his death; and he lived in[R]a separate house, being a leper, for he was cut off from the house of the LORD. And Jotham his son *was* over the king's house judging the people of the land.　　2 Kin. 15:5-7 • [Lev. 13:46]

Death of Uzziah—2 Kin. 15:7

22 Now the rest of the acts of Uzziah, first to last, the prophet[R]Isaiah, the son of Amoz, has written.　　　　　Is. 1:1

23 So Uzziah slept with his fathers, and they buried him with his fathers[R]in the field of the grave which belonged to the kings, for they said, "He is a leper." And Jotham his son became king in his place. 2 Chr. 21:20

CHAPTER 27

The Reign of Jotham—2 Kin. 15:33-38

JOTHAM was twenty-five years old when he became king, and he reigned sixteen years in Jerusalem. And his mother's name was Jerushah the daughter of Zadok.

2 And he did right in the sight of the LORD, according to all that his father Uzziah had done;[R]however he did not enter the temple of the LORD. But the people continued acting corruptly.　　　　　2 Chr. 26:16

3 He built the upper gate of the house of the LORD, and he built extensively the wall of[R]Ophel.　　　2 Chr. 33:14; Neh. 3:26

4 Moreover, he built [R]cities in the hill country of Judah, and he built fortresses and towers on the wooded *hills.*　2 Chr. 11:5

5 He fought also with the king of the Ammonites and prevailed over them so that the Ammonites gave him during that year one hundred talents of silver, ten thousand [9]kors of wheat and ten thousand of barley. The Ammonites also paid him this *amount* in the second and in the third year.

6 So Jotham became mighty because he ordered his ways before the LORD his God.

7 [R]Now the rest of the acts of Jotham, even all his wars and his acts, behold, they are written in the Book of the Kings of Israel and Judah.　　　　　2 Kin. 15:36

8 He was[R]twenty-five years old when he became king, and he reigned sixteen years in Jerusalem.　　　　　2 Chr. 27:1

9 And Jotham slept with his fathers, and they buried him in the city of David; and Ahaz his son became king in his place.

CHAPTER 28

Evaluation of Ahaz—2 Kin. 16:1-4

AHAZ[R] *was* twenty years old when he became king, and he reigned sixteen years in Jerusalem; and[R]he did not do right in the sight of the LORD as David his father *had* done.　　　2 Kin. 16:2-4 • 2 Chr. 27:2

2 [R]But he walked in the ways of the kings of Israel; he also [R]made molten images for the Baals.　　　2 Chr. 22:3 • Ex. 34:17

3 Moreover, [R]he burned incense in the valley of Ben-hinnom, and[R]burned his sons in fire, according to the abominations of the nations whom the LORD had driven out before the sons of Israel. Josh. 15:8 • [Lev. 18:21]

4 And he sacrificed and[R]burned incense on the high places, on the hills, and under every green tree.　　　　　2 Chr. 28:25

Defeat of Judah—2 Kin. 16:5-8; Is. 7:1

5 Wherefore, the LORD his God delivered him into the hand of the king of Aram; and they [T]defeated him and carried away from him a great number of captives, and brought *them* to Damascus. And he was also delivered into the hand of the king of Israel, who [T]inflicted him with heavy casualties.　　smote • smote him with a great smiting

6 For[R]Pekah the son of Remaliah slew in Judah 120,000 in one day, all valiant men, because they had forsaken the LORD God of their fathers.　　　　　2 Kin. 16:5

7 And Zichri, a mighty man of Ephraim, slew Maaseiah the king's son, and Azrikam the ruler of the house and Elkanah the second to the king.

8 And [R]the sons of Israel carried away captive of their brethren 200,000 women, sons, and daughters; and [T]took also a great deal of spoil from them, and they brought the spoil to Samaria.　　Deut. 28:25 • plundered

9 But a prophet of the LORD was there, whose name *was* Oded; and[R]he went out to meet the army which came to Samaria and said to them, "Behold, because the LORD, the God of your fathers,[R]was angry with Ju-

---

[9] I.e., A kor equals approx. 10 bushels

dah, He has delivered them into your hand, and you have slain them in a rage *which* has even reached heaven.   2 Chr. 25:15 • [Is. 47:6]

10 "And now you are proposing to subjugate for yourselves the people of Judah and Jerusalem for male and female slaves. Surely, *do* you not *have* transgressions of your own against the LORD your God?

11 "Now therefore, listen to me and return the captives ^Rwhom you captured from your brothers, ^Rfor the burning anger of the LORD is against you."   2 Chr. 28:8 • James 2:13

12 Then some of the heads of the sons of Ephraim—Azariah the son of Johanan, Berechiah the son of Meshillemoth, Jehizkiah the son of Shallum, and Amasa the son of Hadlai—arose against those who were coming from the battle,

13 and said to them, "You must not bring the captives in here, for you are proposing *to bring* upon us guilt against the LORD adding to our sins and our guilt; for our guilt is great so that *His* burning anger is against Israel."

14 So the armed men left the captives and the spoil before the officers and all the assembly.

15 Then^Rthe men who were designated by name arose, took the captives, and they clothed all their naked ones from the spoil; and they gave them clothes and sandals, fed them and ^Rgave them drink, anointed them *with* oil, led all their feeble ones on donkeys, and brought them to Jericho, the city of palm trees, to their brothers; then they returned to Samaria.   2 Chr. 28:12 • [Prov. 25:21]

16 ^RAt that time King Ahaz sent to the ¹⁰kings of Assyria for help.   2 Kin. 16:7

17 For again the Edomites had come and attacked Judah, and carried away captives.

18 The Philistines also had invaded the cities of the lowland and of the Negev of Judah, and had taken Beth-shemesh, Aijalon, Gederoth, and Soco with its villages, Timnah with its villages, and Gimzo with its villages, and they settled there.

19 For the LORD humbled Judah because of Ahaz king of^RIsrael, for he had brought about a lack of restraint in Judah and was very unfaithful to the LORD.   2 Chr. 21:2

20 So ^RTilgath-pilneser king of Assyria came against him and afflicted him instead of strengthening him.   1 Chr. 5:26

21 Although Ahaz took a portion out of the house of the LORD and out of the palace of the king and of the princes, and gave *it* to the king of Assyria, it did not help him.

Idolatry of Ahaz—2 Kin. 16:12

22 Now in the time of his distress this same King Ahaz^Rbecame yet more unfaithful to the LORD.   Is. 1:5; Jer. 5:3; Rev. 16:11

23 For he sacrificed to the gods of Damas-cus which had ^Tdefeated him, and said, "Because the gods of the kings of Aram helped them, I will sacrifice to them that they may help me." But they became the ^Tdownfall of him and all Israel.   *smitten • stumbling*

24 Moreover, when Ahaz gathered together the utensils of the house of God, he ^Rcut the utensils of the house of God in pieces; and he closed the doors of the house of the LORD, and made altars for himself in every corner of Jerusalem.   2 Kin. 16:17

25 And in every city of Judah he made high places to burn incense to other gods, and provoked the LORD, the God of his fathers, to anger.

Death of Ahaz—2 Kin. 16:20

26 ^RNow the rest of his acts and all his ways, from first to last, behold, they are written in the Book of the Kings of Judah and Israel.   2 Kin. 16:19, 20

27 ^RSo Ahaz slept with his fathers, and they buried him in the city, in Jerusalem, for they did not bring him into the tombs of the kings of Israel; and Hezekiah his son reigned in his place.   2 Kin. 16:20; 2 Chr. 24:25

CHAPTER 29

Evaluation of Hezekiah—2 Kin. 18:2, 3

HEZEKIAH^R became king *when he was* twenty-five years old; and he reigned twenty-nine years in Jerusalem. And his mother's name *was* Abijah, the daughter of Zechariah.   2 Kin. 18:1-3

2 And^Rhe did right in the sight of the LORD, according to all that his father David had done.   2 Chr. 28:1; 34:2

Purification of the Temple

3 In the first year of his reign, in the first month, he^Ropened the doors of the house of the LORD and repaired them. 2 Chr. 28:24; 29:7

4 And he brought in the priests and the Levites, and gathered them into the square on the east.

5 Then he said to them, "Listen to me, O Levites. ^RConsecrate yourselves now, and consecrate the house of the LORD, the God of your fathers, and carry the uncleanness out from the holy place.   2 Chr. 29:15, 34; 35:6

6 "For our fathers have been unfaithful and have done evil in the sight of the LORD our God, and have forsaken Him and turned their faces away from the dwelling place of the LORD, and have turned *their* backs.

7 "They have also shut the doors of the porch and put out the lamps, and have not burned incense or offered burnt offerings in the holy place to the God of Israel.

¹⁰ Ancient versions read *king*

8"Therefore ᴿthe wrath of the LORD was against Judah and Jerusalem, and He has made them an object of terror, of horror, and of ᴿhissing, as you see with your own eyes.   2 Chr. 24:20 • Jer. 25:9, 18

9"For behold, our fathers have fallen by the sword, and our sons and our daughters and our wives are in captivity for this.

10"Now it is in my heart to make a covenant with the LORD God of Israel, that His burning anger may turn away from us.

11"My sons, do not be negligent now, for ᴿthe LORD has chosen you to stand before Him, to minister to Him, and to be His ministers and burn incense."   Num. 3:6; 8:6

12 Then the Levites arose: ᴿMahath, the son of Amasai and Joel the son of Azariah, from the sons of the Kohathites; and from the sons of Merari, Kish the son of Abdi and Azariah the son of Jehallelel; and from the Gershonites, Joah the son of Zimmah and Eden the son of Joah;   2 Chr. 31:13

13 and from the sons of Elizaphan, Shimri and ᴬJeiel; and from the sons of Asaph, Zechariah and Mattaniah;   Jeuel

14 and from the sons of Heman, ᴬJehiel and Shimei; and from the sons of Jeduthun, Shemaiah and Uzziel.   Jehuel, 1 Chr. 15:18, 20

15 And they assembled their brothers, ᴿconsecrated themselves, and went in ᴿto cleanse the house of the LORD, according to the commandment of the king by the words of the LORD.   2 Chr. 29:5 • 1 Chr. 23:28

16 So the priests went in to the inner part of the house of the LORD to cleanse it, and every unclean thing which they found in the temple of the LORD they brought out to the court of the house of the LORD. Then the Levites received it to carry out to ᴿthe Kidron ᴬvalley.   2 Chr. 15:16 • wadi

17 Now they began ᵀthe consecration ᴿon the first day of the first month, and on the eighth day of the month they entered the porch of the LORD. Then they consecrated the house of the LORD in eight days, and finished on the sixteenth day of the first month.   to consecrate • 2 Chr. 29:3

18 Then they went in to King Hezekiah and said, "We have cleansed the whole house of the LORD, the altar of burnt offering with all of its utensils, and the table of showbread with all of its utensils.

19"Moreover, all the utensils which King Ahaz had discarded during his reign in his unfaithfulness, we have prepared and consecrated; and behold, they are before the altar of the LORD."

Restoration of Temple Worship

20 Then King Hezekiah arose early and assembled the princes of the city and went up to the house of the LORD.

21 And they brought seven bulls, seven rams, seven lambs, and seven male goats ᴿfor a sin offering for the kingdom, the sanctuary, and Judah. And he ordered the priests, the sons of Aaron, to offer them on the altar of the LORD.   Lev. 4:3-14

22 So they slaughtered the bulls, and the priests took the blood and sprinkled it on the altar. They also slaughtered the rams and sprinkled the blood on the altar; they slaughtered the lambs also and ᴿsprinkled the blood on the altar.   Lev. 4:18

23 Then they brought the male goats of the sin offering before the king and the assembly, and they laid their hands on them.

24 And the priests slaughtered them and purged the altar with their blood to atone for all Israel, for the king ordered the burnt offering and the sin offering for all Israel.

25 He then stationed the Levites in the house of the LORD with cymbals, with harps, and with lyres, according to the command of David and of Gad the king's seer, and of Nathan the prophet; for the command was from the LORD through His prophets.

26 And the Levites stood with ᴿthe musical instruments of David, and ᴿthe priests with the trumpets.   1 Chr. 23:5 • 2 Chr. 5:12

27 Then Hezekiah gave the order to offer the burnt offering on the altar. When the burnt offering began, the song to the LORD also began with the trumpets, accompanied by the instruments of David, king of Israel.

28 While the whole assembly worshiped, the singers also sang and the trumpets sounded; all this continued until the burnt offering was finished.

29 Now at the completion of the burnt offerings, the king and all who were present with him bowed down and worshiped.

30 Moreover, King Hezekiah and the officials ordered the Levites to sing praises to the LORD with the words of David and Asaph the seer. So they sang praises with joy, and bowed down and worshiped.

31 Then Hezekiah answered and said, "Now that you have consecrated yourselves to the LORD, come near and bring sacrifices and thank offerings to the house of the LORD." And the assembly brought sacrifices and thank offerings, and all those who were willing brought burnt offerings.

32 And the number of the burnt offerings which the assembly brought was 70 bulls, 100 rams, and 200 lambs; all these were for a burnt offering to the LORD.

33 And the consecrated things were 600 bulls and 3,000 sheep.

34 But the priests were too few, so that they were unable to skin all the burnt offerings; therefore their brothers the Levites helped them until the work was completed, and until the other priests had consecrated themselves. For the Levites were more conscientious to consecrate themselves than the priests.

35 And there were also ᴿmany burnt offerings with the fat of the peace offerings and with the libations for the burnt offerings. Thus the service of the house of the LORD was established again.   2 Chr. 29:32

36 Then Hezekiah and all the people rejoiced over what God had prepared for the people, because the thing came about suddenly.

CHAPTER 30

Celebration of the Passover

Now Hezekiah sent to all Israel and Judah and wrote letters also to Ephraim and Manasseh, that they should come to the house of the LORD at Jerusalem to celebrate the Passover to the LORD God of Israel.

2 For the king and his princes and all the assembly in Jerusalem had decided to celebrate the Passover in the second month,

3 since they could not celebrate it at that time, because the priests had not consecrated themselves in sufficient numbers, nor had the people been gathered to Jerusalem.

4 Thus the thing was right in the sight of the king and all the assembly.

5 So they established a decree to circulate a proclamation throughout all Israel from Beersheba even to Dan, that they should come to celebrate the Passover to the LORD God of Israel at Jerusalem. For they had not celebrated *it* in great numbers as it was prescribed.   *voice • written*

6 And the couriers went throughout all Israel and Judah with the letters from the hand of the king and his princes, even according to the command of the king, saying, "O sons of Israel, return to the LORD God of Abraham, Isaac, and Israel, that He may return to those of you who escaped *and* are left from the hand of the kings of Assyria.

7 "And do not be like your fathers and your brothers, who were unfaithful to the LORD God of their fathers, so that He made them a horror, as you see.   Ezek. 20:13

8 "Now do not stiffen your neck like your fathers, but yield to the LORD and enter His sanctuary which He has consecrated forever, and serve the LORD your God, that His burning anger may turn away from you.

9 "For if you return to the LORD, your brothers and your sons will *find* compassion before those who led them captive, and will return to this land. For the LORD your God is gracious and compassionate, and will not turn *His* face away from you if you return to Him."   Deut. 30:2 • [Ex. 34:6, 7; Mic. 7:18]

10 So the couriers passed from city to city through the country of Ephraim and Manasseh, and as far as Zebulun, but they laughed them to scorn, and mocked them.   *runners*

11 Nevertheless some men of Asher, Manasseh, and Zebulun humbled themselves and came to Jerusalem.   2 Chr. 30:18, 21, 25

12 The hand of God was also on Judah to give them one heart to do what the king and the princes commanded by the word of the LORD.   [2 Cor. 3:5; Phil. 2:13; Heb. 13:20, 21]

13 Now many people were gathered at Je-

rusalem to celebrate the Feast of Unleavened Bread in the second month, a very large assembly.   2 Chr. 30:2

14 And they arose and removed the altars which *were* in Jerusalem; they also removed all the incense altars and cast *them* into the brook Kidron.   2 Chr. 28:24 • 2 Chr. 29:16

15 Then they slaughtered the Passover *lambs* on the fourteenth of the second month. And the priests and Levites were ashamed of themselves and consecrated themselves, and brought burnt offerings to the house of the LORD.   2 Chr. 30:2, 3

16 And they stood at their stations after their custom, according to the law of Moses the man of God; the priests sprinkled the blood *which they received* from the hand of the Levites.   2 Chr. 35:10, 15

17 For *there were* many in the assembly who had not consecrated themselves; therefore, the Levites *were* over the slaughter of the Passover *lambs* for everyone who *was* unclean, in order to consecrate *them* to the LORD.   2 Chr. 29:34

18 For a multitude of the people, *even* many from Ephraim and Manasseh, Issachar and Zebulun, had not purified themselves, yet they ate the Passover otherwise than prescribed. For Hezekiah prayed for them, saying, "May the good LORD pardon

19 everyone who prepares his heart to seek God, the LORD God of his fathers, though not according to the purification *rules* of the sanctuary."   2 Chr. 19:3

20 So the LORD heard Hezekiah and healed the people.   James 5:16

21 And the sons of Israel present in Jerusalem celebrated the Feast of Unleavened Bread *for* seven days with great joy, and the Levites and the priests praised the LORD day after day with loud instruments to the LORD.

22 Then Hezekiah spoke encouragingly to all the Levites who showed good insight *in the things* of the LORD. So they ate for the appointed seven days, sacrificing peace offerings and giving thanks to the LORD God of their fathers.   2 Chr. 32:6 • *to the heart of*

Extra Feast Days

23 Then the whole assembly decided to celebrate *the feast* another seven days, so they celebrated the seven days with joy.

24 For Hezekiah king of Judah had contributed to the assembly 1,000 bulls and 7,000 sheep, and the princes had contributed to the assembly 1,000 bulls and 10,000 sheep; and a large number of priests consecrated themselves.   2 Chr. 35:7 • 2 Chr. 29:34

25 And all the assembly of Judah rejoiced, with the priests and the Levites, and all the assembly that came from Israel, both the sojourners who came from the land of Israel and those living in Judah.   2 Chr. 30:11, 18

26 So there was great joy in Jerusalem, because there was nothing like this in Jeru-

salem [R]since the days of Solomon the son of David, king of Israel.　2 Chr. 7:8-10

27 Then [R]the Levitical priests arose and blessed the people; and their voice was heard and their prayer came to His holy dwelling place, to heaven.　2 Chr. 23:18

CHAPTER 31

Destruction of the Idols—2 Kin. 18:4

N<small>OW</small> when all this was finished, all Israel who were present went out to the cities of Judah, broke the pillars in pieces, cut down the [11]Asherim, and pulled down the high places and the altars throughout all Judah and Benjamin, as well as in Ephraim and Manasseh, until they had destroyed them all. Then all the sons of Israel returned to their cities, each to his possession.

Contribution for the Priests and Levites

2 And Hezekiah appointed [R]the divisions of the priests and the Levites by their divisions, each according to his service, *both* the priests and the Levites, for burnt offerings and for peace offerings, to minister and to give thanks and to praise in the gates of the camp of the LORD.　1 Chr. 24:1

3 *He* also *appointed* [R]the king's portion of his goods for the burnt offerings, *namely,* for the morning and evening burnt offerings, and the burnt offerings for the sabbaths and for the new moons and for the fixed festivals, [R]as it is written in the law of the LORD.　2 Chr. 35:7 • Num. 28:1—29:40

4 Also he commanded the people who lived in Jerusalem to give the portion due to the priests and the Levites, that they might devote themselves to the law of the LORD.

5 And as soon as the [T]order spread, the sons of Israel provided in abundance the first fruits of grain, new wine, oil, honey, and of all the produce of the field; and they brought in abundantly the tithe of all.　*word*

6 And the sons of Israel and Judah who lived in the cities of Judah, also brought in the tithe of oxen and sheep, and the tithe of sacred gifts which were consecrated to the LORD their God, and placed *them* in heaps.

7 In the third month they began to [T]make the heaps, and finished *them* by the seventh month.　*found*

8 And when Hezekiah and the rulers came and saw the heaps, they blessed the LORD and [R]His people Israel.　Ps. 33:12; 144:15

9 Then Hezekiah questioned the priests and the Levites concerning the heaps.

10 And Azariah the chief priest [R]of the house of Zadok said to [T]him, "Since the contributions began to be brought into the house of the LORD, we have had enough to eat with plenty left over, for the LORD has blessed His people, and this great quantity is left over."　1 Chr. 6:8, 9 • *him, and he said*

Reorganization of the Priests and Levites

11 Then Hezekiah commanded *them* to prepare [R]rooms in the house of the LORD, and they prepared *them.*　1 Kin. 6:5, 8

12 And they faithfully brought in the contributions and the tithes and the consecrated things; and Conaniah the Levite *was* the officer in charge [T]of them and his brother Shimei *was* second.　2 Chr. 35:9

13 And Jehiel, Azaziah, Nahath, Asahel, Jerimoth, Jozabad, Eliel, Ismachiah, Mahath, and Benaiah *were* overseers [T]under the authority of Conaniah and Shimei his brother by the appointment of King Hezekiah, and Azariah *was* the *chief* officer of the house of God.　*from the hand of*

14 And Kore the son of Imnah the Levite, the keeper of the eastern *gate, was* over the freewill offerings of God, to apportion the contributions for the LORD and the most holy things.

15 And [T]under his authority *were* [R]Eden, Miniamin, Jeshua, Shemaiah, Amariah, and Shecaniah in the cities of the priests, to distribute faithfully *their portions* to their brothers by divisions, whether great or small,　*under his hand* • 2 Chr. 29:12

16 without regard to their genealogical enrollment, to the males from [T]thirty years old and upward—everyone who entered the house of the LORD [R]for his daily obligations—for their work in their duties according to their divisions;　Heb., *three* • Ezra 3:4

17 as well as the priests who were enrolled genealogically according to their fathers' households, and the Levites [R]from twenty years old and upwards, by their duties and their divisions.　1 Chr. 23:24

18 And the genealogical enrollment *included* [T]all their little children, their wives, their sons, and their daughters, for the whole assembly, for they consecrated themselves faithfully in holiness.　*with all*

19 Also for the sons of Aaron the priests *who were* in [R]the pasture lands of their cities, or in each and every city, *there were* men who were designated by name to distribute portions to every male among the priests and to everyone genealogically enrolled among the Levites.　Lev. 25:34; Num. 35:2-5

20 And thus Hezekiah did throughout all Judah; and [R]he did what *was* good, right, and true before the LORD his God.　2 Kin. 20:3; 22:2

21 And every work which he began in the service of the house of God in law and in commandment, seeking his God, he did with all his heart and [R]prospered.　[Deut. 29:9]

---

[11] I.e., wooden symbols of a female deity

CHAPTER 32

Invasion by Assyria
2 Kin. 18:17—19:37; Is. 36:2—37:38

AFTER these acts of faithfulness Sennacherib king of Assyria came and invaded Judah and besieged the fortified cities, and thought to break into them for himself.

2 Now when Hezekiah saw that Sennacherib had come, and that [T]he intended to make war on Jerusalem, *his face for war against*

3 he decided with his officers and his warriors to cut off the *supply of* water from the springs which *were* outside the city, and they helped him.

4 So many people assembled and stopped up all the springs and the stream which flowed [T]through the region, saying, "Why should the kings of Assyria come and find abundant water?"   *in the midst of the land*

5 And he took courage and rebuilt all the wall that had been broken down, and [T]erected towers on it, and *built* another outside wall, and strengthened the Millo *in* the city of David, and made weapons and shields in great number.   *raised on the towers*

6 And he appointed military officers over the people, and gathered them to him in the square at the city gate, and spoke [T]encouragingly to them, saying,   *upon their hearts*

7 "Be[R] strong and courageous, do not fear or be dismayed because of the king of Assyria, nor because of all the multitude which is with him; for the one with us is greater than the one with him.   1 Chr. 22:13

8 "With him is *only* an arm of flesh, but with us is the LORD our God to help us and to fight our battles." And the people relied on the words of Hezekiah king of Judah.

9 After this[R] Sennacherib king of Assyria sent his servants to Jerusalem while he *was* [T]besieging Lachish with all his forces with him, against Hezekiah king of Judah and against all Judah who *were* at Jerusalem, saying,   2 Kin. 18:17 • *against*

10 "Thus says Sennacherib king of Assyria, 'On what are you trusting that you are remaining in Jerusalem under siege?

11 'Is not Hezekiah misleading you to give yourselves over to die by hunger and by thirst, saying, "The LORD our God will deliver us from [T]the hand of the king of Assyria"?   *palm*

12 'Has not the same Hezekiah taken away His high places and His altars, and said to Judah and [T]Jerusalem, "You shall worship before one altar, and on it you shall [T]burn incense"?   *Jerusalem, saying • offer up in smoke*

13 'Do you not know what I and my fathers have done to all the peoples of the lands?[R] Were the gods of the nations of the lands able at all to deliver their land from my hand?   2 Kin. 18:33-35

14 'Who[R] *was there* among all the gods of those nations which my fathers utterly de-

stroyed who could deliver his people out of my hand, that your God should be able to deliver you from my hand?   [Is. 10:9–11]

15 'Now therefore, do not let Hezekiah deceive you or mislead you like this, and do not believe him, for [T]no god of any nation or kingdom was able to deliver his people from my hand or from the hand of my fathers. How much less shall your God deliver you from my hand?' "   Ex. 5:2; Is. 36:18-20; Dan. 3:15

16 And his servants spoke further against the LORD God and against His servant Hezekiah.

17 He also wrote letters to insult the LORD God of Israel, and to speak against Him, saying, "As the gods of the nations of the lands [T]have not delivered their people from my hand, so the God of Hezekiah shall not deliver His people from my hand."   *who have*

18 And [R]they called this out with a loud voice in the language of Judah to the people of Jerusalem who were on the wall, to frighten and terrify them, so that they might take the city.   2 Kin. 18:28

19 And they spoke [T]of the God of Jerusalem as of the gods of the peoples of the earth, the work of men's hands.   *to*

20 But King Hezekiah and Isaiah the prophet, the son of Amoz, prayed about this and cried out to heaven.

21 And the LORD sent an angel who destroyed every mighty warrior, commander and officer in the camp of the king of Assyria. So he returned [T]in shame to his own land. And when he had entered the temple of his god, some of his own children killed him there with the sword.   *in shame of face*

22 So the LORD saved Hezekiah and the inhabitants of Jerusalem from the hand of Sennacherib the king of Assyria, and from the hand of all *others,* and guided them on every side.

Restoration of Hezekiah
2 Kin. 20:1–11; Is. 38:1–8

23 And many were bringing gifts to the LORD at Jerusalem and choice presents to Hezekiah king of Judah, so that he was exalted in the sight of all nations thereafter.

24 In those days Hezekiah became mortally ill; and he prayed to the LORD, and [T]the LORD spoke to him and gave him a sign. *He*

25 But Hezekiah gave no return for the benefit [T]he received, because his heart was [T]proud; therefore wrath came on him and on Judah and Jerusalem.   *to him • high*

26 However, Hezekiah humbled the pride of his heart, both he and the inhabitants of Jerusalem, so that the wrath of the LORD did not come on them in the days of Hezekiah.

Wealth of Hezekiah

27 Now Hezekiah had immense riches and honor; and he made for himself treasur-

ies for silver, gold, precious stones, spices, shields and all kinds of valuable articles,

28 storehouses also for the produce of grain, wine and oil, pens for all kinds of cattle and sheepfolds for the flocks.

29 And he made cities for himself, and acquired flocks and herds in abundance; for God had given him very great wealth.

30 It was Hezekiah who ᴿstopped the upper outlet of the waters of ᴿGihon and directed them to the west side of the city of David. And Hezekiah prospered in all that he did.   2 Kin. 20:20 • 1 Kin. 1:33

Sin of Hezekiah
2 Kin. 20:12–19; Is. 39:1–8

31 And even in the matter of ᴿthe envoys of the rulers of Babylon, who sent to him to inquire of ᴿthe wonder that had happened in the land, God left him alone only ᴿto test him, that He might know all that was in his heart.   2 Kin. 20:12 • Is. 38:7 • [Deut. 8:16]

Death of Hezekiah—2 Kin. 20:20, 21

32 Now the rest of the acts of Hezekiah and his deeds of devotion, behold, they are written in the vision of Isaiah the prophet, the son of Amoz, in the Book of the Kings of Judah and Israel.

33 So Hezekiah slept with his fathers, and they buried him in the ᴬupper section of the tombs of the sons of David; and all Judah and the inhabitants of Jerusalem ᴿhonored him at his death. And his son Manasseh became king in his place.   ascent to • Ps. 112:6

CHAPTER 33

The Reign of Manasseh
2 Kin. 21:1–9, 17, 18

Mᴬɴᴀꜱꜱᴇʜᴿwas twelve years old when he became king, and he reigned fifty-five years in Jerusalem.   2 Kin. 21:1-9

2 Andᴿhe did evil in the sight of the Lord according to the abominations of the nations whom the Lord dispossessed before the sons of Israel.   2 Chr. 28:3; [Jer. 15:4]

3 For he rebuilt the high places which Hezekiah his father had broken down; ᴿhe also erected altars for the Baals and made [12]Asherim, and worshiped all the host of heaven and served them.   Deut. 16:21

4 And he built altars in the house of the Lord of which the Lord had said, "My name shall be in Jerusalem forever."

5 For he built altars for all the host of heaven in ᴿthe two courts of the house of the Lord.   2 Chr. 4:9

6 And he made his sons pass through the fire in the valley of Ben-hinnom; and he practiced witchcraft, used divination, practiced sorcery, and dealt with mediums and spiritists. He did much evil in the sight of the Lord, provoking Him to anger.

7 Then he put the carved image of the idol which he had made in the house of God, of which God had said to David and to Solomon his son, "In this house and in Jerusalem, which I have chosen from all the tribes of Israel, I will put My name forever;

8 and I will not again remove the foot of Israel from the landᴿwhich I have appointed for your fathers, if only they will observe to do all that I have commanded them according to all the law, the statutes, and the ordinances given through Moses."   2 Sam. 7:10

9 Thus Manasseh misled Judah and the inhabitants of Jerusalem to do more evil than the nations whom the Lord destroyed before the sons of Israel.

10 And the Lord spoke to Manasseh and his people, but they paid no attention.

11 ᴿTherefore the Lord brought the commanders of the army of the king of Assyria against them, and they captured Manasseh with [13]hooks, bound him with bronze chains, and took him to Babylon.   Deut. 28:36

12 And when he was in distress, he entreated the Lord his God and humbled himself greatly before the God of his fathers.

13 When he prayed to Him, ᴿHe was moved by his entreaty and heard his supplication, and brought him again to Jerusalem to his kingdom. Then Manassehᴿknew that the Lord was God.   2 Chr. 20 • Dan. 4:32

14 Now after this he built the outer wall of the city of David on the west side of ᴿGihon, in the valley, even to the entrance of the ᴿFish Gate; and he encircled the Ophel with it and made it very high. Then he put army commanders in all the fortified cities of Judah.   1 Kin. 1:33 • Neh. 3:3

15 He also ᴿremoved the foreign gods and the idol from the house of the Lord, as well as all the altars which he had built on the mountain of the house of the Lord and in Jerusalem, and he threw them outside the city.   2 Chr. 33:3-7

16 And he set up the altar of the Lord and sacrificed ᴿpeace offerings and thank offerings on it; and he ordered Judah to serve the Lord God of Israel.   Lev. 7:11-18

17 Neverthelessᴿthe people still sacrificed in the high places, although only to the Lord their God.   2 Chr. 32:12

18 Now the rest of the acts of Manasseh even his prayer to his God, and the words of the seers who spoke to him in the name of the Lord God of Israel, behold, they are among the records of the kings of Israel.

19 His prayer also and ᴿhow God was entreated by him, and all his sin, his unfaithfulness, and the sites on which he built high places and erected the Asherim and the carved images, before he humbled himself,

[12] I.e., wooden symbols of a female deity
[13] I.e., thong put through the nose

behold, they are written in the records of the [T]Hozai.   2 Chr. 33:13 • Gr., reads *seers*
20 So Manasseh slept with his fathers, and they buried him in his own house. And Amon his son became king in his place.

The Reign of Amon—2 Kin. 21:19–26

21 [R]Amon *was* twenty-two years old when he became king, and he reigned two years in Jerusalem.   2 Kin. 21:19-24
22 And he did evil in the sight of the LORD as Manasseh his father[R]had done, and Amon sacrificed to all[R]the carved images which his father Manasseh had made, and he served them.   2 Chr. 33:2-7 • 2 Chr. 34:3, 4
23 Moreover, he did not humble himself before the LORD[R]as his father Manasseh had done, but Amon multiplied guilt. 2 Chr. 33:12
24 Finally his servants conspired against him and put him to death in his own house.
25 But the people of the land[T]killed all the conspirators against King Amon, and the people of the land made Josiah his son king in his place.   smote

CHAPTER 34

Evaluation of Josiah—2 Kin. 22:1, 2

JOSIAH[R]*was* eight years old when he became king, and he reigned thirty-one years in Jerusalem.   2 Kin. 22:1, 2; Jer. 1:2; 3:6
2 And[R]he did right in the sight of the LORD, and walked in the ways of his father David and did not turn aside to the right or to the left.   2 Chr. 29:2

Early Reforms of Josiah

3 For in the eighth year of his reign while he was still a youth, he began to seek the God of his father David; and in the twelfth year he began to purge Judah and Jerusalem of the high places, the Asherim, the carved images, and the molten images.
4 And they tore down the altars of the Baals in his presence, and[R]the incense altars that were high above them he chopped down; also the Asherim, the carved images, and the molten images he broke in pieces and [R]ground to powder and scattered *it* on the graves of those who had sacrificed to them.   2 Kin. 23:4, 5, 11 • Ex. 32:20
5 Then[R]he burned the bones of the priests on their altars, and purged Judah and Jerusalem.   1 Kin. 13:2; 2 Kin. 23:20
6 And[R]in the cities of Manasseh, Ephraim, Simeon, even as far as Naphtali, in their surrounding ruins,   2 Kin. 23:15, 19
7 he also tore down the altars and[R]beat the Asherim and the carved images into powder, and chopped down all the incense altars throughout the land of Israel. Then he returned to Jerusalem.   2 Chr. 31:1

Repair of the Temple—2 Kin. 22:3–7

8 [R]Now in the eighteenth year of his reign, when he had purged the land and the house, he sent Shaphan the son of Azaliah, and Maaseiah an official of the city, and Joah the son of Joahaz the recorder, to repair the house of the LORD his God.   2 Kin. 22:3-20
9 And they came to Hilkiah the high priest and delivered the money that was brought into the house of God, which the Levites, the [T]doorkeepers, had collected [T]from Manasseh and Ephraim, and from all the remnant of Israel, and from all Judah and Benjamin and the inhabitants of Jerusalem.   *guardians of the threshold • from the hand of*
10 Then they gave *it* into the hands of the workmen who had the oversight of the house of the LORD, and the workmen[T]who were working in the house of the LORD used it to restore and repair the house.   *gave*
11 They in turn gave *it* to the carpenters and to the builders to buy quarried stone and timber for couplings and to make beams for the houses[R]which the kings of Judah had let go to ruin.   2 Chr. 33:4-7
12 And the men did the work faithfully with foremen over them to supervise: Jahath and Obadiah, the Levites of the sons of Merari, Zechariah and Meshullam of the sons of the Kohathites, and the Levites, all who were skillful with musical instruments.
13 *They were* also over the burden bearers, and supervised all the workmen from job to job; and *some* of the Levites *were* scribes and officials and gatekeepers.

Discovery of the Law
2 Kin. 22:8—23:20

14 When they were bringing out the money which had been brought into the house of the LORD, Hilkiah the priest found the book of the law of the LORD *given* by Moses.
15 And Hilkiah responded and said to Shaphan the scribe, "I have found the book of the law in the house of the LORD." And Hilkiah gave the book to Shaphan.
16 Then Shaphan brought the book to the king and[T]reported further word to the king, saying, "Everything that was entrusted to your servants they are doing.   *returned*
17 "They have also emptied out the money which was found in the house of the LORD, and have delivered it into the hands of the supervisors and the workmen."
18 Moreover, Shaphan the scribe told the king saying, "Hilkiah the priest gave me a book." And Shaphan read from it in the presence of the king.
19 And it came about when the king heard the words of the law that he tore his clothes.
20 Then the king commanded Hilkiah, Ahikam the son of Shaphan, Abdon the son of Micah, Shaphan the scribe, and Asaiah the king's servant, saying,

21"Go, inquire of the LORD for me and for those who are left in Israel and in Judah, concerning the words of the book which has been found; for ʳgreat is the wrath of the LORD which is poured out on us because our fathers have not observed the word of the LORD, to do according to all that is written in this book."   2 Chr. 29:8

22 So Hilkiah and *those* whom the king had told went to Huldah the prophetess, the wife of Shallum the son of Tokhath, the son of Hasrah, the keeper of the wardrobe (now she lived in Jerusalem in the Second Quarter); and they spoke to her regarding this.

23 And she said to them, "Thus says the LORD, the God of Israel, 'Tell the man who sent you to Me,

24 thus says the LORD, "Behold, ʳI am bringing evil on this place and on its inhabitants, *even* all the curses written in the book which they have read in the presence of the king of Judah.   2 Chr. 36:14-20

25"Becauseʳ they have forsaken Me and have burned incense to other gods, that they might provoke Me to anger with all the works of their hands, therefore My wrath will be poured out on this place, and it shall not be quenched." '   2 Chr. 33:3

26"But to the king of Judah who sent you to inquire of the LORD, thus you will say to him, 'Thus says the LORD God of Israel *regarding* the words which you have heard,

27"Becauseʳ your heart was tender and you humbled yourself before God, when you heard His words against this place and against its inhabitants, and *because* you humbled yourself before Me, tore your clothes, and wept before Me, I truly have heard you," declares the LORD.   2 Kin. 22:19

28"Behold, I will gather you to your fathers and you shall be gathered to your grave in peace, so your eyes shall not see all the evil which I will bring on this place and on its inhabitants." ' " And they brought back word to the king.

29 ʳThen the king sent and gathered all the elders of Judah and Jerusalem.   2 Kin. 23:1-3

30 And the king went up to the house of the LORD and all the men of Judah, the inhabitants of Jerusalem, the priests, the Levites, and all the people, from the greatest to the least; and he read in their hearing all the words of the book of the covenant which was found in the house of the LORD.

31 Then the king ʳstood in his place and ʳmade a covenant before the LORD to walk after the LORD, and to keep His commandments and His testimonies and His statutes with all his heart and with all his soul, to perform the words of the covenant written in this book.   2 Kin. 11:14 · 2 Chr. 23:16; 29:10

32 Moreover, he made all who were present in Jerusalem and Benjamin to stand *with him.* So the inhabitants of Jerusalem did according to the covenant of God, the God of their fathers.

33 And Josiahʳ removed all the abominations from all the lands belonging to the sons of Israel, and made all who were present in Israel to serve the LORD their God. Throughout his ˡlifetime they did not turn from following the LORD God of their fathers.   2 Chr. 34:3-7 · *days*

CHAPTER 35

Celebration of the Passover
2 Kin. 23:21–23

THEN Josiah ʳcelebrated the Passover to the LORD in Jerusalem, andʳthey slaughtered the Passover *animals* on the fourteenth *day* of the first month.   2 Kin. 23:21 · Ex. 12:6

2 And he set the priests in their offices and ʳencouraged them in the service of the house of the LORD.   2 Chr. 29:11

3 He also said toʳthe Levites who taught all Israel *and* who were holy to the LORD, "Put the holy ark in the house which Solomon the son of David king of Israel built;ʳit will be a burden on *your* shoulders no longer. Now serve the LORD your God and His people Israel.   2 Chr. 17:8 · 1 Chr. 23:26

4"And prepare *yourselves* by your fathers' households in your divisions, according to the writing of David king of Israel and according to the writing of his son Solomon.

5"Moreover, ʳstand in the holy place according to the sections of the fathers' households of your brethren the lay people, and according to the Levites, by division of a father's household.   Ezra 6:18

6"Now ʳslaughter the Passover *animals*, ʳsanctify yourselves, and prepare for your brethren to do according to the word of the LORD by Moses."   2 Chr. 35:1 · 2 Chr. 29:5

7 And Josiah contributed to the lay people, to all who were present, flocks of lambs and kids, all for the Passover offerings, numbering 30,000 plus 3,000 bulls; these were from the king's possessions.

8 His officers also contributed a freewill offering to the people, the priests, and the Levites. Hilkiah and Zechariah and Jehiel, ʳthe officials of the house of God, gave to the priests for the Passover offerings 2,600 *from the flocks* and 300 bulls.   2 Chr. 31:13

9 ʳConaniah also, and Shemaiah and Nethanel, his brothers, and Hashabiah and Jeiel and Jozabad, the officers of the Levites, contributed to the Levites for the Passover offerings 5,000 *from the flocks* and 500 bulls.   2 Chr. 31:12

10 So the service was prepared, andʳthe priests stood at their stations and the Levites by their divisions according to the king's command.   2 Chr. 35:5

11 And ˡtheyʳ slaughtered the Passover *animals*, and while the priests sprinkled the blood *received* from their hand, the Levites skinned *them.*   the Levites · 2 Chr. 35:1, 6

12 Then they removed the burnt offerings that *they* might give them to the sections of the fathers' households of the lay people to present to the LORD, as it is written in the book of Moses. *They did* this also with the bulls.

13 So^R they roasted the Passover *animals* on the fire according to the ordinance, and they boiled^R the holy things in pots, in kettles, in pans, and carried *them* speedily to all the lay people.   Ex. 12:8, 9 · Lev. 6:28

14 And afterwards they prepared for themselves and for the priests, because the priests, the sons of Aaron, *were* offering the burnt offerings and the fat until night; therefore the Levites prepared for themselves and for the priests, the sons of Aaron.

15 The singers, the sons of Asaph, *were* also at their stations according to the command of David, Asaph, Heman, and Jeduthun the king's seer; and^R the gatekeepers at each gate did not have to depart from their service, because the Levites their brethren prepared for them.   1 Chr. 25:1 · 1 Chr. 26:12-19

16 So all the service of the LORD was prepared on that day to celebrate the Passover, and to offer burnt offerings on the altar of the LORD according to the command of King Josiah.

17 Thus^R the sons of Israel who were present celebrated the Passover at that time, and the Feast of Unleavened Bread seven days.   Ex. 12:1-20; 2 Chr. 30:21

18 And^R there had not been celebrated a Passover like it in Israel since the days of Samuel the prophet; nor had any of the kings of Israel celebrated such a Passover as Josiah did with the priests, the Levites, all Judah and Israel who were present, and the inhabitants of Jerusalem.   2 Kin. 23:21

19 In the eighteenth year of Josiah's reign this Passover was celebrated.

Death of Josiah—2 Kin. 23:28-30

20 After all this, when Josiah had set the temple in order, Neco king of Egypt came up to make war at Carchemish on the Euphrates, and Josiah went out to engage him.

21 But^T Neco sent messengers to him, saying, "What^R have we to do with each other, O King of Judah? I *am* not *coming* against you today but against the house with which I am at war, and God has ordered me to hurry. Stop for your own sake from *interfering* with God who is with me, that He may not destroy you."   *he* · 2 Chr. 25:19

22 However, Josiah would not turn away from him, but disguised himself in order to make war with him; nor did he listen to the words of Neco from the mouth of God, but came to make war on the plain of Megiddo.

23 And the archers shot King Josiah, and the king said to his servants, "Take me away, for I am badly wounded."

24 So his servants took him out of the chariot and carried him in the second chariot which he had, and brought him to Jerusalem where he died and was buried in the tombs of his fathers. And all Judah and Jerusalem mourned for Josiah.   *and*

25 Then^R Jeremiah chanted a lament for Josiah. And all the male and female singers speak about Josiah in their lamentations to this day. And they made them an ordinance in Israel; behold, they are also written in the Lamentations.   Jer. 22:10; Lam. 4:20

26 Now the rest of the acts of Josiah and his deeds of devotion as written in the law of the LORD,

27 and his acts, first to last, behold, they are written in the Book of the Kings of Israel and Judah.

CHAPTER 36

The Reign of Joahaz
2 Kin. 23:30–33

THEN the people of the land took [14]Joahaz^R the son of Josiah, and made him king in place of his father in Jerusalem. Jer. 22:11

2 Joahaz was twenty-three years old when he became king, and he reigned three months in Jerusalem.

3 Then the King of Egypt deposed him at Jerusalem, and imposed on the land a fine of ^T one hundred talents of silver and^T one talent of gold. $38,400,000 · $5,760,000

The Reign of Jehoiakim
2 Kin. 23:24—24:6

4 And the king of Egypt made Eliakim his brother king over Judah and Jerusalem, and changed his name to Jehoiakim. But ^R Neco took Joahaz his brother and brought him to Egypt.   Jer. 22:10-12

5 ^R Jehoiakim was twenty-five years old when he became king, and he reigned eleven years in Jerusalem; and he did evil in the sight of the LORD his God.   2 Kin. 23:36, 37

6 Nebuchadnezzar king of Babylon came up^R against him and bound him with bronze *chains* to take him to Babylon.   2 Kin. 24:1

7 ^R Nebuchadnezzar also brought *some* of the articles of the house of the LORD to Babylon and put them in his temple at Babylon.   2 Kin. 24:13

8 ^R Now the rest of the acts of Jehoiakim and ^T the abominations which he did, and what was found against him, behold, they are written in the Book of the Kings of Israel and Judah. And Jehoiachin his son became king in his place.   2 Kin. 24:5 · *his*

---

[14] I.e., short form of Jehoahaz

The Reign of Jehoiachin
2 Kin. 24:8–17; Jer. 37:1

9 [R]Jehoiachin was eight years old when he became king, and he reigned three months and ten days in Jerusalem, and he did evil in the sight of the Lord. 2 Kin. 24:8

10 And at the turn of the year King Nebuchadnezzar sent and brought him to Babylon with the valuable articles of the house of the Lord, and he made his kinsman Zedekiah king over Judah and Jerusalem.

Evaluation of Zedekiah
2 Kin. 24:18, 19; Jer. 52:1, 2

11 [R]Zedekiah was twenty-one years old when he became king, and he reigned eleven years in Jerusalem. 2 Kin. 24:18-20

12 And he did evil in the sight of the Lord his God; [R]he did not humble himself before Jeremiah the prophet [T]who spoke for the Lord. 2 Chr. 33:23 • *from the mouth of the Lord*

Destruction of Jerusalem
2 Kin. 24:20—25:21; Jer. 52:3–27

13 And [R]he also rebelled against King Nebuchadnezzar who had made him swear *allegiance* by God. But[R]he stiffened his neck and hardened his heart against turning to the Lord God of Israel. Jer. 52:3 • [2 Chr. 30:8]

14 Furthermore, all the officials of the priests and the people were very unfaithful *following* all the abominations of the nations; and they defiled the house of the Lord which He had sanctified in Jerusalem.

15 And the Lord, the God of their fathers, sent *word* to them again and again by His messengers, because He had compassion on His people and on His dwelling place;

16 but they *continually* [R]mocked the messengers of God, [R]despised His words and scoffed at His prophets, until the wrath of the Lord arose against His people, until there was no remedy. 2 Chr. 30:10 • Prov. 1:24

17 [R]Therefore He brought up against them the king of the Chaldeans who slew their young men with the sword in the house of their sanctuary, and had no compassion on young man or virgin, old man or infirm; He gave *them* all into his hand. 2 Kin. 25:1-7

18 And [a]all the articles of the house of God, great and small, and the treasures of the house of the Lord, and the treasures of the king and of his officers, he brought *them* all to Babylon. 2 Chr. 36:7,10

19 Then they burned the house of God, and broke down the wall of Jerusalem and burned all its fortified buildings with fire, and destroyed all its valuable articles.

20 And those who had escaped from the sword he carried away to Babylon; and they were servants to him and to his sons until the rule of the kingdom of Persia,

21 [R]to fulfill the word of the Lord by the mouth of Jeremiah, until the land had enjoyed its sabbaths. All the days of its desolation it kept sabbath [T]until seventy years were complete. Jer. 29:10 • *to fulfill seventy years*

The Proclamation by Cyrus
to Return to Jerusalem—Ezra 1:1–3

22 [R]Now in the first year of Cyrus king of Persia—in order to fulfill the word of the Lord[R]by the mouth of Jeremiah—the Lord [R]stirred up the spirit of Cyrus king of Persia, so that he sent a proclamation throughout his kingdom, and also *put it* in writing, saying, Ezra 1:1-3 • Jer. 25:12 • Is. 44:28

23 "Thus says Cyrus king of Persia, 'The Lord, the God of heaven, has given me all the kingdoms of the earth, and He has appointed me to build Him a house in Jerusalem, which is in Judah. Whoever there is among you of all His people, may the Lord his God be with him, and let him go up!' "

THE BOOK OF

EZRA

THE BOOK OF EZRA

Ezra continues the Old Testament narrative of Second Chronicles by showing how God fulfills His promise to return His people to the land of promise after seventy years of exile. Israel's "second exodus," this one from Babylon, is less impressive than the return from Egypt because only a remnant chooses to leave Babylon.

Ezra relates the story of two returns from Babylon—the first led by Zerubbabel to rebuild the temple (1—6), and the second under the leadership of Ezra to rebuild the spiritual condition of the people (7—10). Sandwiched between these two accounts is a gap of nearly six decades, during which Esther lives and rules as queen in Persia.

Ezra is the Aramaic form of the Hebrew word *ezer*, "help," and perhaps means "Yahweh helps." Ezra and Nehemiah were originally bound together as one book because Chronicles, Ezra, and Nehemiah were viewed as one continuous history. The Septuagint, a Greek-language version of the Old Testament translated in the third century B.C., calls Ezra-Nehemiah, *Esdras Deuteron*, "Second Esdras." First Esdras is the name of the apocryphal book of Esdras. The Latin title is *Liber Primus Esdrae*, "First Book of Ezra." In the Latin Bible, Ezra is called First Ezra and Nehemiah is called Second Ezra.

THE AUTHOR OF EZRA

Although Ezra is not specifically mentioned as the author, he is certainly the best candidate. Jewish tradition (the Talmud) attributes the book to Ezra, and portions of the book (7:28—9:15) are written in the first person, from Ezra's point of view. The vividness of the details and descriptions favors an author who was an eyewitness of the later events of the book. As in Chronicles, there is a strong priestly emphasis, and Ezra was a direct priestly descendant of Aaron through Eleazar, Phinehas, and Zadok (7:1–5). He studied, practiced, and taught the law of the Lord as an educated scribe (7:1–12). Also according to Second Maccabees 2:13–15, he had access to the library of written documents gathered by Nehemiah. Ezra no doubt used this material in writing Ezra 1—6 as he did in writing Chronicles. Some think that Ezra composed Nehemiah as well by making use of Nehemiah's personal diary.

Ezra was a godly man marked by strong trust in the Lord, moral integrity, and grief over sin. He was a contemporary of Nehemiah

(Neh. 8:1–9; 12:36) who arrived in Jerusalem in 444 B.C. Tradition holds that Ezra was the founder of the Great Synagogue where the canon of Old Testament Scripture was settled. Another tradition says that he collected the biblical books into a unit and that he originated the synagogue form of worship.

Ezra wrote this book probably between 457 B.C. (the events of Ezra 7—10) and 444 B.C. (Nehemiah's arrival in Jerusalem). During the period covered by the Book of Ezra, Gautama Buddha (c. 560–480 B.C.) is in India, Confucius (551–479 B.C.) is in China, and Socrates (470–399 B.C.) is in Greece.

THE TIME OF EZRA

The following table shows the chronological relationship of the books of Ezra, Nehemiah, and Esther:

538–515 B.C.	483–473 B.C.
Zerubbabel	Esther
Ezra 1—6	Book of Esther
First Return	–

457 B.C.	444–c. 425 B.C.
Ezra	Nehemiah
Ezra 7—10	Book of Nehemiah
Second Return	Third Return

These books fit against the background of these Persian kings:

Cyrus	(559–530 B.C.)
Cambyses	(530–522 B.C.)
Smerdis	(522 B.C.)
Darius I	(521–486 B.C.)
Ahasuerus	(486–464 B.C.)
Artaxerxes I	(464–423 B.C.)
Darius II	(423–404 B.C.)

Cyrus the Persian overthrows Babylon in October 539 B.C. and issues his decree allowing the Jews to return in 538 B.C. The temple is begun in 536 B.C. The exile lasts only fifty years after 586 B.C., but the seventy-year figure for the captivity is taken from a beginning date of 606 B.C. when the first deportation to Babylon takes place. The rebuilding of the temple is discontinued in 534 B.C., resumed in 520 B.C., and completed in 515 B.C. It is begun under Cyrus and finished under Darius I. The two intervening kings, Cambyses and Smerdis, are not mentioned in any of these books. The prophets Haggai and Zechariah minister during Zerubbabel's time, about 520 B.C. and in following years. Esther's story fits entirely in

the reign of Xerxes, and Ezra ministers during the reign of Artaxerxes I, as does Nehemiah. There were three waves of deportation to Babylon (606, 597, and 586 B.C.) and three returns from Babylon: 538 B.C. (Zerubbabel), 457 B.C. (Ezra), and 444 B.C. (Nehemiah).

THE CHRIST OF EZRA

Ezra reveals God's continued fulfillment of His promise to keep David's descendants alive. Zerubbabel himself is part of the messianic line as the grandson of Jeconiah (Jehoiachin, 1 Chr. 3:17–19; see Matt. 1:12, 13). There is a positive note of hope in Ezra and Nehemiah because the remnant has returned to the land of promise. In this land the messianic promises will be fulfilled, because they are connected with such places as Bethlehem, Jerusalem, and Zion. Christ will be born in Bethlehem (Mic. 5:2), not in Babylon.

The Book of Ezra as a whole also typifies Christ's work of forgiveness and restoration.

KEYS TO EZRA

Key Word: Temple—The basic theme of Ezra is the restoration of the temple and the spiritual, moral, and social restoration of the returned remnant in Jerusalem under the leadership of Zerubbabel and Ezra. Israel's worship is revitalized and the people are purified. God's faithfulness is seen in the way He sovereignly protects His people through a powerful empire while they are in captivity. They prosper in their exile, and God raises up pagan kings who are sympathetic to their cause and encourage them to rebuild their homeland. God also provides zealous and capable spiritual leaders who direct the return and the rebuilding. He keeps His promise: " 'And I will be found by you,' declares the LORD, 'and I will restore your fortunes and will gather you from all the nations and from

all the places where I have driven you,' declares the LORD, 'and I will bring you back to the place from where I sent you into exile' " (Jer. 29:14).

Key Verses: Ezra 1:3; 7:10—"Whoever there is among you of all His people, may his God be with him! Let him go up to Jerusalem which is in Judah, and rebuild the house of the LORD, the God of Israel; He is the God who is in Jerusalem" (1:3).

"For Ezra had set his heart to study the law of the LORD, and to practice *it,* and to teach *His* statutes and ordinances in Israel" (7:10).

Key Chapter: Ezra 6—Ezra 6 records the completion and dedication of the temple which stimulates the obedience of the remnant to keep the Passover and separate themselves from the "impurity of the nations" (6:21).

SURVEY OF EZRA

Ezra continues the story exactly where Second Chronicles ends and shows how God's promise to bring His people back to their land is fulfilled (Jer. 29:10–14). God is with these people; and although their days of glory seem over, their spiritual heritage still remains and God's rich promises will be fulfilled. Ezra relates the story of the first two returns from Babylon, the first led by Zerubbabel and the second led decades later by Ezra. Its two divisions are the restoration of the temple (1—6) and the reformation of the people (7—10), and they are separated by a fifty-eight-year gap during which the story of Esther takes place.

The Restoration of the Temple (1—6): King Cyrus of Persia overthrows Babylon in 539 B.C. and issues a decree in 538 B.C. that allows the exiled Jews to return to their homeland. Isaiah prophesied two centuries before that the temple would be rebuilt and actually named Cyrus as the one who would bring it about

FOCUS	RESTORATION OF THE TEMPLE		REFORMATION OF THE PEOPLE	
REFERENCE	1:1————————3:1		————7:1————————9:1————————10:44	
DIVISION	FIRST RETURN TO JERUSALEM	CONSTRUCTION OF THE TEMPLE	SECOND RETURN TO JERUSALEM	RESTORATION OF THE PEOPLE
TOPIC	ZERUBBABEL		EZRA	
	FIRST RETURN OF 49,897		SECOND RETURN OF 1,754	
LOCATION	PERSIA TO JERUSALEM		PERSIA TO JERUSALEM	
TIME	22 YEARS (538–516 B.C.)		1 YEAR (458–457 B.C.)	

(Is. 44:28—45:4). Cyrus may have read and responded to this passage.

Out of a total Jewish population of perhaps 2 or 3 million, only 49,897 choose to take advantage of this offer. Only the most committed are willing to leave a life of relative comfort in Babylon, endure a trek of nine hundred miles, and face further hardship by rebuilding a destroyed temple and city. Zerubbabel, a "prince" of Judah (a direct descendant of King David), leads the faithful remnant back to Jerusalem. Those who return are from the tribes of Judah, Benjamin, and Levi; but it is evident that representatives from the other ten tribes eventually return as well. The ten "lost tribes" are not entirely lost.

Zerubbabel's priorities are in the right place: he first restores the altar and the religious feasts before beginning work on the temple itself. The foundation of the temple is laid in 536 B.C., but opposition arises and the work ceases from 534 to 520 B.C. While Ezra 4:1–5, 24 concerns Zerubbabel, 4:6–23 concerns opposition to the building of the wall of Jerusalem some time between 464 and 444 B.C. These verses may have been placed here to illustrate the antagonism to the work of rebuilding. The prophets Haggai and Zechariah exhort the people to get back to building the temple (5:1, 2), and the work begins again under Zerubbabel and Joshua the high priest. Tattenai, a Persian governor, protests to King Darius I about the temple building and challenges their authority to continue. King Darius finds the decree of Cyrus and confirms it, even forcing Tattenai to provide whatever is needed to complete the work. It is finished in 515 B.C.

The Reformation of the People (7—10): A smaller return under Ezra takes place in 457 B.C., eighty-one years after the first return under Zerubbabel. Ezra the priest is given authority by King Artaxerxes I to bring people and contributions for the temple in Jerusalem. God protects this band of less than two thousand men and they safely reach Jerusalem with their valuable gifts from Persia. Many priests but few Levites return with Zerubbabel and Ezra (2:36–42; 8:15–19). God uses Ezra to rebuild the people spiritually and morally. When Ezra discovers that the people and the priests have intermarried with foreign women, he identifies with the sin of his people and offers a great intercessory prayer on their behalf. During the gap of fifty-eight years between Ezra 6 and 7, the people fall into a confused spiritual state and Ezra is alarmed. They quickly respond to Ezra's confession and weeping by making a covenant to put away their foreign wives and to live in accordance with God's law. This confession and response to the Word of God brings about a great revival and changes lives.

OUTLINE OF EZRA

Part One: The Restoration of the Temple of God (1:1—6:22)

Part Two: The Reformation of the People of God (7:1—10:44)

CHAPTER 1

Decree of Cyrus—2 Chr. 36:22, 23

N OW[R] in the first year of Cyrus king of Persia, in order to fulfill the word of the LORD by the mouth of Jeremiah, the LORD stirred up the spirit of Cyrus king of Persia, so that he[R] sent a proclamation throughout all his kingdom, and also *put it* in writing, saying,   2 Chr. 36:22; Jer. 25:12; 29:10 • Ezra 5:13

2 "Thus says Cyrus king of Persia, 'The LORD, the God of heaven, has given me all the kingdoms of the earth, and[R] He has appointed me to build Him a house in Jerusalem, which is in Judah.   Is. 44:28; 45:1, 12, 13

3 'Whoever there is among you of all His people, may his God be with him! Let him go up to Jerusalem which is in Judah, and rebuild the house of the LORD, the God of Israel; He is the God who is in Jerusalem.

4 'And every survivor, at whatever place he may[A] live, let the men of[T] that place support him with silver and gold, with goods and cattle, together with a freewill offering for the house of God which is in Jerusalem.' "   *reside as an alien* • *his*

Gifts from Israel and Cyrus

5 Then the heads of fathers' *households* of Judah and Benjamin and the priests and the Levites arose, even everyone whose spirit God had stirred to go up and rebuild the house of the LORD which is in Jerusalem.

6 And all those about them[T] encouraged[R] them with articles of silver, with gold, with goods, with cattle, and with valuables, aside from all that was given as a freewill offering.   *strengthened their hands* • Neh. 6:9; Is. 35:3

7 Also King Cyrus brought out the articles of the house of the LORD, which Nebuchadnezzar had carried away from Jerusalem and put in the house of his gods;

8 and Cyrus, king of Persia, had them brought out by the hand of Mithredath the [R] treasurer, and he counted them out to Sheshbazzar, the prince of Judah.   Ezra 5:14

9 Now this *was* their number: 30 gold dishes, 1,000 silver dishes, 29 duplicates;

10 30 gold bowls, 410 silver bowls of a second *kind, and* 1,000 other articles.

11 All the articles of gold and silver *numbered* 5,400. Sheshbazzar brought them all up with the exiles who went up from Babylon to Jerusalem.

CHAPTER 2

The Leaders

N OW[R] these are the[T] people of the province who came up out of the captivity of the exiles whom Nebuchadnezzar the king of Babylon had carried away to Babylon, and returned to Jerusalem and Judah, each to his city.   2 Kin. 24:14-16; 25:11 • *sons*

2 These came with Zerubbabel, Jeshua, Nehemiah, Seraiah, Reelaiah, Mordecai, Bilshan, Mispar, Bigvai, Rehum, and Baanah.

The number of the men of the people of Israel:

The People

3 the sons of Parosh, 2,172;

4 the sons of Shephatiah, 372;

5 the sons of[R] Arah, 775;   Neh. 7:10

6 the sons of[R] Pahath-moab of the sons of Jeshua *and* Joab, 2,812;   Neh. 7:11

7 the sons of Elam, 1,254;

8 the sons of Zattu, 945;

9 the sons of Zaccai, 760;

10 the sons of[T] Bani, 642;   In Neh. 7:15, *Binnui*

11 the sons of Bebai, 623;

12 the sons of Azgad, 1,222;

13 the sons of[R] Adonikam, 666;   Ezra 8:13

14 the sons of Bigvai, 2,056;

15 the sons of Adin, 454;

16 the sons of Ater of Hezekiah, 98;

17 the sons of Bezai, 323;

18 the sons of Jorah, 112;

19 the sons of Hashum, 223;

20 the sons of Gibbar, 95;

21 the[T] men of Bethlehem, 123;   *sons*

22 the men of Netophah, 56;

23 the men of Anathoth, 128;

24 the sons of Azmaveth, 42;

25 the sons of[R] Kiriath-arim, Chephirah, and Beeroth, 743;   In Neh. 7:29, *Kiriath-jearim*

26 the men of Ramah and Geba, 621;

27 the men of Michmas, 122;

28 the men of Bethel and Ai, 223;

29 the sons of Nebo, 52;

30 the sons of Magbish, 156;

31 the sons of the other Elam, 1,254;

32 the sons of Harim, 320;

33 the sons of Lod, Hadid, and Ono, 725;

34 the[T] men of Jericho, 345;   *sons*

35 the sons of Senaah, 3,630.

The Priests

36 [R] The priests: the sons of Jedaiah of the house of Jeshua, 973;   1 Chr. 24:7-18

37 the sons of[R]Immer, 1,052;   1 Chr. 24:14
38 [R]the sons of Pashhur, 1,247;   1 Chr. 9:12
39 the sons of[R]Harim, 1,017.   1 Chr. 24:8

The Levites

40 The Levites: the sons of Jeshua and Kadmiel, of the sons of Hodaviah, 74.
41 The singers: the sons of Asaph, 128.
42 The sons of the gatekeepers: the sons of Shallum, the sons of Ater, the sons of Talmon, the sons of Akkub, the sons of Hatita, the sons of Shobai, in all 139.

The Servants

43 The temple servants: the sons of Ziha, the sons of Hasupha, the sons of Tabbaoth,
44 the sons of Keros, the sons of[T]Siaha, the sons of Padon,   In Neh. 7:47, Sia
45 the sons of Lebanah, the sons of Hagabah, the sons of Akkub,
46 the sons of Hagab, the sons of Shalmai, the sons of Hanan,
47 the sons of Giddel, the sons of Gahar, the sons of Reaiah,
48 the sons of Rezin, the sons of Nekoda, the sons of Gazzam,
49 the sons of Uzza, the sons of Paseah, the sons of Besai,
50 the sons of Asnah, the sons of Meunim, the sons of[T]Nephisim, In Neh. 7:52, Nephushesim
51 the sons of Bakbuk, the sons of Hakupha, the sons of Harhur,
52 the sons of[T]Bazluth, the sons of Mehida, the sons of Harsha,   In Neh. 7:54, Bazlith
53 the sons of Barkos, the sons of Sisera, the sons of Temah,
54 the sons of Neziah, the sons of Hatipha.
55 The sons of Solomon's servants: the sons of Sotai, the sons of[T]Hassophereth, the sons of Peruda,   In Neh. 7:57, Sophereth
56 the sons of Jaalah, the sons of Darkon, the sons of Giddel,
57 the sons of Shephatiah, the sons of Hattil, the sons of Pochereth-hazzebaim, the sons of[T]Ami.   In Neh. 7:59, Amon
58 All the[R]temple servants, and the sons of Solomon's servants, were 392.   1 Chr. 9:2

The People

59 Now these are those who came up from Tel-melah, Tel-harsha, Cherub,[T]Addan, and Immer, but they were not able to [T]give evidence of their fathers' households, and their[T]descendants, whether they were of Israel: In Neh. 7:61, Addon • tell • seed
60 the sons of Delaiah, the sons of Tobiah, the sons of Nekoda, 652.

The Priests

61 And of the sons of the priests: the sons of[T]Habaiah, the sons of Hakkoz, the sons of

Barzillai, who took a wife from the daughters of Barzillai the Gileadite, and he was called by their name.   In Neh. 7:63, Hobaiah
62 These searched among their ancestral registration, but they could not be located; [R]therefore they were considered unclean and excluded from the priesthood.   Num. 16:39, 40
63 And the [T]governor said to them that they should not eat from the most holy things until a priest stood up with Urim and Thummim.   Heb., Tirshatha, a Persian title

The People Who Returned

64 The whole assembly numbered 42,360,
65 besides their male and female servants, [T]who numbered 7,337; and they had 200[R]singing men and women.   they were • 2 Chr. 35:25
66 Their horses were 736; their mules, 245;
67 their camels, 435; their donkeys, 6,720.

The Gifts the People Gave

68 And some of the heads of fathers' households, when they arrived at the house of the LORD which is in Jerusalem, offered willingly for the house of God to[T]restore it on its foundation.   establish
69 According to their ability they gave[R]to the treasury for the work 61,000 gold drachmas, and 5,000 silver minas, and 100 priestly garments.   Ezra 8:25-34
70 [R]Now the priests and the Levites, some of the people, the singers, the gatekeepers, and the temple servants lived in their cities, and all Israel in their cities.   1 Chr. 9:2

CHAPTER 3

Spiritual Preparation of the People

NOW when the seventh month came, and the sons of Israel were in the cities, the people gathered together as one man to Jerusalem.
2 Then Jeshua the son of Jozadak and his brothers the priests, and Zerubbabel the son of Shealtiel, and his brothers arose and built the altar of the God of Israel, to offer burnt offerings on it, as it is written in the law of Moses, the man of God.
3 So they set up the altar on its foundation, for[T]they were terrified because of the peoples of the lands; and they offered burnt offerings on it to the LORD, burnt offerings morning and evening.   terror was upon them
4 And they celebrated the [R]Feast of [1]Booths, as it is written, and offered [T]the fixed number of burnt offerings daily, according to the ordinance, as each day required;   Neh. 8:14; Zech. 14:16 • by number
5 and afterward there was a continual burnt offering, also for the new moons and for all the fixed festivals of the LORD that were consecrated, and from everyone who offered a freewill offering to the LORD.

[1] Or, Tabernacles

6 From the first day of the seventh month they began to offer burnt offerings to the LORD, but the foundation of the temple of the LORD had not been laid.

Completion of the Temple Foundation

7 Then they gave money to the masons and carpenters, and [R]food, drink, and oil to the Sidonians and to the Tyrians, to bring cedar wood from Lebanon to the sea at Joppa, according to the permission they had [T]from Cyrus king of Persia.   2 Chr. 2:10 • of

8 Now in the second year of their coming to the house of God at Jerusalem in the second month, Zerubbabel the son of Shealtiel and Jeshua the son of Jozadak and the rest of their brothers the priests and the Levites, and all who came from the captivity to Jerusalem, began the work and appointed the Levites from twenty years and older to oversee the work of the house of the LORD.

9 Then Jeshua with his sons and brothers stood united with Kadmiel and his sons, the sons of Judah and the sons of Henadad with their sons and brothers the Levites, to oversee the workmen in the temple of God.

10 Now when the builders had laid the foundation of the temple of the LORD, the priests stood in their apparel with trumpets, and the Levites, the sons of Asaph, with cymbals, to praise the LORD according to the [T]directions of King David of Israel. hands

11 And [R]they sang, praising and giving thanks to the LORD, saying, "For He is good, for His lovingkindness is upon Israel forever." And all the people shouted with a great shout when they praised the LORD because the foundation of the house of the LORD was laid.   2 Chr. 7:3; Neh. 12:24, 40

12 Yet many of the priests and Levites and heads of fathers' households, the old men who had seen the first [T]temple, wept with a loud voice when the foundation of this house was laid before their eyes, while many shouted aloud for joy;   house

13 so that the people could not distinguish the sound of the shout of joy from the sound of the weeping of the people, for the people shouted with a loud shout, and the sound was heard far away.

CHAPTER 4

Present Opposition Under Darius

NOW when [R]the enemies of Judah and Benjamin heard that [T]the people of the exile were building a temple to the LORD God of Israel,   Ezra 4:7-10 • Ezra 1:11

2 they approached Zerubbabel and the heads of fathers' households, and said to them, "Let us build with you, for we, like you, seek your God; and we have been sacrificing to Him since the days of Esarhaddon king of Assyria, who brought us up here."

3 But Zerubbabel and Jeshua and the rest of the heads of fathers' households of Israel said to them, "You[R] have nothing in common with us in building a house to our God; but we ourselves will together build to the LORD God of Israel, as King Cyrus, the king of Persia has commanded us." Neh. 2:20

4 Then the people of the land [T]discouraged the people of Judah, and frightened them from building,   weakened the hands of

5 and hired counselors against them to frustrate their counsel all the days of Cyrus king of Persia, even until the reign of Darius king of Persia.

Later Opposition Under Ahasuerus

6 Now in the reign of [2]Ahasuerus,[R] in the beginning of his reign, they wrote an accusation against the inhabitants of Judah and Jerusalem.   Esth. 1:1; Dan. 9:1

Later Opposition Under Artaxerxes

7 And in the days of Artaxerxes, Bishlam, Mithredath, Tabeel, and the rest of his colleagues, wrote to Artaxerxes king of Persia; and the text of the letter was written in Aramaic and translated from Aramaic.

8 Rehum the commander and Shimshai the scribe wrote a letter against Jerusalem to King Artaxerxes, as follows—

9 then wrote Rehum the commander and Shimshai the scribe and[R]the rest of their colleagues, the judges and the lesser governors, the officials, the secretaries, the men of Erech, the Babylonians, the men of Susa, that is, the Elamites,   2 Kin. 17:24

10 and the rest of the nations which the great and honorable Osnappar deported and settled in the city of Samaria, and in the rest of the region beyond the [3]River. And now

11 this is the copy of the letter which they sent to him: "To King Artaxerxes: Your servants, the men in the region beyond the River, and now

12 let it be known to the king, that the Jews who came up from you have come to us at Jerusalem; they are rebuilding the rebellious and evil city, and are finishing the walls and repairing the foundations.

13 "Now let it be known to the king, that if that city is rebuilt and the walls are finished, they will not pay tribute, custom, or toll, and it will damage the revenue of the kings.

14 "Now because we [T]are in the service of the palace, and it is not fitting for us to see the king's dishonor, therefore we have sent and informed the king,   eat the salt

15 so that a search may be made in the record books of your fathers. And you will discover in the record books, and learn that that city is a rebellious city and damaging to kings and provinces, and that they have in-

[2] Or, Xerxes
[3] I.e., Euphrates, and so throughout this context

cited revolt within it in past days; therefore that city was laid waste.

16"We inform the king that, if that city is rebuilt and the walls finished, as a result you will have no possession in *the province* beyond the River."

17 *Then* the king sent an answer to Rehum the commander, to Shimshai the scribe, and to the rest of their colleagues who live in Samaria and in the rest of *the provinces* beyond the River: "Peace. And now

18 the document which you sent to us has been translated and read before me. Neh. 8:8

19"And a decree has been issued by me, and a search has been made and it has been discovered that that city has risen up against the kings in past days, that rebellion and revolt have been perpetrated in it,

20 that mighty kings have ruled over Jerusalem, governing all *the provinces* beyond the River, and that tribute, custom, and toll were paid to them. 1 Kin. 4:21; 1 Chr. 18:3 • *been*

21"So, now issue a decree to make these men stop *work*, that the city may not be rebuilt until a decree is issued by me.

22"And beware of being negligent in carrying out this *matter*; why should damage increase to the detriment of the kings?"

23 Then as soon as the copy of King Artaxerxes' document was read before Rehum and Shimshai the scribe and their colleagues, they went in haste to Jerusalem to the Jews and stopped them by force of arms.

Present Interruption
of Construction Under Darius

24 Then work on the house of God in Jerusalem ceased, and it was stopped until the second year of the reign of Darius king of Persia.

CHAPTER 5

Resumption of the Temple Construction
Hab. 1:1; Zech. 1:1

WHEN the prophets, Haggai the prophet and Zechariah the son of Iddo, prophesied to the Jews who were in Judah and Jerusalem, in the name of the God of Israel, who was over them, Hag. 1:1 • Zech. 1:1

2 then Zerubbabel the son of Shealtiel and Jeshua the son of Jozadak arose and began to rebuild the house of God which is in Jerusalem; and the prophets of God were with them supporting them. Ezra 3:2

Opposition by Tattenai

3 At that time Tattenai, the governor of *the province* beyond the River, and Shethar-bozenai and their colleagues came to them and spoke to them thus, "Who issued you a

---

4 Lit., *house*, and so throughout this context

---

decree to rebuild this 4temple and to finish this structure?" Ezra 6:6, 13 • Ezra 1:3; 5:9

4 Then we told them accordingly what the names of the men were who were reconstructing this building. Ezra 5:10

5 But the eye of their God was on the elders of the Jews, and they did not stop them until a report should come to Darius, and then a written reply be returned concerning it. Ezra 7:6, 28

The Letter to Darius

6 *This is* the copy of the letter which Tattenai, the governor of *the province* beyond the River, and Shethar-bozenai and his colleagues the officials, who were beyond the River, sent to Darius the king. Ezra 5:3

7 They sent a report to him in which it was written thus: "To Darius the king, all peace.

8"Let it be known to the king, that we have gone to the province of Judah, to the house of the great God, which is being built with huge stones, and beams are being laid in the walls; and this work is going on with great care and is succeeding in their hands.

9"Then we asked those elders and said to them thus, 'Who issued you a decree to rebuild this temple and to finish this structure?'

10"We also asked them their names so as to inform you, and that we might write down the names of the men who were at their head.

11"And thus they answered us, saying, 'We are the servants of the God of heaven and earth and are rebuilding the temple that was built many years ago, which a great king of Israel built and finished. 1 Kin. 6:1, 38

12 'But because our fathers had provoked the God of heaven to wrath, He gave them into the hand of Nebuchadnezzar king of Babylon, the Chaldean, *who* destroyed this temple and deported the people to Babylon.

13 'However, in the first year of Cyrus king of Babylon, King Cyrus issued a decree to rebuild this house of God. Ezra 1:1

14 'And also the gold and silver utensils of the house of God which Nebuchadnezzar had taken from the temple in Jerusalem, and brought them to the temple of Babylon, these King Cyrus took from the temple of Babylon, and they were given to one whose name was Sheshbazzar, whom he had appointed governor. Ezra 1:7; 6:5 • *that was in*

15 'And he said to him, "Take these utensils, go *and* deposit them in the temple in Jerusalem, and let the house of God be rebuilt in its place." *that is in*

16 'Then that Sheshbazzar came *and* laid the foundations of the house of God in Jerusalem; and from then until now it has been under construction, and it is not *yet* completed.' Ezra 3:8,10 • *that is in* • Ezra 6:15

17"And now, if it pleases the king let a search be conducted in the king's treasure

house, which is there in Babylon, if it be that a decree was issued by King Cyrus to rebuild this house of God at Jerusalem; and let the king send to us his decision concerning this *matter*." Ezra 6:1, 2

CHAPTER 6

Confirmation of the Temple Construction

THEN King Darius issued a decree, and [R]search was made in the [5]archives, where the treasures were stored in Babylon. Ezra 5:17

2 And in [6]Ecbatana in the fortress, which is [R]in the province of Media, a scroll was found and there was written in it as follows: "Memorandum— 2 Kin. 17:6

3"In[R] the first year of King Cyrus, Cyrus the king issued a decree: 'Concerning the house of God at Jerusalem, let the temple, the place where sacrifices are offered, be rebuilt and let its foundations be[A]retained, its height being[T]60 cubits and its width 60 cubits; Ezra 1:1; 5:13 · *Fixed, laid* · 90 ft.

4 with three layers of huge stones, and one layer of timbers. And let the cost be paid from the[T]royal treasury. *king's house*

5 'And also let[R]the gold and silver utensils of the temple of God, which Nebuchadnezzar took from the temple in Jerusalem and brought to Babylon, be returned and [T]brought to their places in the temple in Jerusalem; and you shall put *them* in the house of God.' Ezra 1:7; 5:14 · *go*

6"Now *therefore*, Tattenai, governor of *the province* beyond the River, Shetharbozenai, and[T]your colleagues, the officials of *the provinces* beyond the River,[T]keep away from there. Aram., *their* · *be distant*

7"Leave this work on the house of God alone; let the governor of the Jews and the elders of the Jews rebuild this house of God on its site.

8"Moreover,[R]I issue a decree concerning what you are to do for these elders of Judah in the rebuilding of this house of God: the full cost is to be paid to these people from the royal treasury out of the taxes of *the provinces* beyond the River, and that without delay. Ezra 6:4; 7:14-22

9"And whatever is needed, both young bulls, rams, and lambs for a burnt offering to the God of heaven, and wheat, salt, wine, and anointing oil, as the priests in Jerusalem request, *it* is to be given to them daily without fail,

10 that they may offer [7]acceptable sacrifices to the God of heaven and[R]pray for the life of the king and his sons. Ezra 7:23

11"And I issued a decree that [R]any man who violates this edict, a timber shall be drawn from his house and he shall be impaled on it and his house shall be made a refuse heap on account of this. Ezra 7:26

12"And may the God who has caused His name to dwell there overthrow any king or people who[T]attempts to change *it*, so as to destroy this house of God in Jerusalem. I, Darius, have issued *this* decree, let *it* be carried out with all diligence!" *sends his hand*

Completion of the Temple

13 Then [R]Tattenai, the governor of *the province* beyond the River, Shethar-bozenai, and their colleagues carried out *the decree* with all diligence, just as King Darius had sent. Ezra 6:6

14 And the elders of the Jews were successful in building through the prophesying of Haggai the prophet and Zechariah the son of Iddo. And [T]they finished building according to the command of the God of Israel and the decree of Cyrus, Darius, and Artaxerxes king of Persia. *built and finished*

15 And this temple was completed[T]on the third day of the month Adar; it was the sixth year of the reign of King Darius. *until*

Dedication of the Temple

16 And the sons of Israel, the priests, the Levites, and the rest of the [T]exiles, [R]celebrated the dedication of this house of God with joy. *sons of the captivity* · 1 Kin. 8:63

17 And they offered for the dedication of this temple of God 100 bulls, 200 rams, 400 lambs, and as a sin offering for all Israel[R]12 male goats, corresponding to the number of the tribes of Israel. Ezra 8:35

18 Then they appointed the priests to their divisions and the Levites in their orders for the service of God[T]in Jerusalem, as it is written in the book of Moses. *which is in*

Celebration of the Passover

19 And the exiles observed the Passover on the fourteenth of the first month.

20 For the priests and the Levites had purified themselves together; all of them were pure. Then they slaughtered the Passover *lamb* for all the exiles, both for their brothers the priests and for themselves.

21 And the sons of Israel who returned from exile and[R]all those who had separated themselves from the impurity of the nations of the land to *join* them, to seek the LORD God of Israel, ate the Passover. Neh. 9:2

22 And they observed the Feast of Unleavened Bread seven days with joy, for the LORD had caused them to rejoice, and had turned the heart of the king of Assyria toward them to encourage them in the work of the house of God, the God of Israel.

---

[5] Lit., *house of the books* [6] Aram., *Achmetha*
[7] Lit., *pleasing* or *sweet-smelling sacrifices*

CHAPTER 7

Ezra's Qualifications

N̬OW ᴿafter these things, in the reign of
ᴿArtaxerxes king of Persia, *there went up*
Ezra son of Seraiah, son of Azariah, son of
Hilkiah,   1 Chr. 6:4-14 • Ezra 7:12, 21; Neh. 2:1
  2 son of Shallum, son of Zadok, son of
Ahitub,
  3 son of Amariah, son of Azariah, son of
Meraioth,
  4 son of Zerahiah, son of Uzzi, son of
Bukki,
  5 son of Abishua, son of Phinehas, son of
Eleazar, son of Aaron the chief priest.
  6 This Ezra went up from Babylon, and
he was aᴿscribe skilled in the law of Moses,
which the Lᴏʀᴅ God of Israel had given; and
the king granted him allᵀhe requested because the hand of the Lᴏʀᴅ his God *was*
upon him.   Ezra 7:11, 12, 21 • *his request*
  7 And ᴿsome of the sons of Israel and
some of the priests, the Levites, the singers,
the gatekeepers, and the temple servants
went up to Jerusalem in the seventh year of
King Artaxerxes.   Ezra 8:1-20
  8 And he came to Jerusalem in the fifth
month, which was in the seventh year of the
king.
  9 For on the first of the first monthᵀhe
began to go up from Babylon; and on the
first of the fifth month he came to Jerusalem,ᴿbecause the good hand of his God *was*
upon him.   *was the foundation* • Ezra 7:6; Neh. 2:8
  10 For Ezra had set his heart to study the
law of the Lᴏʀᴅ, and to practice *it*, and to
teach *His* statutes and ordinances in Israel.

Artaxerxes' Letter

  11 Now this is the copy of the decree
which King Artaxerxes gave to Ezra the
priest, the scribe, learned in the words of
the commandments of the Lᴏʀᴅ and His
statutes to Israel:
  12"Artaxerxes,ᴿking of kings, to Ezra the
priest, the scribe of the law of the God of
heaven, perfect *peace*. And now   Ezek. 26:7
  13 ᴿI have issued a decree that any of the
people of Israel and their priests and the Levites in my kingdom who are willing to go
to Jerusalem, may go with you.   Ezra 6:1
  14"Forasmuch as you are sent by the king
and his seven counselors to inquire concerning Judah and Jerusalem according to the
law of your God which is in your hand,
  15 and to bring the silver and gold, which
the king and his counselors have freely offered to the God of Israel,ᴿwhose dwelling is
in Jerusalem,   2 Chr. 6:2; Ezra 6:12; Ps. 135:21
  16 withᴿall the silver and gold which you
shall find in the whole province of Babylon,
alongᴿwith the freewill offering of the people
and of the priests, whoᴿoffered willingly for
the house of their God which is in Jerusalem;   Ezra 8:25 • Ezra 1:4, 6 • 1 Chr. 29:6

  17 with this money, therefore, you shall
diligently buy bulls, rams, and lambs, with
their grain offerings and their libations and
offer them on the altar of the house of your
God which is in Jerusalem.
  18 "And whatever seems good to you and
to your brothers to do with the rest of the
silver and gold, you may do according to the
will of your God.
  19"Also the utensils which are given to
you for the service of the house of your God,
deliver in full before the God of Jerusalem.
  20"And the rest of the needs for the house
of your God, for which you may have occasion to provide,ᴿprovide *for it* from the royal
treasury.   Ezra 6:4
  21"And I, even I King Artaxerxes, issue a
decree to all the treasurers who are *in the
provinces* beyond the River, that whatever
Ezra the priest,ᴿthe scribe of the law of the
God of heaven, may require of you, it shall
be done diligently,   Ezra 7:6
  22 *even* up to 100 talents of silver, 100
kors of wheat, 100 baths of wine, 100 baths
of oil, and saltᵀas needed.   *without prescription*
  23"Whatever isᵀcommanded by the God of
heaven, let it be done with zeal for the
house of the God of heaven,ᴿlest there be
wrath against the kingdom of the king and
his sons.   *from the decree of* • Ezra 6:10
  24"We also inform you that it is not allowed to impose tax, tribute or toll *on* any
of the priests, Levites, singers, doorkeepers,
Nethinim, or servants of this house of God.
  25"And you, Ezra, according to the wisdom of your God which is in your hand,ᴿap-
point magistrates and judges that they may
judge all the people who are in *the province
beyond the River, even* all those who know
the laws of your God; and you may teach
anyone who is ignorant *of them*.   Ex. 18:21
  26"And whoever will not observe the law
of your God and the law of the king, let
judgment be executed upon him strictly,
whether for death or for banishment or for
confiscation of goods or for imprisonment."

Ezra's Response

  27 Blessed be the Lᴏʀᴅ, the God of our fathers,ᴿwho has put *such a thing* as this in the
king's heart, to adorn the house of the Lᴏʀᴅ
which is in Jerusalem,   Ezra 6:22
  28 and has extended lovingkindness to me
before the king and his counselors and before all the king's mighty princes. Thus I
was strengthened according to the hand of
the Lᴏʀᴅ my God upon me, and I gathered
leading men from Israel to go up with me.

CHAPTER 8

Census of the Returning Israelites

N̬OW these are the heads of their fathers'
households and the genealogical enrollment

of those who went up with me from Babylon in the reign of King Artaxerxes:

2 of the sons of Phinehas, Gershom; of the sons of Ithamar, Daniel; of the sons of David,[R]Hattush;   1 Chr. 3:22

3 of the sons of Shecaniah *who was* of the sons of Parosh, Zechariah and with him 150 males *who were in* the genealogical list;

4 of the sons of Pahath-moab, Eliehoenai the son of Zerahiah and 200 males with him;

5 of the sons of Shecaniah, the son of Jahaziel and 300 males with him;

6 and of the sons of Adin, Ebed the son of Jonathan and 50 males with him;

7 and of the sons of Elam, Jeshaiah the son of Athaliah and 70 males with him;

8 and of the sons of Shephatiah, Zebadiah the son of Michael and 80 males with him;

9 of the sons of Joab, Obadiah the son of Jehiel and 218 males with him;

10 and of the sons of Shelomith, the son of Josiphiah and 160 males with him;

11 and of the sons of Bebai, Zechariah the son of Bebai and 28 males with him;

12 and of the sons of Azgad, Johanan the son of Hakkatan and 110 males with him;

13 and of the sons of Adonikam, the last ones, these being their names, Eliphelet, Jeuel, and Shemaiah and 60 males with them;

14 and of the sons of Bigvai, Uthai and [A]Zabbud and 70 males with them.   *Zakkur*

Acquisition of Temple Leadership

15 Now I assembled them at the river that runs to Ahava, where we camped for three days; and when I observed the people and the priests, I did not find any Levites there.

16 So I sent for Eliezer, Ariel, Shemaiah, Elnathan, Jarib, Elnathan, Nathan, Zechariah, and Meshullam,[T]leading men, and for Joiarib and Elnathan, teachers.   *heads*

17 And I sent them to Iddo the[T]leading man at the place Casiphia; and I[T]told them what to say to Iddo *and* his brothers, the temple servants at the place Casiphia, *that is,* to bring ministers to us for the house of our God.   *head • put words in their mouth to say*

18 And[R]according to the good hand of our God upon us they brought us a man of insight of the sons of Mahli, the son of Levi, the son of Israel, namely Sherebiah, and his sons and brothers, 18 men;   Ezra 7:6, 28

19 and Hashabiah and Jeshaiah of the sons of Merari, with his brothers and their sons, 20 men;

20 and 220 of[R]the temple servants, whom David and the princes had given for the service of the Levites, all of them designated by name.   Ezra 2:43; 7:7

Proclamation of a Fast

21 Then I proclaimed[R]a fast there at the river of Ahava, that we might humble ourselves before our God to seek from Him a [T]safe journey for us, our little ones, and all our possessions.   1 Sam. 7:6 • *straight way*

22 For I was ashamed to request from the king troops and horsemen to[T]protect us from the enemy on the way, because we had said to the king, "The hand of our God is favorably disposed to all those who seek Him, but His power and His anger are against all those who forsake Him."   *help*

23 So we fasted and sought our God concerning this *matter,* and He[T]listened[R]to our entreaty.   *was entreated by us • 1 Chr. 5:20*

The Return Is Completed

24 Then I set apart twelve of the leading priests, [R]Sherebiah, Hashabiah, and with them ten of their brothers;   Ezra 8:18, 19

25 and I[R]weighed out to them the silver, the gold, and the utensils, the offering for the house of our God which the king and his counselors and his princes, and all Israel present *there,* had offered.   Ezra 8:33

26 [R]Thus I weighed into their hands 650 talents of silver, and silver utensils *worth* 100 talents, *and* 100 gold talents,   Ezra 1:9-11

27 and 20 gold bowls, *worth*[T]1,000 darics; and two utensils of fine shiny bronze, precious as gold. $1,424,176

28 Then I said to them, "You[R]are holy to the LORD, and the utensils are holy; and the silver and the gold are a freewill offering to the LORD God of your fathers.   Lev. 21:6-8

29"Watch and keep *them*[R]until you weigh *them* before the leading priests, the Levites, and the heads of the fathers' *households* of Israel at Jerusalem, *in* the chambers of the house of the LORD."   Ezra 8:33, 34

30 So the priests and the Levites[R]accepted the weighed out silver and gold and the utensils, to bring *them* to Jerusalem to the house of our God.   Ezra 1:9

31 Then we journeyed from [R]the river Ahava on[R]the twelfth of the first month to go to Jerusalem; and[R]the hand of our God was over us, and He delivered us from the hand of the enemy and the ambushes by the way.   Ezra 8:15, 21 • Ezra 7:9 • Ezra 8:22

32 [R]Thus we came to Jerusalem and remained there three days.   Neh. 2:11

33 And on the fourth day the silver and the gold and the utensils[R]were weighed out in the house of our God into the hand of [R]Meremoth the son of Uriah the priest, and with him *was* Eleazar the son of Phinehas; and with them *were* the Levites, Jozabad the son of Jeshua and Noadiah the son of Binnui.   Ezra 8:30 • Neh. 3:4, 21

34 Everything *was* numbered and weighed, and all the weight was recorded at that time.

35 [R]The exiles who had come from the captivity offered burnt offerings to the God of Israel: 12 bulls for all Israel, 96 rams, 77

lambs, 12 male goats for a sin offering, all as a burnt offering to the LORD.   Ezra 2:1

36 Then they delivered the king's edicts to the king's satraps, and to the governors *in the provinces* beyond the River, and they supported the people and the house of God.

CHAPTER 9

Israel Intermarries

NOW when these things had been completed, the princes approached me, saying, "The people of Israel and the priests and the Levites have not[R]separated themselves from the peoples of the lands, according to their abominations, *those* of the Canaanites, the Hittites, the Perizzites, the Jebusites, the Ammonites, the Moabites, the Egyptians, and the Amorites.   Ezra 6:21; Neh. 9:2

2"For they have taken some of their daughters *as wives* for themselves and for their sons, so that the holy race has intermingled with the peoples of the lands; indeed, the hands of the princes and the rulers have been foremost in this unfaithfulness."

Lamentation of Ezra

3 And when I heard about this matter, I [R]tore my garment and my robe, and pulled some of the hair from my head and my beard, and sat down appalled.   2 Kin. 18:37

4 Then everyone who trembled at the words of the God of Israel on account of the unfaithfulness of the exiles gathered to me, and I sat appalled until the evening offering.

God's Faithfulness

5 But at the evening offering I arose from my[R]humiliation, even with my garment and my robe torn, and I fell on my knees and [R]stretched out my[T]hands to the LORD my God;   *fasting* • Ex. 9:29 • *palms*

6 and I said, "O my God, I am ashamed and embarrassed to lift up my face to Thee, my God, for our iniquities have[T]risen above our heads, and our[R]guilt has grown even to the heavens.   *multiplied over the head* • 2 Chr. 28:9

7"Since[R] the days of our fathers to this day we *have been* in great guilt, and on account of our iniquities we, our kings *and* our priests have been given into the hand of the kings of the lands, to the sword, to captivity, and to plunder and to[T]open shame, as *it is* this day.   2 Chr. 29:6; Ps. 106:6 • *shame of faces*

8"But now for a brief moment grace has been *shown* from the LORD our God, [R]to leave us an escaped remnant and to give us a[R]peg in His holy place, that our God may enlighten our eyes and grant us a little reviving in our bondage.   Ezra 9:13-15 • Is. 22:23

9"For[R]we are slaves; yet in our bondage,

our God has not forsaken us, but[R]has extended lovingkindness to us in the sight of the kings of Persia, to give us reviving to raise up the house of our God, to restore its ruins, and to give us a wall in Judah and Jerusalem.   Neh. 9:36 • Ezra 7:28

Israel's Unfaithfulness

10"And now, our God, what shall we say after this? For we have forsaken Thy commandments,

11 which Thou hast commanded by Thy servants the prophets, saying, 'The land which you are entering to possess is an unclean land with the uncleanness of the peoples of the lands, with their abominations which have filled it from end to end *and* with their impurity.   Ezra 6:21

12 'So now do not[R]give your daughters to their sons nor take their daughters to your sons, and never seek their peace or their prosperity, that you may be strong and eat the good *things* of the land and leave *it* as an inheritance to your sons forever.' [Deut. 7:3]

13"And after all that has come upon us for our evil deeds and[R]our great guilt, since Thou our God hast requited *us* less than our iniquities *deserve,* and hast given us[R]an escaped remnant as this,   Ezra 9:6, 7 • Ezra 9:8

14 [R]shall we again break Thy commandments and intermarry with the peoples who commit these abominations?[R]Wouldst Thou not be angry with us[T]to the point of destruction, until there is no remnant nor any who escape?   Ezra 9:2 • Deut. 9:8, 14 • *to destroy*

15"O LORD God of Israel,[R]Thou art righteous, for we have been left an escaped remnant, as *it is* this day; behold, we are before Thee in our guilt, for no one can stand before Thee because of this."   Neh. 9:33; Dan. 9:7

CHAPTER 10

Israel Laments

NOW[R]while Ezra was praying and making confession, weeping and prostrating himself [R]before the house of God, a very large assembly, men, women, and children, gathered to him from Israel; for the people wept bitterly.   Dan. 9:4, 20 • 2 Chr. 20:9

2 And Shecaniah the son of Jehiel, one of the sons of Elam, answered and said to Ezra, "We have been unfaithful to our God, and have[T]married foreign women from the peoples of the land; yet now there is hope for Israel in spite of this.   *given dwelling to*

The Covenant Is Instituted

3"So now let us make a covenant with our God to put away all the wives and[T]their children, according to the counsel of [8]my lord and of those who tremble at the com-

[8] Or, *the Lord*

mandment of our God; and let it be done according to the law. *that which is born of them*

4 "Arise! For *this* matter is ^Tyour responsibility, but we will be with you; ^Rbe courageous and act."   *upon you • 1 Chr. 28:10*

5 Then Ezra rose and made the leading priests, the Levites, and all Israel, take oath that they would do according to this ^Tproposal; so they took the oath.   *word, thing*

Separation Is Accepted

6 Then Ezra ^Rrose from before the house of God and went into the chamber of Jehohanan the son of Eliashib. Although he went there, ^Rhe did not eat bread, nor drink water, for he was mourning over the unfaithfulness of the exiles.   *Ezra 10:1 • Deut. 9:18*

7 And they made a proclamation throughout Judah and Jerusalem to all the exiles, that they should assemble at Jerusalem,

8 and that whoever would not come within three days, according to the counsel of the leaders and the elders, all his possessions should be forfeited and he himself excluded from the assembly of the exiles.

9 So all the men of Judah and Benjamin assembled at Jerusalem within the three days. It was the ninth month on the twentieth of the month, and all the people sat in the open square *before* the house of God, ^Rtrembling because of this matter and the heavy rain.   *1 Sam. 12:18; Ezra 9:4; 10:3*

10 Then Ezra the priest stood up and said to them, "You have been unfaithful and have married foreign wives adding to the guilt of Israel.

11 "Now, therefore, make confession to the Lord God of your fathers, and do His will; and separate yourselves from the peoples of the land and from the foreign wives."

12 Then all the assembly answered and said with a loud voice, "That's right! As you have said, so it is ^Tour duty to do.   *upon us*

13 "But there are many people, it is the rainy season, and we are not able to stand in the open. Nor *can* the task *be done* in one or two days, for we have transgressed greatly in this matter.

14 "Let our leaders ^Trepresent the whole assembly and let all those in our cities who have married foreign wives come at appointed times, together with the elders and judges of each city, until the ^Rfierce anger of our God on account of this matter is turned away from us."   *stand for • 2 Kin. 23:26*

15 Only Jonathan the son of Asahel and Jahzeiah the son of Tikvah ^Topposed this, with Meshullam and Shabbethai the Levite supporting them.   *stood against*

16 But the exiles did so. And Ezra the priest selected men *who were* heads of fathers' *households* for *each* of their father's households, all of them by name. So they ^Tconvened on the first day of the tenth month to investigate the matter.   *sat*

17 And they finished *investigating* all the men who had married foreign wives by the first of the first month.

Separation of Priests

18 And among the sons of the priests who had married foreign wives were found of the sons of ^RJeshua the son of Jozadak, and his brothers: Maaseiah, Eliezer, Jarib, and Gedaliah.   *Ezra 5:2; Hag. 1:1, 12; 2:4; Zech. 3:1*

19 And they ^Tpledged to put away their wives, and being guilty, *they offered* a ram of the flock for their offense.   *gave their hand*

20 And of the sons of Immer *there were* Hanani and Zebadiah;

21 and of the sons of Harim: Maaseiah, Elijah, Shemaiah, Jehiel, and Uzziah;

22 and of the sons of Pashhur: Elioenai, Maaseiah, Ishmael, Nethanel, Jozabad, and Elasah.

Separation of Levites

23 And of Levites *there were* Jozabad, Shimei, Kelaiah (that is, Kelita), Pethahiah, Judah, and Eliezer.

24 And of the singers *there was* Eliashib; and of the gatekeepers: Shallum, Telem, and Uri.

Separation of People

25 And of Israel, of the sons of Parosh *there were* Ramiah, Izziah, Malchijah, Mijamin, Eleazar, Malchijah, and Benaiah;

26 and of the sons of Elam: Mattaniah, Zechariah, Jehiel, Abdi, Jeremoth, and Elijah;

27 and of the sons of ^RZattu: Elioenai, Eliashib, Mattaniah, Jeremoth, Zabad, and Aziza;   *Ezra 2:8; Neh. 7:13*

28 and of the sons of Bebai: Jehohanan, Hananiah, Zabbai, *and* Athlai;

29 and of the sons of Bani: Meshullam, Malluch, and Adaiah, Jashub, Sheal, *and* Jeremoth;

30 and of the sons of Pahath-moab: Adna, Chelal, Benaiah, Maaseiah, Mattaniah, Bezalel, Binnui, and Manasseh;

31 and *of* the sons of Harim: Eliezer, Isshijah, Malchijah, Shemaiah, Shimeon,

32 Benjamin, Malluch, *and* Shemariah;

33 of the sons of Hashum: Mattenai, Mattattah, Zabad, Eliphelet, Jeremai, Manasseh, *and* Shimei;

34 of the sons of Bani: Maadai, Amram, Uel,

35 Benaiah, Bedeiah, Cheluhi,

36 Vaniah, Meremoth, Eliashib,

37 Mattaniah, Mattenai, Jaasu,

38 Bani, Binnui, Shimei,

39 Shelemiah, Nathan, Adaiah,
40 Machnadebai, Shashai, Sharai,
41 Azarel, Shelemiah, Shemariah,
42 Shallum, Amariah, *and* Joseph.
43 Of the sons of [R]Nebo *there were* Jeiel,

Mattithiah, Zabad, Zebina, Jaddai, Joel, *and* Benaiah.   Num. 32:38; Ezra 2:29
 44 All these had married [R]foreign wives, and some of them had wives *by whom* they had children.   1 Kin. 11:1-3; Ezra 10:3

Weights

Unit	Weight	Equivalents	Translations
Jewish Weights Talent	c. 75 pounds for common talent, c. 150 pounds for royal talent	60 minas; 3,000 shekels	talent, one hundred pounds
Mina	1.25 pounds	50 shekels	maneh, mina
Shekel	c. .4 ounce (11.4 grams) for common shekel c. .8 ounce for royal shekel	2 bekas; 20 gerahs	shekel
Beka	c. .2 ounce (5.7 grams)	½ shekel; 10 gerahs	half-shekel
Gerah	c. .02 ounce (.57 grams)	¹⁄₂₀ shekel	gerah
Roman Weight Litra	12 ounces		pound, pint

Measures of Length

Unit	Length	Equivalents	Translations
Day's journey	c. 20 miles		day's journey, day's walk
Roman mile	4,854 feet	8 stadia	mile
Sabbath day's journey	3,637 feet	6 stadia	a sabbath day's journey
Stadion	606 feet	⅛ Roman mile	mile, stadion
Rod	9 feet (10.5 feet in Ezekiel)	3 paces; 6 cubits	measuring rod
Fathom	6 feet	4 cubits	fathom
Pace	3 feet	⅓ rod; 2 cubits	pace
Cubit	18 inches	½ pace; 2 spans	cubit, yards
Span	9 inches	½ cubit; 3 hand- breadths	span
Handbreadth	3 inches	⅓ span; 4 fingers	handbreadth
Finger	.75 inches	¼ handbreadth	finger

THE BOOK OF
NEHEMIAH

THE BOOK OF NEHEMIAH

Nehemiah, contemporary of Ezra and cupbearer to the king in the Persian palace, leads the third and last return to Jerusalem after the Babylonian exile. His concern for the welfare of Jerusalem and its inhabitants prompts him to take bold action. Granted permission to return to his homeland, Nehemiah challenges his countrymen to arise and rebuild the shattered wall of Jerusalem. In spite of opposition from without and abuse from within, the task is completed in only fifty-two days, a feat even the enemies of Israel must attribute to God's enabling. By contrast, the task of reviving and reforming the people of God within the rebuilt wall demands years of Nehemiah's godly life and leadership.

The Hebrew for Nehemiah is *Nehemyah*, "Comfort of Yahweh." The book is named after its chief character, whose name appears in the opening verse. The combined book of Ezra-Nehemiah is given the Greek title *Esdras Deuteron*, "Second Esdras" (see "The Book of Ezra") in the Septuagint, a third-century B.C. Greek-language translation of the Hebrew Old Testament. The Latin title of Nehemiah is *Liber Secundus Esdrae*, "Second Book of Ezra" (Ezra was the first). At this point, it is considered a separate book from Ezra, and is later called *Liber Nehemiae*, "Book of Nehemiah."

THE AUTHOR OF NEHEMIAH

Clearly, much of this book came from Nehemiah's personal memoirs. The reporting is remarkably candid and vivid. Certainly 1:1—7:5; 12:27-43; and 13:4-31 are the "words of Nehemiah" (1:1). Some scholars think that Nehemiah composed those portions and compiled the rest. Others think that Ezra wrote 7:6—12:26 and 12:44—13:3, and that he compiled the rest making use of Nehemiah's diary. A third view that neither wrote it seems least likely from the evidence. Nehemiah 7:5-73 is almost the same as Ezra 2:1-70, and both lists may have been taken from another record of the same period.

As cupbearer to Artaxerxes I, Nehemiah holds a position of great responsibility. His role of tasting the king's wine to prevent him from being poisoned places Nehemiah in a position of trust and confidence as one of the king's advisers. As governor of Jerusalem from 444 to 432 B.C. (5:14; 8:9; 10:1; 13:6), Nehemiah

demonstrates courage, compassion for the oppressed, integrity, godliness, and selflessness. He is willing to give up the luxury and ease of the palace to help his people. He is a dedicated layman who has the right priorities and is concerned for God's work, who is able to encourage and rebuke at the right times, who is strong in prayer, and who gives all glory and credit to God.

THE TIME OF NEHEMIAH

See "The Time of Ezra," because both Ezra and Nehemiah share the same historical background. The Book of Nehemiah fits within the reign of Artaxerxes I of Persia (464–423 B.C.). Esther is Artaxerxes' stepmother, and it is possible that she is instrumental in Nehemiah's appointment as the king's cupbearer. Nehemiah leaves Persia in the twentieth year of Artaxerxes (2:1), returns to Persia in the thirty-second year of Artaxerxes (13:6), and leaves again for Jerusalem "after some time" (13:6), perhaps about 425 B.C. This book could not have been completed until after his second visit to Jerusalem.

The historical reliability of this book is supported by the Elephantine papyri. These ancient documents mention Sanballat (2:19) and Jehohanan (6:18; 12:23) and indicate that Bigvai replaces Nehemiah as governor of Judah by 410 B.C.

Malachi lives and ministers during Nehemiah's time, and a comparison of the books shows that many of the evils encountered by Nehemiah are specifically denounced by Malachi. The cold-hearted indifference toward God described in both books remains a problem in Israel during the four hundred years before Christ, during which there is no revelation from God.

THE CHRIST OF NEHEMIAH

Like Ezra, Nehemiah portrays Christ in His ministry of restoration. Nehemiah illustrates Christ in that he gives up a high position in order to identify with the plight of his people; he comes with a specific mission and fulfills it; and his life is characterized by prayerful dependence upon God.

In this book, everything is restored except the king. The temple is rebuilt, Jerusalem is reconstructed, the covenant is renewed, and the people are reformed. The messianic line is in-

tact, but the King is yet to come. The decree of Artaxerxes in his twentieth year (2:2) marks the beginning point of Daniel's prophecy of the seventy weeks (see Dan. 9:25–27). "So you are to know and discern *that* from the issuing of a decree to restore and rebuild Jerusalem until Messiah the Prince *there will be* seven weeks and sixty-two weeks; it will be built again, with plaza and moat, even in times of distress" (Dan. 9:25). The Messiah will come at the end of the sixty-nine weeks, and this is exactly fulfilled in A.D. 33 (see "The Christ of Daniel").

KEYS TO NEHEMIAH

Key Word: Jerusalem Walls—While Ezra deals with the religious restoration of Judah, Nehemiah is primarily concerned with Judah's political and geographical restoration. The first seven chapters are devoted to the rebuilding of Jerusalem's walls, because Jerusalem was the spiritual and political center of Judah. Without walls, Jerusalem could hardly be considered a city at all. As governor, Nehemiah also establishes firm civil authority. Ezra and Nehemiah work together to build the people spiritually and morally so that the restoration will be complete.

Key Verses: Nehemiah 6:15, 16; 8:8—"So the wall was completed on the twenty-fifth of *the month* Elul, in fifty-two days. And it came about when all our enemies heard *of it*, and all the nations surrounding us saw *it*, they lost their confidence; for they recognized that this work had been accomplished with the help of our God" (6:15, 16).

"And they read from the book, from the law of God, translating to give the sense so that they understood the reading" (8:8).

Key Chapter: Nehemiah 9—The key to the

Old Testament is the covenant, which is its theme and unifying factor. Israel's history can be divided according to the nation's obedience or disobedience to God's conditional covenant: blessings from obedience and destruction from disobedience. Nehemiah 9 records that upon completion of the Jerusalem wall the nation reaffirmed its loyalty to the covenant.

SURVEY OF NEHEMIAH

Nehemiah is closely associated with the ministry of his contemporary, Ezra. Ezra is a priest who brings spiritual revival; Nehemiah is a governor who brings physical and political reconstruction and leads the people in moral reform. They combine to make an effective team in rebuilding the postexilic remnant. Malachi, the last Old Testament prophet, also ministers during this time to provide additional moral and spiritual direction. The Book of Nehemiah takes us to the end of the historical account in the Old Testament, about four hundred years before the birth of the promised Messiah. Its two divisions are: the reconstruction of the wall (1—7), and the restoration of the people (8—13).

The Reconstruction of the Wall (1—7): Nehemiah's great concern for his people and the welfare of Jerusalem leads him to take bold action. The walls of Jerusalem, destroyed by Nebuchadnezzar in 586 B.C., evidently have been almost rebuilt after 464 B.C. when Artaxerxes I took the throne of Persia (see Ezra 3:6–23). When he hears that opposition led to their second destruction, Nehemiah prays on behalf of his people and then secures Artaxerxes' permission, provision, and protection for the massive project of rebuilding the walls.

The return under Nehemiah in 444 B.C. takes place thirteen years after the return led by

FOCUS	RECONSTRUCTION OF THE WALL		RESTORATION OF THE PEOPLE	
REFERENCE	1:1————————3:1—		—8:1————————11:1———————13:31	
DIVISION	PREPARATION TO RECONSTRUCT THE WALL	RECONSTRUCTION OF THE WALL	RENEWAL OF THE COVENANT	OBEDIENCE TO THE COVENANT
TOPIC	POLITICAL		SPIRITUAL	
	CONSTRUCTION		INSTRUCTION	
LOCATION	JERUSALEM			
TIME	19 YEARS (444 – 425 B.C.)			

Ezra, and ninety-four years after the return led by Zerubbabel. Nehemiah inspects the walls and challenges the people to "arise and build" (2:18). Work begins immediately on the wall and its gates, with people building portions corresponding to where they are living.

However, opposition quickly arises, first in the form of mockery, then in the form of conspiracy when the work is progressing at an alarming rate. Nehemiah overcomes threats of force by setting half of the people on military watch and half on construction. While the external opposition continues to mount, internal opposition also surfaces. The wealthier Jews are abusing and oppressing the people, forcing them to mortgage their property and sell their children into slavery. Nehemiah again deals with the problem by the twin means of prayer and action. He also leads by example when he sacrifices his governor's salary. In spite of deceit, slander, and treachery, Nehemiah continues to trust in God and to press on with singleness of mind until the work is completed. The task is accomplished in an incredible fifty-two days, and even the enemies recognize that it can only have been accomplished with the help of God (6:16).

The Restoration of the People (8—13): The construction of the walls is followed by consecration and consolidation of the people. Ezra the priest is the leader of the spiritual revival

(8—10), reminiscent of the reforms he led thirteen years earlier (Ezra 9 and 10). Ezra stands on a special wooden podium after the completion of the walls and gives the people a marathon reading of the law, translating from the Hebrew into Aramaic so they can understand. They respond with weeping, confession, obedience, and rejoicing. The Levites and priests lead them in a great prayer that surveys God's past work of deliverance and loyalty on behalf of His people, and magnifies God's attributes of holiness, justice, mercy, and love. The covenant is then renewed with God as the people commit themselves to separate from the Gentiles in marriage and to obey God's commandments.

Lots are drawn to determine who will remain in Jerusalem and who will return to the cities of their inheritance. One-tenth are required to stay in Jerusalem, and the rest of the land is resettled by the people and priests. The walls of Jerusalem are dedicated to the Lord in a joyful ceremony accompanied by instrumental and vocal music.

Unfortunately, Ezra's revival is short-lived; and Nehemiah, who returned to Persia in 432 B.C. (13:6), makes a second trip to Jerusalem about 425 B.C. to reform the people. He cleanses the temple, enforces the Sabbath, and requires the people to put away all foreign wives.

OUTLINE OF NEHEMIAH

Part One: The Reconstruction of the Wall (1:1—7:73)

Part Two: The Restoration of the People (8:1—13:31)

CHAPTER 1

Discovery of the Broken Wall

THE words of Nehemiah the son of Haca-liah.

Now it happened in ^{R}the month Chislev, ^{R}*in* the twentieth year, while I was in ^{R}Susa the ^{1}capitol,   Zech. 7:1 • Neh. 2:1 • Esth. 1:2; Dan. 8:2

2 that ^{R}Hanani, one of my brothers, and ^{T}some men from Judah came; and I asked them concerning the Jews who had escaped *and* had survived the captivity, and about Jerusalem.   Neh. 7:2 • *he and some*

3 And they said to me, "The remnant there in the ^{R}province who survived the captivity are in great distress and reproach, and the wall of Jerusalem is broken down and its gates are burned with fire."   Neh. 7:6

Nehemiah Intercedes with God

4 Now it came about when I heard these words, ^{R}I sat down and wept and mourned for days; and I was fasting and praying before the God of heaven.   Ezra 9:3; 10:1

5 And I said, "I beseech Thee, O LORD God of heaven, ^{R}the great and awesome God, who preserves the covenant and lovingkindness for those who love Him and keep His commandments,   Neh. 4:14; 9:32; Dan. 9:4

6 ^{R}let Thine ear now be attentive and Thine eyes open to hear the prayer of Thy servant which I am praying before Thee now, day and night, on behalf of the sons of Israel Thy servants, ^{R}confessing the sins of the sons of Israel which we have sinned against Thee; I and my father's house have sinned.   Dan. 9:17 • Ezra 10:1; Dan. 9:20

7 "We have acted very corruptly against Thee and have not kept the commandments, nor the statutes, nor the ordinances which Thou didst command Thy servant Moses.

8 "Remember the word which Thou didst command Thy servant Moses, saying, 'If ^{R}you are unfaithful I will scatter you among the peoples;   Lev. 26:33

9 ^{R}but if you return to Me and keep My commandments and do them, though those

of you who have been scattered were in the most remote part of the heavens, I ^{R}will gather them from there and will bring them to the place where I have chosen to cause My name to dwell.'   [Deut. 30:2, 3] • Deut. 30:4

10 "And they are Thy servants and Thy people whom Thou didst redeem by Thy great power and by Thy strong hand.

11 "O Lord, I beseech Thee, ^{R}may Thine ear be attentive to the prayer of Thy servant and the prayer of Thy servants who delight to ^{A}revere Thy name, and make Thy servant successful today, and grant him compassion before this man."   Neh. 1:6 • *fear*

Now I was the cupbearer to the king.

CHAPTER 2

Nehemiah Intercedes with Artaxerxes

AND it came about in the month Nisan, ^{R}in the twentieth year of King ^{R}Artaxerxes, that wine *was* before him, and I took up the wine and gave it to the king. Now I had not been sad in his presence.   Neh. 1:1 • Ezra 7:1

2 So the king said to me, "Why is your face sad though you are not sick? ^{R}This is nothing but sadness of heart." Then I was very much afraid.   Prov. 15:13

3 And I said to the king, "Let ^{R}the king live forever. Why should my face not be sad when the city, the place of my fathers' tombs, lies desolate and its gates have been consumed by fire?"   Dan. 2:4 • 2 Kin. 25:8-10

4 Then the king said to me, "What would you request?" ^{R}So I prayed to the God of heaven.   Neh. 1:4

5 And I said to the king, "If it please the king, and if your servant has found favor before you, send me to Judah, to the city of my fathers' tombs, that I may rebuild it."

6 Then the king said to me, the queen sitting beside him, "How long will your journey be, and when will you return?" So it pleased the king to send me, and ^{A}I gave him a definite time.   Neh. 13:6

7 And I said to the king, "If it please the king, let letters be given me ^{R}for the governors *of the provinces* beyond the River, that they may allow me to pass through until I come to Judah,   Ezra 7:21; 8:36

^{1} Or, *palace or citadel*

8 and a letter to Asaph the keeper of the king's forest, that he may give me timber to make beams for the gates of the fortress which is by the ²temple, for the wall of the city, and for the house to which I will go." And the king granted *them* to me because the good hand of my God *was* on me.

Arrival of Nehemiah in Jerusalem

9 Then I came to the governors *of the provinces* beyond the River and gave them the king's letters. Now the king had sent with me officers of the army and horsemen.
10 And when^RSanballat the Horonite and Tobiah the Ammonite ^Tofficial heard *about it*, it was very displeasing to them that someone had come to seek the welfare of the sons of Israel.   Neh. 2:19; 4:1 • *servant*
11 So I^Rcame to Jerusalem and was there three days.   Ezra 8:32

Nehemiah Inspects the Broken Walls

12 And I arose in the night, I and a few men with me. I did not tell anyone what my God was putting into my mind to do for Jerusalem and there was no animal with me except the animal on which I was riding.
13 So I went out at night by^Rthe Valley Gate in the direction of the Dragon's Well and *on* to the ^TRefuse Gate, inspecting the walls of Jerusalem ^Rwhich were broken down and its gates which were consumed by fire.   Neh. 3:13 • *Gate of Ash-heaps* • Neh. 1:3
14 Then I passed on to the Fountain Gate and the King's Pool, but there was no place for^Tmy mount to pass.   *the animal under me*
15 So I went up at night by the^Rravine and inspected the wall. Then I entered the Valley Gate again and returned.   John 18:1
16 And the officials did not know where I had gone or what I had done; nor had I as yet told the Jews, the priests, the nobles, the officials, or the rest who did the work.

Nehemiah Exhorts the People

17 Then I said to them, "You see the bad situation we are in, that^RJerusalem is desolate and its gates burned by fire. Come, let us rebuild the wall of Jerusalem that we may no longer be a reproach."   Neh. 1:3
18 And I told them how the hand of my God had been favorable to me, and also about the king's words which he had spoken to me. Then they said, "Let us arise and build."^RSo they put their hands to the good *work*.   2 Sam. 2:7

Nehemiah Answers the Enemies

19 But when Sanballat the Horonite, and Tobiah the Ammonite ^Tofficial, and^RGeshem the Arab heard *it*,^Rthey mocked us and de-

spised us and said, "What is this thing you are doing? ^RAre you rebelling against the king?"   *servant* • Neh. 6:6 • Neh. 4:1 • Neh. 6:6
20 So I answered them and said to them, "The^R God of heaven will give us success; therefore we His servants will arise and build,^Rbut you have no portion, right, or memorial in Jerusalem."   Ezra 4:3 • Neh. 2:4

CHAPTER 3

Record of the Builders

T HEN^REliashib the high priest arose with his brothers the priests and built^Rthe Sheep Gate; they consecrated it and hung its doors. They consecrated ^Tthe wall to the Tower of the Hundred *and* the Tower of Hananel.   Neh. 3:20; 13:28 • Neh. 3:32 • *it*
2 And next to him ^Rthe men of Jericho built, and next to ^Tthem Zaccur the son of Imri built.   Neh. 7:36 • *him*
3 Now the sons of Hassenaah built^Rthe Fish Gate; they laid its beams and hung its doors with its bolts and bars.   Neh. 12:39
4 And next to them Meremoth the son of Uriah the son of Hakkoz made repairs. And next to him Meshullam the son of Berechiah the son of Meshezabel made repairs. And next to ^Thim Zadok the son of Baana also made repairs.   *them*
5 Moreover, next to ^Thim the Tekoites made repairs, but their nobles did not support the work of their masters.   *them*
6 And Joiada the son of Paseah and Meshullam the son of Besodeiah repaired^Rthe Old Gate; they laid its beams and hung its doors, with its bolts and its bars.   Neh. 12:39
7 Next to them Melatiah the Gibeonite and Jadon the Meronothite, the men of Gibeon and of Mizpah, also made repairs for the official seat of the^Rgovernor *of the province* beyond the River.   Neh. 2:7
8 Next to him Uzziel the son of Harhaiah of the^Rgoldsmiths made repairs. And next to him Hananiah, one of the perfumers, made repairs, and they restored Jerusalem as far as^Rthe Broad Wall.   Neh. 3:31, 32 • Neh. 12:38
9 And next to them Rephaiah the son of Hur,^Rthe official of half the district of Jerusalem, made repairs.   Neh. 3:12, 17
10 Next to them Jedaiah the son of Harumaph made repairs opposite his house. And next to him Hattush the son of Hashabneiah made repairs.
11 Malchijah the son of Harim and Hasshub the son of Pahath-moab repaired another section and the Tower of Furnaces.
12 And next to him Shallum the son of Hallohesh,^Rthe official of half the district of Jerusalem, made repairs, he and his daughters.   Neh. 3:9
13 Hanun and the inhabitants of Zanoah

² Lit., *house*

repaired [R]the Valley Gate. They built it and hung its doors with its bolts and its bars, and [T]a thousand cubits of the wall to the [T]Refuse Gate. Neh. 2:13 • 1500 ft. • *Gate of Ash-heaps*

14 And Malchijah the son of Rechab, the official of the district of [H]Beth-haccherem repaired the Refuse Gate. He built it and hung its doors with its bolts and its bars. Jer. 6:1

15 Shallum the son of Col-hozeh, the official of the district of Mizpah, [R]repaired the Fountain Gate. He built it, covered it, and hung its doors with its bolts and its bars, and the wall of the Pool of Shelah at the king's garden as far as the steps that descend from the city of David. Neh. 2:17

16 After him Nehemiah the son of Azbuk, [R]official of half the district of Beth-zur, made repairs as far as *a point* opposite the tombs of David, and as far as the artificial pool and the house of the mighty men. Neh. 3:9, 12, 17

17 After him the Levites carried out repairs *under* Rehum the son of Bani. Next to him Hashabiah, the official of half the district of Keilah, carried out repairs for his district.

18 After him their brothers carried out repairs *under* Bavvai the son of Henadad, official of *the other* half of the district of Keilah.

19 And next to him Ezer the son of Jeshua, [R]the official of Mizpah, repaired another section, in front of the ascent of the armory [a]at the Angle. Neh. 3:15 • 2 Chr. 26:9

20 After him Baruch the son of Zabbai zealously repaired another section, from the Angle to the doorway of the house of [R]Eliashib the high priest. Neh. 3:1

21 After him Meremoth the son of Uriah the son of Hakkoz repaired another section, from the doorway of Eliashib's house even as far as the end of [T]his house. *Eliashib's*

22 And after him the priests, [R]the men of the ³valley, carried out repairs. Neh. 12:28

23 After [T]them Benjamin and Hasshub carried out repairs in front of their house. After [T]them Azariah the son of Maaseiah, son of Ananiah carried out repairs beside his house. *him*

24 After him Binnui the son of Henadad repaired another section, from the house of Azariah as far as [R]the Angle and as far as the corner. Neh. 3:19

25 Palal the son of Uzai *made repairs* in front of the Angle and the tower projecting from the upper house of the king, which is by [R]the court of the guard. After him Pedaiah the son of Parosh *made repairs*. Jer. 32:2

26 And [R]the temple servants living in [O]Ophel *made repairs* as far as the front of [T]the Water Gate toward the east and the projecting tower. Neh. 7:46 • Neh. 11:21 • Neh. 8:1

27 After him the Tekoites repaired another section in front of the great projecting tower and as far as the wall of Ophel.

28 Above the Horse Gate the priests carried out repairs, each in front of his house.

29 After [T]them Zadok the son of Immer carried out repairs in front of his house. And after him Shemaiah the son of Shecaniah, the keeper of the East Gate, carried out repairs. *him*

30 After him Hananiah the son of Shelemiah, and Hanun the sixth son of Zalaph, repaired another section. After him Meshullam the son of Berechiah carried out repairs in front of his own [A]quarters. *cell*

31 After him Malchijah one of the goldsmiths, carried out repairs as far as the house of the temple servants and of the merchants, in front of the Inspection Gate and as far as the upper room of the corner.

32 And between the upper room of the corner and the Sheep Gate the goldsmiths and the merchants carried out repairs.

CHAPTER 4

Opposition Through Ridicule

NOW it came about that when [R]Sanballat heard that we were rebuilding the wall, he became furious and very angry and mocked the Jews. Neh. 2:10

2 And he spoke in the presence of his brothers and [R]the [A]wealthy *men* of Samaria and said, "What are these feeble Jews doing? Are they going to restore *it* for themselves? Can they offer sacrifices? Can they finish in a day? Can they revive the stones from the [T]dusty rubble even the burned ones?" Ezra 4:9, 10 • *army* • *heaps of dust*

3 Now Tobiah the Ammonite *was* near him and he said, "Even what they are building—if a fox should [T]jump on *it*, he would break their stone wall down!" *go up*

4 [R]Hear, O our God, how we are despised! [R]Return their reproach on their own heads and give them up for plunder in a land of captivity. Ps. 123:3, 4 • Ps. 79:12

5 Do not [T]forgive their iniquity and let not their sin be blotted out before Thee, for they have demoralized the builders. *cover*

6 So we built the wall and the whole wall was joined together to half its *height,* for the people had a [T]mind to work. *heart*

Opposition Through Threat of Attack

7 Now it came about when Sanballat, Tobiah, the Arabs, the Ammonites, and the Ashdodites heard that the [T]repair of the walls of Jerusalem went on, *and* that the breaches began to be closed, they were very angry. *healing*

8 And all of them [R]conspired together to come *and* fight against Jerusalem and to cause a disturbance in it. Ps. 83:3

9 But we prayed to our God, and because

---

³ Lit., *circle;* i.e., lower Jordan valley

of them we^Rset up a guard against them day and night. *Neh. 4:11*

Opposition Through Discouragement

10 Thus ^Tin Judah it was said, *Judah said*
"The strength of the burden bearers is failing,
Yet there is much ^Trubbish; *dust*
And we ourselves are unable
To rebuild the wall."
11 And our enemies said, "They will not know or see until we come among them, kill them, and put a stop to the work."
12 And it came about when the Jews who lived near them came and told us ten times, "They will come up against us from every place where you may turn,"
13 then I stationed *men* in the lowest parts of the space behind the wall, the ^Texposed places, and I ^Istationed the people in families with their swords, spears, and bows. *bare • Neh. 4:17, 18*
14 When I saw *their fear,* I rose and spoke to the nobles, the officials, and the rest of the people: "Do^R not be afraid of them; remember the Lord who is great and awesome, and fight for your brothers, your sons, your daughters, your wives, and your houses." *[Num. 14:9]; Deut. 1:29, 30*
15 And it happened when our enemies heard that it was known to us, and that God had frustrated their plan, then all of us returned to the wall, each one to his work.
16 And it came about from that day on, that half of my servants carried on the work while half of them held the spears, the shields, the bows, and the breastplates; and the captains *were* behind the whole house of Judah.
17 Those who were rebuilding the wall and those who carried burdens took *their* load with one hand doing the work and the other holding a weapon.
18 As for the builders, each *wore* his sword girded at his side as he built, while the trumpeter *stood* near me.
19 And I said to the nobles, the officials, and the rest of the people, "The work is great and extensive, and we are separated on the wall far from one another.
20 "At whatever place you hear the sound of the trumpet, ^Trally to us there. ^ROur God will fight for us." *assemble yourselves • Ex. 14:14*
21 So we carried on the work with half of them holding spears from ^Tdawn until the stars ^Tappeared. *rising of the dawn • came out*
22 At that time I also said to the people, "Let each man with his servant spend the night within Jerusalem so that they may be a guard for us by night and a laborer by day."
23 So neither I, my brothers, my servants, nor the men of the guard who followed me, none of us removed our clothes, each *took* his weapon *even* to the water.

CHAPTER 5

Opposition Through Extortion

NOW^R there was a great outcry of the people and of their wives against their ^RJewish brothers. *Lev. 25:35 • Deut. 15:7*
2 For there were those who said, "We, our sons and our daughters, are many; therefore let us ^Rget grain that we may eat and live." *Hag. 1:6*
3 And there were others who said, "We are mortgaging our fields, our vineyards, and our houses that we might get grain because of the famine."
4 Also there were those who said, "We have borrowed money^Rfor the king's tax *on* our fields and our vineyards. *Ezra 4:13; 7:24*
5 "And now our flesh is like the flesh of our brothers, our children like their children. Yet behold, we are forcing our sons and our daughters to be slaves, and some of our daughters are forced into bondage *already,* and we are helpless because our fields and vineyards belong to others."
6 Then I was very ^Rangry when I had heard their outcry and these words. *Ex. 11:8*
7 And I consulted with myself, and contended with the nobles and the rulers and said to them, "You^Rare exacting usury, each from his brother!" Therefore, I held a great assembly against them. *[Ex. 22:25; Lev. 25:36]*
8 And I said to them, "We according to our ability have ^Tredeemed our Jewish brothers who were sold to the nations; now would you even sell your brothers that they may be sold to us?" Then they were silent and could not find a word *to say.* *bought*
9 Again I said, "The thing which you are doing is not good; should you not walk in the fear of our God because of^Rthe reproach of the nations, our enemies? *Neh. 4:4*
10 "And likewise I, my brothers and my servants, are lending them money and grain. Please, let us leave off this usury.
11 "Please, give back to them this very day their fields, their vineyards, their olive groves, and their houses, also the hundredth *part* of the money and of the grain, the new wine, and the oil that you are exacting from them."
12 Then they said, "We will give *it* back and will require nothing from them; we will do exactly as you say." So I called the priests and took an oath from them that they would do according to this promise.
13 I also shook out the ^Tfront of my garment and said, "Thus may God shake out every man from his house and from his possessions who does not fulfill this ^Tpromise; even thus may he be shaken out and emptied." And all the assembly said, "Amen!" And they praised the LORD. Then the people did according to this promise. *bosom • word*

Nehemiah's Unselfish Example

14 Moreover, from the day that I was ap-

pointed to be their governor in the land of Judah, from the twentieth year to the thirty-second year of King Artaxerxes, *for* twelve years, neither I nor my [T]kinsmen have eaten the governor's food *allowance*.   *brothers*

15 But the former governors who were before me [t]laid burdens on the people and took from them bread and wine besides forty shekels of silver; even their servants domineered the people. But I did not do so because of the fear of God.   *made heavy*

16 And I also [4]applied myself to the work on this wall; we did not buy any land, and all my servants were gathered there for the work.

17 Moreover, [R]there *were* at my table one hundred and fifty Jews and officials, besides those who came to us from the nations that were around us.   1 Kin. 18:19

18 Now that which was prepared for each day was one ox *and* six choice sheep, also birds were prepared for me; and once in ten days all sorts of wine *were furnished* in abundance. Yet for all this I did not demand the governor's food *allowance*, because the servitude was heavy on this people.

19 [R]Remember me, O my God, for good, *according to* all that I have done for this people.   Neh. 13:14, 22, 31

CHAPTER 6

Opposition Through Compromise

Now it came about when it was reported to Sanballat, Tobiah, to Geshem the Arab, and to the rest of our enemies that I had rebuilt the wall, and *that* no breach remained in it, [R]although at that time I had not set up the doors in the gates,   Neh. 3:1, 3

2 that Sanballat and Geshem sent *a message* to me, saying, "Come, let us meet together at [5]Chephirim in the plain of Ono." But they were planning to harm me.

3 So I sent messengers to them, saying, "I am doing a great work and I cannot come down. Why should the work stop while I leave it and come down to you?"

4 And they sent *messages* to me four times in this manner, and I answered them in the same way.

Opposition Through Slander

5 Then Sanballat sent his servant to me in the same manner a fifth time with an open letter in his hand.

6 In it was written, "It is reported among the nations, and Gashmu says, that you and the Jews are planning to rebel; therefore you are rebuilding the wall. And you are to be their king, according to these reports.

7 "And you have also appointed prophets to proclaim in Jerusalem concerning [T]you, 'A

king is in Judah!' And now it will be reported to the king according to these reports. So come now, let us take counsel together."   *you, saying*

8 Then I sent *a message* to him saying, "Such things as you are saying have not been done, but you are [R]inventing them [T]in your own mind."   Job 13:4 • *from your heart*

9 For all of them were *trying* to frighten us, thinking, "They will become discouraged with the work and it will not be done." But now, O God, strengthen my hands.

Opposition Through Treachery

10 And when I entered the house of Shemaiah the son of Delaiah, son of Mehetabel, [R]who was confined at home, he said, "Let us meet together in the house of God, within the temple, and let us close the doors of the temple, for they are coming to kill you, and they are coming to kill you at night."   Jer. 36:5 • *shut up*

11 But I said, "Should a man like me flee? And could one such as I go into the temple [T]to save his life? I will not go in."   *and live*

12 Then I perceived [T]that surely God had not sent him, but he uttered *his* prophecy against me because Tobiah and Sanballat had hired him.   *and behold God*

13 He was hired for this reason, [R]that I might become frightened and act accordingly and sin, so that they might have an evil report in order that they could reproach me.   Neh. 6:6

14 [R]Remember, O my God, Tobiah and Sanballat according to these works of theirs, and also Noadiah [R]the prophetess and the rest of the prophets who were *trying* to frighten me.   Neh. 13:29 • Ezek. 13:17

Completion of the Reconstruction

15 So [R]the wall was completed on the twenty-fifth of *the month* Elul, in fifty-two days.   Neh. 4:1, 2

16 And it came about when all our enemies heard *of it,* and all the nations surrounding us saw *it,* they [T]lost their confidence; for they recognized that this work had been accomplished with the help of our God.   *fell exceedingly in their own eyes*

17 Also in those days many letters went from the nobles of Judah to Tobiah, and Tobiah's *letters* came to them.

18 For many in Judah were bound by oath to him because he was the son-in-law of Shecaniah the son of Arah, and his son Jehohanan had married the daughter of Meshullam the son of Berechiah.

19 Moreover, they were speaking about his good deeds in my presence and reported my words to him. Then Tobiah sent letters to frighten me.

[4] Or, *held fast*   [5] Another reading is, one of *the villages*

CHAPTER 7

Organization of Jerusalem

NOW it came about when [R]the wall was rebuilt and I had set up the doors, and the gatekeepers and the singers and the Levites were appointed,   Neh. 6:1, 15
2 that I put Hanani my brother, and Hananiah the commander of the fortress, in charge of Jerusalem, for he was a faithful man and feared God more than many.
3 Then I said to them, "Do not let the gates of Jerusalem be opened until the sun is hot, and while they are standing *guard,* let them shut and bolt the doors. Also appoint guards from the inhabitants of Jerusalem, each at his post, and each in front of his own house."
4 Now the city was large and spacious, but the people in it were few and the houses were not built.

The Plan

5 Then my God put it into my heart to assemble the nobles, the officials, and the people to be enrolled by genealogies. Then I found the book of the genealogy of those who came up first [T]in which I found the following record: *and I found written in it*
6 [R]These are the [T]people of the province who came up from the captivity of the exiles whom Nebuchadnezzar the king of Babylon had carried away, and who returned to Jerusalem and Judah, each to his city,   Ezra 2:1-70 · *sons*

The Leaders

7 who came with Zerubbabel, Jeshua, Nehemiah, [T]Azariah, Raamiah, Nahamani, Mordecai, Bilshan, Mispereth, Bigvai, Nehum, Baanah.   In Ezra 2:2, *Seraiah*
The number of men of the people of Israel:

The Men of Israel

8 the sons of Parosh, 2,172;
9 the sons of Shephatiah, 372;
10 the sons of Arah, 652;
11 the sons of Pahath-moab of the sons of Jeshua and Joab, 2,818;
12 the sons of Elam, 1,254;
13 the sons of Zattu, 845;
14 the sons of Zaccai, 760;
15 the sons of [T]Binnui, 648; In Ezra 2:10, *Bani*
16 the sons of Bebai, 628;
17 the sons of Azgad, 2,322;
18 the sons of Adonikam, 667;
19 the sons of Bigvai, 2,067;
20 the sons of Adin, 655;
21 the sons of Ater, of Hezekiah, 98;
22 the sons of Hashum, 328;
23 the sons of Bezai, 324;

24 the sons of Hariph, 112;
25 the sons of Gibeon, 95;
26 the men of Bethlehem and Netophah, 188;
27 the men of Anathoth, 128;
28 the men of Beth-azmaveth, 42;
29 the men of [T]Kiriath-jearim, Chephirah, and Beeroth, 743;   In Ezra 2:25, *Kiriath-arim*
30 the men of Ramah and Geba, 621;
31 the men of Michmas, 122;
32 the men of Bethel and Ai, 123;
33 the men of the other Nebo, 52;
34 the sons of the other Elam, 1,254;
35 the sons of Harim, 320;
36 the [T]men of Jericho, 345;   *sons*
37 the sons of Lod, Hadid, and Ono, 721;
38 the sons of Senaah, 3,930.

The Priests

39 The priests: the sons of Jedaiah of the house of Jeshua, 973;
40 the sons of Immer, 1,052;
41 the sons of Pashhur, 1,247;
42 the sons of Harim, 1,017.

The Levites

43 The Levites: the sons of Jeshua, of Kadmiel, of the sons of Hodevah, 74.
44 The singers: the sons of Asaph, 148.
45 The gatekeepers: the sons of Shallum, the sons of Ater, the sons of Talmon, the sons of Akkub, the sons of Hatita, the sons of Shobai, 138.

The Servants

46 The temple servants: the sons of Ziha, the sons of Hasupha, the sons of Tabbaoth,
47 the sons of Keros, the sons of [T]Sia, the sons of Padon,   In Ezra 2:44, *Siaha*
48 the sons of Lebana, the sons of Hagaba, the sons of Shalmai,
49 the sons of Hanan, the sons of Giddel, the sons of Gahar,
50 the sons of Reaiah, the sons of Rezin, the sons of Nekoda,
51 the sons of Gazzam, the sons of Uzza, the sons of Paseah,
52 the sons of Besai, the sons of Meunim, the sons of Nephushesim,
53 the sons of Bakbuk, the sons of Hakupha, the sons of Harhur,
54 the sons of [T]Bazlith, the sons of Mehida, the sons of Harsha,   In Ezra 2:52, *Bazluth*
55 the sons of Barkos, the sons of Sisera, the sons of Temah,
56 the sons of Neziah, the sons of Hatipha.
57 The sons of Solomon's servants: the sons of Sotai, the sons of [T]Sophereth, the sons of Perida,   In Ezra 2:55, *Hassophereth*
58 the sons of Jaala, the sons of Darkon, the sons of Giddel,

59 the sons of Shephatiah, the sons of Hattil, the sons of Pochereth-hazzebaim, the sons of ᵀAmon.   In Ezra 2:57, *Ami*
60 All the temple servants and the sons of Solomon's servants *were* 392.

The Men of Israel

61 And these *were* they who came up from Tel-melah, Tel-harsha, Cherub, Addon, and Immer; but they could not show their fathers' houses or their ᵀdescendants, whether they were of Israel: *seed*
62 the sons of Delaiah, the sons of Tobiah, the sons of Nekoda, 642.

The Priests

63 And of the priests: the sons of ᵀHobaiah, the sons of Hakkoz, the sons of Barzillai, who took a wife of the daughters of Barzillai, the Gileadite, and was named after them.   In Ezra 2:61, *Habaiah*
64 These searched *among* their ancestral registration, but it could not be located; therefore they were considered unclean *and* excluded from the priesthood.
65 And the ᵀgovernor said to them that they should not eat from the most holy things until a priest arose with Urim and Thummim.   Heb., *Tirshatha*, a Persian title

The Total of the Remnant

66 The whole assembly together *was* 42,360,
67 besides their male and their female servants, ᵀof whom *there were* 7,337; and they had 245 male and female singers.   *these*
68 ᴿTheir horses were 736; their mules, 245;   Ezra 2:66

69 *their* camels, 435; *their* donkeys, 6,720.

The Gifts of the Remnant for the Temple

70 And some from among the heads of fathers' *households* gave to the work. The governor gave to the treasury 1,000 gold drachmas, 50 basins, 530 priests' garments.
71 And some of the heads of fathers' *households* gave into the treasury of the workᵀ20,000 gold drachmas, and 2,200 silver minas. $28,483,516
72 And that which the rest of the people gave was 20,000 gold drachmas and 2,000 silver minas, and 67 priests' garments.
73 Now ᵀthe priests, the Levites, the gatekeepers, the singers, some of the people, the temple servants, and all Israel, lived in their cities.   1 Chr. 9:2
And when the seventh month came, the sons of Israel *were* in their cities.

CHAPTER 8

Reading of the Law

AND all the people gathered as one man at the square which was in front of the Water Gate, and they asked Ezra the scribe to bring the book of the law of Moses which the LORD had given to Israel.   *said to*
2 Then Ezra the priest brought the law before the assembly of men, women, and all who *could* listen with understanding, on the first day of the seventh month.

3 And he read from it before the square which was in front ofᴿthe Water Gate from ᵀearly morning until midday, in the presence of men and women, those who could understand; and all the people were attentive to the book of the law.   Neh. 8:1 • *the light*

8:3 Reading God's Word—The person who can read well has a much better opportunity of knowing and understanding God's Word than the person who has to rely upon what others tell him about the Word of God. Reading the Word of God is a very important part of communicating God's Word to God's people. Public Scripture reading was a regular part of the worship services in Israel and in the early church. Today we are blessed above all people in history, for not only does nearly everyone know how to read, but there also are enough copies of the Bible available so that everyone may have a personal copy. Here are some suggestions to aid you in receiving the greatest benefit from reading the Bible:
a. Read the Bible prayerfully. Ask the Spirit of God to meet your heart's need as you read (Page 591—Ps. 119:18).
b. Read the Bible thoughtfully. Think about the meaning and implications of what you are reading.
c. Read the Bible carefully. Take careful note not only of the words that are used but also of how they relate to one another.
d. Read the Bible repeatedly. It may be of great help to read the same portion over daily for a month's time. This is a good way for its words to take root in your heart. If you are reading a short book, read it every day. Divide longer books up into manageable portions of two or three chapters and read that portion through every day.
e. Read the Bible extensively. Sometimes it is of great help to read large portions of the Word of God through at one sitting. If you do this, do it at a time when you are alert and not likely to be disturbed during your reading.
f. Read the Bible regularly. It is good to have a particular time every day when you habitually give yourself to the reading of the Word of God.
g. Read the Bible faithfully. Inevitably there will be days when you will fail to read the Bible. Do not let your momentary lapse discourage you. Faithfully resume your practice of reading God's Word.
h. Read the Bible obediently. Because the Bible is God's Word written to you, it is essential to obey it (Page 75—Ex. 24:3).
Now turn to Page 510—Job 22:22: Memorizing God's Word.

4 And Ezra the scribe stood at a wooden podium which they had made for the purpose. And beside him stood Mattithiah, Shema, Anaiah, Uriah, Hilkiah, and Maaseiah on his right hand; and Pedaiah, Mishael, Malchijah, Hashum, Hashbaddanah, Zechariah, *and* Meshullam on his left hand.

5 And Ezra opened[R]the book in the sight of all the people for he was standing above all the people; and when he opened it, all the people[R]stood up.   Neh. 8:3 • Judg. 3:20

6 Then Ezra blessed the LORD the great God. And all the people answered, "Amen,[R] Amen!" while lifting up their hands; then they bowed low and worshiped the LORD with *their* faces to the ground.   Neh. 5:13

7 Also Jeshua, Bani, Sherebiah, Jamin, Akkub, Shabbethai, Hodiah, Maaseiah, Kelita, Azariah, Jozabad, Hanan, Pelaiah, and the Levites, explained the law to the people while the people *remained* in their place.

8 And they read from the book, from the law of God,[A]translating to give the sense so that they understood the reading.   *explaining*

Israel Celebrates
Her Understanding of the Law

9 Then Nehemiah, who was the[T]governor, and Ezra the priest *and* scribe, and the Levites who taught the people said to all the people, "This day is holy to the LORD your God; do not mourn or weep." For all the people were weeping when they heard the words of the law.   Heb., *Tirshatha,* a Persian title

10 Then he said to them, "Go, eat of the fat, drink of the sweet, and send portions to him who has nothing prepared; for this day is holy to our Lord. Do not be grieved, for the joy of the LORD is your strength."

11 So the Levites calmed all the people, saying, "Be still, for the day is holy; do not be grieved."

12 And all the people went away to eat, to drink, [R]to send portions and to [T]celebrate a great festival, because they understood the words which had been made known to them.   Neh. 8:10 • *make a great rejoicing*

Israel Obeys the Law

13 Then on the second day the heads of fathers' *households* of all the people, the priests, and the Levites were gathered to Ezra the scribe that they might gain insight into the words of the law.

14 And they found written in the law how the LORD had commanded through Moses that the sons of Israel should live in booths during the feast of the seventh month.

15 [R]So they proclaimed and circulated a proclamation in all their cities and in Jerusalem, saying, "Go out to the hills, and bring olive branches, and wild olive branches, myrtle branches, palm branches, and branches of *other* leafy trees, to make booths, as it is written."   Lev. 23:4

16 So the people went out and brought *them* and made booths for themselves, each [R]on his roof, and in their courts, and in the courts of the house of God, and in the square at[R]the Water Gate, and in the square at the Gate of Ephraim.   Jer. 32:29 • Neh. 8:1

17 And the entire assembly of those who had returned from the captivity made booths and lived in[R]them. The sons of Israel had indeed not done so from the days of Joshua the son of Nun to that day. And there was great rejoicing.   *the booths*

18 And he read from the book of the law of God daily, from the first day to the last day. And they celebrated the feast seven days, and on the eighth day *there was* a solemn assembly according to the ordinance.

CHAPTER 9

Spiritual Preparation of Israel

NOW on the twenty-fourth day of[R]this month the sons of Israel assembled [R]with fasting, in sackcloth, and with [d]dirt upon them.   Neh. 8:2 • Ezra 8:23 • 1 Sam. 4:12

2 And the [T]descendants of Israel separated themselves from all foreigners, and stood and[R]confessed their sins and the iniquities of their fathers.   *seed* • Jer. 3:13

8:9 God's Word Convicts—One of the great proofs that the Bible is really God's inspired Word is its unique ability to convict men and women of their sins. Let us consider but a few Old and New Testament examples which demonstrate the lifesaving power of the Scriptures.

Old Testament examples:

a. Josiah, a young and godly Judean king who ruled the Lord's people more than six centuries before Christ, succeeds a wicked ruler who hated righteousness. At the beginning of Josiah's rule a copy of God's Word is found in the temple. When it is read to the king, both he and his people are convicted of their sins in not keeping God's law. A great revival takes place (Page 447—2 Chr. 34:18–21).

b. Nehemiah returns to help the returning Jews rebuild the gates in the Jerusalem wall. This great wall builder thinks the Word of God to be so important that he assembles the people and has the Scriptures read to them for three hours per day. This soon causes them to confess their sins (Page 475—Neh. 9:3).

New Testament examples: Before Jesus left this earth He promised that the Holy Spirit would soon come upon the apostles. "And He, when He comes, will convict the world concerning sin, and righteousness, and judgment" (Page 1083—John 16:8). There are many instances in the New Testament where we see the Holy Spirit using God's Word to convict people of their sin. At Pentecost Peter uses the Scriptures to rebuke Israel for crucifying its Messiah. This sermon results in three thousand souls being convicted and accepting Christ (Page 1096—Acts 2:37, 41).

Now turn to Page 534—Ps. 17:4: God's Word Corrects.

3 While ᴿthey stood in their place, they read from the book of the law of the LORD their God for a fourth of the day; and for *another* fourth they confessed and worshiped the LORD their God.   Neh. 8:4

The Great Deliverances of God

4 ᴿNow on the Levites' platform stood Jeshua, Bani, Kadmiel, Shebaniah, Bunni, Sherebiah, Bani, *and* Chenani, and they cried with a loud voice to the LORD their God.   Neh. 8:7
5 Then the Levites, Jeshua, Kadmiel, Bani, Hashabneiah, Sherebiah, Hodiah, Shebaniah, *and* Pethahiah, said, "Arise, bless the LORD your God forever and ever!
O may Thy glorious name be blessed
And exalted above all blessing and
    praise!
6 "Thouᴿalone art the LORD.   Deut. 6:4
ᴿThou hast made the heavens,   Gen. 1:1
The heaven of heavens with all their
    host,
The earth and all that is on it,
The seas and all that is in them.
Thou dost give life to all of them
And the heavenly host bows down be-
    fore Thee.
7 "Thou art the LORD God,
ᴿWho chose Abram   Gen. 12:1
And brought him out from ᴿUr of the
    Chaldees,   Gen. 11:31
And gave him the name Abraham.
8 "And Thou didst find ᴿhis heart faithful
    before Thee,   Gen. 15:6, 18-21
And didst make a covenant with him
To give *him* the land of the Canaanite,
Of the Hittite and the Amorite,
Of the Perizzite, the Jebusite, and the
    Girgashite—
To give *it* to his ᵀdescendants.   seed
And Thouᴿhast fulfilled Thy promise,
For Thou art righteous.   Josh. 21:43-45

9 "Thouᴿdidst see the affliction of our fa-
    thers in Egypt,   Ex. 3:7
And didst ᴿhear their cry by the ᵀRed
    Sea.   Ex. 14:10-14, 31 • *Sea of Reeds*
10 "Then Thou didst perform signs and
    wonders against Pharaoh,
Against all his servants and all the peo-
    ple of his land;
For Thou didst know that they acted
    arrogantly toward them,
And ᵈdidst make a name for Thyself as
    it is this day.   Ex. 9:16
11 "And ᴿThou didst divide the sea before
    them,   Ex. 14:21
So they passed through the midst of
    the sea on dry ground;
And ᴿtheir pursuers Thou didst hurl into
    the depths,   Ex. 15:1, 5, 10
Like a stone into raging waters.

12 "And with a pillar of cloud ᴿThou didst
    lead them by day,   Ex. 13:21, 22
And with a pillar of fire by night
To light for them the way
In which they were to go.
13 "Then ᴿThou didst come down on Mount
    Sinai,   Ex. 19:11, 18-20
And didst ᴿspeak with them from
    heaven;   Ex. 20:1
Thou didst give to them ᴿjust ordi-
    nances and true laws,   [Ps. 19:7–9]
Good statutes and commandments.
14 "So Thou didst make known to them
    ᴿThy holy sabbath,   Ex. 16:23; 20:8
And didst lay down for them com-
    mandments, statutes, and law,
Through Thy servant Moses.
15 "Thou didst ᴿprovide bread from heaven
    for them for their hunger,   Ex. 16:4
Thou didst bring forth water from a
    rock for them for their thirst,
And Thou didst ᵗtell them to enter in or-
    der to possess   Deut. 1:8, 21
The land which Thou didst ᵀswear to
    give them.   *lift up Thy hand*

The Great Sins of Israel

16 "But they, our fathers, acted arrogantly;
They ⁶became stubborn and would not
    listen to Thy commandments.
17 "And they refused to listen,
And ᴿdid not remember Thy wondrous
    deeds which Thou hadst performed
    among them;   Ps. 78:11, 42-55
So they ⁶became stubborn and ᴿap-
    pointed a leader to return to their
    slavery in Egypt.   Num. 14:4
But Thou art a God of forgiveness,
Gracious and compassionate,
Slow to anger, and abounding in
    lovingkindness;
And Thou didst not forsake them.
18 "Even when they made for themselves
A calf of molten metal
And said, 'This is your God
Who brought you up from Egypt,'
And committed great blasphemies,
19 ᴿThou, in Thy great compassion,
Didst not forsake them in the wilder-
    ness;   Deut. 8:2-4; Neh. 9:27, 31
ᴿThe pillar of cloud did not leave them
    by day,   Neh. 9:12
To guide them on their way,
Nor the pillar of fire by night, to light
    for them the way in which they
    were to go.
20 "And ᴿThou didst give Thy good Spirit to
    instruct them,   Num. 11:17; Neh. 9:30
Thy manna Thou didst not withhold
    from their mouth,
And Thou didst give them water for
    their thirst.
21 "Indeed, ᴿforty years Thou didst provide
    for them in the wilderness *and* they
    were not in want;   Deut. 2:7
Their clothes did not wear out, nor did
    their feet swell.

---

⁶ Lit., *stiffened their neck*

22"Thou didst also give them kingdoms
  and peoples,
  And Thou didst allot *them* to them as a
  ^Tboundary.   *side, corner*
  And they took possession of the land of
  Sihon the king of Heshbon,
  And the land of Og the king of Bashan.
23"And Thou didst make their sons numerous as^Rthe stars of heaven,
  And Thou didst bring them into the
  land   Gen. 15:5; 22:17
  Which Thou hadst told their fathers to
  enter and possess.
24"So^R their sons entered and possessed
  the land.   Josh. 11:23; 21:43
  And ^RThou didst subdue before them
  the inhabitants of the land, the Canaanites,   Josh. 18:1
  And Thou didst give them into their
  hand, with their kings, and the peoples of the land,
  To do with them as they desired.
25"And^Rthey captured fortified cities and a
  ^Tfertile land.   Deut. 3:5 • *fat*
  They took possession of^Rhouses full of
  every good thing,   Deut. 6:11
  Hewn cisterns, vineyards, olive groves,
  Fruit trees in abundance.
  So they ate, were filled, and grew fat,
  And reveled in Thy great goodness.

26"But^R they became disobedient and rebelled against Thee,   Judg. 2:11
  And cast Thy law behind their backs
  And^Rkilled Thy prophets who had admonished them   2 Chr. 36:16
  So that they might return to Thee,
  And ^Rthey committed great ⁷blasphe-
  mies.   Neh. 9:18
27"Therefore Thou didst^Rdeliver them into
  the hand of their oppressors who
  oppressed them,   Judg. 2:14
  But when they cried to Thee^Rin the time
  of their distress,   Deut. 4:29
  Thou didst hear from heaven, and according to Thy great compassion
  Thou didst ^Rgive them deliverers who
  delivered them from the hand of
  their oppressors.   Judg. 2:16
28"But^Ras soon as they had rest, they did
  evil again before Thee;   Judg. 3:11
  Therefore Thou didst abandon them to
  the hand of their enemies, so that
  they ruled over them.
  When they cried again to Thee, Thou
  didst hear from heaven,
  And many times Thou didst rescue
  them according to Thy compassion,
29 And^Radmonished them in order to turn
  them back to Thy law.   Neh. 9:26, 30
  Yet they acted arrogantly and did not
  listen to Thy commandments but
  sinned against Thine ordinances,
  By^Rwhich if a man observes them he
  shall live.   Lev. 18:5

And they ^Tturned^R a stubborn shoulder
  and stiffened their neck, and would
  not listen.   *gave* • Zech. 7:11
30"However,^R Thou didst bear with them
  for many years,   Ps. 95:10; Acts 13:18
  And admonished them by^RThy Spirit
  through Thy prophets,   Neh. 9:20
  Yet they would not give ear.
  Therefore Thou didst give them into
  the hand of the peoples of the
  lands.
31"Nevertheless, in Thy great compassion
  Thou ^Rdidst not make an end of
  them or forsake them,   Jer. 4:27
  For Thou art ^Ra gracious and compassionate God.   Neh. 9:17

Renewal of the Covenant

32"Now therefore, our God,^Rthe great, the
  mighty, and the awesome God, who
  dost keep covenant and lovingkindness,   Neh. 1:5
  Do not let all the hardship seem insignificant before Thee,
  Which has come upon us, our kings,
  our princes, our priests, our prophets, our fathers, and on all Thy people,
  ^RFrom the days of the kings of Assyria
  to this day.   2 Kin. 15:19, 29
33"However,^RThou art just in all that has
  come upon us;   Gen. 18:25; Jer. 12:1
  For Thou hast dealt faithfully, but we
  have acted wickedly.
34"For our kings, our leaders, our priests,
  and our fathers have not kept Thy
  law
  Or paid attention to Thy commandments and Thine admonitions with
  which Thou hast admonished them.
35"But they, in their own kingdom,
  ^RWith Thy great goodness which Thou
  didst give them,   Neh. 9:25
  With the broad and rich land which
  Thou didst set before them,
  Did not serve Thee or turn from their
  evil deeds.
36"Behold,^Rwe are slaves today, Deut. 28:48
  And as to the land which Thou didst
  give to our fathers to eat of its fruit
  and its bounty,
  Behold, we are slaves on it.
37"And ^Rits abundant produce is for the
  kings   Deut. 28:33
  Whom Thou hast set over us because
  of our sins;
  They also rule over our bodies
  And over our cattle as they please,
  So we are in great distress.
38"Now because of all this

---

⁷ Lit., *acts of contempt*

^RWe are making an agreement in writing;   Neh. 10:29
And on the ^Rsealed document *are the names of* our leaders, our Levites *and* our priests."   Neh. 10:1

CHAPTER 10

Ratifiers of the Covenant

NOW on the sealed document *were the names of:* Nehemiah the governor, the son of Hacaliah, and Zedekiah,

2 Seraiah, Azariah, Jeremiah,

3 Pashhur, Amariah, Malchijah,

4 Hattush, Shebaniah, Malluch,

5 Harim, Meremoth, Obadiah,

6 Daniel, Ginnethon, Baruch,

7 Meshullam, Abijah, Mijamin,

8 Maaziah, Bilgai, Shemaiah. These *were* the priests.

9 And the Levites: Jeshua the son of Azaniah, Binnui of the sons of Henadad, Kadmiel;

10 also their brothers Shebaniah, Hodiah, Kelita, Pelaiah, Hanan,

11 Mica, Rehob, Hashabiah,

12 Zaccur, Sherebiah, Shebaniah,

13 Hodiah, Bani, Beninu.

14 The leaders of the people: Parosh, Pahath-moab, Elam, Zattu, Bani,

15 Bunni, Azgad, Bebai,

16 Adonijah, Bigvai, Adin,

17 Ater, Hezekiah, Azzur,

18 Hodiah, Hashum, Bezai,

19 Hariph, Anathoth, Nebai,

20 Magpiash, Meshullam, Hezir,

21 Meshezabel, Zadok, Jaddua,

22 Pelatiah, Hanan, Anaiah,

23 Hoshea, Hananiah, Hasshub,

24 Hallohesh, Pilha, Shobek,

25 Rehum, Hashabnah, Maaseiah,

26 Ahiah, Hanan, Anan,

27 Malluch, Harim, Baanah.

Stipulations of the Covenant

28 Now the rest of the people, the priests, the Levites, the gatekeepers, the singers, the temple servants, and ^Rall those who had separated themselves from the peoples of the lands to the law of God, their wives, their sons and their daughters, all those who had knowledge and understanding,   Neh. 9:2

29 are joining with their ^Tkinsmen, their nobles, and are taking on themselves a curse and an oath to walk in God's law, which was given through Moses, God's servant, and to keep and to observe all the commandments of GOD our Lord, and His ordinances and His statutes;   brothers

30 and ^Rthat we will not give our daughters to the peoples of the land or take their daughters for our sons.   Ex. 34:16; Deut. 7:3

31 As ^Rfor the peoples of the land who bring wares or any grain on the sabbath day to sell, we will not buy from them on the sabbath or a holy day; and we will forego *the crops* the ^Rseventh year and the exaction of every debt.   Neh. 13:15-22 • Ex. 23:10, 11

32 We also placed ourselves under obligation to contribute yearly ^Rone third of a shekel for the service of the house of our God: imposed commandments on us • Ex. 30:11-16

33 for the ^Rshowbread, for the continual grain offering, for the continual burnt offering, the sabbaths, the new moon, for the appointed times, for the holy things and for the sin offerings to make atonement for Israel, and all the work of the house of our God.   Lev. 24:5, 6; 2 Chr. 2:4

34 Likewise ^Rwe cast lots ^Rfor the supply of wood *among* the priests, the Levites, and the people in order that they might bring it to the house of our God, according to our fathers' households, at fixed times annually, to burn on the altar of the LORD our God as it is written in the law;   Neh. 11:1 • Neh. 13:31

35 and in order that they might bring the first fruits of our ground and ^Rthe first fruits of all the fruit of every tree to the house of the LORD annually,   Ex. 23:19; 34:26; Deut. 26:2

36 and bring to the house of our God the first-born of our sons and of our cattle, and the first-born of our herds and our flocks as it is written in the law, for the priests who are ministering in the house of our God.

37 We will also bring the first of our ^Adough, our contributions, the fruit of every tree, the new wine and the oil to the priests at the chambers of the house of our God, and the tithe of our ground to the Levites, for the Levites are they who receive the tithes in all the rural towns.   coarse meal

38 And the priest, the son of Aaron, shall be with the Levites when the Levites receive tithes, and the Levites shall bring up the tenth of the tithes to the house of our God, to the chambers of the storehouse.

39 For the sons of Israel and the sons of Levi shall bring the contribution of the grain, the new wine and the oil, to the chambers; there are the utensils of the sanctuary, the priests who are ministering, the gatekeepers, and the singers. Thus we will not ^Tneglect the house of our God.   forsake

CHAPTER 11

Plan for the Resettlement

NOW ^Rthe leaders of the people lived in Jerusalem, but the rest of the people ^Rcast lots to bring one out of ten to live in Jerusalem, ^Rthe holy city, while nine-tenths *remained* in the *other* cities.   Neh. 7:4 • Neh. 10:34 • Neh. 11:18

2 And the people blessed all the men who volunteered to live in Jerusalem.

Resettlement Within Jerusalem

3 Now these are the heads of the provinces who lived in Jerusalem, but in the

cities of Judah each lived on his own property in their cities—the Israelites, the priests, the Levites, the temple servants and the descendants of Solomon's servants.

4 And some of the sons of Judah and some of the sons of Benjamin lived in Jerusalem. From the sons of Judah: Athaiah the son of Uzziah, the son of Zechariah, the son of Amariah, the son of Shephatiah, the son of Mahalalel, of the sons of Perez;

5 and Maaseiah the son of Baruch, the son of Col-hozeh, the son of Hazaiah, the son of Adaiah, the son of Joiarib, the son of Zechariah, the son of the Shilonite.

6 All the sons of Perez who lived in Jerusalem were 468 able men.

7 Now these are the sons of Benjamin: Sallu the son of Meshullam, the son of Joed, the son of Pedaiah, the son of Kolaiah, the son of Maaseiah, the son of Ithiel, the son of Jeshaiah;

8 and after him Gabbai and Sallai, 928.

9 And Joel the son of Zichri was their overseer, and Judah the son of Hassenuah was second[T] in command of the city.   *over*

10 From the priests: Jedaiah the son of Joiarib, Jachin,

11 Seraiah the son of Hilkiah, the son of Meshullam, the son of Zadok, the son of Meraioth, the son of Ahitub, the leader of the house of God,

12 and their [8]kinsmen who performed the work of the[T]temple, 822; and Adaiah the son of Jeroham, the son of Pelaliah, the son of Amzi, the son of Zechariah, the son of Pashhur, the son of Malchijah,   *house*

13 and his kinsmen, heads of fathers' *households*, 242; and Amashsai the son of Azarel, the son of Ahzai, the son of Meshillemoth, the son of Immer,

14 and their brothers, valiant warriors, 128. And their overseer was Zabdiel, the son of[A]Haggedolim.   *the great ones*

15 Now from the Levites: Shemaiah the son of Hasshub, the son of Azrikam, the son of Hashabiah, the son of Bunni;

16 and Shabbethai and Jozabad, from the leaders of the Levites, who were in charge of the outside work of the house of God;

17 and Mattaniah the son of Mica, the son of Zabdi, the son of Asaph, who was the leader in beginning the thanksgiving at prayer, and Bakbukiah, the second among his brethren; and Abda the son of Shammua, the son of Galal, the son of Jeduthun.

18 All the Levites in[R]the holy city *were* 284.   Neh. 11:1

19 Also the gatekeepers, Akkub, Talmon, and their brethren, who kept watch at the gates, *were* 172.

20 And the rest of Israel, of the priests, *and* of the Levites, *were* in all the cities of Judah, each on his own inheritance.

21 But[R]the temple servants were living in Ophel, and Ziha and Gishpa were[T]in charge of the temple servants.   Neh. 3:26 • *over*

22 Now the overseer of the Levites in Jerusalem was Uzzi the son of Bani, the son of Hashabiah, the son of Mattaniah, the son of Mica, from the sons of Asaph, who were the singers for the service of the house of God.

23 For *there was* a commandment from the king concerning them and a firm regulation for the song leaders day by day.

24 And Pethahiah the son of Meshezabel, of the sons[R]of Zerah the son of Judah, was the king's[T]representative in all matters concerning the people.   Gen. 38:30 • *hand*

Resettlement Outside of Jerusalem

25 Now as for the villages with their fields, some of the sons of Judah lived in Kiriath-arba and its [9]towns, in Dibon and its towns, and in Jekabzeel and its villages,

26 and in Jeshua, in Moladah and Beth-pelet,

27 and in Hazar-shual, in Beersheba and its towns,

28 and in Ziklag, in Meconah and in its towns,

29 and in En-rimmon, in Zorah and in Jarmuth,

30 Zanoah, Adullam, and their villages, Lachish and its fields, Azekah and its towns. So they encamped from Beersheba as far as the valley of Hinnom.

31 The sons of Benjamin also *lived* from Geba *onward*, at Michmash and Aija, at Bethel and its towns,

32 at Anathoth, Nob, Ananiah,

33 Hazor, Ramah, Gittaim,

34 Hadid, Zeboim, Neballat,

35 Lod and Ono, the valley of craftsmen.

36 And from the Levites, *some* divisions in Judah belonged to Benjamin.

CHAPTER 12

*Register of the Priests
and the Levites*

NOW these are[R]the priests and the Levites who came up with Zerubbabel the son of Shealtiel, and Jeshua: Seraiah, Jeremiah, Ezra,   Ezra. 2:1; 7:7

2 Amariah, Malluch, Hattush,

3 Shecaniah, Rehum, Meremoth,

4 Iddo, Ginnethoi, Abijah,

5 Mijamin, Maadiah, Bilgah,

6 Shemaiah and Joiarib, Jedaiah,

7 Sallu, Amok, Hilkiah, and Jedaiah. These were the heads of the priests and their[T]kinsmen in the days of Jeshua. *brothers*

8 And the Levites *were* Jeshua, Binnui, Kadmiel, Sherebiah, Judah, *and* Mattaniah *who was*[T]in charge of the songs of thanksgiving, he and his brothers.   *over*

9 Also Bakbukiah and Unni, their brothers, stood opposite them[R]in *their* service divisions.   Neh. 12:24

---

[8] Lit., *brothers*, and so throughout the ch.
[9] Lit., *daughters*, and so throughout the ch.

10 And Jeshua[T]became the father of Joiakim, and Joiakim[T]became the father of Eliashib, and Eliashib[T]became the father of Joiada,   *begot,* and so in vv. 11, 12
11 and Joiada became the father of Jonathan, and Jonathan became the father of Jaddua.
12 Now in the days of Joiakim the priests, the heads of fathers' *households* were: of Seraiah, Meraiah; of Jeremiah, Hananiah;
13 of Ezra, Meshullam; of Amariah, Jehohanan;
14 of [T]Malluchi, Jonathan; of Shebaniah, Joseph;   In Neh. 12:2, *Malluch*
15 of Harim, Adna; of Meraioth, Helkai;
16 of Iddo, Zechariah; of Ginnethon, Meshullam;
17 of Abijah, Zichri; of Miniamin, of Moadiah, Piltai;
18 of Bilgah, Shammua; of Shemaiah, Jehonathan;
19 of Joiarib, Mattenai; of Jedaiah, Uzzi;
20 of Sallai, Kallai; of Amok, Eber;
21 of Hilkiah, Hashabiah; of Jedaiah, Nethanel.
22 As for the Levites, the heads of fathers' *households* were registered in the days of Eliashib, Joiada, and Johanan, and Jaddua; so *were* the priests in the reign of Darius the Persian.
23 The sons of Levi, the heads of fathers' *households,* were registered in the Book of the Chronicles up to the days of Johanan the son of Eliashib.
24 And the heads of the Levites *were* Hashabiah, Sherebiah, and Jeshua the son of Kadmiel, with their brothers opposite them, [R]to praise *and* give thanks, as prescribed by David the man of God, division corresponding to division.   Neh. 11:17
25 Mattaniah, and Bakbukiah, Obadiah, Meshullam, Talmon, *and* Akkub were gatekeepers keeping watch at[R]the storehouses of the gates.   1 Chr. 26:15
26 These *served* in the days of Joiakim the son of Jeshua, the son of Jozadak, and in the days of[R]Nehemiah the governor and of Ezra the priest *and* scribe.   Neh. 8:9

Dedication of the Jerusalem Wall

27 Now at the dedication of the wall of Jerusalem they sought out the Levites from all their places, to bring them to Jerusalem so that they might celebrate the dedication with gladness, with hymns of thanksgiving and with songs[R]*to the accompaniment* of cymbals, harps, and lyres.   1 Chr. 15:16, 28
28 So the sons of the singers were assembled from the district around Jerusalem, and from the villages of the Netophathites,
29 from Beth-gilgal, and from *their* fields in Geba and Azmaveth, for the singers had built themselves villages around Jerusalem.
30 And the priests and the Levites [ ]purified themselves; they also purified the people, the gates, and the wall.   Neh. 13:22, 30

31 Then I had the leaders of Judah come up on top of the wall, and I appointed two great choirs, the first proceeding to the right on top of the wall toward the Refuse Gate.
32 Hoshaiah and half of the leaders of Judah followed them,
33 with Azariah, Ezra, Meshullam,
34 Judah, Benjamin, Shemaiah, Jeremiah,
35 and some of the sons of the priests with trumpets; *and* Zechariah the son of Jonathan, the son of Shemaiah, the son of Mattaniah, the son of Micaiah, the son of Zaccur, the son of Asaph,
36 and his [T]kinsmen, Shemaiah, Azarel, Milalai, Gilalai, Maai, Nethanel, Judah *and* Hanani,[R]with the musical instruments of David the man of God. And Ezra the scribe went before them.   *brothers* • Neh. 12:24
37 And at the Fountain Gate they went directly up the steps of the city of David by the stairway of the wall above the house of David to the Water Gate on the east.
38 The second [ ]choir proceeded to the left, while I followed them with half of the people on the wall, above the Tower of Furnaces, to the Broad Wall,   *thanksgiving choir*
39 and above[R]the Gate of Ephraim, by[R]the Old Gate, by the Fish Gate, the Tower of Hananel, and the Tower of the Hundred, as far as the Sheep Gate, and they stopped at the Gate of the Guard.   Neh. 8:16 • Neh. 3:6
40 Then the two choirs took their stand in the house of God. So did I and half of the officials with me;
41 and the priests, Eliakim, Maaseiah, Miniamin, Micaiah, Elioenai, Zechariah, and Hananiah, with the trumpets;
42 and Maaseiah, Shemaiah, Eleazar, Uzzi, Jehohanan, Malchijah, Elam, and Ezer. And the singers [ ]sang, with Jezrahiah *their* leader,   *caused their voices to be heard*
43 and on that day they offered great sacrifices and rejoiced because[R]God had given them great joy, even the women and children rejoiced, so that the joy of Jerusalem was heard from afar.   Ps. 9:2; 92:4
44 On that day men were also appointed over the chambers for the stores, the contributions, the first fruits, and the tithes, to gather into them from the fields of the cities the portions required by the law for the priests and Levites; for Judah rejoiced over the priests and Levites who[T]served.   *stood*
45 For they performed the [ ]worship of their God and the service of purification, together with the singers and the gatekeepers[R]in accordance with the command of David *and* of his son Solomon.   *service* • 1 Chr. 25:1
46 For in the days of David and[R]Asaph, in ancient times, *there were* [T]leaders of the singers, songs of praise and hymns of thanksgiving to God.   2 Chr. 29:30 • *heads*
47 And so all Israel in the days of Zerubbabel and Nehemiah gave the portions due the singers and the gatekeepers [ ]as each day required, and[R]set apart the consecrated *portion* for the Levites, and the Levites set

apart the consecrated *portion* for the sons of Aaron.   Neh. 11:23 • Neh. 18:21

CHAPTER 13

Separation from the Heathen

ON that day [R]they read aloud from the book of Moses in the hearing of the people; and there was found written in it that[R]no Ammonite or Moabite should ever enter the assembly of God,   Neh. 9:3 • Deut. 23:3-5

2 because they did not meet the sons of Israel with bread and water, but hired Balaam against them to curse them. However, our God turned the curse into a blessing.

3 So it came about, that when they heard the law, [R]they excluded [R]all foreigners from Israel.   Neh. 9:2; 10:28 • Ex. 12:38

4 Now prior to this, Eliashib the priest, [R]who was appointed over the chambers of the house of our God, being[T]related to Tobiah,   Neh. 2:10; 6:1, 17, 18 • *close to*

5 had prepared a large [A]room for him, where formerly they put the grain offerings, the frankincense, the utensils, and the tithes of grain, wine and oil prescribed for the Levites, the singers and the gatekeepers, and the contributions for the priests.   *chamber*

6 But during all this *time* I was not in Jerusalem, for in [R]the thirty-second year of [R]Artaxerxes king of Babylon I had gone to the king. After some time, however, I asked leave from the king,   Neh. 5:14 • Ezra 6:22

7 and I came to Jerusalem and[A]learned about the evil that Eliashib had done for Tobiah, by preparing a room for him in the courts of the house of God.   *understood*

8 And it was very displeasing to me, so I [R]threw all of Tobiah's household goods out of the room.   John 2:13-16

9 Then I gave an order and[R]they cleansed the rooms; and I returned there the utensils of the house of God with the grain offerings and the frankincense.   2 Chr. 29:5, 15, 16

Restoration of Levitical Support

10 I also [A]discovered that[R]the portions of the Levites had not been given *them*, so that the Levites and the singers who performed the service had[T]gone away, each to his own field.   *knew* • Deut. 12:19; Neh. 10:37 • *fled*

11 So I[T]reprimanded[R]the officials and said, "Why is the house of God forsaken?" Then I gathered them together and restored them to their posts.   *contended with* • Neh. 13:17, 25

12 All Judah then brought the tithe of the grain, wine, and oil into the storehouses.

13 And in charge of the storehouses I appointed Shelemiah the priest, Zadok the scribe, and Pedaiah of the Levites, and in addition to them was Hanan the son of Zaccur, the son of Mattaniah; for they were considered reliable, and it was[T]their task to distribute to their kinsmen.   *on them to*

14 [R]Remember me for this, O my God, and do not blot out my loyal deeds which I have performed for the house of my God and its services.   Neh. 5:19; 13:22, 31

Restoration of the Sabbath

15 In those days I saw in Judah some who were treading wine presses[R]on the sabbath, and bringing in sacks of grain and loading *them* on donkeys, as well as wine, grapes, figs, and all kinds of loads, and they brought *them* into Jerusalem on the sabbath day. So I admonished *them* on the day they sold food.   [Ex. 20:8; 34:21; Deut. 5:12-14; Jer. 17:22]

16 Also men of Tyre were living[T]there *who* imported fish and all kinds of merchandise, and sold *them* to the sons of Judah on the sabbath, even in Jerusalem.   *in it*

17 Then[R][A]reprimanded the nobles of Judah and said to them, "What is this evil thing you are doing,[T]by profaning the sabbath day?   Neh. 13:11, 25 • *contended with* • *and*

18"Did not your fathers do the same so that our God brought on us, and on this city, all this trouble? Yet you are adding to the wrath on Israel by profaning the sabbath."

19 [R]And it came about that just as it grew dark at the gates of Jerusalem before the sabbath, I commanded that the doors should be shut [T]and that they should not open them until after the sabbath. Then I stationed some of my servants at the gates *that* no load should enter on the sabbath day.   Lev. 23:32 • *and commanded*

20 Once or twice the traders and merchants of every kind of merchandise spent the night outside Jerusalem.

21 Then I[T]warned them and said to them, "Why do you spend the night in front of the wall? If you do so again, I will use force against you." From that time on they did not come on the sabbath.   *witnessed against*

22 And I commanded the Levites that [R]they should purify themselves and come as gatekeepers to sanctify the sabbath day. For this also remember me, O my God, and have compassion on me according to the greatness of Thy lovingkindness.   1 Chr. 15:12

Restoration from Mixed Marriages

23 In those days I also saw that the Jews had [T]married[R]women from Ashdod, Ammon, and Moab.   *giving dwelling to* • [Ex. 34:11-16]

24 As for their children, half spoke in the language of Ashdod, and none of them was able to speak the language of Judah, but the language of his own people.

25 So[R]I contended with them and cursed them and struck some of them and pulled out their hair, and made them swear by God, "You shall not give your daughters to their sons, nor take of their daughters for your sons or for yourselves.   Neh. 13:11, 17

26"Did[R]not Solomon king of Israel sin regarding these things? Yet among the many nations there was no king like him, and he was loved by his God, and God made him

king over all Israel; nevertheless the foreign women caused even him to sin.   1 Kin. 11:1

27"Do we then hear about you that you have committed all this great evil by acting unfaithfully against our God by marrying foreign women?"   *It is reported* • [Ezra 10:2]

28 Even one of the sons of Joiada, the son of Eliashib the high priest, was a son-in-law of ^RSanballat the Horonite, so I drove him away from me.   Neh. 2:10, 19; 4:1

29 Remember them, O my God, because they have defiled the priesthood and the covenant of the priesthood and the Levites.

Restoration in Summary

30 ^RThus I purified them from everything foreign and appointed duties for the priests and the Levites, each in his task,   Neh. 10:30

31 and *I arranged* for the supply of wood at appointed times and for the first fruits. Remember me, O my God, for good.

Monies

Unit	Monetary Value	Equivalents	Translations
Jewish Weights			
Talent	gold—$5,760,000¹ silver—$384,000	3,000 shekels; 6,000 bekas	talent, one hundred pounds
Shekel	gold—$1,920 silver—$128	4 days' wages; 2 bekas; 20 gerahs	shekel
Beka	gold—$960 silver—$64	½ shekel; 10 gerahs	beka
Gerah	gold—$96 silver—$6.40	¹⁄₂₀ shekel	gerahs
Persian Coins			
Daric	gold—$1,280² silver—$64	2 days' wages; ½ Jewish silver shekel	daric, drachma
Greek Coins			
Tetradrachma (Stater)	$128	4 drachmas	stater
Didrachma	$64	2 drachmas	two-drachma tax
Drachma	$32	1 day's wage	coin, silver coins
Lepton	$.25	½ of a Roman kodrantes	cents, small copper coin
Roman Coins			
Aureus	$800	25 denarii	gold
Denarius	$32	1 day's wage	denarii
Assarius	$2	¹⁄₁₆ of a denarius	cent
Kodrantes	$.50	¼ of an assarius	cent

¹Value of gold is fifteen times the value of silver.
²Value of gold is twenty times the value of silver.

THE BOOK OF

ESTHER

THE BOOK OF ESTHER

God's hand of providence and protection on behalf of His people is evident throughout the Book of Esther, though His name does not appear once. Haman's plot brings grave danger to the Jews and is countered by the courage of beautiful Esther and the counsel of her wise cousin Mordecai, resulting in a great deliverance. The Feast of Purim becomes an annual reminder of God's faithfulness on behalf of His people.

Esther's Hebrew name was *Hadassah*, "Myrtle" (2:7), but her Persian name *Ester* was derived from the Persian word for "Star" (*stara*). The Greek title for this book is *Esther*, and the Latin title is *Hester*.

THE AUTHOR OF ESTHER

While the author's identity is not indicated in the text, the evident knowledge of Persian etiquette and customs, the palace in Susa, and details of the events in the reign of Ahasuerus indicate that the author lived in Persia during this period. The obvious Jewish nationalism and knowledge of Jewish customs further suggest that the author was Jewish. If this Persian Jew was not an eyewitness, he probably knew people who were. The book must have been written soon after the death of King Ahasuerus (464 B.C.), because 10:2, 3 speaks of his reign in the past tense. Some writers suggest that Mordecai himself wrote the book; this seems unlikely, for although Mordecai did keep records (9:20), 10:2, 3 imply that his career was already over. Nevertheless, the author certainly made use of Mordecai's records and may have had access to the Book of the Chronicles of the Kings of Media and Persia (2:23; 10:2). Ezra and Nehemiah have also been suggested for authorship, but the vocabulary and style of Esther is dissimilar to that found in their books. It seems likely that a younger contemporary of Mordecai composed the book.

THE TIME OF ESTHER

Ahasuerus is the Hebrew name and Xerxes the Greek name of Khshayarsh, king of Persia in 486–464 B.C. According to 1:3, the feast of Xerxes took place in his third year, or 483 B.C. The historian Herodotus refers to this banquet as the occasion of Xerxes' planning for a military campaign against Greece. But in 479 B.C. he was defeated by the Greeks

at Salamis, and Herodotus tells us that he sought consolation in his harem. This corresponds to the time when he held a "contest" and crowned Esther queen of Persia (2:16, 17). Since the events of the rest of the book took place in 473 B.C. (3:7–12), the chronological span is ten years (483–473 B.C.). The probable time of authorship was between 464 B.C. (the end of Xerxes' reign; see 10:2, 3) and about 435 B.C. (the palace at Susa was destroyed by fire during that period, and such an event would probably have been mentioned). The historical and linguistic features of Esther do not support a date later than 400 B.C., as there is no trace of Greek influence.

Xerxes was a boisterous man of emotional extremes, whose actions were often strange and contradictory. This fact sheds light on his ability to sign a decree for the annihilation of the Jews, and two months later to sign a second decree allowing them to overthrow their enemies.

Esther was addressed to the many Jews who did not return to their homeland. Not all the godly people left—some did not return for legitimate reasons. Most were disobedient in staying in Persia. Nevertheless, God continued to care for His people in voluntary exile.

THE CHRIST OF ESTHER

Esther, like Christ, puts herself in the place of death for her people but receives the approval of the king. She also portrays Christ's work as Advocate on our behalf. This book reveals another satanic threat to destroy the Jewish people and thus, the messianic line. God continues to preserve His people in spite of opposition and danger, and nothing can prevent the coming of the Messiah.

KEYS TO ESTHER

Key Word: Providence—The Book of Esther was written to show how the Jewish people were protected and preserved by the gracious hand of God from the threat of annihilation. Although God disciplines His covenant people, He never abandons them. The God of Israel is the sovereign controller of history, and His providential care can be seen throughout this book: He raises a Jewish girl out of obscurity to become the queen of the most powerful empire in the world; He ensures that Mordecai's loyal deed is recorded in the palace records; He guides Esther's admission

to the king's court; He superintends the timing of Esther's two feasts; He is involved in Ahasuerus's insomnia and the cure he uses for it; He sees that Haman's gallows will be utilized in an unexpected way; He gives Esther great favor in the sight of the king; and He brings about the new decree and the eventual victory of the Jews.

Key Verses: Esther 4:14; 8:17—"For if you remain silent at this time, relief and deliverance will arise for the Jews from another place and you and your father's house will perish. And who knows whether you have not attained royalty for such a time as this?" (4:14).

"And in each and every province, and in each and every city, wherever the king's commandment and his decree arrived, there was gladness and joy for the Jews, a feast and a holiday. And many among the peoples of the land became Jews, for the dread of the Jews had fallen on them" (8:17).

Key Chapter: Esther 8—According to the Book of Esther, the salvation of the Jews is accomplished through the second decree of King Ahasuerus, allowing the Jews to defend themselves against their enemies. Chapter 8 records this pivotal event with the accompanying result that "many among the peoples of the land became Jews" (8:17).

SURVEY OF ESTHER

The story of Esther fits between chapters 6 and 7 of Ezra, between the first return led by Zerubbabel and the second return led by Ezra. It provides the only biblical portrait of the vast majority of Jews who choose to remain in Persia rather than return to Palestine. God's guiding and protective hand on behalf of His people is evident throughout this book, even though His name does not appear in it. The clearly emerging message is that God uses ordinary men and women to overcome impossible circumstances to accomplish His gracious purposes. Chapters 1—4 describe the threat to the Jews, and chapters 5—10 describe the triumph of the Jews.

The Threat to the Jews (1—4): The story begins in Ahasuerus's winter palace at Susa. The king provides a lavish banquet and display of royal glory for the people of Susa, and proudly seeks to make Queen Vashti's beauty a part of the program. When she refuses to appear, the king is counseled to depose her and seek another queen, because it is feared that the other women will become insolent if Vashti goes unpunished. Esther later finds favor in the eyes of Ahasuerus and wins the royal "beauty pageant." At her cousin Mordecai's instruction, she does not reveal that she is Jewish. With her help, Mordecai is able to warn the king of an assassination plot, and his deed is recorded in the palace records. Meanwhile, Haman becomes captain of the princes, but Mordecai refuses to bow to him. When he learns that Mordecai is Jewish, Haman plots for a year to eliminate all Jews, as his rage and hatred grow. He casts lots (purim) daily during this period until he determines the best day to have them massacred. Through bribery and lies he convinces Ahasuerus to issue an edict that all Jews in the empire will be slain eleven months hence in a single day. Haman conceives his plot in envy and a vengeful spirit, and he executes it with malicious craft. The decree creates a state of confusion, and Mordecai asks Esther to appeal to the king to spare the Jews. At the peril of her life, Esther decides to see the king and reveal her nationality in a desperate attempt to dissuade Ahasuerus. Mordecai convinces her that she has been called to her high position for this purpose.

The Triumph of the Jews (5—10): After fast-

FOCUS	THREAT TO THE JEWS		TRIUMPH OF THE JEWS	
REFERENCE	1:1 ———————— 2:21 ————————		5:1 ———————— 8:4 ———————— 10:3	
DIVISION	SELECTION OF ESTHER AS QUEEN	FORMULATION OF THE PLOT BY HAMAN	TRIUMPH OF MORDECAI OVER HAMAN	TRIUMPH OF ISRAEL OVER HER ENEMIES
TOPIC	FEASTS OF AHASUERUS		FEASTS OF ESTHER AND PURIM	
	GRAVE DANGER		GREAT DELIVERANCE	
LOCATION	PERSIA			
TIME	10 YEARS (483 – 473 B.C.)			

ing, Esther appears before the king and wisely invites him to a banquet along with Haman. At the banquet she requests that they attend a second banquet, as she seeks the right moment to divulge her request. Haman is flattered but later enraged when he sees Mordecai. He takes his wife's suggestion to build a large gallows for Mordecai (he cannot wait the eleven months for Mordecai to be slain). That night Ahasuerus decides to treat his insomnia by reading the palace records. Reading about Mordecai's deed, he wants him to be honored. Haman, mistakenly thinking the king wants to honor him, tells the king how the honor should be bestowed, only to find out that the reward is for Mordecai. He is humbled and infuriated by being forced to honor the man he loathes. At Esther's second banquet Ahasuerus offers her as much as half of his kingdom for the third time. She then makes her plea for her people and accuses Haman of his treachery. The infuriated king has Haman hanged on the gallows that Haman intended for Mordecai. The gallows, seventy-five feet high, was de-

signed to make Mordecai's downfall a city-wide spectacle, but it ironically provides Haman with unexpected public attention—posthumously.

Persian law sealed with the king's ring (3:12) cannot be revoked, but at Esther's request the king issues a new decree to all the provinces that the Jews may assemble and defend themselves on the day when they are attacked by their enemies. This decree changes the outcome intended by the first order and produces great joy. Mordecai is also elevated and set over the house of Haman. When the fateful day of the two decrees arrives, the Jews defeat their enemies in their cities throughout the Persian provinces, but do not take the plunder. The next day becomes a day of celebration and an annual Jewish holiday called the Feast of Purim. The word is derived from the Assyrian *puru*, meaning "lot," referring to the lots cast by Haman to determine the day decreed for the Jewish annihilation. The narrative closes with the advancement of Mordecai to a position second only to the king.

OUTLINE OF ESTHER

Part One: The Threat to the Jews (1:1—4:17)

Part Two: The Triumph of the Jews (5:1—10:3)

CHAPTER 1

The Banquets of Ahasuerus

NOW it took place in the days of Ahasuerus, the Ahasuerus who reigned from India to [T]Ethiopia over 127 provinces,   *Cush*

2 in those days as King Ahasuerus[R] sat on his royal throne which *was* in [R]Susa the capital,   1 Kin. 1:46 • Neh. 1:1; Dan. 8:2

3 in the third year of his reign,[R] he gave a banquet for all his princes and attendants, the army *officers* of Persia and Media, the nobles, and the princes of his provinces being in his presence.   Esth. 2:18

4 [T]And he displayed the riches of his royal glory and the splendor of his great majesty for many days, 180 days.   *When*

5 And when these days were completed, the king gave a banquet lasting seven days for all the people who were present in Susa the capital, from the greatest to the least, in the court of the garden of the king's palace.

6 *There were hangings of* fine white and violet linen held by cords of fine purple linen on silver rings and marble columns, *and* [R]couches of gold and silver on a mosaic pavement of porphyry, marble, mother-of-pearl, and precious stones.   Ezek. 23:41; Amos 6:4

7 Drinks were served in golden vessels of various kinds, and the royal wine was plentiful according to the king's bounty.

8 And the drinking was *done* according to the law, there was no compulsion, for so the king had given orders to each official of his household that he should do according to the desires of each person.

Refusal of Queen Vashti

9 Queen Vashti also gave a banquet for the women in the [T]palace which belonged to King Ahasuerus.   *royal house*

10 On the seventh day, when the heart of the king was [R]merry with wine, he commanded Mehuman, Biztha, Harbona, Bigtha, Abagtha, Zethar, and Carkas, the seven eunuchs who served in the presence of King Ahasuerus,   Judg. 16:25

11 to bring Queen Vashti before the king with *her* royal [R]crown in order to display her beauty to the people and the princes, for she was beautiful.   Esth. 2:17; 6:8

12 But Queen Vashti refused to come at the king's command delivered by the eunuchs. Then the king became very angry and his wrath burned within him.

Counsel to King Ahasuerus

13 Then the king said to [R]the wise men who understood the times—for it was the custom of the king so *to speak* before all who knew law and justice,   Jer. 10:7; Dan. 2:2

14 and were close to him: Carshena, Shethar, Admatha, Tarshish, Meres, Marsena,

and Memucan, the seven princes of Persia and Media[R] who [T]had access to the king's presence and sat in the first place in the kingdom—   2 Kin. 25:19 • *saw the face of the king*

15 "According to law, what is to be done with Queen Vashti, because she did not [T]obey the command of King Ahasuerus *delivered* by the eunuchs?"   *do*

16 And in the presence of the king and the princes, Memucan said, "Queen Vashti has wronged not only the king but *also* all the princes, and all the peoples who are in all the provinces of King Ahasuerus.

17 "For the queen's conduct will [T]become known to all the women causing them to look with contempt on their husbands by saying, 'King Ahasuerus commanded Queen Vashti to be brought in to his presence, but she did not come.'   *go forth*

18 "And this day the ladies of Persia and Media who have heard of the queen's conduct will speak in *the same way* to all the king's princes, and there will be plenty of contempt and anger.

Commandment of King Ahasuerus

19 "If it pleases the king, let a royal edict be issued by him and let it be written in the laws of Persia and Media so that it cannot be repealed, that Vashti should come no more into the presence of King Ahasuerus, and let the king give her royal position to another who is more worthy than she.

20 "And when the king's edict which he shall make is heard throughout all his kingdom, great as it is, then all women will give honor to their husbands, great and small."

21 And *this* word pleased the king and the princes, and the king did as Memucan proposed.

22 So he sent letters to all the king's provinces, to each province according to its script and to every people according to their language, that every man should be the master in his own house and the one who speaks in the language of his own people.

CHAPTER 2

Decree to Search
for Vashti's Replacement

AFTER these things when the anger of King Ahasuerus had subsided, he remembered Vashti and what she had done and what had been decreed against her.

2 Then the king's attendants, who served him, said, "Let [R]beautiful young virgins be sought for the king.   1 Kin. 1:2

3 "And let the king appoint overseers in [R]all the provinces of his kingdom that they may gather every beautiful young virgin to Susa the capital, to the harem, into the custody of Hegai, the king's eunuch, who was

in charge of the women; and let their cosmetics be given *them*.   Esth. 1:1, 2

4 "Then let the young lady who pleases the king be queen in place of Vashti." And the matter pleased the king, and he did accordingly.

Preparation of Esther

5 *Now* there was a Jew in Susa the capital whose name was [R]Mordecai, the son of Jair, the son of Shimei, the son of Kish, a Benjamite,   Esth. 3:2

6 [R]who had been taken into exile from Jerusalem with the captives who had been exiled with Jeconiah king of Judah, whom Nebuchadnezzar the king of Babylon had exiled.   2 Kin. 24:14, 15; 2 Chr. 36:10

7 And he was bringing up Hadassah, that is Esther, his uncle's daughter, for she had neither father nor mother. Now the young lady was beautiful of form and face, and when her father and her mother died, Mordecai took her as his own daughter.

8 So it came about when the command and decree of the king were heard and [R]many young ladies were gathered to Susa the capital into the custody of [R]Hegai, that Esther was taken to the king's [T]palace into the custody of Hegai, who was in charge of the women.   Esth. 2:3 • Esth. 2:3, 15 • *house*

9 Now the young lady pleased him and found favor with him. So he quickly provided her with her cosmetics and [T]food, gave her seven choice maids from the king's palace, and transferred her and her maids to the best place in the harem.   *portions*

10 Esther did not make known her people or her kindred, for Mordecai had instructed her that she should not make *them* known.

11 And every day Mordecai walked back and forth in front of the court of the harem to learn how Esther was and how she fared.

12 Now when the turn of each young lady came to go in to King Ahasuerus, after the end of her twelve months under the regulations for the women—for the days of their beautification were completed as follows: six months with oil of myrrh and six months with spices and the cosmetics for women—

13 the young lady would go in to the king in this way: anything that she [T]desired was given her to take with her from the harem to the king's palace.   *said*

14 In the evening she would go in and in the morning she would return to the second harem, to the [T]custody of Shaashgaz, the king's eunuch who was in charge of the concubines. She would not again go in to the king unless the king delighted in her and she was summoned by name.   *hand*

Selection of Queen Esther

15 Now when the turn of Esther, [R]the daughter of Abihail the uncle of Mordecai who had taken her as his daughter, came to go in to the king, she did not request anything except what [R]Hegai, the king's eunuch who was in charge of the women, [T]advised. And Esther found favor in the eyes of all who saw her.   Esth. 2:7; 9:29 • Esth. 2:3, 8 • *said*

16 So Esther was taken to King Ahasuerus to his royal palace in the tenth month which is the month Tebeth, in the seventh year of his reign.

17 And the king loved Esther more than all the women, and she found favor and kindness with him more than all the virgins, so that he set the royal crown on her head and made her queen instead of Vashti.

18 Then [R]the king gave a great banquet, Esther's banquet, for all his princes and his servants; he also made a holiday for the provinces and gave gifts [R]according to the king's bounty.   Esth. 1:3 • Esth. 1:7

19 And [R]when the virgins were gathered together the second time, then Mordecai was sitting at the king's gate.   Esth. 2:3, 4

20 [R]Esther had not yet made known her kindred or her people, even as Mordecai had commanded her, for Esther did [T]what Mordecai told her as she had done when under his care.   Esth. 2:10 • *the word of Mordecai*

Mordecai Reveals the Plot
to Murder the King

21 In those days, while Mordecai was sitting at the king's gate, [R]Bigthan and Teresh, two of the king's officials from those who guarded the door, became angry and sought to lay hands on King Ahasuerus.   Esth. 6:2

22 But the plot became known to Mordecai, and he told Queen Esther, and Esther informed the king in Mordecai's name.

23 Now when the plot was investigated and found *to be so,* they were both hanged on a [1]gallows; and it was written in [R]the Book of the Chronicles in the king's presence.   Esth. 10:2

CHAPTER 3

Haman Is Promoted

AFTER these events King Ahasuerus [R]promoted Haman, the son of Hammedatha [R]the Agagite, and advanced him and [T]established his authority over all the princes who *were* with him.   Esth. 5:11 • Esth. 3:10; 8:3 • *set his seat*

The Reason for Haman's Plot

2 And all the king's servants who were at the king's gate bowed down and paid homage to Haman; for so the king had commanded concerning him. But Mordecai neither bowed down nor paid homage.

[1] Lit., *tree*

3 Then the king's servants who were at the king's gate said to Mordecai, "Why are you transgressing the king's command?"

4 Now it was when they had spoken daily to him and he would not listen to them, that they told Haman to see whether Mordecai's reason would stand; for he had told them that he was a Jew.

5 When Haman saw that [R]Mordecai neither bowed down nor paid homage to him, Haman was filled with rage.   Esth. 5:9

6 But he [T]disdained to lay hands on Mordecai alone, for they had told him who the people of Mordecai were; therefore Haman sought to destroy all the Jews, the people of Mordecai, who were throughout the whole kingdom of Ahasuerus.   despised in his eyes

Presentation of the Plot

7 In the first month, which is the month Nisan, in the twelfth year of King Ahasuerus, Pur, that is the lot, was [R]cast before Haman from day to day and from month to month, until the twelfth month, that is [R]the month Adar.   Esth. 9:24-26 • Ezra 6:15

8 Then Haman said to King Ahasuerus, "There is a certain people scattered and dispersed among the peoples in all the provinces of your kingdom; their laws are different from those of all other people, and they do not observe the king's laws, so it is not in the king's interest to let them remain.

9 "If it is pleasing to the king, let it be [T]decreed that they be destroyed, and I will pay ten thousand talents of silver into the hands of those who carry on the king's business, to put into the king's treasuries."   written

Publication of the Decree

10 Then [R]the king took his signet ring from his hand and gave it to Haman, the son of Hammedatha [R]the Agagite, [R]the enemy of the Jews.   Gen. 41:42; Esth. 8:2 • Esth. 3:1 • Esth. 7:6

11 And the king said to Haman, "The silver is [T]yours, and the people also, to do with them as you please."   given to you

12 [R]Then the king's scribes were summoned on the thirteenth day of the first month, and it was written just as Haman commanded to the king's satraps, to the governors who were over each province, and to the princes of each people, each province according to its script, each people according to its language, being written in the name of King Ahasuerus and sealed with the king's signet ring.   Esth. 8:9

13 And letters were sent by [R]couriers to all the king's provinces to destroy, to kill, and to annihilate all the Jews, both young and old, women and children, in one day, the thirteenth day of the twelfth month, which is the month Adar, and to seize their possessions as plunder.   2 Chr. 30:6; Esth. 8:10-14

14 [R]A copy of the edict to be [T]issued as law in every province was published to all the peoples so that they should be ready for this day.   Esth. 8:13, 14 • given

15 The couriers went out impelled by the king's command while the decree was [T]issued in Susa the capital; and while the king and Haman sat down to drink, [R]the city of Susa was in confusion.   given • Esth. 8:15

CHAPTER 4

The Lamentation of the Jews

WHEN Mordecai learned all that had been done, he tore his clothes, put on sackcloth and ashes, and went out into the midst of the city and wailed loudly and bitterly.

2 And he went as far as the king's gate, for no one was to enter the king's gate clothed in sackcloth.

3 And in each and every province where the command and decree of the king came, there was great mourning among the Jews, with fasting, weeping, and wailing; and many lay on sackcloth and ashes.

The Plan of Mordecai

4 Then Esther's maidens and her eunuchs came and told her, and the queen writhed in great anguish. And she sent garments to clothe Mordecai that he might remove his sackcloth from him, but he did not accept them.

5 Then Esther summoned Hathach from the king's eunuchs, whom [T]the king had appointed to attend her, and ordered him to go to Mordecai to learn what this was and why it was.   he

6 So Hathach went out to Mordecai to the city square in front of the king's gate.

7 And Mordecai told him all that had happened to him, and [R]the exact amount of money that Haman had promised to pay to the king's treasuries for the destruction of the Jews.   Esth 3:9

8 He also gave him [R]a copy of the text of the edict which had been issued in Susa for their destruction, that he might show Esther and inform her, and to order her to go in to the king to implore his favor and to plead with him for her people.   Esth. 3:14

9 And Hathach came back and related Mordecai's words to Esther.

10 Then Esther spoke to Hathach and ordered him to reply to Mordecai:

11 "All the king's servants and the people of the king's provinces know that for any man or woman who [R]comes to the king to the inner court who is not summoned, [R]he has but one law, that he be put to death, unless the king holds out to him the golden scepter so that he may live. And I have not been summoned to come to the king for these thirty days."   Esth. 5:1; 6:4 • Dan. 2:9

12 And they related Esther's words to Mordecai.

13 Then Mordecai told *them* to reply to Esther, "Do not imagine that you in the king's palace can escape any more than all the Jews.

14"For if you remain silent at this time, relief and [R]deliverance will arise for the Jews from another place and you and your father's house will perish. And who knows whether you have not attained royalty for such a time as this?"   Lev. 26:42; 2 Kin. 13:5

The Promise of Queen Esther

15 Then Esther told *them* to reply to Mordecai,

16"Go, assemble all the Jews who are found in Susa, and fast for me; [R]do not eat or drink for [R]three days, night or day. I and my maidens also will fast in the same way. And thus I will go in to the king, which is not according to the law; and if I perish, I perish."   Joel 1:14; 2:12 • Esth. 5:1

17 So Mordecai went away and did just as Esther had commanded him.

CHAPTER 5

Esther's First Banquet

NOW it came about on the third day that Esther put on her royal robes and stood in the inner court of the king's palace in front of the king's [T]rooms, and the king was sitting on his royal throne in the throne room, opposite the entrance to the palace.   *house*

2 And it happened when the king saw Esther the queen standing in the court, [R]she obtained favor in his sight; and the king extended to Esther the golden scepter which was in his hand. So Esther came near and touched the top of the scepter.   Esth. 2:9

3 Then the king said to her, "What is *troubling* you, Queen Esther? And what is your request? Even to half of the kingdom it will be given to you."

4 And Esther said, "If it please the king, may the king and Haman come this day to the banquet that I have prepared for him."

5 Then the king said, "Bring Haman quickly that we may do [T]as Esther desires." So the king and Haman came to the banquet which Esther had prepared.   *the word of Esther*

6 And, as they drank their wine at the banquet, [R]the king said to Esther, "What is your petition, for it shall be granted to you. And what is your request? Even to half of the kingdom it shall be done."   Esth. 7:2

7 So Esther answered and said, "My petition and my request is:

8 [R]if I have found favor in the sight of the king, and if it please the king to grant my petition and do [T]what I request, may the king and Haman come to the banquet which I shall prepare for them, and tomorrow I will do as the king says."   Esth. 7:3 • *my request*

Haman Plots to Kill Mordecai

9 Then Haman went out that day glad and pleased of heart; but when Haman saw Mordecai in the king's gate, and that he did not stand up or tremble before him, Haman was filled with anger against Mordecai.

10 Haman controlled himself, however, went to his house, and [T]sent for his friends and his wife Zeresh.   *sent and brought*

11 Then Haman recounted to them the glory of his riches, and the [T]number [R]of his sons, and every *instance* where the king had magnified him, and how he had [T]promoted [R]him above the princes and servants of the king.   *multitude* • Esth. 9:7-10 • *lifted* • Esth. 3:1

12 Haman also said, "Even Esther the queen let no one but me come with the king to the banquet which she had prepared; and [R]tomorrow also I am [T]invited by her with the king.   Esth. 5:8 • *summoned to her*

13"Yet all of this [T]does not satisfy me every time I see Mordecai the Jew sitting at [R]the king's gate."   *is not suitable to me* • Esth. 5:9

14 Then Zeresh his wife and all his friends said to him, "Have [R]a [T]gallows [T]fifty cubits high made and in the morning ask the king to have Mordecai hanged on it, then go joyfully with the king to the banquet." And the [T]advice pleased Haman, so he had the gallows made.   Esth. 6:4; 7:9, 10 • *tree* • 75 ft. • *thing*

CHAPTER 6

King Ahasuerus's Plan to Honor Mordecai

DURING that night [T]the king could not sleep so he gave an order to bring the book of records, the chronicles, and they were read before the king.   *the king's sleep fled*

2 And it was found written what [R]Mordecai had reported concerning Bigthana and Teresh, two of the king's eunuchs who were doorkeepers, that they had sought to lay hands on King Ahasuerus.   Esth. 2:21, 22

3 And the king said, "What honor or dignity has been bestowed on Mordecai for this?" Then the king's servants who attended him said, "Nothing has been done for him."

Haman's Plan to Honor Himself

4 So the king said, "Who is in the court?" Now Haman had just entered the outer court of the king's palace in order to speak to the king about hanging Mordecai on the gallows which he had prepared for him.

5 And the king's servants said to him, "Behold, Haman is standing in the court." And the king said, "Let him come in."

6 So Haman came in and the king said to him, "What is to be done for the man whom the king desires to honor?" And Haman said 'to himself, "Whom would the king desire to honor more than me?"   *in his heart*

7 Then Haman said to the king, "For the man whom the king desires to honor,

8 let them bring a royal robe which the king has worn, and the horse on which the king has ridden, and on whose head a royal crown has been placed;   1 Kin. 1:33

9 and let the robe and the horse be handed over to one of the king's most noble princes and let them array the man whom the king desires to honor and lead him on horseback through the city square, and proclaim before him, 'Thus it shall be done to the man whom the king desires to honor.'"

Haman Is Forced to Honor Mordecai

10 Then the king said to Haman, "Take quickly the robes and the horse as you have said, and do so for Mordecai the Jew, who is sitting at the king's gate; do not fall short in anything of all that you have said."

11 So Haman took the robe and the horse, and arrayed Mordecai, and led him *on horseback* through the city square, and proclaimed before him, "Thus it shall be done to the man whom the king desires to honor."

12 Then Mordecai returned to the king's gate. But Haman hurried home, mourning, with *his* head covered.   2 Sam. 15:30

13 And Haman recounted to Zeresh his wife and all his friends everything that had happened to him. Then his wise men and Zeresh his wife said to him, "If Mordecai, before whom you have begun to fall, is of Jewish origin, you will not overcome him, but will surely fall before him."   Esth. 5:10

14 While they were still talking with him, the king's eunuchs arrived and hastily brought Haman to the banquet which Esther had prepared.   Esth. 5:8

CHAPTER 7

Esther's Second Banquet

Now the king and Haman came to drink *wine* with Esther the queen.

2 And the king said to Esther on the second day also as they drank their wine at the banquet, "What is your petition, Queen Esther? It shall be granted you. And what is your request? Even to half of the kingdom it shall be done."   *at the banquet of wine*

3 Then Queen Esther answered and said, "If I have found favor in your sight, O king, and if it please the king, let my life be given

me as my petition, and my people as my request;   Esth. 5:8; 8:5

4 for we have been sold, I and my people, to be destroyed, to be killed and to be annihilated. Now if we had only been sold as slaves, men and women, I would have remained silent, for the trouble would not be commensurate with the annoyance to the king."   *enemy could not compensate for the loss*

Haman Is Indicted

5 Then King Ahasuerus asked Queen Esther, "Who is he, and where is he, who would presume to do thus?"   *said and said to*

6 And Esther said, "A foe and an enemy, is this wicked Haman!" Then Haman became terrified before the king and queen.

7 And the king arose in his anger from drinking wine *and went* into the palace garden; but Haman stayed to beg for his life from Queen Esther, for he saw that harm had been determined against him by the king.   Esth. 1:12 • *the banquet of wine* • Esth. 1:5

8 Now when the king returned from the palace garden into the place where they were drinking wine, Haman was falling on the couch where Esther was. Then the king said, "Will he even assault the queen with me in the house?" As the word went out of the king's mouth, they covered Haman's face.   *house of the banquet of wine* • Esth. 1:6

Haman Is Hanged

9 Then Harbonah, one of the eunuchs who *were* before the king said, "Behold indeed, the gallows standing at Haman's house fifty cubits high, which Haman made for Mordecai who spoke good on behalf of the king!" And the king said, "Hang him on it."   Esth. 5:14 • 75 ft. • Esth. 2:22

10 So they hanged Haman on the gallows which he had prepared for Mordecai, and the king's anger subsided.   *tree*

CHAPTER 8

Mordecai Is Given Haman's House

On that day King Ahasuerus gave the house of Haman, the enemy of the Jews, to Queen Esther; and Mordecai came before the king, for Esther had disclosed what he was to her.   Esth. 7:6 • Esth. 2:7, 15

2 And the king took off his signet ring which he had taken away from Haman, and gave it to Mordecai. And Esther set Mordecai over the house of Haman.   Esth. 3:10

3 Then Esther spoke again to the king, fell at his feet, wept, and implored him to avert the evil *scheme* of Haman the Agagite and his plot which he had devised against the Jews.

Esther's Petition to King Ahasuerus

4 ^RAnd the king extended the golden scepter to Esther. So Esther arose and stood before the king.   Esth. 4:11; 5:2

5 Then she said, "If^Rit pleases the king and if I have found favor before him and the matter *seems* proper to the king and I am pleasing in his sight, let it be written to revoke the^Rletters devised by Haman, the son of Hammedatha the Agagite, which he wrote to destroy the Jews who are in all the king's provinces.   Esth. 5:8; 7:3 • Esth. 3:13

6"For^Rhow can I endure to see the calamity which shall befall my people, and how can I endure to see the destruction of my kindred?"   Esth. 7:4; 9:1

King Ahasuerus's Counter-Decree

7 So King Ahasuerus said to Queen Esther and to Mordecai the Jew, "Behold, ^RI have given the house of Haman to Esther, and him they have hanged on the gallows because he had stretched out his hands against the Jews.   Esth. 8:1

8"Now you write to the Jews as you see fit, in the king's name, and seal *it* with the king's signet ring; for a decree which is written in the name of the king and sealed with the king's signet ring may not be revoked."

9 So the king's scribes were called at that time in the third month (that is, the month Sivan), on the twenty-third day; and it was written according to all that Mordecai commanded to the Jews, the satraps, the governors, and the princes of the provinces which *extended* from India to Ethiopia, 127 provinces, to every province according to its script, and to every people according to their language, as well as to the Jews according to their script and their language.

10 And he wrote in the name of King Ahasuerus, and sealed it with the king's signet ring, and sent letters by couriers on ^Rhorses, riding on steeds sired by the royal stud.   1 Kin. 4:28

11 ^TIn them the king granted the Jews who were in each and every city the right^Rto assemble and to defend their lives, to destroy, to kill, and to annihilate the entire army of any people or province which might attack them, including children and women, and to plunder their spoil,   Which • Esth. 9:2

12 on^Rone day in all the provinces of King Ahasuerus, the thirteenth *day* of the twelfth month (that is, the month Adar).   Esth. 3:13

13 ^RA copy of the edict to be^Tissued as law in each and every province, was published to all the peoples, so that the Jews should be ready for this day to avenge themselves on their enemies.   Esth. 3:14 • given

14 The couriers, hastened and impelled by the king's command, went out, riding on the royal steeds; and the decree was given out in Susa the capital.

Many Gentiles Are Converted

15 Then Mordecai went out from the presence of the king^Rin royal robes of^Ablue and white, with a large crown of gold and a garment of fine linen and purple; and the city of Susa shouted and rejoiced.   Esth. 5:11 • *violet*

16 For the Jews there was^Rlight and gladness and joy and honor.   Ps. 97:11; 112:4

17 And in each and every province, and in each and every city, wherever the king's commandment and his decree arrived, there was gladness and joy for the Jews, a feast and a^Tholiday. And many among the peoples of the land became Jews, for the dread of the Jews had fallen on them.   *good day*

CHAPTER 9

Victories on the First Day

Now in the twelfth month (that is, the month Adar), on the thirteenth ^Tday when the king's command and edict were about to be executed, on the day when the enemies of the Jews hoped to gain the mastery over them, it was turned to the contrary so that the Jews themselves gained the mastery over those who hated them.   *day in it*

2 ^RThe Jews assembled in their cities throughout all the provinces of King Ahasuerus to lay hands on those who sought their harm; and no one could stand before them, ^Rfor the dread of them had fallen on all the peoples.   Esth. 8:11; 9:15-18 • Esth. 8:17

3 Even all the princes of the provinces, ^Rthe satraps, the governors, and those who were doing the king's business^Tassisted the Jews, because the dread of Mordecai had fallen on them.   Ezra 8:36 • *lifted up*

4 Indeed, Mordecai was great in the king's house, and his fame spread throughout all the provinces; for the man Mordecai ^Rbecame greater and greater.   2 Sam. 3:1

5 Thus^Rthe Jews struck all their enemies with^Tthe sword, killing and destroying; and they did what they pleased to those who hated them.   Esth. 3:13 • *the stroke of*

6 And in Susa the capital the Jews killed and destroyed five hundred men,

7 and Parshandatha, Dalphon, Aspatha,

8 Poratha, Adalia, Aridatha,

9 Parmashta, Arisai, Aridai, and Vaizatha,

10 ^Rthe ten sons of Haman the son of Hammedatha, the Jews' enemy; but they did not lay their hands on the plunder.   Esth. 5:11

11 On that day the number of those who were killed in Susa the capital^Twas reported to the king.   *came*

Victories on the Second Day

12 And the king said to Queen Esther, "The Jews have killed and destroyed five hundred men and the ten sons of Haman in

Susa the capital. What then have they done in the rest of the king's provinces! ^RNow what is your petition? It shall even be granted you. And what is your further request? It shall also be done." Esth. 5:6; 7:2

13 Then said Esther, "If it pleases the king, ^Rlet tomorrow also be granted to Jews who are in Susa to do according to the edict of today; and let Haman's ten sons be hanged on the gallows." Esth. 8:11

14 So the king commanded that it should be done so; and an edict was issued in Susa, and Haman's ten sons were hanged.

15 And the Jews who were in Susa assembled also on the fourteenth day of the month Adar and killed^Rthree hundred men in Susa, but^Rthey did not lay their hands on the plunder. Esth. 9:12 • Esth. 9:10

16 Now^Rthe rest of the Jews who *were* in the king's provinces ^Rassembled, to defend their lives and ^Trid themselves of their enemies, and kill 75,000 of those who hated them; but they did not lay their hands on plunder. Esth. 9:2 • Lev. 26:7, 8 • *have rest from*

The Feast of Purim

17 *This was done* on^Rthe thirteenth day of the month Adar, and ^Ron the fourteenth ^Tday they rested and made it a day of feasting and rejoicing. Esth. 9:1 • Esth. 9:21 • *in it*

18 But the Jews who were in Susa^Rassembled on the thirteenth and^Rthe fourteenth ^Tof the same month, and they rested on the fifteenth day and made it a day of feasting and rejoicing. Esth. 8:11; 9:2 • Esth. 9:21 • *in it*

19 Therefore the Jews of the rural areas, who live in^Rthe rural towns, make the fourteenth day of the month Adar *a* holiday for rejoicing and feasting and sending portions *of food* to one another. Deut. 3:5; Zech. 2:4

20 Then Mordecai recorded these events, and he sent letters to all the Jews who were in all the provinces of King Ahasuerus, both near and far,

21 obliging them to celebrate the fourteenth day of the month Adar, and the fifteenth day of the same month, annually,

22 because on those days the Jews rid themselves of their enemies, and *it was a* month which was turned for them from sorrow into gladness and from mourning into a holiday; that they should make them days of feasting and rejoicing and sending portions *of food* to one another and gifts to the poor.

23 Thus the Jews undertook what they had started to do, and what Mordecai had written to them.

24 For Haman the son of Hammedatha, the Agagite, the adversary of all the Jews, had schemed against the Jews to destroy them, and^Rhad cast Pur, that is the lot, to disturb them and destroy them. Esth. 3:7

25 But when it came^Tto the king's attention, he commanded by letter that his wicked scheme which he had devised against the Jews, should return on his own head, and that he and his sons should be hanged on the ^Tgallows. *before the king, he • tree*

26 Therefore they called these days Purim after the name of Pur. ^TAnd because of the instructions in this letter, both what they had seen in this regard and what had happened to them, *Therefore because of all the words*

27 the Jews established and ^Tmade a custom for themselves, and for their ^Tdescendants, and for all those who allied themselves with them, so that they should not fail to celebrate these two days according to their ^Tregulation, and according to their appointed time annually. *received • seed • writing*

28 So these days were to be remembered and celebrated throughout every generation, every family, every province, and every city; and these days of Purim were not to^Tfail from among the Jews, or their memory fade from their descendants. *pass away*

29 Then Queen Esther, ^Rdaughter of Abihail, with Mordecai the Jew, wrote with full authority to confirm^Rthis second letter about Purim. Esth. 2:15 • Esth. 9:20, 21

30 And he sent letters to all the Jews, to the 127 provinces of the kingdom of Ahasuerus, namely, words of peace and truth,

31 to establish these days of Purim at their appointed times, just as Mordecai the Jew and Queen Esther had established for them, and just as they had established for themselves and for their ^Tdescendants with ^Tinstructions ^Rfor their times of fasting and their lamentations. *seed • words* • Esth. 4:3

32 And the command of Esther established these ^Tcustoms for^RPurim, and it was written in the book. *words* • Esth. 9:26

CHAPTER 10

The Fame of Mordecai

N OW King Ahasuerus laid a tribute on the land and on the coastlands of the sea.

2 And all the^Taccomplishments of his authority and strength, and the full account of the greatness of Mordecai, to which the king ^Tadvanced him, are they not written in the Book of the Chronicles of the Kings of Media and Persia? *doings • made him great*

3 For Mordecai the Jew was^Rsecond *only* to King Ahasuerus and great among the Jews, and in favor with the multitude of his kinsmen, ^Rone who sought the good of his people and one who spoke for the welfare of his whole nation. Gen. 41:43, 44 • Neh. 2:10

THE BOOK OF

JOB

THE BOOK OF JOB

Job is perhaps the earliest book of the Bible. Set in the period of the patriarchs (Abraham, Isaac, Jacob, and Joseph), it tells the story of a man who loses everything—his wealth, his family, his health—and wrestles with the question, Why?

The book begins with a heavenly debate between God and Satan, moves through three cycles of earthly debates between Job and his friends, and concludes with a dramatic "divine diagnosis" of Job's problem. In the end, Job acknowledges the sovereignty of God in his life and receives more than he had before his trials.

Iyyōb is the Hebrew title for this book, and the name has two possible meanings. If derived from the Hebrew word for persecution, it means "Persecuted One." It is more likely that it comes from the Arabic word meaning "To Come Back" or "Repent." If so, it may be defined "Repentant One." Both meanings apply to the book. The Greek title is *Iob*, and the Latin title is *Iob*.

THE AUTHOR OF JOB

The author of Job is unknown, and there are no textual hints as to his identity. Commentators, however, have been generous with suggestions: Job, Elihu, Moses, Solomon, Isaiah, Hezekiah, Jeremiah, Baruch, and Ezra have all been nominated. The non-Hebraic cultural background of this book may point to gentile authorship. The rabbinic traditions are inconsistent but one talmudic tradition suggests that Moses wrote the book. The land of Uz (1:1) is adjacent to Midian, where Moses lived for forty years, and it is conceivable that Moses obtained a record of the dialogue left by Job or Elihu.

THE TIME OF JOB

Lamentations 4:21 locates Uz in the area of Edom, southeast of the Dead Sea. This is also in the region of northern Arabia, and Job's friends come from nearby countries.

It is important to distinguish the date of the events in Job from the date of its writing. Accurate dating of the events is difficult because there are no references to contemporary historical occurrences. However, a number of facts indicate a patriarchal date for Job, perhaps between Genesis 11 and 12 or not long after the time of Abraham: (1) Job lived 140 years *after* the events in the book (42:16); his lifespan must have been close to 200 years. This fits the patriarchal period (Abraham lived 175 years, Gen. 24:7). (2) Job's wealth is measured in terms of livestock (1:3; 42:12) rather than gold and silver. (3) Like Abraham, Isaac, and Jacob, Job is the priest of his family and offers sacrifices. (4) There are no references to Israel, the Exodus, the Mosaic law, or the tabernacle. (5) Fitting Abraham's time, the social unit in Job is the patriarchal family-clan. (6) The Chaldeans who murder Job's servants (1:17) are nomads and have not yet become city-dwellers. (7) Job uses the characteristic patriarchal name for God, *Shaddai* ("the Almighty"), thirty-one times. This early term is found only seventeen times in the rest of the Old Testament. The rare use of Yahweh "the LORD" also suggests a pre-Mosaic date. Ezekiel 14:14, 20 and James 5:11 show that Job was a historical person.

Several theories have been advanced for the date of writing: (1) It was written shortly after the events occurred, perhaps by Job or Elihu. (2) It was written by Moses in Midian (1485–1445 B.C.). (3) It was written in the time of Solomon (c. 950 B.C.). (Job is similar to other wisdom literature of this time; compare the praises of wisdom in Job 28 and Proverbs 8. The problem here is the great time lag of about a thousand years.) (4) It was written during or after the Babylonian captivity.

THE CHRIST OF JOB

Job acknowledges a redeemer (see 19:25–27) and cries out for a mediator (9:33; 25:4; 33:23). The book raises problems and questions which are answered perfectly in Christ who identifies with our sufferings (Heb. 4:15). Christ is the believer's Life, Redeemer, Mediator, and Advocate.

KEYS TO JOB

Key Word: Sovereignty—The basic question of the book is, "Why do the righteous suffer if God is loving and all-powerful?" Suffering itself is not the central theme; rather, the focus is on what Job *learns* from his suffering—the sovereignty of God over all creation. The debate in chapters 3–37 regards whether God would allow this suffering to happen to a person who is innocent. The oversimplified solutions offered by Job's

three friends are simply inadequate. Elihu's claim that God can use suffering to purify the righteous is closer to the mark. The conclusion at the whirlwind is that God is sovereign and worthy of worship in *whatever* He chooses to do. Job must learn to trust in the goodness and power of God in adversity by enlarging his concept of God. Even this "blameless" man (1:1) needs to repent when he becomes proud and self-righteous. He has to come to the end of his own resources, humble himself, and acknowledge the greatness and majesty of the Lord. Job teaches that God is Lord "of those who are in heaven, and on earth, and under the earth" (Phil. 2:10). He is omniscient, omnipotent, and good. As such, His ways are sometimes incomprehensible to men and women, but He can always be trusted. Without the divine perspective in chapters 1 and 2 and in 38—42, chapters 3—37 are a mystery. Job does not have access to chapters 1 and 2, but he is responsible to trust God when all appearances are contrary. Suffering is not always associated with sin; God often sovereignly uses it to test and teach.

Key Verses: Job 13:15; 37:23, 24—"Though He slay me, I will hope in Him. Nevertheless I will argue my ways before Him" (13:15).

"The Almighty—we cannot find Him; He is exalted in power; and He will not do violence to justice and abundant righteousness. Therefore men fear Him; He does not regard any who are wise of heart" (37:23, 24).

Key Chapter: Job 42—The last chapter of the book records the climax of the long and difficult struggle Job has with himself, his wife, his friends, and even his God. Upon Job's full recognition of the utter majesty and sovereignty of the Lord, he repents and no longer demands an answer as to the "why" of his plight.

SURVEY OF JOB

The book of Job concerns the transforming crisis in the life of a great man who lived perhaps four thousand years ago. Job's trust in God (1 and 2) changes to complaining and growing self-righteousness (3—31; see 32:1 and 40:8), but his repentance (42:1-6) leads to his restoration (42:7-17). The trials bring about an important transformation: The man after the process is different from the man before the process. The Book of Job divides into three parts: the dilemma of Job (1 and 2), the debates of Job (3—37), and the deliverance of Job (38—42).

The Dilemma of Job (1 and 2): Job is not a logical candidate for disaster (see 1:1, 8). His moral integrity and his selfless service to God heighten the dilemma. Behind the scene, Satan ("accuser") charges that no one loves God from pure motives, but only for material blessings (1:10). To refute Satan's accusations, God allows him to strike Job with two series of assaults. In his sorrow Job laments the day of his birth but does not deny God (1:21; 2:10).

The Debates of Job (3—37): Although Job's "comforters" reach wrong conclusions, they are his friends: of all who know Job, they are the only ones who come; they mourn with him in seven days of silent sympathy; and they confront Job without talking behind his back. However, after Job breaks the silence, a three-round debate follows in which his friends say Job must be suffering because of his sin. Job's responses to their simplistic assumptions make the debate cycles increase in emotional fervor. He first accuses his friends of judging him, and later appeals to the Lord as his judge and refuge.

Job makes three basic complaints: (1) God does not hear me (13:3, 24; 19:7; 23:3-5;

FOCUS	DILEMMA OF JOB	DEBATES OF JOB					DELIVERANCE OF JOB
REFERENCE	1:1————3:1—	—15:1—	—22:1—	—27:1—		—32:1—	—38:1——42:17
DIVISION	CONTROVERSY OF GOD AND SATAN	FIRST CYCLE OF DEBATE	SECOND CYCLE OF DEBATE	THIRD CYCLE OF DEBATE	FINAL DEFENSE OF JOB	SOLUTION OF ELIHU	CONTROVERSY OF GOD WITH JOB
TOPIC	CONFLICT	DEBATE					REPENTANCE
	PROSE	POETRY					PROSE
LOCATION	LAND OF UZ (NORTH ARABIA)						
TIME	PATRIARCHAL PERIOD (c. 2000 B.C.)						

30:20); (2) God is punishing me (6:4; 7:20; 9:17); and (3) God allows the wicked to prosper (21:7). His defenses are much longer than his friends' accusations; and in the process of defending his innocence, he becomes guilty of self-righteousness.

After Job's five-chapter closing monologue (27—31), Elihu freshens the air with a more perceptive and accurate view than those offered by Eliphaz, Bildad, or Zophar (32—37). He tells Job that he needs to humble himself before God and submit to God's process of purifying his life through trials.

The Deliverance of Job (38—42): After Elihu's preparatory discourse, God Himself ends the debate by speaking to Job from the whirlwind. In His first speech God reveals His power and wisdom as Creator and Preserver of the physical and animal world. Job responds by acknowledging his own ignorance and insignificance; he can offer no rebuttal (40:3–5). In His second speech God reveals His sovereign authority and challenges Job with two illustrations of His power to control the uncontrollable. This time Job responds by acknowledging his error with a repentant heart (42:1–6). If Job cannot understand God's ways in the realm of nature, how then can he understand God's ways in the spiritual realm? God makes no reference to Job's personal sufferings and hardly touches on the real issue of the debate. However, Job catches a glimpse of the divine perspective; and when he acknowledges God's sovereignty over his life, his wordly goods are restored twofold. Job prays for his three friends who have cut him so deeply, but Elihu's speech is never rebuked. Thus, Satan's challenge becomes God's opportunity to build up Job's life. "Behold, we count those blessed who endured. You have heard of the endurance of Job and have seen the outcome of the Lord's dealings, that the Lord is full of compassion and *is* merciful" (James 5:11; see James 1:12).

Part Three: The Deliverance of Job (38:1—42:17)

CHAPTER 1

The Circumstances of Job

THERE was a man in the [R]land of Uz, whose name was [R]Job, and that man was [R]blameless, upright, fearing God, and turning away from evil.   Jer. 25:20 • James 5:11 • Gen. 6:9

2 [R]And seven sons and three daughters were born to him.   Job 42:13

3 [R]His possessions also were 7,000 sheep, 3,000 camels, 500 yoke of oxen, 500 female donkeys, and very many servants; and that man was[R]the greatest of all the[T]men of the east.   Job 42:12 • Job 29:25 • sons

4 And his sons used to go and hold a feast in the house of each one on his day, and they would send and invite their three sisters to eat and drink with them.

5 And it came about, when the days of feasting had completed their cycle, that Job would send and consecrate them, rising up early in the morning and offering[R]burnt offerings according to the number of them all; for Job said, "Perhaps[R]my sons have sinned and [R]cursed God in their hearts." Thus Job did continually.   Gen. 8:20 • Job 8:4 • 1 Kin. 21:10

The First Assault of Satan

6 Now there was a day when the sons of God came to present themselves before the LORD, and [1]Satan also came among them.

7 And the LORD said to Satan, "From where do you come?" Then Satan answered the LORD and said, "From roaming about on the earth and walking around on it."

8 And the LORD said to Satan, "Have you [T]considered[R]My servant Job? For there is no one like him on the earth, a blameless and upright man,[A]fearing God and turning away from evil."   set your heart to • Job 42:7 • revering

9 Then Satan answered the[T]LORD, "Does Job fear God for nothing?   LORD and said

10 "Hast[R]Thou not made a hedge about him and his house and all that he has, on every side? [R]Thou hast blessed the work of his hands, and his[R]possessions have increased in the land. Job 29:2-6 • Job 31:25 • Job 1:3; 31:25

11 "But[R]put forth Thy hand now and[R]touch all that he has; he will surely curse Thee to Thy face."   Job 2:5 • Job 19:21

12 Then the LORD said to Satan, "Behold, all that he has is in your[T]power, only do not put forth your hand on him." So Satan departed from the presence of the LORD.   hand

13 Now it happened on the day when his sons and his daughters were eating and drinking wine in their oldest brother's house,

14 that a messenger came to Job and said, "The oxen were plowing and the[T]donkeys feeding beside them,   female donkeys

15 and[T]the Sabeans[T]attacked and took them. They also[T]slew the servants with the edge of the sword, and[T]I alone have escaped to tell you."   Sheba • fell upon • smote • only alone

16 While he was still speaking, another also came and said, "The[R]fire of God fell from heaven and burned up the sheep and the servants and consumed them, and I alone have escaped to tell you."   Gen. 19:24

17 While he was still speaking, another also came and said, "The[R]Chaldeans formed three bands and made a raid on the camels and took them and[T]slew the servants with

the edge of the sword; and I alone have escaped to tell you." Gen. 11:28, 31 • *smote*

18 While he was still speaking, another also came and said, "Your sons and your daughters were eating and drinking wine in their oldest brother's house,

19 and behold, a great wind came from across the wilderness and struck the four corners of the house, and it fell on the young people and they died; and I alone have escaped to tell you."

20 Then Job arose and [R]tore his robe and shaved his head, and he fell to the ground and worshiped. Gen. 37:29, 34; Josh. 7:6

21 And he said,
"Naked[R] I came from my mother's
   womb, Eccl. 5:15
And naked I shall return there.
The[R] LORD gave and the LORD has
   taken away. [1 Sam. 2:7, 8]; Job 2:10
Blessed be the name of the LORD."

22 [R]Through all this Job did not sin nor did he[T]blame God. Job 2:10 • *ascribe unseemliness to*

CHAPTER 2

The Second Assault of Satan

Again[R]there was a day when the sons of God came to present themselves before the LORD, and Satan also came among them to present himself before the LORD. Job 1:6-8

2 And the LORD said to Satan, "Where have you come from?" Then Satan answered the LORD and said, "From roaming about on the earth, and walking around on it."

3 And the LORD said to Satan, "Have you [T]considered My servant Job? For there is no one like him on the earth, a blameless and upright man fearing God and turning away from evil. And he still holds fast his integrity, although you incited Me against him, to ruin him without cause." *set your heart to*

4 And Satan answered the LORD and said, "Skin for skin! Yes, all that a man has he will give for his life.

5 "However,[R] put forth Thy hand, now, and [R]touch his bone and his flesh; he will curse Thee to Thy face." Job 1:11 • Job 19:20

6 So the LORD said to Satan, "Behold, he is in your[T]power, only spare his life." *hand*

7 Then Satan went out from the presence of the LORD, and smote Job with[R]sore boils from the sole of his foot to the crown of his head. Job 7:5; 13:28; 30:17, 18, 30; Deut. 28:35

8 And he took a potsherd to scrape himself while he was sitting among the ashes.

9 Then his wife said to him, "Do you still hold fast your integrity? Curse God and die!"

10 But he said to her, "You speak as one of the foolish women speaks. [R]Shall we indeed accept good from God and not accept adversity?"[R]In all this Job did not sin with his lips. Job 1:21 • Job 1:22; Ps. 39:1; [James 1:12]

The Arrival of Job's Friends

11 Now when Job's three friends heard of all this adversity that had come upon him, they came each one from his own place, Eliphaz the Temanite, Bildad the Shuhite, and Zophar the Naamathite; and they made an

---

1:21 Response to Suffering—In the hour of suffering the Christian should attempt to determine first of all just why he may be suffering. One can suffer because of his position or his disposition. Peter brings this truth out in his first epistle: "Servants, be submissive to your masters with all respect, not only to those who are good and gentle, but also to those who are unreasonable. For this *finds* favor, if for the sake of conscience toward God a man bears up under sorrows when suffering unjustly" (Page 1262—1 Pet. 2:18, 19).

Suffering is often a two-sided coin. On the one side suffering may be viewed as coming from God to bring out the best in us. See Genesis 22:1, 2, 15–18; Hebrews 11:17. On the other side Satan attempts to use the same temptation and suffering event to bring out the worst in us (Page 1253—James 1:13, 14). Finally, the believer can react to suffering in three different ways:
a. Despise it, that is, treat it too lightly, as did Esau his birthright (Page 1247—Heb. 12:5, 16).
b. Faint under it, that is, treat it too seriously (Page 1247—Heb. 12:5).
c. Be exercised by it, that is, receive instruction from it. This is the reaction desired by God (Page 1247—Heb. 12:11–13).

During this time both Peter and Paul advise us to commit our pain and suffering to God, realizing He is faithful to work out all things for our good and God's glory (Page 1138—Rom. 8:28; Page 1264—1 Pet. 4:19). James tells us to count it all joy when we experience these dark hours (Page 1253—James 1:2).

Now turn to Page 755—Jer. 37:15: Examples of Suffering.

2:7 Purposes of Suffering—Perhaps the most painful question confronting the believer is the problem of suffering. Why does a loving and wise God permit His children to suffer? The Scriptures offer a number of reasons for this.
a. To produce fruit. If we allow suffering to accomplish its purpose, it can bring forth patience (Page 1246—Heb. 10:36; Page 1253—James 1:3), joy (Page 541—Ps. 30:5; 126:6), knowledge (Page 578—Ps. 94:12), and maturity (Page 1264—1 Pet. 5:10).
b. To silence the devil. Satan once accused Job of merely serving God for the material blessings involved. But the Lord allowed the devil to torment Job to demonstrate that His servant loved God because of who He was, and not for what he could get from Him (Page 495—Job 1:9–12; 2:3–7).

appointment together to come to [R]sympathize with him and comfort him.   Job 42:11

12 And when they lifted up their eyes at a distance, and did not recognize him, they raised their voices and wept. And each of them[R]tore his robe, and they[R]threw dust over their heads toward the sky. Job 1:20 • Josh. 7:6

13 [R]Then they sat down on the ground with him for seven days and seven nights with no one speaking a word to him, for they saw that *his* pain was very great.   Gen. 50:10

CHAPTER 3

Job's First Speech

A FTERWARD Job opened his mouth and cursed[T]the day of his *birth*.   *his day*

2 And Job[T]said,   *answered and said*
3 "Let[R]the day perish on which I was to be
   born,   Jer. 20:14-18
   And the night *which* said, 'A [T]boy is
   conceived.'   *man-child*
4 "May that day be darkness;
   Let not God above care for it,
   Nor light shine on it.
5 "Let[R]darkness and black gloom claim it;
   Let a cloud settle on it;   Jer. 13:16
   Let the blackness of the day terrify it.
6 "*As for* that night, let darkness seize it;
   Let it not rejoice among the days of the
   year;
   Let it not come into the number of the
   months.
7 "Behold, let that night be barren;
   Let no joyful shout enter it.
8 "Let those curse it who curse the day,
   Who are prepared to rouse Leviathan.
9 "Let the stars of its twilight be darkened;
   Let it wait for light but have none,
   Neither let it see the breaking dawn;
10 Because it did not shut the opening of
   my *mother's* womb,
   Or hide trouble from my eyes.

11 "Why did I not die[T]at birth, *from the womb*
   Come forth from the womb and expire?
12 "Why did the knees receive me,
   And why the breasts, that I should
   suck?

13 "For now I[R]would have lain down and
   been quiet; Job 3:13-19; 7:8-10, 21; 10:21
   I would have slept then, I would have
   been at rest,
14 With[R]kings and *with* [R]counselors of the
   earth,   Job 12:18 • Job 12:17
   Who rebuilt ruins for themselves;
15 Or with princes[R]who had gold, Job 27:16
   Who were filling their houses *with* silver.
16 "Or like a miscarriage which is [T]discarded, I would not be,   *hidden*
   As infants that never saw light.
17 "There the wicked cease from raging,
   And there the weary are at rest.
18 "The prisoners are at ease together;
   They do not hear the voice of the taskmaster.
19 "The small and the great are there,
   And the slave is free from his master.

20 "Why is[R]light given to him who suffers,
   And life to the bitter of soul; Jer. 20:18
21 Who long for death, but there is none,
   And dig for it more than for [R]hidden
   treasures;   Prov. 2:4
22 Who rejoice greatly,
   They exult when they find the grave?
23 "*Why is light given* to a man[R]whose way
   is hidden,   Job 19:6, 8, 12
   And whom[R]God has hedged in? Job 19:8
24 "For[R]my groaning comes at the sight of
   my food,   Job 6:7; 33:20
   And my cries pour out like water.
25 "For[R]what I fear comes upon me,
   And what I dread befalls me. [Job 9:28]
26 "I am not at ease, nor am I quiet,
   And I am not at rest, but turmoil
   comes."

CHAPTER 4

*Eliphaz Believes
the Innocent Do Not Suffer*

T HEN Eliphaz the Temanite answered,
2 "If one ventures a word with you, will
   you become impatient?
   But who can refrain from speaking?
3 "Behold you have admonished many,
   And you have strengthened weak
   hands.

---

c. To glorify God (Page 1075—John 9:1-3; 11:1-4).
d. To make us like Jesus. "That I may know Him, and the power of His resurrection and the fellowship of His sufferings, being conformed to His death" (Page 1195—Phil. 3:10).
e. To teach us dependence. This is brought out by both Christ (Page 1082—John 15:1-5) and the apostle Paul (Page 1173—2 Cor. 12:1-10).
f. To refine our lives (Page 560—Ps. 66:10-12; Page 622—Prov. 17:3; Page 1260—1 Pet. 1:6, 7).
g. To rebuke our sin (Page 1262—1 Pet. 2:20; 3:17; 4:15). As a faithful earthly father must in love punish his erring child, so does our heavenly Father (Page 1247—Heb. 12:5-9).
h. To enlarge our ministry towards others (Page 1166—2 Cor. 1:3-7). It has been observed that he who has suffered much speaks many languages (understands others).
   Now turn to Page 496—Job 1:21: Response to Suffering.

4"Your words have ^Thelped the tottering
to stand,   *caused*
And you have strengthened ^Tfeeble
knees.   *bowing*
5"But now it has come to you, and you
^Rare impatient;   Job 6:14
It touches you, and you are dismayed.
6"Is not your ²fear^R of God ^Ryour confidence,   Job 1:1 • Prov. 3:26
And the integrity of your ways your
hope?

7"Remember now, ^Rwho *ever* perished
being innocent?   [Job 8:20; 36:6, 7]
Or where were the upright destroyed?
8"According to what I have seen, ^Rthose
who plow iniquity   [Job 15:31, 35]
And those who sow trouble harvest it.
9"By the breath of God they perish,
And ^Rby the ^Tblast of His anger they
come to an end.   Job 40:11-13 • *wind*
10"The^Rroaring of the lion and the voice of
the *fierce* lion,   Job 5:15; Ps. 58:6
And the teeth of the young lions are
broken.
11"The lion perishes for lack of prey,
And the^Rwhelps of the lioness are scattered.   Job 5:4; 20:10; 27:14

12"Now a word ^Rwas brought to me
stealthily,   Job 4:12-17; 33:15-18
And my ear received a whisper of it.
13"Amid disquieting^Tthoughts from the visions of the night,   Job 33:15
When deep sleep falls on men,
14 Dread came upon me, and trembling,
And made all my bones shake.
15"Then a ³spirit passed by my face;
The hair of my flesh bristled up.
16"It stood still, but I could not discern its
appearance;
A form *was* before my eyes;
There was silence, then I heard a voice:
17 'Can mankind be just before God?
Can a man be pure before his Maker?
18 'He puts no trust even in His servants;
And against His angels He charges error.
19 'How much more those who dwell in
^Rhouses of clay,   Job 10:9; 33:6
Whose foundation is in the dust,
Who are crushed before the moth!
20 'Between^Rmorning and evening they are
broken in pieces;   Job 14:2
Unobserved, they perish forever.
21 'Is not their^Rtent-cord plucked up within
them?   Job 8:22
They die, yet^Twithout wisdom.' Job 18:21

CHAPTER 5

Eliphaz Calls Job Foolish

"CALL now, is there anyone who will answer you?
And to which of the^Rholy ones will you
turn?   Job 15:15

2"For^Rvexation slays the foolish man,
And anger kills the simple.   Prov. 12:16
3"I have seen the foolish taking root,
And I cursed his abode immediately.
4"His^Rsons are far from safety,   Job 4:11
They are even ⁴oppressed in the gate,
Neither is there a deliverer.
5"His^Tharvest the hungry devour,   *Whose*
And take it to a *place of* thorns;
And the schemer is eager for their
wealth.
6"For^Raffliction does not come from the
dust,   Job 15:35
Neither does trouble sprout from the
ground,
7 For^Rman is born for trouble,   Job 14:1
As sparks fly upward.

Eliphaz Encourages Job
to Appeal to God

8"But as for me, I would seek God,
And I would place my cause before
God;
9 Who ^Rdoes great and unsearchable
things,   Job 9:10; 37:14, 16; 42:3
^AWonders without number.   *Miracles*
10"He^Rgives rain on the earth, [Job 36:27–29]
And sends water on the fields,
11 So that^THe sets on high those who are
lowly,   Job 22:29; 36:7
And those who mourn are lifted to
safety.
12"He ^Rfrustrates the plotting of the
shrewd,   Ps. 33:10
So that their hands cannot attain success.
13"He ^Rcaptures the wise by their own
shrewdness   [Job 37:24; 1 Cor. 3:19]
And the advice of the cunning is
quickly thwarted.
14"By day they meet with darkness,
And grope at noon as in the night.
15"But He saves from ^Rthe sword of their
mouth,   Job 4:10, 11; Ps. 35:10
And ^Rthe poor from the hand of the
mighty. Job 29:17; 34:28; 36:6, 15; 38:15
16"So the helpless has hope,
And ^Runrighteousness must shut its
mouth.   Ps. 107:42

Eliphaz Encourages Job
to Not Despise God's Discipline

17"Behold, how ^Rhappy is the man whom
God reproves,   Ps. 94:12
So do not despise the^Rdiscipline of the
Almighty.   Job 36:15, 16; [Prov. 3:11]
18"For He inflicts pain, and gives relief;
He wounds, and His hands *also* heal.
19"From six troubles He will deliver you,
Even in seven evil will not touch you.

² Or, *reverence*   ³ Or, *breath passed over*   ⁴ Lit., *crushed*

20"In ^Rfamine He will redeem you from
death, Ps. 33:19; 37:19
And ^Rin war from the power of the
sword. Ps. 144:10
21"You will be^Rhidden from the scourge of
the tongue, Job 5:15; Ps. 31:20
^RNeither will you be afraid of violence
when it comes. Ps. 91:5, 6
22"You will laugh at violence and famine,
^RNeither will you be afraid of ^Twild
beasts. Ps. 91:13 • beasts of the earth
23"For you will be in league with the
stones of the field;
And^Rthe beasts of the field will be at
peace with you. [Is. 11:6–9; 65:25]
24"And you will know that your^Rtent is secure, Job 8:6
For you will visit your abode and fear
no loss.
25"You will know also that your^Tdescend-
ants^Rwill be many, seed • Ps. 112:2
And^Ryour offspring as the grass of the
earth. Is. 44:3, 4; 48:19
26"You will ^Rcome to the grave in full
vigor, Job 42:17
Like the stacking of grain in its season.
27"Behold this, we have investigated it,
thus it is;
Hear it, and know for yourself."

CHAPTER 6

Job's Deep Anguish

THEN Job^Tanswered, answered and said
2"Oh^R that my vexation were actually
weighed, Job 31:6
And laid in the balances together with
my iniquity!
3"For then it would be^Rheavier than the
sand of the seas, Job 23:2
Therefore my words have been rash.
4"For the ^Rarrows of the Almighty are
within me; Job 16:13; Ps. 38:2
^TTheir poison my spirit drinks; Whose
The^Rterrors of God are arrayed against
me. Job 30:15
5"Does the ^Rwild donkey bray over his
grass, Job 39:5-8
Or does the ox low over his fodder?
6"Can something tasteless be eaten without salt,
Or is there any taste in the^Twhite of an
egg? Heb., hallamuth
7"My soul^Rrefuses to touch them; Job 3:24
They are like loathsome food to me.

8"Oh that my request might come to
pass,
And that God would grant my longing!
9"Would that God were^Rwilling to crush
me; Num. 11:15; 1 Kin. 19:4; Job 7:16; 9:21
That He would loose His hand and cut
me off!

10"But it is still my consolation,
And I rejoice in unsparing pain,
That I^Thave not^Tdenied the words of the
Holy One. Job 22:22; 23:11, 12 • hidden
11"What is my strength, that I should
wait?
And what is my end, that I should ^Ten-
dure? prolong my soul
12"Is my strength the strength of stones,
Or is my flesh bronze?
13"Is it that my help is not within me,
And that ^Rdeliverance is driven from
me? Job 26:3

Job Seeks His Friends' Sympathy

14"For the^Rdespairing man there should be
kindness from his friend; Job 4:5
Lest he ^Rforsake the ^Afear of the Almighty. Job 1:5; 15:4 • reverence
15"My brothers have acted^Rdeceitfully like
a^Awadi, Jer. 15:18
Like the torrents of^Awadis which vanish, brook
16 Which are turbid because of ice,
And into which the snow melts.
17"When^Rthey become waterless, they^Aare
silent, Job 24:19 • cease
When it is hot, they vanish from their
place.
18"The paths of their course wind along,
They go up into nothing and perish.
19"The caravans of^RTema looked, Is. 21:14
The travelers of Sheba hoped for them.
20"They^Rwere ^Tdisappointed for they had
trusted, Jer. 14:3 • ashamed
They came there and were confounded.
21"Indeed, you have now become such,
^RYou see a terror and are afraid.Ps. 38:11
22"Have I said, 'Give me something,'
Or, 'Offer a bribe for me from your
wealth,'
23 Or, 'Deliver me from the hand of the
adversary,'
Or, 'Redeem me from the hand of the
tyrants'?

24"Teach me, and^RI will be silent; Ps. 39:1
And show me how I have erred.
25"How painful are honest words!
But what does your argument prove?
26"Do you intend to reprove my words,
When the^Rwords of one in despair belong to the wind? Job 8:2; 15:2; 16:3
27"You would even ^Rcast lots for the ^Ror-
phans, Joel 3:3; Nah. 3:10 • Job 22:9
And^Rbarter over your friend. 2 Pet. 2:3
28"And now please look at me,
And see if I^Rlie to your face. Job 27:4
29"Desist now, let there be no injustice;
Even desist,^Rmy righteousness is yet in
it. Job 13:18; 19:6; 23:10; 27:5, 6; 34:5
30"Is there injustice on my tongue?
Cannot my palate discern calamities?

CHAPTER 7

Job Questions God's Continuing Trials

"Is not man forced to labor on earth,
And *are not* his days like the days of ᴿa
hired man? Job 14:6
2 "As a slave who pants for the shade,
And as a hired man who eagerly waits
for his wages,
3 So am I allotted months of vanity,
And ᴿnights of trouble are appointed
me. Job 16:7
4 "When Iᴿlie down I say, Job 7:13, 14
'When shall I arise?'
But the night continues,
And I am ᵀcontinually tossing until
dawn. *sated with*
5 "Myᴿflesh is clothed with worms and a
crust of dirt; Job 2:7; 17:14
My skin hardens and runs.
6 "My days are ᴿswifter than a weaver's
shuttle, Job 9:25
And come to an end without hope.

7 "Remember that my life is *but* breath,
My eye will not again see good.
8 "The ᴿeye of him who sees me will behold me no more; Job 8:18; 20:9
Thine eyes *will be* on me, butᴿI will not
be. Job 7:21
9 "When a cloud vanishes, it is gone,
Soᴿhe who goes down toᵀSheol does not
come up. Job 3:13-19 • 2 Sam. 12:23
10 "He will not return again to his house,
Nor will his place know him anymore.

11 "Therefore, ᴿI will not restrain my
mouth; Job 10:1; 21:4; 23:2; Ps. 40:9
I will speak in the anguish of my spirit,
I will complain in the bitterness of my
soul.
12 "Am I the sea, or the sea monster,
That Thou dost set a guard over me?
13 "If I say, 'My bed will comfort me,
My couch will ease my complaint,'
14 Then Thou dost frighten me with
dreams
And terrify me by visions;
15 So that my soul would choose suffoca-
tion,
Death rather than myᵀpains. *bones*
16 "I waste away; I will not live forever.
Leave me alone,ᴿfor my days are *but* a
breath. Job 7:7
17 "Whatᴿis man that Thou dost magnify
him, Job 22:2; Ps. 8:4; 144:3; Heb. 2:6
And that Thou ᵀart concerned about
him, *shouldst set Thy heart on*
18 That ᴿThou dost examine him every
morning, Job 14:3
And try him every moment?
19 "Wiltᵀ Thou never turn Thy gaze away
from me, *How long wilt Thou not*
Nor let me alone until I swallow my
spittle?

20 "HaveᴿI sinned? What have I done to
Thee, Job 35:3, 6
Oᴿwatcher of men? Ps. 36:6
Why hast Thou set me as Thy target,
So that I am a burden to myself?
21 "Why then ᴿdost Thou not pardon my
transgression Job 9:28; 10:14
And take away my iniquity?
For now I will lie down in the dust;
And Thou wilt seek me,ᴿbut I will not
be." Job 7:8

CHAPTER 8

Bildad's First Speech

Then Bildad the Shuhite answered,
2 "How long will you say these *things,*
And the ᴿwords of your mouth be a
mighty wind? Job 6:26
3 "Does God pervert justice
Or does ᵀthe Almighty pervert what is
right? Heb., *Shaddai,* also v. 5
4 "If your sons sinned against Him,
Then He delivered them into theᵀpower
of their transgression. *hand*
5 "If you wouldᴿseek God [Job 5:17–27]
And implore the compassion of ᵀthe Almighty, Heb., *Shaddai*
6 If you are pure and upright,
Surely now ᴿHe would rouse Himself
for you Job 22:27; 34:28; Ps. 7:6
And restore your righteous estate.
7 "Though your beginning was insignificant,
Yet your end will increase greatly.

8 "Please inquire of past generations,
And consider the things searched out
by their fathers.
9 "For we are *only* of yesterday and know
nothing,
Because ᴿour days on earth are as a
shadow. Job 14:2
10 "Will they not teach you *and* tell you,
And bring forth words from their
minds?

11 "Can the papyrus grow up without
marsh?
Can the rushes grow without water?
12 "While it is still green *and* not cut down,
Yet it withers before any *other* plant.
13 "So are the paths of all who forget God,
And the hope of the godless will perish,
14 Whose confidence is fragile,
And whose trust a spider'sᵀweb. *house*
15 "Heᵀtrusts in hisᴿhouse, but it does not
stand; *leans on* • Job 8:22; 27:18
He holds fast to it, but it does not endure.
16 "Heᵀthrives before the sun, *is lush*
And hisᴿshoots spread out over his garden. Ps. 80:11

17"His roots wrap around a rock pile,
He[T] grasps a house of stones. Heb., *sees*
18"If he is removed from[R] his place,
Then it will deny him, *saying,* 'I[R] never saw you.' Job 7:10 • Job 7:8
19"Behold, this is the joy of His way;
And out of the dust others will spring.
20"Lo,[R] God will not reject *a man of* integrity, Job 4:7
Nor will He support the evildoers.
21"He will yet fill[R] your mouth with laughter, Job 5:22; Ps. 126:1, 2
And your lips with shouting.
22"Those who hate you will be [R]clothed with shame; Ps. 132:18
And the[R] tent of the wicked will be no more." Job 8:15; 15:34; 18:14; 21:28

CHAPTER 9

Job Argues His Case

THEN Job[T] answered, *answered and said*
2"In truth I know that this is so,
But how can a[R] man be in the right[T] before God? [Job 4:17; 25:4] • *with*
3"If one wished to dispute with Him,
He could not answer Him once in a thousand *times.*
4"Wise in heart and mighty in strength,
Who has defied Him without harm?
5"*It*[R] *is God* who removes the mountains, they know not *how,* [Job 9:5f.; 26:6f.]
When He overturns them in His anger;
6 Who shakes the earth out of its place,
And its[R] pillars tremble; Ps. 75:3
7 Who commands the sun not to shine,
And sets a seal upon the stars;
8 Who alone stretches out the heavens,
And[T] tramples down the waves of the sea; *treads upon the heights of*
9 Who makes the[R] Bear, Orion, and the Pleiades, Job 38:31, 32; Amos 5:8
And the chambers of the south;
10 Who does great things, unfathomable,
And wondrous works without number.
11"Were He to pass by me,[R] I would not see Him; [Job 23:8, 9; 35:14]
Were He to move past *me,* I would not perceive Him.
12"Were He to snatch away, who could[R] restrain Him? Job 10:7; 11:10
Who could say to Him, 'What[R] art Thou doing?' [Is. 45:9]

13"God will not turn back His anger;
Beneath Him crouch the helpers of[R] Rahab. Job 26:12; Ps. 89:10; Is. 30:7; 51:9
14"How then can I answer Him,
And choose my words before Him?
15"For[R] though I were right, I could not[A] answer; Job 9:20, 21 • *plead my case*
I would have to[R] implore the mercy of my judge. Job 8:5
16"If I called and He answered me,
I could not believe that He was listening to my voice.
17"For He bruises me with a tempest,
And multiplies my wounds without cause.
18"He will not allow me to get my breath,
But saturates me with bitterness.
19"If *it is a matter* of power,[R] behold, *He is* the strong one! Job 9:4
And if *it is a matter* of justice, who can summon[T] Him? Heb., *me*
20"Though[R] I am righteous, my mouth will [R]condemn me; Job 9:15 • Job 9:29
Though I am guiltless, He will declare me guilty.
21"I am[R] guiltless; Job 1:1; 12:4; 13:18
I do not take notice of myself;
I[R] despise my life. Job 7:16
22"It is *all* one; therefore I say,
'He [R]destroys the guiltless and the wicked.' Job 10:7, 8
23"If the scourge kills suddenly,
He mocks the despair of the innocent.
24"The earth[R] is given into the hand of the wicked; Job 10:3; 12:6; 16:11
He covers the faces of its judges.
If *it is* not *He,* then who is it?

25"Now[R] my days are swifter than a runner; Job 7:6
They flee away, they see no good.
26"They slip by like[R] reed boats, Is. 18:2
Like an eagle that swoops on its prey.
27"Though I say, 'I will forget[R] my complaint, Job 7:11
I will leave off my *sad* countenance and be cheerful,'
28 I am[R] afraid of all my pains, Job 3:25
I know that Thou wilt not acquit me.
29"I am accounted[R] wicked, [Ps. 37:33]
Why then should I toil in vain?
30"If I should wash myself with snow
And cleanse my hands with lye,
31 Yet Thou wouldst plunge me into the pit,
And my own clothes would abhor me.
32"For *He is*[R] not a man as I am that[R] I may answer Him, Eccl. 6:10 • Job 9:3
That we may go to court together.
33"There is no[R] umpire between us, Is. 1:18
Who may lay his hand upon us both.
34"Let Him remove His rod from me,
And let not dread of Him terrify me.
35"*Then* I would speak and not fear Him;
But I am not like that in myself.

CHAPTER 10

Job Questions His Oppression

"I[T] LOATHE my own life; *My soul loathes*
I will give full vent to my complaint;
I will speak in the bitterness of my soul.

2 "I will say to God, 'Do not condemn me;
Let me know why Thou dost contend
with me.
3 'Is it right for Thee indeed to oppress,
To reject the labor of Thy hands,
And^Tto look favorably on the schemes
of the wicked?   *you shine forth*
4 'Hast Thou eyes of flesh?
Or dost Thou see as a man sees?
5 'Are Thy days as the days of a mortal,
Or^RThy years as man's years, [Job 36:26]
6 That Thou shouldst seek for my guilt,
And search after my sin?
7 'According to Thy knowledge^RI am indeed not guilty;   Job 9:21; 13:18
Yet there is^Rno deliverance from Thy
hand.   Job 9:12; 23:13; 27:22

8 'Thy hands fashioned and made me ^Tal-
together,   *together round about*
^RAnd wouldst Thou destroy me? Job 9:22
9 'Remember now, that Thou hast made
me as^Rclay;   Job 4:19; 33:6
And wouldst Thou^Rturn me into dust
again?   Job 7:21
10 'Didst Thou not pour me out like milk,
And curdle me like cheese;
11 Clothe me with skin and flesh,
And knit me together with bones and
sinews?
12 'Thou hast^Rgranted me life and lovingkindness;   Job 33:4
And Thy care has preserved my spirit.
13 'Yet^Rthese things Thou hast concealed
in Thy heart;   Job 23:13
I know that this is within Thee:
14 If I sin, then Thou wouldst^Rtake note of
me,   Job 7:20
And wouldst not acquit me of my guilt.
15 'If^RI am wicked, woe to me!   Job 10:7
And^Rif I am righteous, I dare not lift up
my head.   Job 6:29
I am sated with disgrace and^Tconscious
of my misery.   *see*
16 'And should *my head* be lifted up,^RThou
wouldst hunt me like a lion; Is. 38:13
And again Thou wouldst show Thy
^Rpower against me.   Job 5:9
17 'Thou dost renew^RThy witnesses against
me,   Ruth 1:21; Job 16:8
And increase Thine anger toward me,
Hardship after hardship is with me.

18 'Why^Rthen hast Thou brought me out of
the womb?   Job 3:11-13
Would that I had died and no eye had
seen me!
19 'I should have been as though I had not
been,
Carried from womb to tomb.'
20 "Would He not let my few days alone?
^TWithdraw^Rfrom me that I may have a
little cheer   *Put* • Job 7:16, 19
21 Before I go—and I shall not return—
^RTo the land of darkness and ^Rdeep
shadow;   Ps. 88:12 • Job 10:22; Ps. 23:4

22 The land of utter gloom as darkness *it-
self,*
Of deep shadow without order,
And which shines as the darkness."

CHAPTER 11

Zophar's First Speech

THEN Zophar the Naamathite answered,
2 "Shall a multitude of words go unanswered,
And a talkative man be acquitted?
3 "Shall your boasts silence men?
And shall you scoff and none rebuke?
4 "For ^Ryou have said, 'My teaching is
pure,   Job 6:10
And I am innocent in your eyes.'
5 "But would that God might speak,
And open His lips against you,
6 And show you the secrets of wisdom!
For sound wisdom has two sides.
Know then that God forgets a part of
your iniquity.

7 "Can you discover the depths of God?
Can you discover the limits of the Almighty?
8 "*They are*^Rhigh as^Tthe heavens, what can
you do? Job 22:12 • *the heights of heaven*
Deeper than ^TSheol,^R what can you
know?   *the nether world* • Job 26:6
9 "Its measure is longer than the earth,
And broader than the sea.
10 "If He passes by or shuts up,
Or calls an assembly,^Rwho can restrain
Him?   Job 9:12
11 "For^RHe knows false men,   Job 34:21-23
And He sees iniquity^Awithout investigating.   *even He does not consider*
12 "And an idiot will become intelligent
When the^Tfoal of a^Rwild donkey is born
a man.   *donkey* • Job 39:5

13 "If you would direct your heart right,
And spread out your hand to Him;
14 If iniquity is in your hand,^Rput it far
away,   Job 22:23
And do not let wickedness dwell in
your tents.
15 "Then, indeed, you could ^Rlift up your
face without *moral* defect, Job 22:26
And you would be steadfast and^Rnot
fear.   Ps. 27:3; 46:2
16 "For you would forget *your* trouble,
As ^Rwaters that have passed by, you
would remember *it.*   Job 22:11
17 "And your ^Tlife would be^Rbrighter than
noonday;   *duration of life* •Job 22:26
Darkness would be like the morning.
18 "Then you would trust, because there is
hope;
And you would look around and rest
securely.
19 "You would^Rlie down and none would
disturb you,   Lev. 26:6; Is. 17:2; Mic. 4:4

And many would entreat your favor.
20"But the eyes of the wicked will fail,
And there will be no escape for them;
And their hope is to breathe their last."

CHAPTER 12

Job Tells His Friends
Only God Knows

Then Job[T]responded,   *answered and said*
2"Truly then[R]you are the people, Job 17:10
And with you wisdom will die!
3"But I have intelligence as well as you;
I am not inferior to you.
And[T]who does not know such things as
these? *with whom is there not like these?*
4"I am a joke to[T]my friends.   *his*
The one who called on God, and He answered him;
The just *and* blameless *man* is a joke.
5"He who is at ease holds calamity in
contempt,
As prepared for those whose feet slip.
6"The tents of the destroyers prosper,
And those who provoke God [R]are secure,   Job 24:23
Whom God brings into [5]their power.

7"But now ask the beasts, and let them
teach you;
And the birds of the heavens, and let
them tell you.
8"Or speak to the earth, and let it teach
you;
And let the fish of the sea declare to
you.
9"Who among all these does not know
That [R]the hand of the Lord has done
this,   Is. 41:20
10 [R]In whose hand is the life of every living
thing,   [Acts 17:28]
And[R]the breath of all mankind? Job 27:3
11"Does not[R]the ear test words,   Job 34:3
As the palate tastes its food?
12"Wisdom is with[R]aged men,   Job 15:10
With long life is understanding.
13"With Him are wisdom and might;
To Him belong counsel and [R]under-
standing.   Job 11:6; 26:12; 32:8; 36:5
14"Behold, He[R]tears down, and it cannot
be rebuilt;   Job 19:10; Is. 25:2
He[T]imprisons[R]a man, and there can be
no release.   *shuts against* • Job 37:7
15"Behold, He [R]restrains the waters, and
they dry up;   Deut. 11:17; [1 Kin. 8:35]
And He[R]sends them out, and they[T]inun-
date the earth.   Gen. 7:11 • *overturn*
16"With Him are strength and sound wisdom,
The[R]misled and the misleader belong to
Him.   Job 13:7, 9
17"He makes counselors walk barefoot,
And makes fools of[R]judges.   Job 9:24

18"He loosens the[A]bond of kings, *discipline*
And binds their loins with a girdle.
19"He makes priests walk barefoot,
And overthrows the secure ones.
20"He deprives the trusted ones of speech,
And[T]takes away the discernment of the
elders.   Job 17:4; 32:9
21"He[R]pours contempt on nobles, Job 34:19
And loosens the belt of the strong.
22"He [R]reveals mysteries from the darkness,   Dan. 2:22; [1 Cor. 4:5]
And brings the deep darkness into
light.
23"He [R]makes the nations great, then destroys them;   Is. 9:3; 26:15
He [A]enlarges the nations, then leads
them away.   *spreads out*
24"He [R]deprives of intelligence the chiefs
of the earth's people,   Job 12:20
And makes them wander in a pathless
waste.
25"They grope in darkness with no light,
And He makes them [R]stagger like a
drunken man.   Is. 24:20

CHAPTER 13

Job Begs God to Speak to Him

"Behold, my eye has seen all *this,*
My ear has heard and understood it.
2"What[R]you know I also know.   Job 12:3
I am not inferior to you.
3"But I would speak to the Almighty,
And I desire to argue with God.
4"But you[R]smear with lies;   Ps. 119:69
You are all worthless physicians.
5"O that you would be completely silent,
And that it would become your wisdom!
6"Please hear my argument,
And listen to the contentions of my
lips.
7"Will you speak what is unjust for God,
And speak what is deceitful for Him?
8"Will you show partiality for Him?
Will you contend for God?
9"Will it be well when He examines you?
Or [R]will you deceive Him as one deceives a man?   Job 12:16
10"He will surely reprove you,
If you secretly[R]show partiality. Job 13:8
11"Will not His majesty terrify you,
And the dread of Him fall on you?
12"Your memorable sayings are proverbs
of ashes,
Your defenses are defenses of clay.

13"Be[R] silent before me so that I may
speak;   Job 13:5
Then let come on me what may.
14"Why should I take my flesh in my
teeth,
And put my life in my[T]hands?   *palm*

[5] Lit., *his*

15"Though^RHe slay me,   Job 7:6
I will hope in Him.
Nevertheless I^Rwill argue my ways^Tbe-
fore Him.   Job 27:5 • to His face
16"This also will be my^Rsalvation,   Job 23:7
For ^Ra godless man may not come before His presence.   Job 34:21-23
17"Listen carefully to my speech,
And let my declaration *fill* your ears.
18"Behold now, I have prepared my case;
I know that I will be vindicated.
19"Who^Rwill contend with me?   Job 7:21
For then I would be silent and die.

20"Only two things do not do to me,
Then I will not hide from Thy face:
21 Remove Thy^Thand from me,   *palm*
And let not the dread of Thee terrify
me.
22"Then call, and^RI will answer;   Job 9:16
Or let me speak, then reply to me.
23"How many are my iniquities and sins?
Make known to me my^Arebellion and
my sin.   *transgression*
24"Why dost Thou^Rhide Thy face,   Ps. 13:1
And consider me Thine enemy?
25"Wilt Thou cause a^Rdriven leaf to tremble?   Lev. 26:36
Or wilt Thou pursue the dry chaff?
26"For Thou dost write ^Rbitter things
against me,   Job 9:18
And dost^Rmake me to inherit the iniquities of my youth.   Ps. 25:7
27"Thou dost put my feet in the stocks,
And dost watch all my paths;
Thou dost 'set a limit for the soles of my
feet,   *carve for*
28 While ^TI am decaying like a ^Rrotten
thing,   *he is* • Job 2:7
Like a garment that is moth-eaten.

CHAPTER 14

Job Mourns That Man
Has Only One Life

"M_{AN,}^R who is born of woman,   Job 5:7
Is short-lived and full of turmoil.
2"Like^Ra flower he comes forth and withers.   Ps. 90:5, 6; 103:15; Is. 40:6, 7
He also flees like ^Ra shadow and does
not remain.   Job 8:9
3"Thou also dost open Thine eyes on him,
And ^Rbring him into judgment with
Thyself.   [Ps. 143:2]
4"Who^Rcan make the clean out of the unclean?   [Job 15:14; 25:4; Ps. 51:5]
No one!
5"Since his days are determined,
The ^Rnumber of his months is with
Thee,   Job 21:21
And his limits Thou hast^Tset so that he
cannot pass.   *made*
6"Turn^RThy gaze from him that he may
^Trest,   Job 7:19; Ps. 39:13 • *cease*

Until he ^Tfulfills his day like a hired
man.   *makes acceptable*

7"For there is hope for a tree,
When it is cut down, that it will sprout
again,
And its shoots will not^Afail.   *cease*
8"Though its roots grow old in the
ground,
And its stump dies in the dry soil,
9 At the scent of water it will flourish
And put forth sprigs like a plant.
10"But^Rman dies and lies prostrate. Job 3:13
Man^Rexpires, and where is he?   Job 13:9
11"*As* water evaporates from the sea,
And a river becomes parched and dried
up,
12 So man lies down and does not rise.
Until the heavens be no more,
He^Twill not awake nor be aroused out
of^This sleep.   *They* • *their*
13"Oh that Thou wouldst hide me in
^TSheol,   *the nether world*
That Thou wouldst conceal me ^Runtil
Thy wrath returns *to Thee,*   Is. 26:20
That Thou wouldst set a limit for me
and remember me!
14"If a man dies, will he live *again?*
All the days of my struggle I will wait,
Until my change comes.
15"Thou wilt call, and I will answer Thee;
Thou wilt long for ^Rthe work of Thy
hands.   Job 10:3
16"For now Thou dost number my steps,
Thou dost not^Robserve my sin.   Job 10:6
17"My transgression is sealed up in a bag,
And Thou dost wrap up my iniquity.

18"But the falling mountain ^Tcrumbles
away,   *withers*
And the rock moves from its place;
19 Water wears away stones,
Its torrents wash away the dust of the
earth;
So Thou dost destroy man's hope.
20"Thou dost forever overpower him and
he^Rdeparts;   Job 4:20; 20:7
Thou dost change his appearance and
send him away.
21"His sons achieve honor, but ^Rhe does
not know *it;*   Eccl. 9:5
Or they become insignificant, but he
does not perceive it.
22"But his^Tbody pains him,   *flesh*
And he mourns only for himself."

CHAPTER 15

Job's Mouth Condemns Him

T_{HEN} Eliphaz the Temanite responded,
2"Should a wise man answer with windy
knowledge,
And fill himself with the east wind?

3"Should he argue with useless talk,
  Or with words which are not profitable?
4"Indeed, you do away with reverence,
  And hinder meditation before God.
5"For your guilt teaches your mouth,
  And you choose the language of[R]the
  crafty.   Job 5:12, 13
6"Your[R]own mouth condemns you, and
  not I;   Job 18:7
  And your own lips testify against you.

7"Were you the first man to be born,
  Or[R]were you brought forth before the
  hills?   Job 38:4, 21; Prov. 8:25
8"Do you hear the secret counsel of God,
  And limit wisdom to yourself?
9"What[R] do you know that we do not
  know?   Job 12:3; 13:2
  What do you understand that[T]we do
  not?   *is not within us?*
10"Both the[R]gray-haired and the aged are
  among us,   Job 12:12; 32:6, 7
  Older than your father.
11"Are[R]the consolations of God too small
  for you,   [Job 5:17–19; 36:15, 16]
  Even the word *spoken* gently with you?
12"Why does your heart carry you away?
  And why do your eyes flash,
13 That you should turn your spirit
  against God,
  And allow *such* words to go out of your
  mouth?

The Wicked Suffer

14"What is man, that he should be pure,
  Or[T]he who is born of a woman, that he
  should be righteous?   Job 25:4
15"Behold, He puts no trust in His[R]holy
  ones,   Job 5:1
  And the[R]heavens are not pure in His
  sight;   Job 25:5
16 How much less one who is[R]detestable
  and corrupt,   Ps. 14:1
  Man, who drinks iniquity like water!
17"I will tell you, listen to me;
  And what I have seen I will also declare;
18 What wise men have told,
  And have not concealed from[R]their fathers,   Job 8:8; 20:4
19 To whom alone the land was given,
  And no alien passed among them.
20"The wicked man writhes[R]in pain all *his*
  days,   Job 15:24
  And[T]numbered are the years stored up
  for the ruthless. *the number of years are*
21"Sounds of terror are in his ears,
  [R]While at peace the destroyer comes
  upon him.   Job 20:21; 1 Thess. 5:3
22"He does not believe that he will[R]return
  from darkness,   Job 15:30
  And he is destined for the sword.
23"He wanders about for food, saying,
  'Where is it?'

He knows that a day of[R]darkness is[T]at
  hand.   Job 15:22, 30 • *ready at his hand*
24"Distress and anguish terrify him,
  They overpower him like a king ready
  for the attack,
25 Because he has stretched out his hand
  against God,
  And conducts himself arrogantly
  against[T]the Almighty.   Heb., *Shaddai*
26"He rushes[T]headlong at Him
  With his massive shield. *with a stiff neck*
27"For he has[R]covered his face with his
  fat,   Ps. 73:7; 119:70
  And made his thighs heavy with flesh.
28"And he has lived in desolate cities,
  In houses no one would inhabit,
  Which are destined to become ruins.
29"He[R]will not become rich, nor will his
  wealth endure;   Job 27:16, 17
  And his grain will not bend down to
  the ground.
30"He will not escape from darkness;
  The[R]flame will wither his shoots,
  And by[T]the breath of His mouth he will
  go away.   Job 15:34 • Job 4:9
31"Let him not[R]trust in emptiness, deceiving himself;   Job 35:13; Is. 59:4
  For emptiness will be his reward.
32"It will be accomplished before his time,
  And his palm branch will not be green.
33"He will drop off his unripe grape like
  the vine,
  And will[R]cast off his flower like the olive tree.   Job 14:2
34"For the company of[R]the godless is barren,   Job 8:13
  And fire consumes[R]the tents of[T]the corrupt.   Job 8:22 • *a bribe*
35"They[R]conceive[A]mischief and bring forth
  iniquity,   Ps. 7:14; Is. 59:4 • *pain*
  And their mind prepares deception."

CHAPTER 16

Job Calls His Friends
Sorry Comforters

THEN Job[T]answered,   *answered and said*
2"I have heard many such things;
  [R]Sorry comforters are you all.   Job 13:4
3"Is there *no* limit to windy words?
  Or what plagues you that you answer?
4"I too could speak like you,
  If I were in your place.
  I could compose words against you,
  And[R]shake my head at you.   Zeph. 2:15
5"I could strengthen you with my mouth,
  And the solace of my lips could lessen
  your pain.

Job Laments His Situation

6"If I speak, my pain is not lessened,
  And if I hold back, what has left me?
7"But now He has[R]exhausted me; Job 7:3
  Thou hast laid waste all my company.

8"And Thou hast shriveled me up,
^RIt has become a witness;   Job 10:17
And my leanness rises up against me,
It testifies to my face.
9"His anger has torn me and^Thunted me
down,   *borne a grudge against me*
He has gnashed at me with His teeth;
My adversary glares at me.
10"They have ^Rgaped at me with their
mouth,   Ps. 22:13
They have ^Tslapped^R me on the cheek
with contempt;   *struck* • Is. 50:6
They have ^Rmassed themselves against
me.   Job 30:12; Ps. 35:15
11"God hands me over to ruffians,
And tosses me into the hands of the
wicked.
12"I was at ease, but He shattered me,
And He has grasped me by the neck
and shaken me to pieces;
He has also set me up as His target.
13"His^Rarrows surround me.
Without mercy He splits my kidneys
open;   Job 6:4; 19:12; 25:3
He pours out my gall on the ground.
14"He^Rbreaks through me with breach after breach;   Job 9:17
He^Rruns at me like a warrior.   Joel 2:7

Job Defends His Innocence

15"I have sewed sackcloth over my skin,
And^Rthrust my horn in the dust. Ps. 7:5
16"My face is flushed from weeping,
And deep darkness is on my eyelids,
17 Although there is no^Rviolence in my
hands,   Is. 59:6; Jon. 3:8
And^Rmy prayer is pure.   Job 27:4

18"O earth, do not cover my blood,
And let there be no *resting* place for
my cry.
19"Even now, behold, ^Rmy witness is in
heaven,   Gen. 31:50; Job 19:25-27
And my^Aadvocate is on high.   *witness*
20"My friends are my scoffers;
My eye^Aweeps to God.   *drips*
21"O that a man might plead with God
As a man with his neighbor!
22"For when a few years are past,
I shall go the way^Tof no return. Job 3:13

CHAPTER 17

God Makes Job a Byword

"MY spirit is broken, my days are extinguished,
The^Tgrave is *ready* for me.   *graves*
2"Surely^Rmockers are with me,
And my eye ^Tgazes on their provocation.   Job 12:4; 17:6 • *lodges*

3"Lay down, now, a pledge^Rfor me with
Thyself;   Ps. 119:122; Is. 38:14

Who is there that will^Tbe my guarantor?   *strike hands with me*
4"For Thou hast^Tkept^Rtheir heart from understanding;   *hidden* • Job 12:20
Therefore Thou wilt not exalt *them.*
5"He who^Rinforms against friends for a
share *of the spoil,*   Lev. 19:13, 16
The^Reyes of his children also shall languish.   Job 11:20

6"But He has made me a^Rbyword of the
people,   Job 17:2
And I am one at whom men spit.
7"My eye has also grown^Rdim because of
grief,   Job 16:16
And all my members are as a shadow.
8"The upright shall be appalled at this,
And the^Rinnocent shall stir up himself
against the godless.   Job 22:19
9"Nevertheless^Rthe righteous shall hold
to his way,   Prov. 4:18
And^Rhe who has clean hands shall grow
stronger and stronger. Job 22:30; 31:7
10"But come again all of you now,
For I ^Rdo not find a wise man among
you.   Job 12:2
11"My ^Rdays are past, my plans are torn
apart,   Job 7:6
Even the wishes of my heart.
12"They make night into day, *saying,*
'The light is near,' in the presence of
darkness.
13"If I look for^RSheol as my home, Job 3:13
I make my bed in the darkness;
14 If I call to the pit, 'You are my father';
To the^Rworm, 'my mother and my sister';   Job 21:26; 25:6
15 Where now is^Rmy hope?   Job 7:6
And who regards my hope?
16"Will it go down with me to Sheol?
Shall we together ^Rgo down into the
dust?"   Job 3:17; 21:33

CHAPTER 18

Bildad's Second Speech

THEN Bildad the Shuhite responded,
2"How long will you hunt for words?
Show understanding and then we can
talk.
3"Why are we^Rregarded as beasts,
As stupid in your eyes?   Ps. 73:22
4"O ^Tyou who tear yourself in your anger—   *he ... tears himself ... his*
For your sake is the earth to be abandoned,
Or the rock to be moved from its
place?

5"Indeed, the ^Rlight of the wicked goes
out,   Job 21:17; Prov. 13:9; 20:20; 24:20
And the flame of his fire gives no light.

6"The light in his tent is darkened,
   And his lamp goes out above him.
7"His vigorous stride is shortened,
   And his own scheme brings him down.
8"For he is ^Rthrown into the net by his
   own feet,   Job 22:10; Ps. 9:15; 35:8
   And he steps on the webbing.
9"A snare seizes *him* by the heel,
   And a trap snaps shut on him.
10"A noose for him is hidden in the
   ground,
   And a trap for him on the path.
11"All around terrors frighten him,
   And^Rharry him at every step.   Job 18:18
12"His strength is^Rfamished,   Is. 8:21
   And calamity is ready at his side.
13"His skin is devoured by disease,
   The first-born of death ^Rdevours his
   ^Alimbs.   Zech. 14:12 • *parts*
14"He is torn from the security of his tent,
   And^Athey march him before the king of
   terrors.   *you or she shall march*
15"There dwells in his tent nothing of his;
   ^RBrimstone is scattered on his habitation.   Ps. 11:6
16"His^Rroots are dried below,   Is. 5:24
   And his branch is cut off above.
17"Memory^R of him perishes from the
   earth,   Job 24:20; [Ps. 34:16]; Prov. 10:7
   And he has no name abroad.
18"He is driven from light into darkness,
   And chased from the inhabited world.
19"He has no^Roffspring or posterity among
   his people,   Job 27:14, 15; Is. 14:22
   Nor any survivor where he sojourned.
20"Those ^Tin the west are appalled at his
   ^Tfate,   *who come after • day*
   And those^Tin the east are seized with
   horror.   *who have gone before*
21"Surely such are the^Rdwellings of the
   wicked,   Job 21:28
   And this is the place of him who does
   not know God."

CHAPTER 19

Job's Response to Bildad

T HEN Job^Tresponded,   *answered and said*
2"How long will you torment^Tme, *my soul*
   And crush me with words?
3"These ten times you have insulted me,
   You are not ashamed to wrong me.
4"Even if I have truly erred,
   My error lodges with me.
5"If indeed you^Rvaunt yourselves against
   me,   Ps. 35:26; 38:16; 55:12, 13
   And prove my disgrace to me,
6 Know then that God has wronged me,
   And has closed His net around me.

7"Behold, ^RI cry, 'Violence!' but I get no
   answer;   Job 9:24; 30:20, 24; Hab. 1:2

I shout for help, but there is no justice.
8"He has^Rwalled up my way so that I cannot pass;   Job 3:23; Lam 3:7, 9
   And He has put darkness on my paths.
9"He has stripped my honor from me,
   And removed the crown from my head.
10"He^Rbreaks me down on every side, and
   I am gone;   Job 12:14
   And He has uprooted my^Rhope^Rlike a
   tree.   Job 7:6 • Job 24:20
11"He has also^Rkindled His anger against
   me,   Job 16:9
   And considered me as His enemy.
12"His^Rtroops come together,   Job 16:13
   And build up their way against me,
   And camp around my tent.

13"He has^Rremoved my brothers far from
   me,   Job 16:7; Ps. 69:8
   And my ^Racquaintances are completely
   estranged from me. Job 16:20; Ps. 88:8
14"My relatives have failed,
   And my^Rintimate friends have forgotten me.   Job 19:19
15"Those who live in my house and my
   maids consider me a stranger.
   I am a foreigner in their sight.
16"I call to my servant, but he does not
   answer,
   I have to implore him with my mouth.
17"My breath is offensive to my wife,
   And I am loathsome to my own brothers.
18"Even young children despise me;
   I rise up and they speak against me.
19"All my^Rassociates abhor me,   Ps. 38:11
   And those I love have turned against
   me.
20"My ^Rbone clings to my skin and my
   flesh,   Job 16:8; 33:21; Ps. 102:5; Lam. 4:8
   And I have escaped *only* by the skin of
   my teeth.
21"Pity me, pity me, O you my friends,
   For the hand of God has struck me.
22"Why do you persecute me as God *does*,
   And are not satisfied with my flesh?

23"Oh that my words were written!
   Oh that they were inscribed in a book!
24"That with an iron stylus and lead
   They were engraved in the rock forever!
25"And as for me, I know that my ^RRe-
   deemer lives,   *Vindicator, defender*
   And ^Aat the last He will take His stand
   on the^Tearth.   *as the Last • dust*
26"Even after my skin is destroyed,
   Yet from my flesh I shall see God;
27 Whom I^Tmyself shall behold, *on my side*
   And whom my eyes shall see and not
   another.
   My^Theart faints within me.   *kidneys*
28"If you say, 'How shall we ^Rpersecute
   him?'   Job 19:22

And 'What pretext for a case against him can we find?'

29 *Then* be afraid of [R]the sword for yourselves,   Job 15:22
For wrath *brings* the punishment of the
sword,
So that you may know [R]there is judgment." Job 22:4; Ps. 1:5; 9:7; [Eccl. 12:14]

CHAPTER 20

Zophar's Second Speech

T HEN Zophar the Naamathite answered,
2 "Therefore my disquieting thoughts
make me respond,   *return*
Even because of my inward agitation.
3 "I listened to [R]the reproof which insults
me,   Job 19:3
And the spirit of my understanding
makes me answer.
4 "Do you know this from [R]of old,   Job 8:8
From the establishment of man on
earth,
5 That the [R]triumphing of the wicked is
short,   Job 8:12, 13; Ps. 37:35, 36
And the joy of the godless momentary?
6 "Though his loftiness [T]reaches [R]the heavens,   *goes up to* • Is. 14:13, 14
And his head touches the clouds,
7 He perishes forever like his refuse;
Those who have seen him [R]will say,
'Where is he?'   Job 7:10; 8:18
8 "He flies away like a [R]dream, and they
cannot find him;   Ps. 73:20; 90:5
Even like a vision of the night he is
[R]chased away.   Job 18:18; 27:21-23
9 "The [R]eye which saw him sees him no
more,   Job 7:8; 8:18
And his place no longer beholds him.
10 "His sons [R]favor the poor,   *seek the favor of*
And his hands give back his wealth.
11 "His bones are full of his youthful vigor,
But it lies down with him in the dust.

12 "Though evil is sweet in his mouth,
And he hides it under his tongue,
13 *Though* he [T]desires it and will not let it
go,   *has compassion on*
But holds it in his [T]mouth,   *palate*
14 *Yet* his food in his stomach is changed
To the venom of cobras within him.
15 "He swallows riches,
But will [R]vomit them up; Job 20:10, 20, 21
God will expel them from his belly.
16 "He sucks the poison of cobras;
The viper's tongue slays him.
17 "He does not look at [R]the streams,
The rivers flowing with honey and
curds.   Job 29:6
18 "He returns what he has attained
And cannot swallow *it;*
As to the riches of his trading,
He cannot even enjoy *them.*
19 "For he has [R]oppressed *and* forsaken the
poor;   Job 24:2-4; 35:9

He has seized a house which he has not
built.

20 "Because he knew no quiet within him
He does not retain anything he desires.
21 "Nothing remains for him to devour,
Therefore [R]his prosperity does not endure.   Job 15:29
22 "In the fulness of his plenty he will be
cramped;
The [R]hand of everyone who suffers will
come *against* him.   Job 5:5
23 "When he [R]fills his belly,   Job 20:13, 14
God will send His fierce anger on him
And will [R]rain *it* on him [R]while he is eating.   Num. 11:18-20, 33 • *as his food*
24 "He may flee from the iron weapon,
But the bronze bow will pierce him.
25 "It is drawn forth and comes out of his
back,
Even the glittering point from his gall.
[R]Terrors come upon him,   Job 18:11, 14
26 Complete [R]darkness is held in reserve
for his treasures,   Job 18:18
And unfanned fire will devour him;
It will consume the survivor in his tent.
27 "The heavens will reveal his iniquity,
And the earth will rise up against him.
28 "The increase of his house will depart;
His possessions will flow away [R]in the
day of His anger.   Job 20:15; 21:30
29 "This is the wicked man's [R]portion from
God,   Job 27:13; 31:2, 3
Even the heritage decreed to him by
God."

CHAPTER 21

Job's Response to Zophar

T HEN Job [T]answered,   *answered and said*
2 "Listen carefully to my speech,
And let this be your *way of* consolation.
3 "Bear with me that I may speak;
Then after I have spoken, you may
[R]mock.   Job 11:3; 17:2
4 "As for me, is my complaint to man?
And why should I not be impatient?
5 "Look at me, and be astonished,
And put *your* hand over *your* mouth.
6 "Even when I remember, I am disturbed,
And horror takes hold of my flesh.
7 "Why [R]do the wicked *still* live,   Job 9:24
Continue on, also become very [R]power-
ful?   Job 12:19
8 "Their [T]descendants [R]are established with
them in their sight,   *seed* • Ps. 17:14
And their offspring before their eyes,
9 Their houses are safe from fear,
Neither is the rod of God on them.
10 "His ox mates without fail;
His cow calves and does not abort.
11 "They send forth their little ones like the
flock,

And their children skip about.
12"They sing to the timbrel and harp
And rejoice at the sound of the flute.
13"They spend their days in prosperity,
And suddenly they go down to Sheol.
14"And they say to God, 'Depart from us!
We do not even desire the knowledge
of Thy ways.
15 'Who^T is the Almighty, that we should
serve Him,   *What* • Heb., *Shaddai*
And what would we gain if we entreat
Him?'   Job 22:17; 34:9
16"Behold, their prosperity is not in their
hand;
The counsel of the wicked is far from
me.   Job 22:18

17"How often is the lamp of the wicked
put out,   Job 18:5, 6
Or *does* their calamity fall on them?
Does God apportion destruction in His
anger?   *He*
18"Are they as straw before the wind,
And like chaff which the storm carries
away?   Ps. 1:4; 35:5; Is. 17:13; Hos. 13:3
19"*You* say, 'God stores away a man's iniquity for his sons.'   [Ex. 20:5] • *his*
Let God repay him so that he may
know *it*.   *Him*
20"Let his own eyes see his decay,
And let him drink of the wrath of the
Almighty.   Rev. 14:10 • Heb., *Shaddai*
21"For what does he care for his household [6]after him,
When the number of his months is cut
off?
22"Can anyone teach God knowledge,
In that He judges those on high?
23"One dies in his full strength,   Job 20:11
Being wholly at ease and satisfied;
24 His sides are filled out with fat,
And the marrow of his bones is moist,
25 While another dies with a bitter soul,
Never even tasting *anything* good.
26"Together they lie down in the dust,
And worms cover them.   Job 24:20

27"Behold, I know your thoughts,
And the plans by which you would
wrong me.
28"For you say, 'Where is the house of the
nobleman,   Job 1:3; 31:37
And where is the tent, the dwelling
places of the wicked?'   Job 8:22
29"Have you not asked wayfaring men,
And do you not recognize their witness?   *signs*
30"For the wicked is reserved for the day
of calamity;   Job 20:29; [Prov. 16:4]
They will be led forth at the day of
fury.   Job 21:17, 20; 40:11
31"Who will confront him with his actions,   *declare his way to his face*
And who will repay him for what he
has done?

32"While he is carried to the grave,
Men will keep watch over *his* tomb.
33"The clods of the valley will gently cover him;   Job 3:22; 17:16 • *be sweet to him*
Moreover, all men will follow after
him,   Job 3:19; 24:24 • *draw*
While countless ones go before him.
34"How then will you vainly comfort me,
For your answers remain *full of* falsehood?"   *faithlessness*

CHAPTER 22

Eliphaz's Third Speech

THEN Eliphaz the Temanite responded,
2"Can a vigorous man be of use to God,
Or a wise man be useful to himself?
3"Is there any pleasure to the Almighty if
you are righteous,   Heb., *Shaddai*
Or profit if you make your ways perfect?
4"Is it because of your reverence that He
reproves you,   *fear*
That He enters into judgment against
you?   Job 14:3; 19:29
5"Is not your wickedness great,   Job 11:6
And your iniquities without end?
6"For you have taken pledges of your
brothers without cause,   Ex. 22:26
And stripped men naked.   Job 31:19, 20
7"To the weary you have given no water
to drink,   Job 31:16, 17
And from the hungry you have withheld bread.   Job 31:31
8"But the earth belongs to the mighty
man,   Job 9:24 • Job 12:19
And the honorable man dwells in it.
9"You have sent widows away empty,
And the strength of the orphans has
been crushed.   *arms* • Job 6:27
10"Therefore snares surround you,   Job 18:8
And sudden dread terrifies you,
11 Or darkness, so that you cannot see,
And an abundance of water covers
you.   Job 38:34; Ps. 69:2; 124:5; Lam. 3:54

12"Is not God *in* the height of heaven?
Look also at the distant stars, how high
they are!   *head, top-most*
13"And you say, 'What does God know?
Can He judge through the thick darkness?
14 'Clouds are a hiding place for Him, so
that He cannot see;   Job 26:9
And He walks on the vault of heaven.'
15"Will you keep to the ancient path
Which wicked men have trod,   Job 34:36
16 Who were snatched away before their
time,   Job 15:32; 21:13, 18
Whose foundations were washed away
by a river?   Is. 28:2 • *poured out*
17"They said to God, 'Depart from us!'
And 'What can the Almighty do to
them?'   Heb., *Shaddai*

[6] I.e., after he dies

18"Yet He ^Rfilled their houses with good things;   Job 12:6
But ^Rthe counsel of the wicked is far from me.   Job 21:16
19"The ^Rrighteous see and are glad,   Ps. 52:6
And the innocent mock them,
20 *Saying,* 'Truly our adversaries are cut off,
And their ^Aabundance ^Rthe fire has consumed.'   *excess* • Job 15:30

21"Yield now and be at peace with Him;
Thereby good will come to you.

22"Please receive ^A instruction ^R from His mouth,   *law* • Job 16:10; 23:12; Prov. 2:6
And establish His words in your heart.

23"If you ^Rreturn to ^tthe Almighty, you will be restored;   Job 8:5 • Heb., *Shaddai*
If you ^Rremove unrighteousness far from your tent,   Job 11:14
24 And place *your* gold in the dust,   *ore*
And *the gold of* Ophir among the stones of the brooks,
25 Then the Almighty will be your gold
And choice silver to you.
26"For then you will ^Rdelight in ^tthe Almighty,   Ps. 37:4 • Heb., *Shaddai*
And lift up your face to God.
27"You will ^Rpray to Him, and ^RHe will hear you;   Job 11:13; 33:26•Job 34:28
And you will pay your vows.
28"You will also decree a thing, and it will be established for you;
And light will shine on your ways.
29"When you are cast down, you will speak with confidence
And the humble person He will save.
30"He will deliver one who is not innocent,
And he will be ^Rdelivered through the cleanness of your hands."   Job 42:7, 8

CHAPTER 23

Job Will Come Forth as Gold

THEN Job ^Treplied,   *answered and said*
2"Even today my complaint is rebellion;
His hand is heavy despite my groaning.
3"Oh that I knew where I might find Him,
That I might come to His seat!

4"I would present *my* case before Him
And fill my mouth with arguments.
5"I would learn the words *which* He would ^Tanswer,   *answer me*
And perceive what He would say to me.
6"Would He contend with me by ^Rthe greatness of *His* power?   Job 9:4
No, surely He would pay attention to me.
7"There the upright would ^Rreason with Him;   Job 13:3
And I ^Awould be delivered forever from my Judge.   *bring forth my justice forever*

8"Behold, I go forward but He is not *there,*
And backward, but I ^Rcannot perceive Him;   Job 9:11; 35:14
9 When He acts on the left, I cannot behold *Him;*
He turns on the right, I cannot see Him.
10"But He knows the way I take;
When He has ^Rtried me, I shall come forth as gold.   [Job 7:18; Ps. 7:9; 11:5]
11"My foot has held fast to His path;
I have kept His way and not turned aside.
12"I have not departed from the command of His lips;
I have treasured the words of His mouth more than my necessary food.
13"But He is unique and who can turn Him?
And *what* His soul desires, that He does.
14"For He performs what is appointed for me,
And many such *decrees* are with Him.
15"Therefore, I would be dismayed at His presence;
When I consider, I am terrified of Him.
16"*It is* God *who* has made my heart faint,
And the Almighty *who* has dismayed me,
17 But I am not silenced by the darkness,
Nor deep gloom *which* covers *me.*

CHAPTER 24

God Seems Indifferent to the Wicked

"WHY^R are times not stored up by the Almighty,   [Acts 1:7]

22:22 Memorizing God's Word—You are not always able to study the Bible by reading it. If you have memorized a portion of the Word of God, you are able to gain insights into its meaning at times when a Bible is not readily available. The Bible recognizes the importance of Scripture memorization. The following benefits can be cited:
a. It keeps the child of God from sinning (Page 591—Ps. 119:11)
b. It provides comfort in times of trouble (Page 532—Ps. 11:52, 92).
c. It stays your mind upon God (Page 550—Ps. 43:3).
d. It provides daily sustenance for the spiritual life (Page 177—Deut. 8:3).
e. It provides continual and ready guidance in all the situations of life (Page 613—Prov. 6:20–23).
f. It provides the basis for formal and informal instruction of your children (Page 175—Deut. 6:6, 7).
Now turn to Page 206—Josh. 1:8: Meditating upon God's Word.

And why do those who know Him not
see[R]His days?   [Is. 2:12]; Jer. 46:10
2"Some[T] remove the landmarks;   *They*
They seize and [A]devour flocks.   *pasture*
3"They drive away the donkeys of the orphans;   Job 6:27
They take the widow's ox for a pledge.
4"They push [R]the needy aside from the
road;   Job 24:14; 29:16; 30:25; 31:19
The[R]poor of the land are made to hide
themselves altogether.   Job 29:12
5"Behold, as[R]wild donkeys in the wilderness   Job 39:5-8
They[R]go forth seeking food in their activity,   Ps. 104:23
As[T]bread for *their* children in the desert.   *his bread*
6"They harvest their fodder in the field,
And they glean the vineyard of the
wicked.
7"They[R] spend the night naked, without
clothing,   Ex. 22:26; Job 22:6
And have no covering against the cold.
8"They are wet with the mountain rains,
And they hug the rock for want of a
shelter.
9"Others[T] snatch the [R]orphan from the
breast,   *They* • Job 6:27
And against the poor they take a
pledge.
10"They cause *the poor* to go about naked
without clothing,
And they take away the sheaves from
the hungry.
11"Within the walls they produce oil;
They tread wine presses but thirst.
12"From the city men groan,
And the souls of the wounded cry out;
Yet God does not pay attention to folly.

13"Others[T]have been with those who rebel
against the light;   *They*
They do not want to know its ways,
Nor abide in its paths.
14"The murderer[R]arises at dawn;   Mic. 2:1
He[R]kills the poor and the needy, Ps. 10:8
And at night he is as a thief.
15"And the eye of the[A]adulterer waits for
the twilight,   Prov. 7:9
Saying, 'No eye will see me.'
And he disguises his face.
16"In the dark they dig into houses,
They[R]shut themselves up by day;
They do not know the light.   [John 3:20]
17"For the morning is the same to him as
thick darkness,
For he is familiar with the[R]terrors of
thick darkness.   Job 15:21

18"They are[A]insignificant[R]on the surface of
the water;   *light* or *swift* •Job 22:11
Their portion is cursed on the earth.
They do not turn toward the vineyards.
19"Drought and heat [A]consume[R] the snow
waters,   *seize* • Job 6:16, 17

So *does* Sheol *those who* have sinned.
20"A[T]mother will forget him;   *womb*
The[R]worm feeds sweetly till he is remembered no more.   Job 21:26
And wickedness will be broken[R]like a
tree.   Job 19:10; Dan. 4:14
21"He wrongs the barren woman,
And does no good for the widow.
22"But He drags off the valiant by[R]His
power;   Job 9:4
He rises, but[R]no one has assurance of
life.   Job 18:20
23"He provides them[R]with security, and
they are supported;   Job 12:6
And His eyes are on their ways.
24"They are exalted a[R]little while, then
they are gone;   Ps. 37:10
Moreover, they are[R]brought low and
like everything gathered up;
Even like the heads of grain they are
cut off.   Job 14:21
25"Now if it is not so,[R]who can prove me a
liar,   Job 6:28; 27:4
And make my speech worthless?"

CHAPTER 25

Bildad's Third Speech

THEN Bildad the Shuhite answered,
2"Dominion and awe belong to Him
Who establishes peace in His heights.
3"Is there any number to His troops?
And upon whom does His light not
rise?
4"How then can a man be just with God?
Or how can he be[R]clean who is born of
woman?   Job 14:4
5"If even the moon has no brightness
And the stars are not pure in His sight,
6 How much less man, *that* maggot,
And the son of man, *that* worm!"

CHAPTER 26

Job's Response to Bildad

THEN Job[T]responded,   *responded and said*
2"What a help you are to the weak!
How you have saved the arm[R]without
strength!   Ps. 71:9
3"What counsel you have given to *one*
without wisdom!
What helpful insight you have abundantly provided!   *made known*
4"To whom have you uttered words?
And whose [T]spirit was expressed
through you?   *breath has gone forth*

5"The[R]departed spirits tremble   Job 3:13
Under the waters and their inhabitants.
6"Naked is Sheol before Him
And [7]Abaddon has no covering.

---

[7] I.e., place of destruction

7"He ᴿstretches out the north over empty
  space,   Job 9:8
And hangs the earth on nothing.
8"He wraps up the waters in His clouds;
And the cloud does not burst under
  them.
9"He obscures the face of the full moon,
And spreads His cloud over it.
10"He has inscribed a ᶜcircle on the surface
  of the waters,   [Job 38:1-11]; Prov. 8:29
At the boundary of light and darkness.
11"The pillars of heaven tremble,
And are amazed at His rebuke.
12"He quieted the sea with His power,
And by His ᴿunderstanding He shat-
  teredᴿRahab.   Job 12:13•Job 9:13
13"By His breath the heavens are cleared;
His hand has pierced ᵗthe fleeing serpent.   Is. 27:1
14"Behold, these are the fringes of His
  ways;
And how faint a word we hear of Him!
But His mightyᵗthunder, who can understand?"   Job 36:29; 37:4, 5

CHAPTER 27

Job Affirms His Righteousness

THEN Job ᴬcontinued his ᴿdiscourse and
said,   *again took up* •Job 13:12; 29:1
2"As God lives, ᴿwho has taken away my
  right,   Job 16:11; 34:5
And the Almighty,ᴿwho has embittered
  my soul,   Job 9:18
3 For as long asᵀlife is in me,   *breath*
And the breath of God is in my nostrils,
4 My lips certainly will not speak unjustly,
Nor will my tongue mutter deceit.
5"Far be it from me that I should declare
  you right;
Till I dieᴿI will not put away my integrity from me.   Job 6:29
6"Iᴿhold fast my righteousness and will
  not let it go.   Job 2:3; 13:18
My heart does not reproach any of my
  days.

7"May my enemy be as the wicked,
And my opponent as the unjust.
8"For what is the hope of the godless
  ᴬwhen he is cut off,   *though he gains*
When God requires hisᵀlife?   *soul*
9"Will Godᴴhear his cry,   Job 35:12, 13
When distress comes upon him?
10"Will he take delight in the Almighty,
Will he call on God at all times?
11"I will instruct you in the power of God;
What is with the Almighty I will not
  conceal.
12"Behold, all of you have seen *it*;
Why then do you act foolishly?

13"This is ᴿthe portion of a wicked man
  from God,   Job 20:29
And the inheritance *which*ᵀtyrants receive from the Almighty.   Job 15:20

14"Though his sons are many, they are
  destinedᴿfor the sword;   Job. 15:22
And his ᴿdescendants will not be satisfied with bread.   Job 20:10
15"His survivors will be buried because of
  the plague,
And ᴬtheir widows will not be able to
  weep.   Heb., *his*
16"Though he piles up silver like dust,
And prepares garments as *plentiful as*
  the clay;
17 He may prepare *it*,ᴿbut the just will
  wear *it*,   Job 20:18-21
And the innocent will divide the silver.
18"He has built his house like the ᴬspider's
  web,   Heb., *moth*
Or as a hut *which* the watchman has
  made.
19"He lies down rich, but never again;
He opens his eyes, and it is no more.
20"Terrors overtake him like a flood;
A tempest steals him away ᴿin the
  night.   Job 20:8; 34:20
21"The east ᴿwind carries him away, and
  he is gone,   Job 21:18
For it whirls him away from his place.
22"For it will hurl at him without sparing;
He ᵀwill surely try to ᴿflee from its
  ᵀpower.   Job 11:20 • *hand*
23"*Men* will clap their hands at him,
And will hiss him from his place.

CHAPTER 28

Job Observes That Man
Cannot Discover Wisdom

"SURELY there is a ⁸mine for silver,
And a place where they refine gold.
2"Iron is taken from the dust,
And from rock copper is smelted.
3"*Man* puts an end to darkness,
And ᴿto the farthest limit he searches
  out   Eccl. 1:13
The rock in gloom and deep shadow.
4"He ᵀsinks a shaft far from habitation,
Forgotten by the foot;   *breaks open*
They hang and swing to and fro far
  from men.
5"The earth, from it comes food,
And underneath it is turned up as fire.
6"Its rocks are the ᴬsource of sapphires,
And its dust *contains* gold.   *place*
7"The path no bird of prey knows,
Nor has the falcon's eye caught sight of
  it.
8"The proud beasts have not trodden it,
Nor has the *fierce* lion passed over it.
9"He puts his hand on the flint;
He ᵀoverturns the mountains at the
  ᵀbase.   *roots*
10"He hews out channels through the
  rocks;
And his eye sees anything precious.

⁸ Or, *source*

11"He dams up the streams from flowing;
And what is hidden he brings out to the
light.

12"But where can wisdom be found?
And where is the place of understanding?
13"Man does not know its value,
Nor is it found in the land of the living.
14"The deep says, 'It is not in me';
And the sea says, 'It is not with me.'
15"Pure^R gold cannot be given in exchange
for it,   Prov. 3:13, 14; 8:10, 11; 16:16
Nor can silver be weighed as its price.
16"It cannot be valued in the gold of
Ophir,
In precious onyx, or sapphire.
17"Gold^R or glass cannot equal it,   Prov. 8:10
Nor can it be exchanged for articles of
fine gold.
18"Coral and crystal are not to be mentioned;
And the acquisition of ^R wisdom is above
that of pearls.   Prov. 8:11
19"The topaz of Ethiopia cannot equal it,
Nor can it be valued in pure gold.
20"Where then does wisdom come from?
And where is the place of understanding?
21"Thus it is hidden from the eyes of all
living,
And concealed from the birds of the
sky.
22"^9Abaddon^R and Death say,   Job 26:6
'With our ears we have heard a report
of it.'

23"God^R understands its way;   Job 9:4
And He knows its place.
24"For He looks to the ends of the earth,
And sees everything under the heavens.
25"When He imparted weight to the wind,
And meted out the waters by measure,
26 When He set a limit for the rain,
And a course for the thunderbolt,
27 Then He saw it and declared it;
He established it and also searched it
out.
28"And to man He said, 'Behold, the^R fear
of the Lord, that is wisdom;
And to depart from evil is understanding.'"   [Ps. 111:10]

CHAPTER 29

Job Remembers His Happy Past

A ND Job again took up his^R discourse and
said,   Num. 23:7; 24:3; Job 13:12; 27:1
2"Oh that I were as in months gone by,

As in the days when God^R watched over
me;   Jer. 31:28
3 When His lamp shone over my head,
And ^R by His light I walked through
darkness;   Job 11:17
4 As I was in ^10 the prime of my days,
When the ^T friendship of God *was* over
my tent;   *counsel*
5 When the Almighty was yet with me,
And my children were around me;
6 When my steps were bathed in butter,
And the ^R rock poured out for me
streams of oil!   Deut. 32:13; Ps. 81:16
7"When I went out to the gate of the city,
When I took my seat in the square;
8 The young men saw me and hid themselves,
And the old men arose *and* stood.
9"The princes ^R stopped talking,   Job 29:21
And put *their* hands on their mouths;
10 The voice of the nobles was hushed,
And their tongue stuck to their palate.
11"For when ^R the ear heard, it called me
blessed;   Job 4:3, 4
And when the eye saw, it gave witness
of me,
12 Because I delivered ^R the poor who cried
for help,   Job 24:4, 9; 34:28; [Prov. 21:13]
And the orphan who had no helper.
13"The blessing of the one ^R ready to perish
came upon me,   Job 31:19
And I made the ^R widow's heart sing for
joy.   Job 22:9
14"I ^R put on righteousness, and it clothed
me;   Job 27:5, 6; Ps. 132:9; Is. 59:17; 61:10
My justice was like a robe and a turban.
15"I was ^R eyes to the blind,   Num. 10:31
And feet to the lame.
16"I was a father to ^R the needy,   Prov. 29:7
And I investigated the case which I did
not know.
17"And I broke the jaws of the wicked,
And snatched the prey from his teeth.
18"Then I thought, 'I shall die in my nest,
And I shall multiply *my* days as the
sand.
19 'My root is spread out to the waters,
And dew lies all night on my branch.
20 'My glory is *ever* new with me,
And my bow is renewed in my hand.'
21"To me ^R they listened and waited, Job 4:3
And kept silent for my counsel.
22"After my words they did not ^R speak
again,   Job 29:10
And my speech dropped on them.
23"And they waited for me as for the rain,
And opened their mouth as for the
spring rain.
24"I smiled on them when they did not believe,
And the light of my face they did not
cast down.
25"I chose a way for them and sat as chief,
And dwelt as a king among the troops,
As one who comforted the mourners.

^9 I.e., Destruction   ^10 Lit., *the days of my autumn*

CHAPTER 30

*Job Describes His Present
Humiliation*

"**B**UT_R now those younger than I
mock me,　　　　　Job 12:4
Whose fathers I disdained to put with
the dogs of my flock.

2"Indeed, what *good was* the strength of
their hands to me?
Vigor had perished from them.

3"From want and famine they are gaunt
Who gnaw the dry ground by night in
waste and desolation,

4 Who pluck ¹¹mallow by the bushes,
And whose food is the root of the
broom shrub.

5"They are driven from the community;
They shout against them as *against* a
thief,

6 So that they dwell in dreadful valleys,
In holes of the earth and of the rocks.

7"Among the bushes they ^cry out;　*bray*
Under the nettles they are gathered together.

8"Fools, even those without a name,
They were scourged from the land.

9"And now I have become their taunt,
I have even become a byword to them.

10"They abhor me *and* stand aloof from
me,
And they do not ᵀrefrain from spitting
at my face.　*withhold spit from my face*

11"Because ^He has loosed His ^bowstring
and afflicted me,　　*they · cord*
They have cast off ᴿthe bridle before
me.　　　　　Ps. 32:9

12"On the right hand their brood arises;
They ᵀthrust aside my feet ᴿand build up
against me their ways of destruction.　　Ps. 140:4, 5 • Job 19:12

13"They ᴿbreak up my path,　　Is. 3:12
They profit ᵀfrom my destruction,　*for*
No one restrains them.

14"As *through* a wide breach they come,
ᵀAmid the tempest they roll on.　*Under*

15"Terrors ᴿare turned against me,　Job 3:25
They pursue my honor as the wind,
And my ^prosperity has passed away
ᴿlike a cloud.　　*welfare* • Hos. 13:3

16"And now ᴿmy soul is poured out ᵀwithin
me; 1 Sam. 1:15; Job 3:24; Is. 53:12 • *upon*
Days of affliction have seized me.

17"At night it pierces my bones within me,
And my gnawing *pains* take no rest.

18"By a great force my garment is ᴿdis-
torted;　　　　　Job 2:7
It binds me about as the collar of my
coat.

19"He has cast me into the ᴿmire,　Ps. 69:2
And I have become like dust and ashes.

20"I ᴿcry out to Thee for help, but Thou
dost not answer me;　　Job 19:7
I stand up, and Thou dost turn Thy attention against me.

21"Thou hast become cruel to me;
With the might of Thy hand Thou dost
ᴿpersecute me.　Job 10:3; 16:9, 14; 19:6

22"Thou dost ᴿlift me up to the wind *and*
cause me to ride;　　Job 9:17; 27:21
And Thou dost dissolve me in a storm.

23"For I know that Thou ᴿwilt bring me to
death　　　　Job 9:22; 10:8
And to the ᴿhouse of meeting for all living.　　　Job 3:19; Eccl. 12:5

24"Yet does not one in a heap of ruins
stretch out *his* hand,
Or in his disaster therefore ᴿcry out for
help?　　　　　Job 19:7

25"Have I not ᴿwept for the ᵀone whose life
is hard?　　Ps. 35:13, 14 • *hard of day*
Was not my soul grieved for ᴿthe
needy?　　　　　Job 24:4

26"When I expected good, then evil came;
When I waited for light, ᴿthen darkness
came.　　　　　Job 19:8

27"I am seething within, and cannot relax;
Days of affliction confront me.

28"I go about mourning without comfort;
I stand up in the assembly *and* ᴿcry out
for help.　　　　　Job 19:7

29"I have become a brother to jackals,
And a companion of ostriches.

30"My skin turns black on me,　*from upon*
And my bones burn with ᵀfever.　*heat*

31"Therefore my ᴿharp ᵀis turned to mourning,　　　　Is. 24:8 • *becomes*
And my flute to the sound of those who
weep.

CHAPTER 31

Innocent of Sensual Sins

"**I** HAVE made a covenant with my eyes;
How then could I gaze at a virgin?

2"And what is the portion of God from
above
Or the heritage of the Almighty from
on high?

3"Is it not ᴿcalamity to the unjust, Job 18:12
And disaster to ᴿthose who work iniquity?　　　　　Job 34:22

4"Does He not ᴿsee my ways,　2 Chr. 16:9
And ᴿnumber all my steps?　　Job 14:16

5"If I have walked with falsehood,
And my foot has hastened after deceit,

6 Let Him ᴿweigh me with ^accurate
scales,　　　Job 6:2, 3 • *just*
And let God know my integrity.

7"If my step has turned from the way,
Or my heart followed my eyes,
Or if any spot has stuck to my hands,

8 Let me ᵀsow and another eat,　Lev. 26:16
And let my ^crops be uprooted. *offspring*

9"If my heart has been ᴿenticed by a
woman,　　　　Job 24:15; 31:1

¹¹ I.e., plant of the salt marshes

Or I have lurked at my neighbor's
doorway,
10 May my wife^Rgrind for another, Is. 47:2
And let others kneel down over her.
11 "For that would be a lustful crime;
Moreover, it would be^Ran iniquity *punishable by* judges.   Job 31:28
12 "For it would be fire that consumes to
^TAbaddon,   place of destruction
And would uproot all my increase.

Innocent of Abusing His Power

13 "If I have^Rdespised the claim of my male
or female slaves   [Deut. 24:14, 15]
When they filed a complaint against
me,
14 What then could I do when God arises,
And when He calls me to account,
what will I answer Him?
15 "Did not^RHe who made me in the womb
make him,   Job 10:3
And the same one fashion us in the
womb?
16 "If I have kept^Rthe poor from *their* desire,   Job 5:16; 20:19
Or have caused the eyes of^Rthe widow
to fail,   [Ex. 22:22–24]; Job 22:9
17 Or have eaten my morsel alone,
And the orphan has not shared it
18 (But from my youth he grew up with
me as with a father,
And from infancy I guided her),
19 If I have seen anyone perish^Rfor lack of
clothing,   Job 22:6; 29:13
Or that the needy had no covering,
20 If his loins have not ^Tthanked me,
And if he has not been warmed with
the fleece of my sheep,   *blessed*
21 If I have lifted up my hand against^Tthe
orphan,   Job 29:12; 31:17
Because I saw ^TI had support ^Rin the
gate,   *my help* · Job 29:7
22 Let my shoulder fall from the socket,
And my arm be broken off ^Tat the elbow.   *from the bone of the upper arm*
23 "For ^Rcalamity from God is a terror to
me,   Job 31:3
And because of^RHis ^Tmajesty I can do
nothing.   Job 13:11 · *exaltation*

Innocent of Trusting in His Wealth

24 "If I have put my confidence *in* gold,
And called fine gold my trust,
25 If I have ^Rgloated because my wealth
was great,   Job 1:3, 10; Ps. 62:10
And because my hand had secured *so*
much;
26 If I have ^Rlooked at the sun when it
shone,   Deut. 4:19; 17:3; Ezek. 8:16
Or the moon going in splendor,
27 And my heart became secretly enticed,
And my hand ^Tthrew a kiss from my
mouth,   *kissed my mouth*

28 That too would have been an iniquity
calling for^Tjudgment,   *judges*
For I would have denied God above.

Innocent of Not Caring for His Enemies

29 "Have I^Rrejoiced at the extinction of my
enemy,   [Prov. 17:5]; 24:17; Obad. 12
Or exulted when evil befell him?
30 "No, I have not allowed my mouth to sin
By asking for his life in^Ra curse. Job 5:3
31 "Have the men of my tent not said,
'Who can ^Tfind one who has not been
satisfied with his meat'?   *give*
32 "The alien has not lodged outside,
For I have opened my doors to the
traveler.
33 "Have I^Rcovered my transgressions like
^AAdam,   [Prov. 28:13] · *mankind*
By hiding my iniquity in my bosom,
34 Because I feared the great multitude,
And the contempt of families terrified
me,
And kept silent and did not go out of
doors?

Job Pleads to Meet God
and Defend Himself

35 "Oh that I had one to hear me!
Behold, here is my ^Tsignature;   *mark*
^RLet the Almighty answer me!   Job 19:7
And the indictment which my^Radversary has written,   Job 27:7
36 Surely I would carry it on my shoulder;
I would bind it to myself like a crown.
37 "I would declare to Him^Rthe number of
my steps;   Job 31:4
Like a prince I would approach Him.

38 "If my land cries out against me,
And its furrows weep together;
39 If I have eaten its fruit without money,
Or have caused its owners to lose their
lives,   *the soul of its owners to expire*
40 Let briars grow instead of wheat,
And stinkweed instead of barley."
The words of Job are ended.

CHAPTER 32

Elihu Intervenes in the Debate

THEN these three men ceased answering
Job, because he was ^Rrighteous in his own
eyes.   Job 10:7; 13:18; 27:5, 6; 31:6
2 But the anger of Elihu the son of Barachel the Buzite, of the family of Ram
burned; against Job his anger burned, because he justified himself before God.
3 And his anger burned against his three
friends because they had found no answer,
and yet had condemned Job.
4 Now Elihu had waited to speak to Job
because they were years older than he.
5 And when Elihu saw that there was no
answer in the mouth of the three men his
anger burned.

6 So Elihu the son of Barachel the Buzite
 ^Tspoke out and said,   *answered*
 "I am young in years and you are old;
   Therefore I was shy and afraid to tell
   you ^Twhat I think.   *my knowledge*
7 "I ^Tthought age should speak,   *said*
   And ^Tincreased years should teach wisdom.   *many*
8 "But it is a spirit in man,
   And the ^Rbreath of the Almighty gives
   them understanding.   [Job 33:4]
9 "The ^Aabundant *in years* may not be
   wise,   *nobles*
   Nor may elders understand justice.
10 "So I ^Asay, 'Listen to me,   *said*
   I too will tell what I think.'

11 "Behold, I waited for your words,
   I listened to your reasonings,
   While you pondered what to say.
12 "I even paid close attention to you,
   ^TIndeed, there was no one who refuted
   Job,   *Behold*
   Not one of you who answered his
   words.
13 "Do ^Tnot say,   *Lest you say*
   'We ^Rhave found wisdom;   [Jer. 9:23]
   God will ^Trout him, not man.' *drive away*
14 "For he has not arranged *his* words
   against me;
   Nor will I reply to him with your ^Targu-
   ments.   *words*

15 "They are dismayed, they answer no
   more;
   Words have failed them.
16 "And shall I wait, because they do not
   speak,
   Because they ^Tstop *and* answer no
   more?   *stand*
17 "I too will answer my share,
   I also will tell my opinion.
18 "For I am full of words;
   The spirit within me constrains me.
19 "Behold, my belly is like unvented wine,
   Like new wineskins it is about to burst.
20 "Let me speak that I may get relief;
   Let me open my lips and answer.
21 "Let me now ^Rbe partial to no one;
   Nor flatter *any* man.   Job 13:8
22 "For I do not know how to flatter,
   Else my Maker would soon take me
   away.

CHAPTER 33

Elihu Challenges Job to Debate

"HOWEVER now, Job, please ^Rhear my
   speech,   Job 13:6
   And listen to all my words.
2 "Behold now, I open my mouth,
   My tongue in my ^Tmouth speaks. *palate*
3 "My words are *from* the uprightness of
   my heart;
   And my lips speak ^Rknowledge sincerely.   Job 6:28; 27:4; 36:4
4 "The Spirit of God has made me,

And the ^Rbreath of ^Tthe Almighty gives
   me life.   Job 27:3 • Heb., *Shaddai*
5 "Refute ^Rme if you can;   Job 33:32
   Array yourselves before me, take your
   stand.
6 "Behold, I belong to God like you;
   I too have been formed out of the clay.
7 "Behold, ^Rno fear of me should terrify
   you,   Job 13:21
   Nor should my pressure weigh heavily
   on you.

Elihu Quotes Job's Complaints

8 "Surely you have spoken in my hearing,
   And I have heard the sound of *your*
   words:
9 'I am ^Rpure, without transgression;
   I am innocent and there ^Ris no guilt in
   me.   Job 9:21 • Job 10:14
10 'Behold, He ^Tinvents pretexts against
   me;   *finds*
   He ^Rcounts me as His enemy. Job 13:24
11 'He ^Rputs my feet in the stocks; Job 13:27
   He watches all my paths.'

Elihu Answers Job's Complaints

12 "Behold, let me ^Ttell you, ^Ryou are not
   right in this,   *answer* • Eccl. 7:20
   For God is greater than man.
13 "Why do you complain against Him,
   That He does not give an account of all
   His doings?
14 "Indeed ^RGod speaks once, Job 33:29; 40:5
   Or twice, *yet* no one notices it.
15 "In a dream, a vision of the night,
   When sound sleep falls on men,
   While they slumber in their beds,
16 Then He opens the ears of men,
   And seals their instruction,
17 That He may turn man aside *from his*
   conduct,
   And ^Tkeep man from pride;   *hide*
18 He keeps back his soul from the pit,
   And his life from passing over into
   Sheol.

19 "Man ^Tis also chastened with ^Rpain on his
   bed,   *He* • Job 30:17
   And with unceasing complaint in his
   bones;
20 So that his life ^Rloathes bread,   Job 3:24
   And his soul favorite food.
21 "His flesh wastes away from sight,
   And his ^Rbones which were not seen
   stick out.   Job 19:20; Ps. 22:17; 102:5
22 "Then his soul draws near to the pit,
   And his life to those who bring death.

23 "If there is an angel *as* mediator for him,
   One out of a thousand,
   To remind a man what is right for him,
24 Then let him be gracious to him, and
   say,

'Deliver him from [R]going down to the
pit,   Job 33:18, 28; Is. 38:17
I have found a [R]ransom';   Ps. 49:7
25 Let his flesh become fresher than in
youth,
Let him return to the days of his youthful vigor;
26 Then he will [R]pray to God, and He will
accept him,   Job 22:27; 34:28; Ps. 50:14
That he may see His face with joy,
And He may restore His righteousness
to man.
27"He will sing to men and say,
'I [R]have sinned and perverted what is
right,   [2 Sam. 12:13; Luke 15:21]
And it is not [R]proper for me.   [Rom. 6:21]
28 'He has redeemed my soul from going
to the pit,
And my life shall see the light.'

29"Behold, God does [R]all these [T]oftentimes
with men,   Eph. 1:11 • twice, three times
30 To bring back his soul from the pit,
That he may be enlightened with the
light of life.
31"Pay attention, O Job, listen to me;
Keep silent and let me speak.
32"*Then* if [T]you have anything to say, answer me;   *there are words*
Speak, for I desire to justify you.
33"If not, [R]listen to me;   Ps. 34:11
Keep silent, and I will teach you wisdom."

CHAPTER 34

Elihu Challenges Job
to Debate Again

THEN Elihu continued and said,
2"Hear my words, you wise men,
And listen to me, you who know.
3"For [R]the ear tests words,   Job 12:11
As the palate tastes food.
4"Let us choose for ourselves what is
right;
Let us know among ourselves what is
good.

Elihu Quotes Job's Complaints

5"For Job has said, 'I am righteous,
But God has taken away my right;
6 Should I lie concerning my right?
My [T]wound is incurable, *though I am*
without transgression.'   *arrow*
7"What man is like Job,
Who drinks up derision like water,
8 Who goes [R]in company with the workers of iniquity,   Job 22:15
And walks with wicked men?
9"For he has said, 'It [R]profits a man nothing   Job 21:15; 35:3; Ps. 50:18
When he is pleased with God.'

Elihu Answers Job's Complaints

10"Therefore, listen to me, you men of understanding.
Far be it from God to do wickedness,
And from the Almighty to do wrong.
11"For He pays a man according to [R]his
work,   Matt. 16:27; Rom. 2:6; [Rev. 22:12]
And makes [T]him find it according to his
way.   *a man*
12"Surely, God will not act wickedly,
And the Almighty will not pervert justice.
13"Who [R]gave Him authority over the
earth?   [Job 38:4]
And who [R]has laid *on Him* the whole
world?   Job 38:5
14"If He should determine to do so,
If He should [R]gather to Himself His
spirit and His breath,   Job 12:10
15 All flesh would perish together,
And man would [R]return to dust. Job 10:9

16"But if *you have* understanding, hear
this;
Listen to the sound of my words.
17"Shall [R]one who hates justice rule?
And [R]will you condemn a righteous
mighty one,   Job 34:30 • Job 40:8
18 Who says to a king, 'Worthless one,'
To nobles, 'Wicked ones';
19 Who shows no partiality to princes,
Nor regards the rich above the poor,
For they all are the work of His hands?
20"In a moment they die, and at midnight
People are shaken and pass away,
And [R]the mighty are taken away without a hand.   Job 12:19

21"For [R]His eyes are upon the ways of a
man,   Job 24:23; 31:4; [Prov. 5:21; 15:3]
And He sees all his steps.
22"There is no darkness or deep shadow
Where the workers of iniquity may
hide themselves.
23"For He does not [R]*need to* consider a
man further,   Job 11:11
That he should go before God in judgment.
24"He breaks in pieces [R]mighty men without inquiry,   Job 12:19
And sets others in their place.
25"Therefore He [R]knows their works,
And He overthrows *them* in the night,
And they are crushed.   Job 34:11
26"He [R]strikes them like the wicked Ps. 9:5
In a public place,
27 Because they [R]turned aside from following Him,   1 Sam. 15:11
And had no regard for any of His ways;
28 So that they caused [T]the cry of the poor
to come to Him,   Job 35:9; James 5:4
And that He might [R]hear the cry of the
afflicted—   [Ex. 22:23]; Job 22:27
29 When He keeps quiet, who then can
condemn?
And when He hides His face, who then
can behold Him,

That is, in regard to both nation and
man?—
30 So that godless men should not rule,
Nor be snares of the people.

31"For has anyone said to God,
'I have borne *chastisement;*
I will not offend *anymore;*
32 Teach Thou me what I do not see;
If I have ^Rdone iniquity,   Job 33:27
I will do it no more'?
33"Shall He recompense on your terms,
because you have rejected *it?*
For you must choose, and not I;
Therefore declare what you know.
34"Men of understanding will say to me,
And a wise man who hears me,
35 'Job speaks without knowledge,
And his words are without wisdom.
36 'Job ought to be tried to the limit,
Because he answers like wicked men.
37 'For he adds^Rrebellion to his sin; Job 23:2
He^Rclaps his hands among us, Job 27:23
And multiplies his words against
God.'"

CHAPTER 35

Elihu's Third Rebuttal

THEN Elihu continued and said,
2"Do you think this is according to ^Rjus-
tice?   Job 27:2
Do you say, 'My righteousness is more
than God's'?
3"For you say, 'What^Radvantage will it be
to You?   Job 34:9
^RWhat profit shall I have, more than if I
had sinned?'   Job 9:30, 31
4"I will answer you,
And your friends with you.
5"Look^Rat the heavens and see; Gen. 15:5
And behold ^Rthe clouds—they are
higher than you.   [Job 22:12]
6"If you have sinned, ^Rwhat do you accomplish against Him?   Job 7:20
And if your transgressions are many,
what do you do to Him?
7"If you are righteous, ^Rwhat do you give
to Him?   Prov. 9:12; [Luke 17:10]
Or what does He receive from your
hand?
8"Your wickedness is for a man like
yourself,
And your righteousness is for a son of
man.

9"Because of the ^Rmultitude of oppressions they cry out;   Ex. 2:23
They cry for help because of the arm^Rof
the mighty.   Job 12:19
10"But ^Rno one says, 'Where is God my
Maker, Job 21:14; 27:10; 36:13; Is. 51:13
Who^Rgives songs in the night, Acts 16:25
11 Who^Rteaches us more than the beasts
of the earth,   Job 36:22; Ps. 94:12

And makes us wiser than the birds of
the heavens?'
12"There^Rthey cry out, but He does not answer   Prov. 1:28
Because of the pride of evil men.
13"Surely^RGod will not listen to ^Aan empty
cry,   Job 27:9; [Prov. 15:29] • *falsehood*
Nor will the Almighty regard it.
14"How much less when ^Ryou say you do
not behold Him,   Job 9:11; 23:8, 9
The^Rcase is before Him, and you must
wait for Him!   Job 31:35
15"And now, because He has not visited *in*
His anger,
Nor has He acknowledged ^Atransgres-
sion well,   *arrogance*
16 So Job opens his mouth ^Temptily; *vainly*
He multiplies words ^Rwithout knowledge."   Job 34:35; 38:2

CHAPTER 36

*Elihu Believes That God
Is Disciplining Job*

THEN Elihu continued and said,
2"Wait for me a little, and I will show you
That there ^Tis yet more to be said in
God's behalf.   *are yet words for God*
3"I will fetch my knowledge from afar,
And I will ascribe^Rrighteousness to my
Maker.   Job 8:3; 37:23
4"For truly ^Rmy words are not false;
One who is ^Rperfect in knowledge is
with you.   Job 33:3 • Job 37:16
5"Behold, God is mighty but does not ^Rde-
spise *any;*   [Ps. 22:24; 69:33]; 102:17
He is ^Rmighty in strength of understanding.   Job 12:13
6"He does not keep the wicked alive,
But gives justice to the afflicted.
7"He does not ^Rwithdraw His eyes from
the righteous;   [Ps. 33:18; 34:15]
But^Rwith kings on the throne Job 5:11
He has seated them forever, and they
are exalted.
8"And if they are bound in fetters,
And are caught in the cords of ^Rafflic-
tion,   Job 36:15, 21
9 Then he declares to them their work
And their transgressions, that they
have magnified themselves.
10"And He opens their ear to instruction,
And ^Rcommands that they return from
evil.   [2 Kin. 17:13]; Job 36:21; Jon. 3:8
11"If they hear and serve *Him,*
They shall end their days in prosperity,
And their years in ^Rpleasures. Ps. 16:11
12"But if they do not hear, they shall ^Tper-
ish by the sword,   *pass away*
And they shall die without knowledge.
13"But the godless in heart lay up anger;
They do not cry for help when He binds
them.
14"They^Adie in youth,   *Their soul dies*
And their life *perishes* among the ^Rcult
prostitutes.   Deut. 23:17

15"He delivers the afflicted in ^Ttheir ^Rafflic-
tion,   *his* • Job 36:8, 21
And ^Ropens their ear ^Ain *time of* oppression.   Job 36:10 • *in adversity*
16"Then indeed, He ^Renticed you from the
mouth of distress,   Hos. 2:14
Instead of it, a broad place with no
constraint;
And that which was set on your table
was full of ^Afatness.   *rich food*

17"But you were full of ^Rjudgment on the
wicked;   Job 22:5, 10, 11
Judgment and justice take hold *of you.*
18"*Beware* lest ^Rwrath entice you to scoffing;   Jon. 4:4, 9
And do not let the greatness of the^Rran-
som turn you aside.   Job 33:24
19"Will your ^Ariches keep *you* from distress,   *cry*
Or all the forces of *your* strength?
20"Do not long for^Rthe night, Job 34:20, 25
When people vanish in their place.
21"Be careful, do^Rnot turn to evil; Job 36:10
For you have preferred this to ^Rafflic-
tion.   Job 36:8, 15; [Heb. 11:25]

*Elihu Reminds Job
of the Greatness of God*

22"Behold, God is exalted in His power;
Who is a^Rteacher like Him?   Job 35:11
23"Who has appointed Him His way,
And who has said, 'Thou^R hast done
wrong'?   [Deut. 32:4]; Job 8:3

24"Remember that you should ^Rexalt His
work,   Ps. 92:5; Rev. 15:3
Of which men have^Rsung.   1 Chr. 16:9
25"All men have seen it;
Man beholds from afar.
26"Behold, God is ^Rexalted, and^Rwe do not
know *Him;*   Job 11:7-9 • 1 Cor. 13:12
The^Rnumber of His years is unsearchable.   Job 10:5; [Ps. 90:2; 102:24, 27]
27"For He draws up the drops of water,
They distill rain from^Tthe mist,   *its*
28 Which the clouds pour down,
They drip upon man abundantly.
29"Can anyone understand the ^Rspreading
of the clouds,   Job 37:11, 16
The thundering of His^Tpavilion? *booth*
30"Behold, He spreads His^Tlightning about
Him,   *light*
And He covers the depths of the sea.
31"For by these He judges peoples;
He^Rgives food in abundance. [Acts 14:17]
32"He covers *His* hands with the lightning,
And commands it to strike the mark.
33"Its^Rnoise declares His presence; Job 37:2
The cattle also, concerning what is
coming up.

CHAPTER 37

"A<small>T</small> this also my heart trembles,
And leaps from its place.

2"Listen closely to the ^Rthunder of His
voice,   Job 36:33; 37:4, 5; Ps. 29:3-9
And the rumbling that goes out from
His mouth.
3"Under the whole heaven He lets it
loose,
And His ^Tlightning to the ^Rends of the
earth.   *light* • Job 28:24; 37:11, 12
4"After it, a voice roars;
He thunders with His majestic voice;
And He does not restrain^Tthe lightnings
when His voice is heard.   *them*
5"God ^Rthunders with His voice wondrously,   Job 26:14
Doing ^Rgreat things which we cannot
comprehend.   Job 5:9; 37:14, 16, 23
6"For to^Rthe snow He says, 'Fall on the
earth,'   Job 38:22
And to the^Tdownpour and the rain, 'Be
strong.' *shower of rain and shower of rains*
7"He seals the hand of every man,
That all men may know His work.
8"Then the beast goes into its^Rlair,
And remains in its^Tden. Job 38:40 • *dens*
9"Out of the south comes the storm,
And out of the north the cold.
10"From the breath of God ice is made,
And the expanse of the waters is frozen.
11"Also with moisture He^Rloads the thick
cloud;   Job 36:27
He disperses the cloud of His lightning.
12"And it changes direction, turning
around by His guidance,
That ^Tit may do whatever He ^Rcom-
mands^Tit   *they* • Job 36:32 • *them*
On the face of the inhabited earth.
13"Whether for ^Tcorrection, ^R or for His
world,   *the rod* • 1 Sam. 12:18, 19
Or for lovingkindness, He causes it to
^Thappen.   *be found*

14"Listen to this, O Job,
Stand and consider the wonders of
God.
15"Do you know how God establishes
them,
And makes the ^Tlightning of His cloud
to shine?   *light*
16"Do you know about the layers of the
thick clouds,
The^Rwonders of one^Rperfect in knowledge,   Job 37:5, 14, 23 • Job 36:4
17 You whose garments are hot,
When the land is still because of the
south wind?
18"Can you, with Him, ^Rspread out the
skies,   Job 9:8; Ps. 104:2; [Is. 45:12]
Strong as a molten mirror? [Jer. 10:12]
19"Teach us what we shall say to Him;
We^Rcannot arrange *our case* because of
darkness.   Job 9:14; [Rom. 8:26]
20"Shall it be told Him that I would speak?
Or should a man say that he would be
swallowed up?

21"And now ᵀmen do not see the light
which is bright in the skies;   *they*
But the wind has passed and cleared
them.

22"Out of the north comes golden *splendor;*
Around God is awesome majesty.

23"The Almighty—we cannot find Him;
He is ᴿexalted in power;   [Job 9:4; 36:5]
And He will not do violence to justice
and abundant righteousness.

24"Therefore men ᴿfear Him;   [Matt. 10:28]
He does not ᴿregard any who are wise
of heart."   [Job 5:13; Matt. 11:25]

CHAPTER 38

*God Questions Job
from the Realm of Creation*

THEN the LORD ᴿanswered Job out of the
whirlwind and said,   Job 40:6

2"Who is this that darkens counsel
By words without knowledge?

3"Now gird up your loins like a man,
And ᴿI will ask you, and you instruct
Me!   Job 42:4

4"Where were you ᴿwhen I laid the foundation of the earth? Job 15:7; Ps. 104:5
Tell *Me,* if you have understanding,

5 Who set its ᴿmeasurements, since you
know?   Prov. 8:29; Is. 40:12
Or who stretched the line on it?

6"On what ᴿwere its bases sunk? Job 26:7
Or who laid its cornerstone,

7 When the morning stars sang together,
And all the ᴿsons of God shouted for
joy?   Job 1:6

8"Or *who* enclosed the sea with doors,
When, bursting forth, it went out from
the womb;

9 When I made a cloud its garment,
And thick darkness its swaddling
band,

10 And I ᴿplaced boundaries on it, Gen. 1:9
And I set a bolt and doors,

11 And I said, 'Thus far you shall come,
but no farther;
And here shall your proud waves stop'?

12"Have you ᴿever in your life commanded
the morning,   *from your days*
And caused the dawn to know its
place;

13 That it might take hold of ᴿthe ends of
the earth,   Job 28:24; 37:3
And the wicked be shaken out of it?

14"It is changed like clay *under* the seal;
And they stand forth like a garment.

15"And ᴿfrom the wicked their light is
withheld,   Job 5:14
And the uplifted arm is broken.

16"Have you entered into ᴿthe springs of
the sea?   Gen. 7:11; 8:2; Prov. 8:24, 28

Or have you walked ᴬin the recesses of
the deep?   *in search of*

17"Have the gates of death been revealed
to you?
Or have you seen the gates of ᴿdeep
darkness?   Job 10:21; 26:6; 34:22

18"Have you understood the ᴬexpanse of
ᴿthe earth?   *width* • Job 28:24
Tell *Me,* if you know all this.

19"Where is the way to the dwelling of
light?
And darkness, where is its place,

20 That you may take it to its territory,
And that you may discern the paths to
its ᵀhome?   *house*

21"You know, for you were born then,
And the number of your days is great!

22"Have you entered the storehouses ᴿof
the snow,   Job 37:6
Or have you seen the storehouses of
the ᴿhail,   Is. 30:30; Ezek. 13:11, 13

23 Which I have reserved for the time of
distress,
For the day of war and battle?

24"Where is the way that ᴿthe light is divided,   Job 26:10
Or the east wind scattered on the
earth?

25"Who has cleft a channel for the flood,
Or a way for the thunderbolt;

26 To bring rain on a land without people,
On a desert without a man in it,

27 To satisfy the waste and desolate land,
And to make the ᴬseeds of grass to
sprout?   *growth*

28"Has ᴿthe rain a father?   Job 36:27, 28
Or who has begotten the drops of dew?

29"From whose womb has come the ice?
And the frost of heaven, who has given
it birth?

30"Water ᵀbecomes hard like stone,
And the surface of the deep is imprisoned.   *hides itself*

31"Can you bind the chains of the
ᴿPleiades,   Job 9:9; Amos 5:8
Or loose the cords of Orion?

32"Can you lead forth a ᶜconstellation in its
season,   *Mazzaroth*
And guide the Bear with her satellites?

33"Do you know the ᴿordinances of the
heavens,   [Ps. 148:6]; Jer. 31:35, 36
Or fix their rule over the earth?

34"Can you lift up your voice to the
clouds,
So that an ᴿabundance of water may
cover you?   Job 22:11; 36:27, 28; 38:37

35"Can you ᴿsend forth lightnings that they
may go   Job 36:32; 37:3
And say to you, 'Here we are'?

36"Who has ᴮput wisdom in the innermost
being,   [Job 9:4; Ps. 51:6; Eccl. 2:26]

Or has given [R]understanding to the
mind?   Job 32:8
37"Who can count the clouds by wisdom,
Or tip the water jars of the heavens,
38 When the dust hardens into a mass,
And the clods stick together?

God Questions Job
from the Realm of Animals

39"Can you hunt the prey for the lion,
Or satisfy the appetite of the young
lions,
40 When they [R]crouch in *their* dens,
And lie in wait in *their* lair?   Job 37:8
41"Who prepares for [R]the raven its nourishment, Ps. 147:9; Matt. 6:26; Luke 12:24
When its young cry to God,
And wander about without food?

CHAPTER 39

"Do you know the time the [T]mountain
goats give birth?   *goats of the rock*
Do you observe the calving of the deer?
2"Can you count the months they fulfill,
Or do you know the time they give
birth?
3"They kneel down, they bring forth their
young,
They get rid of their labor pains.
4"Their offspring become strong, they
grow up in the open field;
They leave and do not return to them.

5"Who sent out the wild donkey free?
And who loosed the bonds of the swift
donkey,
6 To whom I gave [R]the wilderness for a
home,   Job 24:5; Jer. 2:24; Hos. 8:9
And the salt land for his dwelling
place?
7"He scorns the tumult of the city,
The shoutings of the driver he does not
hear.
8"He explores the mountains for his pasture,
And he searches after every green
thing.
9"Will the wild ox consent to serve you?
Or will he spend the night at your manger?
10"Can you bind the wild ox in a furrow
with [T]ropes?   *his rope*
Or will he harrow the valleys after
you?
11"Will you trust him because his strength
is great
And leave your labor to him?
12"Will you have faith in him that he will
return your [T]grain,   *seed*
And gather *it from* your threshing
floor?

13"The ostriches' wings flap joyously
With the pinion and plumage of [12]love,

14 For she abandons her eggs to the earth,
And warms them in the dust,
15 And she forgets that a foot may crush
[T]them,   *it*
Or that a wild beast may trample them.
16"She treats her young [R]cruelly, as if *they*
were not hers;   Lam. 4:3
Though her labor be in vain, *she* is [T]un-
concerned;   *without fear*
17 Because God has made her forget wisdom,
And has not given her a share of understanding.
18"When she lifts herself [A]on high,   *to flee*
She laughs at the horse and his rider.

19"Do you give the horse *his* might?
Do you clothe his neck with a mane?
20"Do you make him leap like the locust?
His majestic snorting is terrible.
21"He paws in the valley, and rejoices in
his strength;
He goes out to meet the weapons.
22"He laughs at fear and is not dismayed;
And he does not turn back from the
sword.
23"The quiver rattles against him,
The flashing spear and javelin.
24"With shaking and rage he [A]races over
the ground;   *swallows up*
And he does not stand still at the voice
of the trumpet.
25"As often as the trumpet *sounds* he
says, 'Aha!'
And he scents the battle from afar,
And thunder of the captains, and the
war cry.

26"Is it by your understanding that the
hawk soars,
Stretching his wings toward the south?
27"Is it at your [T]command that the eagle
mounts up,   *mouth*
And makes [R]his nest on high?   Jer. 49:16
28"On the cliff he dwells and lodges,
Upon the rocky crag, an inaccessible
place.
29"From there he [R]spies out food;   Job 9:26
His eyes see *it* from afar.
30"His young ones also suck up blood;
And where the slain are, there is he."

CHAPTER 40

God Demands an Answer
to His Questions

THEN the LORD said to Job,
2"Will the faultfinder [R]contend with the
Almighty?   Job 9:3; 10:2; 33:13; Is. 45:9
Let him who reproves God answer it."

Job's First Answer to God

3 Then Job answered the LORD and said,
4"Behold, I am insignificant; what can I
reply to Thee?
I [R]lay my hand on my mouth.   Job 21:5

[12] Or, *a stork*

5"Once I have spoken, and[R]I will not an-
    swer;   Job 9:3, 15
Even twice, and I will add no more."

God Tells Job to Save Himself

6 Then the[R]LORD answered Job out of the
storm, and said,   Job 38:1
7"Now gird up your loins like a man;
    I will ask you, and you instruct Me.
8"Will you really annul My judgment?
    Will you[R]condemn Me that you may be
    justified? Job 10:3, 7; 16:11; 19:6; 27:2
9"Or do you have an arm like God,
    And can you[R]thunder with a voice like
    His?   Job 37:5; Ps. 29:3

10"Adorn[R]yourself with eminence and dig-
    nity;   Ps. 93:1; 104:1
    And clothe yourself with honor and
    majesty.
11"Pour out[R]the overflowings of your an-
    ger;   Is. 42:25; [Nah. 1:6, 8]
    And look on everyone who is [R]proud,
    and make him low. Is. 2:12; Dan. 4:37
12"Look on everyone who is proud, *and*
    [R]humble him; 1 Sam. 2:7; [Is. 2:12; 13:11]
    And[tread down the wicked [where they
    stand.   Is. 63:3 • *under them*
13"Hide them in the dust together;
    Bind them in the hidden *place.*
14"Then I will also [confess to you,
    That your own right hand can save
    you.   *praise you*

God Compares the Power of Job
with That of the Behemoth

15"Behold now, [13]Behemoth, which I
    made[as well as you;   *with*
    He eats grass like an ox.
16"Behold now, his strength in his loins,
    And his power in the muscles of his
    belly.
17"He bends his tail like a cedar;
    The sinews of his thighs are knit to-
    gether.
18"His[bones are tubes of bronze;
    His[limbs are like bars of iron.   *bones*

19"He is the first of the ways of God;
    Let his maker bring near his sword.
20"Surely the mountains[R]bring him food,
    And all the beasts of the field play
    there.   Ps. 104:14
21"Under the lotus plants he lies down,
    In the covert of the reeds and the
    marsh.
22"The lotus plants cover him with shade;
    The willows of the brook surround
    him.
23"If a river rages, he is not alarmed;
    He is confident, though the [R]Jordan
    rushes to his mouth.   Gen. 13:10
24"Can anyone capture him [when he is on
    watch,   *in his eyes*

With [barbs can anyone pierce *his*
nose?   *snares*

CHAPTER 41

God Compares the Power of Job
with That of the Leviathan

"CAN you draw out [14]Leviathan[R] with a
    fishhook?   Job 3:8; Ps. 74:14; 104:26
    Or press down his tongue with a cord?
2"Can you put a rope in his nose? Is. 37:29
    Or pierce his jaw with a hook?
3"Will he make many supplications to
    you?
    Or will he speak to you soft words?
4"Will he make a covenant with you?
    Will you take him for a servant for-
    ever?
5"Will you play with him as with a bird?
    Or will you bind him for your maidens?
6"Will the traders bargain over him?
    Will they divide him among the mer-
    chants?
7"Can you fill his skin with harpoons,
    Or his head with fishing spears?
8"Lay your hand on him;
    Remember the battle;[you will not do it
    again!   *do not add*
9"Behold, your expectation is false; *his*
    Will you be laid low even at the sight
    of him?   *he*
10"No one is so fierce that he dares to
    arouse him;   Job 3:8
    Who then is he that can stand before
    Me?
11"Who has [given[R]to Me that I should re-
    pay *him*?   *anticipated* • Rom. 11:35
    Whatever is[under the whole heaven is
    Mine. Ex. 19:5; [Job 9:5-10; 26:6-14]

12"I will not keep silence concerning his
    limbs,
    Or his mighty strength, or his [orderly
    frame.   *graceful*
13"Who can strip off his outer armor?
    Who can come within his double mail?
14"Who can open the doors of his face?
    Around his teeth there is terror.
15"*His* strong scales are *his* pride,
    Shut up *as with* a tight seal.
16"One is so near to another,
    That no air can come between them.
17"They are joined one to another;
    They clasp each other and cannot be
    separated.
18"His sneezes flash forth light,
    And his eyes are like the[R]eyelids of the
    morning.   Job 3:9
19"Out of his mouth go burning torches;
    Sparks of fire leap forth.
20"Out of his nostrils smoke goes forth,
    As *from* a boiling pot and *burning*
    rushes.
21"His breath kindles coals,
    And a flame goes forth from his mouth.

[13] Or, the hippopotamus   [14] Or, the crocodile

22"In his neck lodges strength,
And dismay leaps before him.
23"The folds of his flesh are joined together,
Firm on him and immovable.
24"His heart is as hard as a stone;
Even as hard as a lower millstone.
25"When he raises himself up, the ^mighty
fear;   *gods*
Because of the crashing they are bewildered.
26"The sword that reaches him cannot
avail;
Nor the spear, the dart, or the javelin.
27"He regards iron as straw,
Bronze as rotten wood.
28"The arrow cannot make him flee;
Slingstones are turned into stubble for
him.
29"Clubs are regarded as stubble;
He laughs at the rattling of the javelin.
30"His underparts are *like* sharp pot-
sherds;
He ^spreads out *like* a threshing sledge
on the mire.   *moves across*
31"He makes the depths boil like a pot;
He makes the sea like a jar of ointment.
32"Behind him he makes a wake to shine;
One would think the deep to be gray-
haired.
33"Nothing on ^Tearth is like him,   *dust*
One made without fear.
34"He looks on everything that is high;
He is king over all the sons of pride."

CHAPTER 42

Job Confesses Lack of Understanding

THEN Job answered the LORD, and said,
2"I know that Thou canst do all things,
And that no purpose of Thine can be
thwarted.
3 'Who is this that ^Rhides counsel without
knowledge?'   Job 38:2
"Therefore I have declared that which I
did not understand,
Things ^Rtoo wonderful for me, which I
did not know." [Ps. 40:5; 131:1; 139:6]

Job Repents of His Rebellion

4 'Hear, now, and I will speak;
I will ^Lask Thee, and do Thou instruct
me.'   Job 38:3; 40:7

5"I have ^Rheard of Thee by the hearing of
the ear;   Job 26:14; [Rom. 10:17]
But now my ^Reye sees Thee;   [Eph. 1:17]
6 Therefore I retract,
And I repent in dust and ashes."

*The Deliverance of Job
and His Friends*

7 And it came about after the LORD had
spoken these words to Job, that the LORD
said to Eliphaz the Temanite, "My wrath is
kindled against you and against your two
friends, because you have not spoken of Me
what is right as My servant Job has.
8"Now therefore, take for yourselves
seven bulls and seven rams, and go to My
servant Job, and offer up a burnt offering
for yourselves, and My servant Job will pray
for you. For I will ^Taccept him so that I may
not do with you *according to your* folly, because you have not spoken of Me what is
right, as My servant Job has."   *lift up his face*
9 So Eliphaz the Temanite and Bildad
the Shuhite *and* Zophar the Naamathite
went and did as the LORD told them; and the
LORD ^Taccepted Job.   *lifted up the face of*

10 And the LORD restored the fortunes of
Job when he prayed for his friends, and the
LORD increased all that Job had twofold.
11 Then all his brothers, and all his sisters, and all who had known him before,
came to him, and they ate bread with him in
his house; and they consoled him and comforted him for all the evil that the LORD had
brought on him. And each one gave him one
piece of money, and each a ring of gold.
12 And the LORD blessed the latter *days*
of Job more than his beginning, and he had
14,000 sheep, and 6,000 camels, and 1,000
yoke of oxen, and 1,000 female donkeys.
13 And ^Rhe had seven sons and three
daughters.   Job 1:2
14 And he named the first Jemimah, and
the second Keziah, and the third Keren-
happuch.
15 And in all the land no women were
found so fair as Job's daughters; and their
father gave them inheritance among their
brothers.
16 And after this Job lived 140 years,
and saw his sons, and his grandsons, four
generations.
17 ^RAnd Job died, an old man and full of
days.   Gen. 15:15; 25:8; Job 5:26

THE PSALMS

THE BOOK OF PSALMS

The Book of Psalms is the largest and perhaps most widely used book in the Bible. It explores the full range of human experience in a very personal and practical way. Its 150 "songs" run from the Creation through the patriarchal, theocratic, monarchical, exilic, and postexilic periods. The tremendous breadth of subject matter in the Psalms includes diverse topics such as jubilation, war, peace, worship, judgment, messianic prophecy, praise, and lament. The Psalms were set to the accompaniment of stringed instuments and served as the temple hymnbook and devotional guide for the Jewish people.

The Book of Psalms was gradually collected and originally unnamed, perhaps due to the great variety of material. It came to be known as *Sepher Tehillim*—"Book of Praises"— because almost every psalm contains some note of praise to God. The Septuagint uses the Greek word *Psalmoi* as its title for this book, meaning poems sung to the accompaniment of musical instruments. It also calls it the *Psalterium* (a collection of songs), and this word is the basis for the term *Psalter*. The Latin title is *Liber Psalmorum*, "Book of Psalms."

THE AUTHOR OF PSALMS

Although critics have challenged the historical accuracy of the superscriptions regarding authorship, the evidence is strongly in their favor. Almost half (seventy-three) of the psalms are designated as Davidic: 3—9; 11—32; 34—41; 51—65; 68—70; 86; 101; 103; 108—110; 122; 124; 131; 133; and 138—145. David's wide experience as shepherd, musician, warrior, and king (1011-971 B.C.) is reflected in these psalms. The New Testament reveals that the anonymous psalms 2 and 95 were also written by this king whose name means "Beloved of Yahweh," (Acts 4:25; Heb. 4:7). In addition to the seventy-five by David, twelve were by Asaph, "Collector," a priest who headed the service of music (50; 73—83; Ezra 2:41); ten were by the sons of Korah, "Bald," a guild of singers and composers (42; 44—49; 84; 85; 87; Num. 26:9-11); two were by Solomon, "Peaceful," Israel's most powerful king (72; 127); one was by Moses, "Son of the Water," a prince, herdsman, and deliverer (90); one was by Heman, "Faithful," a wise man (88; 1 Kin. 4:31; 1 Chr. 15:19); and one was by Ethan, "Enduring," a wise man (89; 1 Kin. 4:31, 1 Chr. 15:19). The remaining fifty psalms are anonymous: 1; 2; 10; 33; 43; 66; 67; 71; 91—100; 102; 104—107; 111—121; 123; 125; 126; 128—130; 132; 134—137; and 146—150. Some of the anonymous psalms are traditionally attributed to Ezra.

THE TIME OF PSALMS

The psalms cover a wide time span from Moses (c. 1410 B.C.) to the postexilic community under Ezra and Nehemiah (c. 430 B.C.). Because of their broad chronological and thematic range, the psalms were written to different audiences under many conditions. They therefore reflect a multitude of moods and as such are relevant to every reader.

The five books were compiled over several centuries. As individual psalms were written, some were used in Israel's worship. A number of small collections were independently made, like the pilgrimage songs and groups of Davidic psalms (1—41, 51—70, 138—145). These smaller anthologies were gradually collected into the five books. The last stage was the uniting and editing of the five books themselves. David (1 Chr. 15:16), Hezekiah (2 Chr. 29:30; Prov. 25:1), and Ezra (Neh. 8) were involved in various stages of collecting the psalms. David was the originator of the temple liturgy of which his psalms were a part. The superscriptions of thirteen psalms specify key events in his life: First Samuel 19:11 (Ps. 59); 21:11 (Ps. 56); 21:13 (Ps. 34); 22:1 (Ps. 142); 22:9 (Ps. 52); 23:19 (Ps. 54); 24:3 (Ps. 57); Second Samuel 8:13 (Ps. 60); 12:13 (Ps. 51); 15:16 (Ps. 3); 15:23 (Ps. 63); 16:5 (Ps. 7); 22:2-51 (Ps. 18).

Here are four things to remember when interpreting the psalms: (1) When the superscription gives the historical event, the psalm should be interpreted in that light. When it is not given, there is little hope of reconstructing the historical occasion. Assuming occasions will probably hurt more than help the interpretive process. (2) Some of the psalms are associated with definite aspects of Israel's worship (e.g., 5:7; 66:13; 68:24, 25), and this can help in understanding those psalms. (3) Many of the psalms use definite structure and motifs. (4) Many psalms anticipate Israel's Messiah and are fulfilled in Christ. However, care must be taken not to allegorize them and forget the grammatical-historical method of interpretation.

THE CHRIST OF PSALMS

Many of the psalms specifically anticipated the life and ministry of Jesus
Christ, the One who came centuries later as
the promised Messiah ("Anointed One").

There are five different kinds of messianic
psalms: (1) *Typical Messianic*. The subject of
the psalm is in some respects a type of Christ
(see 34:20; 69:4, 9). (2) *Typical Prophetic*. The
psalmist uses language to describe his present
experience, which points beyond his own life
and becomes historically true only in Christ
(see 22). (3) *Indirectly Messianic*. At the time
of composition the psalm refers to a king or the
house of David in general, but awaits final fulfillment in Christ (see 2; 45; 72). (4) *Purely
Prophetic*. Refers solely to Christ without reference to any other son of David (see 110). (5)
Enthronement. Anticipates the coming of
Yahweh and the consummation of His kingdom, and will be fulfilled in the person of
Christ (see 96—99).

Some of the specific messianic prophecies in
the Book of Psalms include:

Prophecy		Fulfillment
2:7	God will declare Him to be His Beloved Son	Matthew 3:17
8:6	All things will be put under His feet	Hebrews 2:8
16:10	He will be resurrected from the dead	Mark 16:6, 7
22:1	God will forsake Him in His hour of need	Matthew 27:46
22:7, 8	He will be scorned and mocked	Luke 23:35
22:16	His hands and feet will be pierced	John 20:25, 27
22:18	Others will gamble for His garments	Matthew 27:35
34:20	Not a bone of Him shall be broken	John 19:32, 33, 36
35:11	He will be accused by false testimony	Mark 14:57
35:19	He will be hated without a cause	John 15:25
40:7, 8	He will come to do God's will	Hebrews 10:7
41:9	He will be betrayed by a friend	Luke 22:47
45:6	His throne will be forever	Hebrews 1:8
68:18	He will ascend to the right hand of God	Mark 16:19
69:9	Zeal for God's house will consume Him	John 2:17
69:21	He will be given wine and gall to drink	Matthew 27:34
109:4	He will pray for His enemies	Luke 23:34
109:8	His betrayer's office will be fulfilled by another	Acts 1:20
110:1	His enemies will be made subject to Him	Matthew 22:44
110:4	He will be a priest like Melchizedek	Hebrews 5:6
118:22	He will be the chief corner stone	Matthew 21:42
118:26	He will come in the name of the Lord	Matthew 21:9

KEYS TO PSALMS

Key Word: Worship—The central
theme of the Book of Psalms is
worship—God is worthy of all praise because
of who He is, what He has done, and what He
will do. His goodness extends through all time
and eternity. The psalms present personal responses to God as they reflect on His program
for His people. There is a keen desire to see His
program fulfilled and His name extolled.
Many of the psalms survey the Word of God
and the attributes of God, especially during
difficult times. This kind of faith produces
confidence in His power in spite of circumstances.

The psalms were used in the two temples
and some were part of the liturgical service.
They also served as an individual and communal devotional guide.

Key Verses: Psalm 19:14; 145:21—"Let the
words of my mouth and the meditation of my
heart be acceptable in Thy sight, O LORD, my
rock and my Redeemer" (19:14).

"My mouth will speak the praise of the
LORD; and all flesh will bless His holy name
forever and ever" (145:21).

Key Chapter: Psalm 100—So many of the favorite chapters of the Bible are contained in
the Book of Psalms that it is difficult to select
the key chapter among such psalms as Psalms
1; 22; 23; 24; 37; 72; 100; 101; 119; 121; and
150. The two central themes of worship and
praise are beautifully wed in Psalm 100.

SURVEY OF PSALMS

The Psalter is really five books in one,
and each book ends with a doxology
(see chart). The last psalm is the closing doxology for Book 5 and for the Psalter as a whole.
After the psalms were written, editorial superscriptions or instructions were added to 116 of
them. These superscriptions are historically
accurate and are even numbered as the first

verses in the Hebrew text. They designate fifty-seven psalms as *mizmor*, "psalm"—a song accompanied by a stringed instrument. Another twenty-nine are called *shir*, "song", and thirteen are called *maskil*, "contemplative poem." Six are called *miktam*, perhaps meaning "epigram" or "inscription poem." Five are termed *tepillah*, "prayer" (see Hab. 3), and only one is called *tehillah*, "praise" (145). In addition to these technical terms, the psalms can be classified according to certain themes: Creation psalms (8; 19), Exodus psalm (78), penitence psalm (6), pilgrimage psalms (120—134), and messianic psalms (see Christ in Psalms). There are even nine acrostic psalms in which the first verse or line begins with the first letter of the Hebrew alphabet, the next begins with the second, and so on (9; 10; 25; 34; 37; 111; 112; 119; 145).

First Chronicles 16:4 supports another approach to classification: "to celebrate and to thank and praise the LORD God of Israel." This leads to three basic types—lament, thanksgiving, and praise psalms. The following classification further divides the psalms into ten types: (1) *Individual Lament Psalms*: Directly addressed to God, these psalms petition Him to rescue and defend an individual. They have these elements: (a) an introduction (usually a cry to God), (b) the lament, (c) a confession of trust in God, (d) the petition, (e) a declaration or vow of praise. Most psalms are of this type (e.g., 3—7; 12; 13; 22; 25—28; 35; 38—40; 42; 43; 51; 54—57; 59; 61; 63; 64; 69—71; 86; 88; 102; 109; 120; 130; 140—143). (2)*Communal Lament Psalms*: The only difference is

that the nation rather than an individual makes the lament (e.g., 44; 60; 74; 79; 80; 83; 85; 90; and 123). (3) *Individual Thanksgiving Psalms*: The psalmist publicly acknowledges God's activity on his behalf. These psalms thank God for something He has already done or express confidence in what He will yet do. They have these elements: (a) a proclamation to praise God, (b) a summary statement, (c) a report of deliverance, and (d) a renewed vow of praise (e.g., 18; 30; 32; 34; 40; 41; 66; 106; 116; and 138). (4) *Communal Thanksgiving Psalms*: In these psalms the acknowledgement is made by the nation rather than an individual (see 124 and 129). (5) *General Praise Psalms*: These psalms are more general than the thanksgiving psalms. The psalmist attempts to magnify the name of God and boast about His greatness (see 8; 19; 29; 103; 104; 139; 148; 150). The joyous exclamation "hallelujah" ("praise the LORD!") is found in several of these psalms. (6) *Descriptive Praise Psalms*: These psalms praise God for His attributes and acts (e.g., 33; 36; 105; 111; 113; 117; 135; 136; 146; 147). (7) *Enthronement Psalms*: These psalms describe Yahweh's sovereign reign over all (see 47; 93; 96—99). Some anticipate the kingdom rule of Christ. (8) *Pilgrimage Songs*: Also known as Songs of Zion, these psalms were sung by pilgrims traveling up to Jerusalem for the three annual religious feasts of Passover, Pentecost, and Tabernacles (see 43; 46; 48; 76; 84; 87; 120—134). (9) *Royal Psalms*: The reigns of the earthly king and the heavenly King are portrayed in most of these psalms (e.g., 2; 18; 20; 21; 45; 72; 89; 101;

BOOK	BOOK I (1–41)	BOOK II (42–72)	BOOK III (73–89)	BOOK IV (90–106)	BOOK V (107–150)
CHIEF AUTHOR	DAVID	DAVID AND KORAH	ASAPH	ANONYMOUS	DAVID AND ANONYMOUS
NUMBER OF PSALMS	41	31	17	17	44
BASIC CONTENT	SONGS OF WORSHIP	HYMNS OF NATIONAL INTEREST		ANTHEMS OF PRAISE	
TOPICAL LIKENESS TO PENTATEUCH	GENESIS: MAN AND CREATION	EXODUS: DELIVERANCE AND REDEMPTION	LEVITICUS: WORSHIP AND SANCTUARY	NUMBERS: WILDERNESS AND WANDERING	DEUTERONOMY: SCRIPTURE AND PRAISE
CLOSING DOXOLOGY	41:13	72:18, 19	89:52	106:48	150:1–6
POSSIBLE COMPILER	DAVID	HEZEKIAH OR JOSIAH		EZRA OR NEHEMIAH	
POSSIBLE DATES OF COMPILATION	C. 1020–970 B.C.	C. 970–610 B.C.		UNTIL C. 430 B.C.	
SPAN OF AUTHORSHIP	ABOUT 1,000 YEARS (C. 1410–430 B.C.)				

110; 132; and 144). (10) *Wisdom and Didactic Psalms:* The reader is exhorted and instructed in the way of righteousness (see 1; 37; 119).

There is a problem with the so-called imprecatory ("to call down a curse") psalms. These psalms invoke divine judgment on one's enemies (see 7; 35; 40; 55; 58; 59; 69; 79; 109; 137; 139; and 144). Although some of them seem unreasonably harsh, a few things should be kept in mind: (1) they call for divine justice rather than human vengeance; (2) they ask for God to punish the wicked and thus vindicate His righteousness; (3) they condemn sin (in Hebrew thinking no sharp distinction exists

between a sinner and his sin); and (4) even Jesus calls down a curse on several cities and tells His disciples to curse cities that do not receive the gospel (Matt. 10:14, 15).

A number of special musical terms (some obscure) are used in the superscriptions of the psalms. "For the choir director" appears in fifty-five psalms indicating that there is a collection of psalms used by the conductor of music in the temple, perhaps for special occasions. "Selah" is used seventy-one times in the psalms and three times in Habakkuk 3. This word may mark a pause, a musical interlude, or a crescendo.

OUTLINE OF PSALMS

Book One: Psalms 1—41

1. Two Ways of Life Contrasted
2. Coronation of the Lord's Anointed
3. Victory in the Face of Defeat
4. Evening Prayer for Deliverance
5. Morning Prayer for Guidance
6. Prayer for God's Mercy
7. Wickedness Justly Rewarded
8. God's Glory and Man's Dominion
9. Praise for Victory over Enemies
10. Petition for God's Judgment
11. God Tests the Sons of Men
12. The Pure Words of the Lord
13. The Prayer for God's Answer—Now
14. The Characteristics of the Godless
15. The Characteristics of the Godly
16. Eternal Life for One Who Trusts
17. "Hide Me in the Shadow of Thy Wings"
18. Thanksgiving for Deliverance by God
19. The Works and Words of God
20. Boast Not in Chariots and Horses but in God's Name
21. Triumph of the King
22. Psalm of the Cross
23. Psalm of the Divine Shepherd
24. Psalm of the King of Glory
25. Acrostic Prayer for Instruction
26. "Examine Me, O LORD, and Try Me"
27. Trust in the Lord and Be Not Afraid
28. Rejoice Because of Answered Prayer
29. The Powerful Voice of God
30. Praise for Dramatic Deliverance
31. "Let Your Heart Take Courage"
32. The Blessedness of Forgiveness
33. God Considers All Man's Works
34. Seek the Lord
35. Petition for God's Intervention
36. The Excellent Lovingkindness of God
37. "Rest in the LORD"
38. The Heavy Burden of Sin
39. Know the Extent of Man's Days
40. Delight to Do God's Will
41. The Blessedness of Helping the Helpless

Book Two: Psalms 42—72

42. Seek After the Lord
43. "Hope in God"
44. Prayer for Deliverance by God
45. The Psalm of the Great King
46. "God Is Our Refuge and Strength"
47. The Lord Shall Subdue All Nations
48. The Praise of Mount Zion
49. Riches Cannot Redeem
50. The Lord Shall Judge All People
51. Confession and Forgiveness of Sin
52. The Lord Shall Judge the Deceitful
53. A Portrait of the Godless
54. The Lord Is Our Helper
55. "Cast Your Burden upon the LORD"
56. Fears in the Midst of Trials
57. Prayers in the Midst of Perils
58. Wicked Judges Will Be Judged
59. Petition for Deliverance from Violent Men
60. A Prayer for Deliverance of the Nation
61. A Prayer When Overwhelmed
62. Wait for God
63. Thirst for God
64. A Prayer for God's Protection
65. God's Provision Through Nature
66. Remember What God Has Done
67. God Shall Govern the Earth
68. God Is the Father of the Fatherless
69. Petition for God to Draw Near
70. Prayer for the Afflicted and Needy
71. Prayer for the Aged
72. The Reign of the Messiah

Book Three: Psalms 73—89

73. The Perspective of Eternity
74. Request for God to Remember His Covenant
75. "God Is the Judge"
76. The Glorious Might of God
77. When Overwhelmed, Remember God's Greatness
78. God's Continued Guidance in Spite of Unbelief

BOOK 1

PSALM 1

Two Ways of Life Contrasted

HOW blessed is the man who does not
walk in the counsel of the wicked,
Nor stand in the ᴬpath of sinners, *way*
Nor ᴿsit in the seat of scoffers! Jer. 15:17
2 But his ᴿdelight is ᴿin the law of the
LORD,   Ps. 119:14, 16, 35 • [Josh. 1:8]
And in His law he meditates ᴿday and
ᴿnight.   Ps. 25:5 • Ps. 63:5, 6
3 And he will be like a tree *firmly*
planted by ᴬstreams of water, *canals*
Which yields its fruit in its season,
And its ᴬleaf does not wither; *foliage*
And in whatever he does, he prospers.

4 The wicked are not so,
But they are like ᴿchaff which the wind
drives away.   Job 21:18; Is. 17:13
5 Therefore ᴿthe wicked will not stand in
the ᴿjudgment,   Ps. 5:5 • Ps. 9:7, 8

Nor sinners in ᴿthe assembly of the
righteous.   Ps. 89:5, 7
6 For the LORD ᴬknows the way of the
righteous,   *approves; or has regard to*
But the way of the wicked will perish.

PSALM 2

Coronation of the Lord's Anointed

WHY are the nations in an uproar,
And the peoples devising a vain thing?
2 The kings of the earth take their stand,
And the rulers take counsel together
ᴿAgainst the LORD and against His
¹Anointed:ᴿ Ps. 74:18, 23 • [John 1:41]☆
3 "Let us ᴿtear their fetters apart,   Jer. 5:5
And cast away their cords from us!"

4 He who ²sits in the heavens laughs,
The Lord ᴿscoffs at them.   Ps. 59:8
5 Then He will speak to them in His ᴿanger   Ps. 21:8, 9; 76:7

¹ Or, *Messiah*   ² Or, *is enthroned*

And[R]terrify them in His fury: Ps. 78:49
6 "But as for Me, I have installed My King
Upon Zion, My holy mountain."

7 "I will surely tell of the [A]decree of the
     LORD: *decree: The LORD said to Me*
He said to Me, 'Thou art My Son,
Today I have[R]begotten Thee. Luke 1:35 ☆
8 'Ask of Me, and I will surely give the
     [A]nations as Thine inheritance,
And the *very*[R]ends of the earth as Thy
     possession.   *Gentiles* • Ps. 67:7
9 'Thou shalt [3]break[R] them with a [A]rod of
     iron,   Ps. 89:23; 110:5 ☆ • *scepter or staff*
Thou shalt [R]shatter them like [T]earthen-
     ware.' "   Ps. 28:5 • *potter's ware*

10 Now therefore, O kings, [R]show discern-
     ment;   Prov. 8:15; 27:11
Take warning, O [4]judges of the earth.
11 Worship the LORD with reverence,
And rejoice with[R]trembling.   Ps. 119:119
12 Do homage to the Son, lest He become
     angry, and you perish *in* the way,
For His wrath may [5]soon be kindled.
How blessed are all who[R]take refuge in
     Him!   [Ps. 5:11; 34:22]

PSALM 3

Victory in the Face of Defeat

A Psalm of David, when he fled from
Absalom his son.

O LORD, how [R]my adversaries have in-
     creased!   2 Sam. 15:12; Ps. 69:4
Many are rising up against me.
2 Many are saying [A]of my soul,   *to*
"There is no deliverance for him in
     God."   [[6]Selah.

3 But Thou, O LORD, art [R]a shield about
     me,   Ps. 5:12; 28:7
My [R]glory, and the One who[R]lifts my
     head.   Ps. 62:7 • Ps. 9:13; 27:6
4 I was crying to the LORD with my
     voice,
And He answered me from His holy
     mountain.   [Selah.
5 [A]I lay down and slept;   *As for me, I*
I awoke, for the LORD sustains me.
6 I will [R]not be afraid of ten thousands of
     people   Ps. 23:4; 27:3
Who have [R]set themselves against me
     round about.   Ps. 118:10-13

7 Arise, O LORD; [R]save me, O my God!
For Thou[A]hast smitten all my enemies
     on the [A]cheek;   Ps. 6:4 • *dost smite* • *jaw*
Thou[A]hast shattered the teeth of the
     wicked.   *dost shatter*
8 Salvation belongs to the LORD;
Thy blessing *be* upon Thy peo-
     ple!   [Selah.

---

[3] Another reading is *rule*   [4] Or, *leaders*
[5] Or, *quickly, suddenly, easily*
[6] *Selah* may mean: *Pause, Crescendo* or *Musical Interlude*
[7] Or, *meditation*

PSALM 4

Evening Prayer for Deliverance

For the choir director; on stringed
instruments.
A Psalm of David.

A NSWER[R] me when [R]I call, O God of my
     righteousness!   Ps. 3:4 • Ps. 18:6
Thou hast relieved me in my distress;
Be gracious to me and hear my prayer.

2 O sons of men, how long will[R]my[A]honor
     become a reproach?   Ps. 3:3 • *glory*
How long will you love what is worth-
     less and aim at deception?   [Selah.
3 But know that the LORD has [R]set apart
     the godly man for Himself;   Ps. 135:4
The LORD hears when I call to Him.

4 Tremble, and do not sin;
Meditate in your heart upon your bed,
     and be still.   [Selah.
5 Offer the sacrifices of righteousness,
And[R]trust in the LORD.   Ps. 37:3, 5; 62:8

6 Many are saying, "Who[R] will show us
     any good?"   Job 7:7; 9:25
[R]Lift up the light of Thy countenance
     upon us, O LORD!   Num. 6:26; Ps. 80:3
7 Thou hast put gladness in my heart,
More than when their grain and new
     wine abound.
8 In peace I will both lie down and sleep,
For Thou alone, O LORD, dost make me
     to[R]dwell in safety. Deut. 12:10; Ps. 16:9

PSALM 5

Morning Prayer for Guidance

For the choir director; for flute
accompaniment.
A Psalm of David.

G IVE[R]ear to my words, O LORD,   Ps. 54:2
Consider my [7]groaning[R].   Ps. 104:34
2 Heed[A]the sound of my cry for help, my
     King and my God,   Ps. 140:6
For to Thee do I pray.
3 In the morning, O LORD,[A]Thou wilt hear
     my voice;   *mayest Thou hear*
In the morning I will order *my* [A]prayer
     to Thee and *eagerly* watch.   *sacrifice*

4 For Thou art not a God[R]who takes plea-
     sure in wickedness;   [Ps. 11:5; 34:16]
No evil [A]dwells with Thee.   *sojourns*
5 The [R]boastful shall not [A]stand before
     Thine eyes;   Ps. 73:3; 75:4 • Ps. 1:5
Thou dost hate all who do iniquity.
6 Thou [R]dost destroy those who speak
     falsehood;   Ps. 52:4, 5
The LORD abhors[R]the man of bloodshed
     and deceit.   Ps. 55:23
7 But as for me, [R]by Thine abundant
     lovingkindness I will enter Thy
     house,   Ps. 69:13
[A]At Thy holy temple I will[R]bow in rever-
     ence for Thee.   *Toward* • Ps. 138:2

8 O Lord,^Rlead me in Thy righteousness
    because of my foes;   Ps. 31:3
    Make Thy way straight before me.
9 There is^Rnothing^Areliable in^Twhat they
    say;   Ps. 52:3 · *true · his mouth*
    Their inward part is destruction *itself*;
    Their^Rthroat is an open grave; Rom. 3:13
    They flatter with their tongue.
10 Hold them guilty, O God;
    By their own devices let them fall!
    In the multitude of their transgressions
      ^Rthrust them out,   Ps. 36:12
    For they are rebellious against Thee.

11 But let all who^Rtake refuge in Thee^Rbe
    glad,   Ps. 2:12 · Ps. 33:1; 64:10
    Let them ever sing for joy;
    And mayest Thou^Rshelter them, Ps. 12:7
    That those who ^Rlove Thy name may
    exult in Thee.   Ps. 69:36
12 For it is Thou who dost^Rbless the right-
    eous man, O Lord,   [Ps. 29:11]
    Thou dost^Rsurround him with favor as
    with a shield.   Ps. 32:7, 10

PSALM 6

Prayer for God's Mercy

For the choir director; with stringed
instruments,
upon an eight-stringed lyre.
A Psalm of David.

O LORD,^Rdo not rebuke me in Thine an-
    ger,   Ps. 38:1; 118:18
    Nor chasten me in Thy wrath.
2 Be gracious to me, O Lord, for I *am*
    ^Rpining away;   Ps. 102:4, 11
    ^RHeal me, O Lord, for^Rmy bones are dis-
    mayed.   Ps. 41:4 · Ps. 22:14; 31:10
3 And my soul is greatly dismayed;
    But Thou, O Lord—how long? Ps. 90:13

4 Return, O Lord, rescue my ⁸soul;
    Save me because of Thy lovingkind-
    ness.
5 For ^Rthere is no ⁹mention of Thee in
    death;   Ps. 88:10–12; 115:17; [Eccl. 9:10]
    In Sheol who will give Thee thanks?

6 I am^Rweary with my sighing;   Ps. 69:3
    Every night I make my bed swim,
    I dissolve my couch with my tears.
7 My eye has wasted away with grief;
    It has become old because of all my ad-
    versaries.

8 ^RDepart from me, all you who do iniq-
    uity,   Ps. 119:115; Matt. 7:23; Luke 13:27
    For the Lord^Rhas heard the voice of my
    weeping.   Ps. 3:4; 28:6
9 The Lord has heard my supplication,
    The Lord^Rreceives my prayer. Ps. 66:19
10 All my enemies shall^Rbe ashamed and
    greatly dismayed;   Ps. 71:13, 24
    They shall turn back, they shall ^Rsud-
    denly be ashamed.   Ps. 73:19

PSALM 7

Wickedness Justly Rewarded

A ¹⁰Shiggaion of David, which he
sang to the Lord
concerning Cush, a Benjamite.

O LORD my God,^Rin Thee I have taken
    refuge;   Ps. 31:1; 71:1
    Save me from all those who pursue me,
    and^Rdeliver me,   Ps. 31:15
2 Lest he tear ^Amy soul like a lion,   *me*
    ^ADragging me away, while there is none
    to deliver.   *Rending it in pieces, while*

3 O Lord my God, if I have done this,
    If there is injustice in my hands,
4 If I have rewarded evil to my friend,
    Or have ^Rplundered him who without
    cause was my adversary, 1 Sam. 24:7
5 Let the enemy pursue ^Amy soul and
    overtake^A*it*;   *me · me*
    And let him trample my life down to
    the ground,
    And lay my glory in the dust.   [Selah.

6 ^RArise, O Lord, in Thine anger;   Ps. 3:7
    ^RLift up Thyself against the^Rrage of my
    adversaries,   Ps. 94:2 · Ps. 138:7
    And^Rarouse Thyself for me; Thou hast
    appointed judgment. Ps. 35:23; 44:23
7 And let the assembly of the^Rpeoples en-
    compass Thee;   Ps. 22:27
    And over them return Thou on high.
8 The Lord^Rjudges the peoples; [Ps. 96:13]
    ^TVindicate^Rme, O Lord, according to my
    righteousness and my integrity that
    is in me.   *Judge* · [Ps. 18:20; 26:1]
9 O let the evil of the wicked come to an
    end, but establish the righteous;
    For the righteous God^Rtries the hearts
    and ¹¹minds.   Ps. 11:4, 5; Jer. 11:20
10 My^Rshield is^Twith God,   Ps. 18:2 · *upon*
    Who saves the upright in heart.
11 God is a^Rrighteous judge,   Ps. 50:6
    And a God who has^Rindignation every
    day.   Ps. 90:9

12 If ^Ta man ^Rdoes not repent, He will
    sharpen His sword;   *he* · Ps. 58:5
    He has ^Rbent His bow and ^Tmade it
    ready.   Ps. 64:7 · *fixed it*
13 He has also prepared ^Afor Himself
    deadly weapons;   *His deadly weapons*
    He makes His arrows fiery shafts.
14 Behold, he travails with wickedness,
    And he^Rconceives mischief, and brings
    forth falsehood.   Job 15:35; Is. 59:4
15 He has dug a pit and hollowed it out,
    And has^Rfallen into the hole which he
    made.   [Job 4:8]; Ps. 57:6
16 His ^Rmischief will return upon his own
    head,   Esth. 9:25; Ps. 140:9

⁸ Or, *life*   ⁹ Or, *remembrance*
¹⁰ I.e., Dithyrambic rhythm, or, wild, passionate song
¹¹ Lit., *kidneys*, figurative for inner man

And his ^Rviolence will descend upon
¹²his own pate.   Ps. 140:11

17 I will give thanks to the LORD ^Raccord-
ing to His righteousness, [Ps. 71:15f.]
And will ^Rsing praise to the name of the
LORD Most High.   Ps. 9:2; 66:1

PSALM 8

God's Glory and Man's Dominion

For the choir director; on the Gittith.
A Psalm of David.

O LORD, our Lord,
How majestic is Thy name in all the
earth,
Who hast ^Adisplayed^R Thy splendor
above the heavens!   *set* • Ps. 57:5
2 ^RFrom the mouth of infants and nursing
babes Thou hast established
^Astrength,   Matt. 21:16☆ • *a bulwark*
Because of Thine adversaries,
To make ^Rthe enemy and the revengeful
cease.   Ps. 44:16

3 When I ^Aconsider^R Thy heavens, the
work of Thy fingers,   *see* • Ps. 111:2
The moon and the stars, which Thou
hast ^Aordained;   *appointed, fixed*
4 What is man, that Thou ^Adost take
thought of him?   *dost remember him*
And the son of man, that Thou dost
care for him?
5 Yet Thou hast made him a little lower
than ^AGod,   *the angels;* Heb., *Elohim*
And ^Rdost crown him with ^Rglory and
majesty!   Ps. 103:4 • Ps. 21:5
6 Thou dost make him to ^Rrule over the
works of Thy hands;   [Gen. 1:26, 28]
Thou hast put all things under his feet,
7 All sheep and oxen,
And also the ^Abeasts of the field, *animals*
8 The birds of the heavens, and the fish
of the sea,
Whatever passes through the paths of
the seas.

9 ^RO LORD, our Lord,
How majestic is Thy name in all the
earth!   Ps. 8:1

PSALM 9

Praise for Victory over Enemies

For the choir director;
on ¹³Muth-labben. A Psalm of David.

I WILL give thanks to the LORD with all
^Rmy heart;   Ps. 86:12
I will tell of all Thy ^Awonders.   *miracles*

2 I will be glad and ^Rexult in Thee; Ps. 5:11
I will ^Rsing praise to Thy name, O^RMost
High.   Ps. 66:2, 4 • [Ps. 83:18; 92:1]

3 When my enemies turn back,
They stumble and perish before Thee.
4 For Thou hast maintained ^Tmy just
cause;   *my right and my cause*
Thou dost sit on the throne ^Ajudging
righteously.   *a righteous Judge*
5 Thou hast ^Rrebuked the nations; Thou
hast destroyed the wicked; Ps. 119:21
Thou hast ^Rblotted out their name forever and ever.   Ps. 69:28; Prov. 10:7
6 The enemy has come to an end in perpetual ruins,
And Thou hast uprooted the cities;
The very ^Rmemory of them has perished.   [Ps. 34:16]

7 But the^RLORD ¹⁴abides forever; Ps. 10:16
He has established His^Rthrone for judg-
ment,   Ps. 89:14
8 And He will^Rjudge the world in righteousness;   [Ps. 96:13; 98:9]
He will execute judgment for the peoples with equity.
9 ^AThe LORD also will be a stronghold for
the oppressed,   *Let the LORD also be*
A stronghold in times of trouble,
10 And those who^Rknow Thy name will
put their trust in Thee;   Ps. 91:14
For Thou, O LORD, hast not ^Rforsaken
those who seek Thee. Ps. 37:28; 94:14

11 Sing praises to the LORD, who^Rdwells in
Zion;   Ps. 76:2
Declare among the peoples His deeds.
12 For ^RHe who ¹⁵requires blood remembers them;   [Gen. 9:5; Ps. 72:14]
He does not forget ^Rthe cry of the afflicted.   Ps. 9:18
13 Be gracious to me, O LORD;
Behold my affliction from those ^Rwho
hate me,   Ps. 38:19
Thou who^Rdost lift me up from the
gates of death;   Ps. 30:3; 86:13
14 That I may tell of all Thy praises,
That in the gates of the daughter of
Zion
I may rejoice in Thy salvation.
15 The nations have sunk down^Rin the pit
which they have made;   Ps. 7:15, 16
In the ^Rnet which they hid, their own
foot has been caught.   Ps. 57:6
16 The LORD has made Himself known;
He has^Rexecuted judgment.   [Ps. 9:4]
In the work of his own hands the
wicked is snared. [Higgaion Selah.

17 The wicked will^Areturn to Sheol,   *turn*
Even all the nations who forget God.
18 For the ^Rneedy will not always be forgotten,   Ps. 9:12; 12:5
Nor the^Rhope of the afflicted perish forever.   [Ps. 62:5; 71:5]; Prov. 23:18

¹² I.e., the crown of his own head
¹³ I.e., "Death to the Son"   ¹⁴ Or, *sits as king*
¹⁵ I.e., avenges bloodshed

19 Arise, O Lᴏʀᴅ, do not let man prevail;
Let the nations be judged before Thee.
20 Put them ᴿin fear, O Lᴏʀᴅ;   Ps. 14:5
Let the nations know that they are but
men.   [Selah.

PSALM 10

Petition for God's Judgment

Wʜʏ dost Thou stand afar off, O Lᴏʀᴅ?
Why ᴿdost Thou hide ᴬThyself in times of
trouble?   Ps. 13:1; 55:1 · Thine eyes
2 In ᴿpride the wicked ᵀhotly pursue the afflicted;   Ps. 73:6, 8 · burn
ᴬLet them be caught in the plots which
they have devised. They will be caught

3 For the wicked ᴿboasts of his ᴿheart's desire,   Ps. 49:6; 94:3, 4 · Ps. 112:10
And ¹⁶the greedy man curses and
ᴿspurns the Lᴏʀᴅ.   Ps. 10:13
4 The wicked, in the haughtiness of his
countenance, does not seek Him.
All his thoughts are, "There is no God."

5 His ways ᵀprosper at all times; are strong
Thy judgments are on high, ᴮout of his
sight;   Ps. 28:5
As for all his adversaries, he snorts at
them.
6 He says to himself, "I ᴿ shall not be
moved;   Ps. 49:11; [Eccl. 8:11]
ᵀThroughout all generations ᴵI shall not
be in adversity."   To · Rev. 18:7
7 His ᴿmouth is full of curses and deceit
and oppression;   [Rom. 3:14]
ᴿUnder his tongue is mischief and wickedness.   Job 20:12; Ps. 140:3
8 He sits in the ᴿlurking places of the villages;   Ps. 11:2
In the hiding places he ᴿkills the innocent;   Ps. 94:6
His eyes ᵀstealthily watch for the ᴬunfortunate.   lie in wait · poor
9 He lurks in a hiding place as ᴿa lion in
his ᴬlair;   Ps. 17:12 · thicket
He ᴿlurks to catch the afflicted;   Mic. 7:2
He catches the afflicted when he draws
him into his ᴿnet.   Ps. 140:5
10 He ᶜcrouches, he bows down,   is crushed
And the ᴬunfortunate fall ¹⁷by his
mighty ones.   poor
11 He says to himself, "God has forgotten;
He has hidden His face; He will never
see it."

12 Arise, O Lᴏʀᴅ; O God, lift up Thy hand.
ᴿDo not forget the afflicted.   Ps. 9:12
13 Why has the wicked spurned God?
He has said to himself, "Thou wilt not
require it."
14 Thou hast seen it, for Thou hast beheld
ᴿmischief and vexation to ᵀtake it
into Thy hand.   Ps. 10:7 · put, give

The ᴬunfortunate ᴿ commits himself to
Thee;   poor · Ps. 22:11
Thou hast been the ᴿhelper of the orphan.   Ps. 68:5
15 ᴿBreak the arm of the wicked and the
evildoer,   Ps. 37:17
ᴬSeek out his wickedness until Thou
dost find none.   Mayest Thou seek

16 The Lᴏʀᴅ is King forever and ever;
Nations have perished from His land.
17 O Lᴏʀᴅ, Thou hast heard the ᴿdesire of
the ¹⁸humble;   Ps. 9:18
Thou wilt ᵀstrengthen their heart, Thou
wilt incline Thine ear   1 Chr. 29:18
18 To ¹⁹vindicate the ᴿorphan and the ᴿoppressed,   [Ps. 146:9] · Ps. 9:9; 74:21
That man who is of the earth may
cause ᴿterror no more.   Is. 29:20

PSALM 11

God Tests the Sons of Men

For the choir director.
A Psalm of David.

Iɴ the Lᴏʀᴅ I ᴿtake refuge;   Ps. 2:12
How can you say to my soul, "Flee as a
bird to your ᴿmountain;   Ps. 121:1
2 For, behold, the wicked bend the bow,
They ᴬmake ᴿ ready their arrow upon the
string,   fixed · Ps. 64:3
To ᴿshoot in darkness at the upright in
heart.   Ps. 64:4
3 If the ᴿfoundations are destroyed,
What can the righteous do?"   Ps. 82:5

4 The Lᴏʀᴅ is in His ᴿholy temple; the
Lᴏʀᴅ's throne is in heaven;   Mic. 1:2
His ᴿeyes behold, His eyelids test the
sons of men.   [Ps. 33:18; 34:15, 16]
5 The Lᴏʀᴅ ᵀtests the righteous and the
wicked,   Gen. 22:1; Ps. 34:19; James 1:12
And the one who loves violence His
soul hates.
6 Upon the wicked He will rain ²⁰snares;
Fire and brimstone and burning wind
will be the portion of their cup.
7 For the Lᴏʀᴅ is righteous; He loves
ᴬrighteousness;   righteous deeds
The upright will behold His face.

PSALM 12

The Pure Words of the Lord

For the choir director;
upon an eight-stringed lyre.
A Psalm of David.

Hᴇʟᴘ, Lᴏʀᴅ, for ᴿthe godly man ceases to
be,   [Is. 57:1]; Mic. 7:2

¹⁶ Or, blesses the greedy man   ¹⁷ Or, into his claws
¹⁸ Or, afflicted   ¹⁹ Lit., judge   ²⁰ Or, coals of fire

For the faithful disappear from among
the sons of men.
2 They speak falsehood to one another;
With ᴿflattering ᵀlips and with a double
heart they speak.   Ps. 28:3 • *lip*
3 May the LORD cut off all flattering lips,
The tongue that speaks great things;
4 Who ᴿhave said, "With our tongue we
will prevail;   Ps. 73:8, 9
Our lips are ᵀour own; who is lord over
us?"   *with us*
5"Because of the ᴿdevastation of the afflicted, because of the groaning of
the needy,   Ps. 9:9; 10:18
Now ᴿI will arise," says the LORD; "I will
ᴿset him in the safety for which he
longs."   Is. 33:10 • Ps. 34:6; 35:10

6 The words of the LORD are pure words;
As silver ᵀtried in a furnace on the
earth, refined seven times. Prov. 30:5
7 Thou, O LORD, wilt keep them;
Thou wilt ᵀpreserve him from this generation forever.   [Ps. 37:28; 97:10]
8 The wicked strut about on every side,
When ²¹vileness is exalted among the
sons of men.

PSALM 13

The Prayer for God's Answer—Now

For the choir director.
A Psalm of David.

HOW long, O LORD? Wilt Thou ᴿforget me
forever?   Ps. 44:24
How long ᴿwilt Thou hide Thy face from
me?   Job 13:24; Ps. 89:46
2 How long shall I ᴿtake counsel in my
soul,   Ps. 42:4
Having sorrow in my heart all the day?
How long will my enemy be exalted
over me?

3 ᴿConsider *and* answer me, O LORD, my
God;   Ps. 5:1
ᴿEnlighten my eyes, lest I sleep the
sleep of death,   Ezra 9:8; Job 33:30
4 Lest my enemy ᴿsay, "I have overcome
him,"   Ps. 12:4
Lest ᴿmy adversaries rejoice when I am
shaken.   Ps. 25:2; 38:16

5 But I have ᴿtrusted in Thy lovingkindness;   Ps. 52:8
My heart shall rejoice in Thy salvation.
6 I will ᴿsing to the LORD,   Ps. 96:1, 2
Because He has ᴿdealt bountifully with
me.   Ps. 116:7; 119:17; 142:7

²¹ Or, *worthlessness*
²² Or, *restores the fortunes of His people*
²³ I.e., to a fellow Israelite

PSALM 14

The Characteristics of the Godless

For the choir director.
A Psalm of David.

THE fool has ᴿsaid in his heart, "There is no
God."   Ps. 10:4; 53:1
They are corrupt, they have committed
abominable ᵀdeeds;   *doings*
There is ᴿno one who does good. Ps. 14:1
2 The LORD has looked down from
heaven upon the sons of men,
To see if there are any who understand,
Who ᴿseek after God.   1 Chr. 22:19
3 They have all ᵀturned aside; together
they have become corrupt;   Ps. 58:3
There is ᴿno one who does good, not
even one.   Ps. 143:2

4 Do all the workers of wickedness ᴿnot
know,   Ps. 82:5
Who ᴿeat up my people *as* they eat
bread,   Ps. 27:2; Jer. 10:25; Mic. 3:3
And ᴿdo not call upon the Lord? Ps. 79:6
5 There they are in great dread,
For God is with the ᴿrighteous generation.   Ps. 73:15; 112:2
6 You would put to shame the counsel of
the afflicted,
But the LORD is his ᴿrefuge. Ps. 9:9; 40:17

7 Oh, that ᴿthe salvation of Israel would
come out of Zion!   Ps. 53:6
When the LORD ²²restores ᴿHis captive
people,   Ps. 85:1, 2
Jacob will rejoice, Israel will be glad.

PSALM 15

The Characteristics of the Godly

A Psalm of David.

O LORD, who may abide in Thy tent?
Who may dwell on Thy holy hill?
2 He who ᴿwalks with integrity, and
works righteousness,   Is. 33:15
And ᴿspeaks truth in his heart. Eph. 4:25
3 He does not slander with his tongue,
Nor ᴿdoes evil to his neighbor,   Ps. 28:3
Nor ᴿtakes up a reproach against his
friend;   Ex. 23:1
4 In whose eyes a reprobate is despised,
But ᵀwho ᴿhonors those who fear the
LORD;   *he* • Acts 28:10
He ᴿswears to his own hurt, and does
not change;   Judg. 11:35
5 He ᴿdoes not put out his money ²³at interest,   Ex. 22:25; Lev. 25:36; Deut. 23:20
Nor ᴿdoes he take a bribe against the
innocent.   Ex. 23:8; Deut. 16:19
ᴿHe who does these things will never be
shaken.   2 Pet. 1:10

PSALM 16

Eternal Life for One Who Trusts

A [24]Mikhtam of David.

PRESERVE[R]me, O God, for[R]I take refuge in Thee. Ps. 17:8 • Ps. 7:1

2 I said to the LORD, "Thou art my Lord; I[R]have no good besides Thee." Ps. 73:25

3 As for the saints who are in the earth, They are the majestic ones[R]in whom is all my delight. Ps. 119:63

4 The [T]sorrows of those who have bartered for another *god* will be multiplied; sorrows due to idolatry

I shall not pour out their libations of [R]blood, Ps. 106:37, 38

Nor shall I[T]take their names upon my lips. Ex. 23:13; Josh. 23:7

5 The LORD is the[R]portion of my inheritance and my cup; Ps. 73:26; 119:57

Thou dost support my[R]lot. Ps. 125:3

6 The[R]lines have fallen to me in pleasant places; Ps. 78:55

Indeed, my heritage is beautiful to me.

7 I will bless the LORD who has [R]counseled me; Ps. 73:24

Indeed, my [T]mind instructs me in the night. *kidneys,* figurative for inner man

8 [R]I have[R]set the LORD continually before me; Ps. 16:8-11 • Ps. 27:8; 123:1, 2

Because He is[R]at my right hand,[R]I will not be shaken. Ps. 73:23 • [Ps. 112:6]

9 Therefore[R]my heart is glad, and[R]my glory rejoices; Ps. 4:7 • Ps. 30:12

My flesh also will dwell securely.

10 For Thou[R]wilt not abandon my soul to Sheol; [Ps. 49:15; Acts 2:31, 32]☆

Neither wilt Thou[T]allow Thy Holy One to [25]undergo decay. *give*

11 Thou wilt make known to me[R]the path of life; Ps. 139:24; [Matt. 7:14]

In Thy presence is fulness of joy;

In Thy right hand there are[R]pleasures forever. Job 36:11; Ps. 36:7, 8; 46:4

PSALM 17

"Hide Me in the Shadow of Thy Wings"

A Prayer of David.

HEAR a[R]just cause, O LORD,[R]give heed to my cry; Ps. 9:4 • Ps. 61:1; 142:6

[R]Give ear to my prayer, which is not from deceitful lips. Ps. 88:2

2 Let[R]my[T]judgment come forth from Thy presence; Ps. 103:6 • vindication

Let Thine eyes look with equity.

3 Thou hast[T]tried my heart; Ps. 26:1, 2

Thou hast visited *me* by night;

Thou hast [R]tested me and dost find [26]nothing; Job 23:10; Ps. 66:10; Zech. 13:9

I have [R]purposed that my mouth will not transgress. Ps. 39:1

4 As for the deeds of men,[R] by the word of Thy lips Ps. 119:9, 101

I have kept from the[R]paths of the violent. Ps. 10:5-11

5 My steps have held fast to Thy paths. My[R]feet have not slipped. Ps. 18:36; 37:31

6 I have [R]called upon Thee, for Thou wilt answer me, O God; Ps. 86:7; 116:2

[R]Incline Thine ear to me, hear my speech. Ps. 88:2

7 Wondrously show Thy lovingkindness, O [R]Savior of those who take refuge at Thy right hand Ps. 20:6

From those who rise up *against them.*

8 Keep me as [27]the apple of the eye;

Hide me in the shadow of Thy wings,

9 From the wicked who despoil me,

My deadly enemies, who surround me.

10 They have closed their unfeeling *heart*; With their mouth they speak proudly.

11 They have now [R]surrounded us in our steps; Ps. 88:17

[24] Possibly Epigrammatic Poem, or, Atonement Psalm
[25] Or, *see corruption* or *the pit*
[26] Or, *no evil device in me*
[27] Lit., *the pupil, the daughter of the eye*

17:4 God's Word Corrects—There are many symbols for God's Word that can be found in the Bible itself. It can be thought of as a mirror (Page 1253—James 1:23-25), a seed (Page 1261—1 Pet. 1:23), a lamp (Page 593—Ps. 119:105), a sword (Page 1190—Eph. 6:17), and even as food (Page 1241—Heb. 5:12-14). But the Bible also serves as a measuring rod or ruler. Many teachers have used wooden rulers in their classes not only to give the right measurement but, on occasion, to correct a misbehaving pupil. God's Word likewise can do both of these things. It should be used as a standard against which to measure our beliefs. What about certain religious groups which claim Christ was not God, or that the Bible is filled with silly tales? Immediately we can reject such claims by using our divine written ruler to discover that such arguments simply do not measure up.

Sometimes our heavenly teacher, the Father, uses His written ruler to correct us when we are in the wrong. Israel's great king David once experienced this. "Thou hast dealt well with Thy servant, O LORD, according to Thy word. Before I was afflicted I went astray, but now I keep Thy word" (Page 592—Ps. 119:65, 67).

There are times when God's Word can correct believers when they are in honest and unintentional error. Aquila and Priscilla, a godly Christian couple, use the Scriptures to help a powerful young preacher named Apollos (Page 1116—Acts 18:24-26). Paul does the same thing for some former disciples of John the Baptist he meets in the city of Ephesus (Page 1116—Acts 19:1-7).

Now turn to Page 590—Ps. 119:9: God's Word Cleanses.

They set their eyes^Rto cast *us* down to
the ground.   Ps. 37:14

12 He is like a lion that is eager to tear,
And as a young lion^Rlurking in hiding
places.   Ps. 10:9

13 ^RArise, O LORD, confront him,^Rbring him
low;   Ps. 3:7 · Ps. 55:23
^RDeliver my soul from the wicked with
^RThy sword,   Ps. 22:20 · Ps. 7:12
14 From men with Thy hand, O LORD,
From men of the world,^Rwhose portion
is in *this* life;   Ps. 73:3-7; Luke 16:25
And whose belly Thou ^Rdost fill with
Thy treasure;   Ps. 49:6
They are satisfied with children,
And leave their abundance to their
babes.
15 As for me, I shall^Rbehold Thy face in
righteousness;   Ps. 11:7; 16:11; 140:13
I will be satisfied ^Awith Thy likeness
when I awake.   *with* beholding

PSALM 18

Thanksgiving for Deliverance by God

For the choir director. *A Psalm* of
David the servant of the LORD, who
spoke to the LORD the words of this
song in the day that the LORD
delivered him from the hand of all his
enemies and from the hand of Saul.
And he said,

"I LOVE Thee, O LORD, my strength."
2 The LORD is ^Rmy ^Arock and my fortress
and my deliverer,   Ps. 18:31 · *crag*
My God, my rock, in whom I take refuge;
My ^Rshield and the horn of my salvation, my stronghold.   Ps. 28:7; 33:20
3 I call upon the LORD, who is^Rworthy to
be praised,   Ps. 48:1; 96:4; 145:3
And I am saved from my enemies.

4 The cords of death encompassed me,
And the torrents of ²⁸ungodliness^Rterri-
fied me.   *were assailing* or *terrifying*
5 The cords of Sheol surrounded me;
The snares of death confronted me.
6 In my distress I called upon the LORD,
And cried to my God for help;
He heard my voice out of His temple,
And my ^Rcry for help before Him came
into His ears.   Ps. 34:15

7 Then the earth shook and quaked;
And the^Rfoundations of the mountains
were trembling   Ps. 114:4, 6
And were shaken, because He was angry.
8 Smoke went up out of His nostrils,
And fire from His mouth devoured;

Coals were kindled by it.
9 He^Rbowed the heavens also, and came
down   Ps. 144:5
With thick darkness under His feet.
10 And He rode upon a cherub and flew;
And He sped upon the ^Rwings of the
wind.   [Ps. 104:3]
11 He made darkness His hiding place,
His ^Acanopy around Him,   *pavilion*
Darkness of waters, thick clouds of the
skies.
12 From the ^Rbrightness before Him
passed His thick clouds,   Ps. 104:2
Hailstones and^Rcoals of fire.   Ps. 97:3
13 The LORD also^Rthundered in the heavens,   Ps. 29:3; 104:7
And the Most High uttered His voice,
Hailstones and coals of fire.
14 And He ^Rsent out His arrows, and scattered them,   Ps. 144:6; Hab. 3:11
And lightning flashes in abundance,
and^Rrouted them.   *confused*
15 Then the channels of water appeared,
And the foundations of the world were
^Alaid bare   *uncovered*
At Thy^Rrebuke, O LORD,   Ps. 76:6
At the blast of the^Rbreath of Thy nos-
trils.   Ps. 18:8

16 He sent from on high, He took me;
He drew me out of many waters.
17 He^Rdelivered me from my strong enemy,   Ps. 59:1
And from those who hated me, for they
were^Rtoo mighty for me.   Ps. 35:10
18 They confronted me in^Rthe day of my
calamity,   Ps. 59:16
But^Rthe LORD was my stay.   Ps. 16:8
19 He brought me forth also into a^Rbroad
place;   Ps. 4:1; 31:8; 118:5
He rescued me, because^RHe delighted
in me.   Ps. 37:23; 41:11

20 The LORD has ^Rrewarded me according
to my righteousness;   [Job 33:26]
According to the cleanness of my
hands He has recompensed me.
21 For I have kept the ways of the LORD,
And have^Rnot wickedly departed from
my God.   2 Chr. 34:33; Ps. 119:102
22 For all His ordinances were before me,
And I did not put away His ^Rstatutes
from me.   Ps. 119:83
23 I was also ²⁹blameless with Him,
And I kept myself from my iniquity.
24 Therefore the LORD has recompensed
me according to my righteousness,
According to the cleanness of my
hands in His eyes.

25 With^Rthe kind Thou dost show Thyself
kind;   [1 Kin. 8:32; Ps. 62:12; Matt. 5:7]
With the blameless ^RThou dost show
Thyself blameless;   Ps. 18:30
26 With the pure Thou dost show Thyself
^Rpure;   Job 25:5; Hab. 1:13

---

²⁸ Or, *destruction*   ²⁹ Lit., *complete; or, having integrity*

And with the crooked[R]Thou dost show
Thyself [30]astute.   [Lev. 26:23, 24, 27, 28]
27 For Thou dost save an afflicted people;
But haughty eyes Thou dost abase.
28 For Thou dost[R]light my lamp;   Job 18:6
The LORD my God[R]illumines my dark-
ness.   Ps. 27:1
29 For by Thee I can [31]run upon a troop;
And by my God I can leap over a wall.

30 As for God, His way is blameless;
The[R]word of the LORD is tried;   Ps. 12:6
He is a[R]shield to all who take refuge in
Him.   [Ps. 17:7; 91:4]
31 For who is God, but the LORD?
And who is a rock, except our God,
32 The God who girds me with strength,
And makes my way blameless?
33 He makes my feet like hinds' *feet*,
And sets me upon my high places.
34 He[R]trains my hands for battle,   Ps. 144:1
So that my arms can[R]bend a bow of
bronze.   Job 29:20
35 Thou hast also given me[R]the shield of
Thy salvation,   Ps. 33:20
And Thy right hand upholds me;
And Thy gentleness makes me great.
36 Thou dost enlarge my steps under me,
And my[R]feet have not slipped.   *ankles*

37 I [R]pursued my enemies and overtook
them,   [Ps. 44:5]
And I did not turn back[R]until they were
consumed.   Ps. 37:20
38 I shattered them, so that they were[R]not
able to rise;   Ps. 36:12
They fell[R]under my feet.   Ps. 47:3
39 For Thou hast[R]girded me with strength
for battle;
Thou hast subdued under me those
who rose up against me.   Ps. 18:32
40 Thou hast also made my enemies[R]turn
their backs to me,   Ps. 21:12
And I [32]destroyed those who hated me.
41 They cried for help, but there was[R]none
to save,   Ps. 50:22
Even to the LORD, but[R]He did not answer them.   Job 27:9
42 Then I beat them fine as the[R]dust before the wind;   Ps. 83:13
I emptied them out as the mire of the
streets.

43 Thou hast delivered me from the[R]con-
tentions of the people;   2 Sam. 3:1
Thou hast placed me as[R]head of the na-
tions;   2 Sam. 8:1-18; Ps. 89:27
A [R]people whom I have not known
serve me.   Is. 55:5
44 As soon as they hear, they obey me;
Foreigners [33]submit[R]to me.   [Ps. 66:3]
45 Foreigners[R]fade away,   Ps. 37:2
And[R]come trembling out of their[R]for-
tresses.   Mic. 7:17 · *fastnesses*

46 The LORD [R]lives, and blessed be [R]my
rock;   [Job 19:25] · Ps. 18:2
And exalted be[R]the God of my salva-
tion,   Ps. 51:14
47 The God who[R]executes vengeance for
me,   [Ps. 94:1]
And subdues peoples under me.
48 He delivers me from my enemies;
Surely Thou[R]dost lift me above those
who rise up against me; Ps. 27:6; 59:1
Thou dost rescue me from the[R]violent
man.   Ps. 11:5
49 Therefore I will give thanks to Thee
among the nations, O LORD,
And I will sing praises to Thy name.
50 He gives great [34]deliverance[R] to His
king,   Ps. 21:1; 144:10
And shows lovingkindness to [R]His
anointed,   Ps. 28:8
To David and his descendants forever.

PSALM 19

The Works and Words of God

For the choir director.
A Psalm of David.

THE [R]heavens are telling of the glory of
God;   Ps. 8:1; 50:6; [Rom. 1:19, 20]
And their [R]expanse is declaring the
work of His hands.   Gen. 1:6, 7
2 Day to[R]day pours forth speech, Ps. 74:16
And night to night reveals knowledge.
3 There is no speech, nor are there
words;
Their voice is not heard.
4 Their [35]line[R] has gone out through all
the earth,   Rom. 10:18
And their utterances to the end of the
world.
In them He has[R]placed a tent for the
sun,   Ps. 104:2
5 Which is as a bridegroom coming out
of his chamber;
It rejoices as a strong man to run his
course.
6 Its[R]rising is from [T]one end of the heavens,   Ps. 113:3; Eccl. 1:5 · *the*
And its circuit to the [T]other end of
them;   *the ends*
And there is nothing hidden from its
heat.

7 [R]The law of the LORD is [36]perfect[R], restoring the soul;   Ps. 111:7 · Ps. 119:160
The testimony of the LORD is sure,
making wise the simple.
8 The precepts of the LORD are[R]right, rejoicing the heart;   Ps. 119:128
The commandment of the LORD is
[R]pure, enlightening the eyes. Ps. 12:6
9 The fear of the LORD is clean, enduring
forever;

[30] Lit., *twisted*   [31] Or, *crush a troop*   [32] Or, *silenced*
[33] I.e., give feigned obedience   [34] I.e., *victories*
[35] Another reading is *sound*   [36] I.e., *blameless*

The judgments of the LORD are true;
they are righteous altogether.

10 They are more desirable than [R]gold, yes,
than much fine gold;   Ps. 119:72, 127
[R]Sweeter also than honey and the drip-
pings of the honeycomb.   Ps. 119:103

11 Moreover, by them [R]Thy servant is
warned;   [Ps. 17:4]
In keeping them there is great reward.

12 Who can [R]discern *his* errors? Acquit me
of hidden *faults.*   Ps. 40:12; 139:6

13 Also keep back Thy servant [R]from pre-
sumptuous *sins;*   Num. 15:30
Let them not [R]rule over me;   Ps. 119:133
Then I shall be [37]blameless[R],   Ps. 18:32
And I shall be acquitted of [R]great trans-
gression.   Ps. 25:11

14 Let the words of my mouth and [R]the
meditation of my heart   Ps. 104:34
Be acceptable in Thy sight,
O LORD, my rock and my Redeemer.

PSALM 20

*Boast Not in Chariots and Horses
but in God's Name*

For the choir director.
A Psalm of David.

MAY the LORD answer you [R]in the day of
trouble!   Ps. 50:15
May the [R]name of the God of Jacob set
you *securely* on high!   Ps. 91:14

2 May He send you help [R]from the sanctuary,   Ps. 3:4
And [R]support you from Zion!   Ps. 110:2

3 May He [R]remember all your meal offerings,   Acts 10:4
And find your burnt offering acceptable!   [Selah.

4 May He grant you your heart's desire,
And [R]fulfill all your [38]counsel! Ps. 145:19

5 We will sing for joy over your victory,
And in the name of our God we will [R]set
up our banners.   Ps. 60:4
May the LORD fulfill all your petitions.

6 Now [R]I know that the LORD saves His
anointed;   Ps. 41:11
He will [R]answer him from His holy
heaven,   Is. 58:9
With the [R]saving strength of His right
hand.   Ps. 28:8

7 Some *boast* in chariots, and some in
[R]horses;   Ps. 33:17
But [R]we will boast in the name of the
LORD, our God.   [2 Chr. 32:8]

8 They have bowed down and fallen;
But we have risen and stood upright.

9 [R]Save, O LORD;   Ps. 3:7
May the [R]King answer us in the day we
call.   Ps. 17:6

---

[37] Lit., *complete*   [38] Or, *purpose*   [39] Or, *victory*
[40] Lit., *fruit*   [41] Lit., *seed*   [42] Lit., *the hind of the morning*

PSALM 21

Triumph of the King

For the choir director.
A Psalm of David.

O LORD, in Thy strength the king will [R]be
glad,   [Ps. 59:16, 17]
And in Thy [39]salvation how greatly he
will rejoice!

2 Thou hast given him his heart's desire,
And Thou hast not withheld the request of his lips.   [Selah.

3 For Thou [R]dost meet him with the blessings of good things;   Ps. 59:10
Thou dost set a [R]crown of fine gold on
his head.   2 Sam. 12:30

4 He asked life of Thee,
Thou [R]didst give it to him,   Ps. 61:6; 133:3
Length of days forever and ever.

5 His [R]glory is great through Thy [39]salva-
tion,   Ps. 9:14; 20:5
[R]Splendor and majesty Thou dost place
upon him.   Ps. 8:5; 96:6

6 For Thou dost make him [T]most [R]blessed
forever;   *blessings* • 1 Chr. 17:27
Thou dost make him joyful [R]with gladness in Thy presence.   Ps. 43:4

7 For the king trusts in the LORD,
And through the lovingkindness of the
Most High he will not be shaken.

8 Your hand will [R]find out all your enemies;   [Is. 10:10]
Your right hand will find out those who
hate you.

9 You will make them as a fiery oven in
the time [?]of your anger;
The LORD will [R]swallow them up in His
wrath,   *of your presence* • Lam. 2:2
And [R]fire will devour them.   Ps. 50:3

10 Their [40]offspring Thou wilt destroy
from the earth,
And their [41]descendants[R] from among
the sons of men.   Ps. 37:28

11 Though they [T]intended[R] evil against
Thee,   *stretched out* • Ps. 2:1-3
And [R]devised a plot,   Ps. 10:2
They will not succeed.

12 For Thou wilt [R]make them turn their
back;   Ps. 18:40
Thou wilt [T]aim [R]with Thy bowstrings at
their faces.   *make ready* • Ps. 7:12, 13

13 Be Thou exalted, O LORD, in Thy
strength;
We will sing and praise Thy power.

PSALM 22

Psalm of the Cross

For the choir director;
upon [42]Aijeleth Hashshahar.
A Psalm of David.

MY [R]God, my God, why hast Thou forsaken me?   [Matt. 27:46; Mark 15:34] ☆

[R]Far from my deliverance are the words
of my [T]groaning.   Ps. 10:1 • *roaring*

2 O my God, I [T]cry by day, but Thou dost
not answer;   Ps. 42:3; 88:1
And by night, but I have no rest.

3 Yet[R]Thou art holy,   [Ps. 99:9]
O Thou who art enthroned upon the
praises of Israel.

4 In Thee our fathers [R]trusted;   Ps. 78:53
They trusted, and Thou didst [R]deliver
them.   Ps. 107:6

5 To Thee they cried out, and were delivered;
[R]In Thee they trusted, and were not [A]dis-
appointed.   Is. 49:23 • *ashamed*

6 But I am a worm, and not a man,
A [R]reproach of men, and [R]despised by
the people.   Ps. 31:11 • Is. 49:7; 53:3

7 All who see me [A]sneer at me;   *mock me*
They [43]separate with the lip, they [R]wag
the head, *saying,*   Matt. 27:39 ☆

8 "[44]Commit *yourself* to the LORD; [R]let
Him deliver him;   Matt. 27:43 ☆
Let Him rescue him, because He de-
lights in him."

9 Yet Thou art He who [R]didst bring me
forth from the womb;   [Ps. 71:5, 6]
Thou didst make me trust *when* upon
my mother's breasts.

10 Upon Thee I was cast from birth;
Thou hast been my God from my
mother's womb.

11 Be not far from me, for trouble is near;
For there is [R]none to help.   2 Kin. 14:26

12 Many [R]bulls have surrounded me;
Strong *bulls* of [R]Bashan have encircled
me.   Ps. 22:21 • Deut. 32:14; Amos 4:1

13 They open wide their mouth at me,
As a ravening and a roaring lion.

14 I am [R]poured out like water,   Job 30:16
And all my bones are out of joint;
My [R]heart is like wax;   Josh. 7:5; Job 23:16
It is melted within [T]me.   *my inward parts*

15 My strength is dried up like a potsherd,
And my tongue cleaves to my jaws;
And Thou dost [R]lay me [T]in the dust of
death.   Ps. 104:29 • *to*

16 For [R]dogs have surrounded me;
[A]A band of evildoers has encompassed
me;   Ps. 59:6, 7 • *An assembly*
They pierced my hands and my feet.

17 I can count all my bones.
They look, [R]they stare at me; John 19:37 ☆

18 They divide my garments among them,
And for my clothing they cast lots.

19 But Thou, O LORD, be not far off;
O Thou my help, [R]hasten to my assistance.   Ps. 70:5

20 Deliver my [A]soul from the sword,   *life*
My only *life* from the power of the dog.

21 Save me from the [R]lion's mouth; Ps. 22:13
And from the horns of the [R]wild oxen
Thou dost answer me.   Ps. 22:12

22 [R]I will tell of Thy name to my brethren;
In the midst of the assembly I will
praise Thee.   Matt. 4:23; Mark 1:21, 39 ☆

23 You who fear the LORD, praise Him;
All you [T]descendants of Jacob, [R]glorify
Him,   *seed* • Ps. 86:12
And [R]stand in awe of Him, all you de-
scendants of Israel.   Ps. 33:8

24 For He has not despised nor abhorred
the affliction of the afflicted;
Neither has He [R]hidden His face from
him;   Ps. 27:9; 69:17; 102:2
But [R]when he cried to Him for help, He
heard.   Ps. 31:22; Heb. 5:7

25 From Thee *comes* [R]my praise in the
great assembly;   Ps. 35:18; 40:9, 10
I shall [R]pay my vows before those who
fear Him.   Ps. 61:8; Eccl. 5:4

26 The [45]afflicted shall eat and [R]be satis-
fied;   [Ps. 107:9]
Those who seek Him will [R]praise the
LORD.   Ps. 40:16
Let your [R]heart live forever!   Ps. 69:32

27 All the [R]ends of the earth will remember
and turn to the LORD,   [Ps. 2:8; 82:8]
And all the [R]families of the nations will
worship before Thee.   [Ps. 86:9]

28 For the [R]kingdom is the LORD's,   Ps. 47:7
And He [R]rules over the nations.   Ps. 47:8

29 All the [T]prosperous [R]of the earth will eat
and worship,   *fat ones* • Ps. 17:10
All those who [R]go down to the dust will
bow before Him,   Ps. 28:1; [Is. 26:19]
Even he who [A]cannot [R]keep his soul
alive.   *did not* • Ps. 89:48

30 [T]Posterity will serve Him;   *A seed*
It will be told of the Lord to [R]the *coming*
generation.   Ps. 102:18

31 They will come and [R]will declare His
righteousness   Ps. 40:9; 71:18
To a people [R]who will be born, that He
has performed *it.*   Ps. 78:6

PSALM 23

Psalm of the Divine Shepherd

A Psalm of David.

T HE LORD is my [R]shepherd,   Ps. 78:52; 80:1
I [A]shall [R]not want.   *do* • [Phil. 4:19]

2 He makes me lie down in [R]green pastures;   Ps. 65:11-13; Ezek. 34:14
He leads me beside quiet waters.

3 He [R]restores my soul;   Ps. 19:7
He [R]guides me in the [T]paths [R]of righteous-
ness   Ps. 5:8 • *tracks* • Ps. 85:13
For His name's sake.

4 Even though I [R]walk through the [46]val-
ley of the shadow of death, Job 10:21
I fear no [47]evil; for Thou art with me;

---

[43] I.e., make mouths at me
[44] Another reading is *He committed* himself   [45] Or, *poor*
[46] Or, *valley of deep darkness*   [47] Or, *harm*

Thy [R]rod and Thy staff, they comfort
   me.   Mic. 7:14
5 Thou dost [R]prepare a table before me in
   the presence of my enemies;
   Thou hast anointed my head with oil;
   My [R]cup overflows.   Ps. 78:19 • Ps. 16:5
6 [A]Surely [R]goodness and lovingkindness
   will follow me all the days of my
   life,   Only • Ps. 25:7
   And I will [48]dwell in the house of the
   LORD [T]forever.   for length of days

PSALM 24

Psalm of the King of Glory

A Psalm of David.

T HE [R]earth is the LORD's, and [49]all it con-
      tains,   1 Cor. 10:26
   The world, and those who dwell in it.
2 For He has founded it upon the seas,
   And established it upon the rivers.
3 Who may [R]ascend into the [R]hill of the
   LORD?   Ps. 15:1 • Ps. 2:6
   And who may stand in His holy place?
4 He who has [R]clean hands and a [R]pure
   heart,   [Job 17:9] • Ps. 51:10; 73:1
   Who has not [R]lifted up his soul to [A]false-
   hood,   Ezek. 18:15 • in vain
   And has not [R]sworn deceitfully. Ps. 15:4
5 He shall receive a [R]blessing from the
   LORD   [Ps. 115:13]
   And [T]righteousness [R]from the God of his
   salvation.   as vindicated • Ps. 36:10
6 [A]This is the generation of those who
   [R]seek Him,   Such • Ps. 27:4, 8
   Who seek Thy face—even Jacob.
                                   [Selah.

7 [R]Lift up your heads, O gates,   Ps. 118:20
   And be lifted up, O [50]ancient doors,
   That the King of glory may come in!
8 Who is the King of glory?
   The LORD [R]strong and mighty,   Deut. 4:34
   The LORD [R]mighty in battle. [Ex. 15:3, 6]
9 Lift up your heads, O gates,
   And lift them up, O [50]ancient doors,
   That the King of glory may come in!
10 Who is this King of glory?
   The LORD of hosts,
   He is the King of glory.   [Selah.

PSALM 25

Acrostic Prayer for Instruction

A Psalm of David.

T O Thee, O LORD, I [R]lift up my soul. Ps. 86:4
2 O my God, in Thee [R]I trust,   Ps. 31:1
   Do not let me [R]be ashamed;   Ps. 25:20
   Do not let my enemies exult over me.

3 Indeed, [R]none of those who wait for
   Thee will be ashamed;   Ps. 37:9; 40:1
   Those who [R]deal treacherously without
   cause will be ashamed.   Ps. 119:158

4 Make me know Thy ways, O LORD;
   Teach me Thy paths.
5 Lead me in Thy truth and teach me,
   For Thou art the God of my salvation;
   For Thee I [R]wait all the day.   Ps. 40:1
6 [R]Remember, O LORD, Thy compassion
   and Thy lovingkindnesses,   Ps. 98:3
   For they have been [50]from of old.
7 Do not remember the [R]sins of my youth
   or my transgressions; Job 13:26; 20:11
   [R]According to Thy lovingkindness remember Thou me,   Ps. 51:1
   For Thy goodness' sake, O LORD.

8 [R]Good and upright is the LORD;   Ps. 86:5
   Therefore He [R]instructs sinners in the
   way.   Ps. 32:8
9 He leads the [A]humble in justice,   afflicted
   And He teaches the humble His way.
10 All the paths of the LORD are [R]loving-
   kindness and truth   Ps. 40:11
   To [R]those who keep His covenant and
   His testimonies.   Ps. 103:18
11 For [R]Thy name's sake, O LORD,   Ps. 31:3
   Pardon my iniquity, for it is great.

12 Who is the man who fears the LORD?
   He will [R]instruct him in the way he
   should choose.   [Ps. 25:8; 37:23]
13 His soul will abide in [T]prosperity,   good
   And his [51]descendants will [R]inherit the
   [A]land.   Ps. 37:11; 69:36; Matt. 5:5 • earth
14 The [A]secret of the LORD is for those who
   fear Him,   counsel or intimacy
   And He will [R]make them know His covenant.   Gen. 17:1, 2
15 My [R]eyes are continually toward the
   LORD,   [Ps. 123:2; 141:8]
   For He will [T]pluck [R]my feet out of the
   net.   bring out • Ps. 31:4; 124:7

16 Turn to me and be gracious to me,
   For I am [R]lonely and afflicted.   Ps. 143:4
17 The troubles of my heart are enlarged;
   Bring me [R]out of my distresses. Ps. 107:6
18 [R]Look upon my affliction and my [52]trou-
   ble,   2 Sam. 16:12; Ps. 31:7
   And [R]forgive all my sins.   Ps. 103:3
19 Look upon my enemies, for they [R]are
   many;   Ps. 3:1
   And they hate me with violent hatred.
20 [R]Guard my soul and deliver me;   Ps. 86:2
   Do not let me [R]be ashamed, for I take
   refuge in Thee.   Ps. 25:2
21 Let [R]integrity and uprightness preserve
   me,   Ps. 41:12
   For [R]I wait for Thee.   Ps. 25:3
22 [R]Redeem Israel, O God,   [Ps. 130:8]
   Out of all his troubles.

[48] Another reading is return to   [49] Lit., its fulness
[50] Lit., everlasting   [51] Lit., seed   [52] Lit., toil

PSALM 26

"Examine Me, O LORD, and Try Me"

A *Psalm* of David.

V INDICATE [53] me, O LORD, for I have
^Rwalked in my integrity;   2 Kin. 20:3
And I have trusted in the LORD ^Twithout
wavering.   *I do not slide*
2 Examine me, O LORD, and try me;
^RTest my [54]mind and my heart.   Ps. 7:9
3 For Thy ^Rlovingkindness is before my
eyes,   Ps. 48:9
And I have walked in Thy truth.
4 I do not ^Rsit with [55]deceitful men, Ps. 1:1
Nor will I go with ^Rpretenders.   Ps. 28:3
5 I hate the assembly of evildoers,
And I will not sit with the wicked.
6 I shall wash my hands in innocence,
And I will go about ^RThine altar, O
LORD,   Ps. 43:3, 4
7 That I may proclaim with the voice of
^Rthanksgiving,   Ps. 9:1
And declare all Thy ^Awonders.   *miracles*

8 O LORD, I ^Rlove the habitation of Thy
house,   Ps. 27:4
And the place where Thy glory dwells.
9 ^RDo not ^Ttake my soul away *along* with
sinners,   Ps. 28:3 • *gather*
Nor my life with men of bloodshed,
10 In whose hands is a wicked scheme,
And whose right hand is full of bribes.
11 But as for me, I shall ^Rwalk in my integrity;   Ps. 26:1
Redeem me, and be gracious to me.
12 ^RMy foot stands on a level place; Ps. 40:2
In the ^Rcongregations I shall bless the
LORD.   Ps. 22:22

PSALM 27

Trust in the Lord and Be Not Afraid

A *Psalm* of David.

T HE LORD is my light and my salvation;
Whom shall I fear?
The LORD is the ^Adefense of my life;
^RWhom shall I dread?   *refuge* • Ps. 118:6
2 When evildoers came upon me to ^Tde-
vour my flesh,   Ps. 14:4
My adversaries and my enemies, they
^Rstumbled and fell.   John 18:6 ☆
3 Though a host encamp against me,
My heart will not fear;
Though war arise against me,
In *spite of* this I shall be confident.

4 ^ROne thing I have asked from the LORD,
that I shall seek: Ps. 26:8
That I may ^Rdwell in the house of the
LORD all the days of my life, Ps. 23:6
To behold the [56]beauty of the LORD,
And to [57]meditate in His temple.

5 For in the day of trouble He will con-
ceal me in His ^Atabernacle;   *shelter*
In the secret place of His tent He will
^Rhide me;   Ps. 17:8
He will ^Rlift me up on a rock.   Ps. 40:2
6 And now my head will be lifted up
above my enemies around me;
And I will offer in His tent sacrifices
^Twith shouts of joy;   *of shouts*
I will ^Rsing, yes, I will sing praises to the
LORD.   Ps. 13:6

7 ^RHear, O LORD, when I cry with my
voice,   [Ps. 4:3; 61:1]
And be gracious to me and answer me.
8 *When Thou didst say,* "Seek ^RMy face,"
my heart said to Thee,   Ps. 105:4
"Thy face, O LORD, ^RI shall seek." Ps. 34:4
9 ^RDo not hide Thy face from me, Ps. 69:17
Do not turn Thy servant away in anger;
Thou hast been ^Rmy help;   Ps. 40:17
Do not abandon me nor forsake me,
O God of my salvation!
10 For my father and ^Rmy mother have for-
saken me,   Is. 49:15
But ^Rthe LORD will take me up.   Is. 40:11

11 ^RTeach me Thy way, O LORD,   Ps. 25:4
And lead me in a ^Rlevel path,
Because of my foes.   Ps. 5:8; 26:12
12 Do not deliver me over to the ^Tdesire ^Rof
my adversaries;   *soul* • Ps. 41:2
For ^Rfalse witnesses have risen against
me,   Deut. 19:18; Matt. 26:60, 61 ☆
And such as breathe out violence.
13 ^T*I would have despaired* unless I had believed that I would see the good-
ness of the LORD   *Surely I believed*
In the ^Rland of the living.   Job 28:13
14 ^RWait for the LORD;   Ps. 25:3; Prov. 20:22
Be ^Rstrong, and let your heart take courage;
Yes, wait for the LORD.   Ps. 31:24

PSALM 28

Rejoice Because of Answered Prayer

A *Psalm* of David.

T O Thee, O LORD, I call;
My ^Rrock, do not be deaf to me, Ps. 18:2
Lest, if Thou ^Rbe silent to me, Ps. 35:22
I become like those who ^Rgo down to
the pit.   Ps. 88:4; 143:7; Prov. 1:12
2 Hear the voice of my supplications
when I cry to Thee for help,
When I ^Rlift up my hands toward [58]Thy
holy sanctuary.   Lam. 2:19; 1 Tim. 2:8
3 Do not drag me away with the wicked
And with those who work iniquity;
Who speak peace with their neighbors,
While evil is in their hearts.

[53] Lit., *Judge*   [54] Lit., *kidneys,* figurative for inner man
[55] Or, *worthless*   [56] Lit., *delightfulness*   [57] Lit., *inquire*
[58] Lit., *the innermost place of Thy sanctuary*

4 Requite them [R]according to their work
and according to the evil of their
practices;   2 Tim. 4:14; [Rev. 18:6]
Requite them according to the deeds of
their hands;
Repay them their [59]recompense.
5 Because they [R]do not regard the works
of the LORD   Is. 5:12
Nor the deeds of His hands,
He will tear them down and not build
them up.

6 Blessed be the LORD,
Because He [R]has heard the voice of my
supplication.   Ps. 28:2
7 The LORD is my [R]strength and my
[R]shield;   Ps. 18:2; 59:17 • Ps. 3:3
My heart [R]trusts in Him, and I am
helped;   Ps. 13:5; 112:7
Therefore [R]my heart exults,   Ps. 16:9
And with my song I shall thank Him.
8 The LORD is their [R]strength,   Ps. 20:6
And He is a [A]saving defense to His
anointed.   refuge of salvation
9 Save Thy people, and bless [R]Thine inheritance; [Deut. 9:29; 32:9; 1 Kin. 8:51]
Be their [R]shepherd also, and [R]carry them
forever.   Ps. 80:1 • Deut. 1:31

PSALM 29

The Powerful Voice of God

A Psalm of David.

ASCRIBE[R] to the LORD, O [A]sons of the
mighty,   1 Chr. 16:28, 29 • sons of gods
Ascribe to the LORD glory and strength.

2 Ascribe to the LORD the glory[T]due to His
name;   of His name
Worship the LORD in holy array.

3 The [R]voice of the LORD is upon the wa-
ters;   Ps. 104:7
The God of glory [R]thunders, [Job 37:4, 5]
The LORD is over [A]many waters.   great
4 The voice of the LORD is powerful,
The voice of the LORD is majestic.

[59] Or, dealings

5 The voice of the LORD breaks the cedars;
Yes, the LORD breaks in pieces [R]the cedars of Lebanon.   Judg. 9:15; 1 Kin. 5:6
6 And He makes Lebanon [R]skip like a
calf,   Ps. 114:4, 6
And Sirion like a young wild ox.
7 The voice of the LORD hews out [T]flames
of fire.   lightning
8 The voice of the LORD [A]shakes the wilderness;   causes . . . to whirl
The LORD shakes the wilderness of [RT]Ka-
desh.   Num. 13:26
9 The voice of the LORD makes the [R]deer
to calve,   Job 39:1
And strips the forests bare,
And [R]in His temple everything says,
"Glory!"   Ps. 26:8

10 The LORD sat as King at the flood;
Yes, the LORD sits as King forever.
11 [A]The LORD will give [R]strength to His peo-
ple;   May the LORD give • Ps. 28:8
[A]The LORD will bless His people with
[R]peace.   May the LORD bless • [Ps. 37:11]

PSALM 30

Praise for Dramatic Deliverance

A Psalm; a Song at the Dedication of
the House.
A Psalm of David.

I WILL [R]extol Thee, O LORD, for Thou hast
lifted me up,   Ps. 118:28; 145:1
And hast not let my [R]enemies rejoice
over me.   Ps. 25:2; 35:19, 24
2 O LORD my God,
I [R]cried to Thee for help, and Thou didst
[R]heal me.   Ps. 88:13 • Ps. 6:2; 103:3
3 O LORD, Thou hast brought up my soul
from [T]Sheol;   the nether world
Thou hast kept me alive, that I should
not [R]go down to the pit.   Ps. 28:1
4 [R]Sing praise to the LORD, you [R]His godly
ones,   Ps. 149:1 • Ps. 50:5
And give thanks to His holy name.
5 For His anger is but for a moment,
His [R]favor is for a lifetime;   Ps. 118:1
Weeping may last for the night,

29:2 **Worship by Israel**—The central aspect of Israel's worship was the object of their worship, the Lord. While other nations paid homage to many gods (Page 196—Deut. 29:18), only Israel worshiped the one true God (Page 71—Ex. 20:3). This worship could be private (Page 85—Ex. 34:8), as a family (Page 22—Gen. 22:5), or corporate (Page 415—1 Chr. 29:20), as a congregation.

Since so much of the Bible is devoted to Israel's public worship, it deserves special notice. It included offering sacrifices (Page 263—1 Sam. 1:3), adopting a reverent posture (Page 425—2 Chr. 7:6), verbal praise—either spoken (Page 403—1 Chr. 16:36) or sung (Page 557—Ps. 57:7), instrumental praise (Page 605—Ps. 150:3–5), prayer (Page 423—2 Chr. 6:14–42), and the great feasts (Page 117—Lev. 23; 25). One need only read the Psalms to see the excellent form and spirit in which the godly of Israel worshiped.

The first place of worship for the people of Israel was the tabernacle constructed by Moses (Page 76—Ex. 25—27; 30; 31; 35—40) and later the magnificent temple constructed by Solomon (Page 408—1 Chr. 22:5). These structures served to localize the worship of the entire nation. This geographic limitation stands in bold contrast to the privilege of immediate and direct access to God now available to the New Testament believer who himself is the temple of God (Page 1241—Heb. 4:16; Page 1153—1 Cor. 6:19).

Now turn to Page 1101—Acts 7:38: The Meaning of the Church.

But a shout of joy *comes* in the morning.

6 Now as for me, I said in my prosperity,
"I will[R]never be moved." [Ps. 10:6; 62:2, 6]
7 O LORD, by Thy favor Thou hast made
my mountain to stand strong;
Thou didst[R]hide Thy face, I was dismayed. [Deut. 31:17; Ps. 104:29; 143:7]
8 To Thee, O LORD, I called,
And to the LORD I made supplication:
9"What profit is there in my blood, if I[A]go
down to the pit? [Ps. 28:1]
Will the[R]dust praise Thee? Will it declare Thy faithfulness? [Ps. 6:5]

10"Hear, O LORD, and be gracious to me;
O LORD, be Thou my[R]helper." Ps. 27:9
11 Thou hast turned for me[R]my mourning
into dancing; Eccl. 3:4; Jer. 31:4, 13
Thou hast[R]loosed and
girded me with gladness. Is. 20:2
12 That *my*[A]soul[R]may sing praise to Thee,
and not be silent. *glory* · Ps. 16:9
O LORD my God, I will[A]give thanks to
Thee forever. Ps. 44:8

PSALM 31

"Let Your Heart Take Courage"

For the choir director.
A Psalm of David.

IN Thee, O LORD, I have taken refuge;
Let me never[R]be ashamed; Ps. 25:2
In Thy righteousness deliver me.
2 [R]Incline Thine ear to me, rescue me
quickly; Ps. 17:6; 71:2; 86:1; 102:2
Be Thou to me a rock of strength,
A stronghold to save me.
3 For Thou art my rock and my fortress;
For[R]Thy name's sake Thou wilt lead me
and guide me. [Ps. 23:3; 25:11]
4 Thou wilt pull me out of the net which
they have secretly laid for me;
For Thou art my[R]strength. [Ps. 46:1]
5 Into Thy hand I commit my spirit;
Thou hast[R]ransomed me, O LORD, God
of[A]truth. Ps. 55:18; 71:23 · *faithfulness*

6 I hate those who regard vain idols;
But I[R]trust in the LORD. Ps. 52:8
7 I will[R]rejoice and be glad in Thy lovingkindness, Ps. 90:14
Because Thou hast seen my affliction;
Thou hast known the troubles of my
soul,
8 And Thou hast not[R]given me over into
the hand of the enemy; [Deut. 32:30]
Thou hast set my feet in a large place.

9 Be gracious to me, O LORD, for[R]I am in
distress; Ps. 66:14; 69:17
My[R]eye is wasted away from grief, my
soul and my body *also*. Ps. 6:7

10 For my life is spent with[R]sorrow,
And my years with sighing; Ps. 13:2
My[R]strength has failed because of my
iniquity, Ps. 39:11
And[R]my body has wasted away. Ps. 32:3
11 Because of all my adversaries, I have
become a[R]reproach, Ps. 69:19
Especially to my[R]neighbors, Job 19:13
And an object of dread to my acquaintances;
Those who see me in the street flee
from me.
12 I am[R]forgotten as a dead man, out of
mind, Ps. 88:5
I am like a broken vessel.
13 For I have heard the slander of many,
[R]Terror is on every side; Lam. 2:22
While they[R]took counsel together
against me, Ps. 62:4; Matt. 27:1
They schemed to take away my life.

14 But as for me, I trust in Thee, O LORD,
I say, "Thou[A]art my God." Ps. 140:6
15 My[R]times are in Thy hand; Job. 14:5; 24:1
[R]Deliver me from the hand of my enemies, and from those who persecute me. Ps. 143:9
16 Make Thy[R]face to shine upon Thy servant; Num. 6:25; Ps. 4:6; 80:3
[R]Save me in Thy lovingkindness. Ps. 6:4
17 Let me not be[R]put to shame, O LORD,
for I call upon Thee; Ps. 25:2, 20
Let the[R]wicked be put to shame, let
them be silent in Sheol. Ps. 25:3
18 Let the[R]lying lips be dumb, Ps. 109:2
Which[R]speak arrogantly against the
righteous [1 Sam. 2:3]; Ps. 94:4; [Jude 15]
With pride and contempt.

19 How great is Thy[R]goodness,
Which Thou hast stored up for those
who fear Thee, Is. 64:4; [Rom. 2:4]
Which Thou hast wrought for those
who[R]take refuge in Thee, Ps. 5:11
[R]Before the sons of men! Ps. 23:5
20 Thou dost hide them in the[R]secret place
of Thy presence from the[R]conspiracies of man; [Ps. 27:5] · Ps. 37:12
Thou dost keep them secretly in a shelter from the strife of tongues.
21 [R]Blessed be the LORD, Ps. 28:6
For He has made[R]marvelous His
lovingkindness to me in a besieged
[R]city. [Ps. 17:7] · 1 Sam. 23:7; Ps. 87:5
22 As for me,[R]I said in my alarm, Ps. 116:11
"I am cut off from before Thine eyes";
Nevertheless Thou didst[R]hear the voice
of my supplications
When I cried to Thee. Ps. 18:6; 145:19

23 O love the LORD, all you[R]His godly
ones! Ps. 30:4; 37:28; 50:5
The LORD preserves the faithful,
And fully recompenses the proud doer.

24 ^RBe strong, and let your heart take courage,   [Ps. 27:14]
All you who^Ahope in the LORD.   *wait for*

PSALM 32

The Blessedness of Forgiveness

A Psalm of David. A ⁶⁰Maskil.

H^ROW blessed is he whose transgression is
forgiven,   [Ps. 85:2; 103:3]; Rom. 4:7, 8
Whose sin is covered!
2 How blessed is the man to whom the
LORD does not impute iniquity,
And in whose spirit there is no deceit!

3 When I kept silent *about my sin*, my
^Abody wasted away   *bones, substance*
Through my groaning all day long.
4 For day and night^RThy hand was heavy
upon me;   1 Sam. 5:6; Job 23:2; 33:7
My vitality was drained away *as* with
the fever heat of summer.   [Selah.

5 I acknowledged my sin to Thee,
And my iniquity I did not hide;
I said, "I^Rwill confess my transgressions
to the LORD";   [Prov. 28:13]
And Thou didst forgive the guilt of my
sin.   [Selah.

6 Therefore, let everyone who is godly
pray to Thee in a time when Thou
mayest be found;
Surely^Rin a flood of great waters they
shall not reach him. Ps. 46:1-3; Is. 43:2
7 Thou art ^Rmy hiding place; Thou dost
preserve me from trouble;   Ps. 9:9
Thou dost surround me with songs of
deliverance.   [Selah.

8 I will^Rinstruct you and teach you in the
way which you should go;   Ps. 25:8
I will counsel you^Rwith My eye upon
you.   Ps. 33:18
9 Do not be as the horse or as the mule
which have no understanding,
Whose trappings include bit and bridle
to hold them in check,

⁶⁰ Possibly, *Contemplative* or *Didactic*, or *Skillful Psalm*

Otherwise they will not come near to
you.
10 Many are the sorrows of the wicked;
But he who trusts in the LORD, lovingkindness shall surround him.
11 Be ^Rglad in the LORD and rejoice, you
righteous ones,   Ps. 64:10; 68:3; 97:12
And shout for joy, all you who are^Rup-
right in heart.   Ps. 7:10; 64:10

PSALM 33

God Considers All Man's Works

S^RING for joy in the LORD, O you righteous
ones;   Ps. 32:11; Phil. 3:1; 4:4
Praise is becoming to the upright.
2 Give thanks to the LORD with the lyre;
Sing praises to Him with a^Rharp of ten
strings.   Ps. 144:9
3 Sing to Him a^Rnew song;   Ps. 40:3; 96:1
Play skillfully with a shout of joy.
4 For the word of the LORD is upright;
And all His work is *done*^Rin faithfulness.   Ps. 119:90
5 He loves righteousness and justice;
The ^Rearth is full of the lovingkindness
of the LORD.   Ps. 119:64

6 By the^Rword of the LORD the heavens
were made,   Gen. 1:6; [Heb. 11:3]
And ^Rby the breath of His mouth ^Rall
their host.   Ps. 104:30 • Gen. 2:1
7 He gathers the ^Rwaters of the sea together as a heap;   Ex. 15:8; Josh. 3:16
He lays up the deeps in storehouses.
8 Let ^Rall the earth fear the LORD;   Ps. 67:7
Let all the inhabitants of the world
^Rstand in awe of Him.   Ps. 96:9
9 For^RHe spoke, and it was done;   Gen. 1:3
He commanded, and it stood fast.
10 The LORD ^Rnullifies the counsel of the
nations;   [Ps. 2:1-3]; Is. 8:10; 19:3
He frustrates the plans of the peoples.
11 The ^Rcounsel of the LORD stands forever,   Job 23:12; [Prov. 19:21]
The^Rplans of His heart from generation
to generation.   Ps. 40:5; 92:5; 139:17
12 Blessed is the^Rnation whose God is the
LORD,   Ps. 144:15
The people whom He has ^Rchosen for
His own inheritance.   [Ex. 19:5]

32:5 What Should Be Done About Sin—The believer should never condone or attempt to excuse his sin.
There are only two things that he should do about his sin: confess it and forsake it. The Old and New Testament are
agreed on this. David confessed his sin and experienced the Lord's forgiveness. John agrees as he points out: "If
we confess our sins, He is faithful and righteous to forgive us our sins and to cleanse us from all unrighteousness"
(Page 1274—1 John 1:9). To "confess" means *to acknowledge* or *to say the same thing as.* The believer is instructed that he is to say the same thing as God says about his sin, "It is sin." When the believer confesses his sin
he has the assurance that God "is faithful" (He can be counted upon to keep His word) and "just" (He is just in
dealing with our sins because He paid the price for them) "to forgive us our sin and to cleanse us from all unrighteousness." There is no sin too great and no sin too small—God is able to cleanse us completely from anything
that is inconsistent with His own moral character. Having received forgiveness and cleansing, the believer is to
forsake his sin and yield himself completely to God. In doing this the believer is restored to full fellowship with God.
Now turn to Page 1275—1 John 2:15: Temptation by the World.

13 The Lord[R]looks from heaven;　Job 28:24
He [R]sees all the sons of men;　Ps. 11:4
14 From His dwelling place He looks out
On all the inhabitants of the earth,
15 He who fashions the hearts of them all,
He who understands all their works.
16 [R]The king is not saved by a mighty
army;　Ps. 44:6; 60:11
A warrior is not delivered by great
strength.
17 A horse is a false hope for victory;
Nor does it deliver anyone by its great
strength.

18 Behold,[R]the eye of the Lord is on those
who fear Him,　[Job 36:7]; Ps. 32:8
On those who[ ]hope[R]for His lovingkindness,　wait • Ps. 32:10; 147:11
19 To deliver their soul from death,
And to keep them alive in famine.
20 Our soul[R]waits for the Lord;　Is. 8:17
He is our[R]help and our shield.　Ps. 115:9
21 For our heart rejoices in Him,
Because we trust in His holy name.
22 Let Thy lovingkindness, O Lord, be
upon us,
According as we have hoped in Thee.

PSALM 34

Seek the Lord

A *Psalm* of David when he feigned
madness before Abimelech, who drove
him away and he departed.

I WILL bless the Lord at all times;
His [R]praise shall continually be in my
mouth.　Ps. 71:6
2 My soul shall [R]make its boast in the
Lord;　Ps. 44:8; [Jer. 9:24]; 1 Cor. 1:31
The humble shall hear it and rejoice.
3 O[R]magnify the Lord with me,　Luke 1:46
And let us exalt His name together.

4 I [R]sought the Lord, and He answered
me,　[2 Chr. 15:2; Ps. 9:10; Matt. 7:7]
And delivered me from all my fears.
5 They looked to Him and were radiant,
And their faces shall [R]never be
ashamed.　Ps. 25:3
6 This [A]poor man cried and [R]the Lord
heard him,　afflicted • Ps. 34:4
And saved him out of all his troubles.
7 The[R]angel of the Lord encamps around
those who fear Him,
And rescues them.　[Ps. 91:11]; Dan. 6:22

8 O taste and see that the Lord is good;
How[R]blessed is the man who takes refuge in Him!　Ps. 2:12
9 O fear the Lord, you[R]His saints;
For to those who fear Him, there is[R]no
want.　Ps. 31:23 • Ps. 23:1
10 The young lions do lack and suffer hunger;
But they who seek the Lord shall not
be in want of any good thing.

11 Come, you children, listen to me;
I will teach you the fear of the Lord.
12 Who is the man who desires life,
And loves *length of* days that he may
see good?
13 Keep[R]your tongue from evil,　Prov. 13:3
And your lips from speaking deceit.
14 [R]Depart from evil, and do good;　Is. 1:16
Seek peace, and[R]pursue it.　[Heb. 12:14]

15 The [R]eyes of the Lord are toward the
righteous,　Job 36:7; [Ps. 33:18]
And His ears are *open* to their cry.
16 The [R]face of the Lord is against evildoers,　Lev. 17:10; Jer. 44:11; Amos 9:4
To [R]cut off the memory of them from
the earth.　Job 18:17; Ps. 9:6
17 *The righteous* cry and the Lord hears,
And delivers them out of all their troubles.
18 The Lord is near to the brokenhearted,
And saves those who are [61]crushed[R]in
spirit.　Ps. 51:17; [Is. 57:15]

19 [R]Many are the [R]afflictions of the righteous;　Prov. 24:16 • [2 Tim. 3:11f.]
But the Lord[R]delivers him out of them
all.　Ps. 34:4, 6, 17
20 He keeps all his bones;
[R]Not one of them is broken.　John 19:36☆
21 [R]Evil shall slay the wicked;　Prov. 24:16
And those who hate the righteous will
be [A]condemned.　held guilty
22 The Lord[R]redeems the soul of His servants;　1 Kin. 1:29; Ps. 71:23
And none of those who take refuge in
Him will be [A]condemned.　held guilty

PSALM 35

Petition for God's Intervention

A *Psalm* of David.

CONTEND, O Lord, with those who[R]con-
tend with me;　Ps. 18:43; Is. 49:25
Fight against those who[R]fight against
me.　Ps. 56:2
2 Take hold of [62]buckler[R]and shield,
And rise up for my help.　Ps. 91:4
3 Draw also the spear and the battle-axe
to meet those who pursue me;
Say to my soul, "I am your salvation."
4 Let those be [A]ashamed and dishonored
who seek my[A]life;　Ps. 70:2 • soul
Let those be turned back and humiliated who devise evil against me.
5 Let them be like chaff before the wind,
With the angel of the Lord driving
them on.
6 Let their way be dark and slippery,
With the angel of the Lord pursuing
them.

61 Or, *contrite*　62 I.e., small shield

7 For ^Rwithout cause they^Rhid their net for
me;   Ps. 69:4; 109:3; 140:5 • Ps. 9:15
Without cause they dug a pit for my
soul.
8 Let ^Rdestruction come upon him unawares;   Is. 47:11; [1 Thess. 5:3]
And^Rlet the net which he hid catch himself;   Ps. 9:15
Into that very destruction let him fall.

9 And my soul shall rejoice in the LORD;
It shall ^Rexult in His salvation.   Ps. 9:14
10 All my^Rbones will say, "LORD,^Rwho is
like Thee,   Ps. 51:8 • [Ex. 15:11]
Who delivers the afflicted from him
^Rwho is too strong for him,   Ps. 18:17
And^Rthe afflicted and the needy from
him who robs him?"   Ps. 37:14; 109:16
11 ^RMalicious witnesses rise up;
They ask me of things that I do not
know.   Mark 14:57, 58 ☆
12 They^Rrepay me evil for good,   Jer. 18:20
To the bereavement of my soul.
13 But as for me,^Rwhen they were sick, my
clothing was sackcloth;   Job 30:25
I humbled my soul with fasting;
And my prayer kept returning to my
bosom.
14 I went about as though it were my
friend or brother;
I bowed down ^Amourning, as one who
sorrows for a mother. *dressed in black*
15 But at my ⁶³stumbling they rejoiced,
and gathered themselves together;
The smiters whom I did not know gathered together against me,
They slandered me without ceasing.
16 Like godless jesters at a feast,
They gnashed at me with their teeth.

17 Lord, how long wilt Thou look on?
Rescue my soul from their ravages,
My ^Conly *life* from the lions. Ps. 22:20, 21
18 I will^Rgive Thee thanks in the great congregation;   Ps. 22:22
I will ^Rpraise Thee among a mighty
throng.   Ps. 22:25
19 Do not let those who are wrongfully
my enemies rejoice over me;
Neither let those who hate me without
cause ^Awink maliciously. *wink the eye*
20 For they do not speak peace,
But they devise deceitful words against
those who are quiet in the land.
21 And they ^Ropened their mouth wide
against me;   Job 16:10; Ps. 22:13
They said, "Aha, ^Raha, our eyes have
seen it!"   Ps. 40:15; 70:3

22 ^RThou hast seen it, O LORD,^Rdo not keep
silent;   Ex. 3:7; Ps. 10:14 • Ps. 28:1
O Lord, ^Rdo not be far from me. Ps. 10:1
23 Stir up Thyself, and awake to my right,
And to my cause, my God and my
Lord.

24 ^RJudge me, O LORD my God, according
to Thy righteousness;   [Ps. 9:4; 26:1]
And do not let them rejoice over me.
25 Do not let them say in their heart,
"Aha,^Rour desire!"   Ps. 35:21
Do not let them say, "We have ^Rswal-
lowed him up!"   Prov. 1:12; Lam. 2:16
26 Let ^Rthose be ashamed and humiliated
altogether who rejoice at my dis-
tress;   Ps. 40:14
Let those be ^Rclothed with shame and
dishonor who ^Rmagnify themselves
over me.   Ps. 109:29 • Job 19:5

27 Let them^Rshout for joy and rejoice, who
favor my vindication;   Ps. 32:11
And ^Rlet them say continually, "The
LORD be magnified,   Ps. 40:16; 70:4
Who ^Rdelights in the prosperity of His
servant."   Ps. 147:11; 149:4
28 And^Rmy tongue shall declare Thy righteousness   [Ps. 51:14; 71:15, 24]
And Thy praise all day long.

PSALM 36

The Excellent Lovingkindness of God

For the choir director.   *A Psalm* of
David the servant of the LORD.

Transgression speaks to the ungodly
within his heart;
There is no fear of God before his eyes.
2 For it flatters him in his *own* eyes,
Concerning the discovery of his iniquity *and* the hatred *of it.*
3 The ^Rwords of his mouth are wickedness and deceit;   Ps. 10:7; 12:2
He has ^Rceased to ^Abe wise *and* to do
good.   Ps. 94:8 • *understand to do good*
4 He plans wickedness upon his bed;
He sets himself on a ^Rpath that is not
good;   Is. 65:2
He^Rdoes not despise evil.   Ps. 52:3

5 Thy ^Rlovingkindness, O LORD, ^Textends
to the heavens,   Ps. 57:10 • *is in*
Thy faithfulness *reaches* to the skies.
6 Thy righteousness is like the ^Amoun-
tains of God;   *mighty mountains*
Thy judgments are *like* a great deep.
O LORD, Thou ^Rpreservest man and
beast.   Neh. 9:6; Ps. 104:14, 15; 145:16
7 How ^Rprecious is Thy lovingkindness, O
God!   Ps. 40:5; 139:17
And the children of men^Rtake refuge in
the shadow of Thy wings.   Ps. 17:8
8 They ^Rdrink their fill of the ^Aabundance
of Thy house;   Ps. 63:5; 65:4 • *fatness*
And Thou dost give them to drink of
the^Rriver of Thy delights.   Job 20:17
9 For with Thee is the^Rfountain of life;
In Thy light we see light.   [Jer. 2:13]

10 O continue Thy lovingkindness to
^Rthose who know Thee,   [Jer. 22:16]

⁶³ Or, *limping*

And Thy [R]righteousness to the upright in heart.   Ps. 24:5
11 Let not the foot of pride come upon me,
And let not the hand of the wicked drive me away.
12 There the doers of iniquity have fallen;
They have been thrust down and [R]cannot rise.   Ps. 140:10; Is. 26:14

PSALM 37

"Rest in the LORD"

A Psalm of David.

Do not fret because of evildoers,
Be not envious toward wrongdoers.
2 For they will [R]wither quickly like the grass,   Job 14:2; Ps. 90:6; 92:7; James 1:11
And [R]fade like the green herb.   Ps. 129:6
3 [R]Trust in the LORD, and do good;   Ps. 62:8
[R]Dwell in the land and [64]cultivate [R]faithfulness.   [Deut. 30:20] • Ezek. 34:13, 14
4 [R]Delight yourself in the LORD;   Job 22:26
And He will [R]give you the desires of your heart.   [Matt. 7:7, 8]
5 Commit your way to the LORD,
Trust also in Him, and He will do it.
6 And He will bring forth [R]your righteousness as the light,   Ps. 97:11; [Is. 58:8f.]
And your judgment as the noonday.

7 [65]Rest in the LORD and [R]wait [66]patiently for Him;   Ps. 40:1; 62:5; [Lam. 3:26]
[R]Do not fret because of him who prospers in his way,   Ps. 37:1, 8
Because of the man who carries out wicked schemes.
8 Cease from anger, and forsake wrath;
Do not fret, *it leads* only to evildoing.
9 For [R]evildoers will be cut off,   Ps. 37:2, 22
But those who wait for the LORD, they will [R]inherit the land.   [Is. 57:13; 60:21]
10 Yet [R]a little while and the wicked man will be no more;   Job 24:24
And you will look carefully for his place, and he will not be *there*.
11 But the humble will inherit the land,
And will delight themselves in [R]abundant prosperity.   Ps. 72:7

12 The wicked plots against the righteous,
And gnashes at him with his teeth.
13 The Lord [R]laughs at him;   Ps. 2:4
For He sees [R]his day is coming. Job 18:20
14 The wicked have drawn the sword and [R]bent their bow,   Ps. 11:2; Lam. 2:4
To cast down the [R]afflicted and the needy,   Ps. 35:10; 86:1
To [R]slay those who are upright in conduct.   Ps. 11:2
15 Their sword will enter their own heart,
And their [R]bows will be broken. Ps. 46:9

16 Better is the little of the righteous
Than the abundance of many wicked.

17 For the [R]arms of the wicked will be broken;   Job 38:15; Ps. 10:15; Ezek. 30:21
But the LORD sustains the righteous.
18 The LORD [R]knows the days of the [T]blameless;   [Ps. 1:6; 31:7] • *complete;* or, *perfect*
And their inheritance will be forever.
19 They will not be ashamed in the time of evil;
And [R]in the days of famine they will have abundance.   Job 5:20; [Ps. 33:19]
20 But the [R]wicked will perish;   Ps. 73:27
And the enemies of the LORD will be like the [67]glory of the pastures,
They vanish—[R]like smoke they vanish away.   Ps. 68:2; 102:3
21 The wicked borrows and does not pay back,
But the righteous is gracious and gives.
22 For [R]those blessed by Him will [R]inherit the land;   [Prov. 3:33] • Ps. 37:9
But those [R]cursed by Him will be cut off.   Job 5:3

23 [R]The steps of a man are established by the LORD;   1 Sam. 2:9; Ps. 40:2; 66:9
And He [R]delights in his way.   Ps. 147:11
24 When [R]he falls, he shall not be hurled headlong;   Prov. 24:16; Mic. 7:8
Because the LORD is the One [A]who holds his hand. *who sustains him with His hand*
25 I have been young, and now I am old;
Yet [R]I have not seen the righteous forsaken,   Ps. 37:28; Is. 41:17; [Heb. 13:5]
Or his descendants begging bread.
26 All day long he is gracious and lends;
And his descendants are a blessing.

27 [R]Depart from evil, and do good, Ps. 34:14
So you will abide forever.
28 For the LORD loves [T]justice,   *judgment*
And does not forsake His godly ones;
They are [R]preserved forever;   Ps. 31:23
But the [R]descendants [R]of the wicked will be cut off. *seed* • Ps. 21:10; 37:9; Is. 14:20
29 The righteous will inherit the land,
And [A]dwell in it forever.   Ps. 37:18
30 The mouth of the righteous [R]utters wisdom,   Ps. 49:3; Prov. 10:13
And his tongue [R]speaks justice. Ps. 101:1
31 The law of his God is in his heart;
His [R]steps do not slip.   Ps. 26:1; 37:23
32 The wicked spies upon the righteous,
And [A]seeks to kill him.   Ps. 37:14
33 The LORD will [R]not leave him in his hand,   Ps. 31:8; [2 Pet. 2:9]
Or [R]let him be condemned when he is judged.   Ps. 34:22; 109:31
34 Wait for the LORD, and keep His way,
And He will exalt you to inherit the land;
When the [R]wicked are cut off, you will see it.   Ps. 52:5, 6; 91:8

35 I have seen a violent, wicked man

---

[64] Or, *feed securely,* or, *feed on His faithfulness*
[65] Or, *Be still*   [66] Or, *longingly*   [67] I.e., *flowers*

Spreading himself like a^Rluxuriant^Ttree
  in its native soil.   Job 8:16 · *native*
36 Then he passed away, and lo, he was
  no more;
  I sought for him, but he could not be
  found.
37 Mark the ^Tblameless man, and behold
  the upright;   *complete;* or, *perfect*
  For the man of peace will have a ^Tpos-
  terity.^R   *an end* · Is. 57:1, 2
38 But transgressors will be altogether^Rde-
  stroyed;   [Ps. 1:4–6; 37:20, 28]
  The ^Tposterity of the wicked will be ^Tcut
  off.   *end* · Ps. 37:9; 73:17
39 But the ^Rsalvation of the righteous is
  from the LORD;   Ps. 3:8; 62:1
  He is their strength in time of trouble.
40 And^Tthe LORD helps them, and delivers
  them;   Ps. 54:4
  He^Rdelivers them from the wicked, and
  saves them, Ps. 22:4; Is. 31:5; Dan. 3:17
  Because they take refuge in Him.

PSALM 38

The Heavy Burden of Sin

A Psalm of David, for a memorial.

O LORD, rebuke me not in Thy wrath;
  And chasten me not in Thy burning anger.
2 For Thine ^Rarrows have sunk deep into
  me,   Job 6:4
  And^RThy hand has pressed down on
  me.   Ps. 32:4
3 There is ^Rno soundness in my flesh because of Thine indignation;   Is. 1:6
  There is no health^Rin my bones because
  of my sin.   Job 33:19; Ps. 6:2; 31:10
4 For my ^Tiniquities are gone over my
  head;   Ezra 9:6; Ps. 40:12
  As a heavy burden they weigh too
  much for me.
5 My wounds grow foul *and* fester.
  Because of ^Tmy folly,   Ps. 69:5
6 I am bent over and ^Rgreatly bowed
  down;   Ps. 35:14
  I^Rgo mourning all day long.   Job 30:28
7 For my loins are filled with burning;
  And there is no soundness in my flesh.
8 I am benumbed and badly crushed;
  I ^Tgroan^Rbecause of the ^Tagitation of my
  heart.   *roar* · Job 3:24 · *growling*

9 Lord, all my desire is before Thee;
  And my ^Rsighing is not hidden from
  Thee.   Ps. 6:6; 102:5
10 My heart throbs, my strength fails me;
  And the^Rlight of my eyes, even ^Tthat has
  gone from me.   Ps. 6:7 · *they have*
11 My ^Tloved ones and my friends stand
  aloof from my plague;   *lovers*
  And my kinsmen stand afar off.

12 Those who^Rseek my life^Rlay snares *for
  me*;   Ps. 54:3 · Ps. 140:5
  And those who seek to injure me have
  ^Tthreatened destruction,   *spoken*
  And they devise treachery all day long.
13 But I, like a deaf man, do not hear;
  And I am like a ^Tdumb man who does
  not open his mouth. Matt. 27:12–14☆
14 Yes, I am like a man who does not
  hear,
  And in whose mouth are no arguments.
15 For I^Rhope in Thee, O LORD;   *wait for*
  Thou wilt answer, O Lord my God.
16 For I said, "May they not rejoice over
  me,
  Who, when my foot slips, would magnify themselves against me."
17 For I am ^Rready to fall,   Ps. 35:15
  And ^Tmy ⁶⁸sorrow is continually before
  me.   Ps. 13:2
18 For^TI confess my iniquity;   *declare*
  I am full of anxiety because of my sin.
19 But my ^Renemies are vigorous *and*
  ⁶⁹strong;   Ps. 18:17
  And many are those who ^Rhate me
  wrongfully.   Ps. 35:19
20 And those who repay evil for good,
  They^Roppose me, because I follow what
  is good.   Ps. 109:5; 1 John 3:12
21 Do not forsake me, O LORD;
  O my God, do not be far from me!
22 Make^Rhaste to help me,   Ps. 40:13, 17
  O Lord, ^Rmy salvation!   Ps. 27:1

PSALM 39

Know the Extent of Man's Days

For the choir director, for Jeduthun.
  A Psalm of David.

I SAID, "I will^Rguard my ways,   1 Kin. 2:4
  That I may not sin with my tongue;
  I will guard^Rmy mouth as with a muz-
  zle,   Ps. 141:3; [James 3:2]
  While the wicked are in my presence."
2 I was dumb^Tand silent,   *with silence*
  I ⁷⁰refrained *even* from good;
  And my ⁶⁸sorrow grew worse.
3 My^Theart was hot within me;   Ps. 32:4
  While I was musing the fire burned;
  Then I spoke with my tongue:
4 "LORD, make me to know my end,
  And what is the extent of my days,
  Let me know how transient I am.
5 "Behold, Thou hast made^Rmy days *as*
  handbreadths,   Ps. 89:47
  And my ^Rlifetime as nothing in Thy
  sight,   Ps. 144:4
  Surely every man at his best is a mere
  breath.   [Selah.
6 "Surely every man^Rwalks about as ⁷¹a
  phantom;   [1 Cor. 7:31]; James 1:10, 11
  Surely they make an ^Tuproar for nothing;   Ps. 127:2; Eccl. 5:17
  He^Ramasses *riches*, and does not know
  who will gather them.   Ps. 49:10

⁶⁸ Lit., *pain*   ⁶⁹ Or, *numerous*
⁷⁰ Lit., *kept silence*   ⁷¹ Lit., *an image*

7"And now, Lord, for what do I wait?
My^Rhope is in Thee.   Ps. 38:15
8"Deliver me from all my transgressions;
Make me not the^Rreproach of the foolish.   Ps. 44:13; 79:4; 119:22
9"I have become^Rdumb, I do not open my
mouth,   Ps. 39:2
Because it is Thou who hast done *it.*
10"Remove^RThy plague from me;   Job 9:34
Because of the opposition of Thy hand,
I am^Aperishing.   *wasting away*
11"With ^Rreproofs Thou dost chasten a
man for iniquity; Ezek. 5:15; 2 Pet. 2:16
Thou dost^Rconsume as a moth what is
precious to him;   Job 13:28; [Ps. 90:7]
Surely   every   man   is   a   mere
breath.   [Selah.

12"Hear^Rmy prayer, O Lord, and give ear
to my cry;   Ps. 102:1; 143:1
Do not be silent at my tears;   Ps. 56:8
For I am a stranger with Thee,
A sojourner like all my fathers.
13"Turn^RThy gaze away from me, that I
may ⁷²smile *again,*   Job 7:19; 10:20, 21
Before I depart and am no more."

PSALM 40

Delight to Do God's Will

For the choir director.
A Psalm of David.

I WAITED ⁷³patiently for the Lord;
And He inclined to me,^Rand heard my
cry.   Ps. 34:15
2 He brought me up out of the pit of destruction, out of the miry clay;
And^RHe set my feet upon a rock making my footsteps firm.   Ps. 27:5
3 And He put^Ra new song in my mouth, a
song of praise to our God;   [Ps. 32:7]
Many will^Rsee and fear,   Ps. 52:6; 64:9
And will trust in the Lord.

4 How^Rblessed is the man who has made
the Lord his trust,   Ps. 34:8; 84:12
And has not turned to the proud, nor to
those who lapse into falsehood.
5 Many, O Lord my God, are^Rthe won-
ders which Thou hast done, [Job 5:9]
And Thy^Rthoughts toward us;   Is. 55:8
There is none to compare with Thee;
If I would declare and speak of them,
They would be too numerous to count.

6 ^ASacrifice and meal offering Thou hast
not desired;   Blood sacrifice
My ears Thou hast ⁷⁴opened;
Burnt offering and sin offering Thou
hast not required.
7 Then I said, "Behold, I come;
In the scroll of the book it is^Awritten of
me;   *prescribed for*

8 I delight to do Thy will, O my God;
^RThy Law is within my heart."[Ps. 37:31]

9 I have proclaimed glad tidings of righteousness in the great congregation;
Behold, I will not restrain my lips,
O Lord,^RThou knowest.   Josh. 22:22
10 I have^Rnot hidden Thy righteousness
within my heart;   Acts 20:20, 27
I have^Rspoken of Thy faithfulness and
Thy salvation;   Ps. 89:1
I have not concealed Thy lovingkindness and Thy truth from the great
congregation.

11 Thou, O Lord, wilt not withhold Thy
compassion from me;
Thy^Rlovingkindness and Thy truth will
continually preserve me.   Ps. 43:3
12 For evils beyond number have ^Rsur-
rounded me;   Ps. 18:5; 116:3

⁷² Or, *become cheerful*   ⁷³ Or, *intently*
⁷⁴ Lit., *dug,* or possibly, *pierced*

40:8   We Know God's Will Through His Word—Knowing the will of God must not be thought of merely as finding a certain vocation in life. That aspect represents only a small part of God's will. Rather, the will of God is for everyone to live in conformity to His revealed will in His Word.

a. First of all, and most important, the will of God means believing Christ (Page 1071—John 6:40). If we do not take this first step in doing God's will, we will not be saved from judgment (Page 969—Matt. 7:21; 12:50); if we do we will live forever (Page 1275—1 John 2:17).

b. Second, there are clear statements of Scripture which teach that God's will for every Christian includes sancti-fication (Page 1208—1 Thess. 4:13), giving thanks to God (Page 1208—1 Thess. 5:18), doing good (Page 1262—1Pet. 2:15), and suffering for doing the right thing (Page 1263—1 Pet. 3:17).

c. Third, the Bible is God's will and must be applied to our lives (Page 196—Deut. 29:29). This fact involves commands to be obeyed, principles to be followed, prohibitions of things to be avoided, and living examples to be imitated or shunned. An attitude of delightful desire should fill all attempts to do God's will (Page 548—Ps. 40:8). God takes great joy in those who cheerfully do His will.

Although the Bible is a complete revelation of God's will, there are always decisions we must make that are not covered by specific statements of Scripture. In order to know God's will in such instances we must be in fellowship with the Lord (Page 1274—1 John 1:6, 7), seek principles from the Word (Page 1156—1 Cor. 10:6), obtain advice from godly counselors (Page 617—Prov. 11:14; 15:22; 24:6), use common sense, and remember that God works through our own minds and desires to do His will (Page 1194—Phil. 2:13). When none of these principles seem to work, we must simply make the best possible decision, realizing that God will shut the door if it is not His will. Paul, for example, planned to go and see the Roman Christians, although not knowing if God would actually permit it in His will (Page 1144—Rom. 15:22–32). In most cases, however, the believer who thoroughly searches the Word will find the basis for an intelligent decision.

Now turn to Page 199—Deut. 32:7: God's Work in the Past.

My ^Riniquities have overtaken me, so
   that I _Ram not able to see;   Ps. 38:4
They are ^Rmore numerous than the hairs
   of my head;   Ps. 69:4
And my heart has ^Tfailed me.   *forsaken*

13 Be pleased, O LORD, to deliver me;
   Make haste, O LORD, to help me.
14 Let those be ^Rashamed and humiliated
   together   Ps. 35:4, 26; 70:2; 71:13
   Who seek my ⁷⁵life to destroy it;
   Let those be turned back and dishonored
   Who delight ⁷⁶in my hurt.
15 Let those ^Rbe ^Aappalled because of their
   shame   Ps. 70:3 · *desolated*
   Who ^Rsay to me, "Aha, aha!"   Ps. 35:21
16 ^RLet all who seek Thee rejoice and be
   glad in Thee;   Ps. 70:4
   Let those who love Thy salvation ^Rsay
   continually,   Ps. 35:27
   "The LORD be magnified!"
17 Since ^RI am afflicted and needy,   Ps. 70:5
   ^RLet the Lord be mindful of me; 1 Pet. 5:7
   Thou art my help and my deliverer;
   Do not delay, O my God.

PSALM 41

The Blessedness of Helping the Helpless

For the choir director.
A Psalm of David.

H OW blessed is he who ^Rconsiders the
   ^Ahelpless;   Ps. 82:3, 4; [Prov. 14:21] · *poor*
The LORD will deliver him ^Rin a day of
   ^Atrouble.   Ps. 27:5; 37:19 · *evil*
2 The LORD will ^Rprotect him, and keep
   him alive,   Ps. 37:28
   And he shall ^Abe called ^Rblessed upon the
   earth;   *be blessed* · Ps. 37:22
   And ^Rdo not give him over to the desire
   of his enemies.   Ps. 27:12
3 The LORD will sustain him upon his
   sickbed;
   In his illness, Thou dost ⁷⁷restore him
   to health.

4 As for me, I said, "O LORD, be gracious
   to me;
   ^RHeal my soul, for ^RI have sinned against
   Thee."   Ps. 6:2; 103:3; 147:3 · Ps. 51:4
5 My enemies speak evil against me,
   "When will he die, and his name perish?"
6 And ^Awhen he comes to see *me*, he
   speaks ^Tfalsehood;   *if he · emptiness*
   His heart gathers wickedness to itself;
   When he goes outside, he tells it.
7 All who hate me whisper together
   against me;

Against me they ^Rdevise my hurt, *say-*
   ing,   Ps. 56:5
8 "A wicked thing is poured out ^Aupon
   him,   *within*
   That when he lies down, he will ^Rnot
   rise up again."   Ps. 71:10, 11
9 Even my ^Rclose friend, in whom I
   trusted,   Matt. 26:23; Luke 22:21 ☆
   Who ate my bread,
   Has lifted up his heel against me.

10 But Thou, O LORD, be gracious to me,
   and ^Rraise me up,
   That I may repay them.   [Ps. 3:3]
11 By this I know that ^RThou art pleased
   with me,   [Ps. 37:23; 147:11]
   Because ^Rmy enemy does not shout in
   triumph over me.   Ps. 25:2
12 As for me, ^RThou dost uphold me in my
   integrity,   Ps. 18:32; 37:17; 63:8
   And Thou dost set me ^Rin Thy presence
   forever.   [Job 36:7; Ps. 21:6]

13 Blessed be the LORD, the God of Israel,
   From everlasting to everlasting.
   Amen, and Amen.

BOOK 2

PSALM 42

Seek After the Lord

For the choir director.
A Maskil of the sons of Korah.

A S the deer ⁷⁸pants for the water brooks,
   So my soul pants for Thee, O God.
2 My soul ^Rthirsts for God, for the ^Rliving
   God;   Ps. 63:1; 84:2 · Ps. 84:2; Rom. 9:26
   When shall I come and appear before
   God?
3 My ^Rtears have been my food day and
   night,   Ps. 80:5; 102:9
   While *they* ^Rsay to me all day long,
   "Where is your God?" Ps. 79:10; 115:2
4 These things I remember, and I ^Rpour
   out my soul within me.   1 Sam. 1:15
   For I used to go along with the throng
   and ^Alead them in procession to the
   house of God,   *move slowly with them*
   With the voice of joy and thanksgiving,
   a multitude keeping festival.

5 Why are you in despair, O my soul?
   And *why* have you become ^Rdisturbed
   within me?   Ps. 77:3
   ^AHope ^Rin God, for I shall ^Aagain praise
   Him   *Wait for* · Ps. 71:14 · *still*
   For the help of His presence.
6 O my God, my soul is ^Ain despair within
   me;   *sunk down*
   Therefore I ^Rremember Thee from the
   land of the Jordan,   Ps. 61:2

---

⁷⁵ Or, *soul*   ⁷⁶ Or, *to injure me*
⁷⁷ Lit., *turn all his bed*   ⁷⁸ Lit., *longs for*

And the[T]peaks of[R]Hermon, from Mount
Mizar.   *Hermons* • Deut. 3:8
7 Deep calls to deep at the sound of Thy
waterfalls;
All Thy[R]breakers and Thy waves have
rolled over me. Ps. 69:1, 2; 88:7; Jon. 2:3
8 The LORD will [R]command His lovingkindness in the daytime;   Ps. 57:3
And His song will be with me[R]in the
night,   Job 35:10; Ps. 16:7; 63:6; 77:6
A prayer to the God of my life.

9 I will say to God[R]my rock, "Why hast
Thou forgotten me?   Ps. 18:2
Why do I go[R]mourning because of the
oppression of the enemy?"   Ps. 38:6
10 As a shattering of my bones, my adver-
saries revile me,
While they[R]say to me all day long,
"Where is your God?"   Ps. 42:3
11 Why are you in despair, O my soul?
And why have you become disturbed
within me?
Hope in God, for I shall yet praise Him,
The[A]help of my countenance, and my
God.   *saving acts of*

PSALM 43

"Hope in God"

VINDICATE me, O God, and plead my
case against an ungodly nation;
[A]O deliver me from[R]the deceitful and unjust man!   *Mayest Thou* • Ps. 5:6; 38:12
2 For Thou art the[R]God of my strength;
why hast Thou rejected me? Ps. 18:1
Why do I go[R]mourning because of the
oppression of the enemy?   Ps. 42:9

3 O send out Thy[R]light and Thy truth, let
them lead me;   Ps. 36:9
Let them bring me to Thy holy hill,
And to Thy[R]dwelling places.   Ps. 84:1
4 Then I will go to the altar of God,
To God my exceeding[R]joy;   Ps. 21:6
And upon the[R]lyre I shall praise Thee,
O God, my God.   Ps. 33:2; 49:4; 57:8

5 Why are you in despair, O my soul?
And why are you disturbed within me?
[A]Hope in God, for I shall[A]again praise
Him,   *Wait for* • *still*
The[A]help of my countenance, and my
God.   *saving acts of*

PSALM 44

Prayer for Deliverance by God

For the choir director.
A Maskil of the sons of Korah.

O GOD, we have heard with our ears,
Our[R]fathers have told us, [Ex. 12:26, 27]

The work that Thou didst in their days,
In the[R]days of old.   Deut. 32:7; Ps. 77:5
2 Thou with Thine own hand didst[R]drive
out the nations;   Josh. 3:10; Neh. 9:24
Then Thou didst[R]plant them;   Ex. 15:17
Thou didst[R]afflict the peoples, Ps. 135:10
Then Thou didst spread them abroad.
3 For by their own sword they[R]did not
possess the land;   [Deut. 8:17, 18]
And their own arm did not save them;
But Thy right hand, and Thine[R]arm, and
the light of Thy presence,   Ps. 77:15
For Thou didst[R]favor them.   Ps. 106:4

4 Thou art[R]my King, O God;   [Ps. 74:12]
Command[R]victories for Jacob.   *salvation*
5 Through Thee we will[R]push back our
adversaries;   Deut. 33:17; Ps. 60:12
Through Thy name we will trample
down those who rise up against us.
6 For I will[R]not trust in my bow, Ps. 33:16
Nor will my sword save me.
7 But Thou[R]hast saved us from our adversaries,   [Ps. 136:24]
And Thou hast[R]put to shame those who
hate us.   Ps. 53:5
8 In God we have boasted all day long,
And we will give thanks to Thy name
forever.   [Selah.

9 Yet Thou[R]hast rejected *us* and brought
us to dishonor,   Ps. 43:2; 60:1, 10; 74:1
And dost not go out with our armies.
10 Thou dost cause us to[R]turn back from
the adversary;   Lev. 26:17; Josh. 7:8, 12
And those who hate us[R]have taken
spoil for themselves.   Ps. 89:41
11 Thou dost give us as sheep to be eaten,
And hast[R]scattered us among the nations.   Lev. 26:33; Deut. 4:27; 28:64
12 Thou dost sell Thy people cheaply,
And hast not [79]profited by their sale.
13 Thou dost make us a[R]reproach to our
neighbors,   Deut. 28:37; Ps. 79:4; 89:41
A scoffing and a[R]derision to those
around us.   Ps. 80:6; Ezek. 23:32
14 Thou dost make us a[R]byword among
the nations, Job 17:6; Ps. 69:11; Jer. 24:9
A laughingstock among the peoples.
15 All day long my dishonor is before me,
And[T]my humiliation has overwhelmed
me,   *the shame of my face has covered me*
16 Because of the voice of him who[R]re-
proaches and reviles,   Ps. 74:10
Because of the presence of the[R]enemy
and the avenger.   Ps. 8:2

17 All this has come upon us, but we have
[R]not forgotten Thee, Ps. 78:7; 119:61, 83
And we have not[R]dealt falsely with Thy
covenant.   Ps. 78:57
18 Our heart has not turned back,
And our steps[R]have not deviated from
Thy way,   Job 23:11; Ps. 119:51, 157

[79] Or, *set a high price on them*

19 Yet Thou hast ^Rcrushed us in a place of
^Rjackals,   Ps. 51:8; 94:5 • Job 30:29
And covered us with ^Rthe shadow of
death.   Job 3:5; [Ps. 23:4]

20 If we had ^Rforgotten the name of our
God,   Ps. 78:11
Or extended our ^Thands to ^Ra strange
god;   palms • [Deut. 6:14]; Ps. 81:9
21 Would not God ^Rfind this out? [Ps. 139:1]
For He knows the secrets of the heart.
22 But ^Rfor Thy sake we are killed all day
long;   Rom. 8:36
We are considered as ^Rsheep to be
slaughtered.   [Is. 53:7]; Jer. 12:3
23 ^RArouse Thyself, why ^Rdost Thou sleep,
O Lord?   Ps. 7:6 • Ps. 78:65
Awake, do not reject us forever.
24 Why dost Thou ^Rhide Thy face, Job 13:24
And ^Rforget our affliction and our oppression?   Ps. 42:9; Lam. 5:20
25 For our ^Rsoul has sunk down into the
dust;   Ps. 119:25
Our body cleaves to the earth.
26 ^RRise up, be our help,   Ps. 35:2
And ^Rredeem us for the sake of Thy
lovingkindness.   Ps. 6:4; 25:22

PSALM 45

The Psalm of the Great King

For the choir director; according to
the ⁸⁰Shoshannim. A Maskil of the
sons of Korah. A Song of Love.

M Y heart ⁸¹overflows with a good theme;
I address my verses to the King;
My tongue is the pen of a ready writer.
2 Thou art fairer than the sons of men;
Grace is poured ^Aupon Thy lips;   through
Therefore God has ^Rblessed Thee for-
ever.   Ps. 21:6

3 Gird ^RThy sword on Thy thigh, O
^AMighty One,   [Heb. 4:12] • warrior
In Thy splendor and Thy majesty!
4 And in Thy majesty ride on victori-
ously,
For the cause of truth and ^Rmeekness
and righteousness;   Zeph. 2:3
Let Thy ^Rright hand teach Thee ^Aawe-
some things.   Ps. 21:8 • fearful
5 Thine ^Rarrows are sharp;   Ps. 18:14; 120:4
The ^Rpeoples fall under Thee;   Ps. 92:9
Thine arrows are ^Rin the heart of the
King's enemies.   2 Sam. 18:14

6 Thy throne, O God, is forever and ever;
A scepter of ^Ruprightness is the scepter
of Thy kingdom.   [Ps. 98:9]

7 Thou hast ^Rloved righteousness, and
hated wickedness;   [Ps. 11:7; 33:5]
Therefore God, Thy God, has ^Ranointed
Thee   Ps. 2:2
With the oil of joy above Thy fellows.
8 All Thy garments are fragrant with
myrrh and aloes and cassia;
Out of ivory palaces stringed instruments have made Thee glad.
9 Kings' daughters are among ^RThy noble
ladies;   Song 6:8
At Thy ^Rright hand stands the queen in
gold from Ophir.   1 Kin. 2:19

10 Listen, O daughter, give attention and
incline your ear;
^RForget your people and your father's
house;   Deut. 21:13; Ruth 1:16, 17
11 Then the King will desire your beauty;
Because He is your ^RLord, ^Rbow down to
Him.   Gen. 18:12; 1 Pet. 3:6 • Eph. 5:33
12 And the daughter of ^RTyre will come
with a gift;   Ps. 87:4
The ^Rrich among the people will entreat
your favor.   Ps. 22:29; 68:29; 72:10, 11

13 The King's daughter is all glorious
within;
Her clothing is interwoven with gold.
14 She will be ^Rled to the King in embroidered work;   Song 1:4 • Judg. 5:30
The ^Rvirgins, her companions who follow her,   Ps. 45:9
Will be brought to Thee.
15 They will be led forth with gladness
and rejoicing;
They will enter into the King's palace.

16 In place of your fathers will be your
sons;
You shall make them princes in all the
earth.
17 I will cause ^RThy name to be remembered in all generations;   Mal. 1:11
Therefore the peoples ^Rwill give Thee
thanks forever and ever.   Ps. 138:4

PSALM 46

"God Is Our Refuge and Strength"

For the choir director. A Psalm of the
sons of Korah, ⁸²set to Alamoth.
A Song.

G OD is our ^Rrefuge and strength,   Ps. 14:6
⁸³A very present help in trouble.
2 Therefore we will ^Rnot fear, though the
earth should change,   Ps. 23:4; 27:1
And though ^Rthe mountains slip into the
heart of the ^Tsea;   Ps. 18:7 • seas
3 Though its waters roar and foam,
Though the mountains quake at its
swelling pride.   [Selah.

4 There is a ^Rriver whose streams make
glad the city of God,   Ps. 36:8; 65:9

⁸⁰ Possibly, Lilies   ⁸¹ Lit., is astir
⁸² Possibly, for soprano voices
⁸³ Or, Abundantly available for help

The holy ^Rdwelling places of the Most
High.   Ps. 43:3
5 God is^Rin the midst of her, she will not
be moved;   [Deut. 23:14; Is. 12:6]
God will help her ^Twhen morning
dawns.   *at the turning of the morning*
6 The^Anations^Rmade an uproar, the kingdoms tottered;   *Gentiles* • Ps. 2:1, 2
He raised His voice, the earth melted.
7 The LORD of hosts is with us;
The God of Jacob is our stronghold.
[Selah.

8 Come, behold the works of the LORD,
Who has wrought desolations in the
earth.
9 He^Rmakes wars to cease to the end of
the earth;   Is. 2:4; Mic. 4:3
He^Rbreaks the bow and cuts the spear
in two;   1 Sam. 2:4; Ps. 76:3
He^Rburns the chariots with fire.   Is. 9:5
10"Cease ^A*striving* and ^Rknow that I am
God;   *Let go, relax* • [Ps. 100:3]
I will be exalted among the nations, I
will be exalted in the earth."
11 The LORD of hosts is with us;
The God of Jacob is our stronghold.
[Selah.

PSALM 47

The Lord Shall Subdue All Nations

For the choir director.
A Psalm of the sons of Korah.

O^RCLAP your hands, all peoples;   Ps. 98:8
Shout to God with the voice of joy.
2 For the LORD Most High is to be feared,
A great King over all the earth.
3 He^Rsubdues peoples under us,   Ps. 18:47
And nations under our feet.
4 He chooses our inheritance for us,
The glory of Jacob whom He
loves.   [Selah.

5 God has ascended^Awith a shout,   *amid*
The LORD, with the sound of a trumpet.
6 Sing praises to God, sing praises;
Sing praises to our King, sing praises.
7 For God is the King of all the earth;
Sing praises with a skillful psalm.
8 God^Rreigns over the nations, 1 Chr. 16:31
God sits on^RHis holy throne.   Ps. 97:2
9 The^Aprinces of the people have assem-
bled themselves *as* the people of
the God of Abraham;   *nobles*
For the^Rshields of the earth belong to
God;   [Ps. 89:18]
He is highly exalted.

PSALM 48

The Praise of Mount Zion

A Song; a Psalm of the sons of Korah.

G^{REAT} ^Ris the LORD, and greatly to be
praised,   1 Chr. 16:25; Ps. 96:4; 145:3

In the^Rcity of our God, His^Rholy mountain.   Ps. 46:4 • Ps. 2:6; 87:1; Is. 2:3
2 ^RBeautiful in elevation, ^Rthe joy of the
whole earth,   Ps. 50:2 • Lam. 2:15
Is Mount Zion *in* the far north,
The^Rcity of the great King.   Matt. 5:35
3 God, in her palaces,
Has made Himself known as a^Rstrong-
hold.   Ps. 46:7

4 For, lo, the ^Rkings assembled themselves,   2 Sam. 10:6-19
They passed by together.
5 They saw *it*, then they were amazed;
They were terrified, they fled in alarm.
6 Panic seized them there,
Anguish, as of a woman in childbirth.
7 With the^Reast wind   Jer. 18:17
Thou dost break the ships of Tarshish.
8 As we have heard, so have we seen
In the city of the LORD of hosts, in the
city of our God;
God will establish her forever. [Selah.

9 We have thought on^RThy lovingkind-
ness, O God,   Ps. 26:3; 40:10
In the midst of Thy temple.
10 As is Thy^Rname, O God,   [Deut. 28:58]
So is Thy ^Rpraise to the ends of the
earth;   Ps. 65:1, 2; 100:1
Thy right hand is full of righteousness.
11 Let Mount^RZion be glad,   Ps. 97:8
Let the daughters of Judah rejoice,
Because of Thy judgments.
12 Walk about Zion, and go around her;
Count her^Rtowers;   Neh. 3:1, 11, 25-27
13 Consider her^Rramparts;   Ps. 122:7
Go through her palaces;
That you may^Rtell *it* to the next genera-
tion.   [Ps. 78:5-7]
14 For ^Ssuch is God,   *this*
Our God forever and ever;
He will^Rguide us ⁸⁴until death.   Ps. 23:4

PSALM 49

Riches Cannot Redeem

For the choir director.
A Psalm of the sons of Korah.

H^{EAR}^Rthis, all peoples;   Ps. 78:1; Is. 1:2
Give ear, all inhabitants of the world,
2 Both^Rlow and high,   Ps. 62:9
Rich and poor together.
3 My mouth will^Rspeak wisdom; Ps. 37:30
And the meditation of my heart *will be*
^Runderstanding.   [Ps. 119:130]
4 I will incline my ear to a proverb;
I will express my riddle on the harp.

5 Why should I fear in days of adversity,
When the iniquity of my ^Tfoes surrounds me,   *supplanters*
6 Even those who trust in their wealth,

⁸⁴ Some mss. and the Gr. read *forever*

And boast in the abundance of their
  riches?
7 No man can by any means^Rredeem *his*
  brother,   Matt. 25:8, 9
  Or give to God a ransom for him—
8 For the redemption of his soul is costly,
  And he should cease *trying* forever—
9 That he should live on eternally;
  That he should not ⁸⁵undergo decay.

10 For he sees *that even* wise men die;
  The^Rstupid and the senseless alike perish,   Ps. 92:6; 94:8
  And leave their wealth to others.
11 Their ⁸⁶inner^R thought is, *that* their
  houses are forever,   Ps. 64:6
  And their dwelling places to all generations;
  They have^Rcalled their lands after their
  own names.   Gen. 4:17; Deut. 3:14
12 But man in *his* pomp will not endure;
  He is like the beasts that perish.

13 This is the^Rway of those who are foolish,   Jer. 17:11
  And of those after them who approve
  their words.   [Selah.
14 As sheep they are appointed for Sheol;
  Death shall be their shepherd;
  And the^Rupright shall rule over them in
  the morning;   Dan. 7:18; Mal. 4:3
  And their form shall be for ^TSheol to
  consume,   the nether world
  So that they have no habitation.
15 But God will^Rredeem my soul from the
  power of Sheol;   Acts 2:31, 32 ☆
  For He will receive me.   [Selah.

16 Do not be afraid^Rwhen a man becomes
  rich,   [Ps. 37:7]
  When the ⁸⁷glory of his house is increased;
17 For when he dies he will^Rcarry nothing
  away;   Ps. 17:14; 1 Tim. 6:7
  His ⁸⁷glory will not descend after him.
18 Though while he lives he^Rcongratulates
  himself—   Deut. 29:19; Ps. 10:3, 6
  And though *men* praise you when you
  do well for yourself—
19 ^THe shall^Rgo to the generation of his fathers;   *You; or, It* • Gen. 15:15
  They shall never see^Rthe light.   Job 33:30
20 ^RMan in *his* pomp, yet without understanding,   Ps. 49:12 • *honor*
  Is like the^Rbeasts that perish.   *animals*

PSALM 50

The Lord Shall Judge All People

A Psalm of Asaph.

THE^RMighty One, God, the LORD, has spoken,   Josh. 22:22

---

⁸⁵ Or, *see corruption or the pit*
⁸⁶ Some versions read *graves are their houses*
⁸⁷ Or, *wealth*   ⁸⁸ Or, *in My mind*

And summoned the earth^Rfrom the rising of the sun to its setting.   Ps. 113:3
2 Out of Zion, the perfection of beauty,
  God^Rhas shone forth.   Deut. 33:2; Ps. 80:1
3 May our God ^Rcome and not keep silence;   [Ps. 96:13]
  ^RFire devours before Him,   [Ps. 97:3]
  And it is very ^Rtempestuous around
  Him.   Ps. 18:12, 13
4 He summons the heavens above,
  And the earth, to judge His people:
5 "Gather My^Rgodly ones to Me,   Ps. 30:4
  Those who have made a^Rcovenant with
  Me by sacrifice."   2 Chr. 6:11; Ps. 25:10
6 And the^Rheavens declare His righteousness,   [Ps. 89:5; 97:6]
  For God Himself is judge.   [Selah.

7 "Hear, O My people, and I will speak;
  O Israel, I will testify against you;
  I am God,^Ryour God.   Ex. 20:2; Ps. 48:14
8 "I do not reprove you for your sacrifices,
  And your burnt offerings are continually before Me.
9 "I shall take no^Ryoung bull out of your
  house,   Ps. 69:31
  Nor male goats out of your folds.
10 "For every beast of the forest is Mine,
  The cattle on a thousand hills.
11 "I know every bird of the mountains,
  And everything that moves in the field
  is ⁸⁸Mine.
12 "If I were hungry, I would not tell you;
  For the^Rworld is Mine, and ^Tall it contains.   [Deut. 10:14]; Ps. 24:1 • *its fulness*
13 "Shall I eat the flesh of^Tbulls,   *strong ones*
  Or drink the blood of male goats?
14 "Offer to God ^Ra sacrifice of thanksgiving,   Ps. 27:6; Hos. 14:2; Rom. 12:1
  And pay your vows to the Most High;
15 And^Rcall upon Me in the day of trouble;
  I shall^Rrescue you, and you will honor
  Me."   Ps. 91:15; 107:6, 13 • Ps. 81:7

16 But to the wicked God says,
  "What right have you to tell of My statutes,
  And to take ^RMy covenant in your
  mouth?   Is. 29:13
17 "For you^Rhate discipline, [Prov. 5:12; 12:1]
  And you cast My words behind you.
18 "When you see a thief, you^Rare pleased
  with him,   [Rom. 1:32]
  And you associate with adulterers.
19 "You let your mouth loose in evil,
  And your^Rtongue frames deceit. Ps. 36:3
20 "You sit and speak against your brother;
  You slander your own mother's son.
21 "These things you have done, and^RI kept
  silence;   Eccl. 8:11; Is. 42:14; 57:11
  You thought that I was just like you;
  I will^Rreprove you, and state *the case* in
  order before your eyes.   [Ps. 90:8]

22 "Now consider this, you who ^Rforget
  God,   [Job 8:13; Ps. 9:17]

Lest I ^Rtear *you* in pieces, and there be
none to deliver.   Ps. 7:2
23 "He who ^ooffers a sacrifice of thanksgiving honors Me;   Ps. 50:14
And to him who orders *his* way *aright*
I shall show the salvation of God."

PSALM 51

Confession and Forgiveness of Sin

For the choir director.   A Psalm of
David, when Nathan the prophet came
to him, after he had gone in to
Bathsheba.

B<small>E</small> ^Rgracious to me, O God, according to
Thy lovingkindness;   Ps. 4:1; 109:26
According to the greatness of ^RThy
compassion^Rblot out my transgressions.   Ps. 69:16; 106:45 • Ps. 51:9

2 Wash me thoroughly from my iniquity,
And^Rcleanse me from my sin. [Heb. 9:14]

3 For I^Rknow my transgressions, Is. 59:12
And my sin is ever before me.
4 Against Thee, Thee only, I have sinned,
And done what is evil in Thy sight,
So that^RThou ⁸⁹art justified when Thou
dost speak,   Rom. 3:4
And blameless when Thou dost judge.

5 Behold, I was brought forth in iniquity,
And in sin my mother conceived me.
6 Behold, Thou dost desire truth in the
^Ainnermost being,   *inward parts*
And in the hidden part Thou wilt^Rmake
me know wisdom.   [James 1:5]
7 Purify me^Rwith hyssop, and I shall be
clean;   Ex. 12:22; Lev. 14:4; Num. 19:18
^AWash me, and I shall be ^Rwhiter than
snow.   *Mayest Thou wash* • [Is. 1:18]
8 Make me to hear joy and gladness,
Let the^Rbones which Thou hast broken
rejoice.   Ps. 35:10
9 ^RHide Thy face from my sins, [Jer. 16:17]
And blot out all my iniquities.

10 Create in me a clean heart, O God,
And renew a steadfast spirit within me.
11 ^RDo not cast me away from Thy presence,   2 Kin. 13:23; 24:20; Jer. 7:15
And do not take Thy^RHoly Spirit from
me.   Is. 63:10, 11

12 Restore to me the joy of Thy salvation,
And sustain me with a willing spirit.
13 *Then* I will ^Rteach transgressors Thy
ways,   Acts 9:21, 22
And sinners will ⁹⁰be ^Rconverted to
Thee.   [Ps. 22:27]

14 Deliver me from bloodguiltiness, O
God, Thou God of my salvation;
Then my ^Rtongue will joyfully sing of
Thy righteousness.   Ps. 35:28; 71:15
15 O Lord, ^Aopen my lips,   *mayest Thou open*
That my mouth may ^Rdeclare Thy
praise.   Ps. 9:14
16 For Thou ^Rdost not delight in sacrifice,
otherwise I would give it;
Thou art not pleased with burnt offering.   [1 Sam. 15:22]
17 The sacrifices of God are a ^Rbroken
spirit;   Ps. 34:18
A broken and a contrite heart, O God,
Thou wilt not despise.

18 ^RBy Thy favor do good to Zion;   Is. 51:3
^RBuild the walls of Jerusalem.   Ps. 102:16
19 Then Thou wilt delight in ^Arighteous
sacrifices,   *sacrifices of righteousness*
In ^Rburnt offering and whole burnt offering;   Ps. 66:13, 15
Then ^Tyoung bulls will be offered on
Thine altar.   *they will offer young bulls*

PSALM 52

The Lord Shall Judge the Deceitful

For the choir director.   A Maskil of
David, when Doeg the Edomite came
and told Saul, and said to him, "David
has come to the house of Ahimelech."

W<small>HY</small> do you boast in evil, O mighty man?
The^Rlovingkindness of God *endures* all
day long.   Ps. 52:8
2 Your tongue devises^Rdestruction, Ps. 5:9
Like a sharp razor, O worker of deceit.
3 You^Rlove evil more than good,   Ps. 36:4
Falsehood more than speaking what is
right.   [Selah.
4 You love all words that devour,
O^Rdeceitful tongue.   Ps. 120:3

⁸⁹ Or, *mayest be in the right*   ⁹⁰ Or, *turn back*

51:2   What Sin Is—In dealing with sin it is important to know what sin is. If asked to define sin, people will
come up with many different definitions as to what sin is—usually the things that the individual does not like. One
of the most common definitions of sin is *missing the mark*—a failure to live up to an expected standard. The
problem with this definition is that it fails to take into account that when the mark is missed, something is hit.
Another definition of sin is found in First John 3:4, "sin is lawlessness." Put simply according to this verse, sin is
anything that is contrary to what the Word of God commands or forbids. This definition, however, does not take into
account those things about which the Word of God is silent. The best definition for sin is found in First John 5:17,
"All unrighteousness is sin."
     Now turn to Page 706—Is. 59:2: What Sin Does.

5 But God will break you down forever;
  He will snatch you up, and [R]tear you
    away from *your* tent,   Is. 22:18, 19
  And uproot you from the land of the
    living.   [Selah.
6 And the righteous will see and fear,
  And will[R]laugh at him, *saying*, Job 22:19
7 "Behold, the man who would not make
    God his refuge,
  But [R]trusted in the abundance of his
    riches,   Ps. 49:6
  And was strong in his *evil* desire."

8 But as for me, I am like a [R]green olive
    tree in the house of God;   Ps. 92:12
  I [R]trust in the lovingkindness of God
    forever and ever.   Ps. 13:5
9 I will [R]give Thee thanks forever, be-
    cause Thou hast done *it*,   Ps. 30:12
  And I will wait on Thy name,[R]for *it is*
    good, in the presence of Thy godly
    ones.   Ps. 54:6

PSALM 53

A Portrait of the Godless

For the choir director; according to
[91]Mahalath. A Maskil of David.

THE[R]fool has said in his heart, "There is no
    God,"   Ps. 10:4; 14:1-7; 53:1-6
  They are corrupt, and have committed
    abominable injustice;
  There is no one who does good.
2 God has looked down from heaven
    upon the sons of men,
  To see if there is [R]anyone who[A]under-
    stands,   Rom. 3:11 • *acts wisely*
  Who [R]seeks after God.   [2 Chr. 15:2]
3 Every one of them has turned aside; to-
    gether they have become corrupt;
  There is no one who does good, not
    even one.

4 Have the workers of wickedness [R]no
    knowledge,   Jer. 4:22
  Who eat up My people *as though* they
    ate bread,
  And have not called upon God?
5 There they were in great[A]fear[R]*where* no
    fear had been;   *dread* • Prov. 28:1
  For God scattered the bones of him
    who encamped against you;
  You[R]put *them* to shame, because God
    had rejected them.   Ps. 44:7
6 Oh, that[R]the salvation of Israel would
    come out of Zion!   Ps. 14:7
  When God restores His captive people,
  Let Jacob rejoice, let Israel be glad.

PSALM 54

The Lord Is Our Helper

For the choir director; on stringed
instruments. A Maskil of David, when
the Ziphites came and said to Saul, "Is
not David hiding himself among us?"

SAVE me, O God, by Thy name,
  And [92]vindicate me by Thy power.
2 [R]Hear my prayer, O God; Ps. 17:6; 55:1
  Give ear to the words of my mouth.
3 For strangers have risen against me,
  And violent men have sought my life;
  They have not set God before
    them.   [Selah.

4 Behold,[R]God is my helper;   Ps. 30:10
  The Lord is the sustainer of my soul.
5 [93]He will recompense the evil to [A]my
    foes;   *those who lie in wait for me*
  Destroy them in Thy[A]faithfulness. *truth*

6 Willingly I will sacrifice to Thee;
  I will give[R]thanks to Thy name, O LORD,
    for it is good.   Ps. 50:14
7 For [A]He has[R]delivered me from all[A]trou-
    ble;   *His name* • Ps. 34:6 • *distress*
  And my eye has[R]looked *with satisfac-
    tion* upon my enemies.   Ps. 59:10

PSALM 55

"Cast Your Burden upon the LORD"

For the choir director; on stringed
instruments.
A Maskil of David.

GIVE[R]ear to my prayer, O God;   Ps. 54:2
  And [R]do not hide Thyself from my sup-
    plication.   Ps. 27:9
2 Give heed to me, and answer me;
  I am restless in my[A]complaint and [94]am
    surely distracted,   Job 9:27; Ps. 64:1
3 Because of the voice of the enemy,
  Because of the pressure of the wicked;
  For they bring down trouble upon me,
  And in anger they [R]bear a grudge
    against me.   Ps. 71:11; 143:3

4 My heart is in anguish within me,
  And the terrors of [R]death have fallen
    upon me.   Ps. 18:4, 5; 116:3
5 Fear and trembling come upon me;
  And horror has overwhelmed me.
6 And I said, "Oh, that I had wings like a
    dove!
  I would fly away and [95]be at rest.
7 "Behold, I would wander far away,
  I would lodge in the wilderness. [Selah.
8 "I would hasten to my place of refuge
  From the stormy wind *and* tempest."

9 Confuse, O Lord, divide their tongues,
  For I have seen[R]violence and strife in
    the city.   Ps. 11:5; Jer. 6:7

---

[91] I.e., sickness, a sad tone   [92] Lit., *judge*
[93] Lit., *The evil will return*   [94] Or, *I must moan*
[95] Lit., *settle down*

10 Day and night they go around her upon
her walls;
And iniquity and mischief are in her
midst.
11 RDestruction is in her midst; Ps. 5:9
ROppression and deceit do not depart
from her Astreets. Ps. 10:7 • plaza
12 For it isRnot an enemy who reproaches
me, Ps. 41:9
Then I could bear it;
Nor is it one who hates me whoRhas
exalted himself against me, Ps. 35:26
Then I could hide myself from him.
13 But it is you, a man my equal,
My companion and my familiar friend.
14 We who had sweet 96fellowship together,
RWalked in the house of God in the
throng. Ps. 42:4
15 Let death come deceitfully upon them;
Let them go down alive to Sheol,
For evil is in their dwelling, in their
midst.

16 As for me, I shall call upon God,
And the Lord will save me.
17 REvening and morning and at noon, I
will complain and murmur, Ps. 141:2
And He will hear my voice.
18 He will redeem my soul in peace from
the battle which is against me,
For they are many who strive with me.
19 God will hear and Aanswer them— afflict
Even the one who sits enthroned from
of old— [Selah.
With whom there is no change,
And whoRdo not fear God. Ps. 36:1
20 He has put forth his hands against
those who were at peace with him;
He has 97violated his covenant.
21 His speech was smoother than butter,
But his heart was war;
His words wereRsofter than oil, Ps. 12:2
Yet they were drawnRswords. Ps. 57:4

22 RCast your burden upon the Lord, and
He will sustain you; Ps. 37:5; 1 Pet. 5:7
RHe will never allow the righteous toAbe
shaken. Ps. 37:24 • totter
23 But Thou, O God, wilt bring them
down to the pit of destruction;
RMen of bloodshed and deceit will not
live out half their days. Ps. 5:6
But I willRtrust in Thee. Ps. 25:2; 56:3

PSALM 56

Fears in the Midst of Trials

For the choir director; according to
Jonath elem rehokim. A Mikhtam of
David, when the Philistines seized him
in Gath.

BE gracious, O God, for man hasAtrampledR
upon me; snapped at • Ps. 57:3
Fighting all day long he oppresses me.

2 My foes haveAtrampledRupon me all day
long, snapped at • Ps. 35:25; 57:3
For Athey are many who Rfight proudly
against me. many are fighting • Ps. 35:1
3 TWhen I amRafraid, In the day • Ps. 55:4, 5
I willRput my trust in Thee. Ps. 11:1
4 RIn God, whose word I praise, Ps. 56:10f.
In God I have put my trust;
I shall not be afraid.
What can mereTman do to me? flesh
5 All day long they 98distort my words;
All their Athoughts R are against me for
evil. purposes • Ps. 41:7
6 They 99attack,Rthey lurk, Ps. 59:3; 140:2
TheyRwatch myTsteps, Ps. 17:11 • heels
As they have waited to take my life.
7 Because of wickedness, Acast R them
forth, will they have escape? • Ps. 36:12
In anger put down the peoples, O God!

8 ThouRhast taken account of my wanderings; Ps. 139:3
Put myRtears in Thy bottle; 2 Kin. 20:5
Are they not inRThy book? Mal. 3:16
9 Then my enemies willRturn backRin the
day when I call; Ps. 9:3 • Ps. 102:2
This I know, 100that God is for me.
10 In God, whose word I praise,
In the Lord, whose word I praise,
11 In God I have put my 101trust, I shall
not be afraid.
What can man do to me?
12 Thy vows are binding upon me, O God;
I will render thank offerings to Thee.
13 For Thou hast Rdelivered my soul from
death, Ps. 33:19; 49:15; 86:13
Indeed my feet from stumbling,
So that I may walk before God
In the light of theAliving. life

PSALM 57

Prayers in the Midst of Perils

For the choir director; set to
102Al-tashheth. A Mikhtam of David,
when he fled from Saul, in the cave.

BE gracious to me, O God, be gracious to
me,
For my soul takes refuge in Thee;
And in theRshadow of Thy wings I will
take refuge, Ps. 17:8; 36:7; 63:7; 91:4
Until destructionRpasses by. Is. 26:20
2 I will cry to God Most High,
To God who Raccomplishes all things
for me. [Ps. 138:8]
3 He will send from heaven and save me;
He reproaches him who tramples upon
me. [Selah.
God will send forth HisRlovingkindness
and HisAtruth. Ps. 25:10 • faithfulness

96 Lit., counsel 97 Lit., profaned
98 Or, trouble my affairs 99 Or, stir up strife
100 Or, because 101 Or, trust without fear
102 Lit., Do Not Destroy

4 My soul is among R lions;   Ps. 35:17; 58:6
   I must lie among those who breathe
     forth fire,
   Even the sons of men, whose R teeth are
     spears and arrows,   Prov. 30:14
   And their tongue a sharp sword.
5 Be exalted above the heavens, O God;
   Let Thy glory *be* above all the earth.
6 They have ^{103}prepared a R net for my
     steps;   Ps. 10:9; 31:4; 35:7; 140:5
   My soul is R bowed down;   Ps. 145:14
   They R dug a pit before me;   Ps. 7:15
   They *themselves* have fallen into the
     midst of it.   [Selah.

7 R My R heart is steadfast, O God, my heart
     is steadfast;   Ps. 57:7-11 · Ps. 112:7
   I will sing, yes, I will sing praises!
8 Awake, R my glory;   Ps. 16:9; 30:12
   Awake, R harp and lyre,   Ps. 150:3
   I will awaken the dawn!
9 R I will give thanks to Thee, O Lord,
     among the peoples;   Ps. 108:3
   I will sing praises to Thee among the
     T nations.   *peoples*
10 For Thy R lovingkindness is great to the
     heavens,   Ps. 36:5; 103:11; 108:4
   And Thy A truth to the clouds. *faithfulness*
11 Be exalted above the heavens, O God;
   Let Thy glory *be* above all the earth.

PSALM 58

Wicked Judges Will Be Judged

For the choir director; *set to*
Al-tashheth.
A Mikhtam of David.

D O you indeed speak righteousness, O
   ^{104}gods?
   Do you R judge ^{105}uprightly, O sons of
     men?   Ps. 82:2
2 No, in heart you work unrighteousness;
   On earth you R weigh out the violence of
     your hands.   Ps. 94:20; Is. 10:1
3 The wicked are estranged R from the
     womb;   [Ps. 51:5; Is. 48:8]
   These who speak lies R go astray from
     T birth.   [Ps. 53:3] · *the womb*
4 They have venom like the R venom of a
     serpent;   Deut. 32:33; Ps. 140:3
   Like a deaf cobra that stops up its ear,
5 So that it R does not hear the voice of
     A charmers,   Jer. 8:17 · *whisperers*
   Or a skillful caster of spells.

6 O God, R shatter their teeth in their
     mouth;   Job 4:10; Ps. 3:7
   Break out the fangs of the young lions,
     O Lord.
7 Let them A flow away like water that
     runs off;   Josh. 2:11; 7:5; Ps. 112:10

---

103 Or, *spread*   104 Or, *judges*
105 Or, *uprightly the sons of men?*   106 Or, *stir up strife*
107 Many mss. and some ancient versions read *My strength*

When he T aims R his arrows, let them be
   as headless shafts.   *bends* · Ps. 64:3
8 *Let them be* as a snail which T melts
   away as it goes along,   *secretes slime*
   Like the R miscarriages of a woman
   which never see the sun.   Job 3:16
9 Before your R pots can feel *the fire of*
   thorns,   Ps. 118:12; Eccl. 7:6
   He will R sweep them away with a whirlwind, the T green and the burning
   alike.   Ps. 83:15; Prov. 10:25 · *living*

10 The R righteous will rejoice when he R sees
   the vengeance;   Ps. 32:11 · Jer. 11:20
   He will R wash his feet in the blood of the
   wicked.   Ps. 68:23
11 And men will say, "Surely there is a
   T reward for the righteous;   *fruit*
   Surely there is a God who R judges A on
   earth!"   Ps. 9:8; 67:4; 75:7 · *in*

PSALM 59

*Petition for Deliverance
from Violent Men*

For the choir director; *set to*
Al-tashheth. A Mikhtam of
David, when Saul sent *men,*
and they watched the house
in order to kill him.

D ELIVER R me from my enemies, O my
   God;   Ps. 143:9
   Set me *securely* on high away from
     those who rise up against me.
2 Deliver me from those who do iniquity,
   And save me from men of bloodshed.
3 For behold, they have A set an ambush
     for my T life;   *lain in wait · soul*
   A Fierce men ^{106}launch an attack against
     me,   *Strong*
   R Not for my transgression nor for my
     sin, O Lord,   1 Sam. 24:11; Ps. 7:3; 69:4
4 T For no guilt of *mine,* they run and set
     themselves against me. *Without guilt*
   Arouse Thyself to help me, and see!
5 And Thou, R O Lord God of hosts, the
     God of Israel,   Ps. 69:6; 80:4; 84:8
   Awake to T punish all the nations;   *visit*
   Do not be gracious to any *who are*
     treacherous in iniquity.   [Selah.
6 They R return at evening, they howl like
     a R dog,   Ps. 59:14 · Ps. 22:16
   And go around the city.
7 Behold, they R belch forth with their
     mouth;   Ps. 94:4; Prov. 15:2, 28
   R Swords are in their lips,   Prov. 12:18
   For, *they say,* "Who R hears?"   Job 22:13
8 But Thou, O Lord, dost laugh at them;
   Thou dost scoff at all the nations.

9 *Because of* ^{107}his R strength I will watch
     for Thee,   Ps. 18:17
   For God is my R stronghold. [Ps. 9:9; 62:2]
10 My God R in His lovingkindness will
     meet me;   Ps. 21:3

God will let me [R]look *triumphantly*
  upon my foes.   Ps. 54:7
11 Do not slay them,[R]lest my people forget;   Deut. 4:9; 6:12
  [A]Scatter them by Thy power, and bring
  them down,   *Make them wander*
  O Lord,[R]our shield.   Ps. 84:9
12 *On account of* the sin of their mouth
  and the words of their lips,
  Let them even be caught in their pride,
  And on account of [R]curses and [T]lies
  which they utter.   Ps. 10:7 • *lying*
13 [108]Destroy *them* in wrath, [108]destroy
  them, that they may be no more;
  That *men* may[R]know that God[A]rules in
  Jacob,   Ps. 83:18 • *is Ruler*
  To the ends of the earth.   [Selah.
14 And they[R]return at evening, they howl
  like a dog,   Ps. 59:6
  And go around the city.
15 They wander about [109]for food,
  And growl if they are not satisfied.

16 But as for me, I shall [R]sing of Thy
  strength;   Ps. 21:13
  Yes, I shall[R]joyfully sing of Thy loving-
  kindness in the morning,   Ps. 101:1
  For Thou hast been my stronghold,
  And a refuge in the day of my distress.
17 [R]O my strength, I will sing praises to
  Thee;   Ps. 59:9
  For God is my stronghold, the God
  who shows me lovingkindness.

PSALM 60

*A Prayer for Deliverance
of the Nation*

For the choir director; according to
[110]Shushan Eduth. A Mikhtam of
David, to teach; when he struggled
with Aram-naharaim and with Aram-
zobah, and Joab returned, and smote
twelve thousand of Edom in the Valley
of Salt.

O GOD, Thou hast rejected us. Thou hast
  [A]broken us;   *broken out upon us*
  Thou hast been angry; O, restore us.
2 Thou hast made the[A]land[R]quake, Thou
  hast split it open;   *earth* • Ps. 18:7
  [R]Heal its breaches, for it totters. Is. 30:26
3 Thou hast [T]made Thy people experience
  hardship;   *caused Thy people to see*
  Thou hast given us[T]wine to drink that
  makes us stagger.   *wine of staggering*
4 Thou hast given a[R]banner to those who
  fear Thee,   Ps. 20:5; Is. 5:26; 11:12; 13:2
  That it may be displayed because of
  the truth.   [Selah.
5 That Thy beloved may be delivered,
  [R]Save with Thy right hand, and answer
  us!   Ps. 17:7

6 God has spoken in His [111]holiness:
  "I will exult, I will portion out[R]Shechem

and measure out the valley of[R]Suc-
  coth. Josh. 17:7 • Gen. 33:17; Josh. 13:27
7 "Gilead is Mine, and Manasseh is Mine;
  Ephraim also is the helmet of My head;
  Judah is My [112]scepter.[R]   Gen. 49:10
8 "Moab[R]is My washbowl;   2 Sam. 8:2
  Over Edom I shall throw My shoe;
  Shout loud, O [R]Philistia, because of
  Me!"   2 Sam. 8:1

9 Who will bring me into the besieged
  city?
  Who[A]will lead me to Edom?   *has led*
10 Hast not Thou Thyself, O God,[R]rejected
  us?   Ps. 60:1; 108:11
  And [R]wilt Thou not go forth with our
  armies, O God?   Josh. 7:12; Ps. 44:9
11 O give us help against the adversary,
  For deliverance by man is in vain.
12 Through God we shall do valiantly,
  And it is He who will[R]tread down our
  adversaries.   Ps. 44:5; Is. 63:3

PSALM 61

A Prayer When Overwhelmed

For the choir director; on a stringed
instrument.
A Psalm of David.

HEAR[R] my cry, O God;   Ps. 64:1
  [R]Give heed to my prayer.   Ps. 86:6
2 From the [R]end of the earth I call to
  Thee, when my heart is faint;
  Lead me to [T]the rock that is higher
  than I.   Ps. 42:6 • Ps. 18:2; 94:22
3 For Thou hast been a refuge for me,
  A tower of strength against the enemy.
4 Let me dwell in Thy tent forever;
  Let me take refuge in the shelter of Thy
  wings.   [Selah.

5 For Thou hast heard my vows, O God;
  Thou hast given *me* the inheritance of
  those who[R]fear Thy name.   Neh. 1:11
6 Thou wilt prolong the king's life;
  His years will be as many generations.
7 He will abide before God forever;
  Appoint[R]lovingkindness and truth, that
  they may preserve him.   Ps. 40:11
8 So I will[R]sing praise to Thy name forever,   Judg. 5:3; Ps. 30:4; 33:2; 71:22
  That I may pay my vows day by day.

PSALM 62

Wait for God

For the choir director; according to
Jeduthun.
A Psalm of David.

MY soul *waits* in silence for God only;
  From Him[R]is my salvation. Ps. 37:39

---

[108] Lit., *Bring to an end*   [109] Or, *to devour*
[110] Lit., *The lily of testimony*   [111] Or, *sanctuary*
[112] Or, *lawgiver*

2 He only is my rock and my salvation,
  My ^Rstronghold; I shall not be greatly
  shaken.   Ps. 59:17; 62:6

3 How long will you assail a man,
  That you may murder *him,* all of you,
  Like a ^Rleaning wall, like a tottering
  fence?   Is. 30:13
4 They have counseled only to thrust him
  down from his high position;
  They ^Rdelight in falsehood;   Ps. 4:2
  They bless with ^Ttheir mouth,   *his*
  But inwardly they curse.   [Selah.

5 My soul, wait in silence for God only,
  For my hope is from Him.
6 He only is my rock and my salvation,
  My stronghold; I shall not be shaken.
7 On God my ^Rsalvation and my glory
  rest;   [Ps. 85:9; Jer. 3:23]
  The rock of my strength, my ^Rrefuge is
  in God.   [Ps. 46:1]
8 Trust in Him at all times, O people;
  Pour out your heart before Him;
  God is a refuge for us.   [Selah.

9 Men of ^Rlow degree are only vanity, and
  men of rank are a lie;   Ps. 49:2
  In the ^Rbalances they go up;   Is. 40:15
  They are together lighter than breath.
10 ^RDo not trust in oppression,   Is. 30:12
   And do not vainly hope in robbery;
   If riches increase, ^Rdo not set *your* heart
   upon them.   Mark 10:24; Luke 12:15

11 ¹¹³Once God has ^Rspoken;   Job 33:14; 40:5
   ¹¹⁴Twice I have heard this:
   That ^Tpower belongs to God;   Rev. 19:1
12 And lovingkindness is Thine, O Lord,
   For Thou ^Rdost recompense a man according to his work.   Rom. 2:6

PSALM 63

Thirst for God

A Psalm of David, when he was in the
wilderness of Judah.

O GOD, ^RThou art my God; I shall seek
  Thee ¹¹⁵earnestly;   Ps. 118:28
  My soul ^Rthirsts for Thee, my flesh
  ^Tyearns for Thee,   Matt. 5:6 • *faints*
  In a ^Rdry and weary land where there is
  no water.   Ps. 143:6
2 Thus I have ^Rbeheld Thee in the sanctuary,   Ps. 27:4
  To see Thy power and Thy glory.
3 Because Thy ^Rlovingkindness is better
  than life,   [Ps. 69:16]
  My lips will praise Thee.
4 So I will bless Thee as long as I live;
  I will lift up my hands in Thy name.
5 My soul is satisfied as with ¹¹⁶marrow
  and fatness,

And my mouth offers ^Rpraises with joyful lips.   Ps. 71:23

6 When I remember Thee on my bed,
  I meditate on Thee in the night
  watches,
7 For ^RThou hast been my help,   Ps. 27:9
  And in the ^Rshadow of Thy wings I sing
  for joy.   Ps. 17:8
8 My soul ^Tclings ^Tto Thee;   Hos. 6:3 • *after*
  Thy ^Rright hand upholds me.   Ps. 18:35

9 But those who ^Rseek my ^Tlife, to destroy
  it,   Ps. 40:14 • *soul*
  Will go into the depths of the earth.
10 They will be ^Tdelivered over to the
   power of the sword;   *poured out by*
   They will be a ^Tprey for foxes.   *portion*
11 But the king will rejoice in God;
   Everyone who ^Rswears by Him will
   glory,   Deut. 6:13; Is. 45:23; 65:16
   For the ^Rmouths of those who speak lies
   will be stopped.   Job 5:16; Rom. 3:19

PSALM 64

A Prayer for God's Protection

For the choir director.
A Psalm of David.

H EAR my voice, O God, in ^Rmy ¹¹⁷com-
  plaint;   Ps. 55:2
  ^RPreserve my life from dread of the enemy.   Ps. 140:1
2 Hide me from the ^Rsecret counsel of
  evildoers,   Ps. 56:6
  From the tumult of ^Rthose who do iniquity,   Ps. 59:2
3 Who ^Rhave sharpened their tongue like
  a sword.   Ps. 140:3
  They ^Raimed bitter speech *as* their arrow,   Ps. 58:7
4 To ^Rshoot ^Tfrom concealment at the
  blameless;   Ps. 10:8; 11:2 • *in*
  Suddenly they shoot at him, and ^Rdo not
  fear.   [Ps. 55:19]
5 They ^Thold fast to themselves an evil
  purpose;   *make firm*
  They talk of laying snares secretly;
  They say, "Who can see them?"
6 They ¹¹⁸devise injustices, *saying,*
  "We are ^Tready with a well-conceived
  plot";   *complete*
  For the ^Rinward thought and the heart
  of a man are ¹¹⁹deep.   *inward part*

7 But ^RGod ^Awill shoot at them with an ar-
  row;   Ps. 7:12, 13 • *shot*
  Suddenly they will be wounded.
8 So they ^Awill make him stumble;   *made*
  Their own tongue is against them;
  All who see them will shake the head.
9 Then all men ^Awill fear,   *feared*
  And will declare the work of God,

---

¹¹³ Or, *One thing*   ¹¹⁴ Or, *These two things I have heard*
¹¹⁵ Lit., *early*   ¹¹⁶ Lit., *fat*   ¹¹⁷ Or, *concern*
¹¹⁸ Or, *search out*   ¹¹⁹ Or, *unsearchable*

And will consider what He has done.
10 The righteous man will be glad in the
LORD, and will take refuge in Him;
And all the upright in heart will glory.

PSALM 65

God's Provision Through Nature

For the choir director. A Psalm of
David. A Song.

THERE will be silence ^Tbefore Thee, *and*
praise in Zion, O God;   *to*
And to Thee the ^Rvow will be performed.   Ps. 116:18
2 O Thou who dost hear prayer,
To Thee ^Rall ^Tmen come.   [Ps. 86:9] • *flesh*
3 ^RIniquities prevail against me;   Ps. 38:4
As for our transgressions, Thou dost
^Tforgive them.   *cover over, atone for*
4 How ^Rblessed is the one whom Thou
dost ^Rchoose, and bring near *to*
Thee,   Ps. 33:12; 84:4 • Ps. 4:3
To dwell in Thy courts.
We will be ^Rsatisfied with the goodness
of Thy house,   Ps. 36:8
Thy holy temple.

5 By ^Rawesome *deeds* Thou dost answer
us in righteousness, O ^RGod of our
salvation,   Ps. 45:4; 66:3 • Ps. 85:4
Thou who art the trust of all the ends
of the earth and of the farthest sea;
6 Who dost ^Restablish the mountains by
His strength,   Ps. 95:4
Being ^Rgirded with might;   Ps. 93:1
7 Who dost still the roaring of the seas,
The roaring of their waves,
And the ^Rtumult of the peoples.   Ps. 2:1
8 And they who dwell in the ends *of the
earth* stand in awe of Thy signs;
Thou dost make the dawn and the sunset shout for joy.

9 Thou dost visit the earth, and ^Rcause it
to overflow; Lev. 26:4; Job 5:10; Ps. 68:9
Thou dost greatly ^Renrich it;   Ps. 104:24
The stream of God is full of water;
Thou dost prepare their grain, for thus
Thou dost prepare ^Tthe earth.   *it*
10 Thou dost water its furrows abun-
dantly;
Thou dost ^Asettle its ridges;   *smooth*
Thou dost soften it with showers;
Thou dost bless its growth.
11 Thou hast crowned the year ^Twith Thy
^Abounty,^R   *of • goodness • Ps. 104:28*
And Thy paths drip *with* fatness.
12 The pastures of the wilderness drip,
And the ^Rhills gird themselves with re-
joicing.   Ps. 98:8; Is. 55:12
13 The meadows are clothed with flocks,
And the valleys are covered with grain;
They shout for joy, yes, they sing.

PSALM 66

Remember What God Has Done

For the choir director. A Song.
A Psalm.

SHOUT joyfully to God, all the earth;
2 Sing the ^Rglory of His name;   Ps. 79:9
Make His ^Rpraise glorious.   Is. 42:12
3 Say to God, "How ^Rawesome are Thy
works!   Ps. 47:2; 65:5; 145:6
Because of the greatness of Thy power
Thine enemies will ^Tgive feigned
obedience to Thee.   *deceive*
4 "All the earth will worship Thee,
And will ^Rsing praises to Thee;   Ps. 67:4
They will sing praises to Thy
name."   [Selah.

5 Come and see the works of God,
Who is ^Rawesome in *His* deeds toward
the sons of men.   Ps. 106:22
6 He turned the sea into dry land;
They passed through the river on foot;
There let us ^Rrejoice in Him!   Ps. 105:43
7 He rules by His might forever;
His eyes keep watch on the nations;
Let not the rebellious exalt them-
selves.   [Selah.

8 Bless our God, O peoples,
And ^Tsound His praise abroad,   Ps. 98:4
9 Who ^Tkeeps us in life,   *puts our soul in life*
And does not allow our feet to slip.
10 For Thou hast ^Rtried us, O God; Job 23:10
Thou hast ^Rrefined us as silver is refined.   [Is. 48:10; Zech. 13:9; 1 Pet. 1:7]
11 Thou ^Tdidst bring us into the net;
Thou didst lay an oppressive burden
upon our loins.   Lam. 1:13
12 Thou didst make men ^Rride over our
heads;   Is. 51:23
We went through ^Rfire and through water;   Ps. 78:21; Is. 43:2
Yet Thou ^Rdidst bring us out into *a
place of* abundance.   Ps. 18:19
13 I shall ^Rcome into Thy house with burnt
offerings;   Ps. 96:8; Jer. 17:26
I shall ^Rpay Thee my vows,   Ps. 22:25
14 Which my lips uttered
And my mouth spoke when I was ^Rin
distress.   Ps. 18:6
15 I shall ^Roffer to Thee burnt offerings of
fat beasts,   Ps. 51:19
With the smoke of ^Rrams;   Num. 6:14
I shall make *an offering of* bulls with
male goats.   [Selah.

16 Come *and* hear, all who ¹²⁰fear God,
And I will ^Rtell of what He has done for
my soul.   [Ps. 71:15, 24]
17 I cried to Him with my mouth,
And He was extolled with my tongue.
18 If I ¹²¹regard wickedness in my heart,
The Lord ^Awill not hear;   *would*

¹²⁰ Or, *revere*
¹²¹ Or, *had regarded ... would not have heard*

19 But certainly[R]God has heard;   Ps. 18:6
He has given heed to the voice of my
   prayer.
20 [R]Blessed be God,   Ps. 68:35
Who has not turned away my prayer,
Nor His lovingkindness from me.

PSALM 67

God Shall Govern the Earth

For the choir director; with stringed
instruments.
A Psalm. A Song.

GOD be gracious to us and bless us,
And cause His face to shine upon us—
                                    [Selah.
2 That[R]Thy way may be known on the
   earth,   Ps. 98:2; Acts 18:25; Titus 2:11
Thy salvation among all nations.
3 Let the peoples praise Thee, O God;
Let all the peoples praise Thee.
4 Let the [R]nations be glad and sing for
   joy;   Ps. 100:1, 2
For Thou wilt [R]judge the peoples with
   uprightness,   [Ps. 9:8; 96:10, 13; 98:9]
And guide the nations on the
   earth.   [Selah.
5 Let the peoples praise Thee, O God;
Let all the peoples praise Thee.
6 The earth has yielded its produce;
God, our God,[R]blesses us.   Ps. 29:11
7 God blesses us,
   [122]That [R]all the ends of the earth may
   fear Him.   Ps. 22:27; 33:8

PSALM 68

God Is the Father of the Fatherless

For the choir director. A Psalm of
David. A Song.

LET[A] God arise, [A]let His enemies be scattered;   God shall · His enemies shall
And[A]let those who hate Him flee before
   Him.   those who hate Him shall
2 As [R]smoke is driven away, so drive
   them away; Ps. 37:20; Is. 9:18; Hos. 13:3
As[R]wax melts before the fire,   Ps. 22:14
So let the wicked perish before God.
3 But let the[R]righteous be glad; let them
   exult before God;   Ps. 32:11; 97:12
Yes, let them rejoice with gladness.
4 Sing to God, sing praises to His name;
[R]Lift up a song for Him who rides
   through the deserts,   Is. 57:14; 62:10
Whose[R]name is[T]the LORD, and exult before Him.   Ps. 83:18 · Heb., YAH

5 A[R]father of the fatherless and a judge
   [123]for the widows,   [Ps. 10:14; 146:9]
Is God in His holy habitation.
6 God makes a home for the lonely;

He [R]leads out the prisoners into prosperity, [Ps. 69:33; 102:20; 107:10; 146:7]
Only[R]the rebellious dwell in a parched
   land.   Ps. 78:17; 107:34, 40

7 O God, when Thou [R]didst go forth before Thy people,   Ex. 13:21; Ps. 78:14
When Thou didst march through the
   wilderness,   [Selah.
8 The[R]earth quaked;   Ex. 19:18; Judg. 5:4
The[R]heavens also dropped rain at the
   presence of God;   Ps. 18:9; Is. 45:8
[R]Sinai itself quaked at the presence of
   God, the God of Israel.   Ex. 19:18
9 Thou didst[R]shed abroad a plentiful rain,
   O God;   Lev. 26:4; Deut. 11:11; Job 5:10
Thou didst confirm Thine inheritance,
   when it was[T]parched.   weary
10 Thy creatures settled in it;
Thou didst[R]provide in Thy goodness for
   the poor, O God. Ps. 65:9; 74:19; 78:20

11 The Lord gives the[T]command;   word
The[R]women who proclaim the good tidings are a great host: Ex. 15:20
12 "Kings of armies flee, they flee,
And she who remains at home will[R]di-
   vide the spoil!" Judg. 5:30; 1 Sam. 30:24
13 [124]When you lie down [R]among the
   [125]sheepfolds,   Gen. 49:14; Judg. 5:16
You are like the wings of a dove covered with silver,
And its pinions with glistening gold.
14 When the Almighty[T]scattered the kings
   [T]there,   Josh. 10:10 · in it
It was snowing in[R]Zalmon.   Judg. 9:48

15 A[A]mountain[R] of God is the mountain of
   Bashan;   mighty mountain is · Ps. 36:6
A mountain of many peaks is the
   mountain of Bashan.
16 Why do you look with envy, O mountains with many peaks,
At the mountain which God has [R]de-
   sired for His abode?   [Deut. 12:5]
Surely,[R]the LORD will dwell there forever.   Ps. 132:14
17 The [R]chariots of God are [126]myriads,
   thousands upon thousands;
The Lord is among them as at Sinai, in
   holiness.   2 Kin. 6:17
18 Thou hast[R]ascended on high, Thou hast
   led captive Thy captives; Ps. 7:7; 47:5
Thou hast received gifts among men,
Even among the rebellious also, that
   the LORD God may dwell there.

19 Blessed be the Lord, who daily[R]bears
   our burden,   [Ps. 55:22; Is. 46:4]
The God who is our salvation. [Selah.
20 God is to us a God of deliverances;
And[R]to [T]GOD the Lord belong escapes
   from death. [Ps. 49:15] · Heb., YHWH
21 Surely God will[T]shatter the head of His
   enemies,   Ps. 110:6; Hab. 3:13
The hairy crown of him who goes on in
   his guilty deeds.

[122] Or, And let all . . . earth fear Him   [123] Lit., of
[124] Lit., If   [125] Or, cooking stones, or, saddle bags
[126] Lit., twice ten thousand

22 The Lord ^A said, "I ^R will bring *them* back
from Bashan. *says* • Num. 21:33
I will bring *them* back from the depths
of the sea;
23 That ^R your foot may shatter *them* in
blood, Ps. 58:10
The tongue of your dogs *may have* its
portion from *your* enemies."

24 They have seen Thy ^T procession, O God,
The procession of my God, my King,
into the sanctuary. *goings*
25 The ^R singers went on, the musicians after *them*, 1 Chr. 13:8; 15:6; Ps. 47:6
^A In the midst of the maidens beating
tambourines. *The maidens in the midst*
26 Bless God in the congregations,
Even the LORD, *you who are* of the
^R fountain of Israel. Deut. 33:28; Is. 48:1
27 There is Benjamin, the ^A youngest, ^A ruling
them, *smallest* • *their ruler*
The princes of Judah *in* their throng,
The princes of ^R Zebulun, the princes of
Naphtali. Judg. 5:18

28 Your God has commanded your
strength;
Show Thyself strong, O God, who hast
acted ^T on our behalf. *for us*
29 Because of Thy temple at Jerusalem
Kings will bring gifts to Thee.
30 Rebuke the beasts ^R in the reeds, *of*
The herd of ^R bulls with the calves of the
peoples, Ps. 22:12
Trampling under foot the ^T pieces of silver; $128
He has ^R scattered the peoples who delight in war. Ps. 18:14; 89:10
31 Envoys will come out of ^R Egypt; Is. 19:19
^T Ethiopia ^R will quickly stretch out her
hands to God. *Cush* • Is. 45:14

32 Sing to God, O kingdoms of the earth;
Sing praises to the Lord, [Selah.
33 To Him who rides upon the ^T highest
heavens, which are from ancient
times; *heaven of heavens of old*
Behold, He ^T speaks forth with His voice,
a mighty voice. *gives forth*
34 ^R Ascribe strength to God; Ps. 29:1
His majesty is over Israel,
And His strength is in the ^T skies. *clouds*
35 O God, *Thou art* ^R awesome from Thy
^T sanctuary. Deut. 7:21 • *holy places*
The God of Israel Himself gives
strength and power to the people.
^R Blessed be God! Ps. 66:20; 2 Cor. 1:3

PSALM 69

Petition for God to Draw Near

For the choir director; according to
^127 Shoshannim. *A Psalm of David.*

SAVE me, O God,
For the waters have threatened my life.

2 I have sunk in deep ^R mire, and there is
no foothold; Ps. 40:2
I have come into deep waters, and a
^T flood overflows me. *flowing stream*
3 I am ^R weary with my crying; my throat
is parched; Ps. 6:6
My eyes fail while I wait for my God.
4 Those who hate me without a cause are
more than the hairs of my head;
Those who would destroy me are powerful, being wrongfully my enemies,
^R What I did not steal, I then have to restore. Ps. 35:11; Jer. 15:10

5 O God, it is Thou who dost know ^R my
folly, Ps. 38:5
And ^R my wrongs are not hidden from
Thee. Ps. 44:21
6 May those who wait for Thee not be
ashamed through me, O Lord ^T GOD
of hosts; Heb., *YHWH*
May those who seek Thee not be dishonored through me, O God of Israel,
7 Because ^R for Thy sake I have borne reproach; Jer. 15:15; Rom. 15:3 ☆
^R Dishonor has covered my face. Ps. 44:15
8 I have become ^R estranged from my
brothers, Job 19:13–15; Mark 3:21 ☆
And an alien to my mother's sons.
9 For ^R zeal for Thy house has consumed
me, Ps. 119:139; John 2:17
And the reproaches of those who reproach Thee have fallen on me.
10 When I wept in my soul with fasting,
It became my reproach.
11 When I made sackcloth my clothing,
I became ^R a byword to them. 1 Kin. 9:7
12 Those who ^R sit in the gate talk about
me, Gen. 19:1; Ruth 4:1
And I *am* the song of the drunkards.

13 But as for me, my prayer is to Thee, O
LORD, at an acceptable time;
O God, in the ^R greatness of Thy lovingkindness, Ps. 51:1
Answer me with Thy saving truth.
14 Deliver me from the ^R mire, and do not
let me sink; Ps. 69:2
May I be delivered from my foes, and
from the deep waters.
15 May the ^T flood ^R of water not overflow
me, *stream* • Ps. 124:4, 5
And may the deep not swallow me up,
And may the ^R pit not shut its mouth on
me. Num. 16:33; Ps. 28:1; 141:7

16 Answer me, O LORD, for ^R Thy lovingkindness is good; Ps. 63:3; 109:21
^R According to the greatness of Thy
compassion, turn to me, Ps. 51:1
17 And ^R do not hide Thy face from Thy servant, Ps. 27:9; 102:2; 143:7

^127 Or possibly, *Lilies*

For I am ^Rin distress; answer me
quickly.   Ps. 31:9; 66:14

18 Oh draw near to my soul *and* ^Rredeem
it;   2 Sam. 4:9; Ps. 26:11; 49:15
Ransom me because of my enemies!

19 Thou dost know my ^Rreproach and my
shame and my dishonor;   Ps. 22:6
All my adversaries are ¹²⁸before Thee.

20 Reproach has ^Rbroken my heart, and I
am so sick.   Jer. 23:9; Rom. 15:3 ☆
And ^RI looked for sympathy, but there
was none,   Ps. 142:4; Is. 63:5
And for comforters, but I found none.

21 They also gave me ¹²⁹gall for my food,
And for my thirst they ^Tgave me vinegar
to drink.   Matt. 27:34; Mark 15:23, 36 ☆

22 May ^Rtheir table before them become a
snare;   Rom. 11:9, 10
And ^Twhen they are in peace, *may it become* a trap.   *for those who are secure*

23 May their ^Reyes grow dim so that they
cannot see,   Is. 6:10
And make their ^Rloins shake continually.   Dan. 5:6

24 Pour out Thine indignation on them,
And may Thy burning anger overtake
them.

25 May their camp be desolate;
May none dwell in their tents.

26 For they have persecuted him whom
Thou Thyself hast smitten,
And they tell of the pain of those
whom Thou hast ^Twounded.   *pierced*

27 Do Thou add iniquity to their iniquity,
And ^Rmay they not come into ^RThy righteousness.   [Is. 26:10] • Ps. 103:17

28 May they be ^Rblotted out of the ^Rbook of
life,   [Ex. 32:32, 33; Rev. 3:5] • [Rev. 13:8]
And may they not be ^Trecorded ^Rwith the
righteous.   *written* • Luke 10:20

29 But I am ^Rafflicted and in pain;   Ps. 70:5
May Thy salvation, O God, set me *se-
curely* on high.

30 I will ^Rpraise the name of God with
song,   [Ps. 28:7]
And shall ^Rmagnify Him with ^Rthanks-
giving.   Ps. 34:3 • Ps. 50:14

31 And it will ^Tplease the Lord better than
an ox   Ps. 50:13, 14; 51:16
Or a young bull with horns and hoofs.

32 The humble have seen *it and* are glad;
You who seek God, ^Rlet your heart ^Are-
vive.   Ps. 22:26 • *live*

33 For ^Rthe Lord hears the needy,   Ps. 12:5
And ^Rdoes not despise His *who are* prisoners.   [Ps. 68:6]

34 Let heaven and earth praise Him,
The seas and ^Reverything that moves in
them.   Is. 55:12

35 For God will ^Rsave Zion and build the
cities of Judah,   Ps. 46:5; 51:18

---

¹²⁸ Or, known *to Thee*   ¹²⁹ Or, *poison*

That they may dwell there and ^Rpossess
it.   Obad. 17

36 And the ^Tdescendants ^Rof His servants
will inherit it,   *seed* • Ps. 25:13; 102:28
And those who love His name ^Rwill
dwell in it.   [Ps. 37:29]

PSALM 70

Prayer for the Afflicted and Needy

For the choir director. *A Psalm* of
David; for a memorial.

O ^RGOD, *hasten* to deliver me;   Ps. 40:13-17
O Lord, hasten to my help!

2 Let those be ashamed and humiliated
Who seek my ^Alife;   *soul*
Let those be turned back and dishon-
ored
Who delight ^Ain my hurt.   *to injure me*

3 Let those be turned back because of
their shame
Who say, "Aha, aha!"

4 Let all who seek Thee rejoice and be
glad in Thee;
And let those who love Thy salvation
say continually,
"Let God be magnified."

5 But ^RI am afflicted and needy;   Ps. 40:17
^RHasten to me, O God!   Ps. 141:1
Thou art my help and my deliverer;
O Lord, do not delay.

PSALM 71

Prayer for the Aged

In Thee, O Lord, I have taken refuge;
Let me never be ashamed.

2 In Thy righteousness deliver me, and
rescue me;
Incline Thine ear to me, and save me.

3 Be Thou to me a rock of habitation, to
which I may continually come;
Thou hast given ^Rcommandment to save
me,   Ps. 7:6; 42:8
For Thou art my rock and my fortress.

4 ^RRescue me, O my God, out of the hand
of the wicked,   Ps. 140:1, 4
Out of the ^Tgrasp of the wrongdoer and
ruthless man,   *palm*

5 For Thou art my ^Rhope;   Ps. 39:7; Jer. 14:8
O Lord God, *Thou art* my ^Tconfidence
from my youth.   [Ps. 22:9]

6 ^TBy Thee I have been sustained from *my*
birth;   *Upon Thee I have been supported*
Thou art He who ^Rtook me from my
mother's womb;   Job 10:18; [Ps. 22:9]
My praise is continually ^Tof Thee.   *in*

7 I have become a marvel to many;
For Thou art ^Rmy strong refuge.   Ps. 61:3

8 My mouth is filled with Thy praise,

And with Thy glory all day long.

9 Do not cast me off in the ^Rtime of old
age;　　　　　Ps. 71:18; 92:14; Is. 46:4
Do not forsake me when my strength
fails.

10 For my enemies have spoken ^Tagainst
me;　　　　　*with reference to*
And those who^Rwatch for my^Tlife have
consulted together,　　Ps. 56:6 · *soul*

11 Saying, "God^Rhas forsaken him; Ps. 3:2
Pursue and seize him, for there is ^Rno
one to deliver."　　　　Ps. 7:2

12 O God,^Rdo not be far from me; Ps. 10:1
O my God,^Rhasten to my help! Ps. 38:22

13 Let those who are adversaries of my
soul be ashamed *and* consumed;
Let them be covered with reproach and
dishonor, who seek to injure me.

14 But as for me, I will hope continually,
And will ^Tpraise Thee yet more and
more.　　　*add upon all Thy praise*

15 My^Rmouth shall tell of Thy righteous-
ness,　　　　　Ps. 35:28
And of Thy salvation all day long;
For I do not know the sum *of them*.

16 I will come ^Rwith the mighty deeds of
the Lord GOD;　　　Ps. 106:2
I will ^Rmake mention of Thy righteousness, Thine alone.　　Ps. 51:14

17 O God, Thou^Rhast taught me from my
youth;　　　　Deut. 4:5; 6:7
And I still ^Rdeclare Thy wondrous
deeds.　　[Ps. 26:7; 40:5; 119:27]

18 And even when *I am* ^Rold and gray, O
God, do not forsake me,　　Ps. 71:9
Until I^Rdeclare Thy^Tstrength to *this* gen-
eration,　　Ps. 22:31; 78:4, 6 · *arm*
Thy power to all who are to come.

19 ^AFor Thy righteousness, O God, *reaches*
to the^Theavens,　　*And* · *height*
Thou who hast done great things;
O God,^Rwho is like Thee?　Deut. 3:24

20 Thou, who hast ^Rshown ¹³⁰me many
troubles and distresses,　Ps. 60:3
Wilt^Rrevive ¹³⁰me again,　Ps. 80:18; 85:6
And wilt bring ¹³⁰me up again^Rfrom the
depths of the earth.　Ps. 86:13

21 Mayest Thou increase my greatness,
And turn *to* ^Rcomfort me. [Ps. 23:4; 86:17]

22 I will also praise Thee with a harp,
Even Thy^Atruth, O my God;　*faithfulness*
To Thee I will sing praises with the
^Rlyre,　　　Ps. 33:2; 147:7
O Thou^RHoly One of Israel.　Ps. 78:41

23 My lips will^Rshout for joy when I sing
praises to Thee;　Ps. 5:11; 32:11; 132:9
And my ^Rsoul, which Thou hast redeemed.　　[Ps. 34:22; 55:18; 103:4]

24 My ^Rtongue also will utter Thy righteousness all day long;　Ps. 35:28
For they are^Rashamed, for they are humiliated who seek my hurt. Ps. 71:13

PSALM 72

The Reign of the Messiah

A Psalm of Solomon.

GIVE the king Thy judgments, O God,
And ^RThy righteousness to the king's
son.　　　　　Ps. 24:5

2 ^AMay he ^Rjudge Thy people with righteousness,　　*He will judge* · [Is. 9:7] ☆
And ¹³¹Thine afflicted with justice.

3 ^ALet the mountains bring peace to the
people,　　*The mountains will bring*
And the hills in righteousness.

4 ^AMay he ^Rvindicate the afflicted of the
people,　　*He will vindicate* · Is. 11:4 ☆
Save the children of the needy,
And crush the oppressor.

5 ^ALet them fear Thee ^Rwhile the sun endures, *They will fear* · [Ps. 72:17; 89:36] ☆
And as long as the moon, throughout
all generations.

6 ^AMay he come down like rain upon the
mown grass,　　*He will come down*
Like showers that water the earth.

7 In his days may the righteous flourish,
And ^Rabundance of peace till the moon
is no more.　　　Is. 2:4 ☆

8 May he also rule from sea to sea,
And from the River to the ends of the
earth.

9 ^ALet the nomads of the desert bow before him;　　*The nomads . . . will bow*
And his enemies^Rlick the dust. Is. 49:23 ☆

10 Let the kings of^RTarshish and of the islands bring presents;　　2 Chr. 9:21
The kings of ^RSheba and Seba offer
^Agifts.　　Job 6:19; Is. 60:6 · *tribute*

11 And let all kings bow down before him,
All^Rnations serve him. Ps. 138:4; Is. 49:23 ☆

12 For he will ^Rdeliver the needy when he
cries for help,　　Job 29:12; [Ps. 72:4] ☆
The ^Aafflicted also, and him who has no
helper.　　　　*humble*

13 He will have ^Rcompassion on the poor
and needy,　　Prov. 19:17; 28:8
And the lives of the needy he will save.

14 He will ^Trescue their ^Tlife from oppression and violence;　　*redeem* · *soul*
And their blood will be^Rprecious in his
sight;　　1 Sam. 26:21; [Ps. 116:15] ☆

15 So may he live; and may the ^Rgold of
Sheba be given to him;　　Is. 60:6 ☆
And let them pray for him continually;
Let ^Tthem bless him all day long.　*him*

16 May there be abundance of grain in the
earth on top of the mountains;
Its fruit will wave like *the cedars of*
^RLebanon;　　　Ps. 104:16

¹³⁰ Another reading is *us*　　¹³¹ Or, *Thy humble*

And may those from the city flourish
like ᵀvegetation of the earth. Job 5:25
17 May his ᴿname endure forever; Ex. 3:15☆
May his name ᴬincrease ᵀas long as the
sun *shines;*   *sprout forth • before the sun*
And let *men* bless themselves by him;
Let all nations call him blessed.

18 ᴿBlessed be the LORD God, the God of
Israel,   1 Chr. 29:10; Ps. 41:13; 89:52
Who alone ᴿworks wonders.   Ex. 15:11
19 And blessed be His ᴿglorious name for-
ever;   [Neh. 9:5]; Ps. 96:8
And may the whole ᴿearth be filled with
His glory.   Num. 14:21
ᴿAmen, and Amen.   Ps. 41:13

20 The prayers of David the son of Jesse
are ended.

BOOK 3

PSALM 73

The Perspective of Eternity

A Psalm of Asaph.

Surely God is ᴿgood to Israel,   [Ps. 86:5]
To those who are ᴿpure in heart! Ps. 24:4

2 But as for me, ᴿmy feet came close to
stumbling;   Ps. 94:18
My steps had almost slipped.
3 For I was envious of the arrogant,
As I saw the prosperity of the wicked.
4 For there are no pains in their death;
And their ᴬbody is fat.   *belly*
5 They are not in trouble *as other* men;
Nor are they plagued like mankind.
6 Therefore pride is their necklace;
The garment of violence covers them.
7 Their eye ᵀbulges from fatness; *goes forth*
The imaginations of *their* heart run
riot.
8 They ᴿmock, and wickedly speak of oppression;   Ps. 1:1
They ᴿspeak from on high.   2 Pet. 2:18

9 They have ᴿset their mouth ᴬagainst the
heavens,   Rev. 13:6 • *in*
And their tongue ᵀparades through the
earth.   *walks*

10 Therefore ᴬhis people return to this
place;   *His*
And waters of ᴬabundance are ᵀdrunk by
them.   Ps. 23:5 • *drained out*
11 And they say, "How does God know?
And is there knowledge ᵀwith the Most
High?"   *in*
12 Behold, ᴿthese are the wicked;   Ps. 49:6
And always ᴿat ease, they have increased *in* wealth.   Jer. 49:31
13 Surely ᴿin vain I have ᵀkept my heart
pure,   Job 21:15 • *cleansed my heart*
And washed my hands in innocence;
14 For I have been stricken all day long,
And ᴿchastened every morning. Job 33:19

15 If I had said, "I will speak thus,"
Behold, I should have betrayed the
ᴿgeneration of Thy children. [Ps. 14:5]
16 When I pondered to understand this,
It was troublesome in my sight
17 Until I came into the sanctuary of God;
Then I perceived their ᴿend.   [Ps. 37:38]
18 Surely Thou dost set them in ᴿslippery
places;   Ps. 35:6
Thou dost cast them down to ᵀdestruc-
tion.ᴿ   *ruins* • Ps. 35:8; 36:12
19 How they are destroyed in a moment!
They are utterly swept away by ᴿsudden
terrors!   Job 18:11
20 Like a dream when one awakes,
O Lord, when ᴿaroused, Thou wilt despise their form.   Ps. 78:65

21 When my heart was embittered,
And I was pierced ᵀwithin,   *in my kidneys*
22 Then I was senseless and ignorant;
I was *like* a beast before Thee.
23 Nevertheless ᴿI am continually with
Thee;   Ps. 16:8
Thou hast taken hold of my right hand.
24 With Thy counsel Thou wilt guide me,
And afterward receive me to glory.

25 Whom have I in heaven *but Thee?*

73:1   Walking in the Spirit: Confession—An important prerequisite to walking in the Spirit is the confession of sin. Sin must be confessed in order to restore fellowship and to continue receiving God's power (Page 1274—1 John 1:5–10). Confession means that we agree with God about our sin. This involves much more than simply acknowledging the sin. Confession requires an attitude of sorrow for the sin and a willingness to turn from it. It does not mean that we will never commit the same sin again, but it does mean that the attitude of repentance of the sin is present.
   Confession should be made at the moment the Christian becomes aware of sin. Apart from this rule moreover, the Scriptures mention two specific times for confession: before the close of the day (Page 1188—Eph. 4:26) and before the Lord's Supper is observed (Page 1157—1 Cor. 11:27–32). Failure to do the latter is a special cause for discipline from the Lord.
   Confession of sin should involve only those who have knowledge of the sin. This means that private sins should be confessed privately (Page 1274—1 John 1:9); sins between individuals confessed between those involved (Page 967—Matt. 5:23, 24); and public sins confessed publicly (Page 982—Matt. 18:17). Public confession normally is made for the edification of the church (Page 1159—1 Cor. 14:26).
   Now turn to Page 1141—Rom. 12:1–2: Walking in the Spirit: Yielding.

And^besides Thee, I desire nothing on
earth.   *with*
26 My flesh and my heart may fail,
But God is the ^strength of my heart
and my portion forever.   *rock*
27 For, behold, ^those who are far from
Thee will perish;   [Ps. 119:155]
Thou hast ^destroyed all those who are
unfaithful to Thee.   *silenced*
28 But as for me, ^the nearness of God is
my good;   [Heb. 10:22; James 4:8]
I have made the Lord GOD my refuge,
That I may tell of all Thy works.

PSALM 74

*Request for God to Remember
His Covenant*

A Maskil of Asaph.

O GOD, why hast Thou ^rejected *us* forever?   Ps. 44:9; 77:7
Why does Thine anger smoke against
the sheep of Thy^pasture?   *pasturing*
2 Remember Thy congregation, which
Thou hast purchased of old,
Which Thou hast ^redeemed to be the
tribe of Thine inheritance;   Is. 63:9
And this Mount^Zion, where Thou hast
dwelt.   Deut. 32:9; Is. 63:17; Jer. 10:16
3 ^Turn Thy footsteps toward the^perpet-
ual ruins;   *Lift up* • Is. 61:4
The enemy ^has damaged everything
within the sanctuary.   Ps. 79:1
4 Thine adversaries have ^roared in the
midst of Thy meeting place; Lam. 2:7
They have set up their^own ^standards
for signs.   Num. 2:2 • *signs*
5 It seems as if one had lifted up
His ^axe in a forest of trees.   *axes*
6 And now ^all its carved work *altogether*
They smash with hatchet and ^ham-
mers.   *axes*
7 They have^burned Thy sanctuary to the
ground;   *set on fire*
They have^defiled the dwelling place of
Thy name.   Ps. 89:39; Lam. 2:2
8 They said in their heart, "Let us ^com-
pletely subdue them."   *altogether*
They have burned all the meeting
places of God in the land.
9 We do not see our ^signs;   Ps. 78:43
There is no longer any prophet,
Nor is there any among us who knows
^how long.   Ps. 6:3; 79:5; 80:4
10 How long, O God, will the adversary
^revile,   Ps. 44:16; 79:12; 89:51
And the enemy ^spurn Thy name forever?   Lev. 24:16
11 Why ^dost Thou withdraw Thy hand,
even Thy right hand?   Lam. 2:3
From within Thy bosom, destroy *them!*

12 Yet God is ^my king from of old, Ps. 44:4
Who works deeds of deliverance in the
midst of the earth.

13 ^132^Thou didst ^divide the sea by Thy
strength;   Ex. 14:21; Ps. 78:13
Thou didst break the heads of the sea
monsters^in the waters.   *on*
14 ^Thou didst crush the heads of^Levia-
than;   *Thou Thyself* • Ps. 104:26; Is. 27:1
Thou didst give him as food for the
^creatures of the wilderness. *people*
15 ^Thou didst^break open springs and torrents;   *Thou Thyself* • Ex. 17:5, 6
Thou didst ^dry up ever-flowing
streams.   Ex. 14:21, 22; Josh. 2:10; 3:13
16 Thine is the day, Thine also is the night;
^Thou hast prepared the^light and the
sun.   *Thou Thyself* • *luminary*
17 ^Thou hast established all the boundaries of the earth;   *Thou Thyself*
Thou hast made summer and winter.

18 Remember this, O LORD, that the enemy has^reviled;   Ps. 74:10
And a^foolish people has spurned Thy
name.   Deut. 32:6; Ps. 14:1; 39:8; 53:1
19 Do not deliver the soul of Thy ^turtle-
dove to the wild beast;   Song 2:14
^Do not forget the life of Thine afflicted
forever.   Ps. 9:18
20 Consider the^covenant;   Gen. 17:7
For the dark places of the land are full
of the habitations of violence.
21 Let not the ^oppressed return dishonored;   [Ps. 103:6]
Let the ^afflicted and needy praise Thy
name.   [Ps. 35:10; Is. 41:17]

22 Do arise, O God, *and*^plead Thine own
cause;Ps. 43:1; Is. 3:13; 43:26; Ezek. 20:35
Remember how the ^foolish man reproaches Thee all day long. Ps. 14:1
23 Do not forget the voice of Thine^adver-
saries,   Ps. 74:10
The uproar of those who rise against
Thee which ascends continually.

PSALM 75

"God Is the Judge"

For the choir director; *set to*
Al-tashheth.
A Psalm of Asaph, a Song.

WE ^give thanks to Thee, O God, we give
thanks,   Ps. 79:13
For Thy name is^near;   Ps. 145:18
Men declare Thy wondrous works.
2 "When I select an appointed time,
It is I who^judge with equity.   Ps. 9:8
3 "The ^earth and all who dwell in it
^133^melt;   Ps. 46:6; Is. 24:19
It is I who have firmly set its pillars.   [Selah.
4 "I said to the boastful, 'Do not boast,'
And to the wicked, 'Do^not lift up the
horn;   Zech. 1:21

^132^ Or, *Thou Thyself,* and so through v. 17 ^133^ Or, *totter*

5 Do not lift up your horn on high,
Do not speak with insolent pride.' "

6 For not from the east, nor from the west,
Nor from the desert *comes* exaltation;
7 But[R]God is the Judge;   Ps. 50:6
He puts down one, and exalts another.
8 For a[R]cup is in the hand of the LORD,
and the wine foams;   Job 21:20
It is[T]well[R]mixed, and He pours out of this;   *full of mixture* · Prov. 23:30
Surely all the wicked of the earth must drain *and* drink down its dregs.

9 But as for me, I will declare *it* forever;
I will sing praises to the God of Jacob.
10 And all the[R]horns of the wicked[T]He will cut off,   Ps. 101:8; Jer. 48:25 · Heb., *I*
But[T]the horns of the righteous will be lifted up.   1 Sam. 2:1; Ps. 89:17; 92:10

PSALM 76

The Glorious Might of God

For the choir director; on stringed instruments.
A Psalm of Asaph, a Song.

God is[R]known in Judah;   Ps. 48:3
His name is[R]great in Israel.   [Ps. 99:3]
2 And His[T]tabernacle is in Salem;   *shelter*
His dwelling place also is in Zion.
3 There He broke the flaming arrows,
The shield, and the sword, and the weapons of war.   [Selah.

4 Thou art resplendent,
[A]More majestic than the mountains of prey.   *Majestic from the mountains*
5 The stouthearted were plundered;
They sank into sleep;
And none of the warriors could use his hands.
6 At Thy rebuke, O God of Jacob,
Both[T]rider[R]and horse were cast into a dead sleep.   *chariot* · Ex. 15:1, 21
7 Thou, even Thou, art to be feared;
And who may stand in Thy presence when once Thou art angry?

8 Thou didst cause judgment to be heard from heaven;
The earth feared, and was still,
9 When God[R]arose to judgment,   Ps. 9:7, 8
To save all the humble of the earth.   [Selah.
10 For the wrath of man shall praise Thee;
With a remnant of wrath Thou shalt gird Thyself.

11 [R]Make vows to the LORD your God and fulfill *them;*   [Eccl. 5:4–6]

134 Lit., *and did not grow numb*

Let all who are around Him bring gifts to Him who is to be feared.
12 He will cut off the spirit of princes;
He is feared by the kings of the earth.

PSALM 77

When Overwhelmed,
Remember God's Greatness

For the choir director; according to Jeduthun.
A Psalm of Asaph.

My voice *rises* to God, and I will[R]cry aloud;   Ps. 3:4; 142:1
My voice *rises* to God, and He will hear me.
2 In the[R]day of my trouble I sought the Lord;   Ps. 50:15; 86:7
[R]In the night my hand was stretched out [134]without weariness;   Is. 26:9
My soul refused to be comforted.
3 *When* I remember God, then I am[R]disturbed;   Ps. 42:5, 11; 43:5
When I sigh, then my spirit grows faint.   [Selah.
4 Thou hast held my eyelids *open;*
I am so troubled that I cannot speak.
5 I have considered the days of old,
The years of long ago.
6 I will remember my song in the night;
I[R]will meditate with my heart;   Ps. 4:4
And my spirit[T]ponders.   *searched*

7 Will the Lord[R]reject forever?   Ps. 44:9
And will He never be favorable again?
8 Has His [R]lovingkindness ceased forever?   Ps. 89:49
Has *His*[T]promise[R] come to an end forever?   *word* · [2 Pet. 3:9]
9 Has God forgotten to be gracious?
Or has He in anger withdrawn His compassion?   [Selah.
10 Then I said, "It[R]is my grief,   Ps. 31:22
That the[R]right hand of the Most High has changed."   Ps. 44:2, 3

11 I shall remember the [R]deeds of [T]the LORD;   Ps. 105:5; 143:5 · Heb., *YAH*
Surely I will remember Thy wonders of old.
12 I will meditate on all Thy work,
And muse on Thy deeds.
13 Thy way, O God, is[R]holy;   Ps. 63:2; 73:17
What god is great like our God?
14 Thou art the[R]God who workest wonders;   [Ps. 72:18]
Thou hast[R]made known Thy strength among the peoples.   Ps. 106:8
15 Thou hast by Thy[T]power[R]redeemed Thy people,   *arm* · Ex. 6:6; Deut. 9:29
The sons of Jacob and Joseph.   [Selah.

16 The[R]waters saw Thee, O God;   Ex. 14:21

The waters saw Thee, they were in anguish;
The deeps also trembled.

17 The ᴿclouds poured out water; Judg. 5:4
The skies ᴿgave forth a sound; Ps. 68:33
Thy arrows flashed here and there.

18 The ᴿsound of Thy thunder was in the whirlwind; Ps. 18:13; 104:7
The ᴿlightnings lit up the world; Ps. 97:4
The ᴿearth trembled and shook. Ps. 18:7

19 Thy ᴿway was in the sea, Is. 51:10
And Thy paths in the mighty waters,
And Thy footprints may not be known.

20 Thou didst lead Thy people like a flock,
By the hand of Moses and Aaron.

PSALM 78

*God's Continued Guidance
in Spite of Unbelief*

A Maskil of Asaph.

LISTEN, O my people, to my instruction;
ᴿIncline your ears to the words of my mouth. Is. 55:3

2 I will open my mouth in a parable;
I will utter dark sayings of old,

3 Which we have heard and known,
And ᴿour fathers have told us. Ps. 44:1

4 We will ᴿnot conceal them from their children, Ex. 12:26; Deut. 6:7; Job 15:18
But ᴿtell to the generation to come the praises of the Lᴏʀᴅ, Ex. 13:8, 14
And His strength and His ᴿwondrous works that He has done. Ps. 26:7

5 For He established a ᴿtestimony in Jacob, Ps. 19:7; 81:5; Is. 8:20
And appointed a law in Israel,
Which He commanded our fathers,
That they should ᵀteach ᴿthem to their children, *make them known* • Deut. 4:9

6 ᴿThat the generation to come might know, *even* ᴿthe children *yet* to be born, Ps. 102:18 • Ps. 22:31
That they may arise and ᴿtell *them* to their children, Deut. 11:19

7 That they should put their confidence in God,
And not forget the works of God,
But ᴿkeep His commandments, Deut. 4:2

8 And ᴿnot be like their fathers, 2 Chr. 30:7
A stubborn and rebellious generation,
A generation that ᴰdid not ¹³⁵prepare its heart, Job 11:13; Ps. 78:37
And whose spirit was not ᴿfaithful to God. Ps. 51:10

9 The sons of Ephraim ᴬwere archers equipped with bows, *being*
Yet ᴿthey turned back in the day of battle. Judg. 20:39; Ps. 78:57

10 They did not keep the covenant of God,
And refused to walk in His law;

11 And they ᴿforgot His deeds, Ps. 106:13
And His ᴬmiracles that He had shown them. *wonderful works*

12 ᴿHe wrought wonders before their fathers, Ex. chs. 7-12; Ps. 106:22
In the land of Egypt, in the ᴿfield of Zoan. Num. 13:22; Is. 19:11; 30:4

13 He ᴿdivided the sea, and caused them to pass through; Ex. 14:21; Ps. 136:13
And He made the waters stand ᴿup like a heap. Ex. 15:8; Ps. 33:7

14 Then He led them with the cloud by ᴿday, Ex. 13:21; Ps. 105:39
And all the night with a light of fire.

15 He split the rocks in the wilderness,
And gave *them* abundant drink like the ocean depths.

16 He ᴮbrought forth streams also from the rock, Num. 20:8, 10, 11
And caused waters to run down like rivers.

¹³⁵ Or, *put right*

78:4 **History of Israel**—The biblical history of Israel covers 1,800 years and represents a marvelous panorama of God's gracious working through promise, miracle, blessing, and judgment. Israel begins as only a promise to Abraham (Page 14—Gen. 12:2). For over four hundred years the people of Israel rely on that promise, especially during the period of bondage to Egypt. Finally, in God's perfect timing, He brings the nation out of Egypt with the greatest series of miracles known in the entire Old Testament (Page 59—Ex. 7—15). This event is called the Exodus, meaning *a going out*. Since it constitutes the miraculous birth of the nation, it is to this great act of redemption that the nation always looks back as the foremost example of God's care for His people (Page 567—Ps. 77:14-20; 78:12-55; Page 860—Hos. 11:1).

Once God has redeemed Israel He establishes His covenant with them at Mount Sinai (Page 70—Ex. 19:5-8). From that point forward the nation is truly the Lord's possession, and He is their God. The covenant foretells gracious blessings for obedience and severe judgments for disobedience. The rest of Israel's history demonstrates the certainty of that prophecy. Through the periods of conquest, judges, monarchy, exile, restoration, and gentile domination, Israel is blessed when she obeys and judged when she disobeys. The nation is finally destroyed in A.D. 70, although this event is not described in the New Testament. Many prophecies, however, promise a future redemption for Israel (Page 1141—Rom. 11:26).

The practical value of studying Israel's history is threefold:

a. It sets forth examples to be followed or avoided (Page 1156—1 Cor. 10:6).

b. It shows God's control of all historical events, in that He was able to deal with Israel as He chose (Page 568—Ps. 78).

c. It serves as a model for all ages of God's kindness and mercy toward His people (Page 581—Ps. 103:14).
Now turn to Page 182—Deut. 14:2: Purpose of Israel.

17 Yet they still continued to sin against
Him,
To ᴿrebel against the Most High in the
desert.   Deut. 9:22; Is. 63:10; Heb. 3:16
18 And in their heart they ᴿput God to the
test   Ex. 17:6; Deut. 6:16; Ps. 78:41; 95:9
By asking ᵀfood according to their desire.   Num. 11:4
19 Then they spoke against God;
They said, "Can ᴿGod prepare a table in
the wilderness?   Ex. 16:3; Num. 11:4
20 "Behold, He ᴿstruck the rock, so that waters gushed out,   Num. 20:11; Ps. 78:15
And streams were overflowing;
Can He give bread also?
Will He provide meat for His people?"

21 Therefore the Lord heard and ᴬwas full
of wrath,   *became infuriated*
And a fire was kindled against Jacob,
And anger also mounted against Israel;
22 Because they did not believe in God,
And did not trust in His salvation.
23 Yet He commanded the clouds above,
And opened the doors of heaven.
24 And He ᴿrained down manna upon them
to eat,   Ex. 16:4
And gave them food from heaven.
25 Man did eat the bread of angels;
He sent them food in abundance.
26 He ᴿcaused the east wind to blow in the
heavens;   Num. 11:31
And by His ᴬpower He directed the
south wind.   *strength*
27 When He rained ᵀmeat upon them like
the dust,   *flesh*
Even ᴿwinged fowl like the sand of the
seas,   Ex. 16:13; Ps. 105:40
28 Then He let *them* fall in the midst of
ᵀtheir camp,   *His*
Round about their dwellings.
29 So they ate and were well filled;
And their desire He gave to them.
30 Before they had satisfied their desire,
While their food was in their mouths,
31 The anger of God rose against them,
And killed some of their stoutest ones,
And subdued the choice men of Israel.
32 In spite of all this they still sinned,
And ᴿdid not believe in His wonderful
works.   Num. 14:11; Ps. 78:11
33 So He brought their days to an end in
ᵀfutility,   *vanity, a mere breath*
And their years in sudden terror.

34 When He killed them, then they ᴿsought
Him,   Num. 21:7; [Hos. 5:15]
And returned and searched ᴿdiligently
for God;   Ps. 63:1
35 And they remembered that God was
their ᴿrock,   Deut. 32:4
And the Most High God their ᴿRedeemer.   [Deut. 9:26; Ps. 74:2]; Is. 41:14
36 But they ᴿdeceived Him with their
mouth,   Ex. 24:7, 8; Ezek. 33:31
And lied to Him with their tongue.

37 For their heart was not ᴿsteadfast
toward Him,   Ps. 51:10; 78:8; Acts 8:21
Nor were they faithful in His covenant.
38 But He, being compassionate, ᵀforgave
their iniquity, and did not destroy
them;   *covered over, atoned for*
And often He restrained His anger,
And did not arouse all His wrath.
39 Thus ᴴHe remembered that they were
but flesh,   Job 10:9; [Ps. 103:14]
A ᴬwind ᴿthat passes and does not return.   *breath* • Ps. 103:14; [James 4:14]

40 How often they ᴿrebelled against Him in
the wilderness,   Ps. 95:8, 9; Heb. 3:16
And grieved Him in the desert!
41 And again and again they ᴿtempted
God,   Num. 14:22
And pained the Holy One of Israel.
42 They did not remember His power,
The day when He ᴿredeemed them from
the adversary,   Ps. 106:10
43 When He performed His ᴴsigns in
Egypt,   Ps. 105:27
And His marvels in the field of Zoan,
44 And ᴿturned their rivers to blood,
And their streams, they could not
drink.   Ex. 7:20
45 He sent among them swarms of ᴿflies,
which devoured them,   Ps. 105:31
And frogs which destroyed them.
46 He gave also their crops to the ᴿgrass-
hopper,   1 Kin. 8:37; Ps. 105:34
And the product of their labor to the
ᴿlocust.   Ex. 10:14
47 He ᵀdestroyed their vines with ᴴhail-
stones,   *was killing* • Ex. 9:23–25
And their sycamore trees with frost.
48 He gave over their ᴿcattle also to the
hailstones,   Ex. 9:19
And their herds to bolts of lightning.
49 He sent upon them His burning anger,
Fury, and indignation, and trouble,
A band of destroying angels.
50 He leveled a path for His anger;
He did not spare their soul from death,
But gave over their life to the plague,
51 And smote all the first-born in Egypt,
The ᴿfirst *issue* of their virility in the
tents of ᴿHam.   Gen. 49:3 • Ps. 105:23
52 But He ᴮled forth His own people like
sheep,   Ex. 15:22
And guided them in the wilderness ᴵlike
a flock;   Ps. 77:20
53 And He led them ᴴsafely, so that they
did not fear;   Ex. 14:19, 20
But the sea engulfed their enemies.

54 So He brought them to His holy land,
To this ᴬhill country which His right
hand had gained.   *mountain*
55 He also ᴿdrove out the nations before
them,   Josh. 11:16-23; Ps. 44:2
And He ᴿapportioned them for an inheritance by measurement,   Josh. 13:7

And made the tribes of Israel dwell in
their tents.

56 Yet they [136]tempted[R] and rebelled
against the Most High God, Ps. 78:18
And did not keep His testimonies,

57 But turned back and [R]acted treacherously like their fathers; Ezek. 20:27f.
They [R]turned aside like a treacherous
bow.   Hos. 7:16

58 For they[R]provoked Him with their high
places, Deut. 4:25; Judg. 2:12; 1 Kin. 14:9
And aroused His jealousy with their
[R]graven images.   Ex. 20:4; Lev. 26:1

59 When God heard, He [A]was filled with
[R]wrath,   became infuriated · Deut. 1:34
And greatly [R]abhorred Israel; Lev. 26:30

60 So that He [R]abandoned the dwelling
place at Shiloh,   1 Sam. 4:11; Ps. 78:67
The tent which He had pitched among
men,

61 And gave up His strength to captivity,
And His glory[R]into the hand of the adversary.   1 Sam. 4:17

62 He also [R]delivered His people to the
sword,   Judg. 20:21; 1 Sam. 4:10
And [A]was filled with wrath at His inheritance.   became infuriated

63 Fire devoured[A]His young men;   their
And His virgins had no wedding songs.

64 [A]His priests fell by the sword;   their
And His widows could not weep.

65 Then the Lord awoke as *if from* sleep,
Like a warrior overcome by wine.

66 And He [T]drove[R] His adversaries backward;   smote · 1 Sam. 5:6
He put on them an everlasting reproach.

67 He also rejected the tent of Joseph,
And did not choose the tribe of
Ephraim,

68 But chose the tribe of Judah,
Mount[R]Zion which He loved.   [Ps. 87:2]

69 And He [R]built His sanctuary like the
heights,   1 Kin. 6:1-38
Like the earth which He has founded
forever.

70 He also chose David His servant,
And took him from the sheepfolds;

71 From the care of the ewes with suck-
ling lambs He brought him,
To shepherd Jacob His people,
And Israel[R]His inheritance.   1 Sam. 10:1

72 So he shepherded them according to
the[R]integrity of his heart,   1 Kin. 9:4
And guided them with his skillful
hands.

PSALM 79

Avenge the Defilement of Jerusalem

A Psalm of Asaph.

O GOD, the [R]nations have [T]invaded Thine
inheritance;   Lam. 1:10 · come into

They have defiled Thy holy temple;
They have laid Jerusalem in ruins.

2 They have given the [R]dead bodies of
Thy servants for food to the birds
of the heavens,   Deut. 28:26; Jer. 7:33
The flesh of Thy godly ones to the
beasts of the earth.

3 They have poured out their blood like
water round about Jerusalem;
And there was no one to bury them.

4 We have become a [R]reproach to our
neighbors,   Ps. 44:13; 80:6; [Dan. 9:16]
A scoffing and derision to those around
us.

5 [R]How long, O LORD? Wilt Thou be angry
forever? Ps. 13:1; 74:1, 9, 10; 85:5; 89:46
Will Thy jealousy burn like fire?

6 [R]Pour out Thy wrath upon the nations
which do not know Thee,   Ps. 69:24
And upon the kingdoms which do not
call upon Thy name.

7 For they have[R]devoured Jacob,   Ps. 53:4
And laid waste his[T]habitation.   pasture

8 [R]Do not remember the iniquities of *our*
forefathers against us;
Let Thy compassion come quickly to
[T]meet us;   Ps. 106:6; Is. 64:9 · Ps. 21:3
For we are[R]brought very low.   Ps. 116:6

9 [R]Help us, O God of our salvation, for the
glory of Thy name;   2 Chr. 14:11
And deliver us, and forgive our sins,
for Thy name's sake.

10 [R]Why should the nations say, "Where is
their God?"   Ps. 42:10; 115:2
Let there be known among the nations
in our sight,
[R]Vengeance for the blood of Thy servants, which has been shed. Ps. 94:1

11 Let[R]the groaning of the prisoner come
before Thee;   Ps. 102:20
According to the greatness of Thy
[T]power preserve those who are
doomed to die.   arm

12 And return to our neighbors [R]sevenfold
into their bosom Gen. 4:15; Lev. 26:21
[T]The reproach with which they have reproached Thee, O Lord.   Their

13 So we Thy people and the[R]sheep of Thy
[A]pasture   Ps. 74:1; 95:7 · pasturing
Will [R]give thanks to Thee forever;
To all generations we will [R]tell of Thy
praise.   Ps. 44:8 · Ps. 89:1; Is. 43:21

PSALM 80

Israel's Plea for God's Mercy

For the choir director; *set to*
El Shoshannim; Eduth.
A Psalm of Asaph.

OH, give ear,[R]Shepherd of Israel,   Ps. 23:1
Thou who dost lead Joseph like a flock;

[136] Or, *put to the test*

Thou who ^Rart enthroned *above* the cherubim, shine forth!   [Ex. 25:22]

2 Before Ephraim and Benjamin and Manasseh, ^Rstir up Thy power,   Ps. 35:23
And come to save us!

3 O God, ^Rrestore us,   Ps. 60:1; 80:7, 19; 85:4
And cause Thy face to shine *upon us*, ^Aand we will be saved.   *that we may*

4 O^RLORD God *of* hosts,   Ps. 59:5; 84:8
How long wilt Thou^Tbe angry with the prayer of Thy people?   *smoke against*

5 Thou hast fed them with the^Rbread of tears,   Ps. 42:3; 102:9; Is. 30:20
And Thou hast made them to drink tears in large measure.

6 Thou dost make us ¹³⁷an object of contention^Rto our neighbors;   Ps. 44:13
And our enemies laugh among themselves.

7 O God *of* hosts, restore us,
And cause Thy face to shine *upon us*, ¹³⁸and we will be saved.

8 Thou didst remove a vine from Egypt;
Thou didst ^Rdrive out the ^Anations, and didst plant it.   Josh. 13:6 • *Gentiles*

9 Thou didst clear *the ground* before it,
And it ^Rtook deep root and filled the land.   Hos. 14:5

10 The mountains were covered with its shadow;
And the cedars of God with its boughs.

11 It was sending out its branches^Rto the sea,   Ps. 72:8
And its shoots to the River.

12 Why hast Thou ^Rbroken down its ^Ahedges,   Ps. 89:40; Is. 5:5 • *walls, fences*
So that all who pass *that* way pick its *fruit*?

13 A boar from the forest eats it away,
And whatever moves in the field feeds on it.

14 O God *of* hosts, ^Rturn again now, we beseech Thee;   Ps. 90:13
^RLook down from heaven and see, and take care of this vine,   Ps. 102:19

15 Even the ^Ashoot^Rwhich Thy right hand has planted,   *root* • Ps. 80:8
And on the son whom Thou hast ^Astrengthened for Thyself.   *secured*

16 It is burned with fire, it is cut down;
They perish at the^Rrebuke of Thy countenance.   [Ps. 39:11; 76:6]

17 Let^RThy hand be upon the man of Thy right hand,   Ps. 89:21
Upon the son of man whom Thou^Rdidst make strong for Thyself.   Ps. 80:15

18 Then we shall not turn back from Thee;
^RRevive us, and we will call upon Thy name.   [Ps. 71:20]

19 O LORD God of hosts, restore us;
Cause Thy face to shine *upon us*, ^Aand we will be saved.   *that we may*

¹³⁷ Lit., *a strife to*   ¹³⁸ Or, *that we may*

PSALM 81

God's Plea for Israel's Obedience

For the choir director; on the Gittith.
A Psalm of Asaph.

SING^Rfor joy to God our strength;   Ps. 51:14
Shout joyfully to the God of Jacob.

2 Raise a song, strike the timbrel,
The sweet sounding lyre with the harp.

3 Blow the trumpet at the new moon,
At the full moon, on our feast day.

4 For it is a statute for Israel,
An ordinance of the God of Jacob.

5 He established it for a testimony in Joseph,
When he ^Twent^Rthroughout the land of Egypt.   *went out over* • Ex. 11:4
I heard a language that I did not know:

6 "I relieved his shoulder of the burden,
His hands were freed from the basket.

7 "You ^Rcalled in trouble, and I rescued you;   Ex. 2:23; 14:10; Ps. 50:15
I ^Ranswered you in the hiding place of thunder;   Ex. 19:19; 20:18
I proved you at the waters of Meribah.   [Selah.

8 "Hear, O My people, and I will ^Aadmonish you;   *bear witness against*
O Israel, if you would listen to Me!

9 "Let there be no ^Rstrange god among you;   [Ex. 20:3; Deut. 5:7; 32:12]; Ps. 44:20
Nor shall you worship any foreign god.

10 "I, ^T the LORD, am your God,   Ex. 20:2
Who brought you up from the land of Egypt;
Open your mouth wide and I will fill it.

11 "But My people ^Rdid not listen to My voice;   Deut. 32:15; Ps. 106:25
And Israel did not ^Tobey Me.   *yield to*

12 "So I ^Rgave ^Tthem over to the stubbornness of their heart,   [Job 8:4] • *him*
To walk in their own devices.

13 "Oh that My people would listen to Me,
That Israel would walk in My ways!

14 "I would quickly subdue their enemies,
And^Rturn My hand against their adversaries.   Amos 1:8

15 "Those^R who hate the LORD would pretend obedience to Him;   Rom. 1:30
And their time *of punishment* would be forever.

16 "But^T I would feed you with the finest of the wheat;   *He would feed him*
And with^Rhoney from the rock I would satisfy you."   Deut. 32:13

PSALM 82

Rebuke of Israel's Unjust Judges

A Psalm of Asaph.

GOD takes His stand in ^THis own congregation;   *the congregation of God*
He judges in the midst of the rulers.

2 How long will you judge unjustly,
　And　show　partiality　to　the
　wicked?　　　　　　　　　[Selah.
3 Vindicate the weak and fatherless;
　Do justice to the afflicted and destitute.
4 ^RRescue the weak and needy;　Job. 29:12
　Deliver *them* out of the hand of the
　wicked.

5 They^Rdo not know nor do they under-
　stand;　　　Ps. 14:4; Jer. 4:22; Mic. 3:1
　They^Rwalk about in darkness;　Prov. 2:13
　All the^Rfoundations of the earth are
　shaken.　　　　　　　　　　Ps. 11:3
6 ^TI said, "You are gods,　　　*I, on my part*
　And all of you are^Rsons of the Most
　High.　　　　　　　　　　Ps. 89:26
7 "Nevertheless you will die like men,
　And fall like *any* one of the princes."
8 ^RArise, O God, judge the earth!　Ps. 12:5
　For it is Thou who dost^Rpossess all the
　nations.　　　　Ps. 2:8; [Rev. 11:15]

PSALM 83

Plea for God to Destroy
Israel's Enemies

A Song, a Psalm of Asaph.

O GOD,^Rdo not remain quiet;　Ps. 28:1; 35:22
　^RDo not be silent and, O God, do not be
　still.　　　　　　　　　　Ps. 109:1
2 For, behold, Thine enemies^Rmake an
　uproar;　　　　　　Ps. 2:1; Is. 17:12
　And those who hate Thee have^Texalted
　themselves.　　　*lifted up the head*
3 They^Rmake shrewd plans against Thy
　people,　　　　Ps. 64:2; [Is. 29:15]
　And^Aconspire together against Thy
　^Atreasured ones.　*consult · hidden ones*
4 They have said, "Come, and let us wipe
　them out^Tas a nation,　　　*from*
　That the^Aname of Israel be remembered
　no more."　　　Ps. 41:5; Jer. 11:19
5 For they have^Tconspired^Atogether with
　one mind;　Ps. 2:2; Dan. 6:7 · *consulted*
　Against Thee do they make a covenant:
6 The tents of Edom and the Ishmaelites;
　^RMoab, and the Hagrites;　2 Chr. 20:10
7 Gebal, and Ammon, and Amalek;
　Philistia with the inhabitants of Tyre;
8 Assyria also has joined with them;
　They have become a help to the chil-
　dren of Lot.　　　　　　　[Selah.

9 Deal with them as with Midian,
　As^Rwith Sisera *and* Jabin, at the torrent
　of Kishon,　　　Judg. 4:7, 15, 21-24
10 Who were destroyed at En-dor,
　Who became as dung for the ground.
11 Make their nobles like Oreb and Zeeb,
　And all their princes like^RZebah and
　Zalmunna,　　　　　Judg. 8:12, 21
12 Who said, "Let^R us possess for our-
　selves　　　　　　　2 Chr. 20:11
　The^Rpastures of God."　　Ps. 132:13

13 O my God, make them like the
　¹³⁹whirling^Rdust;　　　Is. 17:13
　Like^Rchaff before the wind.　Job 21:18
14 Like^Rfire that burns the forest,　Is. 9:18
　And like a flame that^Rsets the moun-
　tains on fire,　Ex. 19:18; Deut. 32:22
15 So pursue them with Thy tempest,
　And terrify them with Thy storm.
16 ^RFill their faces with dishonor,　Job 10:15
　That they may seek Thy name, O LORD.
17 Let them be^Rashamed and dismayed
　forever;　　　　　Ps. 35:4; 70:2
　And let them be humiliated and perish,
18 That they may^Rknow that Thou alone,
　whose name is the LORD,　Ps. 59:13
　Art the Most High over all the earth.

PSALM 84

The Joy of Dwelling with God

For the choir director; on the Gittith.
A Psalm of the sons of Korah.

H OW lovely are Thy dwelling places,
　O LORD of hosts!
2 My^Rsoul longed and even yearned for
　the courts of the LORD;　Ps. 42:1, 2
　My heart and my flesh sing for joy to
　the^Rliving God.　　　　　Ps. 42:2
3 The bird also has found a house,
　And the swallow a nest for herself,
　where she may lay her young,
　Even Thine altars, O LORD of hosts,
　^RMy King and my God.　　　Ps. 5:2
4 How^Rblessed are those who dwell in
　Thy house!　　　　　　[Ps. 65:4]
　They are ever praising Thee.　[Selah.

5 How　blessed　is　the　man　whose
　^Rstrength is in Thee;　　　Ps. 81:1
　In^Twhose heart are the^Rhighways *to*
　Zion!　*their* · Ps. 86:11; 122:1; Jer. 31:6
6 Passing through the valley of ¹⁴⁰Baca,
　they make it a^Tspring, *place of springs*
　The^Rearly rain also covers it with bless-
　ings.　　　　　[Ps. 107:35; Joel 2:23]
7 They go from strength to strength,
　Every one of them^Rappears before God
　in Zion.　Ex. 34:23; Deut. 16:16; Ps. 42:2

8 O LORD God of hosts, hear my prayer;
　Give ear, O God of Jacob!　[Selah.
9 Behold our^Rshield, O God,　Gen. 15:1
　And look upon the face of ^RThine
　anointed.　2 Sam. 19:21; Ps. 2:2; 132:17
10 For^Ra day in Thy courts is better than a
　thousand *outside*.　　　Ps. 27:4
　I would rather stand at the threshold of
　the house of my God,
　Than dwell in the tents of wickedness.
11 For the LORD God is a sun and shield;
　The LORD gives grace and glory;
　No good thing does He withhold from
　those who walk uprightly.

¹³⁹ Or, *tumbleweed*
¹⁴⁰ Probably, *Weeping* or *Balsam trees*

12 O LORD of hosts,
How[R]blessed is the man who trusts in
Thee!   [Ps. 2:12; 40:4]

PSALM 85

Prayer for Revival

For the choir director.
A Psalm of the sons of Korah.

O LORD, Thou didst show[R]favor to Thy
land;   Ps. 77:7; 106:4
Thou didst [141]restore[R]the captivity of
Jacob.   Ezek. 39:25; Hos. 6:11; Joel 3:1
2 Thou didst[R]forgive the iniquity of Thy
people;   [Num. 14:19]; 1 Kin. 8:34
Thou didst cover all their sin.   [Selah.
3 Thou didst withdraw all Thy fury;
Thou didst[T]turn away from Thy burning anger.   Deut. 13:17; Jon. 3:9

4 Restore us, O God of our salvation,
And[C]cause Thine indignation toward us
to cease.   Dan. 9:16
5 Wilt Thou be angry with us forever?
Wilt Thou prolong Thine anger to 'all
generations?   *generation and generation*
6 Wilt Thou not Thyself revive us again,
That Thy people may rejoice in Thee?
7 Show us Thy lovingkindness, O LORD,
And[R]grant us Thy salvation.   Ps. 106:4

8 I will hear what God the LORD will say;
For He will speak peace to His people,
[T]to His godly ones;   *even to*
But let them not turn back to folly.
9 Surely[R]His salvation is near to those
who [142]fear Him,   Ps. 34:18; Is. 46:13
That glory may dwell in our land.
10 [R]Lovingkindness and[T]truth have met together;   [Ps. 25:10; 89:14] · *faithfulness*
[R]Righteousness and peace have kissed
each other.   Ps. 72:3; [Is. 32:17]
11 [A]Truth springs from the earth;
And righteousness looks down from
heaven.   *Faithfulness*
12 Indeed, [R]the LORD will give what is
good;   [Ps. 84:11; James 1:17]
And our land will yield its produce.
13 Righteousness will go before Him,
And will make His footsteps into a
way.

PSALM 86

"Teach Me Thy Way, O LORD"

A Prayer of David.

INCLINE[R]Thine ear, O LORD, *and* answer
me;   Ps. 17:6; 31:2; 71:2
For I am [R]afflicted and needy.   Ps. 40:17
2 [R]Do preserve my 'soul, for I am a godly
man;   Ps. 25:20 · *life*

O Thou my God, save Thy servant who
[R]trusts in Thee.   Ps. 25:2; 31:14; 56:4
3 Be[R]gracious to me, O Lord,   Ps. 4:1; 57:1
For[R]to Thee I cry all day long.   Ps. 25:5
4 Make glad the soul of Thy servant,
For to Thee, O Lord, I lift up my soul.
5 For Thou, Lord, art[R]good, and[R]ready to
forgive;   Ps. 25:8 · Ps. 130:4
And [R]abundant in lovingkindness to all
who call upon Thee.   Joel 2:13; Jon. 4:2
6 [R]Give ear, O LORD, to my prayer;   Ps. 55:1
And give heed to the voice of my supplications!
7 In [R]the day of my trouble I shall call
upon Thee,   Ps. 50:15; 77:2
For[R]Thou wilt answer me.   Ps. 17:6
8 There is [R]no one like Thee among the
gods, O Lord;   [Ex. 15:11]; 2 Sam. 7:22
Nor are there any works like Thine.
9 [R]All nations whom Thou hast made
shall come and worship before
Thee, O Lord;   Ps. 22:27; 66:4; Rev. 15:4
And they shall glorify Thy name.
10 For Thou art[R]great and doest[A]wondrous
deeds;   Ps. 77:13 · *miracles*
Thou alone[R]art God.   Deut. 6:4; 32:39

11 [R]Teach me Thy way, O LORD;   Ps. 25:5
I will walk in Thy truth;
Unite my heart to fear Thy name.
12 I will [R]give thanks to Thee, O Lord my
God, with all my heart,   Ps. 111:1
And will glorify Thy name forever.
13 For Thy lovingkindness toward me is
great,
And Thou hast delivered my soul from
the [R]depths of Sheol.   *lowest Sheol*

14 O God, arrogant men have [R]risen up
against me,   Ps. 54:3
And[A]a band of violent men have sought
my[R]life,   *an assembly · soul*
And they have not set Thee before
them.
15 But Thou, O Lord, art a God[R]merciful
and gracious,   [Ps. 86:5]
Slow to anger and abundant in lovingkindness and[T]truth.   *faithfulness*
16 Turn to me, and be gracious to me;
Oh grant Thy strength to Thy servant,
And save the son of Thy handmaid.
17 [R]Show me a sign for good,   Judg. 6:17
That those who hate me may [R]see *it*,
and be ashamed,   Ps. 112:10
Because Thou, O LORD,[R]hast helped me
and comforted me.   Ps. 118:13

PSALM 87

Glorious Zion, City of God

A Psalm of the sons of Korah.
A Song.

HIS foundation is in the holy mountains.
2 The LORD loves the gates of Zion

[141] Or, *restore the fortunes*   [142] Or, *reverence*

More than all the *other* dwelling places
of Jacob.
3 Glorious things are spoken of you,
O city of God.   [Selah.
4"I shall mention [143]Rahab and Babylon
among those who know Me;
Behold, Philistia and [R]Tyre with [T]Ethi-
opia: [R]   Ps. 45:12 • *Cush* • Ps. 68:31
'This one was born there.' "
5 But of Zion it shall be said, "This one
and that one were born in her";
And the Most High Himself will [c]estab-
lish her.   Ps. 48:8
6 The LORD shall count when He [R]regis-
ters the peoples,   Ps. 69:28; Is. 4:3
"This one was born there."   [Selah.
7 Then those who sing as well as those
who [c]play the flutes *shall say,* *dance*
"All my springs *of joy* are in you."

PSALM 88

Crying from Deepest Affliction

A Song. A Psalm of the sons of
Korah. For the choir director;
according to Mahalath Leannoth.
A Maskil of Heman the Ezrahite.

O LORD, the [R]God of my salvation, Ps. 24:5
I have [R]cried out by day and in the night
before Thee. Ps. 22:2; 86:3; [Luke 18:7]
2 Let my prayer come before Thee;
[R]Incline Thine ear to my cry!   Ps. 31:2
3 For my soul has had enough troubles,
And my life has drawn near to Sheol.
4 I am reckoned among those who [R]go
down to the pit;   [Ps. 28:1; 143:7]
I have become like a man [R]without
strength,   Job 29:12; Ps. 22:11
5 Forsaken [R]among the dead,   Ps. 31:12
Like the slain who lie in the grave,
Whom Thou dost remember no more,
And they are cut off from Thy hand.
6 Thou hast put me in the lowest pit,
In [b]dark places, in the depths. Ps. 143:3
7 Thy wrath [R]has rested upon me, Ps. 32:4
And Thou hast afflicted me with all
Thy waves.   [Selah.
8 Thou hast removed [R]my acquaintances
far from me;   Job 19:13, 19; Ps. 31:11
Thou hast made me an [144]object [R] of
loathing to them;   Job 30:10
I am shut up and cannot go out.
9 My [c]eye has wasted away because of af-
fliction;   Ps. 6:7; 31:9
I have [c]called upon Thee every day, O
LORD;   Ps. 22:2; 86:3
I have spread out my hands to Thee.

10 Wilt Thou perform wonders for the
dead?
Will the departed spirits rise *and*
praise Thee?   [Selah.
11 Will Thy lovingkindness be declared in
the grave,
Thy faithfulness in Abaddon?

12 Will Thy wonders be made known in
the [R]darkness?   Job 10:21; Ps. 88:6
And Thy righteousness in the land of
forgetfulness?

13 But I, O LORD, have cried out [R]to Thee
for help,   Ps. 30:2
And [R]in the morning my prayer comes
before Thee.   Ps. 5:3; 119:147
14 O LORD, why dost Thou reject my soul?
Why dost Thou hide Thy face from me?
15 I was afflicted and [R]about to die from
my youth on;   Prov. 24:11
I suffer Thy terrors; I am overcome.
16 Thy burning anger has passed over me;
Thy terrors have [A]destroyed me. *silenced*
17 They have [R]surrounded me like water
all day long;   Ps. 118:10-12
They have [R]encompassed me altogether.   Ps. 17:11; 22:12, 16
18 Thou hast removed [R]lover and friend far
from me; Job 19:13; Ps. 88:8; 31:11; 38:11
My acquaintances are *in* darkness.

PSALM 89

*Claiming God's Promises
in Affliction*

A Maskil of Ethan the Ezrahite.

I WILL [R]sing of the lovingkindness of the
LORD forever;   Ps. 59:16; 101:1
To all generations I will make known
Thy faithfulness with my mouth.
2 For I have said, "Lovingkindness [R]will
be built up forever;   Ps. 103:17
In the heavens Thou wilt establish Thy
[R]faithfulness."   Ps. 36:5; [119:90]
3"I have made a covenant with [R]My cho-
sen;   1 Kin. 8:16
I have sworn to David My servant,
4 I will establish your seed forever,
And build up your throne to all genera-
tions."   [Selah.

5 And the [R]heavens will praise Thy wonders, O LORD;   [Ps. 19:1; 97:6]
Thy faithfulness also in [R]the assembly
of the holy ones.   Ps. 149:1
6 For [R]who in the skies is comparable to
the LORD?   Ps. 86:8; 113:5
Who among the [A]sons of the mighty is
like the LORD,   *sons of gods*
7 A God [R]greatly feared in the council of
the holy ones,   Ps. 47:2; 68:35; 76:7, 11
And [R]awesome above all those who are
around Him?   Ps. 96:4
8 O LORD [T]God of hosts, who is like Thee,
O mighty LORD?   Heb., *YAH*
Thy faithfulness also surrounds Thee.
9 Thou dost rule the swelling of the sea;
When its waves rise, Thou [R]dost still
them.   Ps. 65:7; 107:29
10 Thou Thyself didst crush [T]Rahab [R]like
one who is slain;   Egypt • Ps. 87:4

[143] I.e., Egypt   [144] Lit., *abomination to them*

Thou didst scatter Thine enemies with
^TThy mighty arm.   *an arm of might*

11 The^Rheavens are Thine, the earth also is
Thine;   [Gen. 1:1; 1 Chr. 29:11]; Ps. 96:5
The^Rworld and ¹⁴⁵all it contains, Thou
hast founded them.   Ps. 24:1
12 The^Rnorth and the south, Thou hast created them;   Job 26:7
^RTabor and Hermon shout for joy at Thy
name.   Josh. 19:22; Judg. 4:6; Jer. 46:18
13 Thou hast a strong arm;
Thy hand is mighty, Thy^Rright hand is
exalted.   Ps. 98:1; 118:16
14 ^RRighteousness and justice are the foundation of Thy throne;   Ps. 97:2
^RLovingkindness and ^Atruth go before
Thee.   Ps. 85:13 · *faithfulness*
15 How blessed are the people who know
the ¹⁴⁶joyful^Rsound!   Lev. 23:24
O LORD, they walk in the^Rlight of Thy
countenance.   Ps. 4:6; 44:3; 67:1; 80:3
16 In Thy name they rejoice all the day,
And by Thy righteousness they are exalted.
17 For Thou art the glory of ^Rtheir
strength,   [Ps. 28:8]
And by Thy favor our horn is exalted.
18 For our shield belongs to the LORD,
¹⁴⁷And our king to the^RHoly One of Is-
rael.   Ps. 71:22; 78:41

19 ^AOnce Thou didst speak in vision to Thy
godly ones,   *At that time*
And didst say, "I have ^Tgiven help to
one who is mighty;   *placed help upon*
I have exalted one ^Rchosen from the
people.   1 Kin. 11:34; Ps. 78:70
20 "I have found David My servant;
With My holy oil I have anointed him,
21 With whom ^RMy hand will be established;   Ps. 18:35; 80:17
My arm also will strengthen him.
22 "The enemy will not ¹⁴⁸deceive him,
Nor the son of wickedness afflict him.
23 "But I shall ^Rcrush his adversaries before
him,   2 Sam. 7:9; Ps. 18:40
And strike those who hate him.
24 "And My ^Rfaithfulness and My lovingkindness will be with him,   Ps. 89:1
And in My name his^Rhorn will be exalted.   Ps. 132:17
25 "I shall also set his hand on the sea,
And his right hand on the rivers.
26 "He will cry to Me, 'Thou art my Father,
My God, and the rock of my salvation.'
27 "I also shall make him *My* first-born,
The highest of the kings of the earth.
28 "My^Rlovingkindness I will keep for him
forever,   Ps. 89:33

And My^Rcovenant shall be confirmed to
him.   Ps. 89:3, 34
29 "So I will establish his^Tdescendants^Rfor-
ever,   *seed* · Ps. 18:50; 89:4, 36
And his throne as the days of heaven.

30 "If his sons^Rforsake My law,   Ps. 119:53
And do not walk in My judgments,
31 If they ¹⁴⁹violate My statutes,
And do not keep My commandments,
32 Then I will visit their transgression
with the^Rrod,   Job 9:34; 21:9
And their iniquity with stripes.
33 "But I will not break off^RMy lovingkindness from him,   2 Sam. 7:15
Nor deal falsely in My faithfulness.
34 "My covenant I will not^Tviolate,   *profane*
Nor will I alter the utterance of My
lips.
35 "¹⁵⁰Once I have sworn by My holiness;
I will not lie to David.
36 "His descendants shall endure forever,
And his throne as the sun before Me.
37 "It shall be established forever^Rlike the
moon,   Ps. 72:5
And the witness in the sky is faithful."   [Selah.

38 But Thou hast cast off and rejected,
Thou hast been full of wrath ^Aagainst
Thine^Ranointed.   *with* · Ps. 20:6
39 Thou hast^Rspurned the covenant of Thy
servant;   Ps. 78:59; Lam. 2:7
Thou hast^Rprofaned his crown ^Tin the
dust.   Ps. 74:7 · *to the ground*
40 Thou hast broken down all his walls;
Thou hast^Rbrought his strongholds to
ruin.   Lam. 2:2, 5
41 ^RAll who pass along the way plunder
him;   Ps. 80:12
He has become a^Rreproach to his neighbors.   Ps. 44:13; 69:9, 19; 79:4
42 Thou hast^Rexalted the right hand of his
adversaries;   Ps. 13:2
Thou hast made all his enemies rejoice.
43 Thou dost also turn back the edge of
his sword,
And hast not made him stand in battle.
44 Thou hast made his splendor to cease,
And cast his throne to the ground.
45 Thou hast^Rshortened the days of his
youth;   Ps. 102:23
Thou   hast   covered   him   with
shame.   [Selah.

46 ^RHow long, O LORD?   Ps. 13:1; 44:24
Wilt Thou hide Thyself forever?
Will Thy^Rwrath burn like fire?   Ps. 79:5
47 Remember what my span of life is;
For what vanity^AThou hast created all
the sons of men!   *hast Thou . . . men?*
48 What man can live and not see death?
Can he deliver his soul from the power
of Sheol?   [Selah.

¹⁴⁵ Lit., *its fulness*
¹⁴⁶ Or, *blast of the trumpet, shout of joy*
¹⁴⁷ Or, *Even to the Holy One of Israel our King*
¹⁴⁸ Or, *exact usury from him*   ¹⁴⁹ Lit., *profane*
¹⁵⁰ Or, *One thing*

49 Where are Thy former lovingkindnesses, O Lord,
Which Thou didst [R]swear to David in
Thy faithfulness? 2 Sam. 7:15; Jer. 30:9
50 Remember, O Lord, the [R]reproach of
Thy servants;   Ps. 69:9; 74:18, 22
How I do bear in my bosom *the reproach of* all the many peoples,
51 With which [R]Thine enemies have reproached, O LORD,   Ps. 74:10, 18, 22
With which they have reproached the
footsteps of Thine anointed.

52 [R]Blessed be the LORD forever!
Amen and Amen.   Ps. 41:13

BOOK 4

PSALM 90

"Teach Us to Number Our Days"

A Prayer of Moses the man of God.

LORD, Thou hast been our [151]dwelling[R]
place in all generations. [Deut. 33:27]
2 Before the mountains were born,
[A]Or Thou [R]didst give birth to the earth
and the world,   *And* • Gen. 1:1
Even [R]from everlasting to everlasting,
Thou art God.   Ps. 93:2; 102:24, 27

3 Thou dost turn man back into dust,
And dost say, "Return, O children of
men."
4 For a thousand years in Thy sight
Are like yesterday when it passes by,
[A]Or *as* a watch in the night.   *And*
5 Thou hast [?]swept them away like a
flood, they fall asleep;   *flooded*
In the morning they are like grass
which [A]sprouts anew.   *passes away*
6 In the morning it flourishes, and
[?]sprouts anew;   *passes away*
Toward evening it [R]fades, and [R]withers
away. [Ps. 92:7; Matt. 6:30] • James 1:11

7 For we have been [R]consumed by Thine
anger,   Ps. 39:11
And by Thy wrath we have been [A]dis-
mayed.   *terrified*
8 Thou hast [R]placed our iniquities before
Thee,   Ps. 50:21; Jer. 16:17
Our [R]secret *sins* in the light of Thy presence.   Ps. 19:12; Eccl. 12:14
9 For [R]all our days have declined in Thy
fury;   Ps. 78:33
We have finished our years like a sigh.
10 As for the days of our [?]life, [?]they contain
seventy years,   *years • in them are*
Or if due to strength, eighty years,
Yet their pride is *but* labor and sorrow;
For soon it is gone and we fly away.
11 Who [A]understands the [R]power of Thine
anger,   *knows* • [Ps. 76:7]
And Thy fury, according to the fear
[?]that is due Thee?   *of Thee*

12 So teach us to number our days,
That we may [A]present [R]to Thee a heart of
wisdom.   *gain, bring in* • Prov. 2:1-6

13 Do return, O LORD; how long *will it be*?
And be [?]sorry for Thy servants. Ex. 32:12
14 O [R]satisfy us in the morning with Thy
lovingkindness,   [Ps. 36:8; 65:4; 103:5]
That we may [R]sing for joy and be glad
all our days.   Ps. 31:7; 85:6
15 Make us glad [A]according to the days
Thou hast afflicted us, *as many days as*
And the years we have seen [152]evil.
16 Let Thy work appear to Thy servants,
And Thy majesty to their children.
17 And let the [R]favor of the Lord our God
be upon us;   Ps. 27:4
And do [153]confirm [R]for us the work of
our hands;   [Is. 26:12; 1 Cor. 3:7]
Yes, [153]confirm the work of our hands.

PSALM 91

Abiding in
"the Shadow of the Almighty"

HE who dwells in the [R]shelter of the Most
High   Ps. 27:5; 31:20; 32:7
Will abide in the [R]shadow of the Almighty.   Ps. 17:8; 121:5; Is. 25:4; 32:2
2 I will say to the LORD, "My [R]refuge and
my fortress,   Ps. 14:6; 91:9; 94:22
My God, in whom I [R]trust!" Ps. 25:2; 56:4
3 For it is He who delivers you from the
[R]snare of the trapper,   Prov. 6:5
And from the deadly pestilence.
4 He will cover you with His pinions,
And [?]under His wings you may seek refuge;   Ps. 17:8; 36:7; 57:1; 63:7
His [R]faithfulness is a [?]shield and bul-
wark.   Ps. 40:11 • Ps. 35:2

5 You [R]will not be afraid of the terror by
night,   [Job 5:19–23]; Ps. 23:4; 27:1
Or of the arrow that flies by day;
6 Of the [R]pestilence that [A]stalks in darkness,   2 Kin. 19:35; Ps. 91:10 • *walks*
Or of the [R]destruction that lays waste at
noon.   Job 5:22
7 A thousand may fall at your side,
And ten thousand at your right hand;
But it shall not approach you.
8 You will only look on with your eyes,
And see the recompense of the wicked.
9 For you have made the LORD, [R]my refuge,   Ps. 91:2
Even the Most High, [R]your dwelling
place.   Ps. 90:1
10 [R]No evil will befall you,   Prov. 12:21
Nor will any plague come near your
[A]tent.   *dwelling*

---

[151] Or, *hiding place;* some ancient mss. read *place of
refuge* [152] Or, *trouble* [153] Or, *give permanence to*

11 For He will give[R]His angels charge concerning you,   Matt. 4:6; [Heb. 1:14]
To guard you in all your ways.
12 They will bear you up in their hands,
Lest you strike your foot against a
stone.
13 You will tread upon the lion and cobra,
The young lion and the[a]serpent you will
trample down.   *dragon*

14 "Because[R]he has loved Me, therefore I
will deliver him;   Ps. 145:20
I will[R]set him *securely* on high, because
he has known My name.   Ps. 59:1
15 "He will[a]call upon Me, and I will answer
him;   Job 12:4; Ps. 50:15
I will be with him in[a]trouble;   *distress*
I will rescue him, and honor him.
16 "With a long life I will satisfy him,
And let him behold My salvation."

PSALM 92

It Is Good to Praise the Lord

A Psalm, a Song for the Sabbath day.

IT is good to give thanks to the LORD,
And to[R]sing praises to Thy name, O
Most High;   [Ps. 135:3]
2 To[R]declare Thy lovingkindness in the
morning,   Ps. 59:16
And Thy faithfulness[T]by night,   *nights*
3 With the[R]ten-stringed lute, and with
the harp;   1 Sam. 10:5; Ps. 33:2
With resounding music upon the lyre.
4 For Thou, O LORD, hast made me glad
by what Thou hast done,
I will[R]sing for joy at the[R]works of Thy
hands.   Ps. 106:47 • Ps. 8:6

5 How great are Thy works, O LORD!
Thy[a]thoughts are very deep.   *purposes*
6 A senseless man has no knowledge;
Nor does a stupid man understand this:
7 That when the wicked[R]sprouted up like
grass,   Job 12:6; Ps. 90:5
And all who did iniquity flourished,
It *was only* that they might be[R]de-
stroyed forevermore.   [Ps. 37:38]
8 But Thou, O LORD, art on high forever.
9 For, behold, Thine enemies, O LORD,
For, behold, Thine enemies will perish;
All who do iniquity will be scattered.

10 But Thou hast exalted my[R]horn like
that of the wild ox;   Ps. 75:10; 89:17
I have been anointed with fresh oil.
11 And my eye has looked *exultantly*
upon my foes,
My ears hear of the evildoers who rise
up against me.
12 The[R]righteous man will[T]flourish like the
palm tree,   Num. 24:6 • *sprout*
He will grow like a cedar in Lebanon.

13 Planted in the house of the LORD,
They will flourish[R]in the courts of our
God.   Ps. 100:4; 116:19
14 They will still yield fruit in old age;
They shall be [154]full of sap and very
green,
15 To declare that the LORD is upright;
He is my[R]rock, and there is no unrighteousness in Him.   [Deut. 32:4]; Ps. 18:2

PSALM 93

The Majesty of God

THE[R]LORD[a]reigns, He is clothed with majesty;   Ps. 96:10 • *has assumed kingship*
The LORD has[R]clothed and girded Himself with strength;   Ps. 65:6; Is. 51:9
Indeed, the[R]world is firmly established,
it will not be moved.   Ps. 96:10
2 Thy throne is established from of old;
Thou[R]art from everlasting.   [Ps. 90:2]

3 The floods have lifted up, O LORD,
The floods have lifted up their voice;
The floods lift up their pounding
waves.
4 More than the sounds of many waters,
Than the mighty breakers of the sea,
The LORD[a]on high is mighty.   Ps. 65:7
5 Thy testimonies are fully confirmed;
[R]Holiness befits Thy house,   Ps. 29:2; 96:9
O LORD,[T]forevermore.   *for length of days*

PSALM 94

Vengeance Belongs Only to God

O LORD, God of vengeance;
God of vengeance,[R]shine forth!   Ps. 50:2
2 [R]Rise up, O Judge of the earth;   Ps. 7:6
Render recompense to the proud.
3 How long shall the wicked, O LORD,
How long shall the wicked exult?
4 They pour forth *words*, they[R]speak arrogantly;   Ps. 31:18; 75:5
All who do wickedness[R]vaunt themselves.   Ps. 10:3; 52:1
5 They[R]crush Thy people, O LORD,   Is. 3:15
And[a]afflict Thy heritage.   Ps. 79:1
6 They slay the widow and the stranger,
And murder the orphans.
7 And[a]they have said, "The[T]LORD does
not see,   Job 22:13 • Heb., *YAH*
Nor does the God of Jacob pay heed."

8 Pay heed, you[R]senseless among the
people;   Ps. 92:6
And when will you understand, stupid
ones?
9 He who[R]planted the ear, [a]does He not
hear?   [Ex. 4:11; Prov. 20:12] • *can*
He who formed the eye, does He not
see?
10 He who[a]chastens[R]the nations, will He
not rebuke,   *instructs* • Ps. 44:2

154 Lit., *fat and*

Even He who teaches man knowledge?
11 The Lord knows the thoughts of man,
   ^That they are a *mere* breath.   *For*

12 Blessed is the man whom Thou dost
   chasten, O ^TLord,   Heb., *YAH*
   And dost teach out of Thy law;
13 That Thou mayest grant him ^R relief
   from the days of adversity, Job 34:29
   Until a pit is dug for the wicked.
14 For ^R the Lord will not abandon His people,   1 Sam. 12:22; Lam. 3:31; Rom. 11:2
   Nor will He forsake His inheritance.
15 For judgment will again be righteous;
   And all the upright in heart ^T will follow
   it.   *will be after it*
16 Who will ^R stand up for me against evildoers?   Num. 10:35; Is. 28:21; 33:10
   Who will take his stand for me ^a against
   those who do wickedness? Ps. 17:13

17 If the Lord had not been my help,
   My soul would soon have dwelt in *the
   abode* of silence.
18 If I should say, "My foot has slipped,"
   Thy lovingkindness, O Lord, will hold
   me up.
19 When my anxious thoughts ^multiply
   within me,   *are many*
   Thy consolations delight my soul.
20 Can a ^throne ^R of destruction be allied
   with Thee,   *tribunal* • Amos 6:3
   One which devises mischief by decree?
21 They band themselves together against
   the ^c life of the righteous,   *soul*
   And condemn the innocent to death.
22 But the Lord has been my stronghold,
   And my God the rock of my refuge.
23 And He has ^R brought back their wickedness upon them,   Ps. 7:16; 140:9, 11
   And will destroy them in their evil;
   The Lord our God will destroy them.

PSALM 95

Call to Worship the Lord

O COME, let us sing for joy to the Lord;
   Let us shout joyfully to ^R the rock of our
   salvation.   [Ps. 89:26]
2 Let us come before His presence with
   ^thanksgiving;   *a song of thanksgiving*
   Let us shout joyfully to Him ^R with
   psalms.   Ps. 81:2; Eph. 5:19; James 5:13
3 For the Lord is a ^R great God,   Ps. 48:1
   And a great King above all gods,
4 In whose hand are the ^R depths of the
   earth;   Ps. 135:6
   The peaks of the mountains are His
   also.
5 ^T The sea is His, for it was He ^R who made
   it;   *Who has the sea* • Gen. 1:9, 10
   And His hands formed the dry land.

6 Come, let us worship and bow down;
   Let us ^c kneel before the Lord our Maker.   2 Chr. 6:13; Dan. 6:10; [Phil. 2:10]

7 For He is our God,
   And we are the people of His ^T pasture,
   and the sheep of His hand. *pasturing*
   Today, if you would hear His voice,
8 Do not harden your hearts, as at
   ^155 Meribah, ^R   Ex. 17:2-7; Num. 20:13
   As in the day of ^156 Massah ^R in the wilderness;   Ex. 17:7; Deut. 6:16
9 "When your fathers ^R tested Me,
   They tried Me, though they had seen
   My work.   Num. 14:22
10 "For ^R forty years I loathed *that* generation,   Acts 7:36; 13:18; Heb. 3:10, 17
   And said they are a people who err in
   their heart,
   And they do not know My ways.
11 "Therefore I ^R swore in My anger, Heb. 4:3
   Truly they shall not enter into My
   ^R rest."   Deut. 12:9

PSALM 96

Declare the Glory of God

SING ^R to the Lord a new song; 1 Chr. 16:23f.
   Sing to the Lord, all the earth.
2 Sing to the Lord, bless His name;
   ^R Proclaim good tidings of His salvation
   from day to day.   Ps. 71:15
3 Tell of His glory among the nations,
   His wonderful deeds among all the
   peoples.
4 For ^R great is the Lord, and ^R greatly to be
   praised;   Ps. 48:1; 145:3 • Ps. 18:3
   He is to be feared above all gods.
5 For ^R all the gods of the peoples are
   ^A idols,   1 Chr. 16:26 • *non-existent things*
   But the Lord made the heavens.
6 Splendor and majesty are before Him,
   Strength and beauty are in His sanctuary.

7 ^157 Ascribe to the Lord, O ^R families of
   the peoples,   Ps. 22:27
   ^157 Ascribe ^R to the Lord glory and
   strength.   1 Chr. 16:28, 29; Ps. 29:1, 2
8 ^157 Ascribe to the Lord the ^R glory of His
   name;   Ps. 79:9; 115:1
   Bring an ^offering, ^R and come into His
   courts.   *meal offering* • Ps. 45:12; 72:10
9 Worship the Lord in ^158 holy attire;
   Tremble before Him, all the earth.
10 Say among the nations, "The Lord
   reigns;
   Indeed, the ^R world is firmly established,
   it will not be moved;   Ps. 93:1; 97:1
   He will ^R judge the peoples with ^159 equity."   Ps. 9:8; 58:11; 67:4; 98:9

11 Let the ^R heavens be glad, and let the
   earth rejoice;   Ps. 69:34; Is. 49:13
   Let the sea roar, and all it contains;

12 Let the field exult, and all that is in it.
Then all the [R]trees of the forest will sing
for joy   Is. 44:23
13 Before the LORD, for He is coming;
For He is coming to judge the earth.
[R]He will judge the world in righteous-
ness,   [Rev. 19:11]
And the peoples in His faithfulness.

PSALM 97
Rejoice! The Lord Reigns!

THE LORD reigns; let the earth rejoice;
Let the many [160]islands be glad.
2 [R]Clouds and thick darkness surround
Him;   Ex. 19:9; Deut. 4:11; 1 Kin. 8:12
[R]Righteousness and justice are the foundation of His throne.   [Ps. 89:14]
3 [R]Fire goes before Him,   Ps. 18:8; 50:3
And [R]burns up His adversaries round
about.   Mal. 4:1; Heb. 12:29
4 His[R]lightnings lit up the world; Ex. 19:16
The earth saw and[R]trembled.   Ps. 96:9
5 The mountains[R]melted like wax at the
presence of the LORD,   Ps. 46:6
At the presence of the [R]Lord of the
whole earth.   Josh. 3:11
6 The heavens declare His righteousness,
And [R]all the peoples have seen His
glory.   Ps. 98:2; Is. 6:3; 40:5; 66:18

7 Let all those be ashamed who serve
[R]graven images, Ps. 78:58; Is. 42:17; 44:9
Who boast themselves of[R]idols; Jer. 50:2
[R]Worship Him, all you gods.   [Heb. 1:6]
8 Zion heard this and[R]was glad, Ps. 48:11
And the daughters of Judah have re-
joiced
Because of Thy judgments, O LORD.
9 For Thou art the LORD[R]Most High over
all the earth;   Ps. 83:18
Thou art exalted far above all gods.

10 Hate evil, you who love the LORD,
Who[R]preserves the souls of His godly
ones;   Ps. 31:23; 145:20; Prov. 2:8
He[R]delivers them from the hand of the
wicked.   Ps. 37:40; Jer. 15:21; Dan. 3:28
11 [R]Light is sown like seed for the righteous,   Job 22:28; Ps. 112:4; Prov. 4:18
And gladness for the upright in heart.
12 Be [R]glad in the LORD, you righteous
ones;   Ps. 32:11
And give thanks to His holy name.

PSALM 98
Sing a New Song to the Lord
A Psalm.

O SING to the LORD a[R]new song, Ps. 33:3
For He has done wonderful things,
His right hand and His holy arm have
[161]gained the victory for Him.

2 [R]The LORD has made known His salvation;   Is. 52:10
He has [R]revealed His righteousness in
the sight of the nations.   Is. 62:2
3 He has [R]remembered His lovingkindness and His faithfulness to the
house of Israel;   [Luke 1:54, 72]
[R]All the ends of the earth have seen the
salvation of our God.   Ps. 22:27

4 [R]Shout joyfully to the LORD, all the
earth;   Ps. 100:1
[R]Break forth and sing for joy and sing
praises.   Is. 44:23
5 Sing praises to the LORD with the lyre;
With the lyre and the sound of melody.
6 With [R]trumpets and the sound of the
horn   Num. 10:10; 2 Chr. 15:14
[R]Shout joyfully before [R]the King, the
LORD.   Ps. 66:1 • Ps. 47:7

7 Let the sea roar and all it contains,
The world and those who dwell in it.
8 Let the[R]rivers clap their hands; Ps. 93:3
Let the mountains sing together for joy
9 Before the LORD; for He is coming to
judge the earth;   [Ps. 96:13]
He will judge the world with righteousness,
And the peoples with [A]equity. uprightness

PSALM 99
"Exalt the LORD Our God"

THE LORD reigns, let the peoples tremble;
He[T]is enthroned [R]above the cherubim,
let the earth shake!   sits • Ex. 25:22
2 The LORD[A]is great in Zion, in Zion is great
And He is [R]exalted above all the peoples.   [Ps. 97:9; 113:4]
3 Let them praise Thy [R]great and awesome name;   Deut. 28:58; Ps. 76:1
[R]Holy is[A]He.   Lev. 19:2; Josh. 24:19 • it
4 And the strength of the King [R]loves
[162]justice;   Ps. 11:7; 33:5
Thou hast established equity;
Thou hast [R]executed [162]justice and
righteousness in Jacob.   Ps. 103:6
5 [R]Exalt the LORD our God, Ps. 34:3; 107:32
And[R]worship at His footstool; Ps. 132:7
[R]Holy is He.   Ps. 99:3

6 [R]Moses and Aaron were among His
[R]priests,   Jer. 15:1 • Ex. 24:6-8; 29:26
And [R]Samuel was among those who
called on His name;   Jer. 15:1
They called upon the LORD, and He an-
swered them.
7 He spoke to them in the pillar of cloud;
They[R]kept His testimonies,   Ps. 105:28
And the statute that He gave them.
8 O LORD our God, Thou didst [R]answer
them;   Ps. 106:44
Thou wast a forgiving God to them,
And yet an avenger of their evil deeds.
9 Exalt the LORD our God,
And worship at His holy hill;
For holy is the LORD our God.

160 Or, coastlands
161 Or, accomplished salvation   162 Or, judgment

PSALM 100

"Serve the LORD with Gladness"

A Psalm for Thanksgiving.

SHOUT joyfully to the LORD, all the earth.
2 Serve the LORD with gladness;
Come before Him with joyful singing.
3 Know that the LORD Himself is God;
It is He who has ᴿmade us, and ¹⁶³not
we ourselves;   Job 10:3, 8; Ps. 95:6
*We are*ᴿHis people and the sheep of His
pasture.   Ps. 74:1, 2; 95:7; [Is. 40:11]

4 Enter His gates with thanksgiving,
And His courts with praise.
Give thanks to Him; bless His name.
5 Forᴿthe LORD is good;   1 Chr. 16:34
His lovingkindness is everlasting,
And His faithfulness to all generations.

PSALM 101

Commitments of a Holy Life

A Psalm of David.

I WILL sing of lovingkindness and justice,
To Thee, O LORD, I will sing praises.
2 I willᴬgiveᴿheed to the ¹⁶⁴blameless
way.   *behave prudently in* • 1 Sam. 18:5
When wilt Thou come to me?
I will walk within my house in theᴬin-
tegrity of my heart.   *blamelessness*
3 I will set noᴿworthless thing before my
eyes;   Deut. 15:9
I hate the work of those who fall away;
It shall not fasten its grip on me.
4 A perverse heart shall depart from me;
I will know no evil.
5 Whoever secretly slanders his neighbor, him I willᴬdestroy;   *silence*
No one who has aᴿhaughty look and an
arrogant heart will I endure. Ps. 10:4

6 My eyes shall be upon the faithful of
the land, that they may dwell with
me;
He who walks in a ¹⁶⁴blameless way is
the one who will minister to me.
7 He whoᴿpractices deceit shall not dwell
within my house.   Ps. 43:1; 52:2
He who speaks falsehood shall not
maintain his position before me.
8 ᴿEvery morning I will ¹⁶⁵destroy all the
wicked of the land,   Jer. 21:12
So as to cut off from the city of the
LORD all those who do iniquity.

PSALM 102

Prayer of an Overwhelmed Saint

A Prayer of the Afflicted, when he is
faint, and pours out his complaint
before the LORD.

HEARᴿmy prayer, O LORD!   Ps. 39:12; 61:1
And let my cry for help come to Thee.

2 ᴿDo not hide Thy face from me in the
day of my distress;   Ps. 69:17
ᴿIncline Thine ear to me;   Ps. 31:2
In the day when I call ᴿanswer me
quickly.   Ps. 69:17
3 For my daysᴿhave been ᴬconsumed in
smoke,   Ps. 37:20 • *finished*
And myᴿbones have been scorched like
a hearth.   Job 30:30, Lam. 1:13
4 My heart has been smitten like ᵀgrass
and has withered away,   *herbage*
Indeed, I forget to eat my bread.
5 Because of theᵀloudness of my groaning   *voice*
My bones ᵀcling to my flesh. *have cleaved*
6 I resemble a pelican of the wilderness;
I have become like an owl of the waste
places.
7 Iᴿlie awake,   Ps. 77:4
I have become like a lonely bird on a
housetop.

8 My enemies ᴿhave reproached me all
day long;   Ps. 31:11
Those who ᴬderide me have used my
name as a curse.   *made a fool of*
9 For I have eaten ashes like bread,
And mingled my drink with weeping,
10 ᴿBecause of Thine indignation and Thy
wrath;   Ps. 38:3
For Thou hastᴿlifted me up and cast me
away.   Job 27:21; 30:22
11 My days are like a lengthened shadow;
And I wither away like grass.

12 But Thou, O LORD, dost abide forever;
And Thy name to all generations.
13 Thou wilt ᴿarise *and* have ᴿcompassion
on Zion;   [Ps. 12:5; 44:26] • Is. 60:10
For it is time to be gracious to her,
For the appointed time has come.
14 Surely Thy servants ᴬfind pleasure in
her stones,   *have found*
And feel pity for her dust.
15 ᴬSo theᴬnations will fear the name of the
LORD,   *And* • *Gentiles, heathen*
And ᴿall the kings of the earth Thy
glory.   Ps. 138:4
16 For the LORD has built up Zion;
He hasᴿappeared in His glory. [Is. 60:1]
17 He hasᴿregarded the prayer of theᴬdes-
titute,   Neh. 1:6; Ps. 22:24 • *naked*
And has not despised their prayer.

18 ᴬThis will be written for theᴿgeneration
to come;   *Let this be written* • Ps. 22:30
ᴬThat a people yet to be created ᴬmay
praise the LORD.   *And* • *will*
19 For He ᴿlooked down from His holy
height;   Deut. 26:15; Ps. 14:2; 53:2
ᴿFrom heaven the LORD gazedᵀupon the
earth,   Ps. 33:13 • *toward*
20 To hear the groaning of the prisoner;
Toᴿset free ᵀthose who were doomed to
death;   Ps. 146:7 • *the sons of death*

¹⁶³ Some mss. read *His we are*
¹⁶⁴ Or, *way of integrity*   ¹⁶⁵ Or, *silence*

21 That *men* may[R]tell of the name of the
   LORD in Zion,   Ps. 22:22
   And His praise in Jerusalem;
22 When [R]the peoples are gathered to-
   gether, Ps. 22:27; 86:9; Is. 49:22, 23; 60:3
   And the kingdoms, to serve the LORD.

23 He has weakened my strength in the
   way;
   He has[R]shortened my days.   Ps. 39:5
24 I say, "O my God, do not take me away
   in the [T]midst of my days,   *half*
   Thy [R]years are throughout all generations.   Job 36:26; [Ps. 90:2; 102:12]
25 "Of old Thou didst found the earth,
   And the[R]heavens are the work of Thy
   hands.   [Ps. 96:5]
26 "Even [T]they will perish, but Thou dost
   endure;   *They themselves*
   And all of them will wear out like a
   garment;
   Like clothing Thou wilt change them,
   and they will be changed.
27 "But Thou art[T]the[R]same,   *He* • [Is. 41:4]
   And Thy years will not come to an end.
28 "The[R]children of Thy servants will continue,   Ps. 69:36
   And their [T]descendants will be established before Thee."   *seed*

PSALM 103

Bless the Lord, All You People!

A Psalm of David.

B LESS[R]the LORD, O my soul;   Ps. 104:1, 35
   And all that is within me, *bless* His
   [R]holy name.   Ps. 33:21; Ezek. 36:21; 39:7
2 Bless the LORD, O my soul,
   And forget none of His benefits;
3 Who pardons all your iniquities;
   Who[B]heals all your diseases;   [Ex. 15:26]
4 Who redeems your life from the pit;
   Who [R]crowns you with lovingkindness
   and compassion;   [Ps. 5:12]
5 Who [R]satisfies your [166]years with good
   things,   Ps. 107:9; 145:16
   So that your youth is[R]renewed like the
   eagle.   [Is. 40:31]

6 The LORD performs righteous deeds,
   And judgments for all who are [R]op-
   pressed.   Ps. 12:5
7 He made known His ways to Moses,
   His [R]acts to the sons of Israel. Ps. 78:11
8 The LORD is [R]compassionate and gracious,   Neh. 9:17; Ps. 86:15; Jon. 4:2
   [R]Slow to anger and abounding in lovingkindness.   Ps. 145:8; Joel 2:13; Nah. 1:3
9 He will not always strive *with us*;
   Nor will He keep *His anger* forever.
10 He has[R]not dealt with us according to
   our sins,   [Ezra 9:13; Lam. 3:22]

Nor rewarded us according to our iniquities.
11 For as high[R]as the heavens are above
   the earth,   Ps. 36:5; 57:10
   So great is His lovingkindness toward
   those who [167]fear Him.
12 As far as the east is from the west,
   So far has He[R]removed our transgressions from us. [2 Sam. 12:13]; Is. 38:17
13 Just [R]as a father has compassion on *his*
   children,   Mal. 3:17
   So the LORD has compassion on those
   who[A]fear Him.   *revere*
14 For He Himself knows [168]our frame;
   He is mindful that we are *but* dust.

15 As for man, his days are like grass;
   As a [R]flower of the field, so he flourishes.   Job 14:2; James 1:10, 11
16 When the[R]wind has passed over it, it is
   no more;   Is. 40:7
   And its [R]place acknowledges it no
   longer.   Job 7:10; 8:18; 20:9
17 But the[R]lovingkindness of the LORD is
   from everlasting to everlasting on
   those who [167]fear Him,   Ps. 25:6
   And His righteousness [R]to children's
   children, [Ex. 20:6; Deut. 5:10; Ps. 105:8]
18 To those who keep His covenant,
   And who remember His precepts to do
   them.

19 The LORD has established His[R]throne in
   the heavens;   Ps. 11:4
   And His [169]sovereignty rules over all.
20 Bless the LORD, you His angels,
   [R]Mighty in strength, who [R]perform His
   word,   Ps. 29:1; 78:25 • [Matt. 6:10]
   Obeying the voice of His word!
21 Bless the LORD, all you His hosts,
   You who serve Him, doing His will.
22 Bless the LORD, all you works of His,
   In all places of His dominion;
   Bless the LORD, O my soul!

PSALM 104

Psalm Rehearsing Creation

B LESS[R]the LORD, O my soul!   Ps. 103:22
   O LORD my God, Thou art very great;
   Thou art [R]clothed with splendor and
   majesty,   Ps. 93:1
2 Covering Thyself with[R]light as with a
   cloak,   [Dan. 7:9]
   [R]Stretching out heaven like a *tent* curtain.   [Is. 40:22]
3 [170]He [R]lays the beams of His upper
   chambers in the waters;   [Amos 9:6]
   He makes the clouds His chariot;
   He walks upon the wings of the wind;
4 [T]He makes [171]the [R]winds His messengers,   *Who* • Ps. 148:8; Heb. 1:7
   [172]Flaming[R]fire His ministers. 2 Kin. 2:11

5 He[R]established the earth upon its foundations,   Job 38:4; Ps. 24:2

---

166 Or, *desire*   167 Or, *revere*
168 I.e., what we are made of   169 Or, *kingdom*
170 Lit., *Who*, so through v. 4, and vv. 13, 14
171 Or, *His angels, spirits*
172 Or, *His ministers flames of fire*

So that it will not [173]totter forever and ever.

6 Thou [R]didst cover it with the deep as with a garment;　Gen. 1:2
The waters were standing above the mountains.

7 At Thy [R]rebuke they fled;　Ps. 18:15; 106:9
At the [R]sound of Thy thunder they hurried away.　Ps. 29:3; 77:18

8 The mountains rose; the valleys sank down
To the [R]place which Thou didst establish for them.　Ps. 33:7

9 Thou didst set a [R]boundary that they may not pass over;　Job 38:10, 11
That they may not return to cover the earth.

10 He sends forth springs in the valleys;
They flow between the mountains;

11 They [R]give drink to every beast of the field;　Ps. 104:13
The wild donkeys quench their thirst.

12 [A]Beside them the birds of the heavens [R]dwell;　Over, Above · [Matt. 8:20]
They [T]lift up their voices among the branches.　give forth

13 [T]He [R]waters the mountains from His upper chambers;　Who · Ps. 65:9; 147:8
[R]The earth is satisfied with the fruit of His works.　Jer. 10:13

14 [T]He causes the grass to grow for the [A]cattle,　Who · beasts
And vegetation for the labor of man,
So that [A]he may bring forth [T]food from the earth,　He · bread

15 And [R]wine which makes man's heart glad,　Judg. 9:13; Prov. 31:6; Eccl. 10:19
[R]So that he may make his face glisten with oil,　Ps. 23:5; 92:10; 141:5; Luke 7:46
And food which sustains man's heart.

16 The trees of the LORD drink their fill,
The cedars of Lebanon which He planted,

17 Where the birds build their nests,
And the [R]stork, whose home is the [A]fir trees.　Lev. 11:19 · cypress

18 The high mountains are for the [R]wild goats;　Job 39:1
The [R]cliffs are a refuge for the [R]rock badgers.　Prov. 30:26 · Lev. 11:5

19 He made the moon for the seasons;
The sun knows the place of its setting.

20 Thou [R]dost appoint darkness and it becomes night,　[Ps. 74:16; Is. 45:7]
In which all the [R]beasts of the forest [T]prowl about.　[Ps. 50:10] · creep

21 The young lions roar after their prey,
And seek their food from God.

22 When the sun rises they withdraw,
And lie down in their [R]dens.　Job 37:8

23 Man goes forth to [R]his work　Gen. 3:19
And to his labor until evening.

24 O LORD, how many are Thy works!
In wisdom Thou hast made them all;
The earth is full of Thy [174]possessions.

25 There is the sea, great and broad,
In which are swarms without number,
Animals both small and great.

26 There the ships move along,　Ps. 107:23
And [175]Leviathan,[R] which Thou hast formed to sport in it.　Is. 27:1

27 They all [R]wait for Thee,　Ps. 145:15
To [R]give them their food in [176]due season.　Job 36:31; 38:41; Ps. 136:25; 147:9

28 Thou dost give to them, they gather it up;
Thou [R]dost open Thy hand, they are satisfied with good.　[Ps. 145:16]

29 Thou [R]dost hide Thy face, they are dismayed;　Deut. 31:17; Ps. 30:7
Thou [R]dost take away their [177]spirit, they expire,　Job 34:14, 15; Ps. 146:4
And [R]return to their dust.　Job 10:9

30 Thou dost send forth Thy [177]Spirit,[R] they are created;
And Thou dost renew the face of the ground.　[Job 33:4]; Ezek. 37:9

31 Let the [R]glory of the LORD endure forever;　[Ps. 86:12; 111:10]
Let the LORD be glad in His works;

32 He looks at the earth, and it trembles;
He [R]touches the mountains, and they smoke.　Ex. 19:18; Ps. 144:5

33 I will sing to the LORD as long as I live;
I will sing praise to my God while I have my being.

34 Let my meditation be pleasing to Him;
As for me, I shall be glad in the LORD.

35 Let sinners be [R]consumed from the earth,　Ps. 59:13
And let the wicked be no more.
[R]Bless the LORD, O my soul.　Ps. 104:1
[A]Praise [T]the LORD!　Hallelujah! · Heb., YAH

PSALM 105

Remember, God Keeps His Promises

OH [R]give thanks to the LORD, call upon His name;　1 Chr. 16:8–22, 34; Is. 12:4
[R]Make known His deeds among the peoples.　Ps. 145:12

2 Sing to Him, sing praises to Him;
[178]Speak of all His wonders.

3 [A]Glory in His holy name;　Boast
Let the [R]heart of those who seek the LORD be glad.　Ps. 33:21

4 Seek the LORD and His strength;
[R]Seek His face continually.　Ps. 27:8

5 Remember His [T]wonders [R]which He has done,　wonderful acts · Ps. 40:5; 77:11
His marvels, and the judgments [T]uttered by His mouth,　of His mouth

173 Or, *move out of place*
174 Or, *creatures*　175 Or, *a sea monster*
176 Lit., *its appointed time*　177 Or, *breath*
178 Or, *Meditate on*

6 O seed of Abraham, His servant,
　O sons of Jacob, His chosen ones!
7 He is the Lord our God;
　His judgments are in all the earth.

8 He has [R]remembered His covenant for-
　ever,　　　Ps. 105:42; 106:45; Luke 1:72
　The word which He commanded to a
　[R]thousand generations,　　　Deut. 7:9
9 The [R]covenant which He made with
　Abraham, Gen. 12:7; 17:2, 8; [Gal. 3:17]
　And His [R]oath to Isaac.　　　Gen. 26:3
10 Then He [R]confirmed it to Jacob for a
　statute,　　　　　　　　[Gen. 28:13-15]
　To Israel as an everlasting covenant,
11 Saying, "To [R]you I will give the land of
　Canaan　　　　　　　Gen. 13:15; 15:18
　As the portion of your inheritance,"
12 When they were only a [R]few men in
　number,　　　　Gen. 34:30; [Deut. 7:7]
　Very few, and [R]strangers in it. Gen. 23:4
13 And they wandered about from nation
　to nation,
　From *one* kingdom to another people.
14 He permitted no man to oppress them,
　And He reproved kings for their sakes:
15 "Do not touch My anointed ones,
　And do My prophets no harm."

16 And He [R]called for a famine upon the
　land;　　　　　　　　　　Gen. 41:54
　He broke the whole staff of bread.
17 He [R]sent a man before them, [Gen. 45:5]
　Joseph, *who* was sold as a slave.
18 They afflicted his feet with fetters,
　He himself was laid in irons;
19 Until the time that his [R]word came to
　pass,　　　　　　　　　Gen. 40:20, 21
　The word of the Lord tested him.
20 The king sent and released him,
　The ruler of peoples, and set him free.
21 He made him lord of his house,
　And ruler over all his possessions,
22 To [T]imprison his princes at will,　*bind*
　That he might teach his elders wisdom.
23 [R]Israel also came into Egypt;　Acts 7:15
　Thus Jacob [R]sojourned in the land of
　Ham.　　　　　　　　　　Acts 13:17
24 And He [R]caused His people to be very
　fruitful,　　　　　　　　　Ex. 1:7, 9
　And made them stronger than their ad-
　versaries.

25 He [R]turned their heart to hate His peo-
　ple,　　　　　　　　　　Ex. 1:8; 4:21
　To deal craftily with His servants.
26 He [R]sent Moses His servant,　　Ex. 3:10
　And Aaron whom He had chosen.
27 They [T]performed His wondrous acts
　among them,　*set the words of His signs*
　And miracles in the land of Ham.
28 He sent darkness and made *it* dark;
　And they did not [R]rebel against His
　words.　　　　　　　　　　Ps. 99:7

29 He turned their waters into blood,
　And caused their fish to die.
30 Their land swarmed with [R]frogs　Ex. 8:6
　Even in the chambers of their kings.
31 He spoke, and there came a [R]swarm of
　flies　　　　　　　　　　　Ex. 8:21
　And [R]gnats in all their territory. Ex. 8:16
32 He gave them [R]hail for rain,　Ex. 9:23-25
　And flaming fire in their land.
33 He [R]struck down their vines also and
　their fig trees,　　　　　　Ps. 78:47
　And shattered the trees of their terri-
　tory.
34 He spoke, and [R]locusts came, Ex. 10:12f.
　And young locusts, even without num-
　ber,
35 And ate up all vegetation in their land,
　And ate up the fruit of their ground.
36 He also [R]struck down all the first-born
　in their land, Ex. 12:29; 13:15; Ps. 135:8
　The first fruits of all their vigor.

37 Then He brought them out with [R]silver
　and gold;　　　　　　　Ex. 12:35, 36
　And among His tribes there was not
　one who stumbled.
38 Egypt was glad when they departed;
　For the [R]dread of them had fallen upon
　them.　　　　　　　　　　Ex. 15:16
39 He spread a cloud for a [179]covering,
　And [R]fire to illumine by night.　Ex. 40:38
40 They asked, and He brought quail,
　And satisfied them with the [A]bread [R]of
　heaven.　　　*food* • Neh. 9:15; John 6:31
41 He opened the [A]rock, and [R]water flowed
　out;　　　*boulder* • Ex. 17:6; Num. 20:11
　It ran in the dry places *like* a river.
42 For He remembered His holy word
　With Abraham His servant;
43 And He brought forth His people with
　joy,
　His chosen ones with a joyful shout.
44 He [R]gave them also the lands of the [A]na-
　tions,　　　Josh. 11:16-23; 13:7 • *Gentiles*
　That they [R]might take possession of *the
　fruit of* the peoples' labor, Deut. 6:10
45 So that they might keep His statutes,
　And observe His laws,
　[A]Praise [T]the Lord!　*Hallelujah!* • Heb., YAH

PSALM 106

"We Have Sinned"

Praise [A]the [T]Lord!　*Hallelujah!* • Heb., YAH
　Oh [R]give thanks to the Lord, for He is
　good;　　　Ps. 105:1; 107:1; 118:1; 136:1
　For His lovingkindness is everlasting.
2 Who can speak of the [R]mighty deeds of
　the Lord,　　　Ps. 145:4, 12; 150:2
　Or can show forth all His praise?
3 How blessed are those who keep [A]jus-
　tice,　　　　　　　　　　*judgment*
　Who [R]practice righteousness at all
　times!　　　　　　　　　　Ps. 15:2

[179] Or, *curtain*

4 Remember me, O LORD, in *Thy*[R]favor
[T]toward Thy people;   Ps. 44:3 • *of*
Visit me with Thy salvation,
5 That I may see the[R]prosperity of Thy
chosen ones,   Ps. 1:3
That I may[R]rejoice in the gladness of
Thy nation,   Ps. 118:15
That I may[R]glory with Thine [180]inheri-
tance.   Ps. 105:3

6 We have sinned like our fathers,
We have committed iniquity, we have
behaved wickedly.
7 Our fathers in Egypt did not understand Thy[T]wonders;   wonderful acts
They[R]did not remember Thine abundant kindnesses, Judg. 3:7; Ps. 78:11, 42
But[R]rebelled by the sea, at the [181]Red
Sea.   Ex. 14:11, 12; Ps. 78:17
8 Nevertheless He saved them[T]for the
sake of His name,   Ezek. 20:9
That He might make His power known.
9 Thus He[R]rebuked the [181]Red Sea and it
dried up;   Ps. 18:15; 78:13; Is. 50:2
And He[R]led them through the deeps, as
through the wilderness.   Is. 63:11-13
10 So He saved them from the[A]hand of
the one who hated *them*,   power
And[R]redeemed them from the hand of
the enemy.   Ps. 78:42; 107:2
11 And[R]the waters covered their adversaries;   Ex. 14:27, 28; 15:5; Ps. 78:53
Not one of them was left.
12 Then they[R]believed His words; Ex. 14:31
They[R]sang His praise.   [Ex. 15:1–21]

13 They quickly forgot His works;
They did not wait for His counsel,
14 But craved intensely in the wilderness,
And tempted God in the desert.
15 So He gave them their request,
But sent a [A]wasting disease among
them.   leanness into their soul

16 When they became[R]envious of Moses
in the camp,   Num. 16:1-3
And of Aaron, the holy one of the
LORD,
17 The[R]earth opened and swallowed up
Dathan,   Num. 16:32; Deut. 11:6
And engulfed the company of Abiram.
18 And a fire blazed up in their company;
The flame consumed the wicked.

19 They[R]made a calf in Horeb,   Ex. 32:4
And worshiped a molten image.
20 Thus they exchanged their glory
For the image of an ox that eats grass.
21 They[R]forgot God their Savior, Ps. 78:11
Who had done great things in Egypt,
22 [R]Wonders in the land of Ham, Ps. 105:27
And awesome things by the [181]Red
Sea.
23 Therefore[R]He said that He would destroy them,   Ex. 32:10; Deut. 9:14
Had not[R]Moses His chosen one stood in
the breach before Him, Ex. 32:11-14

To turn away His wrath from destroying *them.*
24 Then they despised the pleasant land;
They did not believe in His word,
25 But[R]grumbled in their tents; Num. 14:2
They did not listen to the voice of the
LORD.
26 Therefore He[R]swore to them, [Heb. 3:11]
That He would cast them down in the
wilderness,
27 And that He would [R]cast their seed
among the nations,   Deut. 4:27
And[R]scatter them in the lands. Ps. 44:11

28 They[R]joined themselves also to [A]Baal-
peor,   Num. 25:3 • *Baal of Peor*
And ate sacrifices offered to the dead.
29 Thus they[R]provoked *Him* to anger with
their deeds;   Num. 25:4
And the plague broke out among them.
30 Then Phinehas[R]stood up and inter-
posed;   Num. 25:7
And so the plague was stayed.
31 And it was[R]reckoned to him for righteousness,   Gen. 15:6; Num. 25:11-13
To all generations forever.

32 They also[R]provoked *Him* to wrath at
the waters of [182]Meribah,   Ps. 81:7
So that it[R]went hard with Moses on
their account;   Num. 20:12
33 Because they[R]were rebellious against
[A]His Spirit,   Num. 20:3, 10 • *his spirit*
He spoke rashly with his lips.

34 They did not destroy the peoples,
As the LORD commanded them,
35 But they mingled with the nations,
And learned their[T]practices,   works
36 And[R]served their idols,   Judg. 2:12
Which became a snare to them.
37 They even sacrificed their sons and
their daughters to the demons,
38 And shed[R]innocent blood,   Ps. 94:21
The blood of their [R]sons and their
daughters,   Deut. 18:10
Whom they sacrificed to the idols of
Canaan;
And the land was[R]polluted with the
blood.   [Num. 35:33; Is. 24:5; Jer. 3:1, 2]
39 Thus they became[R]unclean in their
[T]practices,   [Lev. 18:24] • *works*
And played the harlot in their deeds.

40 Therefore the anger of the LORD was
kindled against His people,
And He abhorred His inheritance.
41 Then[R]He gave them into the hand of
the[A]nations;   Judg. 2:14 • *Gentiles*
And those who hated them ruled over
them.
42 Their enemies also oppressed them,
And they were subdued under their
[T]power.   hand
43 Many times He would deliver them;

[180] I.e., people   [181] Lit., *Sea of Reeds*   [182] Lit., *strife*

They, however, were rebellious in their
    ^Rcounsel,   Ps. 81:12
And so sank down in their iniquity.

44 Nevertheless He looked upon their dis-
    tress,
    When He^Rheard their cry;   Judg. 3:9; 6:7
45 And He^Rremembered His covenant for
    their sake,   [Lev. 26:42]; Ps. 105:8
    And ^rrelented according to the great-
    ness of His lovingkindness. *was sorry*
46 He also made them^R*objects* of compas-
    sion   Ezra 9:9; Neh. 1:11; Jer. 42:12
    In the presence of all their captors.

47 ^RSave us, O LORD our God,   1 Chr. 16:35f.
    And gather us from among the nations,
    To give thanks to Thy holy name,
    And ^rglory in Thy praise.   *boast*
48 Blessed be the LORD, the God of Israel,
    From everlasting even to everlasting.
    And let all the people say, "Amen."
    ^APraise the LORD!   *Hallelujah!*

BOOK 5

PSALM 107

God Satisfies the Longing Soul

OH ^Rgive thanks to the LORD, for ^RHe is
    good;   1 Chr. 16:34 • Ezra 3:11; Ps. 100:5
    For His lovingkindness is everlasting.
2 Let the redeemed of the LORD say *so*,
    Whom He has^Rredeemed from the hand
    of the adversary,   Ps. 78:42; 106:10
3 And ^Rgathered from the lands, Deut. 30:3
    From the east and from the west,
    From the north and from the south.

4 They^Rwandered in the wilderness in a
    ^Tdesert region;   Num. 14:33 • *waste*
    They did not find a way to an inhabited
    ^Rcity.   Ps. 107:7, 36
5 *They were* hungry ^Tand thirsty;   *also*
    Their ^Rsoul fainted within them.   Ps. 77:3
6 Then they^Rcried out to the LORD in their
    trouble;   Ps. 50:15; 107:13, 19, 28
    He delivered them out of their dis-
    tresses.
7 He led them also by a straight way,
    To go to an inhabited city.
8 ^RLet them give thanks to the LORD for
    His lovingkindness,   Ps. 107:15, 21, 31
    And for His ^Twonders to the sons of
    men!   *wonderful acts*
9 For He has satisfied the thirsty soul,
    And the^Rhungry soul He has filled with
    what is good.   [Matt. 5:6; Luke 1:53]

10 There were those who dwelt in dark-
    ness and in the shadow of death,
    Prisoners in misery and chains,

11 Because they had^Rrebelled against the
    words of God,   Ps. 78:40; 106:7
    And ^Rspurned the^Rcounsel of the Most
    High.   Prov. 1:25; Is. 5:24 • [Ps. 73:24]
12 Therefore He humbled their heart with
    labor;
    They stumbled and there was^Rnone to
    help.   [Ps. 22:11; 72:12]
13 Then they^Rcried out to the LORD in their
    trouble;   Ps. 107:6
    He saved them out of their distresses.
14 He^Rbrought them out of darkness and
    the shadow of death, Ps. 86:13; 107:10
    And^Rbroke their bands apart. Luke 13:16
15 ^RLet them give thanks to the LORD for
    His lovingkindness,   Ps. 107:8, 21, 31
    And for His ^Twonders to the sons of
    men!   *wonderful acts*
16 For He has shattered gates of bronze,
    And cut bars of iron asunder.

17 Fools, because of their rebellious way,
    And ^Rbecause of their iniquities, were
    afflicted.   [Is. 65:6, 7; Jer. 30:14, 15]
18 Their soul abhorred all kinds of food;
    And they ^Rdrew near to the gates of
    death.   Job 33:22; Ps. 88:3
19 Then they cried out to the LORD in their
    trouble;
    He saved them out of their distresses.
20 He sent His word and healed them,
    And ^Rdelivered *them* from their ¹⁸³de-
    structions. Job 33:28, 30; Ps. 30:3; 49:15
21 ^RLet them give thanks to the LORD for
    His lovingkindness,   Ps. 107:8, 15, 31
    And for His ^Twonders to the sons of
    men!   *wonderful acts*
22 Let them also offer ^Rsacrifices of
    thanksgiving,   Lev. 7:12; Ps. 50:14
    And^Rtell of His works with joyful sing-
    ing.   Ps. 9:11; 73:28; 118:17

23 Those who go down to the sea in ships,
    Who do business on great waters;
24 They have seen the works of the LORD,
    And His wonders in the deep.
25 For He ^Rspoke and raised up a stormy
    wind,   Ps. 105:31, 34
    Which lifted up the waves of the sea.
26 They rose up to the heavens, they went
    down to the depths;
    Their soul melted away in *their* misery.
27 They reeled and ^Rstaggered like a
    drunken man,   Job 12:25; Is. 24:20
    And ¹⁸⁴were at their wits' end.
28 Then they cried to the LORD in their
    trouble,
    And He brought them out of their dis-
    tresses.
29 He ^Rcaused the storm to be still, Ps. 65:7
    So that the waves ^Tof the sea were
    hushed.   *of it*
30 Then they were glad because they were
    quiet;
    So He guided them to their desired ha-
    ven.

¹⁸³ Or, *pits*   ¹⁸⁴ Lit., *all their wisdom was swallowed up*

31 ^{R}Let them give thanks to the LORD for
His lovingkindness,   Ps. 107:8, 15, 21
And for His ^{t}wonders^R to the sons of
men!   wonderful acts • Ps. 78:4; 111:4
32 Let them ^{t}extol Him also in the congregation of the people,   Ps. 34:3; 99:5
And ^{R}praise Him at the seat of the elders.   Ps. 35:18

33 He ^{185}changes rivers into a wilderness,
And springs of water into a thirsty
ground;
34 A fruitful land into a salt waste,
Because of the wickedness of those
who dwell in it.
35 He ^{A}changes ^{R}a ^{t}wilderness into a pool of
water,   turns • [Is. 35:6, 7] • desert
And a dry land into springs of water;
36 And there He makes the hungry to
dwell,
So that they may establish ^{A}an^R inhabited city,   a habitable city • Ps. 107:4, 7
37 And sow fields, and plant vineyards,
And gather a fruitful harvest.
38 Also He blesses them and they ^{R}multi-
ply greatly;   Gen. 12:2; 17:20; Ex. 1:7
And He ^{d}does not let their cattle decrease.   [Deut. 7:14]

39 When they are ^{R}diminished and bowed
down   2 Kin. 10:32; Ezek. 5:11; 29:15
Through oppression, misery, and sorrow,
40 He pours contempt upon princes,
And ^{R}makes them wander ^{R}in a pathless
waste.   Job 12:24 • Deut. 32:10
41 But He ^{R}sets the needy securely on high
away from affliction,   1 Sam. 2:8
And makes his families like a flock.
42 The upright see it, and are glad;
But all ^{R}unrighteousness shuts its
mouth.   Job 5:16; Ps. 63:11; [Rom. 3:19]
43 Who is ^{t}wise? Let him give heed to
these things;   Jer. 9:12; [Hos. 14:9]
And consider the ^{R}lovingkindnesses of
the LORD.   Ps. 107:1

PSALM 108

Awake Early and Praise the Lord

A Song, a Psalm of David.

M Y heart is steadfast, O God;
I will sing, I will sing praises, even with
my ^{t}soul.   glory
2 Awake, harp and lyre!
I will awaken the dawn!
3 I will give thanks to Thee, O LORD,
among the peoples;
And I will sing praises to Thee among
the nations.
4 For Thy ^{R}lovingkindness is great above
the heavens;   Num. 14:18; Deut. 7:9
And Thy truth *reaches* to the skies.
5 Be exalted, O God, above the heavens,
And Thy glory above all the earth.
6 That Thy beloved may be delivered,

Save with Thy right hand, and answer
me!

7 God has spoken in His ^{186}holiness:
"I will exult, I will portion out Shechem,
And measure out the valley of Succoth.
8 "Gilead is Mine, Manasseh is Mine;
Ephraim also is the helmet of My head;
^{t}Judah is My ^{187}scepter.   [Gen. 49:10]
9 "Moab is My washbowl;
Over Edom I shall throw My shoe;
Over Philistia I will shout aloud."

10 ^{R}Who will bring me into the besieged
city?   Ps. 60:9
Who ^{A}will lead me to Edom?   has led
11 Hast not Thou Thyself, O God,^{R}rejected
us?   Ps. 44:9
And wilt Thou not go forth with our
armies, O God?
12 Oh give us help against the adversary,
For deliverance ^{t}by man is in vain.   of
13 ^{A}Through God we shall do valiantly;
And ^{R}it is He who will tread down our
adversaries.   In • Is. 60:12; 63:1-4

PSALM 109

Song of the Slandered

For the choir director.
A Psalm of David.

O GOD ^{R} of my praise,   Deut. 10:21
^{R}Do not be silent!   Ps. 28:1; 83:1
2 For they have opened the wicked and
^{t}deceitful mouth against me;   Ps. 10:7
They have spoken ^{t}against me with a
^{R}lying tongue.   with • Ps. 120:2
3 They have also surrounded me with
^{R}words of hatred,   John 15:23-25 ☆
And fought against me without cause.
4 In return ^{t}for my love they act as my
accusers;   Ps. 38:20
But ^{R}I am *in* prayer.   Ps. 69:13; 141:5
5 Thus they have ^{t}repaid^R me evil for
good,   laid upon me • Ps. 35:12; 38:20
And ^{R}hatred for my love.   [John 7:7; 10:32]

6 Appoint a wicked man over him;
And let an ^{A}accuser^R stand at his right
hand.   adversary, Satan • Zech. 3:1
7 When he is judged, let him ^{R}come forth
guilty;   Ps. 1:5
And let his prayer become sin.
8 Let ^{R}his days be few;   [Ps. 55:23]
Let ^{R}another take his office.   Acts 1:20
9 Let his ^{t}children be fatherless,   Ex. 22:24
And his ^{R}wife a widow.   Jer. 18:21
10 Let his children wander about and beg;
And let them ^{t}seek *sustenance* far from
their ruined homes.   Ps. 37:25
11 Let the creditor seize all that he has;
And let ^{R}strangers plunder the product
of his labor.   Is. 1:7; Lam. 5:2; Ezek. 7:21

^{185} Or, *turns rivers into a desert*
^{186} Or, *sanctuary* ^{187} Or, *lawgiver*

12 Let there be none to ^{T}extend^{R}lovingkind-
 ness to him,   *continue • Ezra 7:28; 9:9*
 Nor^{R}any to be gracious to his fatherless
 children.   Job 5:4; Is. 9:17
13 Let his posterity be cut off;
 In a following generation let their
 ^{R}name be blotted out.   Prov. 10:7

14 Let the iniquity of his fathers be re-
 membered^{T}before the LORD,   *to*
 And do not let the sin of his mother be
 ^{R}blotted out.   Neh. 4:5; Jer. 18:23
15 Let^{R}them be before the LORD continually,   Ps. 90:8; Jer. 16:17
 That He may ^{R}cut off their memory
 from the earth;   Job 18:17; [Ps. 34:16]
16 Because he did not remember to show
 lovingkindness,
 But persecuted the^{R}afflicted and needy
 man,   Ps. 37:14
 And the ^{R}despondent in heart, to put
 them to death.   [Ps. 34:18]
17 He also loved cursing, so ^{R}it came to
 him;   Prov. 14:14; Ezek. 35:9; [Matt. 7:2]
 And he did not delight in blessing, so it
 was far from him.
18 But he ^{R}clothed himself with cursing as
 with his garment,   Ps. 73:6; 109:29
 And it entered into his body like water,
 And like oil into his bones.
19 Let it be to him as ^{R}a garment with
 which he covers himself,   Ps. 73:6
 And for a belt with which he con-
 stantly^{R}girds himself.   2 Sam. 22:40
20 ^{T}Let this be the^{R}reward of my accusers
 from the LORD,   *This is • Ps. 54:5*
 And of those who ^{R}speak evil against
 my soul.   Ps. 41:5; 71:10

21 But Thou, O GOD, the Lord, deal *kindly*
 with me for Thy name's sake;
 Because ^{R}Thy lovingkindness is good,
 deliver me;   [Ps. 69:16]
22 For^{R}I am afflicted and needy,   Ps. 40:17
 And my heart is wounded within me.
23 I am passing ^{R}like a shadow when it
 lengthens;   Ps. 102:11
 I am shaken off like the locust.
24 My knees are weak from fasting;
 And my flesh has grown lean, without
 fatness.
25 I also have become a reproach to them;
 When they see me, they ^{R}wag their
 head.   Lam. 2:15; Matt. 27:39; Mark 15:29

26 ^{R}Help me, O LORD my God;   Ps. 119:86
 Save me according to Thy lovingkindness.
27 ^{A}And let them^{R}know that this is Thy
 hand;   *That they may know • Job 37:7*
 Thou, LORD, hast done it.
28 Let them curse, but do Thou bless;
 When they arise, they shall be
 ashamed,
 But Thy^{R}servant shall be glad.   Is. 65:14
29 ^{A}Let ^{R}my accusers be clothed with dishonor,   *My accusers will be • Job 8:22*

And let them cover themselves with
 their own shame as with a robe.

30 With my mouth I will give thanks
 abundantly to the LORD;
 And in the midst of many^{R}I will praise
 Him.   Ps. 22:22; 35:18; 111:1
31 For He stands ^{R}at the right hand of the
 needy,   [Ps. 16:8; 73:23; 110:5; 121:5]
 To save him from those who^{R}judge his
 soul.   Ps. 37:33

PSALM 110

The Coming of the Priest–King–Judge

A Psalm of David.

T HE^{R}LORD says to my Lord: Acts 2:34, 35
 "Sit ^{R}at My right hand,   [Col. 3:1; Heb. 1:3]
 Until I make^{R}Thine enemies a footstool
 for Thy feet."   [1 Cor. 15:25; Eph. 1:22]
2 The LORD will stretch forth Thy strong
 ^{R}scepter from Zion, *saying,*   [Ps. 45:6]
 "Rule in the midst of Thine enemies."
3 Thy people will volunteer freely in the
 day of Thy power;
 In ^{A}holy array, from the womb of the
 dawn,   *the splendor of holiness*
 Thy youth are to Thee *as* the dew.

4 The LORD has sworn and will not
 ^{T}change His mind,   *be sorry*
 "Thou art a^{R}priest forever
 According to the order of Melchizedek."   [Heb. 5:6, 10; 6:20]☆
5 The Lord is ^{R}at Thy right hand; [Ps. 16:8]
 He^{R}will ^{R}shatter kings in the day of His
 wrath.   Ps. 68:14; 76:12 • *has shattered*
6 He will judge among the nations,
 He^{A}will fill *them* with corpses, *has filled*
 He^{A}will shatter the chief men over a
 broad country.   *has shattered*
7 He will ^{R}drink from the brook by the
 wayside;   Judg. 7:5, 6
 Therefore He will lift up *His* head.

PSALM 111

Praise for God's Tender Care

P RAISE^{A}the LORD!   *Hallelujah! I will*
 I^{R}will give thanks to the LORD with all
 my heart,   Ps. 35:18; 138:1
 In the ^{R}company of the upright and in
 the assembly.   Ps. 89:7; 149:1
2 Great are the works of the LORD;
 They are ^{T}studied^{R}by all who delight in
 them.   *sought out • Ps. 143:5*
3 Splendid and majestic is His work;
 And His ^{R}righteousness endures forever.   Ps. 112:3, 9; 119:142
4 He has made His ^{T}wonders ^{T}to be remembered;   *wonderful acts • a memorial*
 The LORD is^{R}gracious and compassionate.   [Ps. 86:5, 15; 103:8; 145:8]

5 He has ^Rgiven ^Tfood to those who ¹⁸⁸fear
  Him;   [Matt. 6:31-33] • *prey*
  He will ^Rremember His covenant forever.   [Ps. 105:8]
6 He has made known to His people the
  power of His works,
  In giving them the heritage of the nations.

7 The works of His hands are ^Atruth ^R and
  justice;   *faithfulness* • [Rev. 15:3]
  All His precepts are ^Asure.   *trustworthy*
8 They are upheld forever and ever;
  They are performed in ^Atruth ^R and uprightness.   *faithfulness* • Ps. 19:9
9 He has sent redemption to His people;
  He has ordained His covenant forever;
  Holy and awesome is His name.
10 The ¹⁸⁹fear ^R of the LORD is the beginning of wisdom;   Job 28:28; [Prov. 1:7]
  A good understanding have all those
  who do *His commandments*;
  His ^Rpraise endures forever.   Ps. 145:2

PSALM 112

The Blessings of Those Who Fear God

P RAISE ^Athe LORD!   *Hallelujah! Blessed*
  How ^Rblessed is the man who ^Afears the
  LORD,   Ps. 128:1 • *reveres*
  Who greatly ^Rdelights in His commandments.   Ps. 1:2; 119:14, 16
2 His ¹⁹⁰descendants ^Rwill be mighty ^Aon
  earth;   [Ps. 102:28; 127:4] • *in the land*
  The generation of the ^Rupright will be
  blessed.   Ps. 128:4
3 Wealth and riches are in his house,
  And his righteousness endures forever.
4 Light arises in the darkness ^Rfor the upright;   Job 11:17; Ps. 97:11
  He is ^Rgracious and compassionate and
  righteous.   Ps. 37:26
5 It is well with the man who ^Ris gracious
  and lends;   [Ps. 37:21]
  He will ^Amaintain his cause in judgment.   *conduct his affairs with justice*
6 For he will ^Rnever be shaken;   [Ps. 15:5]
  The righteous will be ^Tremembered forever.   *for an eternal remembrance*

7 He will not fear ^Revil tidings; [Prov. 1:33]
  His ^Rheart is steadfast, ^Rtrusting in the
  LORD.   Ps. 57:7; 108:1 • Ps. 56:4
8 His heart is upheld, he will not fear,
  Until he ^Rlooks *with satisfaction* on his
  adversaries.   Ps. 54:7; 59:10
9 He has given freely to the poor;
  His righteousness endures forever;
  His horn will be exalted in honor.

10 The wicked will see it and be vexed;
  He will gnash his teeth and melt away;
  The desire of the wicked will perish.

PSALM 113

The Condescending Grace of God

P RAISE ^Athe LORD!   *Hallelujah! Praise*
  ^RPraise, O servants of the LORD. Ps. 135:1
  Praise the name of the LORD.
2 Blessed be the name of the LORD
  From this time forth and forever.
3 From the rising of the sun to its setting
  The name of the LORD is to be praised.
4 The LORD is high above all nations;
  His ^Rglory is above the heavens. [Ps. 8:1]

5 ^RWho is like the LORD our God,
  Who is enthroned on high,   Ex. 15:11
6 Who ^Rhumbles Himself to behold Ps. 11:4
  The things that are in heaven and in
  the earth?
7 He raises the poor from the dust,
  And lifts the needy from the ash heap,
8 To make *them* sit with ^Aprinces,   *nobles*
  With the princes of His people.
9 He ^Rmakes the barren woman abide in
  the house   1 Sam. 2:5; Ps. 68:6; Is. 54:1
  As a joyful mother of children.
  ^APraise ^Tthe LORD!   *Hallelujah!* • Heb., *YAH*

PSALM 114

In Praise for the Exodus

W HEN Israel went forth from Egypt,
  The house of Jacob from a people of
  ^Rstrange language,   Ps. 81:5
2 Judah became ^RHis sanctuary, Ex. 15:17
  Israel, ^RHis dominion.   Ex. 19:6

3 The ^Rsea looked and fled;   Ex. 14:21
  The ^RJordan turned back.   Josh. 3:13, 16
4 The mountains skipped like rams,
  The hills, like lambs.
5 What ails you, O sea, that you flee?
  O Jordan, that you turn back?
6 O mountains, that you skip like rams?
  O hills, like lambs?

7 Tremble, O earth, before the Lord,
  Before the God of Jacob,
8 Who ^Rturned the rock into a pool of
  water,   Ex. 17:6; Num. 20:11; Ps. 78:15
  The flint into a fountain of water.

PSALM 115

To God Alone Be the Glory

N OT ^Rto us, O LORD, not to us,   [Is. 48:11]
  But ^Rto Thy name give glory   Ps. 29:2
  Because of Thy lovingkindness, be-
  cause of Thy ^Atruth.   *faithfulness*
2 ^RWhy should the nations say,   Ps. 79:10
  "Where, ^Rnow, is their God?" Ps. 42:3, 10

¹⁸⁸ Or, *revere*   ¹⁸⁹ Or, *reverence for*
¹⁹⁰ Lit., *seed*

3 But our God is in the heavens;
He [R]does whatever He pleases.   Ps. 135:6
4 Their [R]idols are silver and gold, Jer. 10:4
The [R]work of man's hands.   Deut. 4:28
5 They have mouths, but they [R]cannot
speak;   Jer. 10:5
They have eyes, but they cannot see;
6 They have ears, but they cannot hear;
They have noses, but they cannot
smell;
7 They have hands, but they cannot feel;
They have feet, but they cannot walk;
They cannot make a sound with their
throat.
8 [R]Those who make them [A]will become
like them,   Ps. 135:18 · *are like them*
Everyone who trusts in them.

9 O [R]Israel, trust in the LORD;   Ps. 118:2
He is their help and their shield.
10 O house of Aaron, trust in the LORD;
He is their help and their shield.
11 You who [191]fear [R]the LORD, trust in the
LORD;   Ps. 22:23; 103:11; 135:20
He is their help and their shield.
12 The LORD [R]has been mindful of us; He
will bless *us*;   Ps. 98:3
He will bless the house of Israel;
He will bless the house of Aaron.
13 He will [R]bless those who [191]fear the
LORD,   Ps. 103:11; 112:1; 128:1
The small together with the great.
14 May the LORD give you increase,
You and your children.
15 May you be blessed of the LORD,
[R]Maker of heaven and earth.   Ps. 96:5

16 The heavens are [R]the heavens of the
LORD;   [Ps. 89:11]
But [R]the earth He has given to the sons
of men.   Ps. 8:6
17 The dead do not praise the LORD,
Nor *do* any who go down into silence;
18 But as for us, we will bless [T]the LORD
From this time forth and forever.
[A]Praise the LORD!   Heb., *YAH* · *Hallelujah!*

PSALM 116

Love the Lord for What He Has Done

I LOVE the LORD, because He hears
My voice *and* my supplications.
2 Because He has inclined His ear to me,
Therefore I shall call *upon Him* as long
as I live.
3 The cords of death encompassed me,
And the [T]terrors of [T]Sheol came upon
me;   *straits* · *the nether world*
I found distress and sorrow.
4 Then [R]I called upon the name of the
LORD: Ps. 18:6; 118:5
"O LORD, I beseech Thee, save my life!"

5 Gracious is the LORD, and righteous;
Yes, our God is [R]compassionate. Ex. 34:6
6 The LORD preserves [R]the simple; Ps. 19:7
I was brought low, and He saved me.
7 Return to your [R]rest, O my soul, Jer. 6:16
For the LORD has [R]dealt bountifully with
you.   Ps. 13:6; 142:7
8 For Thou hast [R]rescued my soul from
death,   Ps. 49:15; 56:13; 86:13
My eyes from tears,
My feet from stumbling.
9 I shall [T]walk before the LORD
In the [T]land of the living.   *lands*
10 I [R]believed when I said,   2 Cor. 4:13
"I am [R]greatly afflicted."   Ps. 88:7
11 I [T]said in my alarm,   Ps. 31:22
"All [R]men are liars."   Ps. 62:9; Rom. 3:4

12 What shall I render to the LORD
For all His benefits toward me?
13 I shall lift up the cup of salvation,
And call upon the name of the LORD.
14 I shall pay my vows to the LORD,
Oh *may it be* [R]in the presence of all His
people.   Ps. 22:25
15 Precious in the sight of the LORD
Is the death of His godly ones.
16 O LORD, surely I am Thy servant,
I am Thy servant, the [T]son of Thy handmaid,   Ps. 86:16
Thou hast [R]loosed my bonds.   Ps. 107:14
17 To Thee I shall offer [A]a sacrifice of
thanksgiving,   Lev. 7:12; Ps. 50:14
And call upon the name of the LORD.
18 I shall pay my vows to the LORD,
Oh *may it be* in the presence of all His
people,
19 In the courts of the LORD's house,
In the midst of you, O Jerusalem.
[A]Praise [T]the LORD!   *Hallelujah!* · Heb., *YAH*

PSALM 117

The Praise of All Nations

PRAISE [R]the LORD, all nations;   Rom. 15:11
Laud Him, all peoples!
2 For His [R]lovingkindness [192]is great
toward us,   Ps. 103:11
And the [A]truth [R]of the LORD is everlasting.   *faithfulness* · [Ps. 100:5; 146:6]
[A]Praise the [T]LORD! Or, *Hallelujah!* · Heb., *YAH*

PSALM 118

Better to Trust God Than Man

GIVE thanks to the LORD, for He is good;
For His lovingkindness is everlasting.
2 Oh let [R]Israel say,   [Ps. 115:9]
"His lovingkindness is everlasting."
3 Oh let the house of Aaron say,
"His lovingkindness is everlasting."
4 Oh let those who [193]fear the LORD say,
"His lovingkindness is everlasting."

[191] Or, *revere*   [192] Lit., *prevails over us*   [193] Or, *revere*

5 From *my* distress I called upon ᵀthe
   LORD;   Heb., *YAH*, also vv. 14, 17, 18, 19
 The LORD answered me *and* ᴿset *me* in a
   large place.   Ps. 18:19
6 The LORD is for me; I will not fear;
   ᴿWhat can man do to me?   Ps. 56:4, 11
7 The LORD is for me ᴿamong those who
   help me;   Ps. 54:4
 Therefore I shall ᴿlook *with satisfaction*
   on those who hate me.   Ps. 54:7
8 It is better to take refuge in the LORD
   Than to trust in man.
9 It is better to take refuge in the LORD
   Than to trust in princes.

10 All nations ᴿsurrounded me;   Ps. 3:6; 88:17
 In the name of the LORD I will surely
   ᴿcut them off.   Ps. 18:40
11 They ᴿsurrounded me, yes, they surrounded me;   Ps. 88:17
 In the name of the LORD I will surely
   cut them off.
12 They surrounded me ᴿlike bees;
 They were extinguished as a ᴿfire of
   thorns;   Deut. 1:44 · Ps. 58:9; Nah. 1:10
 In the name of the LORD I will surely
   cut them off.
13 You ᴿpushed me violently so that I was
   falling,   Ps. 140:4
 But the LORD ᴿhelped me.   Ps. 86:17
14 The LORD is my strength and song,
 And He has become my salvation.

15 The sound of joyful shouting and salvation is in the tents of the righteous;
 The ᴿright hand of the LORD does valiantly.   Ex. 15:6; Ps. 89:13; Luke 1:51
16 The right hand of the LORD is exalted;
 The right hand of the LORD does valiantly.
17 I ᴿshall not die, but live,   [Ps. 6:5; 116:8, 9]
 And tell of the works of the LORD.
18 The LORD has disciplined me severely,
 But He has not given me over to death.

19 Open to me the gates of righteousness;
 I shall enter through them, I shall give
   thanks to the LORD.
20 This is the gate of the LORD;
 The righteous will enter through it.
21 I shall give thanks to Thee, for Thou
   hast ᴿanswered me;   Ps. 116:1; 118:5
 And Thou hast become my salvation.

22 The stone which the builders rejected
 Has become the chief corner *stone.*
23 This is ¹⁹⁴the LORD's doing;
 It is marvelous in our eyes.

24 This is the day which the LORD has
   made;
 Let us ᴿrejoice and be glad in it.   Ps. 31:7
25 O LORD, do save, we beseech Thee;
 O LORD, we beseech Thee, do send
   ᴿprosperity!   Ps. 122:6, 7
26 ᴿBlessed is the one who comes in the
   name of the LORD;   Luke 13:35; 19:38 ☆
 We have ᴿblessed you from the house of
   the LORD.   Ps. 129:8
27 The LORD is God, and He has given us
   ᴿlight;   Esth. 8:16; Ps. 18:28; [1 Pet. 2:9]
 Bind the festival sacrifice with cords ᵀto
   the horns of the altar.   *unto*
28 ᴿThou art my God, and I give thanks to
   Thee;   Ps. 63:1; 140:6
 Thou art my God, I extol Thee.
29 ᴿGive thanks to the LORD, for He is
   good;   Ps. 118:1
 For His lovingkindness is everlasting.

PSALM 119

*An Acrostic in Praise
of the Scriptures*

Aleph.

Hᴏᴡ blessed are those whose way is
   ¹⁹⁵blameless,ᴿ   Ps. 101:2, 6; [Prov. 11:20]
 Who walk in the law of the LORD.
2 How blessed are those who ᴿobserve
   His testimonies,   Ps. 25:10; 99:7; 119:22
 Who seek Him with all *their* heart.
3 They also do no unrighteousness;
 They walk in His ways.
4 Thou hast ordained Thy precepts,
 That we should keep *them* diligently.
5 Oh that my ways may be established
 To ᴿkeep Thy statutes!   Deut. 12:1
6 Then I ᴿshall not be ashamed   Job 22:26
 When I look ᵀupon all Thy commandments.   *to*
7 I shall ᴿgive thanks to Thee with uprightness of heart,   Ps. 119:62
 When I learn Thy righteous judgments.
8 I shall keep Thy statutes;
 Do not ᴿforsake me utterly!   Ps. 38:21

Beth.

9 How can a young man keep his way
   pure?
 By keeping *it* according to Thy word.

10 With all my heart I have sought Thee;

¹⁹⁴ Lit., *from the* LORD
¹⁹⁵ Lit., *complete,* or, *having integrity*

119:9 God's Word Cleanses—One of the pieces of furniture in the Old Testament Tabernacle was called the bronze laver (Page 89—Ex. 38:8). It consisted of a huge upright bronze bowl filled with water, resting upon a pedestal. The priests would often stop at this laver and wash. The Word of God may be thought of in terms of that laver, for it too has the power to cleanse. The Old Testament laver could only remove the physical dirt from human hands, but the Scriptures possess the ability to take away our moral filth (Page 1261—1 Pet. 1:22).

Do not let me[R]wander from Thy commandments.   Ps. 119:21, 118
11 Thy word I have treasured in my heart,
   That I may not sin against Thee.
12 Blessed art Thou, O LORD;
   [R]Teach me Thy statutes. Ps. 119:26, 64, 108
13 With my lips I have[R]told of   Ps. 40:9
   All the ordinances of Thy mouth.
14 I have[R]rejoiced in the way of Thy testimonies,   Ps. 119:111, 162
   [T]As much as in all riches.   As over all
15 I will meditate on Thy precepts,
   And[R]regard Thy ways.   look upon
16 I shall[R]delight in Thy statutes;   Ps. 1:2
   I shall[R]not forget Thy word.   Ps. 119:93

Gimel.

17 Deal bountifully with Thy servant,
   That I may live and keep Thy word.
18 Open my eyes, that I may behold
   Wonderful things from Thy law.
19 I am a[R]stranger in the earth;   Gen. 47:9
   Do not hide Thy commandments from
   me.
20 My soul is crushed with longing
   After Thine ordinances at all times.
21 Thou dost rebuke the arrogant, [A]the
   cursed, Cursed are those who wander ...
   Who[R]wander from Thy commandments.   Ps. 119:10, 118
22 [R]Take away reproach and contempt
   from me,   Ps. 39:8; 119:39
   For I[R]observe Thy testimonies. Ps. 119:2
23 Even though [R]princes sit and talk
   against me,   Ps. 119:161
   Thy servant meditates on Thy statutes.
24 Thy testimonies also are my delight;
   They are my counselors.

Daleth.

25 My[R]soul cleaves to the dust;   Ps. 44:25
   Revive me according to Thy word.
26 I have told of my ways, and Thou hast
   answered me;
   [R]Teach me Thy statutes.   Ps. 25:4; 27:11
27 Make me understand the way of Thy
   precepts,
   So I will meditate on Thy wonders.
28 My soul[T]weeps because of grief;   drops
   Strengthen me according to Thy word.

29 Remove the false way from me,
   And graciously grant me Thy law.
30 I have chosen the faithful way;
   I have [A]placed Thine ordinances before
   me.   accounted Thine ordinances worthy
31 I[R]cleave to Thy testimonies; Deut. 11:22
   O LORD, do not put me to shame!
32 I shall run the way of Thy commandments,
   For Thou wilt[R]enlarge my heart. Is. 60:5

He.

33 [R]Teach me, O LORD, the way of Thy statutes,   Ps. 119:5, 12
   And I shall observe it to the end.
34 [R]Give me understanding, that I may observe Thy law, Ps. 119:27, 73, 125, 144
   And keep it[R]with all my heart. Ps. 191:2
35 Make me walk in the[R]path of Thy commandments,   Ps. 25:4; Is. 40:14
   For I[R]delight in it.   Ps. 112:1; 119:16
36 Incline my heart to Thy testimonies,
   And not to[R]dishonest gain. [Mark 7:21f.]
37 Turn away my [R]eyes from looking at
   vanity,   Is. 33:15
   And[R]revive me in Thy ways.   Ps. 71:20
38 Establish Thy word to Thy servant,
   [T]As that which produces reverence for
   Thee.   Which is for the fear of Thee
39 Turn away my reproach which I dread,
   For Thine ordinances are good.
40 Behold, I long for Thy precepts;
   Revive me through Thy righteousness.

Vav.

41 May Thy[R]lovingkindnesses also come
   to me, O LORD,   Ps. 119:77
   Thy salvation according to Thy word;
42 So I shall have an[R]answer for him who
   reproaches me,   Prov. 27:11
   For I trust in Thy word.
43 And do not take the word of truth utterly out of my mouth,
   For I wait for Thine ordinances.
44 So I will keep Thy law continually,
   Forever and ever.
45 And I will walk[T]at liberty, in a wide place
   For I[R]seek Thy precepts. Ps. 119:94, 155
46 I will also speak of Thy testimonies[R]be-
   fore kings,   Matt. 10:18; Acts 26:1, 2
   And shall not be ashamed.

"If we confess our sins, he is faithful and righteous to forgive us our sins and to cleanse us from all unrighteousness" (Page 1274—1 John 1:9). What areas of my life can the Bible cleanse? It can cleanse me from wrong
thoughts. Sometimes we are tempted to think critically of others; God's Word can prevent this (Page 528—Ps.
1:2). On other occasions fearful thoughts may race through our minds; the Scriptures will prevent this also (Page
206—Josh. 1:8). In fact, the Bible will establish our total thought-life if we but allow it to do so (Page 1196—Phil.
4:8, 9).
   It can cleanse me from wrong words. Of all the Bible authors, James seems to be God's expert on the sins of the
human tongue. In the first chapter of his book he deals with this very thing and shows the absolute necessity of
dependence upon the Scripture to keep our words true (Page 1253—James 1:22–26). See also Psalm 119:172.
   It can cleanse me from wrong actions. Jesus promised us this would be the case: "You are already clean because of the word which I have spoken to you" (Page 1082—John 15:3).
   Finally, God's Word will keep us from wrong thoughts, words, and actions; or else wrong thoughts, words, and
actions will keep us from God's Word.
   Now turn to Page 1074—John 8:31: God's Word Confirms.

47 And I shall ᵀdelightᴿin Thy commandments,   *delight myself* • Ps. 119:16
Which Iᴿlove.   Ps. 119:97, 127, 159
48 And I shall lift up my hands to Thy
commandments,
Which Iᴿlove;   Ps. 119:97, 127, 159
And I will meditate on Thy statutes.

Zayin.

49 Remember the word to Thy servant,
In which Thou hast made me hope.
50 This is my comfort in my affliction,
That Thy word has revived me.
51 The arrogant utterly deride me,
Yet I do not turn aside from Thy law.
52 I have ᴿremembered Thine ordinances
from ¹⁹⁶of old, O LORD,   Ps. 103:18
And comfort myself.
53 Burningᴿindignation has seized me because of the wicked,   Ex. 32:19
Whoᴿforsake Thy law.   Ps. 89:30
54 Thy statutes are my songs
In the house of my pilgrimage.
55 O LORD, Iᴿremember Thy nameᴬin the
night,   Ps. 63:6 • Ps. 42:8
And keep Thy law.
56 This has become mine,
ᴬThat I observe Thy precepts.   *Because*

Heth.

57 The LORD is myᴿportion;   Ps. 16:5
I have promised to keep Thy words.
58 I entreated Thy favor with all *my* heart;
ᴿBe gracious to me according to Thy
ᴬword.   Ps. 41:4; 56:1; 57:1 • *promise*
59 Iᴿconsidered my ways,   Mark 14:72
And turned my feet to Thy testimonies.
60 I hastened and did not delay
To keep Thy commandments.
61 Theᴿcords of the wicked have encircled
me,   Job 36:8; Ps. 140:5
But I have not forgotten Thy law.
62 At ᴿmidnight I shall rise to give thanks
to Thee   Ps. 119:55
Because of Thy righteous ordinances.
63 I am a ᴿcompanion of all those whoᴬfear
Thee,   [Ps. 101:6] • *revere*
And of those who keep Thy precepts.
64 ᴿThe earth is full of Thy lovingkindness,
O LORD;   Ps. 33:5
ᴿTeach me Thy statutes.   Ps. 119:12

Teth.

65 Thou hast dealt well with Thy servant,
O LORD, according to Thy word.
66 Teach me good ᴬdiscernmentᴿ and
knowledge,   *judgment* • Phil. 1:9
For I believe in Thy commandments.
67 Before I was afflicted I went astray,
But now I keep Thy word.
68 Thou artᴿgood and doest good;   Ps. 86:5
ᴿTeach me Thy statutes.   Ps. 119:12
69 The arrogant ¹⁹⁷have ᴿforged a lie
against me;   Job 13:4; Ps. 109:2
With all *my* heart I will ᴿobserve Thy
precepts.   Ps. 119:56

70 Their heart isᴿcovered with fat,   Jer. 5:28
But Iᴿdelight in Thy law.   Ps. 119:16
71 It is good for me that I was afflicted,
That I may learn Thy statutes.
72 The law of Thy mouth is better to me
Than thousands of gold and silver
pieces.

Yodh.

73 ᴿThy hands made me and ¹⁹⁸fashioned
me;   Job 10:8; 31:15; Ps. 100:3; 138:8
ᴿGive me understanding, that I may
learn Thy commandments.   Ps. 119:34
74 May those who ᴿfear Thee ᴿsee me and
be glad,   *revere* • [Ps. 34:2; 35:27; 107:42]
Because Iᴬwait for Thy word.   *hope in*
75 I know, O LORD, that Thy judgments
are righteous,   Ps. 119:138
And thatᴿin faithfulness Thou hast afflicted me.   [Heb. 12:10]
76 O may Thy lovingkindness ᵀcomfort
me,   *be for my comfort*
According to Thy word to Thy servant.
77 Mayᵀ Thy compassion come to me that I
may live,   Ps. 119:41
For Thy law is myᴿdelight.   Ps. 119:16
78 Mayᴿthe arrogant be ashamed, for they
subvert me with a lie;   Jer. 50:32
But I shall meditate on Thy precepts.
79 May those who fear Thee turn to me,
Even those who know Thy testimonies.
80 May my heart beᴿblameless in Thy statutes,   *complete; or, having integrity*
That I may notᴿbe ashamed.   Ps. 119:46

Kaph.

81 My soul languishes for Thy salvation;
Iᴬwait for Thy word.   *hope in*
82 My eyes fail *with longing* for Thy word,
ᵀWhile I say, "When wilt Thou comfort
me?"   *Saying*
83 Though I haveᴿbecome like a wineskin
in the smoke,   Job 30:30
I doᴿnot forget Thy statutes.   Ps. 119:61
84 How many are the ᴿdays of Thy servant?   Ps. 39:4
When wilt Thou ᴿexecute judgment on
those who persecute me?   Rev. 6:10
85 The arrogant have dug pits for me,
Men who are not ᵀin accord with Thy
law.   *according to Thy law*
86 All Thy commandments are faithful;
They have ᴿpersecuted me with a lie;
help me!   Ps. 35:19; 119:78, 161
87 They almost destroyed me on earth,
But as for me, I ᴿdid not forsake Thy
precepts.   Is. 58:2
88 Revive me according to Thy lovingkindness,
So that I may keep the testimony of
Thy mouth.

¹⁹⁶ Or, *everlasting*   ¹⁹⁷ Lit., *besmear me with lies*
¹⁹⁸ Lit., *established*

Lamedh.

89 [R]Forever, O LORD,   Matt. 24:35; [1 Pet. 1:25]
Thy word [199]is settled in heaven.

90 Thy [R]faithfulness *continues* [T]throughout
all generations;   Ps. 36:5; 89:1 • *to*
Thou didst [R]establish the earth, and it
[R]stands.   Ps. 148:6 • Eccl. 1:4

91 They stand this day according to Thine
[R]ordinances,   Jer. 31:35; 33:25
For all things are Thy servants.

92 If Thy law had not been my delight,
Then I would have perished[R]in my affliction.   Ps. 119:50

93 I will never forget Thy precepts,
For by them Thou hast revived me.

94 I am Thine,[R]save me;   Ps. 119:146
For I have sought Thy precepts.

95 The wicked wait for me to destroy me;
I shall diligently consider Thy testimonies.

96 I have seen a limit to all perfection;
Thy commandment is exceedingly
broad.

Mem.

97 O how I[R]love Thy law!   Ps. 119:47, 48, 127
It is my[R]meditation all the day.   Ps. 1:2

98 Thy [R]commandments make me wiser
than my enemies,   Deut. 4:6
For they are ever[A]mine.   *with me*

99 I have more insight than all my teachers,
For Thy testimonies are my [R]medita-
tion.   Ps. 119:15

100 I understand more than the aged,
Because I have observed Thy precepts.

101 I have [R]restrained my feet from every
evil way,   Prov. 1:15
That I may keep Thy word.

102 I have not[R]turned aside from Thine ordinances,   Deut. 17:20; Josh. 23:6
For Thou Thyself hast taught me.

103 How sweet are Thy words to my taste!
Yes, sweeter than honey to my mouth!

104 From Thy precepts I [R]get understanding;   Ps. 119:130
Therefore I hate every false way.

Nun.

105 Thy word is a[R]lamp to my feet,
And a light to my path.   Prov. 6:23

106 I have sworn, and I will confirm it,
That I will keep Thy righteous ordinances.

107 I am exceedingly[R]afflicted;   Ps. 119:25, 50
[A]Revive[R] me, O LORD, according to Thy
word.   *Keep me alive* • Ps. 119:25

108 O accept the [R]freewill offerings of my
mouth, O LORD,   Hos. 14:2; Heb. 13:15
And teach me Thine ordinances.

109 My life is continually [200]in my hand,
Yet I do not[R]forget Thy law.   Ps. 119:16

110 The wicked have laid a snare for me,
Yet I have not [R]gone astray from Thy
precepts.   Ps. 119:10

111 I have [R]inherited Thy testimonies forever,   Deut. 33:4
For they are the joy of my heart.

112 I have [R]inclined my heart to perform
Thy statutes   Ps. 119:36
Forever, *even*[R]to the end.   Ps. 119:33

Samekh.

113 I hate those who are double-minded,
But I love Thy[R]law.   Ps. 119:47

114 Thou art my [R]hiding place and my
shield;   [Ps. 31:20; 32:7; 61:4; 91:1]
I[A]wait for Thy word.   *hope in*

115 [R]Depart from me, evildoers,   Ps. 6:8
That I may [R]observe the commandments of my God.   Ps. 119:22

116 [R]Sustain me according to Thy[A]word, that
I may live;   Ps. 37:17, 24 • *promise*
And do not let me be [A]ashamed of my
hope.   *put to shame because of*

117 Uphold me that I may be[R]safe,   Ps. 12:5
That I may[R]have regard for Thy statutes continually.   Ps. 119:6, 15

118 Thou hast[T]rejected all those who wander from Thy statutes,   *made light of*
For their deceitfulness is useless.

119 Thou hast[T]removed all the wicked of
the earth *like* dross;   *caused to cease*
Therefore I love Thy testimonies.

120 My flesh trembles for fear of Thee,
And I am afraid of Thy judgments.

Ayin.

121 I have done justice and righteousness;
Do not leave me to my oppressors.

122 Be surety for Thy servant for good;
Do not let the arrogant oppress me.

123 My[R]eyes fail *with longing* for Thy salvation,   Ps. 119:82
And for Thy righteous[A]word.   *promise*

124 Deal with Thy servant[R]according to Thy
lovingkindness,   Ps. 51:1; 106:45; 109:26
And[R]teach me Thy statutes.   Ps. 119:12

125 [R]I am Thy servant;[R]give me understanding,   Ps. 116:16 • Ps. 119:27
That I may know Thy testimonies.

126 It is time for the LORD to [R]act,   Jer. 18:23
For they have broken Thy law.

127 Therefore I love Thy commandments
Above gold, yes, above fine gold.

128 Therefore I esteem right all *Thy* precepts concerning everything,
I[R]hate every false way.   Ps. 119:104

Pe.

129 Thy testimonies are wonderful;
Therefore my soul observes them.

130 The unfolding of Thy words gives light;
It gives understanding to the simple.

131 I opened my mouth wide and panted,
For I longed for Thy commandments.

[199] Lit., *stands firm*   [200] I.e., in danger

132 Turn to me and be gracious to me,
After Thy manner ᵀwith those who love
Thy name.   *to*
133 Establish my footsteps in Thy word,
And do not let any iniquity ᴿhave dominion over me. [Ps. 19:13; Rom. 6:12]
134 ᴿRedeem me from the oppression of
man,   Ps. 119:84; 142:6; Luke 1:74
That I may keep Thy precepts.
135 Make Thy face shine upon Thy servant,
And ᴿteach me Thy statutes.   Ps. 119:12
136 My eyes shed streams of water,
Because they do not keep Thy law.

Tsadhe.

137 ᴿRighteous art Thou, O LORD,   Ezra 9:15
And upright are Thy judgments.
138 Thou hast commanded Thy testimonies
in ᴿrighteousness   [Ps. 19:7–9; 119:144]
And exceeding ᴿfaithfulness. Ps. 119:86, 90
139 My zeal has ᵀconsumed me,   *put an end to*
Because my adversaries have forgotten
Thy words.
140 Thy ᴬword is very pure,   *promise*
Therefore Thy servant loves it.
141 I am small and ᴿdespised,   Ps. 22:6
Yet I do not forget Thy precepts.
142 Thy righteousness is an everlasting
righteousness,
And ᵀhThy law is truth.   Ps. 19:9; 119:151
143 Trouble and anguish have ᵀcome upon
me;   *found me*
Yet Thy commandments are my ᴿdelight.   Ps. 119:24
144 Thy testimonies are righteous forever;
Give me understanding that I may live.

Qoph.

145 I cried ᴿwith all my heart; answer me, O
LORD!   Ps. 119:10
I will ᴮobserve Thy statutes. Ps. 119:22, 55
146 I cried to Thee; ᴿsave me,   Ps. 3:7
And I shall keep Thy testimonies.
147 I rise before dawn and cry for help;
I ᴬwait for Thy words.   *hope in*
148 My eyes anticipate the night watches,
That I may meditate on Thy word.
149 Hear my voice ᴿaccording to Thy lovingkindness;   Ps. 119:124
ᴿRevive me, O LORD, according to Thine
ordinances.   Ps. 119:25
150 Those who follow after wickedness
draw near;
They are far from Thy law.
151 Thou art ᴿnear, O LORD, [Ps. 34:18; 145:18]
And all Thy commandments are truth.
152 Of old I have ᴿknown from Thy testimonies,   Ps. 119:125
That Thou hast founded them forever.

Resh.

153 Look upon my affliction and rescue me,
For I do not ᴿforget Thy law. Ps. 119:16

154 Plead my cause and redeem me;
Revive me according to Thy word.
155 Salvation is far from the wicked,
For they do not seek Thy statutes.
156 Great are Thy mercies, O LORD;
Revive me according to Thine ordinances.
157 Many are my ᴿpersecutors and my adversaries,   Ps. 7:1; 119:86, 161
Yet I do not ᴿturn aside from Thy testimonies.   Ps. 119:51
158 I behold the ᴿtreacherous and ᴿloathe
them,   Is. 21:2; 24:16 • Ps. 139:21
Because they do not keep Thy word.
159 Consider how I love Thy precepts;
ᴿRevive me, O LORD, according to Thy
lovingkindness.   Ps. 119:25
160 The ᴿsum of Thy word is truth, Ps. 139:17
And every one of Thy righteous ordinances ᴿis everlasting.   Ps. 119:89, 152

Shin.

161 Princes persecute me without cause,
But my heart ᴿstands in awe of Thy
words.   Ps. 119:120
162 I ᴿrejoice at Thy word,   Ps. 119:14, 111
As one who ᴿfinds great spoil.   Is. 9:3
163 I ᴿhate and despise falsehood,   Ps. 31:6
But I ᴿlove Thy law.   Ps. 119:47
164 Seven times a day I praise Thee,
Because of Thy righteous ordinances.
165 Those who love Thy law have ᴿgreat
peace,   Prov. 3:2; [Is. 26:3; 32:17]
And nothing causes them to stumble.
166 I hope for Thy salvation, O LORD,
And do Thy commandments.
167 My soul keeps Thy testimonies,
And I ᴿlove them exceedingly. Ps. 119:47
168 I ᴿkeep Thy precepts and Thy testimonies,   Ps. 119:22
For all my ways are before Thee.

Tav.

169 Let my cry come before Thee, O LORD;
ᴿGive me understanding ᴿaccording to
Thy word.   Ps. 119:27, 144 • Ps. 119:65
170 Let my supplication come before Thee;
Deliver me according to Thy word.
171 Let my ᴿlips utter praise,   Ps. 51:15; 63:3
For Thou dost teach me Thy statutes.
172 Let my tongue sing of Thy word,
For all Thy ᴿcommandments are righteousness.   Ps. 119:138
173 Let Thy hand be ready to help me,
For I have chosen Thy precepts.
174 I long for Thy salvation, O LORD,
And Thy law is my ᴿdelight. Ps. 119:16, 24
175 Let my ᴿsoul live that it may praise
Thee,   Is. 55:3
And let Thine ordinances help me.
176 I have ᴿgone astray like a lost sheep;
seek Thy servant,   [Is. 53:6]; Jer. 50:6
For I do ᴿnot forget Thy commandments.   Ps. 119:16

PSALM 120

A Cry in Distress

A Song of Ascents.

IN my trouble I cried to the LORD,   Ps. 18:6
And He answered me.
2 Deliver my soul, O LORD, from lying
lips,   Ps. 109:2; [Prov. 12:22]
From a deceitful tongue.   Ps. 52:4
3 What shall be given to you, and what
more shall be done to you,
You deceitful tongue? Ps. 52:4; Zeph. 3:13
4 Sharp arrows of the warrior,   Ps. 45:5
With the *burning* coals of the broom
tree.   Ps. 140:10

5 Woe is me, for I sojourn in Meshech,
For I dwell among the tents of Kedar!
6 Too long has my soul had its dwelling
With those who hate peace.   Ps. 35:20
7 I am *for* peace, but when I speak,
They are for war.   Ps. 55:21

PSALM 121

God Is Our Keeper

A Song of Ascents.

I WILL lift up my eyes to the mountains;
From whence shall my help come?
2 My help *comes* from the LORD, Ps. 124:8
Who made heaven and earth. Ps. 115:15
3 He will not allow your foot to slip;
He who keeps you will not slumber.
4 Behold, He who keeps Israel
Will neither slumber nor sleep.

5 The LORD is your keeper;   Ps. 91:4
The LORD is your shade on your right
hand.   Ps. 16:8; 91:1; Is. 25:4
6 The sun will not smite you by day,
Nor the moon by night.
7 The LORD will 201protect you from all
evil;   Ps. 41:2; 91:10-12
He will keep your soul.
8 The LORD will 201guard your going out
and your coming in   Deut. 28:6
From this time forth and forever.

PSALM 122

"Pray for the Peace of Jerusalem"

A Song of Ascents, of David.

I WAS glad when they said to me,
"Let us go to the house of the LORD."
2 Our feet are standing
Within your gates, O Jerusalem,
3 Jerusalem, that is built Ps. 48:13; 147:2
As a city that is compact together;

201 Or, *keep*

4 To which the tribes go up, even the
tribes of the LORD—   Heb., *YAH*
An ordinance for Israel—   *A testimony*
To give thanks to the name of the
LORD.
5 For there thrones were set for judg-
ment,   Deut. 17:8; 2 Chr. 19:8; Ps. 89:29
The thrones of the house of David.

6 Pray for the peace of Jerusalem:
"May they prosper who love you.
7 "May peace be within your walls,
And prosperity within your palaces."
8 For the sake of my brothers and my
friends,   Ps. 133:1
I will now say, "May peace be within
you."   1 Sam. 25:6; John 20:19
9 For the sake of the house of the LORD
our God
I will seek your good.   Neh. 2:10

PSALM 123

Plea for the Mercy of God

A Song of Ascents.

TO Thee I lift up my eyes, Ps. 121:1; 141:8
O Thou who art enthroned in the heavens!   Ps. 2:4; 11:4
2 Behold, as the eyes of servants *look* to
the hand of their master, Prov. 27:18
As the eyes of a maid to the hand of
her mistress;
So our eyes *look* to the LORD our God,
Until He shall be gracious to us.

3 Be gracious to us, O LORD, be gracious
to us;   Ps. 4:1; 51:1
For we are greatly filled with contempt.   Neh. 4:4; Ps. 119:22
4 Our soul is greatly filled
With the scoffing of those who are at
ease,   Neh. 2:19; Ps. 79:4 • Job 12:5
And with the contempt of the proud.

PSALM 124

God Is on Our Side

A Song of Ascents, of David.

"HAD it not been the LORD who was on
our side,"   Ps. 94:17
Let Israel now say,   Ps. 129:1
2 "Had it not been the LORD who was on
our side,
When men rose up against us;
3 Then they would have swallowed us
alive,   Num. 16:30; Ps. 35:25; 56:1; 57:3
When their anger was kindled against
us;   Gen. 39:19; Ps. 138:7

4 Then the^Rwaters would have engulfed
   us,   Job 22:11; Ps. 18:16; 32:6; 69:2; 144:7
The stream would have 'swept over our
   soul;   *passed over*
5 Then the raging waters would have
   'swept over our soul."   *passed over*

6 Blessed be the LORD,
Who has not given us ^Tto be ^Rtorn by
   their teeth.   *as a prey to* • Ps. 27:2
7 Our soul has ^Rescaped as a bird out of
   the snare of the trapper;   Ps. 141:10
The snare is broken and we have escaped.
8 Our help is in the name of the LORD,
Who^Rmade heaven and earth.   Gen. 1:1

PSALM 125

Trust in the Lord and Abide Forever

A Song of Ascents.

T HOSE who trust in the LORD
Are as Mount Zion, which ^Rcannot be
   moved, but abides forever.   Ps. 46:5
2 As the mountains surround Jerusalem,
So the LORD surrounds His people
From this time forth and forever.
3 For the scepter of wickedness shall not
   rest upon the land of the righteous;
That the righteous^Rmay not put forth
   their hands to do wrong. 1 Sam. 24:10

4 ^RDo good, O LORD, to those who are
   good,   [Ps. 119:68]
And to those who are ^Rupright in their
   hearts.   [Ps. 7:10; 11:2; 32:11; 36:10]
5 But as for those who^Rturn aside to their
   crooked ways, Job 23:11; Ps. 40:4; 101:3
The LORD will lead them away with the
   ^Rdoers of iniquity.   Ps. 92:7; 94:4
^RPeace be upon Israel. Ps. 128:6; Gal. 6:16

PSALM 126

*"Sow in Tears . . . Reap with Joyful
Shouting"*

A Song of Ascents.

W HEN the LORD brought back^Athe captive
   ones of Zion,   *those who returned to*
We were like those who dream.
2 Then our^Rmouth was filled with laughter,   Job 8:21
And our tongue with joyful shouting;
Then they said among the nations,
"The LORD has ^Rdone great things for
   them." 1 Sam. 12:24; Ps. 71:19; Luke 1:49
3 The LORD has done great things for us;
We are^Rglad.   Is. 25:9; Zeph. 3:14

4 Restore our captivity, O LORD,
As the^Tstreams in the South. *stream-beds*

5 Those who sow in^Rtears shall reap with
   joyful shouting.   Ps. 80:5; Jer. 31:9, 16
6 He who goes to and fro weeping, carrying *his* bag of seed,
Shall indeed come again with a shout
   of joy, bringing his sheaves *with
   him.*

PSALM 127

Children Are God's Gift

A Song of Ascents, of Solomon.

U NLESS the LORD builds the house,
They labor in vain who build it;
Unless the LORD guards the city,
The watchman keeps awake in vain.
2 It is vain for you to rise up early,
To^Tretire late,   *delay sitting*
To eat the bread of painful labors;
For He gives to His^Rbeloved^R*even in his*
   sleep.   Ps. 60:5 • Job 11:18, 19

3 Behold, children are a gift of the LORD;
The fruit of the womb is a reward.
4 Like arrows in the hand of a warrior,
So are the children of one's youth.
5 How^Rblessed is the man whose quiver
   is full of them;   Ps. 128:2, 3
^RThey shall not be ashamed,   Prov. 27:11
When they^Rspeak with their enemies in
   the gate.   Is. 29:21; Amos 5:12

PSALM 128

*Blessing on the House
of the God-fearing*

A Song of Ascents.

H OW^Rblessed is everyone who fears the
   LORD,   Ps. 112:1; 119:1
Who^Rwalks in His ways.   Ps. 119:3
2 When you shall ^Reat of the ²⁰²fruit^R of
   your hands,   Is. 3:10 • Ps. 109:11
You will be happy and^Rit will be well
   with you.   Eccl. 8:12; Eph. 6:3
3 Your wife shall be like a fruitful vine,
Within your house,
Your children like^Rolive plants Ps. 52:8
Around your table.
4 Behold, for thus shall the man be
   blessed
Who fears the LORD.

5 ^RThe LORD bless you from Zion, Ps. 134:3
And may you see the prosperity of Je-
   rusalem all the days of your life.
6 Indeed, may you see your^Rchildren's
   children.   Gen. 48:11; 50:23; Job 42:16
^RPeace be upon Israel!   Ps. 125:5

²⁰² Lit., *labor*

PSALM 129

Plea of the Persecuted

A Song of Ascents.

"M^{ANY}[T]times they have persecuted me
from my youth up,"   *Much*
[R]Let Israel now say,   Ps. 124:1

2 "Many[T] times they have persecuted me
from my youth up;   *Much*
Yet they have [R]not prevailed against
me. [Jer. 1:19; 15:20; 20:11]; Matt. 16:18

3 "The plowers plowed upon my back;
They lengthened their furrows."

4 The LORD[R]is righteous;   Ps. 119:137
He has cut in two the [R]cords of the
wicked.   Ps. 140:5

5 May all who[R]hate Zion,   Mic. 4:11
Be put to shame and turned backward,

6 Let them be like[R]grass upon the housetops,   2 Kin. 19:26; Ps. 37:2; Is. 37:27
Which withers before it grows up;

7 With which the reaper does not fill his
[T]hand,   *palm*
Or the binder of sheaves his bosom;

8 Nor do those who pass by say,
"The blessing of the LORD be upon you;
We bless you in the name of the LORD."

PSALM 130

"My Soul Waits for the Lord"

A Song of Ascents.

O[R]UT of the[R]depths I have cried to Thee, O
LORD.   Ps. 42:7; 69:2; Lam. 3:55

2 Lord,[R]hear my voice!   Ps. 64:1; 119:149
Let[R]Thine ears be attentive   Neh. 1:6, 11
To the voice of my supplications.

3 If Thou, [T]LORD, shouldst mark iniquities,   Heb., *YAH*
O Lord, who could[R]stand?   [Nah. 1:6]

4 But there is forgiveness with Thee,
That Thou mayest be[R]feared.   [Jer. 33:8]

5 I wait for the LORD, my soul does wait,
And[T]in His word do I hope.   *for*

6 My soul *waits* for the Lord
More than the watchmen[R]for the morning;   Ps. 63:6; 119:147
Indeed, more than the watchmen for
the morning.

7 O Israel,[R]hope in the LORD;   Ps. 131:3
For with the LORD there is[R]lovingkind-
ness,   [Ps. 86:5; 103:4]
And with Him is abundant redemption.

8 And He will[R]redeem Israel   [Ps. 103:3, 4]
From all his iniquities.

PSALM 131

A Childlike Faith

A Song of Ascents, of David.

O LORD, my heart is not[R]proud, nor my
eyes[A]haughty;   2 Sam. 22:28 •*lofty*

Nor do I[T]involve myself in great matters,   *go after, walk*
Or in things too difficult for me.

2 Surely I have [R]composed and quieted
my soul;   Ps. 62:1
Like a weaned [R]child *rests* [A]against his
mother, [Matt. 18:3; 1 Cor. 14:20] • *upon*
My soul is like a weaned child within
me.

3 O Israel,[R]hope in the LORD   [Ps. 130:7]
From this time forth and forever.

PSALM 132

Trust in the God of David

A Song of Ascents.

R EMEMBER, O LORD, on David's behalf,
All[R]his affliction;   Gen. 49:24; 2 Sam. 16:12

2 How he swore to the LORD,
And vowed to[R]the Mighty One of Jacob,   Gen. 49:24; Is. 49:26; 60:16

3 "Surely I will not enter my house,
Nor lie on my bed;

4 I will not give sleep to my eyes,
Or slumber to my eyelids;

5 Until I find a place for the LORD,
[T]A dwelling place for[R]the Mighty One of
Jacob."   *Dwelling places* • Ps. 132:2

6 Behold, we heard of it in Ephrathah;
We found it in the field of Jaar.

7 Let us go into His dwelling place;
Let us[R]worship at His footstool.   Ps. 5:7

8 Arise, O LORD, to Thy resting place;
Thou and the ark of Thy strength.

9 Let Thy priests be [R]clothed with righteousness;   Job 29:14
And let Thy godly ones sing for joy.

10 For the sake of David Thy servant,
Do not turn away the face of Thine
[R]anointed.   Ps. 2:2; 132:17

11 The LORD has[R]sworn to David,   Ps. 89:3
A truth from which He will not turn
back;
"Of[R]the fruit of your body I will set upon
your throne. 1 Chr. 17:11f.; [2 Chr. 6:16]

12 "If your sons will keep My covenant,
And My testimony which I will teach
them,
Their sons also shall [R]sit upon your
throne forever."   [Luke 1:32; Acts 2:30]

13 For the LORD has [R]chosen Zion;   Ps. 48:1
He has desired it for His habitation.

14 "This is My resting place forever;
Here I will dwell, for I have desired it.

15 "I will abundantly bless her provision;
I will satisfy her needy with bread.

16 "Her [R]priests also I will clothe with salvation;   2 Chr. 6:41; Ps. 132:9
And her godly ones will sing aloud for
joy.

17"There I will cause the ^Rhorn of David to
    spring forth;   Ezek. 29:21; Luke 1:69
I have prepared a ^Rlamp for Mine
    anointed.   1 Kin. 11:36; 15:4; 2 Kin. 8:19
18"His enemies I will clothe with shame;
    But upon himself his ^Rcrown shall
    shine."   Ps. 21:3

PSALM 133

Beauty of the Unity of Brothers

A Song of Ascents, of David.

BEHOLD, how good and how pleasant it is
    For brothers to dwell together in unity!
2 It is like the precious oil upon the head,
Coming down upon the beard,
Even Aaron's beard,
Coming down upon the ^Redge of his
    robes.   Ex. 28:33; 39:24
3 It is like the ^Rdew of Hermon,   Hos. 14:5
Coming down upon the ^Rmountains of
    Zion;   Ps. 48:2; 74:2; 78:68
For there the LORD ^Rcommanded the
    blessing—life forever.   Lev. 25:21

PSALM 134

Praise the Lord in the Evening

A Song of Ascents.

BEHOLD, ^Rbless the LORD, all ^Rservants of
    the LORD,   Ps. 103:21 • Ps. 135:1, 2
Who ^Tserve ^Bby night in the house of the
    LORD!   *stand* • Deut. 10:8; 1 Chr. 23:30
2 Lift up your hands to the sanctuary,
And bless the LORD.
3 May the LORD bless you from Zion,
He who made heaven and earth.

PSALM 135

God Has Done Great Things!

PRAISE ^Athe LORD!   *Hallelujah!* • Heb., YAH
Praise the name of the LORD;
Praise *Him*, O servants of the LORD,
2 You who stand in the house of the
    LORD,
In the courts of the house of our God!
3 Praise the LORD, for the LORD is good;
^RSing praises to His name, ^Rfor it is
    lovely.   Ps. 68:4 • Ps. 147:1
4 For ^Tthe LORD has ^Rchosen Jacob for
    Himself,   Heb., YAH • Deut. 7:6; 10:15
Israel for His ^Bown possession. Titus 2:14

5 For I know that the LORD is great,
And that our Lord is above all gods.
6 Whatever the LORD pleases, He does,
In heaven and in earth, in the seas and
    in all deeps.
7 ^THe causes the vapors to ascend from
    the ends of the earth;   *The one who*

Who makes lightnings for the rain;
Who ^Rbrings forth the wind from His
    treasuries.   Jer. 10:13; 51:16

8 He smote the first-born of Egypt,
^TBoth of man and beast. *From man to beast*
9 ^THe sent signs and wonders into your
    midst, O Egypt,   *The one who*
Upon Pharaoh and all his servants.
10 ^THe smote many nations,
And slew mighty kings,   *The one who*
11 ^RSihon, king of the Amorites, Deut. 29:7
And ^ROg, king of Bashan, Num. 21:33-35
And all the kingdoms of Canaan;
12 And He gave their land as a heritage,
A heritage to Israel His people.
13 Thy name, O LORD, is everlasting,
Thy ^Tremembrance, O LORD, throughout
    all generations.   *memorial • to*
14 For the LORD will judge His people,
And ^Rwill have compassion on His ser-
    vants.   Ps. 90:13; 106:46
15 The ^Ridols of the nations are *but* silver
    and gold,   [Ps. 115:4–8; 135:15–18]
The work of man's hands.
16 They have mouths, but they do not
    speak;
They have eyes, but they do not see;
17 They have ears, but they do not hear;
Nor is there any breath at all in their
    mouths.
18 Those who make them will be like
    them,
Yes, everyone who trusts in them.

19 O house of Israel, bless the LORD;
O house of Aaron, bless the LORD;
20 O house of Levi, bless the LORD;
You ^Rwho ²⁰³revere the LORD, bless the
    LORD.   Ps. 118:4
21 Blessed be the LORD from Zion,
Who ^Rdwells in Jerusalem.   Ps. 132:14
^APraise the LORD!   *Hallelujah!*

PSALM 136

"God's Lovingkindness Is Everlasting"

GIVE thanks to the LORD, for He is good;
    For His lovingkindness is everlasting.
2 Give thanks to the God of gods,
For His lovingkindness is everlasting.
3 Give thanks to the Lord of lords,
For His lovingkindness is everlasting.
4 To Him who alone does great wonders,
For His lovingkindness is everlasting;
5 To Him who ^Rmade the heavens ^Twith
    skill,   Gen. 1:1 • *with understanding*
For His lovingkindness is everlasting;
6 To Him who ^Rspread out the earth
    above the waters,   Gen. 1:2, 6, 9
For His lovingkindness is everlasting;

²⁰³ Or, *fear*

7 To Him who made *the* great lights,
　For His lovingkindness is everlasting:
8 The sun to rule^Aby day,　　*over the*
　For His lovingkindness is everlasting,
9 The moon and stars to rule by night,
　For His lovingkindness is everlasting.

10 To Him who ^Rsmote ^Tthe Egyptians in
　　their first-born,　　*Ex. 12:29 • Egypt*
　For His lovingkindness is everlasting,
11 And ^Rbrought Israel out from their
　　midst,　　*Ex. 12:51; 13:3; Ps. 105:43*
　For His lovingkindness is everlasting,
12 With a ^Tstrong hand and an out-
　　stretched arm, *Ex. 6:1; 13:9; I Kin. 8:42*
　For His lovingkindness is everlasting;
13 To Him who divided the^TRed Sea^Tasun-
　　der,　　*Sea of Reeds • in parts*
　For His lovingkindness is everlasting,
14 And ^Rmade Israel pass through the
　　midst of it,　　*Ex. 14:22; Ps. 106:9*
　For His lovingkindness is everlasting;
15 But He ^Toverthrew Pharaoh and his
　　army in the Red Sea,　　*shook off*
　For His lovingkindness is everlasting.
16 To Him who^Rled His people through the
　　wilderness, *Ex. 13:18; 15:22; Deut. 8:15*
　For His lovingkindness is everlasting;
17 To Him who smote great kings,
　For His lovingkindness is everlasting,
18 And slew ^Tmighty kings,　　*majestic*
　For His lovingkindness is everlasting;
19 Sihon, king of the Amorites,
　For His lovingkindness is everlasting,
20 And^ROg, king of Bashan,　*Num. 21:33-35*
　For His lovingkindness is everlasting,
21 And gave their land as a heritage,
　For His lovingkindness is everlasting,
22 Even a heritage to Israel His servant,
　For His lovingkindness is everlasting.

23 Who remembered us in our low estate,
　For His lovingkindness is everlasting,
24 And has^Rrescued us from our adversar-
　　ies,　　*Judg. 6:9; Neh. 9:28; Ps. 107:2*
　For His lovingkindness is everlasting;
25 Who^Rgives food to all flesh, *[Ps. 104:27]*
　For His lovingkindness is everlasting.
26 Give thanks to the God of heaven,
　For His lovingkindness is everlasting.

PSALM 137

Tears in Exile

BY the^Rrivers of Babylon,　　*Ezek. 1:1, 3*
　There we sat down and^Rwept, *Neh. 1:4*
　When we remembered Zion.
2 Upon the willows in the midst of it
　We^Rhung our^Tharps.　*Job 30:31 • lyres*
3 For there our captors ^Tdemanded of us
　　^Tsongs,　　*asked • words of song*
　And our tormentors mirth, *saying,*
　"Sing us one of the songs of Zion."

4 How can we sing the LORD's song
　In a foreign land?
5 If I^Rforget you, O Jerusalem,　*Is. 65:11*
　May my right hand forget *her skill.*
6 May my^Rtongue cleave to the roof of
　　my mouth,　　*Job 29:10; Ps. 22:15*
　If I do not remember you,
　If I do not^Texalt Jerusalem
　Above my chief joy.　　*cause to ascend*

7 Remember, O LORD, against the sons
　　of^REdom　　*Is. 34:5, 6; Jer. 49:7-22*
　The day of Jerusalem,
　Who said, "Raze it, raze it,
　^RTo its very foundation."　　*[Hab. 3:13]*
8 O daughter of Babylon, you^Adevastated^R
　　one,　*devastator • Is. 13:1-22; 47:1-15*
　How blessed will be the one who^Rre-
　　pays you　*Jer. 50:15, 36, 49; Rev. 18:6*
　With^Tthe recompense with which you
　　have repaid us.　　*your recompense*
9 How blessed will be the one who seizes
　　and^Adashes your little ones *Is. 13:16*
　Against the rock.

PSALM 138

God Answered My Prayer

A Psalm of David.

I WILL give Thee thanks with all my heart;
　I will sing praises to Thee before the
　　^Rgods.　　*[Ps. 95:3; 96:4; 97:7]*
2 I will bow down^Rtoward Thy holy tem-
　　ple,　　*1 Kin. 8:29; Ps. 5:7; 28:2*
　And give thanks to Thy name for Thy
　　lovingkindness and Thy truth;
　For Thou hast magnified Thy^Aword ac-
　　cording to all Thy name.　　*promise*
3 On the day I^Rcalled Thou didst answer
　　me;　　*Ps. 118:5*
　Thou didst make me bold with^Rstrength
　　in my soul.　　*Ps. 28:7; 46:1*

4 ^RAll the kings of the earth will give
　　thanks to Thee, O LORD,　*Ps. 72:11*
　When they have heard the words of
　　Thy mouth.
5 And they will ^Rsing of the ways of the
　　LORD.　　*Ps. 145:7*
　For great is the glory of the LORD.
6 For though the LORD is exalted,
　Yet He^Rregards the lowly; *[James 4:6]*
　But the haughty He knows from afar.

7 Though I walk in the midst of trouble,
　　Thou wilt^Arevive me;　*keep me alive*
　Thou wilt stretch forth Thy hand
　　against the wrath of my enemies,
　And Thy right hand will save me.
8 The LORD will ^Raccomplish what con-
　　cerns me;　　*Ps. 57:2; [Phil. 1:6]*
　Thy^Rlovingkindness, O LORD, is ever-
　　lasting;　　*Ps. 136:1*
　Do not forsake the works of Thy hands.

PSALM 139

"Search Me, O God"

For the choir director.
A Psalm of David.

O LORD, Thou hast [R]searched me and
known *me*.   Ps. 17:3; 44:21; Jer. 12:3

2 Thou dost know [T]when I sit down and
[T]when I rise up;   *my sitting · my rising*
Thou [R]dost understand my thought
from afar.   Ps. 94:11; Is. 66:18; Matt. 9:4

3 Thou dost [ ]scrutinize my [ ]path and my
lying down,   *winnow · journeying*
And art intimately acquainted with all
my ways.

4 [T]Even before there is a word on my
tongue,   *For there is not*
Behold, O LORD, Thou dost know it all.

5 Thou hast [R]enclosed me behind and before,   Ps. 34:7; 125:2
And [R]laid Thy hand upon me.   Job 9:33

6 *Such* [R]knowledge is [ ]too wonderful for
me;   Rom. 11:33 · Job 42:3
It is *too* high, I cannot attain to it.

7 Where can I go from Thy Spirit?
Or where can I flee from Thy presence?

8 If I ascend to heaven, Thou art there;
If I make my bed in [T]Sheol, behold,
Thou art there.   *the nether world*

9 If I take the wings of the dawn,
If I dwell in the remotest part of the
sea,

10 Even there Thy hand will lead me,
And Thy right hand will lay hold of me.

11 If I say, "Surely the [R]darkness will overwhelm me,   Job 22:13
And the light around me will be night,"

12 Even the darkness is not dark to Thee,
And the night is as bright as the day.
Darkness and light are alike *to Thee*.

13 For Thou didst form my inward parts;
Thou didst [R]weave me in my mother's
womb.   [Job 10:11]

14 I will give thanks to Thee, for [204]I am
fearfully and wonderfully made;
[R]Wonderful are Thy works,   Ps. 40:5
And my soul knows it very well.

15 My frame was not hidden from Thee,
When I was made in secret,
And skillfully wrought in the [ ]depths of
the earth.   Ps. 63:9

16 Thine [R]eyes have seen my unformed
substance;   [Job 10:8–10]; Eccl. 11:5
And in Thy book they were all written,
The days that were ordained *for me*,
When as yet there was not one of
them.

17 How precious also are Thy [R]thoughts to
me, O God!   [Ps. 40:5; 92:5]
How vast is the sum of them!

18 If I should count them, they would [ ]out-
number the sand.   Ps. 40:5
When I awake, I am still with Thee.

19 O that Thou wouldst [R]slay the wicked,
O God;   [Is. 11:4]
[R]Depart from me, therefore, [R]men of
bloodshed.   Ps. 6:8; 119:115 · Ps. 5:6

20 For they speak against Thee wickedly,
And Thine enemies [R]take *Thy name* in
vain.   Ex. 20:7; Deut. 5:11

21 Do I not [R]hate those who hate Thee, O
LORD?   2 Chr. 19:2; Ps. 26:5; 31:6
And do I not [R]loathe those who rise up
against Thee?   Ps. 119:158

22 I hate them with the utmost hatred;
They have become my enemies.

23 Search me, O God, and know my heart;
[R]Try me and know my anxious
thoughts;   Prov. 17:3; Jer. 11:20

24 And see if there be any [T]hurtful [R]way in
me,   *way of pain · Ps. 146:9; Prov. 15:9*
And lead me in the everlasting way.

[204] Some ancient versions read *Thou art fearfully
wonderful*

139:14 God's Work in the Present—All people possess an inward desire that their work should have meaning and permanence (Page 576—Ps. 90:16, 17). If man's work is not to be lost in the vastness of eternity, however,
it must conform to the work God has designed for man. This work for the present day can be known only from
God's Word.

According to the Word of God, the primary work of God is for us to believe in Jesus Christ (Page 1071—John
6:29; Page 1136—Rom. 6:17, 18). Apart from entering into this vital relationship with God, man cannot even begin
to work for God. After coming to know Christ, the new Christian discovers God's program for the present from the
Scriptures. It is, first of all, His work in the Christian himself. Regeneration is only the beginning of God's work in
the believer. It actually introduces a process of becoming like Christ which God promises ultimately to bring to
perfection (Page 1193—Phil. 1:6). The Christian's cheerful obedience to God's will as revealed in His Word helps
speed this work along.

Second, no Christian can overlook God's work in the world. Jesus' command to spread the good news of the
gospel to all men appears near the end of all four Gospels and at the beginning of the Book of Acts. God's method
is that men proclaim the gospel and that the Holy Spirit convict (Page 1083—John 16:8–11).

Finally, God's work is in and through the church, the organism ordained by Christ for this age (Page 980—Matt.
16:18). God works in the church through the Spirit and through spiritually gifted people to strengthen and bless it
(Page 1187—Eph. 4:11–13).

Now turn to Page 5—Gen. 2:15–17: The Edenic Covenant.

PSALM 140

Preserve Me from Violence

For the choir director.
A Psalm of David.

RESCUE me, O LORD, from evil men;
Preserve me from ᴿviolent men, Ps. 18:48
2 Who devise evil things in *their* hearts;
They ᴿcontinually stir up wars.   Ps. 56:6
3 They ᴿsharpen their tongues as a serpent;   Ps. 57:4; 64:3
Poison of a viper is under their
lips.   [Selah.

4 ᴿKeep me, O LORD, from the hands of
the wicked;   Ps. 71:4
ᴿPreserve me from violent men, Ps. 140:1
Who have ᴬpurposed to ²⁰⁵trip ᴬup my
feet.   *devised* • Ps. 36:11
5 The proud have ᴿhidden a trap for me,
and cords;   Job 18:9; Ps. 35:7; 141:9
They have spread a net by the wayside;
They have set snares for me.   [Selah.

6 I said to the LORD, "Thou art my God;
ᴿGive ear, O LORD, to the ᴿvoice of my
supplications.   Ps. 143:1 • Ps. 116:1
7 "O GOD the Lord, ᴿthe strength of my salvation,   [Ps. 28:8; 118:14]
Thou hast ᴿcovered my head in the day
of ᴿbattle.   Ps. 144:10 • *weapons*
8 "Do not grant, O LORD, the ᴿdesires of
the wicked;   Ps. 112:10
Do not promote his *evil device, lest*
they be exalted.   [Selah.

9 "As for the head of those who surround
me,
May the ᴿmischief of their lips cover
them.   Ps. 7:16; Prov. 18:7
10 "May burning coals fall upon them;
May they be ᴿcast into the fire, Ps. 21:9
Into ᵀdeep pits from which they ᴿcannot
rise.   *watery* • Ps. 36:12
11 "May a ᵀslanderer not be established in
the earth;   *man of tongue*
ᴿMay evil hunt the violent man
²⁰⁶speedily."   Ps. 34:21

12 I know that the LORD will ᴿmaintain the
cause of the afflicted, 1 Kin. 8:45, 49
And ᴿjustice for the poor. Ps. 12:5; 35:10
13 Surely the ᵀrighteous will give thanks to
Thy name;   Ps. 97:12
The upright will dwell in Thy presence.

PSALM 141

"Set a Guard, O LORD, over My Mouth"

A Psalm of David.

O LORD, I call upon Thee; hasten to me!
ᴿGive ear to my voice when I call to
Thee!   Ps. 5:1; 143:1

²⁰⁵ Lit., *push violently*   ²⁰⁶ Lit., *thrust upon thrust*

2 May my prayer be ᵀcounted as ᴿincense
before Thee;   *fixed* • [Ex. 30:8]
The ᴿlifting up of my hands as the ᴿeve-
ning offering.   [1 Tim. 2:8] • Ex. 29:39
3 Set a guard, O LORD, over my mouth;
Keep watch over the door of my lips.
4 ᴿDo not incline my heart to any evil
thing,   Ps. 119:36
To practice deeds ᵀof wickedness   *in*
With men who ᴿdo iniquity;   Hos. 6:8
And ᴿdo not let me eat of their delicacies.   Prov. 23:6

5 Let the ᴿrighteous smite me ᴬin kindness
and reprove me;   Gal. 6:1 • *lovingly*
It is ᴿoil upon the head; Ps. 23:5; 133:2
Do not let my head refuse it,
For still my prayer is ᴬagainst their
wicked deeds. *in spite of their calamities*
6 Their judges are ᴿthrown down by the
sides of the rock,   2 Chr. 25:12
And they hear my words, for they are
pleasant.
7 As when one ᴿplows and breaks open
the earth,   Ps. 129:3
Our bones have been scattered at the
mouth of ᵀSheol.   *the nether world*

8 For my ᴿeyes are toward Thee, O GOD,
the Lord;   Ps. 25:15; 123:2
In Thee I take refuge; do not ᵀleave me
defenseless.   *pour out my soul*
9 Keep me from the jaws of the trap
which they have set for me,
And from the ᴿsnares of those who do
iniquity.   Ps. 140:5
10 Let the wicked fall into their own nets,
While I pass by ᵀsafely.   *altogether*

PSALM 142

"No One Cares for My Soul"

Maskil of David, when he was in the
cave. A Prayer.

I CRY aloud with my voice to the LORD;
I ᴿmake supplication with my voice to
the LORD.   Ps. 30:8
2 I pour out my complaint before Him;
I declare my trouble before Him.
3 When ᴿmy spirit ᵀwas overwhelmed
within me, Ps. 77:3; 143:4 • *fainted*
Thou didst know my path.
In the way where I walk
They have hidden a trap for me.
4 Look to the right and see;
For there is no one who regards me;
There is no ᴿescape for me;   Job 11:20
ᴿNo one cares for my soul.   Jer. 30:17

5 I cried out to Thee, O LORD;
I said, "Thou art ᴿmy refuge, Ps. 91:2, 9
My portion in the land of the living.
6 "Give ᴿheed to my cry,   Ps. 17:1
For I am ᴿbrought very low;   Ps. 79:8

Deliver me from my persecutors,
For they are too strong for me.
7 "Bring^Rmy soul out of prison,   Ps. 143:11
So that I may give thanks to Thy name;
The righteous will surround me,
For Thou wilt ^Rdeal bountifully with
   me."   Ps. 13:6

PSALM 143

"Teach Me to Do Thy Will"

A Psalm of David.

H EAR my prayer, O LORD,
   ^RGive ear to my supplications!   Ps. 140:6
Answer me in Thy^Rfaithfulness, in Thy
   righteousness!   Ps. 89:1, 2
2 And ^Rdo not enter into judgment with
   Thy servant,   Job 14:3; 22:4
For in Thy sight^Rno man living is righteous. Eccl. 7:20; Rom. 3:10, 20; Gal. 2:16
3 For the enemy has persecuted my soul;
He has crushed my life to the ground;
He^Rhas made me dwell in dark places,
   like those who have long been
   dead.   Ps. 88:6; Lam. 3:6
4 Therefore ^Rmy spirit ^Tis overwhelmed
   within me;   Ps. 77:3; 142:3 • *faints*
My heart is ²⁰⁷appalled within me.

5 I^Rremember the days of old;   Ps. 77:5, 10
I^Rmeditate on all Thy doings;   Ps. 77:12
I muse on the work of Thy hands.
6 I^Rstretch out my hands to Thee; Ps. 88:9
My soul *longs* for Thee, as a parched
   land.   [Selah.

7 ^RAnswer me quickly, O LORD, my^Rspirit
   fails;   Ps. 69:17 • Ps. 73:26; 84:2
^RDo not hide Thy face from me,   Ps. 27:9
Lest I become like^Rthose who go down
   to the pit.   Ps. 28:1; 88:4
8 Let me hear Thy^Rlovingkindness^Rin the
   morning;   Ps. 90:14 • Ps. 46:5
For I trust^Rin Thee;   Ps. 25:2
Teach me the ^Rway in which I should
   walk;   Ps. 27:11; 32:8; 86:11
For to Thee I^Rlift up my soul.   Ps. 25:1
9 Deliver me, O LORD, from my enemies;
I take refuge in Thee.

10 ^RTeach me to do Thy will,
For Thou art my God;   Ps. 25:4, 5; 119:12
Let^RThy good Spirit lead me on level
   ^Tground.   Neh. 9:20 • *land*
11 ^RFor the sake of Thy name, O LORD,^Rre-
   vive me.   Ps. 25:11 • Ps. 119:25
^RIn Thy righteousness bring my soul out
   of trouble.   Ps. 31:1; 71:2
12 And in Thy lovingkindness ^Tcut^Roff my
   enemies,   *silence* • Ps. 54:5
And ^Rdestroy all those who afflict my
   soul;   Ps. 52:5
For^RI am Thy servant.   Ps. 116:16

PSALM 144

"What Is Man?"

A *Psalm* of David.

B LESSED be the LORD,^Rmy rock,   Ps. 18:2
Who trains my hands for war,
And my fingers for battle;
2 My lovingkindness and my fortress,
My stronghold and my deliverer;
My^Rshield and He in whom I take ref-
   uge;   Ps. 3:3; 28:7; 84:9
Who subdues my people under me.
3 O LORD, ^Rwhat is man, that Thou dost
   take knowledge of him?   Heb. 2:6
Or the son of man, that Thou dost think
   of him?
4 ^RMan is like a mere breath;   [Ps. 39:11]
His days are like a passing shadow.

5 ^RBow Thy heavens, O LORD, and^Rcome
   down;   Ps. 18:9 • Is. 64:1
^RTouch the mountains, that they may
   smoke.   Ps. 104:32
6 Flash forth lightning and scatter them;
Send out Thine ^Rarrows and confuse
   them. Ps. 7:13; 58:7; Hab. 3:11; Zech. 9:14
7 Stretch forth Thy hand from on high;
Rescue me and^Rdeliver me out of great
   waters,   Ps. 69:1, 14
Out of the hand of ^Raliens Ps. 18:44; 54:3
8 Whose mouths^Rspeak deceit,   Ps. 12:2
And whose^Rright hand is a right hand
   of falsehood.   Deut. 32:40; Ps. 106:26

9 I will sing a new song to Thee, O God;
Upon a^Rharp of ten strings I will sing
   praises to Thee,   Ps. 33:2
10 Who dost give salvation to kings;
Who ^Rdost rescue David His servant
   from the evil sword.   2 Sam. 18:7
11 Rescue me, and deliver me out of the
   hand of ^Raliens,   Ps. 18:44; 54:3
Whose mouth^Rspeaks deceit,   Ps. 12:2
And whose ^Rright hand is a right hand
   of falsehood.   Gen. 14:22; Deut. 32:40

12 Let our sons in their youth be as
   ^Rgrown-up plants,   [Ps. 92:12–14; 128:3]
And our daughters as ^Rcorner pillars
   fashioned as for a palace;   Song 4:4
13 *Let* our ^Rgarners be full, furnishing every kind of produce,   [Prov. 3:9, 10]
And our flocks bring forth thousands
   and ten thousands in our fields;
14 *Let* our ^Rcattle^Rbear,   Prov. 14:4 • *be laden*
Without mishap and without loss,
Let there be no outcry in our streets!
15 How blessed are the people who are so
   situated;
How^Rblessed are the people whose God
   is the LORD!   [Ps. 33:12]

²⁰⁷ Or, *desolate*

PSALM 145

Testify to God's Great Acts

A Psalm of Praise, of David.

I WILL extol Thee, my God, O King;
And I will^Rbless Thy name forever and
ever.   Ps. 34:1
2 Every day I will bless Thee,
And I will^Rpraise Thy name forever and
ever.   Ps. 71:6
3 ^RGreat is the LORD, and highly to be
praised;   [Ps. 48:1; 86:10; 147:5]
And His greatness is unsearchable.
4 One^Rgeneration shall praise Thy works
to another,   Ps. 22:30, 31; Is. 38:19
And shall declare Thy mighty acts.
5 On the^Rglorious^Asplendor of Thy majesty,   Ps. 145:12 · *majesty of Thy splendor*
And ^Ron Thy wonderful works, I will
meditate.   Ps. 119:27
6 And men shall speak of the^Apower of
Thine awesome acts;   *strength*
And I will tell of Thy greatness.
7 They shall eagerly utter the memory of
Thine^Rabundant goodness,   Ps. 31:19
And shall^Rshout joyfully of Thy righteousness.   Ps. 51:14

8 The LORD is gracious and merciful;
Slow to anger and great in lovingkindness.
9 The LORD is^Rgood to all,   Ps. 100:5; 136:1
And His ^Rmercies are over all His
works.   Ps. 145:15
10 ^RAll Thy works shall give thanks to
Thee, O LORD,   Ps. 19:1; 103:22
And Thy godly ones shall bless Thee.
11 They shall speak of the^Rglory of Thy
kingdom,   Jer. 14:21
And talk of Thy power;
12 To^Rmake known to the sons of men^TThy
mighty acts,   Ps. 105:1 · *His*
And the^Rglory of the majesty of Thy
kingdom.   Ps. 145:5; [Is. 2:10, 19, 21]
13 Thy kingdom is ^Tan everlasting kingdom,   *a kingdom of all ages*
And Thy dominion *endures* throughout
all generations.

14 The LORD ^Rsustains all who fall, Ps. 37:24
And raises up all who are bowed down.
15 The eyes of all^Tlook to Thee,   *wait*
And Thou^Rdost give them their food in
due time.   Ps. 104:27; 136:25
16 Thou^Rdost open Thy hand,   Ps. 104:28
And dost satisfy the desire of every living thing.

17 The LORD is righteous in all His ways,
And kind in all His deeds.
18 The LORD is^Rnear to all who call upon
Him,   [Deut. 4:7]; Ps. 34:18; 119:151
To all who call upon Him in truth.

²⁰⁸ Or, *He is gracious*   ²⁰⁹ Lit., *sorrows*

19 He will^Rfulfill the desire of those who
fear Him;   Ps. 21:2; 37:4
He will also^Rhear their cry and will save
them.   Ps. 10:17; [Prov. 15:29; 1 John 5:14]
20 The LORD keeps all who love Him;
But all the wicked, He will destroy.
21 My^Rmouth will speak the praise of the
LORD;   Ps. 71:8
And ^Rall flesh will bless His holy name
forever and ever.   Ps. 65:2; 150:6

PSALM 146

"Do Not Trust in Princes"

PRAISE^Athe^T LORD!   *Hallelujah!* · Heb., YAH
^RPraise the LORD, O my soul!   Ps. 103:1
2 I will praise the LORD while I live;
I will ^Rsing praises to my God while I
have my being.   Ps. 104:33
3 ^RDo not trust in princes,   Ps. 118:9
In^Tmortal^Rman, in whom there is no salvation.   *a son of man* · Ps. 118:8
4 His ^Rspirit departs, he returns to ^Tthe
earth;   Ps. 104:29 · *his earth*
In that very day his thoughts perish.
5 How^Rblessed is he whose help is the
God of Jacob,   Ps. 144:15; Jer. 17:7
Whose hope is in the LORD his God;
6 Who^Rmade heaven and earth,   Rev. 14:7
The sea and all that is in them;
Who keeps^Afaith forever;   *truth*
7 Who ^Rexecutes justice for the oppressed;   Ps. 103:6
Who^Rgives food to the hungry. Ps. 107:9
The LORD sets the prisoners free.

8 The LORD opens *the eyes of* the blind;
The LORD ^Rraises up those who are
bowed down;   Ps. 145:14
The LORD^Rloves the righteous;   Ps. 11:7
9 The LORD^Aprotects the strangers; *keeps*
He ^Asupports^R the fatherless and the
widow;   *relieves* · Deut. 10:18; Ps. 68:5
But He thwarts the way of the wicked.
10 The LORD will^Rreign forever,   Ex. 15:18
Thy God, O Zion, to all generations.
^APraise the LORD!   *Hallelujah!*

PSALM 147

God Heals the Brokenhearted

PRAISE^Athe^T LORD!   *Hallelujah!* · Heb., YAH
For ^Rit is good to sing praises to our
God;   Ps. 92:1; 135:3
For ²⁰⁸it is pleasant *and* praise is^Rbe-
coming.   Ps. 33:1
2 The LORD^Rbuilds up Jerusalem; Ps. 51:18
He gathers the outcasts of Israel.
3 He heals the^Rbrokenhearted,   Ps. 34:18
And^Rbinds up their ²⁰⁹wounds.   Is. 30:26
4 He counts the number of the stars;
He^Rgives names to all of them. Is. 40:26

5 ^RGreat is our Lord, and abundant in
   strength;   Ps. 48:1; 145:3
  His understanding is infinite.
6 The LORD ²¹⁰supports the afflicted;
  He brings down the wicked to the
  ground.

7 Sing to the LORD with thanksgiving;
  Sing praises to our God on the lyre,
8 Who covers the heavens with clouds,
  Who provides rain for the earth,
  Who ^Rmakes grass to ^Tgrow on the
   mountains.   Job 38:27 • *spring forth*
9 He^Rgives to the beast its food, Ps. 104:27
  And to the young ravens which cry.
10 He does not delight in the strength of
   the^Rhorse;   Ps. 33:17
  He^Rdoes not take pleasure in the legs of
   a man.   [1 Sam. 16:7]
11 The LORD favors those who fear Him,
  ^RThose who wait for His lovingkindness.   [Ps. 33:18]

12 Praise the LORD, O Jerusalem!
  Praise your God, O Zion!
13 For He has strengthened the^Rbars of
   your gates;   Neh. 3:3; 7:3
  He has blessed your sons within you.
14 He makes peace in your borders;
  He ^Rsatisfies you with^Rthe ^Tfinest of the
   wheat.   Ps. 132:15 • Ps. 81:16 • *fat*
15 He sends forth His ^Tcommand to the
   earth;   Job 37:12; Ps. 148:5
  His^Rword runs very swiftly. Ps. 104:4
16 He gives ^Rsnow like wool;   Job 37:6
  He scatters the frost like ashes.
17 He casts forth His ice as fragments;
  Who can stand before His cold?
18 He ^Rsends forth His word and melts
   them;   Ps. 33:9; 107:20; 147:15
  He ^Rcauses His wind to blow and the
   waters to flow.   Ps. 107:25
19 He declares His words to Jacob,
  His ^Rstatutes and His ordinances to Israel.   Mal. 4:4
20 He has not dealt thus with any nation;
  And as for His ordinances, they have
   ^Rnot known them. Ps. 79:6; Jer. 10:25
  ^APraise the LORD!   *Hallelujah!*

PSALM 148

All Creation Praises the Lord

P RAISE^Athe^T LORD! *Hallelujah!* • Heb., *YAH*
  Praise the LORD from the heavens;
  Praise Him^Rin the heights!   Job 16:19
2 Praise Him,^Rall His angels; Ps. 103:20
  Praise Him,^Rall His hosts!   Ps. 103:21
3 Praise Him, sun and moon;
  Praise Him, all stars of light!
4 Praise Him, highest heavens,

And the ^Rwaters that are above the
  heavens!   Gen. 1:7
5 Let them praise the name of the LORD,
  For^RHe commanded and they were created.   Gen. 1:1; Ps. 33:6, 9
6 He has also ^Restablished them forever
   and ever;   Ps. 89:37; [Jer. 31:35, 36]
  He has made a ^Rdecree which will not
   pass away.   Job 38:33

7 Praise the LORD from the earth,
  ^RSea monsters and all deeps; Gen. 1:21
8 Fire and hail, snow and clouds;
  Stormy wind, fulfilling His word;
9 ^RMountains and all hills; Is. 44:23; 49:13
  Fruit^Rtrees and all cedars;   Is. 55:12
10 ^RBeasts and all cattle;   Is. 43:20
  Creeping things and winged fowl;
11 Kings of the earth and all peoples;
  Princes and all judges of the earth;
12 Both young men and virgins;
  Old men and children.

13 Let them praise the name of the LORD,
  For His^Rname alone is exalted; Is. 12:4
  His glory is above earth and heaven.
14 And He has ^Rlifted up a horn for His
   people,   1 Sam. 2:1; Ps. 75:10
  ^RPraise for all His godly ones; Ps. 109:1
  Even for the sons of Israel, a people
   ^Rnear to Him. Lev. 10:3; Eph. 2:17
  ^APraise the LORD!   *Hallelujah!*

PSALM 149

"The LORD Takes Pleasure in His People"

P RAISE^Athe^T LORD! *Hallelujah!* • Heb., *YAH*
  Sing to the LORD a^Rnew song, Ps. 33:3
  And His praise^Rin the congregation of
   the godly ones.   Ps. 35:18; 89:5
2 Let Israel be glad in^Rhis Maker; Ps. 95:6
  Let the sons of Zion rejoice in their
   ^RKing.   Judg. 8:23; Ps. 47:6; Zech. 9:9
3 Let them praise His name with ^Rdanc-
   ing;   2 Sam. 6:14; Ps. 150:4
  Let them sing praises to Him with^Rtim-
   brel and lyre.   Ex. 15:20; Ps. 81:2
4 For the LORD^Rtakes pleasure in His people;   Job 36:11; Ps. 16:11; 35:27; 147:11
  He will^Rbeautify the afflicted ones with
   salvation.   Ps. 132:16; [Is. 61:3]

5 Let the godly ones exult in glory;
  Let them sing for joy on their beds.
6 *Let* the^Rhigh praises of God *be* in their
   ^Tmouth,   Ps. 66:17 • *throat*
  And a two-edged sword in their hand,
7 To execute vengeance on the nations,
  And punishment on the peoples;
8 To bind their kings with chains,
  And their nobles with fetters of iron;
9 To^Rexecute on them the judgment written;   Deut. 7:1, 2; Ezek. 28:26

²¹⁰ Or, *relieves*

This is an honor for all His godly ones.
^APraise the LORD!   *Hallelujah!*

PSALM 150

"Praise the LORD"

P RAISE^Athe^TLORD!   *Hallelujah!* • Heb., YAH
  Praise God in His^Rsanctuary;   Ps. 73:17
  Praise Him in His mighty expanse.

2 Praise Him for His mighty deeds;

Praise Him according to His excellent
  ^Rgreatness.   Deut. 3:24; Ps. 145:3

3 Praise Him with^Rtrumpet sound; Ps. 98:6
  Praise Him with^Rharp and lyre. Ps. 33:2
4 Praise Him with ^Rtimbrel and dancing;
  Praise Him with ^Rstringed instruments
  and^Rpipe.   Ps. 45:8; Is. 38:20 • Gen. 4:21
5 Praise Him with loud cymbals;
  Praise Him with resounding cymbals.
6 Let ^Reverything that has breath praise
  the LORD.   Ps. 103:22; 145:21
  Praise^Tthe LORD!   Heb., YAH

150:1 Praise—To praise God is to acknowledge the glories of His excellent person. It differs somewhat from thanksgiving, which describes what God has done rather than what He is. Here are some facts about praise.
a. God alone is worthy of our praise (Page 535—Ps. 18:3; 113:3).
b. It is His will for us that we praise Him (Page 554—Ps. 50:23; Page 693—Is. 43:21).
c. This praise should be continuous (Page 544—Ps. 34:1; 71:6) and also public (Page 538—Ps. 22:25).
d. We are to praise God for His holiness (Page 434—2 Chr. 20:21), grace (Page 1185—Eph. 1:6), goodness (Page 598—Ps. 135:3), and kindness (Page 599—Ps. 138:2).
e. All nature praises God (Page 604—Ps. 148:7–10).
f. The sun, moon, and stars praise Him (Page 536—Ps. 19:1; 143:3).
g. The angels praise Him (Page 604—Ps. 148:2).
In fact, we are told that on occasion God uses even the wrath of men to praise Him (Page 567—Ps. 76:10). An example of this is seen in the selling of Joseph by his brothers into slavery (Page 38—Gen. 37:28). God later uses this cruel act to promote Joseph as second ruler over all Egypt. As Joseph would remind his brothers: "And as for you, you meant evil against me, *but* God meant it for good in order to bring about this present result, to preserve many people alive" (Page 50—Gen. 50:20).
Now turn to Page 1274—1 John 1:9: Confession.

Jewish Feasts

Feast of	Month on Jewish Calendar	Day	Corresponding Month	References
*Passover (Unleavened Bread)	Nisan	14–21	Mar.–Apr.	Ex. 12:43—13:10; Matt. 26:17–20
*Pentecost (First Fruits or Weeks)	Sivan	6 (50 days after Passover)	May–June	Deut. 16:9–12; Acts 2:1
Trumpets, *Rosh Hashanah*	Tishri	1, 2	Sept.–Oct.	Num. 29:1–6
Day of Atonement, *Yom Kippur*	Tishri	10	Sept.–Oct.	Lev. 23:26–32; Heb. 9:7
*Tabernacles (Booths or Ingathering)	Tishri	15–22	Sept.–Oct.	Neh. 8:13–18; John 7:2
Dedication (Lights), *Hanukkah*	Chislev	25 (8 days)	Nov.–Dec.	John 10:22
Purim (Lots)	Adar	14, 15	Feb.–Mar.	Esth. 9:18–32

*The three major feasts for which all males of Israel were required to travel to the Temple in Jerusalem (Ex. 23:14–19).

THE PROVERBS

THE BOOK OF PROVERBS

The key word in Proverbs is *wisdom*, "the ability to live life skillfully." A godly life in an ungodly world, however, is no simple assignment. Proverbs provides God's detailed instructions for His people to deal successfully with the practical affairs of everyday life: how to relate to God, parents, children, neighbors, and government. Solomon, the principal author, uses a combination of poetry, parables, pithy questions, short stories, and wise maxims to give in strikingly memorable form the common sense and divine perspective necessary to handle life's issues.

Because Solomon, the pinnacle of Israel's wise men, was the principal contributor, the Hebrew title of this book is *Mishle Shelomoh*, "Proverbs of Solomon" (1:1). The Greek title is *Paroimiai Salomontos*, "Proverbs of Solomon." The Latin title *Liber Proverbiorum*, "Book of Proverbs," combines the words *pro* "for" and *verba* "words" to describe the way the proverbs concentrate many words into a few. The Rabbinical writings called Proverbs *Sepher Hokhmah*, "Book of Wisdom."

THE AUTHOR OF PROVERBS

Solomon's name appears at the beginning of the three sections he wrote: 1:1 for chapters 1—9, 10:1 for chapters 10:1—22:16, and 25:1 for chapters 25—29. According to First Kings 4:32, he spoke 3,000 proverbs and 1,005 songs. Only about 800 of his 3,000 proverbs are included in the two Solomonic collections in this book. No man was better qualified than Solomon to be the principal contributor. He asked for wisdom (1 Kin. 3:5–9) and God granted it to him (1 Kin. 4:29–31) to such a degree that people from foreign lands came to hear him speak (1 Kin. 4:34; 10:1–13, 24). His breadth of knowledge, aptitude, skill, and perception were extraordinary. In every area Solomon brought prosperity and glory to Israel until his latter years (cf. 1 Kin. 11:4).

It is likely that Solomon collected and edited proverbs other than his own. According to Ecclesiastes 12:9, "he pondered, searched out and arranged many proverbs." The second collection of Solomonic proverbs in 25—29 was assembled by the scribes of King Hezekiah, because of his interest in spiritually benefiting his subjects with the Word of God. The prophets Isaiah and Micah ministered during Hezekiah's time, and it has been suggested

that they also might have been involved in this collection.

Proverbs 22:17—24:34 consists of "the words of the wise" (22:17; 24:23). Some of these sayings are quite similar to those found in The Wisdom of Amenemope, a document of teachings on civil service by an Egyptian who probably lived between 1000 B.C. and 600 B.C. Wise men of this period went to hear one another, and it is probable that Amenemope borrowed certain aphorisms from Hebrew literature. If the *hakhamim* ("wise men") lived before Solomon's time, he may have been the collector and editor of this series of wise sayings.

There is no biblical information about Agur (30) or Lemuel (31). Agur ben Jakeh (30:1) is simply called an oracle, and Lemuel is called a king and an oracle (31:1). Both have been identified with Solomon, but there is no basis for this suggestion.

THE TIME OF PROVERBS

Proverbs is a collection of topical maxims and is not a historical book. It is a product of the wisdom school in Israel. According to Jeremiah 18:18 and Ezekiel 7:26, three groups communicated to the people on behalf of God: the priests imparted the Law; the prophets communicated the divine word and visions; and the sages, or elders, gave counsel to the people. The sages provided the practical application of godly wisdom to specific problems and decisions. The "Preacher" of Ecclesiastes is a good example of the wisdom school (Eccl. 1:1, 12; 7:27; 12:8–10). *Qoheleth*, or "Preacher," meant "one who addresses an assembly": he presided over a "school" of wise men and "taught the people knowledge" (Eccl. 12:9). "My son" in Proverbs and Ecclesiastes evidently refers to the pupil. This was parallel to Samuel's role of heading Israel's school of prophets.

Wisdom literature is also found in other countries of the ancient Near East. In Egypt, written examples can be found as early as 2700 B.C. Although the style was similar to Israel's wisdom literature, the proverbs and sayings of these countries differed from those of Israel in content because they lacked the character of the righteous standards of the Lord.

Solomon's proverbs were written by 931 B.C., and his proverbs in chapters 25—29 were collected by Hezekiah about 230 years later (Hezekiah reigned from 715 to 686 B.C.). Un-

der Solomon, Israel was at its spiritual, political, and economic summit. Solomon probably wrote his proverbs in his middle years, before his character began to decline into carnality, materialism, and idolatry.

✝ THE CHRIST OF PROVERBS

In Proverbs 8, wisdom is personified and seen in its perfection. It is divine (8:22–31), it is the source of biological and spiritual life (8:35, 36; 3:18), it is righteous and moral (8:8, 9), and it is available to all who will receive it (8:1–6, 32–35). This wisdom became incarnate in Christ "in whom are hidden all the treasures of wisdom and knowledge" (Col. 2:3). "But by His doing you are in Christ Jesus, who became to us wisdom from God, and righteousness and sanctification, and redemption" (1 Cor. 1:30; cf. 1 Cor. 1:22–24).

🗝 KEYS TO PROVERBS

Key Word: Wisdom—Proverbs is one of the few biblical books that clearly spells out its purpose. The purpose statement in 1:2–6 is twofold: (1) to impart moral discernment and discretion (1:3–5), and (2) to develop mental clarity and perception (1:2, 6). The words "wisdom and instruction" in 1:2 complement each other because *wisdom* (*hokhmah*) means "skill," and *instruction* (*musar*) means "discipline." No skill is perfected without discipline, and when a person has skill he has freedom to create something beautiful. Proverbs deals with the most fundamental skill of all: practical righteousness before God in every area of life. This requires knowledge, experience, and a willingness to put God first (see 3:5–7). Chapters 1—9 are designed to create a felt need for wisdom, and

Proverbs as a whole is designed both to prevent and to remedy ungodly life-styles. The book served as a manual to impart the legacy of wisdom, prudence, understanding, discretion, knowledge, guidance, competence, correction, counsel, and truth—from generation to generation.

Key Verses: Proverbs 1:5–7 and 3:5, 6—"A wise man will hear and increase in learning, and a man of understanding will acquire wise counsel, to understand a proverb and a figure, the words of the wise and their riddles. The fear of the LORD is the beginning of knowledge; fools despise wisdom and instruction" (1:5–7).

"Trust in the LORD with all your heart, and do not lean on your own understanding. In all your ways acknowledge Him, and He will make your paths straight" (3:5, 6).

Key Chapter: Proverbs 31—The last chapter of Proverbs is unique in ancient literature, as it reveals a very high and noble view of women. The woman in these verses is: (1) a good woman (31:13, 15, 16, 19, 25), (2) a good wife (31:11, 12, 23, 24), (3) a good mother (31:14, 15, 18, 21, 27), and (4) a good neighbor (31:20–26). Her conduct, concern, speech, and life stand in sharp contrast to the woman pictured in Proverbs 7.

📐 SURVEY OF PROVERBS

Proverbs is the most intensely practical book in the Old Testament because it teaches skillful living in the multiple aspects of everyday life. Its specific precepts include instruction on wisdom and folly, the righteous and the wicked, the tongue, pride and humility, justice and vengeance, the family, laziness and work, poverty and wealth, friends and neighbors, love and lust, anger and strife,

FOCUS	PURPOSE OF PROVERBS	PROVERBS TO YOUTH	PROVERBS OF SOLOMON	PROVERBS OF SOLOMON (HEZEKIAH)	WORDS OF AGUR	WORDS OF LEMUEL
REFERENCE	1:1————1:8—————		10:1————————	25:1———————————	30:1—————————	31:1———31:31
DIVISION	PURPOSE AND THEME	FATHER'S EXHORTATIONS	FIRST COLLECTION OF SOLOMON	SECOND COLLECTION OF SOLOMON	NUMERICAL PROVERBS	VIRTUOUS WIFE
TOPIC	PROLOGUE	PRINCIPLES OF WISDOM			EPILOGUE	
	COMMENDATION OF WISDOM	COUNSEL OF WISDOM			COMPARISONS OF WISDOM	
LOCATION	JUDAH					
TIME	c. 950 – 700 B.C.					

masters and servants, life and death. Proverbs touches upon every facet of human relationships, and its principles transcend the bounds of time and culture.

The Hebrew word for "proverb" (*mashal*) means "comparison, similar, parallel." A proverb uses a comparison or figure of speech to make a pithy but poignant observation. Proverbs have been defined as simple illustrations that expose fundamental realities about life. These maxims are not theoretical but practical; they are easily memorized, based on real-life experience, and designed for use in the mainstream of life. The proverbs are general statements and illustrations of timeless truth, which allow for, but do not condone, exceptions to the rule. The key work is *hokhmah*, "wisdom": it literally means "skill" (in living). Wisdom is more than shrewdness or intelligence. Instead, it relates to practical righteousness and moral acumen. The Book of Proverbs may be divided into six segments: the purpose of Proverbs (1:1-7), the proverbs to the youth (1:8—9:18), the proverbs of Solomon (10:1—24:34), the proverbs of Solomon copied by Hezekiah's men (25:1—29:27), the words of Agur (30:1-33), and the words of King Lemuel (31:1-31).

The Purpose of Proverbs (1:1-7): The brief prologue states the author, theme, and purpose of the book.

The Proverbs to the Youth (1:8—9:18): Following the introduction, there is a series of ten exhortations, each beginning with "My son" (1:8—9:18). These messages introduce the concept of wisdom in the format of a father's efforts to persuade his son to pursue the path of wisdom in order to achieve godly success in life. Wisdom rejects the invitation of crime and foolishness, rewards seekers of wisdom on every level, and wisdom's discipline provides freedom and safety (1—4). Wisdom protects one from illicit sensuality and its consequences, from foolish practices and laziness, and from adultery and the lure of the harlot

(5—7). Wisdom is to be preferred to folly because of its divine origin and rich benefits (8 and 9). There are four kinds of fools, ranging from those who are naive and uncommitted to scoffers who arrogantly despise the way of God. The fool is not mentally deficient; he is self-sufficient, ordering his life as if there were no God.

The Proverbs of Solomon (10:1—24:34): There is a minimal amount of topical arrangement in these chapters. There are some thematic clusters (e.g., 26:1–12, 13–16, 20–22), but the usual units are one-verse maxims. It is helpful to assemble and organize these proverbs according to such specific themes as money and speech. This Solomonic collection consists of 375 proverbs of Solomon. Chapters 10—15 contrast right and wrong in practice, and all but nineteen proverbs use antithetic parallelism, that is, parallels of paired opposite principles. Chapters 16:1—22:16 offer a series of self-evident moral truths, and all but eighteen proverbs use synonymous parallelism, that is, parallels of paired identical or similar principles. The words of wise men (22:17—24:34) are given in two groups. The first group includes thirty distinct sayings (22:17—24:22), and six more are found in the second group (24:23–34).

The Proverbs of Solomon Copied by Hezekiah's Men (25:1—29:27): This second Solomonic collection was copied and arranged by "the men of Hezekiah" (25:1). These proverbs in chapters 25—29 further develop the themes in the first Solomonic collection.

The Words of Agur (30:1-33): The last two chapters of Proverbs form an appendix of sayings by two otherwise unknown sages, Agur and Lemuel. Most of Agur's material is given in clusters of numerical proverbs.

The Words of King Lemuel (31:1-31): The last chapter includes an acrostic of twenty-two verses (the first letter of each verse consecutively follows the complete Hebrew alphabet) portraying a virtuous wife (31:10–31).

OUTLINE OF PROVERBS

CHAPTER 1

The Purpose of Proverbs

T HE[R]proverbs of Solomon[R]the son of David, king of Israel: 1 Kin. 4:32 • Eccl. 1:1
2 To know[R]wisdom and instruction,
To discern the sayings of[R]understanding,   [Prov. 15:33] • Prov. 4:1
3 To receive instruction in wise behavior,
Righteousness, justice and equity;
4 To give prudence to the[T]naive,
To the youth[R]knowledge and discretion,   simple ones • Prov. 2:10, 11; 3:21
5 A wise man will hear and[R]increase in
learning,   Prov. 9:9
And a[R]man of understanding will acquire wise counsel,   Prov. 14:6
6 To understand a proverb and a figure,
The words of the wise and their[R]riddles.   Num. 12:8; Ps. 49:4; 78:2

7 [R]The fear of the LORD is the beginning of
knowledge;   Job 28:28; Ps. 111:10
Fools despise wisdom and instruction.

Obey Parents

8 [R]Hear, my son, your father's instruction,
And [R]do not forsake your mother's
teaching;   Prov. 4:1 • Prov. 6:20

9 Indeed, they are a[R]graceful wreath to
your head,   Prov. 4:9
And ornaments about your neck.

Avoid Bad Company

10 My son, if sinners[R]entice you,
[R]Do not consent.   Prov. 16:29 • Deut. 13:8
11 If they say, "Come with us,
Let us[T]lie in wait for blood,
Let us [R]ambush the innocent without
cause;   Prov. 12:6 • Ps. 10:8; Prov. 1:18
12 Let us[R]swallow them alive like Sheol,
Even whole, as those who[R]go down to
the pit;   Ps. 124:3 • Ps. 28:1
13 We shall find all *kinds* of precious
wealth,
We shall fill our houses with spoil;
14 Throw in your lot with us,
We shall all have one purse,"
15 My son, [R]do not walk in the way with
them.   Ps. 1:1; Prov. 4:14
Keep your feet from their path,
16 For[R]their feet run to evil,   Prov. 6:17, 18
And they hasten to shed blood.
17 Indeed, it is[T]useless to spread the net
In the eyes of any bird;   *in vain*
18 But they lie in wait for their own blood;
They ambush their own lives.
19 So are the ways of everyone who[R]gains
by violence;   Prov. 15:27

1:8   The Role of Children—Both the Old and New Testaments agree that children have only one responsibility in the family—to obey their parents. The admonition of Solomon is more fully explained by Paul in Ephesians 6:1–3: "Children, obey your parents in the Lord, for this is right. Honor your father and mother (which is the first commandment with a promise), that it may be well with you, and that you may live long on the earth." "Children" is an inclusive term. It is not a matter of either sex or age that is involved.

Twice in Scripture God has intervened and directly stated what He would have children do. The last time was nearly two thousand years ago when He gave a revelation to Paul for the church. The first time was nearly thirty-four thousand years ago when He gave a revelation to Moses and Israel in which he commanded, "Honor your father and mother." God's will for children is that they are to obey their parents. The expression "in the Lord" does not limit the responsibility only to the circumstances where the parents are believers. Colossians 3:20 clearly points out that children are to obey their parents "in all things," not just in those things pertaining to Christian living. "In the Lord" more properly is understood to mean by the Lord or because it is the Lord's directive (this is what God says children are to do). "For this is right" indicates that for children to obey their parents is righteous or godlike. Such obedience is perfectly illustrated by God the Son who was completely obedient to God the Father, even though that obedience resulted in His death (Page 1194—Phil. 2:6–8).

Two things are promised to children who obey their parents: it will be well with them—they will have a happy life; and they will have a long life. These are the two things that children want most, and obedience to parents is the only way to assure them. That is why this is the first commandment with promise; from it springs all the other important issues of life. The child who has not learned to obey his parents, who are God's representatives in the family, will not learn to obey God.

Now turn to Page 1190—Eph. 6:4: The Role of the Parents.

It takes away the life of its possessors.

Seek Wisdom

20 ^RWisdom shouts in the street,   Prov. 8:1-3
She^Tlifts her voice in the square;   *gives*
21 At the head of the noisy *streets* she
cries out;
At the entrance of the gates in the city,
she utters her sayings:
22 "How long, O^Tnaive ones, will you love
^Asimplicity?   *simple ones • naivete*
And ^Rscoffers delight themselves in
scoffing,   Ps. 1:1
And fools^Rhate knowledge?   Prov. 1:29
23 "Turn to my reproof,
Behold, I will^Rpour out my spirit on
you;   Is. 32:15; Joel 2:28; [John 7:39]
I will make my words known to you.
24 Because^RI called, and you refused;
I ^Rstretched out my hand, and no one
paid attention;   Is. 65:12 • Is. 65:2
25 And you neglected all my counsel,
And did not want my reproof;
26 I will even laugh at your calamity;
I will mock when your dread comes,
27 When your dread comes like a storm,
And your calamity comes on like a
^Rwhirlwind,
When distress *and* anguish come on
you.   [Prov. 10:25]
28 "Then they will^Rcall on me, but I will not
answer;   1 Sam. 8:18; Job 27:9; 35:12
They will^Rseek me diligently, but they
shall not find me,   Prov. 8:17
29 Because they^Rhated knowledge,
And did not choose the fear of the
LORD.   Job 21:14; Prov. 1:22
30 "They^Rwould not accept my counsel,
They spurned all my reproof.   Ps. 81:11
31 "So they shall ^Reat of the fruit of their
own way,   Job 4:8; Prov. 5:22, 23; 22:8
And be ^Rsatiated with their own devices.   Prov. 14:14
32 "For the^Rwaywardness of the^Tnaive shall
kill them,
And the complacency of fools shall destroy them.   Jer. 2:19 • *simple ones*
33 "But^Rhe who listens to me shall live securely,   Ps. 25:12, 13; Prov. 3:24-26
And shall be at ease from the dread of
evil."

CHAPTER 2

M Y son, if you will^Rreceive my sayings,
And ^Rtreasure my commandments
within you,   [Prov. 4:10] • Prov. 3:1
2 Make your ear attentive to wisdom,
Incline your heart to understanding;
3 For if you cry for discernment,
^TLift your voice for understanding; *Give*
4 If you seek her as^Rsilver,   [Prov. 3:14]
And search for her as for^Rhidden treasures;   Job 3:21; Matt. 13:44

5 Then you will discern the^Rfear of the
LORD,   Prov. 1:7
And discover the knowledge of God.
6 For^Rthe LORD gives wisdom;   1 Kin. 3:12
From His mouth *come* knowledge and
understanding.
7 He stores up sound wisdom for the upright;
He is a^Rshield to those who walk in integrity,   [Ps. 84:11]; Prov. 30:5
8 Guarding the paths of justice,
And He^Rpreserves the way of His godly
ones.   [1 Sam. 2:9]; Ps. 66:9
9 Then you will discern ^Rrighteousness
and justice   Prov. 8:20
And equity *and* every good course.
10 For^Rwisdom will enter your heart,
And ^Rknowledge will be pleasant to
your soul;   [Prov. 14:33] • Prov. 22:18
11 Discretion will^Rguard you,   Prov. 4:6; 6:22
Understanding will watch over you,
12 To^Rdeliver you from the way of evil,
From the man who speaks ^Rperverse
things;   Prov. 28:26 • Prov. 6:12
13 From those who^Rleave the paths of uprightness,   Prov. 21:16
To walk in the ways of darkness;
14 Who^Rdelight in doing evil,   Prov. 10:23
And rejoice in the perversity of evil;
15 Whose paths are^Rcrooked,   Ps. 125:5
And who are devious in their ways;
16 To ^Rdeliver you from the strange
woman,   Prov. 6:24; 7:5
From the^Tadulteress who flatters with
her words;   *strange woman*
17 That leaves the ^Rcompanion of her
youth,   Mal. 2:14, 15
And forgets the covenant of her God;
18 For her house sinks down to death,
And her tracks *lead* to the dead;
19 None who go to her return again,
Nor do they reach the paths of life.
20 So you will^Rwalk in the way of good
men,   Heb. 6:12
And keep to the paths of the righteous.
21 For the upright will live in the land,
And the blameless will remain in it;
22 But^Rthe wicked will be cut off from the
land,   Ps. 37:38; Prov. 10:30
And^Rthe treacherous will be^Ruprooted
from it.   Prov. 11:3 • Deut. 28:63

CHAPTER 3

Benefits of Wisdom

M Y son, do not forget my^Ateaching,   *law*
But let your heart^Rkeep my commandments;   Ex. 20:6; Deut. 30:16
2 For length of days and years of life,
And peace they will add to you.
3 Do not let ^Rkindness and truth leave
you;   2 Sam. 15:20; Prov. 14:22
^RBind them around your neck,   Deut. 6:8
Write them on the tablet of your heart.
4 So you will find favor and^Rgood repute
In the sight of God and man.   Ps. 111:10
5 ^RTrust in the LORD with all your heart,

And [R]do not lean on your own understanding.   [Ps. 37:3, 5] • Prov. 23:4
6 In all your ways acknowledge Him,
And He will make your paths straight.
7 Do not be wise in your own eyes;
Fear the LORD and turn away from evil.
8 It will be healing to your[T]body,   *navel*
And refreshment to your bones.
9 Honor the LORD from your wealth,
And from the first of all your produce;
10 So your[R]barns will be filled with plenty,
And your[R]vats will overflow with new
wine.   Deut. 28:8 • Joel 2:24
11 [R]My son, do not reject the discipline of
the LORD,   [Job 5:17]; Heb. 12:5, 6
Or loathe His reproof,
12 For[R]whom the LORD loves He reproves,
Even[R]as a father, the son in whom he
delights.   Rev. 3:19 • Deut. 8:5

13 [R]How blessed is the man who finds wisdom,   Prov. 8:32, 34
And the man who gains understanding.
14 For its[R]profit is better than the profit of
silver,   Job 28:15-19; Prov. 8:10, 19
And its gain than fine gold.
15 She is[R]more precious than[T]jewels;
And nothing you desire compares with
her.   Job 28:18; Prov. 8:11 • *corals*
16 [R]Long life is in her right hand;   Prov. 3:2
In her left hand are riches and honor.
17 Her[R]ways are pleasant ways,   Matt. 11:29
And all her paths are[R]peace.   Ps. 119:165
18 She is a[T]tree of life to those who take
hold of her,   Gen. 2:9; Prov. 11:30
And happy are all who hold her fast.
19 The LORD [R]by wisdom founded the
earth;   Ps. 104:24; Prov. 8:27
By understanding He [R]established the
heavens.   Prov. 8:27, 28
20 By His knowledge the[R]deeps were broken up,   Gen. 7:11
And the[R]skies drip with dew.   Job 36:28
21 My son,[R]let them not depart from your
sight;   Prov. 4:21
Keep sound wisdom and discretion,
22 So they will be life to your soul,
And[R]adornment to your neck.   Prov. 1:9
23 Then you will[R]walk in your way securely,   Prov. 4:12; 10:9
And your foot will not[R]stumble.   Is. 5:27
24 When you[R]lie down, you will not be
afraid;   Job 11:19; Ps. 3:5
When you lie down, your sleep will be
sweet.
25 Do not be afraid of sudden fear,
Nor of the[T]onslaught[R] of the wicked
when it comes;   *storm* • Job 5:21
26 For the LORD will be[A]your confidence,
And will[R]keep your foot from being
caught.   *at your side* • 1 Sam. 2:9

Be Kind to Others

27 [R]Do not withhold good from[T]those to
whom it is due, [Gal. 6:10] • *its owners*

When it is in your power to do *it.*
28 [R]Do not say to your neighbor, "Go, and
come back,   Lev. 19:13; Deut. 24:15
And tomorrow I will give *it,*"
When you have it with you.
29 [R]Do not devise harm against your neighbor,   Prov. 6:14; 14:22
While he lives in security beside you.
30 [R]Do not contend with a man without
cause,   Prov. 26:17; [Rom. 12:18]
If he has done you no harm.
31 Do not envy a man of violence,
And do not choose any of his ways.
32 For the[R]crooked *man* is an abomination
to the LORD;   Prov. 11:20
But He is intimate with the upright.
33 The[R]curse of the LORD is on the house
of the wicked,   Zech. 5:3, 4; Mal. 2:2
But He [R]blesses the dwelling of the
righteous.   Job 8:6; Ps. 1:3
34 Though He scoffs at the scoffers,
Yet He gives grace to the afflicted.
35 [R]The wise will inherit honor,   Dan. 12:3
But fools[J]display dishonor.   *raise high*

CHAPTER 4

Father Says Get Wisdom

H EAR, O sons, the[R]instruction of a father,
And give attention that you may[T]gain
understanding,   Ps. 34:11 • *know*
2 For I give you[T]sound teaching;   *good*
Do not abandon my[A]instruction.   *law*
3 When I was a son to my father,
[R]Tender and[R]the only son in the sight of
my mother,   1 Chr. 22:5 • Zech. 12:10
4 Then he taught me and said to me,
"Let your heart hold fast my words;
Keep my commandments and live;
5 [R]Acquire wisdom! [R]Acquire understanding!   Prov. 4:7 • Prov. 16:16
Do not forget, nor turn away from the
words of my mouth.
6 "Do not forsake her, and she will guard
you;
Love her, and she will watch over you.
7 "The[A]beginning of wisdom *is:* Acquire
wisdom;   *the primary thing is wisdom*
And with all your acquiring, get understanding.
8 "Prize her, and she will exalt you;
She will honor you if you embrace her.
9 "She will place[R]on your head a garland
of grace;
She will present you with a crown of
beauty."   Prov. 1:9

10 Hear, my son, and accept my sayings,
And the years of your life will be many.
11 I have[R]directed you in the way of wisdom;   1 Sam. 12:23
I have led you in upright paths.
12 When you walk, your[R]steps will not be
impeded;   Job 18:7; Ps. 18:36
And if you run, you will not stumble.

13 Take hold of instruction; do not let go.
Guard her, for she is your life.

Avoid the Wicked

14 [R]Do not enter the path of the wicked,
And do not proceed in the way of evil
men.   [Ps. 1:1]; Prov. 1:15
15 Avoid it, do not pass by it;
Turn away from it and pass on.
16 For they [R]cannot sleep unless they do
evil;   Ps. 36:4; Mic. 2:1
And they are robbed of sleep unless
they make *someone* stumble.
17 For they eat the bread of wickedness,
And drink the wine of violence.
18 But the [R]path of the righteous is like the
[R]light of dawn,   Is. 26:7 • 2 Sam. 23:4
That [R]shines brighter and brighter until
the [R]full day.   Dan. 12:3 • Job 11:17
19 The [R]way of the wicked is like darkness;
They do not know over what they
[A]stumble.   [Job 18:5, 6] • *may stumble*

20 My son, give attention to my words;
Incline your ear to my sayings.
21 Do not let them depart from your sight;
Keep them in the midst of your heart.
22 For they are [R]life to those who find
them,   Prov. 3:22
And health to all [T]their whole body. *his*

Watch Over Your Heart

23 Watch over your heart with all diligence,
For from it *flow* the springs of life.
24 Put away from you a deceitful mouth,
And put devious lips far from you.
25 Let your eyes look directly ahead,
And let your [A]gaze be fixed straight in
front of you.   *eyelids*
26 [R]Watch the path of your feet,   Prov. 5:21
And all your ways will be established.
27 Do not turn to the right nor to the left;
[R]Turn your foot from evil.   Prov. 1:15

CHAPTER 5

Do Not Commit Adultery

MY son, give attention to my wisdom,
Incline your ear to my understanding;
2 That you may observe discretion,
And your lips may reserve knowledge.
3 For the lips of an [T]adulteress [R]drip honey,   *strange woman* • Prov. 2:16; 5:20
And smoother than oil is her speech;
4 But in the end she is [R]bitter as wormwood,   [Eccl. 7:26]
[R]Sharp as a two-edged sword.   Ps. 57:4
5 Her feet [R]go down to death,
Her steps lay hold of Sheol.   Prov. 7:27
6 [T]She does not ponder the path of life;

Her ways are [R]unstable, she does not
know *it.*   *Lest she watch* • 2 Pet. 2:14

7 [R]Now then, *my* sons, listen to me,
And [R]do not depart from the words of
my mouth.   Prov. 7:24 • Ps. 119:102
8 [R]Keep your way far from her,
And do not go near the [R]door of her
house,   Prov. 7:25 • Prov. 9:14
9 Lest you give your vigor to others,
And your years to the cruel one;
10 Lest strangers be filled with your
strength,
And your hard-earned goods *go* to the
house of an alien;
11 And you groan at your latter end,
When your flesh and your body are
consumed;
12 And you say, "How I have [R]hated instruction!   Prov. 1:7, 22, 29
And my heart spurned reproof!
13 "And I have not listened to the voice of
my [R]teachers,   Prov. 1:8
Nor inclined my ear to my instructors!
14 "I was almost in utter ruin
In the midst of the assembly and congregation."

Do Be Faithful to Your Spouse

15 Drink water from your own cistern,
And fresh water from your own well.
16 Should your [R]springs be dispersed
abroad,   Prov. 5:18; 9:17; Song 4:12, 15
Streams of water in the streets?
17 Let them be yours alone,
And not for strangers with you.
18 Let your fountain be blessed,
And rejoice in the wife of your youth.
19 *As* a loving hind and a graceful doe,
Let her breasts satisfy you at all times;
Be exhilarated always with her love.
20 For why should you, my son, be exhilarated with an [R]adulteress,   Prov. 5:3
And embrace the bosom of a foreigner?
21 For the [R]ways of a man are before the
eyes of the LORD,   Job 14:16; 31:4
And He watches all his paths.
22 His [R]own iniquities will capture the
wicked,   Num. 32:23; Ps. 7:15; 9:15
And he will be held with the cords of
his sin.
23 He will [R]die for lack of instruction,
And in the greatness of his folly he will
go astray.   [Job 4:21; 36:12]

CHAPTER 6

Avoid Surety

MY son, if you have become [R]surety for
your neighbor,   Prov. 11:15; 17:18
Have given a pledge for a stranger,
2 *If* you have been snared with the words
of your mouth,

Have been caught with the words of
your mouth,
3 Do this then, my son, and deliver yourself;
Since you have come into the[T]hand of
your neighbor,   *palm*
Go, humble yourself, and importune
your neighbor.
4 Do not give[R]sleep to your eyes,
Nor slumber to your eyelids;   Ps. 132:4
5 Deliver yourself like a gazelle from *the
hunter's* hand,
And like a[R]bird from the hand of the
fowler.   Ps. 91:3; 124:7

Do Not Be Lazy

6 Go to the[R]ant, O sluggard,   Prov. 30:24
Observe her ways and be wise,
7 Which, having[R]no chief,
Officer or ruler,   Prov. 30:27
8 Prepares her food[R]in the summer,
And gathers her provision in the harvest.   Prov. 10:5
9 How long will you lie down, O sluggard?
When will you arise from your sleep?
10"A little sleep, a little slumber,
A little folding of the hands to rest"—
11 [R]And your poverty will come in like a
[T]vagabond,   Prov. 24:34 • *one who walks*
And your need like an armed man.

12 A[R]worthless person, a wicked man,
Is the one who walks with a [R]false
mouth,   Prov. 16:27 • Prov. 4:24; 10:32
13 Who[R]winks with his eyes, who[T]signals
with his feet,   Job 15:12 • *scrapes*
Who points with his fingers;
14 Who *with* [R]perversity in his heart devises evil continually,   Prov. 17:20
Who[T]spreads strife.   *sends out*
15 Therefore[R]his calamity will come suddenly;   Prov. 24:22
Instantly he will be broken, and there
will be[R]no healing.   2 Chr. 36:16

16 There are six things which the LORD
hates,
Yes, seven which are an abomination
[T]to Him: *of His soul*
17 Haughty eyes, a lying tongue,
And hands that shed innocent blood,
18 A heart that devises[R]wicked plans,
Feet that run rapidly to evil,   Gen. 6:5
19 A[T]false witness *who* utters lies,
And one who [T]spreads strife among
brothers.   Ps. 27:12 • *sends out*

Do Not Commit Adultery

20 [R]My son, observe the commandment of
your father,
And do not forsake the [A]teaching of
your mother;   Eph. 6:1 • *law*
21 [R]Bind them continually on your heart;
Tie them around your neck.   Prov. 3:3
22 When you[R]walk about, [T]they will guide
you;
When you sleep, [T]they will watch over
you;
And when you awake, [T]they will talk to
you.   [Prov. 3:23] • *she*

23 For[R]the commandment is a lamp, and
the[A]teaching is light;
And reproofs for discipline are the way
of life,   Ps. 19:8; 119:105 • *law*

24 To[R]keep you from the evil woman,
From the smooth tongue of the [T]adul-
teress.   Prov. 5:3 • *foreign woman*
25 Do not desire her beauty in your heart,
Nor let her catch you with her eyelids.
26 For [T]on account of a harlot *one is reduced* to a loaf of bread,   Prov. 5:9
And [T]an adulteress[R]hunts for the precious life.   *a man's wife* • Prov. 7:23
27 Can a man take fire in his bosom,
And his clothes not be burned?
28 Or can a man walk on hot coals,
And his feet not be scorched?
29 So is the one who[R]goes in to his neighbor's wife;   Ezek. 18:6; 33:26

6:23 Illumination of God's Word—Illumination is the last of three important steps taken by God in communicating His Word to us. The first step was revelation which occurred when God spoke to the Bible authors. The
second step was inspiration, that process whereby God guided them in correctly writing or uttering His message.
But now a third step is needed to provide understanding for men and women as they hear God's revealed and
inspired message. This vital step is illumination, that divine process whereby God causes the written revelation to
be understood by the human heart.
  This third step is needed because unsaved man is blinded both by his fallen, fleshly nature (Page 1150—
1 Cor. 2:14) and by Satan himself (Page 1167—2 Cor. 4:3, 4).
  The Person behind this illumination is the Holy Spirit. Just prior to His crucifixion, Christ promised to send the
Holy Spirit, who would illuminate both unsaved people (Page 1083—John 16:8–11) and Christians (Page 1082—
John 14:26; 16:13, 14).
  An important example of the Holy Spirit's using God's Word to illuminate sinners is seen at Pentecost, where
three thousand people are saved after hearing Simon Peter preach about Christ and the Cross (Page 1096—Acts
2:36–41).
  But Christians also need this illumination to help them fully grasp the marvelous message in God's Word. Paul
tells us that the Holy Spirit will show these tremendous truths to us as we read the Scriptures (Page 1150—1 Cor.
2:10; Page1167—2 Cor. 4:6).
  Now turn to Page 474—Neh. 8:9: God's Word Convicts.

Whoever touches her ^Rwill not ^Tgo unpunished.   Prov. 16:5 · *be innocent*
30 Men do not despise a thief if he steals
To satisfy himself when he is hungry;
31 But when he is found, he must ^Rrepay
sevenfold;
He must give all the ^Asubstance of his
house.   Ex. 22:1-4 · *wealth*
32 The one who commits adultery with a
woman is lacking ^Tsense;   *heart*
He who would destroy himself does it.
33 Wounds and disgrace he will find,
And his reproach will not be blotted
out.
34 For^Rjealousy enrages a man,   Prov. 27:4
And he will not spare in the^Rday of vengeance.   Prov. 11:4
35 He will not accept any ransom,
Nor will he be ^Tcontent though you give
many ^Tgifts.   *willing · bribes*

CHAPTER 7

MY son,^Rkeep my words,
And treasure my commandments
within you.   Prov. 2:1; 6:20
2 ^RKeep my commandments and live,
And my^Tteaching as the ^Aapple of your
eye.   Prov. 4:4 · *law · pupil*
3 ^RBind them on your fingers;   Deut. 6:8
Write them on the tablet of your heart.
4 Say to wisdom, "You are my sister,"
And call understanding *your* intimate
friend;
5 That they may keep you from an ^Tadul-
teress,
From the foreigner who ^Tflatters with
her words.   *strange woman · is smooth*

6 For at the window of my house
I looked out through my lattice,
7 And I saw among the^Tnaive,   *simple ones*
I discerned among the^Tyouths,   *sons*
A young man lacking ^Tsense,   *heart*
8 Passing through the street near ^Rher
corner;   Prov. 7:12
And he takes the way^Tto her house,
9 In the twilight, in the ^Tevening,
In the middle of the night and *in* the
darkness.   *evening of the day*
10 And behold, a woman *comes* to meet
him,
^RDressed as a harlot and cunning of
heart.   Gen. 38:14, 15; 1 Tim. 2:9
11 She is boisterous and rebellious;
Her feet do not remain at home;
12 *She is* now in the streets, now^Rin the
squares,   Prov. 9:14
And^Rlurks by every corner.   Prov. 23:28
13 So she seizes him and kisses him,
^TAnd with a brazen face she says to
him: *She makes bold her face and says*
14 "I was due to offer^Rpeace offerings;
Today I have paid my vows.   Lev. 7:11
15 "Therefore I have come out to meet you,

To seek your presence earnestly, and I
have found you.
16 "I have spread my couch with ^Rcover-
ings,   Prov. 31:22
With colored^Rlinens of Egypt.   Is. 19:9
17 "I have sprinkled my bed
With myrrh, aloes and cinnamon.
18 "Come, let us drink our fill of love until
morning;
Let us delight ourselves with caresses.
19 "For^Tthe man is not at home, *my husband*
He has gone on a long journey;
20 He has taken a bag of money with him,
At full moon he will come home."
21 With her many persuasions she entices
him;
With her ^Tflattering^R lips she seduces
him.   *smooth* · Prov. 5:3; 6:24
22 Suddenly he follows her,
As an ox goes to the slaughter,
Or as *one in* fetters to the discipline of
a fool,
23 Until an arrow pierces through his liver;
As a^Tbird hastens to the snare,
So he does not know that it *will cost
him* his life.   Eccl. 9:12

24 Now therefore, *my* sons,^Rlisten to me,
And pay attention to the words of my
mouth.   Prov. 5:7
25 Do not let your heart^Tturn aside to her
ways,
Do not stray into her paths.   Prov. 5:8
26 For many are the ^Tvictims she has cast
down,   *mortally wounded*
And numerous are all her slain.
27 Her house is the way to Sheol,
Descending to the chambers of death.

CHAPTER 8

Praise of Wisdom

DOES not^Rwisdom call,   Prov. 1:20, 21; 8:1-3
And understanding lift up her voice?
2 On top of^Rthe heights beside the way,
Where the paths meet, she takes her
stand;   Prov. 9:3, 14
3 Beside the^Rgates, at the opening to the
city,
At the entrance of the doors, she cries
out: Job 29:7
4 "To you, O men, I call,
And my voice is to the sons of men.
5 "O ^Tnaive ones, discern^Tprudence;   *simple*
And, O fools, discern^Twisdom.   *heart*
6 "Listen, for I shall speak^Tnoble things;
And the opening of my lips *will pro-
duce* right things.   Prov. 22:20
7 "For my^Tmouth will utter truth;
And wickedness is an abomination to
my lips.   Ps. 37:30; John 8:14; Rom. 15:8
8 "All the utterances of my mouth are in
righteousness;
There is nothing^Rcrooked or perverted
in them.   Deut. 32:5; Prov. 2:15

9 "They are all [R]straightforward to him who understands,
And right to those who [R]find knowledge.   [Prov. 14:6] • Prov. 3:13

10 "Take my [R]instruction, and not silver,
And knowledge rather than choicest gold.   Prov. 3:14, 15; 8:19

11 "For wisdom is better than jewels;
And [a]all desirable things can not compare with her.   corals • Prov. 3:15

12 "I, wisdom, dwell with prudence,
And I find knowledge and discretion.

13 "The fear of the LORD is to hate evil;
Pride and arrogance and the evil way,
And the perverted mouth, I hate.

14 "Counsel is mine and sound wisdom;
I am understanding, power is mine.

15 "By me [R]kings reign,   2 Chr. 1:10; Prov. 29:4
And rulers decree justice.

16 "By me princes rule, and nobles,
All who judge rightly.

17 "I [R]love those who love me;   [1 Sam. 2:30]
And [R]those who diligently seek me will find me.   Prov. 2:4, 5; John 7:37

18 "Riches and honor are with me,
Enduring wealth and righteousness.

19 "My fruit is [R]better than gold, even pure gold,   Job 28:15; Prov. 3:14
And my yield than choicest silver.

20 "I walk in the way of righteousness,
In the midst of the paths of justice,

21 To endow those who love me with wealth,
That I may fill their treasuries.

22 "The LORD possessed me [R]at the beginning of His way,   Ps. 104:24; Prov. 3:19
Before His works [A]of old.   from then

23 "From everlasting I was [A]established,
From the beginning, from the earliest times of the earth.   consecrated

24 "When there were no [R]depths I was [A]brought forth,
When there were no springs abounding with water.   Gen. 1:2; Ex. 15:5 • born

25 "Before the mountains were settled,
Before the hills I was brought forth;

26 While He had not yet made the earth and the [A]fields,   outside places
Nor the first dust of the world.

27 "When He [R]established the heavens, I was there,
When [R]He inscribed a circle on the face of the deep,   Prov. 3:19 • Job 26:10

28 When He made firm the skies above,
When the springs of the deep became [A]fixed,   strong

29 When [R]He set for the sea its boundary,
So that the water should not transgress His [A]command,   Job 38:10 • mouth
When He marked out [R]the foundations of the earth;   Job 38:6; Ps. 104:5

30 Then [R]I was beside Him, as a master workman,   [John 1:2, 3]
And I was daily His delight,
[A]Rejoicing always before Him,   Playing

31 [A]Rejoicing in the world, His earth,
And having [A]my delight in the sons of men.   Playing • Ps. 16:3; John 13:1

32 "Now therefore, O sons, [R]listen to me,
For [R]blessed are they who keep my ways.   Prov. 5:7; 7:24 • Ps. 119:1, 2

33 "Heed [R]instruction and be wise,
And do not neglect it.   Prov. 4:1

34 "Blessed [R]is the man who listens to me,
Watching daily at my gates,
Waiting at my doorposts.   [Prov. 3:13, 18]

35 "For he who finds me finds life,
And obtains favor from the LORD.

36 "But he who [A]sins against me [R]injures himself;   misses me • Prov. 1:31, 32
All those who hate me love death."

CHAPTER 9

W ISDOM has [R]built her house,   [1 Pet. 2:5]
She has hewn out her seven pillars;

2 She has [R]prepared her food, she has [R]mixed her wine;   Matt. 22:4 • Song 8:2
She has also set her table;

3 She has [a]sent out her maidens, she [R]calls
From the [R]tops of the heights of the city: Ps. 68:11 • Prov. 8:1, 2 • Prov. 9:14

4 "Whoever [R]is [a]naive, let him turn in here!"   Prov. 8:5; 9:16 • simple
To him who [R]lacks [T]understanding she says,   Prov. 6:32 • heart

5 "Come, [a]eat of my food,   Song 5:1; Is. 55:1
And drink of the wine I have mixed.

6 "Forsake [a]your folly and [R]live,
And proceed in the way of understanding."   Forsake the simple ones • Prov. 8:35

7 He who [R]corrects a scoffer gets dishonor for himself,   Prov. 23:9
And he who reproves a wicked man gets [T]insults for himself.   a blemish

8 [R]Do not reprove a scoffer, lest he hate you,   Prov. 15:12; Matt. 7:6
[R]Reprove a wise man, and he will love you.   Ps. 141:5; [Prov. 10:8]

9 Give instruction to a wise man, and he will be still wiser,
Teach a righteous man, and he will [R]increase his learning.   Prov. 1:5

10 The [R]fear of the LORD is the beginning of wisdom,   Job 28:28; Ps. 111:10; Prov. 1:7
And the knowledge of the Holy One is understanding.

11 For by me your days will be multiplied,
And years of life will be added to you.

12 If you are wise, you are wise [R]for yourself,   Job 22:2; Prov. 14:14
And if you scoff, you alone will bear it.

Foolish Woman

13 The woman of folly is boisterous,
She is [T]naive, and knows nothing.   simple

14 And she sits at the doorway of her house,

On a seat by the high places of the city,
15 Calling to those who pass by,
Who are making their paths straight:
16 "Whoever is naive, let him turn in here,"
And to him who lacks understanding
she says,   Prov. 9:4 • simple • heart
17 "Stolen water is sweet;
And bread *eaten* in secret is pleasant."
18 But he does not know that the dead are
there,
That her guests are in the depths of
Sheol.   departed spirits • Prov. 7:27

CHAPTER 10

*Proverbs Contrasting
the Godly and the Wicked*

THE proverbs of Solomon.   Prov. 1:1
A wise son makes a father glad,
But a foolish son is a grief to his
mother.   Prov. 15:20; 29:3 • Prov. 17:25
2 Ill-gotten gains do not profit,   Ps. 49:7
But righteousness delivers from death.
3 The LORD will not allow the righteous
to hunger,   soul of the righteous
But He will thrust *aside* the craving of
the wicked.   Ps. 112:10; Prov. 28:9
4 Poor is he who works with a negligent
hand,
But the hand of the diligent makes rich.
5 He who gathers in summer is a son
who acts wisely,
But he who sleeps in harvest is a son
who acts shamefully.
6 Blessings are on the head of the righteous,
But the mouth of the wicked conceals
violence.   Prov. 28:20 • Prov. 10:11
7 The memory of the righteous is
blessed,   Ps. 112:6
But the name of the wicked will rot.
8 The wise of heart will receive commands,   Prov. 9:8; Matt. 7:24
But a babbling fool will be thrown
down.   the foolish of lips
9 He who walks in integrity walks securely,   Ps. 23:4; Prov. 3:23; 28:18
But he who perverts his ways will be
found out.   Prov. 26:26; Matt. 10:26
10 He who winks the eye causes trouble,
And a babbling fool will be thrown
down.   Ps. 35:19 • the foolish of lips
11 The mouth of the righteous is a fountain of life,   Ps. 37:30; Prov. 13:14; 18:4
But the mouth of the wicked conceals
violence.   Prov. 10:6
12 Hatred stirs up strife,
But love covers all transgressions.
13 On the lips of the discerning, wisdom is
found,   [Prov. 10:31]
But a rod is for the back of him who
lacks understanding.   heart
14 Wise men store up knowledge,
But with the mouth of the foolish, ruin
is at hand. Prov. 9:9 • Prov. 10:8, 10; 13:3
15 The rich man's wealth is his fortress,

The ruin of the poor is their poverty.
16 The wages of the righteous is life, *work*
The income of the wicked, punishment.
17 He is *on* the path of life who heeds instruction,
But he who forsakes reproof goes
astray.   Prov. 6:23
18 He who conceals hatred *has* lying lips,
And he who spreads slander is a fool.
19 When there are many words, transgression is unavoidable,   Job 11:2
But he who restrains his lips is wise.
20 The tongue of the righteous is *as*
choice silver,   Prov. 8:19
The heart of the wicked is *worth* little.
21 The lips of the righteous feed many,
But fools die for lack of understanding.
22 It is the blessing of the LORD that
makes rich,   Gen. 24:35; Deut. 8:18
And He adds no sorrow to it.
23 Doing wickedness is like sport to a
fool;
And *so is* wisdom to a man of understanding.   Prov. 2:14; 15:21
24 What the wicked fears will come upon
him,   Job 15:21; Prov. 1:27; Is. 66:4
And the desire of the righteous will be
granted.   Ps. 145:19; [Matt. 5:6]
25 When the whirlwind passes, the
wicked is no more, Job 21:18; Ps. 58:9
But the righteous *has* an everlasting
foundation.   Ps. 15:5; Prov. 12:3
26 Like vinegar to the teeth and smoke to
the eyes,
So is the lazy one to those who send
him.   Prov. 26:6
27 The fear of the LORD prolongs life,
But the years of the wicked will be
shortened.   Prov. 3:2 • days • Ps. 55:23
28 The hope of the righteous is gladness,
But the expectation of the wicked perishes.   Prov. 11:23 • Job 8:13; 11:20
29 The way of the LORD is a stronghold to
the upright,   Prov. 13:6
But ruin to the workers of iniquity.
30 The righteous will never be shaken,
But the wicked will not dwell in the
land.   Ps. 37:29; 125:1 • Prov. 2:22
31 The mouth of the righteous flows with
wisdom,
But the perverted tongue will be cut
out. [Ps. 37:30; Prov. 10:13] • Prov. 17:20
32 The lips of the righteous bring forth
what is acceptable,
But the mouth of the wicked, what is
perverted.   Eccl. 12:10 • Prov. 2:12; 6:12

CHAPTER 11

A FALSE balance is an abomination to
the LORD, Lev. 19:35, 36; Deut. 25:13-16
But a just weight is His delight.
2 When pride comes, then comes dishonor,   Prov. 16:18; 18:12; 29:23
But with the humble is wisdom.

3 The [R]integrity of the upright will guide them, Prov. 13:6
But the [R]falseness of the treacherous will destroy them. Prov. 19:3; 22:12
4 [R]Riches do not profit in the day of wrath, Prov. 10:2; Ezek. 7:19
But righteousness delivers from death.
5 The [R]righteousness of the blameless will smooth his way,
But [R]the wicked will fall by his own wickedness. Prov. 3:6 • Prov. 5:22
6 The righteousness of the upright will deliver them,
But the treacherous will [R]be caught by *their own* greed. Ps. 7:15, 16; 9:15
7 When a wicked man dies, *his* [R]expectation will perish, [Prov. 10:28]
And the hope of strong men perishes.
8 The righteous is delivered from trouble,
But the wicked [T]takes his place. *enters*
9 With *his* [R]mouth the godless man destroys his neighbor, Prov. 16:29
But through knowledge the [R]righteous will be delivered. Prov. 11:6
10 When it [R]goes well with the righteous, the city rejoices,
And when the wicked perish, there is glad shouting. Prov. 28:12
11 By the blessing of the upright a city is exalted,
But by the mouth of the wicked it is torn down.
12 He [T]who despises his neighbor lacks sense,
But a man of understanding keeps silent. *heart*
13 He [R]who goes about as a talebearer reveals secrets, Lev. 19:16; Prov. 20:19
But he who is [T]trustworthy [R]conceals a matter. *faithful of spirit* • Prov. 19:11
14 Where there is no [R]guidance, the people fall, Prov. 15:22; 20:18; 24:6
But in abundance of counselors there is [T]victory. *deliverance*
15 He who is [R]surety for a stranger will surely suffer for it, Prov. 6:1; 27:13
But he who hates going surety is safe.
16 A gracious woman attains honor,
And violent men attain riches.
17 The merciful man does himself good,
But the cruel man does himself harm.
18 The wicked earns deceptive wages,
But he who [R]sows righteousness *gets a* true reward. Hos. 10:12; [Gal. 6:8, 9]
19 He who is steadfast in [T]righteousness *will attain* to life, Prov. 10:16; 12:28
And [R]he who pursues evil *will bring about* his own death. Prov. 21:16
20 The perverse in heart are an abomination to the LORD,
But the [R]blameless in *their* [T]walk are His [R]delight. Ps. 119:1 • *way* • 1 Chr. 29:17
21 [T]Assuredly, the evil man will not go unpunished, *Hand to hand*

But the [T]descendants of the righteous will be delivered. *seed*
22 As a [R]ring of gold in a swine's snout,
So *is* a beautiful woman who lacks [1]discretion. Gen. 24:47
23 The desire of the righteous is only good,
But the [R]expectation of the wicked is wrath. Prov. 10:28; Rom. 2:8, 9
24 There is one who scatters, yet increases all the more,
And there is one who withholds what is justly due, but *it results* only in want.
25 The [T]generous man will be [T]prosperous,
And he who waters will himself be watered. *soul of blessing* • *made fat*
26 He who withholds grain, the [R]people will curse him, Prov. 24:24
But [R]blessing will be on the head of him who [R]sells *it*. Job 29:13 • Gen. 42:6
27 He who diligently seeks good seeks favor,
But [R]he who searches after evil, it will come to him. Esth. 7:10; Ps. 7:15, 16
28 He who [T]trusts in his riches will fall,
But [R]the righteous will flourish like the green leaf. Ps. 49:6 • Ps. 1:3; 92:12
29 He who [T]troubles his own house will [R]inherit wind, Prov. 15:27 • Eccl. 5:16
And [R]the foolish will be servant to the wisehearted. Prov. 14:19
30 The fruit of the righteous is [R]a tree of life, Prov. 3:18
And he who is wise [T]wins souls. *takes*
31 If [T]the righteous will be rewarded in the earth, 2 Sam. 22:21, 25; Prov. 13:21
How much more the wicked and the sinner!

CHAPTER 12

WHOEVER loves [A]discipline loves knowledge, *instruction*
But he who hates reproof is stupid.
2 A [R]good man will obtain favor from the LORD, Prov. 3:4; 8:35
But He will condemn a man [T]who devises evil. *of evil devices*
3 A man will [T]not be established by wickedness,
But the root of the [R]righteous will not be moved. [Prov. 11:5] • [Prov. 10:25]
4 An [A]excellent [R]wife is the crown of her husband, *virtuous* • Prov. 31:11
But she who shames *him* is as [R]rottenness in his bones. Prov. 14:30
5 The thoughts of the righteous are just,
But the counsels of the wicked are deceitful.
6 The [R]words of the wicked lie in wait for blood,
But the [R]mouth of the upright will deliver them. Prov. 11:16 • Prov. 14:3
7 The [R]wicked are overthrown and are no more, Job 34:25; Prov. 10:25

[1] Lit., *taste*

But the ᴿhouse of the righteous will
stand.   [Matt. 7:24–27]

8 A man will be praised according to his
insight,
But one of perverse ᵀmind will be despised.   *heart*

9 Better is he who is lightly esteemed
and has a servant,
Than he who honors himself and lacks
bread.

10 A ᴿrighteous man has regard for the life
of his beast,
But the compassion of the wicked is
cruel.   Deut. 25:4

11 Heᴿwho tills his land will have plenty of
bread,
But he who pursues vain *things* lacks
ᵀsense.   Prov. 28:19 • *heart*

12 The ᴿwicked desires the ᵀbooty of evil
men,
But the root of the righteous ᴿyields
fruit.   Prov. 21:10 • *net* • Prov. 11:30

13 An evil man is ensnared by the transgression of his lips,
But the ᴿrighteous will escape from
trouble.   Prov. 11:8; 21:23; [2 Pet. 2:9]

14 A man will be satisfied with good by
the fruit of his ᵀwords,   *mouth*
And the ᵈdeeds of a man's hands will
return to him.   Job 34:11; Prov. 1:31

15 The ᴿway of a fool is right in his own
eyes,
But a wise man is he who listens to
counsel.   [Prov. 14:12; 16:2; 21:2]

16 A fool's vexation is known at once,
But a prudent man conceals dishonor.

17 He who ᵀspeaks truth tells what is right,
But a false witness, deceit.   *breathes*

18 There is one who ᴿspeaks rashly like the
thrusts of a sword,
But the ᴿtongue of the wise brings healing.   Ps. 57:4 • Prov. 4:22; 15:4

19 Truthful lips will be established forever,
But a ᴿlying tongue is only for a moment.   [Ps. 52:4, 5]; Prov. 19:9

20 Deceit is in the heart of those who devise evil,
But counselors of peace have joy.

21 No harm befalls the righteous,
But the wicked are filled with trouble.

22 ᴿLying lips are an abomination to the
Lord,
But those who deal faithfully are His
delight.   Rev. 22:15

23 A prudent man conceals knowledge,
But the heart of fools proclaims folly.

24 The hand of the diligent will rule,
But the ᵈslack *hand* will be ᴿput to forced
labor.   *slackness* • Gen. 49:15

25 ᴿAnxiety in the heart of a man weighs it
down,   Prov. 15:13
But a ᴿgood word makes it glad.   Is. 50:4

26 The righteous is a guide to his neighbor,

But the way of the wicked leads them
ᵀastray.

27 A ᵀslothful man does not ᴬroast his prey,
But the precious possession of a man *is*
diligence.   *slackness • catch*

28 In the way of righteousness is life,
And in *its* pathway there is no death.

CHAPTER 13

A ᴿWISE son *accepts his* father's discipline,   Prov. 10:1; 15:20
But a scoffer does not listen to rebuke.

2 From the fruit of a man's mouth he ᵀen-
joysᴿgood,   *eats* • Prov. 12:14
But the ᵀdesire of the treacherous is ᴿviolence.   *soul* • Prov. 1:31; Hos. 10:13

3 The one who ᴿguards his mouth preserves his life;   Prov. 18:21; 21:23
The one whoᴿopens wide his lipsᵀcomes
to ruin.   Prov. 18:7; 20:19 • *ruin is his*

4 The soul of the sluggard craves and
gets nothing,
But the soul of the diligent is made fat.

5 A righteous manᴿhates falsehood,
But a wicked man ᴿacts disgustingly
and shamefully.   Col. 3:9 • Prov. 3:35

6 Righteousness ᴿguards the one whose
way is blameless,   Prov. 11:3
But wickedness subverts the sinner.

7 There is one who ᴿpretends to be rich,
but has nothing;   [Luke 12:20, 21]
Another ᵀpretends to be poor, but has
great wealth.   *impoverishes himself*

8 The ransom of a man's life is his riches,
But the poor hears no rebuke.

9 The light of the righteous ²rejoices,
But the lamp of the wicked goes out.

10 Through presumption ᵀcomes nothing
but strife,
But with those who receive counsel is
wisdom.   *gives*

11 Wealth *obtained* by ᵀfraud dwindles,
But the one who gathers by labor increases *it.*   *vanity*

12 Hope deferred makes the heart sick,
But desire fulfilled is a tree of life.

13 The one who despises the word will be
ᵀin debt to it,   *pledged to it*
But the one who fears the commandment will be ᴿrewarded.   Prov. 13:21

14 The ᴬteaching of the wise is a ᴿfountain
of life,   *law* • Prov. 10:11; 14:27
To turn aside from the snares of death.

15 Good understanding produces favor,
But the way of the treacherous is hard.

16 Every ᴿprudent man acts with knowledge,   Prov. 12:23
But a fool ᵀdisplays folly.   *spreads out*

17 A wicked messenger falls into adversity,
But a faithful envoy *brings* healing.

² I.e., shines brightly

18 Poverty and shame *will come* to him
    who ^Rneglects discipline,
    But he who regards reproof will be
    honored.   Prov. 15:5, 32 • *instruction*
19 Desire realized is sweet to the soul,
    But it is an abomination to fools to de-
    part from evil.
20 ^RHe who walks with wise men will be
    wise,
    But the companion of fools will suffer
    harm.   Prov. 2:20; 15:31
21 ^RAdversity pursues sinners,   Ps. 32:10
    But the ^Rrighteous will be rewarded
    with prosperity.   Prov. 11:31; 13:13
22 A good man leaves an inheritance to
    his ^Rchildren's children,   *sons' sons*
    And the ^Rwealth of the sinner is stored
    up for the righteous.   Job 27:16, 17
23 ^RAbundant food *is in* the fallow ground
    of the poor,   Prov. 12:11
    But it is swept away by injustice.
24 He who ^Rspares his rod hates his son,
    But he who loves him ^Rdisciplines him
    diligently.   Prov. 19:18 • Deut. 8:5
25 The ^Rrighteous has enough to satisfy his
    appetite,   Ps. 34:10; 103:5; 132:15
    But the stomach of the wicked is in
    want.

CHAPTER 14

THE ^Rwise woman builds her house,
    But the foolish tears it down with her
    own hands.   Ruth 4:11; Prov. 31:10-27
2 He who ^Rwalks in his uprightness fears
    the LORD,
    But he who is ^Rcrooked in his ways de-
    spises Him.   Prov. 19:1; 28:6 • Prov. 2:15
3 In the mouth of the foolish is a rod ^Tfor
    his back,
    But ^Rthe lips of the wise will preserve
    them.   *of pride* • Prov. 12:6
4 Where no oxen are, the manger is
    clean,
    But much increase *comes* by the
    strength of the ox.
5 A ^Rfaithful witness will not lie,   Rev. 1:5
    But a ^Rfalse witness speaks lies.   Ex. 23:1
6 A scoffer seeks wisdom, and *finds*
    none,
    But knowledge is easy to him who has
    understanding.
7 Leave the ^Rpresence of a fool,   ^T
    Or you will not ^Tdiscern ^Twords of
    knowledge.   Prov. 23:9 • *know* • *lips*
8 The wisdom of the prudent is to under-
    stand his way,
    But the folly of fools is deceit.
9 Fools mock at ^Rsin,
    But ^Ramong the upright there is ^Agood
    will.   *guilt* • Prov. 3:34 • *the favor of God*
10 The heart knows its own bitterness,
    And a stranger does not share its joy.

11 The ^Rhouse of the wicked will be de-
    stroyed,   Job 8:15
    But the tent of the upright will flourish.
12 There ^Ris a way *which seems* right to a
    man,   Prov. 12:15; 16:25
    But its end is the way of death.
13 Even in laughter the heart may be in
    pain,
    And the end of joy may be grief.
14 The backslider in heart will have his ^Rfill
    of his own ways,   Prov. 1:31; 12:21
    But a good man will ^R*be satisfied* ^Twith
    his.   Prov. 12:14; 18:20 • *from himself*
15 The ^Tnaive believes everything,
    But the prudent man considers his
    steps.   *simple*
16 A wise man ^Ris cautious and ^Rturns away
    from evil,   *fears* • Job 28:28; Ps. 34:14
    But a fool is arrogant and careless.
17 A quick-tempered man acts foolishly,
    And a man of evil devices is hated.
18 The ^Tnaive inherit folly,
    But the prudent are crowned with
    knowledge.   *simple*
19 The ^Revil will bow down before the
    good,
    And the wicked at the gates of the
    righteous.   1 Sam. 2:36; Prov. 11:29
20 The poor is hated even by his neighbor,
    But those who love the rich are many.
21 He who ^Rdespises his neighbor sins,
    But ^Rhappy is he who is gracious to the
    ^Tpoor.   Prov. 11:12 • Ps. 41:1 • *afflicted*
22 Will they not go astray who ^Rdevise
    evil?   Ps. 36:4; Prov. 3:29; 12:2; Mic. 2:1
    But kindness and truth *will be to* those
    who devise good.
23 In all labor there is profit,
    But mere talk *leads* only to poverty.
24 The crown of the wise is their riches,
    But the folly of fools is foolishness.
25 A truthful witness saves lives,
    But he who speaks lies is treacherous.
26 In the ³fear ^Rof the LORD there is strong
    confidence,   Prov. 18:10; 19:23; Is. 33:6
    And ^Ahis children will have refuge.   *His*
27 The ³fear of the LORD is a fountain of
    life,
    That one may avoid the snares of
    death.
28 In a multitude of people is a king's
    glory,
    But in the dearth of people is a prince's
    ruin.
29 He who is ^Rslow to anger has great un-
    derstanding,   Prov. 16:32; 19:11; Eccl. 7:9
    But he who is ^Tquick-tempered exalts
    folly.   *short of spirit*
30 A tranquil heart is life to the body,
    But passion is rottenness to the bones.
31 He ^Rwho oppresses the poor reproaches
    his Maker,   Prov. 17:5; Matt. 25:40
    But he who is gracious to the needy
    honors Him.

³ Or, *reverence*

32 The wicked is ^Rthrust down by his ^Awrongdoing,   Prov. 6:15; 24:16 · *calamity*
But the ^Rrighteous has a refuge when he dies.   Gen. 49:18; [Ps. 16:11; 17:15; 37:37]

33 Wisdom rests in the heart of one who has understanding,
But in the ^Tbosom of fools it is made known.   *midst*

34 Righteousness exalts a nation,
But sin is a disgrace to *any* people.

35 The king's favor is toward a ^Rservant who acts wisely,
But his anger is toward him who acts shamefully.   Matt. 24:45, 47; 25:21, 23

CHAPTER 15

A GENTLE answer turns away wrath,
But a harsh word stirs up anger.

2 The ^Rtongue of the wise makes knowledge ^Tacceptable,   Prov. 15:7 · *good*
But the mouth of fools spouts folly.

3 The ^Reyes of the LORD are in every place,   2 Chr. 16:9; Job 31:4; Jer. 16:17
Watching the evil and the good.

4 A soothing tongue is a tree of life,
But perversion in it crushes the spirit.

5 A fool rejects his father's discipline,
But he who regards reproof is prudent.

6 Much wealth is *in* the house of the ^Rrighteous,
But trouble is in the income of the wicked.   Prov. 8:21

7 The lips of the wise spread knowledge,
But the hearts of fools are not so.

8 The ^Rsacrifice of the wicked is an abomination to the LORD,
But ^Rthe prayer of the upright is His delight.   Eccl. 5:1; Is.1:11 · Prov. 15:29

9 The way of the wicked is an abomination to the LORD,
But He loves him who ^Rpursues righteousness.   1 Tim. 6:11

10 Stern discipline is for him who forsakes the way;
He who hates reproof will die.

11 ^TSheol ^Rand Abaddon *lie open* before the LORD,   the nether world · Job 26:6
How much more the hearts of men!

12 A ^Rscoffer does not love one who reproves him,   Prov. 13:1; Amos 5:10
He will not go to the wise.

13 A joyful heart makes a ^Tcheerful face,
But ^Twhen the heart is sad, the spirit is broken.   *good · in sadness of heart*

14 The ^Rmind of the intelligent seeks knowledge,   Prov. 18:15
But the mouth of fools feeds on folly.

15 All the days of the afflicted are bad,
But a ^Tcheerful heart *has* a continual feast.   *good*

16 ^RBetter is a little with the fear of the LORD,   Ps. 37:16; Prov. 16:8; Eccl. 4:6
Than great treasure and turmoil with it.

17 ^RBetter is a ^Adish of ^Avegetables where love is,   Prov. 17:1 · *portion · herbs*
Than a fattened ox and hatred with it.

18 A ^Rhot-tempered man stirs up strife,
But the ^Rslow to anger pacifies contention.   Prov. 16:28; 26:21 · Prov. 14:29

19 The way of the sluggard is as a hedge of thorns,
But the path of the upright is a highway.

20 A wise son makes a father glad,
But a foolish man despises his mother.

21 Folly is joy to him who lacks ^Tsense,
But a man of understanding ^Rwalks straight.   *heart* · Prov. 14:8; Eph. 5:15

22 Without consultation, plans are frustrated,
But with many counselors they ^Asucceed.   *are established*

23 A man has joy in an apt answer,
And how delightful is a timely word!

24 The ^Rpath of life *leads* upward for the wise,
That he may keep away from ^TSheol below.   Prov. 4:18 · *the nether world*

25 The LORD will ^Rtear down the house of the proud,   Prov. 12:7; 14:11
But He will ^Restablish the boundary of the ^Rwidow.   Prov. 23:10 · Ps. 68:5

26 Evil plans are an abomination to the LORD,
But pleasant words are pure.

27 He who ^Rprofits illicitly troubles his own house,   Prov. 1:19; 28:25; 1 Tim. 6:10
But he who hates bribes will live.

28 The heart of the righteous ^Rponders how to answer,   1 Pet. 3:15
But the ^Rmouth of the wicked pours out evil things.   Prov. 10:32; 15:2

29 The LORD is ^Rfar from the wicked,
But He ^Rhears the prayer of the righteous.   Ps. 18:41 · Ps. 145:18, 19

30 Bright eyes gladden the heart;
Good news puts fat on the bones.

31 He whose ear listens to the life-giving reproof
Will dwell among the wise.

32 He who ^Rneglects discipline ^Rdespises himself,   Prov. 1:7; 8:33 · Prov. 8:36
But he who ^Rlistens to reproof acquires ^Tunderstanding.   Prov. 15:5 · *heart*

33 The ^Afear of the LORD is the instruction for wisdom,   *reverence*
And before honor *comes* humility.

CHAPTER 16

*Proverbs Encouraging
Godly Lives*

THE ^Rplans of the heart belong to man,
But the answer of the tongue is from the LORD.   Prov. 16:9; 19:21

2 All the ways of a man are clean in his own sight,
But the LORD weighs the motives.

3 Commit your works to the LORD,
And your plans will be established.

4 The LORD^Rhas made everything for ^its
   own purpose,   Gen. 1:31 • *His*
   Even the wicked for the day of evil.
5 Everyone who is proud in heart is an
   abomination to the LORD;
   Assuredly, he will not be unpunished.
6 By^Rlovingkindness and truth iniquity is
   atoned for,   Dan. 4:27; Luke 11:41
   And by the^fear^Rof the LORD one keeps
   away from evil.   *reverence* • Prov. 8:13
7 When a man's ways are pleasing to the
   LORD,
   He^Rmakes even his enemies to be at
   peace with him.   Gen. 33:4
8 Better is a little with righteousness
   Than great income with injustice.
9 The mind of man plans his way,
   But^Rthe LORD directs his steps. Ps. 37:23
10 A divine ^decision is in the lips of the
    king;   1 Kin. 3:28
    His mouth should not err in judgment.
11 A^just balance and scales belong to the
    LORD;
    All the ^weights of the bag are His ^con-
    cern.   [Prov. 11:1] • *stones* • *work*
12 It is an abomination for kings to com-
    mit wickedness,
    For a ^throne is established on right-
    eousness.   Prov. 25:5
13 Righteous lips are the delight of kings,
    And he who speaks right is loved.
14 The wrath of a king is *as* messengers of
    death,
    But a wise man will appease it.
15 In the light of a king's face is life,
    And his favor is like a cloud with the
    ^spring^rain.   *latter* • Job 29:23
16 How much^Rbetter it is to get wisdom
    than gold!
    And to get understanding is to be cho-
    sen above silver.   Prov. 8:10, 19
17 The^Rhighway of the upright is to depart
    from evil;
    He who watches his way preserves his
    ^life.   Is. 35:8 • *soul*
18 ^RPride *goes* before destruction, Prov. 11:2
    And a haughty spirit before stumbling.
19 It is better to be of a^humble spirit with
    the lowly,   Prov. 3:34; 29:23; Is. 57:15

Than to divide the spoil with the proud.
20 He who gives attention to the word
    shall^Rfind good,   Prov. 19:8
    And ^Rblessed is he who trusts in the
    LORD.   Ps. 2:12; 34:8; Jer. 17:7
21 The ^Rwise in heart will be called dis-
    cerning,   Hos. 14:9
    And sweetness of ^speech increases
    ^persuasiveness.   *lips* • *learning*
22 Understanding is a fountain of life to
    him who has it,
    But the discipline of fools is folly.
23 The ^heart of the wise teaches his
    mouth,   Ps. 37:30; Prov. 15:28
    And adds persuasiveness to his lips.
24 ^RPleasant words are a honeycomb,
    Sweet to the soul and^Rhealing to the
    bones.   Ps. 19:10 • Prov. 4:22; 17:22
25 ^RThere is a way *which seems* right to a
    man,   Prov. 12:15; 14:12
    But its end is the way of death.
26 A worker's appetite works for him,
    For his^hunger urges him *on.*   *mouth*
27 A worthless man digs up evil,
    While his words are as a scorching fire.
28 A perverse man spreads strife,
    And a slanderer separates intimate
    friends.
29 A man of violence ^Rentices his neighbor,
    And leads him in a way that is not
    good.   Prov. 1:10; 12:26
30 He who winks his eyes *does so* to de-
    vise perverse things;
    He who compresses his lips brings evil
    to pass.
31 A gray head is a crown of glory;
    It is found in the way of righteousness.
32 He who is slow to anger is better than
    the mighty,
    And he who rules his spirit, than he
    who captures a city.
33 The^Rlot is cast into the lap,   Prov. 18:18
    But its every decision is from the LORD.

CHAPTER 17

B ETTER^R is a dry morsel and quietness
   with it
   Than a house full of ^feasting with
   strife.   Prov. 15:17 • *sacrifices of strife*
2 A servant who acts wisely will rule
   over a son who acts shamefully,

16:3 Commitment—Dedication is the foundation of commitment. Without it the believer is unable to offer God anything else. Paul explains this dedication process in Romans 12:1 and 2. He emphasizes three things. First, it is our body which is to be dedicated as a living sacrifice to God. Second, we are to avoid being conformed to this world, but strive to be transformed by the Word. Finally, by doing this we can discover God's perfect will for our lives.

After the dedication of our bodies, what are we to commit? We are to commit our salvation to God (Page 1223— 2 Tim. 1:12). Second, we are to commit our works (Page 621—Prov. 16:3). Then, our goals in life are to be given to Him (Page 498—Job 5:8; Page 546—Ps. 37:5). It is difficult but vital to commit our suffering experiences to God (Page 1264—1 Pet. 4:19). Our Lord Jesus did this very thing when He was on earth (Page 1262—1 Pet. 2:23). Finally, in the hour of death we can with confidence commit our very souls to God (Page 542—Ps. 31:5). Paul the apostle assures us that any and all such commitments to the Lord will be accepted and honored. See First Corinthians 15:58.

Now turn to Page 1157—1 Cor. 12:1–10: Using Spiritual Gifts.

And will share in the inheritance among brothers.

3 The [R]refining pot is for silver and the furnace for gold,   Prov. 27:21
But [T]the LORD tests hearts.   1 Chr. 29:17

4 An [R]evildoer listens to wicked lips,
A [T]liar pays attention to a destructive tongue.   Prov. 14:15 • *falsehood*

5 He who mocks the [R]poor reproaches his Maker;   [Prov. 14:31]
He who [R]rejoices at calamity will not go unpunished.   Prov. 24:17; Obad. 12

6 [R]Grandchildren are the crown of old men,   Gen. 48:11; Prov. 13:22
And the glory of sons is their fathers.

7 [T]Excellent [R]speech is not fitting for a fool;   *A lip of abundance* • Prov. 24:7
Much less are lying lips to a prince.

8 A [R]bribe is a [T]charm in the sight of its owner;   Prov. 21:14 • *stone of favor*
Wherever he turns, he prospers.

9 He who [R]covers a transgression seeks love,   Prov. 10:12; [James 5:20; 1 Pet. 4:8]
But he who repeats a matter [R]separates intimate friends.   Prov. 16:28

10 A rebuke goes deeper into one who has understanding
Than a hundred blows into a fool.

11 A rebellious man seeks only evil,
So a cruel messenger will be sent against him.

12 Let a [R]man meet a [R]bear robbed of her cubs,   Prov. 29:9 • 2 Sam. 17:8
Rather than a fool in his folly.

13 He who [R]returns evil for good,   Ps. 35:12
Evil will not depart from his house.

14 The beginning of strife is *like* letting out water,
So [R]abandon the quarrel before it breaks out.   [Prov. 20:3; 25:8]

15 He who [R]justifies the wicked, and he who condemns the righteous,
Both of them alike are an abomination to the LORD.   Ex. 23:7; Prov. 18:5; 24:24

16 Why is there a price in the hand of a fool to [R]buy wisdom,   Prov. 23:23
When [T]he has no sense?   *there is no heart*

17 A [R]friend loves at all times,   Ruth 1:16
And a brother is born for adversity.

18 A man lacking in [T]sense pledges,[R]
And becomes surety in the presence of his neighbor.   *heart* • Prov. 6:1

19 He who [R]loves transgression loves strife;
He who [R]raises his door seeks destruction.   Prov. 29:22 • Prov. 16:18; 29:23

20 He who has a crooked [T]mind [R]finds no good,   *heart* • Prov. 24:20
And he who is [R]perverted in his language falls into evil.   James 3:8

21 He who [R]begets a fool *does so* to his sorrow,   Prov. 10:1; 17:25; 19:13
And the father of a fool has no joy.

22 A joyful heart is good medicine,
But a broken spirit dries up the bones.

23 A wicked man receives a [R]bribe from the bosom   Prov. 17:8

To [R]pervert the ways of justice. Ex. 23:8

24 Wisdom is in the presence of the one who [R]has understanding,
But the [R]eyes of a fool are on the ends of the earth.   Eccl. 2:14

25 A foolish son is a grief to his father,
And bitterness to her who bore him.

26 It is also not good to [R]fine the righteous,
Nor to strike the noble for *their* uprightness.   Prov. 17:15; 18:5

27 He who [R]restrains his words [T]has knowledge,   Prov. 10:19; James 1:19 • *knows*
And he who has a [R]cool spirit is a man of understanding.   Prov. 14:29

28 Even a fool, when he [R]keeps silent, is considered wise;
When he closes his lips, he is *counted* prudent.   Job 13:5

CHAPTER 18

HE who separates himself seeks *his own* desire,
He quarrels against all sound wisdom.

2 A fool does not delight in understanding,
But only in revealing his own mind.

3 When a wicked man comes, contempt also comes,
And with dishonor *comes* reproach.

4 The words of a man's mouth are [R]deep waters;
The fountain of wisdom is a bubbling brook.   Prov. 20:5

5 To [R]show partiality to the wicked is not good,   Lev. 19:15; Deut. 1:17; 16:19
Nor to [R]thrust aside the righteous in judgment.   Ex. 23:2, 6; Prov. 17:26; 31:5

6 A fool's lips [T]bring strife,   *come with*
And his mouth calls for blows.

7 A [R]fool's mouth is his ruin,   Ps. 64:8
And his lips are the snare of his soul.

8 The words of a whisperer are like dainty morsels,
And they go down into the [T]innermost parts of the body. *chambers of the belly*

9 He also who is slack in his work
Is brother to him who destroys.

10 The [R]name of the LORD is a [R]strong tower;   Ex. 3:15 • 2 Sam. 22:2, 3, 33
The righteous runs into it and is safe.

11 A [R]rich man's wealth is his strong city,
And like a high wall in his own imagination.   Prov. 10:15

12 [R]Before destruction the heart of man is haughty,   Prov. 11:2; 16:18; 29:23
But humility *goes* before honor.

13 He who [R]gives an answer before he hears,   Prov. 20:25; John 7:51
It is folly and shame to him.

14 The [R]spirit of a man can endure his sickness,   Prov. 17:22
But a broken spirit who can bear?

15 The [T]mind [R]of the prudent acquires knowledge,   *heart* • Prov. 15:14

And the [R]ear of the wise seeks knowledge.   Prov. 15:31

16 A man's gift makes room for him,
And brings him before great men.

17 The first [T]to plead his case *seems* just,
Until [T]another comes and examines
him.   *in his plea • his neighbor*

18 The lot puts an end to contentions,
And decides between the mighty.

19 A brother offended *is harder to be won*
than a strong city,
And contentions are like the bars of a
castle.

20 With the fruit[R] of a man's mouth his
stomach will be satisfied;   Prov. 12:14
[R]He will be satisfied *with* the product of
his lips.   Prov. 14:14

21 [R]Death and life are in the [T]power of the
tongue,   Prov. 12:13; 13:3 • *hand*
And those who love it will eat its fruit.

22 He who finds a wife finds a good thing,
And obtains favor from the LORD.

23 The poor man utters supplications,
But the rich man answers roughly.

24 A man of *many* friends *comes* to [T]ruin,
But there is a friend who sticks closer
than a brother.   *be broken in pieces*

CHAPTER 19

BETTER is a poor man who [R]walks in his
integrity   Ps. 26:11; Prov. 14:2; 20:7
Than he who is perverse in [T]speech and
is a fool.   *his lips*

2 Also it is not good for a person to be
without knowledge,
And he who makes[R]haste with his feet
[T]errs.   Prov. 21:5; 28:20; 29:20 • *sins*

3 The [R]foolishness of man subverts his
way,   [Prov. 11:3]
And his heart rages against the LORD.

4 [R]Wealth adds many friends,
But a poor man is separated from his
friend.   Prov. 14:20

5 A false witness will not go unpunished,
And he who tells lies will not escape.

6 [R]Many will entreat the favor of a [A]generous man,   [Prov. 29:26] • *noble*
And every man is a friend to him who
[R]gives gifts.   Prov. 18:16; 21:14

7 All the brothers of a poor man hate
him;
How much more do his[R]friends go far
from him!   Ps. 38:11
He [R]pursues *them with* words, *but* they
are [T]gone.   Prov. 18:23 • *not*

8 He who gets [T]wisdom loves his own
soul;
He who keeps understanding will[R]find
good.   *heart* • Prov. 16:20

9 A false witness will not go unpunished,
And he who tells lies will perish.

10 Luxury is[R]not fitting for a fool;
Much less for a [R]slave to rule over
princes.   Prov. 17:7; 26:1 • Prov. 30:22

11 A man's [R]discretion makes him slow to
anger,   Prov. 14:29; 16:32
And it is his glory[T]to overlook a transgression.   [Matt. 5:44]; Eph. 4:32

12 The[R]king's wrath is like the roaring of a
lion,   Prov. 16:14
But his favor is like dew on the grass.

13 A [R]foolish son is destruction to his father,   Prov. 17:25
And the [R]contentions of a wife are a
constant dripping.   Prov. 21:9, 19

14 House and wealth are an[R]inheritance
from fathers,   2 Cor. 12:14
But a prudent wife is from the LORD.

15 Laziness casts into a deep sleep,
And an idle man will suffer hunger.

16 He who [R]keeps the commandment
keeps his soul,
But he who[T]is careless of his ways will
die.   Prov. 13:13; 16:17 • *despises*

17 He who[R]is gracious to a poor man lends
to the LORD,   Deut. 15:7, 8; Prov. 14:31
And He will repay him for his [A]good[R]
deed.   *benefits* • Prov. 12:14; Luke 6:38

18 [R]Discipline your son while there is hope,
And do not desire his death.   Prov. 13:24

19 *A man of* great anger shall bear the
penalty,
For if you rescue *him,* you will only
have to do it again.

20 [R]Listen to counsel and accept discipline,
That you may be wise[T]the rest of your
days.   Prov. 4:1; 8:33 • *in your latter end*

21 Many are the[R]plans in a man's heart,
But the [R]counsel of the LORD, it will
stand.   Prov. 16:1, 9 • [Ps. 33:10, 11]

22 What is desirable in a man is his [4]kindness,
And *it is* better to be a poor man than a
liar.

23 The fear of the LORD *leads* to life,
So that one may sleep satisfied, [T]untouched by evil.   *not visited*

24 The [R]sluggard buries his hand [R]in the
dish,   Prov. 26:15 • Matt. 26:23; Mark 14:20
And will not even bring it back to his
mouth.

25 [R]Strike a scoffer and the [T]naive may become shrewd,   Prov. 21:11 • *simple*
But reprove one who has understanding and he will gain knowledge.

26 He[R]who assaults *his* father *and* drives
his mother away   Prov. 28:24
Is a shameful and disgraceful son.

27 Cease listening, my son, to discipline,
And you will stray from the words of
knowledge.

28 A rascally witness makes a mockery of
justice,
And the mouth of the wicked [A]spreads[R]
iniquity.   *swallows* • Job 15:16

29 Judgments are prepared for[R]scoffers,
And blows for the back of fools. Ps. 1:1

[4] Or, *loyalty*

CHAPTER 20

WINE is a mocker, ^Rstrong drink a brawler,
And whoever^Tis intoxicated by it is not wise.   Prov. 31:4; Is. 5:22; 56:12 • *errs*

2 The terror of a king is like the growling of a lion;
He who provokes him to anger ^Tforfeits^R his own life.   *sins against* • Num. 16:38

3 ^TKeeping^Raway from strife is an honor for a man,   *Ceasing* • Gen. 13:7f.
But any fool will ^Tquarrel.   *burst out*

4 The ^Rsluggard does not plow after the autumn,
So he^Tbegs during the harvest and has nothing.   Prov. 13:4; 21:25 • *asks*

5 A plan in the heart of a man is *like* deep water,
But a man of understanding draws it out.

6 Many a man proclaims his own loyalty,
But who can find a trustworthy man?

7 A righteous man who ^Rwalks in his integrity—   Prov. 19:1
How blessed are his sons after him.

8 A king who sits on the throne of justice
^ADisperses all evil with his eyes.   *Sifts*

9 ^RWho can say, "I have cleansed my heart, [1 Kin. 8:46; 2 Chr. 6:36]; Job 14:4
I am pure from my sin"?

10 ^RDiffering weights and differing measures,
Both of them are abominable to the LORD.   Prov. 11:1; 20:23

11 It is by his deeds that a lad ^Tdistinguishes himself   *makes himself known*
If his conduct is pure and right.

12 The hearing ear and the seeing eye,
The LORD has made both of them.

13 ^RDo not love sleep, lest you become poor;   Prov. 6:9, 10; 19:15; 24:33
Open your eyes, *and* you will be satisfied with^Tfood.   *bread*

14 "Bad, bad," says the buyer;
But when he goes his way, then he boasts.

15 There is gold, and an abundance of ^Ajewels;
But the lips of knowledge are a more precious thing.   *corals*

16 Take his garment when he becomes surety for a stranger;
And for foreigners, hold him in pledge.

17 ^RBread obtained by falsehood is sweet to a man,
But afterward his mouth will be filled with gravel.   Prov. 9:17

18 Prepare plans by consultation,
And make war by wise guidance.

19 He who ^Rgoes about as a slanderer reveals secrets,   Prov. 11:13
Therefore do not associate with ^Ta^R gossip.   *one who opens his lips* • Prov. 13:3

20 He who^Tcurses his father or his mother,
His^Rlamp will go out in time of darkness.   Ex. 21:17; Lev. 20:9 • Job 18:5

21 An inheritance gained hurriedly at the beginning,
Will not be blessed in the end.

22 ^RDo not say, "I will repay evil";
^RWait for the LORD, and He will save you.   Prov. 24:29; [Matt. 5:39] • Ps. 27:14

23 ^TDiffering weights are an abomination to the LORD,   *A stone and a stone*
And a^Rfalse scale is not good.   Prov. 11:1

24 ^RMan's steps are *ordained* by the LORD,
How then can man understand his way?   Prov. 16:9

25 It is a snare for a man to say rashly, "It is holy!"
And after the vows to make inquiry.

26 A^Rwise king winnows the wicked,
And ^Tdrives the ^Rthreshing wheel over them.   Prov. 20:8 • *turns* • Is. 28:27

27 The ^Tspirit^R of man is the lamp of the LORD,   *breath* • 1 Cor. 2:11
Searching all the^Tinnermost parts of his being.   *chambers of the body*

28 ^TLoyalty and truth preserve the king,
And he upholds his throne by ^Trighteousness.   *Covenant loyalty*

29 The glory of young men is their strength,
And the^Ahonor^Rof old men is their gray hair.   *splendor* • Prov. 16:31

30 Stripes that wound scour away evil,
And strokes *reach* the innermost parts.

CHAPTER 21

THE king's heart is *like* channels of water in the hand of the LORD;
He turns it wherever He wishes.

2 ^REvery man's way is right in his own eyes,   Prov. 16:2
But the LORD weighs the hearts.

3 To do^Trighteousness and justice
Is desired by the LORD rather than sacrifice.   Prov. 15:8; 1 Sam. 15:22; Hos. 6:6

4 Haughty eyes and a proud heart,
The lamp of the wicked, is sin.

5 The plans of the^Rdiligent *lead* surely to advantage,   Prov. 10:4; 13:4
But everyone ^Rwho is hasty *comes* surely to poverty.   Prov. 28:22

6 The ^Rgetting of treasures by a lying tongue   Prov. 13:11; 20:21
Is a fleeting vapor, the pursuit of death.

7 The violence of the wicked will drag them away,
Because they refuse to act with justice.

8 The way of a guilty man is^Rcrooked,
But as for the pure, his conduct is upright.   Prov. 2:15

9 It is better to live in a corner of a roof,
Than in a house shared with a contentious woman.

10 The soul of the wicked desires evil;
His neighbor finds no favor in his eyes.

11 When the^Rscoffer is punished, the naive becomes wise;   Prov. 19:25

But when the wise is instructed, he receives knowledge.

12 The righteous one considers the house of the wicked,
Turning the [R]wicked to ruin.   Prov. 14:11
13 He who [R]shuts his ear to the cry of the poor   [Matt. 18:30–34]; 1 John 3:17
Will also cry himself and not be [R]answered.   James 2:13
14 A [R]gift in secret subdues anger,
And a bribe in the bosom, strong wrath.   Prov. 18:16; 19:6
15 The execution of justice is joy for the righteous,
But is terror to the workers of iniquity.
16 A man who wanders from the way of understanding
Will rest in the assembly of the dead.
17 He who [R]loves pleasure *will become* a poor man;
He who loves wine and oil will not become rich.   Prov. 23:21
18 The wicked is a [R]ransom for the righteous,[R]
And the [R]treacherous is in the place of the upright.   Is. 43:3 • Prov. 11:8
19 [R]It is better to live in a desert land,
Than with a contentious and vexing woman.   Prov. 21:9
20 There is precious [R]treasure and oil in the dwelling of the wise,   Prov. 8:21; 22:4
But a foolish man swallows it up.
21 He who [R]pursues righteousness and loyalty   Prov. 15:9; Matt. 5:6; 1 Cor. 15:58
Finds life, righteousness and honor.
22 A [R]wise man scales the city of the mighty,   2 Sam. 5:6-9; Prov. 24:5
And brings down the [T]stronghold in which they trust.   *strength of trust*
23 He who [R]guards his mouth and his tongue,   Prov. 12:13; 13:3; 18:21
Guards his soul from troubles.
24 "Proud," "Haughty," [R]"Scoffer," are his names,   Ps. 1:1; Prov. 1:22; 3:34; 24:9
Who acts with [R]insolent pride.   Is. 16:6
25 The [R]desire of the sluggard puts him to death,   [Prov. 13:4]
For his hands refuse to work;

26 All day long he [T]is craving,   *desires desire*
While the righteous [R]gives and does not hold back.   Matt. 5:42; [Eph. 4:28]
27 The [R]sacrifice of the wicked is an abomination,   Prov. 15:8; Is. 66:3
How much more when he brings it with evil intent!
28 A [R]false witness will perish,
But the man who listens *to the truth* will speak forever.   Prov. 19:5, 9
29 A wicked man [T]shows a bold face,
But as for the upright, he makes his way sure.   *makes firm with his face*
30 There is [R]no wisdom and no understanding   Jer. 9:23; Acts 5:38, 39
And no counsel against the LORD.
31 The [R]horse is prepared for the day of battle,   Ps. 20:7; 33:17; Is. 31:1
But victory belongs to the LORD.

CHAPTER 22

A [R]GOOD name is to be more desired than great riches,   [Prov. 10:7]; Eccl. 7:1
Favor is better than silver and gold.
2 The rich and the poor [T]have a common bond,   *meet together*
The LORD is the maker of them all.
3 The [R]prudent sees the evil and hides himself,   Prov. 14:16; 27:12; Is. 26:20
But the [T]naive go on, and are punished for it.   *simple*
4 The reward of humility *and* the [A]fear of the LORD
Are riches, honor and life.   *reverence*
5 [R]Thorns *and* snares are in the way of the perverse;
He who guards himself will be far from them.   Prov. 15:19

6 [R]Train up a child [T]in the way he should go,
Even when he is old he will not depart from it.   [Eph. 6:4] • *according to his way*

7 The [R]rich rules over the poor,
And the borrower *becomes* the lender's slave.   Prov. 18:23; James 2:6

22:6 A Prescription for Rearing Children—This verse reveals two ingredients in the prescription for rearing children: first, the command, "Train up a child in the way he should go"; and second, the promise, "when he is old he will not depart from it."

The command involves three parts:
a. The concept of training—"Train up." This does not denote corporal punishment but rather includes three ideas: *Dedication*—this is the consistent meaning of the word in its other Old Testament occurrences (Page 187—Deut. 20:5; Page 334—1 Kin. 8:63; Page 425—2 Chr. 7:5). Child training must begin with dedication of the child to God; the parent must realize that the child belongs exclusively to God and is given to the parent only as a stewardship. *Instruction*—this is the meaning of this word as it is used in the Jewish writings; the parents are to instruct or cause their children to learn everything essential in pleasing God. *Motivation*—this is the meaning of the word in Arabic, as it is used to describe the action of a midwife who stimulates the palate of the newborn babe so it will take nourishment. Parents are to create a taste or desire within the child so that he is internally motivated (rather than externally compelled) to do what God wants him to do.
b. The recipient of training—"a child." This is one of seven Hebrew words translated by the English word *child* and would better be translated by our word *dependent*. As long as the child is dependent on his parents he is to be the recipient of training, regardless of his age.
c. The content of the training—"in the way he should go." The thought is that at each stage of his development

(continued on next page)

8 He who sows iniquity will reap vanity,
  And the rod of his fury will perish.
9 He who is generous will be blessed,
  For he gives some of his food to the
  poor.   *has a good eye* • [Prov. 19:17]
10 Drive out the scoffer, and contention
   will go out,   Gen. 21:9, 10; Prov. 18:6
   Even strife and dishonor will cease.
11 He who loves purity of heart   Ps. 24:4
   And whose speech is gracious, the king
   is his friend.   *has grace on his lips*
12 The eyes of the LORD preserve knowledge,
   But He overthrows the words of the
   treacherous man.
13 The sluggard says, "There is a lion outside;   Prov. 26:13
   I shall be slain in the streets!"
14 The mouth of an adulteress is a deep
   pit;   *strange woman* • Prov. 2:16; 5:3; 7:5
   He who is cursed of the LORD will fall
   into it.   [Eccl. 7:26] • *there*
15 Foolishness is bound up in the heart of
   a child;
   The rod of discipline will remove it far
   from him.   [Prov. 13:24; 23:14]
16 He who oppresses the poor to make
   much for himself   Eccl. 5:8
   Or who gives to the rich, will only
   come to poverty.   Prov. 28:22

*Proverbs Concerning
Various Situations*

17 Incline your ear and hear the words of
   the wise,
   And apply your mind to my knowledge;   Prov. 5:1
18 For it will be pleasant if you keep them
   within you,   Prov. 2:10

That they may be ready on your lips.
19 So that your trust may be in the LORD,
   I have taught you today, even you.
20 Have I not written to you excellent
   things   *previous* • Prov. 8:6
   Of counsels and knowledge,

21 To make you know the certainty of the
   words of truth   Luke 1:3, 4 • *truth*
   That you may correctly answer to him
   who sent you?   *return words of truth*

22 Do not rob the poor because he is poor,
   Or crush the afflicted at the gate;
23 For the LORD will plead their case,
   And take the life of those who rob
   them.   Ps. 12:5; 35:10 • *rob the soul*

24 Do not associate with a man *given* to
   anger;
   Or go with a hot-tempered man,
25 Lest you learn his ways,   [1 Cor. 15:33]
   And find a snare for yourself.   *take*

26 Do not be among those who give
   pledges,
   Among those who become sureties for
   debts.   Prov. 17:18 • *strike hands*
27 If you have nothing with which to pay,
   Why should he take your bed from under you?   Ex. 22:26; Prov. 20:16

28 Do not move the ancient boundary
   Which your fathers have set.   Job 24:2

29 Do you see a man skilled in his work?
   He will stand before kings;   Gen. 41:46
   He will not stand before obscure men.

(continued from previous page)
   the parents or guardians are to dedicate, instruct, and motivate the child to do what God evidently has best
   equipped the child to do for Him. This is graphically illustrated by Joshua when he said, "but as for me and my
   house, we will serve the LORD" (Page 227—Josh. 24:15).
   If the command has been kept, the promise can be claimed. The promise includes the time of realization—
"when he is old"—this is best understood as being parallel with "a child," hence, "when he is independent," i.e.,
no longer economically dependent upon his parents, referring to the time when he leaves their home to establish
his own. The promise includes the certainty of realization—"he will not depart from it." If the command has been
kept, the promise will be realized. If the command has not been kept, the promise will not be realized. Rearing
children is not an overnight occurrence; it takes careful forethought and conscious obedience on the part of the
parents.
   Now turn to Page 11—Gen. 9:5: The Origin of Human Government.
   22:21   God's Word Equips—In a general sense it can be said that the Bible was written to convict sinners of
sin and to equip believers for service.
a. It equips for evangelism. Philip the evangelist uses the fifty-third chapter of Isaiah to point the Ethiopian eunuch to Christ in Acts 8:26–35.
b. It equips for counseling others. In his two letters to Timothy, Paul constantly urges this young man to preach the
   Word of God (Page 1217—1 Tim. 1:3, 18; 4:13–15; Page 1224—2 Tim. 2:1, 2, 15). "In pointing out these things
   to the brethren, you will be a good servant of Christ Jesus, *constantly* nourished on the words of the faith and of
   the sound doctrine which you have been following" (Page 1219—1 Tim. 4:6).
c. It equips for using one's spiritual gifts from God. A spiritual gift is an ability given by the Holy Spirit to the
   believer for the purpose of edifying the church and glorifying God. In Ephesians 1:17–19 and 4:7, 11–14 Paul
   says a knowledge of God's Word will provide us with the maturity we need to use our gifts in the most effective
   way.
d. It equips us for doing battle with Satan. In Ephesians 6:10–17 Paul likens the believers' armor to that used by
   Roman foot soldiers. In this comparison the Word of God is likened to the soldier's sword (Page 1190—Eph.
   6:17).
   Now turn to Page 849—Dan. 11:32: We Know God Through His Word.

CHAPTER 23

W HEN you sit down to dine with a ruler,
Consider carefully what is before you;
2 And put a knife to your throat,
If you are a man of *great* appetite.
3 Do not [R]desire his delicacies,   Ps. 141:4
For it is deceptive food.

4 Do not weary yourself to gain wealth,
Cease from your consideration *of it*.
5 When you set your eyes on it, it is
gone.
For [R]*wealth* certainly makes itself
wings,
Like an eagle that flies *toward* the
heavens.   Prov. 27:24; [1 Tim. 6:17]

6 Do not eat the bread of [T]a selfish man,
Or desire his delicacies;   *an evil eye*
7 For as he [T]thinks within himself, so he
is.   *reckons in his soul*
He says to you, "Eat and drink!"
But his heart is not with you.
8 You will [T]vomit up [T]the morsel you have
eaten,   Prov. 25:16 · *your*
And waste your compliments.

9 [R]Do not speak in the [T]hearing of a fool,
For he will [R]despise the wisdom of your
words.   Matt. 7:6 · *ears* · Prov. 1:7

10 Do not move the ancient boundary,
Or go into the fields of the fatherless;
11 For their [R]Redeemer is strong;   Job 19:25
He will plead their case against you.
12 Apply your heart to discipline,
And your ears to words of knowledge.

13 [R]Do not hold back discipline from the
child,
Although you [T]beat him with the rod, he
will not die.   [Prov. 13:24; 19:18] · *smite*
14 You shall [T]beat him with the rod,
And deliver his soul from Sheol.   *smite*

15 My son, if your heart is wise,
My own heart also will be glad;
16 And my inmost being will rejoice,
When your lips speak what is right.

17 Do not let your heart envy sinners,
But *live* in the fear of the LORD always.
18 Surely there is a [T]future,   *latter end*
And your hope will not be cut off.
19 Listen, my son, and [R]be wise,   Prov. 6:6
And direct your heart in the way.
20 Do not be with heavy drinkers of wine,
Or with gluttonous eaters of meat;
21 For the [R]heavy drinker and the glutton
will come to poverty,
And [R]drowsiness will clothe *a man* with
rags.   Prov. 21:17 · Prov. 6:10, 11

22 [R]Listen to your father who begot you,

And [R]do not despise your mother when
she is old.   Prov. 1:8 · Prov. 15:20
23 [R]Buy truth, and do not sell *it*,
Get wisdom and instruction and understanding.   Prov. 4:7; 18:15; [Matt. 13:44]

24 The father of the righteous will greatly
rejoice,
And [R]he who begets a wise son will be
glad in him.   [Prov. 10:1; 15:20; 29:3]
25 Let your [R]father and your mother be
glad,
And let her rejoice who gave birth to
you.   Prov. 27:11

26 [R]Give me your heart, my son,   Prov. 3:1
And let your eyes delight in my ways.
27 For a harlot is a [R]deep pit,   Prov. 22:14
And an [R]adulterous woman is a narrow
well.   *strange* · Prov. 5:20
28 Surely she [R]lurks as a robber,
And increases the [T]faithless among
men.   Prov. 6:26; 7:12 · *treacherous*

29 Who has [R]woe? Who has sorrow?
Who has contentions? Who has com-
plaining?
Who has wounds without cause?
Who has redness of eyes?   Is. 5:11, 22
30 Those who linger long over wine,
Those who go to taste mixed wine.
31 Do not look on the wine when it is red,
When it [R]sparkles in the cup, *gives its eye*
When it [R]goes down smoothly;   Song 7:9
32 At the last it bites like a serpent,
And stings like a [R]viper. Ps. 91:13; Is. 11:8
33 Your eyes will see strange things,
And your [T]mind will [T]utter perverse
things.   *heart* · Prov. 2:12
34 And you will be like one who lies down
in the [T]middle of the sea,
Or like one who lies down on the top of
a [5]mast.   *heart*
35 "They [R]struck me, *but* I did not become
ill;   Prov. 27:22; Jer. 5:3
They beat me, *but* I did not know *it*.
When shall I awake?
I will seek [T]another drink."   *it yet again*

CHAPTER 24

D O not be [R]envious of evil men,   Ps. 37:1
Nor desire to [R]be with them;   Ps. 1:1
2 For their [T]minds devise violence,
And their lips talk of trouble.   *hearts*

3 [R]By wisdom a house is built,   Prov. 9:1
And by understanding it is established;
4 And by knowledge the rooms are filled
With all precious and pleasant riches.

5 A [R]wise man is strong,   Prov. 21:22
And a man of knowledge [T]increases
power.   *strengthens power*

[5] Or, *lookout*

6 For by wise guidance you will[T] wage
    war,   *make battle for yourself*
And[R]in abundance of counselors there is
    victory.   Prov. 11:14

7 Wisdom is[R]too high for a fool,
He does not open his mouth [R]in the
    gate.   Ps. 10:5; Prov. 14:6 • Job 5:4

8 He who[R]plans to do evil,
Men will call him a schemer.   Rom. 1:30
9 The [R]devising of folly is sin,
And the scoffer is an abomination to
    men.   [Matt. 15:19; Acts 8:22]

10 If you [R]are slack in the day of distress,
Your strength is limited.   Deut. 20:8

11 [R]Deliver those who are being taken
    away to death,   Ps. 82:4; Is. 58:6, 7
And those who are staggering to
    slaughter, O hold *them* back.
12 If you say, "See, we did not know
    this,"
Does He not [R]consider *it* [R]who weighs
    the hearts?   Eccl. 5:8 • 1 Sam. 16:7
And [R]does He not know *it* who[R]keeps
    your soul?   Ps. 94:9-11 • Ps. 121:3-8
And will He not[T]render to man accord-
    ing to his work?   *bring back*

13 My son, eat[R]honey, for it is good,
Yes, the[R]honey from the comb is sweet
    to your taste;   Ps. 19:10 • Prov. 16:24
14 Know *that* [R]wisdom is thus for your
    soul;   Prov. 2:10
If you find *it,* then there will be a [T]fu-
    ture[R]   *latter end* • Prov. 23:18
And your hope will not be cut off.

15 [R]Do not lie in wait, O wicked man,
    against the dwelling of the right-
    eous;   Ps. 10:9, 10
Do not [R]destroy his resting place;
16 For a[R]righteous man falls seven times,
    and rises again,   Job 5:19; [Ps. 37:24]

But the[R]wicked stumble in *time of* ca-
    lamity.   Prov. 6:15; 14:32; 24:22

17 [R]Do not rejoice when your enemy falls,
And do not let your heart be glad when
    he stumbles;   Job 31:29; Ps. 35:15, 19
18 Lest the LORD see *it* and be displeased,
And He turn away His anger from him.

19 [R]Do not fret because of evildoers,
Or be envious of the wicked;   Ps. 37:1
20 For[R]there will be no[T]future for the evil
    man;   Job 15:31 • *latter end*
The lamp of the wicked will be put out.

21 My son,[A]fear the LORD and the king;
Do not associate with those who are
    given to change;   *reverence*
22 For their[R]calamity will rise suddenly,
And who knows the ruin *that comes*
    from both of them?   Prov. 24:16

23 These also are[R]sayings of the wise.
To [T]show partiality in judgment is not
    good.   Prov. 1:6; 22:17 • *regard the face*
24 He[R]who says to the wicked, "You are
    righteous,"   Prov. 17:15; Is. 5:23
[R]Peoples will curse him, nations will ab-
    hor him;   Prov. 11:26
25 But [R]to those who rebuke the *wicked*
    will be delight,
And a good blessing will come upon
    them.   Prov. 28:23
26 He kisses the lips
Who gives[A]a right answer.   *an honest*

27 Prepare your work outside,
And[R]make it ready for yourself in the
    field;   Prov. 27:23-27
Afterwards, then, build your house.

28 Do not be a[R]witness against your neigh-
    bor without cause,   Prov. 25:18
And do not deceive with your lips.
29 Do not say, "Thus I shall do to him as
    he has done to me;

24:6 Knowing the Will of God Through Circumstances and Counsel—While the Christian is to live above his circumstances, he is not to be unaware of them. God often works through circumstances in revealing His perfect will for us. Certainly Paul's wonderful statement, "God causes all things to work together for good to those who love God" (Page 1138—Rom. 8:28), takes into account our circumstances. A number of biblical examples can be given to illustrate this.

a. God directed Abraham to substitute a ram, whose horns had somehow become entangled in a thicket, for the life of Isaac (Page 22—Gen. 22:13).
b. God arranged for Pharaoh's daughter to be bathing in the river Nile at the exact time the baby Moses floated by in a little ark of bulrushes (Page 55—Ex. 2:1–10).
c. Paul's young nephew happened to overhear a plot to kill his famous uncle. He then reported it to the authorities, thus saving the apostle's life (Page 1121—Acts 23:12–22).

Surely the above circumstances were providentially arranged. So the Christian should ask, when attempting to discover God's will, "Is the Lord showing me something through my circumstances?"

Counselors also play an important role in finding God's will. "In abundance of counselors there is victory" (Page 628—Prov. 24:6). However, three things must be kept in mind at this point:

a. Counsel must come from a godly source. "*Like* a bad tooth and an unsteady foot is confidence in a faithless man in time of trouble" (Page 629—Prov. 25:19).
b. Sometimes even the godliest person can unknowingly give us wrong advice. Nathan the prophet did this when he encouraged David to build the temple (Page 300—2 Sam. 7:1–13).
c. In the final analysis, each person is responsible for knowing God's revealed purpose for his own life.
   Now turn to Page 782—Lam. 5:20: Occasions of Doubt.

I will [T]render to the man according to
his work."   *bring back*

30 I passed by the field of the sluggard,
And by the vineyard of the man[R]lack-
ing sense;   Prov. 6:32 • *heart*
31 And behold, it was completely [R]over-
grown with thistles,   Gen. 3:18
Its surface was covered with nettles,
And its stone wall was broken down.
32 When I saw, I reflected upon it;
I looked, *and* received instruction.
33 "A[R]little sleep, a little slumber, Prov. 6:10
A little folding of the hands to rest,"
34 Then your poverty will come *as* [A]a robber,   *a vagabond;* lit., *one who walks*
And your want like an armed man.

CHAPTER 25

Relationships with Kings

THESE also are [R]proverbs of Solomon
which the men of Hezekiah, king of Judah,
transcribed.   Prov. 1:1

2 It is the glory of God to[R]conceal a matter,   Deut. 29:29; Rom. 11:33
But the glory of[R]kings is to search out a
matter.   Ezra 6:1
3 *As* the heavens for height and the earth
for depth,
So the heart of kings is unsearchable.
4 Take away the [R]dross from the silver,
And there comes out a vessel for the
[R]smith;   Prov. 26:23 • Mal. 3:2, 3
5 Take away the [R]wicked *from* before the
king,
And his[R]throne will be established in
righteousness.   Prov. 20:8 • Prov. 16:12
6 Do not claim honor in the presence of
the king,
And do not stand in the place of great
men;
7 For[R]it is better that it be said to you,
"Come up here,"   Luke 14:7-11
Than that you should be put lower in
the presence of the prince,
Whom your eyes have seen.

Relationships with Neighbors

8 Do not go out[R]hastily to [T]argue *your*
case;   Prov. 17:14; Matt. 5:25 • *contend*
[T]Otherwise, what will you do in[T]the end,
When your neighbor puts you to
shame?   *Lest • its*
9 [T]Argue your case with your neighbor,
And [R]do not reveal the secret of another,   *Contend •* [Prov. 11:13]
10 Lest he who hears *it* reproach you,
And the evil report about you not[T]pass
away.   *return*

11 *Like* apples of gold in settings of silver
Is a [R]word spoken in [T]right circumstances.   Prov. 15:23 • *its*

12 *Like* [A]an earring of gold and an ornament of fine gold   *a nose ring*
Is a wise reprover to a listening ear.
13 Like the cold of snow in the [T]time of
harvest
Is a [R]faithful messenger to those who
send him,
For he refreshes the soul of his masters.   *day •* Prov. 13:17
14 *Like* clouds and wind without rain
Is a man who boasts of his gifts falsely.
15 By [T]forbearance[R] a ruler may be persuaded,   *length of anger •* Gen. 32:4
And a soft tongue breaks the bone.
16 Have you[R]found honey? Eat *only* [T]what
you need,   Judg. 14:8 • *your sufficiency*
Lest you have it in excess and vomit it.
17 Let your foot rarely be in your neighbor's house,[T]
Lest he become[T]weary of you and hate
you.   *surfeited with*
18 *Like* a club and a [R]sword and a sharp
[R]arrow   Ps. 57:4; Prov. 12:18 • Jer. 9:8
Is a man who bears [R]false witness
against his neighbor.   Ex. 20:16
19 *Like* a bad tooth and [T]an unsteady foot
Is confidence in a[R]faithless man in time
of trouble.   *a slipping foot •* Job 6:15
20 *Like* one who takes off a garment on a
cold day, *or like* vinegar on [T]soda,
Is he who sings songs to [T]a troubled
heart.   *natron • an evil*

Relationships with Enemies

21 [R]If your enemy is hungry, give him food
to eat;   Ex. 23:4, 5; 2 Kin. 6:22
And if he is thirsty, give him water to
drink;
22 For you will[T]heap burning coals on his
head,   *snatch up*
And the LORD will reward you.
23 The north wind brings forth rain,
And a [T]backbiting tongue, an angry
countenance.   *tongue of secrecy*
24 It is[R]better to live in a corner of the roof
Than in a house shared with a contentious woman.   Prov. 21:9

Relationships with Yourself

25 *Like* cold water to a weary soul,
So is good news from a distant land.
26 *Like* a[R]trampled spring and a [T]polluted
well   Ezek. 32:2; 34:18, 19 • *ruined*
Is a righteous man who gives way before the wicked.
27 It is not good to eat much honey,
Nor is it glory to[R]search out [T]one's own
glory.   Prov. 27:2; [Luke 14:11] • *their*
28 *Like* a [R]city that is broken into *and*
without walls   Prov. 16:32
Is a man[T]who has no control over his
spirit.   2 Chr. 32:5; Neh. 1:3

CHAPTER 26

Relationships with Fools

LIKE snow in summer and like[R]rain in harvest,   1 Sam. 12:17
So honor is not fitting for a fool.

2 Like a sparrow in *its* [T]flitting, like a
swallow in *its* flying,   *wandering*
So a [R]curse without cause does not
[T]alight.   Deut. 23:5; 2 Sam. 16:12 • *come*

3 A[R]whip is for the horse, a bridle for the
donkey,   Ps. 32:9
And a rod for the back of fools.

4 [R]Do not answer a fool according to his
folly,   Prov. 23:9; 29:9; Is. 36:21; Matt. 7:6
Lest you also be like him.

5 Answer a fool as his folly *deserves*,
Lest he be wise in his own eyes.

6 He cuts off *his own feet, and* drinks
violence
Who sends a message by the hand of a
fool.

7 *Like* the legs *which* hang down from
the lame,
So is a proverb in the mouth of fools.

8 Like one who binds a stone in a sling,
So is he who gives honor to a fool.

9 *Like* a thorn *which* [T]falls into the hand
of a drunkard,   *goes up*
So is a proverb in the mouth of fools.

10 *Like* an archer who wounds everyone,
So is he who hires a fool or who hires
those who pass by.

11 Like a dog that returns to its vomit
Is a fool who repeats[T]his folly.   *with his*

12 Do you see a man[R]wise in his own
eyes?
[R]There is more hope for a fool than for
him.   Prov. 3:7; 26:5 • Prov. 29:20

Relationships with Sluggards

13 The [R]sluggard says, "There is a lion in
the road!   Prov. 22:13
A lion is[T]in the open square!"   *within*

14 *As* the door turns on its hinges,
So *does* the sluggard on his bed.

15 The [R]sluggard buries his hand in the
dish;
He is weary of bringing it to his mouth
again.   Prov. 19:24

16 The sluggard is wiser in his own eyes
Than seven men who can [T]give a dis-
creet answer.   *return discreetly*

Relationships with Gossips

17 *Like* one who takes a dog by the ears
Is he who passes by *and* meddles with
strife not belonging to him.

18 Like a madman who throws
[R]Firebrands, arrows and death,   Is. 50:11

19 So is the man who[R]deceives his neighbor,   Prov. 24:28
And says, "Was[R]I not joking?"   Eph. 5:4

20 For lack of wood the fire goes out,
And where there is no[R]whisperer, contention quiets down.   Prov. 16:28

21 *Like* charcoal to hot embers and wood
to fire,
So is a [R]contentious man to kindle
strife.   Prov. 15:18; 29:22

22 The [R]words of a whisperer are like
dainty morsels,   Prov. 18:8
And they go down into the [T]innermost
parts of the body. *chambers of the belly*

23 *Like* an earthen [R]vessel overlaid with
silver[R]dross   Matt. 23:27 • Prov. 25:4
Are burning lips and a wicked heart.

24 He who hates disguises *it* with his lips,
But he lays up deceit in his heart.

25 When he[R]speaks graciously, do not believe him,
For there are seven abominations in his
heart.   Ps. 28:3; Prov. 26:23; Jer. 9:8

26 *Though his* hatred [R]covers itself with
guile,
His wickedness will be[R]revealed before
the assembly.   Matt. 23:28 • [Luke 8:17]

27 He who[R]digs a pit will fall into it,
And he who rolls a stone, it will come
back on him.   Esth. 7:10; Prov. 28:10

28 A lying tongue hates those it crushes,
And a flattering mouth works ruin.

CHAPTER 27

*Proverbs Regulating
Various Activities*

DO[R]not boast about tomorrow,
For you[R]do not know what a day may
bring forth.   James 4:13-16 • Luke 12:19

2 Let [R]another praise you, and not your
own mouth;   Prov. 25:27; 2 Cor. 12:11
A stranger, and not your own lips.

3 A stone is heavy and the sand weighty,
But the provocation of a fool is heavier
than both of them.

4 Wrath is fierce and anger is a flood,
But who can stand before jealousy?

5 Better is[R]open rebuke
Than love that is concealed.   Gal. 2:14

6 Faithful are the[R]wounds of a friend,
But [A]deceitful are the[R]kisses of an enemy.   Ps. 141:5 • *excessive* • Matt. 26:49

7 A sated[T]man[T]loathes honey,
But to a famished man any bitter thing
is sweet.   *soul* • *tramples on*

8 Like a[R]bird that wanders from her nest,
So is a man who [R]wanders from his
[T]home.   Prov. 26:2 • Gen. 21:14 • *place*

9 [R]Oil and perfume make the heart glad,
So a [T]man's counsel is sweet to his
friend.   Ps. 23:5; 141:5 • *soul's*

10 Do not forsake your own[R]friend or your
father's friend,   Prov. 18:24
And do not go to your brother's house
in the day of your calamity;
Better is a neighbor who is near than a
brother far away.

11 ^RBe wise, my son, and make my heart glad,   [Prov. 10:1; 23:15; 29:3]
That I may ^Rreply to him who reproaches me.   Ps. 119:42

12 A prudent man sees evil *and* hides himself,
The naive proceed *and* pay the penalty.

13 ^RTake his garment when he becomes surety for a stranger;
And for an^Tadulterous woman hold him in pledge.   Prov. 20:16 · *strange*

14 ^RHe who blesses his friend with a loud voice early in the morning,   Ps. 12:2
It will be reckoned a curse to him.

15 A^Rconstant dripping on a day of steady rain   Prov. 19:13
And a contentious woman are alike;

16 He who would ^Trestrain her ^Trestrains the wind,   *hide(s)*
And grasps oil with his right hand.

17 Iron sharpens iron,
So one man sharpens another.

18 He who tends the ^Rfig tree will eat its fruit;   2 Kin. 18:31; Song 8:12; Is. 36:16
And he who ^Rcares for his master will be honored.   Luke 12:42-44; 19:17

19 As in water face *reflects* face,
So the heart of man *reflects* man.

20 Sheol and Abaddon are never satisfied,
Nor are the eyes of man ever satisfied.

21 The ^Rcrucible is for silver and the furnace for gold,
And a man *is tested* by the praise accorded him.   Prov. 17:3 · Luke 6:26

22 Though you ^Rpound a fool in a mortar with a pestle along with crushed grain,   Prov. 23:35; 26:11; Jer. 5:3
Yet his folly will not depart from him.

23 Know well the ^Tcondition of your flocks,
And pay attention to your herds;   *face*

24 For riches are not forever,
Nor does a ^Rcrown *endure* to all generations.   Job 19:9; Ps. 89:39; Jer. 13:18

25 *When* the grass disappears, the new growth is seen,
And the herbs of the mountains are ^Rgathered in,   Is. 17:5; Jer. 40:10, 12

26 The lambs *will be* for your clothing,
And the goats *will bring* the price of a field,

27 And *there will be* goats' milk enough for your food,
For the food of your household,
And sustenance for your maidens.

CHAPTER 28

T HE wicked flee when no one is pursuing,
But the righteous are bold as a lion.

2 By the transgression of a land ^Rmany are its princes,   1 Kin. 16:8-28
But ^Rby a man of understanding *and* knowledge, so it endures.   Prov. 11:11

3 A ^Rpoor man who oppresses the lowly
Is *like* a driving rain ^Twhich leaves no food.   Matt. 18:28 · *and there is no bread*

4 Those who forsake the law ^Rpraise the wicked,   Ps. 49:18; Rom. 1:32
But those who keep the law ^Rstrive with them.   1 Kin. 18:18; Neh. 13:11, 15

5 Evil men ^Rdo not understand justice,
But those who seek the LORD ^Runderstand all things.   Is. 6:9 · Prov. 2:9

6 ^RBetter is the poor who walks in his integrity,
Than he who is ^Tcrooked though he be rich.   Prov. 19:1 · *perverse of two ways*

7 He who keeps the law is a discerning son,
But he who is a companion of ^Rgluttons humiliates his father.   Prov. 23:20

8 He who increases his wealth by ^Rinterest and usury,   Ex. 22:25; Lev. 25:36
Gathers it ^Rfor him who is gracious to the poor.   Job 27:17; Prov. 13:22; 14:31

9 He who turns away his ear from listening to the law,
Even his prayer is an abomination.

10 He who leads the upright astray in an evil way
Will himself fall into his own pit,
But the blameless will inherit good.

11 The rich man is wise in his own eyes,
But the poor who has understanding ^Tsees through him.   *examines him*

12 When the ^Rrighteous triumph, there is great glory,   Prov. 11:10; 29:2
But when the wicked rise, men ^Thide themselves.   *will be searched for*

13 He who ^Rconceals his transgressions will not prosper,   Job 31:33; Ps. 32:3
But he who ^Rconfesses and forsakes *them* will find compassion.   Ps. 32:5

14 How blessed is the man who ^Tfears always,   Prov. 23:17
But he who ^Rhardens his heart will fall into calamity.   Ps. 95:8; [Rom. 2:5]

15 *Like* a roaring lion and a rushing bear
Is a wicked ruler over a poor people.

16 A^Rleader who is a great oppressor lacks understanding,   Eccl. 10:16; Is. 3:12
But he who hates unjust gain will prolong *his* days.

17 A man who is^Rladen with the guilt of human blood   Gen. 9:6; Ex. 21:14
Will ^Tbe a fugitive until death; let no one support him.   *flee to the pit*

18 He who walks blamelessly will be delivered,
But he who is ^Tcrooked^Rwill fall all at once.   *perverse of two ways* · Prov. 10:27

19 ^RHe who tills his land will ^Rhave plenty of food,   Prov. 12:11 · Prov. 20:13
But he who follows empty *pursuits* will have poverty in plenty.

20 A^Rfaithful man will abound with blessings,   Prov. 10:6; Matt. 24:45; 25:21
But he who ^Rmakes haste to be rich will not go unpunished.   Prov. 20:21; 28:22

21 To ᵀshow partiality is not good,
  ᴿBecause for a piece of bread a man will
  transgress.   *regard the face* • Ezek. 13:19
22 A man with an ᴿevil eye ᴿhastens after
  wealth,   Prov. 23:6 • Prov. 21:5
  And does not know that want will
  come upon him.
23 He who ᴿrebukes a man will afterward
  find *more* favor   Prov. 27:5, 6
  Than he who flatters with the tongue.
24 He who ᴿrobs his father or his mother,
  And says, "It is not a transgression,"
  Is the ᴿcompanion of a man who destroys.   Prov. 19:26 • Prov. 18:9
25 An ᵀarrogant man stirs up strife,
  But he who trusts in the LORD will
  ᵀprosper.   *broad soul • be made fat*
26 He who ᵀtrusts in his own heart is a
  fool,
  But he who walks wisely will be delivered.   Prov. 3:5
27 He who ᴿgives to the poor will never
  want,   Prov. 11:24; 19:17
  But he who ᵀshuts his eyes will have
  many curses.   *hides*
28 When the wicked rise, men hide themselves;
  But when they perish, the righteous increase.

CHAPTER 29

A MAN who hardens *his* neck after ᴿmuch
  reproof   1 Sam. 2:25; 2 Chr. 36:16
  Will ᴿsuddenly be broken ᵀbeyond remedy.   Prov. 6:15 • *and there is no remedy*
2 When the ᴿrighteous increase, the people rejoice,   Esth. 8:15; Prov. 11:10
  But when a wicked man rules, people
  groan.
3 A man who ᴿloves wisdom makes his
  father glad,   Prov. 10:1; 15:20; 27:11
  But he who ᴿkeeps company with harlots wastes *his* wealth.   Prov. 5:10
4 The ᴿking gives stability to the land by
  justice,   2 Chr. 9:8; Prov. 8:15; 29:14
  But a man who takes bribes over-
  throws it.
5 A man who ᵀflatters his neighbor
  Is spreading a net for his steps. Ps. 5:9
6 By transgression an evil man is ᴿen-
  snared,   Prov. 22:5; Eccl. 9:12
  But the righteous sings and rejoices.
7 The ᴿrighteous is concerned for the
  rights of the poor,   Job 29:16; [Ps. 41:1]
  The wicked does not understand *such*
  ᵀconcern.   *knowledge*
8 Scorners ᴿset a city aflame,   Prov. 11:11
  But wise men turn away anger.
9 When a wise man has a controversy
  with a foolish man,
  ᵀThe foolish man either rages or laughs,
  and there is no rest.   *He*
10 Men of ᴿbloodshed hate the blameless,

But the upright ᵀare concerned for his
  life.   Gen. 4:5-8 • *seek his soul*
11 A fool always loses his temper,
  But a wise man holds it back.
12 If a ruler pays attention to falsehood,
  All his ministers *become* wicked.
13 The poor man and the oppressor ᵀhave
  this in common: *meet together*
  The LORD gives ᴿlight to the eyes of
  both.   Ezra 9:8; Ps. 13:3
14 If a king judges the poor with truth,
  His throne will be established forever.
15 The rod and reproof give wisdom,
  But a child who gets his own way
  brings shame to his mother.
16 When the wicked ᴬincrease, transgression increases;   *become great*
  But the righteous will see their fall.
17 ᴿCorrect your son, and he will give you
  comfort;   Prov. 13:24; 29:15
  He will also ᴿdelight your soul. Prov. 10:1
18 Where there is ᴿno ᴬvision, the people
  are unrestrained,   Ps. 74:9 • *revelation*
  But happy is he who keeps the law.
19 A slave will not be instructed by words
  alone;
  For though he understands, there will
  be no response.
20 Do you see a man who is ᴿhasty in his
  words?
  There is ᴿmore hope for a fool than for
  him.   James 1:19 • Prov. 26:12
21 He who pampers his slave from childhood
  Will in the end find him to be a son.
22 An ᴿangry man stirs up strife,
  And a hot-tempered man abounds in
  transgression.   Prov. 15:18; 26:21
23 A man's pride will bring him low,
  But a humble spirit will obtain honor.
24 He who is a partner with a thief hates
  his own life;
  He hears the oath but tells nothing.
25 The fear of man ᵀbrings a snare,
  But he who ᴿtrusts in the LORD will be
  exalted.   *gives* • Ps. 91:1-16; Prov. 18:10
26 ᴿMany seek the ruler's favor,   Prov. 19:6
  But ᴿjustice for man *comes* from the
  LORD.   Is. 49:4; [1 Cor. 4:4]
27 An ᴿunjust man is abominable to the
  righteous,   Ps. 6:8; 139:21, 22; Prov. 12:8
  And he who is ᵁupright in the way is
  abominable to the wicked.   Ps. 69:4

CHAPTER 30

The Words of Agur

T HE words of Agur the son of Jakeh, the
ᴬoracle.
The man declares to Ithiel, to Ithiel and
Ucal: *burden*
2 Surely I am more ᴿstupid than any man,
  And I do not have the understanding of
  a man.   Ps. 49:10; 73:22; [Prov. 12:1]
3 Neither have I learned wisdom,

Nor do I have the ^Rknowledge of the
Holy One.   [Prov. 9:10]
4 Who has ^Rascended into heaven and de-
scended? [Ps. 68:18; John 3:13; Eph. 4:8]
Who has gathered the ^Rwind in His
fists?   Ex. 15:10; Ps. 135:7
Who has ^Rwrapped the waters in ^THis
garment?   Job 26:8; 38:8, 9 · *the*
Who has^Restablished all the ends of the
earth?   Ps. 24:2; Is. 45:18
What is His^Rname or His son's name?
Surely you know!   Rev. 19:12

5 Every^Rword of God is tested;   Ps. 12:6
He is a^Rshield to those who take refuge
in Him.   Ps. 3:3; 84:11; Prov. 2:7
6 ^RDo not add to His words Deut. 4:2; 12:32
Lest He reprove you, and you be
proved a liar.

7 Two things I asked of Thee,
Do not refuse me before I die:
8 Keep deception and ^Tlies far from me,
Give me neither poverty nor riches;
Feed me with the^Rfood that is my por-
tion,   *words of falsehood* · Job 23:12
9 Lest I be^Rfull and deny *Thee* and say,
"Who is the LORD?" Deut. 8:12; 31:20
Or lest I be^Rin want and steal, Prov. 6:30
And profane the name of my God.

10 Do not slander a slave to his master,
Lest he ^Rcurse you and you be found
guilty.   Eccl. 7:21

11 There is a ⁶kind of *man* who^Rcurses his
father,   Ex. 21:17; Prov. 20:20
And does not bless his mother.
12 There is a kind who is^Rpure in his own
eyes,   [Prov. 16:2]; Is. 65:5; Luke 18:11
Yet is not washed from his filthiness.
13 There is a kind—oh how^Rlofty are his
eyes!   Prov. 6:17; Is. 2:11; 5:15
And his eyelids are raised *in arrogance.*   Prov. 6:17; Is. 2:11; 5:15
14 There is a kind of *man* whose^Rteeth are
like swords,   Ps. 57:4
And his^Rjaw teeth *like* knives, Job 29:17
To devour the afflicted from the earth,
And the needy from among men.

15 The leech has two daughters,
"Give," "Give."
There are three things that will not be
satisfied,
Four that will not say, "Enough":
16 Sheol, and the^Rbarren womb, Gen. 30:1
Earth that is never satisfied with water,
And fire that never says, "Enough."
17 The eye that^Rmocks a father, Gen. 9:22
And^Tscorns a mother,   *despises to obey*
The ravens of the valley will pick it out,
And the young eagles will eat it.

⁶ Or, *generation;* so through v. 14

18 There are three things which are too
wonderful for me,
Four which I do not understand:
19 The way of an^Reagle in the sky,
The way of a serpent on a rock,
The way of a ship in the middle of the
sea,   Deut. 28:49; Jer. 48:40; 49:22
And the way of a man with a maid.
20 This is the way of an ^Radulterous
woman: Prov. 5:6
She eats and wipes her mouth,
And says, "I have done no wrong."

21 Under three things the earth quakes,
And under four, it cannot bear up:
22 Under a^Rslave when he becomes king,
And a fool when he is satisfied with
food,   Prov. 19:10; Eccl. 10:7
23 Under an unloved woman when she
gets a husband,
And a maidservant when she supplants
her mistress.

24 Four things are small on the earth,
But they are exceedingly wise:
25 The^Rants are not a strong folk,
But they prepare their food in the summer;   Prov. 6:6
26 The^Rbadgers are not mighty folk,
Yet they make their houses in the
rocks;   Lev. 11:5; Ps. 104:18
27 The locusts have no king,
Yet all of them go out in^Rranks; Joel 2:7
28 The lizard you may grasp with the
hands,
Yet it is in kings' palaces.

29 There are three things which are
stately in *their* march,
Even four which are stately when they
walk:
30 The lion *which* is mighty among beasts
And does not retreat before any,
31 The strutting cock, the male goat also,
And a king *when his* army is with him.

32 If you have been foolish in exalting
yourself
Or if you have plotted *evil,* ^Rput your
hand on your mouth. Job 21:5; 40:4
33 For the^Tchurning of milk produces butter,
And pressing the nose brings forth
blood;
So the ^Tchurning of ^Ranger produces
strife.   *pressing* · Prov. 10:12; 29:22

CHAPTER 31

Wisdom for Leaders

THE words of King Lemuel, the ^Aoracle
which his mother taught him.   *burden*
2 What, O my son?
And what, O^Rson of my womb?
And what, O son of my vows? Is. 49:15

3 ^RDo not give your strength to women,
Or your ways to that which ^Rdestroys
kings.   Prov. 5:9 • Deut. 17:17

4 It is not for^Rkings, O Lemuel,   Eccl. 10:17
It is not for kings to drink wine,
Or for rulers to desire strong drink,

5 Lest they drink and forget what is decreed,
And pervert the ^Trights of all the ^Taf-
flicted.   *judgment • sons of affliction*

6 Give strong drink to him who is ^Rperish-
ing,   Job 29:13
And wine to him whose life is bitter.

7 Let him drink and forget his poverty,
And remember his trouble no more.

8 ^ROpen your mouth for the dumb,   Ps. 82
For the rights of all the unfortunate.

9 Open your mouth, judge righteously,
And defend the rights of the afflicted
and needy.   *judge the afflicted*

Wise Woman

10 An excellent wife, who can find?
For her worth is far above jewels.

11 The heart of her husband trusts in her,
And he will have no lack of gain.

12 She does him good and not evil
All the days of her life.

13 She looks for wool and flax,
And works with her hands in delight.

14 She is like ^Rmerchant ships;   Ezek. 27:25
She brings her food from afar.

15 She ^Rrises also while it is still night,
And gives food to her household,
And portions to her maidens.   Rom. 12:11

16 She considers a field and buys it;
From ^Ther earnings she plants a vineyard.   *the fruit of her palms*

17 She girds^Therself with strength,
And makes her arms strong.   *her loins*

18 She senses that her gain is good;
Her lamp does not go out at night.

19 She stretches out her hands to the distaff,
And her^Thands grasp the spindle.   *palms*

20 She^Textends^Rher hand to the poor;
And she stretches out her hands to the
needy.   *spreads out her palm* • Prov. 22:9

21 She is not afraid of the snow for her
household,
For all her household are ^Rclothed with
scarlet.   2 Sam. 1:24

22 She makes coverings for herself;
Her clothing is fine linen and purple.

23 Her husband is known in the gates,
When he sits among the elders of the
land.   Deut. 16:18; Ruth 4:1, 11

24 She makes ^Rlinen garments and sells
them,   Judg. 14:12
And supplies belts to the tradesmen.

25 Strength and dignity are her clothing,
And she smiles at the future.   *latter days*

26 She^Ropens her mouth in wisdom,
And the^Tteaching of kindness is on her
tongue.   Prov. 10:31 • *law*

27 She looks well to the ways of her
household,
And does not eat the bread of idleness.

28 Her children rise up and bless her;
Her husband *also*, and he praises her,
saying:

29 "Many daughters have done nobly,
But you excel them all."

30 Charm is deceitful and beauty is vain,
But a woman who^Tfears^Rthe LORD, she
shall be praised.   *reverences* • Ps. 112:1

31 Give her the product of her hands,
And let her works praise her in the
gates.   *fruit*

ECCLESIASTES

THE BOOK OF ECCLESIASTES

The key word in Ecclesiastes is *vanity*, the futile emptiness of trying to be happy apart from God. The Preacher (traditionally taken to be Solomon—1:1, 12—the wisest, richest, most influential king in Israel's history) looks at life under the sun (1:9) and, from the human perspective, declares it all to be empty. Power, popularity, prestige, pleasure—nothing can fill the God-shaped void in man's life but God Himself! But once seen from God's perspective, life takes on meaning and purpose, causing Solomon to exclaim, "Eat . . . drink . . . rejoice . . . do good . . . live joyfully . . . fear God . . . keep His commandments!" Skepticism and despair melt away when life is viewed as a daily gift from God.

The Hebrew title *Qoheleth* is a rare term, found only in Ecclesiastes (1:1, 2, 12; 7:27; 12:8–10). It comes from the word *qahal*, "to convoke an assembly, to assemble." Thus, it means "one who addresses an assembly, a preacher." The Septuagint used the Greek word *Ekklesiastes* as its title for this book. Derived from the word *ekklesia*, "assembly, congregation, church," it simply means "preacher." The Latin *Ecclesiastes* means "speaker before an assembly."

THE AUTHOR OF ECCLESIASTES

There are powerful arguments that the author of Ecclesiastes was Solomon.

External Evidence: Jewish talmudic tradition attributes the book to Solomon but suggests that Hezekiah's scribes may have edited the text (see Prov. 25:1). Solomonic authorship of Ecclesiastes is the standard Christian position, although some scholars, along with the Talmud, believe the work was later edited during the time of Hezekiah or possibly Ezra.

Internal Evidence: The author calls himself "the son of David, king in Jerusalem" in 1:1, 12. Solomon was the best qualified Davidic descendant for the quest in this book. He was the wisest man who ever taught in Jerusalem (see 1:16; 1 Kin. 4:29, 30). The descriptions of Qoheleth's exploration of pleasure (2:1–3), impressive accomplishments (2:4–6), and unparalleled wealth (2:7–10) were fulfilled only by King Solomon. The proverbs in this book are similar to those in the Book of Proverbs (e.g., Eccl. 7; 10). According to 12:9, Qoheleth collected and arranged many proverbs, perhaps

referring to the two Solomonic collections in Proverbs. The unity of authorship of Ecclesiastes is supported by the seven references to Qoheleth.

THE TIME OF ECCLESIASTES

Some scholars argue that the literary forms in Ecclesiastes are postexilic, but they are, in fact, unique, and cannot be used in dating this book. The phrase "all who were over Jerusalem before me" in 1:16 has been used to suggest a date after Solomon's time, but there were many kings and wise men in Jerusalem before the time of Solomon. However, Solomon was the only son of David who reigned over Israel from Jerusalem (1:12).

Ecclesiastes was probably written late in Solomon's life, about 935 B.C. If this is so, the great glory that Solomon ushered in early in his reign was already beginning to fade; and the disruption of Israel into two kingdoms would soon take place. Jewish tradition asserts that Solomon wrote Song of Solomon in his youthful years, Proverbs in his middle years, and Ecclesiastes in his latter years. This book may be expressing his regret for his folly and wasted time due to carnality and idolatry (cf. 1 Kin. 11).

There are no references to historical events other than to personal aspects of Qoheleth's life. The location was Jerusalem (1:1, 12, 16), the seat of Israel's rule and authority.

THE CHRIST OF ECCLESIASTES

Ecclesiastes convincingly portrays the emptiness and perplexity of life without a relationship with the Lord. Each person has eternity in his heart (3:11), and only Christ can provide ultimate satisfaction, joy, and wisdom. Man's highest good is found in the "one Shepherd" (12:11) who offers abundant life (John 10:9, 10).

KEYS TO ECCLESIASTES

Key Word: Vanity—Ecclesiastes reports the results of a diligent quest for purpose, meaning, and satisfaction in human life. The Preacher poignantly sees the emptiness and futility of power, popularity, prestige, and pleasure apart from God. The word *vanity* appears nineteen times to express the many things that cannot be understood about life. All earthly goals and ambitions when pursued as ends in themselves lead to dissatisfaction

and frustration. Life "under the sun" (used twenty-nine times) seems to be filled with inequities, uncertainties, changes in fortune, and violations of justice. But Ecclesiastes does not give an answer of atheism or skepticism; God is referred to throughout. In fact, it claims that the search for man's *summum bonum* must end in God. Satisfaction in life can be found only by looking beyond this world. Ecclesiastes gives an analysis of negative themes but it also develops the positive theme of overcoming the vanities of life by fearing a God who is good, just, and sovereign (12:13, 14). Wisdom involves seeing life from a divine perspective and trusting God in the face of apparent futility and lack of purpose. Life is a daily gift from God and it should be enjoyed as much as possible (see 2:24–26; 3:12, 13, 22; 5:18–20; 8:15; 9:7–10; 11:8, 9). Our comprehension is indeed limited, but there are many things we can understand. Qoheleth recognized that ultimately God will judge all people.. Therefore he exhorted: "Fear God and keep His commandments" (12:13).

Key Verses: Ecclesiastes 2:24 and 12:13, 14— "There is nothing better for a man *than* to eat and drink and tell himself that his labor is good. This also I have seen, that it is from the hand of God" (2:24).

"The conclusion, when all has been heard, *is:* fear God and keep His commandments, because this *applies* to every person. For God will bring every act to judgment, everything which is hidden, whether it is good or evil" (12:13, 14).

Key Chapter: Ecclesiastes 12—At the end of the Book of Ecclesiastes, the Preacher looks at life through "binoculars." On the other hand, from the perspective of the natural man who only sees life "under the sun," the conclusion is, "All *is* vanity." Life's every activity, even though pleasant for the moment, becomes purposeless and futile when viewed as an end in itself.

The Preacher carefully documents the latter view with a long list of his own personal pursuits in life. No amount of activities or possessions has satisfied the craving of his heart. Every earthly prescription for happiness has left the same bitter aftertaste. Only when the Preacher views his life from God's perspective "above the sun" does it take on meaning as a precious gift "from the hand of God" (2:24).

Chapter 12 resolves the book's extensive inquiry into the meaning of life with the single conclusion, "fear God and keep His commandments, because this *applies* to every person" (12:13).

SURVEY OF ECCLESIASTES

Ecclesiastes is a profound and problematic book. It is the record of an intense search for meaning and satisfaction in life on this earth, especially in view of all the iniquities and apparent absurdities that surround us. It takes the perspective of the greatest answers that wisdom under the sun can produce. If the Preacher is identified as Solomon, Ecclesiastes was written from a unique vantage point. Possessing the greatest mental, material, and political resources ever combined in one man, he was qualified beyond all others to write this book. Ecclesiastes is extremely difficult to synthesize, and several alternate approaches have been used. The one used here is: the thesis that "all is vanity" (1:1–11), the proof that "all is vanity" (1:12–6:12), the counsel for living with vanity (7:1–12:14).

The Thesis That "All Is Vanity" (1:1-11): After a one-verse introduction, the Preacher states his theme: "Vanity of vanities! All is van-

FOCUS	THESIS: "ALL IS VANITY"		PROOF: "LIFE IS VAIN"			COUNSEL: "FEAR GOD"	
REFERENCE	1:1———1:4———	—1:12———	—3:1———	—7:1———	—10:1———	—12:9———	—12:14
DIVISION	INTRODUCTION OF VANITY	ILLUSTRATIONS OF VANITY	PROOF FROM SCRIPTURE	PROOF FROM OBSERVATIONS	COPING IN A WICKED WORLD	COUNSEL FOR UNCERTAINTY	CONCLUSION: FEAR AND OBEY GOD
TOPIC	DECLARATION OF VANITY		DEMONSTRATION OF VANITY			FROM VANITY	
	SUBJECT		SERMONS			SUMMARY	
LOCATION	UNIVERSE: "UNDER THE SUN"						
TIME	c. 935 B.C.						

ity" (1:2). Life under the sun appears to be futile and perplexing. Verses 3–11 illustrate this theme in the endless and apparently meaningless cycles found in nature and history.

The Proof That "All Is Vanity" (1:12—6:12): The Preacher describes his multiple quest for meaning and satisfaction as he explores his vast personal resources. He begins with wisdom (1:12–18) but finds that "increasing knowledge *results in* increasing pain." Due to his intense perception of reality he experiences just the reverse of "ignorance is bliss." The Preacher moves from wisdom to laughter, hedonism, and wine (2:1–3) and then turns to works, women, and wealth (2:4–11); but all lead to emptiness. He realizes that wisdom is far greater than foolishness, but both seem to lead to futility in view of the brevity of life and universality of death (2:12–17). He concludes by acknowledging that contentment and joy are found only in God.

At this point, Ecclesiastes turns from his situation in life to a philosophical quest; but the conclusion remains the same. The Preacher considers the unchanging order of events and the fixed laws of God. Time is short, and there is no eternity on earth (3:1–15). The futility of death seems to cancel the difference between righteousness and wickedness (3:16–22). Chapters 4 and 5 explore the futility in social relationships (oppression, rivalry, covetousness, power) and in religious relationships (formalism, empty prayer, vows). In addition, the world's offerings produce disappointment, not satisfaction. Ultimate meaning can be found only in God.

The Counsel for Living with Vanity (7:1—12:14): A series of lessons on practical wisdom is given in 7:1—9:12. Levity and pleasure-seeking are seen as superficial and foolish; it is better to have sober depth of thought. Wisdom and self-control provide perspective and strength in coping with life. One should enjoy prosperity and consider in adversity that God made both. Avoid the twin extremes of self-righteousness and immorality. Sin invades all men, and wisdom is cut short by evil and death. The human mind cannot grasp ultimate meaning. Submission to authority helps one avoid unnecessary hardship, but real justice is often lacking on earth. The uncertainties of life and certainty of the grave show that God's purposes and ways often cannot be grasped. One should, therefore, magnify opportunities while they last, because fortune can change suddenly.

Observations on wisdom and folly are found in 9:13—11:6. Wisdom, the most powerful human resource, is contrasted with the meaningless talk and effort of fools. In view of the unpredictability of circumstances, wisdom is the best course to follow in order to minimize grief and misfortune. Wisdom involves discipline and diligence. In 11:7—12:7 the Preacher offers exhortations on using life well. Youth is too brief and precious to be squandered in foolishness or evil. A person should live well in the fullness of each day before God and acknowledge Him early in life. This section closes with an exquisite allegory of old age (12:1–7).

The Preacher concludes that the "good life" is only attained by revering God. Those who fail to take God and His will seriously into account are doomed to lives of foolishness and futility. Life will not wait upon the solution of all its problems; nevertheless, real meaning can be found by looking not "under the sun" but beyond the sun to the "one Shepherd" (12:11).

OUTLINE OF ECCLESIASTES

Part One: The Thesis That "All Is Vanity" (1:1–11)

Part Two: The Proof That "All Is Vanity" (1:12—6:12)

Part Three: The Counsel for Living with Vanity (7:1—12:14)

CHAPTER 1

Introduction of Vanity

THE words of the^RPreacher, the son of David, king in Jerusalem. Eccl. 1:12; 7:27; 12:8-10
2 "¹Vanity of vanities," says the Preacher,
"¹Vanity of vanities! All is vanity."

3 ^RWhat advantage does man have in all
his work Eccl. 2:11; 3:9; 5:16
Which he does under the sun?

Illustrations of Vanity

4 A generation goes and a generation
comes,
But the earth^Tremains forever. *stands*
5 Also,^Rthe sun rises and the sun sets;
And^Thastening to its place it rises there
again. Ps. 19:6 · *panting*
6 ^TBlowing toward the south, *Going*
Then turning toward the north,
The wind continues^Tswirling along;
And on its circular courses the wind re-
turns. *turning*
7 All the rivers^Tflow into the sea,
Yet the sea is not full.
To the place where the rivers flow,
There they flow again. *go*
8 All things are wearisome;
Man is not able to tell *it.*
The eye is not satisfied with seeing,
Nor is the ear filled with hearing.
9 ^RThat which has been is that which will
be, Eccl. 1:10; 2:12; 3:15; 6:10
And that which has been done is that
which will be done.
So, there is nothing new under the sun.
10 Is there anything of which one might
say,
"See this, it is new"?
Already it has existed for ages
Which were before us.

11 There is no ^Rremembrance of ^Tearlier
things; Eccl. 2:16; 9:5 · *first* or *former*
And also of the^Tlater things which will
occur, *latter* or *after*
There will be for them no remembrance
Among those who will come later *still.*

Vanity of Striving After Wisdom

12 I, the^RPreacher, have been king over Israel in Jerusalem. Eccl. 1:1; 7:27; 12:8-10
13 And I^Rset my^Tmind to seek and explore
by wisdom concerning all that has been
done under heaven. *It* is ^Ta grievous task
which God has given to the sons of men to
be afflicted with. Eccl. 1:17 · *heart · an evil*
14 I have seen all the works which have
been done under the sun, and behold, all is
^Avanity and striving after wind. *futility*
15 What is ^Rcrooked cannot be straightened, and what is lacking cannot be
counted. Eccl. 7:13
16 I^Tsaid to myself, "Behold, I have magnified and increased wisdom more than all
who were over Jerusalem before me; and
my mind has observed a wealth of wisdom
and knowledge." *spoke with my heart, saying*
17 And I set my^Tmind to know wisdom
and to know madness and folly; I realized
that this also is striving after wind. *heart*
18 Because ^Rin much wisdom there is
much grief, and increasing knowledge *results in* increasing pain. Eccl. 2:23; 12:12

CHAPTER 2

Vanity of Striving After Pleasure

I SAID^Tto myself, "Come now, I will test
you with pleasure. So enjoy yourself." And
behold, it too was futility. *in my heart*

¹ Or, *Futility of futilities*

2 I said of laughter, "It is madness," and of pleasure, "What does it accomplish?"

3 I explored with my[T]mind *how* to stimulate my body with wine while my[T]mind was guiding *me* wisely, and how to take hold of folly, until I could see what good there is for the sons of men[t]to do under heaven the few years of their lives.   *heart · which they do*

Vanity of Great Accomplishments

4 I enlarged my works: I built houses for myself, I planted vineyards for myself;

5 I made gardens and parks for myself, and I planted in them all kinds of fruit trees;

6 I made ponds of water for myself from which to irrigate a forest of growing trees.

7 I bought male and female slaves, and I had [T]homeborn slaves. Also I possessed flocks and herds larger than all who preceded me in Jerusalem.   *sons of the house*

8 Also, I collected for myself silver and [R]gold, and the treasure of kings and provinces. I provided for myself[R]male and female singers and the pleasures of men—many concubines.   1 Kin. 9:28 · 2 Sam. 19:35

9 Then I became [R]great and increased more than all who preceded me in Jerusalem. My wisdom also stood by me. Eccl. 1:16

10 And[R]all that my eyes desired I did not refuse them. I did not withhold my heart from any pleasure, for my heart was pleased because of all my labor and this was my[T]reward for all my labor.   Eccl. 6:2 · Eccl. 3:22

11 Thus I considered all my activities which my hands had done and the labor which I had [T]exerted, and behold all was [2]vanity and striving after wind and there was no profit under the sun.   *labored to do*

12 So I turned to[R]consider wisdom, madness and folly, for what *will* the man *do* who will come after the king *except*[R]what has already been done?   Eccl. 1:17 · Eccl. 1:9, 10

13 And I saw that[R]wisdom excels folly as light excels darkness.   Eccl. 7:11, 12, 19; 9:18

14 The wise man's eyes are in his head, but the fool walks in darkness. And yet I know that one fate befalls them both.

15 Then I said[t]to myself, "As is the fate of the fool, it will also befall me. Why then have I been extremely wise?" So I said to myself, "This too is vanity."   *in my heart*

16 For there is no lasting remembrance of the wise man *as* with the fool, inasmuch as *in* the coming days all will be forgotten. And how the wise man and the fool alike die!

17 So I[R]hated life, for the work which had been done under the sun was [T]grievous to me; because everything is futility and striving after wind.   Eccl. 4:2, 3 · *evil*

Vanity of Hard Labor

18 Thus I hated [R]all the fruit of my labor for which I had labored under the sun, for I must[R]leave it to the man who will come after me.   Eccl. 1:3; 2:11 · Ps. 39:6; 49:10

19 And who knows whether he will be a wise man or a fool? Yet he will have[T]control over all the fruit of my labor for which I have labored by acting wisely under the sun. This too is[R]vanity.   *dominion* · 1 Tim. 6:10

20 Therefore I[r]completely despaired of all the fruit of my labor for which I had labored under the sun.   *turned aside my heart to despair*

21 When there is a man who has labored with wisdom, knowledge and[R]skill, then he [R]gives his[T]legacy to one who has not labored with them. This too is vanity and a great evil.   Eccl. 4:4 · Eccl. 2:18 · *share*

22 For what does a man get in[a]all his labor and in[T]his striving with which he labors under the sun?   Eccl. 1:3 · *the striving of his heart*

23 Because all his days his task is painful and grievous; even at night his[T]mind[R]does not rest. This too is vanity.   *heart* · Ps. 127:2

Conclusion: Be Content

24 There is[R]nothing better for a man *than* to eat and drink and tell himself that his labor is good. This also I have seen, that it is [R]from the hand of God.   Eccl. 2:3 · Eccl. 3:13

25 For who can eat and who can have enjoyment without Him?

26 For to a person who is good in His sight He has given wisdom and knowledge and joy, while to the sinner He has given the task of gathering and collecting so that he may give to one who is good in God's sight. This too is vanity and striving after wind.

CHAPTER 3

God Predetermines
the Events of Life

THERE is an appointed time for everything. And there is a [R]time for every [T]event under heaven—   Eccl. 3:17; 8:6 · *delight*

2 A time to give birth, and a[R]time to die;
   A time to plant, and a time to uproot what is planted.   Job 14:5; Heb. 9:27

3 A[R]time to kill, and a time to heal;
   A time to tear down, and a time to build up.   Gen. 9:6; 1 Sam. 2:6

4 A time to weep, and a time to laugh;
   A time to mourn, and a time to dance.

5 A time to throw stones, and a time to gather stones;
   A time to embrace, and a time to shun embracing.

6 A time to search, and a time to give up as lost;
   A time to keep, and a time to throw away.

7 A time to tear apart, and a time to sew together;
   A time to [R]be silent, and a time to speak.   Amos 5:13

[2] Or, *futility,* and so throughout this context

8 A time to love, and a time to hate;
 A time for war, and a time for peace.
9 [R]What profit is there to the worker from that in which he toils?   Eccl. 1:3; 2:11; 5:16

God Predetermines
the Conditions of Life

10 I have seen the [R]task which God has given the sons of men with which to occupy themselves.   Eccl. 1:13; 2:26

11 He has made everything [3]appropriate in its time. He has also set eternity in their heart,[A]yet so that man will not find out the work which God has done from the beginning even to the end.   *without which man*

12 I know that there is[R]nothing better for them than to rejoice and to do good in one's lifetime;   Eccl. 2:24

13 moreover, that every man who eats and drinks sees good in all his labor—it is the[R]gift of God.   Eccl. 2:24; 5:19

14 I know that everything God does will remain forever; there is nothing to add to it and there is nothing to take from it, for God has *so* worked that men should fear Him.

15 That[R]which is has been already, and that which will be has already been, for God seeks what has passed by.   Eccl. 1:9; 6:10

God Judges All

16 Furthermore, I have seen under the sun *that* in the place of justice there is[R]wickedness, and in the place of righteousness there is wickedness.   Eccl. 4:1; 5:8; 8:9

17 I said[T]to myself, "God[R]will judge both the righteous man and the wicked man," for a time for every[A]matter and for every deed is there.   *in my heart* • [2 Thess. 1:6–9] • *delight*

18 I said to myself concerning the sons of men, "God has surely tested them in order for them to see that they are but beasts."

19 For the fate of the sons of men and the fate of beasts is the same. As one dies so dies the other; indeed, they all have the same breath and there is no advantage for man over beast, for all is[A]vanity.   *futility*

20 All go to the same place. All came from the[R]dust and all return to the dust.   Gen. 3:19

21 Who knows that the[R]breath of man ascends upward and the breath of the beast descends downward to the earth?   Eccl. 12:7

22 And I have seen that nothing is better than that man should be happy in his activities, for that is his lot. For who will bring him to see what will occur after him?

CHAPTER 4

Evil Oppression

THEN I looked again at all the acts of[R]oppression which were being done under the sun. And behold *I saw* the tears of the oppressed and *that* they had[R]no one to comfort *them;* and on the side of their oppressors

was power, but they had no one to comfort *them.*   Job 35:9; Ps. 12:5 • Jer. 16:7; Lam. 1:9

2 So[R]I congratulated the dead who are already dead more than the living who are still living.   Job 3:11-26; Eccl. 2:17; 7:1

3 But[R]better *off* than both of them is the one who has never existed, who has never seen the evil activity that is done under the sun.   Job 3:11-22; Eccl. 6:3; Luke 23:29

Folly of Hard Work

4 And I have seen that every labor and every skill which is done is *the result of* rivalry between a man and his neighbor. This too is vanity and striving after wind.

5 The fool[R]folds his hands and[R]consumes his own flesh.   Prov. 6:10; 24:33 • Is. 9:20

6 One hand full of rest is better than two fists full of labor and striving after wind.

7 Then I looked again at vanity under the sun.

8 There was a certain man without a[T]dependent, having neither a son nor a brother, yet there was no end to all his labor. Indeed, his eyes were not satisfied with riches *and he never asked,* "And for whom am I laboring and depriving myself of pleasure?" This too is vanity and it is a grievous task. *second*

9 Two are better than one because they have a good return for their labor.

10 For if[T]either of them falls, the one will lift up his companion. But woe to the one who falls when there is not[A]another to lift him up.   *they fall* • *a second*

11 Furthermore, if two lie down together they[R]keep warm, but[R]how can one be warm *alone?*   *have warmth* • 1 Kin. 1:1-4

12 And if[T]one can overpower him who is alone, two can resist him. A cord of three *strands* is not quickly torn apart.   *he*

Transience of Popularity

13 A poor, yet wise lad is better than an old and foolish king who no longer knows *how* to receive[A]instruction.   *warning*

14 For he has come[R]out of prison to become king, even though he was born poor in his kingdom.   Gen. 41:14, 41-43

15 I have seen all the living under the sun throng to the side of the second lad who[T]replaces him.   *stands in his stead*

16 There is no end to all the people, to all who were before them, and even the ones who will come later will not be happy with him, for this too is[R]vanity and striving after wind.   Eccl. 1:14

CHAPTER 5

Insufficiences of Human Religion

GUARD[R]your steps as you go to the house of God, and draw near to listen rather than

---

[3] Lit., *beautiful*

to offer the[R]sacrifice of fools; for they do not know they are doing evil.   Ex. 3:5 • Prov. 15:8

2 Do not be hasty in word or impulsive in thought to bring up a matter in the presence of God. For God is in heaven and you are on the earth; therefore let your words be few.

3 For the dream comes through much[T]effort, and the voice of a[R]fool through many words.   task • Job 11:2; Prov. 15:2; Eccl. 10:14

4 When you[R]make a vow to God, do not be late in paying it, for *He takes* no delight in fools. Pay what you vow!   Ps. 50:14; 76:11

5 It is better that you should not vow than that you should vow and not pay.

6 Do not let your speech cause you to sin and do not say in the presence of the messenger *of God* that it was a mistake. Why should God be angry on account of your voice and destroy the work of your hands?

7 For in many dreams and in many words there is emptiness. Rather, fear God.

Wealth Does Not Satisfy

8 If you see oppression of the poor and denial of justice and righteousness in the province, do not be shocked at the sight, for one official watches over another official, and there are higher officials over them.

9 After all, a king who cultivates the field is an advantage to the land.

10 He who loves money will not be satisfied with money, nor he who loves abundance *with its* income. This too is vanity.

11 When good things increase, those who consume them increase. So what is the advantage to their owners except to look on?

12 The sleep of the working man is[R]pleasant, whether he eats little or much. But the [T]full stomach of the rich man does not allow him to sleep.   Prov. 3:24 • *satiety*

Wealth Brings Difficulties

13 There is a grievous evil *which* I have seen under the sun:[R]riches being[T]hoarded by their owner to his hurt.   Eccl. 6:2 • *guarded*

14 When those riches were lost through a bad investment and he had fathered a son, then there was nothing to support him.

15 As he had come naked from his mother's womb, so will he return as he came. He will[R]take nothing from the fruit of his labor that he can carry in his hand.   Ps. 49:17

16 And this also is a grievous evil—exactly as a man[T]is born, thus will he[T]die. So, [R]what is the advantage to him who[R]toils for the wind?   *comes • go* • Eccl. 1:3 • Prov. 11:29

17 Throughout his life [R]*he* also eats in darkness with[R]great vexation, sickness and anger.   Ps. 127:2 • Eccl. 2:23

Wealth Comes Ultimately from God

18 Here is what I have seen to be good and fitting: to eat, to drink and enjoy oneself in all one's labor in which he toils under the sun *during* the few years of his life which God has given him; for this is his reward.

19 Furthermore, as for every man to whom God has given riches and wealth, He has also[R]empowered him to eat from them and to receive his[A]reward and rejoice in his labor; this is the gift of God.   Eccl. 6:2 • *share*

20 For he will not often[T]consider the years of his life, because God keeps him occupied with the gladness of his heart.   *remember*

CHAPTER 6

No Satisfaction in Wealth

THERE is an evil which I have seen under the sun and it is prevalent among men—

2 a man to whom God has given riches and wealth and honor so that his soul lacks nothing of all that he desires, but God has not empowered him to eat from them, for a foreigner[T]enjoys them. This is[A]vanity and a severe affliction.   *eats from them • futility*

No Satisfaction in Children

3 If a man fathers a hundred *children* and lives many years, however many[T]they be, but his soul is not satisfied with good things, and he does not even have a *proper* [R]burial, *then* I say, "Better the miscarriage than he,   *the days of his years* • Is. 14:20; Jer. 8:2

4 for it comes in futility and goes into obscurity; and its name is covered in obscurity.

5 "It never sees the sun and it never knows *anything;* it is better off than he.

6 "Even if the *other* man lives a thousand years twice and does not [T]enjoy good things—do not all go to one place?"   *see*

No Satisfaction in Labor

7 All a man's labor is for his mouth and yet the[T]appetite is not[T]satisfied.   *soul • filled*

8 For[R]what advantage does the wise man have over the fool? What *advantage* does the poor man have, knowing *how* to walk before the living?   Eccl. 2:15

No Satisfaction in the Future

9 What the eyes see is better than what the soul[T]desires. This too is[R]futility and a striving after wind.   *goes after* • Eccl. 1:14

10 Whatever [R]exists has already been named, and it is known what man is; for he [R]cannot dispute with him who is stronger than he is.   Eccl. 1:9; 3:15 • Prov. 21:30; Is. 45:9

11 For there are many words which increase futility. What *then* is the advantage to a man?

12 For who knows what is good for a man during *his* lifetime, *during* the few[T]years of his futile life? He will [T]spend them like a shadow. For who can tell a man what will be after him under the sun?   *days • do*

CHAPTER 7

Wisdom and Folly Contrasted

A ^RGOOD name is better than a good ointment,   Prov. 22:1
And the ^Rday of *one's* death is better
than the day of one's birth. Eccl. 4:2

2   It is better to go to a house of mourn-
ing
Than to go to a house of feasting,
Because^Tthat is the end of every man,
And the living takes *it* to heart.   death

3   ^RSorrow is better than laughter,
For^Rwhen a face is sad a heart may be
happy.   Eccl. 2:2 • [2 Cor. 7:10]

4   The ^Tmind of the wise is in the house
of mourning,
While the ^Tmind of fools is in the
house of pleasure.   heart

5   It is better to^Rlisten to the rebuke of a
wise man   Ps. 141:5; [Prov. 6:23; 13:18]
Than for one to listen to the song of
fools.

6   For as the^Tcrackling of^Rthorn bushes
under a pot,   *voice* • Ps. 58:9; 118:12
So is the^Rlaughter of the fool,
And this too is futility.   Eccl. 2:2

7   For ^Roppression makes a wise man
mad,   Eccl. 4:1; 5:8
And a bribe corrupts the heart.

8   The^Rend of a matter is better than its
beginning;   Eccl. 7:1
^RPatience of spirit is better than
haughtiness of spirit.   Prov. 14:29

9   Do not be ^Teager in your heart to be
angry,   *hasty in your spirit*
For anger resides in the bosom of
fools.

10 Do not say, "Why is it that the former
days were better than these?"
For it is not from wisdom that you
ask about this.

11 Wisdom along with an inheritance is
good
And an ^Radvantage to those who see
the sun.   Prov. 8:10, 11; Eccl. 2:13

12 For wisdom is^Tprotection *just as* money is^Tprotection.   *in a shadow*
But the advantage of knowledge is
that^Rwisdom preserves the lives of
its possessors.   Prov. 3:18; 8:35

13 Consider the^Rwork of God,
For who is^Rable to straighten what He
has bent?   Eccl. 3:11; 8:17 • Eccl. 1:15

14 ^RIn the day of prosperity be happy,
But^Rin the day of adversity consider—
God has made the one as well as the
other   Eccl. 3:22 • Deut. 8:5; Job 2:10
So that man may not discover any-
thing *that will be* after him.

Wisdom of Moderation

15 I have seen everything during my^Tlife-
time of futility; there is ^Ra righteous man
who perishes in his righteousness, and there
is^Ra wicked man who prolongs *his life* in his
wickedness.   *days* • Eccl. 8:14 • Eccl. 8:12, 13

16 Do not be excessively ^Rrighteous, and
do not^Rbe overly wise. Why should you ruin
yourself?   Prov. 25:16; Phil. 3:6 • Rom. 12:3

17 Do not be excessively wicked, and do
not be a fool. Why should you^Rdie before
your time?   Job 22:16; Ps. 55:23; Prov. 10:27

18 It is good that you grasp one thing, and
also not let go of the other; for the one who
fears God comes forth with both of them.

Strength of Wisdom

19 ^RWisdom strengthens a wise man more
than ten rulers who are in a city.   Eccl. 7:12

20 Indeed, there is not a righteous man on
earth who *continually* does good and who
never sins.

21 Also, do not^Ttake seriously all words
which are spoken, lest you hear your ser-
vant^Rcursing you.   *give your heart to* • Prov. 30:10

22 For you also have realized that you
likewise have many times cursed others.

23 I tested all this with wisdom, *and* I
said, "I will be wise,"^Rbut it was far from
me.   Eccl. 3:11; 8:17

24 What has been is remote and exceed-
ingly^Tmysterious. Who can discover it? *deep*

25 I^Tdirected my^Tmind to know, to investigate, and to seek wisdom and an explana-
tion, and to know the evil of folly and the
foolishness of madness.   *turned about* • *heart*

26 And I discovered more ^Rbitter than
death the woman whose heart is snares and
nets, whose hands are chains. One who is
pleasing to God will escape from her, but
the sinner will be captured by her.   Prov. 5:4

27 "Behold, I have discovered this," says

7:20   Individual Sin—Each individual man, woman, and child who composes mankind is a sinner. Paul points
out in Romans 3:13–16 that "Their throat is an open grave . . . the poison of asps [a small, deadly poisonous
snake] is under their lips; whose mouth is full of cursing and bitterness; their feet are swift to shed blood [consider
the high incidence of violent crime, murder, and abortion that infects our society], destruction and misery are in
their paths [whatever man touches he corrupts]." All of this shows that there is no person that seeks after God and
no person does what is right (Page 1133—Rom. 3:10, 11). Each individual man, woman, and child needs the
righteousness of God. Without God's righteousness no one can ever enter or stand in God's presence. Plainly,
every man, woman, and child needs to have a new life because each is a sinner.
Now turn to Page 1136—Rom. 6:23: New Life: A Free Gift.

the Preacher, "*adding* one thing to another to find an explanation,

28 which[T]I am still seeking but have not found. I have found one man among a thousand, but I have not found a[R]woman among all these.   *my soul still seeks* • 1 Kin. 11:3

29"Behold, I have found only this, that [R]God made men upright, but they have sought out many devices."   Gen. 1:27

CHAPTER 8

Submit to Authority

WHO is like the wise man and who knows the interpretation of a matter? A man's wisdom[R]illumines[T]him and causes his stern face to[A]beam.   Ex. 34:29, 30 • *his face* • *change*

2 I say, "Keep the[T]command of the king because of the oath[T]before God.   *mouth* • *of*

3"Do not be in a hurry[T]to leave him. Do not join in an evil matter, for he will do whatever he pleases."   Eccl. 10:4

4 Since the word of the king is authoritative,[R]who will say to him, "What are you doing?"   Job 9:12; Dan. 4:35

5 He who keeps a *royal* command experiences no[T]trouble, for a wise heart knows the proper time and procedure.   *evil thing*

6 For[R]there is a proper time and procedure for every delight, when a man's trouble is heavy upon him.   Eccl. 3:1, 17

7 If no one[R]knows what will happen, who can tell him when it will happen?   Eccl. 3:22

8 [R]No man has authority to restrain the wind with the wind, or authority over the day of death; and there is no discharge in the time of war, and evil will not deliver [T]those who practice it.   Ps. 49:7 • *its possessors*

9 All this I have seen and applied my [T]mind to every deed that has been done under the sun wherein a man has exercised authority over *another* man to his hurt.   *heart*

Inability to Understand
All God's Doing

10 So then, I have seen the wicked buried, those who used to go in and out from the holy place, and they are[R]*soon* forgotten in the city where they did thus. This too is futility.   Eccl. 1:11; 2:16; 9:5, 15

11 Because the[R]sentence against an evil deed is not executed quickly, therefore[R]the hearts of the sons of men among them are given fully to do evil.   Ex. 34:6 • Eccl. 9:3

12 Although a sinner does evil a hundred *times* and may[R]lengthen his *life*, still I know that it will be well for those who fear God, who fear[T]Him openly.   Eccl. 7:15 • *before Him*

13 But it will not be well for the evil man and he will not lengthen his days like a shadow, because he does not fear God.

14 There is futility which is done on the earth, that is, there are[R]righteous men to whom it[T]happens according to the deeds of the wicked. On the other hand, there are[R]evil

men to whom it[T]happens according to the deeds of the righteous. I say that this too is futility.   Ps. 73:14 • *strikes* • Job 21:7

15 So I commended pleasure, for there is nothing good for a man under the sun except to eat and to drink and to be merry, and this will stand by him in his[T]toils *throughout* the days of his life which God has given him under the sun.   *labor*

16 When I gave my heart to know wisdom and to see the task which has been done on the earth (even though one should[T]never sleep day or night),   *see no sleep in his eyes*

17 and I saw every work of God, *I* concluded that man cannot discover the work which has been done under the sun. Even though man should seek laboriously, he will not discover; and though the wise man should say, "I know," he cannot discover.

CHAPTER 9

Judgment Comes to All Men

FOR I have taken all this to my heart and explain[T]it that righteous men, wise men, and their deeds are in the hand of God. Man does not know whether *it will be*[R]love or hatred; anything awaits him.   *all this* • Eccl. 9:6

2 It is the same for all. There is one fate for the righteous and for the wicked; for the good, for the clean, and for the unclean; for the man who offers a sacrifice and for the one who does not sacrifice. As the good man is, so is the sinner; as the swearer is, so is the one who[T]is afraid to swear.   *fears an oath*

3 This is an evil in all that is done under the sun, that there is[R]one fate for all men. Furthermore,[R]the hearts of the sons of men are full of evil, and[R]insanity is in their hearts throughout their lives. Afterwards they go to the dead.   Eccl. 9:2 • Eccl. 8:11 • Eccl. 1:17

4 For whoever is joined with all the living, there is hope; surely a live dog is better than a dead lion.

5 For the living know they will die; but the dead[R]do not know anything, nor have they any longer a reward, for their[R]memory is forgotten.   Job 14:21 • Ps. 88:12; Eccl. 1:11

6 Indeed their love, their hate, and their zeal have already perished, and they will no longer have a[R]share in all that is done under the sun.   Eccl. 2:10; 3:22

Enjoy Life While You Have It

7 Go *then*, eat your bread in happiness, and drink your wine with a cheerful heart; for God has already approved your works.

8 Let your clothes be white all the time, and let not oil be lacking on your head.

9 Enjoy life with the woman whom you love all the days of your[T]fleeting life which He has given to you under the sun; for this is your reward in life, and in your toil in which you have labored under the sun.   *life of vanity*

10 Whatever your hand finds to do, verily, do *it* with all your might; for there is no ac-

tivity or planning or wisdom in [R]Sheol where you are going. Is. 38:10

11 I again saw under the sun that the [R]race is not to the swift, and the battle is not to the warriors, and neither is bread to the wise, nor wealth to the discerning, nor favor to men of ability; for time and [R]chance overtake them all. Amos 2:14, 15 • 1 Sam. 6:9

12 Moreover, man does not [R]know his time: like fish caught in a treacherous net, and [R]birds trapped in a snare, so the sons of men are ensnared at an evil time when it suddenly falls on them. Eccl. 8:7 • Prov. 7:23

Value of Wisdom

13 Also this I came to see as wisdom under the sun, and it impressed me.

14 There was a small city with few men in it and a great king came to it, surrounded it, and constructed large siegeworks against it.

15 But there was found in it a poor wise man and he [A]delivered the city by his wisdom. Yet [R]no one remembered that poor man. might have delivered • Eccl. 2:16; 8:10

16 So I said, "Wisdom is better than strength." But the wisdom of the poor man is despised and his words are not heeded.

17 The [R]words of the wise heard in quietness are better than the shouting of a ruler among fools. Eccl. 7:5; 10:12

18 Wisdom is better than weapons of war, but one sinner destroys much good.

CHAPTER 10

Wisdom's Characteristics

DEAD flies make a [R]perfumer's oil stink, so a little foolishness is weightier than wisdom and honor. Ex. 30:25

2 A wise man's heart *directs him* toward the right, but the foolish [R]man's heart *directs him* toward the left. Matt. 6:33; Col. 3:1

3 Even when the fool walks along the road his [T]sense is lacking, and he demonstrates to everyone *that* he is a fool. heart

4 If the ruler's [T]temper rises against you, [R]do not abandon your position, because composure allays great offenses. spirit • Eccl. 8:3

5 There is an evil I have seen under the sun, like an error which goes forth from the ruler—

6 folly is set in many exalted places while rich men sit in humble places.

7 I have seen slaves *riding* on horses and princes walking like slaves on the land.

8 [R]He who digs a pit may fall into it, and a [R]serpent may bite him who breaks through a wall. Ps. 7:15; Prov. 26:27 • Amos 5:19

9 He who quarries stones may be hurt by them, and he who splits logs may be endangered by them.

10 If the [T]axe is dull and he does not sharpen *its* edge, then he must [T]exert more strength. Wisdom has the advantage of giving success. iron • strengthen

11 If the serpent bites before being charmed, there is no profit for the charmer.

12 [R]Words from the mouth of a wise man are gracious, while the lips of a [R]fool consume him; Prov. 10:32; 22:11 • Prov. 10:14; 18:7

13 the beginning of his talking is folly, and the end of [T]it is wicked madness. his mouth

14 Yet the [R]fool multiplies words. No man knows what will happen, and who can tell him what will come after him? [Prov. 15:2]

15 The toil of a fool *so* wearies him that he does not *even* know how to go to a city.

Wisdom Related to the King

16 Woe to you, O land, whose king is a lad and whose princes [T]feast in the morning. eat

17 Blessed are you, O land, whose king is of nobility and whose princes eat at the appropriate time—for strength, and not for [R]drunkenness. Prov. 31:4; Is. 5:11

18 Through indolence the rafters sag, and through slackness the house leaks.

19 *Men* prepare a meal for enjoyment, and wine makes life merry, and money [T]is the answer to everything. answers all

20 Furthermore, [R]in your bedchamber do not [R]curse a king, and in your sleeping rooms do not curse a rich man, for a bird of the heavens will carry the sound, and the winged creature will make the matter known. 2 Kin. 6:12; Luke 12:3 • Acts 23:5

CHAPTER 11

Wisdom Related to Business

CAST your bread on the surface of the waters, for you will find it after many days.

2 Divide your portion to seven, or even to eight, for you do not know what [R]misfortune may occur on the earth. Eccl. 11:8; 12:1

3 If the clouds are full, they pour out rain upon the earth; and whether a tree falls toward the south or toward the north, wherever the tree falls, there it [T]lies. is

4 He who watches the wind will not sow and he who looks at the clouds will not reap.

5 Just as you do not [R]know the path of the wind and [R]how bones *are formed* in the womb of the [T]pregnant woman, so you do not know the activity of God who makes all things. John 3:8 • Ps. 139:13-16 • full

6 Sow your seed in the morning, and do not [T]be idle in the evening, for you do not know whether [T]morning or evening sowing will succeed, or whether both of them alike will be good. let down your hand • this or that

Rejoice in Your Youth

7 The light is pleasant, and *it is* good for the eyes to [R]see the sun. Eccl. 6:5; 7:11

8 Indeed, if a man should live many years, let him [R]rejoice in them all, and let him remember the [R]days of darkness, for they shall be many. Everything that is to come *will be* futility. Eccl. 9:7 • Eccl. 12:1

9 Rejoice, young man, during your childhood, and let your heart be pleasant during

the days of young manhood. And follow the
[T]impulses of your heart and the desires of
your eyes. Yet know that God will bring you
to judgment for all these things.   *ways*

10 So, remove vexation from your heart
and put away pain from your body, because
childhood and the prime of life are fleeting.

CHAPTER 12

Remember God in Your Youth

REMEMBER[R]also your Creator in the days
of your youth, before the evil days come and
the years draw near when you will say, "I
have no delight in them";   Neh. 4:14; Ps. 63:6

2 before the[R]sun, the light, the moon, and
the stars are darkened, and clouds return after the rain;   Is. 5:30; 13:10; Ezek. 32:7, 8

3 in the day that the watchmen of the
house tremble, and mighty men[R]stoop, the
grinding ones stand idle because they are
few, and[R]those who look through[A]windows
grow dim;   Ps. 35:14; 38:6 • Gen. 27:1 • *holes*

4 and the doors on the street are shut as
the sound of the grinding mill is low, and
one will arise at the sound of the bird, and
all the daughters of song will sing softly.

5 Furthermore,[T]men are afraid of a high
place and of terrors on the road; the almond
tree blossoms, the grasshopper drags himself along, and the caperberry is ineffective.
For man goes to his eternal home while
mourners go about in the street.   *they*

6 *Remember Him* before the silver cord
is broken and the[R]golden bowl is crushed,
the pitcher by the well is shattered and the
wheel at the cistern is crushed;   Zech. 4:2, 3

7 then the[R]dust will return to the earth as
it was, and the[A]spirit will return to[R]God who
gave it.   Gen. 3:19 • *breath* • Num. 16:22; 27:16

8"Vanity[R]of vanities," says the Preacher,
"all is vanity!"   Eccl. 1:2

Fear God and Keep His Commandments

9 In addition to being a wise man, the
Preacher also taught the people knowledge;
and he pondered, searched out and arranged[R]many proverbs.   1 Kin. 4:32

10 The Preacher sought to find delightful
words and to write words of truth correctly.

11 The[R]words of wise men are like[R]goads,
and masters of *these* collections are like
[T]well-driven nails; they are given by one
Shepherd.   Prov. 1:6 • Acts 2:37 • *planted*

12 But beyond this, my son, be warned:
the[T]writing of[R]many books is endless, and
excessive[R]devotion *to books* is wearying to
the body.   *making* • 1 Kin. 4:32 • Eccl. 1:18

13 The conclusion, when all has been
heard, *is:* fear God and keep His commandments, because this *applies to* every person.

14 For God will bring every act to judgment, everything which is hidden, whether
it is good or evil.

THE SONG OF SOLOMON

📖 THE BOOK OF SONG OF SOLOMON

The Song of Solomon is a love song written by Solomon and abounding in metaphors and oriental imagery. Historically, it depicts the wooing and wedding of a shepherdess by King Solomon, and the joys and heartaches of wedded love.

Allegorically, it pictures Israel as God's espoused bride (Hos. 2:19, 20), and the Church as the bride of Christ. As human life finds its highest fulfillment in the love of man and woman, so spiritual life finds its highest fulfillment in the love of God for His people and Christ for His Church.

The book is arranged like scenes in a drama with three main speakers: the bride (Shulammite), the king (Solomon), and a chorus (daughters of Jerusalem).

The Hebrew title *Shir Hashirim* comes from 1:1, "The song of songs." This is in the superlative and speaks of Solomon's most exquisite song. The Greek title *Asma Asmaton* and the Latin *Canticum Canticorum* also mean "Song of Songs" or "The Best Song." The name *Canticles* ("Songs") is derived from the Latin title. Because Solomon is mentioned in 1:1, the book is also known as the Song of Solomon.

✒️ THE AUTHOR OF SONG OF SOLOMON

Solomonic authorship is rejected by critics who claim it is a later collection of songs. Many take 1:1 to mean "which is about or concerning Solomon." But the internal evidence of the book strongly favors the traditional position that Solomon is its author. Solomon is specifically mentioned seven times (1:1, 5; 3:7, 9, 11; 8:11, 12), and he is identified as the groom. There is evidence of royal luxury and rich imported goods (e.g., 3:6–11). The king by this time also had sixty queens and eighty concubines (6:8). Solomon's harem at its fullest extent reached seven hundred queens and three hundred concubines (1 Kin. 11:3).

First Kings 4:32, 33 says that Solomon composed 1,005 songs and had intimate knowledge of the plant and animal world. This greatest of his songs alludes to twenty-one species of plants and fifteen species of animals. It cites geographical locations in the north and in the south, indicating that they were still one kingdom. For example, 6:4 mentions both Tirzah and Jerusalem, the northern and southern capitals (after Solomon's time, Samaria became the northern capital). Because of the poetic imagery, the Song of Solomon uses

forty-nine words that occur nowhere else in Scripture.

⏳ THE TIME OF SONG OF SOLOMON

This song was written primarily from the point of view of the Shulammite, but Solomon was its author, probably early in his reign, about 965 B.C. There is a problem regarding how a man with a harem of 140 women (6:8) could extol the love of the Shulammite as though she were his only bride. It may be that Solomon's relationship with the Shulammite was the only pure romance he ever experienced. The bulk of his marriages were political arrangements. It is significant that the Shulammite was a vineyard keeper of no great means. This book was also written before Solomon plunged into gross immorality and idolatry. "For it came about when Solomon was old, his wives turned his heart away after other gods; and his heart was not wholly devoted to the LORD his God" (1 Kin. 11:4).

The Shulammite addresses the king as "my beloved" and the king addresses his bride as "my love." The daughters of Jerusalem were probably attendants to the Shulammite. The term *Shulammite* appears only in 6:13, and it may be derived from the town of Shunem which was southwest of the Sea of Galilee in the tribal area of Issachar. The song refers to fifteen geographic locations from Lebanon in the north to Egypt in the south: Kedar (1:5), Egypt (1:9), Engedi (1:14), Sharon (2:1), Jerusalem (2:7), Lebanon (3:9), Mount Gilead (4:1), Amana (4:8), Senir (4:8), Hermon (4:8), Tirzah (6:4), Heshbon (7:4), Damascus (7:4), Carmel (7:5), and Baal-hamon (8:11).

✝️ THE CHRIST OF SONG OF SOLOMON

In the Old Testament, Israel is regarded as the bride of Yahweh (see Is. 54:5, 6; Jer. 2:2; Ezek. 16:8–14; Hos. 2:16–20). In the New Testament, the Church is seen as the bride of Christ (see 2 Cor. 11:2; Eph. 5:23–25; Rev. 19:7–9; 21:9). The Song of Solomon illustrates the former and anticipates the latter.

🔑 KEYS TO SONG OF SOLOMON

Key Word: Love in Marriage—The purpose of this book depends on the viewpoint taken as to its primary thrust. Is it fictional, allegorical, or historical?

(1) *Fictional:* Some hold that this song is a fictional drama that portrays Solomon's attraction and marriage to a poor but beautiful

girl from the country. However, the book gives every indication that the story really happened.

(2) *Allegorical:* In this view, the primary purpose of the song is to illustrate the truth of God's love for His people whether the events were fictional or not. Some commentators insist that the book is indeed historical, but its primary purpose is typical, that is, to present God's love for His bride Israel or Christ's love for His Church. However, this interpretation is subjective and lacking in evidence. In other scriptures the husband and wife relationship is used symbolically (cf. Ezek. 16; 23; Hos. 1—3), but these are always indicated as symbols. This may be an application of the book, but it should not be the primary interpretation.

(3) *Historical:* The Song of Songs is a poetic record of Solomon's actual romance with a Shulammite woman. The various scenes in the book exalt the joys of love in courtship and marriage and teach that physical beauty and sexuality in marriage should not be despised as base or unspiritual. It offers a proper perspective of human love and avoids the extremes of lust and asceticism. Only when sexuality is viewed in the wrong way, as something akin to evil, is an attempt made to allegorize the book. But this is part of God's creation with its related desires and pleasures, and it is reasonable that He would provide us with a guide to a pure sexual relationship between a husband and wife. In fact, the union of the two sexes was originally intended to illustrate the oneness of the Godhead (see Gen. 1:27; 2:24; 1 Cor. 6:16—20). Thus, the Song is a bold and positive endorsement by God of marital love in all its physical and emotional beauty. This interpretation does not mean that the book has no spiritual illustrations and applications. It certainly illustrates God's love for His cove-nant people Israel, and anticipates Christ's love for His bride, the Church.

Key Verses: Song of Solomon 7:10 and 8:7— "I am my beloved's, and his desire is for me" (7:10).

"Many waters cannot quench love, nor will rivers overflow it; if a man were to give all the riches of his house for love, it would be utterly despised" (8:7).

*Key Chapter: Song of Solomon—*Since the whole book is a unity, there is no Key Chapter; rather, all eight chapters beautifully depict the love of a married couple.

SURVEY OF SONG OF SOLOMON

Solomon wrote 1,005 songs (1 Kin. 4:32), but this beautiful eulogy of love stood out among them as the "song of songs" (1:1). The great literary value of this song can be seen in its rich use of metaphor and oriental imagery as it extols the purity, beauty, and satisfaction of love. It is never crass, but often intimate, as it explores the dimensions of the relationship between two lovers: attraction, desire, companionship, pleasure, union, separation, faithfulness, and praise. Like Ecclesiastes, this little book is not easily outlined, and various schemes can be used. It abounds with sudden changes of speakers, and they are not identified. The beginning of love is seen in 1:1—5:1, and the broadening of love is found in 5:2—8:14.

The Beginning of Love (1:1—5:1): King Solomon has a vineyard in the country of the Shulammite (6:13; 8:11). The Shulammite must work in the vineyard with her brothers (1:6; 8:11, 12); and when Solomon visits the area, he wins her heart and eventually takes her to the palace in Jerusalem as his bride. She is tanned from hours of work outside in the vine-

FOCUS	BEGINNING OF LOVE		BROADENING OF LOVE	
REFERENCE	1:1————————3:6	———————5:2———————	——————7:11———————8:14	
DIVISION	FALLING IN LOVE	UNITED IN LOVE	STRUGGLING IN LOVE	GROWING IN LOVE
TOPIC	COURTSHIP	WEDDING	PROBLEM	PROGRESS
	FOSTERING OF LOVE	FULFILLMENT OF LOVE	FRUSTRATION OF LOVE	FAITHFULNESS OF LOVE
LOCATION	ISRAEL			
TIME	c. 1 YEAR			

yard, but she is "most beautiful among women" (1:6, 8).

This song is arranged like scenes in a one-act drama with three main speakers—the bride (the Shulammite), the king (Solomon), and a chorus (the daughters of Jerusalem). It is not always clear who is speaking, but this is a likely arrangement:

The bride: 1:2–4, 5–7, 12–14, 16, 17; 2:1, 3–6, 8–17; 3:1–4; 4:16; 5:2–8, 10–16; 6:2, 3, 11, 12; 7:9–13; 8:1–3, 6, 7, 10–12, 14.

The groom: 1:8–10, 15; 2:2, 7; 3:5; 4:1–15; 5:1; 6:4–10, 13; 7:1–9; 8:4, 5, 13.

The chorus: 1:4, 11; 3:6–11; 5:9; 6:1, 13; 8:5, 8, 9.

Chapters 1—3 give a series of recollections of the courtship: (1) the bride's longing for affection at the palace before the wedding (1:2–8), (2) expressions of mutual love in the banquet hall (1:9—2:7), (3) a springtime visit of the king to the bride's home in the country (2:8–17), (4) the Shulammite's dream of separation from her beloved (3:1–5), and (5) the ornate wedding procession from the bride's home to Jerusalem (3:6–11).

In 4:1—5:1, Solomon praises his bride from head to foot with a superb chain of similes and metaphors. Her virginity is compared to "a garden locked" (4:12), and the garden is entered when the marriage is consummated (4:16—5:1). The union is commended, possibly by God, in 5:1.

The Broadening of Love (5:2—8:14): Some time after the wedding, the Shulammite has a troubled dream (5:2) in the palace while Solomon is away. In her dream Solomon comes to her door, but she answers too late—he is gone. She panics and searches for him late at night in Jerusalem. Upon his return, Solomon assures her of his love and praises her beauty (6:4—7:10). The Shulammite begins to think of her country home and tries to persuade her beloved to return there with her (7:11—8:4). The journey takes place in 8:5–7 and their relationship continues to deepen. Their love will not be overthrown by jealousy or circumstances. At her homecoming (8:8–14) the Shulammite reflects on her brothers' care for her when she was young (8:8, 9). She remains virtuous "I was a wall" (8:10), and is now in a position to look out for her brothers' welfare (8:11, 12). The song concludes with a dual invitation of lover and beloved (8:13, 14).

CHAPTER 1

Bride's Longing for Affection

THE [1]Song of Songs, which is Solomon's.

2"[2]May he kiss me with the kisses of his mouth!
For your love is better than wine.
3"Your oils have a pleasing fragrance,
Your[R]name is *like* purified oil;   Eccl. 7:1
Therefore the[R]maidens love you. *virgins*
4"Draw me after you *and* let us run together!

The [R]king has brought me into his chambers."   Ps. 45:14, 15

"[3]We will rejoice in you and be glad;
We will [T]extol your [R]love more than wine.   *mention with praise* • Song 1:4
Rightly do they love you."

5"[4]I am black but[R]lovely, Song 2:14; 4:3; 6:4
O[R]daughters of Jerusalem, Song 2:7; 3:5
Like the[R]tents of Kedar,
Like the curtains of Solomon. Is. 60:7

[1] Or, *Best of the Songs*   [2] BRIDE   [3] CHORUS   [4] BRIDE

6"Do not stare at me because I am
  ^swarthy,   *black*
For the sun has burned me.
My ^Rmother's sons were angry with me;
They made me ^Rcaretaker of the vine-
  yards,
But I have not taken care of my own
  vineyard.   ^R   Ps. 69:8 · Song 8:11
7"Tell me, O you ^Rwhom my soul loves,
Where do you pasture *your flock*,
Where do you make *it* lie down at
  noon?   Song 3:1-4 · Song 2:16; 6:3
For why should I be like one who veils
  herself
Beside the flocks of your ^Rcompan-
  ions?"   Song 8:13

8"5If you yourself do not know,
^RMost beautiful among women,
Go forth on the trail of the flock,
And pasture your young goats
By the tents of the shepherds.   Song 5:9

Expressions of Mutual Love

9"To^T me, my darling, you are like
My mare among the chariots of Pharaoh.   *I have compared you to*
10"Your ^Rcheeks are lovely with ornaments,   Song 5:13
Your neck with strings of beads."

11"6We will make for you ornaments of
  gold
With beads of silver."

12"4While the king was at his ^table,   *couch*
My perfume gave forth its fragrance.
13"My beloved is to me a pouch of ^Rmyrrh
Which lies all night between my
  breasts.   Ps. 45:8; John 19:39
14"My beloved is to me a cluster of ^Rhenna
  blossoms   Song 4:13
In the vineyards of Engedi."

15"5How^T beautiful you are, my darling,
^THow beautiful you are!   *Behold*
Your ^Reyes are *like* doves."   Song 4:1

16"4How handsome you are, ^Rmy beloved,
And so pleasant!   Song 2:3, 9, 17
Indeed, our couch is luxuriant!
17"The beams of our houses are cedars,
Our rafters, ^cypresses.   *junipers*

CHAPTER 2

"6"4I AM the ^Trose of ^RSharon,   *crocus* · Is. 33:9
The ^Rlily of the valleys."   Song 5:13; 7:2

2"5Like a lily among the thorns,
So is my darling among the maidens."

3"7Like an ^apple^R tree among the trees of
  the forest,   *apricot* · Song 8:5
So is my beloved among the ^Tyoung
  men.   *sons*
In his shade I took great delight and sat
  down,
And his fruit was sweet to my taste.
4"He has brought me to *his* banquet hall,
And his banner over me is love.
5"Sustain me with raisin cakes,
Refresh me with ^apples,   *apricots*
Because ^TI am lovesick.   Song 5:8
6"*Let* his left hand be under my head
And his right hand embrace me."

7"8I ^Radjure you, O ^Rdaughters of Jerusalem,   Song 3:5; 5:8, 9; 8:4 · Song 1:5
By the ^Rgazelles or by the hinds of the
  field,   Prov. 6:5; Song 2:9, 17; 3:5; 8:14
That you will not arouse or awaken *my*
  love,
Until ^she pleases."   *it*

Visit of the King to the Bride's Home

8"7Listen! My beloved!
Behold, he is coming,
Climbing^R on the mountains,
Leaping on the hills!   Song 2:17; Is. 52:7
9"My beloved is like a ^Rgazelle or a young
  ^Tstag.   Prov. 6:5; Song 2:17 · *of the stags*
Behold, he is standing behind our wall,
He is looking through the windows,
He is peering through the lattice.

10"My beloved responded and said to me,
'Arise, my darling, my beautiful one,
And come along.   Song 2:13
11 'For behold, the winter is past,
The rain is over *and* gone.
12 'The flowers have *already* appeared in
  the land;
The time has arrived for ^pruning *the*
  vines,   *singing*
And the voice of the ^Rturtledove has
  been heard in our land.   Gen. 15:9
13 'The fig tree has ripened its figs,
And the ^Rvines in blossom have given
  forth *their* fragrance.
Arise, my darling, my beautiful one,
And come along!' "   Song 7:12
14"O my dove, ^Rin the clefts of the ^rock,
In the secret place of the steep ^path-
  way,   Jer. 48:28 · *crag* · *cliff*
Let me see your ^Tform,   *appearance*
^RLet me hear your voice;   Song 8:13
For your voice is sweet,
And your form is ^Rlovely."   Song 1:5

15"Catch ^Rthe foxes for us,   Ezek. 13:4
The ^little foxes that are ruining the
  vineyards,   *young*
While our vineyards are in blossom."
16"My beloved is mine, and I am his;
He pastures *his flock* among the lilies.
17"Until ^Tthe cool of the day when the
  shadows flee away,   *the day blows*

4 BRIDE   5 BRIDEGROOM
6 CHORUS   7 BRIDE   8 BRIDEGROOM

Turn, my beloved, and be like a gazelle
Or a young stag on the mountains of
^Bether."   *cleavage* or *a kind of spice*

CHAPTER 3

Bride's Dream of Separation

3 ⁹ON my bed night after night I sought
him,
  ^RWhom my soul loves;   Song 1:7
  I sought him but did not find him.
2 'I must arise now and go about the city;
  In the streets and in the squares
  I must seek him whom my soul loves.'
  I sought him but did not find him.
3 "The^R watchmen who make the rounds
  in the city found me,
  And I said, 'Have you seen him whom
  my soul loves?'   Is. 21:6-8, 11, 12
4 "Scarcely^Thad I^Tleft them
  When I found him whom my soul
  loves;   Prov. 8:17 · *passed*
  I^Rheld on to him and would not let him
  go,   Prov. 4:13; Rom. 8:35, 39
  Until I had^Rbrought him to my mother's
  house,   Song 8:2
  And into the room of her who conceived me."

5 "^10I^Radjure you, O daughters of Jerusalem,   Song 2:7; 5:8; 8:4
  By the^Rgazelles or by the hinds of the
  field,   Song 2:7
  That you will not arouse or awaken *my*
  love,
  Until^she pleases."   *it*

Wedding Procession

6 "^11What^Tis this coming up from the wil-
  derness   *Who*
  Like^Rcolumns of smoke,   Ex. 13:21
  Perfumed with ^Rmyrrh and frankin-
  cense,   Song 1:13; 4:6, 14; Matt. 2:11
  With all scented powders of the mer-
  chant?
7 "Behold, it is the *traveling* couch of
  Solomon;
  Sixty mighty men around it,
  Of the mighty men of Israel.
8 "All of them are wielders of the sword,
  ^RExpert in war;   Jer. 50:9
  Each man has his^Rsword at his side,
  Guarding against the ^Tterrors of the
  night.   Ps. 45:3 · *terror in the nights*
9 "King Solomon has made for himself a
  sedan chair
  From the timber of Lebanon.
10 "He made its posts of silver,
  Its^back of gold   *support*
  And its seat of purple fabric,
  With its interior lovingly fitted out
  By the^Rdaughters of Jerusalem. Song 1:5
11 "Go forth, O^Rdaughters of Zion,
  And gaze on King Solomon with the
  ^crown

With which his mother has crowned
  him
On the^Rday of his wedding,
And on the day of his gladness of
  heart."   Is. 3:16, 17 · *wreath* · Is. 62:5

CHAPTER 4

Bride's Beauty Is Praised

4 ¹⁰HOW^Tbeautiful you are, my darling,
  ^THow beautiful you are!   *Behold*
  Your^Reyes are *like* doves^Rbehind your
  veil;   Song 1:15; 5:12 · Song 6:7
  Your^Rhair is like a flock of goats
  That have descended from Mount
  ^RGilead.   Song 6:5 · Mic. 7:14
2 "Your ^Rteeth are like a flock of *newly*
  shorn ewes
  Which have come up from *their* wash-
  ing,
  All of which bear twins,
  And not one among them has^lost her
  young.   Song 6:6 · *miscarried*
3 "Your lips are like a^Rscarlet thread,
  And your^Rmouth is lovely.
  Your temples are like a slice of a pome-
  granate   Josh. 2:18 · Song 5:16
  Behind your veil.
4 "Your neck is like the tower of David
  Built^with rows of stones,   *for an arsenal*
  On which are^Rhung a thousand shields,
  All the round ^Rshields of the mighty
  men.   Ezek. 27:10, 11 · 2 Sam. 1:21
5 "Your^Rtwo breasts are like two fawns,
  Twins of a gazelle,   Song 7:3
  Which^Rfeed among the lilies.   Song 2:16
6 "Until^the^T cool of the day
  When the shadows flee away,
  I will go my way to the mountain of
  myrrh   Song 2:17 · *the day blows*
  And to the hill of frankincense.

7 "You^Rare altogether beautiful, my dar-
  ling,   Song 1:15; Eph. 5:27
  And there is no blemish in you.
8 "*Come* with me from ^RLebanon, *my*
  ^Rbride,   1 Kin. 4:33; Ps. 72:16 · Is. 62:5
  May you come with me from Lebanon.
  ^Journey down from the summit of
  ^RAmana,   *Look* · 2 Kin. 5:12
  From the summit of ^RSenir and Her-
  mon,   Deut. 3:9; 1 Chr. 5:23; Ezek. 27:5
  From the dens of lions,
  From the mountains of leopards.
9 "You have made my heart beat faster,
  ^Rmy sister, *my* bride;   Song 4:10, 12
  You have made my heart beat faster
  with a single *glance* of your eyes,
  With a single strand of your necklace.
10 "How^Rbeautiful is your love, my sister,
  my bride!   Song 7:6

9 BRIDE
10 BRIDEGROOM   11 CHORUS

How much [R]better is your love than wine, Song 1:2, 4
And the[R]fragrance of your oils Song 1:3
Than all *kinds* of [A]spices! *balsam odors*

11 "Your lips, *my* bride, drip honey;
Honey and milk are under your tongue,
And the fragrance of your garments is like the fragrance of Lebanon.

12 "A garden locked is my sister, *my* bride,
A [T]rock garden locked, a [R]spring sealed up. *stone heap* • Prov. 5:15-18

13 "Your shoots are an [A]orchard of [R]pomegranates *park* or *paradise* • Song 6:11
With [R]choice fruits, [B]henna with nard plants, Song 2:3; 4:16; 7:13 • Song 1:14

14 [R]Nard and saffron, calamus and [R]cinnamon, Song 1:12 • Ex. 30:23
With all the trees of frankincense,
[R]Myrrh and aloes, along with all the finest [A]spices. Ps. 45:8 • *balsam odors*

15 "*You are* a garden spring,
A well of [T]fresh water, *living*
And streams *flowing* from Lebanon."

The Marriage Is Consummated

16 "[12]Awake, O north *wind,*
And come, *wind of* the south;
Make my [R]garden breathe out *fragrance,* Song 5:1; 6:2
Let its spices [T]be wafted abroad.
May my beloved come into his garden
And eat its choice fruits!" *flow forth*

CHAPTER 5

"[13]I HAVE [R]come into my garden, [R]my sister, *my* bride; Song 6:2 • Song 4:9
I have gathered my [R]myrrh along with my balsam. Song 1:13; 4:14
I have eaten my honeycomb [T]and my [R]honey; *with* • Song 4:11
I have [R]drunk my wine and my milk.
Eat, [R]friends; Prov. 9:5 • John 3:29
Drink and imbibe deeply, O lovers."

Bride's Second Dream of Separation

2 "[14]I was asleep, but my heart was awake.
A voice! My beloved was knocking:
'Open to me, my sister, my darling,
[R]My dove, my perfect one! Song 2:14; 6:9
For my head is drenched with dew,
My locks with the damp of the night.'

3 "I have [R]taken off my dress, Luke 11:7
How can I put it on *again?*
I have [R]washed my feet, Gen. 19:2
How can I dirty them *again?*

4 "My beloved extended his hand through the opening,

And my feelings were aroused for him.

5 "I arose to open to my beloved;
And my hands dripped with myrrh,
And my fingers with [T]liquid myrrh,
On the handles of the bolt. *passing*

6 "I opened to my beloved,
But my beloved had [R]turned away *and* had gone! Song 6:1
My [T]heart went out *to him* as he [R]spoke.
I [R]searched for him, but I did not find him; *soul* • Song 5:2 • Song 3:1
I called him, but he did not answer me.

7 "The [R]watchmen who make the rounds in the city found me,
They struck me *and* wounded me;
The guardsmen of the walls took away my shawl from me. Song 3:3

Bridegroom's Handsomeness Is Praised

8 "I [R]adjure you, O daughters of Jerusalem, Song 2:7; 3:5
If you find my beloved,
As to what you will tell him:
For [R]I am lovesick." Song 2:5

9 "[15]What kind of beloved is your beloved,
O [R]most beautiful among women?
What kind of beloved is your beloved,
That thus you adjure us?" Song 1:8; 6:1

10 "[14]My beloved is dazzling and ruddy,
Outstanding among ten thousand.

11 "His head is *like* gold, pure gold;
His [R]locks are *like* clusters of dates,
And black as a raven. Song 5:2

12 "His [R]eyes are like doves, Song 1:15; 4:1
Beside streams of water,
Bathed in milk,
And reposed in *their* [R]setting. Ex. 25:7

13 "His cheeks are like a [B]bed of balsam,
Banks of sweet-scented herbs;
His lips are [R]lilies, Song 6:2 • Song 2:1
[R]Dripping with liquid myrrh. Song 5:5

14 "His hands are rods of gold
Set with [R]beryl; Ex. 28:20; 39:13; Ezek. 1:16
His abdomen is carved ivory
Inlaid with [T]sapphires. *lapis lazuli*

15 "His legs are pillars of alabaster
Set on pedestals of pure gold;
His appearance is like Lebanon,
Choice as the [R]cedars. Ezek. 17:23; 31:8

16 "His mouth [R]is *full of* sweetness.
And he is wholly [R]desirable.
This is my beloved and this is my friend, Song 7:9 • 2 Sam. 1:23
O daughters of Jerusalem."

CHAPTER 6

"[16]WHERE has your beloved gone,
O most beautiful among women?
Where has your beloved turned,
That we may seek him with you?"

---

[12] BRIDE   [13] BRIDEGROOM
[14] BRIDE   [15] CHORUS   [16] CHORUS

2"[17]My beloved has gone down to his [R]garden,   Song 4:16; 5:1
To the[R]beds of balsam,   Song 5:13
To[R]pasture *his flock* in the gardens
And gather[R]lilies.   Song 1:7 • Song 2:1
3"[T]I am my beloved's and my beloved is mine,
He who[R]pastures *his flock* among the lilies."   Song 2:16; 7:10 • Song 2:16; 4:5

Bride's Beauty Is Praised

4"[18]You are as beautiful as[R]Tirzah, my darling,   1 Kin. 14:17
As lovely as[R]Jerusalem,   Ps. 48:2; 50:2
As awesome as an army with banners.
5"Turn your eyes away from me,
For they have confused me;
Your hair is like a flock of goats
That have descended from Gilead.
6"Your[R]teeth are like a flock of ewes
Which have come up from *their* washing,
All of which bear twins,
And not one among them has[A]lost her young.   Song 4:2 • *miscarried*
7"Your[R]temples are like a slice of a pomegranate
Behind your veil.   Song 4:3
8"There are sixty[R]queens and eighty concubines,   1 Kin. 11:3
And[A]maidens without number;   *virgins*
9 *But* [R]my dove, my perfect one, is unique;   Song 2:14
She is her mother's[T]only *daughter; one*
She is the pure *child* of the one who bore her.
The [T]maidens [R]saw her and called her blessed,   *daughters* • Gen. 30:13
The queens and the concubines *also,*
and they praised her, *saying,*

10 'Who is this that[T]grows like the dawn,
As beautiful as the full moon,
As pure as the sun,   *looks down*
As awesome as an army with banners?'
11"I went down to the orchard of nut trees
To see the blossoms of the valley,
To see whether the vine had budded
Or the pomegranates had bloomed.
12"Before I was aware, my soul set me
Over the chariots of my noble people."

13"[19]Come back, come back, O Shulammite;
Come back, come back, that we may gaze at you!"

"[20]Why should you gaze at the Shulammite,
As at the dance of the two companies?

CHAPTER 7

"How beautiful are your[T]feet in sandals,
O[R]prince's daughter!   *footsteps* • Ps. 45:13

The curves of your hips are like jewels,
The work of the hands of an artist.
2"Your navel is *like* a round goblet
Which never lacks mixed wine;
Your belly is like a heap of wheat
Fenced about with lilies.
3"Your[R]two breasts are like two fawns,
Twins of a gazelle.   Song 4:5
4"Your[R]neck is like a tower of ivory,
Your eyes *like* the pools in Heshbon
By the gate of Bath-rabbim;   Song 4:4
Your nose is like the tower of Lebanon,
Which faces toward Damascus.
5"Your head[T]crowns you like Carmel,
And the flowing locks of your head are like purple threads;   *is upon*
The king is captivated by *your* tresses.
6"How[R]beautiful and how delightful you are,   Song 1:15, 16; 4:10
My love, with *all* your charms!
7"Your stature is like a palm tree,
And your breasts are *like its* clusters.
8"I said, 'I will climb the palm tree,
I will take hold of its fruit stalks.'
Oh, may your breasts be like clusters of the vine,
And the fragrance of your[T]breath like [A]apples,[R]   *nose* • *apricots* • Song 2:5
9 And your [T]mouth[R] like the best wine!"

"[21]It [R]goes *down* smoothly for my beloved,   *palate* • Song 5:16 • Prov. 23:31
Flowing gently *through* the lips of those who fall asleep.

10"[T]I am my beloved's,   Song 2:16; 6:3
And his[R]desire is for me.   Ps. 45:11

Bride's Desire
to Visit Her Home

11"Come, my beloved, let us go out into the[T]country,   *field*
Let us spend the night in the villages.
12"Let us rise early *and go* to the vineyards;
Let us[R]see whether the vine has budded
And its blossoms have opened,
And whether the pomegranates have bloomed.
There I will give you my love.   Song 6:11
13"The[R]mandrakes have given forth fragrance;   Gen. 30:14
And over our doors are all [R]choice *fruits,*   Song 2:3; 4:13, 16; Matt. 13:52
Both new and old,
Which I have saved up for you, my beloved.

CHAPTER 8

"Oh that you were like a brother to me
Who nursed at my mother's breasts.

[17] BRIDE   [18] BRIDEGROOM
[19] CHORUS   [20] BRIDEGROOM   [21] BRIDE

If I found you outdoors, I would kiss
you;
No one would despise me, either.
2"I would lead you *and*[R]bring you
Into the house of my mother, who used
to instruct me;   Song 3:4
I would give you spiced wine to drink
from the juice of my pomegranates.
3"Let his left hand be under my head,
And his right hand embrace me."

4"[22]I[R]want you to swear, O daughters of
Jerusalem,   Song 2:7; 3:5
[A]Do not arouse or awaken *my* love,
Until she pleases." *Why should you arouse*

Journey and Homecoming

5"[23]Who[R]is this coming up from the wilderness,
Leaning on her beloved?"   Song 3:6

"[22]Beneath the[A]apple[R] tree I awakened
you;
There your mother was in labor with
you,
There she was in labor *and* gave you
birth.   Song 3:6 • *apricot* • Song 2:3
6"Put me like a [24]seal over your heart,
Like a[R]seal on your arm.   Is. 49:16
For love is as strong as death,
[R]Jealousy is as severe as Sheol;
Its flashes are flashes of fire,
The *very* flame of the LORD.   Prov. 6:34
7"Many waters cannot quench love,

22 BRIDEGROOM   23 CHORUS
24 Or, *signet*   25 CHORUS   26 BRIDE   27 BRIDEGROOM

Nor will rivers overflow it;
[R]If a man were to give all the riches of
his house for love,   Prov. 6:35
It would be utterly despised."

8"[25]We have a little sister,
And she[R]has no breasts;   Ezek. 16:7
What shall we do for our sister
On the day when she is spoken for?
9"If she is a wall,
We shall build on her a battlement of
silver;
But if she is a door,
We shall barricade her with[R]planks of
cedar."   1 Kin. 6:15

10"[26]I was a wall, and[R]my breasts were
like towers;
Then I became in his eyes as one who
finds peace.   Ezek. 16:7
11"Solomon had a [R]vineyard at Baal-
hamon;   Eccl. 2:4
He[R]entrusted the vineyard to[R]caretak-
ers;   Matt. 21:33 • Song 1:6
Each one was to bring a [R]thousand
shekels of silver for its fruit. Is. 7:23
12"My very own vineyard is[T]at my disposal;   *before me*
The thousand *shekels* are for you, Solomon,
And two hundred are for those who
take care of its fruit."
13"[27]O you who sit in the gardens,
My[R]companions are listening for your
voice—
[R]Let me hear it!"   Song 1:7 • Song 2:14
14"[26]Hurry,[T] my beloved,   *Flee*
And be like a gazelle or a young stag
On the[R]mountains of spices."   Song 4:6

THE BOOK OF

ISAIAH

THE BOOK OF ISAIAH

Isaiah is like a miniature Bible. The first thirty-nine chapters (like the thirty-nine books of the Old Testament) are filled with judgment upon immoral and idolatrous men. Judah has sinned; the surrounding nations have sinned; the whole earth has sinned. Judgment must come, for God cannot allow such blatant sin to go unpunished forever. But the final twenty-seven chapters (like the twenty-seven books of the New Testament) declare a message of hope. The Messiah is coming as a Savior and a Sovereign to bear a cross and to wear a crown.

Isaiah's prophetic ministry, spanning the reigns of four kings of Judah, covers at least forty years.

Yesha' yahu and its shortened form *yeshaiah* mean "Yahweh Is Salvation." This name is an excellent summary of the contents of the book. The Greek form in the Septuagint is *Hesaias*, and the Latin form is *Esaias* or *Isaias*.

THE AUTHOR OF ISAIAH

Isaiah, the "St. Paul of the Old Testament," was evidently from a distinguished Jewish family. His education is evident in his impressive vocabulary and style. His work is comprehensive in scope and beautifully communicated. Isaiah maintained close contact with the royal court, but his exhortations against alliances with foreign powers were not always well received. This great poet and prophet was uncompromising, sincere, and compassionate. His wife was a prophetess and he fathered at least two sons (7:3; 8:3). He spent most of his time in Jerusalem, and talmudic tradition says his persecutors sawed him in two during the reign of Manasseh (cf. Heb. 11:37).

The unity of this book has been challenged by critics who hold that a "Deutero-Isaiah" wrote chapters 40—66 after the Babylonian captivity. They argue that 1—39 has an Assyrian background, while 40—66 is set against a Babylonian background. But Babylon is mentioned more than twice as often in 1—39 as in 40—66. The only shift is one of perspective from present time to future time. Critics also argue that there are radical differences in the language, style, and theology of the two sections. Actually, the resemblances between 1—39 and 40—66 are greater than the differences. These include similarities in

thoughts, images, rhetorical ornaments, characteristic expressions, and local coloring. It is true that the first section is more terse and rational, while the second section is more flowing and emotional, but much of this is caused by the different subject matter, of condemnation versus consolation. Critics often forget that content, time, and circumstances typically affect any author's style. In addition, there is no theological contradiction between the emphasis on the Messiah as King in 1—39 and as suffering Servant in 40—66. While the thrust is different, the Messiah is seen in both sections as Servant and King. Another critical argument is that Isaiah could not have predicted the Babylonian captivity and the return under Cyrus (mentioned by name in 44 and 45) 150 years in advance. This view is based on the mere assumption that divine prophecy is impossible, rejecting the predictive claims of the book (see 42:9). The theory cannot explain the amazing messianic prophecies of Isaiah that were literally fulfilled in the life of Christ (see "The Christ of Isaiah").

The unity of Isaiah is supported by the book of Ecclesiasticus, the Septuagint, and the Talmud. The New Testament also claims that Isaiah wrote both sections. John 12:37–41 quotes from Isaiah 6:9, 10 and 53:1 and attributes it all to Isaiah. In Romans 9:27 and 10:16–21, Paul quotes from Isaiah 10, 53, and 65 and gives the credit to Isaiah. The same is true of Matthew 3:3 and 12:17–21, Luke 3:4–6, and Acts 8:28.

If 40—66 was written by another prophet after the events took place, it is a misleading and deceptive work. Furthermore, it would lead to the strange conclusion that Israel's greatest prophet is the only writing prophet of the Old Testament to go unnamed.

THE TIME OF ISAIAH

Isaiah's long ministry ranged from about 740 to 680 B.C. (1:1). He began his ministry near the end of Uzziah's reign (790–739 B.C.) and continued through the reigns of Jotham (739–731 B.C.), Ahaz (731–715 B.C.), and Hezekiah (715–686 B.C.). Assyria was growing in power under Tiglath-pileser who turned toward the west after his conquests in the east. He plucked up the small nations that dotted the Mediterranean coast including Israel and much of Judah. Isaiah lived during this time of military threat to Ju-

dah, and warned its kings against trusting in alliances with other countries rather than the power of Yahweh. As a contemporary of Hosea and Micah, he prophesied during the last years of the northern kingdom but ministered to the southern kingdom of Judah who was following the sins of her sister Israel. After Israel's demise in 722 B.C., he warned Judah of judgment not by Assyria but by Babylon, even though Babylon had not yet risen to power.

Isaiah ministered from the time of Tiglath-pileser (745–727 B.C.) to the time of Sennacherib (705–681 B.C.) of Assyria. He outdated Hezekiah by a few years because 37:38 records the death of Sennacherib in 681 B.C. Hezekiah was succeeded by his wicked son Manasseh who overthrew the worship of Yahweh and no doubt opposed the work of Isaiah.

✝ THE CHRIST OF ISAIAH

When he speaks about Christ, Isaiah sounds more like a New Testament writer than an Old Testament prophet. His messianic prophecies are clearer and more explicit than those in any other Old Testament book. They describe many aspects of the person and work of Christ in His first and second advents and often blend the two together. Here are a few of the Christological prophecies with their New Testament fulfillments: 7:14 (Matt. 1:22, 23); 9:1, 2 (Matt. 4:12–16); 9:6 (Luke 2:11; Eph. 2:14–18); 11:1 (Luke 3:23, 32; Acts 13:22, 23); 11:2 (Luke 3:22); 28:16 (1 Pet. 2:4–6); 40:3–5 (Matt. 3:1–3); 42:1–4 (Matt. 12:15–21); 42:6 (Luke 2:29–32); 50:6 (Matt. 26:67; 27:26, 30); 52:14 (Phil. 2:7–11); 53:3 (Luke 23:18; John 1:11; 7:5); 53:4, 5 (Rom. 5:6, 8); 53:7 (Matt. 27:12–14; John 1:29; 1 Pet. 1:18, 19); 53:9 (Matt. 27:57–60); 53:12 (Mark 15:28); 61:1, 2 (Luke 4:17–19, 21). The Old Testament has over three hundred prophecies about the first advent of Christ, and Isaiah contributes a number of them. The odds that even ten of them could be fulfilled by one person is a statistical marvel. Isaiah's messianic prophecies that await fulfillment in the Lord's second advent include: 4:2; 11:2–6, 10; 32:1–8; 49:7; 52:13, 15; 59:20, 21; 60:1–3; 61:2, 3.

Isaiah 52:13—53:12 is the central passage of the consolation section (40—66). Its five stanzas present five different aspects of the saving work of Christ: (1) 52:13–15—His wholehearted sacrifice (burnt offering); (2) 53:1–3—His perfect character (meal offering); (3) 53:4–6—He brought atonement that issues in peace with God (peace offering); (4) 53:7–9—He paid for the transgression of the people (sin offering); (5) 53:10–12—He died for the effects of sin (trespass offering).

🔑 KEYS TO ISAIAH

Key Word: Salvation Is of the Lord— The basic theme of this book is found in Isaiah's name: "Salvation is of the Lord." The word *salvation* appears twenty-seven times in Isaiah but only eight times in all the other prophets combined. Chapters 1—39 portray man's great need for salvation, and chapters 40—66 reveal God's great provision of salvation. Salvation is of God, not man; and He is seen as the supreme Ruler, the sovereign Lord of history, and the only Savior. Isaiah solemnly warns Judah of approaching judgment because of moral depravity, political corruption, social injustice, and especially spiritual idolatry. Because the nation does not turn away from its sinful practice, Isaiah announces the ultimate overthrow of Judah. Nevertheless, God will remain faithful to His covenant by preserving a godly remnant and promises salvation and deliverance through

FOCUS	PROPHECIES OF CONDEMNATION				HISTORICAL PARENTHESIS	PROPHECIES OF COMFORT		
REFERENCE	1:1—————	13:1—————	24:1—————	28:1—————	36:1—————	40:1—————	49:1—————	58:1—66:24
DIVISION	PROPHECIES AGAINST		PROPHECIES OF		HEZEKIAH'S SALVATION, SICKNESS, AND SIN	ISRAEL'S DELIVERANCE	ISRAEL'S DELIVERER	ISRAEL'S GLORIOUS FUTURE
	JUDAH	THE NATIONS	DAY OF LORD	JUDGMENT & BLESSING				
TOPIC	PROPHETIC				HISTORIC	MESSIANIC		
	JUDGMENT				TRANSITION	HOPE		
LOCATION	ISRAEL AND JUDAH							
TIME	c. 740–680 B.C.							

the coming Messiah. The Savior will come out of Judah and accomplish the dual work of redemption and restoration. The Gentiles will come to His light and universal blessing will finally take place.

Key Verses: Isaiah 9:6, 7 and 53:6—"For a child will be born to us, a son will be given to us; and the government will rest on His shoulders; and His name will be called Wonderful Counselor, Mighty God, Eternal Father, Prince of Peace. There will be no end to the increase of *His* government or of peace, on the throne of David and over his kingdom, to establish it and to uphold it with justice and righteousness from then on and forevermore. The zeal of the LORD of hosts will accomplish this" (9:6, 7).

"All of us like sheep have gone astray, each of us has turned to his own way; but the LORD has caused the iniquity of us all to fall on Him" (53:6).

Key Chapter: Isaiah 53—Along with Psalm 22, Isaiah 53 lists the most remarkable and specific prophecies of the atonement of the Messiah. Fulfilling each clear prophecy, the Jewish nation later proved the messiahship of Jesus.

SURVEY OF ISAIAH

Isaiah, the "Shakespeare of the prophets," has often been called the "evangelical prophet" because of his incredibly clear and detailed messianic prophecies. The "gospel according to Isaiah" has three major sections: prophecies of condemnation (1—35), historical parenthesis (36—39), and prophecies of comfort (40—66).

Prophecies of Condemnation (1—35): Isaiah's first message of condemnation is aimed at his own countrymen in Judah (1—12). Chapter 1 is a capsulized message of the entire book. Judah is riddled with moral and spiritual disease; the people are neglecting God as they bow to ritualism and selfishness. But Yahweh graciously invites them to repent and return to Him because this is their only hope of avoiding judgment. Isaiah's call to proclaim God's message is found in chapter 6, and this is followed by the book of Immanuel (7—12). These chapters repeatedly refer to the Messiah (see 7:14; 8:14; 9:2, 6, 7; 11:1, 2) and anticipate the blessing of His future reign.

The prophet moves from local to regional judgment as he proclaims a series of oracles

against the surrounding nations (13—23). The eleven nations are Babylon, Assyria, Philistia, Moab, Damascus (Aram), Ethiopia, Egypt, Babylon (again), Edom, Arabia, Jerusalem (Judah), and Tyre. Isaiah's little apocalypse (24—27) depicts universal tribulation followed by the blessings of the kingdom. Chapters 28—33 pronounce six woes on Israel and Judah for specific sins. Isaiah's prophetic condemnation closes with a general picture of international devastation that will precede universal blessing (34 and 35).

Historical Parenthesis (36—39): This historical parenthesis looks back to the Assyrian invasion of Judah in 701 B.C. and anticipates the coming Babylonian invasion of Judah. Judah escapes captivity by Assyria (36 and 37; 2 Kin. 18 and 19), but they will not escape from the hands of Babylon (38 and 39; 2 Kin. 20). God answers King Hezekiah's prayers and delivers Judah from Assyrian destruction by Sennacherib. Hezekiah also turns to the Lord in his illness and is granted a fifteen-year extension of his life. But he foolishly shows all his treasures to the Babylonian messengers, and Isaiah tells him that the Babylonians will one day carry his treasure and descendants to their land.

Prophecies of Comfort (40—66): Having pronounced Judah's divine condemnation, Isaiah comforts them with God's promises of hope and restoration. The basis for this hope is the sovereignty and majesty of God (40—48). Of the 216 verses in these nine chapters, 115 speak of God's greatness and power. The Creator is contrasted with idols, the creations of men. His sovereign character is Judah's assurance of future restoration. Babylon will indeed carry them off; but Babylon will finally be judged and destroyed, and God's people will be released from captivity.

Chapters 49—57 concentrate on the coming Messiah who will be their Savior and suffering Servant. This rejected but exalted One will pay for their iniquities and usher in a kingdom of peace and righteousness throughout the earth. All who acknowledge their sins and trust in Him will be delivered (58—66). In that day Jerusalem will be rebuilt, Israel's borders will be enlarged, and the Messiah will reign in Zion. God's people will confess their sins and His enemies will be judged. Peace, prosperity, and justice will prevail, and God will make all things new.

OUTLINE OF ISAIAH

CHAPTER 1

The Judgment of Judah

T HE vision of Isaiah the son of Amoz, concerning ᴿJudah and Jerusalem which he saw
during the ᵀreigns of Uzziah, Jotham, Ahaz,
and Hezekiah, kings of Judah.   Is. 2:1 • *days*

2 Listen, O heavens, and hear, O ᴿearth;
  For the LORD speaks,   Mic. 1:2
  "Sons I have reared and brought up,
    But they have revolted against Me.
3 "An ox knows its owner,
  And a donkey its master's manger,
  But Israel ᴿdoes not know,   Jer. 9:3, 6
  My people do not understand."

4 Alas, sinful nation,
People weighed down with iniquity,
[T]Offspring[R]of evildoers,   *Seed • Is. 14:20*
Sons who[R]act corruptly!   Neh. 1:7
They have[R]abandoned the LORD,
They have[R]despised the Holy One of Is-
rael,   Is. 1:28 • Is. 5:24
They have turned away from Him.

5 Where will you be stricken again,
As you[R]continue in *your* rebellion?
The whole head is sick,   Is. 31:6
And the whole heart is faint.
6 [R]From the sole of the foot even to the
head   Job 2:7
There is[R]nothing sound in it,   Ps. 38:3
Only bruises, welts, and raw wounds,
[R]Not pressed out or bandaged,
Nor softened with oil.   Jer. 8:22

7 Your[R]land is desolate,
Your cities are burned with fire,
Your fields—strangers are devouring
them in your presence;
[T]It is desolation, as overthrown by
strangers.   Lev. 26:33; Jer. 44:6 • *And*
8 And the daughter of Zion is left like a
shelter in a vineyard,
Like a watchman's hut in a cucumber
field, like a besieged city.
9 [R]Unless the LORD of hosts   Rom. 9:29
Had left us a few[R]survivors,   Is. 10:20-22
We would be like[R]Sodom,   Gen. 19:24
We would be like Gomorrah.

10 Hear[R]the word of the LORD,   Is. 8:20
You rulers of[R]Sodom;   Is. 3:9; Ezek. 16:49
Give ear to the instruction of our God,
You people of Gomorrah.
11 "What[R]are your multiplied sacrifices to
Me?"   Ps. 50:8; Jer. 6:20; Amos 5:21, 22
Says the LORD.
"I[T]have had enough of burnt offerings of
rams,   *am sated with*
And the fat of fed cattle.
And I take no pleasure in the blood of
bulls, lambs, or goats.
12 "When you come[R]to appear before Me,
Who requires[T]of you this trampling of
My courts?   Ex. 23:17 • *of your hand*
13 "Bring your worthless offerings no
longer,
Incense is an abomination to Me.
[R]New moon and sabbath, the[R]calling of
assemblies—   1 Chr. 23:31 • Ex. 12:16
I cannot[R]endure iniquity and the sol-
emn assembly.   Jer. 7:9, 10
14 "I hate your new moon *festivals* and
your[R]appointed feasts,   Is. 29:1, 2
They have become a burden to Me.
I am[T]weary of bearing *them.*   Is. 7:13
15 "So when you[R]spread out your hands *in*
prayer,   1 Kin. 8:22; Lam. 1:17
[R]I will hide My eyes from you,   Is. 8:17
Yes, even though you[R]multiply prayers,
I will not listen.   Mic. 3:4
Your hands are covered with blood.

16 "Wash[R] yourselves, [R]make yourselves
clean;   Ps. 26:6 • Is. 52:11
[R]Remove the evil of your deeds from
My sight.   Is. 55:7
[R]Cease to do evil,   Jer. 25:5
17 Learn to do good;
[R]Seek justice,   Jer. 22:3; Zeph. 2:3
Reprove the ruthless;
Defend[R]the orphan,
Plead for the widow.   Ps. 82:3

18 "Come now, and [R]let us reason to-
gether,"   Is. 41:1, 21; 43:26; Mic. 6:2
Says the LORD,
"Though[R]your sins are as scarlet,
They will be as white as snow;
Though they are red like crimson,
They will be like wool. Ps. 51:7; [Is. 43:25]
19 "If[T]you consent and obey,   Deut. 28:1
You will eat the best of the land;
20 "But if you refuse and rebel,
You will be[R]devoured by the sword."
Truly, [R]the mouth of the LORD has
spoken.   Is. 3:25 • Mic. 4:4; [Titus 1:2]

21 How the faithful city has become a
[R]harlot,   Is. 57:3-9; Jer. 2:20
She *who* was full of justice!
Righteousness once lodged in her,
But now murderers.
22 Your silver has become dross,
Your drink diluted with water.
23 Your[R]rulers are rebels,   Hos. 5:10; Mic. 7:3
And companions of thieves;
Everyone[R]loves a bribe,   Ex. 23:8; Mic. 7:3
And chases after rewards.
They[R]do not[A]defend the[A]orphan,
Nor does the widow's plea come before
them.   Is. 10:2 • *vindicate • fatherless*

24 Therefore the Lord[T]GOD of hosts,
The Mighty One of Israel declares,
"Ah, I will be relieved of My adver-
saries,   Heb., *YHWH*
And avenge Myself on My foes.
25 "I will also turn My hand against you,
And will[R]smelt away your dross as with
lye,   Ezek. 22:19-22; Mal. 3:3
And will remove all your alloy.
26 "Then I will restore your[R]judges as at
the first,   Is. 60:17
And your counselors as at the begin-
ning;
After that you will be called the[R]city of
righteousness,   Is. 33:5; 60:14; 62:1, 2
A faithful city."

27 Zion will be[R]redeemed with justice,
And her[A]repentant ones with righteousness.   Is. 35:9f.; 62:12; 63:4 • *returnees*
28 But transgressors and sinners will be
[R]crushed together,   Ps. 9:5; [Is. 66:24]
And those who forsake the LORD shall
come to an end.

29 Surely, you will be ashamed of the
   oaks which you have desired,
   And you will be embarrassed at the
   gardens which you have chosen.
30 For you will be like an ^oak whose^R leaf
   fades away,   *terebinth* • Is. 64:6
   Or as a garden that has no water.
31 And the strong man will become tin-
   der,
   His work also a spark.
   Thus they shall both burn together,
   And there will be none to quench *them*.

CHAPTER 2

The Day of the Lord

T HE word which Isaiah the son of Amoz
saw concerning Judah and Jerusalem.
  2 Now it will come about that
    ^R In the last days,   Mic. 4:1-3☆
    The^R mountain of the house of the LORD
    Will be established^T as the chief of the
       mountains,   Is. 27:13; 66:20 • *on*
    And will be raised above the hills;
    And all the nations will stream to it.
  3 And many peoples will come and say,
    ^R "Come, let us go up to the mountain of
       the LORD,   Jer. 50:5☆
    To the house of the God of Jacob;
    That He may teach us ^concerning His
       ways,   *some of*
    And that we may walk in His paths."
    For the^A law will go forth^R from Zion,
    And the word of the LORD from Jerusa-
       lem.   *instruction* • Is. 51:4, 5☆
  4 And He will judge between the nations,
    And will ^render decisions for many
       peoples;   *reprove many*
    And ^R they will hammer their swords
       into plowshares, and their spears
       into pruning hooks.   Is. 32:17, 18☆
    ^R Nation will not lift up sword against
       nation,   Is. 9:5, 7; 11:6-9; Hos. 2:18
    And never again will they learn war.

  5 Come, ^R house of Jacob, and let us walk
    in the light of the LORD.   Is. 58:1
  6 For Thou hast ^R abandoned Thy people,
    the house of Jacob,   Deut. 31:17
    Because they are filled *with influences*
       from the east,
    And *they are* soothsayers^R like the Phi-
       listines,   2 Kin. 1:2
    And they^R strike *bargains* with the chil-
       dren of foreigners.   2 Kin. 16:7, 8
  7 Their land has also been filled with sil-
    ver and gold,
    And there is no end to their treasures;
    Their land has also been filled with
       ^R horses,   Deut. 17:16; Is. 30:16; Mic. 5:10
    And there is no end to their chariots.
  8 Their land has also been^R filled with
    idols;   Is. 10:11
    They worship the work of their hands,
    That which their fingers have made.

  9 So^R the *common* man has been hum-
    bled,   Ps. 49:2; 62:9; Is. 5:15
    And the man *of importance* has been
       abased,
    But^R do not forgive them.   Neh. 4:5
10 Enter the rock and hide in the dust
    From the terror of the LORD and from
       the splendor of His majesty.
11 The proud look of man will be abased,
    And the^R loftiness of man will be hum-
       bled,
    And the LORD alone will be exalted in
       that day.   Ps. 18:27; Is. 13:11; 23:9

12 For the LORD of hosts will have a day
    of reckoning
    Against ^everyone who is proud and
       lofty,   Job 40:11, 12; Is. 24:4, 21; Mal. 4:1
    And against everyone who is lifted up,
    That he may be abased.
13 And *it will be* against all the cedars of
    Lebanon that are lofty and lifted
       up,
    Against all the oaks of Bashan,
14 Against all the^R lofty mountains, Is. 40:4
    Against all the hills that are lifted up,
15 Against every^R high tower,
    Against every fortified wall,   Is. 25:12
16 Against all the ships of Tarshish,
    And against all the beautiful craft.
17 And the pride of man will be humbled,
    And the loftiness of men will be
       abased,
    And the LORD alone will be exalted in
       that day.
18 But the idols will completely vanish.
19 And *men* will ^R go into caves of the
    rocks,   Is. 2:10
    And into holes of the^T ground   *dust*
    Before the terror of the LORD,
    And before the splendor of His maj-
       esty,
    When He arises ^R to make the earth
       tremble.   Ps. 18:7; Is. 2:21; Hag. 2:6, 7
20 In that day men will ^cast away to the
    moles and the^R bats
    Their idols of silver and their idols of
       gold,
    Which they made for themselves to
       worship,   Is. 30:22; 31:7 • Lev. 11:19
21 In order to^R go into the caverns of the
    rocks and the clefts of the cliffs,
    Before the terror of the LORD and the
       splendor of His majesty,
    When He arises to make the earth
       tremble.   Is. 2:19
22 ^T Stop regarding man, whose breath *of*
    life is in his nostrils;   *Cease from man*
    For why should he be esteemed?

CHAPTER 3

F OR behold, the Lord GOD of hosts ^R is
    going to remove from Jerusalem
    and Judah   Lev. 26:26; Is. 5:13; 9:20

Both ^Tsupply and support, the whole
supply of bread,
And the whole supply of water;   *staff*
2 ^RThe mighty man and the warrior,
The judge and the prophet, 2 Kin. 24:14
The diviner and the elder,
3 The captain of fifty and the honorable
man,
The counselor and the expert artisan,
And the skillful enchanter.
4 And I will make mere lads their princes
And ^Tcapricious children will rule over
them,   *arbitrary power will rule*
5 And the people will be ^Roppressed,
Each one by another, and each one by
his ^Rneighbor;   Mic. 7:3-6 · Is. 9:19
The youth will storm against the elder,
And the inferior against the honorable.
6 When a man ^Tlays hold of his brother in
his father's house, *saying,*
"You have a cloak, you shall be our
ruler,
And these ruins will be under your
^Tcharge,"   Is. 4:1 · *hand*
7 On that day will he protest, saying,
"I will not be *your* ^Rhealer,
For in my house there is neither bread
nor cloak;
You should not appoint me ruler of the
people."   Ezek. 34:4; Hos. 5:13
8 For ^RJerusalem has stumbled, and Judah has fallen,   Is. 1:7; 6:11
Because their ^Tspeech and their actions
are against the LORD,   *tongue*
To rebel against His glorious presence.
9 The expression of their faces bears witness against them.
And they display their sin like ^RSodom;
They do not *even* conceal *it.* Gen. 13:13
Woe to ^Tthem!   *their soul*
For they have ^Rbrought evil on themselves.   Prov. 8:36; 15:32; Rom. 6:23
10 Say to the ^Rrighteous that *it will* go well
with them,
For they will eat the fruit of their actions. [Deut. 28:1f.; Eccl. 8:12; Is. 54:17]
11 Woe to the wicked! *It will* go badly
with him,
For ^Twhat ^Rhe deserves will be done to
him.   *the dealing of his hands* · Is. 65:6, 7
12 O My people! Their oppressors ^Aare ^Rchil-
dren,   *deal severely* · Is. 3:4
And women rule over them.
O My people! ^RThose who guide you
lead *you* astray,   Is. 9:16; 28:14, 15
And confuse the direction of your
paths.

13 ^RThe LORD arises to contend,   Is. 66:16
And stands to judge the people.
14 The LORD ^Renters into judgment with
the elders and princes of His peo-
ple,   Job 22:4; Ps. 143:2; Ezek. 20:35, 36
"It is you who have ^Rdevoured the vineyard;   Ps. 14:4; Mic. 3:3
The ^Rplunder of the poor is in your
houses. Job 24:9, 14; Ps. 10:9; Is. 10:1, 2

15 "What do you mean by ^Rcrushing My
people,   Ps. 94:5
And grinding the face of the poor?"
Declares the Lord GOD of hosts.

16 Moreover, the LORD said, "Because the
daughters of Zion are proud,
And walk with ^Theads held high and seductive eyes,   *outstretched necks*
And go along with mincing steps,
And tinkle the bangles on their feet,
17 Therefore the Lord will afflict the scalp
of the daughters of Zion with scabs,
And the LORD will make their foreheads bare."
18 In that day the Lord will take away the
beauty of *their* anklets, headbands, ^Rcrescent
ornaments,   Judg. 8:21, 26
19 dangling earrings, bracelets, veils,
20 ^Rheaddresses, ankle chains, sashes, perfume boxes, amulets,   Ex. 39:28
21 ^Afinger rings, nose rings,   *signet rings*
22 festal robes, outer tunics, cloaks, mon-
ey purses,
23 hand mirrors, undergarments, turbans,
and veils.
24 Now it will come about that instead of
^Asweet ^Rperfume there will be putre-
faction;   *balsam oil* · Esth. 2:12
Instead of a ^Rbelt, a rope;
Instead of ^Rwell-set hair, a ^Rplucked-out
scalp;   1 Pet. 3:3 · Is. 22:12
Instead of fine clothes, a ^Rdonning of
sackcloth;   Is. 15:3; Lam. 2:10
And branding instead of beauty.
25 Your men will fall by the sword,
And your mighty ones in battle.
26 And her ^Tgates will lament and mourn;
And deserted she will ^Rsit on the
ground.   *entrances* · Lam. 2:10

CHAPTER 4

FOR seven women will take hold of ^Rone
man in that day, saying, "We will eat our
own bread and wear our own clothes, only
let us be called by your name; ^Rtake away our
reproach!"   Is. 13:12 · Gen. 30:23; Is. 54:4
2 In that day the ^RBranch of the LORD will
be beautiful and glorious, and the fruit of
the earth *will* be the pride and the adornment of the survivors of Israel. [Is. 11:1; 53:2]
3 And it will come about that he who is
^Rleft in Zion and remains in Jerusalem will be
called ^Rholy—everyone who is recorded for
life in Jerusalem.   Is. 28:5; 46:3 · Is. 52:1; 62:12
4 When the Lord has washed away the
filth of the daughters of Zion, and ^Tpurged
the ^Rbloodshed of Jerusalem from her midst,
by the ^Rspirit of judgment and the spirit of
burning,   *rinsed away* · Is. 1:15 · Is. 28:6
5 then the LORD will create over the
whole area of Mount Zion and over her assemblies a cloud by day, even smoke, and

the brightness of a flaming fire by night; for over all the ᴿglory will be a canopy.   Is. 60:1, 2

6 And there will be a shelter to *give* shade from the heat by day, and refuge and protection from the storm and the rain.

CHAPTER 5

The Parable of the Vineyard

Lᴇᴛ me sing now for my well-beloved
A song of my beloved concerning His vineyard.
My well-beloved had a vineyard on ᵀa fertile hill.   *a horn, the son of fatness*
2 And He dug it all around, removed its stones,
And planted it with ᵀthe ᴿchoicest vine.
And He built a tower in the middle of it,   *a bright red grape* • Jer. 2:21
And hewed out a ˅wine vat in it;
Then He ᴿexpected *it* to produce *good* grapes,   *wine press* • Matt. 21:19
But it produced *only* worthless ones.

3 "And now, O inhabitants of Jerusalem and men of Judah,
Judge between Me and My vineyard.
4 "What more ᵀwas there to do for My vineyard ᵀthat I have not done in it?
Why, when I expected *it* to produce *good* grapes did it produce worth- less ones?   *and I have not done*
5 "So now let Me tell you what I am going to do to My vineyard:
I will ᴿremove its hedge and it will be consumed;   Ps. 89:40
I will ᴿbreak down its wall and it will become trampled ground.   Ps. 80:12
6 "And I will ᴿlay it waste;   2 Chr. 36:19-21
It will not be pruned or hoed,
But briars and thorns will come up.
I will also charge the clouds to ᴿrain no rain on it."   1 Kin. 8:35; 17:1

7 For the ᴿvineyard of the Lᴏʀᴅ of hosts is the house of Israel,   Ps. 80:8-11
And the men of Judah His delightful plant.
Thus He looked for justice, but behold, ᴿbloodshed;   Is. 3:14, 15; 30:12; 59:13
For righteousness, but behold, a cry of distress.

8 Woe to those who ᴿadd house to house *and* join field to field.   Jer. 22:13-17
Until there is no more room,
So that you have to live alone in the midst of the land!
9 In my ears the Lᴏʀᴅ of hosts *has* sworn, "Surely, ᴿmany houses shall become ᴿdesolate,
Even great and fine ones, without oc- cupants.   Is. 6:11, 12 • Matt. 23:38

¹ I.e., Approx. 10½ gal.   ² I.e., Approx. one bu.

10 "For ᴿten acres of vineyard will yield *only* one ¹bath *of wine*,   Lev. 26:26
And a ᴿhomer of seed will yield *but* an ²ephah of grain."   Ezek. 45:11
11 Woe to those who rise early in the morning that they may pursue ᴿstrong drink;   Prov. 23:29, 30
Who stay up late in the evening that wine may inflame them!
12 And their banquets are *accompanied* by lyre and ᴿharp, by tambourine and flute, and by wine;   Amos 6:5, 6
But they ᴿdo not pay attention to the deeds of the Lᴏʀᴅ,
Nor do they consider the work of His hands.   Job 34:27; Ps. 28:5

13 Therefore My people go into exile for their ᴿlack of knowledge;   Hos. 4:6
And ᵀtheir honorable men are famished,
And their multitude is parched with thirst.   *their glory are men of famine*
14 Therefore ᴿSheol has enlarged its ᵀthroat and opened its mouth without mea- sure;   Prov. 30:16; Hab. 2:5 • *appetite*
And Jerusalem's splendor, her multi- tude, her din *of revelry*, and the jubilant within her, descend *into it*.
15 So the *common* man will be humbled, and the man of *importance* abased,
ᴿThe eyes of the proud also will be abased.   Is. 2:11; 10:33
16 But the ᴿLᴏʀᴅ of hosts will be ᴿexalted in judgment,   Is. 28:17 • Is. 2:11, 17
And the holy God will show Himself ᴿholy in righteousness.   Is. 8:13; 29:23
17 ᴿThen the lambs will graze as in their pasture,   Is. 7:25; Mic. 2:12; Zeph. 2:6
And strangers will eat in the waste places of the ᵀwealthy.   *the fat*

18 Woe to those who drag iniquity with the cords of ᵀfalsehood, *worthlessness*
And sin as if with cart ropes;
19 ᴿWho say, "Let Him make speed, let Him hasten His work, that we may see *it*;
And let the purpose of the Holy One of Israel draw near
And come to pass, that we may know *it!*"   Ezek. 12:22; 2 Pet. 3:4
20 Woe to those who ᴿcall evil good, and good evil;   Prov. 17:15; Amos 5:7
Who ᴿsubstitute darkness for light and light for darkness;
Who ᵀsubstitute bitter for sweet, and sweet for bitter!   *set* • Matt. 6:22, 23
21 Woe to those who are ᴿwise in their own eyes,   Prov. 3:7; Rom. 12:16
And clever in their own sight!
22 ᴿWoe to those who are heroes in drink- ing wine,   Prov. 23:20; Is. 5:11; 56:12
And valiant men in mixing strong drink;
23 Who justify the wicked for a bribe,
And take away the ᵀrights of the ones who are in the right!   *righteousness*

24 Therefore,[R]as a tongue of fire consumes
    stubble,   Is. 9:18, 19; Joel 2:5
    And dry grass collapses into the flame,
    So their[R]root will become[R]like rot and
       their blossom blow away as dust;
    For they have rejected the law of the
       LORD of hosts,   Job 18:16 • Hos. 5:12
    And despised the word of the Holy One
       of Israel.
25 On this account the[R]anger of the LORD
    has burned against His people,
    And He has stretched out His hand
    against them and struck them
    down,   2 Kin. 22:13, 17; Is. 66:15
    And the[R]mountains quaked; and their
    corpses[T]lay like refuse in the middle
       of the streets.   Is. 64:3; Jer. 4:24 • were
    For all this His anger is not spent,
    But His hand is still stretched out.

26 He will also lift up a[R]standard to the
    distant nation,   Is. 13:2, 3
    And will whistle for it from the ends of
    the earth;
    And behold, it will [R]come with speed
    swiftly.   Is. 13:4, 5
27 [R]No one in it is weary or stumbles,
    None slumbers or sleeps;   Joel 2:7, 8
    Nor is the[R]belt at its waist undone,
    Nor its sandal strap broken.   Job 12:18
28 [T]Its[R] arrows are sharp, and all its bows
    are bent;   Which, its arrows • Is. 13:18
    The hoofs of its horses[T]seem like flint,
    and its chariot[R]wheels like a whirl-
    wind.   are regarded as • Jer. 4:13
29 Its[R]roaring is like a lioness, and it roars
    like young lions;   Jer. 51:38; Zeph. 3:3
    It growls as it[T]seizes the prey,
    And carries it off with[R]no one to deliver
    it.   Is. 10:6; 49:24, 25 • Is. 42:22
30 And it shall[R]growl over it in that day
    like the roaring of the sea.   Is. 17:12
    If one[R]looks to the land, behold, there is
    darkness and distress;
    Even the light is darkened by its
    clouds.   Joel 2:10; Luke 21:25, 26

CHAPTER 6

The Commission of Isaiah

IN the year of[R]King Uzziah's death,[R]I saw
the Lord sitting on a throne, lofty and exalted, with the train of His robe filling the
temple.   2 Kin. 15:7; 2 Chr. 26:23 • John 12:41
   2 Seraphim stood above Him,[R]each having six wings; with two he covered his face,
and with two he covered his feet, and with
two he flew.   Rev. 4:8

3 And one called out to another and said,
   "Holy, Holy, Holy, is the LORD of hosts,
   The whole earth is full of His glory."

4 And the foundations of the thresholds
trembled at the voice of him who called out,
while the temple was filling with smoke.
   5 Then I said,
   "Woe[R]is me, for I am ruined!   [Ex. 33:20]
   Because I am a man of[R]unclean lips,
   And I live among a[R]people of unclean
    lips;   Ex. 6:12, 30 • Is. 59:3; Jer. 9:3-8
   For my eyes have seen the[R]King, the
    LORD of hosts."   Jer. 51:57
6 Then one of the seraphim flew to me,
with a burning coal in his hand which he
had taken from the[R]altar with tongs. Rev. 8:3
7 And he[T]touched my mouth with it and
said, "Behold, this has touched your lips;
and your iniquity is taken away, and your
sin is[T]forgiven."   Dan. 10:16 • atoned for

8 Then I heard the voice of the Lord, saying, "Whom shall I send, and who will go for
Us?" Then I said, "Here am I. Send me!"

9 And He said, "Go, and tell this people:
   'Keep on[R]listening, but do not perceive;
   Keep on looking, but do not under-
    stand.'   Is. 43:8; Matt. 13:14; Mark 4:12 ☆
10"Render[R]the hearts of this people[T]insen-
    sitive,[R]   Mark 6:1-6 ☆ • fat • Deut. 31:20
   Their ears[T]dull,   heavy

6:3 Holiness of God—Our greatest failing is in not realizing who God is and what His character is like. God is NOT human. He is God, and as such there is an infinite gap between the highest in us and the lowest in God. The gap between God and us is unbridgeable from our side. If the gap is to be bridged, it must be from God's side—for God is holy. To be holy means "to be set apart." God is set apart from the power, practice, and presence of sin, and is set apart to absolute righteousness and goodness. There is no sin in God and God can have nothing to do with sin. If we are to approach God, we must do so on God's terms. Somehow, we must be made holy—just as holy as God is. Any holiness which falls short of God's holiness will not be able to stand in the presence of God. Therefore, because of the holiness of God, we must have a new life in which our sins have been forgiven and done away with so that we actually can be as separated from sin as God is. This is the good news of the gospel—that Christ died for our sins, having taken them upon Himself, and has set us apart from them. This is our position before God which will never change. Because of what God has done, we can enter boldly into the presence of God.
    Now turn to Page 6—Gen. 3:6, 7: Adam's Sin.

6:8 Knowing the Will of God Through Submission to the Spirit—The moment a repenting sinner receives Christ by faith into his heart the Holy Spirit immediately does five things for him:
a. He regenerates the believer, that is, He gives him a new nature (Page 1066—John 3:5, 6; Page 1230—Titus 3:5).
b. He baptizes the believer into the body of Christ (Page 1158—1 Cor. 12:13).
c. He indwells the believer (Page 1137—Rom. 8:9; Page 1153—1 Cor. 6:19).
d. He seals the believer (Page 1185—Eph. 1:13; 4:30).

And their eyes ^Tdim,　　　　*besmeared*
^RLest they see with their eyes,　Jer. 5:21
Hear with their ears,
Understand with their hearts,
And return and be healed."
11 Then I said, "Lord,^Rhow long?" And He
answered,　　　　　　　Ps. 79:5
"Until^Rcities are devastated *and* without
inhabitant,　Lev. 26:31; Is. 1:7; 3:8, 26
Houses are without people,
And the land is utterly desolate,
12 "The LORD has^Rremoved men far away,
And the forsaken places are many in
the midst of the land.　Deut. 28:64
13 "Yet there will be a tenth portion in it,
And it will again be *subject* to burning,
Like a terebinth or an^Roak　Job 14:7
Whose stump remains when it is felled.
The^Rholy seed is its stump."　Deut. 7:6

CHAPTER 7

Sign of Immanuel
2 Kin. 16:5; 2 Chr. 28:5–15

NOW it came about in the days of Ahaz,
the son of Jotham, the son of Uzziah, king of
Judah, that Rezin the king of Aram and Pekah the son of Remaliah, king of Israel,
went up to Jerusalem to *wage* war against
it, but could not ^Tconquer it.　*fight against*
2 When it was reported to_Tthe house of
David, saying, "The Arameans^Thave camped
in Ephraim," his heart and the hearts of his
people shook as the trees of the forest shake
^Twith the wind.　*has settled down on • from before*
3 Then the LORD said to Isaiah, "Go out
now to meet Ahaz, you and your son Shear-
jashub, at the end of the conduit of the upper pool, on the highway to the fuller's field,
4 and say to him, 'Take care, and be
^Rcalm, have no ^Rfear and ^Rdo not be faint-
hearted because of these two stubs of smol-
dering firebrands, on account of the fierce
anger of Rezin and Aram, and the son of
Remaliah.　Ex. 14:13 • Is. 10:24 • Deut. 20:3
5 'Because ^RAram, *with* Ephraim and the
son of Remaliah, has planned evil against
you, saying,　　　　　　Is. 7:2
6 "Let us go up against Judah and^Tterror-
ize it, and make for ourselves a breach in^Tits

³ I.e., God is with us

walls, and set up the son of Tabeel as king in
the midst of it,"　*cause it a sickening dread • it*
7 thus says the Lord GOD, "It^Rshall not
stand nor shall it come to pass.　Acts 4:25, 26
8 "For the head of Aram is^RDamascus and
the head of Damascus is Rezin (now within
another 65 years Ephraim will be shattered,
so that it is no longer a people),　Gen. 14:15
9 and the head of Ephraim is Samaria
and the head of Samaria is the son of Rema-
liah.^RIf you will not believe, you surely shall
not^Alast." ' "　2 Chr. 20:20; Is. 5:24 • *be established*

10 Then the LORD spoke again to Ahaz,
saying,
11 "Ask a^Rsign for yourself from the LORD
your God; make *it* deep as Sheol or high as
^Theaven."　2 Kin. 19:29; Is. 37:30; 38:7, 8 • *heights*
12 But Ahaz said, "I will not ask, nor will I
test the LORD!"
13 Then he said, "Listen now, O^Rhouse of
David! Is it too slight a thing for you to try
the patience of men, that you will^Rtry the
patience of my God as well?　Is. 7:2 • Is. 1:14
14 "Therefore the Lord Himself will give
you a sign: Behold, a^Avirgin will be with
child and bear a son, and she will call His
name ³Immanuel.^R　*maiden* • Is. 8:8, 10 ☆
15 "He will eat^Tcurds and honey ^Tat the time
He knows *enough* to refuse evil and choose
good.　Is. 7:22 • *with respect to his knowing*
16 "For before the boy will know *enough* to
refuse evil and choose good, the land whose
two kings you dread will be forsaken.
17 "The LORD will bring on you, on your
people, and on your father's house such
days as have never come since the day that
^REphraim separated from Judah, the^Rking of
Assyria."　1 Kin. 12:16 • 2 Chr. 28:20; Is. 8:7, 8
18 And it will come about in that day, that
the LORD will whistle for the fly that is in the
remotest part of the rivers of Egypt, and for
the bee that is in the land of Assyria.
19 And they will all come and settle on
the steep^Aravines, on the ledges of the cliffs,
^Ron all the thorn bushes, and on all the^Awater-
ing places.　*wadis* • Is. 7:24, 25 • *pastures*
20 In that day the Lord will^Rshave with a
razor, hired from regions beyond the ^TEu-
phrates (*that is,* with the king of Assyria),
the head and the hair of the legs; and it will
also remove the beard.　2 Kin. 18:13-16 • *River*

---

e. He fills the believer (Page 1095—Acts 2:4; 4:8; 7:55; 13:52).
　All five of these ministries occur often at conversion. The fifth ministry, however, should be asked for as needed.
See Ephesians 5:18; Galatians 5:16. Actually the word *control* is a better term than "fill" in describing this fifth
ministry. It does not mean that we get more of the Spirit, but rather that He gets more of us. The fifth ministry is lost
when the believer either quenches (Page 1209—1 Thess. 5:19) or grieves (Page 1188—Eph. 4:30) the Holy Spirit.
The fifth ministry can be regained by following the command of 1 John 1:9, "If we confess our sins, He is faithful
and righteous to forgive us our sins and to cleanse us from all unrighteousness."
　How can a Christian be certain that he is indeed controlled by the Holy Spirit on a daily basis? First, he must
consecrate his body as a living sacrifice to the Holy Spirit (Page 1141—Rom. 12:1, 2). Second, he must depend
upon the Holy Spirit to convict him of sin (Page 600—Ps. 139:23, 24; 19:12–14). Finally, he must look to the Holy
Spirit for divine power in serving Christ (Page 1094—Acts 1:8; Page 1181—Gal. 5:16, 17; Page 1186—Eph. 3:16).
Now turn to Page 628—Prov. 24:6: Knowing the Will of God Through Circumstances and Counsel.

21 Now it will come about in that day that a man may keep alive a^Rheifer and a pair of sheep;   Is. 14:30; 27:10; Jer. 39:10

22 and it will happen that because of the abundance of the milk produced he will eat curds, for everyone that is left within the land will eat^Rcurds and honey.   Is. 8:15

23 And it will come about in that day, that every place where there used to be a thousand vines, *valued* at a thousand *shekels* of silver, will become^Rbriars and thorns. Is. 5:6

24 *People* will come there with bows and arrows because all the land will be briars and thorns.

25 And as for all the hills which used to be cultivated with the hoe, you will not go there for fear of briars and thorns; but they will become a place for^Tpasturing^Roxen and for sheep to trample.   *sending* • Is. 5:17

CHAPTER 8

Sign of Maher-shalal-hash-baz

THEN the LORD said to me, "Take for yourself a large tablet and write on it^Tin ordinary letters:^RSwift is the booty, speedy is the prey.   *with the stylus of man* • Is. 8:3

2"And I will take to Myself faithful witnesses for testimony, Uriah the priest and Zechariah the son of Jeberechiah."

3 So I approached the prophetess, and she conceived and gave birth to a son. Then the LORD said to me, "Name him [4]Maher-shalal-hash-baz;   Is. 8:1

4 for before the boy knows how to cry out 'My father' or 'My mother,' the wealth of Damascus and the spoil of Samaria will be carried away before the king of Assyria."

5 And again the LORD spoke to me further, saying,

6 "Inasmuch as these people have ^Rrejected the gently flowing waters of Shiloah,   Is. 1:20; 5:24; 7:9; 30:12
And rejoice in^RRezin and the son of Remaliah;   Is. 7:1

7 "Now therefore, behold, the Lord is about to bring on them the^Rstrong and abundant waters of the ^TEuphrates, ^R   Is. 17:12, 13 • *River* • Is. 7:20
Even the^Rking of Assyria and all his glory;   Is. 7:17; 10:5
And it will^Rrise up over all its channels and go over all its banks.   Amos 8:8

8 "Then^Rit will sweep on into Judah, it will overflow and pass through,
It will reach even to the neck;   Is. 10:6
And the spread of its wings will^Tfill the breadth of ^Ayour land, O Immanuel.   *be the fulness of* • *Your*

9 "Be^R broken, O peoples, and be ^Ashattered;   Is. 17:12-14 • *dismayed*
And give ear, all remote places of the earth.

Gird yourselves, yet be shattered;
Gird yourselves, yet be shattered.

10 "Devise^Ra plan but it will be thwarted;
State a^Tproposal, but it will not stand,
For God is with us."   Job 5:12 • *word*

11 For thus the LORD spoke to me with mighty power and instructed me not to walk in the way of this people, saying,

12 "You are not to say, '*It is* a^Rconspiracy!' In regard to all that this people call a conspiracy,   Is. 7:2; 30:1
And you are not to fear^Twhat they fear or be in dread of *it*.   *their fear*

13 "It is the ^RLORD of hosts whom you should regard as holy.   Is. 5:16; 29:23
And He shall be your fear,
And He shall be your dread.

14 "Then He shall become a^Rsanctuary;
But to both the houses of Israel, a ^Rstone to strike and a rock to stumble over,   Is. 4:6 • Luke 2:34; 20:17 ☆
And a snare and a^Rtrap for the inhabitants of Jerusalem.   Is. 24:17, 18

15 "And many will stumble over them,
Then they will fall and be broken;
They will even be snared and caught."

16 Bind up the testimony, seal the ^Alaw among^Rmy disciples.   *teaching* • Is. 50:4

17 And I will^Rwait for the LORD^Rwho is hiding His face from the house of Jacob; I will even look eagerly for Him.   Hab. 2:3 • Is. 1:15

18 ^RBehold, I and the children whom the LORD has given me are for^Rsigns and wonders in Israel from the LORD of hosts, who dwells on Mount Zion.   Heb. 2:13 • Luke 2:34

19 And when they say to you, "Consult^R the mediums and the spiritists who whisper and mutter," should not a people ^Rconsult their God? *Should they consult* the dead on behalf of the living?   Lev. 20:6 • Is. 30:2; 45:11

20 To the^Alaw and to the testimony! If they do not speak according to this word, it is because they have no dawn.   *teaching*

21 And they will pass through^Tthe land hard-pressed and famished, and it will turn out that when they are hungry, they will be enraged and curse^Atheir king and their God as they face upward.   *it* • *by their king*

22 Then they will^Rlook to the earth, and behold, distress and darkness, the gloom of anguish; and *they will be*^Rdriven away into darkness.   Is. 5:30; 59:9; Jer. 13:16 • Is. 8:20

CHAPTER 9

Prophecy of the Messiah's Birth

BUT there will be no *more*^Rgloom for her who was in anguish; in earlier times He ^Rtreated the land of Zebulun and^Rthe land of Naphtali with contempt, but later on He shall make *it* glorious, by the way of the sea, on the other side of Jordan, Galilee of the Gentiles.   Is. 8:22 • 2 Kin. 15:29 • Matt. 4:14–16 ☆

---

[4] I.e., swift is the booty, speedy is the prey

2 [R]The people who walk in darkness
  Will see a great light;   Luke 1:79 ☆
  Those who live in a dark land,
  The light will shine on them.
3 Thou shalt multiply the nation,
  Thou shalt increase their gladness;
  They will be glad in Thy presence
  As with the gladness of harvest,
  As [T]men [R]rejoice when they divide the
  spoil.   they • in • they • 1 Sam. 30:16
4 For [R]Thou shalt break the yoke of their
  burden and the staff on their shoulders,   Is. 10:27; 14:25
  The rod of their oppressor, as [T]at the
  battle of Midian.   in the day of Midian
5 For every boot of the booted warrior in
  the battle tumult,
  And cloak rolled in blood, will be for
  burning, fuel for the fire.

6 For a [R]child will be born to us, a son will
  be given to us;   [Is. 7:14; Luke 2:11] ☆
  And the [R]government will [T]rest on His
  shoulders;   [Matt. 28:18] • be
  And His name will be called [R]Wonderful
  Counselor, Mighty God,   Is. 28:29
  Eternal Father, Prince of Peace.

7 There will be [R]no end to the increase of
  His government or of peace,
  On the [R]throne of David and over his
  kingdom,   Luke 1:32, 33 ☆ • Is. 16:5
  To establish it and to uphold it with
  [R]justice and righteousness   Is. 11:4, 5

From then on and forevermore.
[R]The zeal of the LORD of hosts will accomplish this.   Is. 37:32; 59:17

Judgment on Ephraim

8 The Lord sends a [T]message against Ja-
  cob,
  And it falls on Israel.   *word*
9 And all the people know *it*,
  That is, [R]Ephraim and the inhabitants of
  Samaria,
  Asserting in pride and in [R]arrogance of
  heart: Is. 7:8, 9; 28:1, 3 • Is. 46:12
10 "The bricks have fallen down,
  But we will [R]rebuild with smooth
  stones;   Mal. 1:4
  The sycamores have been cut down,
  But we will replace *them* with cedars."
11 Therefore the LORD raises against them
  adversaries from [R]Rezin,
  And spurs their enemies on,   Is. 7:1, 8
12 The Arameans on the east and the [R]Phi-
  listines on the west;   2 Chr. 28:18
  And they [R]devour Israel with [T]gaping
  jaws.   Ps. 79:7 • the whole mouth
  [R]In *spite of* all this His anger does not
  turn away,   Is. 5:25
  And His hand is still stretched out.

13 Yet the people [R]do not turn back to Him
  who struck them,   Jer. 5:3; Hos. 7:10
  Nor do they seek the LORD of hosts.
14 So the LORD cuts off [R]head and tail from
  Israel,

9:6 The Person of the Son of God—It is crucial to remember that the existence of the Son of God did not commence with His birth in Bethlehem. He is spoken of as the Son before He became a man (Page 665—Is. 9:6; Page 1179—Gal. 4:4). Micah prophesies of His birth, but yet states that "His goings forth are from long ago, from the days of eternity" (Page 893—Mic. 5:2). John says that He existed "in the beginning" before anything was created (Page 1064—John 1:1–3).

Even before He was born of Mary, He appeared to men in the Old Testament as the "Angel of the LORD." It is clear that this Angel is no ordinary angel because He is identified as God (Page 55—Ex. 3:1, 4); He pardons sin (Page 75—Ex. 23:20, 21); and He is worshiped (Page 210—Josh. 5:13–15). While these passages do not say that this member of the Godhead was the preincarnate Christ, we may conclude that they are the same person since their work is the same.

While Christ was preexistent and appeared occasionally to men in the Old Testament, He took on a body perma-nently when He was conceived in Mary's womb. This incomparable event of God's becoming man in Jesus Christ is called the Incarnation. This miracle was prophesied hundreds of years previously (Page 663—Is. 7:14) and was fulfilled historically in Mary in whose womb the Holy Spirit's power conceived a child (Page 964—Matt. 1:23; Page 1026—Luke 1:35). Thus Christ the sinless God-man was qualified to become our Redeemer (Page 1169—2 Cor. 5:21).

Having been born of a woman, Jesus Christ was fully man apart from sin (Page 1064—John 1:14). As a man He experienced the normal physical, mental, social, and spiritual growth as others did (Page 1028—Luke 2:52). He suffered pain, hunger, thirst, fatigue, temptation, pleasure, rest, and even lack of knowledge (Page 1015—Mark 13:32). Because of His complete humanity He can be sympathetic and compassionate toward us (Page 1241—Heb. 4:15).

While Christ was fully man He was also fully God, as these facts indicate: He is called God (Page 1064—John 1:1; Page 1239—Heb. 1:8); He did works that only God could do, such as forgive sins (Page 1001—Mark 2:7) and create (Page 1200—Col. 1:16); He had attributes that only God could have, such as truth (Page 1081—John 14:6) and omniscience (Page 1066—John 2:24, 25); and He claimed equality with God (Page 1077—John 10:30).

The question may then be raised as to whether Christ lost anything of deity when He became a man (Page 1194—Phil. 2:6–8). While there is an inscrutable mystery involved in this unparalleled act of condescension, one can be certain that He lost none of God's attributes, because He was still God (Page 1088—John 20:28). He was fully God and fully man united in one person forever. Even now, at the right hand of God, He is the God-man (Page 1217—1 Tim. 2:5). The great condescension of the Son of God becoming a man serves eternally as a perfect model of humility and self-giving love (Page 1194—Phil. 2:5).

Now turn to Page 1076—John 10:10: The Earthly Life of the Son of God.

Both palm branch and bulrush[R]in a single day.   Is. 19:15 • Rev. 18:8
15 The head is[R]the elder and honorable man,   Is. 3:2, 3
And the prophet who teaches[R]falsehood is the tail.   Is. 28:15; 59:3, 4
16[R]For those who guide this people are leading them astray;   Is. 3:12
And those who are guided by them are [A]brought to confusion.   swallowed up
17 Therefore the Lord does[R]not take pleasure in their young men,   Amos 4:10
[R]Nor does He have pity on their[A]orphans or their widows;   Is. 27:11 • fatherless
For every one of them is[R]godless and an[R]evildoer,   Is. 10:6; 32:6 • Is. 1:4
And every[R]mouth is speaking foolishness.   Matt. 12:34
[R]In spite of all this His anger does not turn away,   Is. 5:25
And His hand is still stretched out.

18[R]For wickedness burns like a fire;
It consumes briars and thorns;
It even sets the thickets of the forest aflame,   Ps. 83:14; [Is. 1:7]
And they roll upward in a column of smoke.
19 By the[R]fury of the LORD of hosts the [R]land is burned up,   Is. 10:6 • Joel 2:3
And the[R]people are like fuel for the fire;
No man spares his brother. Is. 1:31; 24:6
20 And[T]they slice off what is on the right hand but still are hungry,   he slices
And[T]they eat what is on the left hand but they are not satisfied;
Each of them eats the[R]flesh of his own arm.   he eats • Is. 49:26
21 Manasseh devours Ephraim, and Ephraim Manasseh,
[R]And together they are against Judah.
[R]In spite of all this His anger does not turn away,   2 Chr. 28:6, 8 • Is. 5:25
And His hand is still stretched out.

CHAPTER 10

WOE to those who enact evil statutes,
And to those who constantly record [T]unjust decisions,   mischief or misfortune
2 So as[R]to[T]deprive the needy of justice,
And rob the poor of My people of their rights,   Is. 5:23 • turn aside from
In order[R]that widows may be their spoil,   Is. 1:23; 3:14, 15
And that they may plunder the [A]orphans.   fatherless
3 Now[R]what will you do in the[R]day of punishment,   Job 31:14 • Jer. 9:9
And in the devastation which will come[R]from afar?   Is. 5:26
[R]To whom will you flee for help? Is. 20:6
And where will you leave your wealth?

4 Nothing remains but to crouch[T]among the[R]captives   under • Is. 24:22
Or fall among the[R]slain.   Is. 22:2; 34:3
[R]In spite of all this His anger does not turn away,   Is. 5:25
And His hand is still stretched out.

Destruction of Assyria

5 Woe to[R]Assyria, the[R]rod of My anger
And the staff in whose hands is My indignation,   Zeph. 2:13-15 • Jer. 51:20
6 I send it against a[R]godless nation
And commission it against the[R]people of My fury   Is. 9:17 • Is. 9:19
To capture booty and to seize plunder,
And to[T]trample them down like mud in the streets.   make them a trampled place
7 Yet it[R]does not so intend   Gen. 50:20
Nor does it plan so in its heart,
But rather it is[T]its purpose to destroy,
And to cut off many nations.   in its heart
8 For it says, "Are not my princes[T]all kings?   altogether
9"Is not[R]Calno like Carchemish,   Amos 6:2
Or[R]Hamath like Arpad,   Num. 34:8
Or Samaria like[R]Damascus?   2 Kin. 16:9
10"As my hand has reached to the[R]kingdoms of the idols,
Whose graven images were greater than those of Jerusalem and Samaria,   2 Kin. 19:17, 18
11 Shall I not[T]do to Jerusalem and her images
Just as I have done to Samaria and[R]her idols?"   do thus • Is. 2:8
12 So it will be that when the Lord has completed all His work on Mount Zion and on Jerusalem, He will say, "I will punish the fruit of the arrogant heart of the king of Assyria and the pomp of his haughtiness."
13 For[R]he has said,   [2 Kin. 19:22–24]
"By the power of my hand and by my wisdom I did this,
For I have understanding;
And I[R]removed the boundaries of the peoples,   Hab. 2:6-11
And plundered their treasures,
And like a mighty man I brought down their inhabitants,
14 And my hand reached to the riches of the peoples like a[R]nest,
And as one gathers abandoned eggs, I gathered all the earth;
And there was not one that flapped its wing or opened its beak or chirped."   Jer. 49:16; Obad. 4

15 Is the[R]axe to boast itself over the one who chops with it?   Jer. 51:20
Is the saw to exalt itself over the one who wields it?
That would be like[R]a[T]club wielding those who lift it,

Or like ^Ra rod lifting *him who* is not
wood.   Is. 10:5 • *staff* • Is. 10:5

16 Therefore the Lord, the God of hosts,
will send a^Rwasting disease among
his stout warriors;   Ps. 106:15
And under his^Rglory a fire will be kindled like a burning flame.   Is. 8:7

17 And the light of Israel will become a
fire and his Holy One a flame,
And it will burn and devour his thorns
and his briars in a single day.

18 And He will^Rdestroy the glory of his
forest and of his fruitful garden,
both soul and body;
And it will be as when a sick man
wastes away.   Is. 10:33, 34

19 And the^Rrest of the trees of his forest
will be so small in number   Is. 21:17
That a child could write them down.

Remnant of Israel

20 Now it will come about in that day that
the ^Rremnant of Israel, and those of the
house of Jacob^Rwho have escaped, will never again rely^Ron the one who struck them,
but will truly^Rrely on the Lord, the Holy One
of Israel.   Is. 1:9 • Is. 4:2 • 2 Chr. 14:11

21 A^Rremnant will return, the remnant of
Jacob, to the mighty God.   Is. 7:3

22 For^Rthough your people, O Israel, may
be like the sand of the sea,
Only a remnant within them will return;   Rom. 9:27, 28
A^Rdestruction is determined, overflowing with righteousness.   Is. 28:22

23 For a complete destruction, one that is
decreed,^Rthe Lord God of hosts will execute
in the midst of the whole land.   Rom. 9:28

24 Therefore thus says the Lord God of
hosts, "O My people who dwell in^RZion, do
not fear the Assyrian^Twho^Rstrikes you with
the rod and lifts up his staff against you, the
way Egypt *did.*   Ps. 87:5, 6 • *he* • Ex. 5:14-16

25"For in a very little while My indignation *against you* will be spent, and My anger
will be directed to their destruction."

26 And the Lord of hosts will^Rarouse a
scourge against him like the slaughter of
^RMidian at the rock of Oreb; and His staff
will be over the sea, and He will lift it up the
way *He did* in Egypt.   Is. 37:36-38 • Judg. 7:25

27 So it will be in that day, that^Rhis burden
will be removed from your shoulders and
his yoke from your neck, and the yoke will
be broken because of fatness.   the Assyrian

28 He has come against Aiath,
He has passed through^RMigron;
At ^RMichmash he deposited his bag-
gage.   1 Sam. 14:2 • 1 Sam. 13:2, 5

29 They have gone through^Rthe pass, *saying,*   1 Sam. 13:23
"Geba will be our lodging place."

^RRamah is terrified, and Gibeah of Saul
has fled away.   Josh. 18:25; 1 Sam. 7:17

30 Cry aloud with your voice, O daughter
of^RGallim!   1 Sam. 25:44
Pay attention, Laishah *and* wretched
^RAnathoth!   Josh. 21:18; Jer. 1:1

31 Madmenah has fled.
The inhabitants of Gebim have sought
refuge.

32 Yet today he will halt at Nob;
He^Rshakes his fist at the mountain of
the^Rdaughter of Zion, the hill of Jerusalem.   Is. 19:16 • Is. 1:8; Jer. 6:23

33 Behold, the Lord, the God of hosts, will
lop off the boughs with a terrible
crash;
Those also who are^Rtall in stature will
be cut down,   Is. 37:24, 36-38; Ezek. 31:3
And those who are lofty will be abased.

34 And He will cut down the thickets of
the forest with an iron *axe,*
And^RLebanon will fall^Aby the Mighty
One.   Is. 2:13; 33:9 • *as a mighty one*

CHAPTER 11

Restoration of the Messiah's Kingdom

THEN a^Rshoot will spring from the^Rstem of
Jesse,   Is. 4:2; 53:2 • [Is. 9:7; 11:10]
And a^Rbranch from^Rhis roots will bear
fruit.   Is. 6:13; Jer. 23:5☆ • Rev. 5:5

2 And the^RSpirit of the Lord will rest on
Him,   [Is. 42:1; 48:16; 61:1; Matt. 3:16]☆
The spirit of^Rwisdom and understand-
ing,   [1 Cor. 1:30]; Eph. 1:17, 18
The spirit of counsel and^Rstrength,
The spirit of knowledge and the fear of
the Lord.   2 Tim. 1:7

3 And He will delight in the fear of the
Lord,
And He will not judge by what His
eyes^Rsee,
Nor make a decision by what His ears
hear;   John 2:25; 7:24☆

4 But with^Rrighteousness He will judge
the^Rpoor, Is. 9:7; 16:5☆ • Ps. 72:2, 13, 14
And decide with fairness for the ^Raf-
flicted of the earth;   Is. 29:19; 32:7
And He will strike the earth with the
^Rrod of His mouth,   Ps. 2:9; Is. 49:2
And with the^Rbreath of His lips He will
slay the wicked.   Job 4:9; Is. 30:28, 33

5 Also ^Rrighteousness will be the belt
about His loins,
And ^Rfaithfulness the belt about His
waist.   Eph. 6:14 • Is. 25:1

6 And the^Rwolf will dwell with the lamb,
And the leopard will lie down with the
kid,   Is. 65:25
And the calf and the young lion ⁵and
the fatling together;

⁵ Some versions read *will feed together*

And a little boy will lead them.
7 Also the cow and the bear will graze;
Their young will lie down together;
And the lion will eat straw like the ox.
8 And the nursing child will play by the
hole of the cobra,
And the weaned child will put his hand
on the viper's den.
9 They will ^Rnot hurt or destroy in all My
holy mountain,   Job 5:23; Is. 65:25
For the^Rearth will be full of the knowledge of the LORD   Ps. 98:2, 3; Is. 45:6
As the waters cover the sea.

10 Then it will come about in that day
That the^Rnations will resort to the^Rroot
of Jesse,   Luke 2:32 • Is. 11:1☆
Who will stand as a^Asignal^Rfor the peo-
ples;   *standard* • John 3:14, 15; 12:32
And His resting place will be glorious.

11 Then it will happen on that day that the
Lord
Will again recover the second time
with His hand
The^Rremnant of His people, who will
remain,   Is. 10:20-22; 37:4, 31, 32; 46:3
From Assyria, ^REgypt, Pathros, Cush,
Elam, Shinar, Hamath,   Is. 19:21, 22
And from the islands of the sea.
12 And He will lift up a^Rstandard for the
nations,   Is. 11:10
And will^Rassemble the banished ones of
Israel,   Is. 56:8; Zeph. 3:10; Zech. 10:6
And will gather the dispersed of Judah
From the four corners of the earth.
13 Then the^Rjealousy of Ephraim will de-
part,
And those who harass Judah will be
cut off;   Ezek. 37:16, 17, 22; Hos. 1:11
Ephraim will not be jealous of Judah,
And Judah will not harass Ephraim.
14 And they will ^Rswoop down on the
slopes of the Philistines on the
^Rwest;   Jer. 48:40; 49:22 • Is. 9:12
Together they will^Rplunder the sons of
the east;   Jer. 49:28
They will possess^REdom and Moab;
And the sons of Ammon will be^Tsubject
to them.   Amos 9:12 • *their obedience*
15 And the LORD will^Rutterly destroy
The tongue of the Sea of Egypt;
And He will^Rwave His hand over the
^TRiver   Is. 43:16 • Is. 19:16 • Euphrates
With His scorching wind;
And He will strike it into seven
streams,
And make *men* walk over dry-shod.
16 And there will be a^Rhighway from As-
syria   Is. 19:23; 35:8; 40:3; 62:10
For the^Rremnant of His people who will
be left,   Is. 11:11
Just as there was for Israel
In^Rthe day that they came up out of the
land of Egypt.   Ex. 14:26-29

CHAPTER 12

*Thanksgiving in the Messiah's
Kingdom*

THEN you will say on that day,
"I^Rwill give thanks to Thee, O LORD;
For ^Ralthough Thou wast angry with
me,   Ps. 9:1 • Is. 40:1, 2; 54:7-10
Thine anger is turned away,
And Thou dost comfort me.
2 "Behold,^RGod is my salvation,
I will^Rtrust and not be afraid;
For ^Rthe LORD GOD is my strength and
song,   Is. 32:2 • Is. 26:3 • Ex. 15:2
And He has become my salvation."
3 Therefore you will joyously ^Rdraw
water   [John 4:10; 7:37, 38]
From the^Rsprings of salvation. Jer. 2:13
4 And in that day you will^Rsay,
"Give^R thanks to the LORD, call on His
name.   Is. 24:15; 42:12 • Ps. 105:1
^RMake known His deeds among the peo-
ples;   Ps. 145:4
^AMake *them* remember that His name is
exalted."   *Proclaim to* them *that*
5 ^RPraise the LORD in song, for He has
done^Aexcellent things;
Let this be known throughout the
earth.   Ex. 15:1; Ps. 98:1 • *gloriously*
6 ^RCry aloud and shout for joy, O inhabitant of Zion,   Is. 52:9; 54:1; Zeph. 3:14
For^Rgreat in your midst is the Holy One
of Israel.   Is. 1:24; 49:26; 60:16

CHAPTER 13

Prophecies Against Babylon

THE^Aoracle concerning Babylon which^RIsa-
iah the son of Amoz saw.   *burden of* • Is. 1:1
2 ^RLift up a standard on the ⁶bare hill,
Raise your voice to them,   Is. 5:26
^RWave the hand that they may enter the
doors of the nobles.   Is. 10:32; 19:16
3 I have commanded My consecrated
ones,
I have even called My^Rmighty warriors,
My proudly exulting ones,
To *execute* My anger.   Joel 3:11
4 A ^Rsound of tumult on the mountains,
Like that of many people!
A sound of the uproar of kingdoms,
Of nations gathered together!
The LORD of hosts is mustering the
army for battle.   Is. 5:30; 17:12
5 They are coming from a far country
From the^Tfarthest horizons,
The LORD and His instruments of^Rindig-
nation,   *end of heaven* • Is. 10:5
To^Rdestroy the whole land.   Is. 24:1
6 Wail, for the^Rday of the LORD is near!
It will come as destruction from^Tthe Al-
mighty.   Is. 2:12; 10:3 • Heb., *Shaddai*

⁶ Or, *wind-swept mountain*

7 Therefore all hands will fall limp,
And every man's heart will melt.
8 And they will be^Rterrified,
Pains and anguish will take hold of
them;   2 Kin. 19:26; Is. 21:3; Jer. 46:5
They will^Rwrithe like a woman in labor,
They will look at one another in aston-
ishment,   Is. 26:17; Jer. 4:31; John 16:21
Their faces aflame.
9 Behold,^Rthe day of the LORD is coming,
Cruel, with fury and burning anger,
To make the land a desolation;
And He will exterminate its sinners
from it.   Is. 13:6
10 For the^Rstars of heaven and their con-
stellations   Is. 5:30; Ezek. 32:7
Will not flash forth their light;
The sun will be dark when it rises,
And the moon will not shed its light.
11 Thus I will^Rpunish the world for its evil,
And the^Rwicked for their iniquity;
I will also put an end to the arrogance
of the proud,   Is. 26:21 • Is. 3:11; 11:4
And abase the^Rhaughtiness of the^Rruth-
less.   Jer. 48:29 • tyrants, despots
12 I will make mortal man^Rscarcer^Rthan
pure gold,   more precious • Is. 4:1
And mankind than the gold of Ophir.
13 Therefore I shall make the^Rheavens
tremble,   Is. 34:4; 51:6
And^Rthe earth will be shaken from its
place   Is. 2:19; 24:1, 19, 20; Hag. 2:6
At the fury of the LORD of hosts
In the day of His burning anger.
14 And it will be that like a hunted gazelle,
Or like ^Rsheep with none to gather
them,   1 Kin. 22:17; Matt. 9:36
They will each turn to his own people,
And each one flee to his own land.
15 Anyone who is found will be^Rthrust
through,   Is. 14:19; Jer. 50:25; 51:3, 4
And anyone who is captured will fall
by the sword.
16 Their^Rlittle ones also will be dashed to
pieces
Before their eyes;   Hos. 10:14; Nah. 3:10
Their houses will be plundered
And their wives ravished.

17 Behold, I am going to^Rstir up the Medes
against them,   Jer. 51:11; Dan. 5:28
Who will not value silver or^Rtake pleasure in gold,   Prov. 6:34, 35
18 And their bows will mow down the
^Ryoung men,   2 Kin. 8:12; 2 Chr. 36:17
They will not even have compassion on
the fruit of the womb,
Nor will their eye pity^Tchildren.   sons
19 And^RBabylon, the^Rbeauty of kingdoms,
the glory of the Chaldeans' pride,
Will be as when God overthrew Sodom
and Gomorrah.   Is. 21:9 • Dan. 4:30
20 It will^Rnever be inhabited or lived in
from generation to generation;

Nor will the Arab pitch his tent there,
Nor will shepherds make their flocks
lie down there.   Is. 14:23; 34:10-15
21 But ^Rdesert creatures will lie down
there,   Is. 34:11-15; Zeph. 2:14; Rev. 18:2
And their houses will be full of owls,
Ostriches also will live there, and
shaggy goats will frolic there.
22 And^Ahyenas will howl in their fortified
towers   howling creatures
And jackals in their luxurious palaces.
Her fateful time also will soon come
And her days will not be prolonged.

CHAPTER 14

WHEN the LORD will^Rhave compassion on
Jacob, and again ^Rchoose Israel, and settle
them in their own land, then strangers will
join them and attach themselves to the
house of Jacob.   Ps. 102:13 • Is. 41:8, 9; 44:1
2 And the peoples will take them along
and bring them to their place, and the house
of Israel will possess them as an inheritance
in the land of the LORD as male servants and
female servants; and ^Tthey will take their
captors captive, and will rule over their oppressors.   the captors will become their captives
3 And it will be in the day when the LORD
gives you^Rrest from your pain and turmoil
and harsh service in which you have been
enslaved,   Ezra 9:8, 9; Is. 11:10; 40:2; Jer. 30:10
4 that you will^Rtake up this taunt against
the king of Babylon, and say,   Hab. 2:6
"How^Rthe oppressor has ceased,
And how fury has ceased!   Is. 9:4; 16:4
5 "The LORD has broken the staff of the
wicked,
The scepter of rulers
6 Which used to strike the peoples in
fury with unceasing strokes,
Which subdued the nations in anger
with unrestrained persecution.
7 "The whole earth is at rest and is quiet;
They break forth into shouts of joy.
8 "Even the ^Rcypress trees rejoice over
you, and the cedars of Lebanon,
saying,   Is. 55:12; Ezek. 31:16
'Since you were laid low, no tree cutter
comes up against us.'
9 "Sheol from beneath is excited over you
to meet you when you come;
It arouses for you the spirits of the
dead, all the^Tleaders of the earth;
It raises all the kings of the nations
from their thrones.   male goats
10 "They^Rwill all respond and say to you,
'Even you have been made weak as we,
You have become like us.   Ezek. 32:21
11 'Your ^Rpomp and the music of your
harps   Is. 5:14
Have been brought down to Sheol;
Maggots are spread out as your bed beneath you,
And worms are your covering.'

12"How you have fallen from heaven,
O star of the morning, son of the dawn!
You have been cut down to the earth,
You who have weakened the nations!
13"But you said in your heart,
'I will ᴿascend to heaven;   Ezek. 28:2
I will ʳraise my throne above the stars
of God,   Dan. 5:22, 23; 8:10; 2 Thess. 2:4
And I will sit on the mount of assembly
In the recesses of the north.
14 'I will ascend above the heights of the
clouds;
I will make myself like the Most High.'
15"Nevertheless youᴿwill be thrust down
to Sheol,   Ezek. 28:8; Matt. 11:23
To the recesses of the pit.
16"Those who see you will gaze at you,
They willᵀponder over you, saying,
'Is this the man who made the earth
tremble,   show themselves attentive to
Who shook kingdoms,
17 Who made the world like aᴿwilderness
And overthrew its cities,
Whoᴿdid notᵀallow his prisoners to go
home?'   Joel 2:3 • Is. 45:13 • open
18"All the kings of theᵀnations lie in glory,
Each in his ownᵀtomb.   house
19"But you have beenᴿcast out of your
tomb   Is. 22:16-18
Likeᵀa rejected branch,
Clothed with the slain who are pierced
with a sword,   an abhorred branch
Who go down to the stones of theᴿpit,
Like a trampled corpse.   Jer. 41:7, 9
20"You will not be united with them in
burial,
Because you have ruined your country,
You have slain your people.
May theᴿoffspring of evildoers not be
mentioned forever.   Job 18:16, 19
21"Prepare for his sons a place of slaughter
Because of theᴿiniquity of their fathers.
They must not arise and take possession of the earth   Ex. 20:5; Lev. 26:39
And fill the face of the world with
cities."
22"And I will rise up against them," declares the Lᴏʀᴅ of hosts, "and will cut off
from Babylon name and survivors,ᴿoffspring
and posterity," declares the Lᴏʀᴅ.   Is. 47:9
23"I will also make it a possession for the
ᴿhedgehog, and swamps of water, and I will
sweep it with the broom ofᴿdestruction," declares the Lᴏʀᴅ of hosts.   Zeph. 2:14 • Is. 13:6

Prophecies Against Assyria

24 The Lᴏʀᴅ of hosts has sworn saying,
"Surely, ᴿjust as I have intended so it has
happened, and just as I have planned so it
will stand,   Job 23:13; [Is. 46:11; 55:8, 9]; Acts 4:28
25 to break Assyria in My land, and I will
trample him on My mountains. Then his
yoke will be removed from them, and his
burden removed from their shoulder.

26"This is the planᵀdevised against the
whole earth; and this is the hand that is
stretched out against all the nations. planned
27"For the Lᴏʀᴅ of hosts has planned, and
who can frustrate it? And as for His
stretched-out hand, who can turn it back?"

Prophecies Against Philistia

28 In theᴿyear that King Ahaz died this
ᴀoracleᴿcame: 2 Kin. 16:20 • burden • Is. 13:1
29"Do not rejoice, OᴿPhilistia, all of you,
Because the rod thatᴿstruck you is broken;   Is. 2:6; 11:14 • 2 Chr. 26:6
For from the serpent's root aᴿviper will
come out,   Is. 11:8
And its fruit will be a flying serpent.
30"And those who are mostᴿhelpless will
eat,
And the needy will lie down in security;   Is. 3:14, 15; 7:21, 22; 11:4
I will destroy your root with famine,
And it will kill off your survivors.
31"Wail, OᴿgaTe; cry, O city;   Is. 3:26; 24:12
Melt away, O Philistia, all of you;
For smoke comes from the north,
And there is no straggler in his ranks.
32"How then will one answer theᴿmessen-
gers of the nation?   Is. 37:9
Thatᴿthe Lᴏʀᴅ has founded Zion,
And the afflicted of His people will
seek refuge in it."   Ps. 87:1, 5; 102:16

CHAPTER 15

Prophecies Against Moab

Tʜᴇ ᴀoracle concerning Moab.   burden of
Surely in a nightᴿAr of Moab is devastated and ruined;   Num. 21:28
Surely in a night Kir of Moab is devastated and ruined.
2 They have gone up to theᵀtemple and to
ᴿDibon, even to the high places to
weep.   house • Jer. 48:18, 22
Moab wails over Nebo and Medeba;
Everyone's head isᴿbald and every beard
is cut off.   Lev. 21:5; Jer. 48:37
3 In their streets they have girded themselves withᴿsackcloth;   Jon. 3:6-8
On their housetops and in their squares
Everyone is wailing, dissolved in tears.
4 ᴿHeshbon and Elealeh also cry out,
Their voice is heard all the way to Jahaz;   Num. 21:28; 32:3; Jer. 48:34
Therefore the armed men of Moab cry
aloud;
His soul trembles within him.
5 My heart cries out for Moab;
His fugitives are as far asᴿZoar and
Eglath-shelishiyah,   Jer. 48:34
For they go up to theᴿascent of Luhith
weeping;   Jer. 48:5
Surely on the road to Horonaim they
raise a cry of distressᴿover their
ruin.   Is. 59:7; Jer. 4:20

6 For the waters of Nimrim are[T]desolate.
  Surely the grass is withered, the tender
  grass died out,   *desolations*
  There is[R]no green thing.   Joel 1:10-12
7 Therefore the [R]abundance *which* they
  have acquired and stored up
  They carry off over the brook of 'Ara-
  bim.   Is. 30:6; Jer. 48:36 • *the poplars*
8 For the cry of distress has gone around
  the territory of Moab,
  Its wail *goes* as far as Eglaim and its
  wailing even to Beer-elim.
9 For the waters of Dimon are full of
  [T]blood;   Heb., *dam* (a word play)
  Surely I will bring added *woes* upon Dimon,
  A lion upon the fugitives of Moab and
  upon the remnant of the land.

CHAPTER 16

Send[R] the *tribute* lamb to the ruler of the
  land,   2 Kin. 3:4; Ezra 7:17
  From[T]Sela by way of the wilderness to
  the [R]mountain of the daughter of
  Zion.   Petra in Edom • Is. 10:32
2 Then, like 'fleeing[R] birds *or* scattered
  [T]nestlings,   *fluttering* • Prov. 27:8 • *nest*
  The daughters of Moab will be at the
  fords of the[R]Arnon.   Num. 21:13, 14
3 "Give[T]*us* advice, make a decision;   *Bring*
  [T]Cast your shadow like night [T]at high
  noon;   *Set* • *in the midst of the noon*
  [R]Hide the outcasts, do not betray the
  fugitive.   1 Kin. 18:4
4 "Let the outcasts of Moab stay with
  you;
  Be a hiding place to them from the destroyer."
  For the extortioner has come to an end,
  destruction has ceased,
  [R]Oppressors have completely *disappeared* from the land.   Is. 9:4; 14:4
5 A [R]throne will even be established in
  lovingkindness,   [Is. 9:6, 7; 32:1; 55:4]
  And a judge will sit on it in faithfulness
  in the tent of[R]David;   [Is. 9:7]
  Moreover, he will seek justice
  And be prompt in righteousness.

6 [R]We have heard of the pride of Moab,
  an excessive pride;   Jer. 48:29
  Even of his arrogance, pride, and fury;
  His idle boasts are[T]false.   *not so*
7 Therefore Moab shall wail; everyone of
  Moab shall wail.
  You shall moan for the[R]raisin cakes of
  [R]Kir-hareseth   1 Chr. 16:3 • 2 Kin. 3:25
  As those who are utterly stricken.
8 For the fields of Heshbon have with-
  ered, the vines of[R]Sibmah *as well*;
  The lords of the nations have trampled
  down its choice clusters
  Which reached as far as Jazer *and*
  wandered to the deserts; Num. 32:38

[R]Its tendrils spread themselves out *and*
  passed over the sea.   Jer. 48:32
9 Therefore I will[R]weep bitterly for Jazer,
  for the vine of Sibmah;   Jer. 48:32
  I will drench you with my tears, O
  [R]Heshbon and Elealeh;   Is. 15:4
  For the shouting over your [R]summer
  fruits and your harvest has fallen
  away.   Jer. 40:10, 12; 48:32
10 And[R]gladness and joy are taken away
   from the fruitful field;   Is. 24:8
   In the[R]vineyards also there will be no
   cries of joy or jubilant shouting,
   No [R]treader treads out wine in the
   presses,   Amos 5:11, 17 • Job 24:11
   For I have made the shouting to cease.
11 Therefore my[T]heart[R]intones like a harp
   for Moab,   *entrails murmur* • Is. 15:5
   And my[T]inward feelings for Kir-hare-
   seth.   *inward part*
12 So it will come about when Moab[R]pre-
   sents himself, Num. 22:39-41; Jer. 48:35
   When he[R]wearies himself upon *his*[R]high
   place,   1 Kin. 18:29 • Is. 15:2
   And comes to his sanctuary to pray,
   That he will not prevail.
13 This is the word which the LORD spoke
   earlier concerning Moab.
14 But now the LORD speaks, saying,
   "Within three years, as [T]a hired man would
   count them, the glory of Moab will be degraded along with all *his* great population,
   and *his* remnant will be very small *and*[T]im-
   potent."   *the years of a hireling* • *not mighty*

CHAPTER 17

*Prophecies Against Damascus
and Samaria*

The 'oracle concerning Damascus.
   "Behold, Damascus is about to be re-
   moved from being a city,   *burden of*
   And it will become a fallen ruin.
2 "The cities of Aroer are forsaken;
   They will be for flocks[T]to lie down in,
   And there will be[R]no one to frighten
   them.   *and they will lie down* • Mic. 4:4
3 "The 'fortified[R] city will disappear from
   Ephraim,   *fortification* • Is. 7:8, 16; 8:4
   And'sovereignty from Damascus
   And the remnant of Aram;
   They will be like the glory of the sons
   of Israel,"   *royal power, kingdom*
   Declares the LORD of hosts.

4 Now it will come about in that day that
   the glory of Jacob will[T]fade,
   And [R]the fatness of his flesh will become lean.   *become thin* • Is. 10:16
5 It will be[R]even like the reaper gathering
   the standing grain,
   As his arm harvests the ears,
   Or it will be like one gleaning ears of
   grain   Joel 3:13; Matt. 13:30
   In the[R]valley of Rephaim. 2 Sam. 5:18, 22

6 Yet ^Rgleanings will be left in it like the
^Tshaking of an olive tree,
Two *or* three olives on the topmost
bough,   Deut. 4:27; Is. 24:13 • *striking*
Four *or* five on the branches of a fruitful tree,
Declares the LORD, the God of Israel.
7 In that day man will ^Rhave regard for
his Maker,   Is. 10:20; Hos. 3:5; 6:1
And his eyes will look to the Holy One
of Israel.
8 And he will not have regard for the ^Ral-
tars, the work of his hands,   Is. 27:9
Nor will he look to that which his ^Rfin-
gers have made,   Is. 2:8, 20; 30:22
Even the ⁷Asherim and incense stands.
9 In that day their strong cities will be
like forsaken places in the forest,
Or like branches which they abandoned before the sons of Israel;
And ^Tthe land will be a desolation.   *it*
10 For ^Ryou have forgotten the ^RGod of your
salvation   Is. 51:13 • Ps. 68:19
And have not remembered the ^Rrock of
your refuge.   Deut. 32:4, 18, 31; Is. 26:4
Therefore you plant delightful plants
And set them with vine slips of a
strange *god.*
11 In the day that you plant *it* you carefully fence *it* in,
And in the ^Rmorning you bring your
seed to blossom;
But the harvest will ^Rbe a heap
In a day of sickliness and incurable
pain.   Ps. 90:6 • Job 4:8; Hos. 8:7; 10:13

12 Alas, the uproar of many peoples
^RWho roar like the roaring of the seas,
And the rumbling of nations
Who rush on like the ^Rrumbling of
mighty waters!   Is. 5:30 • Ps. 18:4
13 The ^Rnations rumble on like the rumbling of many waters,   Is. 33:3
But He will ^Rrebuke them and they will
flee far away,   Ps. 9:5; Is. 41:11
And be chased ^Rlike chaff in the mountains before the wind,   Job 21:18
Or like whirling dust before a gale.
14 At evening time, behold, *there is* terror!
Before morning ^Rthey are no more.
^TSuch *will be* the portion of those who
plunder us,   2 Kin. 19:35 • *This*
And the lot of those who pillage us.

CHAPTER 18

Prophecies Against Ethiopia

Aʟᴀꜱ, oh land of whirring wings
Which lies beyond the rivers of ⁸Cush,
2 Which sends envoys by the sea,
Even in ^Rpapyrus vessels on the surface
of the waters.   Ex. 2:3
Go, swift messengers, to a nation ^Ttall ^R
and smooth,   *drawn out* • Is. 18:7

To a people feared far and wide,
A powerful and oppressive nation
Whose land the rivers divide.
3 ^RAll you inhabitants of the world and
dwellers on earth,   Ps. 49:1; Mic. 1:2
As soon as a standard is raised on the
mountains, ^Ryou will see *it,*   Is. 26:11
And as soon as the trumpet is blown,
you will hear *it.*
4 For thus the LORD has told me,
"I will look ^Tfrom My ^Rdwelling place
quietly   *in* • Is. 26:21; Hos. 5:15
Like dazzling heat in the ^Tsunshine ^R
Like a cloud of ^Rdew in the heat of harvest."   *light* • 2 Sam. 23:4 • Hos. 14:5
5 For ^Rbefore the harvest, as soon as the
bud blossoms
And the flower becomes a ripening
grape,   Is. 17:10, 11; Ezek. 17:6-10
Then He will cut off the sprigs with
pruning knives
And remove *and* cut away the spreading branches.
6 They will be left together for mountain
birds ^Rof prey,   Is. 46:11; 56:9; Jer. 7:33
And for the beasts of the earth;
And the birds of prey will spend the
summer *feeding* on them,
And all the beasts of the earth will
spend harvest time on them.
7 At that time a gift of homage will be
brought to the LORD of hosts
From a people ^Ttall and smooth,
Even from a people feared ^Tfar and
wide,   *drawn out* • *from it and beyond*
A powerful and oppressive nation,
Whose land the rivers divide—
To the place of the name of the LORD of
hosts, *even* Mount Zion.

CHAPTER 19

Prophecies Against Egypt

Tʜᴇ ʾoracle concerning Egypt.   *burden of*
Behold, the LORD is ^Rriding on a swift
cloud, and is about to come to
Egypt;
The ^Ridols of Egypt will tremble at His
presence,   Ps. 18:9, 10 • Jer. 43:12
And the ^Rheart of the Egyptians will
melt within them.   Josh. 2:11; Is. 13:7
2 "So I will incite Egyptians against Egyptians;
And they will ^Reach fight against his
brother, and each against his neigh-
bor,
City against city, *and* kingdom against
kingdom.   2 Chr. 20:23; Matt. 10:21, 36
3 "Then the spirit of the Egyptians will be
demoralized within them;
And I will confound their strategy,
So that ^Rthey will resort to idols and
ghosts of the dead,   1 Chr. 10:13
And to mediums and spiritists.

⁷ I.e., wooden symbols of a female deity   ⁸ Or, *Ethiopia*

4"Moreover, I will deliver the Egyptians
   into the hand of a[R]cruel master,
And a [A]mighty king will rule over
   them," declares the Lord GOD of
   hosts.   Is. 20:4; Jer. 46:26 • *fierce*

5 [R]And the waters from the sea will dry
   up,   Is. 50:2; Jer. 51:36; Ezek. 30:12
And the river will be parched and dry.
6 And the [T]canals[R]will emit a stench,
The[R]streams of Egypt will thin out and
   dry up;   *rivers* • Ex. 7:18 • Is. 37:25
The reeds and rushes will rot away.
7 The bulrushes by the[R]Nile, by the[A]edge
   of the Nile
And all the sown fields by the Nile
Will become dry, be driven away, and
   be no more.   Is. 23:3, 10 • *mouth*
8 And the[R]fishermen will lament,
And all those who cast a[T]line into the
   Nile will mourn,   Ezek. 47:10 • *hook*
And those who spread nets on the waters will[A]pine away.   *languish*
9 Moreover, the manufacturers of linen
   made from combed flax
And the weavers of white[R]cloth will be
   [T]utterly dejected.   Prov. 7:16 • *ashamed*
10 And the [R]pillars *of Egypt* will be
   crushed;
All the hired laborers will be grieved in
   soul.   Ps. 11:3

11 The princes of Zoan[R]are mere fools;
The advice of Pharaoh's wisest advis-
   ers has become stupid.
How can you *men* say to Pharaoh,
"I am a son of the wise, a son of ancient
   kings"?   Num. 13:22; Ps. 78:12, 43
12 Well then, where are your wise men?
   Please let them tell you,
And let them [A]understand what the
   LORD of hosts   *know*
Has[R]purposed against Egypt.   Is. 14:24
13 The princes of[A]Zoan have acted fool-
   ishly,   *Tanis*
The princes of[R]Memphis are deluded;
Those who are the cornerstone of her
   tribes   Jer. 2:16; 46:14, 19; Ezek. 30:13
Have led Egypt astray.
14 The LORD has mixed within her a spirit
   of[R]distortion;   Prov. 12:8; Matt. 17:17
[R]They have led Egypt astray in all[T]that it
   does,   Is. 3:12; 9:16 • *its work*
As a [R]drunken man [A]staggers in his
   vomit.   Is. 28:7 • *goes astray*
15 And there will be no work for Egypt
[R]Which *its* head or tail, *its* palm branch
   or bulrush, may do.   Is. 9:14, 15
16 In that day the Egyptians will become
like women, and they will tremble and be in
[R]dread because of the[R]waving of the hand of
the LORD of hosts, which He is going to
wave over them.   2 Cor. 5:11 • Is. 11:15
17 And the land of Judah will become a
[A]terror to Egypt; everyone to whom it is men-

tioned will be in dread of it, because of the
purpose of the LORD of hosts which He is
purposing against them.   *cause of shame*
18 In that day five cities in the land of
Egypt will be speaking the language of Canaan and[R]swearing *allegiance* to the LORD of
hosts; one will be called the City of [9]De-
struction.   Is. 45:23; 65:16
19 In that day there will be an[R]altar to the
LORD in the midst of the land of Egypt, and
a pillar to the LORD near its border.   Is. 56:7
20 And it will become a sign and a witness
to the LORD of hosts in the land of Egypt; for
they will cry to the LORD because of oppressors, and He will send them a Savior and a
Champion, and He will deliver them.
21 Thus the LORD will make Himself
known to Egypt, and the Egyptians will
know the LORD in that day. They will even
worship with sacrifice and offering, and will
make a vow to the LORD and perform it.
22 And the LORD will strike Egypt, striking but[R]healing; so they will[R]return to the
LORD, and He will respond to them and will
heal them.   Deut. 32:39; Is. 30:26 • Is. 27:13
23 In that day there will be a[R]highway
from Egypt to Assyria, and the Assyrians
will come into Egypt and the Egyptians into
Assyria, and the Egyptians will[R]worship
with the Assyrians.   Is. 11:16; 35:8 • Is. 27:13
24 In that day Israel will be the third *party*
with Egypt and Assyria, a blessing in the
midst of the earth,
25 whom the LORD of hosts has blessed,
saying, "Blessed is[R]Egypt My people, and
Assyria[R]the work of My hands, and Israel
My inheritance."   Is. 45:14 • Ps. 100:3; Is. 29:23

CHAPTER 20

IN the year that the[T]commander came to
[R]Ashdod, when Sargon the king of Assyria
sent him and he fought against Ashdod and
captured it,   Heb., *Tartan* • 1 Sam. 5:1
2 at that time the LORD spoke through
Isaiah the son of Amoz, saying, "Go and
loosen the [R]sackcloth from your hips, and
take your shoes off your feet." And he did
so, going naked and barefoot.   Zech. 13:4
3 And the LORD said, "Even as My servant Isaiah has gone naked and barefoot
three years as a [A]sign and token against
Egypt and[R]Cush,   *wonder* • Is. 37:9; 43:3
4 so the king of Assyria will lead away
the captives of Egypt and the exiles of Cush,
young and old, naked and barefoot with but-
tocks uncovered, to the shame of Egypt.
5"Then they shall be [R]dismayed and
ashamed because of Cush their hope and
Egypt their[R]boast.   2 Kin. 18:21 • Jer. 9:23, 24
6"So the inhabitants of this coastland
will say in that day, 'Behold, such is our
hope, where we fled[R]for help to be delivered
from the king of Assyria; and we,[R]how shall
we escape?' "   Is. 10:3; 30:7; 31:3 • 1 Thess. 5:3

[9] Some ancient mss. and versions read *the Sun*

CHAPTER 21

Prophecies Against Babylon

THE ᵔoracle^Rconcerning the ¹⁰wilderness^Rof the sea.   *burden of* • Is. 13:1 • Is. 13:20-22; 14:23
As windstorms in the^TNegev sweep on,
It comes from the wilderness, from a terrifying land.   South country
2 A^Rharsh vision has been shown to me;
The^Rtreacherous one still deals treacherously, *and* the destroyer still destroys.   Ps. 60:3 • Is. 24:16; 33:1
Go up,^RElam, lay siege, Media;   Is. 22:6
I have made an end of all^Tthe groaning she has caused.   *her groaning*
3 For this reason my^Rloins are full of anguish;   Is. 13:8; 16:11
Pains have seized me like the pains of a ^Rwoman in labor.   Ps. 48:6; Is. 13:8
I am so bewildered I cannot hear, so terrified I cannot see.
4 My mind reels, horror overwhelms me;
The twilight I longed for has been turned for me into trembling.
5 They set the table, they ¹¹spread out the cloth, they eat, they drink;
"Rise up, captains, oil the shields,"
6 For thus the Lord says to me,
"Go, station the lookout, let him^Rreport what he sees.   2 Kin. 9:17-20
7 "When he sees ᵔriders, horsemen in pairs,
A train of donkeys, a train of camels,
Let him pay close attention, very close attention."   Is. 21:9
8 Then the lookout called,
"O^RLord, I stand continually by day on the watchtower,
And I am stationed every night at my guard post.   Hab. 2:1
9 "Now behold, here comes a troop of riders, horsemen in pairs."
And one answered and said, "Fallen,
fallen is Babylon;   Is. 13:19; 47:5, 9
And all the ^Rimages of her gods are shattered on the ground."   Is. 46:1
10 O my^Tthreshed *people*, and my ^Tafflicted of the threshing floor!
What I have heard from the LORD of hosts,
The God of Israel, I make known to you.   Jer. 51:33; Mic. 4:13 • *son*

Prophecies Against Dumah (Edom)

11 The ᵔoracle concerning^REdom. ^R
One keeps calling to me from ᵔSeir,
"Watchman, ¹²how far gone is the night?   *burden* • Gen. 25:14 • Gen. 32:3
Watchman, ¹²how far gone is the night?"
12 The watchman says,
"Morning comes but also night.
If you would inquire, inquire;
Come back again."

Prophecies Against Arabia

13 The ᵔoracle about Arabia.   *burden*
In the thickets of Arabia you ᵔmust spend the night,   *will spend*
O caravans of^RDedanites.   Ezek. 27:15
14 Bring water ᵀfor the thirsty, ^R   *to meet*
O inhabitants of the land of ᵀTema,
Meet the fugitive with bread.   Job 6:19
15 For they have^Rfled from the swords,
From the drawn sword, and from the bent bow,   Is. 13:14, 15; 17:13
And from the press of battle.
^R16 For thus the Lord said to me, "In a year, as a hired man would count it, all the splendor of Kedar will terminate;   Is. 16:14
17 and the ᵔremainder of the number of bowmen, the mighty men of the sons of Kedar, will be few; for the LORD God of Israel ᵀhas spoken."   Is. 10:19 • Num. 23:19

CHAPTER 22

Prophecies Against Jerusalem

THE ᵔoracle concerning the ^Rvalley of vision.   *burden of* • Ps. 125:2; Jer. 21:13; Joel 3:12
What is the matter with you now, that you have all gone up to the^Rhousetops?   Is. 15:3
2 You who were full of noise,
You boisterous town, you ᵔexultant city;   Is. 23:7; 32:13
Your slain were ^Rnot slain with the sword,   Jer. 14:18; Lam. 2:20
Nor ᵀdid they die in battle.   *dead in battle*
3 ^RAll your rulers have fled together,
And have been captured ᵀwithout the bow;   Is. 21:15 • *from a bow*
All of you who were found were taken captive together,
Though they had fled far away.
4 Therefore I say, "Turn your eyes away from me,
Let me ᵀweep bitterly,   Is. 15:3; Jer. 9:1
Do not ᵀtry to comfort me concerning the destruction of the daughter of my people."   *insist*
5 For the Lord GOD of hosts has a day of panic, subjugation, and confusion
^RIn the valley of vision,   Is. 22:1
A breaking down of walls
And a crying ᵔto the mountain.   *against*
6 And^RElam took up the quiver
With the chariots, ᵀinfantry, *and* horsemen;   Is. 21:2; Jer. 49:35 • *man*
And^RKir uncovered the shield.   Amos 1:5
7 Then your choicest valleys were full of chariots,
And the horsemen took up fixed positions at the gate.

---

¹⁰ Or, *sandy wastes, sea country*
¹¹ Or, *spread out the rugs;* or possibly, *arranged the seating* ¹² Lit., *what is the time of the night?*

8 And He removed the defense of Judah.
In that day you depended on the weapons of the house of the forest,
9 And you saw that the breaches
In the *wall* of the city of David were many;
And you collected the waters of the lower pool.   2 Kin. 20:20; Neh. 3:16
10 Then you counted the houses of Jerusalem,
And you tore down houses to fortify the wall.
11 And you made a reservoir between the two walls   2 Kin. 25:4; Jer. 39:4
For the waters of the old pool.
But you did not depend on Him who made it,   2 Kin. 20:20 • *look to, consider*
Nor did you take into consideration Him who planned it long ago.

12 Therefore in that day the Lord GOD of hosts, called *you* to weeping, to wailing,   Is. 32:11; Joel 1:13; 2:17
To shaving the head, and to wearing sackcloth.   Mic. 1:16
13 Instead, there is gaiety and gladness,
Killing of cattle and slaughtering of sheep,   Is. 5:11, 22; 28:7, 8
Eating of meat and drinking of wine:
"Let us eat and drink, for tomorrow we may die."   Is. 56:12; 1 Cor. 15:32
14 But the LORD of hosts revealed Himself to me,   *in my ears*
"Surely this iniquity shall not be forgiven you   Is. 13:11; 26:21 • *atoned for*
Until you die," says the Lord GOD of hosts.   Is. 65:20

15 Thus says the Lord GOD of hosts,
"Come, go to this steward,
To Shebna, who is in charge of the *royal* household,   2 Kin. 18:18, 26, 37
16 'What right do you have here,
And whom do you have here,
That you have hewn a tomb for yourself here,   2 Sam. 18:18; 2 Chr. 16:14
You who hew a tomb on the height,
You who carve a resting place for yourself in the rock?   *himself*
17 'Behold, the LORD is about to hurl you headlong, O man.
And He is about to grasp you firmly,
18 *And* roll you tightly like a ball,
To be cast into a vast country;
There you will die,   Job 18:18; Is. 17:13
And there your splendid chariots will be,
You shame of your master's house.'
19 "And I will depose you from your office,
And I will pull you down from your station.   Job 40:11, 12; Ezek. 17:24
20 "Then it will come about in that day,
That I will summon My servant Eliakim the son of Hilkiah   2 Kin. 18:18
21 And I will clothe him with your tunic,
And tie your sash securely about him,
I will entrust him with your authority,

And he will become a father to the inhabitants of Jerusalem and to the house of Judah.   *rule* • Gen. 45:8
22 "Then I will set the key of the house of David on his shoulder,   Rev. 3:7
When he opens no one will shut,
When he shuts no one will open.
23 "And I will drive him *like* a peg in a firm place,   Ezra 9:8; Zech. 10:4
And he will become a throne of glory to his father's house.   1 Sam. 2:8
24 "So they will hang on him all the glory of his father's house, offspring and issue, all the least of vessels, from bowls to all the jars.
25 "In that day," declares the LORD of hosts, "the peg driven in a firm place will give way; it will even break off and fall, and the load hanging on it will be cut off, for the LORD has spoken."   Is. 22:23 • Esth. 9:24, 25

CHAPTER 23

Prophecies Against Tyre

THE oracle concerning Tyre.   *burden of*
Wail, O ships of Tarshish,   Is. 2:16
For Tyre is destroyed, without house *or* harbor;   *entering* • Is. 24:10
It is reported to them from the land of Cyprus.   Heb., *Kittim* • Gen. 10:4
2 Be silent, you inhabitants of the coastland,   Is. 47:5
You merchants of Sidon;
Your messengers crossed the sea
3 And *were* on many waters.
The grain of the Nile, the harvest of the River was her revenue;   Heb., *Shihor*
And she was the market of nations.
4 Be ashamed, O Sidon;   Gen. 10:15, 19
For the sea speaks, the stronghold of the sea, saying,
"I have neither travailed nor given birth,
I have neither brought up young men *nor* reared virgins."
5 When the report *reaches* Egypt,
They will be in anguish at the report of Tyre.   Ex. 15:14-16; Josh. 2:9-11
6 Pass over to Tarshish;   Is. 23:1
Wail, O inhabitants of the coastland.
7 Is this your jubilant *city*,   Is. 22:2; 32:13
Whose origin is from antiquity,
Whose feet used to carry her to colonize distant places?   *sojourn afar off*

8 Who has planned this against Tyre, the bestower of crowns,
Whose merchants were princes, whose traders were the honored of the earth?   Ezek. 28:2
9 The LORD of hosts has planned it to defile the pride of all beauty,   Dan. 4:37
To despise all the honored of the earth.
10 Overflow your land like the Nile, O daughter of Tarshish,
There is no more restraint.   *Pass over*

11 He has ^Rstretched His hand out ^Rover the
   sea,   Ex. 14:21; Is. 14:26 • Is. 19:5
   He has ^Rmade the kingdoms tremble;
   The LORD has given a command concerning Canaan to ^Rdemolish its
   strongholds.   Is. 13:13 • Zech. 9:3, 4
12 And He has said, "You ^Rshall exult no
   more, O crushed virgin daughter of
   Sidon.   Ezek. 26:13, 14; Rev. 18:22
   Arise, pass over to ^TCyprus; even there
   you will find no rest."   Heb., *Kittim*
13 Behold, the land of the Chaldeans—
this is the people *which* was not; ^RAssyria appointed it for desert creatures—they
erected their siege towers, they stripped its
palaces, they made it a ruin.   Is. 10:5
14 Wail, O ^Rships of Tarshish,   Is. 2:16
   For your stronghold is destroyed.
15 Now it will come about in that day that
Tyre will be forgotten for ^Rseventy years like
the days of one king. At the end of seventy
years it will happen to Tyre as *in* the song of
the harlot: Jer. 25:11, 22
16 Take *your* harp, walk about the city,
   O forgotten harlot;
   Pluck the strings skillfully, sing many
   songs,
   That you may be remembered.
17 And it will come about at the end of
seventy years that the LORD will visit Tyre.
Then she will go back to her harlot's wages,
and will ^Rplay the harlot with all the kingdoms on the face of the earth.   Ezek. 16:25-29
18 And her ^Rgain and her harlot's wages
will be ^Rset apart to the LORD; it will not be
stored up or hoarded, but her gain will become sufficient food and choice attire for
those who dwell in the presence of the
LORD.   Ps. 72:10, 11; Is. 60:5-9 • Ex. 28:36

CHAPTER 24

Judgments of the Tribulation

BEHOLD, the LORD ^Rlays the earth waste,
devastates it, distorts its surface, and scatters its inhabitants.   Is. 2:19; 13:13; 24:19, 20
2 And the people will be like the priest,
the servant like his master, the maid like her
mistress, the buyer like the seller, the lender
like the borrower, the ^Rcreditor like the
debtor.   Lev. 25:36, 37; Deut. 23:19, 20
3 The earth will be completely laid waste
and completely despoiled, for the LORD has
spoken this word.
4 The earth mourns *and* withers, the
world fades *and* withers, the ^Rexalted of the
people of the earth fade away.   Is. 2:12; 24:21
5 The earth is also polluted by its inhabitants, for they transgressed laws, violated
statutes, broke the everlasting covenant.
6 Therefore, a ^Rcurse devours the earth,
and those who live in it are held guilty.
Therefore, the inhabitants of the earth are
burned, and few men are left.   Josh. 23:15

7 The ^Rnew wine mourns,
   The vine decays,   Is. 16:10; Joel 1:10, 12
   All the merry-hearted sigh.
8 The ^Rgaiety of tambourines ceases,
   The noise of revelers stops,   Is. 5:12, 14
   The gaiety of the harp ceases.
9 They do not drink wine with song;
   ^RStrong drink is ^Rbitter to those who
   drink it.   Is. 5:11, 22 • Is. 5:20
10 The ^Rcity of chaos is broken down;
   ^REvery house is shut up so that none
   may enter.   Is. 34:11 • Is. 23:1
11 There is an ^Routcry in the streets concerning the wine;   Jer. 14:2; 46:12
   All joy turns to gloom.   *is darkened*
   The gaiety of the earth is banished.
12 Desolation is left in the city,
   And the gate is battered to ruins.
13 For ^Rthus it will be in the midst of the
   earth among the peoples,
   As the ^Tshaking of an olive tree,
   As the gleanings when the grape harvest is over.   [Is. 17:6; 27:12] • *striking*
14 ^RThey raise their voices, they shout for
   joy.   Is. 12:6; 48:20; 52:8; 54:1
   They cry out from the ^Twest concerning
   the majesty of the LORD.   *sea*
15 Therefore glorify the LORD in the ^Teast,
   The ^Rname of the LORD, the God of
   Israel   *region of light* • Mal. 1:11
   In the ^Acoastlands of the sea.   *islands*
16 From the ^Rends of the earth we hear
   songs, "Glory ^R to the Righteous
   One,"   Is. 11:12; 42:10 • Is. 28:5; 60:21
   But I say, "Woe ^Tto me! Woe to me!
   Alas for me!   *Wasting to me!*
   The ^Rtreacherous deal treacherously,
   And the treacherous deal very treacherously."   Is. 21:2; 33:1; Jer. 3:20; 5:11
17 ^RTerror and pit and snare
   ^TConfront you, O inhabitant of the
   earth.   Amos 5:19 • *Are upon you*
18 Then it will be that he who flees the
   ^Treport of disaster will fall into the
   pit,   *sound of terror*
   And he who climbs out of the pit will
   be caught in the snare;
   For the windows ^Tabove are opened,
   and the foundations of the earth
   shake.   *from the height;* i.e., heaven
19 ^RThe earth is broken asunder,   Is. 24:1
   The earth is ^Rsplit through,   Deut. 11:6
   The earth is shaken violently.
20 The earth ^Rreels to and fro like a drunkard,   Is. 19:14; 24:1; 28:7
   And it totters like a ^Ashack,   *hut*
   For its transgression is heavy upon it,
   And it will fall, never to rise again.
21 So it will happen in that day,
   That the LORD will punish the host of
   heaven, on high,
   And the kings of the earth, on earth.
22 And ^Rthey will be gathered together
   Like ^Rprisoners in the ^Tdungeon,
   And will be confined in prison;

And after many days they will[R]be punished.　　　Is. 10:4 • *pit* • Ezek. 38:8

23 Then the[R]moon will be abashed and the sun ashamed,　　　Is. 13:10
For the LORD of hosts will reign on Mount Zion and in Jerusalem,
And *His* glory will be before His elders.

CHAPTER 25

*Israel's Praise
for Kingdom Blessings*

O LORD, Thou art[R]my God;
I will exalt Thee, I will give thanks to Thy name;　Ps. 118:28; Is. 7:13; 49:4, 5
For Thou hast[T]worked wonders,
[R]Plans *formed* long ago, with perfect faithfulness.　　Ps. 40:5 • Eph. 1:11

2 For Thou hast made a city into a[R]heap,
A fortified city into a ruin;　Is. 17:1; 26:5
A[R]palace of strangers is a city no more,
It will never be rebuilt.　Is. 13:22; 32:14

3 Therefore a strong people will[R]glorify Thee;
[R]Cities of ruthless nations will revere Thee.　　Is. 24:15 • Is. 13:11

4 For Thou hast been a[R]defense for the helpless,　Is. 14:32; 17:10; 27:5; 33:16
A defense for the needy in his distress,
A[T]refuge from the storm, a shade from the heat;　　Is. 4:6; 32:2
For the breath of the ruthless
Is like a *rain* storm *against* a wall.

5 Like heat in drought, Thou dost subdue the[T]uproar of aliens;　Jer. 51:54-56
Like heat by the shadow of a cloud, the song of the ruthless is silenced.

6 And[R]the LORD of hosts will prepare a lavish banquet for[R]all peoples on this mountain;　Is. 1:19 • [Is. 2:2-4]
A banquet of aged wine, [T]choice pieces with marrow,
And refined, aged wine.　　*fat pieces*

7 And on this mountain He will swallow up the covering[R] which is over all peoples,　　[Eph. 4:18]
Even the veil which is[T]stretched over all nations.　　*woven*

8 He will[T]swallow up death for all time,
And the Lord GOD will[T]wipe tears away from all faces,　[Hos. 13:14] • Is. 30:19
And He will remove the[R]reproach of His people from all the earth;
For the LORD has spoken.　　Ps. 69:9

9 And it will be said in that day,
"Behold,[R]this is our God for whom we have[R]waited that[R]He might save us.
This is the LORD for whom we have waited;　Is. 35:2 • Is. 8:17 • Is. 33:22
[R]Let us rejoice and be glad in His salvation."　Ps. 20:5; Is. 35:1, 2, 10; 65:18

10 For the hand of the LORD will rest on this mountain,

And[R]Moab will be trodden down in his place　　Is. 16:14; Jer. 48:1-47
As straw is trodden down in the water of a manure pile.

11 And he will[T]spread out his hands in the middle of it　Is. 5:25; 14:26
As a swimmer spreads out *his hands* to swim,
But *the Lord* will[R]lay low his pride together with the trickery of his hands.　Job 40:11; Is. 2:10-12, 15-17

12 And the[R]unassailable fortifications of your walls He will bring down,
Lay low, *and* cast to the ground, even to the dust.　Is. 15:1; 25:2; 26:5

CHAPTER 26

Israel's Kingdom Song

I[R]N that day this song will be sung in the land of Judah:　[Is. 4:2; 12:1]
"We have a[R]strong city;　Is. 14:31; 31:5, 9
He sets up walls and ramparts for[T]security;[R]　*salvation* • Is. 60:18

2 "Open the[R]gates, that the[R]righteous nation may enter,　Is. 62:10 • Is. 45:25
The one that remains faithful.

3 "The steadfast of mind Thou wilt keep in perfect[R]peace,　Is. 26:12; 27:5; 57:19
Because he trusts in Thee.

4 "Trust[T]in the LORD forever,　Is. 12:2; 50:10
For in GOD the LORD, *we have* an everlasting[R]Rock.　Is. 17:10; 30:29; 44:8

5 "For He has brought low those who dwell on high, the unassailable city;
He lays it low, He lays it low to the ground, He casts it to the dust.

6 "The[R]foot will trample it,　　Is. 28:3
The feet of the[T]afflicted, the steps of the helpless."　Is. 3:14, 15; 11:4; 29:19

7 The[R]way of the righteous is smooth;
O Upright One,[R]make the path of the righteous level.　Is. 57:2 • Ps. 25:4, 5

8 Indeed, *while following* the way of Thy[R] judgments, O LORD,　Is. 51:4; 56:1
We have waited for Thee eagerly;
[R]Thy name, even Thy[R]memory, is the desire of *our* souls.　Is. 12:4 • Ex. 3:15

9 At night[T]my soul longs for Thee,
Indeed, my spirit within me seeks Thee diligently;　　with *my soul I long*
For when the earth[T]experiences Thy judgments　　*has*
The inhabitants of the world[R]learn righteousness.　Is. 55:6; Hos. 5:15

10 *Though* the wicked is shown favor,
He does not[R]learn righteousness;
He[R]deals unjustly in the land of uprightness,
And does not perceive the majesty of the LORD.　Is. 22:12, 13 • John 5:37, 38

11 O LORD, Thy hand is lifted up *yet* they[R]do not see it.　　Is. 44:9, 18

They see [R]*Thy* zeal for the people and
  are put to shame; Is. 9:7; 37:32; 59:17
Indeed, fire will devour Thine enemies.
12 LORD, Thou wilt establish [R]peace for us,
  Since Thou hast also performed for us
  all our works.   Is. 26:3
13 O LORD our God, [R]other masters besides
  Thee have ruled us;   Is. 2:8; 10:11
  But through Thee alone we [A]confess
  Thy name.   *cause to be remembered*
14 The dead will not live, the [A]departed
  spirits will not rise;   *shades*
  Therefore Thou hast [R]punished and destroyed them,   Is. 10:3
  And Thou hast wiped out all remembrance of them.
15 [R]Thou hast increased the nation, O
  LORD,
  Thou hast increased the nation, Thou
  art glorified;
  Thou hast [R]extended all the borders of
  the land.   Is. 9:3 · Is. 33:17; 54:2, 3
16 O LORD, they sought Thee in distress;
  They could only whisper a prayer,
  Your chastening was upon them.
17 [R]As the pregnant woman approaches
  the time to give birth,
  She writhes *and* cries out in her labor
  pains,   Is. 13:8; 21:3; [John 16:21]
  Thus were we before Thee, O LORD.
18 We were pregnant, we writhed *in
  labor,*
  We [R]gave birth, as it were, *only* to wind.
  We could not accomplish deliverance
  for the earth   Is. 33:11; 59:4
  Nor were [R]inhabitants of the world
  [T]born.   Ps. 17:14 · *fallen*
19 Your [R]dead will live;   [Ezek. 37:1–14]☆
  Their corpses will rise.
  You who lie in the dust, [R]awake and
  shout for joy,   [Eph. 5:14]
  For [T]your dew is as the dew of the
  [A]dawn,   *lights*
  And the earth will [T]give birth to the [A]de-
  parted spirits.   *cause to fall · shades*

20 Come, my people, [R]enter into your
  rooms,   Ex. 12:22, 23; [Ps. 91:1, 4]
  And close your doors behind you;
  Hide for a little while, [R]   [2 Cor. 4:17]
  Until indignation runs *its* course. [R]
21 For behold, the LORD is about to [A]come
  [R]out from His place Mic. 1:3; [Jude 14]
  To [R]punish the inhabitants of the earth
  for their iniquity; Is. 13:11; 30:12-14
  And the earth will [R]reveal her
  bloodshed,   Job 16:18; Luke 11:50
  And will no longer cover her slain.

CHAPTER 27

Israel Blossoms in the Kingdom

IN that day the LORD will punish [R]Leviathan
  the fleeing serpent,
  With His fierce and great and mighty
  sword, Job. 3:8; 41:1; Ps. 74:14; 104:26

Even [A]Leviathan the twisted serpent;
  And [R]He will kill the dragon who *lives* in
  the sea.   *sea monster* · Is. 51:9

2 In that day,
  "A [R]vineyard of wine, sing of it!   Is. 5:7
3 "I, the LORD, am its keeper;
  [R]I water it every moment.   Is. 58:11
  Lest anyone [T]damage it,   *punish*
  I [R]guard it night and day.   1 Sam. 2:9
4 "I have no wrath.
  Should [T]someone give Me [R]briars *and*
  thorns in battle,   *who* · 2 Sam. 23:6
  Then I would [T]step on them, I would
  burn them [T]completely.   *altogether*
5 "Or let him [R]rely on My protection,
  Let him make peace with Me,
  Let him make peace with Me."   Is. 12:2
6 [T]In the days to come Jacob [R]will take
  root,   *Those coming* · Is. 37:31
  Israel will [R]blossom and sprout;
  And they will fill the [T]whole world with
  [R]fruit.   Is. 35:1, 2 · *face of* · Is. 4:2

7 Like the striking of Him who has
  struck them, has He struck them?
  Or like the slaughter of His slain, [T]have
  they been slain?   *he was slain*
8 Thou didst contend with them by ban-
  ishing them, by driving them away.
  With His fierce wind He has expelled
  them on the day of the east wind.
9 Therefore through this Jacob's iniquity
  will be [R]forgiven;   Is. 1:25; 48:10
  And this will be [T]the full price of the
  [T]pardoning of his sin:
  When he makes all the altar stones like
  pulverized chalk stones;
  When Asherim and incense altars will
  not stand.   *all the fruit · removing*
10 For the fortified city is [T]isolated,
  A [T]homestead forlorn and forsaken like
  the desert;   Is. 32:13, 14 · *pasture*
  [R]There the calf will graze,   Is. 17:2
  And there it will lie down and [T]feed on
  its branches.   *consume*
11 When its [R]limbs are dry, they are broken off;   Is. 18:5
  Women come *and* make a fire with
  them.
  For they are not a people of [R]discern-
  ment,   Deut. 32:28; Is. 1:3; 5:13; Jer. 8:7
  Therefore [R]their Maker will not have
  compassion on them.   Deut. 32:18
  And their Creator will not be gracious
  to them.
12 And it will come about in that day, that
the LORD [A]will start *His* threshing from the
flowing stream of the Euphrates to the
brook of Egypt; and you will be gathered up
one by one, O sons of Israel. [Is. 11:11; 17:6]
13 It will come about also in that day that
a great [A]trumpet will be blown; and those
who were perishing in the land of Assyria
and who were scattered in the land of Egypt
will come and worship the LORD in the holy
mountain at Jerusalem. Lev. 25:9; 1 Chr. 15:24

CHAPTER 28

Woe to Ephraim

WOE to the proud crown of the[R]drunkards of Ephraim,   Is. 28:7; Hos. 7:5
And to the fading flower of its glorious beauty,
Which is at the head of the[T]fertile valley   *valley of fatness*
Of those who are overcome with wine!

2 Behold, the Lord has a strong and [R]mighty *agent;*   Is. 8:7; 40:10
As a storm of[R]hail, a tempest of destruction,   Is. 28:17; 30:30; 32:19
Like a storm of[R]mighty overflowing waters,   Is. 8:6, 7; 30:28; Nah. 1:8
He has cast *it* down to the earth with His hand.

3 The proud crown of the drunkards of Ephraim is trodden under foot.

4 And the fading flower of its glorious beauty,
Which is at the head of the[T]fertile valley,   *valley of fatness*
Will be like the[R]first-ripe fig prior to summer;   Hos. 9:10; Mic. 7:1; Nah. 3:12
Which[T]one sees,   *the one seeing sees*
And as soon as it is in his[T]hand,
He swallows it.   *while it is yet • palm*

5 In that day the[R]LORD of hosts will become a beautiful[R]crown
And a glorious diadem to the remnant of His people;   Is. 41:16 • Is. 62:3

6 A[R]spirit of justice for him who sits in judgment,   1 Kin. 3:28; Is. 11:2; 32:15, 16
A strength to those who repel the[T]onslaught at the gate.   *battle*

7 And these also[R]reel with wine and stagger from strong drink: Is. 5:11, 22
[R]The priest and[R]the prophet reel with strong drink,   Is. 24:2 • Is. 9:15
They are confused by wine, they stagger from[R]strong drink;   Hab. 2:15, 16
They reel while[T]having visions,   *seeing*
They totter *when rendering* judgment.

8 For all the tables are full of filthy vomit, without a *single clean* place.

9 "To[R]whom would He teach knowledge?
And to whom would He interpret the message?   Is. 2:3; 28:26; 30:20; 48:17
Those *just* weaned from milk?
Those *just* taken from the breast?

10 "For *He says,*
'Order[R]on order, order on order,
Line on line, line on line,   [2 Chr. 36:15]
A little here, a little there.' "

11 Indeed, He will speak to this people
Through[R]stammering lips and a foreign tongue,   Is. 33:19; 1 Chr. 14:21

12 He who said to them, "Here is [R]rest, give rest to the weary,"
And, "Here is repose," but they would not listen.   Jer. 6:16; [Matt. 11:28, 29]

13 So the word of the LORD to them will be,
"Order on order, order on order,
Line on line, line on line,
A little here, a little there,"
That they may go and[R]stumble backward, be broken, snared, and taken captive.   Is. 8:15; Matt. 21:44

14 Therefore,[R]hear the word of the LORD, O[T]scoffers,
Who rule this people who are in Jerusalem,   Is. 1:10; 28:22 • Is. 29:20

15 Because you have said, "We have made a covenant with death,
And with Sheol we have made a pact.
The overwhelming[A]scourge will not reach us when it passes by,   *flood*
For we have made[R]falsehood our refuge and we have concealed ourselves with deception."   Is. 9:15; 30:9

16 Therefore thus says the Lord GOD,
"Behold,[R] I am laying in Zion a stone, a tested[R]stone,   Rom. 9:33 • Ps. 118:22☆
A costly cornerstone *for* the foundation,[T]firmly placed.   *well-laid*
He who believes *in it* will not be[T]disturbed.   *in a hurry*

17 "And I will make[R]justice the measuring line,   2 Kin. 21:13; Is. 5:16; 30:18; 61:8
And righteousness the level;
Then[R]hail shall sweep away the refuge of lies,   Is. 28:2
And the waters shall overflow the secret place.

18 "And your[R]covenant with death shall be [T]canceled,   Is. 28:15 • *covered over*
And your pact with Sheol shall not stand;
When the[R]overwhelming scourge passes through,   Is. 28:15
Then you become its trampling *place.*

19 "As[T]often as it passes through, it will [T]seize you.   2 Kin. 24:2 • *take*
For[T]morning after morning it will pass through, *anytime* during the day or night.   Is. 50:4
And it will be[T]sheer[R]terror to understand what it means."   *only* • Job 6:4

20 The bed is too short on which to stretch out,
And the[R]blanket is too[T]small to wrap oneself in.   Is. 59:6 • *narrow*

21 For the LORD will rise up as *at* Mount [R]Perazim,   2 Sam. 5:20; 1 Chr. 14:11
He will be stirred up as in the valley of [R]Gibeon;   Josh. 10:10, 12; 2 Sam. 5:25
To do His task, His unusual task,
And to work His work, His[T]extraordinary work.   *work is alien*

22 And now do not carry on as[R]scoffers,
Lest your fetters be made stronger;
For I have heard from the Lord GOD of hosts,   Is. 28:14
Of decisive destruction on all the earth.

23 Give ear and hear my voice,
Listen and hear my words.

24 Does the[T]farmer plow[T]continually to plant seed?

Does he *continually* ^Tturn and harrow
the ground?   *plowman • all day • open*
25 Does he not level its surface,
And sow dill and scatter cummin,
And ^Tplant ^Rwheat in rows,
Barley in its place, and rye within its
^Tarea?   *put • Ex. 9:32 • region*
26 For his God instructs and teaches him
properly.
27 For dill is not threshed with a ^Rthreshing
sledge,
Nor is the cartwheel ^Tdriven over cummin;   [Amos 1:3] • *rolled*
But dill is beaten out with a rod, and
cummin with a club.
28 *Grain for* bread is crushed,
Indeed, he does not continue to thresh
it forever.
Because the wheel of *his* cart and his
horses *eventually* ^Tdamage *it,*
He does not thresh it longer.   *discomfit*
29 This also comes from the LORD of
hosts,
Who has made *His* counsel ^Rwonderful
and *His* wisdom great.   Is. 9:6

CHAPTER 29

Woe to Ariel (Jerusalem)

WOE, O ^TAriel, Ariel the city *where* David
once camped! Lion of God, or, Jerusalem
Add year to year, ^Robserve *your* feasts
on schedule.   Is. 1:14; 5:12; 22:12, 13
2 And I will bring distress to Ariel,
And she shall be *a city of* lamenting
and ^Rmourning;   Is. 3:26; Lam. 2:5
And she shall be like an Ariel to me.
3 And I will ^Rcamp against you ^Tencircling
you,   Luke 19:43, 44 • *like a circle*
And I will set siegeworks against you,
And I will raise up battle towers
against you.
4 Then you shall ^Rbe brought low;
From the earth you shall speak,
And from the dust *where* you are pros-
trate,
Your words *shall come.*
Your voice shall also be like that of a
^Aspirit from the ground,
And your speech shall whisper from
the dust.   Is. 8:19 • *ghost*

5 But the multitude of your ^Tenemies shall
become like fine dust,   *strangers*
And the multitude of the ruthless ones
like the chaff which ^Rblows away;
And it shall happen ^Rinstantly, suddenly.   *passes away* • Is. 17:14; 30:13
6 From the LORD of hosts you will be
^Rpunished with thunder and earth-
quake and loud noise,   Is. 10:3
With whirlwind and tempest and the
flame of a consuming fire.
7 And the ^Rmultitude of all the nations
who wage war against Ariel,

Even all who wage war against her and
her stronghold, and who distress
her,   Mic. 4:11, 12; Zech. 12:9
Shall be like a dream, a ^Rvision of the
night.   Job 20:8; Ps. 73:20; Is. 17:14
8 And it will be as when a hungry man
dreams—
And behold, he is eating;
But when he awakens, his ^Thunger is
not satisfied,
Or as when a thirsty man dreams—
And behold, he is drinking,
But when he awakens, behold, he is
faint,
And his ^Tthirst is not quenched.
^RThus the multitude of all the nations
shall be,   *soul* • Is. 54:17 • *soul*
Who wage war against Mount Zion.

9 ^RBe delayed and wait.   Is. 29:1
Blind yourselves and be blind.
They ^Rbecome drunk, but not with wine;
They stagger, but not with strong
drink.   Is. 51:17, 21, 22; 63:6
10 For the LORD has poured over you a
spirit of deep ^Rsleep,   Ps. 69:23
He has ^Rshut your eyes, the prophets;
And He has covered your heads, the
seers.   Is. 44:18; [2 Thess. 2:9–12]
11 And the entire vision shall be to you
like the words of a sealed book, which when
they give it to the one who ^Tis literate, saying, "Please read this," he will say, "I cannot, for it is sealed."   *knows books*
12 Then the ^Abook will be given to the one
who is illiterate, saying, "Please read this."
And he will say, "I cannot read."   *scroll*
13 Then the Lord said,
"Because ^Rthis people draw near with
their ^Twords   Ezek. 33:31 • *mouth*
And honor Me with their ^Tlip service,
But they remove their hearts far from
Me,   *lips*
And their ^Treverence for Me consists of
tradition learned *by rote,*   *fear of Me*
14 Therefore behold, I will once again deal
^Rmarvelously with this people, won-
drously marvelous;   Is. 6:9, 10; 28:21
And ^Rthe wisdom of their wise men
shall perish,   Is. 44:25; Jer. 8:9; 49:7
And the discernment of their discern-
ing men shall be concealed.

15 Woe to those who deeply hide their
^Tplans from the LORD,   *counsel*
And whose ^Rdeeds are *done* in a dark
place,   Job 22:13; Is. 57:12; Ezek. 8:12
And they say, "Who ^Rsees us?" or "Who
knows us?"   Ps. 94:7; Is. 47:10
16 You turn *things* around!
Shall the potter be considered ^Tas equal
with the clay,   *like*
That ^Twhat is made should say to its
maker, "He did not make me";
Or what is formed say to him who

formed it, "He has no understanding"?   Is. 45:9; 64:8; Jer. 18:1-6

17 Is it not yet just a little while
Before Lebanon will be turned into a
fertile field,
And the fertile field will be considered
as a forest?   And • Ps. 84:6; 107:33, 35
18 And on that day the deaf shall hear
words of a book,   Is. 35:5 • Is. 29:11
And out of their gloom and darkness
the eyes of the blind shall see.
19 The afflicted also shall increase their
gladness in the LORD, [Ps. 25:9; 37:11]
And the needy of mankind shall rejoice
in the Holy One of Israel.   Is. 3:14, 15
20 For the ruthless will come to an end,
and the scorner will be finished,
Indeed all who are intent on doing evil
will be cut off;   Is. 29:5 • watch evil
21 Who cause a person to be indicted by a
word,   bring a person under condemnation
And ensnare him who adjudicates at
the gate,   Amos 5:10
And defraud the one in the right with
meaningless arguments.   confusion
22 Therefore thus says the LORD, who redeemed Abraham, concerning the house of
Jacob,   Is. 41:8; 51:2; 63:16
"Jacob shall not now be ashamed, nor
shall his face now turn pale;
23 But when he sees his children, the
work of My hands, in his midst,
They will sanctify My name;
Indeed, they will sanctify the Holy One
of Jacob,   his children see
And will stand in awe of the God of
Israel.
24 "And those who err in mind will know
the truth,   spirit • understanding
And those who criticize will accept instruction.   murmur • learn

CHAPTER 30

Woe to Egyptian Alliance

"WOE to the rebellious children," declares the LORD,   Is. 1:2, 23; 30:9; 65:2
"Who execute a plan, but not Mine,
And make an alliance, but not of My
Spirit,   pour out a drink offering
In order to add sin to sin;
2 Who proceed down to Egypt,   Is. 31:1
Without consulting Me,
To take refuge in the safety of Pharaoh,
And to seek shelter in the shadow of
Egypt!   Is. 8:19 • My mouth • Is. 36:9
3 "Therefore the safety of Pharaoh will be
your shame,
And the shelter in the shadow of
Egypt, your humiliation.   Jer. 42:18, 22
4 "For their princes are at Zoan,
And their ambassadors arrive at
Hanes.   Is. 19:11

5 "Everyone will be ashamed because of a
people who cannot profit them,
Who are not for help or profit, but for
shame and also for reproach."

6 The oracle concerning the beasts of the
Negev.   burden of • Is. 46:1, 2 • Gen. 12:9
Through a land of distress and anguish,
From where come lioness and lion, viper and flying serpent,   them
They carry their riches on the backs of
young donkeys   Is. 15:7 • shoulders
And their treasures on camels' humps,
To a people who cannot profit them;
7 Even Egypt, whose help is vain and
empty.   Is. 30:5
Therefore, I have called her   this one
"Rahab who has been exterminated."
8 Now go, write it on a tablet before
them
And inscribe it on a scroll,
That it may serve in the time to come
As a witness forever.   Is. 8:1 • be
9 For this is a rebellious people, false
sons,   Is. 30:1 • Is. 28:15; 59:3, 4
Sons who refuse to listen   are not willing
To the instruction of the LORD;   law
10 Who say to the seers, "You must not
see visions";   Is. 29:10
And to the prophets, "You must not
prophesy to us what is right,
Speak to us pleasant words,
Prophesy illusions.   smooth things
11 "Get out of the way, turn aside from the
path,
Let us hear no more about the Holy
One of Israel."   Acts 13:8 • Job 21:14
12 Therefore thus says the Holy One of Israel,
"Since you have rejected this word,
And have put your trust in oppression
and guile, and have relied on them,
13 Therefore this iniquity will be to you
Like a breach about to fall,   Is. 26:21
A bulge in a high wall,
Whose collapse comes suddenly in an
instant.   Is. 29:5; 47:11
14 "And whose collapse is like the smashing of a potter's jar;   Jer. 19:10, 11
So ruthlessly shattered
That a sherd will not be found among
its pieces   Crushed, it will not be spared
To take fire from a hearth,   snatch up
Or to scoop water from a cistern.
15 For thus the Lord GOD, the Holy One of
Israel, has said,
"In repentance and rest you shall be
saved,   returning • Ps. 116:7; Is. 28:12
In quietness and trust is your
strength."   Is. 7:4; 32:17
But you were not willing,
16 And you said, "No, for we will flee on
horses,"
Therefore you shall flee!

"And we will ride on swift *horses*,"
　　Therefore those who pursue you shall
　　　be swift.
17 ᴿOne thousand *shall flee* at the threat of
　　one *man*,　Lev. 26:36; Deut. 28:25; 32:30
　　You shall flee at the threat of five;
　　Until you are left as a ᵀflag on a moun-
　　　tain top,　　　　　　　　　　*pole*
　　And as a signal on a hill.

18 Therefore the LORD ᵀlongsᴿ to be gra-
　　cious to you, ₜ *waits* • Is. 42:14, 16; 48:9
　　And therefore He ᵀwaits on high to have
　　compassion on you.　　　*is on high*
　　For the LORD is aᴿGod of justice;
　　How blessed are all those whoᵀlongᴿfor
　　Him.　　　Is. 5:16; 28:17 • *wait* • Is. 8:17
19 O people in Zion, inhabitant in Jerusalem, you will weep no longer. He will surely
be gracious to you at the sound of your cry;
when He hears it, He will answer you.
20 Although the Lord has given you bread
of privation and water of oppression, *He,*
your Teacher will no longer hide Himself,
but your eyes will behold your Teacher.
21 And your ears will hear a word behind
you, "This is the way, walk in it," whenever
youᴿturn to the right or to the left.　Is. 29:24
22 And you will defile your graven ᴿim-
ages, overlaid with silver, and your molten
images plated with gold. You will scatter
them as an impure thing; *and* say to ᵀthem,
"Beᴿgone!"　　Is. 46:6 • *it "Go out"* • Matt. 4:10
23 Then He will give *you* rain for the seed
which you will sow in the ground, and bread
from the yield of the ground, and it will be
rich and ᵀplenteous; on that day your livestock will graze in a roomy pasture.　　*fat*
24 Also the oxen and the donkeys which
work the ground will eat salted fodder,
whichᵀhas been ᴿwinnowed with shovel and
fork.　　*one winnows* • Matt. 3:12; Luke 3:17
25 And on every lofty mountain and on
every high hill there will be ᵀstreams running
with water on the day of the great slaughter,
when the towers fall.　*canals, streams of water*
26 And the light of the moon will be as the
light of the sun, and the light of the sun will
be seven times *brighter*, like the light of
seven days, on the day the LORD binds up
the ᴿfracture of His people and heals the
bruiseᵀHe has inflicted.　Is. 1:6 • *of His blow*
27 Behold, the name of the LORD comes
　　from a ᵀremote place;　　　*distance*
　　Burning is His anger, and ᵀdense is *His*
　　ᵀsmoke;　　　*heaviness • uplifting*
　　His lips are filled withᴿindignation,
　　And His tongue is like a ᵀconsuming
　　fire;　[Is. 10:5; 13:5; 66:14] • Is. 66:15
28 And Hisᴿbreath is like an overflowing
　　torrent,　　Is. 11:4; 30:33; 2 Thess. 2:8
　　Whichᴿreaches to the neck,　　Is. 8:8
　　To shake the nations back and forth in
　　a ᵀsieve,　　*sifting of the worthless*
　　And to *put* in the jaws of the peoples
　　the bridle which leads to ruin.

29 You will have ᵀsongs as in the night
　　when you keep the festival;
　　And gladness of heart as when one
　　marches to *the sound of* the flute,
　　To go to the mountain of the LORD, to
　　the Rock of Israel.　　　*the song*
30 And the LORD will cause ᵀHis voice of
　　authority to be heard.
　　And the ᵀdescending of His arm to be
　　seen in fierce anger,
　　And *in* the flame of a consuming fire,
　　In cloudburst, downpour, and hail-
　　stones.　*the majesty of His voice • descent*
31 For ᴿat the voice of the LORD ᴿAssyria
　　will be terrified,　Is. 11:4 • Is. 10:12
　　When He strikes with theᵀrod.　Is. 10:26
32 And every ᵀblow of the ᵀrod of punish-
　　ment,　　*passing • staff of foundation*
　　Which the LORD will lay on him,
　　Will be with *the music of* ᵀtambourines
　　and lyres;　　1 Sam. 18:6; Jer. 31:4
　　And in battles, ᴿbrandishing weapons,
　　He will fight them.　　Ezek. 32:10
33 For ¹³Topheth ᴿhas long been ready,
　　Indeed, it has been prepared for the
　　king.　　2 Kin. 23:10; Jer. 7:31; 19:6
　　He has made it deep and large,
　　ᵀA pyre of fire with plenty of wood;
　　The breath of the LORD, like a torrent
　　of brimstone, sets it afire.　　*Its pile*

CHAPTER 31

Wᴼᴱ to those who go down toᴿEgypt for
　　help,　　　Is. 30:2, 7; 36:6
　　And ᴿrely on horses,　Ps. 20:7; 33:17; Is. 2:7
　　And trust in chariots because they are
　　many,
　　And in horsemen because they are
　　very strong,
　　But they do not look to theᴿHoly One of
　　Israel, nor seek the LORD!　Is. 10:17
2 Yet He also is ᴿwise and will ᴿbring
　　disaster,　Is. 28:29; Rom. 16:27 • Is. 45:7
　　And doesᴿnot retract His words,
　　But will arise against the house of ᵀevil-
　　doers,　Num. 23:19 • Is. 1:4; 9:17; 14:20
　　And against the help of theᴿworkers of
　　iniquity.　　Is. 22:14; 32:6
3 Now the Egyptians are ᴿmen, and not
　　God,　　Ezek. 28:9; 2 Thess. 2:4
　　And their ᴿhorses are flesh and not
　　spirit;　　　Is. 36:9
　　So the LORD will stretch out His hand,
　　Andᴿhe who helps will stumble
　　And he who is helped will fall,
　　And all of them will come to an end
　　together.　Is. 30:5, 7; Matt. 15:14

4 For thus says the LORD to me,
　　"As the ᴿlion or the young lion growls
　　over his prey,　Num. 24:9; Hos. 11:10

¹³ I.e., the place of human sacrifice to Molech

Against which a band of shepherds is
called out,
Will not be terrified at their voice, nor
disturbed at their noise,
So will the LORD of hosts come down
to wage[R]war on Mount Zion and on
its hill."   Is. 42:13; Zech. 12:8
5 Like[A]flying birds so the LORD of hosts
will protect Jerusalem.   *hovering*
He will[R]protect and deliver *it;*   Is. 37:35
He will pass over and rescue *it.*
6 Return to Him from whom [T]you have
deeply defected, O sons of Israel. Heb., *they*
7 For in that day every man will cast
away his silver idols and his gold idols,
which your hands have made as a sin.
8 And the [R]Assyrian will fall by a sword
not of man,   Is. 10:12; 14:25; 30:31-33
And a [R]sword not of man will devour
him.   Is. 66:16
So he will[T]not escape the sword,   *flee*
And his young men will become[R]forced
laborers.   Gen. 49:15; Is. 14:2
9"And his[R]rock will pass away because of
panic,   Deut. 32:31, 37
And his princes will be terrified at the
[R]standard,"   Is. 5:26; 13:2; 18:3
Declares the LORD, whose [R]fire is in
Zion and whose furnace is in Jeru-
salem.   Is. 10:16, 17; 30:33; Zech. 2:5

CHAPTER 32

Behold the Coming King

BEHOLD, a[R]king will reign righteously,
And princes will rule justly. [Ps. 72:1-4]
2 And each will be like a[R]refuge from the
wind,   Is. 4:6; 25:4
And a shelter from the storm,
Like [T]streams of water in a dry country,
Like the shade of a [T]huge rock in a
parched land.   *canals • heavy*
3 Then[R]the eyes of those who see will not
be[A]blinded,
And the ears of those who hear will listen.   Is. 29:18 • *turned away*
4 And the [T]mind of the[R]hasty will discern
the [T]truth,   *heart* • Is. 29:24 • *knowledge*
And the tongue of the stammerers will
hasten to speak clearly.
5 No longer will the fool be called noble,
Or the rogue be spoken of *as* generous.
6 For a fool speaks nonsense,
And his heart[A]inclines[R]toward wickedness,   *does* • Prov. 19:3; 24:7-9
To practice [R]ungodliness and to speak
error against the LORD,   Is. 9:17; 10:6
To keep the hungry person unsatisfied
And to withhold drink from the thirsty.
7 As for a rogue, his weapons are evil;
He[R]devises wicked schemes [T]Jer. 5:26-28
To destroy *the* afflicted with [T]slander,
Even though *the* needy one speaks
what is right.   *words of falsehood*

8 But the noble man devises noble plans;
And by noble plans he stands.

9 Rise up you[R]women who are at ease,
And hear my voice;   Is. 47:8; Amos 6:1
[R]Give ear to my word,   Is. 28:23
You complacent daughters.
10 Within a year and *a few* days,
You will be troubled, O complacent
daughters;
[R]For the vintage is ended, Is. 5:5, 6; 7:23
And the *fruit* gathering will not come.
11 [T]Tremble, you *women* who are at ease;
[R]Be troubled, you complacent *daughters;*
[R]Strip, undress, and put *sackcloth* on
your waist,   Is. 22:12 • Is. 47:2
12 [R]Beat your breasts for the pleasant
fields, for the fruitful vine, Nah. 2:7
13 [R]For the land of my people *in which*
thorns *and* briars shall come up;
Yea, for all the joyful houses, *and for*
the jubilant city. Is. 5:6, 10, 17; 27:10
14 Because the palace has been abandoned, the[T]populated city forsaken.
[A]Hill and watch-tower have become
caves forever, *multitude* of *the* • Ophel
A delight for[R]wild donkeys, a pasture
for flocks;   Ps. 104:11; Jer. 14:6
15 Until the[R]Spirit is poured out upon us
from on high,   [Is. 11:2; 44:3; 59:21]
And the wilderness becomes a [R]fertile
field   Ps. 107:35; Is. 29:17; 35:1, 2
And the fertile field is considered as a
forest.
16 Then [R]justice will dwell in the wilderness,
And righteousness will abide in the fertile field.   Is. 33:5; Zech. 8:3
17 And the[A]work of righteousness will be
peace,   Ps. 72:2, 3; 85:8; 119:165; Is. 2:4
And the service of righteousness, quietness and confidence forever.
18 Then my people will live in a[R]peaceful
habitation,   [Is. 26:3, 12]
And in secure dwellings and in undisturbed[R]resting places; Is. 11:10; 14:3
19 And it will[R]hail when the[R]forest comes
down,   Is. 28:2, 17 • Is. 10:18, 19, 34
And the city will be utterly laid low.
20 How[R]blessed will you be, you who sow
beside all waters,   [Eccl. 11:1]
Who[T]let out freely the ox and the donkey.   *send out the foot of the ox*

CHAPTER 33

*Woe to the Destroyer
of Jerusalem (Assyria)*

WOE[T]to you, O destroyer,   Is. 10:6; 21:2
While you were not destroyed;
And he[R]who is treacherous, while *oth-
ers* did not deal treacherously with
him.   Is. 24:16; 48:8
As soon as you shall finish destroying,
[R]you shall be destroyed;   Hab. 2:8

As soon as you shall cease to deal treacherously, *others* shall [R]deal treacherously with you.   Jer. 25:12-14

2 O LORD, [R]be gracious to us; we have waited for Thee.   Is. 30:18, 19
Be Thou their [T]strength[R] every morning,
Our salvation also in the [R]time of distress.   *arm* • Is. 40:10 • Is. 37:3

3 At the [R]sound of the tumult[R]peoples flee;
At the [R]lifting up of Thyself nations disperse.   Is. 17:13; 21:15 • Jer. 25:30, 31

4 And your spoil is gathered *as* the caterpillar gathers;
As locusts rushing about, men rush about on it.

5 The LORD is [R]exalted, for He dwells on high;   Ps. 97:9
He has [R]filled Zion with justice and righteousness.   Is. 1:26; 28:6; 32:16

6 And He shall be the [A]stability[R] of your times,   *faithfulness* • Is. 33:20
A [R]wealth of salvation, wisdom, and [R]knowledge;   Is. 45:17; 51:6 • Is. 11:9
The fear of the LORD is his treasure.

7 Behold, their brave men cry in [T]the streets,   *the outside*
The [A]ambassadors[R] of peace weep bitterly.   *messengers* • 2 Kin. 18:18, 37

8 The highways are desolate, the[R]traveler has ceased,
He has [R]broken the covenant, he has despised the cities,   Is. 35:8 • Is. 24:5
He has no regard for man.

9 [R]The land mourns and pines away,
[R]Lebanon is shamed and withers;
Sharon is like a desert plain,
And Bashan and Carmel [T]lose *their foliage.*   Is. 3:26 • Is. 2:13 • *shake off*

10 "Now [R]I will arise," says the LORD,
"Now I will be exalted, now I will be lifted up.   Ps. 12:5; Is. 2:19, 21

11 "You have conceived [T]chaff, you will give birth to stubble;   *dry grass*
My breath will consume you like a fire.

12 "And the peoples will be burned to lime,
[R]Like cut thorns which are burned in the fire.   2 Sam. 23:6, 7; Is. 10:17; 27:4

13 "You who are far away, [R]hear what I have done;
And you who are near, [T]acknowledge My might."   Ps. 48:10; Is. 49:1 • *know*

14 [R]Sinners in Zion are terrified;   Is. 1:28
[R]Trembling has seized the godless.
"Who among us can live with [R]the consuming fire?   Is. 32:11 • Is. 30:27, 30
Who among us can live with [T]continual [R]burning?"   *everlasting* • Is. 9:18, 19

15 He who [R]walks righteously, and speaks with sincerity,   Ps. 15:2; 24:4
He who rejects [T]unjust gain,
And shakes his hands so that they hold no bribe;   *gain of extortioners*
He who stops his ears from hearing about bloodshed,
And [R]shuts his eyes from looking upon evil;   Ps. 119:37

16 He will dwell on the heights;
[R]His refuge will be the [T]impregnable rock;   Is. 25:4 • *stronghold of rock*
[R]His bread will be given *him;*
His water will be sure.   Is. 49:10

17 Your eyes will see [R]the King in His beauty;   [Is. 6:5; 24:23; 33:21, 22]
They will behold a far-distant land.

18 Your heart will meditate on terror:
"Where is[R]he who counts?   1 Cor. 1:20
Where is he who weighs?
Where is he who counts the towers?"

19 You will no longer see a fierce people,
A people of [T]unintelligible speech which no one comprehends,   *deepness of lip*
Of a stammering tongue [T]which no one understands.   *there is no understanding*

20 [R]Look upon Zion, the city of our appointed feasts;   Ps. 48:12
Your eyes shall see Jerusalem an [R]undisturbed habitation,   Is. 32:18
A tent which shall not be folded,
Its stakes shall never be pulled up
Nor any of its cords be torn apart.

21 But there the majestic *One*, the LORD, shall be for us
A place of [R]rivers *and* wide canals,
On which no boat with oars shall go,
And on which no mighty ship shall pass—   Is. 41:18; 43:19, 20; 48:18; 66:12

22 For the LORD is our[R]judge,   [Is. 2:4; 11:4]
The LORD is [R]our lawgiver,   James 4:12
The LORD is [R]our king;   Is. 33:17; Zech. 9:9
[R]He will save us—   Is. 25:9; 35:4; 49:25, 26

23 Your tackle hangs slack;
It cannot hold the base of its mast firmly,
Nor spread out the sail.
Then the [R]prey of an abundant spoil will be divided;   2 Kin. 7:16
[R]The lame will take the plunder.   Is. 35:6

24 And no resident will say, "I am sick";
The people who dwell [T]there will be [R]forgiven *their* iniquity.   *in it* • Jer. 50:20

CHAPTER 34

Woe to the Nations

DRAW near, [R]O nations, to hear; and listen, O peoples!   Ps. 49:1; Is. 41:1; 43:9
[R]Let the earth and [T]all it contains hear, and the world and all that springs from it.   Deut. 32:1; Is. 1:2 • *its fulness*

2 For the LORD's [R]indignation is against all the nations,   Is. 26:20
And *His* wrath against all their armies;
He has [T]utterly destroyed them,   Is. 13:5
He has given them over to slaughter.

3 So their slain will be thrown out,
And their corpses [T]will give off their stench,   *their stench will go up*
And the mountains will [T]be drenched with their blood.   *dissolve*

4 And ^Rall the host of heaven will ^Twear
   away,   Joel 2:31; Matt. 24:29 • *rot*
   And the ^Rsky will be rolled up like a
   scroll;   Rev. 6:12-14
   All their hosts will also wither away
   As a leaf withers from the vine,
   Or as *one* withers from the fig tree.
5 For^RMy sword is satiated in heaven,
   Behold it shall descend for judgment
   upon^REdom,   Deut. 32:41, 42 • Is. 63:1
   And upon the people whom I have^Rde-
   voted to destruction.   Is. 24:6; 43:28
6 The sword of the LORD is filled with
   blood,
   It is ^Tsated with fat, with the blood of
   lambs and goats,   *made fat*
   With the fat of the kidneys of rams.
   For the LORD has a sacrifice in^RBozrah,
   And a great slaughter in the land of
   ^REdom.   Is. 63:1; Jer. 49:13 • Is. 63:1
7 Wild oxen shall also ^Tfall with them,
   And^Ryoung bulls with strong ones;
   Thus their land shall be ^Tsoaked with
   blood,   *go down* • Jer. 50:27 • Is. 63:6
   And their dust become greasy with fat.
8 For the LORD has a day of ^Rvengeance,
   A year of recompense for the ^Acause of
   Zion.   Is. 13:6; 35:4; 47:3 • *controversy*
9 And ^Tits streams shall be turned into
   pitch,   Edom's
   And its loose earth into^Rbrimstone,
   And its land shall become burning
   pitch.   Deut. 29:23; Ps. 11:6; Is. 30:33
10 It shall ^Rnot be quenched night or day;
   Its smoke shall go up forever;   Is. 1:31
   From ^Rgeneration to generation it shall
   be desolate; Is. 13:20-22; 24:1; 34:10-15
   ^RNone shall pass through it forever and
   ever.   Ezek. 29:11
11 But ^Rpelican^Rand hedgehog shall possess
   it,   *owl* or *jackdaw* • Zeph. 2:14
   And ^Aowl and raven shall dwell in it;
   And He shall stretch over it the^Rline of
   desolation   *great horned owl* • Lam. 2:8
   And the plumb line of emptiness.
12 Its nobles—there is no one there
   Whom they may proclaim king—
   And all its princes shall be nothing.
13 And thorns shall come up in its^Rforti-
   fied towers,   Is. 13:22; 25:2; 32:13
   Nettles and thistles in its fortified
   cities;
   It shall also be a haunt of^Rjackals
   And an abode of ostriches.   Jer. 9:11
14 And the desert creatures shall meet
   with the ^Awolves,   *howling creatures*
   The^Ahairy^Rgoat also shall cry to its kind;
   Yes, the ^Tnight monster shall settle
   there   *demon* • Is. 30:8 • Heb., *Lilith*
   And shall find herself a resting place.
15 The tree snake shall make its nest and
   lay *eggs* there,
   And it will hatch and gather *them* un-
   der its ^Tprotection.   *shade*
   Yes, the^Ahawks shall be gathered there,
   Every one with its kind.   *kites*

16 Seek from the^Rbook of the LORD, and
   read: Is. 30:8
   Not one of these will be missing;
   None will lack its mate.
   For His mouth has commanded,
   And His Spirit has gathered them.
17 And He has cast the^Rlot for them,
   And His hand has divided it to them by
   ^Rline.   Is. 17:13, 14; Jer. 13:25 • Is. 34:11
   They shall possess it forever;
   From ^Rgeneration to generation they
   shall dwell in it.   Is. 34:10

CHAPTER 35

Behold the Coming Kingdom

T HE ^Rwilderness and the desert will be
   glad,   Is. 6:11; 7:21-25; 27:10; 41:18
   And the ^AArabah^R will rejoice and blossom;   *desert* • Is. 41:19; 51:3
   Like the crocus
2 It will^Rblossom profusely [Is. 27:6; 32:15]
   And^Rrejoice with rejoicing and shout of
   joy.   Is. 25:9; 35:10; 55:12, 13; 66:10, 14
   The ^Rglory of Lebanon will be given to
   it,   Is. 60:13
   The majesty of Carmel and Sharon.
   They will see the^Rglory of the LORD,
   The majesty of our God.   Is. 25:9
3 Encourage the ^Texhausted, and
   strengthen the feeble.   *slack hands*
4 Say to those with^Ranxious heart,
   "Take courage, fear not.   Is. 32:4
   Behold, your God will come *with*^Rven-
   geance;
   The recompense of God will come,
   But He will^Rsave you."   Is. 33:22☆
5 Then the ^Reyes of the blind will be
   opened,
   And the ears of the deaf will be un-
   stopped.   [Matt. 11:5]; John 9:6, 7☆
6 Then the^Rlame will leap like a deer,
   And the^Rtongue of the dumb will shout
   for joy.   Matt. 15:30☆ • Luke 11:14
   For waters will break forth in the^Rwil-
   derness   Is. 35:1; 41:18; 43:19; 49:10
   And streams in the^AArabah.   *desert*
7 And the ^Ascorched land will become a
   pool,   *mirage*
   And the thirsty ground ^Rsprings of water;   Is. 49:10
   In the ^Rhaunt of jackals, its resting
   place,   Is. 13:22; 34:13
   Grass *becomes* reeds and rushes.
8 And^Ra highway will be there, ^Ra roadway,   Is. 11:16; 19:23 • Is. 30:21; 51:10
   And it will be called the Highway of
   ^RHoliness.   Is. 4:3; 52:1; Matt. 7:13, 14
   The unclean will not travel on it,
   But it *will* be for him who walks *that*
   way,
   And fools will not wander *on it.*
9 No^Rlion will be there,   Is. 5:29; 30:6
   Nor will any vicious beast go up on it;

^TThese will not be found there.　　　*It*
But the redeemed will walk *there*,
10 And^Rthe ransomed of the LORD will re-
　　turn,　　　　　　　　　　Is. 1:27; 51:11
And come with joyful shouting to Zion,
With everlasting joy upon their heads.
They will find gladness and joy,
And sorrow and sighing will flee away.

CHAPTER 36

Assyria Challenges God
2 Kin. 18:13–37; 2 Chr. 32:1–19

Now^Rit came about in the fourteenth year
of King Hezekiah, Sennacherib king of Assyria came up against all the fortified cities
of Judah and seized them.　　　2 Kin. 18:13
2 And the king of Assyria sent Rabshakeh from Lachish to Jerusalem to King Hezekiah with a large army. And he stood by
the ^Rconduit of the upper pool on the highway of the^Tfuller's field.　　Is. 7:3 • *launderer's*
3 Then^REliakim the son of Hilkiah, who
was over the household, and ^RShebna the
scribe, and Joah the son of Asaph, the recorder, came out to him.　　Is. 22:20 • Is. 22:15
4 Then ^RRabshakeh said to them, "Say
now to Hezekiah, 'Thus says the great king,
the king of Assyria, "What is this confidence that you^Thave?　　2 Kin. 18:19 • *trust*
5"I say, 'Your counsel and strength for
the war are only ^Tempty words.' Now on
whom do you rely, that ^Ryou have rebelled
against me?　　　　*words of lips* • 2 Kin. 18:7
6"Behold, you rely on the ^Rstaff of this
crushed reed, *even* on Egypt; on which if a
man leans, it will go into his^Thand and pierce
it. ^RSo is Pharaoh king of Egypt to all who
rely on him.　　　Ezek. 29:6, 7 • *palm* • Ps. 146:3
7"But if you say to me, 'We trust in the
LORD our God,' is it not He whose high
places and whose altars Hezekiah has taken
away, and has said to Judah and to Jerusalem, 'You shall worship before this altar'?
8"Now therefore, come make a bargain
with my master the king of Assyria, and I
will give you two thousand horses, if you
are able on your part to set riders on them.
9"How then can you ^Trepulse one official
of the least of my master's servants, and
^Trely on Egypt for chariots and for horse-
men?　　　*turn away the face of* • *rely on for yourself*
10"And have I now come up ^Twithout the
LORD's approval against this land to destroy
it? The LORD said to me, 'Go up against this
land, and destroy it.' " ' "　　*without the LORD*
11 Then Eliakim and Shebna and Joah
said to Rabshakeh, "Speak now to your servants in Aramaic, for we^Tunderstand *it*; and
do not speak with us in Judean, in the hearing of the people who are on the wall."　*hear*
12 But Rabshakeh said, "Has my master
sent me only to your master and to you to
speak these words, *and* not to the men who
sit on the wall, *doomed* to eat their own

dung and drink their own urine with you?"
13 Then Rabshakeh stood and cried with
a loud voice in Judean, and said, "Hear the
words of the great king, the king of Assyria.
14"Thus says the king, 'Do not let Hez-
ekiah^Rdeceive you, for he will not be able to
deliver you;　　　　　　　　　　Is. 37:10
15 nor let Hezekiah make you^Rtrust in the
LORD, saying, "The LORD will surely deliver
us, this city shall not be given into the hand
of the king of Assyria."　　Is. 36:18, 20; 37:10, 11
16 'Do not listen to Hezekiah,' for thus
says the king of Assyria, 'Make your peace
with me and come out to me, and eat each
of his vine and each of his fig tree and drink
each of the waters of his own cistern,
17 until I come and take you away to a
land like your own land, a land of grain and
new wine, a land of bread and vineyards.
18 'Beware lest Hezekiah misleads you,
saying, "The LORD will deliver us." Has any
one of the gods of the nations delivered his
land from the hand of the king of Assyria?
19 'Where are the gods of^RHamath and Arpad? Where are the gods of Sepharvaim?
And when have they ^Rdelivered Samaria
from my hand?　　　　　Is. 10:9-11 • 2 Kin. 17:6
20 'Who among all the^Rgods of these lands
have delivered their land from my hand,
that the ^RLORD should deliver Jerusalem
from my hand?' "　　1 Kin. 20:23, 28 • Is. 36:15
21 But they were silent and^aanswered him
not a word; for the king's commandment
was, "Do not answer him."　　[Prov. 9:7, 8; 26:4]
22 Then Eliakim the son of Hilkiah, who
was over the household, and Shebna the
scribe and Joah the son of Asaph, the recorder, came to Hezekiah with their clothes
torn and told him the words of Rabshakeh.

CHAPTER 37

God Destroys Assyria
2 Kin. 19:1–37

And when King Hezekiah heard *it*, he
tore his clothes, covered himself with sackcloth, and entered the house of the LORD.
2 Then he sent^REliakim who was over the
household with ^RShebna the scribe and the
elders of the priests, covered with sackcloth, to ^RIsaiah the prophet, the son of
Amoz.　　Is. 22:20 • Is. 22:15 • Is. 1:1; 20:2
3 And they said to him, "Thus says Hezekiah, 'This day is a day of distress, rebuke,
and rejection; for children have come to
birth, and there is no strength to deliver.
4 'Perhaps the LORD your God will hear
the words of Rabshakeh, whom his master
the king of Assyria has sent to reproach the
living God, and will rebuke the words which
the LORD your God has heard. Therefore, offer a prayer for the remnant that is left.' "
5 So the servants of King Hezekiah came
to Isaiah.

6 And Isaiah said to them, "Thus you shall say to your master, 'Thus says the LORD, "Do^R not be afraid because of the words that you have heard, with which the servants of the king of Assyria have blasphemed Me.   Is. 7:4; 35:4

7 "Behold, I will put a spirit in him so that he shall^R hear a rumor and ^T return to his own land. And I will make him fall by the sword in his own land." ' "   Is. 37:9 • Is. 37:37, 38

8 Then Rabshakeh returned and found the king of Assyria fighting against^T Libnah, for he had heard that ^T the king had left^R Lachish.   Num. 33:20 • he • Josh. 10:31, 32

9 When he heard *them* say concerning Tirhakah king of Cush, "He has come out to fight against you," and when he heard *it* he sent messengers to Hezekiah, saying,

10 "Thus you shall say to Hezekiah king of ^T Judah, 'Do^R not let your God in whom you trust deceive you, saying, "Jerusalem shall not be given into the hand of the king of Assyria."   *Judah, saying* • Is. 36:15

11 'Behold,^R you have heard what the kings of Assyria have done to all the lands, destroying them completely. So will you be ^T spared?   Is. 10:9-11; 36:18-20 • *delivered*

12 'Did the gods of ^T those nations which my fathers have destroyed deliver them, *even* Gozan and Haran and Rezeph and the sons of Eden who *were* in Telassar?   *the*

13 'Where is the king of Hamath, the king of Arpad, the king of the city of Sepharvaim, *and of* Hena and Ivvah?' "

14 Then Hezekiah took the ^T letter from the hand of the messengers and read it, and he went up to the house of the LORD and spread it out before the LORD.   *letters*

15 And Hezekiah prayed to the LORD saying,

16 "O LORD of hosts, the God of Israel,^R who art enthroned *above* the cherubim, Thou art the^R God, Thou alone, of all the kingdoms of the earth. ^R Thou hast made heaven and earth.   Ex. 25:22 • Deut. 10:17 • Is. 42:5; 45:12

17 "Incline Thine ear, O LORD, and hear; open Thine eyes, O LORD, and see; and^R listen to all the words of Sennacherib, who sent *them* to reproach the living God.   Ps. 74:22

18 "Truly, O LORD, the ^R kings of Assyria have devastated all the countries and their lands,   2 Kin. 15:29; 16:9; 17:6, 24; 1 Chr. 5:26

19 and have cast their gods into the fire, for they were not gods but the ^R work of men's hands, wood and stone. So they have ^R destroyed them.   Is. 2:8; 17:8 • Is. 26:14

20 "And now, O LORD our God, ^R deliver us from his hand that ^R all the kingdoms of the earth may know that Thou alone, LORD, art God."   Is. 25:9; 33:22; 35:4 • Ps. 46:10; Is. 37:16

21 Then Isaiah the son of Amoz sent *word* to Hezekiah, saying, "Thus says the LORD, the God of Israel, 'Because you have prayed to Me about Sennacherib king of Assyria,

22 this is the word that the LORD has spoken against him:

"She has despised you and mocked you, The ^R virgin daughter of Zion;   Jer. 14:17 She has ^R shaken *her* head behind you, The daughter of Jerusalem!   Job 16:4

23 "Whom have you^R reproached and blasphemed?   Is. 37:4 And against whom have you raised *your* voice, And^T haughtily lifted up your eyes? Against the Holy One of Israel!   *on high*

24 "Through your servants you have reproached the Lord, And you have said, 'With my many chariots I came up to the heights of the mountains, To the remotest parts of Lebanon; And I cut down its tall ^R cedars *and* its choice cypresses.   Is. 14:8 And I will go to its ^T highest peak, its thickest forest.   *farthest height*

25 'I dug *wells* and drank waters, And with the sole of my feet I dried up All the rivers of^A Egypt.'   *the besieged place*

26 "Have^R you not heard?   Is. 40:21, 28 Long ago I did it, From ancient times I planned it. Now^R I have brought it to pass,   Is. 46:11 That you should turn fortified cities into^R ruinous heaps.   Is. 17:1; 25:2

27 "Therefore their inhabitants were short of strength, They were dismayed and put to shame; They were *as* the^R vegetation of the field and *as* the green herb,   Is. 40:7 As ^T grass on the housetops is scorched before it is grown up.   Ps. 129:6

28 "But I^R know your sitting down, And your going out and your coming in, And your raging against Me.   Ps. 139:1

29 "Because of your raging against Me, And because your ^T arrogance^R has come up to My ears,   *complacency* • Is. 10:12 Therefore I will put My^R hook in your nose,   Ezek. 29:4; 38:4 And My^R bridle in your lips,   Is. 30:28 And I will turn you back^R by the way which you came.   Is. 37:34

30 "Then this shall be the sign for you: ^T you shall eat this year what grows of itself, in the second year what springs from the same, and in the third year sow, reap, plant vineyards, and eat their fruit.   *eating*

31 "And the ^R surviving remnant of the house of Judah shall again take root downward and bear fruit upward.   Is. 4:2; 10:20

32 "For out of Jerusalem shall go forth a ^R remnant, and out of Mount Zion^T survivors. The ^R zeal of the LORD of hosts shall perform this." '   Is. 37:4 • *those who escape* • 2 Kin. 19:31

33 "Therefore, thus says the LORD concerning the king of Assyria, 'He shall not come to this city, or shoot an arrow there; neither shall he come before it with a shield, nor throw up a ^R mound against it.   Jer. 6:6; 32:24

34 'By^R the way that he came, by the same

he shall return, and he shall not come to this city,' declares the LORD.   Is. 37:29

35 'For I will ᴿdefend this city to save itᵀfor My own sake and for My servant David's sake.'"   2 Kin. 20:6; Is. 31:5 • Is. 43:25; 48:9, 11

36 Then the angel of the LORD went out, and struck 185,000 in the camp of the Assyrians; and when men arose early in the morning, behold, all of these were dead.

37 So Sennacherib, king of Assyria, departed and ᵀreturned *home*, and lived at ᴿNineveh.   *went and returned* • Jon. 1:2; 3:3; 4:11

38 And it came about as he was worshiping in the house of Nisroch his god, that Adrammelech and Sharezer his sons killed him with the sword; and they escaped into the land of ᴿArarat. And Esarhaddon his son became king in his place.   Gen. 8:4; Jer. 51:27

CHAPTER 38

Hezekiah's Salvation from Sickness

IN those days Hezekiah became ᵀmortally ill. And Isaiah the prophet the son of Amoz came to him and said to him, "Thus says the LORD, 'Set your house in order, for you shall die and not live.' "   *sick to the point of death*

2 Then Hezekiah turned his face to the wall, and prayed to the LORD,

3 and said, "Remember now, O LORD, I beseech Thee, how I have walked before Thee in truth and with a whole heart, and have done what is good in Thy sight." And Hezekiah wept ᵀbitterly.   *great weeping*

4 Then the word of the LORD came to Isaiah, saying,

5 "Go and say to Hezekiah, 'Thus says the LORD, the God of your father David, "I have heard your prayer, I have seen your tears; behold, I will add fifteen years to your life.

6 "And I will ᴿdeliver you and this city from the hand of the king of Assyria; and I will defend this city." '   Is. 31:5; 37:35

7 "And this shall be the ᴿsign to you from the LORD, that the LORD will do this thing that He has spoken: Judg. 6:17, 21, 36-40

8 "Behold, I will ᴿcause the shadow on the stairway, which has gone down with the sun on the stairway of Ahaz, to go back ten steps." So the ᴿsun's *shadow* went back ten steps on the stairway on which it had gone down.   2 Kin. 20:9-11 • Josh. 10:12-14

9 A writing of Hezekiah king of Judah, after his illness and recovery:

10 I said, "In the middle of myᵀlife   *days* I am to enter the ᴿgates of Sheol; I am to be ᴿdeprived of the rest of my years."   Ps. 107:18 • Job 17:11, 15

11 I said, "I shall not see the LORD, The LORDᴿin the land of the living; I shall look on man no more among the inhabitants of the world.   Ps. 27:13

12 "Like a shepherd's tent my dwelling is pulled up and removed from me;

As aᴿweaver I rolled up my life.   Job 7:6 He ᴿcuts me off from the loom;   Job 6:9 From ᴿday until night Thou dost make an end of me.   Job 4:20; Ps. 73:14

13 "I composed *my soul* until morning. ᴿLike a lion—so He ᴿbreaks all my bones,   Job 10:16 • Ps. 51:8; Dan. 6:24 From ᴿday until night Thou dost make an end of me.   Ps. 32:4

14 "Likeᴿa swallow, *like* a crane, so I twitter;   Job 30:29; Ps. 102:6 Iᴿmoan like a dove;   Ezek. 7:16; Nah. 2:7 My ᴿeyes look wistfully to the heights; O Lord, I am oppressed, be my ᵀsecurity.   Ps. 119:123 • Job 17:3; Ps. 119:122

15 "Whatᴿshall I say?   Ps. 39:9 For He has spoken to me, and He Himself has done it; I shall wander about all my years because of the bitterness of my soul.

16 "O Lord, by *these* things *men* live; And in all these is the life of my spirit; O restore me to health, and let me live!

17 "Lo, for *my own* welfare I had great bitterness; It is Thou who hast kept my soul from the pit of ᴬnothingness,   *destruction* For Thou hast ᴿcast all my sins behind Thy back.   Jer. 31:34; Mic. 7:19

18 "For ᴿSheol cannot thank Thee, Death cannot praise Thee;   [Eccl. 9:10] Those who go down ᴿto the pit cannot hope for Thy faithfulness.   Ps. 28:1

19 "It is the ᴿliving who give thanks to Thee, as I do today;   Ps. 118:17; 119:175 A ᴿfather tells his sons about Thy faithfulness.   Deut. 6:7; 11:19; Ps. 78:5-7

20 "The LORD will surely save me; So we will ᴿplay my songs on stringed instruments   Ps. 33:1-3; 68:24-26 ᴮAll *the* days of our life at the house of the LORD."   Ps. 104:33; 116:2; 146:2

21 Now ᵀIsaiah had said, "Let them take a cake of figs, and apply it to the boil, that he may recover."   2 Kin. 20:7, 8

22 Then Hezekiah had said, "What is the ᴿsign that I shall go up to the house of the LORD?"   Is. 38:7

CHAPTER 39

Hezekiah's Sin

AT ᴿthat time Merodach-baladan son of Baladan, king of Babylon, sent letters and a present to Hezekiah, for he heard that he had been sick and had recovered.   Is. 39:1-8

2 And Hezekiah was pleased, and showed them all his treasure house, the ᴿsilver and the gold and the spices and the precious oil and his whole armory and all that was found in his treasuries. There was nothing in his house, nor in all his dominion, that Hezekiah did not show them.   2 Kin. 18:15, 16

3 Then Isaiah the prophet came to King

Hezekiah and said to him, "What did these men say, and from where have they come to you?" And Hezekiah said, "They have come to me from a far country, from Babylon."

4 And he said, "What have they seen in your house?" So Hezekiah answered, "They have seen all that is in my house; there is nothing among my treasuries that I have not shown them." ^{said}

5 Then Isaiah said to Hezekiah, "Hear the ^Rword of the LORD of hosts,   1 Sam. 15:16

6 'Behold, the days are coming when ^Rall that is in your house, and all that your fathers have laid up in store to this day shall be carried to Babylon; nothing shall be left,' says the LORD.   2 Kin. 24:13; 25:13-15; Jer. 20:5

7 'And *some* of your sons who shall issue from you, whom you shall beget, shall be taken away; and they shall become officials in the palace of the king of Babylon.' "

8 Then Hezekiah said to Isaiah, "The word of the LORD which you have spoken is good." For he ^Tthought, "For there will be peace and truth in my days."   ^{said}

CHAPTER 40

Comfort Because of Israel's Deliverance

"COMFORT,^RO comfort My people," says your God.   Is. 12:1; 49:13; 51:3, 12; 52:9

2 "Speak^Rkindly to Jerusalem,   Zech. 1:13
And call out to her, that her ^Awarfare^R
has ended,   *hard service* • Is. 41:11-13
That her^Riniquity has been removed,
That she has received of the LORD'S
hand   Is. 33:24; 53:5, 6, 11
^RDouble for all her sins."   Jer. 16:18

3 A voice^Ais calling,   *of one calling out*
"Clear^Rthe way for the LORD in the wilderness;   [Mal. 3:1; 4:5, 6]☆
Make smooth in the desert a highway
for our God.

4 "Let every valley be lifted up,
And every mountain and hill be made
low;
And let the rough ground become a
plain,
And the rugged terrain a broad valley;

5 ^AThen the ^Rglory of the LORD will be revealed,   *In order that the* • Is. 6:3
And ^Rall flesh will see *it* together;
For the ^Rmouth of the LORD has spoken."   Joel 2:28 • Is. 1:20; 34:16; 58:14

6 A voice says, "Call out."
Then he answered, "What shall I call
out?"
All flesh is grass, and all its loveliness
is like the flower of the field.

7 The grass withers, the flower fades,
^AWhen the ^Rbreath of the LORD blows
upon it;   *Because* • Job 4:9; 41:21
Surely the people are grass.

8 The grass withers, the flower fades,

But ^Rthe word of our God stands forever.   Is. 55:11; 59:21; Matt. 5:18

9 Get yourself up on a high mountain,
O Zion, bearer of ^Rgood news,
Lift up your voice mightily,   Is. 61:1
O Jerusalem, bearer of good news;
Lift *it* up, do not fear.
Say to the ^Rcities of Judah,   Is. 44:26
"Here^Ris your God!"   Is. 25:9; 35:2

10 Behold, the Lord GOD will come^Rwith
might,   Is. 9:6, 7 ☆
With His arm ruling for Him.
Behold, His reward is with Him,
And His recompense before Him.

11 Like a shepherd He will^Rtend His flock,
In His arm He will gather the lambs,
And carry *them* in His bosom; Mic. 5:4☆
He will gently lead the nursing *ewes*.

Comfort Because of God's Character

12 Who has ^Rmeasured the waters in the
hollow of His hand,   Job 38:8-11
And marked off the heavens by the
^Aspan,   *half cubit;* i.e., 9 in.
And^Tcalculated the dust of the earth by
the measure,
And weighed the mountains in a bal-
ance,   *contained, or, comprehended*
And the hills in a pair of scales?

13 Who has ^Adirected the Spirit of the
LORD,   *measured, marked off*
Or as His counselor has informed Him?

14 ^RWith whom did He consult and *who*
gave Him understanding?   Job 38:4
And *who* taught Him in the path of justice and taught Him knowledge,
And informed Him of the way of understanding?

15 Behold, the ^Rnations are like a drop
from a bucket,   Jer. 10:10
And are regarded as a speck of^Adust on
the scales;   Is. 17:13; 29:5
Behold, He lifts up the^Aislands like fine
dust.   *coastlands*

16 Even Lebanon is not enough to burn,
Nor its^Rbeasts enough for a burnt offering. Ps. 50:9-11; Mic. 6:6, 7; [Heb. 10:5-9]

17 ^RAll the nations are as nothing before
Him,   Is. 29:7
They are regarded by Him as less than
nothing and^Ameaningless.   *void*

18 ^RTo whom then will you liken God?
Or what likeness will you compare
with Him?   Ex. 8:10; 15:11; 1 Sam. 2:2

19 *As for* the^Aidol, a craftsman casts it,
A goldsmith^Rplates it with gold,
And a silversmith *fashions* chains of
silver.   *graven image* • Is. 2:20; 30:22

20 He who is too impoverished for *such*
an offering
Selects a^Rtree that does not rot;
He seeks out for himself a skillful
craftsman   Is. 44:14

To prepare an idol that will not totter.

21 ^RDo you not know? Have you not heard?
Has it not been declared to you from
the beginning?   Ps. 19:1; 50:6; Is. 37:26
Have you not understood ^afrom the
foundations of the earth?   Is. 48:13
22 It is He who ¹⁴sits above the ¹⁵vault^Rof
the earth,   Job 22:14; Prov. 8:27
And its inhabitants are like grasshoppers,   Num. 13:33
Who stretches out the heavens like a
curtain   Job 9:8; Is. 37:16; 42:5; 44:24
And spreads them out like a tent to
dwell in.   Job 36:29; Ps. 18:11; 19:4
23 He it is who reduces rulers to nothing,
Who makes the judges of the earth
meaningless.   Job 12:21 • void
24 ¹⁶Scarcely have they been planted,
¹⁶Scarcely have they been sown,
¹⁶Scarcely has their stock taken root in
the earth,
But He merely blows on them, and
they wither,
And the storm carries them away like
stubble.   Is. 17:13; 41:16
25 "To whom then will you liken Me
That I should be his equal?" says the
Holy One.   Is. 40:18
26 ^RLift up your eyes on high   Is. 51:6
And see who has created these stars,
The One who leads forth their host by
number,   Is. 42:5; 48:12, 13
He calls them all by name;
Because of the greatness of His might
and the strength of His power
Not one of them is missing.   Ps. 89:11-13

27 ^RWhy do you say, O Jacob, and assert,
O Israel,   Is. 49:4, 14
"My way is hidden from the LORD,
And the justice due me escapes the no-
tice of my God"?   passes by my God
28 Do you not know? Have you not heard?
The Everlasting God, the LORD, the
Creator of the ends of the earth
Does not become weary or tired.
His understanding is inscrutable.
29 He gives strength to the weary,
And to him who lacks might He in-
creases power.   Is. 50:4 • Is. 41:10
30 Though youths grow weary and tired,
And vigorous young men stumble
badly,   Jer. 6:11; 9:21 • Is. 9:17
31 Yet those who wait for the LORD
Will gain new strength;   hope in
They will mount up with wings like ea-
gles,   sprout wings • Ex. 19:4 • pinions
They will run and not get tired,
They will walk and not become weary.

CHAPTER 41

Comfort Because of God's Greatness

"COASTLANDS, listen to Me in silence,
And let the peoples gain new strength;

^RLet them come forward, then let them
speak;   Is. 11:11 • Hab. 2:20 • Is. 34:1
Let us come together for judgment.
2 "Who has aroused one from the east
Whom He calls in righteousness to His
feet?   Is. 41:25; 45:1-3 • Is. 42:6 • foot
He delivers up nations before him,
And subdues kings.   2 Chr. 36:23; Ezra 1:2
He makes them like dust with his
sword,   2 Sam. 22:43
As the wind-driven chaff with his bow.
3 "He pursues them, passing on in safety,
By a way he had not been traversing
with his feet.   going
4 "Who has performed and accomplished
it,   Is. 41:26; 44:7; 46:10
Calling forth the generations from the
beginning?
'I, the LORD, am the first, and with the
last, I am He.' "   Is. 43:13; 46:4; 48:12

5 The coastlands have seen and are
afraid;   Is. 41:1; Ezek. 26:15, 16
The ends of the earth tremble;   Ps. 67:7
They have drawn near and have come.
6 Each one helps his neighbor,
And says to his brother, "Be strong!"
7 So the craftsman encourages the
smelter,   Is. 44:12, 13 • Is. 40:19
And he who smooths metal with the
hammer encourages him who beats
the anvil,
Saying of the soldering, "It is good";
And he fastens it with nails,
^RThat it should not totter.   Is. 40:20; 46:7
8 "But you, Israel, My servant,   Is. 42:19
Jacob whom I have chosen,
Descendant of Abraham My friend,
9 "You whom I have taken from the ends
of the earth,   taken hold of • Is. 11:11
And called from its remotest parts,
And said to you, 'You are My servant,
I have chosen you and not rejected
you.   Is. 43:5-7 • Is. 42:1 • Deut. 7:6
10 'Do not fear, for I am with you;   Ps. 27:1
Do not anxiously look about you, for I
am your God.
I will strengthen you, surely I will help
you,   Is. 41:14; 44:2; 49:8
Surely I will uphold you with My righteous right hand.'   Ps. 89:13, 14
11 "Behold, all those who are angered at
you will be shamed and dishonored;
Those who contend with you will be as
nothing, and will perish.   Is. 45:24
12 "You will seek those who quarrel with
you, but will not find them,
Those who war with you will be as
nothing, and non-existent.   Is. 17:14
13 "For I am the LORD your God, who upholds your right hand,
Who says to you, 'Do not fear, I will
help you.'   Is. 42:6; 45:1 • Is. 41:10

¹⁴ Or, is enthroned   ¹⁵ Or, circle   ¹⁶ Or, Not even

14"Do not fear, you^Rworm Jacob, you men
     of Israel;   Job 25:6; Ps. 22:6
  I will help you," declares the Lord,
     "and ^Ryour Redeemer is the Holy
     One of Israel.   [Is. 35:10; 43:14]
15"Behold, I have made you a new, sharp
     threshing sledge with double edges;
  ^RYou will thresh the ^Rmountains, and
     pulverize *them,*   Hab. 3:12 • Jer. 9:10
  And will make the hills like chaff.
16"You will ^Rwinnow them, and the wind
     will carry them away,   Jer. 51:2
  And the storm will scatter them;
  But you will ^Rrejoice in the Lord,
  You will glory in the Holy One of
     Israel.   Is. 25:9; 35:10; 51:3; 61:10☆

17"The afflicted and needy are seeking^Rwa-
     ter, but there is none,
  And their tongue is parched with
     thirst;   Is. 43:20; 44:3; 49:10; 55:1
  I, the Lord, ^Rwill answer them Myself,
  As the God of Israel I ^Rwill not forsake
     them.   Is. 30:19 • Is. 42:16; 62:12
18"I will open ^Rrivers on the bare heights,
  And springs in the midst of the valleys;
  I will make ^Rthe wilderness a pool of
     water,   Is. 30:25; 43:19 • Ps. 107:35
  And the dry land fountains of water.
19"I will put the cedar in the wilderness,
  The acacia, and the ^Rmyrtle, and the
     ^Aolive tree;
  I will place the juniper in the desert,
  Together with the box tree and the cy-
     press,   Is. 35:1; 55:13; 60:13 • *oleaster*
20 That ^Rthey may see and recognize,
  And consider and gain insight as well,
  That the ^Rhand of the Lord has done
     this,
  And the Holy One of Israel has created
     it.   Is. 40:5; 43:10 • Job 12:9; Is. 66:14

21"Present^T your case," the Lord says.
  "Bring forward your strong *arguments,*"
  The King of Jacob says.   *Bring near*
22 ^RLet them bring forth and declare to us
     what is going to take place;
  As for the^Rformer *events,* declare what
     they *were,*   Is. 44:7; 45:21 • Is. 43:9
  That we may consider them, and know
     their outcome;
  Or announce to us what is coming.
23 ^RDeclare the things that are going to
     come afterward,
  That we may know that you are gods;
  Indeed, ^Ado good or evil, that we may
     anxiously look about us and fear to-
     gether.   Is. 42:9; 44:7, 8; 45:3 • Jer. 10:5
24 Behold, you are of ^Rno account,   *nothing*
  And^Ryour work amounts to nothing;
  He who chooses you is an ^Rabomina-
     tion.   Is. 41:29; 37:19 • Prov. 3:32; 28:9

25"I have aroused^Rone from the north, and
     he has come;   Is. 41:2; Jer. 50:3

¹⁷ Another reading is *nothing*

From the rising of the sun he will call
     on My name;
  And he will come upon rulers as *upon*
     ^Rmortar,   2 Sam. 22:43; Is. 10:6
  Even as the potter treads clay."
26 Who has^Rdeclared *this* from the begin-
     ning, that we might know?
  Or from former times, that we may
     say, "*He is* right!"?   Is. 41:22; 44:7
  Surely there was^Rno one who declared,
  Surely there was no one who pro-
     claimed,   Hab. 2:18, 19
  Surely there was no one who heard
     your words.
27"Formerly^R*I* said to Zion, 'Behold, here
     they are.'   Is. 48:3-8
  And to Jerusalem, 'I will give a^Rmes-
     senger of good news.'   Is. 40:9; 44:28
28"But when I look, there is no one,
  And there is no counselor among them
  Who, if I ask, can give an answer.
29"Behold, all of them are ¹⁷false;
  Their works are^Rworthless,
  Their molten images are ^Rwind and
     emptiness.   Is. 44:9 • Jer. 5:13

CHAPTER 42

Comfort Because of God's Servant

"Behold, My Servant, whom I ^Ruphold;
  My chosen one *in whom* My ^Rsoul de-
     lights.   *hold fast* • Mark 1:11; Luke 3:22☆
  I have put My^RSpirit upon Him;
  He will bring forth ^Rjustice to the ^Ana-
     tions.   Matt. 3:16 • Is. 2:4 • *Gentiles*
2"He will not cry out or raise *His* voice,
  Nor make His voice heard in the street.
3"A bruised reed He will not break,
  And a dimly burning wick He will not
     extinguish;
  He will faithfully bring forth justice.
4"He will not be^Rdisheartened or crushed,
  Until He has established justice in the
     earth;   Is. 40:28☆
  And the coastlands will wait expec-
     tantly for His^Alaw."   *instruction*

5 Thus says God the Lord,
  Who ^Rcreated the heavens and
     stretched them out,   Ps. 102:25, 26
  Who spread out the ^Rearth and its ^Aoff-
     spring,   Ps. 24:1, 2; 136:6 • *vegetation*
  Who gives breath to the people on it,
  And spirit to those who walk in it,
6"I am the Lord, I have ^Rcalled you in
     righteousness,   Is. 41:2; Jer. 23:5, 6☆
  I will also ^Rhold you by the hand and
     ^Rwatch over you,   Is. 41:13 • Is. 26:3
  And I will appoint you as a ^Acovenant to
     the people,   Is. 49:8
  As a^Rlight to the nations,   Is. 49:6; 51:4
7 To ^Ropen blind eyes,
  To ^Rbring out prisoners from the dun-
     geon,   Is. 29:18; 35:5☆ • Is. 49:9; 61:1

And those who dwell in darkness from
the prison.

8 "I am the LORD, that is My name;
I will not give My glory to another,
Nor My praise to graven images.   *idols*

9 "Behold, the former things have come to
pass,   Is. 48:3
Now I declare new things;
Before they spring forth I proclaim
them to you."   Is. 43:19; 48:6

10 Sing to the LORD a new song,   Ps. 33:3
Sing His praise from the end of the
earth!   Is. 49:6; 62:11
You who go down to the sea, and all
that is in it.   Ps. 65:5 • Ex. 20:11
You islands and those who dwell on
them.   Is. 42:4

11 Let the wilderness and its cities lift up
their voices,   Is. 32:16; 35:1, 6
The settlements where Kedar inhabits.
Let the inhabitants of Sela sing aloud,
Let them shout for joy from the tops of
the mountains.   Is. 21:16 • Is. 52:7

12 Let them give glory to the LORD,
And declare His praise in the coastlands.   Is. 24:15 • Is. 42:4

13 The LORD will go forth like a warrior,
He will arouse *His* zeal like a man of
war.   Ex. 15:3 • Is. 9:7; 26:11; 37:32
He will utter a shout, yes, He will raise
a war cry.
He will prevail against His enemies.

14 "I have kept silent for a long time,
I have kept still and restrained Myself.
Now like a woman in labor I will groan,
I will both gasp and pant.   Ps. 50:21

15 "I will lay waste the mountains and
hills,   Is. 2:12-16; Ezek. 38:19, 20
And wither all their vegetation;
I will make the rivers into coastlands,
And dry up the ponds.   Is. 44:27; 50:2

16 "And I will lead the blind by a way they
do not know,
In paths they do not know I will guide
them.   Jer. 31:8, 9; Luke 1:78, 79
I will make darkness into light before
them   Is. 29:18; Eph. 5:8
And rugged places into plains.   Is. 40:4
These are the things I will do,
And I will not leave them undone."

17 They shall be turned back and be utter-
ly put to shame,   Ps. 97:7; Is. 1:29
Who trust in idols,   *graven images*
Who say to molten images,
"You are our gods."

18 Hear, you deaf!   Is. 29:18; 35:5
And look, you blind, that you may see.

19 Who is blind but My servant,   Is. 41:8
Or so deaf as My messenger whom I
send?   Is. 44:26
Who is so blind as he that is at peace
with Me,   *the devoted one* • Is. 26:3
Or so blind as the servant of the LORD?

20 You have seen many things, but you do
not observe *them;*   Rom. 2:21
Your ears are open, but none hears.

21 The LORD was pleased for His righteousness' sake
To make the law great and glorious.

22 But this is a people plundered and de-
spoiled;
All of them are trapped in caves,
Or are hidden away in prisons;
They have become a prey with none to
deliver *them,*
And a spoil, with none to say, "Give
them back!"   *holes* • Is. 24:22

23 Who among you will give ear to this?
Who will give heed and listen hereafter?

24 Who gave Jacob up for spoil, and Israel
to plunderers?
Was it not the LORD, against whom we
have sinned,
And in whose ways they were not willing to walk,   Is. 30:15
And whose law they did not obey?

25 So He poured out on him the heat of
His anger
And the fierceness of battle;   Is. 5:25
And it set him aflame all around,
Yet he did not recognize *it;*
And it burned him, but he paid no at-
tention.   *did not lay it to heart*

CHAPTER 43

Comfort Because of Israel's Restoration

BUT now, thus says the LORD, your Cre-
ator, O Jacob,   Is. 43:15
And He who formed you, O Israel,
"Do not fear, for I have redeemed you;
I have called you by name; you are
Mine!   Is. 43:5 • Is. 43:7 • Is. 43:21

2 "When you pass through the waters, I
will be with you;   [Ps. 66:12]; Is. 8:7, 8
And through the rivers, they will not
overflow you.
When you walk through the fire, you
will not be scorched,   Dan. 3:25, 27
Nor will the flame burn you.

3 "For I am the LORD your God,   Ex. 20:2
The Holy One of Israel, your Savior;
I have given Egypt as your ransom,
Cush and Seba in your place.   *Ethiopia*

4 "Since you are precious in My sight,
Since you are honored and I love you,
I will give other men in your place and
other peoples in exchange for your
life.   [Ex. 19:5, 6] • Is. 49:5 • Is. 63:9

5 "Do not fear, for I am with you;
I will bring your offspring from the
east,   Is. 8:10; 43:2 • Is. 41:8; 49:12
And gather you from the west.   Is. 49:12

6 "I will say to the north, 'Give *them* up!'
And to the south, 'Do not hold *them*
back.'   Ps. 107:3

Bring My^Rsons from afar,   2 Cor. 6:18
And My daughters from the ends of the
   earth,   Is. 45:22
7 Everyone who is called by My name,
And whom I have created for My glory,
Whom I have formed, even whom I
   have made."   Is. 56:5 · Is. 44:23; 46:13

8 Bring out the people who are blind,
even though they have eyes,
And the deaf, even though they have
   ears.   Is. 6:9; 42:19; Ezek. 12:2
9 All the nations have gathered together
In order that the peoples may be as-
   sembled.   Is. 34:1; 41:1
Who among them can declare this
And proclaim to us the former things?
Let them present their witnesses that
   they may be justified,   Is. 43:26
Or let them hear and say, "It is true."
10 "You are My witnesses," declares the
LORD,   Is. 44:8
"And My servant whom I have chosen,
In order that you may know and be-
   lieve Me,   Is. 41:8
And understand that I am He.   Is. 41:4
Before Me there was no God formed,
And there will be none after Me.
11 "I, even I, am the LORD;
And there is no savior besides Me.
12 "It is I who have declared and saved and
   proclaimed,
And there was no strange *god* among
   you;
So you are My witnesses," declares the
LORD,
"And I am God.   Deut. 32:16; Ps. 81:9
13 "Even from eternity I am He;   Is. 41:4
And there is none who can deliver out
   of My hand;   Ps. 50:22
I act and who can reverse it?"   Job 9:12

14 Thus says the LORD your Redeemer,
the Holy One of Israel,   Is. 41:14
"For your sake I have sent to Babylon,
And will bring them all down as fugitives,
18Even the Chaldeans, into the ships in
   which they rejoice.   *of their rejoicing*
15 "I am the LORD, your Holy One,
The Creator of Israel, your King."
16 Thus says the LORD,
Who makes a way through the sea
And a path through the mighty waters,
17 Who brings forth the chariot and the
   horse,   Ex. 15:19
The army and the mighty man
(They will lie down together *and* not
   rise again;
They have been quenched *and* extinguished like a wick):   Ps. 118:12

18 "Do not call to mind the former things,
Or ponder things of the past.   Is. 65:17
19 "Behold, I will do something new,
Now it will spring forth;
Will you not be aware of it? [2 Cor. 5:17]
I will even make a roadway in the wil-
   derness,   Ex. 17:6; Num. 20:11
Rivers in the desert.
20 "The beasts of the field will glorify Me;
The jackals and the ostriches;
Because I have given waters in the wil-
   derness   Is. 13:22; 35:7 · Is. 41:17, 18
And rivers in the desert,
To give drink to My chosen people.
21 "The people whom I formed for Myself,
Will declare My praise.   [Luke 1:74, 75]

22 "Yet you have not called on Me, O Jacob;
But you have become weary of Me, O
   Israel.   Mic. 6:3; Mal. 1:13; 3:14
23 "You have not brought to Me the sheep
   of your burnt offerings;   Amos 5:25
Nor have you honored Me with your
   sacrifices.   Zech. 7:5, 6; Mal. 1:6-8
I have not burdened you with offerings,
Nor wearied you with incense.   Lev. 2:1
24 "You have bought Me no sweet cane
   with money,   *calamus* · Ex. 30:23
Neither have you filled Me with the fat
   of your sacrifices;   *saturated*
Rather you have burdened Me with
   your sins,
You have wearied Me with your iniquities.   Ps. 95:10; Is. 1:14; 7:13; Ezek. 6:9

25 "I, even I, am the one who wipes out
   your transgressions for My own
   sake;   Is. 44:22; 55:7 · Is. 37:35; 48:9, 11
And I will not remember your sins.
26 "Put Me in remembrance; let us argue
   our case together,   *Report to Me*
State your *cause*, that you may be
   proved right.   Is. 43:9
27 "Your first forefather sinned,   *father*
And your spokesmen have trans-
   gressed against Me.   *interpreters*
28 "So I will pollute the princes of the
   sanctuary;   *pierce through* · *holy princes*
And I will consign Jacob to the ban,
   and Israel to revilement.   Zech. 8:13

CHAPTER 44

"BUT now listen, O Jacob, My servant;
And Israel, whom I have chosen:
2 Thus says the LORD who made you
And formed you from the womb, who
   will help you,   Is. 44:21, 24 · Is. 41:10
'Do not fear, O Jacob My servant;
And you Jeshurun whom I have cho-
   sen.   Is. 43:5 · Deut. 32:15; 33:5, 26
3 'For I will pour out water on the thirsty
   land   Is. 41:17 · *him who is thirsty*
And streams on the dry ground;

18 Another reading is *As for the Chaldeans, their rejoicing
is turned into lamentations*

I will [R]pour out My Spirit on your [R]off-
　spring,　Is. 32:15; Joel 2:28 • Is. 61:9
And My blessing on your descendants;
4 And they will spring up among the
　grass
Like poplars by streams of water.'
5 "This one will say, 'I am the LORD's';
And that one will call on the name of
　Jacob;
And another will [R]write [A]on his hand,
　'Belonging to the LORD,'
And will name Israel's name with
　honor.　Ex. 13:9; Neh. 9:38 • with

6 "Thus says the LORD, the King of Israel
And his Redeemer, the LORD of hosts:
'I am the [R]first and I am the last,　Is. 41:4
And there is no God besides Me.
7 'And who is like Me? [R]Let him proclaim
　and declare it;
Yes, let him recount it to Me in order,
From the time that I established the
　ancient [A]nation.
And let them declare to them the
　things that are coming
And the events that are going to take
　place.　Is. 41:22, 26 • people
8 'Do not tremble and do not be afraid;
[R]Have I not long since announced it to
　you and declared it?　Is. 42:9; 48:5
And [R]you are My witnesses.　Is. 43:10
Is there any God [R]besides Me,　Joel 2:27
Or is there any other [R]Rock?
I know of none.' "　Is. 17:10; 26:4; 30:29
9 Those who fashion [A]a graven image are
all of them futile, and their precious things
are of no profit; even their own witnesses
fail to see or know, so that they will be [R]put
to shame.　an idol • Ps. 97:7; Is. 42:17; 44:11
10 Who has fashioned a god or cast [A]an
idol to [R]no profit?　a graven image • Is. 41:29
11 Behold, all his companions will be [R]put
to shame, for the craftsmen themselves are
mere men. Let them all assemble themselves, let them stand up, let them tremble,
let them together be put to shame.　Ps. 97:7
12 The man shapes iron into a cutting
tool, and does his work over the coals, [T]fash-
ioning it with hammers, and working it with
his strong arm. He also gets hungry and [T]his
strength fails; he drinks no water and becomes weary.　and fashions • there is no strength
13 Another shapes wood, he extends a
measuring line; he outlines it with red chalk.
He works it with planes, and outlines it with
a compass, and makes it like the form of a
man, like the beauty of [R]man, so that it may
sit in a [R]house.　Ps. 115:5-7 • Judg. 17:4, 5
14 Surely he cuts cedars for himself, and
takes a cypress or an oak, and raises it for
himself among the trees of the forest. He
plants a fir, and the rain makes it grow.
15 Then it becomes something for a man
to burn, so he takes one of them and warms
himself; he also makes a fire to bake bread.
He also [R]makes a god and worships it; he

makes it a graven image, and [R]falls down before it.　Is. 44:17 • 2 Chr. 25:14
16 Half of it he burns in the fire; over this
half he eats meat as he roasts a roast, and is
satisfied. He also warms himself and says,
"Aha! I am warm, I have seen the fire."
17 But the rest of it he [R]makes into a god,
his graven image. He falls down before it
and worships; he also prays to it and says,
"Deliver me, for thou art my god."　Is. 44:15
18 They do not [R]know, nor do they understand, for He has [R]smeared over their eyes so
that they cannot see and their hearts so that
they cannot comprehend.　Is. 1:3 • [Ps. 81:12]
19 And no one [T]recalls, nor is there knowledge or understanding to say, "I have
burned half of it in the fire, and also have
baked bread over its coals. I roast meat and
eat it. Then [A]I make the rest of it into an
abomination, I fall down before a block of
wood!"　returns to his heart • shall I make . . .?
20 He [A]feeds on ashes; a deceived heart has
turned him aside. And he cannot deliver
[T]himself, nor say, "Is there not a lie in my
right hand?"　is a companion of ashes • his soul
21 "Remember [R]these things, O Jacob,
And Israel, for you are [R]My servant;
I have formed you, you are My servant,
O Israel, you will [R]not be forgotten by
　Me.　Zech. 10:9 • Is. 44:1, 2 • Is. 49:15
22 "I have [R]wiped out your transgressions
　like a thick cloud,　Is. 43:25; [Acts 3:19]
And your sins like a [A]heavy mist.　cloud
[R]Return to Me, for I have [R]redeemed
　you."　Is. 31:6; 55:7 • Is. 43:1; 48:20
23 [R]Shout for joy, O heavens, for the LORD
　has done it!　Ps. 69:34; 96:11, 12
Shout joyfully, you lower parts of the
　earth;
[R]Break forth into a shout of joy, you
　mountains,　Ps. 98:7, 8; 148:7, 9
O forest, and every tree in it;
For the LORD has redeemed Jacob
And in Israel He shows forth His glory.

24 Thus says the LORD, your [R]Redeemer,
　and the one who [R]formed you from
　the womb,　Is. 41:14; 43:14 • Is. 44:2
"I, the LORD, am the maker of all things,
Stretching out the heavens by Myself,
And spreading out the earth all alone,
25 Causing the [T]omens of boasters to fail,
[T]Making fools out of diviners,
Causing wise men to draw back,
And [T]turning their knowledge into fool-
　ishness,　signs • He makes • He turns
26 [R]Confirming the word of His servant,
And performing the purpose of His
　messengers.　Zech. 1:6; Matt. 5:18
It is I who says of Jerusalem, 'She shall
　be inhabited!'
And of the [R]cities of Judah, 'They [R]shall
　be built.'　Is. 40:9 • Jer. 32:15, 44
And I will raise up her ruins again.

27"*It is I* who says to the depth of the sea,
  'Be dried up!'
  And I will make your ^{R}rivers dry.
28"*It is I* who says of ^{R}Cyrus, '*He is* My
  shepherd!   Is. 45:1
  And he will perform all My desire.'
  And ^{T}he declares of Jerusalem, 'She ^{R}will
  be built,'   *to say* • 2 Chr. 36:22, 23
  And of the temple, 'Your ^{T}foundation
  will be laid.' "   *You will be founded*

CHAPTER 45

*Comfort Because of God's Use
of Cyrus*

T HUS says the LORD to ^{R}Cyrus His
  anointed,   Is. 44:28
  Whom I have taken by the right ^{R}hand,
  To subdue nations before him,   Is. 41:13
  And ^{T}to loose the loins of kings;
  To open doors before him so that gates
  will not be shut: *I will loose*
2"I will go before you and ^{R}make the
  rough places smooth;   Is. 40:4
  I will shatter the doors of bronze, and
  cut through their iron bars.
3"And I will give you the ^{A}treasures ^{R} of
  darkness,   *hoarded treasures* • Jer. 41:8
  And hidden wealth of secret places,
  In order that you may know that it is I,
  The LORD, the God of Israel, who ^{R}calls
  you by your name.   Ex. 33:12, 17
4"For the sake of ^{R}Jacob My servant,
  And Israel My chosen *one*,   Is. 41:8, 9
  I have also called you by your name;
  I have given you a title of honor
  Though you have not known Me.
5"I am the LORD, and there is no other;
  ^{R}Besides Me there is no God.   Is. 44:6, 8
  I will ^{A}gird ^{R} you, though you have not
  known Me;   *arm* • Ps. 18:39
6 That ^{T}men may know from the rising to
  the setting of the sun   *they*
  That there is no one besides Me.
  I am the LORD, and there is no other,
7 The One ^{R}forming light and ^{R}creating
  darkness,   Is. 42:16 • Ps. 104:20; 105:28
  Causing ^{A}well-being and ^{R}creating calamity;   *peace* • Is. 31:2; 47:11
  I am the LORD who does all these.

8"Drip ^{R} down, O heavens, from above,
  And let the clouds pour down righ-
  teousness;   Ps. 72:6; Hos. 10:12; 14:5
  Let the ^{R}earth open up and salvation
  bear fruit,   Ps. 85:11
  ^{R}And righteousness spring up with it.
  I, the LORD, have created it.   Is. 60:21

9"Woe to *the one* who ^{R}quarrels with his
  ^{T}Maker—   Job 15:25; 40:8, 9 • *Fashioner*
  An earthenware vessel ^{T}among the ves-
  sels of earth!   *with*
  Will the ^{R}clay say to the potter, 'What
  are you doing?'   Is. 29:16; 64:8

Or the thing you are making *say*, 'He
  has no hands'?
10"Woe to him who says to a father,
  'What are you begetting?'
  Or to a woman, 'To what are you ^{T}giv-
  ing birth?' "   *in labor pains with*

11 Thus says the LORD, the Holy One of
  Israel, and his ^{T}Maker: *Fashioner*
  "Ask ^{A}Me about the things to come con-
  cerning My sons,   *Will you ask*
  And you shall commit to Me ^{R}the work
  of My hands.   Is. 19:25; 29:23; 60:21
12"It is I who ^{R}made the earth, and created
  man upon it.   Is. 42:5; 45:18; Jer. 27:5
  I ^{R}stretched out the heavens with My
  hands,   Ps. 104:2; Is. 42:5; 44:24
  And I ordained ^{R}all their host.   Gen. 2:1
13"I have aroused him in ^{R}righteousness,
  And I will ^{R}make all his ways smooth;
  He will build My city, and will let My
  exiles go free,   Is. 41:2 • Is. 45:2
  Without any payment or reward," says
  the LORD of hosts.

14 Thus says the LORD,
  "The ^{T}products of Egypt and the mer-
  chandise of ^{A}Cush   *labor* • *Ethiopia*
  And the Sabeans, men of stature,
  Will ^{R}come over to you and will be
  yours;   Is. 14:1, 2; 49:23; 54:3
  They will walk behind you, they will
  come over in ^{R}chains   Ps. 149:8
  And will ^{R}bow down to you;   Is. 49:23
  They will make supplication to you:
  'Surely, ^{A} God is ^{A}with you, and there is
  none else,   *God is with you alone* • *in*
  No other God.' "
15 Truly, Thou art a God who ^{R}hides Him-
  self,   Ps. 44:24; Is. 1:15; 8:17; 57:17
  O God of Israel, ^{R}Savior!   Is. 43:3
16 They will be ^{R}put to shame and even hu-
  miliated, all of them;   Is. 42:17; 44:9
  The manufacturers of idols will go
  away together in humiliation.
17 Israel has been saved by the LORD
  With an ^{R}everlasting salvation;
  You will not be put to shame or humiliated   Is. 26:4; 51:6; [Rom. 11:26]
  To all eternity.

18 For thus says the LORD, who ^{R}created
  the heavens   Is. 42:5
  (He is the God who ^{R}formed the earth
  and made it,   Is. 45:12
  He established it and did not create it ^{A}a
  ^{R}waste place,   *in vain* • Gen. 1:2
  But formed it to be inhabited),
  "I am the LORD, and there is none else.
19"I ^{R}have not spoken in secret,   Is. 48:16
  In some dark land;
  I did not say to the ^{T}offspring of Jacob,
  'Seek Me in ^{A}a waste place';   *seed* • *vain*
  I, the LORD, speak righteousness
  Declaring things that are upright.

20"Gather ^{R}yourselves and come;   Is. 43:9

Draw near together, you fugitives of
the nations;
^RThey have no knowledge,   Is. 44:18, 19
Who carry about their wooden idol,
And pray to a god who cannot save.
21 "Declare and set forth *your case;*
Indeed, let them consult together.
^RWho has announced this from of old?
Who has long since declared it?
Is it not I, the LORD?   Is. 41:26; 44:7
And there is no other God besides Me,
A righteous God and a^RSavior;
There is none except Me.   Is. 43:3, 11
22 "Turn^Rto Me, and^Rbe saved, all the ends
of the earth;   Num. 21:8, 9 · Is. 30:15
For I am God, and there is no other.
23 "I^Rhave sworn by Myself,   Gen. 22:16
The ^Rword has gone forth from My
mouth in righteousness   Is. 55:11
And will not turn back,
That to Me every knee will bow, every
tongue will swear *allegiance.*
24 "They will say of Me, 'Only^Rin the LORD
are righteousness and strength.'
Men will come to Him,   Jer. 33:16
And ^Rall who were angry at Him shall
be put to shame.   Is. 41:11
25 "In the LORD all the offspring of Israel
Will be justified, and will glory."

CHAPTER 46

Destruction of Babylon's Idols

BEL^R has bowed down, Nebo stoops over;
Their images are *consigned* to the
beasts and the cattle.   Is. 2:18; 21:9
The things ^tthat you carry are burdensome,   *carried by you*
A load for the weary *beast.*
2 They stooped over, they have bowed
down together;
They could not rescue the burden,
But^Ahave themselves^Rgone into captivity.   *their soul has* · Judg. 18:17, 18, 24

3 "Listen^R to Me, O house of Jacob,
And all^Rthe remnant of the house of Is-
rael,   Is. 46:12 · Is. 10:21, 22
You who have been^Rborne by Me from
^tbirth,   Ps. 71:6; Is. 49:1 · *the belly*
And have been carried from the womb;
4 Even to your old age, ^RI ^tshall be the
same,   Is. 41:4; 43:13; 48:12 · *I am He*
And even to your ^tgraying^Ryears I shall
bear *you!*   *gray hairs* · Ps. 71:18
I have ^ddone *it,* and I shall carry *you;*
And I shall bear *you,* and I shall deliver
you.   *made* you

5 "To^R whom would you liken Me,
And make Me equal and compare Me,
That we should be alike?   Is. 40:18, 25
6 "Those who^Rlavish gold from the purse
And weigh silver on the scale
Hire a goldsmith, and he makes it *into*
a god;   Is. 40:19; 41:7; 44:12-17; Jer. 10:4
They^Rbow down, indeed they worship
it.   Is. 44:15, 17

7 "They^Rlift it upon the shoulder and carry
it;   Is. 45:20; 46:1; Jer. 10:5
They set it in its place and it stands
there.
^RIt does not move from its place.
Though one may cry to it, it^Rcannot answer;   Is. 40:20; 41:7 · Is. 41:28
It cannot deliver him from his distress.

8 "Remember this, and be^Tassured;   *firm*
Recall it to mind, you transgressors.
9 "Remember the former things long past,
For I am God, and there is no other;
I am God, and there is no one like Me,
10 Declaring the end from the beginning
And from ancient times things which
have not been done,
Saying, 'My^R purpose will be estab-
lished,   Ps. 33:11; Prov. 19:21
And I will accomplish all My good
pleasure';
11 Calling a^Rbird of prey from the^Reast,
The man of ^TMy purpose from a far
country.   Is. 18:6 · Is. 41:2 · *His*
Truly I have^Rspoken; truly I will bring it
to pass.   Num. 23:19; Is. 14:24; 37:26
I have planned *it, surely* I will do it.

12 "Listen to Me, you stubborn-minded,
Who are far from righteousness.
13 "I^Rbring near My righteousness, it is not
far off;   Is. 51:5; 61:11; [Rom. 3:21]
And My salvation will not delay.
And I will grant salvation in Zion,
And My^Rglory for Israel.   Is. 43:7; 44:23

CHAPTER 47

Destruction of Babylon

"COME down and sit in the dust,
O^Rvirgin daughter of Babylon;
Sit on the ground without a throne,
O daughter of the Chaldeans.   Jer. 46:11
For you shall no longer be called ^tten-
der and delicate.   Deut. 28:56
2 "Take the millstones and grind meal.
Remove your veil, strip off the skirt,
Uncover the leg, cross the rivers.
3 "Your^Rnakedness will be uncovered,
Your shame also will be exposed;
I will ^Rtake vengeance and will not
^tspare a man."   Nah. 3:5 · Is. 34:8 · *meet*
4 Our^RRedeemer, the LORD of hosts is His
name,
The Holy One of Israel.   Is. 41:14
5 "Sit silently, and go into^Rdarkness,
O daughter of the Chaldeans;   Is. 13:10
For you will no more be called
The queen of^Rkingdoms   [Dan. 2:37]
6 "I was angry with My people,
I profaned My heritage,
And gave them into your hand.
You did not show mercy to them,
On the^Raged you made your yoke very
heavy.   Deut. 28:50

7"Yet you said, 'I shall be a ^Rqueen for-
   ever.'   Is. 47:5
These things you did not consider,
Nor remember the outcome of them.

8"Now, then, hear this, you ^Rsensual one,
Who dwells securely,   Is. 22:13; 32:9
Who says in ^Tyour heart,   '*her*
'I am, and there is no one besides me.
I shall ^Rnot sit as a widow,   Rev. 18:7
Nor shall _RI know loss of children.'
9"But these ^Rtwo things shall come on you
   suddenly in one day: Is. 13:16, 18
Loss of children and widowhood,
They shall come on you in full measure
In spite of your many ^Rsorceries,
In spite of the great power of your
   spells.   Is. 47:13; Nah. 3:4; Rev. 18:23
10"And you felt ^Rsecure in your wickedness
   and said,   Ps. 52:7; 62:10; Is. 59:4
'No ^Rone sees me,'   Is. 29:15; Ezek. 8:12; 9:9
Your wisdom and your knowledge,
^Tthey have deluded you;   *it has*
For you have said in your heart,
'I am, and there is no one besides me.'
11"But ^Revil will come on you   Is. 57:1
Which you will not know how to
   charm away;
And disaster will fall on you
For which you cannot atone,
And ^Rdestruction about which you do
   not know   Luke 17:27; 1 Thess. 5:3
Will come on you ^Rsuddenly.   Is. 47:9

12"Stand *fast* now in your ^Rspells
And in your many sorceries
With which you have labored from
   your youth;   Is. 47:9
Perhaps you will be able to profit,
Perhaps you may cause trembling.
13"You are ^Rwearied with your many coun-
   sels;   Jer. 51:58, 64
Let now the ^Rastrologers,   Is. 8:39; 44:25
Those who prophesy by the stars,
Those who predict by the new moons,
Stand up and ^Rsave you from what will
   come upon you.   Is. 47:15
14"Behold, they have become ^Rlike stubble,
^RFire burns them;   Is. 5:24 • [Is. 10:17]
They cannot deliver themselves from
   the power of the flame;
There will be ^Rno coal to warm by,
Nor a fire to sit before!   Is. 44:16
15"So have those become to you with
   whom you have labored,
Who have ^Rtrafficked with you from
   your youth;   Rev. 18:11
Each has wandered in his own ^Tway.
There is none to save you.   *side, region*

CHAPTER 48

Declaration of Judah's Chastening

"HEAR^R this, O house of Jacob, who are
   named Israel   Is. 46:12
And who came forth from the ^Tloins ^Rof
   Judah,   *waters* • Ps. 68:26

Who ^Rswear by the name of the LORD
And invoke the God of Israel,   Is. 45:23
But not in truth nor in righteousness.
2"For they call themselves after the ^Rholy
   city,   Is. 52:1; 64:10
And ^Rlean on the God of Israel;   Jer. 7:4
The LORD of hosts is His name.
3"I ^Rdeclared the former things long ago
And they went forth from My mouth,
   and I proclaimed them.   Is. 41:22
^RSuddenly I acted, and they ^Rcame to
   pass.   Is. 29:5 • Josh. 21:45; Is. 42:9
4"Because I know that you are ^Aobstinate,
And your neck is an iron sinew,   *harsh*
And your ^Rforehead bronze,   Ezek. 3:7-9
5 Therefore I declared *them* to you long
   ago,
Before ^Tthey took place I proclaimed
   them to you,
Lest you should say, 'My ^Ridol has done
   them,   *it* • Jer. 44:15-18
And my graven image and my molten
   image have commanded them.'
6"You have heard; look at all this.
And you, will you not declare it?
I proclaim to you ^Rnew things from this
   time,
Even hidden things which you have not
   known.   Is. 42:9; 43:19
7"They are created now and not long ago;
And before today you have not heard
   them,
Lest you should say, 'Behold, I knew
   them.'
8"You have not ^Rheard, you have not
   known.   Is. 42:25; 47:11; Hos. 7:9
Even from long ago your ear has not
   been open,
Because I knew that you would deal
   very treacherously;
And you have been called a ^Arebel ^Rfrom
^Tbirth.   *transgressor* • Is. 46:8 • *the belly*
9"For ^Rthe sake of My name I ^Rdelay My
   wrath,   Is. 48:11 • Is. 30:18; 65:8
And *for* My praise I restrain *it* for you,
In order not to cut you off.
10"Behold, I have refined you, but ^Rnot as
   silver;   Jer. 9:7; Ezek. 22:18-22
I have tested you in the ^Rfurnace of affliction.   Deut. 4:20; 1 Kin. 8:51; Jer. 11:4
11"For ^RMy own sake, for My own sake, I
   will act;   1 Sam. 12:22; Ps. 25:11; 106:8
For how can *My name* be profaned?
And My ^Rglory I will not give to another.   Deut. 32:26, 27; Is. 42:8

12"Listen to Me, O Jacob, even Israel
^Twhom I called;   *My called one*
^RI am He, ^RI am the first, I am also the
   last.   Is. 41:4; 43:10-13; 46:4 • Rev. 1:17
13"Surely My hand ^Rfounded the earth,
And My right hand spread out the
   heavens;   Ex. 20:11; Ps. 102:25; Is. 42:5
When I ^Rcall to them, they stand together.   Is. 40:26
14"Assemble, ^R all of you, and listen!

ᴿWho among them has declared these
   things?   Is. 43:9; 45:20 • Is. 45:21
The Lᴏʀᴅ loves him; he shall ᴿcarry out
   His good pleasure onᴿBabylon,
And His arm *shall be against* the Chaldeans.   Is. 46:10, 11 • Is. 13:4, 5, 17-19
15"I, even I, have spoken; indeed I have
   ᶜcalled him,
I have brought him, and He will make
   his ways successful.   Is. 41:2; 45:1, 2
16"Comeᴿnear to Me, listen to this:
From the first I haveᴿnot spoken in secret,   Is. 34:1; 41:1; 57:3 • Is. 45:19
ᴿFrom the time it took place, I was
   there.   Is. 43:13
And nowᴿthe Lord Gᴏᴅ has sent Me,
   and His Spirit."   Zech. 2:9, 11

17 Thus says the Lᴏʀᴅ, your ᴿRedeemer,
   the Holy One of Israel;
"I am the Lᴏʀᴅ your God, who teaches
   you to profit,   Is. 41:14; 43:14; 49:7, 26
Whoᴿleads you in the way you should
   go.   Ps. 32:8; Is. 30:21; 49:9, 10
18"If only you had ᴿpaid attention to My
   commandments!   Deut. 5:29; 32:29
Then your ᴬwell-beingᴿwould have been
   like a river,   *peace* • Ps. 119:165
And yourᴿrighteousness like the waves
   of the sea.   Is. 45:8; 61:10, 11; 62:1
19"Your ᴰdescendantsᴿ would have been
   like the sand,   *seed* • Gen. 22:17
And your offspring like its grains;
Their name would never be cut off or
   destroyed from My presence."

20 ᴿGo forth from Babylon! Flee from the
   Chaldeans!   Jer. 50:8; 51:6, 45
Declare with the sound ofᴿjoyful shouting, proclaim this,   Is. 42:10; 49:13
Send it out to the end of the earth;
Say, "Theᴿ Lᴏʀᴅ has redeemed His servant Jacob."   Is. 43:1; 52:9; 63:9
21 And they did not ᴿthirst when He led
   them through the deserts.   Is. 30:25
Heᴿmade the water flow out of the rock
   for them;   Ex. 17:6; Ps. 78:15, 16
He split the rock, andᴿthe water gushed
   forth.   Ps. 78:20; 105:41
22"Thereᴿis no peace for the wicked," says
   the Lᴏʀᴅ.   [Is. 57:21]

CHAPTER 49

The Messiah's Mission

Lɪꜱᴛᴇɴ to Me, Oᴿislands,   Is. 42:4
   And pay attention, you peoples from
   afar.
ᴿThe Lᴏʀᴅ called Me from the womb;
From the ᴛbody of My mother He
   named Me.   Is. 44:2, 24 • *inward parts*
2 And He has made My ᴿmouth like a
   sharp sword;   Rev. 1:16; 2:12 ☆
In the ᴿshadow of His hand He has concealed Me,   Is. 51:16

And He has also made Me a ᴬselect ᴿar-
   row;   *sharpened* • Hab. 3:11
He has hidden Me in His quiver.
3 And He said to Me, "You are My Servant, Israel,   [Zech. 3:8]
In Whom I will show My glory."
4 But I said, "I haveᴿtoiled in vain,
I have spent My strength for nothing
   and vanity;   Is. 65:23
Yet surely the justice *due* to Me is with
   the Lᴏʀᴅ,
And Myᴿreward with My God." Is. 35:4

5 And now says ᴿthe Lᴏʀᴅ, who formed
   Me from the womb to be His Ser-
   vant,   Is. 44:2
To bring Jacob back to Him, in order
   that ᴿIsrael might be gathered to
   Him   Is. 11:12; 27:12; Matt. 23:37 ☆
(For I amᴿhonored in the sight of the
   Lᴏʀᴅ,   Is. 43:4
And My God is Myᴿstrength),   Is. 12:2
6 He says, "It is too ᴛsmall a thing that
   You should be My Servant   *light*
To raise up the tribes of Jacob, and to
   restore theᴿpreserved ones of Israel;
I will also make You aᴿlight ᴬof the na-
   tions   Ps. 37:28; 97:10 • Luke 2:32 ☆ • *to*
So that My salvation may ᴛreach to the
   ᴿend of the earth."   *be* • Is. 48:20
7 Thus says the Lᴏʀᴅ, theᴿRedeemer of
   Israel, *and* its Holy One,   Is. 48:17
To the ᴬdespised One, [Ps. 22:6–8; 69:7–9] ☆
To the One abhorred by the nation,
To the Servant of rulers,
"Kingsᴿshall see and arise,   [Is. 52:15]
Princes shall alsoᴿbow down;   Is. 27:13
Because of the Lᴏʀᴅ who is faithful,
   the Holy One of Israel who has cho-
   sen You."

8 Thus says the Lᴏʀᴅ, "In a ᴿfavorable
   time I have answered You,
And in a day of salvation I have helped
   You;   Ps. 69:13; 2 Cor. 6:2 ☆
And I will keep You andᴿgive You for a
   covenant of the people,   Is. 42:6
To restore the land, to make *them* inherit the desolate heritages;
9 Saying to those who areᴿbound, 'Go
   forth,'   Is. 42:7; 61:1; Luke 4:18 ☆
To those who are in darkness, 'Show
   yourselves.'
Along the roads they will feed,
And their pasture will be on allᴿbare
   heights.   Is. 41:18
10"They willᴿnot hunger or thirst, Is. 33:16
Neither will the scorchingᴿheat or sun
   strike them down;   Rev. 7:16 ☆
ForᴿHe who has compassion on them
   willᴿlead them,   Is. 14:1 • Ps. 23:2
And will guide them toᴿsprings of water.   Is. 35:7; 41:17
11"And I will make allᴿMy mountains a
   road,   Is. 40:4
And My highways will be raised up.
12"Behold, these shall comeᴿfrom afar;

And lo, these *will come* from the north
and from the west,   Is. 49:1; 60:4
And these from the land of Sinim."
13 [R]Shout for joy, O heavens! And rejoice,
O earth!   Is. 44:23
Break forth into joyful shouting, O
mountains!
For the[R]LORD has comforted His people,   Is. 40:1; 51:3, 12
And will[R]have compassion on His afflicted.   Is. 54:7, 8, 10

14 But Zion said, "The LORD has forsaken
me,
And the Lord has forgotten me."
15"Can a woman forget her nursing child,
And have no compassion on the son of
her womb?
Even these may forget, but[R]I will not
forget you.   Is. 44:21
16"Behold, I have [R]inscribed you on the
palms *of My hands;*   Song 8:6
Your walls are continually before Me.
17"Your builders hurry;
Your[R]destroyers and devastators
Will depart from you.   Is. 10:6; 37:18
18"Lift up your eyes and look around;
[R]All of them gather together,[R]they come
to you.   Is. 43:5; 54:7; 60:4 • Is. 49:12
[R]As I live," declares the LORD,   Is. 45:23
"You shall surely put on all of them as
jewels, and bind them on as a bride.
19"For [R]your waste and desolate places,
and your destroyed land—   Is. 1:7
Surely now you will be[R]too cramped
for the inhabitants,   Zech. 10:10
And those who[R]swallowed you will be
far away.   Ps. 56:1, 2
20"The [R]children of [T]whom you were be-
reaved will yet say in your ears,
'The place is too cramped for me;
Make room for me that I may live
here.'   Is. 54:1-3 • *your bereavement*
21 "Then you will [R]say in your heart,
'Who has begotten these for me,
Since I have been bereaved of my chil-
dren,   Is. 29:23; 54:6, 7
And am[R]barren, an [R]exile and a wan-
derer?   Is. 27:10; Lam. 1:1 • Is. 5:13
And who has reared these?
Behold, I was[R]left alone;   Is. 1:8
From where did these come?' "

22 Thus says the Lord GOD,
"Behold, I will lift up My hand to the
nations,
And set up My[R]standard to the peoples;
And they will bring your sons in *their*
bosom,   [Is. 11:10, 12; 18:3; 62:10]
And your daughters will be carried on
their shoulders.
23"And kings will be your guardians,
And their princesses your nurses.
They will[R]bow down to you with their
faces to the earth,   Is. 45:14; 60:14
And[R]lick the dust of your feet;   Ps. 72:9

And *you* will know that I am the LORD;
Those who hopefully[R]wait for Me will
not be put to shame.   Is. 25:9; 26:8

24"Can[R]the prey be taken from the mighty
man,
Or the captives of a tyrant be rescued?"   Matt. 12:29; Luke 11:21
25 Surely, thus says the LORD,
"Even the[R]captives of the mighty man
will be taken away,
And the prey of the tyrant will be rescued;   [Is. 10:6; 14:1, 2]; Jer. 50:33, 34
For I will contend with the one who
contends with you,
And I will[R]save your sons. Is. 25:9; 33:22
26"And I will feed your[R]oppressors with
their[R]own flesh,   Is. 9:4; 14:4 • Is. 9:20
And they will become drunk with their
own blood as with sweet wine;
And all flesh will know that I, the
LORD, am your[R]Savior,   Is. 43:3
And your[R]Redeemer, the Mighty One
of Jacob."   Is. 49:7

CHAPTER 50

The Messiah's Obedience

THUS says the LORD,
"Where is the[R]certificate of divorce,
By which I have sent your mother
away?   Deut. 24:1, 3; Jer. 3:8
Or to whom of My creditors did I[R]sell
you?   Deut. 32:30; 2 Kin. 4:1; Neh. 5:5
Behold, you were sold for your[R]iniqui-
ties,   Is. 52:3; 59:2
And for your transgressions your
mother[R]was sent away.   Jer. 3:8
2"Why was there[R]no man when I came?
When I called, *why* was there none to
answer?   Is. 41:28; 59:16; 66:4
Is My[R]hand so short that it cannot ran-
som?   Gen. 18:14; Num. 11:23; Is. 59:1
Or have I no power to deliver?
Behold, I [R]dry up the sea with My re-
buke,   Ex. 14:21; Is. 19:5; 43:16; 44:27
I[R]make the rivers a wilderness;
Their fish stink for lack of water,
And die of thirst.   Josh. 3:16; Is. 42:15
3"I clothe the heavens with blackness,
And I make sackcloth their covering."

4 The Lord GOD has given Me the tongue
of[R]disciples,   Is. 8:16; 54:13
That I may know how to[R]sustain the
weary one with a word.   Is. 57:19
He awakens *Me*[R]morning by morning,
He awakens My ear to listen as a disciple.   Ps. 5:3; 88:13; 119:147; 143:8
5 The Lord GOD has opened My ear;
And I was[R]not disobedient,
Nor did I turn back. [Phil. 2:8; Heb. 5:8]☆
6 I[R]gave My back to those who strike *Me,*
And My cheeks to those who pluck out
the beard;   Matt. 26:67; 27:30☆

I did not cover My face from humiliation and spitting.

7 For the Lord God[R] helps Me,   Is. 42:1
Therefore, I am[R] not disgraced;
Therefore, I have set My face like[R] flint,
And I know that I shall not be ashamed.   Is. 45:17; 54:4 • Luke 9:51 ☆

8 He who[R] vindicates Me is near;
Who will contend with Me?   Is. 45:25
Let us[R] stand up to each other;
Who has a case against Me?
Let him draw near to Me.   Is. 1:18

9 Behold,[R] the Lord God helps Me;
[R] Who is he who condemns Me?
Behold, they will all wear out like a garment; Is. 41:10; Acts 2:24 ☆ • Is. 54:17
The moth will eat them.

10 Who is among you that fears the Lord,
That obeys the voice of His[R] servant,
That walks in darkness and has no light?   Is. 49:2, 3; 50:4 • Is. 9:2; 26:9
Let him[R] trust in the name of the Lord
and rely on his God.   Is. 12:2; 26:4

11 Behold, all you who[R] kindle a fire,
Who[T] encircle yourselves with firebrands,   Prov. 26:18; Is. 9:18 • gird
Walk in the light of your fire
And among the brands you have set ablaze.
This you will have from My hand;
And you will lie down in torment.

CHAPTER 51

The Messiah's Encouragement to Israel

"Listen to me, you who [R] pursue righteousness,
Who seek the Lord: Ps. 94:15; [Prov. 15:9]
Look to the[R] rock from which you were hewn,   Gen. 17:15-17
And to the[T] quarry from which you were dug.   *excavation of a pit*

2 "Look to[R] Abraham your father,
And to Sarah who gave birth to you in pain;   Is. 29:22; 41:8; 63:16
When *he*[R] *was* one I called him,
Then I blessed him and multiplied him."   Gen. 12:1; 15:5; Deut. 1:10

3 Indeed,[R] the Lord will comfort Zion;
He will comfort all her waste places.
And her wilderness He will make like [R] Eden,   Is. 40:1 • Is. 52:9 • Gen. 2:8
And her desert like the [R] garden of the Lord;   Gen. 13:10
Joy and gladness will be found in her,
Thanksgiving and sound of a melody.

4 "Pay attention to Me, O My people;
And give ear to Me, O My[T] nation;
For a law will go forth from Me, *people*
And I will[T] set My[R] justice for a light of the peoples.   *cause to rest* • Is. 1:27

5 "My[R] righteousness is near, My salvation has gone forth,   Is. 46:13; 54:17
And My[R] arms will judge the peoples;
The[R] coastlands will wait for Me,

And for My [R] arm they will wait expectantly.   Is. 40:10 • Is. 42:4 • Is. 59:16

6 "Lift[R] up your eyes to the sky,   Is. 40:26
Then look to the earth beneath;
For the[R] sky will vanish like smoke,
And the earth will wear out like a garment,   Ps. 102:25, 26; Is. 13:13; 34:4
And its inhabitants will die[A] in like manner,   *like gnats*
But My salvation shall be forever,
And My righteousness shall not wane.

7 "Listen[R] to Me, you who know righteousness,   Is. 51:1
A people in whose heart is My law;
Do not fear the reproach of man,
Neither be dismayed at their revilings.

8 "For the moth will eat them like a garment,   Is. 50:9
And the grub will eat them like wool.
But My righteousness shall be forever,
And My salvation to all generations."

9 [R] Awake, awake, put on strength, O arm of the Lord;   Is. 51:17; 52:1
Awake as in the[R] days of old, the generations of long ago.   Ex. 6:6
[R] Was it not Thou who cut Rahab in pieces,   Job 26:12; Ps. 89:10; Is. 30:7
Who pierced the[R] dragon?   Ps. 74:13

10 Was it not Thou who dried up the sea,
The waters of the great deep;
Who made the depths of the sea a pathway   Is. 11:15, 16; 50:2; 63:11, 12
For the[R] redeemed to cross over?

11 So the[R] ransomed of the Lord will return,   Is. 35:10; Jer. 31:11, 12
And come with joyful shouting to Zion;
And[R] everlasting joy *will be* on their heads.   Is. 60:19; 61:7
They will obtain gladness and joy,
And sorrow and sighing will flee away.

12 "I, even I, am He who[R] comforts you.
Who are you that you are afraid of[R] man who dies,   Is. 51:3 • Ps. 118:6; Is. 2:22
And of the son of man who is made[R] like grass;   Is. 40:6, 7; 1 Pet. 1:24

13 That you have[R] forgotten the Lord your Maker,   Deut. 6:12; 8:11; Is. 17:10
Who[R] stretched out the heavens, Job 9:8
And laid the foundations of the earth;
That you[R] fear continually all day long because of the fury of the oppressor,   Is. 7:4; 10:24
As he makes ready to destroy?
But where is the fury of the oppressor?

14 "The[T] exile[R] will soon be set free, and will not die in the dungeon,[R] nor will his bread be lacking.   *one in chains* • Is. 48:20 • Is. 33:6; 49:10

15 "For I am the Lord your God, who[R] stirs up the sea and its waves roar (the Lord of hosts is His name).   Ps. 107:25; Jer. 31:35

16 "And I have put My words in your mouth, and have covered you with the shadow of My hand, to establish the heavens, to found the earth, and to say to Zion, 'You are My people.' "

17 ᴿRouse yourself! Rouse yourself! Arise,
   O Jerusalem,   Is. 51:9; 52:1
   You who have ᴿdrunk from the LORD's
   hand the cup of His anger;   Is. 29:9
   The ᵀchalice of reeling you have drained
   to the dregs.   *bowl of the cup of reeling*
18 There is ᴿnone to guide her among all
   the sons she has borne;
   Nor is there one to take her by the
   hand among all the sons she has
   reared.   Ps. 88:18; 142:4; Is. 49:21
19 These two things have befallen you;
   Who will mourn for you?
   The ᴿdevastation and destruction, famine and sword;   Is. 8:21; 9:20; 14:30
   How shall I comfort you?
20 Your ᴿsons have fainted,
   They ᴿlie *helpless* at the head of every
   street,   Is. 5:25; Jer. 14:16
   Like an ᴬantelope in a net,   Deut. 14:5
   Full of the wrath of the LORD,
   The ᴿrebuke of your God.   Is. 66:15

21 Therefore, please hear this, you ᴬaf-
   flicted,   Is. 54:11
   Who are drunk, but not with wine:
22 Thus says your Lord, the LORD, even
   your God
   Who ᴿcontends for His people, Jer. 50:34
   "Behold, I have taken out of your hand
   the ᴿcup of reeling;   Is. 51:17
   The chalice of My anger,
   You will never drink it again.
23 "And I will ᴿput it into the hand of your
   tormentors,   Jer. 25:15-17, 26, 28
   Who have said to ᵀyou, 'Lie ᴿdown that
   we may walk over you.'
   You have even made your back like the
   ground,
   And like the street for those who walk
   over *it*."   *your soul* • Josh. 10:24

CHAPTER 52

Aᴡᴀᴋᴇ,ᴿ awake,   Is. 51:9, 17
   Clothe yourself in your strength, O
   Zion;
   Clothe yourself in your ᴿbeautiful gar-
   ments,   1 Chr. 16:29; Ps. 110:3; Is. 49:18
   O Jerusalem, the ᴿholy city. [Rev. 21:2-27]
   For the uncircumcised and the ᴿunclean
   Will no more come into you.   Is. 35:8
2 Shake yourself ᴿfrom the dust, ᴿrise up,
   O captive Jerusalem;   Is. 29:4 • Is. 60:1
   ᴿLoose yourself from the chains around
   your neck,   Is. 9:4; 10:27; 14:25
   O captive daughter of Zion.
3 For thus says the LORD, "You were
   ᴿsold for nothing and you will be ᴿredeemed
   without money."   Ps. 44:12; Jer. 15:13 • Is. 1:27
4 For thus says the Lord GOD, "My peo-
   ple ᴿwent down at the first into Egypt to reside there, then the Assyrian oppressed
   them without cause.   Gen. 46:6
5 "Now therefore, what do I have here,"
   declares the LORD, "seeing that My people
   have been taken away without cause?"
   Again the LORD declares, "Those who rule

over them howl, and My ᴿname is continually
blasphemed all day long.   Ezek. 36:20, 23
6 "Therefore My people shall ᴿknow My
name; therefore in that day I am the one
who is speaking, 'Here I am.'"   Is. 49:23
7 How lovely on the mountains
   Are the feet of him who brings ᴿgood
   news,   Is. 40:9; 61:1; Nah. 1:15
   Who announces ᴬpeace   *well-being*
   And brings good news of ᵀhappiness,
   Who announces salvation,   *good*
   And says to Zion, "Your God reigns!"
8 Listen! Your watchmen lift up *their*
   ᴬvoices,   Is. 62:6
   They shout joyfully together;
   For they will see with their own eyes
   When the LORD restores Zion.
9 ᴿBreak forth, shout joyfully together,
   You ᴬwaste places of Jerusalem;
   For the LORD has comforted His peo-
   ple,   Ps. 98:4; Is. 44:23 • Is. 44:26
   He has ᴿredeemed Jerusalem.   Is. 43:1
10 The LORD has bared His holy ᴬarm
   In the sight of all the nations,   Is. 51:9
   That ᴿall the ends of the earth may see
   The salvation of our God. Is. 45:22; 48:20

11 Depart, depart, go out from there,
   ᴿTouch nothing unclean;   Num. 19:11, 16
   Go out of the midst of her, ᴿpurify your-
   selves,   Lev. 22:2; [Is. 1:16]
   You who carry the vessels of the LORD.
12 But you will not go out in haste,
   Nor will you go as fugitives;   *in flight*
   For the ᴿLORD will go before you,
   And ᴿthe God of Israel *will be* your rear
   guard.   Is. 26:7; 42:16 • Ex. 14:19, 20

The Messiah's Atonement

13 Behold, My servant will prosper,
   He will be high and lifted up, and
   ᴬgreatly ᴿexalted.   *very high* • Phil. 2:9☆
14 Just as many were astonished at you,
   My people,
   So His ᴿappearance was marred more
   than any man,
   And His form more than the sons of
   men.   Is. 53:2, 3☆
15 Thus He will ᴿsprinkle many nations,
   Kings will ᴿshut their mouths on account of Him;   Ezek. 36:25 • Job 21:5
   For ᴿwhat had not been told them they
   will see,   Rom. 15:21; [Eph. 3:5]☆
   And what they had not heard they will
   understand.

CHAPTER 53

Wʜᴏᴿ has believed our message?
   And to whom has the arm of the LORD
   been revealed?   John 12:38☆
2 For He grew up before Him like a ᴿten-
   der ᵀshoot,   Is. 11:1 • *suckling*
   And like a root out of parched ground;
   He has ᴿno *stately* form or majesty
   That we should look upon Him,

Nor appearance that we should [19]be attracted to Him.   Mark 15:32☆
3 He was[R]despised and forsaken of men,
A man of sorrows, and acquainted with grief;   Ps. 22:6; [Is. 49:7]☆ • *pains*
And like one from whom men hide their face,
He was despised, and we did not [R]esteem Him.   [John 1:10, 11]☆

4 Surely our [20]griefs He Himself[R]bore,
And our [A]sorrows He carried;
Yet we ourselves esteemed Him stricken,   [Matt. 8:17]☆ • *pains*
Smitten of[R]God, and afflicted.   John 19:7
5 But He was [21]pierced through for [R]our transgressions,   Is. 53:8; [Heb. 9:28]
He was crushed for[R]our iniquities;
The chastening for our [A]well-being *fell* upon Him,   [1 Cor. 15:3]☆ • *peace*
And by His scourging we are healed.
6 All of us like sheep have gone astray,
Each of us has turned to his own way;
But the Lord has[R]caused the iniquity of us all
To fall on Him.   Heb. 9:28☆

7 He was oppressed and He was afflicted,
Yet He did not[R]open His mouth;
[R]Like a lamb that is led to slaughter,
And like a sheep that is silent before its shearers,   Matt. 26:63☆ • Acts 8:32, 33☆
So He did not open His mouth.
8 By oppression and judgment He was taken away;
And as for His generation, who considered
That He was cut off out of the land of the[A]living,   *life*
For the transgression of my people to whom the stroke *was due?*
9 His grave was assigned with wicked men,
Yet He was with a [R]rich man in His death,   Matt. 27:57–60☆
Because He had done no violence,
Nor was there any deceit in His mouth.

10 But the Lord was pleased
To crush Him, [T]putting *Him* to grief;
If [T]He would render Himself *as* a guilt offering,   *He made Him sick* • *His soul*
He will see[R]*His* offspring,   2 Cor. 5:21☆
He will prolong *His* days,
And the good pleasure of the Lord will prosper in His hand.   *will of*
11 As a result of the anguish of His soul,
He will see *it* and be satisfied;
By His knowledge the Righteous One,
My Servant, will justify the many,
As He will bear their iniquities.
12 Therefore, I will allot Him a [R]portion with the great,   Is. 52:13; [Phil. 2:9–11]
And He will divide the booty with the strong;

Because He poured out [T]Himself[R] to death,   *His soul* • Matt. 26:38, 39, 42
And was[R]numbered with the transgressors;   Mark 15:28; Luke 22:37☆
Yet He Himself bore the sin of many,
And interceded for the transgressors.

CHAPTER 54

*The Messiah's Promise
of Israel's Restoration*

"S HOUT[R] for joy, O barren one, you who have borne no *child;*   Gal. 4:27
Break forth into joyful shouting and cry aloud, you who have not travailed;
For the sons of the desolate one *will be* [R]more numerous
Than the sons of the married woman,"
says the Lord.   1 Sam. 2:5; Is. 49:20
2 "Enlarge[R] the place of your tent;   Is. 33:20
[T]Stretch out the curtains of your dwellings, spare not;   *Let them stretch out*
Lengthen your[R]cords,
And strengthen your pegs.   Ex. 35:18
3 "For you will[R]spread abroad to the right and to the left.   Gen. 28:14; Is. 43:5, 6
And your [T]descendants will[R]possess nations,   *seed* • Is. 14:1, 2
And they will [R]resettle the desolate cities.   Is. 49:19

4 "Fear not, for you will [R]not be put to shame;   Is. 45:17
Neither feel humiliated, for you will not be disgraced;
But you will forget the[R]shame of your youth,   Jer. 31:19
And the reproach of your widowhood you will remember no more.
5 "For your[R]husband is your Maker,
Whose name is the Lord of hosts;
And your[R]Redeemer is the Holy One of Israel,   Jer. 3:14; Hos. 2:19 • Is. 43:14
Who is called the God of all the earth.
6 "For the Lord has called you,
Like a wife [R]forsaken and grieved in spirit,   Is. 49:14-21; 50:1, 2; 62:4
Even like a wife of *one's* youth when she is rejected,"
Says your God.
7 "For a[R]brief moment I forsook you,
But with great compassion I will [R]gather you.   Is. 26:20 • [Is. 11:12; 43:5]
8 "In an[T]outburst of anger   *overflowing*
I hid My face from you for a moment;
But with everlasting lovingkindness I will have compassion on you,"
Says the Lord your[R]Redeemer.   Is. 54:5

9 "For this is like the days of Noah to Me;
When I swore that the waters of Noah
Should[R]not [T]flood the earth again,

[19] Lit., *desire*   [20] Or, *sickness*   [21] Or, *wounded*

So I have sworn that I will not be angry
  with you,   Gen. 9:11 • *cross over*
Nor will I rebuke you.
10"For the [R]mountains may be removed
  and the hills may shake,
But My lovingkindness will not be removed from you,   Ps. 102:26; Is. 51:6
And My [R]covenant of peace will not be
  shaken,"   Ps. 89:34; Is. 55:3; 59:21; 61:8
Says[R]the LORD who has compassion on
  you.   Is. 54:8

11"O [R]afflicted one, storm-tossed, and [R]not
  comforted,   Is. 51:21 • Is. 51:18, 19
Behold, I will set your stones in antimony,
And your foundations I will[R]lay in [A]sap-
  phires.   Is. 14:32; 28:16 • *lapis lazuli*
12"Moreover, I will make your battle-
  ments of [T]rubies,   bright red
And your gates of [A]crystal,   *carbuncles*
And your entire [T]wall of precious
  stones.   *border, boundary*
13"And [R]all your sons will be[A]taught of the
  LORD;   [John 6:45] • *disciples*
And the well-being of your sons will be
  [R]great.   Is. 48:18; 66:12
14"In [R]righteousness you will be established;   Is. 1:26, 27; 9:7; 62:1
You will be far from [R]oppression, for
  you will not fear;   Is. 9:4; 14:4
And from [R]terror, for it will not come
  near you.   Is. 33:18
15"If anyone fiercely assails *you* it will not
  be from Me.
[R]Whoever assails you will fall because
  of you.   Is. 41:11-16
16"Behold, I Myself have created the
  smith who blows the fire of coals,
And brings out a weapon for its work;
And I have created the destroyer to
  ruin.
17"No[R]weapon that is formed against you
  shall prosper;   Is. 17:12-14; 29:8
And [R]every tongue that [T]accuses you in
  judgment you will condemn.
This is the heritage of the servants of
  the LORD,   Is. 50:8, 9 • *rises against*
And their [R]vindication is from Me," declares the LORD.   Is. 45:24; 46:13

CHAPTER 55

*The Messiah's Invitation
to the World*

"Ho! Every one who[R]thirsts, come to the
  waters;   Ps. 42:1, 2; 63:1; 143:6; Is. 41:17
And you who have [R]no [T]money come,
  buy and eat.   Lam. 5:4 • *silver*
Come, buy[R]wine and milk   Song 5:1
Without money and without cost.
2"Why do you spend money for what is
  [R]not bread,

And your wages for what does not satisfy?   Eccl. 6:2; Hos. 8:7
Listen carefully to Me, and[R]eat what is
  good,   Ps. 22:26; Is. 1:19; 62:8, 9
And delight yourself in abundance.
3"Incline your[T] ear and come to Me.
Listen, that[T]you may live;   *your soul*
And I will make [R]an everlasting cov-
  enant with you,   Is. 61:8
According to the [R]faithful mercies
  [T]shown to David. [Acts 13:34] • *of David*
4"Behold, I have made[R]him a witness to
  the peoples,   Ps. 18:43; [Jer. 30:9]
A[R]leader and commander for the peo-
  ples.   [Ezek. 34:24; 37:24, 25; Dan. 9:25]
5"Behold, you will call a [R]nation you do
  not know,   Is. 52:15☆
And a nation which knows you not will
  [R]run to you,   Zech. 8:22
Because of the LORD your God, even
  the Holy One of Israel;
For He has[R]glorified you."   Is. 60:9

6 Seek the LORD while He may be found;
  Call upon Him while He is near.
7 Let the wicked forsake his way,
  And the unrighteous man his thoughts;
  And let him[R]return to the LORD,
  And He will have [R]compassion on him;
  And to our God,   Is. 31:6; 44:22 • Is. 14:1
  For He will abundantly pardon.
8"For My thoughts are not [R]your
  thoughts,   Is. 65:2; 66:18
Neither are[R]your ways My ways," declares the LORD.   [Is. 53:6]
9"For[R]*as* the heavens are higher than the
  earth,   Ps. 103:11
So are My ways higher than your
  ways,
And My thoughts than your thoughts.
10"For as the [R]rain and the snow come
  down from heaven,   Is. 30:23
And do not return there without watering the earth,
And making it bear and sprout,
And furnishing[R]seed to the sower and
  bread to the eater;   2 Cor. 9:10
11 So shall My [T]word be which goes forth
  from My mouth; Is. 45:23; Matt. 24:35
It shall not return to Me empty,
Without [A]accomplishing what I desire,
And without succeeding *in the matter*
  for which I sent it.   Is. 46:10; 53:10
12"For you will go out with[R]joy, Is. 105:43
And be led forth with[R]peace;   Jer. 29:11
The[R]mountains and the hills will break
  forth into shouts of joy before you,
And all the[R]trees of the field will clap
  their hands.   Is. 44:23 • 1 Chr. 16:33
13"Instead of the[T]thorn bush the [R]cypress
  will come up;   Is. 7:19 • Is. 60:13
And instead of the [R]nettle the myrtle
  will come up;   Is. 5:6; 7:24; 32:13
And it will be a[T]memorial to the LORD,
For an everlasting[R]sign which will not
  be cut off."   *name* • Is. 19:20

CHAPTER 56

THUS says the LORD,
"Preserve[R] justice, and do righteous-
ness,   Is. 1:17; 33:5; 61:8
For My salvation is about to come
And My righteousness to be revealed.
2 "How[R]blessed is the man who does this,
And the son of man who[T]takes hold of
it;   Ps. 112:1; 119:1, 2 • Is. 56:4, 6
Who[R]keeps from profaning the sab-
bath,   Ex. 20:8-11; 31:13-17; Is. 56:6
And keeps his hand from doing any
evil."
3 Let not the[R]foreigner who has joined
himself to the LORD say,
"The LORD will surely separate me from
His people."   Is. 14:1; 56:6
Neither let the[R]eunuch say, "Behold, I
am a dry tree."   Jer. 38:7; Acts 8:27
4 For thus says the LORD,
"To the eunuchs who[R]keep My sabbaths,
And choose what pleases Me,   Is. 56:2, 6
And[R]hold fast My covenant,   Is. 56:6
5 To them I will give in My[R]house and
within My[R]walls a memorial,
And a name better than that of sons
and daughters;   Is. 2:2, 3 • Is. 26:1
I will give them an everlasting[R]name
which will not be cut off.   Is. 62:2

6 "Also the[R]foreigners who join themselves to the LORD,   Is. 56:3; 60:10
To minister to Him, and to love the
name of the LORD,
To be His servants, every one who
[R]keeps from profaning the sabbath,
And holds fast My covenant;   Is. 56:2, 4
7 Even [R]those I will bring to My[R]holy
mountain,   [Mic. 4:1, 2] • Is. 11:9; 65:25
And[R]make them joyful in My house of
prayer.   Is. 61:10
Their burnt offerings and their sacrifices will be acceptable on[R]My altar;
For My house will be called a house of
prayer for all the peoples."   Is. 60:7
8 The Lord GOD, who [R]gathers the dispersed of Israel, declares,   Is. 11:12
"Yet *others* I will gather to [T]them, to
those *already* gathered."   *him*

The Messiah's Rebuke of the Wicked

9 All you[R]beasts of the field,
All you beasts in the forest,
Come to eat.   Is. 18:6; 46:11
10 His[R]watchmen are blind,
All of them know nothing.   Ezek. 3:17
All of them are dumb dogs unable to
bark,
Dreamers lying down, who love to
slumber;
11 And the dogs are [T]greedy, they are not
satisfied.   *strong of soul/appetite*

And they are shepherds who have no
understanding;
They have all[R]turned to their own way,
Each one to his unjust gain, to the last
one.   Is. 57:17; Jer. 22:17
12 "Come," *they say*, "let us get [R]wine, and
let us drink heavily of strong drink;
And[R]tomorrow will be like today, only
more so."   Is. 5:11, 12, 22 • Ps. 10:6

CHAPTER 57

THE righteous man perishes, and no man
[R]takes it to heart;   Is. 42:25; 47:7
And devout men are taken away, while
no one understands.
For the righteous man is taken away
from[R]evil,   2 Kin. 22:20; Is. 47:11
2 He enters into peace;
They rest in their[T]beds,
Each one who [R]walked in his upright
way.   graves • Is. 26:7
3 "But come here, you sons of a[R]sorceress,
[R]Offspring of an adulterer and a[R]prosti-
tute.   Mal. 3:5 • Is. 1:4 • Is. 1:21
4 "Against whom do you jest?
Against whom do you open wide your
mouth
And stick out your tongue?
Are you not children of[R]rebellion,
Offspring of deceit,   Is. 48:8
5 *Who* inflame yourselves among the
[A]oaks,   terebinths • Is. 1:29
[R]Under every luxuriant tree,   2 Kin. 16:4
Who[R]slaughter the children in the[A]ra-
vines,   2 Kin. 23:10; Jer. 7:31 • *wadis*
Under the clefts of the crags?
6 "Among the[T]smooth *stones* of the[A]ravine
Is your portion, they are your lot;
Even to them you have poured out a
libation,   symbols of fertility gods • *wadi*
You have made a grain offering.
Shall I relent concerning these things?
7 "Upon a[R]high and lofty mountain
You have[R]made your bed.
You also went up there to offer sacri-
fice.   Jer. 3:6; Ezek. 16:16 • Ezek. 23:41
8 "And behind the door and the doorpost
You have set up your sign;
Indeed, far removed from Me, you
have[R]uncovered yourself;
And have gone up and made your bed
wide.   Ezek. 23:18
And you have made an agreement for
yourselves with them,
You have loved their[A]bed,   *lying down*
You have looked on *their* manhood.
9 "And you have journeyed to the king
with oil
And increased your perfumes;
You have[R]sent your envoys a great distance,   Ezek. 23:16, 40
And made *them* go down to Sheol.
10 "You were tired out by the length of
your road,

Yet you did not say, 'It^Ris hopeless.'
You found renewed strength, Jer. 2:25
Therefore you did not^Afaint. *become sick*

11"Of^Rwhom were you worried and fear-
ful,   Prov. 29:25; Is. 51:12, 13
When you lied, and did^Rnot remember
Me,   Jer. 2:32; 3:21
Nor^Rgive *Me* a thought? Ps. 50:21
Was I not silent even for a long time
So you do not fear Me?
12"I will^Rdeclare your righteousness and
your^Rdeeds, Is. 58:1, 2 • Is. 29:15; 59:6
But they will not profit you.
13"When you cry out,^Rlet your collection
of idols deliver you. Jer. 22:20; 30:14
But the wind will carry all of them up,
And a breath will take *them away.*
But he who^Rtakes refuge in Me shall^Rin-
herit the land, Ps. 37:3, 9 • Is. 49:8
And shall possess My holy mountain."

14 And it shall be said,
"Build^Rup, build up, prepare the way,
Remove *every* obstacle out of the way
of My people." Is. 62:10; Jer. 18:15
15 For thus says the^Rhigh and exalted One
Who ^Alives forever, whose name is
Holy, Is. 52:13 • *dwells in eternity*
"I^Rdwell *on* a high and holy place,
And *also* with the^Rcontrite and lowly of
spirit Is. 33:5; 66:1 • Ps. 34:18; 51:17
In order to revive the spirit of the lowly
And to revive the heart of the contrite.
16"For I will^Rnot contend forever,
^RNeither will I always be angry;
For the spirit would grow faint before
Me, Gen. 6:3 • Ps. 85:5; 103:9
And the^Rbreath *of those whom* I have
made. Is. 42:5
17"Because of the iniquity of his ^Runjust
gain I was angry and struck him;
I hid *My face* and was angry, Jer. 6:13
And he went on^Rturning away, in the
way of his heart. Is. 1:4; Jer. 3:14, 22
18"I have seen his ways, but I will^Rheal
him; Is. 19:22; 30:26; 53:5
I will lead him and^Rrestore comfort to
him and to his mourners, Is. 61:1-3
19 Creating the^Tpraise of the lips.
Peace, peace to him who is far and to
him who is near," *fruit of the lips*
Says the LORD, "and I will heal him."
20 But the^Rwicked are like the tossing sea,
For it cannot be quiet, Job 18:5-14
And its waters toss up refuse and mud.
21"There^Ris no peace," says^Rmy God, "for
the wicked." Is. 48:22; 59:8 • Is. 49:4

CHAPTER 58

Blessings of True Worship

"C^RRY^Rloudly, do not hold back; Is. 40:6
Raise your voice like a trumpet,^R
And declare to My people their^Rtrans-
gression, Is. 43:27; 50:1; 59:12

And to the house of Jacob their sins.
2"Yet they^Rseek Me day by day, and delight to know My ways, Is. 1:11
As a nation that has done^Rrighteous-
ness, Is. 48:1; Jer. 7:9, 10
And^Rhas not forsaken the ordinance of
their God. Is. 1:4, 28; 59:13
They ask Me *for* just decisions,
They delight in the nearness of God.
3 'Why have we^Rfasted and Thou dost not
see? Mal. 3:14; Luke 18:12
Why have we humbled ourselves and
Thou dost not^Tnotice?' *know*
Behold, on the^Rday of your fast you find
your desire, Is. 22:12, 13; Zech. 7:5, 6
And drive hard all your workers.
4"Behold, you fast for contention and
^Rstrife and to strike with a wicked
fist. Is. 3:14, 15; 59:6
You do not fast like *you do* today to
make your voice heard on high.
5"Is it a fast like this which I choose, a
day for a man to humble himself?
Is it for bowing^Tone's head like a reed,
And for spreading out^Rsackcloth and
ashes as a bed? *his* • 1 Kin. 21:27
Will you call this a fast, even an^Rac-
ceptable day to the LORD? Is. 49:8
6"Is this not the fast which I choose,
To^Rloosen the bonds of wickedness,
To undo the bands of the yoke,
And to let the oppressed go free,
And break every yoke? Neh. 5:10-12
7"Is it not to^Rdivide your bread^Twith the
hungry, Job 31:19, 20; Is. 58:10 • *for*
And^Rbring the homeless poor into the
house; Is. 16:3, 4; Heb. 13:2
When you see the^Rnaked, to cover him;
And not to ^Rhide yourself from your
own flesh? Luke 3:11 • Luke 10:31, 32
8"Then your^Rlight will break out like the
dawn,^R Is. 58:10
And your^Rrecovery will speedily spring
forth; Is. 30:26; 33:24; Jer. 30:17; 33:6
And your^Rrighteousness will go before
you; Ps. 85:13; Is. 62:1
The glory of the^RLORD will be your rear
guard. Ex. 14:19; Is. 52:12
9"Then you will ^Rcall, and the LORD will
answer; Ps. 50:15; Is. 55:6; 65:24
You will cry, and He will say, 'Here I
am.'^R
If you ^Rremove the yoke from your
midst, Is. 58:6
The^Tpointing of the finger, and speaking wickedness, *sending out*
10 And if you^Tgive yourself to the hungry,
And satisfy the^Adesire of the afflicted,
Then your^Rlight will rise in darkness,
And your gloom *will become* like midday. *furnish* • *soul* • Is. 42:16; 58:8
11"And the ^RLORD will continually guide
you, Is. 49:10; 57:18
And ^Rsatisfy your ^Adesire in scorched
places, Ps. 107:9; Is. 41:17 • *soul*
And give strength to your bones;

And you will be like a watered garden,
And like a ^Rspring of water whose waters do not ^Afail.   [John 4:14] • *deceive*
12"And those from among you will ^Rrebuild the ancient ruins;   Is. 49:8; 61:4
You will ^Rraise up the age-old foundations;   Is. 44:28
And you will be called the repairer of the ^Rbreach,   Is. 30:13; Amos 9:11
The restorer of the ^Tstreets in which to dwell.   *paths*

13"If because of the sabbath, you ^Rturn your foot   Ex. 31:16, 17; 35:2, 3
From doing your *own* pleasure on My holy day,
And call the sabbath a ^Rdelight, the holy *day* of the LORD honorable,   Ps. 27:4
And shall honor it, desisting from your ^Rown ways,   Is. 55:8
From seeking your *own* pleasure,
And ^Rspeaking your *own* word,   Is. 59:13
14 Then you will take ^Rdelight in the LORD,
And I will make you ride on the heights of the earth;   Job 22:26; Is. 61:10
And I will feed you *with* the heritage of Jacob your father,
For the ^Rmouth of the LORD has spoken."   Is. 1:20; 40:5

CHAPTER 59

Sins of Israel

BEHOLD,^Rthe LORD's hand is not so short
That it cannot save;   Num. 11:23; Is. 50:2
^RNeither is His ear so dull
That it cannot hear.   Ezek. 8:18

2 But your iniquities have made a separation between you and your God,
And your sins have hidden *His* face from you, so that He does not hear.

3 For your hands are defiled with blood,
And your fingers with iniquity;
Your lips have spoken falsehood,
Your tongue mutters wickedness.
4 ^RNo one sues righteously and no one pleads ^Thonestly.   Is. 5:7 • *in truth*
They ^Rtrust in confusion, and speak lies;

They ^Rconceive mischief, and bring forth iniquity.   Jer. 7:4, 8 • Job 15:35
5 They hatch adders' eggs and ^Rweave the spider's web;
He who eats of their eggs dies,
And *from* that which is crushed a snake breaks forth.   Job 8:14
6 Their webs will not become clothing,
Nor will they ^Rcover themselves with their works;   Is. 28:20
Their works are works of iniquity,
And an act of violence is in their hands.
7 ^RTheir feet run to evil,
And they hasten to shed innocent blood;   Prov. 1:16; 6:17; Rom. 3:15-17
^RTheir thoughts are thoughts of iniquity;
Devastation and destruction are in their highways.   Is. 65:2; 66:18
8 They do not know the ^Rway of peace,
And there is no justice in their tracks;
They have made their paths crooked;
Whoever treads on ^Tthem does not know peace.   Luke 1:79 • *it*

9 Therefore, ^Rjustice is far from us,
And righteousness does not overtake us;   Is. 59:14
We ^Rhope for light, but behold, darkness;   Is. 5:30; 8:21, 22
For brightness, but we walk in gloom.
10 We ^Rgrope along the wall like blind men,   Deut. 28:29; Job 5:14
We grope like those who have no eyes;
We ^Rstumble at midday as in the twilight,   Is. 8:14, 15; 28:13
Among those who are vigorous we are ^Rlike dead men.   Lam. 3:6
11 All of us growl like bears,
And ^Rmoan sadly like doves;   Is. 38:14
We hope for justice, but there is none,
For salvation, *but* it is far from us.
12 For our ^Rtransgressions are multiplied before Thee,   Ezra 9:6; Is. 58:1
And our sins ^Ttestify against us;
For our transgressions are with us,
And we know our iniquities: *answer*
13 Transgressing and ^Rdenying the LORD,
And turning away from our God,
Speaking oppression and revolt,
Conceiving *in* and uttering from the heart lying words.   Josh. 24:27

59:2 What Sin Does—Sin, regardless of its degree, always has an effect—separation. Sin separates one from God. This separation from God is death. Adam was told that if he ate of the tree of the knowledge of good and evil that he would die (Page 6—Gen. 3:3). Adam ate of the tree and immediately died spiritually—his soul was separated from God—and he began to die physically. The entrance of sin into the human race brought with it death (Page 1135—Rom. 5:12; 6:23). That man is a sinner is proven by the fact that he dies—where there is death, there is sin. Sin's penalty, death, can be remedied by life—union with God. This is achieved by belief in Jesus, who died to pay the penalty of man's sin (Page 1135—Rom. 5:21). For the one who believes in Jesus, the penalty of sin is broken. Yes, he will die physically (unless he is alive when Jesus returns to take all believers to heaven with Himself, (Page 1208—1 Thess. 5:14–18), but physical death for him is only the doorway into the presence of God. Sin, however, does have an effect upon the believer, for it mars his fellowship with God. Sin in the believer's life is a terrible thing and is not to be tolerated. While it is probable that the believer *will* sin, it is never necessary for him to do so (Page 1274—1 John 2:1).

Now turn to Page 543—Ps. 32:5: What Should Be Done About Sin.

14 And[R]justice is turned back,   Is. 1:21; 5:7
  And[R]righteousness stands far away;
  For truth has stumbled in the street,
  And uprightness cannot enter.   Is. 46:12
15 Yes, truth is lacking;
  And he who turns aside from evil
    [R]makes himself a prey.   Is. 5:23; 10:2

  Now the LORD saw,
  And it was displeasing in His sight that
    there was no justice.   evil
16 And He saw that there was[R]no man,
  And was astonished that there was no
    one to intercede;   Is. 41:28; 63:5
  Then His[R]own arm brought salvation to
    Him;   Ps. 98:1; Is. 52:10; 63:5
  And His righteousness upheld Him.
17 And He put on[R]righteousness like a
    breastplate,   Eph. 6:14
  And a[R]helmet of salvation on His head;
  And He put on[R]garments of vengeance
    for clothing,   Eph. 6:17 • Is. 63:2, 3
  And wrapped Himself with[R]zeal as a
    mantle.   Is. 9:7; 37:32; Zech. 1:14
18 [R]According to their[T]deeds,[T]so He will re-
    pay,   Job 34:11 • recompense • accordingly
  Wrath to His adversaries, recompense
    to His enemies;
  To the coastlands He will[T]make recom-
    pense.   repay
19 So they will fear the name of the LORD
    from the[R]west
  And His glory from the[R]rising of the
    sun,   Is. 49:12 • Ps. 113:3
  For He will come like a rushing stream,
  Which the wind of the LORD drives.
20 "And a Redeemer will come to Zion,
  And to those who turn from transgres-
    sion in Jacob," declares the LORD.

21 "And as for Me, this is My[R]covenant with
them," says the LORD: "My Spirit which is
upon you, and My words which I have put in
your mouth, shall not depart from your
mouth, nor from the mouth of your[T]off-
spring, nor from the mouth of your offspring's offspring," says the LORD, "from
now and forever."   [Jer. 31:31–34] • seed

CHAPTER 60

Glory of Israel in the Kingdom

"ARISE[R], shine; for your[R]light has come,
  And the glory of the LORD has risen
    upon you.   Is. 52:2 • Is. 60:19, 20
2 "For behold,[R]darkness will cover the
    earth,   Is. 58:10; Jer. 13:16; Col. 1:13
  And deep darkness the peoples;
  But the LORD will rise upon you,
  And His glory will appear upon you.
3 "And[R]nations will come to your light,
  And kings to the brightness of your ris-
    ing.   Is. 2:3; 45:14; 49:23; Rev. 21:24 ☆

4 "Lift[T]up your eyes round about, and see;
  They all gather together, they[R]come to
    you.   Is. 11:12; 49:18 • Is. 49:20-22
  Your sons will come from afar,
  And your daughters will be[T]carried in
    the arms.   nursed upon the side
5 "Then you will see and be radiant,
  And your heart will[T]thrill and rejoice;
  Because the[R]abundance of the sea will
    be turned to you,
  The wealth of the nations will come to
    you.   tremble and be enlarged • Is. 23:18
6 "A multitude of camels will cover you,
  The young camels of Midian and
    [R]Ephah;   Gen. 25:4
  All those from[R]Sheba will come;
  They will bring[R]gold and frankincense,
  And will bear good news of the praises
    of the LORD.[R]   Gen. 25:3 • Matt. 2:11
7 "All the flocks of[R]Kedar will be gathered
    together to you,   Gen. 25:13
  The rams of Nebaioth will minister to
    you;
  They will go up with acceptance on My
    [R]altar,   Is. 19:19; 56:7
  And I shall glorify My glorious house.
8 "Who are these who fly like a cloud,
  And like the doves to their lattices?

59:21   Inspiration of God's Word—The word *inspiration* is found but once in the New Testament. This occurs in Second Timothy 3:16, where Paul says "All Scripture *is* inspired by God," literally "God-breathed." Divine inspiration logically follows divine revelation. In revelation God speaks to man's ear while by inspiration He guides the pen to ensure that the imparted message is correctly written down.

There are several ideas about the process of inspiration. One is called the natural theory. This says that the Bible authors were inspired in the same sense that William Shakespeare was inspired. Another theory, called the content theory, suggests that God merely gave the writer the main content or idea, allowing him to choose his own words to express that concept. In contrast Jesus Himself said that the very letters of the words were also chosen by God (Page 966—Matt. 5:18). This position is referred to as the plenary-verbal view, which says that all (plenary) the very words (verbal) of the Bible are inspired by God. Jesus once told the devil that the Christian is to live by each of these inspired words (Page 965—Matt. 4:4). The Bible authors understood that their writings were being guided by the Spirit of God, even as they wrote them. Peter said this was true of the Old Testament authors (Page 1268—2 Pet. 1:20, 21). He then stated his own letters (Page 1260—1 and 2 Pet.) were inspired by God (Page 1269—2 Pet. 3:1, 2). Finally, he pointed out this was also true concerning Paul's writings (Page 1269—2 Pet. 3:15, 16).

One final thing should be said about inspiration. Plenary-verbal inspiration does not guarantee the inspiration of any translation, but only of the original Hebrew and Greek manuscripts.

Now turn to Page 613—Prov. 6:23: Illumination of God's Word.

9"Surely the ^Rcoastlands will wait for Me;
And the ^Rships of Tarshish *will come*
first,   Is. 11:11; 24:15 • Ps. 48:7; Is. 2:16
To ^Rbring your sons from afar,   Is. 14:2
Their silver and their gold with them,
For the name of the LORD your God,
And for the Holy One of Israel because
He has ^Tglorified you.   *beautified*

10"And ^Rforeigners will build up your
walls,   Is. 14:1, 2; 61:5; Zech. 6:15
And their ^Rkings will minister to you;
For in My ^Rwrath I struck you,
And in My favor I have had compassion on you.   Rev. 21:24 • Is. 54:8
11"And your ^Rgates will be open continually;   Is. 26:2; 60:18; 62:10; Rev. 21:25, 26
They will not be closed day or night,
So that *men* may ^Rbring to you the
wealth of the nations,   Is. 60:5
With their kings led in procession.
12"For the nation and the kingdom which
will not serve you will perish,
And the nations will be utterly ruined.
13"The ^Rglory of Lebanon will come to you,
The ^Rjuniper, the box tree, and the cypress together,   Is. 35:2 • Is. 41:19
To beautify the place of My sanctuary;
And I shall make the ^Rplace of My feet
glorious.   1 Chr. 28:2; Ps. 99:5; 132:7
14"And the ^Rsons of those who afflicted you
will come bowing to you,
And all those who despised you will
bow themselves at the soles of your
feet;   Is. 14:1, 2; 45:14, 23; 49:23
And they will call you the ^Rcity of the
LORD,   Is. 1:26
The Zion of the Holy One of Israel.

15"Whereas you have been ^Rforsaken and
^Rhated   Is. 1:7-9; 6:11-13 • Is. 66:5
With no one passing through,
I will make you an everlasting pride,
A joy from generation to generation.
16"You will also ^Rsuck the milk of nations,
And will suck the breast of kings;
Then you will know that I, the LORD,
am your ^RSavior,   Is. 66:11 • Is. 19:20
And your ^RRedeemer, the Mighty One
of Jacob.   Is. 59:20; 63:16
17"Instead of bronze I will bring gold,
And instead of iron I will bring silver,
And instead of wood, bronze,
And instead of stones, iron.
And I will make peace your administrators,
And righteousness your overseers.
18"Violence ^R will not be heard again in
your land,   Is. 54:14
Nor ^Rdevastation or destruction within
your borders;   Is. 51:19
But you will call your ^Rwalls salvation,
and your gates praise.   Is. 26:1
19"No longer will you have the ^Rsun for
light by day,   Rev. 21:23; 22:5

Nor for brightness will the moon give
you light;
But you will have the ^RLORD for an ever-
lasting light,   Is. 2:5; 9:2
And your God for your ^Aglory.   *beauty*
20"Your ^Rsun will set no more,   Is. 30:26
Neither will your moon wane;
For you will have the LORD for an ever-
lasting light,
And the days of your ^Rmourning will be
finished.   Is. 35:10; 65:19; Rev. 21:4
21"Then all your people *will be* righteous;
They will possess the land forever,
The branch of ^TMy planting,   *His*
The ^Rwork of My hands,   Is. 19:25; 29:23
That I may be ^Rglorified.   Is. 61:3
22"The smallest one will become a clan,
And the least one a mighty nation.
I, the LORD, will hasten it in its time."

CHAPTER 61

Advents of the Messiah

T HE ^RSpirit of the Lord GOD is upon me,
Because the LORD has anointed me
To bring good news to the ^Aafflicted;
He has sent me to bind up the broken-
hearted,   Is. 11:2☆ • *humble* • Is. 11:4
To ^Rproclaim liberty to captives,
And freedom to prisoners; Is. 42:7; 49:9☆
2 To ^Rproclaim the favorable year of the
LORD,   Is. 49:8; 60:10
And the day of vengeance of our God;
To ^Rcomfort all who mourn,   Matt. 5:4
3 To grant those who mourn *in* Zion,
Giving them a garland instead of ashes,
The ^Roil of gladness instead of mourn-
ing,
The mantle of praise instead of a spirit
of fainting.   Ps. 23:5; 45:7; 104:15
So they will be called oaks ^R of right-
eousness,
The planting of the LORD, that He may
be glorified.   Is. 60:21; [Jer. 17:7, 8]

4 Then they will ^Rrebuild the ancient ru-
ins,   Is. 49:8; 58:12; Ezek. 36:33
They will raise up the former devasta-
tions,
And they will repair the ruined cities,
The desolations of many generations.
5 And ^Rstrangers will stand and pasture
your flocks,
And foreigners will be your farmers
and your vinedressers. Is. 14:2; 60:10
6 But you will be called the ^Rpriests of the
LORD;
You will be spoken of *as* ^Rministers of
our God.   Is. 66:21 • Is. 56:6
You will eat the wealth of nations,
And in their riches you will boast.
7 Instead of your ^Rshame *you will have a*
^Rdouble *portion,*   Is. 54:4 • Is. 40:2
And *instead of* humiliation they will
shout for joy over their portion.

Therefore they will possess a double
portion in their land,
[R]Everlasting joy will be theirs.   Ps. 16:11
8 For I, the LORD,[R]love justice,   Is. 5:16
I hate robbery[A]in the burnt offering;
And I will faithfully give them their
recompense,   *with iniquity*
And I will make an [R]everlasting covenant with them.   Ps. 105:10; Is. 55:3
9 Then their offspring will be known
among the nations,
And their descendants in the midst of
the peoples.
All who see them will recognize them
Because they are the [R]offspring *whom*
the LORD has blessed.   Is. 44:3

10 I will[R]rejoice greatly in the LORD,
My soul will exult in my God;
For He has clothed me with garments
of salvation,   Is. 12:1, 2; 25:9; 41:16
He has wrapped me with a robe of
righteousness,
As a bridegroom decks himself with a
garland,
And[R]as a bride adorns herself with her
jewels.   Rev. 21:2

11 For as the [R]earth brings forth its
sprouts,   Is. 4:2; 55:10
And as a garden causes the things
sown in it to spring up, [R]
So the Lord GOD will cause [R]righteous-
ness and praise   Ps. 72:3; 85:11
To spring up before all the nations.

CHAPTER 62

Future of Jerusalem

FOR Zion's sake I will not keep silent,
And for Jerusalem's sake I will not
keep quiet,
Until her[R]righteousness goes forth like
brightness,   Is. 1:26; 58:8; 61:11
And her [R]salvation like a torch that is
burning.   Is. 46:13; 52:10
2 And the [R]nations will see your righteousness,   Is. 60:3
And all kings your glory;

And you will be called by a new[R]name,
Which the mouth of the LORD will des-
ignate.   Is. 56:5; 62:4, 12; 65:15
3 You will also be a [R]crown of beauty in
the hand of the LORD,
And a royal[T]diadem in the hand of your
God.   Is. 28:5; Zech. 9:16 • *turban*
4 It will no longer be said to you, [T]"For-
saken,"   Azubah
Nor to your land will it any longer be
said,[T]"Desolate";   Shemamah
But you will be called,[T]"My delight is in
her,"   Hephzibah
And your land, [T]"Married";   Beulah
For the[R]LORD delights in you,   Jer. 32:41
And *to Him* your land will be married.
5 For *as* a young man marries a virgin,
So your sons will marry you;
And *as* the [T]bridegroom rejoices over
the bride,   *exultation of the bridegroom*
So your God will rejoice over you.

6 On your walls, O Jerusalem, I have appointed[R]watchmen;   Is. 52:8; Jer. 6:17
All day and all night they will never
keep silent.
You who[R]remind the LORD, take no rest
for yourselves;   Ps. 74:2; Jer. 14:21
7 And [R]give Him no rest until He establishes   Luke 18:1-8
And makes [R]Jerusalem a praise in the
earth.   Is. 60:18; Jer. 33:9; Zeph. 3:19, 20
8 [R]The LORD has sworn by His right hand
and by His strong arm,   Is. 45:23
"I will [R]never again give your grain *as*
food for your enemies;   Lev. 26:16
Nor will foreigners drink your new
wine, for which you have labored."
9 But those who[R]garner it will eat it, and
praise the LORD;   Is. 65:13, 21-23
And those who gather it will drink it in
the courts of My sanctuary.

10 Go through, go through the gates;
Clear the way[T]for the people;   *of*
[R]Build up, build up the[R]highway;
Remove the stones, lift up a standard
over the peoples.   Is. 57:14 • Is. 11:16
11 Behold, the LORD has proclaimed to the
[R]end of the earth,   Is. 42:10; 49:6

61:10   Christ's Righteousness—One of the most awesome requirements of God made upon men and women is that they be righteous, that is, conform to His ethical and moral standards (Page 533—Ps. 15:2; Page 894—Mic. 6:8). Since God is holy, he cannot allow sinners into his presence (Page 662—Is. 6:3–5). Since all are sinners, they could not be saved apart from the supernatural intervention of God (Page 1133—Rom. 3:10, 23). The righteous demands of God coupled with the inability of man might present an insoluble dilemma. God Himself, however, has graciously solved the problem. He sent Christ, who never sinned, to die for our sins and thus satisfy His own wrath toward us. Simply put, it means that God, at the cross, treated Christ as though He had committed our sins even though He was righteous. On the other hand, when we believe in Christ, He treats us as though we were as righteous as Christ (Page 1169—2 Cor. 5:21). The Bible calls this type of righteousness "reck-oned" (Page 1134—Rom. 4:5). That simply means that God puts to our spiritual account the very worth of Christ, much as though He were a banker adding an inexhaustible deposit to our bank account. There are, sadly, many people who still refuse to believe that such an abundant blessing can be theirs as a free gift (Page 1186—Eph. 2:8, 9). Nevertheless, the Bible clearly urges all men to trust in Jesus Christ as Savior and thus be reckoned as right-eous by God (Page 1134—Rom. 4:24).
Now turn to Page 1276—1 John 3:2: Placed into God's Family.

ᴿSay to the daughter of Zion, "Lo, your
ᴿsalvation comes; Zech. 9:9☆ • Is. 51:5
Behold His reward is with Him, and
His recompense before Him."
12 And they will call them, "Theᴿholy people, Deut. 7:6; Is. 4:3; [1 Pet. 2:9]
The ᴿredeemed of the LORD"; Is. 35:9
And you will be called, "Sought out, a
cityᴿnot forsaken." Is. 41:17; 42:16

CHAPTER 63

Vengeance of God

WHO is this who comes fromᴿEdom,
With ᴬgarments of ᴬglowing colors from
Bozrah, Ps. 137:7 • Is. 63:2 • *crimson*
This One who is majestic in His ap-
parel,
ᵀMarching in the greatness of His
strength? *Inclining*
"It is I who speak in righteousness,
ᴿmighty to save." Zeph. 3:17
2 Why is Your apparel red,
And Your garments like the one who
ᴿtreads in the wine press? Rev. 19:13☆
3 "I ᴿhave trodden the wine trough alone,
And from the peoples there was no
man with Me. Rev. 14:20; 19:15☆
I also ᴮtrod them in My anger, Is. 22:5
And ᴿtrampled them in My wrath;
And ᴿtheir ᵀlifeblood is sprinkled on My
garments, Rev. 19:13 • *juice*
And I ᵀstained all My raiment. *defiled*
4 "For the ᴿday of vengeance was in My
heart, Is. 34:8; 35:4; 61:2; Jer. 51:6
And My year of redemption has come.
5 "And I looked, and there wasᴿno one to
help, Is. 59:16
And I was astonished and there was no
one to uphold;
So My ᴮown arm brought salvation to
Me; Ps. 44:3; Is. 40:10; 52:10
And My wrath upheld Me.
6 "And I ᴿtrod down the peoples in My anger, Is. 22:5; 34:2; 65:12
And made them ᴮdrunk in My wrath,
And I poured out their lifeblood on the
earth." Is. 29:9; 51:17, 21

Prayer of the Remnant

7 I shall make mention of the ᴿlovingkind-
nesses of the LORD, the praises of
the LORD, Ps. 25:6; 92:2; Is. 54:8, 10
According to all that the LORD has
granted us,
And the great ᴮgoodness toward the
house of Israel, 1 Kin. 8:66
Which He has granted them according
to His ᴿcompassion,
And according to the multitude of His
lovingkindnesses. Is. 54:7, 8; Eph. 2:4

8 For He said, "Surely, they are ᴿMy people, Ex. 6:7; Is. 3:15; 51:4
Sons who will not deal falsely."
So He became their ᴿSavior. Is. 60:16☆
9 In all their affliction ᴿHe was afflicted,
And the ᴿangel of His presence saved
them; Judg. 10:16 • Ex. 23:20-23
In His ᴿlove and in His mercy He ᴿredeemed them; Deut. 7:7, 8 • Is. 43:1
And He ᴿlifted them and carried them
all the days of old. Deut. 1:31; 32:10f.
10 But they ᴿrebelled Ps. 78:40; 106:33
And grieved His ᴿHoly Spirit;
Therefore, He turned Himself to become their enemy, Ps. 51:11; Is. 63:11
He fought against them.
11 Then ᴿHis people remembered the days
of old, of Moses. Ps. 106:44, 45
Where is ᴿHe who brought them up out
of the sea with the shepherds of His
flock? Is. 51:10
Where is He who ᴮput His Holy Spirit in
the midst of them, Hag. 2:5
12 Who caused His ᴿglorious arm to go at
the right hand of Moses, Ex. 6:6
Who ᴿdivided the waters before them to
make for Himself an everlasting
name, Ex. 14:21, 22; Is. 11:15; 51:10
13 Who led them through the depths?
Like the horse in the wilderness, they
did not ᴮstumble; Jer. 31:9
14 As the cattle which go down into the
valley,
The Spirit of the LORD gave ᵀthem rest.
So didst Thou lead Thy people, *him*
To make for Thyself a glorious name.

15 ᴿLook down from heaven, and see from
Thy holy and glorious ᴿhabitation;
Where are Thy ᴿzeal and Thy mighty
deeds? Ps. 80:14 • Ps. 68:5 • Is. 9:7
The ᴿstirrings of Thy heart and Thy
compassion are restrained toward
me. Jer. 31:20; Hos. 11:8
16 For Thou art our ᴿFather, though Abraham does not know us, Is. 1:2; 64:8
And Israel does not recognize us.
Thou, O LORD, art our Father,
Our ᴿRedeemer from of old is Thy
name. Is. 41:14; 44:6; 60:16
17 Why, O LORD, dost Thou ᴮcause us to
stray from Thy ways, Is. 30:28
And ᴿharden our heart from fearing
Thee? Is. 29:13, 14
Return for the sake of Thy servants,
the tribes of Thy heritage.
18 Thy holy people possessed Thy sanctuary for a little while,
Our adversaries have trodden *it* down.
19 We have become *like* those over whom
Thou hast never ruled,
Like those who were not called by Thy
name.

CHAPTER 64

O H, that Thou wouldst rend the heavens
   and ᴿcome down,   Ex. 19:18; Ps. 18:9
That the mountains might ᴿquake at
   Thy presence—   Judg. 5:5; Ps. 68:8
2 As fire kindles the brushwood, *as* fire
   causes water to boil—
To make Thy name known to Thine adversaries,
That the ᴿnations may tremble at Thy
   presence!   Ps. 99:1; Jer. 5:22; 33:9
3 When Thou didst ᴿawesome things
   which we did not expect,
Thou didst come down, the mountains
   quaked at Thy presence.   Ps. 65:5
4 For from of old ᴿthey have not heard
   nor perceived by ear,   1 Cor. 2:9
Neither has the eye seen a God besides
   Thee,
Who acts in behalf of the one who
   ᴿwaits for Him.   Is. 25:9; 30:18; 40:31
5 Thou dost ᴿmeet him who rejoices in
   doing righteousness,   Ex. 20:24
Who ᴿremembers Thee in Thy ways.
Behold, ᴿThou wast angry, for we
   sinned,   Is. 26:13; 63:7 • Is. 12:1
We continued in them a long time;
And shall we be saved?
6 For all of us have become like one who
   is ᴿunclean,   Is. 6:5
And all our ᴿrighteous deeds are like a
   filthy garment;   Is. 46:12; 48:1
And all of us ᴿwither like a leaf,
And our ᴿiniquities, like the wind, take
   us away.   Ps. 90:5, 6; Is. 1:30 • Is. 50:1
7 And there is ᴿno one who calls on Thy
   name,   Is. 59:4; Ezek. 22:30
Who arouses himself to take hold of
   Thee;
For Thou hast ᴿhidden Thy face from us,
And hast delivered us into the power of
   our iniquities.   Deut. 31:18; Is. 1:15

8 But now, O LORD, Thou art our Father,
We are the clay, and Thou our potter;
And all of us are the work of Thy hand.
9 Do not be ᴿangry beyond measure, O
   LORD,   Is. 57:17; 60:10
ᴿNeither remember iniquity forever;
Behold, look now, all of us are ᴿThy peo-
   ple.   Is. 43:25 • Ps. 79:13; Is. 63:8
10 Thy ᴿholy cities have become a ᴿwilderness,   Is. 48:2; 52:1 • Is. 1:7; 6:11
Zion has become a wilderness,
Jerusalem a desolation.
11 Our holy and beautiful ᴿhouse,
Where our fathers praised Thee,
Has been burned *by* fire;   2 Kin. 25:9
And ᴿall our precious things have become a ruin.   Lam. 1:7, 10, 11
12 Wilt Thou ᴿrestrain Thyself at these
   things, O LORD?   Ps. 74:10, 11, 18, 19
Wilt Thou keep silent and afflict us beyond measure?

CHAPTER 65

The Lord's Answer to the Remnant

"I PERMITTED Myself to be sought by
    ᴿthose who did not ask *for Me;*
I permitted Myself to be found by
   those who did not seek Me.
I said, 'Here am I, here am I,'
To a nation which ᴿdid not call on My
   name.   Rom. 9:24-26; 10:20 • Is. 63:19
2 "I have spread out My hands all day
   long to a rebellious people,
Who walk *in* the way which is not
   good, following their own thoughts,
3 A people who continually ᴿprovoke Me
   to My face,   Job 1:11; 2:5; Is. 3:8
Offering sacrifices in gardens and
   ᴿburning incense on bricks;   Is. 66:3
4 Who sit among graves, and spend the
   night in secret places;
Who ᴿeat swine's flesh,
And the broth of unclean meat is *in*
   their pots.   Lev. 11:7; Is. 66:3, 17
5 "Who say, 'Keep ᴿ to yourself, do not
   come near me,   Matt. 9:11; Luke 7:39
For I am holier than you!'
These are smoke in My ᴿnostrils,
A fire that burns all the day.   nose
6 "Behold, it is written before Me,
I will not keep silent, but I will repay;
I will even repay into their bosom,
7 Both ᴿtheir own ᴿiniquities and the iniquities of their fathers together,"
   says the LORD.   your • Is. 3:11; 22:14
"Because they have ᴿburned incense on
   the mountains,   Is. 57:7; Hos. 2:13
And scorned Me on the hills,
Therefore I will ᴿmeasure their former
   work into their bosom."   Jer. 5:29

8 Thus says the LORD,
"As the new wine is found in the cluster,
And one says, 'Do not destroy it, for
   there is ᴿbenefit in it,'   *blessing*
So I will act on behalf of My servants
In order not to destroy all of them.
9 "And I will bring forth ᴿoffspring from
   Jacob,   Is. 45:19, 25; Jer. 31:36, 37
And an ᴿheir of My mountains from Ju-
   dah;   Is. 49:8; 60:21; Amos 9:11-15
Even My chosen ones shall inherit it,
And My servants shall dwell there.
10 "And ᴿSharon shall be a pasture land for
   flocks,   Is. 33:9; 35:2
And the ᴿvalley of Achor a resting place
   for herds,   Josh. 7:24, 26; Hos. 2:15
For My people who ᴿseek Me.   Is. 51:1
11 "But you who forsake the LORD,
Who forget My holy mountain,
Who set a table for ᴿFortune,
And who fill *cups* with mixed wine for
   ᴿDestiny,   Heb., *Gad* • Heb., *Meni*
12 I will destine you for the ᴿsword,
And all of you shall bow down to the
   ᴿslaughter.   Is. 27:1; 34:5, 6 • Is. 63:6

Because I called, but you ^Rdid not an-
swer;   2 Chr. 36:15, 16; Prov. 1:24
I spoke, but you did not hear.
And you did evil in My sight,
And chose that in which I did not de-
light."

13 Therefore, thus says the Lord GOD,
"Behold, My servants shall ^Reat, but you
shall be ^Rhungry.   Is. 1:19 • Is. 8:21
Behold, My servants shall ^Rdrink, but
you shall be thirsty.   Is. 41:17, 18
Behold, My servants shall ^Rrejoice, but
you shall be put to shame.   Is. 61:7
14"Behold, My servants shall ^Rshout joyfully with a glad heart,   James 5:13
But you shall ^Rcry out with a ^Theavy
heart,   Is. 13:6; Matt. 8:12 • pain of
And you shall wail with a broken spirit.
15"And you will leave your name for a
^Rcurse to My chosen ones,
And the Lord GOD will slay you.
But My servants will be called by ^Ran-
other name.   Jer. 24:9; 25:18 • Is. 62:2
16"Because he who is blessed in the earth
Shall be blessed by the ^RGod of truth;
And he who swears in the earth
Shall ^Rswear by the God of truth;
Because the former troubles are for-
gotten,
And because they are hidden from My
sight!   Ex. 34:6; Ps. 31:5 • Is. 19:18

Glorious Consummation of History

17"For behold, I create ^Rnew heavens and
a new earth;   Is. 66:22; [2 Pet. 3:13]
And the former things shall not be remembered or come to ^Tmind.   heart
18"But be ^Rglad and rejoice forever in what
I create;   Ps. 98; Is. 12:1, 2; 25:9; 35:10
For behold, I create Jerusalem for rejoicing,
And her people for gladness.
19"I will also ^Rrejoice in Jerusalem, and be
glad in My people;
And there will no longer be heard in
her   Is. 62:4, 5; Jer. 32:41
The voice of ^Rweeping and the sound of
crying.   Is. 25:8; 30:19; 35:10; 51:11
20"No longer will there be in it an infant
who lives but a few days,
Or an old man who does ^Rnot live out
his days;   Deut. 4:40; Job 5:26; Ps. 34:12
For the youth will die at the age of one
hundred
And the ^Rone who does not reach the
age of one hundred   Eccl. 8:12, 13
Shall be thought accursed.
21"And they shall ^Rbuild houses and inhabit them;   Is. 32:18; Amos 9:14
They shall also ^Rplant vineyards and eat
their fruit.   Is. 30:23; 37:30; Jer. 31:5
22"They shall not build, and ^Ranother inhabit,   Is. 62:8, 9

They shall not plant, and another eat;
For as the ^Tlifetime of a tree, so shall be
the days of My people,   days
And My chosen ones shall ^Rwear out the
work of their hands.   Ps. 21:4; 91:16
23"They shall ^Rnot labor in vain,   Is. 55:2
Or bear children for calamity;
For they are the ^Toffspring ^R of those
blessed by the LORD,   seed • Is. 61:9
And their descendants with them.
24"It will also come to pass that before
they call, I will ^Ranswer; and while they are
still speaking, I will hear.   Ps. 91:15; Is. 55:6
25"The ^Rwolf and the lamb shall graze together, and the ^Rlion shall eat straw like the
ox; and dust shall be the serpent's food.
They shall do no evil or harm in all My holy
mountain," says the LORD.   Is. 11:6 • Is. 11:7

CHAPTER 66

THUS says the LORD,
"Heaven ^Ris My throne, and the earth is
My footstool.   1 Kin. 8:27; Ps. 11:4
Where then is a ^Rhouse you could build
for Me?   Jer. 7:4; John 4:20, 21
And where is a place that I may rest?
2"For ^RMy hand made all these things,
Thus all these things came into being,"
declares the LORD.   Is. 40:26
"But to this one I will look,
To him who is humble and ^Rcontrite of
spirit, and who ^Rtrembles at My
word.   [Luke 18:13] • Ps. 119:120; Is. 66:5

3"But he who kills an ox is like one who
slays a man;
He who sacrifices a lamb is like the one
who breaks a dog's neck;
He who offers a grain offering is like
one who offers ^Rswine's blood;
He who burns incense is like the one
who blesses an idol.   Is. 65:4
As they have chosen their own ways,
And their soul delights in their abomi-
nations,
4 So I will ^Rchoose their ^Tpunishments,
And I will bring on them what they
dread.   [Prov. 1:31, 32] • ill treatments
Because I called, but ^Rno one answered;
I spoke, but they did not listen.
And they did ^Revil in My sight,
And chose that in which I did not de-
light."   Prov. 1:24 • 2 Kin. 21:2, 6
5 Hear the word of the LORD, you who
^Rtremble at His word: Is. 66:2
"Your brothers who ^Rhate you, who exclude you for My name's sake,
Have said, 'Let the LORD be glorified,
that we may see your joy.'   Is. 60:15
But they will be put to shame.
6"A voice of uproar from the city, a voice
from the temple,
The voice of the LORD who is ^Rrendering
recompense to His enemies.   Joel 3:7

7"Before she travailed,[R]she brought forth;
Before her pain came,[R]she gave birth to
a boy. Is. 37:3; 54:1 • Rev. 12:5
8"Who[R]has heard such a thing? Who has
seen such things?
Can a land be[T]born in one day?
Can a nation be brought forth all at
once? Is. 64:4 • travailed with
As soon as Zion travailed, she also
brought forth her sons.
9"Shall I bring to the point of birth, and
[R]not give delivery?" says the LORD.
"Or shall I who gives delivery shut the
womb?" says your God. Is. 37:3
10"Be joyful with Jerusalem and rejoice
for her, all you who[R]love her;
Be exceedingly glad with her, all you
who mourn over her, Ps. 26:8; 122:6
11 That you may nurse and[R]be satisfied
with her comforting breasts,
That you may suck and be delighted
with her bountiful bosom." Is. 49:23
12 For thus says the LORD, "Behold, I extend peace to her like a river,
And the[R]glory of the nations like an
overflowing stream; Is. 60:5; 61:6
And you shall[T]be nursed, you shall be
[R]carried on the[T]hip and fondled on
the knees. nurse • Is. 60:4 • side
13"As one whom his mother comforts, so I
will[R]comfort you;
And you shall be comforted in Jerusalem." [2 Cor. 1:3, 4]
14 Then you shall[R]see this, and your[R]heart
shall be glad, Is. 33:20 • Zech. 10:7
And your[R]bones shall flourish like the
new grass; Prov. 3:8; Is. 58:11
And the[R]hand of the LORD shall be
made known to His servants,
But He shall be[R]indignant toward His
enemies. Ezra 7:9; 8:31 • Is. 10:5
15 For behold, the LORD will come in fire
And His[R]chariots like the whirlwind,
To render His anger with fury, Is. 5:28
And His rebuke with flames of fire.
16 For the LORD will execute judgment by
[R]fire Is. 30:30; Ezek. 38:22

And by His[R]sword on all flesh,
And those slain by the LORD will be
many. Is. 65:12; Ezek. 38:21
17"Those who sanctify and purify themselves to go to the[R]gardens, Is. 1:29
[T]Following one in the center, After
Who eat[R]swine's flesh, detestable
things, and mice, Lev. 11:7; Is. 65:4
Shall[R]come to an end altogether," declares the LORD. Is. 1:28, 31
18"For I know their works and their
[R]thoughts;[T]the time is coming to gather all
nations and tongues. And they shall come
and see My glory. Is. 59:7; 65:2 • it is coming
19"And I will set a sign among them and
will send survivors from them to the nations: Tarshish, Put, Lud, Meshech, Rosh,
Tubal, and[T]Javan, to the distant coastlands
that have neither heard My fame nor seen
My glory. And they will[R]declare My glory
among the nations. Greece • 1 Chr. 16:24
20"Then they shall[R]bring all your brethren
from all the nations as a grain offering to the
LORD, on horses, in chariots, in litters, on
mules, and on camels, to My holy mountain
Jerusalem," says the LORD, "just as the sons
of Israel bring their grain offering in a clean
vessel to the house of the LORD. Is. 43:6
21"I will also take some of them for[R]priests
and for Levites," says the LORD. Ex. 19:6
22"For just as the[R]new heavens and the
new earth Is. 65:17; Heb. 12:26, 27
Which I make will endure before Me,"
declares the LORD,
"So your[R]offspring and your[R]name will
endure. John 10:27-29 • Is. 56:5
23"And it shall be from[R]new moon to new
moon Is. 1:13, 14; Ezek. 46:1, 6
And from sabbath to sabbath,
All[T]mankind will come to bow down
before Me," says the LORD. flesh
24"Then they shall go forth and look
On the[R]corpses of the men Is. 5:25; 34:3
Who have[A]transgressed against Me.
For their worm shall not die, rebelled
[R]And their fire shall not be quenched;
And they shall be an abhorrence to all
[T]mankind." Is. 1:31; Matt. 3:12 • flesh

THE BOOK OF

JEREMIAH

THE BOOK OF JEREMIAH

The Book of Jeremiah is the prophecy of a man divinely called in his youth from the priest-city of Anathoth. A heartbroken prophet with a heartbreaking message, Jeremiah labors for more than forty years proclaiming a message of doom to the stiff-necked people of Judah. Despised and persecuted by his countrymen, Jeremiah bathes his harsh prophecies in tears of compassion. His broken heart causes him to write a broken book, which is difficult to arrange chronologically or topically. But through his sermons and signs he faithfully declares that surrender to God's will is the only way to escape calamity.

Yirmeyahu or *Yirmeyah* literally means "Yahweh Throws," perhaps in the sense of laying a foundation. It may effectively mean "Yahweh establishes, appoints, or sends." The Greek form of the Hebrew name in the Septuagint is *Hieremias*, and the Latin form is *Jeremias*.

THE AUTHOR OF JEREMIAH

Jeremiah was the son of Hilkiah the priest and lived just over two miles north of Jerusalem in Anathoth. As an object lesson to Judah he was not allowed to marry (16:2). Because of his radical message of God's judgment through the coming Babylonian invasion, he led a life of conflict. He was threatened in his hometown of Anathoth, tried for his life by the priests and prophets of Jerusalem, put in stocks, forced to flee from King Jehoiakim, publicly humiliated by the false prophet Hananiah, and thrown into a cistern.

The book clearly states that Jeremiah is its author (1:1). Jeremiah dictated all his prophecies to his secretary Baruch from the beginning of his ministry until the fourth year of Jehoiakim. After this scroll was destroyed by the king, Jeremiah dictated a more complete edition to Baruch (see 36—38), and later sections were also composed. Only chapter 52 was evidently not written by Jeremiah. This supplement is almost identical to Second Kings 24:18—25:30, and it may have been added by Baruch.

Daniel alludes to Jeremiah's prophecy of the seventy year captivity (25:11-14; 29:10; Dan. 9:2), and Jeremiah's authorship is also confirmed by Ecclesiasticus, Josephus, and the Talmud. The New Testament makes explicit and implicit references to Jeremiah's proph-

ecy: Matthew 2:17, 18 (31:15); Matthew 21:13; Mark 11:17; Luke 19:4 (7:11); Romans 11:27 (31:33); and Hebrews 8:8-13 (31:31-34).

THE TIME OF JEREMIAH

Jeremiah was a contemporary of Zephaniah, Habakkuk, Daniel, and Ezekiel. His ministry stretched from 627 to about 580 B.C. Josiah, Judah's last good king (640–609 B.C.), instituted spiritual reforms when the Book of the Law was discovered in 622 B.C. Jeremiah was on good terms with Josiah and lamented when he was killed in 609 B.C. by Pharaoh Necho of Egypt. By this time, Babylon had already overthrown Nineveh, the capital city of Assyria (612 B.C.). Jehoahaz replaced Josiah as king of Judah, but reigned only three months before he was deposed and taken to Egypt by Necho. Jehoiakim (609–597 B.C.) was Judah's next king, but he reigned as an Egyptian vassal until 605 B.C., when Egypt was defeated by Babylon at Carchemish. Nebuchadnezzar took Palestine and deported key persons such as Daniel to Babylon. Judah's King Jehoiakim was now a Babylonian vassal, but he rejected Jeremiah's warnings in 601 B.C. and rebelled against Babylon. Jehoiachin became Judah's next king in 597 B.C., but was replaced by Zedekiah three months later when Nebuchadnezzar captured Jerusalem and deported Jehoiachin to Babylon. Zedekiah was the last king of Judah; his attempted alliance with Egypt led to Nebuchadnezzar's occupation and overthrow of Jerusalem in 586 B.C.

Thus, there were three stages in Jeremiah's ministry: (1) From 627 to 605 B.C. he prophesied while Judah was threatened by Assyria and Egypt. (2) From 605 to 586 B.C. he proclaimed God's judgment while Judah was threatened and besieged by Babylon. (3) From 586 to about 580 B.C. he ministered in Jerusalem and Egypt after Judah's downfall.

THE CHRIST OF JEREMIAH

The Messiah is clearly seen in 23:1–8 as the coming Shepherd and righteous Branch who "will reign as king and act wisely and do justice and righteousness in the land. In His days Judah will be saved, and Israel will dwell securely; and this is His name by which He will be called, 'The LORD our righteousness' " (23:5, 6). He will bring in the new cove-

nant (31:31–34), which will fulfill God's covenants with Abraham (Gen. 12:1–3; 17:1–8), Moses and the people (Deut. 28—30), and David (2 Sam. 7:1–17).

The curse on Jehoiachin (Jeconiah, Coniah) in 22:28–30 meant that no physical descendant would succeed him to the throne. Matthew 1:1–17 traces the genealogy of Christ through Solomon and Jeconiah to His legal (but not His physical) father, Joseph. However, no son of Joseph could sit upon the throne of David, for he would be under the curse of Jehoiachin. Luke 3:23–38 traces Christ's lineage backward from Mary (His physical parent) through David's other son, Nathan (3:31), thereby avoiding the curse. The righteous Branch will indeed reign on the throne of David.

KEYS TO JEREMIAH

Key Word: Judah's Last Hour—In Jeremiah, God is seen as patient and holy: He delays judgment and appeals to His people to repent before it is too late. As the object lesson at the potter's house demonstrates, a ruined vessel can be repaired while still wet (18:1–4); but once dried, a marred vessel is fit only for the garbage heap (19:10, 11). God's warning is clear: Judah's time for repentance will soon pass. Because they defy God's words and refuse to repent, the Babylonian captivity is inevitable. Jeremiah lists the moral and spiritual causes for their coming catastrophe, but he also proclaims God's gracious promise of hope and restoration. There will always be a remnant, and God will establish a new covenant.

Key Verses: Jeremiah 7:23, 24 and 8:11, 12—"But this is what I commanded them, saying, 'Obey My voice, and I will be your God, and you will be My people; and you will walk in all the way which I command you, that it may be well with you.' Yet they did not obey or incline their ear, but walked in *their own* counsels *and* in the stubbornness of their evil heart, and went backward and not forward" (7:23, 24).

" 'And they heal the brokenness of the daughter of My people superficially, saying, "Peace, peace," but there is no peace. Were they ashamed because of the abomination they had done? They certainly were not ashamed, and they did not know how to blush; therefore they shall fall among those who fall; at the time of their punishment they shall be brought down,' declares the LORD" (8:11, 12).

Key Chapter: Jeremiah 31—Amid all the judgment and condemnation by Jeremiah are the wonderful promises of Jeremiah 31. Even though Judah has broken the covenants of her great King, God will make a new covenant when He will "put My law within them, and on their heart I will write it; and I will be their God, and they shall be My people" (31:33). The Messiah instituted that new covenant with His death and resurrection (cf. Matt. 26:26–29).

SURVEY OF JEREMIAH

Jeremiah is a record of the ministry of one of Judah's greatest prophets during its darkest days. He is called as a prophet during the reign of Josiah, the last of Judah's good kings. But even Josiah's well-intentioned reforms cannot stem the tide of apostasy. The downhill slide of the nation continues virtually unabated through a succession of four godless kings during Jeremiah's ministry. The people wallow in apostasy and idolatry and grow even more treacherous than Israel was before its captivity (3:11). They pervert the

FOCUS	CALL OF JEREMIAH	PROPHECIES TO JUDAH				PROPHECIES TO THE GENTILES	FALL OF JERUSALEM
REFERENCE	1:1———2:1———	26:1———	30:1———	34:1———	46:1———	52:1—	52:34
DIVISION	PROPHETIC COMMISSION	CONDEMNATION OF JUDAH	CONFLICTS OF JEREMIAH	FUTURE RESTORATION OF JERUSALEM	PRESENT FALL OF JERUSALEM	CONDEMNATION OF NINE NATIONS	HISTORIC CONCLUSION
TOPIC	BEFORE THE FALL				THE FALL	AFTER THE FALL	
	CALL	MINISTRY					RETROSPECT
LOCATION	JUDAH					SURROUNDING NATIONS	BABYLON
TIME	c. 627–580 B.C.						

worship of the true God and give themselves over to spiritual and moral decay. Because they refuse to repent or even listen to God's prophet, the divine cure requires radical surgery. Jeremiah proclaims an approaching avalanche of judgment. Babylon will be God's instrument of judgment, and this book refers to that nation 164 times, more references than in the rest of the Bible.

Jeremiah faithfully proclaims the divine condemnation of rebellious Judah for forty years and is rewarded with opposition, beatings, isolations, and imprisonment. His sympathy and sensitivity cause him to grieve over the rebelliousness and imminent doom of his nation. He often desires to resign from his prophetic office because of the harshness of his message and his reception, but he perseveres to Judah's bitter end. He is the weeping prophet (9:1; 13:17)—lonely, rejected, and persecuted.

Although Jeremiah is not easily arranged chronologically or thematically, its basic message is clear: surrender to God's will is the only way to escape calamity. Judgment cannot be halted, but promises of restoration are sprinkled through the book. Its divisions are: the call of Jeremiah (1); the prophecies to Judah (2—45); the prophecies to the Gentiles (46—51); and the fall of Jerusalem (52).

The Call of Jeremiah (1): Jeremiah is called and sanctified before birth to be God's prophet. This introductory chapter surveys the identification, inauguration, and instructions of the prophet.

The Prophecies to Judah (2—45): Jeremiah's message is communicated through a variety of parables, sermons, and object lessons. The prophet's life becomes a daily illustration to Judah, and most of the book's object lessons are found in this section (13:1–14; 14:1–9; 16:1–9; 18:1–8; 19:1–13; 24:1–10; 27:1–11; 32:6–15; 43:8–13). In a series of twelve graphic messages, Jeremiah lists the causes of Judah's coming judgment. The gentile nations are more faithful to their false gods than Judah is to God. They become a false vine by following idols and are without excuse. The people are condemned for their empty profession, disobedience to God's covenant, and spiritual harlotry. God has bound Judah to Himself;

but like a rotten waistband, they have become corrupt and useless. Jeremiah offers a confession for the people, but their sin is too great; the prophet can only lament for them. As a sign of imminent judgment Jeremiah is forbidden to marry and participate in the feasts. Because the nation does not trust God or keep the Sabbath, the land will receive a sabbath rest when they are in captivity. Jerusalem will be invaded and the rulers and people will be deported to Babylon. Restoration will only come under the new Shepherd, the Messiah, the nation's future King. Jeremiah announces the duration of the captivity as seventy years in contrast to the messages of the false prophets who insist it will not happen.

Because of his message (2:25), Jeremiah suffers misery and opposition (26—45). He is rejected by the prophets and priests who call for his death, but he is spared by the elders and officials. In his sign of the yoke he proclaims the unpopular message that Judah must submit to divine discipline. But he assures the nation of restoration and hope under a new covenant (30—33). A remnant will be delivered and there will be a coming time of blessing. Jeremiah's personal experiences and sufferings are the focal point of 34—45 as opposition against the prophet mounts. Since he is no longer allowed in the temple, he sends his assistant Baruch to read his prophetic warnings. His scroll is burned by Jehoiakim, and Jeremiah is imprisoned. After the destruction of the city, Jeremiah is taken to Egypt by fleeing Jews, but he prophesies that Nebuchadnezzar will invade Egypt as well.

The Prophecies to the Gentiles (46—51): These chapters are a series of prophetic oracles against nine nations: Egypt, Philistia, Moab, Ammon, Edom, Damascus (Syria), Arabia, Elam, and Babylon. Only Egypt, Moab, Ammon, and Elam are given a promise of restoration.

The Fall of Jerusalem (52): Jeremiah's forty-year declaration of doom was finally vindicated in an event so significant that it is recorded in detail four times in the Scriptures (2 Kin. 25; 2 Chr. 36; Jer. 39; 52). In this historical supplement, Jerusalem is captured, destroyed, and plundered. The leaders are killed and the captives taken to Babylon.

OUTLINE OF JEREMIAH

Part One: The Call of Jeremiah (1:1–19)

Part Two: The Prophecies to Judah (2:1—45:5)

Part Three: The Prophecies to the Gentiles (46:1—51:64)

Part Four: The Fall of Jerusalem (52:1-34)

CHAPTER 1

Jeremiah's Call

THE words of [R]Jeremiah, the son of Hil-kiah, of the priests who were in [R]Anathoth in the land of Benjamin,   Ezra 1:1 • Josh. 21:18

2 to whom the word of the LORD came in the days of Josiah, the son of Amon, king of Judah, in the thirteenth year of his reign.

3 It came also in the days of [R]Jehoiakim, the son of Josiah, king of Judah, until the end of the eleventh year of Zedekiah, the son of Josiah, king of Judah, until the exile of Jerusalem in the fifth month.   2 Kin. 23:34

4 Now the word of the LORD came to me saying,

5 "Before I [R]formed you in the womb I
    knew you,   Ps. 139:15, 16
And [R]before you were born I conse-
    crated you;   Is. 49:1, 5; [Luke 1:15]
I have [R]appointed you a prophet to the
    nations."   Jer. 1:10; 25:15-26

6 Then [R]I said, "Alas, Lord GOD!   Ex. 4:10
Behold, I do not know how to speak,
Because [R]I am a youth."   1 Kin. 3:7

7 But the LORD said to me,
"Do not say, 'I am a youth,'
[R]Because everywhere I send you, you
    shall go,   Ezek. 2:3, 4
And [R]all that I command you, you shall
    speak.   Num. 22:20; Jer. 1:17

8 "Do [R]not be afraid of them,
For [R]I am with you to deliver you," de-
    clares the LORD.   Ex. 3:12 • Ezek. 2:6

9 Then the LORD stretched out His hand and [R]touched my mouth, and the LORD said to me,   Is. 6:7; Mark 7:33-35
"Behold, I have [R]put My words in your
    mouth.   Deut. 18:18; Is. 51:16

10 "See, I have appointed you this day over
    the nations and over the kingdoms,
[R]To pluck up and to break down,
To destroy and to overthrow,
To build and to plant."   Jer. 18:7-10

Jeremiah's Signs

11 And the word of the LORD came to me saying, "What do you see, Jeremiah?" And I said, "I see a rod of an almond tree."

12 Then the LORD said to me, "You have seen well, for [R]I am [T]watching over My word to perform it."   Jer. 31:28 • Heb., shoqed

13 And the word of the LORD came to me a second time saying, "What [R]do you see?" And I said, "I see a boiling [R]pot, facing away from the north."   Zech. 4:2 • Ezek. 11:3, 7

14 Then the LORD said to me, "Out [R]of the north the evil [T]will break forth on all the in-habitants of the land.   Is. 41:25 • will be opened

15 "For, behold, I am calling [R]all the fam-ilies of the kingdoms of the north," declares the LORD; "and they will come, and they will [R]set each one his throne at the entrance of the gates of Jerusalem, and against all its walls round about, and against all the [R]cities of Judah.   Jer. 25:9 • Is. 22:7 • Jer. 4:16; 9:11

16 "And I will [T]pronounce My judgments on them concerning all their wickedness, whereby they have forsaken Me and have offered sacrifices to other gods, and wor-shiped the works of their own hands.   speak

Jeremiah's Assurance

17 "Now, [R]gird up your loins, and arise, and speak to them all which I command you. [R]Do not be dismayed before them, lest I dismay you before them.   1 Kin. 18:46 • Ezek. 2:6

18 "Now behold, I have made you today as a fortified city, and as a pillar of iron and as walls of bronze against the whole land, to the kings of Judah, to its princes, to its priests and to the people of the land.

19 "And they will fight against you, but they will not overcome you, for I am with you to deliver you," declares the LORD.

CHAPTER 2

Jeremiah's First Sermon:
Judah Sinned Willfully

NOW the word of the LORD came to me saying,

2 "Go and [R]proclaim in the ears of Jerusa-lem, saying, 'Thus says the LORD,   Is. 58:1
"I remember concerning you the devo-
    tion [R]of your youth,
The love of your betrothals,   Hos. 2:15
[R]Your following after Me in the wilder-
    ness,   Deut. 2:7; Jer. 2:6
Through a land not sown.

3 "Israel was [R]holy to the LORD,   Ex. 19:5, 6
The [R]first of His harvest;   James 1:18
[R]All who ate of it became guilty;
Evil came upon them," declares the
    LORD.' "   Is. 41:11; Jer. 30:16; 50:7

4 Hear the word of the LORD, O house of Jacob, and all the families of the house of Israel.

5 Thus says the LORD,
"What [R]injustice did your fathers find in
    Me,   Is. 5:4; Mic. 6:3
That they went far from Me
And walked after [R]emptiness and be-
    came empty?   Jer. 8:19; Rom. 1:21

6 "And they did not say, 'Where is the
    LORD
Who [R]brought us up out of the land of
    Egypt,   Ex. 20:2; Is. 63:11
Who led us through the wilderness,
Through a land of deserts and of pits,
Through a land of drought and of [R]deep
    darkness,   the shadow of death
Through a land that no one crossed
And where no man dwelt?'

7 "And I brought you into the [R]fruitful
    land,   Deut. 8:7-9; 11:10-12

To eat its fruit and its good things.
But you came and ^Rdefiled My land,
And My inheritance you made an
abomination.   Jer. 3:2; 16:18

8"The^Rpriests did not say, 'Where is the
LORD?'   Jer. 10:21
And those who handle the law^Rdid not
know Me;   Jer. 4:22; Mal. 2:7, 8
The ^Trulers also transgressed against
Me,   *shepherds*
And the^Rprophets prophesied by Baal
And walked after^Rthings that did not
profit.   Jer. 23:13 · Jer. 16:19

9"Therefore I will yet^Rcontend with you,"
declares the LORD,
"And with your sons' sons I will con-
tend.   Jer. 2:35; Ezek. 20:35, 36
10"For cross to the coastlands of ^TKittim
and see,   Cyprus and other islands
And send to ^RKedar and observe
closely,   Ps. 120:5; Is. 21:16; Jer. 49:28
And see if there has been such *a thing*
as this!
11"Has a nation changed gods,
When^Rthey were not gods?
But My people have ^Rchanged their
glory   Is. 37:19 · Ps. 106:20; Rom. 1:23
For that which does not profit.
12"Be appalled,^RO heavens, at this,
And shudder, be very desolate," de-
clares the LORD.   Is. 1:2; Jer. 4:23
13"For My people have committed two
evils:
They have forsaken Me,
The^Rfountain of living waters,
To hew for themselves^Rcisterns,
Broken cisterns,   Ps. 36:9 · Jer. 14:3
That can hold no water.

14"Is Israel^Ra slave? Or is he a homeborn
servant?   Jer. 5:19; 17:4
Why has he become a prey?
15"The young lions have roared at him,
They have^Troared loudly.
And they have^Rmade his land a waste;
His cities have been destroyed, without
inhabitant.   *given their voice* · Jer. 4:7
16"Also the^Amen of^RMemphis and Tahpan-
hes   *sons* · Is. 19:13; Jer. 44:1; Hos. 9:6
Have shaved the crown of your head.
17"Have you not^Rdone this to yourself,
By your forsaking the LORD your God,
When He led you in the way?   Jer. 4:18
18"But now what are you doing ^Ron the
road to Egypt,
To drink the waters of the^TNile?
Or what are you doing on the road to
Assyria,   Is. 30:2 · Heb., *Shihor*
To drink the waters of the Euphrates?
19"Your^Rown wickedness will correct you,
And your ^Rapostasies will reprove you;
Know therefore and see that it is evil
and bitter   Is. 3:9; Jer. 4:18 · Hos. 11:7
For you to forsake the LORD your God,

And the dread of Me is not in you," declares the Lord GOD of hosts.

20"For long ago I^Rbroke your yoke
And tore off your bonds;   Lev. 26:13
But you said, 'I will not serve!'
For on every^Rhigh hill   Deut. 12:2; Is. 57:5
And under every green tree
You have lain down as a harlot.
21"Yet I^Rplanted you a choice vine,
A completely faithful seed.
How then have you turned yourself be-
fore Me   Ex. 15:17; Ps. 44:2; 80:8; Is. 5:2
Into the^Rdegenerate shoots of a foreign
vine?   Is. 5:4
22"Although you^Rwash yourself with lye
And use much soap,   Jer. 4:14
The stain of your iniquity is before
Me," declares the Lord GOD.
23"How can you say, 'I am not defiled,
I have not gone after the Baals'?
Look at your way in the^Tvalley!
Know what you have done!   Jer. 7:31
You are a swift young camel ^Rentan-
gling her ways,   Jer. 2:33, 36; 31:22
24 A^Rwild donkey accustomed to the wil-
derness,
That sniffs the wind in her passion.
In *the time of* her^Theat who can turn
her away?   Jer. 14:6 · *occasion*
All who seek her will not become
weary;
In her month they will find her.
25"Keep your feet from being unshod
And your throat from thirst;
But you said, 'It is^Ahopeless!   *desperate*
No! For I have^Rloved strangers,
And after them I will walk.'   Deut. 32:16

26"As the^Rthief is shamed when he is dis-
covered,   Jer. 48:27
So the house of Israel is shamed;
They, their kings, their princes,
And their priests, and their prophets,
27 Who say to a tree, 'You are my father,'
And to a stone, 'You gave me birth.'
For they have turned *their*^Rback to Me,
And not *their* face;   Jer. 18:17; 32:33
But in the ^Rtime of their^Atrouble they
will say,   Judg. 10:10; Is. 26:16 · *evil*
'Arise and save us.'
28"But where are your^Rgods   Deut. 32:37
Which you made for yourself?
Let them arise, if they can save you
In the time of your^Atrouble;   *evil*
For ^R*according to* the number of your
cities   2 Kin. 17:30, 31; Jer. 11:13
Are your gods, O Judah.

29"Why do you contend with Me?
You have^Rall transgressed against Me,"
declares the LORD.   Jer. 5:1; 6:13
30"In^Rvain I have struck your sons;   Is. 1:5
They accepted no chastening.
Your^Rsword has devoured your proph-
ets   Neh. 9:26; Jer. 26:20-24; Acts 7:52
Like a destroying lion.

31"O generation, heed the word of the LORD.

Have I been a wilderness to Israel,
Or a^Rland of thick darkness?   Is. 45:19
Why do My people say, 'We^Rare free to
roam;   Deut. 32:15; Jer. 2:20, 25
We will come no more to Thee'?
32"Can a virgin forget her ornaments,
Or a bride her attire?
Yet My people have^Rforgotten Me
Days without number.   Ps. 106:21
33"How well you prepare your way
To seek love!
Therefore even the wicked women
You have taught your ways.
34"Also on your skirts is found
The lifeblood of the innocent poor;
You did not find them^Rbreaking in.
But in spite of all these things,   Ex. 22:2
35 Yet you said, 'I am innocent;
Surely His anger is turned away from
me.'
Behold, I will^Renter into judgment with
you   Jer. 25:31
Because you say, 'I have not sinned.'
36"Why do you^Rgo around so much
Changing your way?
Also, ^Ryou shall be put to shame by
Egypt   Jer. 2:23; 31:22 • Is. 30:3
As you were put to shame by Assyria.
37"From this *place* also you shall go out
With your hands on your head;
For the LORD has rejected ^Rthose in
whom you trust,   Jer. 37:7-10
And you shall not prosper with them."

CHAPTER 3

GOD says, "If^Ra husband divorces his wife,
And she goes from him,
And belongs to another man,
Will he still return to her?   Deut. 24:1-4
Will not that land be completely^Apol-
luted?   *alienated*
But you^Rare a harlot *with* many^Tlovers;
Yet you ^Rturn to Me," declares the
LORD.   Jer. 2:20 • *companions* • Jer. 4:1
2"Lift up your eyes to the^Rbare heights
and see;   Deut. 12:2; Jer. 2:20; 3:21; 7:29
Where have you not been violated?
By the roads you have^Rsat for them
Like an Arab in the desert,   Ezek. 16:25
And you have^Rpolluted a land
With your harlotry and with your
wickedness.   Jer. 2:7
3"Therefore the^Rshowers have been with-
held,   Lev. 26:19; Jer. 14:3-6
And there has been no spring rain.
Yet you had a^Rharlot's forehead;
You refused to be ashamed.   Jer. 6:15
4"Have you not just now called to Me,
'My Father, Thou art the^Tfriend^Rof my
^Ryouth?   *leader* • Ps. 71:17 • Jer. 2:2
5 'Will^RHe be angry forever?   Ps. 103:9
Will He^Tbe indignant to the end?'

Behold, you have spoken   *keep it*
And have done evil things,
And you have had your way."

Judah Ignores Israel's Example

6 Then the LORD said to me in the days of
Josiah the king, "Have you seen what faithless Israel did? She^Rwent up on every high
hill and under every green tree, and she was
a harlot there.   Jer. 17:2; Ezek. 23:4-10
7"And^RI thought, 'After she has done all
these things, she will return to Me'; but she
did not return, and her^Rtreacherous sister
Judah saw it.   2 Kin. 17:13 • *said* • Jer. 3:11
8"And I saw that for all the adulteries of
faithless Israel, I had sent her away and^Rgiv-
en her a writ of divorce, yet her^Rtreacherous
sister Judah did not fear; but she went and
was a harlot also.   Is. 50:1 • Ezek. 16:46, 47
9"And it came about because of the light-
ness of her harlotry, that she^Rpolluted the
land and committed adultery with ^Rstones
and trees.   Jer. 2:7; 3:2 • Is. 57:6; Jer. 2:27; 10:8
10"And yet in spite of all this her treacherous sister Judah did not return to Me with
all her heart, but rather in^Rdeception," declares the LORD.   Jer. 12:2; Hos. 7:14

Judah Is Called from Backsliding

11 And the LORD said to me, "Faithless^RIs-
rael has proved herself more righteous than
treacherous Judah.   Ezek. 16:51, 52; 23:11
12"Go, and proclaim these words toward
the north and say,
'Return^R faithless Israel,' declares the
LORD;   Jer. 3:14, 22; Ezek. 33:11
'I will not look upon you in anger.
For I am^Rgracious,' declares the LORD;
'I will not be angry forever.   Ps. 86:15
13 'Only acknowledge^Ryour iniquity,
That you have transgressed against the
LORD your God   Deut. 30:1-3; Jer. 3:25
And have scattered your^Tfavors to the
strangers^Runder every green tree,
And you have not obeyed My voice,'
declares the LORD.   *ways* • Deut. 12:2
14 'Return, O faithless sons,' declares the
LORD;
'For I am a^Rmaster to you,   Jer. 31:32
And I will take you one from a city and
two from a family,
And I will bring you to Zion.'
15"Then I will give you^Rshepherds after
My own heart, who will feed you on knowledge and understanding.   Jer. 23:4; 31:10
16"And it shall be in those days when you
are multiplied and increased in the land,"
declares the LORD, "they shall^Rsay no more,
'The ark of the covenant of the LORD.' And it
shall not come to mind, nor shall they remember it, nor shall they miss *it*, nor shall it
be made again.   Is. 65:17

17"At that time they shall call Jerusalem 'The^R Throne of the LORD,' and^R all the nations will be gathered to it, to Jerusalem, for the ^R name of the LORD; nor shall they^R walk anymore after the stubbornness of their evil heart.　　Jer. 17:12 • Jer. 3:19 • Is. 60:9 • Jer. 11:8

18"In^R those days the house of Judah will walk with the house of Israel, and they will come together^R from the land of the north to the^R land that I gave your fathers as an inheritance.　　Is. 11:13 • Jer. 16:15; 31:8 • Amos 9:15

19"Then I said,

'How^T I would set you among^T My sons,
And give you a pleasant land,　　*the*
The most^R beautiful inheritance of the
　nations!'　　Ps. 16:6
And I said, 'You shall call Me,^R My Father,　　Is. 63:16; Jer. 3:4
And not turn away from following Me.'

20"Surely, as a woman treacherously departs from her^A lover,
So you have^R dealt treacherously with
　Me,　　*companion* • Is. 48:8
O house of Israel," declares the LORD.

21 A voice is heard on the^R bare heights,
The weeping *and* the supplications of
　the sons of Israel;
Because they have perverted their
　way,　　Is. 15:2; Jer. 3:2; 7:29
They have^R forgotten the LORD their
　God.　　Is. 17:10; Jer. 2:32; 13:25

22"Return, O faithless sons,
^R I will heal your faithlessness." Jer. 30:17
"Behold, we come to Thee;
For Thou art the LORD our God.

23"Surely,^R the hills are a deception,
A tumult *on* the mountains.　　Jer. 17:2
Surely, in the^R LORD our God
Is the salvation of Israel. Jer. 17:14; 31:7

24"But^R the shameful thing has consumed the labor of our fathers since our youth, their flocks and their herds, their sons and their daughters.　　Hos. 9:10

25"Let us lie down in our^R shame, and let our humiliation cover us; for we have sinned against the LORD our God, we and our fathers,^R since our youth even to this day. And we have not obeyed the voice of the LORD our God."　　Ezra 9:6, 7 • Jer. 22:21

CHAPTER 4

"I F you will^R return, O Israel," declares the
　LORD,　　Jer. 3:22; 15:19; Joel 2:12
"*Then* you should return to Me.
And^R if you will put away your detested
　things from My presence,
And will not waver,　　Jer. 7:3, 7; 35:15
2 And you will ^R swear, 'As the LORD
　lives,'　　Deut. 10:20; Is. 45:23; 65:16
^R In truth, in justice, and in righteousness;　　Is. 48:1
Then the^R nations will bless themselves
　in Him,　　Jer. 3:17; 12:15, 16; [Gal. 3:8]

And^R in Him they will glory."　　Jer. 9:24

3 For thus says the LORD to the men of
　Judah and to Jerusalem,
"Break up your fallow ground,
And do not sow among thorns.
4"Circumcise^R yourselves to the LORD
And remove the foreskins of your
　heart,　　Deut. 10:16; 30:6; Jer. 9:25, 26
Men of Judah and inhabitants of Jerusalem,
Lest My wrath go forth like fire
And burn with none to quench it,
Because of the evil of your deeds."

Judah's Destruction from the North

5 Declare in Judah and proclaim in Jerusalem, and say,
"Blow^R the trumpet in the land;
Cry aloud and say,　　Jer. 6:1; Hos. 8:1
'Assemble^R yourselves, and let us go
Into the fortified cities.'　　Jer. 8:14
6"Lift up a^R standard toward Zion!
Seek refuge, do not stand *still*, Is. 62:10
For I am bringing^R evil from the north,
And great destruction.　　Jer. 1:14, 15
7"A^R lion has gone up from his thicket,
And a^R destroyer of nations has set out;
He has gone out from his place Jer. 5:6
To^R make your land a waste. Ezek. 26:7f.
Your cities will be ruins　　Jer. 2:15
Without inhabitant.
8"For this,^R put on sackcloth,
Lament and wail;　　Is. 22:12; Jer. 6:26
For the^R fierce anger of the LORD
Has not turned back from us."　　Is. 5:25

9"And it shall come about in that day," declares the LORD, "that the heart of the king and the heart of the princes will fail; and the priests will be appalled, and the ^R prophets will be astounded."　　Ezek. 13:9-16

10 Then I said, "Ah, Lord GOD! Surely Thou hast utterly deceived this people and Jerusalem, saying, 'You will have peace'; whereas a sword touches the^A throat."　　*life*

11 In that time it will be said to this people and to Jerusalem, "A scorching wind from the bare heights in the wilderness in the direction of the daughter of My people—not to winnow, and not to cleanse,

12 a wind too strong for^T this—will come ^T at My command; now I will also pronounce judgments against them.　　*these* • *for Me*

13"Behold, he^R goes up like clouds,　Is. 19:1
And his chariots like the whirlwind;
His horses are swifter than eagles.
Woe to us, for^R we are ruined!"　　Is. 3:8

14 Wash your heart from evil, O Jerusalem,
That you may be saved.
How long will your^R wicked thoughts
Lodge within you?　　Prov. 1:22; Jer. 6:19
15 For a voice declares from^R Dan,

And proclaims wickedness from
Mount Ephraim.   Jer. 8:16
16 "Report *it* to the nations, now!
Proclaim over Jerusalem,
'Besiegers come from a ^Rfar country,
And ^Rlift their voices against the cities
of Judah.   Is. 39:3 • Ezek. 21:22
17 'Like watchmen of a field they are
^Ragainst her round about,
Because she has rebelled against Me,'
declares the Lord.   2 Kin. 25:1, 4
18 "Your^Rways and your deeds   Ps. 107:17
Have^Tbrought these things to you.   *done*
This is your evil. How^Rbitter!   Jer. 2:19
How it has touched your heart!"

19 ^RMy^Tsoul, my^Tsoul! I am in anguish! Oh,
my heart!   Is. 15:5; 16:11 • *inward parts*
My heart is pounding in me;
I cannot be silent,
Because^Ayou have heard, O my soul,
The sound of the trumpet,
The alarm of war.   *I, my soul, heard*
20 Disaster on disaster is proclaimed,
For the whole land is devastated;
Suddenly my^Ttents are devastated,
My curtains in an instant.   Jer. 10:20
21 How long must I see the standard,
And hear the sound of the trumpet?
22 "For^RMy people are foolish,
They know Me not;   Jer. 5:4, 21; 10:8
They are stupid children,
And they have no understanding.
They are shrewd to^Rdo evil,   Jer. 9:3
But to do good they do not know."

23 I looked on the earth, and behold, *it*
was^Aformless^Rand void;
And to the heavens, and they had no
light.   *a waste and emptiness* • Gen. 1:2
24 I looked on the mountains, and behold,
they were^Rquaking,   Is. 5:25; Jer. 10:10
And all the hills moved to and fro.
25 I looked, and behold, there was no
man,
And all the^Rbirds of the heavens had
fled.   Jer. 9:10; 12:4; Zeph. 1:3
26 I looked, and behold,^Athe^Rfruitful land
was a wilderness,
And all its cities were pulled down
Before the Lord, before His fierce anger.   *Carmel* • Jer. 9:10

27 For thus says the Lord,
"The^Rwhole land shall be a desolation,
Yet I will^Rnot execute a complete destruction.   Jer. 12:11, 12 • Jer. 46:28
28 "For this the^Rearth shall mourn,   Hos. 4:3
And the^Rheavens above be dark,
Because I have ^Rspoken, I have purposed,   Joel 2:30, 31 • Jer. 23:20; 30:24
And I will not^Tchange My mind, nor
will I turn from it."   *be sorry*
29 At the sound of the horseman and
bowman^Revery city flees;   2 Kin. 25:4

They ^Rgo into the thickets and climb
among the rocks;   Is. 2:19-21
^REvery city is forsaken,   Jer. 4:7
And no man dwells in them.
30 And you, O desolate one,^Rwhat will you
do?   Is. 10:3; 20:6; Jer. 13:21
Although you dress in scarlet,
Although you decorate *yourself with*
ornaments of gold,
Although you^Renlarge your eyes with
paint,   2 Kin. 9:30; Ezek. 23:40
In vain you make yourself beautiful;
Your lovers^Rdespise you;
They seek your life.   Ezek. 23:9, 10, 22
31 For I heard a^Tcry as of a woman in la-
bor,   *sound*
The anguish as of one giving birth to
her first child,
The cry of the daughter of Zion^Rgasp-
ing for breath,   Is. 42:14
Stretching out her^Thands, *saying,*
"Ah, woe is me, for^TI faint before mur-
derers."   *palms* • *my soul faints*

CHAPTER 5

Judah's Sins

"R OAM^Rto and fro through the streets of
Jerusalem,   2 Chr. 16:9; Dan. 12:4
And look now, and take note.
And seek in her open squares,
If you can^Rfind a man,   Ezek. 22:30
^RIf there is one who does justice, who
seeks truth,   Gen. 18:26, 32
Then I will pardon her.
2 "And ^Ralthough they say, 'As the Lord
lives,'   Is. 48:1; Titus 1:16
Surely they swear falsely."
3 O Lord, do not^RThine eyes look for
^Ttruth?   [2 Chr. 16:9] • *faithfulness*
Thou hast^Rsmitten them,   Is. 1:5; 9:13
But they did not^Aweaken;   *become sick*
Thou hast consumed them,
But they^Rrefused to take correction.
They have made their faces harder
than rock;   Jer. 7:28; 8:5; Zeph. 3:2
They have refused to repent.

4 Then I said, "They are only the poor,
They are foolish;
For they^Rdo not know the way of the
Lord   Is. 27:11; Jer. 8:7; Hos. 4:6
Or the ordinance of their God.
5 "I will go to the great
And will speak to them,
For they know the way of the Lord,
And the ordinance of their God."
But they too, with one accord, have
^Rbroken the yoke
And burst the bonds.   Ex. 32:25; Ps. 2:3
6 Therefore^Ra lion from the forest shall
slay them,   Jer. 4:7
A ^Rwolf of the deserts shall destroy
them,   Ezek. 22:27; Hab. 1:8; Zeph. 3:3

A^Rleopard is watching their cities.
Everyone who goes out of them shall
be torn in pieces,   Hos. 13:7
Because their transgressions are many,
Their apostasies are numerous.

7 "Why should I pardon you?
Your sons have forsaken Me
And^Rsworn by those who are not gods.
When I had fed them to the full,
They committed adultery   Josh. 23:7
And trooped to the harlot's house.

8 "They were well-fed lusty horses,
Each one neighing after his^Rneighbor's
wife.   Jer. 13:27; 29:23; Ezek. 22:11

9 "Shall I not punish ᵗthese *people*," declares the LORD,   *for these things*
"And on a nation such as this
^RShall I not avenge Myself?   Jer. 9:9

10 "Go up through her vine rows and de-
stroy,
But do not execute a complete destruc-
tion;
Strip away her branches,
For they are not the LORD's.

11 "For the^Rhouse of Israel and the house of
Judah   Jer. 3:6, 7, 20
Have dealt very treacherously with
Me," declares the LORD.

12 They have^Rlied about the LORD
And said, "¹Not He;   2 Chr. 36:16
Misfortune will not come on us;
And we will not see sword or famine.

13 "And the^Rprophets are *as* wind,   Job 8:2
And the word is not in them.
Thus it will be done to them!"

14 Therefore, thus says the LORD, the God
of hosts,
"Because you have spoken this word,
Behold, I am^Rmaking My words in your
mouth fire   Is. 24:6; 1:9; 23:29
And this people wood, and it will consume them.

15 "Behold, I am^Rbringing a nation against
you from afar, O house of Israel,"
declares the LORD.   Deut. 28:49
"It is an enduring nation,
It is an ancient nation,
A nation whose^Rlanguage you do not
know,   Is. 28:11
Nor can you understand what they say.

16 "Their^Rquiver is like an open grave,
All of them are mighty men.   Is. 5:28

17 "And they will^Rdevour your harvest and
your food;   Lev. 26:16; Deut. 28:31, 33
They will devour your sons and your
daughters;
They will devour your flocks and your
herds;
They will devour your^Rvines and your
fig trees;   Jer. 8:13
They will demolish with the sword
your^Rfortified cities in which you
trust.   Hos. 8:14

18 "Yet even in those days," declares the
LORD, "I will not make you a complete destruction.

19 "And it shall come about whenᵗthey say,
'Why has the LORD our God done all these
things to us?' then you shall say to them, 'As
you have forsaken Me and served foreign
gods in your land, so you shall serve strangers in a land that is not yours.'   *you*

20 "Declare this in the house of Jacob
And proclaim it in Judah, saying,

21 'Hear this, O foolish and ᵗsenseless peo-
ple,   *without heart*
Who have^Reyes, but see not;   Is. 6:9
Who have ears, but hear not.

22 'Do you not^Rfear Me?' declares the
LORD.   Deut. 28:58; Ps. 119:120; Jer. 2:19
'Do you not tremble in My presence?
For I have^Rplaced the sand as a bound-
ary for the sea,   Job 38:8-11
An eternal decree, so it cannot cross
over it.
Though the waves toss, yet they can-
not prevail;
Though they roar, yet they cannot
cross over it.

23 'But this people has a^Rstubborn and rebellious heart;   Deut. 21:18; Ps. 78:8
They have turned aside and departed.

24 'They do not say in their heart,
"Let us now fear the LORD our God,
Who^Rgives rain in its season,
Both the autumn rain and the spring
rain,   Ps. 147:8; Jer. 3:3; [Matt. 5:45]
Who keeps for us
The appointed weeks of the harvest."

25 'Your ^Riniquities have turned these
away,
And your sins have withheld good
from you.   Jer. 2:17; 4:18

26 'For wicked men are found among My
people,
They^Rwatch like fowlers lying in wait;
They set a trap,   Ps. 10:9; Prov. 1:11
They catch men.

27 'Like a cage full of birds,
So their houses are full of^Rdeceit;
Therefore they have become great and
rich.   Jer. 9:6

28 'They are^Rfat, they are sleek,   Deut. 32:15
They also ²excel in deeds of wicked-
ness;
They do not plead the cause,
The cause of the ᵗorphan,^R that they may
prosper;   *fatherless* • Is. 1:23; Jer. 7:6
And they do not ᵗdefend the rights of
the poor.   *judge*

29 'Shall^R I not punish these *people*?' de-
clares the LORD,   Jer. 5:9; Mal. 3:5
'On a nation such as this
Shall I not avenge Myself?'

30 "An appalling and^Rhorrible thing
Has happened in the land: Jer. 23:14

31 The prophets prophesy falsely,
And the priests rule ᵗon their *own* authority;   *over their own hands*

---

¹ Lit., *He is not*   ² Or, *overlook deeds*

And My people[R]love it so!   Mic. 2:11
But what will you do at the end of it?

CHAPTER 6

Jerusalem to Be Destroyed

"F LEE for safety, O sons of[R]Benjamin,
From the midst of Jerusalem!
Now blow a trumpet in Tekoa,
And raise a signal over [3]Beth-hacce-
    rem;   Josh. 18:28
For evil looks down from the[R]north,
And a great destruction.   Jer. 1:14; 4:6
2 "The comely and dainty one,[T]the daugh-
    ter of Zion, I will cut off.   Jer. 4:31
3 "Shepherds[R] and their flocks will come
    to her,   Jer. 12:10
They will pitch *their* tents around her,
They will pasture each in his place.
4 "Prepare[T]war against her;   *Sanctify*
Arise, and let us[T]attack at[R]noon.
Woe to us, for the day declines,
For the shadows of the evening
    lengthen!   *go up* • Jer. 15:8; Zeph. 2:4
5 "Arise, and let us[T]attack by night   *go up*
And[R]destroy her palaces!"   Is. 32:14
6 For thus says the LORD of hosts,
"Cut[R]down her trees,   Deut. 20:19, 20
And cast up a[R]siege against Jerusalem.
This is the city to be punished,
In whose midst there is only [R]oppres-
    sion.   Jer. 32:24; 33:4 • Jer. 22:17
7 "As a well[T]keeps its waters fresh,
So she[T]keeps fresh her wickedness.
[R]Violence and destruction are heard in
    her;   *keeps cold* • Jer. 20:8
[R]Sickness and wounds are ever before
    Me.   Jer. 30:12, 13
8 "Be[R]warned, O Jerusalem,   Jer. 7:28
Lest I[R]be alienated from you;
Lest I make you a desolation,
A land not inhabited."   Ezek. 23:18

9 Thus says the LORD of hosts,
"They will[R]thoroughly glean as the vine
    the remnant of Israel;
Pass your hand again like a grape gath-
    erer   Jer. 16:16; 49:9; Obad. 5, 6
Over the branches."
10 To whom shall I speak and give warn-
    ing,
That they may hear?
Behold, their[R]ears are closed,   Jer. 5:21
And they cannot listen.
Behold,[R]the word of the LORD has be-
    come a reproach to them;
They have no delight in it.   Jer. 20:8
11 But I am[R]full of the wrath of the LORD:
I am weary with holding *it* in.   Mic. 3:8
"Pour[R]*it* out on the children in the street,
And on the[T]gathering of young men to-
    gether;   Jer. 7:20; 9:21 • *council*
For both husband and wife shall be
    taken,
The aged and the very old.

12 "And their[R]houses shall be turned over
    to others,   Deut. 28:30; Jer. 8:10
Their fields and their wives together;
For I will[R]stretch out My hand
Against the inhabitants of the land,"
    declares the LORD.   Jer. 15:6
13 "For[R]from the least of them even to the
    greatest of them,   Jer. 8:10
Everyone is[R]greedy for gain,
And from the prophet even to the
    priest   Is. 56:11; 57:17; Jer. 8:10; 22:17
Everyone[A]deals falsely.   *make lies*
14 "And they have[R]healed the brokenness
    of My people superficially,
Saying, 'Peace, peace,'
But there is no peace.   Ezek. 13:10
15 "Were they [R]ashamed because of the
    abomination they have done?
They were not even ashamed at all;
They did not even know how to blush.
Therefore they shall fall among those
    who fall;
At the time that I punish them,
They shall be cast down," says the
    LORD.   Jer. 3:3; 8:12

16 Thus says the LORD,
"Stand by the ways and see and ask for
    the[R]ancient paths,   Is. 8:20; Jer. 12:16
Where the good way is, and walk in it;
And you shall find rest for your souls.
But they said, 'We will not walk *in it*.'
17 "And I set watchmen over you, *saying*,
'Listen to the sound of the trumpet!'
But they said, 'We will not listen.'
18 "Therefore hear, O nations,
And know, O congregation, what is
    among them.
19 "Hear, [R] O earth: behold, I am bringing
    disaster on this people,   Jer. 19:3, 15
The[R]fruit of their[A]plans,
Because they have not listened to My
    words,   Prov. 1:31 • *devices*
And as for My law, they have[R]rejected
    it also.   Jer. 8:9
20 "For what purpose does [R]frankincense
    come to Me from Sheba,   Is. 60:6
And the [T]sweet[R] cane from a distant
    land?   *good* • Ex. 30:23
[R]Your burnt offerings are not accept-
    able,   Ps. 40:6; Amos 5:22
And your sacrifices are not pleasing to
    Me."
21 Therefore, thus says the LORD,
"Behold,[R]I am[T]laying stumbling blocks
    before this people.   Is. 8:14 • *giving*
And they will stumble against them,
[R]Fathers and sons together;   Is. 9:14-17
Neighbor and friend will perish."

22 Thus says the LORD,
"Behold, [R]a people is coming from the
    north land,   Jer. 1:15; 10:22; 50:41-43

[3] I.e., house of the vineyard

And a great nation will be aroused
from the remote parts of the earth.
23 "They seize[R]bow and spear;   Is. 13:18
They are cruel and have no mercy;
Their voice[R]roars like the sea,
And they ride on horses,   Is. 5:30
Arrayed as a man for the battle
Against you, O daughter of Zion!"
24 We have[R]heard the report of it;
Our hands are limp. Is. 28:19; Jer. 4:19-21
[R]Anguish has seized us   Jer. 4:31; 13:21
Pain as of a woman in childbirth.
25 [R]Do not go out into the field,   Jer. 14:18
And[R]do not walk on the road,
For the enemy has a sword,   Judg. 5:6
[R]Terror is on every side.   Jer. 20:10; 46:5
26 O daughter of my people,[R]put on sack-
cloth   Jer. 4:8
And[R]roll in ashes;   Jer. 25:34; Mic. 1:10
[R]Mourn as for an only son,
A lamentation most bitter.   [Zech. 12:10]
For suddenly the destroyer
Will come upon us.

27 "I have [R]made you an assayer *and* a
tester among My people,
That you may know and assay their
way."   Jer. 1:18; 15:20
28 All of them are stubbornly rebellious,
[R]Going about as a talebearer.   Jer. 9:4
They are[R]bronze and iron;   Ezek. 22:18
They, all of them, are corrupt.
29 The bellows blow fiercely,
The lead is consumed by the fire;
In vain the refining goes on,
But the wicked are not separated.
30 [R]They call them rejected silver,   Is. 1:22
Because the LORD has rejected them.

CHAPTER 7

Judah's Sin of External Religion

THE word that came to Jeremiah from the
LORD, saying,
2 "Stand in the gate of the LORD's house
and proclaim there this word, and say, 'Hear
the word of the LORD, all you of Judah, who
enter by these gates to worship the LORD!' "
3 Thus says the LORD of hosts, the God
of Israel, "Amend your ways and your
deeds, and I will let you dwell in this place.
4 "Do not trust in deceptive words, saying, 'This is the temple of the LORD, the temple of the LORD, the temple of the LORD.'
5 "For[R]if you truly amend your ways and
your deeds, if you truly practice justice between a man and his neighbor,   Is. 1:19
6 *if* you do not oppress the alien, the[A]or-
phan, or the widow, and do not shed innocent blood in this place, nor[R]walk after other
gods to your own ruin,   *fatherless* • Jer. 13:10
7 then I will let you[R]dwell in this place, in
the[R]land that I gave to your fathers forever
and ever.   Deut. 4:40 • Jer. 3:18

8 "Behold, you are trusting in[R]deceptive
words to no avail.   Jer. 7:4; 28:15
9 "Will you steal, murder, and commit
adultery, and swear falsely, and[A]offer sacrifices to Baal, and walk after[R]other gods that
you have not known,   *burn incense* • Ex. 20:3
10 then[R]come and stand before Me in[R]this
house, which is called by My name, and say,
'We are delivered!'—that you may do all
these abominations?   Ezek. 23:39 • Jer. 32:34
11 "Has[R]this house, which is called by My
name, become a den of robbers in your
sight? Behold,[R]I, even I, have seen *it,*" declares the LORD.   Is. 56:7 • Jer. 29:23
12 "But go now to My place which was in
[R]Shiloh, where I made My name dwell at the
first, and see what I did to it because of the
wickedness of My people Israel.   Judg. 18:31
13 "And now, because you have done all
these things," declares the LORD, "and I
spoke to you,[R]rising up early and[R]speaking,
but you did not hear, and I called you but
you did not answer,   Jer. 7:25 • Jer. 35:17
14 therefore, I will do to the[R]house which
is called by My name, in which you trust,
and to the place which I gave you and your
fathers, as I did to Shiloh.   Deut. 12:5
15 "And I will cast you out of My sight, as I
have cast out all your brothers, all the[T]off-
spring of[R]Ephraim.   *seed* • Ps. 78:67; Hos. 7:13
16 "As for you,[R]do not pray for this people,
and do not lift up cry or prayer for them,
and do not intercede with Me; for I do not
hear you.   Ex. 32:10; Deut. 9:14; Jer. 11:14
17 "Do you not see what they are doing in
the cities of Judah and in the streets of Jerusalem?
18 "The [T]children gather wood, and the fathers kindle the fire, and the women knead
dough to make cakes for the queen of
heaven; and *they*[R]pour out libations to other
gods in order to spite Me.   *sons* • Jer. 19:13
19 "Do[R]they spite Me?" declares the LORD.
"Is it not themselves *they spite,* to[T]their own
[R]shame?"   Job 35:6 • *their faces* • Jer. 9:19
20 Therefore thus says the Lord GOD, "Be-
hold, My [R]anger and My wrath will be
poured out on this place, on man and on
beast and on the[T]trees of the field and on the
fruit of the ground; and it will burn and not
be quenched."   Is. 42:25; Jer. 6:11, 12 • Jer. 8:13
21 Thus says the LORD of hosts, the God
of Israel, "Add your[R]burnt offerings to your
sacrifices and[R]eat flesh.   Is. 1:11 • Ezek. 33:25
22 "For I did not[R]speak to your fathers, or
command them in the day that I brought
them out of the land of Egypt, concerning
burnt offerings and sacrifices.   1 Sam. 15:22
23 "But this is what I commanded them,
saying, 'Obey[R]My voice, and I will be your
God, and you will be My people; and you
will walk in all the way which I command
you, that it may be well with you.'   Ex. 15:26
24 "Yet they did not obey or incline their
ear, but walked in *their own* counsels *and* in
the stubbornness of their evil heart, and
[T]went backward and not forward.   *they were*

25"Since the day that your fathers came out of the land of Egypt until this day, I have ᴿsent you all My servants the prophets, daily rising early and sending *them*.   2 Chr. 36:15

26"Yet they did not listen to Me or incline their ear, but ᴿstiffened their neck; they did evil more than their fathers.   Jer. 17:23; 19:15

27"And you shall ᴿspeak all these words to them, but they will not listen to you; and you shall call to them, but they willᴿnot answer you.   Jer. 1:7; 26:2; Ezek. 2:7 • Zech. 7:13

28"And you shall say to them, 'This is the nation that ᴿdid not obey the voice of the LORD their God or accept correction;ᵀtruthᴿ has perished and has been cut off from their mouth.   Jer. 6:17 • *faithfulness* • Is. 59:14, 15

29 'Cut offᵀyour hair and cast *it* away,
And ᴿtake up a lamentation on the bare
   heights;   *your crown* • Jer. 3:21
For the LORD hasᴿrejected and forsaken
The generation of His wrath.'   Jer. 6:30

30"For the sons of Judah have done that which is evil in My sight," declares the LORD, "they haveᴿset their detestable things in the house which is called by My name, to defile it.   Jer. 32:34, 35; Ezek. 7:20; Dan. 9:27

31"And they have built the high places of Topheth, which is in the valley of the son of Hinnom, to burn their sons and their daughters in the fire, which I did not command, and it did not come into Myᵀmind.   *heart*

32"Therefore, behold, days are coming," declares the LORD, "when it will no more be called Topheth, or the valley of the son of Hinnom, but the valley of the Slaughter; for they will bury in Tophethᴬbecause there is no *other* place.   *until there is no place left*

33"And theᴿdead bodies of this people will be food for the birds of the sky, and for the beasts of the earth; and no one will frighten *them away*.   Deut. 28:26; Ps. 79:2; Jer. 12:9; 19:7

34"Then I will make to ᴿcease from the cities of Judah and from the streets of Jerusalem the voice of joy and the voice of gladness, the voice of the bridegroom and the voice of the bride; for theᴿland will become a ruin.   Is. 24:7, 8; Jer. 16:9 • Lev. 26:33; Is. 1:7

CHAPTER 8

"Aᴛ that time," declares the LORD, "they willᴿbring out the bones of the kings of Judah, and the bones of its princes, and the bones of the priests, and the bones of the prophets, and the bones of the inhabitants of Jerusalem from their graves.   Ezek. 6:5

2"And they will spread them out to the sun, the moon, and to all theᴿhost of heaven, which they have loved, and which they have served, and which they have gone after, and which they have sought, and which they have worshiped. They will not be gathered ᴿor buried;ᴿthey will be as dung on the face of the ground.   Jer. 19:13 • Jer. 22:19 • Ps. 83:10

3"And ᴿdeath will be chosen rather than life by all the remnant that remains of this evil family, that remains in all theᴿplaces to which I have driven them," declares the LORD of hosts.   Job 3:21, 22 • Deut. 30:1, 4

Judah's Judgment Imminent

4"And you shall say to them, 'Thus says the LORD,
"Do *men* fall and not get up again?
Does one turn away and not repent?
5"Why then has this people, Jerusalem,
Turned away in continual apostasy?
Theyᴿhold fast to deceit,   Jer. 5:27; 9:6
Theyᴿrefuse to return.   Jer. 5:3
6"Iᵀhave listened and heard,   Ps. 14:2
They have spoken what is not right;
ᴿNo man repented of his wickedness,
Saying, 'What have I done?'   Mic. 7:2
Everyone turned to his course,
Like a horse charging into the battle.
7"Even the stork in the sky
ᴿKnows her seasons;   Prov. 6:6-8; Is. 1:3
And theᴿturtledove and the swift and
   the thrush   Song 2:12
Observe the time of their migration;
ButᴿMy people do not know
The ordinance of the LORD.   Jer. 5:4

8"Howᴿcan you say, 'We are wise,
And the law of the LORD is with us'?
But behold, the lying pen of the scribes
Has made *it* into a lie.   Job 5:12, 13
9"The wise men areᴿput to shame,
They are dismayed and caught;
Behold, they haveᴿrejected the word of
   the LORD,
And what kind of wisdom do they
   have?   Is. 19:11; Jer. 6:15 • Jer. 6:19
10"Therefore I willᴿgive their wives to others,   Deut. 28:30; Jer. 6:12, 13; 38:22f.
Their fields toᵀnew owners;
Because from the least even to the
   greatest   *possessing ones*
Everyone isᴿgreedy for gain;
From the prophet even to the priest
Everyone practices deceit.   Is. 56:11
11"And they ᴿheal the brokenness of the
   daughter of My people superfi-
   cially,   Jer. 6:14; 14:13, 14; Lam. 2:14
Saying, 'Peace, peace,'
But there is no peace.
12"Were they ᴿashamed because of the
   abomination they had done?   Is. 3:9
They certainly were not ashamed,
And they did not know how to blush;
Therefore they shallᴿfall among those
   who fall;   Is. 9:14; Jer. 6:21; Hos. 4:5
At theᴿtime of their punishment they
   shall be brought down,"
Declares the LORD.   Deut. 32:35; Jer. 10:15

13"I will ᴿsurely snatch them away," de-
   clares the LORD;   Ezek. 22:20, 21
"There will beᴿno grapes on the vine,
Andᴿno figs on the fig tree,
And the leaf shall wither;
And what I have given them shall pass
   away.' "   Jer. 5:17; 7:20 • Luke 13:6

14 Why are we sitting still?
ᴿAssemble yourselves, and let usᴿgo into the fortified cities,
And let us perish there,
Because the Lᴏʀᴅ our God has doomed us   Jer. 4:5 • 2 Sam. 20:6; Jer. 35:11
And given us poisoned water to drink,
For we have sinned against the Lᴏʀᴅ.
15 Weᴿwaited for peace, but no good came;
For a time of healing, but behold, terror!   Jer. 8:11; 14:19
16 FromᴿDan is heard the snorting of his horses;   Judg. 18:29; Jer. 4:15
At the sound of the neighing of hisᴿstallions   Judg. 5:22
The whole land quakes;
For they come andᴿdevour the land and its fulness,   Jer. 3:24; 10:25
The city and its inhabitants.
17"For behold, I am ᴿsending serpents against you,   Num. 21:6; Deut. 32:24
Adders, for which there isᴿno charm,
And they will bite you," declares the Lᴏʀᴅ.   Ps. 58:4, 5

Jeremiah's Lament for Judah

18 Myᴿsorrow is beyond healing,   Is. 22:4
Myᴿheart is faint *within me!*   Lam. 5:17
19 Behold, listen! The cry of the daughter of my people from aᴿdistant land:
"Is the Lᴏʀᴅ not in Zion? Is her King not within her?"   Is. 13:5; 39:3; Jer. 4:16
"Why have they provoked Me with their graven images, with foreign idols?"
20"Harvest is past, summer is ended,
And we are not saved."
21 For theᴿbrokenness of the daughter of my people I am broken;   Jer. 4:19
I mourn, dismay has taken hold of me.
22 Is there noᴿbalm in Gilead?   Gen. 37:25
Is there no physician there?
ᴿWhy then has not theᴬhealth of the daughter of my people ᵀbeen restored?   Jer. 14:19 • *healing* • *gone up*

CHAPTER 9

Oᴴ,ᴿ that my head were waters,
And my eyes a fountain of tears,
That I might weep day and night
For the slain of theᴿdaughter of my people!   Is. 22:4 • Jer. 6:26; 8:21, 22
2 ᴿO that I had in the desert
A wayfarers' lodging place;
That I might leave my people,
And go from them!   Ps. 55:6, 7; 120:5, 6
For all of them areᴿadulterers,   Hos. 4:2
An assembly of treacherous men.
3"And theyᴿbend their tongue *like* their bow;   Ps. 64:3; Is. 59:4; Jer. 9:8
Lies and not truth prevail in the land;
For theyᴿproceed from evil to evil,
And theyᴿdo not know Me," declares the Lᴏʀᴅ.   Jer. 4:22 • Judg. 2:10

4"Let everyoneᴿbe on guard against his neighbor,   Ps. 12:2; Prov. 26:24, 25
Andᴿdo not trust any brother;   Jer. 12:6
Because every brother dealsᵀcraftily,
And every neighbor goes about as a slanderer.   like Jacob (a play on words)
5"And everyoneᴿdeceives his neighbor,
And does not speak the truth,
They have taught their tongue to speak lies;
Theyᴿweary themselves committing iniquity.   Mic. 6:12 • Jer. 12:13; 51:58, 64
6"Yourᴿdwelling is in the midst of deceit;
Through deceit they refuse to know Me," declares the Lᴏʀᴅ.   Ps. 120:5, 6

7 Therefore thus says the Lᴏʀᴅ of hosts,
"Behold, I will refine them and ᴿassay them;   Is. 1:25; Jer. 6:27; Mal. 3:3
Forᴿwhat *else* can I do, because of the daughter of My people?   Hos. 11:8
8"Theirᴿtongue is a deadly arrow;
It speaks deceit;
With his mouth one ᴿspeaks peace to his neighbor,
But inwardly he ᴿsets an ambush for him.   Jer. 9:3 • Ps. 28:3 • Jer. 5:26

Judah's Judgment Is Described

9"Shallᴿ I not punish them for these things?" declares the Lᴏʀᴅ.
"On a nation such as this
Shall I not avenge Myself?   Jer. 5:9, 29

10"For the ᴿmountains I will take up a weeping and wailing,   Jer. 4:24; 7:29
And for the pastures of theᴿwilderness a dirge,   Jer. 4:26; Hos. 4:3
Because they areᴿlaid waste, so that no one passes through,
And the lowing of the cattle is not heard;   Ezek. 14:15; 29:11; 33:28
Both theᴿbirds of the sky and the beasts have fled; they are gone.   Jer. 4:25
11"And I will make Jerusalem aᴿheap of ruins,   Is. 25:2; Jer. 51:37
A haunt ofᴿjackals;   Is. 13:22; 34:13
And I will make the cities of Judah a desolation, without inhabitant."
12 Who is theᴿwise man that may understand this? And *who is* he to whom ᴿthe mouth of the Lᴏʀᴅ has spoken, that he may declare it? ᴿWhy is the land ruined, laid waste like a desert, so that no one passes through?   Ps. 107:43 • Jer. 9:20 • Jer. 23:10
13 And the Lᴏʀᴅ said, "Because they have ᴿforsaken My law which I set before them, and have not obeyed My voice nor walked according to it,   2 Chr. 7:19; Ps. 89:30; Jer. 5:19
14 but have walked after the stubbornness of their heart and after theᴿBaals, as their fathers taught them,"   Jer. 2:8, 23; 23:27
15 therefore thus says the Lᴏʀᴅ of hosts, the God of Israel, "behold, I will feed them,

this people, with wormwood and give them [R]poisoned water to drink. Lam. 3:15

16"And I will scatter them among the nations, whom neither they nor their fathers have known; and I will send the sword after them until I have annihilated them."

17 Thus says the LORD of hosts,
"Consider and call for the [R]mourning women, that they may come;
And send for the wailing women, that they may come! 2 Chr. 35:25

18"And let them make haste, and take up a wailing for us,
That our[R]eyes may shed tears, Is. 22:4
And our eyelids flow with water.

19"For a voice of[R]wailing is heard from Zion, Jer. 7:29; Ezek. 7:16-18
'How[R]are we ruined! Deut. 28:29; Jer. 4:13
We are put to great shame,
For we have[R]left the land,
Because they have cast down our dwellings.' " Jer. 7:15; 15:1

20 Now hear the word of the LORD, O you [R]women, Is. 32:9
And let your ear receive the word of His mouth;
Teach your daughters wailing,
And everyone her neighbor a dirge.

21 For [R]death has come up through our windows; 2 Chr. 36:17; Jer. 15:7; 18:21
It has entered our palaces
To cut off the children from the streets,
The young men from the town squares.

22 Speak, "Thus declares the LORD,
'The corpses of men will fall[R]like dung on the open field, Ps. 83:10; Is. 5:25
And like the sheaf after the reaper,
But no one will gather them.' "

23 Thus says the LORD, "Let[R]not a wise man boast of his wisdom, and let not the mighty man boast of his might, let not a rich man boast of his riches; [Eccl. 9:11]; Is. 47:10

24 but let him who boasts boast of this, that he understands and knows Me, that I am the LORD who exercises lovingkindness, justice, and righteousness on earth; for I delight in these things," declares the LORD.

25"Behold, the days are coming," declares the LORD, "that I will punish all who are circumcised and yet uncircumcised—

26 Egypt, and Judah, and Edom, and the sons of Ammon, and Moab, and[R]all those inhabiting the desert who clip the hair on their temples; for all the nations are uncircumcised, and all the house of Israel are[R]uncircumcised of heart." Jer. 25:23 · Lev. 26:41

CHAPTER 10

Judah's Futile Idolatry

HEAR the word which the LORD speaks to you, O house of Israel.

2 Thus says the LORD,
"Do[R]not learn the way of the nations,
And do not be terrified by the signs of the heavens
Although the nations are terrified by them; [Lev. 18:3; 20:23; Deut. 12:30]

3 For the customs of the peoples are[T]delusion; *vanity*
Because[R]it is wood cut from the forest,
The work of the hands of a craftsman with a cutting tool. Is. 44:9-20

4"They[R]decorate *it* with silver and with gold;
They[R]fasten it with nails and with hammers Is. 40:19 · Is. 40:20; 41:7
So that it will not totter.

5"Like a scarecrow in a cucumber field are they,
And they[R]cannot speak; Ps. 115:5; Is. 46:7
They must be[R]carried,
Because they cannot walk!
Do not fear them, Ps. 115:7; Is. 46:1, 7
For they[R]can do no harm,
Nor can they do any good." Is. 41:23, 24

6 [R]There is none like Thee, O LORD;
Thou art[R]great, and great is Thy name in might. Ex. 15:11 · Ps. 48:1

7 [R]Who would not fear Thee, O[R]King of the nations? Rev. 15:4 · [Ps. 22:28]
Indeed it is Thy due!
For among all the[R]wise men of the nations, Dan. 2:27, 28; [1 Cor. 1:19, 20]
And in all their kingdoms,
There is none like Thee.

8 But they are altogether[R]stupid and foolish Jer. 4:22; 5:4; 10:8
In their discipline of [T]delusion—[T]their idol is wood! *vanities, or idols · it is*

9 Beaten silver is brought from[R]Tarshish,
And gold from Uphaz, Ps. 72:10; Is. 23:6
The work of a craftsman and of the hands of a goldsmith;
Violet and purple are their clothing;
They are all the work of skilled men.

10 But the LORD is the[R]true God; Is. 65:16
He is the[R]living God and the[R]everlasting King. Jer. 4:2 · Ps. 10:16; 29:10
At His wrath the[R]earth quakes,
And the nations cannot[R]endure His indignation. Jer. 4:24; 50:46 · Ps. 76:7

11 Thus you shall say to them, "The[R]gods that did not make the heavens and the earth shall[R]perish from the earth and from under the[R]heavens." Ps. 96:5 · Is. 2:18 · *these heavens*

12 *It is* [R]He who made the earth by His power, Gen. 1:1, 6; Job 38:4-7; Ps. 136:5
Who[R]established the world by His wisdom; Ps. 78:69; Is. 45:18
And by His understanding He has [R]stretched out the heavens. Job 9:8

13 When He utters His[R]voice, *there is* a tumult of waters in the heavens,
And He causes the clouds to ascend from the end of the earth;
He makes lightning for the rain,
And brings out the [R]wind from His storehouses. [Ps. 29:3–9] · Ps. 135:7

14 Every man is^Rstupid, devoid of knowledge;
Every goldsmith is put to shame by his
^Aidols;   Jer. 10:8; 51:17, 18 • *graven image*
For his molten images are deceitful,
And there is no breath in them.
15 They are^Rworthless, a work of mock-
ery;   Is. 41:24; Jer. 8:19; 14:22
In the^Rtime of their punishment they
will perish.   Jer. 8:12; 51:18
16 The portion of Jacob is not like these;
For the^TMaker of all is He,   *Fashioner*
And ^RIsrael is the tribe of His inheri-
tance;   Deut. 32:9; Ps. 74:2
The LORD of hosts is His name.

17 Pick up your bundle from the ground,
You who dwell under siege!
18 For thus says the LORD,
"Behold, I am ^Rslinging out the inhabi-
tants of the land   1 Sam. 25:29
At this time,
And will cause them distress,
That they may^Tbe found."   *find*

Jeremiah's Prayer for Correction

19 Woe is me, because of my^Tinjury!
My wound is incurable.   *breaking*
But I said, "Truly this is a sickness,
And I^Rmust bear it."   Mic. 7:9
20 My^Ttent is destroyed,   Jer. 4:20; Lam. 2:4
And all my ropes are broken;
My^Rsons have gone from me and are no
more.   Jer. 31:15; Lam. 1:5
There is^Rno one to stretch out my tent
again   Is. 51:18
Or to set up my curtains.
21 For the shepherds have become stupid
And^Rhave not sought the LORD;   Jer. 2:8
Therefore they have not prospered,
And ^Rall their flock is scattered. Jer. 23:2
22 The sound of a ^Rreport! Behold, it
comes—   Jer. 4:15
A great commotion^Rout of the land of
the north—   Jer. 1:14; 25:9
To^Rmake the cities of Judah   Jer. 9:11
A desolation, a haunt of jackals.

23 I know, O LORD, that ^Ra man's way is
not in himself;
^RNor is it in a man who walks to direct
his steps.   Prov. 16:1; 20:24 • [Is. 26:7]
24 ^RCorrect me, O LORD, but with justice;
Not with Thine anger, lest Thou^Tbring
me to nothing.   Ps. 6:1 • *diminish me*
25 Pour out Thy wrath on the nations that
^Rdo not know Thee,   1 Thess. 4:5
And on the families that ^Rdo not call
Thy name;   Zeph. 1:6
For they have devoured Jacob;
They have ^Rdevoured him and consumed him,   Jer. 8:16; 50:7, 17
And have laid waste his habitation.

CHAPTER 11

*Judah's Curse
Because of the Broken Covenant*

THE word which came to Jeremiah from
the LORD, saying,
2 "Hear^Rthe words of this ^Rcovenant, and
speak to the men of Judah and to the inhabi-
tants of Jerusalem;   Jer. 11:6 • Ex. 19:5
3 and say to them, 'Thus says the LORD,
the God of Israel, "Cursed is the man who
does not heed the words of this covenant
4 which I commanded your forefathers
in the day that I brought them out of the
land of Egypt, from the iron furnace, saying,
'Listen to My voice, and^Tdo according to all
which I command you; so you shall be My
people, and I will be your God,'   *do them*
5 in order to confirm the ^Roath which I
swore to your forefathers, to give them a
land flowing with milk and honey, as *it is*
this day."'" Then I answered and said,
"Amen,^R O LORD."   Ex. 13:5 • Jer. 28:6
6 And the LORD said to me, "Proclaim all
these words in the cities of Judah and in the
streets of Jerusalem, saying, 'Hear the
words of this covenant and do them.
7 'For I solemnly warned your fathers in
the day that I brought them up from the
land of Egypt, even to this day, warning per-
sistently, saying, "Listen to My voice."
8 'Yet they did not obey or incline their
ear, but walked, each one, in the stubbornness of his evil heart; therefore I brought on
them all the words of this covenant, which I
commanded *them* to do, but they did not.'"
9 Then the LORD said to me, "A conspiracy has been found among the men of Judah
and among the inhabitants of Jerusalem.
10"They have turned back to the iniquities
of their ancestors who^Rrefused to hear My
words, and they have gone after other gods
to serve them; the house of Israel and the
house of Judah have broken My covenant
which I made with their fathers."   Deut. 9:7
11 Therefore thus says the LORD, "Behold
I am bringing disaster on them which they
will not be able to escape; though they will
cry to Me, yet I will not listen to them.
12"Then the cities of Judah and the inhabitants of Jerusalem will ^Rgo and cry to the
gods to whom they burn incense, but they
surely will not save them in the time of their
disaster.   Deut. 32:37; Jer. 44:17
13"For your gods are ^Tas^R many as your
cities, O Judah; and as many as the streets
of Jerusalem are the altars you have set up
to the shameful thing, altars to burn incense
to Baal.   *the number of* • 2 Kin. 23:13; Jer. 2:28
14"Therefore^Rdo not pray for this people,
nor lift up a cry or prayer for them; for I will
^Rnot listen when they call to Me because of
their disaster.   Ex. 32:10; Jer. 7:16 • Ps. 66:18
15"What right has My ^Rbeloved in My
house   Jer. 13:27

When ^Rshe has done many vile deeds?
Can the sacrificial flesh take away
    from you your disaster,   Ezek. 16:25
^TSo *that* you can rejoice?"   *Then*
16 The LORD called your name,
"A ^Rgreen olive tree, beautiful in fruit
    and form";   Ps. 52:8; [Rom. 11:17]
With the noise of a great tumult
He has^Rkindled fire on it,   Ps. 80:16
And its branches are worthless.
17 And the LORD of hosts, who planted
you, has pronounced evil against you because of the evil of the house of Israel and of
the house of Judah, which they have^Adone to
provoke Me by ^Aoffering up sacrifices to
Baal.   *done for themselves • burning incense*

Anathoth's Conspiracy
Against Jeremiah

18 Moreover, the LORD^Rmade it known to
    me and I knew it;   1 Sam. 23:11, 12
Then Thou didst show me their deeds.
19 But I was like a gentle^Rlamb led to the
    slaughter;   Is. 53:7
And I did not know that they had de-
    vised plots against me, *saying,*
"Let us destroy the tree with its^Tfruit,
And^Rlet us cut him off from the^Rland of
    the living,   *bread* • Is. 53:8 • Ps. 52:5
That his ^Rname be remembered no
    more."   Ps. 109:13
20 But, O LORD of hosts, who^Rjudges right-
    eously,   Gen. 18:25; Ps. 7:8; Jer. 20:12
Who^Rtries the^Tfeelings and the heart,
Let me see Thy vengeance on them,
For to Thee have I ^Tcommitted my
    cause.   Jer. 17:10 • *kidneys • revealed*
21 Therefore thus says the LORD concerning the men of Anathoth, who seek your life,
saying, "Do not prophesy in the name of the
LORD, that you might not die at our hand";
22 therefore, thus says the LORD of hosts,
"Behold, I am about to^Rpunish them! The
young men will die by the sword, their sons
and daughters will die by famine;   Jer. 21:14
23 and a remnant will not be left to them,
for I will bring disaster on the men of Anathoth—the year of their punishment."

CHAPTER 12

Jeremiah's Complaint to God

RIGHTEOUS^R art Thou, O LORD, that I
    would plead *my* case with Thee;
Indeed I would^Rdiscuss matters of jus-
    tice with Thee: Ezra 9:15 • Job 13:3
Why has the^Rway of the wicked pros-
    pered?   Jer. 5:27, 28; Hab. 1:4; Mal. 3:15
Why are all those who^Rdeal in treach-
    ery at ease?   Jer. 3:7, 20; 5:11
2 Thou hast^Rplanted them, they have also
    taken root;   Jer. 11:17; 45:4

They grow, they have even produced
    fruit.
Thou art near^Tto their lips   *in their mouth*
But far from their^Tmind.   *kidneys*
3 But Thou^Rknowest me, O LORD;
Thou seest me;   Ps. 139:1-4
And Thou dost^Rexamine my heart's *at-
titude* toward Thee.
Drag them off like sheep for the
    slaughter   Ps. 7:9; 11:5; Jer. 11:20
And ^Tset them apart for a^Rday of car-
    nage!   *sanctify them* • Jer. 17:18; 50:27
4 How long is the^Rland to mourn
And the^Rvegetation of the countryside
    to wither?   Jer. 4:28 • Joel 1:10-17
For the^Rwickedness of those who dwell
    in it,   Ps. 107:34
^RAnimals and birds have been snatched
    away,   Jer. 4:25; 7:20; 9:10; Hos. 4:3
Because *men* have said, "He will not
    see our latter^Rending."   Ezek. 7:2

God's Reply to Jeremiah

5"If you have run with footmen and they
    have tired you out,
Then how can you compete with
    horses?
If you fall down in a land of peace,
How will you do in the^Tthicket^Rof the
    Jordan?   *pride* • Jer. 49:19; 50:44
6"For even your^Rbrothers and the house-
    hold of your father,
Even they have dealt treacherously
    with you,   Job 6:15; Ps. 69:8; Jer. 9:4, 5
Even they have cried aloud after you.
Do not believe them, although they
    may say nice things to you."

7"I have^Rforsaken My house,   Is. 2:6
I have abandoned My inheritance;
I have given the beloved of My soul
Into the hand of her enemies.
8"My inheritance has become to Me
Like a lion in the forest;
She has^Rroared against Me;   Is. 59:13
Therefore I have come to hate her.
9"Is My inheritance like a speckled bird
    of prey to Me?
Are the^Rbirds of prey against her on ev-
    ery side?   2 Kin. 24:2; Ezek. 23:22-25
Go, gather all the^Rbeasts of the field,
Bring them to devour!   Is. 56:9; Jer. 7:33
10"Many^Rshepherds have ruined My^Rvine-
    yard,   Jer. 6:3; 23:1 • Ps. 80:8-16
They have trampled down My field;
They have made My^Rpleasant field
A desolate wilderness.   Jer. 3:19
11"It^Thas been made a desolation,
Desolate, it mourns^Abefore Me;
The whole land has been made deso-
    late,   *One has made it* • *upon*
Because no man lays it to heart.
12"On all the^Abare^Rheights in the wilder-
    ness   *caravan trails* • Jer. 3:2, 21
Destroyers have come,

For a ᴿsword of the LORD is devouring
From one end of the land even to the
ᵀother;   Is. 34:6 • *other end of the land*
There is no peace forᵀanyone.   *all flesh*
13"They have ᴿsown wheat and have
reaped thorns,   Lev. 26:16; Deut. 28:38
They have ᴿstrained themselves ᵀto no
profit.   Is. 55:2 • *they do not profit*
But be ashamed of yourᵀharvest
Because of the ᴿfierce anger of the
LORD."   *products* • Jer. 4:26; 25:37, 38
14 Thus says the LORD concerning all My
ᴿwicked neighbors who strike at the inheritance with which I have endowed My people Israel, "Behold I am about to uproot
them from their land and will uproot the
house of Judah from among them. Jer. 49:1, 7
15"And it will come about that after I have
uprooted them, I will ᴿagain have compassion on them; and I willᴿbring them back,
each one to his inheritance and each one to
his land.   Jer. 48:47; 49:6, 39 • Amos 9:14
16"Then it will come about that if they will
reallyᴿlearn the ways of My people, toᴿswear
by My name, 'As the LORD lives,' even as
they taught My people toᴿswear by Baal,
then they will beᴿbuilt up in the midst of My
people.   Is. 42:6 • [Jer. 4:2] • Jer. 5:7 • Jer. 3:17
17"But if they will not listen, then I will
ᴿuproot that nation, uproot and destroy it,"
declares the LORD.   Ps. 2:8-12; Is. 60:12

CHAPTER 13

Sign of the Ruined Waistband

THUS the LORD said to me, "Go andᴿbuy
yourself a linen waistband, and put it
around your waist, but do not put it in water."   Jer. 13:11
2 So I bought the waistband in accordance with theᴿword of the LORD and put it
around my waist.   Is. 20:2; Ezek. 2:8
3 Then the word of the LORD came to me
a second time, saying,
4"Take the waistband that you have
bought, which is around your waist, and
arise, go to theᴿEuphrates and hide it there
in a crevice of the rock."   Jer. 51:63
5 So I went and hid it by the Euphrates,
ᴿas the LORD had commanded me.   Ex. 40:16
6 And it came about after many days
that the LORD said to me, "Arise, go to the
Euphrates and take from there the waistband which I commanded you to hide
there."
7 Then I went to the Euphrates and dug,
and I took the waistband from the place
where I had hidden it; and lo, the waistband
was ruined, it was totally worthless.
8 Then the word of the LORD came to me,
saying,
9"Thus says the LORD, 'Just so will I destroy theᴿpride of Judah and the great pride
of Jerusalem. Lev. 26:19; [Is. 2:10–17]; Zeph. 3:11
10 'This wicked people, whoᴿrefuse to lis-

ten to My words, who walk in the stubbornness of their hearts and have gone after other gods to serve them and to bow down to
them, let them be just like this waistband,
which is totally worthless.   Num. 14:11
11 'For as the waistband clings to the
waist of a man, so I made the whole household of Israel and the whole household of
Judah cling to Me,' declares the LORD, 'that
they might be for Me a people, forᵀrenown,
forᴿpraise, and for glory; but they ᴿdid not
listen.'   *a name* • Is. 43:21; Jer. 33:9 • Ps. 81:11

Sign of the Wine Jugs

12"Therefore you are to speak this word to
them, 'Thus says the LORD, the God of Israel, "Every jug is to be filled with wine." '
And when they say to you, 'Do we not very
well know that every jug is to be filled with
wine?'
13 then say to them, 'Thus says the LORD,
"Behold I am about to fill all the inhabitants
of this land—the kings that sit for David on
his throne, the priests, the prophets and all
the inhabitants of Jerusalem—with ᴿdrunkenness!   Ps. 60:3; 75:8; Is. 51:17; 63:6; Jer. 25:27
14"And I willᴿdash them against each other, both theᴿfathers and the sons together,"
declares the LORD. "I will not show pity nor
be sorry nor have compassion that I should
not destroy them." ' "   Is. 9:20, 21 • Jer. 6:21
15 Listen and give heed, do not be
        ᴿhaughty,   [Prov. 16:5]; Is. 28:14–22
    For the LORD has spoken.
16 Give glory to the LORD your God,
    Before He bringsᴿdarkness   Is. 5:30
    And before yourᴿfeet stumble
    On the dusky mountains,   Prov. 4:19
    And while you are hoping for light
    He makes it intoᴿdeep darkness,
    And turns *it* into gloom.   Jer. 2:6
17 Butᴿif you will not listen to it,   Mal. 2:2
    My soul will ᴿsob in secret for *such*
        pride;   Ps. 119:136; Luke 19:41, 42
    And my eyes will bitterly weep
    And flow down with tears,
    Because theᴿflock of the LORD has been
        taken captive.   Ps. 80:1; Jer. 23:1, 2
18 Say to theᴿking and the queen mother,
    "Take a lowly seat,   2 Kin. 24:12, 15
    For your beautifulᴿcrown   Ex. 39:28
    Has come down from your head."
19 The ᴿcities of the Negev have been
        locked up,   Jer. 32:44
    And there is no one to open *them*;
    Allᴿudah has been carried into exile,
    Wholly carried into exile.   Jer. 20:4

20"Lift up your eyes and see
    Those comingᴿfrom the north.   Hab. 1:6
    Where is theᴿflock that was given you,
    Your beautiful sheep?   Jer. 13:17; 23:2
21"What will you say when He appoints
        over you—
    And you yourself had taught them—

Former ^Acompanions^R to be head over
you?   *chieftains* • Jer. 2:25; 38:22
Will not^Rpangs take hold of you,
Like a woman in childbirth?   Is. 13:8
22"And if you^Rsay in your heart, Deut. 7:17
   'Why^R have these things happened to
   me?'   Jer. 5:19; 16:10
Because of the^Rmagnitude of your iniq-
   uity   Jer. 2:17-19; 9:2-9
^RYour skirts have been removed, Is. 47:2
And your heels have been exposed.
23"Can^Rthe Ethiopian change his skin
   Or the leopard his spots?   Prov. 27:22
Then you also can do^Rgood   Jer. 4:22
Who are accustomed to do evil.
24"Therefore I will^Rscatter them like drift-
   ing straw   Lev. 26:33; Jer. 9:16
To the desert^Rwind.   Jer. 4:11; 18:17
25"This is your^Rlot, the portion measured
   to you   Job 20:29; Ps. 11:6; Matt. 24:51
From Me," declares the LORD,
   "Because you have^Rforgotten Me
And trusted in falsehood.   Jer. 2:32; 3:21
26"So I Myself have also ^Rstripped your
   skirts off over your face,   Ezek. 23:29
That your shame may be seen.
27"As for your^Radulteries and your *lustful*
   neighings,   Jer. 5:7, 8
The lewdness of your prostitution
On the^Rhills in the field,   Ezek. 6:13
I have seen your abominations.
Woe to you, O Jerusalem!
How long will you remain unclean?"

CHAPTER 14

Judah's Drought Is Described

THAT which came as the word of the
LORD to Jeremiah in regard to the drought:
2"Judah mourns,
   And her^Rgates languish   Is. 3:26
They sit on the ground^Rin mourning,
And the ^Rcry of Jerusalem has as-
   cended.   Jer. 8:21 • Jer. 11:11; 46:12
3"And their nobles have sent their ^Tser-
   vants for water;   *little ones*
They have come to the ^Rcisterns and
   found no water.
They have returned with their vessels
   empty;   2 Kin. 18:31; Jer. 2:13
They have been^Rput to shame and humiliated,   Job 6:20; Ps. 40:14
And they^Rcover their heads. 2 Sam. 15:30
4"Because the ground is cracked,
   For there has been^Rno rain on the land;
The farmers have been put to shame,
They have covered their heads. Jer. 3:3
5"For even the doe in the field has given
   birth only to abandon *her young*,
Because there is^Rno grass.   Is. 15:6
6"And the ^Rwild donkeys stand on the
   bare heights;   Job 39:5, 6; Jer. 2:24
They pant for air like jackals,
Their eyes fail
For there is^Rno vegetation.   Joel 1:18

Jeremiah's First Intercession

7"Although our^Riniquities testify against
   us,   Is. 59:12; Hos. 5:5
O LORD, act for Thy name's sake!
Truly our apostasies have been many,
We have^Rsinned against Thee. Jer. 3:25
8"Thou^RHope of Israel,   Jer. 17:13
Its^RSavior in time of distress,   Is. 43:3
Why art Thou like a stranger in the
   land
Or like a traveler who has pitched his
   tent for the night?
9"Why art Thou like a man dismayed,
   Like a mighty man who^Rcannot save?
Yet Thou art in our midst, O LORD,
And we are called by Thy name;
Do not forsake us!"   Num. 11:23; Is. 50:2
10 Thus says the LORD to this people,
"Even so they have^Rloved to wander; they
have not^Rkept their feet in check. Therefore
the LORD does^Rnot accept them; now He will
remember their iniquity and call their sins
to account."   Jer. 2:25 • Ps. 119:101 • Jer. 6:20
11 So the LORD said to me, "Do^R not pray
for the welfare of this people. Jer. 7:16; 11:14
12"When they fast, I am^Rnot going to listen
to their cry; and when they offer^Rburnt offering and grain offering, I am not going to accept them. Rather I am going to make an
end of them by the^Rsword, famine and pestilence."   Prov. 1:28; [Is. 1:15] • Jer. 6:20 • Jer. 21:9

Jeremiah's Second Intercession

13 But, "Ah, Lord GOD!" I said, "Look, the
prophets are telling them, 'You will not see
the sword nor will you have famine, but I
will give you lasting peace in this place.' "
14 Then the LORD said to me, "The prophets are prophesying falsehood in My name. I
have neither sent them nor commanded
them nor spoken to them; they are prophesying to you a false vision, divination, futility and the deception of their own minds.
15"Therefore thus says the LORD concerning the prophets who are prophesying in My
name, although it was not I who sent
them—yet they keep saying, 'There shall be
no sword or famine in this land'—^Rby sword
and famine those prophets shall^Tmeet their
end!   Jer. 23:15; Ezek. 14:10 • *be finished*
16"The people also to whom they are
prophesying will be ^Rthrown out into the
streets of Jerusalem because of the famine
and the sword; and there will be no one to
^Rbury them—*neither* them, *nor* their wives,
nor their sons, nor their daughters—for I
shall ^Rpour out their *own* wickedness on
them.   Ps. 79:2, 3 • Jer. 8:1, 2 • Prov. 1:31
17"And you will say this word to them,
   'Let^Rmy eyes flow down with tears night
   and day,   Jer. 9:1; 13:17; Lam. 1:16
And let them not cease;
For the virgin^Rdaughter of my people
   has been crushed with a mighty
   blow,   Is. 37:22; Jer. 8:21; Lam. 1:15

With a sorely infected wound.
18 'If I[R]go out to the country,   Lam. 1:20
Behold, those[T]slain with the sword!
Or if I enter the city,   *pierced*
Behold, diseases of famine!
For[R]both prophet and priest   Jer. 6:13
Have gone roving about in the land
    that they do not know.' "

Jeremiah's Third Intercession

19 Hast Thou completely rejected Judah?
Or hast[T]Thou loathed Zion?   *Thy soul*
Why hast Thou stricken us so that we
    [R]are beyond healing?   Jer. 30:13
We[R]waited for peace, but nothing good
    came;   Job 30:26; Jer. 8:15; 1 Thess. 5:3
And for a time of healing, but behold,
    terror!
20 We know our wickedness, O LORD,
The iniquity of our fathers, for[R]we have
    sinned against Thee.   Jer. 8:14; 14:7
21 Do not despise *us*, [R]for Thine own
    name's sake;   Ps. 25:11; Jer. 14:7
Do not disgrace the [R]throne of Thy
    glory;   Jer. 3:17; 17:12
Remember *and* do not annul Thy cov-
    enant with us.
22 Are there any among the[T]idols of the
    nations who give rain?   *vanities*
Or can the heavens grant showers?
Is it not Thou, O LORD our God?
Therefore we hope[R]in Thee,
For Thou art the one who hast done all
    these things.   Lam. 3:26

CHAPTER 15

THEN the LORD said to me, "Even[R]though
Moses and Samuel were to[R]stand before Me,
My[T]heart would not be [T]with this people;
send them away from My presence and let
them go!   Ps. 99:6 · Jer. 15:19 · *soul · toward*
2"And it shall be that when they say to
you, 'Where should we go?' then you are to
tell them, 'Thus says the LORD:
    "Those *destined*[R]for death, to death;
    And those *destined* for the sword, to
        the sword;
    And those *destined* for famine, to fam-
        ine;   Ezek. 5:2, 12; Zech. 11:9; [Rev. 13:10]
    And those *destined* for captivity, to
        captivity." '
3"And I shall [R]appoint over them four
kinds *of doom*," declares the LORD: "the
sword to slay, the dogs to drag off, and the
[R]birds of the sky and the beasts of the earth
to devour and destroy.   Ezek. 14:21 · Jer. 7:33
4"And I shall [R]make them an object of
horror among all the kingdoms of the earth
because of[R]Manasseh, the son of Hezekiah,
the king of Judah, for what he did in Jerusalem.   Lev. 26:33; Jer. 24:9; 29:18 · 2 Chr. 33:1-9

5"Indeed, who will have[R]pity on you, O
    Jerusalem,   Ps. 69:20; Is. 51:19
Or who will[R]mourn for you,   Nah. 3:7
Or who will turn aside to ask about
    your welfare?
6"You who have[R]forsaken Me," declares
    the LORD,   Jer. 6:19; 8:9
"You keep[R]going backward.   Is. 1:4
So I will [R]stretch out My hand against
    you and destroy you;   Jer. 6:12
I am[R]tired of relenting!   Jer. 6:11; 7:16
7"And I will[R]winnow them with a win-
    nowing fork   Ps. 1:4; Jer. 51:2
At the gates of the land;
I will[R]bereave *them* of children, I will
    destroy My people;   Hos. 9:12-16
They did not repent of their ways.
8"Their[R]widows will be more numerous
    before Me   Is. 3:25, 26; 4:1
Than the sand of the seas;
I will bring against them, against the
    mother of a young man,
A [R]destroyer at noonday;   Jer. 22:7
I will suddenly bring down on her
Anguish and dismay.
9"She who bore seven *sons* pines away;
Her breathing is labored.
Her sun has set while it was yet day;
She has been[R]shamed and humiliated.
So I shall [R]give over their survivors to
    the sword
Before their enemies," declares the
    LORD.   Jer. 50:12 · Jer. 21:7

God Encourages Jeremiah

10[R]Woe to me, my mother, that you have
    borne me   Job 3:1, 3; Jer. 20:14
As a[R]man of strife and a man of conten-
    tion to all the land!   Jer. 1:18, 19
I have neither[R]lent, nor have men lent
    money to me,   Lev. 25:36, 37
Yet everyone curses me.
11 The LORD said, "Surely I will [R]set you
    free for *purposes of* good;   Ps. 138:3
Surely I will cause the[R]enemy to make
    supplication to you
In a time of disaster and a time of dis-
    tress.   Jer. 21:2; 37:3; 38:14; 42:2

12"Can anyone smash iron,
Iron from the north, or bronze?
13"Your[R]wealth and your treasures
I will give for booty without cost,
Even for all your sins   Jer. 17:3; 20:5
And within all your borders.
14"Then I will cause your enemies to bring
    [T]it   *your possessions*
Into a[R]land you do not know;   Jer. 16:13
For a[R]fire has been kindled in My an-
    ger,   Deut. 32:22; Ps. 21:9; Jer. 17:4
It will burn upon you."

15[R]Thou who knowest, O LORD,   Jer. 12:3
Remember me, take notice of me,

And[R]take vengeance for me on my persecutors.   Jer. 11:20
Do *not*, in view of Thy patience, take
me away;
Know that[R]for Thy sake I endure re-
proach.   Ps. 44:22; 69:7-9; Jer. 20:8
16 Thy words were found and I ate them,
And Thy words became for me a joy
and the delight of my heart;
For I have been[R]called by Thy name,
O LORD God of hosts.   Jer. 14:9
17 I[R]did not sit in the circle of merrymak-
ers,   Ps. 1:1; Jer. 16:8; 2 Cor. 6:17
Nor did I exult.
Because of Thy hand *upon me* I sat
[R]alone,   Ps. 102:7; Jer. 13:17; Lam. 3:28
For Thou didst fill me with indignation.
18 Why has my pain been perpetual
And my[R]wound incurable, refusing to
be healed?   Job 34:6; Jer. 30:12, 15
Wilt Thou indeed be to me[R]like a de-
ceptive *stream*   Job 6:15, 20; Jer. 14:3
With water that is unreliable?

19 Therefore, thus says the LORD,
"If you return, then I will restore you—
[R]Before Me you will stand;   1 Kin. 17:1
And[R]if you extract the precious from
the worthless,   Jer. 6:29; Ezek. 22:26
You will become[t]My spokesman.
They for their part may turn to you,
But as for you, you must not turn to
them.   *as My mouth*
20"Then I will[R]make you to this people
A fortified wall of bronze;   Jer. 1:18, 19
And though they fight against you,
They will not prevail over you;
For[R]I am with you to save you   Ps. 46:7
And deliver you," declares the LORD.
21"So I will[R]deliver you from the hand of
the wicked,   Ps. 37:40; Is. 49:25
And I will[R]redeem you from the[t]grasp
of the violent."   [Gen. 48:16] • *palm*

CHAPTER 16

Jeremiah Is Not to Marry

THE word of the LORD also came to me
saying,
2"You shall not take a wife for yourself
nor have sons or daughters in this place."
3 For thus says the LORD concerning the
sons and daughters born in this place, and
concerning their[R]mothers who bear them,
and their[R]fathers who beget them in this
land: Jer. 15:8 • Jer. 6:21
4"They will[R]die of deadly diseases, they
[R]will not be lamented or buried; they will be
as dung on the surface of the ground and
come to an end by sword and famine, and
their carcasses will become food for the
[R]birds of the sky and for the beasts of the
earth."   Jer. 15:2 • Jer. 25:33 • Is. 18:6; Jer. 15:3
5 For thus says the LORD, "Do not enter a
house of mourning, or go to lament or to

console them; for I have withdrawn My
peace from this people," declares the LORD,
"My lovingkindness and compassion.
6"Both[R]great men and small will die in
this land; they will not be buried, they will
not be lamented, nor will anyone gash himself or shave his head for them.   2 Chr. 36:17
7"Neither will men break *bread* in
mourning for them, to comfort anyone for
the dead, nor give them a cup of consolation
to drink for anyone's father or mother.
8"Moreover you shall[R]not go into a house
of feasting to sit with them to eat and
drink."   Eccl. 7:2-4; Is. 22:12-14; Jer. 15:17
9 For thus says the LORD of hosts, the
God of Israel: "Behold, I am going to[T]elimi-
nate from this place, before your eyes and in
your time, the voice of rejoicing and the
voice of gladness, the voice of the groom
and the voice of the bride.   *cause to cease*

Judah's Idolatry

10"Now it will come about when you tell
this people all these words that they will say
to you, 'For[R]what reason has the LORD declared all this great calamity against us?
And what is our iniquity, or what is our sin
which we have committed against the LORD
our God?'   Deut. 29:24; 1 Kin. 9:8; Jer. 5:19
11"Then you are to say to them, '*It is*[R]be-
cause your forefathers have forsaken Me,'
declares the LORD, 'and have followed[R]other
gods and served them and bowed down to
them; but Me they have forsaken and have
not kept My law.   Deut. 29:25 • Ps. 106:35-41
12 'You too have done evil, *even*[R]more than
your forefathers; for behold, you are each
one walking according to the[R]stubbornness
of his own[R]evil heart, without listening to
Me.   Jer. 7:26 • [1 Sam. 15:23] • Eccl. 9:3
13 'So I will[R]hurl you out of this land into
the land which you have not known, neither
you nor your fathers; and there you will
[R]serve other gods day and night, for I shall
grant you no favor.'   Deut. 4:26, 27 • Jer. 5:19

God's Promise of Judah's Restoration

14"Therefore behold, days are coming,"
declares the LORD, "when it will no longer
be said, 'As the LORD lives, who brought up
the sons of Israel out of the land of Egypt,'
15 but, 'As the LORD lives, who brought
up the sons of Israel from the[R]land of the
north and from all the countries where He
had banished them.' For I will restore them
to their own land which I gave to their fathers.   Ps. 106:47; Is. 11:11-16; 14:1; Jer. 3:18; 23:8
16"Behold, I am going to send for many
[R]fishermen," declares the LORD, "and they
will fish for them; and afterwards I shall
send for many hunters, and they will hunt
them from every mountain and every hill,
and from the clefts of the rocks.   Amos 4:2

17"For My eyes are on all their ways; they are not hidden from My face, [R]nor is their iniquity concealed from My eyes.   Jer. 2:22

18"And I will first doubly repay their iniquity and their sin, because they have [R]polluted My land; they have filled My inheritance with the carcasses of their detestable idols and with their abominations."   Jer. 2:7

19 O Lord, my [R]strength and my strong-
   hold,   Ps. 18:1, 2; Is. 25:4
   And my refuge in the day of distress,
   To Thee the [R]nations will come
   From the ends of the earth and say,
   "Our fathers have inherited nothing but
      [R]falsehood,   Ps. 22:27 • Is. 44:20
   Futility and things of no profit."
20 Can man make gods for himself?
   Yet they are [R]not gods!   Ps. 115:4-8

21"Therefore behold, I am going to make
   them know—
   This time I will make them know
   My [T]power and My might;   hand
   And they shall [R]know that My name is
      the Lord."   Ps. 83:18; Is. 43:3; Jer. 33:2

CHAPTER 17

Judah's Sins Are Listed

THE [R]sin of Judah is written down with an
   [R]iron stylus;   Jer. 2:22 • Job 19:24
   With a diamond point it is engraved
      upon the tablet of their heart,
   And on the horns of their altars,
2 As they remember their [R]children,
   So they *remember* their altars and their
      [R]Asherim   Jer. 7:18 • Ex. 34:13; Is. 17:8
   By [R]green trees on the high hills. Jer. 3:6
3 O mountain of Mine in the countryside,
   I will [R]give over your wealth and all
      your treasures for booty,
   Your high places for sin throughout
      your borders.   2 Kin. 24:13; Is. 39:4-6
4 And you will, even of yourself, [R]let go of
      your inheritance   Jer. 12:7; Lam. 5:2
   That I gave you;
   And I will make you serve your [R]en-
      emies   Deut. 28:48; Is. 14:3; Jer. 15:14
   In the land which you do not know;
   For you have [R]kindled a fire in My anger
   Which will burn forever.   Jer. 7:20; 15:14

5 Thus says the Lord,
   "Cursed [R]is the man who trusts in man-
      kind   Ps. 146:3; Is. 2:22; 30:1; Ezek. 29:7
   And makes [R]flesh his [T]strength,
   And whose heart turns away from the
      Lord.   2 Chr. 32:8; Is. 31:3 • arm
6"For he will be like a [R]bush in the desert
   And will not see when prosperity
      comes,   Jer. 48:6
   But will live in stony wastes in the wil-
      derness,
   A land of salt without inhabitant.

7"Blessed [R]is the man who trusts in the
   Lord   Ps. 2:12; 34:8; 84:12; Prov. 16:20
   And whose [R]trust is the Lord.   Ps. 40:4
8"For he will be like a [R]tree planted by the
   water,   Ps. 1:3; 92:12-14; Ezek. 31:3-9
   That extends its roots by a stream
   And will not fear when the heat comes;
   But its leaves will be green,
   And it will not be anxious in a year of
      [R]drought   Jer. 14:1-6
   Nor cease to yield fruit.

9"The heart is more [R]deceitful than all else
   And is desperately sick;
   Who can understand it?   [Rom. 7:11]
10"I, the Lord, [R]search the heart,
   I test the [T]mind,   1 Sam. 16:7 • kidneys
   Even [R]to give to each man according to
      his ways,   Jer. 32:19; Rom. 2:6
   According to the results of his deeds.
11"As a partridge that hatches eggs which
      it has not laid,
   So is he who [R]makes a fortune, but un-
      justly;   Jer. 6:13; 8:10; 22:13, 17
   In the midst of his days it will forsake
      him,
   And in [T]the end he will be a fool."   his

12 [R]A glorious throne on high from the be-
      ginning   [Jer. 3:17; 14:21]
   Is the place of our sanctuary.
13 O Lord, the [R]hope of Israel,
   All who [R]forsake Thee will be put to
      shame.   Jer. 14:8; 50:7 • [Is. 1:28]
   Those who turn [T]away on earth will be
      written down,   Heb., away from Me
   Because they have forsaken the foun-
      tain of living water, even the Lord.
14 Heal me, O Lord, and I will be healed;
   [R]Save me and I will be saved,   Ps. 54:1
   For Thou art my [R]praise.   Deut. 10:21
15 Look, they keep [R]saying to me,
   "Where is the word of the Lord?
   Let it come now!"   Is. 5:19; 2 Pet. 3:4
16 But as for me, I have not hurried away
      from *being* a shepherd after Thee,
   Nor have I longed for the woeful day;
   [R]Thou Thyself knowest the utterance of
      my lips
   Was in Thy presence.   Jer. 12:3
17 Do not be a [R]terror to me;
   Thou art my [R]refuge in the day of disas-
      ter.   Ps. 88:15 • Jer. 16:19; Nah. 1:7
18 Let those who persecute me be [R]put to
      shame, but as for me, let me not be
      put to shame;   Ps. 35:4, 26; Jer. 17:13
   Let them be dismayed, but let me not
      be dismayed.
   [R]Bring on them a day of disaster,
   And crush them with twofold destruc-
      tion!   Ps. 35:8

*Jeremiah's Call
for Sabbath Observance*

19 Thus the Lord said to me, "Go and
stand in the public gate, through which the

kings of Judah come in and go out, as well as in all the gates of Jerusalem;

20 and say to them, 'Listen^Rto the word of the LORD,^Rkings of Judah, and all Judah, and all inhabitants of Jerusalem, who come in through these gates: Ezek. 2:7 • Ps. 49:1, 2

21 'Thus says the LORD, "Take heed for yourselves, and^Rdo not carry any load on the sabbath day or bring anything in through the gates of Jerusalem.   Num. 15:32-36

22"And you shall not bring a load out of your houses on the sabbath day nor do any work, but keep the sabbath day holy, as I commanded your^Tforefathers.   *fathers*

23"Yet they^Rdid not listen or incline their ears, but stiffened their necks in order not to listen or take correction.   Jer. 7:24, 28; 11:10

24"But it will come about, if you listen attentively to Me," declares the LORD, "to bring no load in through the gates of this city on the sabbath day, but to keep the sabbath day holy by doing no work on it,

25 then there will come in through the gates of this city kings and princes sitting on the throne of David, riding in chariots and on horses, they and their princes, the men of Judah, and the inhabitants of Jerusalem; and this city will be inhabited forever.

26"They will come in from the^Rcities of Judah and from the environs of Jerusalem, from the land of Benjamin, from the ^Rlowland, from the hill country, and from the ^RNegev, bringing burnt offerings, sacrifices, grain offerings and incense, and bringing sacrifices of thanksgiving to the house of the LORD.   Jer. 32:44 • Zech. 7:7 • Ps. 107:22

27"But if you do not listen to Me to keep the sabbath day holy by not carrying a load and coming in through the gates of Jerusalem on the sabbath day, then I shall kindle a fire in its gates, and it will devour the palaces of Jerusalem and not be quenched." ' "

CHAPTER 18

Sign of the Potter

THE word which came to Jeremiah from the LORD saying,

2"Arise and ^Rgo down to the potter's house, and there I shall announce My words to you."   Jer. 19:1, 2

3 Then I went down to the potter's house, and there he was, making something on the^Twheel.   *pair of stone discs*

4 But the vessel that he was making of clay was spoiled in the hand of the potter; so he remade it into another vessel, as it pleased the potter to make.

5 Then the word of the LORD came to me saying,

6"Can I not, O house of Israel, deal with you as this potter *does*?" declares the LORD. "Behold, like the clay in the potter's hand, so are you in My hand, O house of Israel.

7"At one moment I might speak concern-

ing a nation or concerning a kingdom to^Ruproot, to pull down, or to destroy *it;*   Jer. 1:10

8 ^Rif that nation against which I have spoken turns from its evil, I will ⁴relent^R concerning the calamity I planned to bring on it.   Jer. 7:3–7; 12:16; [Ezek. 18:21] • Ps. 106:45

9"Or at another moment I might speak concerning a nation or concerning a kingdom to^Rbuild up or to plant *it;*   Jer. 1:10; 31:28

10 if it does evil in My sight by not obeying My voice, then I will ⁴think better of the good with which I had promised to bless it.

11"So now then, speak to the men of Judah and against the inhabitants of Jerusalem saying, 'Thus says the LORD, "Behold, I am fashioning calamity against you and devising a plan against you. Oh turn back, each of you from his evil way, and^Treform your ways and your deeds." '   *make good*

12"But^Rthey will say, 'It's hopeless! For we are going to follow our own plans, and each of us will act according to the^Rstubbornness of his evil heart.'   Is. 57:10 • Jer. 7:24; 16:12

13"Therefore thus says the LORD,
   'Ask^Rnow among the nations,   Is. 66:8
   Who ever heard the like of^Tthis?   *these*
   The^Rvirgin of Israel   Jer. 14:17
   Has done a most appalling thing.

14 'Does the snow of Lebanon forsake the
       rock of the open country?
   Or is the cold flowing water *from* a for-
       eign *land* ever snatched away?

15 'For^RMy people have forgotten Me,
   They burn incense^Tto worthless gods
   And they have stumbled from their
       ways,   Jer. 2:32; 3:21 • *to worthlessness*
   From the^Rancient paths,   Jer. 6:16
   To walk in bypaths,
   Not on a^Rhighway,   Is. 57:14; 62:10

16 To make their land a^Rdesolation,
   An *object of* perpetual^Rhissing;
   Everyone who passes by it will be as-
       tonished   Jer. 25:9; 49:13 • 1 Kin. 9:8
   And^Rshake his head.   Is. 37:22; Jer. 48:27

17 'Like an ^Reast wind I will ^Rscatter them
   Before the enemy;   Ps. 48:7 • Job 27:21
   I will show them^RMy back and not *My*
       face   Jer. 2:27; 32:33
   In the day of their calamity.' "

18 Then they said, "Come and let us ^Rdevise plans against Jeremiah. Surely the law is not going to be lost to the priest, nor counsel to the sage, nor the *divine* word to the prophet! Come on and let us ^Rstrike at him with *our* tongue, and let us give no heed to any of his words."   Jer. 11:19 • Ps. 52:2

19 Do give heed to me, O LORD,
   And listen to^Twhat my opponents are
       saying!   *the voice of my opponents*

20 Should good be repaid with evil?
   For they have^Rdug a pit for^Tme.
   Remember how I^Rstood before Thee
   To speak good on their behalf,

---

⁴ Lit., *repent (of)*

So as to turn away Thy wrath from
them.   Ps. 35:7 • *my soul* • Ps. 106:23
21 Therefore, ᴿgive their children over to
famine,   Ps. 109:9-20; Jer. 11:22; 14:16
And deliver them up to the ᵀpower of
the sword;   *hands of*
And let their wives become ᴿchildless
and ᴿwidowed.   Is. 13:18 • Jer. 15:8
Let their men also be smitten to death,
Their ᴿyoung men struck down by the
sword in battle.   Jer. 9:21; 11:22
22 May an ᴿoutcry be heard from their
houses,   Jer. 6:26; 25:34, 36
When Thou suddenly bringest raiders
upon them;
For they have dug a pit to capture me
And hidden snares for my feet.
23 Yet Thou, O Lᴏʀᴅ, knowest
All their ᵀdeadly designs against me;
Do not ᵀforgive their iniquity
Or blot out their sin from Thy sight.
But may they be overthrown before
Thee;   *unto death* • *cover over, atone for*
Deal with them in the ᴿtime of Thine an-
ger!   Jer. 7:20

CHAPTER 19

Sign of the Broken Jar

Tʜᴜs says the Lᴏʀᴅ, "Go and buy a ᴿpot-
ter's earthenware ᴿjar, and *take* some of the
elders of the people and some of the ᴬsenior
priests.   Jer. 18:2 • Jer. 19:10 • *elders of*
2"Then go out to the ᴿvalley of Ben-
hinnom, which is by the entrance of the potsherd gate; and ᴿproclaim there the words
that I shall tell you,   Josh. 15:8 • [Prov. 1:20]
3 and say, 'Hear the word of the Lᴏʀᴅ, O
kings of Judah and inhabitants of Jerusalem: thus says the Lᴏʀᴅ of hosts, the God of
Israel, "Behold I am about to bring a ᴬcalam-
ity upon this place, at which the ears of
everyone that hears of it will tingle. Jer. 6:19
4"Because they have forsaken Me and
have made this an alien place and have
burned ᴬsacrifices in it to ᴮother gods that neither they nor their forefathers nor the kings
of Judah had *ever* known, and *because* they
have filled this place with the ᴿblood of the
innocent   *incense* • Jer. 7:9 • 2 Kin. 21:6, 16
5 and have built the ᴿhigh places of Baal
to burn their ᴿsons in the fire as burnt offerings to Baal, a thing which I never commanded or spoke of, nor did it *ever* enter My
ᵀmind;   Num. 22:41 • 2 Kin. 17:17 • *heart*
6 therefore, behold, ᴿdays are coming,"
declares the Lᴏʀᴅ, "when this place will no
longer be called ᴿTopheth or ᴿthe valley of
Ben-hinnom, but rather the valley of
Slaughter.   Jer. 7:32 • Is. 30:33 • Josh. 15:8
7"And I shall ᴿmake void the counsel of
Judah and Jerusalem in this place, and I

shall cause them to fall by the sword before
their enemies and by the hand of those who
seek their life; and I shall give over their
carcasses as food for the birds of the sky
and the beasts of the earth.   Ps. 33:10, 11
8"I shall also make this city a ᴿdesolation
and an *object of* hissing; everyone who
passes by it will be astonished and hiss because of all its ᵀdisasters.   Jer. 18:16 • *blows*
9"And I shall make them ᴿeat the flesh of
their sons and the flesh of their daughters,
and they will eat one another's flesh in the
siege and in the distress with which their
enemies and those who seek their life will
distress them." '   Lev. 26:29; Deut. 28:53, 55
10"Then you are to break the jar in the
sight of the men who accompany you
11 and say to them, 'Thus says the Lᴏʀᴅ
of hosts, "Just so shall I ᴿbreak this people
and this city, even as one breaks a potter's
vessel, which cannot again be repaired; and
they will ᴿbury in Topheth because there is
no *other* place for burial.   Ps. 2:9 • Jer. 7:32
12"This is how I shall treat this place and
its inhabitants," declares the Lᴏʀᴅ, "so as to
make this city like Topheth.
13"And the houses of Jerusalem and the
houses of the kings of Judah will be defiled
like the place Topheth, because of all the
houses on whose rooftops they burned ᴬsacrifices to all the heavenly host and poured
out libations to other gods." ' "   *incense*
14 Then Jeremiah came from Topheth,
where the Lᴏʀᴅ had sent him to prophesy;
and he stood in the ᴿcourt of the Lᴏʀᴅ's
house and said to all the people: 2 Chr. 20:5
15"Thus says the Lᴏʀᴅ of hosts, the God
of Israel, 'Behold, I am about to bring on
this city and all its towns the entire calamity
that I have declared against it, because they
have ᴿstiffened their necks so ᴿas not to heed
My words.' "   Neh. 9:17, 29; Jer. 7:26 • Ps. 58:4

CHAPTER 20

Jeremiah Is Persecuted by Pashhur

Wʜᴇɴ Pashhur the priest, the son of ᴿIm-
mer, who was ᴿchief officer in the house of
the Lᴏʀᴅ, heard Jeremiah prophesying
these things,   1 Chr. 24:14 • 2 Kin. 25:18
2 Pashhur had Jeremiah the prophet
ᴿbeaten, and put him in the stocks that were
at the upper ᴿBenjamin Gate, which was by
the house of the Lᴏʀᴅ.   Jer. 1:19 • Zech. 14:10
3 Then it came about on the next day,
when Pashhur released Jeremiah from the
stocks, that Jeremiah said to him, "Pashhur
is not the name the Lᴏʀᴅ has ᴿcalled you, but
rather ⁵Magor-missabib.ᴿ   Is. 8:3 • Jer. 6:25
4"For thus says the Lᴏʀᴅ, 'Behold, I am
going to make you a terror to yourself and
to all your friends; and while your eyes look
on, they will fall by the sword of their enemies. So I shall give over all Judah to the
hand of the king of Babylon, and he will car-

⁵ I.e., terror on every side

ry them away as exiles to Babylon and will slay them with the sword.

5 'I shall also give over all the wealth of this city, all its produce, and all its costly things; even all the treasures of the kings of Judah I shall give over to the hand of their enemies, and they will plunder them, take them away, and bring them to Babylon.

6 'And you,^RPashhur, and all who live in your house will go into captivity; and you will enter Babylon, and there you will die, and there you will be buried, you and all your ^Rfriends to whom you have falsely prophesied.'"   Jer. 20:1 • Jer. 20:4; 29:21

Jeremiah Complains to God

7 O LORD, Thou hast deceived me and I was deceived;
Thou hast^Tovercome me and prevailed.
I have become a^Rlaughingstock all day long;   Ezek. 3:14 • Job 12:4
Everyone^Rmocks me.   Ps. 22:7; Jer. 38:19
8 For each time I speak, I cry aloud;
I^Rproclaim violence and destruction,
Because for me the word of the LORD has^Tresulted   Jer. 6:7 • become
In reproach and derision all day long.
9 But if I say, "I will not remember Him
Or speak anymore in His name,"
Then in ^Rmy heart it becomes like a burning fire
Shut up in my bones; Ps. 39:3; Ezek. 3:14
And I am weary of holding it in,
And^RI cannot endure it.   Job 32:18-20
10 For ^RI have heard the whispering of many,   Ps. 31:13
"Terror^Ron every side!   Jer. 6:25
^RDenounce him; yes, let us denounce him!"   Neh. 6:6-13; Is. 29:21; Jer. 18:18
All my^Rtrusted friends,   Ps. 41:9
Watching for my fall, say:
"Perhaps he will be^Tdeceived, so that we may prevail against him   persuaded
And take our revenge on him."
11 But the^RLORD is with me like a dread champion;   Jer. 1:8; 15:20; Rom. 8:31
Therefore my^Rpersecutors will stumble and not prevail.   Deut. 32:35, 36
They will be utterly ashamed, because they have failed,
With an^Reverlasting disgrace that will not be forgotten.   Jer. 23:40
12 Yet, O LORD of hosts, Thou who dost ^Rtest the righteous, Ps. 7:9; 11:5; 17:3
Who seest the mind and the heart;
Let me see Thy vengeance on them;
For to Thee I have set forth my cause.
13 ^RSing to the LORD, praise the LORD!
For He has ^Rdelivered the soul of the needy one   Jer. 31:7 • Ps. 34:6; 69:33
From the hand of evildoers.

14 Cursed be the^Rday when I was born;
Let the day not be blessed when my mother bore me!   Job 3:3-6; Jer. 15:10

15 Cursed be the man who brought the news
To my father, saying,
"A^Tbaby boy has been born to you!"
And made him very happy.   male child
16 But let that man be like the cities
Which the LORD ^Roverthrew without ⁶relenting,   Gen. 19:25
And let him hear an ^Routcry in the morning   Jer. 18:22; 48:3, 4
And a shout of alarm at noon;
17 Because he did not kill me^Tbefore birth,
So that my mother would have been my grave,   from the womb
And her womb ever pregnant.
18 Why did I ever come forth from the womb
To look on trouble and sorrow,
So that my^Rdays have been spent in ^Rshame?   Ps. 90:9 • Ps. 69:19; Jer. 3:25

CHAPTER 21

Message Against Zedekiah

THE word which came to Jeremiah from the LORD when King Zedekiah sent to him Pashhur the son of Malchijah, and Zephaniah the priest, the son of Maaseiah, saying,

2"Please^Rinquire of the LORD on our behalf, for^RNebuchadnezzar king of Babylon is warring against us; perhaps the LORD will deal with us according to all His^Twonderful acts, that the enemy may withdraw from us."   Ex. 9:28 • 2 Kin. 25:1 • miracles

3 Then Jeremiah said to them, "You shall say to Zedekiah as follows:

4 'Thus says the LORD God of Israel, "Behold, I am about to^Rturn back the weapons of war which are in your hands, with which you are warring against the king of Babylon and the Chaldeans who are besieging you outside the wall; and I shall^Rgather them into the center of this city.   Jer. 32:5 • Is. 5:5

5"And I^RMyself shall war against you with an ^Routstretched hand and a mighty arm, even in^Ranger and wrath and great indignation.   Is. 63:10 • Ex. 6:6 • Is. 5:25

6"I shall also strike down the inhabitants of this city, both man and beast; they will die of a great^Rpestilence.   Jer. 14:12; 32:24

7"Then afterwards," declares the LORD, "I^Rshall give over Zedekiah king of Judah and his servants and the people, even those who survive in this city from the pestilence, the sword, and the famine, into the hand of Nebuchadnezzar king of Babylon, and into the hand of their foes, and into the hand of those who seek their lives; and he will strike them down with the edge of the sword. He ^Rwill not spare them nor have pity nor compassion."'   2 Kin. 25:5-7, 18-21 • 2 Chr. 36:17

⁶ Lit., being sorry

8"You shall also say to this people, 'Thus says the LORD, "Behold, I set before you the way of life and the way of death. Is. 1:19, 20

9"He who dwells in this city will die by the sword and by famine and by pestilence; but he who goes out and falls away to the Chaldeans who are besieging you will live, and he will have his own life as booty.

10"For I have set My face against this city for harm and not for good," declares the LORD. "It will be given into the hand of the king of Babylon, and he will burn it with fire." ' evil • Jer. 32:28, 29 • 2 Chr. 36:19

11"Then say to the household of the king of Judah, 'Hear the word of the LORD,

12 O house of David, thus says the LORD: "Administer justice every morning; And deliver the person who has been robbed from the power of his oppressor, Is. 7:2, 13 • in the • hand
That My wrath may not go forth like fire Jer. 4:4; 17:4; Ezek. 20:47, 48
And burn with none to extinguish it, Because of the evil of their deeds.

13"Behold, I am against you, O valley dweller, [Jer. 23:30–32] • Is. 22:1
O rocky plain," declares the LORD, "You men who say, 'Who will come down against us? rock of the level place
Or who will enter into our habitations?'
14"But I shall punish you according to the results of your deeds," declares the LORD, Is. 3:10, 11; Jer. 17:10 • fruit
"And I shall kindle a fire in its forest
That it may devour all its environs." ' "

CHAPTER 22

THUS says the LORD, "Go down to the house of the king of Judah, and there speak this word,

2 and say, 'Hear the word of the LORD, O king of Judah, who sits on David's throne, you and your servants and your people who enter these gates. Is. 9:7; Jer. 22:4, 30; 17:25

3 'Thus says the LORD, "Do justice and righteousness, and deliver the one who has been robbed from the power of his oppressor. Also do not mistreat or do violence to the stranger, the orphan, or the widow; and do not shed innocent blood in this place.

4"For if you men will indeed perform this thing, then kings will enter the gates of this house, sitting in David's place on his throne, riding in chariots and on horses, even the king himself and his servants and his people. Jer. 17:25 • for David

5"But if you will not obey these words, I swear by Myself," declares the LORD, "that this house will become a desolation." ' "

6 For thus says the LORD concerning the house of the king of Judah:
"You are like Gilead to Me, Gen. 37:25
Like the summit of Lebanon;

Yet most assuredly I shall make you like a wilderness, Ps. 107:34; Is. 6:11
Like cities which are not inhabited.
7"For I shall set apart destroyers against you, Is. 10:3-6; Jer. 4:6, 7
Each with his weapons;
And they will cut down your choicest cedars Is. 10:33, 34; 37:24
And throw them on the fire. Jer. 21:14
8"And many nations will pass by this city; and they will say to one another, 'Why has the LORD done thus to this great city?'
9"Then they will answer, 'Because they forsook the covenant of the LORD their God and bowed down to other gods and served them.' " say • 2 Kin. 22:17; 2 Chr. 34:25

Message Against Shallum

10Do not weep for the dead or mourn for him, Eccl. 4:2; Is. 57:1; Jer. 16:7; 22:18
But weep continually for the one who goes away;
For he will never return
Or see his native land. Jer. 25:27; 44:14
11 For thus says the LORD in regard to Shallum the son of Josiah, king of Judah, who became king in the place of Josiah his father, who went forth from this place, "He will never return there; Jehoahaz • 1 Chr. 3:15
12 but in the place where they led him captive, there he will die and not see this land again. 2 Kin. 23:34; Jer. 22:18

Message Against Jehoiakim

13"Woe to him who builds his house without righteousness Mic. 3:10; Hab. 2:9
And his upper rooms without justice,
Who uses his neighbor's services without pay roof chambers
And does not give him his wages,
14 Who says, 'I will build myself a roomy house Is. 5:8
With spacious upper rooms,
And cut out its windows, roof chambers
Paneling it with cedar and painting it bright red.' Paneled • vermilion
15"Do you become a king because you are competing in cedar?
Did not your father eat and drink,
And do justice and righteousness?
Then it was well with him. 2 Kin. 23:25
16"He pled the cause of the afflicted and needy; Ps. 72:1-4, 12, 13
Then it was well.
Is not that what it means to know Me?"
Declares the LORD. 1 Chr. 28:9; Jer. 9:24
17"But your eyes and your heart
Are intent only upon your own dishonest gain, Jer. 6:13; 8:10; [Luke 12:15-20]
And on shedding innocent blood
And on practicing oppression and extortion." 2 Kin. 24:4; Jer. 22:3
18 Therefore thus says the LORD in regard

to ^RJehoiakim the son of Josiah, king of Ju-
dah,   2 Kin. 23:36—24:6; 2 Chr. 36:5
"They will not^Rlament for him: Jer. 22:10
'Alas, my brother!' or, 'Alas, sister!'
They will not lament for him:
'Alas for the master!' or, 'Alas for his
   splendor!'   1 Kin. 13:30
19"He will be ^Rburied with a donkey's
   burial,   1 Kin. 21:23, 24; Jer. 36:30
Dragged off and thrown out beyond
   the gates of Jerusalem.
20"Go up to Lebanon and cry out,
And lift up your voice in Bashan;
Cry out also from ^RAbarim,   Num. 27:12
For all your lovers have been crushed.
21"I spoke to you in your prosperity;
But^Ryou said, 'I will not listen!'
^RThis has been your practice^Rfrom your
   youth,   Jer. 13:10 • Jer. 3:25 • Jer. 3:24
That you have not obeyed My voice.
22"The wind will sweep away all your
   ^Rshepherds,   Jer. 23:1
And your^Rlovers will go into captivity;
Then you will surely be ^Rashamed and
   humiliated   Jer. 30:14 • Is. 65:13
Because of all your wickedness.
23"You who dwell in Lebanon,
Nested in the cedars,
How you will groan when pangs come
   upon you,
Pain like a woman in childbirth!

Message Against Coniah (Jehoiachin)

24"As I live," declares the LORD, "even
though ⁷Coniah the son of Jehoiakim king
of Judah were a signet *ring* on My right
hand, yet I would pull you^Toff;   *off from there*
25 and I shall^Rgive you over into the hand
of those who are seeking your life, yes, into
the hand of those whom you dread, even
into the hand of Nebuchadnezzar king of
Babylon, and into the hand of the Chaldeans.   2 Kin. 24:15, 16; Jer. 21:7; 34:20, 21
26"I shall hurl you and your mother who
bore you into another country where you
were not born, and there you will die.
27"But as for the land to which they desire
to return, they will not return to it.
28"Is this man Coniah a despised, shattered jar?
Or is he an^Rundesirable vessel?
Why have he and his descendants been
   ^Rhurled out
And cast into a^Rland that they had not
   known?   Hos. 8:8 • Jer. 15:1 • Jer. 17:4
29"O^Rland, land, land,   Deut. 4:26; Jer. 6:19
Hear the word of the LORD!
30"Thus says the LORD,
'Write this man down^Rchildless,
A man who will ^Rnot prosper in his
   days;   1 Chr. 3:17 • Jer. 2:37; 10:21
For no man of his ^Rdescendants will
   prosper   Ps. 94:20; Jer. 36:30
Sitting on the throne of David
Or ruling again in Judah.' "

CHAPTER 23

Message of the Righteous King

"WOE to the shepherds who are^Rdestroy-
ing and scattering the^Rsheep of My pasture!"
declares the LORD.   Is. 56:9-12 • Ezek. 34:31
2 Therefore thus says the LORD God of
Israel concerning the shepherds who are
^Ttending My people: "You have scattered My
flock and driven them away, and have not
attended to them; behold, I am about to attend to you for the^Revil of your deeds," declares the LORD.   *shepherding* • Jer. 21:12; 44:22
3"Then I Myself shall^Rgather the remnant
of My flock out of all the countries where I
have driven them and shall bring them back
to their pasture; and they will be fruitful and
multiply.   Is. 11:11, 12, 16; Jer. 31:7, 8; 32:37
4"I shall also raise up shepherds over
them and they will tend them; and they will
not be afraid any longer, nor be terrified,
nor will any be missing," declares the LORD.
5"Behold, the^Rdays are coming," declares
   the LORD,   Jer. 33:14
"When I shall raise up for David a right-
   eous^RBranch;   Matt. 1:1, 6☆
And He will ^Rreign as king and ^Aact
   wisely   Is. 9:7; 52:13 • *succeed*
And^Rdo justice and righteousness in the
   land.   Ps. 72:2; Is. 9:7; 32:1; [Dan. 9:24]
6"In His days Judah will be saved,
And^RIsrael will dwell securely;
And this is His^Rname by which He will
   be called,   Deut. 33:28 • Is. 7:14; 9:6☆
'The^RLORD our righteousness.'   Is. 45:24
7"Therefore behold, *the* days are com-
ing," declares the LORD, "when they will no
longer say, 'As the LORD lives, who brought
up the sons of Israel from the land of Egypt,'
8 but, 'As the LORD lives, who brought
up and led back the descendants of the
household of Israel from *the* north land and
from all the countries where I had driven
them.' Then they will live on their own soil."

Jeremiah's Tenth Sermon:
Against Judah's False Prophets

9 As for the prophets:
My^Rheart is broken within me,
All my bones tremble;
I have become like a drunken man,
Even like a man overcome with wine,
Because of the LORD   Jer. 8:18; Hab. 3:16
And because of His holy words.
10 For the land is full of^Radulterers;
For the land ^Rmourns because of the
   curse.   Jer. 9:2; Hos. 4:2, 3 • Jer. 12:4
The ^Rpastures of the wilderness have
   dried up.   Ps. 107:34; Jer. 9:10
Their course also is evil,
And their might is not right.
11"For^Rboth prophet and priest are pol-
   luted;   Jer. 6:13; Zeph. 3:4

---

⁷ I.e., Jehoiachin

Even in My house I have found their wickedness," declares the LORD.

12"Therefore their way will be like [R]slippery paths to them,   Ps. 35:6
They will be driven away into the [R]gloom and fall down in it;   Is. 8:22
For I shall bring [R]calamity upon them,
The year of their punishment," declares the LORD.   Jer. 11:23

13"Moreover, among the prophets of Samaria I saw an [R]offensive thing:
They prophesied by Baal and led My people Israel astray.   Hos. 9:7, 8

14"Also among the prophets of Jerusalem I have seen a [R]horrible thing:
The committing of [R]adultery and walking in falsehood;   Jer. 5:30 • Jer. 29:23
And they strengthen the hands of [R]evildoers,   Jer. 23:22; Ezek. 13:22, 23
So that no one has turned back from his wickedness.
All of them have become to Me like [R]Sodom,   Jer. 20:16; 49:18; Matt. 11:24
And her inhabitants like Gomorrah.

15"Therefore thus says the LORD of hosts concerning the prophets,
'Behold, I am going to [R]feed them wormwood
And make them drink poisonous water,
For from the prophets of Jerusalem Pollution has gone forth into all the land.'"   Deut. 29:18; Jer. 8:14; 9:15

16 Thus says the LORD of hosts,
"Do not listen to the words of the prophets who are prophesying to you.
They are [R]leading you into futility;
They speak a [R]vision of their own [T]imagination,   Matt. 7:15 • Jer. 14:14 • heart
Not from the mouth of the LORD.

17"They keep saying to those who [R]despise Me,   Mic. 2:11
'The LORD has said, "You [R] will have peace"';   Jer. 8:11; Ezek. 13:10
And as for everyone who walks in the [R]stubbornness of his own heart,
They say, 'Calamity [R] will not come upon you.'   Jer. 13:10 • Amos 9:10

18"But [R]who has stood in the council of the LORD,   Job 15:8, 9; [Jer. 23:22; 1 Cor. 2:16]
That he should see and hear His word?
Who has given [R]heed to His word and listened?   Job 33:31

19"Behold, the [R]storm of the LORD has gone forth in wrath,
Even a whirling tempest;
It will swirl down on the head of the wicked.   Jer. 25:32; 30:23; Amos 1:14

20"The [R]anger of the LORD will not turn back   2 Kin. 23:26, 27; Jer. 30:24
Until He has [R]performed and carried out the purposes of His heart;   Is. 55:11

[R]In the last days you will clearly understand it.   Gen. 49:1

21"I [R]did not send these prophets,
But they ran.   Jer. 14:14; 23:32; 27:15
I did not speak to them,
But they prophesied.

22"But if they had [R]stood in My council,
Then they would have announced My words to My people,   Jer. 9:12; 23:18
And would have turned them back from their evil way
And from the evil of their deeds.

23"Am I a God who is [R]near," declares the LORD,
"And not a God far off?   [Ps. 139:1–10]

24"Can a man [R]hide himself in hiding places,   Job 22:13, 14; [Ps. 139:7–12]
So I do not see him?" declares the LORD.
"Do [R] I not fill the heavens and the earth?" declares the LORD.   Is. 66:1

25"I have [R]heard what the prophets have said who prophesy falsely in My name, saying, 'I had a dream, I had a dream!'   Jer. 8:6

26"How long? Is there anything in the hearts of the prophets who prophesy falsehood, even these prophets of the [R]deception of their own heart,   1 Tim. 4:1, 2

27 who intend to make My people forget My name by their dreams which they relate to one another, just as their fathers [R]forgot My name because of Baal?   Judg. 3:7; 8:33, 34

28"The prophet who has a dream may relate his dream, but let him who has [R]My word speak My word in truth. [R]What does straw have in common with grain?" declares the LORD.   Jer. 9:12, 20 • [1 Cor. 3:12, 13]

29"Is not My word like [R]fire?" declares the LORD, "and like a [R]hammer which shatters a rock?   Jer. 5:14; 20:9 • [2 Cor. 10:4, 5]

30"Therefore behold, [R]I am against the prophets," declares the LORD, "who steal My words from each other.   Deut. 18:20

31"Behold, I am against the prophets," declares the LORD, "who use their tongues and declare, 'The Lord declares.'

32"Behold, I am against those who have prophesied false dreams," declares the LORD, "and related them, and led My people astray by their falsehoods and reckless boasting; yet I did not send them or command them, nor do they furnish this people the slightest benefit," declares the LORD.

33"Now when this people or the prophet or a priest asks you saying, 'What is the [8]oracle [R] of the LORD?' then you shall say to them, 'What oracle?' The LORD declares, 'I shall [R]abandon you.'   Is. 13:1 • Jer. 12:7

34"Then as for the prophet or the priest or the people who say, 'The [R]oracle of the LORD,' I shall bring punishment upon that man and his household.   Lam. 2:14; Zech. 13:3

35"Thus shall each of you say to his neighbor and to his brother, 'What has the LORD answered?' or, 'What has the LORD spoken?'

36"For you will no longer remember the

[8] Or, burden, and so throughout the ch.

oracle of the Lord, because every man's own word will become the oracle, and you have[R]perverted the words of the living God, the Lord of hosts, our God.   [Gal. 1:7, 8]

37"Thus you will say to *that* prophet, 'What has the Lord answered you?' and, 'What has the Lord spoken?'

38"For if you say, 'The oracle of the Lord!' surely thus says the Lord, 'Because you said this word, "The oracle of the Lord!" I have also sent to you, saying, "You shall not say, 'The oracle of the Lord!' " '

39"Therefore behold,[R]I shall surely forget you and cast you away from My presence, along with the city which I gave you and your fathers.   Jer. 7:14, 15; 23:33; Ezek. 8:18

40"And I will put an everlasting[R]reproach on you and an everlasting humiliation which will not be forgotten."   Jer. 20:11; 42:18

CHAPTER 24

Jeremiah's Eleventh Sermon:
The Two Baskets of Figs

AFTER[R]Nebuchadnezzar king of Babylon had carried away captive Jeconiah the son of Jehoiakim, king of Judah, and the officials of Judah with the craftsmen and smiths from Jerusalem and had brought them to Babylon, the Lord showed me: behold, two[R]baskets of figs set before the temple of the Lord!   2 Kin. 24:10-16 • Amos 8:1

2 One basket had very good figs, like [R]first-ripe figs; and the other basket had[R]very bad figs, which could not be eaten due to rottenness.   Mic. 7:1; Nah. 3:12 • Jer. 29:17

3 Then the Lord said to me, "What[R]do you see, Jeremiah?" And I said, "Figs, the good figs, very good; and the bad *figs*, very bad, which cannot be eaten due to rottenness."   Jer. 1:11, 13; Amos 8:2; Zech. 4:2

4 Then the word of the Lord came to me, saying,

5"Thus says the Lord God of Israel, 'Like these good figs, so I will regard as good the captives of Judah, whom I have sent out of this place *into* the land of the Chaldeans.

6 'For I will set My eyes on them for good, and I will[R]bring them again to this land; and I will build them up and not overthrow them, and I will[R]plant them and not pluck *them* up.   Jer. 12:15; 29:10 • Jer. 32:41

7 'And I will give them a heart to know Me, for I am the Lord; and they will be My people, and I will be their God, for they will return to Me with their whole heart.

8 'But like the bad figs which cannot be eaten due to rottenness—indeed, thus says the Lord—so I will abandon Zedekiah king of Judah and his officials, and the remnant of Jerusalem who remain in this land, and the ones who dwell in the land of Egypt.

9 'And I will make them a terror *and an* evil for all the kingdoms of the earth, as a reproach and a proverb, a taunt and a curse in all places where I shall scatter them.

10 'And I will send the[R]sword, the famine, and the pestilence upon them until they are destroyed from the land which I gave to them and their forefathers.' "   Jer. 21:9; 27:8

CHAPTER 25

Jeremiah's Twelfth Sermon:
The Seventy-year Captivity

THE word that came to Jeremiah concerning all the people of Judah, in the[R]fourth year of Jehoiakim the son of Josiah, king of Judah (that was the[R]first year of Nebuchadnezzar king of Babylon),   Jer. 36:1 • Jer. 32:1

2 which Jeremiah the prophet spoke to all the[R]people of Judah and to all the inhabitants of Jerusalem, saying,   Jer. 18:11

3"From the thirteenth year of Josiah the son of Amon, king of Judah, even to this day,[T]these twenty-three years the word of the Lord has come to me, and I have spoken to you[T]again and again, but you have not listened.   *this • rising early and speaking*

4"And the Lord has sent to you all His [R]servants the prophets[T]again and again, but you have not listened nor inclined your ear to hear,   2 Chr. 36:15 • *rising early and sending*

5 saying, 'Turn[R]now everyone from his evil way and from the evil of your deeds, and dwell on the land which the Lord has given to you and your forefathers[R]forever and ever;   2 Kin. 17:13 • Gen. 17:8; Jer. 7:7

6 and do not go after other gods to 'serve them and to worship them, and do not provoke Me to anger with the work of your hands, and I will do you no harm.'   *worship*

7"Yet you have not listened to Me," declares the Lord, "in order that you might [R]provoke Me to anger with the work of your hands to your own harm.   2 Kin. 17:17; 21:15

8"Therefore thus says the Lord of hosts, 'Because you have not obeyed My words,

9 behold, I will send and take all the families of the north,' declares the Lord, 'and *I will send* to Nebuchadnezzar king of Babylon, My servant, and will bring them against this land, and against its inhabitants, and against all these nations round about; and I will[R]utterly destroy them, and[R]make them a horror, and a hissing, and an everlasting desolation.   *put them under the ban* • 1 Kin. 9:7, 8

10 'Moreover, I will[T]take from them the voice of joy and the voice of gladness, the voice of the bridegroom and the voice of the bride, the[R]sound of the millstones and the light of the lamp.   *cause to perish* • Eccl. 12:4

11 'And this whole land shall be a desolation and a horror, and these nations shall serve the king of Babylon seventy years.

12 'Then it will be[R]when seventy years are completed I will[R]punish the king of Babylon and that nation,' declares the Lord, 'for their iniquity, and the land of the Chaldeans; and[R]I will make it an everlasting desolation.   Ezra 1:1; Jer. 29:10 • Is. 13:14 • Is. 13:19

13 'And I will bring upon that land all My words which I have pronounced against it, all that is written in this book, which Jeremiah has prophesied against all the nations.

14 '(For [R]many nations and great kings shall make slaves of them, even them; and I will [R]recompense them according to their deeds, and according to the work of their hands.)' "   Jer. 27:7; 50:9, 41 • Jer. 51:6, 24, 56

15 For thus the LORD, the God of Israel, says to me, "Take this cup of the wine of wrath from My hand, and cause all the nations, to whom I send you, to drink it.

16 "And they shall [R]drink and stagger and go mad because of the sword that I will send among them."   Nah. 3:11

17 Then I took the cup from the LORD's hand, and [R]made all the nations drink, to whom the LORD sent me: Jer. 1:10; 25:28

18 [R]Jerusalem and the cities of Judah, and its kings and its princes, to make them a ruin, a horror, a hissing, and a curse, as it is this day;   Ps. 60:3; Is. 51:17

19 [R]Pharaoh king of Egypt, his servants, his princes, and all his people;   Jer. 46:2-28

20 and all the [A]foreign people, all the kings of the land of Uz, all the kings of the land of the Philistines (even Ashkelon, Gaza, Ekron, and the remnant of Ashdod);   mixed multitude

21 Edom, Moab, and the sons of Ammon;

22 and all the kings of [R]Tyre, all the kings of Sidon, and the kings of the coastlands which are beyond the sea;   Zech. 9:2-4

23 and [R]Dedan, Tema, Buz, and all who [R]cut the corners of their hair;   Is. 21:13 • Jer. 9:26

24 and all the kings of [R]Arabia and all the kings of the [A]foreign [R]people who dwell in the desert;   2 Chr. 9:14 • mixed multitude • Jer. 25:20

25 and all the kings of Zimri, all the kings of Elam, and all the kings of Media;

26 and all the kings of the north, near and far, one with another; and [R]all the kingdoms of the earth which are upon the face of the ground, and the king of [R]Sheshach shall drink after them.   Jer. 25:9; 50:9 • Jer. 51:41

27 "And you shall say to them, 'Thus says the LORD of hosts, the God of Israel, "Drink,[R] be drunk, vomit, fall, and rise no more because of the [R]sword which I will send among you." '   Jer. 25:16; Hab. 2:16 • Ezek. 21:4, 5

28 "And it will be, if they [R]refuse to take the cup from your hand to drink, then you will say to them, 'Thus says the LORD of hosts: "You shall surely drink!   Job 34:33

29 "For behold, I am [R]beginning to work calamity in this city which is called by My name, and shall you be completely free from punishment? You will not be free from punishment; for I am summoning a sword against all the inhabitants of the earth,'" declares the LORD of hosts.'   Prov. 11:31; Is. 10:12

30 "Therefore you shall prophesy against them all these words, and you shall say to them,

'The [R]LORD will [R]roar from on high,

And utter His voice from His holy habitation;   Is. 42:13; Jer. 25:38 • Amos 1:2

He will roar mightily against His [A]fold.

He will shout like those who tread the grapes,   pasture

Against all the inhabitants of the earth.

31 'A clamor has come to the end of the earth,

Because the LORD has [R]a controversy with the nations.   Hos. 4:1; Mic. 6:2

He is entering into [R]judgment with all flesh;   Is. 66:16; Ezek. 20:35, 36; Joel 3:2

As for the wicked, He has given them to the sword,' declares the LORD."

32 Thus says the LORD of hosts,

"Behold, evil is going forth

From [R]nation to nation,   2 Chr. 15:6

And a great storm is being stirred up

From the remotest parts of the earth.

33 "And those slain by the LORD on that day shall be from one end of the earth to the [T]other. They shall not be lamented, gathered, or buried; they shall be like [R]dung on the face of the ground.   other end of the earth • Is. 5:25

34 "Wail, you shepherds, and cry;

And [R]wallow in ashes, you masters of the flock;   Jer. 6:26; Ezek. 27:30

For the days of your slaughter and your dispersions have come,

And you shall fall like a choice vessel.

35 "Flight [R]shall perish from the shepherds,

And escape from the masters of the flock.   [Job 11:20]; Jer. 11:11; Amos 2:14

36 "Hear the sound of the cry of the shepherds,

And the wailing of the masters of the flock!

For the LORD is destroying their pasture,

37 "And the peaceful [A]folds [R]are made silent

Because of the [R]fierce anger of the LORD.   pastures • Jer. 5:17 • Ps. 97:1-3

38 "He has left His hiding place [R]like the lion;   Jer. 4:7; 5:6; Hos. 5:14; 13:7, 8

For their land has become a horror

Because of the fierceness of the [A]oppressing sword,   oppressor

And because of His fierce anger."

CHAPTER 26

Conflict with the Nation

IN the beginning of the reign of [R]Jehoiakim the son of Josiah, king of Judah, this word came from the LORD, saying,   2 Kin. 23:36

2 "Thus says the LORD, 'Stand in the court of the LORD's house, and speak to all the cities of Judah, who have [R]come to worship in the LORD's house, [R]all the words that I have commanded you to speak to them. Do not omit a word!   Deut. 12:5 • Matt. 28:20

3 'Perhaps [R]they will listen and everyone will turn from his evil way, that [R]I may repent of the calamity which I am planning to

do to them because of the evil of their deeds.'   Is. 1:16-19; Jer. 36:3-7 • Jon. 3:8

4"And you will say to them, 'Thus says the LORD, "If^Ryou will not listen to Me, to ^Rwalk in My law, which I have set before you,   Lev. 26:14; 1 Kin. 9:6 • Jer. 32:23; 44:10, 23

5 to listen to the words of^RMy servants the prophets, whom I have been sending to you^tagain and again, but you have not listened;   2 Kin. 9:7 • rising early and sending

6 then I will make this house like^RShiloh, and this city I will make a^Rcurse to all the nations of the earth." ' "   Josh. 18:1 • Jer. 24:9

7 And the priests and the prophets and all the people heard Jeremiah speaking these words in the house of the LORD.

8 And when Jeremiah finished speaking all that the LORD had commanded him to speak to all the people, the priests and the prophets and all the people seized him, saying, "You^Rmust die!   Matt. 21:35, 36; 23:34, 35

9"Why have you prophesied in the name of the LORD saying, 'This house will be like Shiloh, and this city will be^Rdesolate, without inhabitant'?" And^Rall the people gathered about Jeremiah in the house of the LORD.   Jer. 9:11; 33:10 • Acts 3:11; 5:12

10 And when the^Rprinces of Judah heard these things, they came up from the king's house to the house of the LORD and sat in the^Rentrance of the New Gate of the LORD's house.   Jer. 26:21 • Jer. 36:10

11 Then the priests and the prophets ^Rspoke to the officials and to all the people, saying, "A death sentence for this man! For he has prophesied against this city as you have heard in your hearing."   Jer. 18:23

12 Then Jeremiah spoke to all the officials and to all the people, saying, "The^R LORD sent me to prophesy against this house and against this city all the words that you have heard.   Jer. 1:17, 18; 26:15; [Acts 4:19; 5:29]

13"Now therefore amend your ways and your deeds, and obey the voice of the LORD your God; and the LORD will ^tchange His mind about the misfortune which He has pronounced against you.   be sorry for

14"But as for me, behold,^RI am in your hands; do with me as is good and right in your sight.   Jer. 38:5

15"Only know for certain that if you put me to death, you will bring^Rinnocent blood on yourselves, and on this city, and on its inhabitants; for truly the LORD has sent me to you to speak all these words in your hearing."   Num. 35:33; [Prov. 6:16, 17]; Jer. 7:6

16 Then the officials and all the people said to the priests and to the prophets, "No death sentence for this man! For he has spoken to us in the name of the LORD our God."

17 Then^Rsome of the elders of the land rose up and spoke to all the assembly of the people, saying,   Acts 5:34

18"Micah^Rof Moresheth prophesied in the days of Hezekiah king of Judah; and he spoke to all the people of Judah, saying, 'Thus the LORD of hosts has said,   Mic. 1:1

"Zion^Rwill be plowed as a field,   Ps. 79:1
And Jerusalem will become ruins,
And the^Rmountain of the house as the high places of a forest." '   Is. 2:2, 3

19"Did Hezekiah king of Judah and all Judah put him to death? Did he not fear the LORD and entreat the favor of the LORD, and the LORD^tchanged His mind about the misfortune which He had pronounced against them? But we are^Rcommitting a great evil against ourselves."   was sorry for • Jer. 44:7

20 Indeed, there was also a man who prophesied in the name of the LORD, Uriah the son of Shemaiah from^RKiriath-jearim; and he prophesied against this city and against this land words similar to all those of Jeremiah.   Josh. 9:17; 1 Sam. 6:21; 7:2

21 When King Jehoiakim and all his mighty men and all the officials heard his words, then the^Rking sought to put him to death; but Uriah heard it, and he was afraid and fled, and went to Egypt.   2 Chr. 16:10

22 Then King Jehoiakim sent men to Egypt: Elnathan the son of Achbor and certain men with him went into Egypt.

23 And they brought Uriah from Egypt and led him to King Jehoiakim, who slew him with a sword, and cast his dead body into the burial place of the common people.

24 But the hand of^RAhikam the son of Shaphan was with Jeremiah, so that he was^tnot given into the hands of the people to put him to death.   2 Kin. 22:12-14 • 1 Kin. 18:4

CHAPTER 27

Conflict with the False Prophets

I N the beginning of the reign of Zedekiah the son of Josiah, king of Judah, this word came to Jeremiah from the LORD, saying—

2 thus says the LORD to me—"Make for yourself^Rbonds and^Ryokes and put them on your neck,   Jer. 30:8 • Jer. 28:10, 13

3 and send^tword to the king of Edom, to the king of Moab, to the king of the sons of Ammon, to the king of Tyre, and to the king of Sidon by the messengers who come to Jerusalem to Zedekiah king of Judah.   them

4"And command them to go to their masters, saying, 'Thus says the LORD of hosts, the God of Israel, thus you shall say to your masters,

5"I have made the earth, the men and the beasts which are on the face of the earth^Rby My great power and by My outstretched arm, and I will give it to the one who is ^Apleasing in My sight.   Jer. 32:17 • upright

6"And now I^Rhave given all these lands into the hand of Nebuchadnezzar king of Babylon,^RMy servant, and I have given him also the^Rwild animals of the field to serve him.   Jer. 21:7; 22:25 • Is. 44:28 • Jer. 28:14

7"And all the nations shall serve him, and his son, and his grandson, until the time of his own land comes; then many nations and great kings will make him their servant.

8"And it will be, *that* the nation or the kingdom which^Rwill not serve him, Nebuchadnezzar king of Babylon, and which will not put its neck under the yoke of the king of Babylon, I will punish that nation with the sword, with famine, and with pestilence," declares the LORD, "until I have destroyed^Tit by his hand.   Jer. 38:17-19 • *them*

9"But as for you, ^Rdo not listen to your prophets, your diviners, your ^Tdreamers, your soothsayers, or your sorcerers, who speak to you, saying, 'You shall not serve the king of Babylon.'   Deut. 18:10 • *dreams*

10"For they prophesy a^Rlie to you, in order to remove you far from your land; and I will drive you out, and you will perish. Jer. 23:25

11"But the nation which will^Rbring its neck under the yoke of the king of Babylon and serve him, I will^Rlet remain on its land," declares the LORD, "and they will till it and dwell in it." ' "   Jer. 27:2, 8, 12 • Jer. 21:9

12 And I spoke words like all these to Zedekiah king of Judah, saying, "Bring your necks under the yoke of the king of Babylon, and serve him and his people, and live!

13"Why will you^Rdie, you and your people, by the sword, famine, and pestilence, as the LORD has spoken to that nation which will not serve the king of Babylon?   [Prov. 8:36]

14"So ^Rdo not listen to the words of the prophets who speak to you, saying, 'You shall not serve the king of Babylon,' for they prophesy a^Rlie to you;   Jer. 27:9 • Ezek. 13:22

15 for^RI have not sent them," declares the LORD, "but they ^Rprophesy falsely in My name, in order that I may drive you out, and that you may perish, you and the prophets who prophesy to you."   Jer. 23:21 • Jer. 23:25

16 *Then* I spoke to the priests and to all this people, saying, "Thus says the LORD: Do not listen to the words of your prophets who prophesy to you, saying, 'Behold, the^Rvessels of the LORD's house will now shortly be brought again from Babylon'; for they are prophesying a lie to you.   Jer. 28:3; Dan. 1:2

17"Do not listen to them; serve the king of Babylon, and live! Why should this city^Rbecome a ruin?   Jer. 7:34

18"But if they are prophets, and if the word of the LORD is with them, let them now^Rentreat the LORD of hosts, that the vessels which are left in the house of the LORD, in the house of the king of Judah, and in Jerusalem, may not go to Babylon. Jer. 18:20

19"For thus says the LORD of hosts concerning the pillars, concerning the sea, concerning the stands, and concerning the rest of the vessels that are left in this city,

20 which Nebuchadnezzar king of Babylon did not take when he^Rcarried into exile Jeconiah the son of Jehoiakim, king of Judah, from Jerusalem to Babylon, and all the nobles of Judah and Jerusalem. Jer. 22:28

21"Yes, thus says the LORD of hosts, the God of Israel, concerning the vessels that are left in the house of the LORD, and in the house of the king of Judah, and in Jerusalem,

22 'They shall be carried to Babylon, and they shall be there until the day I visit them,' declares the LORD. 'Then I will bring them back and restore them to this place.' "

CHAPTER 28

Conflict with Hananiah

NOW it came about in the same year, in the beginning of the reign of Zedekiah king of Judah, in the fourth year, in the fifth month, that Hananiah the son of Azzur, the prophet, who was from Gibeon, spoke to me in the house of the LORD in the presence of the priests and all the people, saying,

2"Thus^Rsays the LORD of hosts, the God of Israel, 'I have broken the yoke of the king of Babylon.   Jer. 27:12; 28:11

3 'Within two years I am going to bring back to this place ^Rall the vessels of the LORD's house, which Nebuchadnezzar king of Babylon took away from this place and carried to Babylon.   2 Kin. 24:13; 2 Chr. 36:10

4 'I am also going to bring back to this place Jeconiah the son of Jehoiakim, king of Judah, and all the exiles of Judah who went to Babylon,' declares the LORD, 'for I will break the yoke of the king of Babylon.' "

5 Then the prophet Jeremiah spoke to the prophet Hananiah in the presence of the priests and in the presence of all the people who were standing in the house of the LORD,

6 and the prophet Jeremiah said, "Amen! May the LORD do so; may the LORD^Aconfirm your words which you have prophesied to bring back the vessels of the LORD's house and all the exiles, from Babylon to this place.   *fulfill*

7"Yet ^Rhear now this word which I am about to speak in your hearing and in the hearing of all the people!   1 Kin. 22:28

8"The prophets who were before me and before you from ancient times ^Rprophesied against many lands and against great kingdoms, of war and of calamity and of pestilence.   Lev. 26:14-39; 1 Kin. 14:15; Joel 1:20

9"The prophet who prophesies of peace, when the word of the prophet shall come to pass, then that prophet will be known *as* one whom the LORD has truly sent."

10 Then Hananiah the prophet took the ^Ryoke from the neck of Jeremiah the prophet and broke it.   Jer. 27:2

11 And Hananiah spoke in the presence of all the people, saying, "Thus says the LORD, 'Even so will I break within two full years, the yoke of Nebuchadnezzar king of Babylon from the neck of all the nations.' " Then the prophet Jeremiah went his way.

12 And the^Rword of the LORD came to Jeremiah, after Hananiah the prophet had broken the yoke from off the neck of the prophet Jeremiah, saying,   Jer. 1:2

13"Go and speak to Hananiah, saying,

'Thus says the LORD, "You have broken the yokes of wood, but you have made instead of them^Ryokes of iron."   Ps. 107:16; Is. 45:2

14 'For thus says the LORD of hosts, the God of Israel, "I have put a^Ryoke of iron on the neck of all these nations, that they may serve Nebuchadnezzar king of Babylon; and they shall serve him. And I have also given him the beasts of the field." ' "   Deut. 28:48

15 Then Jeremiah the prophet said to Hananiah the prophet, "Listen now, Hananiah, the LORD has not sent you, and you have made this people trust in a lie.

16"Therefore thus says the LORD, 'Behold, I am about to^Tremove you from the face of the earth. This year you are going to die, because you have ^Tcounseled rebellion against the LORD.' "   *send you away • spoken*

17 So Hananiah the prophet died in the same year in the seventh month.

CHAPTER 29

First Letter to the Exiles

NOW these are the words of the^Rletter which Jeremiah the prophet sent from Jerusalem to the rest of the elders of the exile, the priests, the prophets, and all the people whom Nebuchadnezzar had taken into exile from Jerusalem to Babylon.   2 Chr. 30:1, 6

2 (This was after King^RJeconiah and the ^Rqueen mother, the court officials, the princes of Judah and Jerusalem, the craftsmen and the smiths had departed from Jerusalem.)   2 Kin. 24:12-16 • 2 Kin. 24:12, 15

3 *The letter was sent* by the hand of Elasah the son of Shaphan, and Gemariah the son of^RHilkiah, whom Zedekiah king of Judah sent to Babylon to Nebuchadnezzar king of Babylon, saying,   1 Chr. 6:13

4"Thus says the LORD of hosts, the God of Israel, to all the exiles whom I have sent into exile from Jerusalem to Babylon,

5 'Build houses and live in *them;* and plant gardens, and eat their^Tproduce.   *fruit*

6 'Take wives and^Tbecome the fathers of sons and daughters, and take wives for your sons and give your daughters to husbands, that they may bear sons and daughters; and multiply there and do not decrease.   *beget*

7 'And^Rseek the^Awelfare of the city where I have sent you into exile, and^Rpray to the LORD on its behalf; for in its^Awelfare you will have^Awelfare.'   Dan. 4:27 • *peace* • Ezra 6:10

8"For thus says the LORD of hosts, the God of Israel, 'Do not let your^Rprophets who are in your midst and your diviners^Rdeceive you, and do not listen to^Tthe dreams which ^Tthey dream.   Jer. 27:9 • Eph. 5:6 • *your • you*

9 'For they^Rprophesy falsely to you in My name; ^RI have not sent them,' declares the LORD.   Jer. 27:15; 29:21 • Jer. 29:31

10"For thus says the LORD, 'When seventy years have been completed for Babylon, I will visit you and fulfill My good word to you, to bring you back to this place.

11 'For I know the^Rplans that I^Thave for you,' declares the LORD, 'plans for welfare and not for calamity to give you a future and a^Thope.   Ps. 40:5 • *am planning* • Hos. 2:15

12 'Then you will call upon Me and come and pray to Me, and I will listen to you.

13 'And you will seek Me and find *Me,* when you search for Me with all your heart.

14 'And I will be found by you,' declares the LORD, 'and I will restore your^Afortunes and will^Rgather you from all the nations and from all the places where I have driven you,' declares the LORD, 'and I will^Rbring you back to the place from where I sent you into exile.'   *captivity* • Is. 43:5, 6 • Jer. 3:14

15"Because you have said, 'The LORD has raised up prophets for us in Babylon'—

16 for thus says the LORD concerning the king who sits on the throne of David, and concerning all the people who dwell in this city, your brothers who did^Rnot go with you into exile—   Jer. 38:2, 3, 17-23

17 thus says the LORD of hosts, 'Behold, I am sending upon them the^Rsword, famine, and pestilence, and I will make them like ^Rsplit-open figs that cannot be eaten due to rottenness.   Jer. 27:8; 29:18 • Jer. 24:3, 8-10

18 'And I will pursue them with the sword, with famine and with pestilence; and I will ^Rmake them a terror to all the kingdoms of the earth, to be a curse, and a horror, and a hissing, and a reproach among all the nations where I have driven them,   Deut. 28:25

19 because they have^Rnot listened to My words,' declares the LORD, 'which I sent to them again and again by^RMy servants the prophets; but you did not listen,' declares the LORD.   Jer. 6:19 • Jer. 25:4; 26:5; 35:15

20"You, therefore, hear the word of the LORD, all you exiles, whom I have^Rsent away from Jerusalem to Babylon.   Jer. 24:5

21"Thus says the LORD of hosts, the God of Israel, concerning Ahab the son of Kolaiah and concerning Zedekiah the son of Maaseiah, who are prophesying to you falsely in My name, 'Behold, I will deliver them into the hand of Nebuchadnezzar king of Babylon, and he shall slay them before your eyes.

22 'And because of them a curse shall be ^Tused by all the exiles from Judah who are in Babylon, saying, "May the LORD make you like Zedekiah and like Ahab, whom the king of Babylon roasted in the fire,   *taken*

23 because they have acted foolishly in Israel, and have committed adultery with their neighbors' wives, and have spoken words in My name falsely, which I did not command them; and I am He who knows, and am a witness," declares the LORD.' "

Letter from Shemaiah

24 And to^RShemaiah the Nehelamite you shall speak, saying,   Jer. 29:31, 32

25"Thus says the LORD of hosts, the God of Israel, 'Because you have sent^Rletters in your own name to all the people who are in Jerusalem, and to^RZephaniah the son of Ma-

aseiah, the priest, and to all the priests, saying,   Jer. 29:1 • 2 Kin. 25:18; Jer. 37:3; 52:24

26"The LORD has made you priest instead of Jehoiada the priest, to be the[T]overseer in the house of the LORD over every[R]madman who prophesies, to put him in the stocks and in the iron collar,   overseers • 2 Kin. 9:11

27 now then, why have you not rebuked Jeremiah of [R]Anathoth who prophesies to you?   Jer. 1:1

28"For he has sent to us in Babylon, saying, 'The exile will be[R]long;[R]build houses and live in them and plant gardens and eat their [T]produce.' " ' "   Jer. 29:10 • Jer. 29:5 • fruit

29 And Zephaniah the priest read this letter[T]to Jeremiah the prophet.   in the ears of

Second Letter to the Exiles

30 Then came the word of the LORD to Jeremiah, saying,

31"Send to all the exiles, saying, 'Thus says the LORD concerning Shemaiah the Nehelamite, "Because Shemaiah has prophesied to you, although I did not send him, and he has made you trust in a lie,"

32 therefore thus says the LORD, "Behold, I am about to punish Shemaiah the Nehelamite and his[T]descendants; he shall not have anyone living among this people, and he shall not see the good that I am about to do to My people," declares the LORD, "because he has [T]preached[R] rebellion against the LORD." ' "   seed • spoken • Deut. 13:5

CHAPTER 30

Restoration to the Land

THE word which came to Jeremiah from the LORD, saying,

2"Thus says the LORD, the God of Israel, 'Write[R]all the words which I have spoken to you in a book.   Is. 30:8; Jer. 25:13; 36:4, 28, 32

3 'For, behold, days are coming,' declares the LORD, 'when I will restore the [A]fortunes of My people[R]Israel and Judah.' The LORD says, 'I will also bring them back to the land that I gave to their forefathers, and they shall possess it.' "   captivity • Jer. 3:18

4 Now these are the words which the LORD spoke concerning Israel and concerning Judah,

5"For thus says the LORD,
  'I[T]have heard a sound of terror,   We
  Of dread, and there is no peace.

6 'Ask now, and see,
  If a male can give birth.
  Why do I see every man
  With his hands on his loins, [R]as a
    woman in childbirth?   Jer. 4:31; 6:24
  And why have all faces turned pale?

7 'Alas! for that[R]day is great,   [Is. 2:12]
  There is[R]none like it.   Dan. 9:12; 12:1
  And it is the time of Jacob's distress,
  But he will be[R]saved from it.   Jer. 30:10

8 'And it shall come about on that day,'
declares the LORD of hosts, 'that I will break his yoke from off their neck, and will tear off their bonds; and strangers shall no longer make[T]them their slaves.   him their slave

9 'But they shall serve the LORD their God, and[R]David their king, whom I will raise up for them.   Is. 55:3–5; Ezek. 34:23, 24; Hos. 3:5☆

10 'And[R]fear not, O Jacob My servant,' declares the LORD,   Is. 41:13; 43:5; 44:2
  'And do not be dismayed, O Israel;
  For behold, I will save you[R]from afar,
  And your [T]offspring from the land of
    their captivity.   Jer. 23:3, 8 • seed
  And Jacob shall return, and shall be
    [R]quiet and at ease,   Is. 35:9; Jer. 33:16
  And no one shall make him afraid.

11 'For[R]I am with you,' declares the LORD,
    'to save you;   Jer. 1:8, 19
  For I will[R]destroy completely all the nations where I have scattered you,
  Only I will[R]not destroy you completely.
  But I will[R]chasten you justly,
  And will by no means leave you unpunished.'   Jer. 46:28 • Jer. 4:27 • Ps. 6:1

12"For thus says the LORD,
  'Your wound is incurable,
  And your[R]injury is serious.   2 Chr. 36:16

13 'There is no one to plead your cause;
  No healing for your sore,
  [R]No recovery for you.   Jer. 14:19; 46:11

14 'All your[R]lovers have forgotten you,
  They do not seek you;   Jer. 22:20, 22
  For I have [R]wounded you with the
    wound of an enemy,   Lam. 2:4, 5
  With the punishment of a[R]cruel one,
  Because your iniquity is great   Jer. 6:23
  And your[R]sins are numerous.   Jer. 5:6

15 'Why do you cry out over your injury?
  Your pain is incurable.
  Because your iniquity is great
  And your sins are numerous,
  I have done these things to you.

16 'Therefore all who[R]devour you shall be
    devoured;   Jer. 2:3; 8:16; 10:25
  And all your adversaries, every one of
    them,[R]shall go into captivity;
  And those who plunder you shall be for
    plunder,   Is. 14:2; Joel 3:8
  And all who prey upon you I will give
    for prey.

17 'For I will[T]restore you to[A]health
  And I will heal you of your wounds,'
    declares the LORD,
  'Because they have called you an outcast, saying: cause to go up • healing
  "It is Zion; no one cares for her." '

18"Thus says the LORD,
  'Behold, I will restore the[A]fortunes of
    the tents of Jacob   captivity
  And[R]have compassion on his dwelling
    places;   Ps. 102:13
  And the[T]city shall be rebuilt on its ruin,
  And the[R]palace shall stand on its rightful place.   Jer. 31:4, 38–40 • Ps. 122:7

19 'And from them shall proceed^Rthanks-
giving   Is. 12:1; 35:10; 51:3; Jer. 17:26
And the voice of those who ^Amake^R
merry;   *dance* • Ps. 126:1, 2; Is. 51:11
And I will ^Rmultiply them, and they
shall not be diminished;   Jer. 33:22
I will also^Rhonor them, and they shall
not be insignificant.   Is. 55:5; 60:9
20 'Their^T children also shall be as formerly,   *His*
And ^Ttheir congregation shall be ^Restab-
lished before Me;   *his* • [Is. 54:14]
And I will punish all their oppressors.
21 'And ^Ttheir^Rleader shall be one of them,
And their ruler shall come forth from
their midst;   *his* • Jer. 30:9
And I will^Rbring him near, and he shall
approach Me;   Num. 16:5; Ps. 65:4
For who would dare to risk his life to
approach Me?' declares the LORD.
22 'And you shall be^RMy people,   Ex. 6:7
And I will be your God.' "

23 Behold, the^Rtempest of the LORD!
Wrath has gone forth,
A ^Asweeping tempest;   Jer. 23:19 • *raging*
It will burst on the head of the wicked.
24 The ^Rfierce anger of the LORD will not
turn back,
Until He has performed, and until He
has accomplished
The intent of His heart;
In the^Rlatter days you will understand
this.   Jer. 4:8 • Jer. 23:20

CHAPTER 31

Israel Is Restored

" **A**T that time," declares the LORD, "I will
be the^RGod of all the families of Israel, and
they shall be My people."   Jer. 30:22
2 Thus says the LORD,
"The people who survived the sword
Found grace in the wilderness—
Israel, when it went to find its rest."
3 The LORD appeared to ^Thim from afar,
saying,   *me*
"I have ^Rloved you with an everlasting
love;   Deut. 4:37; 7:8; Mal. 1:2
Therefore I have drawn you with
^Rlovingkindness.   Ps. 25:6
4 "Again^RI will build you, and you shall be
rebuilt,   Jer. 24:6; 33:7
O virgin of Israel!
Again you shall ^Atake up your^Rtambou-
rines,   *be adorned with* • Is. 30:32
And go forth to the dances of the
^Rmerrymakers.   Jer. 30:19
5 "Again you shall^Rplant vineyards
On the hills of Samaria;   Ps. 107:37
The planters shall plant
And shall^Tenjoy *them.*   *defile*
6 "For there shall be a day when watch-
men
On the hills of Ephraim shall call out,
'Arise, and^Rlet us go up *to* Zion,
To the LORD our God.' "   [Is. 2:3; Mic. 4:2]

7 For thus says the LORD,
"Sing^Raloud with gladness for Jacob,
And shout among the^Tchiefs^R of the na-
tions;   Jer. 20:13 • *heads* • Is. 61:9
Proclaim, give praise, and say,
'O LORD, ^Rsave Thy people,   Ps. 28:9
The^Rremnant of Israel.'   Jer. 23:3
8 "Behold, I am^Rbringing them from the
north country,   Jer. 3:18; 23:8
And I will^Rgather them from the remote
parts of the earth,   Deut. 30:4; Is. 43:6
Among them the^Rblind and the^Rlame,
The woman with child and she who is
in labor with child, together;
A great ^Acompany, they shall return
here.   Is. 42:16 • Mic. 4:6 • *assembly*
9 "With^Rweeping they shall come,
And by supplication I will lead them;
I will make them walk by ^Tstreams of
waters,   [Ps. 126:5; Jer. 50:4] • Is. 43:20
On a straight path in which they shall
^Rnot stumble;   Is. 63:13
For I am a^Rfather to Israel,   Jer. 3:4, 19
And Ephraim is My first-born."

10 Hear the word of the LORD, O nations,
And declare in the^Rcoastlands afar off,
And say, "He who scattered Israel will
^Rgather him,   Is. 66:19 • Jer. 50:19
And keep him as a^Rshepherd keeps his
flock."   Is. 40:11; Ezek. 34:12
11 For the LORD has ransomed Jacob,
And redeemed him from the hand of
him who was stronger than he.
12 "And they shall^Rcome and shout for joy
on the height of Zion,   Jer. 31:6, 7
And they shall be radiant over the
^Tbounty of the LORD—   *goodness*
Over the^Rgrain, and the new wine, and
the oil,   Hos. 2:22; Joel 3:18
And over the young of the^Rflock and
the herd;   Jer. 31:24; 33:12, 13
And their life shall be like a^Rwatered
garden,   Is. 58:11
And they shall never languish again.
13 "Then the virgin shall rejoice in the
^Rdance,   Judg. 21:21; Ps. 30:11
And the young men and the old, to-
gether,
For I will^Rturn their mourning into joy,
And will comfort them, and give them
joy for their sorrow.   Is. 61:3
14 "And I will ^Rfill the soul of the priests
with ^Aabundance,   *saturate* • *fatness*
And My people shall be satisfied with
My goodness," declares the LORD.

15 Thus says the LORD,
"A voice is heard in^RRamah,   Josh. 18:25
Lamentation *and* bitter weeping.
Rachel is weeping for her children;
She ^Rrefuses to be comforted for her
children,   Gen. 37:35; Ps. 77:2
Because^Rthey are no more." Matt. 2:17 ☆
16 Thus says the LORD,
"Restrain^Ryour voice from weeping,

And your eyes from tears;   Is. 25:8; 30:19
For your[R]work shall be rewarded," declares the LORD,   Ruth 2:12; Heb. 6:10
"And they shall[R]return from the land of
the enemy.   Jer. 30:3; Ezek. 11:17
17"And there is[R]hope for your future," declares the LORD,
"And your children shall return to their
own territory.   Jer. 29:11
18"I have surely heard Ephraim[R]grieving,
'Thou hast[R]chastised me, and I was
chastised,   Jer. 3:21 • Job 5:17
Like an untrained[R]calf;   Hos. 4:16
Bring me back that I may be restored,
For Thou art the LORD my God.
19 'For after I turned back, I[R]repented;
And after I was instructed, I[R]smote on
my thigh;   Ezek. 36:31 • Luke 18:13
I was[R]ashamed, and also humiliated,
Because I bore the reproach of my
youth.'   Jer. 3:25
20"Is[R]Ephraim My dear son?
Is he a delightful child?   Hos. 11:8
Indeed, as often as I have spoken
against him,
I certainly *still* remember him;
Therefore My[T]heart yearns for him," de-
clares the LORD.   *inward parts*

21"Set up for yourself roadmarks,
Place for yourself guideposts;
[R]Direct your mind to the highway,
The way by which you went.
Return, O virgin of Israel,
Return to these your cities.   Jer. 50:5

Judah Is Restored

22"How long will you go here and there,
O[R]faithless daughter?   Jer. 3:6; 49:4
For the LORD has created a new thing
in the earth—
A woman will encompass a man."
23 Thus says the LORD of hosts, the God
of Israel, "Once again they will speak this
word in the land of Judah and in its cities,
when I restore their[A]fortunes,   *captivity*
'The LORD bless you, O[R]abode of righteousness,   Is. 1:26; Jer. 50:7
O[R]holy hill!'   Ps. 48:1; 87:1; [Zech. 8:3]
24"And Judah and all its cities will[R]dwell
together in it, the farmer and they who go
about with flocks.   Jer. 31:12; Ezek. 36:10

25"For I satisfy the weary ones and [T]re-
fresh everyone who languishes."   *fill*
26 At this I [R]awoke and looked, and my
sleep was pleasant to me.   Zech. 4:1
27"Behold, days are coming," declares the
LORD, "when I will [R]sow the house of Israel
and the house of Judah with the seed of man
and with the seed of beast.   Ezek. 36:9, 11
28"And it will come about that as I have
[R]watched over them to pluck up, to break
down, to overthrow, to destroy, and to bring
disaster, so I will watch over them to build
and to plant," declares the LORD.   Jer. 44:27
29"In those days they will not say again,
'The[R]fathers have eaten sour grapes,
And the children's teeth are [A]set on
edge.'   Lam. 5:7; Ezek. 18:2 • *dull*
30"But[R]everyone will die for his own iniquity; each man who eats the sour grapes, his
teeth will be [A]set on edge.   Deut. 24:16 • *dull*

31"Behold,[R] days are coming," declares the
LORD, "when I will make a[R]new covenant
with the house of Israel and with the house
of Judah, Heb. 8:8–12 • [Luke 22:20; 1 Cor. 11:25]☆
32 not like the [R]covenant which I made
with their fathers in the day I[R]took them by
the hand to bring them out of the land of
Egypt, My[R]covenant which they broke, although I was a husband to them," declares
the LORD.   Ex. 19:5 • Deut. 1:31 • Jer. 11:7, 8
33"But[R]this is the covenant which I will
make with the house of Israel after those
days," declares the LORD, "I[R]will put My law
within them, and on their heart I will write
it; and[R]I will be their God, and they shall be
My people.   Jer. 32:40 • [2 Cor. 3:3]☆ • Jer. 24:7
34"And they shall[R]not teach again, each
man his neighbor and each man his brother,
saying, 'Know the LORD,' for they shall all
[R]know Me, from the least of them to the
greatest of them," declares the LORD, "for I
will forgive their iniquity, and their sin I will
remember no more."   1 Thess. 4:9 • Is. 11:9☆

35 Thus says the LORD,
Who[R]gives the sun for light by day,
And the [T]fixed order of the moon and
the stars for light by night,
Who[R]stirs up the sea so that its waves
roar;   Deut. 4:19 • *statutes* • Is. 51:15
The LORD of hosts is His name:
36"If[T]this fixed order departs
From before Me," declares the LORD,

31:31–34 The New Covenant—The New Covenant is the fifth and last of the theocratic covenants (pertaining to the rule of God). Four provisions are made in this covenant: (1) regeneration—God will put His law in their inward parts and write it in their hearts, 31:33; (2) a national restoration—Yahweh will be their God and the nation will be His people, 31:33; (3) personal ministry of the Holy Spirit—they will all be taught individually by God, 31:34; and (4) a full justification—their sins will be forgiven and completely removed, 31:34. The New Covenant is made sure by the blood that Jesus shed on Calvary's cross. That blood which guarantees to Israel this New Covenant also provides for the forgiveness of sins for the believers who comprise the church. Jesus' payment for sins is more than adequate to pay for the sins of all who will believe in Him. The New Covenant is called "new" in contrast to the covenant with Moses which is called "old" (Page 749—Jer. 31:32; Page 1243—Heb. 8:6–13) because it actually accomplishes what the Mosaic Covenant could only point to, that is, the child of God living in a manner that is consistent with the character of God.
Now turn to Page 22—THE CHRISTIAN'S GUIDE: Understanding God's Being.

"Then the offspring of Israel also shall ^Rcease   *these statutes* · Amos 9:8, 9

From being a nation before Me ^Tfor-
ever."   *all the days*

37 Thus says the LORD,
"If ^Tthe heavens above can be measured,
And the foundations of the earth
searched out below,   Is. 40:12
Then I will also ^Rcast off all the offspring
of Israel
For all that they have done," declares
the LORD.   [Rom. 11:2–5, 26, 27]

38 "Behold, days are coming," declares the
LORD, "when the ^Rcity shall be rebuilt for the
LORD from the ^RTower of Hananel to the ^RCor-
ner Gate.   Jer. 30:18 · Neh. 3:1 · 2 Kin. 14:13

39 "And the ^Rmeasuring line shall go out
farther straight ahead to the hill Gareb; then
it will turn to Goah.   Zech. 2:1

40 "And ^Rthe whole valley of the dead bodies and of the ashes, and all the fields as far
as the brook Kidron, to the corner of the
Horse Gate toward the east, shall be holy to
the LORD; it shall not be plucked up, or overthrown anymore forever."   Jer. 7:32; 8:2

CHAPTER 32

Rebuilding of Jerusalem

T HE word that came to Jeremiah from the
LORD in the ^Rtenth year of Zedekiah king of
Judah, which was the eighteenth year of
Nebuchadnezzar.   2 Kin. 25:1, 2; Jer. 39:1, 2

2 Now at that time the army of the king
of Babylon was besieging Jerusalem, and
Jeremiah the prophet was shut up in the
^Rcourt of the guard, which was *in* the house
of the king of Judah,   Neh. 3:25; Jer. 33:1; 37:21

3 because Zedekiah king of Judah had
shut him up, saying, "Why do you prophesy,
saying, 'Thus says the LORD, "Behold, I am
about to give this city into the hand of the
king of Babylon, and he will take it;

4 and Zedekiah king of Judah shall not
escape out of the hand of the Chaldeans, but
he shall surely be given into the hand of the
king of Babylon, and he shall speak with
him face to face, and see him eye to eye;

5 and he shall take Zedekiah to Babylon,
and he shall be there until I visit him," declares the LORD. "If you fight against the
Chaldeans, you shall not succeed" ' ? "

6 And Jeremiah said, "The word of the
LORD came to me, saying,

7 'Behold, Hanamel the son of Shallum
your uncle is coming to you, saying, "Buy
for yourself my field which is at ^RAnathoth,
for you have the ^Rright of redemption to buy
it." '   Jer. 1:1; 11:21 · Lev. 25:25; Ruth 4:3, 4

8 "Then Hanamel my uncle's son came to
me in the ^Rcourt of the guard according to
the word of the LORD and said to me, 'Buy
my field, please, that is at Anathoth, which
is in the land of Benjamin; for you have the
right of possession and the redemption is
yours; buy *it* for yourself.' Then I knew that
this was the word of the LORD.   Jer. 32:2; 33:1

9 "And I bought the field which was at
Anathoth from Hanamel my uncle's son,
and I ^Rweighed out the silver for him, seventeen ^Rshekels of silver.   Gen. 23:16 · Ex. 21:32

10 "And I ^Asigned and sealed the deed, and
called in witnesses, and weighed out the silver on the scales.   *wrote . . . on the document*

11 "Then I took the deeds of purchase,
both the sealed *copy containing* the terms
and conditions, and the open *copy;*

12 and I gave the deed of purchase to Baruch the son of Neriah, the son of Mahseiah,
in the sight of Hanamel my uncle's *son,* and
in the sight of the witnesses who signed the
deed of purchase, before all the Jews who
were sitting in the court of the guard.

13 "And I commanded Baruch in their
presence, saying,

14 'Thus says the LORD of hosts, the God
of Israel, "Take these deeds, this sealed
deed of purchase, and this open deed, and
put them in an earthenware jar, that they
may ^Tlast a long time."   *stand many days*

15 'For thus says the LORD of hosts, the
God of Israel, "Houses and fields and vineyards shall again be bought in this land." '

16 "After I had given the deed of purchase
to Baruch the son of Neriah, then I ^Rprayed
to the LORD, saying,   Gen. 32:9-12; Jer. 12:1

17 'Ah Lord GOD! Behold, Thou hast made
the heavens and the earth by Thy great
power and by Thine outstretched arm!
^RNothing is too difficult for Thee,   Gen. 18:14

18 who ^Rshowest lovingkindness to thousands, but repayest the iniquity of fathers
into the bosom of their children after them,
O ^Rgreat and ^Rmighty God. The LORD of hosts
is His name;   Ex. 20:6 · Ps. 145:3 · Jer. 20:11

19 ^Rgreat in counsel and mighty in deed,
whose ^Reyes are open to all the ways of the
sons of men, ^Rgiving to everyone according
to his ways and according to the fruit of his
deeds;   [Is. 9:6; 28:29] · Job 34:21 · [Matt. 16:27]

20 who hast set signs and wonders in the
land of Egypt, *and* even to this day both in
Israel and among mankind; and Thou hast
made a name for Thyself, as at this day.

21 'And Thou didst bring Thy people Israel
out of the land of Egypt with signs and with
wonders, and with a strong hand and with
an outstretched arm, and with great terror;

22 and gavest them this land, which Thou
didst swear to their forefathers to give
them, a land flowing with milk and honey.

23 'And they came in and took possession
of it, but they ^Rdid not obey Thy voice or
walk in Thy law; they have done nothing of
all that Thou commandedst them to do;
therefore Thou hast made ^Rall this calamity
come upon them.   [Neh. 9:26] · Lam. 1:18

24 'Behold, the siege mounds have reached
the city to take it; and the city is given into
the hand of the Chaldeans who fight against
it, because of the sword, the famine, and the
pestilence; and what Thou hast spoken has
come to pass; and, behold, Thou seest *it.*

25 'And Thou hast said to me, O Lord GOD,

"Buy for yourself the field with money, and call in witnesses"—although the city is given into the hand of the Chaldeans.' "

26 Then the word of the LORD came to Jeremiah, saying,

27 "Behold, I am the LORD, the God of all flesh; is anything too difficult for Me?"

28 Therefore thus says the LORD, "Behold, I am about to ^Rgive this city into the hand of the Chaldeans and into the hand of Nebuchadnezzar king of Babylon, and he shall take it.   2 Kin. 25:11; 2 Chr. 36:17-21; Jer. 19:7-12

29 "And the Chaldeans who are fighting against this city shall enter and ^Rset this city on fire and burn it, with the houses where *people* have offered incense to Baal on their roofs and poured out libations to other gods to provoke Me to anger.   2 Chr. 36:19

30 "Indeed the sons of Israel and the sons of Judah have been doing only evil in My sight from their youth; for the sons of Israel have been only provoking Me to anger by the work of their hands," declares the LORD.

31 "Indeed this city has been to Me *a* ^R*provocation* of My anger and My wrath from the day that they built it, even to this day, that it should be ^Rremoved from before My face,   1 Kin. 11:7, 8 • 2 Kin. 23:27

32 because of all the evil of the sons of Israel and the sons of Judah, which they have done to provoke Me to anger—they, their ^Rkings, their leaders, their priests, their prophets, the men of Judah, and the inhabitants of Jerusalem.   Ezra 9:7; Is. 1:4-6, 23

33 "And they have turned *their* back to Me, and not *their* face; though *I* taught them, ^Rteaching again and again, they would not listen ^Tand receive instruction.   Jer. 7:13 • *to*

34 "But they ^Rput their detestable things in the house which is called by My name, to defile it.   2 Kin. 21:1-7; Jer. 7:30; 19:4-6; Ezek. 8:5

35 "And they built the high places of Baal that are in the valley of Ben-hinnom to cause their sons and their daughters to pass through *the fire* to Molech, which I had not commanded them nor had it ^Tentered My mind that they should do this abomination, to cause Judah to sin.   *come up into My heart*

36 "Now therefore thus says the LORD God of Israel concerning this city of which you say, 'It is ^Rgiven into the hand of the king of Babylon by sword, by famine, and by pestilence.'   Jer. 32:24

37 "Behold, I will ^Rgather them out of all the lands to which I have driven them in My anger, in My wrath, and in great indignation; and I will bring them back to this place and make them dwell in safety.   Deut. 30:3

38 "And they shall be ^RMy people, and I will be their God;   [Jer. 24:7]

39 and I will ^Rgive them one heart and one way, that they may fear Me always, for their own ^Rgood, and for *the good of* their children after them.   2 Chr. 30:12 • Deut. 11:18-21

40 "And I will make an everlasting cov-

⁹ I.e., South country   ¹⁰ I.e., this city

enant with them that I will not turn away from them, to do them good; and I will ^Rput the fear of Me in their hearts so that they will not turn away from Me.   [Jer. 24:7; 31:33]

41 "And I will rejoice over them to do them good, and I will faithfully plant them in this land with all My heart and with all My soul.

42 "For thus says the LORD, 'Just as I brought all this great disaster on this people, so I am going to ^Rbring on them all the good that I am promising them.   Jer. 33:14

43 "And ^Rfields shall be bought in this land of which you say, "It ^Ris a desolation, without man or beast; it is given into the hand of the Chaldeans."   Jer. 32:15, 25 • Jer. 33:10

44 'Men shall buy fields for money, sign and seal deeds, and call in witnesses in the land of Benjamin, in the environs of Jerusalem, in the cities of Judah, in the cities of the hill country, in the cities of the lowland, and in the cities of the ⁹Negev; for I will restore their ^Afortunes,' declares the LORD."   *captivity*

CHAPTER 33

Reconfirming the Covenant

THEN the word of the LORD came to Jeremiah the second time, while he was still confined in the court of the guard, saying,

2 "Thus says the LORD who made ^T*the earth*, the LORD who formed it to establish it, the ^RLORD is His name,   *it* • Ex. 3:15; 6:3

3 'Call to Me, and I will answer you, and I will tell you ^Rgreat and mighty things, ^Rwhich you do not know.'   Jer. 32:17, 27 • Is. 48:6

4 "For thus says the LORD God of Israel concerning the ^Rhouses of this city, and concerning the houses of the kings of Judah, which are broken down *to make a defense* against the ^Rsiege mounds and against the sword,   Is. 32:13, 14 • Ezek. 4:2; 21:22; Hab. 1:10

5 'While *they* are coming to ^Tfight with the Chaldeans, and to fill them with the corpses of men whom I have slain in My anger and in My wrath, and I have ^Rhidden My face from this city because of all their wickedness: Jer. 21:4-7; 32:5 • Jer. 21:10; Mic. 3:4

6 'Behold, I will bring to it ^Rhealth and healing, and I will heal them; and I will reveal to them an ^Aabundance of peace and truth.   Jer. 17:14; 30:17 • Is. 66:12; Gal. 5:22, 23

7 'And I will restore the ^Afortunes of Judah and the fortunes of Israel, and I will ^Rrebuild them as they were at first.   *captivity* • Is. 1:26

8 'And I will cleanse them from all their iniquity by which they have sinned against Me, and I will pardon all their iniquities by which they have sinned against Me, and by which they have transgressed against Me.

9 'And ¹⁰it shall be to Me a name of joy, praise, and glory before all the nations of the earth, which shall hear of all the ^Rgood that I do for them, and they shall ^Rfear and tremble because of all the good and all the peace that I make for it.'   Jer. 24:6 • Ps. 40:3

10 "Thus says the LORD, 'Yet again there

shall be heard in this place, of which you say, "It is a[R]waste, without man and without beast," *that is,* in the cities of Judah and in the streets of Jerusalem that are [R]desolate, without man and without inhabitant and without beast,　　　Jer. 32:43 • Jer. 26:9; 34:22

11 the voice of[R]joy and the voice of gladness, the voice of the bridegroom and the voice of the bride, the voice of those who say,　　　Is. 35:10; 51:3, 11

"Give[R]thanks to the LORD of hosts,
　For the LORD is good,　　2 Chr. 5:13; 7:3
　For His lovingkindness is everlasting";
and of those who bring a[R]thank offering into the house of the LORD. For I will restore the [A]fortunes of the land as they were at first,' says the LORD.　　Jer. 17:26; Heb. 13:15 • *captivity*

12"Thus says the LORD of hosts, 'There shall again be in this place which is waste, [R]without man or beast, and in all its cities, a [A]habitation of shepherds who rest their [R]flocks.　　Jer. 32:43; 36:29 • *pasture* • [Zeph. 2:6, 7]

13 'In the [R]cities of the hill country, in the cities of the lowland, in the cities of the Negev, in the land of Benjamin, in the environs of Jerusalem, and in the cities of Judah, the flocks shall again[R]pass under the hands of the one who numbers them,' says the LORD.　　Jer. 17:26; 32:44 • Lev. 27:32; [Luke 15:4]

14 'Behold, [R]days are coming,' declares the LORD, 'when I will fulfill the good word which I have spoken concerning the house of Israel and the house of Judah.　　Jer. 23:5

15 'In those days and at that time I will cause a[R]righteous Branch of David to spring forth; and He shall execute justice and righteousness on the earth.　　Zech. 3:8; 6:12f. ☆

16 'In those days[R]Judah shall be saved, and Jerusalem shall dwell in safety; and this is *the name* by which she shall be called: the LORD is our righteousness.'　　Is. 45:17, 22☆

17"For thus says the LORD, 'David shall never lack a man to sit on the throne of the house of Israel;

18 and the Levitical priests shall never lack a man before Me to offer burnt offerings, to burn grain offerings, and to prepare sacrifices [T]continually.' "　　*all the days*

19 And the word of the LORD came to Jeremiah, saying,

20"Thus says the LORD, 'If you can[R]break My covenant for the day, and My covenant for the night, so that day and night will not be at their appointed time,　　Jer. 31:35-37

21 then My covenant may also be broken with David My servant that he shall not have a son to reign on his throne, and with the Levitical priests, My ministers.

22 'As the host of heaven cannot be counted, and the sand of the sea cannot be measured, so I will multiply the [T]descendants of David My servant and the [R]Levites who minister to Me.' "　　*seed* • Is. 66:21

23 And the word of the LORD came to Jeremiah, saying,

24"Have you not observed what this people have spoken, saying, 'The two families which the LORD chose, He has rejected them'? Thus they despise My people, no longer are they as a nation in their sight.

25"Thus says the LORD, 'If My [R]covenant *for* day and night *stand* not, *and the* [T]fixed patterns of heaven and earth I have[R]not established,　　Gen. 8:22 • *statutes* • Ps. 74:16, 17

26 then I would reject the[T]descendants of Jacob and David My servant, [T]not taking from his [T]descendants rulers over the [T]descendants of Abraham, Isaac, and Jacob. But I will restore their fortunes and will have mercy on them.' "　　*seed* • *from taking*

CHAPTER 34

Message to Zedekiah

THE word which came to Jeremiah from the LORD, when [R]Nebuchadnezzar king of Babylon and all his army, with [R]all the kingdoms of the earth that were under his dominion and all the peoples, were fighting against Jerusalem and against all its cities, saying,　　2 Kin. 25:1 • Dan. 2:37, 38

2"Thus says the LORD God of Israel, 'Go and speak to Zedekiah king of Judah and say to him: "Thus says the LORD, 'Behold, I am giving this city into the hand of the king of Babylon, and he will burn it with fire.

3 'And you will not escape from his hand, for you will surely be captured and delivered into his hand; and you will[R]see the king of Babylon eye to eye, and he will speak with you[T]face to face, and you will go to Babylon.' " '　　2 Kin. 25:6, 7 • *mouth to mouth*

4"Yet hear the word of the LORD, O Zedekiah king of Judah! Thus says the LORD concerning you, 'You will not die by the sword.

5 'You will die in peace; and as spices were burned for your fathers, the former kings who were before you, so they will [R]burn spices for you; and they will lament for you, "Alas, lord!" ' For I have spoken the word," declares the LORD.　　2 Chr. 16:14; 21:19

6 Then Jeremiah the prophet spoke [R]all these words to Zedekiah king of Judah in Jerusalem　　1 Sam. 3:18; 15:16-24

7 when the army of the king of Babylon was fighting against Jerusalem and against all the remaining cities of Judah, *that is,* Lachish and Azekah, for they *alone* remained as fortified cities among the cities of Judah.

Message to the People

8 The word which came to Jeremiah from the LORD, after King Zedekiah had [R]made a covenant with all the people who were in Jerusalem to [R]proclaim [T]release to them:　　2 Kin. 11:17; 23:2, 3 • Ex. 21:2 • *liberty*

9 that each man should set free his male servant and each man his female servant, a [R]Hebrew man or a Hebrew woman; so that [R]no one should keep them, a Jew his brother, in bondage.　　Gen. 14:13; Ex. 2:6 • Lev. 25:39

10 And all the officials and all the people obeyed, who had entered into the covenant that each man should set free his male servant and each man his female servant, so that no one should keep them any longer in bondage; they obeyed, and set *them free.*

11 But afterward they turned around and took back the male servants and the female servants, whom they had set free, and brought them into subjection for male servants and for female servants.

12 Then the word of the LORD came to Jeremiah from the LORD, saying,

13"Thus says the LORD God of Israel, 'I ᴿmade a covenant with your forefathers in the day that Iᴿbrought them out of the land of Egypt, from the house of bondage, saying,   Ex. 24:3, 7, 8; Deut. 5:2, 3, 27 • Ex. 20:2

14"At the end of seven years each of you shall set free his Hebrew brother, whoᴬhas been sold to you and has served you six years, you shall send him out free from you; but your forefathers did not obey Me, or incline their ear to Me.   *has sold himself*

15"Although recently you *had* turned and done what is right in My sight, each man proclaimingᴿrelease to his neighbor, and you had made a covenant before Me in the house which is called by My name.   *liberty*

16"Yet you turned and profaned My name, and each man took back his male servant and each man his female servant, whom you had set free according to their desire, and you brought them into subjection to be your male servants and female servants." '

17"Therefore thus says the LORD, 'You have not obeyed Me in proclaimingᴬrelease each man to his brother, and each man to his neighbor. Behold, I am proclaiming aᴬrelease to you,' declares the LORD, 'to the ᴿsword, to the pestilence, and to the famine; and I will make you a terror to all the kingdoms of the earth.   *liberty* • Jer. 32:24; 38:2

18 'And I will give the men who have transgressed My covenant, who have not fulfilled the words of the covenant which they made before Me, *when* they cut the calf in two and passed between its parts—

19 the officials of Judah, and the officials of Jerusalem, the court officers, and the priests, and all the people of the land, who passed between the parts of the calf—

20 and I will give them into the hand of their enemies and into the hand of those who ᴿseek their life. And their ᴿdead bodies shall be food for the birds of the sky and the beasts of the earth.   Jer. 11:21 • Deut. 28:26

21 'Andᴿ Zedekiah king of Judah and his officials I will give into the hand of their enemies, and into the hand of those who seek their life, and into the hand of the army of the king of Babylon which hasᴿ gone away from you.   2 Kin. 25:18-21 • Jer. 37:5-11

22 'Behold, I am going to command,' declares the LORD, 'and I will bring them back to this city; and they shall fight against it and take it and burn it with fire; and I will make the cities of Judah a ᴿdesolationᴿwithout inhabitant.' "   Jer. 4:7; 9:11 • Jer. 33:10

CHAPTER 35

Message to the Rechabites

THE word which came to Jeremiah from the LORD in the days ofᴿJehoiakim the son of Josiah, king of Judah, saying,   2 Kin. 23:34-36

2"Go to the house of the Rechabites, and speak to them, and bring them into the house of the LORD, into one of the chambers, and give them wine to drink."

3 Then I took Jaazaniah the son of Jeremiah, son of Habazziniah, and his brothers, and all his sons, and the whole house of the Rechabites,

4 and I brought them into the house of the LORD, into the chamber of the sons of Hanan the son of Igdaliah, the man of God, which was near the chamber of the officials, which was above the chamber of Maaseiah the son of Shallum, the doorkeeper.

5 Then I set before the ᴵmen of the house of the Rechabites pitchers full of wine, and cups; and I said to them, "Drink wine!"   *sons*

6 But they said, "We will not drink wine, for Jonadab the son of Rechab, our father, commanded us, saying, 'You shallᴿnot drink wine, you or your sons, forever.   Num. 6:2-4

7 'And you shall not build a house, and you shall not sow seed, and you shall not plant a vineyard or own one; but in ᴿtents you shall dwell all your days, that you may live ᴿmany days in the land where you ᴿsojourn.'   Gen. 25:27 • Eph. 6:2, 3 • Gen. 36:7

8"And we haveᴿobeyed the voice of Jonadab the son of Rechab, our father, in all that he commanded us, not to drink wine all our days, we, our wives, our sons, or our daughters,   [Prov. 1:8, 9; 4:1, 2, 10; Eph. 6:1; Col. 3:20]

9 nor to build ourselves houses to dwell in; and weᴿdo not have vineyard or field or seed.   [Ps. 37:16]; Jer. 35:7; [1 Tim. 6:6]

10"We have only ᴿdwelt in tents, and have obeyed, and have done according to all that Jonadab our father commanded us.   Jer. 35:7

11"But it came about, when Nebuchadnezzar king of Babylon came up against the land, that we said, 'Come and let us ᴿgo to Jerusalem before the army of the Chaldeans and before the army of the Arameans.' So we have dwelt in Jerusalem."   Jer. 4:5-7; 8:14

12 Then the word of the LORD came to Jeremiah, saying,

13"Thus says the LORD of hosts, the God of Israel, 'Go and say to the men of Judah and the inhabitants of Jerusalem, "Willᴿyou not receive instruction by listening to My words?" declares the LORD.   [Is. 28:9-12]

14"The words of Jonadab the son of Rechab, which he commanded his sons not to drink wine, are observed. So they do not drink *wine* to this day, for they have obeyed their father's command. But I have spoken to you ᴵagain and again; yet you have not listened to Me.   *rising early and speaking*

15"Also I have sent to you all My servants the prophets, sending *them* again and again, saying: 'Turn now every man from his evil way, and amend your deeds, and do not go after other gods to worship them, then you shall dwell in the land which I have given to you and to your forefathers; but you have not inclined your ear or listened to Me.

16 'Indeed, the sons of Jonadab the son of Rechab have observed the command of their father which he commanded them, but this people has not listened to Me.' "'

17"Therefore thus says the LORD, the God of hosts, the God of Israel, 'Behold, I am bringing on Judah and on all the inhabitants of Jerusalem all the disaster that I have pronounced against them; because I spoke to them but they did not listen, and I have called them but they did not answer.' "

18 Then Jeremiah said to the house of the Rechabites, "Thus says the LORD of hosts, the God of Israel, 'Because you have ᴿobeyed the command of Jonadab your father, kept all his commands, and done according to all that he commanded you; Ex. 20:12; Eph. 6:1–3

19 therefore thus says the LORD of hosts, the God of Israel, "Jonadab the son of Rechab ᴿshall not lack a man to stand before Me ᵀalways." ' "   1 Chr. 2:55 • *all the days*

CHAPTER 36

Message of the Scroll

AND it came about in the ᴿfourth year of Jehoiakim the son of Josiah, king of Judah, that this word came to Jeremiah from the LORD, saying,   2 Kin. 24:1; 2 Chr. 36:5-7

2"Take a ᵀscroll and write on it all the words which I have spoken to you concerning Israel, and concerning Judah, and concerning all the nations, from the ᴿday I *first* spoke to you, from the days of Josiah, even to this day.   *scroll of a book* • Jer. 1:2, 3; 25:3

3"Perhaps ᴿthe house of Judah will hear all the calamity which I plan to bring on them, in order that every man will ᵀturn from his evil way; then I will forgive their iniquity and their sin."   Jer. 26:3; 36:7 • [Deut. 30:2, 8]

4 Then Jeremiah called Baruch the son of Neriah, and Baruch wrote at the dictation of Jeremiah all the words of the LORD, which He had spoken to him, on a scroll.

5 And Jeremiah commanded Baruch, saying, "I am ᵀrestricted; I cannot go into the house of the LORD.   *shut up*

6"So you go and read from the scroll which you have written ᵀat my dictation the words of the LORD to the people in the LORD's house on a fast day. And also you shall read them to all *the people of* Judah who come from their cities.   *from my mouth*

7"Perhaps their supplication will ᵀcome before the LORD, and everyone will turn from his evil way, for ᴿgreat is the anger and the wrath that the LORD has pronounced against this people."   *fall* • 2 Kin. 22:13, 17

8 And Baruch the son of Neriah did according to all that Jeremiah the prophet commanded him, reading from the book the words of the LORD in the LORD's house.

9 Now it came about in the ᴿfifth year of Jehoiakim the son of Josiah, king of Judah, in the ninth month, that all the people in Jerusalem and all the people who came from the cities of Judah to Jerusalem proclaimed a ᵀfast before the LORD.   Jer. 36:1 • Jon. 3:5

10 Then Baruch read from the book the words of Jeremiah in the house of the LORD in the chamber of Gemariah the son of Shaphan the ᴿscribe, in the upper court, at the ᴿentry of the New Gate of the LORD's house, to all the people.   Jer. 52:25 • Jer. 26:10

11 Now when ᴿMicaiah the son of Gemariah, the son of Shaphan, had heard all the words of the LORD from the book,   Jer. 36:13

12 he went down to the king's house, into the scribe's chamber. And, behold, all the officials were sitting there—Elishama the scribe, and Delaiah the son of Shemaiah, and Elnathan the son of Achbor, and Gemariah the son of Shaphan, and Zedekiah the son of Hananiah, and all the *other* officials.

13 And Micaiah ᴿdeclared to them all the words that he had heard, when Baruch read from the book to the people.   2 Kin. 22:10

14 Then all the officials sent ᴿJehudi the son of Nethaniah, the son of Shelemiah, the son of Cushi, to Baruch, saying, "Take in your hand the scroll from which you have read to the people and come." So Baruch the son of Neriah ᵀtook the scroll in his hand and went to them.   Jer. 36:21 • Jer. 36:2

15 And they said to him, "Sit down please, and read it to us." So Baruch ᴿread it to them.   Jer. 36:21

16 Now it came about when they had heard all the words, they turned in fear one to another and said to Baruch, "We will surely report all these words to the king."

17 And they asked Baruch, saying, "Tell us please, how did you write all these words? *Was it* at his dictation?"

18 Then Baruch said to them, "He ᴿdictated all these words to me, and I wrote them with ink on the book."   Jer. 36:4

19 Then the officials said to Baruch, "Go, ᴿhide yourself, you and Jeremiah, and do not let anyone know where you are."   1 Kin. 17:3

20 So they went to the ᴿking in the court, but they had deposited the scroll in the chamber of Elishama the scribe, and they reported all the words to the king.   Jer. 36:12

21 Then the king sent Jehudi to get the scroll, and he took it out of the chamber of Elishama the scribe. And Jehudi ᴿread it to the king as well as to all the officials who stood beside the king.   2 Chr. 34:18; Ezek. 2:4, 5

22 Now the king was sitting in the ᴿwinter house in the ninth month, with *a fire* burning in the brazier before him.   Judg. 3:20

23 And it came about, when Jehudi had read three or four columns, *the king* cut it with a scribe's knife and ᴿthrew *it* into the fire that was in the brazier, until all the

scroll was consumed in the fire that was in the brazier. 1 Kin. 22:8, 27; Prov. 1:30; Jer. 36:29

24 Yet the king and all his servants who heard all these words were [R]not afraid, nor did they rend their garments. [Ps. 36:1; 64:5]

25 Even though Elnathan and Delaiah and Gemariah entreated the king not to burn the scroll, he would not listen to them.

26 And the king commanded Jerahmeel the king's son, Seraiah the son of Azriel, and Shelemiah the son of Abdeel to [R]seize Baruch the scribe and Jeremiah the prophet, but the LORD hid them. 1 Kin. 19:1-3, 10, 14

27 Then the word of the LORD came to Jeremiah after the king had burned the scroll and the words which Baruch had written at the dictation of Jeremiah, saying,

28"Take [R]again another scroll and write on it all the former words that were [R]on the first scroll which Jehoiakim the king of Judah burned. Zech. 1:5, 6 • Jer. 36:4, 23

29"And concerning Jehoiakim king of Judah you shall say, 'Thus says the LORD, "You have [R]burned this scroll, saying, 'Why [R] have you written on it [T]that the king of Babylon shall certainly come and destroy this land, and shall make man and beast to cease from it?' " [Deut. 29:19] • Is. 29:21 • saying

30 'Therefore thus says the LORD concerning Jehoiakim king of Judah, "He shall have [R]no one to sit on the throne of David, and his dead body shall be cast out to the heat of the day and the frost of the night. Jer. 22:30

31"I shall also punish him and his [T]descendants and his servants for their iniquity, and I shall bring on them and the inhabitants of Jerusalem and the men of Judah all the calamity that I have declared to them—but they did not listen." ' " seed

32 Then Jeremiah took another scroll and gave it to Baruch the son of Neraiah, the scribe, and he [R]wrote on it at the dictation of Jeremiah all the words of the book which Jehoiakim king of Judah had burned in the fire; and many [T]similar words were added to them. Ex. 4:15, 16; 34:1 • like those

CHAPTER 37

First Interview with Zedekiah
2 Kin. 24:17; 2 Chr. 36:10

NOW Zedekiah the son of Josiah whom Nebuchadnezzar king of Babylon had made king in the land of Judah, reigned as king in place of Coniah the son of Jehoiakim.

2 But [T]neither he nor his servants nor the people of the land listened to the words of the LORD which He spoke through Jeremiah the prophet. 2 Kin. 24:19, 20; 2 Chr. 36:12-16

3 Yet King Zedekiah sent Jehucal the son of Shelemiah, and [R]Zephaniah the son of

Maaseiah, the priest, to Jeremiah the prophet, saying, "Please [R]pray to the LORD our God on our behalf." Jer. 29:25 • Jer. 2:27

4 Now Jeremiah was *still* coming in and going out among the people, for they had not yet [R]put him in the prison. Jer. 32:2, 3

5 Meanwhile, [R]Pharaoh's army had set out from Egypt; and when the Chaldeans who had been besieging Jerusalem heard the report about them, they [R]lifted the *siege* from Jerusalem. 2 Kin. 24:7 • Jer. 37:11

6 Then the word of the LORD came to Jeremiah the prophet, saying,

7"Thus says the LORD God of Israel, 'Thus you are to say to the king of Judah, who sent you to Me to inquire of Me: "Behold, [R]Pharaoh's army which has come out for your assistance is going to return to its own land of Egypt. 2 Kin. 22:18 • Is. 30:1-3

8"The Chaldeans will also [R]return and fight against this city, and they will capture it and burn it with fire." ' Jer. 34:22; 38:23

9"Thus says the LORD, 'Do not [R]deceive yourselves, saying, "The Chaldeans will surely go away from us," for they will not go. Jer. 29:8; Obad. 3; Matt. 24:4, 5; Eph. 5:6

10 'For [R]even if you had defeated the entire army of Chaldeans who were fighting against you, and there were *only* wounded men left among them, each man in his tent, they would rise up and [R]burn this city with fire.' " Lev. 26:36-38; Is. 30:17 • Jer. 37:8

Jeremiah Is Imprisoned in a Dungeon

11 Now it happened, when the army of the Chaldeans had lifted *the siege* from Jerusalem because of Pharaoh's army,

12 that Jeremiah went out from Jerusalem to go to the land of Benjamin in order to [R]take [A]possession of *some* property there among the people. Jer. 32:8 • part in a dividing

13 While he was at the [R]Gate of Benjamin, a captain of the guard whose name was Irijah, the son of Shelemiah the son of Hananiah was there; and he arrested Jeremiah the prophet, saying, "You are [T]going over to the Chaldeans!" Jer. 38:7; Zech. 14:10 • falling

14 But Jeremiah said, "A lie! I am not [T]going over to the Chaldeans"; yet he would not listen to him. So Irijah arrested Jeremiah and brought him to the officials. falling

15 Then the officials were angry at Jeremiah and beat him, and they [R]put him in jail in the house of Jonathan the scribe, which they had made into the prison. Gen. 39:20

16 For Jeremiah had come into the [T]dungeon, that is, the vaulted cell; and Jeremiah stayed there many days. house of the cistern-pit

---

37:15 Examples of Suffering—In the word of God there are four great examples of believers suffering for the sake of righteousness. These are: Joseph, Job, Jeremiah, and Paul.
The sufferings of Joseph: he was hated by his brothers (Page 37—Gen. 37:4, 5, 8); he was sold into slavery
(continued on next page)

Second Interview of Zedekiah

17 Now King Zedekiah sent and took him *out;* and in his palace the king ^Rsecretly asked him and said, "Is there a word from the LORD?" And Jeremiah said, "There is!" Then he said, "You will be given into the hand of the king of Babylon!" 1 Kin. 14:1-4

18 Moreover Jeremiah said to King Zedekiah, *"In* what *way* have I sinned against you, or against your servants, or against this people, that you have put me in prison?

19"Where^R then are your prophets who prophesied to you, saying, 'The ^Rking of Babylon will not come against you or against this land'? Deut. 32:37, 38 • Jer. 27:14

20"But now, please listen, O my lord the king; please let my ^Rpetition ^Tcome before you, and do not make me return to the house of Jonathan the scribe, that I may not die there." Jer. 36:7; 38:26 • *fall*

21 Then King Zedekiah gave commandment, and they committed Jeremiah to the ^Rcourt of the guardhouse and gave him a loaf of^Rbread daily from the bakers' street, until all the bread in the city was ^Rgone. So Jeremiah remained in the court of the guardhouse. Jer. 32:2 • 1 Kin. 17:6 • 2 Kin. 25:3

CHAPTER 38

Jeremiah Is Imprisoned in a Cistern

NOW Shephatiah the son of Mattan, and Gedaliah the son of Pashhur, and Jucal the son of Shelemiah, and Pashhur the son of Malchijah heard the words that Jeremiah was speaking to all the people, saying,

2"Thus says the LORD, 'He who^Rstays in this city will die by the^Rsword and by famine and by pestilence, but he who goes out to the Chaldeans will live and have his *own* life as booty and stay alive.' Jer. 21:9 • Jer. 34:17

3"Thus says the LORD, 'This city will certainly be ^Rgiven into the hand of the army of the king of Babylon, and he will capture it.' " Jer. 21:10; 32:3-5

4 Then the officials said to the king, "Now let this man be put to death, inasmuch as he is discouraging the men of war

who are left in this city and ^Tall the people, by speaking such words to them; for this man is not seeking the well-being of this people, but rather their harm." *the hands of all*

5 So King Zedekiah said, "Behold, he is in your^Thands; for the king^Rcan *do* nothing against you." *hand* • 2 Sam. 3:39

6 Then they took Jeremiah and cast him into the cistern *of* Malchijah the king's son, which was in the court of the guardhouse; and they let Jeremiah down with ropes. Now in the cistern there was no water but only mud, and Jeremiah sank into the mud.

7 But Ebed-melech the Ethiopian, ^Aa ^Reunuch, while he was in the king's palace, heard that they had put Jeremiah into the cistern. Now the king was sitting in the^RGate of Benjamin; *an official* • Jer. 29:2 • Job 29:7

8 and Ebed-melech went out from the king's palace and spoke to the king, saying,

9"My lord the king, these men have acted wickedly in all that they have done to Jeremiah the prophet whom they have cast into the cistern; and he will die right where he is because of the famine, for there is^Rno more bread in the city." Jer. 37:21; 52:6

10 Then the king commanded Ebed-melech the Ethiopian, saying, "Take thirty men from here ^Tunder your authority, and bring up Jeremiah the prophet from the cistern before he dies." *in your hand*

11 So Ebed-melech took the men under his^Tauthority and went into the king's palace to *a place* beneath the storeroom and took from there worn-out clothes and worn-out rags and let them down by ropes into the cistern to Jeremiah. *hand*

12 Then Ebed-melech the Ethiopian said to Jeremiah, "Now put these worn-out clothes and rags under your armpits under the ropes"; and Jeremiah did so.

13 So they pulled Jeremiah up with the ropes and lifted him out of the cistern, and Jeremiah stayed in the ^Rcourt of the guardhouse. Neh. 3:25; Jer. 32:2; 37:21; Acts 23:35

Third Interview of Zedekiah

14 Then King Zedekiah sent and^Thad Jeremiah the prophet brought to him at the third

---

(continued from previous page)

(Page 38—Gen. 37:28); he was severely tempted (Page 39—Gen. 39:7); and he was imprisoned (Page 39—Gen. 39:20).

The sufferings of Job: his oxen and donkeys were stolen and his farmhands killed (Page 495—Job 1:14, 15); his sheep and herdsmen were burned by a fire (Page 495—Job 1:16); his camels were stolen and his servants killed (Page 495—Job 1:17); his sons and daughters died in a windstorm (Page 496—Job 1:18, 19); and he was struck with boils (Page 496—Job 2:7).

The sufferings of Jeremiah: he was persecuted by his own family (Page 730—Jer. 12:6); he was plotted against by his own hometown (Page 730—Jer. 11:18-23); he was rejected and ridiculed by his religious peers (Page 737—Jer. 20:1-3, 7-9); and he was arrested, beaten, and accused of treason (Page 755—Jer. 37:11-16).

The sufferings of Paul: he was plotted against (Page 1104—Acts 9:23, 29; 20:3; 21:30; 23:10, 12; 25:3); he was stoned and left for dead (Page 1110—Acts 14:19); he was subjected to satanic pressure (Page 1207—1 Thess. 2:18); he was beaten and jailed at Philippi (Page 1113—Acts 16:19-24); he was ridiculed (Page 1114—Acts 17:16-18; 26:24); he was falsely accused (Page 1119—Acts 21:21, 28; 24:5-9); he endured a number of violent storms at sea (Page 1173—2 Cor. 11:25; Page 1125—Acts 27:14-20); he was bitten by a serpent (Page 1126—Acts 28:3, 4); and he was forsaken by all (Page 1225—2 Tim. 4:10, 16).

Now turn to Page 379—2 Kin. 23:3: Knowing the Will of God Through the Scriptures.

entrance that is in the house of the LORD; and the king said to Jeremiah, "I am going to [R]ask you something; do not hide anything from me."　　　*took Jeremiah to him* • 1 Kin. 22:16

15 Then Jeremiah said to Zedekiah, "If[R]I tell you, will you not certainly put me to death? Besides, if I give you advice, you will not listen to me."　　　Luke 22:67, 68

16 But King Zedekiah swore to Jeremiah in [R]secret saying, "As the LORD lives, who made this [T]life[R] for us, surely I will not put you to death nor will I give you over to the hand of these men who are seeking your life."　　　Jer. 37:17; John 3:2 • *soul* • Num. 16:22

17 Then Jeremiah said to Zedekiah, "Thus says the LORD God of hosts, the God of Israel, 'If you will indeed go out to the officers of the king of Babylon, then you will live, this city will not be burned with fire, and you and your household will [T]survive.　　*live*

18 'But if you will not go out to the officers of the king of Babylon, then this city will be given over to the hand of the Chaldeans; and they will burn it with fire, and you yourself will not escape from their hand.' "

19 Then King Zedekiah said to Jeremiah, "I dread the Jews who have [R]gone over to the Chaldeans, lest they give me over into their hand and they [R]abuse me."　　*fallen* • Neh. 4:1

20 But Jeremiah said, "They will not give you over. Please [T]obey the LORD in what I am saying to you, that it may go well with you and you may live.　　*listen to the voice of*

21 "But if you keep refusing to go out, this is the word which the LORD has shown me:

22 'Then behold, all of the [R]women who have been left in the palace of the king of Judah are going to be brought out to the officers of the king of Babylon; and those women will say,　Jer. 6:12; 8:10; 43:6 • *princes*

"Your[T] close friends　*The men of your peace*
Have misled and overpowered you;
While your feet were sunk in the mire,
They turned back."

23 'They will also bring out all your wives and your [R]sons to the Chaldeans, and [R]you yourself will not escape from their hand, but will be seized by the hand of the king of Babylon, and this city will be burned with fire.' "　　2 Kin. 25:7; Jer. 39:6; 41:10 • Jer. 38:18

24 Then Zedekiah said to Jeremiah, "Let no man know about these words and you will not die.

25 "But if the officials hear that I have talked with you and come to you and say to you, 'Tell us now what you said to the king, and what the king said to you; do not hide *it* from us, and we will not put you to death,'

26 then you are to say to them, 'I was [T]presenting my petition before the king, not to make me return to the house of Jonathan to die there.' "　　Jer. 37:20

27 Then all the officials came to Jeremiah and questioned him. So he reported to them

in accordance with all these words which the king had commanded; and they ceased speaking with him, since the [T]conversation had not been overheard.　　*word*

28 So Jeremiah [R]stayed in the court of the guardhouse until the day that Jerusalem was captured.　Ps. 23:4; Jer. 15:20, 21; 37:20, 21

CHAPTER 39

Jerusalem Falls
2 Kin. 25:1–12; Jer. 52:4–14

NOW it came about when Jerusalem was captured[R]in the ninth year of Zedekiah king of Judah, in the tenth month, Nebuchadnezzar king of Babylon and all his army came to Jerusalem and laid siege to it;　Jer. 52:4

2 in the eleventh year of Zedekiah, in the fourth month, in the ninth *day* of the month, the city *wall* was[R]breached.　　2 Kin. 25:4

3 Then all the officials of the king of Babylon came in and sat down at the Middle Gate: Nergal-sar-ezer, Samgar-nebu, Sarsekim the [T]Rab-saris, Nergal-sar-ezer *the* Rab-mag, and all the rest of the officials of the king of Babylon.　chief official (Akkad)

4 And it came about, when Zedekiah the king of Judah and all the men of war saw them, that they[R]fled and went out of the city at night by way of the king's garden through the gate between the two walls; and he went out toward the [11]Arabah.　Is. 30:16; Jer. 52:7

5 But the army of the Chaldeans pursued them and overtook Zedekiah in the [R]plains of Jericho; and they seized him and brought him up to Nebuchadnezzar king of Babylon at Riblah in the land of Hamath, and he passed sentence on him.　Josh. 4:13; 5:10

6 Then the[R]king of Babylon slew the sons of Zedekiah[R]before his eyes at Riblah; the king of Babylon also slew all the [R]nobles of Judah.　2 Kin. 25:7 • Deut. 28:34 • Jer. 21:7

7 He then[R]blinded Zedekiah's eyes and bound him in[R]fetters of bronze to bring him to[R]Babylon.　Jer. 52:11 • Judg. 16:21 • Jer. 32:5

8 The Chaldeans also[R]burned with fire the king's palace and the houses of the people, and they[R]broke down the walls of Jerusalem.　2 Kin. 25:9; Jer. 21:10 • 2 Kin. 25:10

9 And as for the rest of the people who were left in the city, the [T]deserters who had gone over to him and[R]the rest of the people who remained, Nebuzaradan the captain of the bodyguard carried *them* into exile in Babylon.　*fallers who had fallen* • Jer. 24:8

10 But some of the [R]poorest people who had nothing, [R]Nebuzaradan the captain of the bodyguard left behind in the land of Judah, and gave them vineyards and fields [T]at that time.　2 Kin. 25:12; Jer. 52:16 • *on that day*

Jeremiah Is Released

11 Now Nebuchadnezzar king of Babylon gave orders about [R]Jeremiah through Nebuzaradan the captain of the bodyguard, saying,　[Job 5:15, 16]; Jer. 1:8; 15:20, 21; Acts 24:23

---

[11] I.e., Jordan valley

12"Take him and[T]look after him, and do nothing harmful to him; but rather deal with him just as he tells you."   *set your eyes on*

13 So Nebuzaradan the captain of the bodyguard sent *word*, along with Nebushazban the Rab-saris, and Nergal-sar-ezer the [T]Rab-mag, and all the leading officers of the king of Babylon;   title of a high official

14 they even sent and took Jeremiah out of the court of the guardhouse and entrusted him to Gedaliah, the son of[R]Ahikam, the son of Shaphan, to take him home. So he stayed among the people.   2 Kin. 22:12, 14

Ebed-melech Is Rewarded

15 Now the word of the LORD had come to Jeremiah while he was[R]confined in the court of the guardhouse, saying,   Jer. 38:28

16"Go and speak to Ebed-melech the Ethiopian, saying, 'Thus says the LORD of hosts, the God of Israel, "Behold, I am about to bring My words on this city for disaster and not for[T]prosperity; and they will[R]take place before you on that day.   good • Ps. 91:8

17"But I will deliver you on that day," declares the LORD, "and you shall not be given into the hand of the men whom you dread.

18"For I will certainly rescue you, and you will not fall by the sword; but you will have your *own* life as booty, because you have trusted in Me," declares the LORD.' "

CHAPTER 40

Ministry to Remnant in Judah

THE word which came to Jeremiah from the LORD after Nebuzaradan captain of the bodyguard had released him from Ramah, when he had taken him bound in chains, among all the exiles of Jerusalem and Judah, who were being exiled to Babylon.

2 Now the captain of the bodyguard had taken Jeremiah and said to him, "The[R]LORD your God promised this calamity against this place;   Lev. 26:14-38; Deut. 28:15-68

3 and the LORD has brought *it* on and done just as He promised. Because you peo-ple[R]sinned against the LORD and did not listen to His voice, therefore this thing has happened to you.   Jer. 50:7; Dan. 9:11; [Rom. 2:5]

4"But now, behold, I am freeing you today from the chains which are on your hands. If you would prefer to come with me to Babylon, come *along*, and I will look after you; but if you would prefer not to come with me to Babylon, never mind. Look, the whole land is before you; go wherever it seems good and right for you to go."

5 As [T]Jeremiah was still not going back, [T]he said, "Go on back then to Gedaliah the son of Ahikam, the son of Shaphan, whom the king of Babylon has[R]appointed over the cities of Judah, and stay with him among the people; or else go anywhere it seems

right for you to go." So the captain of the bodyguard gave him a ration and a gift and let him go.   he • Nebuzaradan • 2 Kin. 25:23

6 Then Jeremiah went to [R]Mizpah to [R]Gedaliah the son of Ahikam and stayed with him among the people who were left in the land.   Judg. 20:1; 21:1; 1 Sam. 7:5 • Jer. 39:14

7 Now all the [A]commanders of the forces that were in the field, they and their men, heard that the king of Babylon had appointed Gedaliah the son of Ahikam over the land and that he had put him in charge of the men, women and [T]children, those of the poorest of the land who had not been exiled to Babylon.   princes • infants

8 So they came to Gedaliah at Mizpah, along with [R]Ishmael the son of Nethaniah, and Johanan and Jonathan the sons of Kareah, and Seraiah the son of Tanhumeth, and the sons of Ephai the Netophathite, and Jezaniah the son of the [R]Maacathite, *both* they and their men.   Jer. 40:14 • Deut. 3:14

9 Then Gedaliah the son of Ahikam, the son of Shaphan, [R]swore to them and to their men, saying, "Do[R] not be afraid of serving the Chaldeans; stay in the land and serve the king of Babylon, that it may go well with you.   1 Sam. 20:16, 17; 2 Kin. 25:24 • Jer. 27:11

10"Now as for me, behold, I am going to stay at Mizpah to stand *for you* before the Chaldeans who come to us; but as for you, gather in wine and summer fruit and oil, and put *them* in your *storage* vessels, and live in your cities that you have taken over."

11 Likewise also all the Jews who were in [R]Moab and among the sons of Ammon and in [R]Edom, and who were in all the *other* countries, heard that the king of Babylon had left a remnant for Judah and that he had appointed over them Gedaliah the son of Ahikam, the son of Shaphan.   Jer. 9:26 • Is. 11:14

12 Then all the Jews[R]returned from all the places to which they had been driven away and came to the land of Judah, to Gedaliah at Mizpah, and gathered in wine and summer fruit in great abundance.   Jer. 43:5

13 Now Johanan the son of Kareah and all the commanders of the forces that were in the field came to Gedaliah at Mizpah,

14 and said to him, "Are you well aware that Baalis the king of the sons of [R]Ammon has sent Ishmael the son of Nethaniah to take your life?" But Gedaliah the son of Ahikam did not believe them.   Jer. 25:21; 41:10

15 Then Johanan the son of Kareah spoke secretly to Gedaliah in Mizpah, saying, "Let me go and kill Ishmael the son of Nethaniah, and not a man will know! Why should he [R]take your life, so that all the Jews who are gathered to you should be scattered and the remnant of Judah perish?"   2 Sam. 21:17

16 But Gedaliah the son of Ahikam said to Johanan the son of Kareah, "Do[R] not do this thing, for you are telling a lie about Ishmael."   Matt. 10:16; 1 Cor. 13:5

CHAPTER 41

Now it came about in the seventh month that Ishmael the son of Nethaniah, the son of Elishama, of the royal ᵀfamily and *one* of the chief officers of the king, along with ten men, came to Mizpah to Gedaliah the son of Ahikam. While they ᴿwere eating bread together there in Mizpah,   *seed* • Ps. 41:9

2 Ishmael the son of Nethaniah and the ten men who were with him arose and ᴿstruck down Gedaliah the son of Ahikam, the son of Shaphan, with the sword and put to death the one whom the king of Babylon had appointed over the land.   2 Sam. 3:27

3 Ishmael also struck down all the Jews who were with him, *that is* with Gedaliah at Mizpah, and the Chaldeans who were found there, the men of war.

4 Now it happened on the ᴬnext day after the killing of Gedaliah, when no one knew about *it*,   *second*

5 that eighty men came from Shechem, from Shiloh, and from Samaria with their beards shaved off and their clothes torn and ᵀtheir bodies gashed, having grain offerings and incense in their hands to bring to the house of the LORD.   *having cut themselves*

6 Then Ishmael the son of Nethaniah went out from Mizpah to meet them, ᴿweeping as he went; and it came about as he met them that he said to them, "Come to Gedaliah the son of Ahikam!"   2 Sam. 3:16; Jer. 50:4

7 Yet it turned out that as soon as they came inside the city, Ishmael the son of Nethaniah and the men that were with him ᴿslaughtered them, *and cast them* into the cistern.   Ps. 55:23; Is. 59:7; Ezek. 22:27; 33:24, 26

8 But ten men who were found among them said to Ishmael, "Do not put us to death; for we have ᴿstores of wheat, barley, oil and honey hidden in the field." So he refrained and did not put them to death along with their companions.   [Is. 45:3]

9 Now as for the cistern where Ishmael had cast all the corpses of the men whom he had struck down because of Gedaliah, it was the one that King Asa had made on account of Baasha, king of Israel; Ishmael the son of Nethaniah filled it with the slain.

10 Then Ishmael took captive all the ᴿremnant of the people who were in Mizpah, the ᴿking's daughters and all the people who were left in Mizpah, whom Nebuzaradan the captain of the bodyguard had put under the charge of Gedaliah the son of Ahikam; thus Ishmael the son of Nethaniah took them captive and proceeded to cross over to the sons of Ammon.   Jer. 40:11, 12 • Jer. 43:6

11 But Johanan the son of Kareah and all the commanders of the forces that were with him heard of all the evil that Ishmael the son of Nethaniah had done.

12 So they took all the men and went to ᴿfight with Ishmael the son of Nethaniah and they found him by the ᴿ ᵀgreat ᵀpool that is in Gibeon.   Gen. 14:14-16 • 2 Sam. 2:13 • *waters*

13 Now it came about, as soon as all the people who were with Ishmael saw Johanan the son of Kareah and the commanders of the forces that were with him, they were glad.

14 So all the people whom Ishmael had taken captive from Mizpah turned around and came back, and went to Johanan the son of Kareah.

15 But Ishmael the son of Nethaniah ᴿescaped from Johanan with eight men and went to the sons of Ammon.   1 Sam. 30:17

16 Then Johanan the son of Kareah and all the commanders of the forces that were with him took from Mizpah all the remnant of the people whom he had recovered from Ishmael the son of Nethaniah, after he had struck down Gedaliah the son of Ahikam, *that is*, the men who were soldiers, *the* women, *the* children, and *the* eunuchs, whom he had brought back from Gibeon.

17 And they went and stayed in ᴿGeruth Chimham, which is beside Bethlehem, in order to proceed into Egypt   2 Sam. 19:37, 38, 40

18 because of the Chaldeans; for they were ᴿafraid of them, since Ishmael the son of Nethaniah had struck down Gedaliah the son of Ahikam, whom the king of Babylon had appointed over the land.   Is. 51:12, 13

CHAPTER 42

Then all the ᴬcommanders of the forces, ᴿJohanan the son of Kareah, Jezaniah the son of Hoshaiah, and all the people both small and great approached   *princes* • Jer. 40:8, 13

2 and said to Jeremiah the prophet, "Please let our petition ᵀcome before you, and ᴿpray for us to the LORD your God, *that is* for all this remnant; because we are left but a ᴿfew out of many, as your own eyes *now* see us,   *fall* • Ex. 8:28 • Lev. 26:22

3 that the LORD your God may tell us the ᴿway in which we should walk and the thing that we should do."   Ps. 86:11; Prov. 3:6

4 Then Jeremiah the prophet said to them, "I have heard *you*. Behold, I am going to pray to the LORD your God in accordance with your words; and it will come about that the whole ᵀmessage which the LORD will answer you I will tell you. I will ᴿnot keep back a word from you."   *word* • Acts 20:20

5 Then they said to Jeremiah, "May the ᴿLORD be a true and faithful witness against us, if we do not act in accordance with the whole ᵀmessage with which the LORD your God will send you to us.   Gen. 31:50 • *word*

6 "Whether *it* is ᵀpleasant or unpleasant, we will listen to the voice of the LORD our God to whom we are sending you, in order that it may go well with us when we listen to the voice of the LORD our God."   *good*

7 Now it came about at the ᴿend of ten days that the word of the LORD came to Jeremiah.　　　　Ps. 27:14; Is. 30:18

8 Then he called for Johanan the son of Kareah, and all the ᴬcommanders of the forces that were with him, and for all the people both small and great,　　*princes*

9 and said to them, "Thus says the LORD the God of Israel, to whom you sent me to present your petition before Him:

10 'If you will indeed stay in this land, then I willᴿbuild you up and not tear you down, and I will plant you and not uproot you; for I shallᴿrelent concerning the calamity that I have inflicted on you.　Jer. 24:6 • [Jer. 18:7, 8]

11 'Doᴿnot be afraid of the king of Babylon, whom you are *now* fearing; do not be afraid of him,' declares the LORD, 'forᴿI am with you to save you and deliver you from his hand.　Jer. 1:8 • Num. 14:9; 2 Chr. 32:7, 8

12 'I will also show you compassion, so thatᴿhe will have compassion on you and restore you to your own soil.　Neh. 1:11

13 'But if you are going to say, "We will ᵀnot stay in this land," so as not to listen to the voice of the LORD your God,　Ex. 5:2

14 saying, "No, but we willᴿgo to the land of Egypt, where we shall not see war orᴿhear the sound of a trumpet or hunger for bread, and we will stay there";　Is. 31:1 • Num. 11:4

15 then ᵀin that case listen to the word of the LORD, O remnant of Judah. Thus says the LORD of hosts, the God of Israel, "If you really set your ᵀmind to enter Egypt, and go in to reside there,　*now therefore • face*

16 then it will come about that the ᴿsword, which you are afraid of will overtake you there in the land of Egypt; and the famine, about which you are anxious, will follow closely after you there *in* Egypt; and you will die there.　Jer. 44:13, 27; Ezek. 11:8

17 "So all the men who set their ᵀmind to go to Egypt to reside there will die by the ᴿsword, by famine, and by pestilence; and they willᴿhave no survivors or refugees from the calamity that I am going to bring on them." ' "　*face* • Jer. 24:10 • Jer. 44:14, 28

18 For thus says the LORD of hosts, the God of Israel, "As My ᴿanger and wrath have been poured out on the inhabitants of Jerusalem, so My wrath will be poured out on you when you enter Egypt. And you will become a ᵀcurse, an object of horror, an imprecation, and a reproach; and you will see this place no more." 2 Chr. 36:16-19 • Deut. 29:21

19 The LORD has spoken to you, O remnant of Judah, "Do notᴿgo into Egypt!" You should clearly ᵀunderstand that today I have testified against you.　Deut. 17:16 • Ezek. 2:5

20 For you have only ᴿdeceived yourselves; for it is you who sent me to the LORD your God, saying, "Pray for us to the LORD our God; and whatever the LORD our God says, tell us so, and we will do it."　Jer. 43:2

21 So, I have told you today, but you have not obeyed the LORD your God, even in whatever He has sent me to *tell* you.

22 Therefore you should now clearly understand that you will ᴿdie by the sword, by famine, and by pestilence, in the place where you wish to go to reside.　Jer. 43:11

CHAPTER 43

Ministry to Remnant in Egypt

BUT it came about, as soon as Jeremiah whom the LORD their God had sent, had ᴿfinished telling all the people all the words of the LORD their God—that is, all these words—　Jer. 26:8; 51:63

2 that Azariah the ᴿson of Hoshaiah, and Johanan the son of Kareah, and all the arrogant men said to Jeremiah, "You are ᵀtelling a lie! The LORD our God has not sent you to say, 'You are not to enter Egypt to reside there';　Jer. 42:1 • 2 Chr. 36:13; Is. 7:9

3 but ᵀBaruch the son of Neriah is inciting you against us to give us over into the hand of the Chaldeans, so they may put us to death or exile us to Babylon."　Jer. 45:1-3

4 So Johanan the son of Kareah and all the ᴬcommanders of the forces, and all the people, did not obey the voice of the LORD, so as to stay in the land of Judah.　*princes*

5 But Johanan the son of Kareah and all the ᴬcommanders of the forces took the ᴿentire remnant of Judah who had returned from all the nations to which they had been driven away, in order to reside in the land of Judah—　*princes* • Jer. 40:11

6 the men, the women, the ᵀchildren, the king's daughters and every person that Nebuzaradan the captain of the bodyguard had left with Gedaliah the son of Ahikam ᵀand grandson of Shaphan, together with ᴿJeremiah the prophet and Baruch the son of Neriah—　*infants • the son* • Eccl. 9:1, 2

7 and they entered the land of Egypt (for they did not obey the voice of the LORD) and went in as far as ᴿTahpanhes.　Jer. 2:16; 44:1

8 Then the word of the LORD came to Jeremiah in ᴿTahpanhes, saying,　Ezek. 30:18

9 "Take *some* large stones in your ᵀhands and hide them in the mortar in the ᴬbrick *terrace* which is at the entrance of Pharaoh's ᵀpalace in Tahpanhes, in the sight of ᵀsome *of the* Jews;　*hand • brickwork • house • men*

10 and say to them, 'Thus says the LORD of hosts, the God of Israel, "Behold, I am going to send and get ᴿNebuchadnezzar the king of Babylon, ᴿMy servant, and I am going to set his throne *right* over these stones that I have hidden; and he will spread his ᴿcanopy over them.　Jer. 25:9, 11 • Is. 44:28 • Ps. 18:11

11 "He will also come and ᵀstrike the land of Egypt; those who are *meant* for death *will be given over* to death, and those for captivity to captivity, and ᴿthose for the sword to the sword.　Is. 19:1-25; Jer. 25:15-19 • Jer. 15:2

12 "And I shall set fire to the temples of the ᴿgods of Egypt, and he will burn them and take them captive. So he will ᴿwrap himself with the land of Egypt as a shepherd wraps

himself with his garment, and he will depart from there safely.   Ex. 12:12 • Ps. 104:2

13"He will also shatter the ^obelisks of Heliopolis, which is in the land of Egypt; and the temples of the gods of Egypt he will burn with fire." ' "   *stone pillars*

CHAPTER 44

THE word that came to Jeremiah for all the Jews living in the land of Egypt, those who were living in Migdol, Tahpanhes, Memphis, and the land of Pathros, saying,

2"Thus says the LORD of hosts, the God of Israel, 'You yourselves have seen all the calamity that I have brought on Jerusalem and all the cities of Judah; and behold, this day they are in ^ruins and no one lives in them,   Is. 6:11; Jer. 4:7; 9:11; 34:22; Mic. 3:12

3 because of their wickedness which they committed so as to provoke Me to anger by continuing to burn ^sacrifices *and* to serve other gods whom they had not known, *neither* they, you, nor your fathers.   *incense*

4 'Yet I sent you all My servants the prophets, again and again, saying, "Oh, do not do this abominable thing which I hate."

5 'But they did not listen or incline their ears to turn from their wickedness, so as not to burn ^sacrifices to other gods.   *incense*

6 'Therefore My ^wrath and My anger were poured out and burned in the ^cities of Judah and in the streets of Jerusalem, so they have become a ruin and a desolation as it is this day.   Is. 51:17-20 • Jer. 7:17, 34

7 'Now then thus says the LORD God of hosts, the God of Israel, "Why are you ^doing great harm to yourselves, so as to ^cut off from you man and woman, child and infant, from among Judah, leaving yourselves without remnant,   Num. 16:38; Jer. 26:19 • Jer. 3:24

8 provoking Me to anger with the works of your hands, burning ^sacrifices to other gods in the land of Egypt, where you are entering to reside, so that you might be cut off and become a curse and a reproach among all the nations of the earth?   *incense*

9"Have you forgotten the ^wickedness of your fathers, the wickedness of the kings of Judah, and the wickedness of their wives, your own wickedness, and the wickedness of your wives, which they committed in the land of Judah and in the streets of Jerusalem?   Jer. 7:9, 10, 17, 18; 44:17, 21

10"But they ^have not become ^contrite even to this day, nor have they feared nor ^walked in My law or My statutes, which I have set before you and before your fathers." '   Jer. 6:15 • *crushed* • Jer. 26:4; 32:23

11"Therefore thus says the LORD of hosts, the God of Israel, 'Behold, I am going to ^set My face against you for ^woe, even to cut off all Judah.   Lev. 17:10; 20:5, 6; 26:17 • *evil*

12 'And I will take away the remnant of Judah who have set their ^mind on entering the land of Egypt to reside there, and they will all ^meet their end in the land of Egypt; they will fall by the sword *and* meet their end by famine. Both small and great will die by the sword and famine; and they will become a curse, an object of horror, an imprecation and a reproach.   *face* • *be finished*

13 'And I will ^punish those who live in the land of Egypt, as I have punished Jerusalem, with the sword, with famine, and with pestilence.   Jer. 11:22; 44:27, 28

14 'So there will be no refugees or survivors for the remnant of Judah who have entered the land of Egypt to reside there and then to return to the land of Judah, to which they are longing to return and live; for none will return except *a few* refugees.' "

15 Then ^all the men who were aware that their wives were burning ^sacrifices to other gods, along with all the women who were standing by, *as* a large assembly, ^including all the people who were living in Pathros in the land of Egypt, responded to Jeremiah, saying,   [Prov. 11:21]; Is. 1:5 • *incense* • *and*

16"As for the ^message ^that you have spoken to us in the name of the LORD, we are not going to listen to you!   *word* • Jer. 43:2

17"But rather we will certainly carry out every word that has proceeded from our mouths, by burning sacrifices to the queen of heaven and pouring out libations to her, just as we ourselves, our forefathers, our kings and our princes did in the cities of Judah and in the streets of Jerusalem; for *then* we had plenty of ^food, and were well off, and saw no ^misfortune.   *bread* • *evil*

18"But since we stopped burning ^sacrifices to the queen of heaven and pouring out libations to her, we have ^lacked everything and have ^met our end by the sword and by famine."   *incense* • Jer. 40:12 • *been finished*

19"And," *said the women*, "when we were burning sacrifices to the queen of heaven, and were pouring out libations to her, was it without our husbands that we made for her *sacrificial* cakes ^in her image and poured out libations to her?"   *to make an image of her*

20 Then Jeremiah said to all the people, to the men and women—even to all the people who were giving him *such* an answer—saying,

21"As for the ^smoking sacrifices that you burned in the cities of Judah and in the ^streets of Jerusalem, you and your forefathers, your kings and your princes, ^and the people of the land, did not the LORD ^remember them, and did not *all this* come into His ^mind?   *incense* • Jer. 11:13 • Amos 8:7 • *heart*

22"So the LORD was no longer able to endure *it*, ^because of the evil of your deeds, because of the abominations which you have committed; thus your land has become a ruin, an object of horror and a curse, without an inhabitant, as *it is* this day.   Jer. 4:4

23"Because you have burned ^sacrifices and have sinned against the LORD and not obeyed the voice of the LORD or walked in His law, His statutes or His testimonies,

therefore this[R]calamity has befallen you, as *it has* this day." *incense* • Neh. 13:18; Jer. 44:2

24 Then Jeremiah said to all the people, including all the women, "Hear[R]the word of the LORD, all Judah who are[R]in the land of Egypt, Jer. 42:15; 44:16 • Jer. 43:7; 44:15, 26

25 thus says the LORD of hosts, the God of Israel, as follows: 'As for you and your wives, you have spoken with your mouths and fulfilled *it* with your hands, saying, "We will certainly perform our vows that we have vowed, to burn sacrifices to the queen of heaven and pour out libations to her."'Go ahead and confirm your vows, and certainly perform your vows!' *Surely cause to stand*

26"Nevertheless[T] hear the word of the LORD, all Judah who are living in the land of Egypt, 'Behold, I have[R]sworn by My great name,' says the LORD, 'never shall My name be invoked again by the mouth of any man of Judah in all the land of Egypt, saying, "As the Lord GOD lives." *Therefore* • Gen. 22:16

27 'Behold, I am watching over them for harm and not for good, and all the men of Judah who are in the land of Egypt will [T]meet their end by the sword and by famine until they are completely gone. *be finished*

28 'And those who escape the sword will return out of the land of Egypt to the land of Judah[T]few in number. Then all the remnant of Judah who have gone to the land of Egypt to reside there will know whose word will stand, Mine or theirs. *men of number*

29 'And this will be the[R]sign to you,' declares the LORD, 'that I am going to punish you in this place, so that you may know that [R]My words will surely stand against you for harm.' Is. 7:11, 14; 8:18 • Prov. 19:21; Is. 40:8

30"Thus says the LORD, 'Behold, I am going to give over[R]Pharaoh Hophra king of Egypt to the hand of his enemies, to the hand of those who seek his life, just as I gave over [R]Zedekiah king of Judah to the hand of Nebuchadnezzar king of Babylon, *who was* his enemy and was seeking his life.'" Jer. 43:9-13 • 2 Kin. 25:4-7; Jer. 34:21

CHAPTER 45

Message to Baruch

*T*HIS is the message which Jeremiah the prophet spoke to Baruch the son of Neriah, when he had written down these words in a book [T]at Jeremiah's dictation, in the fourth year of Jehoiakim the son of Josiah, king of Judah, saying: *from the mouth of Jeremiah*

2"Thus says the LORD the God of Israel to you, O Baruch:

3 'You said, "Ah, woe is me! For the LORD has added sorrow to my pain; I am weary with my groaning and have found no rest."'

4"Thus you are to say to him, 'Thus says the LORD, "Behold, [R]what I have built I am about to tear down, and what I have planted I am about to uproot, that is, the whole land." Is. 5:5; Jer. 1:10; 11:17; 18:7-10; 31:28

5 'But you, are you [R]seeking great things

for yourself? Do not seek *them;* for behold, I am going to[R]bring disaster on all flesh,' declares the LORD, 'but I will[R]give your life to you as booty in all the places where you may go.'" Rom. 12:16 • Jer. 25:31 • Jer. 21:9

CHAPTER 46

Prophecies Against Egypt

*T*HAT which came as the word of the LORD to Jeremiah the prophet [C]concerning the nations. Jer. 1:10; 25:15-38

2 To[R]Egypt, concerning the army of Pharaoh Neco king of Egypt, which was by the Euphrates River at Carchemish, which Nebuchadnezzar king of Babylon defeated in the[R]fourth year of Jehoiakim the son of Josiah, king of Judah: Jer. 46:14 • Jer. 45:1

3"Line[R]up the shield and buckler,
And draw near for the battle! Is. 21:5

4"Harness the horses,
And[A]mount the steeds,
And take your stand with helmets *on!*
Polish the spears, *go up, you horsemen*
Put on the[R]scale-armor! 1 Sam. 17:5, 38

5"Why have I seen *it?*
They are terrified,
They are[R]drawing back, Is. 42:17
And their[R]mighty men are defeated
And have taken refuge in flight,
Without facing back; Is. 5:25; Ezek. 39:18
[R]Terror is on every side!"
Declares the LORD. Jer. 6:25; 20:3; 49:29

6 Let not the[R]swift man flee, Is. 30:16
Nor the mighty man escape;
In the north beside the river Euphrates
They have stumbled and fallen.

7 Who is this that[R]rises like the Nile,
Like the rivers whose waters surge
about? Jer. 47:2

8 Egypt rises like the Nile,
Even like the rivers whose waters
surge about;
And He has said, "I will[R]rise and cover
that land;
I will surely[R]destroy the city and its inhabitants." Is. 37:24 • Is. 10:13

9 Go up, you horses, and[T]drive madly,
you chariots, *act like madmen*
That the mighty men may[T]march forward: *go forth*
Ethiopia and[T]Put,[R] that handle the
shield, Libya (or Somaliland) • Nah. 3:9
And the[T]Lydians,[R] that handle *and* bend
the bow. Heb., *Ludim* • Is. 66:19

10 For[R]that day belongs to the Lord GOD
of hosts, Joel 1:15
A day of[R]vengeance, so as to avenge
Himself on His foes; Jer. 50:15, 18
And the[R]sword will devour and be sati-
ated Deut. 32:42; Is. 31:8; Jer. 12:12
And[T]drink its fill of their blood;
For there will be a[R]slaughter for the
Lord GOD of hosts,
In the land of the north by the river Eu-
phrates. *be saturated with* • Zeph. 1:7

11 Go^Rup to Gilead and obtain balm,
O virgin daughter of Egypt!   Jer. 8:22
In vain have you multiplied^Tremedies;
There is no healing for you.   *healings*
12 The nations have heard of yourshame,
And the earth is full of yourcry *of distress;*   Jer. 2:36; Nah. 3:8-10 • Jer. 14:2
For one^Rwarrior has stumbled overan-
other.   Is. 19:2 • *warrior*
And both of them have fallen down together.
13 *This is* the^Tmessage which the LORD
spoke to Jeremiah the prophet about the
coming of Nebuchadnezzar king of Babylon
to^Rsmite the land of Egypt: *word* • Is. 19:1
14"Declare in Egypt and proclaim in^RMig-
dol,   Jer. 44:1
Proclaim also in Memphis and^RTahpan-
hes;   Jer. 43:8
Say, 'Take your stand and get yourself
ready,
For the^Rsword has devoured those
around you.'   Is. 1:20; Jer. 2:30; 46:10
15"Why have your^Rmighty ones become
prostrate?   Is. 66:15, 16; Jer. 46:5
They do not stand because the LORD
has^Rthrust them down.   Ps. 18:14, 39
16"They have repeatedly^Rstumbled;
Indeed, they have fallen one against
another.   Lev. 26:36, 37; Jer. 46:6
Then they said, 'Get up! And^Rlet us go
back   Jer. 51:9
To our own people and our native land
Away from thesword^Rof the oppressor.'   *oppressing sword* • Jer. 50:16
17"They cried there, 'Pharaoh king of
Egypt *is but*a big noise;   Ex. 15:9, 10
He has let the appointed time pass by!'
18"As I live," declares the^RKing   Jer. 48:15
Whose name is the LORD of hosts,
"Surely one shall come *who looms up*
like^RTabor among the mountains,
Or like Carmel by the sea.   Ps. 89:12
19"Make your baggage ready for^Rexile,
O daughter dwelling in Egypt,   Is. 20:4
For^RMemphis will become a desolation;
It will even be burned down *and*^Tbereft
of inhabitants.   Jer. 46:14 • *without*
20"Egypt is a pretty^Rheifer,   Hos. 10:11
But a horsefly is coming ^Rfrom the
north—it is coming!   Jer. 1:14; 47:2
21"Also hermercenaries in her midst
Are like^Tfattened calves,
For even they too have turned back
and have fled away together;
They did not stand *their ground.*
For the day of their calamity has come
upon them,   2 Sam. 10:6 • *of the stall*
The time of their^Rpunishment.   Mic. 7:4
22"Its sound moves along like a serpent;
For they move on^Alike an army
And come to her as woodcutters with
axes.   *in force*
23"They have cut down her^Rforest," de-
clares the LORD;   Jer. 21:14
"Surely it will no *more* be found,

Even though they are *now* more numerous than^Rlocusts   Judg. 6:5; 7:12
And are without number.
24"The daughter of Egypt has been put to
shame,
Given over to the^Tpower of the^Rpeople
of the north."   *hand* • Jer. 1:15
25 The LORD of hosts, the God of Israel,
says, "Behold, I am going to punish Amon
of^RThebes, and Pharaoh, and Egypt along
with her gods and her kings, even Pharaoh
and those who trust in him.   Ezek. 30:14-16
26"And I shall give them over to the^T
power of those who are seeking their lives,
even into the hand of Nebuchadnezzar king
of Babylon and into the hand of his officers.
Afterwards, however, it will be inhabited as
in the days of old," declares the LORD.   *hand*
27"But as for you, O Jacob My servant,^Rdo
not fear,   Is. 41:13, 14; Jer. 30:10, 11
Nor be dismayed, O Israel!
For, see, I am going to^Rsave you from
afar,   Is. 11:11; Jer. 23:3, 4; 29:14
And your descendants from the land of
their captivity;
And Jacob shall return and be^Rundis-
turbed   Jer. 23:6; 50:19
And secure, with no one making *him*
tremble.
28"O Jacob My servant, do not fear," declares the LORD,
"For^RI am with you.   Ps. 46:7, 11
For I shall make a full end of all the
nations
Where I have driven you,
Yet I shall^Rnot make a full end of you;
But I shall^Rcorrect you properly
And by no means leave you unpun-
ished."   Amos 9:8, 9 • Jer. 10:24

CHAPTER 47

Prophecies Against Philistia

THAT which came as the word of the
LORD to Jeremiah the prophet concerning
the ^RPhilistines, before Pharaoh ^Tconquered
^RGaza.   Jer. 25:20 • *smote* • Amos 1:6; Zeph. 2:4
2 Thus says the LORD:
"Behold, waters are going to rise from
^Rthe north   Is. 14:31; Jer. 1:14; 6:22
And become an overflowing torrent,
And ^Roverflow the land and all its ful-
ness,   Is. 8:7, 8
The city and those who live in it;
And the men will^Rcry out,
And every inhabitant of the land will
wail.   Is. 15:2-5; Jer. 46:12
3"Because of the noise of the galloping^R
hoofs of his stallions,
The tumult of his chariots, *and* the
rumbling of his wheels,   Judg. 5:22
The fathers have not turned back for
their children,
Because of the limpness of *their* hands,
4 On account of the day that is coming
To^Rdestroy all the Philistines,   Is. 14:31

To cut off from [R]Tyre and Sidon
Every ally that is left;
For the LORD is going to destroy the
　Philistines,　　　　　Joel 3:4; Amos 1:9, 10
The remnant of the coastland of [R]Caph-
　tor.　　　　Gen. 10:14; Deut. 2:23; Amos 9:7
5 "Baldness has come upon Gaza;
　[R]Ashkelon has been ruined.　　Amos 1:7, 8
　O remnant of their valley,
　How long will you gash yourself?
6 "Ah, [R]sword of the LORD,　　　　Judg. 7:20
　How long will you not be quiet?
　Withdraw into your sheath;
　Be at rest and stay still.
7 "How can [T]it be quiet,　　　　　　　you
　When the LORD has [R]given it an order?
　Against Ashkelon and against the sea-
　coast—　　　　　　Is. 10:6; Ezek. 14:17
　There He has [R]assigned it."　　　Mic. 6:9

CHAPTER 48

Prophecies Against Moab

CONCERNING [R]Moab.　　Is. 15:1; Ezek. 25:9
Thus says the LORD of hosts, the God
　of Israel,
　"Woe to [R]Nebo, for it has been de-
　stroyed;　　　Num. 32:3, 38; Jer. 48:22
　[R]Kiriathaim has been put to shame, it
　has been captured;　　　　Num. 32:37
　The lofty stronghold has been put to
　shame and [A]shattered.　　　dismayed
2 "There is praise for Moab no longer;
　In [R]Heshbon they have devised calamity
　against her:　　Num. 21:25; Jer. 48:34, 45
　'Come and let us cut her off from being
　a nation!'
　You too, [12]Madmen, will be silenced;
　The sword will follow after you.
3 "The sound of an outcry from [R]Horo-
　naim,　　　　　Is. 15:5; Jer. 48:5, 34
　'Devastation and great destruction!'
4 "Moab is broken,
　Her little ones have sounded out a cry
　of distress.
5 "For by the ascent of [R]Luhith　　Is. 15:5
　They will ascend with continual weep-
　ing;
　For at the descent of Horonaim
　They have heard the [A]anguished cry of
　destruction.　　　distresses of outcry
6 "Flee, [R] save your lives,
　That you may be like a juniper in the
　wilderness.　　　　　　　Jer. 51:6
7 "For because of your [R]trust in your own
　achievements and treasures,
　Even you yourself will be captured;
　And [R]Chemosh will go off into exile
　Together with his priests and his
　princes.　　　　Ps. 52:7 · Num. 21:29
8 "And a destroyer will come to every
　city,
　So that no city will escape;
　The valley also will be ruined,

And the [R]plateau will be destroyed,
As the LORD has said.　　Josh. 13:9, 17, 21
9 "Give [A]wings [R]to Moab,　　　salt · Ps. 11:1
　For she will [A]flee away;　　　fall in ruins
　And her cities will become a [R]desola-
　tion,　　　　　　　　　　Jer. 44:22
　Without inhabitants in them.
10 "Cursed be the one who does the LORD's
　work [R]negligently,
　And cursed be the one who restrains
　his sword from blood.　　　2 Kin. 13:19

11 "Moab has been [R]at ease since his youth;
　He has also been [R]undisturbed on his
　lees,　　　　　Jer. 22:21; Zeph. 1:12
　Neither has he been [R]emptied from ves-
　sel to vessel,　　　　　　Nah. 2:2
　Nor has he gone into exile.
　Therefore he retains his flavor,
　And his aroma has not changed.
12 "Therefore behold, the days are coming," declares the LORD, "when I shall send
to him those who tip vessels, and they will
tip him over, and they will empty his vessels
and shatter [T]his jars.　　　　　　　their
13 "And Moab will be [R]ashamed of Chemosh, as the house of Israel was ashamed of
Bethel, their confidence.　Is. 45:16; Jer. 48:39
14 "How can you say, 'We are [R]mighty war-
　riors,　　　　Ps. 33:16; Is. 10:13-16
　And men valiant for battle'?
15 "Moab has been destroyed, and [T]men
　have gone up to his cities;　one has
　His choicest [T]young men have also gone
　down to the slaughter,"　　warriors
　Declares the [R]King, whose name is the
　LORD of hosts.　　　Jer. 46:18; 51:57
16 "The disaster of Moab will soon come,
　And his calamity has swiftly hastened.
17 "Mourn for him, all you who live around
　him,
　Even all of you who know his name;
　Say, 'How has the mighty [A]scepter [R]been
　broken,
　A staff of splendor!'　　rod · Is. 9:4; 14:5
18 "Come [A]down from your glory　　Is. 47:1
　And sit on the parched ground, in thirst
　O [R]daughter dwelling in [R]Dibon,
　For the destroyer of Moab has come up
　against you,　　Jer. 49:19 · Num. 21:30
　He has ruined your strongholds.
19 "Stand by the road and keep watch,
　O inhabitant of [R]Aroer;　　　Deut. 2:36
　[R]Ask him who flees and her who es-
　capes　　　　　1 Sam. 4:13, 14, 16
　And say, 'What has happened?'
20 "Moab has been put to shame, for it has
　been [A]shattered.　　　　dismayed
　Wail and cry out;
　Declare by the [R]Arnon　　　Num. 21:13
　That Moab has been destroyed.
21 "Judgment has also come upon the
plain, upon Holon, [R]Jahzah, and against
[R]Mephaath,　　Num. 21:23; Is. 15:4 · Josh. 13:18

---

[12] I.e., a city of Moab

22 against Dibon, Nebo, and Beth-dibla-thaim,

23 against Kiriathaim, Beth-gamul, and [R]Beth-meon,   Josh. 13:17

24 against Kerioth, Bozrah, and all the cities of the land of Moab, far and near.

25 "The horn of Moab has been cut off, and his arm broken," declares the LORD.

26 "Make him drunk, for he has become arrogant toward the LORD; so Moab will wallow in his vomit, and he also will become a laughingstock.   *magnified himself against*

27 "Now was not Israel a laughingstock to you? Or was he [A]caught among thieves? For each time you speak about him you [R]shake *your head in scorn.*   *found* • Jer. 18:16

28 "Leave the cities and dwell among the [R]crags,   Judg. 6:2; Is. 2:19; Jer. 49:16
O inhabitants of Moab,
And be like a [A]dove that nests   Ps. 55:6
Beyond the mouth of the chasm.

29 "We [R]have heard of the pride of Moab—
he is very proud—   Is. 16:6; Zeph. 2:8
Of his haughtiness, his pride, his arrogance and his self-exaltation.

30 "I know his [R]fury," declares the LORD,
"But it is futile;
His idle boasts have accomplished nothing.   Is. 37:28

31 "Therefore I shall [R]wail for Moab, Is. 15:5
Even for all Moab shall I cry out;
I will moan for the men of Kir-heres.

32 "More than the weeping for [R]Jazer
I shall weep for you, O vine of Sibmah!
Your tendrils stretched across the sea,
They reached to the sea of Jazer;
Upon your summer fruits and your grape harvest
The destroyer has fallen.   Num. 21:32

33 "So [R]gladness and joy are taken away
From the fruitful field, even from the land of Moab.   Is. 16:10; Jer. 25:10
And I have made the wine to [R]cease
from the wine presses;   Is. 5:10
No one will tread *them* with shouting,
The shouting will not be shouts *of joy.*

34 "From the outcry at Heshbon even to Elealeh, even to Jahaz they have [T]raised their voice, from Zoar even to Horonaim *and to* Eglath-shelishiyah; for even the waters of Nimrim will become desolate.   *given forth*

35 "And I shall make an end of Moab," declares the LORD, "the one who offers *sacrifice* on the high place and the one who [A]burns incense to his gods.   *offers up in smoke*

36 "Therefore My heart [T]wails for Moab like flutes; My heart also [T]wails like flutes for the men of Kir-heres. Therefore they have [R]lost the abundance it produced.   *sounds* • Is. 15:7

37 "For [A]every head is bald and every beard cut short; there are gashes on all the hands and sackcloth on the loins.   Is. 15:2; Jer. 16:6

38 "On all the housetops of Moab and in its streets [T]there is lamentation everywhere; for I have broken Moab like an undesirable vessel," declares the LORD.   *all of it is lamentation*

39 "How [A]shattered it is! How they have wailed! How Moab has turned his back—he is ashamed! So Moab will become a laughingstock and an [R]object of terror to all around him."   *dismayed* • Ezek. 26:16

40 For thus says the LORD,
"Behold, one will [R]fly swiftly like an eagle,   Deut. 28:49; Jer. 49:22; Hos. 8:1
And [R]spread out his wings against Moab.   Is. 8:8

41 "Kerioth has been captured
And the strongholds have been seized,
So the [R]hearts of the mighty men of Moab in that day   Jer. 49:22
Will be like the heart of a [R]woman in labor.   Is. 13:8; 21:3; Mic. 4:9, 10

42 "And Moab will be [R]destroyed from *being* a people   Ps. 83:4; Jer. 48:2
Because he has become [R]arrogant toward the LORD.   Is. 37:23; Jer. 48:26

43 "Terror, [R]pit, and snare are *coming* upon you,
O inhabitant of Moab," declares the LORD.   Is. 24:17, 18; Lam. 3:47

44 "The one who [R]flees from the terror
Will fall into the pit,
And the one who climbs up out of the pit   1 Kin. 19:17; Is. 24:18; Amos 5:19
Will be caught in the snare;
For I shall bring upon her, *even* upon Moab,
The year of their [R]punishment," declares the LORD.   Jer. 46:21

45 "In the shadow of Heshbon
The fugitives stand without strength;
For a fire has gone forth from Heshbon,
And a [R]flame from the midst of Sihon,
And it has devoured the [R]forehead of Moab   Num. 21:28, 29 • Num. 24:17
And the scalps of the riotous revelers.

46 "Woe [R]to you, Moab!   Num. 21:29
The people of [R]Chemosh have perished;
For your sons have been taken away captive,   1 Kin. 11:7; Jer. 48:7
And your daughters into captivity.

47 "Yet I will restore the fortunes of Moab
In the latter days," declares the LORD.
Thus far the judgment on Moab.

CHAPTER 49

Prophecies Against Ammon

CONCERNING the sons of [R]Ammon.
Thus says the LORD: Deut. 23:3, 4
"Does Israel have no sons?
Or has he no heirs?
Why then has Malcam taken possession of Gad
And his people settled in its cities?

2 "Therefore behold, the days are coming," declares the LORD,
"That I shall cause a [A]trumpet [R]blast of war to be heard   *shout of* • Jer. 4:19
Against [R]Rabbah of the sons of Ammon;
And it will become a desolate heap,

And her towns will be set on fire.
Then Israel will take possession of his
  possessors," 2 Sam. 11:1; Ezek. 21:20
Says the LORD.
3"Wail, O^RHeshbon, for ^RAi has been de-
  stroyed! Jer. 48:2 • Josh. 7:2-5; 8:1-29
Cry out, O daughters of Rabbah,
^RGird yourselves with sackcloth and la-
  ment, Is. 32:11; Jer. 48:37
And rush back and forth inside the
  walls;
For Malcam will^Rgo into exile
Together with his priests and his
  princes. Jer. 46:25; 48:7
4"How^Rboastful you are about the val-
  leys! Jer. 9:23
Your valley is flowing *away*,
O^Rbacksliding daughter Jer. 31:22
Who trusts in her^Rtreasures, *saying*,
'Who will come against me?' Ps. 62:10
5"Behold, I am going to bring^Rterror upon
  you," Jer. 48:43f.; 49:29
Declares the Lord GOD of hosts,
"From all *directions* around you;
And each of you will be ^Rdriven out
^Theadlong, Jer. 16:16 • *before him*
With no one to gather the^Rfugitives to-
  gether. Lam. 4:15
6"But afterward I will^Rrestore
The^Afortunes of the sons of Ammon,"
Declares the LORD. Jer. 48:47 • *captivity*

Prophecies Against Edom

7 Concerning^REdom. Gen. 25:30; 32:3
Thus says the LORD of hosts,
"Is there no longer any wisdom in^RTe-
  man?
Has good counsel been lost to the pru-
  dent? Gen. 36:11, 15, 34; Jer. 49:20
Has their wisdom decayed?
8"Flee away, turn back, dwell in the
  depths,
O inhabitants of^RDedan, Is. 21:13
For I^Awill bring the ^Rdisaster of Esau
  upon him *brought* • Jer. 46:21
At the time I^Apunish him. *punished*
9"If^Rgrape gatherers came to you,
Would they not leave gleanings?
If thieves *came* by night,
They would destroy *only*^Tuntil they had
  enough. Obad. 5 • *their sufficiency*
10"But I have^Rstripped Esau bare,
I have uncovered his hiding places
So that he will not be able to conceal
  himself; Jer. 13:26
His^Toffspring has been destroyed along
  with his^Trelatives *seed* • *brothers*
And his neighbors, and he is no more.
11"Leave your^Aorphans^Rbehind, I will keep
  them alive; *fatherless* • Ps. 68:5
And let your widows trust in Me."
12 For thus says the LORD, "Behold, those
^Twho were not sentenced to drink the ^Rcup
will certainly drink *it*, and are you the one
who will be completely acquitted? You will

not be acquitted, but you will certainly
drink *it*. *whose judgment was not to* • Jer. 25:15
13"For I have^Rsworn by Myself," declares
the LORD, "that^RBozrah will become an^Rob-
ject of horror, a reproach, a ruin and a
curse; and all its cities will become perpetual ruins." Is. 45:23 • Gen. 36:33 • Is. 34:9-15
14 I have^Rheard a message from the LORD,
  And an^Renvoy is sent among the na-
    tions, *saying*, Obad. 1-4 • Is. 18:2
"Gather^Ryourselves together and come
  against her, Jer. 50:14
And rise up for battle!"
15"For behold, I have made you small
  among the nations,
Despised among men.
16"As for the terror of you,
The arrogance of your heart has deceived you,
O you who live in the clefts of^Rthe rock,
Who occupy the height of the hill.
Though you make your nest as^Rhigh as
  an eagle's, *Sela* • Is. 14:13-15
I will^Rbring you down from there," declares the LORD. Amos 9:2
17"And Edom will become an object of
horror; everyone who passes by it will be
horrified and will hiss at all its wounds.
18"Like the^Roverthrow of Sodom and Gomorrah with its neighbors," says the LORD,
"no^Rone will live there, nor will a son of man
reside in it. Gen. 19:24, 25 • Job 18:15-18
19"Behold, one will come up like a lion
from the^Tthickets of the Jordan against a pe-
rennially watered pasture; for in an instant I
shall make him run away from it, and whoever is^Rchosen I shall appoint over it. For
who is^Rlike Me, and who will summon Me
into court? And who then is the shepherd
who can stand against Me?" *pride* • Is. 46:9
20 Therefore hear the plan of the LORD
which He has planned against Edom, and
His purposes which He has purposed
against the inhabitants of Teman: surely
they will drag them off, *even* the little ones
of the flock; surely He will make their^Apas-
ture desolate because of them. *habitation*
21 The earth has quaked at the noise of
their downfall. There is an outcry! The noise
of it has been heard at the Red Sea.
22 Behold,^AHe will mount up and swoop
like an eagle, and spread out His wings
^Aagainst Bozrah; and the hearts of the mighty
men of Edom in that day will be like the
heart of a woman in labor. *one* • *over*

Prophecies Against Damascus

23 Concerning^RDamascus. Gen. 14:15; 15:2
"Hamath and Arpad are put to shame,
For they have heard bad news;
They are^Rdisheartened. Ex. 15:15
There is anxiety by the sea,
It^Rcannot be calmed. [Is. 57:20]
24"Damascus has become helpless;
She has turned away to flee,

And panic has gripped her;
ᴿDistress and pangs have taken hold of
her
Like a woman in childbirth.   Is. 13:8
25"How theᴿcity of praise has not been deserted,
The town of My joy!   Jer. 33:9; 51.41
26"Therefore, herᴿyoung men will fall in
her streets,   Jer. 11:22; 50:30
And all the men of war will beˢsilenced
in that day," declares the LORD of
hosts.   *destroyed*
27"And I shall ᴿset fire to the wall of Damascus,   Jer. 43:12; Amos 1:3-5
And it will devour theᴬfortified towers
ofᴿBen-hadad."   *palaces* • 2 Kin. 13:3

Prophecies Against Kedar and Hazor

28 ConcerningᴿKedar and the kingdoms of
Hazor, which Nebuchadnezzar king of
Babylon defeated. Thus says the LORD,
"Arise, go up to Kedar   Gen. 25:13
And devastate the men of the east.
29"They will take away their tents and
their flocks;
They will carry off for themselves
Their tentᴿcurtains, all their goods, and
theirᴿcamels,   Hab. 3:7 • 1 Chr. 5:21
And they will call out to one another,
'Terrorᴿon every side!'   Jer. 46:5
30"Run away, flee! Dwell in the depths,
O inhabitants of Hazor," declares the
LORD;
"For Nebuchadnezzar king of Babylon
has formed a plan against you
And devised a scheme against you.
31"Arise, go up against a nation which is
ᴿat ease,   Judg. 18:7; Is. 47:8
Which lives securely," declares the
LORD.
"It hasᴿno gates or bars;   Is. 42:11
Theyᴿdwell alone.   Num. 23:9; Deut. 33:28
32"And their camels will become plunder,
And the multitude of their cattle for
booty,
And I shall ᴿscatter to all the winds
those whoᴿcut the corners *of their
hair;*   Ezek. 5:10 • Jer. 9:26; 25:23
And I shall bring their disaster from
every side," declares the LORD.
33"And Hazor will become a ᴿhaunt of
jackals,   Is. 13:20-22; Jer. 9:11; 10:22
A desolation forever;
No one will live there,
Nor will a son of man reside in it."

Prophecies Against Elam

34 That which came as the word of the
LORD to Jeremiah the prophet concerning
Elam,ᴿat the beginning of the reign of Zede-
kiah king of Judah, saying,   2 Kin. 24:17, 18
35"Thus says the LORD of hosts,
'Behold, I am going toᴿbreak the bow of
Elam,   Ps. 46:9; Is. 22:6; Jer. 51:56

Theᵀfinest of their might.   *first*
36 'And I shall bring upon Elam theᴿfour
winds   Dan. 7:2; 8:8; Rev. 7:1
From the four ends of heaven,
And shall ᴿscatter them to all these
winds;   Jer. 49:32; Ezek. 5:10; Amos 9:9
And there will be no nation
To which the outcasts of Elam will not
go.
37 'So I shallᴬshatter Elam before their en-
emies   *dismay*
And before those who seek their lives;
And I shallᴿbring calamity upon them,
Even My ᴿfierce anger,' declares the
LORD,   Jer. 6:19 • Jer. 30:24
'And I shall ᴿsend out the sword after
them   Jer. 9:16; 48:2
Until I have consumed them.
38 'Then I shall set My throne in Elam,
And I shall destroyᴬout of it king and
princes,'
Declares the LORD.   *from there*
39 'But it will come about in the last days
That I shall ᴿrestore the ᴬfortunes of
Elam,' "   Jer. 48:47 • *captivity*
Declares the LORD.

CHAPTER 50

Babylon's Defeat

THE word which the LORD spoke concerning ᴿBabylon, the land of the Chaldeans,
through Jeremiah the prophet: Gen. 10:10
2"Declareᴿ and proclaim among the nations.   Jer. 4:16
Proclaim it andᴿlift up a standard.
Do not conceal *it* but say,   Jer. 51:27
'Babylonᴿhas been captured,   Jer. 51:31
Bel has been put to shame,ᵀMarduk has
been shattered;   Heb., *Merodach*
Her images have been put to shame,
her idols have been shattered.'
3"For a nation has come up against her
out of theᴿnorth; it will make her land an
object of horror, and there will be no inhabitant in it. Both man and beast have wandered off, they have gone away!   Is. 13:17
4"In those days and at that time," declares the LORD, "the sons of Israel will
come, *both* they and the sons of Judahᴿas
well; they will go alongᴿweeping as they go,
and it will beᵀthe LORD their God they will
seek.   Is. 11:12, 13 • Ezra 3:12, 13 • Hos. 3:5
5"They will ask for the way to Zion, *turning* their facesᵀin its direction; theyᴬwill
come that they may join themselves to the
LORD *in* an everlasting covenant that will
not be forgotten.   *hither* • *will have come*
6"My people have become lost sheep;
ᴿTheir shepherds have led them astray.
They have made them turn aside *on*
the mountains;   Jer. 23:11-14
They have gone along from mountain
to hill
And have forgotten their resting place.

7"All who came upon them have devoured them;
And their adversaries have said, 'We[R]
are not guilty,　　　　Jer. 2:3; Zech. 11:5
Inasmuch as they have sinned against
the LORD *who is* the[R]habitation of
righteousness,　　　　Jer. 31:23; 40:2, 3
Even the LORD, the[R]hope of their fathers.'　　　　Ps. 22:4; Jer. 14:8; 17:13
8"Wander away from the[R]midst of Babylon,　　　　Is. 48:20; Jer. 51:6; [Rev. 18:4]
And go forth from the land of the Chaldeans;
Be also like male goats[A]at the head of
the flock.　　　　　*in front of*
9"For behold, I am going to[R]arouse and
bring up against Babylon　　Jer. 51:1
A horde of great nations from the land
of the north,
And they will draw up *their* battle lines
against her;
From there she will be taken captive.
Their arrows will be like an expert
warrior
Who does not return empty-handed.
10"And[A]Chaldea will become plunder;
All who plunder her will have enough,"
declares the LORD.　　　*the Chaldeans*

11"Because you are glad, because you are
jubilant,
O you who[R]pillage My heritage,
Because you skip about like a threshing[R]heifer　　　Jer. 12:14 • Jer. 46:20
And neigh like[T]stallions,　　*mighty ones*
12 Your[R]mother will be greatly ashamed,
She who gave you birth will be humiliated.　　　　Jer. 15:9
Behold, *she will be* the least of the nations,
A[R]wilderness, a parched land, and a
desert.　　　　Jer. 22:6; 51:43
13"Because of the indignation of the LORD
she will[R]not be inhabited,　　Jer. 34:22
But she will be[R]completely desolate;
Everyone who passes by Babylon will
be horrified　　　　Jer. 51:26
And will hiss because of all her
wounds.
14"Draw up your battle lines against
Babylon on every side,
All you who[T]bend the bow;
Shoot at her, do not be sparing with
your arrows,　　*tread* (in order to string)
For she has sinned against the LORD.
15"Raise your battle cry against her on every side!
She has[R]given[T]herself up, her pillars
have fallen,　　　1 Chr. 29:24 • *her hand*
Her walls have been torn down.
For this is the[R]vengeance of the LORD:
Take vengeance on her;　　Jer. 46:10
As she has done *to others,* so do to her.
16"Cut off the[R]sower from Babylon,
And the one who wields the sickle at
the time of harvest;　　　Joel 1:11

From before[A]the[R]sword of the oppressor　　　*the oppressing sword* • Jer. 25:38
[R]They will each turn back to his own
people,　　　　Is. 13:14
And they will each flee to his own land.
17"Israel is a scattered[T]flock, the lions
have driven *them* away. The first one *who*
devoured him was the king of Assyria, and
this last one *who* has broken his bones is
Nebuchadnezzar king of Babylon.　　*sheep*
18"Therefore thus says the LORD of hosts,
the God of Israel: 'Behold, I am going to
punish the king of Babylon and his land, just
as I[R]punished the king of Assyria.　Is. 10:12
19 'And I shall bring Israel back to his pasture, and he will graze on Carmel and Bashan, and his[T]desire will be satisfied in the
hill country of Ephraim and Gilead.　　*soul*
20 'In those days and at that time,' declares the LORD, 'search will be made for the
iniquity of Israel, but[T]there will be none; and
for the sins of Judah, but they will not be
found; for I shall pardon those[R]whom I leave
as a remnant.'　　Is. 43:25; [Jer. 31:34] • Is. 1:9

Babylon's Desolation

21"Against the land of [13]Merathaim, go up
against it,
And against the inhabitants of [14]Pekod.[R]　　　　Ezek. 23:23
Slay and[T]utterly destroy them," declares the LORD,　　*put under the ban*
"And do according to all that I have
commanded you.
22"The[R]noise of battle is in the land,
And great destruction.　　　Jer. 4:19-21
23"How the[R]hammer of the whole earth
Has been cut off and broken!
How Babylon has become　　Jer. 51:20-24
An object of horror among the nations!
24"I set a snare for you, and you were also
[R]caught, O Babylon,　　　Dan. 5:30, 31
While you yourself were not aware;
You have been found and also seized
Because you have engaged in[R]conflict
with the LORD."　　　[Job 9:4; 40:2, 9]
25 The LORD has opened His armory
And has brought forth the[R]weapons of
His indignation,　　　　Is. 13:5
For it is a[R]work of the Lord GOD of
hosts　　　Jer. 50:15; 51:12, 25, 55
In the land of the Chaldeans.
26 Come to her from the[T]farthest border;
[R]Open up her barns,　　　*end* • Is. 45:3
Pile her up like heaps
And[T]utterly destroy her,　　Is. 14:23
Let nothing be left to her.
27[R]Put all her young bulls to the sword;
Let them[R]go down to the slaughter!
Woe be upon them, for their[R]day has
come,　　Is. 34:7 • Jer. 48:10 • Jer. 46:21
The time of their punishment.
28 There is a[R]sound of fugitives and refugees from the land of Babylon,

[13] Or, *Double Rebellion*　[14] Or, *Punishment*

To declare in Zion the^Rvengeance of the
   LORD our God,_R   Is. 48:20 • Ps. 149:6-9
Vengeance for His^Rtemple.   Lam. 1:10

29"Summon ¹⁵many against Babylon,
   All those who^Tbend the bow:
   Encamp against her on every side,
   Let there be no escape.
   Repay her according to her work;
   According to all that she has done, *so*
      do to her;   *tread* (in order to string)
   For she has become^Rarrogant against
      the LORD,   Ex. 10:3; Jer. 49:16
   Against the Holy One of Israel.
30"Therefore her^Ryoung men will fall in
      her streets,   Is. 13:17, 18; Jer. 9:21
   And all her men of war will be silenced
      in that day," declares the LORD.
31"Behold,^RI am against you, O^Tarrogant
      one,"   Jer. 21:13; Nah. 2:13 • *arrogance*
   Declares the Lord GOD of hosts,
   "For your day has come,
   The time when I shall punish you.
32"And the^Tarrogant^Rone will stumble and
      fall   *arrogance* • Is. 10:12-15
   With no one to raise him up;
   And I shall set fire to his cities,
   And it will devour all his environs."

33 Thus says the LORD of hosts,
   "The sons of Israel are oppressed,
   And the sons of Judah as well;
   And^Rall who took them captive have
      held them fast,   [Is. 14:17; 58:6]
   They have refused to let them go.
34"Their^RRedeemer is strong, the LORD of
      hosts is His name;   Prov. 23:11
   He will vigorously^Rplead their case,
   So that He may^Rbring rest to^Athe earth,
   But turmoil to the inhabitants of Baby-
      lon.   Mic. 7:9 • Is. 14:3-7 • *their land*
35"A^Rsword against the Chaldeans," de-
      clares the LORD,
   "And against the inhabitants of Baby-
      lon,   Jer. 47:6; Hos. 11:6
   And against her^Rofficials and her^Rwise
      men!   Dan. 5:1, 2 • Dan. 5:7, 8
36"A sword against the^Roracle priests, and
      they will become fools!   Is. 44:25
   A sword against her mighty men, and
      they will be^Ashattered!   *dismayed*
37"A sword against^Ttheir horses and
      against^Ttheir chariots,   *his*
   And against all the^Tforeigners who are
      in the midst of her,   *mixed multitude*
   And they will become^Rwomen!
   A sword against her treasures, and
      they will be plundered!   Jer. 48:41
38"A^Rdrought on her waters, and they will
      be dried up!_R   Is. 44:27; Jer. 51:32, 36
   For it is a land of idols,   Is. 46:1, 6, 7
   And they are mad over fearsome idols.
39"Therefore the^Rdesert creatures will live
      there along with the jackals;
   The ostriches also will live in it,

And it will^Rnever again be inhabited
Or dwelt in from generation to genera-
   tion.   Is. 13:21 • Is. 13:20; Jer. 25:12
40"As when God overthrew^RSodom
   And Gomorrah with its neighbors," de-
      clares the LORD,   Gen. 19:24, 25
   "No man will live there,
   Nor will *any* son of man reside in it.

41"Behold, a people is coming^Rfrom the
      north,   Is. 13:2-5; Jer. 6:22; 50:3, 9
   And a great nation and many kings
   Will be aroused from the remote parts
      of the earth.
42"They seize *their* bow and javelin;
   They are cruel and have no mercy.
   Their^Rvoice roars like the sea,   Is. 5:30
   And they ride on^Rhorses,   Jer. 8:16; 47:3
   Marshalled like a man for the battle
   Against you, O daughter of Babylon.
43"The^Rking of Babylon has heard the re-
      port about them,   Jer. 51:31
   And his hands hang limp;
   ^RDistress has gripped him, Jer. 30:6; 49:24
   Agony like a woman in childbirth.
44"Behold, one will come up like a lion
from the^Tthicket of the Jordan to a peren-
nially watered pasture; for in an instant I
shall make them run away from it, and whoever is_Rchosen I shall appoint over it. For
who is^Rlike Me, and who will summon Me
into court? And who then is the shepherd
who can stand before Me?"   *pride* • Is. 46:9
45 Therefore hear the plan of the LORD
which He has planned against Babylon, and
His purposes which He has purposed
against the land of the Chaldeans: surely
they will drag them off, *even* the little ones
of the flock; surely He will make their^Apas-
ture desolate because of them.   *habitation*
46 At the ^Tshout, "Babylon has been
seized!" the earth is shaken, and an^Routcry
is heard among the nations.   *voice* • Is. 5:7

CHAPTER 51

Babylon's Destiny

THUS says the LORD:
   "Behold, I am going to arouse against
      Babylon
   And against the inhabitants of ¹⁶Leb-
      kamai
   The^Rspirit of a destroyer.   Jer. 4:11, 12
2"And I shall dispatch foreigners to
      Babylon that they may^Rwinnow her
   And may devastate her land;
   For on every side they will be opposed
      to her   Is. 41:16; Jer. 15:7; Matt. 3:12
   In the day of *her* calamity.
3"Let not him who bends his bow bend *it,*
   Nor let him rise up in his scale-armor;
   So do not spare her young men;
   Devote all her army to destruction.
4"And they will fall down^Aslain in the
      land of the Chaldeans,   *wounded*
   And pierced through in their streets."

¹⁵ Another reading is *archers*   ¹⁶ Cryptic name for Chaldea

5 For^Rneither Israel nor Judah has been
^Tforsaken   [Jer. 33:24–26] • *widowed*
By his God, the LORD of hosts,
Although their land is full of guilt
^TBefore the Holy One of Israel.   *From*
6 ^RFlee from the midst of Babylon,
And each of you save his life! Rev. 18:4
Do not be ^Adestroyed in her punish-
ment,   *silenced* or *made lifeless*
For this is the LORD's time of ven-
geance;
He is going to ^Rrender recompense to
her.   Jer. 25:14
7 Babylon has been a golden^Rcup in the
hand of the LORD,
Intoxicating all the earth.   Hab. 2:16
The nations have drunk of her wine;
Therefore the nations are going mad.
8 Suddenly^RBabylon has fallen and been
broken;   Is. 21:9; Jer. 50:2; Rev. 14:8
^RWail over her!   Is. 13:6; Rev. 18:9
^RBring balm for her pain;   Jer. 46:11
Perhaps she may be healed.
9 We applied healing to Babylon, but she
was not healed;
Forsake her and^Rlet us each go to his
own country,   Is. 13:14; Jer. 46:16
For her judgment has ^Rreached to
heaven   Ezra. 9:6; Rev. 18:5
And towers up to the very skies.
10 The LORD has^Rbrought^Tabout our vindication;   Ps. 37:6; Mic. 7:9 • *forth*
Come and let us recount in Zion
The work of the LORD our God!

11 ^RSharpen the arrows, fill the quivers!
The LORD has aroused the spirit of the
kings of the Medes,
Because His purpose is against Baby-
lon to destroy it;   Joel 3:9, 10
For it is the^Rvengeance of the LORD,
vengeance for His temple. Jer. 50:28
12 ^RLift up a signal against the walls of
Babylon;   Is. 13:2; Jer. 50:2; 51:27
Post a strong guard,
Station^Asentries,   *watchmen*
Place men in ambush!
For the LORD has both^Rpurposed and
performed   Jer. 4:28; 23:20; 51:29
What He spoke concerning the inhabi-
tants of Babylon.
13 O you who^Rdwell by many waters,
Abundant in^Rtreasures,
Your end has come,   Rev. 17:1 • Is. 45:3
The measure of your^Tend.   *being cut off*
14 The^RLORD of hosts has sworn by Him-
self: Jer. 49:13
"Surely I will fill you with a^Apopulation
like^Rlocusts,   *mankind* • Jer. 51:27
And they will cry out with shouts of
victory over you."

15 *It is*^RHe who made the earth by His
power,   Gen. 1:1; Jer. 10:12-16; 51:15-19
Who established the world by His wisdom,

And by His understanding He
^Rstretched out the heavens.   Job 9:8
16 When He utters His voice, *there is* a
tumult of waters in the heavens,
And He causes the ^Rclouds to ascend
from the end of the earth;
He makes lightning for the rain,
And brings forth the^Rwind from His
storehouses.   Jer. 10:13 • Jon. 1:4
17 ^RAll mankind is stupid, devoid of knowledge;   [Is. 44:18–20]; Jer. 10:14
Every goldsmith is put to shame by his
^Aidols,   *graven images*
For his molten images are deceitful,
And there is no breath in them.
18 They are^Rworthless, a work of mockery;
In the time of their punishment they
will perish.   Jer. 18:15
19 The portion of Jacob is not like these;
For the^TMaker of all is He,   *Fashioner*
And of the tribe of His inheritance;
The LORD of hosts is His name.
20 *He says,* "You are My^Twar-club, My
weapon of war;   *shatterer* • Is. 10:5
And with you I^Rshatter nations,   Is. 8:9
And with you I destroy kingdoms.
21 "And with you I^Rshatter the horse and
his rider,   Ex. 15:1
22 And with you I shatter the^Rchariot and
its rider,   Ex. 15:4; Is. 43:17
And with you I shatter ^Rman and
woman,   2 Chr. 36:17; Is. 13:15, 16
And with you I shatter old man and
^Ryouth,   Is. 13:18
And with you I shatter young man and
virgin,
23 And with you I shatter the shepherd
and his flock,
And with you I shatter the farmer and
his team,
And with you I shatter governors and
prefects.
24 "But I will repay Babylon and all the in-
habitants of^RChaldea for ^Rall their evil that
they have done in Zion before your eyes,"
declares the LORD.   Jer. 50:10 • Jer. 50:15, 29
25 "Behold, I am against you,^RO destroying
mountain,
Who destroy the whole earth," declares the LORD,   Is. 13:2; Zech. 4:7
"And I will stretch out My hand against
you,
And roll you down from the crags
And I will make you a^Rburnt out mountain.   Rev. 8:8
26 "And they will not take from you *even* a
stone for a corner
Nor a stone for foundations,
But you will be^Rdesolate forever," declares the LORD.   Is. 13:19-22; 50:13

27 Lift up a^Asignal in the land,   *standard*
Blow a trumpet among the nations!
Consecrate the nations against her,
Summon against her the kingdoms of
Ararat, Minni and Ashkenaz;

Appoint a marshal against her,
Bring up the horses like bristly locusts.
28 Consecrate the nations against her,
The kings of the Medes,
^TTheir governors and all^Ttheir prefects,
And every land of their dominion. *Her*
29 So the^Rland quakes and writhes,
For the purposes of the LORD against
Babylon stand,   Jer. 8:16; 10:10; 50:46
To make the land of Babylon
A desolation without inhabitants.
30 The ^Rmighty men of Babylon have
ceased fighting,   Jer. 50:15, 36, 37
They stay in the strongholds;
Their strength is^Texhausted,   *dried up*
They are becoming *like* women;
Their dwelling places are set on fire,
The bars of her *gates* are broken.
31 One^Tcourier runs to meet^Tanother,
And one^Tmessenger to meet^Tanother,
To tell the king of Babylon
That his city has been captured from
end *to end;*   *runner · announcer*
32 The fords also have been seized,
And they have burned the marshes
with fire,
And the men of war are terrified.

33 For thus says the LORD of hosts, the
God of Israel:
"The daughter of Babylon is like a
^Rthreshing floor   Is. 21:10; 41:15, 16
At the time^Tit is stamped firm;
Yet in a little while the time of harvest
will come for her."   *of treading it*

34 "Nebuchadnezzar king of Babylon has
^Rdevoured me *and* crushed me,
He has set me down *like* an^Rempty ves-
sel;   Jer. 50:17 · Is. 24:1-3
He has^Rswallowed me like a monster,
He has filled his stomach with my deli-
cacies;   Job 20:15; Jer. 51:44
He has washed me away.
35 "May the^Rviolence *done* to me and to my
flesh be upon Babylon,"
The ^Tinhabitant of Zion will say;
And, "May my blood be upon the in-
habitants of Chaldea,"
Jerusalem will say.   Ps. 137:8 · *inhabitress*
36 Therefore thus says the LORD,
"Behold, I am going to plead your case
And exact full vengeance for you;
And^RI shall dry up her sea   Jer. 50:38
And make her fountain dry.
37 "And^RBabylon will become a heap *of ruins,* a haunt of jackals,
An^Robject of horror and hissing, without inhabitants.   [Rev. 18:2] · Jer. 25:9
38 "They will roar together like ^Ryoung
lions,   Jer. 2:15
They will growl like lions' cubs.
39 "When they become heated up, I shall
serve *them* their banquet

And^Rmake them drunk, that they may
become jubilant   Jer. 25:27; 48:26
And may sleep a perpetual sleep
And not wake up," declares the LORD.
40 "I shall bring them down like^Alambs^Rto
the slaughter,   *young rams* · Jer. 48:15
Like rams together with male goats.

41 "How ¹⁷Sheshak^Rhas been captured,
And^Rthe praise of the whole earth been
seized!   Jer. 25:26 · Jer. 49:25
How Babylon has become an object of
horror among the nations!
42 "The^Asea^Rhas come up over Babylon;
She has been engulfed with its tumul-
tuous waves.   *broad river* · Dan. 9:26
43 "Her cities have become an ^Robject of
horror,
A parched land and a desert,
A land in which^Rno man lives,
And through which no son of man
passes.   Jer. 50:12 · Is. 13:20; Jer. 2:6
44 "And^RI shall punish Bel in Babylon,
And I shall make what he has swal-
lowed^Rcome out of his mouth;
And the nations will no longer stream
to him.   Is. 46:1; Jer. 50:2 · Ezra 1:7, 8
Even the^Rwall of Babylon has fallen
down!   Jer. 50:15; 51:58

45 "Come forth from her midst, My people,
And each of you save yourselves
From the fierce anger of the LORD.
46 "Now^Rlest your heart grow faint,
And you be afraid at the report that
will be heard in the land—   Is. 43:5
For the report will come^Tone year,
And after that ^Tanother report in an-
other year,   *in the* · *the*
And violence *will be* in the land
With^Rruler against ruler—   Is. 19:2
47 Therefore behold, days are coming
When I shall punish the^Ridols of Baby-
lon;   Is. 21:9; 46:1, 2; Jer. 50:2; 51:52
And her whole land will be ^Rput to
shame,   Jer. 50:12, 35-37
And all her slain will fall in her midst.
48 "Then^Rheaven and earth and all that is in
them   Is. 44:23; 48:20; 49:13; Rev. 18:20
Will shout for joy over Babylon,
For ^Rthe destroyers will come to her
from the north,"   Jer. 50:3
Declares the LORD.

49 ^RIndeed Babylon is to fall *for* the slain of
Israel,   Ps. 137:8; Jer. 50:29
As also for Babylon^Rthe slain of all the
earth have fallen.   Rev. 18:24
50 You^Rwho have escaped the sword,
Depart! Do not stay!   Jer. 44:28
Remember the LORD from afar,
And let Jerusalem come to your mind.
51 ^RWe are ashamed because we have
heard reproach;   Ps. 44:15
Disgrace has covered our faces,

¹⁷ Cryptic name for Babylon

For^Raliens have entered   Ps. 74:3-8
The holy places of the LORD's house.

52"Therefore behold, the days are com-
    ing," declares the LORD,
"When I shall punish her^Ridols,
And the mortally wounded will groan
    throughout her land.   Jer. 50:38
53"Though Babylon should ^Rascend to the
    heavens,   [Is. 14:12–14]; Jer. 49:16
And though she should fortify her lofty
    stronghold,   *the height of her strength*
From^RMe destroyers will come to her,"
    declares the LORD.   Is. 13:3

54 The ^Rsound of an outcry from Babylon,
And of great destruction from the land
    of the Chaldeans!   Jer. 48:3-5
55 For the LORD is going to destroy Baby-
    lon,
And He will make *her* loud^Anoise van-
    ish from her.   *voice*
And their^Rwaves will roar like many
    waters;   Ps. 18:4; 69:2; 124:2, 4, 5
The tumult of their voices ^Tsounds
    forth.   *is given*
56 For the ^Rdestroyer is coming against
    her, against Babylon,   Jer. 51:48, 53
And her mighty men will be captured,
Their^Rbows are shattered;   Ps. 46:9; 76:3
For the LORD is a God of^Rrecompense,
He will fully repay.   Deut. 32:35
57"And I shall^Rmake her princes and her
    wise men drunk,   Jer. 25:27
Her governors, her prefects, and her
    mighty men,
That they may sleep a^Rperpetual sleep
    and not wake up,"   Ps. 76:5, 6
^RDeclares the King, whose name is the
    LORD of hosts.   Jer. 46:18; 48:15
58 Thus says the LORD of hosts,
"The broad^Rwall of Babylon will be com-
    pletely razed,   Jer. 50:15
And her high gates will be set on fire;
So the peoples will^Rtoil for nothing,
And the nations become ^Rexhausted
    only for fire."   Hab. 2:13 • Jer. 9:5
59 The ^Tmessage which Jeremiah the
prophet commanded Seraiah the son of Neriah, the grandson of Mahseiah, when he
went with Zedekiah the king of Judah to
Babylon in the fourth year of his reign.
(Now Seraiah was quartermaster.)   *word*
60 So Jeremiah^Rwrote in a single^Ascroll all
the calamity which would come upon Baby-
lon, *that is,* all these words which have been
written concerning Babylon.   Is. 30:8 • *book*
61 Then Jeremiah said to Seraiah, "As
soon as you come to Babylon, then see that
you read all these words aloud,
62 and say, 'Thou, O LORD, hast^Tpromised
concerning this place to cut it off, so that
there will be nothing dwelling in it,^Twhether
man or beast, but it will be a perpetual desolation.'   *spoken • from man even to beast*
63"And it will come about as soon as you

finish reading this^Ascroll, you will tie a stone
to it and^Rthrow it into the middle of the Euphrates,   *book* • Jer. 19:10, 11; Rev. 18:21
64 and say, 'Just so shall Babylon sink
down and^Rnot rise again, because of the calamity that I am going to bring upon her;
and they will become exhausted.' " Thus far
are the words of Jeremiah.   Nah. 1:8, 9

CHAPTER 52

The Capture of Jerusalem
2 Kin. 24:18—25:30; 2 Chr. 36:11–20;
Jer. 39:1–8

ZEDEKIAH was twenty-one years old
when he became king, and he reigned
eleven years in Jerusalem; and his mother's
name was^RHamutal the daughter of Jeremiah of^RLibnah.   2 Kin. 22:31; 24:18 • 2 Kin. 8:22
2 And he did^Revil in the sight of the LORD
like all that Jehoiakim had done. 2 Chr. 36:12
3 For through the anger of the LORD *this*
came about in Jerusalem and Judah until He
cast them out from His presence. And Zedekiah rebelled against the king of Babylon.
4 Now it came about in the ninth year of
his reign, on the tenth day of the tenth
month, that Nebuchadnezzar king of Babylon came, he and all his army, against Jerusalem, camped against it, and built a^Rsiege
wall all around^Tit.   Jer. 32:24 • *against it*
5 ^RSo the city was under siege until the
eleventh year of King Zedekiah.   2 Kin. 25:2
6 On the ninth day of the fourth month
the famine was so severe in the city that
there was no food for the people of the land.
7 Then the city was broken into, and all
the men of war fled and went forth from the
city at night by way of the gate between the
two walls which *was* by the king's garden,
though the Chaldeans were all around the
city. And they went by way of the Arabah.
8 But the army of the Chaldeans pursued
the king and ^Rovertook Zedekiah in the
^Tplains of Jericho, and all his army was scat-
tered from him.   Jer. 21:7; 32:4; 34:21 • *Arabah*
9 Then they captured the king and
brought him up to the king of Babylon at
Riblah in the land of Hamath; and he^Tpassed
sentence on him.   *spoke judgments with*
10 And the king of Babylon ^Rslaughtered
the sons of Zedekiah before his eyes, and he
also slaughtered all the^Aprinces of Judah in
Riblah.   Jer. 22:30; 39:6 • *commanders*
11 Then he^Rblinded the eyes of Zedekiah;
and the king of Babylon bound him with
bronze fetters and brought him to Babylon,
and put him in prison until the day of his
death.   Jer. 39:7; Ezek. 12:13

The Destruction of Jerusalem

12 Now on the tenth day of the fifth
month, which was the nineteenth year of
King Nebuchadnezzar, king of Babylon,

Nebuzaradan the captain of the bodyguard, [T]who was in the service of the king of Babylon, came to Jerusalem.   *stood before the king*

13 And he[R]burned the house of the LORD, the[R]king's house, and all the houses of Jerusalem; even every large house he burned with fire.   1 Kin. 9:8; 2 Kin. 25:9 • Jer. 39:8

14 So all the army of the Chaldeans who *were* with the captain of the guard broke down all the walls around Jerusalem.

15 Then Nebuzaradan the captain of the guard carried away into exile some of the poorest of the people, the rest of the people who were left in the city, the[T]deserters who had deserted to the king of Babylon, and the rest of the artisans.   *fallers who had fallen*

16 But Nebuzaradan the captain of the guard left some of the poorest of the land to be vinedressers and[A]plowmen.   *unpaid laborers*

17 Now the bronze pillars which belonged to the house of the LORD and the stands and the bronze sea, which were in the house of the LORD, the Chaldeans broke in pieces and carried all their bronze to Babylon.

18 And they also took away the[R]pots, the shovels, the snuffers, the basins, the[A]pans, and all the bronze vessels which were used in *temple* service.   Ex. 27:3 • *spoons* for incense

19 The captain of the guard also took away the bowls, the firepans, the basins, the pots, the lampstands, the[A]pans and the libation bowls, what was fine gold and what was fine silver.   *spoons* for incense

20 The two pillars, the one sea, and the twelve bronze bulls that were under the sea, *and* the stands, which King Solomon had made for the house of the LORD—the bronze of all these vessels was beyond weight.

21 As for the pillars, the[R]height of each pillar was eighteen cubits, and it was twelve cubits in circumference and four fingers in thickness, *and* hollow.   1 Kin. 7:15; 2 Chr. 3:15

22 Now a[R]capital of bronze was on it; and the height of each capital was five cubits, with network and[R]pomegranates upon the capital all around, all of bronze. And the second pillar was like these, including pomegranates.   1 Kin. 7:16 • 1 Kin. 7:20, 42

23 And there were ninety-six exposed pomegranates; all the pomegranates *num-*bered a hundred on the network all around.

The Exile to Babylon

24 Then the captain of the guard took [R]Seraiah the chief priest and Zephaniah the second priest, with the three[T]officers of the temple.   2 Kin. 25:18 • *keepers of the door*

25 He also took from the city one official who was overseer of the men of war, and seven of the king's advisers who were found in the city, and the scribe of the commander of the army who mustered the people of the land, and sixty men of the people of the land who were found in the midst of the city.

26 And Nebuzaradan the captain of the guard took them and[R]brought them to the king of Babylon at Riblah.   2 Kin. 25:20

27 Then the king of Babylon[R]struck them down and put them to death at Riblah in the land of Hamath. So Judah was[R]led away into exile from its land.   2 Kin. 25:21 • Is. 6:11, 12

28 These are the people whom[R]Nebuchadnezzar carried away into exile: in the seventh year 3,023 Jews;   Ezra 2:1; Neh. 7:6

29 in the eighteenth year of Nebuchadnezzar 832 persons from Jerusalem;

30 in the twenty-third year of Nebuchadnezzar, [R]Nebuzaradan the captain of the guard carried into exile 745 Jewish people; there were 4,600 persons in all.   2 Kin. 25:11

The Liberation of Jehoiachin

31 Now it came about in the thirty-seventh year of the exile of Jehoiachin king of Judah, in the twelfth month, on the twenty-fifth of the month, that Evil-merodach king of Babylon, in the *first* year of his reign,[R]showed favor to Jehoiachin king of Judah and brought him out of prison. Ps. 3:3

32 [R]Then he spoke kindly to him and set his throne above the thrones of the kings who *were* with him in Babylon.   2 Kin. 25:28

33 So Jehoiachin changed his prison clothes, and had his meals in the king's presence regularly all the days of his life.

34 And for his allowance, a[R]regular allowance was given him by the king of Babylon, a daily portion all the days of his life until the day of his death.   2 Sam. 9:10; 2 Kin. 25:30

THE LAMENTATIONS
OF JEREMIAH

📖 THE BOOK OF LAMENTATIONS

Lamentations describes the funeral of a city. It is a tear-stained portrait of the once proud Jerusalem, now reduced to rubble by the invading Babylonian hordes. In a five-poem dirge, Jeremiah exposes his emotions. A death has occurred; Jerusalem lies barren.

Jeremiah writes his lament in acrostic or alphabetical fashion. Beginning each chapter with the first letter A (aleph) he progresses verse by verse through the Hebrew alphabet, literally weeping from A to Z. And then, in the midst of this terrible holocaust, Jeremiah triumphantly cries out, "Great is Thy faithfulness" (3:23). In the face of death and destruction, with life seemingly coming apart, Jeremiah turns tragedy into a triumph of faith. God has never failed him in the past. God has promised to remain faithful in the future. In the light of the God he knows and loves, Jeremiah finds hope and comfort.

The Hebrew title of this book comes from the first word of chapters 1, 2, and 4: *Ekah*, "Ah, how!" Another Hebrew word *Ginoth* ("Elegies" or "Lamentations") has also been used as the title because it better represents the contents of the book. The Greek title *Threnoi* means "Dirges" or "Laments," and the Latin title *Threni* ("Tears" or "Lamentations") was derived from this word. The subtitle in Jerome's Vulgate reads: "*Id est lamentationes Jeremiae prophetae*," and this became the basis for the English title "The Lamentations of Jeremiah."

✍ THE AUTHOR OF LAMENTATIONS

The author of Lamentations is unnamed in the book, but internal and external evidence is consistently in favor of Jeremiah.

External Evidence: The universal consensus of early Jewish and Christian tradition attributes this book to Jeremiah. The superscription to Lamentations in the Septuagint says: "And it came to pass, after Israel had been carried away captive, and Jerusalem had become desolate, that Jeremiah sat weeping, and lamented with this lamentation over Jerusalem, saying . . . ." This is also the position of the Talmud, the Aramaic Targum of Jonathan, and early Christian writers, such as Origen and Jerome. In addition, Second Chronicles 35:25 says that "Jeremiah chanted a lament for Josiah." This was an earlier occasion, but Jeremiah was obviously familiar with the lament form.

Internal Evidence: The scenes in this graphic book were clearly portrayed by an eyewitness to Jerusalem's siege and fall soon after the destruction took place (cf. 1:13–15; 2:6, 9; 4:1–12). Jeremiah witnessed the fall of Jerusalem and remained behind after the captives were deported (cf. Jer. 39). Although some critics claim that the style of Lamentations is different from the Book of Jeremiah, the similarities are, in fact, striking and numerous, especially in the poetic sections of Jeremiah. Compare these passages from Lamentations and Jeremiah: 1:2 (Jer. 30:14); 1:15 (Jer. 8:21); 1:16 and 2:11 (Jer. 9:1, 18); 2:22 (Jer. 6:25); 4:21 (Jer. 49:12). The same compassion, sympathy, and grief over Judah's downfall are evident in both books.

⌛ THE TIME OF LAMENTATIONS

The historical background of Lamentations can be found in "The Time of Jeremiah." The book was written soon after Jerusalem's destruction (Jer. 39; 52) at the beginning of the Exile. Nebuchadnezzar laid siege to Jerusalem from January 588 B.C. to July 586 B.C. It fell on July 19, and the city and temple were burned on August 15. Jeremiah probably wrote these five elegies before he was taken captive to Egypt by his disobedient countrymen not long after the destruction (Jer. 43:1–7).

✝ THE CHRIST OF LAMENTATIONS

The weeping prophet Jeremiah is a type of Christ, the Prophet who wept over the same city six centuries later. "O Jerusalem, Jerusalem, who kills the prophets and stones those who are sent to her! How often I wanted to gather your children together, the way a hen gathers her chicks under her wings, and you were unwilling. Behold, your house is being left to you desolate!" (Matt. 23:37, 38). Like Christ, Jeremiah identified himself personally with the plight of Jerusalem and with human suffering caused by sin.

Lamentations also includes elements that typify Christ's life and ministry as the man of sorrows who was acquainted with grief. He was afflicted (1:12; 3:19), despised, and derided by His enemies (2:15, 16; 3:14, 30).

KEYS TO LAMENTATIONS

Key Word: Lamentations—Three themes run through the five laments of Jeremiah. The most prominent is the theme of mourning over Jerusalem's holocaust. The Holy City has been laid waste and desolate: God's promised judgment for sin has come. In his sorrow, Jeremiah speaks for himself, for the captives, and sometimes for the personified city. The second theme is a confession of sin and an acknowledgment of God's righteous and holy judgment upon Judah. The third theme is least prominent but very important: it is a note of hope in God's future restoration of His people. Yahweh has poured out His wrath, but in His mercy He will be faithful to His covenant promises.

Key Verses: Lamentations 2:5, 6 and 3:22, 23—"The Lord has become like an enemy. He has swallowed up Israel; He has swallowed up all its palaces; He has destroyed its strongholds and multiplied in the daughter of Judah mourning and moaning. And He has violently treated His tabernacle like a garden *booth;* He has destroyed His appointed meeting place; the LORD has caused to be forgotten the appointed feast and sabbath in Zion, and He has despised king and priest in the indignation of His anger" (2:5, 6).

"The LORD's lovingkindnesses indeed never cease, for His compassions never fail. *They* are new every morning; great is Thy faithfulness" (3:22, 23).

Key Chapter: Lamentations 3—In the midst of five chapters of ruin, destruction, and utter hopelessness, Jeremiah rises and grasps with strong faith the promises and character of God.

Lamentations 3:22-25 expresses a magnificent faith in the mercy of God—especially when placed against the dark backdrop of chapters 1, 2, 4, and 5.

SURVEY OF LAMENTATIONS

For forty years Jeremiah suffers rejection and abuse for his warnings of coming judgment. When Nebuchadnezzar finally comes and destroys Jerusalem in 586 B.C., a lesser man might say, "I told you so!" But Jeremiah compassionately identifies with the tragic overthrow of Jerusalem and composes five beautiful and emotional lament poems as a requiem for the once proud city. These dirges reflect the tender heart of the man who was divinely commissioned to communicate a harsh message to a sinful and stiff-necked people. The city, the temple, the palace, and the walls have been reduced to rubble and its inhabitants have been deported to distant Babylon. Jeremiah's five mournful poems can be entitled: the destruction of Jerusalem (1), the anger of God (2), the prayer for mercy (3), the siege of Jerusalem (4), and the prayer for restoration (5).

The Destruction of Jerusalem (1): This poem consists of a lamentation by Jeremiah (1:1–11) and a lamentation by the personified Jerusalem (1:12–22). The city has been left desolate because of her grievous sins, and her enemies "mocked at her ruin" (1:7). Jerusalem pleads with God to regard her misery and repay her adversaries.

The Anger of God (2): In his second elegy, Jeremiah moves from Jerusalem's desolation to a description of her destruction. Babylon has destroyed the city, but only as the Lord's instrument of judgment. Jeremiah presents an eyewitness account of the thoroughness and severity of Jerusalem's devastation. Through the Babylonians, God has terminated all religious observances, removed the priests, prophets, and kings, and razed the temple and palaces. Jeremiah grieves over the suffering the people brought on themselves through rebellion

FOCUS	DESTRUCTION OF JERUSALEM	ANGER OF JEHOVAH	PRAYER FOR MERCY	SIEGE OF JERUSALEM	PRAYER FOR RESTORATION
REFERENCE	1:1—————	2:1—————	3:1—————	4:1—————	5:1————5:22
DIVISION	MOURNING CITY	BROKEN PEOPLE	SUFFERING PROPHET	RUINED KINGDOM	PENITENT NATION
TOPIC	GRIEF	CAUSE	HOPE	REPENTANCE	PRAYER
LOCATION	JERUSALEM				
TIME	c. 586 B.C.				

against God, and Jerusalem's supplications complete the lament.

The Prayer for Mercy (3): In the first eighteen verses, Jeremiah enters into the miseries and despair of his people and makes them his own. However, there is an abrupt turn in verses 19–39 as the prophet reflects on the faithfulness and loyal love of the compassionate God of Israel. These truths enable him to find comfort and hope in spite of his dismal circumstances. Jeremiah expresses his deep sorrow and petitions God for deliverance and for God to avenge Jerusalem's misery.

The Siege of Jerusalem (4): The prophet rehearses the siege of Jerusalem and remembers the suffering and starvation of rich and poor. He also reviews the causes of the siege, especially the sins of the prophets and priests and their foolish trust in human aid. This poem closes with a warning to Edom of future punishment and a glimmer of hope for Jerusalem.

The Prayer for Restoration (5): Jeremiah's last elegy is a melancholy description of his people's lamentable state. Their punishment is complete, and Jeremiah prayerfully desires the restoration of his nation.

OUTLINE OF LAMENTATIONS

CHAPTER 1

The Desolation of Jerusalem

Hᴼᵂ ᴿlonely sits the city   Is. 3:26
That was full of people!   Is. 22:2
She has become like a widow   Is. 54:4
Who was *once* ᴿgreat among the nations!   1 Kin. 4:21
She who was a princess among the ᴬprovinces   *districts*
Has become a forced laborer!   Jer. 40:9
2 She ᴿweeps bitterly in the night,   Ps. 6:6
And her tears are on her cheeks;
She has none to comfort her
Among all her ᴿlovers.   Jer. 2:25
All her friends have ᴿdealt treacherously with her;   Ps. 31:11
They have become her enemies.
3 ᴿJudah has gone into exile under affliction,   Jer. 13:19
And under harsh servitude;   *great*
She dwells among the nations,
But she has found no rest;   Lev. 26:39
All her pursuers have overtaken her
In the midst of distress.   *narrow places*
4 The roads of Zion are in mourning
Because no one comes to the appointed feasts.   *to* · Is. 24:4-6

All her gates are ᴿdesolate;   Jer. 9:11
Her priests are groaning,
Her virgins are afflicted,   Lam. 2:10
And she herself ᴬis bitter.   *suffers bitterly*
5 Her adversaries have become her masters,   *head*
Her enemies prosper;   *are at ease*
For the LORD has ᴿcaused her grief
Because of the multitude of her transgressions;   Ps. 90:7, 8; Ezek. 8:17, 18; 9:9
Her little ones have gone away
As captives before the adversary.
6 And all her majesty   Jer. 13:18
Has departed from the daughter of Zion;
Her princes have become like bucks
That have found no pasture;
And they have fled without strength
Before the pursuer.   *gone* · 2 Kin. 25:4, 5
7 In the days of her affliction and homelessness
ᴿJerusalem remembers all her precious things   Ps. 42:4; 77:5-9
That were from the days of old
When her people fell into the hand of the adversary,
And no one helped her.   Jer. 37:7
The adversaries saw her,
They mocked at her ruin.   *cessation*

The Cause of Jerusalem's Desolation

8 Jerusalem sinned [R]greatly,   [Is. 59:2–13]
   Therefore [R]she has become an unclean
      thing.   Lam. 1:17
   All who honored her despise her
   Because they have seen her nakedness;
   Even [R]she herself groans and turns
      away.   Lam. 1:11, 21, 22
9 Her uncleanness was in her skirts;
   She did not consider her future;
   Therefore she has [T]fallen astonishingly;
   She has no comforter.   *come down*
   "See, O LORD, my affliction,
   For the enemy has magnified himself!"
10 The adversary has stretched out his
      hand
   Over all her precious things,
   For she has seen the [R]nations enter her
      sanctuary,   Ps. 74:4–8; Is. 64:10, 11
   The ones whom Thou didst command
   That they should [R]not enter into Thy
      congregation.   Deut. 23:3
11 All her people groan [R]seeking bread;
   They have given their precious things
      for food   Jer. 38:9; 52:6
   To restore their [T]lives themselves.
   "See, O LORD, and look,   *soul*
   For I am [R]despised."   Jer. 15:19

The Contrition of Jerusalem

12 "Is [R]it nothing to all you who pass this
      way?   Jer. 18:16; 48:27
   Look and see if there is any pain like
      my pain
   Which was severely dealt out to me,
   Which the [R]LORD inflicted on the day of
      His fierce anger.   Jer. 30:23, 24
13 "From on high He sent fire into my
      [R]bones,   Job 30:30; Ps. 22:14; Hab. 3:16
   And it prevailed *over them*;
   He has spread a [R]net for my feet;
   He has turned me back;   Job 19:6
   He has made me [R]desolate,   Jer. 44:6
   [A]Faint all day long.   *Sick*
14 "The [R]yoke of my transgressions is
      bound;   [Prov. 5:22]; Is. 47:6
   By His hand they are knit together;
   They have come upon my neck;
   He has made my strength [T]fail; *stumble*
   The Lord [R]has given me into the hands
   Of *those against whom* I am not able to
      stand.   Jer. 32:3, 5; Ezek. 25:4, 7
15 "The [R]Lord has rejected all my strong
      men   Is. 41:2; Jer. 13:24; 37:10
   In my midst;
   He has called an appointed [A]time
      against me   *feast*
   To crush my [R]young men;   Jer. 6:11; 18:21
   The Lord has [R]trodden *as in* a wine
      press   Mal. 4:3
   The virgin daughter of Judah.
16 "For these things I [R]weep;   Jer. 14:17
   [T]My eyes run down with water;
   Because far from me is a comforter,

One who restores my soul;
My children are desolate *My eye, my eye*
Because the enemy has prevailed."
17 Zion [R]stretches out her hands;   [Is. 1:15]
   There is no one to comfort her;
   The LORD has [R]commanded concerning
      Jacob   2 Kin. 24:2–4; Jer. 12:9
   That the ones round about him should
      be his adversaries;
   [R]Jerusalem has become an unclean
      thing among them.   Lam. 1:8
18 "The LORD is [R]righteous;   Ps. 119:75
   For I have [R]rebelled against His [T]com-
      mand;   Jer. 4:17 • *mouth*
   Hear now, all peoples,
   And [R]behold my [A]pain; Lam. 1:12 • *sorrow*
   [R]My virgins and my young men
   Have gone into captivity.   Deut. 28:32, 41
19 "I [R]called to my lovers, *but* they deceived
      me;   Job 19:13–19; Lam. 1:2
   My [R]priests and my elders perished in
      the city,   Jer. 14:15; Lam. 2:20
   While they sought food to restore [T]their
      strength themselves.   *their soul*

The Confession of Jerusalem

20 "See, O LORD, for I am in distress;
   My [R]spirit is greatly troubled;   Is. 16:11
   My heart is overturned within me,
   For I have been very rebellious.
   In the street the sword [T]slays;   *bereaves*
   In the house it is like death.
21 "They have heard that I [R]groan;
   There is no one to comfort me;
   All my enemies have heard of my [T]ca-
      lamity;   Lam. 1:4, 8, 22 • *evil*
   They are glad that Thou hast done *it.*
   Oh, that Thou wouldst bring the day
      which Thou hast proclaimed,
   That they may become like me.
22 "Let all their wickedness come before
      Thee;
   And [R]deal with them as Thou hast dealt
      with me   Neh. 4:4, 5; Ps. 137:7, 8
   For all my transgressions;
   For my groans are many, and my heart
      is faint."

CHAPTER 2

The Anger of God

H OW the Lord has [R]covered the daughter
      of Zion   Ezek. 30:18
   With a cloud in His anger!
   He has cast from heaven to earth
   The [R]glory of Israel,   Is. 64:11
   And has not remembered His [R]footstool
   In the day of His anger.   Ps. 99:5; 132:7
2 The Lord has [R]swallowed up; He has not
      spared   Ps. 21:9; Lam. 3:43
   All the habitations of Jacob.
   In His wrath He has [R]thrown down
   The strongholds of the daughter of Ju-
      dah;   Lam. 2:5; Mic. 5:11, 14

He has ^Rbrought *them* down to the ground;   Is. 25:12; 26:5

He has ^Rprofaned the kingdom and its princes.   Ps. 89:39, 40; Is. 43:28

3 In fierce anger He has cut off
^TAll the strength of Israel;   *Every horn*
He has ^Rdrawn back His right hand
From before the enemy.   Ps. 74:11
And He has ^Rburned in Jacob like a flaming fire   Is. 42:25; Jer. 21:14
Consuming round about.

4 He has bent His ^Rbow like an enemy,
He has set His right hand like an adversary   Job 6:4; 16:13; Lam. 3:12, 13
And slain all that were ^Rpleasant to the eye;   Ezek. 24:25
In the tent of the daughter of Zion
He has poured out His wrath like fire.

5 The Lord has become like an enemy.
He has ^Rswallowed up Israel;   Lam. 2:2
He has swallowed up all its ^Rpalaces;
He has destroyed its strongholds
And ^Rmultiplied in the daughter of Judah   Jer. 52:13; Lam. 2:2 • Jer. 9:17-20
Mourning and moaning.

6 And He has violently treated His ^Ttabernacle like a garden *booth;*   *booth*
He has ^Rdestroyed His appointed ^Ameeting place;   Jer. 52:13 • *feast*
The LORD has ^Rcaused to be forgotten
The appointed feast and sabbath in Zion,   Jer. 17:27; Lam. 1:4
And He has despised king and priest
In the indignation of His anger.

7 The Lord has rejected His altar,
He has abandoned His sanctuary;
He ^Rhas delivered into the hand of the enemy   Jer. 33:4, 5; 52:13
The walls of her palaces.
They have made a ^Rnoise in the house of the LORD   Ps. 74:3-8
As in the day of an appointed feast.

8 The LORD ^Tdetermined to destroy
The wall of the daughter of Zion.
He has stretched out a line,   *thought*
He has not restrained His hand from ^Tdestroying;   *swallowing up*
And He has ^Rcaused rampart and wall to lament;   Is. 3:26; Jer. 14:2
They have languished together.

9 Her ^Rgates have sunk into the ground,
He has destroyed and broken her bars.
Her king and her princes are among the nations;   Neh. 1:3
The ^Rlaw is no more;   Hos. 3:4
Also, her prophets find
^RNo vision from the LORD.   Ezek. 7:26

The Agony of Jerusalem

10 The elders of the daughter of Zion
Sit on the ground, they are silent.
They have thrown ^Rdust on their heads;
They have girded themselves with ^Rsackcloth.   Job 2:12 • Is. 15:3
The ^Rvirgins of Jerusalem   Lam. 1:4

Have bowed their heads to the ground.

11 My eyes fail because of tears,
My ^Rspirit is greatly troubled;   Jer. 4:19
My ^Theart is poured out on the earth,
Because of the destruction of the daughter of my people,   *liver*
When little ones and infants faint
In the streets of the city.

12 They say to their mothers,
"Where ^Ris grain and wine?"   Jer. 5:17
As they faint like a wounded man
In the streets of the city,
As their ^Tlife is poured out
On their mothers' bosom.   Ps. 42:4; 62:8

13 How shall I admonish you?
To what ^Rshall I compare you,
O daughter of Jerusalem?   Lam. 1:12
To what shall I liken you as I comfort you,
O ^Rvirgin daughter of Zion?   Is. 37:22
For your ^Truin is as vast as the sea;
Who can ^Rheal you?   *breaking* • Jer. 8:22

14 Your ^Rprophets have seen for you
False and foolish *visions;*   Jer. 23:25-29
And they have not ^Rexposed your iniquity   Is. 58:1; Ezek. 23:36; Mic. 3:8
So as to restore you from captivity,
But they have seen for you false and misleading ^Toracles.   *burdens*

15 All who pass along the way
Clap their hands *in derision* at you;
They ^Rhiss and shake their heads
At the daughter of Jerusalem,   Ps. 22:7
"Is this the city of which they said,
'The ^Rperfection of beauty,   [Ps. 50:2]
^RA joy to all the earth'?"   [Ps. 48:2]

16 All ^Ryour enemies   Job 16:10; Ps. 22:13
Have opened their mouths wide against you;
They hiss and gnash *their* teeth.
They say, "We have ^Rswallowed *her* up!
Surely this is the ^Rday for which we waited;   Ps. 56:2; 124:3 • Obad. 12-15
We have reached *it,* we have seen *it.*"

17 The LORD has ^Rdone what He purposed;
He has accomplished His word
Which He commanded from days of old.   Jer. 4:28
He has thrown down without sparing,
And He has caused the enemy to ^Rrejoice over you;   Ps. 35:24, 26; 89:42
He has ^Rexalted the ^Tmight of your adversaries.   Lam. 1:5 • *horn*

The Appeal of Jerusalem

18 Their ^Rheart cried out to the Lord,
"O ^Rwall of the daughter of Zion,
Let *your* tears run down like a river day and night;   Ps. 119:145 • Hab. 2:11
Give yourself no relief;
Let your eyes have no rest.

19 "Arise, cry aloud in the ^Rnight   Ps. 42:3
At the beginning of the night watches;
^RPour out your heart like water   Ps. 42:4

Before the presence of the Lord;
Lift up your hands to Him
For the^Rlife of your little ones   Lam. 2:11
Who are^Rfaint because of hunger
At the head of every street."   Is. 51:20
20 See, O LORD, and look!
With whom hast Thou dealt thus?
Should women eat their^Toffspring,
The little ones who were born healthy?
Should priest and prophet be slain
In the sanctuary of the Lord?   *fruit*
21 On the ground in the streets
Lie^Ryoung and old,   2 Chr. 36:17; Jer. 6:11
My^Rvirgins and my young men
Have fallen by the sword.   Ps. 78:62, 63
Thou hast slain *them* in the day of
Thine anger,
Thou hast slaughtered, not sparing.
22 Thou didst call as in the day of an ap-
pointed feast
My^Rterrors on every side;   Ps. 31:13
And there was^Rno one who escaped or
survived   Jer. 11:11
In the day of the LORD'S anger.
Those^Rwhom I bore and reared,
My enemy annihilated them.   Jer. 16:2-4

CHAPTER 3

Jeremiah's Cry of Despair

I AM the man who has seen affliction
Because of the rod of His wrath.
2 He has driven me and made me walk
In^Rdarkness and not in light.   Job 30:26
3 Surely against me He has^Rturned His
hand   Ps. 38:2; Is. 5:25
Repeatedly all the day.
4 He has caused my^Rflesh and my skin to
waste away,   Ps. 31:9, 10; 38:2-8
He has^Rbroken my bones.   Ps. 51:8
5 He has besieged and encompassed me
with bitterness and hardship.
6 In dark places He has made me dwell,
Like those who have long been dead.
7 He has^Rwalled *me* in so that I cannot go
out;   Job 3:23; 19:8
He has made my^Rchain heavy.   Jer. 40:4
8 Even when I cry out and call for help,
He^Rshuts out my prayer.   Job 30:20
9 He has^Rblocked my ways with hewn
stone;   Is. 63:17; Hos. 2:6
He has made my paths crooked.
10 He is to me like a bear lying in wait,
Like a lion in secret places.
11 He has turned aside my ways and^Rtorn
me to pieces;   Job 16:12, 13; Jer. 15:3
He has made me desolate.
12 He^Rbent His bow   Ps. 7:12; Lam. 2:4
And set me as a target for the arrow.
13 He made the^Tarrows of His quiver
To enter into my inward parts.   *sons*
14 I have become a^Rlaughingstock to all
my people,   Ps. 22:6, 7; 123:4; Jer. 20:7

Their *mocking* song all the day.
15 He has^Rfilled me with bitterness,
He has made me drunk with worm-
wood.   Jer. 9:15
16 And He has ^Rbroken my teeth with
^Rgravel;   Ps. 3:7; 58:6 · [Prov. 20:17]
He has made me cower in the dust.
17 And my soul has been rejected^Rfrom
peace;   Is. 59:11; Jer. 12:12
I have forgotten^Thappiness.   *good*
18 So I say, "My strength has perished,
And *so has* my hope from the LORD."

Jeremiah's Confession of Faith

19 Remember my affliction and my ^Awan-
dering, the ^Rwormwood and bitterness.   *bitterness* · Jer. 9:15; Lam. 3:5, 15
20 Surely^Rmy soul remembers   Job 21:6
And is^Rbowed down within me.   Ps. 42:5
21 This I recall to my mind,
Therefore I have^Rhope.   Ps. 130:7
22 The LORD'S lovingkindnesses ^Aindeed
never cease,   *that we are not consumed*
For His compassions never fail.
23 *They* are new^Revery morning;   Is. 33:2
Great is^TThy faithfulness.   Heb. 10:23
24 "The LORD is my portion," says my soul,
"Therefore I have hope in Him."
25 The LORD is good to those who^Rwait for
Him,   Ps. 27:14; Is. 25:9
To the^Tperson who seeks Him.   *soul*
26 *It is* good that he^Rwaits silently
For the salvation of the LORD.   Ps. 37:7
27 *It is* good for a man that he should bear
The yoke in his youth.
28 Let him^Rsit alone and be silent Jer. 15:17
Since He has laid *it* on him.
29 Let him^Tput his mouth in the dust, *give*
Perhaps there is^Rhope.   Jer. 31:17
30 Let him give his cheek to^Tthe smiter;
Let him be filled with reproach.   *his*
31 For the Lord will not reject forever,
32 For if He causes grief,
Then He will have^Rcompassion
According to His abundant lovingkindness.   Ps. 78:38; 106:43-45; Hos. 11:8
33 For He does not afflict^Twillingly,
Or grieve the sons of men. *from His heart*
34 To crush under His feet
All the prisoners of the^Aland,   *earth*
35 To deprive a man of^Rjustice   [Ps. 140:12]
In the presence of the Most High,
36 To^Tdefraud a man in his lawsuit—
Of these things the Lord does not ^Tap-
prove.   *make crooked · see*
37 Who is^Tthere who speaks and it^Rcomes
to pass,   *this* · Ps. 33:9-11
Unless the Lord has commanded *it*?
38 *Is it* not from the mouth of the Most
High
That both good and ill go forth?

39 Why should *any* living ^Amortal, or *any*
man,   *human being*

Offer complaint in view of his sins?

Jeremiah's Condition of Need

40 Let us ^Rexamine and probe our ways,
And let us return to the LORD. Ps. 119:59
41 We lift up our heart ^Tand hands
Toward God in heaven;   *toward our*
42 We have ^Rtransgressed and rebelled,
Thou hast not pardoned.   Neh. 9:26
43 Thou hast covered *Thyself* with ^Ranger
And ^Tpursued us;   Lam. 2:21 • Ps. 83:15
Thou hast slain *and* hast not spared.
44 Thou hast covered Thyself with a cloud
So that no prayer can pass through.
45 *Mere* ^Roffscouring and refuse Thou hast
made us   1 Cor. 4:13
In the midst of the peoples.
46 All our enemies have ^Ropened their
mouths against us.   Job 30:9, 10
47 ^RPanic and pitfall have befallen us,
Devastation and destruction;   Is. 24:17
48 My ^Reyes run down with streams of water   *eye brings* • Ps. 119:136
Because of the destruction of the
daughter of my people.
49 My eyes pour down ^Runceasingly,
Without stopping,   Ps. 77:2; Jer. 14:17
50 Until the LORD ^Rlooks down   Ps. 80:14
And sees from heaven.
51 My eyes bring pain to my soul
Because of all the daughters of my city.
52 My enemies ^Rwithout cause   Ps. 35:7
Hunted me down ^Rlike a bird;   Ps. 11:1
53 They have silenced me in the pit
And have placed a stone on me.
54 Waters flowed ^Tover my head;
I said, "I am cut off!"   Ps. 69:2; Jon. 2:3-5

Jeremiah's Confidence in God

55 I ^Rcalled on Thy name, O LORD,
Out of the lowest pit.   Ps. 130:1; Jon. 2:2
56 Thou hast ^Rheard my voice,   Job 34:28
"Do ^Rnot hide Thine ear from my *prayer*
for relief,   Ps. 55:1
From my cry for help."
57 Thou didst ^Rdraw near when I called on
Thee;   Ps. 145:18
Thou didst say, "Do ^Rnot fear!"   Is. 41:10
58 O Lord, Thou didst ^Rplead my soul's
cause;   Jer. 50:34
Thou hast ^Rredeemed my life.   Ps. 34:22
59 O LORD, Thou hast ^Rseen my oppression;   Jer. 18:19, 20
^RJudge my case.   Ps. 26:1; 43:1
60 Thou hast seen all their vengeance,
All their ^Rschemes against me.   Jer. 11:19
61 Thou hast heard their ^Rreproach, O
LORD,   Ps. 74:18; 89:50; Lam. 5:1
All their schemes against me.
62 The ^Rlips of my assailants and their
whispering   Ps. 59:7, 12; 140:3
Are against me all day long.
63 Look on their sitting and their rising;
^RI am their mocking song.   Job 30:9

64 Thou wilt recompense them, O LORD,
According to the work of their hands.
65 Thou wilt give them ^Ahardness of heart,
Thy curse will be on them.   *insolence*
66 Thou wilt ^Tpursue them in anger and destroy them   Lam. 3:43
From under the heavens of the LORD!

CHAPTER 4

The Conditions During the Siege

Hᴏᴡ dark the gold has become,
How the pure gold has changed!
The sacred stones are poured out
At the ^Tcorner of every street.   *head*
2 The precious sons of Zion,
Weighed against fine gold,
How they are regarded as ^Rearthen jars,
The work of a potter's hands!   Is. 30:14
3 Even ^Tjackals offer the breast,
They nurse their young;   Is. 13:22; 34:13
But the daughter of my people has be-
come ^Tcruel   Is. 49:15; Ezek. 5:10
Like ^Rostriches in the wilderness.
4 The ^Rtongue of the infant cleaves
To the roof of its mouth because of
^Rthirst;   Ps. 22:15 • Jer. 14:3
The little ones ^Rask for bread,   Lam. 2:12
But no one breaks *it* for them.
5 Those who ate ^Rdelicacies   Jer. 6:2
Are desolate in the streets;
Those ^Treared in purple
Embrace ash pits.   *established in crimson*
6 For the ^Ainiquity of the daughter of my
people   *punishment for iniquity*
Is greater than the ^Asin of Sodom,
Which was ^Roverthrown as in a mo-
ment,   *punishment for sin* • Gen. 19:25
And no hands were turned toward her.
7 Her ^Aconsecrated ones were ^Rpurer than
snow,   *Nazirites* • Ps. 51:7
They were whiter than milk;
They were more ruddy *in* ^Tbody than
corals,   *bones*
Their polishing *was* like lapis lazuli.
8 Their appearance is blacker than soot,
They are not recognized in the streets;
Their skin is shriveled on their bones,
It is withered, it has become like wood.
9 Better are those slain with the sword
Than those slain with hunger;
For they pine away, being stricken
For lack of the fruits of the field.
10 The hands of compassionate women
^RBoiled their own children;   Lev. 26:29
They became ^Rfood for them
Because of the destruction of the
daughter of my people.   Deut. 28:53

The Cause of the Siege

11 The LORD has accomplished His wrath,
He has poured out His fierce anger;

And He has kindled a fire in Zion
Which has consumed its foundations.
12 The kings of the earth did not believe,
Nor *did* any of ^Rthe inhabitants of the
world,   Deut. 29:24
That the adversary and the enemy
Could enter the gates of Jerusalem.
13 Because of the sins of her^Rprophets
And the iniquities of her priests,
Who have shed in her midst   Jer. 5:31
The^Rblood of the righteous,   Jer. 2:30
14 They wandered, blind, in the streets;
They were defiled with^Rblood
So that no one could touch their ^Rgar-
ments.   Is. 1:15 • Jer. 2:34
15 "Depart! Unclean!"^Athey cried of them-
selves.   *they* (men) *cried to them*
"Depart, depart, do not touch!"
So they^Rfled and wandered;   Jer. 49:5
Men among the nations said,
"They shall not continue to dwell *with*
us."
16 The presence of the LORD has scattered
them;
He will not continue to regard them.
They did not^Rhonor the priests,
They did not favor the elders. Is. 9:14-16
17 Yet our eyes failed;
Looking for help was useless.
In our watching we have watched
For a nation that could not save.
18 They^Rhunted our steps   Jer. 16:16
So that we could not walk in our
streets;
Our^Rend drew near,   Jer. 5:31
Our days were^Tfinished   *full*
For our end had come.
19 Our pursuers were^Rswifter
Than the eagles of the sky.
They chased us on the mountains;
They waited in ambush for us in the
wilderness.   Is. 5:26-28; 30:16, 17
20 The^Rbreath of our nostrils, the^RLORD'S
anointed,   Gen. 2:7 • 2 Sam. 1:14
Was^Rcaptured in their pits,
Of whom we had said, "Under his
^Rshadow   Jer. 39:5; 52:9 • Dan. 4:12
We shall live among the nations."

The Consequences of the Siege

21 Rejoice and be glad, O daughter of
^REdom,   Ps. 137:7; Jer. 25:21
Who dwells in the land of Uz;
But the^Tcup will come around to you as
well,   Obad. 16
You will become drunk and make
yourself naked.
22 *The punishment* of your iniquity has
been ^Rcompleted, O daughter of
Zion;   [Is. 40:2; Jer. 33:7, 8]
He will exile you no longer.
But He ^Rwill punish your iniquity, O
daughter of Edom;   Jer. 49:10

He will expose your sins!

CHAPTER 5

The Review of the Need for Restoration

Remember, O Lord, what has befallen
us;
Look, and see our^Rreproach! Ps. 44:13-16
2 Our inheritance has been turned over
to strangers,   Is. 1:7; Hos. 8:7, 8
Our^Rhouses to aliens.   Zeph. 1:13
3 We have become orphans^Rwithout a father,   Ex. 22:24; Jer. 15:8; 18:21
Our mothers are like widows.
4 We have to pay for our drinking water,
Our wood comes *to us* at a price.
5 ^TOur pursuers are at our necks;
We are worn out, there is no rest for
us.   *We have been pursued upon*
6 We have submitted to^REgypt *and* Assyria to get enough bread.   Hos. 9:3
7 Our^Rfathers sinned, *and* are no more;
It is we who have borne their iniqui-
ties.   Jer. 14:20; 16:12
8 ^RSlaves rule over us;   Neh. 5:15
There is^Tno one to deliver us from their
hand.   Ps. 7:2; Zech. 11:6
9 We get our bread ^Tat the ^Rrisk of our
lives   *with our soul* • Jer. 40:9-12
^ABecause of the sword in the wilder-
ness.   *In the face of*
10 Our skin has become as hot as an oven,
Because of the burning heat of famine.
11 They ravished the women in Zion,
The virgins in the cities of Judah.
12 Princes were hung by their hands;
^RElders were not respected.   Is. 47:6
13 Young men ^Tworked^R at the grinding
mill;   *carry* • Judg. 16:21
And youths ^Rstumbled under *loads* of
wood.   Jer. 7:18
14 Elders are gone from the gate,
Young men from their^Rmusic.   Is. 24:8
15 The joy of our hearts has^Rceased;
Our dancing has been turned into
mourning.   Jer. 25:10; Amos 8:10

The Repentance of Sin

16 The crown has fallen from our head;
Woe to us, for we have sinned!
17 Because of this our^Rheart is faint;
Because of these things our ^Reyes are
dim;   Is. 1:5 • Job 17:7; Lam. 2:11
18 Because of ^RMount Zion which lies
desolate,   Mic. 3:12
^RFoxes prowl in it.   Neh. 4:3

The Request for Restoration

19 Thou, O LORD, dost^Trule forever;   *sit*

Thy[R]throne is from generation to gen-
eration.   Ps. 45:6

20 Why dost Thou forget us forever;
Why dost Thou forsake us so long?

21 [R]Restore us to Thee, O LORD, that we
may be restored;   Ps. 80:3; Jer. 31:18
Renew[R]our days as of old,   [Is. 60:20–22]
22 Unless Thou hast utterly rejected us,
And art exceedingly angry with us.

5:20 Occasions of Doubt—Doubt may be defined as an uncertainty of belief or lack of confidence in something. Applied to the Christian life, doubt refers to the unbelief in God and His Word that Christians occasionally exhibit. It is possible that in a moment of infirmity a Christian may doubt the existence of God in spite of the fact that it is not reasonable for a person to disbelieve this obvious truth (Page 533—Ps. 14:1). A Christian is more likely to doubt his salvation after sinning or after a spiritual defeat. A misunderstanding of such verses as First John 3:9 contributes to this doubt: "No one who is born of God practices sin." It is crucial to note that this verse speaks of a life-style of sin, not instances of sin.

A Christian may also doubt God's sovereignty or His goodness. In such circumstances as sickness, suffering, injustice, opposition, economic problems, family problems, national calamity, or apparently unanswered prayer, a Christian may be tempted to doubt the goodness of God. One must remember that it is not always possible to discern God's good hand in the affairs of life. The person of faith believes God even when circumstances appear to the contrary.

All doubt may be traced ultimately to unbelief in the Word of God, which affirms beyond question the existence and character of God. To regard doubt as the sin of unbelief and then confess it to God as sin is therefore the first step toward conquering it.

Now turn to Page 903—Hab. 1:2: Sources of Doubt.

The Jewish Calendar

The Jews used two kinds of calendars:
Civil Calendar—official calendar of kings, childbirth, and contracts.
Sacred Calendar—from which festivals were computed.

NAMES OF MONTHS	CORRESPONDS WITH	NO. OF DAYS	MONTH OF CIVIL YEAR	MONTH OF SACRED YEAR	
TISHRI	Sept.–Oct.	30 days	1st	7th	The Jewish day was from sunset to sunset, in 8 equal parts:
HESHVAN	Oct.–Nov.	29 or 30	2nd	8th	
CHISLEV	Nov.–Dec.	29 or 30	3rd	9th	
TEBETH	Dec.–Jan.	29	4th	10th	FIRST WATCH ..... SUNSET TO 9 P.M.
SHEBAT	Jan.–Feb.	30	5th	11th	SECOND WATCH ... 9 P.M. TO MIDNIGHT
ADAR	Feb.–Mar.	29 or 30	6th	12th	THIRD WATCH ..... MIDNIGHT TO 3 A.M.
NISAN	Mar.–Apr.	30	7th	1st	FOURTH WATCH ... 3 A.M. TO SUNRISE
IYAR	Apr.–May	29	8th	2nd	
SIVAN	May–June	30	9th	3rd	FIRST WATCH ..... SUNRISE TO 9 A.M.
TAMMUZ	June–July	29	10th	4th	SECOND WATCH ... 9 A.M. TO NOON
AB	July–Aug.	30	11th	5th	THIRD WATCH ..... NOON TO 3 P.M.
*ELUL	Aug.–Sept.	29	12th	6th	FOURTH WATCH ... 3 P.M. TO SUNSET

*Hebrew months were alternately 30 and 29 days long. Their year, shorter than ours, had 354 days. Therefore, about every 3 years (7 times in 19 years) an extra 29-day-month, VEADAR, was added between ADAR and NISAN.

THE BOOK OF

EZEKIEL

THE BOOK OF EZEKIEL

Ezekiel, a priest and a prophet, ministers during the darkest days of Judah's history: the seventy-year period of Babylonian captivity. Carried to Babylon before the final assault on Jerusalem, Ezekiel uses prophecies, parables, signs, and symbols to dramatize God's message to His exiled people. Though they are like dry bones in the sun, God will reassemble them and breathe life into the nation once again. Present judgment will be followed by future glory so that "you will know that I am the LORD" (6:7).

The Hebrew name *Yehezke'l* means "God Strengthens" or "Strengthened by God." Ezekiel is indeed strengthened by God for the prophetic ministry to which he is called (3:8, 9). The name occurs twice in this book and nowhere else in the Old Testament. The Greek form in the Septuagint is *Iezekiel* and the Latin form in the Vulgate is *Ezechiel*.

THE AUTHOR OF EZEKIEL

Ezekiel, the son of Buzi (1:3), had a wife who died as a sign to Judah when Nebuchadnezzar began his final siege on Jerusalem (24:16–24). Like Jeremiah, he was a priest who was called to be a prophet of the Lord. His prophetic ministry shows a priestly emphasis in his concern with the temple, priesthood, sacrifices, and Shekinah (the glory of God). Ezekiel was privileged to receive a number of visions of the power and plan of God, and he was careful and artistic in his written presentation.

Some objections have been raised, but there is not a good reason to overthrow the strong evidence in favor of Ezekiel's authorship. The first person singular is used throughout the book, indicating that it is the work of a single personality. This person is identified as Ezekiel in 1:3 and 24:24, and internal evidence supports the unity and integrity of Ezekiel's prophetic record. The style, language, and thematic development are consistent throughout the book; and several distinctive phrases are repeated throughout, such as, "You will know that I am the LORD," "son of man," "the word of the LORD came to me," and the "glory of the LORD."

THE TIME OF EZEKIEL

Nebuchadnezzar destroyed Jerusalem in three stages. First, in 605 B.C., he overcame Jehoiakim and carried off key hostages including Daniel and his friends. Second, in 597 B.C., the rebellion of Jehoiakim and Jehoiachin brought further punishment; and Nebuchadnezzar made Jerusalem submit a second time. He carried off ten thousand hostages including Jehoiachin and Ezekiel. Third, in 586 B.C., Nebuchadnezzar destroyed the city after a long siege and disrupted all of Judah. If "thirtieth year" in 1:1 refers to Ezekiel's age, he was twenty-five years old when he was taken to Babylon and thirty years old when he received his prophetic commission (1:2, 3). This means he was about seventeen when Daniel was deported in 605 B.C., so that Ezekiel and Daniel were about the same age. Both men were about twenty years younger than Jeremiah who was ministering in Jerusalem. According to this chronology, Ezekiel was born in 622 B.C., deported to Babylon in 597 B.C., prophesied from 592 B.C. to at least 570 B.C., and died about 560 B.C. Thus, he overlapped the end of Jeremiah's ministry and the beginning of Daniel's ministry. By the time Ezekiel arrived in Babylon, Daniel was already well known; and he is mentioned three times in Ezekiel's prophecy (14:14, 20; 28:3). Ezekiel's Babylonian home was at Tel-abib, the principal colony of Jewish exiles along Nebuchadnezzar's "Grand Canal," the river Chebar (1:1; 3:15, 23).

From 592 to 586 B.C., Ezekiel found it necessary to convince the disbelieving Jewish exiles that there was no hope of immediate deliverance. But it was not until they heard that Jerusalem was destroyed that their false hopes of returning were abandoned.

Ezekiel no doubt wrote this book shortly after the incidents recorded in it occurred. His active ministry lasted for at least twenty-two years (1:2; 29:17), and his book was probably completed by 565 B.C.

THE CHRIST OF EZEKIEL

Ezekiel 17:22–24 depicts the Messiah as a tender twig that becomes a stately cedar on a lofty mountain, as He is similarly called the Branch in Isaiah (11:1), Jeremiah (23:5; 33:15), and Zechariah (3:8; 6:12). The Messiah is the King who has the right to rule (21:26, 27), and He is the true Shepherd who will deliver and feed His flock (34:11–31).

KEYS TO EZEKIEL

Key Word: The Future Restoration of Israel—The broad purpose of Ezekiel is to remind the generation born during the

EZEKIEL 784

Babylonian exile of the cause of Israel's current destruction, of the coming judgment on the gentile nations, and of the coming national restoration of Israel. Central to that hope is the departure of the glory of God from Israel and the prediction of its ultimate return (43:2).

Key Verses: Ezekiel 36:24–26 and 36:33–35—"For I will take you from the nations, gather you from all the lands, and bring you into your own land. Then I will sprinkle clean water on you, and you will be clean; I will cleanse you from all your filthiness and from all your idols. Moreover, I will give you a new heart and put a new spirit within you; and I remove the heart of stone from your flesh and give you a heart of flesh" (36:24–26).

"Thus says the Lord GOD, 'On the day that I cleanse you from all your iniquities, I will cause the cities to be inhabited, and the waste places will be rebuilt. And the desolate land will be cultivated instead of being a desolation in the sight of everyone who passed by. And they will say, "This desolate land has become like the garden of Eden; and the waste, desolate, and ruined cities are fortified *and* inhabited" ' " (36:33–35).

Key Chapter: Ezekiel 37—Central to the hope of the restoration of Israel is the vision of the valley of the dry bones. Ezekiel 37 outlines with clear steps Israel's future.

SURVEY OF EZEKIEL
Ezekiel prophesies among the Jewish exiles in Babylon during the last days of Judah's decline and downfall. His message of judgment is similar to that of his older contemporary Jeremiah, who has remained in Jerusalem. Judah will be judged because of her unfaithfulness, but God promises her future

restoration and blessing. Like Isaiah and Jeremiah, Ezekiel proclaims a message of horror and hope, of condemnation and consolation. But Ezekiel places special emphasis on the glory of Israel's sovereign God, who says, "They shall know that I am the LORD." The book breaks into four sections: the commission of Ezekiel (1—3), the judgment on Judah (4—24), the judgment on the Gentiles (25—32), and the restoration of Israel (33—48).

The Commission of Ezekiel (1—3): God gives Ezekiel an overwhelming vision of His divine glory and commissions him to be His prophet (cf. the experiences of Moses in Ex. 3:1–10, Isaiah in 6:1–10, Daniel in 10:5–14, and John in Rev. 1:12–19). Ezekiel is given instruction, enablement, and responsibility.

The Judgment on Judah (4—24): Ezekiel directs his prophecies against the nation God chose for Himself. The prophet's signs and sermons (4—7) point to the certainty of Judah's judgment. In 8—11, Judah's past sins and coming doom are seen in a series of visions of the abominations in the temple, the slaying of the wicked, and the departing glory of God. The priests and princes are condemned as the glory leaves the temple, moves to the Mount of Olives, and disappears in the east. Chapters 12—24 speak of the causes and extent of Judah's coming judgment through dramatic signs, powerful sermons, and parables. Judah's prophets are counterfeits and her elders are idolators. They have become a fruitless vine and an adulterous wife. Babylon will swoop down like an eagle and pluck them up, and they will not be aided by Egypt. The people are responsible for their own sins, and they are not being unjustly judged for the sins of their ancestors. Judah has been unfaithful, but God promises that her judgment ultimately will be followed by restoration.

FOCUS	COMMISSION OF EZEKIEL		JUDGMENT ON JUDAH	JUDGMENT ON GENTILES	RESTORATION OF ISRAEL	
REFERENCE	1:1———2:1———		—4:1———————	—25:1———————	33:1—————	40:1———48:35
DIVISION	EZEKIEL SEES THE GLORY	EZEKIEL IS COMMISSIONED TO THE WORK	SIGNS, MESSAGES, VISIONS, AND PARABLES OF JUDGMENT	JUDGMENT ON SURROUNDING NATIONS	RETURN OF ISRAEL TO THE LORD	RESTORATION OF ISRAEL IN THE KINGDOM
TOPIC	BEFORE THE SIEGE (c. 592–587 B.C.)			DURING THE SIEGE (c. 586 B.C.)	AFTER THE SIEGE (c. 585–570 B.C.)	
	JUDAH'S FALL			JUDAH'S FOES	JUDAH'S FUTURE	
LOCATION	BABYLON					
TIME	c. 592–570 B.C.					

The Judgment on the Gentiles (25—32): Judah's nearest neighbors may gloat over her destruction, but they will be next in line. They too will suffer the fate of siege and destruction by Babylon. Ezekiel shows the full circle of judgment on the nations that surround Judah by following them in a clockwise circuit: Ammon, Moab, Edom, Philistia, Tyre, and Sidon (25—28). He spends a disproportionate amount of time on Tyre, and many scholars believe that the "king of Tyre" in 28:11-19 may be Satan, the real power behind the nation. Chapters 29—32 contain a series of oracles against Egypt. Unlike the nations in chapters 25—28 that were destroyed by Nebuchadnezzar, Egypt will continue to exist, but as "the lowest of the kingdoms" (29:15). Since that time it has never recovered its former glory or influence.

The Restoration of Israel (33—48): The prophecies in these chapters were given after the overthrow of Jerusalem. Now that the promised judgment has come, Ezekiel's message no longer centers on coming judgment but on the positive theme of comfort and consolation. Just as surely as judgment has come, blessing will also come; God's people will be regathered and restored. The mouth of Ezekiel, God's watchman, is opened when he is told that Jerusalem has been taken. Judah has had false shepherds (rulers), but the true Shepherd will lead them in the future. The vision of the valley of dry bones pictures the reanimation of the nation by the Spirit of God. Israel and Judah will be purified and reunited. There will be an invasion by the northern armies of Gog, but Israel will be saved because the Lord will destroy the invading forces.

In 572 B.C., fourteen years after the destruction of Jerusalem, Ezekiel returns in a vision to the fallen city and is given detailed specifications for the reconstruction of the temple, the city, and the land (40—48). After an intricate description of the new outer court, inner court, and temple (40—42), Ezekiel views the return of the glory of the Lord to the temple from the east. Regulations concerning worship in the coming temple (43—46) are followed by revelations concerning the new land and city (47 and 48).

OUTLINE OF EZEKIEL

Part One: The Commission of Ezekiel (1:1—3:27)

Part Two: Judgment on Judah (4:1—24:27)

CHAPTER 1

Time of the Vision

NOW it came about in the thirtieth year, on the fifth *day* of the fourth month, while I was by the ᴿriver Chebar among the exiles, the ᴿheavens were opened and I saw visions of God.   Ezek. 3:23; 10:15, 20 • Mark 1:10

2 (On the fifth of the month ᵀin the fifth year of King Jehoiachin's exile,   *it was*

3 the word of the LORD came expressly to Ezekiel the priest, son of Buzi, in the land of the Chaldeans by the river Chebar; and there the hand of the LORD came upon him.)

The Four Living Beings

4 And as I looked, behold, a ᴿstorm wind was coming from the north, a great cloud with fire flashing forth continually and a bright light around it, and in its midst something like ᴿglowing metal in the midst of the fire.   Is. 21:1; Jer. 23:19 • Ezek. 1:27; 8:2

5 And within it there were figures resembling four living beings. And this was their appearance: they had human form.

6 Each of them had ᴿfour faces and ᴿfour wings.   Ezek. 1:10; 10:14, 21 • Ezek. 1:23

7 And their legs were straight and their feet were like a calf's hoof, and they gleamed like ᴿburnished bronze.   Dan. 10:6

8 Under their wings on their[R]four sides *were* human hands. As for the faces and wings of the four of them,   Ezek. 1:17

9 their wings touched one another; their *faces* did[R]not turn when they moved, each [R]went straight forward.   Ezek. 1:17 • Ezek. 1:12

10 As for the form of their faces, *each* had the face of a man, all four had the face of a lion on the right and the face of a bull on the left, and all four had the face of an eagle.

11 Such were their faces. Their wings were spread out above; each had two touching another *being,* and[R]two covering their bodies.   Is. 6:2; Ezek. 1:23

12 And[R]each went straight forward; wherever the spirit was about to go, they would go, without turning as they went.   Ezek. 1:9

13 In the midst of the living beings there was something that looked like burning coals of fire,[T]like torches darting back and forth among the living beings. The fire was bright, and lightning was[T]flashing from the fire.   *like the appearance of* • *coming out*

14 And the living beings[R]ran to and fro like bolts of[R]lightning. Zech. 4:10 • [Luke 17:24]

The Four Wheels

15 Now as I looked at the living beings, behold, there was one[R]wheel on the earth beside the living beings,[T]for *each of* the four of them.   Ezek. 1:19-21 • *for his four faces*

16 The appearance of the wheels and their workmanship *was* like sparkling[R]beryl, and all four of them had the same form, their appearance and workmanship *being* as if one wheel were within another.   Ezek. 10:9

17 Whenever they[T]moved, they moved in any of their four[T]directions, without[T]turning as they moved.   *went* • *sides* • Ezek. 1:9, 12

18 As for their rims they were lofty and awesome, and the rims of all four of them were[R]full of eyes round about.   Ezek. 10:12

19 And whenever the living beings [T]moved, the wheels moved with them. And whenever the living beings rose from the earth, the wheels rose *also.*   *went*

20 Wherever the spirit was about to go, they would go in that direction. And the wheels rose close beside them; for the spirit of the living beings *was* in the wheels.

21 Whenever those went, these went; and whenever those stood still, these stood still. And whenever those rose from the earth, the wheels rose close beside them; for the spirit of the living beings *was* in the wheels.

The Firmament

22 Now[R]over the heads of the living beings *there was* something like an expanse, like the awesome gleam of[A]crystal, extended over their heads.   Ezek. 10:1 • *ice*

23 And under the expanse their wings *were stretched out* straight, one toward the other; each one also had[R]two wings covering

their bodies on the one side and on the other.   Ezek. 1:6, 11

24 I also heard the sound of their wings like the sound of abundant waters as they went, like the voice of[T]the Almighty, a sound of tumult like the sound of an army camp; whenever they stood still, they dropped their wings.   Heb., *Shaddai*

25 And there came a voice from above the [R]expanse that was over their heads; whenever they stood still, they dropped their wings.   Ezek. 1:22; 10:1

The Appearance of a Man

26 Now above the expanse that was over their heads there was something resembling a throne, like lapis lazuli in appearance; and on that which resembled a throne, high up, *was* a figure with the appearance of a man.

27 Then I noticed from the appearance of His loins and upward something like glowing metal that looked like fire all around within it, and from the appearance of His loins and downward I saw something like fire; and *there was* a radiance around Him.

28 As the appearance of the rainbow in the clouds on a rainy day, so *was* the appearance of the surrounding radiance. Such *was* the appearance of the likeness of the glory of the LORD. And when I saw *it,* I fell on my face and heard a voice speaking.

CHAPTER 2

Ezekiel Is Sent to Israel

THEN He said to me, "Son of man, stand on your feet that I may speak with you!"

2 And as He spoke to me the[R]Spirit entered me and set me on my feet; and I heard *Him* speaking to me.   Ezek. 3:24; Dan. 8:18

3 Then He said to me, "Son of man, I am sending you to the sons of Israel, to a rebellious people who have[R]rebelled against Me; they and their fathers have transgressed against Me to this very day.   1 Sam. 8:7, 8

4 "And I am sending you to them who are stubborn and obstinate children; and you shall say to them, 'Thus says the Lord GOD.'

5 "As for them, whether they listen or [T]not—for they are a rebellious house—they will[R]know that a prophet has been among them.   *forbear* • Ezek. 33:33; [Luke 10:10, 11]

6 "And you, son of man,[R]neither fear them nor fear their words, though[R]thistles and thorns are with you and though you sit on scorpions; neither fear their words nor be dismayed at their presence, for they are a rebellious house.   Is. 51:12 • [2 Sam. 23:6, 7]

7 "But you shall[R]speak My words to them whether they listen or[T]not, for they are rebellious.   Jer. 1:7, 17; [Ezek. 3:10, 17] • *forbear*

8 "Now you, son of man, listen to what I am speaking to you; do not be rebellious

like that rebellious house. Open your mouth and ^Reat what I am giving you."   Ezek. 3:3

9 Then I looked, behold, a hand was extended to me; and lo, a scroll *was* in it.

10 When He spread it out before me, it was written on the front and back; and written on it were lamentations, mourning and ^Rwoe.   Is. 3:11; Rev. 8:13

CHAPTER 3

THEN He said to me, "Son of man, eat what you find; ^Reat this scroll, and go, speak to the house of Israel."   Ezek. 2:9

2 So I ^Ropened my mouth, and He fed me this scroll.   Jer. 25:17

3 And He said to me, "Son of man, feed your stomach, and fill your body with this scroll which I am giving you." Then I ate it, and it was sweet as honey in my mouth.

Ezekiel Is Instructed
About His Ministry

4 Then He said to me, "Son of man, ^Tgo to the house of Israel and speak with My words to them.   go, come

5"For you are not being sent to a people of ^Runintelligible speech or difficult language, *but* to the house of Israel,   Is. 28:11; 33:19

6 nor to many peoples of unintelligible speech or difficult language, whose words you cannot understand. But I have sent you to them ^Twho should listen to you;   *they*

7 yet the house of Israel will not be willing to listen to you, since they are ^Rnot willing to listen to Me. Surely the whole house of Israel is stubborn and obstinate. 1 Sam. 8:7

8"Behold, I have made your face as hard as their faces, and your forehead as hard as their foreheads.

9"Like ^Temery harder than flint I have made your forehead. Do not be afraid of them or be dismayed before them, though they are a rebellious house."   *corundum*

10 Moreover, He said to me, "Son of man, take into your heart all My words which I shall speak to you, and listen closely.

11"And ^Tgo to the exiles, to the sons of your people, and speak to them and tell them, whether they listen or ^Tnot, 'Thus says the Lord God.' "   *go, come • forbear*

12 Then the ^RSpirit lifted me up, and I heard a great rumbling sound behind me, "Blessed be the glory of the LORD ^{A1}in His place."   Ezek. 3:14; 8:3; Acts 8:39 • *from*

13 And I *heard* the sound of the wings of the living beings touching one another, and the sound of the ^Rwheels beside them, even a great rumbling sound.   Ezek. 1:15; 10:16, 17

14 So the Spirit lifted me up and took me away; and I went embittered in the rage of my spirit, and ^Rthe hand of the LORD was strong on me.   2 Kin. 3:15

15 Then I came to the exiles who lived beside the river Chebar at Tel-abib, and I sat there ^Rseven days where they were living, causing consternation among them. Job 2:13

16 Now it came about ^Rat the end of seven days that the word of the LORD came to me, saying,   Jer. 42:7

17"Son of man, I have appointed you a ^Rwatchman to the house of Israel; whenever you hear a word from My mouth, ^Rwarn them from Me.   Is. 52:8; 56:10 • Hab. 2:1

18"When I say to the wicked, 'You shall surely die'; and you do not warn him or speak out to warn the wicked from his wicked way that he may live, that wicked man shall die in his iniquity, but his ^Rblood I will require at your hand.   Ezek. 3:20; 33:6, 8

19"Yet if you have warned the wicked, and he does not turn from his wickedness or from his wicked way, he shall die in his iniquity; but you have delivered yourself.

20"Again, ^Rwhen a righteous man turns away from his righteousness and commits iniquity, and I place an ^Tobstacle before him, he shall die; since you have not warned him, he shall die in his sin, and his righteous deeds which he has done shall not be remembered; but his blood I will require at your hand.   Ps. 125:5; Ezek. 18:24 • Is. 8:14

21"However, if you have ^Rwarned ^Tthe righteous man that the righteous should not sin, and he does not sin, he shall surely live because he took warning; and you have delivered yourself."   Acts 20:31 • *him, the righteous*

22 And the hand of the LORD was on me there, and He said to me, "Get up, go out to the plain, and there I will speak to you."

23 So I got up and went out to the plain; and behold, the glory of the LORD was standing there, like the glory which I saw by the river Chebar, and I fell on my face.

24 The ^RSpirit then entered me and made me stand on my feet, and He spoke with me and said to me, "Go, shut yourself up in your house.   Ezek. 2:2

25"As for you, son of man, they will put ropes on you and bind you with them, so that you cannot go out among them.

26"Moreover, I will make your tongue stick to the roof of your mouth so that you will be dumb, and cannot be a man who rebukes them, for they are a rebellious house.

27"But ^Rwhen I speak to you, I will open your mouth, and you will say to them, 'Thus says the Lord God.' He who hears, let him hear; and he who refuses, let him refuse; for they are a rebellious house. Ezek. 24:27; 33:22

CHAPTER 4

Sign of the Brick

"NOW you son of man, ^Rget yourself a brick, place it before you, and inscribe a city on it, Jerusalem.   Is. 20:2; Jer. 13:1; 18:2; 19:1

2"Then lay siege against it, build a siege

wall, raise up a ramp, pitch camps, and place battering rams against it all around.

3"Then get yourself an iron plate and set it up as an iron wall between you and the city, and set your face toward it so that it is under siege, and besiege it. This is a ᴿsign to the house of Israel.   Ezek. 12:6, 11; 24:24-27

Sign of Ezekiel's Lying on His Side

4"As for you, lie down on your left side, and lay the iniquity of the house of Israel on it; you shall ᴿbear their iniquity for the number of days that you lie on it.   [Lev. 10:17]

5"For I have assigned you a number of days corresponding to the years of their iniquity, three hundred and ninety days; thus ᴿyou shall bear the iniquity of the house of Israel.   Num. 14:34

6"When you have completed these, you shall lie down a second time, *but* on your right side, and bear the iniquity of the house of Judah; I have assigned it to you for forty days, a day for ᴿeach year.   Rev. 11:2, 3

7"Then you shall set your face toward the siege of Jerusalem with your arm bared, and ᴿprophesy against it.   Ezek. 21:2

8"Now behold, I willᴿput ropes on you so that you cannot turn from one side to the other, until you have completed the days of your siege.   Ezek. 3:25

Sign of the Defiled Bread

9"But as for you, take wheat, barley, beans, lentils, millet and spelt, put them in one vessel and make them into bread for yourself; you shall eat it according to the number of the days that you lie on your side, three hundred and ninety days.

10"And your food which you eat *shall be* ᴿtwenty shekels a day by weight; you shall eat it from time to time.   Ezek. 45:12

11"And the water you drink will be the sixth part of a hin by measure; you shall drink it from time to time.

12"And you shall eat it as a barley cake, having baked *it* in their sight over human ᴿdung."   Is. 36:12

13 Then the LORD said, "Thus shall the sons of Israel eat their bread unclean among the nations where I shall banish them."

14 But I said, "Ah, Lord GOD! Behold, I have never been defiled; for from my youth until now I have never eaten what died of itself or was torn by beasts, nor has any unclean meat ever entered my mouth."

15 Then He said to me, "See, I shall give you cow's dung in place of human dung over which you will prepare your bread."

16 Moreover, He said to me, "Son of man, behold, I am going to break the staff of bread in Jerusalem, and they will eat bread by ᴿweight and with anxiety, and drink water by measure and in horror,   Ezek. 4:10, 11

17 because bread and water will be scarce; and they will be appalled with one another and waste away in their iniquity.

CHAPTER 5

Sign of the Razor and the Hair

"Aˢ for you, son of man, take a sharp sword; take and use it *as* a barber's razor on your head and beard. Then take scales for weighing and divideᵀthe hair.   *them*

2"One third you shall burn in the fire at the center of the city, when theᴿdays of the siege are completed. Then you shall take one third and strike *it* with the sword all around ᵀthe city, and one third you shall scatter to the wind; and I will unsheathe a sword behind them.   Jer. 39:1, 2 • *it*

3"Take also a few in number from them and bind them in the edges of your *robes*.

4"And take again some of them and throw them into the fire, and burn them in the fire; from it a fire willᵀspread to all the house of Israel.   *go out*

Explanation of the Signs

5"Thus says the Lord GOD, 'This isᴿJerusalem; I have set her at the center of the nations, with lands around her.   Jer. 6:6

6 'But she has rebelled against My ordinances more wickedly than the nations and against My statutes more than the lands which surround her; for they haveᴿrejected My ordinances and have not walkedᵀin My statutes.'   Neh. 9:16, 17 • *in them, My statutes*

7"Therefore, thus says the Lord GOD, 'Because you haveᴿmore turmoil than the nations which surround you, and have not walked in My statutes, nor observed My ordinances, nor observed the ordinances of the nations which surround you,'   2 Chr. 33:9

8 therefore, thus says the Lord GOD, 'Behold, I, even I, amᴿagainst you, and I will ᴿexecute judgments among you in the sight of the nations.   Jer. 21:5, 13 • Jer. 24:9

9 'And because of all your abominations, I will do among you what I have not done, and the like of which I will never do again.

10 'Therefore, fathers will eat *their* sons among you, and sons will eat their fathers; for I will execute judgments on you, and scatter all your remnant to every wind.

11 'So as I live,' declares the Lord GOD, 'surely, because you haveᴿdefiled My sanctuary with all your detestable idols and with all your abominations, therefore I will also withdraw, and My eye shall have no pity and I will not spare.   [Jer. 7:9–11]; Ezek. 8:5f.

12 'One third of you will die by plague or be consumed by famine among you, one third will fall by the sword around you, and one third I will scatter to every wind, and I will unsheathe a sword behind them.

13 'Thus My anger will be spent, and I will satisfy My wrath on them, and I shall be ap-

peased; then they will know that I, the LORD, have spoken in My zeal when I have spent My wrath upon them.   *cause to rest*

14 'Moreover, I will make you a desolation and a [R]reproach among the nations which surround you, in the sight of all who pass by.   Ps. 74:3-10; 79:1-4; Ezek. 22:4

15 'So it will be a reproach, a reviling, a warning and an object of horror to the nations who surround you, when I execute judgments against you in anger, wrath, and raging rebukes. I, the LORD, have spoken.

16 'When I send against them the [deadly] arrows of famine which [were] for the destruction of those whom I shall send to destroy you, then I shall also intensify the famine upon you, and break the staff of bread.   *evil · are for destruction, which I will send*

17 'Moreover,[R]I will send on you famine and wild beasts, and they will bereave you of children; plague and bloodshed also will pass through you, and I will bring the sword on you. I, the LORD, have spoken.' "   Rev. 6:8

CHAPTER 6

Destruction of High Places

A ND the word of the LORD came to me saying,

2"Son of man, set your face toward the [R]mountains of Israel, and prophesy against them,   Ezek. 36:1

3 and say, 'Mountains of Israel, listen to the word of the Lord GOD! Thus says the Lord GOD to the mountains, the hills, the ravines and the valleys: "Behold, I Myself am going to bring a sword on you, and[R]I will destroy your high places.   Lev. 26:30

4"So your [R]altars will become desolate, and your incense altars will be smashed; and I shall make your slain fall in front of your idols.   Lev. 26:30; 2 Chr. 14:5; Is. 27:9

5"I shall also lay the dead bodies of the sons of Israel in front of their idols; and I shall scatter your bones around your altars.

6"In all your dwellings, [R]cities will become waste and the high places will be desolate, that your altars may become waste and desolate, your idols may be broken and brought to an end, your incense altars may be cut down, and your works may be blotted out.   Lev. 26:31; Is. 6:11; Ezek. 5:14

7"And the slain will fall among you, and you will know that I am the LORD.

Salvation of the Remnant

8"However, I shall leave a[R]remnant, for you will have those who escaped the sword among the nations when you are scattered among the countries.   Is. 6:13; Jer. 30:11

9"Then those of you who escape will [R]remember Me among the nations to which they will be carried captive, how I have been hurt by their adulterous hearts which turned away from Me, and by their eyes, which played the harlot after their idols; and they will loathe themselves in their own sight for the evils which they have committed, for all their abominations.   [Deut. 4:29]

10"Then they will know that I am the LORD; I have not said in vain[T]that I would inflict this disaster on them." ' to do this evil to

Desolation of the Land

11"Thus says the Lord GOD, 'Clap your hand,[R]stamp your foot, and say, "Alas,[R] because of all the evil abominations of the house of Israel, which will fall by sword, famine, and plague!   Ezek. 25:6 · Ezek. 9:4

12"He who is[R]far off will die by the plague, and he who is near will fall by the sword, and he who remains and is besieged will die by the famine. Thus shall I[R]spend My wrath on them.   Dan. 9:7 · Lam. 4:11, 22; Ezek. 5:13

13"Then you will know that I am the LORD, when their [R]slain are among their idols around their altars, on[R]every high hill, on all the tops of the mountains, under every green tree, and under every leafy oak—the places where they offered soothing aroma to all their idols.   Ezek. 6:4-7 · 1 Kin. 14:23

14"So throughout all their habitations I shall stretch out My hand against them and make the land more desolate and waste than the wilderness toward Diblah; thus they will know that I am the LORD." ' "

CHAPTER 7

Description of the Babylonian Conquest

M OREOVER, the word of the LORD came to me saying,

2"And you, son of man, thus says the Lord GOD to the land of Israel, 'An[R]end! The end is coming on the four corners of the land.   Ezek. 7:3, 5, 6; 11:13; Amos 8:2, 10

3 'Now the end is upon you, and I shall send My anger against you; I shall judge you according to your ways, and I shall bring all your abominations upon you.

4 'For My eye will have no pity on you, nor shall I spare you, but I shall[R]bring your ways upon you, and your abominations will be among you; then you will[R]know that I am the LORD!'   Ezek. 11:21 · Ezek. 6:7, 14

5"Thus says the Lord GOD, 'A disaster, unique disaster, behold it is coming!

6 'An end is coming; the end has come! It has [R]awakened against you; behold, it has come!   Zech. 13:7

7 'Your doom has come to you, O inhabitant of the land. The[R]time has come, the day is near—tumult rather than joyful shouting on the mountains.   Ezek. 7:12; 12:23-25, 28

8 'Now I will shortly pour out My wrath on you, and spend My anger against you,

judge you according to your ways, and bring on you all your abominations.

9 'And My eye will show no pity, nor will I spare. I will [T]repay you according to your ways, while your abominations are in your midst; then you will know that I, the LORD, do the smiting.   *give*

10 'Behold, the day! Behold, it is coming! *Your* doom has gone forth; the[R]rod has budded, arrogance has blossomed.   Ps. 89:32

11 'Violence[T]has grown into a rod of wickedness. None of them *shall remain*, none of their multitude, none of their wealth, nor anything eminent among them.   *has risen*

12 'The [R]time has come, the day has arrived. Let not the [R]buyer rejoice nor the seller mourn; for[R]wrath is against all their multitude.   Ezek. 7:5-7 • Prov. 20:14 • Is. 5:13

13 'Indeed, the seller will not[T]regain what he sold as long as they *both* live; for the vision regarding all their multitude will not[T]be averted, nor will any of them maintain his life by his iniquity.   *return to • return*

14 'They have [R]blown the trumpet and made everything ready, but no one is going to the battle; for My wrath is against all [T]their multitude.   Num. 10:9; Jer. 4:5 • *her*

15 'The sword is outside, and the plague and the famine are within. He who is in the field will die by the sword; famine and the plague will also consume those in the city.

16 'Even when their survivors[R]escape, they will be on the mountains like doves of the valleys, all of them[T]mourning,[R] each over his own iniquity.   Ezra 9:15 • *moaning* • Is. 59:11

17 'All hands will hang limp, and all knees will[T]become like water.   *run with water*

18 'And they will gird themselves with sackcloth, and[R]shuddering will overwhelm them; and shame *will be* on all faces, and baldness on all their heads.   Job 21:6; Ps. 55:5

19 'They shall fling their silver into the streets, and their gold shall become an abhorrent thing; their [R]silver and their gold shall not be able to deliver them in the day of the wrath of the LORD. They cannot satisfy their [T]appetite, nor can they fill their stomachs, for their iniquity has become an occasion of stumbling.   [Prov. 11:4] • *soul*

20 'And they transformed the beauty of His ornaments into pride, and they made the images of their abominations *and* their detestable things with it; therefore I will make it an abhorrent thing to them.

21 'And I shall give it into the hands of the foreigners as plunder and to the wicked of the earth as spoil, and they will profane it.

22 'I shall also turn My[R]face from them, and they will profane My secret place; then robbers will enter and profane it.   Jer. 18:17

23 'Make[R] the chain, for the land is full of [T]bloody crimes, and the city is [R]full of violence.   Jer. 27:2 • *judgment of blood* • Ezek. 8:17

24 'Therefore, I shall bring the worst of the [R]nations, and they will possess their houses. I

shall also make the[R]pride of the strong ones cease, and their [R]holy places will be profaned.   Ezek. 21:31 • Ezek. 33:28 • 2 Chr. 7:20

25 'When anguish comes, they will seek [R]peace, but there will be none.   Ezek. 13:10, 16

26 'Disaster[R] will come upon disaster, and rumor will be *added* to rumor; then they will seek a[R]vision from a prophet, but the[R]law will be lost from the priest and counsel from the elders.   Is. 47:11 • Jer. 21:2 • Ezek. 22:26

27 'The king will mourn, the prince will be clothed with horror, and the hands of the people of the land will tremble. According to their conduct I shall deal with them, and by their judgments I shall judge them. And they will know that I am the LORD.' "

CHAPTER 8

Vision of the Glory of God

AND it came about in the sixth year, on the fifth *day* of the sixth month, as I was sitting in my house with the elders of Judah sitting before me, that the hand of the Lord GOD fell on me there.

2 Then I looked, and behold, a likeness as the appearance of[T]a man; from His loins and downward *there was* the appearance of fire, and from His loins and upward the appearance of brightness, like the appearance of[A]glowing metal.   Heb., *fire • electrum*

3 And He stretched out the form of a hand and caught me by a lock of my head; and the Spirit lifted me up between earth and heaven and brought me in the visions of God to Jerusalem, to the entrance of the [T]north gate of the inner *court*, where the seat of the idol of jealousy, which[R]provokes to jealousy, was *located*.   *facing north* • Ex. 20:4

4 And behold, the[R]glory of the God of Israel *was* there, like the appearance which I saw in the plain.   Ezek. 1:28; 3:22, 23

Idol of Jealousy

5 Then He said to me, "Son of man,[R]raise your eyes, now, toward the north." So I raised my eyes toward the north, and behold, to the north of the altar gate *was* this idol of jealousy at the entrance.   Jer. 3:2

6 And He said to me, "Son of man, do you see what they are doing, the great [R]abominations which the house of Israel are committing here, that I should be far from My sanctuary? But yet you will see still greater abominations."   2 Kin. 23:4, 5

Carvings on the Wall

7 Then He brought me to the entrance of the court, and when I looked, behold, a hole in the wall.

8 And He said to me, "Son of man, now [R]dig through the wall." So I dug through the wall, and behold, an entrance.   Is. 29:15

9 And He said to me, "Go in and see the wicked abominations that they are committing here."

10 So I entered and looked, and behold, every form of creeping things and beasts *and* detestable things, with all the idols of the house of Israel, were carved on the wall all around.

11 And standing in front of them were [R]seventy elders of the house of Israel, with Jaazaniah the son of Shaphan standing among them, each man with his censer in his hand, and the fragrance of the cloud of incense rising.   Num. 11:16, 25; Luke 10:1

12 Then He said to me, "Son of man, do you see what the elders of the house of Israel are committing in the dark, each man in the room of his carved images? For they say, 'The[R]LORD does not see us; the LORD has forsaken the land.'"   Ps. 14:1; Is. 29:15; Ezek. 9:9

Weeping for Tammuz

13 And He said to me, "Yet you will see still greater abominations which they are committing."

14 Then He brought me to the entrance of the [R]gate of the LORD's house which *was* toward the north; and behold, women were sitting there weeping for Tammuz. Ezek. 44:4

Sun Worship

15 And He said to me, "Do you see *this,* son of man? Yet you will see still greater abominations than these."

16 Then He brought me into the inner court of the LORD's house. And behold, at the entrance to the temple of the LORD, between the porch and the altar, *were* about twenty-five men with their backs to the temple of the LORD and their faces toward the east; and they were [T]prostrating themselves eastward toward the sun.   worshiping

17 And He said to me, "Do you see *this,* son of man? Is it too light a thing for the house of Judah to commit the abominations which they have committed here, that they have filled the land with violence and[R]provoked Me repeatedly? For behold, they are putting the twig to their nose.   Jer. 7:18, 19

18"Therefore, I indeed shall deal in wrath. My eye will have no pity nor shall I spare; and[R]though they cry in My ears with a loud voice, yet I shall not listen to them." Is. 1:15

CHAPTER 9

Call to the Six Men

THEN He cried out in my hearing with a loud[T]voice saying, "Draw near,[T]O executioners of the city, each with his destroying weapon in his hand."   Is. 6:8 · *you who punish*

2 And behold, six men came from the direction of the upper gate which faces north, each with his shattering weapon in his hand; and among them was[R]a certain man clothed in linen with a[A]writing case at his loins. And they went in and stood beside the bronze altar.   Lev. 16:4 · *scribal inkhorn*

3 Then the [R]glory of the God of Israel went up from the cherub on which it had been, to the threshold of the[T]temple. And He called to the man clothed in linen at whose loins was the writing case. Ezek. 10:4 · *house*

Command to Slay the Wicked

4 And the LORD said to him, "Go through the midst of the city, *even* through the midst of Jerusalem, and put a[T]mark on the foreheads of the men who sigh and groan over all the abominations which are being committed in its midst."   Ex. 12:7, 13; Ezek. 9:6

5 But to the others He said in my hearing, "Go through the city after him and strike; do not let your eye have pity, and do not spare.

6"Utterly[T] slay old men, young men, maidens, little children, and women, but do not touch any man on whom is the mark; and you shall start from My sanctuary." So they started with the[A]elders who *were* before the[T]temple. To *destruction* · *old men* · *house*

7 And He said to them, "Defile[R]the[T]temple and fill the courts with the slain. Go out!" Thus they went out and struck down *the people* in the city.   2 Chr. 36:17 · *house*

Weeping of Ezekiel

8 Then it came about as they were striking and I *alone* was left, that I fell on my face and cried out[T]saying, "Alas[R] Lord GOD! Art Thou destroying the whole remnant of Israel[T]by pouring out Thy wrath on Jerusalem?"   *and said* · Ezek. 11:13 · *by Thy pouring*

9 Then He said to me, "The iniquity of the house of Israel and Judah is very, very great, and the land is[R]filled with blood, and the city is full of perversion; for they say, 'The LORD has forsaken the land, and the LORD does not see!'   2 Kin. 21:16; Jer. 2:34

10"But as for Me,[R]My eye will have no pity nor shall I spare, but I shall bring their conduct upon their heads."   Is. 65:6; Ezek. 8:18

11 Then behold, the man clothed in linen at whose loins was the writing case [T]reported, saying, "I have done just as Thou hast commanded me."   *brought back word*

CHAPTER 10

Departure of the Glory of God to the Threshold

THEN I looked, and behold, in the[A]expanse[R] that was over the heads of the cherubim

something like a^Rsapphire stone, in appearance resembling a throne, appeared above them.   *firmament* • Ezek. 1:22, 26 • Ex. 24:10

2 And He spoke to the man clothed in linen and said, "Enter between the^Rwhirling wheels under the cherubim, and fill your hands with coals of fire from between the cherubim, and scatter *them* over the city." And he entered in my sight.   Ezek. 1:15-21

3 Now the cherubim were standing on the right side of the temple when the man entered, and the cloud filled the inner court.

4 Then the glory of the LORD went up from the cherub to the threshold of the temple, and the ^Rtemple was filled with the cloud, and the court was filled with the brightness of the glory of the LORD.   Is. 6:1-4

5 Moreover, the sound of the wings of the cherubim was heard as far as the outer court, like the^Rvoice of^TGod Almighty when He speaks.   [Job 40:9] • Heb., *El Shaddai*

6 And it came about when He commanded the man clothed in linen, saying, "Take fire from between the whirling wheels, from between the cherubim," he entered and stood beside a wheel.

7 Then the cherub stretched out his hand from between the cherubim to the fire which *was* between the cherubim, took some and put it into the hands of the one clothed in linen, who took *it* and went out.

8 And the cherubim appeared to have the form of a man's hand under their wings.

Vision of the Wheels and Cherubim

9 Then I looked, and behold, four wheels beside the cherubim, one wheel beside each cherub; and the appearance of the wheels *was* like the gleam of a Tarshish stone.

10 And as for their appearance, all four of them had the same likeness, as if one wheel were within another wheel.

11 When they moved, they went^Rin *any of* their four^Tdirections without turning as they went; but they followed in the direction which^Tthey faced, without turning as they went.   Ezek. 1:17 • *sides* • *the head*

12 And their ^Rwhole body, their backs, their hands, their wings, and the wheels were full of eyes all around, the wheels belonging to all four of them.   Rev. 4:6, 8

13 The wheels were called in my hearing, the whirling wheels.

14 And^Reach one had four faces. The first face *was* the face of a cherub, the second face *was* the face of a man, the third the face of a lion, and the fourth the face of an eagle.   1 Kin. 7:29, 36; Ezek. 1:6, 10; 10:21

15 Then the cherubim rose up. They are the^Rliving beings that I saw by the river Chebar.   Ezek. 1:3, 5

16 Now when the cherubim moved, the wheels would go beside them; also when the cherubim lifted up their wings to rise from the ground, the wheels would not turn from beside them.

17 When ^Tthe cherubim ^Rstood still, the wheels would stand still; and when they rose up, the wheels would rise with them; for the spirit of the living beings *was* in them.   *they* • Ezek. 1:21

18 Then the glory of the LORD departed from the threshold of the temple and stood ^Rover the cherubim.   Ps. 18:10

19 When the cherubim departed, they lifted their wings and rose up from the earth in my sight with the wheels beside them; and they stood still at the entrance of the east gate of the LORD's house. And the glory of the God of Israel hovered over them.

20 These are the living beings that I saw beneath the God of Israel by the river Chebar; so I knew that they *were* cherubim.

21 ^REach one had four faces and each one four wings, and beneath their wings *was* the form of human hands.   Ezek. 1:6, 8; 10:14

22 As for the likeness of their faces, they were the same faces whose appearance I had seen by the river Chebar. Each one went straight ahead.

CHAPTER 11

Vision of the Twenty-five Wicked Rulers

MOREOVER, the Spirit lifted me up and brought me to the east gate of the LORD's house which faced eastward. And behold, *there were* twenty-five men at the entrance of the gate, and among them I saw Jaazaniah son of Azzur and^RPelatiah son of Benaiah, leaders of the people.   Ezek. 11:13

2 And He said to me, "Son of man, these are the men who devise iniquity and^Rgive evil advice in this city,   Jer. 5:5; Mic. 2:1

3 who say, 'Is^Tnot *the time* near to build houses?^AThis^Rcity is the pot and we are the flesh.'   The time *is not near* • This is • Jer. 1:13

4"Therefore,^Rprophesy against them, son of man, prophesy!"   Ezek. 3:4, 17

5 Then the Spirit of the LORD fell upon me, and He said to me, "Say, 'Thus says the LORD, "So you think, house of Israel, for^RI know your^Tthoughts.   Jer. 11:20 • Ezek. 38:10

6"You have multiplied your slain in this city, filling its streets with^Tthem."   *the slain*

7 'Therefore, thus says the Lord GOD, "Your slain whom you have laid in the midst of the city are the flesh, and this *city* is the pot; but I shall bring you out of it.

8"You have ^Rfeared a sword; so I will ^Rbring a sword upon you," the Lord GOD declares.   Prov. 10:24; Is. 66:4 • Job 3:25; Is. 24:17, 18

9"And I shall bring you out of the midst of^Tthe city, and I shall deliver you into the hands of^Rstrangers and^Rexecute judgments against you.   *it* • Deut. 28:36 • Ezek. 5:8; 16:41

10"You will^Rfall by the sword. I shall judge

you to the border of Israel; so you shall know that I am the LORD.   Jer. 52:9, 10

11"This *city* will^Rnot be a pot for you, nor will you be flesh in the midst of it, *but* I shall judge you to the border of Israel.   Ezek. 11:3

12"Thus you will know that I am the LORD; for you have not walked in My statutes nor have you executed My ordinances, but have acted according to the ordinances of the^Rnations around you." ' "   Ezek. 8:10, 14, 16

Promise of the Restoration of the Remnant

13 Now it came about as I prophesied, that Pelatiah son of Benaiah died. Then I fell on my face and cried out with a loud voice and said, "Alas, Lord GOD! Wilt Thou bring the remnant of Israel to a complete end?"

14 Then the word of the LORD came to me, saying,

15"Son of man, your brothers, your^Trelatives, your fellow exiles, and the whole house of Israel, all of them, *are those* to whom the inhabitants of Jerusalem have said, 'Go far from the LORD; this land has been given us as a possession.'   *brothers*

16"Therefore say, 'Thus says the Lord GOD, "Though I had removed them far away among the nations, and though I had scattered them among the countries, yet I was a ^Rsanctuary for them a little while in the countries where they had gone." '   Ps. 31:20; 90:1

17"Therefore say, 'Thus says the Lord GOD, "I shall^Rgather you from the peoples and assemble you out of the countries among which you have been scattered, and I shall give you the land of Israel." ' Jer. 3:12

18"When they come there, they will^Rremove all its^Rdetestable things and all its abominations from it.   Ezek. 37:23 • Ezek. 5:11

19"And I shall give them one heart, and shall put a new spirit within them. And I shall take the heart of stone out of their flesh and give them a heart of flesh,

20 that they may^Rwalk in My statutes and keep My ordinances, and do them. Then they will be^RMy people, and I shall be their God.   Ps. 105:45; Ezek. 36:27 • Ezek. 14:11

21"But as for those whose hearts go after their^Rdetestable things and abominations, I shall bring their conduct down on their heads," declares the Lord GOD.   Jer. 16:18

Departure of the Glory of God from the Mount of Olives

22 Then the cherubim ^Rlifted up their wings with the wheels beside them, and the glory of the God of Israel ^Thovered over them.   Ezek. 10:19 • *over them from above*

23 And the glory of the LORD went up from the midst of the city, and stood over the mountain which is east of the city.

24 And the Spirit lifted me up and brought me in a vision by the Spirit of God

to the exiles^Tin Chaldea. So the vision that I had seen^Tleft me.   Babylonia • *went up from*

25 Then I^Rtold the exiles all the things that the LORD had shown me.   Ezek. 2:7; 3:4, 17, 27

CHAPTER 12

Sign of Baggage for Exile

THEN the word of the LORD came to me saying,

2"Son of man, you live in the midst of the rebellious house, who^Rhave eyes to see but do not see, ears to hear but do not hear; for they are a rebellious house.   Is. 6:9f.; 43:8

3"Therefore, son of man, prepare for yourself baggage for exile and go into exile by day in their sight; even go into exile from your place to another place in their sight. Perhaps they will^Aunderstand though they are a rebellious house.   *see that they are*

4"And bring your baggage out by day in their sight, as baggage for exile. Then you will go out^Rat evening in their sight, as those going into exile.   2 Kin. 25:4; Jer. 39:4

5"Dig a hole through the wall in their sight and^Tgo out through it.   *bring it out*

6"Load *the baggage* on *your* shoulder in their sight, *and* carry *it* out in the dark. You shall cover your face so that you can not see the land, for I have set you as a^Rsign to the house of Israel."   Is. 8:18; 20:3; Ezek. 4:3

7 And I did so, as I had been commanded. By day I brought out my baggage like the baggage of an exile. Then in the evening I dug through the wall with my hands; I went out in the dark *and* carried *the baggage* on *my* shoulder in their sight.

8 And in the morning the word of the LORD came to me, saying,

9"Son of man, has not the house of Israel, the^Rrebellious house, said to you, 'What^Rare you doing?'   Ezek. 2:5-8 • Ezek. 17:12; 20:49; 24:19

10"Say to them, 'Thus says the Lord GOD, "This^Aburden^R concerns the prince in Jerusalem, as well as all the house of Israel who are^Tin it." '   *oracle* • 2 Kin. 9:25 • *in their midst*

11"Say, 'I am^Ta sign to you. As I have done, so it will be done to them; they will go into exile, into captivity.'   *your sign*

12"And the prince who is among them will load *his baggage* on *his* shoulder in the dark and go out. They will dig a hole through the wall to bring *it* out. He will cover his face so that he can not see the landwith *his* eyes.

13"I shall also spread My^Rnet over him, and he will be caught in My snare. And I shall bring him to Babylon in the land of the Chaldeans; yet he will not see it, though he will die there.   Is. 24:17, 18; Ezek. 17:20; 19:8

14"And I shall^Rscatter to every wind all who are around him, his helpers and all his troops; and I shall draw out a sword after them.   2 Kin. 25:4, 5; Ezek. 5:2; 17:21

15"So they will^Rknow that I am the LORD

when I scatter them among the nations, and spread them among the countries. Ezek. 6:7

16"But I shall [T]spare a few of them from the sword, the famine, and the pestilence that they may tell all their abominations among the nations where they go, and may know that I am the LORD." *leave over*

Sign of Quivering

17 Moreover, the word of the LORD came to me saying,

18"Son of man, [R]eat your bread with trembling, and drink your water with quivering and anxiety. Lam. 5:9; Ezek. 4:16

19"Then say to the people of the land, 'Thus says the Lord GOD concerning the inhabitants of Jerusalem in the land of Israel, "They will eat their bread with anxiety and drink their water with horror, because their land will be stripped of its fulness on account of the violence of all who live in it.

20"And the inhabited cities will be laid waste, and the land will be a desolation. So you will know that I am the LORD." ' "

21 Then the word of the LORD came to me saying,

22"Son of man, what is this[R]proverb you *people* have concerning the land of Israel, saying, 'The[R]days are long and every[R]vision fails'? Ezek. 16:44 • Ezek. 11:3 • Ezek. 7:26

23"Therefore say to them, 'Thus says the Lord GOD, "I will make this proverb cease so that they will no longer use it as a proverb in Israel." But tell them, "The[R]days draw near as well as the[T]fulfillment of every vision. Ps. 37:13; Joel 2:1; Zeph. 1:14 • *word*

24"For there will no longer be any[T]false[R] vision or flattering divination within the house of Israel. *vain* • Jer. 14:13-16

25"For I the LORD shall speak, and whatever word I speak will be performed. It will no longer be delayed, for in your days, O rebellious house, I shall speak the word and perform it," declares the Lord GOD.' "

26 Furthermore, the word of the LORD came to me saying,

27"Son of man, behold, the house of Israel is saying, 'The vision that he sees is for [R]many[T]years *from now,* and he prophesies of times far off.' Ezek. 12:22; Dan. 10:14 • *days*

28"Therefore say to them, 'Thus says the Lord GOD, "None of My words will be delayed any longer. Whatever word I speak will be performed," ' " declares the Lord GOD.

CHAPTER 13

Judgment upon False Prophets

THEN the word of the LORD came to me saying,

2"Son of man, prophesy against the prophets of Israel who prophesy, and say to those who prophesy from their own[T]inspiration, 'Listen to the word of the LORD! *heart*

3 'Thus says the Lord GOD, "Woe to the [R]foolish prophets who are following their own spirit and have seen nothing. Lam. 2:14

4"O Israel, your prophets have been like foxes among ruins.

5"You have not [R]gone up into the [R]breaches, nor did you build the wall around the house of Israel to stand in the battle on the day of the LORD. Ps. 106:23 • Is. 58:12

6"They see[T]falsehood and lying divination who are saying, 'The LORD declares,' when the LORD has not sent them; yet they hope for the fulfillment of *their* word. *vanity*

7"Did[R] you not see a false vision and speak a lying divination when you said, 'The LORD declares,' but it is not I who have spoken?" ' " Ezek. 22:28

8 Therefore, thus says the Lord GOD, "Because you have spoken[T]falsehood and seen a lie, therefore behold, I am against you," declares the Lord GOD. *vanity*

9"So My hand will be against the prophets who see false visions and utter lying divinations. They will have no place in the council of My people, nor will they be written down in the register of the house of Israel, nor will they enter the land of Israel, that you may know that I am the Lord GOD.

10"It is definitely because they have[R]misled My people by saying, 'Peace!' when there is[R]no peace. And when anyone builds a wall, behold, they plaster it over with whitewash; Jer. 23:32; 50:6 • Ezek. 7:25; 13:16

11 so tell those who plaster it over with whitewash, that it will fall. A[R]flooding rain will come, and you, O hailstones, will fall; and a violent wind will break out. Ezek. 38:22

12"Behold, when the wall has fallen, will you not be asked, 'Where is the plaster with which you plastered *it?*' "

13 Therefore, thus says the Lord GOD, "I will make a violent wind break out in My wrath. There will also be in My anger a flooding rain and[R]hailstones to consume *it* in wrath. Ex. 9:24, 25; Ps. 18:12, 13; Is. 30:30

14"So I shall tear down the wall which you plastered over with whitewash and bring it down to the ground, so that its[R]foundation is laid bare; and when it falls, you will be[R]consumed in its midst. And you will[R]know that I am the LORD. Mic. 1:6 • Jer. 6:15 • Ezek. 13:9

15"Thus I shall spend My wrath on the wall and on those who have plastered it over with whitewash; and I shall say to you, 'The wall is gone and its plasterers are gone,

16 *along with* the prophets of Israel who prophesy to Jerusalem, and who[R]see visions of peace for her when there is no peace,' declares the Lord GOD. Jer. 6:14; 8:11; Ezek. 13:10

Judgment upon False Prophetesses

17"Now you, son of man, set your face against the daughters of your people who

are^Rprophesying from their own^Tinspiration. Prophesy against them,   Judg. 4:4 • *heart*

18 and say, 'Thus says the Lord GOD, "Woe to the women who sew *magic* bands on^Tall wrists, and make veils for the heads of *persons* of every stature to hunt down lives! Will you hunt down the lives of My people, but preserve the lives *of others* for yourselves? *all joints of the hand;* M.T. reads *of my hands*

19"And^Rfor handfuls of barley and fragments of bread, you have profaned Me to My people to put to death^Asome who should not die and to keep others alive who should not live, by your lying to My people who listen to lies." ' "   Prov. 28:21; Mic. 3:5 • *souls*

20 Therefore, thus says the Lord GOD, "Behold, I am against your *magic* bands by which you hunt^Tlives there as^Abirds, and I will tear them off your arms; and I will let them go, even those lives whom you hunt as birds.   *souls • flying ones*

21"I will also tear off your veils and deliver My people from your hands, and they will no longer be in your hands to be hunted; and you will know that I am the LORD.

22"Because you disheartened the righteous with falsehood when I did not cause him grief, but have^Tencouraged^Rthe wicked not to turn from his wicked way *and* preserve his life,   *strengthen the hands of* • Jer. 23:14

23 therefore, you women will no longer see false visions or practice divination, and I will deliver My people out of your hand. Thus you will know that I am the LORD."

CHAPTER 14

Idolatry of the Elders

THEN some^Relders of Israel came to me and sat down before me.   2 Kin. 6:32

2 And the word of the LORD came to me saying,

3"Son of man, these men have^Rset up their idols in their hearts, and have^Rput right before their faces the stumbling block of their iniquity. Should I be ^Rconsulted by them at all?   Ezek. 20:16 • Ezek. 7:19 • Is. 1:15

4"Therefore speak to them and tell them, 'Thus says the Lord GOD, "Any man of the house of Israel who sets up his idols in his heart, puts right before his face the stumbling block of his iniquity, and *then* comes to the prophet, I the LORD will be brought to give him an answer in^Tthe matter in view of the^Rmultitude of his idols,   *it* • 1 Kin. 21:20-24

5 in order to lay hold of^Tthe hearts of the house of Israel who are^Restranged from Me through all their idols." '   *their* • Zech. 11:8

6"Therefore say to the house of Israel, 'Thus says the Lord GOD, "Repent^Rand turn away from your idols, and turn your faces away from all your abominations.   Is. 2:20

7"For anyone of the house of Israel or of the^Rimmigrants who stay in Israel who separates himself from Me, sets up his idols in his heart, puts right before his face the stumbling block of his iniquity, and *then* comes to the prophet to inquire of Me for himself, I the LORD will be brought to answer him in My own person.   Ex. 12:48; 20:10

8"And I shall set My face against that man and make him a sign and a proverb, and I shall cut him off from among My people. So you will know that I am the LORD.

9"But if the prophet is prevailed upon to speak a word, it is I, the LORD, who have prevailed upon that prophet, and I will stretch out My hand against him and destroy him from among My people Israel.

10"And they will bear *the punishment of* their iniquity; as the iniquity of the inquirer is, so the iniquity of the prophet will be,

11 in order that the house of Israel may no longer stray from Me and no longer defile themselves with all their transgressions. Thus they will be My people, and I shall be their God," ' declares the Lord GOD."

Jerusalem to Be Destroyed

12 Then the word of the LORD came to me saying,

13"Son of man, if a country sins against Me by committing unfaithfulness, and I stretch out My hand against it, destroy its ^Rsupply of bread, send famine against it, and cut off from it both man and beast,   Is. 3:1

14 even *though* these three men, Noah, Daniel, and Job were in its midst, by their *own* righteousness they could *only* deliver themselves," declares the Lord GOD.

15"If I were to cause wild beasts to pass through the land, and they depopulated it, and it became desolate so that no one would pass through it because of the beasts,

16 *though* these three men were in its midst, as I live," declares the Lord GOD, "they could not deliver either *their* sons or *their* daughters. They alone would be delivered, but the country would be desolate.

17"Or *if* I should^Rbring a sword on that country and say, 'Let the sword pass through the country and^Rcut off man and beast from it,'   Lev. 26:25 • Ezek. 25:13

18 even *though* these three men were in its midst, as I live," declares the Lord GOD, "they could not deliver either *their* sons or *their* daughters, but they alone would be delivered.

19"Or *if* I should send a plague against that country and pour out My wrath in blood on it, to cut off man and beast from it,

20 even *though* Noah, Daniel, and Job were in its midst, as I live," declares the Lord GOD, "they could not deliver either *their* son or *their* daughter. They would deliver only themselves by their righteousness."

21 For thus says the Lord GOD, "How

much more when[R] I send My four [T]severe judgments against Jerusalem: sword, famine, wild beasts, and plague to cut off man and beast from it!   Ezek. 5:17; 33:27 • *evil*

22"Yet, behold,[T] survivors will be left in it who will be brought out, *both* sons and daughters. Behold, they are going to come forth to you and you will[R] see their conduct and actions; then you will be comforted for the calamity which I have brought against Jerusalem for everything which I have brought upon it.   *escaped ones* • Ezek. 12:16

23"Then they will comfort you when you see their conduct and actions, for you will know that I have not done in vain whatever I did[A] to it," declares the Lord GOD.   *in*

CHAPTER 15

Parable of the Vine

THEN the word of the LORD came to me saying,

2"Son of man, how is the wood of the vine *better* than any wood of a branch which is among the trees of the forest?

3"Can wood be taken from it to make [T]anything, or can *men* take a peg from it on which to hang any vessel?   *a work*

4"If[A] it has been put into the fire for fuel, *and* the fire has consumed both of its ends, and its middle part has been charred, is it *then* useful for[T]anything?   *Behold* • *a work*

5"Behold, while it is intact, it is not made into[T]anything. How much less, when the fire has consumed it and it is charred, can it still be made into[T]anything!   *a work*

6"Therefore, thus says the Lord GOD, 'As the wood of the vine among the trees of the forest, which I have given to the fire for fuel, so have I given up the inhabitants of Jerusalem;

7 and I[R]set My face against them. *Though* they have[R]come out of the fire, yet the fire will consume them. Then you will know that I am the LORD, when I set My face against them.   Lev. 26:17 • 1 Kin. 19:17; Is. 24:18

8 'Thus I will make the land desolate, because they have[R]acted unfaithfully,' " declares the Lord GOD.   Ezek. 14:13; 17:20

CHAPTER 16

God Has Mercy on Israel

THEN the word of the LORD came to me saying,

2"Son of man,[R]make known to Jerusalem her abominations,   Is. 58:1; Ezek. 20:4; 22:2

3 and say, 'Thus says the Lord GOD to Jerusalem, "Your origin and your birth are from the land of the Canaanite, your father was an Amorite and your mother a Hittite.

4"As for your birth,[R]on the day you were born your navel cord was not cut, nor were you washed with water for cleansing; you were not rubbed with salt or even wrapped in cloths.   Hos. 2:3

5"No eye looked with pity on you to do any of these things for you, to have compassion on you. Rather you were thrown out into the[T]open field, for you were abhorred on the day you were born.   *surface*

6"When I passed by you and saw you squirming in your blood, I said to you *while you were* in your blood, 'Live!' I said to you while you were in your blood, 'Live!'

7"I made you numerous like plants of the field. Then you grew up, became tall, and reached the age for fine ornaments; *your* breasts were formed and your hair had grown. Yet you were naked and bare.

8"Then I passed by you and saw you, and behold, you were at the time for love; so I spread My skirt over you and covered your nakedness. I also swore to you and entered into a covenant with you so that you became Mine," declares the Lord GOD.

9"Then I bathed you with water, washed off your blood from you, and[R]anointed you with oil.   Ruth 3:3

10"I also clothed you with [R]embroidered cloth, and put sandals of porpoise skin on your feet; and I wrapped you with fine linen and covered you with silk.   Ex. 26:36

11"And I adorned you with ornaments, put[R]bracelets on your hands, and a[R]necklace around your neck.   Gen. 24:22, 47 • Gen. 41:42

12"I also put a[R]ring in your nostril, earrings in your ears, and a[R]beautiful crown on your head.   Gen. 24:47; Is. 3:21 • Jer. 13:18

13"Thus you were adorned with gold and silver, and your dress was of fine linen, silk, and embroidered cloth. You ate fine flour, honey, and oil; so you were exceedingly beautiful and advanced to royalty.

14"Then your fame went forth among the nations on account of your beauty, for it was perfect because of My splendor which I bestowed on you," declares the Lord GOD.

Israel Rejects God

15"But you trusted in your beauty and [R]played the harlot because of your fame, and you poured out your harlotries on every passer-by who might be *willing*.   Is. 57:8

16"And you took some of your clothes, made for yourself high places of various colors, and played the harlot on them, which should never come about nor happen.

17"You also took your beautiful [T]jewels[R] *made* of My gold and of My silver, which I had given you, and made for yourself male images that you might play the harlot with them.   *articles of beauty* • Ezek. 16:11, 12

18"Then you took your embroidered cloth and covered them, and offered My oil and My incense before them.

19"Also[R]My bread which I gave you, fine

flour, oil, and honey with which I fed you, [T]you would offer before them for a soothing aroma; so it happened," declares the Lord GOD.   Hos. 2:8 • *and you . . . offer it*

20"Moreover, you took your sons and daughters whom you had borne to Me, and you sacrificed them to idols to be devoured. Were your harlotries so small a matter?

21"You slaughtered [R]My children, and offered them up to [I]idols by causing them to pass through *the fire*.   Ex. 13:2 • *them*

22"And besides all your abominations and harlotries you did not remember the days of [R]your youth, when you were naked and bare and squirming in your blood.   Jer. 2:2

23"Then it came about after all your wickedness ('Woe, woe to you!' declares the Lord GOD),

24 that you built yourself a shrine and made yourself a high place in every square.

25"You built yourself a high place at the top of every street, and made your beauty abominable; and you spread your legs to every passer-by to multiply your harlotry.

26"You also played the harlot with the Egyptians, your lustful neighbors, and multiplied your harlotry to make Me angry.

27"Behold now, I have stretched out My hand against you and diminished your rations. And I delivered you up to the desire of [T]those who hate you, the [R]daughters of the Philistines, who are ashamed of your lewd conduct.   Is. 9:12; Ezek. 16:57

28"Moreover, you played the harlot with the [R]Assyrians because you were not satisfied; you even played the harlot with them and still were not satisfied.   2 Kin. 16:7

29"You also multiplied your harlotry with the land of merchants, Chaldea, yet even with this you were not satisfied." ' "

30"How languishing is your heart," declares the Lord GOD, "while you do all these things, the actions of a bold-faced harlot.

31"When you built your shrine at the beginning of every street and made your high place in every square, in [R]disdaining money, you were not like a harlot.   Is. 52:3

32"You adulteress wife, who takes strangers instead of her husband!

33"Men [T]give gifts to all harlots, but you [R]give your gifts to all your lovers to bribe them to come to you from every direction for your harlotries.   *they* • Ezek. 16:41

34"Thus you are different from those women in your harlotries, in that no one plays the harlot [T]as you do, because you give money and no money is given you; thus you are different."   *after you*

God Punishes Israel

35 Therefore, O harlot, hear the word of the LORD.

36 Thus says the Lord GOD, "Because your lewdness was poured out and your nakedness uncovered through your harlotries with your lovers and with all your detest-able idols, and because of the blood of your sons which you gave to [I]idols,   *them*

37 therefore, behold, I shall [R]gather all your lovers with whom you took pleasure, even all those whom you loved *and* all those whom you hated. So I shall gather them against you from every direction and expose your nakedness to them that they may see all your nakedness. Jer. 13:22, 26; Ezek. 23:9

38"Thus I shall [R]judge you, like women who commit adultery or shed blood are judged; and I shall bring on you the blood of [R]wrath and jealousy.   Ezek. 23:45 • Ps. 79:3, 5

39"I shall also give you into the hands of your lovers, and they will tear down your shrines, demolish your high places, [R]strip you of your clothing, take away your jewels, and will leave you naked and bare.   Hos. 2:3

40"They will [T]incite a crowd against you, and they will stone you and cut you to pieces with their swords.   *bring up an assembly*

41"And they will burn your houses with fire and execute judgments on you in the sight of many women. Then I shall stop you from playing the harlot, and you will also no longer pay [T]your lovers.   *a harlot's hire*

42"So I shall calm My fury against you, and My jealousy will depart from you, and I shall be pacified and angry no more.

43"Because you have [R]not remembered the days of your youth but have enraged Me by all these things, behold, I in turn will bring your conduct down on your own head," declares the Lord GOD, "so that you will not commit this lewdness on top of all your *other* abominations.   Ps. 78:42; 106:13; Ezek. 16:22

44"Behold, everyone who quotes proverbs will quote *this* proverb concerning you, saying, 'Like [T]mother, [T]like daughter.'   *Her*

45"You are the daughter of your mother, who loathed her husband and children. You are also the [R]sister of your sisters, who [R]loathed their husbands and children. Your mother was a Hittite and your father an Amorite.   Ezek. 23:2 • Is. 1:4; Ezek. 23:37-39

46"Now your older sister is Samaria, who lives [T]north of you with her daughters; and your younger sister, who lives south of you, is Sodom with her daughters.   *on your left*

47"Yet you have not merely walked in their ways or done according to their abominations; but, as if that were [R]too little, you acted [R]more corruptly in all your conduct than they.   1 Kin. 16:31 • 2 Kin. 21:9

48"As I live," declares the Lord GOD, "Sodom, your sister, and her daughters, have [R]not done as you and your daughters have done.   Matt. 10:15; 11:23, 24

49"Behold, this was the guilt of your sister Sodom: she and her daughters had arrogance, abundant food, and careless ease, but she did not help the poor and needy.

50"Thus they were haughty and committed [R]abominations before Me. Therefore I removed them when I saw *it*.   Gen. 13:13; 18:20

51"Furthermore, Samaria did not commit half of your sins, for you have multiplied

your abominations more than they. Thus you have made your sisters appear [R]righteous by all your abominations which you have committed. Jer. 3:8-11

52"Also bear your disgrace in that you have made judgment favorable for your sisters. Because of your sins in which you acted more abominably than they, they are more in the right than you. Yes, be also ashamed and bear your disgrace, in that you made your sisters appear righteous.

53"Nevertheless, I will restore their captivity, the captivity of Sodom and her daughters, the captivity of Samaria and her daughters, and [T]along with them your own captivity, *in their midst*

54 in order that you may bear your humiliation, and feel [R]ashamed for all that you have done when you become [R]a consolation to them. Jer. 2:26 • Ezek. 14:22, 23

55"And your sisters, Sodom with her daughters and Samaria with her daughters, will return to their former state, and you with your daughters will *also* return to your former state.

56"As *the name of* your sister Sodom was not heard from your lips in your day of pride,

57 before your [R]wickedness was uncovered,[T]so now you have become the reproach of the daughters of Edom, and of all who are around her, of the daughters of the Philistines—those surrounding *you* who despise you. Ezek. 16:36, 37 • Heb., *as at the time of*

58"You have [R]borne *the penalty of* your lewdness and abominations," the LORD declares. Ezek. 23:49

59 For thus says the Lord GOD, "I will also do with you as you have done, you who have [R]despised the oath by breaking the covenant. Is. 24:5; Ezek. 17:19

God Remembers His Covenant

60"Nevertheless, I will remember My covenant with you in the days of your youth, and I will establish an [R]everlasting covenant with you. Is. 55:3; Jer. 32:38-41; Ezek. 37:26

61"Then you will [R]remember your ways and be ashamed when you receive your sisters, *both* your older and your younger; and I will give them to you as daughters, but not because of your covenant. Jer. 50:4, 5

62"Thus I will establish My covenant with you, and you shall know that I am the LORD,

63 in order that you may [R]remember and be ashamed, and never open your mouth anymore because of your humiliation, when I have forgiven you for all that you have done," the Lord GOD declares. Ezek. 36:31

CHAPTER 17

Parable of the Two Eagles

Now the word of the LORD came to me saying,

2"Son of man, propound a riddle, and speak a parable to the house of Israel,

3 [T]saying, 'Thus says the Lord GOD, "A great eagle with [R]great wings, long pinions and a full plumage of many colors, came to [R]Lebanon and took away the top of the cedar. *and you shall say* • Dan. 4:22 • Jer. 22:23

4"He plucked off the topmost of its young twigs and brought it to a land of merchants; he set it in a city of traders.

5"He also took some of the seed of the land and planted it in [T]fertile [R]soil. He [T]placed *it* beside abundant waters; he set it *like* a willow. *a field of seed* • Deut. 8:7-9 • *took*

6"Then it sprouted and became a low, spreading vine with its branches turned toward him, but its roots remained under it. So it became a vine, and yielded shoots and sent out branches.

7"But there was another great eagle with great wings and much plumage; and behold, this vine bent its roots toward him and sent out its branches toward him from the beds where it was planted, that he might water it.

8"It was planted in good [T]soil beside abundant waters, that it might yield branches and bear fruit, *and* become a splendid vine." ' *field*

9"Say, 'Thus says the Lord GOD, "Will it thrive? Will he not pull up its roots and cut off its fruit, so that it withers—so that all its sprouting leaves wither? And neither by great [T]strength nor by many people can it be raised from its roots *again*. *arm*

10"Behold, though it is planted, will it thrive? Will it not [R]completely wither as soon as the east wind strikes it—wither on the beds where it grew?" ' " Ezek. 19:14; Hos. 13:15

11 Moreover, the word of the LORD came to me saying,

12"Say now to the rebellious house, 'Do you not know what these things *mean?*' Say, 'Behold, the [R]king of Babylon came to Jerusalem, took its king and princes, and brought them to him in Babylon. Ezek. 1:2

13 'And he took one of the royal family and made a covenant with him,[T]putting him under oath. He also took away the mighty of the land, *and caused him to enter into an oath*

14 that the kingdom might be [T]in subjection, not exalting itself, *but* keeping his covenant, that it might continue. *low*

15 'But he [R]rebelled against him by sending his envoys to Egypt that they might give him horses and many [T]troops. Will he succeed? Will he who does such things escape? Can he indeed break the covenant and escape? 2 Kin. 24:20; 2 Chr. 36:13; Jer. 52:3 • *people*

16 'As I live,' declares the Lord GOD, 'Surely in the [T]country of the king who [T]put him on the throne, whose oath he despised, and whose covenant he broke,[R]in Babylon he shall die. *place* • *made him king* • Jer. 52:11

17 'And Pharaoh with *his* mighty army and great company will not [T]help him in the war, when they cast up mounds and build siege walls to cut off many lives. *act with*

18 'Now he despised the oath by breaking the covenant, and behold, he[T]pledged[R]his allegiance, yet did all these things; he shall not escape.'"   *gave his hand* · 1 Chr. 29:24

19 Therefore, thus says the Lord GOD, "As I live, surely My oath which he despised and My covenant which he broke, I will[T]inflict on his head.   *give it*

20"And I will spread My net over him, and he will be caught in My snare. Then I will bring him to Babylon and enter into judgment with him there *regarding* the unfaithful act which he has committed against Me.

21"And all the choice men in all his troops will fall by the sword, and the survivors will be scattered to every wind; and you will know that I, the LORD, have spoken."

22 Thus says the Lord GOD, "I shall also take *a* sprig from the lofty top of the cedar and set *it* out; I shall pluck from the topmost of its young twigs a tender one, and I shall plant *it* on a high and lofty mountain.

23"On the high mountain of Israel I shall plant it, that it may bring forth boughs and bear fruit, and become a stately cedar. And birds of every kind will nest under it; they will nest in the shade of its branches.

24"And all the[R]trees of the field will know that I am the LORD; I bring down the high tree, exalt the low tree, dry up the green tree, and make the dry tree[R]flourish. I am the LORD; I have spoken, and I will perform it."   Ps. 96:12; Is. 55:12 · Amos 9:11

CHAPTER 18

Message of Personal Judgment
for Personal Sin

THEN the word of the LORD came to me saying,
2"What[R]do you mean by using this proverb concerning the land of Israel saying,
'The fathers eat the sour grapes,
But the children's teeth [T]are set on edge'?   Is. 3:15 · *become dull*
3"As I live," declares the Lord GOD, "you are surely not going to use this proverb in Israel anymore.
4"Behold, all[A]souls are Mine; the[A]soul of the father as well as the soul of the son is Mine. The soul who sins will die.   *lives · life*
5"But if a man is righteous, and practices justice and righteousness,
6 and does not [R]eat at the mountain *shrines* or[R]lift up his eyes to the idols of the house of Israel, or[R]defile his neighbor's wife, or approach a woman during her menstrual period—   Ezek. 6:13 · Deut. 4:19 · Ezek. 18:15
7 if a man does not oppress anyone, but restores to the debtor his pledge, does not commit robbery, *but* gives his bread to the hungry, and covers the naked with clothing,
8 if he does not lend *money* on[R]interest or take increase, *if* he keeps his hand from iniquity, *and* [R]executes true justice between man and man,   Ex. 22:25 · Zech. 7:9; 8:16

9 *if* he walks in[R]My statutes and My ordinances so as to deal faithfully—[R]he is righteous *and* will surely[R]live," declares the Lord GOD.   Lev. 18:5 · [Rom. 8:1] · Amos 5:4
10"Then he may[T]have a violent son who sheds blood, and who does any of these things to a brother   *beget*
11 (though he himself did not do any of these things), that is, he even eats at the mountain *shrines*, and[R]defiles his neighbor's wife,   [1 Cor. 6:9]
12 oppresses the[R]poor and needy,[R]commits robbery, does not restore a pledge, but lifts up his eyes to the idols, *and*[R]commits abomination,   Amos 4:1 · Jer. 22:3 · 2 Kin. 21:11
13 he[R]lends *money* on interest and takes increase; will he live? He will not live! He has committed all these abominations, he will surely be put to death; his blood will be [T]on his own head.   Ex. 22:25 · *on him*
14"Now behold, he has a son who has observed all his father's sins which he committed, and observing does not do likewise.
15"He does not eat at the mountain *shrines* or lift up his eyes to the idols of the house of Israel, or defile his neighbor's wife,
16 or oppress anyone, or retain a pledge, or commit robbery, *but* he[R]gives his bread to the hungry, and covers the naked with clothing,   Job 31:16, 20; Ps. 41:1; Is. 58:7, 10
17 he keeps his hand from the poor, does not take interest or increase, *but* executes My ordinances, and walks in My statutes; [R]he will not die for his father's iniquity, he will surely live.   Rom. 2:7
18"As for his father, because he practiced extortion, robbed *his* brother, and did what was not good among his people, behold, he will die for his iniquity.
19"Yet you say, 'Why should the son not bear the punishment for the father's iniquity?' When the son has practiced justice and righteousness, and has observed all My statutes and done them, he shall surely live.
20"The person who[R]sins will die. The son will not bear the punishment for the father's iniquity, nor will the father bear the punishment for the son's iniquity; the righteousness of the righteous will be upon himself, and the wickedness of the wicked will be upon himself.   2 Kin. 14:6; 22:18-20; Ezek. 18:4
21"But if the[R]wicked man turns from all his sins which he has committed and observes all My statutes and practices justice and righteousness, he shall surely live; he shall not die.   Ezek. 18:27, 28; 33:12, 19
22"All[R] his transgressions which he has committed will not be remembered against him; because of his righteousness which he has practiced, he will live.   Is. 43:25; Jer. 50:20
23"Do[R]I have any pleasure in the death of the wicked," declares the Lord GOD, "rather[T] than that he should[R]turn from his ways and live?   [Ezek. 18:32; 33:11] · *is it not* · Ps. 147:11
24"But when a righteous man[T]turns away from his righteousness, commits iniquity,

and does according to all the abominations that a wicked man does, will he live? All his righteous deeds which he has done will not be remembered for his treachery which he has committed and his sin which he has committed; for them he will die.   1 Sam. 15:11

25"Yet you say, 'The^{R}way of the Lord is not right.' Hear now, O house of Israel! Is ^{R}My way not right? Is it not your ways that are not right?   Ezek. 18:29 · Gen. 18:25

26"When a righteous man turns away from his righteousness, commits iniquity, and dies because of it, for his iniquity which he has committed he will die.

27"Again, when a wicked man turns away $^R_C$from his wickedness which he has committed and practices justice and righteousness, he will save his life.   Is. 1:18; 55:7

28"Because he considered and turned away from all his transgressions which he had committed, he shall surely live; he shall not die.

29"But the house of Israel says, 'The way of the Lord is not right.' Are My ways not right, O house of Israel? Is it not your ways that are not right?

30"Therefore I will judge you, O house of Israel, each according to his conduct," declares the Lord GOD. "Repent and turn away from all your transgressions, so that iniquity may not become a stumbling block to you.

31"Cast^{R}away from you all your transgressions which you have committed, and make yourselves a new heart and a new spirit! For why will you die, O house of Israel?   Is. 1:16

32"For I have^{R}no pleasure in the death of anyone who dies," declares the Lord GOD. "Therefore, repent and live."   Ezek. 18:23

CHAPTER 19

Lament for the Princes of Israel

"AS for you, take up a^{R}lamentation for the^{R}princes of Israel,   Ezek. 2:10 · 2 Kin. 23:29
2 and say,

'What was your mother?
A lioness among lions!
She lay down among young lions,
She reared her cubs.
3 'When she brought up one of her cubs,
He became a lion,
And he learned to tear *his* prey;
He devoured men.
4 'Then nations heard about him;
He was captured in their pit,
And they^{R}brought him with hooks
To the land of Egypt.   2 Kin. 23:34
5 'When she saw, as she waited,
That her hope was lost,
She took^{T}another of her cubs   one
And made him a young lion.
6 'And he^{R}walked about among the
lions;   2 Kin. 24:9; 2 Chr. 36:9
He became a young lion,
He learned to tear *his* prey;

He devoured men.
7 'And he destroyed their^{A}fortified tow-
ers   widows
And laid waste their cities;
And the land and its fulness were ap-
palled
Because of the sound of his roaring.
8 'Then nations set against him
On every side from *their* provinces,
And they spread their net over him;
He was captured in their pit.
9 'And^{R}they put him in a cage with
hooks   2 Chr. 36:6
And^{R}brought him to the king of Baby-
lon;   2 Kin. 24:15
They brought him in hunting nets
So that his voice should be heard no
more
On the mountains of Israel.

Parable of the Withered Vine

10 'Your mother was^{R}like a vine in your
vineyard,   Ps. 80:8-11
Planted by the waters;
It was fruitful and full of branches
Because of abundant waters.
11 'And it had^{T}strong branches *fit* for
scepters of rulers,   *rods of her strength*
And its^{R}height was raised above the
clouds   Ezek. 31:3
So that it was seen in its height with
the mass of its branches.
12 'But it was plucked up in fury;
It was cast down to the ground;
And the east wind dried up its fruit.
Its^{R}strong branch was torn off
So that it withered;
The fire consumed it.   Is. 27:11
13 'And now it is planted in the^{R}wilder-
ness,   2 Kin. 24:12-16; Ezek. 19:10; 20:35
In a dry and thirsty land.
14 'And^R_Cfire has gone out from *its* branch;
It has consumed its shoots *and* fruit,
So that there is not in it a strong
branch,   Ezek. 15:4; 20:47, 48
A scepter to rule.'"

This is a lamentation, and has become a lamentation.

CHAPTER 20

In Egypt

NOW it came about in the seventh year, in the fifth *month*, on the tenth of the month, that^{T}certain of the elders of Israel came to inquire of the LORD, and sat before me.   *men*

2 And the word of the LORD came to me saying,

3"Son of man, speak to the elders of Israel, and say to them, 'Thus says the Lord GOD, "Do you come to inquire of Me? As I live," declares the Lord GOD, "I^{R}will not be inquired of by you."'   Ezek. 14:3

4"Will you judge them, will you judge

them, son of man?^RMake them know the abominations of their fathers;   Ezek. 16:2

5 and say to them, 'Thus says the Lord GOD, "On the day when I chose Israel and swore to the^Tdescendants of the house of Jacob and made Myself known to them in the land of Egypt, when I swore to them, saying, I am the LORD your God,   seed

6 on that day I swore to them,^Rto bring them out from the land of Egypt into a land that I had^Tselected for them,^Rflowing with milk and honey, which is the glory of all lands.   Jer. 32:22 • spied out • Ex. 13:5

7"And I said to them, 'Cast^Raway, each of you, the detestable things of his eyes, and do not defile yourselves with the idols of Egypt; I am the LORD your God.'   Ex. 20:4, 5

8"But they rebelled against Me and were not willing to listen to Me;^Tthey did not cast away the detestable things of their eyes, nor did they forsake the idols of Egypt.   each one

Then I^Tresolved to pour out My wrath on them, to accomplish My anger against them in the midst of the land of Egypt.   said

9"But I acted for the sake of My name, that it should not be profaned in the sight of the nations among whom they lived, in whose sight I made Myself known to them by bringing them out of the land of Egypt.

In the Wilderness

10"So I took them out of the land of Egypt and brought them into the wilderness.

11"And I gave them My statutes and informed them of My ordinances, by which, if a man^Tobserves them, he will live.   does

12"And also I gave them My sabbaths to be a^Rsign between Me and them, that they might know that I am the LORD who sanctifies them.   Ex. 31:13, 17; Ezek. 20:20

13"But the house of Israel rebelled against Me in the wilderness. They did not walk in My statutes, and they rejected My ordinances, by which, if a man^Tobserves them, he will live; and My sabbaths they greatly profaned. Then I^Tresolved to^Rpour out My wrath on them in the wilderness, to annihilate them.   does • said • Ex. 32:10; Deut. 9:8

14"But I acted for the sake of My name, that it should not be profaned in the sight of the nations, before whose sight I had brought them out.

15"And also^RI swore to them in the wilderness that I would not bring them into the land which I had given them, flowing with milk and honey, which is the glory of all lands,   Num. 14:30; Ps. 95:11; 106:26

16 because they rejected My ordinances, and as for My statutes, they did not walk in them; they even profaned My sabbaths, for their heart continually went after their idols.

17"Yet My eye spared them rather than destroying them, and I did not cause their ^Rannihilation in the wilderness.   Jer. 4:27; 5:18

18"And I said to their^Tchildren^Rin the wilderness, 'Do not walk in the statutes of your fathers, or keep their ordinances, or defile yourselves with their idols.   sons • Num. 14:31

19 'I am the LORD your God;^Rwalk in My statutes, and keep My ordinances, and^Tobserve them.   Deut. 5:32, 33; 6:1, 2; 8:1, 2 • do

20 'And^Rsanctify My sabbaths; and they shall be a sign between Me and you, that you may know that I am the LORD your God.'   Jer. 17:22

21"But the children rebelled against Me; they did not walk in My statutes, nor were they careful to observe My ordinances, by which, if a man observes them, he will live; they profaned My sabbaths. So I resolved to pour out My wrath on them, to accomplish My anger against them in the wilderness.

22"But I^Twithdrew My hand and acted for the sake of My name, that it should not be profaned in the sight of the nations in whose sight I had brought them out.   Job 13:21

23"Also I swore to them in the wilderness that I would scatter them among the nations and disperse them among the lands,

24 because they had not observed My ordinances, but had rejected My statutes, and had profaned My sabbaths, and their eyes were^Ton the idols of their fathers.   after

25"And I also gave them statutes that were^Rnot good and ordinances by which they could not live;   Ps. 81:12; Is. 66:4

26 and I pronounced them unclean because of their gifts, in that they caused all their first-born to pass through the fire so that I might make them desolate, in order that they might know that I am the LORD." '

In Canaan

27"Therefore, son of man,^Rspeak to the house of Israel, and say to them, 'Thus says the Lord GOD, "Yet in this your fathers have ^Rblasphemed Me by acting treacherously against Me.   Ezek. 2:7; 3:4, 11, 27 • Num. 15:30

28"When I had^Rbrought them into the land which I swore to give to them, then they saw every high hill and every leafy tree, and they offered there their sacrifices, and there they presented the provocation of their offering. There also they made their soothing aroma, and there they poured out their libations.   Josh. 23:3, 14; Neh. 9:22-26; Ps. 78:55

In Ezekiel's Time

29"Then I said to them, 'What is the high place to which you go?' So its name is called ¹Bamah to this day." '

30"Therefore, say to the house of Israel, 'Thus says the Lord GOD, "Will you defile yourselves^Tafter the manner of your^Rfathers and play the harlot after their detestable things?   in the way of • Judg. 2:19; Jer. 7:26

31"And^Twhen you offer your gifts, when you^Rcause your sons to pass through the fire, you are defiling yourselves with all

¹ Or, High Place

your idols to this day. And shall I be inquired of by you, O house of Israel? As I live," declares the Lord GOD, "I will not be inquired of by you.   *in your lifting up* • Jer. 7:31
32"And what comes ^Tinto your mind will not come about, when you say: 'We will be like the nations, like the tribes of the lands, serving wood and stone.'   *upon your spirit*

Message of God's Future Restoration of Israel

33"As I live," declares the Lord GOD, "surely with a mighty hand and with an^Routstretched arm and with wrath poured out, I shall be^Rking over you.   Jer. 21:5 • Jer. 51:57
34"And I shall^Rbring you out from the peoples and gather you from the lands where you are scattered, with a mighty hand and with an outstretched arm and with^R wrath poured out;   Is. 27:12, 13 • Jer. 42:18; 44:6
35 and I shall bring you into the wilderness of the peoples, and there I shall enter into judgment with you face to face.
36"As I^Rentered into judgment with your fathers in the wilderness of the land of Egypt, so I will enter into judgment with you," declares the Lord GOD.   Num. 11:1-35
37"And I shall make you^Rpass under the rod, and I shall bring you into the bond of the covenant;   Lev. 27:32; Jer. 33:13
38 and I shall purge from you the rebels and those who transgress against Me; I shall bring them out of the land where they sojourn, but they will not enter the land of Israel. Thus you will know that I am the LORD.
39"As for you, O house of Israel," thus says the Lord GOD, "Go, serve everyone his idols; but later, you will surely listen to Me, and My holy name you will profane no longer with your gifts and with your idols.
40"For on My holy mountain, on the high mountain of Israel," declares the Lord GOD, "there the whole house of Israel,^Rall of them, will serve Me in the land; there I shall accept them, and there I shall^Aseek your contributions and the choicest of your gifts, with all your holy things.   Is. 66:23 • *require*
41"As^Ta soothing aroma I shall accept you, when I bring you out from the peoples and gather you from the lands where you are scattered; and I shall prove Myself holy among you in the sight of the nations.   *With*
_R42"And^Ryou will know that I am the LORD, when I bring you into the land of Israel, into the land which I swore to give to your forefathers.   Ezek. 36:23; 38:23 • Ezek. 11:17
43"And there you will ^Rremember your ways and all your deeds, with which you have defiled yourselves; and you will loathe yourselves in your own^Tsight for all the evil things that you have done.   Hos. 5:15 • *faces*
44"Then^Ryou will know that I am the LORD when I have dealt with you for My name's sake, not according to your evil ways or according to your corrupt deeds, O house of Israel," declares the Lord GOD.' "   Ezek. 24:24

Sign of the Forest Fire

45 Now the word of the LORD came to me saying,
46"Son of man, set your face toward^ATeman, and speak out against the south, and prophesy against the^Rforest^Tland of the Negev,   *the South* • Is. 30:6-11 • *of the field*
47 and say to the forest of the Negev, 'Hear the word of the LORD: thus says the Lord GOD, "Behold, I am about to kindle a fire in you, and it shall consume every^Tgreen tree in you, as well as every dry tree; the blazing flame will not be quenched, and^Tthe^R whole surface from south to north will be burned by it.   *moist* • *all the faces* • Is. 13:8
48"And all flesh will see that I, the LORD, have kindled it; it shall not be quenched." ' "
49 Then I said, "Ah Lord GOD! They are saying of me, 'Is he not *just* speaking^Rparables?' "   Ezek. 17:2; Matt. 13:13; John 16:25

CHAPTER 21

Sign of the Drawn Sword

AND the word of the LORD came to me saying,
2"Son of man, set your face toward Jerusalem, and speak against the sanctuaries, and prophesy against the land of Israel;
3 and say to the land of Israel, 'Thus says the LORD, "Behold,^RI am against you; and I shall draw My sword out of its sheath and cut off from you the righteous and the wicked.   Jer. 21:13; Ezek. 5:8; Nah. 2:13; 3:5
4"Because I shall cut off from you the righteous and the wicked, therefore My _Rsword shall go forth from its sheath against ^Rall flesh from south *to* north.   Jer. 12:12
5"Thus all flesh will know that I, the LORD, have drawn My sword out of its sheath. It will ^Rnot return *to its sheath* again." '   1 Sam. 3:12; Jer. 23:20; Ezek. 21:30
6"As for you, son of man, groan with breaking ^Theart and bitter grief, groan in their sight.   *loins*
7"And it will come about when they say to you, 'Why do you groan?' that you will say, 'Because of the news that is coming; and every heart will melt, all hands will be feeble, every spirit will faint, and all knees will be weak as water. Behold, it comes and it will happen,' declares the Lord GOD."
8 Again the word of the LORD came to me saying,
9"Son of man, prophesy and say, 'Thus says the LORD.' Say,
    'A^Rsword, a sword sharpened
    And also polished!   Deut. 32:41
10 'Sharpened to make a slaughter,
    Polished^Tto flash like lightning!'
Or shall we rejoice, the rod of My son despising every tree?   *lightning to be to her*
11"And it is given to be polished, that it may be handled; the sword is sharpened and polished, to give it into the hand of the slayer.

12"Cry^Rout and wail, son of man; for it is against My people, it is against all the^Rofficials of Israel. They are delivered over to the sword with My people, therefore strike *your* thigh.   Ezek. 21:6; Joel 1:13 • Ezek. 21:25; 22:6

13"For *there is* a testing; and what if even the^Arod which despises will be no more?" declares the Lord GOD.   *scepter*

14"You therefore, son of man, prophesy, and clap *your* hands together; and let the sword be^Rdoubled the third time, the sword for the slain. It is the sword for the great one slain, which surrounds them,   Lev. 26:21, 24

15 that *their*^Rhearts may melt, and many ^Rfall at all their gates. I have given the glittering sword. Ah! It is made *for striking* like lightning, it is wrapped up *in readiness* for slaughter.   Josh. 2:11 • Is. 59:10; Jer. 13:16; 18:15

16"Show^Ayourself sharp, go to the right; set yourself; go to the left, wherever your ^Tedge is appointed.   *Unite yourself • face*

17"I shall also clap My hands together, and I shall^Tappease^RMy wrath; I, the LORD, have spoken."   *cause to rest • Ezek. 5:13*

Sign of the Double Stroke
of the Sword

18 And the word of the LORD came to me saying,

19"As for you, son of man, make two ways for the sword of the king of Babylon to come; both of them will go out of one land. And^Tmake a signpost;^Tmake it at the head of the way to the city.   *cut out a hand • cut it*

20"You shall^Tmark a way for the sword to come to Rabbah of the sons of Ammon, and to Judah into fortified Jerusalem.   *set*

21"For the king of Babylon stands at the ^Tparting of the way, at the head of the two ways, to use divination; he shakes the arrows, he consults the^Thousehold idols, he looks at the liver.   *mother • Heb., teraphim*

22"Into his right hand came the divination, 'Jerusalem,' to^Rset battering rams, to open the mouth^Tfor slaughter, to lift up the voice with a battle cry, to set battering rams against the gates, to cast up mounds, to build a siege wall.   Ezek. 4:2; 26:9 • *in*

23"And it will be to them like a false divination in their eyes; they have *sworn* solemn oaths. But he^Rbrings iniquity to remembrance, that they may be seized.   Ezek. 21:24

24"Therefore, thus says the Lord GOD, 'Because you have made your iniquity to be remembered, in that your transgressions are uncovered, so that in all your deeds your sins appear—because you have come to remembrance, you will be seized with the hand.

25 'And you, O slain, wicked one, the prince of Israel, whose day has come, in the time of the^Apunishment of the end,'   *iniquity*

26 thus says the Lord GOD, 'Remove the turban, and take off the crown; this will *be*

^Tno more the same. Exalt that which is low, and abase that which is high.   *not this*

27 'A ruin, a ruin, a ruin, I shall make it. This also will be no more, until He comes whose right it is; and I shall give it *to Him*.'

28"And you, son of man, prophesy and say, 'Thus says the Lord GOD concerning the sons of Ammon and concerning their ^Rreproach,' and say: 'A sword, a sword is drawn, polished for the slaughter, to cause it ^Tto ^Rconsume, that it may be like lightning—   Ezek. 36:15 • *to finish* • Is. 31:8

29 while they see for you^Rfalse visions, while they divine lies for you—to place you on the necks of the wicked who are slain, whose day has come, in the time of the^Apunishment of the end.   Ezek. 13:6-9 • *iniquity*

30 'Return^R *it* to its sheath. In the place where you were created, in the land of your origin, I shall judge you.   Jer. 47:6, 7

31 'And I shall pour out My indignation on you; I shall blow on you with the fire of My wrath, and I shall give you into the hand of brutal men,^Askilled in destruction.   *artisans of*

32 'You will be^Tfuel^Tfor the fire; your blood will be in the midst of the land. You will^Rnot be remembered, for I, the LORD, have spoken.' "   *food* • Ezek. 20:47, 48 • Ezek. 25:10

CHAPTER 22

Message of Judgment on Jerusalem

THEN the word of the LORD came to me saying,

2"And you, son of man, will you judge, will you judge the bloody city? Then cause her to know all her abominations.

3"And you shall say, 'Thus says the Lord GOD, "A city^Rshedding blood in her midst, so that her time will come, and that makes idols, contrary to her *interest*, for defilement!   Ezek. 22:6, 27; 23:37, 45

4"You have become^Rguilty by^Tthe blood which you have shed, and defiled by your idols which you have made. Thus you have brought your ^Tday near and have come to your years; therefore I have made you a reproach to the nations, and a mocking to all the lands.   Ezek. 5:14, 15; 16:57 • *your* • *days*

5"Those who are near and those who are far from you will mock you, you of ill repute, full of^Tturmoil.   Is. 22:2

6"Behold, the rulers of Israel, each according to his^Tpower, have been in you for the purpose of shedding blood.   *arm*

7"They have^Rtreated father and mother lightly within you. The alien they have oppressed in your midst; the fatherless and the widow they have wronged in you.   Ex. 20:12

8"You have^Rdespised My holy things and profaned My sabbaths.   Ezek. 22:26

9"Slanderous men have been in you for the purpose of shedding blood, and in you they have eaten at the mountain *shrines*. In

your midst they have ᴿcommitted acts of lewdness. Ezek. 23:29; Hos. 4:2, 10, 14

10"In you ᵀthey have ᴿuncovered *their* fathers' nakedness; in you they have humbled her who was ᴿunclean in her menstrual impurity. *he has* • Lev. 18:8 • Lev. 18:19

11"And one has committed abomination with his ᴿneighbor's wife, and another has lewdly defiled his ᴿdaughter-in-law. And another in you has humbled his sister, his father's daughter. Ezek. 18:11; 33:26 • Lev. 18:15

12"In you they have ᴿtaken bribes to shed blood; you have taken interest and profits, and you have injured your neighbors for gain by oppression, and you have forgotten Me," declares the Lord God. Ex. 23:8

13"Behold, then, I smite My hand at your dishonest gain which you have acquired and at the bloodshed which is among you.

14"Can ᴿyour heart endure, or can your hands be strong, in the days that I shall deal with you?ᴿI, the Lord, have spoken and shall act. Ezek. 21:7 • Ezek. 17:24

15"And I shall ᴿscatter you among the nations, and I shall disperse you through the lands, and I shall ᴿconsume your uncleanness from you. Deut. 4:27; Neh. 1:8 • Ezek. 23:27

16"And you will profane yourself in the sight of the nations, and you will ᴿknow that I am the Lord." ' " Ps. 83:18; Ezek. 6:7

17 And the word of the Lord came to me saying,

18"Son of man, the house of Israel has become ᴿdross to Me; all of them are bronze and tin and iron and lead in the furnace; they are the dross of silver. Ps. 119:119

19"Therefore, thus says the Lord God, 'Because all of you have become dross, therefore, behold, I am going to gather you into the midst of Jerusalem.

20 'As they gather silver and bronze and iron and lead and tin into the furnace to blow fire on it in order to melt *it,* so I shall gather *you* in My anger and in My wrath, and I shall lay you *there* and melt you.

21 'And I shall gather you and blow on you with the fire of My wrath, and you will be melted in the midst of it.

22 'As silver is melted in the furnace, so you will be melted in the midst of it; and you will know that I, the Lord, have ᴿpoured out My wrath on you.' " Ezek. 20:8, 33; Hos. 5:10

23 And the word of the Lord came to me saying,

24"Son of man, say to her, 'You are a land that is ᵀnot cleansed or rained on in the day of indignation.' Is. 9:13; Jer. 2:30; Ezek. 24:13

25"There is a ᴿconspiracy of her prophets in her midst, like a roaring lion tearing the prey. They have ᴿdevoured lives; they have taken treasure and precious things; they have made many ᴿwidows in the midst of her. Jer. 11:9; Hos. 6:9 • Jer. 2:34 • Ezek. 22:7

26"Her priests have done violence to My law and have profaned My holy things; they

have made no distinction between the holy and the profane, and they have not taught the difference between the unclean and the clean; and they hide their eyes from My sabbaths, and I am profaned among them.

27"Her princes within her are like wolves tearing the prey, by shedding blood *and* destroying lives in order to get dishonest gain.

28"And her prophets have smeared whitewash for them, seeing false visions and divining lies for them, saying, 'Thus says the Lord God,' when the Lord has not spoken.

29"The people of the land have practiced ᴿoppression and committed robbery, and they have wronged the poor and needy and have ᴿoppressed the sojourner without justice. Is. 5:7; Ezek. 9:9; 22:7; Amos 3:10 • Ex. 23:9

30"And I searched for a man among them who should build up the wall and stand in the gap before Me for the land, that I should not destroy it; but I found ᵀno one. *not*

31"Thus I have poured out My indignation on them; I have consumed them with the fire of My wrath; their way I have brought upon their heads," declares the Lord God.

CHAPTER 23

Parable of Two Sisters

THE word of the Lord came to me again saying,

2"Son of man, there were ᴿtwo women, the daughters of one mother; Ezek. 16:46

3 and they played the harlot in Egypt. They ᵖplayed the harlot in their youth; there their breasts were pressed, and there their virgin bosom was handled. Lev. 17:7; Jer. 3:9

4"And their names were Oholah the elder and Oholibah her sister. And they became Mine, and they bore sons and daughters. And *as for* their names, Samaria is Oholah, and Jerusalem is Oholibah.

5"And Oholah played the harlot while she was Mine; and she lusted after her lovers, after the Assyrians, *her* neighbors,

6 who were clothed in purple,ᴿgovernors and officials, all of them desirable young men, horsemen riding on horses. Ezek. 23:12

7"And she bestowed her harlotries on them, all of whom *were* the choicest men of Assyria; and with all whom she lusted after, with all their idols she defiled herself.

8"And she did not forsake her harlotries from *the time in* Egypt; for in her youth men had lain with her, and they handled her virgin bosom and poured out their lust on her.

9"Therefore, I gave her into the hand of her lovers, into the hand of the ᵀAssyrians, after whom she lusted. *sons of Asshur*

10"They ᴿuncovered her nakedness; they took her sons and her daughters, but they slew her with the sword. Thus she became a ᵀbyword among women, and they executed judgments on her. Ezek. 16:37, 41 • *name*

11"Now her sister Oholibah saw *this,* yet she was^Rmore corrupt in her lust than she, and her harlotries were more than the harlotries of her sister.   Jer. 3:8-11; Ezek. 16:51

12"She lusted after the ^RAssyrians, governors and officials, the ones near, magnificently dressed, horsemen riding on horses, all of them desirable young men. 2 Kin. 16:7

13"And I saw that she had defiled herself; they both took the same way.   *one*

14"So she increased her harlotries. And she saw men portrayed on the wall, images of the Chaldeans portrayed with vermilion,

15 girded with belts on their loins, with flowing turbans on their heads, all of them looking like officers, like the^TBabylonians *in* Chaldea, the land of their birth. *sons of Babel*

16"And^Twhen she saw them she^Rlusted after them and sent messengers to them in Chaldea.   *at the sight of her eyes* • Ezek. 23:20

17"And the^TBabylonians^R came to her to the bed of love, and they defiled her with their harlotry. And when she had been defiled by them,^Tshe became disgusted with them.   *sons of Babel* • 2 Kin. 24:17 • *her soul*

18"And she uncovered her harlotries and uncovered her nakedness; then ^TI became disgusted with her, as I had become disgusted with her^Rsister.   *My soul* • Ezek. 23:9

19"Yet she multiplied her harlotries, remembering the days of her youth, when she played the harlot in the land of Egypt.

20"And she lusted after their paramours, whose flesh is *like* the flesh of donkeys and whose issue is *like* the issue of horses.

21"Thus you longed for the^Rlewdness of your youth, when the Egyptians handled your bosom because of the breasts of your youth.   Jer. 3:9; Ezek. 23:3

22"Therefore, O Oholibah, thus says the Lord GOD, 'Behold I will arouse your lovers against you, from whom^Tyou were alienated, and I will bring them against you from every side: *your soul was alienated*

23 the Babylonians and all the Chaldeans, Pekod and Shoa and Koa, *and* all the Assyrians with them; desirable young men, governors and officials all of them, officers and men of renown, all of them riding on horses.

24 'And they will come against you with weapons, chariots, and wagons, and with a company of peoples. They will set themselves against you on every side with buckler and shield and helmet; and I shall commit the judgment to them, and they will judge you according to their customs.

25 'And I will set My jealousy against you, that they may deal with you in wrath. They will remove your nose and your ears; and your survivors will fall by the sword. They will take your sons and your daughters; and your survivors will be consumed by the fire.

26 'They will also strip you of your clothes and take away your beautiful jewels.

27 'Thus^RI shall make your lewdness and your harlotry *brought* from the land of Egypt to cease from you, so that you will

not lift up your eyes to them or remember Egypt anymore.'   Ezek. 16:41

28"For thus says the Lord GOD, 'Behold, I will give you into the hand of those whom you hate, into the hand of those from whom ^Tyou were alienated.   *your soul was alienated*

29 'And they will^Rdeal with you in hatred, take all your property, and leave you naked and bare. And the nakedness of your harlotries shall be uncovered, both your lewdness and your harlotries.   Deut. 28:48; Ezek. 23:25

30 'These things will be done to you because you have^Rplayed the harlot with the nations, because you have defiled yourself with their idols.   Ezek. 6:9

31 'You have walked in the way of your sister; therefore I will give^Rher cup into your hand.'   2 Kin. 21:13; Jer. 7:14, 15, Ezek. 23:33

32"Thus says the Lord GOD,
'You will^Rdrink your sister's cup,
Which is deep and wide.   Ps. 60:3
You will be^Rlaughed at and held in derision;   Ezek. 5:14, 15; 16:57; 22:4, 5
It contains much.

33 'You will be filled with^Rdrunkenness
and sorrow,   Jer. 25:15, 16, 27
The cup of horror and desolation,
The cup of your sister Samaria.

34 'And you will^Rdrink it and drain it.
Then you will gnaw its fragments
And tear your breasts;   Ps. 75:8
for I have spoken,' declares the Lord GOD.

35"Therefore, thus says the Lord GOD, 'Because you have forgotten Me and cast Me behind your back, bear now the *punishment* of your lewdness and your harlotries.'"

36 Moreover, the LORD said to me, "Son of man, will you^Rjudge Oholah and Oholibah? Then^Rdeclare to them their abominations.   Jer. 1:10; Ezek. 20:4; 22:2 • Is. 58:1

37"For they have committed adultery, and blood is on their hands. Thus they have committed adultery with their idols and even caused their sons, whom they bore to Me, to pass through *the fire* to them as food.

38"Again, they have done this to Me: they have^Rdefiled My sanctuary on the same day and have profaned My sabbaths.   Ezek. 5:11

39"For when they had slaughtered their children for their idols, they entered My ^Rsanctuary on the same day to profane it; and lo, thus they did within My house.   Jer. 7:9-11

40"Furthermore, they have even sent for men who come from afar, to whom a messenger was sent; and lo, they came—for whom you bathed, painted your eyes, and decorated yourselves with ornaments;

41 and you sat on a splendid^Rcouch with a table arranged before it, on which you had set My incense and My oil.   Esth. 1:6; Is. 57:7

42"And the sound of a^Tcarefree multitude was with her; and drunkards were brought from the wilderness with men of the^Tcommon sort. And they put bracelets on the hands of the women and beautiful crowns on their heads.   *at ease* • *multitude of mankind*

43"Then I said concerning her who was

worn out by adulteries, 'Will they now commit adultery with her when she is *thus*?'

44 "But[A]they went in to her as they would go in to a harlot. Thus they went in to Oholah and to Oholibah, the lewd women.   *And*

45 "But they, righteous men, will [R]judge them with the judgment of adulteresses, and with the judgment of women who shed blood, because they are adulteresses and blood is on their hands.   Ezek. 16:38

46 "For thus says the Lord GOD, 'Bring up a company against them, and give them over to[R]terror and plunder.   Jer. 15:4; 24:9; 29:18

47 'And the company will stone them with stones and cut them down with their swords; they will slay their sons and their daughters and burn their houses with fire.

48 'Thus I shall make lewdness cease from the land, that all women may be admonished and not commit[T]lewdness as you have done.   *according to your lewdness*

49 'And your lewdness [T]will be requited upon you, and you will bear the penalty of *worshiping* your idols; thus you will know that I am the Lord GOD.' "   *they will give*

CHAPTER 24

Parable of the Boiling Pot

A ND the word of the LORD came to me in the ninth year, in the tenth month, on the tenth of the month, saying,

2 "Son of man, write the name of the day, this very day. The king of Babylon[T]has laid siege to Jerusalem this very day.   *leaned on*

3 "And speak a[R]parable to the[R]rebellious house, and say to them, 'Thus says the Lord GOD,   Ps. 78:2; Ezek. 17:2; 20:49 • Ezek. 2:3, 6, 8

"Put on the[R]pot, put *it* on, and also pour water in it;   Ezek. 11:3, 7, 11; 24:6

4   Put[R]in it the pieces,
Every good piece, the thigh, and the shoulder;   Mic. 3:2, 3
Fill *it* with choice bones.

5   "Take the choicest of the flock,
And also pile[T]wood under the pot.
Make it boil vigorously.   *bones*
Also seethe its bones in it."

6   'Therefore, thus says the Lord GOD,
"Woe to the[R]bloody city,   2 Kin. 24:3, 4
To the pot in which there is rust
And whose rust has not gone out of it!
Take out of it piece after piece,
Without making a choice.

7   "For her blood is in her midst;
She placed it on the bare rock;
She did not[R]pour it on the ground
To cover it with dust.   Lev. 17:13

8   "That it may[R]cause wrath to come up to take vengeance,   Is. 26:21
I have put her blood on the bare rock,
That it may not be covered."

9   'Therefore, thus says the Lord GOD,
"Woe[T]to the bloody city!   Ezek. 24:6
I also shall make the pile great.

10   "Heap on the wood, kindle the fire,
[T]Boil the flesh well,   *Complete*
And mix in the spices,
And let the bones be burned.

11   "Then[R]set it empty on its coals,
So that it may be hot,   Mal. 4:1
And its bronze may[T]glow,   *become hot*
And its[R]filthiness may be melted in it,
Its rust consumed.   Ezek. 22:15; 23:27

12   "She has[R]wearied *Me* with toil,
Yet her great rust has not gone from her;   Jer. 9:5
Let her rust *be* in the fire!

13   "In your filthiness is lewdness.
Because I *would* have cleansed you,
Yet you are[R]not clean,   Jer. 6:28-30
You will not be cleansed from your filthiness again,
Until I have spent My wrath on you.

14 "I, the LORD, have spoken; it is coming and I shall act. I shall not relent, and I shall not pity, and I shall not be sorry; according to your ways and according to your deeds I shall judge you," declares the Lord GOD.' "

Sign Through the Death of Ezekiel's Wife

15 And the word of the LORD came to me saying,

16 "Son of man, behold, I am about to take from you the desire of your eyes with a blow; but you shall not mourn, and you shall not weep, and your tears shall not come.

17 "Groan silently; make no mourning for the dead. Bind on your turban, and put your shoes on your feet, and do not cover *your* mustache, and do not eat the bread of men."

18 So I spoke to the people in the morning, and in the evening my wife died. And in the morning I did as I was commanded.

19 And the people said to me, "Will you not tell us what these things that you are doing mean for us?"

20 Then I said to them, "The word of the LORD came to me saying,

21 'Speak to the house of Israel, "Thus says the Lord GOD, 'Behold, I am about to profane My sanctuary, the pride of your power, the[R]desire of your eyes, and the delight of your soul; and your sons and your daughters whom you have left behind will fall by the sword.   Ps. 27:4; 84:1; Ezek. 24:16

22 'And you will do as I have done; you will not cover *your* mustache, and you will not eat the bread of men.

23 'And your turbans will be on your heads and your shoes on your feet. You will not mourn, and you will not weep; but you will rot away in your iniquities, and you will groan[T]to one another.   *a man to his brother*

24 'Thus Ezekiel will be[R]a sign to you; according to all that he has done you will do; when it comes, then you will know that I am the Lord GOD.' "   Ezek. 4:3; Luke 11:29, 30

25 'As for you, son of man, will *it* not be on the day when I take from them their[R]strong-

hold, the joy of their ^pride, the desire of their eyes, and their heart's delight, their sons and their daughters, Ps. 48:2 · *beauty*

26 that on that day he who escapes will come to you with information for *your* ears?

27 'On that day your^mouth will be opened to him who escaped, and you will speak and be dumb no longer. Thus you will be a sign to them, and they will know that I am the LORD.' " Ezek. 3:26; 33:22

CHAPTER 25

Judgment on Ammon

AND the word of the LORD came to me saying,

2"Son of man, set your face toward the ^sons of Ammon, and prophesy against them, Jer. 49:1-6; Amos 1:13-15; Zeph. 2:9

3 and say to the sons of Ammon, 'Hear the word of the Lord GOD! Thus says the Lord GOD, "Because you said,^"Aha!' against My sanctuary when it was profaned, and against the land of Israel when it was made desolate, and against the house of Judah when they went into exile, Ps. 70:2, 3

4 therefore, behold, I am going to give you to the sons of the east for a possession, and they will set their encampments among you and make their dwellings among you; they will eat your fruit and drink your milk.

5"And I shall make^Rabbah a pasture for camels and the sons of Ammon a resting place for flocks. Thus you will know that I am the LORD." Deut. 3:11; 2 Sam. 12:26; Jer. 49:2

6 'For thus says the Lord GOD, "Because you have clapped your hands and stamped your feet and rejoiced with all the scorn of your soul against the land of Israel,

7 therefore, behold, I have^stretched out My hand against you, and I shall give you for spoil to the nations. And I shall cut you off from the peoples and make you perish from the lands; I shall destroy you. Thus you will know that I am the LORD." Zeph. 1:4

Judgment on Moab

8 'Thus says the Lord GOD, "Because ^Moab and Seir say, 'Behold, the house of Judah is like all the nations,' Is. 15:1; Jer. 48:1

9 therefore, behold, I am going to ^deprive the flank of Moab of *its* cities, of its cities which are on its^frontiers, the glory of the land, Beth-jeshimoth, Baal-meon, and ^Kiriathaim, *open · end* · Num. 32:37; Josh. 13:19

10 and I will give it for a possession, along with the sons of Ammon, to the^sons of the east, that the sons of Ammon may not be remembered among the nations. Ezek. 25:4

11"Thus I will execute judgments on Moab, and they will know that I am the LORD."

Judgment on Edom

12 'Thus says the Lord GOD, "Because ^Edom has acted against the house of Judah by taking vengeance, and has incurred grievous guilt, and avenged themselves upon them," 2 Chr. 28:17; Ps. 137:7; Jer. 49:7-22

13 therefore, thus says the Lord GOD, "I will also stretch out My hand against Edom and cut off man and beast from it. And I will lay it waste; from^Teman even to Dedan they will fall by the sword. Gen. 36:34

14"And^I will lay My vengeance on Edom by the hand of My people Israel. Therefore, they will act in Edom^according to My anger and according to My wrath; thus they will know My vengeance," declares the Lord GOD. Is. 11:14 · Ezek. 35:11

Judgment on Philistia

15 'Thus says the Lord GOD, "Because the Philistines have acted in^revenge and have taken vengeance with scorn of soul to destroy with everlasting enmity," Joel 3:4

16 therefore, thus says the Lord GOD, "Behold, I will stretch out My hand against the Philistines, even cut off the Cherethites and destroy the remnant of the seacoast.

17"And I will execute great vengeance on them with wrathful rebukes; and they will ^know that I am the LORD when I lay My vengeance on them." ' " Ps. 9:16

CHAPTER 26

Destruction of Tyre

NOW it came about in the eleventh year, on the first of the month, that the word of the LORD came to me saying,

2"Son of man, because Tyre has said concerning Jerusalem, 'Aha, the gateway of the peoples is broken; it has opened to me. I shall be filled, *now that* she is laid waste,'

3 therefore, thus says the Lord GOD, 'Behold, I am against you, O Tyre, and I will bring up many nations against you, as the ^sea brings up its waves. Is. 5:30; Jer. 50:42

4 'And they will^destroy the walls of Tyre and break down her towers; and I will scrape her debris from her and make her a bare rock. Is. 23:11; Ezek. 26:9; Amos 1:10

5 'She will be a place for the spreading of nets in the midst of the sea, for I have spoken,' declares the Lord GOD, 'and she will become^spoil for the nations. Ezek. 25:7; 29:19

6 'Also her daughters who are on the mainland will be slain by the sword, and they will know that I am the LORD.' "

7 For thus says the Lord GOD, "Behold, I will bring upon Tyre from the north Nebuchadnezzar king of Babylon,^king of kings, with horses, chariots, cavalry, and^a great army. Ezra 7:12 · *an assembly, even many people*

8"He will slay your daughters ^Ton the mainland with the sword; and he will make ^Rsiege walls against you, cast up a mound against you, and raise up a large shield against you.   *in the field* • Jer. 52:4; Ezek. 21:22

9"And the blow of his battering rams he will direct against your walls, and with his axes he will break down your towers.

10"Because of the multitude of his horses, the dust *raised by* them will cover you; your walls will shake at the noise of cavalry and wagons and chariots, when he enters your gates as men enter a city that is breached.

11"With the hoofs of his ^Rhorses he will trample all your streets. He will slay your people with the sword; and your strong pillars will come down to the ground. Is. 5:28

12"Also they will make a spoil of your riches and a prey of your merchandise, break down your walls and destroy your pleasant houses, and throw your stones and your timbers and your debris into the water.

13"So I will ^Tsilence the sound of your songs, and the sound of your ^Rharps will be heard no more. *cause to cease* • Rev. 18:22

14"And I will make you a bare rock; you will be a place for the spreading of nets. You will be built no more, for I the ^RLORD have spoken," declares the Lord GOD. Is. 14:27

15 Thus says the Lord GOD to Tyre, "Shall not the coastlands shake at the sound of your fall when the wounded groan, when the slaughter occurs in your midst?

16"Then all the princes of the sea will go down from their thrones, remove their robes, and strip off their embroidered garments. They will clothe themselves with trembling; they will sit on the ground, tremble every moment, and be appalled at you.

17"And they will take up a ^Rlamentation over you and say to you, Ezek. 19:1, 14; 27:2, 32
'How^Ryou have perished, O inhabited one, Is. 14:12; Jer. 48:39; 50:23
From the seas, O renowned city,
Which was^Rmighty on the sea,
She and her inhabitants, Ezek. 27:3, 10
Who^Timposed^Ther terror *put • their*
On all her inhabitants!
18 'Now the^Rcoastlands will tremble
On the day of your fall; Is. 41:5
Yes, the coastlands which are by the sea
Will be terrified at your passing.' "

19 For thus says the Lord GOD, "When I shall make you a desolate city, like the cities which are not inhabited, when I shall^Rbring up the deep over you, and the great waters will cover you, Is. 8:7, 8; Ezek. 26:3

20 then I shall bring you down with those who go down to the pit, to the people of old, and I shall make you dwell in the lower parts of the earth, like the ancient waste places, with those who go down to the pit, so that you will not^Rbe inhabited; but I shall set glory in the land of the living. *return*

21"I shall^Tbring terrors on you, and you will be no more; though you will be sought,

^Ryou will never be found again," declares the Lord GOD. *give you terrors* • Rev. 18:21

CHAPTER 27

Lament over Tyre

MOREOVER, the word of the LORD came to me saying,

2"And you, son of man,^Rtake up a lamentation over Tyre; Jer. 9:10, 17-20; Ezek. 28:12

3 and say to Tyre,^Rwho dwells at the^Tentrance to the sea, merchant of the peoples to many coastlands, 'Thus says the Lord GOD, "O Tyre, you have said, 'I am perfect in beauty.' Ezek. 28:2 • *entrances*

4 "Your borders are in the heart of the seas;
Your builders have perfected your beauty.

5 "They have^Tmade all *your* planks of fir trees from^RSenir; *built* • Deut. 3:9
They have taken a cedar from Lebanon to make a mast for you.

6 "Of^Roaks from^RBashan they have made your oars; Is. 2:13; Zech. 11:2 • Is. 2:13
With ivory they have^Tinlaid your deck of boxwood from the coastlands of ^RCyprus. *made* • Is. 23:1, 12; Jer. 2:10

7 "Your sail was of fine embroidered linen from Egypt
So that it became your^Adistinguishing mark; *standard*
Your awning was blue and purple from the coastlands of Elishah.

8 "The inhabitants of Sidon and ^RArvad were your rowers; Gen. 10:18
Your wise men, O Tyre, were^Taboard; they were your pilots. *in you*

9 "The elders of^RGebal and her wise men were with you repairing your seams; Josh. 13:5; 1 Kin. 5:18
All the ships of the sea and their sailors were with you in order to deal in your merchandise.

10"Persia^Rand Lud and Put were in your army, your men of war. They hung shield and helmet in you; they set forth your splendor. Ezek. 30:5; 38:5

11"The sons of Arvad and your army were on your walls, *all* around, and the^AGammadim were in your towers. They hung their shields on your walls, *all* around; they perfected your beauty. *valorous ones*

12"Tarshish was your customer because of the abundance of all *kinds* of wealth; with silver, iron, tin, and lead, they paid for your wares.

13"Javan,^RTubal, and Meshech, they were your traders; with the^Rlives of men and vessels of bronze they paid for your merchandise. Gen. 10:2; Is. 66:19; Ezek. 27:19 • Joel 3:3

14"Those from ^RBeth-togarmah gave horses and war horses and mules for your wares. Gen. 10:3; Ezek. 39:6

15"The sons of^RDedan were your traders.

Many coastlands were^Tyour market; ivory tusks and ebony they brought as your payment. Jer. 25:23 · *the market of your hand*

16"Aram was your customer because of the abundance of your goods; they paid for your wares with emeralds, purple, embroidered work, fine linen, coral, and rubies.

17"Judah and the land of Israel, they were your traders; with the wheat of ^RMinnith, ^Tcakes, honey, oil, and balm they paid for your merchandise. Judg. 11:33 · *pannag*

18"Damascus was your customer because of the abundance of your goods, because of the abundance of all *kinds* of wealth, because of the wine of Helbon and white wool.

19"Vedan and Javan paid for your wares from Uzal; wrought iron, cassia, and sweet cane were among your merchandise.

20"Dedan^Rtraded with you in saddlecloths for riding. Gen. 25:3

21"Arabia^Rand all the princes of Kedar, they were^Tyour customers for^Rlambs, rams, and goats; for these they were your customers. Is. 21:13 · *customers of your hand* · Is. 60:7

22"The traders of ^RSheba and Raamah, they traded with you; they paid for your wares with the best of all *kinds* of ^Rspices, and with all *kinds* of precious stones, and gold. Gen. 10:7; Is. 60:6 · Gen. 43:11

23"Haran, Canneh, ^REden, the traders of Sheba, Asshur, *and* Chilmad traded with you. 2 Kin. 19:12; Is. 37:12; Amos 1:5

24"They traded with you in choice garments, in clothes of^Ablue and embroidered work, and in carpets of many colors, *and* tightly wound cords, *which were* among your merchandise. *violet*

25"The^Rships of Tarshish were^Tthe carriers for your merchandise. Is. 2:16 · *your travelers*
And you were filled and were very^Tglorious *honored*
In the heart of the seas.

26"Your rowers have brought you
Into^Rgreat waters; Ezek. 26:19
The^Reast wind has broken you Ps. 48:7
In the heart of the seas.
27"Your wealth, your wares, your merchandise,
Your sailors, and your pilots,
Your repairers of seams, your dealers in merchandise,
And all your men of war who are in you,
With all your company that is in your midst,
Will fall into the heart of the seas
On the day of your overthrow.
28"At the sound of the cry of your pilots
The pasture lands will^Rshake. Ezek. 26:10
29"And all who handle the oar,
The^Rsailors, *and* all the pilots of the sea
Will come down from their ships;
They will stand on the land, Rev. 18:17
30 And they will^Rmake their voice heard over you Is. 23:1-6; Ezek. 26:17

And will cry bitterly.
They will^Rcast dust on their heads,
They will wallow in ashes. 1 Sam. 4:12
31"Also they will make themselves^Rbald for you Is. 15:2; Ezek. 29:18
And^Rgird themselves with sackcloth;
And they will^Rweep for you in bitterness of soul Ezek. 7:18 · Is. 16:9; 22:4
With bitter mourning.
32"Moreover, in their wailing they will take up a^Rlamentation for you
And lament over you:
'Who is like Tyre, Ezek. 26:17; 27:2; 28:12
Like her who is silent in the midst of the sea?
33 'When your wares went out from the seas,
You satisfied many peoples;
With the ^Rabundance of your wealth and your merchandise Ezek. 27:12
You enriched the kings of earth.
34 'Now^Tthat you are broken by the seas
In the depths of the waters, *The time*
Your^Rmerchandise and all your company Zech. 9:3, 4
Have fallen in the midst of you.
35 'All the^Rinhabitants of the coastlands
Are appalled at you, Ezek. 26:16
And their kings are horribly afraid;
They are troubled in countenance.
36 'The merchants among the peoples^Rhiss at you; Jer. 18:16; 19:8; 49:17; 50:13
You have become^Tterrified, *terrors*
And you will be no more.' " ' "

CHAPTER 28

Fall of the King of Tyre

THE word of the LORD came again to me saying,
2"Son of man, say to the^Aleader of Tyre,
'Thus says the Lord GOD, *ruler, prince*
"Because your heart is lifted up
And you have said, 'I^Tam a god,
I sit in the seat of^Agods, Is. 14:14 · *God*
In the heart of the seas';
Yet you are a^Aman and not God,
Although you make your heart like the heart of God— Ps. 9:20; 82:6, 7
3 Behold, you are wiser than^RDaniel;
There is no secret that is a match for you. [Dan. 1:20; 2:20-23, 28; 5:11, 12]
4"By your wisdom and understanding
You have acquired^Rriches for yourself,
And have acquired gold and silver for your treasuries. Zech. 9:2, 3
5"By your great wisdom, by your^Rtrade
You have increased your riches,
And your heart is lifted up because of your riches— Ezek. 27:12; Hos. 12:7
6 Therefore, thus says the Lord GOD,
'Because you have^Rmade your heart
Like the heart of God, Ezek. 28:2
7 Therefore, behold, I will bring^Rstrangers upon you, Ezek. 26:7

The ᴿmost ruthless of the nations.
And they will draw their swords
Against the beauty of your wisdom
And defile your splendor.   Ezek. 30:11
8 'They will bring you down to the pit,
And you will die the ᴿdeath of those
who are slain   Ezek. 27:26, 27, 34
In the heart of the seas.
9 'Will you still say, "I am a god,"
In the presence of your slayer,
Although you are a man and not God,
In the hands of those who wound you?
10 'You will die the death of the ᴿuncircum-
cised 1 Sam. 17:26, 36; Ezek. 31:18; 32:30
By the hand of strangers,
For I have spoken!' declares the Lord
GOD!" ' "
11 Again the word of the LORD came to
me saying,
12 "Son of man, ᴿtake up a lamentation over
the king of Tyre, and say to him, 'Thus says
the Lord GOD,   Ezek. 19:1; 26:17; 27:2
"You had the seal of perfection,
Full of wisdom and perfect in beauty.
13 "You were in ᴿEden, the garden of God;
ᴿEvery precious stone was your cover-
ing: Gen. 2:8 • Ezek. 27:16, 22
The ᴿruby, the topaz, and the diamond;
The beryl, the onyx, and the jasper;
The lapis lazuli, the turquoise, and the
emerald;   Ex. 28:17-20
And the gold, the workmanship of your
ᴬsettings ᴿand sockets,
Was in you.   tambourines • Is. 24:8; 30:32
On the day that you were created
They were prepared.
14 "You were the ᴿanointed cherub who
ᴬcovers,   Ex. 25:17-20 • guards
And I placed you there.
You were on the holy ᴬmountain of God;
You walked in the midst of the ᴿstones
of fire.   Ezek. 20:40 • Ezek. 28:13, 16
15 "You were ᴿblameless in your ways
From the day you were created,
Until unrighteousness was found in
you.   Ezek. 27:3, 4; 28:3-6, 12
16 "By the abundance of your trade
You were internally ᴿfilled with vio-
lence,
And you sinned;   Ezek. 8:17
Therefore I have cast you as profane
From the mountain of God.
And I have destroyed you, O ᴬcovering
cherub,   guardian
From the midst of the stones of fire.
17 "Your heart was lifted up because of
your ᴿbeauty;   Ezek. 27:3, 4; 28:7
You ᴿcorrupted your wisdom by reason
of your splendor.   Is. 19:11
I cast you to the ground;
I put you before ᴿkings,   Ezek. 26:16
That they may see you.
18 "By the multitude of your iniquities,
In the unrighteousness of your trade,
You profaned your sanctuaries.
Therefore I have brought ᴿfire from the
midst of you;   Amos 1:9, 10

It has consumed you,
And I have turned you to ᴿashes on the
earth   Mal. 4:3
In the eyes of all who see you.
19 "All who know you among the peoples
Are appalled at you;
You have become ᵀterrified,   terrors
And you will be ᴿno more." ' "   Jer. 51:64

Judgment on Sidon

20 And the word of the LORD came to me
saying,
21 "Son of man, ᴿset your face toward Si-
don, prophesy against her,   Ezek. 6:2; 25:2
22 and say, 'Thus says the Lord GOD,
"Behold, I am against you, O Sidon,
And I shall ᴬbe glorified in your midst.
Then they will know that I am the
LORD, when I ᴿexecute judgments in
her,   glorify Myself • Ezek. 28:26
And I shall manifest My holiness in
her.
23 "For ᴿI shall send pestilence to her
And blood to her streets,   Ezek. 38:22
And the ᴿwounded will ᴬfall in her midst
By the sword upon her on every side;
Then they will know that I am the
LORD.   Jer. 51:52 • be judged
24 "And there will be no more for the
house of Israel a ᴿprickling brier or a painful
thorn from any round about them who
scorned them; then they will know that I am
the Lord GOD." Num. 33:55; Josh. 23:13; Is. 55:13
25 'Thus says the Lord GOD, "When I
gather the house of Israel from the peoples
among whom they are scattered, and shall
manifest My holiness in them in the sight of
the nations, then they will live in their ᵀland
which I gave to My servant Jacob.   ground
26 "And they will ᴿlive in it securely; and
they will build houses, plant vineyards, and
live securely, when I execute judgments
upon all who scorn them round about them.
Then they will know that I am the LORD
their God." ' "   Jer. 23:6; Ezek. 34:25-28; 38:8

CHAPTER 29

Egypt to Be Desolate

IN the ᴿtenth year, in the tenth *month,* on
the twelfth of the month, the word of the
LORD came to me saying,   Ezek. 26:1; 29:17
2 "Son of man, set your face against ᴿPha-
raoh, king of Egypt, and prophesy against
him and against all Egypt.   Jer. 44:30
3 "Speak and say, 'Thus says the Lord
GOD,
"Behold, I am against you, Pharaoh,
king of Egypt,
The great ᵀmonster ᴿthat lies in the midst
of his ᴿrivers,   tannim • Is. 27:1 • Nile
That ᴿhas said, 'My Nile is mine, and I
myself have made it.'   Ezek. 29:9

4"And I shall put^Rhooks in your jaws,
And I shall make the fish of your^Arivers
cling to your scales.
And I shall bring you up out of the
midst of your rivers,
And all the fish of your rivers will cling
to your scales.   2 Kin. 19:28 • *Nile*
5"And I shall^Rabandon you to the wilderness, you and all the fish of your
^Arivers;   Ezek. 32:4-6 • *Nile*
You will fall on the^Topen field; you will
not be brought together or ^Rgath-
ered.   *faces of the field* • Jer. 8:2; 25:33
I have given you for^Rfood to the beasts
of the earth and to the birds of the
sky.   Jer. 7:33; 34:20; Ezek. 39:4
6"Then all the inhabitants of Egypt will
know that I am the LORD,
Because they have been *only* a staff
made of reed to the house of Israel.
7"When they took hold of you with the
hand,
You^Rbroke and tore all their hands;
And when they leaned on you,
You broke and made all their loins
^Tquake."   2 Kin. 18:21; Is. 36:6 • *stand*
8 'Therefore, thus says the Lord GOD,
"Behold, I shall bring upon you a sword, and
I shall cut off from you man and beast.
9"And the^Rland of Egypt will become a
desolation and waste. Then they will know
that I am the LORD.   Ezek. 29:10-12; 30:7, 8
Because^Tyou^Rsaid, 'The Nile is mine, and I
have made *it*,'   *he* • Prov. 16:18; 18:12; Ezek. 29:3
10 therefore, behold, I am^Ragainst you and
against your^Arivers, and I will make the land
of Egypt an utter waste and desolation,
from Migdol *to* Syene and even to the bor-
der of^TEthiopia.   Ezek. 13:8; 21:3 • *Nile* • *Cush*
11"A man's foot will^Rnot pass through it,
and the foot of a beast will not pass through
it, and it will not be inhabited for forty
years.   Jer. 43:11, 12; 46:19; Ezek. 32:13
12"So I shall make the land of Egypt a
desolation in the midst of desolated lands.
And her cities, in the midst of cities that are
laid waste, will be desolate forty years; and
I shall scatter the Egyptians among the nations and disperse them among the lands."
13 'For thus says the Lord GOD, "At the
end of forty years I shall ^Rgather the Egyptians from the peoples ^Tamong whom they
were scattered.   Is. 19:22; Jer. 46:26 • *where*
14"And I shall turn the fortunes of Egypt
and shall make them return to the land of
^RPathros, to the land of their origin; and there
they will be a lowly kingdom.   Is. 11:11
15"It will be the lowest of the kingdoms;
and it will never again lift itself up above
the nations. And I shall make them so small
that they will not rule over the nations.
16"And it will never again be the confidence of the house of Israel, ^Tbringing to
mind the iniquity of their having turned^Tto
Egypt. Then they will know that I am the
Lord GOD." ' "   *causing to remember* • *after them*

Egypt to Be Taken by Babylon

17 Now in the twenty-seventh year, in the
first *month*, on the first of the month, the
word of the LORD came to me saying,
18"Son of man, Nebuchadnezzar king of
Babylon made his army labor hard against
Tyre; every head was made bald, and every
shoulder was rubbed bare. But he and his
army had no wages from Tyre for the labor
that he had^Tperformed against it."   *labored*
19 Therefore, thus says the Lord GOD,
"Behold, I^Rshall give the land of Egypt to
Nebuchadnezzar king of Babylon. And he
will carry off her^Awealth, and capture her
spoil and seize her plunder; and it will be
wages for his army.   Ezek. 30:10, 24 • *multitude*
20"I have given him the land of Egypt *for*
his labor which he performed, because they
acted for Me," declares the Lord GOD.
21"On that day I shall make a^Rhorn sprout
for the house of Israel, and I shall^Ropen your
mouth in their midst. Then they will know
that I am the LORD."   1 Sam. 2:10 • Ezek. 3:27

CHAPTER 30

Egypt to Be Destroyed

THE word of the LORD came again to me
saying,
2"Son of man, prophesy and say, 'Thus
says the Lord GOD,
"Wail,^R 'Alas for the day!'   Is. 13:6; 15:2
3 "For the day is near,
Even^Rthe day of the LORD is near;
It will be a day of clouds,   Ezek. 7:19
A time *of doom* for the nations.
4 "And a sword will come upon Egypt,
And anguish will be in Ethiopia,
When the slain fall in Egypt,
They take away her^Awealth,   *multitude*
And her foundations are torn down.
5"Ethiopia, Put, Lud, all Arabia, Libya,
and the^Tpeople of the land that is in league
will fall with them by the sword."   *sons*
6 'Thus says the LORD,
"Indeed, those who support^REgypt will
fall,
And the pride of her power will come
down;
From Migdol *to* Syene
They will fall within her by the
sword,"
Declares the Lord GOD.   Is. 20:3-6
7 "And they will be desolate
In the^Rmidst of the desolated lands;
And her cities will be   Jer. 25:18-26
In the midst of the devastated cities.
8 "And they will^Rknow that I am the
LORD,   Ps. 58:11; Ezek. 29:6, 9, 16
When I set a^Rfire in Egypt   Ezek. 22:31
And all her helpers are broken.
9"On that day messengers will go forth
from Me in ships to frighten secure ^TEthi-
opia; and anguish will be on them as on the
day of Egypt; for, behold, it comes!"   *Cush*

10 'Thus says the Lord God,
  "I [R] will also make the ^multitude of
   Egypt cease
   By the hand of Nebuchadnezzar king
   of Babylon.   Ezek. 29:19 • *wealth*
11 "He and his people with him,
   [R]The most ruthless of the nations,
   Will be brought in to destroy the land;
   And they will draw their swords
   against Egypt   Ezek. 28:7
   And fill the land with the slain.
12 "Moreover, I will make the[R]Nile canals
   dry   Ezek. 29:3, 9
   And[R]sell the land into the hands of
   evil men.   Is. 19:4
   And I will make the land desolate,
   And[T]all that is in it,   *her fulness*
   By the hand of strangers; I, the Lord,
   have spoken."

13 'Thus says the Lord God,
   "I will also[R]destroy the idols   Is. 2:18
   And make the images cease from
   Memphis.[R]   Is. 19:13; Jer. 2:16
   And there will no longer be a prince in
   the land of Egypt;
   And I will put fear in the land of
   Egypt.
14 "And I will make[R]Pathros desolate,
   Set a fire in Zoan,   Is. 11:11; Jer. 44:1, 15
   And execute judgments on [2]Thebes.
15 "And I will pour out My wrath on [3]Sin,
   The stronghold of Egypt;
   I will also cut off the multitude of
   ^Thebes.   *No*
16 "And I will set a fire in Egypt;
   ^Sin will writhe in anguish,
   ^Thebes will be breached,
   And [4]Memphis *will have* ^distresses
   daily.   *Pelusium • No • adversaries*
17 "The young men of [5]On[R]and of Pi-
   beseth   Gen. 41:45; 46:20
   Will fall by the sword,
   And the women will go into captivity.
18 "And in[R]Tehaphnehes the day will be
   [R]dark   Jer. 43:8-13 • Ezek. 30:3
   When I[R]break there the yoke bars of
   Egypt.   Lev. 26:13; Is. 10:27; Jer. 27:2
   Then the pride of her power will cease
   in her;
   A cloud will cover her,
   And her daughters will go into captivity.
19 "Thus I will [R]execute judgments on
   Egypt,
   And they will know that I am the
   Lord." ' "   Ezek. 5:8, 15; 25:11; 30:14
20 And it came about in the[R]eleventh year,
in the first *month*, on the seventh of the
month, that the word of the Lord came to
me saying,   Ezek. 26:1; 29:1, 17; 31:1
21 "Son of man, I have[R]broken the arm of
Pharaoh king of Egypt; and, behold, it has
not been bound up[T]for healing or wrapped
with a bandage, that it may be strong to
hold the sword. Ps. 10:15; 37:17 • *to give healing*
22 "Therefore, thus says the Lord God, 'Behold, I am [R]against Pharaoh king of Egypt
and will break his arms, both the strong and
the[R]broken; and I will make the sword fall
from his hand. Jer. 46:25; Ezek. 29:3 • 2 Kin. 24:7
23 'And I will[R]scatter the Egyptians among
the nations and disperse them among the
lands.   Ezek. 29:12; 30:17, 18, 26
24 'For I will[R]strengthen the arms of the
king of Babylon and put My sword in his
hand; and I will break the arms of Pharaoh,
so that he will groan before him with the
groanings of a wounded man.   Zech. 10:12
25 'Thus I will strengthen the arms of the
king of Babylon, but the arms of Pharaoh
will fall. Then they will know that I am the
Lord, when I put My sword into the hand of
the king of Babylon and he[R]stretches it out
against the land of Egypt.   Josh. 8:18
26 'When I scatter the Egyptians among
the nations and disperse them among the
lands, then they will know that I am the
Lord.' "

CHAPTER 31

Egypt Is Cut Down Like Assyria

And it came about in the[R]eleventh year, in
the third *month*, on the first of the month,
that the word of the Lord came to me saying,   Jer. 52:5, 6; Ezek. 30:20; 32:1
2 "Son of man, say to Pharaoh king of
Egypt, and to his[R]multitude, Ezek. 29:19; 30:10
   'Whom are you like in your greatness?
3 'Behold, Assyria *was* a[R]cedar in Lebanon   Is. 10:33, 34; Ezek. 17:3, 4, 22; 31:16
   With beautiful branches and forest
   shade,
   And[T]very[R]high;   *high of stature* • Is. 10:33
   And its top was among the clouds.
4 'The waters made it grow, the[T]deep
   made it high.   *subterranean waters*
   With its rivers it continually[T]extended
   all around its planting place,
   And it sent out its channels to all the
   trees of the field.   *was going*
5 'Therefore[R]its height was loftier than
   all the trees of the field   Dan. 4:11
   And its boughs became many and its
   branches long
   Because of[R]many waters[T]as it spread
   them out.   Ps. 1:3 • *in its sending forth*
6 'All the[R]birds of the heavens nested in
   its boughs,
   And under its branches all the beasts
   of the field gave birth,
   And all great nations lived under its
   shade.   Dan. 4:12, 21; Matt. 13:32
7 'So it was beautiful in its greatness, in
   the length of its branches;
   For its[T]roots extended to many waters.   *root was*
8 'The[R]cedars in God's garden[T]could not
   match it;   Ps. 80:10; Ezek. 31:3 • *did*

[2] Or, *No*   [3] Or, *Pelusium*   [4] Or, *Noph*   [5] Or, *Aven*

The ^cypresses could not compare
with its boughs,   *Phoenician junipers*
And the plane trees^could not match
its branches.   *were not like*
No tree in ^God's garden could compare with it in its beauty.   Ezek. 28:13
9 'I made it beautiful with the multitude
of its branches,
And all the trees of^Eden, which were
in the garden of God, were jealous
of it.   Gen. 2:8, 9; 13:10; Is. 51:3
10 'Therefore, thus says the Lord GOD,
"Because^it is high in stature, and it has set
its top among the ^clouds, and its heart is
haughty in its loftiness,   *you are • thick boughs*
11 therefore, I will give it into the hand of
a ^despot of the nations; he will thoroughly
deal with it. According to its wickedness I
have^driven it away.   *mighty one • Deut. 18:12*
12"And ^alien tyrants of the nations have
cut it down and left it; on the^mountains and
in all the valleys its branches have fallen,
and its boughs have been broken in all the
ravines of the land. And all the peoples of
the earth have^gone down from its shade
and left it.   Ezek. 7:21 • Ezek. 32:5 • Dan. 4:14
13"On its ruin all the^birds of the heavens
will dwell. And all the beasts of the field will
be on its *fallen* branches   Is. 18:6; Ezek. 29:5
14 in order that all the trees by the waters
may not be exalted in their stature, nor set
their top among the clouds, nor their well-
watered mighty ones stand *erect* in their
height. For they have all been given over to
death, to the earth beneath, among the sons
of men, with those who go down to the pit."
15 'Thus says the Lord GOD, "On the day
when it went down to Sheol I^caused lamentations; I closed the deep over it and held
back its rivers. And *its* many waters were
stopped up, and I made Lebanon^mourn for
it, and all the trees of the field wilted away
on account of it.   Ezek. 32:7 • *be darkened*
16"I made the nations quake at the sound
of its fall when I made it go down to Sheol
with those who go down to the pit; and all
the^well-watered trees of Eden, the choicest
and best of^Lebanon, were comforted in the
earth beneath.   *drinkers of water* • Is. 14:8
17"They also went down with it to Sheol
to those who were slain by the sword; and
those who were its^strength lived^under its
shade among the nations.   *arm* • Dan. 4:12
18"To which among the trees of Eden are
you thus equal in glory and greatness? Yet
you will be brought down with the trees of
Eden to the earth beneath; you will lie in the
midst of the uncircumcised, with those who
were slain by the sword. So is Pharaoh and
all his multitude!" ' declares the Lord GOD."

CHAPTER 32

Egypt Is Lamented

AND it came about in the^twelfth year, in
the twelfth *month,* on the first of the month,

that the word of the LORD came to me say-
ing,   Ezek. 30:20; 31:1; 32:17; 33:21
2"Son of man, take up a lamentation over
Pharaoh king of Egypt, and say to him,
'You^compared yourself to a young
lion of the nations,   *were like*
Yet you are like the^monster in the
seas;   Is. 27:1; Ezek. 29:3
And you^burst forth in your rivers,
And muddied the waters with your
feet,   Jer. 46:7, 8
And fouled their rivers.' "
3   Thus says the Lord GOD,
"Now I will spread My net over you
With a company of many peoples,
And they shall lift you up in My net.
4 "And I will leave you on the land;
I will cast you on the open field.
And I will cause all the birds of the
heavens to dwell on you,
And I will satisfy the beasts of the
whole earth^with you.   *from*
5 "And I will lay your flesh^on the moun-
tains,   Ezek. 31:12
And fill the valleys with your refuse.
6 "I will also make the land drink the dis-
charge of your^blood,   Ex. 7:17
As far as the mountains,
And the ravines shall be full of you.
7 "And when I^extinguish you,   Prov. 13:9
I will^cover the heavens, and darken
their^stars;   Is. 34:4 • Is. 13:10
I will cover the sun with a cloud,
And the moon shall not give its light.
8 "All the shining^lights in the heavens
I will darken over you
And will set darkness on your land,"
Declares the Lord GOD.   Gen. 1:14
9"I will also^trouble the hearts of many
peoples, when I ^bring your destruction
among the nations, into lands which you
have not known.   Ezek. 27:29-32 • Ex. 15:14-16
10"And I will make many peoples^appalled
at you, and their kings shall be horribly
afraid of you when I brandish My sword before them; and^they shall tremble every moment, every man for his own life, on the day
of your fall."   Ezek. 27:35 • Ezek. 26:16
11 For ^thus says the Lord GOD, "The
sword of the king of Babylon shall come
upon you.   Jer. 46:26
12"By the swords of the mighty ones I will
cause your multitude to fall; all of them are
^tyrants of the nations,
And they shall^devastate the pride of
Egypt,
And all its multitude shall be destroyed.   Ezek. 28:7 • Ezek. 28:19
13 "I will also destroy all its cattle from
beside many waters;
And^the foot of man shall not muddy
them anymore,
And the hoofs of beasts shall not
muddy them.   Ezek. 29:11
14 "Then I will make their waters settle,

And will cause their rivers to run like
oil,"
Declares the Lord GOD.
15 "When I make the land of Egypt a
^{R}desolation,   Ps. 107:33, 34
And the land is destitute of that
which filled it,
When I smite all those who live in it,
Then they shall^{R}know that I am the
LORD.$_R$ Ex. 7:5; 14:4, 18; Ezek. 6:7
16"This is a^{R}lamentation and they shall
^{A}chant it. The daughters of the nations shall
chant it. Over Egypt and over all her multitude they shall chant it," declares the Lord
GOD.   2 Sam. 1:17; 3:33, 34; 2 Chr. 35:25 • lament

Egypt in Sheol

17 And it came about in the^{R}twelfth year,
on the fifteenth of the month, that the word
of the LORD came to me saying,   Ezek. 31:1
18"Son of man,^{R}wail for the multitude of
Egypt, and^{R}bring it down, her and the
daughters of the powerful nations, to the
^{R}nether world, with those who go down to
the pit;   Is. 16:9 • Jer. 1:10 • Ezek. 31:14, 16, 18
19 'Whom do you surpass in beauty?
   Go down and make your bed with the
   ^{R}uncircumcised.'   Jer. 9:25, 26
20"They shall fall in the midst of those
who are slain by the sword.^{A}She is given
over to the sword; they have drawn her and
all her multitudes away.   *The sword is given*
21"The ^{R}strong among the mighty ones
shall speak of him *and* his helpers from the
midst of Sheol, 'They have gone down, they
lie still, the uncircumcised, slain by the
sword.'   Is. 14:9-12; Ezek. 32:27
22"Assyria^T is there and all her company;
^{T}her graves are round about^{T}her. All of them
are slain, fallen by the sword,   *his • him*
23 whose graves are set in the remotest
parts of the pit, and her company is round
about her grave. All of them are slain, fallen
by the sword, who^{T}spread terror in the land
of the living.   *gave,* and so throughout the ch.
24"Elam is there and all her multitude
around her grave; all of them slain, fallen by
the sword, who went down uncircumcised
to the^{R}lower parts of the earth, who instilled
their terror in the land of the living, and
^{R}bore their disgrace with those who went
down to the pit.   Ezek. 26:20 • Ezek. 16:52, 54
25"They have made a^{R}bed for her among
the slain with all her multitude. Her graves
are around it, they are all uncircumcised,
slain by the sword (although their terror
was^{T}instilled in the land of the living), and
they bore their disgrace with those who go
down to the pit; they were put in the midst
of the slain.   Ps. 139:8 • *given*
26"Meshech, Tubal and all their multitude
are there; their graves^{T}surround them. All of
them were slain by the sword uncircumcised, though they instilled their terror in
the land of the living.   *are around him*
27"Nor do they lie beside the fallen^{A}heroes

of the uncircumcised, who went down to
Sheol with their weapons of war, and whose
swords were laid under their heads; but the
punishment for their iniquity rested on their
bones, though the terror of *these* heroes *was*
once in the land of the living.   *mighty ones*
28"But in the midst of the uncircumcised
you will be broken and lie with those slain
by the sword.
29"There also is^{R}Edom, its kings, and all its
^{A}princes, who^{A}for *all* their might are laid with
those slain by the sword; they will lie with
the uncircumcised, and with those who go
down to the pit.   Is. 34:5-15 • *leaders • in*
30"There also are the^{A}chiefs of the north,
all of them, and all the Sidonians, who in
spite of the terror resulting from their
might, in shame went down with the slain.
So they lay down uncircumcised with those
slain by the sword, and bore their disgrace
with those who go down to the pit.   *princes*
31"These Pharaoh will see, and he will be
^{R}comforted for all his multitude slain by the
sword, *even* Pharaoh and all his army," declares the Lord GOD.   Ezek. 14:22; 31:16
32"Though I instilled a terror of him in the
land of the living, yet he will be made to lie
down among *the* uncircumcised *along* with
those slain by the sword, *even* Pharaoh and
all his multitude," declares the Lord GOD.

CHAPTER 33

*The Appointment of Ezekiel
as Watchman*

AND the word of the LORD came to me
saying,
2"Son of man, speak to the^{R}sons of your
people, and say to them, 'If I bring a sword
upon a land, and the people of the land take
one man from among them and make him
their watchman;   Ezek. 3:11; 33:12, 17, 30; 37:18
3 and he sees the sword coming upon the
land, and he^{R}blows on the trumpet and
warns the people,   Ezek. 33:9; Hos. 8:1; Joel 2:1
4 then he who hears the sound of the
trumpet and^{R}does not take warning, and a
sword comes and takes him away, his^{R}blood
will be on his *own* head.   Jer. 6:17 • [Acts 18:6]
5 'He heard the sound of the trumpet, but
did not take warning; his blood will be on
himself. But had he taken warning, he
would have^{R}delivered his life.   Ex. 9:19-21
6 'But if the watchman sees the sword
coming and does not blow the trumpet, and
the people are not warned, and a sword
comes and takes a person from them, he is
taken away in his iniquity; but his blood I
will require from the watchman's hand.'
7"Now as for you, son of man, I have appointed you a watchman for the house of
Israel; so you will hear a message from My
mouth, and give them warning from Me.
8"When I say to the wicked, 'O wicked
man, you shall^{R}surely die,' and you do not

speak to warn the wicked from his way, that wicked man shall die in his iniquity, but his blood I will require from your hand. Is. 3:11

9"But if you on your part warn a wicked man to turn from his way, and he does not turn from his way, he will die in his iniquity; but you have[R]delivered your life.   Acts 20:26

10"Now as for you, son of man, say to the house of Israel, 'Thus you have spoken, saying, "Surely our transgressions and our sins are upon us, and we are rotting away in them; how then can we[T]survive?"'   live

11"Say to them, 'As I live!' declares the Lord GOD, 'I take no pleasure in the death of the wicked, but rather that the wicked[R]turn from his way and live.[R]Turn back, turn back from your evil ways! Why then will you die, O house of Israel?'   Jer. 31:20 • Ezek. 18:30, 31

12"And you, son of man, say to[T]your fellow citizens, 'The righteousness of a righteous man will not deliver him in the day of his transgression, and as for the wickedness of the wicked, he will not stumble because of it in the day when he turns from his wickedness; whereas a righteous man will not be able to live by his righteousness on the day when he commits sin.'   the sons of your people

13"When I say to the righteous he will surely live, and he so trusts in his righteousness that he[R]commits iniquity, none of his righteous deeds will be remembered; but in that same iniquity of his which he has committed he will die.   Ezek. 18:26; [Heb. 10:38]

14"But when I say to the wicked, 'You will surely die,' and he turns from his sin and practices[R]justice and righteousness,   Mic. 6:8

15 if a wicked man restores a pledge,[R]pays back what he has taken by robbery, walks by the[R]statutes[T]which ensure life without committing iniquity, he will surely live; he shall not die.   Ex. 22:1-4 • Ps. 119:59 • of life

16"None[R]of his sins that he has committed will be remembered against him. He has practiced justice and righteousness; he will surely live.   [Is. 1:18; 43:25]; Ezek. 18:22

17"Yet[T]your fellow citizens say, 'The way of the Lord is not right,' when it is their own way that is not right.   the sons of your people

18"When the righteous turns from his righteousness and[R]commits iniquity, then he shall die in[T]it.   Ezek. 3:20; 18:24 • them

19"But when the wicked turns from his wickedness and practices justice and righteousness, he will live by them.

20"Yet you say, 'The way of the Lord is not right.' O house of Israel, I will judge each of you according to his ways."

21 Now it came about in the twelfth year of our exile, on the fifth of the tenth month, that the refugees from Jerusalem came to me, saying, "The city has been taken."

22 Now the hand of the LORD had been upon me in the evening, before the[T]refugees came. And He opened my mouth[T]at the time they came to me in the morning; so my

mouth was opened, and I was no longer [A]speechless.   refugee • until he came • dumb

23 Then the word of the LORD came to me saying,

24"Son of man, they who[R]live in these waste places in the land of Israel are saying, 'Abraham was only one, yet he possessed the land; so to us who are many the land has been given as a possession.'   Jer. 39:10; 40:7

25"Therefore, say to them, 'Thus says the Lord GOD, "You eat meat with the blood in it, lift up your eyes to your idols as you shed blood. Should you then possess the land?

26"You[T]rely[R]on your sword, you commit abominations, and each of you defiles his neighbor's wife. Should you then possess the land?"'   stand • Mic. 2:1, 2; Zeph. 3:3

27"Thus you shall say to them, 'Thus says the Lord GOD, "As I live, surely those who are in the waste places will fall by the sword, and whoever is in the[T]open field I will give to the beasts to be devoured, and those who are in the strongholds and in the caves will die of pestilence.   surface of the field

28"And I shall make the land a desolation and a waste, and the pride of her power will cease; and the mountains of Israel will be desolate, so that no one will pass through.

29"Then they will know that I am the LORD, when I make the land a desolation and a waste because of all their abominations which they have committed."'

30"But as for you, son of man, your fellow citizens who talk about you by the walls and in the doorways of the houses, speak to one[R] another, each to his brother, saying, 'Come[R] now, and hear what the[T]message is which comes forth from the LORD.'   Is. 29:13 • word

31"And they come to you as people come, and sit before you as My people, and hear your words, but they do not do them, for they do the lustful desires expressed by [R]their[R]mouth, and their heart goes after their [R]gain.   Ps. 78:36, 37; Is. 29:13 • Ezek. 22:13, 27

32"And behold, you are to them like a sensual song by one who has a[R]beautiful voice and plays well on an instrument; for they hear your words, but they do not practice them.   Mark 6:20

33"So when it comes to pass—[T]as surely it will—then they will know that a prophet has been in their midst."   behold, it is coming

CHAPTER 34

The False Shepherds

THEN the word of the LORD came to me saying,

2"Son of man, prophesy against the shepherds of Israel. Prophesy and say to[T]those shepherds, 'Thus says the Lord GOD, "Woe, shepherds of Israel who have been[T]feeding themselves! Should not the shepherds[T]feed the flock?   them, the shepherds • pasturing • pasture

3"You eat the fat and clothe yourselves

with the wool, you slaughter the fat *sheep* without[T]feeding the flock.   *pasturing*

4"Those who are sickly you have not strengthened, the[T] diseased you have not healed,[R]the broken you have not bound up, the scattered you have not brought back, nor have you[R]sought for the lost; but with force and with severity you have dominated them.   *sick* • Zech. 11:16 • Matt. 9:36; 10:6

5"And they were scattered for lack of a shepherd, and they became food for every beast of the field and were scattered.

6"My flock[R]wandered through all the mountains and on every high hill, and[R]My flock was scattered over all the surface of the earth; and there was no one to search or seek *for them.*" ' "   Jer. 40:11, 12 • [John 10:16]

7 Therefore, you shepherds, hear the word of the LORD:

8"As I live," declares the Lord GOD, "surely because My flock has become a [R]prey, My flock has even become food for all the beasts of the field for lack of a shepherd, and My shepherds did not search for My flock, but *rather* the shepherds fed themselves and did not feed My flock;   Acts 20:29

9 therefore, you shepherds, hear the word of the LORD:

10 'Thus says the Lord GOD, "Behold, I am against the shepherds, and I shall demand My sheep[T]from them and make them cease from feeding sheep. So the shepherds will not feed themselves anymore, but I shall deliver My flock from their mouth, that they may not be food for them." ' "   *from their hand*

The True Shepherd

11 For thus says the Lord GOD, "Behold, I Myself will[R]search for My sheep and seek them out.   Ezek. 11:17; 20:41

12"As a shepherd cares for his herd in the day when he is among his scattered sheep, so I will care for My sheep and will deliver them from all the places to which they were scattered on a cloudy and gloomy day.

13"And I will bring them out from the peoples and gather them from the countries and bring them to their own land; and I will[R]feed them on the mountains of Israel, by the [R]streams, and in all the inhabited places of the land.   Ezek. 34:23; 36:29, 30 • Is. 30:25

14"I will feed them in a[R]good pasture, and their grazing ground will be on the mountain heights of Israel. There they will lie down in good grazing ground, and they will feed in[T]rich[R]pasture on the mountains of Israel.   Jer. 31:12-14, 25 • *fat* • Ezek. 28:25, 26

15"I will feed My flock and I will lead them to rest," declares the Lord GOD.

16"I will seek the lost, bring back the scattered, bind up the broken, and strengthen the sick; but the fat and the strong I will destroy. I will feed them with judgment.

17"And as for you, My flock, thus says the Lord GOD, 'Behold, I will[R]judge between one

[A]sheep and another, between the rams and the male goats.   Mal. 4:1; [Matt. 25:32] • *lamb*

18 'Is it too[R]slight a thing for you that you should feed in the good pasture, that you must tread down with your feet the rest of your pastures? Or that you should drink of the clear waters, that you must[T]foul the rest with your feet?   2 Sam. 7:19 • *foul by trampling*

19 'And as for My flock, they must eat what you tread down with your feet, and they must drink what you[T]foul with your feet!' "   *foul by trampling*

20 Therefore, thus says the Lord GOD to them, "Behold, I, even I, will judge between the fat sheep and the lean sheep.

21"Because you push with side and with shoulder, and[R]thrust at all the[A]weak with your horns, until you have scattered them [T]abroad,   Deut. 33:17 • *sick* • *to the outside*

22 therefore, I will deliver My flock, and they will no longer be a prey; and I will judge between one sheep and another.

23"Then I will[R]set over them one[R]shepherd, My servant[R]David, and he will feed them; he will feed them himself and be their shepherd.   [Rev. 7:17] • [Is. 40:11] • Ezek. 37:24

24"And I, the LORD, will be their God, and My servant[R]David will be prince among them; I, the LORD, have spoken.   Is. 55:3

25"And I will make a covenant of peace with them and eliminate harmful beasts from the land, so that they may live securely in the wilderness and sleep in the woods.

26"And I will make them and the places around My hill a[R]blessing. And I will cause showers to come down in their season; they will be showers of blessing.   Gen. 12:2

27"Also the tree of the field will yield its fruit, and the earth will yield its increase, and they will be[R]secure on their land. Then they will know that I am the LORD, when I have[R]broken the bars of their yoke and have delivered them from the hand of those who enslaved them.   Ezek. 38:8, 11 • Lev. 26:13

28"And they will no longer be a prey to the nations, and the beasts of the earth will not devour them; but they will[R]live securely, and no one will make *them* afraid.   Jer. 30:10

29"And I will establish for them a renowned planting place, and they will not again be[T]victims of famine in the land, and they will not[R]endure the insults of the nations anymore.   *those gathered* • Ezek. 36:6, 15

30"Then they will know that[R]I, the LORD their God, am with them, and that they, the house of Israel, are My people," declares the Lord GOD.   Ps. 46:7, 11; Ezek. 14:11; 36:28

31"As for you, My[R]sheep, the[R]sheep of My pasture, you are men, and I am your God," declares the Lord GOD.   Ps. 78:52 • Jer. 23:1

CHAPTER 35

The Judgment of Edom

M OREOVER, the word of the LORD came to me saying,

2"Son of man, set your face against Mount Seir, and prophesy against it,

3 and say to it, 'Thus says the Lord GOD, "Behold, I am against you, Mount Seir, And I will ᴿstretch out My hand against you,   Jer. 6:12; 15:6; Ezek. 25:13
And I will make you aᴿdesolation and a waste.   Jer. 49:13, 17, 18; Ezek. 35:7

4 "I willᴿlay waste your cities, And you will become a desolation. Then you will know that I am the LORD.   Ezek. 6:6; 35:9; Mal. 1:3, 4

5"Because you have had everlasting enmity and haveᵀdelivered the sons of Israel to the power of the sword at the time of their calamity, at the time of theᴬpunishmentᴿof the end,   poured • iniquity • Ezek. 7:2; 21:25, 29

6 therefore, as I live," declares the Lord GOD, "I willᵀgive you over toᵀbloodshed, and bloodshed will pursue you; since you have not hated bloodshed, therefore bloodshed will pursue you.   prepare you for • Is. 63:2-6

7"And I will make Mount Seir a waste and a desolation, and I will cut off from it the one who passes through and returns.

8"And I willᴿfill its mountains with its slain; on your hills and in your valleys and in all your ravines those slain by the sword willᵀfall.   Is. 34:5, 6; Ezek. 31:12 • fall in them

9"I will make you an everlasting desolation, and your cities will not be inhabited. Then you will know that I am the LORD.

10"Because you haveᴿsaid, 'These two nations and these two lands will be mine, and we will possessᵀthem,' although theᴿLORD was there,   Ps. 83:4-12 • it • Zeph. 3:15

11 therefore, as I live," declares the Lord GOD, "I will deal with youᴿaccording to your anger and according to your envy which you showed because of your hatred against them; so I willᴿmake Myself known among them when I judge you.   Ps. 137:7 • Ps. 9:16

12"Then you will know that I, the LORD, have heard all your revilings which you have spoken against the mountains of Israel saying, 'They are laid desolate; they areᴿgiven to us for food.'   Jer. 50:7; Ezek. 36:2

13"And you have ᴿspoken arrogantly against Me and have multiplied your words against Me; I have heard."   Is. 10:13, 14; 36:20

14 'Thus says the Lord GOD, "As all the earth rejoices, I will make you a desolation.

15"As you rejoiced over the inheritance of the house of Israel because it was desolate, so I will do to you. You will be a desolation, O Mount Seir, and all Edom, all of it. Then they will know that I am the LORD." '

CHAPTER 36

Judgment on the Nations

"AND you, son of man, prophesy to the mountains of Israel and say, 'O mountains of Israel, hear the word of the LORD.

2 'Thus says the Lord GOD, "Because the enemy has spoken against you, 'Aha!' and,

'The everlastingᵀheightsᴿhave become our possession,'   Bamoth • Deut. 32:13; Ps. 78:69

3 therefore, prophesy and say, 'Thus says the Lord GOD, "For good cause they have made you desolate and crushed you from every side, that you should become a possession of the rest of the nations, and you have been taken up in theᵀtalk and the whispering of the people." ' "   lip of the tongue

4 'Therefore, Oᴿmountains of Israel, hear the word of the Lord GOD. Thus says the Lord GOD to the mountains and to the hills, to the ravines and to the valleys, to the desolate wastes and to the forsaken cities, which have become aᴿprey and a derision to the rest of the nations which are round about,   Deut. 11:11; Ezek. 36:1, 6 • Ezek. 34:8, 28

5 therefore, thus says the Lord GOD, "Surely in the fire of My jealousy I have spoken against the rest of the nations, and against all Edom, who ᵀappropriated My land for themselves as a possession with wholeheartedᴿjoy and with scorn of soul, to drive it out for a prey."   gave • Mic. 7:8

6 'Therefore, prophesy concerning the land of Israel, and say to the mountains and to the hills, to the ravines and to the valleys, "Thus says the Lord GOD, 'Behold, I have spoken in My jealousy and in My wrath because you haveᴿendured the insults of the nations.'   Ps. 74:10; 123:3, 4; Ezek. 34:29

7"Therefore, thus says the Lord GOD, 'I haveᵀsworn that surely the nations which are around you will themselves endure their insults.   lifted up My hand

Israel Returns to the Lord

8 'But you, O mountains of Israel, you willᴿput forth your branches and bear your fruit for My people Israel; for they will soon come.   Is. 4:2; 27:6; Ezek. 17:23; 34:26-29

9 'For, behold, I am for you, and I will ᴿturn to you, and you shall beᴿcultivated and sown.   Lev. 26:9 • Ezek. 28:26; 34:14; 36:34

10 'And I will multiply men on you,ᴿall the house of Israel, all of it; and theᴿcities will be inhabited, and the waste places will be rebuilt.   Is. 27:6; 49:17-23 • Jer. 31:27, 28; 33:12

11 'And I will multiply on you man and beast; and they will increase and be fruitful; and I will cause you to be inhabited as you wereᴿformerly and willᵀtreat youᴿbetter than at the first. Thus you will know that I am the LORD.   Jer. 30:18 • cause good • Job 42:12

12 'Yes, I will cause men—My people Israel—to walk on you and possess you, so that you will become their inheritance and never again bereave them of children.'

13"Thus says the Lord GOD, 'Because they say to you, "You are a devourer of men and have bereaved your nation of children,"

14 therefore, you will no longer devour men, and no longer bereave your nation of children,' declares the Lord GOD.

15"And I will not let you hearᴿinsults from the nations anymore, nor will you bear dis-

grace from the peoples any longer, nor will you cause your nation to stumble any longer," declares the Lord GOD.' "   Is. 60:14

16 Then the word of the LORD came to me saying,

17"Son of man, when the house of Israel was living in their own land, they^Rdefiled it by their ways and their deeds; their way before Me was like^Rthe uncleanness of a woman in her impurity.   Jer. 2:7 • Lev. 15:19

18"Therefore, I^Rpoured out My wrath on them for the blood which they had shed on the land, because they had defiled it with their idols.   2 Chr. 34:21, 25; Lam. 2:4; 4:11

19"Also I^Rscattered them among the nations, and they were dispersed throughout the lands.^RAccording to their ways and their deeds I judged them.   Amos 9:9 • Ezek. 24:14

20"When they_R came to the nations where they went, they^Rprofaned My holy name, because it was said of them, 'These are the ^Rpeople of the LORD; yet they have come out of His land.'   Is. 52:5; Ezek. 12:16 • Jer. 33:24

21"But I had concern for My^Rholy name, which the house of Israel had profaned among the nations where they went. Is. 48:9

22"Therefore, say to the house of Israel, 'Thus says the Lord GOD, "It is^Rnot for your sake, O house of Israel, that I am about to act, but for My holy name, which you have profaned among the nations where you went.   Deut. 7:7, 8; 9:5, 6; Ezek. 36:32

23"And I will^Rvindicate the holiness of My great name which has been profaned among the nations, which you have profaned in their midst. Then the^Rnations will know that I am the LORD," declares the Lord GOD, "when I prove Myself holy among you in their sight. Is. 5:16; Ezek. 20:41 • Ps. 102:15

24"For I will^Rtake you from the nations, gather you from all the lands, and bring you into your own land.   Is. 43:5, 6; Ezek. 34:13

25"Then I will^Rsprinkle clean water on you, and you will be clean; I will cleanse you from all your^Rfilthiness and from all your ^Ridols.   Num. 19:17-19 • Is. 4:4 • Hos. 14:3, 8

26"Moreover, I will give you a^Rnew heart and put a new spirit within you; and I will remove the heart of stone from your flesh and give you a heart of flesh.   Ps. 51:10

27"And I will put My Spirit within you and cause you to walk in My statutes, and you will be careful to observe My ordinances.

28"And you will live in the land that I gave to your forefathers; so you will be^RMy people, and I will be your God.   Ezek. 14:11

29"Moreover, I will save you from all your uncleanness; and I will call for the grain and multiply it, and I^Rwill not^Tbring a famine on you.   Ezek. 34:27, 29; Hos. 2:21-23 • put

30"And I will^Rmultiply the fruit of the tree and the produce of the field, that you may not receive again the disgrace of famine among the nations.   Lev. 26:4; Ezek. 34:27

31"Then you will ^Rremember your evil ways and your deeds that were not good, and you will loathe yourselves in your own sight for your iniquities and your abominations.   Ezek. 16:61-63; 20:43

32"I am not doing this^Rfor your sake," declares the Lord GOD, "let it be known to you. Be ashamed and confounded for your ways, O house of Israel!"   Deut. 9:5

33 'Thus says the Lord GOD, "On the day that I cleanse you from all your iniquities, I will cause the^Rcities to be inhabited, and the waste places will be rebuilt.   Ezek. 36:10

34"And the desolate land will be cultivated instead of being a desolation in the sight of everyone who passed by.

35"And they will say, 'This desolate land has become like the^Rgarden of Eden; and the waste, desolate, and ruined cities are fortified and inhabited.'   Is. 51:3; Ezek. 31:9; Joel 2:3

36"Then the nations that are left round about you will know that I, the LORD, have rebuilt the ruined places and planted that which was desolate; I, the LORD, have spoken and^Rwill do it."   Ezek. 17:24; 22:14; 37:14

37 'Thus says the Lord GOD, "This also I will let the house of Israel ask Me to do for them: I will increase their men like a flock.

38"Like the flock^Tfor sacrifices, like the flock at Jerusalem during her appointed feasts, so will the waste cities be filled with ^Rflocks of men. Then they will know that I am the LORD." ' "   of holy things • Jer. 23:1

CHAPTER 37

Vision of Dry Bones

THE hand of the LORD was upon me, and He brought me out^Aby the Spirit of the LORD and set me down in the middle of the^Rvalley; and it was full of bones.   in • Jer. 7:32—8:2

2 And He caused me to pass among them round about, and behold, there were very many on the surface of the valley; and lo, they were very dry.

3 And He said to me, "Son of man,^Rcan these bones live?" And I answered, "O Lord GOD,^RThou knowest." Ezek. 26:19 • [1 Sam. 2:6]

4 Again He said to me, "Prophesy over these bones, and say to them, 'O dry bones, ^Rhear the word of the LORD.'   Jer. 22:29

5"Thus says the Lord GOD to these bones, 'Behold, I will cause ⁶breath^Rto enter you that you may come to life.   [Ps. 104:29, 30]

6 'And I will put sinews on you, make flesh grow back on you, cover you with skin, and put breath in you that you may come alive; and you will^Rknow that I am the LORD.' "   Is. 49:23; Ezek. 35:9; Joel 2:27; 3:17

7 So I prophesied as I was commanded; and as I prophesied, there was a^Tnoise, and behold, a rattling; and the bones came together, bone to its bone.   voice; or, thunder

8 And I looked, and behold, sinews were

---

⁶ Or, spirit, and so throughout this context

on them, and flesh grew, and skin covered them; but there was no breath in them.

9 Then He said to me, "Prophesy to the breath, prophesy, son of man, and say to the breath, 'Thus says the Lord GOD, "Come from the four winds, O breath, and breathe on these slain, that they come to life." ' "

10 So I prophesied as He commanded me, and the^Rbreath came into them, and they came to life, and stood on their feet, an^Rexceedingly great army.   Rev. 11:11 • Jer. 30:19

11 Then He said to me, "Son of man, these bones are the whole house of Israel; behold, they say, 'Our^Rbones are dried up, and our hope has perished. We are^Tcompletely^Rcut off.'   Ps. 141:7 • cut off to ourselves • Ps. 88:5

12"Therefore prophesy, and say to them, 'Thus says the Lord GOD, "Behold, I will open your graves and^Rcause you to come up out of your graves, My people; and I will bring you into the land of Israel.   Hos. 13:14

13"Then you will know that I am the LORD, when I have opened your graves and caused you to come up out of your graves, My people.

14"And I will^Rput My ⁷Spirit within you, and you will come to life, and I will place you on your own land. Then you will know that I, the LORD, have spoken and done it," declares the LORD.' "   [Joel 2:28, 29]; Zech. 12:10

Sign of the Two Sticks

15 The word of the LORD came again to me saying,

16"And you, son of man, take for yourself one stick and write on it, 'For^RJudah and for the sons of Israel, his companions'; then take another stick and write on it, 'For Joseph, the stick of Ephraim and all the house of Israel, his companions.'   2 Chr. 10:17

17"Then^Rjoin them for yourself one to another into one stick, that they may become one in your hand.   Is. 11:13; Jer. 50:4

18"And when the sons of your people speak to you saying, 'Will you not declare to us^Rwhat you mean by these?'   Ezek. 12:9

19 say to them, 'Thus says the Lord GOD, "Behold, I will take the stick of Joseph, which is in the hand of Ephraim, and the tribes of Israel, his companions; and I will put them with it, with the stick of Judah, and make them one stick, and they will be one in My hand." '

20"And the sticks on which you write will be in your hand before their eyes.

21"And say to them, 'Thus says the Lord GOD, "Behold, I will take the sons of Israel from among the nations where they have gone, and I will gather them from every side and bring them into their own land;

22 and I will make them one nation in the land, on the mountains of Israel; and one king will be king for all of them; and they will no longer be two nations, and they will no longer be divided into two kingdoms.

23"And they will^Rno longer defile themselves with their idols, or with their detestable things, or with any of their transgressions; but I will deliver them from all their ⁸dwelling places in which they have sinned, and will cleanse them. And they will be My people, and I will be their God.   Ezek. 36:25

24"And My servant David will be king over them, and they will all have one shepherd; and they will walk in My ordinances, and keep My statutes, and observe them.

25"And they shall live on the land that I gave to Jacob My servant, in which your fathers lived; and they will live on it, they, and their sons, and their sons' sons, forever; and ^RDavid My servant shall be their prince forever.   Is. 11:1; Ezek. 37:24; Zech. 6:12☆

26"And I will make a^Rcovenant of peace with them; it will be an^Reverlasting covenant with them. And I will place them and multiply them, and will set My sanctuary in their midst forever.   Ezek. 16:62 • Ps. 89:3, 4; Is. 55:3

27"My^Rdwelling place also will be with them; and^RI will be their God, and they will be My people.   [John 1:14] • [2 Cor. 6:16]

28"And the nations will know that I am the LORD who sanctifies Israel, when My sanctuary is in their midst forever." ' "

CHAPTER 38

Attack by Gog

AND the word of the LORD came to me saying,

2"Son of man, set your face toward Gog of the land of Magog, the^Aprince of Rosh, ^RMeshech, and Tubal, and prophesy against him,   *chief prince of Meshech* • Ezek. 27:13; 38:3

3 and say, 'Thus says the Lord GOD, "Behold, I am against you, O Gog, prince of Rosh, Meshech, and Tubal.

4"And I will turn you about, and put hooks into your jaws, and I will bring you out, and all your army, horses and horsemen, all of them^Asplendidly attired, a great company with buckler and shield, all of them wielding swords;   *clothed in full armor*

5 Persia,^TEthiopia, and Put with them, all of them with shield and helmet;   *Cush*

6 Gomer with all its troops; Beth-togarmah from the remote parts of the north with all its troops—many peoples with you.

7"Be^Rprepared, and prepare yourself, you and all your companies that are assembled about you, and be a guard for them.   Is. 8:9

8"After many days you will be summoned; in the latter years you will come into the land that is restored from the sword, whose inhabitants have been gathered from many^Tnations to the mountains of Israel which had been a continual waste; but^Tits people were brought out from the na-

⁷ Or, breath   ⁸ Another reading is *backslidings*

tions, and they are[R]living securely, all of them. *peoples · it was* · Ezek. 38:11, 14; 39:26

9"And you will go up, you will come[R]like a storm; you will be like a[R]cloud covering the land, you and all your troops, and many peoples with you." Is. 5:28; 21:1 · Ezek. 30:18

10 'Thus says the Lord GOD, "It will come about on that day, that[T]thoughts will come into your mind, and you will[R]devise an evil plan, *words* · Ps. 36:4; Mic. 2:1

11 and you will say, 'I will go up against the land of [9]unwalled[R] villages. I will go against those who are[R]at rest, that live securely, all of them living without walls, and having no bars or gates, Zech. 2:4 · Jer. 49:31

12 to capture spoil and to seize plunder, to turn your hand against the waste places which are *now* inhabited, and against the people who are gathered from the nations, who have acquired cattle and goods, who live at the[T]center of the world.' *navel*

13"Sheba, and Dedan, and the merchants of[R]Tarshish, with all its[A]villages, will say to you, 'Have you come to capture spoil? Have you assembled your company to seize plunder, to carry away silver and gold, to take away cattle and goods, to capture great [R]spoil?' " ' Ezek. 27:12 · *young lions* · Is. 10:6

14"Therefore, prophesy, son of man, and say to Gog, 'Thus says the Lord GOD, "On that day when My people Israel are[R]living securely, will you not know *it*? Ezek. 38:8, 11

15"And[R]you will come from your place out of the remote parts of the north, you and many peoples with you, all of them riding on horses, a great assembly and a mighty army; Ezek. 39:2

16 and you will come up against My people Israel like a cloud to cover the land. It will come about in the last days that I shall bring you against My land, in order that the nations may[R]know Me when I shall be[R]sanctified through you before their eyes, O Gog." Ps. 83:18; Ezek. 36:23 · Is. 5:16; 8:13

Judgment of God

17 'Thus says the Lord GOD, "Are you the one of whom I spoke in former days through My servants the prophets of Israel, who prophesied in those days for *many* years that I would bring you against them?

18"And it will come about on that day, when Gog comes against the land of Israel," declares the Lord GOD, "that My fury will mount up in My[R]anger. Ps. 18:8, 15

19"And in My[R]zeal and in My blazing wrath I declare *that* on that day there will surely be a great[A]earthquake[R]in the land of Israel. Deut. 32:22 · *shaking* · Hag. 2:6, 7, 21

20"And[R]the fish of the sea, the birds of the heavens, the beasts of the field, all the creeping things that creep on the earth, and all the men who are on the face of the earth will shake at My presence; the[R]mountains

also will be thrown down, the steep pathways will[T]collapse, and every wall will fall to the ground. Hos. 4:3 · Zech. 14:4 · *fall*

21"And I shall call for a[R]sword against[T]him on all My mountains," declares the Lord GOD. "Every[R]man's sword will be against his brother. Ezek. 14:17 · Gog · Judg. 7:22

22"And with pestilence and with blood I shall enter into[R]judgment with him; and I shall rain on him, and on his troops, and on the many peoples who are with him,[T]a torrential rain, with[R]hailstones, fire, and brimstone. Jer. 25:31 · *an overflowing* · Ps. 11:6

23"And I shall magnify Myself, sanctify Myself, and[R]make Myself known in the sight of many nations; and they will know that I am the LORD." ' Ps. 9:16; Ezek. 37:28; 38:16

CHAPTER 39

"AND[R]you, son of man, prophesy against Gog, and say, 'Thus says the Lord GOD, "Behold, I am against you, O Gog, prince of Rosh, Meshech, and Tubal; Ezek. 38:2

2 and I shall turn you around, drive you on, take you up from the remotest parts of the north, and bring you against the mountains of Israel.

3"And I shall[R]strike your bow from your left hand, and dash down your arrows from your right hand. Ps. 76:3; Jer. 21:4, 5

4"You shall[R]fall on the mountains of Israel, you and all your troops, and the peoples who are with you; I shall give you as food to every[T]kind of predatory bird and beast of the field. Is. 14:24, 25 · *wing*

5"You will fall on the open field; for it is I who have spoken," declares the Lord GOD.

6"And I shall send fire upon Magog and those who inhabit the coastlands in safety; and they will know that I am the LORD.

7"And My[R]holy name I shall make known in the midst of My people Israel; and I shall not let My holy name be profaned anymore. And the nations will know that I am the LORD, the Holy One in Israel. Ezek. 36:20-22

8"Behold, it is coming and it shall be done," declares the Lord GOD. "That is the day of which I have spoken.

9"Then those who inhabit the cities of Israel will[R]go out, and make[R]fires with the weapons and burn *them*, both shields and bucklers, bows and arrows, war clubs and spears and for seven years they will make fires of them. Is. 66:24 · Josh. 11:6; Ps. 46:9

10"And they will not take wood from the field or gather firewood from the forests, for they will make fires with the weapons; and they will take the spoil of those who despoiled them, and seize the[R]plunder of those who plundered them," declares the Lord GOD. Is. 14:2; 33:1; Mic. 5:8; Hab. 2:8

11"And it will come about on that day that I shall give Gog a burial ground there in Israel, the valley of those who pass by east of the sea, and it will block off the passers-by.

[9] Or, *open country*

So they will bury Gog there with all his multitude, and they will call *it* the valley of °Hamon-gog.   *the multitude of Gog*

12"For seven months the house of Israel will be burying them in order to °cleanse the land.   Deut. 21:23; Ezek. 39:14, 16

13"Even all the people of the land will bury *them;* and it will be °to their °renown *on* the day that I glorify Myself," declares the Lord GOD.   *a memorial for them* • Zeph. 3:19, 20

14"And they will set apart men who will constantly pass through the land, °burying those who were passing through, even those left on the surface of the ground, in order to cleanse it. At the end of seven months they will make a search.   Jer. 14:16

15"And as those who pass through the land pass through and anyone sees a man's bone, then he will °set up a marker by it until the buriers have buried it in the valley of °Hamon-gog.   *build* • *the multitude of Gog*

16"And even *the* name of *the* city will be Hamonah. So they will cleanse the land." '

17"And as for you, son of man, thus says the Lord GOD, 'Speak to every kind of bird and to every beast of the field, "Assemble and come, gather from every side to My sacrifice which I am going to sacrifice for you, as a great sacrifice on the mountains of Israel, that you may eat flesh and drink blood.

18"You shall °eat the flesh of mighty men, and drink the blood of the princes of the earth, as *though they were* °rams, lambs, goats, and bulls, all of them fatlings of °Bashan.   Ezek. 29:5 • Jer. 51:40 • Ps. 22:12

19"So you will eat fat until you are glutted, and drink blood until you are drunk, from My sacrifice which I have sacrificed for you.

20"And you will be glutted at My table with °horses and charioteers, with mighty men and all the men of war," declares the Lord GOD.   Ps. 76:5, 6; Ezek. 38:4; Hag. 2:22

21"And I shall set My °glory among the nations; and all the nations will see My judgment which I have executed, and My hand which I have laid on them.   Ex. 9:16; Is. 37:20

22"And the house of Israel will °know that I am the LORD their God from that day onward.   Jer. 24:7

23"And the nations will know that the house of Israel went into exile for their iniquity because they acted treacherously against Me, and I hid My face from them; so I gave them into the hand of their adversaries, and all of them fell by the sword.

24"According to their uncleanness and according to their transgressions I dealt with them, and I hid My face from them." ' "

25 Therefore thus says the Lord GOD, "Now I shall °restore the fortunes of Jacob, and have mercy on the whole °house of Israel; and I shall be °jealous for My holy name.   *return the captivity* • Jer. 31:1 • Ex. 20:5

26"And they shall [10]forget °their disgrace and all their treachery which they [11]perpetrated against Me, when they °live securely on their *own* land with °no one to make them afraid.   Ezek. 16:63 • 1 Kin. 4:25 • Mic. 4:4

27"When I bring them back from the peoples and gather them from the lands of their enemies, then I shall be sanctified °through them in the sight of the many nations.   *in*

28"Then they will know that I am the LORD their God because I made them go into exile among the nations, and then gathered them *again* to their own land; and I will leave none of them there any longer.

29"And I will not hide My °face from them any longer, for I shall have °poured out My Spirit on the house of Israel," declares the Lord GOD.   Is. 32:15; Ezek. 36:27; 37:14; [Joel 2:28]

CHAPTER 40

Vision of the Man with the Measuring Rod

IN the °twenty-fifth year of our exile, at the beginning of the year, on the tenth of the month, in the fourteenth year after the city was °taken, on that same day the °hand of the LORD was upon me and He brought me there.   Ezek. 32:1, 17; 33:21 • *struck* • Ezek. 1:3

2 In the °visions of God He brought me into the land of Israel, and set me on a very high mountain; and on it to the south *there was* a structure like a city.   Ezek. 1:1; 8:3

3 So He brought me there; and behold, there was a man whose appearance was like the appearance of °bronze, with a line of flax and a °measuring rod in his hand; and he was standing in the gateway.   Ezek. 1:7 • Rev. 11:1

4 And the man said to me, "Son of man, °see with your eyes, hear with your ears, and give attention to all that I am going to show you; for you have been brought here in order to show *it* to you. Declare to the house of Israel all that you see."   Ezek. 2:7, 8; 44:5

The Outer Court

5 And behold, there was a wall on the outside of the temple all around, and in the man's hand was a measuring rod of six cubits, *each of which was* a cubit and a handbreadth. So he measured the thickness of the wall, one rod; and the height, one rod.

6 Then he went to the gate which faced east, went up its steps, and measured the threshold of the gate, one rod in width; and the other threshold *was* one rod in width.

7 And the guardroom *was* one rod long and one rod wide; and *there were* five cubits between the guardrooms. And the threshold of the gate by the porch of the gate °facing inward *was* one rod.   *from the house,* also vv. 8, 9

8 Then he measured the porch of the gate facing inward, one rod.

9 And he measured the porch of the gate, eight cubits; and its side pillars, two cubits. And the porch of the gate was faced inward.

---

[10] Another reading is *bear*   [11] Lit., *did treacherously*

10 And the guardrooms of the gate toward the east *numbered* three on each side; the three of them had the same measurement. The side pillars also had the same measurement on each side.

11 And he measured the width of the ᵀgateway, ten cubits, and the length of the gate, thirteen cubits. ₜ   *entrance of the gate*

12 And *there was* aᵀbarrier *wall* one cubit *wide* in front of the guardrooms on each side; and the guardrooms *were* six cubits *square* on each side.   *border*

13 And he measured the gate from the roof of the one guardroom to the roof of the other, a width of twenty-five cubits from *one* door to *the* door opposite.

14 And he made the side pillars sixty cubits *high;* the gate *extended* round about to the side pillar of theᴿcourtyard.   Ex. 27:9

15 And *from* the front of the entrance gate to the front of the inner porch of the gate *was* fifty cubits.

16 And *there were* shuttered windows *looking* toward the guardrooms, and toward their side pillars within the gate all around, and likewise for the porches. And *there were* windows all around inside; and on *each* side pillar *were* palm tree ornaments.

17 Then he brought me into the outer court, and behold, *there were* chambers and a pavement, made for the court all around; thirty chambersᵀfaced the pavement.   *to*

18 And the pavement (*that is,* the lower pavement) *was* by the side of the gates, corresponding to the length of the gates.

19 Then he measured the width from the front of theᴿlower gate to the front of the exterior of the inner court, a hundred cubits on the east and on the north.   Ezek. 40:23, 27

20 And *as for* theᴿgate of the outer court which faced the north, he measured its length and its width.   Ezek. 40:6

21 Andᵀit had three guardrooms on each side; and its side pillars and its porches had the same measurement as the first gate. Its length *was* fifty cubits, and the width twenty-five cubits.   *its guardrooms were three*

22 And its windows, and its porches, and its palm tree ornaments had the same measurements as the gate which faced toward the east; and it was reached by seven steps, and itsᴬporch *was* in front of them.   *porches*

23 And the inner court had a gate opposite the gate on the north as well as *the gate* on the east; and he measured aᴿhundred cubits from gate to gate.   Ezek. 40:19, 27

24 Then he led me toward the south, and behold, there was aᴿgate toward the south; and he measured itsᴿside pillars and its porches according to those same measurements.   Ezek. 40:6, 20, 35; 46:9 • Ezek. 40:21

25 Andᵀthe gate and its porches had windows all around likeᵀthose other windows; the length *was* fifty cubits and the width twenty-five cubits.   *it • these windows*

26 And *there were* sevenᴿsteps going up to it, and its porches *were* in front of them; and

it had palm tree ornaments on its side pillars, one on each side.   Ezek. 40:6, 22

27 And the inner court had a gate toward the south; and he measured from gate to gate toward the south, a hundred cubits.

The Inner Court

28 Then he brought me to the inner court by the south gate; and he measured the south gateᴿaccording to those same measurements.   Ezek. 40:32, 35

29 Its guardrooms also, its side pillars, and its porches *were* according to those same measurements. Andᵀthe gate and its porches had windows all around; it *was* fifty cubits long and twenty-five cubits wide.   *it*

30 And *there were* porches all around, twenty-five cubits long and five cubits wide.

31 And its porches *were* toward the outer court; and palm tree ornaments *were* on its side pillars, and its stairway had eight steps.

32 And he brought me into the inner court toward the east. And he measured the gate according to those same measurements.

33 Its guardrooms also, its side pillars, and its porches *were* according to those same measurements. Andᵀthe gate and its porches had windows all around; it *was* fifty cubits long and twenty-five cubits wide.   *it*

34 And itsᴿporches *were* toward the outer court; and palm tree ornaments *were* on its side pillars, on each side, and its stairway had eightᴿsteps.   Ezek. 40:16 • Ezek. 40:22, 37

35 Then he brought me to theᴿnorth gate; and he measured *it* according to those same measurements,   Ezek. 40:27, 32; 44:4; 47:2

36 *with* its guardrooms, its side pillars, and its porches. Andᵀthe gate had windows all around; the length *was*ᴿfifty cubits and the width twenty-five cubits.   *it • Ezek. 40:21*

37 And its side pillars *were* toward the outer court; andᴿpalm tree ornaments *were* on its side pillars on each side, and its stairway had eightᴿsteps.   Ezek. 40:16 • Ezek. 40:34

38 And aᴿchamber with its doorway was by the side pillars at the gates; there they rinse the burnt offering.   1 Chr. 28:12

₌39 And in the porch of the gate *were* twoᴿtables on each side, on which to slaughter theᴿburnt offering, the sin offering, and the guilt offering.   ₜEzek. 40:42 • Lev. 1:3-17

40 And on the outerᵀside, as one went up to the gateway toward the north, were two tables; and on the other side of the porch of the gate *were* two tables.   ₜ*shoulder*

41 Four tables *were* on each sideᵀnext to the gate; *or,* eight tables on which they slaughter *sacrifices.*   *by the shoulder of*

42 And for the burnt offering *there were* fourᴿtables ofᵀhewn stone, a cubit and a half long, a cubit and a half wide, and one cubit high, on which they lay the instruments with which they slaughter the burnt offering and the sacrifice.   Ezek. 40:39 • Ex. 20:25

43 And the double ᴬhooks, one handbreadth in length, were installed ᴬin the

house all around; and on the tables *was* the flesh of the offering.   *ledges • inside*

44 And from the outside to the inner gate were chambers for the singers in the inner court, *one of* which was at the^Tside of the north gate, with^Tits front toward the south, and one at the side of the east gate facing toward the north.   *shoulder • their*

45 And he said to me, "This is the^Rchamber which faces toward the south, *intended* for the priests who^Rkeep charge of the^Atemple;   Ezek. 40:17, 38 • 1 Chr. 9:23 • *house*

46 but the^Rchamber which faces toward the north is for the priests who keep charge of the altar. These are the sons of Zadok, who from the sons of Levi come near to the LORD to minister to Him."   Ezek. 40:17, 38

47 And he measured the court, a *perfect* square, a^Rhundred cubits long and a hundred cubits wide; and the altar was in front of the^Ttemple.   Ezek. 40:19, 23, 27 • *house*

The Temple Porch

48 Then he brought me to the^Rporch of the ^Ttemple and measured *each* side pillar of the porch, five cubits on each side; and the width of the gate was three cubits on each side.   1 Kin. 6:3; 2 Chr. 3:4 • *house*

49 The length of the porch was twenty cubits, and the width eleven cubits; and at the ^Rstairway by which it was ascended *were*^Rcolumns belonging to the side pillars, one on each side.   Ezek. 40:31, 34, 37 • 2 Chr. 3:17

CHAPTER 41

The Temple Itself

THEN he brought me to the nave and measured the side pillars; six cubits wide on each side *was* the width of the side pillar.

2 And the width of the entrance *was* ten cubits, and the^Tsides of the entrance were five cubits on each side. And he measured ^Tthe length of the nave, forty cubits, and the width, twenty cubits.   *shoulders • its length*

3 Then he went inside and measured each side pillar of the doorway, two cubits, and the doorway, six cubits *high;* and the width of the doorway, seven cubits.

4 And he measured its length,^Rtwenty cubits, and the width, twenty cubits, before the^Rnave; and he said to me, "This is the most holy *place.*"   1 Kin. 6:20 • 1 Kin. 6:5

5 Then he measured the wall of the temple, six cubits; and the width of the^Rside chambers, four cubits, all around about the house on every side.   1 Kin. 6:5; Ezek. 41:6-11

6 And the side chambers were in three stories,^Tone above another, and^Tthirty in each story; and the side chambers extended to the wall which *stood* on their inward side all around, that they might be fastened, and not be fastened into the wall of the temple *itself.*   *chamber upon chamber • thirty times*

7 And the side chambers surrounding the temple were wider at each successive story. Because the structure surrounding the temple went upward by stages on all sides of the temple, therefore the width of the temple *increased* as it went higher; and thus one went up from the lowest *story* to the highest by way of the second *story.*

8 I saw also that the house had a raised ^Tplatform all around; the foundations of the side chambers were a full rod of six^Along cubits *in height.*   *height • to the joint*

9 The^Tthickness of the outer wall of the side chambers was five cubits. But the^Rfree space between the side chambers belonging to the temple   *width* • Ezek. 41:11

10 and the *outer*^Rchambers *was* twenty cubits in width all around the temple on every side.   Ezek. 40:17

11 And the doorways of the side chambers toward the free space *consisted of* one doorway toward the north and another doorway toward the south; and the width of the free space was five cubits all around.

12 And the building that *was* in front of the separate area at the side toward the west *was* seventy cubits wide; and the wall of the building was five cubits thick all around, and its length *was* ninety cubits.

13 Then he measured the temple, a^Rhundred cubits long; the separate area with the ^Rbuilding and its walls *were* also a hundred cubits long.   Ezek. 40:47 • Ezek. 41:12

14 Also the width of the front of the temple and *that of* the separate^Tareas along the east *side* totaled a hundred cubits.   *area*

15 And he measured the length of the building^Talong the front of the separate area behind it, with a gallery on each side, a hundred cubits; *he* also *measured* the inner nave and the porches of the court.   *to*

16 The thresholds, the^Alatticed windows, and the^Agalleries round about their three stories, opposite the threshold, were paneled with wood all around, and *from* the ground to the windows (but the windows were covered),   *framed • passageways*

17 over the entrance, and to the inner house, and on the outside, and on all the wall all around inside and outside, by measurement.

18 And it was^Tcarved with^Rcherubim and ^Rpalm trees; and a palm tree was between cherub and cherub, and every cherub had two faces,   *made* • Ezek. 41:20, 25 • 2 Chr. 3:5

19 a man's face toward the palm tree on one side, and a young lion's face toward the palm tree on the other side; they were ^Tcarved on all the house all around.   *made*

20 From the ground to above the entrance cherubim and palm trees were^Tcarved, as well as on the wall of the nave.   *made*

21 The^Rdoorposts of the^Rnave were square; as for the front of the sanctuary, the appearance of one doorpost was like that of the other.   1 Kin. 6:33; Ezek. 40:9, 14, 16 • Ezek. 41:1

22 The altar *was* of wood, three cubits high, and its length two cubits; its corners, its[T]base, and its[T]sides *were* of wood. And he said to me, "This is the[R]table that is before the LORD."　　　*length • walls •* Ezek. 23:41; 44:16

23 And the[R]nave and the[R]sanctuary each had a double door.　　Ezek. 41:1 • Ezek. 41:4

24 And each of the doors had two leaves, two [A]swinging leaves; two *leaves* for one door and two leaves for the other.　*turning*

25 Also there were[T]carved on them, on the doors of the nave, cherubim and palm trees like those carved on the walls; and *there was* a[A]threshold of wood on the front of the porch outside.　*made • canopy of wood over*

26 And *there were* latticed windows and palm trees on one side and on the other, on the sides of the porch; thus *were* the side chambers of the house and the thresholds.

CHAPTER 42

The Chamber in the Outer Court

THEN he[R]brought me out into the outer court, the way toward the north; and he brought me to the chamber which *was* opposite the separate area and opposite the building toward the north.　Ezek. 40:17, 28, 48

2 Along the length, *which was* a[R]hundred cubits, *was* the north door; the width *was* fifty cubits.　　　　Ezek. 41:13

3 Opposite the twenty *cubits* which belonged to the inner court, and opposite the [R]pavement which belonged to the outer court, *was* [A]gallery corresponding to gallery in three stories.　Ezek. 40:17 • *passageway*

4 And before the[R]chambers *was* an inner walk ten cubits wide, a way of one *hundred* cubits; and their openings *were* on the north.　　　　　Ezek. 46:19

5 Now the upper chambers *were*[T]smaller because the[A]galleries took more *space* away from them than from the lower and middle ones in the building.　*shorter • passageways*

6 For they *were* in[R]three stories and had no pillars like the pillars of the courts; therefore *the upper chambers* were[A]set back from the ground upward, more than the lower and middle ones.　Ezek. 41:6 • *reduced*

7 As for the outer wall by the side of the chambers, toward the outer court facing the chambers, its length *was* fifty cubits.

8 For the length of the chambers which *were* in the outer court *was* fifty cubits; and behold, *the length of those* facing the temple *was* a[R]hundred cubits.　Ezek. 41:13, 14

9 And below these chambers *was* the[R]entrance on the east side, as one enters them from the outer court.　Ezek. 44:5; 46:19

10 In the[T]thickness of the[R]wall of the court toward the east, facing the[R]separate area and facing the building, *there were* chambers.　*width •* Ezek. 42:7 • Ezek. 42:1, 13

11 And the[R]way in front of them *was* like the appearance of the chambers which *were* on the north, according to their length so was their width; and all their exits *were* both according to their arrangements and openings.　　　　　Ezek. 42:4

12 And corresponding to the openings of the chambers which were toward the south was an opening at the head of the way, the way in front of the[R]wall toward the east, as one enters them.　　　Ezek. 42:7

13 Then he said to me, "The north chambers *and* the south chambers, which are opposite the separate area, they are the[R]holy chambers where the priests who are near to the LORD shall eat the most holy things. There they shall lay the most holy things, the grain offering, the sin offering, and the guilt offering; for the place is holy.　Ex. 29:31

14 "When the priests enter, then they shall not go out into the outer court from the sanctuary[T]without laying there their [R]garments in which they minister, for they are holy. They shall put on other garments; then they shall approach that which is for the people."　*but there they shall lay •* Zech. 3:4, 5

The Place of Separation

15 Now when he had finished measuring the inner house, he brought me out by the way of the[R]gate which faced toward the east, and measured it all around.　Ezek. 40:6

16 He measured on the east side with the measuring reed five hundred reeds, by the [R]measuring reed.　　　　Ezek. 40:3

17 He measured on the north side five hundred reeds by the measuring reed.

18 On the south side he measured five hundred reeds with the measuring reed.

19 He turned to the west side, *and* measured five hundred reeds with the measuring reed.

20 He measured it on the four sides; it had a[R]wall all around, the length five hundred and the width five hundred, to divide between the holy and the profane.　Zech. 2:5

CHAPTER 43

The Return of the Glory of God to the Temple

THEN he led me to the[R]gate, the gate facing toward the east;　Ezek. 10:19; 40:6; 42:15

2 and behold, the glory of the God of Israel was coming from the way of the east. And His voice was like the sound of many waters; and the earth shone with His glory.

3 And *it was* like the appearance of the vision which I saw, like the vision which I saw when He came to destroy the city. And the visions *were* like the vision which I saw by the river Chebar; and I fell on my face.

4 And the glory of the LORD came into

the house by the way of the gate facing toward the^Reast.   Ezek. 10:19; 11:23; 43:2

5 And the Spirit lifted me up and brought me into the inner court; and behold, the glory of the LORD filled the house.

6 Then I heard one speaking to me from the house, while a^Rman was standing beside me.   Ezek. 1:26; 40:3

7 And He said to me, "Son of man, *this is* the place of My^Rthrone and the place of the soles of My feet, where I will dwell among the sons of Israel forever. And the house of Israel will not again defile My holy name, neither they nor their kings, by their harlotry and by the ¹²corpses^Rof their kings ¹³when they die,   Ps. 47:8 • Lev. 26:30

8 by setting their threshold by My threshold, and their door post beside My door post, with *only* the wall between Me and them. And they have^Rdefiled My holy name by their abominations which they have committed. So I have consumed them in My anger.   Ezek. 8:3, 16

9"Now let them put away their harlotry and the ¹²corpses of their kings far from Me; and I will dwell among them forever.

10"As for you, son of man,^Tdescribe^Rthe ^Ttemple to the house of Israel, that they may be ashamed of their iniquities; and let them measure the plan.   *declare* • Ezek. 40:4 • *house*

11"And if they are ashamed of all that they have done, make known to them the ^Adesign of the house, its structure, its exits, its entrances, all its designs, all its statutes, and all its laws. And write *it* in their sight, so that they may observe its whole design and all its statutes, and do them.   *form(s)*

12"This is the^Alaw of the house: its entire ^Tarea on the top of the^Rmountain all around *shall be* most holy. Behold, this is the law of the house.   *instruction for* • *border* • Ezek. 40:2

The Altar of Burnt Offerings

13"And these are the measurements of the altar by cubits (the cubit being a cubit and a handbreadth): the base *shall be* a cubit, and the width a cubit, and its border on its edge round about one span; and this *shall be* the height of the^Abase of the altar.   *lap* • *back*

14"And from the base on the ground to the lower^Rledge *shall be* two cubits, and the width one cubit; and from the smaller ledge to the larger ledge *shall be* four cubits, and the width^Tone cubit.   Ezek. 43:17, 20; 45:19 • *the*

15"And the^Raltar hearth *shall be* four cubits; and from the altar hearth shall extend upwards four^Rhorns.   *ariel* shall • Ex. 27:2

16"Now the^Aaltar hearth *shall be* twelve *cubits* long by twelve wide,^Rsquare in its four sides.   *ariel* shall • Ex. 27:1

17"And the ledge *shall be* fourteen *cubits* long by fourteen wide in its four sides, the border around it *shall be* half a cubit, and its base *shall be* a cubit round about; and its steps shall^Aface the east."   *be on the east side*

18 And He said to me, "Son^Rof man, thus says the Lord GOD, 'These are the statutes for the altar on the day it is built, to offer ^Rburnt offerings on it and to sprinkle blood on it.   Ezek. 2:1 • Ex. 40:29 • [Heb. 9:21, 22]

19 'And you shall give to the Levitical priests who are from the offspring of^RZadok, who draw near to Me to minister to Me,' declares the Lord GOD, 'a^Ryoung bull for a ^Rsin offering.   Ezek. 40:46 • Lev. 4:3 • [Heb. 7:27]

20 'And you shall take some of its blood, and put it on its four^Rhorns, and on the four corners of the ledge, and on the border round about; thus you shall^Rcleanse it and make atonement for it.   Lev. 8:15 • Lev. 16:19

21 'You shall also take the bull for the sin offering; and it *shall be*^Rburned in the appointed place of the house, outside the sanctuary.   Ex. 29:14; Lev. 4:12; Heb. 13:11

22 'And on the second day you shall offer a ^Rmale goat without blemish for a sin offering; and they shall cleanse the altar, as they cleansed *it* with the bull.   Ezek. 43:25

23 'When you have finished cleansing *it,* you shall present a ^Ryoung bull without blemish and a^Rram without blemish from the flock.   Ex. 29:1, 10; Ezek. 45:18 • Ex. 29:1

24 'And you shall present them before the LORD, and the priests shall throw^Rsalt on them, and they shall offer them up as a burnt offering to the LORD.   [Mark 9:49, 50]

25 'For^Rseven days you shall prepare daily a goat for a sin offering; also a young bull and a ram from the flock, without blemish, shall be prepared.   Ex. 29:35-37; Lev. 8:33, 35

26 'For seven days they shall make atonement for the altar and purify it; so shall they ^Tconsecrate it.   *fill its hands*

27 'And when they have completed the days, it shall be that on the^Reighth day and onward, the priests shall^Toffer your burnt offerings on the altar, and your^Rpeace offerings; and I will accept you,' declares the Lord GOD."   Lev. 9:1 • *make* • Lev. 3:1; 17:5

CHAPTER 44

Duties of Temple Priests

THEN He brought me back by the way of the^Router gate of the sanctuary, which faces the east; and it was shut.   Ezek. 40:6, 17; 42:14

2 And the LORD said to me, "This gate shall be shut; it shall not be opened, and no one shall enter by it, for the^RLORD God of Israel has entered by it; therefore it shall be shut.   Ezek. 43:2-4

3"As for the prince, he shall sit in it as prince to eat bread before the LORD; he shall enter by way of the porch of the gate, and shall go out^Tby the same way."   *by his way*

4 Then He brought me by the way of the ^Rnorth gate to the front of the house; and I looked, and behold, the^Rglory of the LORD

¹² Or, *monuments*   ¹³ Or, *in their high places*

filled the house of the LORD, and I[R]fell on my face. Ezek. 40:20, 40 · Is. 6:3, 4 · Ezek. 1:28

5 And the LORD said to me, "Son of man, [T]mark well, see with your eyes, and hear with your ears all that I say to you concerning all the[R]statutes of the house of the LORD and concerning all its laws; and mark well the entrance of the house, with all exits of the sanctuary.   set your heart on · Deut. 12:32

6"And you shall say to the [T]rebellious ones, to the house of Israel, 'Thus says the Lord GOD, "Enough[R] of all your abominations, O house of Israel,   [R]rebellion · Ezek. 45:9

7 when you brought in[R]foreigners,[R]uncircumcised in heart and uncircumcised in flesh, to be in My sanctuary to profane it, even My house, when you offered My food, the fat and the blood; for they made My covenant void—this in addition to all your abominations.   Ex. 12:43-49 · Lev. 26:41

8"And you have not kept charge of My holy things yourselves, but you have set foreigners to keep charge of My sanctuary."

9 'Thus says the Lord GOD, "No foreigner, uncircumcised in heart and uncircumcised in flesh, of all the foreigners who are among the sons of Israel, shall enter My sanctuary.

10"But the Levites who went far from Me, when Israel went astray, who[R]went astray from Me after their idols, shall bear the punishment for their iniquity.   2 Kin. 23:8, 9

11"Yet they shall be[R]ministers in My sanctuary, having oversight at the gates of the house and ministering in the house; they shall slaughter the burnt offering and the sacrifice for the people, and they shall stand before them to minister to them. Num. 3:5-37

12"Because they ministered to them before their idols and became a stumbling block of iniquity to the house of Israel, therefore I have sworn against them," declares the Lord GOD, "that they shall[R]bear the punishment for their iniquity. Ezek. 44:10

13"And they shall[R]not come near to Me to serve as a priest to Me, nor come near to any of My holy things, to the things that are most holy; but they shall[R]bear their shame and their abominations which they have committed.   Num. 18:3 · Ezek. 16:61, 63; 39:26

14"Yet I will[T]appoint them[T]to keep charge of the house, of all its service, and of all that shall be done in it.   give · keepers of the charge

15"But the [R]Levitical priests, the sons of Zadok, who[R]kept charge of My sanctuary when the sons of Israel went astray from Me, shall come near to Me to minister to Me; and they shall stand before Me to offer Me the[R]fat and the blood," declares the Lord GOD.   Jer. 33:18-22 · Num. 18:7 · Lev. 3:16, 17

16"They shall [R]enter My sanctuary; they shall come near to My table to minister to Me and keep My charge.   Num. 18:5, 7, 8

17"And it shall be that when they enter at the gates of the inner court, they shall be clothed with linen garments; and wool shall

not be on them while they are ministering in the gates of the inner court and in the house.

18"Linen[R]turbans shall be on their heads, and linen undergarments shall be on their loins; they shall not gird themselves with anything which makes them sweat.   Is. 3:20

19"And when they go out into the outer court, into the outer court to the people, they shall put off their garments in which they have been ministering and lay them in the holy chambers; then they shall put on other garments that they may not transmit holiness to the people with their garments.

20"Also they shall not shave their heads, yet they shall not let their locks grow long; they shall only trim the hair of their heads.

21"Nor[R]shall any of the priests drink wine when they enter the inner court.   Lev. 10:9

22"And they shall not marry a widow or a divorced woman but shall take virgins from the offspring of the house of Israel, or a widow who is the widow of a priest.

23"Moreover, they shall teach My people the[R]difference between the holy and the profane, and cause them to discern between the unclean and the clean.   Lev. 10:10; Ezek. 22:26

24"And in a dispute[R]they shall take their stand to judge; they shall judge it according to My ordinances. They shall also keep My laws and My statutes in all My appointed feasts, and sanctify My sabbaths. 1 Chr. 23:4

25"And[T]they[R]shall not go to a dead person to defile themselves; however, for father, for mother, for son, for daughter, for brother, or for a sister who has not had a husband, they may defile themselves.   he · Lev. 21:1-4

26"And after he is[R]cleansed, seven days shall [14]elapse for him.   Num. 19:13-19

27"And on the day that he goes into the sanctuary, into the[R]inner court to minister in the sanctuary, he shall offer his sin offering," declares the Lord GOD.   Ezek. 44:17

28"And it shall be with regard to an inheritance for them, that[R]I am their inheritance; and you shall give them no possession in Israel—I am their possession.   Num. 18:20

29"They shall eat the grain offering, the sin offering, and the guilt offering; and every devoted thing in Israel shall be theirs.

30"And the first of all the first fruits of every kind and every contribution of every kind, from all your contributions, shall be for the priests; you shall also give to the priest the first of your[A]dough to cause a blessing to rest on your house.   coarse meal

31"The priests shall not eat any bird or beast that has[R]died a natural death or has been torn to pieces.   Lev. 22:8; Deut. 14:21

CHAPTER 45

Land of the Temple Priests

"AND when you shall divide by lot the land for inheritance, you shall offer an allot-

ment to the LORD, a holy portion of the land; the length shall be the length of 25,000 *cubits*, and the width shall be 10,000. It shall be holy within all its boundary round about.

2"Out of this there shall be for the holy place a square round about five hundred by five hundred *cubits*, and fifty cubits for its ^open space round about.   *pasture land*

3"And from this ^T area you shall measure a length of 25,000 *cubits*, and a width of 10,000 *cubits;* and in it shall be the sanctuary, the most holy place.   *measure*

4"It shall be the holy portion of the land; it shall be for the priests, the ministers of the sanctuary, who come near to minister to the LORD, and it shall be a place for their houses and a holy place for the sanctuary.

5"And *an area* ^R 25,000 *cubits* in length and 10,000 in width shall be for the Levites, the ministers of the house, *and* for their possession cities to dwell in.   Ezek. 48:13

6"And you shall give the ^R city possession of *an area* 5,000 *cubits* wide and 25,000 *cubits* long, alongside the [15]allotment of the holy portion; it shall be for the whole house of Israel.   Ezek. 48:15-18, 30-35

7"And the prince shall have *land* on either side of the holy [15]allotment and the ^T property of the city, adjacent to the holy [15]allotment and the property of the city, on the west side toward the west and on the east side toward the east, and in length comparable to one of the portions, from the west border to the east border.   *possession*

8"This shall be his land for a possession in Israel; so My princes shall no longer ^R oppress My people, but they shall give *the rest of* the land to the house of Israel ^R according to their tribes." [Is. 11:3–5]; Jer. 23:5 • Josh. 11:23

Offerings of the Temple Priests

9 'Thus says the Lord GOD, "Enough, you princes of Israel; put away ^R violence and destruction, and practice justice and righteousness. Stop your expropriations from My people," declares the Lord GOD.   Jer. 6:7

10"You shall have ^R just balances, a just ^R ephah, and a just bath.   Lev. 19:36 • Is. 5:10

11"The ephah and the bath shall be ^T the same quantity, so that the bath may contain a tenth of a ^R homer, and the ephah a tenth of a homer; ^T their standard shall be according to the homer.   *one* • Is. 5:10 • *its measure*

12"And the shekel shall be twenty gerahs; twenty shekels, twenty-five shekels, *and* fifteen shekels shall be your ^T maneh.   *mina*

13"This is the offering that you shall offer: a sixth of an ephah from a homer of wheat; a sixth of an ephah from a homer of barley;

14 and the prescribed portion of oil (*namely,* the bath of oil), a tenth of a bath from *each* kor (*which is* ten baths *or* a homer, for ten baths are a homer);

15 and one sheep from *each* flock of two

hundred from the watering places of Israel—for a grain offering, for a burnt offering, and for peace offerings, to make atonement for them," declares the Lord GOD.

16"All the people of the land shall ^T give to this offering for the prince in Israel.   *be*

17"And it shall be the prince's part *to provide* the burnt offerings, the grain offerings, and the libations, at the feasts, on the new moons, and on the sabbaths, at all the appointed feasts of the house of Israel; he shall provide the sin offering, the grain offering, the burnt offering, and the peace offerings, to make atonement for the house of Israel."

18 'Thus says the Lord GOD, "In the ^R first *month*, on the first of the month, you shall take a young bull ^R without blemish and cleanse the sanctuary.   Ex. 12:2 • Lev. 22:20

19"And the priest shall take some of the blood from the sin offering and put *it* on the door posts of the house, on the ^T four corners of the ledge of the altar, and on the posts of the gate of the inner court.   Lev. 16:18-20

20"And thus you shall do on the seventh *day* of the month for everyone who goes astray or is ^T naive; so you shall make ^R atonement for the house.   *simple* • Ezek. 45:15, 18

21"In the first *month*, on the fourteenth day of the month, you shall have the ^R Passover, a feast of seven days; unleavened bread shall be eaten.   Ex. 12:1-24; Lev. 23:5-8

22"And on that day the prince shall provide for himself and all the people of the land a ^R bull for a sin offering.   Lev. 4:14

23"And *during* the seven days of the feast he shall provide as a burnt offering to the LORD ^R seven bulls and seven rams without blemish on every day of the seven days, and a male goat daily for a sin offering.   Job 42:8

24"And he shall provide as a grain offering an ephah ^T with a bull, an ephah with a ram, and a hin of oil with an ephah.   *for*

25"In the ^R seventh *month*, on the fifteenth day of the month, at the feast, he shall provide like this, seven days ^T for the sin offering, the burnt offering, the grain offering, and the oil."   Num. 29:12-38 • *according to*

CHAPTER 46

'T HUS says the Lord GOD, "The ^R gate of the ^R inner court facing east shall be shut the six working days; but it shall be opened on the sabbath day, and opened on the day of the new moon.   Ezek. 45:19 • Ezek. 8:16; 10:3

2"And the prince shall enter by way of the porch of the gate from outside and stand by the post of the gate. Then the priests shall provide his burnt offering and his peace offerings, and he shall worship at the threshold of the gate and then go out; but the gate shall not be shut until the evening.

3"The ^R people of the land shall also worship at the doorway of that gate before the

[15] Or, *contribution*

LORD on the sabbaths and on the ᴿnew moons.   Luke 1:10 • Ezek. 46:1

4"And the ᴿburnt offering which the prince shall offer to the LORD on the sabbath day shall be six lambs without blemish and a ram without blemish;   Ezek. 45:17

5 and the grain offering shall be an ephahᵀwith the ram, and the grain offering with the lambs as much as he is able to give, and a hin of oil with an ephah.   for

6"And on the day of the ᴿnew moon he shall offer a young bull without blemish, also six lambs and a ram, which shall be without blemish.   Ezek. 46:1

7"And he shall provide a grain offering, an ephahᵀwith the bull, and an ephah with the ram, and with the lambs as much as he is able, and a hin of oil with an ephah.   for

8"And when theᴿprince enters, he shall go in by way of the porch of the gate and go outᵀby the same way.   Ezek. 44:3 • by its way

9"But when the people of the land come ᴿbefore the LORD at the appointed feasts, he who enters by way of the north gate to worship shall go out by way of the south gate. And he who enters by way of the south gate shall go out by way of the north gate. No one shall return by way of the gate by which he entered but shall go straight out. Ps. 84:7

10"And when they go in, the prince shall go inᴿamong them; and when they go out, he shall go out.   2 Sam. 6:14, 15; 1 Chr. 29:20, 22

11"And at the festivals and the appointed feasts the grain offering shall be an ephah ᵀwith a bull and an ephah with a ram, and with the lambs as much as one is able to give, and a hin of oilᵀwith an ephah.   for

12"And when the prince provides a freewill offering, a burnt offering, or peace offerings as a freewill offering to the LORD, the gate facing east shall beᴿopened for him. And he shall provide his burnt offering and his peace offerings as he does on the sabbath day. Then he shall go out, and the gate shall be shut after he goes out.   Ezek. 44:3

13"And you shall provide aᴿlamb a year old without blemish for a burnt offering to the LORD daily;ᴿmorning by morning you shall provide it.   Num. 28:3-5 • Is. 50:4

14"Also you shall provide a grain offering with it morning by morning, a sixth of an ephah, and a third of a hin of oil to moisten the fine flour, a grain offering to the LORD continually by a perpetualᵀordinance. statute

15"Thus they shall provide the lamb, the grain offering, and the oil, morning by morning, for a continual burnt offering."

16 'Thus says the Lord GOD, "If the prince gives aᴿgift out of his inheritance to any of his sons, it shall belong to his sons; it is their possession by inheritance.   2 Chr. 21:3

17"But if he gives a gift from his inheritance to one of his servants, it shall be his until theᴿyear of liberty; then it shall return to the prince. His inheritance shall be only his sons'; it shall belong to them. Lev. 25:10

18"And the prince shall not take from the people's inheritance,ᵀthrusting them out of their possession; he shall give his sons inheritance from his own possession so that My people shall not be scattered, anyone from his possession." ' "   oppressing

19 Then he brought me through the entrance, which was at the side of the gate, into the holy chambers for the priests, which faced north; and behold, there was a place at the extreme rear toward the west.

20 And he said to me, "This is the place where the priests shall boil the guilt offering and the sin offering, and where they shall bake the grain offering, in order that they may not bring them out into the outer court to transmit holiness to the people."

21 Then he brought me out into the outer court and led me across to the four corners of the court; and behold, in every corner of the court there was a small court.

22 In the four corners of the court there were enclosed courts, forty cubits long and thirty wide; these four in the corners were ᵀthe same size.   one measure

23 And there was a row of masonry round about in them, around the four of them, and boiling places were made under the rows round about.

24 Then he said to me, "These are the boiling places where the ministers of the house shall boil the sacrifices of the people."

CHAPTER 47

River from the Temple

THEN he brought me back to theᴿdoor of the house; and behold,ᴿwater was flowing from under the threshold of the house toward the east, for the house faced east. And the water was flowing down from under, from the right side of the house, from south of the altar.   Ezek. 41:2, 23-25 • Ps. 46:4

2 And he brought me out by way of the north gate and led me aroundᵀon the outside to the outer gate by way of the gate that faces east. And behold, water was trickling from the south side.   by way of

3 When the man went out toward the east with a line in his hand, he measured a thousand cubits, and he led me through the water, water reaching the ankles.

4 Again he measured a thousand and led me through the water, water reaching the knees. Again he measured a thousand and led me through the water, water reaching the loins.

5 Again he measured a thousand; and it was a river that I could not ford, for the water had risen, enough water to swim in, a ᴿriver that could not be forded.   Is. 11:9

6 And he said to me, "Son of man, have you seen this?" Then he brought meᵀback to the bank of the river.   and caused me to return

7 Now when I had returned, behold, on the bank of the river there were very many trees on the one side and on the other.

8 Then he said to me, "These waters go out toward the eastern region and go down into the Arabah; then they go toward the sea, being made to flow into the sea, and the waters *of the sea* become^Tfresh.   *healed*

9"And it will come about that every living creature which swarms in every place where the river goes, will live. And there will be very many fish, for these waters go there, and *the others* become fresh; so everything will live where the river goes.

10"And it will come about that^Rfishermen will stand beside it; from^REngedi to Eneglaim there will be a place for the^Rspreading of nets. Their fish will be according to their kinds, like the fish of the Great Sea, very many.   Matt. 4:19 • Gen. 14:7 • Ezek. 26:5, 14

11"But its swamps and marshes will not become fresh; they will be left for salt.

12"And^Rby the river on its bank, on one side and on the other, will grow all *kinds of trees* for food. Their leaves will not wither, and their fruit will not fail. They will bear every month because their water flows from the sanctuary, and their fruit will be for food and their leaves for healing." [Rev. 22:2]

Boundaries of the Land

13 Thus says the Lord GOD, "This *shall be* the^Rboundary by which you shall divide the land for an inheritance among the twelve tribes of Israel; Joseph *shall have two*^Rportions.   Num. 34:2-12 • Gen. 48:5; Ezek. 48:4, 5

14"And you shall divide it for an inheritance, each one equally with the other; for I swore to give it to your forefathers, and this land shall fall to you^Tas an inheritance.   *in*

15"And this *shall be* the boundary of the land: on the^Rnorth side, from the Great Sea *by* the way of Hethlon, to the entrance of ^AZedad,^R   Num. 34:7-9 • *Hamath* • Num. 34:8

16 ^AHamath, Berothah, Sibraim, which is between the border of ^RDamascus and the border of Hamath; Hazer-hatticon, which is by the border of Hauran.   *Zedad* • Gen. 14:15

17"And the boundary shall ^Textend from the sea to^RHazar-enan *at* the border of Damascus, and on the north toward the north is the border of Hamath. This is the north side.   *be* • Num. 34:9

18"And the east side, from between Hauran, Damascus,^RGilead, and the land of Israel, *shall be* the^RJordan; from the *north* border to the eastern sea you shall measure. This is the east side.   Jer. 50:19 • Gen. 13:10, 11

19"And the^Rsouth side toward the south *shall extend* from Tamar as far as the waters of Meribath-kadesh, to the brook *of Egypt, and* to the Great Sea. This is the south side toward the south.   Num. 34:3-5

20"And the west side *shall be* the Great Sea, from the *south* border to a point opposite Lebo-hamath. This is the west side.

21"So you shall divide this land among yourselves according to the tribes of Israel.

22"And it will come about that you shall divide it by^Rlot for an inheritance among yourselves and among the aliens who stay in your midst, who bring forth sons in your midst. And they shall be to you as the native-born among the sons of Israel; they shall be allotted an inheritance with you among the tribes of Israel.   Num. 26:55, 56

23"And it will come about that in the tribe with which the alien stays, there you shall give *him* his inheritance," declares the Lord GOD.

CHAPTER 48

Divisions of the Land

"NOW these are the names of the tribes: from the northern extremity,^Tbeside the way of Hethlon to Lebo-hamath, *as far as* Hazarenan *at* the border of Damascus, toward the north beside Hamath, running from east to west, Dan, one *portion.*   *at the hand of*

2"And beside the border of Dan, from the east side to the west side,^RAsher, one *portion.*   Josh. 19:24-31

3"And beside the border of Asher, from the east side to the west side,^RNaphtali, one portion.   Josh. 19:32-39

4"And beside the border of Naphtali, from the east side to the west side,^RManasseh, one *portion.*   Josh. 13:29-31; 17:1-11

5"And beside the border of Manasseh, from the east side to the west side,^REphraim, one *portion.*   Josh. 16:5-9; 17:8-10, 14-18

6"And beside the border of Ephraim, from the east side to the west side,^RReuben, one *portion.*   Josh. 13:15-21

7"And beside the border of Reuben, from the east side to the west side,^RJudah, one portion.   Josh. 15:1-63; 19:9

8"And beside the border of Judah, from the east side to the west side, shall be the ¹⁶allotment which you shall^Tset apart, 25,000 *cubits* in width, and in length like one of the portions, from the east side to the west side; and the^Rsanctuary shall be in the middle of it.   *offer* • [Is. 12:6; 33:20-22]; Ezek. 45:3, 4

9"The allotment that you shall set apart to the LORD *shall be* 25,000 *cubits* in length, and 10,000 in width.

10"And the holy allotment shall be for these, *namely* for the^Rpriests, toward the north 25,000 *cubits in length,* toward the west 10,000 in width, toward the east 10,000 in width, and toward the south 25,000 in length; and the sanctuary of the LORD shall be in its midst.   Ezek. 44:28; 45:4

11"*It shall be* for the priests who are sanctified of the^Rsons of Zadok, who have kept My charge, who did not go astray when the sons of Israel went astray, as the^RLevites went astray.   Ezek. 40:46 • Ezek. 44:10, 12

12"And it shall be an allotment to them

¹⁶Or, *contribution,* and so throughout this context

from the allotment of the land, a most holy place, by the border of the Levites.

13 "And alongside the border of the priests the Levites *shall have* 25,000 *cubits* in length and 10,000 in width. The whole length *shall be* 25,000 *cubits* and the width 10,000.

14 "Moreover, they shall not sell or exchange any of it, or alienate this choice *portion* of land; for it is holy to the LORD.

15 "And the remainder, 5,000 *cubits* in width and 25,000 in length, shall be for ᴿcommon use for the city, for dwellings and for ^open spaces; and the city shall be in its midst.   *in front* • Ezek. 42:20 • *pasture land*

16 "And these *shall be* its measurements: the north side 4,500 *cubits,* the south side ᴿ4,500 *cubits,* the east side 4,500 *cubits,* and the west side 4,500 *cubits.* ^   Rev. 21:16

17 "And the city shall have^open spaces: on the north 250 *cubits,* on the south 250 *cubits,* on the east 250 *cubits,* and on the west 250 *cubits.*   *pasture land*

18 "And the remainder of the length alongside the holy allotment shall be 10,000 *cubits* toward the east, and 10,000 toward the west; and it shall be^alongside the holy allotment. And its produce shall be food for the workers of the city.   *exactly as*

19 "And the workers of the city, out of all the tribes of Israel, shall cultivate it.

20 "The whole allotment *shall be* 25,000 by 25,000 *cubits;* you shall ᵀset apart the holy allotment, a ᵀsquare, with the ^property of the city.   *offer* • *fourth* • *possession*

21 "And the ᴿremainder *shall be* for the prince, on the one side and on the other of the holy allotment and of the ^property of the city; in front of the 25,000 *cubits* of the allotment toward the east border and westward in front of the 25,000 toward the west border, alongside the portions, *it shall be* for the prince. And the holy allotment and the sanctuary of the house shall be in the middle of it.   Ezek. 34:24; 45:7; 48:22 • *possession*

22 "And exclusive of the ^property of the Levites and the property of the city, *which* are in the middle of that which belongs to the prince, *everything* between the border of Judah and the border of Benjamin shall be for the prince.   *possession*

23 "As for the rest of the tribes: from the east side to the west side, ᴿBenjamin, one *portion.*   Josh. 18:21-28

24 "And beside the border of Benjamin, from the east side to the west side, ᴿSimeon, one *portion.*   Josh. 19:1-9

25 "And beside the border of Simeon, from the east side to the west side, ᴿIssachar, one *portion.*   Josh. 19:17-23

26 "And beside the border of Issachar, from the east side to the west side, ᴿZebulun, one *portion.*   Josh. 19:10-16

27 "And beside the border of Zebulun, from the east side to the west side, ᴿGad, one *portion.*   Josh. 13:24-28

28 "And beside the border of Gad, at the south side toward the south, the border shall be from ᴿTamar to the waters of Meribath-kadesh, to the brook *of Egypt,* to the ᴿGreat Sea.   Gen. 14:7 • Ezek. 47:10, 15, 19, 20

29 "This is the ᴿland which you shall divide by lot to the tribes of Israel for an inheritance, and these are their *several* portions," declares the Lord GOD.   Ezek. 47:13-20

Gates of the City

30 "And these are the exits of the city: on the ᴿnorth side, 4,500 *cubits* by measurement,   Ezek. 48:32, 33, 34

31 ᵀshall be the gates of the city, named for the tribes of Israel, three gates toward the north: the gate of Reuben, one; the gate of Judah, one; the gate of Levi, one.   *and*

32 "And on the east side, 4,500 *cubits,* shall be three gates: the gate of Joseph, one; the gate of Benjamin, one; the gate of Dan, one.

33 "And on the south side, 4,500 *cubits* by measurement,ᵀshall be three gates: the gate of Simeon, one; the gate of Issachar, one; the gate of Zebulun, one.   *and*

34 "On the west side, 4,500 *cubits, shall be* three gates: the gate of Gad, one; the gate of Asher, one; the gate of Naphtali, one.

Name of the City

35 "*The city shall be* 18,000 *cubits* round about; and the ᴿname of the city from *that* day *shall be,* 'The LORD is there.' "   Jer. 23:6

THE BOOK OF

DANIEL

THE BOOK OF DANIEL

Daniel's life and ministry bridge the entire seventy-year period of Babylonian captivity. Deported to Babylon at the age of sixteen, and handpicked for government service, Daniel becomes God's prophetic mouthpiece to the gentile and Jewish world declaring God's present and eternal purpose. Nine of the twelve chapters in his book revolve around dreams, including God-given visions involving trees, animals, beasts, and images. In both his personal adventures and prophetic visions, Daniel shows God's guidance, intervention, and power in the affairs of men.

The name *Daniye'l* or *Dani'el* means "God Is My Judge," and the book is, of course, named after the author and principal character. The Greek form *Daniel* in the Septuagint is the basis for the Latin and English titles.

THE AUTHOR OF DANIEL

Daniel and his three friends were evidently born into noble Judean families and were "youths in whom was no defect, who were good-looking, showing intelligence in every *branch of* wisdom, endowed with understanding, and discerning knowledge" (1:4). He was given three years of training in the best of Babylon's schools (1:5). As part of the reidentification process, he was given a new name that honored one of the Babylonian deities: *Belteshazzar* meant "Bel Protect His Life" (see 1:7; 4:8; Jer. 51:44). Daniel's wisdom and divinely given interpretive abilities brought him into a position of prominence, especially in the courts of Nebuchadnezzar and Darius. He is one of the few well-known Bible characters about whom nothing negative is ever written. His life was characterized by faith, prayer, courage, consistency, and lack of compromise. This "highly esteemed" man (9:23; 10:11, 19) was mentioned three times by his sixth-century B.C. contemporary Ezekiel as an example of righteousness.

Daniel claimed to write this book (12:4), and he used the autobiographical first person from 7:2 onward. The Jewish Talmud agrees with this testimony, and Christ attributed a quote from 9:27 to "Daniel the prophet" (Matt. 24:15).

THE TIME OF DANIEL

Babylon rebelled against the Assyrian Empire in 626 B.C. and overthrew the Assyrian capital of Nineveh in 612 B.C. Baby-

lon became the master of the Middle East when it defeated the Egyptian armies in 605 B.C. Daniel was among those taken captive to Babylon that year when Nebuchadnezzar subdued Jerusalem. He ministered for the full duration of the Babylonian captivity as a prophet and a government official and continued on after Babylon was overcome by the Medes and Persians in 539 B.C. His prophetic ministry was directed to the gentile courts of Babylon (Nebuchadnezzar and Belshazzar) and Persia (Darius and Cyrus), as well as to his Jewish countrymen. Zerubbabel led a return of the Jews to Jerusalem in the first year of Cyrus, and Daniel lived and ministered at least until the third year of Cyrus (536 B.C.; 10:1). Daniel's book was no doubt written by Cyrus's ninth year (c. 530 B.C.). As he predicted, the Persian Empire continued until Alexander the Great (11:2, 3) who extended the boundaries of the Greek Empire as far east as India. The Romans later displaced the Greeks as rulers of the Middle East.

For various reasons, many critics have argued that Daniel is a fraudulent book that was written in the time of the Maccabees in the second century B.C., not the sixth century B.C. as it claims. But their arguments are not compelling:

(1) *The prophetic argument* holds that Daniel could not have made such accurate predictions; it must be a "prophecy after the events." Daniel 11 alone contains over one hundred specific prophecies of historical events that literally came true. The author, the critics say, must have lived at the time of Antiochus Epiphanes (175–163 B.C.) and probably wrote this to strengthen the faith of the Jews. But this argument was developed out of a theological bias that assumes true prophecy cannot take place. It also implies that the work was intentionally deceptive.

(2) *The linguistic argument* claims that the book uses a late Aramaic in 2—7 and that the Persian and Greek words also point to a late date. But recent discoveries show that Daniel's Aramaic is actually a form of the early Imperial Aramaic. Daniel's use of some Persian words is no argument for a late date since he continued living in the Persian period under Cyrus. The only Greek words are names of musical instruments in chapter 3, and this comes as no surprise since there were Greek mercenaries in the Assyrian and Babylonian armies. Far more Greek words would be ex-

pected if the book were written in the second century B.C.

(3) *The historical argument* asserts that Daniel's historical blunders argue for a late date. But recent evidence has demonstrated the historical accuracy of Daniel. Inscriptions found at Haran show that Belshazzar reigned in Babylon while his father Nabonidus was fighting the invading Persians. And Darius the Mede (5:31; 6:1) has been identified as Gubaru, a governor appointed by Cyrus.

THE CHRIST OF DANIEL
Christ is the Great Stone who will crush the kingdoms of this world (2:34, 35, 44), the Son of Man who is given dominion by the Ancient of Days (7:13, 14), and the coming Messiah who will be cut off (9:25, 26). It is likely that Daniel's vision in 10:5–9 was an appearance of Christ (cf. Rev. 1:12–16).

The vision of the sixty-nine weeks in 9:25, 26 pinpoints the coming of the Messiah. The decree of 9:25 took place on March 4, 444 B.C. (Neh. 2:1–8). The sixty-nine weeks of seven years equals 483 years, or 173,880 days (using 360-day prophetic years). This leads to March 29, A.D. 33, the date of the Triumphal Entry. This is checked by noting that 444 B.C. to A.D. 33 is 476 years, and 476 times 365.24219 days per year equals 173,855 days. Adding twenty-five for the difference between March 4 and March 29 gives 173,880 days.

KEYS TO DANIEL
Key Word: God's Program for Israel— Daniel was written to encourage the exiled Jews by revealing God's sovereign program for Israel during and after the period of gentile domination. The "Times of the Gen-

tiles" began with the Babylonian captivity, and Israel would suffer under gentile powers for many years. But this period is not permanent, and a time will come when God will establish the messianic kingdom which will last forever. Daniel repeatedly emphasizes the sovereignty and power of God over human affairs. "The Most High is ruler over the realm of mankind, and bestows it on whomever He wishes" (4:25). The God who directs the forces of history has not deserted His people. They must continue to trust in Him, because His promises of preservation and ultimate restoration are as sure as the coming of the Messiah.

Key Verses: Daniel 2:20–22 and 2:44— "Daniel answered and said, 'Let the name of God be blessed forever and ever, for wisdom and power belong to Him. And it is He who changes the times and the epochs; He removes kings and establishes kings; He gives wisdom to wise men, and knowledge to men of understanding. It is He who reveals the profound and hidden things; He knows what is in the darkness, and the light dwells with Him' " (2:20–22).

"And in the days of those kings the God of heaven will set up a kingdom which will never be destroyed, and *that* kingdom will not be left for another people; it will crush and put an end to all these kingdoms, but it will itself endure forever" (2:44).

Key Chapter: Daniel 9—Daniel's prophecy of the seventy weeks (9:24–27) provides the chronological frame for messianic prediction from the time of Daniel to the establishment of the kingdom on earth. It is clear that the first sixty-nine weeks were fulfilled at Christ's first coming. Some scholars affirm that the last week has not yet been fulfilled because Christ relates its main events to His second coming (Matt. 24:6, 15). Others perceive these words

FOCUS	HISTORY OF DANIEL	PROPHETIC PLAN FOR THE GENTILES				PROPHETIC PLAN OF ISRAEL		
REFERENCE	1:1——————2:1—————————5:1—————		6:1——— 7:1——			8:1 ———— 9:1————— 10:1–12:13		
DIVISION	PERSONAL LIFE OF DANIEL	VISIONS OF NEBUCHADNEZZAR	VISION OF BELSHAZZAR	DECREE OF DARIUS	FOUR BEASTS	VISION OF RAM AND HE-GOAT	VISION OF SEVENTY WEEKS	VISION OF ISRAEL'S FUTURE
TOPIC	DANIEL'S BACKGROUND	DANIEL INTERPRETS OTHERS' DREAMS				ANGEL INTERPRETS DANIEL'S DREAMS		
	HEBREW	ARAMAIC				HEBREW		
LOCATION	BABYLON OR PERSIA							
TIME	c. 605–536 B.C.							

of Christ as applying to the Roman desecration of the temple in A.D. 70.

SURVEY OF DANIEL

Daniel, the "Apocalypse of the Old Testament," presents a surprisingly detailed and comprehensive sweep of prophetic history. After an introductory chapter in Hebrew, Daniel switches to Aramaic in chapters 2—7 to describe the future course of the gentile world powers. Then in 8—12, Daniel reverts back to his native language to survey the future of the Jewish nation under gentile dominion. The theme of God's sovereign control in the affairs of world history clearly emerges and provides comfort to the future church, as well as to the Jews whose nation was destroyed by the Babylonians. The Babylonians, Persians, Greeks, and Romans will come and go, but God will establish His kingdom through His redeemed people forever. Daniel's three divisions are: the personal history of Daniel (1), the prophetic plan for the Gentiles (2—7), and the prophetic plan for Israel (8—12).

The Personal History of Daniel (1): This chapter introduces the book by giving the background and preparation of the prophet. Daniel is deported along with other promising youths and placed in an intensive training program in Nebuchadnezzar's court. Their names and diets are changed so that they will lose their Jewish identification, but Daniel's resolve to remain faithful to the Lord is rewarded. He and his friends are granted wisdom and knowledge.

The Prophetic Plan for the Gentiles (2—7): Only Daniel can relate and interpret Nebuchadnezzar's disturbing dream of the great statue (2). God empowers Daniel to foretell the way in which He will sovereignly raise and depose four gentile empires. The Messiah's kingdom will end the times of the Gentiles.

Because of his position revealed in the dream, Nebuchadnezzar erects a golden image and demands that all bow to it (3). The persecution and preservation of Daniel's friends in the fiery furnace again illustrates the power of God. After Nebuchadnezzar refuses to respond to the warning of his vision of the tree (4), he is humbled until he acknowledges the supremacy of God and the foolishness of his pride. The feast of Belshazzar marks the end of the Babylonian kingdom (5). Belshazzar is judged because of his arrogant defiance of God. In the reign of Darius, a plot against Daniel backfires when he is divinely delivered in the den of lions (6). Daniel's courageous faith is rewarded, and Darius learns a lesson about the might of the God of Israel. The vision of the four beasts (7) supplements the four-part statue vision of chapter 2 in its portrayal of the Babylonian, Persian, Greek, and Roman empires. But once again, "the saints of the Highest One will receive the kingdom and possess the kingdom forever" (7:18).

The Prophetic Plan for Israel (8—12): The focus in chapter 8 narrows to a vision of the ram and goat that shows Israel under the Medo-Persian and Grecian empires. Alexander the Great is the large horn of 8:21 and Antiochus Epiphanes is the small horn of 8:9. After Daniel's prayer of confession for his people, he is privileged to receive the revelation of the seventy weeks, including the Messiah's atoning death (9). This gives the chronology of God's perfect plan for the redemption and deliverance of His people. Following is a great vision that gives amazing details of Israel's future history (10 and 11). Chapter 11 chronicles the coming kings of Persia and Greece, the wars between the Ptolemies of Egypt and the Seleucids of Syria, and the persecution led by Antiochus. God's people will be saved out of tribulation and resurrected (12).

Part Three: The Prophetic Plan for Israel (8:1—12:13)

CHAPTER 1

The Deportation of Daniel
to Babylon

IN the third year of the reign of Jehoiakim king of Judah, Nebuchadnezzar king of Babylon came to Jerusalem and besieged it.

2 And the Lord gave Jehoiakim king of Judah into his hand, along with some of the vessels of the house of God; and he brought them to the land of ᴿShinar, to the house of his ¹god, and he brought the vessels into the treasury of his god.   Dan. 5:2 • Gen. 10:10

3 Then the king ordered Ashpenaz, the chief of his ²officials, to bring in some of the sons of Israel, including some of the ᵀroyal ᴿfamily and of the nobles,   seed of the • Is. 39:7

4 youths in whom was no defect, who were good-looking, showing intelligence in every branch of wisdom, endowed with understanding, and discerning knowledge, and who had ability for serving in the king's court; and he ordered him to teach them the ³literature and language of the Chaldeans.

5 And the king appointed for them a daily ration from the king's choice food and from the wine which he drank, and ap-

pointed that they should be ^educated ᴿthree years, at the end of which they were to ᴿenter the king's personal service.   reared • Dan. 1:19

6 Now among them from the sons of Judah were ᴿDaniel, Hananiah, Mishael and Azariah.   Ezek. 14:14, 20; 28:3; Matt. 24:15

7 Then the commander of the officials assigned new names to them; and to Daniel he assigned the name ᴿBelteshazzar, to Hananiah ᴿShadrach, to Mishael Meshach, and to Azariah Abed-nego.   Dan. 2:26 • Dan. 2:49

The Faithfulness of Daniel
in Babylon

8 But Daniel ᵀmade up his mind that he would not ᴿdefile himself with the king's choice food or with the wine which he drank; so he sought permission from the commander of the officials that he might not defile himself.   set upon his heart • Ezek. 4:13, 14

9 Now God granted Daniel ᵀfavor ᴿand compassion in the sight of the commander of the officials,   lovingkindness • Gen. 39:21

10 and the commander of the officials said to Daniel, "I am afraid of my lord the king, who has appointed your food and your drink; for why should he see your faces looking more haggard than the youths who

---

¹ Or, gods   ² Or, eunuchs, and so throughout the ch.
³ Or, writing

are your own age? Then you would make me forfeit my head to the king."

11 But Daniel said to the overseer whom the commander of the officials had appointed over Daniel, Hananiah, Mishael and Azariah,

12"Please test your servants for ten days, and let us be^Rgiven some vegetables to eat and water to drink.   Dan. 1:16

13"Then let our appearance be^Tobserved in your presence, and the appearance of the youths who are eating the king's choice food; and deal with your servants according to what you see."   *seen*

14 So he listened to them in this matter and tested them for ten days.

15 And at the end of ten days their appearance seemed^Rbetter and^Tthey were fatter than all the youths who had been eating the king's choice food. Ex. 23:25 • *fat of flesh*

16 So the overseer continued to withhold their choice food and the wine they were to drink, and kept giving them vegetables.

The Reputation of Daniel in Babylon

17 And as for these four youths,^RGod gave them knowledge and intelligence in every *branch of*^Aliterature and wisdom; Daniel even understood all *kinds of*^Rvisions and dreams. 1 Kin. 3:12, 28 • *writing* • Dan. 2:19; 7:1

18 Then at the end of the days which the king had^Tspecified^Tfor presenting them, the commander of the officials presented them before Nebuchadnezzar. *said* • *to bring them*

19 And the king talked with them, and out of them all not one was found like Daniel, Hananiah, Mishael and Azariah; so they^Rentered the king's personal service. Gen. 41:46

20 And as for every matter of wisdom^Tand understanding about which the king consulted them, he found them ten times better than all the^Amagicians *and* conjurers who *were* in all his realm. *of* • *soothsayer priests*

21 And Daniel ^Tcontinued until the^Rfirst year of Cyrus the king. *was until* • Dan. 6:28

CHAPTER 2

Nebuchadnezzar Conceals His Dream

Now in the second year of the reign of Nebuchadnezzar, Nebuchadnezzar ^Rhad dreams; and his spirit was troubled and his sleep^Tleft him. Gen. 40:5-8 • *was gone upon him*

2 Then the king gave orders to call in the ⁴magicians, the conjurers, the sorcerers and the ⁵Chaldeans, to tell the king his dreams. So they came in and stood before the king.

3 And the king said to them, "I^Thad a dream, and my spirit^Tis anxious to understand the dream." *dreamed* • *was troubled*

4 Then the Chaldeans spoke to the king

in ^RAramaic: "O king, live forever!^RTell the dream to your servants, and we will declare the interpretation." Ezra 4:7 • Dan. 2:7

5 The king answered and said to the Chaldeans, "The command from me is firm: if you do not make known to me the dream and its interpretation, you will be^Ttorn^Rlimb from limb, and your houses will be made a rubbish heap. *made into limbs* • Dan. 2:21; 3:29

6"But if you declare the dream and its interpretation, you will receive from me^Rgifts and a reward and great honor; therefore declare to me the dream and its interpretation." Dan. 2:48; 5:7, 16, 29

7 They answered a second time and said, "Let the king tell the dream to his servants, and we will declare the interpretation."

8 The king answered and said, "I know for certain that you are^Tbargaining for time, inasmuch as you have seen that the command from me is firm, *buying*

9 that if you do not make the dream known to me, there is only one decree for you. For you have agreed together to speak lying and corrupt^Twords before me until the^Tsituation is changed; therefore tell me the dream, that I may know that you can declare to me its interpretation." *word* • *time*

10 The Chaldeans answered^Tthe king and said, "There is not a man on earth who could declare the matter^Tfor the king, inasmuch as no great king or ruler has *ever* asked anything like this of any^Rmagician, conjurer or Chaldean. *before the* • *of* • Dan. 2:2

11"Moreover, the thing which the king demands is^Adifficult, and there is no one else who could declare it ^Tto the king except ^Rgods, whose^Rdwelling place is not with *mortal flesh*." *rare* • *before* • Gen. 41:39 • Is. 57:15

12 Because of this the king became indignant and very furious, and gave orders to destroy all the wise men of Babylon.

13 So the decree went forth that the wise men should be slain; and they looked for Daniel and his friends to^Tkill *them.* *be killed*

God Reveals the Dream

14 Then Daniel replied with discretion and discernment to Arioch, the captain of the king's^Abodyguard, who had gone forth to slay the wise men of Babylon; *executioners*

15 he answered and said to Arioch, the king's commander, "For what reason is the decree from the king so^Aurgent?" Then Arioch informed Daniel about the matter. *harsh*

16 So Daniel went in and requested of the king that he would^Agive him time, in order that he might declare the interpretation to the king. *appoint a time for him*

17 Then Daniel went to his house and informed his friends,^RHananiah, Mishael and Azariah, about the matter, Dan. 1:6

---

⁴ Or, *soothsayer priests*
⁵ Or, *master astrologers*, and so throughout this context

18 in order that they might^Rrequest compassion from the God of heaven concerning this mystery, so that Daniel and his friends might not be^Rdestroyed with the rest of the wise men of Babylon.   Esth. 4:15 • Gen. 18:28
19 Then the mystery was revealed to Daniel in a night^Rvision. Then Daniel blessed the God of heaven;   Num. 12:6; Job 33:15; Dan. 1:17
20 Daniel answered and said,
     "Let the name of God be^Rblessed forever and ever,   Ps. 103:1, 2; 113: 1, 2
     For ^Rwisdom and power belong to
         Him. [1 Chr. 29:11, 12; Job 12:13, 16–22]
21 "And it is He who^Rchanges the times
         and the epochs;   Ps. 31:15; Dan. 2:9
     He ^Rremoves kings and ^Aestablishes
         kings;   Job 12:18; [Ps. 75:6, 7] • sets up
     He gives^Rwisdom to wise men,
     And knowledge to ^Tmen of understanding.   1 Kin. 3:9, 10; 4:29 • knowers
22 "It is He who^Rreveals the profound and
         hidden things;   Job 12:22; Ps. 25:14
     ^RHe knows what is in the darkness,
     And the light dwells with Him. Is. 45:7
23 "To Thee, O^RGod of my fathers, I give
         thanks and praise, Gen. 31:42; Ex. 3:15
     For Thou hast given me^Rwisdom and
         power;   Dan. 1:17; 2:21
     Even now Thou hast made known to
         me what we^Rrequested of Thee,
     For Thou hast made known to us the
         king's matter."   Ps. 21:2, 4; Dan. 2:18

Daniel Interprets the Dream

24 Therefore, Daniel went in to Arioch, whom the king had appointed to destroy the wise men of Babylon; he went and spoke to him as follows: "Do^R not destroy the wise men of Babylon! Take me^Tinto the king's presence, and I will declare the interpretation to the king."   Dan. 2:12 • in before the king
25 Then Arioch hurriedly brought Daniel into the king's presence and spoke to him as follows: "I have found a man among the^Texiles from Judah who can make the interpretation known to the king!"   sons of the exile of
26 The king answered and said to Daniel, whose name was ^RBelteshazzar, "Are you able to make known to me the dream which I have seen and its interpretation?"   Dan. 1:7
27 Daniel answered before the king and said, "As for the mystery about which the king has inquired, neither^Rwise men, conjurers,^Amagicians, nor diviners are able to declare it to the king.   Dan. 2:2 • soothsayer priests
28"However, there is a God in heaven who reveals mysteries, and He has made known to King Nebuchadnezzar what will take place in the ^Tlatter days. This was your dream and the visions^Tin your mind while on your bed.   end of the days • of your head
29"As for you, O king, while on your bed your thoughts^Tturned to what would take place^Tin the future; and ^RHe who reveals mysteries has made known to you what will take place.   came up • after this • Dan. 2:23, 47

30"But as for me, this mystery has not been revealed to me for any wisdom residing in me more than in any other living man, but for the purpose of making the interpretation known to the king, and that you may understand the thoughts of your mind.
31"You, O king, were looking and behold, there was a single great statue; that statue, which was large and of extraordinary splendor, was standing in front of you, and its appearance was^Rawesome.   Hab. 1:7
32"The^Rhead of that statue was made of fine gold, its breast and its arms of silver, its belly and its thighs of bronze,   Dan. 2:38
33 its legs of iron, its feet partly of iron and partly of clay.
34"You ^Tcontinued looking until a stone was cut out^Rwithout hands, and it struck the statue on its feet of iron and clay, and ^Rcrushed them.   were • Dan. 8:25 • Ps. 2:9
35"Then the iron, the clay, the bronze, the silver and the gold were crushed all at the same time, and became like chaff from the summer threshing floors; and the wind carried them away so that^Rnot a trace of them was found. But the stone that struck the statue became a great^Rmountain and filled the whole earth.   Ps. 37:10 • [Is. 2:2]
36"This was the dream; now we shall tell ^Rits interpretation before the king.   Dan. 2:24
37"You, O king, are the^Rking of kings, to whom the God of heaven has given the ^Akingdom, the^Rpower, the strength, and the glory;   Is. 47:5; Jer. 27:6 • sovereignty • Ps. 62:11
38 and wherever the sons of men dwell, or the^Rbeasts of the field, or the birds of the sky, He has given them into your hand and has caused you to rule over them all. You are the head of gold. Ps. 50:10, 11; Dan. 4:21, 22
39"And after you there will arise another kingdom inferior to you, then another third kingdom of bronze, which will rule over all the earth.
40"Then there will be a^Rfourth kingdom as strong as iron; inasmuch as iron crushes and shatters all things, so, like iron that breaks in pieces, it will crush and break all these in pieces.   Dan. 7:23
41"And in that you saw the feet and toes, partly of potter's clay and partly of iron, it will be a divided kingdom; but it will have in it the toughness of iron, inasmuch as you saw the iron mixed with common clay.
42"And as the toes of the feet were partly of iron and partly of pottery, so some of the kingdom will be strong and part of it will be brittle.
43"And in that you saw the iron mixed with^Tcommon clay, they will combine with one another^Ain the seed of men; but they will not adhere to one another, even as iron does not combine with pottery.   clay of mud • with
44"And in the days of those kings the God of heaven will^Rset up a kingdom which will never be destroyed, and that kingdom will not be left for another people; it will crush

and put an end to all these kingdoms, but it will itself endure forever. $\quad$ Is. 9:7☆

45 "Inasmuch as you saw that a stone was cut out of the mountain without hands and that it crushed the iron, the bronze, the clay, the silver, and the gold, the great God has made known to the king what will take place[T]in the future; so the dream is true, and its interpretation is trustworthy." $\quad$ *after this*

Nebuchadnezzar Promotes Daniel

46 Then King Nebuchadnezzar fell on his face and did[R]homage to Daniel, and gave orders to present to him an offering and[T]fragrant incense. $\quad$ Acts 10:25; 14:13 • *sweet odors*

47 The king answered Daniel and said, "Surely[R]your God is a[R]God of gods and a Lord of kings and a[R]revealer of mysteries, since you have been able to reveal this mystery." $\quad$ Dan. 3:15 • [Deut. 10:17] • Dan. 2:22, 30

48 Then the king[T]promoted Daniel and gave him many great gifts, and he made him ruler over the whole[R]province of Babylon and chief[T]prefect over all the wise men of Babylon. $\quad$ *made great* • Dan. 3:1, 12 • *of the prefects*

49 And Daniel made request of the king, and he[R]appointed[R]Shadrach, Meshach and Abed-nego over the administration of the province of Babylon, while Daniel *was* at the king's[T]court. $\quad$ Dan. 3:12 • Dan. 1:7 • *gate*

CHAPTER 3

Nebuchadnezzar's Image Is Erected

NEBUCHADNEZZAR the king made an [R]image of gold, the height[T] of which *was* sixty [T]cubits *and* its width six[T]cubits; he set it up on the plain of Dura in the province of Babylon. $\quad$ 1 Kin. 12:28 • One cubit equals approx. 18 in.

2 Then Nebuchadnezzar the king sent *word* to assemble the[R]satraps, the prefects and the governors, the counselors, the treasurers, the judges, the magistrates and all the rulers of the provinces to come to the dedication of the image that Nebuchadnezzar the king had set up. $\quad$ Dan. 3:3, 27; 6:1-7

3 Then the satraps, the prefects and the governors, the counselors, the treasurers, the judges, the magistrates and all the rulers of the provinces were assembled for the dedication of the image that Nebuchadnezzar the king had set up; and they stood before the image that Nebuchadnezzar had set up.

4 Then the herald loudly proclaimed: "To you the command is given, O peoples, nations and *men of every*[T]language, $\quad$ *tongue*

5 that at the moment you hear the sound of the horn, flute,[A]lyre, trigon, psaltery, bagpipe, and all kinds of music, you are to fall down and worship the golden image that Nebuchadnezzar the king has set up. $\quad$ *zither*

6 "But whoever does not fall down and worship shall immediately be cast into the midst of a[R]furnace of blazing fire." $\quad$ Jer. 29:22

7 Therefore at that time, when all the peoples heard the sound of the horn, flute, lyre, trigon, psaltery, bagpipe, and all kinds of music, all the peoples, nations and *men of every*[T]language fell down *and* worshiped the golden image that Nebuchadnezzar the king had set up. $\quad$ *tongue*

Daniel's Friends Refuse to Worship

8 For this reason at that time certain Chaldeans came forward and [T]brought charges against the Jews. $\quad$ *ate the pieces of*

9 They responded and said to Nebuchadnezzar the king: "O king, live forever!

10 "You yourself, O king, have made a decree that every man who hears the sound of the horn, flute, lyre, trigon, psaltery, and bagpipe, and all kinds of music, is to fall down and worship the golden image.

11 "But whoever does not fall down and worship shall be cast into the midst of a furnace of blazing fire.

12 "There are certain Jews whom you have [R]appointed over the administration of the province of Babylon, *namely* Shadrach, Meshach and Abed-nego. These men, O king, have disregarded you; they do not serve your gods or worship the golden image which you have set up." $\quad$ Dan. 2:49

Daniel's Friends Trust God

13 Then Nebuchadnezzar in[R]rage and anger gave orders to bring Shadrach, Meshach and Abed-nego; then these men were brought before the king. $\quad$ Dan. 2:12; 3:19

14 Nebuchadnezzar responded and said to them, "Is it true, Shadrach, Meshach and Abed-nego, that you do not serve[R]my gods or worship the golden image that I have set up? $\quad$ Is. 46:1; Jer. 50:2; Dan. 3:1; 4:8

15 "Now if you are ready, at the moment you hear the sound of the horn, flute, lyre, trigon, psaltery, and bagpipe, and all kinds of music, to fall down and worship the image that I have made, *very well*. But if you will not worship, you will[A]immediately be cast into the midst of a furnace of blazing fire; and what god is there who can deliver you out of my hands?" $\quad$ *in the same hour*

16 [R]Shadrach, Meshach and Abed-nego answered and said to the king, "O Nebuchadnezzar, we do not need to give you an answer concerning this matter. $\quad$ Dan. 1:7; 3:12

17 "If[A]it be *so*, our God whom we serve is able to deliver us from the furnace of blazing fire;[A]and He will deliver us out of your hand, O king. $\quad$ *If our God . . . is able* • *then*

18 "But[R]even if *He does* not, let it be known to you, O king, that we are not going to serve your gods or worship the golden image that you have set up." $\quad$ Josh. 24:15

Daniel's Friends Are Protected in the Furnace

19 Then Nebuchadnezzar was filled with ᴿwrath, and his facial expression was altered toward Shadrach, Meshach and Abed-nego. He answered ᵀby giving orders to heat the furnace seven times more than it was usually heated.   Esth. 7:7; Dan. 3:13 • *and ordered to*

20 And he commanded certain valiant warriors who *were* in his army to tie up Shadrach, Meshach and Abed-nego, in order to cast *them* into the furnace of blazing fire.

21 Then these men were tied up in their ᴬtrousers, their ᴬcoats, their caps and their *other* clothes, and were cast into the midst of the furnace of blazing fire.   *cloaks • leggings*

22 For this reason, because the king's ᵀcommand *was* ᴬurgent and the furnace had been made extremely hot, the flame of the fire slew those men who carried up Shadrach, Meshach and Abed-nego.   *word • harsh*

23 But these three men, Shadrach, Meshach and Abed-nego, fell into the midst of the furnace of blazing fire *still* tied up.

24 Then Nebuchadnezzar the king was astounded and stood up in haste; he responded and said to his high officials, "Was it not three men we cast bound into the midst of the fire?" They answered and said to the king, "Certainly, O king."

25 He answered and said, "Look! I see four men loosed *and* ᴿwalking *about* in the midst of the fire ᵀwithout harm, and the appearance of the fourth is like a son of *the* ᴿgods!"   Is. 43:2 • *there is no injury in them* • Jer. 1:8

Daniel's Friends Are Promoted

26 Then Nebuchadnezzar came near to the door of the furnace of blazing fire; he responded and said, "Shadrach, Meshach and ᴿAbed-nego, come out, you servants of the ᴿMost High God, and come here!" Then Shadrach, Meshach and Abed-nego came out of the midst of the fire.   Dan. 3:17; 4:2

27 And the satraps, the prefects, the governors and the king's high officials gathered around *and* saw in regard to these men that the fire had no effect on ᵀthe bodies of these men nor was the hair of their head singed, nor were their trousers damaged, nor had the smell of fire *even* come upon them.   *their*

28 Nebuchadnezzar responded and said, "Blessed be the God of Shadrach, Meshach and Abed-nego, who has sent His angel and delivered His servants who put their trust in Him, violating the king's command, and yielded up their bodies so as not to serve or worship any god except their own God.

29 "Therefore, I make a decree that any people, nation or tongue that speaks anything offensive against the God of Shadrach, Meshach and Abed-nego shall be torn limb

⁶ Or possibly, *the Spirit of the holy God,* and so throughout this context

from limb and their houses reduced to a rubbish heap, inasmuch as there is no other god who is able to deliver in this way."

30 Then the king ᴿcaused Shadrach, Meshach and Abed-nego to prosper in the province of Babylon.   Dan. 2:49; 3:12

CHAPTER 4

Nebuchadnezzar's Proclamation

Nᴇʙᴜᴄʜᴀᴅɴᴇᴢᴢᴀʀ the king to all the peoples, nations, and *men of every* ᵀlanguage that live in all the earth: "May your ᴬpeaceᴿ abound!   *tongue • welfare* or *prosperity* • Ezra 4:17

2 "It has seemed good to me to declare the signs and wonders which the ᴿMost High God has done for me. Dan. 3:26; 4:17, 24, 25, 32

3   "How great are His ᴿsigns,   Ps. 77:19
And how mighty are His wonders!
His ᴿkingdom is an everlasting kingdom,   [Dan. 2:44; 4:34; 6:26]
And His dominion is from generation to generation.

Nebuchadnezzar's Vision

4 "I, Nebuchadnezzar, was at ease in my house and ᴿflourishing in my palace.   Is. 47:7

5 "I saw a dream and it made me fearful; and *these* fantasies *as I lay* on my bed and the visions in my mind kept alarming me.

6 "So I gave orders to ᴿbring into my presence all the wise men of Babylon, that they might make known to me the interpretation of the dream.   Gen. 41:8; Dan. 2:2

7 "Then the magicians, the conjurers, the Chaldeans, and the diviners came in, and I related the dream to them; but they could not make its interpretation known to me.

8 "But finally Daniel came in before me, whose name is ᴿBelteshazzar according to the name of my god, and in whom is ⁶a spirit of the holy gods; and I related the dream ᵀto him, *saying,*   Dan. 1:7; 2:26 • *before*

9 'O Belteshazzar, chief of the magicians, since I know that ᴬa spirit of the holy gods is in you and no mystery baffles you, tell *me* the visions of my dream which I have seen, along with its interpretation.   Gen. 41:38

10 'Now *these were* the visions ᵀin my mind *as I lay* on my bed: I was looking, and behold, *there was* a tree in the midst of the earth, and its height *was* great.   *of my head*

11 'The tree grew large and became strong,
And its height ᴿreached to the sky,
And it *was* visible to the end of the whole earth.   Deut. 9:1; Dan. 4:21, 22

12 'Its foliage *was* ᴿbeautiful and its fruit abundant,   Ezek. 31:7
And in it *was* food for all.
The ᴿbeasts of the field found ᴿshade under it,   Jer. 27:6 • Lam. 4:20
And the ᴿbirds of the sky dwelt in its branches,   Ezek. 17:23; Matt. 13:32

And all ^Tliving creatures fed themselves from it. *flesh*

13 'I was looking in the visions^Tin my mind *as I lay* on my bed, and behold,^Ran *angelic* watcher, a ^Rholy one, descended from heaven. *of my head* • [Dan. 4:17, 23] • Dan. 8:13

14 'He shouted out and spoke as follows: "Chop^R down the tree and cut off its branches, Ezek. 31:10-14; Dan. 4:23

Strip off its foliage and scatter its fruit;

Let the beasts flee from under it,

And the birds from its branches.

15 "Yet^Rleave the stump^Twith its roots in the ground, Job 14:7-9 • *of*

But with a band of iron and bronze *around it*

In the new grass of the field;

And let him be drenched with the dew of heaven,

And let him share with the beasts in the grass of the earth.

16 "Let his^Tmind be changed from *that of* a man,

And let a beast's ^Tmind be given to him, *heart*

And let ^Rseven ^Tperiods of time pass over him. Dan. 4:23, 25, 32 • years

17 "This sentence is by the decree of the *angelic* watchers,

And the decision is a command of the holy ones,

In order that the living may^Rknow

That the Most High is ruler over the realm of mankind, Ps. 9:16; 83:18

And bestows it on whom He wishes,

And sets over it the lowliest of men."

18 'This is the dream *which* I, King Nebuchadnezzar, have seen. Now you, Belteshazzar, tell *me* its interpretation, inasmuch as none of the^Rwise men of my kingdom is able to make known to me the interpretation; but you are able, for a^Rspirit of the holy gods is in you.' Gen. 41:8, 15; Dan. 4:7 • Dan. 4:8, 9

Daniel's Interpretation of the Vision

19"Then Daniel, whose name is Belteshazzar, was appalled for a while as his thoughts alarmed him. The king responded and said, 'Belteshazzar, do not let the dream or its interpretation alarm you.' Belteshazzar answered and said, 'My^Rlord, *if only* the dream applied to those who hate you, and its interpretation to your adversaries! 2 Sam. 18:31

20 'The^Rtree that you saw, which became large and grew strong, whose height reached to the sky and was visible to all the earth, Dan. 4:10-12

21 and whose foliage *was* beautiful and its fruit abundant, and in which *was* food for all, under which the beasts of the field dwelt and in whose branches the birds of the sky lodged—

22 it is you, O king; for you have become great and grown strong, and your majesty has become great and reached to the sky and your dominion to the end of the earth.

23 'And in that the king saw an *angelic* watcher, a holy one, descending from heaven and saying, "Chop down the tree and destroy it; yet leave the stump^Twith its roots in the ground, but with a band of iron and bronze *around it* in the new grass of the field, and let him be drenched with the dew of heaven, and let^Thim share with the beasts of the field until seven^Tperiods of time pass over him"; *of • his portion be with* • years

24 this is the interpretation, O king, and this is the decree of the Most High, which has^Rcome upon my lord the king: Job 40:11

25 that you be^Rdriven away from mankind, and your dwelling place be with the beasts of the field, and you be given grass to eat like cattle and be drenched with the dew of heaven; and seven^Tperiods of time will pass over you, until you recognize that the ^RMost High is ruler over the realm of mankind, and ^Rbestows it on whomever He wishes. Dan. 4:33 • years • Jer. 27:5 • Dan. 2:37

26 'And in that it was commanded to leave the stump^Twith the roots of the tree, your kingdom will be assured to you after you recognize that *it is* Heaven *that* rules. *of*

27 'Therefore, O king, may my advice be pleasing to you:^Rbreak away now from your sins by *doing* righteousness, and from your iniquities by^Rshowing mercy to *the* poor, in case there may be a prolonging of your prosperity.' *redeem now your sins* • Is. 58:6, 7, 10

Nebuchadnezzar's Humiliation

28"All *this*^Rhappened to Nebuchadnezzar the king. Num. 23:19; Zech. 1:6

29"Twelve months later he was walking on the *roof of* the royal palace of Babylon.

30"The king reflected and said, 'Is this not Babylon the great, which I myself have built as a royal residence by the might of my power and for the glory of my majesty?'

31"While the word *was* in the king's mouth, a voice came from heaven, *saying,* 'King Nebuchadnezzar, to you it is declared: sovereignty has been removed from you,

32 and^Ryou will be driven away from mankind, and your dwelling place *will be* with the beasts of the field. You will be given grass to eat like cattle, and seven^Tperiods of time will pass over you, until you recognize that the^RMost High is ruler over the realm of mankind, and bestows it on whomever He wishes.' [Dan. 4:25] • years • Dan. 4:17

33"Immediately the word concerning Nebuchadnezzar was fulfilled; and he was ^Rdriven away from mankind and began eating grass like cattle, and his body was drenched with the dew of heaven, until his hair had grown like eagles' *feathers* and his nails like birds' *claws.* [Dan. 4:25; 5:21]

Nebuchadnezzar's Restoration

34"But at the end of ᵀthat period I, Nebuchadnezzar, raised my eyes toward heaven, and myᵀreason returned to me, and I blessed the Most High and praised and honored Him who lives forever;   *the days • knowledge*
For His dominion is anᴿeverlasting dominion,   Ps. 145:13; Jer. 10:10; Dan. 4:3
And His kingdom *endures* from generation to generation.

35 "And ᴿall the inhabitants of the earth are accounted as nothing,   Ps. 39:5
Butᴿ He does according to His will in the host of heaven   Ps. 33:11; 115:3
And ᴿamong the inhabitants of earth;
Andᴿno one canᵀward off His hand
Or say to Him, 'Whatᴿ hast Thou done?'   Is. 43:13 • *strike against* • Is. 45:9
36"At that time myᵀreason returned to me. And my majesty and splendor were ᵀrestored to me for the glory of my kingdom, and my counselors and my nobles began seeking me out; so I was reestablished in my ᴬsovereignty, and surpassing greatness was added to me.   *knowledge • returning • kingdom*
37"Now I Nebuchadnezzar praise, exalt, and honor the King of heaven, for all His works are true and His ways just, and He is able to humble those who walk in pride."

CHAPTER 5

Belshazzar Defiles
the Temple Vessels

BELSHAZZAR the kingᵀheld a greatᴿfeast for a thousand of his nobles, and he was drinking wine in the presence of the thousand.   *made* • Esth. 1:3; Is. 22:12-14
2 When Belshazzar tasted the wine, he gave orders to bring the gold and silverᴿvessels which Nebuchadnezzar hisᴬfather had taken out of the temple which *was* in Jerusalem, in order that the king and his nobles, his wives, and his concubines might drink from them.   2 Kin. 24:13; 25:15 • *forefather*
3 Then they brought the gold vessels that had been taken out of the temple, the house of God which *was* in Jerusalem; and the king and his nobles, his wives, and his concubines drank from them.
4 They ᴿdrank the wine and praised the gods of ᴿgold and silver, of bronze, iron, wood, and stone.   Is. 42:8; Dan. 5:23 • Is. 40:19

Belshazzar Sees the Handwriting

5 Suddenly the fingers of a man's hand emerged and began writing opposite the lampstand on the plaster of the wall of the king's palace, and the king saw theᴬback of the hand that did the writing.   *palm*
6 Then the king'sᵀface grew pale, and his thoughts alarmed him; and his ᴿhip joints

went slack, and his knees began knocking together.   *brightness changed for him* • Ps. 69:23
7 The king called aloud to bring in the conjurers, the Chaldeans and the diviners. The king spoke and said to the wise men of Babylon, "Any man who can read this inscription and explain its interpretation to me will be clothed with purple, and *have* a necklace of gold around his neck, and have authority as third *ruler* in the kingdom."
8 Then all the king's wise men came in, but they could not read the inscription or make known its interpretation to the king.
9 Then King Belshazzar was greatly ᴿalarmed, hisᴿface grew *even* paler, and his nobles were perplexed.   Job 18:11 • Is. 13:6-8

Daniel Interprets the Handwriting

10 The queen entered the banquet hall because of the words of the king and his nobles; the queen spoke and said, "O king, live forever! Do not let your thoughts alarm you or yourᵀface be pale. *brightness be changed*
11"There is a man in your kingdom in whom is a spirit of the holy gods; and in the days of your father, illumination, insight, and wisdom like the wisdom of the gods were found in him. And King Nebuchadnezzar, your father, your father the king, appointed him chief of theᴬmagicians, conjurers, Chaldeans, *and* diviners. *soothsayer priests*
12"*This was* because an ᴿextraordinary spirit, knowledge and insight, interpretation of dreams, explanation of enigmas, and solving of difficult problems were found in this Daniel, whom the king named Belteshazzar. Let Daniel now be summoned, and he will declare the interpretation." Dan. 5:14
13 Then Daniel was brought in before the king. The king spoke and said to Daniel, "Are you that Daniel who is one of theᵀexiles from Judah, whom my father the king brought from Judah?   *sons of the exile*
14"Now I have heard about you that a spirit of the gods is in you, and that illumination, insight, and extraordinary wisdom have been found in you.
15"Just now theᴿwise men *and* the conjurers were brought in before me that they might read this inscription and make its interpretation known to me, but they ᴿcould not declare the interpretation of theᵀmessage.   Dan. 5:7 • Is. 47:12f.; Dan. 5:8 • *word*
16"But I personally have heard about you, that you are able to give interpretations and solve difficult problems. Now if you are able to read the inscription and make its interpretation known to me, you will be clothed with purple and *wear* a necklace of gold around your neck, and you will have authority as the third *ruler* in the kingdom."
17 Then Daniel answered and said before the king, "Keep your gifts for yourself, or give your rewards to someone else; however, I will read the inscription to the king

and make the interpretation known to him.
18"O^T king, the Most High God granted sovereignty, grandeur, glory, and majesty to Nebuchadnezzar your father. *You, O king*
19"And because of the grandeur which He bestowed on him, all the peoples, nations, and *men of every* language feared and trembled before him; whomever he wished he killed, and whomever he wished he spared alive; and whomever he wished he elevated, and whomever he wished he humbled.
20"But when his heart was^Rlifted up and his spirit became so^Tproud that he behaved arrogantly, he was^Rdeposed from his royal throne, and *his* glory was taken away from him.   Ex. 9:17; Job 15:25 • *strong* • Job 40:11, 12
21"He was also driven away from^Tmankind, and his heart was made like *that of* beasts, and his dwelling place *was* with the wild donkeys. He was given grass to eat like cattle, and his body was drenched with the dew of heaven, until he recognized that the ^RMost High God is ruler over the realm of mankind, and *that* He sets over it whomever He wishes.   *the sons of man* • Ex. 9:14-16
22"Yet you,^Ahis son, Belshazzar, have^Rnot humbled your heart,^Teven though you knew all this,   *descendant* • Ex. 10:3 • *inasmuch as you*
23 but you have^Rexalted yourself against the Lord of heaven; and they have brought the vessels of His house before you, and you and your nobles, your wives and your concubines have been drinking wine from them; and you have praised the gods of silver and gold, of bronze, iron, wood and stone, which do not see, hear or understand. But the God^Rin whose hand are your lifebreath and your^Rways, you have not glorified.   2 Kin. 14:10 • Job 12:10 • Jer. 10:23
24"Then the^Rhand was sent from Him, and this inscription was written out.   Dan. 5:5
25"Now this is the inscription that was written out: 'MENĒ, MENĒ, ^TEKĒL, UPHARSIN.'   *a shekel* from verb "to weigh"
26"This is the interpretation of the^Tmessage: 'MENĒ'—God has numbered your kingdom and^Rput an end to it.   *word* • Is. 13:6
27" 'TEKĒL'—you have been^Rweighed on the scales and found deficient.   Job 31:6
28" 'PERĒS'—your kingdom has been divided and given over to the^RMedes and Persians."   Is. 13:17; 21:2; 45:1, 2; Dan. 5:31; 6:8, 28
29 Then Belshazzar gave orders, and they ^Rclothed Daniel with purple and *put* a necklace of gold around his neck, and issued a proclamation concerning him that he *now* had authority as the^Athird *ruler* in the kingdom.   Dan. 5:7, 16 • *triumvir*

Belshazzar Is Killed

30 That same night^RBelshazzar the Chaldean king was^Rslain.   Dan. 5:1, 2 • Jer. 51:11, 31
31 So^RDarius the Mede received the kingdom at about the age of sixty-two.   Dan. 6:1

CHAPTER 6

Daniel Is Promoted

IT seemed good to Darius to appoint 120 satraps over the kingdom, that they should be in charge of the whole kingdom,
2 and over them three commissioners (of whom Daniel was one), that these satraps might be accountable to them, and that the king might not suffer^Rloss.   Ezra 4:22
3 Then this Daniel began distinguishing himself^Tamong the commissioners and satraps because he possessed an extraordinary spirit, and the king planned to appoint him over the entire kingdom.   *above*

Darius Signs the Foolish Decree

4 Then the commissioners and satraps began trying to find a ground of accusation against Daniel in regard to^Tgovernment affairs; but they could find no ground of accusation or *evidence of* corruption, inasmuch as he was faithful, and no negligence or corruption was *to be* found in him.   *the kingdom*
5 Then these men said, "We shall not find any ground of accusation against this Daniel unless we find *it* against him with regard to the^Rlaw of his God."   Acts 24:13-16, 20
6 Then these commissioners and satraps came by agreement to the king and spoke to him as follows: "King Darius, live forever!
7"All the commissioners of the kingdom, the prefects and the satraps,^Rthe high officials and the governors have^Rconsulted together that the king should establish a statute and enforce an injunction that anyone who makes a petition to any god or man besides you, O king, for thirty days, shall be cast into the lions'^Aden.   Ps. 59:3; 62:4 • *pit*
8"Now, O king, establish the injunction and sign the document so that it may not be changed, according to the law of the Medes and Persians, which may not be revoked."
9 Therefore King Darius ^Rsigned the document, that is, the injunction.   [Ps. 118:9]

Daniel Prays Faithfully

10 Now when Daniel knew that the document was signed, he entered his house (now in his roof chamber he had windows open toward Jerusalem); and he continued kneeling on his knees three times a day, praying and^Rgiving thanks before his God,^Aas he had been doing previously.   1 Thess. 5:17 • *because*
11 Then these men came^Aby^Ragreement and found Daniel making petition and supplication before his God.   *thronging* • Dan. 6:6
12 Then they approached and spoke before the king about the king's injunction, "Did you not sign an injunction that any man who makes a petition to any god or man besides you, O king, for thirty days, is

to be cast into the lions' den?" The king answered and said, "The statement is true, according to the [R]law of the Medes and Persians, which may not be revoked." Esth. 1:19

13 Then they answered and spoke before the king, "Daniel[R], who is one of the [F]exiles from Judah, pays [R]no attention to you, O king, or to the injunction which you signed, but keeps making his petition three times a day." Dan. 2:25 • *sons of the exile* • Acts 5:29

14 Then, as soon as the king heard this statement, he was deeply [R]distressed and set *his* mind on delivering Daniel; and even until sunset he kept exerting himself to rescue him. Mark 6:26

15 Then these men came[A]by agreement to the king and said to the king, "Recognize, O king, that it is a law of the Medes and Persians that no injunction or statute which the king establishes may be changed." *thronging*

Daniel Is Saved in the Lions' Den

16 Then the king gave orders, and Daniel was brought in and[R]cast into the lions' den. The king spoke and said to Daniel, "Your[R] God whom you constantly serve will Himself deliver you." 2 Sam. 3:39 • 2 Cor. 1:10

17 And a[a]stone was brought and laid over the mouth of the den; and the king sealed it with his own signet ring and with the signet rings of his nobles, so that nothing might be changed in regard to Daniel. Matt. 27:66

18 Then the king went off to his palace and spent the night[R]fasting, and no entertainment was brought before him; and his [R]sleep fled from him. 2 Sam. 12:16 • Esth. 6:1

19 Then the king arose with the dawn, at the break of day, and went in haste to the lions' den.

20 And when he had come near the den to Daniel, he cried out with a troubled voice. The king spoke and said to Daniel, "Daniel, servant of the living God, has your God, whom you constantly serve, been[a]able to deliver you from the lions?" Jer. 32:17; Dan. 3:17

21 Then Daniel spoke[a]to the king, "O[R]king, live forever! *with* • Dan. 2:4; 6:6

22"My God [R]sent His angel and shut the lions' mouths, and they have not harmed me, inasmuch as I was found innocent before Him; and also[T]toward you, O king, I have committed no crime." [Heb. 1:14] • *before*

23 Then the king was very pleased and gave orders for Daniel to be taken up out of the den. So Daniel was taken up out of the den, and no injury whatever was found on him, because he had trusted in his God.

24 The king then gave orders, and they brought those men who had maliciously accused Daniel, and they[a]cast them, their[R]children, and their wives into the lions' den; and they had not reached the bottom of the den before the lions overpowered them and crushed all their bones. Esth. 7:10 • Esth. 9:10

Darius's Wise Decree

25 Then Darius the king wrote to all the peoples, nations, and *men of every*[T]language who were living in all the land: "May your [A]peace abound! *tongue* • *welfare or prosperity*

26"I[a]make a decree that in all the dominion of my kingdom men are to fear and tremble before the God of Daniel; Ezra 6:8-12

For He is the[R]living God and[R]enduring
    forever, Rom. 9:26 • Ps. 93:1, 2
And[R]His kingdom is one which will
    not be destroyed, Dan. 2:44; 4:3; 7:14
And His dominion *will be* forever.

27 "He delivers and rescues and performs
    [R]signs and wonders Dan. 4:2, 3
In heaven and on earth,
Who has *also* delivered Daniel from
    the[T]power of the lions." *hand*

28 So this[R]Daniel enjoyed success in the reign of Darius and in the reign of[R]Cyrus the Persian. Dan. 1:21 • 2 Chr. 36:22, 23; Dan. 10:1

CHAPTER 7

Four Beasts

IN the first year of Belshazzar king of Babylon Daniel saw a dream and visions[T]in his mind *as he lay* on his bed; then he wrote the dream down *and* related the *following* [A]summary of it. *of his head* • *beginning* • *words*

2 Daniel said, "I was looking in my vision by night, and behold, the four winds of heaven were stirring up the great sea.

3"And four great beasts were coming up from the sea, different from one another.

4"The first *was* [R]like a lion and had *the* wings of an eagle. I kept looking until its wings were plucked, and it was lifted up from the ground and made to stand on two feet like a man; a human[T]mind also was given to it. Jer. 4:7 • *heart*

5"And behold, another beast, a second one, resembling a bear. And it was raised up on one side, and three ribs *were* in its mouth between its teeth; and thus they said to it, 'Arise, devour much meat!'

6"After this I kept looking, and behold, another one, like a leopard, which had on its back four wings of a bird; the beast also had four heads, and dominion was given to it.

7"After this I kept looking in the night visions, and behold, a[R]fourth beast, dreadful and terrifying and extremely strong; and it had large iron teeth. It devoured and crushed, and trampled down the remainder with its feet; and it was different from all the beasts that were before it, and it had[R]ten horns. Dan. 7:19, 20, 23 • Rev. 12:3; 13:1

8"While I was contemplating the horns, behold, another horn, a little one, came up among them, and three of the first horns were pulled out by the roots before it; and behold, [T]this horn possessed eyes like the

eyes of a man, and ^Ra mouth uttering great boasts.   *in this horn were eyes* • Rev. 13:5, 6

"Ancient of Days"

9 "I kept looking
   Until ^Rthrones were set up,   [Rev. 20:4]
   And the Ancient of Days took *His* seat;
   His ^Rvesture *was* like white snow,
   And the ^Rhair of His head like pure wool.   Mark 9:3 • Rev. 1:14
   His throne *was* ablaze with flames,
   Its wheels *were* a burning fire.
10 "A river of ^Rfire was flowing   Ps. 18:8
   And coming out from before Him;
   ^RThousands upon thousands were attending Him,   Deut. 33:2; 1 Kin. 22:19
   And myriads upon myriads were standing before Him;
   The ^Rcourt sat,   Ps. 96:11-13; Dan. 7:22, 26
   And ^Rthe books were opened.   Dan. 12:1
11 "Then I kept looking because of the sound of the ^Tboastful words which the horn was speaking; I kept looking until the beast was slain, and its body was destroyed and given to the burning ^Tfire.   *great* • *of the fire*
12 "As for the rest of the beasts, their dominion was taken away, but an extension of life was granted to them for an appointed period of time.
13 "I kept looking in the night visions,
   And behold, with the clouds of heaven
   One like a ^RSon of Man was coming,
   And He came up to the Ancient of Days   [Matt. 24:30; 26:64; Mark 13:26]☆
   And was presented before Him.
14 "And to Him was given dominion,
   _RGlory and ^Aa kingdom,   *sovereignty*
   ^RThat all the peoples, nations, and *men* of every ^Tlanguage   Ps. 72:11 • *tongue*
   Might serve Him.
   ^RHis dominion is an everlasting dominion   Mic. 4:7; [Luke 1:33]☆
   Which will not pass away;
   ^RAnd His kingdom is one   Heb. 12:28
   Which will not be destroyed.

Interpretation of the Four Beasts

15 "As for me, Daniel, my spirit was distressed within me, and the ^Rvisions ^Tin my mind kept alarming me.   Dan. 7:1 • *of my head*
16 "I approached one of those who _Rwere ^Rstanding by and began asking him the ^Texact meaning of all this. So he ^Rtold me and made known to me the interpretation of these things: Zech. 1:9 • *truth concerning* • Dan. 8:16
17 'These great beasts, which are four *in number*, are four kings *who* will arise from the earth.
18 'But the ^Tsaints of the Highest One will receive the kingdom and possess the kingdom forever, for all ages to come.'   *holy ones*
19 "Then I desired to know the ^Texact

meaning of the ^Rfourth beast, which was different from all ^Tthe others, exceedingly dreadful, with its teeth of iron and its claws of bronze, *and which* devoured, crushed, and trampled down the remainder with its feet,   *truth concerning* • Dan. 7:7, 8 • *of them*
20 and *the meaning* of the ten horns that *were* on its head, and the other *horn* which came up, and before which three *of them* fell, namely, that horn which had eyes and a mouth uttering great *boasts*, and which was larger in appearance than its associates.
21 "I kept looking, and that horn was ^Rwaging war with the ^Tsaints and overpowering them   Rev. 11:7; 13:7 • *holy ones*
_R22 until the Ancient of Days came, and ^Rjudgment was ^Tpassed in favor of the ^Tsaints of the Highest One, and the time arrived when the ^Tsaints took possession of the kingdom.   [1 Cor. 6:2, 3] • *given for* • *holy ones*

Interpretation of the Fourth Beast

23 "Thus he said: 'The fourth beast will be a fourth kingdom on the earth, which will be different from all the *other* kingdoms, and it will devour the whole earth and tread it down and crush it.
24 'As for the ^Rten horns, out of this kingdom ten kings will arise; and another will arise after them, and he will be different from the previous ones and will subdue three kings.   Dan. 7:7; Rev. 17:12
25 'And he will speak out against the Most High and wear down the ^Tsaints of the Highest One, and he will intend to make alterations in times and in law; and ^Tthey will be given into his hand for a ^Ttime, ^Ttimes, and half a ^Ttime.   *holy ones* • the saints • *year(s)*
26 'But the court will sit *for judgment*, and his dominion will be taken away, annihilated and destroyed ^Tforever.   *to the end*
27 'Then the sovereignty, the dominion, and the greatness of *all* the kingdoms under the whole heaven will be given to the people of the saints of the Highest One; His kingdom *will be* an everlasting kingdom, and all the dominions will serve and obey Him.'
28 "At this point the revelation ended. As for me, Daniel, my thoughts were greatly alarming me and my face grew pale, but I kept the matter ^Tto myself."   *in my heart*

CHAPTER 8

The Ram

IN the third year of the reign of Belshazzar the king a vision appeared to me, ^TDaniel, subsequent to the one which appeared to me ^Tpreviously.   *I, Daniel* • *at the beginning*
2 And I looked in the vision, and it came about while I was looking, that I was in the citadel of Susa, which is in the province of Elam; and I looked in the vision, and I myself was beside the Ulai ^ACanal.   *river*

3 Then I lifted my gaze and looked, and behold, a [R]ram which had two horns was standing in front of the[A]canal. Now the two horns *were*[T]long, but one *was*[T]longer than the other, with the [T]longer one coming up last.   Dan. 8:20 • *river* • *high(er)*

4 I saw the ram butting westward, northward, and southward, and no *other* beasts could stand before him, nor was there anyone to rescue from his[T]power; but he did as he pleased and magnified *himself*.   *hand*

The Male Goat

5 While I was observing, behold, a male goat was coming from the west over the surface of the whole earth without touching the ground; and the[T]goat *had* a[R]conspicuous horn between his eyes.   *buck* • Dan. 8:8, 21

6 And he came up to the ram that had the two horns, which I had seen standing in front of the[A]canal, and rushed at him in his mighty wrath.   *river*

7 And I saw him come beside the ram, and he was enraged at him; and he struck the ram and shattered his two horns, and the ram had no strength to withstand him. So he hurled him to the ground and trampled on him, and there was none to rescue the ram from his[T]power.   *hand*

8 Then the male goat magnified *himself* exceedingly. But as soon as he was mighty, the[R]large horn was broken; and in its place there came up four conspicuous *horns* toward the four winds of heaven. Dan. 8:22

The Small Horn

9 And out of one of them came forth a rather[R]small horn which grew exceedingly great toward the south, toward the east, and toward the [7]Beautiful *Land*.   Dan. 8:23

10 And it grew up to the host of heaven and caused some of the host and some of the[R]stars to fall to the earth, and it[T]trampled them down.   Jer. 48:26 • Dan. 7:7; 8:7

11 It even [R]magnified *itself* [T]to be equal with the[A]Commander of the host; and it removed the[R]regular sacrifice from Him, and the place of His sanctuary was thrown down.   Is. 37:23 • *up to the* • *Prince* • Ezek. 46:14

12 And on account of transgression the host will be given over *to the horn* along with the regular sacrifice; and it will[R]fling truth to the ground and perform *its will* and prosper.   Is. 59:14

The Length of the Vision

13 Then I heard a[R]holy one speaking, and another holy one said to that particular one who was speaking, "How long will the vision *about* the regular sacrifice apply, while the transgression causes horror, so as to allow both the holy place and the host[T]to be trampled?"   Dan. 4:13, 23 • *as a trampling*

[7] I.e., Palestine

14 And he said to me, "For[R]2,300 evenings *and* mornings; then the holy place will be [T]properly restored."   Dan. 7:25; 12:7 • *vindicated*

Interpretation of the Vision

15 And it came about when[R]I, Daniel, had seen the vision, that I sought[T]to understand it; and behold, standing before me was one who looked like a man. Dan. 8:1 • *understanding*

16 And I heard the voice of a man between *the banks of* Ulai, and he called out and said, "Gabriel,[R] give this *man* an understanding of the vision." Dan. 9:21; Luke 1:19, 26

17 So he came near to where I was standing, and when he came I was frightened and [R]fell on my face; but he said to me, "Son of man, understand that the vision pertains to the[R]time of the end."   Ezek. 1:28 • Dan. 8:19

18 Now while he was talking with me, I [R]sank into a deep sleep with my face to the ground; but he touched me and made me stand[T]upright.   Dan. 10:9 • *on my standing*

19 And he said, "Behold, I am going to[R]let you know what will occur at the final period of the indignation, for *it* pertains to the appointed time of the end.   Dan. 8:15-17

Interpretation of the Ram

20"The[R]ram which you saw with the two horns represents the kings of Media and Persia.   Dan. 8:3

Interpretation of the Male Goat

21"And the shaggy goat *represents* the [T]kingdom of Greece, and the large horn that is between his eyes is the first king.   *king*

22"And the [R]broken *horn* and the four horns *that* arose in its place *represent* four kingdoms *which* will arise from *his* nation, although not with his power.   Dan. 8:8

Interpretation of the Small Horn

23 "And in the latter period of their[A]rule, When the transgressors have [T]run their course,   *kingdom* • *finished* A king will arise Insolent and skilled in intrigue.

24 "And his power will be mighty, but not by his *own* power, And he will[A]destroy[R] to an extraordinary degree   *corrupt* • Dan. 8:11-13 And prosper and perform *his will*; He will destroy mighty men and[T]the holy people.   *people of the saints*

25 "And through his shrewdness He will cause deceit to succeed by his [T]influence;   *hand* And he will magnify *himself* in his heart, And he will[A]destroy many while *they are*[A]at ease.   *corrupt* • *secure*

He will even [T]oppose[R] the Prince of
princes,   *stand against* • Dan. 8:11
But he will be broken[R]without human
agency.   Job 34:20; Dan. 2:34, 45
26 "And the vision of the evenings and
mornings
Which has been told is[R]true; Dan. 10:1
But[R]keep the vision secret, Ezek. 12:27
For *it* pertains to many[R]days *in the future.*"   Dan. 10:14

Response of Daniel

27 Then I, Daniel, was exhausted and sick
for days. Then I got up *again* and carried on
the king's business; but I was astounded at
the vision, and there was none to explain *it.*

CHAPTER 9

The Understanding of Daniel

IN the first year of Darius the son of Ahasuerus, of Median descent, who was made
king over the kingdom of the Chaldeans—
2 in the first year of his reign I, Daniel,
observed in the books the number of the
years which was *revealed as* the word of the
LORD to[R]Jeremiah the prophet for the completion of the desolations of Jerusalem,
namely, seventy years.   2 Chr. 36:21; Ezra 1:1

The Intercession of Daniel

3 So I[T]gave my attention to the Lord God
to seek *Him by* prayer and supplications,
with fasting, sackcloth, and ashes. *set my face*
4 And I prayed to the LORD my God and
confessed and said, "Alas, O Lord, the great
and awesome God, who[R]keeps His covenant
and lovingkindness for those who love
Him and keep His commandments, Deut. 7:9

5 [R]we have sinned, committed iniquity,
acted wickedly, and[R]rebelled, even[R]turning
aside from Thy commandments and ordi-
nances.   1 Kin. 8:48 • Lam. 1:18, 20 • Is. 53:6
6"Moreover, we have not[R]listened to Thy

servants the prophets, who spoke in Thy
name to our kings, our princes, our fathers,
and all the people of the land.   2 Chr. 36:16
7"Righteousness belongs to Thee, O
Lord, but to us open shame, as it is this
day—to the men of Judah, the inhabitants
of Jerusalem, and all Israel, those who are
nearby and those who are far away in all the
countries to which Thou hast driven them,
because of their unfaithful deeds which they
have committed against Thee.
8"Open shame belongs to us, O Lord, to
our kings, our princes, and our fathers, because we have sinned against Thee.
9"To the Lord our God belong[R]compas-
sion and forgiveness,[A]for we have[R]rebelled
against Him;   [Neh. 9:17] • *though* • Jer. 14:7
10 nor have we obeyed the voice of the
LORD our God, to walk in His [A]teachings
which He[R]set before us through His servants
the prophets.   *laws* • 2 Kin. 17:13-15; 18:12
11"Indeed all Israel has transgressed Thy
law and turned aside, not obeying Thy
voice; so the[R]curse has been poured out on
us, along with the oath which is written in
the law of Moses the servant of God, for we
have sinned against Him.   Deut. 27:15-26
12"Thus He has confirmed His words
which He had spoken against us and against
our[T]rulers who ruled us, to bring on us great
calamity; for under the whole heaven there
has not been done *anything* like what was
done to Jerusalem.   *judges who judged us*
13"As it is written in the law of Moses, all
this calamity has come on us; yet we have
not[T]sought the favor of the LORD our God by
[R]turning from our iniquity and giving attention to Thy truth. *softened the face of* • Jer. 31:18
14"Therefore, the LORD has kept the calamity in store and brought it on us; for the
LORD our God is righteous with respect to
all His deeds which He has done, but we
have not obeyed His voice.
15"And now, O Lord our God, who hast
brought Thy people out of the[R]land of Egypt
with a mighty hand and hast[R]made a name
for Thyself, as it is this day—we have
sinned, we have been wicked.   Neh. 9:10

9:3, 4 Knowing the Will of God Through Prayer and Fasting—Soon after Israel had invaded Palestine in the
days of Joshua, the Israelites were tricked into signing an unscriptural peace treaty with a group of deceitful pagans. The cause for this tragic error is clearly stated in God's Word, "So the men . . . did not ask for the counsel of
the LORD" (Page 213—Josh. 9:14). These pagans, the Gibeonites, brought only trouble to Israel. See Joshua
10:4-15; Second Samuel 21:1-14.
  It therefore becomes immediately obvious that one of the most important factors in knowing God's will for our
lives is to pray. But "if any of you lacks wisdom, let him ask of God, who gives to all men generously and without
reproach and it will be given to him" (Page 1253—James 1:5). See also Psalms 143:8, 10; James 4:2.
  In the light of these passages it is evident a Christian must pray to know God's will. In other Bible verses fasting
is linked with prayer.
a. Meaning of fasting: To fast is to abstain for a period of time from some important and necessary activity in our
   lives.
b. Purpose of fasting: This is done that we might spend that time in prayer before God.
c. Kinds of fasting: One may, for a time, refrain from sleep (Page 1169—2 Cor. 6:5; 11:27), marital sex (Page
   1153—1 Cor. 7:1-5), or food (Page 965—Matt. 4:1, 2).
d. Examples of biblical fasting: Moses (Page 178—Deut. 9:9, 18, 25-29); Elijah (Page 346—1 Kin. 19:8); Daniel
   (Page 846—Dan. 9:3; 10:3); Ezra (Page 462—Ezra 10:6); Nehemiah (Page 467—Neh. 1:4); and Paul
   (Page1169—2 Cor. 6:5; 11:27).
   Now turn to Page 662—Is. 6:8: Knowing the Will of God Through Submission to the Spirit.

16"O Lord, in accordance with all Thy ^Trighteous acts, let now Thine anger and Thy wrath turn away from Thy city Jerusalem, Thy^Rholy mountain; for because of our sins and the iniquities of our fathers, Jerusalem and Thy people *have become* a reproach to all those around us.   *righteousness* • Ps. 87:1-3

17"So now, our God, listen to the prayer of Thy servant and to his supplications, and for ^TThy sake, O Lord, let Thy face shine on Thy desolate sanctuary.   *the sake of the Lord*

18"O my God, incline Thine ear and hear! Open Thine eyes and see our desolations and the city which is called by Thy name; for we are not^Tpresenting our supplications before Thee on account of any merits of our own, but on account of Thy great compassion.   *causing to fall* • *our righteousnesses*

19"O Lord, hear! O Lord, forgive! O Lord, listen and take action! For Thine own sake, O my God, do not delay, because Thy city and Thy people are called by Thy name."

The Intervention of Gabriel

20 Now while I was speaking and praying, and confessing my sin and the sin of my people Israel, and^Tpresenting my supplication before the LORD my God in behalf of the holy mountain of my God,   *causing to fall*

21 while I was still speaking in prayer, then the man Gabriel, whom I had seen in the vision previously,^Tcame to me in *my* extreme weariness about the time of the^Revening offering.   *was reaching;* or, *touching* • Ezra 9:4

22 And he gave *me* instruction and talked with me, and said, "O Daniel, I have now come forth to give you insight with^Runderstanding.   Dan. 8:16; 10:21; Zech. 1:9

23"At the beginning of your supplications the command was issued, and I have come to tell *you,* for you are^Thighly esteemed; so give heed to the message and gain understanding of the vision.   *desirable;* or, *precious*

The Revelation of the Seventy Weeks

24"Seventy weeks have been decreed for your people and your holy city, to^Afinish the transgression, to make an end of sin, to ^Rmake atonement for iniquity, to bring in everlasting righteousness, to seal up vision and^Tprophecy, and to anoint the most holy place.   *restrain* • [Is. 53:10] • *prophet*

25"So you are to know and discern *that* from the issuing of a^Tdecree to restore and rebuild Jerusalem until Messiah the Prince *there will be* seven weeks and sixty-two weeks; it will be built again, with^Aplaza and moat, even in times of distress.   *word • streets*

26"Then after the sixty-two weeks the ^AMessiah will be^Rcut off and have ^Anothing, and the people of the prince who is to come will destroy the city and the sanctuary. And ^Aits end *will come* with a flood; even to the end there will be war; desolations are determined.   *anointed one* • [Is. 53:8]☆ • *no one* • *his*

27"And he will make a firm covenant with the many for one week, but in the middle of the week he will put a stop to sacrifice and grain offering; and on the wing of^Aabominations *will come* one who ^Amakes desolate, even until a complete destruction, one that is decreed, is poured out on the one who makes desolate."   *detestable things* • *causes horror*

CHAPTER 10

Time of the Vision

IN the third year of^RCyrus king of Persia a ^Tmessage was revealed to Daniel, who was named Belteshazzar; and the^Tmessage was true and *one of* great^Aconflict, but he understood the message and had an understanding of the vision.   Dan. 1:21 • *word • warfare*

2 In those days I, Daniel, had been ^Rmourning for three entire weeks.   Ezra 9:4, 5

3 I did not eat any^Ttasty food, nor did meat or wine enter my mouth, nor did I use any ointment at all, until the entire three weeks were completed.   *bread of desirability*

4 And on the twenty-fourth day of the first month, while I was by the bank of the great river, that is, the^TTigris,   Heb., *Hiddekel*

Vision of the Heavenly Messenger

5 I lifted my eyes and looked, and behold, there was a certain man^Rdressed in linen, whose waist was^Rgirded with *a belt of* pure gold of Uphaz.   Ezek. 9:2 • Rev. 1:13; 15:6

6 His body also was like^Aberyl, his face ^Thad the appearance of lightning, ^Rhis eyes were like flaming torches, his arms and feet like the gleam of polished bronze, and the sound of his words like the sound of a^Atumult.   *yellow serpentine • like* • Rev. 1:14 • *roaring*

7 Now I, Daniel, ^Ralone saw the vision, while the^Rmen who were with me did not see the vision; nevertheless, a great dread fell on them, and they ran away to hide themselves.   2 Kin. 6:17-20 • Acts 9:7

8 So I was left alone and saw this great vision; yet no strength was left in me, for my natural color turned to^Ta deathly pallor, and I retained no strength.   *corruption*

9 But I heard the sound of his words; and as soon as I heard the sound of his words, I ^Rfell into a deep sleep on my face, with my face to the ground.   Gen. 15:12; Job 4:13

Touch of the Heavenly Messenger

10 Then behold, a hand touched me and set me trembling on my hands and knees.

11 And he said to me, "O Daniel, man of ^Thigh esteem, understand the words that I am about to tell you and stand^Tupright, for I have now been sent to you." And when he had spoken this word to me, I stood up trembling.   *desirability • upon your standing*

12 Then he said to me, "Do^Rnot be afraid,

Daniel, for from the first day that you set your heart on understanding *this* and on ᴿhumbling yourself before your God, your words were heard, and I have come in response to your words.   Is. 41:10 • Dan. 9:20-23

13"But the prince of the kingdom of Persia was withstanding me for twenty-one days; then behold, Michael, one of the chief princes, came to help me, for I had been left there with the kings of Persia.

14"Now I have come to give you an understanding of what will happen to your people in theᵀlatter days, for the vision pertains to ᴿthe days yet *future*."   *end of the days* • Dan. 8:26

15 And when he had spoken to me according to these words, I turned my face toward the ground and became speechless.

16 And behold,ᵀone who resembled a human being wasᴿtouching my lips; then I opened my mouth and spoke, and said to him who was standing before me, "O my lord, as a result of the vision anguish has come upon me, and I have retained no strength.   *as a likeness of sons of man* • Is. 6:7

17"Forʰhow can such a servant of my lord talk with such as my lord? As for me, there remains just now no strength in me, nor has any breath been left in me."   Ex. 24:10, 11

*Strengthening
by the Heavenly Messenger*

18 Then *this* one with human appearance touched me again and strengthened me.

19 And he said, "O man ofᵀhigh esteem, do not be afraid. Peaceᵀbe with you; take ᴿcourage and be courageous!" Now as soon as he spoke to me, I received strength and said, "May my lord speak, for you have strengthened me." *desirability* • *to you* • [Is. 35:4]

20 Then he said, "Do youᵀunderstand why I came to you? But I shall now return to fight against the prince of Persia; so I am going forth, and behold, the prince of ᵀGreece is about to come.   *know* • Heb., *Javan*

21"However, I will tell you what is inscribed in the writing of truth. Yet there is no one who stands firmly with me against these *forces* except Michael your prince.

CHAPTER 11

The Rule of Persia

"AND in the first year of Darius the Mede,ᵀI arose to be an encouragement and a protection for him.   *my standing up* was

2"And now I will tell you theᴿtruth. Behold, three more kings are going to ariseᵀin Persia. Then a fourth will gain far more riches than all *of them;* as soon as he becomes strong through his riches, he will arouse the whole *empire* against the realm ofᵀGreece.   Dan. 8:26; 10:1 • *for* • Heb., *Javan*

The Rule of Greece

3"And aᴿmighty king will arise, and he

will rule with great authority andᴿdo as he pleases.   Dan. 8:5, 21 • Dan. 5:19

4"But as soon as he has arisen, his kingdom will be broken up and parceled out toward the fourᵀpoints of the compass, though not to his *own* descendants, nor according to his authority which he wielded; for his sovereignty will be uprooted and *given* to others besides them.   *winds of the heaven*

5"Then theᴿking of the South will grow strong,ᵀalong with *one* of his princesᵀwho will gain ascendancy over him and obtain dominion; his domain *will be* a great dominion *indeed.*   Dan. 11:9, 11, 14, 25 • *and* • *and he*

6"And after some years they will form an alliance, and the daughter of the king of the South will come to the king of the North to carry out a peaceful arrangement. But she will not retain her position of power, nor will he remain with hisᵀpower, but she will be given up, along with those who brought her in, and the one who sired her, as well as he who supported her in *those* times.   *arm*

7"But one of the descendants of her line will arise in his place, and he will come against *their* army and enter theᴿfortress of the king of the North, and he will deal with them and display *great* strength.   Dan. 11:19

8"And also their gods with their metal images *and* their precious vessels of silver and gold he will take into captivity to Egypt, and he on his part will refrain from *attacking* the king of the North for *some* years.

9"Thenᵀthe latter will enter the realm of the king of the South, but will return to his *own* land.   *he will*

10"And his sons willᴬmobilize and assemble a multitude of great forces; and one of them will keep on coming andᴿoverflow and pass through, that he may again wage war up to his *very* fortress.   *wage war* • Jer. 46:7, 8

11"And the king of the South will be enraged and go forth and fightᵀwith the king of the North. Then the latter will raise a great multitude, but *that* multitude will be given into the hand of the *former.*   *with him, with*

12"When the multitude is carried away, his heart will be lifted up, and he will cause tens of thousands to fall; yet he will not prevail.

13"For the king of the North will again raise a greater multitude than the former, andᵀafter anᴿinterval of some years he will press on with a great army and much equipment.   *at the end of the times, years* • Dan. 4:16

14"Now in those times many will rise up against the king of the South; the violent ones among your people will also lift themselves up in order to fulfill the vision, but they willᵀfall down.   *stumble*

15"Then the king of the North will come, cast up a siege mound, and capture a well-fortified city; and the forces of the South will not stand *their ground*, not evenᵀtheir choicest troops, for there will be no strength to make a stand.   *the people of its choice ones*

16"But he who comes against him will^Rdo as he pleases, and^Rno one will *be able to* withstand him; he will also stay *for a time* in the^TBeautiful Land, with destruction in his hand.   Dan. 5:19 • Josh. 1:5 • Palestine

17"And he will set his face to come with the power of his whole kingdom, bringing with him a proposal of peace which he will put into effect; he will also give him the daughter of women to ruin it. But she will not take a stand *for him* or be on his side.

18"Then he will turn his face to the coastlands and capture many. But a commander will put a stop to his scorn against him; moreover, he will repay him for his scorn.

19"So he will turn his face toward the fortresses of his own land, but he will stumble and fall and be^Rfound no more.   Ezek. 26:21

20"Then in his place one will arise who will^Rsend an^Aoppressor through the ⁸Jewel of *his* kingdom; yet within a few days he will be shattered, though neither in anger nor in battle.   Is. 60:17 • *exactor of tribute*

21"And in his place a despicable person will arise, on whom the honor of kingship has not been conferred, but he will come in a time of tranquility and^Rseize the kingdom by intrigue.   2 Sam. 15:6

22"And the overflowing ^Rforces will be flooded away before him and shattered, and also the prince of the covenant.   Dan. 9:26

23"And after an alliance is made with him he will practice deception, and he will go up and gain power with a small *force of* people.

24"In a time of tranquility he will enter the richest *parts* of the^Arealm, and he will accomplish what his fathers never did, nor his^Tancestors; he will distribute plunder, booty, and possessions among them, and he will

devise his schemes against strongholds, but *only* for a time.   *province • fathers' fathers*

25"And he will stir up his strength and ^Tcourage against the^Rking of the South with a large army; so the king of the South will mobilize an extremely large and mighty army for war; but he will not stand, for schemes will be devised against him.   *heart* • Dan. 11:5

26"And those who eat his choice food will ^Tdestroy him, and his army will^Roverflow, but many will fall down slain.   *break* • Dan. 11:10

27"As for both kings, their hearts will be *intent* on ^Revil, and they will^Rspeak lies *to each other* at the same table; but it will not succeed, for the^Rend is still *to come* at the appointed time.   Ps. 52:1 • Ps. 12:2 • Dan. 8:19

28"Then he will return to his land with much plunder; but his heart will be *set* against the holy covenant, and he will take action and *then* return to his *own* land.

29"At the appointed time he will return and come into the South, but this last time it will not turn out the way it did before.

30"For ships of^TKittim^R will come against him; therefore he will be disheartened, and will return and become enraged at the holy covenant and take action; so he will come back and show regard for those who forsake the holy covenant. Cyprus • Num. 24:24; Is. 23:1

31"And forces from him will arise, desecrate the sanctuary fortress, and do away with the regular sacrifice. And they will set up the^Rabomination of desolation.   Dan. 9:27

32"And by^Rsmooth *words* he will^Aturn to godlessness those who act wickedly toward the covenant, but the people who know their God will display^Rstrength and take action.   Dan. 11:21, 34 • *pollute those* • Mic. 5:7-9

33"And those who have insight among the people will give understanding to the many;

⁸ Lit., *adornment;* i.e., probably Jerusalem and its temple

11:32 We Know God Through His Word—One of the most vital teachings of Scripture is that God can be known. The highest knowledge to which men and women can attain is a personal knowledge of God (Page 728—Jer. 9:24). Since all men are sinners they do not naturally possess this knowledge (Page 1133—Rom. 3:10, 11), even though they know that He exists (Page 533—Ps. 14:1; Page 1132—Rom. 1:19, 20). Knowing that God exists is not the same as knowing God personally, just as knowing about the President does not mean that you necessarily know him personally. This knowledge of God is crucial, however, since to know God personally is to be saved and have eternal life (Page 1084—John 17:3). People should rejoice in the fact that God earnestly wants them to attain this knowledge. That is why He has spoken to us in His Word, revealing Himself and disclosing the means by which we may know Him.

While God surely can be known, there is always more to be learned about Him. There are many Scriptures which teach that our knowledge of God is partial. It is said to be "too wonderful" (Page 600—Ps. 139:6), "unsearchable" (Page 603—Ps. 145:3; Page 1141—Rom. 11:33), and "infinite" (Page 604—Ps. 147:5). Since our knowledge of God is incomplete, we must increase it through spiritual growth. Paul, for example, prays to know God better (Page 1195—Phil. 3:10). We are even commanded to grow in the knowledge of Christ (Page 1270—2 Pet. 3:18). The development of one's intimate knowledge of God constitutes one of the greatest delights of the Christian life.

The Bible also reveals that God cannot be known personally apart from His Word. It contains the gospel which must be believed (Page 1185—Eph. 1:13), and the gospel brings forth saving faith in itself (Page 1140—Rom. 10:17). The gospel can therefore be called "the power of God for salvation" (Page 1132—Rom. 1:16). The part that the Scriptures and the gospel contained within them play in bringing men to know God is described in three important illustrations: the gospel is the agent of the new birth (Page 1253—James 1:18), that is, it is like the implanted seed without which the conception of new life cannot occur; it is also a cleansing agent through which God gives the believing sinner a spiritual bath that results in salvation (Page 1189—Eph. 5:26); and the Scriptures are like an educator bringing the wisdom that leads to salvation (Page 1225—2 Tim. 3:15).

Now turn to Page 548—Ps. 40:8: We Know God's Will Through His Word.

yet they will fall by sword and by flame, by captivity and by plunder, for *many* days.

34"Now when they fall they will be granted a little help, and many will^Rjoin with them in^Rhypocrisy.   Matt. 7:15 • Dan. 11:21, 32

35"And some of those who have insight will fall, in order to refine, purge, and make them^Tpure, until the end time; because *it is* still *to come* at the appointed time.   *white*

Prophecy of the Willful King

36"Then the king will do as he pleases, and he will exalt and magnify himself above every god, and will speak ^Tmonstrous things against the God of gods; and he will prosper until the indignation is finished, for that which is decreed will be done.   *extraordinary*

37"And he will show no regard for the ^Agods of his fathers or for the desire of women, nor will he show regard for any *other* god; for he will magnify himself above *them* all.   *God*

38"But^Tinstead he will honor a god of fortresses, a god whom his fathers did not know; he will honor *him* with gold, silver, costly stones, and treasures.   *in his place*

39"And he will take action against the strongest of fortresses with *the help of* a foreign god; he will give great honor to those who acknowledge *him,* and he will cause them to rule over the many, and will parcel out land for a price.

40"And at the end time the^Rking of the South will collide with him, and the^Rking of the North will storm against him with chariots, with horsemen, and with many ships; and he will enter countries, overflow *them,* and pass through.   Dan. 11:11 • Dan. 11:7, 13

41"He will also enter the Beautiful Land, and many *countries* will fall; but these will be rescued out of his hand: Edom, Moab and the foremost of the sons of Ammon.

42"Then he will stretch out his hand against *other* countries, and the land of Egypt will not escape.

43"But he will gain control over the hidden treasures of gold and silver, and over all the precious things of Egypt; and Libyans and Ethiopians *will follow* at his heels.

44"But rumors from the East and from the North will disturb him, and he will go forth with great wrath to destroy and ^Tannihilate many.   *devote to destruction*

45"And he will pitch the tents of his royal pavilion between the seas and the beautiful ^RHoly Mountain; yet he will come to his end, and no one will help him.   Is. 11:9; 27:13; 65:25

CHAPTER 12

Prophecy of the Great Time of Distress

"NOW at that time Michael, the great prince who stands *guard* over the sons of your people, will arise. And there will be a time of distress such as never occurred since there was a nation until that time; and at that time your people, everyone who is found written in the book, will be rescued.

Prophecy of the Resurrections

2"And^Rmany of those who sleep in the dust of the ground will awake, these to everlasting life, but the others to disgrace *and* everlasting^Tcontempt.   Is. 26:19 • *abhorrence*

3"And^Athose who have^Rinsight will shine brightly like the brightness of the^Aexpanse of heaven, and those who lead the many to righteousness, like the stars forever and ever.   *the instructors will* • Dan. 11:33 • *firmament*

Sealing of the Book

4"But as for you, Daniel, conceal these words and seal up the book until the^Rend of time; ^Rmany will go back and forth, and knowledge will increase."   Dan. 8:17 • Is. 11:9

Questions Regarding the Great Time of Distress

5 Then I, Daniel, looked and behold, two others were standing, one on this bank of the river, and the other on that bank of the river.

6 And^Rone said to the man^Rdressed in linen, who was above the waters of the river, "How^Rlong *will it be* until the end of *these* wonders?"   Dan. 8:16 • Ezek. 9:2 • Dan. 8:13

7 And I heard the man dressed in linen, who was above the waters of the river,^Tas he raised his right hand and his left toward heaven, and swore by Him who lives forever that it would be for a^Ttime, times, and half *a time;* and as soon as they finish shattering the ^Tpower of the holy people, all these *events* will be completed.   *and* • year(s) • *hand*

8 As for me, I heard but could not understand; so I said, "My lord, what *will be* the ^Aoutcome of these *events?*"   *final end*

9 And he said, "Go *your way,* Daniel, for *these* words are concealed and^Rsealed up until the end time.   Dan. 12:4

10"Many will be purged, purified and refined; but the wicked will act wickedly, and none of the wicked will understand, but those who have insight will understand.

11"And from the time that the regular sacrifice is abolished, and the abomination of desolation is set up, *there will be* 1,290 days.

12"How blessed is he who keeps waiting and attains to the^R1,335 days!   Rev. 11:2; 12:6

13"But as for you, go *your way* to the^Tend; then you will enter into^Rrest and rise *again* for your^Rallotted portion at the end of the ^Tage."   end of your life • Is. 57:2 • Ps. 16:5 • *days*

THE BOOK OF

HOSEA

THE BOOK OF HOSEA

Hosea, whose name means "Salvation," ministers to the northern kingdom of Israel (also called Ephraim, after its largest tribe). Outwardly, the nation is enjoying a time of prosperity and growth; but inwardly, moral corruption and spiritual adultery permeate the people. Hosea, instructed by God to marry a woman named Gomer, finds his domestic life to be an accurate and tragic dramatization of the unfaithfulness of God's people. During his half century of prophetic ministry, Hosea repeatedly echoes his threefold message: God abhors the sins of His people; judgment is certain; but God's loyal love stands firm.

The names Hosea, Joshua, and Jesus are all derived from the same Hebrew root word. The word *hoshea* means "salvation," but "Joshua" and "Jesus" include an additional idea: "Yahweh Is Salvation" (see "The Book of Joshua"). As God's messenger, Hosea offers the possibility of salvation if only the nation will turn from idolatry back to God.

Israel's last king, Hoshea, has the same name as the prophet even though the English Bible spells them differently. Hosea in the Greek and Latin is *Osee*.

THE AUTHOR OF HOSEA

Few critics refute the claim in 1:1 that Hosea is the author of this book. His place of birth is not given, but his familiarity and obvious concern with the northern kingdom indicate that he lived in Israel, not Judah. This is also seen when he calls the king of Samaria "our king" (7:5). Hosea was the son of Beeri (1:1), husband of Gomer (1:3), and father of two sons and a daughter (1:4, 6, 9). Nothing more is known of him since he is not mentioned elsewhere in the Bible.

Hosea had a real compassion for his people, and his personal suffering because of Gomer gave him some understanding of God's grief over their sin. Thus, his words of coming judgment were passionately delivered but tempered with a heart of tenderness. He upbraids his people for their lying, murder, insincerity, ingratitude, idolatry, and covetousness with cutting metaphors and images; but his messages are punctuated with consolation and future hope.

THE TIME OF HOSEA

Hosea addressed the northern kingdom of Israel (5:1), often called Ephraim after the largest tribe (5:3, 5, 11, 13). According to 1:1, he ministered during the reigns of Uzziah (767–739 B.C.), Jotham (739–731 B.C.), Ahaz (731–715 B.C.), and Hezekiah (715–686 B.C.), kings of Judah. When Hosea began his ministry, Jeroboam II (782–753 B.C.) was still reigning in Israel. This makes Hosea a younger contemporary of Amos, another prophet to the northern kingdom. Hosea was also a contemporary of Isaiah and Micah who ministered to the southern kingdom. Hosea's long career continued after the time of Jeroboam II and spanned the reigns of the last six kings of Israel from Zechariah (753–752 B.C.) to Hoshea (732–722 B.C.). Hosea evidently compiled this book during the early years of Hezekiah, and his ministry stretched from about 755 B.C. to about 710 B.C. The Book of Hosea represents approximately forty years of prophetic ministry.

When Hosea began his ministry, Israel was enjoying a temporary period of political and economic prosperity under Jeroboam II. However, the nation began to crumble after Tiglath-pileser III (745–727 B.C.) strengthened Assyria. The reigns of Israel's last six kings were relatively brief since four were murdered and a fifth was carried captive to Assyria. Confusion and decline characterized the last years of the northern kingdom, and her people refused to heed Hosea's warning of imminent judgment. The people were in a spiritual stupor, riddled with sin and idolatry.

THE CHRIST OF HOSEA

Matthew 2:15 applies Hosea 11:1 to Christ in Egypt: "When Israel *was* a youth I loved him, and out of Egypt I called My son." Matthew quotes the second half of this verse to show that the Exodus of Israel from Egypt as a new nation was a prophetic type of Israel's Messiah who was also called out of Egypt in His childhood. Both Israel and Christ left Palestine to take refuge in Egypt.

Christ's identification with our plight and His loving work of redemption can be seen in Hosea's redemption of Gomer from the slave market.

KEYS TO HOSEA

Key Word: The Loyal Love of God for Israel—The themes of chapters 1—3 echo throughout the rest of the book. The harlotry of Gomer (1) illustrates the sin of Israel (4—7); the degradation of Gomer (2) represents the judgment of Israel (8—10); and Hosea's redemption of Gomer (3) pictures the restoration of Israel (11—14). More than any other Old Testament prophet, Hosea's personal experiences illustrate his prophetic message. In his relationship to Gomer, Hosea portrays God's faithfulness, justice, love, and forgiveness toward His people. The theme of God's holiness is developed in contrast to Israel's corruption and apostasy. Hosea utters about 150 statements concerning the sins of Israel, and more than half deal specifically with idolatry. The theme of God's justice is contrasted with Israel's lack of justice. There has never been a good king in Israel, and judgment is long overdue. The theme of God's love is seen in contrast to Israel's hardness and empty ritual. God's loyal love is unconditional and ceaseless; in spite of Israel's manifold sins, God tries every means to bring His people back to Himself. He pleads with the people to return to Him, but they will not. "Return, O Israel, to the LORD your God, for you have stumbled because of your iniquity" (14:1).

Key Verses: Hosea 4:1; 11:7-9— "Listen to the word of the LORD, O sons of Israel, for the LORD has a case against the inhabitants of the land, because there is no faithfulness or kindness or knowledge of God in the land" (4:1).

"So My people are bent on turning from Me. Though they call them to *the One* on high, none at all exalts *Him*. How can I give you up, O Ephraim? How can I surrender you, O Israel? How can I make you like Admah? How can I treat you like Zeboiim? My heart is turned over within Me, all My compassions are kindled. I will not execute My fierce anger; I will not destroy Ephraim again. For I am God and not man, the Holy One in your midst, and I will not come in wrath" (11:7-9).

Key Chapter: Hosea 4—The nation of Israel has left the knowledge of the truth and followed the idolatrous ways of their pagan neighbors. Central to the book is Hosea 4:6— "My people are destroyed for lack of knowledge. Because you have rejected knowledge, I also will reject you from being My priest. Since you have forgotten the law of your God, I also will forget your children."

SURVEY OF HOSEA

Hosea is called by God to prophesy during Israel's last hours, just as Jeremiah will prophesy years later to the crumbling kingdom of Judah. As one commentator has noted, "What we see in the prophecy of Hosea are the last few swirls as the kingdom of Israel goes down the drain." This book represents God's last gracious effort to plug the drain. Hosea's personal tragedy is an intense illustration of Israel's national tragedy. It is a story of one-sided love and faithfulness that represents the relationship between Israel and God. As Gomer is married to Hosea, so Israel is betrothed to God. Both relationships gradually disintegrate—Gomer runs after other men, and Israel runs after other gods. Israel's spiritual adultery is illustrated in Gomer's physical adultery. The development of the book can be traced in two parts: the adulterous wife and faithful husband (1—3) and the adulterous Israel and faithful Lord (4—14).

The Adulterous Wife and Faithful Husband (1—3): Hosea marries a woman named Gomer who bears him three children appropriately

FOCUS	ADULTEROUS WIFE AND FAITHFUL HUSBAND			ADULTEROUS ISRAEL AND FAITHFUL LORD			
REFERENCE	1:1————2:2————3:1————			4:1—————	6:4————	9:1————	11:1———14:9
DIVISION	PROPHETIC MARRIAGE	APPLICATION OF GOMER TO ISRAEL	RESTORATION OF GOMER	SPIRITUAL ADULTERY OF ISRAEL	REFUSAL OF ISRAEL TO REPENT	JUDGMENT OF ISRAEL BY GOD	RESTORATION OF ISRAEL TO GOD
TOPIC	MARRIAGE OF HOSEA			MESSAGE OF HOSEA			
	PERSONAL			NATIONAL			
LOCATION	NORTHERN KINGDOM OF ISRAEL						
TIME	c. 755—710 B.C.						

named by God as signs to Israel. Jezreel, Lo-ruhamah, and Lo-ammi mean "God Scatters," "Not Pitied," and "Not My People." Similarly, God will judge and scatter Israel because of her sin.

Gomer seeks other lovers and deserts Hosea. In spite of the depth to which her sin carries her, Hosea redeems her from the slave market and restores her.

The Adulterous Israel and Faithful Lord (4—14): Because of his own painful experience, Hosea can feel some of the sorrow of God over the sinfulness of His people. His loyal love for Gomer is a reflection of God's concern for Israel. However, Israel has fallen into the dregs of sin and is hardened against God's gracious last appeal to return. The people have flagrantly violated all of God's commandments,

and they are indicted by the holy God for their crimes. Even now God wants to heal and redeem them (7:1, 13), but in their arrogance and idolatry they rebel.

Chapters 9 and 10 give the verdict of the case God has just presented. Israel's disobedience will lead to her dispersion. "For they sow the wind" (4—7), "and they reap the whirlwind" (8—10). Israel spurns repentance, and the judgment of God can no longer be delayed.

God is holy (4—7) and just (8—10), but He is also loving and gracious (11—14). God must discipline, but because of His endless love, He will ultimately save and restore His wayward people. "How can I give you up, O Ephraim? . . . I will heal their apostasy, I will love them freely, for My anger has turned away from them" (11:8; 14:4).

CHAPTER 1

*The Introduction
to the Book of Hosea*

THE word of the LORD which came to[R]Hosea the son of Beeri, during the days of Uzziah, Jotham, Ahaz, *and* Hezekiah, kings of Judah, and during the days of Jeroboam the son of Joash, king of Israel. Rom. 9:25

Hosea's Marriage to Gomer

2 When the LORD first spoke through Hosea, the LORD said to Hosea, "Go, take to yourself a wife of harlotry, and *have* children of harlotry; for the land commits flagrant harlotry, forsaking the LORD." Hos. 3:1

---

¹ I.e., she has not obtained compassion

The Children of Hosea and Gomer

3 So he went and took Gomer the daughter of Diblaim, and she conceived and[R]bore him a son. Ezek. 23:4

4 And the LORD said to him, "Name him [R]Jezreel; for yet a little while, and I will punish the house of Jehu for the bloodshed of Jezreel, and[R]I will put an end to the kingdom of the house of Israel. Hos. 2:22 • 2 Kin. 15:8-10

5"And it will come about on that day, that I will[R]break the bow of Israel in the[R]valley of Jezreel." Jer. 49:35 • Josh. 17:16

6 Then she conceived again and gave birth to a daughter. And[R]the LORD said to him, "Name her ¹Lo-ruhamah, for I will no longer have compassion on the house of Israel, that I should ever forgive them. *He*

7"But I will have compassion on the house of Judah and deliver them by the

LORD their God, and will not deliver them by bow, sword, battle, horses, or horsemen."

8 When she had weaned Lo-ruhamah, she conceived and gave birth to a son.

9 And [T]the LORD said, "Name him [2]Lo-ammi, for you are not My people and I am not [T]your God."   *He · yours*

The Application
of Future Restoration

10 Yet the number of the sons of Israel
Will be like the [R]sand of the sea,
Which cannot be measured or numbered;   Gen. 22:17; 32:12; Jer. 33:22
And [R]it will come about that, in the place   Rom. 9:26
Where it is said to them,
"You are [T]not My people,"
It will be said to them,   Is. 65:1; Hos. 1:9
"You are the sons of the living God."
11 And the [R]sons of Judah and the sons of Israel will be gathered together,
And they will appoint for themselves [R]one leader,   Is. 11:12 · Jer. 30:21
And they will go up from the land,
For great will be the day of Jezreel.

CHAPTER 2

SAY to your brothers, "[3]Ammi," and to your sisters, "[4]Ruhamah."

Israel's Sin of Spiritual Adultery

2 "Contend with your mother, [R]contend,
For she is [R]not my wife, and I am not her husband;   Ezek. 23:45 · Is. 50:1
And let her put away her [R]harlotry from her face,   Jer. 3:1, 9, 13
And her adultery from between her breasts,
3 Lest I strip her [R]naked   Ezek. 16:7, 22, 39
And expose her as on the [R]day when she was born.   Ezek. 16:4
I will also [R]make her like a wilderness,
Make her like desert land,   Is. 32:13, 14
And slay her with [R]thirst.   Amos 8:11-13
4 "Also, I will have no compassion on her children,
Because they are children of harlotry.
5 "For their mother has [R]played the harlot;
She who conceived them has acted shamefully.   Is. 1:21; Jer. 2:25; 3:1, 2
For she said, 'I will go after my lovers,
Who [R]give *me* my bread and my water,
My wool and my flax, my [R]oil and my drink.'   Jer. 44:17; Hos. 2:12 · Hos. 2:8

Judgment of God

6 "Therefore, behold, I will [R]hedge up her way with [R]thorns,   Job 19:8 · Hos. 9:6
And I will build a wall against her so that she cannot find her paths.

7 "And she will [R]pursue her lovers, but she will not overtake them;   Hos. 5:13
And she will seek them, but will not find *them.*
Then she will say, 'I [R]will go back to my [R]first husband,   Luke 15:17 · Jer. 2:2
For it was [R]better for me then than now!'   Jer. 14:22; Hos. 13:6

8 "For she does [R]not know that it was [R]I who gave her the grain, the new wine, and the oil,   Is. 1:3 · Ezek. 16:19
And lavished on her silver and gold,
Which they [A]used for Baal.   *made into the*
9 "Therefore, I will [T]take back My grain at [T]harvest time   Hos. 8:7; 9:2 · *its time*
And My new wine in its season.
I will also take away My wool and My flax
Given to cover her nakedness.
10 "And then I will [R]uncover her lewdness
In the sight of her lovers,   Ezek. 16:37
And no one will rescue her out of My hand.
11 "I will also [R]put an end to all her gaiety,
Her [R]feasts, her [R]new moons, her sabbaths,   Jer. 7:34 · Hos. 3:4 · Is. 1:13, 14
And all her festal assemblies.
12 "And I will [R]destroy her vines and fig trees,   Jer. 5:17; 8:13
Of which she said, 'These are my wages
Which my lovers have given me.'
And I will [R]make them a forest,   Is. 5:5
And the [R]beasts of the field will devour them.   Hos. 13:8
13 "And I will punish her for the [R]days of the Baals   Hos. 4:13; 11:2
When she used to [A]offer [R]sacrifices to them   *burn incense* · Jer. 7:9
And [R]adorn herself with her [A]earrings and jewelry,   Ezek. 16:12 · *nose rings*
And follow her lovers, so that she [R]forgot Me," declares the LORD.   Hos. 4:6

Restoration of Israel

14 "Therefore, behold, I will allure her,
Bring her into the wilderness,
And speak [T]kindly to her.   *upon her heart*
15 "Then I will give her her [R]vineyards from there,   Ezek. 28:25, 26
And [R]the valley of Achor as a door of hope.   Josh. 7:26
And she will [A]sing there as in the days of her youth,   *give answer* · Jer. 2:1-3
As in the [R]day when she came up from the land of Egypt.   Hos. 11:1; 12:9, 13
16 "And it will come about in that day," declares the LORD,
"That you will call Me [5]Ishi
And will no longer call Me [6]Baali.

[2] I.e., not my people   [3] I.e., my people
[4] I.e., she has obtained compassion   [5] I.e., my Husband
[6] I.e., my Master, or, my Baal

17"For ^{R}I will remove the names of the
Baals from her mouth,
So that they will be mentioned by their
names no more. Ex. 23:13
18"In that day I will also make a covenant
for them
With the^{R}beasts of the field, Is. 11:6-9
The birds of the sky,
And the creeping things of the ground.
And I will ^{T}abolish the bow, the sword,
and war from the land, break
And will make them lie down in safety.
19"And I will betroth you to Me forever;
Yes, I will betroth you to Me in^{R}right-
eousness and in justice, Is. 1:27
In lovingkindness and in compassion,
20 And I will betroth you to Me in faithfulness.
Then you will^{R}know the LORD. Hos. 6:6

21"And it will come about in that day that
^{R}I will respond," declares the LORD.
"I will respond to the heavens, and they
will respond to the earth, Is. 55:10
22 And the earth will respond to the grain,
to the new wine, and to the oil,
And they will respond to ^{7}Jezreel.
23"And I will ^{R}sow her for Myself in the
land. Jer. 31:27
I will also have compassion on her who
had not obtained compassion,
And I will say to^{T}those who were^{R}not
My people, Heb., Lo-ammi • Hos. 1:9
'You are My people!'
And they will say, 'Thou art my God!' "

CHAPTER 3

The Restoration of Gomer to Hosea

THEN the LORD said to me, "Go again,
love a woman who is loved by her^{T}husband,
yet an adulteress, even as the LORD loves
the sons of Israel, though they turn to other
gods and love raisin cakes." companion
2 So I^{R}bought her for myself for fifteen
shekels of silver and a homer and a^{T}half of
barley. Ruth 4:10 • Heb., lethech
3 Then I said to her, "You shall^{R}stay with
me for many days. You shall not play the
harlot, nor shall you have a^{A}man; so I will
also be toward you." Deut. 21:13 • husband
4 For the sons of Israel will remain for
many days without king or prince, without
sacrifice or sacred pillar, and without^{R}ephod
or^{T}household idols. Ex. 28:4-12 • Heb., teraphim
5 Afterward the sons of Israel will return
and seek the LORD their God and David their
king; and they will come trembling to the
LORD and to His goodness in the last days.

^{7} I.e., God sows

CHAPTER 4

Rejection of the Knowledge of God

LISTEN^{R}to the word of the LORD, O sons of
Israel, Hos. 5:1
For the LORD has a^{R}case against the inhabitants of the land, Hos. 12:2
Because there is ^{R}no ^{A}faithfulness or
^{A}kindness Is. 59:4 • truth • loyalty
Or knowledge of God in the land.
2 There is swearing, ^{R}deception, murder,
stealing, and adultery. Hos. 7:3
They employ violence, so that
bloodshed follows bloodshed.
3 Therefore the land^{R}mourns, Is. 24:4; 33:9
And everyone who lives in it languishes
Along with the beasts of the field and
the birds of the sky;
And also the fish of the sea disappear.

4 Yet let no one^{T}find^{R}fault, and let none
offer reproof; contend • Amos 5:10, 13
For your people are like those who
^{R}contend with the priest. Deut. 17:12
5 So you will^{R}stumble by day, Ezek. 14:3, 7
And the prophet also will stumble with
you by night;
And I will destroy your mother.
6 ^{R}My people are destroyed for lack of
knowledge. Is. 5:13
Because you have^{R}rejected knowledge,
I also will^{R}reject you from being My
priest. Hos. 4:14; Mal. 2:7 • Zech. 11:8, 9
Since you have^{R}forgotten the^{R}law of
your God, Hos. 2:13; 8:14 • Hos. 8:1, 12
I also will forget your children.

7 The more they^{R}multiplied, the more
they sinned against Me; Hos. 10:1
I will change their glory into shame.
8 They^{R}feed on the^{A}sin of My people,
And^{R}direct their desire toward their iniquity. Hos. 10:13 • sin offering • Is. 56:11
9 And it will be, like people,^{R}like priest;
So I will punish them for their ways,
And repay them for their deeds. Is. 24:2
10 And^{R}they will eat, but not have enough;
They will^{R}play the harlot, but not increase, Lev. 26:26; Is. 65:13 • Hos. 7:4
Because they have^{T}stopped giving heed
to the LORD. forsaken giving heed

11 Harlotry, wine, and new wine take
away the^{T}understanding. heart

Idolatry of Israel

12 My people ^{R}consult their wooden idol,
and their diviner's wand informs
them; Is. 44:19; Jer. 2:27
For a spirit of harlotry has led them
astray,
And they have played the harlot, de-
parting^{T}from their God. from under

13 They offer sacrifices on the[R]tops of the
   mountains   Jer. 3:6
   And[A]burn[R]incense on the hills,
   [R]Under oak, poplar, and terebinth,
   Because their shade is pleasant.
   Therefore your daughters play the har-
   lot,   *offer sacrifices* • Hos. 2:13 • Jer. 2:20
   And your brides commit adultery.
14 I will not punish your daughters when
   they play the harlot
   Or your[R]brides when they commit adul-
   tery,   *daughters-in-law*
   For *the men* themselves go apart with
   harlots
   And offer sacrifices with[R]temple prosti-
   tutes;   Deut. 23:17
   So the people without understanding
   are[T]ruined.   *thrust down*

15 Though you, Israel, play the harlot,
   Do not let Judah become guilty;
   Also do not go to[R]Gilgal,   Hos. 9:15
   Or go up to Beth-aven,
   [R]And take the oath: Jer. 5:2; Amos 8:14
   "As the LORD lives!"
16 Since Israel is[R]stubborn   Ps. 78:8
   Like a stubborn heifer,
   Can the LORD now pasture them
   Like a lamb in a large field?
17 Ephraim is joined to[R]idols;   Hos. 13:2
   [R]Let him alone.   Ps. 81:12; Hos. 4:4
18 Their liquor gone,
   They play the harlot continually;
   Their[T]rulers dearly love shame. *shields*
19 [R]The wind wraps them in its wings,
   And they will be ashamed because of
   their sacrifices.   Hos. 12:1; 13:15

CHAPTER 5

Judgment of Israel

HEAR this, O priests!
   Give heed, O house of Israel!
   Listen, O house of the king!
   For the judgment applies to you,
   For you have been a[R]snare at Mizpah,
   And a net spread out on Tabor. Hos. 9:8
2 And the revolters have[A]gone deep in
   depravity,   *waded deep in slaughter*
   But I will chastise all of them.
3 I[R]know Ephraim, and Israel is not hid-
   den from Me;   Amos 3:2; 5:12
   For now, O Ephraim, you have played
   the harlot,
   Israel has defiled itself.
4 Their deeds will not allow them
   To return to their God.
   For a spirit of harlotry is within them,
   And they do not know the LORD.
5 Moreover, the[R]pride of Israel testifies
   against him,   Hos. 7:10
   And Israel and Ephraim stumble in
   their iniquity;

   Judah also has stumbled with them.
6 They will [R]go with their flocks and
   herds   Hos. 8:13; Mic. 6:6, 7
   To seek the LORD, but they will[R]not find
   Him;   Prov. 1:28; Is. 1:15; Jer. 14:12
   He has[R]withdrawn from them. Ezek. 8:6
7 They have[R]dealt treacherously against
   the LORD,   Is. 48:8; Jer. 3:20; Hos. 6:7
   For they have borne[T]illegitimate[R] children.   *strange* • Hos. 2:4
   Now the[R]new moon will devour them
   with their[T]land.   Hos. 2:11 • *portions*

8 Blow the horn in[R]Gibeah, Hos. 9:9; 10:9
   The trumpet in Ramah.
   Sound an alarm at Beth-aven:
   "Behind[R]you, Benjamin!"   Judg. 5:14
9 Ephraim will become a[R]desolation in
   the[R]day of rebuke; Is. 28:1-4 • Is. 37:3
   Among the tribes of Israel I[R]declare
   what is sure.   Is. 46:10; Zech. 1:6
10 The princes of Judah have become like
   those who[R]move a boundary;
   On them I will[R]pour out My wrath[R]like
   water.   Deut. 19:14 • Ezek. 7:8 • Ps. 32:6
11 Ephraim is[R]oppressed, crushed in judgment,   Deut. 28:33
   Because he was determined to[A]follow
   man's command.   *follow nothingness*
12 Therefore I am like a[A]moth to Ephraim,
   And like rottenness to the house of Judah.   [Ps. 39:11; Is. 51:8]
13 When Ephraim saw his sickness,
   And Judah his[A]wound,   *ulcer*
   Then Ephraim went to[R]Assyria Hos. 7:11
   And sent to[A]King Jareb. *the avenging king*
   But he is unable to heal you,
   Or to cure you of your wound.
14 For I *will be*[R]like a lion to Ephraim,
   And like a young lion to the house of
   Judah.   Ps. 7:2; Hos. 13:7, 8; Amos 3:4
   [R]I, even I, will tear to pieces and go
   away,   Ps. 50:22
   I will carry away, and there will be
   [R]none to deliver.   Mic. 5:8

Eventual Restoration of Israel

15 I will go away *and* return to My place
   Until they[A]acknowledge their guilt and
   seek My face;   *bear their punishment*
   In their affliction they will earnestly
   [R]seek Me.   Ps. 50:15; 78:34; Jer. 2:27

CHAPTER 6

"COME,[R] let us return to the LORD.
   For He has torn *us*, but[R]He will heal us;
   He has[T]wounded *us*, but He will ban-
   dage us.   Jer. 50:4 • Jer. 30:17 • *struck*
2 "He will[R]revive us after two days;
   He will[R]raise us up on the third day

That we may live before Him. 1 Cor. 15:4
3 "So let us[R]know, let us press on to know
the LORD. Is. 2:3; Mic. 4:2
His [R]going forth is as certain as the
dawn; Ps. 19:6; Mic. 5:2
And He will come to us like the[R]rain,
Like the spring rain watering the
earth." Job 29:23; Ps. 72:6; Joel 2:23

Willful Transgression of the Covenant

4 What shall I do with you, O[R]Ephraim?
What shall I do with you, O Judah?
For your [A]loyalty is like a morning
cloud, Hos. 7:1; 11:8 • *lovingkindness*
And like the dew which goes away
early.
5 Therefore I have[R]hewn *them* in pieces
by the prophets; 1 Sam. 15:32, 33
I have slain them by the[R]words of My
mouth; [Jer. 23:29]
And the judgments on you are *like* the
light that goes forth.
6 For[R]I delight in loyalty[R]rather than sacrifice, Matt. 9:13; 12:7 • Is. 1:11
And in the knowledge of God rather
than burnt offerings.
7 But[R]like [A]Adam they have transgressed
the covenant; Job 31:33 • *men*
There they have [R]dealt treacherously
against Me. Hos. 5:7
8 Gilead is a city of wrongdoers,
Tracked with bloody *footprints.*
9 And as[R]raiders wait for a man, Hos. 7:1
So a band of priests[R]murder on the way
to Shechem; Jer. 7:9, 10; Hos. 4:2
Surely they have committed crime.
10 In the house of Israel I have seen a[R]hor-
rible thing; Jer. 5:30, 31; 23:14
Ephraim's[R]harlotry is there, Israel has
defiled itself. Hos. 5:3
11 Also, O Judah, there is a[R]harvest appointed for you, Jer. 51:33; Joel 3:13
When I[R]restore the fortunes of My people. Zeph. 2:7

CHAPTER 7

Willful Refusal to Return to the Lord

W HEN I[R]would heal Israel, Ezek. 24:13
The iniquity of Ephraim is uncovered,
And the evil deeds of Samaria,
For they deal[R]falsely; Hos. 4:2
The thief enters in,
[R]Bandits raid outside, Hos. 6:9
2 And they do not [T]consider in their
hearts *say to their heart*
That I[R]remember all their wickedness.
Now their deeds are all around them;
They are before My face. Jer. 14:10; 17:1

3 [R]With their wickedness they make the
[R]king glad, [Rom. 1:32] • Jer. 28:1-4
And the princes with their[R]lies. Hos. 4:2
4 They are[R]all adulterers Jer. 9:2; 23:10
Like an oven heated by the baker,
Who ceases to stir up *the fire*
From the kneading of the dough until it
is leavened.
5 On the [T]day of our king, the princes[R]be-
came sick with the heat of wine;
He stretched out his hand with scoff-
ers, a festive occasion • Is. 28:1, 7
6 For their hearts are like an[R]oven
As they approach their [T]plotting;
Their anger [T]smolders all night,
In the morning it burns like a flaming
fire. Ps. 21:9 • *ambush* • *sleeps*
7 All of them are hot like an oven,
And they consume their[R]rulers;
All their kings have fallen.
None of them calls on Me. Hos. 13:10

8 Ephraim [R]mixes himself with the [T]na-
tions; Ps. 106:35 • *peoples*
Ephraim has become a cake not
turned.
9 [R]Strangers devour his strength, Hos. 8:7
Yet he[R]does not know *it*; Hos. 4:6
Gray hairs also are sprinkled on him,
Yet he does not know *it.*
10 Though the [R]pride of Israel testifies
against him, Hos. 5:5
Yet[R]they have neither returned to the
LORD their God, Is. 9:13
Nor have they sought Him, for all this.
11 So Ephraim has become like a silly
dove,[R]without [T]sense; Hos. 4:6 • *heart*
They call to Egypt, they go to Assyria.
12 When they go, I will [R]spread My net
over them; Ezek. 12:13
I will bring them down like the birds of
the sky.
I will chastise them in accordance with
the proclamation to their assembly.
13 [R]Woe to them, for they have [R]strayed
from Me! Hos. 9:12 • Jer. 14:10
Destruction is theirs, for they have rebelled against Me!
I[R]would redeem them, but they speak
lies against Me. Jer. 51:9; Hos. 7:1
14 And[T]they do not cry to Me from their
heart Job 35:9-11; Hos. 8:2; Zech. 7:5
When they wail on their beds;
For the sake of grain and new wine
they assemble themselves,
They[R]turn away from Me. Hos. 13:16
15 Although I trained *and* strengthened
their arms,
Yet they devise evil against Me.
16 They turn, *but* not[A]upward,
They are like a deceitful bow;
Their princes will fall by the sword
Because of the [T]insolence of their
tongue. *to the Most High • indignation*
This *will be* their[R]derision in the land of
Egypt. Ezek. 23:32; Hos. 9:3, 6

CHAPTER 8

Willful Idolatry

PUT the trumpet to your^Tlips!   *palate*
Like an eagle *the enemy comes*^Ragainst
    the house of the LORD,   Deut. 28:49
Because they have ^Rtransgressed My
    covenant,   Hos. 6:7
And rebelled against My^Rlaw.   Hos. 4:6
2 ^RThey cry out to Me,   Ps. 78:34; Hos. 7:14
"My God, we of Israel know Thee!"
3 Israel has rejected the good;
    The enemy will pursue him.
4 ^RThey have set up kings, but not by Me;
    They have appointed princes, but I did
        not know *it*.   2 Kin. 15:13; Hos. 13:10
    With their ^Rsilver and gold they have
        made idols for themselves, Hos. 2:8
    That^Tthey might be cut off.   *he*
5 ^AHe has rejected your calf, O Samaria,
        saying,   *Your calf has rejected you*
    "My anger burns against them!"
    How long will they be incapable of^Rin-
        nocence?   Ps. 19:13; Jer. 13:27
6 For from Israel is even this!
    A ^Rcraftsman made it, so it is not God;
    Surely the calf of Samaria will be bro-
        ken to^Apieces.   Hos. 13:2 • *splinters*
7 For^Rthey sow the wind,   Prov. 22:8
    And they reap the^Rwhirlwind.   Is. 66:15
    The standing grain has no heads;
    It yields^Rno^Agrain.   Hos. 2:9 • *meal*
    Should it yield, strangers would swal-
        low it up.

8 Israel is^Rswallowed up;   2 Kin. 17:6
    They are now among the nations
    Like a vessel in which no one delights.
9 For they have gone up to Assyria,
    Like a wild donkey all alone;
    Ephraim has hired^Tlovers.   *loves*
10 Even though they hire *allies* among the
        nations,
    Now I will^Rgather them up;   Ezek. 16:37
    And they will begin to^Adiminish
    Because of the burden of the^Rking of
        princes.   *suffer for awhile* • Is. 10:8

11 Since Ephraim has^Rmultiplied altars for
        sin,   Hos. 10:1
    They have become altars of sinning for
        him.
12 Though^RI wrote for him ten thousand
        precepts of My law,   [Deut. 4:6, 8]
    They are regarded as a strange thing.
13 As for My^Rsacrificial gifts,   Hos. 5:6
    They^Rsacrifice the flesh and eat *it*,
    But the LORD has taken no delight in
        them.   Jer. 6:20; 7:21
    Now He will remember their iniquity,
    And^Rpunish *them* for their sins; Hos. 4:9
    They will return to^REgypt.   Hos. 9:3, 6

14 For Israel has^Rforgotten his Maker and
        ^Rbuilt palaces;   Hos. 2:13 • Is. 9:9, 10
    And Judah has multiplied fortified
        cities,
    But I will send a fire on its cities that it
        may consume its palatial dwellings.

CHAPTER 9

Judgment of Dispersion

DO not rejoice, O Israel,^Twith exultation
    like the^Tnations!   *to • peoples*
    For you have played the harlot,^Tforsak-
        ing your God.   *away from your God*
    You have loved *harlots'* earnings on
        every threshing floor.
2 Threshing floor and wine press will^Rnot
        feed them,   Hos. 2:9
    And the new wine will fail^Tthem.   *her*
3 They will not remain in ^Rthe LORD's
        land,   Lev. 25:23; Jer. 2:7
    But Ephraim will return to^REgypt,
    And in ^RAssyria they will eat^Runclean
        food.   Hos. 7:16 • Hos. 7:11 • Ezek. 4:13
4 They will not pour out libations of^Rwine
        to the LORD,   Ex. 29:40
    Their sacrifices will not please Him.
    Their bread will ^Tbe like ^Amourners'
        bread;   *be to them • bread of misfortune*
    All who eat of it will be^Rdefiled,
    For their bread will be for^Tthemselves
        alone;   Hag. 2:13, 14 • *their appetite*
    It will not enter the house of the LORD.
5 ^RWhat will you do on the day of the ap-
        pointed festival   Is. 10:3; Jer. 5:31
    And on the day of the ^Rfeast of the
        LORD?   Hos. 2:11; Joel 1:13
6 For behold, they will go because of de-
        struction;
    Egypt will gather them up, ^RMemphis
        will bury them. Is. 19:13; Jer. 2:16; 44:1
    Weeds will take over their treasures of
        silver;
    ^RThorns *will be* in their tents.   Is. 5:6; 7:23

7 The days of punishment have come,
    The days of retribution have come;
    ^ALet Israel know *this*!   *Israel will know it*
    The prophet is a^Rfool,   [Ezek. 13:3, 10]
    The^Tinspired man is demented,
    Because of the grossness of your^Riniq-
        uity,   *man of the spirit* • Ezek. 14:9, 10
    And *because* your hostility is *so* great.
8 Ephraim *was* a watchman with my
        God, a prophet;
    Yet the snare of a bird catcher is in all
        his ways,
    And there is *only* hostility in the house
        of his God.
9 They have gone deep in depravity
    As in the days of^RGibeah;   Judg. 19:12
    He will^Rremember their iniquity,
    He will punish their sins.   Hos. 7:2; 8:13

Judgment of Barrenness

10 I found Israel like [R]grapes in the wilderness;   Mic. 7:1
I saw your forefathers as the [R]earliest fruit on the fig tree in its first *season*.   Jer. 24:2
But they came to [R]Baal-peor and devoted themselves to [8]shame,
And they became as detestable as that which they loved.   Num. 25:1-5

11 As for Ephraim, their [R]glory will fly away like a bird—   Hos. 4:7; 10:5
No birth, no pregnancy, and no conception!

12 Though they bring up their children,
Yet I will bereave them [T]until not a man is left.   *without a man*
Yes, [R]woe to them indeed when I depart from them!   Deut. 31:17; Hos. 7:13

13 Ephraim, as I have seen,
Is planted in a pleasant meadow like [R]Tyre;   Ezek. 26:1-21
But Ephraim will bring out his children for slaughter.

14 Give them, O LORD—what wilt Thou give?
Give them a [R]miscarrying womb and dry breasts.   Hos. 9:11

15 All their evil is at [T]Gilgal;   Hos. 4:15; 12:11
Indeed, I came to hate them there!
Because of the [R]wickedness of their deeds   Hos. 4:9; 7:2; 12:2
I will drive them out of My house!
I will love them no more;
All their princes are [R]rebels.   Is. 1:23

16 [R]Ephraim is stricken, their root is dried up,   Hos. 5:11
They will bear [R]no fruit.   Hos. 8:7
Even though they bear children,
I will slay the [R]precious ones of their womb.   Ezek. 24:21

17 My God will cast them away
Because they have [R]not listened to Him;
And they will be [R]wanderers among the nations.   Hos. 4:10 · Hos. 7:13

CHAPTER 10

Judgment of Destruction

ISRAEL is a [A]luxuriant vine;   *degenerate*
He produces fruit for himself.
The more his fruit,
The more altars he [R]made;   Jer. 2:28
The [A]richer his land,   *better*
The better he made the *sacred* pillars.

2 Their heart is [T]faithless;   *smooth*
Now they must bear their guilt.
[T]The LORD will break down their altars
And destroy their *sacred* pillars.   *He*

3 Surely now they will say, "We have [R]no king,   Ps. 12:4; Is. 5:19
For we do not revere the LORD.
As for the king, what can he do for us?"

4 They speak *mere* words,
With [R]worthless oaths they make covenants;   Ezek. 17:13-19; Hos. 4:2
And judgment sprouts like poisonous weeds in the furrows of the field.

5 The inhabitants of Samaria will fear
For the [C]calf of Beth-aven.   Heb., *calves*
Indeed, its people will mourn for it,
And its idolatrous priests [A]will cry out over it,   who *used to rejoice over*
Over its [R]glory, since it has departed from it.   Hos. 9:11

6 The thing itself will be carried to [R]Assyria   Hos. 11:5
As tribute to [R]King Jareb;   Hos. 5:13
Ephraim will [T]be seized with shame,
And Israel will be ashamed of its [R]own counsel.   *receive shame* · Is. 30:3

7 Samaria will be cut off *with* her king,
Like a stick on the surface of the water.

8 Also the [R]high places of Aven, the sin of Israel, will be destroyed;   Hos. 4:13
[R]Thorn and thistle will grow on their altars,   Is. 32:13; Hos. 9:6; 10:2
Then they will [R]say to the mountains, "Cover us!" And to the hills, "Fall on us!"   Is. 2:19; Luke 23:30; Rev. 6:16

9 From the days of Gibeah you have sinned, O Israel;
There they stand!
Will not the battle against the sons of iniquity overtake them in Gibeah? [R]

10 When it is My [A]desire, I will [A]chastise [R] them;   Ezek. 5:13 · *bind* · Hos. 4:9
And [R]the peoples will be gathered against them   Jer. 16:16
When they are bound for their double guilt.

11 And Ephraim is a trained [R]heifer that loves to thresh,   [Jer. 50:11; Hos. 4:16]
But I will [C]come over her fair neck *with a yoke*;   Jer. 28:14
I will harness Ephraim,
Judah will plow, Jacob will harrow for himself.

12 Sow with a view to righteousness,
Reap in accordance with [A]kindness;   *loyalty*
Break up your fallow ground,
For it is time to [R]seek the LORD
Until He [R]comes to [A]rain righteousness on you.   Hos. 12:6 · Hos. 6:3 · *teach*

13 You have [R]plowed wickedness, you have reaped injustice,   Prov. 22:8
You have eaten the fruit of lies.
Because you have trusted in your way, in your [R]numerous warriors, Ps. 33:16

14 Therefore, a tumult will arise among your people,
And all your [R]fortresses will be destroyed,   Is. 17:3

As Shalman destroyed Beth-arbel on
    the day of battle,
When [R]mothers were dashed in pieces
    with *their* children.   Hos. 13:16
15 Thus it will be done to you at Bethel
    because of your great wickedness.
    At dawn the king of Israel will be com-
    pletely cut off.

CHAPTER 11

God's Love for Israel

W HEN Israel *was* a youth I loved him,
    And out of Egypt I called My son.
2 The more they called them,
    The more they went from them;
    They kept sacrificing to the Baals
    And [R]burning incense to idols. Jer. 18:15
3 Yet it is I who taught Ephraim to walk,
    [T]I took them in My arms; Heb., *He . . . His*
    But they did not know that I [R]healed
    them.   Ps. 107:20; Jer. 30:17
4 I [R]led them with cords of a man, with
    bonds of love,   Jer. 31:2, 3
    And [R]I became to them as one who lifts
    the yoke from their jaws; Lev. 26:13
    And I bent down *and* fed them.

5 [T]They will not return to the land of
    Egypt;   *He*
    But Assyria—he will be [T]their king, *his*
    Because they refused to return *to* Me.
6 And the [R]sword will whirl against their
    cities,   Hos. 13:16
    And will demolish their gate bars
    And [R]consume *them* because of their
    [R]counsels.   Lam. 2:9 • Hos. 4:16, 17
7 So My people are bent on [R]turning from
    Me.   Jer. 3:6, 7; 8:5
    Though [T]they call [T]them to *the One* on
    high,   God's prophets • *him;* i.e., Israel
    None at all exalts *Him.*

8 How can I give you up, O Ephraim?
    How can I surrender you, O Israel?
    How can I [T]make you like Admah?
    How can I treat you like Zeboiim?
    My heart is turned over within Me,
    All my compassions are kindled. *give*
9 I will not execute My fierce anger;
    I will not destroy Ephraim again.
    For [R]I am God and not man, the Holy
    One in your midst,   Num. 23:19
    And I will not come in [T]wrath. *excitement*
10 They will [R]walk after the LORD, Hos. 3:5
    He will [R]roar like a lion; Is. 31:4; [Joel 3:16]
    Indeed He will roar,
    And *His* sons will come [R]trembling from
    the west.   Is. 66:2, 5
11 They will come trembling like birds
    from [R]Egypt,   Is. 11:11
    And like [R]doves from the land of As-
    syria;   Is. 60:8; Hos. 7:11
    And I will [R]settle them in their houses,
    declares the LORD.   Ezek. 28:25, 26

12 Ephraim surrounds Me with [R]lies,
    And the house of Israel with deceit;
    Judah is also unruly against God,
    Even against the Holy One who is
    faithful.   Hos. 4:2; 7:3

CHAPTER 12

Israel's Continuing Sin

E PHRAIM feeds on [R]wind,   Jer. 22:22
    And pursues the [R]east wind continually;
    He multiplies lies and violence.
    Moreover, [T]he makes a covenant with
    Assyria,   Gen. 41:6 • *they make*
    And oil is carried to Egypt.
2 The LORD also has a [A]dispute with Ju-
    dah,   Hos. 4:1; Mic. 6:2
    And will punish Jacob [R]according to his
    ways;   Hos. 4:9; 7:2
    He will repay him according to his
    deeds.
3 In the womb he [T]took his brother by the
    heel,   Gen. 25:26
    And in his maturity he [R]contended with
    God.   Gen. 32:28
4 Yes, he wrestled with the angel and
    prevailed;
    He wept and sought His favor.
    He found Him at [R]Bethel, [Gen. 28:13–19]
    And there He spoke with him.
5 Even the LORD, the God of hosts;
    The LORD is His [T]name.   *memorial*
6 Therefore, return to your God,
    Observe [A]kindness and justice, *loyalty*
    And wait for your God continually.
7 A [A]merchant, in whose hands are false
    [R]balances,   *Canaanite* • Prov. 11:1
    He loves to oppress.
8 And Ephraim said, "Surely I have be-
    come [R]rich,   Ps. 62:10; Hos. 13:6
    I have found wealth for myself;
    In all my labors they will find in me
    No iniquity, which *would be* sin."
9 But I *have been* the LORD your God
    since the land of Egypt;
    I will make you [R]live in tents again,
    As in the days of the appointed festi-
    val.   Lev. 23:42
10 I have also spoken to the prophets,
    And I [T]gave numerous visions;
    And through the prophets I gave [R]par-
    ables.   *multiplied the vision* • Ezek. 17:2
11 Is there iniquity in Gilead?
    Surely they are worthless.
    In Gilgal they sacrifice bulls,
    Yes, [R]their altars are like the stone
    heaps   Hos. 8:11; 10:1, 2
    Beside the furrows of the field.

12 Now Jacob fled to the [T]land of Aram,
    And Israel worked for a wife, *field*
    And for a wife he kept *sheep.*
13 But by a [R]prophet the LORD brought Is-
    rael from Egypt,   Is. 63:11-14

And by a prophet he was kept.
14 [R]Ephraim has provoked to bitter anger;
So his Lord will leave his[R]bloodguilt on
him,   2 Kin. 17:7-18 • Ezek. 18:10-13
And bring back his reproach to him.

CHAPTER 13

WHEN[R] Ephraim [A]spoke, *there was* trembling.   Job 29:21 • *spoke with trembling*
He[R]exalted himself in Israel,   Judg. 8:1
But through [R]Baal he [A]did wrong and
died.   Hos. 2:8-17; 11:2 • *became guilty*
2 And now they sin more and more,
And make for themselves[R]molten im-
ages,   Is. 46:6; Jer. 10:4; Hos. 2:8
Idols skillfully made from their silver,
All of them the work of craftsmen.
They say of them, "Let the men who
sacrifice kiss the[R]calves!"   Hos. 8:5, 6
3 Therefore, they will be like the[R]morn-
ing cloud,   Hos. 6:4
And like dew which [T]soon disappears,
Like chaff which is blown away from
the threshing floor,   *goes away early*
And like smoke from a chimney.

4 Yet I *have been* the[R]LORD your God
Since the land of Egypt;   Hos. 12:9
And you were not to know[R]any god ex-
cept Me,   Ex. 20:3; 2 Kin. 18:35
For there is no savior besides Me.
5 I[A]cared for you in the wilderness, *knew*
[R]In the land of drought.   Deut. 8:15
6 As *they had* their pasture, they became
[R]satisfied,   Deut. 8:12, 14; Jer. 5:7
And being satisfied, their[R]heart became
proud;   Hos. 7:14
Therefore, they[R]forgot Me. Hos. 2:13; 4:6
7 So I will be[R]like a lion to them;
Like a[R]leopard I will[A]lie in wait by the
wayside.   Hos. 5:14 • Jer. 5:6 • *watch*
8 I will encounter them [R]like a bear
robbed of her cubs,   2 Sam. 17:8
And I will tear open[T]their chests;
There I will also devour them like a
lioness,   *the enclosure of their heart*
As a wild beast would tear them.

9 *It is* your destruction, O Israel,
[A]That *you are* against Me, against your
[R]help.   *But in Me is your help* • Deut. 33:26
10 Where now is your[R]king   2 Kin. 17:4
That he may save you in all your cities,
And your [R]judges of whom you [T]re-
quested,   1 Sam. 8:5, 6 • *said*
"Give me a king and princes"?
11 I gave you a king in My anger,
And took him away in My wrath.

12 The iniquity of Ephraim is bound up;
His sin is[R]stored up.   Deut. 32:34, 35
13 The pains of[R]childbirth come upon him;
He is[R]not a wise son,   Is. 13:8 • Hos. 5:4

For it is not the time that he should de-
lay at the opening of the womb.
14 Shall I[R]ransom them from the[T]power of
Sheol?   Ps. 49:15; Ezek. 37:12, 13 • *hand*
Shall I redeem them from death?
[R]O Death, where are your thorns?
O Sheol, where is your sting?
[R]Compassion will be hidden from My
sight. [1 Cor. 15:55] • Jer. 20:16; 31:35-37

15 Though he flourishes among the[A]reeds,
An[R]east wind will come,
The wind of the LORD coming up from
the wilderness;   *brothers* • Gen. 41:6
And his fountain will[R]become dry,
And his spring will be dried up;
It will[R]plunder *his* treasury of every
precious article.   Jer. 51:36 • Jer. 20:5
16 Samaria will be held[R]guilty,   Hos. 10:2
For she has rebelled against her God.
They will fall by the[R]sword,   Hos. 11:6
Their little ones will be [R]dashed in
pieces,   Hos. 10:14
And their pregnant [R]women will be
ripped open.   2 Kin. 15:16

CHAPTER 14

God's Promise to Restore Israel

RETURN,[R] O Israel, to the LORD your God,
For you have stumbled[A]because of your
[R]iniquity.   Hos. 6:1; 10:12 • *in* • Hos. 4:8
2 Take words with you and return to the
LORD.
Say to Him, "Take[R] away all iniquity,
And receive *us* graciously,   Mic. 7:18, 19
That we may[R]present the fruit of our
lips.   [Heb. 13:15]
3 "Assyria will not save us,
We will[R]not ride on horses;   Is. 31:1
Nor will we say again, 'Our god,'
To the[R]work of our hands;   Hos. 4:12
For in Thee the orphan finds mercy."

4 I will[R]heal their apostasy,   Is. 57:18
I will[R]love them freely,   Zeph. 3:17
For My anger has[R]turned away from
them.   Is. 12:1
5 I will be like the[R]dew to Israel; Is. 26:19
He will blossom like the[R]lily,   Matt. 6:28
And he will[T]take root like *the cedars of*
[R]Lebanon.   *strike his roots* • Is. 35:2
6 His shoots will[T]sprout,   *go*
And his[A]beauty will be like the[R]olive
tree,   *splendor* • Jer. 11:16
And his fragrance like *the cedars of*
[R]Lebanon.   Song 4:11
7 Those who live in his shadow
Will[A]again raise grain,
And they will blossom like the vine.
His renown *will be* like the wine of
Lebanon.   *return, they will raise grain*

8 O Ephraim, what more have I to do
with [R] idols?   Job 34:32; Hos. 14:3
It is I who answer and look after [T] you.
I am like a luxuriant cypress;   *him*
From [R] Me comes your fruit.   Ezek. 17:23

9 [R] Whoever is wise, let him understand
these things;   Ps. 107:43; Jer. 9:12
Whoever is discerning, let him know
them.
For the ways of the LORD are right,
And the righteous will walk in them,
But transgressors will stumble in them.

THE BOOK OF

JOEL

THE BOOK OF JOEL

Disaster strikes the southern kingdom of Judah without warning. An ominous black cloud descends upon the land—the dreaded locusts. In a matter of hours, every living green thing has been stripped bare. Joel, God's spokesman during the reign of Joash (835–796 B.C.), seizes this occasion to proclaim God's message. Although the locust plague has been a terrible judgment for sin, God's future judgments during the day of the Lord will make that plague pale by comparison. In that day, God will destroy His enemies, but bring unparalleled blessing to those who faithfully obey Him.

The Hebrew name *Yo'el* means "Yahweh Is God." This name is appropriate to the theme of the book, which emphasizes God's sovereign work in history. The courses of nature and nations are in His hand. The Greek equivalent is *Ioel*, and the Latin is *Joel*.

THE AUTHOR OF JOEL

Although there are several other Joels in the Bible, the prophet Joel is known only from this book. In the introductory verse, Joel identifies himself as the son of Pethuel (1:1), meaning "Persuaded of God." His frequent references to Zion and the house of the Lord (1:9, 13, 14; 2:15–17, 23, 32; 3:1, 5, 6, 16, 17, 20, 21) suggest that he probably lived not far from Jerusalem. Because of his statements about the priesthood in 1:13, 14 and 2:17, some think Joel was a priest as well as a prophet. In any case, Joel was a clear, concise, and uncompromising preacher of repentance.

THE TIME OF JOEL

Since this book includes no explicit time references, it cannot be dated with certainty. Some commentators assign a late date (usually postexilic) to Joel for these reasons: (1) It does not mention the northern kingdom and indicates it was written after the 722 B.C. demise of Israel. (2) The references to priests but not kings fit the postexilic period. (3) Joel does not refer to Assyria, Aram, or Babylon, perhaps because these countries have already been overthrown. (4) If Joel 3:2 refers to the Babylonian captivity, this also supports the postexilic date. (5) The mention of the Greeks in 3:6 argues for a late date.

Commentators who believe Joel was written in the ninth century B.C. answer the above arguments in this way: (1) Joel's failure to mention the northern kingdom is an argument from silence. His prophecy was directed to Judah, not Israel. (2) Other early prophets omit references to a king (Obadiah, Jonah, Nahum, and Habakkuk). This also fits the political situation during 841–835 B.C. when Athaliah usurped the throne upon the death of her son Ahaziah. Joash, the legitimate heir to the throne, was a minor and protected by the high priest Jehoiada. When Athaliah was removed from power in 835, Joash came to the throne but ruled under the regency of Jehoiada. Thus, the prominence of the priests and lack of reference to a king in Joel fit this historical context. (3) It is true that Joel does not refer to Assyria or Babylon, but the countries Joel mentions are more crucial. They include Phoenicia, Philistia, Egypt, and Edom—countries prominent in the ninth century but not later. Assyria and Babylon are not mentioned because they had not yet reached a position of power. Also, if Joel was postexilic, a reference to Persia would be expected. (4) Joel 3:2 does not refer to the Babylonian captivity but to an event that has not yet occurred. (5) Greeks are mentioned in Assyrian records from the eighth century B.C. It is just an assumption to state that the Hebrews had no knowledge of the Greeks at an early time.

Evidence also points to a sharing of material between Joel and Amos (cf. Joel 3:16 and Amos 1:2; Joel 3:18 and Amos 9:13). The context of the books suggests that Amos, an eighth-century prophet, borrowed from Joel. Also, Joel's style is more like that of Hosea and Amos than of the postexilic writers. The evidence seems to favor a date of about 835 B.C. for Joel. Since Joel does not mention idolatry, it may have been written after the purge of Baal worship and most other forms of idolatry in the early reign of Joash under Jehoiada the priest. As an early prophet of Judah, Joel would have been a contemporary of Elisha in Israel.

THE CHRIST OF JOEL

Christ promised to send the Holy Spirit after His ascension to the Father (John 16:7–15; Acts 1:8). When this was fulfilled on the day of Pentecost, Peter said, "But this is what was spoken of through the prophet Joel" (Joel 2:28–32; Acts 2:16–21). Joel also portrays Christ as the One who will judge the

nations in the Valley of Jehoshaphat in 3:2, 12.

KEYS TO JOEL

Key Word: The Great and Terrible Day of the Lord—The key theme of Joel is the day of the Lord in retrospect and prospect. Joel uses the terrible locust plague that has recently occurred in Judah to illustrate the coming day of judgment when God will directly intervene in human history to vindicate His righteousness. This will be a time of unparalleled retribution upon Israel (2:1-11) and the whole nation (3:1-17), but this time will culminate in great blessing and salvation for all who trust in the Lord (2:18-32; 3:18-21). "And it will come about that whoever calls on the name of the LORD will be delivered" (2:32).

Joel is written as a warning to the people of Judah of their need to turn humbly to the Lord with penitent hearts (2:12-17) so that God can bless rather than buffet them. If they continue to spurn God's gracious call to repentance, judgment will be inevitable. Joel stresses the sovereign power of God over nature and nations, and points out how God uses nature to get the attention of people.

Key Verses: Joel 2:11, 28, 29—"And the LORD utters His voice before His army; surely His camp is very great, for strong is He who carries out His word. The day of the LORD is indeed great and very awesome, and who can endure it?" (2:11).

"And it will come about after this that I will pour out My Spirit on all mankind; and your sons and daughters will prophesy, your old men will dream dreams, your young men will see visions. And even on the male and female servants I will pour out My Spirit in those days" (2:28, 29).

Key Chapter: Joel 2—The prophet calls for Judah's repentance and promises God's repentance (2:13, 14) from His planned judgment upon Judah if they do indeed turn to Him. Though the offer is clearly given, Judah continues to rebel against the Lord, and judgment is to follow. In that judgment, however, is God's promise of His later outpouring, fulfilled initially on the day of Pentecost (Acts 2:16ff.) and ultimately when Christ returns for the culmination of the day of the Lord.

SURVEY OF JOEL

The brief book Joel develops the crucial theme of the coming day of the Lord (1:15; 2:1, 2, 11, 31; 3:14, 18). It is a time of awesome judgment upon people and nations that have rebelled against God. But it is also a time of future blessing upon those who have trusted in Him. The theme of disaster runs throughout the book (locust plagues, famine, raging fires, invading armies, celestial phenomena), but promises of hope are interspersed with the pronouncements of coming judgment. The basic outline of Joel is: the day of the Lord in retrospect (1:1-20) and the day of the Lord in prospect (2:1—3:21).

The Day of the Lord in Retrospect (1:1-20): Joel begins with an account of a recent locust plague that has devastated the land. The black cloud of insects has stripped the grapevines and fruit trees and ruined the grain harvest. The economy has been brought to a further standstill by a drought and the people are in a desperate situation.

The Day of the Lord in Prospect (2:1—3:21): Joel makes effective use of this natural catastrophe as an illustration of a far greater judgment to come. Compared to the terrible day of the Lord, the destruction by the locusts will seem insignificant. The land will be invaded

FOCUS	DAY OF THE LORD IN RETROSPECT		DAY OF THE LORD IN PROSPECT	
REFERENCE	1:1————1:13		2:1————2:28	3:21
DIVISION	PAST DAY OF THE LOCUST	PAST DAY OF THE DROUGHT	IMMINENT DAY OF THE LORD	ULTIMATE DAY OF THE LORD
TOPIC	HISTORICAL INVASION		PROPHETIC INVASION	
	PAST JUDGMENT ON JUDAH		FUTURE JUDGMENT AND RESTORATION OF JUDAH	
LOCATION	SOUTHERN KINGDOM OF JUDAH			
TIME	c. 835 B.C.			

by a swarming army; like locusts they will be speedy and voracious. The desolation caused by this army will be dreadful: "The day of the LORD is indeed great and very awesome, and who can endure it?" (2:11).

Even so, it is not too late for the people to avert disaster. The prophetic warning is designed to bring them to the point of repentance (2:12-17). " 'Yet even now,' declares the LORD, 'return to Me with all your heart, and with fasting, weeping, and mourning' " (2:12). But God's gracious offer falls on deaf ears.

Ultimately, the swarming, creeping, stripping, and gnawing locusts (1:4; 2:25) will come again in a fiercer form. But God promises that judgment will be followed by great blessing in a material (2:18-27) and spiritual (2:28-32) sense.

These rich promises are followed by a solemn description of the judgment of all nations in the valley of decision (3:14) in the end times. The nations will give an account of themselves to the God of Israel who will judge those who have rebelled against Him. God alone controls the course of history. "Then you will know that I am the LORD your God, dwelling in Zion My holy mountain" (3:17). Joel ends with the kingdom blessings upon the remnant of faithful Judah: "But Judah will be inhabited forever, and Jerusalem for all generations" (3:20).

OUTLINE OF JOEL

CHAPTER 1

The Past Day of the Locust

T HE^Rword of the LORD that came to ^RJoel, the son of Pethuel. Jer. 1:2 • Acts 2:16

2 ^RHear this, O^Relders,   Hos. 4:1 • Job 8:8
And listen, all inhabitants of the land.
^RHas *anything like* this happened in
your days   Jer. 30:7; Joel 2:2
Or in your fathers' days?

3 ^RTell your sons about it, Ex. 10:2; Ps. 78:4
And *let* your sons *tell* their sons,
And their sons the next generation.

4 What the^Rgnawing locust has left, the
swarming locust has eaten; Joel 2:25
And what the swarming locust has left,
the creeping locust has eaten;
And what the creeping locust has left,
the stripping locust has eaten.

5 Awake,^Rdrunkards, and weep;   Joel 3:3
And wail, all you wine drinkers,
On account of the sweet wine
That is cut off from your mouth.

6 For a^Rnation has invaded my land,
Mighty and without number;   Joel 2:2
^RIts teeth are the teeth of a lion, Rev. 9:8
And it has the fangs of a lioness.

7 It has^Rmade my vine a waste, Amos 4:9
And my fig tree^Asplinters.   *a stump*
It has stripped them bare and cast
them away;

Their branches have become white.

8 Wail like a virgin girded with sackcloth
For the bridegroom of her youth.

9 The^Rgrain offering and the libation are
cut off   Hos. 9:4; Joel 1:13; 2:14
From the house of the LORD.
The^Rpriests mourn,   Joel 2:17
The ministers of the LORD.

10 The field is ruined,
The land mourns,
For the grain is ruined,
The new wine dries up,
Fresh oil^Afails.   *wastes away*

11 ^RBe ashamed, O farmers,   Amos 5:16
Wail, O vinedressers,
For the wheat and the barley;
Because the^Rharvest of the field is destroyed.   Is. 17:11; Jer. 9:12

12 The^Rvine dries up,   Joel 1:10; Hab. 3:17
And the fig tree^Tfails;   *wastes away*
The^Rpomegranate, the palm also, and
the^Aapple tree,   Hag. 2:19 • *apricot*
All the trees of the field dry up.
Indeed,^Rrejoicing dries up   Jer. 48:33
From the sons of men.

The Past Day of the Drought

13 ^RGird yourselves *with* sackcloth, Jer. 4:8
And lament, O priests;
^RWail, O ministers of the altar! Jer. 9:10

Come,^Rspend the night in sackcloth,
O ministers of my God,   1 Kin. 21:27
For the grain offering and the libation
Are withheld from the house of your
    God.
14 ^RConsecrate a fast,   Joel 2:15, 16
Proclaim a^Rsolemn assembly;
Gather the elders   Lev. 23:36
And all the inhabitants of the land
To the house of the LORD your God,
And^Rcry out to the LORD.   Jon. 3:8
15 ^RAlas for the day!   [Is. 13:9; Jer. 30:7]
For the^Rday of the LORD is near,
And it will come as destruction from
    the ^TAlmighty.   Joel 2:1 • Heb., *Shaddai*
16 Has not^Rfood been cut off before our
    eyes,   Is. 3:7; Amos 4:6
Gladness and^Rjoy from the house of our
    God?   Deut. 12:7; Ps. 43:4
17 The seeds shrivel under their^Aclods;
The storehouses are desolate,   *shovels*
The barns are torn down,
For the grain is dried up.
18 How^Rthe beasts groan! 1 Kin. 8:5; Jer. 12:4
The herds of cattle wander aimlessly
Because there is no pasture for them;
Even the flocks of sheep suffer.
19 ^RTo Thee, O LORD, I cry;   Mic. 7:7
For^Rfire has devoured the pastures of
    the wilderness,   Jer. 9:10; Amos 7:4
And the flame has burned up all the
    trees of the field.
20 Even the beasts of the field^Tpant^R for
    Thee;   *long for* • Ps. 104:21; Joel 1:18
For the^Rwater brooks are dried up,
And fire has devoured the pastures of
    the wilderness.   1 Kin. 17:7; 18:5

CHAPTER 2

Prophecy of the Imminent Invasion of Judah

BLOW^Ra trumpet in Zion,   Jer. 4:5; Joel 2:15
And sound an alarm on My holy moun-
    tain!
Let all the inhabitants of the land trem-
    ble,
For the^Rday of the LORD is coming;
Surely it is near, Joel 1:15; 2:11, 31; 3:14
2 A day of^Rdarkness and gloom, Joel 2:10
A day of clouds and thick darkness.
As the dawn is spread over the moun-
    tains,
So there is a great and mighty people;
There has^Rnever been *anything* like it,
Nor will there be again after it Joel 1:2
To the years of many generations.
3 A^Rfire consumes before them,   Is. 9:18
And behind them a flame burns.
The land is^Rlike the garden of Eden be-
    fore them,   Is. 51:3; Ezek. 36:35
But a desolate wilderness behind them,
And nothing at all escapes them.
4 Their ^Rappearance is like the appear-
    ance of horses;   Rev. 9:7
And like war horses, so they run.

5 With a^Rnoise as of chariots   Rev. 9:9
They leap on the tops of the mountains,
Like the ^Tcrackling of a flame of fire
    consuming the stubble,   *noise*
Like a mighty people arranged for bat-
    tle.
6 Before them the people are in anguish;
All faces^Aturn pale.   *become flushed*
7 They run like mighty men;
They climb the wall like soldiers;
And they each march^Tin line, *in his ways*
Nor do they deviate from their paths.
8 They do not crowd each other;
They march everyone in his path.
When they^Tburst through the^Tdefenses,
They do not break ranks.   *fall* • *weapon*
9 They rush on the city,
They run on the wall;
They climb into the^Rhouses,   Ex. 10:6
They^Renter through the windows like a
    thief.   Jer. 9:21; John 10:1
10 Before them the earth^Rquakes, Joel 3:16
The heavens tremble,
The sun and the moon grow dark,
And the stars lose their brightness.
11 And the LORD^Rutters His voice before
    ^RHis army;   Ps. 46:6; Is. 13:4 • Joel 2:25
Surely His camp is very great,
For^Rstrong is he who carries out His
    word.   Jer. 50:34; Rev. 18:8
The ^Rday of the LORD is indeed great
    and very awesome,   Jer. 30:7; Joel 1:15
And^Rwho can endure it?   Ezek. 22:14

Conditional Promise of the Salvation of Judah

12 "Yet even now," declares the LORD,
    "Return^Rto Me with all your heart,
And with^Rfasting, weeping, and mourn-
    ing;   Ezek. 33:11; Hos. 12:6 • Dan. 9:3
13 And^Rrend your heart and not^Ryour gar-
    ments." [Is. 57:15] • 2 Sam. 1:11; Job 1:20
Now return to the LORD your God,
For He is^Rgracious and compassionate,
Slow to anger, abounding in loving-
    kindness,   [Ex. 34:6]
And^Rrelenting of evil.   Jer. 18:8; 42:10
14 Who knows^Rwhether He will *not* turn
    and relent,   Jer. 26:3; Jon. 3:9
And leave a blessing behind Him,
Even^Ra grain offering and a libation
For the LORD your God?   Joel 1:9, 13
15 ^RBlow a trumpet in Zion,   2 Kin. 10:20
^RConsecrate a fast, proclaim a solemn
    assembly,   Joel 1:14
16 Gather the people,^Rsanctify the congre-
    gation,   1 Sam. 16:5; 2 Chr. 29:5
Assemble the elders,
Gather the children and the nursing in-
    fants.
Let the ^Rbridegroom come out of his
    room   Ps. 19:5
And the bride out of her *bridal* cham-
    ber.
17 Let the priests, the LORD'S ministers,
Weep^Rbetween the porch and the altar,

And let them say, "Spare[R] Thy people,
O LORD,   Ezek. 8:16 • Ex. 32:11, 12
And do not make Thine inheritance a
[R]reproach,   Ps. 44:13; 74:10
A byword among the nations.
Why should they among the peoples
    say,
'Where[R] is their God?' "   Ps. 42:10; 79:10

18 Then the LORD[A] will be[R] zealous for His
    land,   was zealous • Zech. 1:14; 8:2
And will have pity on His people.
19 And the LORD[A] will answer and say to
    His people,   answered and said
    "Behold, I am going to[R] send you grain,
    new wine, and oil, Jer. 31:12; Hos. 2:21
And you will be satisfied in full with
    [T]them;   it
And I will never again make you a re-
    proach among the nations.
20 "But I will remove the[R] northern army
    far from you,   Jer. 1:14, 15
And I will drive it into a parched and
    desolate land,
And its vanguard into the[R] eastern sea,
And its rear guard into the[R] western
    sea.   Zech. 14:8 • Deut. 11:24
And its[R] stench will arise and its foul
    smell will come up,   Is. 34:3
For it has done great things."

21 [R]Do not fear, O land, rejoice and be
    glad,   Is. 54:4; Jer. 30:10; Zeph. 3:16, 17
For the LORD has done great things.
22 Do not fear, beasts of the field,
For the[R] pastures of the wilderness have
    turned green,   Ps. 65:12, 13
For the tree has borne its fruit,
The fig tree and the vine have yielded
    [T]in full.   their wealth
23 So rejoice, O[R] sons of Zion,   Ps. 149:2
And[R] be glad in the LORD your God;
For He has[R] given you the [1]early rain for
    your vindication. Is. 12:2-6 • Is. 41:16
And He has poured down for you the
    rain,
The [1]early and [2]latter rain as before.
24 And the threshing floors will be full of
    grain,
And the vats will[R] overflow with the
    new wine and oil.   Lev. 26:10
25 "Then I will make up to you for the
    years
That the swarming[R] locust has eaten,
The creeping locust, the stripping lo-
    cust, and the gnawing locust,
My great army which I sent among
    you.   Joel 1:4-7; 2:2-11
26 "And you shall have plenty to[R] eat and be
    satisfied, Lev. 26:5; Deut. 11:15; Is. 62:9
And[R] praise the name of the LORD your
    God,   Deut. 12:7; Ps. 67:5-7
Who has[R] dealt wondrously with you;

Then My people will[R] never be put to
    shame.   Ps. 126:2, 3; Is. 25:1 • Is. 45:17
27 "Thus you will[R] know that I am in the
    midst of Israel,   Lev. 26:11, 12
And that I am the LORD your God
And there is[R] no other;   [Is. 45:5, 6]
And My people will never be[R] put to
    shame.   Is. 49:23

*Last Events Before the Terrible Day
of the Lord*

28 "And it will come about after this
That I will[R] pour out My Spirit on all
    [T]mankind;   Is. 32:15; 44:3 • flesh
And your sons and daughters will
    prophesy,
Your old men will dream dreams,
Your young men will see visions.
29 "And even on the[R] male and female ser-
    vants   [1 Cor. 12:13; Gal. 3:28]
I will pour out My Spirit in those days.
30 "And I will[R] display wonders in the sky
    and on the earth,   Matt. 24:29
Blood, fire, and columns of smoke.
31 "The[R] sun will be turned into darkness,
And the moon into blood,   Is. 13:10; 34:4
Before the[R] great and awesome day of
    the LORD comes.   Is. 13:9; [Mal. 4:1, 5]
32 "And it will come about that[R] whoever
    calls on the name of the LORD
Will be delivered;   Acts 2:21; Rom. 10:13
For[R] on Mount Zion and in Jerusalem
There will be those who[R] escape,
As the LORD has said,   Is. 46:13 • Is. 4:2
Even among the[R] survivors whom the
    LORD calls.   Is. 11:11; Jer. 31:7

CHAPTER 3

Judgments on the Gentiles

"FOR behold,[R] in those days and at that
    time,   Jer. 30:3; Ezek. 38:14
When I[R] restore the fortunes of Judah
    and Jerusalem,   Jer. 16:15
2 I will[R] gather all the nations,   Is. 66:18
And bring them down to the valley of
    [T]Jehoshaphat.   YHWH judges
Then I will[R] enter into judgment with
    them there   Is. 66:16; Jer. 25:31
On behalf of My people and My inheri-
    tance, Israel,
Whom they have[R] scattered among the
    nations;   Jer. 50:17; Ezek. 34:6
And they have divided up My land.
3 "They have also cast lots for My people,
[T]Traded[R] a boy for a harlot,
And sold a girl for wine that they may
    drink.   Given • Amos 2:6
4 "Moreover, what are you to Me, O Tyre,
Sidon, and all the regions of Philistia? Are
you rendering Me a recompense? But if you
do recompense Me, swiftly and speedily I
will return your recompense on your head.

---

[1] I.e., autumn   [2] I.e., spring

5"Since you have ᴿtaken My silver and My
gold, brought My precious ᵀtreasures to your
temples,   2 Kin. 12:18; 2 Chr. 21:16 · *goodly things*
6 and sold the sons of Judah and Jerusa-
lem to the ᵀGreeks in order to remove them
far from their territory,   *sons of Javan*
7 behold, I am going to arouse them
from the place where you have sold them,
and return your recompense on your head.
8"Also I will ᴿsell your sons and your
daughters into the hand of the sons of Judah, and they will sell them to the ᴿSabeans,
to a distant nation," for the LORD has spoken.   Is. 14:2; 60:14 · Job 1:15; Ps. 72:10
9 ᴿProclaim this among the nations:
ᴿPrepare a war; ᴿrouse the mighty men!
Let all the soldiers draw near, let them
come up!   Jer. 51:27 · Jer. 6:4 · Is. 8:9
10 ᴿBeat your plowshares into swords,
And your pruning hooks into spears;
ᴿLet the weak say, "I am a mighty
man."   [Is. 2:4; Mic. 4:3] · Zech. 12:8
11 ᴬHasten ᴿand come, all you surrounding
nations,   *Lend aid* · Ezek. 38:15, 16
And gather yourselves there.
Bring down, O LORD, Thy mighty ones.
12 Let the nations be aroused
And come up to the ᴿvalley of ᵀJehosha-
phat,   Joel 3:2, 14 · *YHWH judges*
For there I will sit to ᴿjudge   Is. 2:4; 3:13
All the surrounding nations.
13 Put in the sickle, for the ᴿharvest is ripe.
Come, ᴬtread, for the ᴿwine press is full;
The vats overflow, for their wickedness
is great. Hos. 6:11 · Rev. 14:19 · [Is. 63:3]
14 Multitudes, multitudes in the ᴿvalley of
ᵀdecision!   Joel 3:2, 12 · *God's verdict*
For the ᴿday of the LORD is near in the
valley of decision.   Joel 1:15; 2:1, 11
15 The ᴿsun and moon grow dark,   Joel 2:10

And the stars lose their brightness.

Restoration of Judah

16 And the LORD ᴿroars from Zion
And ᴿutters His voice from Jerusalem,
And the ᴿheavens and the earth trem-
ble.   Amos 1:2 · Joel 2:11 · Joel 2:10
But the LORD is a refuge for His people
And a stronghold to the sons of Israel.
17 Then you will ᴿknow that I am the LORD
your God,   Joel 2:27
Dwelling in Zion My ᴿholy mountain.
So Jerusalem will be holy, [Is. 11:9; 56:7]
And ᴿstrangers will pass through it no
more.   Is. 52:1; Nah. 1:15

18 And it will come about in that day
That the ᴿmountains will drip with
sweet wine,   Amos 9:13
And the hills will flow with milk,
And all the ᴿbrooks of Judah will flow
with water;   Is. 30:25; 35:6
And a ᴿspring will go out from the
house of the LORD,   Ezek. 47:1-12
To water the valley of ᴬShittim. *acacias*
19 Egypt will become a waste,
And Edom will become a desolate wilderness,
Because of the ᴿviolence done to the
sons of Judah,   Obad. 10
In whose land they have shed innocent
blood.
20 But Judah will be inhabited forever,
And Jerusalem for all generations.
21 And I will ᴿavenge their blood which I
have not avenged,   Is. 4:4
For the LORD dwells in Zion.

THE BOOK OF

AMOS

THE BOOK OF AMOS

Amos prophesies during a period of national optimism in Israel. Business is booming and boundaries are bulging. But below the surface, greed and injustice are festering. Hypocritical religious motions have replaced true worship, creating a false sense of security and a growing callousness to God's disciplining hand. Famine, drought, plagues, death, destruction—nothing can force the people to their knees.

Amos, the farmer-turned-prophet, lashes out at sin unflinchingly, trying to visualize the nearness of God's judgment and mobilize the nation to repentance. The nation, like a basket of rotting fruit, stands ripe for judgment because of its hypocrisy and spiritual indifference.

The name *Amos* is derived from the Hebrew root *amas*, "to lift a burden, to carry." Thus, his name means "Burden" or "Burden-Bearer." Amos lives up to the meaning of his name by bearing up under his divinely given burden of declaring judgment to rebellious Israel. The Greek and Latin titles are both transliterated in English as *Amos*.

THE AUTHOR OF AMOS

The only Old Testament appearance of the name *Amos* is in this book. (He should not be confused with Amoz, the father of Isaiah.) Concerning his background, Amos said, "I am not a prophet, nor am I the son of a prophet; for I am a herdsman and a grower of sycamore figs" (7:14). But he was gripped by God and divinely commissioned to bring his prophetic burden to Israel (3:8; 7:15). He came from the rural area of Tekoa in Judah, twelve miles south of Jerusalem, where he tended a special breed of small sheep that produced wool of the best quality. As a grower of sycamore figs, he had to puncture the fruit before it ripened to allow the insects inside to escape. Amos lived a disciplined life, and his knowledge of the wilderness often surfaces in his messages (cf. 3:4, 5, 12; 5:8, 19; 9:9). Amos was from the country, but he was well-educated in the Scriptures. His keen sense of morality and justice is obvious, and his objective appraisal of Israel's spiritual condition was not well received, especially since he was from Judah. He delivered his message in Bethel because it was the residence of the king of Israel and a center of idolatry. His frontal attack on the greed, injustice, and self-righteousness of the people of the northern kingdom made his words unpopular.

THE TIME OF AMOS

Amos prophesied "in the days of Uzziah king of Judah, and in the days of Jeroboam son of Joash, king of Israel, two years before the earthquake" (1:1). Uzziah reigned from 767 to 739 B.C. and Jeroboam II reigned from 782 to 753 B.C., leaving an overlap from 767 to 753 B.C. Over two hundred years later, Zechariah referred to this earthquake in Uzziah's reign (Zech. 14:5). Amos 7:11 anticipates the 722 B.C. Assyrian captivity of Israel and indicates that at the time of writing, Jeroboam II was not yet dead. Thus, Amos prophesied in Bethel about 755 B.C. Astronomical calculations indicate that a solar eclipse took place in Israel on June 15, 763 B.C. This event was probably fresh in the minds of Amos's hearers (see 8:9).

Amos ministered after the time of Obadiah, Joel, and Jonah and just before Hosea, Micah, and Isaiah. At this time Uzziah reigned over a prosperous and militarily successful Judah. He fortified Jerusalem and subdued the Philistines, the Ammonites, and the Edomites. In the north, Israel was ruled by the capable King Jeroboam II. Economic and military circumstances were almost ideal, but prosperity only increased the materialism, immorality, and injustice of the people (2:6–8; 3:10; 4:1; 5:10–12; 8:4–6). During these years, Assyria, Babylon, Aram, and Egypt were relatively weak. Thus, the people of Israel found it hard to imagine the coming disaster predicted by Amos. However, it was only three decades until the downfall of Israel.

THE CHRIST OF AMOS

The clearest anticipation of Christ in Amos is found at the end of the book. He has all authority to judge (1:11—9:10), but He will also restore His people (9:11–15).

KEYS TO AMOS

Key Word: The Judgment of Israel— The basic theme of Amos is the coming judgment of Israel because of the holiness of Yahweh and the sinfulness of His covenant

people. Amos unflinchingly and relentlessly visualizes the causes and course of Israel's quickly approaching doom. God is gracious and patient, but His justice and righteousness will not allow sin to go unpunished indefinitely. The sins of Israel are heaped as high as heaven: empty ritualism, oppression of the poor, idolatry, deceit, self-righteousness, arrogance, greed, materialism, and callousness. The people have repeatedly broken every aspect of their covenant relationship with God. Nevertheless, God's mercy and love are evident in His offer of deliverance if the people will only turn back to Him. God graciously sends Amos as a reformer to warn the people of Israel of their fate if they refuse to repent. But they reject his plea, and the course of judgment cannot be altered.

Key Verses: Amos 3:1, 2; 8:11, 12—"Hear this word which the LORD has spoken against you, sons of Israel, against the entire family which He brought up from the land of Egypt, 'You only have I chosen among all the families of the earth; therefore, I will punish you for all your iniquities' " (3:1, 2).

" 'Behold, days are coming,' declares the Lord GOD, 'when I will send a famine on the land, not a famine for bread or a thirst for water, but rather for hearing the words of the LORD. And people will stagger from sea to sea, and from the north even to the east; they will go to and fro to seek the word of the LORD, but they will not find *it*' " (8:11, 12).

Key Chapter: Amos 9—Set in the midst of the harsh judgments of Amos are some of the greatest prophecies of restoration of Israel anywhere in Scripture. Within the scope of just five verses the future of Israel becomes clear, as the Abrahamic, Davidic, and Palestinian covenants are focused on their climactic fulfillment in the return of the Messiah.

SURVEY OF AMOS

Amos's message of the coming doom of the northern kingdom of Israel seems preposterous to the people. Unsurprisingly, Amos's earnest and forceful message against Israel's sins and abuses is poorly received. The prophet of Israel's Indian summer presents a painfully clear message: "Prepare to meet your God, O Israel" (4:12). The four divisions of Amos are: the eight prophecies (1:1—2:16), the three sermons (3:1—6:14), the five visions (7:1—9:10), and the five promises (9:11–15).

The Eight Prophecies (1:1—2:16): Amos is called by God to the unenviable task of leaving his homeland in Judah to preach a harsh message of judgment to Israel. Each of his eight oracles in chapters 1 and 2 begins with the statement "For three transgressions of . . . and for four." The fourth trangression is equivalent to the last straw; the iniquity of each of the eight countries is full. Amos begins with the nations that surround Israel as his catalog of catastrophes gradually spirals in on Israel herself. Seven times God declares, "I will send fire" (1:4, 7, 10, 12, 14; 2:2, 5), a symbol of judgment.

The Three Sermons (3:1—6:14): In these chapters, Amos delivers three sermons, each beginning with the phrase "Hear this word" (3:1; 4:1; 5:1). The first sermon (3) is a general pronouncement of judgment because of Israel's iniquities. The second sermon (4) exposes the crimes of the people and describes the ways God has chastened them in order to draw them back to Himself. Five times He says, "Yet you have not returned to Me" (4:6, 8, 9, 10, 11). The third sermon (5 and 6) lists the sins of the house of Israel and calls the people to repent. But they hate integrity, justice, and com-

FOCUS	EIGHT PROPHECIES	THREE SERMONS	FIVE VISIONS	FIVE PROMISES
REFERENCE	1:1—————————	3:1———————	7:1————————	9:11————————9:15
DIVISION	JUDGMENT OF ISRAEL AND SURROUNDING NATIONS	SIN OF ISRAEL: PRESENT, PAST, AND FUTURE	PICTURES OF THE JUDGMENT OF ISRAEL	RESTORATION OF ISRAEL
TOPIC	PRONOUNCEMENTS OF JUDGMENT	PROVOCATIONS FOR JUDGMENT	FUTURE OF JUDGMENT	PROMISES AFTER JUDGMENT
		JUDGMENT		HOPE
LOCATION	SURROUNDING NATIONS	NORTHERN KINGDOM OF ISRAEL		
TIME	c. 760 – 753 B.C.			

passion, and their refusal to turn to Yahweh will lead to their exile. Although they arrogantly wallow in luxury, their time of prosperity will suddenly come to an end.

The Five Visions (7:1—9:10): Amos's three sermons are followed by five visions of coming judgment upon the northern kingdom. The first two judgments of locusts and fire do not come to pass because of Amos's intercession. The third vision of the plumb line is followed by the only narrative section in the book (7:10–17). Amaziah, the priest of Bethel, wants Amos to go back to Judah. The fourth vision pictures Israel as a basket of rotten fruit, overripe for judgment. The fifth vision is a relentless portrayal of Israel's unavoidable judgment.

The Five Promises (9:11–15): Amos has hammered upon the theme of divine retribution with oracles, sermons, and visions. Nevertheless, he ends his book on a note of consolation, not condemnation. God promises to reinstate the Davidic line, to renew the land, and to restore the people.

CHAPTER 1

Introduction to Amos

THE words of Amos, who was among the sheepherders from Tekoa, which he envisioned in visions concerning Israel in the days of ᴿUzziah king of Judah, and in the days of Jeroboam son of Joash, king of Israel, two years before the earthquake.   Is. 1:1
2 And he said,
  "The ᴿLORD roars from Zion,   Jer. 25:30
  And from Jerusalem He utters His voice;
  And the shepherds' ᴿpasture grounds mourn,   Jer. 12:4; Joel 1:18, 19
  And the summit of Carmel dries up."

Judgment on Damascus

3 Thus says the LORD,
  "For ᴿthree transgressions of ᴿDamascus
    and for four   Amos 2:1, 4, 6 • Is. 8:4
  I will not revoke its *punishment*,
  Because they threshed Gilead with *implements* of sharp iron.
4 "So I will send fire upon the house of Hazael,

  And it will consume the citadels of
    ᴿBen-hadad.   1 Kin. 20:1; 2 Kin. 6:24
5 "I will also ᴿbreak the *gate* bar of Damascus,   Jer. 51:30; Lam. 2:9
  And cut off the inhabitant from the ᴬvalley of Aven,   *Baalbek*
  And him who holds the scepter, from Beth-eden;
  So the people of Aram will go exiled to
    ᴿKir,"   2 Kin. 16:9; Amos 9:7
  Says the LORD.

Judgment on Gaza

6 Thus says the LORD,
  "For three transgressions of ᴿGaza and
    for four   1 Sam. 6:17; Jer. 47:1, 5
  I will not revoke its *punishment*,
  Because they deported an entire population
  To ᴿdeliver *it* up to Edom.   Ezek. 35:5
7 "So I will send fire upon the wall of Gaza,
  And it will consume her citadels.
8 "I will also cut off the inhabitant from
    ᴿAshdod,   2 Chr. 26:6; Amos 3:9
  And him who holds the scepter, from
    ᴿAshkelon;   Jer. 47:5; Zeph. 2:4

I will even^Tunleash My^Tpower upon Ekron,   *cause to return • hand*
And the remnant of the^RPhilistines will perish,"   Is. 14:29-31; Jer. 47:1-7
Says the Lord^TGOD.   Heb., *YHWH*

Judgment on Tyre

9 Thus says the LORD,
"For three transgressions of^RTyre and for four   Is. 23:1-18; Jer. 25:22
I will not revoke its *punishment*,
Because they delivered up an entire population to Edom
And did not remember *the* covenant of ^Tbrotherhood.^R   *brothers* • 1 Kin. 9:11-14
10"So I will ^Rsend fire upon the wall of Tyre,   Zech. 9:4
And it will consume her citadels."

Judgment on Edom

11 Thus says the LORD,
"For three transgressions of^REdom and for four   Is. 34:5, 6; 63:1-6; Jer. 49:7-22
I will not revoke its *punishment*,
Because he^Rpursued his brother with the sword,   Num. 20:14-21; 2 Chr. 28:17
While he stifled his compassion;
His anger also tore continually,
And he maintained his fury forever.
12"So I will send fire upon^RTeman,
And it will consume the citadels of Bozrah."   Jer. 49:7, 20; Obad. 9

Judgment on Ammon

13 Thus says the LORD,
"For three transgressions of the sons of ^RAmmon and for four   Ezek. 21:28-32
I will not revoke its *punishment*,
Because they^Rripped open the pregnant women of Gilead   2 Kin. 15:16
In order to^Renlarge their borders. Is. 5:8
14"So I will kindle a fire on the wall of ^RRabbah,   Deut. 3:11; 1 Chr. 20:1
And it will consume her citadels
Amid war cries on the day of battle
And a storm on the day of tempest.
15"Their^Rking will go into exile,   Jer. 49:3
He and his princes together," says the LORD.

CHAPTER 2
Judgment on Moab

THUS says the LORD,
"For three transgressions of^RMoab and for four   Is. 15:1—16:14; Jer. 48:1-47
I will not revoke its *punishment*,

Because he ^Rburned the bones of the king of Edom to lime.   2 Kin. 3:26, 27
2"So I will send fire upon Moab,
And it will consume the citadels of^RKerioth;   Jer. 48:24, 41
And Moab will die amid^Rtumult,
With ^Awar cries and the sound of a trumpet.   Jer. 48:45 • *shouts*
3"I will also cut off the^Ajudge^Rfrom her midst,   *executive officer* • Amos 5:7
And slay all her ^Rprinces with him," says the LORD.   Job 12:21; Is. 40:23

Judgment on Judah

4 Thus says the LORD,
"For three transgressions of^RJudah and for four   2 Kin. 17:19; Hos. 12:2
I will not revoke its *punishment*,
Because they^Rrejected the law of the LORD   Judg. 2:17-20; 2 Kin. 22:11-17
And have not kept His statutes;
Their lies also have led them astray,
Those after which their fathers walked.
5"So I will^Rsend fire upon Judah,
And it will consume the citadels of Jerusalem."   Jer. 17:27; 21:10; Hos. 8:14

Judgment on Israel

6 Thus says the LORD,
"For three transgressions of^RIsrael and for four   2 Kin. 18:11, 12
I will not revoke its *punishment*,
Because they ^Rsell the righteous for money   Joel 3:3; Amos 5:11, 12; 8:6
And the needy for a pair of sandals.
7"These who^Apant after the *very* dust of the earth on the head of the^Rhelpless   *trample* • Amos 8:4; Mic. 2:2, 9
Also turn aside the way of the humble;
And a^Rman and his father^Tresort to the same girl   Hos. 4:14 • *go*
In order to profane My holy name.
8"And on garments^Rtaken as pledges they stretch out beside every altar,
And in the house of their God they ^Rdrink the wine of those who have been fined.   Ex. 22:26 • Amos 4:1; 6:6

9"Yet it was I who destroyed the^RAmorite before them,   Num. 21:23-25; Josh. 10:12
^TThough his^Rheight *was* like the height of cedars   *Whose height* • Num. 13:32
And he *was* strong as the oaks;
I even destroyed his^Rfruit above and his root below.   Ezek. 17:9; [Mal. 4:1]
10"And it was I who^Rbrought you up from the land of Egypt,   Ex. 12:51; 20:2
And I led you in the wilderness^Rforty years   Deut. 2:7
^TThat you might take possession of the land of the Amorite.   *To possess*
11"Then I^Rraised up some of your sons to be prophets   Deut. 18:18; Jer. 7:25

And some of your young men to be
   ^{R}Nazirites.   Num. 6:2, 3; Judg. 13:5
Is this not so, O sons of Israel?" de-
   clares the LORD.
12"But you made the Nazirites drink wine,
   And you commanded the prophets saying, 'You shall not prophesy!'
13"Behold, I am^{A}weighted^{R}down beneath
   you   tottering • Is. 1:14
As a wagon^{A}is weighted down when
   filled with sheaves.   totters
14"Flight^{A}will perish from the swift,
   And the stalwart will not strengthen
   his power,   A place of refuge
Nor the mighty man save his^{T}life.   soul
15"He who^{R}grasps the bow will not stand
   his ground,   Jer. 51:56; Ezek. 39:3
The swift of foot will not escape,
   Nor will he who rides the^{R}horse save
   his^{T}life.   Is. 31:3 • soul
16"Even the^{T}bravest among the warriors
   will flee naked in that day," declares the LORD.   stout of heart

CHAPTER 3

Israel's Judgment Is Deserved (Present)

H EAR this word which the LORD has spoken against you, sons of Israel, against the
entire^{T}family^{R}which^{T}He brought up from the
land of Egypt,   nation • Jer. 8:3; 13:11 • I

2"You^{R}only have I^{T}chosen among all the
   families of the earth;   Ex. 19:5 • known
Therefore, I will^{T}punish^{R}you for all your
   iniquities."   visit • Dan. 9:12; [Rom. 2:9]

3 Do two men walk together unless they
   have made an appointment?
4 Does a^{R}lion roar in the forest when he
   has no prey?   Ps. 104:21; Hos. 5:14
   Does a young lion growl from his den
   unless he has captured *something*?
5 Does a bird fall into a trap on the
   ground when there is no bait in it?
   Does a trap spring up from the earth
   when it captures nothing at all?
6 If a^{R}trumpet is blown in a city will not
   the people tremble?   Jer. 4:5, 19, 21
   If a^{R}calamity occurs in a city has not
   the LORD done it?   Is. 14:24-27; 45:7

7 ^{A}Surely the Lord GOD does nothing   *For
   Unless He^{R}reveals His secret counsel
   To His servants the prophets.   Gen. 6:13
8 A^{R}lion has roared! Who will not fear?
   The Lord GOD has spoken!^{R}Who can
   but prophesy?   Amos 1:2 • Jer. 20:9
9 Proclaim on the citadels in Ashdod and
on the citadels in the land of Egypt and say,
"Assemble yourselves on the mountains of
Samaria and see *the* great tumults within
her and *the* oppressions in her midst.
10"But they do not know how to do what
is right," declares the LORD, "these who
^{R}hoard up ^{T}violence and devastation in their
citadels."   Hab. 2:8-10 • *the booty from violence*

Israel's Judgment Is Described (Present)

11 Therefore, thus says the Lord GOD,
   "An ^{R}enemy, even one surrounding the
   land,   Amos 6:14
Will pull down your strength from you
   And your citadels will be looted."
12 Thus says the LORD,
   "Just as the shepherd^{A}snatches from the
   lion's mouth a couple of legs or a
   piece of an ear,   *delivers*
So will the sons of Israel dwelling in
   Samaria be^{A}snatched away—
With *the* corner of a bed and the^{T}cover
   of a couch!   *delivered • damask*
13"Hear and^{R}testify against the house of
   Jacob,"   Ezek. 2:7
Declares the Lord GOD, the God of
   hosts.
14"For on the day that I punish Israel's
   transgressions,
I will also punish the altars of Bethel;
   The horns of the altar will be cut off,
   And they will fall to the ground.
15"I will also smite the^{A}winter house to-
   gether with the summer house;
The houses of^{T}ivory will also perish
   And the^{R}great houses will come to an
   end,"   *autumn • ivory inlay • Amos 2:5*
Declares the LORD.

CHAPTER 4

Israel's Judgment Is Deserved (Past)

H EAR this word, you cows of^{R}Bashan who
are on the^{R}mountain of Samaria,

3:2 **Selection of Israel**—The selection of Israel as a special nation to God was part of God's plan (Page
1140—Rom. 11:2). Historically, the selection of Israel began with the Lord's promise to Abraham, "I will make you
a great nation" (Page 14—Gen. 12:2). The name Israel actually comes from the new name which God gave to
Abraham's grandson, Jacob. It was occasioned by Jacob's spiritual victory at the ford of Jabbok (Page 33—Gen.
32:28). This fact explains why his descendants are often called the children of Israel.
   The motivation for the Lord's choice of Israel as His select nation did not lie in any special attraction it possessed. Its people were, in fact, the least in number among all the nations (Page 176—Deut. 7:6-8). Rather, the
Lord chose them because of His love for them and because of His covenant with Abraham. This fact does not
mean that God did not love other nations, because it was through Israel that He intended to bring forth the Savior
and to bless the entire world (Page 14—Gen. 12:3).
   Now turn to Page 568—Ps. 78:4: History of Israel.

Who oppress the poor, who crush the
needy,   Ps. 22:12 • Amos 3:9; 6:1
Who say to ^Tyour husbands, "Bring
now, that we may drink!" *their lords*
2 The Lord GOD has ^Rsworn by His^Rholi-
ness,   Amos 6:8; 8:7 • Ps. 89:35
"Behold, the days are coming upon you
When ^Tthey will take you away with
^Rmeat hooks,   *he* • Is. 37:29; Ezek. 38:4
And the last of you with fish hooks.
3 "You will ^Rgo out *through* breaches *in
the walls,*
Each one straight before her,
And you will be cast to Harmon," declares the LORD.   Jer. 52:7

4 "Enter Bethel and transgress;
In Gilgal multiply transgression!
^RBring your sacrifices every morning,
Your tithes every three days. Num. 28:3
5 "Offer^T a thank offering also from that
which is leavened,   *Offer up in smoke*
And proclaim^Rfreewill offerings, make
them known.   Lev. 22:18-21
For so you^Rlove *to do,* you sons of Is-
rael,"   Jer. 7:9, 10; Hos. 9:1, 10
Declares the Lord GOD.

Israel's Judgment Is Demonstrated (Past)

6 "But I gave you also^Rcleanness of teeth
in all your cities   Is. 3:1; Jer. 14:18
And lack of bread in all your places,
Yet you have^Rnot returned to Me," declares the LORD.   Jer. 5:3; Hag. 2:17
7 "And furthermore, I^Rwithheld the rain
from you Deut. 11:17; 2 Chr. 7:13; Is. 5:6
While *there were* still three months until harvest.
Then I would send rain on one city
And on^Ranother city I would not send
rain;   Ex. 9:4, 26; 10:22, 23
One part would be rained on,
While the part not rained on would dry
up.
8 "So two or three cities would stagger to
another city to drink water,
But would^Rnot be satisfied; Ezek. 4:16, 17
Yet you have^Rnot returned to Me," declares the LORD.   Jer. 3:7
9 "I^Rsmote you with scorching *wind* and
mildew;   Deut. 28:22; Hag. 2:17
And the^Rcaterpillar was devouring
Your many gardens and vineyards, fig
trees and olive trees;   Amos 7:1, 2
Yet you have not returned to Me," declares the LORD.
10 "I sent a^Rplague among you after the
manner of Egypt;   Ex. 9:3; Lev. 26:25
I slew your young men by the sword
along with your captured horses,
And I made the^Rstench of your camp
rise up in your nostrils;   Joel 2:20
Yet you have^Rnot returned to Me," declares the LORD.   Is. 9:13

11 "I overthrew you as ^RGod overthrew
Sodom and Gomorrah, Gen. 19:24, 25
And you were like a^Rfirebrand snatched
from a blaze;   Zech. 3:2
Yet you have^Rnot returned to Me," de-
clares the LORD.   Jer. 23:14

Israel's Judgment Is Described (Past)

12 "Therefore, thus I will do to you, O Is-
rael;
Because I shall do this to you,
Prepare to meet your God, O Israel."
13 For behold, He who forms mountains
and^Rcreates the wind   Jer. 10:13
And ^Rdeclares to man what are His
thoughts,   Dan. 2:28, 30
He who makes dawn into darkness
And^Rtreads on the high places of the
earth,   Mic. 1:3
The LORD God of hosts is His name.

CHAPTER 5

Israel's Judgment Is Deserved (Future)

HEAR this word which I take up for you
as a^Rdirge, O house of Israel.   Jer. 7:29
2 She has fallen, she will^Rnot rise again—
The^Rvirgin Israel.   Amos 8:14 • Jer. 14:17
She *lies* neglected on her land;
There is^Rnone to raise her up. Jer. 50:32
3 For thus says the Lord GOD,
"The city which goes forth a thousand
strong
Will have a^Rhundred left,   Is. 6:13
And the one which goes forth a hun-
dred *strong*
Will have^Rten left to the house of Is-
rael."   Amos 6:9

4 For thus says the LORD to the house of
Israel,
"Seek Me^Rthat you may live.   [Is. 55:3]
5 "But do not^Tresort to Bethel,   *seek*
And do not come to^RGilgal,   1 Sam. 7:16
Nor cross over to^RBeersheba; Amos 8:14
For Gilgal will certainly go into captiv-
ity,
And Bethel will come to trouble.
6 "Seek the LORD that you may live,
Lest He break forth like a^Rfire,^RO house
of Joseph,   [Deut. 4:24] • *in the house*
And it consume with none to quench *it*
for Bethel,
7 *For* those who turn^Rjustice into wormwood   Amos 2:3; 5:12; 6:12
And ^Tcast righteousness down to the
earth."   *they have put down*

8 He who made the^RPleiades and Orion
And^Rchanges deep darkness into morning,   Job 9:9; 38:31 • Job 12:22; 38:12
^TWho also darkens day *into* night,

Who[R]calls for the waters of the sea
And pours them out on the surface of
the earth, *And He darkened* • Ps. 104:6-9
The[R]LORD is His name.   Amos 4:13
9 It is He who[R]flashes forth *with* destruction upon the strong,   Amos 2:14
So that [R]destruction comes upon the
fortress.   Mic. 5:11

10 They hate him who reproves in the
[T]gate,   the place where court was held
And they[R]abhor him who speaks *with*
integrity.   Is. 59:15; Jer. 17:16-18
11 Therefore, because you[A]impose heavy
rent on the poor   *trample upon*
And exact a tribute of grain from them,
Though you have built[R]houses of well-
hewn stone,   Amos 3:15; 6:11
Yet you will not live in them;
You have planted pleasant vineyards,
yet you will not drink their wine.
12 For I know your transgressions are
many and your sins are great,
You who[R]distress the righteous *and* accept bribes,   Is. 1:23; 5:23; Amos 2:6
And turn aside the poor in the gate.
13 Therefore, at[T]such a time the prudent
person[R]keeps silent, for it is an evil
time.   *that time* • Eccl. 3:7; Hos. 4:4

14 Seek good and not evil, that you may
live;
And thus may the LORD God of hosts
be with you,
[R]Just as you have said!   Mic. 3:11
15 [R]Hate evil, love good, Ps. 97:10; Rom. 12:9
And establish justice in the gate!
Perhaps the LORD God of hosts
[R]May be gracious to the [R]remnant of
Joseph.   Joel 2:14 • Mic. 5:3, 7, 8

The First Woe of Judgment

16 Therefore, thus says the LORD God of
hosts, the Lord,
"There is wailing in all the plazas,
And in all the streets they say, 'Alas!
Alas!'
They also call the farmer to mourning
And[T]professional mourners to lamenta-
tion.   *those who know lamentation*
17"And in all the[R]vineyards *there is* wail-
ing,   Is. 16:10; Jer. 48:33
Because I shall pass through the midst
of you," says the LORD.

18 Alas, you who are longing for the[R]day
of the LORD,   Is. 5:19; Jer. 30:7
For what purpose *will* the day of the
LORD *be* to you?
It *will be* darkness and not light;
19 As when a man[R]flees from a lion,
And a bear meets him, Jer. 15:2, 3; 48:44
[A]Or goes home, leans his hand against
the wall,   *Then*
And a snake bites him.

20 *Will* not the day of the LORD *be*[R]dark-
ness instead of light,   Is. 13:10
Even gloom with no brightness in it?

21"I hate, I[R]reject your festivals, Is. 1:11-16
Nor do I[R]delight in your solemn assemblies.   Lev. 26:31; Jer. 14:12; Hos. 5:6
22"Even though you[R]offer up to Me burnt
offerings and your grain offerings,
I will not accept *them*;   Mic. 6:6, 7
And I will not *even* look at the[R]peace
offerings of your fatlings.   Amos 4:5
23"Take away from Me the noise of your
songs;
I will not even listen to the sound of
your harps.
24"But let[R]justice roll down like waters
And righteousness like an ever-flowing
stream.   Jer. 22:3; Ezek. 45:9; Mic. 6:8
25"Did[R]you present Me with sacrifices and
grain offerings in the wilderness for forty
years, O house of Israel?   Acts 7:42, 43
26"You also carried along Sikkuth your
king and Kiyyun, your images, the star of
your gods which you made for yourselves.
27"Therefore, I will make you go into exile
beyond Damascus," says the LORD, whose
name is the God of hosts.

CHAPTER 6

The Second Woe of Judgment

WOE[R]to those who are at ease in Zion,
And to those who *feel* secure in the
mountain of Samaria,   Is. 32:9-11
The[R]distinguished men of the foremost
of nations,   Ex. 19:5; Amos 3:2
To whom the house of Israel comes.
2 Go over to[R]Calneh and look,   Is. 10:9
And go from there to [R]Hamath the
great,   1 Kin. 8:65; 2 Kin. 18:34; Is. 10:9
Then go down to[R]Gath of the Philis-
tines.   1 Sam. 5:8; 2 Chr. 26:6
Are they better than these kingdoms,
Or is their territory greater than yours?
3 Do you[R]put off the day of calamity,
And would you[R]bring near the seat of
violence?   Is. 56:12 • Amos 3:10

4 Those who recline on beds of ivory
And sprawl on their[R]couches, Amos 3:12
And eat lambs from the flock
And calves from the midst of the stall,
5 Who improvise to the sound of the
harp,
And like David have composed [R]songs
for themselves,   1 Chr. 15:16; 23:5
6 Who drink wine from[T]sacrificial bowls
While they anoint themselves with the
finest of oils,   *sprinkling basins*
Yet they have not[R]grieved over the ruin
of Joseph.   Ezek. 9:4
7 Therefore, they will now[R]go into exile
at the head of the exiles,   Amos 7:11

And the sprawlers' ^banqueting will
^Tpass away.   *cultic feasts • turn aside*

8 The Lord GOD has ^Rsworn by Himself,
the LORD God of hosts has de-
clared: Jer. 22:5; 51:14
"I loathe the arrogance of Jacob,
And I ^Tdetest his citadels;   *hate*
Therefore, I will ^Rdeliver up *the* city and
^Tall it contains."   Hos. 11:6 • *its fulness*
9 And it will be, if ^Tten men are left in one
house, they will die.   Amos 5:3
10 Then one's ^Auncle, or his ^Tundertaker,
will lift him up to carry out *his* bones from
the house, and he will say to the one who is
in the innermost part of the house, "Is anyone else with you?" And that one will say,
"No one." Then he will ^Tanswer, "Keep quiet.
For the name of the LORD is not to be mentioned."   *beloved one • one who burns him • say*
11 For behold, the LORD is going to command that the great house be smashed to
pieces and the small house to fragments.
12 Do horses run on rocks?
Or does one plow them with oxen?
Yet you have turned ^Rjustice into poison,   1 Kin. 21:7-13
And the fruit of righteousness into
¹wormwood,
13 You who rejoice in ²Lo-debar,
^TAnd say, "Have we not ^Rby our *own*
strength taken ³Karnaim for ourselves?"   *Who • Ps. 75:4, 5; Is. 28:14, 15*
14"For behold, ^RI am going to raise up a
nation against you,   Jer. 5:15
O house of Israel," declares the LORD
God of hosts,
"And they will afflict you from the ^Ren-
trance of Hamath
To the brook of the Arabah.   2 Kin. 14:25

CHAPTER 7

Vision of the Locusts

THUS the Lord GOD showed me, and behold, He was forming a locust-swarm ^Twhen
the spring crop began to sprout. And behold, the spring crop *was* after the king's
mowing.   *at the beginning of the coming up of*
2 And it came about, ^Twhen it had ^Rfin-
ished eating the vegetation of the land, that
I said,   *if • Ex. 10:15*
"Lord ^RGOD, please pardon!   Jer. 14:7, 20
^THow can Jacob stand,   *As who*
For he is ^Tsmall?"   Is. 37:4; Jer. 42:2
3 The LORD ^Cchanged His mind about this.
"It shall not be," said the LORD. *relented*

Vision of the Fire

4 Thus the Lord GOD showed me, and behold, the Lord GOD was calling to contend
with them by fire, and it consumed the great
deep and began to consume the farm land.

5 Then I said,
"Lord ^RGOD, please stop! Ps. 85:4; Joel 2:17
How can Jacob stand, for he is small?"
6 The LORD ^Cchanged ^RHis mind about this.
"This too shall not be," said the Lord
GOD.   *relented • Amos 7:3; Jon. 3:10*

Vision of the Plumb Line

7 Thus He showed me, and behold, the
Lord was standing by a ^Tvertical wall, with a
plumb line in His hand.   *wall of a plumb line*
8 And the LORD said to me, "What ^Rdo
you see, Amos?" And I said, "A plumb line."
Then the Lord said,   Jer. 1:11; Amos 8:2
"Behold I am about to put a plumb line
In the midst of My people Israel.
I will ^Tspare them no longer.   *pass him by*
9"The ^Rhigh places of Isaac will be desolated   Gen. 46:1; Hos. 10:8; Mic. 1:5
And the ^Rsanctuaries of Israel laid
waste.   Lev. 26:31; Is. 63:18; Jer. 51:51
Then shall I rise up against the house
of Jeroboam with the sword."

Opposition of Amaziah (Historical Parenthesis)

10 Then Amaziah, the priest of Bethel,
sent *word* to ^RJeroboam, king of Israel, saying, "Amos has conspired against you in the
midst of the house of Israel; the land is unable to endure all his words.   2 Kin. 14:23, 24
11"For thus Amos says, 'Jeroboam will die
by the sword and Israel will certainly go
from its land into exile.'"
12 Then Amaziah said to Amos, "Go,^R you
seer, flee away to the land of Judah, and
there eat bread and there do your prophesying!   Matt. 8:34
13"But ^Rno longer prophesy at Bethel, for it
is a ^Rsanctuary of the king and a royal ^Tresi-
dence."   Amos 2:12 • 1 Kin. 12:29, 32 • *house*
14 Then Amos answered and said to Amaziah, "I am not a prophet, nor am I the ^Rson
of a prophet; for I am a herdsman and a
^Agrower of sycamore figs.   1 Kin. 20:35 • *nipper*
15"But the LORD took me from ^Tfollowing
the flock and the LORD said to me, 'Go
prophesy to My people Israel.'   *behind*
16"And now hear the word of the LORD:
you are saying, 'You ^Rshall not prophesy
against Israel nor shall you ^Tspeak against
the house of Isaac.'   Amos 2:12; 7:13 • *flow*
17"Therefore, thus says the LORD, 'Your
wife will become a harlot in the city, your
sons and your daughters will fall by the
sword, your land will be parceled up by a
measuring line, and you yourself will die
upon ^Runclean soil. Moreover, Israel will certainly go from its land into exile.'"   Hos. 9:3

---

¹ I.e., *bitterness*   ² Lit., *a thing of nothing*
³ Lit., *a pair of horns*

CHAPTER 8

Vision of the Summer Fruit

THUS the Lord GOD showed me, and behold, *there was* a basket of summer fruit. 2 And He said, "What do you see, Amos?" And I said, "A basket of summer fruit." Then the LORD said to me, "The ᴿend has come for My people Israel. I will ᵀspare them no longer.   Ezek. 7:2, 3, 6 • *pass him by*
3"The songs of the palace will turn to wailing in that day," declares the Lord GOD. "Many *will be* the corpses; in every place they will cast them forth in ᴬsilence."   *hush!*

4 Hear this, you who trample the needy, to do away with the humble of the land,
 5 saying,
   "When will the new moon ᵀbe over,
   So that we may sell grain,   *pass by*
   And the ᴿsabbath, that we may open the
      wheat *market*,   Ex. 31:13-17; Neh. 13:15
   To make the ᵀbushel smaller and the
      shekel bigger,   *ephah*
   And to cheat with dishonest scales,
 6 So as to ᴿbuy the helpless for ᵀmoney
   And the needy for a pair of sandals,
   And *that* we may sell the refuse of the
      wheat?"   Amos 2:6 • *silver*

7 The LORD has ᴿsworn by the ᴿpride of Jacob,   Amos 4:2 • Deut. 33:26; Ps. 68:34
   "Indeed, I will ᴿnever forget any of their
      deeds.   Ps. 10:11; Hos. 7:2; 8:13
8"Because of this will not the land ᴿquake
   And everyone who dwells in it ᴿmourn?
   Indeed, all of it will ᴿrise up like the
      Nile,   Ps. 18:7 • Hos. 4:3 • Jer. 46:7, 8
   And it will be tossed about,
   And subside like the Nile of Egypt.
9"And it will come about in that day,"
   declares the Lord GOD,
   "That I shall make the ᴿsun go down at
      noon   Job 5:14; Is. 13:10; Jer. 15:9
   And ᴿmake the earth dark in ᵀbroad day-
      light.   Is. 59:9, 10 • *a day of light*
10"Then I shall ᴿturn your festivals into
      mourning   Job 20:23; Amos 5:21
   And all your songs into ᴬlamentation;
   And I will bring ᴿsackcloth on every-
      one's loins   *a dirge* • Ezek. 7:18; 27:31
   And baldness on every head.
   And I will make it ᴿlike *a time of*
      mourning for an only son,   Jer. 6:26
   And the end of it will be like a bitter
      day.

11"Behold, days are coming," declares the
      Lord GOD,
   "When I will send a famine on the land,
   Not a famine for bread or a thirst for
      water,
   But rather ᴿfor hearing the words of the
      LORD.   1 Sam. 3:1; 2 Chr. 15:3; Ps. 74:9
12"And people will stagger from sea to
      sea,

   And from the north even to the east;
   They will go to and fro to ᴿseek the
      word of the LORD,   Ezek. 20:3, 31
   But they will not find *it.*
13"In that day the beautiful ᴿvirgins
   And the young men will ᴿfaint from
      thirst.   Lam. 1:18 • Is. 41:17; Hos. 2:3
14"*As for* those who swear by the ᴬguilt ᴿof
      Samaria,   *Ashimah* • Hos. 8:5
   Who say, 'As your god lives, O Dan,'
   And, 'As the way of Beersheba lives,'
   They will fall and not rise again."

CHAPTER 9

Vision of the Smitten Capitals
of the Door

I SAW the Lord standing beside the ᴿaltar,
   and He said,   Amos 3:14
   "Smite the capitals so that the ᴿthresh-
      olds will shake,   Zeph. 2:14
   And ᴿbreak them on the heads of them
      all!   Ps. 68:21; Hab. 3:13
   Then I will ᴿslay the rest of them with
      the sword;   Amos 7:17
   They will ᴿnot have a fugitive who will
      flee,   Jer. 11:11
   Or a refugee who will escape.
2"Though they dig into ᴿSheol,   Ps. 139:8
   From there shall My hand take them;
   And though they ascend to heaven,
   From there will I bring them down.
3"And though they hide on the summit of
      Carmel,
   I will ᴿsearch them out and take them
      from there;   Jer. 16:16
   And though they ᴿconceal themselves
      from My sight on the floor of the
      sea,   [Job 34:22; Ps. 139:9, 10]
   From there I will command the ᴿserpent
      and it will bite them.   Is. 27:1
4"And though they go into ᴿcaptivity be-
      fore their enemies,   Lev. 26:33
   From there I will command the sword
      that it slay them,
   And I will ᴿset My eyes against them for
      evil and not for good."   Lev. 17:10

5 And the Lord GOD of hosts,
   The One who ᴿtouches the land so that
      it melts,   Ps. 104:32; 144:5; Is. 64:1
   And all those who dwell in it mourn,
   And all of it rises up like the Nile
   And subsides like the Nile of Egypt;
6 The One who builds His ᴬupper ᴿcham-
      bers in the heavens,   *stairs* • Ps. 104:3
   And has founded His vaulted dome
      over the earth,
   He who ᴿcalls for the waters of the sea
   And ᴿpours them out on the face of the
      earth,   Amos 5:8 • Ps. 104:6
   ᴿThe LORD is His name.   Amos 4:13

7"Are you not as the sons of ᴿEthiopia to
      Me,   2 Chr. 14:9, 12; Is. 20:4; 43:3

O sons of Israel?" declares the LORD.
"Have I not brought up Israel from the
land of Egypt,
And the Philistines from Caphtor and
the Arameans from^RKir?   2 Kin. 16:9
8"Behold, the^Reyes of the Lord GOD are
on the sinful kingdom,   Jer. 44:27
And I will^Rdestroy it from the face of
the earth;   Amos 7:17; 9:10
Nevertheless, I will^Rnot totally destroy
the house of Jacob,"   Jer. 5:10; 30:11
Declares the LORD.
9"For behold, I am commanding,
And I will^Rshake the house of Israel
among all nations Is. 30:28; Luke 22:31
As *grain* is shaken in a sieve,
But not a kernel will fall to the ground.
10"All the^Rsinners of My people will die by
the sword,   Is. 33:14; Zech. 13:8
Those who say, 'The^Rcalamity will not
overtake or confront us.'   Amos 6:3

The Five Promises of
The Restoration of Israel

11"In that day I will raise up the fallen
^booth of David,   *shelter* or *tabernacle*
And wall up its^Rbreaches;   Ps. 80:12

I will also raise up its ruins,
And rebuild it as in the days of old;
12^RThat they may possess the remnant of
^REdom   Obad. 19 • Num. 24:18; Is. 11:14
And all the^nations who are^Rcalled by
My name,"   *Gentiles* • Is. 43:7
Declares the LORD who does this.

13"Behold, days are coming," declares the
LORD,
"When the^Rplowman will overtake the
reaper   Lev. 26:5
And the treader of grapes him who
sows seed;
When the^Rmountains will drip sweet
^Rwine,   Joel 3:18 • Gen. 49:11
And all the hills will be dissolved.
14"Also I will^Rrestore the^captivity of My
people Israel,   Is. 60:4 • *fortunes*
And they will^Rrebuild the ruined cities
and live *in them*,   Is. 61:4; 65:21
They will also ^Rplant vineyards and
drink their wine,   Jer. 24:6; 31:28
And make gardens and eat their fruit.
15"I will also plant them on their land,
And^Rthey will not again be rooted out
from their land   Ezek. 34:28; 37:25
Which I have given them,"
Says the LORD your God.

OBADIAH

THE BOOK OF OBADIAH

A struggle that began in the womb between twin brothers, Esau and Jacob, eventuates in a struggle between their respective descendants, the Edomites and the Israelites. For the Edomites' stubborn refusal to aid Israel, first during the time of wilderness wandering (Num. 20:14–21) and later during a time of invasion, they are roundly condemned by Obadiah. This little-known prophet describes their crimes, tries their case, and pronounces their judgment: total destruction.

The Hebrew name *Obadyah* means "Worshiper of Yahweh" or "Servant of Yahweh." The Greek title in the Septuagint is *Obdiou*, and the Latin title in the Vulgate is *Abdias*.

THE AUTHOR OF OBADIAH

Obadiah was an obscure prophet who probably lived in the southern kingdom of Judah. Nothing is known of his hometown or family, but it is not likely that he came out of the kingly or priestly line, because his father is not mentioned (1:1). There are thirteen Obadiahs in the Old Testament, and some scholars have attempted to identify the author of this book with one of the other twelve. Four of the better prospects are: (1) the officer in Ahab's palace who hid God's prophets in a cave (1 Kin. 18:3); (2) one of the officials sent out by Jehoshaphat to teach the law in the cities of Judah (2 Chr. 17:7); (3) one of the overseers who took part in repairing the temple under Josiah (2 Chr. 34:12); or (4) a priest in the time of Nehemiah (Neh. 10:5).

THE TIME OF OBADIAH

Obadiah mentions no kings, so verses 10–14 provide the only historical reference point to aid in determining the book's time and setting. However, scholars disagree about which invasion of Jerusalem Obadiah had in mind. There are four possibilities: (1) In 926 B.C., Shishak of Egypt plundered the temple and palace of Jerusalem in the reign of Rehoboam (1 Kin. 14:25, 26). At this time, Edom was still subject to Judah. This does not fit Obadiah 10–14, which indicates that Edom was independent of Judah. (2) During the reign of Jehoram (848–841 B.C.), the Philistines and Arabians invaded Judah and looted the palace (2 Chr. 21:16, 17). Edom revolted during the reign of Jehoram and became a bitter antagonist (2 Kin. 8:20–22; 2 Chr. 21:8–20). This fits the description of Obadiah. (3) In 790

B.C., King Jehoash of Israel invaded Judah (2 Kin. 14; 2 Chr. 25). However, Obadiah in verse 11 calls the invaders "strangers." This would be an inappropriate term for describing the army of the northern kingdom. (4) In 586 B.C., Nebuchadnezzar of Babylon defeated and destroyed Jerusalem (2 Kin. 24 and 25).

The two best candidates are (2) and (4). Obadiah 10–14 seems to fit (2) better than (4) because it does not indicate the total destruction of the city, which took place when Nebuchadnezzar burned the palace and temple and razed the walls. And Nebuchadnezzar certainly would not have "cast lots for Jerusalem" (11) with anyone. Also, all of the other prophets who speak of the destruction of 586 B.C. identify Nebuchadnezzar and the Babylonians as the agents; but Obadiah leaves the enemy unidentified. For these and other reasons, it appears likely that the plundering of Jerusalem written of in Obadiah was by the Philistines between 848 and 841 B.C. This would make the prophet a contemporary of Elisha, and Obadiah would be the earliest of the writing prophets, predating Joel by a few years.

The history of Edom began with Esau who was given the name Edom ("Red") because of the red stew for which he traded his birthright. Esau moved to the mountainous area of Seir and absorbed the Horites, the original inhabitants. Edom refused to allow Israel to pass through their land on the way to Canaan. The Edomites opposed Saul and were subdued under David and Solomon. They fought against Jehoshaphat and successfully rebelled against Jehoram. They were again conquered by Judah under Amaziah, but they regained their freedom during the reign of Ahaz. Edom was later controlled by Assyria and Babylon; and in the fifth century B.C. the Edomites were forced by the Nabataeans to leave their territory. They moved to the area of southern Palestine and became known as Idumeans. Herod the Great, an Idumean, became king of Judea under Rome in 37 B.C. In a sense, the enmity between Esau and Jacob was continued in Herod's attempt to murder Jesus. The Idumeans participated in the rebellion of Jerusalem against Rome and were defeated along with the Jews by Titus in A.D. 70. Ironically, the Edomites applauded the destruction of Jerusalem in 586 B.C. (see Ps. 127:7) but died trying to defend it in A.D. 70. After that time they were never heard of again. As Obadiah predicted, they would be "cut off forever" (10);

"there will be no survivor of the house of Esau" (18).

✝ THE CHRIST OF OBADIAH

Christ is seen in Obadiah as the Judge of the nations (15 and 16), the Savior of Israel (17–20), and the Possessor of the kingdom (21).

🗝 KEYS TO OBADIAH

Key Word: The Judgment of Edom— The major theme of Obadiah is a declaration of Edom's coming doom because of its arrogance and cruelty to Judah: "I will make you small among the nations" (2); "The arrogance of your heart has deceived you" (3); "O how you will be ruined!" (5); "O how Esau will be ransacked" (6); "Then your mighty men will be dismayed, O Teman" (9); "you will be covered *with* shame" (10); "you will be cut off forever" (10); "As you have done, it will be done to you" (15). Even the last few verses, which primarily deal with Israel, speak of Edom's downfall (17–21). The secondary theme of Obadiah is the future restoration of Israel and faithfulness of Yahweh to His covenant promises. God's justice will ultimately prevail.

Key Verses: Obadiah 10 and 21—"Because of violence to your brother Jacob, you will be covered *with* shame, and you will be cut off forever" (10).

"The deliverers will ascend Mount Zion to judge the mountain of Esau, and the kingdom will be the LORD's" (21).

🅰 SURVEY OF OBADIAH

Obadiah is the shortest book in the Old Testament (twenty-one verses), but it carries one of the strongest messages of

judgment in the Old Testament. For Edom there are no pleas to return, no words of consolation or hope. Edom's fate is sealed, and there are no conditions for possible deliverance. God will bring total destruction upon Edom, and there will be no remnant. Obadiah is Edom's day in court, complete with Edom's arraignment, indictment, and sentence. This prophet of poetic justice describes how the Judge of the earth will overthrow the pride of Edom and restore the house of Jacob. The two sections of Obadiah are: the judgment of Edom (1–18) and the restoration of Israel (19–21).

The Judgment of Edom (1–18): The first section of Obadiah makes it clear that the coming overthrow of Edom is a certainty, not a condition. Edom is arrogant (3) because of its secure position in Mount Seir, a mountainous region south of the Dead Sea. Its capital city of Sela (Petra) is protected by a narrow canyon that prevents invasion by an army. But God says this will make no difference. Even a thief does not take everything, but when God destroys Edom it will be totally ransacked. Nothing will avert God's complete judgment. Verses 10–14 describe Edom's major crime of gloating over the invasion of Jerusalem. Edom rejoiced when foreigners plundered Jerusalem, and became as one of them. On the day when she should have been allied with Judah, she instead became an aggressor against Judah. Edom will eventually be judged during the coming Day of the Lord when Israel "will be a fire . . . but the house of Esau *will be* as stubble" (18).

The Restoration of Israel (19–21): The closing verses give hope to God's people that they will possess not only their own land, but also that of Edom and Philistia.

FOCUS	JUDGMENT OF EDOM			RESTORATION OF ISRAEL
REFERENCE	1————————10	————————15	————————19	————————21
DIVISION	PREDICTIONS OF JUDGMENT	REASONS FOR JUDGMENT	RESULTS OF JUDGMENT	POSSESSION OF EDOM BY ISRAEL
TOPIC	DEFEAT OF ISRAEL			VICTORY OF ISRAEL
	PREDICTION OF JUDGMENT			PREDICTION OF POSSESSION
LOCATION	EDOM AND ISRAEL			
TIME	c. 840 B.C.			

OUTLINE OF OBADIAH

The Predictions of Judgment on Edom

THE vision of Obadiah.
Thus says the Lord GOD concerning
[R]Edom—   Jer. 49:7-22
[R]We have heard a report from the LORD,
And an[R]envoy has been sent among the
nations saying,   Obad. 1-4 • Is. 18:2
"Arise[R]and let us go against her for bat-
tle"—   Jer. 6:4, 5
2"Behold, I will make you[R]small among
the nations;   Num. 24:18; Is. 23:9
You are greatly despised.
3"The[R]arrogance of your heart has de-
ceived you,   Is. 16:6; Jer. 49:16
You who live in the clefts of[T]the[R]rock,
In the loftiness of your dwelling place,
Who say in your heart,   Sela • 2 Kin. 14:7
'Who will bring me down to earth?'
4"Though you[R]build high like the eagle,
Though you set your nest among the
[R]stars,   Job 20:6, 7 • Is. 14:12-15
From there I will bring you down," de-
clares the LORD.
5"If[T]thieves came to you,   Jer. 49:9
If robbers by night—
O how you will be ruined!—
Would they not steal *only*[T]until they
had enough?   *their sufficiency*
If grape gatherers came to you,
Would they not leave *some* gleanings?
6"O how Esau will be ransacked,
And his hidden treasures searched out!
7"All the[R]men allied with you   Jer. 30:14
Will send you forth to the border,
And the men at peace with you
Will deceive you and overpower you.
They who eat your[R]bread   Ps. 41:9
Will set an ambush for you.
(There is no understanding in him.)
8"Will I not on that day," declares the
LORD,
"Destroy[R]wise men from Edom Is. 29:14
And understanding from the mountain
of Esau?
9"Then your mighty men will be dis-
mayed, O[R]Teman,   Job 2:11; Jer. 49:7
In order that everyone may be[R]cut off
from the mountain of Esau by
slaughter.   Is. 34:5-8; 63:1-3; Obad. 5

The Reasons for the Judgment on Edom

10"Because of[R]violence to your brother Jacob,   Gen. 27:41; Ezek. 25:12; Joel 3:19

You will be covered *with* shame,
And you will be cut off forever.
11"On the day that you[R]stood aloof,
On the day that strangers carried off
his wealth,   Ps. 83:5, 6; 137:7; Amos 1:6
And foreigners entered his gate
And[R]cast lots for Jerusalem—   Joel 3:3
You too were as one of them.
12"Do not[T]gloat over your brother's day,
The day of his misfortune.   *look on*
And[R]do not rejoice over the sons of Ju-
dah   Prov. 17:5; Ezek. 35:15; 36:5
In the day of their destruction;
Yes, do not[T]boast   *make your mouth large*
In the day of *their* distress.
13"Do not enter the gate of My people
In the[R]day of their disaster.   Ezek. 35:5
Yes, you, do not[T]gloat over their calam-
ity   *look on*
In the day of their disaster.
And do not[R]loot their wealth Ezek. 35:10
In the day of their disaster.
14"And do not[R]stand at the fork of the
road   Is. 16:3, 4
To cut down their fugitives;
And do not imprison their survivors
In the day of their distress.

The Results of the Judgment on Edom

15"For the[R]day of the LORD draws near on
all the nations.   Ezek. 30:3; Joel 1:15
[R]As you have done, it will be done to
you.   Hab. 2:8
Your[R]dealings will return on your own
head.   Ezek. 35:11
16"Because just as you[R]drank on[R]My holy
mountain,   Jer. 49:12 • Joel 3:17
All the nations will drink continually.
They will drink and[T]swallow,   *stagger*
And become as if they had never existed.
17"But on Mount[R]Zion there will be those
who escape,   Is. 4:2, 3
And it will be holy.
And the house of Jacob will[R]possess
their possessions.   Is. 14:1, 2
18"Then the house of Jacob will be a[R]fire
And the house of Joseph a flame;
But the house of Esau *will be* as stub-
ble.
And they[T]will set[T]them on fire and con-
sume[T]them,   Is. 5:24 • the people of Esau
So that there will be[R]no survivor of the
house of Esau,"   Jer. 11:23; Amos 1:8
For the LORD has spoken.

The Possession of Edom by Israel

19 Then *those of* the [1]Negev will[R]possess
the mountain of Esau,   Is. 11:14
And *those of* the [2]Shephelah the[R]Philis-
tine *plain*;   Is. 11:14
Also, they will[R]possess the territory of
Ephraim and the territory of Samaria,   Jer. 31:5; 32:44
And Benjamin *will possess* Gilead.
20 And the exiles of this host of the sons
of Israel,

Who are *among* the Canaanites as far
as[R]Zarephath,   1 Kin. 17:9; Luke 4:26
And the exiles of Jerusalem who are in
Sepharad
Will possess the cities of the Negev.
21 The deliverers will ascend Mount Zion
To judge the mountain of Esau,
And the kingdom will be the LORD's.

---

[1] I.e., South country   [2] I.e., the foothills

THE BOOK OF

JONAH

THE BOOK OF JONAH

Nineveh is northeast; Tarshish is west. When God calls Jonah to preach repentance to the wicked Ninevites, the prophet knows that God's mercy may follow. He turns down the assignment and heads for Tarshish instead. But once God has dampened his spirits (by tossing him out of the boat and into the water) and has demonstrated His protection (by moving him out of the water and into the fish), Jonah realizes God is serious about His command. Nineveh must hear the word of the Lord; therefore Jonah goes. Although the preaching is a success, the preacher comes away angry and discouraged and must learn firsthand of God's compassion for sinful men.

Yonah is the Hebrew word for "dove." The Septuagint hellenized this word into *Ionas*, and the Latin Vulgate used the title *Jonas*.

THE AUTHOR OF JONAH

The first verse introduces Jonah as "the son of Amittai." Nothing more would be known about him were it not for another reference to him in Second Kings 14:25 as a prophet in the reign of Jeroboam II of Israel. Under Jeroboam, the borders of Israel were expanded "according to the word of the LORD, the God of Israel, which He spoke through His servant Jonah the son of Amittai, the prophet, who was of Gath-hepher." Gath-hepher was three miles north of Nazareth in lower Galilee, making Jonah a prophet of the northern kingdom. The Pharisees were wrong when they said, "Search, and see that no prophet arises out of Galilee" (John 7:52), because Jonah was a Galilean. One Jewish tradition says that Jonah was the son of the widow of Zarephath whom Elijah raised from the dead (1 Kin. 17:8–24).

Some critics claim that Jonah was written during the fifth to third centuries B.C. as a historical fiction to oppose the "narrow nationalism" of Ezra and Nehemiah by introducing universalistic ideas. They say an anonymous writer created this work to counteract the Jewish practice of excluding the Samaritans from worship and of divorcing foreign wives. To support this view, it is noted that the book is written in the third person with no claim that Jonah wrote it. The use of Aramaic words and the statement that "Nineveh was an exceed-

ingly great city" (3:3) indicate a late date after Nineveh's fall in 612 B.C.

Conservative scholars refute this claim with these arguments: (1) The idea of God's inclusion of the Gentiles in His program is found elsewhere in the Scripture (cf. Gen. 9:27; 12:3; Lev. 19:33, 34; 1 Sam. 2:10; Is. 2:2; Joel 2:28–32). (2) Aramaic words occur in early as well as late Old Testament books. Aramaic is found in Near Eastern texts as early as 1500 B.C. (3) The fact that the book does not explicitly say that it was written by Jonah is an argument from silence. (4) Use of the third-person style was common among biblical writers. (5) The text in 3:3 literally means "had become." At the time of the story, Nineveh had already become a very large city. (6) Jonah was a historical prophet (2 Kin. 14:25), and there are no hints that the book is fictional or allegorical. (7) Christ supported the historical accuracy of the book (Matt. 12:39–41).

THE TIME OF JONAH

Jonah was a contemporary of Jeroboam II of Israel (782–753 B.C.) who ministered after the time of Elisha and just before the time of Amos and Hosea. Israel under Jeroboam II was enjoying a period of resurgence and prosperity (see "The Time of Amos"). Conditions looked promising after many bleak years, and nationalistic fervor was probably high. During these years, Assyria was in a period of mild decline. Weak rulers had ascended the throne, but Assyria remained a threat. By the time of Jonah, Assyrian cruelty had become legendary. Graphic accounts of their cruel treatment of captives have been found in ancient Assyrian records, especially from the ninth and seventh centuries B.C. The repentance of Nineveh probably occurred in the reign of Ashurdan III (773–755 B.C.). Two plagues (765 and 759 B.C.) and a solar eclipse (763 B.C.) may have prepared the people for Jonah's message of judgment.

THE CHRIST OF JONAH

Jonah is the only prophet whom Jesus likened to Himself. "But He answered and said to them, 'An evil and adulterous generation craves for a sign; and *yet* no sign shall be given to it but the sign of Jonah the prophet; for just as Jonah was three days and three nights in the belly of the sea monster, so

shall the Son of Man be three days and three nights in the heart of the earth. The men of Nineveh shall stand up with this generation at the judgment, and shall condemn it because they repented at the preaching of Jonah; and behold, something greater than Jonah is here' " (Matt. 12:39–41). Jonah's experience is a type of the death, burial, and resurrection of Christ. (The Hebrew idiom, "three days and three nights," only requires a portion of the first and third days.)

KEYS TO JONAH

Key Word: The Revival in Nineveh— God's loving concern for the Gentiles is not a truth disclosed only in the New Testament. More than seven centuries before Christ, God commissioned the Hebrew prophet Jonah to proclaim a message of repentance to the Assyrians. Jewish nationalism, however, blinded both God's prophets and covenant people to God's worldwide purpose of salvation. The story of Jonah is one of the clearest demonstrations of God's love and mercy for all mankind in the entire Scriptures.

Key Verses: Jonah 2:8, 9; 4:2—"Those who regard vain idols forsake their faithfulness, but I will sacrifice to Thee with the voice of thanksgiving. That which I have vowed I will pay. Salvation is from the LORD" (2:8, 9).

"And he prayed to the LORD and said, 'Please LORD, was not this what I said while I was still in my *own* country? Therefore, in order to forestall this I fled to Tarshish, for I knew that Thou art a gracious and compassionate God, slow to anger and abundant in lovingkindness, and one who relents concerning calamity' " (4:2).

Key Chapter: Jonah 3—The third chapter of Jonah records perhaps the greatest revival of all time as the people of Nineveh "believed in

God; and they called a fast" and cried out to God.

SURVEY OF JONAH

Jonah is an unusual book because of its message and messenger. Unlike other Old Testament books, it revolves exclusively around a gentile nation. God is concerned for the Gentiles as well as for His covenant people Israel. But God's messenger is a reluctant prophet who does not want to proclaim his message for fear that the Assyrians will respond and be spared by the compassionate God of Israel. Of all the people and things mentioned in the book—the storm, the lots, the sailors, the fish, the Ninevites, the plant, the worm, and the east wind—only the prophet himself fails to obey God. All these were used to teach Jonah a lesson in compassion and obedience. The four chapters divide: the first commission of Jonah (1 and 2) and the second commission of Jonah (3 and 4).

The First Commission of Jonah (1 and 2): This chapter records the commission of Jonah (1:1, 2), the disobedience of Jonah (1:3), and the judgment on Jonah (1:4–17). Jonah does not want to see God spare the notoriously cruel Assyrians. To preach a message of repentance to them would be like helping Israel's enemy. In his patriotic zeal, Jonah put his country before his God and refused to represent Him in Nineveh. Instead of going five hundred miles northeast to Nineveh, Jonah attempts to go two thousand miles west to Tarshish (Spain). But the Lord uses a creative series of countermeasures to accomplish His desired result. Jonah's efforts to thwart God's plan are futile.

God prepares a "great fish" to preserve Jonah and deliver him on dry land. The fish and its divinely appointed rendezvous with the sinking prophet become a powerful reminder

FOCUS	FIRST COMMISSION OF JONAH				SECOND COMMISSION OF JONAH			
REFERENCE	1:1————1:4———2:1———2:10———				3:1———3:5———4:1——4:4——4:11			
DIVISION	DISOBEDIENCE TO THE FIRST CALL	JUDGMENT ON JONAH EXACTED	PRAYER OF JONAH IN THE FISH	DELIVERANCE OF JONAH FROM THE FISH	OBEDIENCE TO THE SECOND CALL	JUDGMENT ON NINEVEH AVERTED	PRAYER OF JONAH	REBUKE OF JONAH
TOPIC	GOD'S MERCY UPON JONAH				GOD'S MERCY UPON NINEVEH			
	"I WON'T GO."		"I WILL GO."		"I'M HERE."		"I SHOULDN'T HAVE COME."	
LOCATION	THE GREAT SEA				THE GREAT CITY			
TIME	c. 760 B.C.							

to Jonah of the sovereignty of God in every circumstance. While inside the fish (2), Jonah utters a declarative praise psalm which alludes to several psalms that were racing through his mind (Ps. 3:8; 31:22; 42:7; 69:1). In his unique "prayer closet," Jonah offers thanksgiving for his deliverance from drowning. When he acknowledges that "Salvation is from the LORD" (2:9), he is finally willing to obey and be used by God. After he is cast up on the shore, Jonah has a long time to reflect on his experiences during his eastward trek of five hundred miles to Nineveh.

The Second Commission of Jonah (3 and 4): Jonah obeys his second commission to go to Nineveh (3:1–4) where he becomes "a sign to the Ninevites" (Luke 11:30). The prophet is a walking object lesson from God, his skin no doubt bleached from his stay in the fish. As he proceeds through the city, his one-sentence sermon brings incredible results: it is the most effective evangelistic effort in history. Jonah's

words of coming judgment are followed by a proclamation by the king of the city to fast and repent. Because of His great mercy, God "relented concerning the calamity which He had declared He would bring upon them" (3:10).

In the final chapter, God's love and grace are contrasted with Jonah's anger and lack of compassion. He is unhappy with the good results of his message because he knows God will now spare Nineveh. God uses a plant, a worm, and a wind to teach Jonah a lesson in compassion. Jonah's emotions shift from fierce anger (4:1), to despondency (4:3), then to great joy (4:6), and finally to despair (4:8). In a humorous but meaningful account, Jonah is forced to see that he has more concern for a plant than for hundreds of thousands of people (if 120,000 children are in mind in 4:11, the population of the area may have been 600,000). Jonah's lack of a divine perspective makes his repentance a greater problem than the repentance of Nineveh.

CHAPTER 1

The Disobedience to the First Call

THE word of the LORD came to [R]Jonah the son of Amittai saying,   Luke 11:29, 30, 32

2 "Arise, go to [R]Nineveh the great city, and cry against it, for their wickedness has come up before Me."   Gen. 10:11; 2 Kin. 19:36

3 But Jonah rose up to flee to [R]Tarshish from the presence of the LORD. So he went down to Joppa, found a ship which was going to Tarshish, paid the fare, and went down into it to go with them to Tarshish from the presence of the LORD.   Is. 23:1, 6, 10

The Great Storm

4 And the LORD hurled a great wind on the sea and there was a great storm on the sea so that the ship was about to break up.

5 Then the sailors became afraid, and every man cried to his god, and they threw the [T]cargo which was in the ship into the sea to lighten *it* [T]for them. But Jonah had gone below into the hold of the ship, lain down, and fallen sound asleep.   *vessels • from upon them*

6 So the captain approached him and said, "How is it that you are sleeping? Get up, [R]call on your god. Perhaps *your* [R]god will be concerned about us so that we will not perish."   Ps. 107:28 • 2 Sam. 12:22; Amos 5:15

7 And each man said to his mate, "Come, let us cast lots so we may learn on whose account this calamity *has struck* us." So they cast lots and the lot fell on Jonah.

8 Then they said to him, "Tell us, now! On whose account *has* this calamity *struck* us? What is your [R]occupation? And where do you come from? What is your country? From what people are you?"   Gen. 47:3

9 And he said to them, "I am a Hebrew, and I fear the LORD God of heaven who [R]made the sea and the dry land."   [Neh. 9:6]

10 Then the men became extremely frightened and they said to him, "How could you do this?" For the men knew that he was [R]fleeing from the presence of the LORD, because he had told them.   Job 27:22; Jon. 1:3

11 So they said to him, "What should we do to you that the sea may become calm [T]for us?"—for the sea was becoming increasingly stormy.   *from upon us*

12 And he said to them, "Pick me up and

throw me into the sea. Then the sea will become calm ᵀfor you, for I know that ᴿon account of me this great storm *has come* upon you." *from upon you* • 2 Sam. 24:17; 1 Chr. 21:17

13 However, the men ᵀrowed *desperately* to return to land but they could not, for the sea was becoming *even* stormier against them. *dug their oars into the water*

14 Then they called on the LORD and said, "We earnestly pray, O LORD, do not let us perish on account of this man's life and do not put innocent blood on us; for Thou, O LORD, hast done as Thou hast pleased."

15 So they picked up Jonah, threw him into the sea, and the sea stopped its raging.

16 Then the men feared the LORD greatly, and they offered a sacrifice to the LORD and made ᴿvows. *Ps. 50:14; 66:13, 14*

The Great Salvation of Jonah
by the Fish

17 And the LORD appointed a great fish to swallow Jonah, and Jonah was in the stomach of the fish three days and three nights.

CHAPTER 2

The Prayer of Jonah

THEN Jonah prayed to the LORD his God from the stomach of the fish,

2 and he said,
"I ᵀcalled out of my distress to the LORD,
And He answered me. *1 Sam. 30:6*
I cried for help from the ᵀdepth of
ᴿSheol; *belly* • *Ps. 18:5, 6; 86:13; 88:1-7*
Thou didst hear my voice.

3"For Thou hadst ᴿcast me into the deep,
Into the heart of the seas, *Lam. 3:54*
And the current engulfed me.
All Thy ᴿbreakers and billows passed
over me. *Ps. 42:7*

4"So I said, 'I have been ᴿexpelled from
ᵀThy sight. *Ps. 31:22* • *before Thine eyes*
Nevertheless I will look again ᵀtoward
Thy holy temple.' *2 Chr. 6:38; Ps. 5:7*

5"Water ᴿencompassed me to the ʲpoint of
death. *Lam. 3:54* • *soul*
The great deep ᵀengulfed me, *surrounded*
Weeds were wrapped around my head.

6"I ᴿdescended to the roots of the mountains. *Ps. 18:5; 116:3*
The earth with its ᴿbars *was* around me
forever, *[Is. 38:10; Matt. 16:18]*
But Thou hast brought up my life from
ᴬthe pit, O LORD my God. *corruption*

7"While I was ᴿfainting away, *Ps. 142:3*
I ᵀremembered the LORD; *Ps. 77:10, 11*
And my ᴿprayer came to Thee, *Ps. 18:6*
Into ᴿThy holy temple. *Mic. 1:2; Hab. 2:20*

8"Those who regard ᵀvain idols
Forsake their faithfulness, *empty vanities*

9 But I will ᴿsacrifice to Thee *Ps. 50:14, 23*
With the voice of thanksgiving.
That which I have vowed I will pay.
ᴿSalvation is from the LORD." *Ps. 3:8*

The Deliverance of Jonah

10 Then the LORD commanded the fish, and it vomited Jonah up onto the dry land.

CHAPTER 3

The Obedience to the Second Call

NOW the word of the LORD came to Jonah the second time, saying,

2"Arise, go to ᴿNineveh the great city and ᴿproclaim to it the proclamation which I am going to tell you." *Zeph. 2:13* • *Jer. 1:17*

3 So Jonah arose and went to Nineveh according to the word of the LORD. Now Nineveh was ¹an ᴿexceedingly great city, a three days' walk. *Jon. 1:2; 4:11*

4 Then Jonah began to go through the city one day's walk; and he ᴿcried out and said, "Yet forty days and Nineveh will be overthrown." *[Matt. 12:41; Luke 11:32]*

The Great Fast

5 Then the people of Nineveh believed in God; and they called a fast and put on sackcloth from the greatest to the least of them.

6 When the word reached the king of Nineveh, he arose from his throne, laid aside his robe from him, covered *himself* with sackcloth, and sat on the ᴬashes. *dust*

7 And he issued a ᴿproclamation and it said, "In Nineveh by the decree of the king and his nobles: Do not let man, beast, herd, or flock taste a thing. Do not let them eat or drink water. *2 Chr. 20:3; Ezra 8:21; Jon. 3:5*

8"But both man and beast must be covered with sackcloth; and let ᵀmen ᴿcall on God earnestly that each may turn from his wicked way and from the violence which is in ᵀhis hands. *them* • *Ps. 130:1* • *their*

9"Who ᴿknows, God may turn and relent, and withdraw His burning anger so that we shall not perish?" *2 Sam. 12:22; Joel 2:14*

The Great Salvation of Nineveh
by God

10 When God saw their deeds, that they ᴿturned from their wicked way, then God relented concerning the calamity which He had declared He would ᵀbring upon them. And He did not do *it*. *1 Kin. 21:27-29* • *do*

CHAPTER 4

The Prayer of Jonah

BUT it greatly displeased Jonah, and he became ᴿangry. *Matt. 20:15; Luke 15:28*

2 And he prayed to the LORD and said, "Please LORD, was not this what I said while

¹ Lit., *a great city to God*

I was still in my *own* country? Therefore,[T] in order to forestall this I fled to Tarshish, for I knew that Thou art a gracious and compassionate God, slow to anger and abundant in lovingkindness, and one who relents concerning calamity.   *I was beforehand in fleeing*

3 "Therefore now, O LORD, please[R] take my [T]life from me, for death is[R] better to me than life."   1 Kin. 19:4 • *soul* • Eccl. 7:1

The Rebuke of Jonah by God

4 And the LORD said, "Do you have good reason to be angry?"

5 Then Jonah went out from the city and sat east of it. There he made a shelter for himself and sat under it in the shade until he could see what would happen in the city.

6 So the LORD God appointed a plant and it grew up over Jonah to be a shade over his head to deliver[T] him from his discomfort. And Jonah was extremely happy about the plant.   *greatly*

7 But God appointed a worm when dawn came the next day, and it attacked the plant and it[R] withered.   Joel 1:12

8 And it came about when the sun came up that God appointed a scorching [R]east wind, and the sun beat down on Jonah's head so that he became faint and begged with *all* his soul to die, saying, "Death is better to me than life."   Ezek. 19:12; Hos. 31:15

9 Then God said to Jonah, "Do you have good reason to be angry about the plant?" And he said, "I have good reason to be angry, even to death."

10 Then the LORD said, "You had compassion on the plant for which you did not work, and *which* you did not cause to grow, which came up[T] overnight and perished overnight.   *a son of a night*

11 "And should I not have compassion on Nineveh, the great city in which there are more than 120,000 persons who do not know *the difference* between their right and left hand, as well as many animals?"

THE BOOK OF

MICAH

THE BOOK OF MICAH

Micah, called from his rustic home to be a prophet, leaves his familiar surroundings to deliver a stern message of judgment to the princes and people of Jerusalem. Burdened by the abusive treatment of the poor by the rich and influential, the prophet turns his verbal rebukes upon any who would use their social or political power for personal gain. One-third of Micah's book exposes the sins of his countrymen; another third pictures the punishment God is about to send; and the final third holds out the hope of restoration once that discipline has ended. Through it all, God's righteous demands upon His people are clear: "to do justice, to love kindness, and to walk humbly with your God" (6:8).

The name *Michayahu* ("Who Is Like Yahweh?") is shortened to *Michaia*. In 7:18, Micah hints at his own name with the phrase "Who is a God like Thee?" The Greek and Latin titles of this book are *Michaias* and *Micha*.

THE AUTHOR OF MICAH

Micah's hometown of Moresheth-gath (1:14) was located about twenty-five miles southwest of Jerusalem on the border of Judah and Philistia, near Gath. Like Amos, Micah was from the country. His family and occupation are unknown, but Moresheth was in a productive agricultural belt. Micah was not as aware of the political situation as Isaiah or Daniel, but he showed a profound concern for the sufferings of the people. His clear sense of prophetic calling is seen in 3:8: "On the other hand I am filled with power—with the Spirit of the LORD—and with justice and courage to make known to Jacob his rebellious act, even to Israel his sin."

THE TIME OF MICAH

The first verse indicates that Micah prophesied in the days of Jotham (739–731 B.C.), Ahaz (731–715 B.C.), and Hezekiah (715–686 B.C.), kings of Judah. Although Micah deals primarily with Judah, he also addresses the northern kingdom of Israel and predicts the fall of Samaria (1:6). Much of his ministry, therefore, took place before the Assyrian captivity of Israel in 722 B.C. His strong denunciations of idolatry and immorality also suggest that his ministry largely preceded the sweeping religious reforms of Hezekiah. Thus,

Micah's prophecies ranged from about 735 to 710 B.C. He was a contemporary of Hosea in the northern kingdom and of Isaiah in the court of Jerusalem.

After the prosperous reign of Uzziah in Judah (767–739 B.C.), his son, Jotham, came to power and followed the same policies (739–731 B.C.). He was a good king, although he failed to remove the idolatrous high places. Under the wicked King Ahaz (731–715 B.C.), Judah was threatened by the forces of Assyria and Aram. Hezekiah (715–686 B.C.) opposed the Assyrians and successfully withstood an Assyrian siege with the help of God. He was an unusually good king who guided the people of Judah back to a proper course in their walk with God.

During the ministry of Micah, the kingdom of Israel continued to crumble inwardly and outwardly until its collapse in 722 B.C. The Assyrian Empire under Tiglath-pileser III (745–727 B.C.), Shalmaneser V (727–722 B.C.), Sargon II (722–705 B.C.), and Sennacherib (705–681 B.C.) reached the zenith of its power and became a constant threat to Judah. Babylon was still under Assyrian domination, and Micah's prediction of future Babylonian captivity for Judah (4:10) must have seemed unlikely.

THE CHRIST OF MICAH

Micah 5:2 is one of the clearest and most important of all Old Testament prophecies: "But as for you, Bethlehem Ephrathah, *too* little to be among the clans of Judah, from you One will go forth for Me to be ruler in Israel. His goings forth are from long ago, from the days of eternity." This prophecy about the birthplace and eternity of the Messiah was made seven hundred years before His birth. The chief priests and scribes paraphrased this verse in Matthew 2:5, 6 when questioned about the birthplace of the Messiah. Micah 2:12, 13; 4:1–8; and 5:4, 5 offer some of the best Old Testament descriptions of the righteous reign of Christ over the whole world.

KEYS TO MICAH

Key Word: The Judgment and Restoration of Judah—Micah exposes the injustice of Judah and the righteousness and justice of Yahweh. About one-third of the book indicts Israel and Judah for specific sins, in-

cluding oppression; bribery among judges, prophets, and priests; exploitation of the powerless; covetousness; cheating; violence; and pride. Another third of Micah predicts the judgment that will come as a result of those sins. The remaining third of the book is a message of hope and consolation. God's justice will triumph and the divine Deliverer will come. True peace and justice will prevail only when the Messiah reigns. The "kindness and severity of God" (Rom. 11:22) are illustrated in Micah's presentation of divine judgment and pardon. This book emphasizes the integral relationship between true spirituality and social ethics. Micah 6:8 summarizes what God wants to see in His people: justice and equity tempered with mercy and compassion, as the result of a humble and obedient relationship with Him.

Key Verses: Micah 6:8; 7:18—"He has told you, O man, what is good; and what does the LORD require of you but to do justice, to love kindness, and to walk humbly with your God?" (6:8).

"Who is a God like Thee, who pardons iniquity and passes over the rebellious act of the remnant of His possession? He does not retain His anger forever, because He delights in unchanging love" (7:18).

Key Chapters: Micah 6, 7—The closing section of Micah describes a courtroom scene. God has a controversy against His people, and He calls the mountains and hills together to form the jury as He sets forth His case. The people have replaced heartfelt worship with empty ritual, thinking that this is all God demands. They have divorced God's standards of justice from their daily dealings in order to cover their unscrupulous practices. They have failed to realize what the Lord requires of man. There can only be one verdict: guilty.

Nevertheless, the book closes on a note of hope. The same God who executes judgment also delights to extend mercy. "Who is a God like Thee, who pardons iniquity and passes over the rebellious act of the remnant of His possession? He does not retain His anger forever, because He delights in unchanging love" (7:18). No wonder the prophet exclaims, "But as for me, I will watch expectantly for the LORD; I will wait for the God of my salvation. My God will hear me" (7:7).

SURVEY OF MICAH

Micah is the prophet of the downtrodden and exploited people of Judean society. He prophesies during a time of great social injustice and boldly opposes those who impose their power upon the poor and weak for selfish ends. Corrupt rulers, false prophets, and ungodly priests all become targets for Micah's prophetic barbs. Micah exposes judges who are bought by bribes and merchants who use deceptive weights. The pollution of sin has permeated every level of society in Judah and Israel. The whole earth is called to witness God's indictment against His people (1:2; 6:1, 2), and the guilty verdict leads to a sentence of destruction and captivity. However, while the three major sections begin with condemnation (1:2—2:11; 3:6), they all end on a clear note of consolation (2:12, 13; 4; 5; 7). After sin is punished and justice is established, "He will again have compassion on us; He will tread our iniquities under foot. Yes, Thou wilt cast all their sins into the depths of the sea" (7:19). The three sections of Micah are: the prediction of judgment (1—3), the prediction of restoration (4 and 5), and the plea for repentance (6 and 7).

The Prediction of Judgment (1—3): Micah

FOCUS	PREDICTION OF JUDGMENT		PREDICTION OF RESTORATION			PLEA FOR REPENTANCE		
REFERENCE	1:1———3:1———4:1———			4:6———5:2———		6:1———	6:10———7:7———7:20		
DIVISION	JUDGMENT OF PEOPLE	JUDGMENT OF LEADERSHIP	PROMISE OF COMING KINGDOM	PROMISE OF COMING CAPTIVITIES	PROMISE OF COMING KING	FIRST PLEA OF GOD	SECOND PLEA OF GOD	PROMISE OF FINAL SALVATION
TOPIC	PUNISHMENT		PROMISE			PARDON		
	RETRIBUTION		RESTORATION			REPENTANCE		
LOCATION	JUDAH—ISRAEL							
TIME	c. 735—710 B.C.							

begins by launching into a general declaration of the condemnation of Israel (Samaria) and Judah (Jerusalem). Both kingdoms will be overthrown because of their rampant treachery. Micah uses a series of wordplays on the names of several cities of Judah in his lamentation over Judah's coming destruction (1:10–16). This is followed by some of the specific causes for judgment: premeditated schemes, covetousness, and cruelty. Nevertheless, God will regather a remnant of His people (2:12, 13). The prophet then systematically condemns the princes (3:1–4) and the prophets (3:5–8) and concludes with a warning of coming judgment (3:9–12).

The Prediction of Restoration (4 and 5): Micah then moves into a two-chapter message of hope, which describes the reinstitution of the kingdom (4:1–5) and the intervening captivity of the kingdom (4:6—5:1), concluding with the coming Ruler of the Kingdom (5:2–15). The prophetic focus gradually narrows from the nations to the remnant to the King.

The Plea for Repentance (6 and 7): In His two controversies with His people, God calls them into court and presents an unanswerable case against them. The people have spurned God's grace, choosing instead to revel in wickedness. Micah concludes with a sublime series of promises that the Lord will pardon their iniquity and renew their nation in accordance with His covenant.

OUTLINE OF MICAH

CHAPTER 1

Introduction to the Book of Micah

T HE word of the LORD which came *to* Micah of Moresheth in the days of Jotham, Ahaz, *and* Hezekiah, kings of Judah, which he saw concerning Samaria and Jerusalem.

Judgment on Samaria

2 Hear, O peoples, all of ^Tyou;   *them*
  Listen, O earth and all it contains,
  And let the Lord GOD be a ⁴witness
    against you,   Is. 50:7
  The Lord from His holy temple.
3 For behold, the LORD is ^Rcoming forth
    from His place.   Is. 26:21
  He will come down and tread on the
    high places of the ⁴earth.   *land*
4 ^RThe mountains will melt under Him,
  And the valleys will be split,   Ps. 97:5
  Like wax before the fire,
  Like water poured down a steep place.
5 All this is for the rebellion of Jacob
  And for the sins of the house of Israel.
  What is the rebellion of Jacob?
  Is it not ^RSamaria?   Is. 7:9; Amos 8:14

What is the high ¹place of Judah?   *places*
Is it not Jerusalem?
6 For I will make Samaria a heap of ruins
  ^Tin the open country,   *of the field*
  Planting places for a vineyard.
  I will ^Rpour her stones down into the
    valley,   Lam. 4:1
  And will lay bare her foundations.
7 All of her idols will be smashed,
  All of her earnings will be burned with
    fire,
  And all of her images I will make desolate,
  For she collected *them* from a ^Rharlot's
    earnings,   Deut. 23:18; Is. 23:17
  And to the earnings of a harlot they
    will return.

8 Because of this I must lament and wail,
  I must go ^Rbarefoot and naked;   Is. 32:11
  I must make a lament like the jackals
  And a mourning like the ostriches.

Judgment on Judah

9 For her ^Twound is incurable,   *wounds*
  For ^Rit has come to Judah;   2 Kin. 18:13

It has reached the ^Rgate of my people,
Even to Jerusalem.   Mic. 1:12
10 ^RTell it not in Gath,   2 Sam. 1:20
Weep not at all.
At ¹Beth-le-aphrah roll yourself in the
dust.
11 ^TGo on your way, inhabitant of ²Sha-
phir, in ^Rshameful nakedness.
The inhabitant of ³Zaanan does not es-
cape.   Go into captivity • Ezek. 23:29
The lamentation of ⁴Beth-ezel: "He
will take from you its support."
12 For the inhabitant of ⁵Maroth
Becomes weak waiting for good,
Because a calamity has come down
from the LORD
To the ^Rgate of Jerusalem.   Mic. 1:9
13 Harness the chariot to the team of
horses,
O inhabitant of ^RLachish—   Josh. 10:3
She was the beginning of sin
To the daughter of Zion—
Because in you were found
The ^Rrebellious acts of Israel.   Mic. 1:5
14 Therefore, you will give parting gifts
On behalf of Moresheth-gath;
The houses of ^RAchzib *will* become a
^Rdeception   Josh. 15:44 • Jer. 15:18
To the kings of Israel.
15 Moreover, I will bring on you
The one who takes possession,
O inhabitant of ⁶Mareshah.   Josh. 15:44
The glory of Israel will enter Adullam.
16 Make yourself ^Rbald and cut off your
hair,   Is. 22:12
Because of the children of your delight;
Extend your baldness like the eagle,
For they will go from you into exile.

CHAPTER 2

Cause of the Judgment

W OE to those who scheme iniquity,
Who work out evil on their beds!
When morning comes, they do it,
For it is in the power of their hands.
2 They covet fields and then seize *them*,
And houses, and take *them* away.
They ^Trob a man and his house,   *oppress*
A man and his inheritance.
3 Therefore, thus says the LORD,
"Behold, I am ^Rplanning against this fam-
ily a calamity   Deut. 28:48; Jer. 18:11
From which you ^Rcannot remove your
necks;   Lam. 1:14; 5:5
And you will not walk haughtily,
For it will be an ^Revil time.   Amos 5:13
4 "On that day they will ^Rtake up against
you a ^ttaunt   Hab. 2:6 • *proverb*
And utter a bitter lamentation *and* say,
'We are completely destroyed!

He exchanges the portion of my peo-
ple;
How He removes it from me!
To the apostate He ^Rapportions our
fields.'   Jer. 6:12; 8:10
5 "Therefore, you will have no one
^Tstretching ^a a measuring line
For you by lot in the assembly of the
LORD.   *casting* • Num. 34:13, 16-29

6 'Do not speak out,' *so* they speak out.
But if ^Tthey do not speak out concerning
these things,   God's prophets
Reproaches will not be turned back.
7 "Is it being said, O house of Jacob:
'Is the Spirit of the LORD impatient?
Are these His doings?'
Do not My words ^Rdo good   Jer. 15:16
To the one ^Rwalking uprightly?   Ps. 15:2
8 "Recently My people have arisen as an
^Tenemy—   *And yesterday* • Jer. 12:8
You strip the robe off the garment,
From unsuspecting passers-by,
From those returned from war.
9 "The women of My people you evict,
Each *one* from her pleasant house.
From her children you take My ^Tsplen-
dor forever.   Ezek. 39:21; Hab. 2:14
10 "Arise and go,
For this is no place ^Rof rest   Deut. 12:9
Because of the ^Runcleanness that brings
on destruction,   Ps. 106:38
A painful destruction.
11 "If a man walking after wind and ^Rfalse-
hood   Jer. 5:31
Had told lies *and said,*
'I will ^Tspeak out to you concerning ^Rwine
and liquor,'   *flow* • Is. 28:7
He would be spokesman to this people.

Promise of Future Restoration

12 "I will surely assemble all ^Rof you, Jacob,
I will surely gather the ^Rremnant of Is-
rael.   Mic. 5:7, 8
I will put them together like sheep in
the fold;
Like a flock in the midst of its pasture
They will be noisy with men.
13 "The breaker goes up before them;
They break out, pass through the gate,
and go out by it.
So their king goes on before them,
And the LORD at their head."

CHAPTER 3

Judgment on Rulers

A ND I said,
"Hear now, heads of Jacob
And rulers of the house of Israel.
Is it not for you to know justice?
2 "You who hate good and love evil,

¹ I.e., house of dust   ² I.e., pleasantness
³ I.e., going out   ⁴ I.e., house of removal
⁵ I.e., bitterness   ⁶ I.e., possession

Who tear off their skin from them
And their flesh from their bones,
3 And who [R]eat the flesh of my people,
Strip off their skin from them,   Ps. 14:4
Break their bones,
And [R]chop *them* up as for the pot
And as meat in a kettle." Ezek. 11:3, 6, 7
4 Then they will [T]cry out to the LORD,
But He will not answer them.   Ps. 18:41
Instead, He will [R]hide His face from
   them at that time,   Deut. 31:17
Because they have [R]practiced evil
   deeds.   Is. 3:11; Mic. 7:13

Judgment on Prophets

5 Thus says the LORD concerning the
   prophets
Who [R]lead my people astray;   Is. 3:12
When they have *something* to bite with
   their teeth,
They [R]cry, "Peace,"   Jer. 6:14
But against him who puts nothing in
   their mouths,
They declare holy war.
6 Therefore *it will be* [R]night for you—
   without vision,   Is. 8:20-22; 29:10-12
And darkness for you—without divina-
   tion.
The [R]sun will go down on the prophets,
And the day will become dark over
   them.   Is. 59:10
7 The seers will be [R]ashamed   Zech. 13:4
And the diviners will be embarrassed.
Indeed, they will all cover *their* mouths
Because there is no answer from God.
8 On the other hand [R]I am filled with
   power—   Is. 61:1, 2; Jer. 1:18
With the Spirit of the LORD—
And with justice and courage
To [R]make known to Jacob his rebellious
   act,   Is. 58:1
Even to Israel his sin.

Promise of Future Judgment

9 Now hear this, [R]heads of the house of
   Jacob   Mic. 1:1
And rulers of the house of Israel,
Who [R]abhor justice   Ps. 58:1, 2; Is. 1:23
And twist everything that is straight,
10 Who build Zion with bloodshed
And Jerusalem with violent injustice.
11 Her leaders pronounce [R]judgment for a
   bribe,   Is. 1:23; Mic. 7:3
Her [R]priests instruct for a price,   Jer. 6:13
And her prophets divine for money.
Yet they lean on the LORD saying,
"Is [R]not the LORD in our midst?   Is. 48:2
Calamity will not come upon us."
12 Therefore, on account of you,
[R]Zion will be plowed as a field,   Jer. 26:18
Jerusalem will become a heap of ruins,
And the mountain of the temple *will*
   become high places of a forest.

CHAPTER 4

The Promise of the Coming Kingdom

AND it will come about in the last days
That the [R]mountain of the house of the
   LORD   Ezek. 43:12; [T]Mic. 3:12; Zech. 8:3
Will be established [T]as the chief of the
   mountains.   *on*
It will be raised above the hills,
And the peoples will stream to it.
2 And many nations will come and say,
"Come [R]and let us go up to the mountain
   of the LORD   Is. 2:3; Jer. 31:6
And to the house of the God of Jacob,
That He may teach us about His ways
And that we may walk in His paths."
For from Zion will go forth the law,
Even the word of the LORD from Jeru-
   salem.
3 And He will [R]judge between many peo-
   ples   Is. 2:4; 11:3-5
And render decisions for mighty, [T]dis-
   tant nations.   *at a distance*
Then they will hammer their swords
[R]into plowshares   Joel 3:10
And their spears into pruning hooks;
Nation will not lift up sword against
   nation,
And never again will they [T]train for
   war.   *learn*
4 And each of them will [R]sit under his
   vine   1 Kin. 4:25; Zech. 3:10
And under his fig tree,
With no one to make *them* afraid,
For the [R]mouth of the LORD of hosts has
   spoken.   Is. 1:20; 40:5
5 Though all the peoples walk
Each in the name of his god,
As for us, [R]we will walk   Zech. 10:12
In the name of the [R]LORD our God for-
   ever and ever.   Josh. 24:15; Is. 26:8, 13

The Promise
of the Coming Captivities

6 "In that day," declares the LORD,
"I will assemble the [R]lame,   Zeph. 3:19
And [R]gather the outcasts,   Ps. 147:2
Even those whom I have afflicted.
7 "I will make the lame a remnant,
And the outcasts a strong nation,
And the [R]LORD will reign over them in
   Mount Zion   Is. 24:23
From now on and forever.
8 "And as for you, tower of the flock,
[T]Hill of the daughter of Zion,
To you it will come—   Heb., *Ophel of*
Even the [T]former dominion will come,
The kingdom of the daughter of Jeru-
   salem.   Is. 1:26; [Zech. 9:10]

9 "Now, why do you cry out loudly?
Is there no king among you,
Or has your counselor perished,

That agony has gripped you like a woman in childbirth?

10 "Writhe[R] and labor to give birth,   Mic. 5:3
Daughter of Zion,
Like a woman in childbirth,
For now you will go out of the city,
Dwell in the field,
And go to Babylon.
[R]There you will be rescued;   Is. 43:14
There the LORD will redeem you
From the hand of your enemies.

11 "And now[R] many nations have been assembled against you   Is. 5:25-30
Who say, 'Let her be polluted,
And let our eyes gloat over Zion.'

12 "But they do not[R]know the thoughts of the LORD,   Ps. 147:19, 20
And they do not understand His purpose;
For He has gathered them like sheaves to the threshing floor.

13 "Arise and thresh, daughter of Zion,
For your horn I will make iron
And your hoofs I will make bronze,
That you may pulverize many peoples,
That you may[R]devote to the LORD their unjust gain   Is. 60:9
And their wealth to the Lord of all the earth.

CHAPTER 5

"NOW muster yourselves in troops, daughter of troops;
[T]They have laid siege against us; *He has*
With a rod they will[R]smite the judge of Israel on the cheek.   Mark 15:19☆

Birth of the Messiah

2 "But as for you, Bethlehem Ephrathah,
Too little to be among the clans of Judah,
From[R]you One will go forth for Me to be ruler in Israel. Is. 11:1; Luke 2:4–7☆
His goings forth are from long ago,
From the days of eternity."

Rejection of the Messiah

3 Therefore, He will[R]give them *up* until the time   Hos. 11:8; Mic. 4:10; 7:13
When she[R]who is in labor has borne a child.   Mic. 4:9, 10
Then the remainder of His brethren
Will return to the sons of Israel.

Work of the Messiah

4 And He will arise and[R]shepherd *His* flock   [Is. 40:11; 49:9]
In the strength of the LORD,
In the majesty of the name of the LORD His God.
And they will[A]remain,   *live* in safety

Because[T]at that time He will be great
To the[R]ends of the earth.   *now* • Is. 45:22

5 And this One[R]will be *our* peace. [Is. 9:6]
When the Assyrian invades our land,
When he tramples on our citadels,
Then we will raise against him
Seven shepherds and eight leaders of men.

6 And they will[R]shepherd the land of Assyria with the sword,   Nah. 2:11-13
The land of Nimrod at its entrances;
And He will[R]deliver *us* from the Assyrian   Is. 14:25; 37:36, 37
When he attacks our land
And when he tramples our territory.

7 Then the[R]remnant of Jacob   Mic. 2:12
Will be among many peoples
Like[R]dew from the LORD,   Deut. 32:2
Like[R]showers on vegetation   Ps. 72:6
Which do not wait for man
Or delay for the sons of men.

8 And the remnant of Jacob
Will be among the nations,
Among many peoples
[R]Like a lion among the beasts of the forest,   Gen. 49:9; Num. 24:9
Like a young lion among flocks of sheep,
Which, if he passes through,
Tramples down and[R]tears,   Hos. 5:14
And there is[R]none to rescue.   Ps. 50:22

9 Your hand will be[R]lifted up against your adversaries,   Ps. 10:12; 21:8
And all your enemies will be cut off.

10 "And it will be in that day," declares the LORD,
"That[R] I will cut off your[R]horses from among you   Zech. 9:10 • Deut. 17:16
And destroy your chariots.

11 "I will also cut off the cities of your land
And tear down all your fortifications.

12 "I will cut off[R]sorceries from your hand,
And you will have fortunetellers no more.   Deut. 18:10-12; Is. 2:6; 8:19

13 "I[R]will cut off your carved images
And your *sacred* pillars from among you,   Is. 2:18; 17:8; Ezek. 6:9
So that you will no longer bow down
To the work of your hands.

14 "I will root out your[R]Asherim from among you   Ex. 34:13; Is. 17:8; 27:9
And destroy your cities.

15 "And I will[R]execute vengeance in anger and wrath   Is. 1:24; 65:12
On the nations which have not obeyed."

CHAPTER 6

God Pleads

HEAR now what the LORD is saying,
"Arise, plead your case[T]before the mountains,   *with*
And let the hills hear your voice.

2"Listen, you mountains, to the indict-
ment of the LORD,
And you enduring ^Rfoundations of the
earth,   2 Sam. 22:16; Ps. 104:5
Because the ^RLORD has a case against
His people;   [Is. 1:18]; Hos. 4:1; 12:2
Even with Israel He will dispute.
3"My^R people, ^Rwhat have I done to you,
And^Rhow have I wearied you? Answer
Me.   Ps. 50:7 • Jer. 2:5 • Is. 43:22
4"Indeed, I^Rbrought you up from the land
of Egypt   Ex. 12:51; 20:2
And^Rransomed you from the house of
slavery,   Deut. 7:8
And I sent before you^RMoses, Aaron,
and Miriam.   Ex. 4:10-16; Ps. 77:20
5"My people, remember now
What^RBalak king of Moab counseled
And what Balaam son of Beor an-
swered him,   Num. 22:5, 6
And from^RShittim to Gilgal,   Num. 25:1
In order^Tthat you might know the righteous acts of the LORD."   to know

Micah Replies

6 ^RWith what shall I come to the LORD
And bow myself before the God on
high?   Ps. 40:6-8
Shall I come to Him with^Rburnt offer-
ings,   Ps. 51:16, 17
With yearling calves?
7 Does the LORD take delight in ^Rthou-
sands of rams,   Ps. 50:9; Is. 1:1
In ten thousand rivers of oil?
Shall I present my^Rfirst-born for my re-
bellious acts,   Lev. 18:21; 20:1-5
The fruit of my body for the sin of my
soul?
8 He has told you, O man, what is good;
And what does the LORD require of you
But to do justice, to love kindness,
And to walk humbly with your God?

9 The voice of the LORD will call to the
city—
And it is sound wisdom to fear Thy
name:
"Hear, O tribe. Who has appointed ^Tits
time?   it

God Pleads

10"Is there yet a man in the wicked house,
Along with treasures of wickedness,
And a short measure that is cursed?
11"Can I justify wicked^Rscales   Lev. 19:36
And a bag of deceptive weights?
12"For the rich men of the^Tcity are full of
^Rviolence,   her • Is. 1:23; 5:7
Her residents speak^Rlies,   Hos. 7:13
And their^Rtongue is deceitful in their
mouth.   Is. 3:8

13"So also I will make you^Rsick, striking
you down,   Mic. 1:9
Desolating you because of your sins.
14"You will eat, but you will^Rnot be satisfied,   Is. 9:20
And your ⁷vileness will be in your
midst.
You will try to remove for safekeeping,
But you will^Rnot preserve anything,
And what you do preserve I will give to
the sword.   Is. 30:6
15"You will sow but you will not reap.
You will tread the olive but will not
anoint yourself with oil;
And the grapes, but you will^Rnot drink
wine.   Amos 5:11; Zeph. 1:13
16"The statutes of^ROmri   1 Kin. 16:25, 26
And all the works of the house of^RAhab
are observed;   1 Kin. 16:29-33
And in their devices you^Rwalk. Jer. 7:24
Therefore, I will give you up for ^Tde-
struction   Jer. 18:16; Mic. 6:13
And ^Tyour inhabitants for derision,   her
And you will bear the^Rreproach of My
people." Ps. 44:13; Jer. 51:51; Hos. 12:14

CHAPTER 7

Micah Replies

WOE is me! For I am
Like the fruit pickers and the ^Rgrape
gatherers.   Is. 24:13
There is not a cluster of grapes to eat,
Or a first-ripe fig which^TI crave. my soul
2 The ^Rgodly person has ^Rperished from
the land,   loyal • Is. 57:1
And there is no upright person among
men.
All of them lie in wait for bloodshed;
Each of them hunts the other with a
^Rnet.   Jer. 5:26; Hos. 5:1
3 Concerning evil, both hands do it well.
The prince asks, also the judge, for a
^Rbribe,   Amos 5:12; Mic. 3:11
And a great man speaks the desire of
his soul;
So they weave it together.
4 The best of them is like a briar,
The most upright like a thorn hedge.
The day when you post a watchman,
Your^Rpunishment will come.   Is. 10:3
Then their confusion will occur.
5 Do not^Rtrust in a neighbor;   Jer. 9:4
Do not have confidence in a friend.
From her who lies in your bosom
Guard^Tyour lips.   openings of your mouth
6 For ^Rson treats father contemptuously,
Daughter rises up against her mother,
Daughter-in-law against her mother-in-
law;   Matt. 10:21, 35; Luke 12:53
^RA man's enemies are the men of his
own household.   Matt. 10: 36

⁷ Or possibly, garbage or excreta

The Promise of Final Salvation

7 But as for me, I will[R]watch expectantly
   for the LORD;   Hab. 2:1
I will wait for the God of my salvation.
My[R]God will hear me.   [Ps. 4:3]
8 Do not rejoice over me, O my enemy.
   Though I fall I will[R]rise;   Amos 9:11
   Though I dwell in darkness, the LORD is
   a[R]light for me.   Is. 9:2

9 I will bear the indignation of the LORD
   Because I have sinned against Him,
   Until He[R]pleads my case and executes
      justice for me.   Jer. 50:34
   He will bring me out to the light,
   And I will see His righteousness.
10 Then my enemy will see,
   And shame will cover her who[R]said to
      me,   Joel 2:17
   "Where is the LORD your God?"
   My eyes will look on her;
   [T]At that time she will [T]be trampled
      down,   Now • become a trampled place
   Like mire of the streets.
11 It will be a day for[R]building your walls.
   On that day will your boundary be ex-
      tended.   Is. 54:11; [Amos 9:11]
12 It will be a day when[T]they will[R]come to
      you   he • [Is. 19:23–25; 60:4, 9]
   From Assyria and the cities of Egypt,
   From Egypt even to the[T]Euphrates,
   Even from sea to sea and mountain to
      mountain.   River
13 And the earth will become[R]desolate be-
      cause of her inhabitants,   Jer. 25:11
   On account of the fruit of their deeds.

14 [R]Shepherd Thy people with Thy scepter,

The flock of Thy possession   Ps. 95:7
Which dwells by itself in the wood-
   land,
In the midst of [A]a fruitful field.   Carmel
Let them feed in Bashan and Gilead
[R]As in the days of old.   Amos 9:11
15 "As in the days when you came out
      from the land of Egypt,
   I will show[T]you miracles."   him
16 Nations[R]will see and be ashamed
   Of all their might.   Is. 26:11
   They will [R]put their hand on their
      mouth,   Mic. 3:7
   Their ears will be deaf.
17 They[R]will lick the dust like a serpent,
   Like[R]reptiles of the earth.   Deut. 32:24
   They will come[R]trembling out of their
      [T]fortresses;   Ps. 18:45 • fastnesses
   To the LORD our God they will come in
      [T]dread,   Is. 25:3; 59:19
   And they will be afraid before Thee.
18 Who is a God like Thee, who[R]pardons
      iniquity   Ex. 34:7, 9; Is. 43:25
   And passes over the rebellious act of
      the remnant of His possession?
   He does not retain His anger forever,
   Because He [R]delights in [A]unchanging
      love.   Jer. 32:41 • lovingkindness
19 He will again have compassion on us;
   He will tread our iniquities under foot.
   Yes, Thou wilt[R]cast all their sins
   Into the depths of the sea.   [Jer. 31:34]
20 Thou wilt give truth to Jacob
   And unchanging love to Abraham,
   Which Thou didst[R]swear to our forefa-
      thers   [Deut. 7:8, 12]; Luke 1:72 ☆
   From the days of old.

THE BOOK OF
NAHUM

📖 THE BOOK OF NAHUM

"And from everyone who has been given much shall much be required" (Luke 12:48). Nineveh had been given the privilege of knowing the one true God. Under Jonah's preaching this great gentile city had repented, and God had graciously stayed His judgment. However, a hundred years later, Nahum proclaims the downfall of this same city. The Assyrians have forgotten their revival and have returned to their habits of violence, idolatry, and arrogance. As a result Babylon will so destroy the city that no trace of it will remain—a prophecy fulfilled in painful detail.

The Hebrew word *nahum* ("comfort, consolation") is a shortened form of Nehemiah ("Comfort of Yahweh"). The destruction of the capital city of Assyria is a message of comfort and consolation to Judah and all who live in fear of the cruelty of the Assyrians. The title of this book in the Greek and Latin Bibles is *Naoum* and *Nahum*.

✍️ THE AUTHOR OF NAHUM

The only mention of Nahum in the Old Testament is found in 1:1 where he is called an Elkoshite. At least four locations have been proposed for Elkosh: (1) A sixteenth-century tradition identifies Elkosh with Al-qush in Iraq, north of the site of Nineveh on the Tigris River. (2) Jerome believed that Elkesi, a city near Ramah in Galilee, was Elkosh because of the similarity of the consonants. (3) Capernaum means "City of Nahum" (*Kephar-nahum*), and many believe that the name Elkosh was changed to Capernaum in Nahum's honor. (4) Most conservative scholars believe that Elkosh was a city of southern Judah (later called Elcesei) between Jerusalem and Gaza. This would make Nahum a prophet of the southern kingdom and may explain his interest in the triumph of Judah (1:15; 2:2).

⏳ THE TIME OF NAHUM

The fall of Nineveh to the Babylonians in 612 B.C. is seen by Nahum as a future event. Critics who deny predictive prophecy naturally date Nahum after 612 B.C., but this is not based upon exegetical or historical considerations. Nahum 3:8–10 refers to the fall of Thebes as a recent event, so this book must be dated after 664 B.C., the year when

this took place. Thus, Nahum can safely be placed between 663 and 612 B.C. Thebes was restored a decade after its defeat, and Nahum's failure to mention this restoration has led several scholars to the conclusion that Nahum was written before 654 B.C. The fact that Nahum mentions no king in the introduction to his book (1:1) may point to the reign of the wicked King Manasseh (686–642 B.C.).

The conversion of the Ninevites in response to Jonah's message of judgment took place about 760 B.C. The revival was evidently short-lived, because the Assyrians soon returned to their ruthless practices. In 722 B.C., Sargon II of Assyria destroyed Samaria, the capital of the northern kingdom of Israel, and scattered the ten tribes. Led by Sennacherib, the Assyrians also came close to capturing Jerusalem in the reign of King Hezekiah in 701 B.C. By the time of Nahum (c. 660 B.C.), Assyria reached the peak of its prosperity and power under Ashurbanipal (669–633 B.C.). This king extended Assyria's influence farther than had any of his predecessors. Nineveh became the mightiest city on earth with walls 100 feet high and wide enough to accommodate three chariots riding abreast. Dotted around the walls were huge towers that stretched an additional 100 feet above the top of the walls. In addition, the walls were surrounded by a moat 150 feet wide and 60 feet deep. Nineveh appeared impregnable and could withstand a 20-year siege. Thus, Nahum's prophecy of Nineveh's overthrow seemed unlikely indeed.

Assyrian power faded under Ashurbanipal's sons, Ashuretililani (633–629 B.C.) and Sinshar-ishkun (629–612 B.C.). Nahum predicted that Nineveh would end "with an overflowing flood" (1:8), and this is precisely what occurred. The Tigris River overflowed its banks and the flood destroyed part of Nineveh's wall. The Babylonians invaded through this breach in the wall, plundered the city, and set it on fire. Nahum also predicted that Nineveh would "be hidden" (3:11). After its destruction in 612 B.C. the site was not discovered until A.D. 1842.

✝️ THE CHRIST OF NAHUM

While there are no direct messianic prophecies in Nahum, the divine attributes in 1:2–8 are consistent with Christ's work as the Judge of the nations in His second advent.

KEYS TO NAHUM

Key Word: The Judgment of Nineveh—
If ever a city deserved the title "Here to Stay," Nineveh was that city. The great city appeared invincible. But into the scene steps Nahum—a prophet of God's judgment—to declare that Nineveh will fall. Less than half a century later, the prediction of God's spokesman comes true as the great city topples before the Babylonian onslaught, never again to be rebuilt.

Key Verses: Nahum 1:7, 8; 3:5-7—"The LORD is good, a stronghold in the day of trouble, and He knows those who take refuge in Him. But with an overflowing flood He will make a complete end of its site, and will pursue His enemies into darkness" (1:7, 8).

" 'Behold, I am against you,' declares the LORD of hosts; 'and I will lift up your skirts over your face, and show to the nations your nakedness and to the kingdoms your disgrace. I will throw filth on you and make you vile, and set you up as a spectacle. And it will come about that all who see you will shrink from you and say, "Nineveh is devastated! Who will grieve for her?" Where will I seek comforters for you?' " (3:5-7).

Key Chapter: Nahum 1—The first chapter of Nahum records the principles of divine judgment resulting in the decree of the destruction of Nineveh and the deliverance and celebration of Judah. Beginning with 1:9, the single thrust of Nahum's prophecy is the retribution of God upon the wickedness of Nineveh. Nineveh's judgment is irreversibly decreed by the righteous God who will no longer delay His wrath. Assyria's arrogance and cruelty to other nations will come to a sudden end: her power will be useless against the mighty hand of Yahweh.

Nahum 1:2-8 portrays the patience, power,

holiness, and justice of the living God. He is slow to wrath, but God settles His accounts in full. This book concerns the downfall of Assyria, but it is written for the benefit of the surviving kingdom of Judah (Israel had already been swallowed up by Assyria). The people in Judah who trust in the Lord will be comforted to hear of God's judgment upon the proud and brutal Assyrians (1:15; 2:2).

SURVEY OF NAHUM

When God finally convinces His prophet Jonah to preach to the people of Nineveh, the whole city responds with repentance and Nineveh escapes destruction. The people humble themselves before the one true God, but their humility soon changes to arrogance as Assyria reaches its zenith as the most powerful empire in the world. About a century after the preaching of Jonah, God calls Nahum to proclaim the coming destruction of Nineveh. This time there will be no escape, because their measure of wickedness is full. Unlike Jonah, Nahum does not go to the city but declares his oracle from afar. There is no hope of repentance. Nineveh's destruction is decreed (1), described (2), and deserved (3).

The Destruction of Nineveh Is Decreed (1): Nahum begins with a very clear description of the character of Yahweh. Because of His righteousness, He is a God of vengeance (1:2). God is also characterized by patience (1:3) and power (1:3-6). He is gracious to all who respond to Him, but those who rebel against Him will be overthrown (1:7, 8). God is holy, and Nineveh stands condemned because of her sins (1:9-14). Nothing can stand in the way of judgment, and this is a message of comfort to the people of Judah (1:15). The threat of Assyrian invasion will soon be over.

FOCUS	DESTRUCTION OF NINEVEH DECREED		DESTRUCTION OF NINEVEH DESCRIBED		DESTRUCTION OF NINEVEH DESERVED	
REFERENCE	1:1————————1:9————		2:1————————2:3————		3:1————————3:12————3:19	
DIVISION	GENERAL PRINCIPLES OF DIVINE JUDGMENT	DESTRUCTION OF NINEVEH AND DELIVERANCE OF JUDAH	THE CALL TO BATTLE	DESCRIPTION OF THE DESTRUCTION OF NINEVEH	REASONS FOR THE DESTRUCTION OF NINEVEH	INEVITABLE DESTRUCTION OF NINEVEH
TOPIC	VERDICT OF VENGEANCE		VISION OF VENGEANCE		VINDICATION OF VENGEANCE	
	WHAT GOD WILL DO		HOW GOD WILL DO IT		WHY GOD WILL DO IT	
LOCATION	IN JUDAH AGAINST NINEVEH, CAPITAL OF ASSYRIA					
TIME	C. 660 B.C.					

The Destruction of Nineveh Is Described (2): Assyria will be conquered, but Judah will be restored (2:1, 2). Nahum's description of the siege of Nineveh (2:3–7) and the sack of Nineveh (2:8–13) is one of the most vivid portraits of battle in Scripture. The storming warriors and chariots can almost be seen as they enter the city through a breach in the wall. As the Ninevites flee in terror, the invading army plunders the treasures of the city. Nineveh is burned and cut off forever.

The Destruction of Nineveh Is Deserved (3): Nahum closes his brief book of judgment with God's reasons for Nineveh's coming overthrow. The city is characterized by cruelty and corruption (3:1–7). Just as Assyria crushed the Egyptian capital city of Thebes (No-amon), Assyria's capital city will also be destroyed (3:8–10). Nineveh is fortified so well that defeat seems impossible, but God proclaims that its destruction is inevitable (3:11–19). None of its resources can deter divine judgment.

OUTLINE OF NAHUM

CHAPTER 1

God's Vengeance in Judgment

T HE ¹oracle^R of Nineveh. The book of the vision of Nahum the Elkoshite.   Is. 13:1; 19:1

2 A ^{R}jealous and avenging God is the LORD;   Ex. 20:5; Josh. 24:19
The LORD is avenging and wrathful.
The LORD takes ^{R}vengeance on His adversaries,   Ps. 94:1
And He reserves wrath for His enemies.

God's Power in Judgment

3 The LORD is ^{R}slow to anger and great in power,   Ex. 34:6, 7; Neh. 9:17; Ps. 103:8
And the LORD will by no means leave *the guilty* unpunished.
In whirlwind and storm is His way,
And ^{R}clouds are the dust beneath His feet.   Ps. 104:3; Is. 19:1
4 He rebukes the sea and makes it dry;
He dries up all the rivers.
^{R}Bashan and Carmel wither;   Is. 33:9
The blossoms of Lebanon wither.
5 Mountains quake because of Him,
And the hills ^{R}dissolve;   Mic. 1:4
Indeed the earth is ^{R}upheaved by His presence,   Is. 24:1, 20
The world and all the inhabitants in it.
6 Who can stand before His indignation?
Who can endure the ^{R}burning of His anger?   Is. 13:13
His wrath is poured out like fire,

And the rocks are broken up by Him.
7 The LORD is ^{R}good,   Ps. 25:8; 37:39, 40
A stronghold in the day of trouble,
And ^{R}He knows those who take refuge in Him.   Ps. 1:6; John 10:14; 2 Tim. 2:19
8 But with an ^{R}overflowing flood Amos 8:8
He will make a complete end of its site,
And will pursue His enemies into ^{R}darkness.   Is. 13:9, 10

The Destruction of Nineveh and Deliverance of Judah

9 Whatever you devise against the LORD,
He will make a complete end of it.
Distress will not rise up twice.
10 Like tangled ^{R}thorns,   2 Sam. 23:6; Mic. 7:4
And like those who are ^{R}drunken with their drink,   Is. 56:12; Nah. 3:11
They are ^{R}consumed   Mal. 4:1
As stubble completely withered.
11 From you has gone forth
One who plotted evil against the LORD,
A ^{A}wicked counselor. *worthless:* Heb., *Belial*
12 Thus says the LORD,
"Though they are at full *strength* and likewise many,
Even so, they will be ^{R}cut off and pass away.   Is. 10:16-19, 33, 34
Though I have afflicted you,
I will afflict you ^{R}no longer.   Lam. 3:31, 32
13 "So now, I will ^{R}break his yoke bar from upon you,   Is. 9:4; 10:27; Jer. 2:20
And I will tear off your shackles."

¹ Or, *burden*

14 The LORD has issued a command con-
cerning you: the king of Nineveh
"Your name will no longer be perpet-
uated. *No more of your name will be sown*
I will cut off idol and image
From the house of your gods.
I will prepare your grave, Ezek. 32:22, 23
For you are contemptible."

15 Behold, on the mountains the feet of
him who brings good news,
Who announces peace!   Rom. 10:15
Celebrate your feasts, O Judah;
Pay your vows.
For never again will the wicked one
pass through you;   Is. 52:1; Joel 3:17
He is cut off completely.   Is. 29:7, 8

CHAPTER 2

The Call to Battle

THE one who scatters has come up
against you.   *your face*
Man the fortress, watch the road;
Strengthen your back, summon all
your strength.   *Make strong your loins*
2 For the LORD will restore the splendor
of Jacob   Is. 60:15
Like the splendor of Israel,
Even though devastators have devastated them
And destroyed their vine branches.

The Destruction of Nineveh

3 The shields of his mighty men are col-
ored red,   those attacking Nineveh
The warriors are dressed in scarlet,
The chariots are *enveloped* in flashing
steel   *fire of steel*
When he is prepared *to march*,
And the cypress *spears* are brandished.
4 The chariots race madly in the streets,
They rush wildly in the squares,
Their appearance is like torches,
They dash to and fro like lightning
flashes.   *broad places*
5 He remembers his nobles;   Nah. 3:18
They stumble in their march, Jer. 46:12
They hurry to her wall,
And the mantelet is set up.
6 The gates of the rivers are opened,
And the palace is dissolved.
7 And it is fixed:
She is stripped, she is carried away,
And her handmaids are moaning like
the sound of doves,   Is. 38:14; 59:11
Beating on their breasts.   *hearts*

8 Though Nineveh *was* like a pool of wa-
ter throughout her days,
Now they are fleeing;
"Stop, stop,"

But no one turns back.   Jer. 46:5; 47:3
9 Plunder the silver!
Plunder the gold!   Rev. 18:12, 16
For there is no limit to the treasure—
Wealth from every kind of desirable
object.
10 She is emptied! Yes, she is desolate
and waste!   Is. 24:1; 34:10-13; Nah. 2:2
Hearts are melting and knees knock-
ing!   Ps. 22:14; Is. 13:7, 8; Ezek. 21:7
Also anguish is in the whole body,
And all their faces are grown pale!
11 Where is the den of the lions
And the feeding place of the young
lions,   Is. 5:29
Where the lion, lioness, and lion's cub
prowled,
With nothing to disturb *them*?
12 The lion tore enough for his cubs,
Killed *enough* for his lionesses,
And filled his lairs with prey *Strangled*
And his dens with torn flesh.
13 "Behold, I am against you," declares the
LORD of hosts. "I will burn up her chariots in
smoke, a sword will devour your young
lions, I will cut off your prey from the land,
and no longer will the voice of your messengers be heard."   Jer. 21:13; Ezek. 5:8; Nah. 3:5

CHAPTER 3

Nineveh's Great Ungodliness

WOE to the bloody city, completely full of
lies *and* pillage;   Ezek. 24:6, 9
Her prey never departs.
2 The noise of the whip,   Job 39:22-25
The noise of the rattling of the wheel,
Galloping horses,
And bounding chariots!   *skipping*
3 Horsemen charging,
Swords flashing, spears gleaming,
Many slain, a mass of corpses, Is. 34:3
And countless dead bodies— Ezek. 39:4
They stumble over the dead bodies!
4 *All* because of the many harlotries of
the harlot,   Ezek. 16:25-29; Rev. 17:1, 2
The charming one, the mistress of sor-
ceries,   Is. 47:9, 12, 13
Who sells nations by her harlotries
And families by her sorceries. Rev. 18:3
5 "Behold, I am against you," declares the
LORD of hosts;   Jer. 50:31; Ezek. 26:3
"And I will lift up your skirts over your
face,   *uncover your* · Is. 47:2, 3
And show to the nations your naked-
ness   Ezek. 16:37
And to the kingdoms your disgrace.
6 "I will throw filth on you *detestable things*
And make you vile,   Job 30:8; Mal. 2:9
And set you up as a spectacle. Is. 14:16
7 "And it will come about that all who see
you

Will [T]shrink from you and say,　　*flee*
'Nineveh is devastated!
[R]Who will grieve for her?'　　Is. 51:19
Where will I seek comforters for you?''

Comparison of Nineveh to No-amon

8 Are you better than [2]No-amon,
　Which was situated by the [R]waters of
　　the Nile,　　Is. 19:6-8
　With water surrounding her,
　Whose rampart *was* [T]the sea,　*the Nile*
　Whose wall *consisted* of the sea?
9 [R]Ethiopia was *her* might,　　Is. 20:5
　And Egypt too, without limits.
　Put and [R]Lubim were among [T]her help-
　　ers.　　2 Chr. 12:3; 16:8 • *your*
10 Yet she [R]became an exile,　Is. 19:4; 20:4
　She went into captivity;
　Also her [R]small children were dashed to
　　pieces　Ps. 137:9; Is. 13:16; Hos. 13:16
　[R]At the head of every street;　Lam. 2:19
　They [R]cast lots for her honorable men,
　And all her great men were bound with
　　fetters.　　Joel 3:3; Obad. 11
11 You too will become [R]drunk,　Is. 49:26
　You will be [R]hidden.　Is. 2:10, 19; Hos. 10:8
　You too will search for a refuge from
　　the enemy.

Nineveh's Strongholds Are Weak

12 All your fortifications are [R]fig trees with
　　[T]ripe fruit—　　Rev. 6:13 • *first fruits*
　When shaken, they fall into the eater's
　　mouth.
13 Behold, your people are [R]women in your
　　midst!　　Is. 19:16; Jer. 50:37; 51:30
　The gates of your land are [R]opened wide
　　to your enemies;　Is. 45:1, 2; Nah. 2:6
　Fire consumes your gate bars.

14 Draw for yourself water for the siege!
　[R]Strengthen your fortifications!　Nah. 2:1
　Go into the clay and tread the mortar!
　Take hold of the brick mold!
15 There fire will consume you,
　The sword will cut you down;
　It will consume you as the locust *does*.

Multiply yourself like the creeping lo-
　cust,
Multiply yourself like the swarming lo-
　cust.

Nineveh's Leaders Are Weak

16 You have increased your [R]traders more
　　than the stars of heaven—　Is. 23:8
　The creeping locust [T]strips and flies
　　away.　　*strips vegetation; or, molts*
17 Your [R]guardsmen are like the swarming
　　locust.　　*officials* • Rev. 9:7
　Your [R]marshals are like hordes of grass-
　　hoppers　　Jer. 51:27
　Settling in the stone walls on a cold
　　day.
　The sun rises and they flee,
　And the place where they are is not
　　known.
18 Your shepherds are [R]sleeping, O king of
　　Assyria;　Ps. 76:5, 6; Is. 56:10; Jer. 51:57
　Your [T]nobles are lying down.　Nah. 2:5
　Your people are [R]scattered on the
　　mountains,　　1 Kin. 22:17; Is. 13:14
　And there is no one to regather *them*.
19 There is no relief for your breakdown,
　Your [R]wound is incurable.　　Jer. 30:12
　All who hear [T]about you　　*your report*
　Will clap *their* hands over you,
　For on whom has not your evil passed
　　continually?

[2] I.e., the city of Amon: Thebes

THE BOOK OF

HABAKKUK

THE BOOK OF HABAKKUK

Habakkuk ministers during the "death throes" of the nation of Judah. Although repeatedly called to repentance, the nation stubbornly refuses to change her sinful ways. Habakkuk, knowing the hardheartedness of his countrymen, asks God how long this intolerable condition can continue. God replies that the Babylonians will be His chastening rod upon the nation—an announcement that sends the prophet to his knees. He acknowledges that the righteous in any generation shall live by faith (2:4), not by sight. Habakkuk concludes by praising God's wisdom even though he doesn't fully understand God's ways.

Habaqquq is an unusual Hebrew name derived from the verb *habaq*, "embrace." Thus his name probably means "One Who Embraces" or "Clings." At the end of his book this name becomes appropriate because Habakkuk chooses to cling firmly to God regardless of what happens to his nation (3:16–19). The Greek title in the Septuagint is *Ambakouk*, and the Latin title in Jerome's Vulgate is *Habacuc*.

THE AUTHOR OF HABAKKUK

In the introduction to the book (1:1) and in the closing psalm (3:1), the author identifies himself as Habakkuk the prophet. This special designation seems to indicate that Habakkuk was a professional prophet. The closing statement at the end of the psalm ("For the choir director, on my stringed instruments") suggests that Habakkuk may have been a priest connected with the temple worship in Jerusalem. He mentions nothing of his genealogy or location, but speculative attempts have been made to identify him with certain unnamed Old Testament characters. In the apocryphal book of Bel and the Dragon, Daniel is rescued a second time by the prophet Habakkuk.

THE TIME OF HABAKKUK

The only explicit time reference in Habakkuk is to the Babylonian invasion as an imminent event (1:6; 2:1; 3:16). Some scholars suggest Habakkuk was written during the reign of Manasseh (686–642 B.C.) or Amon (642–640 B.C.) because of the list of Judah's sins in 1:2–4. However, the description of the Chaldeans indicate that Babylon had become a world power; and this was not true in the time of Manasseh when Babylon was under the thumb of Assyria. It is also unlikely that this prophecy took place in the time of King Josiah (640–609 B.C.), because the moral and spiritual reforms of Josiah do not fit the situation in 1:2–4. The most likely date for the book is in the early part of Jehoiakim's reign (609–597 B.C.). Jehoiakim was a godless king who led the nation down the path of destruction (cf. 2 Kin. 23:34—24:5; Jer. 22:17).

The Babylonians began to rise in power during the reign of Nabopolassar (626–605 B.C.), and in 612 B.C. they destroyed the Assyrian capital of Nineveh. By the time of Jehoiakim, Babylon was the uncontested world power. Nabopolassar's successor, Nebuchadnezzar, came to power in 605 B.C. and carried out successful military expeditions in the west, advancing into Palestine and Egypt. Nebuchadnezzar's first invasion of Judah occurred in his first year, when he deported ten thousand of Jerusalem's leaders to Babylon. The nobles who oppressed and extorted from the poor were the first to be carried away. Since Habakkuk prophesied prior to the Babylonian invasion, the probable date for this book is about 607 B.C.

THE CHRIST OF HABAKKUK

The word *salvation* appears three times in 3:13, 18 and is the root word from which the name *Jesus* is derived (cf. Matt. 1:21). When He comes again, "the earth will be filled with the knowledge of the glory of the LORD, as the waters cover the sea" (2:14).

KEYS TO HABAKKUK

Key Word: "The Righteous Will Live by His Faith"—The circumstances of life sometimes appear to contradict God's revelation concerning His power and purposes. Habakkuk struggles in his faith when he sees men flagrantly violate God's law and distort justice on every level, without fear of divine intervention. He wants to know why God allows this growing iniquity to go unpunished. When God reveals His intention to use Babylon as His rod of judgment, Habakkuk is even more troubled, because that nation is more corrupt than Judah. God's answer satisfies Habakkuk that he can trust Him even in the worst of circumstances because of His match-

less wisdom, goodness, and power. God's plan is perfect, and nothing is big enough to stand in the way of its ultimate fulfillment. In spite of appearances to the contrary, God is still on the throne as the Lord of history and the Ruler of the nations. God may be slow to wrath, but all iniquity will be punished eventually. He is the worthiest object of faith, and the righteous man will trust in Him at all times.

Key Verses: Habakkuk 2:4; 3:17–19— "Behold, as for the proud one, his soul is not right within him; but the righteous will live by his faith" (2:4).

"Though the fig tree should not blossom, and there be no fruit on the vines, *though* the yield of the olive should fail, and the fields produce no food, though the flock should be cut off from the fold, and there be no cattle in the stalls, yet I will exult in the LORD, I will rejoice in the God of my salvation. The Lord GOD is my strength, and He has made my feet like hinds' *feet*, and makes me walk on my high places" (3:17–19).

Key Chapter: Habakkuk 3—The Book of Habakkuk builds to a triumphant climax reached in the last three verses (3:17–19). The beginning of the book and the ending stand in stark contrast: mystery to certainty, questioning to affirming, and complaint to confidence. Chapter 3 is one of the most majestic of all Scriptures and records the glory of God in past history and in future history (prophecy).

SURVEY OF HABAKKUK

Habakkuk is a freethinking prophet who is not afraid to wrestle with issues that test his faith. He openly and honestly directs his problems to God and waits to see how He will respond to his probing questions. After two rounds of dialogue with the Lord, Habakkuk's increased understanding of the per-

son, power, and plan of God cause him to conclude with a psalm of unqualified praise. The more he knows about the Planner, the more he can trust His plans. No matter what God brings to pass, "the righteous will live by his faith" (2:4). The two divisions of this book are: the problems of Habakkuk (1 and 2) and the praise of Habakkuk (3).

The Problems of Habakkuk (1 and 2): Habakkuk's first dialogue with God takes place in 1:1–11. In 1:1–4, the prophet asks God how long He will allow the wickedness of Judah to go unpunished. The people of Judah sin with impunity, and justice is perverted. God's startling answer is given in 1:5–11: He is raising up the fierce Babylonians as His rod of judgment upon sinful Judah. The Chaldeans will come against Judah swiftly, violently, and completely. The coming storm from the east will be God's answer to Judah's crimes.

This answer leads to Habakkuk's second dialogue with God (1:12—2:20). The prophet is more perplexed than ever and asks how the righteous God can punish Judah with a nation that is even more wicked (1:12—2:1). Will the God whose eyes are too pure to approve evil reward the Babylonians for their cruelty and idolatry? Habakkuk stands upon a watchtower to wait for God's reply. The Lord answers with a series of five woes—of greed and aggression (2:5–8), exploitation and extortion (2:9–11), violence (2:12–14), immorality (2:15–17), and idolatry (2:18–20). God is aware of the sins of the Babylonians, and they will not escape His terrible judgment. But Judah is guilty of the same offenses and stands under the same condemnation. Yahweh concludes His answer with a statement of His sovereign majesty: "But the LORD is in His holy temple. Let all the earth be silent before Him" (2:20).

FOCUS	PROBLEMS OF HABAKKUK				PRAISE OF HABAKKUK
REFERENCE	1:1————————1:5————————		1:12————————2:2————————		3:1————————3:19
DIVISION	FIRST PROBLEM OF HABAKKUK	FIRST REPLY OF GOD	SECOND PROBLEM OF HABAKKUK	SECOND REPLY OF GOD	PRAYER OF PRAISE OF HABAKKUK
TOPIC	FAITH TROUBLED				FAITH TRIUMPHANT
	WHAT GOD IS DOING				WHO GOD IS
LOCATION	THE NATION OF JUDAH				
TIME	c. 607 B.C.				

The Praise of Habakkuk (3): Habakkuk begins by questioning God, but he concludes his book with a psalm of praise for the person (3:1–3), power (3:4–12), and plan (3:13–19) of God. He now acknowledges God's wisdom in the coming invasion of Judah, and although it terrifies him, he will trust the Lord. God's creative and redemptive work in the past gives the prophet confidence in the divine purposes, and hope at a time when he would otherwise despair. "Yet I will exult in the LORD, I will rejoice in the God of my salvation" (3:18).

OUTLINE OF HABAKKUK

CHAPTER 1

The First Problem of Habakkuk

THE ¹oracle^R which Habakkuk the prophet saw.   Is. 13:1; Nah. 1:1

2 ^RHow long, O LORD, will I call for help,
And Thou wilt not hear?   Ps. 13:1, 2
I cry out to Thee, "Violence!"
Yet Thou dost^Rnot save.   Jer. 14:9

3 Why dost Thou make me see iniquity,
And cause *me* to look on wickedness?
Yes, ^Rdestruction and violence are before me;   Jer. 20:8
Strife exists and contention arises.

4 Therefore, the^Rlaw is ignored Ps. 58:1, 2
And justice is never upheld.
For the wicked surround the righteous;
Therefore, justice comes out perverted.

God's First Reply

5 "Look among the nations! Observe!
Be astonished!^RWonder!   Is. 29:9
Because *I* am doing^Rsomething in your
days—   Is. 29:14; Ezek. 12:22-28

¹ Or, *burden*

You would not believe if you were told.
6 "For behold, I am^Rraising up the Chaldeans,   2 Kin. 24:2; Jer. 4:11–13
That^Tfierce and impetuous people *bitter*
Who march throughout the earth
To ^Tseize^Rdwelling places which are not
theirs.   *take possession of* • Jer. 8:10
7 "They are dreaded and^Rfeared. Is. 18:2, 7
Their justice and ^Tauthority originate
with themselves.   *eminence*
8 "Their horses are swifter than leopards
And keener than wolves in the evening.
Their horsemen come galloping,
Their horsemen come from afar;
They fly like an^Reagle swooping *down*
to devour.   Ezek. 17:3; Hos. 8:1
9 "All of them come for violence.
Their horde of faces *moves* forward.
They collect captives like sand.
10 "They^Rmock at kings,   2 Chr. 36:6, 10
And rulers are a laughing matter to
them.
They^Rlaugh at every fortress,   Is. 10:9
And heap up rubble to capture it.
11 "Then they will sweep through *like* the
^Rwind and pass on.   Jer. 4:11, 12
But they will be held^Rguilty,   Jer. 2:3
They whose strength is their god."

1:2 Sources of Doubt—One of the most potent sources of doubt is introduced in the early chapters of Genesis. It is Satan himself who causes Eve to doubt God by questioning His Word: "Indeed, has God said, 'You shall not eat from any tree of the garden?' " (Page 6—Gen. 3:1). Satan even tries to get the long-suffering Job to curse God (Page 495—Job 1:11). Satan is said to be seeking to devour Christians (Page 1264—1 Pet. 5:8). This statement must not be taken literally, but means that Satan wants to devour the Christian's commitment to God and testimony before others. One way he does this is by introducing doubt into the mind.
    The world system is another source of doubt. Since it has its own set of values and objectives that are opposed to God, it also has its own worldly wisdom (Page 1150—1 Cor. 2:6). This wisdom stands in direct opposition to the wisdom of God taught by the Holy Spirit (Page 1150—1 Cor. 2:13). It is clearly revealed, for example, in the opposition of the evolutionary theory to the truth of the creation of man (Page 1220—1 Tim. 6:20).
    Probably the greatest source of doubt Christians face is simply their own spiritual immaturity. James traces doubting in prayer to double-mindedness and instability (Page 1253—James 1:8). Paul explains that when Christians doubt sound doctrine, it is because they are children in the faith and thus are easily deceived (Page 1187—Eph. 4:14). Conquering this kind of doubt demands a growing, obedient relationship with God.
    Now turn to Page 345—1 Kin. 18:21: Cure for Doubt.

The Second Problem of Habakkuk

12 Art Thou not from everlasting,
O LORD, my God, my Holy One?
We will not die.
Thou, O LORD, hast ᴿappointed them to
judge;   Is. 10:5, 6; Mal. 3:5
And Thou, O ᴿRock, hast established
them to correct.   Deut. 32:4
13 *Thine* eyes are too pure to ᵀapprove evil,
And Thou canst not look on wicked-
ness *with favor.*   *look at*
Why dost Thou look with favor
On those who deal treacherously?
Why art Thou ᴿsilent when the wicked
ᴿswallow up   Ps. 50:21 • Ps. 35:25
Those more righteous than they?
14 *Why* hast Thou made men like the fish
of the sea,
Like creeping things without a ruler
over them?
15 *The Chaldeans* ᴿbring all of them up
with a hook,   Jer. 16:16; Amos 4:2
Drag them away with their net,
And gather them together in their fishing net.
Therefore, they rejoice and are glad.
16 Therefore, they offer a sacrifice to their
net.
And burn incense to their fishing net;
Because through these things their
catch is ᵀlarge,   *fat; or, plentiful*
And their food is ᵀplentiful.   *the fat portion*
17 Will they therefore empty their net
And continually ᴿslay nations without
sparing?   Is. 14:5, 6

CHAPTER 2

I WILL ᴿstand on my guard post   Is. 21:8
And station myself on the rampart;
And I will ᴿkeep watch to see ᵀwhat He
will speak to me,   Ps. 5:3 • Ps. 85:8
And how I may reply ᵀwhen I am re-
proved.   *upon my reproof*

God's Second Reply

2 Then the LORD answered me and said,
"Record ᴿthe vision   Deut. 27:8; Rom. 15:4
And inscribe *it* on tablets,
That the one who reads it may run.
3 "For the vision is yet for the ᵃappointed
time;   Dan. 8:17, 19; 10:14
It ᵀhastens toward the goal, and it will
not ᴬfail.   *pants • lie*
Though it tarries, ᴿwait for it;   Ps. 27:14
For it will certainly come, it ᴿwill not
delay.   Ezek. 12:25; [Heb. 10:37]
4 "Behold, as for the ᴿproud one,   Ps. 49:18
His soul is not right within him;
But the righteous will live by his faith.
5 "Furthermore, ᴿwine betrays the ᴿhaughty
man,   Prov. 20:1 • Prov. 21:24
So that he does not stay at home.
He enlarges his appetite like Sheol,
And he is like death, never satisfied.

He also gathers to himself all nations
And collects to himself all peoples.

6 "Will not all of these ᴿtake up a taunt-
song against him,   Is. 14:4-10
Even mockery *and* insinuations
against him,
And say, 'Woe ᴿto him who increases
what is not his—   Hab. 2:12
For how long—
And makes himself rich with loans?'
7 "Will not ᵀyour creditors ᴿrise up suddenly,   *those who bite you* • Prov. 29:1
And those who ᵀcollect from you
awaken?   *violently shake you*
Indeed, you will become plunder for
them.
8 "Because you have ᴿlooted many nations,
All the remainder of the peoples will
loot you—   Is. 33:1; Jer. 27:7; Zech. 2:8
Because of human bloodshed and vio-
lence done to the land,
To the town and all its inhabitants.

9 "Woe to him who gets ᴿevil gain for his
house   Jer. 22:13; Ezek. 22:27
To ᴿput his nest on high   Jer. 49:16
To be delivered from the hand of calamity!
10 "You have devised a ᴿshameful thing for
your house   2 Kin. 9:26; Nah. 1:14
By cutting off many peoples;
So you are sinning against yourself.
11 "Surely the ᴿstone will cry out from the
wall,   Josh. 24:27; Luke 19:40
And the rafter will answer it from the
ᵀframework.   *wood*

12 "Woe to him who ᴿbuilds a city with
bloodshed   Mic. 3:10; Nah. 3:1
And founds a town with violence!
13 "Is it not indeed from the LORD of hosts
That peoples ᴿtoil for fire,   Is. 50:11
And nations grow weary for nothing?
14 "For the earth will be ᴿfilled   [Ps. 22:27]
With the knowledge of the glory of the
LORD,
As the waters cover the sea.

15 "Woe to you who make ᵀyour neighbors
drink,   *his neighbor*
Who mix in your venom even to make
them drunk
So as to look on their nakedness!
16 "You will be filled with disgrace rather
than honor.
Now you yourself ᴿdrink and expose
your *own* nakedness.   Lam. 4:21
The ᴿcup in the LORD's right hand will
come around to you,   Jer. 25:15, 17
And ᴿutter disgrace *will come* upon
your glory.   Nah. 3:6
17 "For the ᴿviolence done to Lebanon will
ᵀoverwhelm you,   Joel 3:19 • *cover*
And the devastation of *its* beasts by
which you terrified them,
Because of human bloodshed and ᴿviolence done to the land,   Jer. 51:35

To the town and all its inhabitants.

18 "What profit is the ^Aidol when its maker
has carved it,   *a graven image*
Or an image, a teacher of falsehood?
For *its* maker ^Rtrusts in his *own* handi-
work   Ps. 115:4, 8
When he fashions speechless idols.
19 "Woe to him who ^Rsays to a *piece of*
wood, 'Awake!'   Jer. 2:27, 28; 10:3
To a dumb stone, 'Arise!'
And that is *your* teacher?
Behold, it is overlaid with ^Rgold and sil-
ver,   Ps. 135:15-18; Jer. 10:4, 9, 14
And there is no breath at all inside it.
20 "But the LORD is in His holy temple.
Let all the earth be silent before Him.''

CHAPTER 3

Habakkuk Prays for God's Mercy

A PRAYER of Habakkuk the prophet, according to ²Shigionoth.
2 LORD, I have ^Rheard ^Athe report about
Thee *and* I fear.   Job 42:5 • *Thy report*
O LORD, ^Rrevive Thy work in the midst
of the years,   Ps. 71:20; 85:6
In the midst of the years make it
known;
In wrath remember ^Amercy.   *compassion*

The Glory of the Person of God

3 God comes from ^RTeman,   Jer. 49:7
And the Holy One from Mount Pa-
ran.   [Selah.
His splendor covers the heavens,
And the earth is full of His praise.
4 *His* radiance is like the sunlight;
He has rays *flashing* from His hand,
And there is the hiding of His power.

The Power of the Saving Acts of God

5 Before Him goes pestilence,
And plague comes after Him. *at His feet*
6 He stood and surveyed the earth;
He looked and startled the nations.
Yes, the perpetual mountains were
shattered,
The ancient hills collapsed.
His ways are ^Reverlasting.   Hab. 1:12
7 I saw the tents of Cushan under ^Adis-
tress,   Ex. 15:14-16
The tent curtains of the land of ^RMidian
were trembling.   Num. 31:7, 8

8 Did the LORD rage against the rivers,
Or *was* Thine anger against the rivers,
Or *was* Thy wrath against the sea,

That Thou didst ride on Thy horses,
On Thy ^Rchariots of salvation?   Ps. 68:17
9 Thy ^Rbow was made bare,   Ps. 7:12, 13
The rods of chastisement were
sworn.   [Selah.
Thou didst cleave the earth with rivers.
10 The mountains saw Thee *and* quaked;
The downpour of waters swept by.
The deep ^Ruttered forth its voice,
It lifted high its hands.   Ps. 93:3; 98:7, 8
11 Sun *and* moon stood in their places;
They went away at the ^Rlight of Thine
arrows,   Ps. 18:14
At the radiance of Thy gleaming spear.
12 In indignation Thou didst ^Amarch
through the earth;   Ps. 68:7
In anger Thou didst ^Atrample ^Rthe na-
tions.   *thresh* • Is. 41:15; Jer. 51:33
13 Thou didst go forth for the ^Rsalvation of
Thy people,   Ex. 15:2; 2 Sam. 5:20
For the salvation of Thine anointed.
Thou didst strike the ^Rhead of the house
of the evil   Ps. 68:21; 110:6
To lay him open from thigh to
neck.   [Selah.
14 Thou didst pierce with his own ^Tspears
The head of his throngs.   *shafts*
They stormed in to scatter ^Tus;   *me*
Their exultation *was* like those
Who devour the oppressed in secret.
15 Thou didst ^Rtread on the sea with Thy
horses,   Ps. 77:19; Hab. 3:8
On the ^Rsurge of many waters.   Ex. 15:8

Habakkuk Trusts in God's Salvation

16 I heard and my inward parts trembled,
At the sound my lips quivered.
Decay enters my ^Rbones,   Job 30:17, 30
And in my place I tremble.
Because I must ^Rwait quietly for the day
of distress,   Luke 21:19
^AFor the people to arise *who* will invade
us.   *To come upon the people who will*
17 Though the ^Rfig tree should not blos-
som,   Joel 1:10-12; Amos 4:9
And there be no fruit on the vines,
Though the yield of the ^Rolive should
fail,   Mic. 6:15
And the fields produce no food,
Though the ^Rflock should be cut off
from the fold,   Joel 1:18
And there be no cattle in the stalls,
18 Yet I will ^Rexult in the LORD,   Ex. 15:1, 2
I will ^Rrejoice in the ^RGod of my salvation.   Ps. 46:1-5; Phil. 4:4 • Ps. 25:5
19 The Lord GOD is my strength,
And ^RHe has made my feet like hinds'
feet,   2 Sam. 22:34
And makes me walk on my ^Rhigh
places.   Deut. 33:29

For the choir director, on my stringed
instruments.

² I.e., A highly emotional poetic form

THE BOOK OF
ZEPHANIAH

THE BOOK OF ZEPHANIAH

During Judah's hectic political and religious history, reform comes from time to time. Zephaniah's forceful prophecy may be a factor in the reform that occurs during Josiah's reign—a "revival" that produces outward change, but does not fully remove the inward heart of corruption which characterizes the nation. Zephaniah hammers home his message repeatedly that the day of the Lord, judgment day, is coming when the malignancy of sin will be dealt with. Israel and her gentile neighbors will soon experience the crushing hand of God's wrath. But after the chastening process is complete, blessing will come in the person of the Messiah, who will be the cause for praise and singing.

Tsephan-yah means "Yahweh Hides" or "Yahweh Has Hidden." Zephaniah was evidently born during the latter part of the reign of King Manasseh. His name may mean that he was "hidden" from Manasseh's atrocities. The Greek and Latin title is *Sophonias*.

THE AUTHOR OF ZEPHANIAH

The first verse is very unusual in that Zephaniah traces his lineage back four generations to Hezekiah. This is probably Hezekiah the king of Judah, since this would best explain the genealogy. If Zephaniah was the great-great-grandson of the godly King Hezekiah, he was the only prophet of royal descent. This may have given the prophet freer access to the court of King Josiah in whose reign he ministered. Because Zephaniah used the phrase "this place" (1:4) to refer to Jerusalem and was quite familiar with its features (cf. 1:9, 10; 3:1–7), he was probably an inhabitant of Judah's royal city.

THE TIME OF ZEPHANIAH

Zephaniah solves the dating problem by fixing his prophecy "in the days of Josiah the son of Amon, king of Judah" (1:1). Josiah reigned from 640 to 609 B.C., and 2:13 indicates that the destruction of Nineveh (612 B.C.) was still a future event. Thus, Zephaniah's prophecy can be dated between 640 and 612 B.C.

However, the sins catalogued in 1:3–13 and 3:1–7 indicate a date prior to Josiah's reforms when the sins from the reigns of Manasseh and Amon still predominated. It is therefore likely that Zephaniah's ministry played a significant role in preparing Judah for the revivals that took place in the reign of the nation's last righteous king. Josiah became king of Judah at the age of eight, and by the age of sixteen his heart had already begun to turn toward God. His first reform took place in the twelfth year of his reign (628 B.C., 2 Chr. 34:3–7) when he tore down all the altars of Baal, destroyed the foreign incense altars, burned the bones of the false prophets on their altars, and broke the Asherim (carved images) and molten images in pieces. Six years later (622 B.C.), Josiah's second reform was kindled when Hilkiah the priest found the Book of the Law in the temple (2 Chr. 34:8—35:19). Thus, Zephaniah's prophecy can be dated more precisely as occurring between 630 and 625 B.C.

The evil reigns of Manasseh and Amon (a total of fifty-five years) had such a profound effect upon Judah that it never recovered. Josiah's reforms were too little and too late, and the people reverted to their crass idolatry and teaching soon after Josiah was gone. As a contemporary of Jeremiah and Habakkuk, Zephaniah was one of the eleventh-hour prophets to Judah.

THE CHRIST OF ZEPHANIAH

Jesus alluded to Zephaniah on two occasions (cf. Zeph. 1:3; Matt. 13:41 and cf. Zeph. 1:15; Matt. 24:29). Both of these passages about the day of the Lord are associated with Christ's second advent. Although the Messiah is not specifically mentioned in Zephaniah, it is clear that He is the One who will fulfill the great promises of 3:9–20. He will gather His people and reign in victory: "The LORD has taken away *His* judgments against you, He has cleared away your enemies. The King of Israel, the LORD, is in your midst; you will fear disaster no more" (3:15).

KEYS TO ZEPHANIAH

Key Word: The Day of the Lord— Zephaniah discusses the day of the Lord and describes the coming day of judgment upon Judah and the nations. God is holy and must vindicate His righteousness by calling all the nations of the world into account before Him. The sovereign God will judge not only His own people but also the whole world: no one escapes from His authority and domin-

ion. The day of the Lord will have universal impact. To some degree, that day has already come for Judah and all the nations mentioned in 2:4–15, but there is also a future aspect, when all the earth will be judged. Zephaniah 3:9–20 speaks of another side of the day of the Lord: it will be a day of blessing after the judgment is complete. A righteous remnant will survive and all who call upon Him, Jew or Gentile, will be blessed. God will regather and restore His people, and there will be worldwide rejoicing.

Zephaniah is also written as a warning to Judah and as a call to repentance (2:1–3). God wants to spare the people, but they ultimately reject Him. His judgment will be great; but God promises His people a future day of hope and joy. Wrath and mercy, severity and kindness, cannot be separated in the character of God.

Key Verses: Zephaniah 1:14, 15; 2:3—"Near is the great day of the LORD, near and coming very quickly; listen, the day of the LORD! In it the warrior cries out bitterly. A day of wrath is that day, a day of trouble and distress, a day of destruction and desolation, a day of darkness and gloom, a day of clouds and thick darkness" (1:14, 15).

"Seek the LORD, all you humble of the earth who have carried out His ordinances; seek righteousness, seek humility. Perhaps you will be hidden in the day of the LORD'S anger" (2:3).

Key Chapter: Zephaniah 3—The last chapter of Zephaniah records the two distinct parts of the day of the Lord: judgment and restoration. Following the conversion of the nation, Israel finally is fully restored. Under the righteous rule of God, Israel fully inherits the blessings contained in the biblical covenants.

SURVEY OF ZEPHANIAH

On the whole, Zephaniah is a fierce and grim book of warning about the coming day of the Lord. Desolation, darkness, and ruin will strike Judah and the nations because of the wrath of God upon sin. Zephaniah looks beyond judgment, however, to a time of joy when God will cleanse the nations and restore the fortunes of His people Israel. The book begins with God's declaration, "I will completely remove all *things* from the face of the earth" (1:2); but it ends with this promise, "At that time I will bring you in" and "restore your fortunes before your eyes" (3:20). Zephaniah moves three times from the general to the specific: (1) from universal judgment (1:1–3) to judgment upon Judah (1:4—2:3); (2) from judgment upon surrounding nations (2:4–15) to judgment upon Jerusalem (3:1–7); (3) from judgment and cleansing of all nations (3:8–10) to restoration of Israel (3:11–20). The two broad divisions of the book are: the judgment in the day of the Lord (1:1—3:8), and the salvation in the day of the Lord (3:9–20).

The Judgment in the Day of the Lord (1:1—3:8): The prophetic oracle begins with an awesome statement of God's coming judgment upon the entire earth because of the sins of men (1:2, 3). Zephaniah then concentrates on the judgment of Judah (1:4–18), listing some of the offenses that will cause it to come. Judah is polluted with idolatrous priests who promote the worship of Baal and nature, and her officials and princes are completely corrupt. Therefore, the day of the Lord is imminent; and it will be characterized by terror, desolation, and distress. However, by His grace, Yahweh appeals to His people to repent and humble themselves to avert the coming disaster before it is too late (2:1–3).

FOCUS	JUDGMENT IN THE DAY OF THE LORD					SALVATION IN THE DAY OF THE LORD	
REFERENCE	1:1———1:4———	2:4————	3:1————	3:8———	3:9———	3:14——3:20	
DIVISION	JUDGMENT ON THE WHOLE EARTH	JUDGMENT ON THE NATION OF JUDAH	JUDGMENT ON THE NATIONS SURROUNDING JUDAH	JUDGMENT ON THE CITY OF JERUSALEM	JUDGMENT ON THE WHOLE EARTH	PROMISE OF CONVERSION	PROMISE OF RESTORATION
TOPIC	DAY OF WRATH					DAY OF JOY	
	JUDGMENT ON JUDAH					RESTORATION FOR JUDAH	
LOCATION	JUDAH AND THE NATIONS						
TIME	c. 630 B.C.						

Zephaniah pronounces God's coming judgment upon the nations that surround Judah (2:4–15). He looks in all four directions: Philistia (west), Moab and Ammon (east), Ethiopia (south), and Assyria (north). Then he focuses on Jerusalem, the center of God's dealings (3:1–7). Jerusalem is characterized by spiritual rebellion and moral treachery. "She heeded no voice; she accepted no instruction. She did not trust in the LORD; she did not draw near to her God" (3:2).

The Salvation in the Day of the Lord (3:9–20):

After a broad statement of the judgment of all nations (3:8), Zephaniah changes the tone of the remainder of his book to blessing; for this, too, is an aspect of the day of the Lord. The nation will be cleansed and will call on the name of the Lord (3:9, 10). The remnant of Israel will be regathered, redeemed, and restored (3:11–20). They will rejoice in their Redeemer, and He will be in their midst. Zephaniah opens with idolatry, wrath, and judgment, but closes with true worship, rejoicing, and blessing.

OUTLINE OF ZEPHANIAH

CHAPTER 1

The Judgment on the Whole Earth

THE word of the LORD which came to Zephaniah son of Cushi, son of Gedaliah, son of Amariah, son of Hezekiah, in the days of Josiah son of Amon, king of Judah,

2 "I will completely ᴿremove all *things* From the face of the ᵀearth," declares the LORD.   Gen. 6:7; Jer. 7:20 • *ground*

3 "I will remove ᴿman and beast; Is. 6:11, 12 I will remove the ᴿbirds of the sky And the fish of the sea,   Jer. 4:25; 9:10 And the ruins along with the wicked; And I will cut off man from the face of the earth," declares the LORD.

Causes of the Judgment

4 "So I will ᴿstretch out My hand against Judah   Jer. 6:12; Ezek. 6:14 And against all the inhabitants of Jerusalem.

And I will ᴿcut off the remnant of Baal from this place,   Mic. 5:13 *And* the names of the ᴿidolatrous priests along with the priests.   2 Kin. 23:5

5 "And those who bow down on the housetops to the host of heaven, And those who bow down *and* swear to the LORD and *yet* swear by ᴿMilcom,   1 Kin. 11:5, 33; Jer. 49:1

6 And those who have ᴿturned back from following the LORD,   Is. 1:4; Hos. 7:10 And those who have ᴿnot sought the LORD or inquired of Him."   Is. 9:13

7 ᵀBe silent before the Lord GOD!   *Hush* For the day of the LORD is near, For the LORD has prepared a sacrifice, He has consecrated His guests.

8 "Then it will come about on the day of the LORD's sacrifice, That I will ᴿpunish the princes, the king's sons,   Is. 24:21; Hab. 1:10 And all who clothe themselves with ᴿforeign garments.   Is. 2:6

9 "And I will punish on that day all who leap on the *temple* threshold, Who fill the house of their ᴬlord with violence and deceit.   *Lord*

10 "And on that day," declares the LORD, "There will be the sound of a cry from the ᴿFish Gate,   2 Chr. 33:14; Neh. 3:3 A wail from the ¹Second Quarter, And a loud crash from the hills.

11 "Wail, O inhabitants of the ¹Mortar, For all the ᴬpeople of ᴿCanaan will be silenced;   *merchant people will•*Zeph. 2:5 All who weigh out silver will be cut off.

12 "And it will come about at that time That I will ᴿsearch Jerusalem with lamps,   Jer. 16:16, 17; Ezek. 9:4-11 And I will punish the men

¹ I.e., a district of Jerusalem

Who are [R]stagnant in spirit,   Jer. 48:11
Who say in their hearts,
'The LORD will not do good or evil!'
13 "Moreover, their wealth will become
    [R]plunder,   Jer. 15:13; 17:3
And their houses desolate;
Yes,[R]they will build houses but not in-
    habit *them*,   Amos 5:11; Mic. 6:15
And plant vineyards but not drink their
    wine."

Description of the Judgment

14 Near is the great day of the LORD,
   Near and coming very quickly;
   Listen, the day of the LORD!
   In it the warrior cries out bitterly.
15 A day of wrath is that day,
   A day of trouble and distress,
   A day of destruction and desolation,
   A day of darkness and gloom,
   A day of clouds and thick darkness,
16 A day of trumpet and battle cry,
   Against the [R]fortified cities   Is. 2:12-15
   And the high corner towers.
17 And I will bring [R]distress on men,
   So that they will walk [R]like the blind,
   Because they have sinned against the
       LORD;   Jer. 10:18 • Deut. 28:29
   And their [R]blood will be poured out like
       dust,   Ezek. 24:7, 8
   And their [R]flesh like dung.   Jer. 8:2; 9:22
18 Neither their [R]silver nor their gold
   Will be able to deliver them   Ezek. 7:19
   On the day of the LORD's wrath;
   And [R]all the earth will be devoured
   In the fire of His jealousy,   Zeph. 3:8
   For He will make a complete end,
   Indeed a terrifying one,
   Of all the inhabitants of the earth.

CHAPTER 2

Call to Repentance

GATHER   yourselves   together,   yes,
    [R]gather,   2 Chr. 20:4; Joel 1:14
O nation without [A]shame,   *longing*
2 Before the decree [T]takes effect—   *is born*
The day passes like the chaff—
Before the [R]burning anger of the LORD
    comes upon you,   Lam. 4:11; Nah. 1:6
Before the [R]day of the LORD's anger
    comes upon you.   Zeph. 1:18
3 [R]Seek the LORD,   Ps. 105:4; Amos 5:6
All you [R]humble of the earth   Ps. 22:26
Who have carried out His ordinances;
Seek righteousness, seek humility.
Perhaps you will be [R]hidden   Is. 26:20
In the day of the LORD's anger.

Judgment Against Philistia (West)

4 For [R]Gaza will be abandoned,

And Ashkelon a desolation;
Ashdod will be driven out at noon,
And Ekron will be uprooted.   Zech. 9:5-7
5 Woe to the inhabitants of the seacoast,
The nation of the [2]Cherethites!
The word of the LORD is against you,
O Canaan, land of the Philistines;
And I will [R]destroy you,   Is. 14:29, 30
So that there will be no inhabitant.
6 So the seacoast will be pastures,
With [A]caves for shepherds and folds for
    flocks.   *meadows* or *wells*
7 And the coast will be
For the remnant of the house of Judah,
They will [R]pasture on it.   Is. 32:14
In the houses of Ashkelon they will lie
    down at evening;
For the LORD their God will [R]care for
    them   Ex. 4:31; Ps. 80:14
And [R]restore their fortune.   Jer. 32:44

*Judgment Against Moab and Ammon
(East)*

8 "I have heard the [T]taunting of Moab
And the [R]revilings of the sons of Am-
    mon,   *reproach* • Ezek. 25:3
With which they have [T]taunted My peo-
    ple   *reproached*
And [b]become arrogant against their ter-
    ritory.   *made* themselves *great*
9 "Therefore, as I live," declares the LORD
    of hosts,
The God of Israel,
"Surely Moab will be like Sodom,
And the sons of [R]Ammon like Gomor-
    rah—   Jer. 49:1-6; Ezek. 25:1-10
A place possessed by nettles and salt
    pits,
And a perpetual desolation.
The remnant of My people will [R]plunder
    them,   Is. 11:14
And the remainder of My nation will
    inherit them."
10 This they will have in return for their
    [R]pride, because they have taunted and [T]be-
come arrogant against the people of the
LORD of hosts.   Is. 16:6 • *made* themselves *great*
11 The LORD will be terrifying to them, for
He will starve all the gods of the earth; and
all the coastlands of the nations will bow
down to Him, everyone from his *own* place.

Judgment Against Ethiopia (South)

12 "You also, O [R]Ethiopians, will be slain by
    My sword."   Is. 18:1-7; 20:4, 5

Judgment Against Assyria (North)

13 And He will [R]stretch out His hand
    against the north   Is. 14:26; Zeph. 1:4
   And destroy [R]Assyria,   Is. 10:16; Mic. 5:6
   And He will make [R]Nineveh a desola-
       tion,   Nah. 3:7
   Parched like the wilderness.

[2] I.e., a segment of the Philistines with roots in Crete

14 And flocks will lie down in her midst,
   All beasts which range in herds;
   Both the pelican and the hedgehog
   Will lodge in the tops of her pillars;
   [T]Birds will sing in the window,   *A voice*
   Desolation *will be* on the threshold;
   For He has laid bare the cedar work.
15 This is the[R]exultant city   Is. 22:2
   Which[R]dwells securely,   Is. 32:9, 11
   Who says in her heart,
   "I am, and there is no one besides me."
   How she has become a[R]desolation,
   A resting place for beasts!   Is. 32:14
   Everyone who passes by her will hiss
   And wave his hand *in contempt.*

CHAPTER 3

Jerusalem's Injustice

W OE to her who is[R]rebellious and defiled,
   The[R]tyrannical city!   Jer. 5:23 • Jer. 6:6
2 She[R]heeded no voice;   Jer. 7:23-28
   She[R]accepted no instruction. 2 Tim. 3:16
   She did not trust in the LORD;
   She did not draw near to her God.
3 Her [R]princes within her are roaring
      lions,   Ezek. 22:27
   Her judges are wolves at evening;
   They leave nothing for the morning.
4 Her prophets are[R]reckless, treacherous
      men;   Judg. 9:4
   Her[R]priests have profaned the sanctu-
      ary.   Ezek. 22:26; Mal. 2:7, 8
   They have done violence to the law.

The Lord's Justice

5 The LORD is righteous within her;
   He will[R]do no injustice.   Ps. 92:15
   [R]Every morning He brings His justice to
      light;   Job 7:18
   He does not fail.
   But the unjust knows no shame.
6 "I have cut off nations;
   Their corner towers are in ruins.
   I have made their streets desolate,
   With no one passing by;
   Their[R]cities are laid waste,   Lev. 26:31
   Without a man, without an inhabitant.
7 "I said, 'Surely you will revere Me,
   [R]Accept instruction.'   Job 36:10; Ps. 32:8
   So her dwelling will[R]not be cut off
   According to all that I have appointed
      concerning her.   Jer. 7:7
   But they were eager to[R]corrupt all their
      deeds.   Hos. 9:9

The Judgment on the Whole Earth

8 "Therefore,[R]wait for Me," declares the
   LORD,   Ps. 27:14; Is. 30:18; Hab. 2:3
   "For the day when I rise up to the prey.
   Indeed, My decision is to [R]gather na-
      tions,   Ezek. 38:14-23; Joel 3:2

To assemble kingdoms,
   To pour out on them My indignation,
   All My burning anger;
   For[R]all the earth will be devoured
   By the fire of My zeal.   Zeph. 1:18

The Promise of Conversion

9 "For then I will[T]give to the peoples[R]puri-
      fied lips,   *change* • Is. 19:18; 57:19
   That all of them may[R]call on the name
      of the LORD,   Hab. 2:14; Zeph. 2:11
   To serve Him shoulder to shoulder.
10 "From beyond the rivers of Ethiopia
   My[A]worshipers, My dispersed ones,
   Will bring My offerings.   *suppliants*
11 "In that day you will[T]feel no shame
   Because of all your deeds   Joel 2:26, 27
   By which you have rebelled against
      Me;
   For then I will remove from your midst
   Your[R]proud, exulting ones,   Is. 2:12; 5:15
   And you will never again be haughty
   On My[R]holy mountain.   Ezek. 20:40
12 "But I will leave among you
   A[R]humble and lowly people,   Is. 14:30
   And they will[R]take refuge in the name
      of the LORD.   Is. 14:32; 50:10; Nah. 1:7
13 "The remnant of Israel will do no wrong
   And[R]tell no lies,   Zech. 8:3, 16; Rev. 14:5
   Nor will a deceitful tongue
   Be found in their mouths;
   For they shall feed and lie down
   With no one to make them tremble."

The Promise of Restoration

14 Shout for joy, O daughter of Zion!
   [R]Shout *in triumph,* O Israel!   Zech. 9:9
   Rejoice and exult with all *your* heart,
   O daughter of Jerusalem!
15 The LORD has taken away [R]His judg-
      ments against you,   [John 5:30]
   He has cleared away your enemies.
   The King of Israel, the LORD, is[R]in your
      midst;   Ezek. 37:26-28; Zeph. 3:5
   You will fear disaster no more.
16 In that day it will be said to Jerusalem:
   "Do[R]not be afraid, O Zion;   Is. 35:3, 4
   Do not let your hands fall limp.
17 "The LORD your God is in your midst,
   A[T]victorious warrior.   *A warrior who saves*
   He will exult over you with joy,
   He will be quiet in His love,
   He will rejoice over you with shouts of
      joy.
18 "I will gather those who [R]grieve about
      the appointed feasts—   Ps. 42:2-4
   They[T]came from you, O Zion;   *were*
   The reproach *of exile* is a burden on
      [T]them.   *her*
19 "Behold, I am going to deal at that time
   With all your[R]oppressors,   Is. 60:14
   I will save the[R]lame [Ezek. 34:16; Mic. 4:6]
   And gather the outcast,

And I will turn their [R]shame into praise
and renown   Ezek. 16:27, 57
In all the earth.
20"At that time I will bring you in,
Even at the time when I gather you together;

Indeed, I will give you [R]renown and
praise   Deut. 26:18, 19; Is. 56:5; 66:22
Among all the peoples of the earth,
When I [R]restore your fortunes before
your eyes," Jer. 29:14; Joel 3:1; Zeph. 2:7
Says the LORD.

THE BOOK OF
HAGGAI

THE BOOK OF HAGGAI

With the Babylonian exile in the past, and a newly returned group of Jews back in the land, the work of rebuilding the temple can begin. However, sixteen years after the process is begun, the people have yet to finish the project, for their personal affairs have interfered with God's business. Haggai preaches a fiery series of sermonettes designed to stir up the nation to finish the temple. He calls the builders to renewed courage in the Lord, renewed holiness of life, and renewed faith in God who controls the future.

The etymology and meaning of *haggay* is uncertain, but it is probably derived from the Hebrew word *hag*, "festival." It may also be an abbreviated form of *haggiah*, "festival of Yahweh." Thus, Haggai's name means "Festal" or "Festive," possibly because he was born on the day of a major feast, such as Tabernacles (Haggai's second message takes place during that feast, 2:1). The title in the Septuagint is *Aggaios* and in the Vulgate it is *Aggaeus*.

THE AUTHOR OF HAGGAI

Haggai's name is mentioned nine times (1:1, 3, 12, 13; 2:1, 10, 13, 14, 20); the authorship and date of the book are virtually uncontested. The unity of theme, style, and dating is obvious. Haggai is known only from this book and from two references to him in Ezra 5:1 and 6:14. There he is seen working alongside the younger prophet Zechariah in the ministry of encouraging the rebuilding of the temple. Haggai returned from Babylon with the remnant under Zerubbabel and evidently lived in Jerusalem. Some think 2:3 may mean that he was born in Judah before the 586 B.C. Captivity and was one of the small company who could remember the former temple before its destruction. This would mean Haggai was about seventy-five when he prophesied in 520 B.C. It is equally likely, however, that he was born in Babylon during the Captivity.

THE TIME OF HAGGAI

In 538 B.C. Cyrus of Persia issued a decree allowing the Jews to return to their land and rebuild their temple. The first return was led by Zerubbabel, and in 536 B.C. work on the temple began. Ezra 4—6 gives the background to the Book of Haggai and describes how the Samaritans hindered the building of the temple and wrote a letter to the Persian king. This opposition only added to the growing discouragement of the Jewish remnant. Their initial optimism upon returning to their homeland was dampened by the desolation of the land, crop failure, hard work, hostility, and other hardships. They gave up the relative comfort of Babylonian culture to pioneer in a land that seemed unproductive and full of enemies. Finding it easier to stop building than to fight their neighbors, the work on the temple ceased in 534 B.C. The pessimism of the people led to spiritual lethargy, and they became preoccupied with their own building projects. They used political opposition and a theory that the temple was not to be rebuilt until some later time (perhaps after Jerusalem was rebuilt) as excuses for neglecting the house of the Lord.

It was in this context that God called His prophets Haggai and Zechariah to the same task of urging the people to complete the temple. Both books are precisely dated: Haggai 1:1, September 1, 520 B.C.; Haggai 1:15, September 24, 520 B.C.; Haggai 2:1, October 21, 520 B.C.; Zechariah 1:1, November, 520 B.C.; Haggai 2:10, 20, December 24, 520 B.C.; Zechariah 1:7, February 24, 519 B.C.; Zechariah 7:1, December 4, 518 B.C. Zechariah's prophecy commenced between Haggai's second and third messages. Thus, after fourteen years of neglect, work on the temple was resumed in 520 B.C. and was completed in 516 B.C. (Ezra 6:15). The Talmud indicates that the ark of the covenant, the Shekinah glory, and the Urim and Thummim were not in the rebuilt temple.

Darius I (521–486 B.C.) was king of Persia during the ministries of Haggai and Zechariah. He was a strong ruler who consolidated his kingdom by defeating a number of revolting nations.

THE CHRIST OF HAGGAI

The promise of Haggai 2:9 points ahead to the crucial role the second temple is to have in God's redemptive plan. Herod the Great later spent a fortune on the project of enlarging and enriching this temple, and it was filled with the glory of God incarnate every time Christ came to Jerusalem.

The Messiah is also portrayed in the person of Zerubbabel: "I will take you, Zerubbabel . . . and I will make you like a signet *ring*, for I have chosen you" (2:23). Zerubbabel becomes the center of the Messianic line and is like a signet ring, sealing both branches together.

```
          ──────DAVID──────
SOLOMON                    NATHAN

       ZERUBBABEL

(Matt. 1:12)              (Luke 3:27)

JOSEPH                       MARY
```

KEYS TO HAGGAI

Key Word: The Reconstruction of the Temple—Haggai's basic theme is clear: the remnant must reorder its priorities and complete the temple before it can expect the blessing of God upon its efforts. Because of spiritual indifference the people fail to respond to God's attempts to get their attention. In their despondency they do not realize that their hardships are divinely given symptoms of their spiritual disease. Haggai brings them to an understanding that circumstances become difficult when people place their own selfish interests before God's. When they put God first and seek to do His will, He will bring His people joy and prosperity.

Key Verses: Haggai 1:7, 8 and 2:7–9—"Thus says the LORD of hosts, 'Consider your ways! Go up to the mountains, bring wood and rebuild the temple, that I may be pleased with it and be glorified,' says the LORD" (1:7, 8).

" 'And I will shake all the nations; and they will come with the wealth of all nations; and I will fill this house with glory,' says the LORD of hosts. 'The silver is Mine, and the gold is Mine,' declares the LORD of hosts. 'The latter glory of this house will be greater than the former,' says the LORD of hosts, 'and in this place I shall give peace,' declares the LORD of hosts" (2:7–9).

Key Chapter: Haggai 2—Verses 6–9 record

some of the most startling prophecies in Scripture: "I am going to shake the heavens and the earth, the sea also and the dry land" (the tribulation) and "they will come with the wealth of all nations" and "in this place I shall give peace" (the second coming of the Messiah).

SURVEY OF HAGGAI

Haggai is second only to Obadiah in brevity among Old Testament books, but this strong and frank series of four terse sermons accomplishes its intended effect. The work on the temple has ceased, and the people have become more concerned with the beautification of their own houses than with the building of the central sanctuary of God. Because of their misplaced priorities, their labor is no longer blessed by God. Only when the people put the Lord first by completing the task He has set before them will His hand of blessing once again be upon them. Haggai acts as God's man in God's hour, and his four messages are: the completion of the latter temple (1:1–15), the glory of the latter temple (2:1–9), the present blessings of obedience (2:10–19), and the future blessings of promise (2:20–23).

The Completion of the Latter Temple (1:1–15): When the remnant returns from Babylon under Zerubbabel, they begin to rebuild the temple of the Lord. However, the work soon stops and the people find excuses to ignore it as the years pass. They have no problem in building rich dwellings for themselves ("paneled houses," 1:4) while they claim that the time for building the temple has not yet come (1:2). God withdraws His blessing and they sink into an economic depression. However, they do not recognize what is happening because of their indifference to God and indulgence of self; so God communicates directly to the remnant through His prophet Haggai. Zerubbabel the governor, Joshua the high priest, and all the

FOCUS	COMPLETION OF THE LATTER TEMPLE	GLORY OF THE LATTER TEMPLE	PRESENT BLESSING OF OBEDIENCE	FUTURE BLESSING THROUGH PROMISE
REFERENCE	1:1	2:1	2:10	2:20 ─── 2:23
DIVISION	"CONSIDER YOUR WAYS . . . MY HOUSE WHICH LIES DESOLATE.	"THE LATTER GLORY OF THIS HOUSE WILL BE GREATER."	"FROM THIS DAY ON I WILL BLESS YOU."	"I AM GOING TO SHAKE THE HEAVENS AND THE EARTH."
TOPIC	THE TEMPLE OF GOD		THE BLESSINGS OF GOD	
	FIRST REBUKE (PRESENT)	FIRST ENCOURAGEMENT (FUTURE)	SECOND REBUKE (PRESENT)	SECOND ENCOURAGEMENT (FUTURE)
LOCATION	JERUSALEM			
TIME	SEPTEMBER 1 520 B.C.	OCTOBER 21 520 B.C.	DECEMBER 24 520 B.C.	DECEMBER 24 520 B.C.

people respond; and twenty-three days later they again begin to work on the temple.

The Glory of the Latter Temple (2:1–9): In a few short weeks, the enthusiasm of the people sours into discouragement; the elders remember the glory of Solomon's temple and bemoan the puniness of the present temple (see Ezra 3:8–13). Haggai's prophetic word of encouragement reminds the people of God's covenant promises in the past (2:4, 5), and of His confident plans for the future (2:6–9): "The latter glory of this house will be greater than the former" (2:9).

The Present Blessings of Obedience (2:10–19): Haggai's message to the priests illustrates the concept of contamination (2:11–13) and applies it to the nation (2:14–19). The Lord requires holiness and obedience, and the contamination of sin blocks the blessing of God. Because the people have obeyed God in building the temple, they will be blessed from that day forward.

The Future Blessings Through Promise (2:20–23): On the same day that Haggai addresses the priests, he gives a second message to Zerubbabel. God will move in judgment, and in His power He will overthrow the nations of the earth (2:21, 22). At that time, Zerubbabel, a symbol of the Messiah to come, will be honored.

OUTLINE OF HAGGAI

CHAPTER 1

The Temple Is Not Complete—Ezra 5:1

IN the second year of Darius the king, on the first day of the sixth month, the word of the LORD came by the prophet Haggai to Zerubbabel the son of Shealtiel, ᴿgovernor of Judah, and to Joshua the son of Jehozadak, the high priest saying,   1 Kin. 10:15; Ezra. 5:3

2 "Thus says the LORD of ᵗhosts, 'This people says, "The time has not come, *even* the time for the house of the LORD to be rebuilt." ' "   *hosts, saying*

3 Then the word of the LORD came by Haggai the prophet saying,

4 "Is it time for you yourselves to dwell in your paneled houses while this house ᴿ*lies* desolate?"   Jer. 33:10, 12; Hag. 1:9

5 Now therefore, thus says the LORD of hosts, "Consider' your ways! *Set your heart on*

6 "You have sown much, but harvest little; *you* eat, but *there is* not enough to be satisfied; *you* drink, but *there is* not enough to become drunk; *you* put on clothing, but no one is warm *enough*; and he who earns, earns wages *to put* into a purse with holes."

The Temple Must Be Completed

7 Thus says the LORD of hosts, "Considerᵀ your ways!   *Set your heart on*

8 "Go up to the ᵀmountains, bring wood and ᴿrebuild the ᵀtemple, that I may be pleased with it and be glorified," says the LORD.   *mountain* • 1 Kin. 6:1 • *house*

9 "Youᴿ look for much, but behold, *it comes* to little; when you bring *it* home, ᴿblow it *away*. Why?" declares the LORD of hosts, "Because of My house which *lies* desolate, while each of you runs to his own house.   Prov. 27:20; Eccl. 1:8 • Is. 40:7

10 "Therefore, because of you the ᴿsky has withheld ᵗits dew, and the earth has withheld its produce.   Deut. 28:23, 24 • *from dew*

11 "And I called for aᴿdrought on the land, on the mountains, on the grain, on the new wine, on the oil, on what the ground produces, on men, on cattle, and on all the labor of ᵗyour hands."   Jer. 14:2-6 • *the palms*

12 Then ᴿZerubbabel the son of Shealtiel, and Joshua the son of Jehozadak, the high priest, with all the remnant of the people, obeyed the voice of the LORD their God and the words of Haggai the prophet, as the LORD their God had sent him. And the people showed reverence for the LORD.   Hag. 1:1

13 Then Haggai, the ᴿmessenger of the LORD, spokeᴬby the commission of the LORD to the people saying, " 'I am with you,' declares the LORD."   Is. 44:26 • *the message*

14 So the LORD stirred up the spirit of Zerubbabel the son of Shealtiel, governor of Judah, and the spirit of Joshua the son of Jehozadak, the high priest, and the spirit of all the remnant of the people; and they came andᴿworked on the house of the LORD of hosts, their God,   Ezra 5:2; Neh. 4:6

15 on the twenty-fourth day of the sixth month in the second year of Darius the king.

CHAPTER 2

The Latter Temple Is Not as Glorious as the First

ON the twenty-first of the seventh month, the word of the LORD came by[R]Haggai the prophet saying,   Hag. 1:1

2 "Speak now to Zerubbabel the son of Shealtiel, governor of Judah, and to Joshua the son of Jehozadak, the high priest, and to the[R]remnant of the people saying,   Hag. 1:12

3 'Who is left among you who saw this [T]temple in its former glory? And how do you see it now? Does it not [T]seem to you like nothing in comparison?   *house • in your eyes*

The Latter Temple Will Be More Glorious than the First

4 'But now[T]take courage, Zerubbabel,' declares the LORD, 'take courage also, Joshua son of Jehozadak, the high priest, and all you people of the land take courage,' declares the LORD, 'and work; for I am with you,' says the LORD of hosts.   *be strong*

5 'As for the[T]promise which I made you when you came out of Egypt, My Spirit is abiding in your midst; do not fear!'   *word*

6 "For thus says the LORD of hosts, 'Once[R] more [T]in a little while, I am going to shake the heavens and the earth, the sea also and the dry land.   Heb. 12:26 • *it is a little*

7 'And I will shake [R]all the nations; and they will come with the wealth of all nations; and I will fill this house with glory,' says the LORD of hosts. [Dan. 2:44]; Joel 3:9, 16

8 'The [R]silver is Mine, and the gold is Mine,' declares the LORD of hosts.   Is. 60:17

9 'The latter [R]glory of this house will be greater than the former,' says the LORD of hosts, 'and in this place I shall give peace,' declares the LORD of hosts."   [Zech. 2:5]

The Disobedience of the Remnant

10 On the [R]twenty-fourth of the ninth *month*, in the second year of Darius, the word of the LORD came to Haggai the prophet saying,   Hag. 2:20

11 "Thus says the LORD of hosts, 'Ask[R]now the priests *for* a[T]ruling: Deut. 17:8-11 • *law*

12 'If a man carries holy meat in the[T]fold of his garment, and touches bread with [T]this fold, or cooked food, wine, oil, or any *other* food, will it become holy?' " And the priests answered and said, "No."   *wing • his wing*

13 Then Haggai said, "If[R] one who is unclean from a[T]corpse touches any of these, will *the latter* become unclean?" And the priests answered and said, "It will become unclean."   Lev. 22:4-6; Num. 19:22 • *soul*

14 Then Haggai answered and said, " 'So[R] is this people. And so is this nation before Me,' declares the LORD, 'and so is every work of their hands; and what they offer there is unclean.   [Prov. 15:8; Is. 1:11-15]

The Obedience of the Remnant

15 'But now, do[T]consider from this day onward: before one stone was placed on another in the temple of the LORD, *set your heart*

16 [T]from that time *when* one came to a *grain* heap of twenty *measures*, there would be only ten; and *when* one came to the wine vat to draw fifty[A]measures, there would be *only* twenty.   *since they were • troughs full*

17 'I smote you *and* every work of your hands with blasting wind, mildew, and hail; [A]yet you *did* not *come back* to Me,' declares the LORD.   *but what did we have in common?*

18 'Do[T]consider from this day onward, from the twenty-fourth day of the ninth *month;* from the day when the temple of the LORD was founded, consider: *set your heart*

19 'Is the seed still in the barn? Even including the vine, the fig tree, the pomegranate, and the olive tree, it has not borne *fruit.* Yet from this day on I will bless *you.*' "

The Future Destruction of the Nations

20 Then the word of the LORD came a second time to Haggai on the [R]twenty-fourth *day* of the month saying,   Hag. 2:10

21 "Speak to Zerubbabel governor of Judah saying, 'I am going to[T]shake the heavens and the earth.   Hag. 2:6; [Heb. 12:26, 27]

22 'And I will overthrow the thrones of kingdoms and destroy the power of the kingdoms of the [A]nations; and I will overthrow the chariots and their riders, and the horses and their riders will go down, everyone by the sword of another.'   *Gentiles*

The Future Recognition of Zerubbabel

23 'On that day,' declares the LORD of hosts, 'I will take you, Zerubbabel, son of Shealtiel, my servant,' declares the LORD, 'and I will make you like a[A]signet[R]ring, for[R]I have chosen you,' " declares the LORD of hosts.   *seal* • Song 8:6; Jer. 22:24 • Is. 42:1; 43:10

THE BOOK OF

ZECHARIAH

THE BOOK OF ZECHARIAH

For a dozen years or more, the task of rebuilding the temple has been half completed. Zechariah is commissioned by God to encourage the people in their unfinished responsibility. Rather than exhorting them to action with strong words of rebuke, Zechariah seeks to encourage them to action by reminding them of the future importance of the temple. The temple must be built, for one day the Messiah's glory will inhabit it. But future blessing is contingent upon present obedience. The people are not merely building a building; they are building the future. With that as their motivation, they can enter into the building project with wholehearted zeal, for their Messiah is coming.

Zekar-yah means "God Remembers" or "God Has Remembered." This theme dominates the whole book: Israel will be blessed because Yahweh remembers the covenant He made with the fathers. The Greek and Latin version of his name is *Zacharias*.

THE AUTHOR OF ZECHARIAH

Zechariah ("God Remembers") was a popular name shared by no fewer than twenty-nine Old Testament characters. It may have been given out of gratitude for God's gift of a baby boy. Like his predecessors, Jeremiah and Ezekiel, Zechariah was of priestly lineage as the son of Berechiah and grandson of Iddo (1:1, 7; Ezra 5:1; 6:14; Neh. 12:4, 16). He was born in Babylon and was brought by his grandfather to Palestine when the Jewish exiles returned under Zerubbabel and Joshua the high priest. If he was the "young man" of 2:4, he was called to prophesy at an early age in 520 B.C. According to Jewish tradition, Zechariah was a member of the Great Synagogue that collected and preserved the canon of revealed Scripture. Matthew 23:35 indicates he was "murdered between the temple and the altar" in the same way that an earlier Zechariah was martyred (see 2 Chr. 24:20, 21). The universal testimony of Jewish and Christian tradition affirms Zechariah as the author of the entire book.

THE TIME OF ZECHARIAH

Zechariah was a younger contemporary of Haggai the prophet, Zerubbabel the governor, and Joshua the high priest. The historical setting for chapters 1—8 (520–518 B.C.) is identical to that of Haggai (see "The Time of Haggai"). Work was resumed on the temple in 520 B.C., and the project was completed in 516 B.C. Chapters 9—14 are undated, but stylistic differences and references to Greece indicate a date of between 480 and 470 B.C. This would mean that Darius I (521–486 B.C.) had passed from the scene and had been succeeded by Xerxes (486–464 B.C.), the king who deposed Queen Vashti and made Esther queen of Persia.

THE CHRIST OF ZECHARIAH

Very clear messianic passages abound in this book. Christ is portrayed in His two advents as both Servant and King, Man and God. The following are a few of Zechariah's explicit anticipations of Christ: the angel of the Lord (3:1, 2); the righteous Branch (3:8; 6:12, 13), the stone with seven eyes (3:9); the King-Priest (6:13); the humble King (9:9, 10); the cornerstone, tent peg, and battle bow (10:4); the good Shepherd who is rejected and sold for thirty shekels of silver, the price of a slave (11:4–13); the pierced One (12:10); the cleansing fountain (13:1); the smitten Shepherd who is abandoned (13:7); the coming Judge and righteous King (14).

KEYS TO ZECHARIAH

Key Word: Prepare for the Messiah— The first eight chapters frequently allude to the temple and encourage the people to complete their great work on the new sanctuary. As they build the temple, they are building their future, because that very structure will be used by the Messiah when He comes to bring salvation. Zechariah eloquently attests to Yahweh's covenant faithfulness toward Israel through the work of the Messiah, especially in chapters 9—14. This book outlines God's program for His people during the times of the Gentiles until the Messiah comes to deliver them and reign upon the earth. This hope of glory provides a source of reassurance to the Jewish remnant at a time when circumstances are trying. Zechariah also seeks to promote spiritual revival so that the people will call upon the Lord with humble hearts and commit their ways to Him.

Key Verse: Zechariah 8:3; 9:9—"Thus says the LORD, 'I will return to Zion and will dwell in the midst of Jerusalem. Then Jerusalem will be called the City of Truth, and the mountain

of the LORD of hosts *will be called* the Holy Mountain' " (8:3).

"Rejoice greatly, O daughter of Zion! Shout *in triumph*, O daughter of Jerusalem! Behold, your king is coming to you; He is just and endowed with salvation, humble, and mounted on a donkey, even on a colt, the foal of a donkey" (9:9).

Key Chapter: Zechariah 14—Zechariah builds to a tremendous climax in the fourteenth chapter where he discloses the last siege of Jerusalem, the initial victory of the enemies of Israel, the cleaving of the Mount of Olives, the Lord's defense of Jerusalem with His visible appearance on Olivet, judgment on the confederated nations, the topographical changes in the land of Israel, the Feast of Tabernacles, and the ultimate holiness of Jerusalem and her people.

SURVEY OF ZECHARIAH

Zechariah uses a series of eight visions, four messages, and two burdens to portray God's future plans for His covenant people. The first eight chapters were written to encourage the remnant while they were rebuilding the temple; the last six chapters were written after the completion of the temple to anticipate Israel's coming Messiah. Zechariah moves from gentile domination to messianic rule, from persecution to peace, and from uncleanness to holiness. The book divides into: the eight visions (1—6), the four messages (7 and 8), and the two burdens (9—14).

The Eight Visions (1—6): The book opens with an introductory appeal to the people to repent and return to God, unlike their fathers who rejected the warnings of the prophets (1:1-6). A few months later, Zechariah has a series of eight night visions, evidently in one troubled night (February 15, 519 B.C.; 1:7). The angel who speaks with him interprets the visions, but some of the symbols are not explained. The visions mix the work of the Messiah in both advents, and like the other prophets, Zechariah sees only the peaks of God's program without the intervening valleys. The first five are visions of comfort, and the last three are visions of judgment: (1) The horseman among the myrtle trees—God will rebuild Zion and His people (1:7-17). (2) The four horns and craftsmen—Israel's oppressors will be judged (1:18-21). (3) The man with a measuring line—God will protect and glorify Jerusalem (2:1-13). (4) The cleansing of Joshua the high priest—Israel will be cleansed and restored by the coming Branch (3:1-10). (5) The golden lampstand—God's Spirit is empowering Zerubbabel and Joshua (4:1-14). (6) The flying scroll—individual sin will be judged (5:1-4). (7) The woman in the basket—national sin will be removed (5:5-11). (8) The four chariots—God's judgment will descend on the nations (6:1-8). The crowning of Joshua (6:9-15) anticipates the coming of the Branch who will be King and Priest (the composite crown).

The Four Messages (7 and 8): In response to a question about the continuation of the fasts (7:1-3), God gives Zechariah a series of four messages: (1) a rebuke of empty ritualism (7:4-7); (2) a reminder of past disobedience (7:8-14); (3) the restoration and consolation of Israel (8:1-17); and (4) the recovery of joy in the kingdom (8:18-23).

The Two Burdens (9—14): The first burden (9—11) concerns the first advent and rejection of Israel's coming King. Alexander the Great will conquer Israel's neighbors, but will spare

FOCUS	EIGHT VISIONS			FOUR MESSAGES	TWO BURDENS	
REFERENCE	1:1———1:7———		6:9———7:1———		9:1———12:1———14:21	
DIVISION	CALL TO REPENTANCE	EIGHT VISIONS	CROWNING OF JOSHUA	QUESTION OF THE FASTS	FIRST BURDEN: REJECTION OF THE MESSIAH	SECOND BURDEN: REIGN OF THE MESSIAH
TOPIC	PICTURES			PROBLEM	PREDICTION	
	ISRAEL'S FORTUNE			ISRAEL'S FASTINGS	ISRAEL'S FUTURE	
LOCATION	JERUSALEM					
TIME	WHILE BUILDING THE TEMPLE (520–518 B.C.)				AFTER BUILDING THE TEMPLE (c. 480–470 B.C.)	

Jerusalem (9:1–8) which will be preserved for her King (the Messiah; 9:9, 10). Israel will succeed against Greece (the Maccabean revolt; 9:11–17), and although they will later be scattered, the Messiah will bless them and bring them back (10:1—11:3). Israel will reject her Shepherd-King and be led astray by false shepherds (11:4–17). The second burden (12—14)

concerns the second advent of Christ and the acceptance of Israel's King. The nations will attack Jerusalem, but the Messiah will come and deliver His people (12). They will be cleansed of impurity and falsehood (13), and the Messiah will come in power to judge the nations and reign in Jerusalem over the whole earth (14).

CHAPTER 1

The Call to Repentance—Ezra 5:1

IN the eighth month of the second year of ^R Darius, the word of the LORD came to Zechariah the prophet, the son of Berechiah, the son of Iddo saying,   Ezra 4:24; 6:15

2 "The LORD was very ^a angry with your fathers. 2 Chr. 36:16; Jer. 44:6; Ezek. 8:18; Zech. 1:15

3 "Therefore say to them, 'Thus says the LORD of hosts, "Return ^R to Me," declares the LORD of hosts, "that I may return to you," says the LORD of hosts. Is. 31:6; 44:22; Mal. 3:7

4 "Do not be ^R like your fathers, to whom the former prophets proclaimed, saying, 'Thus says the LORD of hosts, "Return now from your evil ways and from your evil deeds." ' But they did not listen or give heed to Me," declares the LORD. Ps. 78:8; 106:6, 7

5 "Your fathers, where are they? And the ^R prophets, do they live forever? John 8:52

6 "But did not My words and My statutes, which I commanded My servants the prophets, ^R overtake your fathers? Then they repented and said, 'As the LORD of hosts purposed to do to us in accordance with our ways and our deeds, so He has dealt with us.' " '" Jer. 12:16, 17; 44:28, 29; Amos 9:10

The Horses Among the Myrtle Trees

7 On the twenty-fourth day of the eleventh month, which is the month Shebat, in

the second year of Darius, the word of the LORD came to Zechariah the prophet, the son of Berechiah, the son of Iddo, as follows:

8 I saw at night, and behold, a man was riding on a ^R red horse, and he was standing among the ^R myrtle trees which were in the ravine, with red, sorrel, and white horses behind him. Zech. 6:2; [Rev. 6:4] • [Neh. 8:15]

9 Then I said, "My ^t lord, what are these?" And the ^R angel who was speaking with me said to me, "I will show you what these are." Zech. 1:19; 4:4, 5, 13; 6:4 • Zech. 2:3; 5:5

10 And the man who was standing among the myrtle trees answered and said, "These are those whom the LORD has sent to ^t patrol ^R the earth." walk about through • [Job 1:7]

11 So they answered the angel of the LORD who was standing among the myrtle trees, and said, "We have ^t patrolled the earth, and behold, all the earth is ^t peaceful and quiet." walked about through • sitting

12 Then the angel of the LORD answered and said, "O LORD of hosts, how long wilt Thou have no compassion for Jerusalem and the cities of Judah, with which Thou hast been indignant these seventy years?"

13 And the LORD answered the angel who was speaking with me with ^t gracious words, ^R comforting words. good • Is. 40:1, 2; 57:18

14 So the angel who was speaking with me said to me, "Proclaim, ^R saying, 'Thus says the LORD of hosts, "I am exceedingly jealous for Jerusalem and Zion. Is. 40:2, 6

15"But I am very angry with the nations who are at ease; for while I was only a little angry, they furthered the disaster."

16 'Therefore, thus says the LORD, "I will [R]return to Jerusalem with compassion; My house will be built in it," declares the LORD of hosts, "and a measuring line will be stretched over Jerusalem." '   [Is. 54:8–10]

17"Again, proclaim, saying, 'Thus says the LORD of hosts, "My [R]cities will again overflow with prosperity, and the LORD will again [R]comfort Zion and again choose Jerusalem." ' "   Is. 44:26; 61:4 • [Is. 51:3]

The Four Horns and Four Craftsmen

18 Then I lifted up my eyes and looked, and behold, *there were* four horns.

19 So I said to the angel who was speaking with me, "What are these?" And he answered me, "These are the [R]horns which have scattered Judah, Israel, and Jerusalem."   1 Kin. 22:11; Ps. 75:4, 5; Amos 6:13

20 Then the LORD showed me four [R]craftsmen.   Is. 44:12; 54:16

21 And I said, "What are these coming to do?" And he said, "These are the [R]horns which have scattered Judah, so that no man lifts up his head; but these *craftsmen* have come to terrify them, to [R]throw down the horns of the nations who have lifted up *their* horns against the land of Judah in order to scatter it."   Zech. 1:19 • Ps. 75:10

CHAPTER 2

The Man with the Measuring Line

THEN I lifted up my eyes and looked, and behold, *there was* a man with a [R]measuring line in his hand.   Jer. 31:39

2 So I said, "Where are you going?" And he said to me, "To measure Jerusalem, to see how wide it is and how long it is."

3 And behold, the [R]angel who was speaking with me was going out, and another angel was coming out to meet him,   Zech. 1:9

4 and said to him, "Run, speak to that [R]young man, saying, 'Jerusalem will be inhabited without walls, because of the multitude of men and cattle within it.   1 Tim. 4:12

5 'For I,' declares the LORD, 'will be a [R]wall of fire [T]around her, and I will be the glory in her midst.' "   [Is. 4:5; 26:1; 60:18] • *to her*

6 "Ho[T] there! [R]Flee from the land of the north," declares the LORD, "for I have dispersed you as the four winds of the heavens," declares the LORD.   Ho! ho! • Jer. 3:18

7"Ho, Zion! [R]Escape, you who are living with the daughter of Babylon."   Is. 48:20

8 For thus says the LORD of hosts, "After [A]glory He has sent me against the nations which plunder you, for he who touches you, touches the [T]apple of His eye.   *the glory* • *pupil*

9"For behold, I will [R]wave My hand over them, so that they will be [R]plunder for their slaves. Then you will know that the LORD of hosts has sent Me.   Is. 19:16 • Is. 14:2

10"Sing for joy and be glad, O daughter of Zion; for behold I am coming and I will dwell in your midst," declares the LORD.

11"And [R]many nations will join themselves to the LORD in that day and will become My people. Then I will [R]dwell in your midst, and you will know that the LORD of hosts has sent Me to you.   Mic. 4:2 • Zech. 2:5, 10

12"And the LORD will [A]possess[R] Judah as His portion in the holy land, and will again choose Jerusalem.   *inherit* • [Deut. 32:9]

13"Be silent, all flesh, before the LORD; for He is aroused from His holy habitation."

CHAPTER 3

The Cleansing of Joshua,
the High Priest

THEN he showed me [R]Joshua the high priest standing before the angel of the LORD, and [A]Satan standing at his right hand to accuse him.   Ezra 5:2 • the *Adversary* or *Accuser*

2 And the LORD said to Satan, "The[T] LORD rebuke you, Satan! Indeed, the LORD who has chosen Jerusalem rebuke you! Is this not a brand plucked from the fire?"   [Jude 9]

3 Now Joshua was clothed with filthy garments and standing before the angel.

4 And he spoke and said to those who were standing before him saying, "Remove[R] the filthy garments from him." Again he said to him, "See, I have taken your iniquity away from you and [T]will clothe you with festal robes."   Is. 43:25; Ezek. 36:25 • *to clothe*

5 Then I said, "Let them put a clean [R]turban on his head." So they put a clean turban on his head and clothed him with garments, while the angel of the LORD was standing by.   Job 29:14; Is. 3:23

6 And the angel of the LORD admonished Joshua saying,

7"Thus says the LORD of hosts, 'If you will walk in My ways, and if you will perform My service, then you will also govern My house and also have charge of My courts, and I will grant you [T]free access among these who are standing *here.*   *goings*

8 'Now listen, Joshua the high priest, you and your friends who are sitting in front of you—indeed they are men who are a symbol, for behold, I am going to bring in [R]My servant the [T]Branch.   Is. 42:1☆ • *Sprout*

9 'For behold, the stone that I have set before Joshua; on one stone are seven eyes. Behold, I will engrave an inscription on it,' declares the LORD of hosts, 'and I will remove the iniquity of that land in one day.

10 'In that day,' declares the LORD of hosts, 'every one of you will invite his neighbor to *sit* under *his* [R]vine and under *his* fig tree.' "   1 Kin. 4:25; Is. 36:16; Mic. 4:4

CHAPTER 4

The Golden Lampstand and Olive Trees

THEN the angel who was speaking with me returned, and [R]roused me as a man who is awakened from his sleep.   1 Kin. 19:5-7

2 And he said to me, "What[R] do you see?" And I said, "I see, and behold, a lampstand all of gold with its bowl on the top of it, and its[R] seven lamps on it with seven spouts belonging to each of the lamps which are on the top of it;　　　Jer. 1:13; Zech. 5:2 • [Rev. 4:5]

3 also[R] two olive trees by it, one on the right side of the bowl and the other on its left side."　　　Zech. 4:11; Rev. 11:4

4 Then I answered and said to the angel who was speaking with me saying, "What are these,[R] my lord?"　　　Zech. 1:9; 4:5, 13; 6:4

5 So[R] the angel who was speaking with me answered and said to me, "Do[R] you not know what these are?" And I said, "No, my lord."　　　Zech. 1:9; 4:1 • Zech. 4:13

6 Then he answered and said to me, "This is the word of the LORD to[R] Zerubbabel saying, 'Not by might nor by power, but by My Spirit,' says the LORD of hosts.　　Ezra 5:2

7 'What are you, O great[R] mountain? Before Zerubbabel *you will become* a plain; and he will bring forth the top stone with shouts of "Grace, grace to it!" ' "　　Ps. 114:4, 6

8 Also the word of the LORD came to me saying,

9 "The hands of Zerubbabel have laid the foundation of this house, and his hands will finish *it*. Then you will know that the LORD of hosts has sent me to[T] you.　　*you* (plural)

10 "For who has despised the day of[R] small things? But these seven will be glad when they see the[T] plumb line in the hand of Zerubbabel—*these are* the eyes of the LORD which range to and fro throughout the earth."　　Neh. 4:2-4; Amos 7:2, 5 • *plummet stone*

11 Then I answered and said to him, "What are these[R] two olive trees on the right of the lampstand and on its left?"　　Rev. 11:4

12 And I answered the second time and said to him, "What are the two olive ^branches which are beside the two golden pipes, which empty the golden *oil* from themselves?"　　　*clusters*

13 So he answered me saying, "Do[R] you not know what these are?" And I said, "No, [R] my lord."　　　Zech. 4:5 • Zech. 4:4, 5

14 Then he said, "These are the two [T] anointed ones, who are standing by the Lord of the whole earth."　　　*sons of fresh oil*

CHAPTER 5

The Flying Scroll

THEN I lifted up my eyes again and looked, and behold, *there was* a flying scroll.

2 And he said to me, "What[R] do you see?" And I answered, "I see a flying scroll; its length is twenty[T] cubits and its width ten cubits."　　Zech. 4:2 • One cubit equals approx. 18 in.

3 Then he said to me, "This is the [R] curse that is going forth over the face of the whole ^land; surely everyone who steals will be purged away according to[T] the writing on one side, and everyone who swears will be purged away according to the writing on the other side.　　Is. 24:6; 43:28; Jer. 26:6 • *earth* • *it*

4 "I will[R] make it go forth," declares the LORD of hosts, "and it will enter the house of the thief and the house of the one who swears falsely by My name; and it will spend the night within that house and consume it with its timber and stones."　　Mal. 3:5

The Woman in the Ephah

5 Then the angel who was speaking with me went out, and said to me, "Lift up now your eyes, and see what this is, going forth."

6 And I said, "What is it?" And he said, "This is the ephah going forth." Again he said, "This is their appearance in all the land

7 (and behold, a lead cover was lifted up); and this is a woman sitting inside the ephah."

8 Then he said, "This is[R] Wickedness!" And he threw her down into the middle of the ephah and cast the lead weight on its [T] opening.　　Hos. 12:7; Amos 8:5; Mic. 6:11 • *mouth*

9 Then I lifted up my eyes and looked, and there two women were coming out with the wind in their wings; and they had wings like the wings of a[R] stork, and they lifted up the ephah between the earth and the heavens.　　Lev. 11:13, 19; Ps. 104:17; Jer. 8:7

10 And I said to the angel who was speaking with me, "Where are they taking the ephah?"

11 Then he said to me, "To build a[T] temple for her in the land of[R] Shinar; and when it is prepared, she will be set there on her own pedestal."　　*house* • Gen. 10:10; 11:2; 14:1

CHAPTER 6

The Four Chariots

NOW I lifted up my eyes again and looked, and behold, four chariots were coming forth from between the two mountains; and the mountains *were* bronze mountains.

2 With the first chariot *were* red horses, with the second chariot black horses,

3 with the third chariot[R] white horses, and with the fourth chariot strong[R] dappled horses.　　Rev. 6:2 • Rev. 6:8

4 Then I spoke and said to the angel who was speaking with me, "What[R] are these, my lord?"　　　Zech. 1:9

5 And the angel answered and said to me, "These are the[R] four spirits of heaven, going forth after standing before the Lord of all the earth,　Dan. 7:2; 11:4; Matt. 24:31; Rev. 7:1

6 with one of which the black horses are going forth to the north country; and the white ones go forth after them, while the dappled ones go forth to the south country.

7 "When the strong ones went out, they were eager to go to[T] patrol the earth." And He said, "Go, patrol the earth." So they patrolled the earth.　　*walk about through*

8 Then He cried out to me and spoke to me saying, "See, those who are going to the land of the north have[R] appeased My wrath in the land of the north."　　Ezek. 5:13; 24:13

The Crowning of Joshua

9 The[R] word of the LORD also came to me saying,   Zech. 1:1; 7:1; 8:1

10 "Take[R] *an offering* from the exiles, from Heldai, Tobijah, and Jedaiah; and you go the same day and enter the house of Josiah the son of Zephaniah, where they have arrived from Babylon.   Ezra 7:14-16; 8:26-30; Jer. 28:6

11 "And take silver and gold, make an *ornate* crown, and set *it* on the head of Joshua the son of Jehozadak, the high priest.

12 "Then say to him, 'Thus says the LORD of hosts, "Behold, a man whose name is [T]Branch,[R] for He will[T]branch out from where He is; and He will build the temple of the LORD.   *Sprout* • Is. 4:2; 11:1; Jer. 23:5☆ • *sprout up*

13 "Yes, it is He who will build the temple of the LORD, and He who will bear the honor and sit and rule on His throne. Thus, He will be a priest on His throne, and the counsel of peace will be between the two offices." '

14 "Now the [R]crown will become a reminder in the temple of the LORD to Helem, Tobijah, [T]Jedaiah, and Hen the son of Zephaniah.   Zech. 6:11 • Josiah

15 "And those who are far off will come and build the temple of the LORD." Then you will know that the LORD of hosts has sent me to you. And it will take place, if you completely obey the LORD your God.

CHAPTER 7

The Question of Fasting

THEN it came about in the fourth year of King Darius, that the word of the LORD came to Zechariah on the fourth *day* of the ninth month, *which is*[R]Chislev.   Neh. 1:1

2 Now *the town of* Bethel had sent Sharezer and Regemmelech and their men to [T]seek the favor of the LORD,   *soften the face of*

3 speaking to the priests who belong to the house of the LORD of hosts, and to the prophets saying, "Shall I weep in the fifth month [T]and abstain, as I have done these many years?"   *abstaining; or, dedicating myself*

Rebuke of Hypocrisy

4 Then the word of the LORD of hosts came to me saying,

5 "Say to all the people of the land and to the priests, 'When you fasted and mourned in the fifth and seventh months [T]these [R]seventy years, was it actually for[R]Me that you fasted?   *and these* • Zech. 1:12 • [Is. 1:11, 12; 58:5]

6 'And when you eat and drink, do you not eat for yourselves and do you not drink for yourselves?

7 'Are not *these* the words which the LORD proclaimed by the former prophets, when Jerusalem was inhabited and[A]prosperous with its cities around it, and the Negev and the foothills were inhabited?' "   *at ease*

---

¹ Or, *squares*

Repent of Disobedience

8 Then the word of the LORD came to Zechariah saying,

9 "Thus has the LORD of hosts said, 'Dispense true justice, and practice [R]kindness and compassion each to his brother; Job 6:14

10 and[R]do not oppress the widow or the [A]orphan, the[A]stranger or the poor; and do not devise evil in your hearts against one another.'   Ex. 22:22 • *fatherless* • *resident alien*

11 "But they refused to pay attention, and [T]turned a stubborn shoulder and [T]stopped their ears from hearing.   *gave* • *made heavy*

12 "And they made their[R]hearts *like* [T]flint so that they could not hear the law and the words which the LORD of hosts had sent by His Spirit through the former prophets; therefore great wrath came from the LORD of hosts.   2 Chr. 36:13 • *corundum* • *from hearing*

13 "And it came about that just as [R]He called and they would not listen, so [R]they called and I would not listen," says the LORD of hosts;   Jer. 11:10, 14; 14:12 • Prov. 1:24-28

14 "but I scattered them with a storm wind among all the nations whom they have not known. Thus the land is desolated behind them, so that no one went back and forth, for they made the pleasant land desolate."

CHAPTER 8

Restoration of Israel

THEN the word of the LORD of hosts came saying,

2 "Thus says the LORD of hosts, 'I am[R]exceedingly jealous for Zion, yes, with great wrath I am jealous for her.'   Zech. 1:14

3 "Thus says the LORD, 'I will return to Zion and will dwell in the midst of Jerusalem. Then Jerusalem will be called the City of Truth, and the mountain of the LORD of hosts *will be called* the Holy Mountain.'

4 "Thus says the LORD of hosts, 'Old men and old women will again sit in the ¹streets of Jerusalem, each man with his staff in his hand because of[T]age.   *the multitude of days*

5 'And the ¹streets of the city will be filled with [R]boys and girls playing in its ¹streets.'   Jer. 30:19, 20; 31:12, 13

6 "Thus says the LORD of hosts, 'If it is[R]too difficult in the sight of the remnant of this people in those days, will it also be too difficult in My sight?' declares the LORD of hosts.   *wonderful* • Ps. 118:23; 126:1-3

7 "Thus says the LORD of hosts, 'Behold, I am going to save My people from the land of the east and from the land of the west;

8 and I will bring them *back*, and they will live in the midst of Jerusalem, and they will be My people and I will be their God in [A]truth and righteousness.'   *faithfulness*

9 "Thus says the LORD of hosts, 'Let your hands be[R]strong, you who are listening in these days to these words from the mouth of the prophets, *those* who *spoke* in the day that the foundation of the house of the LORD

of hosts was laid, to the end that the temple might be built.   1 Chr. 22:13; Is. 35:4; Hag. 2:4

10 'For before those days there was no wage for man or any wage for animal; and for him who went out or came in there was no peace because of [R]his enemies, and I set all men one against another.   *the adversary*

11 'But now I will [R]not [T]treat the remnant of this people as in the former days,' declares the LORD of hosts.   [Ps. 103:9] • *be to the*

12 'For *there will be* [R]peace for the seed: the vine will yield its fruit, the land will yield its produce, and the heavens will give their dew; and I will cause the remnant of this people to inherit all these *things.*   Lev. 26:3-6

13 'And it will come about that just as you were a [R]curse among the nations, O house of Judah and house of Israel, so I will save you that you may become a blessing. Do not fear; let your hands be strong.'   Jer. 29:18

14 "For thus says the LORD of hosts, 'Just as I purposed to do harm to you when your fathers provoked Me to wrath,' says the LORD of hosts, 'and I have not relented,

15 so I have again purposed in these days to [R]do good to Jerusalem and to the house of Judah. Do not fear!   Jer. 29:11; [Mic. 7:18–20]

16 'These are the things which you should do: speak the [R]truth to one another; judge with truth and judgment for peace in your [2]gates.   [Prov. 12:17–19; Zech. 8:3; Eph. 4:25]

17 'Also let none of you [R]devise evil in your heart against another, and do not love [T]perjury; for all these are what I hate,' declares the LORD."   Prov. 3:29; Jer. 4:14 • *false oath*

Rejoice in Israel's Future

18 Then the word of the LORD of hosts came to me saying,

19 "Thus says the LORD of hosts, 'The fast of the [R]fourth, the fast of the fifth, the fast of the seventh, and the fast of the tenth *months* will become joy, gladness, and [A]cheerful feasts for the house of Judah; so love truth and peace.'   2 Kin. 25:3, 4 • *goodly*

20 "Thus says the LORD of hosts, '*It will* yet *be* that [R]peoples will come, even the inhabitants of many cities.   Ps. 117:1; Jer. 16:19

21 'And the inhabitants of one will go to another saying, "Let us go at once to entreat the favor of the LORD, and to seek the LORD of hosts; [A]I will also go."   *let me go too*

22 'So many peoples and mighty nations will come to seek the LORD of hosts in Jerusalem and to entreat the favor of the LORD.'

23 "Thus says the LORD of hosts, 'In those days ten men from all the [1]nations will grasp the garment of a Jew saying, "Let us go with you, for we have heard that God is with you." ' "   *languages of the nations*

CHAPTER 9

Judgment on Surrounding Nations

THE [A]burden of the word of the LORD is against the land of Hadrach, with [R]Damascus

as its resting place (for the eyes of men, especially of all the tribes of Israel, are toward the LORD),   *oracle* • Is. 17:1; Jer. 49:23-27

2 And [R]Hamath also, which borders on it;   Jer. 49:23
Tyre and Sidon, [A]though [T]they are very wise.   *because* • *they think they are*

3 For Tyre built herself a fortress
And piled up silver like dust,
And gold like the mire of the streets.

4 Behold, the Lord will dispossess her
And cast her wealth into the sea;
And she will be consumed with fire.

5 Ashkelon will see *it* and be afraid.
Gaza too will writhe in great pain;
Also Ekron, for her expectation has been confounded.
Moreover, the king will perish from Gaza,
And Ashkelon will not be inhabited.

6 And a [T]mongrel race will dwell in [A]Ashdod,   *bastard will* • Amos 1:8; Zeph. 2:4
And I will cut off the pride of the Philistines.

7 And I will remove their blood from their mouth,
And their detestable things from between their teeth.
Then they also will be a remnant for our God,
And be like a [A]clan in Judah,   *chief*
And Ekron like a Jebusite.

8 But I will camp around My house because of an army,
Because of [R]him who passes by and returns;   Is. 52:1
And [R]no oppressor will pass over them anymore,   Is. 54:14; 60:18
For now I have seen with My eyes.

First Coming of the Messiah

9 Rejoice [R]greatly, O daughter of Zion!
Shout *in triumph*, O daughter of Jerusalem!   Matt. 21:4, 5☆
Behold, your king is coming to you;
He is [A]just and endowed with salvation,   *vindicated and victorious*
Humble, and mounted on a donkey,
Even on a colt, the foal of a donkey.

Second Coming of the Messiah

10 And I will [R]cut off the chariot from Ephraim,   Hos. 1:7
And the horse from Jerusalem;
And the bow of war will be cut off.
And He will speak [R]peace to the nations;   Mic. 4:2–4☆
And His [R]dominion will be from sea to sea,   Ps. 72:8; Is. 60:12
And from the [3]River to the ends of the earth.

[2] I.e., the place where court was held
[3] I.e., Euphrates

11 As for you also, because of the[R]blood of My covenant with you,   Heb. 10:2
I have set your[R]prisoners free from the waterless pit.   Is. 24:22; 51:14

12 Return to the stronghold, O prisoners [T]who have the hope;   *of the hope*
This very day I am declaring that I will restore[R]double to you.   Is. 61:7

13 For I will bend Judah as My bow,
I will fill the bow with Ephraim.
And I will stir up your sons, O Zion,
against your sons, O Greece;
And I will make you like a[R]warrior's sword.   Ps. 45:3

14 Then the LORD will appear over them,
And His[R]arrow will go forth like lightning;   Ps. 18:14; Hab. 3:11
And the Lord GOD will blow the[R]trumpet,   Is. 27:13
And will march in the[R]storm winds of the south.   [Is. 21:1; 66:15]

15 The LORD of hosts will defend them.
And they will[R]devour, and trample on the sling stones;   Zech. 12:6
And they will drink, *and* be[R]boisterous as with wine;   Ps. 78:65
And they will be filled like a *sacrificial* basin,
Drenched like the corners of the altar.

16 And the LORD their God will [R]save them in that day   Jer. 31:10, 11
As the flock of His people;
For *they are as* the stones of a crown,
[A]Sparkling in His land.   *Displayed over*

17 For what [T]comeliness and[R]beauty *will* be[T]theirs!   *goodness* • Ps. 27:4 • *his*
Grain will make the young men flourish, and new wine the virgins.

CHAPTER 10

ASK[R]rain from the LORD at the time of the spring rain—   [Joel 2:23]
The LORD who [R]makes the [A]storm clouds;   Jer. 10:13 • *thunderbolts*
And He will give them [R]showers of rain, vegetation in the field to *each* man.   Is. 30:23

2 For the teraphim speak iniquity,
And the diviners see lying visions,
And tell[R]false dreams;   Jer. 23:32
They comfort in vain.
Therefore *the people* [T]wander like [R]sheep,   *journey* • Ezek. 34:5, 8; Matt. 9:36
They are afflicted, because there is no shepherd.

3 "My[R]anger is kindled against the shepherds,   Jer. 25:34-36
And I will punish the male goats;
For the LORD of hosts has visited His flock, the house of Judah,
And will make them like His majestic horse in battle.

4 "From [T]them will come the [R]cornerstone,   *him* • Luke 20:17; Eph. 2:20
From them the tent peg,

From them the bow of battle,
From them every[A]ruler, *all* of them together.   *oppressor*

5 "And they will be as mighty men,
[R]Treading down *the enemy* in the mire of the streets in battle;   2 Sam. 22:43
And they will fight, for the LORD *will be* with them;
And the[R]riders on horses will be put to shame.   Amos 2:15; Hag. 2:22

6 "And I shall [R]strengthen the house of Judah,   Zech. 10:12
And I shall save the house of Joseph,
And I shall[R]bring them back,   Zech. 8:8
Because I have had [R]compassion on them;   Is. 54:8; Zech. 1:16
And they will be as though I had[R]not rejected them,   Is. 54:4
For I am the LORD their God, and I will[R]answer them.   Zech. 13:9

7 "And Ephraim will be like a mighty man,
And their heart will be glad as if *from* wine;
Indeed, their[R]children will see *it* and be glad,   Is. 54:13; Ezek. 37:25
Their heart will rejoice in the LORD.

8 "I will[R]whistle for them to gather them together,   Is. 5:26; 7:18, 19
For I have redeemed them;
And they will be as numerous as they [T]were before.   *were numerous*

9 "When I[T]scatter them among the peoples,   *sow*
They will[R]remember Me in far countries,   1 Kin. 8:47, 48; Ezek. 6:9
And they with their children will live and come back.

10 "I will[R]bring them back from the land of Egypt,   Is. 11:11
And gather them from Assyria;
And I will bring them into the land of [R]Gilead and Lebanon,   Jer. 50:19
Until no *room* can be found for them.

11 "And He will pass through the[R]sea *of* distress,   Is. 51:9, 10
And strike the waves in the sea,
So that all the depths of the[R]Nile will dry up;   Is. 19:5-7
And the pride of [R]Assyria will be brought down,   Zeph. 2:13
And the scepter of Egypt will depart.

12 "And I shall [R]strengthen them in the LORD,   Zech. 10:6
And in His name[R]they will walk," declares the LORD.   Mic. 4:5

CHAPTER 11

Rejection of the Messiah

OPEN your doors, O Lebanon,
That a fire may feed on your cedars.

2 Wail, O [A]cypress, for the cedar has fallen,   *juniper*
Because the glorious *trees* have been destroyed;

Wail, O oaks of Bashan,
For the impenetrable forest has come
down.
3 There is a sound of the shepherds'
^Rwail,   Jer. 25:34-36
For their glory is ruined;
There is a ^Rsound of the young lions'
roar,   Jer. 2:15; 50:44
For the pride of the Jordan is ruined.
4 Thus says the LORD my God, "Pasture
the flock *doomed* to^Rslaughter.   Ps. 44:22
5"Those who buy them slay them and^Tgo
unpunished, and *each of* those who sell
them says, 'Blessed be the LORD, for I have
become rich!' And their own shepherds
have no pity on them.   *are not held guilty*
6"For I shall^Rno longer have pity on the
inhabitants of the land," declares the LORD;
"but behold, I shall^Rcause the men to^Tfall,
each into another's ^Tpower and into the
power of his king; and they will strike the
land, and I shall not deliver *them* from their
power."   Jer. 13:14 • Is. 9:19-21 • *find • hand*
7 So I pastured the flock *doomed* to
slaughter, hence the afflicted of the flock.
And I took for myself two staffs: the one I
called^AFavor, and the other I called^AUnion;
so I pastured the flock.   *Pleasantness • Cords*
8 Then I annihilated the three shepherds
in ^Rone month, for my soul was impatient
with them, and their soul also^Awas weary of
me.   Hos. 5:7 • *detested*
9 Then I said, "I will not pasture you.
What is to die, let it die, and what is to be
annihilated, let it be annihilated; and let
those who are left eat one another's flesh."
10 And I took my staff,^AFavor, and cut it in
pieces, to break my covenant which I had
made with all the peoples.   *Pleasantness*
11 So it was^Abroken on that day, and ⁴thus
the^Rafflicted of the flock who were watching
me realized that it was the word of the
LORD.   *annulled* • Zeph. 3:12
12 And I said to them, "If it is good in
your sight, give *me* my wages; but if not,
never mind!" So they weighed out^Rthirty
shekels of silver as my wages.   Matt. 27:9☆
13 Then the LORD said to me, "Throw it to
the^Rpotter, *that* magnificent price at which I
was valued by them." So I took the thirty
shekels of silver and threw them to the potter in the house of the LORD.   Matt. 27:3-10☆
14 Then I cut my second staff,^AUnion, in
pieces, to^Rbreak the brotherhood between
Judah and Israel.   *Cords* • Is. 9:21; Zech. 11:6
15 And the LORD said to me, "Take again
for yourself the equipment of a^Afoolish^Rshep-
herd.   *useless* • Is. 6:10-12; Zech. 11:17
16"For behold, I am going to raise up a
shepherd in the land who will^Rnot care for
the perishing, seek the scattered, heal the
broken, or sustain the one standing, but will
^Rdevour the flesh of the fat *sheep* and tear off
their hoofs.   Jer. 23:2 • Ezek. 34:2-6
17 "Woe^Tto the worthless shepherd
Who leaves the flock!   Jer. 23:1
A^Rsword will be on his arm

And on his right eye!   Jer. 50:35-37
His arm will be totally withered,
And his right eye will be blind."

CHAPTER 12

Physical Salvation of Judah

THE ⁵burden of the word of the LORD concerning Israel.
Thus declares the LORD who ^Rstretches
out the heavens,^Rlays the foundation of the
earth, and forms the spirit of man within
him,   Is. 42:5; 44:24; Jer. 51:15 • Job 26:7
2"Behold, I am going to make Jerusalem
a cup^Tthat causes reeling to all the peoples
around; and when the siege is against Jerusalem, it will also be against Judah. *of reeling*
3"And it will come about in that day that
I will make Jerusalem a heavy stone for all
the peoples; all who lift it will be^Rseverely
^Tinjured. And all the nations of the earth will
be gathered against it.   Matt. 21:44 • *scratched*
4"In that day," declares the LORD, "I will
strike every horse with bewilderment, and
his rider with madness. But I will watch
over the house of Judah, while I strike every
horse of the peoples with blindness.
5"Then the clans of Judah will say in
their hearts, 'A^Tstrong support for us are the
inhabitants of Jerusalem through the LORD
of hosts, their God.'   *My strength is*
6"In that day I will make the clans of Judah like a^Rfirepot among pieces of wood and
a flaming torch among sheaves, so they will
consume on the right hand and on the left
all the surrounding peoples, while the inhabitants of Jerusalem again dwell on their
own sites in Jerusalem.   Is. 10:17, 18; Obad. 18
7"The LORD also will^Rsave the tents of Judah first in order that the glory of the house
of^RDavid and the glory of the inhabitants of
Jerusalem may not be magnified above Ju-
dah.   Jer. 30:18 • [Amos 9:11]
8"In that day the LORD will defend the
inhabitants of Jerusalem, and the one who
is feeble among them in that day will be like
David, and the house of David *will be* like
God, like the angel of the LORD before them.
9"And it will come about in that day that
I will ^Tset about to destroy all the nations
that come against Jerusalem.   *seek to*

Spiritual Salvation of Judah

10"And I will pour out on the house of David and on the inhabitants of Jerusalem, the
Spirit of grace and of supplication, so that
they will ^Rlook on Me whom they have
pierced; and they will mourn for Him, as
one mourns for an only son, and they will
weep bitterly over Him, like the bitter weeping over a first-born.   John 19:34; 20:27☆
11"In that day there will be great^Rmourn-

---

⁴ Another reading is *the sheep dealers who*   ⁵ Or, *oracle*

ing in Jerusalem, like the mourning of Hadadrimmon in the plain of Megiddo.   Rev. 1:7

12"And the land will mourn, every family by itself; the family of the house of David by itself, and their wives by themselves; the family of the house of Nathan by itself, and their wives by themselves;

13 the family of the house of Levi by itself, and their wives by themselves; the family of the Shimeites by itself, and their wives by themselves;

14 all the families that remain, every family by itself, and their wives by themselves.

CHAPTER 13

"IN that day a fountain will be opened for the house of David and for the inhabitants of Jerusalem, for sin and for impurity.

2"And it will come about in that day," declares the LORD of hosts, "that I will[R]cut off the names of the idols from the land, and they will no longer be remembered; and I will also remove the prophets and the unclean spirit from the land.   Ex. 23:13; Hos. 2:17

3"And it will come about that if anyone still[R]prophesies, then his father and mother who gave birth to him will say to him, 'You shall not live, for you have spoken falsely in the name of the LORD'; and his father and mother who gave birth to him will pierce him through when he prophesies.   Jer. 23:34

4"Also it will come about in that day that the prophets will each be ashamed of his vision when he prophesies, and they will not put on a hairy robe in order to deceive;

5 but he will say, 'I am not a prophet; I am a tiller of the ground, for a man sold me as a slave in my youth.'

6"And one will say to him, [R]"What are these wounds between your arms?' Then he will say, 'Those with which I was wounded in the house of my friends.'   John 20:25, 27☆

7 "Awake, O[R]sword, against My Shepherd,   Jer. 47:6; Ezek. 21:3-5
And against the man, My[R]Associate,"
Declares the LORD of hosts.   Ps. 2:2
"Strike[R] the Shepherd that the sheep may be scattered;   Matt. 26:56☆
And I will[R]turn My hand[A]against the little ones.   Is. 1:25 • upon

8 "And it will come about in all the land,"
Declares the LORD,
"That[R]two parts in it will be cut off and perish;   Is. 6:13; Ezek. 5:2-4, 12
But the third will be left in it.

9 "And I will bring the third part through the[R]fire,   Is. 48:10; Mal. 3:3
Refine them as silver is refined,
And test them as gold is tested.
They will[R]call on My name,   Zech. 12:10
And I will[R]answer them;   Jer. 29:11-13
I will say, 'They are[R]My people,'
And they will say, 'The LORD is my God.' "   Hos. 2:23

CHAPTER 14

Final Siege of Jerusalem

BEHOLD, a[R]day is coming for the LORD when the spoil taken from you will be divided among you.   [Is. 13:6, 9; Joel 2:1; Mal. 4:1]

2 For I will[R]gather all the nations against Jerusalem to battle, and the city will be captured, the[R]houses plundered, the women ravished, and half of the city exiled, but the rest of the people will not be cut off from the city.   Zech. 12:2, 3 • Is. 13:16

Second Coming of the Messiah

3 Then the LORD will[R]go forth and fight against those nations, as when He fights on a day of battle.   His day of fighting

4 And in that day His feet will stand on the Mount of Olives, which is in front of Jerusalem on the east; and the Mount of Olives will be split in its middle from east to west by a very large valley, so that half of the mountain will move toward the north and the other half toward the south.

5 And you will flee by the valley of My mountains, for the valley of the mountains will reach to Azel; yes, you will flee just as you fled before the[R]earthquake in the days of Uzziah king of Judah. Then the LORD, my God, will come, and all the holy ones with[T]Him!   Is. 29:6 • Heb., Thee

6 And it will come about in that day that there will be no light; the[T]luminaries will dwindle.   glorious ones will congeal

7 For it will be[R]a unique day which is known to the LORD, neither day nor night, but it will come about that at evening time there will be light.   [Jer. 30:7]; Amos 8:9

8 And it will come about in that day that[R]living waters will flow out of Jerusalem, half of them toward the eastern sea and the other half toward the western sea; it will be in summer as well as in winter.   [Rev. 22:1, 2]

Kingdom of the Messiah

9 And the LORD will be king over all the earth; in that day the LORD will be the only[R]one, and His name the only one.   [Deut. 6:4]

10 All the[R]land will be changed into a plain from[R]Geba to Rimmon south of Jerusalem; but[T]Jerusalem will rise and remain on its site from Benjamin's Gate as far as the place of the First Gate to the Corner Gate, and from the Tower of Hananel to the king's wine presses.   1 Kin. 15:22 • it

11 And[T]people will live in it, and there will be[R]no more curse, for Jerusalem will[R]dwell in security.   they • [Rev. 22:3] • Ezek. 34:25-28

12 Now this will be the plague with which the LORD will strike all the peoples who have gone to war against Jerusalem; their

flesh will rot while they stand on their feet, and their eyes will rot in their sockets, and their tongue will rot in their mouth.

13 And it will come about in that day that a great panic from the LORD will [T]fall on them; and they will seize one another's hand, and the hand of one will be lifted against the hand of another.   *be among*

14 And Judah also will fight at Jerusalem; and the [R]wealth of all the surrounding nations will be gathered, gold and silver and garments in great abundance.   Is. 23:18

15 So also like this [R]plague, will be the plague on the horse, the mule, the camel, the donkey, and all the cattle that will be in those camps.   Zech. 14:12

16 Then it will come about that any who are left of all the nations that went against Jerusalem will go up from year to year to worship the King, the LORD of hosts, and to celebrate the [R]Feast of Booths.   Lev. 23:34-44

17 And it will be that whichever of the families of the earth does not go up to Jerusalem to worship the King, the LORD of hosts, there will be no rain on them.

18 And if the family of Egypt does not go up or enter, then no *rain will fall* on them; it will be the [R]plague with which the LORD smites the nations who do not go up to celebrate the Feast of Booths.   Zech. 14:12, 15

19 This will be the [T]punishment of Egypt, and the punishment of all the nations who do not go up to celebrate the Feast of Booths.   *sin*

20 In that day there will *be inscribed* on the bells of the horses, "HOLY TO THE LORD." And the cooking pots in the LORD's house will be like the bowls before the altar.

21 And every cooking pot in Jerusalem and in Judah will be holy to the LORD of hosts; and all who sacrifice will come and take of them and boil in them. And there will no longer be a [A]Canaanite in the house of the LORD of hosts in that day.   *merchant*

The Jewish Calendar

The Jews used two kinds of calendars:

Civil Calendar—official calendar of kings, childbirth, and contracts.

Sacred Calendar—from which festivals were computed.

NAMES OF MONTHS	CORRESPONDS WITH	NO. OF DAYS	MONTH OF CIVIL YEAR	MONTH OF SACRED YEAR	
TISHRI	Sept.–Oct.	30 days	1st	7th	The Jewish day was from sunset to sunset, in 8 equal parts:
HESHVAN	Oct.–Nov.	29 or 30	2nd	8th	
CHISLEV	Nov.–Dec.	29 or 30	3rd	9th	
TEBETH	Dec.–Jan.	29	4th	10th	**FIRST WATCH** ..... SUNSET TO 9 P.M.
SHEBAT	Jan.–Feb.	30	5th	11th	**SECOND WATCH** ... 9 P.M. TO MIDNIGHT
ADAR	Feb.–Mar.	29 or 30	6th	12th	**THIRD WATCH** ..... MIDNIGHT TO 3 A.M.
NISAN	Mar.–Apr.	30	7th	1st	**FOURTH WATCH** ... 3 A.M. TO SUNRISE
IYAR	Apr.–May	29	8th	2nd	
SIVAN	May–June	30	9th	3rd	**FIRST WATCH** ..... SUNRISE TO 9 A.M.
TAMMUZ	June–July	29	10th	4th	**SECOND WATCH** ... 9 A.M. TO NOON
AB	July–Aug.	30	11th	5th	**THIRD WATCH** ..... NOON TO 3 P.M.
*ELUL	Aug.–Sept.	29	12th	6th	**FOURTH WATCH** ... 3 P.M. TO SUNSET

*Hebrew months were alternately 30 and 29 days long. Their year, shorter than ours, had 354 days. Therefore, about every 3 years (7 times in 19 years) an extra 29-day-month, VEADAR, was added between ADAR and NISAN.

THE BOOK OF

MALACHI

THE BOOK OF MALACHI

Malachi, a prophet in the days of Nehemiah, directs his message of judgment to a people plagued with corrupt priests, wicked practices, and a false sense of security in their privileged relationship with God. Using the question-and-answer method, Malachi probes deeply into their problems of hypocrisy, infidelity, mixed marriages, divorce, false worship, and arrogance. So sinful has the nation become that God's words to the people no longer have any impact. For four hundred years after Malachi's ringing condemnations, God remains silent. Only with the coming of John the Baptist (3:1) does God again communicate to His people through a prophet's voice.

The meaning of the name *Mal'aki* ("My Messenger") is probably a shortened form of *Mal'ak-ya*, "Messenger of Yahweh," and it is appropriate to the book which speaks of the coming of the "messenger of the covenant" ("messenger" is mentioned three times in 2:7; 3:1). The Septuagint used the title *Malachias* even though it also translated it "by the hand of his messenger." The Latin title is *Maleachi.*

THE AUTHOR OF MALACHI

The only Old Testament mention of Malachi is in 1:1. The authorship, date, and unity of Malachi have never been seriously challenged. The unity of the book can be seen in the dialectic style that binds it together. Nothing is known of Malachi (not even his father's name), but a Jewish tradition says that he was a member of the Great Synagogue (see "The Author of Zechariah").

THE TIME OF MALACHI

Although an exact date cannot be established for Malachi, internal evidence can be used to deduce an approximate date. The Persian term for governor, *pechah* (1:8; cf. Neh. 5:14; Hag. 1:1, 14; 2:21), indicates that this book was written during the Persian domination of Israel (539–333 B.C.). Sacrifices were being offered in the temple (1:7–10; 3:8), which was rebuilt in 516 B.C. Evidently many years had passed since the offerings were instituted, because the priests had grown tired of them and corruptions had crept into the system. In addition, Malachi's oracle was inspired by the same problems that Nehemiah faced: corrupt priests (1:6–2:9; Neh. 13:1–9), neglect of tithes and offerings (3:7–12; Neh. 13:10–13), and intermarriage with pagan wives (2:10–16; Neh. 13:23–28). Nehemiah came to Jerusalem in 444 B.C. to rebuild the city walls, thirteen years after Ezra's return and reforms (457 B.C.). Nehemiah returned to Persia in 432 B.C., but came back to Palestine about 425 B.C. and dealt with the sins described in Malachi. It is therefore likely that Malachi proclaimed his message while Nehemiah was absent between 432 B.C. and 425 B.C., almost a century after Haggai and Zechariah began to prophesy (520 B.C.).

THE CHRIST OF MALACHI

The Book of Malachi is the prelude to four hundred years of prophetic silence, broken finally by the words of the next prophet, John the Baptist: "Behold, the Lamb of God who takes away the sin of the world!" (John 1:29). Malachi predicts the coming of the messenger who will clear the way before the Lord (3:1; cf. Is. 40:3). John the Baptist later fulfills this prophecy, but the next few verses (3:2–5) jump ahead to Christ in His second advent. This is also true of the prophecy of the appearance of "Elijah the prophet" (4:5). John the Baptist was this Elijah (Matt. 3:3; 11:10–14; 17:9–13; Mark 1:3; 9:10, 11; Luke 1:17; 3:4; John 1:23), but Elijah will also appear before the second coming of Christ.

KEYS TO MALACHI

Key Word: An Appeal to Backsliders— The divine dialogue in Malachi's prophecy is designed as an appeal to break through the barrier of Israel's disbelief, disappointment, and discouragement. The promised time of prosperity has not yet come, and the prevailing attitude that it is not worth serving God becomes evident in their moral and religious corruption. However, God reveals His continuing love in spite of Israel's lethargy. His appeal in this oracle is for the people and priests to stop and realize that their lack of blessing is not caused by God's lack of concern, but by their disobedience of the covenant law. When they repent and return to God with sincere hearts, the obstacles to the flow of divine blessing will be removed. Malachi also reminds the people that a day of reckoning will surely come when God will judge the righteous and the wicked.

Key Verses: Malachi 2:17—3:1; 4:5, 6— "You have wearied the LORD with your words.

Yet you say, 'How have we wearied *Him*?' In that you say, 'Everyone who does evil is good in the sight of the LORD, and He delights in them,' or, 'Where is the God of justice?' "

" 'Behold, I am going to send My messenger, and he will clear the way before Me. And the Lord, whom you seek, will suddenly come to His temple; and the messenger of the covenant, in whom you delight, behold, He is coming,' says the LORD of hosts" (2:17—3:1).

"Behold, I am going to send you Elijah the prophet before the coming of the great and terrible day of the LORD. And he will restore the hearts of the fathers to *their* children, and the hearts of the children to their fathers, lest I come and smite the land with a curse" (4:5, 6).

Key Chapter: Malachi 3—The last book of the Old Testament concludes with a dramatic prophecy of the coming of the Lord and John the Baptist: "I am going to send My messenger, and he will clear the way before Me" (3:1). Israel flocked to the Jordan four hundred years later when "The voice of one crying in the wilderness, 'Make ready the way of the LORD' " (Matt. 3:3) appeared, breaking the long silence of prophetic revelation. Malachi 3 and 4 record the coming of the Messiah and His forerunner.

SURVEY OF MALACHI

The great prophecies of Haggai and Zechariah are not yet fulfilled, and the people of Israel become disillusioned and doubtful. They begin to question God's providence as their faith imperceptibly degenerates into cynicism. Internally, they wonder whether it is worth serving God after all. Externally, these attitudes surface in mechanical observances, empty ritual, cheating on tithes and of-

ferings, and crass indifference to God's moral and ceremonial law. Their priests are corrupt and their practices wicked, but they are so spiritually insensitive that they wonder why they are not being blessed by God.

Using a probing series of questions and answers, God seeks to pierce their hearts of stone. In each case the divine accusations are denied: How has God loved us? (1:2-5); How have we (priests) despised God's name? (1:6—2:9); How have we (people) profaned the covenant? (2:10-16); How have we wearied God? (2:17—3:6); How have we robbed God? (3:7-12); How have we spoken against God? (3:13-15). In effect, the people sneer, "Oh, come on now: it's not that bad!" However, their rebellion is quiet, not open. As their perception of God grows dim, the resulting materialism and externalism become settled characteristics that later grip the religious parties of the Pharisees and Sadducees. In spite of all this, God still loves His people and once again extends His grace to any who will humbly turn to Him. Malachi explores: the privilege of the nation (1:1-5), the pollution of the nation (1:6—3:15) and the promise of the nation (3:16—4:16).

The Privilege of the Nation (1:1–5): The Israelites blind themselves to God's love for them. Wallowing in the problems of the present, they are forgetful of God's works for them in the past. God gives them a reminder of His special love by contrasting the fates of Esau (Edom) and Jacob (Israel).

The Pollution of the Nation (1:6—3:15): The priests have lost all respect for God's name and in their greed offer only diseased and imperfect animals on the altar. They have more respect for the Persian governor than they do for the living God. Moreover, God is withholding

FOCUS	PRIVILEGE OF THE NATION	POLLUTION OF THE NATION		PROMISE TO THE NATION		
REFERENCE	1:1————————1:6	————————2:10	————————3:16	————————4:1	————————4:4	————4:6
DIVISION	LOVE OF GOD FOR THE NATION	SIN OF THE PRIESTS	SIN OF THE PEOPLE	BOOK OF REMEMBRANCE	COMING OF CHRIST	COMING OF ELIJAH
TOPIC	PAST	PRESENT		FUTURE		
	CARE OF GOD	COMPLAINT OF GOD		COMING OF GOD		
LOCATION		JERUSALEM				
TIME		c. 432—425 B.C.				

His blessings from them because of their disobedience to God's covenant and their insincere teaching.

The people are indicted for their treachery in divorcing the wives of their youth in order to marry foreign women (2:10–16). In response to their questioning the justice of God, they receive a promise of the Messiah's coming but also a warning of the judgment that He will bring (2:17—3:6). The people have robbed God of the tithes and offerings due Him, but God is ready to bless them with abundance if they will put Him first (3:7–12). The final problem is the arrogant challenge to the character of God (3:13–15), and this challenge is answered in the remainder of the book.

The Promises to the Nation (3:16—4:6): The Lord assures His people that a time is coming when the wicked will be judged and those who fear Him will be blessed. The day of the Lord will reveal that it is not "vain to serve God" (3:14).

Malachi ends on the bitter word "curse." Although the people are finally cured of idolatry, there is little spiritual progress in Israel's history. Sin abounds, and the need for the coming Messiah is greater than ever.

OUTLINE OF MALACHI

CHAPTER 1

The Privilege of the Nation

THE [T] oracle of the word of the LORD to Israel through [A] Malachi.   *burden • My messenger*

2 "I have loved you," says the LORD. But you say, "How hast Thou loved us?" "*Was* not Esau Jacob's brother?" declares the LORD. "Yet I [R] have loved Jacob;   Rom. 9:13

3 but I have hated Esau, and I have [R] made his mountains a desolation, and *appointed* his inheritance for the jackals of the wilderness."   Jer. 49:10, 16-18; Ezek. 35:3, 4, 7, 8, 15

4 Though Edom says, "We have been [R] beaten down, but we will return and build up the ruins"; thus says the LORD of hosts, "They may build, but I will tear down; and *men* will call them the [T] wicked territory, and the people toward whom the LORD is indignant forever."   Jer. 5:17 • *border of wickedness*

5 And your eyes will see this and you will say, "The LORD [A] be magnified beyond the [A] border of Israel!"   *will be great • territory*

The Priests Despise the Name of the Lord

6 " 'A son honors *his* father, and a servant his master. Then if I am a father, where is My honor? And if I am a master, where is My respect?' says the LORD of hosts to you, O priests who despise My name. But you say, 'How have we despised Thy name?'

7 "*You* are presenting defiled [T] food [R] upon My altar. But you say, 'How have we defiled Thee?' In that you say, 'The table of the LORD is to be despised.'   *bread • Lev. 3:11*

8 "But when you present the [R] blind for sacrifice, is it not evil? And when you present the lame and sick, is it not evil? Why not offer it to your governor? Would he be pleased with you? Or would he receive you kindly?" says the LORD of hosts.   Lev. 22:22

9 "But now [T] will you not entreat God's favor, that He may be gracious to us? [T] With such an offering on your part, will He receive any of you kindly?" says the LORD of hosts.   *entreat, please • This has been from your hand*

10 "Oh that there were one among you who would [R] shut the [A] gates, that you might not uselessly kindle *fire on* My altar! I am not pleased with you," says the LORD of hosts, "nor [R] will I accept an offering from you.   Is. 1:13 • *doors* • Hos. 5:6 • *your hand*

11 "For from the rising of the sun, even to its setting, My name *will be* great among the nations, and in every place incense is going to be offered to My name, and a grain offering *that is* pure; for My name *will be* great among the nations," says the LORD of hosts.

12 "But you are profaning it, in that you say, 'The table of the Lord is defiled, and as for its fruit, its food is to be despised.'

13 "You also say, 'My, how tiresome it is!' And you disdainfully sniff at it," says the LORD of hosts, "and you bring what was

taken by robbery, and *what is* lame or sick; so you bring the offering! Should I receive that from your hand?" says the LORD.

14"But cursed be the swindler who has a male in his flock, and vows it, but sacrifices a blemished animal to the Lord, for I am a great King," says the LORD of hosts, "and My name is feared among the nations."

CHAPTER 2

The Lord Curses the Priests

"AND now, this commandment is for you, O priests.

2"If you do ᴿnot listen, and if you do not take it to heart to give honor to My name," says the LORD of hosts, "then I will send the curse upon you, and I will curse your blessings; and indeed, I have ᴿcursed them *already*, because you are not taking *it* to heart. [Lev. 26:14, 15; Deut. 28:15] • Mal. 3:9

3"Behold, I am going to rebuke your offspring, and I will spread ᴬrefuse on your faces, the refuse of your feasts; and you will be taken away ᵀwith it. *seed • vomit • to*

4"Then you will know that I have sent this commandment to you, ᴬthat My covenant may ᵀcontinue with Levi," says the LORD of hosts. *to be My covenant with • be*

5"My covenant with him was *one of* life and peace, and I gave them to him *as an object of* ᴿreverence; so he ᴬrevered Me, and stood in awe of My name. *fear • feared*

6"True ᴬinstruction was in his mouth, and unrighteousness was not found on his lips; he ᴿwalked with Me in peace and uprightness, and he turned many back from iniquity. *Law of truth • Deut. 33:8, 9; Ps. 37:37*

7"For the lips of a priest should preserve ᴿknowledge, and ᵀmen should seek ᴬinstruction from his mouth; for he is the messenger of the LORD of hosts. *Lev. 10:11 • they • law*

8"But as for you, you have turned aside from the way; you have caused many to ᴿstumble ᴬby the instruction; you have ᴬcorrupted the covenant of Levi," says the LORD of hosts. *Jer. 18:15 • in the law • violated*

9"So I also have made you despised and abased ᵀbefore all the people, just as you are not keeping My ways, but are showing ᴿpartiality in the ᴬinstruction. *to • Mic. 3:11 • law*

The People Commit Idolatry

10"Do we not all have one father? Has not one God created us? Why do we deal treacherously each against his brother so as to profane the covenant of our fathers?

11"Judah has dealt ᴿtreacherously, and an abomination has been committed in Israel and in Jerusalem; for Judah has profaned the sanctuary of the LORD ᴬwhich He loves, and has married the daughter of a foreign god. *Jer. 3:7-9 • in that he has loved and married*

12"*As* for the man who does this, may the LORD cut off from the tents of Jacob *everyone* who awakes and answers, or who presents an offering ᵀto the LORD of hosts.

13"And this is ᴬanother thing you do: you cover the altar of the LORD with tears, with weeping and with groaning, because He no longer regards the offering or accepts *it with* favor from your hand. *second*

The People Divorce

14"Yet you say, 'For what reason?' Because the LORD has been a witness between you and the ᴿwife of your youth, against whom you have dealt ᵀtreacherously, though she is your companion and your wife by covenant. *Is. 54:6 • Jer. 9:2; Mal. 3:5*

15"But not one has ᴿdone *so* who has a remnant of the Spirit. And what did *that* one *do* while he was seeking a godly ᵀoffspring? Take heed then, to your spirit, and let no one deal treacherously against the wife of your youth. *Matt. 19:4, 5 • seed*

16"For ᵀI hate ᵀdivorce," says the LORD, the God of Israel, "and him who covers his garment with wrong," says the LORD of hosts. "So take heed to your spirit, that you do not deal treacherously." *He hates • sending away*

The Lord Will Judge at His Coming

17 You have ᴿwearied the LORD with your words. Yet you say, "How have we wearied Him?" In that you say, "Everyone ᴿwho does evil is good in the sight of the LORD, and He ᴿdelights in them," or, "Where is the God of justice?" *Is. 43:22, 24 • Is. 5:20 • Job 9:24*

CHAPTER 3

"BEHOLD, ᴿ I am going to send My ᴬmessenger, and he will ᴬclear the way before Me. And the Lord, whom you seek, will suddenly come to His temple; ᴬand the messenger of the covenant, in whom you delight, behold, He is coming," says the LORD of hosts. *Matt. 11:10, 14 ☆ • angel • prepare • even*

2"But who can endure the day of His coming? And who can stand when He appears? For He is like a ᴿrefiner's fire and like ᵀfullers' soap. *[Matt. 3:10–12] • laundrymen's*

2:10 God the Father of All—The Fatherhood of God applies in a general sense to everyone since all men and women are created by God in His image. Thus their creaturehood is derived from His Fatherhood. This fact is demonstrated by Hebrews 12:9, which speaks of God as "the Father of spirits" (cf. Page 145—Num. 16:22; Page 645—Eccl. 12:7). Paul even agrees with a heathen poet that all men are God's offspring (Page 1115—Acts 17:28). He does not mean, of course, that everyone will have eternal life but that all men and women are the offspring of God in their created natures. James says that men still bear this image (Page 1255—James 3:9).

3"And He will sit as a smelter and purifier of silver, and He will [R]purify the sons of Levi and refine them like gold and silver, so that they may present to the LORD [A]offerings in righteousness.   Is. 1:25 • *grain offerings*

4"Then the offering of Judah and Jerusalem will be pleasing to the LORD, as in the days of old and as in former years.

5"Then I will draw near to you for judgment; and I will be a swift witness against the sorcerers and against the adulterers and against those who swear falsely, and against those who oppress the wage earner in his wages, the widow and the [']orphan, and those who turn aside the alien, and do not fear Me," says the LORD of hosts.   *fatherless*

The People Rob God

6"For [A]I, the LORD, [R]do not change; therefore you, O sons of Jacob, are not consumed.   *I am the LORD; I do not* • [James 1:17]

7"From the [R]days of your fathers you have turned aside from My statutes, and have not kept *them*. Return to Me, and I will return to you," says the LORD of hosts. "But you say, 'How shall we return?'   Jer. 7:25, 26; 16:11, 12

8"Will a man ¹rob God? Yet you are robbing Me! But you say, 'How have we robbed Thee?' In tithes and [A]offerings.   *heave offerings*

9"You are cursed with a curse, for you are ¹robbing Me, the whole nation *of you*!

10"Bring [R]the whole tithe into the storehouse, so that there may be [']food in My house, and test Me now in this," says the LORD of hosts, "if I will not open for you the windows of heaven, and pour out for you a blessing until ²it overflows.   Lev. 27:30 • *prey*

11"Then I will rebuke the devourer for you, so that it may not destroy the fruits of the ground; nor will your vine in the field cast *its* grapes," says the LORD of hosts.

12"And [R]all the nations will call you blessed, for you shall be a [R]delightful land," says the LORD of hosts.   Is. 61:9 • Is. 62:4

The People Doubt
the Character of God

13"Your words have been [T]arrogant against Me," says the LORD. "Yet you say, 'What have we spoken against Thee?'   *strong*

14"You have said, 'It is [R]vain to serve God;

¹ Or, *defraud(ing)*   ² Or, *there is not room enough*
³ Or, *revere(d)*

and what profit is it that we have kept His charge, and that we have walked in mourning before the LORD of hosts?   Jer. 2:25; 18:12

15 'So now we call the arrogant blessed; not only are the doers of wickedness built up, but they also test God and escape.' "

The Rewards of the Book
of Remembrance

16 Then those who ³feared the LORD spoke to one another, and the LORD [R]gave attention and heard *it*, and a [R]book of remembrance was written before Him for those who ³fear the LORD and who esteem His name.   Ps. 34:15; Jer. 31:18-20 • Is. 4:3; Dan. 12:1

17"And they will be Mine," says the LORD of hosts, "on the day that I [T]prepare *My* own possession, and I will spare them as a man spares his own son who serves him."   *make*

18 So you will again [R]distinguish between the righteous and the wicked, between one who serves God and one who does not serve Him.   [Gen. 18:25]; Amos 5:15

CHAPTER 4

The Rewards of the Coming of Christ

"FOR behold, the day is coming, [R]burning like a furnace; and all the arrogant and every evildoer will be chaff; and the day that is coming will set them ablaze," says the LORD of hosts, "so that it will leave them neither root nor branch."   [2 Pet. 3:7]

2"But for you who ³fear My name the [R]sun of righteousness will rise with healing in its wings; and you will go forth and skip about like calves from the stall.   2 Sam. 23:4; Is. 30:26

3"And you will [R]tread down the wicked, for they shall be ashes under the soles of your feet on the day [A]which I am preparing," says the LORD of hosts.   Job 40:12 • *when I act*

The Prophecy of the Coming of Elijah

4"Remember [R]the law of Moses My servant, *even the* statutes and ordinances which I commanded him in Horeb for all Israel.   Deut. 4:23; 8:11, 19

5"Behold, I am going to send you [R]Elijah the prophet before the coming of the great and terrible day of the LORD. [Mark 9:11-13]☆

6"And he will [']restore the hearts of the fathers to *their* children, and the hearts of the children to their fathers, lest I come and [R]smite the land with a curse."   *turn* • Is. 11:4☆

God is also the Father of all as sustainer of life. Every person is an object of His fatherly care (Page 981—Matt. 18:10) and a candidate for His Kingdom (Page 1049—Luke 18:16). Furthermore, God is not willing that any should perish (Page 982—Matt. 18:14; Page 1217—1 Tim. 2:4). Even when men and women reject God He still provides for them as He does believers with rain, fruitful seasons, food, and gladness (Page 968—Matt. 5:45; Page 1110—Acts 14:17).

Now turn to Page 965—Matt. 3:17: God the Father of Christ.

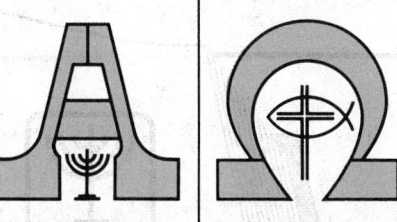

Introduction to the Visual Survey of the Bible

The book introductions in **The Open Bible** provide background information and a survey of each book. But this Visual Survey of the Bible takes a further step by giving a perspective on the whole of Scripture.

Take a moment to familiarize yourself with the first chart, which compares the Old and New Testaments. Note particularly the time-line at the bottom of the page. This time-line divides the Old Testament into five periods and the New Testament into two. It is the key to the rest of the charts.

As you look through the following pages, notice that each chart has its own time-line containing both biblical and extrabiblical events. The maps portray the major movement of each period; the boxes present the key topics. The charts also summarize the themes of the Old Testament poetic and prophetic books, and the themes of the New Testament Epistles.

The ten Life Applications are an important part of this Survey. Based on the flow of each period, they crystallize the central spiritual truths of Scripture. Each principle leads into the next, and all of them relate to your own life.

VISUAL SURVEY...

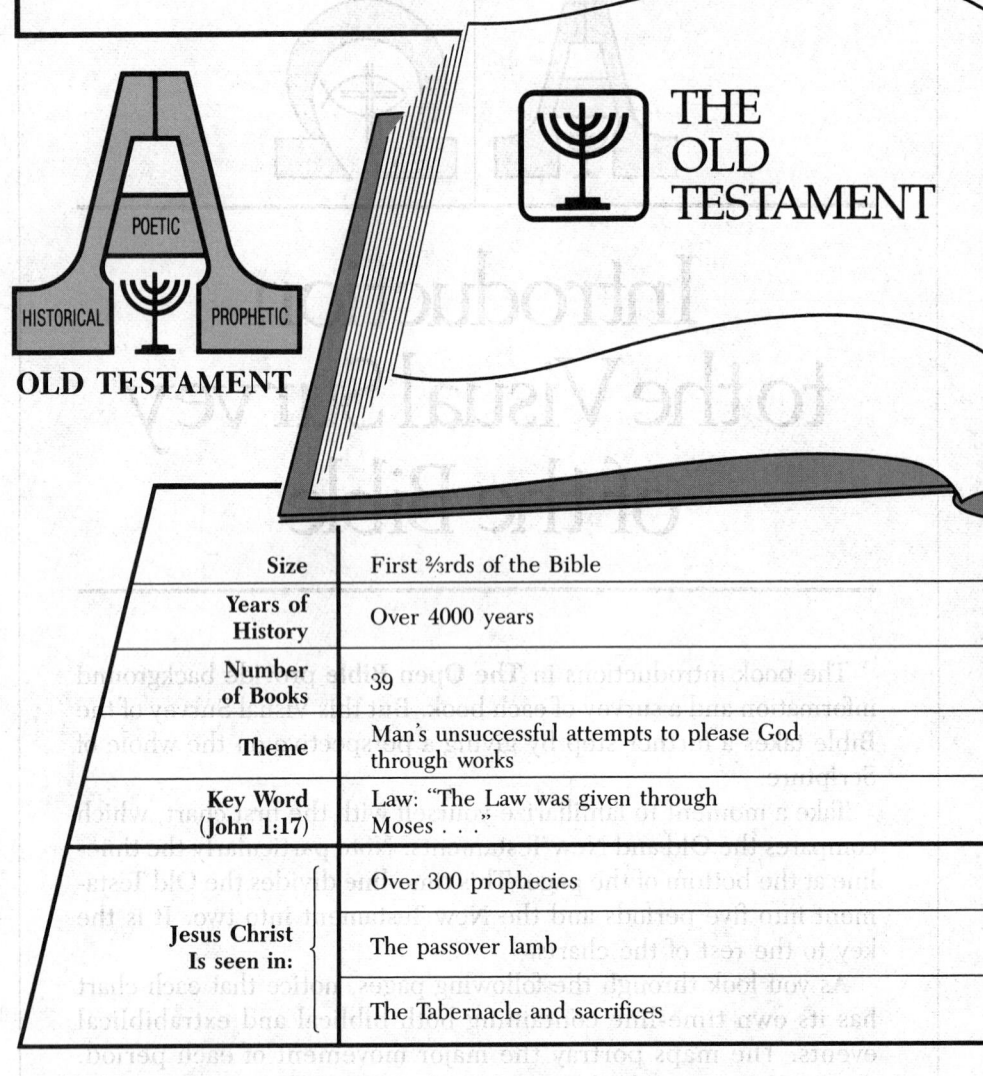

OLD TESTAMENT

THE OLD TESTAMENT

Size	First ⅔rds of the Bible
Years of History	Over 4000 years
Number of Books	39
Theme	Man's unsuccessful attempts to please God through works
Key Word (John 1:17)	Law: "The Law was given through Moses . . ."
Jesus Christ Is seen in:	Over 300 prophecies
	The passover lamb
	The Tabernacle and sacrifices

Adam		Noah	Abraham	Moses	David	Ezra
Before 4000 B.C.		?	2000 B.C.	1500 B.C.	1000 B.C.	500 B.C.

History of the Early World		History of Israel			
Pre-Flood	After the Flood	The People	The Land	The Kingdom	The Remnant
11 Chapters (Gen. 1—11)		Over 38 Books (Gen. 12—Mal.)			

934

...OF THE BIBLE

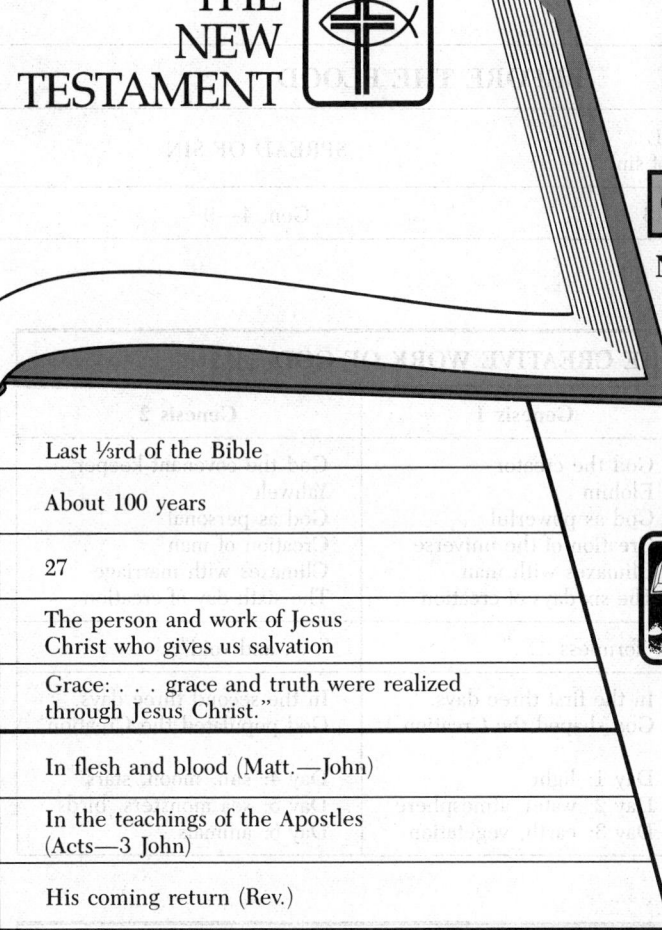

THE NEW TESTAMENT

NEW TESTAMENT

ACTS

GOSPELS

EPISTLES

Last ⅓rd of the Bible

About 100 years

27

The person and work of Jesus Christ who gives us salvation

Grace: . . . grace and truth were realized through Jesus Christ."

In flesh and blood (Matt.—John)

In the teachings of the Apostles (Acts—3 John)

His coming return (Rev.)

"Thy word I have treasured in my heart, that I may not sin against Thee."
Psalms 119:11

Throughout this visual survey, the symbol above will focus on a key principle of life change that grows out of that section of the Bible survey.

Jesus		Peter	Paul	John

4 B.C.   A.D. 33   A.D. 100

History of the Messiah	History of the Early Church		
The Life of Christ	In all Jerusalem	In all Judea & Samaria	To all the Earth
(Matt.—John)	(Acts—Rev.)		

935

HISTORY OF THE EARLY WORLD

Adam

Before
4000 B.C.

BEFORE THE FLOOD

CREATION (Origin of man)	FALL (Origin of sin)	SPREAD OF SIN
Gen. 1; 2	Gen. 3	Gen. 4—9

THE CREATIVE WORK OF GOD

	Genesis 1	Genesis 2
Creation Accounts	God the creator Elohim God as powerful Creation of the universe Climaxes with man The six days of creation	God the covenant-keeper Yahweh God as personal Creation of man Climaxes with marriage The sixth day of creation
Genesis 1:2	"formless . . ."	". . . and void"
Six Days of Creation	In the first three days, God shaped the Creation Day 1: light Day 2: water, atmosphere Day 3: earth, vegetation	In the second three days, God populated the Creation Day 4: sun, moon, stars Day 5: sea monsters, birds Day 6: animals

TEMPTATION: THE TWO ADAMS CONTRASTED

1 John 2:16	Genesis 3:6 (First Adam)	Luke 4:1–13 (Second Adam—Christ)
"the lust of the flesh"	"the tree was good for food"	"tell this stone to become bread"
"the lust of the eyes"	"it was a delight to the eyes"	"he [devil] . . . showed Him all the kingdoms"
"the boastful pride of life"	"the tree was desirable to make one wise"	"throw Yourself down from here"

Noah			Abraham
2500 B.C. ?			2000 B.C.

AFTER THE FLOOD

FLOOD (Judgment of sin)	SPREAD OF NATIONS
Gen. 6—9	Gen. 10—11

AGES OF THE PATRIARCHS
(Before and after the Flood)

The patriarchs who lived before the Flood had an average life span of about 900 years (Gen. 5). The ages of post-Flood patriarchs dropped rapidly and gradually leveled off (Gen. 11). Some suggest that this is due to major environmental changes brought about by the Flood.

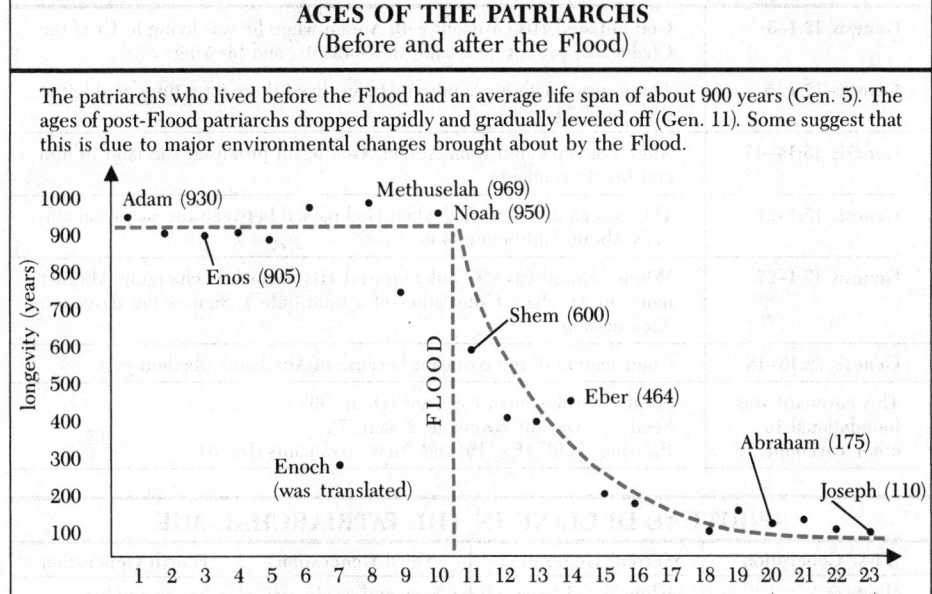

Principle: Righteousness is creative; sin is destructive (Gen. 2:17; Rom. 6:23).

Practice: Genesis 1—11, the prologue not only to Genesis, but to the entire Bible, begins with the ordered and life-giving activity of the holy Creator. The fall of man and the consequent spread of sin stand in stark contrast to the work of God and illustrate the disorder and death that always accompanies rebellion against the purposes of the Lord. God is not mocked; in a moral and spiritual universe, sin must be judged. What must you do, according to Romans 3:21–26, to escape the condemnation of your Creator?

937

HISTORY OF ISRAEL:

Abraham	Joseph
2000 B.C.	1975 B.C.

THE PEOPLE

THE PATRIARCHS	BONDAGE IN EGYPT

2135	1991	Jacob	1790
Birth of	Beginning of	Enters Egypt	Code of
Abraham	Egyptian	with His Family	Hammurabi
	Middle Kingdom		

THE ABRAHAMIC COVENANT

Genesis 12:1–3	God initiated His covenant with Abram when he was living in Ur of the Chaldeans, promising a land, descendants, and blessing.
Genesis 12:4, 5	Abram went with his family to Haran, lived there for a time, and left at the age of 75.
Genesis 13:14–17	After Lot separated from Abram, God again promised the land to him and his descendants.
Genesis 15:1–21	This covenant was ratified when God passed between the sacrificial animals Abram laid before God.
Genesis 17:1–27	When Abram was 99 God renewed His covenant, changing Abram's name to Abraham ("the father of a multitude"). Sign of the covenant: circumcision.
Genesis 22:15–18	Confirmation of the covenant because of Abraham's obedience.
This covenant was foundational to other covenants.	Land: Palestinian covenant (Deut. 30). Seed: Davidic covenant (2 Sam. 7). Blessing: "old" (Ex. 19) and "new" covenants (Jer. 31).

SPIRITUAL DECLINE IN THE PATRIARCHAL AGE

First Generation	Second Generation	Third Generation	Fourth Generation
Abraham	Ishmael and Isaac	Esau and Jacob	Joseph and his eleven brothers
Abraham: man of faith believed God	Ishmael: not son of promise Isaac: called on God believed God	Esau: unspiritual little faith Jacob: at first compromised, later turned to the Lord	Joseph: man of God showed faith Brothers: treachery, immorality, lack of separation from Canaanites
Abraham: built altars to God (Gen. 12:7, 8; 13:4, 18; 22:9)	Isaac: built an altar to God (Gen. 26:25)	Jacob: built altars to God (Gen. 33:20; 35:1, 3, 7)	No altars were built to God in the fourth generation

```
                                                    ┌──────────┐
                                                    │  Moses   │
                                                    └──────────┘
                                                   1500 B.C.
```

(430 years until Exodus, Ex. 12:40; Gal. 3:17)

c. 1750	1570	1525	1445
Beginning of Hittite Empire	Beginning of Egyptian New Kingdom	Birth of Moses	The Exodus

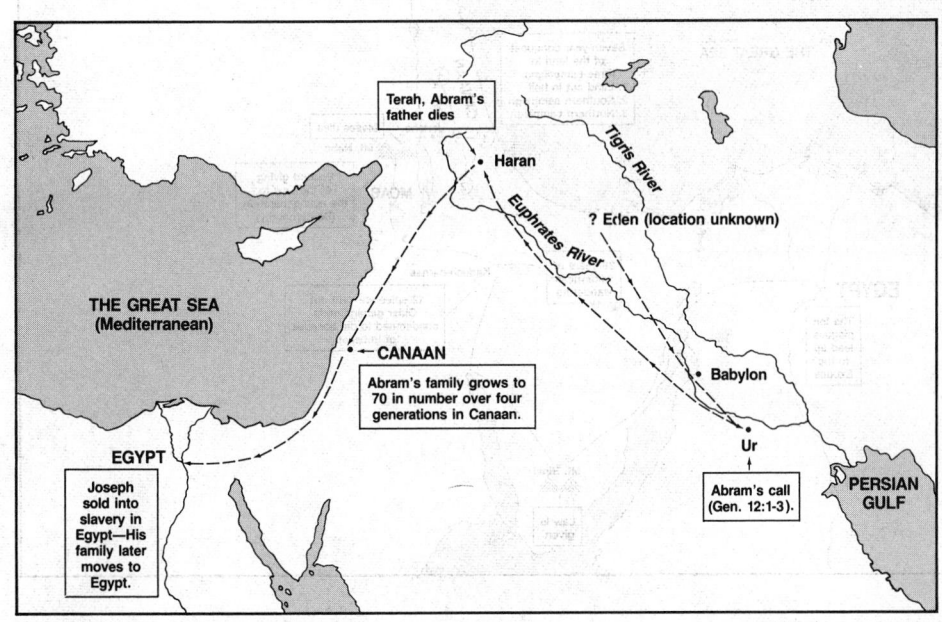

Terah, Abram's father dies

Haran

Tigris River

? Eden (location unknown)

Euphrates River

THE GREAT SEA (Mediterranean)

CANAAN

Abram's family grows to 70 in number over four generations in Canaan.

Babylon

EGYPT

Joseph sold into slavery in Egypt—His family later moves to Egypt.

Ur

Abram's call (Gen. 12:1-3).

PERSIAN GULF

Principle: The destructiveness of sin is overcome by a faith that takes God at His word in spite of appearances and circumstances to the contrary (Gen. 15:6; John 3:16; Heb. 11:8–22).

Practice: Beginning in Genesis 12, God drew forth a man who would be the father of the people from whom and to whom the Messiah would come. Abraham became a friend of God through faith. In spite of appearances to the contrary, he went to a land he had not seen, believed God's promise of a son, and offered up that son at the same area where God's own Son would be crucified. Because he believed God, his faith was accounted to him for righteousness. In the same way, you can enter into a relationship with God by placing your trust in the person and work of His Son. Have you made that decision?

939

POETIC

HISTORICAL | PROPHETIC

Moses
1500 B.C.

→ Shang Dynasty c. 1000 →
→ Mycenaean Civilization c. 1100 →

THE LAND

EXODUS	CONQUEST	PERIOD OF THE JUDGES

1445   1405   1398
1450 ——————— 1423   Reign of Amenhotep II of Egypt

THE GREAT SEA

Seven-year conquest of the land in three campaigns:
1. Land cut in half
2. Southern campaign
3. Northern campaign

CANAAN

Jericho   Moses dies
  Mt. Nebo

Second giving of the Law to the new generation (Deuteronomy)

MOAB

38 years of wilderness wandering

Kadesh-barnea

12 spies are sent out. Older generation is condemned to die because of unbelief.

EGYPT

The ten plagues lead up to the Exodus

Mt. Sinai

Law is given.

Principle: Revelation demands obedience, and obedience brings blessing (Deut. 6:1–15; Josh. 1:8; John 15:12–17).

Practice: After redeeming His people from bondage, the Lord spoke to them in power and glory at Mt. Sinai. The revelation of the Mosaic law required a response of obedience. Their success as individuals and as a nation would depend on the degree of their conformity to God's moral, civil, and ceremonial law. Likewise, disobedience would lead to disaster (e.g., the wilderness wandering and servitude in the time of the Judges). As believers in Christ, our success is measured by the degree of our conformity to His character. To what extent is Christ the Lord of your life?

THE LAND		2000	1500	1000	500	Christ
		People	Land	Kingdom	Remnant	

	Samuel	David
	1105–1020	1000 B.C.
	c. 1100 Greek Dark Ages $\longrightarrow$	

1191	1043
Gideon beats Midianites	Saul anointed King

THE LAW

After their deliverance from Egyptian bondage, the children of Israel needed to learn to walk with their God. The Law was given to instruct the people about the person and the ways of their Redeemer so that they could be set apart to a life of holiness and obedience, not to save anyone but to reveal the people's need to trust in the Lord. As Paul told the Galatians, "Wherefore the law was our schoolmaster to bring us unto Christ, that we might be justified by faith (Gal. 3:24).

The Law combines poetry, salvation history, legislation, and exhortation. The three major divisions of the Law (Deut. 4:44) are the testimonies (moral duties), the statutes (ceremonial duties), and the judgments or ordinances (civil and social duties). The moral portion of the Law is summarized in the Ten Commandments (Ex. 20:1–17; Deut. 5:6–21):

THE TEN COMMANDMENTS (Moral Law)

1–4	Duties to God	"Thou shalt love the Lord thy God" (Matt. 22:37).
5–10	Duties to man	"Thou shalt love thy neighbour" (Matt. 22:39).

THE JUDGES: A CASE STUDY IN DISOBEDIENCE

Each of the seven cycles found in Judges 3:5—16:31 has five steps: sin, servitude, supplication, salvation, and silence. The cycles connect as a descending spiral of sin (2:19), with Israel vacillating between obedience and apostasy.

Cycle	Oppressor	Years of Oppression	Judge/Deliverer	Years of Peace
1. (3:7–11)	Mesopotamians	8	Othniel	40
2. (3:12–30)	Moabites	18	Ehud	80
(3:31)	Philistines		Shamgar	
3. (4:1—5:31)	Canaanites	20	Deborah/Barak	40
4. (6:1—8:32)	Midianites	7	Gideon	40
5. (8:33—10:5)	Abimelech	3	Tola/Jair	45
6. (10:6—12:15)	Ammonites	18	Jephthah/Ibzan/Elon/Abdon	6/7/10/8
7. (13:1—16:31)	Philistines	40	Samson	20

941

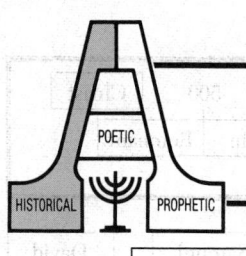

HISTORY OF ISRAEL:

POETIC
HISTORICAL · PROPHETIC

David	Solomon		Elijah	Elisha		Homer (Iliad & Odyssey)
1000 B.C.			852			c. 800

THE KINGDOM

UNITED KINGDOM	DIVIDED KINGDOM
1043 931	
Samuel anoints Saul	ISRAEL: 10 Tribes (North-Samaria)

SAUL	DAVID	SOLOMON	← Civil War Divides Kingdom
			JUDAH: 2 Tribes (South-Jerusalem)

THE LIFE OF DAVID: A Man after God's own heart

1041 B.C.				1011			971 B.C.
		DAVID'S 70 YEARS					
David as Subject (30 Years)				David as King (40 Years)			
As a son to his father	As a servant to King Saul			King over the South	King over all 12 tribes		
	His rise over Saul	Rejected by Saul	Refuge with Philistines	Growing ↗	Growing ↘		
	17–18	19–26	27–31	↗ Success		Crisis ↘	
Psalms	1 Samuel			2 Samuel			1 Kings
23	17	19:1–10	31	7	11 14–18 24		2:10

David the Shepherd · Kills Goliath · Protected by Jonathan · Saul and Jonathan killed at Gilboa · Promise of Christ · Sins with Bathsheba · Absalom's Rebellion · David's Census · David Dies

---

Principle: Obedience grows out of a heart for God (Deut. 6:5; 1 Sam. 13:14; 1 Chr. 28:9; Acts 13:22).

Practice: Saul and David are a study in contrasts. The key to Saul's failure was his lack of a heart for God; the key to David's greatness was his obvious love for the Lord. David's relationship with God became the standard by which all the kings of Judah would be measured. To know God is to love Him, and to love Him is to desire to obey Him. Read Psalms 23 as a model of a man who was intimate with God. What are the things that may be hindering your growth in the knowledge of God?

THE KINGDOM

	2000	1500	1000	500	Christ
	People	Land	Kingdom	Remnant	

Rome Founded
753

Births of Buddha, Confucius
563   551

Ezra

500 B.C.

	EXILE	RETURN

722   586   516

← Assyria Conquers Israel

Babylon Conquers Judah →

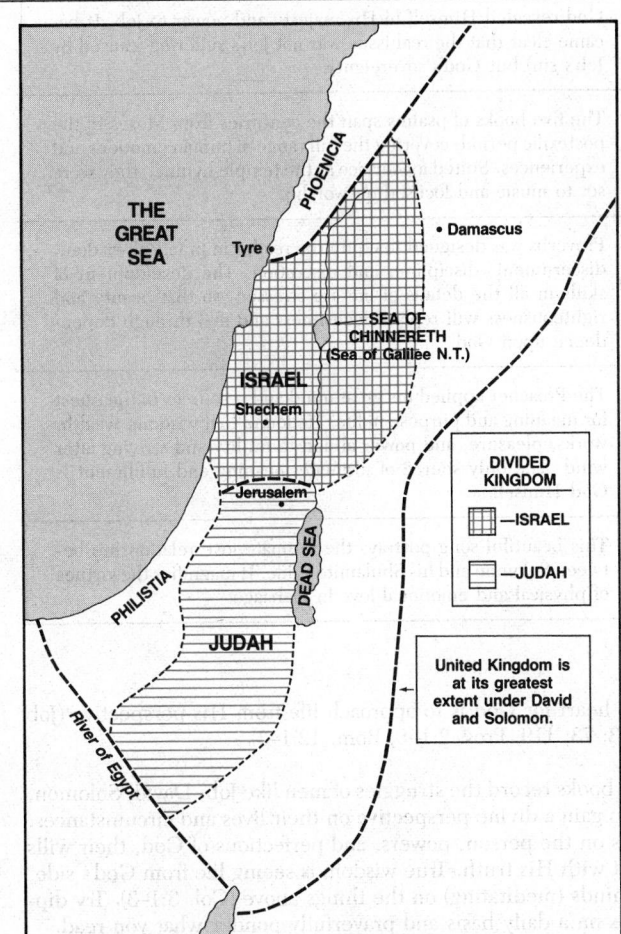

THE GREAT SEA

PHOENICIA

Tyre

• Damascus

SEA OF CHINNERETH
(Sea of Galilee N.T.)

ISRAEL

Shechem

Jerusalem

DEAD SEA

PHILISTIA

JUDAH

River of Egypt

DIVIDED KINGDOM

▦ —ISRAEL

▤ —JUDAH

United Kingdom is at its greatest extent under David and Solomon.

KINGS OF ISRAEL
1. Jeroboam I
2. Nadab
3. Baasha
4. Elah
5. Zimri
6. Omri
7. Ahab
8. Ahaziah
9. Jehoram
10. Jehu
11. Jehoahaz
12. Jehoash
13. Jeroboam II
14. Zechariah
15. Shallum
16. Menahem
17. Pekahiah
18. Pekah
19. Hoshea

KINGS OF JUDAH
1. Rehoboam
2. Abijam
3. Asa
4. Jehoshaphat
5. Jehoram
6. Ahaziah
7. Athaliah
8. Joash
9. Amaziah
10. Azariah
11. Jotham
12. Ahaz
13. Hezekiah
14. Manasseh
15. Amon
16. Josiah
17. Jehoahaz
18. Jehoiakim
19. Jehoiachin
20. Zedekiah

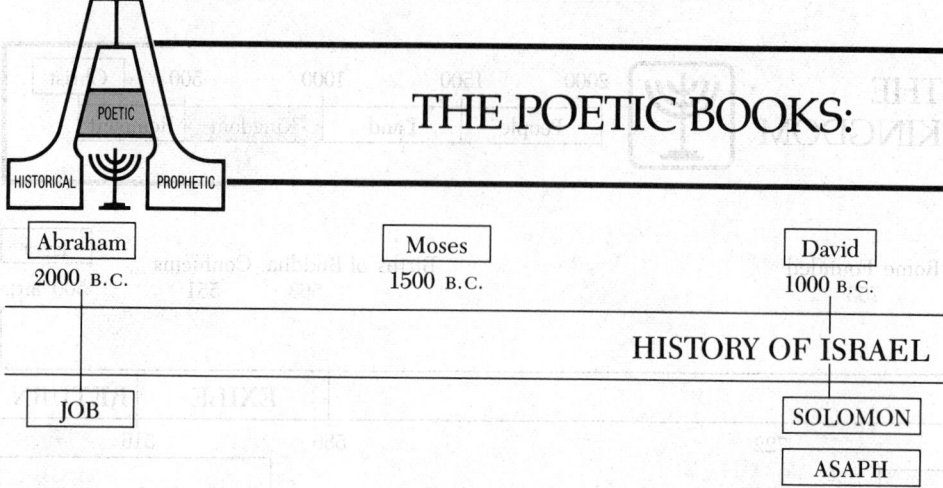

THE POETIC BOOKS:

POETIC	
HISTORICAL	PROPHETIC

Abraham	Moses	David
2000 B.C.	1500 B.C.	1000 B.C.

HISTORY OF ISRAEL

JOB		SOLOMON
		ASAPH

THEMES OF THE POETIC BOOKS

BOOK	KEY WORD	THEME
Job	Sovereignty	God revealed Himself in His majesty and power to Job. It became clear that the real issue was not Job's suffering (caused by Job's sin) but God's sovereignty.
Psalms	Worship	The five books of psalms span the centuries from Moses to the postexilic period, covering the full range of human emotions and experiences. Suited for service as the temple hymnal, they were set to music and focused on worship.
Proverbs	Wisdom	Proverbs was designed to equip the reader in practical wisdom, discernment, discipline, and discretion. The development of skills in all the details of life are stressed, so that beauty and righteousness will replace foolishness and evil through dependence upon God.
Ecclesiastes	Vanity	The Preacher applied his great mind and resources to the quest for meaning and purpose in life. He found that wisdom, wealth, works, pleasure, and power all led to futility and striving after wind. The only source of ultimate meaning and fulfillment is God Himself.
Song of Solomon	Love in Marriage	This beautiful song portrays the intimate love relationship between Solomon and his Shulamite bride. It magnifies the virtues of physical and emotional love in marriage.

Principle: To have a heart for God is to approach life from His perspective (Job 42:1–6; Ps. 1; 19; 63; 73; 119; Prov. 2:1–9; Rom. 12:1–3).

Practice: The poetic books record the struggles of men like Job, David, Solomon, Asaph, and others to gain a divine perspective on their lives and circumstances. As they learned to set their minds on the person, powers, and perfections of God, their wills and emotions came into alignment with His truth. True wisdom is seeing life from God's side, and this is rooted in setting our minds (meditating) on the things above (Col. 3:1–3). Try dipping into the Psalms and Proverbs on a daily basis and prayerfully ponder what you read.

THE HEART OF THE JEWS

THE PATH TO TRUE SUCCESS	
Question	**Principle**
1. What is wisdom?	Wisdom is the key to a life of beauty, fulfillment, and purpose (Prov. 3:15–18). Wisdom is the skill in the art of living life with every area under the dominion of God. It is the ability to use the best means at the best time to accomplish the best ends.
2. How do we pursue wisdom?	The treasure of wisdom rests in the hands of God. Since it comes from above (Prov. 2:6; cf. James 3:17), we cannot attain it apart from Him.
3. What are the conditions for attaining wisdom?	True wisdom can only be gained by cultivating the fear of the Lord (Job 28:28; Ps. 86:11; 111:10; Prov. 1:7; 9:10).
4. What is the fear of the Lord?	To fear God is to have an attitude of awe and humility before Him (Prov. 15:33). It is to recognize Him as our Creator and our complete dependence upon Him in every activity of our lives.
5. Why have so few people developed this fear of God?	The temporal value system of this world is based on what is seen, while the eternal value system of Scripture is based on what is unseen (2 Cor. 4:16–18; 5:7). The former exerts a powerful influence upon us, and we struggle with giving up the seen for the unseen.
6. What can enable us to choose the eternal value system?	This choice is based on faith (believing God in spite of appearances and circumstances), and faith is based on trust.
7. How do we grow in faith?	Our ability to trust God is directly proportional to our knowledge of God. The better we know Him, the more we can trust Him.
8. How can we increase in our knowledge of God?	We become intimate with God as we talk with Him in prayer and listen to His voice in Scripture. The better we know God, the more we love Him and want to respond to His desires for our lives. Faith in God is simply trusting Him as a person, and trust is manifested in action.

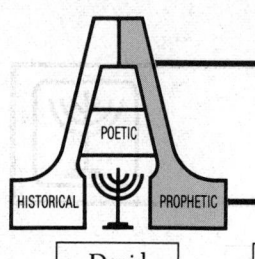

POETIC
HISTORICAL   PROPHETIC

THE PROPHETIC BOOKS:

David		Elijah	Elisha		Zerubbabel	Ezra	Nehemiah
1000 B.C.		852			500		

THE KINGDOM

UNITED KINGDOM	DIVIDED KINGDOM	EXILE	RETURN

	ISRAEL	← 722	70 Years in Babylon	3 stage return
UNITED KINGDOM	← 931			1st Zerubbabel
		586 →		2nd Ezra
	JUDAH			3rd Nehemiah

PROPHETS BEFORE THE EXILE		EXILE PROPHETS	PROPHETS AFTER THE EXILE
To Israel:	To Judah:	To Jews in Babylon:	To the Remnant after returning:
Amos (760)	Joel (835)	Daniel (605)	
Hosea (755)	Isaiah (740)	Ezekiel (592)	Haggai (520)
	Micah (735)		Zechariah (520)
To Nineveh:	Zephaniah (630)		Malachi (432)
	Jeremiah (627)		
Jonah (760)	Habakkuk (607)		
Nahum (660)	Lamentations (586)		
To Edom:			
Obadiah (840)			

Principle: God's disciplines are designed to restore a heart for Himself (Jer. 17:5, 7; Joel 2:12, 13; Heb. 12:5–11).

Practice: God had to discipline His people because of their moral and spiritual rebellion and their refusal to heed the warnings of His prophets. Reproof is designed to bring repentance and repentance brings restoration. The same prophets who pronounced the condemnation of God also announced the consolation of God. Similarly, because God loves us, He must sometimes chasten us as His children to train us in the ways of righteousness. How do you respond during these times? Are you teachable or intractable?

THE HOPE OF THE JEWS

Christ
4 B.C.

THE REMNANT

400 YEARS UNTIL CHRIST

415

THEMES OF THE PROPHETIC BOOKS

The Major Prophets

BOOK	KEY WORD	THEME
Isaiah	Salvation Is of the Lord	Twofold message of condemnation (1–39) and consolation (40–66). God's judgment on the sins of Judah, the surrounding nations, and the world, followed by future salvation and restoration.
Jeremiah	Judah's Last Hour	Declaration of certain judgment of God against Judah. God promises to establish a new covenant with His people.
Lamentations	Lamentations	This beautifully structured series of five lament poems is a funeral dirge for the fallen city of Jerusalem.
Ezekiel	Future Restoration	Ministry to the Jewish captives in Babylon before and after the fall of Jerusalem. The fate of Judah's foes and an apocalyptic vision of Judah's future.
Daniel	God's Program for Israel	Outlines God's plan for the gentile nations (2–7) and portrays Israel during the time of gentile domination (8–12).

The Minor Prophets

BOOK	KEY WORD	THEME
Hosea	God's Love for Israel	The story of Hosea and his faithless wife illustrates the loyal love of God and the spiritual adultery of Israel.
Joel	Day of the Lord	A recent locust plague illustrates the far more terrifying day of the Lord. God appeals to the people to repent in order to avert the coming disaster.
Amos	Judgment of Israel	In eight pronouncements of judgment, Amos spirals around the surrounding countries before landing on Israel. He lists the sins of Israel and calls for repentance.
Obadiah	Judgment of Edom	Condemns the nation of Edom (descended from Esau) for refusing to act as a brother toward Judah (descended from Jacob).
Jonah	Revival in Nineveh	The repentant response of the people of Nineveh to Jonah's one-line prophetic message caused the God of mercy to spare the city.
Micah	Judgment and Restoration of Judah	In spite of divine retribution against the corruption of Israel and Judah, God's covenant with them will be fulfilled in Messiah's future kingdom.
Nahum	Judgment of Nineveh	About 125 years after Nineveh repented under the preaching of Jonah, Micah predicted the destruction of the city because of its idolatry and brutality.
Habakkuk	Live by Faith	Troubled with God's plan to use the Babylonians as His rod of judgment on Judah, Habakkuk praises the Lord after gaining a better perspective on His power and purposes.
Zephaniah	Day of the Lord	The coming day of the Lord is a time of awesome judgment followed by great blessing. Judah stands condemned, but God will restore the fortunes of the remnant.
Haggai	Reconstruction of the Temple	After the Babylonian exile, Haggai urges the Jews to put God first and finish the Temple they had begun so that they can enjoy God's blessing.
Zechariah	Prepare for the Messiah	Like Haggai, Zechariah exhorts the Jews to complete the construction of the Temple. He relates it to the coming of Messiah in a series of visions and messianic prophecies.
Malachi	Appeal to Backsliders	The spiritual climate of the people had grown cold, and Malachi rebukes them for their religious and social compromise. If they return to God with sincere hearts, they will be blessed.

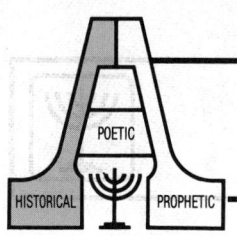

POETIC

HISTORICAL   PROPHETIC

HISTORY OF ISRAEL: THE REMNANT

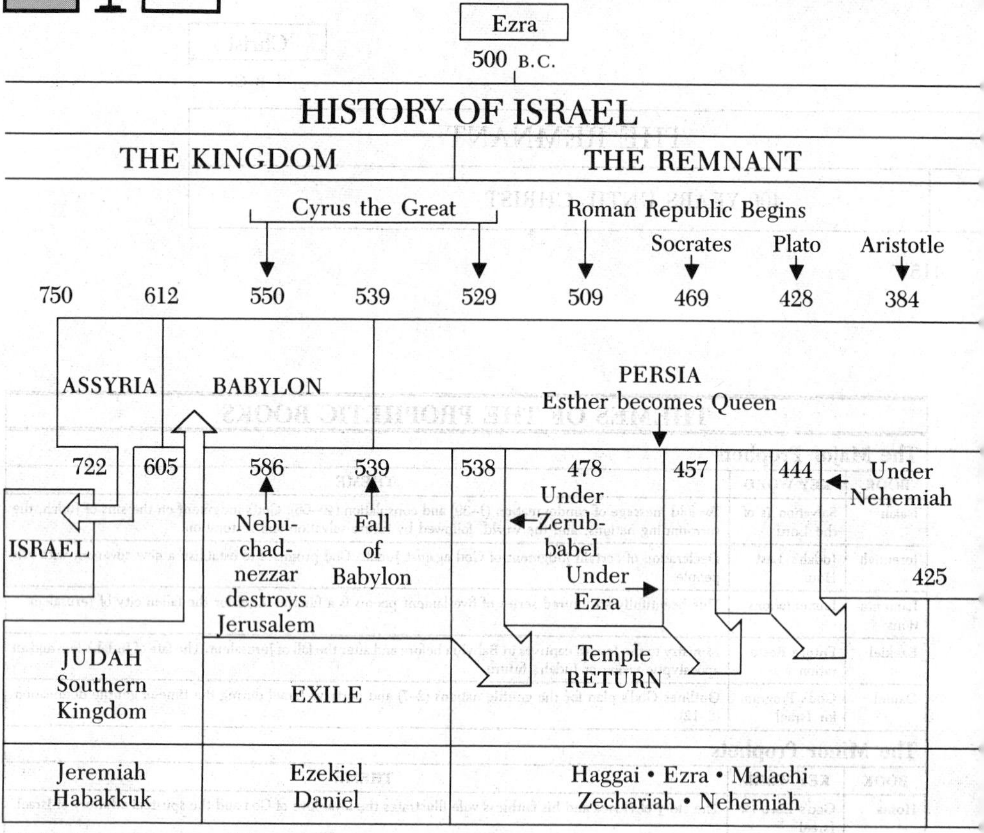

Ezra

500 B.C.

HISTORY OF ISRAEL

THE KINGDOM	THE REMNANT

Cyrus the Great · · · · · · · Roman Republic Begins

Socrates   Plato   Aristotle

750	612	550	539	529	509	469	428	384

| ASSYRIA | BABYLON | | | | PERSIA | | | |
| | | | | | Esther becomes Queen | | | |

722	605	586	539	538	478	457	444	Under Nehemiah
					Under Zerubbabel			
ISRAEL		Nebu-chad-nezzar destroys Jerusalem	Fall of Babylon		Under Ezra			425

JUDAH Southern Kingdom	EXILE			Temple RETURN			

Jeremiah Habakkuk	Ezekiel Daniel	Haggai • Ezra • Malachi Zechariah • Nehemiah

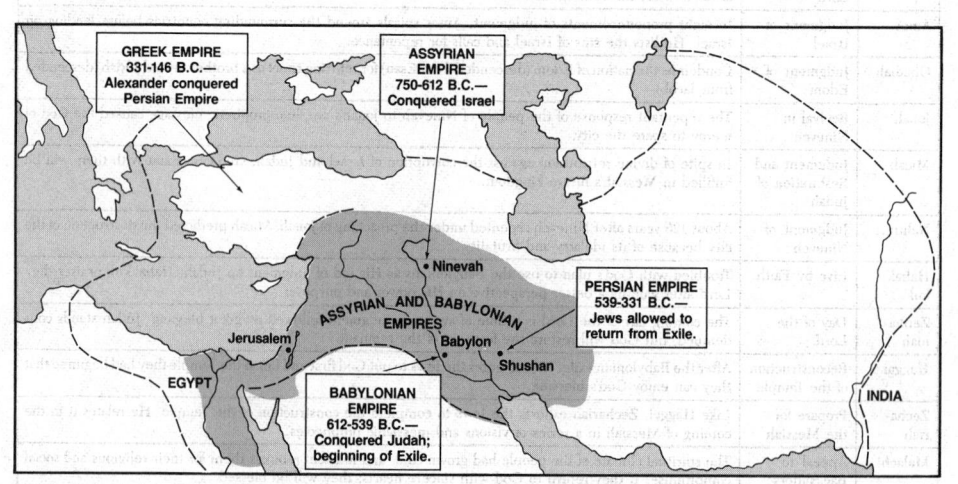

GREEK EMPIRE
331-146 B.C.—
Alexander conquered
Persian Empire

ASSYRIAN
EMPIRE
750-612 B.C.—
Conquered Israel

• Ninevah

PERSIAN EMPIRE
539-331 B.C.—
Jews allowed to
return from Exile.

ASSYRIAN AND BABYLONIAN
EMPIRES

Jerusalem •   Babylon •
• Shushan

EGYPT

INDIA

BABYLONIAN
EMPIRE
612-539 B.C.—
Conquered Judah;
beginning of Exile.

948

Bridging the Testaments

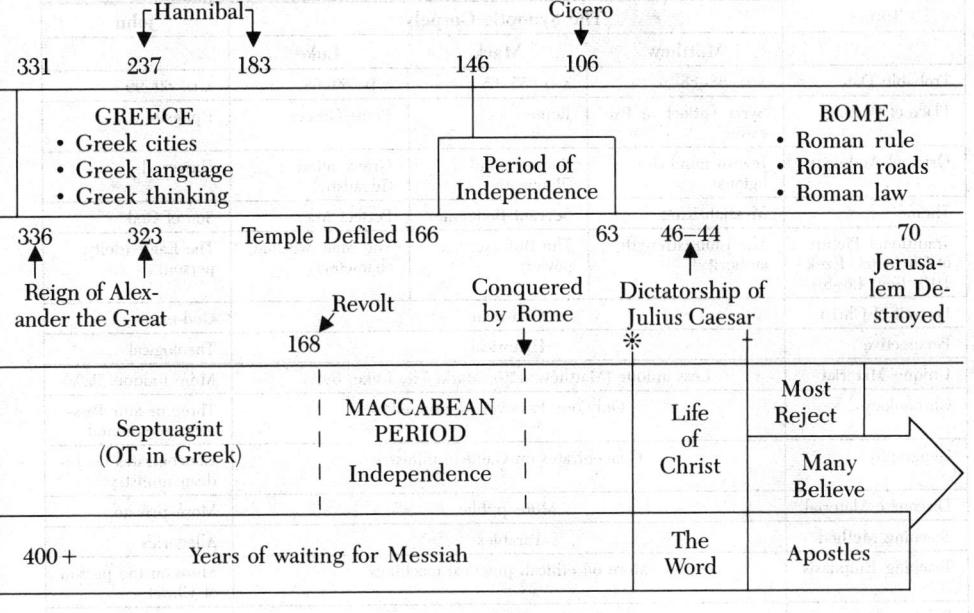

	500	Christ	A.D. 100
Kingdom	The Remnant		

	Christ	
4 B.C.	A.D. 33	A.D. 100
	Life of Christ	History of the Early Church

	Hannibal		Cicero	
331	237	183	146	106

GREECE		ROME
• Greek cities		• Roman rule
• Greek language	Period of Independence	• Roman roads
• Greek thinking		• Roman law

336	323	Temple Defiled 166		63	46–44	70
Reign of Alexander the Great		Revolt 168		Conquered by Rome	Dictatorship of Julius Caesar ✳	Jerusalem Destroyed

Septuagint (OT in Greek)	MACCABEAN PERIOD	Life of Christ	Most Reject
	Independence		Many Believe
400+ Years of waiting for Messiah		The Word	Apostles

![icon]

Principle: True restoration results from being molded by the Word within rather than the world without (Ezra 7:10; 9:10–15; Is. 46:3, 4; Acts 7:51–53).

Practice: Even after the chastening of the Exile, most of the returning Jews became enmeshed once again in the affairs of the world and neglected their relationship with God. For some, the problem was external religiosity without internal reality; for others, the problem was being more influenced by culture than Scripture. God has always had to work with a faithful minority who love Him enough to stand against the tide of the world system. Is your quality of life different from that of those who love the world more than the Lord?

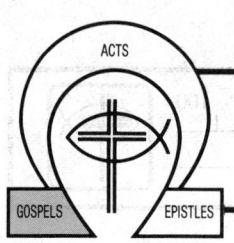

ACTS

GOSPELS   EPISTLES

THE LIFE OF CHRIST:

4 B.C.   A.D. 9 (Temple Discussion)

EARLY CHILDHOOD	YEARS AT NAZARETH (Luke 2:51, 52)

Birth   Luke 2:41–50

THE GOSPELS COMPARED AND CONTRASTED

Topics	The Synoptic Gospels			John
	Matthew	Mark	Luke	
Probable Date	A.D. 58–68	A.D. 55–65	A.D. 60–68	A.D. 80–90
Place of Writing	Syria Antioch or Palestine	Rome	Rome/Greece	Ephesus
Original Audience	Jewish mind (Religious)	Roman mind (Pragmatic)	Greek mind (Idealistic)	Universal
Theme	Messiah-King	Servant-Redeemer	Perfect Man	Son of God
Traditional Picture of Christ (cf. Ezek. 1:10; Rev. 4:6–8)	The Lion (strength, authority)	The Bull (service, power)	The Man (wisdom, character)	The Eagle (deity, person)
Portrait of Christ	God-man			God-man
Perspective	Historical			Theological
Unique Material	Less unique (Matthew, 42%; Mark, 7%; Luke, 59%)			More unique (92%)
Chronology	Only one Passover mentioned			Three or four Passovers mentioned
Geography	Concentrates on Galilean ministry			Concentrates on Judean ministry
Discourse Material	More public			More private
Teaching Method	Parables			Allegories
Teaching Emphasis	More on ethical, practical teachings			More on the person of Christ
Relationship to Other Gospels	Complementary			Supplementary

CHRIST'S PUBLIC MINISTRY

Masses drawn to His miracles and teachings →

Popularity peaks
Leaders attribute His miracles

A.D. 29	30	31
Opening events	Early Judaean ministry	Great Galilean ministry
Year of curious acceptance		Year of growing hostility

↑ Baptized by John Matt. 3

↑ First miracle John 2

↑ Nicodemus learns of new birth John 3

↑ Woman at well John 4

↑ Rejected at Nazareth Luke 4

↑ Apostles selected Mark 3

↑ Sermon on Mount Matt. 5—7

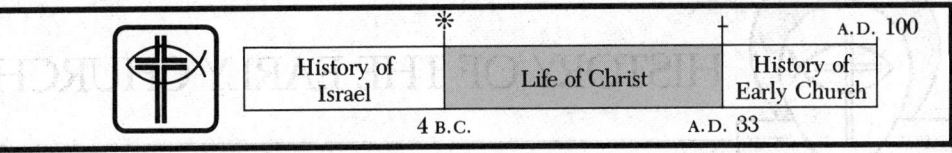
A.D. 29   A.D. 33

PUBLIC MINISTRY

Principle: Jesus, the living Word, lives His life in and through us as we walk in dependence upon Him (John 1:11, 12; 10:10; 15:4, 5; Gal. 2:20).

Practice: In Christ, God personally revealed Himself in human flesh: to see Him is to see God (John 12:45; 14:9), to know Him is to know God (John 8:19), to receive Him is to receive God (Mark 9:37), to honor Him is to honor God (John 5:23), and to reject Him is to reject God (Luke 10:16). He is the vine, the source of life; we are the branches, the channels of life. It is only as we draw our life from Him that we bear lasting fruit. To what extent are you looking to Jesus as the true source of your security, significance, and fulfillment?

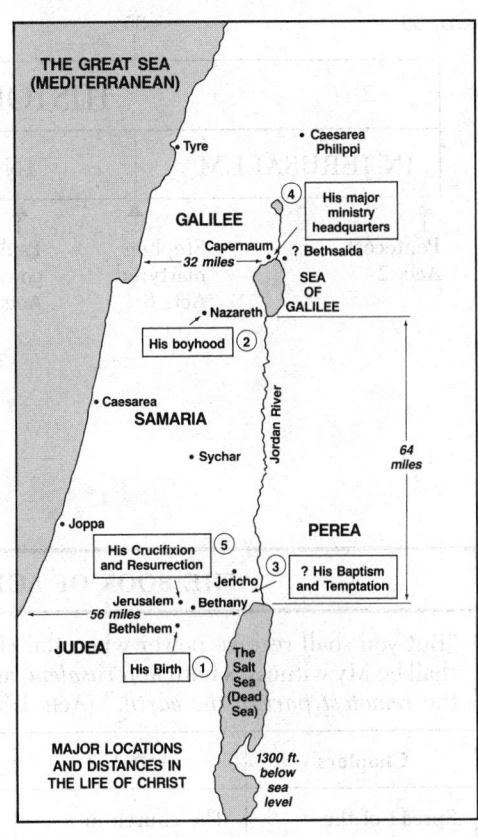

THE GREAT SEA (MEDITERRANEAN)

Tyre

Caesarea Philippi

GALILEE

④ His major ministry headquarters

Capernaum — 32 miles → ? Bethsaida

SEA OF GALILEE

Nazareth

His boyhood ②

Caesarea

SAMARIA

Sychar

Jordan River

64 miles

Joppa

His Crucifixion and Resurrection ⑤

PEREA

Jericho

③ ? His Baptism and Temptation

Jerusalem • Bethany
56 miles
Bethlehem

JUDEA

His Birth ①

The Salt Sea (Dead Sea)

1300 ft. below sea level

MAJOR LOCATIONS AND DISTANCES IN THE LIFE OF CHRIST

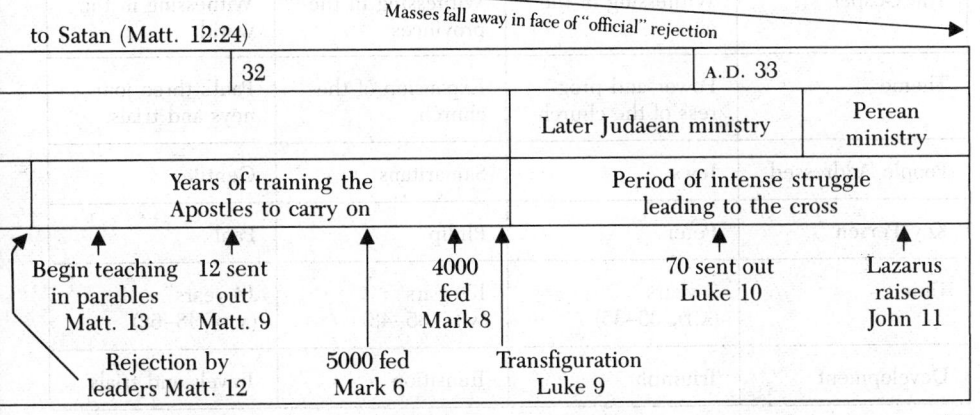

to Satan (Matt. 12:24)

Masses fall away in face of "official" rejection

32	A.D. 33	
	Later Judaean ministry	Perean ministry
Years of training the Apostles to carry on	Period of intense struggle leading to the cross	

Begin teaching in parables Matt. 13   12 sent out Matt. 9   4000 fed Mark 8   70 sent out Luke 10   Lazarus raised John 11

Rejection by leaders Matt. 12   5000 fed Mark 6   Transfiguration Luke 9

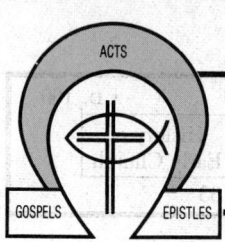

HISTORY OF THE EARLY CHURCH:

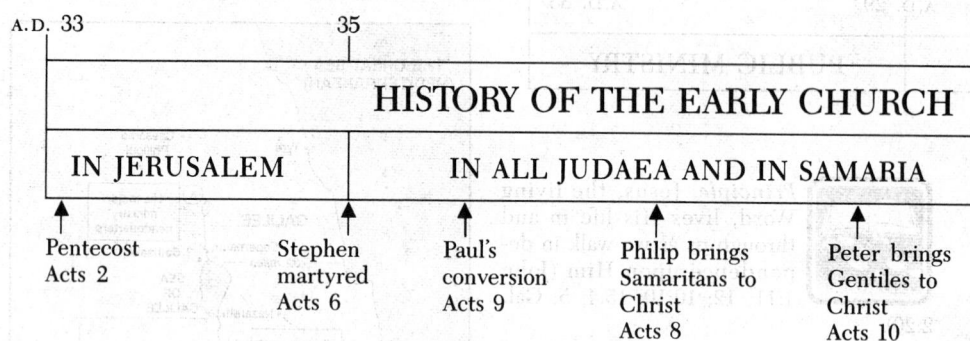

A.D. 33   35

HISTORY OF THE EARLY CHURCH

| IN JERUSALEM | IN ALL JUDAEA AND IN SAMARIA |

Pentecost
Acts 2

Stephen
martyred
Acts 6

Paul's
conversion
Acts 9

Philip brings
Samaritans to
Christ
Acts 8

Peter brings
Gentiles to
Christ
Acts 10

THE BOOK OF ACTS IN OVERVIEW

"But you shall receive power when the Holy Spirit has come upon you; and you shall be My witnesses both in *Jerusalem*, and in all *Judea* and *Samaria*, and even to the *remotest part of the earth*." (Acts 1:8).

Chapters	Acts 1–7	Acts 8–12	Acts 13–28
Spread of the Church	The church in Jerusalem	The church in all Judea and Samaria	The church to all the earth
The Gospel	Witnessing in the city	Witnessing in the provinces	Witnessing in the world
Theme	Power and progress of the church	Expansion of the church	Paul's three journeys and trials
People Addressed	Jews	Samaritans	Gentiles
Key Person	Peter	Philip	Paul
Time	2 years (A.D. 33–35)	13 years (A.D. 35–48)	14 years (A.D. 48–62)
Development	Triumph	Transition	Travels and trials

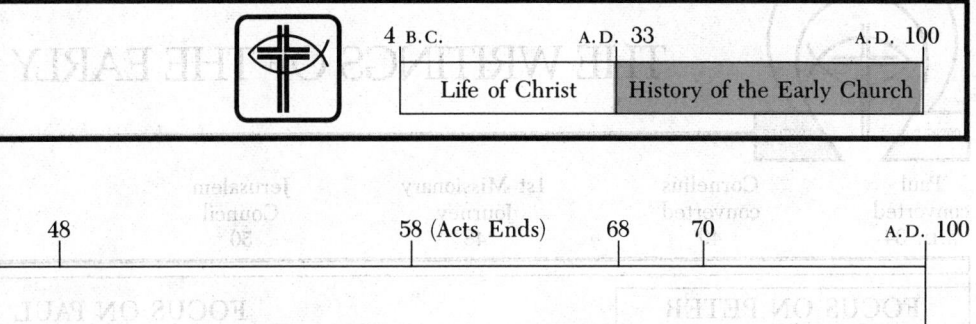

4 B.C.	A.D. 33	A.D. 100
	Life of Christ	History of the Early Church

48	58 (Acts Ends)	68	70	A.D. 100

UNTO THE UTTERMOST PART OF THE EARTH

Missionary Journeys	Paul Imprisoned	Peter Executed	Jerusalem Destroyed	John Dies
Jerusalem Council Acts 15			Paul Executed	

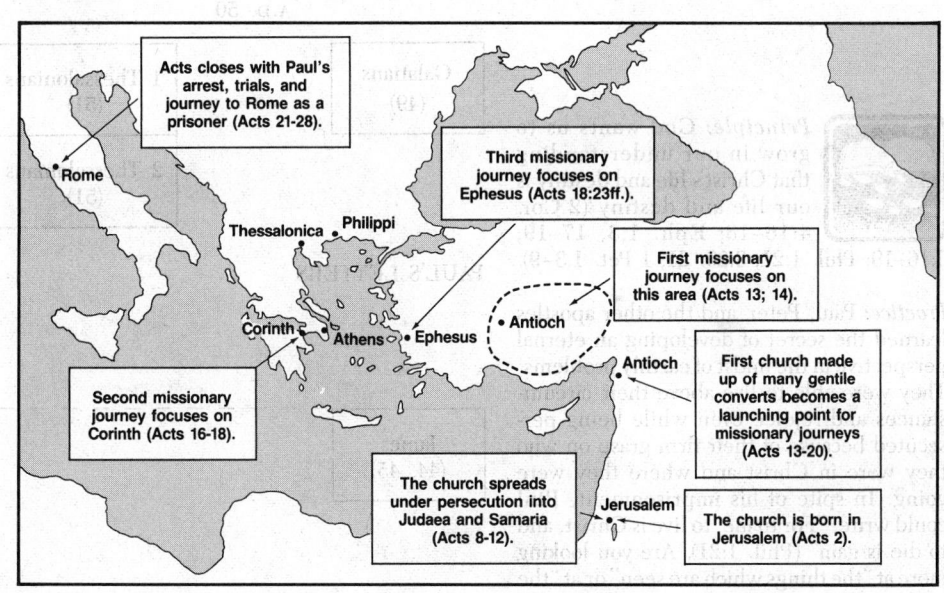

Acts closes with Paul's arrest, trials, and journey to Rome as a prisoner (Acts 21-28).

Rome

Third missionary journey focuses on Ephesus (Acts 18:23ff.).

Thessalonica   Philippi

First missionary journey focuses on this area (Acts 13; 14).

Corinth   Athens   Ephesus   • Antioch

Antioch

First church made up of many gentile converts becomes a launching point for missionary journeys (Acts 13-20).

Second missionary journey focuses on Corinth (Acts 16-18).

The church spreads under persecution into Judaea and Samaria (Acts 8-12).

Jerusalem

The church is born in Jerusalem (Acts 2).

Principle: Christ's life is reproduced in others when we take the initiative to witness in the power of the Holy Spirit (Matt. 28:18–20; Acts 1:8; Col. 4:2–6).

Practice: The Book of Acts records the spread of the gospel from the city of Jerusalem to the whole province of Judea and Samaria, and ultimately through the Roman Empire and beyond. These first-century Christians were sold out for the cause of Christ and transformed their world as their lives became living epistles of the Good News. God has called us to a life-style of evangelism in which we build relationships with non-Christians. These friendships in turn become natural bridges for communicating the gospel. Take a close look at Colossians 4:2–6 to learn how to become more effective as an instrument of the Holy Spirit to reproduce the life of Christ in others.

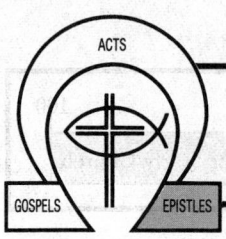

THE WRITINGS OF THE EARLY

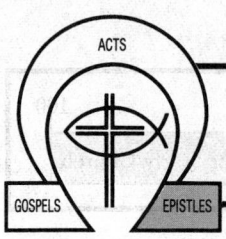

Paul converted A.D. 34	Cornelius converted 40	1st Missionary Journey 48	Jerusalem Council 50

FOCUS ON PETER		FOCUS ON PAUL

PAUL THE LEARNER

PAUL THE MISSIONARY

Paul spends nearly 3 years at Damascus and 10 years in obscurity in Tarsus before he is ready for mission work.	1st Journey	The Jerusalem Council Acts 15	2nd Journey

A.D. 50

Principle: God wants us to grow in our understanding that Christ's life and destiny is our life and destiny (2 Cor. 4:16–18; Eph. 1:3, 17–19; 3:16–19; Phil. 1:21; 3:20, 21; 1 Pet. 1:3–9).

Practice: Paul, Peter, and the other apostles learned the secret of developing an eternal perspective in the midst of earthly problems. They were able to live above their circumstances and rejoice even while being persecuted because of their firm grasp on who they were in Christ and where they were going. In spite of his imprisonment, Paul could write, "For to me, to live is Christ, and to die is gain" (Phil. 1:21). Are you looking more at "the things which are seen" or at "the things which are not seen"? The former are temporary, but the latter are eternal (2 Cor. 4:18).

Galatians (49)

1 Thessalonians (51)

2 Thessalonians (51)

PAUL'S LETTERS

James (44, 45)

LETTERS BY OTHERS

GOSPELS & ACTS

Matthew (c. 40's)

CHURCH

	A.D. 33	49		A.D. 100
		James	John	

| Paul
imprisoned
58 | Peter
executed
64 | Paul
executed
68 | Jerusalem
destroyed
70 | John
dies
A.D. 100 |

FOCUS ON JOHN

PAUL THE PRISONER

3rd Journey	1st Imprisonment	Freedom	2nd Imprisonment	JOHN'S WRITINGS
1 Corinthians (56)	Ephesians (60)	1 Timothy (62)	2 Timothy (67)	
2 Corinthians (56)	Colossians (61)	Titus (66)		
Romans (56, 57)	Philemon (61)			
	Philippians (62)			
		1 Peter (64)	Hebrews (66–69)	1 John (85–90)
		2 Peter (64)	Jude (75)	2 John (85–90)
				3 John (85–90)
				Revelation (95–96)
	Acts (62)			
	Luke (58–60)	Mark (60)		John (65–70)

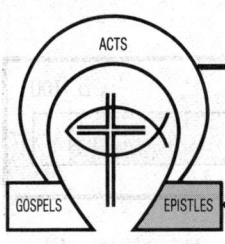

ACTS

GOSPELS   EPISTLES

THE THEMES OF THE NEW TESTAMENT LETTERS

PAUL'S LETTERS TO CHURCHES

BOOK	KEY WORD	THEME
Romans	Righteousness of God	Portrays the gospel from condemnation to justification to sanctification to glorification (1–8). Presents God's program for Jews and Gentiles (9–11) and practical exhortations for believers (12–16).
1 Corinthians	Correction of Carnal Living	Corrects problems of factions, immorality, lawsuits, and abuse of the Lord's Supper (1–6). Replies to questions concerning marriage, meat offered to idols, public worship, and the Resurrection (7–16).
2 Corinthians	Paul Defends His Ministry	Defends Paul's apostolic character, call, and credentials. The majority had repented of their rebellion against Paul, but there was still an unrepentant minority.
Galatians	Freedom from the Law	Refutes the error of legalism that had ensnared the churches of Galatia. Demonstrates the superiority of grace over law, and magnifies the life of liberty over legalism and license.
Ephesians	Building the Body of Christ	Extols the believer's position in Christ (1–3), and exhorts the readers to maintain a spiritual walk that is based upon their spiritual wealth (4–6).
Philippians	To Live Is Christ	Paul speaks of the latest developments in his imprisonment and urges his readers to a life-style of unity, humility, and godliness.
Colossians	The Preeminence of Christ	Demonstrates the preeminence of Christ in creation, redemption, and the relationships of life. The Christian is complete in Christ and needs nothing else.
1 Thessalonians	Holiness in Light of Christ's Return	Paul commends the Thessalonians for their faith and reminds them of his motives and concerns on their behalf. He exhorts them to purity of life and teaches them about the coming of the Lord.
2 Thessalonians	Understanding the Day of the Lord	Paul corrects false conclusions about the day of the Lord, explains what must precede this awesome event, and exhorts his readers to remain diligent.

PAUL'S LETTERS TO PEOPLE

BOOK	KEY WORD	THEME
1 Timothy	Leadership Manual for Churches	Paul counsels Timothy on the problems of false teachers, public prayer, the role of women, and the requirements for elders and deacons.
2 Timothy	Endurance in Ministry	A combat manual designed to build up and encourage Timothy to boldness and steadfastness in view of the hardships of the spiritual warfare.
Titus	Conduct Manual for Churches	Lists the requirements for elders and instructs Titus in his duties relative to the various groups in the churches.
Philemon	Forgiveness from Slavery	Paul appeals to Philemon to forgive Onesimus and to regard him no longer as a slave but as a brother in Christ.

LETTERS FROM OTHERS

BOOK	KEY WORD	THEME
Hebrews	Superiority of Christ	Demonstrates the superiority of Christ's person, priesthood, and power over all that preceded Him to encourage the readers to mature and to become stable in their faith.
James	Faith that Works	A practical catalog of the characteristics of true faith written to exhort James' Hebrew-Christian readers to examine the reality of their own faith.
1 Peter	Suffering for Christ	Comfort and counsel to those who were being maligned for their faith in Christ. They are encouraged to develop an attitude of submission in view of their suffering.
2 Peter	Guard Against False Prophets	Copes with internal opposition in the form of false teachers who were enticing believers into their errors of belief and conduct. Appeals for growth in the true knowledge of Christ.
1 John	Fellowship with God	Explores the dimensions of fellowship between redeemed people and God. Believers must walk in His light, manifest His love, and abide in His life.
2 John	Avoid Fellowship with False Teachers	John commends his readers for remaining steadfast in apostolic truth and reminds them to walk in love and avoid false teachers.
3 John	Enjoy Fellowship with the Brethren	John thanks Gaius for his support of traveling teachers of the truth, in contrast to Diotrephes, who rejected them and told others to do the same.
Jude	Contend for the Faith	This expose of false teachers reveals their conduct and character and predicts their judgment. Jude encourages his readers to build themselves up in the truth and contend earnestly for the faith.
Revelation	Revelation of the Coming Christ	The glorified Christ gives seven messages to the church (1–3). Visions of unparalleled judgment upon rebellious mankind are followed by the Second Advent (4–19). The Apocalypse concludes with a description of the new heaven and new earth and the marvels of the new Jerusalem (20–22).

The

New Testament

of

The
Open
Bible®
EXPANDED
EDITION

New American Standard Bible

The

New Testament

of

The
Open
Bible®

EXPANDED
EDITION

New American Standard Bible

THE GOSPEL ACCORDING TO

MATTHEW

THE BOOK OF MATTHEW

Matthew is the gospel written by a Jew to Jews about a Jew. Matthew is the writer, his countrymen are the readers, and Jesus Christ is the subject. Matthew's design is to present Jesus as the King of the Jews, the long-awaited Messiah. Through a carefully selected series of Old Testament quotations, Matthew documents Jesus Christ's claim to be Messiah. His genealogy, baptism, messages, and miracles all point to the same inescapable conclusion: Christ is King. Even in His death, seeming defeat is turned to victory by the Resurrection, and the message again echoes forth: the King of the Jews lives.

At an early date this gospel was given the title *Kata Matthaion*, "According to Matthew." As this title suggests, other gospel accounts were known at that time (the word *gospel* was added later). Matthew ("Gift of the Lord") was also surnamed Levi (Mark 2:14; Luke 5:27).

THE AUTHOR OF MATTHEW

The early church uniformly attributed this gospel to Matthew, and no tradition to the contrary ever emerged. This book was known early and accepted quickly. In his Ecclesiastical History (A.D. 323), Eusebius quoted a statement by Papias (c. A.D. 140) that Matthew wrote *logia* ("sayings") in Aramaic. No Aramaic gospel of Matthew has been found, and it is evident that Matthew is not a Greek translation of an Aramaic original. Some believe that Matthew wrote an abbreviated version of Jesus' sayings in Aramaic before writing his gospel in Greek for a larger circle of readers.

Matthew, the son of Alphaeus (Mark 2:14), occupied the unpopular post of tax collector in Capernaum for the Roman government. As a publican he was no doubt disliked by his Jewish countrymen. When Jesus called him to discipleship (9:9–13; Mark 2:14; Luke 5:27, 28), his quick response probably meant that he had already been stirred by Jesus' public preaching. He gave a large reception for Jesus in his house so that his associates could meet Jesus. He was chosen as one of the twelve apostles, and the last appearance of his name in the Bible is in Acts 1:13. Matthew's life from that point on is veiled in tradition.

THE TIME OF MATTHEW

Like all the gospels, Matthew is not easy to date: suggestions have ranged from A.D. 40 to 140. The expression "to this day" (27:8; 28:15) indicates that a substantial period of time has passed since the events described in the book, but they also point to a date prior to the destruction of Jerusalem in A.D. 70. The Olivet Discourse (24—25) also anticipates this event. The strong Jewish flavor of this gospel is another argument for a date prior to A.D. 70. If Matthew depended on Mark's gospel as a source, the date of Mark would determine the earliest date for Matthew. The likely time frame for this book is A.D. 58–68. It may have been written in Palestine or Syrian Antioch.

THE CHRIST OF MATTHEW

Matthew presents Jesus as Israel's promised messianic King (1:23; 2:2, 6; 3:17; 4:15–17; 21:5, 9; 22:44, 45; 26:64; 27:11, 27–37). The phrase "the kingdom of heaven" appears twenty-eight times in Matthew but nowhere else in the New Testament. To show that Jesus fulfills the qualifications for the Messiah, Matthew uses more Old Testament quotations and allusions than any other book (almost 130). Often used in this gospel is the revealing phrase "that what was spoken through the prophets might be fulfilled," which appears nine times in Matthew and not once in the other gospels. Jesus is the climax of the prophets (12:39, 40; 13:13–15, 35; 17:5–13), "the Son of Man" (24:30ff.), the "Servant" of the Lord (12:17–21), and the "Son of David" (the Davidic reference occurs nine times in Matthew, but only six times in all of the other gospels).

KEYS TO MATTHEW

Key Word: Jesus the King—A Jewish tax collector named Matthew writes to a Jewish audience to convince them that the King of the Jews has come. By quoting repeatedly from the Old Testament, Matthew validates Christ's claims that He is, in fact, the prophesied Messiah (the Anointed One) of Israel. Everything about this King is unique: His miraculous birth and obscure yet carefully prophesied birthplace, His flight into Egypt, His announcement by John, His battle with

Satan in the wilderness, all support the only possible conclusion—Jesus is the culmination of promises delivered by the prophets over a period of a thousand years. Thus God's redemptive plan is alive and well, even after four hundred years of prophetic silence.

Key Verses: Matthew 16:16–19 and 28:18–20—"And Simon Peter answered and said, 'Thou art the Christ, the Son of the living God.' And Jesus answered and said to him, 'Blessed are you, Simon Barjona, because flesh and blood did not reveal *this* to you, but My Father who is in heaven. And I also say to you that you are Peter, and upon this rock I will build My church; and the gates of Hades shall not overpower it. I will give you the keys of the kingdom of heaven; and whatever you shall bind on earth shall be bound in heaven, and whatever you shall loose on earth shall be loosed in heaven' " (16:16–19).

"And Jesus came up and spoke to them, saying, 'All authority has been given to Me in heaven and on earth. Go therefore and make disciples of all the nations, baptizing them in the name of the Father and the Son and the Holy Spirit, teaching them to observe all that I commanded you; and lo, I am with you always, even to the end of the age' " (28:18–20).

Key Chapter: Matthew 12—The turning point of Matthew comes in the twelfth chapter when the Pharisees, acting as the leadership of the nation of Israel, formally reject Jesus Christ as the Messiah, saying that His power comes not from God but from Satan. Christ's ministry changes immediately with His new teaching of parables, increased attention given to His disciples, and His repeated statement that His death is now near.

SURVEY OF MATTHEW

The Old Testament prophets predicted and longed for the coming of the Anointed One who would enter history to bring redemption and deliverance. The first verse of Matthew succinctly announces the fulfillment of Israel's hope in the coming of Christ: "The book of the genealogy of Jesus Christ, the son of David, the son of Abraham." Matthew was placed first in the canon of New Testament books by the early church because it is a natural bridge between the Testaments. This gospel describes the person and work of Israel's messianic King. An important part of Matthew's structure is revealed in the phrase "when Jesus had finished" (7:28; 11:1; 13:53; 19:1; 26:1), which is used to conclude the five key discourses of the book: the Sermon on the Mount (5:3—7:27), Instruction of the Disciples (10:5–42), Parables of the Kingdom (13:3–52), Terms of Discipleship (18:3–35), and the Olivet Discourse (24:4—25:46). Matthew can be outlined as follows: the presentation of the King (1:1—4:11); the proclamation of the King (4:12—7:29); the power of the King (8:1—11:1); the progressive rejection of the King (11:2—16:12); the preparation of the King's disciples (16:13—20:28); the presentation and rejection of the King (20:29—27:66); the proof of the King (28:1–20).

The Presentation of the King (1:1–4:11): The promise to Abraham was that "in you all the families of the earth shall be blessed" (Gen. 12:3). Jesus Christ, the Savior of the world, is "the son of Abraham" (1:1). However, He is also "the son of David"; and as David's direct descendant, He is qualified to be Israel's King. The magi know that the

FOCUS	OFFER OF THE KING			REJECTION OF THE KING			
REFERENCE	1:1————4:12————		8:1——11:2————		16:13————	20:29————	28:1——28:20
DIVISION	PRESENTATION OF THE KING	PROCLAMATION OF THE KING	POWER OF THE KING	PROGRESSIVE REJECTION OF THE KING	PREPARATION OF THE KING'S DISCIPLES	PRESENTATION AND REJECTION OF THE KING	PROOF OF THE KING
TOPIC	TEACHING THE THRONGS			TEACHING THE TWELVE			
	CHRONOLOGICAL	THEMATIC		CHRONOLOGICAL			
LOCATION	BETHLEHEM AND NAZARETH	GALILEE			JUDEA		
TIME	c. 4 B.C.—A.D. 33						

"King of the Jews" (2:2) has been born and come to worship Him. John the Baptist, the messianic forerunner who breaks the four hundred years of prophetic silence, also bears witness of Him (cf. Mal. 3:1). The sinlessness of the King is proved when He overcomes the satanic temptations to disobey the will of the Father.

The Proclamation of the King (4:12—7:29): In this section, Matthew uses a topical rather than a chronological arrangement of his material in order to develop a crucial pattern in Christ's ministry. The words of the Lord are found in the Sermon on the Mount (5—7). This discourse requires less than fifteen minutes to read, but its brevity has not diminished its profound influence on the world. The Sermon on the Mount presents new laws and standards for God's people.

The Power of the King (8:1—11:1): The works of the Lord are presented in a series of ten miracles (8 and 9) that reveal His authority over every realm (disease, demons, death, and nature). Thus, the words of the Lord are supported by His works; His claims are verified by His credentials.

The Progressive Rejection of the King (11:2—16:12): Here we note a series of reactions to Christ's words and works. Because of increasing opposition, Jesus begins to spend propor-
tionately more time with His disciples as He prepares them for His coming death and departure.

The Preparation of the King's Disciples (16:13—20:28): In a series of discourses, Jesus communicates the significance of accepting or rejecting His offer of righteousness. His teaching in 16:13—21:11 is primarily directed to those who accept Him.

The Presentation and Rejection of the King (20:29—27:66): The majority of Christ's words in this section are aimed at those who reject their King. The Lord predicts the terrible judgment that will fall on Jerusalem, resulting in the dispersion of the Jewish people. Looking beyond these events (fulfilled in A.D. 70), He also describes His second coming as the Judge and Lord of the earth.

The Proof of the King (28): Authenticating His words and works are the empty tomb, resurrection, and appearances, all proving that Jesus Christ is indeed the prophesied Messiah, the very Son of God.

Christ's final ministry in Judea (beginning in 19:1) reaches a climax at the cross as the King willingly gives up His life to redeem sinful persons. Jesus endures awesome human hatred in this great demonstration of divine love (cf. Rom. 5:7, 8). His perfect sacrifice is acceptable, and this gospel concludes with His glorious resurrection.

OUTLINE OF MATTHEW

Part Three: The Power of the King (8:1—11:1)

Part Four: The Progressive Rejection of the King (11:2—16:12)

Part Five: The Preparation of the King's Disciples (16:13—20:28)

Part Six: The Presentation and Rejection of the King (20:29—27:66)

CHAPTER 1

Genealogy of Christ
*Ruth 4:18–22; 1 Chr. 1:34, 2:1–15;
Luke 3:31–34*

THE book of the genealogy of Jesus Christ, ᴿthe son of David, ᴿthe son of Abraham.   Ps. 132:11; [Rom. 1:3]★ • Matt. 1:1–6

2 To ᴿAbraham was born Isaac; and to Isaac, Jacob; and to Jacob, ¹Judah and his brothers;   Gen. 12:7★

3 and to Judah were born Perez and Zerah by Tamar; and to Perez was born Hezron; and to Hezron, ᵀRam;   Gr., Aram

4 and to Ram was born Amminadab; and to Amminadab, Nahshon; and to Nahshon, Salmon;

5 and to Salmon was born Boaz by Rahab; and to Boaz was born Obed by Ruth; and to Obed, ⁹Jesse;   Is. 11:1, 10★

6 and to Jesse was born David the king.
And to Davidᴿwas born Solomon by her *who had been the wife* of Uriah; 2 Sam. 12:24

7 and to Solomonᴿwas born Rehoboam; and to Rehoboam, Abijah; and to Abijah, ᵀAsa;   1 Chr. 3:10ff. • Gr., Asaph

8 and to Asa was born Jehoshaphat; and to Jehoshaphat, ᵀJoram; and to Joram, Uzziah;   Gr., Jehoram

9 and to Uzziah was born Jotham; and to Jotham, Ahaz; and to Ahaz, Hezekiah;

10 and to Hezekiah was born Manasseh; and to Manasseh, ᵀAmon; and to Amon, Josiah;   Gr., Amos

11 and to Josiah were bornᴬJeconiah and his brothers, at the time of theᴿdeportation to Babylon.   Jehoiachin • 2 Kin. 24:14; Matt. 1:17

12 And after the deportation to Babylon, to Jeconiah was born ᵀShealtiel; and to Shealtiel, Zerubbabel;   Gr., Salathiel

13 and to Zerubbabel was born Abiud; and to Abiud, Eliakim; and to Eliakim, Azor;

14 and to Azor was born Zadok; and to Zadok, Achim; and to Achim, Eliud;

15 and to Eliud was born Eleazar; and to Eleazar, Matthan; and to Matthan, Jacob;

16 and to Jacob was born Joseph the husband of Mary, by whom was born Jesus, who is calledᵀChrist.   the Messiah

17 Therefore all the generations from Abraham to David are fourteen generations; and from David to the deportation to Babylon fourteen generations; and from the deportation to Babylon to *the time of*ᵀChrist fourteen generations.   the Messiah

Birth of Christ

18 Now the birth of Jesus Christ was as follows. When Hisᴿmother Mary had been betrothed to Joseph, ᴿbefore they came together she wasᴿfound to be with child by the Holy Spirit.   Luke 1:27 • Is. 7:14★ • Luke 1:35

---

¹ Gr., *Judas*. Names of Old Testament characters will be given in their Old Testament form.

19 And Joseph her husband, being a righteous man, and not wanting to disgrace her, desired ²to^Rput her away secretly. John 8:4, 5

20 But when he had considered this, behold, an angel of the Lord appeared to him in a dream, saying, "Joseph,^R son of David, do not be afraid to take Mary as your wife; for that which has been ³conceived in her is of the Holy Spirit. Luke 2:4

21 "And she will bear a Son; and you shall call His name Jesus, for it is He who^Rwill save His people from their sins." Rom. 5:19☆

22 Now all this^Rtook place that what was spoken by the Lord through the prophet might be fulfilled, saying,   has taken place

23 "BEHOLD,^R THE VIRGIN SHALL BE WITH CHILD, AND SHALL BEAR A SON, AND THEY SHALL CALL HIS NAME IMMANUEL," which translated means, "GOD WITH US." Is. 7:4★

24 And Joseph arose from his sleep, and did as the angel of the Lord commanded him, and took her as his wife,

25 and ⁴kept her a virgin until she ^Rgave birth to a Son; and ^Rhe called His name Jesus. Luke 2:7 • Matt. 1:21; Luke 2:21★

CHAPTER 2

Visit of Wise Men

NOW after Jesus was^Rborn in Bethlehem of Judea in the days of^RHerod the king, behold, ⁵magi from the east arrived in Jerusalem, saying, Mic. 5:2★ • Luke 1:5

2 "Where is He who has been born^RKing of the Jews? For we saw His star in the east, and have come to worship Him." Jer. 23:5★

3 And when Herod the king heard it, he was troubled, and all Jerusalem with him.

4 And gathering together all the chief priests and scribes of the people, he began to inquire of them where the ^TChrist was to be born. the Messiah

5 And they said to him, "In^RBethlehem of Judea, for so it has been written ^Tby the prophet, John 7:42★ • through

6 'AND^R YOU, BETHLEHEM, LAND OF JUDAH, Mic. 5:2; John 7:42

ARE BY NO MEANS LEAST AMONG THE LEADERS OF JUDAH;

FOR^ROUT OF YOU SHALL COME FORTH A RULER, Gen. 49:10★

WHO WILL ^RSHEPHERD MY PEOPLE ISRAEL.'" John 21:16

7 Then Herod secretly called the magi, and ascertained from them^Tthe time the star appeared. the time of the appearing star

8 And he sent them to Bethlehem, and said, "Go and make careful search for the Child; and when you have found Him, report to me, that I too may come and worship Him."

9 And having heard the king, they went

---

their way; and lo, the star, which they had seen in the east, went on before them, until it came and stood over where the Child was.

10 And when they saw the star, they rejoiced exceedingly with great joy.

11 And they came into the house and saw the Child with Mary His mother; and they fell down and worshiped Him; and opening their treasures they presented to Him gifts of gold and frankincense and myrrh.

12 And having been warned by God in a dream not to return to Herod, they departed for their own country by another way.

Flight into Egypt

13 Now when they had departed, behold, an^Rangel of the Lord *appeared^Rto Joseph in a dream, saying, "Arise and take the Child and His mother, and flee to Egypt, and remain there until I tell you; for ^RHerod is going to search for the Child to destroy Him." Acts 5:19; 10:7 • Matt. 2:12, 19 • Matt. 2:16☆

14 And he arose and took the Child and His mother by night, and departed for Egypt;

15 and was there until the death of Herod, that what was spoken by the Lord through the prophet might be fulfilled, saying, "OUT^R OF EGYPT DID I CALL MY SON." Hos. 11:1★

Herod Kills the Children

16 Then when Herod saw that he had been tricked by^Rthe magi, he became very enraged, and sent and^Rslew all the male children who were in Bethlehem and in all its environs, from two years old and under, according to the time which he had ascertained from the magi. Matt. 2:1 • Is. 59:7

17 Then that which was spoken through Jeremiah the prophet was fulfilled, saying,

18 "A VOICE WAS HEARD IN RAMAH,
WEEPING AND GREAT MOURNING,
RACHEL WEEPING FOR HER CHILDREN;
AND SHE REFUSED TO BE COMFORTED,
BECAUSE THEY WERE NO MORE."

Jesus Returns to Nazareth
Luke 2:39

19 But when Herod was dead, behold, an angel of the Lord *appeared^Rin a dream to Joseph in Egypt, saying, Matt. 1:20; 2:12, 13, 22

20 "Arise and take the Child and His mother, and go into the land of Israel; for those who sought the Child's life are dead."

21 And he arose and took the Child and His mother, and came into the land of Israel.

22 But when he heard that Archelaus was reigning over Judea in place of his father Herod, he was afraid to go there. And being ^Rwarned by God in a dream, he departed for the regions of Galilee, Matt. 2:12, 13, 19

23 and came and resided in a city called ^RNazareth, ^Rthat what was spoken through the prophets might be fulfilled, "He shall be called a Nazarene." Luke 1:26 • Judg. 13:5★

---

² Or, to divorce her   ³ Lit., begotten
⁴ Lit., was not knowing her
⁵ Pronounced may-ji, a caste of wise men specializing in astrology, medicine and natural science

CHAPTER 3

The Person of John the Baptist
Mark 1:2–6; Luke 3:3–6

NOW ᴿin those days John the Baptist *came,^preaching in the wilderness of Judea, saying, Matt. 3:1-12 · *proclaiming as a herald*

2 "Repent, for theᴿkingdom ofʰheavenʳis at hand." Mal. 4:5, 6★ · *the heavens* · *has come near*

3 For this is theᴿone referred toʳby Isaiah the prophet, saying, Luke 1:17 · *through*

"THEᴿVOICE OF ONE CRYING IN THE WILDERNESS, Is. 40:3★
'MAKE READY THE WAY OF THE LORD,
MAKE HIS PATHS STRAIGHT!' "

4 Now John himself had ᵗaᵗ garment of camel's hair, and a leather belt about his waist; and his food was locusts and wild honey. *his garment* · 2 Kin. 1:8; Zech. 13:4

5 Then Jerusalemᴿwas going out to him, and all Judea, and allʰthe district around the Jordan; Mark 1:5 · Luke 3:3

6 and they were beingʳbaptized by him in the Jordan River, as they confessed their sins. Matt. 3:11, 13-16; Mark 1:5; John 1:25, 26; 3:23

The Preaching of John the Baptist
Mark 1:7–9; Luke 3:7–9, 16, 17

7 But when he saw many of the Pharisees and Sadducees coming for baptism, he said to them, "You brood of vipers, who warned you to flee from the wrath to come?

8 "Thereforeᴿ bring forth fruit ʰin keeping with repentance; Luke 3:8 · Acts 26:20

9 and do not suppose that you can say to yourselves, 'Weᴿ have Abraham for our father'; for I say to you, that God is able from these stones to raise up children to Abraham. Luke 3:8; 16:24; John 8:33, 39, 53; Acts 13:26

10 "Andʰthe axe is already laid at the root of the trees;ᴿevery tree therefore that does not bear good fruit is cut down and thrown into the fire. Luke 3:9 · Ps. 92:12-14

11 "As for me,ᴿI baptize you ⁶with water for repentance, but He who is coming after

me is mightier than I, and I am not fit to remove His sandals; He will baptize you with the Holy Spirit and fire. Acts 2:4, 33☆

12 "And His winnowing fork is in His hand, and He will thoroughly clear His threshing floor; and He willʳgather His wheat into the barn, but He will burn up the chaff with unquenchable fire." Matt. 13:30

Baptism of Jesus
Mark 1:9–11; Luke 3:21–23

13 ᴿThen Jesus *arrivedᴿfrom Galilee at the Jordan *coming* to John, to be baptized by him. Matt. 3:13-17; John 1:31-34 · Matt. 2:22

14 But John tried to prevent Him, saying, "I have need to be baptized by You, and do You come to me?"

15 But Jesus answering said to him, "Permit *it* at this time; for in this way it is fitting for usᴿto fulfill all righteousness." Then He *permitted Him. Ps. 40:7, 8; John 4:34; 8:29

16 And after being baptized, Jesus went up immediately from the water; and behold, the heavens were opened, and^heᴿsaw the Spirit of God descending as a dove, *and* coming upon Him, He · Is. 11:2; 42:1; 61:1★

17 and behold, a voice out of the heavens, saying, "Thisᴿis ⁷My beloved Son, in whom I am well-pleased." Ps. 2:7; Is. 42:1; Matt. 12:18

CHAPTER 4

First Temptation
Mark 1:12, 13; Luke 4:1–4

THEN Jesus was led up by the Spirit into the wilderness to be tempted by the devil.

2 And after He had fasted forty days and forty nights, He ⁸then became hungry.

3 And the tempter came and said to Him, "If You are the Son of God, command that these stones becomeʳbread." *loaves*

4 But He answered and said, "It is written, 'MANᴿSHALL NOT LIVE ON BREAD ALONE, BUT ON EVERY WORD THAT PROCEEDS OUT OF THE MOUTH OF GOD.' " Deut. 8:3

---

⁶ The Gr. here can be translated *in, with* or *by*
⁷ Lit., *My Son, the Beloved* ⁸ Lit., *later, afterward*

3:17 God the Father of Christ—Every new Christian eventually wonders in what sense God may be called the Father of Christ and Christ the Son of God. The answer to this question is not a simple one. First, one must recognize that the title Son of God does not speak of physical nature, for God is spirit (Page 1067—John 4:24), and Christ was the Son of God before He assumed a human body in Bethlehem (Page 1066—John 3:16; Page 1179—Gal. 4:4). Passages which use terms implying physical origin must be taken in a figurative sense (Page 1239—Heb. 1:5).

Second, the title expresses a unique relationship. Christ distinguished His sonship from that of His disciples (Page 1087—John 20:17). He was begotten of God in a sense that no one else is (Page 1064—John 1:14; 3:16). Some call it "eternal generation," signifying the timelessness of this "God from God" relationship.

Third, the title describes a relationship of equality. The Son of God is no less than God. When Jesus claimed to be "one" with the Father, He was speaking of a unity of "substance" with the Father and thus equality in all the attributes of deity (Page 1077—John 10:30). The Jews certainly understood this claim, for they took up stones to stone Him, protesting that "You, . . . make Yourself out *to be* God" (Page 1077—John 10:33).

Fourth, the title especially emphasizes Christ's role as the revealer of God. He alone possesses the knowledge of the Father (Page 1081—John 14:6–9; Page 1274—1 John 1:2) and He is the sole mediator of that knowledge (Page 1217—1 Tim. 2:5). Therefore no one can know the Father except through the Son (Page 1081—John 14:6). The narrowness of this way to God should be a sober incentive to take to all the world the message that the Son of God has come to impart to every person the life of the Father.

Now turn to Page 1137—Rom. 8:15: God the Father of Believers.

Second Temptation
Luke 4:9–12

5 Then the devil *took Him into*ᴿ*the holy city; and he had Him stand on the pinnacle of the temple,   Neh. 11:1, 18; Matt. 27:53

6 and *said to Him, "If You are the Son of God throw Yourself down; for it is written,

'Heᴿ will give His angels charge
    concerning You';   Ps. 91:11, 12★
and
'On *their* hands they will bear You
    up,
Lest You strike Your foot against
    a stone.' "

7 Jesus said to him, "On the other hand, it is written, 'Youᴿshall not ⁹put the Lord your God to the test.' "   Deut. 6:16

Third Temptation
Mark 1:13; Luke 4:5–8, 13

8 Again, the devil *took Him to a very high mountain, and *showed Him all the kingdoms of the world, and their glory;

9 and he said to Him, "Allᴿ these things will I give You, if You fall down and worship me."   1 Cor. 10:20f.

10 Then Jesus *said to him, "Begone, Satan! For it is written, 'You shall worship the Lord your God, and ^serve Him only.' "   *fulfill religious duty to Him*

11 Then the devil *left Him; and behold, angels came and *began* to minister to Him.

Jesus Begins His Ministry
Mark 1:14, 15; Luke 4:14, 31

12 Now when He heard that ᴿJohn had ᵀbeen taken into custody, He withdrew into Galilee;   Matt. 14:3 • *been delivered up*

13 and leaving Nazareth, He came and settled in Capernaum, which is by the sea, in the region of Zebulun and Naphtali.

14 *This was* to fulfill what was spoken through Isaiah the prophet, saying,

15 "Theᴿ land of Zebulun and the land
    of Naphtali,   Is. 9:1, 2★
^By the way of the sea, beyond the
    Jordan, Galilee of the ¹⁰Gen-
    tiles—   *Toward the sea*

16 "The people who were sitting in
    darkness saw a great light,
And to those who were sitting in
    the land and shadow of death,
Upon them a light dawned."

17 ᴿFrom that time Jesus began to^preach and say, "Repent, for the kingdom of heaven is at hand."   Mark 1:14, 15 • *proclaim*

Jesus Calls His First Disciples
Mark 1:16–20

18 And walking by the Sea of Galilee, He saw two brothers, Simon who was called

Peter, and Andrew his brother, casting a net into the sea; for they were fishermen.

19 And He *said to them, "Follow Me, and I will make you fishers of men."

20 And they immediately left the nets, and followed Him.

21 And going on from there He saw two other brothers, 'James the *son* of Zebedee, and'John his brother, in the boat with Zebedee their father, mending their nets; and He called them.   *Jacob* • Gr., *Joannes*

22 And they immediately left the boat and their father, and followed Him.

Jesus Ministers in Galilee
Mark 1:39; Luke 4:44

23 And *Jesus* was going about in all Galilee, teaching in their synagogues, and proclaiming the gospel of the kingdom, and ᴿhealing every kind of disease and every kind of sickness among the people.   Ps. 22:22★

24 And the news about Him went outᴿinto all Syria; and they brought to Him all who were ill, taken with various diseases and pains, demoniacs,ᵀepileptics, paralytics; and He healed them.   Mark 7:26 • *moon-smitten*

25 And great multitudes followed Him from Galilee and Decapolis and Jerusalem and Judea and *from* beyond the Jordan.

CHAPTER 5

The Beatitudes
Luke 6:20–26

And when He saw the multitudes, He went up on the^mountain; and after He sat down, His disciples came to Him.   *hill*

2 Andᴿopening His mouth He *began* to teach them, saying,   Matt. 13:35; Acts 8:35

3 "Blessedᴿare the poor in spirit, for theirs is the kingdom of heaven.   Matt. 5:3-12

4 "Blessed areᴿthose who mourn, for they shall be comforted.   Is. 61:2; [John 16:20]

5 "Blessed areᴿthe ¹¹gentle, for they shall inherit the earth.   Ps. 37:11

6 "Blessed are ᴿthose who hunger and thirst for righteousness, for they shall be satisfied.   [Is. 55:1, 2; John 4:14; 6:48ff.; 7:37]

7 "Blessed areᴿthe merciful, for they shall receive mercy.   Prov. 11:17; [Matt. 6:14]

8 "Blessed are^the pure in heart, forᴿthey shall see God.   Ps. 24:4 • 1 John 3:2; Rev. 22:4

9 "Blessed are the peacemakers, forᴿthey shall be called sons of God.   [Matt. 5:45]

10 "Blessed are those who have beenᴿpersecuted for the sake of righteousness, for theirs is the kingdom of heaven.   1 Pet. 3:14

11 "Blessed are you when *men* cast insults at you, and persecute you, and say all kinds of evil against you falsely, on account of Me.

12 "Rejoice, and be glad, for your reward

⁹ Or, *tempt . . . God*   ¹⁰ Or, *nations*   ¹¹ Or, *humble, meek*

in heaven is great, for so they persecuted the prophets who were before you.

The Similitudes

13"You are the salt of the earth; but[R]if the salt has become tasteless, how will it be made salty *again*? It is good for nothing anymore, except to be thrown out and trampled under foot by men.   Luke 14:34f.

14"You are the light of the world. A city set on a[A]hill cannot be hidden.   *mountain*

15"Nor[R]do *men* light a lamp, and put it under the peck-measure, but on the lampstand; and it gives light to all who are in the house.   Mark 4:21; Luke 8:16; 11:33; Phil. 2:15

16"Let your light shine before men in such a way that they may see your good works, and glorify your Father who is in heaven.

Jesus Fulfills the Law

17"Do not think that I came to abolish the [R]Law or the Prophets; I did not come to abolish, but to fulfill.   Matt. 7:12

18"For truly I say to you,[R]until heaven and earth pass away, not the smallest letter or stroke shall pass away from the Law, until all is accomplished.   Matt. 24:35; Luke 16:17

19"Whoever then annuls one of the least of these commandments, and so teaches [T]others, shall be called least in the kingdom of heaven; but whoever [T]keeps and teaches *them*, he shall be called great in the kingdom of heaven.   *the men • does*

Murder

20"For I say to you, that unless your[R]righteousness surpasses *that* of the scribes and Pharisees, you shall not enter the kingdom of heaven.   Luke 18:11, 12

21"You have heard that [T]the ancients were told, 'YOU SHALL NOT COMMIT MURDER' and 'Whoever commits murder shall be [12]liable to the court.'   *it was said to the ancient*

22"But I say to you that everyone who is angry with his brother[13] shall be [A]guilty before[R]the court; and whoever shall say to his brother, '[14]Raca,' shall be [A]guilty before [15]the supreme court; and whoever shall say, 'You fool,' shall be guilty *enough to go* into the [16]fiery hell.   *liable to • Deut. 16:18*

23"If therefore you are presenting your offering at the altar, and there remember that your brother has something against you,

24 leave your [A]offering there before the altar, and go your way; first be [R]reconciled to your brother, and then come and present your offering.   *gift • [Rom. 12:17, 18]*

25"Make friends quickly with your opponent at law while you are with him on the way, in order that your opponent may not deliver you to the judge, and the judge to the officer, and you be thrown into prison.

26"Truly I say to you,[R]you shall not come out of there, until you have paid up the last [17]cent.   Luke 12:59

Adultery

27"You[R] have heard that it was said, 'YOU SHALL NOT COMMIT ADULTERY';   Matt. 5:21, 33

28 but I say to you, that everyone who looks on a woman[A]to lust for her has committed adultery with her already in his heart.   2 Sam. 11:2-5; Matt. 15:19; James 1:14, 15

29"And if your right eye makes you[T]stumble, tear it out, and throw it from you; for it is better for you that one of the parts of your body perish, than for your whole body to be thrown into hell.   *cause to sin*

30"And if your right hand makes you [T]stumble, cut it off, and throw it from you; for it is better for you that one of the parts of your body perish, than for your whole body to go into hell.   *cause to sin*

Divorce

31"And it was said, 'WHOEVER[T]SENDS HIS WIFE AWAY,[R]LET HIM GIVE HER A CERTIFICATE OF DIVORCE';   *puts away • Deut. 24:1, 3*

32[R]but I say to you that everyone who divorces his wife, except for *the* cause of unchastity, makes her commit adultery; and whoever marries a divorced woman commits adultery.   [Matt. 19:9; Mark 10:11f.]

Vows

33"Again, you have heard that [T]the ancients were told, 'YOU SHALL NOT MAKE FALSE VOWS, BUT SHALL FULFILL YOUR VOWS TO THE LORD.'   *it was said to the ancients*

34"But I say to you, make no oath at all, either by heaven, for it is the throne of God,

35 or by the earth, for it is the[R]footstool of His feet, or[A]by Jerusalem, for it is THE CITY OF THE GREAT KING.   Is. 66:1 • *toward*

36"Nor shall you make an oath by your head, for you cannot make one hair white or black.

37"But let your statement be, 'Yes, yes' *or* 'No, no'; and anything beyond these is [A]of [R]evil.   *from the evil one • Matt. 6:13; 13:19, 38*

Retaliation

38"You have heard that it was said, 'AN EYE FOR AN EYE, AND A TOOTH FOR A TOOTH.'

39"But I say to you, do not resist him who is evil; but whoever slaps you on your right cheek, turn to him the other also.

40"And if anyone wants to sue you, and take your [18]shirt, let him have your [19]coat also.

---

[12] Or, *guilty before*
[13] Some mss. insert here: *without cause*
[14] Aramaic for *empty-head* or, *good for nothing*
[15] Lit., *the Sanhedrin*   [16] Lit., *Gehenna of fire*
[17] Lit., *quadrans* (equaling two lepta or mites), i.e., 1/64 of a denarius   [18] Or, *tunic*; i.e., garment worn next to the body
[19] Or, *cloak*; i.e., outer garment

41 "And whoever shall force you to go one mile, go with him two.

42 "Give[R] to him who asks of you, and do not turn away from him who wants to borrow from you.   Deut. 15:7-11; Luke 6:34f.

Love
Luke 6:27, 32

43 "You[R] have heard that it was said, 'YOU[R] SHALL LOVE YOUR NEIGHBOR, and hate your enemy.'   Matt. 5:21, 27 • Lev. 19:18

44 "But I say to you, love your enemies, and pray for those who persecute you

45 in order that you may[A] be[R] sons of your Father who is in heaven; for He causes His sun to rise on *the* evil and *the* good, and sends rain on *the* righteous and *the* unrighteous.   *show yourselves to be* • Matt. 5:9

46 "For[R] if you love those who love you, what reward have you? Do not even the tax-gatherers do the same?   Luke 6:32

47 "And if you greet your brothers only, what do you do more *than others*? Do not even the Gentiles do the same?

48 "Therefore[R] you are to be perfect, as your heavenly Father is perfect.   Lev. 19:2

CHAPTER 6

Almsgiving

"BEWARE of practicing your righteousness before men[A] to be noticed by them; otherwise you have no reward with your Father who is in heaven.   Matt. 6:5, 16; 23:5

2 "When therefore you[A] give alms, do not sound a trumpet before you, as the hypocrites do in the synagogues and in the streets, that they[R] may be honored by men. Truly I say to you, they have their reward in full.   *do an act of charity* • Matt. 6:5, 16; 23:5

3 "But when you give alms, do not let your left hand know what your right hand is doing

4 that your[A] alms may be in secret; and[R] your Father who sees in secret will repay you.   *deeds of charity* • Jer. 17:10; Matt. 6:6, 18

Prayer
Luke 11:2-4

5 "And when you pray, you are not to be as the hypocrites; for they love to stand and pray in the synagogues and on the street corners, in order to be seen by men. Truly I say to you, they have their reward in full.

6 "But you, when you pray,[R] go into your inner room, and when you have shut your door, pray to your Father who is in secret, and[T] your Father who sees in secret will repay you.   Matt. 26:36-39 • Matt. 6:4, 18

7 "And when you are praying, do not use meaningless repetition, as the Gentiles do, for they suppose that they will be heard for their[R] many words.   1 Kin. 18:26f.

8 "Therefore do not be like them; for[R] your

Father knows what you need, before you ask Him.   Ps. 38:9; Luke 12:30

9 "Pray,[R] then, in this way: *Luke 11:2-4*
'Our Father who art in[T] heaven,
Hallowed be Thy name.   *the heavens*

10 'Thy[R] kingdom come.   Matt. 3:2; 4:17
Thy will be done,
On earth as it is in heaven.

11 'Give us this day our daily bread.

12 'And[R] forgive us our debts, as we also have forgiven our debtors.   Ex. 34:7

13 'And do not lead us into temptation, but deliver us from evil. [For Thine is the kingdom, and the power, and the glory, forever. Amen.]'

14 "For[R] if you forgive men for their transgressions, your heavenly Father will also forgive you. [Matt. 7:2]; Mark 11:25f.; [Eph. 4:32]

15 "But[R] if you do not forgive men, then your Father will not forgive your transgressions.   Matt. 18:35

Fasting

16 "And whenever you fast, do not put on a gloomy face as the hypocrites *do*, for they neglect their appearance in order to be seen fasting by men. Truly I say to you, they have their reward in full.

17 "But you, when you fast,[R] anoint your head, and wash your face   2 Sam. 12:20

18 so that you may not be seen fasting by men, but by your Father who is in secret; and your[R] Father who sees in secret will repay you.   Matt. 6:4, 6

Wealth
Luke 11:34-36; 12:22-34

19 "Do not lay up for yourselves treasures upon earth, where moth and rust destroy, and where thieves break in and steal.

20 "But lay up for yourselves[R] treasures in heaven, where neither moth nor rust destroys, and where thieves do not break in or steal;   Matt. 19:21; Luke 12:33; 1 Tim. 6:19

21 for[R] where your treasure is, there will your heart be also.   Luke 12:34

22 "The[R] lamp of the body is the eye; if therefore your eye is[C] clear, your whole body will be full of light.   Matt. 6:22, 23 • *healthy*

23 "But if[T] your eye is bad, your whole body will be full of darkness. If therefore the light that is in you is darkness, how great is the darkness!   Matt. 20:15; Mark 7:22

24 "No one can serve two masters; for either he will hate the one and love the other, or he will hold to one and despise the other. You cannot serve God and [20] mammon.

25 "For this reason I say to you, do not be anxious for your life, *as to* what you shall eat, or what you shall drink; nor for your body, *as to* what you shall put on. Is not life more than food, and the body than clothing?

26 "Look[R] at the birds of the[T] air, that they

[20] Or, *riches*

do not sow, neither do they reap, nor gather into barns, and *yet* your heavenly Father feeds them. Are you not worth much more than they? Ps. 104:27; Luke 12:24 • *heaven*

27 "And which of you by being anxious can add a *single* cubit to his life's span? 1.5 ft.

28 "And why are you[R]anxious about clothing? Observe how the lilies of the field grow; they do not toil nor do they spin, Matt. 6:25

29 yet I say to you that even[R]Solomon in all his glory did not clothe himself like one of these. 1 Kin. 10:4-7; 2 Chr. 9:4-6, 20-22

30 "But if God so arrays the grass of the field, which is *alive* today and tomorrow is thrown into the furnace, *will He* not much more *do so for* you, O men of little faith?

31 "Do not be anxious then, saying, 'What shall we eat?' or 'What shall we drink?' or 'With what shall we clothe ourselves?'

32 "For all these things the Gentiles eagerly seek; for[R]your heavenly Father knows that you need all these things. Matt. 6:8

33 "But[A]seek first[A]His kingdom and His righteousness; and all these things shall be added to you. *continually seek* • *the kingdom*

34 "Therefore do not be anxious for tomorrow; for tomorrow will care for itself. *Each* day has enough trouble of its own.

CHAPTER 7

Judging—Luke 6:37-42

"DO not judge lest you be judged.

2 "For in the way you judge, you will be judged; and[R]by your standard of measure, it will be measured to you. Mark 4:24; Luke 6:38

3 "And why do you[R]look at the speck that is in your brother's eye, but do not notice the log that is in your own eye? Rom. 2:1

4 "Or how[T]can you say to your brother, 'Let me take the speck out of your eye,' and behold, the log is in your own eye? *will*

5 "You hypocrite, first take the log out of your own eye, and then you will see clearly to take the speck out of your brother's eye.

6 "Do[R] not give what is holy to dogs, and do not throw your pearls before swine, lest they trample them under their feet, and turn and tear you to pieces. Matt. 15:26

"Ask, and It Shall Be Given"
Luke 11:9-13

7 "Ask,[A] and it shall be given to you;[A]seek, and you shall find; knock, and it shall be opened to you. *Keep asking* • *keep seeking*

8 "For everyone who asks receives, and he who seeks finds, and to him who knocks it shall be opened.

9 "Or what man is there among you,[T]when his son shall ask him for a loaf, will give him a stone? *whom*

10 "Or[T]if he shall ask for a fish, he will not give him a snake, will he? *also*

11 "If you then, being evil, know how to give good gifts to your children, how much

more shall your Father who is in heaven give what is good to those who ask Him!

Golden Rule
Luke 6:31

12 "Therefore, however you want people to treat you,[A]so treat them, for this is the Law and the Prophets. *you, too, do so for*

Two Ways of Life

13 "Enter[R]by the narrow gate; for the gate is wide, and the way is broad that leads to destruction, and many are those who enter by it. Luke 13:24

14 "For the gate is small, and the way is narrow that leads to life, and few are those who find it.

False and True Teaching
Luke 6:43-45

15 "Beware of the[R]false prophets, who come to you in sheep's clothing, but inwardly are ravenous wolves. Matt. 24:11, 24

16 "You will[A]know them by their fruits. Grapes are not gathered from thorn *bushes,* nor figs from thistles, are they? *recognize*

17 "Even so, every good tree bears good fruit; but the bad tree bears bad fruit.

18 "A good tree cannot produce bad fruit, nor can a bad tree produce good fruit.

19 "Every tree that does not bear good fruit is cut down and thrown into the fire.

20 "So then, you will[A]know them[R]by their fruits. *recognize* • Matt. 7:16; 12:33; Luke 6:44

True Way into the Kingdom
Luke 6:46

21 "Not[R] everyone who says to Me, 'Lord, Lord,' will enter the kingdom of heaven; but he who does the will of My Father who is in heaven. Luke 6:46

22 "Many will say to Me on that day, 'Lord, Lord, did we not prophesy in Your name, and in Your name cast out demons, and in Your name perform many miracles?'

23 "And then I will declare to them, 'I never knew you;[R]DEPART FROM ME, YOU WHO PRACTICE LAWLESSNESS.' Ps. 6:8; [Matt. 25:41]☆

Parable of the Two Builders
Luke 6:47-49

24 "Therefore[R]everyone who hears these words of Mine, and[T]acts upon them, may be compared to a wise man, who built his house upon the rock. Matt. 16:18 • *does*

25 "And the rain descended, and the[T]floods came, and the winds blew, and burst against that house; and *yet* it did not fall, for it had been founded upon the rock. *rivers*

26 "And everyone who hears these words of Mine, and does not[T]act upon them, will be

like a foolish man, who built his house upon the sand.   *do*
27"And the rain descended, and the⸀floods came, and the winds blew, and burst against that house; and it fell, and great was its fall."   *rivers*

Response to the Sermon

28 ⸀The result was that when Jesus had finished these words, the multitudes were amazed at His teaching;   *And it came to pass*
29 for He was teaching them as one having authority, and not as their scribes.

CHAPTER 8

The Leper Is Cleansed
Mark 1:40–44; Luke 5:12–14

AND when He had come down from the mountain, great multitudes followed Him.
2 And behold, a leper came to Him, and bowed down to Him, saying, "Lord, if You are willing, You can make me clean."
3 And He stretched out His hand and touched him, saying, "I am willing; be cleansed." And immediately his⸀leprosy was cleansed.   Matt. 11:5; Luke 4:27
4 And Jesus *said to him, "See that you tell no one; but go, show yourself to the priest, and present the ⸀offering that Moses commanded, for a testimony to them."   *gift*

The Centurion's Servant Is Healed
Luke 7:1–10

5 And when He had entered Capernaum, a centurion came to Him, entreating Him,
6 and saying, "Lord,⸀ my servant is lying paralyzed at home, suffering great pain." *Sir*
7 And He *said to him, "I will come and heal him."
8 But the centurion answered and said, "Lord,⸀ I am not worthy for You to come under my roof, but just say the word, and my ⸀servant will be healed.   *Sir • boy*
9"For I, too, am a man under⸀authority, with soldiers under me; and I say to this one, 'Go!' and he goes, and to another, 'Come!' and he comes, and to my slave, 'Do this!' and he does *it*."   [Mark 1:27; Luke 9:1]
10 Now when Jesus heard *this*, He marveled, and said to those who were following, "Truly I say to you, I have not found such great faith with anyone in Israel.
11"And I say to you, that many⸀shall come from east and west, and ²¹recline *at the table* with Abraham, and Isaac, and Jacob, in the kingdom of heaven;   Is. 49:12; 59:19☆
12 but⸀the sons of the kingdom shall be cast out into⸀the outer darkness; in that place there shall be weeping and gnashing of teeth."   [Matt. 13:38] • Matt. 22:13
13 And Jesus said to the centurion, "Go your way; let it be done to you⸀as you have believed." And the ⸀servant was healed that *very* hour.   [Matt. 9:22, 29] • *boy*

Peter's Mother-in-law Is Healed
Mark 1:29–34; Luke 4:38–41

14 ⸀And when Jesus had come to Peter's ^home, He saw his mother-in-law lying sick in bed with a fever.   Matt. 8:14-16 • *house*
15 And He touched her hand, and the fever left her; and she arose, and^waited on Him.   *served*
16 And when evening had come, they brought to Him many ⸀who were demon-possessed; and He cast out the spirits with a word, and healed all who were ill Matt. 4:24
17 in order that what was spoken through Isaiah the prophet might be fulfilled, saying, ⸀"HE HIMSELF TOOK OUR INFIRMITIES, AND CARRIED AWAY OUR DISEASES."   Is. 53:4

Demands of Discipleship
Luke 9:57–62

18 Now when Jesus saw a crowd around Him,⸀He gave orders to depart to the other side.   Mark 4:35; Luke 8:22
19 ⸀And a certain scribe came and said to Him, "Teacher, I will follow You wherever You go."   Matt. 8:19-22; *Luke 9:57-60*
20 And Jesus *said to him, "The foxes have holes, and the birds of the ^air *have* ^nests; but the Son of Man has nowhere to lay His head."   *sky • roosting places*
21 And another of the disciples said to Him, "Lord, permit me first to go and bury my father."
22 But Jesus *said to him, "Follow Me; and allow the dead to bury their own dead."

The Sea Is Stilled
Mark 4:35–41; Luke 8:22–25

23 ⸀And when He got into the boat, His disciples followed Him. Matt. 8:23-27; *Mark 4:36-41*
24 And behold, there arose a great storm in the sea, so that the boat was covered with the waves; but He Himself was asleep.
25 And they came to *Him*, and awoke Him, saying, "Save⸀us, Lord; we are perishing!"   Matt. 8:2; 9:18
26 And He *said to them, "Why are you timid, ⸀you men of little faith?" Then He arose, and rebuked the winds and the sea; and it became perfectly calm.   Matt. 6:30
27 And the men marveled, saying, "What kind of a man is this, that even the winds and the sea obey Him?"

Demons Are Cast into Swine
Mark 5:1–17; Luke 8:26–37

28 ⸀And when He had come to the other side into the country of the Gadarenes, two men who were demon-possessed met Him as they were coming out of the tombs; *they*

²¹ Or, *dine*

were so exceedingly violent that no one could pass by that road.   Matt. 8:28-34
29 And behold, they cried out, saying, "What do we have to do with You, Son of God? Have You come here to torment us before the time?"   the appointed time of judgment
30 Now there was at a distance from them a herd of many swine feeding.
31 And the demons *began* to entreat Him, saying, "If You are *going to* cast us out, send us into the herd of swine."
32 And He said to them, "Begone!" And they came out, and went into the swine, and behold, the whole herd rushed down the steep bank into the sea and perished in the waters.
33 And the herdsmen ran away, and went to the city, and reported everything, including the *incident* of the demoniacs.   *and*
34 And behold, the whole city came out to meet Jesus; and when they saw Him, they entreated *Him* to depart from their region.

CHAPTER 9

The Paralytic Is Forgiven
Mark 2:1-12; Luke 5:17-26

AND getting into a boat, He crossed over, and came to His own city.   Matt. 4:13
2 And behold, they were bringing to Him a paralytic, lying on a bed; and Jesus seeing their faith said to the paralytic, "Take courage, My son, your sins are forgiven."   *child*
3 And behold, some of the scribes said to themselves, "This *fellow* blasphemes."
4 And Jesus knowing their thoughts said, "Why are you thinking evil in your hearts?   Matt. 12:25; Luke 6:8; 9:47
5 "For which is easier, to say, 'Your sins are forgiven,' or to say, 'Rise, and walk'?
6 "But in order that you may know that the Son of Man has authority on earth to forgive sins"—then He *said to the paralytic—"Rise, take up your bed, and go home."   Matt. 8:20 • Matt. 4:24; 9:2
7 And he rose, and went home.   *departed*
8 But when the multitudes saw *this,* they were filled with awe, and glorified God, who had given such authority to men.   *afraid*

Matthew Is Called
Mark 2:14; Luke 5:27, 28

9 And as Jesus passed on from there, He saw a man, called Matthew, sitting in the tax office; and He *said to him, "Follow Me!" And he rose, and followed Him.

The Disciples Eat with Sinners
Mark 2:15-17; Luke 5:29-32

10 And it happened that as He was reclining *at the table* in the house, behold many tax-gatherers and sinners came and were dining with Jesus and His disciples.

11 And when the Pharisees saw *this,* they said to His disciples, "Why is your Teacher eating with the tax-gatherers and sinners?"
12 But when He heard this, He said, "It is not those who are healthy who need a physician, but those who are sick.   Mark 2:17
13 "But go and learn what *this* means, 'I DESIRE COMPASSION, AND NOT SACRIFICE,' for I did not come to call the righteous, but sinners."   Matt. 12:7 • Hos. 6:6 • *mercy*

The Disciples Do Not Fast
Mark 2:18-22; Luke 5:33-39

14 Then the disciples of John *came to Him, saying, "Why do we and the Pharisees fast, but Your disciples do not fast?"
15 And Jesus said to them, "The attendants of the bridegroom cannot mourn as long as the bridegroom is with them, can they? But the days will come when the bridegroom is taken away from them, and then they will fast.   *sons of the bridal-chamber*
16 "But no one puts a patch of unshrunk cloth on an old garment; for the patch pulls away from the garment, and a worse tear results.   *that which is put on • that which fills up*
17 "Nor do *men* put new wine into old wineskins; otherwise the wineskins burst, and the wine pours out, and the wineskins are ruined; but they put new wine into fresh wineskins, and both are preserved."

Life Is Restored
Mark 5:21-43; Luke 8:40-56

18 While He was saying these things to them, behold, there came a *synagogue* official, and bowed down before Him, saying, "My daughter has just died; but come and lay Your hand on her, and she will live."
19 And Jesus rose and *began* to follow him, and *so did* His disciples.
20 And behold, a woman who had been suffering from a hemorrhage for twelve years, came up behind Him and touched the fringe of His cloak;   *outer garment*
21 for she was saying to herself, "If I only touch His garment, I shall get well." *in herself*
22 But Jesus turning and seeing her said, "Daughter, take courage; your faith has made you well." And at once the woman was made well.   *saved you • from that hour*
23 And when Jesus came into the official's house, and saw the flute-players, and the crowd in noisy disorder,   *ruler's • Jer. 9:17*
24 He *began* to say, "Depart; for the girl has not died, but is asleep." And they *began* laughing at Him.   John 11:13; Acts 20:10
25 But when the crowd had been put out, He entered and took her by the hand; and the girl arose.   Acts 9:40 • *was raised up*
26 And this news went out into all that land.   Matt. 4:24; 14:1; Mark 1:28, 45; Luke 4:14

Sight Is Restored

27 And as Jesus passed on from there, two blind men followed Him, crying out,

²² I.e., more than

and saying, "Have mercy on us, ʀSon of David!" Matt. 1:1; 12:23; 15:22

28 And after He had come into the house, the blind men came up to Him, and Jesus *said to them, "Do you believe that I am able to do this?" They *said to Him, "Yes, Lord."

29 Then He touched their eyes, saying, "Be it done to you according to your faith."

30 And their eyes were opened. And Jesus ʀsternly warned them, saying, "See here, let no one know about this!" Matt. 8:4

31 But they went out, and ʀspread the news about Him in all that land. Matt. 4:24

Speech Is Restored

32 And as they were going out, behold, ʀa dumb man, demon-possessed, ᵀwas brought to Him. Matt. 12:22, 24 · they brought

33 And after the demon was cast out, the dumb man spoke; and the multitudes marveled, saying, "Nothingʀ like this ᵀwas ever seen in Israel." Mark 2:12 · ever appeared

34 But the Pharisees were saying, "He ʀcasts out the demons by the ruler of the demons." Matt. 12:24; Mark 3:22; Luke 11:15

The Need for Delegation of Power

35 And Jesus was going about all the cities and the villages, ʀteaching in their synagogues, and proclaiming the gospel of the kingdom, and healing every kind of disease and every kind of sickness. Mark 1:14

36 And seeing the multitudes, He felt compassion for them, because they were ᴬdistressed and ᵀdowncast like sheepᵀwithout a shepherd. harassed · thrown down · not having

37 Then He *said to His disciples, "The harvest is plentiful, but the workers are few.

38 "Therefore beseech the Lord of the harvest to send out workers into His harvest."

CHAPTER 10

The Twelve Apostles Are Sent
Mark 6:7; Luke 9:1

AND having summoned His twelve disciples, He gave them authority over unclean spirits, to cast them out, and to heal every kind of disease and every kind of sickness.

2 Now the names of the twelve apostles are these: The first, Simon, who is called Peter, and Andrew his brother; and ᴬJames the son of Zebedee, and John his brother; Jacob

3 Philip andᵀBartholomew; Thomas and Matthew the tax-gatherer; James the son of Alphaeus, and Thaddaeus; son of Talmai

4 Simon the ᴬZealot, and Judas Iscariot, the one who betrayed Him. Cananaean

The Twelve Apostles Are Instructed
Mark 6:8–13; Luke 9:2–6; 12:2–10

5 ʀThese twelve Jesus sent out after instructing them, saying, "Do not ᴬgo in the way of the Gentiles, and do not enter any city of the Samaritans; Luke 9:2 · go off to

6 but rather ᴬgo to ʀthe lost sheep of the house of Israel. proceed · Matt. 15:24

7 "And as you ᴬgo, preach, saying, 'The kingdom of heaven is at hand.' proceed

8 "Heal the sick, raise the dead, cleanse the lepers, cast out demons; freely you received, freely give.

9 "Doʀ not acquire gold, or silver, or copperᵀfor your money belts, Mark 6:8-11 · into

10 or a bag for your journey, or even two ᴬtunics, or sandals, or a staff; for the worker is worthy of his support. inner garments

11 "And into whatever city or village you enter, inquire who is worthy in it; and abide there until you go away.

12 "And as you enter the ᴬhouse, ʀgive it your greeting. household · 1 Sam. 25:6

13 "And if the house is worthy, let your greeting of peace come upon it; but if it is not worthy, let your greeting of peace return to you.

14 "And whoever does not receive you, nor heed your words, as you go out of that house or that city, ʀshake off the dust of your feet. Acts 13:51

15 "Truly I say to you, it will be more tolerable for the land of Sodom and Gomorrah in the day of judgment, than for that city.

16 "Behold, ʀ I send you out as sheep in the midst of wolves; therefore be shrewd as serpents, and innocent as doves. Luke 10:3

17 "But beware of men; for they will deliver you up to the ʀcourts, and scourge you in their synagogues; Matt. 5:22

18 and you shall even be brought before governors and kings for My sake, as a testimony to them and to the Gentiles.

19 "Butʀ when they deliver you up, do not become anxious about how or what you will speak; for it shall be given you in that hour what you are to speak. Matt. 10:19-22

20 "For it is not you who speak, but it is the Spirit of your Father who speaks in you.

21 "And brother will deliver up brother to death, and a father his child; and children will rise up against parents, and ᴬcause them to be put to death. put them to death

22 "And you will be hated by all on account of My name, but it is the one who has endured to the end who will be saved.

23 "But whenever they persecute you in this city, flee to the next; for truly I say to you, you shall not finish going through the cities of Israel, until the Son of Man comes.

24 "A ᴬdisciple is not above his teacher, nor a slave above his master. pupil

25 "It is enough for the disciple that he become as his teacher, and the slave as his master. If they have called the head of the house ᴬBeelzebul, how much more the members of his household! Beezebul

26 "Therefore do not fear them, for there is nothing covered that will not be revealed, and hidden that will not be known.

27"What I tell you in the darkness, speak in the light; and what you hear *whispered* in *your* ear, proclaim upon the housetops.

28"And do not fear those who kill the body, but are unable to kill the soul; but rather[R]fear Him who is able to destroy both soul and body in[T]hell.   Heb. 10:31 • *Gehenna*

29"Are[R]not two sparrows sold for a [23]cent? And *yet* not one of them will fall to the ground apart from your Father.   Luke 12:6

30"But[R]the very hairs of your head are all numbered. 1 Sam. 14:45; 2 Sam. 14:11; Luke 21:18

31"Therefore do not fear;[R]you are of more value than many sparrows.   Matt. 12:12

32"Everyone therefore who shall confess [T]Me before men, I will also confess him before My Father who is in heaven.   *in Me*

33"But [R]whoever shall deny Me before men, I will also deny him before My Father who is in heaven.   [Mark 8:38; Luke 9:26]

34"Do[R]not think that I came to[T]bring peace on the earth; I did not come to bring peace, but a sword.   *Luke 12:51-53 • cast*

35"For I came to[R]SET A MAN AGAINST HIS FATHER, AND A DAUGHTER AGAINST HER MOTHER, AND A DAUGHTER-IN-LAW AGAINST HER MOTHER-IN-LAW;   Mic. 7:6; Matt. 10:21☆

36 and[R]A MAN'S ENEMIES WILL BE THE MEMBERS OF HIS HOUSEHOLD. Mic. 7:6; Matt. 10:21☆

37"He[R] who loves father or mother more than Me is not worthy of Me; and he who loves son or daughter more than Me is not worthy of Me.   Deut. 33:9; Luke 14:26

38"And he who does not take his cross and follow after Me is not worthy of Me.

39"He[R]who has found his[A]life shall lose it, and he who has lost his life for My sake shall find it.   Mark 8:35; John 12:25 • *soul*

40"He[R]who receives Me receives Me, and [R]he who receives Me receives Him who sent Me.   Matt. 18:5; Luke 10:16 • Luke 9:48; John 12:44

41"He[R]who receives a prophet in *the* name of a prophet shall receive a prophet's reward; and he who receives a righteous man in the name of a righteous man shall receive a righteous man's reward.   Matt. 25:44

42"And whoever in the name of a disciple gives to one of these[T]little ones even a cup of cold water to drink, truly I say to you he shall not lose his reward."   *humble*

CHAPTER 11

AND it came about that when Jesus had finished giving instructions to His twelve disciples, He departed from there to teach and[A]preach in their cities.   *proclaim*

Rejection of John the Baptist
Luke 7:19-30

2 [R]Now when[R]John in prison heard of the works of Christ, he sent *word* by his disciples,   Matt. 11:2-19 • Mark 6:17; Luke 9:7ff.

3 and said to Him, "Are You[R]the [T]Expected One, or shall we look for someone else?"   John 6:14; Heb. 10:37 • *Coming One*

4 And Jesus answered and said to them, "Go and report to John[R]what you hear and see: Is. 29:18, 19; 35:4-6★

5 *the* BLIND RECEIVE SIGHT and *the* lame walk, *the* lepers are cleansed and *the* deaf hear, and *the* dead are raised up, and *the* POOR HAVE THE GOSPEL PREACHED TO THEM.

6"And blessed is he [T]who keeps from [A]stumbling over Me."   *whoever • taking offense at*

7 And as these were going *away*, Jesus began to speak to the multitudes about John, "What did you go out into the wilderness to look at? A reed shaken by the wind?

8"But what did you go out to see? A man dressed in soft *clothing*? Behold, those who wear soft *clothing* are in kings' palaces.

9"But[A] why did you go out? To see [R]a prophet? Yes, I say to you, and one who is more than a prophet.   *Well then • Luke 1:76*

10"This is the one about whom it[T]is written,   *has been written*

'BEHOLD[R] I SEND MY MESSENGER BEFORE YOUR FACE, Mal. 3:1; Mark 1:2★
WHO WILL PREPARE YOUR WAY BEFORE YOU.'

11"Truly, I say to you, among those born of women there has not arisen *anyone* greater than John the Baptist; yet he who is [T]least in the kingdom of heaven is greater than he.   *less*

12"And from the days of John the Baptist until now the kingdom of heaven suffers violence, and violent men take it by force.

13"For all the prophets and the Law prophesied until John.

14"And if you care to accept *it*, he himself is Elijah, who[A]was to come.   *is to come*

15"He who has ears to hear, let him hear.

Rejection by Jesus' Generation
Luke 7:31-35

16"But to what shall I compare this generation? It is like children sitting in the market places, who call out to the other *children*,

17 and say, 'We played the flute for you, and you did not dance; we sang a dirge, and you did not[T]mourn.'   *beat the breast*

18"For John came neither eating nor drinking, and they say, 'He has a demon!'

19"The Son of Man came eating and drinking, and they say, 'Behold, a gluttonous man and a [A]drunkard, a friend of tax-gatherers and sinners!' [T]Yet wisdom is vindicated by her deeds."   *wine-drinker • And*

Rejection of Chorazin,
Bethsaida, and Capernaum
Luke 10:12-15

20 Then He began to reproach the cities in which most of His[A]miracles were done, because they did not repent.   *works of power*

21"Woe to you, Chorazin! Woe to you, [R]Bethsaida! For if the[A]miracles had occurred

[23] Gr., *assarion*, the smallest copper coin

in Tyre and Sidon which occurred in you, they would have repented long ago in sackcloth and ashes.   Mark 6:45 • *works of power*

22"Nevertheless I say to you, ^Rit shall be more tolerable for Tyre and Sidon in *the* day of judgment, than for you.   Matt. 10:15

23"And you, Capernaum, will not be exalted to heaven, will you? You shall descend to Hades; for if the 'miracles had occurred in Sodom which occurred in you, it would have remained to this day.   *works of power*

24"Nevertheless I say to you that it shall be more tolerable for the land of Sodom in *the* day of judgment, than for you."

Invitation to Come to Jesus

25 ^RAt that ^time Jesus answered and said, "I praise Thee, O Father, Lord of heaven and earth, that Thou didst hide these things from *the* wise and intelligent and didst reveal them to babes.   Matt. 11:25-27 • *occasion*

26"Yes, ^RFather, for thus it was well-pleasing in Thy sight.   Luke 22:42; 23:34; John 11:41

27"All things have been handed over to Me by My Father; and no one knows the Son, except the Father; nor does anyone know the Father, except the Son, and anyone to whom the Son wills to reveal *Him.*

28"Come to Me, all who are weary and heavy-laden, and I will give you rest.

29"Take My yoke upon you, and ^Rlearn from Me, for I am gentle and humble in heart; and ^RYOU SHALL FIND REST FOR YOUR SOULS.   [John 13:15; Eph. 4:20] • *Jer. 6:16*

30"For ^RMy yoke is ^easy, and My load is light."   [1 John 5:3] • *kindly or pleasant*

CHAPTER 12

Controversy over Sabbath-labor
Mark 3:23-28; Luke 6:1-5

AT^R that ^time Jesus went on the Sabbath through the grainfields, and His disciples became hungry and began to pick the heads of *grain* and eat.   Matt. 12:1-8 • *occasion*

2 But when the Pharisees saw it, they said to Him, "Behold, Your disciples do what is not lawful to do on a Sabbath."

3 But He said to them, "Have you not read what David did, when he became hungry, he and his companions;

4 how he entered the house of God, and they ate the ^consecrated bread, which was not lawful for him to eat, nor for those with him, but for the priests alone?   *showbread*

5"Or have you not read in the Law, that on the Sabbath the priests in the temple break the Sabbath, and are innocent?

6"But I say to you, that something ^Rgreater than the temple is here.   [2 Chr. 6:18]

7"But if you had known what this 'means, 'I DESIRE ^COMPASSION, AND NOT A SACRIFICE,' you would not have condemned the innocent.   *is* • [Hos. 6:6] • *mercy*

8"For ^Rthe Son of Man is Lord of the Sabbath."   Matt. 8:20; 12:32, 40

Controversy over Sabbath-healing
Mark 3:1-5; Luke 6:6-10

9 ^RAnd departing from there, He went into their synagogue.   Matt. 12:9-14; *Mark 3:1-6*

10 And behold, *there was* a man with a withered hand. And they questioned Him, saying, "Is^R it lawful to heal on the Sabbath?"—in order that they might accuse Him.   Matt. 12:2; Luke 13:14; 14:3; John 5:10

11 And He said to them, "What^R man shall there be ^among you, who shall have one sheep, and if it falls into a pit on the Sabbath, will he not take hold of it, and lift it out?   Luke 14:5 • *of*

12"Of^R how much more value then is a man than a sheep! So then, it is lawful to do^T good on the Sabbath."   Luke 14:1-6 • *well*

13 Then He *said to the man, "Stretch out your hand!" And he stretched it out, and it was restored to normal, like the other.

Pharisees Plan to Destroy Christ
Mark 3:6-12; Luke 6:11

14 But the Pharisees went out, and ^Rcounseled together against Him, *as to* how they might destroy Him.   Matt. 26:4; Mark 14:1

15 But Jesus, ^Taware of *this*, withdrew from there. And many followed Him, and ^RHe healed them all,   *knowing* • Matt. 4:23

16 and ^Rwarned them not to ^make Him known,   Matt. 8:4; 9:30 • *reveal who He was*

17 in order that what was spoken through Isaiah the prophet, might be fulfilled, saying,

18 "BEHOLD, ^R MY ^TSERVANT WHOM I HAVE
    CHOSEN;   Is. 42:1 ★ • *Child*
   MY BELOVED IN WHOM MY SOUL ^is
    WELL-PLEASED;   *took pleasure*
   I WILL PUT MY SPIRIT UPON HIM,
   AND HE SHALL PROCLAIM 'JUSTICE TO
    THE GENTILES.   *judgment*

19 "HE^R WILL NOT QUARREL, NOR CRY OUT;
   NOR WILL ANYONE HEAR HIS VOICE IN
    THE STREETS.   Is. 42:2 ★

20 "A^R BATTERED REED HE WILL NOT BREAK
    OFF,   Is. 42:3 ★
   AND A SMOLDERING WICK HE WILL NOT
    PUT OUT,
   UNTIL HE LEADS JUSTICE TO VICTORY.

21 "AND^R IN HIS NAME THE ^GENTILES WILL
    HOPE."   Is. 42:4 ★; Rom. 15:12 • *nations*

Pharisees Blaspheme the Holy Spirit
Mark 3:22-27; Luke 11:17-23

22 ^RThen there was brought to Him a demon-possessed man *who was* blind and dumb, and He healed him, so that the dumb man spoke and saw.   Matt. 12:22, 24

23 And all the multitudes were amazed, and *began* to say, "This *man* cannot be the ^RSon of David, can he?"   Matt. 9:27

24 But when the Pharisees heard it, they said, "This man casts out demons only by

^ABeelzebul the ruler of the demons   *Beezebul*
25 And knowing their thoughts He said to them, "Any^Tkingdom divided against itself is laid waste; and any city or house divided against itself shall not stand.   *Every*
26"And if^RSatan casts out Satan, he^Tis divided against himself; how then shall his kingdom stand?   Matt. 4:10; 13:19 • *was*
27"And if I by Beelzebul cast out demons, by whom do your sons cast them out? Consequently they shall be your judges.
28"But^Rif I cast out demons by the Spirit of God, then the kingdom of God has come upon you.   [1 John 3:8]
29"Or how can anyone enter the strong man's house and carry off his property, unless he first binds the strong *man*? And then he will plunder his house.
30"He^Rwho is not with Me is against Me; and he who does not gather with Me scatters.   [Mark 9:40; Luke 9:50; 11:23]

Pharisees Commit the Unpardonable Sin
Mark 3:28, 29

31"Therefore^R I say to you, any sin and blasphemy shall be forgiven men, but blasphemy against the Spirit shall not be forgiven.   Matt. 12:31, 32; Mark 3:28-30; Luke 12:10
32"And whoever shall speak a word against the Son of Man, it shall be forgiven him; but whoever shall speak against the Holy Spirit, it shall not be forgiven him, either in this age, or in the *age* to come.
33"Either make the tree good, and its fruit good; or make the tree bad, and its fruit bad; for the tree is known by its fruit.
34"You^R brood of vipers, how can you, being evil, speak ^Twhat is good? ^RFor the mouth speaks out of that which fills the heart.   Matt. 3:7 • *good things* • Is. 32:6
35"The good man out of *his* good treasure brings forth^Twhat is good; and the evil man out of *his* evil treasure brings forth^Twhat is evil.   *good things* • *evil things*
36"And I say to you, that every careless word that men shall speak, they shall render account for it in the day of judgment.
37"For^Aby your words you shall be justified, and^Aby your words you shall be condemned."   *in accordance with*

Pharisees Demand a Sign
Luke 11:24-26, 29-32

38 Then some of the scribes and Pharisees answered Him, saying, "Teacher, we want to see a ^Asign from You."   *attesting miracle*
39 But He answered and said to them, "An evil and adulterous generation craves for a sign; and *yet* no sign shall be given to it but the sign of Jonah the prophet;
40 for just as JONAH WAS THREE DAYS AND THREE NIGHTS IN THE BELLY OF THE SEA MONSTER, so shall the Son of Man be three days and three nights in the heart of the earth.
41"The^R men of Nineveh shall stand up with this generation at the judgment, and shall condemn it because they repented at the preaching of Jonah; and behold, something greater than Jonah is here.   Jon. 1:2
42"The^RQueen of *the* South shall rise up with this generation at the judgment and shall condemn it, because she came from the ends of the earth to hear the wisdom of Solomon; and behold, something greater than Solomon is here.   1 Kin. 10:1; 2 Chr. 9:1
43"Now when the unclean spirit goes out of a man, it passes through waterless places, seeking rest, and does not find *it.*
44"Then it says, 'I will return to my house from which I came'; and when it comes, it finds it unoccupied, swept, and put in order.
45"Then it goes, and takes along with it seven other spirits more wicked than itself, and they go in and live there; and^Rthe last state of that man becomes worse than the first. That is the way it will also be with this evil generation."   [Heb. 6:4-8; 2 Pet. 2:20]

Jesus and the True Brothers
Mark 3:31-35

46 ^RWhile He was still speaking to the multitudes, behold, His ^Rmother and brothers were standing outside, seeking to speak to Him.   Luke 8:19-21 • Matt. 1:18
47 And someone said to Him, "Behold, Your mother and Your brothers are standing outside seeking to speak to You."
48 But He answered the one who was telling Him and said, "Who is My mother and who are My brothers?"
49 And stretching out His hand toward His disciples, He said, "Behold, My mother and My brothers!
50"For whoever does the will of My Father who is in heaven, he is My brother and sister and mother."

CHAPTER 13

Parable of the Soils
Mark 4:1-20; Luke 8:4-15

O N that day Jesus went out of^Rthe house, and was sitting by the sea.   Matt. 9:28; 13:36
2 And great multitudes gathered to Him, so that^RHe got into a boat and sat down, and the whole multitude was standing on the beach.   Luke 5:3
3 And He spoke many things to them in ^Rparables, saying, "Behold, the sower went out to sow;   Matt. 13:10ff.; Mark 4:2ff.
4 and as he sowed, some *seeds* fell beside the road, and the birds came and ate them up.
5"And others fell upon the rocky places, where they^Tdid not have much soil; and immediately they sprang up, because they had no depth of soil.   *were not having*
6"But when the sun had risen, they were scorched; and because they had no root, they withered away.
7"And others fell among the thorns, and the thorns came up and choked them out.

8"And others fell on the good soil, and *yielded a crop, some a[R]hundredfold, some sixty, and some thirty.　Gen. 26:12; Matt. 13:23

9"He[R]who has ears, let him hear." Rev. 2:7

10 And the disciples came and said to Him, "Why do You speak to them in parables?"

11 And He answered and said to them, "To[R]you it has been granted to know the mysteries of the kingdom of heaven, but to them it has not been granted. [1 John 2:20, 27]

12"For[R]whoever has, to him shall *more be given, and he shall have an abundance; but whoever does not have, even what he has shall be taken away from him.　Luke 8:18

13"Therefore I speak to them in parables; because while[R]seeing they do not see, and while hearing they do not hear, nor do they understand.　Deut. 29:4; Is. 42:19, 20; Jer. 5:21

14"And[T]in their case the prophecy of Isaiah is being fulfilled, which says,　for them

'YOU[R]WILL KEEP ON HEARING, BUT WILL
　　NOT UNDERSTAND;　Is. 6:9; Mark 4:12★
AND[T]YOU WILL KEEP ON SEEING, BUT
　　WILL NOT PERCEIVE;　seeing you will see
15　[R]FOR THE HEART OF THIS PEOPLE HAS
　　BECOME DULL,　Ps. 119:70; Is. 6:10★
AND WITH THEIR EARS THEY SCARCELY
　　HEAR,
AND THEY HAVE CLOSED THEIR EYES
LEST THEY SHOULD SEE WITH THEIR
　　EYES,
AND HEAR WITH THEIR EARS,
AND UNDERSTAND WITH THEIR HEART
　　AND RETURN,
AND I SHOULD HEAL THEM.'

16"But blessed are your eyes, because they see; and your ears, because they hear.

17"For truly I say to you, that[R]many prophets and righteous men desired to see what you see, and did not see it; and to hear what you hear, and did not hear it. John 8:56

18"Hear then the parable of the sower.

19"When anyone hears the word of the kingdom, and does not understand it, the evil one comes and snatches away what has been sown in his heart. This is the one on whom seed was sown beside the road.

20"And the one on whom seed was sown on the rocky places, this is the man who hears the word, and immediately receives it with joy;

21 yet he has no firm root in himself, but is only temporary, and when affliction or persecution arises because of the word, immediately he[T]falls away.　is caused to stumble

22"And the one on whom seed was sown among the thorns, this is the man who hears the word, and the worry of[R]the[A]world, and the deceitfulness of riches choke the word, and it becomes unfruitful.　Gal. 1:4 • age

23"And the one on whom seed was sown on the good soil, this is the man who hears the word and understands it; who indeed bears fruit, and brings forth, some a hundredfold, some sixty, and some thirty."

Parable of the Wheat and Tares

24 He presented another parable to them, saying, "The[R] kingdom of heaven [T]may be compared to a man who sowed good seed in his field.　Matt. 13:31, 33 • was compared to

25"But while men were sleeping, his enemy came and sowed [24]tares also among the wheat, and went away.

26"But when the [T]wheat sprang up and bore grain, then the tares became evident also.　grass

27"And the slaves of the landowner came and said to him, 'Sir, did you not sow good seed in your field? [T]How then does it have tares?'　From where

28"And he said to them, 'An [T]enemy has done this!' And the slaves *said to him, 'Do you want us, then, to go and gather them up?'　enemy man

29"But he *said, 'No; lest while you are gathering up the tares, you may root up the wheat with them.

30 'Allow both to grow together until the harvest; and in the time of the harvest I will say to the reapers, "First gather up the tares and bind them in bundles to burn them up; but gather the wheat into my barn." ' "

Parable of the Mustard Seed
Mark 4:30–32; Luke 13:18, 19

31 He presented another parable to them, saying, "The[R] kingdom of heaven is like [R]a mustard seed, which a man took and sowed in his field;　Luke 13:18, 19 • Luke 17:6

32 and this is smaller than all other seeds; but when it is full grown, it is larger than the garden plants, and becomes a tree, so that [R]THE BIRDS OF THE [A]AIR come and NEST IN ITS BRANCHES."　Ezek. 17:23; Ps. 104:12 • sky

Parable of the Leaven
Luke 13:20, 21

33 He spoke another parable to them, "The kingdom of heaven is like leaven, which a woman took, and hid in three[T]pecks of meal, until it was all leavened."　Gr., sata

34 All these things Jesus spoke to the multitudes in parables, and He did not speak to them without a parable,

35 so that what was spoken through the prophet might be fulfilled, saying,
　"I WILL OPEN MY MOUTH IN PARABLES;
　I WILL UTTER THINGS HIDDEN SINCE
　　THE FOUNDATION OF THE WORLD."

Parable of the Tares Explained

36 Then He left the multitudes, and went into[R]the house. And His disciples came to Him, saying, "Explain to us the parable of the[R]tares of the field."　Matt. 13:1 • darnel

37 And He answered and said, "The one who sows the good seed is the Son of Man,

38 and the field is the world; and as for

---

[24] Or, darnel, a weed resembling wheat

the good seed, these are [R]the sons of the kingdom; and the tares are[R]the sons of the evil *one;*   Matt. 8:12 • Acts 13:10; [1 John 3:10]
39 and the enemy who sowed them is the devil, and the harvest is the^end of the age; and the reapers are angels.   *consummation*
40 "Therefore just as the tares are gathered up and burned with fire, so shall it be at the ^end of the age.   *consummation*
41 "The Son of Man will send forth His angels, and they will gather out of His kingdom ^all stumbling blocks, and those who commit lawlessness, *everything that is offensive*
42 and[R]will cast them into the furnace of fire; in that place^there shall be weeping and gnashing of teeth.   Matt. 13:50 • Matt. 8:12
43 "Then THE RIGHTEOUS WILL SHINE FORTH AS THE SUN in the kingdom of their Father. He who has ears, let him hear.

Parable of the Hidden Treasure

44 "The kingdom of heaven is like a treasure hidden in the field, which a man found and hid; and from joy over it he goes and sells all that he has, and buys that field.

Parable of the Pearl of Great Value

45 "Again,[R]the kingdom of heaven is like a merchant seeking fine pearls,   Matt. 13:24
46 and upon finding one pearl of great value, he went and sold all that he had, and bought it.

Parable of the Dragnet

47 "Again,[R]the kingdom of heaven is like a dragnet cast into the sea, and gathering *fish* of every kind;   Matt. 13:44
48 and when it was filled, they drew it up on the beach; and they sat down, and gathered the good *fish* into containers, but the bad they threw away.
49 "So it will be at the end of the age; the angels shall come forth, and ^take out the wicked from among the righteous, *separate*
50 and[R]will cast them into the furnace of fire;[R]there shall be weeping and gnashing of teeth.   Matt. 13:42 • Matt. 8:12

Parable of the Head of the Household

51 "Have you understood all these things?" They *said to Him, "Yes."
52 And He said to them, "Therefore every scribe who has become a disciple of the kingdom of heaven is like a head of a household, who brings forth out of his treasure things new and old."
53 [R]And it came about that when Jesus had finished these parables, He departed from there.   Matt. 7:28

Rejection at Nazareth
Mark 6:1–6

54 And coming to His home town He *began*[R]teaching them in their synagogue, so

that they became astonished, and said, "Where *did* this man *get* this wisdom, and *these* miraculous powers?   Ps. 22:22★
55 "Is not this the carpenter's son? Is not His mother called Mary, and His brothers, James and Joseph and Simon and Judas?
56 "And[R]His sisters, are they not all with us? Where then *did* this man *get* all these things?"   Mark 6:3
57 And they [T]took offense at Him. But Jesus said to them, "A prophet is not without honor except in his home town, and in his own household." *were being made to stumble*
58 And He did not do many^miracles there because of their unbelief. *works of power*

CHAPTER 14

Present Response to Jesus
Mark 6:14–16; Luke 9:7–9

A[R]T^that^time Herod the tetrarch heard the news about Jesus,   *Luke 9:7-9 • occasion*
2 and said to his servants, "This[R]is John the Baptist;^he has risen from the dead; and that is why miraculous powers are at work in him."   Mark 6:14; Luke 9:7 • *he, himself*

Recount of the Murder of
John the Baptist
Mark 6:17–29

3 For when[R]Herod had John arrested, he bound him, and put him[R]in prison on account of[R]Herodias, the wife of his brother Philip.   Mark 8:15 • Matt. 4:12 • Luke 3:19f.
4 For John had been saying to him, "It[R]is not lawful for you to have her." Lev. 18:16
5 And although he wanted to put him to death, he feared the multitude, because[T]they regarded him as a prophet. *they were holding*
6 But when Herod's birthday [T]came, the daughter of Herodias danced [T]before *them* and pleased Herod. *occurred • in the midst*
7 Thereupon he promised with an oath to give her whatever she asked.
8 And having been prompted by her mother, she *said, "Give me here on a platter the head of John the Baptist."
9 And although he was grieved, the king commanded *it* to be given because of his oaths, and because of his dinner guests.
10 And he sent and had John beheaded in the prison.
11 And his head was brought on a platter and given to the girl; and she brought *it* to her mother.
12 And his disciples came and took away the body and buried[T]it; and they went and reported to Jesus.   *him*

Jesus Feeds 5,000
Mark 6:31–44; Luke 9:11–17;
John 6:1–13

13 Now when Jesus heard *it,* He withdrew from there in a boat, to a lonely place by Himself; and when the multitudes heard *of this,* they followed Him on foot from the cities.

14 And when He went ᵀashore, He saw a great multitude, and felt compassion for them, and healed their sick.   *out*

15 And when it was evening, the disciples came to Him, saying, "The place is desolate, and the time is already past; so send the multitudes away, that they may go into the villages and buy food for themselves."

16 But Jesus said to them, "They do not need to go away; you give them *something* to eat!"

17 And they *said to Him, "We have here only ᴿfive loaves and two fish."   Matt. 16:9

18 And He said, "Bring them here to Me."

19 And ordering the multitudes to recline on the grass, He took the five loaves and the two fish, and looking up toward heaven, He ᴿblessed *the food*, and breaking the loaves He gave them to the disciples, and the disciples *gave* to the multitudes,   1 Sam. 9:13

20 And they all ate, and were satisfied. And they picked up what was left over of the broken pieces, twelve full baskets.

21 And there were about five thousand men who ate, aside from women and children.

Jesus Walks on Water
Mark 6:45-52; John 6:14-21

22 ᴿAnd immediately He ᵀmade the disciples get into the boat, and go ahead of Him to the other side, while He sent the multitudes away.   *Mark 6:45-51 • compelled*

23 And after He had sent the multitudes away,ᴿHe went up to the mountain by Himself to pray; and when it was evening, He was there alone.   Mark 6:46; Luke 6:12; 9:28

24 But the boat was already many ²⁵stadia away from the land, ᵇbattered by the waves; for the wind was contrary.   *tormented*

25 And in the ²⁶fourth watch of the night He came to them, walking on the sea.

26 And when the disciples saw Him walking on the sea, they were frightened, saying, "It is a ghost!" And they cried out for fear.

27 But immediately Jesus spoke to them, saying, "Takeᴿ courage, it is I; ᴿdo not be afraid."   Matt. 9:2 • John 6:20; Rev. 1:17

28 And Peter answered Him and said, "Lord, if it is You, command me to come to You on the water."

29 And He said, "Come!" And Peter got out of the boat, and walked on the water and came toward Jesus.

30 But seeing the wind, he became afraid, and beginning to sink, he cried out, saying, "Lord, save me!"

31 And immediately Jesus stretched out His hand and took hold of him, and *said to him, "Oᴿ you of little faith, why did you doubt?"   Matt. 6:30; 8:26; 16:8

32 And when they got into the boat, the wind stopped.

33 And those who were in the boat worshiped Him, saying, "You are certainly ᴿGod's Son!"   Matt. 4:3

Jesus Heals Many
Mark 6:53-56

34 And when they had crossed over, they came toᵀland at Gennesaret.   *the land*

35 And when the men of that place recognized Him, they sent into all that surrounding district and brought to Him all who were sick;   *knew*

36 and they *began* to entreat Him that they might just touch ᴿthe fringe of His cloak; and as many as ᴿtouched *it* were cured.   Matt. 9:20 • Matt. 9:21; Mark 3:10

CHAPTER 15

Debate over Tradition
Mark 7:1-23

THENᴿsome Pharisees and scribes *came to Jesus from Jerusalem, saying,   Matt. 15:1

2"Why do Your disciples transgress the tradition of the elders? For theyᴿdo not wash their hands when they eat bread." Luke 11:38

3 And He answered and said to them, "And why doᴬyou yourselves transgress the commandment of God for the sake of your tradition?   *you also*

4"For God said, 'HONORᴿ YOUR FATHER AND MOTHER,' and, 'HE WHO SPEAKS EVIL OF FATHER OR MOTHER, LET HIM ᵀBE PUT TO DEATH.'   Ex. 20:12; [Deut. 5:16] • *die the death*

5"But you say, 'Whoever shall say to *his* father or mother, "Anything of mine you might have been helped by has beenᴬgiven to God,"   *a gift, an offering*

6 he is not to honor his father ²⁷or his mother²⁸.' And *thus* you invalidated the word of God for the sake of your tradition.

7"You hypocrites, rightly did Isaiah prophesy of you, saying,

8 'THISᴿ PEOPLE HONORS ME WITH THEIR
     LIPS,   Is. 29:13
     BUT THEIR HEART IS FAR AWAY FROM
     ME.

9 'BUT IN VAIN DO THEY WORSHIP ME,
     TEACHING ASᴿDOCTRINES THE PRECEPTS
     OF MEN.' "   [Col. 2:22]

10 And after He called the multitude to Him, He said to them, "Hear, and understand.

11"Notᴿwhat enters into the mouth defiles the man, but what proceeds out of the mouth, this defiles the man."   [1 Tim. 4:3]

12 Then the disciples *came and *said to Him, "Do You know that the Pharisees were offended when they heard this statement?"

13 But He answered and said, "Everyᴿ plant which My heavenly Father did not plant shall be rooted up.   [John 15:2; 1 Cor. 3:9]

14"Let them alone; they are blind guides ²⁹of the blind. And if a blind man guides a blind man, both will fall into a pit."

---

²⁵ A stadion was about 600 feet   ²⁶ I.e., 3-6 a.m.
²⁷ Many mss. do not contain *or his mother*
²⁸ I.e., by supporting them with it
²⁹ Some mss. do not contain *of the blind*

15 And Peter answered and said to Him, "Explain^Rthe parable to us."   Matt. 13:36

16 And He said, "Are you still lacking in understanding also?

17"Do you not understand that everything that goes into the mouth passes into the ^Tstomach, and is eliminated?   belly

18"But^Rthe things that proceed out of the mouth come from the heart, and those defile the man.   [Matt. 12:34]; Mark 7:20

19"For^R out of the heart come evil thoughts, murders, adulteries, fornications, thefts, false witness, slanders.   [Gal. 5:19ff.]

20"These are the things which defile the man; but to eat with unwashed hands does not defile the man."

Jesus Heals the Gentile Woman's Daughter
Mark 7:24–30

21 ^RAnd Jesus went away from there, and withdrew into the district of ^RTyre and ^RSidon.   Matt. 15:21-28; Mark 7:24-30 • Matt. 11:21

22 And behold, a Canaanite woman came out from that region, and began to cry out, saying, "Have mercy on me, O Lord,^RSon of David; my daughter is cruelly ^Rdemon-possessed."   Matt. 9:27 • Matt. 4:24

23 But He did not answer her a word. And His disciples came to Him and kept asking Him, saying, "Send her away, for she is shouting out after us."

24 But He answered and said, "I was sent only to the lost sheep of the house of Israel."

25 But she came and began to bow down before Him, saying, "Lord, help me!"

26 And He answered and said, "It is not ^Agood to take the children's bread and throw it to the dogs."   proper

27 But she said, "Yes, Lord;^Tbut even the dogs feed on the crumbs which fall from their masters' table."   for

28 Then Jesus answered and said to her, "O woman,^Ryour faith is great; be it done for you as you wish." And her daughter was healed^Tat once.   Matt. 9:22 • from that hour

Jesus Heals Many
Mark 7:31–37

29 And departing from there, Jesus went along by the Sea of Galilee, and having gone up to the mountain, He was sitting there.

30 And great multitudes came to Him, bringing with them those who were lame, crippled, blind, dumb, and many others, and they laid them down at His feet; and ^RHe healed them,   Matt. 4:23

31 so that the multitude marveled as they saw the dumb speaking, the crippled restored, and the lame walking, and the blind seeing; and they glorified the God of Israel.

Jesus Feeds 4,000
Mark 8:1–10

32 And Jesus called His disciples to Him, and said, "I feel compassion for the multitude, because they^Thave remained with Me

now three days and have nothing to eat; and I do not wish to send them away hungry, lest they faint on the way."   are remaining

33 And the disciples *said to Him, "Where would we get so many loaves in a desolate place to satisfy such a great multitude?"

34 And Jesus *said to them, "How many loaves do you have?" And they said, "Seven, and a few small fish."

35 And He directed the multitude to ^Tsit down on the ground;   recline

36 and He took the seven loaves and the fish; and giving thanks, He broke them and started giving them to the disciples, and the disciples in turn, to the multitudes.

37 And they all ate, and were satisfied, and they picked up what was left over of the broken pieces, seven large baskets full.

38 And those who ate were four thousand men, besides women and children.

39 And sending away the multitudes, He got into^Rthe boat, and came to the region of ^RMagadan.   Mark 3:9 • Mark 8:10

CHAPTER 16

Debate over a Sign from Heaven
Mark 8:11, 12

AND the Pharisees and Sadducees came up, and testing Him asked Him to show them a^Asign from heaven.   attesting miracle

2 But He answered and said to them, "When^Rit is evening, you say, 'It will be fair weather, for the sky is red.'   Luke 12:54f.

3"And in the morning, 'There will be a storm today, for the sky is red and threatening.' ^RDo you know how to discern the ^Tappearance of the sky, but cannot discern the signs of the times?   Luke 12:56 • face

4"An evil and adulterous generation seeks after a^Asign; and a sign will not be given it, except the sign of Jonah." And He left them, and went away.   attesting miracle

Withdrawal of Jesus
Mark 8:13–21

5 And the disciples came to the other side and had forgotten to take bread.

6 And Jesus said to them, "Watch out and^Rbeware of the^Aleaven of the Pharisees and Sadducees."   Mark 8:15 • yeast

7 And they began to discuss among themselves, saying, "It is because we took no bread."

8 But Jesus, aware of this, said, "You men of little faith, why do you discuss among yourselves that you have no bread?

9"Do you not yet understand or remember the five loaves of the five thousand, and how many baskets you took up?

10"Or^Rthe seven loaves of the four thousand, and how many large baskets you took up?   Matt. 15:34-38

11"How is it that you do not understand

that I did not speak to you concerning bread? But beware of the ᴬleaven of the Pharisees and Sadducees."   *yeast*

12 Then they understood that He did not say to beware of the leaven of bread, but of the teaching of the ᴿPharisees and Sadducees.   Matt. 3:7; 5:20; 16:6, 11

Revelation of the Person of the King
Mark 8:27–30; Luke 9:18–21

13 ᴿNow when Jesus came into the district of Caesarea Philippi, He *began* asking His disciples, saying, "Who do people say that the Son of Man is?"   Mark 8:27-29

14 And they said, "Some *say* John the Baptist; and others, ᵀElijah; but still others, Jeremiah, or one of the prophets."   Gr., *Elias*

15 He *said to them, "But who do you say that I am?"

16 And Simon Peter answered and said, "Thou art ᵀthe Christ, the Son of the living God."   the Messiah

17 And Jesus answered and said to him, "Blessed are you, Simon ᵀBarjona, because flesh and blood did not reveal *this* to you, but My Father who is in heaven.   son of Jonah

Revelation of the Church

18 "And I also say to you that you are ᵀPeter, and upon this rock I will ᴷbuild My church; and the gates of Hades shall not overpower it.   Gr., *Petros*, a stone • Acts 2:41, 47 ☆

19 "I will give you ᴿthe keys of the kingdom of heaven; and ᴿwhatever you shall bind on earth shall be bound in heaven, and whatever you shall loose on earth shall be loosed in heaven."   Is. 22:22 • John 20:23

20 Then He warned the disciples that they should tell no one that He was the Christ.

Revelation of Jesus' Death
Mark 8:31–33; Luke 9:22

21 From that time Jesus Christ began to show His disciples that He must go to Jerusalem, and suffer many things from the elders and chief priests and scribes, and be killed, and be raised up on the third day.

22 And Peter took Him aside and began to rebuke Him, saying, "God forbid *it*, Lord! This shall never ᵀhappen to You."   be

23 But He turned and said to Peter, "Get behind Me, Satan! You are a stumbling block to Me; for you are not setting your mind on God's interests, but man's."

Revelation of Jesus' Reward
Mark 8:34–37; Luke 9:23–25

24 Then Jesus said to His disciples, "If anyone wishes to come after Me, let him deny himself, and ᴿtake up his cross, and follow Me.   Matt. 10:38; Luke 14:27

25 "For ᴿwhoever wishes to save his ᴬlife shall lose it; but whoever loses his life for My sake shall find it.   Matt. 10:39 • *soul*

26 "For what will a man be profited, if he gains the whole world, and forfeits his soul? Or what will a man give in exchange for his soul?

The Prophecy of the Second Coming
Mark 8:38—9:1; Luke 9:26, 27

27 "For the ᴿSon of Man is going to come in the glory of His Father with His angels; and WILL THEN RECOMPENSE EVERY MAN ACCORDING TO HIS ᵀDEEDS.   Matt. 8:20 • *doing*

28 "Truly I say to you, there are some of those who are standing here who shall not taste death until they see the ᴿSon of Man coming in His kingdom."   Matt. 8:20

CHAPTER 17
The Transfiguration
Mark 9:2–13; Luke 9:28–36;
2 Pet. 1:17, 18

AND ᴿsix days later Jesus *took with Him Peter and ᴶJames and John his brother, and *brought them up to a high mountain by themselves.   Matt. 17:1-8 • *Jacob*

2 And He was transfigured before them; and His face shone like the sun, and His garments became as white as light.

3 And behold, Moses and Elijah appeared to them, talking with Him.

4 And Peter answered and said to Jesus, "Lord, it is good for us to be here; if You wish, ᴿI will make three ᴬtabernacles here, one for You, and one for Moses, and one for Elijah."   Mark 9:5; Luke 9:33 • *sacred tents*

5 While he was still speaking, behold, a bright cloud overshadowed them; and behold, ᴿa voice out of the cloud, saying, "This is My beloved Son, with whom I am well-pleased; listen to Him!"   Is. 42:1; Luke 3:22 ★

6 And when the disciples heard *this*, they fell on their faces and were much afraid.

7 And Jesus came to *them* and touched them and said, "Arise, and ᴿdo not be afraid."   Matt. 14:27

8 And lifting up their eyes, they saw no one, except Jesus Himself alone.

16:18 The Origin of the Church—The church was a mystery (i.e., hidden, not revealed) in the Old Testament. It was first prophesied in these words spoken to Peter, "upon this rock I will build My church." In this prophecy there is a play on the word *rock* which also happens to be Peter's name. Jesus said, "you are Peter" (masculine, *petros*) and "upon this rock (feminine, *petra*) I will build My church." But when did the church actually begin? Again, many suggestions are offered for varying reasons. The simplest view is to understand the New Testament church as beginning on the Day of Pentecost in response to Peter's pentecostal sermon when "there were added that day about three thousand souls" (Page 1096—Acts 2:41). This group became "the church," and God added to their number daily those who were saved.

Now turn to Page 1186—Eph. 3:21: The Purpose of the Church.

9 ᴿAnd as they were coming down from the mountain, Jesus commanded them, saying, "Tell the vision to no one until the Son of Man has risen from the dead." *Mark 9:9-13*

10 And His disciples asked Him, saying, "Why then do the scribes say that ᴿElijah must come first?" *Mal. 4:5; Matt. 11:14; 16:14*

11 And He answered and said, "Elijah is coming and will restore all things;

12 but I say to you, that Elijah already came, and they did not recognize him, but did ᵀto him whatever they wished. So also the Son of Man is going to suffer ᵀat their hands." *in him;* or, *in his case • by them*

13 Then the disciples understood that He had spoken to them about John the Baptist.

Instruction About Faith
Mark 9:14-29; Luke 9:37-42

14 ᴿAnd when they came to the multitude, a man came up to Him, falling on his knees before Him, and saying, *Matt. 17:14-19*

15 "Lord, have mercy on my son, for he is a lunatic, and is very ill; for he often falls into the fire, and often into the water. *Sir*

16 "And I brought him to Your disciples, and they could not cure him."

17 And Jesus answered and said, "O unbelieving and perverted generation, how long shall I be with you? How long shall I put up with you? Bring him here to Me."

18 And Jesus rebuked him, and the demon came out of him, and the boy was cured ᵀat once. *from that hour*

19 Then the disciples came to Jesus privately and said, "Why could we not cast it out?"

20 And He *said to them, "Because of the littleness of your faith; for truly I say to you, ᴿif you have faith as a mustard seed, you shall say to this mountain, 'Move from here to there,' and it shall move; and nothing shall be impossible to you. *Mark 11:23f.*

21 ["³⁰Butᴿ this kind does not go out except by prayer and fasting."] *Mark 9:29*

Instruction About Jesus' Death
Mark 9:30-32; Luke 9:43-45

22 ᴿAnd while they were gathering together in Galilee, Jesus said to them, "The Son of Man is going to be^delivered into the hands of men; *Matt. 26:57☆ • betrayed*

23 andᴿthey will kill Him, and He will be raised on the third day." And they were deeply grieved. *Mark 15:37☆*

Instruction About Taxes

24 And when they had come to Capernaum, those who collected ᴿthe ³¹two-drachma *tax* came to Peter, and said, "Does your teacher not pay the ³¹two-drachma *tax*?" *Ex. 30:13; 38:26*

25 He *said, "Yes." And when he came into the house, Jesus^spoke to him first, saying, "What do you think, Simon? From whom do the kings of the earth collect customs or poll-tax, from their sons or from strangers?" *anticipated what he was going to say,*

26 And upon his saying, "From strangers," Jesus said to him, "Consequently the sons are^exempt. *free*

27 "But, lest we give them offense, go to the sea, and throw in a hook, and take the first fish that comes up; and when you open its mouth, you will find a ³²stater. Take that and give it to them for you and Me."

CHAPTER 18
Instruction About Humility
Mark 9:33-37; Luke 9:46-48

AT that ᵀtime the disciples came to Jesus, saying, "Who then is ᵀgreatest in the kingdom of heaven?" *hour • greater*

2 And He called a child to Himself and set him ᵀbefore them, *in their midst*

3 and said, "Truly I say to you, unless you are converted and become like children, you shall not enter the kingdom of heaven.

4 "Whoever then humbles himself as this child, he is the greatest in the kingdom of heaven.

5 "And whoever receives one such child in My name receives Me;

Punishment of Offenders
Mark 9:42-48

6 but whoever causes one of these little ones who believe in Me to stumble, it is better for him that a heavy millstone be hung around his neck, and that he be drowned in the depth of the sea.

7 "Woe to the world because of *its* stumbling blocks! For it is inevitable that stumbling blocks come; but woe to that man through whom the stumbling block comes!

8 "And ᴿif your hand or your foot causes you to stumble, cut it off and throw it from you; it is better for you to enter life crippled or lame, than having two hands or two feet, to be cast into the eternal fire. *Mark 9:43*

9 "And ᴿif your eye causes you to stumble, pluck it out, and throw it from you. It is better for you to enter life with one eye, than having two eyes, to be cast into the ᵀfiery hell. *Mark 9:47 • Gehenna of fire*

10 "See that you do not despise one of these little ones, for I say to you, that ᴿtheir angels in heaven continually behold the face of My Father who is in heaven. *Acts 12:15*

Parable of the Lost Sheep
Luke 15:4-7

11 ["³³Forᴿ the Son of Man has come to save that which was lost.] *Luke 19:10*

---

³⁰ Many mss. do not contain this verse
³¹ Equivalent to two denarii or two days' wages paid as a temple tax   ³² Or, *shekel*, worth four drachmas
³³ Most ancient mss. do not contain this verse

12"What do you think?ᴿIf any manᴧhas a hundred sheep, and one of them has gone astray, does he not leave the ninety-nine on the mountains and go and search for the one that is straying?   *Luke 15:4-7 • comes to have*

13"And if it turns out that he finds it, truly I say to you, he rejoices over it more than over the ninety-nine which have not gone astray.

14"Thus it is not *the* willᵀof your Father who is in heaven that one of these little ones perish.   *before*

The Offended Brother

15"Andᴿif your brother sins³⁴, go and re-prove him in private; if he listens to you, you have won your brother.   *Luke 17:3; [Gal. 6:1]*

16"But if he does not listen *to you*, take one or two more with you, so thatᴿBY THE MOUTH OF TWO OR THREE WITNESSES EVERY ᵀFACT MAY BE CONFIRMED.   *Heb. 10:28 • word*

17"And if he refuses to listen to them, tell it to the church; and if he refuses to listen even to the church, let him be to you asᵀa Gentile and a tax-gatherer.   *the*

18"Truly I say to you,ᴿwhatever you shall ᴧbind on earth shall be bound in heaven; and whatever youᴧloose on earth shall be loosed in heaven.   [John 20:23] • *forbid • permit*

19"Again I say to you, that if two of you agree on earth about anything that they may ask,ᴿit shall be done for them ᴿby My Father who is in heaven.   *Matt. 7:7 • from*

20"For where two or three have gathered together in My name, ᴿthere I am in their midst."   *Matt. 28:20*

Instruction About Forgiveness

21 Then Peter came and said to Him, "Lord, ᴿhow often shall my brother sin against me and I forgive him? Up toᴿseven times?"   *Matt. 18:15 • Luke 17:4*

22 Jesus *said to him, "I do not say to you, up to seven times, but up toᴿseventy times seven.   *Gen. 4:24*

23"For this reason the kingdom of heaven may be compared to a certain king who wished to settle accounts with his slaves.

24"And when he had begun to settle *them*, there was brought to him one who owed him ³⁵ten thousand talents.

25"But since he did not have *the means* to repay, his lord commanded him to be sold, along with his wife and children and all that he had, and repayment to be made.

26"The slave therefore falling down,ᴿpros-trated himself before him, saying, 'Have pa-tience with me, and I will repay you every-thing.'   *Matt. 8:2*

27"And the lord of that slave felt compas-sion and released him andᴿforgave him the ᴧdebt.   *Luke 7:42 • loan*

28"But that slave went out and found one of his fellow slaves who owed him a hun-dred ³⁶denarii; and he seized him and *began*

to choke *him*, saying, 'Pay back what you owe.'

29"So his fellow slave fell down and *began* to entreat him, saying, 'Have patience with me and I will repay you.'

30"He was unwilling however, but went and threw him in prison until he should pay back what was owed.

31"So when his fellow slaves saw what had happened, they were deeply grieved and came and reported to their lord all that had happened.

32"Then summoning him, his lord *said to him, 'You wicked slave, I forgave you all that debt because you entreated me.

33'Shouldᴿyou not also have had mercy on your fellow slave, even as I had mercy on you?'   *Matt. 6:12; [Eph. 4:32]*

34"And his lord, moved with anger, handed him over to the torturers until he should repay all that was owed him.

35"So shall My heavenly Father also do to you, if each of you does not forgive his brother fromᵀyour heart."   *your hearts*

CHAPTER 19

Instruction About Divorce
Mark 10:1–16; Luke 18:15–17

AND ᴿit came about that when Jesus had finished these words, He departed from Galilee, and came into the region of Judea beyond the Jordan;   *Matt. 7:28*

2 and great multitudes followed Him, andᴿHe healed them there.   *Matt. 4:23*

3 And *some* Pharisees came to Him, test-ing Him, and saying, "Is it lawful *for a man* to divorce his wife for any cause at all?"

4 And He answered and said, "Have you not read,ᴿthat He who created *them* from the beginning MADE THEM MALE AND FE-MALE,   *Gen. 1:27; 5:2*

5 and said, 'FORᴿTHIS CAUSE A MAN SHALL LEAVE HIS FATHER AND MOTHER, AND SHALL CLEAVE TO HIS WIFE; ANDᴿTHE TWO SHALL BE-COME ONE FLESH'?   *Gen. 2:24 • [1 Cor. 6:16]*

6"Consequently they are no longer two, but one flesh. What therefore God has joined together, let no man separate."

7 They *said to Him, "Whyᵀthen did Mo-ses command to GIVE HER A CERTIFICATE OF DIVORCE AND SEND *her* AWAY?"   *Deut. 24:1-4*

8 He *said to them, "Becauseᴧ of your hardness of heart, Moses permitted you to divorce your wives; but from the beginning it has not been this way.   *With reference to*

9"And I say to you,ᴿwhoever divorces his wife, except for immorality, and marries an-other woman commits adultery."   [Matt. 5:32]

10 The disciples *said to Him, "If the rela-tionship of the man with his wife is like this, it is better not to marry."

11 But He said to them, "Notᴿall men *can*

³⁴ Many mss. add here: *against you*
³⁵ About $10,000,000 in silver content but worth much more in buying power
³⁶ The denarius was equivalent to one day's wage

accept this statement, but *only* those to whom it has been given.   [1 Cor. 7:7ff.]

12 "For there are eunuchs who were born that way from their mother's womb; and there are eunuchs who were made eunuchs by men; and there are *also* eunuchs who made themselves eunuchs for the sake of the kingdom of heaven. He who is able to accept *this*, let him accept *it*."

13 Then *some* children were brought to Him so that He might lay His hands on them and pray; and the disciples rebuked them.

14 But Jesus said, "Let ᴿthe children alone, and do not hinder them from coming to Me; for the kingdom of heaven belongs to such as these."   Mark 10:15

15 And after laying His hands on them, He departed from there.

Rich Young Ruler
Mark 10:17–27; Luke 18:18–27

16 ᴿAnd behold, one came to Him and said, "Teacher, what good thing shall I do that I may obtain eternal life?"   *Luke 18:18-30*

17 And He said to him, "Why are you asking Me about what is good? There is *only* One who is good; but if you wish to enter into life, keep the commandments."

18 He *said to Him, "Which ones?" And Jesus said, "Youᴿ SHALL NOT COMMIT MURDER; You SHALL NOT COMMIT ADULTERY; You SHALL NOT STEAL; You SHALL NOT BEAR FALSE WITNESS;   Ex. 20:13-16; Deut. 5:17-20

19 ᴿHONOR YOUR FATHER AND MOTHER; and ᴿYOU SHALL LOVE YOUR NEIGHBOR AS YOURSELF."   Ex. 20:12; Deut. 5:16 · Lev. 19:18

20 The young man *said to Him, "All these things I have kept; what am I still lacking?"

21 Jesus said to him, "If you wish to be ᴬcomplete, go *and* sell your possessions and give to *the* poor, and you shall have treasure in heaven; and come, follow Me."   *perfect*

22 But when the young man heard this statement, he went away grieved; for he was one who owned much property.

23 And Jesus said to His disciples, "Truly I say to you,ᴿit is hard for a rich man to enter the kingdom of heaven."   Luke 18:24

24 "And again I say to you,ᴿit is easier for a camel to go through the eye of a needle, than for a rich man to enter the kingdom of God."   Mark 10:25; Luke 18:25

25 And when the disciples heard *this,* they were very astonished and said, "Then who can be saved?"

26 And looking upon *them* Jesus said to them, "Withᴿ men this is impossible, but with God all things are possible."   Gen. 18:14

The Apostles' Reward
Mark 10:28–30; Luke 18:28–30

27 Then Peter answered and said to Him, "Behold, we have left everything and fol-

lowed You; what then will there be for us?"

28 And Jesus said to them, "Truly I say to you, that you who have followed Me, in the regeneration when the Son of Man will sit on ᵀHis glorious throne, you also shall sit upon twelve thrones, judging the twelve tribes of Israel.   *the throne of His glory*

29 "And everyone who has left houses or brothers or sisters or father or mother³⁷ orᴬ children or farms for My name's sake, shall receive many times as much, and shall inherit eternal life.   Many mss. add *or wife*

30 "Butᴿmany *who are* first will be last; and *the* last, first.   Mark 10:31; Luke 13:30

CHAPTER 20

Parable of the Laborers—Mark 10:31

"FOR the kingdom of heaven is like ᵀa landowner who went out early in the morning to hire laborers for his vineyard.   *a man*

2 "And when he had agreed with the laborers for a ³⁸denarius for the day, he sent them into his vineyard.

3 "And he went out about the ³⁹third hour and saw others standing idle in the market place;

4 and to those he said, 'You too go into the vineyard, and whatever is right I will give you.' And *so* they went.

5 "Again he went out about the ⁴⁰sixth and the ninth hour, and did the same thing.

6 "And about the ⁴¹eleventh *hour* he went out, and found others standing; and he *said to them, 'Why have you been standing here idle all day long?'

7 "They *said to him, 'Because no one hired us.' He *said to them, 'You too go into the vineyard.'

8 "And when evening had come, the owner of the vineyard *said to his foreman, 'Call the laborers and pay them their wages, beginning with the last *group* to the first.'

9 "And when those *hired* about the eleventh hour came, each one received a ³⁸denarius.

10 "And when those *hired* first came, they thought that they would receive more; and they also received each one a ³⁸denarius.

11 "And when they received it, they grumbled at the landowner,

12 saying, 'These last men have worked *only* one hour, and you have made them equal to us who have borne the burden and theᴿscorching heat of the day.'   Jon. 4:8

13 "But he answered and said to one of them, 'Friend, I am doing you no wrong; did you not agree with me for a ³⁸denarius?

14 'Take what is yours and go your way, but I wish to give to this last man the same as to you.

15 'Is it not lawful for me to do what I wish with what is my own? Or is your eye ᵀenvious because I am generous?'   *evil*

16 "Thusᴿthe last shall be first, and the first last."   Matt. 19:30; Mark 10:31; Luke 13:30

---

³⁷ Many mss. add here, *or wife*
³⁸ The denarius was equivalent to one day's wage
³⁹ I.e., 9 a.m.   ⁴⁰ I.e., Noon and 3 p.m.   ⁴¹ I.e., 5 p.m.

Instruction About Jesus' Death
Mark 10:32–34; Luke 18:31–34

17 ᴿAnd as Jesus was about to go up to Jerusalem, He took the twelve *disciples* aside by themselves, and on the way He said to them,   Matt. 20:17-19; Mark 10:32-34; Luke 18:31-33

18"Behold, we are going up to Jerusalem; and the Son of Manᴿwill be^delivered to the chief priests and scribes, and they will condemn Him to death, Matt. 26:46, 66☆ • *betrayed*

19 and will deliver Him to the Gentiles to mock and scourge and crucify *Him,* and on the third day He will be raised up."

Instruction About Ambition
Mark 10:35–45

20 Then the mother of the sons of Zebedee came to Him with her sons, bowing down, and making a request of Him.

21 And He said to her, "What do you wish?" She *said to Him, "Command that in Your kingdom these two sons of mine may sit, one on Your right and one on Your left."

22 But Jesus answered and said, "You do not know what you are asking for. Are you able to drink the cup that I am about to drink?" They *said to Him, "We are able."

23 He *said to them, "My cup you shall drink; but to sit on My right and on *My* left, this is not Mine to give, but it is for those for whom it has been prepared by My Father."

24 And hearing *this,* the ten became indignant with the two brothers.

25 ᴿBut Jesus called them to Himself, and said, "You know that the rulers of the Gentiles lord it over them, and *their* great men exercise authority over them.   Luke 22:25-27

26"It is not so among you, ᴿbut whoever wishes to become great among you shall be your servant,   Mark 9:35; 10:43; Luke 22:26

27 and whoever wishes to be first among you shall be your slave;

28 just as ᴿthe Son of Man did not come to be served, but to serve, and ᴿto give His^life a ransom for many." Matt. 8:20 • Is. 53:12☆ • *soul*

The Blind Men Recognize the King
Mark 10:46–52; Luke 18:35–43

29 And as they were going out from Jericho, a great multitude followed Him.

30 And behold, two blind men sitting by the road, hearing that Jesus was passing by, cried out, saying, "Lord,ᴿhave mercy on us, ᴿSon of David!"   Matt. 20:31 • Matt. 9:27

31 And the multitude sternly told them to be quiet; but they cried out all the more, saying, "Lord, have mercy on us,ᴿSon of David!"   Matt. 9:27

32 And Jesus stopped and called them, and said, "What do you want Me to do for you?"

33 They *said to Him, "Lord, *we want* our eyes to be opened."

34 And moved with compassion, Jesus touched their eyes; and immediately they regained their sight and followed Him.

CHAPTER 21

The Triumphal Entry
Mark 11:1–10; Luke 19:29–38;
John 12:12–15

Aᴿ Nᴰwhen they had approached Jerusalem and had come to Bethphage, to ᴿthe Mount of Olives, then Jesus sent two disciples,   Matt. 21:1-9 • John 8:1; Acts 1:12

2 saying to them, "Go into the village opposite you, and immediately you will find a donkey tied *there* and a colt with her; untie *them,* and bring *them* to Me.

3"And if anyone says something to you, you shall say, 'The Lord has need of them,' and immediately he will send them."

4 ᴿNow this took place that what was spoken through the prophet might be fulfilled, saying,   Luke 19:35-38; John 12:12-15

5 "ᴿSAY TO THE DAUGHTER OF ZION,
'BEHOLD YOUR KING IS COMING TO YOU,
GENTLE, AND MOUNTED ON A DONKEY,
EVEN ON A COLT, THE FOAL OF A BEAST
OF BURDEN.' "   Is. 62:11; Zech. 9:9★

6 And the disciples went and did just as Jesus had directed them,

7 and brought the donkey and the colt, and laid on them their garments,ᵀon which He sat.   *on them*

8 And most of the multitudeᴿspread their garments in the road, and others were cutting branches from the trees, and spreading them in the road.   2 Kin. 9:13

9 And the multitudes going before Him, and those who followed after were crying out,ᴿsaying,   Ps. 118:26; Matt. 23:39★

"Hosanna to the Son of David;
BLESSED IS HE WHO COMES IN THE
NAME OF THE LORD;
Hosannaᴿin the highest!"   Luke 2:14

10 And when He had entered Jerusalem, all the city was stirred, saying, "Who is this?"

11 And the multitudes were saying, "This isᴿthe prophet Jesus, fromᴿNazareth in Galilee."   Mark 6:15; [Acts 3:22f.; 7:37] • Matt. 2:23

The Cleansing of the Temple
Mark 11:15–17; Luke 19:45, 46

12 ᴿAnd Jesus entered the temple and cast out all those who were buying and selling in the temple, and overturned the tables of the moneychangers and the seats of those who were sellingᵀdoves.   Mal. 3:1★ • *the doves*

13 And He *said to them, "It is written, 'MYᴿ HOUSE SHALL BE CALLED A HOUSE OF PRAYER'; but you are making it aᴿROBBERS' ᵀDEN."   Is. 56:7 • Jer. 7:11 • *cave*

14 And *the* blind and *the* lame came to Him in the temple, and He healed them.

15 But when the chief priests and the scribes saw the wonderful things that He had done, and the children who were crying out in the temple and saying, "Hosanna to the Son of David," they became indignant,

16 and said to Him, "Do You hear what these are saying?" And Jesus *said to them, "Yes; have you never read, 'OUT^R OF THE MOUTH OF INFANTS AND NURSING BABES THOU HAST PREPARED PRAISE FOR THY-SELF'?"   Ps. 8:2; Matt. 11:25 ★
17 And He left them and went out of the city to^RBethany, and lodged there. Luke 19:29

Cursing of the Fig Tree
Mark 11:11–14, 20–24

18 ^RNow in the morning, when He returned to the city, He became hungry. Matt. 21:18-22
19 And seeing a lone fig tree by the road, He came to it, and found nothing on it except leaves only; and He *said to it, "No longer shall there ever be any fruit from you." And at once the fig tree withered.
20 And seeing this, the disciples marveled, saying, "How did the fig tree wither at once?"
21 And Jesus answered and said to them, "Truly I say to you,^Rif you have faith, and do not doubt, you shall not only do what was done to the fig tree, but even if you say to this mountain, 'Be taken up and cast into the sea,' it shall happen.   Luke 17:6; James 1:6
22 "And ^Rall things you ask in prayer, believing, you shall receive."   Matt. 7:7

Question of Jesus' Authority
Mark 11:27–33; Luke 20:1–18

23 ^RAnd when He had come into the temple, the chief priests and the elders of the people came to Him ^Ras He was teaching, and said, "By what authority are You doing these things, and who gave You this authority?"   Matt. 21:23-27; Luke 20:1-8 • Matt. 26:55
24 And Jesus answered and said to them, "I will ask you one^Tthing too, which if you tell Me, I will also tell you by what authority I do these things.   word
25 "The baptism of John was from what source, from heaven or from men?" And they began reasoning among themselves, saying, "If we say, 'From heaven,' He will say to us, 'Then why did you not believe him?'
26"But if we say, 'From men,' we fear the multitude; for they all hold John to be ^Ra prophet."   Matt. 11:9; Mark 6:20
27 And answering Jesus, they said, "We do not know." He also said to them, "Neither will I tell you by what authority I do these things.

Parable of the Two Sons

28 "But what do you think? A man had two ^Tsons, and he came to the first and said, 'Son, go work today in the vineyard.'   children
29 "And he answered and said, 'I will, sir'; and he did not go.
30 "And he came to the second and said ^Tthe same thing. But he answered and said, 'I

will not'; yet he afterward regretted it and went.   likewise
31 "Which of the two did the will of his father?" They *said, "The latter." Jesus *said to them, "Truly I say to you that the tax-gatherers and harlots^Awill get into the kingdom of God before you.   are getting into
32 "For John came to you in the way of righteousness and you did not believe him; but the tax-gatherers and harlots did believe him; and you, seeing this, did not even feel remorse afterward so as to believe him.

Parable of the Landowner
Mark 12:1–12; Luke 20:9–19

33 "Listen to another parable. There was a ^Tlandowner who PLANTED A VINEYARD AND PUT A WALL AROUND IT AND DUG A WINE PRESS IN IT, AND BUILT A TOWER, and rented it out to^Avine-growers, and went on a journey.   a man, a householder • tenant farmers
34 "And when the harvest time approached, he ^Rsent his slaves to the vine-growers to receive his produce.   Matt. 22:3
35 "And the vine-growers took his slaves and beat one, and killed another, and stoned a third.
36 "Again he^Rsent another group of slaves larger than the first; and they did^Tthe same thing to them.   Matt. 22:4 • likewise
37 "But afterward he sent his son to them, saying, 'They will respect my son.'
38 "But when the vine-growers saw the son, they said among themselves, 'This is the heir; come, let us kill him, and seize his inheritance.'
39 "And they took him, and threw him out of the vineyard, and killed him.
40 "Therefore when the^Towner of the vineyard comes, what will he do to those vine-growers?"   lord
41 They *said to Him, "He will bring those wretches to a wretched end, and^Rwill rent out the vineyard to other vine-growers, who will pay him the proceeds at the proper seasons."   [Matt. 8:11f.; Acts 13:46; 18:6; 28:28]
42 Jesus *said to them, "Did you never read in the Scriptures,
     'THE^R STONE WHICH THE BUILDERS RE-
     JECTED,   Ps. 118:22f.; Acts 4:11 ★
     THIS BECAME THE CHIEF CORNER stone;
     THIS CAME ABOUT FROM THE LORD,
     AND IT IS MARVELOUS IN OUR EYES'?
43 "Therefore I say to you, the kingdom of God will be taken away from you, and be given to a nation producing the fruit of it.
44 "And^Rhe who falls on this stone will be broken to pieces; but on whomever it falls, it will scatter him like dust."   Is. 8:14, 15 ★
45 And when the chief priests and the Pharisees heard His parables, they understood that He was speaking about them.
46 And when they sought to seize Him, they ^Rfeared the multitudes, because they held Him to be a prophet.   Matt. 21:26

CHAPTER 22

Parable of the Marriage Feast

A^ND Jesus answered and spoke to them again in parables, saying,

2 "The kingdom of heaven may be compared to ^a king, who ^gave a wedding feast for his son.   *a man, a king • made*

3 "And he ^sent out his slaves to call those who had been invited to the wedding feast, and they were unwilling to come. Matt. 21:34

4 "Again he ^sent out other slaves saying, 'Tell those who have been invited, "Behold, I have prepared my dinner; my oxen and my fattened livestock are *all* butchered and everything is ready; come to the wedding feast." '   Matt. 21:36

5 "But they paid no attention and went their way, one to his own ^farm, another to his business,   *field*

6 and the rest seized his slaves and mistreated them and killed them.

7 "But the king was enraged and sent his armies, and destroyed those murderers, and set their city on fire.

8 "Then he *said to his slaves, 'The wedding is ready, but those who were invited were not worthy.

9 'Go therefore to ^the main highways, and as many as you find *there*, invite to the wedding feast.'   Ezek. 21:21; Obad. 14

10 "And those slaves went out into the streets, and gathered together all they found, both evil and good; and the wedding hall was filled with dinner guests.

11 "But when the king came in to look over the dinner guests, he saw there ^a man not dressed in wedding clothes,   Zech. 3:3, 4

12 and he *said to him, 'Friend, how did you come in here^ without wedding clothes?' And he was speechless.   *not having*

13 "Then the king said to the servants, 'Bind him hand and foot, and cast him into ^the outer darkness; in that place there shall be weeping and gnashing of teeth.'

14 "For many are ^called, ^but few *are* chosen."   *invited* • Matt. 24:22; 2 Pet. 1:10; Rev. 17:14

Conflict with Pharisees and Herodians
Mark 12:13–17; Luke 20:20–26

15 ^Then the Pharisees went and counseled together how they might trap Him^ in what He said.   Mark 12:13-17 • *in word*

16 And they *sent their disciples to Him, along with the ^Herodians, saying, "Teacher, we know that You are truthful and teach the way of God in truth, and defer to no one; for You are not partial to any.   Mark 3:6; 8:15

17 "Tell us therefore, what do You think? Is it ^lawful to give a ^poll-tax to Caesar, or not?"   *permissible* • Matt. 17:25

18 But Jesus perceived their ^malice, and said, "Why are you testing Me, you hypocrites?   *wickedness*

19 "Show Me the coin *used* for the poll-tax." And they brought Him a denarius.

20 And He *said to them, "Whose likeness and inscription is this?"

21 They *said to Him, "Caesar's." Then He *said to them, "Then^ render to Caesar the things that are Caesar's; and to God the things that are God's."   Luke 20:25; [Rom. 13:7]

22 And hearing *this*, they marveled, and ^leaving Him, they went away.   Mark 12:12

Conflict with Sadducees
Mark 12:18–27; Luke 20:27–40

23 ^On that day *some* ^Sadducees (who say there is no resurrection) came to Him and questioned Him,   Matt. 22:23-33 • Matt. 3:7

24 saying, "Teacher, Moses said, 'IF^ A MAN DIES, HAVING NO CHILDREN, HIS BROTHER AS NEXT OF KIN SHALL MARRY HIS WIFE, AND RAISE UP AN OFFSPRING TO HIS BROTHER.'   Deut. 25:5

25 "Now there were seven brothers with us; and the first married and died, and having no offspring left his wife to his brother;

26 so also the second, and the third, down to the seventh.

27 "And last of all, the woman died.

28 "In the resurrection therefore whose wife of the seven shall she be? For they all had her."

29 But Jesus answered and said to them, "You are mistaken, not ^understanding the Scriptures, or the power of God.   *knowing*

30 "For in the resurrection they neither marry, nor are given in marriage, but are like angels in heaven.

31 "But regarding the resurrection of the dead, have you not read that which was spoken to you by God, saying,

32 'I AM THE GOD OF ABRAHAM, AND THE GOD OF ISAAC, AND THE GOD OF JACOB'? He is not the God of the dead but of the living."

33 And when the multitudes heard *this*, they were astonished at His teaching.

The Greatest Commandment
Mark 12:28–34

34 ^But when the Pharisees heard that He had put the Sadducees to silence, they gathered themselves together.   Luke 10:25-37

35 And one of them, ⁴²a^ lawyer, asked Him *a question*, testing Him,   Luke 7:30; 10:25

36 "Teacher, which is the great commandment in the Law?"

37 And He said to him, " 'YOU^ SHALL LOVE THE LORD YOUR GOD WITH ALL YOUR HEART, AND WITH ALL YOUR SOUL, AND WITH ALL YOUR MIND.'   Deut. 6:5

38 "This is the great and ^foremost commandment.   *first*

39 "The second is like it, 'YOU^ SHALL LOVE YOUR NEIGHBOR AS YOURSELF.'   Lev. 19:18

40 "On^ these two commandments depend the whole Law and the Prophets."   Matt. 7:12

⁴² I.e., an expert in the Mosaic law

The Son of David
Mark 12:35–37; Luke 20:41–44

41 Now while the Pharisees were gathered together, Jesus asked them a question, **42** saying, "What do you think about the Christ, whose son is He?" They *said to Him, "*The son* of David."   the Messiah

43 He *said to them, "Then how does David in the Spirit call Him 'Lord,' saying,

44 THE LORD SAID TO MY LORD,   Ps. 110:1
  "SIT AT MY RIGHT HAND,
  UNTIL I PUT THINE ENEMIES BENEATH
    THY FEET"?

45 "If David then calls Him 'Lord,' how is He his son?"

46 And [R]no one was able to answer Him a word, nor did anyone dare from that day on to ask Him another question. Luke 14:6; 20:40

CHAPTER 23

Jesus Characterizes the Pharisees
Mark 12:38–40; Luke 20:45–47

T HEN [R] Jesus spoke to the multitudes and to His disciples, Matt. 23:1-7; *Mark 12:38, 39*

2 saying, "The [R] scribes and the Pharisees have seated themselves in the chair of Moses;   Deut. 33:3f.; Ezra 7:6, 25; Neh. 8:4

3 therefore all that they tell you, do and observe, but do not do according to their deeds; for they say *things*, and do not do *them*.

4 "And [R] they tie up heavy loads, and lay them on men's shoulders; but they themselves are unwilling to move them with *so much as* a finger.   Luke 11:46; Acts 15:10

5 "But they do all their deeds [T] to be noticed by men; for they [R] broaden their [43] phylacteries, and lengthen the tassels *of their garments*.   [Matt. 6:1, 5, 16] • Ex. 13:9

6 "And they [R] love the place of honor at banquets, and the chief seats in the synagogues,   Luke 11:43; 14:7; 20:46

7 and respectful greetings in the market places, and being called by men, Rabbi.

8 "But do not be called Rabbi; for One is your Teacher, and you are all brothers.

9 "And do not call *anyone* on earth your father; for [R] One is your Father, He who is in heaven.   Matt. 6:9; 7:11

10 "And do not be called [A] leaders; for One is your Leader, *that is*, Christ.   teachers

11 "But [R] the greatest among you shall be your servant.   Matt. 20:26

12 "And [R] whoever exalts himself shall be humbled; and whoever humbles himself shall be exalted.   Luke 14:11; 18:14

Jesus Condemns the Pharisees

13 "But woe to you, scribes and Pharisees, hypocrites, because you shut off the king-

dom of heaven [T] from men; for you do not enter in yourselves, nor do you allow those who are entering to go in.   in front of

14 [" [44] Woe to you, scribes and Pharisees, hypocrites, because [R] you devour widows' houses, even while for a pretense you make long prayers; therefore you shall receive greater condemnation.] Mark 12:40; Luke 20:47

15 "Woe to you, scribes and Pharisees, hypocrites, because you travel about on sea and land to make one [A] proselyte; and when he becomes one, you make him twice as much a son of hell as yourselves.   convert

16 "Woe to you, blind guides, who say, 'Whoever swears by the [A] temple, that is nothing; but whoever swears by the gold of the [A] temple, he is obligated.'   sanctuary

17 "You fools and blind men; which is [T] more important, the gold, or the [A] temple that sanctified the gold?   greater • sanctuary

18 "And, 'Whoever swears by the altar, *that* is nothing, but whoever swears by the [A] offering upon it, he is obligated.'   gift

19 "You blind men, [R] which is [T] more important, the [A] offering or the altar that sanctifies the [A] offering?   Ex. 29:37 • greater • gift

20 "Therefore he who swears, swears *both* by the altar and by everything on it.

21 "And he who swears by the [A] temple, swears *both* by [the] temple and by Him who [R] dwells within it.   sanctuary • it • Ps. 26:8

22 "And he who swears by heaven, [R] swears *both* by the throne of God and by Him who sits upon it.   Is. 66:1; Matt. 5:34

23 "Woe [R] to you, scribes and Pharisees, hypocrites! For you tithe mint and dill and [A] cummin, and have neglected the weightier provisions of the law: justice and mercy and faithfulness; but these are the things you should have done without neglecting the others.   Luke 11:42 • Similar to caraway seeds

24 "You [R] blind guides, who strain out a gnat and swallow a camel!   Matt. 23:16

25 "Woe to you, scribes and Pharisees, hypocrites! For you clean the outside of the cup and of the dish, but inside they are full [A] of robbery and self-indulgence.   as a result of

26 "You blind Pharisee, first clean the inside of the cup and of the dish, so that the outside of it may become clean also.

27 "Woe [R] to you, scribes and Pharisees, hypocrites! For you are like whitewashed tombs which on the outside appear beautiful, but inside they are full of dead men's bones and all uncleanness.   Acts 23:3

28 "Even so you too outwardly appear righteous to men, but inwardly you are full of hypocrisy and lawlessness.

29 "Woe [R] to you, scribes and Pharisees, hypocrites! For you build the tombs of the prophets and adorn the monuments of the righteous,   Luke 11:47f.

30 and say, 'If we had been *living* in the days of our fathers, we would not have been partners with them in *shedding* the blood of the prophets.'

---

[43] I.e., small boxes containing Scripture texts worn for religious purposes
[44] This verse not found in the earliest mss.

31 "Consequently you bear witness against yourselves, that you are ^Asons of those who murdered the prophets.　　　*descendants*

32 "Fill^T up then the measure *of the guilt of* your fathers.　　　　　*And fill up*

33 "You serpents, you brood of vipers, how shall you escape the sentence of hell?

34 "Therefore^R, behold, I am sending you prophets and wise men and scribes; some of them you will kill and crucify, and some of them you will scourge in your synagogues, and persecute from city to city, Matt. 23:34-36

35 that upon you may fall *the guilt of* all the righteous blood shed on earth, from the blood of righteous Abel to the blood of Zechariah, the son of Berechiah, whom you murdered between the temple and the altar.

36 "Truly I say to you, all these things shall come upon^R this generation.　　　Matt. 10:23

Jesus Laments over Jerusalem

37 "O^R Jerusalem, Jerusalem, who kills the prophets and stones those who are sent to her! How often I wanted to gather your children together, the way a hen gathers her chicks under her wings, and you^R were unwilling.　　　Matt. 23:37-39 • Is. 49:5 ★

38 "Behold,^R your house is being left to you desolate!　　　　　Jer. 22:5 ★

39 "For I say to you, from now on you shall not see Me until you say, 'BLESSED IS HE WHO COMES IN THE NAME OF THE LORD!' "

CHAPTER 24

The Temple to Be Destroyed
Mark 13:1, 2; Luke 21:5, 6

AND Jesus came out from the temple and was going away when His disciples came up to point out the temple buildings to Him.

2 And He answered and said to them, "Do you not see all these things? Truly I say to you, not one stone here shall be left upon another, which will not be torn down."

The Disciples' Two Questions
Mark 13:3, 4; Luke 21:7

3 And as He was sitting on the Mount of Olives, the disciples came to Him privately, saying, "Tell us, when will these things be, and what *will be* the sign of Your coming, and of the ^Aend of the age?"　　*consummation*

The Tribulation
Mark 13:5-23; Luke 21:5-24

4 And Jesus answered and said to them, "See^R to it that no one misleads you. Jer. 29:8

5 "For^R many will come in My name, saying, 'I am the ^TChrist,' and will mislead many.　　Matt. 24:11, 24; Acts 5:36f. • Messiah

6 "And you will be hearing of ^Rwars and rumors of wars; see that you are not frightened, for *those things* must take place, but *that* is not yet the end.　　　[Rev. 6:4]

7 "For^R nation will rise against nation, and kingdom against kingdom, and in various places there will be ^Rfamines and earthquakes.　　2 Chr. 15:6 • Acts 11:28; Rev. 6:5, 6

8 "But^R all these things are *merely* the beginning of birth pangs.　　　Luke 21:12-24

9 "Then they will deliver you to tribulation, and will kill you, and you will be hated by all nations on account of My name.

10 "And at that time many will ^Rfall^R away and will deliver up one another and hate one another.　　*be caused to stumble* • Matt. 11:6

11 "And many ^Rfalse prophets will arise, and will mislead many.　　Matt. 7:15; 24:24

12 "And because lawlessness is increased, most people's love will grow cold.

13 "But^R the one who endures to the end, he shall be saved.　　　　Matt. 10:22

14 "And this ^Rgospel of the kingdom shall be preached in the whole ^Tworld for a witness to all the nations, and then the end shall come.　　Matt. 4:23 • *inhabited earth*

15 "Therefore when you see the ABOMINATION OF DESOLATION which was spoken of through Daniel the prophet, standing in the holy place (let the reader understand),

16 then let those who are in Judea flee to the mountains;

17 let him who is on^R the housetop not go down to get the things out that are in his house;　　1 Sam. 9:25; 2 Sam. 11:2; Matt. 10:27

18 and let him who is in the field not turn back to get his cloak.

19 "But woe to those who are with child and to those who nurse babes in those days!

20 "But pray that your flight may not be in the winter, or on a Sabbath;

21 for then there will be a ^Rgreat tribulation, such as has not occurred since the beginning of the world until now, nor ever shall.　　Dan. 12:1; Joel 2:2; Matt. 24:29

22 "And unless those days had been cut short, no ^Tlife would have been saved; but for ^Rthe sake of the ^Relect those days shall be cut short.　　*flesh* • Matt. 22:14 • *chosen ones*

23 "Then if anyone says to you, 'Behold, here is the ^TChrist,' or 'There^T *He is*,' do not believe *him*.　　　Messiah • *here*

24 "For false Christs and false prophets will arise and will show great ^Asigns and wonders, so as to mislead, if possible, even the ^Aelect.　　*attesting miracles* • *chosen ones*

25 "Behold, I have told you in advance.

26 "If therefore they say to you, 'Behold, He is in the wilderness,' do not go forth, *or*, 'Behold, He is in the inner rooms,' do not believe *them*.

The Second Coming
Mark 13:24-27; Luke 21:25-28

27 "For just as the lightning comes from the east, and flashes even to the west, so shall the coming of the Son of Man be.

28 "Wherever^R the corpse is, there the ^Avultures will gather.　　Ezek. 39:17 • *eagles*

29 "But immediately after the tribulation of those days THE SUN WILL BE DARKENED,

AND THE MOON WILL NOT GIVE ITS LIGHT, AND THE STARS WILL FALL from the sky, and the powers of the heavens will be shaken,

30 and then the sign of the Son of Man will appear in the sky, and then all the tribes of the earth will mourn, and they will see the SON OF MAN COMING ON THE CLOUDS OF THE SKY with power and great glory.

31"And He will send forth His angels with A GREAT TRUMPET and THEY WILL GATHER TOGETHER His elect from the four winds, from one end of the sky to the other.

Parable of the Fig Tree
Mark 13:28–31; Luke 21:29–33

32"Now learn the parable from the fig tree: when its branch has already become tender, and puts forth its leaves, you know that summer is near;

33 even so you too, when you see all these things, recognize that^AHe is near, *right* at the ^Tdoor.   *know • it • doors*

34"Truly I say to you,^Rthis 'generation will not pass away until all these things take place.   [Matt. 10:23; 16:28; 23:36] • *race*

35"Heaven^Rand earth will pass away, but My words shall not pass away.   Mark 13:31

Illustration of the Days of Noah
Mark 13:32–37; Luke 21:34–36

36"But^Rof that day and hour no one knows, not even the angels of heaven, nor the Son, but the Father alone.   Mark 13:32

37"For the^Rcoming of the Son of Man will be just like the days of Noah.   [Matt. 16:27]

38"For as in those days which were before the flood they were eating and drinking, they were marrying and giving in marriage, until the day that Noah entered the ark,

39 and they did not^Tunderstand until the flood came and took them all away; so shall the coming of the Son of Man be.   *know*

40"Then there shall be two men in the field; one will be taken, and one will be left.

41"Two women *will be* grinding at the mill; one will be taken, and one will be left.

42"Therefore be on the alert, for you do not know which day your Lord is coming.

43"But^Tbe sure of this, that if the head of the house had known at what time of the night the thief was coming, he would have been on the alert and would not have allowed his house to be broken into.   *know this*

44"For this reason^Ryou be ready too; for the Son of Man is coming at an hour when you do not think *He will*.   Matt. 24:42, 43; 25:10

Illustration of the Two Servants
Luke 12:41–48

45"Who^R then is the faithful and sensible slave whom his 'master put in charge of his household to give them their food at the proper time?   Matt. 24:45-51 • *lord*

46"Blessed is that slave whom his 'master finds so doing when he comes.   *lord*

47"Truly I say to you, that^Rhe will put him in charge of all his possessions.   Matt. 25:21

48"But if that evil slave says in his heart, 'My master is not coming for a long time,'

49 and shall begin to beat his fellow slaves and eat and drink with drunkards;

50 the ^Amaster of that slave will come on a day when he does not expect *him* and at an hour which he does not know,   *lord*

51 and shall cut him in pieces and assign him a place with the hypocrites; weeping shall be there and the gnashing of teeth.

CHAPTER 25

Parable of the Ten Virgins

"THEN^Rthe kingdom of heaven will be comparable to ten virgins, who took their ^Rlamps, and went out to meet the bridegroom.   Matt. 13:24 • John 18:3

2"And five of them were foolish, and five were^Rprudent.   Matt. 7:24; 10:16; 25:2ff.

3"For when the foolish took their lamps, they took no oil with them,

4 but the^Rprudent took oil in flasks along with their lamps.   Matt. 7:24; 10:16; 25:2ff.

5"Now while the bridegroom was delaying, they all got drowsy and *began* to sleep.

6"But at midnight there was a shout, 'Behold, the bridegroom! Come out to meet *him*.'

7"Then all those virgins rose, and trimmed their lamps.

8"And the foolish said to the prudent, 'Give us some of your oil, for our lamps are going out.'

9"But the^Rprudent answered, saying, 'No, there will not be enough for us and you *too;* go instead to the dealers and buy *some* for yourselves.'   Matt. 7:24; 10:16; 25:2ff.

10"And while they were going away to make the purchase, the bridegroom came, and those who were ready went in with him to the wedding feast; and the door was shut.

11"And later the other virgins also came, saying, 'Lord, lord, open up for us.'

12"But he answered and said, 'Truly I say to you, I do not know you.'

13"Be^R on the alert then, for you do not know the day nor the hour.   Matt. 24:42ff.

Parable of the Talents

14"For *it is* just like a man *about* to go on a journey, who called his own slaves, and entrusted his possessions to them.

15"And to one he gave five^Rtalents, to another, two, and to another, one, each according to his own ability; and he^Rwent on his journey.   Matt. 18:24 • Matt. 21:33

16"Immediately the one who had received the five^Rtalents went and traded with them, and gained five more talents.   Luke 19:13

17"In the same manner the one who *had received* the two *talents* gained two more.

18"But he who received the one *talent*

went away and dug in the ground, and hid his master's money.   *lord's*

19 "Now after a long time the master of those slaves *came and *settled[R] accounts with them.   Matt. 18:23

20 "And the one who had received the five [R]talents came up and brought five more talents, saying, 'Master, you entrusted five talents to me; see, I have gained five more talents.'   Matt. 18:24; Luke 19:13

21 "His master said to him, 'Well done, good and [R]faithful slave; you were faithful with a few things, I will[R]put you in charge of many things, enter into the joy of your [A]master.'   [Matt. 24:45, 47] • [Luke 12:44] • *lord*

22 "The one also who *had received* the two [R]talents came up and said, 'Master, you entrusted to me two talents; see, I have gained two more talents.'   Luke 19:13

23 "His master said to him, 'Well done, good and [R]faithful slave; you were faithful with a few things, I will put you in charge of many things; enter into the joy of your master.'   Matt. 24:45, 47; 25:21

24 "And the one also who had received the one [R]talent came up and said, 'Master, I knew you to be a hard man, reaping where you did not sow, and gathering where you scattered no *seed.*   Matt. 18:24; Luke 19:13

25 'And I was afraid, and went away and hid your talent in the ground; see, you have what is yours.'

26 "But his master answered and said to him, 'You wicked, lazy slave, you knew that I reap where I did not sow, and gather where I scattered no *seed.*

27 'Then you ought to have put my money in the bank, and on my arrival I would have received my *money* back with interest.

28 'Therefore take away the talent from him, and give it to the one who has the ten talents.'

29 "For to everyone who has shall *more* be given, and he shall have an abundance; but from the one who does not have, even what he does have shall be taken away.

30 "And cast out the worthless slave into [R]the outer darkness; in that place there shall be weeping and gnashing of teeth. Matt. 8:12

Judgment of the Gentiles

31 "But when the[R]Son of Man comes in His glory, and all the angels with Him, then He will sit on His glorious throne.   Matt. 16:27f.

32 "And all the nations will be[R]gathered before Him; and He will separate them from one another, as the shepherd separates the sheep from the goats; Matt. 13:49; [2 Cor. 5:10]

33 and He will put the sheep[R]on His right, and the goats on the left.   1 Kin. 2:19; Ps. 45:9

34 "Then the King will say to those on His right, 'Come, you who are blessed of My Father,[R]inherit the kingdom prepared for you from the foundation of the world. [1 Cor. 6:9]

35 'For [R]I was hungry, and you gave Me

something to eat; I was thirsty, and you gave Me drink;[R]I was a stranger, and you invited Me in;   Is. 58:7; Ezek. 18:7 • Job 31:32

36 [R]naked, and you clothed Me; I was sick, and you[R]visited Me; I was in prison, and you came to Me.'   Is. 58:7; Ezek. 18:7 • [James 1:27]

37 "Then the righteous will answer Him, saying, 'Lord, when did we see You hungry, and feed You, or thirsty, and give You drink?

38 'And when did we see You a stranger, and invite You in, or naked, and clothe You?

39 'And when did we see You sick, or in prison, and come to You?'

40 "And the King will answer and say to them, 'Truly I say to you, to the extent that you did it to one of these brothers of Mine, *even* the least *of them,* you did it to Me.'

41 "Then He will also say to those on His left, 'Depart[R] from Me, accursed ones, into the eternal fire which has been prepared for the devil and his angels;   Matt. 7:23

42 for I was hungry, and you gave Me *nothing* to eat; I was thirsty, and you gave Me nothing to drink;

43 I was a stranger, and you did not invite Me in; naked, and you did not clothe Me; sick, and in prison, and you did not visit Me.'

44 "Then they themselves also will answer, saying, 'Lord, when did we see You hungry, or thirsty, or a stranger, or naked, or sick, or in prison, and did not take care of You?'

45 "Then He will answer them, saying, 'Truly I say to you, to the extent that you did not do it to one of the least of these, you did not do it to Me.'

46 "And these will go away into [R]eternal punishment, but the righteous into [R]eternal life."   [Dan. 12:2; John 5:29] • Matt. 19:29

CHAPTER 26

The Religious Leaders Plot to Kill Jesus
Mark 14:1, 2; Luke 22:1, 2

AND[R] it came about that when Jesus had finished all these words, He said to His disciples,   Matt. 7:28

2 "You[R]know that after two days the Passover is coming, and the Son of Man is *to be* delivered up for crucifixion."   Matt. 26:2-5

3 Then the chief priests and the elders of the people were gathered together in the court of the high priest, named Caiaphas;

4 and they [R]plotted together to seize Jesus by stealth, and kill *Him.*   Matt. 12:14

5 But they were saying, "Not during the festival, lest a riot occur among the people."

Mary Anoints Jesus for Burial
Mark 14:3-9; Luke 12:2-8

6 [R]Now when Jesus was in Bethany, at the home of Simon the leper,   Matt. 26:6-13

7 [R]a woman came to Him with an alabas-

ter vial of very costly perfume, and she poured it upon His head as He reclined *at the table.*   Luke 7:37f.

8 But the disciples were indignant when they saw *this,* and said, "Why this waste?

9 "For this *perfume* might have been sold for a high price and *the money* given to the poor."

10 But Jesus, aware of this, said to them, "Why do you bother the woman? For she has done a good deed to Me.

11 "For the poor you have with you always; but you do not always have Me.

12 "For when she poured this perfume upon My body, she did it[R]to prepare Me for burial.   John 19:40

13 "Truly I say to you,[R]wherever this gospel is preached in the whole world, what this woman has done shall also be spoken of in memory of her."   Mark 14:9

Judas Agrees to Betray Jesus
Mark 14:10, 11; Luke 22:3–6

14 [R]Then one of the twelve, named Judas Iscariot, went to the chief priests, *Luke 22:3-6*

15 and said, "What are you willing to give me to deliver Him up to you?" And they weighed out to him thirty pieces of silver.

16 And from then on he *began* looking for a good opportunity to betray Him.

The Passover Is Prepared
Mark 14:12–16; Luke 22:7–13

17 [R]Now on the first *day* of Unleavened Bread the disciples came to Jesus, saying, "Where do You want us to prepare for You to eat the Passover?"   *Luke 22:7-13*

18 And He said, "Go into the city to a certain man, and say to him, 'The Teacher says, "My time is at hand; I *am* to keep the Passover at your house with My disciples." ' "

19 And the disciples did as Jesus had directed them; and they prepared the Passover.

The Passover Is Celebrated
Mark 14:17–21; Luke 22:14, 21–23;
John 13:21, 22

20 [R]Now when evening had come, He was reclining *at the table* with the twelve disciples.   Matt. 26:20-24; Mark 14:17-21

21 And as they were eating, He said, "Truly[R]I say to you that one of you will betray Me."   Luke 22:21-23; John 13:21f.

22 And being deeply grieved, they [A]each one began to say to Him, "Surely not I, Lord?"   *one after another*

23 And He answered and said, "He[R] who dipped his hand with Me in the bowl is the one who will betray Me.   Ps. 41:9 ★

24 "The Son of Man *is* to go, just as it is written of Him; but woe to that man by whom the Son of Man is betrayed! It would have been good[T]for that man if he had not been born."   *for him if that man had not been born*

25 And [R]Judas, who was betraying Him, answered and said, "Surely it is not I,

[R]Rabbi?" He *said to him, "You have said *it* yourself."   Matt. 26:14 • Matt. 23:7; 26:49

The Lord's Supper Is Instituted
Mark 14:22–25; Luke 22:19, 20;
1 Cor. 11:23–26

26 And while they were eating, Jesus took *some* bread, and [T]after a blessing, He broke *it* and gave *it* to the disciples, and said, "Take, eat; this is My body."   *having blessed*

27 And when He had taken a cup and given thanks, He gave *it* to them, saying, "Drink from it, all of you;

28 for[R]this is My blood of the covenant, which is poured out for[R]many for forgiveness of sins.   [Ex. 24:8; Heb. 9:20] • Matt. 20:28

29 "But I say to you, I will not drink of this fruit of the vine from now on until that day when I drink it new with you in My Father's kingdom."

Peter's Denial Is Predicted
Mark 14:26–31; Luke 22:34, 39;
John 13:37, 38

30 [R]And after singing a hymn, they went out to the Mount of Olives.   Mark 14:26-31

31 Then Jesus *said to them, "You will all [A]fall[R]away because of Me this night, for it is written, 'I[R]WILL STRIKE DOWN THE SHEPHERD, AND THE SHEEP OF THE FLOCK SHALL BE SCATTERED.'   *stumble* • [Matt. 11:6] • Zech. 13:7 ☆

32 "But after I have been raised,[R]I will go before you to Galilee."   Matt. 28:7, 10, 16 ☆

33 But Peter answered and said to Him, "*Even* though all may[A]fall away because of You, I will never fall away."   *stumble*

34 Jesus said to him, "Truly[R]I say to you that this *very* night, before a cock crows, you shall deny Me three times." Matt. 26:75 ☆

35 Peter *said to Him, "Even[R] if I have to die with You, I will not deny You." All the disciples said the same thing too.   John 13:37

Jesus' Three Prayers
Mark 14:32–42; Luke 22:40–46

36 [R]Then Jesus *came with them to a place called[R]Gethsemane, and *said to His disciples, "Sit here while I go over there and pray."   Matt. 26:36-46 • Luke 22:39; John 18:1

37 And He took with Him[R]Peter and the two sons of Zebedee, and began to be grieved and distressed.   Matt. 4:21; 17:1

38 Then He *said to them, "My[R] soul is deeply grieved, to the point of death; remain here and keep watch with Me."   John 12:27

39 And He went a little beyond *them,* and fell on His face and prayed, saying, "My Father, if it is possible, let this cup pass from Me; yet not as I will, but as Thou wilt."

40 And He *came to the disciples and *found them sleeping, and *said to Peter, "So, you *men* could not[T]keep watch with Me for one hour?"   Matt. 26:38

41 "Keep[R] watching and praying, that you may not enter into temptation; the spirit is willing, but the flesh is weak."   Matt. 26:38

42 He went away again a second time and prayed, saying, "My Father, if this ᴿcannot pass away unless I drink it, ᴿThy will be done."   Matt. 20:22 • Is. 50:5 ★

43 And again He came and found them sleeping, for their eyes were heavy.

44 And He left them again, and went away and prayed a third time, saying the same thing once more.

45 Then He *came to the disciples, and *said to them, "Areᴬ you still sleeping and taking your rest? Behold, the hour is at hand and the Son of Man is being betrayed into the hands of sinners. *Keep on sleeping therefore*

46 "Arise, let us be going; behold, the one whoᴿbetrays Me is at hand!"   Matt. 26:21 ★

Jesus' Betrayal and Arrest
Mark 14:43–52; Luke 22:47–53;
John 18:1–11

47 And while He was still speaking, behold, Judas, one of the twelve, came up, ᴬaccompanied by a great multitude with swords and clubs, from the chief priests and elders of the people.   *and with him*

48 Now he who was betraying Him gave them a sign, saying, "Whomever I shall kiss, He is the one; seize Him."

49 And immediately he went to Jesus and said, "Hail, Rabbi!" and kissed Him.

50 And Jesus said to him, "Friend, do what you have come for." Then they came and laid hands on Jesus and seized Him.

51 And behold, one of those who were with Jesusᵀreached and drew out his sword, and struck the slave of the high priest, and ᵀcut off his ear.   *extended the hand • took off*

52 Then Jesus *said to him, "Put your sword back into its place; for all those who take up the sword shall perish by the sword.

53 "Or do you think that I cannot appeal to My Father, and He will at once put at My disposal more than twelve ⁴⁵legionsᴿ of ᴿangels?   Mark 5:9, 15; Luke 8:30 • Matt. 4:11

54 "How then shall the Scriptures be fulfilled, that it must happen this way?"

55 At that time Jesus said to the multitudes, "Have you come out with swords and clubs to arrest Me as against a robber?ᴿEvery day I used to sit in the temple teaching and you did not seize Me.   Mark 12:35; 14:49

56 "But all this has taken place that the Scriptures of the prophets may be fulfilled." Then all the disciples left Him and fled.

Two False Witnesses
Mark 14:53–65; Luke 22:54, 55, 63–65;
John 18:12, 18, 24

57 ᴿAnd those who had seized Jesus led Him away to ᴿCaiaphas, the high priest, where the scribes and the elders were gathered together.   Matt. 26:57-68 • Matt. 26:3

58 But Peter also was following Him at a distance as far as the courtyard of the high priest, and entered in, and sat down with the ᴬofficers to see the outcome.   *servants*

59 Now the chief priests and the whole ᴬCouncil kept trying to obtain false testimony against Jesus, in order that they might put Him to death;   *Sanhedrin*

60 and they did not find *any*, even though ᴿmany false witnesses came forward. But later on two came forward,   Ps. 27:12 ★

61 and said, "This man stated, 'I am able to destroy theᴬtemple of God and to rebuild itᴬin three days.'"   *sanctuary • after*

62 And the high priest stood up and said to Him, "Do You make no answer? What is it that these men are testifying against You?"

63 But Jesus kept silent. And the high priest said to Him,ᴿ"I adjure You by the living God, that You tell us whether You are the Christ, the Son of God."   Is. 53:7 ★

64 Jesus *said to him, "You have said it *yourself*; nevertheless I tell you, ᴬhereafter you shall see THE SON OF MAN SITTING AT THE RIGHT HAND OF POWER, and COMING ON THE CLOUDS OF HEAVEN."   *from now on*

65 Then the high priest tore his robes, saying, "He has blasphemed! What further need do we have of witnesses? Behold, you have now heard the blasphemy;

66 what do you think?" They answered and said, "He is deserving of death!"

67 ᴿThen they spat in His face and beat Him with their fists; and others ᴬslapped Him,   Is. 50:6 ★ • *beat Him with rods*

68 and said, "Prophesy to us, You Christ; who is the one who hit You?"   *the Messiah*

Three Denials of Peter
Mark 14:66–72; Luke 22:55–62;
John 18:15–18, 25–27

69 ᴿNow Peter was sitting outside in the ᴿcourtyard, and a certain servant-girl came to him and said, "You too were with Jesus the Galilean."   Matt. 26:69-75 • Matt. 26:3

70 But he denied *it* before them all, saying, "I do not know what you are talking about."

71 And when he had gone out to the gateway, another *servant-girl* saw him and *said to those who were there, "This man was with Jesus of Nazareth."

72 And again he denied *it* with an oath, "I do not know the man."

73 And a little later the bystanders came up and said to Peter, "Surely you too are one of them;ᴿfor the way you talkᵀgives you away."   Mark 14:70 • *makes you evident*

74 Then he began to curse and swear,"ᴿI do not know the man!" And immediately a cock crowed.   Matt. 26:34 ★

75 And Peter remembered the word which Jesus had said, "Beforeᴬa cock crows, you will deny Me three times." And he went out and wept bitterly.   Matt. 26:34

---

⁴⁵ A legion equaled 6,000 troops

CHAPTER 27

Jesus Is Delivered to Pilate
Mark 15:1; Luke 22:66; 23:1; John 18:28

NOW[R] when morning had come, [R]all the chief priests and the elders of the people took counsel against Jesus to put Him to death;   Mark 15:1 • Ps. 2:2★
2 and they bound Him, and led Him away, and [R]delivered Him up to [R]Pilate the governor.   Matt. 20:19★ • Luke 3:1; 13:1; 23:12

Judas Repents
Acts 1:18, 19

3 Then when Judas, who had betrayed Him, saw that He had been condemned, he felt remorse and returned the thirty pieces of silver to the chief priests and elders,
4 saying, "I have sinned by betraying innocent blood." But they said, "What is that to us?[R]See *to that* yourself!"   Matt. 27:24
5 And he threw the pieces of silver into the sanctuary and [R]departed; and he went away and hanged himself.   Luke 18:7; 26:24★
6 And the chief priests took the pieces of silver and said, "It is not lawful to put them into the temple treasury, since it is the price of blood."
7 And they counseled together and with [T]the money bought the Potter's Field as a burial place for strangers.   *them*
8 For this reason that field has been called the Field of Blood to this day.
9 Then that which was spoken through Jeremiah the prophet was fulfilled, saying, "AND[R] THEY TOOK THE THIRTY PIECES OF SILVER, THE PRICE OF THE ONE WHOSE PRICE HAD BEEN SET by the sons of Israel;   Zech. 11:12★
10 AND THEY GAVE THEM FOR THE POTTER'S FIELD, AS THE LORD DIRECTED ME."

Jesus Is Examined
Mark 15:2–5; Luke 23:2–5;
John 18:29–38

11 [R]Now Jesus stood before the governor, and the governor questioned Him, saying, "Are You the King of the Jews?" And Jesus said to him, "*It is as* you say."   Matt. 27:11-14
12 And while He was being accused by the chief priests and elders,[R]He made no answer.   Matt. 26:63; John 19:9
13 Then Pilate *said to Him, "Do You not hear how many things they testify against You?"
14 [R]And He did not answer him with regard to even a *single* charge, so that the governor was quite amazed.   Ps. 38:13, 14★

Barabbas Is Freed
Mark 15:6–14; Luke 23:17–23;
John 18:39, 40

15 [R]Now at *the* feast the governor was accustomed to release for the multitude *any* one prisoner whom they wanted.   *Mark 15:6*

16 And they were holding at that time a notorious prisoner, called Barabbas.
17 When therefore they were gathered together, Pilate said to them, "Whom do you want me to release for you? Barabbas, or Jesus[R]who is called Christ?"   Matt. 1:16; 27:22
18 For he knew that because of envy they had delivered Him up.
19 And [R]while he was sitting on the judgment seat, his wife sent to him, saying, "Have nothing to do with that righteous Man; for [T]last night I suffered greatly in a dream because of Him."   Acts 12:21 • *today*
20 But the chief priests and the elders persuaded the multitudes to [R]ask for Barabbas, and to put Jesus to death.   Acts 3:14
21 But the governor answered and said to them, "Which of the two do you want me to release for you?" And they said, "Barabbas."
22 Pilate *said to them, "Then what shall I do with Jesus[R]who is called Christ?" They all *said, "Let Him be crucified!"   Matt. 1:16
23 And he said, "Why, what evil has He done?" But they kept shouting all the more, saying, "Let Him be crucified!"
24 And when Pilate saw that he was accomplishing nothing, but rather that [R]a riot was starting, he took water and [R]washed his hands in front of the multitude, saying, "I am innocent of this Man's blood; see *to that* yourselves."   Matt. 26:5 • Deut. 21:6-8
25 And all the people answered and said, "His blood *be* on us and on our children!"

Jesus Is Scourged
Mark 15:15–17; Luke 23:24, 25;
John 19:16

26 Then he released Barabbas[A]for them; but after having Jesus [R]scourged, he delivered Him to be crucified.   *to them* • Is. 50:6★
27 Then the soldiers of the governor took Jesus into the Praetorium and gathered the whole Roman[A]cohort around Him.   *battalion*
28 And they stripped Him, and[R]put a scarlet robe on Him.   Mark 15:17; John 19:2

Jesus Is Led to Golgotha
Mark 15:18–22; Luke 23:26–33;
John 19:17

29 [R]And after weaving a crown of thorns, they put it on His head, and a [A]reed in His right hand; and they kneeled down before Him and mocked Him, saying, "Hail, King of the Jews!"   Ps. 69:19; Is. 53:3★ • *staff*
30 And they spat on Him, and took the reed and *began* to beat Him on the head.
31 And after they had mocked Him, they took His robe off and put His garments on Him, and led Him away to crucify *Him*.
32 [R]And as they were coming out, they found a man of [R]Cyrene named Simon, [T]whom they pressed into service to bear His cross.   Matt. 27:32 • Acts 2:10; 6:9 • *this one*
33 [R]And when they had come to a place called [R]Golgotha, which means Place of a Skull,   Matt. 27:34-44 • Luke 23:33

Jesus Is Crucified
Mark 15:23–32; Luke 23:33–43;
John 19:18–24

34 ᴿthey gave Himᴿwine to drink mingled with gall; and after tasting *it*, He was unwilling to drink.   Ps. 69:21★ • Mark 15:23

35 And when they had crucified Him,ᴿthey divided up His garments among themselves, castingᵀlots;   Ps. 22:18★ • *a lot*

36 and sitting down, they *began to* ᴿkeep watch over Him there.   Ps. 22:17; Matt. 27:54★

37 And they put up above His head the charge against Himᵀwhich read, "THIS IS JESUS THE KING OF THE JEWS."   *written*

38 ᴿAt that time two robbers *were crucified with Him, one on the right and one on the left.   Is. 53:9★

39 And those passing by were hurling abuse at Him,ᴿwagging their heads, Ps. 22:7★

40 and saying, "Youᴿwho *are going to* destroy the temple and rebuild it in three days, save Yourself! If You are the Son of God, come down from the cross."   Matt. 26:61

41 In the same way the chief priests also, along with the scribes and elders, were ᴿmocking *Him*, and saying,   Matt. 20:19★

42"He saved others; He cannot save Himself.ᴿHe is the King of Israel; let Him now come down from the cross, and we shall believe in Him.   Ps. 22:6; 69:9★

43"Heᴿ TRUSTS IN GOD; LET HIM DELIVER *Him* now, IF HE TAKES PLEASURE IN HIM; for He said, 'I am the Son of God.'"   Ps. 22:8☆

44 ᴿAnd the robbers also who had been crucified with Him were casting the same insult at Him.   Luke 23:39-43

Jesus Dies
Mark 15:33–37; Luke 23:44–46;
John 19:28–30

45 Now from the ⁴⁶sixth hour darkness fell upon all the land until the ⁴⁷ninth hour.

46 And about the ninth hour Jesus cried out with a loud voice, saying, "ELI, ELI, LAMA SABACHTHANI?" that is, "MY GOD, MY GOD, WHY HAST THOU FORSAKEN ME?"

47 And some of those who were standing there, when they heard it, *began* saying, "This man is calling for Elijah."

48 And immediately one of them ran, and taking a sponge, he filled it with sour wine, and put it on a reed, and gave Him a drink.

49 But the rest *of them* said, "Let us see whether Elijah will come to save Him."⁴⁸

50 And Jesus cried out again with a loud voice, and yielded up *His* spirit.

Signs Accompanying Jesus' Death
Mark 15:38–41; Luke 23:45, 47–49

51 And behold, the veil of the temple was torn in two from top to bottom, and the earth shook; and the rocks were split,

52 and the tombs were opened; and many bodies of the ᴬsaints who had ᴿfallen asleep were raised;   *holy ones* • Acts 7:60

53 and coming out of the tombs after His

resurrection they enteredᴿthe holy city and appeared to many.   Matt. 4:5

54 Now the centurion, and those who were with him keeping guard over Jesus, when they saw the earthquake and the things that were happening, became very frightened and said, "Truly this wasᴬthe Son of God!"   *a son of God or a son of a god*

55 And many women were there looking on from a distance, who had followed Jesus from Galilee, ᴬministering to Him,   *waiting on*

56 among whom was ᴿMary Magdalene, *along with* Mary the mother of James and Joseph, and the mother of the sons of Zebedee.   Matt. 28:1

Jesus Is Buried
Mark 15:42–47; Luke 23:50–55;
John 19:38–42

57 ᴿAnd when it was evening, there came a rich man from Arimathea, named Joseph, who himself had also become a disciple of Jesus.   Matt. 27:57-61; Mark 15:42-47

58 This man went to Pilate and asked for the body of Jesus. Then Pilate ordered *it* to be given over *to him*.

59 And Joseph took the body and wrapped it in a clean linen cloth,

60 andᴿlaid it in his own new tomb, which he had hewn out in the rock; and he rolledᴿa large stone against the entrance of the tomb and went away.   Is. 53:9★ • Mark 16:4

61 And Mary Magdalene was there, and the other Mary, sitting opposite the grave.

62 Now on the next day, which is *the one* after the preparation, the chief priests and the Pharisees gathered together with Pilate,

63 and said, "Sir, we remember that when He was still alive that deceiver said, 'Afterᴿ three days I *am to* rise again.'   Matt. 16:21

64"Therefore, give orders for the grave to be made secure until the third day, lest the disciples come and steal Him away and say to the people, 'He has risen from the dead,' and the last deception will be worse than the first."

65 Pilate said to them, "You have a guard; go, make it *as* secure as you know how."

66 And they went and made the grave secure, and along withᴿthe guard they set a seal on the stone.   Matt. 27:65; 28:11

CHAPTER 28

The Empty Tomb
Mark 16:1–8; Luke 24:1–11

NOW ᴿafter the Sabbath, as it began to dawn toward the first *day* of the week, Mary Magdalene and the other Mary came to look at the grave.   Matt. 28:1-8; Mark 16:1-8

2 And behold, a severe earthquake had occurred, for ᴿan angel of the Lord descended from heaven and came and rolled away the stone and sat upon it.   Luke 24:4

⁴⁶ I.e., noon   ⁴⁷ I.e., 3 p.m.
⁴⁸ Some early mss. add: *And another took a spear and pierced His side, and there came out water and blood.* (cf. John 19:34)

3 And[R]his appearance was like lightning, and his garment as white as snow;   Dan. 7:9

4 and the guards shook for fear of him, and became like dead men.

5 And the angel answered and said to the women, "Do[AR]not be afraid; for I know that you are looking for Jesus who has been crucified.   *Stop being afraid* • Matt. 14:27; 28:10

6 "He is not here, for He has risen,[R]just as He said. Come, see the place where He was lying.   Matt. 12:40; 16:21; 27:63★

7 "And go quickly and tell His disciples that He has risen from the dead; and behold, He is going before you into Galilee, there you will see Him; behold, I have told you."

8 And they departed quickly from the tomb with fear and great joy and ran to report it to His disciples.

The Appearance of Jesus to the Women

9 And behold, Jesus met them and greeted them. And they came up and took hold of His feet and worshiped Him.

10 Then Jesus *said to them, "Do[AR]not be afraid; go and take word to My brethren to leave for Galilee, and there they shall see Me."   *Stop being afraid* • Matt. 14:27; 28:5

The Bribery of the Soldiers

11 Now while they were on their way, behold, some of[R]the guard came into the city and reported to the chief priests all that had happened.   Matt. 27:65, 66

12 And when they had assembled with the elders and counseled together, they gave a large sum of money to the soldiers,

13 and said, "You are to say, 'His disciples came by night and stole Him away while we were asleep.'

14 "And if this should come to the governor's ears, we will win him over and [T]keep you out of trouble."   *make you free from care*

15 And they took the money and did as they had been instructed; and[R]this story was widely [R]spread among the Jews, *and is* [R]to this day.   Luke 2:34★ • Matt. 9:31 • Matt. 27:8

The Appearance of Jesus to the Disciples

16 But the eleven disciples proceeded [R]to Galilee, to the mountain which Jesus had designated.   Matt. 26:32; 28:7, 10; Mark 15:41; 16:7

17 And when they saw Him, they worshiped *Him*; but some were doubtful.

The Great Commission

18 And Jesus came up and spoke to them, saying, "All[R]authority has been given to Me in heaven and on earth. [Dan. 7:13f.]; Rom. 14:9

19 "Go therefore and make disciples of all the nations, baptizing them in the name of the Father and the Son and the Holy Spirit,

20 teaching them to observe all that I commanded you; and lo, I am with you [T]always, even to the end of the age."   *all the days*

28:19 Sharing Our Faith: Why?—There are at least six compelling reasons for sharing our faith in Christ with those who have not experienced new life in Christ.

a. Because God has commanded us to do so. The final words of Jesus while on earth (Page 1094—Acts 1:8) and also the Bible (Page 1308—Rev. 22:17) speak concerning this.

b. Because it demonstrates our love for God. Christ said that if we truly loved Him we would keep His commandments (Page 1081—John 14:15).

c. Because all are lost (Page 1133—Rom. 3:10, 23).

d. Because our sharing is God's chosen method to tell all people. He could have used angels, but He didn't. Only redeemed sinners can tell lost sinners about Christ. See Romans 10:14–17; Acts 8:3.

e. Because God desires to save all people (Page 1098—Acts 4:12; Page 1269—2 Pet. 3:9; Page 1217—1 Tim. 2:4).

f. Because someone once shared his faith with us. It may have been a faithful Bible teacher, or a godly pastor, or a praying parent. In other words, they have the right to expect that we will do for others what they have done for us.

Now turn to Page 1160—1 Cor. 15:3, 4: Sharing Our Faith: What?

THE GOSPEL ACCORDING TO

MARK

THE BOOK OF MARK

The message of Mark's gospel is captured in a single verse: "For even the Son of Man did not come to be served, but to serve, and to give His life a ransom for many" (10:45). Chapter by chapter, the book unfolds the dual focus of Christ's life: service and sacrifice.

Mark portrays Jesus as a Servant on the move, instantly responsive to the will of the Father. By preaching, teaching, and healing, He ministers to the needs of others even to the point of death. After the resurrection, He commissions His followers to continue His work in His power—servants following in the steps of the perfect Servant.

The ancient title for this gospel was *Kata Markon*, "According to Mark." The author is best known by his Latin name *Marcus*, but in Jewish circles he was called by his Hebrew name *John*. Acts 12:12, 25 and 15:37 refer to him as "John, who was also called Mark."

THE AUTHOR OF MARK

According to Acts 12:12, Mark's mother Mary had a large house that was used as a meeting place for believers in Jerusalem. Peter apparently went to this house often because the servant girl recognized his voice at the gate (Acts 12:13–16). Barnabas was Mark's cousin (Col. 4:10), but Peter may have been the person who led him to Christ (Peter called him "my son, Mark" in 1 Pet. 5:13). It was this close association with Peter that lent apostolic authority to Mark's gospel, since Peter was evidently Mark's primary source of information. It has been suggested that Mark was referring to himself in his account of "a certain young man" in Gethsemane (14:51, 52). Since all the disciples had abandoned Jesus (14:50), this little incident may have been a firsthand account.

Barnabas and Saul took Mark along with them when they returned from Jerusalem to Antioch (Acts 12:25) and again when they left on the first missionary journey (Acts 13:5). However, Mark left early and returned to Jerusalem (Acts 13:13). When Barnabas wanted to bring Mark on the second missionary journey, Paul's refusal led to a disagreement. The result was that Barnabas took Mark to Cyprus and Paul took Silas through Syria and Cilicia (Acts 15:36–41). Nevertheless, Paul wrote that Mark was with him during his first Roman imprisonment (Col. 4:10; Philem. 24) about twelve years later, so there must have been a reconciliation. In fact, at the end of his life Paul sent for Mark, saying, "he is useful to me for service" (2 Tim. 4:11).

The early church uniformly attested that Mark wrote this gospel. Papias, Irenaeus, Clement of Alexandria, and Origen are among the church fathers who affirmed Marcan authorship.

THE TIME OF MARK

Many scholars believe that Mark was the first of the four gospels, but there is uncertainty over its date. Because of the prophecy about the destruction of the temple (13:2), it should be dated before A.D. 70, but early traditions disagree as to whether it was written before or after the martyrdom of Peter (c. A.D. 64). The probable range for this book is A.D. 55–65.

Mark was evidently directed to a Roman readership and early tradition indicates that it originated in Rome. This may be why Mark omitted a number of items that would not have been meaningful to Gentiles, such as the genealogy of Christ, fulfilled prophecy, references to the Law, and certain Jewish customs that are found in other gospels. Mark interpreted Aramaic words (3:17; 5:41; 7:34; 15:22) and used a number of Latin terms in place of their Greek equivalents (4:21; 6:27; 12:14, 42; 15:15, 16, 39).

THE CHRIST OF MARK

The Lord is presented as an active, compassionate, and obedient Servant who constantly ministers to the physical and spiritual needs of others. Because this is the story of a Servant, Mark omits Jesus' ancestry and birth and moves right into His busy public ministry. The distinctive word of this book is *euthus*, translated "immediately," and it appears more often in this compact gospel (forty times) than in the rest of the New Testament. Christ is constantly moving toward a goal that is hidden to almost all. Mark clearly shows the power and authority of this unique Servant, identifying Him as no less than the Son of God (1:1, 11; 3:11; 5:7; 9:7; 13:32; 14:61; 15:39).

KEYS TO MARK

Key Word: Jesus the Servant—Even in the first verse it is obvious that this gospel centers on the person and mission of the Son of God. Mark's theme is captured well in

10:45 because Jesus is portrayed in this book as a Servant and as the Redeemer of men (cf. Phil. 2:5-11). Like the other gospels, Mark is not a biography but a topical narrative. Mark juxtaposes Christ's teachings and works to show how they authenticate each other. Miracles are predominant in this book (there are eighteen), and they are used to demonstrate not only the power of Christ but also His compassion. Mark shows his gentile readers how the Son of God—rejected by His own people—achieves ultimate victory through apparent defeat. There was no doubt an evangelistic purpose behind this gospel as Mark directed his words to a gentile audience that knew little about Old Testament theology.

Key Verses: Mark 10:43-45 and 8:34-37— "But it is not so among you, but whoever wishes to become great among you shall be your servant; and whoever wishes to be first among you shall be slave of all. For even the Son of Man did not come to be served, but to serve, and to give His life a ransom for many" (10:43-45).

"And He summoned the multitude with His disciples, and said to them, 'If anyone wishes to come after Me, let him deny himself, and take up his cross, and follow Me. For whoever wishes to save his life shall lose it; but whoever loses his life for My sake and the gospel's shall save it. For what does it profit a man to gain the whole world, and forfeit his soul? For what shall a man give in exchange for his soul?' " (8:34-37).

Key Chapter: Mark 8—As in Matthew, Mark's gospel contains a pivotal chapter showing the change of emphasis in Jesus' ministry. In Matthew it is chapter 12; in Mark it is chapter 8. The pivotal event lies in Peter's confession, "Thou art the Christ." That faith-inspired response triggers a new phase in both the content and the course of Jesus' ministry. Until this point He has sought to validate His claims as Messiah. But now He begins to fortify His men for His forthcoming suffering and death at the hands of the religious leaders. Jesus' steps begin to take Him daily closer to Jerusalem—the place where the Perfect Servant will demonstrate the full extent of His servanthood.

SURVEY OF MARK

Mark, the shortest and simplest of the four gospels, gives a crisp and fast-moving look at the life of Christ. With few comments, Mark lets the narrative speak for itself as it tells the story of the Servant who constantly ministers to others through preaching, healing, teaching, and, ultimately, His own death. Mark traces the steady building of hostility and opposition to Jesus as He resolutely moves toward the fulfillment of His earthly mission. Almost forty percent of this gospel is devoted to a detailed account of the last eight days of Jesus' life, climaxing in His resurrection. The Lord is vividly portrayed in this book in two parts: to serve (1—10); to sacrifice (11—16).

To Serve (1—10): Mark passes over the birth and early years of Jesus' life and begins with the events that immediately precede the inauguration of His public ministry—His baptism by John and His temptation by Satan (1:1-13). The first four chapters emphasize the words of the Servant while chapters 5—7 accent His works. However, in both sections there is a frequent alternation between Christ's message and miracles in order to reveal His person and power. Though He has come to serve others, Jesus' authority prevails over many realms.

Although Jesus has already been teaching and testing His disciples (see ch. 4), His minis-

FOCUS	TO SERVE			TO SACRIFICE	
REFERENCE	1:1————————2:13————————		8:27——————11:1————————		16:1————16:20
DIVISION	PRESENTATION OF THE SERVANT	OPPOSITION TO THE SERVANT	INSTRUCTION BY THE SERVANT	REJECTION OF THE SERVANT	RESURRECTION OF THE SERVANT
TOPIC	SAYINGS AND SIGNS			SUFFERINGS	
	c. 3 YEARS		c. 6 MONTHS	8 DAYS	
LOCATION	GALILEE AND PERAEA			JUDEA AND JERUSALEM	
TIME	c. A.D. 29—33				

try with them becomes more intense from this point on as He begins to prepare them for His departure. The religious leaders are growing more antagonistic, and Christ's "hour" is only about six months away. Mark 8:31 is the pivotal point in the gospel as the Son of Man speaks clearly to His disciples about His coming death and resurrection. The disciples struggle with this difficult revelation, but Jesus' steps head inexorably to Jerusalem.

To Sacrifice (11—16): Mark allots a dispro-

portionate space to the last weeks of the Servant's redemptive ministry. During the last seven days in Jerusalem, hostility from the chief priests, scribes, elders, Pharisees, Herodians, and Sadducees reaches crisis proportions as Jesus publicly refutes their arguments in the temple. After His last supper with the disciples, Jesus offers no resistance to His arrest, abuse, and agonizing crucifixion. His willingness to bear countless human sins is the epitome of servanthood.

OUTLINE OF MARK

Part Five: The Resurrection of the Servant (16:1–20)

CHAPTER 1

The Forerunner of the Servant
Matt. 3:1–11; Luke 3:3–16; John 1:19–34

THE beginning of the gospel of Jesus Christ, ¹the[R] Son of God.   Matt. 4:3
2 As it is written in Isaiah the prophet, "BEHOLD[R], I SEND MY MESSENGER BE-FORE YOUR FACE,   Mal. 3:1★
WHO WILL PREPARE YOUR WAY;
3 THE[R] VOICE OF ONE CRYING IN THE WIL-DERNESS,   Is. 40:3; Matt. 3:3★
'MAKE READY THE WAY OF THE LORD,
MAKE HIS PATHS STRAIGHT.' "
4 John the Baptist appeared in the wilderness ²preaching[R] a baptism of repentance for the forgiveness of sins.   Acts 13:24
5 And all the country of Judea was going out to him, and all the people of Jerusalem; and they were being baptized by him in the Jordan River, confessing their sins.
6 And John was clothed with camel's hair and *wore* [R]a leather belt around his waist, and [T]his diet was locusts and wild honey.   2 Kin. 1:8 • *he was eating*
7 And he was ^preaching, and saying, "After me One is coming who is mightier than I, and I am not fit to stoop down and untie the thong of His sandals.   *proclaiming*
8 "I baptized you ³with water; but He will baptize you ³with the Holy Spirit."

The Baptism of the Servant
Matt. 3:13–17; Luke 3:21–23

9 And it came about in those days that Jesus came from Nazareth in Galilee, and was baptized by John in the Jordan.

10 And immediately coming up out of the water, He saw the heavens opening, and the Spirit like a dove descending upon Him;
11 and a voice came out of the heavens: "Thou[R] art My beloved Son, in Thee I am well-pleased."   [Ps. 2:7]; Is. 42:1★

The Temptation of the Servant
Matt. 4:1–11; Luke 4:1–13

12 [R]And immediately the Spirit *impelled Him *to go* out into the wilderness.   *Luke 4:1*
13 And He was in the wilderness forty days being tempted by [R]Satan; and He was with the wild beasts, and the angels were ministering to Him.   Matt. 4:10

The Work of the Servant
Matt. 4:12–17; Luke 4:14, 15

14 [R]And after John had been [T]taken into custody, Jesus came into Galilee, preaching the gospel of God,   Matt. 4:12 • *delivered up*
15 and saying, "The time is fulfilled, and the kingdom of God is at hand; repent and ^believe in the gospel."   *put your trust in*

The First Disciples Are Called
Matt. 4:18–22

16 [R]And as He was going along by the Sea of Galilee, He saw Simon and Andrew, the brother of Simon, casting a net in the sea; for they were fishermen.   Mark 1:16-20
17 And Jesus said to them, "Follow Me, and I will make you become fishers of men."
18 And they immediately left the nets and followed Him.
19 And going on a little farther, He saw ^James the *son* of Zebedee, and John his brother, who were also in the boat mending the nets.   *Jacob*
20 And immediately He called them; and they left their father Zebedee in the boat

¹ Many mss. do not contain *the Son of God*
² Or, *proclaiming*
³ The Gr. here can be translated *in, with* or *by*

with the hired servants, and went away[T]to follow Him.   *after Him*

Demons Are Cast Out
Luke 4:31–37

21 [R]And they *went into Capernaum; and immediately on the Sabbath He entered the synagogue and *began* to teach.   *Luke 4:31-37*

22 And[R]they were amazed at His teaching; for He was teaching them as *one* having authority, and not as the scribes.   *Matt. 7:28*

23 And just then there was in their synagogue a man with an unclean spirit; and he cried out,

24 saying, "What[R]do we have to do with You, Jesus [4]of[R]Nazareth? Have You come to destroy us? I know who You are—the Holy One of God!"   *Matt. 8:29 • Matt. 2:23; Mark 10:47*

25 And Jesus rebuked him, saying, "Be quiet, and come out of him!"

26 And throwing him into convulsions, the unclean spirit cried out with a loud voice, and came out of him.

27 And they were all[R]amazed, so that they debated among themselves, saying, "What is this? A new teaching with authority! He commands even the unclean spirits, and they obey Him."   *Mark 10:24, 32; 16:5, 6*

28 And immediately the news about Him went out everywhere into all the surrounding district of Galilee.

Peter's Mother-in-law Is Healed
Matt. 8:14, 15; Luke 4:38, 39

29 [R]And immediately after they had come out of the synagogue, they came into the house of Simon and Andrew, with [J]James and John.   *Mark 1:29-31; Matt. 8:14, 15 • Jacob*

30 Now Simon's mother-in-law was lying sick with a fever; and immediately they *spoke to Him about her.

31 And He came to her and raised her up, taking her by the hand, and the fever left her, and she [5]waited on them.

Many Healings
Matt. 8:16, 17, 4:23; Luke 4:40–44

32 [R]And[R]when evening had come, after the sun had set, they *began* bringing to Him all who were ill and those who were demon-possessed.   *Mark 1:32-34 • Luke 4:40*

33 And the whole[R]city had gathered at the door.   *Mark 1:21*

34 And He[R]healed many who were ill with various diseases, and cast out many demons; and He was not permitting the demons to speak, because they [6]knew who He was.   *Matt. 4:23*

35 [R]And in the early morning, while it was still dark, He arose and went out and departed to a lonely place, and[R]was praying there.   *Luke 4:42, 43 • Matt. 14:23; Luke 5:16*

36 And Simon and his companions hunted for Him;

37 and they found Him, and *said to Him, "Everyone is looking for You."

38 And He *said to them, "Let us go somewhere else to the towns nearby, in order that I may[A]preach there also; for that is what I came out for."   *proclaim*

39 And He went into their synagogues throughout all Galilee,[A]preaching and casting out the demons.   *proclaiming*

A Leper Is Cleansed
Matt. 8:1–4; Luke 5:12–16

40 [R]And a leper *came to Him, beseeching Him and falling on his knees before Him, and saying to Him, "If You are willing, You can make me clean."   *Mark 1:40-44; Matt. 8:2-4*

41 And moved with compassion, He stretched out His hand, and touched him, and *said to him, "I am willing; be cleansed."

42 And immediately the leprosy left him and he was cleansed.

43 And He sternly warned him and immediately sent him away,

44 and He *said to him, "See[R]that you say nothing to anyone; but go, show yourself to the priest and[R]offer for your cleansing what Moses commanded, for a testimony to them."   *Matt. 8:4 • Lev. 14:1-32*

45 But he went out and began to[R]proclaim it freely and to spread the news about, to such an extent that Jesus could no longer publicly enter a city, but [7]stayed out in unpopulated areas; and[R]they were coming to Him from everywhere.   *Luke 5:15 • Luke 5:17*

CHAPTER 2

A Paralytic Is Healed
Matt. 9:1–8; Luke 5:17–26

Aᴺᴰ when He had come back to Capernaum several days afterward, it was heard that He was at home.

2 And[R]many were gathered together, so that there was no longer room, even near the door; and He was speaking the word to them.   *Mark 1:45; 2:13*

3 [R]And they *came, bringing to Him a paralytic, carried by four men.   *Luke 5:18-26*

4 And being unable to [T]get to Him because of the crowd, they removed the roof [T]above Him; and when they had dug an opening, they let down the pallet on which the paralytic was lying.   *bring to • where He was*

5 And Jesus seeing their faith *said to the paralytic, "My [8]son,[R]your sins are forgiven."   *Matt. 9:2*

6 But there were some of the scribes sitting there and reasoning in their hearts,

[4] Lit., *the Nazarene*   [5] Or, *served*
[6] Some mss. read: *knew Him to be Christ*   [7] Lit., *was*
[8] Lit., *child*

7"Why does this man speak that way? He is blaspheming; [R]who can forgive sins [T]but God alone?"   Is. 43:25 • *if not one, God*

8 And immediately Jesus, aware [T]in His spirit that they were reasoning that way within themselves, *said to them, "Why are you reasoning about these things in your hearts?   *by*

9"Which is easier, to say to the[R]paralytic, 'Your sins are forgiven'; or to say, 'Arise, and take up your pallet and walk'? Matt. 4:24

10"But in order that you may know that the Son of Man has authority on earth to forgive sins"—He *said to the paralytic—

11"I say to you, rise, take up your pallet and go home."

12 And he rose and immediately took up the pallet and went out in the sight of all; so that they were all amazed and[R]were glorifying God, saying, "We[R]have never seen anything like this."   Matt. 9:8 • Matt. 9:33

Call of Matthew
Matt. 9:9–13; Luke 5:27–32

13 And He went out again by the seashore; and[R]all the multitude were coming to Him, and He was teaching them.   Mark 1:45

14 [R]And as He passed by, He saw[R]Levi the *son* of Alphaeus sitting in the tax office, and He *said to him, "Follow Me!" And he rose and followed Him.   Mark 2:14-17 • Matt. 9:9

15 And it came about that He was reclining *at the table* in his house, and many tax-gatherers and sinners were dining with Jesus and His disciples; for there were many of them, and they were following Him.

16 And when[R]the scribes of the Pharisees saw that He was eating with the sinners and tax-gatherers, they *began* saying to His disciples, "Why is He eating and drinking with tax-gatherers and sinners?"   Luke 5:30

17 And hearing this, Jesus *said to them, "*It is* not those who are healthy who need a physician, but those who are sick; I did not come to call the righteous, but sinners."

Parable of Cloth and Wineskins
Matt. 9:14–17; Luke 5:33–39

18 [R]And John's disciples and the Pharisees were fasting; and they *came and *said to Him, "Why do John's disciples and the disciples of the Pharisees fast, but Your disciples do not fast?"   Mark 2:18-22; Luke 5:33-38

19 And Jesus said to them, "While the bridegroom is with them,[T]the attendants of the bridegroom do not fast, do they? So long as they have the bridegroom with them, they cannot fast.   *sons of the bridal-chamber*

20"But the[R]days will come when the bridegroom is taken away from them, and then they will fast in that day.   Luke 17:22

21"No one sews a patch of unshrunk cloth on an old garment; otherwise [T]the patch pulls away from it, the new from the old, and a worse tear results.   *that which fills up*

22"And no one puts new wine into old [T]wineskins; otherwise the wine will burst the skins, and the wine is lost, and the skins *as well;* but one puts new wine into fresh wineskins."   skins used as bottles

Controversy over Sabbath-work
Matt. 12:1–8; Luke 6:1–5

23 [R]And it came about that He was passing through the grainfields on the Sabbath, and His disciples began to make their way along while picking the heads *of grain.*   Matt. 12:1-8

24 And the Pharisees were saying to Him, "See here,[R]why are they doing what is not lawful on the Sabbath?"   Matt. 12:2

25 And He *said to them, "Have you never read what David did when he was in need and became hungry, he and his companions:

26 how he entered the house of God in the time of Abiathar *the* high priest, and ate the consecrated bread, which is not lawful for *anyone* to eat except the priests, and he gave *it* also to those who were with him?"

27 And He was saying to them, "The Sabbath[4]was made[T]for man, and not man for the Sabbath.   *came into being • for the sake of*

28"Consequently, the Son of Man is Lord even of the Sabbath."

CHAPTER 3

Controversy over Sabbath-healing
Matt. 12:9–13; Luke 6:6–10

AND He entered again into a synagogue; and a man was there with a withered hand.

2 And[R]they were watching Him *to see* if He would heal him on the Sabbath, in order that they might accuse Him.   Luke 6:7; 14:1

3 And He *said to the man with the withered hand, "Rise and *come* forward!"

4 And He *said to them, "Is it lawful on the Sabbath to do good or to do harm, to save a life or to kill?" But they kept silent.

5 And after[R]looking around at them with anger, grieved at their hardness of heart, He *said to the man, "Stretch out your hand." And he stretched it out, and his hand was restored.   Luke 6:10

Pharisees Counsel to Destroy Jesus
Matt. 12:14–16; Luke 6:11

6 [R]And the Pharisees went out and immediately *began* taking counsel with the[R]Herodians against Him, *as to* how they might destroy Him.   Ps. 2:2★ • Matt. 22:16; Mark 12:13

7 And Jesus withdrew to the sea with His disciples; and a great multitude from Galilee followed; and *also* from Judea,

8 and from Jerusalem, and from Idumea, and beyond the Jordan, and the vicinity of Tyre and Sidon, a great multitude heard of all that He was doing and came to Him.

9 [R]And He told His disciples that a boat should stand ready for Him because of the multitude, in order that they might not crowd Him; Mark 4:1; Luke 5:1-3

10 for He had healed many, with the result that all those who had afflictions pressed about Him in order to touch Him.

11 And whenever the unclean spirits beheld Him, they would fall down before Him and cry out, saying, "You are [R]the Son of God!" Matt. 4:3

12 And He earnestly warned them not to [A]make Him known. *reveal who He was*

Selection of the Twelve—Luke 6:12–16

13 And He *went up to[R]the mountain and *summoned those whom He Himself wanted, and they came to Him. Luke 6:12

14 And He appointed twelve[9], that they might be with Him, and that He might send them out to preach,

15 and to have authority to cast out the demons.

16 And He appointed the twelve: [R]Simon (to whom He gave the name Peter), Acts 1:13

17 and [A]James, the *son* of Zebedee, and John the brother of James (to them He gave the name Boanerges, which means, "Sons of Thunder"); *Jacob*

18 and Andrew, and Philip, and Bartholomew, and Matthew, and Thomas, and [A]James the *son* of Alphaeus, and Thaddaeus, and Simon the[A]Zealot; *Jacob • Cananaean*

19 and Judas Iscariot, who also betrayed Him.

Opposition of His Friends

20 And He *came [10]home, and the multitude *gathered again, to such an extent that they could not even eat[T]a meal. *bread*

21 And when[R]His own [11]people heard *of this*, they went out to take custody of Him; for they were saying, "He[R] has lost His senses." Mark 3:31f. • John 10:20; Acts 26:24

Scribes Commit the Unpardonable Sin
Matt. 12:24–32; Luke 11:17–23

22 And the scribes who came down from Jerusalem were saying, "He is possessed by [A]Beelzebul," and "He casts out the demons by the ruler of the demons." *Beezebul*

23 [R]And He called them to Himself and began speaking to them in parables, "How can Satan cast out Satan? Luke 11:17-22

24 "And if a kingdom is divided against itself, that kingdom cannot stand.

25 "And if a house is divided against itself, that house will not be able to stand.

26 "And if[R]Satan has risen up against himself and is divided, he cannot stand, but[T]he is finished! Matt. 4:10 • *he has an end*

27 "But[R]no one can enter the strong man's house and plunder his property unless he

first binds the strong man, and then he will plunder his house. [Is. 49:24, 25]

28 "Truly[R]I say to you, all sins shall be forgiven the sons of men, and whatever blasphemies they utter; Matt. 12:31, 32; Mark 3:28-30

29 but [R]whoever blasphemes against the Holy Spirit never has forgiveness, but is guilty of an eternal sin"— Luke 12:10

30 because they were saying, "He has an unclean spirit."

New Relationships Are Defined
Matt. 12:46–50; Luke 8:19–21

31 [R]And His mother and His brothers *arrived, and standing outside they sent word to Him, and called Him. Luke 8:19-21

32 And a multitude was sitting around Him, and they *said to Him, "Behold, Your mother and Your brothers[12] are outside looking for You."

33 And answering them, He *said, "Who are My mother and My brothers?"

34 And looking about on those who were sitting around Him, He *said, "Behold[R] My mother and My brothers! Matt. 12:49

35 "For whoever does the will of God, he is My brother and sister and mother."

CHAPTER 4

Parable of the Soils
Matt. 13:1–23; Luke 8:4–15

AND He began to teach again by the sea. And such a very great multitude[T]gathered to Him that He got into a boat in the sea and sat down; and the whole multitude was by the sea on the land. *is gathered*

2 And He was teaching them many things in[R]parables, and was saying to them in His teaching, Matt. 13:3ff.; Mark 3:23; 4:2ff.

3 "Listen *to this!* Behold, the sower went out to sow;

4 and it came about that as he was sowing, some *seed* fell beside the road, and the birds came and ate it up.

5 "And other *seed* fell on the rocky *ground* where it did not have much soil; and immediately it sprang up because it had no depth of soil.

6 "And after the sun had risen, it was scorched; and because it had no root, it withered away.

7 "And other *seed* fell among the thorns, and the thorns came up and choked it, and it yielded no crop.

8 "And other *seeds* fell into the good soil and as they grew up and increased, they yielded a crop and produced thirty, sixty, and a hundredfold."

9 And He was saying, "He[R]who has ears to hear, let him hear." Matt. 11:15; Mark 4:23

10 And as soon as He was alone,[T]His fol-

[9] Some early mss. add: *whom He named apostles*
[10] Lit., *into a house* [11] Or, *kinsmen*
[12] Later mss. add: *and Your sisters*

lowers, along with the twelve, *began* asking Him *about* the parables.   *those about Him*

11 And He was saying to them, "To you has been given the mystery of the kingdom of God; but[R]those who are outside get everything[R]in parables,   [Col. 4:5] • Mark 3:23; 4:2

12 in order that[R]WHILE SEEING, THEY MAY SEE AND NOT PERCEIVE; AND WHILE HEARING, THEY MAY HEAR AND NOT UNDERSTAND LEST THEY RETURN AND BE FORGIVEN."   Jer. 5:21

13 [R]And He *said to them, "Do you not understand this parable? And how will you understand all the parables?   Mark 4:13-20

14 "The sower sows the word.

15 "And these are the ones who are beside the road where the word is sown; and when they hear, immediately [R]Satan comes and takes away the word which has been sown in them.   [1 Pet. 5:8]

16 "And in a similar way these are the ones on whom seed was sown on the rocky *places*, who, when they hear the word, immediately receive it with joy;

17 and they have no *firm* root in themselves, but are *only* temporary; then, when affliction or persecution arises because of the word, immediately they fall away.

18 "And others are the ones on whom seed was sown among the thorns; these are the ones who have heard the word,

19 and the worries of[R]the [13]world, and the deceitfulness of riches, and the desires for other things enter in and choke the word, and it becomes unfruitful.   [Rom. 12:2]

20 "And those are the ones on whom seed was sown on the good soil; and they hear the word and accept it, and [R]bear fruit, thirty, sixty, and a hundredfold."   [Rom. 7:4]

Parable of the Lamp
Luke 8:16–18

21 And He was saying to them, "A lamp is not brought to be put under a peck-measure, is it, or under a bed? Is it not *brought* to be put on the lampstand?

22 "For[R]nothing is hidden, except to be revealed; nor has *anything* been secret, but that it should come to light.   Luke 8:17; 12:2

23 "If[R]any man has ears to hear, let him hear."   Matt. 11:15; 13:9, 43; Mark 4:9; Luke 8:8

24 And He was saying to them, "Take care what you listen to.[R]By your standard of measure it shall be measured to you; and more shall be given you besides.   Luke 6:38

25 "For whoever has, to him shall *more* be given; and whoever does not have, even what he has shall be taken away from him."

Parable of the Growing Seed

26 And He was saying, "The kingdom of God is like a man who casts seed upon the soil;

27 and goes to bed at night and gets up by day, and the seed sprouts up and grows—how, he himself does not know.

28 "The soil produces crops by itself; first the blade, then the head, then the mature grain in the head.

29 "But when the crop permits, he immediately[T]puts[R]in the sickle, because the harvest has come."   *sends forth* • [Joel 3:13]

Parable of the Mustard Seed
Matt. 13:31–35

30 [R]And He said, "How shall we [14]picture the kingdom of God, or by what parable shall we present it?   Mark 4:30-32

31 "*It is* like a mustard seed, which, when sown upon the soil, though it is smaller than all the seeds that are upon the soil,

32 yet when it is sown, grows up and becomes larger than all the garden plants and forms large branches; so that THE BIRDS OF THE [15]AIR can NEST UNDER ITS SHADE."

33 And with many such parables He was speaking the word to them as they were able to hear it;

34 and He did not speak to them[R]without a parable; but He was explaining everything privately to His own disciples.   Matt. 13:34

The Sea Is Stilled
Matt. 8:23–27; Luke 8:22–25

35 [R]And on that day, when evening had come, He *said to them, "Let us go over to the other side."   Mark 4:35-41; Luke 8:22, 25

36 And leaving the multitude, they *took Him along with them, just as He was, in the boat; and other boats were with Him.

37 And there *arose a fierce gale of wind, and the waves were breaking over the boat so much that the boat was already filling up.

38 And He Himself was in the stern, asleep on the cushion; and they *awoke Him and *said to Him, "Teacher, do You not care that we are perishing?"

39 And being aroused, He rebuked the wind and said to the sea, "Hush, be still." And the wind died down and[T]it became perfectly calm.   *a great calm occurred*

40 And He said to them, "Why are you so timid? How is it that you have no faith?"

41 And they became very much afraid and said to one another, "Who then is this, that even the wind and the sea obey Him?"

CHAPTER 5

Demons Are Cast into Swine
Matt. 8:28–34; Luke 8:26–39

AND they came to the other side of the sea, into the country of the Gerasenes.

---

[13] Or, *age*   [14] Lit., *compare*   [15] Or, *sky*

2 And when He had come out of [R]the boat, immediately a man from the tombs with an unclean spirit met Him, Mark 3:9; 4:1

3 and he had his dwelling among the tombs. And no one was able to bind him anymore, even with a chain;

4 because he had often been bound with shackles and chains, and the chains had been torn apart by him, and the shackles broken in pieces, and no one was strong enough to subdue him.

5 And constantly night and day, among the tombs and in the mountains, he was crying out and gashing himself with stones.

6 And seeing Jesus from a distance, he ran up and bowed down before Him;

7 and crying out with a loud voice, he *said, "What[R] do I have to do with You, Jesus, Son of the Most High God? I implore You by God, do not torment me!" Matt. 8:29

8 For He had been saying to him, "Come out of the man, you unclean spirit!"

9 And He was asking him, "What is your name?" And he *said to Him, "My name is [R]Legion; for we are many." Luke 8:30

10 And he *began* to entreat Him earnestly not to send them out of the country.

11 Now there was a big herd of swine feeding there on the mountain.

12 And *the demons* entreated Him, saying, "Send us into the swine so that we may enter them."

13 And He gave them permission. And coming out, the unclean spirits entered the swine; and the herd rushed down the steep bank into the sea, about two thousand *of them;* and they were drowned in the sea.

14 And their herdsmen ran away and reported it in the city and *out* in the country. And *the people* came to see what it was that had happened.

15 And they *came to Jesus and *observed the man who had been demon-possessed sitting down, clothed and in his right mind, the very man who had had the "legion"; and they became frightened.

16 And those who had seen it described to them how it had happened to the demon-possessed man, and *all* about the swine.

17 And they began to[R]entreat Him to depart from their region. Matt. 8:34; Acts 16:39

18 [R]And as He was getting into the boat, the man who had been demon-possessed was entreating Him that he might [T]accompany Him. Mark 5:18-20 • *be with Him*

19 And He did not let him, but He *said to him, "Go home to your people and report to them [16]what great things the Lord has done for you, and *how* He had mercy on you."

20 And he went away and began to proclaim in Decapolis what great things Jesus had done for him; and everyone marveled.

Jairus Pleads for His Daughter
Matt. 9:18, 19; Luke 8:41, 42

21 [R]And when Jesus had crossed over again in the boat to the other side, a great multitude gathered about Him; and He [T]stayed by the seashore. *was*

22 And one of [R]the synagogue [A]officials named Jairus *came up, and upon seeing Him, *fell at His feet, Matt. 9:18 • *rulers*

23 and *entreated Him earnestly, saying, "My little daughter is at the point of death; *please* come and lay Your hands on her, that she may[T]get well and live." *be saved*

24 And He went off with him; and a great multitude was following Him and pressing in on Him.

A Woman Is Healed
Matt. 9:20–22; Luke 8:43–48

25 And a woman who had had a hemorrhage for twelve years,

26 and had endured much at the hands of many physicians, and had spent all that she had and was not helped at all, but rather had grown worse,

27 after hearing about Jesus, came up in the crowd behind *Him,* and touched His [A]cloak. *outer garment*

28 For she [T]thought, "If I just touch His garments, I shall get well." *was saying*

29 And immediately the flow of her blood was dried up; and she felt in her body that she was healed of her[R]affliction. Mark 3:10

30 And immediately Jesus, perceiving in Himself that [R]the power *proceeding* from Him had gone forth, turned around in the crowd and said, "Who touched My garments?" Luke 5:17

31 And His disciples said to Him, "You see the multitude pressing in on You, and You say, 'Who touched Me?' "

32 And He looked around to see the woman who had done this.

33 But the woman fearing and trembling, aware of what had happened to her, came and fell down before Him, and told Him the whole truth.

34 And He said to her, "Daughter, your faith has[T]made you well; go in peace, and be healed of your affliction." *saved you*

Jairus's Daughter Is Healed
Matt. 9:23–26; Luke 8:49–56

35 While He was still speaking, they *came from the *house of* the[R]synagogue official, saying, "Your daughter has died; why trouble the Teacher anymore?" Mark 5:22

36 But Jesus, overhearing what was being spoken, *said to the synagogue official, "Do not be afraid *any longer,* only believe."

37 And He allowed no one to follow with Him, except[R]Peter and [A]James and John the brother of James. Matt. 17:1; 26:37 • *Jacob*

38 And they *came to the house of the [R]synagogue official; and He *beheld a com-

[16]Or, *everything that*

motion, and *people* loudly weeping and wailing. Mark 5:22

39 And entering in, He *said to them, "Why make a commotion and weep? The child has not died, but is asleep."

40 And they *began* laughing at Him. But putting them all out, He *took along the child's father and mother and His own companions, and *entered *the room* where the child was.

41 And taking the child by the hand, He *said to her, "Talitha kum!" (which translated means, "Little girl, ᴿI say to you, arise!"). Luke 7:14; Acts 9:40

42 And immediately the girl rose and *began* to walk; for she was twelve years old. And immediately they were completely astounded.

43 And He gave them strict orders that no one should know about this; and He said that *something* should be given her to eat.

CHAPTER 6

Jesus Is Rejected at Nazareth
Matt. 13:54–58

Aᴺᴰ He went out from there, and He *came into ᴬHis home town; and His disciples *followed Him. *His own part of the country*

2 And when the Sabbath had come, He began to teach in the synagogue; and the many listeners were astonished, saying, "Where did this man *get* these things, and what is *this* wisdom given to Him, and such miracles as these performed by His hands?

3 "Is not this the carpenter, the son of Mary, and brother of James, and Joses, and Judas, and Simon? Are not His sisters here with us?" And they took offense at Him.

4 And Jesus said to them, "A prophet is not without honor except in ᴬhis home town and among his *own* relatives and in his *own* household." *his own part of the country*

5 And He could do no ᴬmiracle there except that He laid His hands upon a few sick people and healed them. *work of power*

6 And He wondered at their unbelief. ᴿAnd He was going around the villages teaching. Matt. 9:35; Mark 1:39; 10:1; Luke 13:22

Twelve Are Sent to Serve
Matt. 10:1–42; Luke 9:1–6

7 ᴿAndᴿHe *summoned the twelve and began to send them out in pairs; and He was giving them authority over the unclean spirits; Mark 6:7-11 · Mark 3:13

8 and He instructed them that they should take nothing for *their* journey, except a mere staff; no bread, noᴬbag, no money in their belt; *knapsack or beggar's bag*

9 but ᵀto wear sandals; and *He added,* "Do not put on two ¹⁷tunics." *being shod with*

10 And He said to them, "Wherever you enter a house, stay there until you ᵀleave town. *go out from there*

11 "And any place that does not receive you or listen to you, as you go out from there, shake off the dust from the soles of your feet for a testimony against them."

12 And they went out and ᴬpreached that *men* should repent. *proclaimed as a herald*

13 And they were casting out many demons andᴿwere anointing with oil many sick people and healing them. [James 5:14]

John the Baptist Is Murdered
Matt. 14:1–12; Luke 9:7–9

14 And King Herod heard *of it,* for His name had become well known; and *people* were saying, "John the Baptist has risen from the dead, and that is why these miraculous powers are at work in Him."

15 But others were saying, "He isᴿElijah." And others were saying, "*He is* a prophet, like one of the prophets *of old.*" Mark 8:28

16 But when Herod heard *of it,* he kept saying, "John, whom I beheaded, has risen!"

17 For Herod himself had sent and had John arrested and bound in prison on account of Herodias, the wife of his brother Philip, because he had married her.

18 For John had been saying to Herod, "Itᴿ is not lawful for you to have your brother's wife." Matt. 14:4

19 And ᴿHerodias had a grudge against him and wanted to put him to death and could not *do so;* Matt. 14:3

20 for Herod was afraid of John, knowing that he was a righteous and holy man, and kept him safe. And when he heard him, he was very perplexed; ᵀbut he ᵀused to enjoy listening to him. *and · was hearing him gladly*

21 And a strategic day came when Herod on his birthdayᴿgave a banquet for his lords and military commanders and the leading menᴿof Galilee; Esth. 1:3; 2:18 · Luke 3:1

22 and when the daughter of ᴿHerodias herself came in and danced, she pleased Herod and his dinner guests; and the king said to the girl, "Ask me for whatever you want and I will give it to you." Matt. 14:3

23 And he swore to her, "Whatever you ask of me, I will give it to you; up toᴿhalf of my kingdom." Esth. 5:3, 6; 7:2

24 And she went out and said to her mother, "What shall I ask for?" And she said, "The head of John the Baptist."

25 And immediately she came in haste before the king and asked, saying, "I want you to give me right away the head of John the Baptist on a platter."

26 And although the king was very sorry, *yet* because of his oaths and because ofᵀhis dinner guests, he was unwilling to refuse her. *those reclining at the table*

27 And immediately the king sent an executioner and commanded *him* to bring *back*

¹⁷ Or, *inner garments*

his head. And he went and had him beheaded in the prison,

28 and brought his head on a platter, and
gave it to the girl; and the girl gave it to her
mother.

29 And when his disciples heard *about
this,* they came and took away his body and
laid it in a tomb.

Twelve Return
Luke 9:10

30 ᴿAnd the apostles *gathered together
with Jesus; and they reported to Him all
that they had done and taught.　　Luke 9:10

31 And He *said to them, "Come away by
yourselves to a lonely place and rest a
while." (For there were many *people* coming and going, andᴿthey did not even have
time to eat.)　　　　　　　　　　Mark 3:20

Five Thousand Are Fed
Matt. 14:13–21; Luke 9:11–17;
John 6:1–14

32 ᴿAnd they went away in the boat to a
lonely place by themselves.　　Mark 6:32-44

33 And *the people* saw them going, and
many recognized *them,* and they ran there
together on foot from all the cities, and got
there ahead of them.

34 And when He went ᵀashore, Heᴿsaw a
great multitude, and He felt compassion for
them because they were like sheep without
a shepherd; and He began to teach them
many things.　　　　　　　out • Matt. 9:36

35 And when it was already quite late, His
disciples came up to Him and *began* saying,
"The place is desolate and it is already quite
late;

36 send them away so that they may go
into the surrounding countryside and villages and buy themselves ᵀsomething to
eat."　　　　　　　　what they may eat

37 But He answered and said to them,
"You give them *something* to eat!" ᴿAnd
they *said to Him, "Shall we go and spend
two hundred ¹⁸denarii on bread and give
them *something* to eat?"　　　　John 6:7

38 And He *said to them, "How many
loaves do you have? Go look!" And when
they found out, they *said, "Five and two
fish."

39 And He commanded them all to recline
by groups on the green grass.

40 And they reclined in companies of hundreds and of fifties.

41 And He took the five loaves and the
two fish, and looking up toward heaven, He
ᴿblessed *the food* and broke the loaves and
He kept giving *them* to the disciples to set
before them; and He divided up the two fish
among them all.　　　　　　Matt. 14:19

42 And they all ate and were satisfied.

43 And they picked up twelve full baskets
of the broken pieces, and also of the fish.

44 And there wereᴿfive thousand men who
ate the loaves.　　　　　　　Matt. 14:21

Jesus Walks on Water
Matt. 14:22–33; John 6:15–21

45 And immediately He made His disciples get into the boat and go ahead of *Him*
to the other side to Bethsaida, while He
Himself was sending the multitude away.

46 And after ᴿbidding them farewell, He
departed to the mountain to pray. 2 Cor. 2:13

47 And when it was evening, the boat was
in the midst of the sea, and He *was* alone on
the land.

48 And seeing them ᵀstraining at the oars,
for the wind was against them, at about the
ᵀfourth watch of the night, He *came to
them, walking on the sea; and He intended
to pass by them.　　harassed in rowing • 3-6 a.m.

49 But when they saw Him walking on the
sea, they supposed that it was a ghost, and
cried out;

50 for they all saw Him and wereᴬfright-
ened. But immediately He spoke with them
and *said to them, "Takeᴿcourage; it is I, do
not be afraid."　　　　troubled • Matt. 9:2

51 And He got intoᴿthe boat with them,
and the wind stopped; and they were greatly
astonished,　　　　　　　　Mark 6:32

52 for ᴿthey had not gained any insight
from the *incident of* the loaves, but their
heart was hardened.　　　　Mark 8:17ff.

Jesus Heals at Gennesaret
Matt. 14:34–36

53 ᴿAnd when they had crossed over they
came to land at Gennesaret, and moored to
the shore.　　　Mark 6:53-56; John 6:24, 25

54 And when they had come out of the
boat, immediately *the people* recognized
Him,

55 and ran about that whole country and
began to carry about on their pallets those
who were sick, toᴬthe place they heard He
was.　　　where they were hearing that He was

56 And wherever He entered villages, or
cities, or countryside, they were laying the
sick in the market places, and entreating
Him that they might justᴿtouchᴿthe fringe of
His cloak; and as many as touched it were
being cured.　　　Mark 3:10 • Matt. 9:20

CHAPTER 7

Pharisees and Defilement
Matt. 15:1–20

Aᴺᴰᴿ the Pharisees and some of the
scribes gathered together around Him when
they had come from Jerusalem,　　Mark 7:1-23

2 and had seen that some of His disciples
were eating their bread withᴿimpure hands,
that is, unwashed.　　　Matt. 15:2; Mark 7:5

3 (For the Pharisees and all the Jews do
not eat unless they ᵀcarefully wash their
hands, *thus* observing theᴿtraditions of the
elders;　　　　　　with the fist • Gal. 1:14

¹⁸ The denarius was equivalent to one day's wage

4 and *when they come* from the market place, they do not eat unless they˄cleanse themselves; and there are many other things which they have received in order to observe, such as the washing of cups and pitchers and copper pots.)   *sprinkle*

5 And the Pharisees and the scribes *asked Him, "Why do Your disciples not walk according to the tradition of the elders, but eat their bread with impure hands?"

6 And He said to them, "Rightly did Isaiah prophesy of you hypocrites, as it is written,

'THIS[R] PEOPLE HONORS ME WITH THEIR
    LIPS,   Is. 29:13★
BUT THEIR HEART IS FAR AWAY FROM
    ME.

7 'BUT IN VAIN DO THEY WORSHIP ME,
TEACHING AS DOCTRINES THE PRECEPTS
    OF MEN.'

8"Neglecting the commandment of God, you hold to the[R]tradition of men."   Mark 7:3

9 He was also saying to them, "You nicely set aside the commandment of God in order to keep your[R]tradition.   Gal. 1:14

10"For Moses said, 'HONOR[R] YOUR FATHER AND YOUR MOTHER'; and, 'HE WHO SPEAKS EVIL OF FATHER OR MOTHER, LET HIM[T]BE PUT TO DEATH';   Ex. 20:12 • *die the death*

11 but you say, 'If a man says to *his* father or *his* mother, anything of mine you might have been helped by is[R]Corban (that is to say, [19]given *to God*),'   Lev. 1:2; Matt. 27:6

12 you no longer permit him to do anything for *his* father or *his* mother;

13 *thus* invalidating the word of God by your [R]tradition which you have handed down; and you do many things such as that."   Mark 7:3, 5, 8, 9; Gal. 1:14

14 And after He called the multitude to Him again, He *began* saying to them, "Listen to Me, all of you, and understand:

15 there is nothing outside the man which going into him can defile him; but the things which proceed out of the man are what defile the man.

16 ['[20]If any man has ears to hear, let him hear."]

17 And when leaving the multitude, He had entered[R]the house, His disciples questioned Him about the parable.   Mark 2:1; 3:20

18 And He *said to them, "Are you so lacking in understanding also? Do you not understand that whatever goes into the man from outside cannot defile him;

19 because it does not go into his heart, but into his stomach, and is eliminated?" (*Thus He* declared[R]all foods clean.)   Col. 2:16

20 And He was saying, "That[R]which proceeds out of the man, that is what defiles the man.   Matt. 15:18; Mark 7:23

21"For from within, out of the heart of men, proceed the evil thoughts, fornications, thefts, murders, adulteries,

[19] Or, *a gift, an offering*
[20] Many mss. do not contain this verse
[21] Some early mss. add: *and Sidon*   [22] Lit., *Greek*

22 deeds of coveting *and* wickedness, *as well as* deceit, sensuality, [T]envy, slander, pride *and* foolishness.   *an evil eye*

23"All these evil things proceed from within and defile the man."

Syrophoenician's Daughter Is Healed
Matt. 15:21–28

24 And from there He arose and went away to the region of Tyre[21]. And when He had entered a house, He wanted no one to know *of it;* yet He could not escape notice.

25 But after hearing of Him, a woman whose little daughter had an unclean spirit, immediately came and fell at His feet.

26 Now the woman was a [22]Gentile, of the Syrophoenician race. And she kept asking Him to cast the demon out of her daughter.

27 And He was saying to her, "Let the children be satisfied first, for it is not˄good to take the children's bread and throw it to the dogs."   *proper*

28 But she answered and *said to Him, "Yes, Lord, *but* even the dogs under the table feed on the children's crumbs."

29 And He said to her, "Because of this [T]answer go your way; the demon has gone out of your daughter."   *word*

30 And going back to her home, she found the child[T]lying on the bed, the demon having departed.   *thrown*

Deaf and Dumb Man Is Healed

31 And again He went out from the region of Tyre, and came through Sidon to the Sea of Galilee, within the region of Decapolis.

32 And they *brought to Him one who was deaf and spoke with difficulty, and they *entreated Him to lay His hand upon him.

33 And He took him aside from the multitude by himself, and put His fingers into his ears, and after spitting, He touched his tongue *with the saliva;*

34 and looking up to heaven with a deep sigh, He *said to him, "Ephphatha!" that is, "Be opened!"

35 And his ears were opened, and the˄impediment of his tongue was removed, and he *began* speaking plainly.   *bond*

36 And He gave them orders not to tell anyone; but the more He ordered them, the more widely they continued to proclaim it.

37 And they were utterly astonished, saying, "He has done all things well; He makes even the deaf to hear, and the dumb to speak."

CHAPTER 8

Four Thousand Are Fed
Matt. 15:32–38

IN those days again, when there was a great multitude and they had nothing to eat, He called His disciples and *said to them,

2 "I feel compassion for the multitude because they have remained with Me now three days, and have nothing to eat;

3 and if I send them away hungry to their home, they will faint on the way; and some of them have come from a distance."

4 And His disciples answered Him, "Where will anyone be able to *find enough to* satisfy these men with ᵀbread here in a desolate place?"   *loaves*

5 And He was asking them, "How many loaves do you have?" And they said, "Seven."

6 And He *directed the multitude to ᵀsit down on the ground; and taking the seven loaves, He gave thanks and broke them, and started giving them to His disciples to ᵀserve to them, and they served them to the multitude.   *recline • set before*

7 They also had a few small fish; and after He had blessed them, He ordered these to be ᵀserved as well.   *set before them*

8 And they ate and were satisfied; and they picked up seven large baskets full of what was left over of the broken pieces.

9 And about four thousand were *there*; and He sent them away.

Pharisees Seek a Sign
Matt. 15:39—16:4

10 And immediately He entered the boat with His disciples, and came to the district ofᴿDalmanutha.   Matt. 15:39

11 And the Pharisees came out and began to argue with Him, seeking from Him aᴬsign from heaven, to test Him.   *attesting miracle*

12 And sighing deeply ᴬin His spirit, He *said, "Why does this generation seek for a sign? Truly I say to you, no sign shall be given to this generation."   *to Himself*

13 And leaving them, He again embarked and went away to the other side.

Disciples Do Not Understand
Matt. 16:5–12

14 And they had forgotten to take bread; and ᵀdid not have more than one loaf in the boat with them.   *were not having*

15 And He was giving orders to them, saying, "Watch out! Beware of the leaven of the Pharisees and the leaven of Herod."

16 And they *began* to discuss with one another the *fact* that they had no bread.

17 And Jesus, aware of this, *said to them, "Why do you discuss *the fact* that you have no bread? Do you not yet see or understand? Do you have a hardened heart?

18 "HAVINGᴿ EYES, DO YOU NOT SEE? AND HAVING EARS, DO YOU NOT HEAR? And do you not remember,   Jer. 5:21; Ezek. 12:2; Mark 4:12

19 when I brokeᴿthe five loaves for the five thousand, how manyᴿbaskets full of broken pieces you picked up?" They *said to Him, "Twelve."   Mark 6:41-44 • Matt. 14:20

20 "And when *I broke* ᴿthe seven for the four thousand, how many large baskets full of broken pieces did you pick up?" And they *said to Him, "Seven."   Mark 8:6-9

21 And He was saying to them, "Doᴿyou not yet understand?"   [Mark 6:52]

A Blind Man Is Healed

22 And they *came to ᴿBethsaida. And they *brought a blind man to Him, and *entreated Him to touch him.   Mark 6:45

23 And taking the blind man by the hand, Heᴿbrought him out of the village; and after spitting on his eyes, and ᴿlaying His hands upon him, He asked him, "Do you see anything?"   Mark 7:33 • Mark 5:23

24 AndᴬHe looked up and said, "I see men, for ᴬI am seeing *them* like trees, walking about."   *gained sight • they look to me*

25 Then again He laid His hands upon his eyes; and he looked intently and was restored, and *began* to see everything clearly.

26 And He sent him to his home, saying, "Do not even enterᴿthe village."   Mark 8:23

Peter's Confession of Christ
Matt. 16:13–23; Luke 9:18–22

27 ᴿAnd Jesus went out, along with His disciples, to the villages ofᴿCaesarea Philippi; and on the way He questioned His disciples, saying to them, "Who do people say that I am?"   Mark 8:27-29 • Matt. 16:13

28 ᴿAnd they told Him, saying, "John the Baptist; and others *say* Elijah; but others, one of the prophets."   Mark 6:14; Luke 9:7, 8

29 And He *continued* by questioning them, "But who do you say that I am?"ᴿPeter *answered and *said to Him, "Thou art ᵀthe Christ."   John 6:68, 69 • the Messiah

30 And ᴿHe ᴬwarned them to tell no one about Him.   Matt. 8:4 • *strictly admonished*

31 And He began to teach them that the Son of Man must suffer many things and be rejected by the elders and the chief priests and the scribes, and be ᴿkilled, and after three days rise again.   Luke 24:46 ☆

32 And He was stating the matterᴿplainly. And Peter took Him aside and began to rebuke Him.   John 10:24; 11:14; 16:25, 29; 18:20

33 But turning around and seeing His disciples, He rebuked Peter, and *said, "Get behind Me, Satan; for you are not setting your mind on ²³God's interests, but man's."

Cost of Discipleship
Matt. 16:24–27; Luke 9:22–26

34 And He summoned the multitude with His disciples, and said to them, "If anyone wishes to come after Me, let him deny himself, and take up his cross, and follow Me.

35 "For whoever wishes to save his life shall lose it; but whoever loses his life for My sake and the gospel's shall save it.

²³ Lit., *the things of God*

36"For what does it profit a man to gain the whole world, and forfeit his soul?

37"For what shall a man give in exchange for his soul?

38"For whoever is ashamed of Me and My words in this adulterous and sinful generation, the Son of Man will also be ashamed of him when He comes in the glory of His Father with the holy angels."

CHAPTER 9

The Transfiguration
Matt. 16:28—17:3; Luke 9:27–36

AND He was saying to them, "Truly^RI say to you, there are some of those who are standing here who shall not taste death until they see the kingdom of God after it has come with power."   Acts 7:55, 56☆

2 ^RAnd six days later, Jesus *took with Him ^RPeter and 'James and John, and *brought them up to a high mountain by themselves. And He was transfigured before them;   Mark 9:2-8 · Mark 5:37 · *Jacob*

3 and^RHis garments became radiant and exceedingly white, as no launderer on earth can whiten them.   Matt. 28:3

4 And Elijah appeared to them along with Moses; and they were talking with Jesus.

5 And Peter answered and *said to Jesus, "Rabbi, it is good for us to be here; and let us make three tabernacles, one for You, and one for Moses, and one for Elijah."

6 For he did not know what to answer; for they became terrified.

7 Then a cloud formed, overshadowing them, and a voice came out of the cloud, "This is My beloved Son, listen to Him!"

8 And all at once they looked around and saw no one with them anymore, except Jesus alone.

9 And as they were coming down from the mountain, He gave them orders not to relate to anyone what they had seen, until the Son of Man should rise from the dead.

10 And they ᴬseized upon that statement, discussing with one another what rising from the dead might mean.   *kept to themselves*

11 And they asked Him, saying, "Why is it that the scribes say that^RElijah must come first?"   Mal. 4:5; Matt. 11:14

12 And He said to them, "Elijah does first come and restore all things. And yet how is it written of^Rthe Son of Man that^RHe should suffer many things and be treated with contempt?   Ps. 22:6; Is. 53:3☆ · Matt. 16:21; 26:24

13"But I say to you, that Elijah has indeed come, and they did to him whatever they wished, just as it is written of him."

Demon-possessed Son Is Delivered
Matt. 17:14–21; Luke 9:37–42

14 And when they came *back* to the disci-

ples, they saw a large crowd around them, and *some* scribes arguing with them.

15 And immediately, when the entire crowd saw Him, they were^Ramazed, and *began* running up to greet Him.   Mark 14:33

16 And He asked them, "What are you discussing with them?"

17 And one of the crowd answered Him, "Teacher, I brought You my son, possessed with a spirit which makes him mute;

18 andᴬwhenever it seizes him, it dashes him *to the ground* and he foams *at the mouth*, and grinds his teeth, and stiffens out. And I told Your disciples to cast it out, and they could not *do it*."   *wherever*

19 And He *answered them and *said, "O unbelieving generation, how long shall I be with you? How long shall I put up with you? Bring him to Me!"

20 And they brought^Tthe boy to Him. And when he saw Him, immediately the spirit threw him into a convulsion, and falling to the ground, he *began* rolling about and foaming *at the mouth*.   *him*

21 And He asked his father, "How long has this been happening to him?" And he said, "From childhood.

22"And it has often thrown him both into the fire and into the water to destroy him. But if You can do anything, take pity on us and help us!"

23 And Jesus said to him, " 'If You can!' ^RAll things are possible to him who believes."   Matt. 17:20; John 11:40

24 Immediately the boy's father cried out and *began* saying, "I do believe; help my unbelief."

25 And when Jesus saw that a crowd was ᴬrapidly gathering, He rebuked the unclean spirit, saying to it, "You deaf and dumb spirit, I command you, come out of him and do not enter him again."   *running together*

26 And after crying out and throwing him into terrible convulsions, it came out; and *the boy* became so much like a corpse that most *of them* said, "He is dead!"

27 But Jesus took him by the hand and raised him; and he got up.

28 And when He had come into *the* house, His disciples *began* questioning Him privately, "Why could we not cast it out?"

29 And He said to them, "This kind cannot come out by anything but prayer."[24]

Jesus Foretells His Death
Matt. 17:22, 23; Luke 9:43–45

30 And from there they went out and *began* to go through Galilee, and He was unwilling for anyone to know *about it*.

31 For He was teaching His disciples and telling them, "The Son of Man is to be [25]delivered into the hands of men, and they will kill Him; and when He has been killed, He will^Rrise three days later."   Luke 24:46☆

32 But they did not understand *this* statement, and they were afraid to ask Him.

---

[24] Many mss. add: *and fasting*   [25] Or, *betrayed*

Attitude of Servanthood
Matt. 18:1–5; Luke 9:46–50

33 ᴿAnd they came to Capernaum; and when He ᵀwas in the house, He *began* to question them, "What were you discussing on the way?"   Mark 9:33-37 • *had come*

34 But they kept silent, for on the way ᴿthey had discussed with one another which *of them was* the greatest.   Matt. 18:4

35 And sitting down, He called the twelve and *said to them, "Ifᴿanyone wants to be first, ʜe shall be last of all, and servant of all."   Matt. 20:26; Luke 22:26 • *let him be*

36 And taking a child, He set himᵀbefore them, and taking him in His arms, He said to them,   *in their midst*

37"Whoever receivesᵀone child like this in My name receives Me; and whoever receives Me does not receive Me, but Him who sent Me."   *one of such children*

38 ᴿJohn said to Him, "Teacher, we saw someone casting out demons in Your name, and we tried to hinder him because he was not following us."   Mark 9:38-40; *Luke 9:49*

39 But Jesus said, "Do not hinder him, for there is no one who shall perform a miracle in My name, and be able soon afterward to speak evil of Me.

40"For he who is not against us is ²⁶for us.

41"For whoever gives you a cup of water to drinkᵀbecause of your name as *followers* of Christ, truly I say to you, he shall not lose his reward.   *in a name that you are Christ's*

Warning About Hell
Matt. 18:6–9

42"And whoever causes one of theseᵀlittle ones who believe to stumble, it would be better for him if, with a heavy millstone hung around his neck, heᵀhad been cast into the sea.   humble • *has been cast*

43"And if your hand causes you to stumble, cut it off; it is better for you to enter life crippled, than having your two hands, to go into hell, into the unquenchable fire,

44 [²⁷where THEIR WORM DOES NOT DIE, AND ᵀHE FIRE IS NOT QUENCHED.]

45"And if your foot causes you to stumble, cut it off; it is better for you to enter life lame, than having your two feet, to be cast intoᵀhell,ᴿ   Gr., *Gehenna* • Matt. 5:22

46 [²⁷where THEIR WORM DOES NOT DIE, AND THE FIRE IS NOT QUENCHED.]

47"And if your eye causes you to stumble, cast it out; it is better for you to enter the kingdom of God with one eye, than having two eyes, to be cast intoᵀhell,   Gr., *Gehenna*

48 ᴿwhere THEIR WORM DOES NOT DIE, AND THE FIRE IS NOT QUENCHED.   Is. 66:24

49"For everyone will be salted with fire.

50"Salt is good; but if the salt becomes unsalty, with what will you ᵀmake it salty *again*? Have salt in yourselves, and be at peace with one another."   *season it*

CHAPTER 10

Marriage and Divorce
Matt. 19:1–9

Aᴺᴰᴿrising up, He *went from there to the region of Judea, and beyond the Jordan; and crowds *gathered around Him again, and, according to His custom, He once more *began* to teach them.   Mark 10:1-12; *Matt. 19:1-9*

2 And *some* Pharisees came up to Him, testing Him, and *began* to question Him whether it was lawful for a man to divorce a wife.

3 And He answered and said to them, "What did Moses command you?"

4 And they said, "Mosesᴿ permitted *a man* TO WRITE A CERTIFICATE OF DIVORCE ANDᐱSEND *her* AWAY."   Matt. 5:31 • *divorce her*

5 But Jesus said to them, "Becauseᴬᴿof your hardness of heart he wrote you this commandment.   *With reference to* • Matt. 19:8

6"But ᴿfrom the beginning of creation, *God* MADE THEM MALE AND FEMALE. 2 Pet. 3:4

7"FORᴿTHIS CAUSE A MAN SHALL LEAVE HIS FATHER AND MOTHER,²⁸   Gen. 2:24

8 ᴿAND THE TWO SHALL BECOME ONE FLESH; consequently they are no longer two, but one flesh.   Gen. 2:24

9"What therefore God has joined together, let no man separate."

10 And in the house the disciples *began* questioning Him about this again.

11 And He *said to them, "Whoeverᴿdivorces his wife and marries another woman commits adultery against her;   [Matt. 5:32]

12 andᴿif she herself divorces her husband and marries another man, she is committing adultery."   1 Cor. 7:11, 13

Children and the Kingdom
Matt. 19:13–15; Luke 18:15–17

13 ᴿAnd they were bringing children to Him so that He might touch them; and the disciples rebuked them.   Luke 18:15-17

14 But when Jesus saw this, He was indignant and said to them, "Permit the children to come to Me; do not hinder them; for the kingdom of God belongs to such as these.

15"Truly I say to you,ᴿwhoever does not receive the kingdom of God like a child shall not enter it *at all.*"   [1 Cor. 14:20; 1 Pet. 2:2]

16 And Heᴿtook them in His arms and *began* blessing them, laying His hands upon them.   Mark 9:36

Rich Young Ruler
Matt. 19:16–22; Luke 18:18–23

17 ᴿAnd as He was setting out on a journey, a man ran up to Him andᴿknelt before

---

²⁶ Or, *on our side*
²⁷ Vv. 44 and 46, which are identical with v. 48, are not found in the best ancient mss.
²⁸ Some mss. add: *and shall cleave to his wife*

Him, and *began* asking Him, "Good Teacher, what shall I do to inherit eternal life?"   Mark 10:17-31 • Mark 1:40

18 And Jesus said to him, "Why do you call Me good? No one is good except God alone.

19"You know the commandments, 'Do[R] NOT MURDER, DO NOT COMMIT ADULTERY, DO NOT STEAL, DO NOT BEAR FALSE WITNESS, Do not defraud, HONOR YOUR FATHER AND MOTHER.' "   Ex. 20:12-16; Deut. 5:16-20

20 And he said to Him, "Teacher, I have kept all these things from my youth up."

21 And looking at him, Jesus felt a love for him, and said to him, "One thing you lack: go and sell all you possess, and give to the poor, and you shall have [R]treasure in heaven; and come, follow Me."   Matt. 6:20

22 But at these words^his face fell, and he went away grieved, for he was one who owned much property.   *he became gloomy*

Difficulty of Riches
Matt. 19:23-26; Luke 18:24-27

23 And Jesus, looking around, *said to His disciples, "How[R]hard it will be for those who are wealthy to enter the kingdom of God!"   Matt. 19:23

24 And the disciples[R]were amazed at His words. But Jesus *answered again and *said to them, "Children, how hard it is [29]to enter the kingdom of God!   Mark 1:27

25"It is easier for a camel to go through the eye of[T]a needle than for a rich man to enter the kingdom of God."   *the*

26 And they were even more astonished and said to Him, "Then who can be saved?"

27 Looking upon them, Jesus *said, "With[R] men it is impossible, but not with God; for all things are possible with God."   Matt. 19:26

Eternal Reward
Matt. 19:27-30; Luke 18:28-30

28 Peter began to say to Him, "Behold, we have left everything and followed You."

29 Jesus said, "Truly I say to you,[R]there is no one who has left house or brothers or sisters or mother or father or children or farms, for My sake and for the gospel's sake,   [Matt. 6:33; 19:29]; Luke 18:29f.

30 but that he shall receive a hundred times as much now in [T]the present age, houses and brothers and sisters and mothers and children and farms, along with persecutions; and in[R]the age to come, eternal life.   *this time* • Matt. 12:32

[29] Later mss. insert: *for those who trust in wealth*
[30] Or, *betrayed*

31"But[R]many *who are* first, will be last; and the last, first." Matt. 19:30; 20:16; Luke 13:30

Coming Crucifixion
Matt. 20:17-19; Luke 18:31-34

32 And they were on the road, going up to Jerusalem, and Jesus was walking on ahead of them; and they[R]were amazed, and those who followed were fearful. And again He took the twelve aside and began to tell them what was going to happen to Him,   Mark 1:27

33 *saying,* "Behold, we are going up to Jerusalem, and the Son of Man[R]will be [30]delivered to the chief priests and the scribes; and they will condemn Him to death, and will deliver Him to the Gentiles.   Mark 14:53, 64☆

34"And they will mock Him and spit upon Him, and scourge Him, and kill *Him,* and three days later He will rise again."

"Whoever Wishes to Become Great"
Matt. 20:20-28

35 [R]And [A]James and John, the two sons of Zebedee, *came up to Him, saying to Him, "Teacher, we want You to do for us whatever we ask of You."   Mark 10:35-45 • *Jacob*

36 And He said to them, "What do you want Me to do for you?"

37 And they said to Him, "Grant[T]that we may sit in Your glory, one on Your right, and one on *Your* left."   *Give to us*

38 But Jesus said to them, "You do not know what you are asking for. Are you able [R]to drink the cup that I drink, or[R]to be baptized with the baptism with which I am baptized?"   Matt. 20:22 • Luke 12:50

39 And they said to Him, "We are able." And Jesus said to them, "The cup that I drink[R]you shall drink; and you shall be baptized with the baptism with which I am baptized.   Acts 12:2; Rev. 1:9

40"But to sit on My right or on *My* left, this is not Mine to give;[R]but it is for those for whom it has been prepared."   Matt. 13:11

41 And hearing this, the ten began to feel indignant with [A]James and John.   *Jacob*

42 And calling them to Himself, Jesus *said to them, "You know that those who are recognized as rulers of the Gentiles lord it over them; and their great men exercise authority over them.

43"But it is not so among you,[R]but whoever wishes to become great among you shall be your servant;   Matt. 20:26; Luke 22:26

44 and whoever wishes to be first among you shall be slave of all.

45"For even the Son of Man did not come to be served, but to serve, and to give[R]His^life a ransom for many."   Is. 53:12☆ • *soul*

10:45   The Ministry of the Son of God—The ministry of Christ is threefold:
a.   He is Savior. The title *Savior* implies many important and interrelated truths: the need of sinful men to be saved (Page 1217—1 Tim. 1:15); the qualifications of Christ as God–man to be our Savior (Page 1077—John 10:18); the humiliating death He experienced to become our Savior (Page 1086—John 19:18); the victorious, bodily

(continued on next page)

Blind Bartimaeus Is Healed
Matt. 20:29–34; Luke 18:35–43

46 ᴿAnd they *came to Jericho. And as He was going out from Jericho with His disciples and a great multitude, a blind beggar *named* Bartimaeus, the son of Timaeus, was sitting by the road. Mark 10:46-52; *Luke 18:35-43*
47 And when he heard that it was Jesus the Nazarene, he began to cry out and say, "Jesus, Son of David, have mercy on me!"
48 And many were sternly telling him to be quiet, but he kept crying out all the more, "Son of David, have mercy on me!"
49 And Jesus stopped and said, "Call him here." And they *called the blind man, saying to him, "Takeᴿcourage, arise! He is calling for you."   Matt. 9:2
50 And casting aside his cloak, he jumped up, and came to Jesus.
51 And answering him, Jesus said, "What do you want Me to do for you?" And the blind man said to Him, "³¹Rabboniᴿ, *I want* to regain my sight!"   Matt. 23:7; John 20:16
52 And Jesus said to him, "Go your way; your faith hasᵀmade you well." And immediately he regained his sight and *began* following Him on the road.   *saved you*

<h3 style="text-align:center">CHAPTER 11</h3>

The Triumphal Entry
Matt. 21:1–11; Luke 19:29–40

Aɴᴅ as they *approached Jerusalem, at Bethphage and Bethany, near the Mount of Olives, He *sent two of His disciples,
2 and *said to them, "Go into the village opposite you, and immediately as you enter it, you will find a colt tied *there,* on which no one yet has ever sat; untie it and bring it here.
3"And if anyone says to you, 'Why are you doing this?' you say, 'The Lord has need of it'; and immediately heᵀwill send it back here."   *sends*
4 And they went away and found a colt

tied at the door outside in the street; and they *untied it.
5 And some of the bystanders were saying to them, "What are you doing, untying the colt?"
6 And they spoke to them just as Jesus had told *them,* and they gave them permission.
7 ᴿAnd they *brought the colt to Jesus and put their garments on it; andᴿHe sat upon it.   Matt. 21:4–9; Mark 11:7-10 • Zech. 9:9★
8 And many spread their garments in the road, and others *spread* leafy branches which they had cut from the fields.
9 And those who went before, and those who followed after, were crying out,
    ᴿ"Hosanna!   Ps. 118:26★
    ᴿBʟᴇssᴇᴅ ɪs Hᴇ ᴡʜᴏ ᴄᴏᴍᴇs ɪɴ ᴛʜᴇ
        ɴᴀᴍᴇ ᴏғ ᴛʜᴇ Lᴏʀᴅ;   Matt. 21:9
10 Blessed *is* the coming kingdom of our
        father David;
    Hosannaᴿin the highest!"   Matt. 21:9
11 AndᴿHe entered Jerusalem *and came* into the temple; and after looking all around, He departed for Bethany with the twelve, since it was already late.   Matt. 21:12

A Fig Tree Is Cursed
Matt. 21:18, 19

12 And on the next day, when they had departed from Bethany, He became hungry.
13 And seeing at a distance a fig tree in leaf, He went *to see* if perhaps He would find anything on it; and when He came to it, He found nothing but leaves, for it was not the season for figs.
14 And He answered and said to it, "May no one ever eat fruit from you again!" His disciples were listening.

The Temple Is Cleansed
Matt. 21:12, 13; Luke 19:45, 46

15 ᴿAnd they *came to Jerusalem. And He entered the temple and began to cast out

³¹ I.e., My Master

(continued from previous page)
   resurrection He experienced as a sure guarantee of our salvation (Page 1160—1 Cor. 15:13–22); and the glorious results of salvation (Page 1069—John 5:24). It is no wonder that in light of these precious realities Paul speaks of Christ as "our great God and Savior" (Page 1230—Titus 2:13).
b. He is High Priest. The high priest was of supreme importance in the Old Testament. It was on the basis of his mediation for the people before God on the Day of Atonement that they were brought near to God and protected from judgment (Page 111—Lev. 16:16). Therefore his qualifications were exacting: appointed by God, physically perfect, ceremonially pure, etc. (Page 115—Lev. 21). Jesus is eminently qualified to be our High Priest: He was appointed by God (Page1241—Heb. 5:5); He is eternal (Page 1243—Heb. 7:24, 25); He is sinless (Page 1243—Heb. 7:26); His offering was final (Page 1245—Heb. 9:28); and His mediation is effective (Page 1138—Rom. 8:34; Page 1243—Heb. 7:25; Page 1274—1 John 2:1). As the only qualified High Priest for men and women, Jesus Christ thus constitutes the only way to God (Page 1217—1 Tim. 2:5).
c. He is King. The position of king implies sovereign authority and rule over all. The Scriptures clearly teach that this right belongs only to Jesus Christ who is called "Lord of lords and King of kings" (Page 1304—Rev. 17:14; 19:16). This title means that He is destined to rule as king and that every knee must ultimately bow and acknowledge His authority (Page 1194—Phil. 2:10). Those who acknowledge Christ as King and Lord in this life will reign with Him; those who do not will be judged by Him (Page 1306—Rev. 20:11–15). The weight of eternity hangs on this solemn decision.
   Now turn to Page 1187—Eph. 4:3: The Person of the Holy Spirit.

those who were buying and selling in the temple, and overturned the tables of the moneychangers and the seats of those who were selling doves;   John 2:13-16 • Mal. 3:1★

16 and He would not permit anyone to carry[T]goods through the temple.   *a vessel*

17 And He *began* to teach and say to them, "Is it not written, 'MY HOUSE SHALL BE CALLED A HOUSE OF PRAYER FOR ALL THE NATIONS'? But you have made it a ROBBERS' [T]DEN."   *cave*

18 And the chief priests and the scribes heard *this*, and[R]*began* seeking how to destroy Him; for they were afraid of Him, for [R]all the multitude was astonished at His teaching.   Matt. 21:46 • Matt. 7:28

19 And whenever evening came, [T]they would go out of the city.   Jesus and His disciples

Power of Faith
Matt. 21:20-22

20 [R]And as they were passing by in the morning, they saw the fig tree withered from the roots *up*.   Mark 11:12-14, 20-24

21 And being reminded, Peter *said to Him, "Rabbi,[R] behold, the fig tree which You cursed has withered."   Matt. 23:7

22 And Jesus *answered saying to them, "Have[R]faith in God.   Matt. 17:20; 21:21f.

23 "Truly[R]I say to you, whoever says to this mountain, 'Be taken up and cast into the sea,' and does not doubt in his heart, but believes that what he says is going to happen, it shall be *granted* him.   [1 Cor. 13:2]

24 "Therefore I say to you,[R]all things for which you pray and ask, believe that you have received them, and they shall be *granted* you.   Matt. 7:7f.

Necessity of Forgiveness

25 "And whenever you stand praying, forgive, if you have anything against anyone; so that your Father also who is in heaven may forgive you your transgressions.

26 ["[32]But[R] if you do not forgive, neither will your Father who is in heaven forgive your transgressions."]   Matt. 6:15; 18:35

Question of Authority
Matt. 21:23-27; Luke 20:1-8

27 And they *came again to Jerusalem. [R]And as He was walking in the temple, the chief priests, and scribes, and elders *came to Him,   Matt. 21:23-27; Luke 20:1-8

28 and *began* saying to Him, "By what authority are You doing these things, or who gave You this authority to do these things?"

29 And Jesus said to them, "I will ask you one question, and you answer Me, and *then* I will tell you by what authority I do these things.

30 "Was the baptism of John from heaven, or from men? Answer Me."

31 And they *began* reasoning among themselves, saying, "If we say, 'From heaven,' He will say, 'Then why did you not believe him?'

32 "But shall we say, 'From men'?"—they were afraid of the multitude, for all considered John to have been a prophet indeed.

33 And answering Jesus, they *said, "We do not know." And Jesus *said to them, "Neither[T]will I tell you by what authority I do these things."   *do I tell*

CHAPTER 12

Parable of the Vineyard Owner
Matt. 21:33-46; Luke 20:9-19

AND[R]He began to speak to them in parables: "A man PLANTED A VINEYARD, AND PUT A[A]WALL AROUND IT, AND DUG A VAT UNDER THE WINE PRESS, AND BUILT A TOWER, and rented it out to [33]vine-growers and went on a journey.   Mark 3:23; 4:2ff. • *fence*

2 "And at the *harvest* time he sent a slave to the vine-growers, in order to receive *some* of the produce of the vineyard from the vine-growers.

3 "And they took him, and beat him, and sent him away empty-handed.

4 "And again he sent them another slave, and they wounded him in the head, and treated him shamefully.

5 "And he sent another, and that one they killed; and *so with* many others, beating some, and killing others.

6 "He had one more *to send*, a beloved son; he sent him last *of all* to them, saying, 'They will respect my son.'

7 "But those vine-growers said to one another, 'This is the heir; come, let us kill him, and the inheritance will be ours!'

8 "And they took him, and killed him, and threw him out of the vineyard.

9 "What will the [T]owner of the vineyard do? He will come and destroy the vine-growers, and will give the vineyard to others.   *lord*

10 "Have you not even read this Scripture: 'THE[R] STONE WHICH THE BUILDERS REJECTED,   Ps. 118:22★
THIS BECAME THE CHIEF CORNER *stone;*

11 THIS CAME ABOUT FROM THE LORD,
AND IT IS MARVELOUS IN OUR EYES'?"

12 And[R]they were seeking to seize Him; and *yet* they feared the multitude; for they understood that He spoke the parable against them. And *so*[R]they left Him, and went away.   Mark 11:18 • Matt. 22:22

Question of Taxes
Matt. 22:15-22; Luke 20:20-26

13 [R]And they *sent some of the Pharisees and[R]Herodians to Him, in order to trap Him in a statement.   Mark 12:13-17 • Matt. 22:16

[32] Many mss. do not contain this verse
[33] Or, *tenant farmers*, also vv. 2, 7, 9

14 And they *came and *said to Him, "Teacher, we know that You are truthful, and defer to no one; for You are not partial to any, but teach the way of God in truth. Is it lawful to pay a poll-tax to Caesar, or not?

15"Shall we pay, or shall we not pay?" But He, knowing their hypocrisy, said to them, "Why are you testing Me? Bring Me a ³⁴denarius to look at."

16 And they brought one. And He *said to them, "Whose likeness and inscription is this?" And they said to Him, "Caesar's."

17 And Jesus said to them, "Render to Caesar the things that are Caesar's, and to God the things that are God's." And they ^were amazed at Him.   were greatly marveling

Question of the Resurrection
Matt. 22:23–33; Luke 20:27–40

18 ᴿAnd some Sadducees (who say that there is no resurrection) *came to Him, and began questioning Him, saying, Mark 12:18-27

19"Teacher, Moses wrote for us thatᴿIF A MAN'S BROTHER DIES, and leaves behind a wife, AND LEAVES NO CHILD, HIS BROTHER SHOULD TAKE THE WIFE, AND RAISE UP OFFSPRING TO HIS BROTHER.   Deut. 25:5

20"There were seven brothers; and the first took a wife, and died, leaving no offspring.

21"And the second one took her, and died, leaving behind no offspring; and the third likewise;

22 and soᵀall seven left no offspring. Last of all the woman died also.   the seven

23"In the resurrection, ³⁵when they rise again, which one's wife will she be? Forᵀall seven had her as wife."   the seven

24 Jesus said to them, "Is this not the reason you are mistaken, that you do not^understand the Scriptures, or the power of God?   know

25"For when they rise from the dead, they neither marry, nor are given in marriage, but are like angels in heaven.

26"But regarding the fact that the dead rise again, have you not read in the book of Moses, ᴿin the passage about the burning bush, how God spoke to him, saying, 'I AM THE GOD OF ABRAHAM, AND THE GOD OF ISAAC, AND THE GOD OF JACOB'?   Luke 20:37

27"He is not the God of the dead, but of the living; you are greatly mistaken."

Question of the Greatest Commandment
Matt. 22:34–40

28 And one of the scribes came and heard them arguing, and recognizing that He had answered them well, asked Him, "What commandment is the foremost of all?"

29 Jesus answered, "The foremost is, 'HEARᴿ O ISRAEL! THE LORD OUR GOD IS ONE LORD;   Deut. 6:4

30 ᴿAND YOU SHALL LOVE THE LORD YOUR GOD WITH ALL YOUR HEART, AND WITH ALL YOUR SOUL, AND WITH ALL YOUR MIND, AND WITH ALL YOUR STRENGTH.'   Deut. 6:5

31"The second is this, 'YOU SHALL LOVE YOUR NEIGHBOR AS YOURSELF.' There is no other commandment greater than these."

32 And the scribe said to Him, "Right, Teacher, You have truly stated thatᴿHE IS ONE; AND THERE IS NO ONE ELSE BESIDES HIM;   Deut. 4:35

33 ᴿAND TO LOVE HIM WITH ALL THE HEART AND WITH ALL THE UNDERSTANDING AND WITH ALL THE STRENGTH, AND TO LOVE ONE'S NEIGHBOR AS HIMSELF, is much more than all burnt offerings and sacrifices."   Deut. 6:5

34 And when Jesus saw that he had answered intelligently, He said to him, "You are not far from the kingdom of God." ᴿAnd after that, no one would venture to ask Him any more questions.   Matt. 22:46

Jesus Questions the Leaders
Matt. 22:41–45; Luke 20:41–44

35 ᴿAnd Jesus answering began to say, as He taught in the temple, "How is it that the scribes say thatᵀthe Christ is the son of David?   Mark 12:35-37 • the Messiah

36"David himself said in the Holy Spirit, 'THEᴿLORD SAID TO MY LORD,   Ps. 110:1
"SIT AT MY RIGHT HAND,
UNTIL I PUT THINE ENEMIES BENEATH THY FEET."'

37"David himself calls Him 'Lord'; and so in what sense is He his son?" Andᴿthe great crowd enjoyed listening to Him.   John 12:9

Jesus Condemns the Leaders
Matt. 23:1–14; Luke 20:45—21:4

38 ᴿAnd in His teaching He was saying: "Beware of the scribes who like to walk around in long robes, and like respectful greetings in the market places,   Mark 12:38-40

39 and chief seats in the synagogues, and places of honor at banquets,

40 who devour widows' houses, and for appearance's sake offer long prayers; these will receive greater condemnation."

41 ᴿAnd He sat down opposite the treasury, and began observing how the multitude were puttingᵀmoney into the treasury; and many rich people were putting in large sums.   Luke 21:1-4 • copper coins

42 And a poor widow came and put in two small copper coins, which amount to a cent.

43 And calling His disciples to Him, He said to them, "Truly I say to you, this poor widow put in more than allᵀthe contributors to the treasury;   those who were putting in

44 for they all put in out of their^surplus, but she, out of her poverty, put in all she owned, all she had to live on."   abundance

---

³⁴ The denarius was equivalent to one day's wage
³⁵ Most ancient mss. do not contain when they rise again

CHAPTER 13

Questions from the Disciples
Matt. 24:1–3; Luke 21:5–7

A ND[R] as He was going out of the temple, one of His disciples *said to Him, "Teacher, behold [36]what wonderful stones and what wonderful buildings!"   Mark 13:1-37; *Matt. 24*

2 And Jesus said to him, "Do you see these great buildings? [R]Not one stone shall be left upon another which will not be torn down."   Luke 19:44

3 And as He was sitting on[R]the Mount of Olives opposite the temple, Peter and [A]James and John and Andrew were questioning Him privately,   Matt. 21:1 • *Jacob*

4"Tell us, when will these things be, and what *will be* the [A]sign when all these things are going to be fulfilled?"   *attesting miracle*

The Tribulation
Matt. 24:4–26; Luke 21:8–24

5 And Jesus began to say to them, "See to it that no one misleads you.

6"Many will come in My name, saying, 'I[R] am *He!*' and will mislead many.   John 8:24

7"And when you hear of wars and rumors of wars, do not be frightened; *those things* must take place; but *that is* not yet the end.

8"For nation will arise against nation, and kingdom against kingdom; there will be earthquakes in various places; there will *also* be famines. These things are *merely* the beginning of birth pangs.

9"But[T]be on your guard; for they will deliver you to *the* courts, and you will be flogged in *the* synagogues, and you will stand before governors and kings for My sake, as a testimony to them. *look to yourselves*

10"And[R]the gospel must first be preached to all the nations.   Matt. 24:14

11"And when they[T]arrest you and deliver you up, do not be anxious beforehand about what you are to say, but say whatever is given you in that hour; for it is not you who speak, but *it is* the Holy Spirit.   *lead*

12"And brother will deliver brother to death, and a father *his* child; and children will rise up against parents and[T]have them put to death.   *put them to death*

13"And [R]you will be hated by all on account of My name, but the one who endures to the end, he shall be saved.   Matt. 10:22

14"But when you see the ABOMINATION OF DESOLATION standing where it should not be (let the reader understand), then let those who are in Judea flee to the mountains.

15"And[R]let him who is on the housetop not go down, or enter in, to get anything out of his house;   Luke 17:31

16 and let him who is in the field not turn back to get his cloak.

17"But woe to those who are with child and to those who nurse babes in those days!

18"But pray that it may not happen in the winter.

19"For those days will be a *time of* tribulation such as has not occurred[R]since the beginning of the creation which God created, until now, and never shall.   Dan. 12:1

20"And unless the Lord had shortened *those* days, no[T]life would have been saved; but for the sake of the[A]elect whom He chose, He shortened the days.   *flesh • chosen ones*

21"And then if anyone says to you, 'Behold, here is[T]the Christ'; or, 'Behold, *He is* there'; do not believe *him;*   the Messiah

22 for false Christs and false prophets will arise, and will show signs and wonders, in order, if possible, to lead the elect astray.

23"But take heed; behold, I have told you everything in advance.

The Second Coming
Matt. 24:29–31; Luke 21:25–28

24"But in those days, after that tribulation, THE SUN WILL BE DARKENED, AND THE MOON WILL NOT GIVE ITS LIGHT,

25 AND THE STARS WILL BE FALLING from heaven, and the powers that are in the heavens will be shaken.

26"And then they will see[R]THE SON OF MAN [R]COMING IN CLOUDS with great power and glory.   [Dan. 7:13] • [Matt. 16:27; Mark 8:38] ☆

27"And then He will send forth the angels, and will gather together His elect from the four winds, [R]from the farthest end of the earth, to the farthest end of heaven. Zech. 2:6

Parable of the Fig Tree
Matt. 24:32–35

28"Now learn the parable from the fig tree: when its branch has already become tender, and puts forth its leaves, you know that summer is near.

29"Even so, you too, when you see these things happening,[T]recognize that[A]He is near, *right* at the door.   *know • it*

30"Truly I say to you, this [37]generation will not pass away until all these things take place.

31"Heaven and earth will pass away, but My words will not pass away.

Exhortation to Be Alert
Matt. 24:36–51; Luke 21:34–36

32"But[R]of that day or hour no one knows, not even the angels in heaven, nor the Son, but the Father *alone.*   Matt. 24:36; Acts 1:7

33"Take heed, keep on the alert; for you do not know when the *appointed* time is.

34"*It is* like a man, away on a journey, *who* upon leaving his house and[T]putting his slaves in charge, *assigning* to each one his task, also commanded the doorkeeper to stay on the alert.   *giving the authority to*

[36] Lit., *how great*   [37] Or, *race*

35"Therefore, be on the alert—for you do not know when the master of the house is coming, whether in the evening, at midnight, at cockcrowing, or in the morning—
36 lest he come suddenly and find you ^Rasleep. [Rom. 13:11]
37"And what I say to you I say to all, 'Be^R on the alert!' "   Matt. 24:42; Mark 13:35

CHAPTER 14

Leaders Plot to Kill Jesus
Matt. 26:1–5; Luke 22:1, 2

N^ROW the Passover and Unleavened Bread was two days off; and the chief priests and the scribes were seeking how to seize Him by stealth, and kill *Him;*   Mark 14:1
2 for they were saying, "Not during the festival, lest there be a riot of the people."

Mary Anoints Jesus
Matt. 26:6–13; John 12:2–8

3 ^RAnd while He was in ^RBethany at the home of Simon the leper, and reclining *at the table,* there came a woman with an alabaster vial of very costly perfume of pure nard; *and* she broke the vial and poured it over His head.   Mark 14:3-9 • Matt. 21:17
4 But some were indignantly *remarking* to one another, "Why has this perfume been wasted?
5"For this perfume might have been sold for over three hundred ³⁸denarii, and *the money* given to the poor." And they were scolding her.
6 But Jesus said, "Let her alone; why do you bother her? She has done a good deed to Me.
7"For the poor you always have with you, and whenever you wish, you can do them good; but you do not always have Me.
8"She has done what she could; she has anointed My body beforehand for the burial.
9"And truly I say to you, ^Rwherever the gospel is preached in the whole world, that also which this woman has done shall be spoken of in memory of her."   Matt. 26:13

Judas Plans to Betray Jesus
Matt. 26:14–16; Luke 22:3–6

10 And Judas Iscariot, who was one of the twelve, went off to the chief priests, in order to^Abetray Him to them.   *deliver Him up*
11 And they were glad when they heard *this,* and promised to give him money. And he *began* seeking how to betray Him at an opportune time.

The Passover Is Prepared
Matt. 26:17–19; Luke 22:7–13

12 ^RAnd on the first day of Unleavened Bread, when the Passover *lamb* was being

sacrificed, His disciples *said to Him, "Where do You want us to go and prepare for You to eat the Passover?"   Mark 14:12-16
13 And He *sent two of His disciples, and *said to them, "Go into the city, and a man will meet you carrying a pitcher of water; follow him;
14 and wherever he enters, say to the owner of the house, 'The Teacher says, "Where is My guest room in which I may eat the Passover with My disciples?" '
15"And he himself will show you a large upper room furnished *and* ready; and prepare for us there."
16 And the disciples went out, and came to the city, and found *it* just as He had told them; and they prepared the Passover.

The Passover Is Celebrated
Matt. 26:20–25; Luke 22:14–16; John 13:21–30

17 ^RAnd when it was evening He *came with the twelve.   Mark 14:17-21; Luke 22:14
18 And as they were reclining *at the table* and eating, Jesus said, "Truly I say to you that one of you will^Abetray Me—one^R who is eating with Me."   *deliver Me up* • Ps. 41:9☆
19 They began to be grieved and to say to Him one by one, "Surely not I?"
20 And He said to them, "*It* is one of the twelve, one who dips with Me in the bowl.
21"For the Son of Man *is* to go, just as it is written of Him; but woe to that man by whom the Son of Man is betrayed! It would have been good^Tfor that man if he had not been born."   *for him if that man had not been born*

The Lord's Supper Is Instituted
Matt. 26:26–29; Luke 22:17–23

22 And while they were eating, He took *some* bread, and^Tafter a blessing He broke *it;* and gave *it* to them, and said, "Take *it;* this is My body."   *having blessed*
23 And when He had taken a cup, *and* given thanks, He gave *it* to them; and they all drank from it.
24 And He said to them, "This is My^Rblood of the ^Rcovenant, which is poured out for many.   Ex. 24:8 • [Jer. 31:31–34]
25"Truly I say to you, I shall never again drink of the fruit of the vine until that day when I drink it new in the kingdom of God."

Jesus Predicts Peter's Denial
Matt. 26:30–35; Luke 22:31–39; John 13:36–38

26 ^RAnd after singing a hymn, they went out to the Mount of Olives.   Matt. 26:30
27 And Jesus *said to them, "You will all ^Afall away, because it is written, 'I^R WILL STRIKE DOWN THE SHEPHERD, AND THE SHEEP SHALL BE SCATTERED.'   *stumble* • Zech. 13:7

³⁸ The denarius was equivalent to one day's wage

28"But after I have been raised,ᴿI will go before you to Galilee."   Matt. 28:16
29 But Peter said to Him, "*Even* though all may^fall away, yet I will not."   *stumble*
30 And Jesus *said to him, "Truly I say to you, that you yourself ᵀthisᴿ very night, before a cock crows twice, shall three times deny Me."   *today, on this night* • Matt. 26:34 ☆
31 But *Peter* kept saying insistently, "*Even* if I have to die with You, I will not deny You!" And they all were saying the same thing, too.

Jesus Prays In Gethsemane
Matt. 26:36–46; Luke 22:39–46

32 ᴿAnd they *came to a place named Gethsemane; and He *said to His disciples, "Sit here until I have prayed."   Mark 14:32-42
33 And He *took with Him Peter and ^James and John, and began to be veryᴿ distressed and troubled.   *Jacob* • Mark 9:15
34 And He *said to them, "Myᴿ soul is deeply grieved to the point of death; remain here and keep watch."   Matt. 26:38; John 12:27
35 And He went a little beyond *them*, and ᵀfell to the ground, and *began* to pray that if it were possible, the hour mightᵀ pass Him by.   *was falling • pass from Him*
36 And He was saying, "Abba!ᴿFather! All things are possible for Thee; remove this cup from Me;ᴿyet not what I will, but what Thou wilt."   Rom. 8:15; Gal. 4:6★ • Matt. 26:39
37 And He *came and *found them sleeping, and *said to Peter, "Simon, are you asleep? Could you not keep watch for one hour?

38"KeepᴿWatching and praying, that you may not come into temptation; the spirit is willing, but the flesh is weak."   Matt. 26:41

39 And again He went away and prayed, saying the sameᵀwords.   *word*
40 And again He came and found them sleeping, for their eyes were very heavy; and they did not know what to answer Him.
41 And He *came the third time, and *said to them, "Are you still sleeping and taking your rest? It is enough; the hour has come; behold, the Son of Man is being^betrayed into the hands of sinners. *delivered up*
42"Arise, let us be going; behold, the one who betrays Me is at hand!"   Matt. 26:21★

Judas Betrays Jesus
Matt. 26:47–56; Luke 22:47–53;
John 18:1–11

43 And immediately while He was still speaking, Judas, one of the twelve, *came up, ᵀaccompanied by a multitude with swords and clubs, from the chief priests and the scribes and the elders.   *and with him*
44 Now he who was betraying Him had given them a signal, saying, "Whomever I shall kiss, He is the one; seize Him, and lead Him away ᵀunder guard."   *safely*
45 And after coming, he immediately went to Him, saying, "Rabbi!" ᴿand kissed Him.   Matt. 23:7
46 And they laid hands on Him, and seized Him.
47 But a certain one of those who stood by drew his sword, and struck the slave of the high priest, andᵀcut off his ear.   *took off*
48 And Jesus answered and said to them, "Have you come out with swords and clubs to arrest Me, as against a robber?
49"Every day I was with you in the temple teaching, and you did not seize Me; but^this *has happened* that the Scriptures might be fulfilled."   *let the Scriptures be fulfilled*
50 And they all left Him and fled.
51 And a certain young man was following Him, wearing *nothing but* a linen sheet over *his* naked *body;* and they *seized him.
52 But he left the linen sheet behind, and escaped naked.

The Sanhedrin Tries Jesus
Matt. 26:57–68; Luke 22:54, 55,
63–65; John 18:12, 18, 24

53 And they led Jesus away to the high priest; and all the chief priests and the elders and the scribes *gathered together.
54 And Peter had followed Him at a distance, right into the courtyard of the high priest; and he was sitting with the^officers, and warming himself at the fire.   *servants*

14:38 Temptation by the Flesh—*Flesh* in the Bible often means something other than the substance of the human body. It is used constantly to refer to the carnal, sinful principle within man that is opposed to God (Page 1137—Rom. 8:7). The actions produced by the flesh are given in detail in Galatians 5:19–21. Among these are all types of sexual immorality, impurity, hatred, anger, false religions, envy, and drunkenness. A person whose life is characterized by these sins cannot be a true Christian and is under the wrath of God (Page 1181—Gal. 5:21; Page 1185—Eph. 2:3).
Though the flesh is not eradicated for the Christian, he does not have to obey it (Page 1136—Rom. 7:15–25). He possesses a new nature empowered by the Holy Spirit. Since the flesh and the Spirit are totally opposed to each other, the one whom the believer allows to dominate him will take charge in his life and produce its own fruit. The solution to the urges of the flesh lies in acknowledging that the power of sin was nullified by Jesus' death (Page 1135—Rom. 6:11) and in living under the control of the Spirit's power (Page 1181—Gal. 5:16). The latter is a moment-by-moment dependence in faith on the Spirit's power. The believer must choose by an act of his will to benefit from the Spirit's enablement.
Now turn to Page 435—2 Chr. 21:1: Temptation by Satan.

55 Now the chief priests and the whole [39]Council[R] kept trying to obtain testimony against Jesus to put Him to death; and they were not finding any.   Matt. 5:22

56 For many were giving false testimony against Him, and *yet* their testimony was not consistent.

57 And some stood up and *began* to give false testimony against Him, saying,

58 "We heard Him say, 'I will destroy this temple made with hands, and in three days I will build another made without hands.'"

59 And not even in this respect was their testimony consistent.

60 And the high priest stood up *and came* forward and questioned Jesus, saying, "Do You make no answer? What is it that these men are testifying against You?"

61 But He kept silent, and made no answer. Again the high priest was questioning Him, and [T]saying to Him, "Are You the Christ, the Son of the Blessed *One?*"   says

62 And Jesus said, "I am; and you shall see[E]THE SON OF MAN SITTING AT THE RIGHT HAND OF POWER, and [R]COMING WITH THE CLOUDS OF HEAVEN."   Ps. 110:1 • Dan. 7:13

63 And[R]tearing his clothes, the high priest *said, "What further need do we have of witnesses?   Num. 14:6; Matt. 26:65; Acts 14:14

64 "You have heard the blasphemy; how does it seem to you?" And they all condemned Him to be deserving of death.

65 And some began to[R]spit at Him, and[^]to blindfold Him, and to beat Him with their fists, and to say to Him, "Prophesy!" And the officers[^]received Him with slaps *in the face*.   Is. 50:6 ★ • *cover over His face* • *treated*

Peter Denies Jesus
Matt. 26:69–75; Luke 22:55–62;
John 18:15–18, 25–27

66 [R]And as Peter was below in[R]the courtyard, one of the servant-girls of the high priest *came,   Mark 14:66-72 • Mark 14:54

67 and seeing Peter[R]warming himself, she looked at him, and *said, "You, too, were with Jesus the Nazarene."   Mark 14:54

68 But he denied *it*, saying, "I neither know nor understand what you are talking about." And he went out onto the porch.[40]

69 And the maid saw him, and began once more to say to the bystanders, "This is *one* of them!"

70 But again[R]he was denying it. And after a little while the bystanders were again saying to Peter, "Surely you are *one* of them, for you are a Galilean too."   Mark 14:68

71 But he began to curse and swear, "I do not know this man you are talking about!"

72 And immediately a cock crowed a second time. And Peter remembered how Jesus had made the remark to him, "Before[R]a cock crows twice, you will deny Me three times." And he began to weep.   Mark 14:30, 68 ★

CHAPTER 15

Pilate Tries Jesus
Matt. 27:1, 2, 11–23;
Luke 23:1–5, 13–23; John 18:28—19:15

AND early in the morning the chief priests with the elders and scribes, and the whole [41]Council, immediately held a consultation; and binding Jesus, they led Him away, and [R]delivered Him up to Pilate.   Is. 53:7 ★

2 [R]And Pilate questioned Him, "Are You the King of the Jews?" And answering He *said to him, "It is *as* you say."   Mark 15:2-5

3 And the chief priests *began* to accuse Him[^]harshly.   *of many things*

4 And Pilate was questioning Him again, saying, "Do You make no answer? See how many charges they bring against You!"

5 But Jesus[R]made no further answer; so that Pilate was amazed.   Ps. 38:13, 14 ★

6 [R]Now at *the* feast he used to release for them *any* one prisoner whom they requested.   Mark 15:6-15; Luke 23:18-25

7 And the man named Barabbas had been imprisoned with the insurrectionists who had committed murder in the insurrection.

8 And the multitude went up and began asking him *to do* as he had been accustomed to do for them.

9 And Pilate answered them, saying, "Do you want me to release for you the King of the Jews?"

10 For he was aware that the chief priests had delivered Him up because of envy.

11 But the chief priests stirred up the multitude [R]to ask him to release Barabbas for them instead.   Acts 3:14

12 And answering again, Pilate was saying to them, "Then what shall I do with Him whom you call the King of the Jews?"

13 And they shouted [^]back, "Crucify Him!"   *again*

14 But Pilate was saying to them, "Why, what evil has He done?" But they shouted all the more, "Crucify Him!"

Jesus Is Beaten
Matt. 27:26–34; Luke 23:24–32;
John 19:16–22

15 And wishing to satisfy the multitude, Pilate released Barabbas for them, and after having Jesus[R]scourged, he delivered *Him* to be crucified.   Matt. 27:26

16 And the soldiers took Him away into the [^]palace (that is, the Praetorium), and they *called together the whole *Roman* [42]cohort.   *court*

17 And they *dressed Him up in purple, and after weaving a crown of thorns, they put it on Him;

[39] Or, *Sanhedrin*   [40] Later mss. add: *and a cock crowed*
[41] Or, *Sanhedrin*   [42] Or, *battalion*

18 and they began to acclaim Him, "Hail, King of the Jews!"

19 And they kept[R] beating His head with a [43]reed, and spitting at Him, and kneeling and bowing before Him.   Is. 52:14; Mic. 5:1 ★

20 And after they had[R]mocked Him, they took the purple off Him, and put His garments on Him. And they *led Him out to crucify Him.   Ps. 69:19; Is. 53:3; Luke 18:32 ★

21 'And they *pressed into service a passer-by coming from the country, Simon of Cyrene (the father of Alexander and Rufus), to bear His cross.   Mark 15:21; Matt. 27:32

22 [R]And they *brought Him to the place [R]Golgotha, which is translated, Place of a Skull.   Mark 15:22-32 · Luke 23:33; John 19:17

23 And they tried to give Him wine mixed with myrrh; but He did not take it.

Jesus Is Crucified
Matt. 27:35–56; Luke 23:33–49; John 19:18, 23–30

24 [R]And they *crucified Him, and *divided up His garments among themselves, casting [T]lots for them, *to decide* what each should take.   Ps. 22:16–18 ★ · *a lot upon*

25 And it was the [44]third[R]hour[T]when they crucified Him.   Mark 15:33 · *and*

26 And the inscription of the charge against Him [T]read, "THE[R] KING OF THE JEWS."   *had been inscribed* · Matt. 27:37

27 And they *crucified two robbers with Him, one on His right and one on His left.

28 [[45]And the Scripture was fulfilled which says, [R]"And He was numbered with transgressors."]   Is. 53:12; Luke 22:37 ★

29 And those passing by were hurling abuse at Him,[R]wagging their heads, and saying, "Ha! You who *are going to* destroy the temple and rebuild it in three days, Ps. 22:7 ★

30 [R]save Yourself, and come down from the cross!"   Ps. 22:8 ★

31 In the same way the chief priests also, along with the scribes, were mocking *Him* among themselves and saying, "He[R] saved others; He cannot save Himself.   Ps. 69:19 ★

32 "Let *this* Christ,[R]the King of Israel, now come down from the cross, so that we may see and believe!" And[R]those who were crucified with Him were casting the same insult at Him.   Ps. 22:8 ★ · Matt. 27:44; Mark 15:27

33 [R]And when the [46]sixth hour had come, darkness[ʌ]fell over the whole land until the [47]ninth hour. Amos 8:9; Mark 15:33-41 ★ · *occurred*

34 And at the ninth hour Jesus cried out with a loud voice, "ELOI, ELOI, LAMA SABACHTHANI?" which is translated, "MY GOD, MY GOD, WHY HAST THOU FORSAKEN ME?"

35 And when some of the bystanders heard[R]it, they *began* saying, "Behold, He is calling for Elijah."   Ps. 22:1 ★

36 And someone ran and filled a sponge with sour wine, put it on a reed, and gave Him a drink, saying, "Let us see whether Elijah will come to take Him down."

37 [R]And Jesus uttered a loud cry, and breathed His last.   Matt. 17:23 ★

38 [R]And the veil of the temple was torn in two from top to bottom.   Zech. 11:10, 11 ★

39 And when the centurion, who was standing[ʌ]right in front of Him, saw the way He breathed His last, he said, "Truly this man was the Son of God!"   *opposite Him*

40 And there were also *some* women looking on from a distance, among whom *were* Mary Magdalene, and Mary the mother of James the Less and Joses, and Salome.

41 And when He was in Galilee, they used to follow Him and [ʌ]minister to Him; and *there were* many other women who had come up with Him to Jerusalem.   *wait on*

Jesus Is Buried
Matt. 27:57–61; Luke 23:50–55; John 19:38–42

42 [R]And when evening had already come, because it was the preparation day, that is, the day before the Sabbath,   Mark 15:42-47

43 Joseph of Arimathea came, a prominent member of the Council, who himself was waiting for the kingdom of God; and he gathered up courage and went in before Pilate, and asked for the body of Jesus.

44 And Pilate wondered if He was dead by this time, and summoning the centurion, he questioned him as to whether He was already dead.

45 And ascertaining this from the centurion, he granted the body to Joseph.

46 And *Joseph* bought a linen cloth, took Him down, wrapped Him in the linen cloth, and [R]laid Him in a tomb which had been hewn out in the rock; and he rolled a stone against the entrance of the tomb. Matt. 26:12

47 And [R]Mary Magdalene and Mary the *mother* of Joses were looking on *to see* where He was laid. Matt. 27:56; Mark 15:40; 16:1

CHAPTER 16

The Resurrection of Jesus
Matt. 28:1–8; Luke 24:1–9

AND[R] when the Sabbath was over, Mary Magdalene, and Mary the *mother* of [ʌ]James, and Salome, bought spices, that they might come and anoint Him.   Mark 16:1-8 · *Jacob*

2 And very early on the first day of the week, they *came to the tomb when the sun had risen.

3 And they were saying to one another, "Who will roll away[R]the stone for us from the entrance of the tomb?"   Mark 15:46; 16:4

4 And looking up, they *saw that the stone had been rolled away,[T]although it was extremely large.   *for*

5 And entering the tomb, they saw a

---

[43] Or, *staff* (made of a reed)   [44] I.e., 9 a.m.
[45] Many mss. do not contain this verse
[46] I.e., noon   [47] I.e., 3 p.m.

young man sitting at the right, wearing a white robe; and they were amazed.

6 And he *said to them, "Do[R] not be amazed; you are looking for Jesus the Nazarene, who has been crucified. He has[R]risen; He is not here; behold, *here is* the place where they laid Him.   Mark 9:15 • Hos. 6:2★

7 "But go, tell His disciples and Peter, 'He is going before you into Galilee; there you will see Him, just as He said to you.' "

8 And they went out and fled from the tomb, for trembling and astonishment had gripped them; and they said nothing to anyone, for they were afraid.

The Appearances of Jesus
Luke 24:13–48; John 20:1–10

9 [[48]Now after He had risen early on the first day of the week, He first appeared to [R]Mary Magdalene, from whom He had cast out seven demons.   Matt. 27:56; John 20:14

10 [R]She went and reported to those who had been with Him, while they were mourning and weeping.   John 20:18

11 And when they heard that He was alive, and had been seen by her, [R]they refused to believe it.   Matt. 28:17; Mark 16:13, 14

12 And after that, He appeared in a different form to two of them, while they were walking along on their way to the country.

13 And they went away and reported it to the others, but they[R]did not believe them either.   Matt. 28:17; Mark 16:11, 14; Luke 24:11, 41

14 And afterward [R]He appeared to the eleven themselves as they were reclining *at the table;* and He reproached them for their unbelief and hardness of heart, because

they had not believed those who had seen Him after He had risen.   John 21:1, 14

15 And He said to them, "Go into all the world and preach the gospel to all creation.

16 "He[R]who has believed and has been baptized shall be saved; but he who has disbelieved shall be condemned.   Acts 16:31

17 "And these^signs will accompany those who have believed: [R]in My name they will cast out demons, they will speak with new tongues;   *attesting miracles* • Mark 9:38

18 they will[R]pick up serpents, and if they drink any deadly *poison,* it shall not hurt them; they will[R]lay hands on the sick, and they will recover."   Luke 10:19 • Mark 5:23

The Ascension of Jesus
Luke 24:49–53; Acts 1:9

19 So then, when the Lord Jesus had[R]spoken to them, He [R]was received up into heaven, and[R]sat down at the right hand of God.   Acts 1:3 • Is. 9:7★ • [Ps. 110:1]

20 And they went out and preached everywhere, while the Lord worked with them, and confirmed the word by the^signs that followed.]   *attesting miracles*

[[49]*And they promptly reported all these instructions to Peter and his companions. And after that, Jesus Himself sent out through them from east to west the sacred and imperishable proclamation of eternal salvation.*]

[48] Some of the oldest mss. do not contain vv. 9–20
[49] A few later mss. and versions contain this paragraph, usually after verse 8; a few have it at the end of chapter.

The Jewish Calendar

The Jews used two kinds of calendars:
Civil Calendar—official calendar of kings, childbirth, and contracts.
Sacred Calendar—from which festivals were computed.

NAMES OF MONTHS	CORRESPONDS WITH	NO. OF DAYS	MONTH OF CIVIL YEAR	MONTH OF SACRED YEAR	
TISHRI	Sept.–Oct.	30 days	1st	7th	
HESHVAN	Oct.–Nov.	29 or 30	2nd	8th	The Jewish day was from sunset to sunset, in 8 equal parts:
CHISLEV	Nov.–Dec.	29 or 30	3rd	9th	
TEBETH	Dec.–Jan.	29	4th	10th	FIRST WATCH ..... SUNSET TO 9 P.M.
SHEBAT	Jan.–Feb.	30	5th	11th	SECOND WATCH ... 9 P.M. TO MIDNIGHT
ADAR	Feb.–Mar.	29 or 30	6th	12th	THIRD WATCH ..... MIDNIGHT TO 3 A.M.
NISAN	Mar.–Apr.	30	7th	1st	FOURTH WATCH ... 3 A.M. TO SUNRISE
IYAR	Apr.–May	29	8th	2nd	
SIVAN	May–June	30	9th	3rd	FIRST WATCH ..... SUNRISE TO 9 A.M.
TAMMUZ	June–July	29	10th	4th	SECOND WATCH ... 9 A.M. TO NOON
AB	July–Aug.	30	11th	5th	THIRD WATCH ..... NOON TO 3 P.M.
*ELUL	Aug.–Sept.	29	12th	6th	FOURTH WATCH ... 3 P.M. TO SUNSET

*Hebrew months were alternately 30 and 29 days long. Their year, shorter than ours, had 354 days. Therefore, about every 3 years (7 times in 19 years) an extra 29-day-month, VEADAR, was added between ADAR and NISAN.

THE GOSPEL ACCORDING TO

LUKE

THE BOOK OF LUKE

Luke, a physician, writes with the compassion and warmth of a family doctor as he carefully documents the perfect humanity of the Son of Man, Jesus Christ. Luke emphasizes Jesus' ancestry, birth, and early life before moving carefully and chronologically through His earthly ministry. Growing belief and growing opposition develop side by side. Those who believe are challenged to count the cost of discipleship. Those who oppose will not be satisfied until the Son of Man hangs lifeless on a cross. But the resurrection insures that His purpose will be fulfilled: "to seek and to save that which was lost" (19:10).

Kata Loukon, "According to Luke," is the ancient title that was added to this gospel at a very early date. The Greek name *Luke* appears only three times in the New Testament (Col. 4:14; 2 Tim. 4:11; Philem. 24).

THE AUTHOR OF LUKE

It is evident from the prologues to Luke and Acts (Luke 1:1–4; Acts 1:1–5) that both books were addressed to Theophilus as a two-volume work (Luke is called "the first account"). Acts begins with a summary of Luke and continues the story from where the Gospel of Luke concludes. The style and language of both books are quite similar. The "we" portions of Acts (Acts 16:1–17; 20:5—21:18; 27:1—28:16) reveal that the author was a close associate and traveling companion of Paul. Because all but two of Paul's associates are named in the third person, the list can be narrowed to Titus and Luke. Titus has never been seriously regarded as a possible author of Acts, and Luke best fits the requirements. He was with Paul during his first Roman imprisonment, and Paul referred to him as "Luke, the beloved physician" (Col. 4:14; cf. Philem. 24). During his second Roman imprisonment, Paul wrote "Only Luke is with me" (2 Tim. 4:11), an evidence of Luke's loyalty to the apostle in the face of profound danger.

Luke may have been a Hellenistic Jew, but it is more likely that he was a Gentile (this would make him the only gentile contributor to the New Testament). In Colossians 4:10–14, Paul lists three fellow workers who are "from the circumcision" (vv. 10, 11) and then includes Luke's name with two Gentiles (vv. 12–14). Luke's obvious skill with the Greek language

and his phrase "their own language" in Acts 1:19 also imply that he was not Jewish. It has been suggested that Luke may have been a Greek physician to a Roman family who at some point was set free and given Roman citizenship. Another guess is that he was the "brother" referred to in Second Corinthians 8:18, 19. Ancient traditions (including the Muratorian Fragment, Irenaeus, Tertullian, Clement of Alexandria, Origen, Eusebius, and Jerome) strongly support Luke as the author of Luke and Acts. Tradition also says that Luke was from Syrian Antioch, remained unmarried, and died at the age of eighty-four.

THE TIME OF LUKE

Luke was not an eyewitness of the events in his gospel, but he relied on the testimony of eyewitnesses and written sources (1:1–4). He carefully investigated and arranged his material and presented it to Theophilus ("Friend of God"). The title "most excellent," or "most noble" (see Acts 23:26; 24:3; 26:25), indicates that Theophilus was a man of high social standing. He probably assumed responsibility for publishing Luke and Acts so that they would be available to gentile readers. Luke translates Aramaic terms with Greek words and explains Jewish customs and geography to make his gospel more intelligible to his original Greek readership. During Paul's two-year Caesarean imprisonment, Luke may have traveled in Palestine to gather information from eyewitnesses of Jesus' ministry. The date of this gospel depends on that of Acts since this was the first volume (see "The Time of Acts"). If Luke was written during Paul's first imprisonment in Rome it would be dated in the early 60's. However, it may have been given final form in Greece. In all probability, its publication preceded the destruction of Jerusalem (A.D. 70).

THE CHRIST OF LUKE

The humanity and compassion of Jesus are repeatedly stressed in Luke's gospel. Luke gives the most complete account of Christ's ancestry, birth, and development. He is the ideal Son of Man who identified with the sorrow and plight of sinful men in order to carry our sorrows and offer us the priceless gift of salvation. Jesus alone fulfills the Greek ideal of human perfection.

KEYS TO LUKE

Key Word: Jesus the Son of Man—Luke clearly states his purpose in the prologue of his gospel: ". . . to write *it* out for you in consecutive order . . . so that you might know the exact truth about the things you have been taught" (1:3, 4). Luke wanted to create an accurate, chronological, and comprehensive account of the unique life of Jesus the Christ to strengthen the faith of gentile believers and stimulate saving faith among nonbelievers. Luke also had another purpose, and that was to show that Christ was not only divine but also human. Luke portrays Christ in His fullest humanity by devoting more of his writing to Christ's feelings and humanity than any other gospel.

Key Verses: Luke 1:3, 4 and 19:10—"It seemed fitting for me as well, having investigated everything carefully from the beginning, to write *it* out for you in consecutive order, most excellent Theophilus; so that you might know the exact truth about the things you have been taught" (1:3, 4).

"For the Son of Man has come to seek and to save that which was lost" (19:10).

Key Chapter: Luke 15—Captured in the three parables of the Lost Sheep, Lost Coin, and Lost Son is the crux of this gospel: that God through Christ has come to seek and to save that which was lost.

SURVEY OF LUKE

Luke builds the gospel narrative on the platform of historical reliability. His emphasis on chronological and historical accuracy makes this the most comprehensive of the four gospels. This is also the longest and most literary gospel, and it presents Jesus Christ as the Perfect Man who came to seek

and to save sinful men. This book can be divided into four sections: the introduction of the Son of Man (1:1—4:13); the ministry of the Son of Man (4:14—9:50); the rejection of the Son of Man (9:51—19:27); the crucifixion and resurrection of the Son of Man (19:28—24:53).

The Introduction of the Son of Man (1:1—4:13): Luke places a strong emphasis on the ancestry, birth, and early years of the Perfect Man and of His forerunner John the Baptist. Their infancy stories are intertwined as Luke records their birth announcements, advents, and temple presentations. Jesus prepares over thirty years (summarized in one verse, 2:52) for a public ministry of only three years. The ancestry of the Son of Man is traced back to the first man Adam, and His ministry commences after His baptism and temptation.

The Ministry of the Son of Man (4:14—9:50): The authority of the Son of Man over every realm is demonstrated in 4:14—6:49. In this section His authority over demons, disease, nature, the effects of sin, tradition, and all people is presented as a prelude to His diverse ministry of preaching, healing, and discipling (7:1—9:50).

The Rejection of the Son of Man (9:51—19:27): The dual response of growing belief and growing rejection has already been introduced in the gospel (cf. 4:14 and 6:11), but from this time forward the intensity of opposition to the ministry of the Son of Man increases. When the religious leaders accuse Him of being demonized, Jesus pronounces a series of divine woes upon them (11). Knowing that He is on His last journey to Jerusalem, Jesus instructs His disciples on a number of practical matters including prayer, covetousness, faithfulness, repentance, humility, disciple-

FOCUS	INTRODUCTION OF THE SON OF MAN	MINISTRY OF THE SON OF MAN	REJECTION OF THE SON OF MAN	CRUCIFIXION AND RESUR-RECTION OF THE SON OF MAN
REFERENCE	1:1——————4:14		——9:51——————19:28	———————24:53
DIVISION	ADVENT	ACTIVITIES	ANTAGONISM AND ADMONITION	APPLICATION AND AUTHENTICATION
TOPIC	SEEKING THE LOST		SAVING THE LOST	
	MIRACLES PROMINENT		TEACHING PROMINENT	
LOCATION	ISRAEL	GALILEE	ISRAEL	JERUSALEM
TIME	c. 4 B.C.–A.D. 33			

ship, evangelism, money, forgiveness, service, thankfulness, the second advent, and salvation (12:1—19:27).

The Crucifixion and Resurrection of the Son of Man (19:28—24:53): After His triumphal entry into Jerusalem, Jesus encounters the opposition of the priests, Sadducees, and scribes and predicts the overthrow of Jerusalem (19:28—21:38). The Son of Man instructs His disciples for the last time before His betrayal in Gethsemane. The three religious and three civil trials culminate in His crucifixion. The glory and foundation of the Christian message is the historical resurrection of Jesus Christ. The Lord conquers the grave as He has promised, and appears on a number of occasions to His disciples before His ascension to the Father.

OUTLINE OF LUKE

Part One: The Introduction of the Son of Man (1:1—4:13)

Part Two: The Ministry of the Son of Man (4:14—9:50)

Part Three: The Rejection of the Son of Man (9:51—19:27)

Part Four: The Crucifixion and Resurrection of the Son of Man (19:28—24:53)

CHAPTER 1

The Purpose and Method of Luke's Gospel

INASMUCH as many have undertaken to compile an account of the things accomplished among us,

2 just as those who from the beginning were eyewitnesses and servants of the ¹word have handed them down to us,

3 it seemed fitting for me as well, having investigated everything carefully from the beginning, to write *it* out for you in consecutive order, most excellent Theophilus;

4 so that you might know the exact truth about the things you have been taught.

Zacharias Ministers in the Temple

5 In the days of Herod, king of Judea, there^Twas a certain priest named ^TZacharias, of the division of ²Abijah; and he had a wife ³from the daughters of Aaron, and her name was Elizabeth.   *came into being* • Zechariah

6 And they were both ^Rrighteous in the sight of God, walking ^Rblamelessly in all the commandments and requirements of the Lord.   Gen. 7:1; Acts 2:25; 8:21 • Phil. 2:15; 3:6

7 And they had no child, because Elizabeth was barren, and they were both advanced in^Tyears.   *days*

8 Now it came about, while he was performing his priestly service before God in the *appointed* order of his division,

9 according to the custom of the priestly office, he was chosen by lot to enter the temple of the Lord and burn incense.

10 And the whole multitude of the people were in prayer^Routside at the hour of the incense offering.   Lev. 16:17

An Angel Announces the Birth of John the Baptist

11 And^Ran angel of the Lord appeared to him, standing to the right of the altar of incense.   Luke 2:9; Acts 5:19

12 And Zacharias was troubled when he saw *him*, and fear ᵃgripped him.   *fell upon*

13 But the angel said to him, "Do not be afraid, Zacharias, for your petition has been heard, and your wife Elizabeth will bear you a son, and you will give him the name John.

14 "And you will have joy and gladness, and many will rejoice at his birth.

15 "For he will be great in the sight of the Lord, and he will drink no wine or liquor; and he will be filled with the Holy Spirit, ^Twhile yet in his mother's womb.   *even from*

16 "And he will^Rturn back many of the sons of Israel to the Lord their God.   Matt. 3:2, 6

17 "And it is he who will ^Rgo *as a forerunner* before Him in the spirit and power of ^RElijah, ^RTO TURN THE HEARTS OF THE FATHERS BACK TO THE CHILDREN, and the disobedient to the attitude of the righteous; so as to make ready a people prepared for the Lord."   Luke 1:76 • Matt. 11:14 • Mal. 4:5, 6☆

Zacharias Is Unable to Speak

18 And Zacharias said to the angel, "How shall I know this *for certain*? For I am an old man, and my wife is advanced in years."

19 And the angel answered and said to him, "I am Gabriel, who stands in the presence of God; and I have been sent to speak to you, and to bring you this good news.

20 "And behold, you shall be silent and unable to speak until the day when these things take place, because you did not believe my words, which shall be fulfilled in their proper time."

21 And the people were waiting for Zacharias, and were wondering at his delay in the temple.

22 But when he came out, he was unable to speak to them; and they realized that he had seen a vision in the temple; and he kept making signs to them, and remained mute.

23 And it came about, when the days of his priestly service were ended, that he went back home.

24 And after these days Elizabeth his wife became pregnant; and she^Tkept herself in seclusion for five months, saying,   *was hidden*

25 "This is the way the Lord has dealt with me in the days when He looked *with favor* upon *me*, to^Rtake away my disgrace among men."   Gen. 30:23; Is. 4:1; 25:8

Gabriel Announces Christ's Birth

26 Now in the sixth month the angel^RGabriel was sent from God to a city in Galilee, called^RNazareth,   Luke 1:19 • Matt. 2:23

27 to a virgin engaged to a man whose name was Joseph, of the descendants of David; and the virgin's name was Mary.

28 And coming in, he said to her, "Hail, favored one! The Lord *is* with you."⁴

29 But she ^Rwas greatly troubled at *this* statement, and kept pondering what kind of salutation this might be.   Luke 1:12

30 And the angel said to her, "Do^Rnot be afraid, Mary; for you have found favor with God.   Matt. 14:27; Luke 1:13

31 "And behold, you will conceive in your womb, and bear a son, and you^Rshall name Him Jesus.   Is. 7:14; Matt. 1:21, 25; Luke 2:21☆

32 "He will be great, and will be called the Son of the Most High; and the Lord God will give Him the throne of His father David;

33 "and He will reign over the house of Jacob forever; ^Rand His kingdom will have no end."   Matt. 1:1 • 2 Sam. 7:13, 16; Ps. 89:36, 37☆

Mary Miraculously Conceives

34 And Mary said to the angel, "How can this be, since I^Tam a virgin?"   *know no man*

---

¹ I.e., gospel   ² Gr., *Abia*   ³ I.e., of priestly descent
⁴ Later mss. add: *you are blessed among women*

35 And the angel answered and said to her, "The Holy Spirit will come upon you, and the power of the Most High will overshadow you; and for that reason the holy offspring shall be called the Son of God.

36 "And behold, even your relative Elizabeth has also conceived a son in her old age; and [T]she who was called barren is now in her sixth month.   *this is the sixth month to her who*

37 "For [T]nothing[R] will be impossible with God."   *not any word* • Gen. 18:14; Jer. 32:17

38 And [T]Mary said, "Behold, the [5]bondslave of the Lord; be it done to me according to your word." And the angel departed from her.   Gr., *Miriam;* i.e., Miriam: so throughout Luke

Mary Visits Elizabeth

39 Now [T]at this time Mary arose and went with haste to [R]the hill country, to a city of Judah,   *in these days* • Josh. 20:7; 21:11

40 and entered the house of Zacharias and greeted Elizabeth.

41 And it came about that when Elizabeth heard Mary's greeting, the baby leaped in her womb; and Elizabeth was [R]filled with the Holy Spirit.   Luke 1:67; Acts 2:4; 4:8; 9:17

42 And she cried out with a loud voice, and said, "Blessed among women *are* you, and blessed *is* the fruit of your womb!

43 "And how has it *happened* to me, that the mother of my Lord should come to me?

44 "For behold, when the sound of your greeting reached my ears, the baby leaped in my womb for joy.

45 "And [R]blessed *is* she who believed that there would be a fulfillment of what had been spoken to her by the Lord."   Luke 1:20

46 And Mary said:
"My [R]soul exalts the Lord,   Luke 1:46-53

47 "And [R]my spirit has rejoiced in [R]God my Savior.   Ps. 35:9 • 1 Tim. 1:1; 2:3

48 "For He has had regard for the humble state of His [T]bondslave;   *female slave*
For behold, from this time on all generations will count me blessed.

49 "For the Mighty One has done great things for me;
And holy is His name.

50 "AND [R]HIS MERCY IS UPON GENERATION AFTER GENERATION   Ps. 103:17
TOWARD THOSE WHO FEAR HIM.

51 "He [R]has done [T]mighty deeds with His arm;   Ps. 98:1; 118:15 • *might*
He has scattered *those who were* proud in the thoughts of their heart.

52 "He has brought down rulers from *their* thrones,
And has [R]exalted those who were humble.   Job 5:11

53 "HE [R]HAS FILLED THE HUNGRY WITH GOOD THINGS;   Ps. 107:9
And sent away the rich empty-handed.

54 "He has given help to Israel His servant,
In remembrance of His mercy,

55 [R]As He spoke to our fathers,   Gen. 17:19
[R]To Abraham and his [T]offspring forever."   Gen. 17:7 • *seed*

56 And Mary stayed with her about three months, and *then* returned to her home.

Elizabeth Gives Birth to John

57 Now the time had come for Elizabeth to give birth, and she brought forth a son.

58 And her neighbors and her relatives heard that the Lord had [T]displayed [R]His great mercy toward her; and they were rejoicing with her.   *magnified* • Gen. 19:19

59 And it came about that on [R]the eighth day they came to circumcise the child, and they were going to call him Zacharias, [T]after his father.   Gen. 17:12 • *after the name of*

60 And his mother answered and said, "No indeed; but he shall be called John."

61 And they said to her, "There is no one among your relatives who is called by that name."

62 And they [R]made signs to his father, as to what he wanted him called.   Luke 1:22

63 And he asked for a tablet, and wrote as follows, "His [R]name is John." And they were all astonished.   Luke 1:13, 60

64 [R]And at once his mouth was opened and his tongue *loosed,* and he *began* to speak in praise of God.   Luke 1:20

65 And fear came on all those living around them; and all these matters were being talked about in all [R]the hill country of Judea.   Luke 1:39

66 And all who heard them kept them in mind, saying, "What then will this child *turn out to* be?" For [R]the hand of the Lord was certainly with him.   Acts 11:21

Zacharias Prophesies of John's Ministry

67 And his father Zacharias [R]was filled with the Holy Spirit, and [R]prophesied, saying: Luke 1:41; Acts 2:4, 8; 9:17 • Joel 2:28

68 "Blessed *be* the Lord God of Israel,
For He has visited us and accomplished redemption for His people,

69 And has raised up a [R]horn of salvation for us   1 Sam. 2:1, 10; Ps. 18:2
In the house of David His servant—

70 [R]As He spoke by the mouth of His holy prophets from of old—   Rom. 1:2

71 [A]Salvation FROM OUR ENEMIES,
And FROM THE HAND OF ALL WHO HATE US;   *Deliverance*

72 To show mercy toward our fathers,
And to remember His holy covenant,

73 [R]The oath which He swore to Abraham our father,   Gen. 22:16ff.; [Heb. 6:13]

74 To grant us that we, being delivered from the hand of our enemies,
Might serve Him without fear,

[5] I.e., female slave

75 ᴿIn holiness and righteousness before
   Him all our days.   [Eph. 4:24]
76 "And you, child, will be called the
   ᴿprophet of the Most High; Matt. 11:9
   For you will go on BEFORE THE LORD
   TO PREPARE HIS WAYS;
77 To give to His people the knowledge
   of salvation
   By the forgiveness of their sins,
78 Because of the tender mercy of our
   God,
   With whichᴿthe Sunrise from on high
   shall visit us,   [Mal. 4:2; Eph. 5:14]
79 ᴿTo SHINE UPON THOSE WHO SIT IN
   DARKNESS AND THE SHADOW OF
   DEATH,   Is. 9:2
   To guide our feet into the ᴿway of
   peace."   Is. 59:8; John 14:27; 16:33☆
80 ᴿAnd the child continued to grow, and
to become strong in spirit, and he lived in
the deserts until the day of his public appearance to Israel.   Luke 2:40

CHAPTER 2

Christ Is Born

Now it came about in those days that a
decree went out from Caesar Augustus, that
a census be taken of all ⁶the inhabited earth.
2 This was the first census taken while
⁷Quirinius was governor ofᴿSyria. Matt. 4:24
3 And all were proceeding to register for
the census, everyone to his own city.
4 And Joseph also went up from Galilee,
from the city of Nazareth, to Judea, to the
city of David, which is calledᴿBethlehem, be-
causeᴴhe was of the house and family of David,   Mic. 5:2★ • Luke 1:27
5 in order to register, along with Mary,
who was engaged to him, and was with
child.
6 And it came about that while they
were there, the days were completed for her
to give birth.
7 And she gave birth to her first-born
son; and she wrapped Him in cloths, and
laid Him in a ᴬmanger, because there was no
room for them in the inn.   feeding trough

The Angels Announce Jesus
to the Shepherds

8 And in the same region there were
some shepherds staying out in the fields,
and keeping watch over their flock by night.
9 And ᴿan angel of the Lord suddenly
ᴿstood before them, and the glory of the Lord
shone around them; and they were terribly
frightened.   Luke 1:11 • Luke 24:4; Acts 12:7
10 And the angel said to them, "Do not be
afraid; for behold, I bring you good news of
a great joy which shall be for all the people;
11 for today in the city of David there has

been born for you aᴿSavior, who is ⁸Christ
the Lord.   Is. 9:6; Matt. 1:21★
12"Andᴿthis will be a sign for you: you will
find a baby wrapped in cloths, and lying in a
ᴬmanger."   2 Kin. 19:29 • feeding trough
13 And suddenly there appeared with the
angel a multitude of the heavenly host
praising God, and saying,
14 "Gloryᴿto God in the highest, Matt. 21:9
   And on earth peace among men ⁹with
   whom He is pleased."

The Shepherds Visit Jesus

15 And it came about when the angels had
gone away from them into heaven, that the
shepherds began saying to one another,
"Let us go straight to Bethlehem then, and
see this thing that has happened which the
Lord has made known to us."
16 And they came in haste and found their
way to Mary and Joseph, and the baby as
He lay in theᴬmanger.   feeding trough
17 And when they had seen this, they
made known the statement which had been
told them about this Child.
18 And all who heard it wondered at the
things which were told them by the shepherds.
19 But Maryᴿtreasured up all these things,
pondering them in her heart.   Luke 2:51
20 And the shepherds went back, glorifying and praising God for all that they had
heard and seen, just as had been told them.

Christ Is Circumcised

21 And when eight days were completed
before His circumcision, His name was then
called Jesus, the name given by the angel
before He was conceived in the womb.
22 ᴿAnd when the days for their purification according to the law of Moses were
completed, they brought Him up to Jerusalem to present Him to the Lord   Lev. 12:6-8
23 (as it is written in the Law of the Lord,
"EVERYᴿ first-born MALE THAT OPENS THE
WOMB SHALL BE CALLED HOLY TO THE
LORD"),   Ex. 13:2, 12; Num. 3:13; 8:17
24 and to offer a sacrifice according to
what was said in the Law of the Lord, "Aᴿ
PAIR OF TURTLEDOVES, OR TWO YOUNG PI-
GEONS."   Lev. 5:11; 12:8

Simeon's Prophecy

25 And behold, there was a man in Jerusalem whose name was Simeon; and this man
was ᴿrighteous and devout, ᴿlooking for the
consolation of Israel; and the Holy Spirit
was upon him.   Luke 1:6 • Mark 15:43
26 ᴿAnd it had been revealed to him by the
Holy Spirit that he would not see death before he had seen the Lord's Christ. Luke 2:30
27 And he came in the Spirit into the temple; and when the parents brought in the
child Jesus,ᵀto carry out for Him the custom
of the Law,   to do for Him according to

⁶ I.e., the Roman empire   ⁷ Gr., Kyrenios
⁸ I.e., Messiah
⁹ Lit., of good pleasure; or possibly, of good will

28 then he took Him into his arms, and blessed God, and said,

29 "Now Lord, Thou dost let Thy bond-servant depart
In peace, according to Thy word;

30 For my eyes have seen Thy salvation,

31 Which Thou hast prepared in the presence of all peoples,

32 ^RA LIGHT ^AOF REVELATION TO THE GEN-TILES,   Is. 9:2; 42:6☆ • *for*
And the glory of Thy people Israel."

33 And His father and ^Rmother were amazed at the things which were being said about Him.   Matt. 12:46

34 And Simeon blessed them, and said to Mary His mother, "Behold, this *Child* is appointed for^Rthe fall and rise of many in Israel, and for a sign to be opposed— 1 Pet. 2:7

35 and a sword will pierce even your own soul—to the end that thoughts from many hearts may be revealed."

Anna's Testimony

36 And there was a prophetess, ^AAnna the daughter of Phanuel, of the tribe of Asher. She was advanced in ^Tyears, having lived with a husband seven years after her ^Tmarriage,   *Hannah • days • virginity*

37 and then as a widow to the age of eighty-four. And she never left the temple, serving night and day with ^Rfastings and prayers.   Luke 5:33; Acts 13:3; 14:23; 1 Tim. 5:5

38 And at that very moment she came up and *began* giving thanks to God, and continued to speak of Him to all those who were looking for the redemption of Jerusalem.

Jesus Returns to Nazareth
Matt. 2:19-23

39 And when they had performed everything according to the Law of the Lord, they returned to Galilee, to ^Rtheir own city of Nazareth.   Matt. 2:23; Luke 1:26; 2:51; 4:16

40 ^RAnd the Child continued to grow and become strong, increasing in wisdom; and the grace of God was upon Him.   Luke 1:80

Jesus Celebrates the Passover

41 And His parents used to go to Jerusalem every year at the Feast of the Passover.

42 And when He became twelve, they went up *there* according to the custom of the Feast;

43 and as they were returning, after spending the ^Rfull number of days, the boy Jesus stayed behind in Jerusalem. And His parents were unaware of it,   Ex. 12:15

44 but supposed Him to be in the caravan, and went ^Ta day's journey; and they *began* looking for Him among their relatives and acquaintances.   20 mi.

45 And when they did not find Him, they returned to Jerusalem, looking for Him.

46 And it came about that after three days they found Him in the temple, sitting in the midst of the teachers, both listening to them, and asking them questions.

47 And all who heard Him were amazed at His understanding and His answers.

48 And when they saw Him, they were astonished; and His mother said to Him, "Son, why have You treated us this way? Behold, Your father and I have been anxiously looking for You."

49 And He said to them, "Why is it that you were looking for Me? Did you not know that I had to be in My Father's *house?*"

50 And they did not understand the statement which He had made to them.

Jesus Grows in Wisdom

51 And He went down with them, and came to Nazareth; and He continued in subjection to them; and His mother ^Ttreasured all *these* things in her heart.   *was treasuring*

52 And Jesus kept increasing in wisdom and stature, and in favor with God and men.

CHAPTER 3

The Ministry of John the Baptist
Matt. 3:1-12; Mark 1:2-8; John 1:19-31

NOW in the fifteenth year of the reign of Tiberius Caesar, when Pontius Pilate was governor of Judea, and Herod was tetrarch of Galilee, and his brother Philip was tetrarch of the region of Ituraea and Trachonitis, and Lysanias was tetrarch of Abilene,

2 in the high priesthood of Annas and Caiaphas, the word of God came to John, the son of Zacharias, in the wilderness.

3 And he came into all the district around the Jordan, preaching a baptism of repentance for the forgiveness of sins;

4 as it is written in the book of the words of Isaiah the prophet,
"THE^R VOICE OF ONE CRYING IN THE WIL-DERNESS,   Is. 40:3★
'MAKE READY THE WAY OF THE LORD,
MAKE HIS PATHS STRAIGHT.

5 ^REVERY RAVINE SHALL BE FILLED UP,
AND EVERY MOUNTAIN AND HILL SHALL BE BROUGHT LOW;
AND THE CROOKED SHALL BECOME STRAIGHT,   Is. 40:4★
AND THE ROUGH ROADS SMOOTH;

6 ^RAND ALL ^AFLESH SHALL SEE THE SALVA-TION OF GOD.' "   Is. 40:5★ • *mankind*

7 He therefore *began* saying to the multitudes who were going out to be baptized by him, "You^Rbrood of vipers, who warned you to flee from the wrath to come?   Matt. 12:34

8 "Therefore bring forth fruits in keeping with repentance, and ^Rdo not begin to say ^Ato yourselves, 'We^Rhave Abraham for our father,' for I say to you that God is able from these stones to raise up children to Abraham.   Luke 5:21 • *in* • John 8:33

9 "And also the axe is already laid at the root of the trees; ^Revery tree therefore that

does not bear good fruit is cut down and thrown into the fire."   Matt. 7:19; Luke 13:6-9

10 And the multitudes were questioning him, saying, "Then what shall we do?"

11 And he would answer and say to them, "Let the man who has two tunics [R] share with him who has none; and let him who has food do likewise.'   Is. 58:7; 1 Tim. 6:17; James 2:14-20

12 And some [10]tax-gatherers [R] also came to be baptized, and they said to him, "Teacher, what shall we do?"   Luke 7:29

13 And he said to them, "Collect no more than what you have been ordered to."

14 And some [11]soldiers were questioning him, saying, "And what about us, what shall we do?" And he said to them, "Do not take money from anyone by force, or [R]accuse anyone falsely, and [R]be content with your wages."   Ex. 20:16; 23:1 • [Phil. 4:11]

15 Now while the people were in a state of expectation and all were [A]wondering in their hearts about John, as to whether he might be [T]the Christ,   reasoning or debating • the Messiah

16 John answered and said to them all, "As for me, I baptize you with water; but One is coming who is mightier than I, and I am not fit to untie the thong of His sandals; He will baptize you [T]with the Holy Spirit and fire.   The Gr. here can be translated in, with or by

17 "And His [R]winnowing fork is in His hand to thoroughly clear His threshing floor, and to gather the wheat into His barn; but He will burn up the chaff with [A]unquenchable fire."   Is. 30:24 • Mark 9:43, 48

18 So with many other exhortations also he preached the gospel to the people.

19 But when Herod the tetrarch was reproved by him on account of Herodias, his brother's wife, and on account of all the wicked things which Herod had done,

20 he added this also to them all, that [R]he locked John up in prison.   John 3:24

The Baptism of Christ
Matt. 3:13–17; Mark 1:9–11;
John 1:32–34

21 [R]Now it came about when all the people were baptized, that Jesus also was baptized, and while He was [R]praying, heaven was opened,   Luke 3:21 • Matt. 14:23; Luke 5:16

22 and the Holy Spirit descended upon Him in bodily form like a dove, and a voice came out of heaven, "Thou [R]art My beloved Son, in Thee I am well-pleased."   Ps. 2:7

The Genealogy of Christ Through Mary
Gen. 5:1–32; 11:10–26; Ruth 4:18–22;
1 Chr. 1:1–4, 24–27, 34; 2:1–15;
Matt. 1:2–6

23 And [R]when He began His ministry, Jesus Himself was about thirty years of age, [T]being supposedly the son of Joseph, the son of Eli,   Matt. 4:17 • as it was being thought

24 the son of Matthat, the son of Levi, the son of Melchi, the son of Jannai, the son of Joseph,

25 the son of Mattathias, the son of Amos, the son of Nahum, the son of [A]Hesli, the son of Naggai,   Also spelled Esli

26 the son of Maath, the son of Mattathias, the son of Semein, the son of Josech, the son of Joda,

27 the son of Joanan, the son of Rhesa, [R]the son of Zerubbabel, the son of [T]Shealtiel, the son of Neri,   Matt. 1:12 • Gr., Salathiel

28 the son of Melchi, the son of Addi, the son of Cosam, the son of Elmadam, the son of Er,

29 the son of [T]Joshua, the son of Eliezer, the son of Jorim, the son of Matthat, the son of Levi,   Gr., Jesus

30 the son of Simeon, the son of [T]Judah, the son of Joseph, the son of Jonam, the son of Eliakim,   Gr., Judas

31 the son of Melea, the son of Menna, the son of Mattatha, the son of Nathan, [R]the son of David,   Is. 9:7 ★

32 [R]the son of Jesse, the son of Obed, the son of Boaz, the son of [T]Salmon, the son of [T]Nahshon,   Is. 11:1, 10 ★ • Gr., Sala • Gr., Naasson

33 the son of Amminadab, the son of Admin, the son of [T]Ram, the son of Hezron, the son of Perez, the son of Judah,   Gr., Arni

34 the son of Jacob, the son of Isaac, [R]the son of Abraham, the son of Terah, the son of Nahor,   Gen. 11:26-30; 1 Chr. 1:24-27; Luke 3:34-36

35 the son of Serug, the son of [T]Reu, the son of Peleg, the son of [T]Heber, the son of Shelah,   Gr., Ragau • Gr., Eber

36 the son of Cainan, the son of Arphaxad, the son of Shem, [R]the son of Noah, the son of Lamech,   Luke 3:36-38; Gen. 5:3-32

37 the son of Methuselah, the son of Enoch, the son of Jared, the son of Mahalaleel, the son of Cainan,

38 the son of Enosh, the son of Seth, the son of Adam, the son of God.

CHAPTER 4

The Temptation of Christ
Matt. 4:1–11; Mark 1:12, 13

AND [R] Jesus, full of the Holy Spirit, returned from the Jordan and was led about by the Spirit in the wilderness   Luke 4:1-13

2 for [R]forty days, being tempted by the devil. And He ate nothing during those days; and when they had ended, He became hungry.   Ex. 34:28; 1 Kin. 19:8

3 And the devil said to Him, "If You are the Son of God, tell this stone to become bread."

4 And Jesus answered him, "It is written, 'MAN [R] SHALL NOT LIVE ON BREAD ALONE.' "   Deut. 8:3

5 [R]And he led Him up and showed Him all the kingdoms of [T]the world in a moment of time.   Matt. 4:8-10 • the inhabited earth

6 And the devil said to Him, "I will give

---

[10] I.e., Collectors of Roman taxes for profit
[11] I.e., men in active military service

You all this domain and[T]its glory;[R]for it has been handed over to me, and I give it to whomever I wish.   *their* • 1 John 5:19

7"Therefore if You[A]worship before me, it shall all be Yours."   *bow down*

8 And Jesus answered and said to him, "It is written, 'YOU SHALL WORSHIP THE LORD YOUR GOD AND SERVE HIM ONLY.' "

9 [R]And he led Him to Jerusalem and had Him stand on the pinnacle of the temple, and said to Him, "If You are the Son of God, throw Yourself down from here;   Matt. 4:5-7

10 for it is written,

'HE WILL GIVE HIS ANGELS CHARGE
   CONCERNING YOU TO GUARD YOU,'

11 and,

'ON[R]*their* HANDS THEY WILL BEAR YOU
   UP,   Ps. 91:11, 12★
LEST YOU STRIKE YOUR FOOT AGAINST
   A STONE.' "

12 And Jesus answered and said to him, "It is said, 'YOU[R]SHALL NOT [12]PUT THE LORD YOUR GOD TO THE TEST.' "   Deut. 6:16

13 And when the devil had finished every temptation, he departed from Him until an opportune time.

Acceptance Throughout Galilee
Matt. 4:12; Mark 1:14

14 And Jesus returned to Galilee in the power of the Spirit; and news about Him spread through all the surrounding district.

15 And He *began*[R]teaching in their synagogues and was praised by all.   Is. 52:13★

Rejection at Nazareth

16 And He came to Nazareth, where He had been brought up; and as was His custom,[R]He entered the synagogue on the Sabbath, and stood up to read.   Ps. 22:22★

17 And the book of the prophet Isaiah was handed to Him. And He opened the book, and found the place where it was written,

18 "THE SPIRIT OF THE LORD IS UPON ME,
   BECAUSE HE ANOINTED ME TO PREACH
      THE GOSPEL TO THE POOR.
   HE HAS SENT ME TO PROCLAIM RE-
      LEASE TO THE CAPTIVES,
   AND RECOVERY OF SIGHT TO THE BLIND,
   TO SET FREE THOSE WHO ARE DOWN-
      TRODDEN,

19 [R]TO PROCLAIM THE FAVORABLE YEAR OF
      THE LORD."   Is. 61:1, 2★

20 And He [R]closed the[A]book, and gave it back to the attendant, and sat down; and the eyes of all in the synagogue were fixed upon Him.   Luke 4:17 • *scroll*

21 And He began to say to them, "Today this Scripture has been fulfilled in your [T]hearing."   *ears*

22 And all were[A]speaking well of Him, and wondering at the gracious words which were falling from His lips; and they were saying, "Is this not Joseph's son?"   *testifying*

23 And He said to them, "No doubt you will quote this proverb to Me, 'Physician,

heal yourself! Whatever we heard was done [R]at Capernaum, do here in[R]your home town as well.' "   Matt. 4:13 • Mark 6:1; Luke 2:39

24 And He said, "Truly I say to you, no prophet is welcome in his home town.

25"But I say to you in truth, there were many widows in Israel[R]in the days of Elijah, when the sky was shut up for three years and six months, when a great famine came over all the land;   1 Kin. 17:1; 18:1; James 5:17

26 and yet Elijah was sent to none of them, but only to Zarephath, *in the land* of Sidon, to a woman who was a widow.

27"And there were many lepers in Israel in the time of Elisha the prophet; and none of them was cleansed, but [R]only Naaman the Syrian."   2 Kin. 5:1-14

28 And all in the synagogue were filled with rage as they heard these things;

29 and they rose up and [R]cast Him out of the city, and led Him to the brow of the hill on which their city had been built, in order to throw Him down the cliff.   Num. 15:35

30 But [R]passing through their midst, He went His way.   John 10:39

Demons Are Cast Out
Mark 1:21-28

31 And[R]He came down to[R]Capernaum, a city of Galilee. And He was teaching them on the Sabbath;   Luke 4:31-37 • Matt. 4:13

32 and they were amazed at His teaching, for His message was with authority.

33 And there was a man in the synagogue possessed by the spirit of an unclean demon, and he cried out with a loud voice,

34"Ha![A]What[R]do we have to do with You, Jesus of Nazareth? Have You come to destroy us? I know who You are—the Holy One of God!"   *Let us alone* • Matt. 8:29

35 And Jesus [R]rebuked him, saying, "Be quiet and come out of him!" And when the demon had thrown him down in *their* midst, he came out of him without doing him any harm.   Matt. 8:26; Mark 4:39; Luke 4:39, 41; 8:24

36 And amazement came upon them all, and they *began* discussing with one another saying, "What is this message? For[R]with authority and power He commands the unclean spirits, and they come out."   Luke 4:32

37 And[R]the report about Him was getting out into every locality in the surrounding district.   Luke 4:14

Peter's Mother-in-law Is Healed
Matt. 8:14, 15; Mark 1:29-31

38 [R]And He arose and *left* the synagogue, and entered Simon's home. Now Simon's mother-in-law was[R]suffering from a high fever; and they made request of Him on her behalf.   Matt. 8:14; Luke 4:38, 39 • Matt. 4:24

39 And standing over her, He rebuked the

[12] Or, *tempt . . . God*

fever, and it left her; and she immediately arose and ^waited on them. *served*

Jesus Ministers Throughout Galilee
Matt. 4:23–25; 8:16, 17; Mark 1:32–39

40 ᴿAnd while the sun was setting, all who had any sick with various diseases brought them to Him; and laying His hands on every one of them, He was healing them. Luke 4:40
41 And demons also were coming out of many, crying out and saying, "You are the Son of God!" And rebuking them, He would not allow them to speak, because they knew Him to be ᵀthe Christ. *the Messiah*
42 ᴿAnd when day came, He departed and went to a lonely place; and the multitudes were searching for Him, and came to Him, and tried to keep Him from going away from them. *Mark 1:35–38; Luke 4:42, 43*
43 But He said to them, "I must preach the kingdom of God to the other cities also, ᴿfor I was sent for this purpose." Mark 1:38
44 And He kept on preaching in the synagoguesᴿof ¹³Judea. Matt. 4:23

CHAPTER 5

The First Disciples Are Called

Nᴼᵂᴿit came about that while the multitude were pressing around Him and listening to the word of God, He was standing by the lake of Gennesaret; Matt. 4:18-22
2 and He saw two boats lying at the edge of the lake; but the fishermen had gotten out of them, and were washing their nets.
3 And ᴿHe got into one of the boats, which was Simon's, and asked him to put out a little way from the land. And He sat down and *began* teaching the multitudes from the boat. Matt. 13:2; Mark 3:9, 10; 4:1
4 And when He had finished speaking, He said to Simon, "Put out into the deep water and let down your nets for a catch."
5 And Simon answered and said, "Master, we worked hard all night and caught nothing, but at Your^bidding I will let down the nets." Luke 8:24 • John 21:3 • *word*
6 And when they had done this, ᴿthey enclosed a great quantity of fish; and their nets *began* to break; John 21:6
7 and they signaled to their partners in the other boat, for them to come and help them. And they came, and filled both of the boats, so that they began to sink.
8 But when Simon Peter saw *that,* he fell down at Jesus' ᵀfeet, saying, "Depart from me, for I am a sinful man, O Lord!" *knees*
9 For amazement had seized him and all his companions because of the catch of fish which they had taken;
10 and so also ^James and John, sons of Zebedee, who were partners with Simon. And Jesus said to Simon, "Do not fear, from now on you will be catching men." *Jacob*

---

¹³ I.e., the country of the Jews (including Galilee); some mss. read *Galilee*

11 And when they had brought their boats to land, ᴿthey left everything and followed Him. Matt. 4:20, 22; 19:29; Mark 1:18, 20

A Leper Is Cleansed
Matt. 8:2–4; Mark 1:40–45

12 ᴿAnd it came about that while He was in one of the cities, behold, *there was* a man full of leprosy; and when he saw Jesus, he fell on his face and implored Him, saying, "Lord, if You are willing, You can make me clean." Matt. 8:2–4; Mark 1:40–44; Luke 5:12–14
13 And He stretched out His hand, and touched him, saying, "I am willing; be cleansed." And immediately the leprosy left him.
14 And He ordered him to tell no one, "But go and ᴿshow yourself to the priest, and make an offering for your cleansing, just as Moses commanded, for a testimony to them." Lev. 13:49; 14:2ff.
15 But ᴿthe news about Him was spreading even farther, and great multitudes were gathering to hear *Him* and to be healed of their sicknesses. Matt. 9:26

A Paralytic Is Healed
Matt. 9:1–8; Mark 2:1–12

16 But He Himself would *often* slip away to the^wilderness and pray. *lonely places*
17 And it came about ᵀone day that He was teaching; and ᴿthere were *some* Pharisees and teachers of the law sitting *there,* who had come from every village of Galilee and Judea and *from* Jerusalem; and the power of the Lord was *present* for Him to perform healing. *on one of the days* • Matt. 15:1
18 And behold, *some* men *were* carrying on a^bed a man who was paralyzed; and they were trying to bring him in, and to set him down in front of Him. *stretcher*
19 And not finding any *way* to bring him in because of the crowd, they went up on ᴿthe roof and let him downᴿthrough the tiles with his stretcher, right in the center, in front of Jesus. Matt. 24:17 • Mark 2:4
20 And seeing their faith, He said, "Friendᵀ your sins are forgiven you." *Man*
21 And the scribes and the Pharisees ᴿbegan to reason, saying, "Whoᴿ is this *man* who speaks blasphemies? Who can forgive sins, but God alone?" Luke 3:8 • Luke 7:49
22 But Jesus, ^aware of their reasonings, answered and said to them, "Why are you reasoning in your hearts? *perceiving*
23 "Which is easier, to say, 'Your sins have been forgiven you,' or to say, 'Rise and walk'?
24 "But in order that you may know that the Son of Man has authority on earth to forgive sins,"—He said to theᴿparalytic—"I say to you, rise, and take up your stretcher and go home." Matt. 4:24
25 And at once he rose up before them, and took up what he had been lying on, and went home, ᴿglorifying God. Matt. 9:8

26 And they were all seized with astonishment and *began* [R]glorifying God; and they were filled with fear, saying, "We have seen remarkable things today."   Matt. 9:8

Matthew Is Called
Matt. 9:9; Mark 2:13, 14

27 [R]And after that He went out, and noticed a [14]tax-gatherer named[R]Levi, sitting in the tax office, and He said to him, "Follow Me."   Luke 5:27-39 • Matt. 9:9
28 And he [R]left everything behind, and rose and *began* to follow Him.   Luke 5:11

Jesus Eats with Sinners
Matt. 9:10-13; Mark 2:15-17

29 And Levi gave a big reception for Him in his house; and there was a great crowd of tax-gatherers and other *people* who were reclining *at the table* with them.   banquet
30 And[R]the Pharisees and their scribes *began* grumbling at His disciples, saying, "Why do you eat and drink with the tax-gatherers and sinners?"   Mark 2:16; Luke 15:2
31 And Jesus answered and said to them, "It is not those who are well who need a physician, but those who are sick.   Mark 2:17
32 "I have not come to call the righteous but sinners to repentance."

Jesus Teaches About Fasting
Matt. 9:14, 15; Mark 2:18-20

33 And they said to Him, "The disciples of John often fast and offer prayers; the *disciples* of the Pharisees also do the same; but Yours eat and drink."   likewise
34 And Jesus said to them, "You cannot make the attendants of the bridegroom fast while the bridegroom is with them, can you?
35 "But[R] the days will come; and when the bridegroom is taken away from them, then they will fast in those days."   Matt. 9:15

Parable of the Cloth and Wineskins
Matt. 9:16, 17; Mark 2:21, 22

36 And He was also telling them a parable: "No one tears a piece from a new garment and puts it on an old garment; otherwise he will both tear the new; and the piece from the new will not match the old.
37 "And no one puts new wine into old wineskins; otherwise the new wine will burst the skins, and it will be spilled out, and the skins will be ruined.
38 "But new wine must be put into fresh wineskins.
39 "And no one, after drinking old *wine* wishes for new; for he says, 'The old is good enough.'"

CHAPTER 6

Jesus Works on the Sabbath
Matt. 12:1-8; Mark 2:23-28

N OW[R]it came about that on a *certain* Sabbath He was passing through *some* grain-fields; and His disciples [R]were picking and eating the heads *of grain*, rubbing them in their hands.   Luke 6:1-5 • Deut. 23:25
2 But some of the Pharisees said, "Why do you do what[R]is not lawful on the Sabbath?"   Matt. 12:2
3 And Jesus answering them said, "Have you not even read what David did when he was hungry, he and those who were with him,   1 Sam. 21:6
4 how he entered the house of God, and took and ate the [15]consecrated bread which [R]is not lawful for any to eat except the priests alone, and gave it to his companions?"   Lev. 24:9
5 And He was saying to them, "The Son of Man is Lord of the Sabbath."

Jesus Heals on the Sabbath
Matt. 12:9-14; Mark 3:1-6

6 [R]And it came about on another Sabbath, that He entered the synagogue and was teaching; and there was a man there whose right hand was withered.   Luke 6:6-11
7 And the scribes and the Pharisees[R]were watching Him closely, *to see* if He healed on the Sabbath, in order that they might find *reason* to accuse Him.   Mark 3:2
8 But He knew[T]what they were thinking, and He said to the man with the withered hand, "Rise and come forward!" And he rose and came forward.   their thoughts
9 And Jesus said to them, "I ask you, is it lawful on the Sabbath to do good, or to do harm, to save a life, or to destroy it?"
10 And after looking around at them all, He said to him, "Stretch out your hand!" And he did *so;* and his hand was restored.
11 But they themselves were filled with [T]rage, and discussed together what they might do to Jesus.   folly

Selection of the Twelve Apostles
Mark 3:13-19

12 And it was[T]at this time that He went off to the mountain to pray, and He spent the whole night in prayer to God.   in these days
13 And when day came,[R]He called His disciples to Him; and chose twelve of them, whom He also named as apostles: Acts 1:13
14 Simon, whom He also named Peter, and Andrew his brother; and [A]James and John; and Philip and Bartholomew;   Jacob
15 and[R]Matthew and Thomas; James *the son* of Alphaeus, and Simon who was called the Zealot;   Matt. 9:9
16 Judas *the son* of James, and Judas Iscariot, who became a traitor.
17 And He [R]descended with them, and stood on a level place; and *there was* [A]a great multitude of His disciples, and a great throng of people from all Judea and Jerusalem and the coastal region of[R]Tyre and Sidon,   Luke 6:12 • Matt. 4:25 • Matt. 11:21

[14] I.e., Collector of Roman taxes for profit
[15] Or, *showbread,* lit., *loaves of presentation*

18 who had come to hear Him, and to be healed of their diseases; and those who were troubled with unclean spirits were being cured.

19 And all the multitude were trying to ^Rtouch Him, for ^Rpower was coming from Him and healing *them* all.   Matt. 9:21 • Luke 5:17

The Beatitudes
Matt. 5:1–12

20 And turning His gaze on His disciples, He *began* to say, "Blessed *are* you *who are* poor, for yours is the kingdom of God.

21 "Blessed *are* you who hunger now, for you shall be satisfied. Blessed *are* you who weep now, for you shall laugh.

22 "Blessed^R are you when men hate you, and ^Rostracize you, and cast insults at you, and spurn your name as evil, for the sake of the Son of Man.   [1 Pet. 4:14] • John 9:22

23 "Be glad in that day, and ^Rleap *for joy*, for behold, your reward is great in heaven; for in the same way their fathers used to ^Ttreat the prophets.   [Mal. 4] • *do to*

24 "But woe to ^Ryou who are rich, for you are receiving your comfort in full. Luke 16:25

25 "Woe to you who are well-fed now, for you shall be hungry. Woe *to you* who laugh now, for you shall mourn and weep.

26 "Woe *to you* when all men speak well of you, for in the same way their fathers used to ^Ttreat the false prophets.   *do to*

Rules of Kingdom Life
Matt. 5:39–48; 7:1, 2, 12

27 "But I say to you who hear, love your enemies, do good to those who hate you,

28 bless those who curse you, pray for those who ^Amistreat you.   *revile*

29 "Whoever hits you on the cheek, offer him the other also; and whoever takes away your ^Acoat, do not withhold your shirt from him either.   *cloak*

30 "Give to everyone who asks of you, and whoever takes away what is yours, do not demand it back.

31 "And just as you want people to ^Ttreat you, ^Ttreat them in the same way.   *do to*

32 "And ^Rif you love those who love you, what credit is *that* to you? For even sinners love those who love them.   Matt. 5:46

33 "And if you do good to those who do good to you, what credit is *that* to you? For even sinners do the same.

34 "And ^Rif you lend to those from whom you expect to receive, what credit is *that* to you? Even sinners lend to sinners, in order to receive back the same *amount*. Matt. 5:42

35 "But ^Rlove your enemies, and do good, and lend, expecting nothing in return; and your reward will be great, and you will be sons of the Most High; for He Himself is kind to ungrateful and evil *men*.   Luke 6:27

36 "Be ^Amerciful, just as your Father is merciful.   *Become*

37 "And^R do not judge and you will not be judged; and do not condemn, and you will not be condemned; ^Tpardon, and you will be pardoned.   Luke 6:37-42 • *release*

38 "Give, and it will be given to you; ^Rgood measure, pressed down, shaken together, running over, they will pour into your lap. For by your standard of measure it will be measured to you in return."   Mark 4:24

Parable of the Blind Leading the Blind
Matt. 7:3–5, 16–18

39 And He also spoke a parable to them: "A blind man cannot guide a blind man, can he? Will they not both fall into a pit?

40 "A ^Apupil is not above his teacher; but everyone, after he has been fully trained, will be like his teacher.   *disciple*

41 "And why do you look at the speck that is in your brother's eye, but do not notice the log that is in your own eye?

42 "Or how can you say to your brother, 'Brother, let me take out the speck that is in your eye,' when you yourself do not see the log that is in your own eye? You hypocrite, first take the log out of your own eye, and then you will see clearly to take out the speck that is in your brother's eye.

43 "For there is no good tree which produces bad fruit; nor, ^Ton the other hand, a bad tree which produces good fruit.   *again*

44 "For each tree is known by its own fruit. For men do not gather figs from thorns, nor do they pick grapes from a briar bush.

45 "The good man out of the good ^Atreasure of his heart brings forth what is good; and the evil *man* out of the evil *treasure* brings forth what is evil; for his mouth speaks from that which fills his heart.   *treasury, storehouse*

Parable of the Two Foundations
Luke 7:21–27

46 "And ^Rwhy do you call Me, 'Lord, Lord,' and do not do what I say? Mal. 1:6; Matt. 7:21

47 "Everyone who comes to Me, and hears My words, and ^Tacts upon them, I will show you whom he is like: *does*

48 he is like a man building a house, who dug deep and laid a foundation upon the rock; and when a flood rose, the torrent burst against that house and could not shake it, because it had been well built.

49 "But the one who has heard, and has not acted *accordingly*, is like a man who built a house upon the ground without any foundation; and the ^Ttorrent burst against it and immediately it collapsed, and the ruin of that house was great."   *river*

CHAPTER 7

A Centurion's Servant Is Healed
Matt. 8:5–13

W HEN^R He had completed all His discourse in the hearing of the people, ^RHe went to Capernaum.   Matt. 7:28 • Luke 7:1-10

2 And a certain centurion's slave, ^Twho was highly regarded by him, was sick and about to die.   *to whom he was honorable*

3 And when he heard about Jesus, ^Rhe sent some Jewish elders asking Him to come and save the life of his slave. Matt. 8:5

4 And when they had come to Jesus, they earnestly entreated Him, saying, "He is worthy for You to grant this to him;

5 for he loves our nation, and it was he who built us our synagogue."

6 Now Jesus *started* on His way with them; and when He was already not far from the house, the centurion sent friends, saying to Him, "Lord, do not trouble Yourself further, for I am not worthy for You to come under my roof;   *Sir*

7 for this reason I did not even consider myself worthy to come to You, but *just* say the word, and my servant will be healed.

8 "For I, too, am a man under authority, with soldiers under me; and I say to this one, 'Go!' and he goes; and to another, 'Come!' and he comes; and to my slave, 'Do this!' and he does it."

9 Now when Jesus heard this, He marveled at him, and turned and said to the multitude that was following Him, "I say to you, ^Rnot even in Israel have I found such great faith."   Matt. 8:10; Luke 7:50

10 And when those who had been sent returned to the house, they found the slave in good health.

A Widow's Son Is Raised

11 And it came about soon afterwards, that He went to a city called Nain; and His disciples were going along with Him, ^Taccompanied by a large multitude.   *and*

12 Now as He approached the gate of the city, behold, ^Ta dead man was being carried out, the only son of his mother, and she was a widow; and a sizeable crowd from the city was with her.   *one who had died*

13 And when ^Rthe Lord saw her, He felt compassion for her, and said to her, "Do^Anot weep."   Luke 7:19; 10:1; 11:1 • *Stop weeping*

14 And He came up and touched the coffin; and the bearers came to a halt. And He said, "Young man, I say to you, arise!"

15 And the dead man sat up, and began to speak. And *Jesus* gave him back to his mother.   *corpse*

16 And fear gripped them all, and they *began* glorifying God, saying, "A great prophet has arisen among us!" and, "God has^Avisited His people!"   *cared for*

John's Questions Are Answered
Matt. 11:2-6

17 ^RAnd this report concerning Him went out all over Judea, and in all the surrounding district.   Matt. 9:26

18 ^RAnd the disciples of John reported to him about all these things.   Luke 7:18-35

19 And summoning ^Ttwo of his disciples, John sent them to the Lord, saying, "Are You the ^TExpected One, or do we look for someone else?"   *a certain two • Coming One*

20 And when the men had come to Him, they said, "John the Baptist has sent us to You, saying, 'Are You the ^TExpected One, or do we look for someone else?' "   *Coming One*

21 At that ^Tvery time He ^Rcured many *people* of diseases and ^Rafflictions and evil spirits; and He granted sight to many *who were* blind.   *hour* • Matt. 4:23 • Mark 3:10

22 And He answered and said to them, "Go and report to John what you have seen and heard: *the* BLIND RECEIVE SIGHT, *the* lame walk, *the* lepers are cleansed, and *the* deaf hear, *the* dead are raised up, *the* POOR HAVE THE GOSPEL PREACHED TO THEM.

23 "And ^Rblessed is he ^Twho keeps from stumbling over Me."   Ps. 2:12★ • *whoever*

Jesus Praises John
Matt. 11:7-15

24 And when the messengers of John had left, He began to speak to the multitudes about John, "What did you go out into the wilderness to look at? A reed shaken by the wind?

25 "But what did you go out to see? A man dressed in soft clothing? Behold, those who are splendidly clothed and live in luxury are *found* in royal palaces.   *Well then, what*

26 "But what did you go out to see? A prophet? Yes, I say to you, and one who is more than a prophet.

27 "This is the one about whom it ^Tis written,   *has been written*

    'BEHOLD, ^R I SEND MY MESSENGER BEFORE YOUR FACE,   Mal. 3:1★
    WHO WILL PREPARE YOUR WAY BEFORE YOU.'

28 "I say to you, among those born of women, there is no one greater than John; yet he who is ^Tleast in the kingdom of God is greater than he."   *less*

29 And when all the people and the ¹⁶taxgatherers heard *this*, they ^Aacknowledged ^RGod's justice, having been baptized with the baptism of John.   *justified God* • Luke 7:35

30 But the Pharisees and the ¹⁷lawyers rejected God's purpose for themselves, not having been baptized by ^TJohn.   *him*

Jesus Criticizes His Generation
Matt. 11:16-19

31 "To what then shall I compare the men of this generation, and what are they like?

32 "They are like children who sit in the market place and call to one another; and they say, 'We played the flute for you, and you did not dance; we sang a dirge, and you did not weep.'

¹⁶ I.e., Collectors of Roman taxes for profit
¹⁷ I.e., experts in the Mosaic law

33"For John the Baptist has come ᴿeating no bread and drinking no wine; and you say, 'He has a demon!' Luke 1:15

34"The Son of Man has come eating and drinking; and you say, 'Behold, a gluttonous man, and a ᴬdrunkard, a friend of tax-gatherers and sinners!' *wine-drinker*

35"Yetᵀ wisdom ᴿis vindicated by all her children." *And · Luke 7:29*

A Woman Anoints Jesus' Feet

36 Now one of the Pharisees was requesting Him to ᵀdine with him. And He entered the Pharisee's house, and reclined *at the table.* *eat*

37 And behold, there was a woman in the city who was a ᵀsinner; and when she learned that He was reclining *at the table* in the Pharisee's house, she brought an alabaster vial of perfume, *an immoral woman*

38 and standing behind *Him* at His feet, weeping, she began to wet His feet with her tears, and kept wiping them with the hair of her head, and kissing His feet, and anointing them with the perfume.

39 Now when the Pharisee who had invited Him saw this, he said to himself, "If this man were a prophet He would know who and what sort of person this woman is who is touching Him, that she is a sinner."

The Parable of the Two Debtors

40 And Jesus answered and said to him, "Simon, I have something to say to you." And heᵀreplied, "Say it, Teacher." *says*

41"A certain moneylender had two debtors: one owed five hundred ¹⁸denarii,ᴿ and the other fifty. Matt. 18:28; Mark 6:37

42"When they were unable to repay, he graciously forgave them both. Which of them therefore will love him more?"

43 Simon answered and said, "I suppose the one whom he forgave more." And He said to him, "You have judged correctly."

44 And turning toward the woman, He said to Simon, "Do you see this woman? I entered your house; you gave Me no water for My feet, but she has wet My feet with her tears, and wiped them with her hair.

45"Youᴿgave Me no kiss; but she, since the time I came in, ᵀhas not ceased to kiss My feet. 2 Sam. 15:5 · *was not ceasing*

46"You did not anoint My head with oil, but she anointed My feet with perfume.

47"For this reason I say to you, her sins, which are many, have been forgiven, for she loved much; but he who is forgiven little, loves little."

48 And He said to her, "Yourᴿ sins have been forgiven." Matt. 9:2; Mark 2:5, 9

49 And those who were reclining *at the table* with Him began to say to themselves,

"Who is this *man* who even forgives sins?"

50 And He said to the woman, "Yourᴿfaith has saved you; go in peace." Matt. 9:22

CHAPTER 8

Certain Women Minister to Christ

Aɴᴅ it came about soon afterwards, that He *began* going about from one city and village to another, ᴿproclaiming and preaching the kingdom of God; and the twelve were with Him, Matt. 4:23

2 and *also* ᴿsome women who had been healed of evil spirits and sicknesses: Mary who was called Magdalene, from whom seven demons had gone out, Matt. 27:55

3 and Joanna the wife of Chuza,ᴿHerod's steward, and Susanna, and many others who were contributing to their support out of their private means. Matt. 14:1

Parable of the Soils
Matt. 13:1–23; Mark 4:1–20

4 ᴿAnd when a great multitude were coming together, and those from the various cities were journeying to Him, He spoke by way of a parable: Matt. 13:2–9; Luke 8:4–8

5"The sower went out to sow his seed; and as he sowed, some fell beside the road; and it was trampled under foot, and the birds of the ᵀair ate it up. *heaven*

6"And other *seed* fell on rocky *soil,* and as soon as it grew up, it withered away, because it had no moisture.

7"And other *seed* fell among the thorns; and the thorns grew up with it, and choked it out.

8"And other *seed* fell into the good soil, and grew up, and produced a crop a hundred times as great." As He said these things, He would call out, "Heᴿwho has ears to hear, let him hear." Matt. 11:15; Mark 7:16

9 And His disciples *began* questioning Him as to what this parable might be.

10 And He said, "To you it has been granted to know the mysteries of the kingdom of God, but to the rest *it is* in parables, in orderᴿthat sᴇᴇɪɴɢ ᴛʜᴇʏ ᴍᴀʏ ɴᴏᴛ sᴇᴇ, ᴀɴᴅ ʜᴇᴀʀɪɴɢ ᴛʜᴇʏ ᴍᴀʏ ɴᴏᴛ ᴜɴᴅᴇʀsᴛᴀɴᴅ. Is. 6:9

11"Now the parable is this:ᵀthe seed is the word of God. [1 Pet. 1:23]

12"And those beside the road are those who have heard; then the devil comes and takes away the word from their heart, so that they may not believe and be saved.

13"And those on the rocky *soil are* those who, when they hear, receive the word with joy; and these have no *firm* root; ᵀthey believe for a while, and in time of temptation fall away. *who believe*

14"And the *seed* which fell among the thorns, these are the ones who have heard, and as they go on their way they are choked with worries and riches and pleasures of *this* life, and bring no fruit to maturity.

¹⁸ The denarius was equivalent to one day's wage

15 "And the *seed* in the good soil, these are the ones who have heard the word in an honest and good heart, and hold it fast, and bear fruit with ^perseverance.   *steadfastness*

Parable of the Lamp
Mark 4:21-25

16 "Now no one after lighting a lamp covers it over with a container, or puts it under a bed; but he puts it on a lampstand, in order that those who come in may see the light.
17 "For nothing is hidden that shall not become evident, nor *anything* secret that shall not be known and come to light.
18 "Therefore take care how you listen;^for whoever has, to him shall *more* be given; and whoever does not have, even what he ^thinks he has shall be taken away from him."   Matt. 13:12; 25:29 • *seems to have*

Christ's True Brothers
Matt. 12:46-50; Mark 3:31-35

19 ^RAnd His mother and brothers came to Him, and they were unable to get to Him because of the crowd.   Luke 8:19-21
20 And it was reported to Him, "Your mother and Your brothers are standing outside, wishing to see You."
21 But He answered and said to them, "My mother and My brothers are these^who hear the word of God and do it."   Luke 11:28

The Storm Is Stilled
Matt. 8:23-27; Mark 4:35-41

22 ^RNow it came about on one of *those* days, that He and His disciples got into a boat, and He said to them, "Let us go over to the other side of ^the lake." And they launched out.   Luke 8:22-25 • Luke 5:1f.
23 But as they were sailing along He fell asleep; and a fierce gale of wind descended upon ^the lake, and they *began* to be swamped and to be in danger.   Luke 5:1f.; 8:22
24 And they came to Him and woke Him up, saying, "Master, Master, we are perishing!" And being aroused, He rebuked the wind and the surging waves, and they stopped, and ^it became calm.   *a calm occurred*
25 And He said to them, "Where is your faith?" And they were fearful and amazed, saying to one another, "Who then is this, that He commands even the winds and the water, and they obey Him?"

Demons Are Cast into Swine
Matt. 8:28-34; Mark 5:1-20

26 And they sailed to the country of the Gerasenes, which is opposite Galilee.
27 And when He had come out onto the land, He was met by a certain man from the city who was possessed with demons; and who had not put on any clothing for a long

time, and was not living in a house, but in the tombs.
28 And seeing Jesus, he cried out and fell before Him, and said in a loud voice, "What^R do I have to do with You, Jesus, Son of^the Most High God? I beg You, do not torment me."   Matt. 8:29 • Mark 5:7
29 For He^had been commanding the unclean spirit to come out of the man. For it had seized him many times; and he was bound with chains and shackles and kept under guard; and *yet* he would burst his fetters and be driven by the demon into the desert.   *was commanding*
30 And Jesus asked him, "What is your name?" And he said,^"'Legion''; for many demons had entered him.   Matt. 26:53
31 And they were entreating Him not to command them to depart into the abyss.
32 Now there was a herd of many swine feeding there on the mountain; and *the demons* entreated Him to permit them to enter the swine. And He gave them permission.
33 And the demons came out from the man and entered the swine; and the herd rushed down the steep bank into^the lake, and were drowned.   Luke 5:1f.; 8:22
34 And when the herdsmen saw what had happened, they ran away and reported it in the city and *out* in the country.
35 And *the people* went out to see what had happened; and they came to Jesus, and found the man from whom the demons had gone out, sitting down ^at the feet of Jesus, clothed and in his right mind; and they became frightened.   Luke 10:39
36 And those who had seen it reported to them how the man who was demon-possessed had been^made well.   *saved*
37 And all the people of the country of the Gerasenes and the surrounding district asked Him to depart from them; for they were gripped with great fear; and He got into a boat, and returned.
38 ^RBut the man from whom the demons had gone out was begging Him that he might ^accompany Him; but He sent him away, saying,   Luke 8:38, 39 • *be with*
39 "Return to your house and describe what great things God has done for you." And he went away, proclaiming throughout the whole city what great things Jesus had done for him.
40 ^RAnd as Jesus returned, the multitude welcomed Him, for they had all been waiting for Him.   Matt. 9:1; Mark 5:21

A Woman with Issue Is Healed
Matt. 9:18-22; Mark 5:21-34

41 And behold, there came a man named Jairus, and he was an official of the synagogue; and he fell at Jesus' feet, and *began* to entreat Him to come to his house;
42 for he had an ^only daughter, about twelve years old, and she was dying. But as

He went, the multitudes were pressing against Him.   *only begotten*

43 And a woman who had a hemorrhage for twelve years, [19]and could not be healed by anyone,

44 came up behind Him, and touched the fringe of His ˆcloak; and immediately her hemorrhage stopped.   *outer garment*

45 And Jesus said, "Who is the one who touched Me?" And while they were all denying it, Peter said, "Master, the multitudes are crowding and pressing upon You."

46 But Jesus said, "Someone did touch Me, for I was aware that ˮpower had gone out of Me."   Luke 5:17

47 And when the woman saw that she had not escaped notice, she came trembling and fell down before Him, and declared in the presence of all the people the reason why she had touched Him, and how she had been immediately healed.

48 And He said to her, "Daughter, your faith has made you well; go in peace."

Jairus's Daughter Is Raised
Matt. 9:23–26; Mark 5:35–43

49 While He was still speaking, someone *came from *the house of* the synagogue official, saying, "Your daughter has died; do not trouble the Teacher anymore." Luke 8:41

50 But when Jesus heard *this,* He answered him, "Do not be afraid *any longer;* only believe, and she shall be made well."

51 And when He had come to the house, He did not allow anyone to enter with Him, except Peter and John and James, and the girl's father and mother.

52 Now they were all weeping and lamenting for her; but He said, "Stop weeping, for she has not died, but is asleep."

53 And they *began* laughing at Him, knowing that she had died.

54 He, however, took her by the hand and called, saying, "Child, arise!"

55 And her spirit returned, and she rose immediately; and He gave orders for *something* to be given her to eat.

56 And her parents were amazed; but He ˮinstructed them to tell no one what had happened.   Matt. 8:4

CHAPTER 9

Twelve Are Sent to Preach
Matt. 10:1–14; 14:1–14;
Mark 6:7–16, 30–34

AND ˮHe called the twelve together, and gave them power and authority over all the demons, and to heal diseases.   Matt. 10:5

2 And He sent them out to proclaim the kingdom of God, and to perform healing.

3 And He said to them, "Take nothing for *your* journey, neither a staff, nor aˆbag, nor bread, nor money; and do not *even* have two tunics apiece.   *knapsack* or *beggar's bag*

4 "And whatever house you enter, stay there, and take your leave from there.

5 "And as for those who do not receive you, as you go out from that city, ˮshake off the dust from your feet as a testimony against them."   Luke 10:11; Acts 13:51

6 And departing, they *began* going about among the villages, ˮpreaching the gospel, and healing everywhere.   Mark 6:12

7 ˮNow Herod the tetrarch heard of all that was happening; and he was greatly perplexed, because it was said by some that John had risen from the dead,   Luke 9:7-9

8 and by some thatˮElijah had appeared, and by others, that one of the prophets of old had risen again.   Matt. 16:14

9 And Herod said, "I myself had John beheaded; but who is this man about whom I hear such things?" Andˮhe kept trying to see Him.   Luke 23:8

10 And when the apostles returned, they gave an account to Him of all that they had done. And taking them with Him, He withdrew by Himself to a city called Bethsaida.

11 But the multitudes were aware of this and followed Him; and welcoming them, He *began* speaking to them about the kingdom of God and curing those who had need of healing.

Five Thousand Are Fed
Matt. 14:15–21; Mark 6:35–44;
John 6:1–14

12 And the day began to decline, and the twelve came and said to Him, "Send the multitude away, that they may go into the surrounding villages and countryside and find lodging and get something to eat; for here we are in a desolate place."

13 But He said to them, "You give them *something* to eat!" And they said, "We have no more than five loaves and two fish, unless perhaps we go and buy food for all these people."

14 (For there were about five thousand men.) And He said to His disciples, "Have them recline *to eat*ˮin groups of about fifty each."   Mark 6:39

15 And they did so, and had them all recline.

16 And He took the five loaves and the two fish, and looking up to heaven, He blessed them, and broke *them,* and kept giving *them* to the disciples to set before the multitude.

17 And they all ate and were satisfied; and the broken pieces which they had left over were picked up, twelve baskets *full.*

Peter's Confession of Faith
Matt. 16:13–21; Mark 8:27–31

18 ˮAnd it came about that while He was

---

[19] Some mss. add *who had spent all her living upon physicians*

praying alone, the disciples were with Him. and He questioned them, saying, "Who do the multitudes say that I am?"   Luke 9:18-20

19 And they answered and said, "John the Baptist, and others *say* Elijah; but others, that one of the prophets of old has risen again."

20 And He said to them, "But who do you say that I am?" And Peter answered and said, "The[T]Christ of God."   Messiah

21 But He[R]warned them, and instructed *them* not to tell this to anyone,   Matt. 8:4

22 saying, "The[R] Son of Man must suffer many things, and be rejected by the elders and chief priests and scribes, and be killed, and be raised up on the third day." Luke 9:44

True Cost of Discipleship
Matt. 16:24-27; Mark 9:34-38

23 And He was saying to *them* all, "If[R]anyone wishes to come after Me, let him deny himself, and take up his cross daily, and follow Me.   Matt. 10:38; Luke 14:27

24"For whoever wishes to save his life shall lose it, but whoever loses his life for My sake, he is the one who will save it.

25"For what is a man profited if he gains the whole world, and[R]loses or forfeits himself?   [Heb. 10:34]

26"For[R]whoever is ashamed of Me and My words, of him will the Son of Man be ashamed when He comes in His glory, and *the glory* of the Father and of the holy angels.   Matt. 10:33; Luke 12:9

The Transfiguration
Matt. 16:28—17:9; Mark 9:1-9;
2 Pet. 1:17, 18

27"But I say to you truthfully, [R]there are some of those standing here who shall not taste death until they see the kingdom of God."   Matt. 16:28; Acts 7:55, 56☆

28 [R]And some eight days after these sayings, it came about that He took along[R]Peter and John and James, and went up to the mountain to pray.   Luke 9:28-36 • Matt. 17:1

29 And while He was praying, the appearance of His face became different, and His clothing *became* white *and* gleaming.

30 And behold, two men were talking with Him; and they were Moses and Elijah,

31 who, appearing in[g]glory, were speaking of His departure which He was about to accomplish at Jerusalem.   *splendor*

32 Now Peter and his companions[R]had been overcome with sleep; but when they were fully awake, they saw His glory and the two men standing with Him.   Mark 14:40

33 And it came about, as[T]these were parting from Him, Peter said to Jesus, "Master, it is good for us to be here; and let us make three[A]tabernacles: one for You, and one for Moses, and one for Elijah"—not realizing what he was saying.   *they • sacred tents*

34 And while he was saying this, a cloud formed and *began* to overshadow them; and they were afraid as they entered the cloud.

35 And[R]a voice came out of the cloud, saying, "This[R]is My Son, *My* Chosen One; listen to Him!"   2 Pet. 1:17f. • [Is. 42:1]★

36 And when the voice[T]had spoken, Jesus was found alone. And they kept silent, and reported to no one in those days any of the things which they had seen.   *occurred*

Demoniac Son Is Healed
Matt. 17:14-18; Mark 9:14-27

37 And it came about on the next day, that when they had come down from the mountain, a great multitude met Him.

38 And behold, a man from the multitude shouted out, saying, "Teacher, I beg You to look at my son, for he is my only *boy,*

39 and behold, a spirit seizes him, and he suddenly screams, and it throws him into a convulsion with foaming *at the mouth,* and as it mauls him, it scarcely leaves him.

40"And I begged Your disciples to cast it out, and they could not."

41 And Jesus answered and said, "O unbelieving and perverted generation, how long shall I be with you, and put up with you? Bring your son here."

42 And while he was still approaching, the demon[A]dashed him *to the ground,* and threw him into a convulsion. But Jesus rebuked the unclean spirit, and healed the boy, and gave him back to his father.   *tore him*

Christ Prophesies His Coming Death
Matt. 17:22, 23; Mark 9:30-32

43 And they were all amazed at the greatness of God.

But while everyone was marveling at all that He was doing, He said to His disciples,

44"Let these words sink into your ears;[R]for the Son of Man is going to be[A]delivered into the hands of men." Luke 9:22; 22:54☆ • *betrayed*

45 But[R]they[T]did not understand this statement, and it was concealed from them so that they might not perceive it; and they were afraid to ask Him about this statement.   Mark 9:32 • *were not knowing*

True Greatness
Matt. 18:1-5; Mark 9:33-40

46 And an argument arose among them as to which of them might be the greatest.

47 But Jesus, knowing[T]what they were thinking in their heart, took a child and stood him by His side,   *the reasoning*

48 and said to them, "Whoever receives this child in My name receives Me; and whoever receives Me receives Him who sent Me; for he who is[A]least among you, this is the one who is great."   *lowliest*

49 And John answered and said, "Master, we saw someone casting out demons in

Your name; and we tried to hinder him because he does not follow along with us."

50 But Jesus said to him, "Do not hinder *him;* [R]for he who is not against you is [A]for you."   Matt. 12:30; Luke 11:23 • *on your side*

Samaria Rejects Christ

51 And it came about, when the days were approaching for His ascension, that He resolutely set His face to go to Jerusalem;

52 and He sent messengers on ahead of Him. And they went, and entered a village of the [R]Samaritans, to [A]make arrangements for Him.   Matt. 10:5; Luke 10:33 • *prepare*

53 And they did not receive Him, because [T]He was journeying with His face toward Jerusalem.   *His face was proceeding toward*

54 And when His disciples [R]James and John saw *this,* they said, "Lord, do You want us to command fire to come down from heaven and consume them?" Mark 3:17

55 But He turned and rebuked them, [and said, "You do not know what kind of spirit you are of;

56 for the Son of Man did not come to destroy men's lives, but to save them."] And they went on to another village.

True Cost of Discipleship
Matt. 8:18–22

57 And [A]as they were going along the road, [R]someone said to Him, "I will follow You wherever You go."   Luke 9:51 • Luke 9:57

58 And Jesus said to him, "The foxes have holes, and the birds of the [A]air *have* [A]nests, but the Son of Man has nowhere to lay His head."   *sky* • *roosting-places*

59 And He said to another, "Follow[R]Me." But he said, "Permit[20] me first to go and bury my father."   Matt. 8:22

60 But He said to him, "Allow the dead to bury their own dead; but as for you, go and proclaim everywhere the kingdom of God."

61 And another also said, "I will follow You, Lord; but[R]first permit me to say goodbye to those at home."   1 Kin. 19:20

62 But Jesus said to him, "No one, after putting his hand to the plow and looking back, is fit for the kingdom of God."

CHAPTER 10

Mission of the Seventy

N OW after this[R]the Lord appointed seventy others, and sent them two and two ahead of Him to every city and place where He Himself was going to come.   Luke 7:13

2 And He was saying to them, "The[R] harvest is plentiful, but the laborers are few; therefore beseech the Lord of the harvest to send out laborers into His harvest. John 4:35

3 "Go your ways;[R]behold, I send you out as lambs in the midst of wolves. Matt. 10:16

4 "Carry no purse, no bag, no shoes; and greet no one on the way.

5 "And whatever house you enter, first say, 'Peace *be* to this house.'

6 "And if a [T]man of peace is there, your peace will rest upon him; but if not, it will return to you.   *son*

7 "And stay in [A]that house, eating and drinking what they give you; for the laborer is worthy of his wages. Do not keep moving from house to house.   *the house itself*

8 "And whatever city you enter, and they receive you, eat what is set before you;

9 and heal those in it who are sick, and say to them, 'The[R]kingdom of God has come near to you.'   Matt. 3:2; 10:7; Luke 10:11

10 "But whatever city you enter and they do not receive you, go out into its streets and say,

11 'Even[R]the dust of your city which clings to our feet, we wipe off *in protest* against you; yet[T]be sure of this, that the kingdom of God has come near.'   Matt. 10:14 • *know*

12 "I say to you, it will be more tolerable in that day for Sodom, than for that city.

13 "Woe to you, Chorazin! Woe to you, Bethsaida! For if the[A]miracles had been performed in Tyre and Sidon which occurred in you, they would have repented long ago, sitting in sackcloth and ashes. *works of power*

14 "But it will be more tolerable for Tyre and Sidon in the judgment, than for you.

15 "And you, [R]Capernaum, will not be exalted to heaven, will you? You will be brought down to Hades! Is. 14:13-15; Matt. 4:13

16 "The one who listens to you listens to Me, and[R]the one who rejects you rejects Me; and he who rejects Me rejects the One who sent Me."   John 12:48; 1 Thess. 4:8

Return of the Seventy

17 And the [A]seventy returned with joy, saying, "Lord, even the demons are subject to us in Your name." Some mss. read *seventy-two*

18 And He said to them, "I was watching Satan fall from heaven like lightning.

19 "Behold, I have given you authority to [R]tread upon serpents and scorpions, and over all the power of the enemy, and nothing shall injure you.   Ps. 91:13; Mark 16:18

20 "Nevertheless do not rejoice in this, that the spirits are subject to you, but rejoice that your names are recorded in heaven."

21 At that very[T]time He rejoiced greatly in the Holy Spirit, and said, 'I [A]praise Thee, O Father, Lord of heaven and earth, that Thou didst hide these things from *the* wise and intelligent and didst reveal them to babes. Yes, Father, for thus it was well-pleasing in Thy sight.   *hour* • *acknowledge*

22 "All things have been handed over to Me by My Father, and no one knows who the Son is except the Father, and who the

---

[20] Some mss. add *Lord*

Father is except the Son, and anyone to whom the Son wills to reveal *Him*."

23 *And turning to the disciples, He said privately, "Blessed *are* the eyes which see the things you see, *Matt. 13:16, 17; Luke 10:23, 24*

24 for I say to you, that many prophets and kings wished to see the things which you see, and did not see *them*, and to hear the things which you hear, and did not hear *them*."

How to Inherit Eternal Life

25 And behold, a certain lawyer stood up and put Him to the test, saying, "Teacher, what shall I do to inherit eternal life?"

26 And He said to him, "What is written in the Law? How does it read to you?"

27 And he answered and said, "You᷎ SHALL LOVE THE LORD YOUR GOD WITH ALL YOUR HEART, AND WITH ALL YOUR SOUL, AND WITH ALL YOUR STRENGTH, AND WITH ALL YOUR MIND; AND YOUR NEIGHBOR AS YOUR-SELF."   *Lev. 19:18; Deut. 6:5*

28 And He said to him, "You have answered correctly; ᴿDO THIS, AND YOU WILL LIVE."   *Lev. 18:5; Ezek. 20:11; Matt. 19:17*

Parable of the Good Samaritan

29 But wishing to justify himself, he said to Jesus, "And who is my neighbor?"

30 Jesus replied and said, "A certain man was going down from Jerusalem to Jericho; and he fell among robbers, and they stripped him and ᵀbeat him, and went off leaving him half dead.   *laid blows upon*

31 "And by chance a certain priest was going down on that road, and when he saw him, he passed by on the other side.

32 "And likewise a Levite also, when he came to the place and saw him, passed by on the other side.

33 "But a certainᴿSamaritan, who was on a journey, came upon him; and when he saw him, he felt compassion,   *Matt. 10:5; Luke 9:52*

34 and came to him, and bandaged up his wounds, pouring oil and wine on *them;* and he put him on his own beast, and brought him to an inn, and took care of him.

35 "And on the next day he took out two ²¹denarii and gave them to the innkeeper and said, 'Take care of him; and whatever more you spend, when I return, I will repay you.'

36 "Which of these three do you think proved to be a neighbor to the man who fell into the robbers' *hands?*"

37 And he said, "The one who showed mercy toward him." And Jesus said to him, "Go and do ᴬthe same."   *likewise*

Mary and Martha Are Contrasted

38 Now as they were traveling along, He entered a certain village; and a ᵀwoman named ᴿMartha welcomed Him into her home.   *certain woman • Luke 10:40f.*

39 And she had a sister calledᴿMary, who moreover was listening to the Lord's word, ᴿseated at His feet.   *Luke 10:42 • Luke 8:35*

40 But Martha was distracted with ᵀall her preparations; and she came up *to Him,* and said, "Lord, do You not care that my sister has left me to do all the serving alone? Then tell her to help me."   *much service*

41 But the Lord answered and said to her, "Martha,ᴿ Martha, you are worried and bothered about so many things;   *Luke 10:38, 40*

42 ᴿbut *only* a few things are necessary, ᵀreally *only* one, for Mary has chosen the good part, which shall not be taken away from her."   *[Ps. 27:4; John 6:27] • or*

CHAPTER 11

The Lord's Prayer
Matt. 6:9–13

A̲ND it came about that while He was praying in a certain place, after He had finished, one of His disciples said to Him, "Lord, teach us to pray just as John also taught his disciples."

2 And He said to them, "Whenᴿyou pray, say: *Matt. 6:9–13; Luke 11:2–4*
'Father,²² hallowed be Thy name.
Thy kingdom come.

3 'Give us each day our daily bread.

4 'And forgive us our sins,
For we ourselves also forgive every-
     one who is indebted to us.
And lead us not into temptation.' "

Parable of the Persistent Friend

5 And He said to them, "Supposeᵀ one of you shall have a friend, and shall go to him at midnight, and say to him, 'Friend, lend me three loaves;   *Which one of you*

6 for a friend of mine has come to me from a journey, and I have nothing to set before him';

7 and from inside he shall answer and say, 'Do not bother me; the door has already been shut and my children and I are in bed; I cannot get up and give you *anything.*'

8 "I tell you, even though he will not get up and give him *anything* because he is his friend, yet because of his persistence he will get up and give him as much as he needs.

9 "And I say to you, ask, and it shall be given to you; seek, and you shall find; knock, and it shall be opened to you.

10 "For everyone who asks, receives; and he who seeks, finds; and to him who knocks, it shall be opened.

Parable of the Good Father
Matt. 7:7–11

11 "Now suppose one of you fathers is

---

²¹ The denarius was equivalent to one day's wage
²² Some mss. insert phrases from Matt. 6:9-13 to make the two passages closely similar

asked by his son for a fish; he will not give him a snake instead of a fish, will he?

12 "Or if he is asked for an egg, he will not give him a scorpion, will he?

13 "If you then, being evil, know how to give good gifts to your children, how much more shall your heavenly Father give the Holy Spirit to those who ask Him?"

Christ Heals the Demoniac

14 And He was casting out a demon, and it was dumb; and it came about that when the demon had gone out, the dumb man spoke; and the multitudes marveled.

Christ's Power Not from Satan
Matt. 12:25–30, 43–45; Mark 3:22–27

15 But some of them said, "He casts out demons[R]by[R]Beelzebul, the ruler of the demons."   Matt. 9:34 • Matt. 10:25

16 And others,[T]to test Him, were demanding of Him a sign from heaven.   were testing

17 But He knew their thoughts, and said to them, "Any[T]kingdom divided against itself is laid waste; and a house divided against[T]itself falls.   every • a house

18 "And if Satan also is divided against himself, how shall his kingdom stand? For you say that I cast out demons by Beelzebul.

19 "And if I by Beelzebul cast out demons, by whom do your sons cast them out? Consequently they shall be your judges.

20 "But if I cast out demons by the[R]finger of God, then[R]the kingdom of God has come upon you.   Ex. 8:19 • Matt. 3:2

21 "When[T]a strong man, fully armed, guards his own homestead, his possessions are[T]undisturbed;   the • in peace

22 but when someone stronger than he attacks him and overpowers him, he takes away from him all his armor on which he had relied, and distributes his plunder.

23 "He[R]who is not with Me is against Me; and he who does not gather with Me, scatters.   Matt. 12:30; Mark 9:40

24 "When the unclean spirit goes out of a man, it passes through waterless places seeking rest, and not finding any, it says, 'I will return to my house from which I came.'

25 "And when it comes, it finds it swept and put in order.

26 "Then it goes and takes along seven other spirits more evil than itself, and they go in and live there; and the last state of that man becomes worse than the first."

27 And it came about while He said these things, one of the women in the crowd raised her voice, and said to Him, "Blessed[R] is the womb that bore You, and the breasts at which You nursed."   Luke 23:29

28 But He said, "On the contrary, blessed are[R]those who hear the word of God, and observe it."   [Luke 8:21]

Christ's Only Sign Is Jonah
Matt. 12:39–42

29 And as the crowds were increasing, He began to say, "This generation is a wicked generation; it seeks for a[A]sign, and yet no sign shall be given to it[R]but the sign of Jonah.   attesting miracle • Luke 24:46; Acts 10:40☆

30 "For just as[R]Jonah became a sign to the Ninevites,[R]so shall the Son of Man be to this generation.   Jon. 3:4 • 1 Cor. 15:4☆

31 "The[R]Queen of the South shall rise up with the men of this generation at the judgment and condemn them, because she came from the ends of the earth to hear the wisdom of Solomon; and behold, something greater than Solomon is here.   1 Kin. 10:1-10

32 "The men of Nineveh shall stand up with this generation at the judgment and condemn it, because[R]they repented at the preaching of Jonah; and behold, something greater than Jonah is here.   Jon. 3:5

Parable of the Lighted Lamp

33 "No[R] one, after lighting a lamp, puts it away in a cellar, nor under a peck-measure, but on the lampstand, in order that those who enter may see the light.   Matt. 5:15

34 "The lamp of your body is your eye; when your eye is[A]clear, your whole body also is full of light; but when it is bad, your body also is full of darkness.   healthy

35 "Then watch out that the light in you may not be darkness.

36 "If therefore your whole body is full of light, with no dark part in it, it shall be wholly illumined, as when the lamp illumines you with its rays."

"Woes" on the Pharisees

37 Now when He had spoken, a Pharisee *asked Him to have lunch with him; and He went in, and reclined at the table.

38 And when the Pharisee saw it, he was surprised that He had not first[T]ceremonially washed before the meal.   baptized

39 But the Lord said to him, "Now you Pharisees clean the outside of the cup and of the platter; but[T]inside of you, you are full of robbery and wickedness.   your inside is full

40 "You[R]foolish ones, did not He who made the outside make the inside also? Luke 12:20

41 "But give that which is within as charity, and then all things are clean for you.

42 "But[R]woe to you Pharisees! For you[R]pay tithe of mint and rue and every kind of garden herb, and yet disregard justice and the love of God; but these are the things you should have done without neglecting the others.   Matt. 23:23 • Lev. 27:30; Luke 18:12

43 "Woe to you Pharisees! For you love the front seats in the synagogues, and the respectful greetings in the market places.

44 "Woe to you! For you are like[A]concealed

tombs, and the people who walk over *them* are unaware *of it."*   indistinct, unseen

"Woes" on the Lawyers

45 And one of the [23]lawyers[R] *said to Him in reply, "Teacher, when You say this, You insult us too."*   Matt. 22:35; Luke 11:46, 52

46 But He said, "Woe to you[R]lawyers as well! For [R]you weigh men down with burdens hard to bear,[T]while you yourselves will not even touch the burdens with one of your fingers.   Matt. 22:35 • Matt. 23:4 • *and*

47 "Woe[R]to you! For you build the[A]tombs of the prophets, and *it was* your fathers *who* killed them.   Matt. 23:29ff. • *monuments to*

48 "Consequently, you are witnesses and approve the deeds of your fathers; because it was they who killed them, and you build *their tombs.*

49 "For this reason also the wisdom of God said, 'I will send to them prophets and apostles, and *some* of them they will kill and *some* they will[A]persecute,   *drive out*

50 in order that the blood of all the prophets, shed since the foundation of the world, may be charged against this generation,

51 from[R]the blood of Abel to the blood of Zechariah, who perished between the altar and the house *of God;* yes, I tell you, it shall be charged against this generation.'   Gen. 4:8

52 "Woe to you[R]lawyers! For you have taken away the key of knowledge; you did not enter in yourselves, and those who were entering in you hindered."   Matt. 22:35

53 And when He left there, the scribes and the Pharisees began to be very hostile and to question Him closely on many subjects,

54 [R]plotting against Him, to catch *Him* in something He might say.   Mark 3:2; Luke 20:20

CHAPTER 12

Christ Warns About Hypocrisy
Matt. 10:26–33

UNDER these circumstances, after [T]so many thousands of the multitude had gathered together that they were stepping on one another, He began saying to His disciples first *of all,* "Beware of the leaven of the Pharisees, which is hypocrisy.   *myriads*

2 "But there is nothing covered up that will not be revealed, and hidden that will not be known.

3 "Accordingly, whatever you have said in the dark shall be heard in the light, and what you have whispered in the inner rooms shall be proclaimed upon the housetops.

4 "And I say to you, My friends, do not be afraid of those who kill the body, and after that have no more that they can do.

5 "But I will warn you whom to fear: fear the One who after He has killed has authority to cast into hell; yes, I tell you, fear Him!

6 "Are not five sparrows sold for two [T]cents? And *yet* not one of them is forgotten before God.   the smallest of copper coins

7 "Indeed,[R] the very hairs of your head are all numbered. Do not fear; you are of more value than many sparrows.   Matt. 10:30

8 "And I say to you, everyone who confesses Me before men, the Son of Man shall confess him also before the angels of God;

9 but he who denies Me before men shall be denied before the angels of God.

10 "And everyone who will speak a word against the Son of Man, it shall be forgiven him; but he who blasphemes against the Holy Spirit, it shall not be forgiven him.

11 "And when they bring you before [R]the synagogues and the rulers and the authorities, do not become anxious about how or what you should speak in your defense, or what you should say;   Matt. 10:17

12 for the Holy Spirit will teach you in that very hour what you ought to say."

Parable of the Rich Fool

13 And someone [T]in the crowd said to Him, "Teacher, tell my brother to divide the *family* inheritance with me."   *out of*

14 But He said to him, "Man, who appointed Me a judge or arbiter over you?"

15 And He said to them, "Beware, and be on your guard against every form of greed; for not *even* when one has an abundance does his life consist of his possessions."

16 And He told them a parable, saying, "The land of a certain rich man was very productive.

17 "And he began reasoning to himself, saying, 'What shall I do, since I have no place to store my crops?'

18 "And he said, 'This is what I will do: I will tear down my barns and build larger ones, and there I will store all my grain and my goods.

19 'And I will say to my soul, "Soul,[R]you have many goods laid up for many years *to come;* take your ease, eat, drink *and* be merry." '   Eccl. 11:9

20 "But God said to him, 'You fool! This *very* night[T]your soul is required of you; and *now* who will own what you have prepared?'   *they are demanding your soul from you*

21 "So is the man who lays up treasure for himself, and is not rich toward God."

Seek the Kingdom of God
Matt. 6:25–33

22 And He said to His disciples, "For this reason I say to you, do not be anxious for *your* life, *as to* what you shall eat; nor for your body, *as to* what you shall put on.

23 "For life is more than food, and the body than clothing.

24 "Consider the ravens, for they neither

[23] I.e., experts in the Mosaic law

sow nor reap; and they have no storeroom nor barn; and *yet* God feeds them; how much more valuable you are than the birds!

25 "And which of you by being anxious can add a *single* [24]cubit to his [25]life's span?

26 "If then you cannot do even a very little thing, why are you anxious about other matters?

27 "Consider the lilies, how they grow; they neither toil nor spin; but I tell you, even [R]Solomon in all his glory did not clothe himself like one of these.   1 Kin. 10:4-7; 2 Chr. 9:3-6

28 "But if God so arrays the grass in the field, which is *alive* today and tomorrow is thrown into the furnace, how much more *will He clothe* you, O men of little faith!

29 "And do not seek what you shall eat, and what you shall drink, and do not [R]keep worrying.   Matt. 6:31

30 "For all these things the nations of the world eagerly seek; but your Father knows that you need these things.

31 "But seek for His kingdom, and [R]these things shall be added to you.   Matt. 6:33

32 "Do[R] not be afraid, [R]little flock, for your Father has chosen gladly to give you the kingdom.   Matt. 14:27 • Is. 40:11; Zech. 13:7☆

33 "Sell[R]your possessions and give to charity; make yourselves purses which do not wear out, [R]an unfailing treasure in heaven, where no thief comes near, nor moth destroys.   Matt. 19:21 • Matt. 6:20; Luke 12:21

34 "For [R]where your treasure is, there will your heart be also.   Matt. 6:21

Parable of the Expectant Steward

35 "Be[T]dressed in readiness, and *keep* your lamps alight.   *Let your loins be girded*

36 "And be like men who are waiting for their master when he returns from the wedding feast, so that they may immediately open *the door* to him when he comes and knocks.

37 "Blessed are those slaves whom the master shall find [R]on the alert when he comes; truly I say to you, that [R]he will gird himself *to serve*, and have them recline *at the table*, and will come up and wait on them.   Matt. 24:42 • Luke 17:8; John 13:4

38 "Whether[R] he comes in the [26]second watch, or even in the [27]third, and finds *them* so, blessed are those *slaves*.   Matt. 24:43

39 "And[T]be sure of this, that if the head of the house had known at what hour the thief was coming, he would not have allowed his house to be[T]broken into.   *know • dug through*

40 "You[R]too, be ready; for the Son of Man is coming at an hour that you do not [T]expect."   Mark 13:33; [Luke 21:36] • *think, suppose*

Parable of the Faithful Steward
Matt. 24:45-51

41 And Peter said, "Lord, are You ad-

dressing this parable to us, or[R]to everyone *else* as well?"   Luke 12:47, 48

42 And the Lord said, "Who then is the faithful and sensible steward, whom his master will put in charge of his servants, to give them their rations at the proper time?

43 "Blessed is that slave whom his [A]master finds so doing when he comes.   *lord*

44 "Truly I say to you, that he will put him in charge of all his possessions.

45 "But if that slave says in his heart, 'My master will be a long time in coming,' and begins to beat the slaves, *both* men and women, and to eat and drink and get drunk;

46 the master of that slave will come on a day when he does not expect *him*, and at an hour he does not know, and will cut him in pieces, and assign him a place with the unbelievers.

47 "And that slave who knew his master's will and did not get ready or act in accord with his will, shall receive many lashes,

48 but the one who did not know *it*, and committed deeds worthy of [T]a flogging, will receive but few. And from everyone who has been given much shall much be required; and to whom they entrusted much, of him they will ask all the more.   *blows*

Christ Warns of the Costs of Discipleship

49 "I have come to cast fire upon the earth; and how I wish it were already kindled!

50 "But I have a baptism to undergo, and how distressed I am until it is accomplished!

51 "Do[R] you suppose that I came to grant peace on earth? I tell you, no, but rather division;   Matt. 10:34-36; Luke 12:51-53

52 for from now on five *members* in one household will be divided, three against two, and two against three.

53 "They will be divided, father against son, and son against father; mother against daughter, and daughter against mother; mother-in-law against daughter-in-law, and daughter-in-law against mother-in-law."

Christ Warns of
Not Discerning the Times

54 And He was also saying to the multitudes, "When[R]you see a cloud rising in the west, immediately you say, 'A shower is coming,' and so it turns out.   Matt. 16:2f.

55 "And when *you see* a south wind blowing, you say, 'It will be a[R]hot day,' and it turns out *that way*.   Matt. 20:12

56 "You hypocrites![R]You know how to analyze the appearance of the earth and the sky, but[T]why do you not analyze this present time?   Matt. 16:3 • *how*

57 "And[R]why do you not even on your own initiative judge what is right?   Luke 21:30

58 "For while you are going with your opponent to appear before the magistrate, on

your way *there* make an effort to settle with him, in order that he may not drag you before the judge, and the judge turn you over to the constable, and the constable throw you into prison.   *be released from him*

59"I say to you, you shall not get out of there until you have paid the very last cent."

CHAPTER 13

Christ Teaches on Repentance

NOW on the same occasion there were some present who reported to Him about the Galileans, whose blood Pilate had mingled with their sacrifices.   *shed along with*

2 And He answered and said to them, "Do you suppose that these Galileans were *greater* sinners than all *other* Galileans, because they suffered this *fate*?   John 9:2f.

3"I tell you, no, but, unless you repent, you will all likewise perish.   *are repentant*

4"Or do you suppose that those eighteen on whom the tower in Siloam fell and killed them, were *worse* culprits than all the men who live in Jerusalem?   *debtors*

5"I tell you, no, but unless you repent, you will all likewise perish."

6 And He *began* telling this parable: "A certain man had a fig tree which had been planted in his vineyard, and he came looking for fruit on it, and did not find any.

7"And he said to the vineyard-keeper, 'Behold, for three years I have come looking for fruit on this fig tree without finding any. Cut it down! Why does it even use up the ground?'   *and I do not find* • Matt. 3:10; 7:19

8"And he answered and said to him, 'Let it alone, sir, for this year too, until I dig around it and put in fertilizer;

9 and if it bears fruit next year, *fine;* but if not, cut it down.' "

Christ Heals the Crippled Woman

10 And He was teaching in one of the synagogues on the Sabbath.   Matt. 4:23

11 And behold, there was a woman who for eighteen years had had a sickness caused by a spirit; and she was bent double, and could not straighten up at all. Luke 13:16

12 And when Jesus saw her, He called her over and said to her, "Woman, you are freed from your sickness."

13 And He laid His hands upon her; and immediately she was made erect again, and *began* glorifying God.   Mark 5:23 • Matt. 9:8

14 And the synagogue official, indignant because Jesus had healed on the Sabbath, *began* saying to the multitude in response, "There are six days in which work should be done; therefore come during them and get healed, and not on the Sabbath day."

15 But the Lord answered him and said,

"You hypocrites, does not each of you on the Sabbath untie his ox or his donkey from the stall, and lead him away to water *him?*

16"And this woman, a daughter of Abraham as she is, whom Satan has bound for eighteen long years, should she not have been released from this bond on the Sabbath day?"   Luke 19:9 • Matt. 4:10; Luke 13:11

17 And as He said this, all His opponents were being humiliated; and the entire multitude was rejoicing over all the glorious things being done by Him.   Luke 18:43

Parable of the Mustard Seed
Matt. 13:31, 32; Mark 4:30–32

18 Therefore He was saying, "What is the kingdom of God like, and to what shall I compare it?   Luke 13:18, 19 • Matt. 13:24

19"It is like a mustard seed, which a man took and threw into his own garden; and it grew and became a tree; and THE BIRDS OF THE AIR NESTED IN ITS BRANCHES."   *sky*

Parable of the Leaven
Matt. 13:33–35

20 And again He said, "To what shall I compare the kingdom of God?   Matt. 13:24

21"It is like leaven, which a woman took and hid in three pecks of meal, until it was all leavened."   Luke 13:20, 21 • Gr., *sata*

The Way into the Kingdom

22 And He was passing through from one city and village to another, teaching, and proceeding on His way to Jerusalem.

23 And someone said to Him, "Lord, are there *just* a few who are being saved?" And He said to them,

24"Strive to enter by the narrow door; for many, I tell you, will seek to enter and will not be able.   [Matt. 7:13] • *able, once*

25"Once the head of the house gets up and shuts the door, and you begin to stand outside and knock on the door, saying, 'Lord, open up to us!' then He will answer and say to you, 'I do not know where you are from.'

26"Then you will begin to say, 'We ate and drank in Your presence, and You taught in our streets';   Luke 3:8

27 and He will say, 'I tell you, I do not know where you are from; DEPART FROM ME, ALL YOU EVILDOERS.'   Luke 13:25

28"There will be weeping and gnashing of teeth there when you see Abraham and Isaac and Jacob and all the prophets in the kingdom of God, but yourselves being cast out.   Matt. 8:12; 22:13; 25:30

29"And they will come from east and west, and from north and south, and will recline *at the table* in the kingdom of God.

30"And behold, *some* are last who will be first and *some* are first who will be last."

Christ Mourns over Jerusalem

31 Just at that time some Pharisees came up, saying to Him, "Go away and depart from here, for Herod wants to kill You."

32 And He said to them, "Go and tell that fox, 'Behold, I cast out demons and perform cures today and tomorrow, and ᴿthe third day I reach My goal.'   Luke 24:46☆

33"Nevertheless ᴿI must journey on today and tomorrow and the next *day;* for it cannot be that a ᴿprophet should perish outside of Jerusalem.   John 11:9 • Matt. 21:11

34"O ᴿJerusalem, Jerusalem, *the city* that kills the prophets and stones those sent to her! How often I wanted to gather your children together, ᴿjust as a hen *gathers* her brood under her wings, and you would not have it!   Luke 13:34, 35 • Matt. 23:37

35"Behold, ᴿyour house is left to you *desolate;* and I say to you, you shall not see Me until *the time* comes when you say, 'BLESSED ᴿIS HE WHO COMES IN THE NAME OF THE LORD!' "   Jer. 22:5☆ • Ps. 118:26; Matt. 21:9

CHAPTER 14

Instruction on the Sabbath

Aɴᴅ it came about when He went into the house of one of the ᵀleaders of the Pharisees on *the* Sabbath to eat bread, that they were watching Him closely. members of the Sanhedrin

2 And ᵀthere, in front of Him was a certain man suffering from dropsy.   *behold*

3 And Jesus answered and spoke to the ᴿlawyers and Pharisees, saying, "Is it lawful to heal on the Sabbath, or not?"   Matt. 22:35

4 But they kept silent. And He took hold of him, and healed him, and sent him away.

5 And He said to them, "Which one of you shall have a ᵃson or an ox fall into a well, and will not immediately pull him out on a Sabbath day?"   Some ancient mss. read *donkey*

6 And they could make no reply to this.

Parable of the Ambitious Guest

7 And He *began* speaking a parable to the invited guests when He noticed how ᴿthey had been picking out the places of honor *at the table;* saying to them,   Matt. 23:6

8"When you are invited by someone to a wedding feast, do not ᵀtake the place of honor, lest someone more distinguished than you may have been invited by him,   *recline at*

9 and he who invited you both shall come and say to you, 'Give place to this man,' and then ᴿin disgrace you ᵀproceed to occupy the last place.   Luke 3:8 • *begin*

10"But when you are invited, go and recline at the last place, so that when the one who has invited you comes, he may say to

you, 'Friend, move up higher'; then you will have honor in the sight of all whoᵀare at the table with you.   *recline at the table*

11"For ᴿeveryone who exalts himself shall be humbled, and he who humbles himself shall be exalted."   2 Sam. 22:28; Prov. 29:23

12 And He also went on to say to the one who had invited Him, "When you give a luncheon or a dinner, do not invite your friends or your brothers or your relatives or rich neighbors, lest they also invite you in return, and repayment come to you.

13"But when you give a reception, invite *the* poor, *the* crippled, *the* lame, *the* blind,

14 and you will be ᵃblessed, since they ᵃdo not have *the means* to repay you; for you will be repaid at the resurrection of the righteous."   *happy • are unable to*

Parable of the Great Supper

15 And when one of those who were reclining *at the table* with Him heard this, he said to Him, "Blessed ᴿis everyone who shall eat bread in the kingdom of God!"   Rev. 19:9

16 But He said to him, "Aᴿ certain man was giving a big dinner, and he invited many;   Matt. 22:2-14; Luke 14:16-24

17 and at the dinner hour he sent his slave to say to those who had been invited, 'Come; for everything is ready now.'

18"But they all alike began to make excuses. The first one said to him, 'I have bought a piece of land and I need to go out and look at it; please consider me excused.'

19"And another one said, 'I have bought five yoke of oxen, and I am going to try them out; please consider me excused.'

20"And another one said, 'I have married a wife, and for that reason I cannot come.'

21"And the slave came *back* and reported this to his master. Then the head of the household became angry and said to his slave, 'Go out at once into the streets and lanes of the city and bring in here the poor and crippled and blind and lame.'

22"And the slave said, 'Master, what you commanded has been done, and still there is room.'

23"And the master said to the slave, 'Go out into the highways and along the hedges, and compel *them* to come in, that my house may be filled.

24 'For I tell you, none of those men who were invited shall taste of my dinner.' "

Christ Teaches on Discipleship

25 Now great multitudes were going along with Him; and He turned and said to them,

26"If ᴿanyone comes to Me, and does not ²⁸hate his own father and mother and wife and children and brothers and sisters, yes, and even his own life, he cannot be My disciple.   Matt. 10:37

---
²⁸ I.e., by comparison of his love for Me

27 "Whoever does not carry his own cross and come after Me cannot be My disciple.

28 "For which one of you, when he wants to build a tower, does not first sit down and calculate the cost, to see if he has enough to complete it?

29 "Otherwise, when he has laid a foundation, and is not able to finish, all who observe it begin to ridicule him,

30 saying, 'This man began to build and was not able to finish.'

31 "Or what king, when he sets out to meet another king in battle, will not first sit down and take ᴿcounsel whether he is strong enough with ten thousand *men* to encounter the one coming against him with twenty thousand?   Prov. 20:18

32 "Or else, while the other is still far away, he sends ᵃa delegation and asks terms of peace.   *an embassy*

33 "So therefore, no one of you can be My disciple who ᴿdoes not give up all his own possessions.   Phil. 3:7; [Heb. 11:26]

34 "Therefore, salt is good; but ᵀif even salt has become tasteless, with what will it be seasoned?   Matt. 5:13; [Mark 9:50]

35 "It is useless either for the soil or for the manure pile; ᵀit is thrown out. He who has ears to hear, let him hear."   *they throw it out*

CHAPTER 15

Parable of the Lost Sheep
Matt. 18:12–14

NOW all the tax-gatherers and the sinners were coming near Him to listen to Him.

2 And both the Pharisees and the scribes *began* to grumble, saying, "This man receives sinners and eats with them."

3 And He told them this parable, saying,

4 "What ᴿman among you, if he has a hundred sheep and has lost one of them, does not leave the ninety-nine in the ᵀopen pasture, and go after the one which is lost, until he finds it?   Matt. 18:12-14 · *wilderness*

5 "And when he has found it, he lays it on his shoulders, rejoicing.

6 "And when he comes home, he calls together his friends and his neighbors, saying to them, 'Rejoice with me, for I have found my sheep which was lost!'

7 "I tell you that in the same way, there will be *more* joy in heaven over one sinner who repents, than over ninety-nine righteous persons who need no repentance.

Parable of the Lost Coin

8 "Or what woman, if she has ten ᵀsilver coins and loses one coin, does not light a lamp and sweep the house and search carefully until she finds it?   Gr., *drachmas*

9 "And when she has found it, she calls together her ᵀfriends and neighbors, saying, 'Rejoice with me, for I have found the coin which I had lost!'   *women friends and neighbors*

10 "In the same way, I tell you, there is joy ᴿin the presence of the angels of God over one sinner who repents." Matt. 10:32; Luke 15:7

Parable of the Lost Son

11 And He said, "A certain man had two sons;

12 and the younger of them said to his father, 'Father, give me ᴿthe share of the estate that falls to me.' And he divided his ᵀwealth between them.   Deut. 21:17 · *living*

13 "And not many days later, the younger son gathered everything together and went on a journey into a distant country, and there he squandered his estate with loose living.

14 "Now when he had spent everything, a severe famine occurred in that country, and he began to be in need.

15 "And he went and attached himself to one of the citizens of that country, and he sent him into his fields to feed swine.

16 "And he was longing to fill his stomach with the pods that the swine were eating, and no one was giving *anything* to him.

17 "But when he came to ᵀhis senses, he said, 'How many of my father's hired men have more than enough bread, but I am dying here with hunger!   *himself*

18 'I will get up and go to my father, and will say to him, "Father, I have sinned against heaven, and ᵀin your sight;   *before you*

19 I am no longer worthy to be called your son; make me as one of your hired men."'

20 "And he got up and came to ᵀhis father. But while he was still a long way off, his father saw him, and felt compassion *for him*, and ran and ᵀembraced him, and kissed him.   *his own · fell on his neck*

21 "And the son said to him, 'Father, I have sinned against heaven and in your sight; I am no longer worthy to be called your son.'

22 "But the father said to his slaves, 'Quickly bring out ᴿthe best robe and put it on him, and ᴿput a ring on his hand and sandals on his feet;   Zech. 3:4 · Gen. 41:42

23 and bring the fattened calf, kill it, and let us eat and be merry;

24 for this son of mine was dead, and has come to life again; he was lost, and has been found.' And they began to be merry.

25 "Now his older son was in the field, and when he came and approached the house, he heard music and dancing.

26 "And he summoned one of the servants and *began* inquiring what these things might be.

27 "And he said to him, 'Your brother has come, and your father has killed the fat-

tened calf, because he has received him back safe and sound.'

28 "But he became angry, and was not willing to go in; and his father came out and *began* entreating him.

29 "But he answered and said to his father, 'Look! For so many years I have been serving you, and I have never ᴬneglected a command of yours; and *yet* you have never given me aᴬkid, that I might be merry with my friends;   *disobeyed • young goat*

30 but when this son of yours came, who has devoured your ᵗwealth with harlots, you killed the fattened calf for him.'   *living*

31 "And he said to him, 'My child, youᵀhave always been with me, and all that is mine is yours.   *are always with me*

32 'Butᵀwe had to be merry and rejoice, for this brother of yours was ᴿdead and *has begun* to live, and *was* lost and has been found.' "   *it was necessary • Luke 15:24*

CHAPTER 16

Parable of the Unjust Servant

Nᴏᴡ He was also saying to the disciples, "There was a certain rich man who had a steward, and this *steward* was ᴬreported to him as squandering his possessions.   *accused*

2 "And he called him and said to him, 'What is this I hear about you? Give an account of your stewardship, for you can no longer be steward.'

3 "And the steward said to himself, 'What shall I do, since my ᴬmaster is taking the stewardship away from me? I am not strong enough to dig; I am ashamed to beg.   *lord*

4 'I know what I shall do, so that when I am removed from the stewardship, they will receive me into their homes.'

5 "And he summoned each one of his master's debtors, and he *began* saying to the first, 'How much do you owe my master?'

6 "And he said, 'Aᴬ hundred measures of oil.' And he said to him, 'Take your bill, and sit down quickly and write fifty.'   *600 gal.*

7 "Then he said to another, 'And how much do you owe?' And he said, 'Aᵀhundred measures of wheat.' He *said to him, 'Take your bill, and write eighty.'   *65.2 bushels*

8 "And his ᴬmaster praised the unrighteous steward because he had acted shrewdly; for the sons of this age are more shrewd in relation to their own ᴵkind than the sons of light.   *lord • generation*

9 "And I say to you, make friends for yourselves by means of the ²⁹mammon of unrighteousness; that when it fails, they may receive you into the eternal dwellings.

10 "Heᴿ who is faithful in a very little thing is faithful also in much; and he who is unrighteous in a very little thing is unrighteous also in much.   *Matt. 25:21, 23*

11 "If therefore you have not been faithful

²⁹ Or, *riches*

in the *use of* unrighteous ᴬmammon, who will entrust the true *riches* to you?   *riches*

12 "And if you have not been faithful in the *use of* that which is another's, who will give you that which is your own?

13 "Noᴬservant can serve two masters; for either he will hate the one, and love the other, or else he will hold to one, and despise the other. You cannot serve God and ᴬmammon."   *house-servant • riches*

Christ Warns the Pharisees

14 Now the Pharisees, who wereᴿlovers of money, were listening to all these things, and they were scoffing at Him.   *2 Tim. 3:2*

15 And He said to them, "You are those who justify yourselvesᵀin the sight of men, but God knows your hearts; for that which is ᵀhighly esteemed among men is detestable in the sight of God.   *before men • high*

16 "Theᴿ Law and the Prophets *were proclaimed* until John; since then the gospel of the kingdom of God is preached, and everyone is forcing his way into it.   *Matt. 11:12f.*

17 "But it is easier for heaven and earth to pass away than for one ᵀstroke of a letter of the Law to fail.   *projection of a letter*

Christ Teaches on Divorce

18 "Everyoneᴿ who divorces his wife and marries another commits adultery; and he who marries one who is divorced from a husband commits adultery.   *1 Cor. 7:10, 11*

Parable of the Rich Man and Lazarus

19 "Now there was a certain rich man, and he habitually dressed in purple and fine linen, gaily living in splendor every day.

20 "And a certain poor man named Lazarus was laid at his gate, covered with sores,

21 and longing to be fed with the *crumbs* which were falling from the rich man's table; besides, even the dogs were coming and licking his sores.

22 "Now it came about that the poor man died and he was carried away by the angels to ᴿAbraham's bosom; and the rich man also died and was buried.   *John 1:18; 13:23*

23 "And in ᴿHades he lifted up his eyes, being in torment, and *saw Abraham far away, and Lazarus in his bosom.   *Matt. 11:23*

24 "And he cried out and said, 'Fatherᴿ Abraham, have mercy on me, and send Lazarus, that he may dip the tip of his finger in water and cool off my tongue; for I am in agony in this flame.'   *Luke 3:8; 16:30; 19:9*

25 "But Abraham said, 'Child, remember that ᴿduring your life you received your good things, and likewise Lazarus bad things; but now he is being comforted here, and you are in agony.   *Luke 6:24*

26 'Andᵀbesides all this, between us and you there is a great chasm fixed, in order that those who wish to come over from here

to you may not be able, and *that* none may cross over from there to us.' *in all these things*

27"And he said, 'Then I beg you, Father, that you send him to my father's house—

28 for I have five brothers—that he may [R]warn them, lest they also come to this place of torment.'   Acts 2:40; 8:25; 10:42; 18:5; 20:21ff.

29"But Abraham *said, 'They have Moses and the Prophets; let them hear them.'

30"But he said, 'No,[R]Father Abraham, but if someone goes to them from the dead, they will repent!'   Luke 3:8; 16:24; 19:9

31"But he said to him, 'If they do not listen to Moses and the Prophets, neither will they be persuaded if someone rises from the dead.' "

CHAPTER 17

Christ Teaches Concerning Stumbling Blocks

AND He said to His disciples, "It is inevitable that stumbling blocks should come, but woe to him through whom they come!

2"It would be better for him if a millstone were hung around his neck and he were thrown into the sea, than that he should cause one of these little ones to stumble.

3"Be on your guard! If your brother sins, rebuke him; and if he repents, forgive him.

4"And if he sins against you seven times a day, and returns to you seven times, saying, 'I repent,'[T]forgive him."   *you shall forgive*

5 And[R]the apostles said to[T]the Lord, "Increase our faith!"   Mark 6:30 • Luke 7:13

6 And the Lord said, "If you had faith like a mustard seed, you would say to this mulberry tree, 'Be uprooted and be planted in the sea'; and it would obey you.

7"But which of you, having a slave plowing or tending sheep, will say to him when he has come in from the field, 'Come immediately and[T]sit down to eat'?   *recline*

8"But will he not say to him, 'Prepare something for me to eat, and *properly*[T]clothe yourself and serve me until I have eaten and drunk; and[T]afterward you will eat and drink'?   *gird • after these things*

9"He does not thank the slave because he did the things which were commanded, does he?

10"So you too, when you do all the things which are commanded you, say, 'We are unworthy slaves; we have done *only* that which we ought to have done.' "

Christ Cleanses Ten Lepers

11 And it came about while He was[R]on the way to Jerusalem, that He was passing between Samaria and Galilee.   Luke 9:51

12 And as He entered a certain village, ten leprous men who[R]stood at a distance met Him;   Lev. 13:45f.

13 and they raised their voices, saying, "Jesus,[R]Master, have mercy on us!" Luke 5:5

14 And when He saw them, He said to them, "Go[R] and show yourselves to the priests." And it came about that as they were going, they were cleansed. Lev. 14:1-32

15 Now one of them, when he saw that he had been healed, turned back, [R]glorifying God with a loud voice,   Matt. 9:8

16 and he fell on his face at His feet, giving thanks to Him. And he was a Samaritan.

17 And Jesus answered and said, "Were there not ten cleansed? But the nine—where are they?

18"Was no one found who turned back to give glory to God, except this foreigner?"

19 And He said to him, "Rise, and go your way; your faith [30]has made you well."

Christ Teaches on the Second Coming

20 Now having been questioned by the Pharisees as to when the kingdom of God was coming, He answered them and said, "The kingdom of God is not coming with [T]signs to be observed;   *observation*

21 nor will they say, 'Look, here *it is!*' or, 'There *it is!*' For behold, the kingdom of God is[A]in your midst."   *within you*

22 And He said to the disciples, "The[R]days shall come when you will long to see one of the days of the Son of Man, and you will not see it.   Matt. 9:15; Mark 2:20; Luke 5:35

23"And[R]they will say to you, 'Look there! Look here!' Do not go away, and do not run after *them.*   Matt. 24:23; Mark 13:21; [Luke 21:8]

24"For just as the lightning, when it flashes out of one part[T]of the sky, shines to the other part[T]of the sky, so will the Son of Man be in His day.   *under heaven*

25"But[R] first He must suffer many things and be rejected by this generation. Luke 9:22

26"And[R]just as it happened[R]in the days of Noah, so it shall be also in the days of the Son of Man: Luke 17:26, 27 • [Gen. 6:5–8]

27 they were eating, they were drinking, they were marrying, they were being given in marriage, until the day that Noah entered the ark, and the flood came and destroyed them all.

28"It was the same as happened in the days of Lot: they were eating, they were drinking, they were buying, they were selling, they were planting, they were building;

29 but on the day that Lot went out from Sodom it rained fire and[A]brimstone from heaven and destroyed them all.   *sulphur*

30"It will be just the same on the day that the Son of Man[R]is revealed.   1 John 2:28

31"On that day, let not the one who is[R]on the housetop and whose goods are in the house go down to take them away; and likewise let not the one who is in the field turn back.   Matt. 24:17, 18; Mark 13:15f.; Luke 21:21

[30] Or, *has saved you*

32 "Remember[R]Lot's wife.   Gen. 19:26
33 "Whoever[R] seeks to keep his life shall lose it, and whoever loses *his life* shall preserve it.   Matt. 10:39 • *soul*
34 "I tell you, on that night there will be two men in one bed; one will be taken, and the other will be left.
35 "There[R] will be two women grinding at the same place; one will be taken, and the other will be left.   Matt. 24:41
36 ["Two[31] men will be in the field; one will be taken and the other will be left."]
37 And answering they *said to Him, "Where, Lord?" And He said to them, "Where[R] the body is, there also will the vultures be gathered."   Matt. 24:28 • *eagles*

CHAPTER 18

Parable of the Woman and the Judge

NOW He was telling them a parable to show that at all times they[R] ought to pray and not to lose heart,   Luke 11:5-10
2 saying, "There was in a certain city a judge who did not fear God, and did not[R] respect man.   Luke 18:4; 20:13; Heb. 12:9
3 "And there was a widow in that city, and she kept coming to him, saying, 'Give me legal protection from my opponent.'
4 "And for a while he was unwilling; but afterward he said to himself, 'Even though I do not fear God nor[R] respect man,   Luke 18:2
5 yet because this widow bothers me, I will give her legal protection, lest by continually coming she wear me out.' "
6 And[R] the Lord said, "Hear what the unrighteous judge *said;   Luke 7:13
7 now shall not God[R] bring about justice for His elect, who cry to Him day and night, and will He delay long over them?   Rev. 6:10
8 "I tell you that He will bring about justice for them speedily. However, when the Son of Man comes,[R] will He find faith on the earth?"   Luke 17:26ff. • *the faith*

Parable of the Pharisee and the Tax-gatherer

9 And He also told this parable to certain ones who[R] trusted in themselves that they were righteous, and[R] viewed others with contempt: Luke 16:15 • Rom. 14:3, 10
10 "Two men went up into the temple to pray, one a Pharisee, and the other a tax-gatherer.   Collector of Roman taxes for profit
11 "The Pharisee stood and was praying thus to himself, 'God, I thank Thee that I am not like other people: swindlers, unjust, adulterers, or even like this tax-gatherer.
12 'I[R] fast twice a week; I pay tithes of all that I get.'   Matt. 9:14 • Luke 11:42
13 "But the tax-gatherer,[R] standing some

distance away, was even unwilling to lift up his eyes to heaven, but was beating his breast, saying, 'God, be[A] merciful to me, the sinner!'   Matt. 6:5; Mark 11:25 • *propitious*
14 "I tell you, this man went down to his house justified rather than the other;[R] for everyone who exalts himself shall be humbled, but he who humbles himself shall be exalted."   Matt. 23:12; Luke 14:11

Christ Blesses the Children
Matt. 19:13–15; Mark 10:13–16

15 [R]And they were bringing even their babies to Him so that He might touch them, but when the disciples saw it, they *began* rebuking them.   Matt. 19:13-15; Luke 18:15-17
16 But Jesus called for them, saying, "Permit the children to come to Me, and do not hinder them, for the kingdom of God belongs to such as these.
17 "Truly I say to you,[R] whoever does not receive the kingdom of God like a child shall not enter it *at all.*"   1 Cor. 14:20; 1 Pet. 2:2

Rich Young Ruler
Matt. 19:16–26; Mark 10:17–27

18 [R]And a certain ruler questioned Him, saying, "Good Teacher, what shall I do to inherit eternal life?"   Mark 10:17-30
19 And Jesus said to him, "Why do you call Me good? No one is good except God alone.
20 "You know the commandments, 'Do NOT COMMIT ADULTERY, DO NOT MURDER, DO NOT STEAL, DO NOT BEAR FALSE WITNESS, HONOR YOUR FATHER AND MOTHER.' "
21 And he said, "All these things I have kept from *my* youth."
22 And when Jesus heard *this*, He said to him, "One thing you still lack;[R] sell all that you possess, and distribute it to the poor, and you shall have[R] treasure in heaven; and come, follow Me."   Matt. 19:21 • Matt. 6:20
23 But when he had heard these things, he became very sad; for he was extremely rich.
24 And Jesus looked at him and said, "How[T] hard it is for those who are wealthy to enter the kingdom of God!   Mark 10:23f.
25 "For it is easier for a camel to[T] go through the eye of a needle, than for a rich man to enter the kingdom of God."   *enter*
26 And they who heard it said, "Then[T] who can be saved?"   *And*
27 But He said, "The[R] things impossible with men are possible with God." Matt. 19:26

Christ Will Reward Sacrifice
Matt. 19:27–29; Mark 10:28–30

28 And Peter said, "Behold, we have left our own *homes*, and followed You."
29 And He said to them, "Truly I say to you,[R] there is no one who has left house or

---

[31] Many mss. do not contain this verse

wife or brothers or parents or children, for the sake of the kingdom of God,   Matt. 6:33

30 who shall not receive many times as much at this time and in [R]the age to come, eternal life."   Matt. 12:32

Christ Foretells His
Death and Resurrection
Matt. 20:17–19; Mark 10:32–34

31 [R]And He took the twelve aside and said to them, "Behold, we are going up to Jerusalem, and all things which are written through the prophets about the Son of Man will be accomplished.   *Matt. 20:17–19*

32 "For [R]He will be delivered to the Gentiles, and will be mocked and mistreated and spit upon,   Matt. 16:21; Mark 15:19☆

33 [R]and after they have scourged Him, they will kill Him; and the third day He will rise again."

34 And [R]they understood none of these things, and this saying was hidden from them, and they did not comprehend the things that were said.   Mark 9:32; Luke 9:45

Christ Heals Bartimaeus
Matt. 20:29–34; Mark 10:46–52

35 [R]And it came about that as He was approaching Jericho, a certain blind man was sitting by the road, begging.   Luke 18:35-43

36 Now hearing a multitude going by, he *began* to inquire what this might be.

37 And they told him that Jesus of Nazareth was passing by.

38 And he called out, saying, "Jesus, [R]Son of David, have mercy on me!"   Luke 18:39

39 And those who led the way were sternly telling him to be quiet; but he kept crying out all the more, "Son[R] of David, have mercy on me!"   Luke 18:38

40 And Jesus [T]stopped and commanded that he be brought to Him; and when he had come near, He questioned him,   *stood*

41 "What do you want Me to do for you?" And he said, "Lord, *I want* to regain my sight!"

42 And Jesus said to him, "Receive your sight; your faith has made you well."

43 And immediately he regained his sight, and *began* following Him, [R]glorifying God; and when [R]all the people saw it, they gave praise to God.   Matt. 9:8 • Luke 9:43; 13:17; 19:37

CHAPTER 19

Christ Abides with Zaccheus

AND He [R]entered and was passing through Jericho.   Luke 18:35

2 And behold, there was a man called by the name of Zaccheus; and he was a chief tax-gatherer, and he was rich.

3 And he was trying to see who Jesus was, and he was unable because of the crowd, for he was small in stature.

4 And he ran on ahead and climbed up into a sycamore tree in order to see Him, for He was about to pass through that way.

5 And when Jesus came to the place, He looked up and said to him, "Zaccheus, hurry and come down, for today I must stay at your house."

6 And he hurried and came down, and received Him [T]gladly.   *rejoicing*

7 And when they saw it, they all *began* to grumble, saying, "He has gone to be the guest of a man who is a sinner."

8 And Zaccheus [T]stopped and said to [R]the Lord, "Behold, Lord, half of my possessions I will give to the poor, and if I have defrauded anyone of anything, I will give back four times as much."   *stood* • Luke 7:13

9 And Jesus said to him, "Today salvation has come to this house, because he, too, is [R]a son of Abraham. Luke 3:8; 13:16; Rom. 4:16

10 "For [R]the Son of Man has come to seek and to save that which was lost." Matt. 18:11

Christ Gives the Parable of the
Ten Minas

11 And while they were listening to these things, He went on to tell a parable, because [R]He was near Jerusalem, and they supposed that [R]the kingdom of God was going to appear immediately.   Luke 9:51 • Luke 17:20

12 He said therefore, "A certain nobleman went to a distant country to receive a kingdom for himself, and *then* return.

13 "And he called ten of his slaves, and gave them ten [32]minas, and said to them, 'Do business *with this* until I come *back*.'

14 "But his citizens hated him, and sent [A]a delegation after him, saying, 'We do not want this man to reign over us.'   *an embassy*

15 "And it came about that when he returned, after receiving the kingdom, he ordered that these slaves, to whom he had given the money, be called to him in order that he might know what business they had done.

16 "And the first appeared, saying, 'Master, your mina has made ten minas more.'

17 "And he said to him, 'Well done, good slave, because you have been [R]faithful in a very little thing, be in authority over ten cities.'   Luke 16:10

18 "And the second came, saying, 'Your mina, [T]master, has made five minas.'   *lord*

19 "And he said to him also, 'And you are to be over five cities.'

20 "And another came, saying, 'Master, behold your mina, which I kept put away in a handkerchief;

21 for I was afraid of you, because you are an exacting man; you take up what you did not lay down, and reap what you did not sow.'

[32] A mina is equal to about 100 days' wages or nearly $20

22 "He *said to him, 'By[T] your own words I will judge you, you worthless slave. Did you know that I am an exacting man, taking up what I did not lay down, and reaping what I did not sow?   *Out of your own mouth*

23 'Then[T] why did you not put the money in the bank, and having come, I would have collected it with interest?'   *And*

24 "And he said to the bystanders, 'Take the mina away from him, and give it to the one who has the ten minas.'

25 "And they said to him, 'Master, he has ten minas *already*.'

26 "I[R] tell you, that to everyone who has shall *more* be given, but from the one who does not have, even what he does have shall be taken away. Matt. 13:12; Mark 4:25; Luke 8:18

27 "But these enemies of mine, who did not want me to reign over them, bring them here and slay them in my presence."

The Triumphal Entry
Matt. 21:1-9; Mark 11:1-10;
John 12:12-19

28 And after He had[R] said these things, He was going on ahead, [R]ascending to Jerusalem.   Mark 10:32 • Luke 9:51

29 And it came about that when He approached Bethphage and Bethany, near the mount that is called [A]Olivet, He sent two of the disciples,   *hill • Olive Grove*

30 saying, "Go into the village opposite *you*, in which as you enter you will find a colt tied, on which no one yet has ever sat; untie it, and bring it *here*.

31 "And if anyone asks you, 'Why are you untying it?' thus shall you speak, 'The Lord has need of it.' "

32 And those who were sent went away and found it just as He had told them.

33 And as they were untying the colt, its [T]owners said to them, "Why are you untying the colt?"   *lords*

34 And they said, "The Lord has need of it."

35 And they brought it to Jesus, [R]and they threw their garments on the colt, and put Jesus *on it*.   Matt. 21:4-9; Luke 19:35-38

36 And as He was going, they were spreading their garments in the road.

37 And as He was now approaching, near the descent of [R]the Mount of Olives, the whole multitude of the disciples began to praise God joyfully with a loud voice for all the miracles which they had seen, Matt. 21:1

38 saying,
"BLESSED[R] IS THE King WHO COMES IN
THE NAME OF THE LORD; Ps. 118:26★
Peace in heaven and[R]glory in the highest!"   Matt. 21:9; Luke 2:14

39 [R]And some of the Pharisees[R]in the multitude said to Him, "Teacher, rebuke Your disciples."   Matt. 21:15f. • *from*

40 And He answered and said, "I tell you, if these become silent,[R]the stones will cry out!"   Hab. 2:11

41 And when He approached, He saw the city and[R]wept over it,   Luke 13:34, 35

42 saying, "If you had known in this day, even you, the things which make for peace! But now they have been hidden from your eyes.

43 "For the days shall come upon you when your enemies will[T]throw up a bank before you, and surround you, and hem you in on every side,   *and* • Eccl. 9:14

44 and will level you to the ground and your children within you, and[R]they will not leave in you one stone upon another, because you did not recognize[T]the time of your visitation."   Matt. 24:2 • 1 Pet. 2:12

Cleansing the Temple
Matt. 21:12, 13; Mark 11:15-17

45 [R]And He entered the temple and began to cast out those who were selling, Mal. 3:1★

46 saying to them, "It is written, 'AND MY HOUSE SHALL BE A HOUSE OF PRAYER,' but you have[R]made it a ROBBERS' DEN."   *cave*

47 And[R]He was teaching daily in the temple; but the chief priests and the scribes and the leading men among the people were trying to destroy Him,   Matt. 26:55; Luke 21:37

48 and they could not find [T]anything that they might do, for all the people were hanging upon His words.   *what they might do*

CHAPTER 20

Religious Leaders Question
Christ's Authority
Matt. 21:23-27; Mark 11:27-33

AND[R] it came about on one of the days while [R]He was teaching the people in the temple and preaching the gospel, that the chief priests and the scribes with the elders confronted *Him*,   Luke 20:1-8 • Matt. 26:55

2 and they spoke, saying to Him, "Tell us by what authority You are doing these things, or who is the one who gave You this authority?"

3 And He answered and said to them, "I shall also ask you a[T]question, and you tell Me: *word*

4 "Was the baptism of John from heaven or from men?"

5 And they reasoned among themselves, saying, "If we say, 'From heaven,' He will say, 'Why did you not believe him?'

6 "But if we say, 'From men,' all the people will stone us to death, for they are convinced that John was a[T]prophet." Matt. 11:9

7 And they answered that they did not know where *it came* from.

8 And Jesus said to them, "Neither[T]will I tell you by what authority I do these things."   *do I tell*

Parable of the Vineyard Owner
Matt. 21:33-44; Mark 12:1-11

9 And He began to tell the people this

parable: "A man planted a vineyard and rented it out to ^Avine-growers, and went on a journey for a long time.   *tenant farmers*

10"And at the *harvest* time he sent a slave to the vine-growers, in order that they might give him *some* of the produce of the vineyard; but the vine-growers beat him and sent him away empty-handed.

11"And he proceeded to send another slave; and they beat him also and treated him shamefully, and sent him away empty-handed.

12"And he proceeded to send a third; and this one also they wounded and cast out.

13"And the owner of the vineyard said, 'What shall I do? I will send my beloved son; perhaps they will respect him.'   *lord*

14"But when the vine-growers saw him, they reasoned with one another, saying, 'This is the heir; let us kill him that the inheritance may be ours.'

15"And they threw him out of the vineyard and killed him. What, therefore, will the owner of the vineyard do to them?

16"He will come and ^Rdestroy these vine-growers and will give the vineyard to others." And when they heard it, they said, "May^Rit never be!"   Matt. 21:41 • Rom. 3:4

17 But He looked at them and said, "What then is this that is written,

'THE^R STONE WHICH THE BUILDERS RE-
JECTED,   Ps. 118:22★
THIS BECAME ^RTHE CHIEF CORNER
stone'?   Eph. 2:20; 1 Pet. 2:6

18"Everyone^R who falls on that stone will be broken to pieces; but on whomever it falls, it will scatter him like dust." Matt. 21:44

Herodians Question Tribute Money
Matt. 21:45, 46; 22:15–22;
Mark 12:12–17

19 And the scribes and the chief priests ^Rtried to lay hands on Him that very hour, and they feared the people; for they understood that He spoke this parable against them.   Luke 19:47

20 And they watched Him, and sent spies who^Tpretended to be righteous, in order that they might catch Him in some statement, so as to deliver Him up to the rule and the authority of the governor.   *feigned themselves*

21 And they questioned Him, saying, "Teacher, we know that You speak and teach correctly, and You are not partial to any, but teach the way of God in truth.

22"Is it^Alawful for us^Rto pay taxes to Caesar, or not?"   *permissible* • Matt. 17:25

23 But He detected their trickery and said to them,

24"Show Me a ³³denarius. Whose^Tlikeness and inscription does it have?" And they said, "Caesar's."   *image*

25 And He said to them, "Then^Rrender to Caesar the things that are Caesar's, and to God the things that are God's." Mark 12:17

26 And they were unable to^Tcatch^RHim in a saying in the presence of the people; and marveling at His answer, they became silent.   *take hold of His saying* • Luke 11:54

Sadducees Question Resurrection
Matt. 22:23–32; Mark 12:18–27

27 ^RNow there came to Him some of the ^RSadducees (who say that there is no resurrection),   Luke 20:27-40 • Acts 23:8

28 and they questioned Him, saying, "Teacher, Moses wrote for us that ^RIF A MAN'S BROTHER DIES, having a wife, AND HE IS CHILDLESS, HIS BROTHER SHOULD TAKE THE WIFE AND RAISE UP OFFSPRING TO HIS BROTHER.   Deut. 25:5

29"Now there were seven brothers; and the first took a wife, and died childless;

30 and the second

31 and the third took her; and in the same way all seven died, leaving no children.

32"Finally the woman died also.

33"In the resurrection therefore, which one's wife will she be? For ^Tall seven had her as wife."   *the*

34 And Jesus said to them, "The sons of this age marry and are given in marriage,

35 but those who are considered worthy to attain to ^Rthat age and the resurrection from the dead, neither marry, nor are given in marriage;   Matt. 12:32; Luke 16:8

36 for neither can they die anymore, for they are like angels, and are ^Rsons of God, being sons of the resurrection.   1 John 3:1

37"But that the dead are raised, even Moses showed, in ^Rthe *passage about the burning* bush, where he calls the Lord THE GOD OF ABRAHAM, AND THE GOD OF ISAAC, AND THE GOD OF JACOB.   Mark 12:26

38"Now^RHe is not the God of the dead, but of the living; for all live to Him." Matt. 22:32

Christ Questions the Scribes
Matt. 22:41—23:14; Mark 12:35–40

39 And some of the scribes answered and said, "Teacher, You have spoken well."

40 For they did not have courage to question Him any longer about anything.

41 And He said to them, "How *is it that* they say ³⁴the Christ is David's son?

42"For David himself says in the book of Psalms,

'THE^RLORD SAID TO MY LORD,   Ps. 110:1☆
"SIT AT MY RIGHT HAND,

43 ^RUNTIL I MAKE THINE ENEMIES A FOOT-
STOOL FOR THY FEET." '

44"David therefore calls Him 'Lord,' and how is He his son?"

45 ^RAnd while all the people were listening, He said to the disciples,   Luke 20:45-47

46"Beware of the scribes,^Rwho like to walk around in long robes, and love respectful

---

³³ The denarius was equivalent to one day's wage
³⁴ I.e., the Messiah

greetings in the market places, and chief seats in the synagogues, and places of honor at banquets,   Luke 11:43; 14:7

47 who devour widows' houses, and for appearance's sake offer long prayers; these will receive greater condemnation."

CHAPTER 21

Christ Teaches on the Widow's Gift
Mark 12:41–44

A^{R}ND He looked up and saw the rich putting their gifts into the treasury.   Luke 21:1-4

2 And He saw a certain poor widow putting in two small copper coins.   Gr., *lepta*

3 And He said, "Truly I say to you, this poor widow put in more than all *of them;*

4 for they all out of their surplus put into the offering; but she out of her poverty put in all that she had to live on."   *abundance*

The Disciples' Two Questions
Matt. 24:1–3; Mark 13:1–4

5 ^{R}And while some were talking about the temple, that it was adorned with beautiful stones and votive gifts, He said,   Luke 21:5-36

6"*As for* these things which you are looking at, the days will come in which ^{R}there will not be left one stone upon another which will not be torn down."   Luke 19:44

7 And they questioned Him, saying, "Teacher, when therefore will these things be? And what *will be* the sign when these things are about to take place?"

Signs of Christ's Coming
Matt. 24:4–13; Mark 13:5–13

8 And He said, "See to it that you be not misled; for many will come in My name, saying, 'I am He,' and, 'The time is at hand'; do not go after them.   John 8:24

9"And when you hear of wars and disturbances, do not be terrified; for these things must take place first, but the end *does* not *follow* immediately."

10 Then He continued by saying to them, "Nation will rise against nation, and kingdom against kingdom,

11 and there will be great earthquakes, and in various places plagues and famines; and there will be terrors and great signs from heaven.   *attesting miracles*

12"But before all these things, they will lay their hands on you and will persecute you, delivering you to the synagogues and prisons, bringing you before kings and governors for My name's sake.   *being brought*

13"It will lead to an opportunity for your testimony.   [Phil. 1:12] • *a testimony for you*

14"So make up your minds not to prepare beforehand to defend yourselves;   Luke 12:11

15 for I will give you utterance and wisdom which none of your opponents will be able to resist or refute.   *a mouth*

16"But you will be delivered up even by parents and brothers and relatives and friends, and they will put *some* of you to death,

17 and you will be hated by all on account of My name.

18"Yet not a hair of your head will perish.

19"By^R your endurance you will gain your ^{A}lives.   Matt. 10:22; 24:13; Rom. 2:7 • *soul*

Destruction of Jerusalem
Matt. 24:15–21; Mark 13:14–19

20"But when you see Jerusalem ^{R}surrounded by armies, then recognize that her desolation is at hand.   Luke 19:43 • *know*

21 "Then let those who are in Judea flee to the mountains, and let those who are in the midst of the city depart, and let not those who are in the country enter the city;

22 because these are ^{R}days of vengeance, in order that all things which are written may be fulfilled. Is. 63:4; [Dan. 9:24–27]; Hos. 9:7

23"Woe to those who are with child and to those who nurse babes in those days; for there will be great distress upon the ^{A}land, and wrath to this people,   *earth*

24 and they will fall by ^{R}the edge of the sword, and will be led captive into all the nations; and Jerusalem will be trampled under foot by the Gentiles until the times of the Gentiles be fulfilled.   Gen. 34:26; Ex. 17:13

The Second Coming
Matt. 24:29–31; Mark 13:24–27

25"And there will be ^{A}signs in sun and moon and stars, and upon the earth dismay among nations, in perplexity at the roaring of the sea and the waves,   *attesting miracles*

26 men fainting from fear and the expectation of the things which are coming upon the world; for the powers of ^{A}the heavens will be shaken.   *inhabited earth • heaven*

27"And^{R}then they will see THE SON OF MAN COMING IN A CLOUD with power and great glory.   [Matt. 16:27] • Dan. 7:13; Rev. 1:7

28"But when these things begin to take place, straighten up and lift up your heads, because your redemption is drawing near."

Parable of the Fig Tree
Matt. 24:32–35; Mark 13:28–31

29 And He told them a parable: "Behold the fig tree and all the trees;

30 as soon as they put forth *leaves*, you see it and know for yourselves that summer is now near.   Luke 12:57

31"Even so you, too, when you see these things happening, recognize that ^{R}the kingdom of God is near.   *know* • Matt. 3:2

32"Truly I say to you, this generation will not pass away until all things take place.

33"Heaven^R and earth will pass away, but My words will not pass away.   [Matt. 5:18]

Warning to Be Alert for His Coming
Matt. 24:36–44; Mark 13:32–37

34 "Be on guard, that your hearts may not be weighted down with dissipation and drunkenness and the worries of life, and that day come on you suddenly like a trap; **35** for it will come upon all those who dwell on the face of all the earth. **36** "But[R]keep on the alert at all times, praying in order that you may have strength to escape all these things that are about to take place, and to [R]stand before the Son of Man." Mark 13:33 • Luke 1:19; Rev. 7:9 **37** Now [T]during the day He was teaching in the temple, but [T]at evening He would go out and spend the night on [T]the mount that is called Olivet. days • nights • the hill **38** And all the people would get up [T]early in the morning to come to Him in the temple to listen to Him. John 8:2

CHAPTER 22

Judas Agrees to Betray Christ
Matt. 26:1–5, 14–16;
Mark 14:1, 2, 10, 11

Now[R] the Feast of Unleavened Bread, which is called the[R]Passover, was approaching. Ex. 12:1–27; Luke 22:1 • John 11:55; 13:1 **2** And the chief priests and the scribes were seeking how they might put Him to death; for they were afraid of the people. **3** [R]And Satan entered into Judas who was called Iscariot, [T]belonging to the number of the twelve. Luke 22:3-6 • being of **4** And he went away and discussed with the chief priests and [R]officers how he might betray Him to them. 1 Chr. 9:11; Acts 4:1 **5** And they were glad, and agreed to give him money. **6** And he consented, and began seeking a good opportunity to betray Him to them [T]apart from the multitude. without a disturbance

The Upper Room Is Prepared
Matt. 26:17–19; Mark 14:12–16

7 [R]Then came the first day of Unleavened Bread on which[R]the Passover lamb had to be sacrificed. Luke 22:7-13 • Mark 14:12 **8** And He sent [R]Peter and John, saying, "Go and prepare the Passover for us, that we may eat it."Acts 3:1, 11; 4:13, 19; 8:14; Gal. 2:9 **9** And they said to Him, "Where do You want us to prepare it?" **10** And He said to them, "Behold, when you have entered the city, a man will meet you carrying a pitcher of water; follow him into the house that he enters. **11** "And you shall say to the owner of the house, 'The Teacher says to you, "Where is the guest room in which I may eat the Passover with My disciples?" ' **12** "And he will show you a large, furnished, upper room; prepare it there."

13 And they departed and found everything just as He had told them; and they prepared the Passover.

The Passover Is Celebrated
Matt. 26:20, 29; Mark 14:17, 25

14 [R]And when the hour had come He reclined at the table, and the apostles with Him. Matt. 26:20; Mark 14:17 **15** And He said to them, "I have earnestly desired to eat this Passover with you before I suffer; **16** for I say to you, I shall never again eat it until it is fulfilled in the kingdom of God." **17** [R]And when He had taken a cup and given thanks, He said, "Take this and share it among yourselves; Matt. 26:26-29; Luke 22:17-20 **18** for [T]I say to you, I will not drink of the fruit of the vine from now on until the kingdom of God comes." Matt. 26:29; Mark 14:25

The Lord's Supper Is Instituted
Matt. 26:26–28; Mark 14:22–24

19 And when He had taken some bread and[R]given thanks, He broke it, and gave it to them, saying, "This is My body [35]which is given for you; do this in remembrance of Me." Matt. 14:19 **20** And in the same way He took the cup after they had eaten, saying, "This cup which is[R]poured out for you is the new covenant in My blood. Matt. 26:28; Mark 14:24

Christ Predicts His Betrayer
Matt. 26:21–25; Mark 14:18–21;
John 13:21–26

21 "But[R]behold, the hand of the one betraying Me is with Me on the table. Luke 22:21-23 **22** "For indeed, the Son of Man is going[R]as it has been determined; but woe to that man by whom He is betrayed!" Acts 2:23; 4:28 **23** And they began to discuss among themselves which one of them it might be who was going to do this thing.

The Disciples Argue
over Who Is the Greatest

24 And there arose also[R]a dispute among them as to which one of them was regarded to be greatest. Mark 9:34; Luke 9:46 **25** [R]And He said to them, "The kings of the Gentiles lord it over them; and those who have authority over them are called 'Benefactors.' Matt. 20:25-28; Luke 22:25-27 **26** "But not so with you, but let him who is the greatest among you become as the youngest, and the leader as the servant. **27** "For who is greater, the one who reclines at the table, or the one who serves? Is it not the one who reclines at the table? But I am among you as the one who serves.

[35] Some ancient mss. do not contain the remainder of v. 19 nor any of v. 20

28"And you are those who have stood by Me in My^Rtrials; [Heb. 2:18; 4:15]

29 and just as My Father has granted Me a^Rkingdom, I grant you [Matt. 5:3; 2 Tim. 2:12]

30 that you may eat and drink at My table in My kingdom, and you will sit on thrones judging the twelve tribes of Israel.

Christ Predicts Peter's Denial
Matt. 26:31–35; Mark 14:27–31; John 13:36–38

31 "Simon, Simon, behold, Satan has demanded *permission* to sift you like wheat;

32 but I^Rhave prayed for you, that your faith may not fail; and you, when once you have turned again, ^Rstrengthen your brothers." [John 17:9, 15] • John 21:15–17

33 And he said to Him, "Lord, with You I am ready to go both to prison and to death!"

34 And He said, "I say to you, Peter, the cock will not crow today until you have denied three times that you know Me."

Christ Predicts Coming Conflict

35 And He said to them, "When^R I sent you out without purse and bag and sandals, you did not lack anything, did you?" And they said, "No, nothing." Matt. 10:9f.; Mark 6:8

36 And He said to them, "But now, let him who has a purse take it along, likewise also a bag, and let him who has no sword sell his ^Arobe and buy one. *outer garment*

37 "For I tell you, that this which is written must be fulfilled in Me, 'AND^R HE WAS NUMBERED WITH TRANSGRESSORS'; for that which refers to Me has *its* fulfillment." Is. 53:12☆

38 And they said, "Lord, look, here are two ^Rswords." And He said to them, "It is enough." Luke 22:36, 49

Christ Prays in Gethsemane
Matt. 26:36–46; Mark 14:32–42; John 18:1

39 ^RAnd He came out and proceeded as was His custom to the Mount of Olives; and the disciples also followed Him. Matt. 26:30

40 ^RAnd when He arrived at the place, He said to them, "Pray^Rthat you may not enter into temptation." Luke 22:40–46 • Matt. 6:13

41 And He withdrew from them about a stone's throw, and He^Rknelt down and *began* to pray, Matt. 26:39; Mark 14:35; Luke 18:11

42 saying, "Father, if Thou art willing, remove this^Rcup from Me;^Ryet not My will, but Thine be done." Matt. 20:22 • Is. 50:5★

43 Now an^Rangel from heaven appeared to Him, strengthening Him. Matt. 4:11

44 And^Rbeing in agony He was praying very fervently; and His sweat became like drops of blood, falling down upon the ground. [Heb. 5:7]

45 And when He rose from prayer, He came to the disciples and found them sleeping from sorrow,

46 and said to them, "Why are you sleeping? Rise and^Rpray that you may not enter into temptation." Luke 22:40

Judas Betrays Christ
Matt. 26:47–56; Mark 14:43–50; John 18:2–11

47 While He was still speaking, behold, a multitude *came*, and the one called Judas, one of the twelve, was preceding them; and he approached Jesus to kiss Him.

48 But Jesus said to him, "Judas, are you betraying the Son of Man with a kiss?"

49 And when those who were around Him saw what was going to happen, they said, "Lord, shall we strike with the sword?"

50 And a certain one of them struck the slave of the high priest and cut off his right ear.

51 But Jesus answered and said, "Stop! No more of this." And He touched his ear and healed him.

52 And Jesus said to the chief priests and officers of the temple and elders who had come against Him, "Have you come out with swords and clubs as against a robber?

53 "While I was with you daily in the temple, you did not lay hands on Me; but this hour and the power of darkness are yours."

Peter Denies Christ
Matt. 26:57, 58, 69–75; Mark 14:53, 54, 66–72; John 18:15–18, 25–27

54 ^RAnd having arrested Him, they led Him *away*, and brought Him to the house of the high priest; but^RPeter was following at a distance. Matt. 26:57 • Matt. 26:58; Mark 14:54

55 And after they had kindled a fire in the middle of the courtyard and had sat down together, Peter was sitting among them.

56 And a certain servant-girl, seeing him as he sat in the firelight, and looking intently at him, said, "This man was with Him too."

57 But he denied *it*, saying, "Woman, I do not know Him."

58 And a little later,^Ranother saw him and said, "You are *one* of them too!" But Peter said, "Man, I am not!" John 18:26

59 And after about an hour had passed, another man *began* to insist, saying, "Certainly this man also was with Him,^Rfor he is a Galilean too." Matt. 26:73; Mark 14:70

60 But Peter said, "Man, I do not know what you are talking about." And^Rimmediately, while he was still speaking, a cock crowed. Luke 22:34; John 13:38★

61 And the Lord turned and looked at Peter. And Peter remembered the word of the Lord, how He had told him, "Before a cock crows today, you will deny Me three times."

62 And he went out and wept bitterly.

Christ Is Beaten
Matt. 26:67, 68; Mark 14:65

63 ^RAnd the men who were holding ^TJesus in custody were mocking Him, and beating Him,　　Ps. 69:19; Is. 50:6; 52:14 ★ • *Him*
64 and they blindfolded Him and were asking Him, saying, "Prophesy,^R who is the one who hit You?"　　Matt. 26:68; Mark 14:65
65 And they were saying many other things against Him,^Rblaspheming.　Is. 53:3 ★

The Sanhedrin Tries Christ
Matt. 27:1; Mark 15:1

66 ^RAnd when it was day, the ³⁶Council of elders of the people assembled, both chief priests and scribes, and they led Him away to their council *chamber,* saying,　John 18:28
67"If^RYou are the ^TChrist, tell us." But He said to them, "If I tell you, you will not believe;　Matt. 26:63-66; Mark 14:61-63 • *Messiah*
68 and if I ask a question, you will not answer.
69"But^Rfrom now on^RTHE SON OF MAN WILL BE SEATED AT THE RIGHT HAND of the power OF GOD."　　Heb. 1:3☆ • Ps. 110:1
70 And they all said, "Are You^Rthe Son of God, then?" And He said to them,^R "Yes,^T I am."　Matt. 4:3 • Luke 1:35 ★ • *You say that I am*
71 And they said, "What further need do we have of testimony? For we have heard it ourselves from His own mouth."

CHAPTER 23

Pilate Tries Christ
Matt. 27:2, 11–14; Mark 15:1–5;
John 18:28–38

T HEN the whole body of them arose and ^Rbrought Him before Pilate.　Luke 18:32 ★
2 And they began to accuse Him, saying, "We found this man misleading our nation and forbidding to pay taxes to Caesar, and saying that He Himself is Christ, a King."
3 And Pilate asked Him, saying, "Are You the King of the Jews?" And He answered him and said, "*It is as you say.*"
4 And Pilate said to the chief priests and the multitudes, "I find no guilt in this man."
5 But they kept on insisting, saying, "He stirs up the people, teaching all over Judea, ^Rstarting from Galilee, even as far as this place."　　Matt. 4:12
6 But when Pilate heard it, he asked whether the man was a Galilean.
7 And when he learned that He belonged to Herod's jurisdiction, he sent Him to ^RHerod, who himself also was in Jerusalem ^Tat that time.　Matt. 14:1; Mark 6:14 • *in these days*

Herod Tries Christ

8 Now Herod was very glad when he saw Jesus; for ^Rhe had wanted to see Him for a long time, because he had been hearing about Him and was hoping to see some ^Asign performed by Him.　Luke 9:9 • *attesting miracle*
9 And he questioned Him at some length; but He answered him nothing.
10 And the chief priests and the scribes were standing there, accusing Him vehemently.
11 ^RAnd Herod with his soldiers, after treating Him with contempt and mocking Him, dressed Him in a gorgeous robe and sent Him back to Pilate.　Ps. 69:19; Is. 53:3 ★
12 Now Herod and Pilate became friends with one another that very day; for before they had been at enmity with each other.

Pilate Again Tries Christ
Matt. 27:15–26; Mark 15:6–15;
John 18:39—19:16

13 And Pilate summoned the chief priests and the ^Rrulers and the people,　Luke 23:35
14 and said to them, "You brought this man to me as one who ^Rincites the people to rebellion, and behold, having examined Him before you, I ^Rhave found no guilt in this man regarding the charges which you make against Him.　Luke 23:2 • Luke 23:4
15"No, nor has ^RHerod, for he sent Him back to us; and behold, nothing deserving death has been done by Him.　Luke 9:9
16"I will therefore ^Rpunish Him and release Him."　　Mark 15:15; Luke 23:22; John 19:1
17 [³⁷Now he was obliged to release to them at the feast one prisoner.]
18 But^Rthey cried out all together, saying, "Away with this man, and release for us Barabbas!"　　Is. 53:3; Acts 3:14 ★
19 (He was one who had been thrown into prison for a certain insurrection made in the city, and for murder.)
20 And Pilate, wanting to release Jesus, addressed them again,
21 but they kept on calling out, saying, "Crucify, crucify Him!"
22 And he said to them the third time, "Why, what evil has this man done? I have found in Him no guilt *demanding* death; I will therefore punish Him and release Him."
23 But they were insistent, with loud voices asking that He be crucified. And their voices *began* to prevail.
24 And Pilate pronounced sentence that their demand should be granted.
25 And he released the man they were asking for who had been thrown into prison for insurrection and murder, but he delivered Jesus to their will.

Christ Is Crucified
Matt. 27:31–56; Mark 15:20–41;
John 19:16–30

26 ^RAnd when they led Him away, they laid hold of one Simon of Cyrene, coming in

³⁶ Or, *Sanhedrin*
³⁷ Many mss. do not contain this verse

from the country, and placed on him the cross to carry behind Jesus.   Luke 23:26

27 And there were following Him a great multitude of the people, and of women who were mourning and lamenting Him.

28 But Jesus turning to them said, "Daughters of Jerusalem, stop weeping for Me, but weep for yourselves and for your children.

29"For behold, the days are coming when they will say, 'Blessed[R] are the barren, and the wombs that never bore, and the breasts that never nursed.'   Matt. 24:19; Luke 11:27

30"Then they will begin TO 'SAY TO THE MOUNTAINS, 'FALL ON US,' AND TO THE HILLS, 'COVER US.'   Is. 2:19, 20; Hos. 10:8; Rev. 6:16

31"For if they do these things in the green tree, what will happen in the dry?"

32 [R]And two others also, who were criminals, were being led away to be put to death with Him.   Matt. 27:38; Mark 15:27; John 19:18

33 And when they came to the place called 'The Skull, there[R] they crucified Him and the criminals, one on the right and the other on the left.   Calvary · Ps. 22:16-18 ★

34 But Jesus was saying, "Father, forgive them; for they do not know what they are doing." And they cast lots, dividing up His garments among themselves.   [Matt. 11:25]

35 [R]And the people stood by, looking on. And even the[R] rulers were sneering at Him, saying, "He saved others; let Him save Himself if this is the 'Christ of God, His Chosen One."   Ps. 22:7, 8 ★ · Luke 23:13 · Messiah

36 And the soldiers also mocked Him, coming up to Him, offering Him sour wine,

37 and saying, "If[R] You are the King of the Jews, save Yourself!"   Matt. 27:43

38 Now there was also an inscription above Him, "THIS[R] IS THE KING OF THE JEWS."   Matt. 27:37; Mark 15:26; John 19:19

39 And one of the criminals who were hanged there was 'hurling abuse at Him, saying, "Are[R] You not the 'Christ? Save Yourself and us!"   blaspheming · Ps. 22:8 ★ · Messiah

40 But the other answered, and rebuking him said, "Do you not even fear God, since you are under the same sentence of condemnation?

41"And we indeed justly, for we are receiving what we deserve for our deeds; but this man has done nothing wrong."

42 And he was saying, "Jesus, remember me when You come 'in Your kingdom!"   into

43 And He said to him, "Truly I say to you, today you shall be with Me in [R]Paradise."   [2 Cor. 12:4; Rev. 2:7]

44 [R]And it was now about 38the sixth hour, and darkness 'fell over the whole land until 39the ninth hour,   Amos 8:9 ★ · occurred

45 the sun 'being obscured; and the veil of the temple was torn in two.   failing

46 And Jesus, crying out with a loud voice, said, "Father,[R] INTO THY HANDS I COMMIT MY SPIRIT." [R]And having said this, He breathed His last.   Ps. 31:5 · Matt. 17:23 ★

47 Now when the centurion saw what had happened, he began praising God, saying, "Certainly this man was 'innocent." righteous

48 And all the multitudes who came together for this spectacle, when they observed what had happened, began to return, [R]beating their breasts.   John 16:20-22 ★

49 [R]And all His acquaintances and the women who accompanied Him from Galilee, were standing at a distance, seeing these things.   Matt. 27:55f.; Mark 15:40f.; Luke 8:2

Christ Is Buried
Matt. 27:57-61; Mark 15:42-47;
John 19:38-42

50 [R]And behold, a man named Joseph, who was a member of the Council, a good and righteous man   Matt. 27:57-61; Luke 23:50-56

51 (he had not consented to their plan and action), *a man* from Arimathea, a city of the Jews, who was [R]waiting for the kingdom of God;   Mark 15:43; Luke 2:25

52 [R]this man went to Pilate and asked for the body of Jesus.   Is. 53:9 ★

53 And he took it down and wrapped it in a linen cloth, and laid Him in a tomb cut into the rock, where no one had ever lain.

54 And it was the preparation day, and the Sabbath was about to 'begin.   dawn

55 Now the women who had come with Him out of Galilee followed after, and saw the tomb and how His body was laid.

In the Grave

56 And they returned and [R]prepared spices and perfumes. And[R] on the Sabbath they rested according to the commandment.   Mark 16:1 · Deut. 5:14

CHAPTER 24

The Resurrection
Matt. 28:1-8; Mark 16:1-8; John 20:1-10

BUT[R] on the first day of the week, at early dawn, they came to the tomb, bringing the spices which they had prepared.   Luke 24:1-10

2 And they found the stone rolled away from the tomb,

3 but when they entered, they did not find the body of[R] the Lord Jesus.   Acts 1:21

4 And it happened that while they were perplexed about this, behold, two men suddenly stood near them in dazzling apparel;

5 and as *the women* were terrified and bowed their faces to the ground, *the men* said to them, "Why do you seek the living One among the dead?

6"He is not here, but He has risen.[R] Re-

---

38 I.e., 12 noon   39 I.e., 3 p.m.

member how He spoke to you while He was still in Galilee,   Matt. 16:21; Mark 8:31 ★

7 saying that the Son of Man must be delivered into the hands of sinful men, and be crucified, and the third day rise again."

8 And they remembered His words,

9 and returned from the tomb and reported all these things to the eleven and to all the rest.

10 Now they were [R]Mary Magdalene and Joanna and Mary the *mother* of James; also the other women with them were telling these things to the apostles.   Matt. 27:56

11 And these words appeared to them as nonsense, and they would not believe them.

12 [[40]But Peter arose and [R]ran to the tomb; stooping and looking in, he *saw the linen wrappings [A]only; and he went away to his home, marveling at that which had happened.]   John 20:3-6 • *by themselves*

Christ Appears on
the Road to Emmaus
Mark 16:12, 13

13 And behold, two of them were going that very day to a village named Emmaus, which was [41]about seven miles from Jerusalem.

14 And they were conversing with each other about all these things which had taken place.

15 And it came about that while they were conversing and discussing, Jesus Himself approached, and *began* traveling with them.

16 But their eyes [T]were prevented from recognizing Him.   *were being prevented*

17 And He said to them, "What are these words that you are exchanging with one another as you are walking?" And they stood still, looking sad.

18 And one of them, named Cleopas, answered and said to Him, "Are You[A]the only one visiting Jerusalem and unaware of the things which have happened here in these days?"   *visiting Jerusalem alone*

19 And He said to them, "What things?" And they said to Him, "The things about [R]Jesus the Nazarene, who was a [R]prophet mighty in deed and word in the sight of God and all the people,   Mark 1:24 • Matt. 21:11

20 and how the chief priests and our [R]rulers delivered Him up to the sentence of death, and crucified Him.   Luke 23:13

21 "But we were hoping that it was He who was going to [R]redeem Israel. Indeed, besides all this, it is the third day since these things happened.   Luke 1:68

22 "But also some women among us amazed us. [R]When they were at the tomb early in the morning,   Luke 24:1ff.

23 and did not find His body, they came, saying that they had also seen a vision of angels, who said that He was alive.

24 "And some of those who were with us went to the tomb and found it just exactly as the women also had said; but Him they did not see."

25 And He said to them, "O foolish men and slow of heart to believe in all that [R]the prophets have spoken!   Matt. 26:24

26 "Was [R]it not necessary for the Christ to suffer these things and to enter into His glory?"   Luke 24:7, 44ff.; [Heb. 2:10] • *Messiah*

27 And beginning [T]with [R]Moses and [T]with all the prophets, He explained to them the things concerning Himself in all the Scriptures.   *from* • [Gen. 3:15; 12:3; Num. 21:9]

28 And they approached the village where they were going, and [R]He acted as though He would go farther.   Mark 6:48

29 And they urged Him, saying, "Stay with us, for it is *getting* toward evening, and the day[T]is now nearly over." And He went in to stay with them.   *has now declined*

30 And it came about that when He had reclined *at the table* with them, He took the bread and [R]blessed *it*, and breaking *it*, He *began* giving *it* to them.   Matt. 14:19

31 And their [R]eyes were opened and they recognized Him; and He vanished from [T]their sight.   Luke 24:16 • *them*

32 And they said to one another, "Were not our hearts burning within us while He was speaking to us on the road, while He was explaining the Scriptures to us?"

The Proof of His Resurrection
Mark 16:4; John 20:19–23; 1 Cor. 15:5

33 And they arose that very hour and returned to Jerusalem, and [R]found gathered together the eleven and [R]those who were with them,   Mark 16:13 • Acts 1:14

34 saying, "The [R]Lord has really risen, and has appeared to Simon."   Luke 24:6

35 And they *began* to relate their experiences on the road and how He was recognized by them in the breaking of the bread.

36 And while they were telling these things, He Himself stood in their midst.[42]

37 But they were startled and frightened and thought that they were seeing a spirit.

38 And He said to them, "Why are you troubled, and why do doubts arise in your [T]hearts?   *heart*

39 "See [R]My hands and My feet, that it is I Myself; [R]touch Me and see, for a spirit does not have flesh and bones as you see that I have."   John 20:20, 27 • John 20:27

40 [[43]And when He had said this, He showed them His hands and His feet.]

41 And while they still could not believe *it* for joy and were marveling, He said to them, "Have you anything here to eat?"

42 And they gave Him a piece of a broiled fish;

[40] Some ancient mss. do not contain v. 12
[41] I.e., 60 stadia, one stadion was about 600 feet
[42] Some ancient mss. insert *And He says to them, "Peace be to you."*   [43] Many mss. do not contain this verse

43 and He took it and ate *it* before them.

The Great Commission
Acts 1:3–8

44 Now He said to them, "These are My words which I spoke to you while I was still with you, that all things which are written about Me in the Law of Moses and the Prophets and the Psalms must be fulfilled."
45 Then He [R]opened their [T]minds to understand the Scriptures,   Luke 24:32 • *mind*
46 and He said to them, "Thus [R]it is written, that the Christ should suffer and rise again from the dead the third day; Hos. 6:2 ★
47 and that repentance for forgiveness of

[44] Some mss. add *and was carried up into heaven*
[45] Some mss. insert *worshiped Him, and*

sins should be proclaimed in His name to all the nations, beginning from Jerusalem.
48 "You are witnesses of these things.

The Ascension
Mark 16:19; Acts 1:9

49 "And behold, [R]I am sending forth the promise of My Father upon you; but you are to stay in the city [R]until you are clothed with power from on high."   [John 14:26] • Acts 2:4 ☆
50 And He led them out as far as [R]Bethany, and He lifted up His hands and blessed them.   Matt. 21:17; Acts 1:12
51 And it came about that while He was blessing them, He parted from them.[44]
52 And they[45] returned to Jerusalem with great joy,
53 and were continually in the temple, [T]praising God.   *blessing*

Unit	Monetary Value	Equivalents	Translations
Jewish Weights			
Talent	gold—$5,760,000[1] silver—$384,000	3,000 shekels; 6,000 bekas	talent, one hundred pounds
Shekel	gold—$1,920 silver—$128	4 days' wages; 2 bekas; 20 gerahs	shekel
Beka	gold—$960 silver—$64	½ shekel; 10 gerahs	beka
Gerah	gold—$96 silver—$6.40	¹⁄₂₀ shekel	gerahs
Persian Coins			
Daric	gold—$1,280[2] silver—$64	2 days' wages; ½ Jewish silver shekel	daric, drachma
Greek Coins			
Tetradrachma (Stater)	$128	4 drachmas	stater
Didrachma	$64	2 drachmas	two-drachma tax
Drachma	$32	1 day's wage	coin, silver coins
Lepton	$.25	½ of a Roman kodrantes	cents, small copper coin
Roman Coins			
Aureus	$800	25 denarii	gold
Denarius	$32	1 day's wage	denarii
Assarius	$2	¹⁄₁₆ of a denarius	cent
Kodrantes	$.50	¼ of an assarius	cent

<h2 style="text-align:center">Monies</h2>

[1]Value of gold is fifteen times the value of silver.
[2]Value of gold is twenty times the value of silver.

JOHN

THE BOOK OF JOHN

Just as a coin has two sides, both valid, so Jesus Christ has two natures, both valid. Luke presents Christ in His humanity as the Son of Man; John portrays Him in His deity as the Son of God. John's purpose is crystal clear: to set forth Christ in His deity in order to spark believing faith in his readers. John's gospel is topical, not primarily chronological, and it revolves around seven miracles and seven "I am" statements of Christ.

Following an extended eyewitness description of the Upper Room meal and discourse, John records events leading up to the Resurrection, the final climactic proof that Jesus is who He claims to be—the Son of God.

The title of the Fourth Gospel follows the same format as the titles of the synoptic Gospels: *Kata Ioannen*, "According to John." As with the others, the word "Gospel" was later added. *Ioannes* is derived from the Hebrew name *Johanan*, "Yahweh Has Been Gracious."

THE AUTHOR OF JOHN

Jesus nicknamed John and his brother, James, "Sons of Thunder" (Mark 3:17). Their father was Zebedee, and their mother, Salome, served Jesus in Galilee and was present at His crucifixion (Mark 15:40, 41). John was evidently among the Galileans who followed John the Baptist until they were called to follow Jesus at the outset of His public ministry (1:19–51). These Galileans were later called to become full-time disciples of the Lord (Luke 5:1–11), and John was among the twelve men who were selected to be apostles (Luke 6:12–16). After Christ's ascension, John became one of the "pillars" of the church in Jerusalem along with James and Peter (Gal. 2:9). He is mentioned three times by name in Acts (3:1; 4:13; 8:14), each time in association with Peter. Tradition says that John later went to Ephesus (perhaps just before the destruction of Jerusalem). He was eventually exiled by the Romans for a time to the island of Patmos (Rev. 1:9).

The author of this gospel is identified only as the disciple "whom Jesus loved" (13:23; 19:26; 20:2; 21:7, 20). His knowledge of Palestinian geography and Jewish customs makes it clear that he was a Palestinian Jew, and his meticulous attention to numbers (2:6; 6:13, 19; 21:8, 11) and names (1:45; 3:1; 11:1; 18:10) indicates that he was an eyewitness. This fits his own claim to be a witness of the events he described (1:14; 19:35; 21:24, 25). The disciple "whom Jesus loved" was part of the inner circle of disciples and was closely associated with Peter. The synoptic Gospels name this inner circle as Peter, James, and John. Since Peter is separate from the beloved disciple, only James and John are left. James was martyred too early to be the author (Acts 12:1, 2), so the Apostle John was the author of this gospel. This conclusion from internal evidence is consistent with the external testimony of the early church. Irenaeus (c. A.D. 185) was a disciple of Polycarp who was in turn a disciple of the Apostle John. In his *Against Heresies*, Irenaeus bore witness to Johannine authorship of this gospel and noted that John lived until the time of the emperor Trajan (A.D. 98–117). Clement of Alexandria, Theophilus of Antioch, Origen, and others also ascribe this book to John.

THE TIME OF JOHN

In spite of the strong internal and external testimony supporting Johannine authorship of this gospel, theological assumptions have motivated a number of critics to deny this claim. Until recently it was popular to propose a second-century date for this book. The discovery of the John Rylands Papyrus 52 containing portions of John 18:31–33, 37, 38 has overthrown this conjecture. This fragment has been dated at about A.D. 135, and a considerable period of time must have been required for John's gospel to be copied and circulated before it reached Egypt, where this papyrus was found.

On the other hand, John was written after the last of the synoptic Gospels (c. A.D. 66–68). His familiarity with the topography of Jerusalem (e.g., 5:2; 19:13) does not necessarily require a date before A.D. 70. Since John's three epistles and Revelation were written after his gospel, the probable range for this work is A.D. 60–90. By this time, John would have been one of the last surviving eyewitnesses of the Lord. According to tradition, John wrote this gospel in Ephesus.

THE CHRIST OF JOHN

This book presents the most powerful case in all the Bible for the deity of the incarnate Son of God. "The man who is called Jesus" (9:11) is also "the Holy One of God" (6:69). The deity of Christ can be seen in His

seven "I am" statements: "I am the bread of life" (6:35, 48); "I am the light of the world" (8:12; 9:5); "I am the door" (10:7, 9); "I am the good shepherd" (10:11, 14); "I am the resurrection and the life" (11:25); "I am the way, the truth, and the life" (14:6); "I am the true vine" (15:1-5). The seven signs (1—12) and the five witnesses (5:30-40) also point to His divine character. On certain occasions, Jesus equates Himself with the Old Testament "I AM," or Yahweh (see 4:25, 26; 8:24, 28, 58; 13:19; 18:5, 6, 8). Some of the most crucial affirmations of His deity are in 1:1; 8:58; 10:30; 14:9; 20:28.

The Word was God (1:1), but the Word also became flesh (1:14). The humanity of Jesus can be seen in His weariness (4:6), thirst (4:7), dependence (5:19), grief (11:35), troubled soul (12:27), and His anguish and death (19).

KEYS TO JOHN

Key Word: Believe That Jesus Is the Son of God—The Fourth Gospel has the clearest statement of purpose in the Bible: "but these have been written that you may believe that Jesus is the Christ, the Son of God; and that believing you may have life in His name" (20:31). John selected the signs he used for the specific purpose of creating intellectual ("that you may believe") and spiritual ("that believing you may have life") conviction about the Son of God. The key verb in John is "believe," and requires both knowledge (8:32; 10:38) and volition (1:12; 3:19; 7:17).

The predominant theme of this gospel is the dual response of faith and unbelief to the person of Jesus Christ. Those who place their faith in the Son of God have eternal life, but those who reject Him are under the condemnation of God (3:36; 5:24-29; 10:27-29): this is the basic issue. John 1:11, 12 summarizes

the responses of accepting or rejecting the Son of God that are traced through the rest of the book. The rejection of Jesus by His own people can be seen over and over in chapters 2 through 19 ("those who were His own did not receive Him"), but John also lists a number of men and women who believed in Him ("But as many as received Him").

Key Verses: John 1:11-13 and 20:30, 31—"He came to His own, and those who were His own did not receive Him. But as many as received Him, to them He gave the right to become children of God, *even* to those who believe in His name, who were born not of blood, nor of the will of the flesh, nor of the will of man, but of God" (1:11-13).

"Many other signs therefore Jesus also performed in the presence of the disciples, which are not written in this book; but these have been written that you may believe that Jesus is the Christ, the Son of God; and that believing you may have life in His name" (20:30, 31).

Key Chapter: John 3—John 3:16 is without doubt the most quoted and preached verse in all of Scripture. Captured in it is the gospel in its clearest and simplest form: that salvation is a gift of God and is obtainable only through belief. The conversation with Nicodemus and the testimony of John the Baptist provide the setting that clearly points out that being "born again" is the only way to find the "kingdom of God."

SURVEY OF JOHN

This most unusual gospel, with its distinct content and style, serves as a supplement to the three synoptics. It is easily the simplest and yet the most profound of the gospels, and for many people it is the greatest and most powerful. John writes his gospel for the

FOCUS	INCARNATION OF THE SON OF GOD	PRESENTATION OF THE SON OF GOD	OPPOSITION TO THE SON OF GOD	PREPARATION OF THE DISCIPLES	CRUCIFIXION AND RESURRECTION OF THE SON OF GOD
REFERENCE	1:1————————1:19————————5:1————————13:1————————18:1————21:25				
DIVISION	INTRODUCTION TO CHRIST	REVELATION OF CHRIST	REJECTION OF CHRIST	REVELATION OF CHRIST	REJECTION OF CHRIST
TOPIC	SEVEN MIRACLES			UPPER ROOM DISCOURSE	SUPREME MIRACLE
	THAT YOU MIGHT BELIEVE			THAT YOU MIGHT HAVE LIFE	
LOCATION	ISRAEL				
TIME	A FEW YEARS			A FEW HOURS	A FEW WEEKS

specific purpose of bringing people to spiritual life through belief in the person and work of Jesus Christ. The five basic sections of this gospel are: the incarnation of the Son of God (1:1–18); the presentation of the Son of God (1:19—4:54); the opposition to the Son of God (5:1—12:50); the preparation of the disciples by the Son of God (13:1—17:26); the crucifixion and resurrection of the Son of God (18:1—21:25).

The Incarnation of the Son of God (1:1–18): This prologue introduces the rest of the book and gives the background for the historical narrative that follows. It dates the nature of Jesus, introduces His forerunner, clarifies His mission, and notes the rejection and acceptance He will find during His ministry.

The Presentation of the Son of God (1:19—4:54): In this section Christ is under careful consideration and scrutiny by Israel. He is introduced by John the Baptist who directs his own disciples to Christ. Shortly the author begins listing the seven signs, which continue through the next section. John carefully selects seven miracles out of the many that Christ accomplished (cf. John 21:25) in order to build a concise case for His deity. They are called signs because they symbolize the life-changing results of belief in Jesus—(1) water to wine: the ritual of law is replaced by the reality of grace (2:1–11); (2) healing the nobleman's son: the gospel brings spiritual restoration (4:46–54); (3) healing the paralytic: weakness is replaced by strength (5:1–16); (4) feeding the multitude: Christ satisfies spiritual hunger (6:1–13); (5) walking on water: the Lord transforms fear to faith (6:16–21); (6) sight to the man born blind: Jesus overcomes darkness and brings in light (9:1–7); (7) raising of Lazarus: the gospel brings people from death to life (11:1–44). These signs combine to show that Jesus is indeed the Son of God.

The Opposition to the Son of God (5:1—12:50): John's unusual pattern in these chapters is to record the reactions of belief and disbelief after the performance of one miracle before moving to the next. In a series of growing confrontations, John portrays the intense opposition that will culminate in the Lord's final rejection on the cross. Even though many people received Him, the inevitable crucifixion is foreshadowed in several places (2:4, 21, 22; 7:6, 39; 11:51, 52; 12:16).

The Preparation of the Disciples by the Son of God (13:1—17:26): John surveys the incarnation and public ministry of Jesus in twelve chapters, but radically changes the pace in the next five chapters to give a detailed account of a few crucial hours. In this clear and vivid recollection of Jesus' last discourse to His intimate disciples, John captures the Lord's words of comfort and assurance to a group of fearful and confused followers. Jesus knows that in less than twenty-four hours He will be on the cross. Therefore, His last words speak of all the resources that will be at the disciples' disposal after His departure. They will be indwelled and empowered by the Triune Godhead. The Upper Room Discourse contains the message of the epistles in capsule form as it reveals God's pattern for Christian living. In it the key themes of servanthood, the Holy Spirit, and abiding in Christ are developed.

The Crucifixion and Resurrection of the Son of God (18:1—21:25): After recording Christ's high priestly prayer on behalf of His disciples and all who believe in Him "through their word" (17), John immediately launches into a dramatic description of Christ's arrest and trials before Annas, Caiaphas, and Pilate. In His crucifixion, Jesus willingly fulfills John the Baptist's prophetic words: "Behold, the Lamb of God who takes away the sin of the world!" (1:29). John closes his profound gospel with a particulary detailed account of the post-resurrection appearances of the Lord. The Resurrection is the ultimate sign that points to Jesus as the Son of God.

CHAPTER 1

The Deity of Christ

I N ᴿ the beginning was ᴿ the Word, and the Word was ᴿ with God, and the Word was God. Gen. 1:1 • [John 1:14] • [John 17:5; 1 John 1:2]

2 He was in the beginning with God.

The Preincarnate Work of Christ

3 ᴿAll things came into being ᴬby Him, and apart from Him nothing came into being that has come into being.   John 1:10 • through

4 ᴿIn Him was life, and the life was ᴿthe light of men.   [John 5:26; 11:25] • John 8:12; 9:5

5 And the light shines in the darkness, and the darkness did not ¹comprehend it.

The Forerunner of Christ

6 There ²came a man, sent from God, whose name was ᴿJohn.   Matt. 3:1

7 ᵀHe came ᴿfor a witness, that he might bear witness of the light, that all might believe through him.   This one • John 1:15, 19, 32

8 ᵀHe was not the light, but came that he might bear witness of the light.   That one

The Rejection of Christ

9 There was the true light ³which, coming into the world, enlightens every man.

10 He was in the world, and ᴿthe world was made through Him, and the world did not know Him.   1 Cor. 8:6; Col. 1:16; Heb. 1:2

11 He came to His ⁴own, and those who were His own did not receive Him.

The Acceptance of Christ

12 But as many as received Him, to them He gave the right to become children of God, even to those who believe in His name,

13 ᴿwho were ᴬborn not of ᵀblood, nor of the will of the flesh, nor of the will of man, but of God.   [1 John 2:29; 3:9] • begotten • bloods

The Incarnation of Christ

14 And the Word became flesh, and dwelt among us, and we beheld His glory, glory as of ᴬthe only begotten from the Father, full of grace and truth.   unique, only one of His kind

15 John *bore witness of Him, and cried out, saying, "This was He of whom I said, 'He who comes after me has a higher rank than I, ᴿfor He existed before me.' " John 1:30

16 For of His fulness ᵀwe have all received, and grace upon grace.   we all received

17 For ᴿthe Law was given through Moses; ᴿgrace and ᴿtruth were realized through Jesus Christ.   John 7:19 • John 1:14 • [John 8:32; 14:6]

18 ᴿNo man has seen God at any time; the only begotten ⁵God, who is in the bosom of the Father, He has explained Him.   Ex. 33:20

John's Witness to the Priests and Levites
Matt. 3:1–12; Mark 1:2–8; Luke 3:3–16

19 And this is the witness of John, when the Jews sent to him priests and Levites from Jerusalem to ask him, "Who are you?"

20 And he confessed, and did not deny, and he confessed, "I am not the Christ."

21 And they asked him, "What then? Are you Elijah?" And he *said, "I am not." "Are you the Prophet?" And he answered, "No."

22 They said then to him, "Who are you, so that we may give an answer to those who sent us? What do you say about yourself?"

23 He said, "I am ᴿA VOICE OF ONE CRYING IN THE WILDERNESS, 'MAKE STRAIGHT THE WAY OF THE LORD,' as Isaiah the prophet said."   Is. 40:3; Matt. 3:3; Mark 1:3; Luke 3:4 ★

24 Now they had been sent from the Pharisees.

25 And they asked him, and said to him, "Why then are you baptizing, if you are not the Christ, nor Elijah, nor the Prophet?"

26 John answered them saying, "I ᵀbaptize in water, but among you stands One whom you do not know.   Matt. 3:11; Mark 1:8

27"It is He who comes after me, the thong of whose sandal I am not worthy to untie."

28 These things took place in Bethany beyond the Jordan, where John was baptizing.

John's Witness at Christ's Baptism
Matt. 3:13–17; Mark 1:9–11;
Luke 3:21, 22

29 The next day he *saw Jesus coming to him, and *said, "Behold, the Lamb of God who takes away the sin of the world!

30"This is He on behalf of whom I said, 'After me comes a Man who has a higher rank than I, for He existed before me.'

31"And I did not recognize ᵀHim, but in or-

---

¹ Or, overpower   ² Or, came into being
³ Or, which enlightens every man coming into the world
⁴ Or, own things, possessions, domain
⁵ Some later mss. read Son

der that He might be manifested to Israel, I came baptizing [6]in water." *as the Messiah*

32 And John bore witness saying, "I have beheld the Spirit descending as a dove out of heaven, and He remained upon Him.

33 "And I did not recognize Him, but He who sent me to baptize [6]in water said to me, 'He upon whom you see[R]the Spirit descending and remaining upon Him, this is the one who baptizes in the Holy Spirit.' Is. 42:1 ★

34 "And I have seen, and have borne witness that this is[R]the Son of God." Luke 1:35 ★

Andrew and Peter Follow Christ

35 Again[R]the next day John was standing [T]with two of his disciples, John 1:29 • *and*

36 and he looked upon Jesus as He walked, and *said, "Behold, [R]the Lamb of God!" John 1:29

37 And the two disciples heard him speak, and they followed Jesus.

38 And Jesus turned, and beheld them following, and *said to them, "What do you seek?" And they said to Him, "Rabbi[R](which translated means Teacher), where are You staying?" Matt. 23:7f.; John 1:49

39 He *said to them, "Come, and you will see." They came therefore and saw where He was staying; and they stayed with Him that day, for it was about the [7]tenth hour.

40 [R]One of the two who heard John *speak,* and followed Him, was Andrew, Simon Peter's brother. Matt. 4:18-22; Mark 1:16-20

41 He *found first his own brother Simon, and *said to him, "We have found the Messiah" (which translated means Christ).

42 He brought him to Jesus. Jesus looked at him, and said, "You are Simon the son of [T]John; you shall be called Cephas" (which is translated Peter). Gr., *Joannes*

Philip and Nathanael Follow Christ

43 The next day He purposed to go forth into [R]Galilee, and He *found Philip. And Jesus *said to him, "Follow Me." Matt. 4:12

44 Now[R]Philip was from Bethsaida, of the city of Andrew and Peter. John 1:44-48; 6:5, 7

45 Philip *found Nathanael and *said to him, "We have found Him of whom Moses in the Law and *also* the Prophets wrote, Jesus of Nazareth, the son of Joseph."

46 And Nathanael *said to him, "Can[R]any good thing come out of Nazareth?" Philip *said to him, "Come and see." John 7:41, 52

47 Jesus saw Nathanael coming to Him, and *said of him, "Behold, an[R]Israelite indeed, in whom is no guile!" [Rom. 9:4]

48 Nathanael *said to Him, "How do You know me?" Jesus answered and said to him, "Before[R]Philip called you, when you were under the fig tree, I saw you." Matt. 10:3

49 Nathanael answered Him, "Rabbi,[R] You are[R]the Son of God; You are the[R]King of Israel." John 1:38 • John 1:34 • Ps. 2:7 ★

50 Jesus answered and said to him, "Because I said to you that I saw you under the fig tree, do you believe? You shall see greater things than these."

51 And He *said to him, "Truly, truly, I say to you, you shall see the heavens opened, and the angels of God ascending and descending on the Son of Man."

CHAPTER 2

Christ Changes Water to Wine

AND on[R]the third day there was a wedding in Cana of Galilee, and the[R]mother of Jesus was there; John 1:29, 35, 43 • Matt. 12:46

2 and Jesus also was invited, and His[R]disciples, to the wedding. John 1:40-49; 2:12, 17, 22

3 And when the wine gave out, the mother of Jesus *said to Him, "They have no wine."

4 And Jesus *said to her, "Woman, what do I have to do with you? My hour has not yet come."

5 His [R]mother *said to the servants, "Whatever He says to you, do it." Matt. 12:46

6 Now there were six stone waterpots set there[R]for the Jewish custom of purification, containing twenty or thirty gallons each. [Mark 7:3f.]; John 3:25

7 Jesus *said to them, "Fill the waterpots with water." And they filled them up to the brim.

8 And He *said to them, "Draw *some* out now, and take it to the [8]headwaiter." And they took it *to him.*

9 And when the headwaiter tasted the water[R]which had become wine, and did not know where it came from (but the servants who had drawn the water knew), the headwaiter *called the bridegroom, John 4:46

10 and *said to him, "Every man serves the good wine first, and when *men* have drunk freely, *then* that which is poorer; you have kept the good wine until now."

The Disciples Believe

11 This beginning of His[R]signs Jesus did in Cana of Galilee, and manifested His glory, and His disciples believed in Him. John 2:23

12 After this He went down to [R]Capernaum, He and His[R]mother, and *His* brothers, and His [R]disciples; and there they stayed a few days. Matt. 4:13 • Matt. 12:46 • John 2:2

Christ Cleanses the Temple

13 And the Passover of the Jews was at hand, and Jesus went up to Jerusalem.

14 [R]And He found in the temple those who

---

[6] The Gr. here can be translated *in, with* or *by*
[7] Perhaps 10 a.m. (Roman time)
[8] Or, *steward*

were selling oxen and sheep and doves, and the moneychangers seated.   Mal. 3:1★

15 And He made a scourge of cords, and drove *them* all out of the temple, with the sheep and the oxen; and He poured out the coins of the moneychangers, and overturned their tables;

16 and to those who were selling [R]the doves He said, "Take these things away; stop making[R]My Father's house a house of merchandise."   Matt. 21:12 • Luke 2:49

17 His [R]disciples remembered that it was written, "ZEAL[R] FOR THY HOUSE WILL CONSUME ME."   John 2:2 • Ps. 69:9★

18 The Jews therefore answered and said to Him, "What[R]sign do You show to us, seeing that You do these things?"   Matt. 12:38

19 Jesus answered and said to them, "Destroy[R]this temple, and in three days I will raise it up."   Matt. 26:61; 27:40; Acts 10:40 ☆

20 The Jews therefore said, "It took forty-six years to build this[A]temple, and will You raise it up in three days?"   *sanctuary*

21 But He was speaking of[R]the[A]temple of His body.   [1 Cor. 6:19] • *sanctuary*

22 When therefore He was raised from the dead, His disciples remembered that He said this; and they believed the Scripture, and the word which Jesus had spoken.

23 Now when He was in Jerusalem at[R]the Passover, during the feast, many believed in His name, [R]beholding His signs which He was doing.   John 2:13 • John 2:11

24 But Jesus, on His part, was not entrusting Himself to them, for He knew all men,

25 and because He did not need anyone to bear witness concerning man[R]for He Himself knew what was in man.   Matt. 9:4

CHAPTER 3

Christ Witnesses to Nicodemus

NOW there was a man of the Pharisees, named Nicodemus, a ruler of the Jews;

2 this man came to Him by night, and said to Him, "Rabbi, we know that You have come from God *as* a teacher; for no one can do these[A]signs that You do unless [R]God is with him."   *attesting miracles* • Acts 2:22

3 Jesus answered and said to him, "Truly, truly, I say to you, unless one is born again, he cannot see the kingdom of God."

4 Nicodemus *said to Him, "How can a man be born when he is old? He cannot enter a second time into his mother's womb and be born, can he?"

5 Jesus answered, "Truly, truly, I say to you, unless one is born of[R]water and the Spirit, he cannot enter into[R]the kingdom of God.   [Ezek. 36:25–27]; Eph. 5:26 • Matt. 19:24

6"That which is born of the flesh is flesh, and that which is born of the Spirit is spirit.★

7"Do not marvel that I said to you, 'You must be born[A]again.'   *from above*

8"The wind blows where it wishes and you hear the sound of it, but do not know where it comes from and where it is going; so is everyone who is born of the Spirit."

9 Nicodemus answered and said to Him, "How can these things be?"

10 Jesus answered and said to him, "Are you[R]the teacher of Israel, and do not understand these things?   Luke 2:46; 5:17; Acts 5:34

11"Truly, truly, I say to you,[R]we speak that which we know, and[R]bear witness of that which we have seen; and you do not receive our witness.   John 1:18; 7:16f. • John 3:32

12"If I told you earthly things and you do not believe, how shall you believe if I tell you heavenly things?

13"And[R]no one has ascended into heaven, but He who descended from heaven, *even* [R]the Son of Man.   Deut. 30:12 • Matt. 8:20

14"And as[R]Moses lifted up the serpent in the wilderness, even so must the Son of Man be lifted up;   Num. 21:9 • John 8:28; 19:18☆

15 that whoever [9]believes may [R]in Him have eternal life.   John 20:31; [1 John 5:11–13]

16"For God so loved the world, that He gave His[A]only begotten Son, that whoever believes in Him should not perish, but have eternal life.   *unique, only one of His kind*

17"For God did not send the Son into the world[R]to judge the world, but that the world should be saved through Him.   Luke 19:10 ☆

18"He who believes in Him is not judged; he who does not believe has been judged already, because he has not believed in the name of the only begotten Son of God.

19"And this is the judgment, that[R]the light is come into the world, and men loved the darkness rather than the light; for [R]their deeds were evil.   [John 1:4; 8:12; 9:5] • John 7:7

20"For[R]everyone who does evil hates the light, and does not come to the light, lest his deeds should be exposed.   John 3:20, 21

21"But he who practices the truth comes to the light, that his deeds may be manifested as having been wrought in God."

John the Baptist Witnesses Concerning Christ

22 After these things Jesus and His[R]disciples came into the land of Judea, and there He was spending time with them and[R]baptizing.   John 2:2 • John 4:1, 2

23 And John also was baptizing in Aenon near Salim, because there was [r]much water there; and they were coming and were being baptized.   *many waters*

24 For[R]John had not yet been thrown into prison.   Matt. 4:12; 14:3; Mark 6:17; Luke 3:20

25 There arose therefore a discussion on the part of John's disciples with a Jew about [R]purification.   John 2:6

26 And they came to John and said to him, "Rabbi,[R] He who was with you beyond the Jordan, to whom you[R]have borne witness, behold, He is baptizing, and all are coming to Him."   Matt. 23:7; John 3:2 • John 1:7

[9] Some mss. read *believes in Him may have eternal life*

27 John answered and said, "A[R] man can receive nothing, unless it[R] has been given him from heaven.   1 Cor. 4:7 • [James 1:17]

28 "You yourselves bear me witness, that I said, 'I[T] am not the [']Christ,' but, 'I have been sent before Him.'   John 1:20, 23 • Messiah

29 "He who has the bride is the bridegroom; but the friend of the bridegroom, who stands and hears him, rejoices greatly because of the bridegroom's voice. And so this[R] joy of mine has been made full.   Phil. 2:2

30 "He must increase, but I must decrease.

31 "He[']who comes from above is above all, [R] he who is of the earth is from the earth and speaks of the earth. He who comes from heaven is above all.   Matt. 28:18 • 1 Cor. 15:47

32 "What He has seen and heard, of that He[R] bears witness;[R] and no man receives His witness.   John 3:11 • Is. 53:1, 3 ★

33 "He who has received His witness has set his seal to *this*, that God is true.

34 "For He whom God has[R] sent speaks the words of God;[R] for He gives the Spirit without measure.   Deut. 18:18 ★ • Luke 4:18

35 "The Father loves the Son, and[R] has given all things into His hand.   Matt. 11:27

36 "He who[R] believes in the Son has eternal life; but he who[R] does not['] obey the Son shall not see life, but the wrath of God abides on him."   John 3:16 • Acts 14:2; Heb. 3:18 • *believe*

CHAPTER 4

Christ Witnesses to the Woman at the Well

WHEN therefore the Lord knew that the Pharisees had heard that Jesus was making and baptizing more disciples than John

2 (although [R] Jesus Himself was not baptizing, but His disciples were),   John 3:22, 26

3 He left [']Judea, and departed[']again into Galilee.   John 3:22 • John 2:11f.

4 And He had to pass through Samaria.

5 So He *came to a city of [R] Samaria, called Sychar, near the parcel of ground that Jacob gave to his son Joseph;   Luke 9:52

6 and Jacob's well was there. Jesus therefore, being wearied from His journey, was sitting thus by the well. It was about [10] the sixth hour.

7 There *came a woman of Samaria to draw water. Jesus *said to her, "Give Me a drink."

8 For His [R] disciples had gone away into [R] the city to buy food.   John 2:2 • John 4:5, 39

9 The[R] Samaritan woman therefore *said to Him, "How is it that You, being a Jew, ask me for a drink since I am a Samaritan woman?" (For[R] Jews have no dealings with Samaritans.)   Luke 9:52 • Ezra 4:3-6, 11ff.

10 Jesus answered and said to her, "If you knew the gift of God, and who it is who says to you, 'Give Me a drink,' you would have asked Him, and He would have given you [R] living water."   Jer. 2:13; John 4:14; 7:37f.

[10] Perhaps 6 p.m. (Roman time)

11 She *said to Him, "Sir,['] You have nothing to draw with and the well is deep; where then do You get that living water?   Lord

12 "You are not greater than our father Jacob, are You, who[R] gave us the well, and drank of it himself, and his sons, and his cattle?"   John 4:6

13 Jesus answered and said to her, "Everyone who drinks of this water shall thirst again;

14 but whoever drinks of the water that I shall give him shall never thirst; but the water that I shall give him shall become in him a well of water springing up to eternal life."

15 The woman *said to Him, "Sir,['] give[R] me this water, so I will not be thirsty, nor come all the way here to draw."   Lord • [John 6:35]

16 He *said to her, "Go, call your husband, and come here."

17 The woman answered and said, "I have no husband." Jesus *said to her, "You have well said, 'I have no husband';

18 for you have had five husbands, and the one whom you now have is not your husband; this you have said truly."

19 The woman *said to Him, "Sir,['] I perceive that You are a prophet.   Lord

20 "Our fathers worshiped in this mountain, and you *people* say that in Jerusalem is the place where men ought to worship."

21 Jesus *said to her, "Woman, believe Me,[R] an hour is coming when[R] neither in this mountain, nor in Jerusalem, shall you worship the Father.   John 4:23; 5:25, 28 • [Mal. 1:11]

22 "You worship that which you do not know; we worship that which we know, for [R] salvation is from the Jews.   [Is. 2:3; Rom. 3:1f.]

23 "But an hour is coming, and now is, when the true worshipers shall worship the Father in spirit and truth; for such people the Father seeks to be His worshipers.

24 "God is spirit, and those who worship Him must worship in spirit and truth."

25 The woman *said to Him, "I know that [R] Messiah is coming (He[R] who is called Christ); when that One comes, He will declare all things to us."   Dan. 9:25; John 1:41 ★ • Matt. 1:16

26 Jesus *said to her, "I[T] who speak to you am *He*."   John 8:24, 28, 58; 9:37; 13:19

Christ Witnesses to the Disciples

27 And at this point His [R] disciples came, and they marveled that He had been speaking with a woman; yet no one said, "What do You seek?" or, "Why do You speak with her?"   John 4:8

28 So the woman left her waterpot, and went into the city, and *said to the men,

29 "Come, see a man who told me all the things that I *have* done; [R] this is not [T] the Christ, is it?"   Matt. 12:23 • the Messiah

30 They went out of the city, and were coming to Him.

31 In the meanwhile the disciples were requesting Him, saying, "Rabbi, eat."

32 But He said to them, "I have food to eat that you do not know about."

33 The [R]disciples therefore were saying to one another, "No one brought Him *anything* to eat, did he?"   Luke 6:13-16; John 1:40-49; 2:2

34 Jesus *said to them, "My food is to [R]do the will of Him who sent Me, and to [R]accomplish His work.   John 5:30; 6:38 • John 5:36

35 "Do you not say, 'There are yet four months, and *then* comes the harvest'? Behold, I say to you, lift up your eyes, and look on the fields, that they are white for harvest.

36 "Already he who reaps is receiving [R]wages, and is gathering [R]fruit for life eternal; that he who sows and he who reaps may rejoice together.   [Prov. 11:18] • Rom. 1:13

37 "For in this *case* the saying is true, 'One [R] sows, and another reaps.'   Job 31:8; Mic. 6:15

38 "I sent you to reap that for which you have not labored; others have labored, and you have entered into their labor."

Christ Witnesses to the Samaritans

39 And from that city many of the Samaritans believed in Him because of the word of the woman who testified, "He told me all the things that I *have* done."

40 So when the Samaritans came to Him, they were asking Him to stay with them; and He stayed there two days.

41 And many more believed because of His word;

42 and they were saying to the woman, "It is no longer because of what you said that we believe, for we have heard for ourselves and know that this One is indeed [R]the Savior of the world."   Matt. 1:21; Luke 2:11; John 1:29

Christ Is Received by the Galileans

43 And after [R]the two days He went forth from there into Galilee.   John 4:40

44 For Jesus Himself testified that a prophet has no honor in his own country.

45 So when He came to Galilee, the Galileans received Him, having seen all the things that He did in Jerusalem at the feast; for they themselves also went to the feast.

Christ Heals the Nobleman's Son

46 He came therefore again to [R]Cana of Galilee where He had made the water wine. And there was a certain royal official, whose son was sick at Capernaum.   John 2:1

47 When he heard that Jesus had come [R]out of Judea into Galilee, he went to Him, and was requesting *Him* to come down and heal his son; for he was at the point of death.   John 4:3, 54

48 Jesus therefore said to him, "Unless

you *people* see [A]signs and wonders, you *simply* will not believe."   *attesting miracles*

49 The royal official *said to Him, "Sir, [A] come down before my child dies."   *Lord*

50 Jesus *said to him, "Go your way; your son lives." The man believed the word that Jesus spoke to him, and he started off.

51 And as he was now going down, *his* slaves met him, saying that his [A]son was living.   *boy*

52 So he inquired of them the hour when he began to get better. They said therefore to him, "Yesterday at the [11]seventh hour the fever left him."

53 So the father knew that *it was* at that hour in which Jesus said to him, "Your son lives" and he himself believed, and [R]his whole household.   Acts 11:14

54 This is again a second [A]sign that Jesus performed, when He had [R]come out of Judea into Galilee.   *attesting miracle* • John 4:45f.

CHAPTER 5

Christ Heals the Paralytic Man

AFTER these things there was [12]a feast of the Jews, and Jesus went up to Jerusalem.

2 Now there is in Jerusalem by the sheep gate a pool, which is called in [T]Hebrew Bethesda, having five porticoes.   Jewish Aramaic

3 In these lay a multitude of those who were sick, blind, lame, and withered, [[13]waiting for the moving of the waters;

4 for an angel of the Lord went down at certain seasons into the pool, and stirred up the water; whoever then first, after the stirring up of the water, stepped in was made well from whatever disease with which he was afflicted.]

5 And a certain man was there, who had been thirty-eight years in his sickness.

6 When Jesus saw him lying there, and knew that he had already been a long time *in that condition*, He *said to him, "Do you wish to get well?"

7 The sick man answered Him, "Sir, I have no man to put me into the pool when the water is stirred up, but while I am coming, another steps down before me."

8 Jesus *said to him, "Arise, [R] take up your pallet, and walk."   Matt. 9:6; Mark 2:11

9 And immediately the man became well, and took up his pallet and *began* to walk.

Now it was the Sabbath on that day.

Christ Heals on the Sabbath

10 Therefore [R]the Jews were saying to him who was cured, "It is the Sabbath, and [R]it is not permissible for you to carry your pallet."   John 1:19; 5:15, 16, 18 • Luke 6:2; John 7:23

---

[11] Perhaps 7 p.m. (Roman time)
[12] Many mss. read *the feast*, i.e., the Passover
[13] Many mss. do not contain the remainder of v. 3 nor v. 4

11 But he answered them, "He who made me well was the one who said to me, 'Take up your pallet and walk.' "

12 They asked him, "Who is the man who said to you, 'Take up *your pallet,* and walk'? "

13 But he who was healed did not know who it was; for Jesus had slipped away while there was a crowd in *that* place.

14 Afterward Jesus *found him in the temple, and said to him, "Behold, you have become well; do not [R]sin anymore, so that nothing worse may befall you." Mark 2:5

15 The man went away, and told the Jews that it was Jesus who had made him well.

16 And for this reason[R]the Jews were persecuting Jesus, because He was doing these things on the Sabbath. John 1:19; 5:10, 15, 18

Equality with God in Nature

17 But He answered them, "My Father is working until now, and I Myself am working."

18 For this cause therefore[R]the Jews were seeking all the more to kill Him, because He not only was breaking the Sabbath, but also was calling God His own Father, making Himself equal with God. John 1:19; 5:15, 16

Equality with God in Power

19 Jesus therefore answered and was saying to them, "Truly, truly, I say to you,[R]the Son can do nothing of Himself, unless *it is* something He sees the Father doing; for whatever *the Father* does, these things the Son also does in like manner. Matt. 26:39

20 "For the Father loves the Son, and shows Him all things that He Himself is doing; and[R]greater works than these will He show Him, that you may marvel. John 14:12

21 "For just as the Father raises the dead and[R]gives them life, even so the Son also gives life to whom He wishes. Rom. 4:17; 8:11

Equality with God in Authority

22 "For not even the Father judges anyone, but He has given all judgment to the Son, 23 in order that all may honor the Son, even as they honor the Father.[R]He who does not honor the Son does not honor the Father who sent Him. Luke 10:16; 1 John 2:23

24 "Truly, truly, I say to you, he who hears My word, and[R]believes Him who sent Me, has eternal life, and[R]does not come into judgment, but has[R]passed out of death into life. John 3:18; 12:44 • John 3:18 • [1 John 3:14]

25 "Truly, truly, I say to you,[R]an hour is coming and now is, when the dead shall hear the voice of the Son of God; and those who[R]hear shall live. John 4:21, 23 • John 6:60

26 "For just as the Father has life in Himself, even so He[R]gave to the Son also to have life in Himself; John 1:4; 6:57

27 and He gave Him authority to execute judgment, because He is *the* Son of Man.

28 "Do not marvel at this; for[R]an hour is coming, in which[R]all who are in the tombs shall hear His voice, John 4:21 • John 11:24

29 and shall come forth;[R]those who did the good *deeds* to a resurrection of life, those who committed the evil *deeds* to a resurrection of judgment. Dan. 12:2; Matt. 25:46

30 "I can do nothing on My own initiative. As I hear, I judge; and My judgment is just, because I do not seek My own will, but[R]the will of Him who sent Me. John 4:34; 6:38

Witness of John the Baptist

31 "If I *alone* bear witness of Myself, My testimony is not true.

32 "There is[R]another who bears witness of Me, and I know that the testimony which He bears of Me is true. John 5:37

33 "You have sent to John, and he[R]has borne witness to the truth. John 1:7, 15, 19, 32

34 "But[R]the witness which I receive is not from man, but I say these things that you may be saved. John 5:32; 1 John 5:9

35 "He was[R]the lamp that was burning and was shining and you[R]were willing to rejoice for a while in his light. 2 Pet. 1:19 • Mark 1:5

Witness of the Works of Christ

36 "But the witness which I have is greater than *that* of John; for[R]the works which the Father has given Me to accomplish, the very works that I do, bear witness of Me, that the Father[R]has sent Me. Matt. 11:4 • John 3:17

Witness of the Father

37 "And the Father who sent Me,[R]He has borne witness of Me. You have neither

---

5:24 Everlasting Life—One benefit of finding new life in Christ is called in the Bible "everlasting [eternal] life." The character of this great reality may be summarized by carefully looking at each word. The word *life* stresses the quality of this new relationship to God (Page 1076—John 10:10). It does not mean, of course, that we are not physically alive before salvation; it simply stresses the fact that we enter a new, personal relationship with God that gives us a fullness of spiritual vitality that we lacked before (Page 1084—John 17:3).

The word *everlasting* emphasizes life without end. Though it will not be completely fulfilled until our future bodily redemption (Page 1138—Rom. 8:23), it is still a present possession that can never perish (Page 1077—John 10:28).

Everlasting life must not be conceived of as an exclusively future possession. Rather its possession is clearly seen in our actions. Thus, "no murderer has eternal life abiding in him" (Page 1276—1 John 3:15). Indeed, love is the confirming evidence that we do in fact have eternal life (Page 1276—1 John 3:14).

The greatness of this spiritual reality constitutes a wonderful incentive to vigorously proclaim the gospel to those who are still dead in "trespasses and sins" (Page 1185—Eph. 2:1).

Now turn to Page 1168—2 Cor. 5:17: New Nature.

heard His voice at any time, nor seen His form.   Matt. 3:17; Mark 1:11; Luke 3:22; 24:27
38"And you do not have[R]His word abiding in you, for you do not believe Him whom He [R]sent.   1 John 2:14 • John 3:17

Witness of the Scriptures

39"[14]You search the Scriptures, because you think that in them you have eternal life; and it is these that bear witness of Me;
40 and you are unwilling to come to Me, that you may have life.
41"I do not receive glory from men;
42 but I know you, that you do not have the love of God in yourselves.
43"I have come in My Father's name, and you do not receive Me; if another shall come in his own name, you will receive him.
44"How can you believe, when you [R]receive [A]glory from one another, and you do not seek[R]the glory that is from the one and only God? John 5:41 • honor or fame • [Rom. 2:29]
45"Do not think that I will accuse you before the Father; the one who accuses you is Moses, in whom you have set your hope.
46"For if you believed Moses, you would believe Me; for[R]he wrote of Me.   Luke 24:27
47"But if you do not believe his writings, how will you believe My words?"

CHAPTER 6

Christ Feeds 5,000
Matt. 14:13–21; Mark 6:31–44;
Luke 9:11–17

AFTER these things [R]Jesus went away to the other side of[R]the Sea of Galilee (or Tiberias).   Mark 6:32-44; Luke 9:10-17 • Matt. 4:18
2 And a great multitude was following Him, because they were seeing the [A]signs[R] which He was performing on those who were sick.   attesting miracles • John 2:11, 23; 3:2
3 And Jesus went up on the mountain, and there He sat with His disciples.
4 Now [R]the Passover, the feast of the Jews, was at hand.   Deut. 16:1; John 2:13
5 Jesus therefore lifting up His eyes, and seeing that a great multitude was coming to Him, *said to[R]Philip, "Where are we to buy bread, that these may eat?"   John 1:43
6 And this He was saying to[R]test him; for He Himself knew what He was intending to do.   2 Cor. 13:5; Rev. 2:2
7 Philip answered Him, "Two hundred [15]denarii worth of bread is not sufficient for them, for everyone to receive a little."
8 One of His [R]disciples, Andrew, Simon Peter's brother, *said to Him,   John 2:2
9"There is a lad here who has five barley loaves and two[R]fish, but what are these for so many people?"   John 6:11; 21:9, 10, 13
10 Jesus said, "Have the people [T]sit down." Now there was much grass in the

place. So the men [T]sat down, in number about[R]five thousand.   recline(d) • Matt. 14:21
11 Jesus therefore took the loaves; and [R]having given thanks, He distributed to those who were seated; likewise also of the[R]fish as much as they wanted.   Matt. 15:36 • John 6:9
12 And when they were filled, He *said to His [R]disciples, "Gather up the leftover fragments that nothing may be lost."   John 2:2
13 And so they gathered them up, and filled twelve[R]baskets with fragments from the five barley loaves, which were left over by those who had eaten.   Matt. 14:20
14 When therefore the people saw the sign which He had performed, they said, "This is of a truth[R]the Prophet who is to come into the world."   Deut. 18:18 ★

Christ Walks on the Water
Matt. 14:22–33; Mark 6:45–52

15 Jesus therefore perceiving that they were[A]intending to come and take Him by force, to make Him king, withdrew again to the mountain by Himself alone.   about
16 Now when evening came, His[R]disciples went down to the sea,   John 2:2
17 and after getting into a boat, they started to cross the sea[R]to Capernaum. And it had already become dark, and Jesus had not yet come to them.   Mark 6:45; John 6:24, 59
18 And the sea began to be stirred up because a strong wind was blowing.
19 When therefore they had rowed about [T]three or four miles, they *beheld Jesus walking on the sea and drawing near to the boat; and they were frightened. 25 or 30 stadia
20 But He *said to them, "It is I; [']do[R]not be afraid."   stop fearing • Matt. 14:27
21 They were willing therefore to receive Him into the boat; and immediately the boat was at the land to which they were going.

"I Am the Bread of Life"

22 The next day[R]the multitude that stood on the other side of the sea saw that there was no other small boat there, except one, and that Jesus[R]had not entered with His disciples into the boat, but that His disciples had gone away alone.   John 6:2 • John 6:15ff.
23 There came other small boats from Tiberias near to the place where they ate the bread after the Lord had given thanks.
24 When the multitude therefore saw that Jesus was not there, nor His disciples, they themselves got into the small boats, and came to Capernaum, seeking Jesus.
25 And when they found Him on the other side of the sea, they said to Him, "Rabbi,[R] when did You get here?"   Matt. 23:7
26 Jesus answered them and said, "Truly,

---

[14] Or, (a command) Search the Scriptures!
[15] The denarius was equivalent to one day's wage

truly, I say to you, you seek Me, not because you saw [R]signs, but because you ate of the loaves, and were filled.   John 6:2, 14, 30

27"Do not [R]work for the food which perishes, but for the food which endures to eternal life, which [R]the Son of Man shall give to you, for on Him the Father, *even* God,[R]has set His seal."   Is. 55:2 • Matt. 8:20 • John 3:33

28 They said therefore to Him, "What shall we do, that we may work the works of God?"

29 Jesus answered and said to them, "This is [R]the work of God, that you believe in Him whom He has sent."   1 John 3:23; Rev. 2:26

30 They said therefore to Him, "What [R] then do You do for a [R]sign, that we may see, and believe You? What work do You perform?   Matt. 12:38 • John 6:2, 14, 26

31"Our fathers ate the manna in the wilderness; as it is written, 'He[R] GAVE THEM BREAD OUT OF HEAVEN TO EAT.' "   Ps. 78:24

32 Jesus therefore said to them, "Truly, truly, I say to you, it is not Moses who has given you the bread out of heaven, but it is My Father who gives you the true bread out of heaven.

33"For the bread of God is [16]that which [R]comes down out of heaven, and gives life to the world."   John 6:41, 50

34 They said therefore to Him, "Lord, evermore[R]give us this bread."   John 4:15

35 Jesus said to them, "I am the bread of life; he who comes to Me shall not hunger, and he who believes in Me shall never thirst.

36"But[R]I said to you, that you have seen Me, and yet do not believe.   John 6:26

37"All[R]that the Father gives Me shall come to Me, and the one who comes to Me I will certainly not cast out.   John 6:39; 17:2, 24

38"For I have come down from heaven, [R]not to do My own will, but[R]the will of Him who sent Me.   Matt. 26:39 • John 4:34; 5:30

39"And this is the will of Him who sent Me, that of all that He has given Me I lose nothing, but raise it up on the last day.

40"For this is the will of My Father, that everyone who[R]beholds the Son and believes in Him, may have eternal life; and I Myself will raise him up on the last day."   John 12:45

41 The Jews therefore were grumbling about Him, because He said, "I am the bread that came down out of heaven."

42 And they were saying, "Is[R] not this Jesus, the son of Joseph, whose father and mother we know? How does He now say, 'I have come down out of heaven'?"   Luke 4:22

43 Jesus answered and said to them, "Do not grumble among yourselves.

44"No one can come to Me, unless the Father who sent Me[R]draws him; and I will[R]raise him up on the last day.   Jer. 31:3 • John 6:39

45"It is written[R]in the prophets, 'AND[R]THEY SHALL ALL BE [R]TAUGHT OF GOD.' Everyone

who has heard and learned from the Father, comes to Me.   Acts 7:42 • Is. 54:13 ★ • Phil. 3:15

46"Not[R]that any man has seen the Father, except the One who is from God; He has seen the Father.   John 1:18

47"Truly, truly, I say to you, he who believes[R]has eternal life.   John 3:36; 5:24; 6:51, 58

48"I[R]am the bread of life.   John 6:35, 51

49"Your[R]fathers ate the manna in the wilderness, and they died.   John 6:31, 58

50"This is the bread which [R]comes down out of heaven, so that one may eat of it and [R]not die.   John 6:33 • John 3:36; 5:24; 6:47, 51, 58

51"I am the living bread that came down out of heaven; if anyone eats of this bread, [R]he shall live forever; and the bread also which I shall give[R]for the life of the world is [R]My flesh."   John 3:36 • John 1:29 • John 6:53-56

52 The Jews therefore [R]began to argue with one another, saying, "How can this man give us *His* flesh to eat?"   John 9:16

53 Jesus therefore said to them, "Truly, truly, I say to you, unless you eat the flesh of [R]the Son of Man and drink His blood, you have no life in yourselves.   Matt. 8:20

54"He who eats My flesh and drinks My blood has eternal life, and I will[R]raise him up on the last day.   John 6:39

55"For My flesh is true food, and My blood is true drink.

56"He who eats My flesh and drinks My blood[R]abides in Me, and I in him.   John 15:4f.

57"As the[R]living Father sent Me, and I live because of the Father, so he who eats Me, he also shall live because of Me.   Matt. 16:16

58"This is the bread which came down out of heaven; not as the fathers ate, and died, he who eats this bread shall live forever."

59 These things He said[R]in the synagogue, as He taught in Capernaum.   Matt. 4:23

Rejection by Many Followers

60 Many therefore of His [R]disciples, when they heard *this* said, "This is a difficult statement; who can listen to it?"   John 2:2

61 But Jesus,[R]conscious that His disciples grumbled at this, said to them, "Does this [R]cause you to stumble?   John 6:64 • Matt. 11:6

62"*What* then if you should behold [R]the Son of Man [R]ascending where He was before?   Matt. 8:20 • Mark 16:19; Acts 1:9 ✩

63"It is the Spirit who gives life; the flesh profits nothing;[R]the words that I have spoken to you are spirit and are life. [John 6:68]

64"But there are some of you who do not believe." For Jesus knew from the beginning who they were who did not believe, and who it was that would betray Him.

65 And He was saying, "For this reason I have [R]said to you, that no one can come to Me, unless[R]it has been granted him from the Father."   John 6:37, 44 • Matt. 13:11; John 3:27

66 As a result of this many of His [R]disciples[R]withdrew, and were not walking with Him anymore.   John 2:2; 7:3 • John 6:60, 64

---

[16] Or, *He who comes*

Confession by Peter

67 Jesus said therefore to the twelve, "You do not want to go away also, do you?" 68 ᴿSimon Peter answered Him, "Lord, to whom shall we go? You haveᴿwords of eternal life.   Matt. 16:16 · John 6:63; 12:49f.; 17:8 69"And we have believed and have come to know that You are the Holy One of God." 70 Jesus answered them, "DidᴿI Myself not choose you,ᴿthe twelve, and *yet* one of you is a devil?"   John 15:16, 19 · Matt. 10:2 71 Now He meant Judasᵗ*the son* of Simon Iscariot, for he, one of the twelve,^was going to betray Him.   John 12:4 · *was intending to*

CHAPTER 7

Christ's Brothers Do Not Believe

Aɴᴅ after these things Jesusᴿwas walking in Galilee; for He was unwilling to walk in Judea, becauseᴿthe Jewsᴿwere seeking to kill Him.   John 4:3; 6:1 · John 1:19 · John 5:18 2 Now the feast of the Jews,ᴿthe Feast of Booths, was at hand. Lev. 23:34; Deut. 16:13, 16 3 His ᴿbrothers therefore said to Him, "Depart from here, and go into Judea, that Yourᴿdisciples also may behold Your works which You are doing.   Matt. 12:46 · John 6:60 4"For no one does anything in secret, ᵀwhen he himself seeks to be *known* publicly. If You do these things, show Yourself to the world."   *and* 5 For not even Hisᴿbrothers were believing in Him.   Ps. 69:8; Mic. 7:6★ 6 Jesus therefore *said to them, "Myᴿ time is not yet at hand, but your time is always opportune. Matt. 26:18; John 2:4; 7:8, 30 7"Theᵗworld cannot hate you; but it hates Me because I testify of it, thatᴿits deeds are evil.   John 15:18f. · John 3:19f. 8"Go up to the feast yourselves; I do not go up to this feast becauseᴿMy time has not yet fully come."   John 7:6 9 And having said these things to them, He stayed in Galilee.

Christ Secretly Goes to the Feast

10 But when Hisᴿbrothers had gone up to the feast, then He Himself also went up, not publicly, but as it were, in secret. Mark 3:21 11 ᴿThe Jews thereforeᴿwere seeking Him at the feast, and were saying, "Where is He?"   John 7:13, 15, 35 · John 11:56 12 And there was much grumbling among the multitudes concerning Him;ᴿsome were saying, "He is a good man"; others were saying, "No, on the contrary, He leads the multitude astray."   John 7:40-43 13 Yet no one was speaking openly of Him forᵗfear of the Jews. [John 9:22; 12:42]

Christ's Authority from the Father

14 But when it was now the midst of the feast Jesusᴿwent up into the temple, and *began to*ᴿteach. Ps. 22:22★ · Matt. 26:55; John 7:28 15 The Jews therefore were marveling, saying, "How has this manᴿbecome learned, having never been educated?"   Acts 26:24 16 Jesus therefore answered them, and said, "Myᴿteaching is not Mine, but His who sent Me.   John 3:11 17"If any man is willing to do His will, he shall know of the teaching, whether it is of God, or *whether* I speak from Myself. 18"He who speaks from himself seeks his own glory; but He who is seeking the glory of the one who sent Him, He is true, and there is no unrighteousness in Him. 19"Didᴿnot Moses give you the Law, and *yet* none of you carries out the Law? Why do youᴿseek to kill Me?"   John 1:17 · Mark 11:18 20 The multitude answered, "You^have a demon! Who seeks to kill You?" *are demented* 21 Jesus answered and said to them, "I did one ᵗdeed, and you all marvel. 22"On this accountᴿMoses has given you circumcision (not because it is from Moses, but fromᴿthe fathers), and on *the* Sabbath you circumcise a man.   Lev. 12:3 · Acts 7:8 23"If a man receives circumcision on *the* Sabbath that the Law of Moses may not be broken, are you angry with Me because I made an entire man well on *the* Sabbath? 24"Do notᴿjudge according to appearance, but judge with righteous judgment." Is. 11:3

Christ's Origin from the Father

25 Therefore some of the people of Jerusalem were saying, "Is this not the man whom they are seeking to kill? 26"And look, He is speaking publicly, and they are saying nothing to Him.ᴿThe rulers do not really know that this isᵗthe Christ, do they?   Luke 23:13; John 3:1 · the Messiah 27"However,ᴿwe know where this man is from; but whenever the Christ may come, no one knows where He is from."   John 6:42 28 Jesus therefore cried out in the temple, teaching and saying, "You both know Me and know where I am from; and I have not come of Myself, but He who sent Me is true, whom you do not know. John 6:42; 7:14f.; 9:29 29"I know Him; becauseᴿI am from Him, andᴿHe sent Me."   John 6:46 · John 3:17 30 They were seeking therefore to seize Him; and no man laid his hand on Him, because Hisᴿhour had not yet come.   John 7:6 31 Butᴿmany of the multitude believed in Him; and they were saying, "When ᵀthe Christ shall come, He will not perform more ^signs than those which this man has, will He?"   John 2:23 · the Messiah · *attesting miracles*

Christ's Departure to the Father

32 The Pharisees heard the multitude muttering these things about Him; and the chief priests and the Pharisees sentᴿofficers toᴿseize Him.   Matt. 26:58 · Matt. 12:14

33 Jesus therefore said, "For[R]a little while longer I am with you, then[R]I go to Him who sent Me.   Mark 16:19; Acts 1:9☆ • John 14:12, 28
34 "You shall seek Me, and shall not find Me; and where I am, you cannot come."
35 The Jews therefore said to one another, "Where does this man intend to go that we shall not find Him? He is not intending to go to[R]the Dispersion among[R]the Greeks, and teach the Greeks, is He?   [Is. 11:12] • Acts 14:1
36 "What is this statement that He said, 'You[R]will seek Me, and will not find Me; and where I am, you cannot come'?"   John 7:34

Christ Reveals the "Living Water"

37 Now on[R]the last day, the great *day* of the feast, Jesus stood and cried out, saying, "If[R]any man is thirsty, let him come to Me and drink.   Num. 29:35; Neh. 8:18 • John 4:10, 14
38 "He who believes in Me, as the Scripture said, 'From[T]his innermost being shall flow rivers of living water.'"   *out of his belly*
39 But this He spoke of the Spirit, whom those who believed in Him were to receive; for[R]the Spirit was not yet *given*, because Jesus was not yet glorified.   Acts 1:4f.; 2:4, 33

Israel Is Divided over Christ

40 *Some* of the multitude therefore, when they heard these words, were saying, "This certainly is[R]the Prophet."   Matt. 21:11; John 1:21
41 Others were saying, "This is [T]the Christ." Still others were saying, "Surely[R] the Christ is not going to come from Galilee, is He?   the Messiah • John 1:46; 7:52
42 "Has not the Scripture said that the Christ comes from[R]the offspring of David, and from Bethlehem, the village where David was?"   Ps. 89:4; Mic. 5:2; Matt. 1:1; 2:5f.
43 So[R]there arose a division in the multitude because of Him.   John 9:16; 10:19
44 And some of them wanted to seize Him, but no one laid hands on Him.

The Sanhedrin Is Confused over Christ

45 The officers therefore came to the chief priests and Pharisees, and they said to them, "Why did you not bring Him?"
46 The officers answered, "Never did a man speak the way this man speaks."
47 The Pharisees therefore answered them, "You[R]have not also been led astray, have you?   John 7:12
48 "No one of[R]the rulers or Pharisees has believed in Him, has he?   Luke 23:13
49 "But this multitude which does not know the Law is accursed."
50 Nicodemus *said to them (he who came to Him before, being one of them),
51 "Our[R]Law does not judge a man, unless it first hears from him and knows what he is doing, does it?"   Ex. 23:1; Deut. 17:6; 19:15

[17] John 7:53–8:11 is not found in most of the old mss.
[18] Many ancient mss. read *the Father who sent Me*

52 They answered and said to him, "You[R] are not also from Galilee, are you? Search, and see that no prophet arises out of Galilee."   John 1:46; 7:41
53 [[17]And everyone went to his home.

CHAPTER 8

A Woman Is Caught in Adultery

BUT Jesus went to the Mount of Olives.
2 And early in the morning He came again into the temple, and all the people were coming to Him; and[R]He sat down and *began* to teach them.   Matt. 26:55; John 8:20
3 And the scribes and the Pharisees *brought a woman caught in adultery, and having set her in the midst,
4 they *said to Him, "Teacher, this woman has been caught in adultery, in the very act.
5 "Now in the Law[R]Moses commanded us to stone such women; what then do You say?"   Lev. 20:10; Deut. 22:22f.
6 And they were saying this, testing Him, in order that they might have grounds for accusing Him. But Jesus stooped down, and with His finger wrote on the ground.
7 But when they persisted in asking Him, [R]He straightened up, and said to them, "He who is without sin among you, let him *be the* first to throw a stone at her."   John 8:10
8 And again He stooped down, and wrote on the ground.
9 And when they heard it, they *began* to go out one by one, beginning with the older ones, and He was left alone, and the woman, where she was, in the midst.
10 And [R]straightening up, Jesus said to her, "Woman, where are they? Did no one condemn you?"   John 8:7
11 And she said, "No one, [A]Lord." And Jesus said, "Neither do I condemn you; go your way. From now on sin no more."]   *Sir*

"I Am the Light of the World"

12 Again therefore Jesus spoke to them, saying, "I[R]am the light of the world; he who follows Me shall not walk in the darkness, but shall have the light of life."   John 1:4; 9:5
13 The Pharisees therefore said to Him, "You[R]are bearing witness of Yourself; Your witness is not[T]true."   John 5:31 • *valid*
14 Jesus answered and said to them, "Even if I bear witness of Myself, My witness is true; for I know where I came from, and where I am going; but you do not know where I come from, or where I am going.
15 "You people judge according to the flesh;[R]I am not judging anyone.   [John 3:17]
16 "But even[R]if I do judge, My judgment is true; for I am not alone *in it*, but I and [18]He who sent Me.   John 5:30
17 "Even in your law it has been written, that the testimony of two men is true.

18"I am He who bears witness of Myself, and [R]the Father who sent Me bears witness of Me."   John 5:37; 1 John 5:9

19 And so they were saying to Him, "Where is Your Father?" Jesus answered, "You know neither Me, nor My Father; [R]if you knew Me, you would know My Father also."   John 7:28; 8:55; 14:7, 9; 16:3

20 These words He spoke in [R]the treasury, as [R]He taught in the temple; and no one seized Him, because [R]His hour had not yet come.   Mark 12:41, 43 • John 7:14 • John 7:30

21 He said therefore again to them, "I go away, and [R]you shall seek Me, and shall die in your sin; [R]where I am going, you cannot come."   John 7:34 • Mark 16:19; Acts 1:9 ☆

22 Therefore [R]the Jews were saying, "Surely He will not kill Himself, will He, since He says, 'Where [R]I am going, you cannot come'?"   John 1:19; 8:48, 52, 57 • John 7:35

23 And He was saying to them, "You are from below, I am from above; [R]you are of this world, I am not of this world.   1 John 4:5

24"I said therefore to you, that you [R]shall die in your sins; for unless you believe that I am He, you shall die in your sins."   John 8:21

25 And so they were saying to Him, "Who are You?" Jesus said to them, "What have I been saying to you from the beginning?

26"I have many things to speak and to judge concerning you, but [R]He who sent Me is true; and the things which I heard from Him, these I speak to the world."   John 3:33

27 They did not realize that He had been speaking to them about the Father.

28 Jesus therefore said, "When you [R]lift up the Son of Man, then you will know that [R]I am He, and [R]I do nothing on My own initiative, but I speak these things as the Father taught Me.   John 3:14 • Luke 21:8 • John 3:11

29"And He who sent Me is with Me; He [A]has not left Me alone, for I always do the things that are pleasing to Him."   *did not leave*

30 As He spoke these things, [R]many came to believe in Him.   John 7:31

31 Jesus therefore was saying to those Jews who had believed Him, "If [R]you abide in My word, then you are truly [R]disciples of Mine;   John 15:7; 2 John 9 • John 2:2

32 and [R]you shall know the truth, and the truth shall make you free."   [John 1:14, 17]

33 They answered Him, "We [R]are Abraham's offspring, and have never yet been enslaved to anyone; how is it that You say, 'You shall become free'?"   [Matt. 3:9]; Luke 3:8

34 Jesus answered them, "Truly, truly, I say to you, [R]everyone who commits sin is the slave of sin.   Rom. 6:16; 2 Pet. 2:19

35"And the slave does not remain in the house forever; the son does remain forever.

36"If therefore the Son [R]shall make you free, you shall be free indeed.   John 8:32

37"I know that you are Abraham's offspring; yet you seek to kill Me, because My word [A]has no place in you.   *makes no progress*

38"I speak the things which I have seen with My Father; therefore you also do the things which you heard from your father."

39 They answered and said to Him, "Abraham is [R]our father." Jesus *said to them, "If [R]you are Abraham's children, do the deeds of Abraham.   John 8:37 • [Gal. 3:7]

40"But as it is, you are seeking to kill Me, a man who has told you the truth, which I heard from God; this Abraham did not do.

41"You are doing the deeds of [R]your father." They said to Him, "We were not born of fornication; [R]we have one Father, even God."   John 8:38, 44 • Deut. 32:6; Is. 63:16; 64:8

42 Jesus said to them, "If God were your Father, [R]you would love Me; [R]for I proceeded forth and have come from God, for I have not even come on My own initiative, but [A]He sent Me.   1 John 5:1 • John 13:3 • *that One*

43"Why do you not understand [A]what I am saying? It is because you cannot [R]hear My word.   *My mode of speaking* • John 5:25

44"You are of your father the devil, and you want to do the desires of your father. He was a murderer from the beginning, and does not stand in the truth, because there is no truth in him. Whenever he speaks [A]a lie, he speaks from his own nature; for he is a liar, and the father of [A]lies.   *the lie* • *it*

45"But because [R]I speak the truth, you do not believe Me.   John 18:37

46"Which one of you convicts Me of sin? If I speak truth, why do you not believe Me?

8:31   God's Word Confirms—To confirm means to fully establish a truth or fact. The Bible should be used to confirm the truth in our own hearts.

a. It confirms our salvation. Often Christians are troubled with doubts about their conversion experience. Did God really save them when they asked Him to do so? Are they still saved today? A number of verses may be used to confirm our salvation. One of the strongest is Jesus' own words in the Gospel of John: "Truly, truly, I say to you, he who hears My word, and believes Him who sent Me, has eternal life, and does not come into judgment, but has passed out of death into life" (Page 1069—John 5:24). Compare John 3:16; 6:27, 35, 37, 40; 10:27–29; Romans 8:1.

b. It confirms the hand of God in all of life's bitter disappointments. Undoubtedly a most important verse of reassurance and comfort in the hour of great need is Romans 8:28: "And we know that God causes all things to work together for good to those who love God, to those who are called according to His purpose."

c. It confirms our forgiveness when we sin. Sometimes believers carry with them an unnecessary burden of guilt over past sins and failures. Even though these have been confessed, they have difficulty believing God has truly forgiven and cleansed them. But time and again the Bible assures us that all confessed sin is instantly and eternally forgiven. (Page 543—Ps. 32:5; 103:12; Page 688—Is. 38:17).
Now turn to Page 626—Prov. 22:21: God's Word Equips.

47 "He^R who is of God hears the words of God; for this reason you do not hear *them,* because you are not of God."   1 John 4:6

48 The Jews answered and said to Him, "Do we not say rightly that You are a ^RSamaritan and have a demon?"   Matt. 10:5

49 Jesus answered, "I do not^Rhave a demon; but I honor My Father, and you dishonor Me.   John 7:20

50 "But^RI do not seek My glory; there is One who seeks and judges.   John 5:41; 8:54

51 "Truly, truly, I say to you, if anyone keeps My word he shall never see death."

52 The Jews said to Him, "Now we know that You^Rhave a demon. Abraham died, and the prophets *also;* and You say, 'If anyone ^Rkeeps My word, he shall never ^Rtaste of death.'   John 7:20 • John 8:55; 14:23 • John 8:51

53 "Surely You^Rare not greater than our father Abraham, who died? The prophets died too; whom do You make Yourself out *to be*?"   John 4:12

54 Jesus answered, "If^R I glorify Myself, My glory is nothing; ^Rit is My Father who glorifies Me, of whom you say, 'He is our God';   John 8:50 • John 7:39

55 and^Ryou have not come to know Him, but I know Him; and if I say that I do not know Him, I shall be a liar like you, but I do know Him, and keep His word.   John 8:19

56 "Your father Abraham rejoiced to see My day, and he saw *it* and was glad."

57 ^RThe Jews therefore said to Him, "You are not yet fifty years old, and have You seen Abraham?"   John 1:19

58 Jesus said to them, "Truly, truly, I say to you, before Abraham was born, I am."

59 Therefore they picked up stones to throw at Him; but Jesus^Thid Himself, and went out of the temple.   *was hidden*

CHAPTER 9

Christ Heals the Blind Man

AND as He passed by, He saw a man blind from birth.

2 And His disciples asked Him, saying, "Rabbi, who sinned, this man or his^Rparents, that he should be born blind?"   Ex. 20:5

3 Jesus answered, "*It was* neither *that* this man sinned, nor his parents; but *it was* in order^Rthat the works of God might be displayed in him.   John 11:4

4 "We must work the works of Him who sent Me,^Ras long as it is day; night is coming, when no man can work.   John 7:33; 11:9; 12:35

5 "While I am in the world, I am^Rthe light of the world."   Matt. 5:14; [John 1:4; 8:12; 12:46]

6 When He had said this, He^Rspat on the ground, and made clay of the spittle, and applied the clay to his eyes,   Mark 7:33; 8:23

7 and said to him, "Go, wash in^Rthe pool of Siloam" (which is translated, Sent). And

so he went away and ^Rwashed, and ^Rcame *back* seeing.   Is. 8:6 • 2 Kin. 5:13f. • Is. 29:18

8 The neighbors therefore, and those who previously saw him as a beggar, were saying, "Is not this the one who used to^Rsit and beg?"   Acts 3:2, 10

9 Others were saying, "This is he," *still* others were saying, "No, but he is like him." He kept saying, "I am the one."

10 Therefore they were saying to him, "How then were your eyes opened?"

11 He answered, "The man who is called Jesus made clay, and anointed my eyes, and said to me, 'Go to^RSiloam, and wash'; so I went away and washed, and I received sight."   John 9:7

12 And they said to him, "Where is He?" He *said, "I do not know."

13 They *brought to the Pharisees him who was formerly blind.

14 Now it was a Sabbath on the day when Jesus made the clay, and opened his eyes.

15 ^RAgain, therefore, the Pharisees also were asking him how he received his sight. And he said to them, "He applied clay to my eyes, and I washed, and I see."   John 9:10

16 Therefore some of the Pharisees were saying, "This man is not from God, because He does not keep the Sabbath." But others were saying, "How can a man who is a sinner perform such^Asigns?" And there was a division among them.   *attesting miracles*

17 They *said therefore to the blind man ^Ragain, "What do you say about Him, since He opened your eyes?" And he said, "He is a ^Rprophet."   John 9:15 • Deut. 18:15; Matt. 21:11

18 The Jews therefore did not believe *it* of him, that he had been blind, and had received sight, until they called the parents of the very one who had received his sight,

19 and questioned them, saying, "Is this your son, who you say was born blind? Then how does he now see?"

20 His parents answered them and said, "We know that this is our son, and that he was born blind;

21 but how he now sees, we do not know; or who opened his eyes, we do not know. Ask him; he is of age, he shall speak for himself."

22 His parents said this because they ^Rwere afraid of the Jews; for the Jews had already agreed, that if anyone should confess Him to be^TChrist, he should be put out of the synagogue.   John 7:13 • the Messiah

23 For this reason his parents said, "He^Ris of age; ask him."   John 9:21

24 So a second time they called the man who had been blind, and said to him, "Give^R glory to God; we know that^Rthis man is a sinner."   Josh. 7:19; Ezra 10:11 • John 9:16

25 He therefore answered, "Whether He is a sinner, I do not know; one thing I do know, that, whereas I was blind, now I see."

26 They said therefore to him, "What did He do to you? How did He open your eyes?"

27 He answered them, "I[R]told you already, and you did not listen; why do you want to hear *it* again? You do not want to become His disciples too, do you?"   John 9:15

28 And they reviled him, and said, "You are His disciple, but [R]we are disciples of Moses.   John 5:45; Rom. 2:17

29"We know that God has spoken to Moses; but as for this man,[R]we do not know where He is from."   John 8:14

30 The man answered and said to them, "Well, here is an amazing thing, that you do not know where He is from, and *yet* He opened my eyes.

31"We know that[R]God does not hear sinners; but if anyone is God-fearing, and does His will, He hears him. Is. 1:15; [James 5:16ff.]

32"Since the beginning of time it has never been heard that anyone opened the eyes of a person born blind.

33"If[R] this man were not from God, He could do nothing."   John 3:2; 9:16

34 They answered and said to him, "You were born entirely in sins, and are you teaching us?" And they put him out.

35 Jesus heard that they had[R]put him out; and finding him, He said, "Do you believe in the[R]Son of Man?"   John 9:22, 34 • Matt. 4:3

36 He answered and said, "And who is He,[A]Lord, that I may believe in Him?"   *Sir*

37 Jesus said to him, "You have both seen Him, and[R]He is the one who is talking with you."   John 4:26

38 And he said, "Lord, I believe." And he [R]worshiped Him.   Matt. 8:2

39 And Jesus said, "For[R]judgment I came into this world, that those who do not see may see; and that[R]those who see may become blind." [John 3:19; 5:22, 27] • Matt. 13:13

40 Those of the Pharisees who were with Him heard these things, and said to Him, "We[R]are not blind too, are we?" [Rom. 2:19]

41 Jesus said to them, "If[R]you were blind, you would have no sin; but since you say, 'We see,' your sin remains.   John 15:22, 24

CHAPTER 10

"I Am the Good Shepherd"

"TRULY, truly, I say to you, he who does not enter by the door into the fold of the sheep, but climbs up some other way, he is[R]a thief and a robber.   John 10:8

2"But he who enters by the door is [R]a shepherd of the sheep.   John 10:11f.

3"To him the doorkeeper opens, and the sheep hear his voice, and he calls his own sheep by name, and leads them out.

4"When he puts forth all his own, he goes before them, and the sheep follow him because they know[R]his voice.   John 10:5, 16, 27

5"And a stranger they simply will not follow, but will flee from him, because they do not know the voice of strangers."

6 This [R]figure of speech Jesus spoke to them, but they did not understand what those things were which He had been saying to them.   John 16:25, 29; 2 Pet. 2:22

7 Jesus therefore said to them again, "Truly, truly, I say to you, I am[R]the door of the sheep.   John 10:1f., 9

8"All who came before Me are [R]thieves and robbers, but the sheep did not hear them.   Jer. 23:1f.; Ezek. 34:2ff.; John 10:1

9"I[R]am the door; if anyone enters through Me, he shall be saved, and shall go in and out, and find pasture.   John 10:1f., 9

10"The thief comes only to steal, and kill, and destroy; I came that they[R]might have life, and might have *it* abundantly.   John 5:40

11"I am the good shepherd; the good shepherd lays down His life for the sheep.

12"He who is a hireling, and not a [R]shep-

10:10 The Earthly Life of the Son of God—Since the gospel narratives are mainly concerned with Jesus' earthly ministry, it is important that the main aspects of His teaching be recognized. The most important of these are: the kingdom of God (Page 966—Matt. 5—7; 24—25); His divine authority over men (Page 970—Matt. 7:28, 29; Page 1001—Mark 2:10); His own role as God and Messiah demonstrated by miracles and signs (Page 980—Matt. 16:15—20); the significance of His death and resurrection (Page 980—Matt. 16:21; Page 1058—Luke 24:26); the relationship which His disciples and subsequent believers are to share with Him (Page 1080—John 13—16); and the urgency of His commission to believers to make disciples (Page 995—Matt. 28:19, 20).

Of the many events of His earthly life the most significant, without a doubt, are His death and resurrection. On these two pivotal, historical incidents rest the validity of the entire Christian faith (Page 1160—1 Cor. 15:14). It is vital then to understand the nature of these two events. The death of Christ was first of all a humiliating physical death (Page 1086—John 19:18, 33). More than that, for a brief time it constituted a spiritual separation from God (Page 994—Matt. 27:46). Within this moment there occurred the inexplicable mystery of the Father punishing the Son for the sins of the world (Page 1263—1 Pet. 3:18; Page 1169—2 Cor. 5:21). This event, though it was the greatest crime of human history, was in the plan of God (Page 1095—Acts 2:23), and thus became the basis of salvation for sinners (Page 702—Is. 53:5).

The power of the death of Christ would be nullified without His bodily resurrection. Though it does not justify us, the resurrection demonstrated that His death, by which believing sinners are justified, was valid (Page 1160—1 Cor. 15:12—20). While skeptics have denied the bodily resurrection of Christ, the historical evidence for it is overwhelming: the many separate accounts of post-resurrection appearances, the empty tomb, and the transformed disciples. Every life that has been dramatically and wonderfully changed by believing in Christ since the first century is a testimony to its historical reality. Furthermore, it is the power of the resurrection that marvelously empowers Christians today to live the Christian life (Page 1185—Eph. 1:19, 20; Page 1195—Phil. 3:10).

Now turn to Page 1011—Mark 10:45: The Ministry of the Son of God.

herd, who is not the owner of the sheep, beholds the wolf coming, and leaves the sheep, and flees, and the wolf snatches them, and scatters *them*.   John 10:2

13"*He flees* because he is a hireling, and is not concerned about the sheep.

14"I am the[R]good shepherd; and I know My own, and My own know Me,   Is. 40:11★

15 even as [R]the Father knows Me and I know the Father; and[R]I lay down My life for the sheep.   Matt. 11:27 • Matt. 27:50☆

16"And I have[R]other sheep, which are not of this fold; I must bring them also, and they shall hear My voice; and they shall become one flock *with* one shepherd.   Is. 42:6; 56:8★

17"For this reason the Father loves Me, because I[R]lay down My life that I may take it again.   John 10:11, 15, 18

18"No one [19]has taken it away from Me, but I lay it down on My own initiative. I have authority to lay it down, and I have authority to take it up again. This commandment I received from My Father."

19[R]There arose a division again among the Jews because of these words.   John 7:43; 9:16

20 And many of them were saying, "He [R]has a demon and[R]is insane. Why do you listen to Him?"   John 7:20 • Mark 3:21

21 Others were saying, "These are not the sayings of one demon-possessed. A demon cannot open the eyes of the blind, can he?"

The Opposition at the Feast of Dedication in Jerusalem

22 At that time the Feast of the Dedication took place at Jerusalem;

23 it was winter, and Jesus was walking in the temple in the portico of Solomon.

24 The Jews therefore gathered around Him, and were saying to Him, "How long will You keep us in suspense? If You are[R]the Christ, tell us plainly."   the Messiah

25 Jesus answered them, "I[R]told you, and you do not believe;[R]the works that I do in My Father's name, these bear witness of Me.   John 8:56, 58 • John 5:36; 10:38

26"But you do not believe, because[R]you are not of My sheep.   [John 8:47]

27"My sheep[R]hear My voice, and I know them, and they follow Me;   John 10:4, 16

28 and I give[R]eternal life to them, and they shall never perish; and no one shall snatch them out of My hand.   John 17:2f.; 1 John 2:25

29"[20]My Father, who has given *them* to Me, is greater than all; and no one is able to snatch *them* out of the Father's hand.

30"I[R]and the Father are one."   John 17:21ff.

31 The Jews[R]took up stones again to stone Him.   John 8:59

32 Jesus answered them, "I showed you many good works from the Father; for which of them are you stoning Me?"

33 The Jews answered Him, "For a good work we do not stone You, but for[R]blas-

phemy; and because You, being a man, make Yourself out *to be* God."   Lev. 24:16

34 Jesus answered them, "Has it not been written in your Law, 'I SAID, YOU ARE GODS'?

35"If he called them gods, to whom the word of God came (and the Scripture cannot be broken),

36 do you say of Him, whom the Father [R]sanctified and[R]sent into the world, 'You are blaspheming,' because I said, 'I[R]am the Son of God'?   Jer. 1:5 • John 3:17 • John 5:17f.

37"If[R]I do not do the works of My Father, do not believe Me;   John 10:25; 15:24

38 but if I do them, though you do not believe Me, believe[R]the works, that you may know and understand that the Father is in Me, and I in the Father."   John 10:25; 14:11

39 Therefore they were seeking again to seize Him, and He eluded their grasp.

40 And He went away again beyond the Jordan to the place where John was first baptizing, and He was staying there.

41 And many came to Him and were saying, "While John performed no [R]sign, yet [R]everything John said about this man was true."   John 2:11 • [John 1:27, 30, 34; 3:27–30]

42 And many believed in Him there.

CHAPTER 11

Christ Raises Lazarus

Now a certain man was sick, Lazarus of [R]Bethany, the village of Mary and her sister [R]Martha.   Matt. 21:17; John 11:18 • Luke 10:38

2 And it was the Mary who anointed the Lord with ointment, and wiped His feet with her hair, whose brother Lazarus was sick.

3 The sisters therefore sent to Him, saying, "Lord,[R] behold, [R]he whom You love is sick."   Luke 7:13 • John 11:5, 11, 36

4 But when Jesus heard it, He said, "This sickness is not unto death, but for[R]the glory of God, that the Son of God may be glorified by it."   John 9:3; 10:38; 11:40

5 Now Jesus loved[R]Martha, and her sister, and Lazarus.   John 11:1

6 When therefore He heard that he was sick, He stayed then two days *longer* in the place where He was.

7 Then after this He *said to the disciples, "Let[R]us go to Judea again."   John 10:40

8 The disciples *said to Him, "Rabbi, the Jews were just now seeking[R]to stone You, and are You going there again?"   John 8:59

9 Jesus answered, "Are[R]there not twelve hours in the day? If anyone walks in the day, he does not stumble, because he sees the light of this world.   Luke 13:33; John 9:4; 12:35

10"But if anyone walks in the night, he stumbles, because the light is not in him."

11 This He said, and after that He *said to them, "Our[R]friend Lazarus[R]has fallen asleep; but I go, that I may awaken him out of sleep."   John 11:3 • Mark 5:39; John 11:13

12 The disciples therefore said to Him,

---

[19] Many Gr. mss. read *takes*
[20] Some early mss. read *What My Father has given Me is greater than all*

"Lord, if he has fallen asleep, he will ᵀre-cover."   *be saved*

13 Now ᴿJesus had spoken of his death, but they thought that He was speaking of ᵀliteral sleep.   Matt. 9:24 • *the slumber of sleep*

14 Then Jesus therefore said to them plainly, "Lazarus is dead,

15 and I am glad for your sakes that I was not there, so that you may believe; but let us go to him."

16 Thomas therefore, who is called Didymus, said to *his* fellow disciples, "Let us also go, that we may die with Him."

17 So when Jesus came, He found that he had already been in the tomb four days.

18 Now Bethany was near Jerusalem, about ᵀtwo miles off;   15 stadia (9,090 ft.)

19 and many of ᴿthe Jews had come to ᴿMartha and Mary, to console them concerning *their* brother.   John 1:19; 11:8 • John 11:1

20 ᴿMartha therefore, when she heard that Jesus was coming, went to meet Him; but Mary still sat in the house.   Luke 10:38-42

21 Martha therefore said to Jesus, "Lord,ᴿif You had been here, my brother would not have died.   John 11:32, 37

22 "Even now I know that ᴿwhatever You ask of God, God will give You."   [John 9:31]

23 Jesus *said to her, "Your brother shall rise again."

24 Martha *said to Him, "Iᵀknow that he will rise again in the resurrection on the last day."   [Dan. 12:2; John 5:28f.; Acts 24:15]

25 Jesus said to her, "Iᴿam the resurrection and the life; he who believes in Me shall live even if he dies,   John 1:4; 5:26; 6:39f.

26 and everyone who lives and believes in Me shall never die. Do you believe this?"

27 She *said to Him, "Yes, Lord; I have believed that You are the Christ, the Son of God, *even* He who comes into the world."

28 And when she had said this, sheᴿwent away, and called Mary her sister, saying secretly, "Theᴿ Teacher is here, and is calling for you."   John 11:30 • Mark 14:14; Luke 22:11

29 And when she heard it, she *arose quickly, and was coming to Him.

30 Now Jesus had not yet come into the village, butᴿwas still in the place where Martha met Him.   John 11:20

31 The Jews then who were with her in the house, and consoling her, when they saw that Mary rose up quickly and went out, followed her, supposing that she was going to the tomb toᵀweep there.   *wail*

32 Therefore, when Mary came where Jesus was, she saw Him, and fell at His feet, saying to Him, "Lord,ᴿ if You had been here, my brother would not have died."   John 11:2

33 When Jesus therefore saw herᵀweeping, and the Jews who came with her, *also* weeping, He was deeply moved in spirit, andᵀwas troubled,   *wailing • troubled Himself*

34 and said, "Where have you laid him?" They *said to Him, "Lord, come and see."

35 Jesus ᴿwept.   Luke 19:41; John 11:33

36 And soᴿthe Jews were saying, "Behold how Heᵀloved him!"   John 11:19 • *was loving*

37 But some of them said, "Could not this man, who opened the eyes of him who was blind, have kept this man also from dying?"

38 Jesus therefore again being deeply moved within, *came to the tomb. Now it was a cave, and a stone was lying against it.

39 Jesus *said, "Remove the stone." Martha, the sister of the deceased, *said to Him, "Lord, by this timeᵀthere will be a stench, for he has been *dead* four days."   *he stinks*

40 Jesus *said to her, "Didᴿ I not say to you, if you believe, you will see the glory of God?"   [John 11:4, 23ff.]

41 And so they removed the stone. And Jesus raised His eyes, and said, "Father, I thank Thee that Thou heardest Me.

42 "And I knew that Thou hearest Me always; but ᴿbecause of the people standing around I said it, that they may believe that ᴿThou didst send Me."   John 12:30 • John 3:17

43 And when He had said these things, He cried out with a loud voice, "Lazarus, come forth."

44 He who had died came forth, ᴿbound hand and foot with wrappings; andᴿhis face was wrapped around with a cloth. Jesus *said to them, "Unbind him, and let him go."   John 19:40 • John 20:7

The Pharisees Plan to Kill Christ

45 Many therefore of the Jews,ᴿwho had come to Mary and ᴿbeheld what He had done, believed in Him.   John 11:19 • John 2:23

46 But some of them went away to the ᴿPharisees, and told them the things which Jesus had done.   John 7:32, 45; 11:57

47 Therefore the chief priests and the Pharisees convened a council, and were saying, "What are we doing? For this man is performing manyˢsigns.   *attesting miracles*

48 "If we let Him *go on* like this, all men will believe in Him, and the Romans will come and take away both ourᴿplace and our nation."   Matt. 24:15

49 But a certain one of them, Caiaphas, ᴿwho was high priest that year, said to them, "You know nothing at all,   John 11:51; 18:13

50 nor do you take into account thatᴿit is expedient for you that one man should die for the people, and that the whole nation should not perish."   John 18:14

51 Now this he did not sayᵀon his own initiative; butᴿbeing high priest that year, he prophesied that Jesus was going to die for the nation,   *from himself* • John 18:13

52 and not for the nation only, but that He might also gather together into one the children of God who are scattered abroad.

53 So from that day on theyᴿplanned together to kill Him.   Matt. 26:4

54 Jesus thereforeᴿno longer continued to walk publicly among the Jews, but went away from there to the country near the wil-

derness, into a city called Ephraim; and there He stayed with the disciples.   John 7:1

55 Now [R]the Passover of the Jews was at hand, and many went up to Jerusalem out of the country before the Passover, [R]to purify themselves.   Luke 22:1; John 2:13 • Num. 9:10

56 Therefore they were seeking for Jesus, and were saying to one another, as they stood in the temple, "What do you think; that He will not come to the feast at all?"

57 Now [R]the chief priests and the Pharisees had given orders that if anyone knew where He was, he should report it, that they might seize Him.   John 11:47

CHAPTER 12

Mary Anoints Christ
Matt. 26:6–12; Mark 14:3–8

JESUS, therefore, six days before the Passover, came to Bethany where Lazarus was, whom Jesus had raised from the dead.

2 So they made Him a supper there, and Martha was serving; but Lazarus was one of those reclining *at the table* with Him.

3 Mary therefore took a pound of very costly [R]perfume of pure nard, and anointed the feet of Jesus, and wiped His feet with her hair; and the house was filled with the fragrance of the perfume.   Mark 14:3

4 But Judas Iscariot, one of His disciples, who was intending to betray Him, *said,

5 "Why was this perfume not sold for [21]three hundred denarii, and given to poor *people?*"

6 Now he said this, not because he was concerned about the poor, but because he was a thief, and as he had the money box, he used to pilfer what was put into it.

7 Jesus therefore said, "Let her alone, in order that she may keep [22]it for [R]the day of My burial.   John 19:40

8 "For the poor you always have with you, but you do not always have Me."

9 The [R]great multitude therefore of the Jews learned that He was there; and they came, not for Jesus' sake only, but that they might also see Lazarus, [R]whom He raised from the dead.   Mark 12:37 • John 11:43f.

10 But the chief priests took counsel that they might put Lazarus to death also;

11 because [R]on account of him [R]many of the Jews were going away, and were believing in Jesus.   John 11:45f.; 12:18 • John 7:31; 11:42

The Triumphal Entry
Matt. 21:1–9; Mark 11:1–10;
Luke 19:29–38

12 On the next day the great multitude who had come to the feast, when they heard that Jesus was coming to Jerusalem,

13 took the branches of the palm trees, and went out to meet Him, and *began to* cry out, "Hosanna! [R]BLESSED IS HE WHO COMES IN THE NAME OF THE LORD, even the [R]King of Israel."   Ps. 118:26★ • John 1:49

14 And Jesus, finding a young donkey, sat on it; as it is written,

15 "FEAR [R]NOT, DAUGHTER OF ZION; BEHOLD, YOUR KING IS COMING, SEATED ON A DONKEY'S COLT."   Zech. 9:9★

16 These things His disciples did not understand at the first; but when Jesus [R]was glorified, then they remembered that these things were written of Him, and that they had done these things to Him.   John 7:39

17 And so [R]the multitude who were with Him when He called Lazarus out of the tomb, and raised him from the dead, were bearing Him witness.   John 11:42

18 For this cause also the multitude went and met Him, because they heard that He had performed this [A]sign.   *attesting miracle*

19 The Pharisees therefore said to one another, "You see that you are not doing any good; look, the world has gone after Him."

20 Now there were certain [R]Greeks among those who were going up to worship at [R]the feast;   John 7:35 • John 12:1

21 these therefore came to Philip, who was from Bethsaida of Galilee, and *began to* ask him, saying, "Sir, we wish to see Jesus."

22 Philip *came and *told [R]Andrew; Andrew and Philip *came, and they *told Jesus.   John 1:44

The Messiah Teaches

23 And Jesus *answered them, saying, "The [R]hour has come [R]for the Son of Man to be glorified.   John 13:1 • Acts 3:13☆

24 "Truly, truly, I say to you, [R]unless a grain of wheat falls into the earth and dies, it remains by itself alone; but if it dies, it bears much fruit.   [Rom. 14:9]; 1 Cor. 15:36

25 "He [R]who loves his [A]life loses it; and he who [R]hates his life in this world shall keep it to life eternal.   Mark 8:35 • *soul* • Luke 14:26

26 "If anyone serves Me, let him follow Me; and [R]where I am, there shall My servant also be; if anyone serves Me, the Father will [R]honor him.   John 14:3; 17:24 • 1 Sam. 2:30; Ps. 91:15

27 "Now [R] My soul has become troubled; and what shall I say, 'Father, [R] save Me from [R]this hour'? But for this purpose I came to this hour.   Mark 14:34 • Matt. 11:25 • John 12:23

28 "Father, glorify Thy name." There came therefore a voice out of heaven: "I have both glorified it, and will glorify it again."

29 The multitude therefore, who stood by and heard it, were saying that it had thundered; others were saying, "An [R] angel has spoken to Him."   Acts 23:9

30 Jesus answered and said, "This [R]voice has not come for My sake, but for your sakes.   John 11:42

31 "Now judgment is upon this world; now the ruler of this world shall be cast out.

[21] Equivalent to 11 months' wages
[22] I.e., The custom of anointing for burial

32"And I, if I^Rbe lifted up from the earth, will draw all men to Myself."   John 3:14; 8:28

33 But He was saying this to indicate the kind of death by which He was to die.

34 The multitude therefore answered Him, "We have heard out of the Law that ^Tthe Christ is to remain forever; and how can You say, 'The Son of Man must be lifted up'? Who is this Son of Man?"   the Messiah

35 Jesus therefore said to them, "For a little while longer the light is among you. Walk while you have the light, that darkness may not overtake you; he who walks in the darkness does not know where he goes.

36"While you have the light,^Rbelieve in the light, in order that you may become^Rsons of light."   John 12:46 • Luke 16:8; John 8:12

These things Jesus spoke, and He departed and^Thid Himself from them.   was hidden

37 But though He had performed so many ^Asigns before them, yet they were not believing in Him;   attesting miracles

38 that the word of Isaiah the prophet might be fulfilled, which he spoke, "LORD,^R WHO HAS BELIEVED OUR REPORT? AND TO WHOM HAS THE ARM OF THE LORD BEEN REVEALED?"   Is. 53:1; Rom. 10:16★

39 For this cause they could not believe, for Isaiah said again,

40"HE HAS BLINDED THEIR EYES, AND HE ^RHARDENED THEIR HEART; LEST THEY SEE WITH THEIR EYES, AND PERCEIVE WITH THEIR HEART, AND ^TBE CONVERTED, AND I HEAL THEM." Mark 6:52 • should be turned; i.e., turn about

41 These things Isaiah said, because he saw His glory, and he spoke of Him.

42 Nevertheless many even of the rulers believed in Him, but because of the Pharisees they were not confessing Him, lest they should be put out of the synagogue;

43 for they loved the approval of men rather than the approval of God.

44 And Jesus cried out and said, "He^Rwho believes in Me does not believe in Me, but in Him who sent Me.   Matt. 10:40; [John 5:24]

45"And^Rhe who beholds Me beholds the One who sent Me.   [John 14:9]

46"I^R have come as light into the world, that everyone who believes in Me may not remain in darkness.   John 1:4; 3:19; 8:12; 9:5

47"And if anyone hears My sayings, and does not keep them, I do not judge him; for ^RI did not come to judge the world, but to save the world.   John 3:17; 8:15f.

48"He who rejects Me, and does not receive My sayings, has one who judges him; ^Rthe word I spoke is what will judge him at ^Rthe last day.   Deut. 18:18f. • Acts 17:31

49"For I did not speak ^Ton My own initiative, but the Father Himself who sent Me ^Rhas given Me commandment, what to say, and what to speak.   of Myself • John 14:31; 17:8

50"And I know that His commandment is eternal life; therefore the things I speak, I speak just as the Father has told Me."

CHAPTER 13

Christ Washes the Disciples' Feet

NOW before the Feast of the Passover, Jesus knowing that His hour had come that He should depart out of this world to the Father, having loved His own who were in the world, He loved them to the end.

2 And during supper,^Rthe devil having already put into the heart of Judas Iscariot, the son of Simon, to betray Him,   John 6:70

3 Jesus,^Rknowing that the Father had given all things into His hands, and that^RHe had come forth from God, and was going back to God,   John 3:35 • John 8:42

4 *rose from supper, and *laid aside His garments; and taking a towel, He ^Rgirded Himself about.   Luke 12:37; 17:8

5 Then He *poured water into the basin, and began to^Rwash the disciples' feet, and to wipe them with the towel with which He was girded.   Gen. 18:4; 19:2; 43:24; Judg. 19:21

6 And so He *came to Simon Peter. He *said to Him, "Lord, do You wash my feet?"

7 Jesus answered and said to him, "What I do you do not realize now, but you shall understand^Rhereafter."   John 13:12ff.

8 Peter *said to Him, "Never shall You wash my feet!" Jesus answered him, "If I do not wash you, you have no part with Me."

9 Simon Peter *said to Him, "Lord, not my feet only, but also my hands and my head."

10 Jesus *said to him, "He who has bathed needs only to wash his feet, but is completely clean; and^Ryou are clean, but not all of you."   [John 15:3; Eph. 5:26]

11 For^RHe knew the one who was betraying Him; for this reason He said, "Not all of you are clean."   John 6:64; 13:2

12 And so when He had washed their feet, and^Rtaken His garments, and reclined at the table again, He said to them, "Do you know what I have done to you?   John 13:4

13"You call Me Teacher and^RLord; and^Tyou are right, for so I am.   Phil. 2:11 • you say well

14"If I then, ^Rthe Lord and the Teacher, washed your feet, you also ought to wash one another's feet.   John 11:2; [1 Cor. 12:3]

15"For I gave you ^Ran example that you also should do as I did to you.   1 Pet. 5:3

16"Truly, truly, I say to you, a slave is not greater than his master; neither is one who is sent greater than the one who sent him.

17"If you know these things, you are ^Rblessed if you do them. Luke 11:28; [James 1:25]

18"I do not speak of all of you. I know the ones I have chosen; but it is that the Scripture may be fulfilled, 'HE WHO EATS MY BREAD HAS LIFTED UP HIS HEEL AGAINST ME.'

19"From now on^RI am telling you before it comes to pass, so that when it does occur, you may believe that I am He.   John 14:29

20"Truly, truly, I say to you, ^Rhe who receives whomever I send receives Me; and he who receives Me receives Him who sent Me."   Matt. 10:40; Mark 9:37; Luke 9:48; 10:16

Christ Announces Judas, the Betrayer
Matt. 26:21, 22; Mark 14:18, 19;
Luke 22:21–23

21 When Jesus had said this, He became troubled in spirit, and testified, and said, "Truly, truly, I say to you, that ᴿone of you will ᴬbetray Me."   John 18:2✩ • *deliver Me up*
22 The disciples *began* looking at one another, ᴿat a loss *to know* of which one He was speaking.   Luke 22:21ff.; John 13:18, 21, 26
23 There was reclining on Jesus' breast one of His disciples, whom Jesus loved.
24 Simon Peter therefore *gestured to him, and *said to him, "Tell *us* who it is of whom He is speaking."
25 He, ᴿleaning back thus on Jesus' breast, *said to Him, "Lord, who is it?"   John 21:20
26 Jesus therefore *answered, "That is the one for whom I shall dip the morsel and give it to him." So when He had dipped the morsel, He *took and *gave it to Judas, ᴿ*the son* of Simon Iscariot.   John 6:71
27 And after the morsel, ᴿSatan then entered into him. Jesus therefore *said to him, "What you do, do quickly."   Matt. 4:10
28 Now no one of those reclining *at the table* knew for what purpose He had said this to him.
29 For some were supposing, because Judas ᴿhad the money box, that Jesus was saying to him, "Buy the things we have need of ᴿfor the feast"; or else, that he should give something to the poor.   John 12:6 • John 13:1
30 And so after receiving the morsel he went out immediately; and it was night.

Christ Announces His Departure

31 When therefore he had gone out, Jesus *said, "Now ᴬis the Son of Man glorified, and ᴿGod is glorified in Him;   *was* • [1 Pet. 4:11]
32 if God is glorified in Him, ᴿGod will also glorify Him in Himself, and will glorify Him immediately.   John 17:1
33 "Little children, I am with you a little while longer. You shall seek Me; and as I said to the Jews, I now say to you also, 'Where I am going, you cannot come.'
34 "A new commandment I give to you, that you love one another, even as I have loved you, that you also love one another.
35 "By ᴿthis all men will know that you are My disciples, if you have love for one another."   1 John 3:14; 4:20

Christ Foretells Peter's Denial
Matt. 26:34, 35; Mark 14:30, 31;
Luke 22:33, 34

36 Simon Peter *said to Him, "Lord, where are You going?" Jesus answered, "Where ᴿI go, you cannot follow Me now; but you shall follow later."   John 13:33; 14:2; 16:5

---

37 Peter *said to Him, "Lord, why can I not follow You right now? ᴿI will lay down my life for You."   *Matt. 26:33-35; Mark 14:29-31*
38 Jesus *answered, "Will you lay down your life for Me? Truly, truly, I say to you, ᴿa cock shall not crow, until you deny Me three times.   Mark 14:30; John 18:27✩

CHAPTER 14

Christ Comforts His Disciples

"LET ᴿnot your heart be troubled; ²³believe in God, believe also in Me. [John 14:27]
2 "In My Father's house are many dwelling places; if it were not so, I would have told you; for I go to prepare a place for you.
3 "And if I go and prepare a place for you, I will come again, and receive you to Myself; that where I am, *there* you may be also.
4 "²⁴And you know the way where I am going."

Christ Answers Thomas

5 ᴿThomas *said to Him, "Lord, we do not know where You are going, how do we know the way?"   John 11:16
6 Jesus *said to him, "I am ᴿthe way, and ᴿthe truth, and the life; no one comes to the Father, but through Me.[Rom. 5:2] • [John 1:14]
7 "If you had known Me, you would have known My Father also; from now on you ᴿknow Him, and have seen Him."   1 John 2:13

Christ Answers Philip

8 ᴿPhilip *said to Him, "Lord, show us the Father, and it is enough for us."   John 1:43
9 Jesus *said to him, "Have I been so long with you, and *yet* you have not come to know Me, Philip? ᴿHe who has seen Me has seen the Father; how do you say, 'Show us the Father'?   John 1:14; 12:45; Col. 1:15; Heb. 1:3
10 "Do you not believe that ᴿI am in the Father, and the Father is in Me? ᴿThe words that I say to you I do not speak on My own initiative, but the Father abiding in Me does His works.   John 10:38 • Deut. 18:18; John 5:19★
11 "Believe Me that ᴿI am in the Father, and the Father in Me; otherwise believe on account of the works themselves.   John 10:38
12 "Truly, truly, I say to you, he who believes in Me, the works that I do shall he do also; and ᴿgreater *works* than these shall he do; because I go to the Father.   John 4:37f.
13 "And ᴿwhatever you ask in My name, that will I do, that ᴿthe Father may be glorified in the Son.   Matt. 7:7 • John 13:31
14 "If you ask Me anything ᴿin My name, I will do *it.*   John 15:16; 16:23f.
15 "If ᴿyou love Me, you will keep My commandments.   John 14:21, 23; 15:10; 1 John 5:3
16 "And I will ask the Father, and ᴿHe will give you another ᴿHelper, that He may be with you forever;   Acts 2:4, 33✩ • [John 15:26]
17 *that is* ᴿthe Spirit of truth, ᴿwhom the world cannot receive, because it does not

---

²³ Or, *you believe in God*
²⁴ Many ancient authorities read *And where I go you know, and the way you know*

behold Him or know Him, *but* you know Him because He abides with you, and will be in you. [John 15:26; 16:13] • [1 Cor. 2:14]

18"I will not leave you as orphans;[R]I will come to you. [John 14:3, 28]

19"After[R] a little while the world will behold Me no more; but you *will* behold Me; because I live, you shall live also. John 7:33

20"In that day you shall know that I am in My Father, and you in Me, and I in you.

21"He[R] who has My commandments and keeps them, he it is who loves Me; and[R]he who loves Me shall be loved by My Father, and I will love him, and will[R]disclose Myself to him." 2 John 6 • [John 14:23] • Ex. 33:18f.

Christ Answers Judas

22 [R]Judas (not Iscariot) *said to Him, "Lord, what then has happened[R]that You are going to disclose Yourself to us, and not to the world?" Luke 6:16 • Acts 10:40, 41

23 Jesus answered and said to him, "If anyone loves Me, he will keep My word; and My Father will love him, and We will come to him, and make Our abode with him.

24"He who does not love Me [R]does not keep My words; and[R]the word which you hear is not Mine, but the Father's who sent Me. John 14:23 • John 7:16; 14:10

25"These things I have spoken to you, while abiding with you.

26"But the[R]Helper, the Holy Spirit, whom the Father will send in My name, He will teach you all things, and bring to your remembrance all that I said to you. John 14:16

27"Peace[R]I leave with you; My peace I give to you; not as the world gives, do I give to you. Let not your heart be troubled, nor let it be fearful. Luke 1:79; [John 16:33; 20:19]★

28"You[R] heard that I said to you, 'I go away, and[R]I will come to you.' If you loved Me, you would have rejoiced, because[R]I go to the Father; for the Father is greater than I. John 14:2-4 • John 14:3, 18 • John 14:12

29"And now [R]I have told you before it comes to pass, that when it comes to pass, you may believe. John 13:19

30"I will not speak much more with you, for[R]the ruler of the world is coming, and he has nothing in Me; [John 12:31]

31 but that the world may know that I love the Father, and as[R]the Father gave Me commandment, even so I do. Arise,[R]let us go from here. Is. 50:5; John 10:18★ • John 13:1; 18:1

CHAPTER 15

The Relationship of Believers to Christ

"I[R] AM the true vine, and My Father is the [R]vinedresser. Ps. 80:8ff.; Is. 5:1ff. • Rom. 11:17

2"Every branch in Me that does not bear fruit, He takes away; and every *branch* that bears fruit, He [25]prunes it, that it may bear more fruit.

3"You[R] are already clean because of the word which I have spoken to you. Eph. 5:26

4"Abide[R] in Me, and I in you. As the branch cannot bear fruit of itself, unless it abides in the vine, so neither *can* you, unless you abide in Me. John 6:56; 15:4-7

5"I am the vine, you are the branches; he who abides in Me, and I in him, he[R]bears much fruit; for apart from Me you can do nothing. John 15:16

6"If anyone does not abide in Me, he is [R]thrown away as a branch, and dries up; and they gather them, and cast them into the fire, and they are burned. John 15:2

7"If you abide in Me, and My words abide in you,[R]ask whatever you wish, and it shall be done for you. Matt. 7:7; John 15:16

8"By[R]this is My Father glorified, that you bear much fruit, and so[R]prove to be My disciples. [Matt. 5:16] • John 8:31

9"Just as[R]the Father has loved Me, I have also loved you; abide in My love. John 3:35

10"If[R] you keep My commandments, you will abide in My love; just as[R]I have kept My Father's commandments, and abide in His love. John 14:15 • John 8:29

11"These[R]things I have spoken to you, that My joy may be in you, and *that* your [R]joy may be made full. John 17:13 • John 3:29

The Relationship of Believers to Each Other

12"This is My commandment, that you love one another, just as I have loved you.

13"Greater love has no one than this, that one lay down his life for his friends.

14"You are My[R]friends, if[R]you do what I command you. Luke 12:4 • [Matt. 12:50]

15"No longer do I call you slaves, for the slave does not know what his master is doing; but I have called you friends, for[R]all things that I have heard from My Father I have made known to you. John 8:26; 16:12

16"You did not choose Me, but I chose you, and appointed you, that you should go and bear fruit, and *that* your fruit should remain, that[R]whatever you ask of the Father in My name, He may give to you. John 14:13

17"This[R]I command you, that you love one another. John 15:12

The Relationship of Believers to the World

18"If[R]the world hates you, you know that it has hated Me before *it hated* you. John 7:7

19"If you were of the world, the world would love its own; but because you are not of the world, but I chose you out of the world, therefore the world hates you.

20"Remember the word that I said to you, 'A[R] slave is not greater than his master.' If they persecuted Me,[R]they will also persecute you; if they[R]kept My word, they will keep yours also. Matt. 10:24 • 2 Cor. 4:9 • John 8:51

[25] Lit., *cleanses*

21"But all these things they will do to you ᴿfor My name's sake, because they do not know the One who sent Me.   Matt. 10:22; 24:9

22"If ᴿI had not come and spoken to them, they would not have ᵀsin, but now they have no excuse for their sin.   John 9:41 • guilt

23"He who hates Me hates My Father also.

24"If I had not done among them the works which no one else did, they would not have ᵀsin; but now they have both seen and hated Me and My Father as well.   guilt

25"But *they have done this* in order that the word may be fulfilled that is written in their ᴿLaw, 'THEYᴿ HATED ME WITHOUT A CAUSE.'   John 10:34 • Ps. 35:19; 69:4 ★

The Promise of the Holy Spirit

26"When the Helper comes, whom I will send to you from the Father, *that is* ᴿthe Spirit of truth, who proceeds from the Father, He will bear witness of Me, [John 14:17]

27 and you *will* bear witness also, because you have been with Me from the beginning.

CHAPTER 16

"THESE things I have spoken to you, that you may be kept from ᴿstumbling.   Matt. 11:6

2"They will ᴿmake you outcasts from the synagogue, but ᴿan hour is coming for everyone ᴿwho kills you to think that he is offering service to God.   John 9:22 • John 4:21 • Rev. 6:9

3"And these things they will do, because they have not known the Father, or Me.

4"But these things I have spoken to you, ᴿthat when their hour comes, you may remember that I told you of them. And these things I did not say to you ᴿat the beginning, because I was with you.   John 13:19 • Luke 1:2

5"But now ᴿI am going to Him who sent Me; and none of you asks Me, 'Where ᴿare You going?'   John 7:33 • John 13:36; 14:5

6"But because I have said these things to you, ᴿsorrow has filled your heart.   John 14:1

7"But I tell you the truth, it is to your advantage that I go away; for if I do not go away, the Helper shall not come to you; but if I go, ᴿI will send Him to you.   Acts 2:33 ☆

8"And He, when He comes, ᴿwill convict the world concerning sin, and righteousness, and judgment;   Acts 2:37 ☆

9 concerning sin, ᴿbecause they do not believe in Me;   John 15:22, 24

10 and concerning ᴿrighteousness, because ᴿI go to the Father, and you no longer behold Me;   Acts 3:14; 7:52; 17:31; [1 Pet. 3:18] • John 16:5

11 and concerning judgment, because the ruler of this world has been judged.

12"I have many more things to say to you, but you cannot bear *them* now.

13"But when He, the Spirit of truth, comes, He will guide you into all the truth; for He will not speak on His own initiative, but whatever He hears, He will speak; and He will disclose to you what is to come.

14"He shall ᴿglorify Me; for He shall take of Mine, and shall disclose *it* to you.   John 7:39

15"All ᴿthings that the Father has are Mine; therefore I said, that He takes of Mine, and will disclose *it* to you.   John 17:10

The Predictions of Christ's Death and Resurrection

16"A ᴿlittle while, and you will no longer behold Me; and again a little while, and ᴿyou will see Me."   John 19:42; 20:19 ☆ • John 16:22

17 *Some* of His disciples therefore said to one another, "What is this thing He is telling us, 'A ᴿlittle while, and you will not behold Me; and again a little while, and you will see Me'; and, 'because ᴿI go to the Father'?"   John 16:16 • John 16:5

18 And so they were saying, "What is this that He says, 'A little while'? We do not know what He is talking about."

19 ᴿJesus knew that they wished to question Him, and He said to them, "Are you deliberating together about this, that I said, 'A little while, and you will not behold Me, and again a little while, and you will see Me'?   Mark 9:32; John 6:61

20"Truly, truly, I say to you, that ᵀyou will weep and lament, but the world will rejoice; you will be sorrowful, but ᴿyour sorrow will be turned to joy.   Mark 16:10 • John 20:20 ☆

21"Whenever ᴿa woman is in travail she has sorrow, because her hour has come; but when she gives birth to the child, she remembers the anguish no more, for joy that a child has been born into the world.   Is. 13:8

22"Therefore ᴿyou too now have sorrow; but ᵀI will see you again, and your heart will rejoice, and no one takes your joy away from you.   John 16:6 • John 20:20 ☆

23"And in that day you will ᵀask Me no question. Truly, truly, I say to you, if you shall ask the Father for anything, He will give it to you in My name. *question Me nothing*

24"Until now you have asked for nothing in My name; ask, and you will receive, that your ᵀjoy may be made full.   John 3:29; 15:11

25"These things I have spoken to you in figurative language; an hour is coming when I will speak no more to you in figurative language, but will tell you plainly of the Father.

26"In ᴿthat day you will ask in My name, and I do not say to you that I will request the Father on your behalf;   John 14:20; 16:23

27 for the Father Himself loves you, because you have loved Me, and ᴿhave believed that I came forth from the Father.   John 2:11

28"I ᴿcame forth from the Father, and have come into the world; I am leaving the world again, and going to the Father."   John 8:42

29 His disciples *said, "Lo, now You are speaking plainly, and are not using ᴿa ᵀfigure of speech.   Matt. 13:34; John 10:6; 16:25 • *proverb*

30"Now we know that You know all things, and have no need for anyone to question You; by this we ᴿbelieve that You ᴿcame from God."   John 2:11; 16:27 • John 8:42

31 Jesus answered them, "Do you now believe?

32 "Behold, an hour is coming, and has *already* come, for[R]you to be scattered, each to [R]his own *home*, and to leave Me alone; and *yet* [R]I am not alone, because the Father is with Me.   Zech. 13:7☆ • John 19:27 • John 8:29

33 "These things I have spoken to you, that [R]in Me you may have peace. In the world you have tribulation, but[R]take courage; I have overcome the world."   John 14:27 • Matt. 9:2

CHAPTER 17

Christ Prays for Himself

THESE things Jesus spoke; and[R]lifting up His eyes to heaven, He said, "Father, the hour has come; [R]glorify Thy Son, that the Son may glorify Thee,   John 11:41 • John 7:39

2 even as Thou gavest Him authority over all mankind, that to all whom Thou hast given Him, He may give eternal life.

3 "And this is eternal life, that they may know Thee,[R]the only true God, and Jesus Christ whom Thou hast sent.   John 5:44

4 "I[R]glorified Thee on the earth,[R]having accomplished the work which Thou hast given Me to do.   Is. 50:5; John 13:31★ • Luke 22:37

5 "And now, glorify Thou Me together with Thyself, Father, with the glory which I had with Thee before the world was.

Christ Prays for His Disciples

6 "I manifested Thy name to the men whom Thou gavest Me out of the world; [R]Thine they were, and Thou gavest them to Me, and they have kept Thy word. John 17:9

7 "Now they have come to know that everything Thou hast given Me is from Thee;

8 for[R]the words which Thou gavest Me I have given to them; and they received *them*, and truly understood that[R]I came forth from Thee, and they believed that Thou didst send Me.   Deut. 18:18; John 6:68★ • John 8:42

9 "I ask on their behalf; I do not ask on behalf of the world, but of those whom Thou hast given Me; for they are Thine;

10 and [R]all things that are Mine are Thine, and Thine are Mine; and I have been glorified in them.   John 16:15

11 "And I am no more in the world; and *yet* they themselves are in the world, and I come to Thee. Holy Father, keep them in Thy name, *the name* which Thou hast given Me, that they may be one, even as We *are*.

12 "While I was with them, I was keeping them in Thy name[R]which Thou hast given Me; and I guarded them, and not one of them perished but the son of perdition, that the Scripture might be fulfilled.   John 17:6

13 "But now I come to Thee; and these things I speak in the world, that they may have My joy made full in themselves.

14 "I have given them Thy word; and the world has hated them, because they are not of the world, even as I am not of the world.

15 "I do not ask Thee to take them out of the world, but to keep them[A]from[A]the[R] evil one.   *out of* the power of • *evil* • Matt. 5:37

16 "They[R]are not of the world, even as I am not of the world.   John 17:14

17 "Sanctify[R]them in the truth; Thy word is truth.   John 15:3

18 "As Thou didst send Me into the world, I also have sent them into the world.

19 "And for their sakes I[R]sanctify Myself, that they themselves also may be[R]sanctified [R]in truth.   John 15:13 • John 15:3 • 2 Cor. 7:14

Christ Prays for All Believers

20 "I do not ask in behalf of these alone, but for those also who believe in Me through their word;

21 that they may all be one;[R]even as Thou, Father, *art* in Me, and I in Thee, that they also may be in Us; that the world may believe that Thou didst send Me.   John 10:38

22 "And the[R]glory which Thou hast given Me I have given to them; that they may be one, just as We are one;   John 1:14; 17:24

23 I in them, and Thou in Me, that they may be perfected in unity, that the world may know that Thou didst send Me, and didst love them, even as Thou didst love Me.

24 "Father, I desire that they also, whom Thou hast given Me, be with Me where I am, in order that they may behold My glory, which Thou hast given Me; for Thou didst love Me before the foundation of the world.

25 "O righteous Father,[T]although[T]the world has not known Thee, yet I have known Thee; and these have known that[R]Thou didst send Me;   *and* • John 7:29; 15:21 • John 3:17

26 and[R]I have made Thy name known to them, and will make it known; that[R]the love wherewith Thou didst love Me may be in them, and I in them."   John 17:6 • John 15:9

CHAPTER 18

The Arrest of Christ
Matt. 26:47-56; Mark 14:43-52;
Luke 22:47-53

WHEN Jesus had spoken these words,[R]He went forth with His disciples over the[T]ravine of the Kidron, where there was [R]a garden, into which He Himself entered, and His disciples.   Luke 22:39 • *winter-torrent* • Matt. 26:36

2 Now Judas also, who was betraying Him, knew the place; for Jesus had often met there with His disciples.

3 Judas then, having received[d]the *Roman* cohort, and officers from the chief priests and the Pharisees, *came there with lanterns and torches and weapons.   John 18:12

4 Jesus therefore, knowing all the things

that were coming upon Him, went forth, and *said to them, "Whom do you seek?"

5 They answered Him, "Jesus the Nazarene." He *said to them, "I am *He.*" And Judas also who was betraying Him, was standing with them.

6 When therefore He said to them, "I am *He,*" they drew back, and fell to the ground.

7 Again therefore He asked them, "Whom[R] do you seek?" And they said, "Jesus the Nazarene."   John 18:4

8 Jesus answered, "I told you that I am *He*; if therefore you seek Me, let these go their way,"

9 that the word might be fulfilled which He spoke, "Of[R] those whom Thou hast given Me I lost not one."   [John 17:12]

10 Simon Peter therefore[B] having a sword, drew it, and struck the high priest's slave, and cut off his right ear; and the slave's name was Malchus.   Matt. 26:51

11 Jesus therefore said to Peter, "Put the sword into the sheath; the cup which the Father has given Me, shall I not drink it?"

First Jewish Trial Before Annas
Matt. 26:69, 70; Mark 14:66–68;
Luke 22:55–57

12 So the Roman [A]cohort and the commander, and the officers of the Jews, arrested Jesus and bound Him,   *battalion*

13 and led Him to [B]Annas first; for he was father-in-law of [R]Caiaphas, who was high priest that year.   Luke 3:2 • John 11:49, 51

14 Now Caiaphas was the one who had advised the Jews that it was expedient for one man to die on behalf of the people.

15 And[R] Simon Peter was following Jesus, and *so was* another disciple. Now that disciple was known to the high priest, and entered with Jesus into[R] the court of the high priest,   Matt. 26:58; Mark 14:54 • Matt. 26:3

16 but Peter was standing at the door outside. So the other disciple, who was known to the high priest, went out and spoke to the doorkeeper, and brought in Peter.

17 The slave-girl therefore who kept the door *said to Peter, "You are not also *one* of this man's disciples, are you?" He *said, "I am not."

18 Now the slaves and the officers were standing *there,* having made[R] a charcoal fire, for it was cold and they were warming themselves; and Peter also was with them, standing and warming himself.   John 21:9

19 [R]The high priest therefore questioned Jesus about His disciples, and about His teaching.   Mark 14:55-65; Luke 22:63-71

20 Jesus answered him, "I [R]have spoken openly to the world; I always[t] taught in [s]synagogues, and in the temple, where all the Jews come together; and I spoke nothing in secret.   John 7:26 • Matt. 4:23 • *the synagogue*

21 "Why do you question Me? Question

those who have heard what I spoke to them; behold, these know what I said."

22 And when He had said this, one of the [R]officers standing by[R] gave Jesus a blow, saying, "Is that the way You answer the high priest?"   John 18:3 • Job 16:10; Lam. 3:30 ★

23 [R]Jesus answered him, "If I have spoken wrongly, bear witness of the wrong; but if rightly, why do you strike Me?"   Matt. 5:39

Second Jewish Trial Before Caiaphas
Matt. 26:57–68, 73–75; Mark 14:53–65,
70–72; Luke 22:59–65

24 [R]Annas therefore sent Him bound to Caiaphas the high priest.   John 18:13

25 Now Simon Peter was standing and warming himself. They said therefore to him, "You are not also *one* of His disciples, are you?" He denied *it,* and said, "I am not."

26 One of the slaves of the high priest, being a relative of the one[R] whose ear Peter cut off, *said, "Did I not see you in[R] the garden with Him?"   John 18:10 • John 18:1

27 [R]Peter therefore denied *it* again; and immediately a cock crowed.   Matt. 26:34 ★

First Roman Trial Before Pilate
Matt. 27:2, 11–14; Mark 15:1–5;
Luke 23:1–5

28 They *led Jesus therefore from Caiaphas into the [26]Praetorium, and it was early; and they themselves did not enter into the Praetorium in order that they might not be defiled, but might eat the Passover.

29 [R]Pilate therefore went out to them, and *said, "What accusation do you bring against this Man?"   Mark 15:2-5; Luke 23:2, 3

30 They answered and said to him, "If this Man were not an evildoer, we would not have delivered Him up to you."

31 Pilate therefore said to them, "Take Him yourselves, and judge Him according to your law." The Jews said to him, "We are not permitted to put anyone to death,"

32 that [R]the word of Jesus might be fulfilled, which He spoke, signifying by what kind of death He was about to die. John 3:14

33 Pilate therefore[R] entered again into the [26]Praetorium, and summoned Jesus, and said to Him, "Are[R] You the King of the Jews?"   John 18:28, 29 • Luke 23:3; John 19:12

34 Jesus answered, "Are you saying this [t]on your own initiative, or did others tell you about Me?"   *from yourself*

35 Pilate answered, "I am not a Jew, am I? Your own nation and the chief priests delivered You up to me; what have You done?"

36 Jesus answered, "My[R] kingdom[A] is not of this world. If My kingdom were of this world, then My servants would be fighting, that I might not be delivered up to the Jews; but as it is, My kingdom is not [27]of this realm."   Luke 17:21 • *is not derived from*

37 Pilate therefore said to Him, "So You are a king?" Jesus answered, "You say *correctly* that I am a king. For this I have been

born, and for this I have come into the world, to bear witness to the truth. Everyone who is of the truth hears My voice."

38 Pilate *said to Him, "What is truth?" And when he had said this, he [R]went out again to the Jews, and *said to them, "I [R]find no guilt in Him."   John 18:33; 19:4 • John 19:4, 6

Second Roman Trial Before Pilate
Matt. 27:15–31; Mark 15:6–20;
Luke 23:13–25

39 "But [R]you have a custom, that I should release someone [A]for you at the Passover; do you wish then that I release for you the King of the Jews?"   Luke 23:18-25 • *to you*

40 Therefore they cried out again, saying, "Not [R]this Man, but Barabbas." Now Barabbas was a robber.   Is. 53:3; Acts 3:14 ★

CHAPTER 19

THEN [R]Pilate therefore took Jesus, and [A]scourged Him.   Is. 50:6 ★ • *had Him scourged*

2 [R]And the soldiers wove a crown of thorns and put it on His head, and arrayed Him in a purple robe;   Matt. 27:27-30

3 and they *began* to come up to Him, and say, "Hail, [R] King of the Jews!" and to give Him blows *in the face.*   Matt. 27:29; Mark 15:18

4 And Pilate [R]came out again, and *said to them, "Behold, I am bringing Him out to you, that you may know that [R]I find no guilt in Him."   John 18:33, 38 • Luke 23:4; John 18:38

5 Jesus therefore came out, wearing the crown of thorns and the purple robe. And *Pilate* *said to them, "Behold, the Man!"

6 When therefore the chief priests and the [R]officers saw Him, they cried out, saying, "Crucify, crucify!" Pilate *said to them, "Take Him yourselves, and crucify Him, for [R]I find no guilt in Him."   John 18:3 • Luke 23:4

7 The Jews answered him, "We have a law, and by that law [R]He ought to die because He [R]made Himself out *to be* the Son of God."   Matt. 20:18 ★ • • John 5:18

8 When Pilate therefore heard this statement, he was the more afraid;

9 and he entered into the [28]Praetorium again, and *said to Jesus, "Where are You from?" But Jesus gave him no answer.

10 Pilate therefore *said to Him, "You do not speak to me? Do You not know that I have authority to release You, and I have authority to crucify You?"

11 Jesus answered, "You would have no authority over Me, unless it had been given you from above; for this reason he who delivered Me up to you has *the* greater sin."

12 As a result of this Pilate made efforts to release Him, but the Jews cried out, saying, "If you release this Man, you are no friend of Caesar; everyone who makes himself out *to be* a king opposes Caesar."

13 When Pilate therefore heard these words, he brought Jesus out, and sat down on the judgment seat at a place called The Pavement, but in Hebrew, Gabbatha.

14 Now it was [R]the day of preparation for the Passover; it was about the [29]sixth [R]hour. And he *said to the Jews, "Behold, [R]your King!"   Matt. 27:62 • Matt. 27:45 • John 19:19, 21

15 They therefore cried out, "Away [R]with Him, away with Him, crucify Him!" Pilate *said to them, "Shall I crucify your King?" The chief priests answered, "We have no king but Caesar."   Is. 53:3 ★

16 So he then [R]delivered Him to them to be crucified.   Matt. 27:26; Mark 15:15; Luke 23:25

The Crucifixion of Christ
Matt. 27:23–38, 48, 50; Mark 15:21–26,
36, 37; Luke 23:26–33, 38, 46

17 They took Jesus therefore, and He went out, bearing His own cross, to the place called the Place of a Skull, which is called in [T]Hebrew, Golgotha.   Jewish Aramaic

18 There they [R]crucified Him, and with Him two other men, one on either side, and Jesus in between.   Ps. 22:16; Matt. 20:19; 26:2 ★

19 And Pilate wrote an inscription also, and put it on the cross. And it was written, "JESUS [R]THE NAZARENE, [R]THE KING OF THE JEWS."   Matt. 27:37 • John 19:14, 21

20 Therefore this inscription many of the Jews read, for the place where Jesus was crucified was near the city; and it was written in Hebrew, Latin, *and* in Greek.

21 And so the chief priests of the Jews were saying to Pilate, "Do not write, 'The [R] King of the Jews'; but that He said, 'I am [R]King of the Jews.' "   John 19:14, 19

22 Pilate answered, "What [R]I have written I have written."   Gen. 43:14; Esth. 4:16

23 The soldiers therefore, when they had crucified Jesus, took His outer garments and made [R]four parts, a part to every soldier and *also* the [30]tunic; now the tunic was seamless, woven in one piece.   Acts 12:4

24 They said therefore to one another, "Let us not tear it, but cast [T]lots for it, *to decide* whose it shall be"; that the Scripture might be fulfilled, "THEY [R]DIVIDED MY OUTER GARMENTS AMONG THEM, AND THEY CAST LOTS."   *a lot* • Ps. 22:18 ★

25 Therefore the soldiers did these things. [R]But there were standing by the cross of Jesus His mother, and His mother's sister, Mary the *wife* of [R]Clopas, and [R]Mary Magdalene.   Luke 2:35 ★ • Luke 24:18 • Luke 8:2

26 When Jesus therefore saw His mother, and [R]the disciple whom He loved standing nearby, He *said to His mother, "Woman, behold, your son!"   John 13:23 • John 2:4

27 Then He *said to the disciple, "Behold, your mother!" And from that hour the disciple took her into his own *household.*

28 After this, Jesus, [R]knowing that all things had already been accomplished, in

---

[28] I.e., governor's official residence
[29] Perhaps 6 a.m. (Roman time)
[30] Gr., *khiton*, the garment worn next to the skin

order that the Scripture might be fulfilled, *said, "I am thirsty."   John 13:1 • Ps. 22:15★

29 A jar full of sour wine was standing there; so they put a sponge full of the sour wine upon a branch of hyssop, and brought it up to His mouth.   Ps. 69:21★

30 When Jesus therefore had received the sour wine, He said, "It is finished!" And He bowed His head, and gave up His spirit.

31 The Jews therefore, because it was the day of preparation, so that the bodies should not remain on the cross on the Sabbath (for that Sabbath was a high day), asked Pilate that their legs might be broken, and that they might be taken away.

32 The soldiers therefore came, and broke the legs of the first man, and of the other man who was crucified with Him; John 19:18

33 but coming to Jesus, when they saw that He was already dead, they did not break His legs;   Ps. 34:20★

34 but one of the soldiers pierced His side with a spear, and immediately there came out blood and water.   [1 John 5:6, 8]

35 And he who has seen has borne witness, and his witness is true; and he knows that he is telling the truth, so that you also may believe.   John 15:27; 21:24

36 For these things came to pass, that the Scripture might be fulfilled, "NOT A BONE OF HIM SHALL BE BROKEN."   Ps. 34:20★ • crushed

37 And again another Scripture says, "THEY SHALL LOOK ON HIM WHOM THEY PIERCED."   Zech. 12:10; Rev. 1:7★

The Burial of Christ
*Matt. 27:57–60; Mark 15:42–46;
Luke 23:50–54*

38 And after these things Joseph of Arimathea, being a disciple of Jesus, but a secret one, for fear of the Jews, asked Pilate that he might take away the body of Jesus; and Pilate granted permission. He came therefore, and took away His body. Is. 53:9★

39 And Nicodemus came also, who had first come to Him by night; bringing a mixture of myrrh and aloes, about a hundred pounds weight.   Ps. 45:8 • 100 litras (12 oz. each)

40 And so they took the body of Jesus, and bound it in linen wrappings with the spices, as is the burial custom of the Jews.

41 Now in the place where He was crucified there was a garden; and in the garden a new tomb, in which no one had yet been laid.   Is. 53:9; Matt. 27:60★ • Luke 23:53

42 Therefore on account of the Jewish day of preparation, because the tomb was nearby, they laid Jesus there.   Mark 14:8★

CHAPTER 20

The Resurrection of Christ
Matt. 28:1–8; Mark 16:1–8; Luke 24:1–12

NOW on the first day of the week Mary Magdalene *came early to the tomb, while it *was still dark, and *saw the stone already taken away from the tomb.   John 19:25; 20:18

2 And so she *ran and *came to Simon Peter, and to the other disciple whom Jesus loved, and *said to them, "They have taken away the Lord out of the tomb, and we do not know where they have laid Him."

3 Peter therefore went forth, and the other disciple, and they were going to the tomb.

4 And the two were running together; and the other disciple ran ahead faster than Peter, and came to the tomb first;

5 and stooping and looking in, he *saw the linen wrappings lying there; but he did not go in.   John 20:11 • John 19:40

6 Simon Peter therefore also *came, following him, and entered the tomb; and he *beheld the linen wrappings lying there,

7 and the face-cloth, which had been on His head, not lying with the linen wrappings, but rolled up in a place by itself.

8 So the other disciple who had first come to the tomb entered then also, and he saw and believed.   John 20:4

9 For as yet they did not understand the Scripture, that He must rise again from the dead.   Matt. 22:29; John 2:22 • Luke 24:26ff., 46

10 So the disciples went away again to their own homes.   Luke 24:12

Christ Appears to Mary Magdalene

11 But Mary was standing outside the tomb weeping; and so, as she wept, she stooped and looked into the tomb; John 20:5

12 and she *beheld two angels in white sitting, one at the head, and one at the feet, where the body of Jesus had been lying.

13 And they *said to her, "Woman, why are you weeping?" She *said to them, "Because they have taken away my Lord, and I do not know where they have laid Him."

14 When she had said this, she turned around, and *beheld Jesus standing there, and did not know that it was Jesus.

15 Jesus *said to her, "Woman, why are you weeping? Whom are you seeking?" Supposing Him to be the gardener, she *said to Him, "Sir, if you have carried Him away, tell me where you have laid Him, and I will take Him away."   John 20:13

16 Jesus *said to her, "Mary!" She *turned and *said to Him in Hebrew, "Rabboni!" (which means, Teacher).   John 5:2

17 Jesus *said to her, "Stop clinging to Me, for I have not yet ascended to the Father; but go to My brethren, and say to them, 'I ascend to My Father and your Father, and My God and your God.' " Acts 1:9☆

18 Mary Magdalene *came, announcing to the disciples, "I have seen the Lord," and that He had said these things to her.

Christ Appears to the Disciples
(Thomas Absent)
Mark 16:14; Luke 24:36–43

19 When therefore it was evening, on that day, the first day of the week, and when the

doors were shut where the disciples were, for fear of the Jews, [R]Jesus came and stood in their midst, and *said to them, "Peace[T] be with you."   John 16:16 ★ • *Peace to you

20 And when He had said this,[R]He showed them both His hands and His side. The disciples therefore[R]rejoiced when they saw the Lord.   Luke 24:39, 40; John 19:34 • John 16:20, 22 ★

21 Jesus therefore said to them again, "Peace[R] be with you;[a]as the Father has sent Me, I also send you."   Luke 24:36 • John 17:18

22 [R]And when He had said this, He breathed on them, and *said to them, "Receive the Holy Spirit.   John 16:20–22 ★

23"If you forgive the sins of any, *their sins have been forgiven them;* if you retain the *sins* of any, they have been retained."

24 But[R]Thomas, one of[R]the twelve, called [T]Didymus, was not with them when Jesus came.   John 11:16 • John 6:67 • the Twin

25 The other disciples therefore were saying to him, "We have seen the Lord!" But he said to them, "Unless I shall see in His hands the imprint of the nails, and put my finger into the place of the nails, and put my hand into His side, I will not believe."

Christ Appears to the Disciples
(Thomas Present)
1 Cor. 15:5

26 And [a]after eight days again His disciples were inside, and Thomas with them. Jesus *came, the doors having been [a]shut, and stood in their midst, and said, "Peace[R] be with you."   *a week later* • *locked* • Luke 24:36

27 Then He *said to Thomas, "Reach here your finger, and see My hands; and reach here your hand, and put it into My side; and be not unbelieving, but believing."

28 Thomas answered and said to Him, "My Lord and my God!"

29 Jesus *said to him, "Because you have seen Me, have you believed? Blessed *are* they who did not see, and *yet* believed."

The Purpose of John's Gospel

30 Many other [R]signs therefore Jesus also performed in the presence of the disciples, which are not written in this book;   John 2:11

31 but these have been written that you may believe that Jesus is[T]the Christ,[R]the Son of God; and that believing you may have life in His name.   the Messiah • Matt. 4:3

CHAPTER 21

Christ Appears to the Seven Disciples

AFTER these things Jesus [a]manifested[R] Himself again to the disciples at the[R]Sea of Tiberias, and He manifested *Himself* in this way.   *made Himself visible* • Mark 16:12 • John 6:1

2 There were together Simon Peter, and Thomas called [T]Didymus, and Nathanael of Cana in Galilee, and the *sons* of Zebedee, and two others of His disciples.   the Twin

3 Simon Peter *said to them, "I am going fishing." They *said to him, "We will also come with you." They went out, and got into the boat; and[R]that night they caught nothing.   Luke 5:5

4 But when the day was now breaking, Jesus stood on the beach; yet the disciples did not[R]know that it was Jesus.   Luke 24:16

5 Jesus therefore *said to them, "Children,[R]you do not have any fish, do you?" They answered Him, "No."   Luke 24:41

6 And He said to them, "Cast[R]the net on the right-hand side of the boat, and you will find *a catch*." They cast therefore, and then they were not able to haul it in because of the great number of fish.   Luke 5:4ff.

7 [R]That disciple therefore whom Jesus [T]loved *said to Peter, "It is the Lord." And so when Simon Peter heard that it was the Lord, he put his outer garment on (for he was stripped *for work*), and threw himself into the sea.   John 13:23; 21:20 • *was loving*

8 But the other disciples came in the little boat, for they were not far from the land, but about [T]one hundred yards away, dragging the net *full* of fish.   200 cubits

9 And so when they got out upon the land, they *saw a charcoal fire *already* laid, and[R]fish placed on it, and bread.   John 6:9, 11

10 Jesus *said to them, "Bring some of the fish which you have now caught."

11 Simon Peter went up, and drew the net to land, full of large fish, a hundred and fifty-three; and although there were so many, the net was not torn.

12 Jesus *said to them, "Come *and* have [R]breakfast." None of the disciples ventured to question Him, "Who are You?" knowing that it was the Lord.   John 21:15

13 Jesus *came and *took[R]the bread, and *gave them, and the fish likewise.   John 21:9

14 This is now the third time that Jesus [a]was manifested to the disciples, after He was raised from the dead.   *made Himself visible*

Christ Speaks to Peter

15 So when they had finished breakfast, Jesus *said to Simon Peter, "Simon, *son* of John, do you[T]love Me more than these?" He *said to Him, "Yes, Lord; You know that I [T]love You." He *said to him, "Tend [R]My lambs.   Gr., agapao • Gr., phileo • Luke 12:32

16 He *said to him again a second time, "Simon, *son* of John, do you[T]love Me?" He *said to Him, "Yes, Lord; You know that I [T]love You." He *said to him, "Shepherd[R]My sheep."   Gr., agapao • Gr., phileo • Rev. 7:17

17 He *said to him the third time, "Simon, *son* of John, do you[T]love Me?" Peter was grieved because He said to him[R]the third time, "Do you love Me?" And he said to Him, "Lord,[R]You know all things; You know that I love You." Jesus *said to him, "Tend My sheep.   Gr., phileo • John 13:38 • John 16:30

18"Truly, truly, I say to you, when you were younger, you used to gird yourself, and walk wherever you wished; but when you grow old, you will stretch out your hands, and someone else will gird you, and bring you where you do not wish to go."

19 Now this He said,[R]signifying by what kind of death he would glorify God. And when He had spoken this, He *said to him, "Follow[R]Me!"   John 12:33 • [Matt. 8:22; 16:24]

20 Peter, turning around, *saw the[R]disciple whom Jesus loved following *them;* the one who also had[R]leaned back on His breast at the supper, and said, "Lord, who is the one who betrays You?"   John 21:7 • John 13:25

21 Peter therefore seeing him *said to Jesus, "Lord, and what about this man?"

22 Jesus *said to him, "If I want him to remain[R]until I come, what *is that* to you? You[R]follow Me!"   James 5:7 • [Matt. 8:22; 16:24]

23 This saying therefore went out among the brethren that that disciple would not die; yet Jesus did not say to him that he would not die, but *only,* "If I want him to remain until I come, what *is that* to you?"

The Conclusion of John's Gospel

24 This is the disciple who[R]bears witness of these things, and wrote these things; and we know that his witness is true.   John 15:27

25 And there are also[R]many other things which Jesus did, which if they *were written in detail, I suppose that even the world itself *would not contain the books which *were written.   John 20:30

Measures of Length

Unit	Length	Equivalents	Translations
Day's journey	c. 20 miles		day's journey, day's walk
Roman mile	4,854 feet	8 stadia	mile
Sabbath day's journey	3,637 feet	6 stadia	a sabbath day's journey
Stadion	606 feet	⅛ Roman mile	mile, stadion
Rod	9 feet (10.5 feet in Ezekiel)	3 paces; 6 cubits	measuring rod
Fathom	6 feet	4 cubits	fathom
Pace	3 feet	⅓ rod; 2 cubits	pace
Cubit	18 inches	½ pace; 2 spans	cubit, yards
Span	9 inches	½ cubit; 3 handbreadths	span
Handbreadth	3 inches	⅓ span; 4 fingers	handbreadth
Finger	.75 inches	¼ handbreadth	finger

THE
ACTS OF THE APOSTLES

THE BOOK OF ACTS

Jesus' last recorded words have come to be known as the Great Commission: "You shall be My witnesses both in Jerusalem, and in all Judea and Samaria, and even to the remotest part of the earth" (1:8). The Book of Acts, written by Luke, is the story of the men and women who took that commission seriously and began to spread the news of a risen Savior to the most remote corners of the known world.

Each section of the book (1—7; 8—12; 13—28) focuses on a particular audience, a key personality, and a significant phase in the expansion of the gospel message.

As the second volume in a two-part work by Luke, this book probably had no separate title. But all available Greek manuscripts designate it by the title *Praxeis*, "Acts," or by an expanded title like "The Acts of the Apostles." *Praxeis* was commonly used in Greek literature to summarize the accomplishments of outstanding men. While the apostles are mentioned collectively at several points, this book really records the acts of Peter (1—12) and of Paul (13—28).

THE AUTHOR OF ACTS

Acts 1:1 refers Theophilus to "The first account," that is, the Gospel of Luke. (See "The Author of Luke" for the internal and external support for Lucan authorship of Luke.) Luke's source for the "we" sections in this book (16:10–17; 20:5—21:18; 27:1—28:16) was his own memory if not some kind of diary. For the remainder of this book, Luke no doubt followed the same careful investigative procedures that he used in writing his gospel (Luke 1:1–4). As a close traveling companion of Paul, Luke had access to the principal eyewitness for chapters 13—28. It is also likely that he had opportunities to interview such key witnesses in Jerusalem as Peter and John for the information in chapters 1—12. Acts 15:23–29 and 23:26–30 indicate that Luke may have used written documents as well.

THE TIME OF ACTS

Suggested dates for the writing of Acts range from A.D. 62 to the middle of the second century. Twentieth-century archaeological discoveries have strikingly confirmed the trustworthiness and precision of Luke as an historian and show that his work should be dated in the first century. Luke's perplexingly abrupt ending with Paul awaiting trial in Rome has led many to believe that Acts was completed prior to Paul's trial (A.D. 62). If it was written after this crucial event, why didn't Luke mention the outcome? Luke may have had a reason, but the simplest explanation of his silence is that Paul had not yet stood before Caesar. Acts gives no hint of the persecution under Nero (A.D. 64), Paul's death (A.D. 68), or the destruction of Jerusalem (A.D. 70).

THE CHRIST OF ACTS

The resurrected Savior is the central theme of the sermons and defenses in Acts. The Old Testament Scriptures, the historical resurrection, the apostolic testimony, and the convicting power of the Holy Spirit all bear witness that Jesus is both Lord and Christ (see Peter's sermons in 2:22—36 and 10:34—43). "Of Him all the prophets bear witness that through His name everyone who believes in Him receives forgiveness of sins" (10:43). "And there is salvation in no one else; for there is no other name under heaven that has been given among men, by which we must be saved" (4:12).

KEYS TO ACTS

Key Word: The Growth of the Church—While there are four accounts of the life of Jesus, this is the only book that carries on the story from His ascension to the period of the New Testament epistles. Thus, Acts is the historical link between the gospels and the epistles. Because of Luke's strong emphasis on the ministry of the Holy Spirit, this book could be regarded as "The Acts of the Spirit of Christ Working in and Through the Apostles." As a missionary himself, Luke's interest in the progressive spread of the gospel is obviously reflected in this apostolic history. Luke was personally involved as a participant in this story, so it was not written from a detached point of view.

From a theological standpoint, Acts was written to trace the development of the body of Christ over the one-generation transition from a primarily Jewish to a predominantly gentile membership. This apologetic work presents Christianity as distinct from Judaism but also as its fulfillment.

Key Verses: Acts 1:8 and 2:42–47—"But you shall receive power when the Holy Spirit has

come upon you; and you shall be My witnesses both in Jerusalem, and in all Judea and Samaria, and even to the remotest part of the earth" (1:8).

"And they were continually devoting themselves to the apostles' teaching and to fellowship, to the breaking of bread and to prayer. And everyone kept feeling a sense of awe; and many wonders and signs were taking place through the apostles. And all those who had believed were together, and had all things in common; and they *began* selling their property and possessions, and were sharing them with all, as anyone might have need. And day by day continuing with one mind in the temple, and breaking bread from house to house, they were taking their meals together with gladness and sincerity of heart, praising God, and having favor with all the people. And the Lord was adding to their number day by day those who were being saved" (2:42–47).

Key Chapter: Acts 2—Chapter 2 records the earth-changing events of the Day of Pentecost when the Holy Spirit comes, fulfilling Christ's promise to wait until the Holy Spirit arrives to empower and direct the witness. The Spirit transforms a small group of fearful men into a thriving, worldwide Church that is ever moving forward and fulfilling the Great Commission.

SURVEY OF ACTS

Luke begins the Book of Acts where he left off in his gospel. Acts records the initial fulfillment of the Great Commission of Matthew 28:19, 20 as it traces the beginning and growth of the New Testament church (this growth pattern can be seen in 1:15; 2:41, 47; 4:4; 5:14; 6:7; 9:31; 12:24; 13:49; 16:5; 19:20). Acts traces important events in the early history of Christianity from the ascen-sion of Christ to the outpouring of the Holy Spirit to the rapid progress of the gospel, beginning in Jerusalem and spreading throughout the Roman Empire.

Acts is a pivotal book of transitions: from the Gospels to the Epistles (history), from Judaism to Christianity (religion), from law to grace (divine dealing), from Jews alone to Jews and Gentiles (people of God), and from kingdom to church (program of God).

The three movements in Acts follow its key verse (1:8): witness in Jerusalem (1:1—8:4); witness in Judea and Samaria (8:5—12:25); witness to the remotest part of the earth (13—28).

Witness in Jerusalem (1:1—8:4): After appearing to His disciples "over *a period of* forty days" (1:3), the Lord tells them to wait in Jerusalem for the fulfillment of His promise concerning the Holy Spirit. Ten days after His ascension, this promise is significantly fulfilled as the disciples are suddenly empowered and filled with the Holy Spirit. The disciples are transformed and filled with courage to proclaim the brand new message of the resurrected Savior. Peter's powerful sermon, like all the sermons in Acts, is built upon the Resurrection, and 3,000 persons respond with saving faith. After dramatically healing a man who was lame from birth, Peter delivers a second crucial message to the people of Israel resulting in thousands of additional responses. The religious leaders arrest the apostles, and this gives Peter an opportunity to preach a special sermon to them.

The enthusiasm and joy of the infant church are marred by internal and external problems. Ananias and Sapphira receive the ultimate form of discipline because of their treachery, and the apostles are imprisoned and persecuted because of their witness. Seven men, in-

FOCUS	WITNESS IN JERUSALEM		WITNESS IN JUDEA AND SAMARIA	WITNESS TO THE REMOTEST PART OF THE EARTH	
REFERENCE	1:1————————3:1—————		8:5————————	13:1————21:17————	28:31
DIVISION	POWER OF THE CHURCH	PROGRESS OF THE CHURCH	EXPANSION OF THE CHURCH	PAUL'S THREE JOURNEYS	PAUL'S TRIALS
TOPIC	JEWS		SAMARITANS	GENTILES	
	PETER		PHILIP	PAUL	
LOCATION	JERUSALEM		JUDEA AND SAMARIA	UTTERMOST PART	
TIME	2 YEARS (A.D.33–35)		13 YEARS (A.D. 35–48)	14 YEARS (A.D. 48–62)	

cluding Stephen and Philip, are selected to assist the apostles. Stephen is brought before the Sanhedrin; in his defense, Stephen surveys the Scriptures to prove that the Man they condemned and killed was the Messiah Himself. The members of the Sanhedrin react to Stephen's words by dragging him out of the city and making him the first Christian martyr.

Witness in Judea and Samaria (8:5—12:25): Philip goes to the province of Samaria and successfully proclaims the new message to a people hated by the Jews. Peter and John confirm his work and exercise their apostolic authority by imparting the Holy Spirit to these new members of the body of Christ. God sovereignly transforms Saul the persecutor into Paul the apostle to the Gentiles, but He uses Peter to introduce the gospel to the Gentiles. In a special vision Peter realizes that Christ has broken down the barrier between Jew and Gentile. After Cornelius and other Gentiles come to Christ through his preaching, Peter convinces the Jewish believers in Jerusalem that "the Gentiles also had received the word of God" (11:1). Even while experiencing more and more persecution, the church continues to increase, spreading throughout the Roman Empire.

Witness to the Remotest Part of the Earth (13—28): Beginning with chapter 13, Luke switches the focus of Acts from Peter to Paul. Antioch in Syria gradually replaces Jerusalem as the headquarters of the church, and all three of Paul's missionary journeys originate from that city. The first journey (A.D. 48–49) concentrates on the Galatian cities of Pisidian, Antioch, Iconium, Lystra, and Derbe. After this journey, a council is held among the apostles and elders of the church in Jerusalem to determine that the gentile converts need not submit to the law of Moses. The second missionary journey (A.D. 50–52) brings Paul once again to the Galatian churches, and then for the first time on to Macedonia and Greece. Paul spends much of his time in the cities of Philippi, Thessalonica, and Corinth, and later returns to Jerusalem and Antioch. In his third missionary journey (A.D. 53–57), Paul spends almost three years in the Asian city of Ephesus before visiting Macedonia and Greece for the second time. Although he is warned not to go to Jerusalem, Paul cannot be dissuaded.

It is not long before Paul is falsely accused of bringing Gentiles into the temple. Only the Roman commander's intervention prevents his being killed by the mob. Paul's defense before the people and before the Sanhedrin evokes violent reactions. When the commander learns of a conspiracy to assassinate Paul, he sends his prisoner to Felix, the governor in Caesarea. During his two-year imprisonment there (A.D. 57–59), Paul defends the Christian faith before Felix, Festus, and Agrippa. His appeal to Caesar requires a long voyage to Rome, where he is placed under house arrest until his trial.

OUTLINE OF ACTS

Part One: The Witness in Jerusalem (1:1—8:4)

Part Two: The Witness in Judea and Samaria (8:5—12:25)

CHAPTER 1

Prologue to Acts

THE first account I composed, Theophilus, about all that Jesus began to do and teach, 2 until the day when He was taken up, after He had by the Holy Spirit given orders to the apostles whom He had chosen.

Appearances of the Resurrected Christ
Luke 24:44–49

3 To 'these He also presented Himself alive, after His suffering, by many convincing proofs, appearing to them over *a period of* forty days, and speaking of the things concerning the kingdom of God.   *whom*
4 And gathering them together, He commanded them not to leave Jerusalem, but to wait for what the Father had promised, "Which," *He said,* "you heard of from Me;
5 for John baptized with water, but you shall be baptized with the Holy Spirit 'not many days from now."   *after these many days*
6 And so when they had come together, they were asking Him, saying, "Lord, is it at this time You are restoring the kingdom to Israel?"   Matt. 17:11; Mark 9:12; Luke 17:20; 19:11
7 He said to them, "It is not for you to know times or epochs which the Father has fixed by His own authority;   Matt. 24:36

8 but you shall receive power when the Holy Spirit has come upon you; and you shall be My witnesses both in Jerusalem, and in all Judea and Samaria, and even to the remotest part of the earth."   [Acts 2:1–4]

Ascension of Christ
Mark 16:19; Luke 24:50, 51

9 And after He had said these things, He was lifted up while they were looking on, and a cloud received Him out of their sight.
10 And as they were gazing intently into the sky while He was departing, behold, two men in white clothing stood beside them;

11 and they also said, "Men of Galilee, why do you stand looking into the sky? This Jesus, who has been taken up from you into heaven, will come in just the same way as you have watched Him go into heaven."

Anticipation of the Spirit
Luke 24:52

12 Then they returned to Jerusalem from the 'mount called Olivet, which is near Jerusalem, a Sabbath day's journey away.   *hill*
13 And when they had entered, they went up to 'the upper room, where they were staying; that is, Peter and John and 'James and Andrew, Philip and Thomas, Bartholomew and Matthew, 'James *the son* of Alphaeus, and Simon the Zealot, and 'Judas *the son* of 'James.   Mark 14:15; Luke 22:12 • *Jacob* • John 14:22
14 These all with one mind were continually devoting themselves to prayer, along with 'the women, and Mary the mother of Jesus, and with His brothers.   *certain women*

Appointment of Matthias
Matt. 27:7, 8

15 And 'at this time Peter stood up in the midst of the brethren (a gathering of about one hundred and twenty 'persons was there together), and said,   *in these days* • *names*
16 "Brethren, the Scripture had to be fulfilled, which the Holy Spirit foretold by the mouth of David concerning Judas, who became a guide to those who arrested Jesus.
17 "For he was counted among us, and received his portion in this ministry."
18 (Now this man 'acquired a field with the price of his wickedness; and falling headlong, he burst open in the middle and all his bowels gushed out.   Matt. 27:3-10
19 And it became known to all who were living in Jerusalem; so that in 'their own language that field was called Hakeldama, that is, Field of Blood.)   Matt. 27:8; Acts 21:40
20 "For it is written in the book of Psalms, 'LET' HIS HOMESTEAD BE MADE DESOLATE,   Ps. 69:25

1:8 Empowered by God—One of the most common excuses for not becoming a Christian is the fear of failure to live the Christian life. Besides overlooking the fact that men cannot be saved on the basis of good works (Page 1230—Titus 3:5), this objection neglects the truth that God provides the power to live the Christian life. Before Christ was crucified He promised the coming of the Holy Spirit to help believers (Page 1083—John 16:13, 14). The subsequent events of the Book of Acts supply ample evidence of the fulfillment of this prophecy (Page 1097—Acts 4:7, 33; 6:8).

The power of the Holy Spirit was not designed solely for the first-century church. Rather, all Christians are indwelt by the Spirit and thus have His power available (Page 1153—1 Cor. 6:19). However, living the Christian life under the Spirit's power must not be thought of as simply allowing the Spirit to take control while the believer does nothing. The believer still must live the Christian life, though he does it through the Spirit's power. Romans 8:13 says, "if by the Spirit you are putting to death the deeds of the body, you will live." It is you who are to put to death the sinful deeds of the body, but you are to do it through the Spirit's power.

The Christian who struggles in his own strength to live the Christian life will fail. He must by faith appropriate daily the power of the Holy Spirit (Page 1137—Rom. 8:4, 5). Described practically, this means that the believer trusts the Spirit to empower him in specific instances such as sharing his faith with others, resisting temptation, being faithful, etc. There is no *secret formula* that makes the Spirit's power available. It is simply a reliance on the Spirit to help.

Now turn to Page 1229—Titus 1:2: Promise of God.

AND^RLET NO MAN DWELL IN IT';
and,   Ps. 109:8 ★
'HIS OFFICE LET ANOTHER MAN TAKE.'
21 "It is therefore necessary that of the men who have accompanied us all the time that^Rthe Lord Jesus went in and out ^Tamong us—   Luke 24:3 · *to us*
22 beginning ^Twith the baptism of John, until the day that He was taken up from us—one of these should become a^Rwitness with us of His resurrection."   *from* · Acts 1:8
23 And they put forward two men, Joseph called Barsabbas (who was also called Justus), and^RMatthias.   Acts 1:26
24 And they ^Rprayed, and said, "Thou, Lord, ^Rwho knowest the hearts of all men, show which one of these two Thou hast chosen   Acts 6:6; 13:3; 14:23 · 1 Sam. 16:7; Jer. 17:10
25 to ^Toccupy this ministry and ^aapostleship from which Judas turned aside to go to his own place."   *take the place of* · Gal. 2:8
26 And they ^Tdrew lots for them, and the lot fell ^Ato Matthias; and he was ^Tnumbered with the eleven apostles.   *gave · upon · chosen*

CHAPTER 2

Filling with the Holy Spirit

AND when the day of Pentecost had come, they were all together in one place.
2 And suddenly there came from heaven a noise like a violent, rushing wind, and it filled^Rthe whole house where they were sitting.   Acts 4:31
3 And there appeared to them tongues as of fire distributing themselves, and ^Tthey ^Arested on each one of them.   *it · sat*
4 And they were all^Rfilled with the Holy Spirit and began to ^Rspeak with other tongues, as the Spirit was giving them utterance.   Acts 1:5, 8 · Mark 16:17 ★

Speaking with Other Tongues

5 Now there were Jews living in Jerusalem, ^Rdevout men, from every nation under heaven.   Luke 2:25; Acts 8:2
6 And when this sound occurred, the multitude came together, and were bewildered, because they were each one hearing them speak in his own^Alanguage.   *dialect*
7 And they were amazed and marveled, saying, "Why, ^T are not all these who are speaking^RGalileans?   *Behold* · Matt. 26:73
8 "And how is it that we each hear *them* in our own ^Alanguage ^Tto which we were born?   *dialect · in*
9 "Parthians and Medes and Elamites, and residents of Mesopotamia, Judea and ^RCappadocia, Pontus and Asia,   1 Pet. 1:1
10 Phrygia and Pamphylia, Egypt and the districts of Libya around Cyrene, and visi-

tors from Rome, both Jews and ¹proselytes,
11 Cretans and Arabs—we hear them in our *own* tongues speaking of the mighty deeds of God."
12 And^Rthey all continued in amazement and great perplexity, saying to one another, "What does this mean?"   Acts 2:7
13 But others were mocking and saying, "They are full of ^Asweet wine."   *new wine*

Peter Explains Pentecost

14 But Peter, taking his stand with ^Rthe eleven, raised his voice and declared to them: "Men of Judea, and all you who live in Jerusalem, let this be known to you, and give heed to my words.   Acts 1:26
15 "For these men are not drunk, as you suppose, ^Rfor it is *only* the ²third hour of the day;   1 Thess. 5:7
16 but this is what was spoken of through the prophet Joel:
17   'AND^R IT SHALL BE IN THE LAST DAYS,'
         God says,
      'THAT I WILL POUR FORTH OF MY SPIRIT
         UPON ALL^TMANKIND;
      AND YOUR SONS AND YOUR DAUGHTERS
         SHALL PROPHESY,
      AND YOUR YOUNG MEN SHALL SEE VISIONS,
      AND YOUR OLD MEN SHALL DREAM
         DREAMS;   Joel 2:28-32 · *flesh*
18   EVEN UPON MY BONDSLAVES, BOTH
         MEN AND WOMEN,
      I WILL IN THOSE DAYS POUR FORTH OF
         MY SPIRIT
      And they shall prophesy.
19   'AND I WILL GRANT WONDERS IN THE
         SKY ABOVE,
      AND SIGNS ON THE EARTH BENEATH,
      BLOOD, AND FIRE, AND VAPOR OF
         SMOKE.
20   'THE SUN SHALL BE TURNED INTO DARKNESS,
      AND THE MOON INTO BLOOD,
      BEFORE THE GREAT AND GLORIOUS DAY
         OF THE LORD SHALL COME.
21   'AND IT SHALL BE, THAT ^REVERYONE
         WHO CALLS ON THE NAME OF THE
         LORD SHALL BE SAVED.'   Rom. 10:13
22 "Men of Israel, listen to these words: Jesus the Nazarene, a man attested to you by God with miracles and wonders and signs which God performed through Him in your midst, just as you yourselves know—
23 this *Man*, delivered up by the predetermined plan and foreknowledge of God, ^Ryou nailed to a cross by the hands of godless men and put *Him* to death.   Luke 23:33; 24:20
24 "And God raised Him up again, putting an end to the agony of death, since it was impossible for Him to be held in its power.
25 "For David says of Him,
      'I^RWAS ALWAYS BEHOLDING THE LORD
         IN MY PRESENCE;

---

¹ I.e., Gentile converts to Judaism   ² I.e., 9 a.m.

For He is at my right hand, that I may not be shaken.   Ps. 16:8–11 ★

26 'Therefore my heart was glad and my tongue exulted;

Moreover my flesh also will abide in hope;

27 Because Thou wilt not abandon my soul to ^RHades,   Matt. 11:23; Acts 2:31

Nor 'allow Thy Holy One to 'undergo decay.   *give • see corruption*

28 'Thou hast made known to me the ways of life;

Thou wilt make me full of gladness with Thy presence.'

29"Brethren^T, I may confidently say to you regarding the^Rpatriarch David that he both died and was buried, and his tomb is^Twith us to this day.   *Men brothers • Heb. 7:4 • among*

30"And so, because he was a prophet, and knew that^RGod had sworn to him with an oath to seat *one*^Tof his descendants upon his throne,   Ps. 132:11 ★ • *of the fruit of his loins*

31 he looked ahead and spoke of the resurrection of ³the Christ, that^RHe was neither abandoned to Hades, nor did His flesh^Tsuffer decay.   Ps. 16:10 ★ • *see corruption*

32"This Jesus ^RGod raised up again, to which we are all witnesses.   Ps. 68:18 ★

33"Therefore having been exalted^Ato the right hand of God, and^Rhaving received from the Father^Rthe promise of the Holy Spirit, He has^Rpoured forth this which you both see and hear.   *by* • Ps. 16:11 ★ • Gal. 3:14 • Acts 2:17

34"For it was not David who ascended into^Theaven, but he himself says: *the heavens*

'The^RLord said to my Lord,   Ps. 110:1 ★

"Sit at My right hand,

35 Until I make Thine enemies a footstool for Thy feet." '

36"Therefore let all the house of Israel know for certain that God has made Him both^RLord and^TChrist—this Jesus^Rwhom you crucified."   Luke 2:11 • *Messiah* • Acts 2:23

37 Now when they heard *this*, they were ^Apierced^Rto the heart, and said to Peter and the rest of the apostles, "Brethren, what shall we do?"   *smitten in conscience* • John 16:8 ★

38 And Peter *said* to them, "Repent^R and let each of you be^Rbaptized in the name of Jesus Christ for the forgiveness of your sins; and you shall receive the gift of the Holy Spirit. [Acts 3:19; 5:31; 20:21] • Acts 8:12, 16; 22:16

39"For the promise is for you and your children, and for all who are far off, as many as the Lord our God shall call to Himself."

40 And with many other words he solemnly^Rtestified and kept on exhorting them, saying, "Be^A saved from this^Rperverse generation!"   Luke 16:28 • *Escape* • Deut. 32:5

41 So then, those who had received his word were baptized; and there were added that day about three thousand ⁴souls.

Practices of the Early Church

42 And they were ^Rcontinually devoting themselves to the apostles' teaching and to fellowship, to ^Rthe breaking of bread and 'to prayer.   Acts 1:14 • [1 Cor. 10:16] • *the prayers*

43 And everyone kept feeling a sense of awe; and many^Rwonders and signs were taking place through the apostles.⁵   Acts 2:22

44 And all those who had believed ⁶were together, and had all things in common;

45 and they *began* selling their property and possessions, and were sharing them with all, as anyone might have need.

46 And day by day continuing with one mind in the temple, and breaking bread^Afrom house to house, they were taking their^Tmeals together with gladness and sincerity of heart,   *in the various private homes • food*

47 praising God, and^Rhaving favor with all the people. And the Lord was adding^Tto their number day by day^Rthose who were being saved.   Acts 5:13 • *together* • 1 Cor. 1:18

CHAPTER 3

Peter Heals the Lame Man

Now^RPeter and John were going up to the temple at the ⁷ninth *hour*, ^Rthe hour of prayer.   Acts 3:3, 4, 11 • Matt. 27:45; Acts 10:30

2 And a certain man who had been lame from his mother's womb was being carried along, whom they^Rused to set down every day at the gate of the temple which is called Beautiful, in order to beg ⁸alms of those who were entering the temple.   Luke 16:20

3 And when he saw ^RPeter and John about to go into the temple, he *began* asking to receive alms.   Luke 22:8; Acts 3:1, 4, 11

³ I.e., the Messiah   ⁴ I.e., persons
⁵ Some ancient mss. add *in Jerusalem; and great fear was upon all*   ⁶ Some ancient mss. do not contain *were*
⁷ I.e., 3 p.m.   ⁸ Or, *a gift of charity*

2:42–47 Benefits of Participation in the Local Church—The benefits of participation in a local church are immediately apparent. This passage records the first meeting of the first local church. From this passage seven benefits of participation in the local church are immediately apparent: instruction—"continually devoting themselves to the apostles' teaching"; fellowship—"and to fellowship"; observance of the ordinances—"breaking of bread"; corporate prayer—"to prayer"; effective outreach—"everyone kept feeling a sense of awe"; common cause—"had all things in common"; and mutual assistance—"were sharing them with all, as anyone might have need." In addition to these, four other benefits of participation in the local church are clear: worship (Page 1117—Acts 20:7); discipline (Page 982—Matt. 18:15–17; Page 1174—2 Cor. 13:1–10); pastoral oversight (Page 1264—1 Pet. 5:1–3); and obedience to God's command (Page 1245—Heb. 10:25). Participation in the local church is not optional for the child of God. It is imperative and yields eternal benefits.
Now turn to Page 995—Matt. 28:19: Sharing Our Faith: Why?

4 And Peter, along with John, fixed his gaze upon him and said, "Look at us!"

5 And he *began* to give them his attention, expecting to receive something from them.

6 But Peter said, "I do not possess silver and gold, but what I do have I give to you: [R]In the name of Jesus Christ the Nazarene—walk!"   Acts 2:22; 3:16; 4:10

7 And seizing him by the right hand, he raised him up; and immediately his feet and his ankles were strengthened.

8 [R]And[T]with a leap, he stood upright and *began* to walk; and he entered the temple with them, walking and leaping and praising God.   Acts 14:10 · *leaping up*

9 And [R]all the people saw him walking and praising God;   Acts 4:16, 21

10 and they were taking note of him as being the one who used to[R]sit at the Beautiful Gate of the temple to *beg* alms, and they were filled with wonder and amazement at what had happened to him.   John 9:8; Acts 3:2

11 And while he was clinging to[R]Peter and John, all the people ran together to them at the so-called [A]portico[R] of Solomon, full of amazement.   Luke 22:8 · *colonnade* · Acts 5:12

Peter's Second Sermon

12 But when Peter saw *this*, he replied to the people, "Men of Israel, why do you marvel at this, or why do you gaze at us, as if by our own power or piety we had made him walk?

13"The God of Abraham, Isaac, and Jacob, the God of our fathers, has glorified His[A]servant Jesus, *the one* whom you delivered up, and disowned in the presence of Pilate, when he had decided to release Him.   *Child*

14"But you disowned[R]the Holy and Righteous One, and[R]asked for a murderer to be granted to you,   Mark 1:24 · Luke 23:18, 25

15 but put to death the[A]Prince of life, *the one* whom God raised from the dead, *a fact* to which we are witnesses.   *Author*

16"And on the basis of faith[R]in His name, *it is* the name of [T]Jesus which has strengthened this man whom you see and know; and the faith which *comes* through Him has given him this perfect health in the presence of you all.   Acts 3:6 · *His*

17"And now, brethren, I know that you acted[R]in ignorance, just as your[R]rulers did also.   Acts 13:27; 26:9; Eph. 4:18 · Luke 23:13

18"But the things which[R]God announced beforehand by the mouth of all the prophets, that His [A]Christ should suffer, He has thus fulfilled.   Ps. 22; Is. 53:3★ · *Anointed One*

19"Repent[R]therefore and return, that your sins may be wiped away, in order that[T]times of refreshing may come from the presence of the Lord;   [Acts 2:38; 26:20] · 2 Thess. 1:7

[R]20 and that He may send Jesus, the[A]Christ appointed for you,   *Anointed One* · Mal. 3:1★

21 whom heaven must receive until the [T]period of restoration of all things about which God spoke by the mouth of His holy prophets from ancient time.   *periods, times*

22"Moses said, 'THE[R] LORD GOD SHALL RAISE UP FOR YOU A PROPHET LIKE ME FROM YOUR BRETHREN; TO HIM YOU SHALL GIVE HEED in everything He says to you. Acts 7:37

23 'And it shall be that every soul that does not heed that prophet shall be utterly destroyed from among the people.'

24"And likewise, all the prophets who have spoken, from Samuel and *his* successors onward, also announced these days.

25"It is you who are the sons of the prophets, and of the covenant which God made with your fathers, saying to Abraham, 'AND[R] IN YOUR SEED ALL THE FAMILIES OF THE EARTH SHALL BE BLESSED.' Gen. 12:3; 18:18★

26"For you first, God raised up His Servant, and sent Him to bless you by turning every one *of you* from your wicked ways."

CHAPTER 4

Peter and John Are Put into Custody

AND as they were speaking to the people, the priests and the captain of the temple *guard*, and the Sadducees, came upon them,

2 being greatly disturbed because they were teaching the people and proclaiming in Jesus the resurrection from the dead.

3 And they laid hands on them, and[R]put them in jail until the next day, for it was already evening.   Acts 5:18

4 But many of those who had heard the [A]message believed; and the number of the men came to be about five thousand.   *word*

Peter Preaches to the Sanhedrin

5 And it came about on the next day, that their[R]rulers and elders and scribes were gathered together in Jerusalem;   Luke 23:13

6 and Annas the high priest *was there*, and Caiaphas and John and Alexander, and all who were of high-priestly descent.

7 And when they had placed them in the center, they *began to* inquire, "By what power, or in what name, have you done this?"

8 Then Peter,[A]filled[R]with the Holy Spirit, said to them, "Rulers[R]and elders of the people,   *having just been filled* · Acts 2:4 · Acts 4:5

9 if we are on trial today for [R]a benefit done to a sick man,[A]as to how this man has been made well,   Acts 3:7f. · *by whom*

10 let it be known to all of you, and to all the people of Israel, that[A]by[R]the name of Jesus Christ the Nazarene, whom you crucified, whom God raised from the dead—[A]by [A]this *name* this man stands here before you in good health.   *in* · Acts 2:22; 3:6 · *him*

11"He[T] is the [R]STONE WHICH WAS REJECTED by you, THE BUILDERS, *but* WHICH BECAME THE VERY CORNER *stone*. *This One* · Ps. 118:22★

12"And there is salvation in^Rno one else; for there is no other name under heaven that has been given among men, by which we must be saved."   [Matt. 1:21; Acts 10:43]

Sanhedrin Commands Peter Not to Preach

13 Now as they observed the ^Rconfidence of Peter and John, and understood that they were uneducated and untrained men, they were marveling, and *began* to recognize them as having been with Jesus.   Acts 4:31
14 And seeing the man who had been healed standing with them, they had nothing to say in reply.
15 But when they had ordered them to go aside out of the^ACouncil,^R they *began* to confer with one another,   Sanhedrin • Matt. 5:22
16 saying, "What^Rshall we do with these men? For the fact that a^Rnoteworthy^Amiracle has taken place through them is apparent to all who live in Jerusalem, and we cannot deny it.   John 11:47 • Acts 3:7-10 • *sign*
17"But in order that it may not spread any further among the people, let us warn them to speak no more to any man in this name."
18 And when they had summoned them, they ^Rcommanded them not to speak or teach at all in the name of Jesus.   Acts 5:28f.
19 But^RPeter and John answered and said to them, "Whether^Rit is right in the sight of God to give heed to you rather than to God, you be the judge;   Acts 4:13 • Acts 5:28f.
20 for^Rwe cannot stop speaking what we have seen and heard."   1 Cor. 9:16
21 And when they had threatened them further, they let them go (finding no basis on which they might punish them) on account of the people, because they were all glorifying God for what had happened;
22 for the man was more than forty years old on whom this ^Amiracle of healing had been performed.   *sign*

Apostles' Prayer for Boldness

23 And when they had been released, they went to their own *companions*, and reported all that the chief priests and the elders had said to them.
24 And when they heard *this*, they lifted their voices to God with one accord and said, "O Lord, it is Thou who DIDST MAKE THE HEAVEN AND THE EARTH AND THE SEA, AND ALL THAT IS IN THEM,
25 who ^Rby the Holy Spirit, *through* the mouth of our father David Thy servant, didst say,

'WHY^RDID THE ⁹GENTILES RAGE,
AND THE PEOPLES DEVISE FUTILE
THINGS?   Acts 1:16 • Ps. 2:1★
26 'THE^RKINGS OF THE EARTH^ATOOK THEIR
STAND,   Ps. 2:2★ • *approached*
AND THE RULERS WERE GATHERED TO-
GETHER

AGAINST THE LORD, AND AGAINST HIS
^ACHRIST.'   *AnointedOne;* i.e., Messiah
27"For truly in this city there were gathered together against Thy holy ^Aservant Jesus, whom Thou didst anoint, both Herod and Pontius Pilate, along with the^AGentiles and the peoples of Israel,   *Child • nations*
28 to do whatever Thy hand and^RThy purpose predestined to occur.   Acts 2:23
29"And now, Lord, take note of their threats, and grant that Thy bond-servants may speak Thy word with all confidence,
30 while Thou dost extend Thy hand to heal, and ^Asigns and wonders take place through the name of Thy holy ^Aservant^R Jesus."   *attesting miracles • Child* • Acts 3:13
31 And when they had prayed, the^Rplace where they had gathered together was shaken, and they were all filled with the Holy Spirit, and *began* to speak the word of God with^Rboldness.   Acts 2:1 • Acts 4:13; 14:3

Early Church Voluntarily Shares

32 And the congregation of those who believed were of one heart and soul; and not one *of them* ^Tclaimed that anything belonging to him was his own; but all things were common property to them.   *was saving*
33 And ^Rwith great power the apostles were giving^Rwitness to the resurrection of the Lord Jesus, and abundant grace was upon them all.   [Acts 1:8] • Luke 24:48
34 For there was not a needy person among them, for all who were owners of land or houses^Rwould sell them and bring the proceeds of the sales,   [Matt. 19:21]
35 and^Rlay them at the apostles' feet; and they would be ^Rdistributed to each, as any had need.   Acts 4:37; 5:2 • Acts 2:45; 6:1
36 And Joseph, a Levite of Cyprian birth, who was also called Barnabas by the apostles (which translated means, Son of ^AEncouragement),   *Exhortation* or *Consolation*
37 and who owned a tract of land, sold it and brought the money and ^Rlaid it at the apostles' feet.   Acts 4:35; 5:2

CHAPTER 5

Ananias and Sapphira Lie

BUT a certain man named Ananias, with his wife Sapphira, sold a piece of property,
2 and kept back *some* of the price for himself, with his wife's^Afull knowledge, and bringing a portion of it, he ^Rlaid it at the apostles' feet.   *collusion* • Acts 4:35, 37
^R 3 But Peter said, "Ananias, why has Satan filled your heart^Rto lie to the Holy Spirit, and to^Rkeep back *some* of the price of the land?   John 13:2, 27 • Acts 5:4, 9 • Acts 5:2

⁹ Or, *nations*

4"While it remained *unsold,* did it not remain your own? And after it was sold, was it not under your control? Why is it that you have^conceived this deed in your heart? You have not lied to men, but to God."   *placed*

5 And as he heard these words, Ananias fell down and breathed his last; and great fear came upon all who heard of it.

6 And the^Tyoung men arose and^Rcovered him up, and after carrying him out, they buried him.   *younger* · John 19:40

7 Now there elapsed an interval of about three hours, and his wife came in, not knowing what had happened.

8 And Peter responded to her, "Tell me whether you sold the land^Tfor^Rsuch and such a price?" And she said, "Yes, that was the price."   *for so much* · Acts 5:2

9 Then Peter *said* to her, "Why is it that you have agreed together to^Rput^Rthe Spirit of the Lord to the test? Behold, the feet of those who have buried your husband are at the door, and they shall carry you out *as well."*   Acts 15:10 · Acts 5:3, 4

10 And she ^Rfell immediately at his feet, and breathed her last; and the young men came in and found her dead, and they carried her out and buried her beside her husband.   Ezek. 11:13; Acts 5:5

11 And ^Rgreat fear came upon the whole church, and upon all who heard of these things.   Acts 2:43; 5:5

Apostles' Mighty Miracles

12 And^Tat the hands of the apostles many signs and wonders were taking place among the people; and they were all with one accord in Solomon's portico.   *through*

13 But none of the rest dared to associate with them; however, ^Rthe people^Theld them in high esteem.   Acts 2:47; 4:21 · *were holding*

14 And all the more^Rbelievers in the Lord, multitudes of men and women, were constantly added to *their number;*   2 Cor. 6:15

15 to such an extent that they even carried the sick out into the streets, and laid them on cots and pallets, so that when Peter came by, ^Rat least his shadow might fall on any one of them.   Acts 19:12

16 And also the^Tpeople from the cities in the vicinity of Jerusalem were coming together, bringing people who were sick ^10or afflicted with unclean spirits; and they were all being healed.   *multitude*

Apostles Are Miraculously Freed from Prison

17 But the high priest rose up, along with all his associates (that is the sect of the Sadducees), and they were filled with jealousy;

18 and they laid hands on the apostles, and^Rput them in a public jail.   Acts 4:3

19 But ^Ran angel of the Lord during the

---

night opened the gates of the prison, and taking them out he said,   Matt. 1:20, 24

20"Go your way, stand and^speak to the people in the temple^Tthe whole message of this Life."   *continue to speak* · *all the words*

21 And upon hearing *this,* they entered into the temple^Rabout daybreak, and *began* to teach. Now when the high priest and his associates had come, they called the^Council together, even all the Senate of the sons of Israel, and sent *orders* to the prison house for them to be brought.   John 8:2 · *Sanhedrin*

22 But^Rthe officers who came did not find them in the prison; and they returned, and reported back,   Matt. 26:58; Acts 5:26

23 saying, "We found the prison house locked quite securely and the guards standing at the doors; but when we had opened up, we found no one inside."

24 Now when the captain of the temple *guard* and the chief priests heard these words, they were greatly perplexed about them as to what would come of this.

25 But someone came and reported to them, "Behold, the men whom you put in prison are standing in the temple and teaching the people!"

26 Then the captain went along with the officers and *proceeded* to bring them *back* without violence (for they were afraid of the people, lest they should be stoned).

27 And when they had brought them, they stood them^Tbefore^Rthe Council. And the high priest questioned them,   *in* · Acts 5:21, 34, 41

28 saying, "We gave you^Rstrict orders not to continue teaching in this name, and behold, you have filled Jerusalem with your teaching, and ^Rintend to bring this man's blood upon us."   Acts 4:18 · Matt. 23:35; 27:25

Apostles Preach to the Council

29 But Peter and the apostles answered and said, "We^Rmust obey God rather than men.   Acts 4:19

30"The^RGod of our fathers^Rraised up Jesus, whom you had put to death by hanging Him on a^Tcross.   Acts 3:13 · Acts 2:24 · *wood*

31 "He is the one whom God exalted^Tto His right hand as a^Prince and a^Savior, to grant ^Rrepentance to Israel, and forgiveness of sins.   *by* · *Leader* · Luke 2:11 · Luke 24:47

32"And we are witnesses^11 of these things; and^Rso *is* the Holy Spirit, whom God has given to those who obey Him."   John 15:26

Gamaliel's Advice

33 But when they heard this, they were ^Rcut^Tto the quick and were intending to slay them.   Acts 2:37; 7:54 · *in their hearts*

34 But a certain Pharisee named ^RGamaliel, a^Rteacher of the Law, respected by all the people, stood up in^Rthe Council and gave

---

^10 Lit., *and*   ^11 Some mss. add *in Him,* or, *of Him*

orders to put the men outside for a short time. Acts 22:3 • Luke 2:46; 5:17 • Acts 5:21

35 And he said to them, "Men of Israel, take care what you propose to do with these men.

36 "For some time ago Theudas rose up, claiming to be somebody; and a group of about four hundred men joined up with him. And he was slain; and all who followed him were dispersed and came to nothing.

37 "After this man Judas of Galilee rose up in the days of the census, and drew away *some* people after him, he too perished, and all those who followed him were scattered.

38 "And so in the present case, I say to you, stay away from these men and let them alone, for if this plan or ªaction should ᴿbe of men, it will be overthrown; *work* • Mark 11:30

39 but if it is of God, you will not be able to overthrow them; or else you may even be found ᵀfighting against God." [Prov. 21:30]

Apostles Are Beaten

40 And they took his advice; and after calling the apostles in, they flogged them and ordered them to speak no more in the name of Jesus, and *then* released them.

41 So they went on their way from the presence of the Council, rejoicing that they had been considered worthy to suffer shame for ᵀHis name. *the name* (par excellence)

42 And every day, in the temple and from house to house, they kept right on teaching and preaching Jesus *as* the ᵀChrist. Messiah

CHAPTER 6

Deacons Are Appointed

Nowᵀat this time while the disciples were increasing *in number,* a complaint arose on the part of the ¹²Hellenistic *Jews* against the *native*ᴿHebrews, because their widows were being overlooked in ᴿthe daily serving *of food.* *in these days* • 2 Cor. 11:22 • Acts 4:35

2 And the twelve summoned the ªcongregation of the disciples and said, "It is not desirable for us to neglect the word of God in order to serve tables. *multitude*

3 "But select from among you, ᴿbrethren, seven men of good reputation, ᴿfull of the Spirit and of wisdom, whom we may put in charge of this task. John 21:23 • Acts 2:4

4 "But we will devote ourselves to prayer, and to the ªministry of the word." *service*

5 And the statement found approval with the whole ᵀcongregation; and they chose Stephen, a man full of faith and of the Holy Spirit, and Philip, Prochorus, Nicanor, Timon, Parmenas and ᵀNicolas, a ¹³proselyte from Antioch. *multitude* • Gr., *Nikolaos*

6 And these they brought before the apostles; and after ᴿpraying, they ᴿlaid their hands on them. Acts 1:24 • Num. 8:10

7 And ᴿthe word of God kept on spreading; and the number of the disciples continued to increase greatly in Jerusalem, and a great many of the priests were becoming obedient to ᴿthe faith. Acts 12:24 • Gal. 1:23

8 And Stephen, full of grace and power, was performing great ᴿwonders and ªsigns among the people. John 4:48 • *attesting miracles*

Stephen Is Brought Before the Council

9 But some men from what was called the Synagogue of the Freedmen, *including* both Cyrenians and Alexandrians, and some from Cilicia and ᵀAsia, rose up and argued with Stephen. *west coast province of Asia Minor*

10 And *yet* they were unable to cope with the wisdom and the Spirit with which he was speaking.

11 Then they secretly induced men to say, "We have heard him speak blasphemous words against Moses and *against* God."

12 And they stirred up the people, the elders and the scribes, and they came upon him and dragged him away, and brought him ᵀbefore the ªCouncil. *into* • *Sanhedrin*

13 And they put forward false witnesses who said, "This man incessantly speaks against this holy place, and the Law;

14 for we have heard him say that ᴿthis Nazarene, Jesus, will destroy this place and alter ᴿthe customs which Moses handed down to us." Matt. 26:61 • Acts 15:1; 21:12

15 And fixing their gaze on him, all who were sitting in the ªCouncil ᴿsaw his face like the face of an angel. *Sanhedrin* • Matt. 5:22

CHAPTER 7

Stephen Preaches to the Council

Andᴺᴰ the high priest said, "Are these things so?"

2 And he said, "Hear me, brethren and fathers! The God of glory appeared to our father Abraham when he was in Mesopotamia, before he lived in ᵀHaran, Gr., *Kharran*

3 and said to him, 'DEPART FROM YOUR COUNTRY AND YOUR RELATIVES, AND COME INTO THE LAND THAT I WILL SHOW YOU.'

4 "Then he departed from the land of the Chaldeans, and settled in Haran. And from there, after his father died, God removed him into this country in which you are now living.

5 "And He gave him no inheritance in it, not even a foot of ground; and *yet,* even when he had no child, ᴿHe promised that HE WOULD GIVE IT TO HIM AS A POSSESSION, AND TO HIS OFFSPRING AFTER HIM. Gen. 12:7; 13:15

6 "But God spoke to this effect, that his OFFSPRING WOULD BE ALIENS IN A FOREIGN

¹² I.e., non-Palestinian Jews who normally spoke Greek
¹³ I.e., a Gentile convert to Judaism

LAND, AND THAT THEY WOULD BE ENSLAVED AND MISTREATED FOR FOUR HUNDRED YEARS.

7 " 'AND WHATEVER NATION TO WHICH THEY SHALL BE IN BONDAGE I MYSELF WILL JUDGE,' said God, 'AND [R]AFTER THAT THEY WILL COME OUT AND [14]SERVE ME IN THIS PLACE.'   Ex. 3:12

8 "And He gave him the covenant of circumcision; and so *Abraham* became the father of Isaac, and circumcised him on the eighth day; and Isaac *became the father of* Jacob, and Jacob *of* the twelve patriarchs.

9 "And the patriarchs[R]became jealous of Joseph and sold him into Egypt. And *yet* God was with him,   Gen. 37:11, 28; 39:2, 21f.

10 and rescued him from all his afflictions, and [R]granted him favor and wisdom in the sight of Pharaoh, king of Egypt; and he made him governor over Egypt and all his household.   Gen. 39:21; 41:40-46; Ps. 105:21

11 "Now a famine came over all Egypt and Canaan, and great affliction *with it;* and our fathers[T]could find no food.   *were not finding*

12 "But[R]when Jacob heard that there was grain in Egypt, he sent our fathers *there* the first time.   Gen. 42:2

13 "And on the second *visit* [R]Joseph made himself known to his brothers, and Joseph's family was disclosed to Pharaoh. Gen. 45:1-4

14 "And Joseph sent *word* and invited Jacob his father and all his relatives to come to him,[R]seventy-five persons *in all.*   Ex. 1:5

15 "And Jacob went down to Egypt and *there* passed away, he and our fathers.

16 "And *from there* they were removeJ to Shechem, and laid in the tomb which Abraham had purchased for a sum of money from the sons of Hamor in Shechem.

17 "But as the[R]time of the promise was approaching which God had assured to Abraham,[R]the people increased and multiplied in Egypt,   Gen. 15:13 • Ex. 1:7f.

18 until THERE AROSE ANOTHER KING OVER EGYPT WHO KNEW NOTHING ABOUT JOSEPH.

19 "It was he who took shrewd advantage of our race, and mistreated our fathers so that they would [A]expose their infants and they would not survive.   *put out to die*

20 "And it was at this time that[R]Moses was born; and he was lovely[T]in the sight of God; and he was nurtured three months in his father's home.   Ex. 2:2; Heb. 11:23 • *to God*

21 "And after he had been exposed, Pharaoh's daughter[A]took him away, and nurtured him as her own son.   *adopted him*

22 "And Moses was educated in all [R]the learning of the Egyptians, and he was a man of power in words and deeds.   1 Kin. 4:30

[14] Or, *worship*

23 "But when he was approaching the age of forty, [R]it entered his [T]mind to visit his brethren, the sons of Israel.   Ex. 2:11f. • *heart*

24 "And when he saw one *of them* being treated unjustly, he defended him and took vengeance for the oppressed by striking down the Egyptian.

25 "And he[T]supposed that his brethren understood that God was granting them[A]deliverance[T]through him; but they did not understand.   *was thinking • salvation • through his hand*

26 "And[R]on the following day he appeared to them as they were fighting together, and he tried to reconcile them in peace, saying, 'Men, you are brethren, why do you injure one another?'   Ex. 2:13f.

27 "But the one who was injuring his neighbor pushed him away, saying, 'WHO MADE YOU A RULER AND JUDGE OVER US?

28 'YOU DO NOT MEAN TO KILL ME AS YOU KILLED THE EGYPTIAN YESTERDAY, DO YOU?'

29 "And at this remark MOSES FLED, AND BECAME AN ALIEN IN THE LAND OF MIDIAN, where he became the father of two sons.

30 "And after forty years had passed, [R]AN ANGEL APPEARED TO HIM IN THE WILDERNESS OF MOUNT Sinai, IN THE FLAME OF A BURNING THORN BUSH.   Ex. 3:1f.; Is. 63:9

31 "And when Moses saw it, he *began* to marvel at the sight; and as he approached to look *more* closely, there came the voice of the Lord:

32 'I[R] AM THE GOD OF YOUR FATHERS, THE GOD OF ABRAHAM AND ISAAC AND JACOB.' And Moses shook with fear and would not venture to look.   Ex. 3:6; [Matt. 22:32]

33 "BUT[R]THE LORD SAID TO HIM, 'TAKE[R]OFF THE SANDALS FROM YOUR FEET, FOR THE PLACE ON WHICH YOU ARE STANDING IS HOLY GROUND.   Ex. 3:5 • Josh. 5:15

34 'I HAVE CERTAINLY SEEN THE OPPRESSION OF MY PEOPLE IN EGYPT, AND HAVE HEARD THEIR GROANS, AND I HAVE COME DOWN TO DELIVER THEM; [T]COME NOW, AND I WILL SEND YOU TO EGYPT.'   *and now hither!*

35 "This Moses whom they disowned, saying, 'WHO MADE YOU A RULER AND A JUDGE?' is the one whom God sent *to be* both a ruler and a deliverer with the help of the angel who appeared to him in the thorn bush.

36 "This[R] man led them out, performing wonders and signs in the land of Egypt and in the Red Sea and in the [R]wilderness for forty years.   Ex. 12:41 • Acts 7:42

37 "This is the Moses who said to the sons of Israel, 'GOD SHALL RAISE UP FOR YOU A PROPHET LIKE ME FROM YOUR BRETHREN.'

38 "This is the one who was in the congregation in the wilderness together with the

---

7:38 The Meaning of the Church—In modern English the word *church* is used in five ways: (1) a building designated as a place of worship, i.e., a church building; (2) all who profess faith in Christ regardless of particular theological beliefs; (3) a denomination; (4) a single organized Christian group, i.e., a local church; and (5) the Body of Christ, i.e., the universal church. While all of these are legitimate uses for modern English, the word

(continued on next page)

angel who was speaking to him on Mount Sinai, and *who was* with our fathers; and he received living oracles to pass on to you.

39"And our fathers were unwilling to be obedient to him, but repudiated him and in their hearts turned back to Egypt,

40 SAYING TO AARON, 'MAKE FOR US GODS WHO WILL GO BEFORE US; FOR THIS MOSES WHO LED US OUT OF THE LAND OF EGYPT—WE DO NOT KNOW WHAT HAPPENED TO HIM.'

41"And at that time they made a calf and brought a sacrifice to the idol, and were rejoicing in the works of their hands.

42"But God turned away and delivered them up to ^Aserve the host of heaven; as it is written in the book of the prophets, 'IT WAS NOT TO ME THAT YOU OFFERED VICTIMS AND SACRIFICES FORTY YEARS IN THE WILDERNESS, WAS IT, O HOUSE OF ISRAEL?   *worship*

43 'YOU^RALSO TOOK ALONG THE TABERNACLE OF MOLOCH AND THE STAR OF THE GOD ROMPHA, THE IMAGES WHICH YOU MADE TO WORSHIP THEM. I ALSO WILL REMOVE YOU BEYOND BABYLON.'   Amos 5:26, 27

44"Our fathers had the tabernacle of testimony in the wilderness, just as He who spoke to Moses directed *him* to make it according to the pattern which he had seen.

45"And having received it in their turn, our fathers^Rbrought it in with 'Joshua upon dispossessing the^Anations whom God drove out before our fathers, until the time of David.   Josh. 3:14ff.; 18:1 • Gr., *Jesus* • *Gentiles*

46"And *David* found favor in God's sight, and ^Rasked that he might find a dwelling place for the ¹⁵God of Jacob.   2 Sam. 7:1-16

47"But it was^RSolomon who built a house for Him.   1 Kin. 6:1-38; 8:20; 2 Chr. 3:1-17

48"However, ^Rthe Most High does not dwell in *houses* made by *human* hands; as the prophet says: Luke 1:32

49 'HEAVEN^RIS MY THRONE,
    AND EARTH IS THE FOOTSTOOL OF MY
       FEET;
    WHAT KIND OF HOUSE WILL YOU BUILD
       FOR ME?' says the Lord;
    'OR WHAT PLACE IS THERE FOR MY RE-
       POSE?   Is. 66:1; Matt. 5:34f.

50 'WAS^R IT NOT MY HAND WHICH MADE
    ALL THESE THINGS?'   Is. 66:2

51"You men who are^Rstiff-necked and uncircumcised in heart and ears are always resisting the Holy Spirit; you are doing just as your fathers did.   Ex. 32:9; 33:3, 5; Lev. 26:41

52"Which one of the prophets did your fathers not persecute? And they killed those who had previously announced the coming of the Righteous One, whose betrayers and murderers^Ryou have now become;   Acts 3:14

53 you who received the law as^Rordained by angels, and *yet* did not keep it." Heb. 2:2

54 Now when they heard this, they were ^Rcut^Tto the quick, and they *began* gnashing their teeth at him.   Acts 5:33 • *in their hearts*

55 But being ^Rfull of the Holy Spirit, he ^Rgazed intently into heaven and saw the glory of God, and Jesus standing at the right hand of God;   Acts 2:4 • John 11:41

56 and he said, "Behold, I see the heavens opened up and^Rthe Son of Man standing at the right hand of God."   Matt. 8:20

57 But they cried out with a loud voice, and covered their ears, and they rushed upon him with one impulse.

58 And when they had^Rdriven him out of the city, they *began* stoning *him*, and the witnesses laid aside their robes at the feet of a young man named Saul.   Lev. 24:14, 16

59 And they went on stoning Stephen as he ^Rcalled upon *the Lord* and said, "Lord Jesus, receive my spirit!" Acts 9:14, 21; 22:16

60 And^Rfalling on his knees, he cried out with a loud voice, "Lord,^Rdo not hold this sin against them!" And having said this, he^Afell asleep.   Luke 22:41 • Matt. 5:44 • *expired*

CHAPTER 8

Saul Persecutes the Church

AND^RSaul was in hearty agreement with putting him to death.   Acts 7:58; 22:20; 26:10

And on that day a great persecution arose against the church in Jerusalem; and they were all scattered throughout the regions of Judea and Samaria, except the apostles.

2 And *some* devout men buried Stephen, and made loud lamentation over him.

3 But ^RSaul *began* ravaging the church, entering house after house; and^Rdragging off men and women, he would put them in prison.   1 Cor. 15:9; Gal. 1:13; Phil. 3:6 • James 2:6

¹⁵ The earliest mss. read *house* instead of *God;* the Septuagint reads *God*

(continued from previous page)

church is used in the New Testament in only the last two senses—a local church, or the Body of Christ, the universal church. At its root, the word *church* means a "called-out group." It is used of the nation Israel (Acts 7:38) which was a group of people who were called out of the rest of the people of the world to have a special national relationship to God. It is used of a local church (Page 1206—1 Thess. 1:1, church of the Thessalonians; Page 1294—Rev. 2:1, church of Ephesus, etc.), and of the universal church, the Body of Christ (Page 1200—Col. 1:18). The universal church comprises all believers from the Day of Pentecost until the time God takes the church out of the world, and at which time His program for the church will be complete. The local church is a local, visible, temporal manifestation of the universal church. At one point in history the local and universal churches were identical (Page 1096—Acts 2:41). The universal church will not meet until "we all get to heaven" and once in session will never cease.

Now turn to Page 980—Matt. 16:18: The Origin of the Church.

4 Therefore, those who had been scattered went about preaching the word.

Philip Witnesses to the Samaritans

5 And[R]Philip went down to the city of Samaria and *began* proclaiming [T]Christ to them.   Acts 6:5; 8:26, 30 • the Messiah

6 And the multitudes with one accord were giving attention to what was said by Philip, as they heard and saw the [A]signs which he was performing.   *attesting miracles*

7 For *in the case of* many who had unclean spirits, they were coming out *of them* shouting with a loud voice; and many who had been paralyzed and lame were healed.

8 And there was[R]much rejoicing in that city.   John 4:40-42; Acts 8:39

9 Now there was a certain man named Simon, who formerly was practicing magic in the city, and astonishing the people of Samaria, claiming to be someone great;

10 and they all, from smallest to greatest, were giving attention to him, saying, "This[R] man is what is called the Great Power of God."   Acts 14:11; 28:6

11 And they were giving him attention because he had for a long time astonished them with his[R]magic arts.   Acts 8:9; 13:6

12 But when they believed Philip preaching the good news about the kingdom of God and the name of Jesus Christ, they were being baptized, men and women alike.

13 And even Simon himself believed; and after being baptized, he continued on with Philip; and as he observed[R]signs and [R]great miracles taking place, he was constantly amazed.   Acts 8:6 • Acts 19:11

14 Now when the apostles in Jerusalem heard that Samaria had received the word of God, they sent them Peter and John,

15 who came down and prayed for them, that they might receive the Holy Spirit.

16 For He had[R]not yet fallen upon any of them; they had simply been baptized[T]in the name of the Lord Jesus.   Matt. 28:19 • *into*

17 Then they[R]*began* laying their hands on them, and they were [R]receiving the Holy Spirit.   Mark 5:23; Acts 6:6 • Acts 2:4

18 Now when Simon saw that the Spirit was bestowed through the laying on of the apostles' hands, he offered them money,

19 saying, "Give this authority to me as well, so that everyone on whom I lay my hands may receive the Holy Spirit."

20 But Peter said to him, "May your silver perish with you, because you thought you could obtain the gift of God with money!

21"You have [R]no part or portion in this [A]matter, for your heart is not[R]right before God.   Deut. 10:9 • *teaching; lit., word* • Ps. 78:37

22"Therefore repent of this wickedness of yours, and pray the Lord that if possible, the intention of your heart may be forgiven you.

23"For I see that you are in the gall of bitterness and in the bondage of iniquity."

[16] Many mss. do not contain this verse

24 But Simon answered and said, "Pray to the Lord for me yourselves, so that nothing of what you have said may come upon me."

25 And so, when they had solemnly[R]testified and spoken[R]the word of the Lord, they started back to Jerusalem, and were[R]preaching the gospel to many villages of the Samaritans.   Luke 16:28 • Acts 13:12 • Acts 8:40

Philip Witnesses to the Ethiopian Treasurer

26 But [R]an angel of the Lord spoke to Philip saying, "Arise and go south to the road that descends from Jerusalem to Gaza." (This is a desert *road*.)   Acts 5:19; 8:29

27 And he arose and went; and behold, there was an Ethiopian eunuch, a court official of Candace, queen of the Ethiopians, who was in charge of all her treasure; and he had come to Jerusalem to worship.

28 And he was returning and sitting in his chariot, and was reading the prophet Isaiah.

29 And[R]the Spirit said to Philip, "Go up and join this[A]chariot."   Heb. 3:7 • *carriage*

30 And when Philip had run up, he heard him reading Isaiah the prophet, and said, "Do you understand what you are reading?"

31 And he said, "Well, how could I, unless someone guides me?" And he invited Philip to come up and sit with him.

32 Now the passage of Scripture which he was reading was this:

"HE[R] WAS LED AS A SHEEP TO SLAUGH-
     TER;   Is. 53:7
AND AS A LAMB BEFORE ITS SHEARER IS
     SILENT,
SO HE DOES NOT OPEN HIS MOUTH.

33 "IN[R] HUMILIATION HIS JUDGMENT WAS
     TAKEN AWAY;   Is. 53:8
WHO SHALL[A]RELATE HIS[A]GENERATION?
FOR HIS LIFE IS REMOVED FROM THE
     EARTH."   *describe* • *family* or *origin*

34 And the eunuch answered Philip and said, "Please *tell me*, of whom does the prophet say this? Of himself, or of someone else?"

35 And Philip[R]opened his mouth, and[R]beginning from this Scripture he [R]preached Jesus to him.   Matt. 5:2 • Acts 17:2 • Acts 5:42

36 And as they went along the road they came to some water; and the eunuch *said,* "Look! Water! [R]What prevents me from being baptized?"   Acts 10:47

37 [16]And Philip said, "If you believe with all your heart, you may." And he answered and said, "I believe that Jesus Christ is the Son of God."]

38 And he ordered the chariot to stop; and they both went down into the water, Philip as well as the eunuch; and he baptized him.

39 And when they came up out of the water, [R]the Spirit of the Lord snatched Philip away; and the eunuch saw him no more, but went on his way rejoicing.   Ezek. 3:12, 14; 8:3

40 But Philip[A]found himself at Azotus; and as he passed through he[R]kept preaching the

gospel to all the cities, until he came to ^RCaesarea.   *was found* • Acts 8:25 • Acts 9:30

CHAPTER 9

Saul Is Converted and Blinded
Acts 22:4–11; 26:13–18

NOW Saul, still ^Rbreathing ^Tthreats and murder against the disciples of the Lord, went to the high priest,   Acts 8:3 • *threat*

2 and asked for letters from him to ^Rthe synagogues at ^RDamascus, so that if he found any belonging to ^Rthe Way, both men and women, he might bring them bound to Jerusalem.   Matt. 10:17 • Gen. 14:15 • John 14:6

3 And it came about that as he journeyed, he was approaching Damascus, and ^Rsuddenly a light from heaven flashed around him;   1 Cor. 15:8

4 and ^Rhe fell to the ground, and heard a voice saying to him, "Saul, Saul, why are you persecuting Me?"   Acts 22:7; 26:14

5 And he said, "Who art Thou, Lord?" And He *said*, "I am Jesus whom you are persecuting,

6 but rise, and enter the city, and ^Rit shall be told you what you must do."   Acts 9:16

7 And the men who traveled with him ^Rstood speechless, ^Rhearing the ^Avoice, but seeing no one.   Acts 26:14 • John 12:29f. • *sound*

8 And Saul got up from the ground, and though his eyes were open, he ^Tcould see nothing; and leading him by the hand, they brought him into Damascus.   *was seeing*

9 And he was three days without sight, and neither ate nor drank.

Saul Is Filled with the Spirit

10 Now there was a certain disciple at Damascus, named Ananias; and the Lord said to him in ^Ra vision, "Ananias." And he said, "Behold, *here am* I, Lord."   Acts 10:3, 17, 19

11 And the Lord *said* to him, "Arise and go to the street called Straight, and inquire at the house of Judas for a man from Tarsus named Saul, for behold, he is praying,

12 and he has seen [17]in a vision a man named Ananias come in and lay his hands on him, so that he might regain his sight."

13 But Ananias answered, "Lord, I have heard from many about this man, ^Rhow much harm he did to ^RThy ^Asaints at Jerusalem;   Acts 8:3 • Acts 9:32, 41; 26:10 • *holy ones*

14 and here he ^Rhas authority from the chief priests to bind all who ^Rcall upon Thy name."   Acts 9:2, 21 • Acts 7:59

15 But the Lord said to him, "Go, for ^Rhe is a chosen [18]instrument of Mine, to bear My name before ^Rthe Gentiles and ^Rkings and the sons of Israel;   Eph. 3:7 • Rom. 1:5 • 2 Tim. 4:17

16 for ^RI will show him how much he must suffer for My name's sake."   Acts 20:23

17 And Ananias departed and entered the

house, and after ^Rlaying his hands on him said, "Brother ^RSaul, the Lord Jesus, who appeared to you on the road by which you were coming, has sent me so that you may regain your sight, and be ^Rfilled with the Holy Spirit."   Acts 6:6 • Acts 2:13 • Acts 2:4

18 And immediately there fell from his eyes something like scales, and he regained his sight, and he arose and was baptized;

19 and he took food and was strengthened.

Now ^Rfor several days he was with the disciples who were at Damascus,   Acts 26:20

Saul Preaches at Damascus

20 and immediately he *began* to proclaim Jesus ^Rin the synagogues, ^Tsaying, "He is ^Rthe Son of God."   Acts 13:5, 14 • *that* • Matt. 4:3

21 And all those hearing him continued to be amazed, and were saying, "Is this not he who in Jerusalem ^Rdestroyed those who ^Rcalled on this name, and *who* had come here for the purpose of bringing them bound before the chief priests?"   Acts 8:3 • Acts 9:14

22 But Saul kept increasing in strength and confounding the Jews who lived at Damascus by proving that this *Jesus* is the ^TChrist.   Messiah

Saul Witnesses in Jerusalem

23 And when many days had elapsed, the Jews plotted together to do away with him,

24 but ^Rtheir plot became known to Saul. And ^Rthey were also watching the gates day and night so that they might put him to death;   Acts 20:3, 19; 23:12, 30 • 2 Cor. 11:32f.

25 but his disciples took him by night, and let him down through *an opening in* the wall, lowering him in a large basket.

26 And ^Rwhen he had come to Jerusalem, he was trying to associate with the disciples; and they were all afraid of him, not believing that he was a disciple.   Acts 26:20

27 But ^RBarnabas took hold of him and brought him to the apostles and described to them how he had ^Rseen the Lord on the road, and that He had talked to him, and how at Damascus he had spoken out boldly in the name of Jesus.   Acts 4:36 • Acts 9:3-6

28 And he was with them ^Tmoving about freely in Jerusalem, speaking out boldly in the name of the Lord.   *going in and going out*

29 And he was talking and arguing with the ^RHellenistic *Jews;* but they were attempting to put him to death.   Acts 6:1

30 But when ^Rthe brethren learned *of it,* they brought him down to Caesarea and sent him away to Tarsus.   Acts 1:15

31 So ^Rthe church throughout all Judea and Galilee and Samaria ^Tenjoyed peace, being built up; and, going on in the fear of the

[17] Some mss. do not contain *in a vision*   [18] Or, *vessel*

Lord and in the comfort of the Holy Spirit, it continued to increase.   Acts 5:11 • *was having*

Peter Heals Aeneas at Lydda

32 Now it came about that as Peter was traveling through all *those parts,* he came down also to the saints who lived at Lydda.
33 And there he found a certain man named Aeneas, who had been bedridden eight years, for he was paralyzed.
34 And Peter said to him, "Aeneas, Jesus Christ heals you; arise, and make your bed." And immediately he arose.
35 And all who lived at[T]Lydda and Sharon saw him, and they turned to the Lord.   *Lod*

Peter Raises Dorcas at Joppa

36 Now in Joppa there was a certain disciple named Tabitha (which translated *in Greek* is called [A]Dorcas); this woman was abounding with deeds of kindness and charity, which she continually did.   *Gazelle*
37 And it came about[T]at that time that she fell sick and died; and when they had washed her body, they laid it in an [R]upper room.   *in those days* • Acts 1:13; 9:39
38 And since Lydda was near [R]Joppa, the disciples, having heard that Peter was there, sent two men to him, entreating him, "Do not delay to come to us."   Ezra 3:7; Jon. 1:3
39 And Peter arose and went with them. And when he had come, they brought him into the upper room; and all the [R]widows stood beside him weeping, and showing all the [19]tunics and garments that Dorcas used to make while she was with them.   Acts 6:1
40 But Peter [R]sent them all out and[R]knelt down and prayed, and turning to the body, he said, "Tabitha,[R] arise." And she opened her eyes, and when she saw Peter, she sat up.   Matt. 9:25 • Luke 22:41; Acts 7:60 • Mark 5:41
41 And he gave her his hand and raised her up; and calling the [A]saints and[R]widows, he presented her alive.   *holy ones* • Acts 6:1
42 And it became known all over [R]Joppa, and many believed in the Lord.   Josh. 19:46
43 And it came about that he stayed many days in Joppa with a certain tanner, Simon.

CHAPTER 10

Cornelius Sends for Peter

NOW there was a certain man at Caesarea named Cornelius, a centurion of what was [R]called the Italian [20]cohort,   Matt. 27:27
2 a devout man, and[R]one who feared God with all his household, and [R]gave many [21]alms to the *Jewish* people, and prayed to God continually.   [Acts 10:22, 35] • Luke 7:4f.
3 About[R]the [22]ninth hour of the day he clearly saw[R]in a vision[R]an angel of God who had *just* come in to him, and said to him, "Cornelius!"   Acts 3:1 • Acts 9:10 • Acts 5:19
4 And [R]fixing his gaze upon him and being much alarmed, he said, "What is it, Lord?" And he said to him, "Your prayers and [23]alms[R]have ascended[R]as a memorial before God.   Acts 3:4 • Rev. 8:4 • Matt. 26:13
5 "And now dispatch *some* men to[R]Joppa, and send for a man *named* Simon, who is also called Peter;   Acts 9:36
6 he is staying with a certain tanner *named* Simon, whose house is by the sea."
7 And when the angel who was speaking to him had departed, he summoned two of his servants and a devout soldier of those who were in constant attendance upon him,
8 and after he had explained everything to them, he sent them to[R]Joppa.   Acts 9:36

Peter Sees the Great Sheet

9 And on the next day, as they were on their way, and approaching the city, Peter went up on[R]the housetop about[R]the [24]sixth hour to pray.   Zeph. 1:5 • Ps. 55:17; Acts 10:3
10 And he became hungry, and was desiring to eat; but while they were making preparations, he[R]fell into a trance;   Acts 11:5; 22:17
11 and he *beheld[R]the[A]sky opened up, and a certain [25]object like a great sheet coming down, lowered by four corners to the ground,   John 1:51 • *heaven*
12 and there were in it all *kinds* of four-footed animals and [26]crawling creatures of the earth and birds of the[A]air.   *heaven*
13 And a voice came to him, "Arise, Peter, [A]kill and eat!"   *sacrifice*
14 But Peter said, "By no means, Lord, for [R]I have never eaten anything[A]unholy and unclean."   Ezek. 4:14; Dan. 1:8 • *profane; lit., common*
15 And again a voice *came* to him a second time, "What[R] God has cleansed, no longer consider[T]unholy." [Titus 1:15] • *common*
16 And this happened three times; and immediately the[A]object was taken up into the [A]sky.   *vessel • heaven*
17 Now while Peter was greatly perplexed [T]in mind as to what[R]the vision which he had seen might be, behold, [R]the men who had been sent by Cornelius, having asked directions for Simon's house, appeared at the gate;   *himself* • Acts 10:3 • Acts 10:8
18 and calling out, they were asking whether Simon, who was also called Peter, was[A]staying there.   *lodging*
19 And while Peter was reflecting on[R]the vision, the Spirit said to him, "Behold, three men are looking for you.   Acts 10:3
20 "But arise, go downstairs, and accompany them[T]without misgivings; for I have sent them Myself."   *doubting nothing*
21 And Peter went down to the men and

---

[19] Or, *inner garments*   [20] Or, *battalion*
[21] Or, *gifts of charity*   [22] I.e., 3 p.m.
[23] Or, *deeds of charity*   [24] I.e., noon   [25] Or, *vessel*
[26] Or possibly, *reptiles*

said, "Behold, I am the one you are looking for; what is the reason for which you have come?"
22 And they said, "Cornelius, a centurion, a righteous and God-fearing man well spoken of by the entire nation of the Jews, was *divinely* directed by a^aholy angel to send for you *to come* to his house and hear ^ra message from you."   Luke 9:26 · *words*

Peter Preaches to the Gentiles

23 And so he invited them in and gave them lodging.
And on the next day he arose and went away with them, and some of the brethren from ^RJoppa accompanied him.   Acts 9:36
24 And on the following day he entered ^RCaesarea. Now Cornelius was waiting for them, and had called together his relatives and close friends.   Acts 8:40; 10:1
25 And when it came about that Peter entered, Cornelius met him, and fell at his feet and^Rworshiped *him*.   Matt. 8:2
26 But Peter raised him up, saying, "Stand^Rup; I too am *just* a man."   Acts 14:15
27 And as he talked with him, he entered, and^Tfound many people assembled.   *finds*
28 And he said to them, "You yourselves know how unlawful it is for a man who is a Jew to associate with a foreigner or to visit him; and *yet* God has shown me that I should not call any man unholy or unclean.
29"That is why I came without even raising any objection when I was sent for. And so I ask for what reason you have sent for me."
30 And Cornelius said, "Four^Rdays ago to this hour, I was praying in my house during the ²⁷ninth hour; and behold, a man stood before me in shining garments, Acts 10:9, 22f.
31 and he *said, 'Cornelius, your prayer has been heard and your^Aalms have been remembered before God.   *deeds of charity*
32 'Send therefore to ^RJoppa and invite Simon, who is also called Peter, to come to you; he is^Astaying at the house of Simon *the tanner by the sea.*'   John 4:9; 18:28 · *lodging*
33"And so I sent to you immediately, and you have^Tbeen kind enough to come. Now then, we are all here present before God to hear all that you have been commanded by the Lord."   *done well in coming*
34 And opening his mouth, Peter said: "I most certainly understand *now* that^RGod is not one to show partiality,   Deut. 10:17
35 but in every nation the man who^Afears^R Him and^Tdoes what is right, is welcome to Him.   *reverences* · Acts 10:2 · *works righteousness*
36"The word which He sent to the sons of Israel, preaching^Apeace through Jesus Christ (He is Lord of all)—   *the gospel of peace*
37 you yourselves know the thing which took place throughout all Judea, starting from Galilee, after the baptism which John proclaimed.

38"*You know of* Jesus of Nazareth, how God anointed Him with the Holy Spirit and with power, and *how* He went about doing good, and healing all who were oppressed by the devil; for God was with Him.
39"And we are witnesses of all the things He did both in the land of the Jews and in Jerusalem. And they also put Him to death by hanging Him on a^Tcross.   *wood*
40"God raised Him up on the third day, and granted that He should become visible,
41 ^Rnot to all the people, but to witnesses who were chosen beforehand by God, *that is*, to us, who ate and drank with Him after He arose from the dead. John 14:19, 22; 15:27 ★
42"And He ordered us to^Apreach to the people, and solemnly to testify that this is the One who has been appointed by God as Judge of the living and the dead.   *proclaim*
43"Of Him all the prophets bear witness that through His name everyone who believes in Him receives forgiveness of sins."

Gentiles Are Converted and Speak in Tongues

44 While Peter was still speaking these words, the Holy Spirit fell upon all those who were listening to the^Tmessage.   *word*
45 And all the circumcised believers who had come with Peter were amazed, because the gift of the Holy Spirit had been^Rpoured out upon the Gentiles also.   Acts 2:33, 38
46 For they were hearing them^Rspeaking with tongues and exalting God. Then Peter answered,   Mark 16:17; Acts 2:4; 19:6
47"Surely no one can refuse the water for these to be baptized who^Ahave received the Holy Spirit just as we *did*, can he?" Acts 2:4
48 And he^Rordered them to be baptized in the name of Jesus Christ. Then they asked him to stay on for a few days. 1 Cor. 1:14-17

CHAPTER 11

Peter Defends His Ministry to the Gentiles

NOW the apostles and the brethren who were throughout Judea heard that the Gentiles also had received the word of God.
2 And when Peter came up to Jerusalem, ^Tthose who were circumcised took issue with him, *those of the circumcision;* i.e., Jewish Christians
3 saying, "You^Awent to uncircumcised men and ate with them."   *entered the house of*
4 But Peter began *speaking* and proceeded to explain to them ^Rin orderly sequence, saying,   Luke 1:3
5"I^Twas in the city of Joppa praying; and in a trance I saw a vision, a certain^Aobject coming down like a great sheet lowered by four corners from^Athe sky; and it came right down to me,   Acts 10:9-32 · *vessel* · *heaven*

²⁷ I.e., 3 to 4 p.m.

6 and when I had fixed my gaze upon it and was observing it [T]I saw the four-footed animals of the earth and the wild beasts and the [28]crawling creatures and the birds of the [A]air.   *and I saw · heaven*

7"And I also heard a voice saying to me, 'Arise, Peter; [k]kill and eat.'   *sacrifice*

8"But I said, 'By no means, Lord, for nothing [A]unholy or unclean has ever entered my mouth.'   *profane; lit., common*

9"But a voice from heaven answered a second time, 'What God has cleansed, no longer [T]consider unholy.'   *make common*

10"And this happened three times, and everything was drawn back up into the sky.

11"And behold, at that moment three men appeared before the house in which we were *staying*, having been sent to me from [R]Caesarea.   Acts 8:40

12"And the Spirit told me to go with them [A]without misgivings. And these six brethren also went with me, and we entered the man's house.   *without making any distinction*

13"And he reported to us how he had seen the angel standing in his house, and saying, 'Send to Joppa, and have Simon, who is also called Peter, brought here;

14 and he shall speak [R]words to you by which you will be saved, you and [R]all your household.'   Acts 10:22 · John 4:53; Acts 10:2

15"And as I began to speak, [n]the Holy Spirit fell upon them, just [R]as He did upon us at the beginning.   Acts 10:44 · Acts 2:4

16"And I remembered the word of the Lord, how He used to say, 'John[R] baptized with water, but you shall be baptized[A]with the Holy Spirit.'   Acts 1:5 · *in*

17"If God therefore gave to them the same gift as *He gave* to us also after believing in the Lord Jesus Christ, who was I that I could[A]stand in God's way?"   *prevent God*

18 And when they heard this, they[T]quieted down, and glorified God, saying, "Well then, God has granted to the Gentiles also the repentance *that leads* to life."   *became silent*

The Witness of the Antioch Church

19 So then those who were scattered because of the persecution that arose in connection with Stephen made their way to Phoenicia and Cyprus and Antioch, speaking the word to no one except to Jews alone.

20 But there were some of them, men of Cyprus and [R]Cyrene, who came to Antioch and *began* speaking to the [29]Greeks also, preaching the Lord Jesus.   Matt. 27:32

21 And [R]the hand of the Lord was with them, and [R]a large number who believed turned to the Lord.   Luke 1:66 · Acts 2:47

22 And the[T]news about them reached the ears of the church at Jerusalem, and they sent Barnabas off[T]to Antioch.   *word · as far as*

23 Then when he had come and witnessed the grace of God, he rejoiced and *began* to encourage them all with [T]resolute heart to remain *true* to the Lord;   *purpose of heart*

24 for he was a good man, and full of the Holy Spirit and of faith. And considerable numbers were[T]brought to the Lord.   *added*

25 And he left for Tarsus to look for Saul;

26 and when he had found him, he brought him to Antioch. And it came about that for an entire year they[A]met with the church, and taught considerable [T]numbers; and the disciples were first called Christians in Antioch.   *were gathered together · multitude*

27 Now at this time some prophets came down from Jerusalem to [R]Antioch.   Acts 6:5

28 And one of them named Agabus stood up and *began* to indicate[A]by the Spirit that there would certainly be a great famine all over the [T]world. And this took place in the reign of Claudius.   *through · inhabited earth*

29 And in the proportion that any of the disciples had means, each of them determined to send *a contribution* for the[T]relief of the brethren living in Judea.   *service*

30 And this they did, sending it in charge of Barnabas and Saul to the[R]elders.   3 John 1

CHAPTER 12

Herod Kills James

NOW about that time[T]Herod the king laid hands on some who belonged to the church, in order to mistreat them.   Herod Agrippa I

2 And he[R]had James the brother of John put to death with a sword.   Matt. 4:21; 20:23

Peter Is Miraculously Released from Prison

3 And when he saw that it pleased the Jews, he proceeded to arrest Peter also. Now[T]it was during[R]the days of Unleavened Bread.   *they were the days · Ex. 12:15; 23:15*

4 And when he had seized him, he put him in prison, delivering him to four squads of soldiers to guard him, intending after the Passover to bring him out before the people.

5 So Peter was kept in the prison, but prayer for him was being made fervently by the church to God.

6 And on the very night when Herod was about to bring him forward, Peter was sleeping between two soldiers,[R]bound with two chains; and guards in front of the door were watching over the prison.   Acts 21:33

7 And behold,[R]an angel of the Lord suddenly[R]appeared, and a light shone in the cell; and he struck Peter's side and roused him, saying, "Get up quickly." And his chains fell off his hands.   Acts 5:19 · Luke 2:9; 24:4

8 And the angel said to him, "Gird yourself and[T]put on your sandals." And he did so. And he *said to him, "Wrap your cloak around you and follow me."   *bind*

---

[28] Or possibly, *reptiles*
[29] Some mss. read *Greek-speaking Jews*

9 And he went out and continued to follow, and he did not know that what was being done by the angel was real, but thought he was seeing[R]a vision.   Acts 9:10

10 And when they had passed the first and second guard, they came to the iron gate that leads into the city, which[R]opened for them by itself; and they went out and went along one street; and immediately the angel departed from him.   Acts 5:19; 16:26

11 And when Peter came to himself, he said, "Now I know for sure that the Lord has sent forth His angel and rescued me from the hand of Herod and from all that the Jewish people were expecting."

12 And when he realized this, he went to the house of Mary, the mother of John who was also called Mark, where many were gathered together and were praying.

13 And when he knocked at the door of the gate,[R]a servant-girl named Rhoda came to answer.   John 18:16f.

14 And when she recognized Peter's voice, because of her joy she did not open the gate, but ran in and announced that Peter was standing in front of the gate.

15 And they said to her, "You are out of your mind!" But she kept insisting that it was so. And they kept saying, "It is[R]his angel."   [Matt. 18:10]

16 But Peter continued knocking; and when they had opened the door, they saw him and were amazed.

17 But[R]motioning to them with his hand to be silent, he described to them how the Lord had led him out of the prison. And he said, "Report these things to [A]James and [R]the brethren." And he departed and went to another place.   Acts 13:16 • Jacob • Acts 1:15

18 Now when day came, there was no small disturbance among the soldiers as to what could have become of Peter.

19 And when Herod had searched for him and had not found him, he examined the guards and ordered that they be led away to execution. And he went down from Judea to Caesarea and was spending time there.

Herod Blasphemes and Dies

20 Now he was very angry with the people of Tyre and Sidon; and with one accord they came to him, and having won over Blastus the king's chamberlain, they were asking for peace, because[R]their country was fed by the king's country.   Ezra 3:7; Ezek. 27:17

21 And on an appointed day Herod, having put on his royal apparel, took his seat on the [A]rostrum and began delivering an address to them.   judgment seat

22 And the people kept crying out, "The voice of a god and not of a man!"

23 And immediately an angel of the Lord struck him because he did not give God the glory, and he was eaten by worms and died.

24 But[R]the word of the Lord continued to grow and to be multiplied.   Acts 6:7; 19:20

25 And Barnabas and Saul returned from Jerusalem when they had fulfilled their[T]mission, taking along with them[R]John, who was also called Mark.   ministry • Acts 12:12

CHAPTER 13

Barnabas and Saul Are Sent from Antioch

NOW there were at[R]Antioch, in the[R]church that was there,[R]prophets and teachers: Barnabas, and Simeon who was called Niger, and Lucius of Cyrene, and Manaen who had been brought up with Herod the tetrarch, and Saul.   Acts 11:19 • Acts 11:26 • Acts 11:27

2 And while they were ministering to the Lord and fasting, the Holy Spirit said, "Set apart for Me Barnabas and Saul for the work to which I have called them."

3 Then, when they had fasted and[R]prayed and [R]laid their hands on them, [R]they sent them away.   Acts 1:24 • Acts 6:6 • Acts 13:4

Preaching in the Synagogues

4 So, being[R]sent out by the Holy Spirit, they went down to Seleucia and from there they sailed to[R]Cyprus.   Acts 13:2f. • Acts 4:36

5 And when they reached Salamis, they began to proclaim the word of God in[R]the synagogues of the Jews; and they also had [R]John as their helper.   Acts 9:20 • Acts 12:12

Controversy with Bar-Jesus

6 And when they had gone through the whole island as far as Paphos, they found a certain [R]magician, a Jewish false prophet whose name was Bar-Jesus,   Acts 8:9

7 who was with the[R]proconsul, Sergius Paulus, a man of intelligence. This man summoned Barnabas and Saul and sought to hear the word of God.   Acts 13:8, 12; 18:12

8 But Elymas the[R]magician (for thus his name is translated) was opposing them, seeking to turn the[R]proconsul away from[R]the faith.   Acts 8:9 • Acts 13:7, 12 • Acts 6:7

9 But Saul, who was also known as Paul, [A]filled[R] with the Holy Spirit, fixed his gaze upon him,   having just been filled • Acts 2:4; 4:8

10 and said, "You who are full of all deceit and fraud, you[R]son of the devil, you enemy of all righteousness, will you not cease to make crooked [R]the straight ways of the Lord?   Matt. 13:38; John 8:44 • Hos. 14:9

11 "And now, behold,[R]the hand of the Lord is upon you, and you will be blind and not see the sun for a time." And immediately a mist and a darkness fell upon him, and he went about seeking those who would lead him by the hand.   Job 19:21; Ps. 32:4; Heb. 10:31

12 Then the[R]proconsul believed when he

saw what had happened, being amazed at the teaching of the Lord.   Acts 13:7, 8; 18:12

13 Now Paul and his companions put out to sea from [R]Paphos and came to [R]Perga in Pamphylia; and John left them and returned to Jerusalem.   Acts 13:6 · Acts 14:25

Paul Preaches on First Sabbath

14 But going on from Perga, they arrived at Pisidian Antioch, and on the Sabbath day they went into the synagogue and sat down.

15 And after the reading of the Law and the Prophets the synagogue officials sent to them, saying, "Brethren, if you have any word of exhortation for the people, say it."

16 And Paul stood up, and [R]motioning with his hand, he said,   Acts 12:17

"Men of Israel, and [R]you who fear God, listen: Acts 10:2; 13:26

17 "The God of this people Israel chose our fathers, and made the people great during their stay in the land of Egypt, and with an uplifted arm He led them out from it.

18 "And for a period of about forty years He put up with them in the wilderness.

19 "And when He had destroyed seven nations in the land of Canaan, He distributed their land as an inheritance—*all of which took* about four hundred and fifty years.

20 "And after these things He [R]gave *them* judges until Samuel the prophet.   Judg. 2:16

21 "And then they asked for a king, and God gave them Saul the son of Kish, a man of the tribe of Benjamin, for forty years.

22 "And after He had removed him, He raised up David to be their king, concerning whom He also testified and said, 'I HAVE FOUND DAVID the son of Jesse, A MAN AFTER MY HEART, who will do all My[T]will.'   *wills*

23 "From[R]the offspring of this man, according to promise, God has brought to Israel[R]a Savior, Jesus,   Matt. 1:1 ★ · Luke 2:11; John 4:42

24 after John had proclaimed before [T]His coming a baptism of repentance to all the people of Israel.   *the face of His entering*

25 "And while John was completing his course, [R]he kept saying, 'What do you suppose that I am? I am not *He.* But behold, one is coming after me the sandals of whose feet I am not worthy to untie.'   Mark 1:7; Luke 3:16

26 "Brethren, sons of Abraham's family, and those among you who fear God, to us the word of this salvation is sent out.

27 "For those who live in Jerusalem, and their rulers, recognizing neither Him nor the [T]utterances of [R]the prophets which are [R]read every Sabbath, fulfilled *these* by condemning *Him.*   *voices* · Luke 24:27 · Acts 13:15

28 "And though they found no ground for *putting Him to* death, they[R]asked Pilate that He be[T]executed.   Matt. 27:22, 23 · *destroyed*

29 "And when they had carried out all that was written concerning Him,[R]they took Him down from the [T]cross and [R]laid Him in a tomb.   Luke 23:53 · *wood* · Matt. 27:57-61

30 "But God raised Him from the dead;

31 and for many days He appeared to those who came up with Him from Galilee to Jerusalem, the very ones who are now [R]His witnesses to the people.   Luke 24:48

32 "And we preach to you the good news of the[R]promise made to the fathers,   Heb. 1:5

33 that God has fulfilled this *promise* to our children in that He raised up Jesus, as it is also written in the second Psalm, 'THOU ART MY SON; TODAY I HAVE BEGOTTEN THEE.'

34 "*And as for the fact* that He raised Him up from the dead, no more to return to decay, He has spoken in this way: 'I WILL GIVE YOU THE HOLY *and* SURE *blessings* OF DAVID.'

35 "Therefore He also says in another *Psalm,* 'THOU WILT NOT [R]ALLOW THY HOLY ONE TO UNDERGO DECAY.'   Ps. 16:10 ★

36 "For David, after he had served the purpose of God in his own generation, [R]fell asleep, and was laid among his fathers, and [T]underwent decay;   1 Kin. 2:10 · *saw corruption*

37 but He whom God [R]raised did not [T]undergo decay.   Acts 2:24 · *see corruption*

38 "Therefore let it be known to you, brethren, that[R]through [T]Him forgiveness of sins is proclaimed to you,   Luke 24:47 · *this One*

39 and through Him [R]everyone who believes is [T]freed from all things, from which you could not be[T]freed through the Law of Moses.   Acts 10:43; [Rom. 3:28; 10:4] · *justified*

40 "Take [R]heed therefore, so that the thing spoken of [R]in the Prophets may not come upon *you:*   Luke 24:44; John 6:45; Acts 7:42

41   'BEHOLD,[R] YOU SCOFFERS, AND MARVEL, AND[T]PERISH;   Hab. 1:5 · *disappear*
     FOR I AM ACCOMPLISHING A WORK IN YOUR DAYS,
     A WORK WHICH YOU WILL NEVER BELIEVE, THOUGH SOMEONE SHOULD DESCRIBE IT TO YOU.' "

42 And as [T]Paul and Barnabas were going out, [T]the people kept begging that these [T]things might be spoken to them the next [R]Sabbath.   *they were · they · words* · Acts 13:14

43 Now when *the meeting of* the synagogue had broken up, many of the Jews and of the God-fearing proselytes followed Paul and Barnabas, who, speaking to them, were urging them to continue in the grace of God.

Paul Preaches on Second Sabbath

44 And the next Sabbath nearly the whole city assembled to hear the word of God.

45 But when [R]the Jews saw the crowds, they were filled with jealousy, and *began* contradicting the things spoken by Paul, and were[A]blaspheming.   1 Thess. 2:16 · *reviling*

46 And Paul and Barnabas spoke out boldly and said, "It was necessary that the word of God should be spoken to you[R]first; since you repudiate it, and judge yourselves unworthy of eternal life, behold, [R]we are turning to the Gentiles.   Acts 3:26 · Acts 18:6

47 "For thus the Lord has commanded us,

'I[R] HAVE PLACED YOU AS A [R]LIGHT FOR THE GENTILES,   Is. 42:6★ • Luke 2:32 THAT YOU SHOULD BRING SALVATION TO THE END OF THE EARTH.'"

48 And when the Gentiles heard this, they *began* rejoicing and glorifying the word of the Lord; and as many as [R]had been appointed to eternal life believed.   Rom. 8:28ff.

49 And [R]the word of the Lord was being spread through the whole region.   Acts 13:12

50 But the Jews aroused the [A]devout women of prominence and the leading men of the city, and instigated a persecution against Paul and Barnabas, and drove them out of their [T]district.   *worshiping • boundaries*

Ministry at Iconium

51 But [R]they shook off the dust of their feet *in protest* against them and went to [R]Iconium.   [Luke 9:5; 10:11] • Acts 14:1, 19, 21; 16:2

52 And the disciples were continually filled with joy and with the Holy Spirit.

CHAPTER 14

AND it came about that in Iconium[R]they entered the synagogue of the Jews together, and spoke in such a manner [R]that a great multitude believed, both of Jews and of [R]Greeks.   Acts 13:5 • Acts 2:47 • John 7:35

2 But the Jews who disbelieved stirred up the [T]minds of the Gentiles, and embittered them against the brethren.   *souls*

3 Therefore they spent a long time *there* speaking boldly *with reliance* upon the Lord, who was bearing witness to the word of His grace, granting that [A]signs and wonders be done by their hands.   *attesting miracles*

4 But the multitude of the city was divided; and some [T]sided with the Jews, and some with[R]the apostles.   *were* • Acts 14:14

5 And when an attempt was made by both the Gentiles and the Jews with their rulers, to mistreat and to stone them,

A Lame Man Is Healed

6 they became aware of it and fled to the cities of Lycaonia, [R]Lystra and Derbe, and the surrounding region;   Acts 14:8, 21

7 and there they continued to[R]preach the gospel.   Acts 14:15, 21; 16:10

8 And at[R]Lystra there was sitting[R]a certain man, without strength in his feet, lame from his mother's womb, who had never walked.   Acts 14:6, 21; 16:1f. • Acts 3:2

9 This man was listening to Paul as he spoke, who,[R]when he had fixed his gaze upon him, and had seen that he had[R]faith to be[T]made well,   Acts 3:4 • Matt. 9:28 • *saved*

10 said with a loud voice, "Stand upright on your feet." [R]And he leaped up and *began* to walk.   Acts 3:8

Paul and Barnabas Are Deified

11 And when the multitudes saw what Paul had done, they raised their voice, saying in the [R]Lycaonian language, "The[R] gods have become like men and have come down to us."   Acts 14:6 • Acts 8:10; 28:6

12 And they *began* calling Barnabas, Zeus, and Paul, Hermes, because he was[T]the chief speaker.   *the leader of the speaking*

13 And the priest of Zeus, whose *temple* was[T]just outside the city, brought oxen and garlands to the gates, and wanted to offer sacrifice with the crowds.   *in front of*

14 But when the apostles, Barnabas and Paul, heard of it, they tore their robes and rushed out into the crowd, crying out

15 and saying, "Men, why are you doing these things? We are also men of the same nature as you, and preach the gospel to you in order that you should turn from these [30]vain[R]things to a[R]living God, WHO MADE THE HEAVEN AND THE EARTH AND THE SEA, AND ALL THAT IS IN THEM.   Jer. 8:19 • Ps. 146:6

16 "And in the generations gone by He permitted all the nations to go their own ways;

17 and yet[R]He did not leave Himself without witness, in that He did good and[R]gave you rains from heaven and fruitful seasons, [T]satisfying your hearts with food and gladness."   Rom. 1:19f. • Deut. 11:14 • *filling*

18 And *even* saying these things, they with difficulty restrained the crowds from offering sacrifice to them.

Paul Is Stoned

19 But Jews came from Antioch and Iconium, and having won over the multitudes, they stoned Paul and[T]dragged him out of the city, supposing him to be dead. *were dragging*

20 But while[R]the disciples stood around him, he arose and entered the city. And the next day he went away with Barnabas to [R]Derbe.   Acts 11:26; 14:22, 28 • Acts 14:6

Ministry on the Return Trip

21 And after they had[R]preached the gospel to that city and had [R]made many disciples, they returned to Lystra and to[R]Iconium and to Antioch,   Acts 14:7 • Acts 2:47 • Acts 13:51

22 strengthening the souls of the disciples, encouraging them to continue in the faith, and *saying*, "Through many tribulations we must enter the kingdom of God."

23 And when[R]they had appointed elders for them in every church, having prayed with fasting, they commended them to the Lord in whom they had believed.   2 Cor. 8:19

24 And they passed through[R]Pisidia and came into[R]Pamphylia.   Acts 13:14 • Acts 13:13

[30] I.e., idols

25 And when they had spoken the word in ᴿPerga, they went down to Attalia;　Acts 13:13

Report on the First Missionary Journey

26 and from there they sailed to ᴿAntioch, from ᴿwhich they had been commended to the grace of God for the work that they had ᵀaccomplished.　Acts 11:19 • Acts 13:3 • *fulfilled*

27 And when they had arrived and gathered the church together, they *began* toᴿreport all things that God had done with them and ᵀhow He had opened a ᴿdoor of faith to the Gentiles.　Acts 15:3, 4, 12 • *that* • Col. 4:3

28 And they spent ᵀa long time with ᴿthe disciples.　*not a little* • Acts 11:26; 14:22

CHAPTER 15

Debate over Gentiles Keeping the Law

AND some men came down from Judea and *began* teaching the brethren, "Unless you are circumcised according to the custom of Moses, you cannot be saved."

2 And when Paul and Barnabas had ᵀgreat dissension and debate with them, ᴬ*the brethren* determined that Paul and Barnabas and certain others of them should go up to Jerusalem to the apostles and elders concerning this issue.　*not a little* • *it was determined*

3 Therefore, being sent on their way by the church, they were passing through both Phoenicia and Samaria, describing in detail the conversion of the Gentiles, and were bringing great joy to all the brethren.

4 And when they arrived at Jerusalem, they were received by the church and ᴿthe apostles and the elders, and they reported all that God had done with them.　Acts 11:30

5 But certain ones of ᴿthe sect of the ᴿPharisees who had believed, stood up, saying, "It is necessary toᴿcircumcise them, and to direct them to observe the Law of Moses."　Acts 5:17 • Matt. 3:7 • 1 Cor. 7:18

Peter Preaches Salvation Through Grace

6 And the apostles and the elders came together toᵀlook into this matter.　*see about*

7 And after there had been much debate, Peter stood up and said to them, "Brethren, you know thatᵀin the early days God made a choice among you, that by my mouth the Gentiles should hear the word ofᴿthe gospel and believe.　*from days of old* • Acts 20:24

8 "And God, ᴿwho knows the heart, bore witness to them, giving them the Holy Spirit, just as He also did to us;　Acts 1:24

9 and He made no distinction between us and them, cleansing their hearts by faith.

10 "Now therefore why do you put God to the test by placing upon the neck of the disciples a yokeᴿwhichᴿneither our fathers nor we have been able to bear?　Matt. 23:4

11 "But we believe that we are saved throughᴿthe grace of the Lord Jesus, in the same way as they also are."　Rom. 3:24; 5:15

Paul and Barnabas Testify

12 And all the multitude kept silent, and they were listening to Barnabas and Paul as they wereᴿrelating whatᴿsigns and wonders God had done through them among the Gentiles.　Acts 14:27; 15:3, 4 • John 4:48

James Proves Gentiles Are Free from the Law

13 And after they had stopped speaking, ᴬJamesᴿ answered, saying, "Brethren, listen to me.　*Jacob* • Acts 12:17

14 "Simeon has related how God first concerned Himself about taking from among the Gentiles a people for His name.

15 "And with this the words ofᴿthe Prophets agree, just as it is written,　Acts 13:40

16 'AFTER THESE THINGS I will return,
　AND I WILL REBUILD THEᴬTABERNACLE
　　OF DAVID WHICH HAS FALLEN,
　AND I WILL REBUILD ITS RUINS,
　AND I WILL RESTORE IT,　*tent*

17 IN ORDER THAT THE REST OFᵀMANKIND
　MAY SEEK THE LORD,　*men*
　AND ALL THE GENTILES ᴿWHO ARE
　　CALLED BY MY NAME,'　Deut. 28:10

18 SAYS THE LORD, WHO MAKES THESE
　THINGS KNOWN FROM OF OLD.

19 "Therefore it isᴿmy judgment that we do not trouble those who are turning to God from among the Gentiles,　Acts 15:28; 21:25

20 but that we write to them that they abstain fromᵀthings contaminated by idols and fromᴿfornication and from what is strangled and from blood.　*the pollutions of* • Lev. 18:6-23

21 "For ᴿMoses from ancient generations has in every city those who preach him, since he is read in the synagogues every Sabbath."　Acts 13:15; 2 Cor. 3:14f.

The Council Sends an Official Letter

22 Then it seemed good to ᴿthe apostles and the elders, with the whole church, to choose men from among them to send to ᴿAntioch with Paul and Barnabas—Judas called Barsabbas, and Silas, leading men among the brethren,　Acts 15:2 • Acts 11:20

23 and they sent this letter by them,
　"The apostles and the brethren who
　are elders, to the brethren in Antioch and Syria and Cilicia who are
　from the Gentiles, greetings.

24 "Since we have heard thatᵀsome ᵀof our number to whom we gave no instruction have ᴿdisturbed you with *their* words, unsettling your souls,　Acts 15:1 • *from us* • Gal. 1:7

25 it seemed good to us, having ^Abecome of one mind, to select men to send to you with our beloved Barnabas and Paul,   *met together*

26 men who have ^Trisked^R their lives for the name of our Lord Jesus Christ.   *given over* • Acts 9:23ff.; 14:19

27 "Therefore we have sent ^RJudas and ^RSilas, who themselves will also report the same things by word *of mouth.*   Acts 15:22, 32 • Acts 15:22

28 "For it seemed good to ^Rthe Holy Spirit and to^Rus to lay upon you no greater burden than these essentials: Acts 5:32; 15:8 • Acts 15:19, 25

29 that you abstain from^Rthings sacrificed to idols and from^Rblood and from ^Rthings strangled and from ^Rfornication; if you keep yourselves free from such things, you will do well. Farewell."   Acts 15:20

Report to Antioch

30 So, when they were sent away, ^Rthey went down to Antioch; and having gathered the ^Acongregation together, ^Cthey delivered the letter.   Acts 15:22f. • *multitude*

31 And when they had read it, they rejoiced because of its encouragement.

32 And ^RJudas and Silas, also being prophets themselves, ^Aencouraged and strengthened ^Rthe brethren with a lengthy message.   Acts 15:22, 27 • *exhorted* • Acts 15:1

33 And after they had spent time *there,* they were sent away from the brethren in peace to those who had sent them out.

34 [³¹But it seemed good to Silas to remain there.]

35 But^RPaul and Barnabas stayed in Antioch, teaching and preaching, with many others also, the word of the Lord. Acts 12:25

Contention over John Mark

36 And after some days Paul said to Barnabas, "Let us return and visit the brethren in every city in which we proclaimed the word of the Lord, *and see* how they are."

37 And Barnabas was desirous of taking John, called Mark, along with them also.

38 But Paul kept insisting that they should not take him along who had^Rdeserted them ^Tin Pamphylia and had not gone with them to the work.   Acts 13:13 • *from*

39 And there arose such a sharp disagreement that they separated from one another, and Barnabas took ^RMark with him and sailed away to^RCyprus.   Acts 12:12 • Acts 4:36

40 But Paul chose ^RSilas and departed, being ^Rcommitted by the brethren to the grace of the Lord.   Acts 15:22 • Acts 11:23

41 And he was traveling through Syria and Cilicia, strengthening the churches.

CHAPTER 16
Derbe and Lystra:
Timothy Is Circumcised

AND he came also to^RDerbe and to^RLystra. And behold, a certain disciple was there, named^RTimothy, the son of a Jewish woman who was a believer, but his father was a Greek,   Acts 14:6 • Acts 17:14f.; 18:5; 19:22; 20:4

2 and he was well spoken of by the brethren who were in Lystra and Iconium.

3 Paul wanted this man to^Tgo with him; and he^Rtook him and circumcised him because of the Jews who were in those parts, for they all knew that his father was a Greek.   *go out* • Gal. 2:3

4 Now while they were passing through the cities, they were delivering^Rthe decrees, which had been decided upon by^Tthe apostles and elders who were in Jerusalem, for them to observe.   Acts 15:28f. • Acts 15:2

5 So the churches were being strengthened^Ain the faith, and were^Rincreasing in number daily.   *in faith* • Acts 2:47

Troas: Macedonian Call

6 And they passed through the Phrygian and Galatian region, having been forbidden by the Holy Spirit to speak the word in Asia;

7 and when they had come to Mysia, they were trying to go into Bithynia, and the Spirit of Jesus did not permit them;

8 and passing^Aby^RMysia, they came down to^RTroas.   *through* • Acts 16:7 • Acts 16:11

9 And a vision appeared to Paul in the night: a certain man of Macedonia was standing and appealing to him, and saying, "Come over to Macedonia and help us."

10 And when he had seen the vision, immediately we sought to^Tgo into Macedonia, concluding that God had called us to^Rpreach the gospel to them.   *go out* • Acts 14:7

Lydia Is Converted

11 Therefore putting out to sea from ^RTroas, we ran ^Ra straight course to Samothrace, and on the day following to Neapolis;   Acts 16:8; 20:5f.; 2 Cor. 2:12 • Acts 21:1

12 and from there to^RPhilippi, which is a leading city of the district of^RMacedonia, a *Roman* colony; and we were staying in this city for some days.   Acts 20:6 • Acts 16:9, 10

13 And on the Sabbath day we went outside the gate to a riverside, where we were supposing that there would be a place of prayer; and we sat down and began speaking to the women who had assembled.

14 And a certain woman named Lydia, from the city of^RThyatira, a seller of purple fabrics, a worshiper of God, was listening; and the Lord opened her heart to respond to the things spoken by Paul. Rev. 1:11; 2:18, 24

³¹ Many mss. do not contain this verse

15 And when she and ᴿher household had been baptized, she urged us, saying, "If you have judged me to be faithful to the Lord, come into my house and stay." And she prevailed upon us.   Acts 11:14

A Spirit of Divination Is Cast Out

16 And it happened that as we were going to ᴿthe place of prayer, a certain slave-girl having ᵏa spirit of divination met us, who was bringing her masters much profit by fortunetelling.   Acts 16:13 · 2 Kin. 21:6
17 Following after Paul and us, she kept crying out, saying, "These men are bondservants of the Most High God, who are proclaiming to you the way of salvation."
18 And she continued doing this for many days. But Paul was greatly annoyed, and turned and said to the spirit, "I command youᴿin the name of Jesus Christ to come out of her!" And it came out at that veryᵀmoment.   Mark 16:17 · hour
19 But when her masters saw that their hope of profit wasᵀgone, they seized Paul and Silas and dragged them into the market place before the authorities,   gone out
20 and when they had brought them to the chief magistrates, they said, "These men are throwing our city into confusion, being Jews,
21 andᴿare proclaiming customs which it is not lawful for us to accept or to observe, beingᴿRomans."   Esth. 3:8 · Acts 16:12
22 And the crowd rose up together against them, and the chief magistrates tore their robes off them, and proceeded to order ᵀthem to be beaten with rods.   to beat with rods
23 And when they had inflicted many blows upon them, they threw them into prison, commanding ᴿthe jailer to guard them securely;   Acts 16:27, 36
24 and he, having received such a command, threw them into the inner prison, and fastened their feet inᴿthe stocks.   Job 13:27

Philippian Jailer Is Converted

25 But about midnight ᴿPaul and Silas were praying andᴿsinging hymns of praise to God, and the prisoners were listening to them;   Acts 16:19 · Eph. 5:19
26 and suddenlyᴿthere came a great earthquake, so that the foundations of the prison house were shaken; and immediatelyᴿall the doors were opened, and everyone's chains were unfastened.   Acts 4:31 · Acts 12:10
27 And whenᴿthe jailer had been roused out of sleep and had seen the prison doors opened, he drew his sword and was aboutᴿto kill himself, supposing that the prisoners had escaped.   Acts 16:23, 36 · Acts 12:19
28 But Paul cried out with a loud voice, saying, "Do yourself no harm, for we are all here!"
29 And he called for lights and rushed in and, trembling with fear, he fell down beforeᴿPaul and Silas,   Acts 16:19
30 and after he brought them out, he said, "Sirs, what must I do to be saved?"

31 And they said, "Believeᴿ in the Lord Jesus, and you shall be saved, you andᴿyour household."   [Mark 16:16] · Acts 11:14; 16:15

32 And they spoke the word of the Lord to him together with all who were in his house.
33 And he took themᴿthat very hour of the night and washed their wounds, and immediately he was baptized, he and all his household.   Acts 16:25
34 And he brought them into his house and set ᵀfood before them, and rejoiced greatly, having believed in God with ᴿhis whole household.   a table · Acts 11:14; 16:15

Paul Is Released from Prison

35 Now when day came, the chief magistrates sent their policemen, saying, "Release those men."
36 And ᴿthe jailer reported these words to Paul, saying, "The chief magistrates have sent to release you. Now therefore, come out and goᴿin peace."   Acts 16:27 · Acts 15:33
37 But Paul said to them, "They have beaten us in public without trial,ᴿmen who are Romans, and have thrown us into prison; and now are they sending us away

---

16:31 New Life: Received by Faith—The words spoken to the Philippian jailer are the best news human ears have ever heard, for they clearly tell how we receive God's gift of eternal life. When we receive God's gift of eternal life we are said to be "saved." The basic concept underlying "salvation" or "being saved" is deliverance. We are delivered from the penalty of sin (death, separation from God) and from the power of sin. Ultimately we will be delivered from the very presence of sin and will be delivered into the very presence of God. We receive new life by faith—believing that Jesus died for our sins, that His death was in our place, and that His payment for sin is fully acceptable in God's sight. Faith can be summarized in the acrostic:

F orsaking
A ll
I
T ake
H im

We are to forsake all (repent of our sins) and to take Him (by faith turn to God for our salvation) (Page 1118—Acts 20:21).

Now turn to Page 1069—John 5:24: Everlasting Life.

secretly? No indeed! But let them come themselves and bring us out." Acts 22:25-29

38 And the policemen reported these words to the chief magistrates. And ^Rthey were afraid when they heard that they were Romans, Acts 22:29

39 and they came and appealed to them, and when they had brought them out, they kept begging them to leave the city.

40 And they went out of the prison and entered *the house of* Lydia, and when they saw ^Rthe brethren, they ^Aencouraged them and departed. Acts 1:15; 16:2 • *exhorted*

CHAPTER 17

Thessalonica: "Upset the World"

Now when they had traveled through Amphipolis and Apollonia, they came to ^RThessalonica, where there was a synagogue of the Jews. Acts 17:11, 13; 20:4; 27:2; Phil. 4:16

2 And according to Paul's custom, he went to them, and for three Sabbaths reasoned with them from the Scriptures,

3 ^Texplaining and giving evidence that the Christ had to suffer and rise again from the dead, and *saying*, "This Jesus whom I am proclaiming to you is the Christ." *opening*

4 And some of them were persuaded and joined Paul and Silas, ^Talong with a great multitude of the God-fearing Greeks and a number of the leading women. *and a great*

5 But ^Rthe Jews, becoming jealous and taking along some wicked men from the market place, formed a mob and set the city in an uproar; and coming upon the house of ^RJason, they were seeking to bring them out to the people. Acts 17:13 • Acts 17:6, 7, 9

6 And when they did not find them, they *began* ^Rdragging Jason and some brethren before the city authorities, shouting, "These men who have upset ³²the^Rworld have come here also; Acts 16:19f. • Matt. 24:14; Acts 17:31

7 ^Tand Jason ^Rhas welcomed them, and they all act contrary to the decrees of Caesar, saying that there is another king, Jesus." *whom Jason has welcomed* • Luke 10:38

8 And they stirred up the crowd and the city authorities who heard these things.

9 And when they had received a^Apledge from ^RJason and the others, they released them. *bond* • Acts 17:5

Berea: Many Receive the Word

10 And the brethren immediately sent Paul and Silas away by night to Berea; ^Tand when they arrived, they went into the synagogue of the Jews. *who when . . . arrived went*

11 Now these were more noble-minded than those in Thessalonica, ^Tfor they received the word with ^Tgreat eagerness, examining the Scriptures daily, *to see* whether these things were so. *who received* • *all*

12 ^RMany of them therefore believed,^Talong with a number of prominent Greek^Rwomen and men. Acts 2:47 • *and not a few* • Acts 13:50

13 But when the Jews of ^RThessalonica found out that the word of God had been proclaimed by Paul in^RBerea also, they came there likewise, agitating and stirring up the crowds. Acts 17:1 • Acts 17:10; 20:4

14 And then immediately the brethren sent Paul out to go as far as the sea; and Silas and^RTimothy remained there. Acts 16:1

15 Now those who conducted Paul brought him as far as Athens; and receiving a command for Silas and Timothy to come to him as soon as possible, they departed.

Athens: Paul's Sermon on Mars' Hill

16 Now while Paul was waiting for them at ^RAthens, his spirit was being provoked within him as he was beholding the city full of idols. Acts 17:15, 21f.; 18:1; 1 Thess. 3:1

17 So he was reasoning in the synagogue with the Jews and^Rthe God-fearing *Gentiles*, and in the market place every day with those who happened to be present. Acts 17:4

18 And also some of the Epicurean and Stoic philosophers were ^Aconversing with him. And some were saying, "What would this idle babbler wish to say?" Others, "He seems to be a proclaimer of strange ^Tdeities,"—because he was preaching Jesus and the resurrection. *disputing* • *demons*

19 And they took him and brought him^Ato the Areopagus, saying, "May we know what this new teaching is ^Twhich you are proclaiming? *before* • *which is being spoken by you*

20 "For you are bringing some strange things to our ears; we want to know therefore what these things mean."

21 (Now all the Athenians and the strangers^Rvisiting there used to spend their time in nothing other than telling or hearing something new.) Acts 2:10

22 And Paul stood in the midst of the Areopagus and said, "Men of Athens, I observe that you are very religious in all respects.

23 "For while I was passing through and examining the objects of your worship, I also found an altar with this inscription, 'TO AN UNKNOWN GOD.' What therefore you worship in ignorance, this I proclaim to you.

24 "The^R God who made the world and all things in it, since He is^RLord of heaven and earth, does not^Rdwell in temples made with hands; Is. 42:5 • Ps. 115:16 • 1 Kin. 8:27

25 neither is He served by human hands, ^Ras though He needed anything, since He Himself gives to all life and breath and all things; Job 22:2; Ps. 50:10-12

26 and^RHe made from ³³one, every nation of mankind to live on all the face of the earth, having ^Rdetermined *their* appointed

³² Lit., *the inhabited earth*
³³ Some later mss. read *one blood*

times, and the boundaries of their habitation, Mal. 2:10 · Deut. 32:8; Job 12:23

27 that they should seek God, if perhaps they might grope for Him and find Him, though He is not far from each one of us;

28 for in Him we live and move and [r]exist, as even some of your own poets have said, 'For we also are His offspring.' *are*

29 "Being then the offspring of God, we [r]ought not to think that the Divine Nature is like gold or silver or stone, an image formed by the art and thought of man. Is. 40:18ff.

30 "Therefore having overlooked the times of ignorance, God is now declaring to men that all everywhere should repent,

31 because He has fixed a day in which He will judge [r]the world in righteousness through a Man whom He has appointed, having furnished proof to all men by raising Him from the dead." *the inhabited earth*

32 Now when they heard of [r]the resurrection of the dead, some *began* to sneer, but others said, "We shall hear you [r]again concerning this." Acts 17:18, 31 · *also again*

33 So Paul went out of their midst.

34 But some men joined him and believed, among whom also were Dionysius the [r]Areopagite and a woman named Damaris and others with them. Acts 17:19, 22

CHAPTER 18

Paul Works with Aquila and Priscilla

AFTER these things he left [r]Athens and went to [r]Corinth. Acts 17:15 · Acts 18:8; 19:1

2 And he found a certain Jew named Aquila, a native of Pontus, having recently come from Italy with his wife Priscilla, because Claudius had commanded all the Jews to leave Rome. He came to them,

3 and because he was of the same trade, he stayed with them and they were working; for by trade they were tent-makers.

Jews Reject Paul

4 And he was reasoning [r]in the synagogue every Sabbath and trying to persuade [r]Jews and Greeks. Acts 9:20; 18:19 · Acts 14:1

5 But when [r]Silas and Timothy came down from [r]Macedonia, Paul *began* devoting himself completely to the word, solemnly testifying to the Jews that Jesus was the [r]Christ. Acts 15:22; 16:1 · Acts 16:9 · Messiah

6 And when they resisted and blasphemed, he [r]shook out his garments and said to them, "Your [r]blood *be* upon your own heads! I am clean. From now on I shall go to the Gentiles." Neh. 5:13 · 2 Sam. 1:16

Crispus, the Gentile, Is Converted

7 And he departed from there and went to the house of a certain man named Titius

Justus, [r]a worshiper of God, whose house was next to the synagogue. Acts 13:43; 16:14

8 And [r]Crispus, [r]the leader of the synagogue, believed in the Lord [r]with all his household, and many of the Corinthians when they heard were believing and being baptized. 1 Cor. 1:14 · Mark 5:22 · Acts 11:14

9 And the Lord said to Paul in the night by a vision, "Do not be afraid *any longer*, but go on speaking and do not be silent;

10 for I am with you, and no man will attack you in order to harm you, for I have many people in this city."

11 And he settled *there* a year and six months, teaching the word of God among them.

Gallio Will Not Try Paul

12 But while Gallio was [r]proconsul of [r]Achaia, the Jews with one accord rose up against Paul and brought him before the judgment seat, Acts 13:7 · Acts 18:27; 19:21

13 saying, "This man persuades men to worship God contrary to the law."

14 But when Paul was about to [r]open his mouth, Gallio said to the Jews, "If it were a matter of wrong or of vicious crime, O Jews, it would be reasonable for me to put up with you; Matt. 5:2

15 but if there are [r]questions about words and names and your own law, look after it yourselves; I am unwilling to be a judge of these matters." Acts 23:29; 25:19

16 And he drove them away from [r]the judgment seat. Matt. 27:19

17 And they all took hold of [r]Sosthenes, [r]the leader of the synagogue, and *began* beating him in front of the judgment seat. And Gallio was not concerned about any of these things. 1 Cor. 1:1 · Acts 18:8

Return Trip to Antioch

18 And Paul, having remained many days longer, took leave of the brethren and put out to sea for Syria, and with him were Priscilla and [r]Aquila. In Cenchrea he had his hair cut, for he was keeping a vow. Acts 18:2, 26

19 And they came to Ephesus, and he left them there. Now he himself entered the synagogue and reasoned with the Jews.

20 And when they asked him to stay for a longer time, he did not consent,

21 but [r]taking leave of them and saying, "I will return to you again [r]if God wills," he set sail from Ephesus. Mark 6:46 · Rom. 1:10

22 And when he had landed at [r]Caesarea, he went up and greeted the church, and went down to [r]Antioch. Acts 8:40 · Acts 11:19

Galatia and Phrygia:
Strengthening the Disciples

23 And having spent some time *there*, he departed and passed successively through

the ᴿGalatian region and Phrygia, strengthening all the disciples.   Acts 16:6

Apollos Teaches Effectively

24 Now a certain Jew named ᴮApollos, an
ᴿAlexandrian by birth, ᴬan eloquent man,
came to Ephesus; and he was mighty in the
Scriptures.   Titus 3:13 • Acts 6:9 • *a learned man*
25 This man had been instructed in the
way of the Lord; and being fervent in spirit,
he was speaking and teaching accurately
the things concerning Jesus, being acquainted only with the baptism of John;
26 and he began to speak out boldly in the
synagogue. But when ᴮPriscilla and Aquila
heard him, they took him aside and explained to him ᴿthe way of God more accurately.   Acts 18:2, 18 • Acts 18:25
27 And when he wanted to go across to
Achaia, the brethren encouraged him and
wrote to the disciples to welcome him; and
when he had arrived, he helped greatly
those who had believed through grace;
28 for he powerfully refuted the Jews in
public, demonstratingᴮby the Scriptures that
Jesus was the ᵀChrist.   Acts 8:35 • Messiah

CHAPTER 19

Disciples of John
Receive the Holy Spirit

AND it came about that while ᴮApollos was
atᴿCorinth, Paul having passed through the
upper country came toᴿEphesus, and found
some disciples,   Titus 3:13 • Acts 18:1 • Eph. 1:1
2 and he said to them, "Did you receive
the Holy Spirit when you believed?" And
they *said* to him, "No, we have not even
heard whether there is a Holy Spirit."
3 And he said, "Into what then were you
baptized?" And they said, "Intoᴿ John's baptism."   Luke 7:29; Acts 18:25
4 And Paul said, "Johnᴮbaptized with the
baptism of repentance, telling the peopleᴿto
believe in Him who was coming after him,
that is, in Jesus."   Mark 1:4, 7, 8 • John 1:7
5 And when they heard this, they were
baptizedᵀin the name of the Lord Jesus. *into*
6 And when Paul hadᵈlaid his hands upon
them, the Holy Spirit came on them, and
they *began* ᴮspeaking with tongues and
ᴮprophesying.   Acts 6:6 • Acts 2:4 • Acts 13:1
7 And there were in all about twelve
men.

Paul Teaches in Tyrannus's School

8 And he entered ᴿthe synagogue and
continued speaking out boldly for three
months, reasoning and persuading *them*
about the kingdom of God.   Acts 9:20; 18:26
9 But when some were becoming hardened and disobedient, speaking evil of the

Way before the multitude, he withdrew
from them and took away the disciples, reasoning daily in the school of Tyrannus.
10 And this took place forᴿtwo years, so
that all who lived in Asia heard the word of
the Lord, both Jews and Greeks.   Acts 19:8

Miracles Are Performed at Ephesus

11 And God was performing extraordinary miracles by the hands of Paul,
12 ᴿso that handkerchiefs or aprons were
even carried from his body to the sick, and
the diseases left them andᴿthe evil spirits
went out.   Acts 5:15 • Mark 16:17
13 But also some of the Jewish exorcists,
who went from place to place, attempted to
name over those who had the evil spirits the
name of the Lord Jesus, saying, "I adjure
you by Jesus whom Paul preaches."
14 And seven sons of one Sceva, a Jewish
chief priest, were doing this.
15 And the evil spirit answered and said
to them, "I recognize Jesus, and I know
about Paul, but who are you?"
16 And the man, in whom was the evil
spirit, leaped on them and subdued all of
them and overpowered them, so that they
fled out of that house naked and wounded.
17 And this became known to all, both
Jews and Greeks, who lived inᴿEphesus; and
fear fell upon them all and the name of the
Lord Jesus was being magnified.   Acts 18:19
18 Many also of those who had believed
kept coming, confessing and disclosing their
practices.
19 And many of those who practiced magic brought their books together and *began*
burning them in the sight of all; and they
counted up the price of them and found it
fifty thousandᴿpieces of silver.   Luke 15:8
20 So the word of the Lordᴿwas growing
mightily and prevailing.   Acts 6:7; 12:24

Timothy and Erastus Are Sent to Macedonia

21 Now after these things were finished,
Paul purposed in theᴬspirit to go to Jerusalem after he had passed through Macedonia
and Achaia, saying, "After I have been
there, I must also see Rome."   *Spirit*
22 And having sent into Macedonia two of
those who ministered to him, Timothy and
Erastus, he himself stayed in ᵀAsia for a
while.   *west coast province of Asia Minor*

Demetrius Causes Uproar
at Ephesus

23 And about that time there arose no
small disturbance concerning the Way.
24 For a certain man named Demetrius, a
silversmith, who made silver shrines of Artemis,ᴿwas bringing no littleᴬbusiness to the
craftsmen;   Acts 16:16, 19f. • *profit*
25 these he gathered together with the
workmen of similar *trades,* and said, "Men,

you know that our prosperity⊤depends upon this business. *is from*

26 "And you see and hear that not only in Ephesus, but in almost all of Asia, this Paul has persuaded and turned away a considerable number of people, saying that gods made with hands are no gods *at all.*

27 "And not only is there danger that this trade of ours fall into disrepute, but also that the temple of the great goddess Artemis be regarded as worthless and that she whom all of ᴿAsia and the ⊤world worship should even be dethroned from her magnificence." Acts 19:10 · *the inhabited earth*

28 And when they heard *this* and were filled with rage, they *began* crying out, saying, "Great is Artemis of the Ephesians!"

29 And the city was filled with the confusion, and they rushed with one accord into the theater,⊤dragging along Gaius and Aristarchus, Paul's traveling ᴿcompanions from Macedonia. *having dragged* · Acts 13:5; 19:22

30 And when Paul wanted to go into the assembly, the disciples would not let him.

31 And also some of the ³⁴Asiarchs who were friends of his sent to him and repeatedly urged him not to⊤venture into the theater. *give himself*

32 So then, some were shouting one thing and some another, for the assembly was in confusion, and the majority did not know for what cause they had come together.

33 And some of the crowd concluded *it was* Alexander, since the Jews had put him forward; and having ᴿmotioned with his hand, Alexander was intending to make a defense to the⊤assembly. Acts 12:17 · *people*

34 But when they recognized that he was a Jew, a *single* outcry arose from them all as they shouted for about two hours, "Great is Artemis of the Ephesians!"

35 And after quieting the multitude, the town clerk *said, "Men of Ephesus, what man is there after all who does not know that the city of the Ephesians is guardian of the temple of the great Artemis, and of the *image* which fell down from heaven?

36 "Since then these are undeniable facts, you ought to keep calm and to do nothing rash.

37 "For you have brought these men *here* who are neitherᴿrobbers of temples nor blasphemers of our goddess. Rom. 2:22

38 "So then, if Demetrius and the craftsmen who are with him have a complaint against any man, the courts are in session andᴿproconsuls are *available*; let them bring charges against one another. Acts 13:7

39 "But if you want anything beyond this, it shall be settled in the lawful assembly.

40 "For indeed we are in danger of being accused of a riot in connection with today's affair, since there is no *real* cause *for it;* and in this connection we shall be unable to account for this disorderly gathering."

³⁴ I.e., political or religious officials of the province of Asia

41 And after saying this he dismissed the ⊤assembly. Gr., ekklesia

CHAPTER 20

Macedonia: Three Months of Ministry

AND after the uproar had ceased, Paul sent for the disciples and when he had exhorted them and taken his leave of them, he departed to go toᴿMacedonia. Acts 16:9; 20:3

2 And when he had gone through those districts and had given them much exhortation, he came to Greece.

3 And *there* he spent three months, and when a plot was formed against him by the Jews as he was about to set sail for Syria, he determined to return through Macedonia.

4 And he was accompanied by Sopater ofᴿBerea, *the son* of Pyrrhus; and by Aristarchus and Secundus of the Thessalonians; and Gaius of Derbe, and Timothy; and Tychicus and Trophimus of Asia. Acts 17:10

5 But these had gone on ahead and were waiting forᴿus at Troas. Acts 16:10; 20:5-15

Troas: Eutychus Falls from Loft

6 Andᴿwe sailed from Philippi after the days of Unleavened Bread, and came to them atᴿTroas within five days; and there we stayed seven days. Acts 16:10 · Acts 16:8

7 And onᴿthe first day of the week, when we were gathered together to break bread, Paul *began* talking to them, intending to depart the next day, and he prolonged his⊤message until midnight. 1 Cor. 16:2 · *word, speech*

8 And there were many lamps in the upper room where we were gathered together.

9 And there was a certain young man named Eutychus sitting ˒on the window sill, sinking into a deep sleep; and as Paul kept on talking, he was overcome by sleep and fell down from the third floor, and was picked up dead. *at the window*

10 But Paul went down and fell upon him and after embracing him, he said, "Do not be troubled, for his life is in him."

11 And when he had gone *back* up, and hadᴿbroken the bread and⊤eaten, he talked with them a long while, until daybreak, and so departed. Acts 2:42; 20:7 · *tasted*

12 And they took away the boy alive, and were⊤greatly comforted. *not moderately*

Miletus: Paul Bids Farewell to Ephesian Elders

13 But we, going ahead to the ship, set sail for Assos, intending from there to take Paul on board; for thus he had arranged it, intending himself to go˒by land. *on foot*

14 And when he met us at Assos, we took him on board and came to Mitylene.

15 And sailing from there, we arrived the

following day opposite Chios; and the next day we crossed over to Samos; and the day following we came to^RMiletus.   Acts 20:17

16 For Paul had decided to sail past Ephesus in order that he might not have to spend time in ^TAsia; for he was hurrying to be in Jerusalem, if possible, on the day of Pentecost.   *west coast province of Asia Minor*

17 And from Miletus he sent to Ephesus and called to him the elders of the church.

18 And when they had come to him, he said to them,

"You yourselves know,^Rfrom the first day that I set foot in Asia, how I was with you the whole time,   Acts 18:19; 19:1, 10; 20:4, 16

19 serving the Lord with all humility and with tears and with trials which came upon me through^Rthe plots of the Jews;   Acts 20:3

20 how I did not shrink from declaring to you anything that was profitable, and teaching you publicly and from house to house,

21 solemnly ^Rtestifying to both Jews and Greeks of repentance toward God and faith in our Lord Jesus Christ.   Luke 16:28; Acts 18:5

22 "And now, behold, bound in^Aspirit, I am on my way to Jerusalem, not knowing what will happen to me there,   *the Spirit*

23 except that ^Rthe Holy Spirit solemnly testifies to me in every city, saying that bonds and afflictions await me.   Acts 8:29

24 "But I do not consider my life of any account as dear to myself, in order that I may finish my course, and the ministry which I received from the Lord Jesus, to testify solemnly of the gospel of the grace of God.

25 "And now, behold, I know that all of you, among whom I went about preaching the kingdom, will see my face no more.

26 "Therefore I testify to you this day, that I am innocent of the blood of all men.

27 "For I^Rdid not shrink from declaring to you the whole purpose of God.   Acts 20:20

28 "Be on guard for yourselves and for all ^Rthe flock, among which the Holy Spirit has made you^Aoverseers, to shepherd the church of God which He^Tpurchased with His own blood.   Acts 20:29; 1 Pet. 5:2f. • *bishops* • *acquired*

29 "I know that after my departure^Rsavage wolves will come in among you, not sparing ^Rthe flock;   Ezek. 22:27; Matt. 7:15 • John 21:15-17

30 and from among your own selves men will arise, speaking perverse things, to draw away^Rthe disciples after them.   Acts 11:26

31 "Therefore be on the alert, remembering that night and day for a period of ^Rthree years I did not cease to admonish each one ^Rwith tears.   Acts 19:8, 10; 24:17 • Acts 20:19

32 "And now I commend you to God and to the word of His grace, which is able to build *you* up and to give *you* the inheritance among all those who are sanctified.

33 "I^Rhave coveted no one's silver or gold or clothes.   1 Cor. 9:4-18; 2 Cor. 11:7-12; 12:14-18

34 "You yourselves know that^Rthese hands ministered to my *own* needs and to the^Rmen who were with me.   Acts 18:3 • Acts 19:22

35 "In everything I showed you that by working hard in this manner you must help the weak and remember the words of the Lord Jesus, that He Himself said, 'It is more blessed to give than to receive.' "

36 And when he had said these things, he knelt down and prayed with them all.

37 And they *began* to weep aloud and embraced Paul, and repeatedly kissed him,

38 ^Tgrieving especially over the word which he had spoken, that they should see his face no more. And they were accompanying him to the ship.   *suffering pain*

CHAPTER 21

Tyre: Paul Is Warned About Jerusalem

A<small>ND</small> when it came about that we had parted from them and had set sail, we ran^Ra straight course to Cos and the next day to Rhodes and from there to Patara;   Acts 16:11

2 and having found a ship crossing over to Phoenicia, we went aboard and set sail.

3 And when we had come in sight of^RCyprus, leaving it on the left, we kept sailing to Syria and landed at Tyre; for there the ship was to unload its cargo.   Acts 4:36; 21:16

4 And after looking up^Rthe disciples, we stayed there seven days; and they kept telling Paul^Rthrough the Spirit not to set foot in Jerusalem.   Acts 11:26; 21:16 • [Acts 20:23; 21:11]

5 And when it came about that^Tour days there were ended, we departed and started on our journey, while they all, with wives and children,^Rescorted us until *we were* out of the city. And after kneeling down on the beach and praying, we said farewell to one another.   *we had completed the days* • Acts 15:3

6 Then we went on board the ship, and they returned^Rhome again.   John 19:27

Caesarea: Agabus's Prediction

7 And when we had finished the voyage from^RTyre, we arrived at Ptolemais; and after greeting ^Rthe brethren, we stayed with them for a day.   Acts 12:20 • Acts 1:15; 21:17

8 And on the next day we departed and came to^RCaesarea; and entering the house of Philip the evangelist, who was one of the seven, we stayed with him.   Acts 8:40; 21:16

9 Now this man had four virgin daughters who were^Rprophetesses.   Luke 2:36

10 And as we were staying there for some days, a certain prophet named ^RAgabus came down from Judea.   Acts 11:28

11 And coming to us, he took Paul's belt and bound his own feet and hands, and said, "This is what the Holy Spirit says: 'In this way the Jews at Jerusalem will ^Rbind him and deliver him into the hands of the Gentiles.' "   Acts 9:16; 21:33

12 And when we had heard this, we as

well as the local residents *began* begging him[R]not to go up to Jerusalem.   Acts 21:15

13 Then Paul answered, "What are you doing, weeping and breaking my heart? For [R]I am ready not only to be bound, but even to die at Jerusalem for[R]the name of the Lord Jesus."   Acts 20:24 • Acts 5:41; 9:16

14 And since he would not be persuaded, we fell silent, remarking, "The[R] will of the Lord be done!"   Luke 22:42

15 And after these days we got ready and started on our way up to Jerusalem.

16 And *some* of the disciples from Caesarea also came with us, taking us to Mnason of[R]Cyprus, a disciple of long standing with whom we were to lodge.   Acts 4:36; 21:3

Paul Conforms to Jewish Customs

17 And when we had come to Jerusalem, [R]the brethren received us gladly.   Acts 1:15

18 And now the following day Paul went in with us to ᵀJames,[R] and all[R]the elders were present.   Jacob • Acts 12:17 • Acts 11:30

19 And after he had greeted them, he[R]*began* to relate one by one the things which God had done among the Gentiles through his[R]ministry.   Acts 14:27 • Acts 1:17

20 And when they heard it they *began* glorifying God; and they said to him, "You see, brother, how many thousands there are among the Jews of those who have believed, and they are all zealous for the Law;

21 and they have been told about you, that you are teaching all the Jews who are among the Gentiles to forsake Moses, telling them not to circumcise their children nor to walk according to the customs.

22"What, then, is *to be done*? They will certainly hear that you have come.

23"Therefore do this that we tell you. We have four men who are under a vow;

24 take them and [R]purify yourself along with them, andᵀpay their expenses in order that they may shave their[T]heads; and all will know that there is nothing to the things which they have been told about you, but that you yourself also walk orderly, keeping the Law.   Acts 21:26; 24:18 • *spend on them* • *head*

25"But concerning the Gentiles who have believed, we wrote, having decided that they should abstain fromᵀmeat sacrificed to idols and from blood and from what is strangled and from fornication."   *the thing*

26 Then Paul took the men, and the next day, [R]purifying himself along with them, [R]went into the temple, giving notice of the completion of the days of purification, until the sacrifice was offered for each one of them.   Acts 21:24; 24:18 • Num. 6:13; Acts 24:18

Paul's Arrest

27 And when[R]the seven days were almost

³⁵ I.e., chiliarch, in command of one thousand troops

over, the Jews from Asia, upon seeing him in the temple, *began* to stir up all the multitude and laid hands on him,   Num. 6:9, 13-20

28 crying out, "Men of Israel, come to our aid![R] This is the man who preaches to all men everywhere against our people, and the Law, and this place; and besides he has even brought Greeks into the temple and has[R]defiled this holy place."   Acts 6:13 • [Matt. 24:15]

29 For they had previously seen[R]Trophimus the[R]Ephesian in the city with him, and they supposed that Paul had brought him into the temple.   Acts 20:4 • Acts 18:19

30 And all the city was aroused, and the people rushed together; and taking hold of Paul, they dragged him out of the temple; and immediately the doors were shut.

31 And while they were seeking to kill him, a report came up to the ³⁵commander of the[R]Roman^cohort that all Jerusalem was in confusion.   Acts 10:1 • *battalion*

32 And at once he took along *some* soldiers and centurions, and ran down to them; and when they saw the commander and the soldiers, they stopped beating Paul.

33 Then the commander came up and took hold of him, and ordered him to be bound with two chains; and he *began* asking who he was and what he had done.

34 But among the crowd some were shouting one thing *and* some another, and when he could not find out the[T]facts on account of the uproar, he ordered him to be brought into the barracks.   *certainty*

35 And when he got to the stairs, it so happened that he was carried by the soldiers because of the violence of the mob;

36 for the multitude of the people kept following behind, crying out, "Away[R] with him!"   Luke 23:18; John 19:15; Acts 22:22

37 And as Paul was about to be brought into the barracks, he said to the commander, "May I say something to you?" And he *said, "Do you know Greek?

38"Then you are not the Egyptian who some ᵀtime ago stirred up a revolt and led the four thousand men of the Assassins out [R]into the wilderness?"   *days* • Matt. 24:26

39 But Paul said, "I am a Jew of Tarsus in Cilicia, a citizen of no insignificant city; and I beg you, allow me to speak to the people."

Paul's Defense Before the Crowd
Acts 9:1-8, 17, 18; 26:13-18

40 And when he had given him permission, Paul, standing on the stairs, motioned to the people with his hand; and when there was a great hush, he spoke to them in the ᵀHebrew dialect, saying,   *Jewish Aramaic*

CHAPTER 22

"**B**RETHREN[R] and fathers, hear my defense which I now *offer* to you."   Acts 7:2

2 And when they heard that he was ad-

dressing them in the Hebrew dialect, they became even more quiet; and he *said,

3 "I am a Jew, born in Tarsus of Cilicia, but brought up in this city, educated ᵀunder Gamaliel, ᴿstrictly according to the law of our fathers, being zealous for God, just as you all are today.   at the feet of · Acts 23:6; 26:5

4 "And ᴿI persecuted this ᴿWay to the death, binding and putting both men and women into prisons,   Acts 8:3 · Acts 9:2

5 as also the high priest and all the Council of the elders ᵀcan testify. From them I also received letters to the brethren, and started off for Damascus in order to bring even those who were there to Jerusalem as prisoners to be punished.   testifies for me

6 "And ᴿit came about that as I was on my way, approaching Damascus about noontime, a very bright light suddenly flashed from heaven all around me,   Acts 9:3-8

7 and I fell to the ground and heard a voice saying to me, 'Saul, Saul, why are you persecuting Me?'

8 "And I answered, 'Who art Thou, Lord?' And He said to me, 'I am ᴿJesus the Nazarene, whom you are persecuting.'   Acts 26:9

9 "And those who were with me ᴿbeheld the light, to be sure, but did not ᴬunderstand the voice of the One who was speaking to me.   Acts 26:13 · hear (with comprehension)

10 "And I said, 'What shall I do, Lord?' And the Lord said to me, 'Arise and go on into Damascus; and there you will be told of all that has been appointed for you to do.'

11 "But since Iᴿcould not see because of the ᴬbrightness of that light, I was led by the hand by those who were with me, and came into Damascus.   Acts 9:8 · glory

12 "And a certain Ananias, a man who was devout by the standard of the Law, and well spoken of by all the Jews who lived there,

13 came to me, and standing near said to me, 'Brother Saul, receive your sight!' And at that very time I looked up at him.

14 "And he said, 'The God of our fathers has appointed you to know His will, and to see the Righteous One, and to hear an ᴬutterance from His mouth.   message; lit., voice

15 'For you will be a witness for Him to all men of what you have seen and heard.

16 'And now why do you delay? ᴿArise, and be baptized, and ᴿwash away your sins, calling on His name.'   Acts 9:18 · Acts 2:38

17 "And it came about when I ᴿreturned to Jerusalem and was praying in the temple, that I ᴿfell into a trance,   Acts 9:26 · Acts 10:10

18 and I saw Him saying to me, 'Make ᴿhaste, and get out of Jerusalem quickly, because they will not accept your testimony about Me.'   Acts 9:29

19 "And I said, 'Lord, they themselves understand that in one synagogue after another ᴿI used to imprison and ᴿbeat those who believed in Thee.   Acts 8:3; 22:4 · Matt. 10:17

20 'And when the blood of Thy witness Stephen was being shed, I also was standing by, approving, and watching out for the cloaks of those who were slaying him.'

21 "And He said to me, 'Go! For I will send you far away ᴿto the Gentiles.' "   Acts 9:15

22 And they listened to him up to this statement, and then they raised their voices and said, "Away ᴿwith such a fellow from the earth, for ᴿhe should not be allowed to live!"   Acts 21:36; 1 Thess. 2:16 · Acts 25:24

23 And as they were crying out and ᴿthrowing off their cloaks and ᴿtossing dust into the air,   Acts 7:58 · 2 Sam. 16:13

Paul's Defense Before the Centurion

24 the ³⁶commander ordered him to be brought into ᴿthe barracks, stating that he should be examined by scourging so that he might find out the reason why they were shouting against him that way.   Acts 21:34

25 And when they stretched him out with thongs, Paul said to the centurion who was standing by, "Is it lawful for you to scourge a man who is a Roman and uncondemned?"

26 And when the centurion heard this, he went to the commander and told him, saying, "What are you about to do? For this man is a Roman."

27 And the commander came and said to him, "Tell me, are you a Roman?" And he said, "Yes."

28 And the commander answered, "I acquired this citizenship with a large sum of money." And Paul said, "But I was actually born a citizen."

29 Therefore those who were about to examine him immediately let go of him; and the commander also was afraid when he found out that he was a Roman, and because he had ᵀput him in chains.   bound him

Paul's Defense Before the Sanhedrin

30 But on the next day, ᴿwishing to know for certain why he had been accused by the Jews, he ᴿreleased him and ordered the chief priests and all the ᴬCouncil to assemble, and brought Paul down and set him before them.   Acts 23:28 · Acts 21:33 · Sanhedrin

CHAPTER 23

AND Paul, looking intently at the ᴬCouncil, said, "Brethren, I have ᴬlived my life with a perfectly good conscience before God up to this day."   Sanhedrin · conducted myself as a citizen

2 And the high priest ᴿAnanias commanded those standing beside him ᴿto strike him on the mouth.   Acts 24:1 · John 18:22

3 Then Paul said to him, "God is going to strike you, ᴿyou whitewashed wall! And do

---

³⁶ I.e., chiliarch, in command of one thousand troops

you[R]sit to try me according to the Law, and in violation of the Law order me to be struck?"   Matt. 23:27 • Deut. 25:2; John 7:51

4 But the bystanders said, "Do you revile God's high priest?"

5 And Paul said, "I was not aware, brethren, that he was high priest; for it is written, 'YOU[R] SHALL NOT SPEAK EVIL OF A RULER OF YOUR PEOPLE.'"   Ex. 22:28

6 But perceiving that one part were Sadducees and the other Pharisees, Paul *began* crying out in the Council, "Brethren, I am a Pharisee, a son of Pharisees; I am on trial for the hope and resurrection of the dead!"

7 And as he said this, there arose a dissension between the Pharisees and Sadducees; and the assembly was divided.

8 For the Sadducees say that there is no resurrection, nor an angel, nor a spirit; but the Pharisees acknowledge them all.

9 And there arose a great uproar; and some of [R]the scribes of the Pharisaic party stood up and *began* to argue heatedly, saying, "We[R] find nothing wrong with this man; [R]suppose a spirit or an angel has spoken to him?"   Mark 2:16 • Acts 23:29 • John 12:29

10 And as a great dissension was developing, the [37]commander was afraid Paul would be torn to pieces by them and ordered the troops to go down and take him away from them by force, and bring him into[R]the barracks.   Acts 21:34; 23:16, 32

11 But on the night *immediately* following, the Lord stood at his side and said, "Take courage; for as you have [R]solemnly witnessed to My cause at Jerusalem, so you must witness at Rome also."   Luke 16:28

Jews' Plan to Kill Paul

12 And when it was day, the Jews formed a [A]conspiracy and bound themselves under an oath, saying that they would neither eat nor drink until they had killed Paul.   *mob*

13 And there were more than forty who formed this plot.

14 And they came to the chief priests and the elders, and said, "We have[R]bound ourselves under a solemn oath to taste nothing until we have killed Paul.   Acts 23:12, 21

15 "Now, therefore, you and the Council notify the commander to bring him down to you, as though you were going to determine his case by a more thorough investigation; and we for our part are ready to slay him before he comes near *the place*."

16 But the son of Paul's sister heard of their ambush, and he came and entered[T]the barracks and told Paul.   Acts 21:34; 23:10, 32

17 And Paul called one of the centurions

to him and said, "Lead this young man to the commander, for he has something to report to him."

18 So he took him and led him to the commander and *said, "Paul[T]the prisoner called me to him and asked me to lead this young man to you since he has something to tell you."   [Eph. 3:1]

19 And the commander took him by the hand and stepping aside, *began* to inquire of him privately, "What is it that you have to report to me?"

20 And he said, "The[R] Jews have agreed to ask you to bring Paul down tomorrow to[R]the [A]Council, as though they were going to inquire somewhat more thoroughly about him.   Acts 23:14f. • Acts 22:30 • *Sanhedrin*

21 "So do not[T]listen to them, for more than forty of them are[T]lying in wait for him who have bound themselves under a curse not to eat or drink until they slay him; and now they are ready and waiting for the promise from you."   *be persuaded by them* • Luke 11:54

22 Therefore the commander let the young man go, instructing him, "Tell no one that you have notified me of these things."

Paul's Rescue

23 And he called to him two of the centurions, and said, "Get two hundred soldiers ready by [38]the third hour of the night to proceed to [R]Caesarea, [T]with seventy soldiers and two hundred spearmen."   Acts 8:40 • *and*

24 *They were* also to provide mounts to put Paul on and bring him safely to[R]Felix the governor.   Acts 23:26, 33; 24:1, 3, 10; 25:14

25 And he wrote a letter having this form:

26 "Claudius Lysias, to the most excellent governor Felix, greetings.

27 "When this man was arrested by the Jews and was about to be slain by them, I came upon them with the troops and rescued him, having learned that he was a Roman.

28 "And wanting to ascertain the charge for which they were accusing him, I[R]brought him down to their[A]Council;   Acts 23:10 • *Sanhedrin*

29 and I found him to be accused over questions about their Law, but[T]under no accusation deserving death or[T]imprisonment.   *having • bonds*

30 "And when I was [R]informed that there would be a plot against the man, I sent him to you at once, also instructing his accusers to [T]bring charges against him before you."   Acts 23:20f. • *speak against him*

31 So the soldiers, in accordance with their orders, took Paul and brought him by night to Antipatris.

32 But the next day, leaving[R]the horsemen to go on with him, they returned to[R]the barracks.   Acts 23:23 • Acts 23:10

33 And when these had come to[R]Caesarea

---

[37] I.e., chiliarch, in command of one thousand troops
[38] I.e., 9 p.m.

and delivered the letter to the governor, they also presented Paul to him.   Acts 8:40

Paul Is Tried Before Felix

34 And when he had read it, he asked from what [R]province he was; and when he learned that he was from Cilicia,   Acts 25:1

35 he said, "I will give you a hearing after your accusers arrive also," giving orders for him to be kept in Herod's [39]Praetorium.

CHAPTER 24

AND after five days the high priest Ananias came down with some elders, [T]with a certain [A]attorney *named* Tertullus; and they [A]brought charges to the governor against Paul.   *and · orator · presented their evidence or case*

2 And after *Paul* had been summoned, Tertullus began to accuse him, saying *to the governor,*

"Since we have through you attained much peace, and since by your providence reforms are being carried out for this nation,

3 we acknowledge *this* in every way and everywhere, [R]most excellent Felix, with all thankfulness.   Acts 23:26; 26:25

4"But, that I may not weary you any further, I beg you [T]to grant us, by your kindness, a brief hearing.   *to hear . . . briefly*

5"For we have found this man a real pest and a fellow who stirs up dissension among all the Jews throughout [40]the world, and a ringleader of the sect of the Nazarenes.

6"And he even tried to [T]desecrate the temple; and [T]then we arrested him. [[41]And we wanted to judge him according to our own Law.   Acts 21:28 · *also*

7"But Lysias the commander came along, and with much violence took him out of our hands,

8 ordering his accusers to come before you.] And by examining him yourself concerning all these matters, you will be able to ascertain the things of which we accuse him."

9 And the Jews also joined in the attack, asserting that these things were so.

10 And when [R]the governor had nodded for him to speak, Paul responded: Acts 23:24

"Knowing that for many years you have been a judge to this nation, I cheerfully make my defense,

11 since you can take note of the fact that no more than [R]twelve days ago I went up to Jerusalem to worship.   Acts 21:18, 27; 24:1

12"And neither in the temple, nor in the synagogues, nor in the city *itself* did they find me carrying on a discussion with anyone or causing [T]a riot.   *an attack of a mob*

13"Nor [R]can they prove to you *the charges* of which they now accuse me.   Acts 25:7

14"But this I admit to you, that according to the Way which they call a sect I do serve

[T]the God of our fathers, believing everything that is in accordance with the Law, and that is written in the Prophets;   *the ancestral god*

15 having a hope in God, which [R]these men cherish themselves, that there shall certainly be a resurrection of both the righteous and the wicked.   [Dan. 12:2; John 5:28f.]

16"In view of this, [R]I also do my best to maintain always a blameless conscience *both* before God and before men.   Acts 23:1

17"Now [R]after several years I [R]came to bring [42]alms to my nation and to present offerings;   Acts 20:31 · Acts 11:29f.; Rom. 15:25-28

18 in which they found me *occupied* in the temple, having been [R]purified, without *any* [R]crowd or uproar. But *there were* certain Jews from Asia—   Acts 21:26 · Acts 24:12

19 who ought to have been present before you, and to [R]make accusation, if they should have anything against me.   Acts 23:30

20"Or else let these men themselves tell what misdeed they found when I stood before [R]the [A]Council,   Matt. 5:22 · *Sanhedrin*

21 other than for this one statement which [R]I shouted out while standing among them, 'For the resurrection of the dead I am on trial before you today.' "   [Acts 23:6; 24:15]

22 But Felix, having a more exact knowledge about [R]the Way, put them off, saying, "When Lysias the [43]commander comes down, I will decide your case."   Acts 24:14

23 And he gave orders to the centurion for him to be [R]kept in custody and *yet* have *some* freedom, and not to prevent any of his friends from ministering to him.   Acts 23:35

24 But some days later, Felix arrived with Drusilla, his [T]wife who was a Jewess, and sent for Paul, and heard him *speak* about [R]faith in Christ Jesus.   *own wife* · Acts 20:21

25 And as he was discussing [R]righteousness, [R]self-control and the judgment to come, Felix became frightened and said, "Go away for the present, and when I find time, I will summon you."   Titus 2:12 · Gal. 5:23

26 At the same time too, he was hoping that [R]money would be given him by Paul; therefore he also used to send for him quite often and converse with him.   Acts 24:17

27 But after two years had passed, Felix [T]was succeeded by Porcius Festus; and wishing to do the Jews a favor, Felix left Paul imprisoned.   *received a successor, Porcius Festus*

CHAPTER 25

Paul Is Tried Before Festus

FESTUS therefore, having arrived in [R]the province, three days later went up to Jerusalem from [R]Caesarea.   Acts 23:34 · Acts 8:40

2 And the chief priests and the leading

---
[39] I.e., governor's official residence
[40] Lit., *the inhabited earth*
[41] Many mss. do not contain the remainder of v. 6, v. 7, nor the first part of v. 8   [42] Or, *gifts to charity*
[43] I.e., chiliarch, in command of one thousand troops

men of the Jews [R]brought charges against Paul; and they were urging him,   Acts 24:1

3 requesting a concession against Paul, that he might[T]have him brought to Jerusalem (at the same time, setting an ambush to kill him on the way).   send for him to Jerusalem

4 Festus then answered that Paul was being kept in custody at Caesarea and that he himself was about to leave shortly.

5 "Therefore," he[T] *said, "let the influential men among you go there with me, and if there is anything wrong[T]about the man, let them prosecute him."   go down • in • accuse

6 And after he had spent not more than eight or ten days among them, he went down to[R]Caesarea; and on the next day he took his seat on[R]the tribunal and ordered Paul to be brought.   Acts 8:40 • Matt. 27:19

7 And after he had arrived, the Jews who had come down from Jerusalem stood around him, bringing [R]many and serious charges against him[R]which they could not prove;   Acts 24:5f. • Acts 24:13

8 while Paul said in his own defense, "I[R] have committed no offense either against the Law of the Jews or against the temple or against Caesar."   Acts 6:13; 24:12; 28:17

9 But Festus, wishing to do the Jews a favor, answered Paul and said, "Are you willing to go up to Jerusalem and[T]stand trial before me on these charges?"   be judged

10 But Paul said, "I am standing before Caesar's[R]tribunal, where I ought to be tried. I have done no wrong to the Jews, as you also very well know.   Matt. 27:19; Acts 25:6, 17

11 "If then I am a wrongdoer, and have committed anything worthy of death, I do not refuse to die; but if none of those things is true of which these men accuse me, no one can hand me over to them. I[R]appeal to Caesar."   Acts 25:21, 25; 26:32; 28:19

12 Then when Festus had conferred with his council, he answered, "You have appealed to Caesar, to Caesar you shall go."

13 Now when several days had elapsed, King Agrippa and Bernice arrived at Caesarea, and paid their respects to Festus.

14 And while they were spending many days there, Festus laid Paul's case before the king, saying, "There is a certain man[R]left a prisoner by Felix;   Acts 24:27

15 and when I was at Jerusalem, the chief priests and the elders of the Jews[R]brought charges against him, asking for a sentence of condemnation upon him.   Acts 24:1; 25:2

16 "And I[R]answered them that it is not the custom of the Romans to hand over any man before the accused meets his accusers face to face, and has an opportunity to make his defense against the charges.   Acts 25:4f.

17 "And so after they had assembled here, I made no delay, but on the next day took my seat on[R]the tribunal, and ordered the man to be brought.   Matt. 27:19; Acts 25:6, 10

18 "And when the accusers stood up, they began bringing charges against him not of such crimes as I was expecting;

19 but they simply had some points of disagreement with him about their own [T]religion and about a certain dead man, Jesus, whom Paul asserted to be alive.   superstition

20 "And[R]being at a loss how to investigate [T]such matters, I asked whether he was willing to go to Jerusalem and there stand trial on these matters.   Acts 25:9 • these

21 "But when Paul[R]appealed to be held in custody for [44]the Emperor's decision, I ordered him to be kept in custody until I send him to Caesar."   Acts 25:11f.

22 And Agrippa said to Festus, "I also would like to hear the man myself." "Tomorrow," he *said, "you shall hear him."

Paul Is Tried Before Agrippa

23 And so, on the next day when Agrippa had come[T]together with Bernice, amid great pomp, and had entered the auditorium [45]accompanied by the commanders and the prominent men of the city, at the command of Festus, Paul was brought in.   and Bernice

24 And Festus *said, "King Agrippa, and all you gentlemen here present with us, you behold this man about whom[R]all the people of the Jews appealed to me, both at Jerusalem and here, loudly declaring that he ought not to live any longer.   Acts 25:2, 7

25 "But I found that he had committed [R]nothing worthy of death; and since he himself[R]appealed to the Emperor, I decided to send him.   Luke 23:4; Acts 23:29 • Acts 25:11f.

26 "Yet I have nothing definite about him to write to my lord. Therefore I have brought him before you all and especially before you, King Agrippa, so that after the investigation has taken place, I may have something to write.

27 "For it seems absurd to me in sending a prisoner, not to indicate also the charges against him."

CHAPTER 26

AND [R]Agrippa said to Paul, "You are permitted to speak for yourself." Then Paul stretched out his hand and proceeded to make his defense: Acts 9:15

2 "In regard to all the things of which I am accused by the Jews, I consider myself fortunate, King Agrippa, that I am about to make my defense before you today;

3 especially because you are an expert in all customs and questions among the Jews; therefore I beg you to listen to me patiently.

4 "So then, all Jews know[R]my manner of life from my youth up, which from the beginning was spent among my own nation and at Jerusalem;   Gal. 1:13f.; Phil. 3:5

5 since they have known about me for a long time previously, if they are willing to

---

[44] Lit., the Augustus' (in this case Nero)   [45] Lit., and with

testify, that I lived *as* a Pharisee according to the strictest 'sect of our religion.　Acts 15:5

6"And now I am 'standing trial ᴿfor the hope of ᴿthe promise made by God to our fathers;　　　*being tried* • Acts 24:15 • Acts 13:32

7 *the promise* to which our twelve tribes hope to attain, as they earnestly serve God night and day. And for this ᴿhope, O King, I am being accused by Jews.　Acts 24:15; 28:20

8"Why is it considered incredible among you *people* if God does raise the dead?

9"So then, ᴿI thought to myself that I had to do many things hostile to ᴿthe name of Jesus of Nazareth.　John 16:2 • John 15:21

10"And this is 'just what I did in Jerusalem; not only did I lock up many of the ᴬsaints in prisons, having received authority from the chief priests, but also when they were being put to death I 'cast my vote against them.　*also* • *holy ones* • Acts 22:20

11"And ᴬas I punished them often in all the synagogues, I tried to force them to blaspheme; and being furiously enraged at them, I kept pursuing them ᴿeven to ᴬforeign cities.　　Matt. 10:17 • Acts 22:5 • *outlying*

12"While thus engaged ᴬas I was journeying to Damascus with the authority and commission of the chief priests,　Acts 9:3-8

13 at midday, O King, I saw on the way a light from heaven, 'brighter than the sun, shining all around me and those who were journeying with me.　*above the brightness of*

14"And when we had ᴿall fallen to the ground, I heard a voice saying to me in the 'Hebrew dialect, 'Saul, Saul, why are you persecuting Me? It is hard for you to kick against the goads.'　Acts 9:7 • Jewish Aramaic

15"And I said, 'Who art Thou, Lord?' And the Lord said, 'I am Jesus whom you are persecuting.

16 'But arise, and stand on your feet; for this purpose I have appeared to you, to appoint you a minister and a witness not only to the things which you have seen, but also to the things in which I will appear to you;

17 ᴿdelivering you 'from the *Jewish* people and from the Gentiles, to whom I am sending you,　Jer. 1:8, 19 • 1 Chr. 16:35; Acts 9:15

18 to ᴿopen their eyes so that they may turn from ᴿdarkness to light and from the dominion of Satan to God, in order that they may receive forgiveness of sins and an inheritance among those who have been sanctified by faith in Me.'　Is. 35:5 • John 1:5

19"Consequently, King Agrippa, I did not prove disobedient to the heavenly vision,

20 but *kept* declaring both ᴿto those of Damascus first, and *also* at Jerusalem and *then* throughout all the region of Judea, and *even* to the Gentiles, that they should repent and turn to God, performing deeds ᴿappropriate to repentance.　Acts 9:19ff. • Matt. 3:8

21"For this reason *some* Jews seized me in the temple and tried to put me to death.

22"And so, having obtained help from

God, I stand to this day ᴿtestifying both to small and great, stating nothing but what ᴿthe Prophets and Moses said was going to take place;　Luke 16:28 • Acts 10:43; 24:14

23 that the Christ was to suffer, *and* that by reason of *His* resurrection from the dead He should be the first to proclaim light both to the *Jewish* people and to the Gentiles."

24 And while *Paul* was saying this in his defense, Festus *said in a loud voice, "Paul, you are out of your mind! 'Your great learning is driving you mad."　*The many letters*

25 But Paul *said, "I am not out of my mind, most excellent Festus, but I utter words 'of sober truth.　*of truth and rationality*

26"For the king ᴬknows about these matters, and I speak to him also with confidence, ᴬsince I am persuaded that none of these things escape his notice; for this has not been done in a corner.　*understands* • *for*

27"King Agrippa, do you believe the Prophets? I know that you do."

28 And Agrippa *replied* to Paul, "In ᴬ a short time you ᴬwill persuade me to 'become a Christian."　*With a little* • *try to convince* • *make*

29 And Paul *said,* "I' would to God, that whether ᴬin a short or long time, not only you, but also all who hear me this day, might become such as I am, except for these chains."　*I would pray to* • *with a little or with much*

30 And ᴿthe king arose and the governor and Bernice, and those who were sitting with them,　Acts 25:23

31 and when they had drawn aside, they *began* talking to one another, saying, "This ᴿ man is not doing anything worthy of death or 'imprisonment."　Acts 23:29 • *bonds*

32 And Agrippa said to Festus, "This man might have been ᴿset free if he had not ᴿappealed to Caesar."　Acts 28:18 • Acts 25:11

CHAPTER 27

Paul's Witness During the Shipwreck

AND when it was decided that we should sail for Italy, they proceeded to deliver Paul and some other prisoners to a centurion of the Augustan [46]cohort named Julius.

2 And embarking in an Adramyttian ship, which was about to sail to the regions along the coast of ᴿAsia, we put out to sea, accompanied by ᴿAristarchus, a Macedonian of Thessalonica.　Acts 2:9 • Acts 19:29

3 And the next day we put in at ᴿSidon; and Julius ᴿtreated Paul with consideration and allowed him to go to his friends and receive care.　Matt. 11:21 • Acts 27:43

4 And from there we put out to sea and sailed under the shelter of ᴿCyprus because the winds were contrary.　Acts 4:36

[46] Or, *battalion*

5 And when we had sailed through the sea along the coast of [R]Cilicia and Pamphylia, we landed at Myra in Lycia. Acts 6:9

6 And there the centurion found an [R]Alexandrian ship sailing for [R]Italy, and he put us aboard it.   Acts 28:11 • Acts 18:2; 27:1

7 And when we had sailed slowly for a good many days, and with difficulty had arrived off Cnidus, since the wind did not permit us to go farther, we sailed under the shelter of [R]Crete, off Salmone;   Titus 1:5, 12

8 and with difficulty [R]sailing past it we came to a certain place called Fair Havens, near which was the city of Lasea. Acts 27:13

9 And when considerable time had passed and the voyage was now dangerous, since even [R]the [47]fast was already over, Paul began to admonish them,   Lev. 16:29-31

10 and said to them, "Men, I perceive that the voyage will certainly be attended with damage and great loss, not only of the cargo and the ship, but also of our lives."

11 But the centurion was more persuaded by the pilot and the [c]captain of the ship, than by what was being said by Paul.   owner

12 And because the harbor was not suitable for wintering, the majority reached a decision to put out to sea from there, if somehow they could reach Phoenix, a harbor of [R]Crete, facing southwest and northwest, and spend the winter there.   Acts 2:11

13 And when a moderate south wind came up, supposing that they had gained their purpose, they weighed anchor and began sailing along Crete, close inshore.

14 But before very long there [R]rushed down from [T]the land a violent wind, called [48]Euraquilo;   Mark 4:37 • it

15 and when the ship was caught in it, and could not face the wind, we gave way to it, and let ourselves be driven along.

16 And running under the shelter of a small island called Clauda, we were scarcely able to get the ship's boat under control.

17 And after they had hoisted it up, they used [T]supporting cables in undergirding the ship; and fearing that they might [R]run aground on the shallows of Syrtis, they let down the sea anchor, and so let themselves be driven along.   helps • Acts 27:26, 29

18 The next day as we were being violently storm-tossed, [t]they began to jettison the cargo;   they were doing a throwing out

19 and on the third day they threw the ship's tackle overboard with their own hands.

20 And since neither sun nor stars appeared for many days, and no small storm was assailing us, from then on all hope of our being saved was gradually abandoned.

21 And [T]when they had gone a long time without food, then Paul stood up in their midst and said, "Men, you ought to have followed my advice and not to have set sail from Crete, and incurred this damage and loss.   there being much abstinence from food

22 "And yet now I urge you to keep up your courage, for there shall be no loss of life among you, but only of the ship.

23 "For this very night [R]an angel of the God to whom I belong and [R]whom I serve [R]stood before me,   Acts 5:19 • Rom. 1:9 • 2 Tim. 4:17

24 saying, 'Do not be afraid, Paul; [R]you must stand before Caesar; and behold, God has granted you [R]all those who are sailing with you.'   Acts 23:11 • Acts 27:31, 42, 44

25 "Therefore, keep up your courage, men, for I believe God, that [T]it will turn out exactly as I have been told.   it will be

26 "But we must [R]run aground on a certain [R]island."   Acts 27:17, 29 • Acts 28:1

27 But when the fourteenth night had come, as we were being driven about in the Adriatic Sea, about midnight the sailors began to surmise that [T]they were approaching some land.   some land was approaching them

28 And they took soundings, and found it to be [T]twenty fathoms; and a little farther on they took another sounding and found it to be [T]fifteen fathoms.   120 ft. • 90 ft.

29 And fearing that we might [R]run aground somewhere on the [T]rocks, they cast four anchors from the stern and wished for daybreak.   Acts 27:17, 26 • rough places

30 And as the sailors were trying to escape from the ship, and had let down the ship's boat into the sea, on the pretense of intending to lay out anchors from the bow,

31 Paul said to the centurion and to the soldiers, "Unless these men remain in the ship, you yourselves cannot be saved."

32 Then the soldiers cut away the ropes of the ship's boat, and let it fall away.

33 And until the day was about to dawn, Paul was encouraging them all to take some food, saying, "Today is the fourteenth day that you have been constantly watching and going without eating, having taken nothing.

34 "Therefore I encourage you to take some food, for this is for your preservation; for [R]not a hair from the head of any of you shall perish."   [Matt. 10:30]

35 And having said this, he took bread and gave thanks to God in the presence of all; and he broke it and began to eat.

36 And all of them were encouraged, and they themselves also took food.

37 And all of us in the ship were two hundred and seventy-six [T]persons.   souls

38 And when they had eaten enough, they began to lighten the ship by [R]throwing out the wheat into the sea.   Jon. 1:5; Acts 27:18

39 And when day came, they could not recognize the land; but they did observe a certain bay with a beach, and they resolved to [49]drive the ship onto it if they could.

---

[47] I.e., Day of Atonement in September or October
[48] I.e., a northeaster
[49] Some ancient mss. read bring the ship safely ashore

40 And casting off the anchors, they ^left them in the sea while at the same time they were loosening the ropes of the rudders, and hoisting the foresail to the wind, they were heading for the beach.   *were leaving*

41 But striking a^reef where two seas met, they ran the vessel aground; and the prow stuck fast and remained immovable, but the stern *began* to be broken up by the force of the waves.   *place*

42 And the soldiers' plan was to ^kill the prisoners, that none *of them* should swim away and escape;   Acts 12:19

43 but the centurion, ^wanting to bring Paul safely through, kept them from their intention, and commanded that those who could swim should^jump overboard first and get to land,   Acts 27:3 · *cast themselves*

44 and the rest *should follow*, some on planks, and others on various things from the ship. And thus it happened that^they all were brought safely to land.   Acts 27:22, 31

CHAPTER 28

Paul's Witness on Malta

A̲ND when they had been brought safely through, ^then we found out that^the island was called Malta.   Acts 27:39 · Acts 27:26

2 And the ^natives showed us extraordinary kindness; for because of the rain that had set in and because of the cold, they kindled a fire and received us all.   *barbarians*

3 But when Paul had gathered a bundle of sticks and laid them on the fire, a viper came out^because of the heat, and fastened on his hand.   *from the heat*

4 And when the^natives saw the creature hanging from his hand, they *began* saying to one another, "Undoubtedly this man is a murderer, and though he has been saved from the sea,^justice has not allowed him to live."   *barbarians* · personification of a goddess

5 However^he shook the creature off into the fire and suffered no harm.   Mark 16:18

6 But they were expecting that he was about to swell up or suddenly fall down dead. But after they had waited a long time and had seen nothing unusual happen to him, they changed their minds and^*began* to say that he was a god.   Acts 14:11

7 Now in the neighborhood of that place were lands belonging to the leading man of the island, named Publius, who welcomed us and entertained us courteously three days.

8 And it came about that the father of Publius was lying *in bed* afflicted with *recurrent* fever and dysentery; and Paul went in *to see* him and after he had prayed, he laid his hands on him and healed him.

9 And after this had happened, the rest of the people on the island who had diseases were coming to him and getting cured.

10 And they also honored us with many marks of respect; and when we were setting sail, they supplied *us* with all we needed.

11 And at the end of three months we set sail on^an Alexandrian ship which had wintered at the island, and which had the Twin Brothers for its figurehead.   Acts 27:6

12 And after we put in at Syracuse, we stayed there for three days.

13 And from there we sailed around and arrived at Rhegium, and a day later a south wind sprang up, and on the second day we came to Puteoli.

14 ^There we found *some* brethren, and were invited to stay with them for seven days; and thus we came to Rome.   *where*

15 And the ^brethren, when they heard about us, came from there as far as the Market of Appius and Three Inns to meet us; and when Paul saw them, he thanked God and took courage.   Acts 1:15; 10:23; 11:1, 12, 29

Paul's Witness in Rome

16 And when we entered Rome, Paul was ^allowed to stay by himself, with the soldier who was guarding him.   Acts 24:23

17 And it happened that after three days he called together those who were the leading men of the Jews, and when they had come together, he *began* saying to them, "Brethren, though I had done nothing against our people, or the customs of our fathers, yet I was delivered prisoner from Jerusalem into the hands of the Romans.

18 "And when they had examined me, they were willing to release me because there was no ground for putting me to death.

19 "But when the Jews objected, I was forced to appeal to Caesar; not that I had any accusation against my nation.

20 "For this reason therefore, I^requested to see you and to speak with you, for I am wearing this chain for the sake of the hope of Israel."   *invited you to see me and speak with me*

21 And they said to him, "We have neither received letters from Judea concerning you, nor have any of^the brethren come here and reported or spoken anything bad about you.   Acts 3:17; 22:5; 28:14; Rom. 9:3

22 "But we desire to hear from you what ^your views are; for concerning this^sect, it is known to us that^it is spoken against everywhere."   *you think* · Acts 24:14 · 1 Pet. 2:12

23 And when they had set a day for him, they came to him at^his lodging in large numbers; and he was explaining to them by solemnly^testifying about the kingdom of God, and trying to persuade them concerning Jesus,^from both the Law of Moses and from the Prophets, from morning until evening.   Philem. 22 · Luke 16:28 · Acts 8:35

24 And some were being persuaded by the things spoken, but others would not believe.

25 And when they did not agree with one another, they *began* leaving after Paul had

spoken one *parting* word, "The Holy Spirit rightly spoke through[R]Isaiah the prophet to your fathers,　　Is. 6:9, 10

26 saying,

'GO[R]TO THIS PEOPLE AND SAY,　Is. 6:9 ★
"YOU[T]WILL KEEP ON HEARING, BUT WILL NOT UNDERSTAND;　*with a hearing*
AND [T]YOU WILL KEEP ON SEEING, BUT WILL NOT PERCEIVE; *seeing you will see*

27 [R]FOR THE HEART OF THIS PEOPLE HAS BECOME DULL,　Is. 6:10 ★
AND WITH THEIR EARS THEY SCARCELY HEAR,
AND THEY HAVE CLOSED THEIR EYES;
LEST THEY SHOULD SEE WITH THEIR EYES,
AND HEAR WITH THEIR EARS,

AND UNDERSTAND WITH THEIR HEART AND RETURN,
AND I SHOULD HEAL THEM." '

28"Let it be known to you therefore, that this salvation of God has been sent[R]to the Gentiles; they will also listen." Is. 42:1; 49:6 ★

29 [[50]And when he had spoken these words, the Jews departed, having a great dispute among themselves.]

30 And he stayed two full years[^]in his own rented quarters, and was welcoming all who came to him,　*at his own expense*

31 [^]preaching the kingdom of God, and teaching concerning the Lord Jesus Christ with all openness, unhindered.　*proclaiming*

[50] Many mss. do not contain this verse

Jewish Feasts

Feast of	Month on Jewish Calendar	Day	Corresponding Month	References
*Passover (Unleavened Bread)	Nisan	14–21	Mar.–Apr.	Ex. 12:43— 13:10; Matt. 26:17–20
*Pentecost (First Fruits or Weeks)	Sivan	6 (50 days after Passover)	May–June	Deut. 16:9–12; Acts 2:1
Trumpets, *Rosh Hashanah*	Tishri	1, 2	Sept.–Oct.	Num. 29:1–6
Day of Atonement, *Yom Kippur*	Tishri	10	Sept.–Oct.	Lev. 23:26–32; Heb. 9:7
*Tabernacles (Booths or Ingathering)	Tishri	15–22	Sept.–Oct.	Neh. 8:13–18; John 7:2
Dedication (Lights), *Hanukkah*	Chislev	25 (8 days)	Nov.–Dec.	John 10:22
Purim (Lots)	Adar	14, 15	Feb.–Mar.	Esth. 9:18–32

*The three major feasts for which all males of Israel were required to travel to the Temple in Jerusalem (Ex. 23:14–19).

THE EPISTLE OF PAUL TO THE

ROMANS

THE BOOK OF ROMANS

Romans, Paul's greatest work, is placed first among his thirteen epistles in the New Testament. While the four Gospels present the words and works of Jesus Christ, Romans explores the significance of His sacrificial death. Using a question-and-answer format, Paul records the most systematic presentation of doctrine in the Bible. Romans is more than a book of theology; it is also a book of practical exhortation. The good news of Jesus Christ is more than facts to be believed; it is also a life to be lived—a life of righteousness befitting the person "justified as a gift by His [God's] grace through the redemption which is in Christ Jesus" (3:24).

Although some manuscripts omit "in Rome" in 1:7, 15, the title *Pros Romaious*, "To the Romans," has been associated with the epistle almost from the beginning.

THE AUTHOR OF ROMANS

All critical schools agree on the Pauline authorship (1:1) of this foundation book. The vocabulary, style, logic, and theological development are consistent with Paul's other epistles. Paul dictated this letter to a secretary named Tertius (16:22), who was allowed to add his own greeting.

The problem arises not with the authorship but with the disunity of the epistle. Some Latin (but no Greek) manuscripts omit 15:1—16:24, and the closing doxology (16:25–27) is placed at the end of chapter 14 in some manuscripts. These variations have led some scholars to conclude that the last two chapters were not originally part of the epistle, or that Paul issued it in two editions. However, most scholars believe that chapter 15 fits in logically with the rest of the epistle. There is more debate over chapter 16, because Paul greets by name twenty-six persons in a church he has never visited. Some scholars contend that it was a separate letter, perhaps written to Ephesus, that was appended to this epistle. Such a letter would be surprising, to say the least (nothing but greetings), especially in the ancient world. It is simpler to understand the list of greetings as Paul's effort as a stranger to the Roman church to list his mutual friends. Paul met these people in the cities of his missionary journeys. Significantly, the only other Pauline epistle that lists individual greetings was addressed to the believers at Colossae, another church Paul had never visited. It may be that this portion was omitted from some copies of Romans because it did not seem relevant.

THE TIME OF ROMANS

Paul did not found the church at Rome, and the tradition that Peter was its founder is contrary to the evidence. It is possible that it began when some of the Jews and proselytes to Judaism who became followers of Christ on the day of Pentecost (cf. Acts 2:10) returned to Rome, but it is more likely that Christians from churches established by Paul in Asia, Macedonia, and Greece settled in Rome and led others to Christ. According to this epistle, Gentiles were predominant in the church at Rome (1:13; 11:13, 28–31; 15:15, 16), but there were also Jewish believers (2:17—3:8; 3:21—4:1; 7:1–14; 14:1—15:12).

Rome was founded in 753 B.C., and by the time of Paul it was the greatest city in the world with over one million inhabitants (one inscription says over four million). It was full of magnificent buildings, but the majority of people were slaves: opulence and squalor coexisted in the Imperial City. The church in Rome was well known (1:8), and it had been established for several years by the time of this letter (see 14:14; 15:23). The believers there were probably numerous, and evidently they met in several places (16:1–16). The historian Tacitus referred to the Christians who were persecuted under Nero in A.D. 64 as "an immense multitude." The gospel filled the gap left by the practically defunct polytheism of Roman religion.

Paul wrote Romans in A.D. 57, near the end of his third missionary journey (Acts 18:23—21:14; cf. Rom. 15:19). It was evidently written during his three-month stay in Greece (Acts 20:3–6), more specifically, in Corinth. Paul was staying with Gaius of Corinth (16:23; cf. 1 Cor. 1:14), and he also mentioned "Erastus, the city treasurer" (16:23). A first-century inscription in Corinth mentions him: "Erastus, the commissioner of public works, laid this pavement at his own expense." Paul's collection from the churches of Macedonia and Achaia for the needy Christians in Jerusalem was complete (15:26), and he was ready to deliver it (15:25). Instead of sailing directly to Jerusalem, Paul avoided a plot by the Jews by first going north to Philippi. He evidently gave

this letter to Phoebe from the church at Cenchrea, near Corinth, and she carried it to Rome (16:1, 2).

✝ THE CHRIST OF ROMANS

Paul presents Jesus Christ as the second Adam whose righteousness and substitutionary death have provided justification for all who place their faith in Him. He offers His righteousness as a gracious gift to sinful men, having borne God's condemnation and wrath for their sinfulness. His death and resurrection are the basis for the believer's redemption, justification, reconciliation, salvation, and glorification.

🔑 KEYS TO ROMANS

Key Word: The Righteousness of God— The theme of Romans is found in 1:16, 17: God offers the gift of His righteousness to everyone who comes to Christ by faith. Paul writes Romans to reveal God's sovereign plan of salvation (1—8), to show how Jews and Gentiles fit into that plan (9—11), and to exhort them to live righteous and harmonious lives (12—16). In his sweeping presentation of God's plan of salvation, Paul moves from condemnation to glorification and from positional truth to practical truth. Key words, such as righteousness, faith, law, all, and sin each appear at least sixty times in this epistle.

Key Verses: Romans 1:16, 17 and 3:21-25— "For I am not ashamed of the gospel, for it is the power of God for salvation to everyone who believes, to the Jew first and also to the Greek. For in it *the* righteousness of God is revealed from faith to faith; as it is written, 'But the righteous *man* shall live by faith' " (1:16, 17).

"But now apart from the Law *the* righteousness of God has been manifested, being witnessed by the Law and the Prophets, even *the* righteousness of God through faith in Jesus Christ for all those who believe; for there is no distinction; for all have sinned and fall short of the glory of God, being justified as a gift by His grace through the redemption which is in Christ Jesus; whom God displayed publicly as a propitiation in His blood through faith. *This was* to demonstrate His righteousness, because in the forbearance of God He passed over the sins previously committed" (3:21-25).

Key Chapters: Romans 6—8— Foundational to all teaching on the spiritual life is the central passage of Romans 6—8. The answers to the questions of how to be delivered from sin, how to live a balanced life under grace, and how to live the victorious Christian life through the power of the Holy Spirit are all contained here. Many consider this to be the principal passage on conforming to the image of Jesus Christ.

📐 SURVEY OF ROMANS

The poet Samuel Taylor Coleridge regarded Romans as "the most profound book in existence," and the commentator Godet called it "the cathedral of the Christian faith." Because of its majestic declaration of the divine plan of salvation, Martin Luther wrote: "This epistle is the chief part of the New Testament and the very purest gospel . . . . It can never be read or pondered too much, and the more it is dealt with the more precious it becomes, and the better it tastes." The four Gospels present the words and works of the Lord Jesus, but Romans, "The Gospel According to Paul," delves more into the significance of His death and resurrection. The theology of Romans is balanced by practical exhortation, because Paul sees the believer's position as the basis for his practice. The theme of righteous-

FOCUS	REVELATION OF GOD'S RIGHTEOUSNESS			VINDICATION OF GOD'S RIGHTEOUSNESS			APPLICATION OF GOD'S RIGHTEOUSNESS	
REFERENCE	1:1————3:21————6:1————			9:1————9:30————11:1————			12:1————14:1——16:27	
DIVISION	NEED FOR GOD'S RIGHTEOUSNESS	IMPUTATION OF GOD'S RIGHTEOUSNESS	DEMONSTRATION OF GOD'S RIGHTEOUSNESS	ISRAEL'S ELECTION	ISRAEL'S PRESENT: REJECTION	ISRAEL'S FUTURE: RESTORATION	CHRISTIAN DUTIES	CHRISTIAN LIBERTIES
TOPIC	SIN	SALVATION	SANCTIFICATION	SOVEREIGNTY			SERVICE	
	DOCTRINAL						BEHAVIORAL	
LOCATION	PROBABLY WRITTEN IN CORINTH							
TIME	C. A.D. 57							

ness that runs through the book is reflected in the following outline: the revelation of the righteousness of God (1—8); the vindication of the righteousness of God (9—11); the application of the righteousness of God (12—16).

The Revelation of the Righteousness of God (1—8): The prologue (1:1-17) consists of a salutation (1:1-7), a statement of Paul's desire to minister in Rome (1:8-15), and the theme of the book (1:16, 17). This two-verse theme is the basic text of Romans because it combines the three crucial concepts of salvation, righteousness, and faith.

In 1:18—3:20, Paul builds a solid case for the condemnation of all people under the holy God. The Gentiles are without excuse because they have suppressed the knowledge of God they received from nature and their conscience (1:18-32; their seven-step regression is traced in 1:21-31). The Jews are also under the condemnation of God, and Paul overcomes every objection they could raise to this conclusion (2:1—3:8). God judges according to truth (2:2-5), works (2:6-10), and impartiality (2:11-16), and both the moral and religious Jews fail to meet His standard. Paul concludes his discussion of the reasons for the guilt of the Jews by reminding them they do not obey the Law (2:17-29) nor believe the Oracles of God (3:1-8). The divine verdict (3:9-20) is universal: "all have sinned and fall short of the glory of God" (3:23).

The section on justification (3:21—5:21) centers on and develops the theme of God's provision for man's need. The first eleven verses are the core of the book (3:21-31), revealing that in Christ, God is both Judge and Savior. Justification is by grace (the source of salvation; 3:21-24), by blood (the basis of salvation; 3:25, 26), and by faith (the condition of salvation; 3:27-31).

Chapter 4 illustrates the principle of justification by faith apart from works in the life of Abraham. Justification results in reconciliation between God and man (5:1-11). It is brought about by the love of God which is causeless (5:6), measureless (5:7, 8), and unconditional (5:9-11). In 5:12-21 Paul con-

trasts the two Adams and the opposite results of their two acts. The righteousness of the second Adam is imputed to all who trust in Him, leading to reconciliation.

Chapter 6 describes the believer's relationship to sin: in his position he is dead to the principle of sin (6:1-14) and the practice of sin (6:15-23). The reality of identification with Christ is the basis for the sanctified Christian life. After describing the Christian's emancipation from the law (7), Paul looks at the work of the Holy Spirit who indwells and empowers every believer (8:1-17). The next major topic after condemnation, justification, and sanctification is glorification (8:18-39). All Christians can anticipate a time when they will be perfectly conformed to Jesus Christ not only in their position (present) but also in their practice (the future resurrection).

The Vindication of the Righteousness of God (9—11): It appears that God has rejected His people, Israel, but it is really Israel who has rejected her Messiah. God's rejection of Israel is only partial (there is a spiritual remnant that has trusted in Christ) and temporary (they will be grafted back, 11:23-27). Paul appropriately quotes frequently from the Old Testament in this section, and he emphasizes that God will be faithful to His covenant promises and restore Israel.

The Application of the Righteousness of God (12—16): Paul recognizes that behavior must be built upon belief, and this is why the practical exhortations of this epistle appear after his teaching on the believer's position in Christ. The salvation described in the first eleven chapters should transform a Christian's life in relation to God (12:1, 2), society (12:3-21), higher powers (13:1-7); and one's neighbors (13:8-14). In chapters 14 and 15 the apostle discusses the whole concept of Christian liberty, noting its principles (14) and its practice (15:1-13). A changed life is not a condition for salvation, but it should be the natural outcome of saving faith. The epistle closes with Paul's statement of his plans (15:14-33), a long series of personal greetings (16:1-16), and an admonition followed by a doxology (16:17-27).

OUTLINE OF ROMANS

Part One: The Revelation of the Righteousness of God (1:1—8:39)

CHAPTER 1

Introduction

PAUL, a bond-servant of Christ Jesus, ᵀcalled *as* an apostle,ᴿset apart forᴿthe gospel of God,   *a called apostle* · Acts 9:15 · Mark 1:14

2 which He promised beforehand through His prophets in the holy Scriptures,

3 concerning His Son, who was born ofᴿa descendant of David according to the flesh,   Is. 9:7; Gal. 4:4 ★

4 who was declaredᴿthe Son of God with power ¹by the resurrection from the dead, according to the ᴬspirit of holiness, Jesus Christ our Lord,   Ps. 2:7; 16:10, 11 ★ · *spirit*

5 through whom we have received grace and ᴿapostleship ᵀto bring about *the* ᴿobedience of faith among all the Gentiles, for His name's sake,   Acts 1:25 · *for obedience* · Acts 6:7

6 among whom you also are theᴿcalled of Jesus Christ;   Jude 1; Rev. 17:14

7 to all who areᴿbeloved of God in Rome, called *as* ᴬsaints: ᴿGrace to you and peace from God our Father and the Lord Jesus Christ.   Rom. 5:5ff. · *holy ones* · Eph. 1:2

8 First, ᴿI thank my God through Jesus Christ for you all, because ᴿyour faith is being proclaimed throughout the whole world.   1 Cor. 1:4 · Acts 28:22; Rom. 16:19

9 ForᴿGod, whom Iᴿserve in my spirit in the *preaching of the* gospel of His Son, is my witness *as to* how unceasinglyᴿI make mention of you,   Rom. 9:1 · Acts 24:14 · Eph. 1:16

10 always in my prayers making request, if perhaps now at last byᵀthe will of God I may succeed in coming to you.   Acts 18:21

11 ForᴿI long to see you in order that I may impart some spiritual gift to you, that you may be established;   Acts 19:21

12 that is, that I may be encouraged together with you *while* among you, each of us by the other's faith, both yours and mine.

13 AndᴿI do not want you to be unaware, ᴿbrethren, that often I have planned to come to you (and have been prevented thus far) in order that I might obtain someᴿfruit among you also, even as among the rest of the Gentiles.   Rom. 11:25 · Acts 1:15 · John 4:36; 15:16

14 ᴿI am ²under obligation both to Greeks and toᴿbarbarians, both to the wise and to the foolish.   1 Cor. 9:16 · Acts 28:2

15 Thus, for my part, I am eager to preach the gospel to you also who are in Rome.

¹ Or, *as a result of*   ² Lit., *debtor*

16 For I am not [R]ashamed of the gospel, for it is the power of God for salvation to everyone who believes, to the [R]Jew first and also to [R]the Greek.   Mark 8:38 • Rom. 2:9 • John 7:35

17 For in it the righteousness of God is revealed from faith to faith; as it is written, "BUT [A] THE RIGHTEOUS man SHALL LIVE BY FAITH."   But he who is righteous by faith shall live.

Reason for Gentile Guilt

18 For [R]the wrath of God is revealed from heaven against all ungodliness and unrighteousness of men, who [R]suppress the truth [A]in unrighteousness,   Rom. 5:9 • 2 Thess. 2:6f. • by

19 because [R]that which is known about God is evident [A]within them; for God made it evident to them.   [Acts 14:17; 17:24ff.] • among

20 For since the creation of the world His invisible attributes, His eternal power and divine nature, have been clearly seen, [R]being understood through what has been made, so that they are without excuse.   Jer. 5:21f.

21 For even though they knew God, they did not [3]honor Him as God, or give thanks; but they became futile in their speculations, and their foolish heart was darkened.

22 [R]Professing to be wise, they became fools,   Jer. 10:14; [1 Cor. 1:20]

23 and exchanged the glory of the incorruptible God for an image in the form of corruptible man and of birds and four-footed animals and [4]crawling creatures.

Results of Gentile Guilt

24 Therefore God gave them over in the lusts of their hearts to impurity, that their bodies might be dishonored among them.

25 For they exchanged the truth of God for [a] lie, and worshiped and served the creature rather than the Creator, who is blessed [T]forever. Amen.   the lie • unto the ages

26 For this reason God gave them over to [R]degrading passions; for their women exchanged the natural function for that which is [T]unnatural,   1 Thess. 4:5 • against nature

27 and in the same way also the men abandoned the natural function of the woman and burned in their desire toward one another, men with men committing indecent acts and receiving in their own persons the due penalty of their error.

28 And just as they did not see fit [T]to acknowledge God any longer, God gave them over to a depraved mind, to do those things which are not proper,   to have God in knowledge

29 being filled with all unrighteousness, wickedness, greed, evil; full of envy, murder, strife, deceit, malice; they are gossips,

30 slanderers, [A]haters of God, insolent, arrogant, boastful, inventors of evil, [R]disobedient to parents,   hateful to God • 2 Tim. 3:2

31 without understanding, untrustworthy, [A]unloving, unmerciful;   2 Tim. 3:3

32 and, although they know the ordinance of God, that those who practice such things are worthy of [R]death, they not only do the same, but also [A]give hearty approval to those who practice them.   [Rom. 6:21] • Luke 11:48

CHAPTER 2

Jews Are Judged According to Truth

THEREFORE you are [R]without excuse, [R]every man of you who passes judgment, for in that [A]you judge another, you condemn yourself; for you who judge practice the same things.   [Rom. 1:20] • Luke 12:14 • 2 Sam. 12:5–7

2 And we know that the judgment of God [T]rightly falls upon those who practice such things.   is according to truth against

3 And do you suppose this, O man, when you pass judgment upon those who practice such things and do the same yourself, that you will escape the judgment of God?

4 Or do you think lightly of the riches of His kindness and [R]forbearance and [R]patience, not knowing that the kindness of God leads you to repentance?   [Rom. 3:25] • [1 Tim. 1:16]

5 But because of your stubbornness and unrepentant heart you are storing up wrath for yourself in the day of wrath and revelation of the righteous judgment of God,

Jews Are Judged by Their Works

6 [R]who WILL RENDER TO EVERY MAN ACCORDING TO HIS DEEDS: Ps. 62:12; Prov. 24:12

7 to those who by perseverance in doing good seek for [R]glory and honor and immortality, [R]eternal life;   Heb. 2:7 • Matt. 25:46

8 but to those who are selfishly ambitious and do not obey the truth, but obey unrighteousness, wrath and indignation.

9 There will be tribulation and distress [T]for every soul of man who does evil, of the Jew first and also of the Greek,   upon

10 but [R]glory and honor and peace to every man who does good, to the Jew [R]first and also to the Greek.   [1 Pet. 1:7] • Rom. 2:9

Jews Are Judged with Impartiality

11 For there is no partiality with God.

12 For all who have sinned [A]without the Law will also perish without the Law; and all who have sinned [A]under the Law will be judged by the Law;   without law • under law

13 for [R]not the hearers [A]of the Law are [A]just before God, but the doers [A]of the Law will be justified.   Matt. 7:21, 24ff. • of law • righteous

14 For when Gentiles who do not have [A]the Law do [T]instinctively [R]the things of the Law,

---

[3] Lit., glorify   [4] Or possibly, reptiles

these, not having ^the Law, are a law to themselves,   *law • by nature* • Rom. 1:19; 2:15

15 in that they show the work of the Law written in their hearts, their conscience bearing witness, and their thoughts alternately accusing or else defending them,

16 on the day when, ᴿaccording to my gospel, ᴿGod will judge the secrets of men through Christ Jesus.   1 Cor. 15:1 • Acts 10:42

Jews Do Not Obey the Law

17 But if you bear the name "Jew," and rely upon the Law, and boast in God,

18 and know *His* will, and ᴿapprove the things that are essential, being instructed out of the Law,   Phil. 1:10

19 and are confident that you yourself are a guide to the blind, a light to those who are in darkness,

20 a corrector of the foolish, a teacher of the immature, having in the Law the embodiment of knowledge and of the truth,

21 you, therefore, who teach another, do you not teach yourself? You who preach that one should not steal, do you steal?

22 You who say that one should not commit adultery, do you commit adultery? You who abhor idols, do you rob temples?

23 You who ᴿboast ^in the Law, through your breaking the Law, do you dishonor God?   Mic. 3:11; John 5:45; Rom. 2:17 • *in law*

24 For ᴿthe ᴿname of God is blasphemed among the Gentiles ᴿbecause of you," just as it is written.   Ezek. 36:20ff. • 2 Pet. 2:2

25 For indeed circumcision is of value, if you practice ^the Law; but if you are a transgressor ^of the Law, your circumcision has become uncircumcision.   *law • of law*

26 If therefore ᴿthe ᵀuncircumcised man ᴿkeeps the requirements of the Law, will not his uncircumcision be regarded as circumcision?   Eph. 2:11 • *uncircumcision* • Rom. 2:25

27 And will not he who is physically uncircumcised, if he keeps the Law, will he not judge you who ᵀthough having the letter *of the Law* and circumcision are a transgressor ^of the Law?   *through the letter • of law*

28 For ᴿhe is not a Jew who is one outwardly; neither is circumcision that which is outward in the flesh.   John 8:39; Rom. 2:17; 9:6

29 But he is a Jew who is one inwardly; and circumcision is that which is of the heart, by the Spirit, not by the letter; and his praise is not from men, but from God.

CHAPTER 3

Jews Do Not Believe the Oracles

THEN what advantage has the Jew? Or what is the benefit of circumcision?

2 Great in every respect. First of all, that they were entrusted with the oracles of God.

3 What then? If ᵀsome ^did not believe, their unbelief will not nullify the faithfulness of God, will it?   Heb. 4:2 • *were unfaithful*

4 ᴿMay it never be! Rather, let God be found true, though every man *be found* ᴿa liar, as it is written,   Luke 20:16 • Ps. 116:11
"That ᴿThou mightest be justified in Thy words,   Ps. 51:4
And mightest prevail when Thou ^art judged."   *dost enter into judgment*

5 But if our unrighteousness ^demonstrates the righteousness of God, ᴿwhat shall we say? The God who inflicts wrath is not unrighteous, is He? (I ᴿam speaking in human terms.)   *commends* • Rom. 4:1 • Rom. 6:19

6 ᴿMay it never be! For otherwise how will God judge the world?   Luke 20:16

7 But if through my lie the truth of God abounded to His glory, ᴿwhy am I also still being judged as a sinner?   Rom. 9:19

8 And why not *say* (as we are slanderously reported and as some affirm that we say), "Let ᴿus do evil that good may come"? ᵀTheir condemnation is just.   Rom. 6:1 • *Whose*

Conclusion: All Are Guilty Before God

9 What then? Are we better than they? Not at all; for we have already charged that both Jews and Greeks are all under sin;

10 as it is written,
"There ᴿis none righteous, not even one;   Ps. 14:1-3; 53:1-3
11 There is none who understands,
There is none who seeks for God;
12 All have turned aside, together they have become useless;
There is none who does good,
There is not even one."
13 "Their ᴿthroat is an open grave,
With their tongues they keep deceiving,"   Ps. 5:9
"The ᴿpoison of asps is under their lips";   Ps. 140:3
14 "Whose ᴿmouth is full of cursing and bitterness";   Ps. 10:7
15 "Their feet are swift to shed blood,
16 Destruction and misery are in their paths,
17 And the path of peace have they not known."
18 "There ᴿis no fear of God before their eyes."   Ps. 36:1

19 Now we know that whatever the ᴿLaw says, it speaks to ᴿthose who are ᵀunder the Law, that every mouth may be closed, and ᴿall the world may become accountable to God;   John 10:34 • Rom. 2:12 • *in* • Rom. 3:9

20 because ᴿby the works ^of the Law no flesh will be justified in His sight; for ^through the Law *comes* the knowledge of sin.   Ps. 143:2; [Acts 13:39] • *of law • through law*

Description of Righteousness

21 But now apart from the Law *the* righteousness of God has been manifested, being witnessed by the Law and the Prophets,

22 even *the* [R]righteousness of God through faith in Jesus Christ for all those who believe; for there is no distinction;   Rom. 1:17
23 for [A]all [R]have sinned and fall short of the glory of God,   *all sinned* • Rom. 3:9
24 being justified as a gift [R]by His grace through [T]the redemption which is in Christ Jesus; [Eph. 2:8] • 1 Cor. 1:30; [Eph. 1:7; Col. 1:14]
25 whom God displayed publicly as a propitiation [A]in His blood through faith. *This was* to demonstrate His righteousness, because in the forbearance of God He passed over the sins previously committed;   *by*
26 for the demonstration, *I say*, of His righteousness at the present time, that He might be just and the justifier of the one who [T]has faith in Jesus.   *is of the faith of Jesus.*
27 Where then is [R]boasting? It is excluded. By [R]what kind of law? Of works? No, but by a law of faith.   Rom. 2:17, 23; 4:2 • Rom. 9:31
28 For we maintain that a man is justified by faith apart from works [A]of the Law. *of law*
29 Or [R]is God *the God* of Jews only? Is He not *the God* of Gentiles also? Yes, of Gentiles also,   Acts 10:34f.; Rom. 9:24; Gal. 3:28
30 since indeed God who will justify the [T]circumcised [T]by faith and the uncircumcised through faith is one.   *circumcision* • *out of*
31 Do we then nullify [A]the Law through faith? [R]May it never be! On the contrary, we [B]establish the Law.   *law* • Rom. 3:4 • Matt. 5:17

CHAPTER 4

Abraham's Righteousness Apart from Works

WHAT then shall we say that Abraham, [A]our forefather according to the flesh, has found? *our forefather, has found according to the flesh*
2 For if Abraham was justified by works, he has something to boast about; but [R]not [T]before God.   1 Cor. 1:31 • *toward*
3 For what does the Scripture say? "AND [R]ABRAHAM BELIEVED GOD, AND IT WAS RECKONED TO HIM AS RIGHTEOUSNESS." James 2:23
4 Now to the one who works, his wage is not reckoned as a favor, but as what is due.
5 But to the one who does not work, but believes in Him who justifies the ungodly, his faith is reckoned as righteousness,
6 just as David also speaks of the blessing upon the man to whom God reckons righteousness apart from works:
7 "BLESSED [R]ARE THOSE WHOSE LAWLESS DEEDS HAVE BEEN FORGIVEN, Ps. 32:1 AND WHOSE SINS HAVE BEEN COVERED.
8 "BLESSED [R]IS THE MAN WHOSE SIN THE LORD WILL NOT [T]TAKE [R]INTO ACCOUNT." Ps. 32:2 • *reckon* • 2 Cor. 5:19

Abraham's Righteousness Apart from Circumcision

9 Is this blessing then upon [T]the circumcised, or upon [T]the uncircumcised also? For we say, "FAITH WAS RECKONED TO ABRAHAM AS RIGHTEOUSNESS." *circumcision* • *uncircumcision*

10 How then was it reckoned? While he was [T]circumcised, or [T]uncircumcised? Not while circumcised, but while [T]uncircumcised;   *in circumcision* • *in uncircumcision*
11 and he received the sign of circumcision, a seal of the righteousness of the faith which he had while uncircumcised, that he might be the father of [R]all who believe without being circumcised, that righteousness might be reckoned to them,   Rom. 3:22; 4:16
12 and the father of circumcision to those who not only are of the circumcision, but who also follow in the steps of the faith of our father Abraham which he had while uncircumcised.

Abraham's Righteousness Apart from the Law

13 For the promise to Abraham or to his [T]descendants that he would be heir of the world was not [T]through the Law, but through the righteousness of faith.   *seed* • *through law*
14 For [R]if those who are [A]of the Law are heirs, faith is made void and the promise is nullified;   Gal. 3:18 • *of law*
15 for [R]the Law brings about wrath, but [R]where there is no law, neither is there violation.   Rom. 7:7; 1 Cor. 15:56; Gal. 3:10 • Rom. 3:20

Abraham's Righteousness Was by Faith

16 For this reason *it is* by faith, that *it might be* in accordance with grace, in order that the promise may be certain to all the descendants, not only to those who are of the Law, but also to those who are of the faith of Abraham, who is the father of us all,
17 (as it is written, "A FATHER OF MANY NATIONS HAVE I MADE YOU") in the sight of Him whom he believed, *even* God, who gives life to the dead and [R]calls into being that which does not exist.   Is. 48:13; 51:2
18 In hope against hope he believed, in order that he might become a father of many nations, according to that which had been spoken, "SO SHALL YOUR DESCENDANTS BE."
19 And without becoming weak in faith he contemplated his own body, now as good as dead since he was about a hundred years old, and the deadness of Sarah's womb;
20 yet, with respect to the promise of God, he did not waver in unbelief, but grew strong in faith, [R]giving glory to God, Matt. 9:8
21 and being fully assured that what He had promised, He was able also to perform.
22 Therefore also [R]IT WAS RECKONED TO HIM AS RIGHTEOUSNESS.   Gen. 15:6; Rom. 4:3
23 Now [R]not for his sake only was it written, that it was reckoned to him, Rom. 15:4
24 but for our sake also, to whom it will be reckoned, as those who believe in Him who raised Jesus our Lord from the dead,
25 *He* who was [R]delivered up because of our transgressions, and was [R]raised because of our justification.   Is. 53:4, 5 • [Rom. 5:18]

CHAPTER 5

Peace with God

THEREFORE[R] having been justified by faith,[A]we have peace with God through our Lord Jesus Christ,   Rom. 3:28 • *let us have*

2 through whom also we have [R]obtained our introduction by faith into this grace[R]in which we stand; and[A]we exult in hope of the glory of God. [Eph. 2:18] • 1 Cor. 15:1 • *let us exult*

Joy in Tribulation

3 And not only this, but[A]we also exult in our tribulations, knowing that tribulation brings about perseverance;   *let us also exult*

4 and perseverance, [R]proven character; and proven character, hope;   Phil. 2:22

5 and hope[R]does not disappoint, because the love of God has been[R]poured out within our hearts through the Holy Spirit who was given to us.   Ps. 119:116 • Acts 2:33; Gal. 4:6

6 For while we were still helpless, at the right time Christ died for the ungodly.

7 For one will hardly die for a righteous man; though perhaps for the good man someone would dare even to die.

8 But God [R]demonstrates [R]His own love toward us, in that while we were yet sinners, Christ died for us.   Rom. 3:5 • Is. 53:5 ★

Salvation from God's Wrath

9 Much more then, having now been justified[A]by His blood, we shall be saved from the wrath *of God* through Him.   *in*

10 For if while we were[A]enemies, we were reconciled to God through the death of His Son, much more, having been reconciled, we shall be saved[A]by His life.   Rom. 11:28 • *in*

11 [R]And not only this,[A]but we also exult in God through our Lord Jesus Christ, through whom we have now received[R]the reconciliation.   Rom. 5:3 • *but also exulting* • Rom. 5:10

Contrast of Righteousness and Condemnation

12 Therefore, just as through[R]one man sin entered into the world, and[R]death through sin, and so death spread to all men, because all sinned—   Gen. 2:17 • Rom. 6:23

13 for until the Law sin was in the world; but sin is not imputed when there is no law.

14 Nevertheless death reigned from Adam until Moses, even over those who had not sinned[R]in the likeness of the offense of Adam, who is a [5]type[R] of Him who was to come.   Hos. 6:7 • [1 Cor. 15:45]

15 But the free gift is not like the transgression. For if by the transgression of the one the many died, much more did the grace of God and the gift by the grace of the one Man, Jesus Christ, abound to the many.

16 And the gift is not like *that which came* through the one who sinned; for on

the one hand the judgment *arose* from one *transgression* resulting in condemnation, but on the other hand the free gift *arose* from many transgressions[T]resulting in justification. *to condemnation* • *to an act of righteousness*

17 For if by the transgression of the one, death reigned[R]through the one, much more those who receive the abundance of grace and of the gift of righteousness will reign in life through the One, Jesus Christ.   Gen. 2:17

18 So then as through one transgression there resulted condemnation to all men, even so through one act of righteousness there resulted justification of life to all men.

19 For as through the one man's disobedience the many were made sinners, even so through[R]the obedience of the One the many will be made righteous.   [Is. 53:11, 12] ★

20 And[A]the Law came in that the transgression might increase; but where sin increased, grace abounded all the more,   *law*

21 that, as sin reigned in death, even so grace might reign through righteousness to eternal life through Jesus Christ our Lord.

CHAPTER 6

Believer's Death to Sin in Principle

WHAT shall we say then? Are we to continue in sin that grace might increase?

2 May it never be! How shall we who [R]died to sin still live in it?   [Col. 2:20]

3 Or do you not know that all of us who have been[R]baptized into Christ Jesus have been baptized into His death?   [Matt. 28:19]

4 Therefore we have been buried with Him through baptism into death, in order that as Christ was raised from the dead through the [R]glory of the Father, so we too might walk in newness of life.   John 11:40

5 For [R]if we have become[A]united with *Him* in the likeness of His death, certainly we shall be also[A]*in the likeness* of His resurrection,   Col. 2:12 • *united with the likeness* • *with*

6 knowing this, that our old[T]self was crucified with *Him*, that our body of sin might be[A]done away with, that we should no longer be slaves to sin;   *man* • *made powerless*

7 for he who has died is freed from sin.

8 Now if we have died with Christ, we believe that we shall also live with Him,

9 knowing that Christ, having been raised from the dead, is never to die again; death no longer is master over Him.

10 For the death that He died, He died to sin, once for all; but the life that He lives, He lives to God.

11 Even so consider yourselves to be dead to sin, but alive to God in Christ Jesus.

12 Therefore do not let sin reign in your mortal body that you should obey its lusts,

13 and do not go on presenting[T]the members of your body to sin *as*[A]instruments of unrighteousness; but[R]present yourselves to God as those alive from the dead, and your members *as*[A]instruments of righteousness to God.   *your members to sin* • *weapons* • Rom. 12:1

---

[5] Or, *foreshadowing*

14 For sin shall not be master over you, for you are not under law, but under grace.

Believer's Death to Sin in Practice

15 What then? [R]Shall we sin because we are not under law but under grace? [R]May it never be!   Rom. 6:1 • Luke 20:16; Rom. 6:2

16 Do you not know that when you present yourselves to someone *as* slaves for obedience, you are slaves of the one whom you obey, either of sin resulting in death, or of obedience resulting in righteousness?

17 But thanks be to God that though you were slaves of sin, you became obedient from the heart to that [R]form of teaching to which you were committed,   2 Tim. 1:13

18 and having been [R]freed from sin, you became slaves of righteousness.   John 8:32

19 I am speaking in human terms because of the weakness of your flesh. For just [R]as you presented your members *as* slaves to impurity and to lawlessness, [T]resulting in *further* lawlessness, so now present your members *as* slaves to righteousness, resulting in sanctification.   Rom. 6:13 • *to lawlessness*

20 For when you were slaves of sin, you were free in regard to righteousness.

21 Therefore what [T]benefit were you then [T]deriving [T]from the things of which you are now ashamed? For the outcome of those things is [R]death.   *fruit • having • in* • Rom. 1:32

22 But now having been freed from sin and enslaved to God, you [T]derive your [T]benefit, [T]resulting in sanctification, and the outcome, eternal life.   *have • fruit • to sanctification*

23 For the wages of [R]sin is death, but the free gift of God is [R]eternal life in Christ Jesus our Lord.   [Rom. 1:32; 5:12] • Matt. 25:46

CHAPTER 7

Dead to the Law but Alive to God

OR do you not know, [R]brethren (for I am speaking to those who know the law), that the law has jurisdiction over a person as long as he lives?   Rom. 1:13

2 For [R]the married woman is bound by law to her husband while he is living; but if her husband dies, she is released from the law concerning the husband.   1 Cor. 7:39

3 So then if, while her husband is living, she is joined to another man, she shall be called an adulteress; but if her husband dies,

she is free from the law, so that she is not an adulteress, though she is joined to another man.

4 Therefore, my brethren, you also were [R]made to die to the Law through the body of Christ, that you might be joined to another, to Him who was raised from the dead, that we might bear fruit for God.   Rom. 6:2; 7:6

5 For while we were in the flesh, the sinful passions, which were *aroused* by the Law, were at work [R]in the members of our body to bear fruit for death.   Rom. 6:13, 21, 23

6 But now we have been released from the Law, having died to that by which we were bound, so that we serve in newness of the [6]Spirit and not in oldness of the letter.

Law Cannot Deliver from Sin

7 What shall we say then? Is the Law sin? May it never be! On the contrary, I would not have come to know sin except [A]through the Law; for I would not have known about coveting if the Law had not said, "YOU SHALL NOT COVET."   *through law*

8 But sin, [R]taking opportunity [T]through the commandment, produced in me *coveting* of every kind; for apart [A]from the Law sin *is* dead.   Rom. 7:11 • Rom. 3:20; 7:11 • *lust • from law*

9 And I was once alive apart [A]from the Law; but when the commandment came, sin became alive, and I died;   *from law*

10 and this commandment, which was [T]to [R]result in life, proved [T]to result in death for me;   *to life* • Lev. 18:5; Luke 10:28 • *to death*

11 for sin, [R]taking opportunity [R]through the commandment, [R]deceived me, and through it killed me.   Rom. 7:8 • Rom. 3:20; 7:8 • Gen. 3:13

12 So then, the Law is holy, and the commandment is holy and righteous and good.

13 Therefore did that which is good become a *cause of* death for me? [R]May it never be! Rather it was sin, in order that it might be shown to be sin by effecting my death through that which is good, that through the commandment sin might become utterly sinful.   Luke 20:16

14 For we know that the Law is spiritual; but I am of flesh, sold into bondage to sin.

15 For that which I am doing, [R]I do not understand; for I am not practicing [R]what I *would* like to do, but I am doing the very thing I hate.   John 15:15 • Rom. 7:19; [Gal. 5:17]

[6] Or, *spirit*

6:23 New Life: A Free Gift—You can work for sin but it is a cruel master. When it pays you off, its wage is death—separation from God forever. In stark contrast, God does not pay wages. He has a free gift to offer—eternal life. There is nothing that one can do to earn this gift. If one could earn it, it would not be a gift; it would be wages. Eternal life is just that—eternal—it never ceases. The basic concept underlying life is *union*. There are three kinds of life mentioned in the Bible: (1) physical life—union of the soul with the body; (2) spiritual life—union of the soul with God; and (3) eternal life—eternal union of the soul with God. Jesus said, "My sheep hear My voice . . . and I give eternal life to them, and they shall never perish" (Page 1077—John 10:27, 28). The gift of God is eternal life. One receives this gift when he believes in Jesus as his own personal Savior. Having eternal life, he will never perish.

Now turn to Page 1200—Col. 1:22: New Life: Based on Christ's Death.

16 But if I do the very thing I do not wish *to do,* I agree with[R]the Law, *confessing* that it is good.   Rom. 7:12; 1 Tim. 1:8

17 So now, [R]no longer am I the one doing it, but sin which indwells me.   Rom. 7:20

18 For I know that nothing good dwells in me, that is, in my[R]flesh; for the wishing is present in me, but the doing of the good *is* not.   John 3:6; Rom. 7:25; 8:3

19 For[R]the good that I wish, I do not do; but I practice the very evil that I do not wish.   Rom. 7:15

20 But if I am doing the very thing I do not wish,[R]I am no longer the one doing it, but sin which dwells in me.   Rom. 7:17

21 I find then the principle that evil is present in me, the one who wishes to do good.

22 For I joyfully concur with the law of God[A]in[R]the inner man, *concerning* • [2 Cor. 4:16]

23 but I see a different law in the members of my body, waging war against the law of my mind, and making me a prisoner of the law of sin which is in my members.

24 Wretched man that I am! Who will set me free from the body of this death?

25 [R]Thanks be to God through Jesus Christ our Lord! So then, on the one hand I myself with my mind am serving the law of God, but on the other, with my flesh[R]the law of sin.   1 Cor. 15:57 • Rom. 7:21, 23; 8:2

CHAPTER 8

The Spirit Delivers from the Power of the Flesh

THERE is therefore now no condemnation for those who are[R]in Christ Jesus. Rom. 8:9f.

2 For[R]the law of the Spirit of life in[R]Christ Jesus[R]has set [7]you free from the law of sin and of death. [1 Cor. 15:45] • Rom. 8:1 • John 8:32

3 For what the Law could not do, [7]weak as it was through the flesh, God *did:* sending His own Son in the likeness of [8]sinful flesh

[7] Some ancient mss. read *me*
[8] Some ancient mss. read *because of*

and *as an offering* for sin, He condemned sin in the flesh, *wherein it was weak • flesh of sin*

4 in order that the [R]requirement of the Law might be fulfilled in us, who [R]do not walk according to the flesh, but according to the Spirit.   Luke 1:6; Rom. 2:26 • Gal. 5:16, 25

5 For those who are according to the flesh set their minds on the things of the flesh, but those who are according to the Spirit, the things of the Spirit.

6 [R]For the mind set on the flesh is [R]death, but the mind set on the Spirit is life and peace.   Gal. 6:8 • Rom. 6:21; 8:13

7 because the mind set on the flesh is [R]hostile toward God; for it does not subject itself to the law of God, for it is not even able *to do so;*   James 4:4

8 and those who are[R]in the flesh cannot please God.   Rom. 7:5

9 However, you are not in the flesh but in the Spirit, if indeed the Spirit of God dwells in you. But if anyone does not have the Spirit of Christ, he does not belong to Him.

10 And[R]if Christ is in you, though the body is dead because of sin, yet the spirit is [A]alive because of righteousness.   John 17:23 • *life*

11 But if the Spirit of Him who [R]raised Jesus from the dead dwells in you,[R]He who raised Christ Jesus from the dead will also give life to your mortal bodies [8]through His Spirit who indwells you.   Acts 2:24 • John 5:21

The Spirit Gives Sonship

12 So then, brethren, we are under obligation, not to the flesh, to live according to the flesh—

13 for[R]if you are living according to the flesh, you[A]must die; but if by the Spirit you are[R]putting to death the deeds of the body, you will live.   Rom. 8:6 • *are about to* • [Col. 3:5]

14 For all who are being led by the Spirit of God, these are[R]sons of God.   John 1:12

15 For you have not received a spirit of slavery leading to fear again, but you have received [A]a spirit of adoption as sons by which we cry out, "Abba! Father!" *the Spirit*

8:15 God the Father of Believers—God is the Father of all who believe in Christ in a special sense not shared by unbelievers. God is called their Father, first of all, because they have a new standing before Him. While unbelievers are the offspring of God because He created them (Page 1115—Acts 17:28, 29), they do not have the standing of sons. Their standing is rather as condemned sinners before God the Judge (Page 1066—John 3:18; Page 1306—Rev. 20:11). When a person believes in Christ as Savior, his estate is wonderfully changed from grim condemnation to privileged sonship. This new standing grants to all believers the legal right and spiritual privileges of divine sonship: "heirs of God and fellow heirs with Christ" (Page 1138—Rom. 8:17).

God is the Father of believers also in the sense that He gives them new life (Page 1066—John 3:3). This relationship then is a family one involving many of the same realities that exist between an earthly father and child; birth of the child (Page 1066—John 3:3); partaking of the father's nature (Page 1268—2 Pet. 1:4); the father's care for the child (Page 969—Matt. 6:32, 33; 7:9–11); and the father's discipline of the child (Page 1247—Heb. 12:6–8). Furthermore, this new Father-child relationship carries with it new brothers and sisters (Page 1248—Heb. 13:1).

To obtain God as Father is not a result of one's own merit but a result of Christ's. The one who believes in Christ as Savior enters into the blessed Father-child relationship with God solely on the grounds of Christ's sonship (Page 1138—Rom. 8:17; Page 1240—Heb. 2:17). It is the grand privilege and calling of those who know God as Father to graciously invite unbelievers to meet God as Father and not as Judge.

Now turn to Page 665—Is. 9:6: The Person of the Son of God.

16 The Spirit Himself bears witness with our spirit that we are children of God,

17 and if children,[R]heirs also, heirs of God and fellow heirs with Christ,[R]if indeed we suffer with *Him* in order that we may also be glorified with *Him*.　Acts 20:32 • 2 Cor. 1:5, 7

The Spirit Assures of Future Glory

18 For I consider that the sufferings of this present time[R]are not worthy to be compared with the[R]glory that is to be revealed to us.　2 Cor. 4:17 • [Col. 3:4; Titus 2:13]

19 For the[R]anxious longing of the creation waits eagerly for[R]the revealing of the[R]sons of God.　Phil. 1:20 • Rom. 8:18; [1 John 3:2] • Hos. 1:10

20 For the creation was subjected to[R]futility, not of its own will, but because of Him who subjected it, [9]in hope　Ps. 39:5f.; Eccl. 1:2

21 that the creation itself also will be set free from its slavery to corruption into the freedom of the glory of the children of God.

22 For we know that the whole creation [R]groans and suffers the pains of childbirth together until now.　Jer. 12:4, 11

23 And not only this, but also we ourselves, having the first fruits of the Spirit, even we ourselves groan within ourselves, [R]waiting eagerly for *our* adoption as sons, the redemption of our body.　Rom. 8:15, 19, 25

24 For in hope we have been saved, but [R]hope that is seen is not hope; for [10]why does one also hope for what he sees?　Rom. 4:18

25 But if we hope for what we do not see, with perseverance we wait eagerly for it.

26 And in the same way the Spirit also helps our weakness; for [R]we do not know how to pray as we should, but[R]the Spirit Himself intercedes for *us* with groanings too deep for words;　Matt. 20:22 • John 14:16

27 and He who searches the hearts knows what[R]the mind of the Spirit is, because He [R]intercedes for the [A]saints according to *the will of* God.　Rom. 8:6 • Rom. 8:34 • *holy ones*

28 And we know that [11]God causes [A]all things to work together for good to those who love God, to those who are [R]called according to *His* purpose.　Rom. 8:32 • Rom. 8:30

29 For whom He [R]foreknew, He also predestined *to become*[A]conformed to the image of His Son, that He might be the first-born among many brethren;　Rom. 11:2 • [Phil. 3:21]

30 and whom He [R]predestined, these He also[R]called; and whom He called, these He also justified; and whom He justified, these He also glorified.　Rom. 9:23 • Rom. 8:28; 9:24

The Spirit Assures of Final Victory

31 What then shall we say to these things? [R]If God *is* for us, who *is* against us?　Ps. 118:6

32 He who did not spare His own Son, but delivered Him up for us all, how will He not also with Him freely give us all things?

33 Who will bring a charge against God's elect?[R]God is the one who justifies;　Is. 50:8f.

34 who is the one who[R]condemns? Christ Jesus is He who died, yes, rather who was [12]raised, who is at the right hand of God, who also intercedes for us.　Rom. 8:1

35 Who shall separate us from the love of [13]Christ? Shall [R]tribulation, or distress, or [R]persecution, or [R]famine, or [R]nakedness, or [R]peril, or sword?　Rom. 2:9 • 1 Cor. 4:11

36 Just as it is written,

"FOR[R] THY SAKE WE ARE BEING PUT TO
　DEATH ALL DAY LONG;
WE WERE CONSIDERED AS SHEEP TO BE
　SLAUGHTERED."　Ps. 44:22; Acts 20:24

37 But in all these things we overwhelmingly conquer through Him who loved us.

38 For I am convinced that neither [R]death, nor life, nor [R]angels, nor principalities, nor [R]things present, nor things to come, nor powers,　1 Cor. 3:22 • [1 Cor. 15:24] • 1 Cor. 3:22

39 nor height, nor depth, nor any other created thing, shall be able to separate us from [R]the love of God, which is [R]in Christ Jesus our Lord.　Rom. 5:8 • Rom. 8:1

CHAPTER 9

Paul's Sorrow

I[R] AM telling the truth in Christ, I am not lying, my conscience bearing me witness in the Holy Spirit,　Rom. 1:9; Gal. 1:20; 1 Tim. 2:7

2 that I have great sorrow and unceasing grief in my heart.

3 For[T]I could wish that I myself were[R]accursed, *separated* from Christ for the sake of my brethren, my kinsmen [R]according to the flesh,　Ex. 32:32 • *pray* • 1 Cor. 12:3 • Eph. 6:5

4 who are Israelites, to whom belongs [R]the adoption as sons and the glory and the covenants and the giving of the Law and the *temple* service and the promises,　[Rom. 8:15]

5 whose are the fathers, and from whom is the Christ according to the flesh, who is over all,[R]God blessed forever. Amen. Col. 2:9

God's Sovereignty

6 But *it is* not as though[R]the word of God has failed. For they are not all Israel who are *descended* from Israel;　Num. 23:19

7 neither are they all children [R]because they are[R] Abraham's [T]descendants, but: "THROUGH[R] ISAAC YOUR [T]DESCENDANTS WILL BE NAMED."　[John 8:33, 39] • *seed* • Gen. 21:12

8 That is, it is not the children of the flesh who are[R]children of God, but the[R]children of the promise are regarded as [T]descendants.　Rom. 8:14 • Rom. 4:13, 16 • *seed*

9 For this is a word of promise: "AT THIS

---

[9] Some ancient mss. read *in hope; because the creation*
[10] Some ancient mss. read *who hopes for what he sees?*
[11] Some ancient mss. read *all things work together for good*
[12] Some ancient mss. read *raised from the dead*
[13] Some ancient mss. read *God*

TIME I WILL COME, AND SARAH SHALL HAVE A SON."   Gen. 18:10

10 And not only this, but there was [R]Rebekah also, when she had conceived *twins* by one man, our father Isaac;   Gen. 25:21

11 for though *the twins* were not yet born, and had not done anything good or bad, in order that [R]God's purpose according to *His* choice might stand, not because of works, but because of Him who calls,   [Rom. 4:17]

12 it was said to her, "THE[R] OLDER WILL SERVE THE YOUNGER."   Gen. 25:23

13 Just as it is written, "JACOB[R] I LOVED, BUT ESAU I HATED."   Mal. 1:2f.

14 [R]What shall we say then?[R]There is no injustice with God, is there?[R]May it never be!   Rom. 3:5 · 2 Chr. 19:7 · Luke 20:16

15 For He says to Moses, "I[R] WILL HAVE MERCY ON WHOM I HAVE MERCY, AND I WILL HAVE COMPASSION ON WHOM I HAVE COMPASSION."   Ex. 33:19

16 So then it *does* not *depend* on the man who wills or the man who[R]runs, but on[R]God who has mercy.   Gal. 2:2 · Eph. 2:8

17 For the Scripture says to Pharaoh, "FOR THIS VERY PURPOSE I RAISED YOU UP, TO DEMONSTRATE MY POWER IN YOU, AND THAT MY NAME MIGHT BE PROCLAIMED [T]THROUGHOUT THE WHOLE EARTH."   *in*

18 So then He has mercy on whom He desires, and He hardens whom He desires.

19 You will say to me then, "Why does He still find fault? For who resists His will?"

20 On the contrary, who are you, O man, who answers back to God? [R]The thing molded will not say to the molder, "Why did you make me like this," will it? Is. 29:16; 45:9

21 Or does not the potter have a right over the clay, to make from the same lump one vessel [T]for honorable use, and another [T]for common use?   *for honor · for dishonor*

22 What if God, although willing to demonstrate His wrath and to make His power known, endured with much patience vessels of wrath[R]prepared for destruction? [1 Pet. 2:8]

23 And *He did so* in order that He might make known[R]the riches of His glory upon vessels of mercy, which He[R]prepared beforehand for glory,   Rom. 2:4 · [Rom. 8:29f.]

24 *even* us, whom He also[R]called,[R]not from among Jews only, but also from among Gentiles.   [Rom. 8:28] · Rom. 3:29

25 As He says also in Hosea,
"I[R]WILL CALL THOSE WHO WERE NOT MY PEOPLE, 'MY PEOPLE,'
AND HER WHO WAS NOT BELOVED, 'BELOVED.' "   Hos. 2:23; 1 Pet. 2:10

26 "AND[R] IT SHALL BE THAT IN THE PLACE WHERE IT WAS SAID TO THEM, 'YOU ARE NOT MY PEOPLE,'   Hos. 1:10
THERE THEY SHALL BE CALLED SONS OF [R]THE LIVING GOD."   Matt. 16:16

27 And Isaiah cries out concerning Israel, "THOUGH THE NUMBER OF THE SONS OF ISRAEL BE AS THE SAND OF THE SEA, IT IS[T]THE REMNANT THAT WILL BE SAVED;   Rom. 11:5

28 FOR THE LORD WILL EXECUTE HIS WORD UPON THE EARTH, [T]THOROUGHLY AND [T]QUICKLY."   *finishing it · cutting it short*

29 And just as Isaiah foretold,
"EXCEPT THE LORD OF [T]SABAOTH HAD LEFT TO US A POSTERITY,   Hosts
[R]WE WOULD HAVE BECOME AS SODOM, AND WOULD HAVE [T]RESEMBLED GOMORRAH."   Deut. 29:23 · *been made like*

Israel Seeks Righteousness by Works

30 [R]What shall we say then? That Gentiles, who did not pursue righteousness, attained righteousness, even [R]the righteousness which is[T]by faith; Rom. 9:14 · [Gal. 2:16] · *out of*

31 but Israel, pursuing a law of righteousness, did not[R]arrive at *that* law.   [Gal. 5:4]

32 Why? Because *they did* not *pursue it* by faith, but as though *it were* by works. They stumbled over the stumbling stone,

33 just as it is written,
[R]"BEHOLD, I LAY IN ZION A STONE OF STUMBLING AND A ROCK OF OFFENSE, AND HE WHO BELIEVES IN HIM WILL NOT BE DISAPPOINTED."   Ps. 118:22 ★

CHAPTER 10

Israel Rejects Christ

BRETHREN, my heart's desire and my prayer to God for them is for *their* salvation.

2 For I bear them witness that they have [R]a zeal for God, but not in accordance with knowledge.   Acts 21:20

3 For not knowing about [R]God's righteousness, and [R]seeking to establish their own, they did not subject themselves to the righteousness of God. [Rom. 1:17] · Rom. 10:2f.

4 For Christ is the end of the law for righteousness to everyone who believes.

5 For Moses writes that the man who practices the righteousness which is based on law shall live[T]by that righteousness. *by it*

6 But[T]the righteousness [T]based on faith speaks thus, "DO NOT SAY IN YOUR HEART, 'WHO WILL ASCEND INTO HEAVEN?' (that is, to bring Christ down),   Rom. 9:30 · *out of, from*

7 or 'WHO WILL DESCEND INTO THE [R]ABYSS?' (that is, to[T]bring Christ up from the dead)."   Luke 8:31 · [Heb. 13:20]

8 But what does it say? "THE[R] WORD IS NEAR YOU, IN YOUR MOUTH AND IN YOUR HEART"—that is, the word of faith which we are preaching,   Deut. 30:14

9 [T]that [R]if you confess with your mouth Jesus *as* Lord, and[R]believe in your heart that God raised Him from the dead, you shall be saved;   *because* · Matt. 10:32 · Acts 16:31

10 for with the heart man believes, resulting in righteousness, and with the mouth he confesses,[T]resulting in salvation.   *to salvation*

11 For the Scripture says, "WHOEVER BELIEVES IN HIM WILL NOT BE DISAPPOINTED."

12 For^Rthere is no distinction between Jew and Greek; for the same *Lord* is^RLord of ^Rall, abounding in riches for all who call upon Him;　　　Rom. 3:22, 29 • Acts 10:36 • Rom. 3:29

13 for "WHOEVER^R WILL CALL UPON THE NAME OF THE LORD WILL BE SAVED." Joel 2:32

14 How then shall they call upon Him in whom they have not believed? And how shall they believe in Him ^Rwhom they have not heard? And how shall they hear without ^Ra preacher?　Eph. 2:17; 4:21 • Acts 8:31; Titus 1:3

15 And how shall they preach unless they are sent? Just as it is written, "HOW BEAUTIFUL ARE THE FEET OF THOSE WHO BRING GLAD TIDINGS OF GOOD THINGS!"　*preach the gospel*

Israel Rejects the Prophets

16 However, they did not all heed the^Tglad tidings; for Isaiah says, "LORD,^R WHO HAS BELIEVED OUR REPORT?"　*gospel* • John 12:38 ★

17 So faith *comes* from hearing, and hearing by the word of Christ.

18 But I say, surely they have never heard, have they? Indeed they have;
"THEIR^R VOICE HAS GONE OUT INTO ALL THE EARTH,　Ps. 19:4; Rom. 1:8; Col. 1:6
AND THEIR WORDS TO THE ENDS OF THE ^AWORLD."　*inhabited earth*

19 But I say, surely Israel did not know, did they? At the first Moses says,
"I WILL ^RMAKE YOU JEALOUS BY THAT WHICH IS NOT A NATION,　Rom. 11:11
BY A NATION WITHOUT UNDERSTANDING WILL I ANGER YOU."

20 And Isaiah is very bold and says,
"I^R WAS FOUND BY THOSE WHO SOUGHT ME NOT,　Is. 65:1; Rom. 9:30
I BECAME MANIFEST TO THOSE WHO DID NOT ASK FOR ME."

21 But as for Israel He says, "ALL^R THE DAY LONG I HAVE STRETCHED OUT MY HANDS TO A DISOBEDIENT AND OBSTINATE PEOPLE." Is. 65:2

CHAPTER 11

Israel's Rejection Is Not Total

I SAY then, God has not rejected His people, has He? May it never be! For I too am an Israelite, ^Ta descendant of Abraham, of the tribe of Benjamin.　*of the seed of Abraham*

2 God has not rejected His people whom He foreknew. Or do you not know what the Scripture says in *the passage about* Elijah, how he pleads with God against Israel?

3 "Lord, ^RTHEY HAVE KILLED THY PROPHETS, THEY HAVE TORN DOWN THINE ALTARS, AND I ALONE AM LEFT, AND THEY ARE SEEKING MY LIFE."　1 Kin. 19:10, 14

4 But what ^Tis the divine response to him? "I^R HAVE KEPT for Myself SEVEN THOUSAND MEN WHO HAVE NOT BOWED THE KNEE TO BAAL."　*says* • 1 Kin. 19:18

5 In the same way then, there has also come to be at the present time a remnant according to *God's* gracious choice.

6 But^Rif it is by grace, it is no longer on the basis of works, otherwise grace is no longer grace.　Rom. 4:4

7 What then? That which^RIsrael is seeking for, it has not obtained, but ^Tthose who were chosen obtained it, and the rest were ^Rhardened;　Rom. 9:31 • *the election* • Mark 6:52

8 just as it is written,
"GOD^R GAVE THEM A SPIRIT OF STUPOR, EYES TO SEE NOT AND EARS TO HEAR NOT,　Is. 29:10
DOWN TO THIS VERY DAY."

9 And David says,
"LET^R THEIR TABLE BECOME A SNARE AND A TRAP,　Ps. 69:22 ★
AND A STUMBLING BLOCK AND A RETRIBUTION TO THEM.

10 "LET^T THEIR EYES BE DARKENED TO SEE NOT,　Ps. 69:23 ★
AND BEND THEIR BACKS FOREVER."

Purpose of Israel's Rejection

11 I say then, they did not stumble so as to fall, did they? May it never be! But by their transgression salvation *has come* to the Gentiles, to make them jealous.

12 Now if their transgression be riches for the world and their failure be^Rriches for the Gentiles, how much more will their ^Afulfillment be!　Is. 8:14, 15; Hos. 1:10, 23 ★ • *fulness*

13 But I am speaking to you who are Gentiles. Inasmuch then as^RI am an apostle of Gentiles, I magnify my ministry,　Acts 9:15

14 if somehow I might ^Rmove to jealousy ^Tmy ^Tfellow countrymen and save some of them.　Rom. 11:11 • Gen. 29:14 • *flesh*

15 For if their rejection be the ^Rreconciliation of the world, what will *their* acceptance be but life from the dead?　Rom. 5:11

16 And if the^Rfirst piece *of dough* be holy, the lump is also; and if the root be holy, the branches are too.　Num. 15:18ff.; Neh. 10:37

17 But if some of the^Rbranches were broken off, and ^Ryou, being a wild olive, were grafted in among them and became partaker with them of the^Trich root of the olive tree,　Jer. 11:16 • [Eph. 2:11ff.] • *root of the fatness*

18 do not be arrogant toward the branches; but if you are arrogant, *remember that*^Rit is not you who supports the root, but the root *supports* you.　John 4:22

19 You will say then, "Branches were broken off so that I might be grafted in."

20 Quite right, they were broken off for their unbelief, but you stand by your faith. ^RDo not be conceited, but fear;　Rom. 12:16

21 for if God did not spare the natural branches, neither will He spare you.

22 Behold then the kindness and severity of God; to those who fell, severity, but to you, God's kindness, if you continue in His kindness; otherwise you also will be cut off.

23 And they also,[R]if they do not continue in their unbelief, will be grafted in; for God is able to graft them in again.   2 Cor. 3:16

24 For if you were cut off from what is by nature a wild olive tree, and were grafted contrary to nature into a cultivated olive tree, how much more shall these who are the natural *branches* be grafted into their own olive tree?

Promise of Israel's Restoration

25 For I do not want you, brethren, to be uninformed of this mystery, lest you be wise in your own estimation, that a partial hardening has happened to Israel until the [R]fulness of the Gentiles has come in;   Luke 21:24

26 and thus all Israel will be saved; just as it is written,
"THE[R] DELIVERER WILL COME FROM ZION,   Is. 59:20
HE WILL REMOVE UNGODLINESS FROM JACOB."

27 "AND[R] THIS IS [T]MY COVENANT WITH THEM,   Is. 59:21 · *the covenant from Me*
WHEN I TAKE AWAY THEIR SINS."

28 From the standpoint of the gospel they are [R]enemies for your sake, but from the standpoint of God's choice they are beloved for the sake of the fathers;   Rom. 5:10

29 for the gifts and the [R]calling of God [R]are irrevocable.   Rom. 8:28; 1 Cor. 1:26 · Heb. 7:21

30 For just as you once were disobedient to God, but now have been shown mercy because of their disobedience,

31 so these also now have been disobedient, in order that because of the mercy shown to you they also may now be shown mercy.

32 For [R]God has shut up all in disobedience that He might show mercy to all.   Rom. 3:9

Israel's Restoration:
The Occasion for Glorifying God

33 Oh, the depth of the riches[A]both of the [R]wisdom and knowledge of God! How unsearchable are His judgments and unfathomable His ways!   *and the wisdom* · Eph. 3:10

34 For WHO HAS KNOWN THE MIND OF THE LORD, OR WHO BECAME HIS COUNSELOR?

35 Or WHO HAS FIRST GIVEN TO HIM THAT IT MIGHT BE PAID BACK TO HIM AGAIN?

36 For[R]from Him and through Him and to Him are all things. To Him *be* the glory[T]forever. Amen.   [1 Cor. 8:6]; Col. 1:16 · *to the ages*

CHAPTER 12

Responsibilities Toward God

I URGE you therefore, brethren, by the mercies of God, to present your bodies a living and holy sacrifice, acceptable to God, which is your spiritual service of worship.

2 And do not be conformed to this[A]world, but be transformed by the[R]renewing of your mind, that you may prove what the will of God is, that which is good and[A]acceptable and perfect.   *age* · Eph. 4:23 · *well-pleasing*

Responsibilities Toward Society

3 For through the grace given to me I say to every man among you not to think more highly of himself than he ought to think; but to think so as to have sound judgment, as God has allotted to each a measure of faith.

4 For[R]just as we have many members in one body and all the members do not have the same function, 1 Cor. 12:12–14; [Eph. 4:4, 16]

5 so we, [R]who are many, are[R]one body in Christ, and individually members one of another.   [1 Cor. 10:17, 33] · 1 Cor. 12:20, 27; Eph. 4:12

6 And since we have gifts that differ according to the grace given to us, *let each exercise them accordingly:* if prophecy, according to the proportion of his faith;

7 if [A]service, in his serving; or he who teaches, in his teaching;   *office of service*

12:1 Walking in the Spirit: Yielding—Confession of sin in itself is not enough to enable the believer to automatically walk in the Spirit. He must then become a yielded instrument for God's service. What is to be yielded is simply himself (Page 1135—Rom. 6:13; Page 1255—James 4:7). This involves both the body (Rom. 12:1; Page 1153—1 Cor. 6:20) and the mind (Rom. 12:2), since it is with the body that actions conceived in the mind are carried out and with the mind that they are formulated. Stated another way, that which is conceived in the mind is carried out in the body; thus, one's whole being must be presented by a decisive act of the will to God for His service. Yielding must not be thought of simply as a willingness to do some specific thing. Rather, it consists of dedication by a person to do whatever God commands.

Yielding leads not only to dedication but also can result in separation: "do not be conformed to this world" (Rom. 12:2). Since the world is resolutely opposed to God, one cannot revel in its lusts and at the same time do the will of God (Page 1275—1 John 2:15–17). The same word translated "conformed" here can be translated "fashioning." So the concept of separation involves being "unfashionable" in spirit, thought, values, and actions according to the world's standards.

Finally, yielding includes transformation of the mind. This work is said to be accomplished through a lifetime of "renewing" the mind. Man's mind has been darkened by sin (Page 1137—Rom. 8:7; Page 1200—Col. 1:21) and must be brought to the place where it thinks as God thinks (Page 1188—Eph. 4:23). This renewing is said to come especially through prayer to God in everything (Page 1195—Phil. 4:6, 7) and through constant meditation on the Word of God (Page 590—Ps. 119:1). This transformation is a lifelong process that will not be completed until we are with Christ (Page 1193—Phil. 1:6; Page 1276—1 John 3:2). Along life's way, however, it brings a peace and delight that can only come from having embraced the mind of Christ.

Now turn to Page 1188—Eph. 5:18: Walking in the Spirit: Filling.

8 or he who [R]exhorts, in his exhortation; he who gives, with [14]liberality; he who [A]leads, with diligence; he who shows mercy, with cheerfulness. Acts 4:36; 11:23 • *gives aid*

9 Let [R]love be without hypocrisy. Abhor what is evil; cling to what is good. 2 Cor. 6:6

10 Be [R]devoted to one another in brotherly love; [c]give preference to one another in honor; John 13:34 • *outdo one another in showing honor*

11 not lagging behind in diligence, fervent in spirit, [R]serving the Lord; Acts 20:19

12 [R]rejoicing in hope, persevering in tribulation, [R]devoted to prayer, Rom. 5:2 • Acts 1:14

13 contributing to the needs of the [A]saints, [T]practicing hospitality. *holy ones • pursuing*

14 [R]Bless those who persecute [15]you; bless and curse not. [Matt. 5:44]; Luke 6:28; 1 Cor. 4:12

15 [R]Rejoice with those who rejoice, and weep with those who weep. Job 30:25

16 [R]Be of the same mind toward one another; [R]do not be haughty in mind, but associate with the lowly. Do not be wise in your own estimation. Rom. 15:5 • Rom. 11:20

17 Never pay back evil for evil to anyone. Respect what is right in the sight of all men.

18 If possible, so far as it depends on you, [R]be at peace with all men. Mark 9:50

19 [R]Never take your own revenge, beloved, but [T]leave room for the wrath of God, for it is written, "VENGEANCE IS MINE, I WILL REPAY," says the Lord. Prov. 20:22 • *give a place*

20 "BUT [T] IF YOUR ENEMY IS HUNGRY, FEED HIM, AND IF HE IS THIRSTY, GIVE HIM A DRINK; FOR IN SO DOING YOU WILL HEAP BURNING COALS UPON HIS HEAD." 2 Kin. 6:22; Prov. 25:21f.

21 Do not be overcome by evil, but overcome evil with good.

CHAPTER 13

Responsibilities Toward Higher Powers

LET every [A]person be in subjection to the governing authorities. For there is no authority except [T]from God, and those which exist are established by God. *soul • by*

2 Therefore he who resists authority has opposed the ordinance of God; and they who have opposed will receive condemnation upon themselves.

3 For rulers are not a cause of fear for good behavior, but for evil. Do you want to have no fear of authority? Do what is good, and you will have praise from the same;

4 for it is a minister of God to you for good. But if you do what is evil, be afraid; for it does not bear the sword for nothing; for it is a minister of God, an [R]avenger who brings wrath upon the one who practices evil. 1 Thess. 4:6

5 Wherefore it is necessary to be in subjection, not only because of wrath, but also [R]for conscience' sake. Eccl. 8; [1 Pet. 2:13, 19]

6 For because of this you also pay taxes, for *rulers* are servants of God, devoting themselves to this very thing.

7 Render to all what is due them: tax to whom tax *is due;* custom to whom custom; fear to whom fear; honor to whom honor.

Responsibilities Toward Neighbors

8 Owe nothing to anyone except to love one another; for [T]he who loves [T]his neighbor has fulfilled *the* law. Matt. 7:12 • *the other*

9 For this, "YOU SHALL NOT COMMIT ADULTERY, YOU SHALL NOT MURDER, YOU SHALL NOT STEAL, YOU SHALL NOT COVET," and if there is any other commandment, it is summed up in this saying, "YOU [R] SHALL LOVE YOUR NEIGHBOR AS YOURSELF." Lev. 19:18

10 Love does no wrong to a neighbor; love therefore is the fulfillment of *the* law.

11 And this *do,* knowing the time, that it is [a]already the hour for you to [R]awaken from sleep; for now [16]salvation is nearer to us than when we believed. [2 Pet. 3:9] • Mark 13:37

12 The night is almost gone, and the day is at hand. Let us therefore lay aside the deeds of darkness and put on the armor of light.

13 Let us [T]behave properly as in the day, [R]not in carousing and drunkenness, not in sexual promiscuity and sensuality, not in strife and jealousy. *walk* • Luke 21:34; Gal. 5:21

14 But [R]put on the Lord Jesus Christ, and make no provision for the flesh [R]in regard to *its* lusts. Job 29:14; [Gal. 3:27] • [Gal. 5:16]

[14] Or, *simplicity*   [15] Some ancient mss. do not contain *you*
[16] Or, *our salvation is nearer than when*

13:1–4 The Function of Human Government—The general function of human government, as instituted by God, may be said to be threefold: to protect, punish, and promote.
a. The Function of Protection: The moment Adam sinned it was obvious that civilizations would need some form of restraint and rule to protect citizens from themselves. An example of this function is seen in Acts 21:27–37 where Roman soldiers step in and save Paul from being murdered by his own enraged countrymen in Jerusalem.
b. The Function of Punishment: Both Paul and Peter bring this out. Paul writes that duly appointed human officials are to be regarded as God's servants to "bear the sword," that is, to impose punishment upon criminals (vv. 3, 4). Peter tells us that governors are "sent by him for the punishment of evildoers" (Page 1262—1 Pet. 2:13, 14).
c. The Function of Promotion: Human government is to promote the general welfare of the community where its laws are in effect. Paul commands us to pray for human leaders "that we may lead a tranquil and quiet life in all godliness and dignity" (Page 1217—1 Tim. 2:1, 2).
Now turn to Page 1262—1 Pet. 2:13: Our Responsibility to Human Government.

CHAPTER 14

Principles of Christian Liberty

N OW ^Raccept the one who is^Rweak in faith, *but* not for *the purpose of* passing judgment on his opinions.   Acts 28:2 • Rom. 14:2; 15:1

2 ^ROne man has faith that he may eat all things, but he who is^Rweak eats vegetables *only.*   [Rom. 14:14] • 1 Cor. 8:9ff.; 9:22

3 Let not him who eats regard with contempt him who does not eat, and let not him who does not eat^Rjudge him who eats, for God has^Raccepted him.   [Col. 2:16] • Acts 28:2

4 Who are you to judge the ^Aservant of another? To his own [†]master he stands or falls; and stand he will, for the Lord is able to make him stand.   *house-servant • lord*

5 ^ROne man [†]regards one day above another, another regards every day *alike.* Let each man be ^Rfully convinced in his own mind.   Gal. 4:10 • *judges* • Luke 1:1; Rom. 4:21

6 He who observes the day, observes it for the Lord, and he who eats, [†]does so for the Lord, for he^Rgives thanks to God; and he who eats not, for the Lord he does not eat, and gives thanks to God.   *eats* • Matt. 14:19

7 For not one of us^Rlives for himself, and not one dies for himself; Rom. 8:38f.; Gal. 2:20

8 for if we live, we live for the Lord, or if we die, we die for the Lord; therefore whether we live or die, we are the Lord's.

9 For to this end^RChrist died and lived *again,* that He might be^RLord both of the dead and of the living. [Rev. 1:18] • [Matt. 28:18]

10 But you, why do you judge your brother? Or you again, why do you regard your brother with contempt? For we shall all stand before the judgment seat of God.

11 For it is written,
"AS I LIVE, SAYS THE LORD,^REVERY KNEE
   SHALL BOW TO ME,   [Phil. 2:10f.]
AND EVERY TONGUE SHALL ^AGIVE
   PRAISE TO GOD."   *confess*

12 So then ^Reach one of us shall give account of himself to God.   [Matt. 12:36; 16:27]

13 Therefore let us not^Rjudge one another anymore, but rather determine this—[†]not to put an obstacle or a stumbling block in a brother's way.   Matt. 7:1; Rom. 14:3 • 1 Cor. 8:13

14 I know and am convinced in the Lord Jesus that[†]nothing is unclean in itself; but to him who^Rthinks anything to be unclean, to him it is unclean.   Rom. 14:2, 20 • 1 Cor. 8:7

15 For if because of food your brother is hurt, you are no longer[†]walking according to love.^RDo not destroy with your food him for whom Christ died.   Eph. 5:2 • Rom. 14:20

16 Therefore do not let what is for you a good thing be[†]spoken of as evil; *blasphemed*

17 for the kingdom of God is not eating and drinking, but righteousness and^Rpeace and joy in the Holy Spirit.   Rom. 15:13

18 For he who in this *way* serves Christ is acceptable to God and approved by men.

19 So then ¹⁷let us ^Rpursue the things which make for peace and the^Rbuilding up of one another.   Rom. 12:18 • 1 Cor. 10:23; 14:3f., 26

20 ^RDo not tear down the work of God for the sake of food. All things indeed are clean, but they are evil for the man who eats [†]and gives offense.   Rom. 14:15 • *with offense*

21 ^RIt is good not to eat meat or to drink wine, or *to do anything* by which your brother stumbles.   1 Cor. 8:13

22 The faith which you have, have[†]as your own conviction before God. Happy is he who^Rdoes not condemn himself in what he approves.   *according to yourself* • 1 John 3:21

23 But he who doubts is condemned if he eats, because *his eating is* not from faith; and whatever is not from faith is sin.

CHAPTER 15

Practices of Christian Liberty

N OW we who are strong ought to bear the weaknesses of^Rthose without strength and not *just* please ourselves.   Rom. 14:1; [Gal. 6:2]

2 Let each of us please his neighbor for his good, to his^Redification.   1 Cor. 10:23; 14:3f.

3 For even^RChrist did not please Himself; but as it is written, "THE^R REPROACHES OF THOSE WHO REPROACHED THEE FELL UPON ME."   [2 Cor. 8:9] • Ps. 69:7, 9, 20 ★

4 For whatever was written in earlier times was written for our instruction, that through perseverance and the encouragement of the Scriptures we might have hope.

5 Now may the God[†]who gives perseverance and encouragement grant you[†]to be of the same mind with one another according to Christ Jesus;   *of perseverance* • Rom. 12:16

6 that with one accord you may with one voice glorify[†]the God and Father of our Lord Jesus Christ.   *mouth* • Rev. 1:6

7 Wherefore, accept one another, just as Christ also accepted us to the glory of God.

8 For I say that Christ has become a servant to^Rthe circumcision on behalf of the truth of God to confirm^Rthe promises *given* to the fathers,   Matt. 15:24 • [Rom. 4:16]

9 and for^Rthe Gentiles to glorify God for His mercy; as it is written,   Rom. 3:29; 11:30f.
"THEREFORE I WILL ^AGIVE PRAISE TO
   THEE AMONG THE GENTILES,   *confess*
AND I WILL SING TO THY NAME."

10 And again he says,
"REJOICE, O GENTILES, WITH HIS PEO-
   PLE."   Deut. 32:43

11 And again,
"PRAISE^R THE LORD ALL YOU GENTILES,
AND LET ALL THE PEOPLES PRAISE
   HIM."   Ps. 117:1

12 And again Isaiah says,
"THERE^R SHALL COME ^RTHE ROOT OF
   JESSE,   Is. 11:10 ★ • Rev. 5:5; 22:16

---

¹⁷ Many ancient mss. read *we pursue*

AND HE WHO ARISES TO RULE OVER
THE GENTILES,
IN HIM SHALL THE GENTILES HOPE."
13 Now may the God of hope fill you with
all[R]joy and peace in believing, that you may
abound in hope[R]by the power of the Holy
Spirit.   Rom. 14:17 • Rom. 15:19; 1 Cor. 2:4

Paul's Purpose for Writing

14 And concerning you, my brethren, I
myself also am convinced that you yourselves are full of [R]goodness, filled with [R]all
knowledge, and able also to admonish one
another.   Eph. 5:9 • 1 Cor. 1:5; 8:1, 7, 10; 12:8; 13:2
15 But I have written very boldly to you
on some points, so as to remind you again,
because of [R]the grace that was given me
[A]from God,   Rom. 12:3 • by God
16 to be [R]a minister of Christ Jesus to the
Gentiles, ministering as a priest the [R]gospel
of God, that my [b]offering of the Gentiles
might become acceptable, sanctified by the
Holy Spirit.   Acts 9:15 • Rom. 1:1 • Rom. 12:1
17 Therefore in Christ Jesus I have found
[R]reason for boasting in [R]things pertaining to
God.   Phil. 3:3 • Heb. 2:17; 5:1
18 For I will not presume to speak of anything except what[R]Christ has accomplished
through me, resulting in the obedience of
the Gentiles by word and deed,   Acts 15:12
19 in the power of signs and wonders, in
the power of the Spirit; so that from Jerusalem and round about as far as Illyricum I
have fully preached the gospel of Christ.
20 And thus I aspired to[R]preach the gospel, not where Christ was already named,
[R]that I might not build upon another man's
foundation; Rom. 1:15 • 1 Cor. 3:10; [2 Cor. 10:15f.]
21 but as it is written,
"THEY[R] WHO HAD NO NEWS OF HIM
SHALL SEE,   Is. 52:15
AND THEY WHO HAVE NOT HEARD
SHALL UNDERSTAND."

Paul's Plans for Traveling

22 For this reason[R]I have often been hindered from coming to you;   Rom. 1:13
23 but now, with no further place for me
in these regions, and since I have had for
many years a longing to come to you
24 whenever I go to Spain—for I hope to
see you in passing, and to be helped on my
way there by you, when I have first enjoyed
your company[T]for a while—   in part

25 but now,[R]I am going to Jerusalem [R]serv-
ing the [A]saints.   Acts 19:21 • Acts 24:17 • holy ones
26 For Macedonia and [R]Achaia have been
pleased to make a contribution for the poor
among the saints in Jerusalem.   Acts 18:12
27 Yes, they were pleased to do so, and
they are indebted to them. For[R]if the Gentiles have shared in their spiritual things,
they are indebted to minister to them also in
material things.   1 Cor. 9:11
28 Therefore, when I have finished this,
and[R]have put my seal on this fruit of theirs, I
will go on by way of you to Spain. John 3:33
29 And I know that when[R]I come to you, I
will come in the fulness of the blessing of
Christ.   Acts 19:21; [Rom. 1:10f.; 15:23, 32]
30 Now I urge you, brethren, by our Lord
Jesus Christ and by[R]the love of the Spirit, to
[R]strive together with me in your prayers to
God for me,   Gal. 5:22 • 2 Cor. 1:11; Col. 4:12
31 that I may be[R]delivered from those who
are disobedient in Judea, and that my [R]ser-
vice for Jerusalem may prove acceptable to
the [R]saints;   2 Cor. 1:10 • Rom. 15:25f. • Acts 9:13
32 so that[R]I may come to you in joy by[R]the
will of God and find refreshing rest in your
company.   Rom. 15:23 • Acts 18:21; Rom. 1:10
33 Now[R]the God of peace be with you all.
Amen.   Rom. 16:20; 2 Cor. 13:11; Phil. 4:9

CHAPTER 16

Paul's Praise and Greetings

I[R]COMMEND to you our sister Phoebe,
who is a [A]servant of the church which is at
[R]Cenchrea;   2 Cor. 3:1 • deaconess • Acts 18:18
2 that you receive her in the Lord in a
manner worthy of the saints, and that you
help her in whatever matter she may have
need of you; for she herself has also been a
helper of many, and of myself as well.
3 Greet [R]Prisca and Aquila, my fellow
workers in[R]Christ Jesus,   Acts 18:2 • Rom. 8:1
4 who for my life risked their own necks,
to whom not only do I give thanks, but also
all the churches of the Gentiles;

5 also greet the church that is in their
house. Greet Epaenetus, my beloved, who is
the first convert to Christ from Asia.

6 Greet Mary, who has worked hard for
you.
7 Greet Andronicus and [A]Junias, my kins-

16:5 **Definition of the Local Church**—The local church is a geographically located, temporally limited, and
visibly evident manifestation of the universal church, the body of Christ. In the early New Testament days the local
church met in the Jewish synagogue and had a very simple organization (Page 1254—James 2:2). A little later the
church met in the homes of believers (Rom. 16:5), and it was not uncommon to have a number of churches in an
area (Page 1177—Gal. 1:2). The idea of meeting in a building constructed for that exclusive purpose is a post-New
Testament idea. (For a more complete discussion of the church turn to Page 1101 and read Acts 7:38 and The
Christian's Guide: The Meaning of the Church.)
Now turn to Page 1245—Heb. 10:25: The Reason for Participation in the Local Church.

men, and my[R]fellow prisoners, who are outstanding among the apostles, who also were in Christ before me.　　*Junia* (fem.) • Col. 4:10

8 Greet Ampliatus, my beloved in the Lord.

9 Greet Urbanus, our fellow worker [R]in Christ, and Stachys my beloved.　[2 Cor. 5:17]

10 Greet Apelles, the approved[R]in Christ. Greet those who are of the *household* of Aristobulus.　　[Rom. 8:11ff.]; 16:3, 7, 9

11 Greet Herodion, my [R]kinsman. Greet those of the *household* of Narcissus, who are in the Lord.　　　Rom. 9:3; 16:7, 21

12 Greet Tryphaena and Tryphosa, workers in the Lord. Greet Persis the beloved, who has worked hard in the Lord.

13 Greet[R]Rufus, a choice man in the Lord, also his mother and mine.　　Mark 15:21

14 Greet Asyncritus, Phlegon, Hermes, Patrobas, Hermas and the brethren with them.

15 Greet Philologus and Julia, Nereus and his sister, and Olympas, and all [R]the saints who are with them.　　　Rom. 16:2, 14

16 [R]Greet one another with a holy kiss. All the churches of Christ greet you. 1 Cor. 16:20

17 Now I urge you, brethren, keep your eye on those who cause dissensions and hindrances contrary to the teaching which you learned, and[R]turn away from them. Gal. 1:8f.

18 Many mss. do not contain this verse

18 For such men are slaves, not of our Lord Christ but of their own appetites; and by their smooth and flattering speech they deceive the hearts of the unsuspecting.

19 For the report of your obedience has reached to all; therefore I am rejoicing over you, but[R]I want you to be wise in what is good, and innocent in what is evil.　Jer. 4:22

20 And the God of peace will soon crush Satan under your feet.

The grace of our Lord Jesus be with you.

21 Timothy my fellow worker greets you, and *so do* Lucius and [R]Jason and[R]Sosipater, my kinsmen.　　Acts 17:5 • Acts 20:4

22 I, Tertius, who [R]write this letter, greet you in the Lord.　　1 Cor. 16:21; Gal. 6:11

23 Gaius, host to me and to the whole church, greets you. Erastus, the city treasurer greets you, and Quartus, the brother.

24 [[18]The grace of our Lord Jesus Christ be with you all. Amen.]

25 Now to Him who is able to establish you according to my gospel and the preaching of Jesus Christ, according to the revelation of[R]the mystery which has been kept secret for[R]long ages past,　Matt. 13:35 • Titus 1:2

26 but now is manifested, and by [R]the Scriptures of the prophets, according to the commandment of the eternal God, has been made known to all the nations, *leading* to [R]obedience of faith;　　Rom. 1:2 • Rom. 1:5

27 to the only wise God, through Jesus Christ, be the glory forever. Amen.

CORINTHIANS

THE BOOK OF
FIRST CORINTHIANS

Corinth, the most important city in Greece during Paul's day, was a bustling hub of worldwide commerce, degraded culture, and idolatrous religion. There Paul founded a church (Acts 18:1–17), and two of his letters are addressed "to the church of God which is at Corinth."

First Corinthians reveals the problems, pressures, and struggles of a church called out of a pagan society. Paul addresses a variety of problems in the life-style of the Corinthian church: factions, lawsuits, immorality, questionable practices, abuse of the Lord's Supper, and spiritual gifts. In addition to words of discipline, Paul shares words of counsel in answer to questions raised by the Corinthian believers.

The oldest recorded title of this epistle is *Pros Korinthious A*, in effect, the "First to the Corinthians." The *A* was no doubt a later addition to distinguish this book from Second Corinthians.

THE AUTHOR OF
FIRST CORINTHIANS

Pauline authorship of First Corinthians is almost universally accepted. Instances of this widely held belief can be found as early as A.D. 95, when Clement of Rome wrote to the Corinthian church and cited this epistle in regard to their continuing problem of factions among themselves.

THE TIME OF
FIRST CORINTHIANS

Corinth was a key city in ancient Greece until it was destroyed by the Romans in 146 B.C. Julius Caesar rebuilt it as a Roman colony in 46 B.C. and it grew and prospered, becoming the capital of the province of Achaia. Its official language was Latin, but the common language remained Greek. In Paul's day Corinth was the metropolis of the Peloponnesus, since it was strategically located on a narrow isthmus between the Aegean Sea and the Adriatic Sea that connects the Peloponnesus with northern Greece. Because of its two seaports it became a commercial center, and many small ships were rolled or dragged across the Corinthian isthmus to avoid the dangerous 200-mile voyage around southern Greece. Nero and others attempted

to build a canal at the narrowest point, but this was not achieved until 1893. The city was filled with shrines and temples, but the most prominent was the Temple of Aphrodite on top of a 1,800-foot promontory called the Acrocorinthus. Worshipers of the "goddess of love" made free use of the 1,000 Hieroduli (consecrated prostitutes). This cosmopolitan center thrived on commerce, entertainment, vice, and corruption; pleasure-seekers came there to spend money on a holiday from morality. Corinth became so notorious for its evils that the term *Korinthiazomai* ("to act like a Corinthian") became a synonym for debauchery and prostitution.

In Paul's day the population of Corinth was approximately 700,000, about two-thirds of whom were slaves. The diverse population produced no philosophers, but Greek philosophy influenced any speculative thought that was there. In spite of these obstacles to the gospel, Paul was able to establish a church in Corinth on his second missionary journey (3:6, 10; 4:15; Acts 18:1–7). Persecution in Macedonia drove him south to Athens, and from there he proceeded to Corinth. He made tents with Aquila and Priscilla and reasoned with the Jews in the synagogue. Silas and Timothy joined him (they evidently brought a gift from Philippi; 2 Cor. 11:8, 9; Phil. 4:15), and Paul began to devote all his time to spreading the gospel. Paul wrote First and Second Thessalonians, moved his ministry from the synagogue to the house of Titius Justus because of opposition, and converted Crispus, the leader of the synagogue. Paul taught the Word of God in Corinth for eighteen months in A.D. 51 and 52. After Paul's departure, Apollos came from Ephesus to minister in the Corinthian church (3:6; Acts 18:24–28).

When Paul was teaching and preaching in Ephesus during his third missionary journey, he was disturbed by reports from the household of Chloe concerning quarrels in the church at Corinth (1:11). The church sent a delegation of three men (16:17), who apparently brought a letter that requested Paul's judgment on certain issues (7:1). Paul wrote this epistle as his response to the problems and questions of the Corinthians (he had already written a previous letter; 5:9). It may be that the men who came from Corinth took this letter back with them. Paul was planning to leave Ephesus (16:5–8), indicating that First Corinthians was written in A.D. 56.

✝ THE CHRIST OF FIRST CORINTHIANS

This book proclaims the relevance of Christ Jesus to every area of the believer's life. He "became to us wisdom from God, and righteousness and sanctification, and redemption" (1:30), and these are the themes Paul addresses in this epistle.

🔑 KEYS TO FIRST CORINTHIANS

Key Word: Correction of Carnal Living—The basic theme of this epistle is the application of Christian principles to carnality in the individual as well as in the church. The cross of Christ is a message that is designed to transform the lives of believers and make them different as people and as a corporate body from the surrounding world. However, the Corinthians are destroying their Christian testimony because of immorality and disunity. Paul writes this letter as his corrective response to the news of problems and disorders among the Corinthians. It is designed to refute improper attitudes and conduct and to promote a spirit of unity among the brethren in their relationships and worship. Paul's concern as their spiritual father (4:14, 15) is tempered with love, and he wants to avoid visiting them "with a rod" (4:21).

Key Verses: First Corinthians 6:19, 20 and 10:12, 13—"Or do you not know that your body is a temple of the Holy Spirit who is in you, whom you have from God, and that you are not your own? For you have been bought with a price: therefore glorify God in your body" (6:19, 20).

"Therefore let him who thinks he stands take heed lest he fall. No temptation has over taken you but such as is common to man; and God is faithful, who will not allow you to be tempted beyond what you are able, but with the temptation will provide the way of escape also, that you may be able to endure it" (10:12, 13).

Key Chapter: First Corinthians 13—Read at weddings and often the text for sermons, First Corinthians 13 has won the hearts of people across the world as the best definition of "love" ever penned. Standing in stark contrast to the idea that love is an emotion, that one can fall into or fall out of love, this chapter clearly reveals that true love is primarily an action. This is why when "God so loved the world, that He gave" (John 3:16).

🅰 SURVEY OF FIRST CORINTHIANS

Through the missionary efforts of Paul and others, the church has been established in Corinth, but Paul finds it very difficult to keep Corinth out of the church. The pagan life-style of Corinth exerts a profound influence upon the Christians in that corrupt city—problems of every kind plague them. In this disciplinary letter, Paul is forced to exercise his apostolic authority as he deals firmly with problems of divisiveness, immorality, lawsuits, selfishness, abuses of the Lord's Supper and spiritual gifts, and denials of the Resurrection. This epistle is quite orderly in its approach as it sequentially addresses a group of problems that have come to Paul's attention. Paul also gives a series of perspectives on various questions and issues raised by the Corinthians in a letter. He uses the introductory words "Now concerning" or "Now" to delineate those topics (7:1, 25; 8:1; 11:2; 12:1; 15:1; 16:1). The three divisions of First Corinthians are: answer to Chloe's report of divisions (1—4); answer to report of fornication (5 and 6); and answer to letter of questions (7—16).

Answer to Chloe's Report of Divisions (1—4): Personality cults centering around Paul, Apol-

FOCUS	ANSWER TO CHLOE'S REPORT OF DIVISIONS		ANSWER TO REPORT OF FORNICATION			ANSWER TO LETTER OF QUESTIONS				
REFERENCE	1:1————1:18—		5:1——6:1——	6:12————	7:1——	8:1———	11:2——	15:1—	16:1——	16:24
DIVISION	REPORT OF DIVISIONS	REASON FOR DIVISIONS	INCEST	LITIGATION	IMMORALITY	MARRIAGE	OFFERINGS TO IDOLS	PUBLIC WORSHIP	RESUR-RECTION	COLLECTION FOR JERUSALEM
TOPIC	DIVISIONS IN THE CHURCH		DISORDER IN THE CHURCH			DIFFICULTIES IN THE CHURCH				
	CONCERN		CONDEMNATION			COUNSEL				
LOCATION	WRITTEN IN EPHESUS									
TIME	C. A.D. 56									

los, and Peter have led to divisions and false pride among the Corinthians (1). It is not their wisdom or cleverness that has brought them to Christ, because divine wisdom is contrary to human wisdom. The truth of the gospel is spiritually apprehended (2). Factions that exist among the saints at Corinth are indications of their spiritual immaturity (3). They should pride themselves in Christ, not in human leaders who are merely His servants (4).

Answer to Report of Fornication (5 and 6): The next problem Paul addresses is that of incest between a member of the church and his stepmother (5). The Corinthians have exercised no church discipline in this matter, and Paul orders them to remove the offender from their fellowship until he repents. Another source of poor testimony is the legal action of believer against believer in civil courts (6:1–8). They must learn to arbitrate their differences within the Christian community. Paul concludes this section with a warning against immorality in general (6:9–20).

Answer to Letter of Questions (7—16): In these chapters the apostle Paul gives authoritative answers to thorny questions raised by the Corinthians. His first counsel concerns the issues of marriage, celibacy, divorce, and remarriage (7). The next three chapters are related to the problem of meat offered to idols (8:1—11:1). Paul illustrates from his own life the twin principles of Christian liberty and the law of love, and he concludes that believers must sometimes limit their liberty for the sake of weaker brothers (cf. Rom. 14). The apostle then turns to matters concerning public worship, including improper observance of the Lord's Supper and the selfish use of spiritual gifts (11:2—14:40). Gifts are to be exercised in love for the edification of the whole body. The Corinthians also have problems with the Resurrection, which Paul seeks to correct (15). His historical and theological defense of the Resurrection includes teaching on the nature of the resurrected body. The Corinthians probably have been struggling over this issue because the idea of a resurrected body is disdainful in Greek thought. The epistle closes with Paul's instruction for the collection he will make for the saints in Jerusalem (16:1–4), followed by miscellaneous exhortations and greetings (16:5–24).

OUTLINE OF FIRST CORINTHIANS

Part One: In Answer to Chloe's Report of Divisions (1:1—4:21)

Part Two: In Answer to Reports of Fornication (5:1—6:20)

Part Three: In Answer to the Letter of Questions (7:1—16:24)

CHAPTER 1

Greetings of Grace

PAUL, ᴿcalled *as* an apostle of Jesus Christ ᵀby the will of God, and ᴿSosthenes our brother,   Rom. 1:1 • *through* • Acts 18:17

2 to the church of God which is at Corinth, to those who have been sanctified in Christ Jesus, saints by calling, with all who in every place call upon the name of our Lord Jesus Christ, their *Lord* and ours:

3 ᴿGrace to you and peace from God our Father and the Lord Jesus Christ.   Rom. 1:7

Prayer of Thanksgiving

4 ᴿI thank ¹my God always concerning you, for the grace of God which was given you in Christ Jesus,   Rom. 1:8

5 that in everything you were enriched in Him, in all speech and all knowledge,

6 even as the testimony concerning Christ was confirmedᴬin you,   *among*

7 so that you are not lacking in any gift, ᴿawaiting eagerly the revelation of our Lord Jesus Christ,   Luke 17:30; Rom. 8:19; [2 Pet. 3:12]

8 ᴿwho shall also confirm you to the end, blameless in ᴿthe day of our Lord Jesus Christ.   Phil. 1:6; Col. 2:7 • Luke 17:24, 30

9 God is faithful, through whom you were ᴿcalled intoᴿfellowship with His Son, Jesus Christ our Lord.   Rom. 8:28 • 1 John 1:3

Report of Divisions

10 Now I exhort you, brethren, by the name of our Lord Jesus Christ, that you all agree, and there be noᵀdivisions among you, but you beᴬmade complete in the same mind and in the same judgment.   *schisms • united*

11 For I have been informed concerning you, my brethren, by Chloe's *people*, that there are quarrels among you.

12 Now I mean this, that each one of you is saying, "I am of Paul," and "I of Apollos," and "I of Cephas," and "I of Christ."

13 Has Christ been divided? Paul was not crucified for you, was he? Or were youᴿbaptizedᵀin the name of Paul?   [Matt. 28:19] • *into*

14 ²I thank God that I baptized none of you exceptᴿCrispus and Gaius,   Acts 18:8

15 that no man should say you were baptizedᵀin my name.   *into*

16 Now I did baptize also theᴿhousehold of Stephanas; beyond that, I do not know whether I baptized any other. 1 Cor. 16:15, 17

17 ᴿFor Christ did not send me to baptize, but to preach the gospel, not inᵀcleverness of speech, that the cross of Christ should not be made void.   Acts 10:48 • *wisdom*

The Gospel Is Not Earthly Wisdom

18 For the word of the cross is to those who are perishing foolishness, but to us who are being saved it is the power of God.

19 For it is written,
"Iᴿ WILL DESTROY THE WISDOM OF THE
WISE,   Is. 29:14
AND THE CLEVERNESS OF THE CLEVER I
WILL SET ASIDE."

20 Where is the wise man? Where is the scribe? Where is the debater of ᴿthis age? Has not Godᴿmade foolish the wisdom ofᶠᵗhe world?   Matt. 13:22 • Rom. 1:20ff. • John 12:31

21 For since in the wisdom of God the world through its wisdom did not *come to* know God, ᴿGod was well-pleased through the foolishness of theᵀmessage preached to save those who believe.   Luke 12:32 • *preaching*

22 For indeed Jews ask for ᴬsigns, and Greeks search for wisdom;   *attesting miracles*

23 but we preach ³Christᴿ crucified, ᴿto Jews a stumbling block, and to Gentiles ᴿfoolishness,   Gal. 3:1 • [1 Pet. 2:8] • 1 Cor. 1:18

24 but to those who areᴿthe called, both Jews and Greeks, Christᴿthe power of God and the wisdom of God.   Rom. 8:28 • Rom. 1:16

25 Because theᴿfoolishness of God is wiser than men, andᴿthe weakness of God is stronger than men.   1 Cor. 1:18, 21, 23 • 2 Cor. 13:4

26 For consider your calling, brethren, that there were not many wise according to the flesh, not many mighty, not many noble;

27 but God has chosen the foolish things of the world to shame the wise, and God has chosen the weak things of the world to shame the things which are strong,

28 and the base things ofᴿthe world and the despised, God has chosen,ᴿthe things that are not, that He mightᴿnullify the things that are,   1 Cor. 1:20 • Rom. 4:17 • Job 34:19

29 that no man should boast before God.

30 But ᵀby His doing you are in Christ Jesus, who became to us wisdom from God, ᴬand righteousness and ᴿsanctification, and redemption,   *of Him • both* • 1 Cor. 1:2; 6:11

---

¹ Some ancient mss. do not contain *my*
² Some ancient mss. read *I give thanks that*   ³ I.e., Messiah

31 that, just as it is written, "LET[R]HIM WHO BOASTS, BOAST IN THE LORD."   Jer. 9:23f.

CHAPTER 2

AND when I came to you, brethren, I[R]did not come with superiority of speech or of wisdom, proclaiming to you[R]the [4]testimony of God.   [1 Cor. 1:17; 2:4, 13] • [1 Cor. 2:7]

2 For I determined to know nothing among you except [R]Jesus Christ, and Him crucified.   1 Cor. 1:23; Gal. 6:14

3 And I was with you in[R]weakness and in fear and in much trembling.   1 Cor. 4:10

4 And my [T]message and my preaching were [R]not in persuasive words of wisdom, but in demonstration of[R]the Spirit and of power,   word • 1 Cor. 1:17; 2:1 • Rom. 15:19

5 that your faith should not rest on the wisdom of men, but on the power of God.

The Gospel Is Heavenly Wisdom

6 Yet we do speak wisdom among those who are[R]mature; a wisdom, however, not of this age, nor of the rulers of this age, who are[R]passing away;   [Eph. 4:13] • 1 Cor. 1:28

7 but we speak God's wisdom in a[R]mystery, the hidden wisdom, which God predestined before the ages to our glory;   1 Cor. 2:1

8 the wisdom[R]which none of the rulers of [R]this age has understood; for if they had understood it, they would not have crucified the Lord of glory;   1 Cor. 1:26; 2:6 • Matt. 13:22

9 but just as it is written,

"THINGS[R]WHICH EYE HAS NOT SEEN AND
     EAR HAS NOT HEARD,   Is. 64:4; 65:17
AND which HAVE NOT ENTERED THE
     HEART OF MAN,
ALL THAT GOD HAS PREPARED FOR
     THOSE WHO LOVE HIM."

10 [5]For to us God revealed them[R]through the Spirit; for the Spirit searches all things, even the depths of God.   John 14:26

11 For who among men knows the thoughts of a man except the [R]spirit of the man, which is in him? Even so the thoughts of God no one knows except the Spirit of God.   [Prov. 20:27]

12 Now we[R]have received, not the spirit of [R]the world, but the Spirit who is from God, that we might know the things freely given to us by God,   [Rom. 8:15] • 1 Cor. 1:27

13 which things we also speak, [R]not in words taught by human wisdom, but in those taught by the Spirit, combining spiritual thoughts with spiritual words. 1 Cor. 1:17

14 But [A]a [R]natural man does not accept the things of the Spirit of God; for they are foolishness to him, and he cannot understand them, because they are spiritually[A]appraised.   an unspiritual • 1 Cor. 15:44 • examined

15 But he who is [R]spiritual appraises all things, yet he himself is appraised by no man.   1 Cor. 3:1; 14:37; Gal. 6:1

16 For WHO HAS KNOWN THE MIND OF THE LORD, THAT HE SHOULD INSTRUCT HIM? But [R]we have the mind of Christ.   [John 15:15]

CHAPTER 3

AND I, brethren, could not speak to you as to[R]spiritual men, but as to[R]men of flesh, as to [R]babes in Christ.   Gal. 6:1 • Rom. 7:14 • Heb. 5:13

2 I gave you milk to drink, not solid food; for you were not yet able to receive it. Indeed, even now you are not yet able,

3 for you are still fleshly. For since there is [R]jealousy and strife among you, are you not fleshly, and are you not walking[T]like mere men?   Rom. 13:13 • according to man

4 For when[R]one says, "I am of Paul," and another, "I am of Apollos," are you not mere[R]men?   1 Cor. 1:12 • 1 Cor. 3:3

Ministers Are Fellow Workers with God

5 What then is Apollos? And what is Paul?[R]Servants through whom you believed, even [R]as the Lord gave opportunity to each one.   Rom. 15:16; Eph. 3:7 • Rom. 12:6; 1 Cor. 3:10

6 I planted, [R]Apollos watered, but God was causing the growth.   Acts 18:24-27

7 So then neither the one who plants nor the one who waters is anything, but God who causes the growth.

8 Now he who plants and he who waters are one; but each will receive his own[A]reward according to his own labor.   wages

9 For we are God's fellow workers; you are God's[A]field, God's building.   cultivated land

10 According to the grace of God which was given to me, as a wise master builder[R]I laid a foundation, and [R]another is building upon it. But let each man be careful how he builds upon it.   Rom. 15:20 • 1 Thess. 3:2

11 For no man can lay a[R]foundation other than the one which is laid, which is Jesus Christ.   Is. 28:16; Eph. 2:20; 1 Pet. 2:4ff.

12 Now if any man builds upon the foundation with gold, silver, [A]precious stones, wood, hay, straw,   costly

13 each man's work will become evident; for[R]the day will show it, because it is to be revealed with fire; and the fire itself will test the quality of each man's work.   Matt. 10:15

14 If any man's work which he has built upon it remains, he shall receive a reward.

15 If any man's work is burned up, he shall suffer loss; but he himself shall be saved, yet[R]so as through fire.   Ps. 66:10, 12

16 [R]Do you not know that[R]you are a[A]temple of God, and that the Spirit of God dwells in you? [Rom. 6:16] • Rom. 8:9; Eph. 2:21f. • sanctuary

17 If any man destroys the[A]temple of God, God will destroy him, for the temple of God is holy, and that is what you are.   sanctuary

[4] Some ancient mss. read mystery
[5] Some ancient mss. use But

Ministers Are Accountable to God

18 ^RLet no man deceive himself.^RIf any man among you thinks that he is wise in^Rthis age, let him become foolish that he may become wise.   Is. 5:21 • 1 Cor. 8:2; Gal. 6:3 • 1 Cor. 1:20

19 For^Rthe wisdom of this world is foolishness before God. For it is written, *"He is*^RTHE ONE WHO CATCHES THE WISE IN THEIR CRAFTINESS"*;*   1 Cor. 1:20 • Job 5:13

20 and again, "THE^RLORD KNOWS THE REASONINGS of the wise, THAT THEY ARE USELESS."   Ps. 94:11

21 So then^Rlet no one boast in men. For^Rall things belong to you,   1 Cor. 4:6 • Rom. 8:32

22 whether Paul or Apollos or Cephas or the world or life or death or things present or things to come; all things belong to you,

23 and^Ryou belong to Christ; and ^RChrist belongs to God.   1 Cor. 15:23 • 1 Cor. 11:3; 15:28

CHAPTER 4

LET a man regard us in this manner, as ^Rservants of Christ, and^Rstewards of^Rthe mysteries of God.   Luke 1:2 • Titus 1:7 • Rom. 11:25

2 In this case, moreover, it is required^Tof stewards that one be found trustworthy.   *in*

3 But to me it is a very small thing that I should be examined by you, or by *any* human^Tcourt; in fact, I do not even examine myself.   *day*

4 For I am conscious of nothing against myself, yet I am not by this acquitted; but the one who examines me is the Lord.

5 Therefore do not go on passing judgment before ⁶the time, *but wait* until the Lord comes who will both bring to light the things hidden in the darkness and disclose the motives of *men's* hearts; and then each man's praise will come to him from God.

Misunderstanding of Paul's Ministry

6 Now these things, brethren, I have figuratively applied to myself and Apollos for your sakes, that in us you might learn not to exceed what is written, in order that no one of you might become^Tarrogant in behalf of one against the other.   *puffed up*

7 For who regards you as superior? And ^Rwhat do you have that you did not receive? But if you did receive it, why do you boast as if you had not received it?   Rom. 12:3, 6

8 You are ^Ralready filled, you have already become rich, you have become kings without us; and *I* would indeed that you had become kings so that we also might reign with you.   Rev. 3:17f.

9 For, I think, God has exhibited us apostles last of all, as men condemned to death; because we^Rhave become a spectacle to the world, both to angels and to men.   Heb. 10:33

10 We are^Rfools for Christ's sake, but^Ryou are prudent in Christ; we are weak, but you are strong; you are distinguished, but we are without honor.   Acts 17:18; 26:24 • 1 Cor. 1:19f.

11 To this present hour we are both hungry and thirsty, and are poorly clothed, and are roughly treated, and are homeless;

12 and we toil, working with our own hands; when we are^Rreviled, we bless; when we are persecuted, we endure;   1 Pet. 3:9

13 when we are slandered, we try to^Aconciliate; we have^Rbecome as the scum of the world, the dregs of all things, *even* until now.   *console* • Lam. 3:45

14 I do not write these things to^Rshame you, but to admonish you as my beloved ^Rchildren.   1 Cor. 6:5; 15:34 • 2 Cor. 6:13; 12:14

15 For if you were to have countless^Rtutors in Christ, yet *you would* not *have* many fathers; for in Christ Jesus I became your father through the gospel.   Gal. 3:24f

16 I exhort you therefore, be^Rimitators of me.   [1 Cor. 11:1]; Phil. 3:17; 4:9; [1 Thess. 1:6]

17 For this reason I have sent to you Timothy, who is my ^Rbeloved and faithful child in the Lord, and he will remind you of my ways which are in Christ, just as I teach everywhere in every church.   1 Tim. 1:2, 18

18 Now some have become ^Tarrogant, as though I were not coming to you.   *puffed up*

19 But I will come to you soon, if the Lord wills, and I shall find out, not the words of those who are arrogant, but their power.

20 For the kingdom of God does^Rnot consist in^Twords, but in power.   1 Cor. 2:4 • *word*

21 What do you desire? ^RShall I come to you with a rod or with love and a spirit of gentleness?   2 Cor. 1:23; 2:1, 3; 12:20; 13:2, 10

CHAPTER 5

Deliver the Fornicators for Discipline

IT is actually reported that there is immorality among you, and immorality of such a kind as does not exist even among the Gentiles, that someone has his father's wife.

2 And you ^Rhave become ^Tarrogant, and have not mourned instead, in order that the one who had done this deed might be removed from your midst.   1 Cor. 4:6 • *puffed up*

3 For I, on my part, though ^Rabsent in body but present in spirit, have already judged him who has so committed this, as though I were present.   Col. 2:5; 1 Thess. 2:17

4 In the name of our Lord Jesus, when you are assembled, and I with you in spirit, with the power of our Lord Jesus,

5 *I have decided* to^Rdeliver such a one to ^RSatan for the destruction of his flesh, that his spirit may be saved in^Rthe day of the Lord ⁷Jesus.   Prov. 23:14 • Matt. 4:10 • 1 Cor. 1:8

6 ^RYour boasting is not good.^RDo you not know that^aa little leaven leavens the whole lump *of dough*?   1 Cor. 5:2 • Rom. 6:16 • Hos. 7:4

7 Clean out the old leaven, that you may

---

⁶ I.e., the appointed time of judgment
⁷ Some ancient mss. do not contain *Jesus*

be a new lump, just as you are *in fact* unleavened. For Christ our[R]Passover also has been sacrificed.   Mark 14:12; 1 Pet. 1:19

8 Let us therefore celebrate the feast,[R]not with old leaven, nor with the leaven of malice and wickedness, but with the unleavened bread of sincerity and truth.   Deut. 16:3

Separate Yourselves from Immoral Believers

9 I wrote you in my letter[R]not to associate with immoral people;   2 Cor. 6:14

10 I *did* not at all *mean* with the immoral people of this world, or with the covetous and swindlers, or with idolaters; for then you would have to go out of the world.

11 But actually, I wrote to you not to associate with any so-called brother if he should be an immoral person, or covetous, or an idolater, or a reviler, or a drunkard, or a swindler—not even to eat with such a one.

12 For what have I to do with judging[R]outsiders? [R]Do you not judge those who are within *the church*?   [Mark 4:11] • 1 Cor. 5:3-5

13 But those who are outside, God[A]judges. [R]REMOVE THE WICKED MAN FROM AMONG YOURSELVES.   *will judge* • Deut. 13:5; 17:7, 12

CHAPTER 6

Concerning Litigation Between Believers

DOES any one of you, when he has a[T]case against his neighbor, dare to go to law before the unrighteous, and [R]not before the [A]saints?   *matter* • Matt. 18:17 • *holy ones*

2 Or do you not know that the saints will judge the world? And if the world is judged by you, are you not competent to[A]constitute the smallest law courts?   *try the trivial cases?*

3 [R]Do you not know that we shall judge angels? How much more, matters of this life?   Rom. 6:16

4 If then you have law courts dealing with matters of this life, [A]do you appoint them as judges who are of no account in the church?   *apoint them . . . church*

5 I say *this* to your shame. *Is it so, that* there is not among you one wise man who will be able to decide between his brethren?

6 but brother goes to law with brother, and that before[R]unbelievers?   2 Cor. 6:14f.

7 Actually, then, it is already a defeat for you, that you have lawsuits with one another.[R]Why not rather be wronged? Why not rather be defrauded?   Matt. 5:39f.

8 On the contrary, you yourselves wrong and defraud, and that *your* brethren.

9 Or do you not know that the unrighteous shall not[R]inherit the kingdom of God? [R]Do not be deceived; neither fornicators, nor idolaters, nor adulterers, nor [8]effeminate, nor homosexuals,   Acts 20:32 • Luke 21:8

10 nor thieves, nor *the* covetous, nor drunkards, nor revilers, nor swindlers, shall [R]inherit the kingdom of God.   1 Cor. 15:50

11 And such were some of you; but you were washed, but you were sanctified, but you were justified in the name of the Lord Jesus Christ, and in the Spirit of our God.

Warning Against Sexual Immorality

12 [R]All things are lawful for me, but not all things are profitable. All things are lawful for me, but I will not be mastered by anything.   1 Cor. 10:23

13 Food is for the stomach, and the stomach is for food; but God will do away with both[T]of them. Yet the body is not for immorality, but for the Lord; and[R]the Lord is for the body.   *it and them* • [Gal. 5:24; Eph. 5:23]

14 Now God has not only raised the Lord, but will also raise us up through His power.

15 Do you not know that your bodies are members of Christ? Shall I then take away the members of Christ and make them members of a harlot? May it never be!

[8] I.e., effeminate by perversion

6:11 Changed Life—The first stanza of a famous Christian song begins: "What a wonderful change in my life has been wrought since Jesus came into my heart."

Without doubt the greatest proof of the new birth is a changed life. The child of God now suddenly loves the following:

a. He loves Jesus. Before conversion the sinner might hold Christ in high esteem, but after conversion he loves the Savior (Page 1277—1 John 5:1, 2).

b. He loves the Bible. We should love God's Word as the psalmist did in Psalm 119. He expresses his great love for God's Word no less than 17 times! See verses 24, 40, 47, 48, 72, 97, 103, 111, 113, 127, 129, 140, 143, 159, 162, 165, 168.

c. He loves other Christians. "We know that we have passed out of death into life, because we love the brethren" (Page 1276—1 John 3:14).

d. He loves his enemies. See Matthew 5:43–45.

e. He loves the souls of all people. Like Paul, he too can cry out for the conversion of loved ones. "Brethren, my heart's desire and my prayer to God for them is for *their* salvation" (Page 1139—Rom. 10:1). See also Second Corinthians 5:14.

f. He loves the pure life. John says if one loves the world, the love of the Father is not in him (Page 1275—1 John 2:15–17). See also First John 5:4.

g. He loves to talk to God. "Speaking to one another in psalms and hymns and spiritual songs, singing and making melody with your heart to the Lord" (Page 1188—Eph. 5:19).

Now turn to Page 23—THE CHRISTIAN'S GUIDE: Growing in the New Life.

16 Or[R]do you not know that the one who joins himself to a harlot is one body *with her*? For He says, "THE[R] TWO WILL BECOME ONE FLESH."   1 Cor. 6:3 • Gen. 2:24; Matt. 19:5

17 But the one who joins himself to the Lord is[R]one spirit *with Him.*   [John 17:21–23]

18 Flee immorality. Every *other* sin that a man commits is outside the body, but the immoral man sins against his own body.

A 19 Or do you not know that your body is a temple of the Holy Spirit who is in you, whom you have from[A]God, and that you are not your own?   *sanctuary • God? And you . . . own*

20 For you have been bought with a price: therefore glorify God in[R]your body. Phil. 1:20

CHAPTER 7

Principles for Married Life

Now concerning the things about which you wrote, it is[R]good for a man not to touch a woman.   1 Cor. 7:8, 26

2 But because of immoralities, let each man have his own wife, and let each woman have her own husband.

3 Let the husband[T]fulfill his duty to his wife, and likewise also the wife to her husband.   *render*

4 The wife does not have authority over her own body, but the husband *does*; and likewise also the husband does not have authority over his own body, but the wife *does.*

5 [R]Stop depriving one another, except by agreement for a time that you may devote yourselves to prayer, and [T]come together again lest[R]Satan tempt you because of your lack of self-control.   Ex. 19:15 • *be* • Matt. 4:10

6 But this I say by way of concession,[R]not of command.   2 Cor. 8:8

⁹ Some ancient mss. read *For*
¹⁰ Some ancient mss. read *you*

7 ⁹Yet I wish that all men were[R]even as I myself am. However,[R]each man has his own gift from God, one in this manner, and another in that.   1 Cor. 7:8; 9:5 • Matt. 19:11f.

8 But I say to the unmarried and to widows that it is[R]good for them if they remain [R]even as I.   1 Cor. 7:1, 26 • 1 Cor. 7:7; 9:5

9 But if they do not have self-control,[R]let them marry; for it is better to marry than to [T]burn.   1 Tim. 5:14 • burn with passion

Principles for the Married Believer

10 But to the married I give instructions, [R]not I, but the Lord, that the wife should not [T]leave her husband   Mark 10:2-12 • *depart from*

11 (but if she does leave, let her remain unmarried, or else be reconciled to her husband), and that the husband should not[A]send his away.   *leave his wife*

12 But to the rest[R]I say, not the Lord, that if any brother has a wife who is an unbeliever, and she consents to live with him, let him not[A]send her away.   1 Cor. 7:6 • *leave her*

13 And a woman who has an unbelieving husband, and he consents to live with her, let her not send her husband away.

14 For the unbelieving husband is sanctified through his wife, and the unbelieving wife is sanctified through[T]her believing husband; for otherwise your children are unclean, but now they are holy.   *the brother*

15 Yet if the unbelieving one leaves, let him leave; the brother or the sister is not under bondage in such *cases,* but God has called ¹⁰us[T]to[R]peace.   *in* • Rom. 14:19

16 For how do you know, O wife, whether you will[R]save your husband? Or how do you know, O husband, whether you will save your wife?   Rom. 11:14; 1 Pet. 3:1

Principle of Abiding in God's Call

17 Only,[R]as the Lord has assigned to each one, as God has called each, in this manner let him walk. And[R]thus I direct in [R]all the churches.   Rom. 12:3 • 1 Cor. 4:17 • 1 Cor. 11:16

6:19 The Work of the Holy Spirit in Christian Living—As a loving and wise mother tenderly watches over her child, so the Holy Spirit cares for the children of God.

a. The Holy Spirit indwells Christians. The Bible teaches that all believers are indwelt by the Holy Spirit (1 Cor. 6:19). The purpose of this indwelling ministry is to control the newly created nature given at conversion (Page 1168—2 Cor. 5:17; Page 1186—Phil. 3:16).

b. The Holy Spirit fills believers. We are admonished to "be filled with the Spirit" (Page 1188—Eph. 5:18). The word "fill" means to be controlled. The filling does not mean that the Christian gets more of the Holy Spirit, but rather, He gets more of us!

c. The Holy Spirit sanctifies the believer (Page 1144—Rom. 15:16; Page 1212—2 Thess. 2:13).

d. The Holy Spirit produces fruit in the life of the believer. This fruit is described by Paul: "But the fruit of the Spirit is love, joy, peace, patience, kindness, goodness, faithfulness, gentleness, self-control" (Page 1181—Gal. 5:22, 23).

e. The Holy Spirit imparts gifts to Christians (Page 1141—Rom. 12:6–8; Page 1157—1 Cor. 12:1–11; Page 1187—Eph. 4:7–12). A spiritual gift is an ability imparted to every Christian (Page 1153—1 Cor. 7:7; Page 1264—1 Pet. 4:10). The purpose of these gifts is twofold, namely, to glorify God (Page 1296—Rev. 4:11) and to edify the body of Christ (Page 1187—Eph. 4:12, 13).

f. The Holy Spirit teaches believers. He will instruct us in all spiritual things as we read the Word of God (Page 1082—John 14:26) and abide in the Son of God (Page 1276—1 John 2:24–27).
Now turn to Page 23—THE CHRISTIAN'S GUIDE: Beginning the New Life.

18 Was any man called *already* circumcised? Let him not become uncircumcised. Has anyone been called in uncircumcision? ᴿLet him not be circumcised. Acts 15:1ff.

19 Circumcision is nothing, and uncircumcision is nothing, but *what matters is* the keeping of the commandments of God.

20 ᴿLet each man remain in that ᵀcondition in which he was called.   1 Cor. 7:24 • *calling*

21 Were you called while a slave? Do not worry about it; but if you are able also to become free, rather ᵀdo that.   *use*

22 For he who was called in the Lord while a slave, is ᴿthe Lord's freedman; likewise he who was called while free, is ᴿChrist's slave.   [John 8:32] • Eph. 6:6; Col. 3:24

23 ᴿYou were bought with a price; do not become slaves of men.   1 Cor. 6:20

24 Brethren, ᴿlet each man remain with God in that *condition* in which he was called.   1 Cor. 7:20

Principles for the Unmarried

25 Now concerning virgins I have ᴿno command of the Lord, but I give an opinion as one who ᴿby the mercy of the Lord is trustworthy.   1 Cor. 7:6 • 2 Cor. 4:1; 1 Tim. 1:13, 16

26 I think then that this is good in view of the ^present distress, that it is good for a man ᵀto remain as he is.   *impending* • *so to be*

27 Are you bound to a wife? Do not seek to be released. Are you released from a wife? Do not seek a wife.

28 But if you should marry, you have not sinned; and if a virgin should marry, she has not sinned. Yet such will have trouble in this life, and I am trying to spare you.

29 But this I say, brethren, ᴿthe time has been shortened, so that from now on those who have wives should be as though they had none;   [Rom. 13:11f.]; 1 Cor. 7:31

30 and those who weep, as though they did not weep; and those who rejoice, as though they did not rejoice; and those who buy, as though they did not possess;

31 and those who use the world, as though they did not make full use of it; for the form of this world is passing away.

32 But I want you to be free from concern. One who is ᴿunmarried is concerned about the things of the Lord, how he may please the Lord;   1 Tim. 5:5

33 but one who is married is concerned about the things of the world, how he may please his ¹¹wife,

34 and *his interests* are divided. And the woman who is unmarried, and the virgin, is concerned about the things of the Lord, that she may be holy both in body and spirit; but one who is married is concerned about the things of the world, how she may please her husband.

35 And this I say for your own benefit; not to put a restraint upon you, but ᵀto promote what is seemly, and *to secure* undistracted devotion to the Lord.   *for what is seemly*

36 But if any man thinks that he is acting unbecomingly toward his virgin *daughter,* if she should be of full age, and if it must be so, let him do what he wishes, he does not sin; let ᵀher marry.   *them*

37 But he who stands firm in his heart, ᵀbeing under no constraint, but has authority ᵀover his own will, and has decided this in his own heart, to keep his own virgin *daughter,* he will do well.   *having no necessity* • *pertaining to*

38 So then both he who gives his own virgin *daughter* in marriage does well, and he who does not give her in marriage will do better.

Principles for Remarriage

39 ᴿA wife is bound as long as her husband lives; but if her husband ᵀis dead, she is free to be married to whom she wishes, only in the Lord.   Rom. 7:2 • *has fallen asleep*

40 But ᴿin my opinion she is happier if she remains as she is; and I think that I also have the Spirit of God.   1 Cor. 7:6, 25

CHAPTER 8

Principles of Liberty and the Weaker Brother

NOW concerning ᴿthings sacrificed to idols, we know that we all have ᴿknowledge. Knowledge ᵀmakes arrogant, but love ᴿedifies.   Acts 15:20 • 1 Cor. 8:7 • *puffs up* • Rom. 14:19

2 ᴿIf anyone supposes that he knows anything, he has not yet ᴿknown as he ought to know;   1 Cor. 3:18 • [1 Cor. 13:8–12; 1 Tim. 6:4]

3 but if anyone loves God, he ᴿis known by Him.   Ps. 1:6; Jer. 1:5; Amos 3:2; [Rom. 8:29]

4 Therefore concerning the eating of things sacrificed to idols, we know that ¹²there is no such thing as an idol in the world, and that there is no God but one.

5 For even if there are so-called gods whether in heaven or on earth, as indeed there are many gods and many lords,

6 yet for us there is *but* one God, ᴿthe Father, ᴿfrom whom are all things, and we *exist* for Him; and ᴿone Lord, Jesus Christ, ᴿby whom are all things, and we *exist* through Him.   Eph. 4:6 • Rom. 11:36 • Eph. 4:5 • [Col. 1:16]

7 However not all men ᴿhave this knowledge; but ᴿsome, being accustomed to the idol until now, eat *food* as if it were sacrificed to an idol; and their conscience being weak is defiled.   1 Cor. 8:4ff. • Rom. 14:14, 22f.

8 But food will not commend us to God; we are neither ᵀthe worse if we do not eat, nor ᵀthe better if we do eat.   *lacking* • *abounding*

9 But ᴿtake care lest this ᵀliberty of yours

---

¹¹ Some mss. read *wife. And there is a difference also between the wife and the virgin. One who is unmarried is concerned . . .*   ¹² I.e., has no real existence

somehow become a stumbling block to the [R]weak.   Gal. 5:13 • *right* • Rom. 14:1; 1 Cor. 8:10f.

10 For if someone sees you, who have [R]knowledge, dining in an idol's temple, will not his conscience, if he is weak, be strengthened to eat [R]things sacrificed to idols?   1 Cor. 8:4ff. • Acts 15:20; 1 Cor. 8:1, 4, 7

11 For through[R]your knowledge he who is weak[R]is ruined, the brother for whose sake Christ died.   1 Cor. 8:4ff. • Rom. 14:15, 20

12 And thus, by sinning against the brethren and wounding their conscience when it is weak, you sin[R]against Christ.   Matt. 25:45

13 Therefore, if food causes my brother to stumble, I will never eat meat again, that I might not cause my brother to stumble.

CHAPTER 9

Paul Lists His Rights as a Minister

AM I not free? Am I not an apostle? Have I not[R]seen Jesus our Lord? Are you not[R]my work in the Lord?   Acts 9:3, 17 • 1 Cor. 3:6; 4:15

2 If to others I am not an apostle, at least I am to you; for you are the[R]seal of my[R]apostleship in the Lord.   John 3:33 • Acts 1:25

3 My defense to those who examine me is this:

4 [R]Do we not have a right to eat and drink?   1 Cor. 9:14; [1 Thess. 2:6, 9]; 2 Thess. 3:8f.

5 Do we not have a right to take along a [T]believing wife, even as the rest of the apostles, and the[R]brothers of the Lord, and[R]Cephas?   *sister, as wife* • Matt. 12:46 • Matt. 8:14

6 Or do only[T]Barnabas and I not have a right to refrain from working?   *I and Barnabas*

7 Who at any time serves[R]as a soldier at his own expense? Who[R]plants a vineyard, and does not eat the fruit of it? Or who tends a flock and does not[T]use the milk of the flock?   2 Cor. 10:4 • 1 Cor. 3:6, 8 • *eat of*

8 I am not speaking these things according to[T]human judgment, am I? Or does not the Law also say these things?   *man*

9 For it is written in the Law of Moses, "YOU[R]SHALL NOT MUZZLE THE OX WHILE HE IS THRESHING." God is not concerned about [R]oxen, is He?   Deut. 25:4; 1 Tim. 5:18 • Deut. 22:1-4

10 Or is He speaking altogether for our sake? Yes,[R]for our sake it was written, because[R]the plowman ought to plow in hope, and the thresher *to thresh* in hope of sharing *the crops.*   Rom. 4:23f. • 2 Tim. 2:6

11 [R]If we sowed spiritual things in you, is it too much if we should reap material things from you?   Rom. 15:27; 1 Cor. 9:14

12 If others share the right over you, do we not more? Nevertheless, we[R]did not use this right, but we endure all things,[R]that we may cause no hindrance to the[R]gospel of Christ.   Acts 18:3 • 2 Cor. 6:3 • 1 Cor. 4:15; 9:14

13 Do you not know that those who perform sacred services eat the *food* of the

temple, *and* those who attend regularly to the altar have their share with the altar?

14 So also[R]the Lord directed those who proclaim the[R]gospel to[R]get their living from the gospel.   Luke 10:7 • 1 Cor. 4:15 • Luke 10:8

Paul Limits His Rights for Ministry

15 But I have used none of these things. And I am not writing these things that it may be done so in my case; for it would be better for me to die than have any man make[R]my boast an empty one.   2 Cor. 11:10

16 For if I preach the gospel, I have nothing to boast of, for I am under compulsion; for woe is me if I do not preach the gospel.

17 For if I do this voluntarily, I have a[R]reward; but if against my will, I have a[R]stewardship entrusted to me.   John 4:36 • 1 Cor. 4:1

18 What then is my[R]reward? That, when I preach the gospel, I may offer the gospel without charge, so as[R]not to make full use of my right in the gospel.   John 4:36 • 1 Cor. 7:31

19 For though I am[R]free from all *men,* I have made myself[R]a slave to all, that I might [R]win the more.   1 Cor. 9:1 • Gal. 5:13 • 1 Pet. 3:1

20 And to the Jews I became as a Jew, that I might win Jews; to those who are under[A]the Law, as under the Law, though not being myself under the Law, that I might win those who are under the Law;   *law*

21 to those who are without law, as without law, though not being without the law of God but under the law of Christ, that I might win those who are without law.

22 To the[R]weak I became weak, that I might win the weak; I have become [R]all things to all men,[R]that I may by all means save some.   Rom. 14:1 • 1 Cor. 10:33 • Rom. 11:14

23 And I do all things for the sake of the gospel, that I may become a fellow partaker of it.

24 Do you not know that those who run in a race all run, but *only* one receives the prize? Run in such a way that you may win.

25 And everyone who [R]competes in the games exercises self-control in all things. They then *do it* to receive a perishable wreath, but we an imperishable.   [Eph. 6:12]

26 Therefore I[R]run in such a way, as not without aim; I box in such a way, as not [R]beating the air;   Gal. 2:2; 2 Tim. 4:7 • 1 Cor. 14:9

27 but I buffet my body and make it my slave, lest possibly, after I have preached to others, I myself should be disqualified.

CHAPTER 10

Warning Against Forfeiting Liberty

FOR I do not want you to be unaware, brethren, that our fathers were all under the cloud, and all passed through the sea;

2 and all [13]were[R]baptized into Moses in the cloud and in the sea;   Rom. 6:3; 1 Cor. 1:13

[13] Some ancient mss. read *received baptism*

3 and all ate the same spiritual food;

4 and all^{R}drank the same spiritual drink, for they were drinking from a spiritual rock which followed them; and the rock was ^{T}Christ.   Ex. 17:6; Num. 20:11 • the Messiah

5 Nevertheless, with most of them God was not well-pleased; for^{R}they were laid low in the wilderness.   Num. 14:29ff.; Heb. 3:17

6 Now these things happened as^{R}examples for us, that we should not crave evil things, as they also craved.   1 Cor. 10:11

7 And do not be^{R}idolaters, as some of them were; as it is written, "THE^{R}PEOPLE SAT DOWN TO EAT AND DRINK, AND STOOD UP TO ^{R}PLAY."   Ex. 32:4; 1 Cor. 5:11 • Ex. 32:6 • Ex. 32:19

8 Nor let us act immorally, as^{R}some of them^{T}did, and^{R}twenty-three thousand fell in one day. Num. 25:1ff. • acted immorally • Num. 25:9

9 Nor let us try the Lord, as^{R}some of them^{T}did, and were destroyed by the serpents.   Num. 21:5f. • made trial

10 Nor grumble, as some of them^{T}did, and were destroyed by the destroyer.   grumbled

11 Now these things happened to them as an^{R}example, and^{R}they were written for our instruction, upon whom^{R}the ends of the ages have come.   1 Cor. 10:6 • Rom. 4:23 • Rom. 13:11

12 Therefore let him who^{R}thinks he stands take heed lest he fall.   Rom. 11:20; 2 Pet. 3:17

13 No temptation has overtaken you but such as is common to man; and God is faithful, who will not allow you to be tempted beyond what you are able, but with the temptation will provide the way of escape also, that you may be able to endure it.

Exhortation to Use Liberty to Glorify God

14 Therefore, my^{R}beloved, flee from^{R}idolatry.   Heb. 6:9 • 1 Cor. 10:7, 19f.; 1 John 5:21

15 I speak as to wise men; you judge what I say.

16 Is not the^{R}cup of blessing which we bless a sharing in the blood of Christ? Is not the^{T}bread which we break a sharing in the body of Christ?   Luke 22:20; 1 Cor. 11:25 • loaf

17 Since there is one^{T}bread, we^{R}who are many are one body; for we all partake of the one bread.   loaf • Rom. 12:5; 1 Cor. 12:12f., 27

18 Look at the nation Israel; are not those who eat the sacrifices sharers in the altar?

19 What do I mean then? That a thing sacrificed to idols is anything, or^{R}that an idol is anything?   1 Cor. 8:4

20 No, but I say that the things which the Gentiles sacrifice, they^{R}sacrifice to demons, and not to God; and I do not want you to become sharers in demons.   Gal. 4:8; Rev. 9:20

21 ^{R}You cannot drink the cup of the Lord and the cup of demons; you cannot partake of the table of the Lord and^{R}the table of demons.   2 Cor. 6:16 • Is. 65:11

22 Or do we provoke the Lord to jealousy? We are not stronger than He, are we?

23 ^{R}All things are lawful, but not all things are profitable. All things are lawful, but not all things^{R}edify.   1 Cor. 6:12 • Rom. 14:19

24 Let no one^{R}seek his own good, but that of his^{A}neighbor.   2 Cor. 12:14 • the other

25 ^{R}Eat anything that is sold in the meat market, without asking questions for conscience' sake;   Acts 10:15; 1 Cor. 8:7

26 ^{R}FOR THE EARTH IS THE LORD'S, AND ^{T}ALL IT CONTAINS.   Ps. 24:1; 50:12 • its fulness

27 If ^{R}one of the unbelievers invites you, and you wish to go,^{R}eat anything that is set before you, without asking questions for conscience' sake.   1 Cor. 5:10 • Luke 10:8

28 But^{R}if anyone should say to you, "This is meat sacrificed to idols," do not eat it, for the sake of the one who informed you, and for conscience' sake;   [1 Cor. 8:7, 10–12]

29 I mean not your own conscience, but the other man's; for ^{R}why is my freedom judged by another's conscience?   Rom. 14:16

30 If I partake with thankfulness,^{R}why am I slandered concerning that for which I^{R}give thanks?   1 Cor. 9:1 • Rom. 14:6

31 Whether, then, you eat or drink or whatever you do, do all to the glory of God.

32 ^{R}Give no offense either to Jews or to Greeks or to the church of God;   Acts 24:16

33 just as I also please all men in all things, not seeking my own profit, but the profit of the many, that they may be saved.

CHAPTER 11

B E^{R}imitators of me, just as I also am of Christ.   1 Cor. 4:16; Phil. 3:17

Principles of Public Prayer

2 Now I praise you because you remember me in everything, and hold firmly to the traditions, just as I delivered them to you.

3 But I want you to understand that Christ is the ^{R}head of every man, and^{R}the man is the head of a woman, and God is the head of Christ.   Col. 1:18 • [Eph. 5:23]

4 Every man who has something on his head while praying or^{R}prophesying, disgraces his head.   Acts 13:1; 1 Thess. 5:20

5 But every woman who has her head uncovered while praying or prophesying, disgraces her head; for she is one and the same with her whose head is shaved.

6 For if a woman does not cover ^{T}her head, let her also^{T}have her hair cut off; but if it is disgraceful for a woman to have her hair cut off or her head shaved, let her cover her head.   herself • shear herself

7 For a man ought not to have his head covered, since he is the image and glory of God; but the woman is the glory of man.

8 For man ^{T}does not originate from woman, but woman from man;   is not from

9 for indeed man was not created for the woman's sake, but ^{R}woman for the man's sake.   Gen. 2:18

10 Therefore the woman ought to have a symbol of authority on her head, because of the angels.

11 However, in the Lord, neither is woman[T]independent of man, nor is man independent of woman.   *without*

12 For as the woman[T]originates from the man, so also the man *has his birth* through the woman; and [R]all things [T]originate [R]from God.   *is* • 2 Cor. 5:18 • *are* • Rom. 11:36

13 [R]Judge[T]for yourselves: is it proper for a woman to pray to God *with head* uncovered?   Luke 12:57 • *in*

14 Does not even nature itself teach you that if a man has long hair, it is a dishonor to him,

15 but if a woman has long hair, it is a glory to her? For her hair is given to her for a covering.

16 But if one is inclined to be contentious, [R]we have no [T]other practice, nor have [R]the churches of God.   1 Cor. 4:5 • *such* • 1 Cor. 7:17

Rebuke of Disorders at the Lord's Supper

17 But in giving this instruction,[R]I do not praise you, because you come together not for the better but for the worse. 1 Cor. 11:2, 22

18 For, in the first place, when you come together as a church, I hear that divisions exist among you; and in part, I believe it.

19 For there must also be factions among you, in order that those who are approved may have become evident among you.

20 Therefore when you meet together, it is not to eat the Lord's Supper,

21 for in your eating each one takes his own supper first; and one is hungry and[R]another is drunk.   Jude 12

22 What! Do you not have houses in which to eat and drink? Or do you despise the church of God, and shame those who have nothing? What shall I say to you? Shall I praise you? In this I will not praise you.

23 For [R]I received from the Lord that which I also delivered to you, that[R]the Lord Jesus in the night in which He was betrayed took bread;   Gal. 1:12; Col. 3:24 • 1 Cor. 11:23-25

24 and when He had given thanks, He broke it, and said, "This is My body, which [14]is for you; do this in remembrance of Me."

25 In the same way *He took* the cup also, after supper, saying, "This cup is the new covenant in My blood; do this, as often as you drink *it*, in remembrance of Me."

26 For as often as you eat this bread and drink the cup, you proclaim the Lord's death[R]until He comes.   John 21:22; 1 Cor. 4:5

27 Therefore whoever eats the bread or drinks the cup of the Lord in an unworthy

[14] Some ancient mss. read *is broken*

manner, shall be[R]guilty of the body and the blood of the Lord.   Heb. 10:29

28 But let a man examine himself, and so let him eat of the bread and drink of the cup.

29 For he who eats and drinks, eats and drinks judgment to himself, if he does not judge the body rightly.

30 For this reason many among you are weak and sick, and a number[R]sleep. Acts 7:60

31 But if we judged ourselves rightly, we should not be judged.

32 But when we are judged, we are disciplined by the Lord in order that we may not be condemned along with the world.

33 So then, my brethren, when you come together to eat, wait for one another.

34 If anyone is [R]hungry, let him eat at home, so that you may not come together for judgment. And the remaining matters I shall arrange when I come.   1 Cor. 11:21

CHAPTER 12

Test of the Spirit's Control

N OW concerning [R]spiritual *gifts,* brethren, I do not want you to be unaware. 1 Cor. 12:4

2 You know that when you were pagans, *you were*[R]led astray to the[R]dumb idols, however you were led.   1 Thess. 1:9 • Jer. 10:5

3 Therefore I make known to you, that no one speaking by the Spirit of God says, "Jesus is accursed"; and no one can say, "Jesus is Lord," except by the Holy Spirit.

Diversity of the Gifts

4 Now there are[R]varieties of gifts, but the same Spirit.   Rom. 12:6f.; 1 Cor. 12:11; Eph. 4:4ff.

5 And there are varieties of ministries, and the same Lord.

6 And there are varieties of effects, but the same[R]God who works all things in all persons.   1 Cor. 15:28; Eph. 1:23; 4:6

7 But to each one is given the manifestation of the Spirit for the common good.

8 For to one is given the word of wisdom through the Spirit, and to another the word of knowledge according to the same Spirit;

9 to another faith by the same Spirit, and to another gifts of healing by the one Spirit,

10 and to another the[R]effecting of miracles, and to another prophecy, and to another the distinguishing of spirits, to another *various* kinds of tongues, and to another the interpretation of tongues.   *effects*

11 But one and the same Spirit works all these things, [R]distributing to each one individually just as He wills.   1 Cor. 12:4

12:1–10 Using Spiritual Gifts—Spiritual gifts are discussed in detail in four passages of the New Testament: Romans 12:3–8; First Corinthians 12:1–10, 28–31; Ephesians 4:11, 12; and First Peter 4:10, 11. These lists are to be regarded as representative of spiritual gifts. Spiritual gifts are those gifts given by the Spirit of God for the accomplishment of God's purpose in the world and for the edification of the church, the body of Christ. Two things are important to remember concerning spiritual gifts: (1) every believer has been given spiritual gifts (Page 1141— Rom. 12:5, 6; 1 Cor. 12:7; Page 1264—1 Pet. 4:10); and (2) the gifts belong to God and are given for the believer to use for the glory of God (Page 1264—1 Pet. 4:11).
Now turn to Page 1180—Gal. 5:13: Serving.

Importance of All Gifts

12 For even[R]as the body is one and *yet* has many members, and all the members of the body, though they are many, are one body, [R]so also is Christ.   Rom. 12:4f. • 1 Cor. 12:27

13 For[A]by one Spirit we were all baptized into one body, whether Jews or Greeks, whether slaves or free, and we were all made to[R]drink of one Spirit.   *in* • [John 7:37–39]

14 For[R]the body is not one member, but many.   1 Cor. 12:20

15 If the foot should say, "Because I am not a hand, I am not *a part* of the body," it is not for this reason[T]any the less *a part* of the body.   *not* a part

16 And if the ear should say, "Because I am not an eye, I am not *a part* of the body," it is not for this reason[T]any the less *a part* of the body.   *not* a part

17 If the whole body were an eye, where would the hearing be? If the whole were hearing, where would the sense of smell be?

18 But now God has[R]placed the members, each one of them, in the body,[R]just as He desired.   1 Cor. 12:28 • Rom. 12:6; 1 Cor. 12:11

19 And if they were all one member, where would the body be?

20 But now[R]there are many members, but one body.   1 Cor. 12:12, 14

21 And the eye cannot say to the hand, "I have no need of you"; or again the head to the feet, "I have no need of you."

22 On the contrary, it is much truer that the members of the body which seem to be weaker are necessary;

23 and those *members* of the body, which we [A]deem less honorable, [A]on these we bestow more abundant honor, and our unseemly *members come to* have more abundant seemliness,   *think to be* • *these we clothe with*

24 whereas our seemly *members* have no need *of it.* But God has *so* composed the body, giving more abundant honor to that *member* which lacked,

25 that there should be no [T]division in the body, but *that* the members should have the same care for one another.   *schism*

26 And if one member suffers, all the members suffer with it; if *one* member is honored, all the members rejoice with it.

27 Now you are [R]Christ's body, and [R]individually members of it.   1 Cor. 1:2 • Eph. 5:30

28 And God has[T]appointed in the church, first[R]apostles, second prophets, third teachers, then [A]miracles, then gifts of healings, helps, administrations, *various* kinds of tongues.   *set some in* • Eph. 4:11 • *works of power*

29 All are not apostles, are they? All are not prophets, are they? All are not teachers, are they? All are not *workers of*[A]miracles, are they?   *works of power*

30 All do not have gifts of healings, do they? All do not speak with tongues, do they? All do not interpret, do they?

31 But earnestly desire the greater gifts. And I show you a still more excellent way.

CHAPTER 13

Exercise Gifts with Love

IF I speak with the tongues of men and of angels, but do not have love, I have become a noisy gong or a[R]clanging cymbal.   Ps. 150:5

2 And if I have *the gift of* prophecy, and know all mysteries and all knowledge; and if I have all faith, so as to remove mountains, but do not have love, I am nothing.

3 And if I[R]give all my possessions to feed *the poor,* and if I[R]deliver my body [15]to be burned, but do not have love, it profits me nothing.   Matt. 6:2 • Dan. 3:28

4 Love[R]is patient, love is kind, *and*[R]is not jealous; love does not brag *and* is not[R]arrogant,   Prov. 10:12; 17:9 • Acts 7:9 • 1 Cor. 4:6

5 does not act unbecomingly; it[R]does not seek its own, is not provoked, does not take into account a wrong *suffered,*   1 Cor. 10:24

6 [R]does not rejoice in unrighteousness, but rejoices with the truth;   2 Thess. 2:12

7 [A]bears all things, believes all things, hopes all things, endures all things.   *covers*

8 Love never fails; but if *there are gifts of* [T]prophecy, they will be done away; if *there are* tongues, they will cease; if *there is* knowledge, it will be done away.   *prophecies*

9 For we[R]know in part, and we prophesy in part;   1 Cor. 8:2; 13:12

10 but when the perfect comes, the partial will be done away.

11 When I was a child, I used to speak as a child, think as a child, reason as a child; when I became a man, I did away with childish things.

12 For now we see in a mirror[T]dimly, but then face to face; now I know in part, but then I shall know fully just as I also[R]have been fully known.   *in a riddle* • 1 Cor. 8:3

13 But now abide faith, hope, love, these three; but the greatest of these is love.

CHAPTER 14

Superiority of Prophecy

PURSUE[R]love, yet desire earnestly [R]spiritual *gifts,* but especially that you may [R]prophesy.   1 Cor. 16:14 • 1 Cor. 12:1 • 1 Cor. 13:2

2 For one who[R]speaks in a tongue does not speak to men, but to God; for no one [T]understands, but[A]in *his* spirit he speaks mysteries.   1 Cor. 12:10, 28, 30 • *hears* • *by the Spirit*

3 But one who prophesies speaks to men for[R]edification and[R]exhortation and consolation.   Rom. 14:19; 1 Cor. 14:5, 12, 17 • Acts 4:36

4 One who [R]speaks in a tongue [R]edifies himself; but one who[R]prophesies edifies the church.   Mark 16:17 • Rom. 14:19 • 1 Cor. 13:2

5 Now I wish that you all spoke in tongues, but [R]*even* more that you would

[15] Some ancient mss. read *that I may boast*

prophesy; and greater is one who prophesies than one who speaks in tongues, unless he interprets, so that the church may receive[R]edifying.   Num. 11:29 • 1 Cor. 14:4, 12, 17

6 But now, brethren, if I come to you speaking in tongues, what shall I profit you, unless I speak to you either by way of[R]revelation or of[R]knowledge or of prophecy or of [R]teaching?   1 Cor. 14:26 • 1 Cor. 12:8 • Rom. 6:17

Gift of Tongues

7 Yet *even* lifeless things, either flute or harp, in producing a sound, if they do not produce a distinction in the tones, how will it be known what is played on the flute or on the harp?

8 For if the bugle produces an indistinct sound, who will prepare himself for battle?

9 So also you, unless you utter by the tongue speech that is clear, how will it be known what is spoken? For you will be [R]speaking into the air.   1 Cor. 9:26

10 There are, perhaps, a great many kinds of [T]languages in the world, and no *kind* is without meaning.   *voices*

11 If then I do not know the meaning of the language, I shall be to the one who speaks a barbarian, and the one who speaks will be a barbarian[^to me.   *in my estimation*

12 So also you, since you are zealous of [T]spiritual *gifts*, seek to abound for the[R]edification of the church.   *spirits* • 1 Cor. 14:4, 5, 17

13 Therefore let one who speaks in a tongue pray that he may interpret.

14 For if I pray in a tongue, my spirit prays, but my mind is unfruitful.

15 What is *the outcome* then? I shall pray with the spirit and I shall pray with the mind also; I shall[R]sing with the spirit and I shall sing with the mind also.   Eph. 5:19

16 Otherwise if you bless [A]in the spirit *only,* how will the one who fills the place of the[T]ungifted say the "Amen" at your giving of thanks, since he does not know what you are saying?   *with the* • unversed in spiritual gifts

17 For you are giving thanks well enough, but the other man is not[R]edified.   Rom. 14:19

18 I thank God, I speak in tongues more than you all;

19 however, in the church I desire to speak five words with my mind, that I may instruct others also, rather than ten thousand words in a tongue.

20 Brethren, [R]do not be children in your thinking; yet in evil[R]be babes, but in your thinking be mature.   Eph. 4:14 • Rom. 16:19

21 In[R]the Law it is written, "BY[R] MEN OF STRANGE TONGUES AND BY THE LIPS OF STRANGERS I WILL SPEAK TO THIS PEOPLE, AND EVEN SO THEY WILL NOT LISTEN TO ME," says the Lord.   John 10:34 • Is. 28:11f.

22 So then tongues are for a sign, not to those who believe, but to unbelievers; but [R]prophecy *is for a sign*, not to unbelievers, but to those who believe.   1 Cor. 14:1

23 If therefore the whole church should assemble together and all speak in tongues, and ungifted men or unbelievers enter, will they not say that[R]you are mad?   Acts 2:13

24 But if all prophesy, and an unbeliever or an ungifted man enters, he is convicted by all, he is called to account by all;

25 [R]the secrets of his heart are disclosed; and so he will[R]fall on his face and worship God,[R]declaring that God is certainly among you.   John 4:19 • Luke 17:16 • Is. 45:14

Exercising Gifts in Public Worship

26 What is *the outcome* then, brethren? When you assemble, each one has a psalm, has a teaching, has a revelation, has a tongue, has an[R]interpretation. Let all things be done for edification.   1 Cor. 12:10; 14:5, 13

27 If anyone speaks in a tongue, *it should be* by two or at the most three, and *each* in turn, and let one[R]interpret;   1 Cor. 12:10; 14:5

28 but if there is no interpreter, let him keep silent in the church; and let him speak to himself and to God.

29 And let two or three prophets speak, and let the others[R]pass judgment.   1 Cor. 12:10

30 But if a revelation is made to another who is seated, let the first keep silent.

31 For you can all prophesy one by one, so that all may learn and all may be exhorted;

32 and the spirits of prophets are subject to prophets;

33 for God is not *a God* of confusion but of peace, as in all the churches of the saints.

34 Let the women [R]keep silent in the churches; for they are not permitted to speak, but let them subject themselves, just as[R]the Law also says.   1 Cor. 11:5 • 1 Cor. 14:21

35 And if they desire to learn anything, let them ask their own husbands at home; for it is improper for a woman to speak in church.

36 Was it from you that the word of God *first* went forth? Or has it come to you only?

37 [R]If anyone thinks he is a prophet or [R]spiritual, let him recognize that the things which I write to you[R]are the Lord's commandment.   2 Cor. 10:7 • 1 Cor. 2:15 • [1 John 4:6]

38 But if anyone [16]does not recognize *this,* he is not recognized.

39 Therefore, my brethren, [R]desire earnestly to [R]prophesy, and do not forbid to speak in tongues.   1 Cor. 12:31 • 1 Cor. 13:2; 14:1

40 But[R]let all things be done properly and in an orderly manner.   1 Cor. 14:33

CHAPTER 15

Fact of Christ's Resurrection

NOW I make known to you, brethren, the gospel which I preached to you, which also you received, in which also you stand,

2 by which also you are saved, if you hold fast[T]the word which I preached to you, unless you believed in vain.   *to what word I*

---

[16] Some ancient mss. read *is ignorant, let him be ignorant*

3 For I delivered to you as of first importance what I also received, that Christ died
for our sins according to the Scriptures,
4 and that He was buried, and that He
was[R]raised on the third day[R]according to the
Scriptures,   Matt. 6:21; John 2:20ff. • Ps. 16:8ff. ★

5 and that[R]He appeared to[R]Cephas, then
to the twelve.   Luke 24:34 • 1 Cor. 1:12
6 After that He appeared to more than
five hundred brethren at one time, most of
whom remain until now, but some [R]have
fallen asleep;   Acts 7:60; 1 Cor. 15:18, 20
7 then He appeared to[T]James,[R]then to[R]all
the apostles;   Jacob • Acts 12:17 • Luke 24:33
8 and last of all, as it were to one untimely born, He appeared to me also.
9 For I am[R]the least of the apostles, who
am not fit to be called an apostle, because I
persecuted the church of God.   2 Cor. 12:11
10 But by[R]the grace of God I am what I
am, and His grace toward me did not prove
vain; but I[R]labored even more than all of
them, yet[R]not I, but the grace of God with
me.   Rom. 12:3 • 2 Cor. 11:23 • 1 Cor. 3:6; 2 Cor. 3:5
11 Whether then it was I or they, so we
preach and so you believed.

Importance of Christ's Resurrection

12 Now if Christ is preached, that He has
been raised from the dead, how do some
among you say that there[R]is no resurrection
of the dead?   Acts 17:32; 23:8; [2 Tim. 2:18]
13 But if there is no resurrection of the
dead, not even Christ has been raised;
14 and if Christ has not been raised, then
our preaching is vain, your faith also is vain.
15 Moreover we are even found to be false
witnesses of God, because we witnessed
^against God that He[R]raised [17]Christ, whom
He did not raise, if in fact the dead are not
raised.   concerning • Acts 2:24
16 For if the dead are not raised, not even
Christ has been raised;
17 and if Christ has not been raised, your
faith is worthless; you are still in your sins.
18 Then those also who[R]have fallen asleep
in Christ have perished. 1 Cor. 15:6; Rev. 14:13
19 If we have hoped in Christ in this life
only, we are of all men most to be pitied.

Order of the Resurrections

20 But now Christ[R]has been raised from
the dead, the[R]first fruits of those who[R]are
asleep.   1 Pet. 1:3 • 1 Cor. 15:23 • 1 Thess. 4:16
21 For since by a man came death, by a
man also came the resurrection of the dead.
22 For as in Adam all die, so also in[T]Christ
all shall be made alive.   the Messiah
23 But each in his own order: Christ[R]the
first fruits, after that those who are Christ's
at[R]His coming,   Acts 26:23 • 1 Thess. 2:19
24 then comes the end, when He delivers
up [R]the kingdom to the God and Father,
when He has abolished[R]all rule and all authority and power.   [Dan. 2:44] ☆ • Rom. 8:38
25 For He must reign[R]until He has put all
His enemies under His feet.   Matt. 22:44 ☆
26 The last enemy that will be[R]abolished is
death.   [2 Tim. 1:10; Rev. 20:14; 21:4] ☆
27 For[R]HE HAS PUT ALL THINGS IN SUBJEC-
TION UNDER HIS FEET. But when He says,
"All[R]things are put in subjection," it is evident that He is excepted who put all things
in subjection to Him.   Ps. 8:6 ☆ • Matt. 11:27
28 And when[R]all things are subjected to
Him, then the Son Himself also will be subjected to the One who subjected all things
to Him, that God may be all in all. Phil. 3:21

*Moral Implications
of Christ's Resurrection*

29 Otherwise, what will those do who are
baptized for the dead? If the dead are not
raised at all, why then are they baptized for
them?
30 Why are we also in danger every hour?
31 I protest, brethren, by the boasting in
you, which I have in Christ Jesus our Lord,[R]I
die daily.   Rom. 8:36
32 If from human motives I fought with
wild beasts at Ephesus, what does it profit
me? If the dead are not raised,[R]LET US EAT
AND DRINK, FOR TOMORROW WE DIE. Is. 22:13
33 [R]Do not be deceived: "Bad company
corrupts good morals."   1 Cor. 6:9
34 Become sober-minded as you ought,
and stop sinning; for some have no knowledge of God. I speak this to your shame.

[17] I.e., the Messiah

15:3, 4 Sharing Our Faith: What?—Before discussing just what is to be shared concerning our faith, let us
mention a few things we are not to do. We are not commanded to force Christian standards upon the unbelieving
world (Page 1152—1 Cor. 5:12). We are not to confuse people by allowing them to believe that church membership, tithing, or any good works are somehow connected with becoming a Christian (Page 1186—Eph. 2:8–10).
   Actually, we have but one thing to share with the unsaved, and that is the gospel of Christ. According to Paul it
involves the death and resurrection of Christ (1 Cor. 15:1–4). A plan for sharing your faith might be as follows:
a. God's Word says all are sinners, condemned to hell (Page 702—Is. 53:6; Page 1133—Rom. 3:10, 11, 23; 5:8,
   12; Page 1306—Rev. 20:15).
b. There is nothing a lost person can do on his own to save himself (Page 711—Is. 64:6; Page 1186—Eph. 2:9).
c. Christ was born, crucified, and resurrected to save lost people from their sin (Page 1066—John 3:16; Page
   1217—1 Tim. 1:15).
d. To be saved a sinner must believe God's Word and invite Christ into his heart by faith (Page 1069—John 5:24;
   Page 1113—Acts 16:31).
   Now turn to Page 1206—1 Thess. 1:5: Sharing Our Faith: How?

Bodies of the Resurrected Dead

35 But ᴿsomeone will say, "How areᴿthe dead raised? And with what kind of body do they come?"   Rom. 9:19 • Ezek. 37:3
36 You fool! That which youᴿsow does not come to life unless it dies;   John 12:24
37 and that which you sow, you do not sow the body which is to be, but a bare grain, perhaps of wheat or of ᵀsomething else.   *some of the rest*
38 But God gives it a body just as He wished, andᴿto each of the seeds a body of its own.   Gen. 1:11
39 All flesh is not the same flesh, but there is one *flesh* of men, and another flesh of beasts, and another flesh of birds, and another of fish.
40 There are also heavenly bodies and earthly bodies, but the glory of the heavenly is one, and the *glory* of the earthly is another.
41 There is one glory of the sun, and another glory of the moon, and another glory of the stars; for star differs from star in glory.
42 So also is the resurrection of the dead. It is sownᵀa perishable *body*, it is raisedᵀan imperishable *body*; *in corruption • in incorruption*
43 it is sown in dishonor, it is raised in ᴿglory; it is sown in weakness, it is raised in power;   [Phil. 3:21; Col. 3:4]
44 it is sown a natural body, it is raised a ᴿspiritual body. If there is a natural body, there is also a spiritual *body*.   1 Cor. 15:50
45 So also it is written, "The first MAN, Adam, BECAME A LIVING SOUL." The last Adam *became* aᴿlife-giving spirit.   John 5:21
46 However, the spiritual is not first, but the natural; then the spiritual.
47 The first man is from the earth,ᵀearthy; the second man is from heaven.   *made of dust*
48 As is the earthy, so also are those who are earthy; and as is the heavenly,ᴿso also are those who are heavenly.   Phil. 3:20f.
49 And just as we haveᴿborne the image of the earthy, ¹⁸weᴿshall also bear the image of the heavenly.   Gen. 5:3 • Rom. 8:29
50 Now I say this, brethren, that flesh and blood cannotᴿinherit the kingdom of God; nor doesᵀthe perishable inheritᵀthe imperishable.   1 Cor. 6:9 • *corruption • incorruption*

Bodies of the Translated Living

51 Behold, I tell you a mystery; we shall not all sleep, but we shall all be changed,
52 in a moment, in the twinkling of an eye, at the last trumpet; for the trumpet will sound, and the dead will be raisedᵀimperishable, and we shall be changed.   *incorruptible*
53 For thisᵀperishable must put onᵀthe imperishable, and thisᴿmortal must put on immortality.   *corruptible • incorruption • 2 Cor. 5:4*

54 But when this perishable will have put on the imperishable, and this mortal will have put on immortality, then will come about the saying that is written, "DEATHᴿIS SWALLOWED UP in victory.   Is. 25:8
55 "Oᴿ DEATH, WHERE IS YOUR VICTORY? O DEATH, WHERE IS YOUR STING?"   Hos. 13:14
56 The sting ofᵀdeath is sin, andᴿthe power of sin is the law;   Rom. 5:12 • [Rom. 3:20; 4:15]
57 but thanks be to God, who gives us the victory through our Lord Jesus Christ.
58 Therefore, my beloved brethren, be steadfast, immovable, always abounding in ᴿthe work of the Lord, knowing that your toil is not *in* vain in the Lord.   1 Cor. 16:10

CHAPTER 16

Counsel Concerning the Collection for Jerusalem

NOW concerning the collection for the saints, asᴮI directed the churches ofᴿGalatia, so do you also.   1 Cor. 4:17 • Acts 16:6
2 Onᴿthe first day of every week let each one of youᵀput aside and save, as he may prosper, thatᴿno collections be made when I come.   Acts 20:7 • *put by himself* • 2 Cor. 9:4f.
3 And when I arrive,ᴿwhomever you may approve, I shall send them with letters to carry your gift to Jerusalem;   2 Cor. 3:1; 8:18f.
4 and if it is fitting for me to go also, they will go with me.

Conclusion

5 But I ᴿshall come to you after I go throughᴿMacedonia, for Iᴬam going through Macedonia;   1 Cor. 4:19 • Rom. 15:26 • Acts 19:21
6 and perhaps I shall stay with you, or even spend the winter, that you mayᴿsend me on my way wherever I may go.   Acts 15:3
7 For I do not wish to see you nowᴿ*just* in passing; for I hope to remain with you for some time, if the Lord permits.   2 Cor. 1:15f.
8 But I shall remain inᴿEphesus untilᴿPentecost;   Acts 18:19 • Acts 2:1
9 for aᴿwide doorᵀfor effective *service* has opened to me, andᴿthere are many adversaries.   Acts 14:27 • *and* • Acts 19:9
10 Now if Timothy comes, see that he is with you without cause to be afraid; for he is doing the Lord's work, as I also am.
11 ᴿLet no one therefore despise him. But ᴿsend him on his wayᴿin peace, so that he may come to me; for I expect him with the brethren.   Titus 2:15 • Acts 15:3 • Acts 15:33
12 But concerning ᴿApollos our brother, I encouraged him greatly to come to you with the brethren; and it was not at all *his* desire to come now, but he will come when he has opportunity.   Acts 18:24; 1 Cor. 1:12; 3:5f.
13 ᴿBe on the alert, stand firm in the faith, act like men,ᴿbe strong.   Matt. 24:42 • Eph. 3:16
14 Let all that you do be done in love.
15 Now I urge you, brethren (you know the household of Stephanas, thatᵀthey were

---

¹⁸ Some ancient mss. read *let us also*

the first fruits of [R]Achaia, and that they have devoted themselves for [R]ministry to the saints),   *it was* • Acts 18:12 • Rom. 15:31

16 that[R]you also be in subjection to such men and to everyone who helps in the work and labors.   1 Thess. 5:12; Heb. 13:17

17 And I rejoice over the^coming of Stephanas and Fortunatus and Achaicus; because they have ^supplied what was lacking on your part.   *presence* • *made up for your absence*

18 For they have refreshed my spirit and yours. Therefore acknowledge such men.

19 The churches of Asia greet you. Aquila and Prisca greet you heartily in the Lord, with the church that is in their house.

20 All the brethren greet you. [R]Greet one another with a holy kiss.   Rom. 16:16

21 The greeting is in my own hand—Paul.

22 If anyone does not love the Lord, let him be accursed.[T]Maranatha.   Lord come!

23 [R]The grace of the Lord Jesus be with you.   Rom. 16:20

24 My love be with you all in Christ Jesus. Amen.

CORINTHIANS

THE BOOK OF SECOND CORINTHIANS

Since Paul's first letter, the Corinthian church had been swayed by false teachers who stirred the people against Paul. They claimed he was fickle, proud, unimpressive in appearance and speech, dishonest, and unqualified as an apostle of Jesus Christ. Paul sent Titus to Corinth to deal with these difficulties, and upon his return, rejoiced to hear of the Corinthians' change of heart. Paul wrote this letter to express his thanksgiving for the repentant majority and to appeal to the rebellious minority to accept his authority. Throughout the book he defends his conduct, character, and calling as an apostle of Jesus Christ.

To distinguish this epistle from First Corinthians, it was given the title *Pros Korinthious B*, the "Second to the Corinthians." The *A* and *B* were probably later additions to *Pros Korinthious*.

THE AUTHOR OF SECOND CORINTHIANS

External and internal evidence amply support the Pauline authorship of this letter. As with Romans, the problem of Second Corinthians is with its lack of unity, not with its authorship. Many critics theorize that chapters 10—13 were not a part of this letter in its original form because their tone contrasts with that of chapters 1—9. It is held that the sudden change from a spirit of joy and comfort to a spirit of concern and self-defense points to a "seam" between two different letters. Many hypotheses have been advanced to explain the problem, but the most popular is that chapters 10—13 belong to a lost letter referred to in 2:4. Several problems arise with these attempts to dissect Second Corinthians. Chapters 10—13 do not fit Paul's description of the "lost" letter of 2:4 because they are firm but not sorrowful and because they do not refer to the offender about whom that letter was written (2:5–11). Also, this earlier material would have been appended at the beginning of Second Corinthians, not at the end. There is simply no external (manuscripts, church fathers, tradition) or internal basis for challenging the unity of this epistle. The difference in tone between 1—9 and 10—13 is easily explained by the change in focus from the repentant majority to the rebellious minority.

THE TIME OF SECOND CORINTHIANS

Part of the background of Second Corinthians can be found in "The Time of First Corinthians." Paul was in Ephesus when he wrote First Corinthians and expected Timothy to visit Corinth and return to him (1 Cor. 16:10, 11). Timothy apparently brought Paul a report of the opposition that had developed against him in Corinth, and Paul made a brief and painful visit to the Corinthians (this visit is not mentioned in Acts, but it can be inferred from 2 Cor. 2:1; 12:14; 13:1, 2). Upon returning to Ephesus, Paul regretfully wrote his sorrowful letter to urge the church to discipline the leader of the opposition (2:1–11; 7:8). Titus carried this letter. Paul, anxious to learn the results, went to Troas and then to Macedonia to meet Titus on his return trip (2:12, 13; 7:5–16). Paul was greatly relieved by Titus's report that the majority of the Corinthians had repented of their rebelliousness against Paul's apostolic authority. However, a minority opposition still persisted, evidently led by a group of Judaizers (10—13). There in Macedonia Paul wrote Second Corinthians and sent it with Titus and another brother (8:16–24). This took place late in A.D. 56, and the Macedonian city from which it was written may have been Philippi. Paul then made his third trip to Corinth (12:14; 13:1, 2; Acts 20:1–3) where he wrote his letter to the Romans.

There is an alternate view that the anguished letter of 2:4 and 7:8 is in fact First Corinthians and not a lost letter. This would require that the offender of Second Corinthians 2:5–11 and 7:12 be identified with the offender of First Corinthians 5.

THE CHRIST OF SECOND CORINTHIANS

Christ is presented as the believer's comfort (1:5), triumph (2:14), Lord (4:5), light (4:6), judge (5:10), reconciliation (5:19), substitute (5:21), gift (9:15), owner (10:7), and power (12:9).

KEYS TO SECOND CORINTHIANS

Key Word: Paul's Defense of His Ministry—The major theme of Second Corinthians is Paul's defense of his apostolic credentials and authority. This is especially evident in the portion directed to the still rebel-

lious minority (10—13), but the theme of vindication is also clear in chapters 1—9. Certain false apostles had mounted an effective campaign against Paul in the church at Corinth, and Paul was forced to take a number of steps to overcome the opposition. This epistle expresses the apostle's joy over the triumph of the true gospel in Corinth (1—7), and it acknowledges the godly sorrow and repentance of the bulk of the believers. It also urges the Corinthians to fulfill their promise of making a liberal contribution for the poor among the Christians in Judea (8:9). This collection would not only assist the poor, but it would also demonstrate the concern of gentile Christians in Macedonia and Achaia for Jewish Christians in Judea, thus displaying the unity of Jews and Gentiles in the body of Christ.

The opposition addressed in chapters 10—13 apparently consists of Jews (Palestinian or Hellenistic; 11:22) who claim to be apostles (11:5, 13; 12:11) but who preach a false gospel (11:4) and are enslaving in their leadership (11:20). Chapters 10—13 are intended to expose these "false apostles" (11:13) and defend Paul's God-given authority and ministry as an apostle of Jesus Christ.

Key Verses: Second Corinthians 4:5, 6 and 5:17-19—"For we do not preach ourselves but Christ Jesus as Lord, and ourselves as your bond-servants for Jesus' sake. For God, who said, 'Light shall shine out of darkness,' is the One who has shone in our hearts to give the light of the knowledge of the glory of God in the face of Christ" (4:5, 6).

"Therefore if any man is in Christ, *he is* a new creature; the old things passed away; behold, new things have come. Now all *these* things are from God, who reconciled us to Himself through Christ, and gave us the ministry of reconciliation, namely, that God was in

Christ reconciling the world to Himself, not counting their trespasses against them, and He has committed to us the word of reconciliation" (5:17-19).

Key Chapters: Second Corinthians 8 and 9—Chapters 8 and 9 are really one unit and comprise the most complete revelation of God's plan for giving found anywhere in the Scriptures. Contained therein are the principles for giving (8:1-6), the purposes for giving (8:7-15), the policies to be followed in giving (8:16—9:5), and the promises to be realized in giving (9:6-15).

SURVEY OF SECOND CORINTHIANS

Second Corinthians describes the anatomy of an apostle. The Corinthian church has been swayed by false teachers who have stirred the people against Paul, especially in response to First Corinthians, Paul's disciplinary letter. Throughout this letter (Second Corinthians) Paul defends his apostolic conduct, character, and call. The three major sections are: Paul's explanation of his ministry (1—7); Paul's collection for the saints (8 and 9); and Paul's vindication of his apostleship (10—13).

Paul's Explanation of His Ministry (1—7): After his salutation and thanksgiving for God's comfort in his afflictions and perils (1:1-11), Paul explains why he has delayed his planned visit to Corinth. It is not a matter of vacillation: the apostle wants them to have enough time to repent (1:12—2:4). Paul graciously asks them to restore the repentant offender to fellowship (2:5-13). At this point, Paul embarks on an extended defense of his ministry in terms of his message, circumstances, motives, and conduct (2:14—6:10). He then admon-

FOCUS	EXPLANATION OF PAUL'S MINISTRY			COLLECTION FOR THE SAINTS		VINDICATION OF PAUL'S APOSTLESHIP		
REFERENCE	1:1———2:14———6:11———			8:1———8:7———		10:1———11:1———12:14–13:14		
DIVISION	HIS CHANGE OF PLANS	PHILOSOPHY OF MINISTRY	EXHORTATIONS TO THE CORINTHIANS	EXAMPLE OF THE MACEDONIANS	EXHORTATION TO THE CORINTHIANS	ANSWERS HIS ACCUSERS	DEFENDS HIS APOSTLESHIP	ANNOUNCES HIS UPCOMING VISIT
TOPIC	CHARACTER OF PAUL			COLLECTION FOR SAINTS		CREDENTIALS OF PAUL		
	EPHESUS TO MACEDONIA: CHANGE OF ITINERARY			MACEDONIA: PREPARATION FOR VISIT		TO CORINTH: IMMINENT VISIT		
LOCATION	WRITTEN IN MACEDONIA							
TIME	C. A.D. 56							

ishes the believers to separate themselves from defilement (6:11—7:11), and expresses his comfort at Titus's news of their change of heart (7:2–16).

Paul's Collection for the Saints (8 and 9): This is the longest discussion of the principles and practice of giving in the New Testament. The example of the Macedonians' liberal giving for the needy brethren in Jerusalem (8:1–6) is followed by an appeal to the Corinthians to keep their promise by doing the same (8:7—9:15). In this connection, Paul commends the messengers he has sent to Corinth to make arrangments for the large gift they have promised. Their generosity will be more than amply rewarded by God.

Paul's Vindication of His Apostleship (10—13): Paul concludes this epistle with the defense of his apostolic authority and credentials that is directed to the still rebellious minority in the Corinthian church. His meekness in their presence in no way diminishes his authority as an apostle (10). To demonstrate his apostolic credentials, Paul is forced to boast about his knowledge, integrity, accomplishments, sufferings, visions, and miracles (11:1—12:13). He reveals his plans to visit them for the third time and urges them to repent so that he will not have to use severity when he comes (12:14—13:10). The letter ends with an exhortation, greetings, and a benediction (13:11–14).

OUTLINE OF SECOND CORINTHIANS

Part One: Paul's Explanation of His Ministry (1:1—7:16)

Part Two: Paul's Collection for the Saints (8:1—9:15)

Part Three: Paul's Vindication of His Apostleship (10:1—13:14)

CHAPTER 1

Paul's Thanksgiving to God

P AUL, an apostle of Christ Jesus by the will of God, and Timothy *our* brother, to the church of God which is at Corinth with all the saints who are throughout Achaia:

2 ᴿGrace to you and peace from God our Father and the Lord Jesus Christ.   Rom. 1:7

3 ᴿBlessed *be* the God and Father of our Lord Jesus Christ, the Father of mercies and ᴿGod of all comfort;   Eph. 1:3 • Rom. 15:5

4 who comforts us in all our affliction so that we may be able to comfort those who are in any affliction with the comfort with which we ourselves are comforted by God.

5 For just ᴿas the sufferings of Christ are ᵀours in abundance, so also our comfort is abundant through Christ.   Phil. 3:10 • *to us*

6 But if we are afflicted, it is ᴿfor your comfort and salvation; or if we are comforted, it is for your comfort, which is effective in the patient enduring of the same sufferings which we also suffer;   2 Tim. 2:10

7 and our hope for you is firmly grounded, knowing that ᴿas you are sharers of our sufferings, so also you are *sharers* of our comfort.   [Rom. 8:17]

Paul's Trouble in Asia

8 For we do not want you to be unaware, brethren, of our affliction which came *to us* in ᵀAsia, that we were burdened excessively, beyond our strength, so that we despaired even of life;   west coast province of Asia Minor

9 ᵀindeed, we had the sentence of death within ourselves in order that we should not trust in ourselves, but in God who raises the dead;   *but we ourselves*

10 who ᴿdelivered us from so great a *peril* of death, and will deliver *us*, He ᴿon whom we have set our hope. And He will yet deliver us,   Rom. 15:31 • 1 Tim. 4:10

11 you also joining in ᴿhelping us through your prayers, that thanks may be given by ᴿmany persons on our behalf for the favor bestowed upon us through *the prayers of* many.   Rom. 15:30; Phil. 1:19 • 2 Cor. 4:15; 9:11f.

Paul's Original Plan

12 For our ᵀproud confidence is this, the testimony of ᴿour conscience, that in holiness and godly sincerity, not in fleshly wisdom but in the grace of God, we have conducted ourselves in the world, and especially toward you.   *boasting* • Acts 23:1

13 For we write nothing else to you than what you read and understand, and I hope you will understand ᴿuntil the end;   1 Cor. 1:8

14 just as you also partially did understand us, that we are your reason to be proud as you also are ours, in ᴿthe day of our Lord Jesus.   1 Cor. 1:8

15 And in this confidence I intended at first to come to you, that you might ᵀtwice receive a blessing;   *have a second grace*

16 ᵀthat is, to pass ᵀyour way into Macedonia, and again from Macedonia to come to you, and by you to be ᴿhelped on my journey to Judea.   *and* • *through you into* • 1 Cor. 16:6, 11

17 Therefore, I was not vacillating when I intended to do this, was I? Or that which I purpose, do I purpose ᴿaccording to the flesh, that with me there should be yes, yes and no, no *at the same time*?   2 Cor. 10:2f.; 11:18

18 But as ᴿGod is faithful, ᴿour word to you is not yes and no.   1 Cor. 1:9 • 2 Cor. 2:17

19 For the Son of God, Christ Jesus, who was preached among you by us—by me and ᴿSilvanus and Timothy—was not yes and no, but is yes ᴴin Him.   Acts 15:22 • [Heb. 13:8]

20 For ᴿas many as may be the promises of God, ᴿin Him they are yes; wherefore also by Him is ᴿour Amen to the glory of God through us. [Rom. 15:8] • [Heb. 13:8] • 1 Cor. 14:16

21 Now He who establishes us with you in Christ and ᴿanointed us is God, 1 John 2:20, 27

22 who also sealed us and gave *us* the Spirit in our hearts as a ᴬpledge. *down payment*

Paul's Change of Plans

23 But I call God as witness to my soul, that to spare you I came no more to Corinth.

24 Not that we lord it over your faith, but are workers with you for your joy; for in your faith you are ᴿstanding firm.   Rom. 11:20

CHAPTER 2

B UT I determined this ᴬfor my own sake, that I ᴿwould not come to you in sorrow again.   *as far as I am concerned* • 1 Cor. 4:21

2 For if I ᴿcause you sorrow, who then makes me glad but the one whom I made sorrowful?   2 Cor. 7:8

3 And this is the very thing I ᴿwrote you, lest, when I came, I should have sorrow from those who ought to make me rejoice; having confidence in you all, that my joy would be *the joy* of you all. [2 Cor. 2:9; 7:8, 12]

4 For out of much affliction and anguish of heart I ᴿwrote to you with many tears; not that you should be made sorrowful, but that you might know the love which I have especially for you.   [2 Cor. 2:9; 7:8, 12]

Paul's Appeal to Forgive

5 But ᴿif any has caused sorrow, he has caused sorrow not to me, but in some degree—in order not to say too much—to all of you.   [1 Cor. 5:1f.]

6 Sufficient for such a one is this punishment which was *inflicted by* the majority,

7 so that on the contrary you should rather ᴿforgive and comfort *him*, lest somehow such a one be overwhelmed by excessive sorrow.   Gal. 6:1; Eph. 4:32

8 Wherefore I urge you to reaffirm *your* love for him.

9 For to this end also I wrote that I might ᵀput you to the test, whether you are obedient in all things.   *know the proof of you*

10 But whom you forgive anything, I *forgive* also; for indeed what I have forgiven, if I have forgiven anything, *I did it* for your sakesᴿin the presence of Christ,   1 Cor. 5:4

11 in order that no advantage be taken of us byᴿSatan; forᴿwe are not ignorant of his schemes.   Matt. 4:10 • Luke 22:31; 2 Cor. 4:4

12 Now when I came toᴿTroas for the gospel of Christ and when aᴿdoor was opened for me in the Lord,   Acts 16:8 • Acts 14:27

13 I had no rest for my spirit, not finding ᴿTitus my brother; but taking my leave of them, I went on to Macedonia.   2 Cor. 7:6, 13f.

Christ Causes Us to Triumph

14 But thanks be to God, who always leads us in His triumph in Christ, and manifests through us the sweet aroma of the ᴿknowledge of Him in every place.   1 Cor. 12:8

15 For we are aᴿfragrance of Christ to God among those who are being saved and among those who are perishing;   Ezek. 20:41

16 to the one an aroma from death to death, to the other an aroma from life to life. And who is adequate for these things?

17 For we are not like many, ¹peddling the word of God, butᴿas from sincerity, but as from God, we speak in Christᴿin the sight of God.   1 Cor. 5:8; 1 Pet. 4:11 • 2 Cor. 12:19

CHAPTER 3

Changed Lives Prove Ministry

Aᴿᴿ we beginning to commend ourselves again? Or do we need, as some, letters of commendation to you or from you?

2 ᴿYou are our letter, written in our hearts, known and read by all men; 1 Cor. 9:2

3 being manifested that you are a letter of Christ,ᵀcared for by us, written not with ink, but with the Spirit of the living God, not on tablets of stone, but onᴿtablets of human hearts.   *served* • Prov. 3:3; 7:3

4 And suchᴿconfidence we have through Christ toward God.   Eph. 3:12

5 Not that we are adequate in ourselves to consider anything as *coming* from ourselves, but our adequacy is from God,

New Covenant Is the Basis of Ministry

6 who also made us adequate *as*ᴿservants of aᴿnew covenant, not ofᵀthe letter, but of the Spirit; for the letter kills, but the Spirit gives life.   1 Cor. 3:5 • Jer. 31:31 • Rom. 2:29

7 But if the ministry of death, in letters engraved on stones, came ᴬwith glory, so that the sons of Israel could not look intently at the face of Moses because of the glory of his face, fading *as* it was,   *in glory*

8 how shall the ministry of the Spirit fail to be even more with glory?

9 For if ᴿthe ministry of condemnation has glory, much more does the ministry of righteousness abound in glory. Heb. 12:18-21

10 For indeed what had glory, in this case has no glory on account of the glory that surpasses *it*.

11 For if that which fades away *was*ᵀwith glory, much more that which remains *is* in glory.   *through*

12 ᴿHaving therefore such a hope, we use great boldness in *our* speech,   2 Cor. 7:4

13 and *are* not as Moses,ᴿwho used to put a veil over his face that the sons of Israel might not look intently at the end of what was fading away.   Ex. 34:33-35; 2 Cor. 3:7

14 But their minds wereᴿhardened; for until this very day at the reading of the old covenant the same veil remains unlifted, because it is removed in Christ.   Is. 29:10 ★

15 But to this day whenever Moses is read, a veil lies over their heart;

16 ᴿbut whenever a man turns to the Lord, the veil is taken away.   Ex. 34:34; Rom. 11:23

17 Now the Lord is the Spirit; and where the Spirit of the Lord is, *there* is liberty.

18 But we all, with unveiled faceᴿbeholding as in a mirror theᴿglory of the Lord, are being ᴿtransformed into the same image from glory to glory, just as from the Lord, the Spirit. 1 Cor. 13:12 • John 17:22 • [Rom. 8:29]

CHAPTER 4

Christ Is the Theme of Ministry

Tᴴᴱᴿᴱꜰᴼᴿᴱ, since we have this ministry, as we received mercy, we do not lose heart,

2 but we have renounced theᴿthings hidden because of shame, not walking in craftiness orᴿadulterating the word of God, but by the manifestation of truth commending ourselves to every man's conscience in the sight of God.   Rom. 6:21 • 2 Cor. 2:17

3 And even if our gospel is veiled, it is veiledᵀto those who are perishing,   *in*

4 in whose case the god of this world has blinded the minds of the unbelieving, that they might not see the light of the gospel of the glory of Christ, who is the image of God.

5 For we do not preach ourselves but Christ Jesus as Lord, and ourselves as your bond-servantsᴬfor Jesus' sake.   *through Jesus*

6 For God, who said, "Lightᴿshall shine out of darkness," is the One who hasᴿshone in our hearts to give theᴿlight of the knowledge of the glory of God in the face of Christ.   Gen. 1:3 • 2 Pet. 1:19 • Acts 26:18

7 But we have this treasure in ᴿearthen vessels, that the surpassing greatness ofᴿthe power may be of God and not from ourselves;   Job 4:19; 10:9; 2 Tim. 2:20 • Judg. 7:2

Trials Abound in the Ministry

8 *we are* afflicted in every way, but not crushed; perplexed, but not despairing;

---

¹ Or, *corrupting*

9 persecuted, but not [R]forsaken; [R]struck down, but not destroyed; [Heb. 13:5] • Mic. 7:8

10 [R]always carrying about in the body the dying of Jesus, that the life of Jesus also may be manifested in our body.   Rom. 6:5

11 For we who live are constantly being delivered over to death for Jesus' sake, that the life of Jesus also may be manifested in our mortal flesh.

12 So death works in us, but life in you.

13 But having the same [R]spirit of faith, according to what is written, "I [R] BELIEVED, THEREFORE I SPOKE," we also believe, therefore also we speak;   1 Cor. 12:9 • Ps. 116:10

14 knowing that He who raised the Lord Jesus [R]will raise us also with Jesus and will [R]present us with you. 1 Thess. 4:14 • [Luke 21:36]

15 For all things are [R]for your sakes, that the grace which is spreading to more and more people may cause the giving of thanks to abound to the glory of God.   Rom. 8:28

Motivation of External Perspective

16 Therefore we do not lose heart, but though our outer man is decaying, yet our inner man is being renewed day by day.

17 For momentary, [R]light affliction is producing for us an eternal weight of glory far beyond all comparison,   Rom. 8:18

18 while we [R]look not at the things which are seen, but at the things which are not seen; for the things which are seen are temporal, but the things which are not seen are eternal.   Rom. 8:24; [2 Cor. 5:7; Heb. 11:1, 13]

CHAPTER 5
Motivation of the Future Presence
of Christ

FOR we know that if the earthly [R]tent which is our house is torn down, we have a building from God, a house not made with hands, eternal in the heavens.   2 Pet. 1:13f.

2 For indeed in this *house* we [R]groan, longing to be [R]clothed with our dwelling from heaven;   Rom. 8:23 • 1 Cor. 15:53f.

3 inasmuch as we, having put it on, shall not be found naked.

4 For indeed while we are in this tent, we groan, being burdened, because we do not want to be unclothed, but to be [R]clothed, in order that what is [R]mortal may be swallowed up by life.   2 Cor. 5:2 • 1 Cor. 15:54

5 Now He who prepared us for this very purpose is God, who [R]gave to us the Spirit as a^pledge. Rom. 8:23; [2 Cor. 1:22] • *down payment*

6 Therefore, being always of good courage, and knowing that while we are at home in the body we are absent from the Lord—

7 for we walk by faith, not by sight—

8 we are of good courage, I say, and prefer rather to be absent from the body and [R]to be at home with the Lord.   [John 12:26]

Motivation of Future Reward

9 Therefore also we have as our ambition, whether at home or absent, to be [R]pleasing to Him.   Rom. 14:18; Col. 1:10; 1 Thess. 4:1

10 For we must all appear before [R]the judgment seat of Christ, that each one may be recompensed for [T]his deeds in the body, according to what he has done, whether good or bad.   Eph. 6:8 ☆ • *the things through the body*

Motivation of the Love of Christ

11 Therefore knowing the fear of the Lord, we persuade men, but we are made manifest to God; and I hope that we are made manifest also in your consciences.

12 We are not [R]again commending ourselves to you but *are* giving you an [R]occasion to be proud of us, that you may have *an answer* for those who take pride in appearance, and not in heart.   2 Cor. 3:1 • Phil. 1:26

13 For if we are beside ourselves, it is for God; if we are of sound mind, it is for you.

14 For the love of Christ [R]controls us, having concluded this, that [R]one died for all, therefore all died;   Acts 18:5 • [Rom. 5:15; 6:6f.]

15 and He died for all, that they who live should no longer [R]live for themselves, but for Him who died and rose again on their behalf.   Rom. 14:7-9

16 Therefore from now on we recognize no man according to the flesh; even though we have known Christ according to the flesh, yet now we know *Him thus* no longer.

Motivation of the Message
of Reconciliation

17 Therefore if any man is in Christ, *he is* [R]a new creature; the old things passed away; behold, new things have come.   John 3:3

5:17 New Nature—The term *new nature* refers to the spiritual transformation that occurs within the inner man when a person believes in Christ as Savior. The Christian is now a *new man* as opposed to the *old man* that he was before he became a Christian (Page 1135—Rom. 6:6; Page 1186—Eph. 2:15; 4:22–24; Page 1201—Col. 3:9, 10). This concept of *newness* may be traced to an important choice between two Greek words, both meaning "new." One word means "new" in the sense of renovation (to repair), the other in the sense of fresh existence. It is the latter that is used to describe the Christian. He is not the old man renovated or refreshed; he is a brand-new man with a new family, a new set of values, new motivations, and new possessions.

The old man is still present in the new life and expresses himself in corrupting deeds such as lying (Page 1188—Eph. 4:22; Page 1201—Col. 3:9). The new man, to be visible, must be *put on* as one would put on a new suit of clothes (Page 1201—Col. 3:10). In other words, the new nature must be cultivated or nurtured by spiritual decisiveness to grow in Christ. We must not revert to putting on the *old suit* of the former life; rather, we must continue to grow in this new life (Page 1188—Eph. 5:8).

18 Now ^Rall *these* things are from God, ^Rwho reconciled us to Himself through Christ, and gave us the^Rministry of reconciliation,   1 Cor. 11:12 · Rom. 5:10 · 1 Cor. 3:5

19 namely, that God was in Christ reconciling the world to Himself, not counting their trespasses against them, and He has committed to us the word of reconciliation.

20 Therefore, we are ^Rambassadors for Christ, as though God were entreating through us; we beg you on behalf of Christ, be^Rreconciled to God.   Eph. 6:20 · Rom. 5:10

21 He made Him who knew no sin *to be*^Rsin on our behalf, that we might become the righteousness of God in Him.   [Rom. 3:25]★

CHAPTER 6

Giving No Offense in the Ministry

A ND^Rworking together *with Him,*^Rwe also urge you not to receive^Rthe grace of God in vain—   1 Cor. 3:9 · 2 Cor. 5:20 · Acts 11:23

2 for He says, "AT^RTHE ACCEPTABLE TIME I LISTENED TO YOU,   Is. 49:8★ AND ON THE DAY OF SALVATION I HELPED YOU"; behold, now is "THE ACCEPTABLE TIME," behold, now is "THE DAY OF SALVATION"—

3 giving no cause for offense in anything, in order that the ministry be not discredited,

4 but in everything ^Rcommending ourselves as ^Aservants of God,^Rin much endurance, in afflictions, in hardships, in distresses,   Rom. 3:5 · *ministers* · 2 Cor. 4:8-11; 6:4ff.

5 in beatings, in imprisonments, in tumults, in labors, in sleeplessness, in hunger,

6 in purity, in knowledge, in patience, in kindness, in the Holy Spirit, in genuine love,

7 in^Rthe word of truth, in the power of God; by the weapons of righteousness for the right hand and the left,   2 Cor. 2:17; 4:2

8 by glory and dishonor, by^Revil report and good report; *regarded* as^Rdeceivers and yet^Rtrue;   Rom. 3:8 · Matt. 27:63 · 2 Cor. 1:18; 4:2

9 as unknown yet well-known, as^Rdying yet behold,^Rwe live; as^Apunished yet not put to death,   Rom. 8:36 · 2 Cor. 1:8, 10 · *disciplined*

10 as sorrowful yet always ^Rrejoicing, as poor yet making many rich, as having nothing yet possessing all things.   Phil. 2:17; 4:4

Paul's Appeal for Reconciliation

11 Our mouth has spoken freely to you, O Corinthians, our heart is opened wide.

12 You are not restrained^Aby us, but you are restrained in your own affections.   *in us*

13 Now in a like exchange—I speak as to ^Rchildren—open wide *to us* also.   1 Cor. 4:14

Paul's Appeal for Separation from Unbelievers

14 Do not be^Tbound together with unbelievers; for what partnership have righteousness and lawlessness, or what fellowship has light with darkness?   *unequally yoked*

15 Or what^Rharmony has Christ with^TBelial, or what has a believer in common with an unbeliever?   1 Cor. 10:21 · Gr., *Beliar*

16 Or what agreement has the temple of God with idols? For we are^Rthe temple of the living God; just as God said, [1 Cor. 3:16; 6:19] "I WILL ^RDWELL IN THEM AND ^RWALK AMONG THEM;   [John 14:23] · Rev. 2:1 AND I WILL BE THEIR GOD, AND THEY SHALL BE MY PEOPLE.

17 "Therefore,^R COME^R OUT FROM THEIR MIDST AND BE SEPARATE," says the Lord.   Is. 52:11 · Rev. 18:4 "AND DO NOT TOUCH WHAT IS UNCLEAN; And I will welcome you.

18 "And^RI will be a father to you,   Hos. 1:10 And you shall be^Rsons and daughters to Me,"   [Rom. 8:14] Says the Lord Almighty.

CHAPTER 7

T HEREFORE, having these promises, beloved,^Rlet us cleanse ourselves from all defilement of flesh and spirit, perfecting holiness in the fear of God.   1 Pet. 1:15f.

Paul's Meeting with Titus

2 ^RMake room for us *in your hearts;* we wronged no one, we corrupted no one, we took advantage of no one.   2 Cor. 6:12f.; 12:15

3 I do not speak to condemn you; for I have said before that you are^Rin our hearts to die together and to live together.   Phil. 1:7

4 Great is my confidence^Tin you, great is my boasting on your behalf; I am filled with ^Rcomfort. I am overflowing with^Rjoy in all our affliction.   *to* · [2 Cor. 1:4] · [2 Cor. 6:10]

5 For even when we came into^RMacedonia our flesh had no rest, but we were^Rafflicted on every side:^Rconflicts without, fears within.   Rom. 15:26 · 2 Cor. 4:8 · Deut. 32:25

6 But God, who comforts the^Adepressed, comforted us by the coming of Titus; *humble*

7 and not only by his coming, but also by the comfort with which he was comforted in you, as he reported to us your longing, your mourning, your zeal for me; so that I rejoiced even more.

Corinthians' Response to Paul's Letter

8 For though I^Rcaused you sorrow by my letter, I do not regret it; though I did regret

---

it—*for* I see that that letter caused you sorrow, though only for a while—   2 Cor. 2:2

9 I now rejoice, not that you were made sorrowful, but that you were made sorrowful to *the point of* repentance; for you were made sorrowful according to *the will of* God, in order that you might not suffer loss in anything through us.

10 For the sorrow that is according to *the will of* God produces a[R]repentance without regret, *leading* to salvation; but the sorrow of the world produces death.   Acts 11:18

11 For behold what earnestness this very thing, this [T]godly sorrow, has produced in you: what vindication of yourselves, what indignation, what fear, what longing, what zeal, what avenging of wrong! In everything you[R]demonstrated yourselves to be innocent in the matter.   *sorrow according to God* • Rom. 3:5

12 So although[R]I wrote to you *it was* not for the sake of[R]the offender, nor for the sake of the one offended, but that your earnestness on our behalf might be made known to you in the sight of God.   2 Cor. 2:3 • 1 Cor. 5:1f.

13 For this reason we have been comforted.

And besides our comfort, we rejoiced even much more for the joy of Titus, because his spirit has been refreshed by you all.

14 For if in anything I have[R]boasted to him about you, I was not put to shame; but as we spoke all things to you in truth, so also our boasting before[R]Titus proved to be *the* truth.   Phil. 1:26; 2 Thess. 1:4 • 2 Cor. 2:13; 7:6, 13

15 And his[T]affection abounds all the more toward you, as he remembers the obedience of you all, how you received him with[R]fear and trembling.   *inward parts* • 1 Cor. 2:3

16 I rejoice that in everything[R]I have confidence in you.   2 Cor. 2:3

CHAPTER 8

Example of the Macedonians

NOW, brethren, we *wish to* make known to you the grace of God which has been given in the churches of[R]Macedonia,   Acts 16:9

2 that in a great ordeal of affliction their abundance of joy and their deep poverty overflowed in the wealth of their liberality.

3 For I testify that [R]according to their ability, and beyond their ability *they gave* of their own accord,   1 Cor. 16:2; 2 Cor. 8:11

4 begging us with much entreaty for the [R]favor of participation in the[T]support of the [A]saints,   Acts 24:17 • *service to the saints* • *holy ones*

5 and *this*, not as we had[T]expected, but they first[R]gave themselves to the Lord and to us by the will of God.   *hoped* • 2 Cor. 8:1

6 Consequently we urged Titus that as he had previously[R]made a beginning, so he would also complete in you[R]this gracious work as well.   2 Cor. 8:10 • Acts 24:17

Example of Christ

7 But just as you[R]abound[R]in everything, in faith and utterance and knowledge and in all earnestness and in the [2]love we inspired in you, *see* that you[R]abound in this gracious work also.   2 Cor. 9:8 • Rom. 15:14; 1 Cor. 1:5

8 I am not speaking *this* as a command, but as proving through the earnestness of others the sincerity of your love also.

9 For you know the grace of our Lord Jesus Christ, that though He was rich, yet for your sake He became poor, that you through His poverty might become rich.

Purpose of Giving

10 And I[R]give *my* opinion in this matter, for this is to your advantage, who were the first to begin a year ago not only to do *this*, but also to desire *to do it*.   1 Cor. 7:25, 40

11 But now finish [T]doing it also; that just as *there was* the[R]readiness to desire it, so *there may be* also the completion of it by your ability.   *the doing* • [2 Cor. 8:12, 19; 9:2]

12 For if the readiness is present, it is acceptable according to what *a man* has, not according to what he does not have.

13 For *this* is not for the ease of others *and* for your affliction, but by way of equality—

14 at this present time your abundance *being a supply* for their want, that their abundance also may become *a supply* for your want, that there may be equality;

15 as it is written, "HE[R] WHO *gathered* MUCH DID NOT HAVE TOO MUCH, AND HE WHO *gathered* LITTLE HAD NO LACK."   Ex. 16:18

Policies in Giving

16 But[R]thanks be to God, who[R]puts the same earnestness on your behalf in the heart of Titus.   2 Cor. 2:14 • Rev. 17:17

17 For he not only accepted our[R]appeal, but being himself very earnest, he has gone to you of his own accord.   2 Cor. 8:6; 12:18

18 And we have sent along with him the brother whose fame in *the things of* the gospel *has spread* through all the churches;

19 and not only *this*, but he has also been appointed by the churches to travel with us in this gracious work, which is being administered by us for the glory of the Lord Himself, and *to show* our[R]readiness,   2 Cor. 8:11

20 [T]taking precaution that no one should discredit us in our administration of this generous gift;   *avoiding this*

[2] Lit., *love from us in you; some ancient mss. read your love for us*

21 for we have regard for what is honorable, not only in ᴿthe sight of the Lord, but also in the sight of men.   Prov. 3:4; Rom. 14:18

22 And we have sent with them our brother, whom we have often tested and found diligent in many things, but now even more diligent, because of *his* great confidence in you.

23 As for Titus, *he is* my partner and fellow worker ᵀamong you; as for our ᴿbrethren, *they are* ᵀmessengers of the churches, a glory to Christ.   *for you* • 2 Cor. 8:18, 22 • *apostles*

24 Therefore openly before the churches show them the proof of your love and of our ᴿreason for boasting about you.   2 Cor. 7:4

CHAPTER 9

Readiness in Giving

FOR it is superfluous for me to write to you about this ministry to the saints;

2 for I know your readiness, of which I boast about you to the ᴿMacedonians, *namely,* that ᴿAchaia has been prepared since last year, and your zeal has stirred up most of them.   Rom. 15:26 • Acts 18:12

3 But I have sent the brethren, that our ᴿboasting about you may not be made empty in this case, that, ᴿas I was saying, you may be prepared;   2 Cor. 7:4 • 1 Cor. 16:2

4 lest if any ᴿMacedonians come with me and find you unprepared, we (not to speak of you) should be put to shame by this confidence.   Rom. 15:26

5 So I thought it necessary to urge the brethren that they would go on ahead to you and arrange beforehand your previously promised ᵀbountiful gift, that the same might be ready as a bountiful gift, and not ᵀaffected by covetousness.   *blessing* • *as covetousness*

Principles in Giving

6 Now this *I say,* he who sows sparingly shall also reap sparingly; and he who sows bountifully shall also reap bountifully.

7 Let each one *do* just as he has purposed in his heart; not grudgingly or under compulsion; for God loves a cheerful giver.

Promises from Giving

8 And ᴿGod is able to make all grace abound to you, that always having all sufficiency in everything, you may have an abundance for every good deed;   [Eph. 3:20]

9 as it is written,
   "Heᴿ SCATTERED ABROAD, HE GAVE TO
     THE POOR,   Ps. 112:9
   HIS RIGHTEOUSNESS ABIDES FOREVER."

10 Now He who supplies seed to the sower and bread for food, will supply and multiply your seed for sowing and ᴿincrease the harvest of your righteousness;   Hos. 10:12

11 you will be ᴿenriched in everything for all liberality, which through us is producing ᴿthanksgiving to God.   1 Cor. 1:5 • 2 Cor. 1:11

12 For the ministry of this service is not only fully supplying ᴿthe needs of the ᴬsaints, but is also overflowing through many thanksgivings to God.   2 Cor. 8:14 • *holy ones*

13 Because of the proof given by this ministry they will glorify God for *your* obedience to your confession of the gospel of Christ, and for the liberality of your ᴬcontribution to them and to all,   *sharing with them*

14 while they also, by prayer on your behalf, yearn for you because of the surpassing grace of God in you.

15 ᴿThanks be to God for His indescribable ᴿgift!   2 Cor. 2:14 • Rom. 5:15f.

CHAPTER 10

The Charge of Cowardice Is Answered

NOW I, Paul, myself urge you by the meekness and gentleness of Christ—I who am ᵀmeek when face to face with you, but bold toward you when absent!   *lowly*

2 I ask that ᴿwhen I am present I may not be bold with the confidence with which I propose to be courageous against ᴿsome,

---

9:6–8 Giving—There is no better indicator of growth in the new life than in the area of giving. This passage deals with the attitude one should have in his giving—it should be cheerful. When giving is cheerful, it will also be generous. The important rule of thumb is not how much is given, but how much is left after the giving. God is not primarily occupied with the amount of the gift, but with the motive that lies behind it. All the money in the world belongs to God. My gift to Him does not make Him any richer; it makes me richer spiritually because of the realization that everything I have is His and that I am giving because I love Him and want to give.

The formula for giving is found in First Corinthians 16:2 where three principles can be seen: (1) my giving is to be regular, "on the first day of every week" (2) my giving is to be systematic, "let each one of you put aside and save"; and (3) my giving is to be proportionate, "as he may prosper."

Failure to give of the money which God has given is a serious matter. The person who fails to honor God with his money actually robs God (Page 931—Mal. 3:8), not because it impoverishes God but because it denies the God-ordained means for the support of His work and His ministers. For the child of God who honors God with his money God promises abundant blessing (Page 931—Mal. 3:10; Page 1033—Luke 6:38) and the provision of his every need (Page 1196—Phil. 4:19). Giving, then, is a key to growth in the new life.

Now turn to Page 402—1 Chr. 16:29: The Meaning of Worship.

who regard us as if we walked\[R\]according to the flesh.   1 Cor. 4:21 • 1 Cor. 4:18f. • Rom. 8:4

The Charge of Walking in the Flesh Is Answered

3 For though we walk in the flesh, we do not war\[R\]according to the flesh,   Rom. 8:4

4 for the weapons of our warfare are not of the flesh, but\[A\]divinely powerful for the destruction of fortresses.   *mighty before God*

5 *We are* destroying speculations and every lofty thing raised up against the knowledge of God, and *we are* taking every thought captive to the obedience of Christ,

6 and we are ready to punish all disobedience, whenever \[R\]your obedience is complete.   2 Cor. 2:9

7 You are looking at \[T\]things as they are outwardly. If anyone is confident in himself that he is Christ's, let him consider this again within himself, that just as he is Christ's, so also are we. *what is before your face*

8 For even if I should boast somewhat further about our authority, which the Lord gave for building you up and not for destroying you, I shall not be put to shame,

9 \[T\]for I do not wish to seem as if I would terrify you by my letters.   *that I may not seem*

The Charge of Personal Weakness Is Answered

10 For they say, "His letters are weighty and strong, but his personal presence is unimpressive, and his speech contemptible."

11 Let such a person consider this, that what we are in word by letters when absent, such persons *we are* also in deed when present.

12 For we are not bold to class or compare ourselves with\[A\]some of those who\[R\]commend themselves; but when they measure themselves by themselves, and compare themselves with themselves, they are without understanding.   *any* • 2 Cor. 3:1; 10:18

13 But we will not boast beyond *our* measure, but\[R\]within the measure of the sphere which God apportioned to us as a measure, to reach even as far as you.   Rom. 12:3

14 For we are not overextending ourselves, as if we did not reach to you, for\[R\]we were the first to come even as far as you in the\[R\]gospel of Christ;   1 Cor. 3:6 • 2 Cor. 2:12

15 not boasting beyond *our* measure, *that is*, in other men's labors, but with the hope that as your faith grows, we shall be, within our sphere, enlarged even more by you,

16 so as to preach the gospel even to the regions beyond you, *and* not to boast \[T\]in what has been accomplished in the sphere of another.   *to the things prepared in the*

17 But\[R\]HE WHO BOASTS, LET HIM BOAST IN THE LORD.   Jer. 9:24; 1 Cor. 1:31

18 For not he who commends himself is approved, but whom the Lord commends.

CHAPTER 11

Paul's Declaration of His Apostleship

I WISH that you would\[R\]bear with me in a little foolishness; but\[A\]indeed you are bearing with me.   2 Cor. 11:4, 16 • *do indeed bear with me*

2 For I am jealous for you with a godly jealousy; for I\[R\]betrothed you to one husband, that to Christ I might\[A\]present you *as a* pure virgin.   Hos. 2:19f.; [Eph. 5:26f.] • 2 Cor. 4:14

3 But I am afraid, lest as the\[R\]serpent deceived Eve by his craftiness, your minds should be led astray from the simplicity and purity *of devotion* to Christ.   Gen. 3:4, 13

4 For if one comes and preaches another Jesus whom we have not preached, or you receive a different spirit which you have not received, or a different gospel which you have not accepted, you bear *this* beautifully.

5 For I consider myself not in the least inferior to the most eminent apostles.

6 But even if I am\[R\]unskilled in speech, yet I am not so in\[R\]knowledge; in fact, in every way we have\[R\]made *this* evident to you in all things.   [1 Cor. 1:17] • [1 Cor. 12:8] • 2 Cor. 4:2

7 Or\[R\]did I commit a sin in humbling myself that you might be exalted, because I preached the\[R\]gospel of God to you\[R\]without charge?   2 Cor. 12:13 • Rom. 1:1 • Acts 18:3

8 I robbed other churches,\[R\]taking wages *from them* to serve you;   1 Cor. 4:12; 9:6

9 and when I was present with you and was in need, I was not a burden to anyone; for when the brethren came from Macedonia, they fully supplied my need, and in everything I kept myself from being a burden to you, and will continue to do so.

10 \[R\]As the truth of Christ is in me, \[R\]this boasting of mine will not be stopped in the regions of Achaia.   Rom. 1:9; 9:1 • 1 Cor. 9:15

11 Why?\[R\]Because I do not love you?\[R\]God knows I *do*!   2 Cor. 12:15 • 2 Cor. 2:17; 11:31

12 But what I am doing, I will continue to do, \[R\]that I may cut off opportunity from those who desire an opportunity to be\[T\]regarded just as we are in the matter about which they are boasting.   1 Cor. 9:12 • *found*

13 For such men are\[R\]false apostles,\[R\]deceitful workers, disguising themselves as apostles of Christ.   Acts 20:30; Gal. 1:7; 2:4 • Phil. 3:2

14 And no wonder, for even Satan disguises himself as an\[R\]angel of light.   Col. 1:12

15 Therefore it is not surprising if his servants also disguise themselves as servants of righteousness; \[R\]whose end shall be according to their deeds.   Rom. 2:6; 3:8

Paul's Sufferings Support His Apostleship

16 \[R\]Again I say, let no one think me foolish; but if *you do*, receive me even as foolish, that I also may boast a little.   2 Cor. 11:1

17 That which I am speaking, I am not speaking as the Lord would, but as in foolishness, in this confidence of boasting.

18 Since ᴿmany boast ᴿaccording to the flesh, I will boast also. [Phil. 3:3ff.] · 2 Cor. 5:16

19 For you,ᴿbeing *so* wise, bear with the foolish gladly.   1 Cor. 4:10

20 For you bear with anyone if he enslaves you, if heᴿdevours you, if he takes advantage of you, if he ᴿexalts himself, if he hits you in the face.   Mark 12:40 · 2 Cor. 10:5

21 To *my* shame I *must* say that we have been weak *by comparison.* But in whatever respect anyone *else* is bold (I speak in foolishness), I am just as bold myself.

22 Are theyᴿHebrews?ᴿSo am I. Are they Israelites? So am I. Are theyᵀdescendants of Abraham? So am I.   Acts 6:1 · Phil. 3:5 · *seed*

23 Are they servants of Christ? (I speak as if insane) I more so; in far more labors, in far more imprisonments, beaten times without number, often in danger of death.

24 Five times I received from the Jews ᴿthirty-nine *lashes.*   Deut. 25:3

25 Three times I was ᴿbeaten with rods, once I wasᴿstoned, three times I was shipwrecked, a night and a day I have spent in the deep.   Acts 16:22 · Acts 14:19

26 *I have been* on frequent journeys, in dangers from rivers, dangers from robbers, dangers from myᴿcountrymen, dangers from the Gentiles, dangers in the city, dangers in the wilderness, dangers on the sea, dangers amongᴿfalse brethren;   Acts 9:23 · Gal. 2:4

27 *I have been* in labor and hardship, ᵀthrough many sleepless nights, in hunger and thirst, often without food, in cold and ᵀexposure.   *often in wakefulness · nakedness*

28 Apart from *such*ᴬexternal things, there is the daily pressure upon me *of* concern for all the churches.   *the things unmentioned*

29 Who is weak without my being weak? Who isᵀled into sinᵀwithout my intense concern?   *made to stumble · and I do not burn*

30 If I have to boast, I will boast of what pertains to myᴿweakness.   1 Cor. 2:3

31 The God and Father of the Lord Jesus, ᴿHe who is blessed forever,ᴿknows that I am not lying.   Rom. 1:25 · 2 Cor. 11:11

32 InᴿDamascus the ethnarch under Aretas the king was guarding the city of the Damascenes in order to seize me,   Acts 9:2

33 and I was let down in a basketᴿthrough a windowᵀin the wall, and *so* escaped his hands.   Acts 9:25 · *through*

CHAPTER 12

Vision of Paradise

Bᴏᴀsᴛɪɴɢ is necessary, though it is not profitable; but I will go on to visions and ᴿrevelationsᴬof the Lord.   1 Cor. 14:6 · *from*

2 I know a man in Christ who fourteen years ago—whether in the body I do not know, or out of the body I do not know, God

knows—such a man wasᴿcaught up to the ᴿthird heaven.   Acts 8:39 · Deut. 10:14; Ps. 148:4

3 And I know how such a man—whether in the body or apart from the body I do not know,ᴿGod knows—   2 Cor. 11:11

4 wasᴿcaught up intoᴿParadise, and heard inexpressible words, which a man is not permitted to speak.   Ezek. 8:3 · Luke 23:43

5 ᴿOn behalf of such a man will I boast; but on my own behalf I will not boast, except in regard to *my* weaknesses.   2 Cor. 12:1

6 For if I do wish to boast I shall not be ᴿfoolish,ᴿfor I shall be speaking the truth; but I refrain *from this,* so that no one may credit me with more than he sees *in* me or hears from me.   2 Cor. 5:13; 11:16f. · 2 Cor. 7:14

Thorn in the Flesh

7 And because of the surpassing greatness of theᴿrevelations, for this reason, to keep me from exalting myself, there was given me aᵀthorn in the flesh, aᴿmessenger of Satan to buffet me—to keep me from exalting myself!   2 Cor. 12:1 · Hos. 2:6 · Job 2:6

8 Concerning this I entreated the Lord three times that it might depart from me.

9 And He has said to me, "My grace is sufficient for you, for ³power is perfected in weakness." Most gladly, therefore, I will ratherᴿboast about my weaknesses, that the power of Christ may dwell in me.   2 Cor. 12:5

10 Therefore ᴿI am well content with weaknesses, with ᴬinsults, with distresses, with persecutions, with difficulties, for Christ's sake; forᴿwhen I am weak, then I am strong.   [Rom. 5:3] · *mistreatment* · 2 Cor. 13:4

Paul's Signs Support His Apostleship

11 I have become foolish; you yourselves compelled me. Actually I should have been commended by you, for in no respect was I inferior to theᴬmost eminent apostles, even though I am a nobody.   *super-apostles*

12 The signs of a true apostle were performed among you with all perseverance, by signs and wonders and miracles.

13 For in what respect were you treated as inferior to the rest of the churches, except that I myself did not become a burden to you? Forgive meᴿthis wrong!   [2 Cor. 11:7]

Paul's Concern Not to Be a Financial Burden

14 Here for this third time I am ready to come to you, and I will not be a burden to you; for Iᴿdo not seek what is yours, but you; forᴿchildren are not responsible to save up for *their* parents, butᴿparents for *their* children. [1 Cor. 10:24, 33] · 1 Cor. 4:14f. · [Prov. 19:14]

15 And I will ᴿmost gladly spend and be

³ Later mss. read *My power*

expended for your souls. If I love you the more, am I to be loved the less?   Rom. 9:3

16 But be that as it may, I[R]did not burden you myself; nevertheless, crafty fellow that I am, I took you in by deceit.   2 Cor. 11:9

17 [R]Certainly I have not taken advantage of you through any of those whom I have sent to you, have I?   2 Cor. 9:5

18 I urged Titus *to go,* and sent the brother with him. Titus did not take any advantage of you, did he? Did we not[T]conduct ourselves[*]in the same spirit *and walk* in the same steps?   *walk • by the same Spirit*

Paul's Concern Not to Find Them Carnal

19 All this time[*]you have been thinking that we are defending ourselves to you. *Actually,* it is in the sight of God that we have been speaking in Christ; and all for your upbuilding, beloved.   *have you been thinking . . . ?*

20 For I am afraid that perhaps when I come I may find you to be not what I wish and may be found by you to be not what you wish; that perhaps *there may be*[R]strife, jealousy, angry tempers, disputes, slanders, gossip, arrogance, disturbances;   1 Cor. 1:11

21 I am afraid that when I come again my God may humiliate me before you, and I may mourn over many of those who have sinned in the past and not repented of the [R]impurity,[T]immorality and sensuality which they have practiced.   Col. 3:5 • sexual immorality

CHAPTER 13

Paul's Warning to Examine Yourselves

THIS is the third time I am coming to you. EVERY[T]FACT IS TO BE CONFIRMED BY THE TESTIMONY OF TWO OR THREE WITNESSES.   *word*

2 I have previously said when present

---

[4] Some early mss. read *with Him*

---

the second time, and though now absent I say in advance to those who have sinned in the past and to all the rest as well, that if I come again, I will not spare *anyone,*

3 since you are seeking for proof of the Christ who speaks in me, and who is not weak toward you, but mighty in you.

4 For indeed He was[R]crucified because of weakness, yet He lives because of the power of God. For we also are weak [4]in Him, yet we shall live with Him because of the power of God *directed* toward you.   Phil. 2:7f.

5 [R]Test yourselves *to see* if you are in the faith;[R]examine yourselves! Or do you not recognize this about yourselves, that Jesus Christ is in you—unless indeed you[T]fail the test?   John 6:6 • 1 Cor. 11:28 • *are unapproved*

6 But I trust that you will realize that we ourselves do not fail the test.

7 Now we pray to God that you do no wrong; not that we ourselves may appear approved, but that you may do what is right, even though we should[T]appear unapproved.   *be as*

8 For we can do nothing against the truth, but *only* for the truth.

9 For we rejoice when we ourselves are weak but you are strong; this we also pray for, that you be[R]made complete.   2 Cor. 13:11

10 For this reason I am writing these things while absent, in order that when present I may not use severity, in accordance with the authority which the Lord gave me, for building up and not for tearing down.

Conclusion

11 Finally, brethren, rejoice, [*]be made complete, be comforted, be like-minded, live in peace; and the God of love and peace shall be with you.   *put yourselves in order*

12 Greet one another with a holy kiss.

13 All the[*]saints greet you.   *holy ones*

14 The grace of the Lord Jesus Christ, and the love of God, and the[R]fellowship of the Holy Spirit, be with you all.   Phil. 2:1

THE EPISTLE OF PAUL TO THE

GALATIANS

THE BOOK OF GALATIANS

The Galatians, having launched their Christian experience by faith, seem content to leave their voyage of faith and chart a new course based on works—a course Paul finds disturbing. His letter to the Galatians is a vigorous attack against the gospel of works, and a defense of the gospel of faith.

Paul begins by setting forth his credentials as an apostle with a message from God: blessing comes from God on the basis of faith, not law. The law declares men guilty and imprisions them; faith sets men free to enjoy liberty in Christ. But liberty is not license. Freedom in Christ means freedom to produce the fruits of righteousness through a Spirit-led life-style.

The book is called *Pros Galatas*, "To the Galatians," and it is the only letter of Paul that is specifically addressed to a number of churches ("to the churches of Galatia," 1:2). The name *Galatians* was given to this Celtic people because they originally lived in Gaul before their migration to Asia Minor.

THE AUTHOR OF GALATIANS

The Pauline authorship and the unity of this epistle are virtually unchallenged. The first verse clearly identifies the author as "Paul, an apostle" as does 5:2, "Behold I, Paul, say to you." In fact, Paul actually wrote Galatians (6:11), instead of dictating it to a secretary, as was his usual practice.

THE TIME OF GALATIANS

The term *Galatia* was used in an ethnographic sense (that is cultural and geographic origin) and in a political sense. The original ethnographic sense refers to the central part of Asia Minor where these Celtic tribes eventually settled after their conflicts with the Romans and Macedonians. Later, in 189 B.C. Galatia came under Roman domination, and in 25 B.C. Augustus declared it a Roman province. The political or provincial Galatia included territory to the south that was not originally considered part of Galatia (for example, the cities of Pisidian Antioch, Iconium, Lystra, and Derbe). There are two theories regarding the date and setting of Galatians.

The *North Galatian Theory* holds that Paul was speaking of Galatia in its earlier, more restricted sense. According to this theory, the churches of Galatia were north of the cities Paul visited on his first missionary journey. Paul visited the ethnographic Galatia (the smaller region to the North) for the first time on his second missionary journey, probably while he was on his way to Troas (Acts 16:6). On his third missionary journey, Paul revisited the Galatian churches he had established (Acts 18:23) and wrote this epistle either in Ephesus (A.D. 53–56) or in Macedonia (A.D. 56).

According to the *South Galatian Theory*, Paul was referring to Galatia in its wider political sense as a province of Rome. This means that the churches he had in mind in this epistle were in the cities he evangelized during his first missionary journey with Barnabas (Acts 13:13—14:23). This was just prior to the Jerusalem Council (Acts 15), so the Jerusalem visit in Galatians 2:1–10 must have been the Acts 11:27–30 famine-relief visit. Galatians was probably written in Syrian Antioch in A.D. 49 just before Paul went to the Council in Jerusalem.

Paul wrote this epistle in response to a report that the Galatian churches were suddenly taken over by the false teaching of certain Judaizers who professed Jesus yet sought to place gentile converts under the requirements of the Mosaic Law (1:7; 4:17, 21; 5:2–12; 6:12, 13).

THE CHRIST OF GALATIANS

Christ has freed the believer from bondage to the law (legalism) and to sin (license) and has placed him in a position of liberty. The transforming provides for the believer's deliverance from the curse of sin, law, and self (1:4; 2:20; 3:13; 4:5; 5:24; 6:14).

KEYS TO GALATIANS

Key Word: Freedom from the Law— This epistle shows that the believer is no longer under the law but is saved by faith alone. It has been said that Judaism was the cradle of Christianity, but also that it was very nearly its grave as well. God raised up Paul as the Moses of the Christian church to deliver them from this bondage. Galatians is the Christian's Declaration of Independence. The power of the Holy Spirit enables the Christian to enjoy freedom within the law of love.

Key Verses: Galatians 2:20, 21 and 5:1—"I have been crucified with Christ; and it is no longer I who live, but Christ lives in me; and the *life* which I now live in the flesh I live by the faith in the Son of God, who loved me, and

delivered Himself up for me. I do not nullify the grace of God; for if righteousness *comes* through the Law, then Christ died needlessly" (2:20, 21).

"It was for freedom that Christ set us free; therefore keep standing firm and do not be subject again to a yoke of slavery" (5:1).

Key Chapter: Galatians 5—The impact of the truth concerning freedom is staggering: freedom must not be used as "an opportunity for the flesh, but through love serve one another" (5:13). This chapter records the power, "walk by the Spirit" (5:16), and the results, "the fruit of the Spirit" (5:22), of that freedom.

SURVEY OF GALATIANS

The Epistle to the Galatians has been called "the Magna Carta of Christian liberty." It is Paul's manifesto of justification by faith, and the resulting liberty. Paul directs this great charter of Christian freedom to a people who are willing to give up the priceless liberty they possess in Christ. The oppressive theology of certain Jewish legalizers has been causing the believers in Galatia to trade their freedom in Christ for bondage to the law. Paul writes this forceful epistle to do away with the false gospel of works and demonstrate the superiority of justification by faith. This carefully written polemic approaches the problem from three directions: the gospel of grace defended (1 and 2), the gospel of grace explained (3 and 4), and the gospel of grace applied (5 and 6).

The Gospel of Grace Defended (1 and 2): Paul affirms his divinely given apostleship and presents the gospel (1:1–5) because it has been distorted by false teachers among the Galatians (1:6–10). Paul launches into his biographical argument for the true gospel of justification by faith in showing that he received his message not from men but directly from God (1:11–24). When he submits his teaching of Christian liberty to the apostles in Jerusalem, they all acknowledge the validity and authority of his message (2:1–10). Paul also must correct Peter on the matter of freedom from the law (2:11–21).

The Gospel of Grace Explained (3 and 4): In this section Paul uses eight lines of reasoning to develop his theological defense of justification by faith: (1) The Galatians began by faith, and their growth in Christ must continue to be by faith (3:1–5). (2) Abraham was justified by faith, and the same principle applies today (3:6–9). (3) Christ has redeemed all who trust in Him from the curse of the law (3:10–14). (4) The promise made to Abraham was not nullified by the law (3:15–18). (5) The law was given to drive men to faith, not to save them (3:19–22). (6) Believers in Christ are adopted sons of God and are no longer bound by the law (3:23—4:7). (7) The Galatians must recognize their inconsistency and regain their original freedom in Christ (4:8–20). (8) Abraham's two sons allegorically reveal the superiority of the Abrahamic promise to the Mosaic Law (4:21–31).

The Gospel of Grace Applied (5 and 6): The Judaizers seek to place the Galatians under bondage to their perverted gospel of justification by law, but Paul warns them that law and grace are two contrary principles (5:1–12). So far, Paul has been contrasting the liberty of faith with the legalism of law, but at this point he warns the Galatians of the opposite extreme of license or antinomianism (5:13—6:10). The Christian is not only set free from the bondage of law, but he is also free of the bondage of sin because of the power of the indwelling Spirit. Liberty is not an excuse to indulge in the deeds

FOCUS	GOSPEL OF GRACE DEFENDED		GOSPEL OF GRACE EXPLAINED		GOSPEL OF GRACE APPLIED	
REFERENCE	1:1————2:1————		3:1————4:1————		5:1————6:1————6:18	
DIVISION	PAUL'S APOSTLESHIP	PAUL'S AUTHORITY	BONDAGE OF LAW	FREEDOM OF GRACE	FRUIT OF THE SPIRIT	FRUITS OF THE SPIRIT
TOPIC	BIOGRAPHICAL EXPLANATION		DOCTRINAL EXPOSITION		PRACTICAL EXHORTATION	
	AUTHENTICATION OF LIBERTY		ARGUMENTATION FOR LIBERTY		APPLICATION OF LIBERTY	
LOCATION	SOUTH GALATIAN THEORY: SYRIAN ANTIOCH NORTH GALATIAN THEORY: EPHESUS OR MACEDONIA					
TIME	SOUTH GALATIAN THEORY: A.D. 49 NORTH GALATIAN THEORY: A.D. 53—56					

of the flesh; rather, it provides the privilege of bearing the fruit of the Spirit by walking in dependence upon Him. This letter closes with a contrast between the Judaizers—who are mo-

tivated by pride and a desire to avoid persecution—and Paul, who has suffered for the true gospel, but boasts only in Christ (6:11–18).

OUTLINE OF GALATIANS

CHAPTER 1

Salutation: The Ground of Grace

PAUL, an apostle (not *sent* from men, nor through the agency of man, but [R]through Jesus Christ, and God the Father, who raised Him from the dead), Acts 9:15; 20:24

2 and all the brethren who are with me, to[R]the churches of Galatia: Acts 16:6

3 [R]Grace to you and peace from God our Father, and the Lord Jesus Christ, Rom. 1:7

4 who gave Himself for our sins, that He might deliver us out of this present evil age, according to the will of our God and Father,

5 [R]to whom *be* the glory forevermore. Amen. Rom. 11:36

Situation: The Departure from Grace

6 I am amazed that you are so quickly deserting Him who called you[T]by the grace of Christ, for a different gospel; *in*

7 which is *really* not another; only there are some who are[R]disturbing you, and want to distort the gospel of Christ. Acts 15:24

8 But even though we, or an angel from heaven, should preach to you a gospel contrary to that which we have preached to you, let him be[T]accursed. Gr., anathema

9 As we have said before, so I say again now, if any man is preaching to you a gospel [A]contrary to that which you received, let him be[T]accursed. *other than, more than* • Gr., anathema

Gospel of Grace Is Given by Divine Revelation

10 For am I now seeking the favor of men, or of God? Or am I striving to please men? If I were still trying to please men, I would not be a[R]bond-servant of Christ. Rom. 1:1; Phil. 1:1

11 For[R]I would have you know, brethren, that the gospel which was preached by me is[R]not according to man. Rom. 2:16 • 1 Cor. 3:4

12 For[R]I neither received it from man, nor was I taught it, but *I received it* through a [R]revelation of Jesus Christ. Gal. 1:1 • Gal. 1:16

13 For you have heard of[R]my former manner of life in Judaism, how I used to persecute [R]the church of God beyond measure, and tried to destroy it; Acts 26:4f. • 1 Cor. 10:32

14 and I was advancing in Judaism beyond many of my contemporaries among my[T]countrymen, being more extremely zealous for my ancestral traditions. *race*

15 But when He who had set me apart, *even* from my mother's womb, and [R]called me through His grace, was pleased Jer. 1:5

16 to reveal His Son in me, that I might preach Him among the Gentiles, I did not immediately consult with flesh and blood,

17 [R]nor did I go up to Jerusalem to those who were apostles before me; but I went away to Arabia, and returned once more to [R]Damascus. Acts 9:19-22 • Acts 9:2

18 Then three years later I went up to Jerusalem to[R]become acquainted with Cephas, and stayed with him fifteen days. *visit Cephas*

19 But I did not see any other of the apostles except ᴬJames, the Lord's brother. *Jacob*
20 (Now in what I am writing to you, I assure you before God that I am not lying.)
21 Then ᴿI went into the regions of ᴿSyria and ᴿCilicia. Acts 9:30 • Acts 15:23, 41 • Acts 6:9
22 And I was *still* unknown by sight to the churches of Judea which were in Christ;
23 but only, they kept hearing, "He who once persecuted us is now preaching the faith which he once tried to destroy."
24 And they ᴿwere glorifying God ᵀbecause of me. Matt. 9:8 • *in me*

CHAPTER 2

Gospel of Grace Is Approved
by Jerusalem Leadership

THEN after an interval of fourteen years I went up again to Jerusalem with ᴿBarnabas, taking ᴿTitus along also. Acts 4:36 • 2 Cor. 2:13
2 And ᵀit was because of a revelation that I went up; and I submitted to them the gospel which I preach among the Gentiles, but *I did so* in private to those who were of reputation, for fear that I might be running, or had run, in vain. *according to revelation I went up*
3 But not even ᴿTitus who was with me, though he was a Greek, was ᴿcompelled to be circumcised. 2 Cor. 2:13; Gal. 2:1 • Acts 16:3
4 But *it was* because of the false brethren who ᴿhad sneaked in to spy out our ᴿliberty which we have in Christ Jesus, in order to bring us into bondage. Jude 4 • [James 1:25]
5 But we did not yield in subjection to them for even an hour, so that ᴿthe truth of the gospel might remain with you. Gal. 1:6
6 But from those who were of high ᴿreputation (what they were makes no difference to me; God ᵀshows no partiality)—well, those who were of reputation contributed nothing to me. Gal. 2:9 • *does not receive a face*
7 But on the contrary, seeing that I had been entrusted with the ᴿgospel ᵀto the uncircumcised, just as Peter *had been* to the circumcised Acts 9:15 • *of the uncircumcision*
8 (for He who effectually worked for Peter in his ᴿapostleship ᵀto the circumcised effectually worked for me also to the Gentiles), Acts 1:25 • *of the circumcision*
9 and recognizing the grace that had been given to me, ᴬJames and Cephas and John, who were reputed to be pillars, gave to me and Barnabas the right ᵀhand of fellowship, that we *might* go to the Gentiles, and they to the circumcised. *Jacob • hands*
10 *They* only *asked* us to remember the poor—the very thing I also was eager to do.

Gospel of Grace Is Vindicated
by Rebuking Peter

11 But when ᴿCephas came to Antioch, I opposed him to his face, because he ᴬstood condemned. Gal. 1:18 • *was to be condemned*

12 For prior to the coming of certain men from ᴬJames, he used to ᴿeat with the Gentiles; but when they came, he *began* to withdraw and hold himself aloof, fearing the party of the circumcision. *Jacob • Acts 11:3*
13 And the rest of the Jews joined him in hypocrisy, with the result that even Barnabas was carried away by their hypocrisy.
14 But when I saw that they were not straightforward about the truth of the gospel, I said to Cephas in the presence of all, "If you, being a Jew, live like the Gentiles and not like the Jews, how *is it that* you compel the Gentiles to live like Jews?
15 "We *are* Jews by nature, and not ᴿsinners from among the Gentiles; 1 Sam. 15:18
16 nevertheless knowing that a man is not justified by the works of the Law but through faith in Christ Jesus, even we have believed in Christ Jesus, that we may be justified by faith in Christ, and not by the works of the Law; since by the works of the Law shall no ᴬflesh be justified. *mortal man*
17 "But if, while seeking to be justified in Christ, we ourselves have also been found ᴿsinners, is Christ then a minister of sin? ᴿMay it never be! Gal. 2:15 • Luke 20:16; Gal. 3:21
18 "For if I rebuild what I have *once* destroyed, I prove myself to be a transgressor.
19 "For through ᴬthe Law I ᴿdied to ᵀthe Law, that I might live to God. *law • Rom. 6:2*
20 "I have been crucified with Christ; and it is no longer I who live, but Christ lives in me; and the *life* which I now live in the flesh I live by faith in the Son of God, who loved me, and delivered Himself up for me.
21 "I do not nullify the grace of God; for ᴿif righteousness *comes* through ᴬthe Law, then Christ died needlessly." Gal. 3:21 • *law*

CHAPTER 3

Holy Spirit Is Given by Faith, Not by Works

YOU foolish Galatians, who has bewitched you, before whose eyes Jesus Christ was publicly portrayed *as* crucified?
2 This is the only thing I want to find out from you: did you receive the Spirit by the works of the Law, or by hearing with faith?
3 Are you so foolish? Having begun ᴬby the Spirit, are you now ᴬbeing perfected by the flesh? *with • ending with*
4 Did you suffer so many things in vain— ᴬif indeed it was in vain? 1 Cor. 15:2
5 Does He then, who provides you with the Spirit and works ᴬmiracles among you, do it by the works of the Law, or by ᵀhearing with faith? *works of power • the hearing of faith*

Abraham Was Justified by Faith,
Not by Works

6 Even so Abraham BELIEVED GOD, AND IT WAS RECKONED TO HIM AS RIGHTEOUSNESS.

7 Therefore,[T]be sure that it is those who are of faith who are sons of Abraham. *know*

8 And the Scripture, foreseeing that God [T]would justify the [T]Gentiles by faith, preached the gospel beforehand to Abraham, *saying,* "ALL[R] THE NATIONS SHALL BE BLESSED IN YOU." *justifies • nations • Gen. 12:3*

9 So then [R]those who are of faith are blessed with Abraham, the believer. *Gal. 3:7*

Christ Redeems Us From the Curse of the Law

10 For as many as are of the works of[A]the Law are under a curse; for it is written, "CURSED[R]IS EVERYONE WHO DOES NOT ABIDE BY ALL THINGS WRITTEN IN THE BOOK OF THE LAW, TO PERFORM THEM." *law • Deut. 27:26*

11 Now that no one is justified[A]by[A]the Law before God is evident; for, "THE RIGHTEOUS MAN SHALL LIVE BY FAITH." *in • law*

12 [A]However, the Law is not[A]of faith; on the contrary, "HE WHO PRACTICES THEM SHALL LIVE[A]BY THEM." *And • based on • in*

13 Christ[R]redeemed us from the curse of the Law, having become a curse for us—for it is written, "CURSED IS EVERYONE WHO HANGS ON A[T]TREE"— *Gal. 4:5 • wood*

14 in order that in Christ Jesus the blessing of Abraham might[A]come to the Gentiles, so that we might receive[R]the promise of the Spirit through faith. *occur • Is. 49:6; Acts 2:33★*

Abrahamic Covenant Is Not Voided by the Law

15 Brethren, I speak in terms of human relations: even though it is *only* a man's covenant, yet when it has been ratified, no one sets it aside or adds[A]conditions to it. *a codicil*

16 Now the promises were spoken [R]to Abraham and to his seed. He does not say, "And to seeds," as *referring* to many, but *rather* to one, "And[R]to your seed," that is, Christ. *Gen. 12:3; [Rom. 4:13, 16; 9:4]★ • Acts 3:25*

17 What I am saying is this: the Law, which came[R]four hundred and thirty years later, does not invalidate a covenant previously ratified by God, so as to nullify the promise. *Gen. 15:13f.; Ex. 12:40; Acts 7:6*

18 For[R]if the inheritance is[T]based on law, it is no longer[T]based on a promise; but[R]God has granted it to Abraham by means of a promise. *Rom. 4:14 • out of, from • Heb. 6:14*

Law Given to Drive Us to Faith

19 Why the Law then? It was added because of transgressions, having been ordained through angels by the [T]agency of a mediator, until the seed should come to whom the promise had been made. *hand*

20 Now a mediator is not [T]for one *party* only; whereas God is *only* one. *of one*

21 Is the Law then contrary to the promises of God? May it never be! For if a law had been given which was able to impart

life, then righteousness[A]would indeed have been[T]based on law. *would indeed be • out of, from*

22 But the Scripture has shut up all men under sin, that the promise by faith in Jesus Christ might be given to those who believe.

Believers Are Free from the Law

23 But before faith came, we were kept in custody under the law, being shut up to the faith which was later to be revealed.

24 Therefore the Law has become our[T]tutor *to lead us* to Christ, that[R]we may be justified by faith. *child-conductor • [Gal. 2:16]*

25 But now that faith has come, we are no longer under a[T]tutor. *child-conductor*

26 For you are all [R]sons of God through faith in[R]Christ Jesus. *[Rom. 8:14] • Gal. 3:28*

27 For all of you who were baptized into Christ have clothed yourselves with Christ.

28 There is neither Jew nor Greek, there is neither slave nor free man, there is [T]neither male nor female; for [R]you are all one in Christ Jesus. *not male and female • John 17:11*

29 And if you belong to Christ, then you are Abraham's[T]offspring, heirs according to [R]promise. *seed • Gen. 12:3; Gal. 3:18; 4:28★*

CHAPTER 4

NOW I say, as long as the heir is a child, he does not differ at all from a slave although he is [T]owner of everything, *lord*

2 but he is under guardians and[A]managers until the date set by the father. *stewards*

3 So also we, while we were children, were held[R]in bondage under the [R]elemental things of the world. *Gal. 2:4 • Gal. 4:9; Col. 2:8*

4 But when[R]the fulness of the time came, God sent forth His Son,[R]born of a woman, born under[A]the Law, *Mark 1:15★ • Is. 7:14★ • law*

5 in order that He might redeem those who were under[A]the Law, that we might receive the adoption as[R]sons. *law • Gal. 3:26*

6 And because you are sons, God has sent forth the Spirit of His Son into our hearts, crying, "Abba![R]Father!" *Mark 14:36*

7 Therefore you are no longer a slave, but a son; and[R]if a son, then an heir[T]through God. *[Rom. 8:17] • through the gracious act of*

8 However at that time, when you did not know God, you were slaves to[R]those which by nature are no gods. *2 Chr. 13:9*

9 But now that you have come to know God, or rather to be known by God, how is it that you turn back again to the weak and worthless [R]elemental things, to which you desire to be enslaved all over again? *Gal. 4:3*

10 You[R]observe days and months and seasons and years. *Rom. 14:5; Col. 2:16*

11 I fear for you, that perhaps I have labored[A]over you in vain. *for*

Galatians Receive Blessings by Faith, Not by the Law

12 I beg of you,[R]brethren,[R]become as I *am,*

for I also *have become* as you *are.* You have done me no wrong;　　Gal. 6:18 • 2 Cor. 6:11, 13

13 but you know that it was because of a [T]bodily illness that I preached the gospel to you the[A]first time;　*weakness of the flesh • former*

14 and that which was a trial to you in my [T]bodily condition you did not despise or [T]loathe, but you received me as an angel of God, as Christ Jesus *Himself. flesh • spit out at*

15 Where then is that sense of blessing you had? For I bear you witness, that if possible, you would have plucked out your eyes and given them to me.

16 Have I therefore become your enemy [R]by telling you the truth?　　Amos 5:10

17 They eagerly seek you, not commendably, but they wish to shut you out, in order that you may seek them.

18 But it is good always to be eagerly sought in a commendable manner, and[R]not only when I am present with you.　Gal. 4:13f.

19 My children, with whom I am again in labor until Christ is formed in you—

20 but I could wish to be present with you now and to change my tone, for[R]I am perplexed about you.　　2 Cor. 4:8

Law and Grace Cannot Coexist

21 Tell me, you who want to be under law, do you not[R]listen to the law?　　Luke 16:29

22 For it is written that Abraham had two sons,[R]one by the bondwoman and[R]one by the free woman.　　Gen. 16:15 • Gen. 21:2

23 But the son by the bondwoman was born according to the flesh, and the son by the free woman through the promise.

24 [T]This is allegorically speaking: for these *women* are two covenants, one *proceeding* from Mount Sinai bearing children[T]who are to be slaves; she is Hagar.　*Which • into slavery*

25 Now this Hagar is Mount Sinai in Arabia, and corresponds to the present Jerusalem, for she is in slavery with her children.

26 But[R]the Jerusalem above is free;[T]she is our mother.　Heb. 12:22; Rev. 3:12; 21:2 • *which*

27 For it is written,

"REJOICE,[R] BARREN WOMAN WHO DOES NOT BEAR;　　Is. 54:1

BREAK FORTH AND SHOUT, YOU WHO ARE NOT IN LABOR;

FOR MORE ARE THE CHILDREN OF THE DESOLATE

THAN OF THE ONE WHO HAS A HUSBAND."

28 And you brethren,[R]like Isaac, are[R]children of promise.　　Gal. 4:23 • Rom. 9:7ff.

29 But as at that time[R]he who was born according to the flesh[R]persecuted him *who*

was born according to the Spirit, [R]so it is now also.　Gal. 4:23 • Gen. 21:9 • Gal. 5:11

30 But what does the Scripture say? "CAST[R]OUT THE BONDWOMAN AND HER SON,　　Gen. 21:10, 12

FOR [R]THE SON OF THE BONDWOMAN SHALL NOT BE AN HEIR WITH THE SON OF THE FREE WOMAN."　　[John 8:35]

31 So then, brethren, we are not children of a bondwoman, but of the free woman.

CHAPTER 5

Position of Liberty: Stand Fast

IT was for freedom that Christ set us free; therefore keep standing firm and do not be subject again to a[R]yoke of slavery.　Gal. 2:4

2 Behold I,[R]Paul, say to you that if you receive [R]circumcision, Christ will be of no benefit to you.　2 Cor. 10:1 • Acts 15:1; Gal. 5:3

3 And I testify again to every man who receives circumcision, that he is under obligation to[R]keep the whole Law.　[Rom. 2:25]

4 You have been severed from Christ, you who[A]are seeking to be justified by law; you have fallen from grace.　　*would be*

5 For we through the Spirit, by faith, are waiting for the hope of righteousness.

6 For in Christ Jesus neither circumcision nor uncircumcision means anything, but[R]faith working through love.　1 Thess. 1:3

7 You were[R]running well; who hindered you from obeying the truth?　　Gal. 2:2

8 This persuasion *did* not *come* from [R]Him who calls you.　[Rom. 8:28]; Gal. 1:6

9 [R]A little leaven leavens the whole lump of dough.　　1 Cor. 5:6

10 I have confidence[T]in you in the Lord, that you will adopt no other view; but the one who is [R]disturbing you shall bear his judgment, whoever he is.　*toward • Gal. 1:7*

11 But I, brethren, if I still preach circumcision, why am I still[R]persecuted? Then[R]the stumbling block of the cross has been abolished.　Gal. 4:29; 6:12 • Rom. 9:33; [1 Cor. 1:23]

12 Would that those who are troubling you would even mutilate themselves.

Practice of Liberty: Love One Another

13 For you were called to freedom, brethren;[R]only *do* not *turn* your freedom into an opportunity for the flesh, but through love [R]serve one another.　1 Cor. 8:9 • 1 Cor. 9:19

5:13 Serving—God intended that the Christian life should be dynamic, not static. We should sit under the teaching of the Word of God, understand and apply its meaning and implications, and serve God and our fellow believers. The Spirit of God has given us spiritual gifts, but those gifts are worthless unless they are put to use in the service of God and His church. Paul often uses the figure of the human body to show the dependence of the members of the body upon one another and the importance of each member serving the other (Page 1141—Rom.

14 For[R]the whole Law is fulfilled in one word, in the *statement*, "YOU SHALL LOVE YOUR NEIGHBOR AS YOURSELF."   Rom. 13:8, 10

15 But if you[R]bite and devour one another, take care lest you be consumed by one another.   Gal. 5:20; Phil. 3:2

Conflict Between the Spirit and the Flesh

16 But I say, walk by the Spirit, and you will not carry out the desire of the flesh.

17 For[R]the flesh[T]sets its desire against the Spirit, and the Spirit against the flesh; for these are in opposition to one another, so that you may not do the things that you [T]please.   Rom. 7:18, 23; 8:5ff. • *lusts against • wish*

18 But if you are[R]led by the Spirit,[R]you are not under the Law.   Rom. 8:14 • [Rom. 6:14; 7:4]

Works of the Flesh

19 Now the deeds of the flesh are evident, which are: immorality, impurity, sensuality,

20 idolatry,[R]sorcery, enmities,[R]strife, jealousy, outbursts of anger, disputes, dissensions,[A]factions,   Rev. 21:8 • 2 Cor. 12:20 • *heresies*

21 envying,[R]drunkenness, carousing, and things like these, of which I forewarn you just as I have forewarned you that those who practice such things shall not[R]inherit the kingdom of God.   Rom. 13:13 • 1 Cor. 6:9

Fruit of the Spirit

22 But[R]the fruit of the Spirit is[R]love, joy, peace, patience, kindness, goodness, faithfulness,   Matt. 7:16ff. • [Rom. 5:1-5; 1 Cor. 13:4]

23 gentleness, [R]self-control; against such things[R]there is no law.   Acts 24:25 • Gal. 5:18

24 Now those who[T]belong to Christ Jesus have [R]crucified the flesh with its passions and desires.   *are of Christ Jesus* • Rom. 6:6

25 If we live by the Spirit, let us also[A]walk [R]by the Spirit.   *follow the Spirit* • Gal. 5:16

26 Let us not become boastful, challenging one another, envying one another.

CHAPTER 6

Bear One Another's Burdens

BRETHREN, even if a man is caught in any trespass, you who are spiritual, restore such a one in a spirit of gentleness; *each one* looking to yourself, lest you too be tempted.

[1] Some ancient mss. read *have been*

2 [R]Bear one another's burdens, and thus fulfill[R]the law of Christ.   Rom. 15:1 • Rom. 8:2

3 For if anyone thinks he is something when he is nothing, he deceives himself.

4 But let each one [R]examine his own work, and then he will have *reason for* [R]boasting in regard to himself alone, and not in regard to another.   1 Cor. 11:28 • Phil. 1:26

5 For each one shall bear his own load.

Do Not Lose Heart in Doing Good

6 And let the one who is taught the word share all good things with him who teaches.

7 Do[R] not be deceived, [R]God is not mocked; for[R]whatever a man sows, this he will also reap.   1 Cor. 6:9 • Job 13:9 • 2 Cor. 9:6

8 For the one who sows to his own flesh shall from the flesh reap[R]corruption, but[R]the one who sows to the Spirit shall from the Spirit reap eternal life.   1 Cor. 15:42 • Rom. 8:11

9 And[R]let us not lose heart in doing good, for in due time we shall reap if we[R]do not grow weary.   1 Cor. 15:58; 2 Cor. 4:1 • Matt. 10:22

10 So then, while we have opportunity, let us do good to all men, and especially to those who are of the household of the faith.

Motives of the Circumcised

11 See with what large letters I[A]am writing to you with my own hand.   *have written*

12 Those who desire to make a good showing in the flesh try to compel you to be circumcised, simply that they may not be persecuted[A]for the cross of Christ. *because of*

13 For those who [1]are circumcised do not even[R]keep[T]the Law themselves, but they desire to have you circumcised, that they may [R]boast in your flesh.   Rom. 2:25 • *law* • Phil. 3:3

Motives of the Apostle Paul

14 But may it never be that I should boast, except in the cross of our Lord Jesus Christ, through[A]which the world has been crucified to me, and[R]I to the world. *whom* • [Rom. 6:2, 6]

15 For neither is circumcision anything, nor uncircumcision, but a new creation.

16 And those who will[A]walk by this rule, peace and mercy *be* upon them, and upon the[R]Israel of God.   *follow this rule* • [Rom. 9:6]

17 From now on let no one cause trouble for me, for I bear on my body the[R]brandmarks of Jesus.   Is. 44:5; Ezek. 9:4; [2 Cor. 4:10]

18 The grace of our Lord Jesus Christ be [R]with your spirit, brethren. Amen.   2 Tim. 4:22

12:4, 5; Page 1158—1 Cor. 12:12–31). While some members of the body have more prominent places of service than others, all are equally important. The worst thing that can happen to the human body is for one of its members to become nonfunctioning. Paralysis, sickness, deterioration, and sometimes death occur when a body member ceases to serve the other members of the body in the particular way that God intended. To maintain strength, health, and vitality, every member of the body must function and serve all the other members of the body. This is also true of the spiritual or new life. We will grow in the new life, become strong, and maintain good spiritual health as we use the talents and abilities that God has given us to meet the needs of the other members of the body.
Now turn to Page 1171—2 Cor. 9:6–8: Giving.

EPHESIANS

THE BOOK OF EPHESIANS

Ephesians is addressed to a group of believers who are rich beyond measure in Jesus Christ, yet living as beggars, and only because they are ignorant of their wealth. Since they have yet to accept their wealth, they relegate themselves to living as spiritual paupers. Paul begins by describing in chapters 1—3 the contents of the Christian's heavenly "bank account": adoption, acceptance, redemption, forgiveness, wisdom, inheritance, the seal of the Holy Spirit, life, grace, citizenship—in short, every spiritual blessing. Drawing upon that huge spiritual endowment, the Christian has all the resources needed for living "to the praise of the glory of His grace" (1:6). Chapters 4—6 resemble an orthopedic clinic, where the Christian learns a spiritual walk rooted in his spiritual wealth. "For we are His workmanship, created in Christ Jesus [1—3] for good works, . . . that we should walk in them [4—6]" (2:10).

The traditional title of this epistle is *Pros Ephesious*, "To the Ephesians." Many ancient manuscripts, however, omit *en Epheso*, "at Ephesus," in 1:1. This has led a number of scholars to challenge the traditional view that this message was directed specifically to the Ephesians. The encyclical theory proposes that it was a circular letter sent by Paul to the churches of Asia. It is argued that Ephesians is really a Christian treatise designed for general use: it involves no controversy and deals with no specific problems in any particular church. This is also supported by the formal tone (no terms of endearment) and distant phraseology ("having heard of the faith," 1:15; if they "have heard" of his message, 3:2). These things seem inconsistent with the relationship Paul must have had with the Ephesians after a ministry of almost three years among them. On the other hand, the absence of personal greetings is not a support for the encyclical theory because Paul would have done this to avoid favoritism. The only letters that greet specific people are Romans and Colossians, and they were addressed to churches Paul had not visited. Some scholars accept an ancient tradition that Ephesians is Paul's letter to the Laodiceans (Col. 4:16), but there is no way to be sure. If Ephesians began as a circular letter, it eventually became associated with Ephesus, the foremost of the Asian churches. Another plausible option is that this epistle was directly addressed to the Ephesians, but written in such a way as to make it helpful for all the churches in Asia.

THE AUTHOR OF EPHESIANS

All internal (1:1) and external evidence strongly supports the Pauline authorship of Ephesians. In recent years, however, critics have turned to internal grounds to challenge this unanimous ancient tradition. It has been argued that the vocabulary and style are different from other Pauline epistles, but this overlooks Paul's flexibility under different circumstances (cf. Rom. and 2 Cor.). The theology of Ephesians in some ways reflects a later development, but this must be attributed to Paul's own growth and meditation on the church as the body of Christ. Since the epistle clearly names the author in the opening verse, it is not necessary to theorize that Ephesians was written by one of Paul's pupils or admirers, such as Timothy, Luke, Tychicus, or Onesimus.

THE TIME OF EPHESIANS

At the end of his second missionary journey, Paul visited Ephesus where he left Priscilla and Aquila (Acts 18:18-21). This strategic city was the commercial center of Asia Minor, but heavy silting required a special canal to be maintained so that ships could reach the harbor. Ephesus was a religious center as well, famous especially for its magnificent temple of Diana (Roman name) or Artemis (Greek name), a structure considered to be one of the seven wonders of the ancient world (cf. Acts 19:35). The practice of magic and the local economy were clearly related to this temple. Paul remained in Ephesus for nearly three years on his third missionary journey (Acts 18:23—19:41); the Word of God was spread throughout the province of Asia. Paul's effective ministry began to seriously hurt the traffic in magic and images, leading to an uproar in the huge Ephesian theater. Paul then left for Macedonia, but afterward he met with the Ephesian elders while on his way to Jerusalem (Acts 20:17-38).

Paul wrote the "Prison Epistles" (Ephesians, Philippians, Colossians, and Philemon) during his first Roman imprisonment in A.D. 60–62. These epistles all refer to his imprisonment (Eph. 3:1; 4:1; 6:20; Phil. 1:7, 13, 14; Col. 4:3, 10, 18; Philem. 9, 10, 13, 23), and fit well

against the background in Acts 28:16–31. This is especially true of Paul's references to the "praetorian guard" (governor's official residential guard, Phil. 1:13) and "Caesar's household" (Phil. 4:22). Some commentators believe that the imprisonment in one or more of these epistles refers to Paul's Caesarean imprisonment or to a hypothetical Ephesian imprisonment, but the weight of evidence favors the traditional view that they were written in Rome. Ephesians, Colossians, and Philemon were evidently written about the same time (cf. Eph. 6:21, 22 with Col. 4:7–9) in A.D. 60–61. Philippians was written in A.D. 62, not long before Paul's release.

THE CHRIST OF EPHESIANS

Paul's important phrase "in Christ" (or its equivalent) appears about thirty-five times, more than in any other New Testament book. The believer is in Christ (1:1), in the heavenly places in Christ (1:3), chosen in Him (1:4), adopted through Christ (1:5), in the Beloved (1:6), redeemed in Him (1:7), given an inheritance in Him (1:11), given hope in Him (1:12), sealed in Him (1:13), made alive together with Christ (2:5), raised and seated with Him (2:6), created in Christ (2:10), brought near by the blood of Christ (2:13), growing in Christ (2:21), a partaker of the promise in Christ (3:6), and given access through faith in Him (3:12).

KEYS TO EPHESIANS

Key Word: Building the Body of Christ—Ephesians focuses on the believer's responsibility to walk in accordance with his heavenly calling in Christ Jesus (4:1). Ephesians was not written to correct specific errors in a local church, but to prevent prob-lems in the church as a whole by encouraging the body of Christ to maturity in Him. It was also written to make believers more aware of their position in Christ because this is the basis for their practice on every level of life.

Key Verses: Ephesians 2:8–10 and 4:1–3— "For by grace you have been saved through faith; and that not of yourselves, it is the gift of God; not as a result of works, that no one should boast. For we are His workmanship, created in Christ Jesus for good works, which God prepared beforehand, that we should walk in them" (2:8–10).

"I, therefore, the prisoner of the Lord, entreat you to walk in a manner worthy of the calling with which you have been called, with all humility and gentleness, with patience, showing forbearance to one another in love, being diligent to preserve the unity of the Spirit in the bond of peace" (4:1–3).

Key Chapter: Ephesians 6—Even though the Christian is blessed "with every spiritual blessing in the heavenly places in Christ" (1:3), spiritual warfare is still the daily experience of the Christian while in the world. Chapter 6 is the clearest advice for how to "be strong in the Lord, and in the strength of His might" (6:10).

SURVEY OF EPHESIANS

Paul wrote this epistle to make Christians more aware of their position in Christ and to motivate them to draw upon their spiritual source in daily living: "Walk in a manner worthy of the calling with which you have been called" (4:1; see 2:10). The first half of Ephesians lists the believer's heavenly possessions: adoption, redemption, inheritance, power, life, grace, citizenship, and the love of Christ. There are no imperatives in chapters 1—3, which focus only on divine gifts. But chapters 4—6 include thirty-five di-

FOCUS	THE POSITION OF THE CHRISTIAN				THE PRACTICE OF THE CHRISTIAN			
REFERENCE	1:1————	1:15————	1:24————	3:14—	4:1————	4:17————	5:22————	6:10———6:24
DIVISION	PRAISE FOR REDEMPTION	PRAYER FOR REVELATION	POSITION OF THE CHRISTIAN	PRAYER FOR REALIZATION	UNITY IN THE CHURCH	HOLINESS IN LIFE	RESPONSIBIL-ITIES AT HOME AND WORK	CONDUCT IN THE CONFLICT
TOPIC	BELIEF				BEHAVIOR			
	PRIVILEGES OF THE CHRISTIAN				RESPONSIBILITIES OF THE CHRISTIAN			
LOCATION	ROME							
TIME	A.D. 60-61							

rectives in the last half of Ephesians that speak of the believer's responsibility to conduct himself according to his individual calling. So Ephesians begins in heaven, but concludes in the home and in all other relationships of daily life. The two divisions are: the position of the Christian (1:1—3:21) and the practice of the Christian (4:1—6:20).

The Position of the Christian (1:1—3:21): After a two-verse prologue, in one long Greek sentence Paul extols the triune God for the riches of redemption (1:3-14). This hymn to God's grace praises the Father for choosing us (1:3-6), the Son for redeeming us (1:7-12), and the Spirit for sealing us (1:13, 14). The saving work of each divine Person is to the praise of the glory of His grace (1:6, 12, 14). Before continuing, Paul offers the first of two very significant prayers (1:15-23; cf. 3:14-21). Here he asks that the readers receive spiritual illumination so that they may come to perceive what is, in fact, true. Next, Paul describes the power of God's grace by contrasting their former condition with their present spiritual life in Christ, a salvation attained not by human works but by divine grace (2:1-10). This redemption includes Jews, yet also extends to those Gentiles who previously were "strangers to the covenants of promise" (2:12). In Christ, the two for the first time have become members of one body (2:11-22). The truth that Gentiles would become "fellow heirs and fel-

low members of the body" (3:6) was formerly a mystery that has now been revealed (3:1-13). Paul's second prayer (3:14-21) expresses his desire that the readers be strengthened with the power of the Spirit and fully apprehend the love of Christ.

The Practice of the Christian (4:1—6:20): The pivotal verse of Ephesians is 4:1, because it draws a sharp line between the doctrinal and the practical divisions of this book. There is a cause and effect relationship between chapters 1—3 and 4—6 because the spiritual walk of a Christian must be rooted in his spiritual wealth. As Paul emphasized in Romans, behavior does not determine blessing; instead, blessing should determine behavior.

Because of the unity of all believers in the body of Christ, growth and maturity come from "the proper working of each individual part" (4:16). This involves the exercise of spiritual gifts in love. Paul exhorts the readers to "lay aside the old self" (4:22) and "put on the new self" (4:24) that will be manifested by a walk of integrity in the midst of all people. They are also to maintain a walk of holiness as children of light (5:1-21). Every relationship (wives, husbands, children, parents, slaves, masters) must be transformed by their new life in Christ (5:22—6:9). Paul's colorful description of the spiritual warfare and the armor of God (6:10-20) is followed by a word about Tychicus and then a benediction (6:21-24).

OUTLINE OF EPHESIANS

Part One: The Position of the Christian (1:1—3:21)

Part Two: The Practice of the Christian (4:1—6:24)

CHAPTER 1

Salutation from Paul

PAUL, an apostle of Christ Jesus by the will of God, to the saints who are [1]at Ephesus, and *who are* faithful in Christ Jesus:
2 [R]Grace to you and peace from God our Father and the Lord Jesus Christ.   Rom. 1:7

Chosen by the Father

3 [R]Blessed *be* the God and Father of our Lord Jesus Christ, who has blessed us with every spiritual blessing in [R]the heavenly *places* in Christ,   2 Cor. 1:3 • Eph. 1:20; 2:6
4 just as He chose us in Him before the foundation of the world, that we should be holy and blameless before [2]Him. In love
5 He predestined us to adoption as sons through Jesus Christ to Himself, according to the[T]kind intention of His will, *good pleasure*
6 [R]to the praise of the glory of His grace, which He freely bestowed on us in[R]the Beloved.   Eph. 1:12, 14 • Matt. 3:17

Redeemed by the Son

7 In[T]Him we have redemption through His blood, the forgiveness of our trespasses, according to the riches of His grace,   *whom*
8 which He[T]lavished upon us. In all wisdom and insight   *made abundant toward*
9 He[T]made known to us the mystery of His will, according to His kind intention which He purposed in Him   *making known*
10 with a view to an administration[T]suitable to[R]the fulness of the times, *that is,*[R]the summing up of all things in Christ, things[T]in the heavens and things upon the earth. In Him   *of* • Mark 1:15 • Eph. 3:15; Phil. 2:9f. • *upon*
11 [T]also we have obtained an inheritance, having been [R]predestined according to His purpose who works all things after the counsel of His will,   *in whom also* • Eph. 1:5
12 to the end that we who were the first to hope in [3]Christ should be[R]to the praise of His glory.   Eph. 1:6, 14

Sealed by the Spirit

13 In Him, you also, after listening to the message of truth, the gospel of your salvation—having also believed, you were sealed in Him with the Holy Spirit of promise,
14 who is[A]given as a pledge of our inheritance, with a view to the [R]redemption of [R]God's own possession, to the praise of His glory.   *a down payment* • Eph. 1:7 • Eph. 1:11

[1] Some ancient mss. do not contain *at Ephesus*
[2] Or, *Him, in love.* [3] I.e., the Messiah
[4] Many ancient mss. do not contain *your love*
[5] Some ancient mss. read *in Christ*

Prayer for Revelation

15 For this reason I too, having heard of the faith in the Lord Jesus which *exists* among you, and [4]your love for all the saints,
16 do not cease giving thanks for you, while making mention *of you* in my prayers;
17 that the God of our Lord Jesus Christ, the Father of glory, may give to you a spirit of wisdom and of[R]revelation in the[A]knowledge of Him.   1 Cor. 14:6 • *true knowledge*
18 *I pray that*[R]the eyes of your heart[T]may be enlightened, so that you may know what is the[R]hope of His calling, what are the riches of the glory of His inheritance in the [A]saints,   Acts 26:18 • *being* • Eph. 4:4 • *holy ones*
19 and what is the surpassing greatness of His power toward us who believe.[R]*These are* in accordance with the working of the [R]strength of His might   Eph. 3:7 • Eph. 6:10
20 which He brought about in Christ, when He [R]raised Him from the dead, and [R]seated Him at His right hand in[R]the heavenly *places,*   Acts 2:24 ★ • Mark 16:19 • Eph. 1:3
21 far above [R]all rule and authority and power and dominion, and every[R]name that is named, not only in[R]this age, but also in the one to come.   Matt. 28:18 • John 17:11 • Eph. 2:2
22 And He[R]put all things in subjection under His feet, and gave Him as[R]head over all things to the church,   Dan. 7:13, 14 • 1 Cor. 11:3
23 which is His body, the[R]fulness of Him who fills[R]all in all.   John 1:16 • Col. 3:11

CHAPTER 2

Old Condition: Dead to God

AND you[T]were dead[A]in your trespasses and sins,   *being* • *by reason of*
2 in which you[R]formerly walked according to the[T]course of this world, according to [R]the prince of the power of the air, of the spirit that is now working in the sons of disobedience.   Rom. 13:13 • *age* • [John 12:31]
3 Among them we too all formerly lived in the lusts of our flesh,[T]indulging the desires of the flesh and of the[T]mind, and were [R]by nature [R]children of wrath, even as the rest.   *doing* • *thoughts* • Rom. 2:14 • Rom. 5:9

New Condition: Alive to God

4 But God, being rich in mercy, because of His great love with which He loved us,
5 even when we were dead in our transgressions, made us alive together [5]with Christ (by grace you have been saved),
6 and[R]raised us up with Him, and[R]seated us with Him in [R]the heavenly *places,* in Christ Jesus,   Col. 2:12 • Eph. 1:20 • Eph. 1:3
7 in order that in the ages to come He might show the surpassing riches of His grace in kindness toward us in Christ Jesus.

8 For by grace you have been saved through faith; and that not of yourselves, *it is* the gift of God;

9 [R]not as a result of works, that[R]no one should boast. Rom. 3:28; [2 Tim. 1:9] • 1 Cor. 1:29

10 For we are His workmanship, created in Christ Jesus for[R]good works, which God [R]prepared beforehand, that we should[R]walk in them.   [Titus 2:14] • Eph. 1:4 • Eph. 4:1

Reconciliation of Jews and Gentiles

11 Therefore remember, that [R]formerly you, the Gentiles in the flesh, who are called [R]"Uncircumcision" by the so-called "Circumcision," *which is* performed in the flesh by human hands— Rom. 13:13 • [Rom. 2:28f.]

12 *remember* that you were at that time separate from Christ, [A]excluded from the commonwealth of Israel, and strangers to the covenants of promise, having no hope and without God in the world.   *alienated*

13 But now in Christ Jesus you who formerly were far off[T]have been brought near by the blood of Christ.   *became; or, were made*

14 For He Himself is[R]our peace, who made both *groups into* one, and broke down the barrier of the dividing wall,   Is. 9:6★

15 by abolishing in His flesh the enmity, *which is* the Law of commandments *contained* in ordinances, that in Himself He might[T]make the two into[R]one new man, *thus* establishing[R]peace,   *create* • Gal. 3:28 • Is. 9:6

16 and might[R]reconcile them both in one body to God through the cross,[A]by it having put to death the enmity. [Col. 1:20] • *in Himself*

17 AND[R]HE CAME AND PREACHED[R]PEACE TO YOU WHO WERE FAR AWAY, AND PEACE TO THOSE WHO WERE NEAR; Is. 57:19 • Acts 10:36

18 for through Him we both have our access in[R]one Spirit to the Father. 1 Cor. 12:13

19 So then you are no longer strangers and aliens, but you are fellow citizens with the saints, and are of God's household,

20 having been built upon the foundation of the apostles and prophets, Christ Jesus Himself being the[R]corner *stone*, Ps. 118:22★

21 [R]in whom the whole building, being fitted together is growing into[R]a holy[T]temple in the Lord; Eph. 4:15f. • 1 Cor. 3:16f. • *sanctuary*

22 in whom you also are being built together into a dwelling of God in the Spirit.

CHAPTER 3

Revelation of the Mystery of the Church

FOR this reason I, Paul, the prisoner of Christ Jesus for the sake of you Gentiles—

2 if indeed you have heard of the[R]stewardship of God's grace which was given to me for you; Eph. 1:10; 3:9; Col. 1:25; 1 Tim. 1:4

3 that [R]by revelation there was [R]made known to me[R]the mystery, as I wrote before in brief. Gal. 1:12 • Eph. 1:9; 3:4 • [Rom. 11:25]

4 [T]And by referring to this, when you read you can understand my insight [T]into the mystery of Christ, *To which, when you read* • *in*

5 which in other generations was not made known to the sons of men, as it has now been revealed to His holy[A]apostles and prophets[A]in the Spirit;   1 Cor. 12:28 • *by*

6 *to be specific*, that the Gentiles are fellow heirs and fellow members of the body, and [R]fellow partakers of the promise in Christ Jesus through the gospel,   Eph. 5:7

7 of which I was made a[R]minister, according to the gift of[R]God's grace which was given to me[R]according to the working of His power.   1 Cor. 3:5 • Acts 9:15 • Eph. 1:19; 3:20

8 To me, the very least of all[A]saints, this grace was given, to preach to the Gentiles the unfathomable riches of Christ, *holy ones*

9 and to bring to light what is the administration of the mystery which for ages has been hidden in God, who created all things;

10 in order that the manifold[R]wisdom of God might now be made known through the church to the[R]rulers and the authorities in the heavenly *places*. [Rom. 11:33] • Eph. 1:21

11 *This was* in accordance with the [T]eternal purpose which He[A]carried out in Christ Jesus our Lord,   *purpose of the ages* • *formed*

12 in whom we have boldness and confident access through faith[T]in Him.   *of Him*

13 Therefore I ask[A]you not to lose heart at my tribulations on your behalf,[T]for they are your glory.   *that I may not lose* • *which are*

Prayer for Realization

14 For this reason, I[R]bow my knees before the Father,   Phil. 2:10

15 from whom[A]every family in heaven and on earth derives its name,   *the whole*

16 that He would grant you, according to [R]the riches of His glory, to be[R]strengthened with power through His Spirit in[R]the inner man; Eph. 1:18; 3:8 • 1 Cor. 16:13 • Rom. 7:22

17 so that Christ may dwell in your hearts through faith; *and* that you, being[R]rooted and[R]grounded in love,   1 Cor. 3:6 • Col. 1:23

18 may be able to comprehend with [R]all the saints what is[R]the breadth and length and height and depth,   Eph. 1:15 • Job 11:8f.

19 and to know the love of Christ which surpasses knowledge, that you may be[R]filled up to all the fulness of God.   Col. 2:10

20 [R]Now to Him who is[R]able to do exceeding abundantly beyond all that we ask or think, [R]according to the power that works within us,   Rom. 16:25 • 2 Cor. 9:8 • Eph. 3:7

21 to Him *be* the glory in the church and in Christ Jesus to all generations[T]forever and ever. Amen.   *of the age of the ages*

3:21 The Purpose of the Church—The ultimate purpose of the church is to bring honor and glory to its head, Jesus Christ. It does this as it fulfills its two purposes related to God's program for the world.

CHAPTER 4
Exhortation to Unity

I, THEREFORE, the prisoner of the Lord, entreat you to walk in a manner worthy of the calling with which you have been called,
2 with all[R]humility and gentleness, with patience, showing forbearance to one another[R]in love,   Col. 3:12f. • Eph. 1:4

3 being diligent to preserve the unity of the Spirit in the[R]bond of peace.   Col. 3:14f.

Explanation of Unity

4 There is[R]one body and one Spirit, just as also you were called in one[R]hope of your calling;   1 Cor. 12:4ff.; Eph. 2:16, 18 • Eph. 1:18
5 one Lord, one faith, one baptism,
6 one God and Father of all[R]who is over all and through all and in all.   Rom. 11:36

Means for Unity: The Gifts

7 But to each one of us grace was given according to the measure of Christ's gift.
8 Therefore[A]it says,   He
"WHEN[R]HE ASCENDED ON HIGH, Ps. 68:18
HE[R]LED CAPTIVE A HOST OF CAPTIVES,
AND HE GAVE GIFTS TO MEN."   Col. 2:15
9 (Now this expression, "He ascended," what does it mean except that He also had descended into the lower parts of the earth?
[R] 10 He who descended is Himself also He who ascended far above all the heavens, that He might fill all things.)   [John 20:17]

11 And He[R]gave some as apostles, and some as prophets, and some as evangelists, and some as pastors and teachers,   Eph. 4:8

Purpose of the Gifts

12 [R]for the equipping of the[A]saints for the work of service, to the building up of the body of Christ;   2 Cor. 13:9 • holy ones
13 until we all attain to the unity of the faith, and of the[A]knowledge of the Son of God, to a mature man, to the measure of the stature [T]which belongs to the [R]fulness of Christ.   true knowledge • of the fulness • John 1:16
14 As a result, we are no longer to be children, tossed here and there by waves, and carried about by every wind of doctrine, by the trickery of men, by craftiness[T]in deceitful scheming; with regard to the scheming of deceit
15 but[A]speaking the truth in love, we are to grow up in all aspects into Him, who is the head, even Christ,   holding to or walking in
16 from whom the whole body, being fitted and held together[T]by that which every joint supplies, according to the proper working of each individual part, causes the growth of the body for the building up of itself in love.   through every joint of the supply

Put Off the Old Self

17 This I say therefore, and affirm together with the Lord, [R]that you walk no longer just as the Gentiles also walk, in the [R]futility of their mind,   Eph. 2:2; 4:22 • Rom. 1:21

The one purpose of the church, as it relates to the world, is evangelism. This program is spelled out in the Great Commission (Page 995—Matt. 28:19, 20), which has never been rescinded. The program is to "make disciples of all the nations." The way this is to be done is twofold: by "baptizing them in the name of the Father and the Son and the Holy Spirit," and by "teaching them to observe all that I commanded you." Baptism is not an optional afterthought. It is a vital part of evangelism and making disciples. By baptism, one indicates that he has been identified with Christ in His death, burial, and resurrection (i.e., he is a member of the universal church, the body of Christ) and wishes to be identified with the local church. A responsible parent not only brings a child into the world, but also provides what is necessary for the child's growth. So in the church, teaching must accompany evangelism so that the child of God can learn all that God expects of him and has provided for him.
Another purpose of the church, as it relates to the world, is edification. According to Ephesians 4:12 the saints need to be edified (built up) for two goals: "for the equipping of the saints for the work of service." The believers who comprise the church's membership need to be built up so that they may realize all that God has provided for Christian living and that they may come to spiritual maturity. They also need to be equipped to perform that work in the body of Christ that God wants them to perform. In a real sense each member of the church is to be a Christian worker so that the work that God wants to perform through the local church can be accomplished.
Now turn to Page 1218—1 Tim. 3:1–13: The Offices of the Church.

4:3 The Person of the Holy Spirit—One of the most serious errors in the minds of many people concerning the Holy Spirit is that He is simply a principle or an influence. On the contrary, the Holy Spirit is as much a person (individual existence of a conscious being) as the Father and the Son.
a. The personality of the Holy Spirit. The Bible speaks of the mind (Page 1138—Rom. 8:27) and will (Page 1157—1 Cor. 12:11) of the Holy Spirit. He is often described as speaking directly to men in the Book of Acts. During Paul's second missionary journey the apostle was forbidden by the Spirit to visit a certain mission field (Page 1112—Acts 16:6, 7) and then was instructed to proceed toward another field of service (Page 1112—Acts 16:10). It was God's Spirit who spoke directly to Christian leaders in the Antioch church, commanding them to send Paul and Barnabas on their first missionary journey (Page 1108—Acts 13:2).
b. The deity of the Holy Spirit. He is not only a real person, but He is also God. As is God the Father, He too is everywhere at once (Page 600—Ps. 139:7). As the Son is eternal, the Holy Spirit has also existed forever (Page 1244—Heb. 9:14). He is often referred to as God in the Bible. See Acts 5:3, 4. Finally, the Holy Spirit is equal with the Father and Son. This is seen during the baptism of Christ (Page 965—Matt. 3:16, 17) and is mentioned by Jesus Himself just prior to His ascension from the Mount of Olives (Page 995—Matt. 28:19, 20).
Now turn to Page 1230—Titus 3:5: The Work of the Holy Spirit in Salvation.

18 being darkened in their understanding, ᴬexcluded from the life of God, because of the ignorance that is in them, because of the hardness of their heart;　　　*alienated*

19 and they, havingᴿbecome callous,ᴿhave given themselves over toᴿsensuality, for the practice of every kind of impurity with greediness.　　1 Tim. 4:2 • Rom. 1:24 • Col. 3:5

20 But you did not ᴿlearn ᵀChrist in this way,　　[Matt. 11:29] • the Messiah

21 if indeed you have heard Him and have been taught in Him, just as truth is in Jesus,

22 that, in reference to your former manner of life, youᴿlay aside the oldᵀself, which is being corrupted in accordance with the ᴿlusts of deceit,　　Eph. 4:25, 31 • *man* • 2 Cor. 11:3

Put On the New Self

23 and that you beᴿrenewed in the spirit of your mind,　　[Rom. 12:2]

24 and put on the newᵀself, which in *the likeness of God has* been created in righteousness and holiness of the truth.　　*man*

25 Therefore, ᴿlaying aside falsehood, ᴿSPEAK TRUTH, EACH ONE *of you,* WITH HIS NEIGHBOR, for we areᴿmembers of one another.　　Eph. 4:22, 31 • Zech. 8:16 • [Rom. 12:5]

26 ᴿBE ANGRY, AND *yet* DO NOT SIN; do not let the sun go down on your anger,　　Ps. 4:4

27 and do notᴿgive the devilᵀan opportunity.　　[Rom. 12:19; James 4:7] • *a place*

28 Let him who steals steal no longer; but rather ᴿlet him labor, ᴿperforming with his own hands what is good,ᴿin order that he may have *something* to share with him who has need.　　Acts 20:35 • 1 Thess. 4:11 • 1 Thess. 4:12

29 Let no ᵀunwholesome word proceed from your mouth, but only such *a word* as is good forᴿedificationᵀaccording to the need of *the moment,* that it may give grace to those who hear.　　*rotten* • [Eccl. 10:12] • *of the need*

Grieve Not the Holy Spirit

30 And ᴿdo not grieve the Holy Spirit of God,ᵀby whom you wereᴿsealed for the day of redemption.　　Is. 63:10 • *in* • John 3:33

31 ᴿLet all bitterness and wrath and anger and clamor and slander be put away from you, along with allᴿmalice.　　Col. 3:8 • 1 Pet. 2:1

32 And ᴿbe kind to one another, tenderhearted, forgiving each other, just as God in Christ also has forgiven ⁶you.　　1 Pet. 3:8

CHAPTER 5

THEREFOREᴿbe imitators of God, as beloved children; [Matt. 5:48]; Luke 6:36; Eph. 4:32

2 andᴿwalk in love, just as Christ also loved ⁶you, and gave Himself up for us, an offering and a sacrifice to Godᵀas a fragrant aroma.　　Rom. 14:15 • *for an odor of fragrance*

3 But do not let immoralityᵀor any impurity or greed even be named among you, as is proper amongᴬsaints;　　*and all • holy ones*

4 and *there must be no*ᴿfilthiness and silly talk, or coarse jesting, which are not fitting, but rather giving of thanks.　　Matt. 12:34

5 For this you know with certainty, that ᴿno immoral or impure person or covetous man, who is an idolater, has an inheritance in the kingdom of Christ and God.　　1 Cor. 6:9

6 ᴿLet no one deceive you with empty words, for because of these thingsᴿthe wrath of God comes uponᴿthe sons of disobedience.　　Col. 2:8 • Rom. 1:18; Col. 3:6 • Eph. 2:2

7 Therefore do not be ᴿpartakers with them;　　[Eph. 3:6]

8 for ᴿyou were formerly ᴿdarkness, but now you are light in the Lord; walk asᴿchildren of light　　Eph. 2:2 • Acts 26:18 • Luke 16:8

9 (for the fruit of the light *consists* in all goodness and righteousness and truth),

10 ᵀtryingᴿto learn what is pleasing to the Lord.　　*proving what* • [Rom. 12:2]

11 Andᴿdo not participate in the unfruitful ᴿdeeds ofᴿdarkness, but instead evenᴬexpose them;　　1 Cor. 5:9 • Rom. 13:12 • Acts 26:18 • *reprove*

12 for it is disgraceful even to speak of the things which are done by them in secret.

Walk as Children of Light

13 But all things become visible when they areᴬexposed by the light, for everything that becomes visible is light.　　*reproved*

14 For this reasonᴬit says,　　*He* "Awakeᴿ, sleeper,　　Is. 26:19; [Rom. 13:11] ★ And arise fromᴿthe dead,　　Eph. 2:1 And Christ will shine on you."

15 ThereforeᵀTbe careful how you walk, not as unwise men, but as wise,　　*look carefully*

16 ᵀmaking the most of your time, because ᴿthe days are evil.　　*redeeming the time* • [Gal. 1:4]

17 So then do not be foolish, butᴿunderstand what the will of the Lord is.　　Rom. 12:2

Be Filled with the Spirit

18 And do not get drunk with wine,ᵀfor that isᴿdissipation, but beᴿfilled with the Spirit,　　*in which is* • Titus 1:6 • Luke 1:15

19 speaking to one another in psalms and

⁶ Some ancient mss. read *us*

5:18 Walking in the Spirit: Filling—To be filled with the Spirit is to be controlled by the Spirit and is therefore crucial to successfully living the Christian life. Unlike the indwelling of the Spirit, filling is a repeated experience. This is underscored by the use of the present tense ("be filled") as well as by biblical examples of Christians who were filled more than once (Page 1095—Acts 2:4; 4:31). Just as important, we must observe that filling is a command to be obeyed, not an option.

hymns and spiritual songs, singing and making melody with your heart to the Lord;

20 ᴿalways giving thanks for all things in the name of our Lord Jesus Christ to ᵀGod, even the Father;   Rom. 1:8 • *the God and Father*

21 ᵀand be subject to one another in the ^fear of Christ.   *being subject • reverence*

Wives: Submit to Your Husbands

22 Wives, ᴿ*be subject* to your own husbands, ᴿas to the Lord.   1 Cor. 14:34f. • Eph. 6:5

23 For the husband is the head of the wife, as Christ also is the head of the church, He Himself *being* the Savior of the body.

24 But as the church is subject to Christ, so also the wives *ought to be* to their husbands in everything.

Husbands: Love Your Wives

25 ᴿHusbands, love your wives, just as Christ also loved the church and ᴿgave Himself up for her;   Eph. 5:28, 33 • Eph. 5:2

26 that He might sanctify her, having ᴿcleansed her by the ᴿwashing of water with ᴿthe word,   2 Pet. 1:9 • Acts 22:16 • [John 15:3]

27 that He might present to Himself the church ᵀin all her glory, having no spot or wrinkle or any such thing; but that she should be holy and blameless.   *glorious*

28 So husbands ought also to ᴿlove their own wives as their own bodies. He who loves his own wife loves himself;   Eph. 5:25

29 for no one ever hated his own flesh, but nourishes and cherishes it, just as Christ also *does* the church,

30 because we are members of His body.

31 ᴿFOR THIS CAUSE A MAN SHALL LEAVE HIS FATHER AND MOTHER, AND SHALL CLEAVE TO HIS WIFE; AND THE TWO SHALL BECOME ONE FLESH.   Gen. 2:24; Matt. 19:5; Mark 10:7f.

32 This mystery is great; but I am speaking with reference to Christ and the church.

33 Nevertheless let each individual among you also ᴿlove his own wife even as himself; and *let* the wife *see to it* that she ᵀrespect her husband.   Eph. 5:25, 28; 1 Pet. 3:7 • *fear*

CHAPTER 6

Children: Obey Your Parents

CHILDREN, ᴿ obey your parents in the Lord, for this is right.   Prov. 6:20; 23:22

2 ᴿHONOR YOUR FATHER AND MOTHER (which is the first commandment with a promise),   Ex. 20:12; Deut. 5:16

3 THAT IT MAY BE WELL WITH YOU, AND THAT YOU MAY LIVE LONG ON THE EARTH.

The next most important question is: How can someone be filled with the Spirit? The prerequisites are simply confession of sin and yielding to God. The former means to agree with God about the person's sin; the latter means primarily dedication of himself to God. As the believer chooses to obey in these areas, he is filled with the Spirit and enabled to manifest Christlike character. This obedience may be accompanied by prayer but is not necessarily so.

The certainty of being filled with the Spirit may be confirmed by the believer's faith and life. The believer must, of course, believe God's Word that meeting the conditions will result in the filling. The Spirit-filled person will exhibit the Christlike character described in Galatians 5:22, 23 as the fruit of the Spirit. Included in that list are all the vibrant, attractive qualities desired by all Christians. How delightful it is that any Christian may possess them and be transformed by the filling of the Spirit.

Now turn to Page 24—THE CHRISTIAN'S GUIDE: Facing Problems in the New Life.

5:25 The Relationship of the Church to Christ—The wonderful relationship that exists between Christ and the church was initiated by Christ who loved the church and gave Himself for it. The intimacies of that relationship are described with seven figures:

a. "The shepherd and the sheep" emphasizes both the warm leadership and protection of Christ and the helplessness and dependency of believers (Page 1076—John 10:1–18).

b. "The vine and the branches" points out the necessity for Christians to depend on Christ's sustaining strength for growth (Page 1082—John 15:1–8).

c. "Christ as high priest" and "the church as a kingdom of priests" stresses the joyful worship, fellowship, and service which the church can render to God through Christ (Page 1241—Heb. 5:1–10; 7:1; 8:6; Page 1261—1 Pet. 2:5–9; Page 1293—Rev. 1:6).

d. "The cornerstone and building stones" accents the foundational value of Christ to everything the church is and does, as well as Christ's value to the unity of believers. Love is to be the mortar which solidly holds the living stones together (Page 1150—1 Cor. 3:9; 13:1–13; Page 1186—Eph. 2:19–22; Page 1261—1 Pet. 2:5).

e. "The head and many-membered body" is frequently used in Scripture to illustrate several tremendous truths: the church is a vibrant organism, not merely an organization; it draws its vitality and direction from Christ, the head; and each believer has a unique and necessary place in its growth (Page 1158—1 Cor. 12:12, 13, 27; Page 1187—Eph. 4:4).

f. "The last Adam and new creation" presents Christ as the initiator of a new creation of believers as Adam was of the old creation (Page 1160—1 Cor. 15:22, 45; Page 1168—2 Cor. 5:17).

g. "The bridegroom and bride" beautifully emphasizes the intimate fellowship and co-ownership existing between Christ and the church (Eph. 5:25–33; Page 1305—Rev. 19:7, 8; 21:9).

You have now completed The Christian's Guide to the New Life.

4 And,[R] fathers, do not provoke your children to anger; but bring them up in the discipline and instruction of the Lord.   Col. 3:21

Service on the Job

5 Slaves, be obedient to those who are your [T]masters according to the flesh, with fear and trembling, in the sincerity of your heart, as to Christ;   earthly masters, with fear
6 not [T]by way of eyeservice, as menpleasers, but as slaves of Christ, doing the will of God from the[T]heart.   according to · soul
7 With good will[T]render service, as to the Lord, and not to men,   rendering
8 knowing that whatever good thing each one does, this he will receive back from the Lord, whether slave or free.
9 And, masters, do the same things to them, and give up threatening, knowing that [R]both their Master and yours is in heaven, and there is no partiality with Him.   Col. 4:1

Put On the Armor of God

10 Finally,[R]be strong in the Lord, and in the strength of His might.   1 Cor. 16:13
11 [R]Put on the full armor of God, that you may be able to stand firm against the [R]schemes of the devil.   [Rom. 13:12] · Eph. 4:14
12 For our struggle is not against flesh and blood, but against the rulers, against the powers, against the world forces of this [R]darkness, against the spiritual forces of wickedness in the heavenly places.   Col. 1:13
13 Therefore, take up[R]the full armor of God, that you may be able to[R]resist in[R]the evil day, and having done everything, to stand firm.   Eph. 6:11 · [James 4:7] · Eph. 5:16
14 Stand firm therefore, [R]HAVING GIRDED

7 Some ancient mss. read I may speak it boldly

YOUR LOINS WITH TRUTH, and HAVING PUT ON THE BREASTPLATE OF RIGHTEOUSNESS, Is. 11:5
15 and having shod YOUR FEET WITH THE PREPARATION OF THE GOSPEL OF PEACE;
16 in addition to all, taking up the shield of faith with which you will be able to extinguish all the flaming missiles of the evil one.
17 And take[R]THE HELMET OF SALVATION, and the [R]sword of the Spirit, which is[R]the word of God.   Is. 59:17 · Is. 49:2 · Eph. 5:26

Pray for Boldness

18 With all[R]prayer and petition[T]pray at all times in the Spirit, and with this in view,[T]be on the alert with all perseverance and petition for all the saints,   Phil. 4:6 · praying · being
19 and[R]pray on my behalf, that utterance may be given to me in the opening of my mouth, to make known with[R]boldness the mystery of the gospel,   Col. 4:3 · 2 Cor. 3:12
20 for which I am an ambassador in [T]chains; that [7]in proclaiming it I may speak boldly,[R]as I ought to speak.   a chain · Col. 4:4

Conclusion

21 [R]But that you also may know about my circumstances, how I am doing,[R]Tychicus, [R]the beloved brother and faithful minister in the Lord, will make everything known to you.   Eph. 6:21, 22 · Acts 20:4 · Col. 4:7
22 And I have sent him to you for this very purpose, so that you may know about us, and that he may comfort your hearts.
23 [R]Peace be to the brethren, and[R]love with faith, from God the Father and the Lord Jesus Christ.   Rom. 15:33 · Gal. 5:6; 1 Thess. 5:8
24 Grace be with all those who love our Lord Jesus Christ with a love incorruptible.

6:4 The Role of the Parents—The father is the parent responsible for setting the pattern for the child's obedience in the family. Any disciplining the mother does is an extension of the father's authority in the home. The husband and father must take leadership in this area of the family, and the wife and mother must be in submission. The father's responsibility is set forth in two ways: First, what the father is not to do—"do not provoke your children to anger." He is not to over-discipline them or reign in terror, with the result that the child can only react in a blind outbreak of rage. Second, what the father is to do—"but bring them up in the discipline and instruction of the Lord." To "bring them up" involves three ideas:
a. It is a continuous job. As long as the child is a dependent, the father is to be responsible for providing for the child so that he becomes what God wants him to be.
b. It is a loving job. To "bring up" means literally to nourish tenderly; children should be objects of tender, loving care.
c. It is a twofold job involving nurture (lit., child-training)—all that a child needs for his development physically, mentally, and spiritually, and admonition (lit., corrective) discipline of the Lord.
   The father is God's constituted home authority who is to discipline the child when he does not obey as God intends. The father who does not discipline his children is a father who is undisciplined himself and disobedient to God's will. A child's disobedience is not to be tolerated. See Exodus 21:15–17; Deuteronomy 21:18–21; Proverbs 13:24; 19:18; 22:15; 23:13, 14; 29:15–17.
   Now turn to Page 625—Prov. 22:6: A Prescription for Rearing Children.

PHILIPPIANS

THE BOOK OF PHILIPPIANS

Paul writes a thank-you note to the believers at Philippi for their help in his hour of need, and he uses the occasion to send along some instruction on Christian unity. His central thought is simple: Only in Christ are real unity and joy possible. With Christ as your model of humility and service, you can enjoy a oneness of purpose, attitude, goal, and labor—a truth which Paul illustrates from his own life, and one the Philippians desperately need to hear. Within their own ranks, fellow workers in the Philippian church are at odds, hindering the work in proclaiming new life in Christ. Because of this, Paul exhorts the church to "stand firm . . . live in harmony . . . rejoice in the Lord always . . . by prayer and supplication with thanksgiving let your requests be made known . . . and the peace of God . . . shall guard your hearts and minds in Christ Jesus" (4:1, 2, 4, 6, 7).

This epistle is called *Pros Philippesious*, "To the Philippians." The church at Philippi was the first church Paul founded in Macedonia.

THE AUTHOR OF PHILIPPIANS

The external and internal evidence for the Pauline authorship of Philippians is very strong, and there is scarcely any doubt that anyone but Paul wrote it.

THE TIME OF PHILIPPIANS

In 356 B.C., King Philip of Macedonia (the father of Alexander the Great) took this town and expanded it, renaming it Philippi. The Romans captured it in 168 B.C.; and in 42 B.C., the defeat of the forces of Brutus and Cassius by those of Anthony and Octavian (later Augustus) took place outside the city. Octavian turned Philippi into a Roman colony (cf. Acts 16:12) and a military outpost. The citizens of this colony were regarded as citizens of Rome and given a number of special privileges. Because Philippi was a military city and not a commercial center, there were not enough Jews for a synagogue when Paul came (Acts 16:13).

Paul's "Macedonian Call" in Troas during his second missionary journey led to his ministry in Philippi with the conversion of Lydia and others. Paul and Silas were beaten and imprisoned, but this resulted in the conversion of the Philippian jailer. The magistrates were placed in a dangerous position by beating Roman citizens without a trial (Acts 16:37–40),

and that embarrassment may have prevented future reprisals against the new Christians in Philippi. Paul visited the Philippians again on his third missionary journey (Acts 20:1, 6). When they heard of his Roman imprisonment, the Philippian church sent Epaphroditus with financial help (4:18); they had helped Paul in this way on at least two other occasions (4:16). Epaphroditus almost died of an illness, yet remained with Paul long enough for the Philippians to receive word of his malady. Upon his recovery, Paul sent this letter back with him to Philippi (2:25–30).

Silas, Timothy, Luke, and Paul first came to Philippi in A.D. 51, eleven years before Paul wrote this letter. Philippians 1:13 and 4:22 suggest that it was written from Rome, although some commentators argue for Caesarea or Ephesus. Paul's life was at stake, and he was evidently awaiting the verdict of the Imperial Court (2:20–26).

THE CHRIST OF PHILIPPIANS

The great *kenosis* passage is one of several portraits of Christ in this epistle. In chapter 1, Paul sees Christ as his life ("For to me, to live is Christ," 1:21). In chapter 2, Christ is the model of true humility ("Have this attitude in yourselves which was also in Christ Jesus," 2:5). Chapter 3 presents Him as the One ("who will transform the body of our humble state into conformity with the body of His glory," 3:21). In chapter 4, He is the source of Paul's power over circumstances ("I can do all things through Him who strengthens me," 4:13).

KEYS TO PHILIPPIANS

Key Word: To Live Is Christ—Central to Philippians is the concept of "For to me, to live is Christ, and to die is gain" (1:21). Every chapter resounds with the theme of the centrality of Jesus in the Christian's life. High points include the following: "Have this attitude in yourselves, which was also in Christ Jesus" (2:5); "I count all things to be loss in view of the surpassing value of knowing Christ Jesus" (3:8); and "I can do all things through Him who strengthens me" (4:13).

Key Verses: Philippians 1:21 and 4:12—"For to me, to live is Christ, and to die is gain" (1:21).

"I know how to get along with humble means, and I also know how to live in prosperity; in any and every circumstance I have

learned the secret of being filled and going hungry, both of having abundance and suffering need" (4:12).

Key Chapter: Philippians 2—The grandeur of the truth of the New Testament seldom exceeds the revelation of the humility of Jesus Christ when He left heaven to become a servant of man. Christ is clearly the Christian's example, and Paul encourages "Have this attitude in yourselves which was also in Christ Jesus" (2:5).

SURVEY OF PHILIPPIANS

Philippians is the epistle of joy and encouragement in the midst of adverse circumstances. Paul freely expresses his fond affection for the Philippians, appreciates their consistent testimony and support, and lovingly urges them to center their actions and thoughts on the pursuit of the person and power of Christ. Paul also seeks to correct the problems of disunity and rivalry (2:2–4) and to prevent the problems of legalism and antinomianism (3:1–19). Philippians focuses on: Paul's account of his present circumstances (1); Paul's appeal to have the attitude of Christ (2); Paul's appeal to have the knowledge of Christ (3); Paul's appeal to have the peace of Christ (4).

Paul's Account of His Present Circumstances (1): Paul's usual salutation (1:1, 2) is followed by his thanksgiving, warm regard, and prayer on behalf of the Philippians (1:3–11). For years, they have participated in the apostle's ministry, and he prays for their continued growth in the real knowledge of Christ. Paul shares the circumstances of his imprisonment and rejoices in the spread of the gospel in spite of and because of his situation (1:12–26). As he considers the outcome of his approaching trial, he expresses his willingness to "depart and be with Christ" (1:23) or to continue in

ministry. Paul encourages the Philippians to remain steadfast in the face of opposition and coming persecution (1:27–30).

Paul's Appeal to Have the Attitude of Christ (2): Paul exhorts the Philippians to have a spirit of unity and mutual concern by embracing the attitude of humility (2:1–4), the greatest example of which is the incarnation and crucifixion of Christ (2:5–11). The *kenosis* or "emptying," of Christ does not mean that He divested Himself of His deity, but that He withheld His preincarnate glory and voluntarily restricted His use of certain attributes (e.g., omnipresence and omniscience). Paul asks the Philippians to apply this attitude to their lives (2:12–18), and he gives two more examples of sacrifice, the ministries of Timothy and Epaphroditus (2:19–30).

Paul's Appeal to Have the Knowledge of Christ (3): It appears that Paul is about to close his letter ("Finally, my brethren," 3:1) when he launches into a warning about the continuing problem of legalism (3:1–9). Paul refutes this teaching with revealing autobiographical details about his previous attainment in Judaism. Compared to the goal of knowing Christ, those pursuits are as nothing. True righteousness is received through faith, not by mechanical obedience to any law. Paul yearns for the promised attainment of the resurrected body.

Paul's Appeal to Have the Peace of Christ (4): In a series of exhortations, Paul urges the Philippians to have peace with the brethren by living a life-style of unity, prayerful dependence, and holiness (4:13). In 4:4–9, Paul describes the secrets of having the peace of God as well as peace with God. He then rejoices over their gift, but explains that the power of Christ enables him to live above his circumstances (4:10–20). This joyous letter from prison closes with greetings and a benediction (4:21–23).

FOCUS	ACCOUNT OF CIRCUMSTANCES	THE MIND OF CHRIST	THE KNOWLEDGE OF CHRIST	THE PEACE OF CHRIST
REFERENCE	1:1——————————2:1		——————3:1———————	4:1——————————4:23
DIVISION	PARTAKE OF CHRIST	PEOPLE OF CHRIST	PURSUIT OF CHRIST	POWER OF CHRIST
TOPIC	SUFFERING	SUBMISSION	SALVATION	SANCTIFICATION
	EXPERIENCE	EXAMPLES	EXHORTATION	
LOCATION	ROME			
TIME	C. A.D. 62			

OUTLINE OF PHILIPPIANS

CHAPTER 1

Paul's Prayer of Thanksgiving

PAUL and Timothy, bond-servants of Christ Jesus, to all the saints in Christ Jesus who are in Philippi, including the overseers and deacons: *holy ones* • Acts 16:12 • Acts 20:28

2 Grace to you and peace from God our Father and the Lord Jesus Christ.

3 I thank my God in all my remembrance of you,   Rom. 1:8

4 always offering prayer with joy in my every prayer for you all,   Rom. 1:9

5 in view of your participation in the gospel from the first day until now.

6 For I am confident of this very thing, that He who began a good work in you will perfect it until the day of Christ Jesus.

7 For it is only right for me to feel this way about you all, because I have you in my heart, since both in my imprisonment and in the defense and confirmation of the gospel, you all are partakers of grace with me.

8 For God is my witness, how I long for you all with the affection of Christ Jesus.

9 And this I pray, that your love may abound still more and more in real knowledge and all discernment,   1 Thess. 3:12

10 so that you may approve the things that are excellent, in order to be sincere and blameless until the day of Christ;

11 having been filled with the fruit of righteousness which *comes* through Jesus Christ, to the glory and praise of God.

Paul's Afflictions Promote the Gospel

12 Now I want you to know, brethren, that my circumstances have turned out for the greater progress of the gospel,

13 so that my imprisonment in *the cause of* Christ has become well known through-

out the whole ¹praetorian guard and to everyone else,   *bonds* • Acts 28:30

14 and that most of the brethren, trusting in the Lord because of my imprisonment, have far more courage to speak the word of God without fear.   *bonds* • Acts 4:31; 2 Cor. 3:12

15 Some, to be sure, are preaching Christ even from envy and strife, but some also from good will;   2 Cor. 11:13

16 ²the latter *do it* out of love, knowing that I am appointed for the defense of the gospel;   Phil. 1:5, 7, 12, 27; 2:22; 4:3, 15

17 the former proclaim Christ out of selfish ambition, rather than from pure motives, thinking to cause me distress in my imprisonment.   *not sincerely* • bonds

18 What then? Only that in every way, whether in pretense or in truth, Christ is proclaimed; and in this I rejoice, yes, and I will rejoice.

Paul's Afflictions Exalt the Lord

19 For I know that this shall turn out for my deliverance through your prayers and the provision of the Spirit of Jesus Christ,

20 according to my earnest expectation and hope, that I shall not be put to shame in anything, but *that* with all boldness, Christ shall even now, as always, be exalted in my body, whether by life or by death.

21 For to me, to live is Christ, and to die is gain.   [Gal. 2:20]

22 But if I am to live on in the flesh, this will mean fruitful labor for me; and I do not know which to choose.   *what I shall choose*

23 But I am hard-pressed from both *directions,* having the desire to depart and be with Christ, for *that* is very much better;

24 yet to remain on in the flesh is more necessary for your sake.

25 And convinced of this, I know that I shall remain and continue with you all for your progress and joy in the faith,

26 so that your proud confidence in me may abound in Christ Jesus through my coming to you again.   2 Cor. 5:12; 7:4; Phil. 2:16

¹ Or, *governor's palace*
² Some later mss. reverse the order of vv. 16 and 17

Paul's Exhortation to the Afflicted

27 Only conduct yourselves in a manner worthy of the gospel of Christ; so that whether I come and see you or remain absent, I may hear of you that you are standing firm in one spirit, with one mind striving together for the faith of the gospel;

28 in no way alarmed by *your* opponents—which is a ᴿsign of destruction for them, but of salvation for you, and that *too*, from God.   2 Thess. 1:5

29 For to you ᴿit has been granted for Christ's sake, not only to believe in Him, but also to suffer for His sake,   [Matt. 5:11, 12]

30 experiencing the same conflict which you saw in me, and now hear *to be* in me.

CHAPTER 2

Paul's Exhortation to Humility

IF therefore there is any encouragement in Christ, if there is any consolation of love, if there is any fellowship of the Spirit, if any ᵀaffection and compassion,   *inward parts*

2 make my joy complete by being of the same mind, maintaining the same love, united in spirit, intent on one purpose.

3 Do nothing fromᴬselfishness or empty conceit, but with humility of mind letᴿeach of you regard one another as more important than himself;   *contentiousness* • Rom. 12:10

4 ᴿdo not *merely* look out for your own personal interests, but also for the interests of others.   Rom. 15:1f.

Christ's Example of Humility

5 Have this attitudeᴬin yourselves which was also inᴿChrist Jesus,   *among* • Phil. 1:1

6 who, although Heᴿexisted in the form of God,ᴿdid not regard equality with God a thing to be grasped,   John 1:1 • John 5:18

7 but ³emptiedᴿHimself, taking the form of aᴿbond-servant, *and* being made in the likeness of men.   2 Cor. 8:9 • Matt. 20:28

8 And being found in appearance as a man, He humbled Himself by becomingᴿobedient to the point of death, even deathᵀon a cross.   Matt. 26:39; John 10:18; [Rom. 5:19] • *of*

9 Therefore also Godᴿhighly exalted Him, and bestowed on Him ᴿthe name which is above every name,   Matt. 28:18★ • Eph. 1:21

10 that at the name of Jesus EVERY KNEE SHOULD BOW, of those who are in heaven, and on earth, and under the earth,

11 and that every tongue should confess that Jesus Christ isᴿLord, to the glory of God the Father.   John 13:13; [Rom. 10:9; 14:9]

12 So then, my beloved, just as you have always obeyed, not as in my presence only, but now much more in my absence, work out your salvation with fear and trembling;

13 for it is ᴿGod who is at work in you,

both to will and to workᴿfor *His* good pleasure.   Rom. 12:3; 1 Cor. 12:6; 15:10 • Eph. 1:5

14 Do all things withoutᴿgrumbling or disputing;   1 Cor. 10:10; 1 Pet. 4:9

15 that you mayᴬprove yourselves to be blameless and innocent, children of God above reproach in the midst of a crooked and perverse generation, among whom you appear as lights in the world,   *become*

16 holding fast the word of life, so that in the day of Christ I may have cause to glory because I did not run in vain nor toil in vain.

Paul's Example of Humility

17 But even if I am beingᴿpoured out as a drink offering uponᴿthe sacrifice and service of your faith, I rejoice and share my joy with you all.   2 Cor. 12:15; 2 Tim. 4:6 • Rom. 15:16

18 And you too, *I urge you*, rejoice in the same way and share your joy with me.

Timothy's Example of Humility

19 But I hopeᴬin the Lord Jesus to ᴿsend ᴿTimothy to you shortly, so that I also may be encouraged when I learn of your condition.   *trusting in* • Phil. 2:23 • Phil. 1:1

20 For I have no one *else*ᴿof kindred spirit who will genuinely be concerned for your welfare.   1 Cor. 16:10; 2 Tim. 3:10

21 For they allᴿseek after their own interests, not those of Christ Jesus.   Phil. 2:4

22 But you know of his proven worth that he served with me in the furtherance of the gospel like a child *serving* his father.

23 ᴿTherefore I hope to send him immediately, as soon as I see how things go with me;   Phil. 2:19

24 andᴿI trust in the Lord that I myself also shall be coming shortly.   Phil. 1:25

Epaphroditus's Example of Humility

25 But I thought it necessary to send to you Epaphroditus, my brother and fellow worker and fellow soldier, who is also your messenger and minister to my need;

26 because he was longing ⁴for you all and was distressed because you had heard that he was sick.

27 For indeed he was sick to the point of death, but God had mercy on him, and not on him only but also on me, lest I should have sorrow upon sorrow.

28 Therefore I have sent him all the more eagerly in order that when you see him again you may rejoice and I may be less concerned *about you*.

29 Thereforeᴿreceive him in the Lord with all joy, andᴿhold men like him in high regard;   Rom. 16:2 • 1 Cor. 16:18

³ I.e., laid aside His privileges
⁴ Some ancient mss. read *to see you all*

30 because he came close to death for the work of Christ, risking his life to complete what was deficient in your service to me.

CHAPTER 3

Warning Against Confidence in the Flesh

FINALLY, my brethren, rejoice in the Lord. To write the same things *again* is no trouble to me, and it is a safeguard for you.

2 Beware of the dogs, beware of the evil workers, beware of the false circumcision;

3 for[R]we are the *true*[T]circumcision, who worship in the Spirit of God and glory in Christ Jesus and put no confidence in the flesh, Rom. 2:29; 9:6; [Gal. 6:15] • Gr., peritome

4 although [R]I myself might have confidence even in the flesh. If anyone else has a mind to put confidence in the flesh, I far more: 2 Cor. 5:16; 11:18

5 circumcised the eighth day, of the nation of Israel, of the tribe of Benjamin, a Hebrew of Hebrews; as to the Law, a Pharisee;

6 as to zeal,[R]a persecutor of the church; as to the righteousness which is in the Law, found blameless. Acts 8:3; 22:4, 5; 26:9-11

7 But[R]whatever things were gain to me, those things I have counted as loss for the sake of Christ. [Luke 14:33]

8 More than that, I count all things to be loss in view of the surpassing value of [T]knowing[R]Christ Jesus my Lord, for whom I have suffered the loss of all things, and count them but rubbish in order that I may gain Christ, *the knowledge of* • Rom. 8:39; Phil. 1:1

9 and may be found in Him, not having[R]a righteousness of my own derived from *the* Law, but that which is through faith in Christ, the righteousness which *comes* from God on the basis of faith, Rom. 10:5

Exhortation to Know Christ

10 that I may know Him, and the power of His resurrection and the fellowship of His sufferings, being conformed to His death;

11 [T]in order that I may[R]attain to the resurrection from the dead. *if somehow* • Acts 26:7

12 Not that I have already obtained *it*, or have already become perfect, but I press on in [T]order that I may lay hold of that [A]for which also I [R]was laid hold of by Christ Jesus. *if I may even* • *because also* • Acts 9:5f.

13 Brethren, I do not regard myself as having laid hold of *it* yet; but one thing *I do*: [R]forgetting what *lies* behind and reaching forward to what *lies* ahead, Luke 9:62

14 I press on toward the goal for the prize of the upward call of God in Christ Jesus.

15 Let us therefore, as many as are[A]perfect, have this attitude; and if in anything you have a different attitude,[R]God will reveal that also to you; *mature* • [John 6:45]

16 however, let us keep living by that same *standard* to which we have attained.

Warning Against Living for the Flesh

17 Brethren,[R]join in following my example, and observe those who walk according to the pattern you have in us. 1 Cor. 4:16; 11:1

18 For many walk, of whom I often told you, and now tell you even weeping, *that they are* enemies of the cross of Christ,

19 whose end is destruction, whose god is *their*[T]appetite, and *whose*[R]glory is in their shame, who[R]set their minds on earthly things. *belly* • Rom. 6:21 • Rom. 8:5f.; Col. 3:2

20 For our[T]citizenship is in heaven, from which also we eagerly[R]wait for a Savior, the Lord Jesus Christ; *commonwealth* • 1 Cor. 1:7

21 who will transform [A]the body of our humble state into conformity with[A]the body of His glory, by the exertion of the power that He has even to subject all things to Himself. *our lowly body* • *His glorious body*

CHAPTER 4

Peace with the Brethren

THEREFORE, my beloved brethren[T]whom I long *to see*, my joy and crown, so stand firm in the Lord, my beloved. *and longed for*

2 I urge Euodia and I urge Syntyche to live in harmony in the Lord.

3 Indeed, true comrade, I ask you also to help these women who have shared my struggle in *the cause of* the gospel, together with Clement also, and the rest of my[R]fellow workers, whose[R]names are in the book of life. Phil. 2:25 • Luke 10:20

Peace with the Lord

4 [R]Rejoice in the Lord always; again I will say, rejoice! Phil. 3:1

5 Let your forbearing *spirit* be known to all men.[R]The Lord is[A]near. Heb. 10:37 • *at hand*

6 Be anxious for nothing, but in everything by [R]prayer and supplication with thanksgiving let your requests be made known to God. Eph. 6:18; 1 Tim. 2:1; 5:5

4:6 Thanksgiving—The importance and spiritual benefits of thanksgiving in our prayer life cannot be overemphasized. The Bible tells us God resists the proud, but gives grace to the humble (Page 1255—James 4:6). But the question is: How do you become humble? It is done by being thankful! A good rule is to be anxious (worried) for nothing (Phil. 4:6), be prayerful in all things (Page 1208—1 Thess. 5:18), and be thankful for everything. It was the sin of thanklessness that caused the ancient world to plunge into the terrible depths of sexual depravity (Page

(continued on next page)

7 And the peace of God, which surpasses all[T]comprehension, shall guard your hearts and your minds in Christ Jesus.   *mind*

8 Finally, brethren, whatever is true, whatever is honorable, whatever is right, whatever is pure, whatever is lovely, whatever is[A]of good repute, if there is any excellence and if anything worthy of praise, let your mind dwell on these things.   *attractive*

9 The things you have learned and received and heard and seen[R]in me, practice these things; and[R]the God of peace shall be with you.   Phil. 3:17 • Rom. 15:33

Peace in All Circumstances

10 But I rejoiced in the Lord greatly, that now at last[R]you have revived your concern for me; indeed, you were concerned *before*, but you lacked opportunity.   2 Cor. 11:9

11 Not that I speak[T]from want; for I have learned to be[A]content in whatever circumstances I am.   *according to • self-sufficient*

12 I know how to get along with humble means, and I also know how to live in prosperity; in any and every circumstance I have learned the secret of being filled and going hungry,[R]both of having abundance and[R]suffering need.   1 Cor. 4:11 • 2 Cor. 11:9

13 I can do all things[T]through Him who [R]strengthens me.   *in* • [2 Cor. 12:9; Eph. 3:16]

14 Nevertheless, you have done well to [R]share *with me* in my affliction.   Heb. 10:33

15 And you yourselves also know, Philippians, that at the[R]first preaching of the gospel, after I departed from Macedonia, no church shared with me in the matter of giving and receiving but you alone;   Phil. 1:5

16 for even in[R]Thessalonica you sent *a gift* more than once for my needs.   Acts 17:1

17 [R]Not that I seek the gift itself, but I seek for the[T]profit which increases to your account.   1 Cor. 9:11f.; 2 Cor. 9:5 • *fruit*

18 But I have received everything in full, and have an abundance; I am amply supplied, having received from Epaphroditus what you have sent, a fragrant aroma, an acceptable sacrifice, well-pleasing to God.

19 And my God shall supply[A]all your needs according to His[R]riches in glory in Christ Jesus.   *every need of yours* • Rom. 2:4

Conclusion

20 Now to[R]our God and Father *be* the glory forever and ever. Amen.   Gal. 1:4

21 Greet every saint in Christ Jesus.[R]The brethren who are with me greet you. Gal. 1:2

22 All the [R]saints greet you, especially those of Caesar's household.   Acts 9:13

23 [R]The grace of the Lord Jesus Christ[R]be with your spirit.   Rom. 16:20 • 2 Tim. 4:22

(continued from previous page)

1132—Rom. 1:21). In the Old Testament a special group of priests was appointed to do nothing else but praise and thank the Lord (Page 444—2 Chr. 31:2).

There are two main things we are to thank God for:

a. We are to thank Him for His work in Creation. David reminds us concerning this area of thanksgiving in Psalm 100. Later, John the apostle tells us we will thank God for His work in Creation throughout all eternity. Note the words of this song of praise: "Worthy art Thou, our Lord and our God, to receive glory and honor and power; for Thou didst create all things, and because of Thy will they existed, and were created" (Page 1296—Rev. 4:11).

b. We are to thank Him for His work in redemption. John also informs us that our second song in heaven will feature thanksgiving for God's work in redemption: "And they sang a new song, saying, 'Worthy art Thou to take the book, and to break its seals; for Thou wast slain, and didst purchase for God with Thy blood *men* from every tribe and tongue and people and nation'" (Page 1296—Rev. 5:9).

Now turn to Page 621—Prov. 16:3: Commitment.

COLOSSIANS

THE BOOK OF COLOSSIANS

If Ephesians can be labeled the epistle portraying the "Church of Christ," then Colossians must surely be the "Christ of the Church." Ephesians focuses on the Body; Colossians focuses on the Head. Like Ephesians, the little Book of Colossians divides neatly in half with the first portion doctrinal (1 and 2) and the second practical (3 and 4). Paul's purpose is to show that Christ is pre-eminent—first and foremost in everything—and the Christian's life should reflect that priority. Because believers are rooted in Him, alive in Him, hidden in Him, and complete in Him, it is utterly inconsistent for them to live life without Him. Clothed in His love, with His peace ruling in their hearts, they are equipped to make Christ first in every area of life.

This epistle became known as *Pros Kolossaeis*, "To the Colossians," because of 1:2. Paul also wanted it to be read in the neighboring church at Laodicea (4:16).

THE AUTHOR OF COLOSSIANS

The external testimony to the Pauline authorship of Colossians is ancient and consistent, and the internal evidence also is very good. It not only claims to be written by Paul (1:1, 23; 4:18), but the personal details and close parallels with Ephesians and Philemon make the case even stronger. Nevertheless, the authenticity of this letter has been challenged on the internal grounds of vocabulary and thought. In its four chapters, Colossians uses fifty-five Greek words that do not appear in Paul's other epistles. However, Paul commanded a wide vocabulary; and the circumstances and subject of this epistle, especially the references to the Colossian heresy, account for these additional words. The high Christology of Colossians has been compared to John's later concept that Christ is the Logos (cf. 1:15–23 and John 1:1–18), with the conclusion that these concepts were too late for Paul's time. However, there is no reason to assume that Paul was unaware of Christ's work as creator, especially in view of Philippians 2:5–11. It is also wrong to assume that the heresy refuted in Colossians 2 refers to the fully developed form of Gnosticism that did not appear until the second century. The parallels only indicate that Paul was dealing with an early form of Gnosticism.

THE TIME OF COLOSSIANS

Colossae was a minor city about one hundred miles east of Ephesus in the region of the seven Asian churches of Revelation 1—3. Located in the fertile Lycus Valley by a mountain pass on the road from Ephesus to the East, Colossae once was a populous center of commerce, famous for its glossy black wool. By the time of Paul, it had been eclipsed by its neighboring cities, Laodicea and Hierapolis (cf. 4:13), and was on the decline. Apart from this letter, Colossae exerted almost no influence on early church history. It is evident from 1:4–8 and 2:1 that Paul had never visited the church at Colossae, which was founded by Epaphras. On his third missionary journey, Paul devoted almost three years to an Asian ministry centered in Ephesus (cf. Acts 19:10; 20:31), and Epaphras probably came to Christ during this time. He carried the gospel to the cities in the Lycus Valley and years later came to visit Paul in his imprisonment (4:12, 13; Philem. 23).

Colossians, Philemon, and Ephesians were evidently written about the same time and under the same circumstances, judging by the overlapping themes and personal names (cf. Col. 4:9–17 and Philem. 2, 10, 23, 24). Although Caesarea and Ephesus have been suggested as the location of authorship, the bulk of the evidence indicates that Paul wrote all four Prison Epistles during his first Roman imprisonment (see "The Time of Ephesians" and "The Time of Philippians"). If so, Paul wrote it in A.D. 60 or 61 and sent it with Tychicus and the converted slave Onesimus to Colossae (4:7–9; see Eph. 6:21; Philem. 10–12).

Epaphroditus's visit and report about the conditions in Colossae prompted this letter. Although the Colossians had not yet succumbed (2:1–5), an encroaching heresy was threatening the predominantly gentile (1:21, 27; 2:13) Colossian church. The nature of this heresy can only be deduced from Paul's incidental references to it in his refutation in 2:8–23. It was apparently a religious system that combined elements from Greek speculation (2:4, 8–10), Jewish legalism (2:11–17), and Oriental mysticism (2:18–23). It involved a low view of the body (2:20–23) and probably nature as a whole. Circumcision, dietary regulations, and ritual observances were included in this system, which utilized asceticism, worship of angels as intermediaries, and mystical

experiences as an approach to the spiritual realm. Any attempt to fit Christ into such a system would undermine His person and redemptive work.

THE CHRIST OF COLOSSIANS

This singularly Christological book is centered on the cosmic Christ—"the head over all rule and authority" (2:10), the Lord of creation (1:16, 17), and the Author of reconciliation (1:20–22; 2:13–15). He is the basis for the believer's hope (1:5, 23, 27), the source of the believer's power for a new life (1:11, 29), the believer's Redeemer and Reconciler (1:14, 20–22; 2:11–15), the embodiment of full deity (1:15, 19; 2:9), the Creator and Sustainer of all things (1:16, 17), the Head of the church (1:18), the resurrected God-Man (1:18; 3:1), and the all-sufficient Savior (1:26; 2:3, 10; 3:1–4).

KEYS TO COLOSSIANS

Key Word: The Preeminence of Christ—The resounding theme in Colossians is the preeminence and sufficiency of Christ in all things. The believer is complete in Him alone and lacks nothing because "in Him all the fulness of Deity dwells in bodily form" (2:9); He has "all the treasures of wisdom and knowledge" (2:3). There is no need for speculation, mystical visions, or ritualistic regulations as though faith in Christ were insufficient. Paul's predominant purpose, then, is to refute a threatening heresy that is devaluing Christ. This false teaching is countered by a positive presentation of His true attributes and accomplishments. A proper view of Christ is the antidote for heresy. Paul also writes this epistle to encourage the Colossians to "continue in the faith firmly established and steadfast" (1:23), so that they will grow

and bear fruit in the knowledge of Christ (1:10). A firm adherence to the true gospel will give them stability and resistance to opposing influences.

Key Verses: Colossians 2:9, 10 and 3:1, 2—"For in Him all the fulness of Deity dwells in bodily form, and in Him you have been made complete, and He is the head over all rule and authority" (2:9, 10).

"If then you have been raised up with Christ, keep seeking the things above, where Christ is, seated at the right hand of God. Set your mind on the things above, not on the things that are on earth" (3:1, 2).

Key Chapter: Colossians 3—Chapter 3 links the three themes of Colossians (see "Key Word") together showing their cause and effect relationships. Because the believer is risen with Christ (3:1–4), he is to put off the old man and put on the new (3:5–17), which will result in holiness in all relationships (3:18–25).

SURVEY OF COLOSSIANS

Colossians is perhaps the most Christ-centered book in the Bible. In it Paul stresses the preeminence of the person of Christ and the completeness of the salvation He provides, in order to combat a growing heresy that is threatening the church at Colossae. This heresy seeks to devaluate Christ by elevating speculation, ritualism, mysticism, and asceticism. But Christ, the Lord of creation and Head of the Body, is completely sufficient for every spiritual and practical need of the believer. The last half of this epistle explores the application of these principles to daily life, because doctrinal truth (1 and 2) must bear fruit in practical conduct (3 and 4). The two major topics are: supremacy of Christ (1 and 2) and submission to Christ (3 and 4).

Supremacy of Christ (1 and 2): Paul's greet-

FOCUS	SUPREMACY OF CHRIST			SUBMISSION TO CHRIST		
REFERENCE	1:1 ——— 1:15 ——— 2:4 ———			3:1 ——— 3:5 ——— 4:7 ——— 4:18		
DIVISION	INTRODUCTION	PREEMINENCE OF CHRIST	FREEDOM IN CHRIST	POSITION OF THE BELIEVER	PRACTICE OF THE BELIEVER	CONCLUSION
TOPIC	DOCTRINAL			PRACTICAL		
	WHAT CHRIST DID FOR US			WHAT CHRIST DOES THROUGH US		
LOCATION	ROME					
TIME	A.D. 60–61					

ing (1:1, 2) is followed by an unusually extended thanksgiving (1:3–8) and prayer (1:9–14) on behalf of the believers at Colossae. Paul expresses his concern that the Colossians come to a deeper understanding of the person and power of Christ. Even here Paul begins to develop his major theme of the preeminence of Christ, but the most potent statement of this theme is in 1:15–23. He is supreme both in creation (1:15–18) and in redemption (1:19–23), and this majestic passage builds a positive case for Christ as the most effective refutation of the heresy that will be exposed in chapter 2. Paul describes his own ministry of proclaiming the mystery of "Christ in you, the hope of glory" (1:27) to the Gentiles and assures his readers that although he has not personally met them, he strongly desires that they become deeply rooted in Christ alone, who is preeminent in the Church (1:24—2:3). This is especially important in view of false teachers who would defraud them through enticing rationalisms (2:4–7), vain philosophy (2:8–10),

legalistic rituals (2:11–17), improper mysticism (2:18, 19), and useless asceticism (2:20–23). In each case, Paul contrasts the error with the corresponding truth about Christ.

Submission to Christ (3 and 4): The believer's union with Christ in His death, resurrection, and exaltation is the foundation upon which his earthly life must be built (3:1–4). Because of his death with Christ, the Christian must regard himself as dead to the old sins and put them aside (3:5–11); because of his resurrection with Christ, the believer must regard himself as alive to Him in righteousness and put on the new qualities that are prompted by Christian love (3:12–17). Turning from the inward life (3:1–17) to the outward life (3:18—4:6), Paul outlines the transformation that faith in Christ should make in relationships inside and outside the home. This epistle concludes with a statement concerning its bearers (Tychicus and Onesimus), greetings and instructions, and a farewell note (4:7–18).

OUTLINE OF COLOSSIANS

Part One: The Supremacy of Christ in the Church (1:1—2:23)

Part Two: The Submission to Christ in the Church (3:1—4:18)

CHAPTER 1

Paul's Greeting to the Colossians

PAUL, an apostle of Jesus Christ by the will of God, and Timothy our brother,

2 to the ᴬsaints and faithful brethren in Christ *who are* at Colossae: Grace to you and peace from God our Father.   *holy ones*

Paul's Thanksgiving for the Colossians

3 ᴿWe give thanks to God,ᴿthe Father of our Lord Jesus Christ, praying always for you,   Rom. 1:8 • Rom. 15:6; 2 Cor. 1:3

4 since we heard of your faith in Christ

Jesus and the love which you haveᴬforᴿall theᴬsaints;   *toward* • Eph. 6:18 • *holy ones*

5 because of the hope laid up for you in heaven, of which you previously heard in the word of truth,ᴬthe gospel,   *of the gospel*

6 which has come to you, just as in all the world also it is constantly bearing fruit and increasing, even as *it has been doing* in you also since the day you heard *of it* and understood the grace of God in truth;

7 just as you learned *it* from Epaphras, our beloved fellow bond-servant, who is a faithful servant of Christ on ¹our behalf,

8 and he also informed us of yourᴿlove in the Spirit.   Rom. 15:30

¹ Some later mss. read *your*

Paul's Prayer for the Colossians

9 For this reason also, since the day we heard *of it,* we have not ceased to pray for you and to ask that you may be filled with the ^knowledge of His will in all spiritual wisdom and understanding, *real knowledge*

10 so that you may^walk in a manner worthy of the Lord, to please *Him* in all respects, bearing fruit in every good work and increasing in the knowledge of God; Eph. 4:1

11 strengthened with all power, according to His glorious might, for the attaining of all steadfastness and patience; joyously

12 giving thanks to the Father, who has qualified us^to share in the inheritance of the^saints in light. *unto the portion of · holy ones*

13 For He delivered us from the^domain of darkness, and transferred us to the kingdom of^His beloved Son, *authority · the Son of His love*

14 ^in whom we have redemption, the forgiveness of sins. Rom. 3:24; Eph. 1:7

Christ Is Preeminent in Creation

15 And He is the image of the invisible God, the first-born of all creation.

16 For by Him all things were created, *both* in the heavens and on earth, visible and invisible, whether thrones or dominions or rulers or authorities—all things have been created^by Him and for Him. *through*

17 And He^is before all things, and in Him all things hold together. *has existed prior to*

18 He is also ^head of the body, the church; and He is the beginning, the first-born from the dead; so that He Himself might come to have first place in everything. Eph. 1:22

Christ Is Preeminent in Redemption

19 For it was^the *Father's* good pleasure for all the fulness to dwell in Him, Eph. 1:5

20 and through Him to reconcile all things to Himself, having made peace through the blood of His cross; through Him, *I say,* whether things on earth or things in heaven.

21 And although you were^formerly alienated and hostile in mind, *engaged* in evil deeds, Rom. 5:10; [Eph. 2:3, 12]

22 yet He has now^reconciled you in His fleshly body through death, in order to present you before Him holy and blameless and beyond reproach— 2 Cor. 5:18; [Eph. 2:16]

23 if indeed you continue in the faith firmly established and steadfast, and not moved away from the hope of the gospel that you have heard, which was proclaimed in all creation under heaven, and of which I, Paul,^was made a minister. *became*

Christ Is Preeminent in the Church

24 ^Now I rejoice in my sufferings for your sake, and in my flesh I^do my share on behalf of His body (which is the church) in filling up that which is lacking in Christ's afflictions. [Rom. 8:17] · *representatively . . . fill up*

25 Of *this church* I^was made a minister according to the^stewardship from God bestowed on me for your benefit, that I might ^fully carry out the *preaching of* the word of God, *became* · Eph. 3:2 · *make full the word of God*

26 *that is,* the mystery which has been hidden from the *past* ages and generations; but has now been manifested to His saints,

27 to whom^God willed to make known what is the riches of the glory of this mystery among the Gentiles, which is Christ in you, the hope of glory. Matt. 13:11

28 And we proclaim Him, ^admonishing every man and teaching every man^with all wisdom, that we may present every man ^complete in Christ. Acts 20:31 · *in · perfect*

29 And for this purpose also I labor, striving according to His^power, which^mightily works within me. *working · in power*

CHAPTER 2

FOR I want you to know how great a struggle I have on your behalf, and for those who are at Laodicea, and for all those who have not personally seen my face,

2 that their hearts may be encouraged, having been knit together in love, and *attaining* to all the wealth^that comes from the full assurance of understanding, *resulting* in a true knowledge of God's mystery, *that is,* Christ *Himself,* *of the full assurance*

3 in whom are hidden all^the treasures of wisdom and knowledge. Is. 11:2; [Rom. 11:33]

Freedom from Enticing Words

4 I say this in order that no one may delude you with persuasive argument.

5 For even though I am absent in body, nevertheless I am with you in spirit, rejoicing^to see your good discipline and the stability of your faith in Christ. *and seeing*

1:22 New Life Based on Christ's Death—Salvation is free, but it is not cheap. Salvation is a gift and costs me nothing, but it cost God everything—it cost Jesus His life. The wages of sin is death (separation from God). God's gift is eternal life (eternal union of the soul with God). This is possible because of the death of Jesus on Calvary's cross (Page 1136—Rom. 6:23). Jesus actually took sin's penalty for every man, woman, and child who ever has lived or ever will live. As He hung upon the cross He cried, "Eli, Eli, lama sabachthani?" Being interpreted, He cried, "My God, My God, why hast Thou forsaken Me?" (Page 994—Matt. 27:46). Jesus was separated from God the Father so that you and I do not have to be. This is the heart of the atonement. The marvel of it all is that He did this while we were His enemies: "But God demonstrates His own love toward us, in that while we were yet sinners, Christ died for us" (Page 1135—Rom. 5:8).
Now turn to Page 1113—Acts 16:31: New Life: Received by Faith.

6 As you therefore have received Christ Jesus the Lord, *so* walk in Him,

7 having been firmly ᴿrooted *and now* being built up in Him and established ²inᴬyour faith, just as you were instructed, *and* overflowing with gratitude.   Eph. 3:17 • *by*

Freedom from Vain Philosophy

8 See to it that no one takes you captive through philosophy and empty deception, according to the tradition of men, according to the elementary principles of the world, ᵀrather than according to Christ.   *and not*

9 For in Him all the ᴿfulness of Deity dwells in bodily form,   2 Cor. 5:19; Col. 1:19

10 and in Him you have been madeᴬcomplete, and He is the headᵀover allᴿrule and authority;   *full • of •* [Eph. 3:10]; Col. 2:15

Freedom from the Judgment of Men

11 and in Himᴿyou were also circumcised with a circumcision made without hands, in the removal of the body of the flesh by the circumcision of Christ;   [Rom. 2:29]; Eph. 2:11

12 having beenᴿburied with Him in baptism, in which you were also raised up with Him through faith in the working of God, who raised Him from the dead.   Rom. 6:4f.

13 And when you were dead ᴬin your transgressions and the uncircumcision of your flesh, Heᴿmade you alive together with Him, having forgiven us all our transgressions,   *by reason of •* Eph. 2:5; [Col. 2:12]

14 having canceled out the certificate of debt consisting of decrees against us *and* which was hostile to us; and He has taken it out of the way, having nailed it to the cross.

15 When He had disarmed theᴿrulers and authorities, He made a public display of them, having triumphed over them through ᴬHim.   [John 12:31; 1 Cor. 15:24] • *it*

16 Therefore let no one act as your judge in regard to food or drink or in respect to a festival or a new moon or a Sabbath day—

17 things which are ᴿa *mere* shadow of what is to come; but theᵀsubstanceᵀbelongs to Christ.   Heb. 8:5; 10:1 • *body • of Christ*

Freedom from Improper Worship

18 Let no one keep defrauding you of your prize by delighting inᴬself-abasement and the worship of the angels, taking his stand on *visions* he has seen, inflated without cause by his fleshly mind,   *humility*

19 and not holding fast to the head, from whom the entire body, being supplied and held together by the joints and ligaments, grows with a growth which is from God.

Freedom from the Doctrine of Men

20 If you have died with Christᵀto the elementary principles of the world, why, as if you were living in the world, do you submit yourself to decrees, such as,   *from*

21 "Do not handle, do not taste, do not touch!"

22 (which all *refer to* things destined to perish with the using)—in accordance with the commandments and teachings of men?

23 These are matters which have, to be sure, the appearance of wisdom in ᴿself-made religion and self-abasement and severe treatment of the body, *but are* of no value against fleshly indulgence.   Col. 2:18

CHAPTER 3
The Position of the Believer

IF then you have been ᴿraised up with Christ, keep seeking the things above, where Christ is,ᴿseated at the right hand of God.   Col. 2:12 • Ps. 110:1; Mark 16:19 ★

2 ᴬSet your mind on the things above, not on the things that are on earth.   *Be intent on*

3 For you haveᴿdied and your life is hidden with Christ in God.   [Rom. 6:2; 2 Cor. 5:14]

4 When Christ, ᴿwho is our life, is revealed,ᴿthen you also will be revealed with Him in glory.   [John 11:25; Gal. 2:20] • 1 Cor. 1:7

Put Off the Old Man

5 Therefore consider the members of your earthly body as dead toᵀimmorality, impurity, passion, evil desire, and greed, whichᵀamounts to idolatry.   *fornication • is*

6 For it is on account of these things that ᴿthe wrath of God will come,³   Rom. 1:18

7 and ᴿin them you also once walked, when you were living in them.   [Eph. 2:2]

8 But now you also,ᴿput them all aside: ᴿanger, wrath, malice, slander, *and* abusive speech from your mouth. Eph. 4:22 • Eph. 4:31

9 Do not lie to one another, since you laid aside the old self with its *evil* practices,

10 and have put on the new self who is being renewed to a true knowledge according to the image of the One who created him

11 —a *renewal* in whichᴿthere is no *distinction between* Greek and Jew, ᴿcircumcised and uncircumcised, barbarian, Scythian, slave and freeman, butᴿChrist is all, and in all.   Rom. 10:12 • 1 Cor. 7:19 • Eph. 1:23

Put On the New Man

12 And so, as those who have beenᴿchosen of God, holy and beloved, put on a heart of compassion, kindness, humility, gentleness and patience;   Luke 18:7

13 ᴿbearing with one another, andᴿforgiving each other, whoever has a complaint against anyone; just as the Lord forgave you, so also should you.   Eph. 4:2 • Rom. 15:7

14 And beyond all these things *put on* love, which is the perfect bond of unity.

---

² Or, by
³ Some early mss. add *upon the sons of disobedience*

15 And let the peace of Christ rule in your hearts, to which┬indeed you were called in ᴿone body; and be thankful.   *also* • Eph. 2:16

16 Let the word of ⁴Christ richly dwell within you, with all wisdom teaching and admonishing one another with psalms *and* hymns *and* spiritual songs, singing with thankfulness in your hearts to God.

17 And whatever you do in word or deed, *do* all in the name of the Lord Jesus, giving thanks through Him to God the Father.

Holiness in Family Life

18 ᴿWives, be subject to your husbands, as is fitting in the Lord.   Eph. 5:22-6:9

19 ᴿHusbands, love your wives, and do not be embittered against them.   [1 Pet. 3:7]

20 ᴿChildren, be obedient to your parents in all things, for this is well-pleasing┬to the Lord.   Eph. 6:1 • *in*

21 Fathers, do not ⁵exasperate your children, that they may not lose heart.

Holiness in Work Life

22 Slaves, in all things obey those who are your masters on earth, not with external service, as those who *merely* please men, but with sincerity of heart, fearing the Lord.

23 Whatever you do, do your work heartily, as for the Lord rather than for men;

24 knowing that from the Lord you will receive the reward ofᴿthe inheritance. It is the Lord Christ whom you serve.   Acts 20:32

25 For he who does wrong will receive the consequences of the wrong which he has done, andᴿthat without partiality. Deut. 10:17

CHAPTER 4

Mᴀꜱᴛᴇʀꜱ, grant to your slaves justice and fairness,ᴿknowing that you too have a Master in heaven.   Eph. 6:9

Holiness in Public Life

2 Devote yourselves to prayer, keeping alert in it with *an attitude of* thanksgiving;

3 praying at the same timeᴿfor us as well, that God may open up to us aᴿdoor forᴿthe word, so that we may speak forth the mystery of Christ, for which I have also been imprisoned;   Eph. 6:19 • Acts 14:27 • 2 Tim. 4:2

4 in order that I may make it clearᴿin the way I ought to speak.   Eph. 6:20

5 ┬Conduct yourselves with wisdom toward ᴿoutsiders, ┬making the most of the opportunity. *Walk* • Mark 4:11 • *redeeming the time*

6 ᴿLet your speech always beᴬwith grace, seasoned, *as it were*, withᴿsalt, so that you may know how you should respond to each person.   Eph. 4:29 • *gracious* • Mark 9:50

Commendation of Tychicus

7 As to all my affairs,ᴿTychicus, ourᴿbeloved brother and faithful servant and fellow bond-servant in the Lord, will bring you information.   Acts 20:4; 2 Tim. 4:12 • Eph. 6:21

8 ᴿFor I have sent him to you for this very purpose, that you may know *about* our circumstances and that he may ᴿencourage your hearts;   Eph. 6:22 • Col. 2:2

9 ┬and with him Onesimus, *our* faithful and beloved brother, who is one of your *number.* They will inform you about the whole situation here.   *along with Onesimus*

Greetings from Paul's Friends

10 Aristarchus, my fellow prisoner, sends you his greetings; and *also* Barnabas' cousin Mark (about whom you received instructions: if he comes to you, welcome him);

11 and *also* Jesus who is called Justus; these are the only ᴿfellow workers for the kingdom of Godᴿwho are from the circumcision; and they have proved to be an encouragement to me.   Rom. 16:3 • Acts 11:2

12 Epaphras, who is one of your number, a bondslave of Jesus Christ, sends you his greetings, always laboring earnestly for you in his prayers, that you may stand perfect and fully assured in all the will of God.

13 For I bear him witness that he has a deep concern for you and for those who are inᴿLaodicea and Hierapolis.   Col. 2:1; 4:15f.

⁴ Some mss. read *the Lord;* others read *God*
⁵ Some early mss. read *provoke to anger*

3:19 The Role of the Husband—Paul tells the husband to love his wife (Page 1189—Eph. 5:25), while Peter tells the husband to dwell together with his wife (Page1263—1 Pet. 3:7). The husband cannot live with his wife as Peter says unless he loves her in the way Paul means. The love that the husband is commanded to have for the wife is not primarily sexual or emotional (though both of those concepts are involved); it is a love that loves in spite of the response (or lack of it) in the one loved. It is the kind of love that God has for the world (Page 1066—John 3:16) and is the fruit of the Spirit (Page 1181—Gal. 5:22). A husband can only love his wife properly if he is a Christian and under the control of the Holy Spirit.

The two responsibilities the husband has in the family are to dwell with his wife according to knowledge, and to render to his wife the honor which is due her because she is his wife. To "dwell together" with his wife means that the husband must take his wife into *every* aspect of his life. There are to be no areas of his life where there are signs that say, "Private, husband only—wife keep out."

The husband is to perform his two duties for a spiritual purpose: "That your prayers may not be hindered." The man who is not taking his wife into every aspect of his life and rendering to her the honor which is due her because she is his wife cannot communicate with her in the way that God intended; hence, he cannot communicate with God either. To make sure that the channel of communication with God is open, the husband must make sure that the channel of communication with his wife is open. Only in this way can he truly love his wife as God intended and manifest his headship properly.

Now turn to Page 609—Prov. 1:8: The Role of Children.

14 [R]Luke, the beloved physician, sends you his greetings, and *also* Demas.   2 Tim. 4:11

Introductions Regarding This Letter

15 Greet the brethren who are in Laodicea and also [6]Nympha and the church that is in her house.

[6] Or, *Nymphas* (masc.)

16 And when this letter is read among you, have it also read in the church of the Laodiceans; and you, for your part read my letter *that is coming* from Laodicea.

17 And say to Archippus, "Take heed to the ministry which you have received in the Lord, that you may fulfill it." *continually fulfill*

18 I, Paul, write this greeting with my own hand. Remember my imprisonment. Grace be with you.

THESSALONIANS

THE BOOK OF FIRST THESSALONIANS

Paul has many pleasant memories of the days he spent with the infant Thessalonian church. Their faith, hope, love, and perseverance in the face of persecution are exemplary. Paul's labors as a spiritual parent to the fledgling church have been richly rewarded, and his affection is visible in every line of his letter.

Paul encourages them to excel in their new-found faith, to increase in their love for one another, and to rejoice, pray, and give thanks always. He closes his letter with instruction regarding the return of the Lord, whose advent signifies hope and comfort for believers both living and dead.

Because this is the first of Paul's two canonical letters to the church at Thessalonica, it received the title *Pros Thessalonikeis A*, the "First to the Thessalonians."

THE AUTHOR OF FIRST THESSALONIANS

First Thessalonians went unchallenged as a Pauline epistle until the nineteeth century, when radical critics claimed that its dearth of doctrinal content made its authenticity suspect. But this is a weak objection on two counts: (1) the proportion of doctrinal teaching in Paul's epistles varies widely, and (2) 4:13—5:11 is a foundational passage for New Testament eschatology (future events). Paul had quickly grounded the Thessalonians in Christian doctrine, and the only problematic issue when this epistle was written concerned the matter of Christ's return. The external and internal evidence points clearly to Paul.

THE TIME OF FIRST THESSALONIANS

In Paul's time, Thessalonica was the prominent seaport and the capital of the Roman province of Macedonia. This prosperous city was located on the Via Egnatia, the main road from Rome to the East, within sight of Mount Olympus, legendary home of the Greek pantheon. Cassander expanded and strengthened this site around 315 B.C. and renamed it after his wife, the half-sister of Alexander the Great. The Romans conquered Macedonia in 168 B.C. and organized it into a single province twenty-two years later with Thessalonica as the capital city. It became a "free city" under Augustus with its own authority to appoint a governing board of magistrates who were called "politarchs." The strategic location assured Thessalonica of commercial success, and it boasted a population of perhaps 200,000 in the first century. Thessalonica survives under the shortened name Salonika.

Thessalonica had a sizable Jewish population, and the ethical monotheism of Judaism attracted many Gentiles who had become disenchanted with Greek paganism. These God-fearers quickly responded to Paul's reasoning in the synagogue when he ministered there on his second missionary journey (Acts 17:10). The Jews became jealous of Paul's success and organized a mob to oppose the Christian missionaries. Not finding Paul and Silas, they dragged Jason, Paul and Silas's host, before the politarchs, and accused him of harboring traitors of Rome. The politarchs extracted a pledge guaranteeing the departure of Paul and Silas, who left that night for Berea. After a time, the Thessalonian Jews raised an uproar in Berea so that Paul departed for Athens, leaving orders for Silas and Timothy to join him there (Acts 17:11–16). Because of Luke's account in Acts some scholars have reasoned that Paul was in Thessalonica for less than a month ("three Sabbaths," 17:2), but other evidence suggests a longer stay: (1) Paul received two separate offerings from Philippi, 100 miles away, while he was in Thessalonica (Phil. 4:15, 16). (2) According to 1:9 and 2:14–16, most of the Thessalonian converts were Gentiles who came out of idolatry. This would imply an extensive ministry directed to the Gentiles after Paul's initial work with the Jews and gentile God-fearers. (3) Paul worked "night and day" (2:9; 2 Thess. 3:7–9) during his time there. He may have begun to work immediately, but Paul supported himself by tent-making, which took many hours away from his ministry, requiring a longer stay to accomplish the extensive ministry of evangelism and teaching that took place in that city. After Silas and Timothy met Paul in Athens (3:1, 2), he sent Timothy to Thessalonica (Silas also went back to Macedonia, probably Philippi), and his assistants later rejoined him in Corinth (Acts 18:5; cf. 1 Thess. 1:1 where Silas is called Silvanus). There he wrote this epistle in A.D. 51 as his response to Timothy's good report.

THE CHRIST OF FIRST THESSALONIANS

Christ is seen as the believer's hope of salvation both now and at His coming. When He returns, He will deliver (1:10; 5:4–11), reward (1:19), perfect (3:13), resurrect (4:13–18), and sanctify (5:23) all who trust Him.

KEYS TO FIRST THESSALONIANS

Key Word: Holiness in Light of Christ's Return—Throughout this letter is an unmistakable emphasis upon steadfastness in the Lord (3:8) and a continuing growth in faith and love in view of the return of Christ (1:3–10; 2:12–20; 3:10–13; 4:1—5:28). The theme is not only the returning of Christ, but also the life of the believer in every practical relationship, each aspect of which can be transformed and illuminated by the glorious prospect of His eventual return.

Key Verses: First Thessalonians 3:12, 13 and 4:16–18—"And may the Lord cause you to increase and abound in love for one another, and for all men, just as we also *do* for you; so that He may establish your hearts unblamable in holiness before our God and Father at the coming of our Lord Jesus with all His saints" (3:12, 13).

"For the Lord Himself will descend from heaven with a shout, with the voice of *the* archangel, and with the trumpet of God; and the dead in Christ shall rise first. Then we who are alive and remain shall be caught up together with them in the clouds to meet the Lord in the air, and thus we shall always be with the Lord. Therefore comfort one another with these words" (4:16–18).

Key Chapter: First Thessalonians 4—Chapter 4 includes the central passage of the epistles on the coming of the Lord when the dead in Christ shall rise first, and those who remain are caught up together with them in the clouds.

SURVEY OF FIRST THESSALONIANS

After Paul's forced separation from the Thessalonians, he grows increasingly concerned about the progress of their faith. His great relief upon hearing Timothy's positive report prompts him to write this warm epistle of commendation, exhortation, and consolation. They are commended for remaining steadfast under afflictions, exhorted to excel still more in their Christian walk, and consoled concerning their loved ones who have died in Christ. The theme of the coming of the Lord recurs throughout this epistle, and 4:13—5:11 is one of the fullest New Testament developments of this crucial truth. The two major sections of First Thessalonians are: Paul's personal reflections of the Thessalonians (1—3) and Paul's instructions for the Thessalonians (4 and 5).

Paul's Personal Reflections on the Thessalonians (1—3): Paul's typical salutation in the first verse combines the customary Greek ("grace") and Hebrew ("peace") greetings of his day and enriches them with Christian content. The opening chapter is a declaration of thanksgiving for the Thessalonians' metamorphosis from heathenism to Christian hope. Faith, love, and hope (1:3) properly characterize the new lives of these believers. In 2:1–16, Paul reviews his brief ministry in Thessalonica and defends his conduct and motives, apparently to answer enemies who are trying to impugn his character and message. He sends Timothy to minister to them and is greatly relieved when Timothy reports the stability of their faith and love (2:17—3:10). Paul

FOCUS	REFLECTIONS ON THE THESSALONIANS			INSTRUCTIONS TO THE THESSALONIANS			
REFERENCE	1:1———2:1	———2:17	———4:1	———4:13	———5:1	———5:12	—5:28
DIVISION	COMMENDATION FOR GROWTH	FOUNDING OF THE CHURCH	STRENGTHENING OF THE CHURCH	DIRECTION FOR GROWTH	THE DEAD IN CHRIST	THE DAY OF THE LORD	HOLY LIVING
TOPIC	PERSONAL EXPERIENCE			PRACTICAL EXHORTATION			
	LOOKING BACK			LOOKING FORWARD			
LOCATION	WRITTEN IN CORINTH						
TIME	C. A.D. 51						

therefore closes this historical section with a prayer that their faith may continue to deepen (3:11–13).

Paul's Instructions to the Thessalonians (4 and 5): The apostle deftly moves into a series of exhortations and instructions by encouraging the Thessalonians to continue progressing. He reminds them of his previous teaching on sexual and social matters (4:1–12), since these gentile believers lack the moral upbringing in the Mosaic Law provided in the Jewish community. Now rooted in the Word of God (2:13), the readers must resist the constant pressures of a pagan society.

Paul has taught them about the return of Christ, and they have become distressed over the deaths of some among them. In 4:13–18, Paul comforts them with the assurance that all who die in Christ will be resurrected at His *parousia* ("presence," "coming," "advent"). The apostle continues his discourse on eschatology by describing the coming day of the Lord (5:1–11). In anticipation of this day, believers are to be "alert and sober" (5:6) as "sons of light" (5:5) who are destined for salvation, not wrath. Paul requests the readers to deal with integrity toward one another and to continue growing spiritually (5:12–22). The epistle closes with a wish for their sanctification, three requests, and a benediction (5:23–28).

OUTLINE OF FIRST THESSALONIANS

CHAPTER 1

Paul's Commendation for Their Growth

PAUL and ^RSilvanus and ^RTimothy to the church of the Thessalonians in God the Father and the Lord Jesus Christ: Grace to you and peace.   2 Cor. 1:19 • Acts 16:1

2 We give thanks to God always for all of you, making mention *of you* in our prayers;

3 constantly bearing in mind your work of faith and labor of love and steadfastness of hope^Tin our Lord Jesus Christ in the presence of our God and Father,   *of*

4 knowing,^Rbrethren beloved by God,^R*His* choice of you;   Rom. 1:7 • 2 Pet. 1:10

5 for our gospel did not come to you in word only, but also in power and in the Holy Spirit and with full conviction; just as you know what kind of men we ^Tproved to be among you for your sake.   *became*

6 You also became imitators of us and of the Lord, having received the word in much tribulation with the joy of the Holy Spirit,

7 so that you became an example to all the believers in Macedonia and in Achaia.

8 For^Rthe word of the Lord has sounded forth from you, not only in Macedonia and Achaia, but also in every place your faith toward God has gone forth, so that we have no need to say anything. Col. 3:16; 2 Thess. 3:1

9 For they themselves report about us what kind of a ^Treception we had with you, and how you turned to God from idols to serve a living and true God,   *entrance*

1:5 Sharing Our Faith: How?—In order to share our faith successfully, we must keep the following rules in mind.
a. First, we must be clean vessels. God reminds Isaiah the prophet of this, "Purify yourselves, you who carry the vessels of the LORD" (Page 701—Is. 52:11). David the sinner prays for forgiveness and cleansing. Upon receiving this he states, "*Then* I will teach transgressors Thy ways, and sinners will be converted to Thee" (Page 554—Ps. 51:13). While God does not demand golden or silver vessels, He does require clean ones.
b. We must be able to clearly give out the simple facts of the gospel without getting bogged down with profound theological concepts. Philip the evangelist demonstrated how to do this when he dealt with a sinner in the desert. "And Philip opened his mouth, and beginning from this Scripture he preached Jesus to him" (Page 1103—Acts 8:35).
c. We must avoid arguments and stick to the basic issues of man's sin and Christ's blood. Often unbelievers will attempt to sidestep the gospel by asking unrelated questions, such as "Where did Cain get his wife?"
d. We must use the Word of God. Paul's tremendous success as an evangelist can be linked directly to his constant use of God's Word. See Acts 17:2; 18:28; Second Timothy 2:15; 3:14–17.
e. We must depend upon the Spirit of God. See John 3:15; Acts 6:10; First Corinthians 2:4.
Now turn to Page 1225—2 Tim. 4:2: Sharing Our Faith: When?

10 and to[R]wait for His Son from[T]heaven, whom He raised from the dead, *that is* Jesus, who[R]delivers us from the wrath to come.   [Matt. 16:27f.] • *the heavens* • Rom. 5:9

CHAPTER 2

Paul's Founding of the Church

F[OR] you yourselves know, brethren, that our coming to you was not in vain,

2 but after we had already suffered and been[R]mistreated in Philippi, as you know, we had the boldness in our God to speak to you the[R]gospel of God amid much[A]opposition.   Acts 14:5 • Rom. 1:1 • *struggle, conflict*

3 For our exhortation does not *come* from error or impurity or by way of deceit;

4 but just as we have been approved by God to be entrusted with the gospel, so we speak,[R]not as pleasing men but God, who [A]examines our hearts.   Gal. 1:10 • *approves*

5 For we never came [T]with flattering speech, as you know, nor with a pretext for greed—God is witness—   *in a word of flattery*

6 nor did we seek glory from men, either from you or from others, even though as apostles of Christ we might have [A]asserted our authority.   *been burdensome*

7 But we proved to be [1]gentle [T]among you, as a nursing *mother* tenderly cares for her own children.   *in the midst of you*

8 Having thus a fond affection for you, we were well-pleased to[R]impart to you not only the gospel of God but also our own [A]lives, because you had become[T]very dear to us.   2 Cor. 12:15 • *souls* • *beloved*

9 For you recall, brethren, our labor and hardship, *how* working night and day so as not to be a burden to any of you, we proclaimed to you the gospel of God.

10 You are witnesses, and *so is* God, how devoutly and uprightly and blamelessly we [T]behaved toward you believers;   *became*

11 just as you know how we *were* exhorting and encouraging and imploring each one of you as a father *would* his own children,

12 so that you may[R]walk in a manner worthy of the God who[R]calls you into His own kingdom and glory.   Eph. 4:1 • Rom. 8:28

13 And for this reason we also constantly thank God that when you received from us the word of God's message, you accepted *it* not *as* the word of men, but *for* what it really is, the word of God, which also performs its work in you who believe.

14 For you, brethren, became imitators of the churches of God in Christ Jesus that are in Judea, for you also endured the same sufferings at the hands of your own countrymen, even as they *did* from the Jews,

15 who both killed the Lord Jesus and the prophets, and drove us out. They are not pleasing to God, but hostile to all men,

16 hindering us from speaking to the Gentiles[R]that they might be saved; with the result that they always fill up the measure of their sins. But[R]wrath has come upon them [2]to the utmost.   1 Cor. 10:33 • 1 Thess. 1:10

Satan Hinders Paul

17 But we, brethren, having been bereft of you for a short while—in [T]person, not in [T]spirit—were all the more eager with great desire to see your face.   *face* • *heart*

18 [A]For we wanted to come to you—I, Paul, [T]more than once—and *yet* Satan thwarted us.   *Because* • *both once and twice*

19 For who is our hope or joy or crown of exultation? Is it not even you, in the presence of our Lord Jesus at His coming?

20 For you are our glory and joy.

CHAPTER 3

Paul Sends Timothy

T[HEREFORE][R]when we could endure *it* no longer, we thought it best to be left behind at [R]Athens alone;   1 Thess. 3:5 • Acts 17:15f.

2 and we sent[R]Timothy, our brother and God's fellow worker in the gospel of Christ, to strengthen and encourage you as to your faith,   2 Cor. 1:1; Col. 1:1

3 so that no man may be disturbed by these afflictions; for you yourselves know that we have been destined for this.

4 For indeed when we were with you, we *kept* telling you in advance that we were going to suffer affliction; [T]and so it came to pass,[T]as you know.   *just as* • *and*

5 For this reason,[R]when I could endure *it* no longer, I also sent to[A]find out about your faith, for fear that[R]the tempter might have tempted you, and our labor should be in vain.   Phil. 2:19 • *to know, to ascertain* • Matt. 4:3

Timothy's Encouraging Report

6 But now that[R]Timothy has come to us from you, and has brought us good news of your faith and love, and that you always think kindly of us, longing to see us just as we also long to see you,   Acts 18:5

7 for this reason, brethren, in all our distress and affliction we were comforted about you through your faith;

8 for now we *really* live, if you[R]stand firm in the Lord.   1 Cor. 6:13

9 For what thanks can we render to God for you in return for all the joy with which we rejoice before our God on your account,

10 as we night and day keep praying most earnestly that we may see your face, and may complete what is lacking in your faith?

Paul's Desire to Visit Them

11 Now may our God and Father Himself and Jesus our Lord direct our way to you;

12 and may the Lord cause you to in-

[1] Some ancient mss. read *babes*
[2] Or, *forever;* or, *altogether*

crease and abound in love for one another, and for all men, just as we also *do* for you;

13 so that He may^Restablish your hearts unblamable in holiness before our God and Father at the^coming of our Lord Jesus with all His^saints.   1 Cor. 1:8 • *presence* • *holy ones*

CHAPTER 4

Directions for Growth

FINALLY then,^Rbrethren, we request and exhort you in the Lord Jesus, that, as you received from us *instruction* as to how you ought to^Rwalk and^Rplease God (just as you actually do ³walk), that you may excel still more.   Gal. 6:1 • Eph. 4:1 • 2 Cor. 5:9

2 For you know what commandments we gave you ⁴by *the authority of* the Lord Jesus.

3 For this is the will of God, your sanctification; *that is,* that you^Rabstain from^sexual immorality;   1 Cor. 6:18 • *fornication*

4 that each of you know how to possess his own ⁵vessel in sanctification and honor,

5 not in^Tlustful passion, like the Gentiles who^Rdo not know God;   *passion of lust* • Gal. 4:8

6 *and* that no man transgress and ^Rdefraud his brother^Rin the matter because the Lord is *the* avenger in all these things, just as we also^Rtold you before and solemnly warned *you.*   1 Cor. 6:8 • 2 Cor. 7:11 • Luke 16:28

7 For God has not called us for the purpose of impurity, but in sanctification.

8 Consequently, he who rejects *this* is not rejecting man but the God who^Rgives His Holy Spirit to you.   Rom. 5:5; [2 Cor. 1:22]

9 Now as to the^Rlove of the brethren, you ^Rhave no need for *anyone* to write to you, for you yourselves are^Rtaught by God to love one another;   John 13:34 • 2 Cor. 9:1 • John 6:45

10 for indeed you do practice it toward all the brethren who are in all Macedonia. But we urge you, brethren, to excel still more,

11 and to make it your ambition^Rto lead a quiet life and^Rattend to your own business and^Rwork with your hands, just as we commanded you;   2 Thess. 3:12 • 1 Pet. 4:15 • Acts 18:3

12 so that you may behave properly toward outsiders and not be in any need.

Revelation Concerning the Dead in Christ

13 But^Rwe do not want you to be uninformed, brethren, about those who are asleep, that you may not grieve, as do the rest who have no hope.   Rom. 1:13

14 For if we believe that Jesus died and rose again, even so God will bring with Him those who have fallen asleep in Jesus.

15 For this we say to you by the word of the Lord, that we who are alive,^Tand remain until the coming of the Lord, shall not precede those who have fallen asleep.   *who*

16 For the Lord Himself will descend from heaven with a shout, with the voice of *the* archangel, and with the trumpet of God; and the dead in Christ will rise first.

17 Then we who are alive^Tand remain shall be caught up together with them in the clouds to meet the Lord in the air, and thus we shall always be with the Lord.   *who*

18 Therefore comfort one another with these words.

CHAPTER 5

Description of the Day of the Lord

NOW as to the^Rtimes and the epochs, brethren, you^Rhave no need of anything to be written to you.   Acts 1:7 • 1 Thess. 4:9

2 For you yourselves know full well that the day of the Lord^Twill come^Rjust like a thief in the night.   *is coming* • Luke 21:34

3 While they are saying, "Peace^R and safety!" then ^destruction ^Twill come upon them suddenly like birth pangs upon a woman with child; and they shall not escape.   Jer. 6:14 • *sudden destruction* • *is at hand*

4 But you, brethren, are not in^Rdarkness, that the day should overtake you like a thief;   Acts 26:18; 1 John 2:8

5 for you are all sons of light and sons of day. We are not of night nor of darkness;

6 so then let us not sleep as others do, but let us be alert and ⁶sober.

7 For those who sleep do their sleeping at night, and those who get drunk get^Rdrunk at night.   Acts 2:15; 2 Pet. 2:13

8 But since^Rwe are of *the* day, let us^Rbe ⁶sober, having put on the^Rbreastplate of faith and love, and as a helmet, the hope of salvation.   1 Thess. 5:5 • 1 Pet. 1:13 • Eph. 6:14

9 For God has not destined us for^Rwrath, but for^Robtaining salvation through our Lord Jesus Christ,   1 Thess. 1:10 • [2 Thess. 2:13f.]

10 ^Rwho died for us, that whether we are awake or asleep, we may live together with Him.   [Rom. 14:9]

11 Therefore^encourage one another, and ^Rbuild up one another, just as you also are doing.   *comfort* • Eph. 4:29

Instruction for Holy Living

12 But we request of you, brethren, that you^Tappreciate those who diligently labor among you, and have charge over you in the Lord and give you instruction,   *know*

13 and that you esteem them very highly in love because of their work.^RLive in peace with one another.   Mark 9:50

14 And we urge you, brethren, admonish the unruly, encourage the fainthearted, help the weak, be patient with all men.

15 See that^Rno one repays another with evil for evil, but always ^Rseek after that which is good for one another and for all men.   Matt. 5:44; Rom. 12:17 • Rom. 12:9; Gal. 6:10

16 ^RRejoice always;   Phil. 4:4

17 ^Rpray without ceasing;   Eph. 6:18

18 in everything^Rgive thanks; for this is God's will for you in Christ Jesus.   Eph. 5:20

---

³ Or, *conduct yourselves*   ⁴ Lit., *through the Lord*
⁵ I.e., *body; or possibly, wife*   ⁶ Or, *self-controlled*

19 ᴿDo not quench the Spirit;   [Eph. 4:30]
20 do not despise prophetic ⁷utterances.
21 Butᴿexamine everything *carefully*; hold
fast to that which is good;   1 Cor. 14:29
22 abstain from every ⁸form of evil.

Conclusion

23 Now ᴿmay the God of peace ᴿHimself
sanctify you entirely; and may your spirit

⁷ Or, *gifts*   ⁸ Or, *appearance*
⁹ Some mss. add *also*

and soul and body be preserved complete,
without blame at the coming of our Lord
Jesus Christ.   Rom. 15:33 • 1 Thess. 3:11
24 ᴿFaithful is He who calls you, and He
also will bring it to pass.   1 Cor. 1:9
25 Brethren,ᴿpray for us.⁹   Eph. 6:19
26 Greet all the brethren with a holy kiss.
27 I adjure you by the Lord toᴿhave this
letter read to all the brethren.   Col. 4:16
28 ᴿThe grace of our Lord Jesus Christ be
with you.   Rom. 16:20; 2 Thess. 3:18

THE SECOND EPISTLE OF PAUL TO THE

THESSALONIANS

THE BOOK OF SECOND THESSALONIANS

Since Paul's first letter, the seeds of false doctrine have been sown among the Thessalonians, causing them to waver in their faith. Paul removes these destructive seeds and again plants the seeds of truth. He begins by commending the believers on their faithfulness in the midst of persecution and encouraging them that present suffering will be repaid with future glory. Therefore, in the midst of persecution, expectation can be high.

Paul then deals with the central matter of his letter: a misunderstanding spawned by false teachers regarding the coming day of the Lord. Despite reports to the contrary, that day has not yet come, and Paul recounts the events that must first take place. Laboring for the gospel, rather than lazy resignation, is the proper response.

As the second letter in Paul's Thessalonian correspondence, this was entitled *Pros Thessalonikeis B*, the "Second to the Thessalonians."

THE AUTHOR OF SECOND THESSALONIANS

The external attestation to the authenticity of Second Thessalonians as a Pauline epistle is even stronger than that for First Thessalonians. Internally, the vocabulary, style, and doctrinal content support the claims in 1:1 and 3:17 that it was written by Paul.

THE TIME OF SECOND THESSALONIANS

See "The Time of First Thessalonians" for the background to the Thessalonian correspondence. This letter was probably written a few months after First Thessalonians, while Paul was still in Corinth with Silas and Timothy (1:1; cf. Acts 18:5). The bearer of the first epistle may have brought Paul an update on the new developments, prompting him to write this letter. They were still undergoing persecution, and the false teaching about the day of the Lord led some of them to overreact by giving up their jobs. The problem of idleness recorded in First Thessalonians 4:11, 12 had become more serious (3:6–15). By this time, Paul was beginning to see the opposition he would face in his ministry in Corinth (3:2; see Acts 18:5–10).

THE CHRIST OF SECOND THESSALONIANS

The return of Christ is mentioned more times (318) in the New Testament than any other doctrine, and this is certainly the major concept in chapters 1 and 2 of this epistle. The return of the Lord Jesus is a reassuring and joyful hope for believers, but His revelation from heaven holds awesome and terrifying implications for those who have not trusted in Him (1:6–10; 2:8–12).

KEYS TO SECOND THESSALONIANS

Key Word: Understanding the Day of the Lord—The theme of this epistle is an understanding of the day of the Lord and the resulting life-style changes. The doctrinal error of chapter 2 has been causing the practical error that Paul seeks to overcome in chapter 3. Some of the believers have abandoned their work and have begun to live off others, apparently assuming that the end is at hand. Paul commands them to follow his example by supporting themselves and instructs the rest of the church to discipline them if they fail to do so.

Key Verses: Second Thessalonians 2:2, 3 and 3:4, 5—"That you may not be quickly shaken from your composure or be disturbed either by a spirit or a message or a letter as if from us, to the effect that the day of the Lord has come. Let no one in any way deceive you, for *it will not come* unless the apostasy comes first, and the man of lawlessness is revealed, the son of destruction" (2:2, 3).

"And may the Lord direct your hearts into the love of God and into the steadfastness of Christ. Now we command you, brethren, in the name of our Lord Jesus Christ, that you keep aloof from every brother who leads an unruly life and not according to the tradition which you received from us" (3:5, 6).

Key Chapter: Second Thessalonians 2—The second chapter is written to correct the fallacious teaching that the day of the Lord has already come upon the Thessalonian church. This teaching, coupled with the afflictions they have been suffering, is causing a great disturbance among the believers who wonder when their "gathering together to Him" (2:1; 1 Thess. 4:13–18) will take place. Paul makes it clear that certain identifiable events will precede that day and that those events have not yet occurred.

SURVEY OF SECOND THESSALONIANS

This epistle is the theological sequel to First Thessalonians, which developed the theme of the coming day of the Lord (1 Thess. 5:1–11). However not long after the Thessalonians receive that letter, they fall prey to false teaching or outright deception, thinking the day of the Lord has already begun. Paul writes this brief letter to correct the error and also to encourage those believers whose faith is being tested by the difficulties presented by persecution. He also reproves those who have decided to cease working because they believe the coming of Christ is near. Second Thessalonians deals with Paul's encouragement in persecution (1); Paul's explanation of the day of the Lord (2); and Paul's exhortation to the church (3).

Paul's Encouragement in Persecution (1): After his two-verse salutation, Paul gives thanks for the growing faith and love of the Thessalonians and assures them of their ultimate deliverance from those who are persecuting them (1:3–10). They are encouraged to patiently endure their afflictions, knowing that the Lord Jesus will judge their persecutors when He is "revealed from heaven with His mighty angels in flaming fire" (1:7). Before Paul moves to the next topic, he concludes this section with a prayer for the spiritual welfare of his readers (1:11, 12).

Paul's Explanation of the Day of the Lord (2): Because of the severity of their afflictions, the Thessalonians have become susceptible to false teaching (and possibly a fraudulent letter in the name of Paul), claiming that they are already in the day of the Lord (2:1, 2). This was particularly disturbing because Paul's previous letter had given them the comforting hope that they were not destined for the wrath of that day (1 Thess. 5:9). Paul therefore assures them that the day of the Lord is yet in the future and will not arrive unannounced. Paul then concludes with a word of encouragement and a benedictory prayer of comfort before moving to his next topic (2:13–17).

Paul's Exhortation to the Church (3:1–18): Paul requests the Thessalonian church to pray on his behalf and to wait patiently for the Lord (3:1–5). Having thus commended, corrected, and comforted his readers, the tactful apostle closes his letter with a sharp word of command to those who have been using the truth of Christ's return as an excuse for disorderly conduct (3:6–15; cf. 1 Thess. 4:11, 12). The doctrine of the Lord's return requires a balance betwen waiting and working. It is a perspective that should encourage holiness, not idleness. This final section, like the first two, closes on a benedictory note (3:16–18).

FOCUS	ENCOURAGEMENT IN PERSECUTION			EXPLANATION OF THE DAY OF THE LORD		EXHORTATION TO THE CHURCH	
REFERENCE	1:1————1:5————1:11			2:1————2:13		3:1————3:6————3:18	
DIVISION	THANKSGIVING FOR GROWTH	ENCOURAGEMENT IN PERSECUTION	PRAYER FOR BLESSING	EVENTS PRECEDING	COMFORT OF THE BELIEVER	WAIT PATIENTLY	WITHDRAW
TOPIC	DISCOURAGED BELIEVERS			DISTURBED BELIEVERS		DISOBEDIENT BELIEVERS	
	THANKSGIVING FOR THEIR LIFE			INSTRUCTION OF THEIR DOCTRINE		CORRECTION OF THEIR BEHAVIOR	
LOCATION	WRITTEN IN CORINTH						
TIME	C. A.D. 51						

OUTLINE OF SECOND THESSALONIANS

CHAPTER 1

Thanksgiving for Their Growth

PAUL and Silvanus and ᴿTimothy to the church of the Thessalonians in God our Father and the Lord Jesus Christ: Acts 16:1

2 ᴿGrace to you and peace from God the Father and the Lord Jesus Christ.   Rom. 1:7

3 We ought alwaysᴿto give thanks to God for you,ᴿbrethren, as is *only* fitting, because your faith is greatly enlarged, and the love of each one of you toward one another grows *ever* greater;   Rom. 1:8 • 1 Thess. 4:1

4 therefore, we ourselvesᴿspeak proudly of you amongᴿthe churches of God for your ^perseverance and faith in the midst of all your persecutions and afflictions which you endure.   2 Cor. 7:4 • 1 Cor. 7:17 • *steadfastness*

Encouragement in Their Persecution

5 *This is* aᴿplain indication of God's righteous judgment so that you may be considered worthy of the kingdom of God, for which indeed you are suffering.   Phil. 1:28

6 For after all it is *only* just for God to repay with affliction those who afflict you,

7 and *to give* relief to you who are afflicted and to us as well when the Lord Jesus shall be revealed from heaven with His mighty angelsᴿin flaming fire,   Ex. 3:2

8 dealing out retribution to those whoᴿdo not know God and to those who do not obey the gospel of our Lord Jesus.   Gal. 4:8

9 And these will pay the penalty of eternal destruction, away from the presence of the Lord and from the glory of His power,

10 when He comes to be glorified in His ^saints on that day, and to be marveled at among all who have believed—for our testimony to you was believed.   *holy ones*

Prayer for God's Blessing

11 To this end also we pray for you always that our God may count you worthy of your calling, and fulfill every desire for goodness and the work of faith with power;

12 in order that the name of our Lord Jesus may be glorified in you, and you in Him, according to the grace of our God and ^the Lord Jesus Christ.   omit, the

CHAPTER 2

The Events Preceding the Day of the Lord

NOW we request you, brethren, with regard to the coming of our Lord Jesus Christ, and our gathering together to Him,

2 that you may not be quickly shaken from yourᵀcomposure or be disturbed either by aᴿspirit or aᵀmessage or aᴿletter as if from us, to the effect that the day of the Lord has come.   *mind* • 1 Cor. 14:32 • *word* • 2 Thess. 3:17

3 ᴿLet no one in any way deceive you, for *it will not come* unless the ¹apostasy comes

first, and theᴿman of lawlessness is revealed, the son of destruction,   Eph. 5:6 • Dan. 7:25

4 who opposes and exalts himself above ᴿevery so-called god or object of worship, so that he takes his seat in the temple of God, displaying himself as being God.   1 Cor. 8:5

5 Do you not remember that while I was still with you, I was telling you these things?

6 And you know what restrains him now, so that in his time he may be revealed.

7 For the mystery of lawlessness is already at work; only he who now restrains *will do so* until he is taken out of the way.

8 And then that lawless one will be revealed whom the Lord will slay with the breath of His mouth and bring to an end by the appearance of His^coming;   *presence*

9 *that is*, the one whose coming is in accord with the activity of Satan, with all power and signs and false wonders,

10 and with all the deception of wickedness forᴿthose who perish, because they did not receive the love ofᴿthe truth so as to be saved.   1 Cor. 1:18 • 2 Thess. 2:12, 13

11 And for this reason Godᵀwill send upon them a deluding influence so that they might believe^what is false,   *sends • the lie*

12 in order that they all may be ^judged who did not believe the truth, butᵀtook pleasure in wickedness.   *condemned • approved*

The Comfort of the Believer on the Day of the Lord

13 But we should always give thanks to God for you, brethren beloved by the Lord, because God has chosen you ²from the beginning for salvation through sanctification by the Spirit and faith in the truth.

14 And it was for this He ᴿcalled you through our gospel, that you may gain the glory of our Lord Jesus Christ.   1 Thess. 2:12

15 So then, brethren,ᴿstand firm andᴿhold to the traditions which you were taught, whetherᴿby word *of mouth* or by letterᵀfrom us.   1 Cor. 16:13 • 1 Cor. 11:2 • 2 Thess. 2:2 • *of*

16 ᴿNow may our Lord Jesus Christ Himself and God our Father, who has loved us and given us eternal comfort and good hope by grace,   1 Thess. 3:11

17 comfort andᴿstrengthen your hearts in every good work and word.   2 Thess. 3:3

CHAPTER 3

Wait Patiently for Christ

FINALLY, brethren, pray for us that the word of the Lord may spread rapidly and be glorified, just as *it did* also with you;

2 and that we may be delivered from perverse and evil men; for not all have faith.

3 Butᴿthe Lord is faithful, andᵀHe will strengthen and protect you^from ᴿthe evil *one*.   1 Cor. 1:9 • *will • from evil* • [Matt. 5:37]

¹ Or, *falling away* from the faith
² Some ancient mss. read *first fruits*

4 And we have confidence in the Lord concerning you, that you are doing and will *continue to* do what we command.

5 And may the Lord[R]direct your hearts into the love of God and into the steadfastness of Christ. 1 Thess. 3:11

Withdraw from the Disorderly

6 Now we command you, brethren, in the name of our Lord Jesus Christ, that you [A]keep aloof from every brother who leads an unruly life and not according to the tradition which you received from us. *avoid*

7 For you yourselves know how you ought to [T]follow[R] our example, because we did not act in an undisciplined manner among you, *imitate us* · 1 Thess. 1:6; 2 Thess. 3:9

8 nor did we eat anyone's bread without paying for it, but with labor and hardship we *kept* working night and day so that we might not be a burden to any of you;

9 not because we do not have[R]the right *to this,* but in order to offer ourselves [R]as a model for you, that you might[T]follow our example. 1 Cor. 9:4ff. · 2 Thess. 3:7 · *imitate us*

10 For even[R]when we were with you, we used to give you this order: if anyone will not work, neither let him eat. 1 Thess. 3:4

11 For we hear that some among you are leading an undisciplined life, doing no work at all, but acting like[R]busybodies. 1 Tim. 5:13

12 Now such persons we command and exhort in the Lord Jesus Christ to work in quiet fashion and eat their own bread.

13 But as for you,[R]brethren,[R]do not grow weary of doing good. 1 Thess. 4:1 · 2 Cor. 4:1

14 And if anyone does not obey our [T]instruction in this letter, take special note of that man and do not associate with him, so that he may be put to shame. *word*

15 And yet[R]do not regard him as an enemy, but admonish him as a brother. Gal. 6:1

Conclusion

16 Now may the Lord of peace Himself continually grant you peace in every circumstance. The Lord be with you all!

17 I, Paul, write this greeting with my own hand, and this is a distinguishing mark in every letter; this is the way I write.

18 [R]The grace of our Lord Jesus Christ be with you all. Rom. 16:20; 1 Thess. 5:28

TIMOTHY

THE BOOK OF FIRST TIMOTHY
Paul, the aged and experienced apostle, writes to the young pastor Timothy who is facing a heavy burden of responsibility in the church at Ephesus. The task is challenging: false doctrine must be erased, public worship safeguarded, and mature leadership developed. In addition to the conduct of the church, Paul talks pointedly about the conduct of the minister. Timothy must be on his guard lest his youthfulness become a liability, rather than an asset, to the gospel. He must be careful to avoid false teachers and greedy motives, pursuing instead righteousness, godliness, faith, love, perseverance, and the gentleness that befits a man of God.

The Greek title for this letter is *Pros Timotheon A*, the "First to Timothy." *Timothy* means "honoring God" or "honored by God," and probably was given to him by his mother Eunice.

THE AUTHOR OF FIRST TIMOTHY
Since the early nineteenth century, the Pastoral Epistles have been attacked more than any other Pauline epistles on the issue of authenticity. The similarity of these epistles requires that they be treated as a unit in terms of authorship because they stand or fall together.

The external evidence solidly supports the conservative position that Paul wrote the letters to Timothy and Titus. Postapostolic church fathers, such as Polycarp and Clement of Rome, allude to them as Paul's writing. In addition, these epistles are identified as Pauline by Irenaeus, Tertullian, Clement of Alexandria, and the Muratorian Canon. Only Romans and First Corinthians have better attestation among the Pauline epistles.

Suggestions of an author other than Paul are supported wholly on the basis of internal evidence. Even though these letters claim to be written by Paul (1:1; 2 Tim. 1:1; Titus 1:1), critics assert that they are "pious forgeries" that appeared in the second century. There are several problems with this: (1) Pseudonymous writing was unacceptable to Paul (see 2 Thess. 2:2; 3:17) and to the early church, which was very sensitive to the problem of forgeries. (2) The adjective *pious* should deceive no one: a forgery was as deliberately deceptive then as it is now. (3) The many personal facts and names that appear in the Pastoral Epistles would have been avoided by a forger who would have taken refuge in vagueness. Nor would a forger have used expressions like those in 1:13, 15 if he had been an admirer of Paul. The doctrinal teaching and autobiographical details (cf. 1:12–17; 2:7; 2 Tim. 1:8–12; 4:9–22; Titus 1:5; 3:12, 13) fit very well with "Paul, the aged" (Philem. 9). (4) What purpose or advantage would these epistles serve as forgeries written years later? There are too many personal elements, and the doctrinal refutations do not refer to second-century Gnosticism. (5) The style and content of the postapostolic writings or apocryphal books differ greatly with these three letters.

THE TIME OF FIRST TIMOTHY
Pauline authorship of the Pastoral Epistles requires Paul's release from his Roman imprisonment (Acts 28), the continuation of his missionary endeavors, and his imprisonment for a second time in Rome. Unfortunately, the order of events can only be reconstructed from hints, because there is no concurrent history paralleling Acts to chronicle the last years of the apostle. The following reconstruction, therefore, is only tentative:

As he anticipated in Philippians (1:19, 25, 26; 2:24), Paul was released from his first Roman imprisonment. It is possible that his Jewish accusers decided not to appear at his trial before Caesar. In fulfillment of his promise to the Philippians (Phil. 2:19–23), he sends Timothy to Philippi to relate the good news. Paul himself went to Ephesus (in spite of his earlier expectations in Acts 20:38) and to other Asian churches like Colossae (see Philem. 22). When Timothy rejoined him in Ephesus, Paul instructed his assistant to "remain on at Ephesus" (1:3) while he journeyed to Macedonia. When he saw that he might be delayed in Macedonia, Paul wrote First Timothy, perhaps from Philippi (3:14, 15). After he saw Timothy in Ephesus, the apostle journeyed on to the island of Crete where, after a period of ministry, he left Titus to continue the work (Titus 1:5). In Corinth, Paul decided to write a letter to Titus because Zenas and Apollos were making a journey that would take them by way of Crete (Titus 3:13). He instructed Titus to join him in Nicopolis after the arrival of his replacement in Crete, Artemas or Tychicus (Titus 3:12).

If he went to Spain as he had planned (Rom.

15:24, 28), Paul probably departed with Titus for that western province after his winter in Nicopolis. Early church tradition holds that Paul did go to Spain. Before the end of the first century, Clement of Rome said that Paul "reached the limits of the West" (I Clement 5:7). Since he was writing from Rome, he evidently had Spain in mind. Paul may have been in Spain from A.D. 64 to 66. He returned to Greece and Asia—to Corinth, Miletus, and Troas (2 Tim. 4:13, 20)—and may have been arrested in Troas where he left his valuable books and parchments (2 Tim. 4:13, 15).

Now that Christianity had become an illegal religion in the Empire (the burning of Rome took place in A.D. 64), Paul's enemies were able to successfully accuse him. He was imprisoned in A.D. 67 and wrote Second Timothy from his Roman cell after his first defense before the Imperial Court (2 Tim. 1:8, 17; 2:9; 4:16, 17). He was delivered from condemnation, but he held no hope of release and expected to be executed (2 Tim. 4:6–8, 18). He urged Timothy to come before that happened (2 Tim. 4:9, 21); and, according to tradition, the apostle was beheaded west of Rome on the Ostian Way.

Paul wrote First Timothy from Macedonia in A.D. 62 or 63 while Timothy was serving as his representative in Ephesus and perhaps in other churches in the province of Asia. Timothy was to appoint elders, combat false doctrine, and supervise church life as an apostolic representative.

THE CHRIST OF FIRST TIMOTHY

Christ is the "one mediator also between God and men" (2:5), "who was revealed in the flesh, was vindicated in the Spirit, beheld by angels, proclaimed among the nations, believed on in the world, taken up in glory" (3:16). He is the source of spiritual strength, faith, and love (1:12, 14). He "came

into the world to save sinners" (1:15) and "gave Himself as a ransom for all" (2:6) as "the Savior of all men, especially of believers" (4:10).

KEYS TO FIRST TIMOTHY

Key Word: Leadership Manual for Church Organization—The theme of this epistle is Timothy's organization and oversight of the Asian churches as a faithful minister of God. Paul writes this letter as a reference manual for leadership so that Timothy will have effective guidance for his work during Paul's absence in Macedonia (3:14, 15). Paul wants to encourage and exhort his younger assistant to become an example to others, exercise his spiritual gifts, and "fight the good fight of faith" (6:12; cf. 1:18; 4:12–16; 6:20). Timothy's personal and public life must be above reproach and he must be ready to deal with matters of false teaching, organization, discipline, proclamation of the Scriptures, poverty and wealth, and the roles of various groups. Negatively, he is to refute error (1:7–11; 6:3–5); positively, he is to teach the truth (4:13–16; 6:2, 17, 18).

Key Verses: First Timothy 3:15, 16 and 6:11, 12—"But in case I am delayed, *I write* so that you may know how one ought to conduct himself in the household of God, which is the church of the living God, the pillar and support of the truth. And by common confession great is the mystery of godliness: He who was revealed in the flesh, was vindicated in the Spirit, beheld by angels, proclaimed among the nations, believed on in the world, taken up in glory" (3:15, 16).

"But flee from these things, you man of God; and pursue righteousness, godliness, faith, love, perseverance *and* gentleness. Fight the good fight of faith; take hold of the eternal life to which you were called, and you made

FOCUS	DOCTRINE	PUBLIC WORSHIP	FALSE TEACHERS	CHURCH DISCIPLINE	PASTORAL MOTIVES
REFERENCE	1:1————————2:1———		——4:1————————5:1—		————6:1————6:21
DIVISION	PROBLEM OF FALSE DOCTRINE	PUBLIC WORSHIP AND LEADERSHIP	PRESERVE TRUE DOCTRINE	PRESCRIPTIONS FOR WIDOWS AND ELDERS	PASTORAL MOTIVATIONS
TOPIC	WARNING	WORSHIP	WISDOM	WIDOWS	WEALTH
	DANGERS OF FALSE DOCTRINE	DIRECTIONS FOR WORSHIP	DEFENSE AGAINST FALSE TEACHERS	DUTIES TOWARD OTHERS	DEALINGS WITH RICHES
LOCATION	WRITTEN IN MACEDONIA				
TIME	C. A.D. 62-63				

the good confession in the presence of many witnesses" (6:11, 12).

Key Chapter: First Timothy 3—Listed in chapter 3 are the qualifications for the leaders of God's church, the elders and deacons. Notably absent are qualities of worldly success or position. Instead, Paul enumerates character qualities demonstrating that true leadership emanates from our walk with God rather than from achievements or vocational success.

SURVEY OF FIRST TIMOTHY

Paul's last three recorded letters, written near the end of his full and fruitful life, were addressed to his authorized representatives Timothy and Titus. These were the only letters Paul wrote exclusively to individuals (Philemon was addressed primarily to its namesake, but also to others), and they were designed to exhort and encourage Timothy and Titus in their ministry of solidifying the churches of Ephesus and Crete. In the eighteenth century, these epistles came to be known as the Pastoral Epistles even though they do not use any terms, such as shepherd, pastor, flock, or sheep. Still, this title is appropriate for First Timothy and Titus, since they focus on the oversight of church life. It is less appropriate in the case of Second Timothy, which is a more personal than church-oriented letter. The Pastoral Epistles abound with principles for leadership and righteous living.

In his first letter to Timothy, Paul seeks to guide his younger and less experienced assistant in his weighty responsibility as the overseer of the work at Ephesus and other Asian cities. He writes, in effect, a challenge to Timothy to fulfill the task before him: combating false teaching with sound doctrine, developing qualified leadership, teaching God's Word, and encouraging Christian conduct. Because of the personal and conversational character of this letter, it is loosely structured around five clear charges that end each section (1:18-20; 3:14-16; 4:11-20; 5:21-25; 6:20, 21): Paul's charge concerning doctrine (1); Paul's charge concerning public worship (2 and 3); Paul's charge concerning false teachers (4); Paul's charge concerning church discipline (5); and Paul's charge concerning pastoral motives (6).

Paul's Charge Concerning Doctrine (1): After his greetings (1:1, 2), Paul warns Timothy about the growing problem of false doctrines, particularly as they relate to the misuse of the Mosaic Law (1:3-11). The aging apostle then recounts his radical conversion to Christ and subsequent calling to the ministry (1:12-17). Timothy, too, has received a divine calling, and Paul charges him to fulfill it without wavering in doctrine or conduct (1:18-20).

Paul's Charge Concerning Public Worship (2 and 3): Turning his attention to the church at large, Paul addresses the issues of church worship and leadership. Efficacious public prayer should be a part of worship, and Paul associates this with the role of men in the church (2:1-8). He then turns to the role of women (2:9-15), wherein he emphasizes the importance of the inner quality of godliness. In 3:1-7, Paul lists several qualifications for overseers or bishops. The word for "overseer" (*episkopos*) is used synonymously with the word for "elder" (*presbuteros*) in the New Testament, because both originally referred to the same office (see Acts 20:17, 28; Titus 1:5, 7). The qualifications for the office of deacon (*diakonos*, "servant") are listed in 3:8-13.

Paul's Charge Concerning False Teachers (4): Timothy obviously had difficulties with some of the older men (5:1) who had left the faith. Paul carefully advises on the issues of marriage, food, and exercise. The closing charge exhorts Timothy not to neglect the spiritual gift given to him.

Paul's Charge Concerning Church Discipline (5): One of the most difficult pastoral duties for the young minister is to lead in the exercise of church discipline. Commencing with the general advice of treating all members of the church as family (5:1, 2), Paul concentrates on the two special areas of widows and elders, focusing on Timothy's responsibility and providing practical instruction.

Paul's Charge Concerning Pastoral Motives (6): In addition, the insidious doctrine was being taught that godliness will eventually result in material blessing. Paul, in no uncertain terms, states, "flee from these things" (6:11). The book closes with an extended charge (6:11-21), which is supplemented by an additional charge that Timothy is to give to the wealthy of this age (6:17-19).

OUTLINE OF FIRST TIMOTHY

CHAPTER 1

Paul's Past Charge to Timothy

PAUL, an apostle of Christ Jesus according to the commandment of God our Savior, and of Christ Jesus, *who is* our hope;

2 to ᴿTimothy, *my* true child in *the* faith: Grace, mercy *and* peace from God the Father and Christ Jesus our Lord.   Acts 16:1

3 As I urged you ᵀupon my departure to Macedonia, remain on at Ephesus, in order that you may instruct certain men not to teach strange doctrines,   *while departing*

4 nor to pay attention to myths and endless genealogies, which give rise to mere speculation rather than *furthering* the administration of God which is by faith.

5 But the goal of our ᵀinstruction is love from a pure heart and a good conscience and a sincereᴿfaith.   *commandment* • 2 Tim. 1:5

6 For some men, straying from these things, have turned aside toᴿfruitless discussion,   Titus 1:10

7 wanting to be teachers of the Law, even though they do not understand either what they are saying or the matters about which they make confident assertions.

8 But we know thatᴿthe Law is good, if one uses it lawfully,   Rom. 7:12, 16

9 realizing the fact thatᴿlaw is not made for a righteous man, but for those who are lawless andᴿrebellious, for theᴿungodly and sinners, for the unholy and profane, for those who kill their fathers or mothers, for murderers   Gal. 5:23 • Titus 1:6, 10 • 1 Pet. 4:18

10 and immoral men and homosexuals and kidnappers and liars and perjurers, and whatever else is contrary to sound teaching,

11 according toᴿthe glorious gospel ofᴿthe blessed God, with which I have been ᴿentrusted.   2 Cor. 4:4 • 1 Tim. 6:15 • Gal. 2:7

Christ's Past Charge to Paul

12 I thank Christ Jesus our Lord, who has strengthened me, because He considered me faithful, putting me into service;

13 even though I was formerly a blasphemer and aᴿpersecutor and a violent aggressor. And yet I was shown mercy, because I acted ignorantly in unbelief;   Acts 8:3

14 and the ᴿgrace of our Lord was more than abundant, with the faith and love which are *found* in Christ Jesus.   Rom. 5:20

15 ᴿIt is a trustworthy statement, deserving full acceptance, thatᴿChrist Jesus came into the world to save sinners, among whom I am foremost *of all*.   1 Tim. 3:1; 4:9 • Is. 53:5 ★

16 And yet for this reason I found mercy, in order that in me as the foremost, Jesus Christ might demonstrate His perfect patience, as an example for thoseᴬwho would believe in Him for eternal life.   *destined to*

17 Now to the King eternal, immortal, invisible, the only God, *be* honor and glory ᵀforever and ever. Amen.   *to the ages of the ages*

First Charge: Fight the Good Fight

18 This command I entrust to you, Timothy, my son, in accordance with the prophecies previously made concerning you, that by them you may fight the good fight,

19 keeping faith and a good conscience, which some have rejected and suffered shipwreck in regard to their faith.

20 ᵀAmong these are Hymenaeus and ᴿAlexander, whom I have delivered over to Satan, so that they may beᴿtaught not to blaspheme.   *Of* • 2 Tim. 4:14 • 1 Cor. 11:32

CHAPTER 2

Prayer in Public Worship

FIRST of all, then, I urge thatᴿentreaties *and* prayers, petitions *and* thanksgivings, be made on behalf of all men,   Eph. 6:18

2 for kings and all who are in authority, in order that we may lead a tranquil and quiet life in all godliness and dignity.

3 This is good and acceptable in the sight ofᴿGod our Savior,   Luke 1:47; 1 Tim. 1:1; 4:10

4 who desires all men to be saved and to come to the knowledge of the truth.

5 For there isᴿone God, and ᴿone mediator also between God and men, the ᴿman Christ Jesus,   Rom. 3:30 • 1 Cor. 8:6 • Matt. 1:1

6 who gave Himself as a ransom for all, the testimony *borne* at the proper time.

7 And for this I was appointed a ᴬpreacher and an apostle (I am telling the truth, I am not lying) as a teacher of the Gentiles in faith and truth.   *herald*

8 Therefore [R]I want the men in every place to pray, lifting up holy hands, without wrath and dissension.   Phil. 1:12; 1 Tim. 5:14

Women in Public Worship

9 Likewise, *I want* women to adorn themselves with proper clothing, modestly and discreetly, not with braided hair and gold or pearls or costly garments;

10 but rather by means of good works, as befits women making a claim to godliness.

11 [R]Let a woman quietly receive instruction with entire submissiveness.   1 Cor. 14:34

12 [R]But I do not allow a woman to teach or exercise authority over a man, but to remain quiet.   1 Cor. 14:34; Titus 2:5

13 [R]For it was Adam who was first^created, *and* then Eve.   Gen. 2:7, 22; 3:16 • *formed*

14 And *it was* not Adam *who* was deceived, but[R]the woman being quite deceived, fell into transgression.   Gen. 3:6, 13

15 But *women* shall be[T]preserved through the bearing of children if they continue in [R]faith and love and sanctity with ^self-restraint.   *saved* • 1 Tim. 1:14 • *discretion*

CHAPTER 3

Qualifications of Bishops

I[T] is a trustworthy statement: if any man aspires to the [R]office of^overseer, it is a fine work he desires *to do*.   Acts 20:28 • *bishop*

2 [T]An overseer, then, must be above reproach,[R]the husband of one wife,[R]temperate, prudent, respectable, [R]hospitable, able to teach,   *The* • Titus 1:6 • 1 Tim. 3:8 • 1 Pet. 4:9

3 not addicted to wine[T]or pugnacious, but gentle, uncontentious,[R]free from the love of money.   *not* • 1 Tim. 3:8; 6:10

4 *He must be* one who[R]manages his own household well, keeping his children under control with all dignity   1 Tim. 3:12

5 (but if a man does not know how to manage his own household, how will he take care of^the church of God?);   1 Tim. 3:15

6 *and* not a new convert, lest he become conceited and fall into the[R]condemnation[T]incurred by the devil.   1 Tim. 3:7 • *of the devil*

7 And he must [R]have a good reputation with [R]those outside *the church*, so that he may not fall into reproach and[R]the snare of the devil.   2 Cor. 8:21 • Mark 4:11 • 1 Tim. 6:9

Qualifications of Deacons

8 Deacons likewise *must be* men of dignity, not double-tongued, [T]or addicted to much wine or fond of sordid gain,   *not*

9 [R]*but* holding to the mystery of the faith with a clear conscience.   1 Tim. 1:5, 19

10 And[R]let these also first be tested; then let them serve as deacons if they are beyond reproach.   1 Tim. 5:22

11 [T]Women *must* likewise *be* dignified, not malicious gossips, but temperate, faithful in all things.   either deacons' wives or deaconesses

12 Let deacons be husbands of *only* one wife, *and* [T]good managers of *their* children and their own households.   *managing well*

13 For those who have served well as deacons[R]obtain for themselves a[T]high standing and great confidence in the faith that is in Christ Jesus.   Matt. 25:21 • *good*

Second Charge:
Conduct Yourself in the
Household of God

14 I am writing these things to you, hoping to come to you before long;

15 but[T]in case I am delayed, *I write* so that you may know how one ought to conduct himself in[R]the household of God, which is the church of the living God, the pillar and support of the truth.   *if I delay* • 1 Cor. 3:16

16 And by common confession great is [R]the mystery of godliness: Rom. 16:25

[1]He who was revealed in the flesh,
Was^vindicated in the Spirit,   *justified*
[R]Beheld by angels,   Luke 2:13
Proclaimed among the nations,
[R]Believed on in the world,   2 Thess. 1:10
[R]Taken up in glory.   [Mark 16:19]

CHAPTER 4

Description of False Teachers

B[UT][R]the Spirit explicitly says that in later times some will fall away from the faith,

[1] Some later mss. read God

3:1–13 The Offices of the Church—The New Testament uses four terms to describe the leadership of the church: (1) "elder" (Gr., *presbuteros*) which places emphasis upon the authority that the leadership has to teach or rule in the church; (2) "bishop" (Gr., *episkopos*—overseer) which emphasizes the fact that the leadership is charged with overseeing the local church and as such is responsible for the spiritual well-being of those in the church; (3) "pastor" (Gr., *poimen*—shepherd) which places emphasis upon the responsibility of the leadership of the church to shepherd the flock. No shepherd has ever given birth to his sheep. It is the responsibility of those in leadership to do for the sheep what they cannot do for themselves and to make sure that they are in good spiritual condition so that they can do what comes naturally, that is, beget other sheep; (4) "deacon" (Gr., *diakonos*—minister) which places emphasis upon the attitude that the leaders are to have in their leading. They are not to "lord it over" the flock, but are to realize that they are the ministers or servants of those whom the Lord has put under their care.

The function of the office of elder is twofold: (1) teaching and (2) ruling (Page 1219—1 Tim. 5:17). An elder is to be able to teach his people what the Word of God teaches and to give direction as to how that is to be accomplished in and through the local church.

The qualifications for the office of deacon are essentially the same as those for the elder except that the deacon need not be "able to teach." The deacons are to be spiritual and in tune with the elders and seek to assist them in implementing the goals that the elders feel the Spirit of God is leading them to pursue through the local church.

Now turn to Page 1189—Eph. 5:25–29: The Relationship of the Church to Christ.

paying attention to[R]deceitful spirits and doctrines of demons,   [John 16:13] • 1 John 4:6

2 by means of the hypocrisy of liars [R]seared in their own conscience as with a branding iron,   Eph. 4:19

3 *men* who forbid marriage *and advocate* abstaining from foods, which God has created to be gratefully shared in by those who believe and know the truth.

4 For[R]everything created by God is good, and nothing is to be rejected, if it is[R]received with gratitude;   1 Cor. 10:26 • Rom. 14:6

5 for it is sanctified by means of [R]the word of God and prayer.   Gen. 1:25, 31

Instruction for the True Teacher

6 In pointing out these things to the brethren, you will be a good servant of Christ Jesus, *constantly* nourished on the words of the faith and of the[T]sound doctrine which you have been following.   *good*

7 But have nothing to do with[R]worldly[R]fables fit only for old women. On the other hand, discipline yourself for the purpose of [R]godliness;   1 Tim. 1:9 • 1 Tim. 1:4 • 1 Tim. 4:8

8 for [R]bodily discipline is only of little profit, but godliness is profitable for all things, since it holds promise for the present life and *also* for the *life* to come.   Col. 2:23

9 [R]It is a trustworthy statement deserving full acceptance.   1 Tim. 1:15

10 For it is for this we labor and strive, because we have fixed[R]our hope on the living God, who is[R]the Savior of all men, especially of believers.   2 Cor. 1:10 • John 4:42

Third Charge: Do Not Neglect the Gift

11 Prescribe and teach these things.

12 Let no one look down on your youthfulness, but *rather* in speech, conduct,[R]love, faith *and* purity, show yourself[R]an example ^of those who believe. 1 Tim. 1:14 • Titus 2:7 • *to*

13 [R]Until I come, give attention to the *pub-*lic[R]reading *of Scripture*, to exhortation and teaching.   1 Tim. 3:14 • 2 Tim. 3:15ff.

14 Do not neglect the spiritual gift within you, which was bestowed upon you through prophetic utterance with the laying on of hands by the^presbytery.   *board of elders*

15 Take pains with these things; be *absorbed* in them, so that your progress may be evident to all.

16 Pay close attention to yourself and to your teaching; persevere in these things; for as you do this you will insure salvation both for yourself and for those who hear you.

CHAPTER 5

How to Treat All People

Do not sharply rebuke an [R]older man, but *rather* appeal to *him* as a father, *to*[R]the younger men as brothers,   Titus 2:2 • Titus 2:6

2 the older women as mothers, *and* the younger women as sisters, in all purity.

How to Treat Widows

3 Honor widows who are widows indeed;

4 but if any widow has children or grandchildren, [R]let them first learn to practice piety in regard to their own family, and to make some return to their parents; for this is acceptable in the sight of God. [Eph. 6:2]

5 Now she who is a[R]widow indeed, and who has been left alone has fixed her hope on God, and continues in entreaties and prayers night and day.   Acts 6:1; 9:39, 41

6 But she who gives herself to wanton pleasure is dead even while she lives.

7 Prescribe these things as well, so that they may be above reproach.

8 But if anyone does not provide for his own, and especially for those of his household, he has[R]denied the faith, and is worse than an unbeliever.   2 Pet. 2:1; Jude 4

9 Let a widow be[R]put on the list only if she is not less than sixty years old, *having been* the wife of one man,   1 Tim. 5:16

10 having a reputation for good works; *and* if she has brought up children, if she has shown hospitality to strangers, if she has washed the^saints' feet, if she has assisted those in distress, *and* if she has devoted herself to every good work. *holy ones*

11 But refuse *to put* younger widows *on the list*, for when they feel[R]sensual desires in disregard of Christ, they want to get married,   Rev. 18:7

12 *thus* incurring condemnation, because they have set aside their previous pledge.

13 And at the same time they also learn *to be* idle, as they go around from house to house; and not merely idle, but also[R]gossips and busybodies, talking about [R]things not proper *to mention*.   3 John 10 • Titus 1:11

14 Therefore, I want younger *widows* to get married, bear children, keep house, *and* give the enemy no occasion for reproach;

15 for some[R]have already turned aside to follow[R]Satan.   1 Tim. 1:20 • Matt. 4:10

16 If any woman who is a believer has *dependent* widows, let her assist them, and let not the church be burdened, so that it may assist those who are widows indeed.

How to Treat Elders

17 Let[R]the elders who[R]rule well be considered worthy of double honor, especially those who work hard [T]at preaching and teaching.   Acts 11:30 • Rom. 12:8 • *in word*

18 For the Scripture says, "YOU[R] SHALL NOT MUZZLE THE OX WHILE HE IS THRESHING," and "The[R] laborer is worthy of his wages."   Deut. 25:4 • Matt. 10:10; Luke 10:7

19 Do not receive an accusation against an[R]elder except on the basis of[R]two or three witnesses.   Acts 11:30 • Deut. 17:6; 19:15

20 Those who continue in sin,[R]rebuke in the presence of all,[R]so that the rest also may be fearful *of sinning*.   Gal. 2:14 • 2 Cor. 7:11

Fourth Charge:
Maintain the Principle
Without Bias

21 ᴿI solemnly charge you in the presence of God and of Christ Jesus and of *His* chosen angels, to maintain these *principles* without bias, doing nothing in a *spirit of* partiality. Luke 9:26; 1 Tim. 6:13; 2 Tim. 2:14; 4:1

22 Do not lay hands upon anyone *too* hastily and thus share *responsibility for* the sins of others; keep yourself free from sin.

23 No longer drink water *exclusively,* but ᴿuse a little wine for the sake of your stomach and your frequent ailments.   1 Tim. 3:8

24 The sins of some men are quite evident, going before them to judgment; for others, their *sins*ᴿfollow after.   Rev. 14:13

25 Likewise also, deeds that are good are quite evident, andᴿthose which are otherwise cannot be concealed.   Prov. 10:9

CHAPTER 6

Exhortation to Slaves

L ET all who are under the yoke as slaves regard their own masters as worthy of all honor soᴿthat the name of God and *our* doctrine may not be spoken against.   Titus 2:5

2 And let those who have believers as their masters not be disrespectful to them because they are brethren, but let them serve them all the more, because those who partake of the benefit are believers and beloved. Teach and preach these *principles.*

Exhortation to Godliness
with Contentment

3 If anyone advocates a different doctrine, and does not agree with sound words, those of our Lord Jesus Christ, and with the doctrine conforming to godliness,

4 he is conceited *and* understands nothing; but heᵀhas a morbid interest in controversial questions and disputes about words, out of which arise envy, strife, abusive language, evil suspicions,   *is sick about*

5 and constant friction betweenᴿmen of depraved mind and deprived of the truth, whoᴿsuppose thatᴬgodliness is a means of gain.   2 Tim. 3:8 • Titus 1:11 • *religion*

6 ᴿBut godliness *actually* is a means of great gain, when accompanied byⁿcontentment.   Luke 12:15-21 • Phil. 4:11; Heb. 13:5

7 Forᴿwe have brought nothing into the world, ²so we cannot take anything out of it either.   Job 1:21; Eccl. 5:15

8 And if weᴿhave food and covering, with these we shall be content.   Prov. 30:8

9 ᴿBut those who want to get rich fall into temptation and ᴿa snare and many foolish and harmful desires which plunge men into ruin and destruction.   Prov. 15:27 • 1 Tim. 3:7

10 For the love of money is a root of all ᵀsorts of evil, and some by longing for it have wandered away from the faith, and pierced themselves with many a pang.   *the evils*

11 But flee from these things, you man of God; and pursue righteousness, godliness, faith, love, perseverance *and* gentleness.

12 Fight the good fight ofᴿfaith; take hold of the eternal life to which you were called, and you made the good confession in the presence of many witnesses.   1 Tim. 1:19

13 ᴿI charge you in the presence of God, whoᴬgives life to all things, and of Christ Jesus, who testified the good confession before Pontius Pilate,   1 Tim. 5:21 • *preserves alive*

14 that you keep the commandment without stain or reproach until theᴿappearing of our Lord Jesus Christ,   [2 Thess. 2:8]

15 which He will bring about at the proper time—He who is the blessed and only Sovereign, the King of kings and Lord of lords;

16 who alone possesses immortality and ᴿdwells in unapproachable light; whom no man has seen or can see. To Him *be* honor and eternal dominion! Amen.   Ps. 104:2

Exhortation to the Rich

17 Instruct those who are rich inᴿthis present worldᴿnot to be conceited or to fix their hope on the uncertainty of riches, but on God, who richly supplies us with all things to enjoy.   Matt. 12:32 • Ps. 62:10

18 *Instruct them* to do good, to be rich in ᴿgoodᴬworks,ᴿto be generous and ready to share,   1 Tim. 5:10 • *deeds* • Rom. 12:8

19 ᴿstoring up for themselves the treasure of a good foundation for the future, so that they mayᴿtake hold of that which is life indeed.   [Matt. 6:20] • 1 Tim. 6:12

Fifth Charge:
Guard What Has Been Entrusted

20 O Timothy, guard what has been entrusted to you, avoiding worldly *and* empty chatter *and* the opposing arguments of what is falsely called "knowledge"—

21 which some have professedᵀand thus gone astrayᵀfrom the faith.   *concerning*
Grace be with you.

² Later mss. read *it is clear that*

TIMOTHY

THE BOOK OF SECOND TIMOTHY

Prison is the last place from which to expect a letter of encouragement, but that is where Paul's second letter to Timothy originates. He begins by assuring Timothy of his continuing love and prayers, and reminds him of his spiritual heritage and responsibilities. Only the one who perseveres, whether as a soldier, athlete, farmer, or minister of Jesus Christ, will reap the reward. Paul warns Timothy that his teaching will come under attack as men desert the truth for ear "itching" words (4:3). But Timothy has Paul's example to guide him and God's Word to fortify him as he faces growing opposition and glowing opportunities in the last days.

Paul's last epistle received the title *Pros Timotheon B*, the "Second to Timothy." When Paul's epistles were collected together the *B* was probably added to distinguish this letter from the first letter he wrote to Timothy.

THE AUTHOR OF SECOND TIMOTHY

Since the Pastoral Epistles have to be treated as a unit on the matter of authorship, see "The Author of First Timothy" for comments on the origin of Second Timothy.

Timothy's name is found more often in the salutations of the Pauline epistles than any other (2 Cor.; Phil.; Col.; 1 and 2 Thess.; 1 and 2 Tim.; Philem.). His father was a Greek (Acts 16:1), but his Jewish mother Eunice and grandmother Lois reared him in the knowledge of the Hebrew Scriptures (1:5; 3:15). Timothy evidently became a convert of Paul (1 Cor. 4:17; 1 Tim. 1:2; 2 Tim. 1:2) when the apostle was in Lystra on his first missionary journey (Acts 14:8–20). When he visited Lystra on his second missionary journey, Paul decided to take Timothy along with him and circumcised him because of the Jews (Acts 16:1–3). Timothy was ordained to the ministry (1 Tim. 4:14; 2 Tim. 1:6) and served as a devoted companion and assistant to Paul in Troas, Berea, Thessalonica, and Corinth (Acts 16—18; 1 Thess. 3:1, 2). During the third missionary journey, Timothy labored with Paul and ministered for him as his representative in Ephesus, Macedonia, and Corinth. He was with Paul during his first Roman imprisonment and evidently went to Philippi (2:19–23) after Paul's release. Paul left him in Ephesus to supervise the work there (1 Tim. 1:3) and

years later summoned him to Rome (4:9, 21). According to Hebrews 13:23, Timothy was imprisoned and released, but the passage does not say where. Timothy was sickly (1 Tim. 5:23), timid (1:7), and youthful (1 Tim. 4:12), but he was a gifted teacher who was trustworthy and diligent.

THE TIME OF SECOND TIMOTHY

For a tentative reconstruction of the events following Paul's first Roman imprisonment, see "The Time of First Timothy." The cruel and unbalanced Nero, emperor of Rome from A.D. 54 to 68, was responsible for the beginning of the Roman persecution of Christians. Half of Rome was destroyed in July A.D. 64 by a fire, and mounting suspicion that Nero was responsible for the conflagration caused him to use the unpopular Christians as his scapegoat. Christianity thus became a *religio illicito*, and persecution of those who professed Christ became severe. By the time of Paul's return from Spain to Asia in A.D. 66, his enemies were able to use the official Roman position against Christianity to their advantage. Fearing for their own lives, the Asian believers failed to support Paul after his arrest (1:15) and no one supported him at his first defense before the Imperial Court (4:16). Abandoned by almost everyone (4:10, 11), the apostle found himself in circumstances very different from those of his first Roman imprisonment (Acts 28:16–31). At that time he was merely under house arrest, people could freely visit him, and he had the hope of release. Now he was in a cold Roman cell (4:13), regarded "as a criminal" (2:9), and without hope of acquittal in spite of the success of his initial defense (4:6–8, 17, 18). Under these conditions, Paul wrote this epistle in the fall of A.D. 67, hoping that Timothy would be able to visit him before the approaching winter (4:21). Timothy evidently was in Ephesus at the time of this letter (see 1:18; 4:19), and on his way to Rome he would go through Troas (4:13) and Macedonia. Priscilla and Aquila (4:19) probably returned from Rome (Rom. 16:3) to Ephesus after the burning of Rome and the beginning of the persecution. Tychicus may have been the bearer of this letter (4:12).

THE CHRIST OF SECOND TIMOTHY

Christ Jesus appeared on earth, "abolished death, and brought life and immortality

to light through the gospel" (1:10). He rose from the dead (2:8) and provides salvation and "eternal glory" (2:10); for if believers "died with Him" they will "also live with Him" (2:11). All who love His appearing will receive the "crown of righteousness" (4:8) and "reign with Him" (2:12).

KEYS TO SECOND TIMOTHY

Key Word: Endurance in the Pastoral Ministry—In this letter, Paul commissions Timothy to faithfully endure and carry on the work that the condemned apostle must now relinquish. This set of instructions exhorts Timothy to use the Word of God constantly in order to overcome growing obstacles to the spread of the gospel. Timothy is in great need of encouragement because of the hardships he is facing, and Paul uses this letter to instruct him about handling persecution from the secular authorities, and dissension and deception from within the church. As a spiritual father, Paul urges his young helper to overcome his natural timidity and boldly proclaim the gospel, even if it means that he will suffer for doing so.

Key Verses: Second Timothy 2:3, 4 and 3:14–17—"Suffer hardship with *me*, as a good soldier of Christ Jesus. No soldier in active service entangles himself in the affairs of everyday life, so that he may please the one who enlisted him as a soldier" (2:3, 4).

"You, however, continue in the things you have learned and become convinced of, knowing from whom you have learned *them;* and that from childhood you have known the sacred writings which are able to give you the wisdom that leads to salvation through faith which is in Christ Jesus. All Scripture is inspired by God and profitable for teaching, for reproof, for correction, for training in

righteousness; that the man of God may be adequate, equipped for every good work" (3:14–17).

Key Chapter: Second Timothy 2—The second chapter of Second Timothy ought to be required daily reading for every pastor and full-time Christian worker. Paul lists the keys to an enduring successful ministry: (1) a reproducing ministry (1 and 2), an enduring ministry (3–13), a studying ministry (14–18), and a holy ministry (19–26).

SURVEY OF SECOND TIMOTHY

Paul knows as he writes this final epistle that his days on earth are quickly drawing to a close. About to relinquish his heavy burdens, the godly apostle seeks to challenge and strengthen his somewhat timid but faithful associate, Timothy, in his difficult ministry in Ephesus. In spite of Paul's bleak circumstances, this is a letter of encouragement that urges Timothy on to steadfastness in the fulfillment of his divinely appointed task. Paul calls Timothy a "good soldier of Christ Jesus" (2:3), and it is clear from the sharp imperatives that this letter is really a combat manual for use in the spiritual warfare: "kindle afresh" (1:6); "do not be ashamed" (1:8, 12, 13); "join with *me* in suffering" (1:8); "Retain the standard" (1:13); "guard . . . the treasure" (1:14); "be strong" (2:1); "suffer hardship" (2:3); "be diligent to present yourself approved" (2:15); "flee . . . pursue" (2:22); "refuse"(2:23); "be on guard" (4:15). Central to everything in Second Timothy is the sure foundation of the Word of God. Paul focuses on the need to persevere in present testings (1 and 2), and to endure in future testings (3 and 4).

Persevere in Present Testings (1 and 2): After his salutation to his "beloved son" (1:2), Paul expresses his thanksgiving for Timothy's "sin-

FOCUS	PERSEVERE IN PRESENT TESTINGS			ENDURE IN FUTURE TESTINGS		
REFERENCE	1:1————1:6———————2:1			——3:1————————4:1————4:6————4:22		
DIVISION	THANKSGIVING FOR TIMOTHY'S FAITH	REMINDER OF TIMOTHY'S RESPONSIBILITY	CHARACTERISTICS OF A FAITHFUL MINISTER	APPROACHING DAY OF APOSTASY	CHARGE TO PREACH THE WORD	APPROACHING DEATH OF PAUL
TOPIC	POWER OF THE GOSPEL		PERSEVERANCE OF THE GOSPEL	PROTECTOR OF THE GOSPEL	PROCLAMATION OF THE GOSPEL	
	REMINDER		REQUIREMENTS	RESISTANCE	REQUESTS	
LOCATION	ROMAN PRISON					
TIME	C. A.D. 67					

cere faith" (1:5). He then encourages Timothy to stand firm in the power of the gospel and to overcome any fear in the face of opposition. At personal risk, Onesiphorus boldly sought out Paul in Rome, but most of the Asian Christians failed to stand behind Paul at the time of his arrest. Timothy must remain faithful and not fear possible persecution. Paul then exhorts his spiritual son to reproduce in the lives of others what he has received in Christ (four generations are mentioned in 2:2). He is responsible to work hard and discipline himself like a teacher, a soldier, a farmer, a workman, a vessel, and a servant, following the example of Paul's perseverance (2:1–13). In his dealings with others, Timothy must not become entangled in false speculation, foolish quarrels, or youthful lusts, which would hamper his effectiveness. As he pursues "righteousness, faith, love *and* peace" (2:22) he must know how to graciously overcome error.

Endure in Future Testings (3 and 4): Paul anticipates a time of growing apostasy and wickedness when men and women will be increasingly susceptible to empty religiosity and false teaching (3:1–9). Arrogance and godlessness will breed further deception and persecution, but Timothy must not waiver in using the Scripture to combat doctrinal error and moral evil (3:10–17). The Scriptures are inspired ("God-breathed") and with them Timothy is equipped to carry out the ministry to which he was called. Paul's final exhortation to Timothy (4:1–5) is a classic summary of the task of the man of God to proclaim the gospel in spite of opposing circumstances. This very personal letter closes with an update of Paul's situation in Rome along with certain requests (4:6–22). Paul longs to see Timothy before the end, and he also needs certain articles, especially "the parchments" (probably portions of the Old Testament Scriptures).

OUTLINE OF SECOND TIMOTHY

CHAPTER 1

Thanksgiving for Timothy's Faith

PAUL, ᴿan apostle of ᴿChrist Jesus ᵀby the will of God, according to the promise of life in Christ Jesus,   2 Cor. 1:1 • Gal. 3:26 • *through*

2 to ᴿTimothy, my beloved ᵀson: Grace, mercy *and* peace from God the Father and Christ Jesus our Lord.   Acts 16:1 • *child*

3 I thank God, whom I serve with a clear conscienceᵀthe way my forefathers did, as I constantly remember you in my ^prayers night and day,   *from my forefathers* • *petitions*

4 longing to see you, even as I recall your tears, so that I may be filled with joy.

5 For I am mindful of the sincere faith within you, which first dwelt in your grandmother Lois, andᴿyour mother Eunice, and I am sure that *it is* in you as well.   Acts 16:1

Reminder of Timothy's Responsibility

6 And for this reason I remind you to

kindle afresh the gift of God which is in you through the laying on of my hands.

7 For God has not given us a ᴿspirit of timidity, but of power and love and ^discipline.   John 14:27; Rom. 8:15 • *sound judgment*

8 Therefore do not be ashamed of the testimony of our Lord, or of me His prisoner; but join with *me* in suffering for the gospel according to the power of God,

9 who hasᴿsaved us, and called us with a holyᴿcalling,ᴿnot according to our works, but according to His own purpose and grace which was granted us in Christ Jesus from all eternity,   Rom. 11:14 • Rom. 11:29 • Eph. 2:9

10 but now has been revealed by the appearing of our Savior Christ Jesus, who abolished death, and brought life and immortality to light through the gospel,

11 ᴿfor which I was appointed a preacher and an apostle and a teacher.   1 Tim. 2:7

12 For this reason I also suffer these things, but I am not ashamed; for I know ᴿwhom I have believed and I am convinced

that He is able to guard what I have entrusted to Him^until that day.   Titus 3:8 • *for*

13 Retain the standard of sound words which you have heard from me, in the faith and love which are in Christ Jesus.

14 Guard, through the Holy Spirit who ^Rdwells in us, the^Ttreasure which has been entrusted to *you*.   Rom. 8:9 • *good deposit*

15 You are aware of the fact that all who are in Asia turned away from me, among whom are Phygelus and Hermogenes.

16 The Lord grant mercy to the house of Onesiphorus for he often refreshed me, and was not ashamed of my^Tchains;   *chain*

17 but when he was in Rome, he eagerly searched for me, and found me—

18 the Lord grant to him to find mercy from the Lord on^Rthat day—and you know very well what services he rendered at^REphesus.   1 Cor. 1:8; 3:13 • Acts 18:19; 1 Tim. 1:3

CHAPTER 2

Discipling Teacher

YOU therefore, my ^Tson, be strong in the grace that is in^RChrist Jesus.   *child* • 2 Tim. 1:1

2 And the things^Rwhich you have heard from me in the presence of many witnesses, these entrust to faithful men, who will be able to teach others also.   2 Tim. 1:13

Single-minded Soldier

3 ^RSuffer hardship with *me*, as a good^Rsoldier of Christ Jesus.   2 Tim. 1:8 • 1 Cor. 9:7

4 No soldier in active service^Rentangles himself in the affairs of everyday life, so that he may please the one who enlisted him as a soldier.   2 Pet. 2:20

5 And also if anyone competes as an athlete, he does not win the prize unless he competes according to the rules.

Enduring Farmer

6 The hard-working farmer ought to be the first to receive his share of the crops.

7 Consider what I say, for the Lord will give you understanding in everything.

8 Remember Jesus Christ,^Rrisen from the dead,^Rdescendant of David,^Raccording to my gospel,   Acts 2:24 • Matt. 1:1 • Rom. 2:16

9 ^Tfor which I suffer hardship even to^Rimprisonment as a criminal; but the word of God is not imprisoned.   *in which* • Phil. 1:7

10 For this reason I endure all things for the sake of those who are chosen, that they also may obtain the salvation which is in Christ Jesus *and* with *it* eternal glory.

11 ^RIt is a trustworthy statement:
For^Rif we died with Him, we shall also
live with Him;   1 Tim. 1:15 • Rom. 6:8

12 If we endure,^Rwe shall also reign with
Him;   [Matt. 19:28]

If we deny Him, He also will deny us;

13 If we are faithless, He remains faithful; for He cannot deny Himself.

Diligent Workman

14 Remind *them* of these things, and solemnly charge *them* in the presence of God not to wrangle about words, which is useless, *and leads* to the ruin of the hearers.

15 Be diligent to^Rpresent yourself approved to God as a workman who does not need to be ashamed, handling accurately the^Rword of truth.   Rom. 6:13 • Eph. 1:13

16 But avoid worldly *and* empty chatter, for it will lead to further ungodliness,

17 and their ^Ttalk will spread like [1]gangrene. Among them are ^RHymenaeus and Philetus,   *word* • 1 Tim. 1:20

18 *men* who have gone astray from the truth saying that ^Rthe resurrection has already taken place, and thus they upset^Rthe faith of some.   1 Cor. 15:12 • 1 Tim. 1:19

19 Nevertheless, the ^Rfirm foundation of God stands, having this seal, "The Lord knows those who are His," and, "Let everyone who names the name of the Lord abstain from wickedness." Is. 28:16f.; 1 Tim. 3:15

Sanctified Vessel

20 Now in a large house there are not only gold and silver vessels, but also vessels of wood and of earthenware, and^Rsome to honor and some to dishonor.   Rom. 9:21

21 Therefore, if a man cleanses himself from ^Rthese *things*, he will be a vessel for honor, sanctified, useful to the Master, prepared for every good work.   1 Tim. 6:11

22 Now^Rflee from youthful lusts, and pursue righteousness, ^Rfaith, love *and* peace, with those who^Rcall on the Lord from a pure heart.   1 Tim. 6:11 • 1 Tim. 1:14 • Acts 7:59

23 But refuse foolish and ignorant speculations, knowing that they produce quarrels.

Gentle Servant

24 And^Rthe Lord's bond-servant must not be quarrelsome, but be kind to all, able to teach, patient when wronged,   1 Tim. 3:3

25 ^Rwith gentleness correcting those who are in opposition,^Rif perhaps God may grant them repentance leading to^Rthe knowledge of the truth,   Gal. 6:1 • Acts 8:22 • 1 Tim. 2:4

26 and they may come to their senses *and* escape from the snare of the devil, having been held captive by him to do his will.

CHAPTER 3

Coming of Apostasy

BUT realize this, that^Rin the last days difficult times will come.   1 Tim. 4:1

---

[1] Or, *cancer*

2 For men will be lovers of self, lovers of money, boastful, arrogant, revilers, disobedient to parents, ungrateful, unholy,

3 ᴿunloving, irreconcilable,ᴿmalicious gossips, without self-control, brutal,ᵀhaters of good,   Rom. 1:31 • 1 Tim. 3:11 • *not loving good*

4 treacherous, reckless, conceited, lovers of pleasure rather than lovers of God;

5 holding to a form of ᴬgodliness, although they have denied its power; and ᴿavoid such men as these.   *religion* • Matt. 7:15

6 For among them are those whoᴬenter into households and captivateᴿweak women weighed down with sins, led on byᴿvarious impulses,   *creep into* • 1 Tim. 5:6 • Titus 3:3

7 always learning and never able to come to the knowledge of the truth.

8 And just as ᴿJannes and Jambres ᴿopposed Moses, so these *men* also oppose the truth, men of depraved mind, rejected as regards the faith.   Ex. 7:11 • Acts 13:8

9 But they will not make further progress; for theirᴿfolly will be obvious to all, as also that of those *two* came to be.   Luke 6:11

Confronting Apostasy

10 But you ᴿfollowed my teaching, conduct, purpose, faith, patience, love,ᴬperseverance,   Phil. 2:20, 22; 1 Tim. 4:6 • *steadfastness*

11 persecutions, *and* sufferings, such as happened to me at Antioch, at Iconium *and* at Lystra; what persecutions I endured, and out of them all the Lord delivered me!

12 And indeed, all who desire to live godly in Christ Jesusᴴwill be persecuted.   Acts 14:22

13 But evil men and impostors ᴿwill proceed *from bad* to worse, ᴿdeceiving and being deceived.   2 Tim. 2:16 • Titus 3:3

14 You, however,ᴿcontinue in the things you have learned and become convinced of, knowing from whom you have learned *them*;   2 Tim. 1:13; Titus 1:9

15 and that from childhood you have known the sacred writings which are able to give you the wisdom that leads to salvation through faith which is in Christ Jesus.

16 ²All Scripture is inspired by God and

² Or possibly, *Every Scripture inspired by God is also profitable*

profitable for teaching, for reproof, for correction, for training in righteousness;

17 thatᴿthe man of God may be adequate, equipped for every good work.   1 Tim. 6:11

CHAPTER 4

Charge to Preach the Word

I SOLEMNLY charge *you* in the presence of God and of Christ Jesus, who is toᴿjudge the living and the dead, and by Hisᴿappearing and His kingdom: Acts 10:42 • 2 Thess. 2:8

2 preach the word; be ready in season *and* out of season; reprove, rebuke, exhort, withᵀgreat patience and instruction.   *all*

3 Forᴿthe time will come when they will not endureᴿsound doctrine; but *wanting* to have their ears tickled, they will accumulate for themselves teachers in accordance to their own desires;   2 Tim. 3:1 • 1 Tim. 1:10

4 and will turn away their ears from the truth, and will turn aside to myths.

5 But you, be sober in all things,ᴿendure hardship, do the work of anᴿevangelist, fulfill your ministry.   2 Tim. 1:8 • Acts 21:8

Paul's Hope in Death

6 For I am already beingᴿpoured out as a drink offering, and the time ofᴿmy departure has come.   Phil. 2:17 • [Phil. 1:23]; 2 Pet. 1:14

7 I have fought the good fight, I have finished the course, I have kept the faith;

8 in the future thereᴿis laid up for me the crown of righteousness, which the Lord, the righteous Judge, will award to me on that day; and not only to me, but also to all who have loved His appearing.   Col. 1:5; [1 Pet. 1:4]

Paul's Situation in Prison

9 Make every effort to come to me soon;

10 for Demas, having loved this present ᴬworld, has deserted me and gone to Thessalonica; Crescens *has* gone to Galatia, Titus to Dalmatia.   *age*

4:2 Sharing Our Faith: When?—A famous evangelist once ended a revival meeting in Chicago by advising the unbelievers who were present that night to go home and seriously consider the claims of the gospel, and then return on the following night prepared to make a decision for Christ. But on that same night, October 8, 1871, the tragic Chicago fire broke out. Before it was finally extinguished nearly four miles of buildings were consumed, along with 250 human fatalities. The evangelist then vowed never to end a service without giving an invitation to accept Christ immediately.

The question as to when we should share our faith is directly tied to when a sinner should accept Christ. The Bible is clear that God's accepted time is today. See Hebrews 3:15; 4:7; Second Corinthians 6:2; Isaiah 55:6. The reason for this is very simple—a sinner has no assurance whatsoever that he will live to see tomorrow. See Proverbs 27:1; Luke 12:19; James 4:13–15.

Thus, we are to witness any time, all the time, in any place and in all places. The apostle Paul shows us how this should be done. He witnesses everywhere, in a prison at midnight (Page 1113—Acts 16:25–31), and even on a sinking ship during a dark and stormy day (Page 1125—Acts 27:20–25).

Now turn to Page 565—Ps. 73:1: Walking in the Spirit: Confession.

11 [R]Only [R]Luke is with me. Pick up [R]Mark and bring him with you, for he is useful to me for service.　2 Tim. 1:15 · Col. 4:14 · Acts 12:12

12 But Tychicus I have sent to Ephesus.

13 When you come bring the cloak which I left at [R]Troas with Carpus, and the books, especially the parchments.　Acts 16:8

14 [R]Alexander the coppersmith did me much harm; the Lord will repay him according to his deeds.　Acts 19:33; 1 Tim. 1:20

15 Be on guard against him yourself, for he vigorously opposed our [T]teaching.　words

16 At my first defense no one supported me, but all deserted me; [R]may it not be counted against them.　Acts 7:60; [1 Cor. 13:5]

17 But the Lord stood with me, and strengthened me, in order that through me the proclamation might be fully accomplished, and that all the Gentiles might hear; and I was delivered out of the lion's mouth.

18 The Lord will deliver me from every evil deed, and will [A]bring me safely to His heavenly kingdom; to [T]Him *be* the glory forever and ever. Amen.　*save me for · Whom*

Paul's Closing Greetings

19 Greet Prisca and [R]Aquila, and the household of Onesiphorus.　Acts 18:2

20 [R]Erastus remained at Corinth, but Trophimus I left sick at Miletus.　Acts 19:22

21 Make every effort to come before winter. Eubulus greets you, also Pudens and Linus and Claudia and all the brethren.

22 [R]The Lord be with your spirit. [R]Grace be with you.　Gal. 6:18; Phil. 4:23 · Col. 4:18

THE EPISTLE OF PAUL TO

TITUS

THE BOOK OF TITUS

Titus, a young pastor, faces the unenviable assignment of setting in order the church at Crete. Paul writes advising him to appoint elders, men of proven spiritual character in their homes and businesses, to oversee the work of the church. But elders are not the only individuals in the church who are required to excel spiritually. Men and women, young and old, each have their vital functions to fulfill in the church if they are to be living examples of the doctrine they profess. Throughout his letter to Titus, Paul stresses the necessary, practical working out of salvation in the daily lives of both the elders and the congregation. Good works are desirable and profitable for all believers.

This third Pastoral Epistle is simply titled *Pros Titon*, "To Titus." Ironically, this was also the name of the Roman general who destroyed Jerusalem in A.D. 70 and succeeded his father Vespasian as emperor.

THE AUTHOR OF TITUS

Since the Pastoral Epistles have to be treated as a unit on the matter of authorship, see "The Author of First Timothy" for the authorship of Titus.

Titus is not mentioned in Acts, but the thirteen references to him in the Pauline epistles make it clear that he was one of Paul's closest and most trusted companions. This convert of Paul ("my true child in a common faith," Titus 1:4) was probably from Syrian Antioch, if he was one of the disciples of Acts 11:26. Paul brought this uncircumcised Greek believer to Jerusalem (Gal. 2:3) where he became a test case on the matter of Gentiles and liberty from the law. Years later when Paul set out from Antioch on his third missionary journey (Acts 18:22), Titus must have accompanied him because he was sent by the apostle to Corinth on three occasions during that time (2 Cor. 2:12, 13; 7:5-7, 13-15; 8:6, 16-24). He is not mentioned again until Paul leaves him in Crete to carry on the work (Titus 1:5). He was with Paul during his second Roman imprisonment but left to go to Dalmatia (2 Tim. 4:10), possibly on an evangelistic mission. Paul spoke of this reliable and gifted associate as his "brother" (2 Cor. 2:13), his "partner and fellow worker" (2 Cor. 8:23), and his "child" (1:4). He lauded Titus's character and conduct in Second Corinthians 7:13-15 and 8:16, 17.

THE TIME OF TITUS

For a tentative reconstruction of the events following Paul's first Roman imprisonment, see "The Time of First Timothy."

The Mediterranean island of Crete is 156 miles long and up to 30 miles wide, and its first-century inhabitants were notorious for untruthfulness and immorality (1:12, 13). "To act the Cretan" became an idiom meaning "to play the liar." A number of Jews from Crete were present in Jerusalem at the time of Peter's sermon on the Day of Pentecost (Acts 2:11), and some of them may have believed in Christ and introduced the gospel to their countrymen. Certainly Paul would not have had opportunity to do evangelistic work during his brief sojourn in Crete while he was en route to Rome (Acts 27:7-13). The apostle spread the gospel in the cities of Crete after his release from Roman imprisonment and left Titus there to finish organizing the churches (1:5). Because of the problem of immorality among the Cretans, it was important for Titus to stress the need for righteousness in Christian living. False teachers, especially "those of the circumcision" (1:10), were also misleading and divisive. Paul wrote this letter about A.D. 63, perhaps from Corinth, taking advantage of the journey of Zenas and Apollos (3:13), whose destination would take them by way of Crete. Paul was planning to spend the winter in Nicopolis (western Greece), and he urged Titus in this letter to join him there upon his replacement by Artemas or Tychicus (3:12). Paul may have been planning to leave Nicopolis for Spain in the spring, and he wanted his useful companion Titus to accompany him.

THE CHRIST OF TITUS

The deity and redemptive work of Christ are beautifully stated in 2:13, 14: "Looking for the blessed hope and the appearing of the glory of our great God and Savior, Christ Jesus; who gave Himself for us, that He might redeem us from every lawless deed and purify for Himself a people for His own possession, zealous for good deeds."

KEYS TO TITUS

Key Word: Conduct Manual for Church Living—This brief letter focuses on Titus's role and responsibility in the organization and supervision of the churches in Crete. It is written to strengthen and exhort

Titus to firmly exercise his authority as an apostolic representative to churches that need to be put in order, refuting false teachers and dissenters and replacing immoral behavior with good deeds. Paul uses this letter to remind Titus of some of the details related to his task, including the qualifications for elders and the behavior expected of various groups in the churches. Paul includes three doctrinal sections in this letter to stress that proper belief (orthodoxy) gives the basis for proper behavior (orthopraxy).

Key Verses: Titus 1:5 and 3:8—"For this reason I left you in Crete, that you might set in order what remains, and appoint elders in every city as I directed you" (1:5).

"This is a trustworthy statement; and concerning these things I want you to speak confidently so that those who have believed God may be careful to engage in good deeds. These things are good and profitable for men" (3:8).

Key Chapter: Titus 2—Summarized in Titus 2 are the key commands to be obeyed which insure godly relationships within the church. Paul includes all categories of people instructing them to show "all good faith that they may adorn the doctrine of God our Savior in every respect" (2:10).

SURVEY OF TITUS

Titus, like First Timothy, was written by Paul after his release from Roman imprisonment and was also written to an associate who was given the task of organizing and supervising a large work as an apostolic representative. Paul left Titus on the island of Crete to "set in order what remains, and appoint elders in every city" (1:5). Not long after Paul's departure from Crete, he wrote this letter to encourage and assist Titus in his task. It stresses sound doctrine and warns against

those who distort the truth, but it also is a conduct manual that emphasizes good deeds and the proper conduct of various groups within the churches. This epistle falls into two major sections: appoint elders (1); set things in order (2 and 3).

Appoint Elders (1): The salutation to Titus is actually a compact doctrinal statement, which lifts up "His word" as the source of the truth that reveals the way to eternal life (1:1-4). Paul reminds Titus of his responsibility to organize the churches of Crete by appointing elders (also called overseers; see 1:5, 7) and rehearses the qualifications these spiritual leaders must meet (1:5-9). This is especially important in view of the disturbances that are being caused by false teachers who are upsetting a number of the believers with their Judaic myths and commandments (1:10-16). The natural tendency toward moral laxity among the Cretans coupled with that kind of deception is a dangerous force that must be overcome by godly leadership and sound doctrine.

Set Things in Order (2 and 3): Titus is given the charge to "speak the things which are fitting for sound doctrine" (2:1), and Paul delineates Titus's role with regard to various groups in the church, including older men, older women, young women, young men, and bondslaves (2:2-10). The knowledge of Christ must affect a transformation in each of these groups so that their testimony will "adorn the doctrine of God" (2:10). The second doctrinal statement of Titus (2:11-14) gives the basis for the appeals Paul has just made for righteous living. God in His grace redeems believers from being slaves of sin, assuring them the "blessed hope" of the coming of Christ that will eventually be realized. Paul urges Titus to authoritatively proclaim these truths (2:15).

In chapter 3, Paul moves from conduct in

FOCUS	APPOINT ELDERS		SET THINGS IN ORDER	
REFERENCE	1:1————————1:10		——————2:1——————————3:1——————————3:15	
DIVISION	ORDAIN QUALIFIED ELDERS	REBUKE FALSE TEACHERS	SPEAK SOUND DOCTRINE	MAINTAIN GOOD WORKS
TOPIC	PROTECTION OF SOUND DOCTRINE		PRACTICE OF SOUND DOCTRINE	
	ORGANIZATION	OFFENDERS	OPERATION	OBEDIENCE
LOCATION	PROBABLY WRITTEN IN CORINTH			
TIME	C. A.D. 63			

groups (2:1–10) to conduct in general (3:1–11). The behavior of believers as citizens must be different than the behavior of unbelievers because of their regeneration and renewal by the Holy Spirit. The third doctrinal statement in this book (3:4–7) emphasizes the kindness, love, and mercy of God who saves us "not on the basis of deeds which we have done in right-eousness" (3:5). Nevertheless, the need for good deeds as a result of salvation is stressed six times in the three chapters of Titus (1:16; 2:7, 14; 3:1, 8, 14). Paul exhorts Titus to deal firmly with dissenters who would cause factions and controversies (3:9–11) and closes the letter with three instructions, a greeting, and a benediction (3:12–15).

OUTLINE OF TITUS

CHAPTER 1

Introduction

PAUL, a bond-servant of God, and an apostle of Jesus Christ, for the faith of those chosen of God and the knowledge of the truth which is according to godliness,

2 in the hope of eternal life, which God, who cannot lie, promised long ages ago,

3 but at the proper time manifested, *even* His word, in the proclamation with which I was entrusted according to the commandment of ᴿGod our Savior; Luke 1:47; 1 Tim. 1:1

4 to Titus, my true childᵀin a common faith: Grace and peace from God the Father and Christ Jesus our Savior. *according to*

Ordain Qualified Elders

5 For this reason I left you inᴿCrete, that youᴿ might ᴿset in order what remains, and appointᴿelders in every city as I directed you, Acts 27:7 • Acts 14:23 • Acts 11:30

6 *namely,*ᴿif any man be above reproach, theᴿhusband of one wife, having children who believe, not accused ofᴿdissipation or rebellion. 1 Tim. 3:2-4 • 1 Tim. 3:2 • Eph. 5:18

7 For the overseer must be above reproach as God's steward, not self-willed, not quick-tempered, not addicted to wine, not pugnacious, not fond of sordid gain,

8 but hospitable, loving what is good, sensible, just, devout, self-controlled,

9 holding fast the faithful word which is in accordance with the teaching, that he may be able both to exhort in sound doctrine and to refute those who contradict.

Reprove False Teachers

10 For there are many rebellious men, empty talkers and deceivers, especially ᴿthose of the circumcision, Acts 11:2

11 who must be silenced because they are upsetting ᴿwhole families, teaching ᴿthings they should not *teach,*ᴿfor the sake of sordid gain. 1 Tim. 5:4 • 1 Tim. 5:13 • 1 Tim. 6:5

12 One of themselves, a prophet of their own, said, "Cretansᴿare always liars, evil beasts, lazy gluttons." Acts 2:11; 27:7

13 This testimony is true. For this cause ᴿreprove them ᴿseverely in the faith, 1 Tim. 5:20 • 2 Cor. 13:10

14 not paying attention to Jewishᴿmyths

1:2 Promise of God—Often the Christian will doubt his salvation simply because he does not feel saved, not understanding that the basis for that salvation is the promise of God and not emotional feelings. In fact, the entire Trinity is involved in this.
a. The promise and work of the Father in our salvation. He has promised to graciously accept in Christ all repenting sinners (Page 1185—Eph. 1:6; Page 1201—Col. 3:3). This means a Christian has the right to be in heaven someday, for he is in Christ. God guarantees to us that He will work out all things for our good (Page 1138—Rom. 8:28).
b. The promise and work of the Son. He has promised us eternal life (Page 1069—John 5:24) and abundant life (Page 1076—John 10:10). This covers not only our final destiny in heaven, but also our present Christian service here on earth. He is, in fact, right now praying for us and ministering to us at His Father's right hand (Page 1243—Heb. 8:1; 9:24).
c. The promise and work of the Holy Spirit. The Holy Spirit is said to indwell the believer (Page 1081—John 14:16). In addition, He places all believing sinners into the body of Christ, thus assuring us of union with God Himself (Page 1158—1 Cor. 12:13).
Now turn to Page 1277—1 John 3:24: Witness of the Spirit.

and[R]commandments of men who[R]turn away from the truth. 1 Tim. 1:4 • Col. 2:22 • 2 Tim. 4:4

15 [R]To the pure, all things are pure; but to those who are defiled and unbelieving, nothing is pure, but both their[R]mind and their conscience are defiled. Luke 11:41 • 1 Tim. 6:5

16 [R]They profess to know God, but by *their* deeds they[R]deny *Him*, being detestable and [R]disobedient, and worthless [R]for any good deed. 1 John 2:4 • 1 Tim. 5:8 • Titus 3:3 • 2 Tim. 3:17

CHAPTER 2

Speak Sound Doctrine

BUT as for you, speak the things which are fitting for[R]sound doctrine. Titus 1:9

2 [R]Older men are to be temperate, dignified, sensible,[R]sound in faith, in love, in^perseverance. Philem. 9 • Titus 1:13 • *steadfastness*

3 Older women likewise are to be reverent in their behavior,[R]not malicious gossips, nor[R]enslaved to much wine, teaching what is good, 1 Tim. 3:11 • 1 Tim. 3:8

4 that they may ^encourage the young women to love their husbands, to love their children, *train*

5 *to be* sensible, pure,[R]workers at home, kind, being[R]subject to their own husbands, [R]that the word of God may not be dishonored. 1 Tim. 5:14 • Eph. 5:22 • 1 Tim. 6:1

6 Likewise urge [R]the young men to be ^sensible; 1 Tim. 5:1 • *sensible in all things; show*

7 in all things show yourself to be[R]an example of good deeds, *with* [T]purity in doctrine, dignified, 1 Tim. 4:12 • *uncorruptness*

8 sound *in* speech which is beyond reproach, in order[R]that the opponent may be put to shame, having nothing bad to say about us. 2 Thess. 3:14; 1 Pet. 2:12

9 Urge[R]bondslaves to be subject to their own masters in everything, to be well-pleasing, not[T]argumentative, Eph. 6:5 • *contradicting*

10 not pilfering, but showing all good faith that they may adorn the doctrine of [R]God our Savior in every respect. Titus 1:3

11 For the grace of God has [R]appeared, bringing salvation to all men, 2 Tim. 1:10

12 instructing us to deny ungodliness and worldly desires and to live sensibly, righteously and godly in the present age,

13 looking for the blessed hope and the appearing of the glory of our great God and Savior, Christ Jesus;

14 who[R]gave Himself for us, that He might redeem us from every lawless deed and purify for Himself a people for His own possession, zealous for good deeds. Is. 53:12★

15 These things speak and[R]exhort and reprove with all [T]authority. [R]Let no one disregard you. 1 Tim. 4:13 • *command* • 1 Tim. 4:12

CHAPTER 3

Engage in Good Deeds

REMIND them[R]to be subject to rulers, to authorities, to be obedient, to be[R]ready for every good deed, [Rom. 13:1] • 2 Tim. 2:21

2 to malign no one,[R]to be uncontentious, gentle,[R]showing every consideration for all men. 1 Tim. 3:3; 1 Pet. 2:18 • 2 Tim. 2:25

3 For we also once were foolish ourselves, [R]disobedient, deceived, enslaved to [R]various lusts and pleasures, spending our life in malice and envy, hateful, hating one another. Titus 1:16 • 2 Tim. 3:6; Titus 2:12

4 But when the kindness of God our Savior and *His* love for mankind appeared,

5 He saved us, not on the basis of deeds which we have done in righteousness, but [R]according to His mercy, by the[R]washing of regeneration and [R]renewing by the Holy Spirit, Eph. 2:4 • John 3:5 • [Rom. 12:2]

6 [R]whom He poured out upon us richly through Jesus Christ our Savior, Rom. 5:5

7 that being justified by His grace we might be made heirs^according to *the* hope of eternal life. *of eternal life according to hope*

8 [R]This is a trustworthy statement; and concerning these things I[R]want you to speak confidently, so that those who have believed God may be careful to [R]engage in good deeds. These things are good and profitable for men. 1 Tim. 1:15 • 1 Tim. 2:8 • Titus 2:7, 14; 3:14

9 But shun[R]foolish controversies and[R]genealogies and strife and disputes about the Law; for they are[R]unprofitable and worthless. 1 Tim. 2:23 • 1 Tim. 1:4 • 2 Tim. 2:14

10 [R]Reject a[R]factious man after a first and second warning, 2 John 10 • Rom. 16:17

3:5 **The Work of the Holy Spirit in Salvation**—There are three wonderful works performed by the Holy Spirit in preparing unsaved people to become Christians.

a. The work of the Holy Spirit in restraining. Satan would enjoy nothing more than to destroy people before they make their decision to accept Christ as Savior. But the Holy Spirit prevents this from occurring (Page 707—Is. 59:19).

b. The work of the Holy Spirit in convicting. Mankind's sin and righteousness are exposed by the Holy Spirit (Page 1083—John 16:8). There are two well-known examples of sinners being convicted by the Holy Spirit in the Book of Acts. Felix, a Roman governor, actually trembles under conviction as he hears Paul preach (Page 1122—Acts 24:25). The other case involves King Agrippa who responds to a gospel message by saying: "In a short time you will persuade me to become a Christian" (Page 1124—Acts 26:28).

c. The work of the Holy Spirit in regenerating. When a repenting sinner accepts Christ as Savior he is given a new nature by the Holy Spirit. See Second Corinthians 5:17. Jesus carefully explained this ministry of the Holy Spirit to Nicodemus (Page 1066—John 3:3–7).

Now turn to Page 1153—1 Cor. 6:19: The Work of the Holy Spirit in Christian Living.

11 knowing that such a man is perverted and is sinning, being self-condemned.

Conclusion

12 When I send Artemas or [R]Tychicus to you,[R]make every effort to come to me at Nicopolis, for I have decided to[R]spend the winter there.   Acts 20:4 · 2 Tim. 4:9 · 2 Tim. 4:21

13 Diligently help Zenas the [R]lawyer and [R]Apollos on their way so that nothing is lacking for them.   Matt. 22:35.· Acts 18:24; 1 Cor. 16:12

14 And let our *people* also learn to engage in good[A]deeds to meet pressing needs, that they may not be unfruitful.   *occupations*

15 [R]All who are with me greet you. Greet those who love us in *the* faith.

[R]**Grace** be with you all.   Acts 20:34 · Col. 4:18

PHILEMON

📖 THE BOOK OF PHILEMON

Does Christian brotherly love really work, even in situations of extraordinary tension and difficulty? Will it work, for example, between a prominent slave owner and one of his runaway slaves? Paul had no doubt! He writes a "postcard" to Philemon, his beloved brother and fellow worker, on behalf of Onesimus—a deserter, thief, and formerly worthless slave, but now Philemon's brother in Christ. With much tact and tenderness, Paul asks Philemon to receive Onesimus back with the same gentleness with which he would receive Paul himself. Any debt Onesimus owes, Paul promises to make good. Knowing Philemon, Paul is confident that brotherly love and forgiveness will carry the day.

Since this letter is addressed to Philemon in verse 1, it becomes known as *Pros Philemona*, "To Philemon." Like First and Second Timothy and Titus, it is addressed to an individual, but unlike the Pastoral Epistles, Philemon is also addressed to a family and a church (v. 2).

✒️ THE AUTHOR OF PHILEMON

The authenticity of Philemon was not called into question until the fourth century, when certain theologians concluded that its lack of doctrinal content made it unworthy of the apostle Paul. But men like Jerome and Chrysostom soon vindicated this epistle, and it was not challenged again until the nineteenth century. Some radical critics who denied the authenticity of Colossians also turned against the Pauline authorship of Philemon because of the close connection between the two epistles (e.g., the same people are associated with Paul in both letters: cf. Col. 4:9, 10, 12, 14 with Philem. 10, 23, 24). The general consensus of scholarship, however, recognized Philemon as Paul's work. There could have been no doctrinal motive for its forgery, and it is supported externally by consistent tradition and internally by no less than three references to Paul (vv. 1, 9, 19).

⌛ THE TIME OF PHILEMON

Reconstructing the background of this letter, it appears that a slave named Onesimus had robbed or in some other way wronged his master Philemon and had escaped. He had made his way from Colossae to Rome where he had found relative safety among the masses in the Imperial City. Some-

how Onesimus had come into contact with Paul: it is possible that he had even sought out the apostle for help (Onesimus no doubt had heard Philemon speak of Paul). Paul had led him to Christ (v. 10), and although Onesimus had become a real asset to Paul, both knew that as a Christian, Onesimus had a responsibility to return to Philemon. That day came when Paul wrote his epistle to the Colossians. Tychicus was the bearer of that letter. Paul decided to send Onesimus along with Tychicus to Colossae (Col. 4:7–9; Philem. 12), knowing that it would be safer, in view of slave-catchers, to send Onesimus with a companion.

Philemon is one of the four Prison Epistles (see Ephesians, Philippians, and especially "The Time of Colossians" for background). It was written in A.D. 60 or 61 and dispatched at the same time as Colossians during Paul's first Roman imprisonment (see vv. 1, 9, 10, 13, 23). Philemon 22 reflects Paul's confident hope of release: "prepare me a lodging; for I hope that through your prayers I shall be given to you."

Philemon was a resident of Colossae (Col. 4:9, 17; Philem. 1, 2) and a convert of Paul (v. 19), perhaps through an encounter with Paul in Ephesus during Paul's third missionary journey. Philemon's house was large enough to serve as the meeting place for the church there (v. 2). He was benevolent to other believers (vv. 5–7), and his son Archippus evidently held a position of leadership in the church (Col. 4:17; Philem. 2). Philemon may have had other slaves in addition to Onesimus, and he was not alone as a slave owner among the Colossian believers (Col. 4:1). Thus this letter and his response would provide guidelines for other master-slave relationships.

According to Roman law, runaway slaves such as Onesimus could be severely punished or condemned to a violent death. It is doubtful that Onesimus would have returned to Philemon even with this letter if he had not become a believer in Christ.

✝️ THE CHRIST OF PHILEMON

The forgiveness that the believer finds in Christ is beautifully portrayed by analogy in Philemon. Onesimus, guilty of a great offense (vv. 11, 18), is motivated by Paul's love to intercede on his behalf (vv. 10–17). Paul lays aside his rights (v. 8) and becomes Onesimus's substitute by assuming his debt (vv. 18, 19). By Philemon's gracious act,

Onesimus is restored and placed in a new relationship (vv. 15, 16). In this analogy, we are as Onesimus. Paul's advocacy before Philemon is parallel to Christ's work of mediation before the Father. Onesimus was condemned by law but saved by grace.

KEYS TO PHILEMON
Key Word: Forgiveness from Slavery— Philemon develops the transition from bondage to brotherhood that is brought about by Christian love and forgiveness. Just as Philemon was shown mercy through the grace of Christ, so he must graciously forgive his repentant runaway who has returned as a brother in Christ. Paul writes this letter as his personal appeal that Philemon receive Onesimus even as he would receive Paul. This letter is also addressed to other Christians in Philemon's circle, because Paul wants it to have an impact on the Colossian church as a whole.

Key Verses: Philemon 16, 17—"No longer as a slave, but more than a slave, a beloved brother, especially to me, but how much more to you, both in the flesh and in the Lord. If then you regard me a partner, accept him as *you would* me" (vv. 16, 17).

SURVEY OF PHILEMON
The briefest of Paul's epistles (only 334 words in the Greek text) is a model of courtesy, discretion, and loving concern for the forgiveness of one who would otherwise face the sentence of death. This tactful and highly personal letter can be divided into three components: prayer of thanksgiving for Philemon (vv. 1–7); petition of Paul for Onesimus (vv. 8–16); promise of Paul to Philemon (vv. 17–25).

Prayer of Thanksgiving for Philemon (vv. 1–7): Writing this letter as a "prisoner of Christ Jesus," Paul addresses it personally to Philemon (a Christian leader in Colossae), to Apphia and Archippus (evidently Philemon's wife and son), as well as to the church that meets in Philemon's house. The main body of this compact letter begins with a prayer of thanksgiving for Philemon's faithfulness and love.

Petition of Paul for Onesimus (vv. 8–16): Basing his appeal on Philemon's character, Paul refuses to command Philemon to pardon and receive Onesimus. Instead, Paul seeks to persuade his friend of his Christian responsibility to forgive even as he was forgiven by Christ. Paul urges Philemon not to punish Onesimus but to receive him "no longer as a slave" but as "a beloved brother" (v. 16).

Promise of Paul to Philemon (vv. 17–25): Paul places Onesimus's debt on his account, but then reminds Philemon of the greater spiritual debt which Philemon himself owes as a convert to Christ (vv. 17–19).

Paul closes this effective epistle with a hopeful request (v. 22), greetings from his companions (vv. 23, 24), and a benediction (v. 25). The fact that it was preserved indicates Philemon's favorable response to Paul's pleas.

FOCUS	PRAYER OF THANKSGIVING	PETITION FOR ONESIMUS	PROMISE TO PHILEMON
REFERENCE	1 —————— 8	—————— 17	—————— 25
DIVISION	COMMENDATION OF PHILEMON'S LOVE	INTERCESSION FOR ONESIMUS	CONFIDENCE IN PHILEMON'S OBEDIENCE
TOPIC	PRAISE OF PHILEMON	PLEA OF PAUL	PLEDGE OF PAUL
	CHARACTER OF PHILEMON	CONVERSION OF ONESIMUS	CONFIDENCE OF PAUL
LOCATION	ROME		
TIME	c. A.D. 60–61		

OUTLINE OF PHILEMON

The Prayer of Thanksgiving for Philemon

PAUL, a prisoner of Christ Jesus, and Timothy[T]our brother, to Philemon our beloved *brother* and fellow worker, *the*

2 and to Apphia[T]our sister, and to [R]Archippus our fellow soldier, and to the church in your house: *the* • Col. 4:17

3 [R]Grace to you and peace from God our Father and the Lord Jesus Christ. Rom. 1:7

4 [R]I thank my God always, making mention of you in my prayers, Rom. 1:8f.

5 because I hear of your love, and of the faith which you have toward the Lord Jesus, and toward all the[A]saints; *holy ones*

6 *and I pray* that the fellowship of your faith may become effective [1]through the [R]knowledge of every good thing which is in [2]you for Christ's sake. Phil. 1:9; [Col. 1:9; 3:10]

7 For I have come to have much joy and comfort in your love, because the[T]hearts of the[A]saints have been refreshed through you, brother. *inward parts • holy ones*

The Petition of Paul for Onesimus

8 Therefore, though I have[T]enough confidence in Christ to order you *to do* that which is[R]proper, *much* • Eph. 5:4

9 yet for love's sake I rather appeal *to you*—since I am such a person as Paul,[A]the aged, and now also [R]a prisoner of [R]Christ Jesus— *an ambassador* • Philem. 1 • Gal. 3:26

10 I[R]appeal to you for my child, whom I have begotten in my[T]imprisonment, [3]Onesimus, Rom. 12:1 • *bonds*

11 who formerly was useless to you, but now is useful both to you and to me.

12 And I have sent him back to you in person, that is, *sending* my very heart,

13 whom I wished to keep with me, that in your behalf he might minister to me in my[T]imprisonment for the gospel; *bonds*

14 but without your consent I did not want to do anything, that your goodness should[R]not be as it were by compulsion, but of your own free will. 2 Cor. 9:7; 1 Pet. 5:2

15 For perhaps [R]he was for this reason parted *from you* for a while, that you should have him back forever, Gen. 45:5, 8

16 [R]no longer as a slave, but more than a slave, [R]a beloved brother, especially to me, but how much more to you, both in the flesh and in the Lord. [1 Cor. 7:22] • Matt. 23:8

The Promise of Paul to Philemon

17 If then you regard me a[R]partner, accept him as *you would* me. 2 Cor. 8:23

18 But if he has wronged you in any way, or owes you anything, charge that to my account;

19 [R]I, Paul, am writing this with my own hand, I will repay it (lest[R]I should[T]mention to you that you owe to me even your own self as well). 1 Cor. 16:21 • 2 Cor. 9:4 • *say*

20 Yes, brother, let me benefit from you in the Lord; refresh my heart in Christ.

21 [R]Having confidence in your obedience, I write to you, since I know that you will do even more than what I say. 2 Cor. 2:3

22 And at the same time also prepare me a lodging; for [R]I hope that through your prayers I shall be given to you. Phil. 1:25; 2:24

23 [R]Epaphras, my[R]fellow prisoner in Christ Jesus, greets you, Col. 1:7 • Rom. 16:7

24 *as do*[R]Mark, [R]Aristarchus, Demas, Luke, my fellow workers. Acts 12:12, 25 • Acts 19:29

25 [R]The grace of the Lord Jesus Christ be [R]with your spirit.[4] Gal. 6:18 • 2 Tim. 4:22

---

[1] Or, *in* [2] Some ancient mss. read *us* [3] I.e., useful
[4] Some ancient mss. add *Amen*

HEBREWS

THE BOOK OF HEBREWS

Many Jewish believers, having stepped out of Judaism into Christianity, want to reverse their course in order to escape persecution by their countrymen. The writer of Hebrews exhorts them to "press on to maturity" (6:1). His appeal is based on the superiority of Christ over the Judaic system. Christ is better than the angels, for they worship Him. He is better than Moses, for He created him. He is better than the Aaronic priesthood, for His sacrifice was once for all time. He is better than the Law, for He mediates a better covenant. In short, there is more to be gained in Christ than to be lost in Judaism. Pressing on in Christ produces tested faith, self-discipline, and a visible love seen in good works.

Although the King James Version uses the title "The Epistle of Paul the Apostle to the Hebrews," there is no early manuscript evidence to support it. The oldest and most reliable title is simply *Pros Ebraious*, "To Hebrews."

THE AUTHOR OF HEBREWS

Like the ancestry of Melchizedek, the origin of Hebrews is unknown. Uncertainty plagues not only its authorship, but also where it was written, its date, and its readership. The question of authorship delayed its recognition in the West as part of the New Testament canon in spite of early support by Clement of Rome. Not until the fourth century was it generally accepted as authoritative in the western church, when the testimonies of Jerome and Augustine settled the issue. In the eastern church, there was no problem of canonical acceptance because it was regarded as one of the "fourteen" epistles of Paul. The issue of its canonicity was again raised during the Reformation, but the spiritual depth and quality of Hebrews bore witness to its inspiration, despite its anonymity.

Hebrews 13:18–24 tells us that this book was not anonymous to the original readers; they evidently knew the author. For some reason, however, early church tradition is divided over the identity of the author. Part of the church attributed it to Paul; others preferred Barnabas, Luke, or Clement; and some chose anonymity. Thus, external evidence will not help determine the author. Internal evidence must be the final court of appeal, but here, too, the results are ambiguous. Some aspects of the language, style, and theology of Hebrews are very similar to Paul's epistles, and the author also refers to Timothy (13:23). However, significant differences have led the majority of biblical scholars to reject Pauline authorship of this book: (1) The Greek style of Hebrews is far more polished and refined than that found in any of Paul's recognized epistles. (2) In view of Paul's consistent claims to be an apostle and an eyewitness of Christ, it is very doubtful that he would have used the phraseology found in 2:3: "After it was at the first spoken through the Lord, it was confirmed to us by those who heard." (3) The lack of Paul's customary salutation, which includes his name, goes against the firm pattern found in all his other epistles. (4) While Paul used both the Hebrew text and the Septuagint to quote from the Old Testament, the writer of Hebrews apparently did not know Hebrew and quoted exclusively from the Septuagint. (5) Paul's common use of compound titles to refer to the Son of God is not followed in Hebrews, which usually refers to Him as Christ, Jesus, and Lord. (6) Hebrews concentrates on Christ's present priestly ministry, but Paul's writings have very little to say about the present work of Christ. Thus, Hebrews appears not to have been written by Paul although the writer shows a Pauline influence. The authority of Hebrews in no way depends upon Pauline authorship, especially since it does not claim to have been written by Paul.

Tertullian referred to Barnabas as the author of Hebrews, but it is unlikely that this resident of Jerusalem (Acts 4:36, 37) would include himself as one of those who relied on others for eyewitness testimony about Jesus (2:3). Other suggestions include Luke, Clement of Rome, Apollos, Silvanus (Silas), Philip, and even Priscilla. Some of these are possibilities, but we must agree with the third-century theologian Origen who wrote: "Who it was that really wrote the Epistle, God only knows."

THE TIME OF HEBREWS

Because of the exclusive use of the Septuagint (Greek translation of the Hebrew Old Testament) and the elegant Greek style found in Hebrews, some recent scholars have argued that this book was written to a

gentile readership. However, the bulk of the evidence favors the traditional view that the original recipients of this letter were Jewish Christians. In addition to the ancient title "To Hebrews," there is also the frequent use of the Old Testament as an unquestioned authority, the assumed knowledge of the sacrificial ritual, and the many contrasts between Christianity and Judaism, which are designed to prevent the readers from lapsing into Judaism.

Many places have been suggested for the locality of the readers, but this letter's destination cannot be determined with any certainty. In the past, Jerusalem was most frequently suggested, but this view is hindered by four problems: (1) It is unlikely that a book addressed to Palestineans would quote exclusively from the Septuagint rather that the Hebrew Old Testament. (2) Palestinian believers were poor (Rom. 15:26), but these readers were able to financially assist other Christians (6:10). (3) Residents of Jerusalem would not be characterized by the description in 2:3 because some would have been eyewitnesses of the ministry of Christ. (4) "You have not yet resisted to the point of shedding blood" (12:4) does not fit the situation in Jerusalem. The majority view today is that the recipients of Hebrews probably lived in Rome. The statement "Those from Italy greet you" in 13:24 seems to suggest that Italians away from Italy are sending their greetings home.

The recipients of this letter were believers (3:1) who had come to faith through the testimony of eyewitnesses of Christ (2:3). They were not novices (5:12), and they had successfully endured hardships because of their stand for the gospel (10:32–34). Unfortunately, they had become "dull of hearing" (5:11) and were in danger of drifting away (2:1; 3:12). This made them particularly susceptible to the re-newed persecutions that were coming upon them (12:4–12), and the author found it necessary to check the downward spiral with "this word of exhortation" (13:22). While there is disagreement over the specific danger involved, the classic position that the readers were on the verge of lapsing into Judaism to avoid persecution directed at Christians seems to be supported by the whole tenor of the book. Hebrews' repeated emphasis on the superiority of Christianity over Judaism would have been pointless if the readers were about to return to Gnosticism or heathenism.

The place of writing is unknown, but a reasonable estimate of the date can be made. Hebrews was quoted in A.D. 95 by Clement of Rome, but its failure to mention the ending of the Old Testament sacrificial system in the destruction of Jerusalem in A.D. 70 indicates that it was written prior to that date. Timothy was still alive (13:23), persecution was mounting, and the old Jewish system was about to be removed (12:26, 27). All this suggests a date between A.D. 64 and 68.

✝ THE CHRIST OF HEBREWS

Christ is our eternal High Priest according to the order of Melchizedek. He identified with man in His incarnation and offered no less a sacrifice than Himself on our behalf.

Hebrews presents Christ as the divine-human Prophet, Priest, and King. His deity (1:1–3, 8) and humanity (2:9, 14, 17, 18) are asserted with equal force, and over twenty titles are used to describe His attributes and accomplishments (e.g., heir of all things, Apostle and High Priest, mediator, author and perfecter of faith). He is superior to all who went before and offers the supreme sacrifice, priesthood, and covenant.

FOCUS	CHRIST'S PERSON			CHRIST'S WORK			THE WALK OF FAITH		
REFERENCE	1:1——1:4	——3:1	——4:14	——8:1	——9:1	——10:19	——12:1	——13:1–13:25	
DIVISION	CHRIST OVER PROPHETS	CHRIST OVER ANGELS	CHRIST OVER MOSES	PRIEST-HOOD	COVENANT	SANCTUARY AND SACRIFICE	ASSURANCE OF FAITH	ENDURANCE OF FAITH	EXHORTATION TO LOVE
TOPIC	MAJESTY OF CHRIST			MINISTRY OF CHRIST			MINISTERS FOR CHRIST		
	DOCTRINE						DISCIPLINE		
LOCATION	PLACE OF WRITING UNKNOWN								
TIME	c. A.D. 64–68								

KEYS TO HEBREWS

Key Word: The Superiority of Christ—
The basic theme of Hebrews is found in the word "better," describing the superiority of Christ in His person and work (1:4; 6:9; 7:19, 22; 8:6; 9:23; 10:34; 11:16, 35, 40; 12:24). The words "perfect" and "heavenly" are also prominent. He offers a better revelation, position, priesthood, covenant, sacrifice, and power. The writer develops this theme to prevent the readers from giving up the substance for the shadow by abandoning Christianity and retreating into the old Judaic system. This epistle is also written to exhort them to become mature in Christ and to put away their spiritual dullness and degeneration. Thus, it places heavy stress on doctrine, concentrating on Christology and soteriology (salvation).

Key Verses: Hebrews 4:14–16 and 12:1, 2— "Since then we have a great high priest who has passed through the heavens, Jesus the Son of God, let us hold fast our confession. For we do not have a high priest who cannot sympathize with our weaknesses, but one who has been tempted in all things as *we are, yet* without sin. Let us therefore draw near with confidence to the throne of grace, that we may receive mercy and may find grace to help in time of need" (4:14–16).

"Therefore since we have so great a cloud of witnesses surrounding us, let us also lay aside every encumbrance and the sin which so easily entangles us, and let us run with endurance the race that is set before us, fixing our eyes on Jesus, the author and perfecter of faith, who for the joy set before Him endured the cross, despising the shame, and has sat down at the right hand of the throne of God" (12:1, 2).

*Key Chapter: Hebrews 11—*The hall of fame of the Scriptures is located in Hebrews 11 and records those who willingly took God at His word even when there was nothing to cling to but His promise. Inherent to all those listed is the recognition that "without faith it is impossible to please *Him*, for he who comes to God must believe that He is, and *that* He is a rewarder of those who seek Him" (Heb. 11:6).

SURVEY OF HEBREWS

Hebrews stands alone among the New Testament Epistles in its style and approach, and it is the only New Testament book whose authorship remains a real mystery. This profound work builds a case for the superiority of Christ through a cumulative argument in which Christ is presented as "better" in every respect. In His person He is better than the angels, Moses, and Joshua; and in His per-

formance He provides a better priesthood, covenant, sanctuary, and sacrifice. Evidently, the readers are in danger of reverting to Judaism because of the suffering they are beginning to experience for their faith in Christ. However, by doing so, they would be retreating from the substance back into the shadow. In addition to his positive presentation of the supremacy of Christ, the writer intersperses five solemn warnings about the peril of turning away from Christ (2:1-4; 3:7—4:13; 5:11—6:20; 10:19-39; 12:25-29). These parenthetical warnings include cautions against neglect (2:1-4) and refusal (12:25-29). After using the Old Testament to demonstrate the superiority of Christ's person (1:1—4:13) and the superiority of Christ's work (4:14—10:18), the writer applies these truths in a practical way to show the superiority of the Christian's walk of faith (10:19—13:25).

The Superiority of Christ's Person (1:1—4:13): Instead of the usual salutation, this epistle immediately launches into its theme—the supremacy of Christ even over the Old Testament prophets (1:1-3). Christianity is built upon the highest form of divine disclosure: the personal revelation of God through His incarnate Son. Christ is therefore greater than the prophets, and He is also greater than the angels, the mediators of the Mosaic Law (1:4—2:18; see Acts 7:53; Heb. 2:2). This is seen in His name, His position, His worship by the angels, and His incarnation. The Son of God partook of flesh and blood and was "made like His brethren in all things" (2:17) in order to bring "many sons to glory" (2:10). Christ is also superior to Moses (3:1-6), for Moses was a servant in the house of God, but Christ is the Son over God's household. Because of these truths, the readers are exhorted to avoid the divine judgment that is visited upon unbelief (3:7—4:13). Their disbelief had prevented the generation of the Exodus from becoming the generation of the conquest, and the rest that Christ offers is so much greater than what was provided by Joshua. The readers are therefore urged to enter the eternal rest that is possessed by faith in Christ.

The Superiority of Christ's Work (4:14—10:18): The high priesthood of Christ is superior to the Aaronic priesthood (4:14—7:28). Because of His incarnation, Christ can "sympathize with our weaknesses," having been "tempted in all things as *we are, yet* without sin" (4:15). Christ was not a Levite, but He qualified for a higher priesthood according to the order of Melchizedek. The superiority of Melchizedek to Levi is seen in the fact that

Levi, in effect, paid tithes through Abraham to Melchizedek (7:9, 10). Abraham was blessed by Melchizedek, and "the lesser is blessed by the greater" (7:7). The parenthetical warning in 5:11—6:20 exhorts the readers to "press on to maturity" by moving beyond the basics of salvation and repentance.

By divine oath (7:21), Christ has become a permanent and perfect high priest and "the mediator of a better covenant" (8:6). The new covenant has made the old covenant obsolete (8:6–13). Our great high priest similarly ministers "through the greater and more perfect tabernacle, not made with hands, that is to say, not of this creation" (9:11). And unlike the former priests, He offers Himself as a sinless and voluntary sacrifice once and for all (9:1—10:18).

The Superiority of the Christian's Walk of Faith (10:19—13:25): The author applies what he has been saying about the superiority of Christ by warning his readers of the danger of discarding their faith in Christ (10:19–39). The faith that the readers must maintain is defined in 11:1–3 and illustrated in 11:4–40. The triumphs and accomplishments of faith in the lives of Old Testament believers should encourage the recipients of "something better" (11:40) in Christ to fix their "eyes on Jesus, the author and perfecter of faith" (12:2). Just as Jesus endured great hostility, those who believe in Him will sometimes have to endure divine discipline for the sake of holiness (12:1–29).

The readers are warned not to turn away from Christ during such times, but to place their hope in Him. The character of their lives must be shaped by their dedication to Christ (13:1–19), and this will be manifested in their love of each other through their hospitality, concern, purity, contentment, and obedience. The author concludes this epistle with one of the finest benedictions in Scripture (13:20, 21) and some personal words (13:22–25).

OUTLINE OF HEBREWS

Part One: The Superiority of Christ's Person (1:1—4:13)

Part Two: The Superiority of Christ's Work (4:14—10:18)

Part Three: The Superiority of the Christian's Walk of Faith (10:19—13:25)

CHAPTER 1

The Superiority of Christ over the Prophets

GOD, after He[R]spoke long ago to the fathers in the prophets in many portions and in many ways,   John 9:29; 16:13; Heb. 2:2f.

2 [A]in[R] these last days has spoken to us in *His* Son, whom He appointed heir of all things, through whom also He made the [T]world.   *at the end of these days* · Matt. 13:39 · ages

3 [T]And He is the radiance of His glory and the exact representation of His nature, and upholds all things by the word of His power. When He had made purification of sins, He [R]sat down at the right hand of the Majesty on high;   *Who being* · Ps. 68:18; 110:1; Mark 16:19 ★

Christ Is Superior Because of His Deity

4 having become as much better than the angels, as He has inherited a more excellent [R]name than they.   Eph. 1:21; [Phil. 2:9]

5 For to which of the angels did He ever say,
"THOU[R]ART MY SON, Ps. 2:7; Acts 13:33 ★
TODAY I HAVE BEGOTTEN THEE"?
And again,
"I[R]WILL BE A FATHER TO HIM, 2 Sam. 7:14
AND HE SHALL BE A SON TO ME"?

6 And when He again [R]brings the firstborn into the world, He says,   Heb. 10:5
"AND[R] LET ALL THE ANGELS OF GOD
WORSHIP HIM."   Ps. 97:7

7 And of the angels He says,
"WHO MAKES HIS ANGELS WINDS,
AND HIS MINISTERS A FLAME OF FIRE."

8 But of the Son *He says*,
"THY[R]THRONE, O GOD, IS FOREVER AND
EVER,   Ps. 45:6 ★
AND THE RIGHTEOUS SCEPTER IS THE
SCEPTER OF [1]HIS KINGDOM.

9 "THOU[R] HAST LOVED RIGHTEOUSNESS
AND HATED LAWLESSNESS; Ps. 45:7
THEREFORE GOD, THY GOD, HATH
[R]ANOINTED THEE
WITH THE OIL OF GLADNESS ABOVE
THY COMPANIONS."   Is. 61:1, 3 ★

10 And,
"THOU[R] LORD, IN THE BEGINNING DIDST
LAY THE FOUNDATION OF THE EARTH,
AND THE HEAVENS ARE THE WORKS OF
THY HANDS;   Ps. 102:25

[1] Some mss. read *Thy*

11 [R]THEY WILL PERISH, BUT THOU REMAINEST;   Ps. 102:26
[R]AND THEY ALL WILL BECOME OLD AS A
GARMENT,   Is. 51:6; Heb. 8:13

12 [R]AND AS A MANTLE THOU WILT ROLL
THEM UP;   Ps. 102:26
AS A GARMENT THEY WILL ALSO BE
CHANGED.
BUT THOU ART[R]THE SAME, Heb. 13:8
AND THY YEARS WILL NOT COME TO AN
END."

13 But to which of the angels has He ever said,
"SIT[R]AT MY RIGHT HAND, Ps. 110:1
[R]UNTIL I MAKE THINE ENEMIES Josh. 10:24
A FOOTSTOOL FOR THY FEET"?

14 Are they not all ministering spirits, sent out to render service for the sake of those who will inherit[R]salvation? Heb. 2:3

CHAPTER 2

First Warning: Danger of Neglect

FOR this reason we must pay much closer attention to what we have heard, lest we drift away *from it.*

2 For if the word spoken through angels proved[A]unalterable, and every transgression and disobedience received a just [R]recompense,   *steadfast* · [Heb. 10:35; 11:26]

3 how shall we escape if we neglect so great a salvation? [T]After it was at the first spoken through the Lord, it was confirmed to us by those who heard,   *Which was*

4 God also bearing witness with them, both by signs and wonders and by various miracles and by [T]gifts of the Holy Spirit according to His own will.   *distributions*

Christ Is Superior Because of His Humanity

5 For He did not subject to angels [T]the[R] world to come, concerning which we are speaking.   *the inhabited earth* · Matt. 24:14

6 But one has testified[R]somewhere, saying,   Heb. 4:4
"WHAT[R]IS MAN, THAT THOU REMEMBEREST HIM?   Ps. 8:4
OR THE SON OF MAN, THAT THOU ART
CONCERNED ABOUT HIM?

7 "THOU[R] HAST MADE HIM FOR A LITTLE
WHILE LOWER THAN THE ANGELS;

Thou hast crowned him with glory
  and honor,   Ps. 8:5, 6
2And hast appointed him over the
  works of Thy hands;
8 RThou hast put all things in subjection under his feet."   Ps. 8:6
For in subjecting all things to him, He left
nothing that is not subject to him. But now
we do not yet see all things subjected to
him.

9 But we do see Him who has been made
Afor a little while lower than the angels,
namely, Jesus, because of the suffering of
death crowned with glory and honor, that
by the grace of God He mightRtaste death
for everyone.   a little lower • Matt. 16:28

10 ForRit was fitting for Him, for whom
are all things, and through whom are all
things, in bringing many sons to glory, to
perfect theAauthorRof their salvation through
sufferings.   Luke 24:26 • leader • Acts 3:15

11 For both He whoRsanctifies and those
who areAsanctified are all from one Father;
for which reason He is not ashamed to call
them brethren,   Heb. 13:12 • being sanctified

12 saying,
  "IR will proclaim Thy name to My
    brethren,   Ps. 22:22
  In the midst of theTcongregation I
    will sing Thy praise."   church

13 And again,
  "IR will put My trust in Him."
And again,
  "Behold,R I and the children whom
    God has given Me."   Is. 8:18

14 Since then the children share inTflesh
and blood, He Himself likewise also partook
of the same, that through death He might
render powerless him who had the power of
death, that is, the devil;   blood and flesh

15 and might deliver those who through
Rfear of death were subject to slavery all
their lives.   Is. 42:7; 49:9, 61:1; [Rom. 8:15] ★

16 For assuredly He does not give help to
angels, but He gives help to the descendant
of Abraham.

17 Therefore, HeT had to be made like His
brethren in all things, that He might become
a merciful and faithful high priest in things
pertaining to God, to make propitiation for
the sins of the people.   was obligated to be

18 For since He Himself was tempted in
that which He has suffered, He is able to
come to the aid of those who are tempted.

CHAPTER 3

Christ Is Superior to Moses in His Work

Therefore, holy brethren, partakers of
a heavenly calling, consider Jesus, the
Apostle and High Priest of our confession.

2 He was faithful to Him who appointed
Him, as Moses also was in all His House.

3 RFor He has been counted worthy of
more glory than Moses, by just so much as
the builder of the house has more honor
than the house.   2 Cor. 3:7-11

4 For every house is built by someone,
but the builder of all things is God.

Christ Is Superior to Moses in His Person

5 Now Moses was faithful in all His
house as a servant, for a testimony of those
things which were to be spoken later;

6 but Christ was faithful as a Son over
His house whose house we are, if we hold
fast our confidence and the boast of our
Rhope firm until the end.   Heb. 6:11; 7:19

Danger of Hardening the Heart

7 Therefore, just as the Holy Spirit says,
  "Today if you hear His voice,
8 RDo not harden your hearts as
    when they provoked Me,   Ps. 95:8
  As in the day of trial in the wil-
    derness,
9 RWhere your fathers tried Me by
    testing Me,   Ps. 95:9-11
  And saw My works for Rforty
    years.   Acts 7:36
10 "ThereforeR I was angry with this
    generation,   Ps. 95:10
  And said, 'They always go astray
    in their heart;
  And they did not know My ways';
11 RAs I swore in My wrath,   Ps. 95:11
    'They shall not enter My rest.' "

12 Take care, brethren, lest there should
be in any one of you an evil, unbelieving
heart, in falling away from the living God.

13 But Rencourage one another day after
day, as long as it is still called "Today," lest
any one of you be hardened by theRdeceitful-
ness of sin.   Heb. 10:24f. • Eph. 4:22

14 For we have become partakers of
Christ, if we hold fast the beginning of our
assurance firm until the end;

15 while it is said,
  "TodayR if you hear His voice, Ps. 95:7
    Do not harden your hearts, as
      when they provoked Me."

16 For whoR provoked Him when they had
heard? Indeed, did not all those who came
out of Egypt led by Moses?   Jer. 32:29; 44:3, 8

17 And with whom was He angry for forty
years? Was it not with those who sinned,
whose bodies fell in the wilderness?

18 And to whom did He swearR that they
should not enter His rest, but to those who
wereR disobedient?   Num. 14:23 • Rom. 11:30-32

19 And so we see that they were not able
to enter because ofRunbelief.   John 3:18, 36

---

2 Some ancient mss. do not contain And . . . hands

CHAPTER 4

Challenge to Enter His Rest

THEREFORE, let us fear lest, while a promise remains of entering His rest, any one of you should seem to have ᴿcome short of it.   2 Cor. 6:1; [Gal. 5:4]; Heb. 12:15

2 For indeed we have had good news preached to us, just as they also; but ᴿthe word ᵀthey heard did not profit them, because it was not united by faith in those who heard.   Rom. 10:17; Gal. 3:2 · *of hearing*

3 ³For we who have believed enter that rest, just as He has said,

"As ᴿI swore in My wrath,
They shall not enter My rest,"

although His works were finished from the foundation of the world.   Ps. 95:11; Heb. 3:11

4 For He has thus said somewhere concerning the seventh *day*, "And God rested on the seventh day from all His works";

5 and again in this *passage*, "They ᴿshall not enter My rest."   Ps. 95:11; Heb. 3:11

6 Since therefore it remains for some to enter it, and those who formerly had good news preached to them failed to enter because of ᴿdisobedience,   Heb. 3:18; 4:11

7 He again fixes a certain day, "Today," saying ᴬthrough David after so long a time just ᴿas has been said before,   *in* · Heb. 3:7f.

"Today ᴿif you hear His voice, Ps. 95:7
Do not harden your hearts."

8 For ᴿif ᵀJoshua had given them rest, He would not have spoken of another day after that.   Josh. 22:4 · *Jesus*

9 There remains therefore a Sabbath rest for the people of God.

10 For the one who has entered His rest has himself also ᴿrested from his works, as ᴿGod did from His.   Rev. 14:13 · Gen. 2:2

11 Let us therefore be diligent to enter that rest, lest anyone fall through *following* the same ᴿexample of disobedience. 2 Pet. 2:6

12 For ᴿthe word of God is living and active and sharper than any two-edged ᴿsword, and piercing as far as the division of soul and spirit, of both joints and marrow, and able to judge the thoughts and intentions of the heart.   Jer. 23:29 · Eph. 6:17

13 And ᴿthere is no creature hidden from His sight, but all things are ᴿopen and laid bare to the eyes of Him with whom we have to do.   2 Chr. 16:9; Ps. 33:13-15 · Job 26:6

Christ Is Superior in His Position

14 Since then we have a great ᴿhigh priest who has ᴿpassed through the heavens, Jesus ᴿthe Son of God, let us hold fast our confession.   Heb. 2:17 · [Eph. 4:10] · Matt. 4:3

15 For we do not have ᴿa high priest who cannot sympathize with our weaknesses, but one who has been tempted in all things as *we are,* yet without sin.   Heb. 2:17

16 Let us therefore ᴿdraw near with ᴿconfidence to the throne of grace, that we may receive mercy and may find grace to help in time of need.   Heb. 7:19 · Heb. 3:6

CHAPTER 5

Aaronic Priesthood

FOR every high priest ᴿtaken from among men is appointed on behalf of men in things pertaining to God, in order to offer both gifts and sacrifices for sins;   Ex. 28:1

2 ᵀhe can deal gently with the ignorant and misguided, since he himself also is beset with weakness;   *being able to*

3 and because of it he is obligated to offer *sacrifices* ᴿfor sins, ᴿas for the people, so also for himself.   [1 Cor. 15:3] · Lev. 9:7

4 And ᴿno one takes the honor to himself, but *receives it* when he is called by God, even ᴿas Aaron was.   Num. 16:40 · Ex. 28:1

Melchizedekian Priesthood

5 So also Christ ᴿdid not glorify Himself so as to become a ᴿhigh priest, but He who ᴿsaid to Him,   John 8:54 · Heb. 2:17 · Heb. 1:1, 5

"Thou ᴿart My Son,   Ps. 2:7 ★
Today I have begotten Thee";

6 just as He says also in another *passage*,

"Thou ᴿart a priest forever Ps. 110:4 ★
According to ᴿthe order of Melchizedek."   Heb. 5:10; 6:20; 7:11, 17

7 In the days of His flesh, ᵀHe offered up both prayers and supplications with loud crying and tears to the One able to save Him ᴬfrom death, and He was heard because of His piety.   *who having offered up* · *out of*

8 Although He was ᴿa Son, He learned ᴿobedience from the things which He suffered.   Heb. 1:2 · Phil. 2:8

9 And having been made ᴿperfect, He became to all those who obey Him the source of eternal salvation,   Heb. 2:10

10 being designated by God as ᴿa high priest according to ᴿthe order of Melchizedek.   Heb. 2:17; 5:5 · Ps. 110:4 ★ Heb. 5:6; 6:20

Dullness of Hearing

11 Concerning ⁴him we have much to say, and *it is* hard to explain, since you have become dull of hearing.

12 For though by this time you ought to be teachers, you have need again for someone to teach you the elementary principles of the oracles of God, and you have come to need milk and not solid food.

13 For everyone who partakes *only* of milk is not accustomed to the word of righteousness, for he is a ᴿbabe.   1 Cor. 3:1; 14:20

³ Some ancient mss. read *Therefore*   ⁴ Or, *Him; or, this*

14 But solid food is for [R]the mature, who because of practice have their senses trained to discern good and evil.   1 Cor. 2:6

CHAPTER 6

Need for Maturity

THEREFORE leaving the [T]elementary teaching about the [T]Christ, let us press on to maturity, not laying again a foundation of repentance from dead works and of faith toward God,   *word of the beginning* • Messiah

2 of [R]instruction about washings, and laying on of hands, and the resurrection of the dead, and eternal judgment.   John 3:25

3 And this we shall do, if God permits.

4 For in the case of those who have once been [R]enlightened and have tasted of the heavenly gift and have been made partakers of the Holy Spirit,   [2 Cor. 4:4, 6]

5 and [R]have tasted the good word of God and the powers of the age to come, 1 Pet. 2:3

6 and *then* have fallen away, it is impossible to renew them again to repentance, since they again crucify to themselves the Son of God, and put Him to open shame.

7 For ground that drinks the rain which often falls upon it and brings forth vegetation useful to those for whose sake it is also tilled, receives a blessing from God;

8 but if it yields thorns and thistles, it is worthless and close [T]to being cursed, and [T]it ends up being burned.   *to a curse* • *its end*

Exhortation to Maturity

9 But, [R]beloved, we are convinced of better things concerning you, and things that [A]accompany salvation, though we are speaking in this way.   1 Cor. 10:14 • *belong to*

10 For God is not unjust so as to forget your work and the love which you have shown toward His name, in having ministered and in still ministering to the saints.

11 And we desire that each one of you show the same diligence so as to realize the full assurance of hope until the end,

12 that you may not be sluggish, but [R]imitators of those who through faith and patience inherit the promises.   Heb. 13:7

13 For [R]when God made the promise to Abraham, since He could swear by no one greater, He swore by Himself,   Gal. 3:15, 18

14 saying, "I [R]WILL SURELY BLESS YOU, AND I WILL SURELY MULTIPLY YOU."   Gen. 22:17

15 And thus, [R]having patiently waited, he obtained the promise.   Gen. 12:4; 21:5

16 For men swear by one greater *than themselves*, and with them an oath *given* as confirmation is an end of every dispute.

17 [A]In the same way God, desiring even more to show to the heirs of the promise the unchangeableness of His purpose, [A]interposed with an oath,   *Therefore God* • *guaranteed*

18 in order that by two unchangeable things, in which [R]it is impossible for God to lie, we may have strong encouragement, we who have fled for refuge in laying hold of the hope set before us.   Num. 23:19; Titus 1:2

19 [T]This hope we have as an anchor of the soul, a *hope* both sure and steadfast and one which enters within the veil,   *Which we have*

20 where Jesus has entered as a forerunner for us, having become a high priest forever according to the order of Melchizedek.

CHAPTER 7

Description of Melchizedek

FOR this [R]Melchizedek, king of Salem, priest of the Most High God, who met Abraham as he was returning from the slaughter of the kings and blessed him,   Gen. 14:18-20

2 to whom also Abraham apportioned a tenth part of all *the spoils*, was first of all, by the translation *of his name*, king of righteousness, and then also king of Salem, which is king of peace.

3 Without father, without mother, without genealogy, having neither beginning of days nor end of life, but made like the Son of God, he abides a priest perpetually.

Superiority of Melchizedek

4 Now observe how great this man was to whom Abraham, the [R]patriarch, gave a tenth of the choicest spoils.   Acts 2:29; 7:8f.

5 And those indeed of the sons of Levi who receive the priest's office have commandment [T]in the Law to collect a tenth from the people, that is, from their brethren, although these [T]are descended from Abraham.   *according to* • *have come out of the loins of*

6 But the one [R]whose genealogy is not traced from them collected a tenth from Abraham, and [R]blessed the one who [R]had the promises.   Heb. 7:3 • Heb. 7:1f. • [Rom. 4:13]

7 But without any dispute the lesser is blessed by the greater.

8 And in this case mortal men receive tithes, but in that case one *receives them*, of whom it is witnessed that he lives on.

9 And, so to speak, through Abraham even Levi, who received tithes, paid tithes,

10 for he was still in the loins of his father when Melchizedek met him.

Imperfection of Aaronic Priesthood

11 Now if perfection was through the Levitical priesthood (for on the basis of it the people received the Law), what further need *was there* for another priest to arise accord-

ing to the order of Melchizedek, and not be designated according to the order of Aaron?

12 For when the priesthood is changed, of necessity there takes place a change of law also.

13 For^R the one concerning whom ^R these things are spoken belongs to another tribe, from which no one has officiated at the altar.   Heb. 7:14 • Heb. 7:11

14 For it is evident that our Lord^T was^R descended from Judah, a tribe with reference to which Moses spoke nothing concerning priests.   *rose from* • Num. 24:17; Is. 11:1; Mic. 5:2★

15 And this is clearer still, if another priest arises according to the likeness of Melchizedek,

16 who has become *such* not on the basis of a law of ^R physical requirement, but according to the power of ^R an indestructible life.   Heb. 9:10 • Heb. 9:14

17 For it is witnessed *of Him*,

"THOU^R ART A PRIEST FOREVER Ps. 110:4★
ACCORDING TO THE ORDER OF MEL-
    CHIZEDEK."

18 For, on the one hand, there is a setting aside of a former commandment^R because of its weakness and uselessness   [Rom. 8:3]

19 (for ^R the Law made nothing perfect), and on the other hand there is a bringing in of a better hope, through which we draw near to God.   [Acts 13:39]; Rom. 3:20; Gal. 2:16

20 And inasmuch as *it was* not without an oath

21 (for they indeed became priests without an oath, but He with an oath through the One who said to Him,

"The^R LORD HAS SWORN   Ps. 110:4
AND WILL NOT CHANGE HIS MIND,
'THOU ART A PRIEST FOREVER' ");

22 so much the more also Jesus has become the guarantee of a better covenant.

23 And the *former* priests, on the one hand, existed in greater numbers, because they were prevented by death from continuing,

24 but He, on the other hand, because He abides^R forever, holds His priesthood permanently. Is. 9:7; John 12:34; Rom. 9:5; Heb. 7:23f., 28

25 Hence, also, He is able to save^A forever those who^R draw near to God through Him, since He always lives to make intercession for them.   *completely* • Heb. 7:19

26 For it was fitting that we should have such a^R high priest,^R holy, innocent, undefiled, separated from sinners and exalted above the heavens;   Heb. 2:17 • [2 Cor. 5:21]

27 who does not need daily, like those high priests, to ^R offer up sacrifices, first for His own sins, and then for the *sins* of the people, because this He did once for all when He offered up Himself.   Heb. 5:1

28 For the Law appoints men as high priests^R who are weak, but the word of the oath, which came after the Law, *appoints* a Son, made perfect forever.   Heb. 5:2

CHAPTER 8

A Better Covenant

NOW the main point in what has been said *is this*: we have such a high priest, who has taken His seat at the right hand of the throne of the Majesty in the heavens,

2 a minister^A in the sanctuary, and^A in the true^A tabernacle, which the Lord^R pitched, not man.   *of* • *sacred tent* • Ex. 33:7

3 For every^R high priest is appointed^R to offer both gifts and sacrifices; hence it is necessary that this *high priest* also have something to offer.   Heb. 2:17 • [Rom. 4:25]

4 Now if He were on earth, He would not be a priest at all, since there are those who offer the gifts according to the Law;

5 who serve a copy and shadow of the heavenly things, just as Moses was warned *by God* when he was about to erect the tabernacle; for, "SEE," He says, "THAT YOU MAKE all things ACCORDING TO THE PATTERN WHICH WAS SHOWN YOU ON THE MOUNTAIN."

6 But now He has obtained a more excellent ministry, by as much as He is also the mediator of a better covenant, which has been enacted on better promises.

A New Covenant

7 For ^R if that first *covenant* had been faultless, there would have been no occasion sought for a second.   Heb. 7:11

8 For finding fault with them, He says,
"BEHOLD,^R DAYS ARE COMING, SAYS THE
    LORD,   Jer. 31:31★
^T WHEN I WILL EFFECT A NEW COVENANT
WITH THE HOUSE OF ISRAEL AND WITH
    THE HOUSE OF JUDAH;   *And*

9 ^R NOT LIKE THE COVENANT WHICH I
    MADE WITH THEIR FATHERS
ON THE DAY WHEN I TOOK THEM BY
    THE HAND
TO LEAD THEM OUT OF THE LAND OF
    EGYPT;
FOR THEY DID NOT CONTINUE IN MY
    COVENANT,
AND I DID NOT CARE FOR THEM, SAYS
    THE LORD. Ex. 19:5; Deut. 5:2; Jer. 31:32

10 "FOR^R THIS IS THE COVENANT THAT I
    WILL MAKE WITH THE HOUSE OF IS-
    RAEL   Jer. 31:33; Rom. 11:27; Heb. 10:16
AFTER THOSE DAYS, SAYS THE LORD:
I WILL PUT MY LAWS INTO THEIR
    MINDS,
AND I WILL WRITE THEM^R UPON THEIR
    HEARTS.   2 Cor. 3:3
AND I WILL BE THEIR GOD,
AND THEY SHALL BE MY PEOPLE.

11 "AND^R THEY SHALL NOT TEACH EVERY-
    ONE HIS FELLOW CITIZEN,   Jer. 31:34
AND EVERYONE HIS BROTHER, SAYING,
    'KNOW THE LORD,'
FOR^R ALL SHALL KNOW ME,

From the least to the greatest of
them. Is. 54:13; John 6:45; [1 John 2:27]
12 "For[R]I will be merciful to their iniquities,   Is. 43:25; Jer. 31:34; 50:20
[R]And I will remember their sins no
more."   Heb. 10:17
13 ^When He said, "A new *covenant*," He
has made the first obsolete. But whatever is
becoming obsolete and growing old is^ready
to disappear.   *In His saying • near*

CHAPTER 9

Old Covenant's Sanctuary

Now even the first *covenant* had[R]regula-
tions of divine worship and[R]the earthly sanctuary.   Heb. 9:10 • Ex. 25:8; [Heb. 8:2; 9:11, 24]
2 For there was a tabernacle prepared,
the[T]outer one, in which *were* the lampstand
and the table and the [T]sacred bread; this is
called the holy place. *first • loaves of presentation*
3 And behind[R]the second veil, there was
a^tabernacle which is called the[R]Holy of Holies,   Ex. 26:31-33; 40:3 • *sacred tent* • Ex. 26:33
4 having a golden ^altar of incense and
the ark of the covenant covered on all sides
with gold, in which *was* a golden jar holding
the manna, and Aaron's rod which budded,
and the tables of the covenant.   *censer*
5 And above it *were* the cherubim of glory overshadowing the mercy seat; but of
these things we cannot now speak in detail.

Old Covenant's Sacrifice

6 Now when these things have been thus
prepared, the priests[R]are continually entering the[T]outer^tabernacle, performing the divine worship, Num. 18:2-6; 28:3 • *first • sacred tent*
7 but into[R]the second only the high priest
enters, once a year, not without *taking*
blood, which he offers for himself and for
the[T]sins of the people committed in ignorance.   Heb. 9:3 • *ignorance of the people*
8 [R]The Holy Spirit *is* signifying this,[R]that
the way into the holy place has not yet been
disclosed, while the[T]outer tabernacle is still
standing,   Heb. 3:7 • [John 14:6] • *first*
9 which *is* a symbol for the present time.
Accordingly[R]both gifts and sacrifices are offered which[R]cannot make the worshiper perfect in conscience,   Heb. 5:1 • Heb. 7:19
10 since they *relate* only to food and drink
and various washings, regulations for the
body imposed until a time of reformation.

New Covenant's Sanctuary

11 But when Christ appeared *as* a high
priest of the good things [5]to come, *He entered* through the greater and more perfect
^tabernacle, not made with hands, that is to
say, not of this creation;   *sacred tent*

New Covenant's Sacrifice

12 and not through the blood of goats and
calves, but through His own blood, He entered the holy place once for all,[R]having obtained eternal redemption.   [Dan. 9:24] ★
13 For if[R]the blood of goats and bulls and
[R]the ashes of a heifer sprinkling those who
have been defiled, sanctify for the[T]cleansing
of the flesh,   Lev. 16:15 • Num. 19:9, 17f. • *purity*
14 how much more will the blood of
Christ, who through the eternal Spirit [R]of-
fered Himself without blemish to God,
cleanse your conscience from dead works to
serve the living God?   Is. 53:12 ★
15 And for this reason[R]He is the[R]mediator
of a new covenant, in order that since a
death has taken place for the redemption of
the transgressions that were *committed* under the first covenant, those who have been
called may receive the promise of the eternal inheritance.   Rom. 3:24 • 1 Tim. 2:5
16 For where a^covenant is, there must of
necessity[T]be the death of the one who made
it.   *testament • be brought*
17 For a covenant is valid *only* when[T]men
are dead, [6]for it is never in force while the
one who made it lives.   *over the dead*
18 Therefore even the first *covenant* was
not inaugurated without blood.
19 For when every commandment had
been[R]spoken by Moses to all the people according to the Law, he took the blood of the
calves and the goats, with water and scarlet
wool and hyssop, and sprinkled both the
book itself and all the people,   Heb. 1:1
20 saying, "This is the blood of the covenant which God commanded you."
21 And in the same way he[R]sprinkled both
the^tabernacle and all the vessels of the ministry with the blood.   Ex. 24:6; 40:9 • *sacred tent*
22 And according to the^Law, one may[R]al-
most *say*, all things are cleansed with blood,
and without shedding of blood there is no
forgiveness.   *Law, almost all things* • Lev. 5:11f.
23 Therefore it was necessary for the copies of the things in the heavens to be
cleansed with these, but the heavenly things
themselves with better sacrifices than these.
24 For Christ [R]did not enter a holy place
made with hands, a *mere* copy of the true
one, but into heaven itself, now to appear in
the presence of God for us;   Heb. 4:14; 9:12
25 nor was it that He should offer Himself
often, as the high priest enters the holy
place year by year with blood not his own.
26 Otherwise, He would have needed to
suffer often since the foundation of the
world; but now once at the consummation
of the ages He has been manifested to put
away sin by the sacrifice of Himself.
27 And inasmuch as it is [T]appointed for
men to die once and after this[R]comes judgment,   *laid up*

[5] Some ancient mss. read *that have come*
[6] Some ancient mss. read *for is it then . . . lives?*

28 so Christ also, having been offered once to bear the sins of many, shall appear a second time for salvation without *reference to* sin, to those who eagerly await Him.

CHAPTER 10

For the Law, since it has *only* a shadow of the good things to come *and* not the very form of things, [7]can never by the same sacrifices year by year, which they offer continually, make perfect those who draw near.

2 Otherwise, would they not have ceased to be offered, because the worshipers, having once been cleansed, would no longer have had[R]consciousness of sins?   [1 Pet. 2:19]

3 But in[T]those *sacrifices* there is a reminder of sins year by year.   *them there is*

4 For it is[R]impossible for the blood of bulls and goats to take away sins.   Heb. 10:1

5 Therefore, [R]when He comes into the world, He says,   Heb. 1:6

"SACRIFICE[R] AND OFFERING THOU HAST NOT DESIRED,   Ps. 40:6★

BUT[R]A BODY THOU HAST PREPARED FOR ME;   Heb. 2:14; 5:7; 1 Pet. 2:24

6 [R]IN WHOLE BURNT OFFERINGS AND *sacrifices* FOR SIN THOU HAST TAKEN NO PLEASURE.   Ps. 40:6★

7 "THEN[R]I SAID, 'BEHOLD, I HAVE COME (IN[R]THE ROLL OF THE BOOK IT IS WRITTEN OF ME)   Ps. 40:7, 8★ • Ezra 6:2

TO DO THY WILL, O GOD.' "

8 After saying above, "SACRIFICES[R] AND OFFERINGS AND [R]WHOLE BURNT OFFERINGS AND *sacrifices*[R]FOR SIN THOU HAST NOT DESIRED, NOR HAST THOU TAKEN PLEASURE *in them*" (which are offered according to the Law),   Ps. 40:6★ • Mark 12:33 • Rom. 8:3

9 then He said, "BEHOLD,[R] I HAVE COME TO DO THY WILL." He takes away the first in order to establish the second.   Ps. 40:7, 8★

10 By[T]this will we have been[R]sanctified through the offering of the body of Jesus Christ once for all.   *which* • Is. 53:12★

11 And every priest stands daily ministering and offering time after time the same sacrifices, which can never take away sins;

12 but He, having offered one sacrifice for [A]sins for all time,[R]SAT DOWN AT THE RIGHT HAND OF GOD,   *sins, forever sat down* • Heb. 1:3

13 waiting from that time onward[R]UNTIL HIS ENEMIES BE MADE A FOOTSTOOL FOR HIS FEET.   Ps. 110:1; Heb. 1:13★

14 For by one offering He has perfected for all time those who are sanctified.

[7] Some ancient mss. read *they can*

15 And[R]the Holy Spirit also bears witness to us; for after saying,   Heb. 3:7

16 "THIS[R] IS THE COVENANT THAT I WILL MAKE WITH THEM   Jer. 31:33★

AFTER THOSE DAYS, SAYS THE LORD:

I WILL PUT MY LAWS UPON THEIR HEART,

AND UPON THEIR MIND I WILL WRITE THEM,"

He then says,

17 "AND[R]THEIR SINS AND THEIR LAWLESS DEEDS   Jer. 31:34; Heb. 8:12★

I WILL REMEMBER NO MORE."

18 Now where there is forgiveness of these things, there is no longer *any* offering for sin.

Hold Fast the Confession of Faith

19 Since therefore, brethren, we[R]have confidence to[R]enter the holy place by the blood of Jesus,   Heb. 3:6 • Heb. 9:25

20 by[R]a new and living way which He inaugurated for us through[R]the veil, that is, His flesh,   Heb. 9:8 • Heb. 6:19; 9:3

21 and since *we have*[R]a great priest[R]over the house of God,   Ps. 110:4 • 1 Tim. 3:15

22 let us draw near with a[T]sincere heart in full assurance of faith, having our hearts sprinkled *clean* from an evil conscience and our bodies washed with pure water.   *true*

23 Let us hold fast the[R]confession of our [R]hope without wavering, for He who promised is faithful;   Heb. 3:1 • Heb. 3:6

24 and let us consider how to stimulate one another to love and good deeds,

25 not forsaking our own assembling together, as is the habit of some, but[R]encouraging *one another*; and all the more, as you see the day drawing near.   Heb. 3:13

Fourth Warning: Danger of Shrinking Back

26 For if we go on sinning willfully after receiving the knowledge of the truth, there no longer remains a sacrifice for sins,

27 but a certain terrifying expectation of judgment, and[R]THE FURY OF A FIRE WHICH WILL CONSUME THE ADVERSARIES. 2 Thess. 1:7

28 [R]Anyone who has set aside the Law of Moses dies without mercy on *the testimony of* two or three witnesses.   Deut. 17:2-6; 19:15

29 [R]How much severer punishment do you think he will deserve[R]who has trampled under foot the Son of God, and has regarded as unclean[R]the blood of the covenant by which

---

10:25 The Reason for Participation in the Local Church—The ultimate reason that we should participate in a local church is because it is specifically commanded by God. Even in New Testament days there were those who yielded to the temptation of absenting themselves from the worship services of the local church. The writer of Hebrews points out that members of a local church have an obligation to one another. They are to provoke one another to good works and to exhort one another to live consistent lives worthy of God. This can best be done within the context of a local church; so believers are commanded not to forsake the assembling of themselves together.

Now turn to Page 1096—Acts 2:42–47: Benefits of Participation in the Local Church.

he was sanctified, and has insulted the Spirit of grace? Heb. 2:3 · Heb. 6:6 · Matt. 26:28

30 For we know Him who said, "VENGEANCE IS MINE, I WILL REPAY." And again, "THE LORD WILL JUDGE HIS PEOPLE."

31 It is a[R]terrifying thing to fall into the hands of the living God.   2 Cor. 5:11

32 But remember[R]the former days,[T]when, after being enlightened, you endured a great conflict of sufferings,   Heb. 5:12 · in which

33 partly, by being[R]made a public spectacle through reproaches and tribulations, and partly by becoming[R]sharers with those who were so treated.   1 Cor. 4:9 · 1 Thess. 2:14

34 For you[R]showed sympathy to the prisoners, and accepted[R]joyfully the seizure of your property, knowing that you have for yourselves[R]a better possession and an abiding one.   Heb. 13:3 · Matt. 5:12 · Heb. 9:15

35 Therefore, do not throw away your confidence, which has a great reward.

36 For you have need of endurance, so that when you have done the will of God, you may receive what was promised.

37   FOR YET IN A VERY LITTLE WHILE,
     [R]HE WHO IS COMING WILL COME, AND
     WILL NOT DELAY.   Hab. 2:3☆

38   [R]BUT MY RIGHTEOUS ONE SHALL LIVE BY
     FAITH;   Rom. 1:17
     AND IF HE SHRINKS BACK, MY SOUL
     HAS NO PLEASURE IN HIM.

39 But we are not of those who shrink back to destruction, but of those who have faith to the preserving of the soul.

CHAPTER 11

Definition of Faith

NOW faith is the assurance of things hoped for, the conviction of things not seen.

2 For by it the[R]men of old [T]gained approval.   Heb. 1:1 · obtained a testimony

3 By faith we understand that the[T]worlds were prepared[R]by the word of God, so that what is seen was not made out of things which are visible.   ages · Ps. 33:6, 9; Heb. 6:5

Abel

4 By faith Abel offered to God a better sacrifice than Cain, through which he obtained the testimony that he was righteous, God testifying about his gifts, and through faith, though he is dead, he still speaks.

Enoch

5 By faith Enoch was taken up so that he should not [R]see death; AND HE WAS NOT FOUND BECAUSE GOD TOOK HIM UP; for he obtained the witness that before his being taken up he was pleasing to God.   Luke 2:26

6 And without faith it is impossible to please Him, for he who[R]comes to God must believe that He is, and that He is a rewarder of those who seek Him.   Heb. 7:19

Noah

7 By faith [R]Noah, being warned by God about things not yet seen, in reverence prepared an ark for the salvation of his household, by which he condemned the world, and became an heir of the righteousness which is according to faith.   Gen. 6:13-22

Abraham and Sarah

8 By faith Abraham, when he was called, obeyed by going out to a place which he was to receive for an inheritance; and he went out, not knowing where he was going.

9 By faith he lived as an alien in[R]the land of promise, as in a foreign land,[R]dwelling in tents with Isaac and Jacob, fellow heirs of the same promise;   Acts 7:5 · Gen. 12:8; 13:3

10 for he was looking for the city which has foundations, whose architect and builder is God.

11 By faith even [R]Sarah herself received ability to conceive, even beyond the proper time of life, since she considered Him[R]faithful who had promised;   Gen. 17:19 · Heb. 10:23

12 therefore, also, there was born of one man, and him as good as dead [T]at that, as many descendants AS THE STARS OF HEAVEN IN NUMBER, AND INNUMERABLE AS THE SAND WHICH IS BY THE SEASHORE.   in these things

13 [R]All these died in faith, without receiving the promises, but having seen them and having welcomed them from a distance, and having confessed that they were strangers and exiles on the earth.   Matt. 13:17

14 For those who say such things make it clear that they are seeking a country of their own.

15 And indeed if they had been thinking of that country from which they went out, they would have had opportunity to return.

16 But as it is, they desire a better country, that is a[R]heavenly one. Therefore God is not ashamed to be called their God; for He has prepared a city for them.   2 Tim. 4:18

17 By faith[R]Abraham, when he was tested, offered up Isaac; and he who had[R]received the promises was offering up his only begotten son;   Gen. 22:1-10 · Heb. 11:13

18 it was he to whom it was said, "IN[R] ISAAC YOUR [T]DESCENDANTS SHALL BE CALLED."   Gen. 21:12; Rom. 9:7★ · seed

19 [T]He considered that God is able to raise men even from the dead; from which he also received him back as a type.   Considering

Isaac

20 By faith[R]Isaac blessed Jacob and Esau, even regarding things to come.   Gen. 27:27-29

Jacob

21 By faith Jacob, as he was dying, blessed each of the sons of Joseph, and worshiped, leaning on the top of his staff.

Joseph

22 By faith ᴿJoseph, when he was dying, made mention of the exodus of the sons of Israel, and gave orders concerning his bones.   Gen. 50:24f.; Ex. 13:19

Moses' Parents

23 By faith Moses, when he was born, was hidden for three months by his parents, because they saw he was a beautiful child; and they were not afraid of the king's edict.

Moses

24 By faith Moses,ᴿwhen he had grown up, refused to be called the son of Pharaoh's daughter;   Ex. 2:10, 11ff.
25 choosing rather toᴿendure ill-treatment with the people of God, than to enjoy the passing pleasures of sin;   Heb. 11:37
26 considering the reproach of Christ greater riches than the treasures of Egypt; for he was looking to theᴿreward.   Heb. 2:2
27 By faith heᴿleft Egypt, not fearing the wrath of the king; for he endured, as seeing Him who is unseen.   Ex. 2:15; 12:50f.; 13:17f.
28 By faith he kept the Passover and the sprinkling of the blood, so that he who destroyed the first-born might not touch them.
29 By faith they passed through the Red Sea as though *they were passing* through dry land; and the Egyptians, when they attempted it, were ᵀdrowned.   *swallowed up*

Joshua and Rahab

30 By faithᴿthe walls of Jericho fell down, ᴿafter they had been encircled for seven days.   Josh. 6:20 • Josh. 6:15f.
31 By faith Rahab the harlot did not perish along with those who were disobedient, after she had welcomed the spies in peace.

Many Other Heroes of Faith

32 And what more shall I say? For time will fail me if I tell ofᴿGideon, Barak, Samson, Jephthah, ofᴿDavid and Samuel and the prophets,   Judg. 6—8 • 1 Sam. 16:1, 13
33 who by faith conquered kingdoms, performed *acts of* righteousness, obtained promises, shut the mouths of lions,
34 quenched the power of fire,ᴿescaped the edge of the sword, from weakness were made strong, became mighty in war, put foreign armies to flight.   1 Sam. 18:11; 19:10
35 Women received *back* their dead by resurrection; and others were tortured, not accepting their release, in order that they might obtain a better resurrection;
36 and othersᵀexperienced mockings and scourgings, yes, alsoᴿchains and imprisonment.   *received the trial of* • Gen. 39:20

37 They wereᴿstoned, they were sawn in two, [8]they were tempted, they were put to death with the sword; they went about in sheepskins, in goatskins, being destitute, afflicted, ill-treated   1 Kin. 21:13; 2 Chr. 24:21
38 (*men* of whom the world was not worthy), wandering in deserts and mountains and caves and holes in the ground.
39 And all these, having ᵀgained approval through their faith, did not receive ᵀwhat was promised,   *obtained a testimony* • *the promise*
40 because God had'provided something better for us, so that apart from us they should not be made perfect.   *foreseen*

CHAPTER 12

Example of Christ's Endurance

THEREFORE, since we have so great a cloud of witnesses surrounding us, let us alsoᴿlay aside every encumbrance, and the sin which so easily entangles us, and let us ᴿrun withᴿendurance the race that is set before us,   Rom. 13:12 • 1 Cor. 9:24 • Heb. 10:36
2 fixing our eyes on Jesus, the author and perfecter of faith,ᴿwho for the joy set before Him endured the cross, despising the shame, andᴿhas sat down at the right hand of the throne of God. Ps. 69:7, 19★ • Ps. 68:18★
3 For consider Him who has endured such hostility by sinners against Himself, so that you may not grow weary ᵀandᴿ lose heart.   *fainting in your souls* • Gal. 6:9
4 ᴿYou have not yet resistedᵀto the point of shedding blood in your striving against sin;   Heb. 10:32ff.; 13:13 • *as far as blood*

Exhortation to Endure God's Chastening

5 and you have forgotten the exhortation which is addressed to you as sons,
"MYᴿSON, DO NOT REGARD LIGHTLY THE
    DISCIPLINE OF THE LORD,   Job 5:17
NORᴿFAINT WHEN YOU ARE REPROVED
    BY HIM;   Heb. 12:3
6   ᴿFOR THOSEᴿWHOM THE LORD LOVES HE
    DISCIPLINES,
AND HE SCOURGES EVERY SON WHOM
    HE RECEIVES."   Prov. 3:12 • Ps. 119:75
7 It is for discipline that you endure; God deals with you as with sons; for what son is there whom *his* father does not discipline?
8 But if you are without discipline, of which all have become partakers, then you are illegitimate children and not sons.
9 Furthermore, we hadᵀearthly fathers to discipline us, and we respected them; shall we not much rather be subject to the Father of spirits, and live?   *fathers of our flesh*
10 For theyᵀdisciplined us for a short time as seemed best to them, but He *disciplines us* for *our* good,ᴿthat we may share His holiness.   *were discipling* • [2 Pet. 1:4]
11 All discipline for the moment seems not to be joyful, but sorrowful; yet to those

---

[8] Some mss. do not contain *they were tempted*

who have been trained by it, afterwards it yields the peaceful fruit of righteousness.

12 Therefore, strengthen the hands that are weak and the knees that are feeble,

13 and make straight paths for your feet, so that *the limb* which is lame may not be put out of joint, but rather be healed.

14 [R]Pursue peace with all men, and the [R]sanctification without which no one will see the Lord. Rom. 14:19 • [Rom. 6:22]

15 See to it that no one[R]comes short of the grace of God; that no root of bitterness springing up causes trouble, and by it many be defiled; 2 Cor. 6:1; Gal. 5:4; Heb. 4:1

16 that *there be* no[R]immoral or godless person like Esau, who sold his own birthright for a *single* meal. Heb. 13:4

17 For you know that even afterwards, when he desired to inherit the blessing, he was rejected, for he found no place for repentance, though he sought for it with tears.

18 For you have not come to *a mountain* that may be touched and to a blazing fire, and to darkness and gloom and whirlwind,

19 and to the blast of a trumpet and the sound of words which *sound was such that* those who heard begged that no further word should be spoken to them.

20 For they could not bear the command, "IF[R]EVEN A BEAST TOUCHES THE MOUNTAIN, IT WILL BE STONED." Ex. 19:12f.

21 And so terrible was the sight, *that* Moses said, "I[R] AM FULL OF FEAR and trembling." Deut. 9:19

22 But you have come to Mount Zion and to the city of the living God, the heavenly Jerusalem, and to myriads of angels,

23 to the general assembly and church of the first-born who are enrolled in heaven, and to God, the Judge of all, and to the spirits of righteous men made perfect,

24 and to Jesus, the mediator of a new covenant, and to the sprinkled blood, which speaks better than *the blood* of Abel.

Fifth Warning: Danger of Refusing God

25 [R]See to it that you do not refuse Him who is speaking. For if those[T]did not escape when they refused him who warned *them* on earth, much[T]less *shall* we *escape* who turn away from Him who *warns* from heaven. Heb. 3:12 • *were not escaping* • *more*

26 And [R]His voice shook the earth then, but now He has promised, saying, "YET ONCE MORE I WILL SHAKE NOT ONLY THE EARTH, BUT ALSO THE HEAVEN." Ex. 19:18

27 And this *expression*, "Yet once more," denotes[R]the removing of those things which can be shaken, as of created things, in order that those things which cannot be shaken may remain. [Is. 34:4; 54:10; 65:17; Rom. 8:19, 21]

28 Therefore, since we receive a kingdom which cannot be shaken, let us show gratitude, by which we may offer to God an acceptable service with reverence and awe;

29 for our God is a consuming fire.

CHAPTER 13

Love in the Social Realm

LET love of the brethren continue.

2 Do not neglect to[R]show hospitality to strangers, for by this some have entertained angels without knowing it. Matt. 25:35

3 [R]Remember[R]the prisoners, as though in prison with them, and those who are ill-treated, since you yourselves also are in the body. Col. 4:18 • Matt. 25:36

4 [R]Let marriage *be held* in honor among all, and let the *marriage* bed *be* undefiled; [R]for fornicators and adulterers God will judge. 1 Cor. 7:38; 1 Tim. 4:3 • 1 Cor. 6:9

5 Let your character be[R]free from the love of money, being content with what you have; for He Himself has said, "I WILL NEVER DESERT YOU, NOR WILL I EVER FORSAKE YOU," Eph. 5:3; Col. 3:5; 1 Tim. 3:3

6 so that we confidently say,
"THE[R]LORD IS MY HELPER, I WILL NOT BE AFRAID. Ps. 118:6
WHAT SHALL MAN DO TO ME?"

Love in the Religious Realm

7 Remember those who led you, who spoke the word of God to you; and considering the[A]result of their conduct,[R]imitate their faith. *end of their life* • Heb. 6:12

8 [R]Jesus Christ *is* the same yesterday and today, *yes* and forever. 2 Cor. 1:19; Heb. 1:12

9 Do not be carried away by varied and strange teachings; for it is good for the heart to be strengthened by grace, not by foods, through which those who[T]were thus occupied were not benefited. *walked*

10 We have an altar,[R]from which those [R]who serve the[A]tabernacle have no right to eat. 1 Cor. 10:18 • Heb. 8:5 • *sacred tent*

11 For[R]the bodies of those animals whose blood is brought into the holy place by the high priest *as an offering* for sin, are burned outside the camp. Ex. 29:14; Lev. 4:12, 21

12 Therefore Jesus also,[R]that He might sanctify the people[R]through His own blood, suffered outside the gate. Eph. 5:26 • Heb. 9:12

13 Hence, let us go out to Him outside the camp, bearing His reproach.

14 For here[R]we do not have a lasting city, but we are seeking [R]the city which is to come. Heb. 10:34; 12:27 • [Heb. 2:5; 11:10]

15 [R]Through Him then, let us continually offer up a[R]sacrifice of praise to God, that is,

---

13:15 The Expressions of Worship—Since worship encompasses thought, feeling, and deed, there are many expressions of it. Worship especially includes praise and thanksgiving which may be expressed privately or publicly, either by grateful declarations (Heb. 13:15) or by joyful singing (Page 580—Ps. 100:2; Page 1188—Eph.

the fruit of lips that [T]give thanks to His
name.   [1 Pet. 2:5] • Lev. 7:12 • *confess*

16 And do not neglect doing good and
[R]sharing; for [R]with such sacrifices God is
pleased.   Rom. 12:13 • Phil. 4:18

17 [R]Obey your leaders, and submit *to them*;
for they keep watch over your souls, as
those who will give an account. Let them do
this with joy and not with grief, for this
would be unprofitable for you.   1 Cor. 16:16

Conclusion

18 Pray for us, for we are sure that we
have a good conscience, desiring to conduct
ourselves honorably in all things.
19 And I urge *you* all the more to do this,
that I may be restored to you the sooner.

20 Now the God of peace, who[R]brought up
from the dead the great Shepherd of the
sheep[A]through the blood of the eternal covenant, *even* Jesus our Lord,   Acts 2:24 ★ • *in*
21 equip you in every good thing to do His
will, working in us that which is pleasing in
His sight, through Jesus Christ, to whom *be*
the glory forever and ever. Amen.
22 But[R]I urge you, brethren,[A]bear with[T]this
word of exhortation, for I have written to
you briefly.   Acts 13:15 • *listen to* • *the*
23 Take notice that[R]our brother Timothy
has been released, with whom, if he comes
soon, I shall see you.   Acts 16:1; Col. 1:1
24 Greet all of your leaders and all the
[A]saints. Those from Italy greet you.   *holy ones*
25 [R]Grace be with you all.   Col. 4:18

5:19; Page 1202—Col. 3:16). Portions of early Christian hymns of worship actually may be preserved in the New
Testament (Page 1218—1 Tim. 3:16; Page 1224—2 Tim. 2:11–13).
    One very important expression of worship for the church is remembering the death of Christ through the Lord's
Supper (Page 1157—1 Cor. 11:26). The Lord's Supper was instituted by Christ Himself (Page 991—Matt. 26:26–
28) and judged by Paul not to be taken lightly (Page 1157—1 Cor. 11:28–32).
    Since worship means giving something to God, the cheerful giving of money to God's work is certainly an act of
worship (Page 1171—2 Cor. 9:7). The giving of one's time to the Lord's work may be considered worship as well.
The use of one's spiritual gifts in ministry to the body of Christ constitutes an example of worship as service (Page
1157—1 Cor. 12), as does faithfully occupying a church office (Page 1187—Eph. 4:11; Page 1218—1 Tim. 3:1–
13; Page 1229—Titus 1:5–9). Ministry in edifying saints and evangelizing sinners both likewise constitute services
of worship.
    The single most important act of worship for the Christian is the unqualified presentation of himself to God as an
obedient servant. This dedication involves the body and the mind (Page 1141—Rom. 12:1, 2): the body because it
contains the tools by which the will of God is carried out; the mind because it coordinates the actions to be executed by the body. When these are gladly devoted to God, they become instruments by which He effects His will
on the earth. Such faithful and joyous service makes one's entire life a performance of worship.
    Now turn to Page 424—2 Chr. 7:3: The Reasons for Worship.

THE EPISTLE OF

JAMES

THE BOOK OF JAMES

Faith without works cannot be called faith. Faith without works is dead, and a dead faith is worse than no faith at all. Faith must work; it must produce; it must be visible. Verbal faith is not enough; mental faith is insufficient. Faith must be there, but it must be more. It must inspire action. Throughout his epistle to Jewish believers, James integrates true faith and everyday practical experience by stressing that true faith must manifest itself in works of faith.

Faith endures trials. Trials come and go, but a strong faith will face them head-on and develop endurance. Faith understands temptations. It will not allow us to consent to our lust and slide into sin. Faith obeys the Word. It will not merely hear and not do. Faith produces doers. Faith harbors no prejudice. For James, faith and favoritism cannot coexist. Faith displays itself in works. Faith is more than mere words; it is more than knowledge; it is demonstrated by obedience; and it overtly responds to the promises of God. Faith controls the tongue. This small but immensely powerful part of the body must be held in check. Faith can do it. Faith acts wisely. It gives us the ability to choose wisdom that is heavenly and to shun wisdom that is earthly. Faith produces separation from the world and submission to God. It provides us with the ability to resist the devil and humbly draw near to God. Finally, faith waits patiently for the coming of the Lord. Through trouble and trial it stifles complaining.

The name *Iakobos* (James) in 1:1 is the basis for the early title *Iakobou Epistole*, "Epistle of James." *Iakobos* is the Greek form of the Hebrew name Jacob, a Jewish name common in the first century.

THE AUTHOR OF JAMES

Four men are named James in the New Testament: (1) James, the father of Judas (not Iscariot), is mentioned twice (Luke 6:16; Acts 1:13) as the father of one of the twelve disciples, but is otherwise completely unknown. (2) James, the son of Alphaeus (Matt. 10:3; Mark 3:18; Luke 6:15; Acts 1:13), elsewhere called James the Less (Mark 15:40), was one of the twelve disciples. Apart from being listed with the other disciples, this James is completely obscure, and it is doubtful that he is the authoritative figure be-

hind the epistle. Some attempts have been made to identify this James with the Lord's brother (Gal. 1:19), but this view is difficult to reconcile with the gospel accounts. (3) James, the son of Zebedee and brother of John (Matt. 4:21; 10:2; 17:1; Mark 3:17; 10:35; 13:3; Luke 9:54; Acts 1:13), was one of Jesus' intimate disciples, but his martyrdom by A.D. 44 (Acts 12:2) makes it very unlikely that he wrote this epistle. (4) James, the Lord's brother (Matt. 13:55; Mark 6:3; Gal. 1:19), was one of the "pillars" in the church in Jerusalem (Acts 12:17; 15:13–21; 21:18; Gal. 2:9, 12). Tradition points to this prominent figure as the author of the epistle, and this best fits the evidence of Scripture. There are several clear parallels between the language of the letter drafted under his leadership in Acts 15:23–29 and the Epistle of James (e.g., the unusual word *chairein*, "greeting," is found only in Acts 15:23; 23:26; and James 1:1). The Jewish character of this epistle with its stress upon the law, along with the evident influence by the Sermon on the Mount (e.g., 4:11, 12; 5:12), complement what we know about James "the Just" from Scripture and early tradition.

It has been argued that the Greek of this epistle is too sophisticated for a Galilean such as James, but this assumes that he never had the opportunity or aptitude to develop proficiency in Koine ("common") Greek. As a prominent church leader, it would have been to his advantage to become fluent in the universal language of the Roman Empire.

For various reasons, some assert that James was a stepbrother of Jesus by a previous marriage of Joseph, or that the "brothers" of Jesus mentioned in Matthew 13:55 and Mark 6:3 were really His cousins. However, the most natural understanding of the gospel accounts is that James was the half-brother of Jesus, being the offspring of Joseph and Mary after the birth of Jesus (Matt. 1:24, 25). He apparently did not accept the claims of Jesus until the Lord appeared to him after His resurrection (1 Cor. 15:7). He and his brothers were among the believers who awaited the coming of the Holy Spirit on the day of Pentecost (Acts 1:14). It was not long before he became an acknowledged leader of the Jerusalem church (Acts 12:17; Gal. 2:9, 12), and he was a central figure in the Jerusalem Council in Acts 15. Even after Paul's third missionary journey, James continued to observe the Mosaic Law as a tes-

timony to other Jews (Acts 21:18-25). Early tradition stresses his Jewish piety and his role in bringing others to an understanding of Jesus as the Messiah. He suffered a violent martyr's death not long before the fall of Jerusalem.

The brevity and limited doctrinal emphasis of James kept it from wide circulation; and by the time it became known in the church as a whole, there was uncertainty about the identity of the James in 1:1. Growing recognition that it was written by the Lord's brother led to its acceptance as a canonical book.

THE TIME OF JAMES

James is addressed "to the twelve tribes who are dispersed abroad" (1:1), and it is apparent from verses like 1:19 and 2:1, 7 that this greeting refers to Hebrew Christians outside of Palestine. Their place of meeting is called a "synagogue" in the Greek text of 2:2, and the whole epistle reflects Jewish thought and expressions (e.g., 2:19, 21; 4:11, 12; 5:4, 12). There are no references to slavery or idolatry, and this also fits an originally Jewish readership.

These Jewish believers were beset with problems that were testing their faith, and James was concerned that they were succumbing to impatience, bitterness, materialism, disunity, and spiritual apathy. As a resident of Jerusalem and a leader of the church, James no doubt had frequent contact with Jewish Christians from a number of Roman provinces. He therefore felt a responsibility to exhort and encourage them in their struggles of faith.

According to Josephus, James was martyred in A.D. 62. (Hegesippus, quoted in Eusebius, fixed the date of James's death at A.D. 66.) Those who accept him as the author of this epistle have proposed a date of writing ranging from A.D. 45 to the end of his life. However, several factors indicate that this letter may have been the earliest writing of the New Testament (c. A.D. 46-49): (1) There is no mention of gentile Christians or their relationship to Jewish Christians as would be expected in a later epistle. (2) Apart from references to the person of Christ, there is practically no distinctive theology in James, suggesting an early date when Christianity was viewed in terms of Messianic Judaism. (3) The allusions to the teachings of Christ have such little verbal agreement with the synoptic Gospels that they probably preceded them. (4) James uses the word "synagogue" (assembly, 2:2) in addition to "church" and indicates a very simple organization of elders and masters, that is, teachers (3:1; 5:14), which was patterned after the early synagogue. (5) James does not mention the issues involved in the Acts 15 Council in Jerusalem (A.D. 49).

THE CHRIST OF JAMES

In 1:1 and 2:1 James refers to the "Lord Jesus Christ," and in 5:7, 8 he anticipates "the coming of the Lord." Compared to other New Testament writers, James says little about Christ, and yet his speech is virtually saturated with allusions to the teaching of Christ. The Sermon on the Mount is especially prominent in James's thinking (there are fifteen indirect references; e.g., James 1:2 and Matt. 5:10-12; James 1:4 and Matt. 5:48; James 2:13 and Matt. 6:14, 15; James 4:11 and Matt. 7:1, 2; James 5:2 and Matt. 6:19). This epistle portrays Christ in the context of early Messianic Judaism.

KEYS TO JAMES

Key Word: Faith That Works—Throughout his epistle, James develops the theme of the characteristics of true faith. He effectively uses these characteristics as a series

FOCUS	TEST OF FAITH		CHARACTERISTICS OF FAITH	TRIUMPH OF FAITH		
REFERENCE	1:1————1:13————1:19————			———5:7——5:13————————		—5:19————5:20
DIVISION	PURPOSE OF TESTS	SOURCE OF TEMPTATION	OUTWARD DEMONSTRATION OF INNER FAITH	ENDURES WAITING	PRAYS FOR AFFLICTED	CONFRONTS SIN
TOPIC	DEVELOPMENT OF FAITH		WORKS OF FAITH	POWER OF FAITH		
	RESPONSE OF FAITH		REALITY OF FAITH	REASSURANCE OF FAITH		
LOCATION	PROBABLY JERUSALEM					
TIME	c. A.D. 46—49					

of tests to help his readers evaluate the quality of their relationship to Christ. The purpose of this work is not doctrinal or apologetic but practical. James seeks to challenge these believers to examine the quality of their daily lives in terms of attitudes and actions. A genuine faith will produce real changes in a person's conduct and character, and the absence of change is a symptom of a dead faith.

Key Verses: James 1:19–22 and 2:14–17— "*This* you know, my beloved brethren. But let everyone be quick to hear, slow to speak *and* slow to anger; for the anger of man does not achieve the righteousness of God. Therefore putting aside all filthiness and *all* that remains of wickedness, in humility receive the word implanted, which is able to save your souls. But prove yourselves doers of the word, and not merely hearers who delude themselves" (1:19–22).

"What use is it, my brethren, if a man says he has faith, but he has no works? Can that faith save him? If a brother or sister is without clothing and in need of daily food, and one of you says to them, 'Go in peace, be warmed and be filled,' and yet you do not give them what is necessary for *their* body, what use is that? Even so faith, if it has no works, is dead, *being* by itself" (2:14–17).

Key Chapter: James 1—One of the most difficult areas of the Christian life is that of testings and temptations. James reveals our correct response to both: to testings, count them all joy; to temptations, realize that God is not their source.

SURVEY OF JAMES

James is the Proverbs of the New Testament because it is written in the terse moralistic style of wisdom literature. It is evident that James was profoundly influenced by the Old Testament (especially by its wisdom literature) and by the Sermon on the Mount. But James's impassioned preaching against inequity and social injustice also earns him the title of the Amos of the New Testament. Because of the many subjects in this epistle, it is difficult to outline; suggestions have ranged from no connection between the various topics to a unified scheme. The outline used here is: the test of faith (1:1–18); the characteristics of faith (1:19—5:6); and the triumph of faith (5:7–20).

The Test of Faith (1:1–18): The first part of this epistle develops the qualities of genuine faith in regard to trials and temptations. After a one-verse salutation to geographically dispersed Hebrew Christians (1:1), James quickly introduces his first subject, outward tests of faith (1:2–12). These trials are designed to produce mature endurance and a sense of dependence upon God, to whom the believer turns for wisdom and enablement. Inward temptations (1:13–18) do not come from the One who bestows "Every good thing" (1:17). These solicitations to evil must be checked at an early stage or they may result in disastrous consequences.

The Characteristics of Faith (1:19—5:6): A righteous response to testing requires that one be "quick to hear, slow to speak *and* slow to anger" (1:19), and this broadly summarizes the remainder of the epistle. Quickness of hearing involves an obedient response to God's Word (1:19–27). True hearing means more than mere listening; the Word must be received and applied. After stating this principle (1:21, 22), James develops it with an illustration (1:23–25) and an application (1:26, 27). A genuine faith should produce a change in attitude from partiality to the rich to a love for the poor as well as the rich (2:1–13). True faith should also result in actions (2:14–26). In Romans 4, Paul used the example of Abraham to show that justification is by faith, not by works. But James says that Abraham was justified by works (2:21). In spite of the apparent contradiction, Romans 4 and James 2 are really two sides of the same coin. In context, Paul is writing about justification before God while James writes of the evidence of justification before men. A faith that produces no change is not saving faith.

Moving from works to words, James shows how a living faith controls the tongue ("slow to speak," 1:19). The tongue is small, but it has the power to accomplish great good or equally great evil. Only the power of God applied by an active faith can tame the tongue (3:1–12). Just as there are wicked and righteous uses of the tongue, so there are demonic and divine manifestations of wisdom (3:13–18). James contrasts seven characteristics of human wisdom with seven qualities of divine wisdom.

The strong pulls of worldliness (4:1–12) and wealth (4:13—5:6) create conflicts that are harmful to the growth of faith. The world system is at enmity with God, and the pursuit of its pleasures produces covetousness, envy, fighting, and arrogance (4:1–6). The believer's only alternative is submission to God out of a humble and repentant spirit. This will produce a transformed attitude toward others as well (4:7–12). This spirit of submission and humility should be applied to any attempts to

accrue wealth (4:13–17), especially because wealth can lead to pride, injustice, and selfishness (5:1–6).

The Triumph of Faith (5:7–20): James encourages his readers to patiently endure the sufferings of the present life in view of the future prospect of the coming of the Lord (5:7–12). They may be oppressed by the rich or by other circumstances, but as the example of Job

teaches, believers can be sure that God has a gracious purpose in His dealings with them. James concludes his epistle with some practical words on prayer and restoration (5:13–20). The prayers of righteous men (e.g., elders in local churches) are efficacious for the healing and restoration of believers. When sin is not dealt with, it can contribute to illness and even death.

CHAPTER 1

The Purpose of Tests

JAMES, a bond-servant of God and [R]of the Lord Jesus Christ, to the twelve tribes who are dispersed abroad, greetings.   2 Pet. 1:1

2 Consider it all joy, my brethren, when you encounter various[A]trials,   *temptations*

3 knowing that[R]the testing of your faith produces[A]endurance.   1 Pet. 1:7 • *steadfastness*

4 And let endurance have *its* perfect[T]result, that you may be[A]perfect and complete, lacking in nothing.   *work • mature*

5 But if any of you[R]lacks wisdom, let him ask of God, who gives to all men generously and[T]without reproach, and it will be given to him.   1 Kin. 3:9ff.; Prov. 2:3-6 • *does not reproach*

6 But let him[R]ask in faith[R]without any doubting, for the one who doubts is like the surf of the sea[R]driven and tossed by the wind.   Matt. 21:21 • [Mark 11:23] • Matt. 14:28–31

7 For let not that man expect that he will receive anything from the Lord,

8 *being* a[A]double-minded[R] man, unstable in all his ways.   *doubting, hesitating •* James 4:8

9 [R]But let the brother of humble circumstances glory in his high position; Luke 14:11

10 and *let* the rich man *glory* in his humiliation, because[R]like [T]flowering grass he will pass away.   [1 Cor. 7:31] • *the flower of the grass*

11 For the sun rises with [T]a scorching wind, and withers the grass; and its flower falls off, and the beauty of its appearance is destroyed; so too the rich man in the midst of his pursuits will fade away.   *the*

12 Blessed is a man who perseveres under trial; for once he has been approved, he will receive the crown of life, which *the Lord* has promised to those who love Him.

[1] Or, *Know* this

The Source of Temptations

13 Let no one say when he is tempted, "I[R] am being tempted[T]by God"; for God cannot be tempted[T]by evil, and He Himself does not tempt anyone.   Gen. 22:1 • *from • of evil things*

14 But each one is tempted when he is carried away and enticed by his own lust.

15 Then[R]when lust has conceived, it gives birth to sin; and when sin is accomplished, it brings forth death.   Job 15:35; Ps. 7:14; Is. 59:4

16 [R]Do not be deceived,[R]my beloved brethren.   1 Cor. 6:9 • Acts 1:15; James 1:2, 19

17 Every good thing bestowed and every perfect gift is from above, coming down from the Father of lights,[R]with whom there is no variation, or shifting shadow.   Mal. 3:6

18 In the exercise of His will He brought us forth by the word of truth, so that we might be, [T]as it were, the first fruits [T]among His creatures.   *a certain first fruits • of*

Faith Obeys the Word

19 [1]*This* you know, my beloved brethren. But let everyone be quick to hear,[R]slow to speak *and* slow to anger;   Prov. 10:19; 17:27

20 for[R]the anger of man does not achieve the righteousness of God.   [Matt. 5:22]

21 Therefore putting aside all filthiness and *all*[T]that remains of wickedness, in humility receive the word implanted, which is able to save your souls.   *abundance of malice*

22 [R]But prove yourselves doers of the word, and not merely hearers who delude themselves.   Luke 6:46–49; [Rom. 2:13]

23 For if anyone is a hearer of the word and not a doer, he is like a man who looks at his natural face[R]in a mirror;   1 Cor. 13:12

24 for *once* he has looked at himself and gone away, [T]he has immediately forgotten what kind of person he was.   *and he*

25 But one who looks intently at the perfect law, the *law* of liberty, and abides by it, not having become a forgetful hearer but[T]an effectual doer, this man shall be blessed in [T]what he does. *a doer of a work • his doing*

26 If anyone thinks himself to be religious, and yet does not[R]bridle his tongue but deceives his *own* heart, this man's religion is worthless. Ps. 39:1; 141:3; [James 3:2–12]

27 This is pure and undefiled religion in the sight of *our* God and Father, to visit orphans and widows in their distress, *and* to keep oneself unstained by the world.

CHAPTER 2

Faith Removes Discrimination

M Y brethren,[R]do not hold your faith in our [R]glorious Lord Jesus Christ with *an attitude of* personal favoritism. Heb. 12:2 • Acts 7:2

2 For if a man comes into your[A]assembly with a gold ring and dressed in[A]fine clothes, and there also comes in a poor man in[R]dirty clothes, *synagogue • bright •* Zech. 3:3f.

3 and you[T]pay special attention to the one who is wearing the fine clothes, and say, "You sit here in a good place," and you say to the poor man, "You stand over there, or sit down by my footstool," *look upon*

4 have you not made distinctions among yourselves, and become judges [R]with evil [T]motives? Luke 18:6; John 7:24 • *reasonings*

5 Listen, my beloved brethren: did not God choose the poor[T]of this world *to be* rich in faith and heirs of the kingdom which He promised to those who love Him? *to the*

6 But you have dishonored the poor man. Is it not the rich who oppress you and personally drag you into[T]court? *courts*

7 [R]Do they not blaspheme the fair name by which you have been called? Acts 11:26

8 If, however, you[R]are fulfilling the[A]royal law, according to the Scripture, "YOU SHALL LOVE YOUR NEIGHBOR AS YOURSELF," you are doing well. Matt. 7:12 • *law of* our King

9 But if you [R]show partiality, you are committing sin *and* are convicted by the [A]law as transgressors. Acts 10:34 • *Law*

10 For whoever keeps the whole[A]law and yet[R]stumbles in one *point,* he has become [R]guilty of all. *Law •* James 3:2 • Matt. 5:19

11 For He who said, "DO NOT COMMIT ADULTERY," also said, "DO NOT COMMIT MURDER." Now if you do not commit adultery, but do commit murder, you have become a transgressor of the[A]law. *Law*

12 So speak and so act, as those who are to be judged by *the* law of liberty.

13 For[R]judgment *will be* merciless to one who has shown no mercy; mercy[T]triumphs over judgment. Prov. 21:13 • *boasts against*

Faith Proves Itself by Works

14 What use is it,[R]my brethren, if a man says he has faith, but he has no works? Can [T]that faith save him? James 1:16 • *the*

15 [R]If a brother or sister is without clothing and in need of daily food, Matt. 25:35f.

16 and one of you says to them, "Go[R]in peace, be warmed and be filled," and yet you do not give them what is necessary for *their* body, what use is that? [1 John 3:17f.]

17 Even so[R]faith, if it has no works, is dead, *being* by itself. [Gal. 5:6]; James 2:20, 26

18 [R]But someone[T]may *well* say, "You have faith, and I have works; show me your faith without the works, and I will show you my faith by my works." Rom. 9:19 • *will*

19 You believe that [2]God is one. You do well; the demons also believe, and shudder.

20 But are you willing to recognize,[R]you foolish fellow, that faith without works is useless? Rom. 9:20; 1 Cor. 15:36

21 [R]Was not Abraham our father justified by works, when he offered up Isaac his son on the altar? Gen. 22:9, 10, 12, 16-18

22 You see that faith was working with his works, and[A]as a result of the works, faith was[A]perfected; *by the deeds • completed*

23 and the Scripture was fulfilled which says, "AND ABRAHAM BELIEVED GOD, AND IT WAS RECKONED TO HIM AS RIGHTEOUSNESS," and he was called the friend of God.

24 You see that a man is justified by works, and not by faith alone.

25 And in the same way was not[R]Rahab the harlot also justified by works,[R]when she received the messengers and sent them out by another way? Heb. 11:31 • Josh. 2:4, 6, 15

26 For just as the body without *the* spirit is dead, so also faith without works is dead.

CHAPTER 3

Faith Controls the Tongue

L ET not many of *you* become teachers, my brethren, knowing that as such we shall incur a[A]stricter judgment. *greater condemnation*

2 For we all[R]stumble in many *ways.* [R]If anyone does not stumble in[T]what he says, he is a perfect man, able to bridle the whole body as well. James 2:10 • [Matt. 12:34–37] • *word*

3 Now[R]if we put the bits into the horses' mouths so that they may obey us, we direct their entire body as well. Ps. 32:9

4 Behold, the ships also, though they are so great and are driven by strong winds, are still directed by a very small rudder, wherever the inclination of the pilot desires.

5 So also the tongue is a small part of the body, and *yet* it[R]boasts of great things.[R]Behold, how great a forest is set aflame by such a small fire! Ps. 12:3f.; 73:8f. • Prov. 26:20f.

6 And the tongue is a fire, the *very* world of iniquity; the tongue is set among our members as that which defiles the entire body, and sets on fire the course of our[A]life, and is set on fire by hell. *existence, origin*

[2] Or, *there is one God*

7 For every species of beasts and birds, of reptiles and creatures of the sea, is tamed, and has been tamed by the human ᵀrace.   *nature*

8 But no one can tame the tongue; *it is a* restless evil *and* full of deadly poison.

9 With it we blessᴿ*our* Lord and Father; and with it we curse men, who have been made in the likeness of God;   James 1:27

10 from the same mouth come *both* blessing and cursing. My brethren, these things ought not to be this way.

11 Does a fountain send out from the same opening *both* fresh and bitter *water*?

12 ᴿCan a fig tree, my brethren, produce olives, or a vine produce figs? Neither *can* salt water produce fresh.   Matt. 7:16

Faith Produces Wisdom

13 Who among you is wise and understanding? Let him show by his good behavior his deeds in the gentleness of wisdom.

14 But if you have bitter jealousy andᴬselfish ambition in your heart, do not be arrogant and *so* lie against the truth.   *strife*

15 This wisdom is not that which comes down from above, but is ᴿearthly, ᴬnatural, demonic.   1 Cor. 2:6; 3:19 • *unspiritual*

16 For whereᴿjealousy and selfish ambition exist, there is disorder and every evil thing.   Rom. 2:8; 2 Cor. 12:20

17 But the wisdom from above is first pure, then peaceable, gentle, ᴬreasonable, full of mercy and good fruits, unwavering, without hypocrisy.   *willing to yield*

18 And theᵀseed whose fruit is righteousness is sown in peaceᴬby those who make peace.   *fruit of righteousness • for*

CHAPTER 4

Faith Produces Humility

WHAT is the source of quarrels and conflicts among you? Is not the source your pleasures that wage war in your members?

2 You lust and do not have; *so* you commit murder. And you are envious and cannot obtain; *so* you fight and quarrel. You do not have because you do not ask.

3 You ask and do not receive, because you ask with wrong motives, so that you may spend *it*ᵀon your pleasures.   *in*

4 You ᴿadulteresses, do you not know that friendship with the world is hostility toward God? Therefore whoever wishes to be a friend of the world makes himself an enemy of God.   Jer. 2:2; Ezek. 16:32

5 Or do you think that the Scripture speaks to no purpose: "³Heᵀjealously desires ᴿthe Spirit which He has made to dwell in us"?   *desires to jealousy • 1 Cor. 6:19*

6 Butᴿ He gives a greater grace. Therefore *it* says, "GOD IS OPPOSED TO THE PROUD, BUT GIVES GRACE TO THE HUMBLE."   Is. 54:7f.

³ Or, *The Spirit which He has made to dwell in us jealously desires us*

7 ᴿSubmit therefore to God. Resist the devil and he will flee from you.   1 Pet. 5:6

8 ᴿDraw near to God and He will draw near to you. ᴿCleanse your hands, you sinners; and purify your hearts, you doubleminded.   2 Chr. 15:2; Zech. 1:3 • Job 17:9; Is. 1:16

9 ᴿBe miserable and mourn and weep; let your laughter be turned into mourning, and your joy to gloom.   Prov. 14:13; Luke 6:25

10 ᴿHumble yourselves in the presence of the Lord, and He will exalt you.   Job 5:11

11 ᴿDo not speak against one another, ᴿbrethren. He who speaks against a brother, or judges his brother, speaks against the law, and judges the law; but if you judge the law, you are not a doer of the law, but a judge *of it*.   2 Cor. 12:20; James 5:9 • James 1:16

12 There is *only* one Lawgiver and Judge, the One who is able to save and to destroy; but who are you who judge your neighbor?

Faith Produces Dependence on God

13 ᴿCome now, you who say, "Today or tomorrow, we shall go to such and such a city, and spend a year there and engage in business and make a profit."   James 5:1

14 ᵀYet you do not know what your life will be like tomorrow. ᴿYou are *just* a vapor that appears for a little while and then vanishes away.   *Who do not • Job 7:7; Ps. 39:5*

15 Instead, *you ought* to say, "If the Lord wills, we shall live and also do this or that."

16 But as it is, you boast in your ᴬarrogance; all such boasting is evil.   *pretensions*

17 Therefore, ᴿto one who knows the ᴬright thing to do, and does not do it, to him it is sin.   [Luke 12:47]; John 9:41 • *good*

CHAPTER 5

COME now, you rich, weep and howl for your miseries which are coming upon you.

2 ᴿYour riches have rotted and your garments have become moth-eaten.   Job 13:28

3 Your gold and your silver have rusted; and their rust will be a witness against you and will consume your flesh like fire. It isᴿin the last days that you have stored up your treasure!   James 5:7, 8

4 Behold, the pay of the laborers who mowed your fields, *and* which has been withheld by you, cries out *against you*; and the outcry of those who did the harvesting has reached the ears of the Lord of Sabaoth.

5 You have lived luxuriously on the earth and led a life of wanton pleasure; you have fattened your hearts in a day of slaughter.

6 You have condemned and put to death the righteous *man;* he does not resist you.

Faith Endures Awaiting Christ's Return

7 Be patient, therefore, brethren, until the coming of the Lord. Behold, the farmer waits for the precious produce of the soil,

being patient about it, until^it gets^R the early and late rains.   *he •* Deut. 11:14

8 ^R You too be patient; strengthen your hearts, for ^R the coming of the Lord is ^R at hand.   Luke 21:19 • John 21:22 • Rom. 13:11

9 Do not ^T complain, brethren, against one another, that you yourselves may not be judged; behold, the Judge is standing ^T right at the ^T door.   *groan • before • doors*

10 As an example, ^R brethren, of suffering and patience, take the prophets who spoke in the name of the Lord.   James 4:11; 5:7, 9

11 Behold, we count those blessed who endured. You have heard of the endurance of Job and have seen the ^T outcome of the Lord's dealings, that the Lord is full of compassion and *is* merciful.   *end of the Lord*

12 But above all, my brethren, do not swear, either by heaven or by earth or with any other oath; but ^T let your yes be yes, and your no, no; so that you may not fall under judgment.   *let yours be the yes, yes, and the no, no*

Faith Prays for the Afflicted

13 Is anyone among you ^R suffering? Let him pray. Is anyone cheerful? Let him ^R sing praises.   James 5:10 • 1 Cor. 14:15; Col. 3:16

14 Is anyone among you sick? Let him call for the elders of the church, and let them pray over him, ^T anointing him with oil in the name of the Lord;   *having anointed*

15 and the prayer ^T offered in faith will ⁴restore the one who is sick, and the Lord will raise him up, and if he has committed sins, ^T they will be forgiven him.   *of • it*

16 Therefore, confess your sins to one another, and pray for one another, so that you may be healed. The effective prayer of a righteous man can accomplish much.

17 Elijah was a man with a nature like ours, and he prayed ^T earnestly that it might not rain; and it did not rain on the earth for three years and six months.   *with prayer*

18 And he ^R prayed again, and ^R the ^T sky ^T poured rain, and the earth produced its fruit.   1 Kin. 18:42 • 1 Kin. 18:45 • *heaven • gave*

Faith Confronts the Erring Brother

19 My brethren, if any among you strays from the truth, and one turns him back,

20 let him know that he who turns a sinner from the error of his way will ^R save his soul from death, and will ^R cover a multitude of sins.   Rom. 11:14; 1 Cor. 1:21 • Prov. 10:12

⁴ Or, *save*

THE FIRST EPISTLE OF

PETER

THE BOOK OF FIRST PETER

Persecution can cause either growth or bitterness in the Christian life. Response determines the result. In writing to Jewish believers struggling in the midst of persecution, Peter encourages them to conduct themselves courageously for the Person and program of Christ. Both their character and conduct must be above reproach. Having been born again to a living hope, they are to imitate the Holy One who has called them. The fruit of that character will be conduct rooted in submission: citizens to government, servants to masters, wives to husbands, husbands to wives, and Christians to one another. Only after submission is fully understood does Peter deal with the difficult area of suffering. The Christians are not to be "surprised at the fiery ordeal among you, which comes upon you for your testing, as though some strange thing were happening to you" (4:12), but are to rejoice as partakers of the suffering of Christ. That response to life is truly the climax of one's submission to the good hand of God.

This epistle begins with the phrase *Petros apostolos Iesou Christou*, "Peter, an apostle of Jesus Christ." This is the basis of the early title *Petrou A*, the "First of Peter."

THE AUTHOR OF FIRST PETER

The early church universally acknowledged the authenticity and authority of First Peter. The internal evidence supports this consistent external testimony in several ways. The apostle Peter's name is given in 1:1, and there are definite similarities between certain phrases in this letter and Peter's sermons as recorded in the Book of Acts (cf. 1 Pet. 1:20 and Acts 2:23; 1 Pet. 4:5 and Acts 10:42). Twice in Acts Peter used the Greek word *xylon*, "wood, tree," to speak of the cross, and this distinctive use is also found in First Peter (see Acts 5:30; 10:39; 1 Pet. 2:24). The epistle contains a number of allusions to events in the life of Christ that held special significance for Peter (e.g., 2:23; 3:18; 4:1; 5:1; cf. 5:5 and John 13:4).

Nevertheless, critics since the nineteenth century have challenged the authenticity of First Peter on several grounds. Some claim that 1:1, 2 and 4:12—5:14 were later additions that turned an anonymous address or a baptismal sermon into a Petrine epistle. Others argue that the sufferings experienced by readers of this letter must refer to the persecution of Christians that took place after the time of Peter in the reigns of the emperors Domitian (A.D. 81–96) and Trajan (A.D. 98–117). There is no basis for the first argument, and the second argument falsely assumes that Christians were not being reviled for their faith during the life of Peter. Another challenge asserts that the quality of the Greek of this epistle is too high for a Galilean like Peter. But Galileans were bilingual (Aramaic and Greek), and writers such as Matthew and James were skillful in their use of Greek. It is also likely that Peter used Silvanus as his scribe (5:12; Paul calls him Silvanus in 2 Cor. 1:19; 1 Thess. 1:1; 2 Thess. 1:1; Luke calls him Silas in Acts 15:40—18:5), and Silvanus may have smoothed out Peter's speech in the process.

THE TIME OF FIRST PETER

This letter is addressed "to those who reside as aliens," or more literally, "sojourners of the dispersion" (1:1). This, coupled with the injunction to keep their behavior "excellent among the Gentiles" (2:12), gives the initial appearance that the bulk of the readers are Hebrew Christians. A closer look, however, forms the opposite view that most of these believers were Gentiles. They were called "out of darkness" (2:9), and they "once were not a people," but now they "are the people of God" (2:10). Their former "way of life inherited from [their] forefathers" was characterized by ignorance and futility (1:14, 18; cf. Eph. 4:17). Because they no longer engage in debauchery and idolatry, they are maligned by their countrymen (4:3, 4). These descriptions do not fit a predominantly Hebrew Christian readership. Though Peter was an apostle "to the circumcised" (Gal. 2:9), he also ministered to Gentiles (Acts 10:34–48; Gal. 2:12), and a letter like this would not be beyond the scope of his ministry.

This epistle was addressed to Christians throughout Asia Minor, indicating the spread of the gospel in regions not evangelized when Acts was written (Pontus, Cappadocia, Bithynia; 1:1). It is possible that Peter visited and ministered in some of these areas, but there is no evidence. He wrote this letter in response to the news of growing opposition to the believers in Asia Minor (1:6; 3:13–17; 4:12–19; 5:9, 10). Hostility and suspicion were mounting against Christians in the empire,

and they were being reviled and abused for their life-styles and subversive talk about another Kingdom. Christianity had not yet received the official Roman ban, but the stage was being set for the persecution and martyrdom of the near future.

Peter's life was dramatically changed after the Resurrection, and he occupied a central role in the early church and in the spread of the gospel to the Samaritans and Gentiles (Acts 2—10). After the Jerusalem Council in Acts 15, little is recorded of Peter's activities. He evidently traveled extensively with his wife (1 Cor. 9:5) and ministered in various Roman provinces. According to tradition, Peter was crucified upside down in Rome prior to Nero's death in A.D. 68.

This epistle was written from Babylon (5:13), but scholars are divided as to whether this refers literally to Babylon in Mesopotamia or symbolically to Rome. There is no tradition that Peter went to Babylon, and in his day it had few inhabitants. On the other hand, tradition consistently indicates that Peter spent the last years of his life in Rome. As a center of idolatry, the term "Babylon" was an appropriate figurative designation for Rome (cf. the later use of Babylon in Rev. 17; 18). Peter used other figurative expressions in this epistle, and it is not surprising that he would do the same with Rome. His mention of Mark (5:13) also fits this view because Mark was in Rome during Paul's first imprisonment (Col. 4:10). This epistle was probably written shortly before the outbreak of persecution under Nero in A.D. 64.

THE CHRIST OF FIRST PETER
This epistle presents Christ as the believer's example and hope in times of suffering in a spiritually hostile world. He is the basis for the Christian's "living hope" and

"inheritance" (1:3, 4), and the love relationship available with Him by faith is a source of inexpressible joy (1:8). His suffering and death provide redemption for all who trust in Him: "and He Himself bore our sins in His body on the cross, that we might die to sin and live to righteousness; for by His wounds you were healed" (2:24; cf. 1:18, 19; 3:18). Christ is the Chief Shepherd and Guardian of believers (2:25; 5:4), and when He appears, those who know Him will be glorified.

KEYS TO FIRST PETER
Key Word: Suffering for the Cause of Christ—The basic theme of First Peter is the proper response to Christian suffering. Knowing that his readers will be facing more persecution than ever before, Peter writes this letter to give them a divine perspective on these trials so that they will be able to endure them without wavering in their faith. They should not be surprised at their ordeal because the One they follow also suffered and died (2:21; 3:18; 4:1, 12–14). Rather, they should count it a privilege to share the sufferings of Christ. Peter therefore exhorts them to be sure that their hardships are not being caused by their own wrongdoings, but for their Christian testimony. They are not the only believers who are suffering (5:9), and they must recognize that God brings these things into the lives of His children, not as a punishment but as a stimulus to "perfect . . . you" in Christ (5:10). Peter wants to overcome the attitudes of bitterness and anxiety, replacing them with dependence on and confidence in God.

Another theme is stated in 5:12: "I have written to you briefly, exhorting and testifying that this is the true grace of God." In this epistle, Peter frequently speaks of the believer's position in Christ and future hope, and he

FOCUS	SALVATION OF THE BELIEVER		SUBMISSION OF THE BELIEVER	SUFFERING OF THE BELIEVER			
REFERENCE	1:1———1:13———		2:13———————	3:13———3:18———		4:7———	5:1———5:14
DIVISION	SALVATION OF THE BELIEVER	SANCTIFICA- TION OF THE BELIEVER	GOVERNMENT, BUSINESS, MARRIAGE, AND ALL OF LIFE	CONDUCT IN SUFFERING	CHRIST'S EXAMPLE OF SUFFERING	COMMANDS IN SUFFERING	MINISTER IN SUFFERING
TOPIC	BELIEF OF CHRISTIANS		BEHAVIOR OF CHRISTIANS	BUFFETING OF CHRISTIANS			
	HOLINESS		HARMONY	HUMILITY			
LOCATION	EITHER ROME OR BABYLON						
TIME	C. A.D. 63–64						

does so to remind his readers that they are merely sojourners on this planet: their true destiny is eternal glory "at the revelation of His glory" (4:13). The grace of God in their salvation (1:1—2:10) shall give them an attitude of submission (2:11—3:12) in the context of suffering for the name of Christ (3:13—5:14).

Key Verses: First Peter 1:10-12 and 4:12, 13—"As to this salvation, the prophets who prophesied of the grace that *would come* to you made careful search and inquiry, seeking to know what person or time the Spirit of Christ within them was indicating as He predicted the sufferings of Christ and the glories to follow. It was revealed to them that they were not serving themselves, but you, in these things which now have been announced to you through those who preached the gospel to you by the Holy Spirit sent from heaven—things into which angels long to look" (1:10-12).

"Beloved, do not be surprised at the fiery ordeal among you, which comes upon you for your testing, as though some strange thing were happening to you; but to the degree that you share the sufferings of Christ, keep on rejoicing; so that also at the revelation of His glory, you may rejoice with exultation" (4:12, 13).

Key Chapter: First Peter 4—Central in the New Testament revelation concerning how to handle persecution and suffering caused by one's Christian testimony is First Peter 4. Not only is Christ's suffering to be our model (4:1, 2), but also we are to rejoice in that we can share in His suffering (4:12-14).

SURVEY OF FIRST PETER

Peter addresses this epistle to "aliens" in a world that is growing increasingly hostile to Christians. These believers are beginning to suffer because of their stand for Christ, and Peter uses this letter to give them counsel and comfort by stressing the reality of their living hope in the Lord. By standing firm in the grace of God (5:12) they will be able to endure their "fiery ordeal" (4:12), knowing that there is a divine purpose behind their pain. This letter logically proceeds through the themes of: the salvation of the believer (1:1—2:12); the submission of the believer (2:13—3:12); and the suffering of the believer (3:13—5:14).

The Salvation of the Believer (1:1—2:12): Addressing his letter to believers in several Roman provinces, Peter briefly describes the saving work of the triune Godhead in his salutation (1:1, 2). He then extols God for the riches of this salvation by looking in three tem-

poral directions (1:3-12). First, Peter anticipates the future realization of the Christian's manifold inheritance (1:3-5). Second, he looks at the present joy that this living hope produces in spite of various trials (1:6-9). Third, he reflects upon the prophets of the past who predicted the gospel of God's grace in Christ (1:10-12).

The proper response to this salvation is the pursuit of sanctification or holiness (1:13—2:10). This involves a purifying departure from conformity with the world to godliness in behavior and love. With this in mind, Peter exhorts his readers to "grow in respect to salvation" (2:2) by applying the "living and abiding word of God" (1:23) and acting as a holy priesthood of believers.

The Submission of the Believer (2:13—3:12): Peter turns to the believer's relationships in the world and appeals for an attitude of submission as the Christlike way to harmony and true freedom. Submission for the Lord's sake to those in governmental (2:13-17) and social (2:18-20) authority will foster a good testimony to outsiders. Before moving on to submission in marital relationships (3:1-7), Peter again picks up the theme of Christian suffering (mentioned in 1:6, 7 and 2:12, 18-20) and uses Christ as the supreme model: He suffered sinlessly, silently, and as a substitute for the salvation of others (2:21-25; cf. Is. 52:13—53:12). Peter summarizes his appeal for Christlike submission and humility in 3:8-12.

The Suffering of the Believer (3:13—5:14): Anticipating that growing opposition to Christianity will require a number of his readers to defend their faith and conduct, Peter encourages them to be ready to do so in an intelligent and gracious way (3:13-16). Three times he tells them that if they must suffer, it should be for righteousness' sake and not as a result of sinful behavior (3:17; see 2:20; 4:15, 16). The end of this chapter (3:18-22) is an extremely difficult passage to interpret, and several options have been offered. Verses 19 and 20 may mean that Christ, during the period between His death and resurrection, addressed demonic spirits or the spirits of those who were alive before the Flood. Another interpretation is that Christ preached through Noah to his pre-Flood contemporaries.

As believers in Christ, the readers are no longer to pursue the lusts of the flesh as they did formerly, but rather the will of God (4:1-6). In view of the hardships that they may suffer, Peter exhorts them to be strong in their mutual love and to exercise their spiritual gifts in the power of God so that they will be built

up (4:7–11). They should not be surprised when they are slandered and reviled for their faith because the sovereign God has a purpose in all things, and the time of judgment will come when His name and all who trust in Him will be vindicated (4:12–19). They must therefore "entrust their souls to a faithful Creator in doing what is right" (4:19).

In a special word to the elders of the churches in these Roman provinces, Peter urges them to be diligent but gentle shepherds over the flocks that have been divinely placed under their care (5:1–4). The readers as a whole are told to clothe themselves with humility toward one another and toward God who will exalt them at the proper time (5:5–7). They are to resist the adversary in the sure knowledge that their calling to God's eternal glory in Christ will be realized (5:8–11). Peter ends his epistle by stating his theme ("the true grace of God") and conveying greetings and a benediction (5:12–14).

OUTLINE OF FIRST PETER

Part One: The Salvation of the Believer (1:1—2:12)

Part Two: The Submission of the Believer (2:13—3:12)

Part Three: The Suffering of the Believer (3:13—5:14)

CHAPTER 1

Salutation

PETER,[R] an apostle of Jesus Christ, to those who reside as aliens, scattered throughout Pontus, Galatia, Cappadocia, Asia, and Bithynia, who are chosen   2 Pet. 1:1

2 according to the foreknowledge of God the Father, by the sanctifying work of the Spirit, that you may obey Jesus Christ and be[R]sprinkled with His blood: May grace and peace be yours in fullest measure. Is. 52:15 ★

Hope for the Future

3 [R]Blessed be the God and Father of our Lord Jesus Christ, who according to His great mercy has caused us to be born again to a living hope through the resurrection of Jesus Christ from the dead,   2 Cor. 1:3

4 to *obtain* an[R]inheritance *which is* imperishable and undefiled and will not fade away, reserved in heaven for you, Rom. 8:17

Trials for the Present

5 who are[R]protected by the power of God through faith for a salvation ready to be revealed in the last time.   [John 10:28; Phil. 4:7]

6 In this you greatly rejoice, even though now for a little while, if necessary, you have been distressed by various[t]trials, *temptations*

7 that the^proof of your faith, *being* more precious than gold which[t]is perishable, even though tested by fire, may be found to result in praise and glory and honor at the revelation of Jesus Christ;   *genuineness · perishes*

8 and[R]though you have not seen Him, you[R]love Him, and though you do not see Him now, but believe in Him, you greatly rejoice with joy inexpressible and [t]full of glory,   John 20:29 · Eph. 3:19 · *glorified*

9 obtaining as[R]the outcome of your faith the salvation of [1]your souls.   [Rom. 6:22]

Anticipation in the Past

10 As to this salvation, the prophets who prophesied of the grace that *would come* to you made careful search and inquiry,

11 [t]seeking to know what person or time the Spirit of Christ within them was indicat-

---

[1] Some ancient mss. do not contain *your*

ing as He predicted the sufferings of Christ and the glories[T]to follow.   *inquiring • after these*

12 It was revealed to them that they were not serving themselves, but you, in these things which now have been announced to you through those who[R]preached the gospel to you by the Holy Spirit sent from heaven—things into which angels long to [A]look.   *1 Pet. 1:25; 4:6 • gain a clear glimpse*

"Be Holy"

13 Therefore, gird your minds for action, [T]keep sober *in spirit,* fix your hope completely on the grace to be brought to you at the revelation of Jesus Christ.   *be sober*

14 As [T]obedient children, do not be conformed to the former lusts *which were yours* in your ignorance,   *children of obedience*

15 but like the Holy One who called you, be holy yourselves also in all *your* behavior;

16 because it is written, "YOU[R] SHALL BE HOLY, FOR I AM HOLY."   Lev. 11:44f.; 19:2; 20:7

17 And if you address as Father the One who impartially judges according to each man's work, conduct yourselves in fear during the time of your stay *upon earth*;

18 knowing that you were not[A]redeemed[R] with perishable things like silver or gold from your futile way of life inherited from your forefathers,   *ransomed • Is. 52:3★*

19 but with precious[R]blood, as of a[R]lamb unblemished and spotless, *the blood of* Christ.   Acts 20:28 • Is. 53:7★; Heb. 9:14

20 For He was [R]foreknown before the foundation of the world, but has appeared in these last times for the sake of you   Eph. 1:4

21 who through Him are[R]believers in God, who raised Him from the dead and [R]gave Him glory, so that your faith and[R]hope are in God.   Rom. 4:24 • Heb. 2:9 • 1 Pet. 1:3

"Love One Another"

22 Since you have [R]in obedience to the truth purified your souls for a[T]sincere love of the brethren, fervently love one another from [2]the heart,   *1 Pet. 1:2 • unhypocritical*

23 for you have been [R]born again [R]not of seed which is perishable but imperishable, *that is,* through the living and abiding[R]word of God.   John 3:3 • John 1:13 • Heb. 4:12

24 For,
    "ALL[R]FLESH IS LIKE GRASS,   Is. 40:6ff.
    AND ALL ITS GLORY LIKE THE FLOWER
       OF GRASS.
    THE GRASS WITHERS,
    AND THE FLOWER FALLS OFF,

25 [R]BUT THE WORD OF THE LORD ABIDES
     FOREVER."   Is. 40:8

---

[2] Some mss. read *a clean heart*
[3] I.e., Christ's coming again in judgment

And this is[R]the word which was[T]preached to you.   Heb. 6:5 • *preached as good news to you*

CHAPTER 2

"Long for the Pure Milk of the Word"

THEREFORE,[R]putting aside all[A]malice and all guile and hypocrisy and envy and all slander,   Eph. 4:22, 25, 31 • *wickedness*

2 like newborn babes, long for the[A]pure milk of the word, that by it you may grow in respect to salvation,   *unadulterated*

3 if you have[R]tasted[T]the kindness of the Lord.   Heb. 6:5 • *that the Lord is kind*

"Offer Up Spiritual Sacrifices"

4 And coming to Him as to a living stone, [R]rejected by men, but[T]choice and precious in the sight of God,   1 Pet. 2:7 • *chosen; or, elect*

5 you also, as living stones, are being built up as a spiritual house for a holy priesthood, to offer up spiritual sacrifices acceptable to God through Jesus Christ.

6 For *this* is contained in Scripture:
    "BEHOLD[R]I LAY IN ZION A CHOICE STONE,
       A PRECIOUS CORNER *stone,*   Is. 28:16★
    AND HE WHO BELIEVES IN [A]HIM SHALL
       NOT BE DISAPPOINTED."   *it*

7 This precious value, then, is for you who believe. But for those who disbelieve,
    "THE[R] STONE WHICH THE BUILDERS [R]RE-
       JECTED,   Ps. 118:22★ • 1 Pet. 2:4
    THIS BECAME THE VERY CORNER
       stone,"

8 and,
    "A[R] STONE OF STUMBLING AND A ROCK OF
       OFFENSE";   Is. 8:14★
[R]for they stumble because they are disobedient to the word,[R]and to this *doom* they were also appointed.   1 Cor. 1:23 • Rom. 9:22

9 But you are [R]A CHOSEN RACE, A royal [R]PRIESTHOOD, A [R]HOLY NATION, A PEOPLE FOR *God's* OWN POSSESSION, that you may proclaim the excellencies of Him who has called you out of darkness into His marvelous light;   Is. 43:20f. • 1 Pet. 2:5 • Ex. 19:6

10 [R]for you once were NOT A PEOPLE, but now you are THE PEOPLE OF GOD; you had NOT RECEIVED MERCY, but now you have RECEIVED MERCY.   Hos. 1:10; 2:23; Rom. 9:25; 10:19

"Abstain from Fleshly Lusts"

11 [R]Beloved, I urge you as aliens and strangers to abstain from fleshly lusts, which wage war against the soul.   Heb. 6:9

12 Keep your behavior excellent among the Gentiles, so that in the thing in which they slander you as evildoers, they may on account of your good deeds, as they observe *them,* glorify God in the day of [3]visitation.

Submission to the Government

13 [R]Submit yourselves for the Lord's sake to every human institution, whether to a king as the one in authority,   [Rom. 13:1]

14 or to governors as sent[T]by him[R]for the punishment of evildoers and the praise of those who do right.   *through* • Rom. 13:4

15 For [R]such is the will of God that by doing right you may[R]silence the ignorance of foolish men.   [1 Pet. 3:17] • 1 Pet. 2:12

16 *Act* as[R]free men, and do not use your freedom as a covering for evil, but *use it* as [R]bondslaves of God.   [John 8:32] • Rom. 6:22

17 Honor all men; love the brotherhood, fear God, honor the[A]king.   *emperor*

Submission in Business

18 [R]Servants, be submissive to your masters with all respect, not only to those who are good and gentle, but also to those who are[A]unreasonable.   Eph. 6:5 • *perverse*

19 For this *finds*[A]favor, if for the sake of conscience toward God a man bears up under sorrows when suffering unjustly.   *grace*

20 For what credit is there if, when you sin and are harshly treated, you endure it with patience? But if when you do what is right and suffer *for it* you patiently endure it, this *finds* favor with God.

21 For[R]you have been called for this purpose, [R]since Christ also suffered for you, leaving you an example for you to follow in His steps,   Acts 14:22 • 1 Pet. 3:18; 4:1, 13

22 WHO[R]COMMITTED NO SIN, NOR WAS ANY DECEIT FOUND IN HIS MOUTH;   Is. 53:9 ★

23 [T]and while being[R]reviled, He did not revile in return; while suffering, He uttered no threats, but kept entrusting *Himself* to Him who judges righteously;   *who* • Is. 53:7 ★

24 and He Himself bore our sins in His body on the cross, that we might die to sin and live to righteousness; for[R]by His wounds you were healed.   Is. 53:5 ★

25 For you were continually straying like sheep, but now you have returned to the Shepherd and Guardian of your souls.

CHAPTER 3

Submission in Marriage

IN[R]the same way, you wives,[R]be submissive to your own husbands so that even if any *of them* are disobedient to the word, they may be won without a word by the behavior of their wives,   1 Pet. 3:7 • Eph. 5:22

2 as they observe your chaste and [T]respectful behavior.   *with fear*

3 [R]And let not your adornment be *merely* external—braiding the hair, and wearing gold jewelry, or putting on dresses; 1 Tim. 2:9

4 but *let it be* [R]the hidden person of the heart, with the imperishable quality of a gentle and quiet spirit, which is precious in the sight of God.   Rom. 7:22

5 For in this way in former times the holy women also, [R]who hoped in God, used to adorn themselves, being submissive to their own husbands.   1 Tim. 5:5; 1 Pet. 1:3

2:13 Our Responsibility to Human Government—It is impossible for a believer to be a good Christian and a bad citizen at the same time. As children of God our responsibility to human government is threefold:

a. We are to recognize and accept that the powers that be are ordained by God. "Let every person be in subjection to the governing authorities. For there is no authority except from God, and those which exist are established by God" (Page 1142—Rom. 13:1). This truth applies even to atheistic human governments unless, of course, the law is anti-scriptural. In that situation the believer must obey God rather than man (Page 1098—Acts 4:18–20). In fact, when Paul wrote those words in Romans 13:1, the evil emperor Nero was on the throne. See also Titus 3:1.

b. We are to pay our taxes to human government (Page 981—Matt. 17:24–27; 22:21; Page 1142—Rom. 13:7).

c. We are to pray for the leaders in human government. "First of all, then, I urge that entreaties *and* prayers, petitions *and* thanksgivings, be made on behalf of all men, for kings and all who are in authority, in order that we may lead a tranquil and quiet life in all godliness and dignity. This is good and acceptable in the sight of God our Savior" (Page 1217—1 Tim. 2:1–3).

Paul exhorts us to pray for those who are in authority that we may lead a quiet life. We are to pray that they hold their offices in godliness and honesty (Page 1217—1 Tim. 2:1–3).

Now turn to Page 873—Amos 3:2: Selection of Israel.

3:1-6 The Role of the Wife—In this passage the wife's only responsibility in the family is to "be submissive" to her husband. A woman is to be in submission to her husband, not to mankind in general. To be in subjection to her husband does not imply any kind of natural inferiority on the part of the wife to the husband. In marriage two people become one. Therefore there are two intellects, two sets of emotions, and two wills that have been joined to constitute one. To keep the union from fracturing and destroying itself, one of those persons is charged with leadership in the relationship, and one is charged with submission.

The wife's submission to her husband is her "adornment," which makes her truly beautiful (3:3). This inner beauty is of great value in God's sight (3:4). The believing women of the Old Testament who hoped to be the human channel for the Messiah to come into the world made themselves beautiful by being in subjection to their own husbands. This is supremely illustrated in the relationship between Sarah and Abraham. Wives are exhorted to do what Sarah did, to be in subjection to their husbands, letting the consequences rest with God, and thus become Sarah's daughters (3:6). For the wife who will do this God promises that, if her husband is either an unbeliever or out of fellowship with God, her subjection can be the very means God will use to bring her husband into a proper relationship with God (3:1, 2). The wife's subjection may lead to the husband's salvation.

Now turn to Page 1202—Col. 3:19: The Role of the Husband.

6 Thus Sarah obeyed Abraham, [R]calling him lord, and you have become her children if you do what is right[T]without being frightened by any fear.   Gen. 18:12 • *and are not*

7 [R]You husbands likewise, live with your wives in an understanding way, as with a weaker [R]vessel, since she is a woman; and grant her honor as a fellow heir of the grace of life, so that your prayers may not be hindered.   [Eph. 5:25]; Col. 3:19 • 1 Thess. 4:4
8 [A]To sum up, [R]let all be harmonious, sympathetic, brotherly, kindhearted, and humble in spirit;   *Finally* • Rom. 12:16

Submission in All of Life

9 not returning evil for evil, or insult for insult, but[T]giving a blessing instead; for you were called for the very purpose that you might inherit a blessing.   *blessing instead*
10 For,

"LET[R]HIM WHO MEANS TO LOVE LIFE AND
    SEE GOOD DAYS   Ps. 34:12, 13
REFRAIN HIS TONGUE FROM EVIL AND
    HIS LIPS FROM SPEAKING GUILE.
11 "AND[R] LET HIM TURN AWAY FROM EVIL
    AND DO GOOD;   Ps. 34:14
LET HIM SEEK PEACE AND PURSUE IT.
12 "FOR[R] THE EYES OF THE LORD ARE UPON
    THE RIGHTEOUS,   Ps. 34:15, 16
AND HIS EARS ATTEND TO THEIR
    PRAYER,
BUT THE FACE OF THE LORD IS AGAINST
    THOSE WHO DO EVIL."

Conduct in Suffering

13 And[R]who is there to harm you if you prove zealous for what is good?   Prov. 16:7
14 But even if you should[R]suffer for the sake of righteousness, *you are* blessed. AND DO NOT FEAR THEIR [T]INTIMIDATION, AND DO NOT BE TROUBLED,   [Matt. 5:10] • *fear*
15 but [4]sanctify Christ as Lord in your hearts, always *being* ready to make a defense to everyone who asks you to give an account for the hope that is in you, yet with gentleness and[A]reverence;   *fear*
16 [T]and keep a good conscience so that in the thing in which you are slandered, those

who revile your good behavior in Christ may be put to shame.   *having a good*

17 For it is better, if[T]God should will it so, that you suffer for doing what is right rather than for doing what is wrong.   *the will of God*

Christ's Example of Suffering

18 For[R]Christ also died for sins[R]once for all, *the* just for *the* unjust, in order that He might bring us to God, having been put to death in the flesh, but made alive in the [A]spirit;   1 Pet. 2:21 • Heb. 9:26, 28 • *Spirit*
19 in[A]which also He went and made proclamation to the spirits *now* in prison,   *whom*
20 who once were disobedient, when the [R]patience of God kept waiting in the days of Noah, during the construction of the ark, in which a few, that is, eight persons, were brought safely through *the* water.   Rom. 2:4
21 [R]And corresponding to that, baptism now saves you—[B]not the removal of dirt from the flesh, but an appeal to God for a good conscience—through the resurrection of Jesus Christ,   Acts 16:33 • [Heb. 9:14]
22 who is at the right hand of God, having gone into heaven, after angels and authorities and powers had been subjected to Him.

CHAPTER 4

THEREFORE, since [R]Christ has [5]suffered in the flesh, arm yourselves also with the same purpose, because he who has suffered in the flesh has ceased from sin,   1 Pet. 2:21
2 [R]so as to live[R]the rest of the time in the flesh no longer for the lusts of men, but for the will of God.   [Rom. 6:2] • 1 Pet. 1:14
3 For the time already past is sufficient *for you* to have carried out the desire of the Gentiles, having pursued a course of sensuality, lusts, drunkenness, carousals, drinking parties and abominable idolatries.
4 And in *all* this, they are surprised that you do not run with *them* into the same excess of dissipation, and they malign *you*;
5 but they shall give account to Him who is ready to judge the living and the dead.

---

[4] I.e., set apart   [5] I.e., suffered death

3:17 Kinds of Suffering—There are three basic kinds of suffering, all of which can bring about much pain and discomfort to the believer.
a. Physical suffering. This, of course, occurs when a part of our body is injured or begins to malfunction, resulting in a disharmony between it and the rest of the body. Several factors can be involved in physical suffering. It can be caused by an accident or by carelessness (Page 298—2 Sam. 4:4). It can be due to birth deformities (Page 1075—John 9:1). It can result from internal disorders (Page 1037—Luke 8:43). Finally, physical suffering may actually be caused by Satan (Page 496—Job 2:7; Page 1044—Luke 13:16).
b. Mental suffering. In many ways this suffering is even more intense than physical suffering. Justified or unjustified concern over some matter can easily produce mental anguish. Paul himself experienced "fear and trembling" and "anguish of heart" (Page 1150—1 Cor. 2:3; Page 1166—2 Cor. 1:8; 2:4, 13; 7:5).
c. Spiritual suffering. Spiritual suffering can come from the world (Page 1275—1 John 2:15–17), the flesh (Page 1137—Rom. 7:18–24), or the devil. Often it is the latter. See Acts 13:8–11; 16:16–18; First Thessalonians 2:18. Now turn to Page 496—Job 2:7: Purposes of Suffering.

6 For [R]the gospel has for this purpose been preached even to those who are dead, that though they are judged in the flesh as men, they may live in the spirit according to *the will of* God.   1 Pet. 1:12; 3:19

Commands in Suffering

7 The end of all things [T]is at hand; therefore, be of sound judgment and sober *spirit* for the purpose of prayer.   *has come near*

8 Above all,[R]keep fervent in your love for one another, because [R]love covers a multitude of sins.   1 Pet. 1:22 • [Prov. 10:12]

9 [R]Be hospitable to one another without [R]complaint.   Heb. 13:2 • Phil. 2:14

10 As each one has received a *special* gift, employ it in serving one another, as good stewards of the manifold grace of God.

11 [R]Whoever speaks, *let him speak,* as it were, the utterances of God; whoever serves, *let him do so* as [T]by the strength which God supplies; so that in all things God may be glorified through Jesus Christ, to whom belongs the glory and dominion forever and ever. Amen.   1 Thess. 2:4 • *from*

12 Beloved, do not be surprised at the fiery ordeal among you, which comes upon you for your testing, as though some strange thing were happening to you;

13 but to the degree that you [R]share the sufferings of Christ, keep on rejoicing; so that also at the revelation of His glory, you may rejoice with exultation.   2 Cor. 1:5

14 If you are reviled [T]for the name of Christ, you are blessed, because the Spirit of glory and of God rests upon you.   *in*

15 By no means let any of you suffer as a murderer, or thief, or evildoer, or a[T]troublesome meddler;   *one who oversees others' affairs*

16 but if *anyone suffers* as a[R]Christian, let him not feel ashamed, but in that name let him[R]glorify God.   James 2:7 • 1 Pet. 4:11

17 For *it is* time for judgment to begin with the household of God; and if *it begins* with us first, what *will be* the outcome for those who do not obey the gospel of God?

18 AND IF IT IS WITH DIFFICULTY THAT THE RIGHTEOUS IS SAVED, WHAT WILL BECOME OF THE[R]GODLESS MAN AND THE SINNER? 1 Tim. 1:9

19 Therefore, let those also who suffer according to the will of God entrust their souls to a faithful Creator in doing what is right.

CHAPTER 5

Elders, Shepherd the Flock

THEREFORE,[R] I exhort the elders among you, as *your* fellow elder and witness of the sufferings of Christ, and a partaker also of the glory that is to be revealed,   Acts 11:30

2 shepherd[R]the flock of God among you, exercising oversight[R]not under compulsion, but voluntarily, according to *the will of* God; and[R]not for sordid gain, but with eagerness;   John 21:16 • Philem. 14 • 1 Tim. 3:8

3 nor yet as lording it over[T]those allotted to your charge, but[A]proving to be examples to the flock.   *the allotments • becoming*

4 And when the Chief [R]Shepherd appears, you will receive the [R]unfading [T]crown of glory.   1 Pet. 2:25 • 1 Pet. 1:4 • *wreath*

Saints, Humble Yourselves

5 [R]You younger men, likewise, be subject to your elders; and all of you, clothe yourselves with humility toward one another, for GOD IS OPPOSED TO THE PROUD, BUT GIVES GRACE TO THE HUMBLE.   Luke 22:26; 1 Tim. 5:1

6 [R]Humble yourselves, therefore, under the mighty hand of God, that He may exalt you at the proper time,   Matt. 23:12; Luke 14:11

7 casting all your[R]anxiety upon Him, because He cares for you.   Ps. 55:22; Matt. 6:25

8 Be of sober *spirit,* be on the alert. Your adversary, the devil, prowls about like a roaring lion, seeking someone to devour.

9 [T]But resist him, firm in *your* faith, knowing that the same experiences of suffering are being accomplished by your brethren who are in the world.   *whom resist*

Benediction

10 And after you have suffered[R]for a little while, the[R]God of all grace, who[R]called you to His eternal glory in Christ, will Himself perfect, confirm, strengthen *and* establish you.   1 Pet. 1:6 • 1 Pet. 4:10 • 1 Cor. 1:9

11 [R]To Him *be* dominion forever and ever. Amen.   Rom. 11:36; 1 Pet. 4:11

12 Through Silvanus, our faithful brother (for so I regard *him*), I have written to you briefly, exhorting and testifying that this is the true grace of God. Stand firm in it!

13 [6]She who is in Babylon, chosen together with you, sends you greetings, and *so does* my son,[R]Mark.   Acts 12:12, 25; 15:37, 39

14 Greet one another with a kiss of love. Peace be to you all who are in Christ.

[6] Some mss. read *The church which*

THE SECOND EPISTLE OF

PETER

THE BOOK OF SECOND PETER

First Peter deals with problems from the outside; Second Peter deals with problems from the inside. Peter writes to warn the believers about the false teachers who are peddling damaging doctrine. He begins by urging them to keep close watch on their personal lives. The Christian life demands diligence in pursuing moral excellence, knowledge, self-control, perseverance, godliness, brotherly kindness, and selfless love. By contrast, the false teachers are sensual, arrogant, greedy, and covetous. They scoff at the thought of future judgment and live their lives as if the present would be the pattern for the future. Peter reminds them that although God may be long-suffering in sending judgment, ultimately it will come. In view of that fact, believers should live lives of godliness, blamelessness, and steadfastness.

The statement of authorship in 1:1 is very clear: "Simon Peter, a bond-servant and apostle of Jesus Christ." To distinguish this epistle from the first by Peter it was given the Greek title *Petrou B*, "Second of Peter."

THE AUTHOR OF SECOND PETER

No other book in the New Testament poses as many problems of authenticity as does Second Peter. Unlike First Peter, this letter has very weak external testimony, and its genuineness is hurt by internal difficulties as well. Because of these obstacles, many scholars reject the Petrine authorship of this epistle, but this does not mean that there is no case for the opposite position.

External Evidence: The external testimony for the Petrine authorship of Second Peter is weaker than that for any other New Testament book, but by the fourth century it became generally recognized as an authentic work of the apostle Peter. There are no undisputed second-century quotations from Second Peter, but in the third century it is quoted in the writings of several church fathers, notably Origen and Clement of Alexandria. Third-century writers were generally aware of Second Peter and respected its contents, but it was still cataloged as a disputed book. The fourth century saw the official acknowledgment of the authority of Second Peter in spite of some lingering doubts. For several reasons Second Peter was not quickly accepted as a canonical book: (1) Slow circulation kept it from being widely

known. (2) Its brevity and contents greatly limited the number of quotations from it in the writings of early church leaders. (3) The delay in recognition meant that Second Peter had to compete with several later works which falsely claimed to be Petrine (e.g., the Apocalypse of Peter). (4) Stylistic differences between First and Second Peter also raised doubts.

Internal Evidence: On the positive side, Second Peter bears abundant testimony to its apostolic origin. It claims to be by "Simon Peter" (1:1), and 3:1 says "This is now, beloved, the second letter I am writing to you." The writer refers to the Lord's prediction about the apostle's death in 1:14 (cf. John 21:18, 19) and says he was an eyewitness of the Transfiguration (1:16–18). As an apostle (1:1), he places himself on an equal level with Paul (3:15). There are also distinctive words that are found in Second Peter and in Peter's sermons in Acts, as well as unusual words and phrases shared by First and Second Peter.

On the negative side, a number of troublesome areas challenge the traditional position: (1) There are differences between the style and vocabulary of First and Second Peter. The Greek of Second Peter is rough and awkward compared to that of First Peter, and there are also differences in informality and in the use of the Old Testament. But these differences are often exaggerated, and they can be explained by Peter's use of Silvanus as his secretary for First Peter and his own hand for Second Peter. (2) It is argued that Second Peter used a passage from Jude to describe false teachers, and that Jude was written after Peter's death. However, this is a debated issue, and it is possible that Jude quoted from Peter or that both used a common source (see "The Author of Jude"). (3) The reference to a collection of Paul's letters (3:15, 16) implies a late date for this epistle. But it is not necessary to conclude that all of Paul's letters were in mind here. Peter's contact with Paul and his associates no doubt made him familiar with several Pauline epistles. (4) Some scholars claim that the false teaching mentioned in Second Peter was a form of Gnosticism that emerged after Peter's day, but there is insufficient evidence to support this stand.

The alternative to Petrine authorship is a later forgery done in the name of Peter. Even the claim that Second Peter was written by a

disciple of Peter cannot overcome the problem of misrepresentation. In addition Second Peter is clearly superior to any pseudonymous writings. In spite of the external and internal problems, the traditional position of Petrine authorship overcomes more difficulties than any other option.

THE TIME OF SECOND PETER

Most scholars regard 3:1 ("This is . . . the second letter I am writing to you") as a reference to First Peter. If this is so, Peter had the same readers of Asia Minor in mind (see "The Time of First Peter"), although the more general salutation in 1:1 would also allow for a wider audience. Peter wrote this epistle in response to the spread of heretical teachings which were all the more insidious because they emerged from within the churches. These false teachers perverted the doctrine of justification and promoted a rebellious and immoral way of life.

This epistle was written just before the apostle's death (1:14), probably from Rome. His martyrdom took place between A.D. 64 and 66 (if Peter were alive in 67 when Paul wrote Second Timothy during his second Roman imprisonment, it is likely that Paul would have mentioned him).

THE CHRIST OF SECOND PETER

Apart from the first verse of his epistle, Peter employs the title *Lord* every time he names the Savior. The Lord Jesus Christ is the source of full knowledge and power for the attainment of spiritual maturity (1:2, 3, 8; 3:18). Peter recalls the glory of His transfiguration on the holy mountain and anticipates His *parousia*, "coming," when the whole world, not just three men on a mountain, will behold His glory.

KEYS TO SECOND PETER

Key Word: Guard Against False Teachers—The basic theme that runs through Second Peter is the contrast between the knowledge and practice of truth versus falsehood. This epistle is written to expose the dangerous and seductive work of false teachers, and to warn believers to be on their guard so that they will not be "carried away by the error of unprincipled men" (3:17). It is also written to exhort the readers to "grow in the grace and knowledge of our Lord and Savior Jesus Christ" (3:18), because this growth into Christian maturity is the best defense against spiritual counterfeits. This letter serves to remind its readers of the foundational elements in the Christian life from which they must not waver (1:12, 13; 3:1, 2). This includes the certainty of the Lord's return in power and judgment.

Key Verses: Second Peter 1:20, 21 and 3:9–11—"But know this first of all, that no prophecy of Scripture is *a matter* of one's own interpretation, for no prophecy was ever made by an act of human will, but men moved by the Holy Spirit spoke from God" (1:20, 21).

"The Lord is not slow about His promise, as some count slowness, but is patient toward you, not wishing for any to perish but for all to come to repentance. But the day of the Lord will come like a thief, in which the heavens will pass away with a roar and the elements will be destroyed with intense heat, and the earth and its works will be burned up. Since all these things are to be destroyed in this way, what sort of people ought you to be in holy conduct and godliness" (3:9–11).

Key Chapter: Second Peter 1—The Scripture clearest in defining the relationship between God and man on the issue of inspiration is contained in 1:19–21. Three distinct principles surface: (1) that the interpretation of Scrip-

FOCUS	CULTIVATION OF CHRISTIAN CHARACTER		CONDEMNATION OF FALSE TEACHERS			CONFIDENCE IN CHRIST'S RETURN	
REFERENCE	1:1————1:15—		—2:1————	2:4————	2:10———	3:1————	—3:8————3:18
DIVISION	GROWTH IN CHRIST	GROUNDS OF BELIEF	DANGER	DESTRUCTION	DESCRIPTION	MOCKERY IN THE LAST DAYS	DAY OF THE LORD
TOPIC	TRUE PROPHECY		FALSE PROPHETS			PROPHECY: DAY OF THE LORD	
	HOLINESS		HERESY			HOPE	
LOCATION	PROBABLY ROME						
TIME	c. A.D. 64–66						

tures is not limited to a favored elect but is open for all who are "handling accurately the word of truth" (2 Tim. 2:15); (2) that the divinely inspired prophet did not initiate the Scripture himself; and (3) that the Holy Spirit (not the emotion or circumstances of the moment) moved holy men.

ⒶSURVEY OF SECOND PETER

Peter wrote his first epistle to encourage his readers to respond properly to external opposition. His second epistle focuses on internal opposition caused by false teachers whose "destructive heresies" (2:1) can seduce believers into error and immorality. While First Peter speaks of the new birth through the living Word, Second Peter stresses the need for growth in the grace and knowledge of Christ. The best antidote for error is a mature understanding of the truth. Second Peter divides into three parts: cultivation of Christian character (1); condemnation of false teachers (2); and confidence of Christ's return (3).

Cultivation of Christian Character (1): Peter's salutation (1:1, 2) is an introduction to the major theme of chapter 1, that is, the true knowledge of Jesus Christ. The readers are reminded of the "precious and magnificent promises" that are theirs because of their calling to faith in Christ (1:3, 4). They have been called away from the corruption of the world to conformity with Christ, and Peter urges them to progress by forging a chain of eight Christian virtues from faith to love (1:5-7). If a believer does not transform profession into practice, he becomes spiritually useless, perverting the purpose for which he was called (1:8-11).

This letter was written not long before Peter's death (1:14) to remind believers of the riches of their position in Christ and their responsibility to hold fast to the truth (1:12-21). Peter knew that his departure from this earth was imminent, and he left this letter as a written legacy. As an eyewitness of the life of Christ (he illustrates this with a portrait of the Transfiguration in 1:16-18), Peter affirms the authority and reliability of the prophetic word. The clearest biblical description of the divine-human process of inspiration is found in 1:21: "men moved by the Holy Spirit spoke from God."

Condemnation of False Teachers (2): Peter's discussion of true prophecy leads him to an extended denunciation of false prophecy in the churches. These false teachers were especially dangerous because they arose within the church and undermined the confidence of believers (2:1-3). Peter's extended description of the characteristics of these false teachers (2:10-22) exposes the futility and corruption of their strategies. Their teachings and lifestyles reek of arrogance and selfishness, but their crafty words are capable of enticing immature believers.

Confidence of Christ's Return (3): Again Peter states that this letter is designed to stir up the minds of his readers "by way of reminder" (3:1; cf. 1:13). This very timely chapter is designed to remind them of the certain truth of the imminent *parousia* (this Greek word, used in 3:4, 12, refers to the second coming or advent of Christ) and to refute those mockers who will deny this doctrine in the last days. These scoffers will claim that God does not powerfully intervene in world affairs, but Peter calls attention to two past and one future divinely induced catastrophic events: the Creation, the Flood, and the dissolution of the present heavens and earth (3:1-7). It may appear that the promise of Christ's return will not be fulfilled, but this is untrue for two reasons: God's perspective on the passing of time is quite unlike that of men, and the apparent delay in the *parousia* is due to His patience in waiting for more individuals to come to a knowledge of Christ (3:8, 9). Nevertheless, the day of consummation will come, and all the matter of this universe will evidently be transformed into energy from which God will fashion a new cosmos (3:10-13).

In light of this coming day of the Lord, Peter exhorts his readers to live lives of holiness, steadfastness, and growth (3:14-18). He mentions the letters of "our beloved brother Paul" and significantly places them on a level with the Old Testament Scriptures (3:15, 16). After a final warning about the danger of false teachers, the epistle closes with an appeal to growth, and a doxology.

OUTLINE OF SECOND PETER

CHAPTER 1

Salutation

[1] SIMON PETER, a bond-servant and apostle of Jesus Christ, to those who have received[R] a faith of the same[A] kind as ours,[A] by the righteousness of our God and Savior, Jesus Christ: Titus 1:4 • *value* • *in*
2 [R]Grace and peace be multiplied to you in[R]the knowledge of God and of Jesus our Lord;   Rom. 1:7 • Phil. 3:8; 2 Pet. 1:3, 8

Growth in Christ

3 seeing that His divine power has granted to us everything pertaining to life and godliness, through the true knowledge of Him who called us[A] by His own glory and [A]excellence.   possibly, *to* • *virtue*
4 For by these He has granted to us His precious and magnificent promises, in order that by them you might become[R]partakers of *the* divine nature, having escaped the corruption that is in the world by lust. 1 John 3:2
5 Now for this very reason also, applying all diligence, in your faith[R]supply moral[A]excellence, and in *your* moral excellence, [R]knowledge;   2 Pet. 1:11 • *virtue* • Col. 2:3
6 and in *your* knowledge, [R]self-control, and in *your* self-control, perseverance, and in *your* perseverance, godliness;   Acts 24:25
7 and in *your* godliness, brotherly kindness, and in *your* brotherly kindness, love.
8 For if these *qualities* are yours and are increasing, they render you neither useless nor[R]unfruitful in the true[R]knowledge of our Lord Jesus Christ.   Col. 1:10 • [John 17:3]
9 For he who lacks these *qualities* is [R]blind or short-sighted, having forgotten *his* purification from his former sins. 1 John 2:11
10 Therefore, brethren, be all the more diligent to make certain about His calling and choosing you; for as long as you practice these things, you will never stumble;
11 for in this way the entrance into[R]the eternal kingdom of our [R]Lord and Savior Jesus Christ will be[R]abundantly supplied to you.   2 Tim. 4:18 • 2 Pet. 2:20 • [Rom. 2:4]
12 Therefore, [R]I shall always be ready to remind you of these things, even though you *already* know *them*, and have been established in[R]the truth which is present with *you*.   Phil. 3:1; 1 John 2:21 • Col. 1:5f.; [2 John 2]
13 And I consider it[R]right, as long as I am in[R]this *earthly* dwelling, to stir you up by way of reminder,   Phil. 1:7 • [2 Cor. 5:1, 4]
14 knowing that the laying aside of my *earthly* dwelling is imminent, as also our Lord Jesus Christ has made clear to me.

Experience of the Transfiguration
Matt. 17:5; Mark 9:7; Luke 9:35

15 And I will also be diligent that at any time after my[R]departure you may be able to call these things to mind.   Luke 9:31
16 For we did not follow cleverly devised tales when we made known to you the power and coming of our Lord Jesus Christ, but we were eyewitnesses of His majesty.
17 For when He received honor and glory from God the Father, such an[T]utterance as this was[T]made to Him by the Majestic Glory, "This is My beloved Son with whom I am well-pleased"—   *voice* • *borne*
18 and we ourselves heard this[T]utterance made from heaven when we were with Him on the[R]holy mountain.   *voice borne* • Ex. 3:5

Certainty of the Scriptures

19 And *so* we have[R]the prophetic word *made* more sure, to which you do well to pay attention as to a lamp shining in a dark place, until the day dawns and the morning star arises in your hearts.   1 Pet. 1:10f.
20 But [R]know this first of all, that [R]no prophecy of Scripture is *a matter* of one's own interpretation,   2 Pet. 3:3 • [Rom. 12:6]
21 for[R]no prophecy was ever made by an act of human will, but men moved by the Holy Spirit spoke from God.   [2 Tim. 3:16]

CHAPTER 2

Danger of False Teachers

BUT[R]false prophets also arose among the people, just as there will also be false teachers among you, who will secretly introduce destructive heresies, even denying the Master who bought them, bringing swift destruction upon themselves.   Deut. 13:1ff.
2 And many will follow their[R]sensuality, and because of them[R]the way of the truth will be maligned;   Gen. 19:5ff. • Acts 16:17
3 and in *their*[R]greed they will[R]exploit you with[R]false words; their judgment from long ago is not idle, and their destruction is not asleep.   1 Tim. 6:5 • 2 Cor. 2:17 • Rom. 16:18

Destruction of False Teachers

4 For[R]if God did not spare angels when they sinned, but cast them into hell and [R]committed them to pits of darkness, reserved for judgment;   Jude 6 • Rev. 20:1f.
5 and did not spare[R]the ancient world, but preserved[R]Noah, a [A]preacher of righteousness, with seven others, when He brought a flood upon the world of the ungodly;   Ezek. 26:20 • 1 Pet. 3:20 • *herald*
6 and if He[R]condemned the cities of Sodom and Gomorrah to destruction by reducing *them* to ashes, having made them an[R]example to those who would [R]live ungodly thereafter;   Gen. 19:24 • Is. 1:9 • Jude 15
7 and if He[R]rescued righteous Lot, oppressed by the[R]sensual conduct of[R]unprincipled men   Gen. 19:16 • Gen. 19:5ff. • 2 Pet. 3:17
8 (for by what he saw and heard *that* [R]righteous man, while living among them,

[1] Most early mss. read *Simeon*

felt *his* righteous soul tormented day after day with *their* lawless deeds),   Heb. 11:4

9 [R]*then* the Lord knows how to rescue the godly from[Λ]temptation, and to keep the unrighteous under punishment for the[R]day of judgment,   1 Cor. 10:13 • *trial* • Jude 6

Description of False Teachers

10 and especially those who indulge the flesh in *its* corrupt desires and despise authority. Daring, self-willed, they do not tremble when they revile angelic majesties,

11 whereas angels who are greater in might and power do not bring a reviling judgment against them before the Lord.

12 But these, like unreasoning animals, born as creatures of instinct to be captured and killed, reviling where they have no knowledge, will in the destruction of those creatures also be destroyed,

13 suffering wrong as[R]the wages of doing wrong. They count it a pleasure to[R]revel in the daytime. They are stains and blemishes, reveling in their [2]deceptions, as they carouse with you,   2 Pet. 2:15 • Rom. 13:13

14 having eyes full of adultery and that never cease from sin, [R]enticing [R]unstable souls, having a heart trained in greed, accursed children;   2 Pet. 2:18 • James 1:8

15 forsaking[R]the right way they have gone astray, having followed[R]the way of Balaam, the *son* of Beor, who loved the wages of unrighteousness,   Acts 13:10 • Num. 22:5, 7

16 but he received a rebuke for his own transgression;[R]*for* a dumb donkey, speaking with a voice of a man, restrained the madness of the prophet.   Num. 22:21, 23, 28, 30ff.

17 These are [R]springs without water, and mists driven by a storm, for whom the black darkness has been reserved.   Jude 12

18 For speaking out [R]arrogant *words* of [R]vanity they entice by fleshly desires, by sensuality, those who barely escape from the ones who live in error,   Jude 16 • Eph. 4:17

19 promising them freedom while they themselves are slaves of corruption; for[R]by what a man is overcome, by this he is enslaved.   John 8:34; Rom. 6:16

20 For if after they have[R]escaped the defilements of the world by[R]the knowledge of the Lord and Savior Jesus Christ, they are again entangled in them and are overcome, the last state has become worse for them than the first.   2 Pet. 2:18 • 2 Pet. 1:2

21 [R]For it would be better for them not to have known the way of righteousness, than having known it, to turn away from the holy commandment delivered to them. Ezek. 18:24

22 It has happened to them according to the true proverb, "A[R] DOG RETURNS TO ITS OWN VOMIT," and, "A sow, after washing, *returns* to wallowing in the mire." Prov. 26:11

---

[2] Some ancient mss. read *love feasts*, (cf. Jude 12)
[3] Some ancient mss. read *discovered*

CHAPTER 3
Mockery in the Last Days

THIS is now, beloved, the second letter I am writing to you in which I am stirring up your sincere mind by way of reminder,

2 that you should[R]remember the words spoken beforehand by the holy prophets and the commandment of the Lord and Savior *spoken* by your apostles.   Jude 17

3 [R]Know this first of all, that in the last days mockers will come with *their* mocking, following after their own lusts,   2 Pet. 1:20

4 and saying, "Where[R]is the promise of His coming? For *ever* since the fathers fell asleep, all continues just as it was from the beginning of creation."   Is. 5:19; Jer. 17:15

5 For when they maintain this, it escapes their notice that[R]by the word of God *the* heavens existed long ago and *the* earth was formed out of water and by water,   Heb. 11:3

6 through which the world at that time was destroyed, being flooded with water.

7 But[R]the present heavens and earth by His word are being reserved for[R]fire, kept for the day of judgment and destruction of ungodly men.   2 Pet. 3:10, 12 • Is. 66:15

Manifestation of the Day of the Lord

8 But do not let this one *fact* escape your notice,[R]beloved, that with the Lord one day is as a thousand years, and[R]a thousand years as one day.   2 Pet. 3:1 • Ps. 90:4

9 [R]The Lord is not slow about His promise, as some count slowness, but is patient toward you, not wishing for any to perish but for all to come to repentance.   Hab. 2:3

10 But the[R]day of the Lord will come like a thief, in which the heavens will pass away with a roar and the elements will be destroyed with intense heat, and the earth and its works will be [3]burned up.   Matt. 24:43☆

Maturity in View of the Day of the Lord

11 Since all these things are to be destroyed in this way, what sort of people ought you to be in holy conduct and godliness,

12 looking for and hastening the coming of the day of God, on account of which the heavens will be destroyed by burning, and the elements will melt with intense heat!

13 But according to His[R]promise we are looking for new heavens and a new earth, in which righteousness dwells.   Is. 65:17; 66:22

14 [R]Therefore, beloved, since you look for these things, be diligent to be found by Him in peace, spotless and blameless, 1 Cor. 15:58

15 and regard the[R]patience of our Lord *to be* salvation; just as also [R]our beloved brother Paul, according to the wisdom given him, wrote to you,   2 Pet. 3:9 • Acts 9:17

16 as also in all *his* letters, speaking in them of[R]these things, [R]in which are some

things hard to understand, which the untaught and unstable distort, as *they do* also the rest of the Scriptures, to their own destruction. 2 Pet. 3:14 · Heb. 5:11

17 You therefore, beloved, knowing this beforehand, be on your guard lest, being carried away by the error of unprincipled men, you fall from your own steadfastness,

18 but grow in the grace and ᵏknowledge of ourᵃLord and Savior Jesus Christ. To Him *be* the glory, both now and to the day of eternity. Amen. 2 Pet. 1:2 · 2 Pet. 1:11

THE FIRST EPISTLE OF
JOHN

THE BOOK OF FIRST JOHN

God is light; God is love; and God is life. John is enjoying a delightful fellowship with that God of light, love, and life, and he desperately desires that his spiritual children enjoy the same fellowship.

God is light. Therefore, to engage in fellowship with Him we must walk in light and not in darkness. As we walk in the light, we will regularly confess our sins, allowing the blood of Christ to continually cleanse us. Christ will act as our defense attorney before the Father. Proof of our "walk in the light" will be keeping the commandments of God and replacing any hatred we have toward our brother with love. Two major roadblocks to hinder this walk will be falling in love with the world and falling for the alluring lies of false teachers.

God is love. Since we are His children we must walk in love. In fact, John says that if we do not love, we do not know God. Additionally, our love needs to be practical. Love is more than just words; it is actions. Love is giving, not getting. Biblical love is unconditional in its nature. It is an "in spite of" love. Christ's love fulfilled those qualities and when that brand of love characterizes us, we will be free of self-condemnation and experience confidence before God.

God is life. Those who fellowship with Him must possess His quality of life. Spiritual life begins with spiritual birth. Spiritual birth occurs through faith in Jesus Christ. Faith in Jesus Christ infuses us with God's life—eternal life. Therefore, one who walks in fellowship with God will walk in light, love, and life.

Although the apostle John's name is not found in this book, it was given the title *Ioannou A*, "First of John."

THE AUTHOR OF FIRST JOHN

The external evidence for the authorship of First John shows that from the beginning it was universally received without dispute as authoritative. It was used by Polycarp (who knew John in his youth) and Papias in the early second century, and later in that century Irenaeus (who knew Polycarp in his youth) specifically attributed it to the apostle John. All the Greek and Latin church fathers accepted this epistle as Johannine.

The internal evidence supports this universal tradition because the "we" (apostles), "you" (readers), and "they" (false teachers)

phraseology places the writer in the sphere of the apostolic eyewitness (cf. 1:1–3; 4:14). John's name was well known to the readers, and it was unnecessary for him to mention it. The style and vocabulary of First John are so similar to those of the Fourth Gospel that most scholars acknowledge these books to be by the same hand (see "The Author of John"). Both share many distinctively Johannine phrases, and the characteristics of limited vocabulary and frequent contrast of opposites are also common to them. Even so, some critics have assailed this conclusion on various grounds, but the theological and stylistic differences are not substantial enough to overcome the abundant similarities.

The traditional view is also rejected by those who hold that the Fourth Gospel and these three epistles were written by John the "elder" or "presbyter," who is to be distinguished from John the apostle. But the only basis for this distinction is Eusebius's interpretation in his *Ecclesiastical History* (A.D. 323) of a statement by Papias. Eusebius understood the passage to refer to two distinct Johns, but the wording does not require this; the elder John and the apostle John may be one and the same. Even if they were different, there is no evidence for contradicting the consistent acknowledgment by the early church that this book was written by the apostle John.

THE TIME OF FIRST JOHN

In Acts 8:14, John is associated with "the apostles in Jerusalem," and Paul calls him one of the "pillars" of the Jerusalem church in Galatians 2:9. Apart from Revelation 1, the New Testament is silent about his later years, but early Christian tradition uniformly tells us that he left Jerusalem (probably not long before its destruction in A.D. 70) and that he ministered in and around Ephesus. The seven churches in the Roman province of Asia, mentioned in Revelation 2 and 3, were evidently a part of this ministry. Although there is no address in First John, it is likely that the apostle directed this epistle to the Asian churches that were within the realm of his oversight.

The believers in these congregations were well established in Christian truth, and John wrote to them not as novices but as brethren grounded in apostolic doctrine (2:7, 18–27; 3:11). The apostle does not mention his own

affairs, but his use of such terms of address as "beloved" and "my little children" gives this letter a personal touch that reveals his close relationship to the original recipients. First John was probably written in Ephesus after the Gospel of John, but the date cannot be fixed with certainty. No persecution is mentioned, suggesting a date prior to A.D. 95 when persecution broke out during the end of Domitian's reign (A.D. 81–96).

Advanced in years, John wrote this fatherly epistle out of loving concern for his "children," whose steadfastness in the truth was being threatened by the lure of worldliness and the guile of false teachers. The Gnostic heresy taught that matter is inherently evil, and a divine being therefore could not take on human flesh. This resulted in the distinction between the man Jesus and the spiritual Christ who came upon Jesus at His baptism but departed prior to His crucifixion. Another variation was Docetism (from *dokeo*, "to seem"), the doctrine that Christ only seemed to have a human body. The result in both cases was the same—a flat denial of the incarnation.

The Gnostics also believed that their understanding of the hidden knowledge (*gnosis*) made them a kind of spiritual elite, who were above the normal distinctions of right and wrong. This led in most cases to deplorable conduct and complete disregard for Christian ethics.

THE CHRIST OF FIRST JOHN

The present ministry of Christ is portrayed in 1:5—2:22. His blood continually cleanses the believer from all sin, and He is our righteous Advocate before the Father. This epistle places particular stress on the incarnation of God the Son and the identity of Jesus as the Christ (2:22; 4:2, 3), in refutation

of Gnostic doctrine. Jesus Christ "came by water and blood" (5:6). He was the same indivisible person from the beginning (His baptism) to the end (His crucifixion) of His public ministry.

KEYS TO FIRST JOHN

Key Word: Fellowship with God—The major theme of First John is fellowship with God. John wants his readers to have assurance of the indwelling God through their abiding relationship with Him (2:28; 5:13). Belief in Christ should be manifested in the practice of righteousness and love for the brethren, which in turn produces joy and confidence before God. John writes this epistle to encourage this kind of fellowship and to emphasize the importance of holding fast to apostolic doctrine.

First John is also written to refute the destructive teachings of the Gnostics by stressing the reality of the incarnation and the emptiness of profession without practice. These antichrists fail the three tests of righteous living, love for the brethren, and belief that Jesus is the Christ, the incarnate God-man.

Key Verses: First John 1:3, 4 and 5:11–13—"What we have seen and heard we proclaim to you also, that you also may have fellowship with us; and indeed our fellowship is with the Father, and with His Son Jesus Christ. And these things we write, so that our joy may be made complete" (1:3, 4).

"And the witness is this, that God has given us eternal life, and this life is in His Son. He who has the Son has the life; he who does not have the Son of God does not have the life. These things I have written to you who believe in the name of the Son of God, in order that you may know that you have eternal life" (5:11–13).

FOCUS	BASIS OF FELLOWSHIP		BEHAVIOR OF FELLOWSHIP	
REFERENCE	1:1————————2:15————		————2:28————————5:4————5:21	
DIVISION	CONDITIONS FOR FELLOWSHIP	CAUTIONS TO FELLOWSHIP	CHARACTERISTICS OF FELLOWSHIP	CONSEQUENCES OF FELLOWSHIP
TOPIC	MEANING OF FELLOWSHIP		MANIFESTATIONS OF FELLOWSHIP	
	ABIDING IN GOD'S LIGHT		ABIDING IN GOD'S LOVE	
LOCATION	WRITTEN IN EPHESUS			
TIME	C. A.D. 90			

Key Chapter: First John 1—The two central passages for continued fellowship with God are John 15 and First John 1. John 15 relates the positive side of fellowship, that is, abiding in Christ. First John 1 unfolds the other side, pointing out that when Christians do not abide in Christ, they must seek forgiveness before fellowship can be restored.

SURVEY OF FIRST JOHN

John writes his first epistle at a time when apostolic doctrine is being challenged by a proliferation of false teachings. Like Second Peter and Jude, First John has a negative and a positive thrust: it refutes erroneous doctrine and encourages its readership to walk in the knowledge of the truth. John lists the criteria and characteristics of fellowship with God and shows that those who abide in Christ can have confidence and assurance before Him. This simply written but profound work develops the meaning of fellowship in the basis of fellowship (1:1—2:27) and the behavior of fellowship (2:28—5:21).

The Basis of Fellowship (1:1—2:27): John's prologue (1:1-4) recalls the beginning of apostolic contact with Christ. It relates his desire to transmit this apostolic witness to his readers so that they may share the same fellowship with Jesus Christ, the personification of life. This proclamation is followed by a description of the conditions of fellowship (1:5—2:14).

The readers' sins have been forgiven and they enjoy fellowship with God. As a result, they know "Him who has been from the beginning" and are strengthened to overcome the temptations of the evil one (2:12-14). The cautions to fellowship are both practical (the lusts of the corrupt world system which opposes God, 2:15-17) and doctrinal (the teachings of those who differentiate between Jesus and the Christ, 2:18-23). In contrast to these antichrists, the readers have the knowledge of the truth and an anointing from the Holy One. Therefore, it would be foolish for them to turn away from the teachings of the apostles to the innovations of the antichrists. The antidote to these heretical teachings is abiding in the apostolic truths that they "heard from the beginning," which are authenticated by the anointing they have received (2:24-27).

The Behavior of Fellowship (2:28—5:21): The basic theme of First John is summarized in 2:28—assurance through abiding in Christ. The next verse introduces the motif of regeneration, and 2:29—3:10 argues that regeneration is manifested in the practice of righteousness. Because we are children of God

through faith in Christ, we have a firm hope of being fully conformed to Him when He appears (3:1-3). Our present likeness to Christ places us in a position of incompatability with sin, because sin is contrary to the person and work of Christ (3:4-6). The concept in 3:6 does not contradict 1:8 because it is saying that the abider, insofar as he abides, does not sin. When the believer sins, he does not reflect the regenerate new man but Satan, the original sinner (3:7-10).

Regeneration is shown in righteousness (2:29—3:10), and righteousness is manifested in love (3:10-23). The apostle uses the example of Cain to illustrate what love is not: hatred is murdering in spirit, and it arises from the worldly sphere of death. John then uses the example of Christ to illustrate what love is: love is practiced in self-sacrifice, not mere profession. This practical expression of love results in assurance before God and answered prayers because the believer is walking in obedience to God's commands to believe in Christ and love one another.

In 3:24 John introduces two important motifs, which are developed in 4:1-16: the indwelling God, and the Spirit as a mark of this indwelling. The Spirit of God confesses the incarnate Christ and confirms apostolic doctrine (4:1-6). The mutual abiding of the believer in God and God in the believer is manifested in love for others, and this love produces a divine and human fellowship that testifies to and reflects the reality of the incarnation (4:7-16). It also anticipates the perfect fellowship to come and creates a readiness to face the One from whom all love is derived (4:17-19).

John joins the concepts he has presented into a circular chain of six links that begins with love for the brethren (4:20—5:17): (1) Love for believers is the inseparable product of love for God (4:20—5:1). (2) Love for God arises out of obedience to His commandments (5:2, 3). (3) Obedience to God is the result of faith in His Son (5:4, 5). (4) This faith is in Jesus, who was the Christ not only at His baptism (the water), but also at His death (the blood; 5:6-8). (5) The divine witness to the person of Christ is worthy of complete belief (5:9-13). (6) This belief produces confident access to God in prayer (5:14-17). Since intercessory prayer is a manifestation of love for others, the chain has come full circle.

The epilogue (5:18-21) summarizes the conclusions of the epistle in a series of three certainties: (1) Sin is a threat to fellowship, and it should be regarded as foreign to the believer's position in Christ (cf. Rom. 6). (2) The be-

liever stands with God against the satanic world system. (3) The incarnation produces true knowledge and communion with Christ.

Since He is the true God and eternal life, the one who knows Him should avoid the lure of any substitute.

OUTLINE OF FIRST JOHN

Part One: The Basis of Fellowship (1:1—2:27)

Part Two: The Behavior of Fellowship (2:28—5:21)

CHAPTER 1

Introduction

W HAT was from the beginning, what we have ᴿheard, what we have seen with our eyes, what we beheld and our hands handled, concerning the Word of Life—Acts 4:20

2 and ᴿthe life was manifested, and we have seen and bear witness and proclaim to you the eternal life, which was with the Father and was manifested to us—　John 1:4

3 what we have ᴿseen and ᴿheard we proclaim to you also, that you also may have fellowship with us; and indeed our fellowship is with the Father, and with His Son Jesus Christ.　　　　John 19:35 • Acts 4:20

4 And these things we write, so that our ᴿjoy may be made complete.　　　John 3:29

Walk in the Light

5 And this is the message we have heard from Him and announce to you, that God is light, and in Him there is no darkness at all.

6 ᴿIf we say that we have fellowship with

Him and yet walk in the darkness, we lie and do not practice the truth;　　[John 8:12]

7 but if weᴿwalk in the light asᴿHe Himself is in the light, we have fellowship with one another, and the blood of Jesus His Son cleanses us from all sin.　　Is. 2:5 • 1 Tim. 6:16

Confession of Sin

8 ᴿIf we say that we have no sin, we are deceiving ourselves, and theᴿtruth is not in us.　　　　　　Job 15:14 • John 8:44; 1 John 2:4

9 ᴿIf we confess our sins, He is faithful and righteous to forgive us our sins and to cleanse us from all unrighteousness.　Ps. 32:5

10 If we say that we have not sinned, we make Him a liar, and His word is not in us.

CHAPTER 2

M Yᴿ little children, I am writing these things to you that you may not sin. And if anyone sins, we have an ¹Advocate with the Father, Jesus Christ the righteous;　John 13:33

¹ Gr., *Paracletos*, one called alongside to help

1:9 Confession—One of the most remarkable chapters in the Old Testament is Psalm 51. This Psalm contains the actual words of confession uttered by King David after his great sins of adultery and murder (Page 303—2 Sam. 11).

This prayer can serve as a pattern to the Christian when he is guilty of sin in his life today.

a. David begins his prayer by freely admitting his sin (Page 554—Ps. 51:3, 4). This honesty is vital in our confession. God will graciously forgive all our sins, but not on account of our excuses.

b. He then displays real sorrow over his sin (Page 554—Ps. 51:17). Paul writes (Page 1170—2 Cor. 7:10) that the main characteristic of true confession is godly sorrow.

c. He asks God's forgiveness (Page 554—Ps. 51:1, 7–9).

d. He believes that God has heard him and will restore him (Page 554—Ps. 51:12–15).

In the New Testament the most important single verse concerning confession is First John 1:9. In essence John tells us the means of forgiveness and cleansing is the blood of Christ, while the method of this forgiveness and cleansing is the confession of the Christian.

Like David, we must admit our sin, regret the actions of our sin, plead the blood of Christ, and believe that God has indeed done what He promised, namely, to cleanse us from sin and restore us to fellowship and service.

Now turn to Page 263—1 Sam. 1:17: Petition.

2 and He Himself is the^propitiation for our sins; and not for ours only, but also for *those of* the whole world.   *satisfaction*

Obedience to His Commandments

3 And ᴿby this we know that we have come to ᴿknow Him, if we keep His commandments.   1 John 2:5 • 1 John 2:4; 3:6; 4:7f.

4 The one who says, "Iᴿ have come to ᴿknow Him," and does not keep His commandments, is aᴿliar, and the truth is not in him;   Titus 1:10 • 1 John 3:6 • 1 John 1:6

5 but whoever ᴿkeeps His word, in him the love of God has truly been perfected. By this we know that we are in Him: John 14:23

6 the one who says he ᴿabides in Him ᴿought himself to walk in the same manner as He walked.   [John 15:4] • John 13:15

Love for One Another

7 Beloved, I am not writing a new commandment to you, but an old commandment which youᵀhave had from the beginning; the old commandment is the word which you have heard.   *were having*

8 On the other hand, I am writing a new commandment to you, which is true in Him and in you, because the darkness is passing away, and the true light is already shining.

9 The one who says he is in the light and yetᴿhates hisᴿbrother is in the darkness until now.   1 John 2:11 • Acts 1:15; 1 John 3:10

10 ᴿThe one who loves his brother abides in the light and there is no cause for stumbling in him.   John 11:9; 1 John 2:10, 11

11 But the one whoᴿhates his brother is in the darkness and walks in the darkness, and does not know where he is going because the darkness has blinded his eyes.   1 John 2:9

12 I am writing to you,ᴿlittle children, because ᴿyour sins are forgiven you for His name's sake.   1 John 2:1 • Acts 13:38

13 I am writing to you, fathers, because you know Himᴿwho has been from the be-ginning. I am writing to you, young men, be-cause ᴿyou have overcome the evil one. I have written to you, children, because you know the Father.   1 John 1:1 • John 16:33

14 I have written to you, fathers, because you know Himᴿwho has been from the be-ginning. I have written to you, young men, because you are ᴿstrong, and the word of God abides in you, and you have overcome the evil one.   1 John 1:1 • Eph. 6:10

Love of the World

15 <u>Do not loveᴿthe world, nor the things in the world. If anyone loves the world, the love of the Father is not in him.</u>   [Rom. 12:2]

16 For all that is in the world,ᴿthe lust of the flesh and the lust of the eyes and the boastful pride of life, is not from the Father, but is from the world.   Rom. 13:14; Eph. 2:3

17 Andᴿthe world is passing away, and *also* its lusts; but the one whoᴿdoes the will of God abides forever.   1 Cor. 7:31 • Mark 3:35

Spirit of the Antichrist

18 Children,ᴿit is the last hour; and just as you heard that antichrist is coming, even now many antichrists have arisen; from this we know that it is the last hour.   Rom. 13:11

19 ᴿThey went out from us, but they were not *really* of us; for if they had been of us, they would have remained with us; but *they went out*, in order that it might be shown that they all are not of us.   Acts 20:30

20 ᵀBut you have an anointing from the Holy One, and you all know.   *And*

21 I have not written to you because you do not know the truth, but because you do know it, and because no lie is of the truth.

22 Who is the liar butᴿthe one who denies that Jesus is theᵀChrist? This is the anti-christ, the one who denies the Father and the Son.   1 John 4:3 • Messiah

23 ᴿWhoever denies the Son does not have the Father; the one who confesses the Son has the Father also.   John 8:19; 16:3; 17:3

2:15 Temptation by the World—The term *world* does not always refer to the universe as created by God. It often is used to describe the community of sinful humanity that possesses a spirit of rebellion against God (Page 1278—1 John 5:19). Because of its opposition to God, the world values those things which are contrary to God's will: "the lust of the flesh and the lust of the eyes and the boastful pride of life" (1 John 2:16). Its temptations to the believer are thus twofold: lust for the sensual and pride in mastery of his own life.

The attraction of the world is amplified by Satan who is head of its system. He is called the "ruler of this world" (Page 1079—John 12:31; 14:30; 16:11), and the whole world is said to be under his power (Page 1278—1 John 5:19).

Some of the tragic effects that love of the world will produce in the believer's life are:
a. A turning away from the Lord's work and other believers (Page 1225—2 Tim. 4:10);
b. Alienation from God (Page 1255—James 4:4);
c. Corrupting sins (Page 1268—2 Pet. 1:4; 1 John 2:15–17);
d. Deception by false teachers (Page 1277—1 John 4:1; Page 1281—2 John 7).

The solution to the love of the world is to have a greater love for the Father (1 John 2:15). The Christian who seeks daily to please God in everything and who strives for spiritual growth through prayer, study of God's Word, and witnessing need not fall prey to the temptations of the world.

Now turn to Page 1017—Mark 14:38: Temptation by the Flesh.

24 As for you, let that abide in you which you heard from the beginning. If what you heard from the beginning abides in you, you also will abide in the Son and in the Father.

25 And this is the promise which He Himself[T]made to us: eternal life.　　*promised us*

26 These things I have written to you concerning those who are trying to deceive you.

27 And as for you, the anointing which you received from Him abides in you, and you have no need for anyone to teach you; but as His anointing teaches you about all things, and is true and is not a lie, and just as it has taught you, you abide in Him.

Purity of Life

28 And now, little children, abide in Him, so that when He appears, we may have confidence and not [T]shrink away from Him in shame at His coming.　　*be put to shame from Him*

29 If you know that He is righteous, you know that everyone also who practices righteousness is[A]born of Him.　　*begotten*

CHAPTER 3

SEE how[R]great a love the Father has bestowed upon us, that we should be called children of God; and *such* we are. For this reason the world does not know us, because it did not know Him.　　[John 3:16]

2 [R]Beloved, now we are [R]children of God, and it has not appeared as yet what we shall be. We know that, when He [R]appears, we shall be like Him, because we shall see Him just as He is. 1 John 2:7 • [John 1:12] • Luke 17:30

3 And everyone who has this hope *fixed* on Him purifies himself, just as He is pure.

Practice of Righteousness

4 Everyone who practices sin also practices lawlessness; and sin is lawlessness.

5 And you know that He[R]appeared in order to[R]take away sins; and in Him there is no sin.　　1 John 1:2; 3:8 • John 1:29

6 No one who abides in Him sins; no one who sins has seen Him or knows Him.

7 [R]Little children, let no one deceive you; the one who practices righteousness is righteous, just as He is righteous;　1 John 2:1

8 the one who practices sin is[R]of the devil; for the devil[T]has sinned from the beginning.[R]The Son of God appeared for this purpose, that He might destroy the works of the devil.　　Matt. 13:38 • *sins* • Matt. 4:3

9 No one who is born of God practices sin, because His seed abides in him; and he cannot sin, because he is born of God.

10 By this the children of God and the [R]children of the devil are obvious: anyone who does not practice righteousness is not of God, nor the one who[R]does not love his [R]brother.　Matt. 13:38 • Rom. 13:8ff. • 1 John 2:9

11 [R]For this is the message[R]which you have heard from the beginning, that we should love one another;　1 John 1:5 • 1 John 2:7

12 not as Cain, *who* was of the evil one, and slew his brother. And for what reason did he slay him? Because his deeds were evil, and his brother's were righteous.

Love in Deed and Truth

13 Do not marvel, brethren, if[R]the world hates you.　　[John 15:18; 17:14]

14 We know that we have passed out of death into life, because we love the brethren. He who does not love abides in death.

15 Everyone who[R]hates his brother is a murderer; and you know that no murderer has eternal life abiding in him.　　Matt. 5:21f.

16 We know love by this, that[R]He laid down His life for us; and we ought to lay down our lives for the brethren.　John 10:11

17 But whoever has the world's goods, and beholds his brother in need and closes his[T]heart[T]against him, how does the love of God abide in him?　　*inward parts* • *from*

3:2 **Placed into God's Family**—In a general sense all men and women are the offspring of God in that He is the Creator (Page 1115—Acts 17:28, 29). This relationship, however, is not sufficient to offset the penalty of sin, because all persons are sinners separated from God (Page 1134—Rom. 3:23). Therefore, for a sinful person to become a child of God, a miraculous transformation must take place. The Bible refers to this change as being "born again" (Page 1066—John 3:3). When an individual places his faith in Christ as Savior, he is born again into a new, spiritual, family relationship with God (Page 1179—Gal. 3:26). He gains God as Father (Page 1187—Eph. 4:6) and other Christians as brothers and sisters (Page 1240—Heb. 3:1). It is significant to note that the term "love of the brethren," which Christians are commanded to have for each other (Page 1248—Heb. 13:1), is never used in the Greek language to refer to loving others as though they were your brothers. Rather, it is always used of loving those who actually are your brothers. So it is in the Christian faith: we actually are brothers and sisters with other Christians.

Not only are Christians the children of God by spiritual birth; they are adopted as well (Page 1185—Eph. 1:5). This figure implies a dramatic transformation of status from slave to son (Page 1179—Gal. 4:1-5). One is no longer in bondage to the master but becomes a free son possessing all the rights and privileges of sonship. One of these benefits is the right to call God *Abba,* an affectionate term meaning "father" (Page 1137—Rom. 8:15). This marvelous relationship carries responsibilities with it, as well as privileges. Everyone who has the hope of having his sonship perfected someday is presently purifying his own life. Since he bears the family relationship to God, he must also exhibit the family character.

Now turn to Page 1094—Acts 1:8: Empowered by God.

18 Little children, let us not love with word or with tongue, but in deed and truth.

19 We shall know by this that we are of the truth, and shall^assure our heart^before Him,   *persuade • before Him; because if our heart*

20 in whatever our heart condemns us; for God is greater than our heart, and knows all things.

21 Beloved, if our heart does not condemn us, we have confidence^before God;   *toward*

22 and^whatever we ask we receive from Him, because we^keep His commandments and do^the things that are pleasing in His sight.   Job 22:26f. • 1 John 2:3 • John 8:29

23 And this is His commandment, that we ^believe in the name of His Son Jesus Christ, and love one another, just as He commanded us.   *believe the name*

24 And the one who^keeps His commandments abides in Him, and He in him. And we know by this that He abides in us, by the Spirit whom He has given us.   1 John 2:3

CHAPTER 4

Testing the Spirits

B ELOVED,^ do not believe every spirit, but test the spirits to see whether they are from God; because many false prophets have gone out into the world.   3 John 11

2 By this you know the Spirit of God:^every spirit that confesses that Jesus Christ has come in the flesh is from God; 1 Cor. 12:3

3 and every spirit that^does not confess Jesus is not from God; and this is the *spirit* of the^antichrist, of which you have heard that it is coming, and now it is already in the world.   1 John 2:22 • 1 John 2:18, 22

4 You are from God, little children, and have overcome them; because greater is He who is in you than he who is in the world.

5 ^They are from the world; therefore they speak *as* from the world, and the world listens to them.   John 15:19; 17:14, 16

6 ^We are from God; he who knows God listens to us; he who is not from God does not listen to us. By this we know the spirit of truth and the spirit of error.   John 8:23

Love as Christ Loved

7 Beloved, let us love one another, for love is from God; and everyone who loves is ^born of God and knows God.   *begotten*

8 The one who does not love does not know God, for^God is love.   1 John 4:7, 16

9 By this the love of God was manifested ^in us, that God has sent His^only begotten Son into the world so that we might live through Him.   *in our case • unique*

10 In this is love,^not that we loved God, but that He loved us and sent His Son *to be* the propitiation for our sins.   Rom. 5:8, 10

11 ^Beloved, if God so loved us, we also ought to love one another.   1 John 2:7

12 ^No one has beheld God at any time; if we love one another, God abides in us, and His love is perfected in us.   John 1:18

13 ^By this we know that we abide in Him and He in us, because He has given us of His Spirit.   Rom. 8:9; 1 John 3:24

14 And we have beheld and^bear witness that the Father has sent the Son *to be* the Savior of the world.   John 15:27; 1 John 1:2

15 ^Whoever confesses that ^Jesus is the Son of God, God abides in him, and he in God.   1 John 2:23 • [Rom. 10:9]; 1 John 3:23

16 And we have come to know and have believed the love which God has^for us. God is love, and the one who abides in love abides in God, and God abides in him.   *in*

17 By this,^love is perfected with us, that we may have^confidence in the day of judgment; because as He is, so also are we in this world.   1 John 2:5; 4:12 • 1 John 2:28

18 There is no fear in love; but ^perfect love casts out fear, because fear ^involves punishment, and the one who fears is not perfected in love.   [Rom. 8:15] • *has*

19 We love, because He first loved us.

20 If someone says, "I love God," and hates his brother, he is a liar; for the one who does not love his brother whom he has seen, cannot love God whom he has not seen.

21 And^this commandment we have from Him, that the one who loves God should love his brother also.   Lev. 19:18; [Matt. 5:43f.]

CHAPTER 5

W HOEVER believes that Jesus is the ^2Christ is born of God; and whoever loves the Father loves the *child* born of Him.

^2 I.e., Messiah

3:24 Witness of the Spirit—While it is true that one need not always feel spiritual to have new life in Christ, nevertheless, feelings and emotions do play a vital role in our salvation. Both Paul (Page 1138—Rom. 8:16) and John (1 John 3:24) inform us we can experience that inner witness of the Holy Spirit to our spirit. What does this mean? It means we can enjoy the quiet confidence given by the Spirit that we have indeed passed from death unto life. It means we can now approach the mighty Creator of the vast universe and refer to Him as Abba, Father (Page 1137—Rom. 8:15). *Abba* is a very personal and intimate term for one's father. Prior to Pentecost only Christ had used the title for God (Page 1017—Mark 14:36). It is almost akin to our modern title *daddy*, or *papa*. It not only means we can approach the throne of grace with a holy boldness (Page 1241—Heb. 4:16), but we can also experience the blessing of knowing that the Father will hear and answer our prayers (1 John 3:22).

The apostle Paul experiences this witness during a crisis in his life while preaching in Corinth. See Acts 18:9, 10.

Now turn to Page 1152—1 Cor. 6:11: Changed Life.

2 ᴿBy this we know thatᴿwe love the children of God, when we love God andᵀobserve His commandments. 1 John 2:5 · 1 John 3:14 · *do*

3 Forᴿthis is the love of God, that we keep His commandments; and His commandments are not burdensome. John 14:15

Victory over the World

4 For whatever is ^born of God overcomes the world; and this is the victory that has overcome the world—our faith. *begotten*

5 And who is the one who overcomes the world, but he whoᴿbelieves that Jesus is the Son of God? 1 John 4:15; 5:1

Assurance of Salvation

6 This is the one who came by water and blood, Jesus Christ; notᵀwith the water only, but with the water and with the blood. *in*

7 And it isᴿthe Spirit who bears witness, because the Spirit is the truth. John 15:26

8 For there are three that bear witness, ³the Spirit and the water and the blood; and the three areᵀin agreement. *for the one thing*

9 ᴿIf we receive the witness of men, the witness of God is greater; for the witness of God is this, thatᴿHe has borne witness concerning His Son. John 5:34 · John 5:32, 37

10 The one who believes in the Son of God ᴿhas the witness in himself; the one who does not believe God has made Him a liar, because he has not believed in the witness that God has borne concerning His Son. Gal. 4:6

11 And the witness is this, that God has given usᴿeternal life, andᴿthis life is in His Son. John 3:36; 1 John 1:2 · John 1:4

12 ᴿHe who has the Son has the life; he who does not have the Son of God does not have the life. [John 3:15f., 36]

13 ᴿThese things I have written to you who ᴿbelieve in the name of the Son of God, in order that you may know that you have eternal life. John 20:31 · 1 John 3:23

Guidance in Prayer

14 And this is the confidence which we haveᵀbefore Him, that, if we ask anything according to His will, He hears us. *toward*

15 And if we know that He hears us *in* whatever we ask, we know that we have the requests which we have asked from Him.

16 If anyone sees his brotherᵀcommitting a sin not *leading* to death,ᴿhe shall ask and God will for him give life to those who commit sin not *leading* to death. There is a sin *leading* to death; I do not say that he should make request for this. *sinning* · James 5:15

17 ᴿAll unrighteousness is sin, and there is a sin not *leading* to death. 1 John 3:4

Freedom from Habitual Sin

18 ᴿWe know thatᴿno one who is^born of God sins; but He who was born of God keeps him and the evil one does not touch him. 1 John 5:15 · 1 John 3:9 · *begotten*

19 ᴿWe know thatᴿwe are of God, and the whole world lies in *the power of* the evil one. 1 John 5:15, 18, 20 · 1 John 4:6

20 Andᴿwe know thatᴿthe Son of God has come, and has given us understanding, in order that we might know Him who is true, and we are in Him who is true, in His Son Jesus Christ. This is the true God and eternal life. 1 John 5:15 · John 8:42; 1 John 5:5

21 ᴿLittle children, guard yourselves from ᴿidols. 1 John 2:1 · 1 Cor. 10:7, 14

³ A few late mss. read *in heaven, the Father, the Word, and the Holy Spirit, and these three are one. And there are three that bear witness on earth, the Spirit*

THE SECOND EPISTLE OF

JOHN

THE BOOK OF SECOND JOHN
"Let him who thinks he stands take heed lest he fall" (1 Cor. 10:12). These words of the apostle Paul could well stand as a subtitle for John's little epistle. The recipients, a chosen lady and her children, were obviously standing. They were walking in truth, remaining faithful to the commandments they had received from the Father. John is deeply pleased to be able to commend them. But he takes nothing for granted. Realizing that standing is just one step removed from falling, he hesitates not at all to issue a reminder: love one another. The apostle admits that this is not new revelation, but he views it sufficiently important to repeat. Loving one another, he stresses, is equivalent to walking according to God's commandments.

John indicates, however, that this love must be discerning. It is not a naive, unthinking, open to anything and anyone kind of love. Biblical love is a matter of choice; it is dangerous and foolish to float through life with undiscerning love. False teachers abound who do not acknowledge Christ as having come in the flesh. It is false charity to open the door to false teaching. We must have fellowship with God. We must have fellowship with Christians. But we must not have fellowship with false teachers.

The "elder" of verse 1 has been traditionally identified with the apostle John, resulting in the Greek title *Ioannou B*, "Second of John."

THE AUTHOR OF SECOND JOHN
Because of the similarity of the contents and circumstances of Second and Third John, the authorship of both will be considered here. These letters were not widely circulated at the beginning because of their brevity and their specific address to a small number of people. This limited circulation, combined with the fact that they have few distinctive ideas to add that are not found in First John, meant that they were seldom quoted in the patristic writings of the early church. Their place in the canon of New Testament books was disputed for a time, but it is significant that there was no question in the minds of those church fathers who lived closest to the time of John that these two epistles were written by the apostle. The second-century writers Irenaeus and Clement of Alexandria entertained no other view. Only as the details of

their origin were forgotten did doubts arise, but the positive evidence in their favor eventually won for them the official recognition of the whole church.

It is obvious that the recipients of Second and Third John well knew the author's identity, although he did not use his name. Instead, he designated himself in the first verse of both letters as "the elder." This is not an argument against the Johannine authorship of Second and Third John, since the context of these epistles reveals that his authority was far greater than that of an elder in a local church. The apostle Peter also referred to himself as an elder (1 Pet. 5:1), and John uses the distinguishing term "the elder."

The similarity of style, vocabulary, structure, and mood between Second and Third John makes it clear that these letters were written by the same author. In addition, both (especially Second John) bear strong resemblances to First John and to the Fourth Gospel. Thus, the external and internal evidence lends clear support to the traditional view that these epistles were written by the apostle John.

THE TIME OF SECOND JOHN
The identification of the original readers of this epistle is difficult because of disagreement regarding the interpretation of "the chosen lady and her children" (v.1). Some scholars believe the address should be taken literally to refer to a specific woman and her children, while others prefer to take it as a figurative description of a local church.

The evidence is insufficient for a decisive conclusion, but in either case, the readers were well-known to John and probably lived in the province of Asia, not far from Ephesus. If the figurative view is taken, "the children of your chosen sister" (v.13) refers to the members of a sister church.

In his first epistle, John wrote that a number of false teachers had split away from the church ("They went out from us, but they were not *really* of us," 1 John 2:19). Some of these became traveling teachers who depended on the hospitality of individuals while they sought to infiltrate churches with their teachings.

Judging by the content and circumstances of Second John, it was evidently contemporaneous with First John or was written slightly later. It was probably written about A.D. 90. All three of John's epistles may have been writ-

ten in Ephesus (see "The Time of First John").

THE CHRIST OF SECOND JOHN

John refutes the same error regarding the person of Christ in this epistle as he did in his first epistle. Again he stresses that those "who do not acknowledge Jesus Christ *as* coming in the flesh" (v.7) are deceivers who must be avoided. One must abide "in the teaching of Christ" (v.9) to have a relationship with God. The doctrine of the person and work of Jesus Christ affects every other area of theology.

KEYS TO SECOND JOHN

Key Word: Avoid Fellowship with False Teachers—The basic theme of this brief letter is steadfastness in the practice and purity of the apostolic doctrine that the readers "have heard from the beginning" (v.6). John writes it as a reminder to continue walking in obedience to God's commandment to love one another (practical exhortation, vv.4–6). His primary purpose is to deliver a warning not to associate with or assist teachers who do not acknowledge the truth about Jesus Christ (doctrinal exhortation, vv.7–11).

It has been suggested that Second and Third John were written as cover letters for First John to provide a personal word to a church (2 John) and to Gaius (3 John) that would supplement the longer epistle. However, there is no way to be sure.

Key Verses: Second John 9, 10—"Anyone who goes too far and does not abide in the teaching of Christ, does not have God; the one who abides in the teaching, he has both the Father and the Son. If anyone comes to you and does not bring this teaching, do not receive him into *your* house, and do not give him a greeting" (vv.9, 10).

SURVEY OF SECOND JOHN

This brief letter has much in common with First John, including a warning about the danger of false teachers who deny the incarnation of Jesus Christ. John encourages the readers to continue walking in love but exhorts them to be discerning in their expression of love. Second John breaks with two parts: abide in God's commandments (vv.1–6) and abide not with false teachers (vv.7–13).

Abide in God's Commandments (vv.1–6): The salutation (vv.1–3) centers on the concept of abiding in the truth (mentioned four times in these three verses). The recipients are loved for their adherence to the truth by "all who know the truth." The apostle commends his readers on their walk in truth in obedience to God's commandment (v.4), and reminds them that this commandment entails the practice of love for one another (vv.5, 6). The divine command is given in verse 5 and the human response follows in verse 6.

Abide Not with False Teachers (vv.7–13): Moving from the basic test of Christian behavior (love for the brethren) to the basic test of Christian belief (the person of Christ), John admonishes the readers to beware of deceivers "who do not acknowledge Jesus Christ *as* coming in the flesh" (vv.7–9). In no uncertain terms, the apostle enjoins the readers to deny even the slightest assistance or encouragement to itinerant teachers who promote an erroneous view of Christ (and hence of salvation; vv.10, 11).

This letter closes with John's explanation of its brevity: he anticipates a future visit during which he will be able to "speak face to face" with his readers (v.12). The meaning of the greeting in verse 13 relates to the interpretation of verse 1.

FOCUS	ABIDE IN GOD'S COMMANDMENTS			ABIDE NOT WITH FALSE TEACHERS		
REFERENCE	1 —————— 4	——————	5 ——————	7 ——————	10 ——————	12 ———— 13
DIVISION	SALUTATION	WALK IN TRUTH	WALK IN LOVE	DOCTRINE OF FALSE TEACHERS	AVOID THE FALSE TEACHERS	BENEDICTION
TOPIC	WALK IN COMMANDMENTS			WATCH FOR COUNTERFEITS		
	PRACTICE THE TRUTH			PROTECT THE TRUTH		
LOCATION	WRITTEN IN EPHESUS					
TIME	C. A.D. 90					

Salutation

THE[R]elder to the chosen lady and her children, whom I love in truth; and not only I, but also all who know the truth,   Acts 11:30

2 for[R]the sake of the truth which abides in us and will be with us forever: 2 Pet. 1:12

3 [R]Grace, mercy *and* peace will be with us, from God the Father and from Jesus Christ, the Son of the Father, in truth and love.   Rom. 1:7; 1 Tim. 1:2

Walk in Truth

4 [R]I was very glad to find *some* of your children walking in truth, just as we have received commandment *to do* from the Father.   3 John 3f.

Walk in Love

5 And now I ask you, lady,[R]not as writing to you a new commandment, but the one which we have had from the beginning, that we[R]love one another.   1 John 2:7 • [John 13:34]

6 And this is love, that we walk according to His commandments. This is the commandment, just as you have heard from the beginning, that you should walk in it.

Doctrine of the False Teachers

7 For[R]many deceivers have gone out into the world, those who do not acknowledge Jesus Christ *as* coming in the flesh. This is the deceiver and the antichrist.   1 John 2:26

8 Watch yourselves, that you might not lose what^we have accomplished, but that you may receive a full reward.   *you*

9 Anyone who goes too far and does not abide in the teaching of Christ, does not have God; the one who abides in the teaching, he has both the Father and the Son.

Avoid the False Teachers

10 If anyone comes to you and does not bring this teaching, do not receive him into *your* house, and do not give him a greeting;

11 for the one who gives him a greeting [R]participates in his evil deeds.   Eph. 5:11

Benediction

12 Having many things to write to you, I do not want to *do so* with paper and ink; but I hope to come to you and speak face to face, that^your joy may be made full.   *our*

13 The children of your [R]chosen sister greet you.   2 John 1

JOHN

THE BOOK OF THIRD JOHN

In First John the apostle discusses fellowship with God; in Second John he forbids fellowship with false teachers; and in Third John he encourages fellowship with Christian brothers. Following his expression of love for Gaius, John assures him of his prayers for his health and voices his joy over Gaius's persistent walk in truth and for the manner in which he shows hospitality and support for missionaries who have come to his church. The phrase "send them on their way" means to provide help for the missionaries' endeavors. Included in this help can be food, money, arrangements for companions, and means of travel. By supporting these men who are ministering for Christ, Gaius has become a fellow worker of the truth.

But not everyone in the church feels the same way. Diotrephes's heart is one hundred and eighty degrees removed from Gaius's heart. He is no longer living in love. Pride has taken precedence in his life. He has refused a letter John has written for the church, fearing that his authority might be superseded by that of the apostle. He also has accused John of evil words and refused to accept missionaries. He forbids others to do so and even expels them from the church if they disobey him. John uses this negative example as an opportunity to encourage Gaius to continue his hospitality. Demetrius has a good testimony and may even be one of those turned away by Diotrephes. He is widely known for his good character and his loyalty to the truth. Here he is well commended by John and stands as a positive example for Gaius.

The Greek titles of First, Second, and Third John are *Ioannou A, B,* and *G.* The *G* is gamma, the third letter of the Greek alphabet; *Ioannou G* means "Third of John."

THE AUTHOR OF THIRD JOHN

The authorship of Second and Third John was considered together because the contents and circumstances of both books are similar (see "The Author of Second John"). Although the external evidence for Second and Third John is limited (there is even less for Third John than for Second John), what little there is consistently points to the apostle John as author. The internal evidence is stronger, and it, too, supports the apostolic origin of both letters.

THE TIME OF THIRD JOHN

The parallels between Second and Third John suggest that these epistles were written at about the same time (A.D. 90). Early Christian writers are unified in their testimony that the headquarters of John's later ministry was in Ephesus, the principal city of the Roman province of Asia (see "The Time of First John"). John evidently commissioned a number of traveling teachers to spread the gospel and to solidify the Asian churches, and these teachers were supported by believers who received them into their homes.

Third John, probably delivered by Demetrius, was occasioned by the report of some of these emissaries (called "brethren" in this letter), who returned to the apostle and informed him of the hospitality of Gaius and the hostility of Diotrephes. The arrogant Diotrephes seized the reins of an Asian church and vaunted himself as its preeminent authority. He maligned John's authority and rejected the teachers sent out by John, expelling those in his church who wanted to receive them.

Gaius was a common name in the Roman Empire, and three other men by that name are mentioned in the New Testament: (1) Gaius, one of Paul's traveling companions from Macedonia (Acts 19:29); (2) Gaius of Derbe (Acts 20:4); and (3) Gaius, Paul's host in Corinth, one of the few Corinthians Paul baptized (Rom. 16:23; 1 Cor. 1:14). The Gaius of Third John evidently lived in Asia, and it is best to distinguish him from these other men.

In verse 9, John alludes to a previous letter that Diotrephes had spurned. This may have been First or Second John, but it is more likely a letter that has been lost or perhaps destroyed by Diotrephes.

THE CHRIST OF THIRD JOHN

Unlike First and Second John, Third John makes no mention of the name of Jesus Christ. But verse 7 says "they went out for the sake of the Name," an indirect reference to our Lord (cf. Acts 5:41, where the identical Greek construction is used to refer back to "the name of Jesus" in Acts 5:40). The concept of truth runs throughout this letter, and Christ is the source and incarnation of truth, as is obvious from John's other writings.

KEYS TO THIRD JOHN

Key Word: Enjoy Fellowship with the Brethren—The basic theme of this letter is to enjoy and continue to have fellowship (hospitality) with fellow believers, especially full-time Christian workers. This is contrasted between the truth and servanthood of Gaius and the error and selfishness of Diotrephes. Moving through Third John, five specific purposes can be discerned from its contents: (1) to commend Gaius for his adherence to the truth and his hospitality to the emissaries sent out by John (vv. 1–6); (2) to encourage Gaius to continue his support of these brethren (vv. 6–8); (3) to rebuke Diotrephes for his pride and misconduct (vv. 9–11); (4) to provide a recommendation for Demetrius (v. 12); and (5) to inform Gaius of John's intention to visit and straighten out the difficulties (vv. 10, 13, 14).

Key Verse: Third John 11—"Beloved, do not imitate what is evil, but what is good. The one who does good is of God; the one who does evil has not seen God" (v. 11).

SURVEY OF THIRD JOHN

Third John is the shortest book in the Bible, but it is very personal and vivid. It offers a stark contrast between two men who respond in opposite ways to the itinerant teachers who have been sent out by the apostle. The faithful Gaius responds with generosity and hospitality, but the faithless Diotrephes responds with arrogance and opposition. Thus, John writes this letter to commend Gaius for walking in the truth (vv. 1–8) and to condemn Diotrephes for walking in error (vv. 9–14).

Commendation of Gaius (vv. 1–8): The "elder" writes to one of his beloved "children" whose godly behavior has given the apostles great joy (vv. 1–4). The "brethren," upon returning to John, have informed him of Gaius's faithfulness, love, and generosity in their behalf. The apostle acknowledges these actions and urges Gaius to continue supporting traveling teachers and missionaries who go out "for the sake of the Name" (vv. 5–8).

Condemnation of Diotrephes (vv. 9–14): The epistle suddenly shifts to a negative note as John describes a man whose actions are diametrically opposed to those of Gaius (vv. 9–11). Diotrephes boldly rejects John's apostolic authority and refuses to receive the itinerant teachers sent out by the apostle. Diotrephes evidently has been orthodox in his doctrine, but his evil actions indicate a blindness to God in his practice.

By contrast, John gives his full recommendation to Demetrius, another emissary and probably the bearer of this letter to Gaius (v. 12). John expresses his hope of a personal visit in the closing remarks (vv. 13, 14), as he does in Second John.

FOCUS	COMMENDATION OF GAIUS			CONDEMNATION OF DIOTREPHES		
REFERENCE	1 —————— 2 ————— 5			———— 9 ————— 12		———— 13 ———— 14
DIVISION	SALUTATION	GODLINESS OF GAIUS	GENEROSITY OF GAIUS	PRIDE OF DIOTREPHES	PRAISE FOR DEMETRIUS	BENEDICTION
TOPIC	SERVANTHOOD			SELFISHNESS		
	DUTY OF HOSPITALITY			DANGER OF HAUGHTINESS		
LOCATION	WRITTEN IN EPHESUS					
TIME	c. A.D. 90					

OUTLINE OF THIRD JOHN

Salutation

THE[R]elder to the beloved[R]Gaius, whom I love in truth.   2 John 1 • Acts 19:29; 20:4

Godliness of Gaius

2 Beloved, I pray that in all respects you may prosper and be in good health, just as your soul prospers.

3 For I [R]was very glad when brethren came and bore witness to your truth, *that is,* how you are walking in truth.   2 John 4

4 I have no greater joy than this, to hear of[R]my children walking in the truth. Gal. 4:19

Generosity of Gaius

5 Beloved, you are acting faithfully in whatever you accomplish for the brethren, and especially *when they are* strangers;

6 and they bear witness to your love before the church; and you will do well to[R]send them on their way in a manner[R]worthy of God.   Acts 15:3 • Col. 1:10; 1 Thess. 2:12

7 For they went out for the sake of the Name, accepting nothing from the Gentiles.

8 Therefore we ought to ^support such men, that we may be fellow workers^with the truth.   *receive such men as guests • for*

Pride of Diotrephes

9 I wrote something to the church; but Diotrephes, who loves to be first among them, does not accept[T]what we say.   *us*

10 For this reason,[R]if I come, I will call attention to his deeds which he does, unjustly accusing us with wicked words; and not satisfied with this, neither does he himself[R]receive the brethren, and he forbids those who desire *to do so,* and puts *them* out of the church.   2 John 12 • 2 John 10; 3 John 5

11 Beloved, [R]do not imitate what is evil, but what is good.[R]The one who does good is of God;[R]the one who does evil has not seen God.   Ps. 34:14 • 1 John 2:29 • 1 John 3:6

Praise for Demetrius

12 Demetrius [R]has received a good testimony from everyone, and from the truth itself; and we also bear witness, and you know that our witness is true.   1 Tim. 3:7

Benediction

13 [R]I had many things to write to you, but I am not willing to write *them* to you with pen and ink;   2 John 12

14 but I hope to see you shortly, and we shall speak face to face. [R]Peace *be* to you. The friends greet you. Greet the friends[R]by name.   John 20:19, 21, 26; Eph. 6:23 • [John 10:3]

THE EPISTLE OF

JUDE

THE BOOK OF JUDE
Fight! Contend! Do battle! When apostasy arises, when false teachers emerge, when the truth of God is attacked, it is time to fight for the faith. Only believers who are spiritually "in shape" can answer the summons. At the beginning of his letter Jude focuses on the believers' common salvation, but then feels compelled to challenge them to contend for the faith. The danger is real. False teachers have crept into the church, turning God's grace into unbounded license to do as they please. Jude reminds such men of God's past dealings with unbelieving Israel, disobedient angels, and wicked Sodom and Gomorrah. In the face of such danger Christians should not be caught off guard. The challenge is great, but so is the God who is able to keep them from stumbling.

The Greek title *Iouda*, "Of Jude," comes from the name *Ioudas* which appears in verse 1. This name, which can be translated Jude or Judas, was popular in the first century because of Judas Maccabaeus (died 160 B.C.), a leader of the Jewish resistance against Syria during the Maccabean revolt.

THE AUTHOR OF JUDE
In spite of its limited subject matter and size, Jude was accepted as authentic and quoted by early church fathers. There may be some older allusions, but undisputed references to this epistle appear in the last quarter of the second century. It was included in the Muratorian Canon (c. A.D. 170) and accepted as part of Scripture by early leaders, such as Tertullian and Origen. Nevertheless, doubts arose concerning the place of Jude in the canon because of its use of the Apocrypha. It was a disputed book in some parts of the church, but it eventually won universal recognition.

The author identifies himself as "a bondservant of Jesus Christ, and brother of James" (v. 1). This designation, combined with the reference in verse 17 to the apostles, makes it unlikely that this is the apostle Jude, called "Judas *the son* of James" in Luke 6:16 and in Acts 1:13. This leaves the traditional view that Jude was one of the Lord's brothers, called Judas in Matthew 13:55 and Mark 6:3 (see "The Author of James"). His older brother James (note his position on the two lists) was the famous leader of the Jerusalem church (Acts 15:13–21) and author of the epistle that bears his name. Like his brothers, Jude did not believe in Jesus before the Resurrection (John 7:1–9; Acts 1:14). The only other biblical allusion to him is in First Corinthians 9:5 where it is recorded that "the brothers of the Lord" took their wives along on their missionary journeys (the Judas of Acts 15:22, 32 may be another reference to him). Extrabiblical tradition adds nothing to our limited knowledge of Jude.

THE TIME OF JUDE
Jude's general address does not mark out any particular circle of readers, and there are no geographical restrictions. Nevertheless, he probably had in mind a specific region that was being troubled by false teachers. There is not enough information in the epistle to settle the question of whether his readers were predominately Jewish or gentile Christians (there was probably a mixture of both). In any case, the progress of the faith in their region was threatened by a number of apostates who rejected Christ in practice and principle. These proud libertines were especially dangerous because of their deceptive flattery (v. 16) and infiltration of Christian meetings (v. 12). They perverted the grace of God (v. 4) and caused divisions in the church (v. 19).

Jude's description of these heretics is reminiscent of that found in Second Peter and leads to the issue of the relationship between the two epistles (see "The Author of Second Peter"). The strong similarity between Second Peter 2:1—3:4 and Jude 4–18 can hardly be coincidental, but the equally obvious differences rule out the possibility that one is a mere copy of the other. It is also doubtful that both authors independently drew from an unknown third source, so the two remaining options are that Peter used Jude or Jude used Peter. Both views have their advocates, and a number of arguments have been raised in support of either side. But two arguments for the priority of Second Peter are so strong that they tip the scales in favor of this position: (1) A comparison of the two books shows that Second Peter anticipates the future rise of apostate teachers (2 Pet. 2:1, 2; 3:3) while Jude records the historical fulfillment of Peter's words (Jude 4, 11, 12, 17, 18); (2) Jude directly quotes Second Peter 3:3 and acknowledges it as a quote from the apostles (cf. 1 Tim. 4:1; 2 Tim. 3:1).

Because of the silence of the New Testament and tradition concerning Jude's later years, we cannot know where this epistle was written. Nor is there any way to be certain of its date. Assuming the priority of Second Peter (A.D. 64–66), the probable range is A.D. 66–80. (Jude's silence concerning the destruction of Jerusalem does not prove that he wrote this letter before A.D. 70.)

THE CHRIST OF JUDE

In contrast to those who stand condemned by their licentiousness and denial of Christ (v. 4), the believer is "kept for Jesus Christ" (v. 1). Jude tells his readers to "keep yourselves in the love of God, waiting anxiously for the mercy of our Lord Jesus Christ to eternal life" (v. 21). But at the same time, the Lord "is able to keep you from stumbling and to make you stand in the presence of His glory blameless with great joy" (v. 24).

KEYS TO JUDE

Key Word: Contend for the Faith—
This epistle is intensely concerned with the threat of heretical teachers in the church and the believer's proper response to that threat. The contents reveal two major purposes: first, to condemn the practices of the ungodly libertines who were infesting the churches and corrupting the believers; and second, to counsel the readers to stand firm, grow in their faith, and contend for the truth. Jude says little about the actual doctrines of these "hidden reefs," but they may have held to an antinomian version of Gnosticism (see "The Time of First John"). The readers are encouraged to reach out to those who have been misled by these men.

Key Verse: Jude 3—"Beloved, while I was making every effort to write you about our common salvation, I felt the necessity to write to you appealing that you contend earnestly for the faith which was once for all delivered to the saints" (v. 3).

SURVEY OF JUDE

A surprisingly large number of the Pauline and non-Pauline epistles confront the problem of false teachers, and almost all of them allude to it. But Jude goes beyond all other New Testament epistles in its relentless and passionate denunciation of the apostate teachers who have "crept in unnoticed." With the exception of its salutation (vv. 1, 2) and doxology (vv. 24, 25), the entire epistle revolves around this alarming problem. Combining the theme of Second Peter with the style of James, Jude is potent in spite of its brevity. This urgent letter has four major sections: purpose of Jude (vv. 1–4); description of false teachers (vv. 5–16); defense against false teachers (vv. 17–23); and doxology of Jude (vv. 24,25).

Purpose of Jude (vv. 1–4): Jude addresses his letter to believers who are "called," "beloved," and "kept," and wishes for them the threefold blessing of mercy, peace, and love (vv. 1, 2). Grim news about the encroachment of false teachers in the churches has impelled Jude to put aside his commentary on salvation to write this timely word of rebuke and warning (vv. 3, 4). In view of apostates who turn the grace of our God into licentiousness and deny Christ, it is crucial that believers "contend earnestly for the faith."

Description of False Teachers (vv. 5–16): Jude begins his extended exposé of the apostate teachers by illustrating their ultimate doom with three examples of divine judgment from the Pentateuch (vv. 5–7).

Like unreasoning animals, these apostates are ruled by the things they revile, and they are destroyed by the things they practice (vv. 8–

FOCUS	PURPOSE	DESCRIPTION OF FALSE TEACHERS			DEFENSE AGAINST FALSE TEACHERS	DOXOLOGY
REFERENCE	1————5	————8	————14	——17	——24	——25
DIVISION	INTRODUCTION	PAST JUDGMENT	PRESENT CHARACTERISTICS	FUTURE JUDGMENT	DUTY OF BELIEVERS	CONCLUSION
TOPIC	REASON TO CONTEND				HOW TO CONTEND	
	ANATOMY OF APOSTASY				ANTIDOTE FOR APOSTASY	
LOCATION	UNKNOWN					
TIME	C. A.D. 66–80					

10). Even the archangel Michael is more careful in his dealings with superhuman powers than are these arrogant men. He compares these men to three spiritually rebellious men from Genesis (Cain) and Numbers (Balaam and Korah) who incurred the condemnation of God (v. 11). Verses 12 and 13 succinctly summarize their character with five highly descriptive metaphors taken from nature. After affirming the judgment of God upon such ungodly men with a quote from the noncanonical book of Enoch (vv. 14, 15), Jude catalogs some of their practices (v. 16).

Defense Against False Teachers (vv. 17–23): This letter has been exposing apostate teachers (vv. 8, 10, 12, 14, 16), but now Jude directly addresses his readers ("But you, beloved, ought to remember" v. 17). He reminds them of the apostolic warning that such men would come (vv. 17–19) and encourages them to protect themselves against the onslaught of apostasy (vv. 20, 21). The readers must become mature in their own faith so that they will be able to rescue those who are enticed or already ensnared by error (vv. 22, 23).

Doxology of Jude (vv. 24, 25): Jude closes with one of the greatest doxologies in the Bible. It emphasizes the power of Christ to keep those who trust in Him from being overthrown by error.

Purpose of Jude

JUDE,[T] a bond-servant of Jesus Christ, and brother of [A]James, to those who are the called, beloved in God the Father, and kept for Jesus Christ: Gr., *Judas • Jacob*
2 [R]May mercy and peace and love[R]be multiplied to you.   Gal. 6:16 • 1 Pet. 1:2; 2 Pet. 1:2
3 [R]Beloved, while I was making every effort to write you about our[R]common salvation, I felt the necessity to write to you appealing that you contend earnestly for the faith which was once for all delivered to the [A]saints.   Heb. 6:9 • Titus 1:4 • *holy ones*
4 For certain persons have crept in unnoticed, those who were long beforehand [A]marked out for this condemnation, ungodly persons who turn the grace of our God into licentiousness and deny our only Master and Lord, Jesus Christ.   *written about*

Past Judgment of False Teachers

5 Now I desire to [R]remind you, though [R]you know all things once for all, that [1]the Lord, after saving a people out of the land of Egypt, subsequently destroyed those who did not believe.   2 Pet. 1:12f. • 1 John 2:20
6 And angels who did not keep their own domain, but abandoned their proper abode, He has kept in eternal bonds under darkness for the judgment of the great day.
7 Just as[R]Sodom and Gomorrah and the cities around them, since they in the same way as these indulged in gross immorality and went after strange flesh, are exhibited as an example, in undergoing the punishment of eternal fire.   Gen. 19:24f.; 2 Pet. 2:6

Present Characteristics of False Teachers

8 Yet in the same manner these men, also by dreaming, defile the flesh, and reject authority, and revile angelic majesties.
9 But [R]Michael the archangel, when he disputed with the devil and argued about the body of Moses, did not dare pronounce against him a railing judgment, but said, "The Lord rebuke you."   Dan. 10:13, 21; 12:1
10 But[R]these men revile the things which they do not understand; and [R]the things which they know by instinct, like unreasoning animals, by these things they are [T]destroyed.   2 Pet. 2:12 • Phil. 3:19 • *corrupted*
11 Woe to them! For they have gone[R]the way of Cain, and for pay they have rushed headlong into the error of Balaam, and perished in the rebellion of Korah.   Gen. 4:3-8
12 These men are those who are[A]hidden reefs in your love feasts when they feast with you without fear, caring for themselves; clouds without water, carried along by winds; autumn trees without fruit,[T]doubly dead, uprooted;   *stains • twice*
13 [R]wild waves of the sea, casting up their own[A]shame like foam; wandering stars, for whom the black darkness has been reserved forever.   Is. 57:20 • *shameless deeds*

Future Judgment of False Teachers

14 And about these also[R]Enoch, *in* the seventh *generation* from Adam, prophesied, saying, "Behold, the Lord came with many thousands of His holy ones,   Zech. 14:5☆

---

[1] Some ancient mss. read *Jesus*

15 to execute judgment upon all, and to convict all the ungodly of all their ungodly deeds which they have done in an ungodly way, and of all the harsh things which ungodly sinners have spoken against Him."

16 These are grumblers, finding fault, following after their own lusts;ᵀthey speak arrogantly, flattering people for the sake of *gaining an* advantage.   *their mouth speaks*

Defense Against False Teachers

17 But you,ᴿbeloved, ought to remember the words that were spoken beforehand by the apostles of our Lord Jesus Christ, Jude 3

18 that they were saying to you, "Inᴿthe last time there shall be mockers, following after their own ungodly lusts."   Acts 20:29

19 These are the ones who cause divisions, worldly-minded, devoid of the Spirit.

20 But you,ᴿbeloved,ᴿbuilding yourselves up on your most holy faith; praying in the Holy Spirit;   Jude 3 • Col. 2:7; 1 Thess. 5:11

21 keep yourselves in the love of God, ᴿwaiting anxiously for the mercy of our Lord Jesus Christ to eternal life.   Titus 2:13

22 And have mercy on some, who are doubting;

23 save others,ᴿsnatching them out of the fire; and on some have mercy with fear, ᴿhating even the garment polluted by the flesh.   Amos 4:11 • [Zech. 3:3f.]; Rev. 3:4

Doxology of Jude

24 ᴿNow to Him who is able to keep you from stumbling, and toᴿmake you stand in the presence of His glory blameless with great joy,   Rom. 16:25 • [2 Cor. 4:14]

25 to the only God our Savior, through Jesus Christ our Lord, *be* glory, majesty, dominion and authority, before all time and now andᵀforever. Amen.   *to all the ages*

Measures of Length

Unit	Length	Equivalents	Translations
Day's journey	c. 20 miles		day's journey, day's walk
Roman mile	4,854 feet	8 stadia	mile
Sabbath day's journey	3,637 feet	6 stadia	a sabbath day's journey
Stadion	606 feet	⅛ Roman mile	mile, stadion
Rod	9 feet (10.5 feet in Ezekiel)	3 paces; 6 cubits	measuring rod
Fathom	6 feet	4 cubits	fathom
Pace	3 feet	⅓ rod; 2 cubits	pace
Cubit	18 inches	½ pace; 2 spans	cubit, yards
Span	9 inches	½ cubit; 3 handbreadths	span
Handbreadth	3 inches	⅓ span; 4 fingers	handbreadth
Finger	.75 inches	¼ handbreadth	finger

THE

REVELATION TO JOHN

(The Apocalypse)

THE BOOK OF REVELATION

Just as Genesis is the book of beginnings, Revelation is the book of consummation. In it, the divine program of redemption is brought to fruition, and the holy name of God is vindicated before all creation. Although there are numerous prophecies in the Gospels and Epistles, Revelation is the only New Testament book that focuses primarily on prophetic events. Its title means "unveiling" or "disclosure." Thus, the book is an unveiling of the character and program of God. Penned by John during his exile on the island of Patmos, Revelation centers around visions and symbols of the resurrected Christ, who alone has authority to judge the earth, to remake it, and to rule it in righteousness.

The title of this book in the Greek text is *Apokalypsis Ioannou*, "Revelation of John." It is also known as the Apocalypse, a transliteration of the word *apokalypsis*, meaning "unveiling," "disclosure," or "revelation." Thus, the book is an unveiling of that which otherwise could not be known. A better title comes from the first verse: *Apokalypsis Iesou Christou*, "Revelation of Jesus Christ." This could be taken as a revelation which came from Christ or as a revelation which is about Christ—both are appropriate. Because of the unified contents of this book, it should not be called Revelations.

THE AUTHOR OF REVELATION

The style, symmetry, and plan of Revelation show that it was written by one author, four times named "John" (1:1, 4, 9; 22:8; see "The Author of John"). Because of its contents and its address to seven churches, Revelation quickly circulated and became widely known and accepted in the early church. It was frequently mentioned and quoted by second- and third-century Christian writers and was received as part of the canon of New Testament books. From the beginning, Revelation was considered an authentic work of the apostle John, the same John who wrote the gospel and three epistles. This was held to be true by Justin Martyr, the Shepherd of Hermas, Melito, Irenaeus, the Muratorian Canon, Tertullian, Clement of Alexandria, Origen, and others.

This view was seldom questioned until the middle of the third century when Dionysius presented several arguments against the apostolic authorship of Revelation. He observed a clear difference in style and thought between Revelation and the books that he accepted as Johannine, and concluded that the Apocalypse must have been penned by a different John. Indeed, the internal evidence does pose some problems for the traditional view: (1) The Greek grammar of Revelation is not on par with the Fourth Gospel or the Johannine Epistles. (2) There are also differences in vocabulary and expressions used. (3) The theological content of this book differs from John's other writings in emphasis and presentation. (4) John's other writings avoid the use of his name, but it is found four times in this book. While these difficulties exist, two things should be kept in mind: (1) There are a number of remarkable similarities between the Apocalypse and the other books traditionally associated with the apostle John (e.g., the distinctive use of terms, such as "word," "lamb," and "true," and the careful development of conflicting themes, such as light and darkness, love and hatred, good and evil). (2) Many of the differences can be explained by the unusual circumstances surrounding this book. The apocalyptic subject matter demands a different treatment, and John received the contents not by reflection but by a series of startling and ecstatic visions. It is also possible that John used a secretary who smoothed out the Greek style of his other writings, and that his exile on Patmos prevented the use of such a scribe when he wrote Revelation.

Thus, the internal evidence, while problematic, need not overrule the early and strong external testimony to the apostolic origin of this important book. The author was obviously well-known to the recipients in the seven Asian churches, and this fits the unqualified use of the name John and the uniform tradition about his ministry in Asia. Alternate suggestions, such as John the Elder or a prophet named John, create more problems than they solve.

THE TIME OF REVELATION

John directed this prophetic word to seven selected churches in the Roman province of Asia (1:3, 4). The messages to these churches in chapters 2 and 3 begin with Ephesus, the most prominent, and continue in a

clockwise direction until Laodicea is reached. It is likely that this book was initially carried along this circular route. While each of these messages had particular significance for these churches, they were also relevant for the church as a whole ("He who has an ear, let him hear what the Spirit says to the churches").

John's effective testimony for Christ led the Roman authorities to exile him to the small, desolate island of Patmos in the Aegean Sea (1:9). This island of volcanic rock was one of several places to which the Romans banished criminals and political offenders.

Revelation was written at a time when Roman hostility to Christianity was erupting into overt persecution (1:9; 2:10, 13). Some scholars believe that it should be given an early date during the persecution of Christians under Nero after the A.D. 64 burning of Rome. The Hebrew letters for Nero Caesar (*Neron Kesar*) add up to 666, the number of the beast (13:18), and there was a legend that Nero would reappear in the East after his apparent death (cf. Rev. 13:3, 12, 14). This kind of evidence is weak, and a later date near the end of the reign of the emperor Domitian (A.D. 81–96) is preferable for several reasons: (1) This was the testimony of Irenaeus (disciple of Polycarp who was a disciple of John) and other early Christian writers. (2) John probably did not move from Jerusalem to Ephesus until about A.D. 67, shortly before the Roman destruction of Jerusalem in A.D. 70. The early dating would not give him enough time to have established an ongoing ministry in Asia by the time he wrote this book. (3) The churches of Asia appear to have been in existence for a number of years, long enough for some to reach a point of complacency and decline (cf. 2:4; 3:1, 15–18). (4) The deeds of Domitian are more relevant than those of Nero

to the themes of the Apocalypse. Worship of deceased emperors had been practiced for years, but Domitian was the first emperor to demand worship while he was alive. This led to a greater clash between the state and the church, especially in Asia, where the worship of Caesar was widely practiced. The persecution under Domitian presaged the more severe persecutions to follow.

Thus, it is likely that John wrote this book in A.D. 95 or 96. The date of his release from Patmos is unknown, but he was probably allowed to return to Ephesus after the reign of Domitian. Passages such as 1:11; 22:7, 9, 10, 18, 19 suggest that the book was completed before John's release.

✝ THE CHRIST OF REVELATION

Revelation has much to say about all three Persons of the Godhead, but it is especially clear in its presentation of the awesome resurrected Christ who has received all authority to judge the earth. He is called Jesus Christ (1:1), the faithful witness, the firstborn of the dead, the ruler of the kings of the earth (1:5), the first and the last (1:17), the living One (1:18), the Son of God (2:18), holy and true (3:7), the Amen, the faithful and true Witness, the Beginning of the creation of God (3:14), the Lion that is from the tribe of Judah, the Root of David (5:5), a Lamb (5:6), Faithful and True (19:11), The Word of God (19:13), KING OF KINGS, AND LORD OF LORDS (19:16), the Alpha and the Omega (22:13), the bright morning star (22:16), and the Lord Jesus (22:21).

This book is indeed "The Revelation of Jesus Christ" (1:1) since it comes from Him and centers on Him. It begins with a vision of His glory, wisdom, and power (1), and portrays His authority over the entire church (2; 3). He

FOCUS	"THINGS WHICH YOU HAVE SEEN"	"THINGS WHICH ARE"	"THINGS WHICH SHALL TAKE PLACE"				
REFERENCE	1:1————2:1————4:1————6:1————19:7————20:1————21:1—22:21						
DIVISION	THE LORD JESUS CHRIST	SEVEN CHURCHES	THE JUDGE	TRIBULATION	SECOND COMING	MILLENNIUM	ETERNAL STATE
TOPIC	VISION OF CHRIST		VISION OF CONSUMMATION				
	THEOPHANY	TALKS	TRIBULATIONS		TRUMPETS		TOGETHER
LOCATION	WRITTEN ON THE ISLAND OF PATMOS						
TIME	C. A.D. 95—96						

is the Lamb who was slain and declared worthy to open the book of judgment (5). His righteous wrath is poured out upon the whole earth (6—18), and He returns in power to judge His enemies and to reign as the Lord over all (19; 20). He will rule forever over the heavenly city in the presence of all who know Him (21; 22).

The Scriptures close with His great promise: "And behold, I am coming quickly" (22:7, 12). "Yes, I am coming quickly. Amen. Come, Lord Jesus" (22:20).

KEYS TO REVELATION

Key Word: The Revelation of the Coming of Christ—The purposes for which Revelation was written depend to some extent on how the book as a whole is interpreted. Because of its complex imagery and symbolism, Revelation is the most difficult biblical book to interpret, and there are four major alternatives: (1) The symbolic or idealist view maintains that Revelation is not a predictive prophecy, but a symbolic portrait of the cosmic conflict of spiritual principles. (2) The preterist view (the Latin word *praeter* means "past") maintains that it is a symbolic description of the Roman persecution of the church, emperor worship, and the divine judgment of Rome. (3) The historicist view approaches Revelation as an allegorical panorama of the history of the (western) church from the first century to the Second Advent. (4) The futurist view acknowledges the obvious influence that the first-century conflict between Roman power and the church had upon the themes of this book. It also accepts the bulk of Revelation (4—22) as an inspired look into the time immediately preceding the Second Advent (the "Tribulation," usually seen as seven years; 6—18), and extending from the return of Christ to the creation of the new cosmos (19—22).

Advocates of all four interpretive approaches to Revelation agree that it was written to assure the recipients of the ultimate triumph of Christ over all who rise up against Him and His saints. The readers were facing dark times of persecution, and even worse times would follow. Therefore they needed to be encouraged to persevere by standing firm in Christ in view of God's plan for the righteous and the wicked. This plan is especially clear in the stirring words of the epilogue (22:6–21). The book was also writen to challenge complacent Christians to stop compromising with the world. According to futurists, Revelation serves the additional purpose of providing a perspective on end-time events that would

have meaning and relevance to the spiritual lives of all succeeding generations of Christians.

Key Verses: Revelation 1:19 and 19:11–15— "Write therefore the things which you have seen, and the things which are, and the things which shall take place after these things" (1:19).

"And I saw heaven opened; and behold, a white horse, and He who sat upon it *is* called Faithful and True; and in righteousness He judges and wages war. And His eyes *are* a flame of fire, and upon His head *are* many diadems; and He has a name written *upon Him* which no one knows except Himself. And *He is* clothed with a robe dipped in blood; and His name is called The Word of God. And the armies which are in heaven, clothed in fine linen, white *and* clean, were following Him on white horses. And from His mouth comes a sharp sword, so that with it He may smite the nations; and He will rule them with a rod of iron; and He treads the wine press of the fierce wrath of God, the Almighty" (19:11–15).

Key Chapters: Revelation 19—22—When the end of history is fully understood, its impact radically affects the present. In Revelation 19—22 the plans of God for the last days and for all of eternity are recorded in explicit terms. Careful study of and obedience to them will bring the blessings that are promised (1:3). Uppermost in the mind and deep in the heart should be guarded the words of Jesus, "Behold, I am coming quickly."

SURVEY OF REVELATION

Revelation is written in the form of apocalyptic literature (cf. Daniel and Zechariah) by a prophet (10:11; 22:9) and refers to itself as a prophetic book (1:3; 22:7, 10, 18, 19). The three major movements in this profound unveiling are captured in 1:19: "the things which you have seen" (1); "the things which are" (2 and 3); and "the things which shall take place" (4—22).

"The Things Which You Have Seen" (1): Revelation contains a prologue (1:1–3) before the usual salutation (1:4–8). The Revelation was received by Christ from the Father and communicated by an angel to John. This is the only biblical book that specifically promises a blessing to those who read it (1:3), but it also promises a curse to those who add to or detract from it (22:18, 19). The salutation and closing benediction show that it was originally written as an epistle to seven Asian churches.

A rich theological portrait of the triune God (1:4–8) is followed by an overwhelming the-

ophany (visible manifestation of God) in 1:9–20. The omnipotent and omniscient Christ who will subjugate all things under His authority is the central figure in this book.

"The Things Which Are" (2 and 3): The messages to the seven churches (2 and 3) refer back to an aspect of John's vision of Christ and contain a command, a commendation and/or condemnation, a correction, and a challenge.

"The Things Which Shall Take Place" (4—22): John is translated into heaven where he is given a vision of the divine majesty. In it, the Father ("One sitting on the throne") and the Son (the Lion/Lamb) are worshiped by the twenty-four elders, the four living creatures, and the angelic host because of who they are and what they have done (creation and redemption; 4 and 5).

Three cycles of seven judgments in chapters 6—16 consist of seven seals, seven trumpets, and seven bowls. There is a prophetic insert between the sixth and seventh seal and trumpet judgments and an extended insert between the trumpet and bowl judgments. Because of the similarity of the seventh judgment in each series, it is possible that the three sets of judgments take place concurrently or with some overlap so that they all terminate with the return of Christ. An alternate approach views them as three consecutive series of judgments, so that the seventh seal is the seven trumpets and the seventh trumpet is the seven bowls.

The seven seals (6:1—8:5) include war, the famine and death that are associated with war, and persecution. The prophetic insert between the sixth and seventh seals (7) describes the protective sealing of 144,000 "sons of Israel," 12,000 from every tribe. It also looks ahead to the multitudes from every part of the earth "who come out of the great tribulation." The catastrophic events in most of the trumpet judgments are called "woes" (8:2—11:19). The prophetic interlude between the sixth and seventh trumpets (10:1—11:14) adds more details about the nature of the tribulation period and mentions a fourth set of seven judgments (the "seven peals of thunder") which would have extended it if they had not been withdrawn. Two unnamed witnesses minister during the last three-and-a-half years of the tribulation (forty-two months or 1,260 days). At the end of their ministry they are overcome by the beast, but their resurrection and ascension confounds their enemies.

Chapters 12—14 contain a number of miscellaneous prophecies that are inserted between the trumpet and bowl judgments to give further background on the time of tribulation. In chapter 12 a woman gives birth to a male child, who is caught up to God. The woman flees into the wilderness and is pursued by a dragon, who is cast down to earth. Chapter 13 gives a graphic description of the beast and his false prophet, both empowered by the dragon. The first beast is given political, economic, and religious authority; and because of his power and the lying miracles performed by the second beast, he is worshiped as the ruler of the earth. Chapter 14 contains a series of visions including the 144,000 at the end of the tribulation, the fate of those who follow the beast, and the outpouring of the wrath of God.

The seven bowl judgments of chapter 16 are prefaced by a heavenly vision of the power, holiness, and glory of God in chapter 15.

Chapters 17 and 18 anticipate the final downfall of Babylon, the great harlot sitting upon a scarlet-colored beast.

The marriage banquet of the Lamb is ready and the King of Kings, Lord of Lords leads the armies of heaven into battle against the beast and his false prophet. They are cast into a lake of fire (19).

In chapter 20 the dragon—Satan—is bound for a thousand years. He is cast into a bottomless pit. During this one thousand-year period Christ reigns over the earth with His resurrected saints, but by the end of this millennium, many have been born who refuse to submit their hearts to Christ. At the end of the thousand years, Satan is released and a final battle ensues. This is followed by the judgment at the great white throne.

A new universe is created, this time unspoiled by sin, death, pain, or sorrow. The new Jerusalem, described in 21:9—22:5, is shaped like a gigantic cube, 1,500 miles in length, width, and height (the most holy place in the Old Testament tabernacle and the temple was also a perfect cube). Its multicolored stones will reflect the glory of God, and it will continually be filled with light. But the greatest thing of all is that believers will be in the presence of God "and they shall see His face."

Revelation concludes with an epilogue (22:6–21), which reassures the readers that Christ is coming quickly (22:7, 12, 20) and invites all who wish to "take the water of life without cost" (22:17) to come to the Alpha and Omega, the Bright Morning Star.

OUTLINE OF REVELATION

CHAPTER 1

Introduction

THE Revelation of Jesus Christ, which God gave Him to show to His bond-servants, the things which must shortly take place; and He sent and^communicated *it* by His angel to His bond-servant John, *signified*

2 who bore witness to^Rthe word of God and to^Rthe testimony of Jesus Christ, *even to* all that he saw.   Rev. 1:9; 6:9 • 1 Cor. 1:6

3 ^RBlessed is he who reads and those who hear the words of the prophecy, and^heed the things which are written in it; for the time is near.   Luke 11:28; Rev. 22:7 • *keep*

4 ^RJohn to^Rthe seven churches that are in Asia: Grace to you and peace, from Him who is and who was and who is to come; and from the seven Spirits who are before His throne;   Rev. 1:1, 9; 22:8 • Rev. 1:11

5 and from Jesus Christ,^Rthe faithful witness, the first-born of the dead, and the^Rruler of the kings of the earth. To Him who loves us, and released us from our sins^by His blood,   Ps. 89:27★ • 1 Cor. 15:20; [Col. 1:18] • *in*

6 and He has made us *to be* a^Rkingdom, priests to^His God and Father; to Him *be* the glory and the dominion forever and ever. Amen.   Ex. 19:6; Is. 61:6 • *God and His Father*

7 ^RBEHOLD, HE IS COMING WITH THE

CLOUDS, and ^Revery eye will see Him, even those who pierced Him; and all the tribes of the earth will mourn over Him. Even so. Amen.   Dan. 7:13 • Zech. 12:10–14 ☆

8 "I am ^Rthe Alpha and the Omega," says the Lord God, "who is and who was and who is to come, the Almighty."   Is. 41:4

Revelation of Christ

9 ^RI, John, your brother and fellow partaker in the tribulation and kingdom and perseverance *which are* in Jesus, was on the island called Patmos, because of the word of God and the testimony of Jesus.   Rev. 1:1

10 I was ¹in ^Rthe Spirit on ^Rthe Lord's day, and I heard behind me a loud voice like *the sound* of a trumpet,   Rev. 4:2 • Acts 20:7

11 saying, "Write ^Rin a ^Abook what you see, and send *it* to the seven churches: to Ephesus and to Smyrna and to Pergamum and to Thyatira and to Sardis and to Philadelphia and to Laodicea."   Rev. 1:2, 19 • *scroll*

12 And I turned to see the voice that was speaking with me. And having turned I saw ^Rseven golden lampstands;   Zech. 4:2; Rev. 1:20

13 and ^Rin the middle of the lampstands one like ²a son of man, clothed in a robe reaching to the feet, and girded across His breast with a golden girdle.   Rev. 2:1

14 And His head and His ^Rhair were white like white wool, like snow; and His eyes were like a flame of fire;   Dan. 7:9

15 and His ^Rfeet *were* like burnished bronze, when it has been caused to glow in a furnace, and His ^Rvoice *was* like the sound of many waters.   Ezek. 1:7 • Ezek. 1:24; 43:2

16 And in His right hand He held seven stars; and ^Rout of His mouth came a sharp two-edged sword; and His face was like the sun shining in its strength.   Is. 49:2 ☆

17 And when I saw Him, I ^Rfell at His feet as a dead man. And He ^Rlaid His right hand upon me, saying, "Do not be afraid; I am the first and the last,   Dan. 8:17 • Dan. 8:18

18 and the living One; and I ^rwas dead, and behold, I am alive forevermore, and I have the keys of death and of Hades.   *became*

19 "Write ^Rtherefore ^Rthe things which you have seen, and the things which are, and the things which shall take place ^Rafter these things.   Rev. 1:11 • Rev. 1:12-16 • Rev. 4:1

20 "As for the ^Rmystery of the ^Rseven stars which you saw in My right hand, and the seven golden lampstands: the seven stars are the angels of the seven churches, and the seven lampstands are the seven churches.   Rom. 11:25 • Rev. 1:16; 2:1; 3:1

CHAPTER 2

Message to Ephesus

"TO the angel of the church in ^REphesus write: Rev. 1:11

The One who holds the seven stars in His right hand, the One who walks among the seven golden lampstands, says this:

2 'I ^Rknow your deeds and your toil and perseverance, and that you cannot endure evil men, and you put to the test those who call themselves apostles, and they are not, and you found them *to be* false;   Rev. 2:19

3 and you have perseverance and have endured ^Rfor My name's sake, and have not grown weary.   John 15:21

4 'But I have *this* against you, that you have ^Rleft your first love.   Jer. 2:2; Matt. 24:12

5 'Remember therefore from where you have fallen, and repent and do the ʳdeeds you did at first; or else I am coming to you, and will remove your lampstand out of its place—unless you repent.   *first deeds*

6 'Yet this you do have, that you hate the deeds of the Nicolaitans, which I also hate.

7 'He who has an ear, let him hear what the Spirit says to the churches. To him who overcomes, I will grant to eat of the tree of life, which is in the Paradise of God.'

Message to Smyrna

8 "And to the angel of the church in ^RSmyrna write:

The first and the last, who ^rwas dead, and has come to life, says this: Rev. 1:11 • *became*

9 'I know your ^Rtribulation and your poverty (but you are rich), and the blasphemy by those who say they are Jews and are not, but are a synagogue of Satan.   Rev. 1:9

10 'Do not fear what you are about to suffer. Behold, the devil is about to cast some of you into prison, that you may be ^Rtested, and you will have tribulation ^Rten days. Be faithful until death, and I will give you the crown of life.   Rev. 3:10 • Dan. 1:12, 14

11 'He ^Rwho has an ear, let him hear what the Spirit says to the churches. ^RHe who overcomes shall not be hurt by the ^Rsecond death.'   Matt. 11:15 • Rev. 2:7 • Rev. 20:6

Message to Pergamum

12 "And to the angel of the church in ^RPergamum write:

The One who has ^Rthe sharp two-edged sword says this: Rev. 1:11 • Is. 49:2 ☆

13 'I know where you dwell, where Satan's throne is; and you hold fast My name, and did not deny My faith, even in the days of Antipas, My witness, My faithful one, who was killed among you, where Satan dwells.

14 'But ^RI have a few things against you, because you have there some who hold the teaching of Balaam, who kept teaching Balak to put a stumbling block before the sons of Israel, to eat things sacrificed to idols, and to commit *acts of* immorality.   Rev. 2:20

¹ Or, *in spirit*   ² Or, *the Son of Man*

15 'Thus you also have some who in the same way hold the teaching of the[R]Nicolaitans.   Rev. 2:6

16 'Repent[R]therefore; or else I am coming to you quickly, and I will make war against them with the sword of My mouth.   Rev. 2:5

17 'He who has an ear, let him hear what the Spirit says to the churches. To him who overcomes, to him I will give *some* of the hidden manna, and I will give him a white stone, and a new name written on the stone which no one knows but he who receives it.'

Message to Thyatira

18 "And to the angel of the church in[R]Thyatira write:

The Son of God, who[T]has eyes like a flame of fire, and His feet are like burnished bronze, says this: Rev. 1:11; 2:24 • *His eyes*

19 'I know your deeds, and your love and faith and service and perseverance, and that your deeds of late are greater than at first.

20 'But[R]I have *this* against you, that you tolerate the woman [R]Jezebel, who calls herself a prophetess, and she teaches and leads My bond-servants astray, so that they commit *acts of* immorality and eat things sacrificed to idols.   Rev. 2:14 • 1 Kin. 16:31

21 'And I gave her time to repent; and she does not want to repent of her immorality.

22 'Behold,[T]I will cast her[T]upon a bed *of sickness,* and those who commit adultery with her into great tribulation, unless they repent of [3]her deeds.   *I cast* • *into*

23 'And I will kill her children with[A]pestilence; and all the churches will know that I am He who searches the[T]minds and hearts; and I will give to each one of you according to your deeds.   *death* • *kidneys,* i.e., inner man

24 'But I say to you, the rest who are in [R]Thyatira, who do not hold this teaching, who have not known the[R]deep things of Satan, as they call them—I place no other burden on you.   Rev. 2:18 • 1 Cor. 2:10

25 'Nevertheless[R]what you have, hold fast [R]until I come.   Rev. 3:11 • John 21:22

26 'And he who overcomes, and he who keeps My deeds until the end, TO HIM I WILL GIVE AUTHORITY OVER THE[A]NATIONS;   *Gentiles*

27 [R]AND HE SHALL RULE THEM WITH A ROD OF IRON, AS THE VESSELS OF THE POTTER ARE BROKEN TO PIECES, as I also have received *authority* from My Father;   Ps. 2:8, 9 ☆

28 and I will give him the morning star.

29 'He[R]who has an ear, let him hear what the Spirit says to the churches.'   Rev. 2:7

CHAPTER 3

Message to Sardis

"AND to the angel of the church in[R]Sardis write: Rev. 1:11

He who has the seven Spirits of God, and the seven stars, says this: 'I know your

---

3 Some mss. read *their*
4 Or, *deeds (behold . . . shut), that you*
5 I.e., origin or source

deeds, that you have a name that you are alive, but you are dead.

2 'Wake up, and strengthen the things that remain, which were about to die; for I have not found your deeds completed in the sight of My God.

3 'Remember[R]therefore[T]what you have received and heard; and keep *it,* and repent. If therefore you will not wake up, I will come like a thief, and you will not know at what hour I will come upon you.   Rev. 2:5 • *how*

4 'But you have a few[T]people[R]in [R]Sardis who have not soiled their garments; and they will walk with Me in white; for they are worthy.   *names* • Rev. 11:13 • Rev. 1:11

5 'He[R] who overcomes shall thus be clothed in[R]white garments; and I will not erase his name from the book of life, and I will confess his name before My Father, and before His angels.   Rev. 2:7 • Rev. 3:4

6 'He[R]who has an ear, let him hear what the Spirit says to the churches.'   Rev. 2:7

Message to Philadelphia

7 "And to the angel of the church in[R]Philadelphia write:

[R]He who is holy,[R]who is true, who has the key of David, who opens and no one will shut, and who shuts and no one opens, says this: Rev. 1:11 • Rev. 6:10 • 1 John 5:20

8 'I know your [4]deeds. Behold, I have put before you an open door which no one can shut, because you have a little power, and have kept My word, and have not denied My name.

9 'Behold, I[T]will cause *those* of the synagogue of Satan, who say that they are Jews, and are not, but lie—behold, I will make them to come and bow down at your feet, and to know that I have loved you.   *give*

10 'Because you have kept the word of My [A]perseverance, I also will keep you from the hour of testing, that *hour* which is about to come upon the whole world, to test those who dwell upon the earth.   *steadfastness*

11 'I[T]am coming quickly;[R]hold fast what you have, in order that no one take your [R]crown.   Rev. 1:3 • Rev. 2:25 • [Rev. 2:10]

12 'He[R]who overcomes, I will make him a pillar in the temple of My God, and he will not go out from it anymore; and I will write upon him the name of My God, and the name of the city of My God, the new Jerusalem, which comes down out of heaven from My God, and My new name.   Rev. 3:5

13 'He[R]who has an ear, let him hear what the Spirit says to the churches.'   Rev. 3:6

Message to Laodicea

14 "And to the angel of the church in[R]Laodicea write:

The Amen, the faithful and true Witness, the [5]Beginning of the creation of God, says this: Rev. 1:11

15 'I^Rknow your deeds, that you are neither cold nor hot;^RI would that you were cold or hot.   Rev. 3:1 • Rom. 12:11

16 'So because you are lukewarm, and neither hot nor cold, I will^Tspit you out of My mouth.   *vomit*

17 'Because you say, "I^Ram rich, and have become wealthy, and have need of nothing," and you do not know that you are wretched and miserable and poor and blind and naked,   Hos. 12:8; Zech. 11:5; [Matt. 5:3]

18 I advise you to^Rbuy from Me gold refined by fire, that you may become rich, and white garments, that you may clothe yourself, and *that* the shame of your nakedness may not be revealed; and eye salve to anoint your eyes, that you may see.   Matt. 13:44

19 'Those whom I love, I reprove and discipline; be zealous therefore, and repent.

20 'Behold, I stand^Rat the door and knock; if anyone hears My voice and opens the door, I will come in to him, and will dine with him, and he with Me.   James 5:9

21 'He^Rwho overcomes, I will grant to him ^Rto sit down with Me on My throne, as I also overcame and sat down with My Father on His throne.   Rev. 2:7 • Matt. 19:28 ☆

22 'He^Rwho has an ear, let him hear what the Spirit says to the churches.' "   Rev. 2:7

CHAPTER 4

The Throne of God

AFTER these things I looked, and behold, ^Ra door *standing* open in heaven, and the first voice which I had heard, like *the sound* of a trumpet speaking with me,^Tsaid, "Come up here, and I will show you what must take place after these things."   Ezek. 1:1 • *saying*

2 Immediately I was ⁶in the Spirit; and behold, a throne was standing in heaven, and One sitting on the throne.

3 And He who was sitting *was* like a jasper stone and a sardius in appearance; and *there was* a^Rrainbow around the throne, like an emerald in appearance.   *halo*

4 And ^Raround the throne *were*^Rtwenty-four thrones; and upon the thrones *I saw* ^Rtwenty-four elders sitting, clothed in white garments, and golden crowns on their heads.   Rev. 4:6 • Rev. 11:16 • Rev. 4:10

5 And from the throne proceed^Rflashes of lightning and sounds and peals of thunder. And *there were*^Rseven lamps of fire burning before the throne, which are^Rthe seven Spirits of God;   Ex. 19:16 • Ex. 25:37 • [Rev. 1:4]

6 and before the throne *there was*, as it were, a sea of glass like crystal; and in the center and around the throne, four living creatures full of eyes in front and behind.

7 ^RAnd the first creature *was* like a lion, and the second creature like a calf, and the third creature had a face like that of a man, and the fourth creature *was* like a flying eagle.   Ezek. 1:10; 10:14

8 And the^Rfour living creatures, each one of them having^Rsix wings, are full of eyes around and within; and day and night they do not cease to say,   Ezek. 1:5 • Is. 6:2

"HOLY, HOLY, HOLY, *is* THE LORD GOD, THE ALMIGHTY, who was and who is and who is to come."

9 And when the living creatures give glory and honor and thanks to Him who^Rsits on the throne, to^RHim who lives forever and ever,   Ps. 47:8; Is. 6:1 • Deut. 32:40; Dan. 4:34

10 the^Rtwenty-four elders will ^Rfall down before Him who^Rsits on the throne, and will worship Him who lives forever and ever, and will cast their crowns before the throne, saying,   Rev. 4:4 • Rev. 5:8 • Ps. 47:8

11 "Worthy art Thou, our Lord and our God, to receive glory and honor and power; for Thou didst create all things, and because of Thy will they ^Texisted, and were created."   *were*

CHAPTER 5

The Sealed Book

AND I saw in the right hand of Him who sat on the throne a book written inside and on the back, sealed up with seven seals.

2 And I saw a strong angel proclaiming with a loud voice, "Who is worthy to open the^book and to break its seals?"   *scroll*

3 And no one in heaven, or on the earth, or under the earth, was able to open the ^book, or to look into it.   *scroll*

4 And I *began* to weep greatly, because no one was found worthy to open the^book, or to look into it;   *scroll*

5 and one of the elders *said to me, "Stop weeping; behold, the^RLion that is from the tribe of Judah, the Root of David, has overcome so as to open the^book and its seven seals."   Gen. 49:9, 10 ★ • *scroll*

6 And I saw ⁷between the throne (with the four living creatures) and the elders a Lamb standing, as if slain, having seven horns and seven eyes, which are the seven Spirits of God, sent out into all the earth.

7 And He came, and He took *it* out of the right hand of Him who sat on the throne.

8 And when He had taken the book, the four living creatures and the twenty-four elders fell down before the Lamb, having each one a harp, and golden bowls full of incense, which are the prayers of the^saints. *holy ones*

9 And they *sang a new song, saying,

"Worthy art Thou to take the^book, and to break its seals; for Thou wast slain, and didst purchase for God with Thy blood *men* from every tribe and tongue and people and nation.   *scroll*

⁶ Or, *in spirit*
⁷ Lit., *in the middle of the throne and of the four living creatures, and in the middle of the elders*

10 "And Thou hast made them *to be* a kingdom and priests to our God; and they will reign upon the earth."

11 And I looked, and I heard the voice of many angels[R]around the throne and the living creatures and the elders; and the number of them was myriads of myriads, and thousands of thousands,   Rev. 4:4

12 saying with a loud voice,
"Worthy[R]is the[R]Lamb that was slain to receive power and riches and wisdom and might and honor and glory and blessing."   Rev. 1:6 • Is. 53:7★

13 And [R]every created thing which is in heaven and on the earth and under the earth and on the sea, and all things in them, I heard saying,   Phil. 2:10
"To Him who[R]sits on the throne, and to the[R]Lamb, *be* blessing and honor and glory and dominion forever and ever."   Rev. 5:1 • John 1:29

14 And the[R]four living creatures kept saying,[R]"Amen." And the elders fell down and worshiped.   Rev. 4:6 • 1 Cor. 14:16

CHAPTER 6

First Seal

AND I saw when the[R]Lamb broke one of the seven seals, and I heard one of the four living creatures saying as with a voice of thunder, "Come."   [John 1:29; Rev. 5:6, 12f.]

2 And I looked, and behold, a [R]white horse, and he who sat on it had a bow; and a crown was given to him; and he went out conquering, and to conquer.   Zech. 1:8; 6:3f.

Second Seal

3 And when He broke the second seal, I heard the [R]second living creature saying, "Come."[A]   Rev. 4:7 • Some mss. add *and see*

4 And another,[R]a red horse, went out; and to him who sat on it, it was granted to [R]take peace from the earth, and that *men* should slay one another; and a great sword was given to him.   Zech. 1:8 • Matt. 10:34

Third Seal

5 And when He broke the third seal, I heard the [R]third living creature saying, "Come." And I looked, and behold, a[R]black horse; and he who sat on it had a pair of scales in his hand.   Rev. 4:7 • Zech. 6:2

6 And I heard as it were a voice in the center of the[R]four living creatures saying, "A [8]quart of wheat for a [9]denarius, and three quarts of barley for a denarius; and do not harm the oil and the wine."   Rev. 4:6f.

[8] Gr., *choenix*; i.e., a dry measure almost equal to a quart
[9] The denarius was equivalent to one day's wage
[10] I.e., chiliarchs, in command of one thousand troops

Fourth Seal

7 And when He broke the fourth seal, I heard the voice of the fourth living creature saying, "Come."[A]   Some mss. add *and see*

8 And I looked, and behold, an [A]ashen horse; and he who sat on it had the name Death; and Hades was following with him. And authority was given to them over a fourth of the earth, to kill with sword and with famine and with[A]pestilence and by the wild beasts of the earth.   *sickly pale • death*

Fifth Seal

9 And when He broke the fifth seal, I saw [R]underneath the[R]altar the souls of those who had been slain because of the word of God, and because of the testimony which they had maintained;   Ex. 29:12 • Rev. 14:18

10 and they cried out with a loud voice, saying, "How[R]long, O[A]Lord, holy and true, wilt Thou refrain from judging and avenging our blood on those who dwell on the earth?"   Zech. 1:12 • *Master*

11 And[R]there was given to each of them a white robe; and they were told that they should rest for a little while longer, until *the number of* their fellow servants and their brethren who were to be killed even as they had been, should be completed also.   Rev. 3:4

Sixth Seal

12 And I looked when He broke the sixth seal, and there was a great[R]earthquake; and the[R]sun became black as[R]sackcloth *made* of hair, and the whole moon became like blood;   Matt. 24:7 • Is. 13:10 • Is. 50:3

13 and [R]the stars of the sky fell to the earth, as a fig tree casts its unripe figs when shaken by a great wind. Matt. 24:29; Mark 13:25

14 And the sky was split apart like a scroll when it is rolled up; and every mountain and island were moved out of their places.

15 And [R]the kings of the earth and the great men and the [10]commanders and the rich and the strong and every slave and free man, hid themselves in the caves and among the rocks of the mountains;   Is. 2:10f.

16 and they *said to the mountains and to the rocks, "Fall on us and hide us from the [T]presence of Him who sits on the throne, and from the wrath of the Lamb;   *face*

17 for [R]the great day of their wrath has come; and who is able to stand?"   Jer. 30:7

CHAPTER 7

144,000 Jews

AFTER this I saw[R]four angels standing at the[R]four corners of the earth, holding back [R]the four winds of the earth, so that no wind should blow on the earth or on the sea or on any tree.   Rev. 9:14 • Is. 11:12 • Dan. 7:2

2 And I saw another angel ascending

from the rising of the sun, having the seal of the living God; and he cried out with a loud voice to the four angels to whom it was granted to harm the earth and the sea,

3 saying, "Do[R]not harm the earth or the sea or the trees, until we have [R]sealed the bond-servants of our God on their [R]fore-heads."   Rev. 6:6 • John 3:33 • Ezek. 9:4

4 And I heard the[R]number of those who were sealed, [R]one hundred and forty-four thousand sealed from every tribe of the sons of Israel: Rev. 9:16 • Rev. 14:1, 3

5 from the tribe of Judah, twelve thousand *were* sealed, from the tribe of Reuben twelve thousand, from the tribe of Gad twelve thousand,

6 from the tribe of Asher twelve thousand, from the tribe of Naphtali twelve thousand, from the tribe of Manasseh twelve thousand,

7 from the tribe of Simeon twelve thousand, from the tribe of Levi twelve thousand, from the tribe of Issachar twelve thousand,

8 from the tribe of Zebulun twelve thousand, from the tribe of Joseph twelve thousand, from the tribe of Benjamin, twelve thousand *were* sealed.

Great Multitude of Gentiles

9 After these things I looked, and behold, a great multitude, which no one could count, from[R]every nation and *all* tribes and peoples and tongues, standing [R]before the throne and before the Lamb, clothed in white robes, and palm branches *were* in their hands;   Rev. 5:9 • Rev. 7:15

10 and they cry out with a loud voice, saying,

"Salvation[R] to our God who sits on the throne, and to the Lamb."   Ps. 3:8; Rev. 12:10

11 And all the angels were standing [R]around the throne and *around* the elders and the[R]four living creatures; and they fell on their faces before the throne and worshiped God,   Rev. 4:4 • Rev. 4:6

12 saying,

"Amen[R] blessing[R] and glory and wisdom and thanksgiving and honor and power and might, *be* to our God forever and ever. Amen."   Rev. 5:14 • Rev. 5:12

13 And one of the elders[R]answered, saying to me, "These who are clothed in the[R]white robes, who are they, and from where have they come?"   Acts 3:12 • Rev. 7:9

14 And I said to him, "My lord, you know." And he said to me, "These are the ones who come out of the great tribulation, and they have washed their robes and made them white in the blood of the Lamb.

15 "For this reason, they are [R]before the throne of God; and they[R]serve Him day and night in His[t]temple; and He who sits on the throne shall spread His tabernacle over them.   Rev. 7:9 • Rev. 4:8f. • *sanctuary*

16 "They [R]shall hunger no more, neither

thirst anymore; neither shall the sun[T]beat down on them, nor any heat;   Is. 49:10 ☆ • *fall*

17 for the Lamb in the center of the throne [R]shall be their shepherd, and shall guide them to springs of the water[R]of life; and God shall wipe every tear from their eyes."   Ps. 23:1f.; [John 10:11, 14] ☆ • [John 4:14]

CHAPTER 8

Seventh Seal

AND when He broke the [R]seventh seal, there was silence in heaven for about half an hour.   Rev. 5:1; 6:1, 3, 5, 7, 9, 12

2 And I saw[R]the seven angels who stand before God; and seven[R]trumpets were given to them.   Rev. 1:4 • 1 Cor. 15:52; 1 Thess. 4:16

3 And another angel came and stood at the altar, holding a golden censer; and much incense was given to him, that he might add it to the prayers of all the saints upon the golden altar which was before the throne.

4 And[R]the smoke of the incense,[a]with the prayers of the saints, went up before God out of the angel's hand.   Ps. 141:2 • *for*

5 And the angel took the censer; and he [R]filled it with the fire of the altar and[R]threw it to the earth; and there followed peals of thunder and sounds and flashes of lightning and an earthquake.   Lev. 16:12 • Ezek. 10:2

First Trumpet

6 [R]And the seven angels who had the seven trumpets prepared themselves to sound them.   Rev. 8:2

7 And the first sounded, and there came [R]hail and fire, mixed with blood, and they were thrown to the earth; and[R]a third of the earth was burned up, and a third of the trees were burned up, and all the green grass was burned up.   Ex. 9:23ff. • Zech. 13:8, 9; Rev. 8:7-12

Second Trumpet

8 And the second angel sounded, and *something* like a great [R]mountain burning with fire was thrown into the sea; and a third of the sea became blood;   Jer. 51:25

9 and [R]a third of the creatures, which were in the sea and had life, died; and a third of the ships were destroyed.   Zech. 13:8

Third Trumpet

10 And the third angel sounded, and a great star[R]fell from heaven, burning like a torch, and it fell on a third of the rivers and on the springs of waters;   Is. 14:12; Rev. 6:13

11 and the name of the star is called Wormwood; and a third of the waters became wormwood; and many men died from the waters, because they were made bitter.

Fourth Trumpet

12 And the fourth angel sounded, and a [R]third of the sun and a third of the moon and a third of the stars were smitten, so that a

third of them might be darkened and the day might not shine for a third of it, and the night in the same way. Zech. 13:8, 9; Rev. 8:7-12

13 And I looked, and I heard [T]an eagle flying in midheaven, saying with a loud voice, "Woe, woe, woe, to those who dwell on the earth, because of the remaining blasts of the trumpet of the three angels who are about to sound!"   *one eagle*

CHAPTER 9

Fifth Trumpet

AND the[R]fifth angel sounded, and I saw a star from heaven which had fallen to the earth; and the key of the[T]bottomless pit was given to him.   Rev. 8:2 • *shaft of the abyss*

2 And he opened the bottomless pit; and smoke went up out of the pit, like the smoke of a great furnace; and the sun and the air were darkened by the smoke of the pit.

3 And out of the smoke came forth[R]locusts[T]upon the earth; and power was given them, as the [R]scorpions of the earth have power.   Rev. 9:7 • *into* • Ezek. 2:6

4 And they were told that they should not [R]hurt the [R]grass of the earth, nor any green thing, nor any tree, but only the men who do not have the seal of God on their foreheads.   Rev. 6:6 • Rev. 8:7

5 And [T]they were not permitted to kill anyone, but to torment for five months; and their torment was like the torment of a scorpion when it stings a man. *it was given to them*

6 And in those days[R]men will seek death and will not find it; and they will long to die and death flees from them.   Job 3:21; 7:15

7 And the[T]appearance of the locusts was like horses prepared for battle; and on their heads, as it were, crowns like gold, and their faces were like the faces of men. *appearances*

8 And they had hair like the hair of women, and their[R]teeth were like *the teeth* of lions.   Joel 1:6

9 And they had breastplates like breastplates of iron; and the[R]sound of their wings was like the sound of chariots, of many horses rushing to battle. Jer. 47:3; Joel 2:5

10 And they have tails like[R]scorpions, and stings; and in their tails is their power to hurt men for five months.   2 Chr. 10:11, 14

11 They have as king over them, the angel of the[R]abyss; his name in[R]Hebrew is [11]Abaddon, and in the Greek he has the name[T]Apollyon.   Luke 8:31 • John 5:2 • *destroyer*

12 [R]The first woe is past; behold, two woes are still coming after these things.   Rev. 8:13

Sixth Trumpet

13 And the sixth angel sounded, and I heard[T]a voice from the [12]four horns of the golden altar which is before God,   *one voice*

14 one saying to the sixth angel who had

the trumpet, "Release the four angels who are bound at the great river Euphrates."

15 And the four angels, who had been prepared for the hour and day and month and year, were[R]released, so that they might kill a third of[T]mankind.   Rev. 20:7 • *men*

16 And the number of the armies of the horsemen was[R]two hundred million;[R]I heard the number of them.   Rev. 5:11 • Rev. 7:4

17 And[T]this is how I saw in the vision the horses and those who sat on them: *the riders* had breastplates *the color* of fire and of hyacinth and of[A]brimstone; and the heads of the horses are like the heads of lions; and out of their mouths proceed fire and smoke and brimstone.   *thus I saw* • *sulphur*

18 A[R]third of[T]mankind was killed by these three plagues, by the fire and the smoke and the[A]brimstone, which proceeded out of their mouths.   Rev. 8:7 • *men* • *sulphur*

19 For the power of the horses is in their mouths and in their tails; for their tails are like serpents and have heads; and with them they do harm.

20 And the rest of mankind, who were not killed by these plagues, did not repent of the works of their hands, so as not to worship demons, and the idols of gold and of silver and of brass and of stone and of wood, which can neither see nor hear nor walk;

21 and they[R]did not repent of their murders nor of their sorceries nor of their immorality nor of their thefts.   Rev. 9:20

CHAPTER 10

Little Book

AND I saw another[R]strong angel[R]coming down out of heaven, clothed with a cloud; and the rainbow was upon his head, and his face was like the sun, and his feet like pillars of fire;   Rev. 5:2 • Rev. 18:1; 20:1

2 and he had in his hand a little book which was open. And he placed his right foot on the sea and his left on the land;

3 and he cried out with a loud voice,[R]as when a lion roars; and when he had cried out, the[R]seven peals of thunder[R]uttered their voices.   Is. 31:4 • Ps. 29:3-9 • *spoke*

4 And when the seven peals of thunder had spoken, I was about to write; and I heard a voice from heaven saying, "Seal up the things which the seven peals of thunder have spoken, and do not write them."

5 And the angel whom I saw standing on the sea and on the land[R]lifted up his right hand to heaven,   Deut. 32:40; Dan. 12:7

6 and swore by Him who lives forever and ever, WHO CREATED HEAVEN AND THE THINGS IN IT, AND THE EARTH AND THE THINGS IN IT, AND THE SEA AND THE THINGS IN IT, that there shall be delay no longer,

7 but in the days of the voice of the seventh angel, when he is about to sound, then the mystery of God is finished, as He preached to His servants the prophets.

[11] I.e., destruction
[12] Some ancient mss. do not contain *four*

8 And [R]the voice which I heard from heaven, *I heard* again speaking with me, and saying, "Go, take the^book which is open in the hand of the angel who stands on the sea and on the land."   Rev. 10:4 · *scroll*

9 And I went to the angel, telling him to give me the little book. And he *said to me, "Take[R] it, and eat it; and it will make your stomach bitter, but in your mouth it will be sweet as honey."   Jer. 15:16; Ezek. 2:8; 3:1-3

10 And I took the little book out of the angel's hand and ate it, and it was in my mouth sweet as honey; and when I had eaten it, my stomach was made bitter.

11 And they *said to me, "You must prophesy again concerning[R] many peoples and nations and tongues and kings." Rev. 5:9

CHAPTER 11

Two Witnesses

AND there was given me a[T]measuring rod like a staff;[T]and someone said, "Rise and measure the temple of God, and the altar, and those who worship in it.   *reed · saying*

2"And[T]leave out the [R]court which is outside the'temple, and do not measure it, for it has been given to the nations; and they will tread under foot the holy city for forty-two months.   *throw out · Ezek. 40:17 · sanctuary*

3"And I will grant *authority* to my two [R]witnesses, and they will prophesy for'twelve hundred and sixty days, clothed in sackcloth."   Rev. 1:5; 2:13 · Dan. 7:25

4 These are the [R]two olive trees and the two lampstands that stand before the Lord of the earth.   Ps. 52:8; Jer. 11:16; Zech. 4:3, 11, 14

5 And if anyone desires to harm them, [R]fire proceeds out of their mouth and devours their enemies; and if anyone would desire to harm them,[R]in this manner he must be killed.   2 Kin. 1:10-12 · Num. 16:29, 35

6 These have the power to[R]shut up the sky, in order that rain may not fall during the days of their prophesying; and they have power over the waters to turn them into blood, and to smite the earth with every plague, as often as they desire.   Luke 4:25

7 And when they have finished their testimony,[R]the beast that comes up out of the abyss will make war with them, and overcome them and kill them.   Rev. 13:1ff.; 17:8

8 And their dead [13]bodies *will lie in* the street of the[R]great city which [14]mystically is called [R]Sodom and Egypt, where also their Lord was crucified.   Rev. 14:8 · Is. 1:9, 10

9 And those from[R]the peoples and tribes and tongues and nations *will* look at their dead [13]bodies for three and a half days, and [T]will not permit their dead bodies to be laid in a tomb.   Rev. 5:9; 10:11 · *do not permit*

10 And[R]those who dwell on the earth *will* rejoice over them and make merry; and they will[R]send gifts to one another, because these two prophets tormented those who dwell on the earth.   Rev. 3:10 · Neh. 8:10, 12

11 And after the three and a half days the breath of life from God came into them, and they stood on their feet; and great fear fell upon those who were beholding them.

12 And they heard a loud voice from heaven saying to them, "Come[R] up here." And they went up into heaven in the cloud, and their enemies beheld them.   Rev. 4:1

13 And in that hour there was a great [R]earthquake, and a tenth of the city fell; and seven thousand people were killed in the earthquake, and the rest were terrified and gave glory to the God of heaven.   Rev. 6:12

14 The second[R] woe is past; behold, the third woe is coming quickly.   Rev. 8:13; 9:12

Seventh Trumpet

15 And the seventh angel sounded; and there arose loud voices in heaven, [R]saying, "The kingdom of the world has become *the kingdom* of our Lord, and of His [15]Christ; and He will reign forever and ever." Ps. 89:27

16 And the twenty-four elders, who[R]sit on their thrones before God, fell on their faces and worshiped God,   Matt. 19:28; Rev. 4:4

17 saying, "We give Thee thanks,[R]O Lord God, the Almighty, who art and who wast, because Thou hast taken Thy great power and[T]hast begun to reign.   Rev. 1:8 · *didst reign*

18"And the nations were enraged, and Thy wrath came, and the time *came* for the dead to be judged, and *the time* to give their reward to Thy bond-servants the prophets and to the ^saints and to those who fear Thy name, the small and the great, and to destroy those who destroy the earth." *holy ones*

19 And the ^temple of God which is in heaven was opened; and the ark of His covenant appeared in His temple, and there were flashes of lightning and sounds and peals of thunder and an earthquake and a great[T]hailstorm.   *sanctuary · hail*

CHAPTER 12

The Woman

AND a great[R]sign appeared[R]in heaven: a woman clothed with the sun, and the moon under her feet, and on her head a crown of twelve stars;   Matt. 24:30 · Rev. 11:19

2 and she was with child; and she *cried out, being in labor and in pain to give birth.

3 And[R]another sign appeared in heaven: and behold, a great red[R]dragon having seven heads and ten horns, and on his heads *were* seven diadems.   Rev. 12:1 · Is. 27:1; Rev. 12:4

4 And his tail *swept away a [R]third of the stars of heaven, and[R]threw them to the earth. And the [R]dragon stood before the woman who was about to give birth, so that when she gave birth he might devour her child.   Rev. 8:7 · Dan. 8:10 · Is. 27:1

[13] Some ancient mss. read *body*   [14] Lit., *spiritually*
[15] I.e., Messiah

5 And she gave birth to a son, a male *child*, who is to ᴿrule all the^nations with a rod of iron; and her child was caught up to God and to His throne.   Ps. 2:9☆ • *Gentiles*

6 And the woman fled into the wilderness where she *had a place prepared by God, so that there ᵀshe might be nourished for ᴿone thousand two hundred and sixty days.   *they may nourish her for* • Rev. 11:3; 13:5

The War in Heaven

7 And there was war in heaven, Michael and his angels waging war with the dragon. And the dragon and his angels waged war,

8 and they were not strong enough, and there was no longer a place found for them in heaven.

9 And the great dragon was thrown down, the serpent of old who is called the devil and Satan, who deceives the whole world; he was thrown down to the earth, and his angels were thrown down with him.

10 And I heard a loud voice in heaven, saying,

"Now the salvation, and the power, and the kingdom of our God and the authority of His Christ have come, for the accuser of our brethren has been thrown down, who accuses them before our God day and night.

11 "And they ᴿovercame him because of the blood of the Lamb and because of the word of their testimony, and they did not love their life even to death.   John 16:33; 1 John 2:13

12 "For this reason, rejoice, O heavens and you who ^dwell in them. Woe to the earth and the sea, because the devil has come down to you, having great wrath, knowing that he has *only* a short time."   *tabernacle*

The War on Earth

13 And when the dragon saw that he was thrown down to the earth, he persecuted the woman who gave birth to the male *child*.

14 And the ᴿtwo wings of the great eagle were given to the woman, in order that she might fly into the wilderness to her place, where she *was nourished for a time and times and half a time, from the ᵀpresence of the serpent.   Ex. 19:4; Deut. 32:11 • *face*

15 And the ᴿserpent ᵀpoured water like a river out of his mouth after the woman, so that he might cause her to be swept away with the flood.   Gen. 3:1 • *threw*

16 And the earth helped the woman, and the earth opened its mouth and drank up the river which the dragon ᵀpoured out of his mouth.   *threw*

17 And the dragon was enraged with the woman, and went off to ᴿmake war with the rest of her ᴿoffspring, who keep the commandments of God and hold to the testimony of Jesus.   Rev. 11:7 • Gen. 3:15

CHAPTER 13

The Beast Out of the Sea

Aɴᴅ he stood on the sand of the ᵀseashore. And I saw a beast coming up out of the sea, having ten horns and seven heads, and on his horns *were* ten diadems, and on his heads *were* blasphemous names.   *sea*

2 And the beast which I saw was ᴿlike a leopard, and his feet were *like those* of a bear, and his mouth like the mouth of a lion. And the dragon gave him his power and his throne and great authority.   Dan. 7:6; Hos. 13:7

3 And *I saw* one of his heads as if it had been ᵀslain, and his fatal wound was healed. And the whole earth was amazed *and followed* after the beast;   *smitten to death*

4 and they worshiped the ᴿdragon, because he gave his authority to the beast; and they worshiped the beast, saying, "Who ᴿis like the beast, and who is able to wage war with him?"   Rev. 12:3 • Ex. 15:11; Is. 46:5

5 And there was given to him a mouth speaking ᵀarrogant words and blasphemies; and authority to ᵀact for forty-two months was given to him.   *great things* • *do*

6 And he opened his mouth in blasphemies against God, to blaspheme His name and His tabernacle, *that is*,ᴿthose who ᵀdwell in heaven.   Rev. 7:15; 12:12 • *tabernacle*

7 And it was given to him to make war with the saints and to overcome them; and authority over every tribe and people and tongue and nation was given to him.

8 And all who ᴿdwell on the earth will worship him, *everyone* whose name has not been [16]written from the foundation of the world in the book of life of the Lamb who has been slain.   Rev. 3:10; 13:12, 14

9 If anyone has an ear, let him hear.

10 If anyone [17]*is destined* for captivity, to captivity he goes; if anyone kills with the sword, with the sword he must be killed. Here is the perseverance and the faith of the saints.

The Beast Out of the Earth

11 And I saw another beast coming up out of the earth; and he ᵀhad two horns like a lamb, and he spoke as a dragon.   *was having*

12 And he ᴿexercises all the authority of the first beast ^in his presence. And he makes the earth and those who dwell in it to worship the first beast, whose fatal wound was healed.   Rev. 13:4 • *by his authority*

13 And he performs great signs, so that he even makes fire come down out of heaven to the earth in the presence of men.

14 And he deceives those who dwell on the earth because of the signs which it was given him to perform in the presence of the beast, telling those who dwell on the earth to make an image to the beast who *had the wound of the sword and has come to life.

15 And there was given to him to give breath to the image of the beast, that the

[16]Or, *written in the book . . . slain from the foundation of the world*   [17]Or, leads *into captivity*

image of the beast might even [18]speak and cause[R]as many as do not worship the image of the beast to be killed.   Dan. 3:3ff.

16 And he causes all, the small and the great, and the rich and the poor, and the free men and the slaves, to be given a mark on their right hand, or on their forehead,

17 and he provides that no one should be able to buy or to sell, except the one who has the[R]mark, either the name of the beast or the number of his name.   Gal. 6:17; Rev. 7:3

18 Here is wisdom. Let him who has understanding calculate the number of the beast, for the number is that of a man; and his number is [19]six hundred and sixty-six.

CHAPTER 14

The 144,000

AND I looked, and behold,[R]the Lamb was standing on Mount Zion, and with Him one hundred and forty-four thousand, having His name and the name of His Father written on their foreheads.   Rev. 5:6

2 And I heard a voice from heaven, like [R]the sound of many waters and like the [R]sound of loud thunder, and the voice which I heard was like the sound of harpists playing on their harps.   Rev. 1:15 · Rev. 6:1

3 And they *sang[R]a new song before the throne and before the four living creatures and the elders; and no one could learn the song except the one hundred and forty-four thousand who had been purchased from the earth.   Rev. 5:9

4 These are the ones who have not been defiled with women, for they [20]have kept themselves chaste. These are the ones who follow the Lamb wherever He goes. These have been purchased from among men as first fruits to God and to the Lamb.

5 And[R]no lie was found in their mouth; they are blameless.   Ps. 32:2; Zeph. 3:13

The Three Angels' Announcements

6 And I saw another angel flying in midheaven, having an eternal gospel to preach to those who live on the earth, and to every nation and tribe and tongue and people;

7 and he said with a loud voice, "Fear[R] God, and give Him glory, because the hour of His judgment has come; and worship Him who made the heaven and the earth and sea and springs of waters."   Rev. 15:4

8 And another angel, a second one, followed, saying, "Fallen, fallen is[R]Babylon the great, she who has made all the nations drink of the wine of the^passion of her immorality."   Is. 21:9 · Dan. 4:30 · wrath

9 And another angel, a third one, followed them, saying with a loud voice, "If anyone[R]worships the beast and his[R]image, and receives a[R]mark on his forehead or upon his hand,   Rev. 13:12 · Rev. 13:14f. · Rev. 13:16

10 he also will drink of the[R]wine of the wrath of God, which is mixed [T]in full

strength in the cup of His anger; and he will be tormented with fire and brimstone in the presence of the holy angels and in the presence of the Lamb.   Is. 51:17 · unmixed

11 "And the[R]smoke of their torment goes up forever and ever; and[R]they have no rest day and night, those who worship the beast and his image, and whoever receives the mark of his name."   Rev. 18:9 · Rev. 4:8

12 Here is the^perseverance of the^saints who keep the commandments of God and their faith in Jesus.   steadfastness · holy ones

13 And I heard a voice from heaven, saying, "Write, 'Blessed[R]are the dead who die in the Lord from now on!' " "Yes," says the Spirit, "that they may rest from their labors, for their deeds follow with them."   Rev. 20:6

The Harvest Judgment

14 And I looked, and behold, a white cloud, and sitting on the cloud was one like [21]a son of man, having a golden crown on His head, and a sharp sickle in His hand.

15 And another angel came out of the ^temple, crying out with a loud voice to Him who sat on the cloud, "Put[T] in your sickle and reap, because the hour to reap has come, because the harvest of the earth is ripe."   sanctuary · Send forth

16 And He who sat on the cloud [T]swung His sickle over the earth; and the earth was reaped.   cast

17 And another angel came out of the ^temple which is in heaven,[T]and he also had a sharp sickle.   sanctuary · having himself also

18 And another angel,[R]the one who has power over fire, came out from the altar; and he called with a loud voice to him who had the sharp sickle, saying, "Put[T] in your sharp sickle, and gather the clusters[T]from the vine of the earth, because her grapes are ripe."   Rev. 16:8 · Send forth · of

19 And the angel swung his sickle to the earth, and gathered the clusters from the vine of the earth, and threw them into the great wine press of the wrath of God.

20 And[R]the wine press was trodden outside the city, and blood came out from the wine press, up to the horses' bridles, for a distance of [22]two hundred miles.   Is. 63:3

CHAPTER 15

Preparation for the Bowl Judgments

AND I saw[R]another sign in heaven, great and marvelous, seven angels who had seven plagues, which are the last, because in them the wrath of God is finished.   Rev. 12:1, 3

2 And I saw, as it were, a[R]sea of glass mixed with fire, and those who had[R]come off victorious from the [R]beast and from his image and from the number of his name,

[18] Some ancient mss. read speak, and he will cause
[19] Some mss. read 616   [20] Lit., are chaste men
[21] Or, the Son of Man
[22] Lit., sixteen hundred stadia. A stadion was about six hundred feet.

standing on the sea of glass, holding harps of God.   Rev. 4:6 • Rev. 12:11 • Rev. 13:1

3 And they *sang the[R]song of Moses[R]the bond-servant of God and the song of the Lamb, saying,   Ex. 15:1ff. • Josh. 22:5
"Great and marvelous are Thy works,
[R]O Lord God, the Almighty;   Hos. 14:9
Righteous and true are Thy ways,
Thou [R]King of the [23]nations. 1 Tim. 1:17
4 "Who[R]will not fear, O Lord, and glorify Thy name?   Jer. 10:7; Rev. 14:7
For Thou alone art holy;
For [R]ALL THE NATIONS WILL COME AND WORSHIP BEFORE THEE,   Ps. 86:9
For Thy[A]righteous[R]acts have been revealed."   judgments • Rev. 19:8
5 After these things I looked, and [R]the [A]temple of the tabernacle of testimony in heaven was opened,   Rev. 11:19 • sanctuary
6 and the [R]seven angels who had the seven plagues [R]came out of the [A]temple, clothed in [24]linen, clean and bright, and girded around their breasts with golden girdles.   Rev. 15:1 • Rev. 14:15 • sanctuary
7 And one of the [R]four living creatures gave to the[R]seven angels seven[R]golden bowls full of the wrath of God, who lives forever and ever.   Rev. 4:6 • Rev. 15:1 • Rev. 5:8
8 And the[A]temple was filled with[R]smoke from the glory of God and from His power; and no one was able to enter the temple until the seven plagues of the seven angels were finished.   sanctuary • Lev. 16:2

CHAPTER 16

First Bowl

AND I heard a loud voice from[R]the[A]temple, saying to the seven angels, "Go and pour out the seven bowls of the wrath of God into the earth."   Rev. 11:19 • sanctuary
2 And the first angel went and poured out his bowl[R]into the earth; and it became a loathsome and malignant[R]sore upon the men who had the mark of the beast and who worshiped his image.   Rev. 8:7 • Ex. 9:9-11

Second Bowl

3 And the second angel poured out his bowl[R]into the sea, and it became blood like that of a dead man; and every living [25]thing in the sea died.   Ex. 7:17-21; Rev. 8:8f.; 11:6

Third Bowl

4 And the third angel poured out his bowl into the[R]rivers and the springs of waters; and [26]they became blood.   Rev. 8:10
5 And I heard the angel of the waters saying, "Righteous[R]art Thou, [R]who art and who wast, O Holy One, because Thou didst judge these things;   John 17:25 • Rev. 11:17

6 for they poured out the blood of saints and prophets, and Thou hast given them blood to drink. They[T]deserve it."   are worthy
7 And I heard[R]the altar saying, "Yes, O [R]Lord God, the Almighty, true and righteous are Thy judgments."   Rev. 6:9 • Rev. 1:8

Fourth Bowl

8 And the fourth angel poured out his bowl upon[R]the sun;[R]and it was given to it to scorch men with fire.   Rev. 6:12 • Rev. 14:18
9 And men were scorched with fierce heat; and they blasphemed the name of God who has the power over these plagues; and they did not repent, so as to give Him glory.

Fifth Bowl

10 And the fifth angel poured out his bowl upon the[R]throne of the beast; and his kingdom became darkened; and they gnawed their tongues because of pain,   Rev. 13:2
11 and they blasphemed the God of heaven because of their pains and their sores; and they did not repent of their deeds.

Sixth Bowl

12 And the sixth angel poured out his bowl upon the [R]great river, the Euphrates; and its water was dried up, that the way might be prepared for the kings from the [T]east.   Rev. 9:14 • rising of the sun
13 And I saw coming out of the mouth of the dragon and out of the mouth of the beast and out of the mouth of the false prophet, three unclean spirits like frogs;
14 for they are [R]spirits of demons, performing signs, which go out to the kings of the whole [T]world, to gather them together for the war of the great day of God, the Almighty.   1 Tim. 4:1 • inhabited earth
15 ("Behold, I am coming like a thief. Blessed is the one who stays awake and keeps his garments, lest he walk about naked and[T]men see his shame.")   they
16 And they[R]gathered them together to the place which[R]in Hebrew is called [27]Har-[R]Magedon.   Rev. 19:19 • Rev. 9:11 • Judg. 5:19

Seventh Bowl

17 And the seventh angel poured out his bowl upon[R]the air; and a loud voice came out of the[A]temple from the throne, saying, "It is done."   [Eph. 2:2] • sanctuary
18 And there were flashes of[R]lightning and sounds and peals of thunder; and there was [R]a great earthquake,[R]such as there had not been since man came to be upon the earth, so great an earthquake was it, and mighty.   Rev. 4:5 • Rev. 6:12 • Dan. 12:1
19 And[R]the great city was split into three parts, and the cities of the[A]nations fell. And Babylon the great was remembered before God, to give her the cup of the wine of His fierce wrath.   Rev. 11:8 • Gentiles
20 And [R]every island fled away, and the mountains were not found.   Rev. 6:14; 20:11

---

[23] Some ancient mss. read ages
[24] Some mss. read stone
[25] Lit., soul. Some ancient mss. read thing, the things in the sea. [26] Some ancient mss. read it became
[27] Some authorities read Armageddon

21 And huge hailstones, about ²⁸one hundred pounds each, *came down from heaven upon men; and men blasphemed God because of the plague of the hail, because its plague *was extremely severe.

CHAPTER 17

Great Harlot Is Described

AND^Rone of the^Rseven angels who had the ^Rseven bowls came and spoke with me, saying, "Come here, I shall show you the judgment of the great harlot who sits on many waters,   Rev. 1:1; 21:9 · Rev. 15:1 · Rev. 15:7

2 with whom^Rthe kings of the earth committed *acts of* immorality, and those who dwell on the earth were made drunk with the wine of her immorality."   Rev. 2:22; 18:3, 9

3 And he carried me away ²⁹in the Spirit into a wilderness; and I saw a woman sitting on a scarlet beast, full of blasphemous names, having seven heads and ten horns.

4 And the woman was clothed in purple and scarlet, and^Tadorned with gold and precious stones and pearls, having in her hand a gold cup full of abominations and of the unclean things of her immorality,   *gilded*

5 and upon her forehead a name *was* written, a ^Rmystery, "BABYLON^R THE GREAT, THE MOTHER OF HARLOTS AND OF THE ABOMINATIONS OF THE EARTH."   2 Thess. 2:7; Rev. 1:20 · Rev. 14:8

6 And I saw the woman drunk with^Rthe blood of the^Asaints, and with the blood of the witnesses of Jesus. And when I saw her, I wondered greatly.   Rev. 16:6 · *holy ones*

Great Harlot Is Destroyed

7 And the angel said to me, "Why^Tdo you wonder? I shall tell you the^Rmystery of the woman and of the beast that carries her, which has the seven heads and the ten horns.   *have you wondered* · 2 Thess. 2:7

8"The beast that you saw was and is not, and is about to come up out of the abyss and ³⁰to go to destruction. And those who dwell on the earth will wonder, whose name has not been written in the book of life from the foundation of the world, when they see the beast, that he was and is not and will come.

9"Here^R is the mind which has wisdom. The ^Rseven heads are seven mountains on which the woman sits,   Rev. 13:18 · Rev. 17:3

10 and they are seven ^Rkings; five have fallen, one is, the other has not yet come; and when he comes, he must remain a little while.   Rev. 10:11

11"And the beast which^Rwas and is not, is himself also an eighth, and is *one* of the seven, and he goes to destruction. Rev. 13:3

12"And the^Rten horns which you saw are ten kings, who have not yet received a kingdom, but they receive authority as kings with the beast for one hour.   Dan. 7:24

13"These have one purpose and they give their power and authority to the beast.

14"These will wage^Rwar against the Lamb, and the Lamb will^Rovercome them, because He is Lord of lords and King of kings, and those who are with Him *are the* called and chosen and faithful."   Rev. 16:14 · Rev. 3:21

15 And he *said to me, "The waters which you saw where the harlot sits, are peoples and multitudes and nations and tongues.

16"And the ten horns which you saw, and the beast, these will hate the harlot and will make her desolate and naked, and will eat her flesh and will burn her up with fire.

17"For God has put it in their hearts to execute His^Apurpose^Tby having a common purpose, and by giving their kingdom to the beast, until the words of God should be fulfilled.   *mind · even to do one mind and to give*

18"And the woman whom you saw is^Rthe great city, which^Treigns over the kings of the earth."   Rev. 11:8; 16:19 · *has a kingdom*

CHAPTER 18

Babylon the Great Is Destroyed

AFTER these things I saw another^Rangel ^Rcoming down from heaven, having great authority, and the earth was^Rillumined with his glory.   Rev. 17:1 · Rev. 10:1 · Ezek. 43:2

2 And he cried out with a mighty voice, saying, "Fallen, fallen is Babylon the great! And she^Rhas become a dwelling place of demons and a^Aprison of every unclean spirit, and a prison of every unclean and hateful bird.   Is. 21:9 · Is. 13:21f.; 34:11 · *haunt*

3"For all the nations ³¹have drunk of the wine of the^Tpassion of her immorality, and the kings of the earth have committed *acts of* immorality with her, and the merchants of the earth have become rich by the ^Twealth of her sensuality."   *wrath · power*

4 And I heard another voice from heaven, saying, "Come out of her, my people, that you may not participate in her sins and that you may not receive of her plagues;

5 for her sins have^Tpiled^Rup as high as heaven, and God has^Rremembered her iniquities.   *joined together* · Jer. 51:9 · Rev. 16:19

6"Pay her back even as she has paid, and ^Tgive back *to her* double according to her deeds; in the cup which she has mixed, mix twice as much for her.   *double* to her

7"To the degree that she glorified herself and lived sensuously, to the same degree give her torment and mourning; for she says in her heart, 'I SIT *as* A QUEEN AND I AM NOT A WIDOW, and will never see mourning.'

8"For this reason in one day her plagues will come, pestilence and mourning and famine, and she will be burned up with fire; for the Lord God who judges her is strong.

²⁸ Lit., *the weight of a talent*   ²⁹ Or, *in spirit*
³⁰ Some ancient mss. read *he goes*
³¹ Many ancient mss. read *have fallen by*

Earth Mourns Babylon's Destruction

9"And the kings of the earth, who committed *acts of* immorality and lived sensuously with her, will weep and lament over her when they see the smoke of her burning,

10 standing at a distance because of the fear of her torment, saying, 'Woe, woe, the great city, Babylon, the strong city! For in one hour your judgment has come.'

11"And the[R]merchants of the earth weep and mourn over her, because no one buys their cargoes any more; Ezek. 27:9-25; Rev. 18:3

12 cargoes of gold and silver and precious [T]stones and pearls and fine linen and purple and silk and scarlet, and every *kind of* citron wood and every article of ivory and every article *made* from very costly wood and bronze and iron and marble,   *stone*

13 and cinnamon and [T]spice and incense and perfume and frankincense and wine and olive oil and fine flour and wheat and cattle and sheep, and *cargoes* of horses and chariots and slaves and human lives. Gr., amomum

14"And the fruit you long for has gone from you, and all things that were luxurious and splendid have passed away from you and *men* will no longer find them.

15"The[R]merchants of[R]these things, who became rich from her, will stand at a distance because of the fear of her torment, weeping and mourning,   Rev. 18:3 • Rev. 18:12

16 saying, 'Woe, woe, the great city, she who was clothed in fine linen and purple and scarlet, and[T]adorned with gold and precious stones and pearls;   *gilded*

17 for in[R]one hour such great wealth has been laid waste!' And every shipmaster and every[T]passenger and sailor, and as many as make their living by the sea, stood at a distance,   Rev. 18:10 • *one who sails anywhere*

18 and were[R]crying out as they[R]saw the smoke of her burning, saying, 'What *city* is like the great city?'   Ezek. 27:30 • Rev. 18:9

19"And they threw[R]dust on their heads and were crying out, weeping and mourning, saying, 'Woe,[R] woe, the great city, in which all who had ships at sea became rich by her[T]wealth, for in one hour she has been laid waste!'   Josh. 7:6 • Rev. 18:10 • *costliness*

Heaven Rejoices Babylon's Destruction

20"Rejoice[R] over her, O heaven, and you [A]saints and apostles and prophets, because God has pronounced judgment for you against her."   Jer. 51:48 • *holy ones*

21 And[T]a[R]strong angel took up a stone like a great millstone and threw it into the sea, saying, "Thus will Babylon, the great city, be thrown down with violence, and will not be found any longer.   *one* • Rev. 5:2; 10:1

22"And[R]the sound of harpists and musicians and flute-players and trumpeters will not be heard in you any longer; and no craftsman of any craft will be found in you

any longer; and the sound of a mill will not be heard in you any longer;   Ezek. 26:13

23 and the light of a lamp will not shine in you any longer; and the voice of the bridegroom and bride will not be heard in you any longer; for your merchants were the great men of the earth, because all the nations were deceived by your sorcery.

24"And in her was found the[R]blood of prophets and of[A]saints and of all who have been slain on the earth."   Rev. 16:6 • *holy ones*

CHAPTER 19

AFTER these things I heard, as it were, a [R]loud voice of a great multitude in heaven, saying,   Jer. 51:48

"Hallelujah! Salvation and glory and power belong to our God;

2 BECAUSE HIS JUDGMENTS ARE TRUE AND RIGHTEOUS; for He has judged the great harlot who was corrupting the earth with her immorality, and HE HAS AVENGED THE BLOOD OF HIS BOND-SERVANTS ON HER."

3 And a second time they said, "Hallelujah![R] HER[R] SMOKE RISES UP FOREVER AND EVER."   Rev. 19:1, 4, 6 • Is. 34:10; Rev. 14:11

4 And the[R]twenty-four elders and the [R]four living creatures fell down and worshiped God who sits on the throne saying, "Amen. Hallelujah!"   Rev. 4:4 • Rev. 4:6

5 And a voice came from the throne, saying,

"Give[R]praise to our God, all you His bondservants,[R]you who fear Him, the small and the great."   Ps. 22:23; 115:13; 134:1 • Rev. 11:18

6 And I heard, as it were,[R]the voice of a great multitude and as[R]the sound of many waters and as the sound of mighty peals of thunder, saying,   Jer. 51:48 • Ezek. 1:24

"Hallelujah! For the Lord our God, the Almighty, reigns.

Marriage Supper of the Lamb

7"Let us rejoice and be glad and[R]give the glory to Him, for[R]the marriage of the Lamb has come and His[T]bride has made herself ready."   Rev. 11:13 • Matt. 22:2 • *wife*

8 And it was given to her to clothe herself in fine linen, bright *and* clean; for the fine linen is the righteous acts of the saints.

9 And[R]he *said to me, "Write, 'Blessed are those who are invited to the marriage supper of the Lamb.'" And he *said to me, "These are true words of God."   Rev. 17:1

10 And[R]I fell at his feet to worship him. [R]And he *said to me, "Do not do that; I am a fellow servant of yours and your brethren who hold the testimony of Jesus; worship God. For the testimony of Jesus is the spirit of prophecy."   Rev. 22:8 • Acts 10:26

Second Coming of Christ

11 And I saw[R]heaven opened; and behold, a white horse, and He who sat upon it *is*

called Faithful and True; and in righteousness He judges and wages war.   Ezek. 1:1

12 And His^Reyes *are* a flame of fire, and upon His head *are* many diadems; and He has a name written *upon Him* which no one knows except Himself.   Dan. 10:6; Rev. 1:14 ☆

13 And *He is* clothed with a^Rrobe dipped in blood; and His name is called^RThe Word of God.   Is. 63:3 ☆ • [John 1:1]

14 And the armies which are in heaven, clothed in^Rfine linen, white *and* clean, were following Him on white horses.   Rev. 19:8

15 And from His mouth comes a sharp sword, so that with it He may smite the nations; and He will^Arule them with a rod of iron; and He treads the wine press of the fierce wrath of God, the Almighty.   *shepherd*

16 And on His robe and on His thigh He has ^Ra name written, "KING OF KINGS, AND LORD OF LORDS."   Rev. 2:17; 19:12

17 And I saw an angel standing in the sun; and he cried out with a loud voice, saying to all the birds which fly in midheaven, "Come, assemble for the great supper of God;

18 in order that you may^Reat the flesh of kings and the flesh of [32]commanders and the flesh of mighty men and the flesh of horses and of those who sit on them and the flesh of all men, both free men and slaves, and small and great."   Ezek. 39:18-20

19 And I saw^Rthe beast and the kings of the earth and their armies, assembled to make war against Him who sat upon the horse, and against His army.   Rev. 16:16 ☆

20 And the beast was seized, and with him the^Rfalse prophet who performed the signs in his presence, by which he deceived those who had received the mark of the beast and those who worshiped his image; these two were thrown alive into the lake of fire which burns with brimstone.   Rev. 16:13

21 And the rest were killed with the sword which^Rcame from the mouth of Him who sat upon the horse, and all the birds were filled with their flesh.   Rev. 19:15

CHAPTER 20

Satan Is Bound 1,000 Years

AND I saw^Ran angel coming down from heaven, having the key of the abyss and a great chain^Tin his hand.   Rev. 10:1 • *upon*

2 And he laid hold of the^Rdragon, the serpent of old, who is the devil and Satan, and bound him for a thousand years,   Gen. 3:1

3 and threw him into the abyss, and shut *it* and sealed *it* over him, so that he should not deceive the nations any longer, until the thousand years were completed; after these things he must be released for a short time.

Saints Reign 1,000 Years

4 And I saw^Rthrones, and^Rthey sat upon them, and judgment was given to them. And I *saw* the souls of those who had been be-

headed because of the testimony of Jesus and because of the word of God, and those who had not worshiped the beast or his image, and had not received the mark upon their forehead and upon their hand; and they came to life and reigned with Christ for a thousand years.   Dan. 7:9 • Matt. 19:28

5 The rest of the dead did not come to life until the thousand years were completed.^RThis is the first resurrection. Phil. 3:11

6 ^RBlessed and holy is the one who has a part in the first resurrection; over these the second death has no power, but they will be priests of God and of Christ and will reign with Him for a thousand years.   Rev. 14:13

Satan Is Released and Leads Rebellion

7 And when the thousand years are completed, Satan will be ^Rreleased from his prison,   Rev. 20:2f.

8 and will come out to deceive the nations which are in the four corners of the earth, Gog and Magog, to gather them together for the war; the number of them is like the sand of the^Tseashore.   *sea*

9 And they came up on the broad plain of the earth and surrounded the camp of the saints and the beloved city, and fire came down from heaven and devoured them.

Satan Is Tormented Forever

10 And^Rthe devil who deceived them was thrown into the lake of fire and brimstone, where the beast and the false prophet are also; and they will be tormented day and night forever and ever.   Rev. 20:2f.

Great White Throne Judgment

11 And I saw a great white ^Rthrone and Him who sat upon it, from whose ^Tpresence earth and heaven fled away, and no place was found for them.   Rev. 4:2 • *face*

12 And I saw the dead, the^Rgreat and the small, standing before the throne, and ^Abooks were opened; and another^Abook was opened, which is *the book* of life; and the dead were judged from the things which were written in the books, according to their deeds.   Rev. 11:18 • *scrolls • scroll*

13 And the sea gave up the dead which were in it, and^Rdeath and Hades^Rgave up the dead which were in them; and they were judged, every one of *them*^Raccording to their deeds.   1 Cor. 15:26 • Is. 26:19 • Rev. 2:23

14 And^Rdeath and Hades were thrown into ^Rthe lake of fire. This is the second death, the lake of fire.   1 Cor. 15:26 • Rev. 19:20; 20:10

15 And if^Tanyone's name was not found written in^Rthe book of life, he was thrown into the lake of fire.   *anyone was* • Rev. 3:5

---

[32] I.e., chiliarchs, in command of one thousand troops

CHAPTER 21

New Heaven and Earth Are Created

AND I saw a new heaven and a new earth; for the first heaven and the first earth passed away, and there is no longer any sea.

New Jerusalem Descends

2 And I saw [R]the holy city, [R]new Jerusalem, [R]coming down out of heaven from God, made ready as a bride adorned for her husband.   Is. 52:1 • Rev. 3:12 • Heb. 11:10
3 And I heard a loud voice from the throne, saying, "Behold, the tabernacle of God is among men, and He shall dwell among them, and they shall be His people, and God Himself shall be among them,[33]
4 and He shall [R]wipe away every tear from their eyes; and there shall no longer be any death; there shall no longer be any mourning, or crying, or pain; the first things have passed away."   Is. 25:8; Rev. 7:17☆
5 And [R]He who sits on the throne said, "Behold, I am [R]making all things new." And He *said, "Write, for these words are faithful and true."   Rev. 4:9 • 2 Cor. 5:17
6 And He said to me, "It [T]is done. I am the [R]Alpha and the Omega, the beginning and the end. I will give to the one who thirsts from the spring of the water of life without cost.   They are • Rev. 1:8
7 "He [R]who overcomes shall inherit these things, and [R]I will be his God and he will be My son.   Rev. 2:7 • 2 Sam. 7:14; Ps. 89:26f. ☆
8 "But [R] for the cowardly and [^]unbelieving and abominable and murderers and immoral persons and sorcerers and idolaters and all liars, their part will be in the lake that burns with fire and brimstone, which is the second death."   1 Cor. 6:9 • untrustworthy

New Jerusalem Is Described

9 [R]And one of the seven angels who had the seven bowls [T]full of the seven last plagues, came and spoke with me, saying, "Come here, I shall show you the bride, the wife of the Lamb."   Rev. 17:1 • who were full
10 And [R]he carried me away [34]in the Spirit to a great and high mountain, and showed me the holy city, Jerusalem, coming down out of heaven from God,   Ezek. 40:2; Rev. 17:3
11 having [R]the glory of God. Her [T]brilliance was like a very costly stone, as a stone of crystal-clear jasper.   Is. 60:1f. • luminary
12 [T]It had a great and high wall, with [R] twelve gates, and at the gates twelve angels; and names were written on them, which are those of the twelve tribes of the sons of Israel.   having • Ezek. 48:31-34
13 There were three gates on the east and three gates on the north and three gates on the south and three gates on the west.
14 And the wall of the city had [R]twelve foundation stones, and on them were the twelve names of the [R]twelve apostles of the Lamb.   Heb. 11:10 • Acts 1:26
15 And the one who spoke with me had a [T]gold measuring rod to measure the city, and its gates and its wall.   measure, a gold reed
16 And the city is laid out as a square, and its length is as great as the width; and he measured the city with the [T]rod, [35]fifteen hundred miles; its length and width and height are equal.   reed
17 And he measured its wall, [36]seventy-two yards, according to [R]human [T]measurements, which are also [R]angelic measurements.   Deut. 3:11 • measure • Rev. 21:9
18 And the material of the wall was [R]jasper; and the city was [R]pure gold, like [T]clear glass.   Rev. 21:11 • Rev. 21:21 • pure
19 [R]The foundation stones of the city wall were adorned with every kind of precious stone. The first foundation stone was jasper; the second, sapphire; the third, chalcedony; the fourth, emerald;   Ex. 28:17-20; Is. 54:11f.
20 the fifth, sardonyx; the sixth, sardius; the seventh, chrysolite; the eighth, beryl; the ninth, topaz; the tenth, chrysoprase; the eleventh, jacinth; the twelfth, amethyst.
21 And the twelve [R]gates were twelve pearls; each one of the gates was a single pearl. And the street of the city was pure gold, like transparent glass.   Rev. 21:12, 15, 25
22 And I saw [R]no [^]temple in it, for the Lord God, the Almighty, and the Lamb, are its temple.   Matt. 24:2; John 4:23☆ • sanctuary
23 And the city [R]has no need of the sun or of the moon to shine upon it, for [R]the glory of God has illumined it, and its lamp is the [R]Lamb.   Is. 24:23☆ • Rev. 21:11 • Rev. 5:6
24 And [R]the nations shall walk by its light, and the kings of the earth [T]shall bring their glory into it.   Is. 60:3, 5☆ • bring
25 And in the daytime (for [R]there shall be no night there) [R]its gates shall never be closed;   Zech. 14:7 • Rev. 21:12, 15
26 and [R]they shall bring the glory and the honor of the nations into it;   Is. 49:23; 60:16
27 and nothing unclean and no one who practices abomination and lying, shall ever come into it, but only those whose names are written in the Lamb's book of life.

CHAPTER 22

AND he showed me a [R]river of the water of life, clear as crystal, coming from the throne of God and of [37]the Lamb,   Zech. 14:8☆
2 in the middle of its street. And on either side of the river was the tree of life, bearing twelve [38]kinds of fruit, yielding its fruit every month; and the leaves of the tree were for the healing of the nations.

---

[33] Some ancient mss. add, and be their God
[34] Or, in spirit
[35] Lit., twelve thousand stadia; a stadion was about 600 ft.
[36] Lit., one hundred forty-four cubits
[37] Or, the Lamb. In the middle of its street, and on either side of the river, was   [38] Or, crops of fruit

REVELATION 22 1308

3 And ᴿthere shall no longer be any curse; and ᴿthe throne of God and of the Lamb shall be in it, and His bond-servants shall ᴿserve Him; Zech. 14:11☆ • Ezek. 48:35☆ • Rev. 7:15

4 and they shall ᴺsee His face, and His name *shall be* on their foreheads. Matt. 5:8☆

5 And there shall no longer be *any* night; and they ᵀshall not have need of the light of a lamp nor the light of the sun, because the Lord God shall illumine them; and they shall reign forever and ever. *do not have*

Conclusion

6 And ᴿhe said to me, "These ᴿ words are faithful and true"; and the Lord, the God of the spirits of the prophets, sent His angel to show to His bond-servants the things which must shortly take place. Rev. 1:1 • Rev. 19:9

7 And behold, ᴿI am coming quickly. Blessed is he who ᴬheeds the words of the prophecy of this book." Rev. 1:3 • *keeps*

8 And ᴿI, John, am the one who heard and saw these things. And when I heard and saw, I fell down to worship at the feet of the angel who showed me these things. Rev. 1:1

9 And he *said to me, "Do not do that; I am a fellow servant of yours and of your brethren the prophets and of those who heed the words of this book; worship God."

10 And he *said to me, "Do ᴿ not seal up ᴿthe words of the prophecy of this book, for the time is near. Dan. 8:26 • Rev. 1:11; 22:9

11"Let ᴿ the one who does wrong, still do wrong; and let the one who is filthy, still be filthy; and let the one who is righteous, still practice righteousness; and let the one who is holy, still keep himself holy." Ezek. 3:27

12"Behold, I am coming quickly, and My reward *is* with Me, ᴿto render to every man according to what he has done. Is. 40:10☆

13"I am the Alpha and the Omega, the first and the last, the beginning and the end."

14 Blessed are those who ᴿwash their robes, that they may have the right to ᴿthe tree of life, and may enter by the gates into the city. Rev. 7:14 • Gen. 2:9; 3:22

15 Outside are the ᴰdogs and the sorcerers and the immoral persons and the murderers and the idolaters, and everyone who loves and practices lying. Deut. 23:18

16"I, Jesus, have sent My angel to testify to you these things ᴬfor the churches. I am the root and the offspring of David, the bright morning star." Rev. 1:1 • *concerning*

17 And the ᴿSpirit and the ᴿbride say, "Come." And let the one who hears say, "Come." And let the one who is thirsty come; let the one who wishes take the water of life without cost. Rev. 2:7 • [Rev. 21:2]

18 I testify to everyone who hears the words of the prophecy of this book: if anyone adds to them, God shall add to him the plagues which are written in this book;

19 and if anyone ᴿtakes away from the ᴿwords of the book of this prophecy, God shall take away his part from the tree of life and ᵀfrom the holy city, which are written in this book. Deut. 4:2 • Rev. 22:7 • *out of*

20 He who ᴿtestifies to these things says, "Yes, ᴿI am coming quickly." Amen. Come, Lord Jesus. Rev. 1:2 • Rev. 22:7

21 ᴿThe grace of the Lord Jesus be with ³⁹all. Amen. Rom. 16:20

³⁹ Some ancient mss. read *the saints*

Harmony of the Gospels

Date	Event	Location	Matthew	Mark	Luke	John	Related References
	Luke's Introduction				1:1–4		Acts 1:1
	Pre-fleshly state of Christ					1:1–18	Heb. 1:1–14
	Genealogy of Jesus Christ		1:1–17		3:23–38		Ruth 4:18–22
							1 Chr. 1:1–4

BIRTH, INFANCY, AND ADOLESCENCE OF JESUS AND JOHN THE BAPTIST IN 17 EVENTS

Date	Event	Location	Matthew	Mark	Luke	John	Related References
7 B.C.	(1) Announcement of Birth of John	Jerusalem (Temple)			1:5–25		Num. 6:3
7 or 6 B.C.	(2) Announcement of Birth of Jesus to the Virgin	Nazareth			1:26–38		Is. 7:14
c. 5 B.C.	(3) Song of Elizabeth to Mary	{Hill Country {of Judah			1:39–45		
	(4) Mary's Song of Praise				1:46–56		Ps. 103:17
5 B.C.	(5) Birth, Infancy, and Purpose for Future of John the Baptist	Judea			1:57–80		Mal. 3:1
	(6) Announcement of Jesus' Birth to Joseph	Nazareth	1:18–25				Is. 9:6, 7
5–4 B.C.	(7) Birth of Jesus Christ	Bethlehem	1:24, 25		2:1–7		Is. 7:14
	(8) Proclamation by the Angels	{Near {Bethlehem			2:8–14		1 Tim. 3:16
	(9) The Visit of Homage by Shepherds	Bethlehem			2:15–20		
	(10) Jesus' Circumcision	Bethlehem			2:21		Lev. 12:3
4 B.C.	(11) First Temple Visit with Acknowledgments by Simeon and Anna	Jerusalem			2:22–38		Ex. 13:2 Lev. 12
	(12) Visit of the Wise Men	{Jerusalem & {Bethlehem	2:1–12				Num. 24:17
	(13) Flight to Egypt and Slaughter of Innocents	{Bethlehem, {Jerusalem & {Egypt	2:13–18				Jer. 31:15
	(14) From Egypt to Nazareth with Jesus		2:19–23		2:39		
Afterward A.D. 7–8	(15) Childhood of Jesus	Nazareth			2:40, 51		
	(16) Jesus, 12 Years Old, Visits the Temple	Jerusalem			2:41–50		Deut. 16:1–8
Afterward	(17) 18-Year Account of Jesus' Adolescence and Adulthood	Nazareth			2:51, 52		1 Sam. 2:26

TRUTHS ABOUT JOHN THE BAPTIST

Date	Event	Location	Matthew	Mark	Luke	John	Related References
c. A.D. 25–27	John's Ministry Begins	Judean Wilderness	3:1	1:1–4	3:1, 2	1:19–28	Mal. 3:1
	Man and Message		3:2–12	1:2–8	3:3–14		Is. 40:3
	His Picture of Jesus		3:11, 12	1:7, 8	3:15–18	1:26, 27	Acts 2:38
	His Courage		14:4–12		3:19, 20		

BEGINNING OF JESUS' MINISTRY IN 12 EVENTS

Date	Event	Location	Matthew	Mark	Luke	John	Related References
c. A.D. 27	(1) Jesus Baptized	Jordan River	3:13–17	1:9–11	3:21–23	1:29–34	Ps. 2:7
	(2) Jesus Tempted	Wilderness	4:1–11	1:12, 13	4:1–13		Ps. 91:11
	(3) Calls First Disciples	Beyond Jordan				1:35–51	
	(4) The First Miracle	Cana in Galilee				2:1–11	
	(5) First Stay in Capernaum	(Capernaum is "His" city)				2:12	
A.D. 27	(6) First Cleansing of the Temple	Jerusalem				2:13–22	Ps. 69:9
	(7) Received at Jerusalem	Judea				2:23–25	
	(8) Teaches Nicodemus about Second Birth	Judea				3:1–21	Num. 21:8, 9
	(9) Co-Ministry with John	Judea				3:22–30	

Date	Event	Location	Matthew	Mark	Luke	John	Related References
A.D. 27	(10) Leaves for Galilee	Judea	4:12	1:14	4:14	4:1–4	
	(11) Samaritan Woman at Jacob's Well	Samaria				4:5–42	Josh. 24:32
	(12) Returns to Galilee			1:15	4:15	4:43–45	

A.D. 27–29	THE GALILEAN MINISTRY OF JESUS IN 55 EVENTS						

Date	Event	Location	Matthew	Mark	Luke	John	Related References
A.D. 27	(1) Healing of the Royal Official's Son	Cana				4:46–54	
	(2) Rejected at Nazareth	Nazareth			4:16–30		Is. 61:1, 2
	(3) Moved to Capernaum	Capernaum	4:13–17				Is. 9:1, 2
	(4) Four Become Fishers of Men	Sea of Galilee	4:18–22	1:16–20	5:1–11		Ps. 33:9
	(5) Demoniac Healed on the Sabbath Day	Capernaum		1:21–28	4:31–37		
	(6) Peter's Mother-in-Law Cured, Plus Others	Capernaum	8:14–17	1:29–34	4:38–41		Is. 53:4
c. A.D. 27	(7) First Preaching Tour of Galilee	Galilee	4:23–25	1:35–39	4:42–44		
	(8) Leper Cleansed and Response Recorded	Galilee	8:1–4	1:40–45	5:12–16		Lev. 13:49
	(9) Paralytic Healed	Capernaum	9:1–8	2:1–12	5:17–26		Rom. 3:23
	(10) Matthew's Call and Reception Held	Capernaum	9:9–13	2:13–17	5:27–32		Hos. 6:6
	(11) Disciples Defended via a Parable	Capernaum	9:14–17	2:18–22	5:33–39		
A.D. 28	(12) Goes to Jerusalem for Second Passover; Heals Lame Man	Jerusalem				5:1–47	Ex. 20:10
	(13) Plucked Grain Precipitates Sabbath Controversy	En Route to Galilee	12:1–8	2:23–28	6:1–5		Deut. 5:14
	(14) Withered Hand Healed Causes Another Sabbath Controversy	Galilee	12:9–14	3:1–6	6:6–11		
	(15) Multitudes Healed	Sea of Galilee	12:15–21	3:7–12	6:17–19		
	(16) Twelve Apostles Selected After a Night of Prayer	Near Capernaum		3:13–19	6:12–16		
	(17) Sermon on the Mt.	Near Capernaum	5:1—7:29		6:20–49		
	(18) Centurion's Servant Healed	Capernaum	8:5–13		7:1–10		Is. 49:12, 13
	(19) Raises Widow's Son from Dead	Nain			7:11–17		Job 19:25
	(20) Jesus Allays John's Doubts	Galilee	11:2–19		7:18–35		Mal. 3:1
	(21) Woes Upon the Privileged		11:20–30				Gen. 19:24
	(22) A Sinful Woman Anoints Jesus	Simon's House, Capernaum			7:36–50		
	(23) Another Tour of Galilee	Galilee			8:1–3		
	(24) Jesus Accused of Blasphemy	Capernaum	12:22–37	3:20–30	11:14–23		
	(25) Jesus' Answer to a Demand for a Sign	Capernaum	12:38–45		11:24–26; 29–36		
	(26) Mother, Brothers Seek Audience	Capernaum	12:46–50	3:31–35	8:19–21		
	(27) Famous Parables of Sower, Seed, Tares, Mustard Seed, Leaven, Treasure, Pearl, Dragnet, Lamp Told	By Sea of Galilee	13:1–52	4:1–34	8:4–18		Joel 3:13
	(28) Sea Made Serene	Sea of Galilee	8:23–27	4:35–41	8:22–25		
	(29) Gadarene Demoniac Healed	E. Shore of Galilee	8:28–34	5:1–20	8:26–39		
	(30) Jairus's Daughter Raised and Woman with Hemorrhage Healed		9:18–26	5:21–43	8:40–56		
	(31) Two Blind Men's Sight Restored		9:27–31				

Date	Event	Location	Matthew	Mark	Luke	John	Related References
A.D. 28	(32) Mute Demoniac Healed		9:32–34				
	(33) Nazareth's Second Rejection of Christ	Nazareth	13:53–58	6:1–6			
	(34) Twelve Sent Out		9:35— 11:1	6:6–13	9:1–6		1 Cor. 9:14
	(35) Fearful Herod Beheads John	Galilee	14:1–12	6:14–29	9:7–9		
Spring A.D. 29	(36) Return of 12, Jesus Withdraws, 5000 Fed	{Near {Bethsaida	14:13–21	6:30–44	9:10–17	6:1–14	
	(37) Walks on the Water	Sea of Galilee	14:22–33	6:45–52		6:15–21	
	(38) Sick of Gennesaret Healed	Gennesaret	14:34–36	6:53–56			
	(39) Peak of Popularity Passes in Galilee	Capernaum				{6:22–71 {7:1	Is. 54:13
A.D. 29	(40) Traditions Attacked		15:1–20	7:1–23			Ex. 21:17
	(41) Aborted Retirement in Phoenicia: Syro-Phoenician Healed	Phoenicia	15:21–28	7:24–30			
	(42) Afflicted Healed	Decapolis	15:29–31	7:31–37			
	(43) 4000 Fed	Decapolis	15:32–39	8:1–9			
	(44) Pharisees Increase Attack	Magdala	16:1–4	8:10–13			
	(45) Disciples' Carelessness Condemned; Blind Man Healed		16:5–12	8:14–26			Jer. 5:21
	(46) Peter Confesses Jesus is the Christ	{Near {Caesarea {Philippi	16:13–20	8:27–30	9:18–21		
	(47) Jesus Foretells His Death	{Caesarea {Philippi	16:21–26	8:31–37	9:22–25		
	(48) Kingdom Promised		16:27, 28	9:1	9:26, 27		Prov. 24:12
	(49) The Transfiguration	{Mountain {Unnamed	17:1–13	9:2–13	9:28–36		Is. 42:1
	(50) Epileptic Healed	{Mt. of Transfiguration	17:14–21	9:14–29	9:37–42		
	(51) Again Tells of Death, Resurrection	Galilee	17:22, 23	9:30–32	9:43–45		
	(52) Taxes Paid	Capernaum	17:24–27				Ex. 30:11–15
	(53) Disciples Contend About Greatness; Jesus Defines; also Patience, Loyalty, Forgiveness	Capernaum	18:1–35	9:33–50	9:46–62		
	(54) Jesus Rejects Brothers' Advice	Galilee				7:2–9	
c. Sept. A.D. 29	(55) Galilee Departure and Samaritan Rejection		19:1		9:51–56	7:10	

A.D. 29–30   LAST JUDEAN AND PEREAN MINISTRY OF JESUS IN 42 EVENTS

Date	Event	Location	Matthew	Mark	Luke	John	Related References
Oct. A.D. 29	(1) Feast of Booths	Jerusalem				{7:2, { 11–52	
	(2) Forgiveness of Adulteress	Jerusalem				{7:53— { 8:11	Lev. 20:10
A.D. 29	(3) Christ—the Light of the World	Jerusalem				8:12–20	
	(4) Pharisees Can't Meet the Prophecy Thus Try to Destroy the Prophet	{Jerusalem— {Temple				8:12–59	Is. 6:9
	(5) Man Born Blind Healed; Following Consequences	Jerusalem				9:1–41	
	(6) Parable of the Good Shepherd	Jerusalem				10:1–21	
	(7) The Service of the Seventy	{Probably {Judea			10:1–24		
	(8) Lawyer Hears the Story of the Good Samaritan	Judea (?)			10:25–37		
	(9) The Hospitality of Martha and Mary	Bethany			10:38–42		
	(10) Another Lesson on Prayer	Judea (?)			11:1–13		

Date	Event	Location	Matthew	Mark	Luke	John	Related References
A.D. 29	(11) Accused of Connection with Beelzebul				11:14–36		
	(12) Judgment Against Lawyers and Pharisees				11:37–54		Mic. 6:8
	(13) Jesus Deals with Hypocrisy, Covetousness, Worry, and Alertness				12:1–59		Mic. 7:6
	(14) Repent or Perish				13:1–5		
	(15) Barren Fig Tree				13:6–9		
	(16) Crippled Woman Healed on Sabbath				13:10–17		Deut. 5:12–15
	(17) Parables of Mustard Seed and Leaven	{Probably Perea			13:18–21		
Winter A.D. 29	(18) Feast of Dedication	Jerusalem				10:22–39	Ps. 82:6
	(19) Withdrawal Beyond Jordan					10:40–42	
	(20) Begins Teaching Return to Jerusalem with Special Words About Herod	Perea			13:22–35		Ps. 6:8
	(21) Meal with a Pharisee Ruler Occasions Healing Man with Dropsy: Parables of Ox, Places of Honor, and Big Dinner				14:1–24		
	(22) Demands of Discipleship	Perea			14:25–35		
	(23) Parables of Lost Sheep, Coin, Son				15:1–32		1 Pet. 2:25
	(24) Parables of Unrighteous Steward, Rich Man and Lazarus				16:1–31		
	(25) Lessons on Service, Faith, Influence				17:1–10		
	(26) Resurrection of Lazarus	{Perea to Bethany				11:1–44	
	(27) Reaction to It: Withdrawal of Jesus					11:45–54	
A.D. 30	(28) Begins Last Journey to Jerusalem via Samaria & Galilee	{Samaria, Galilee			17:11		
	(29) Cleanses Ten Lepers				17:12–19		Lev. 13:45, 46
	(30) Lessons on the Coming Kingdom				17:20–37		Gen. 6—7
	(31) Parables: Persistent Widow, Pharisee and Tax-gatherer				18:1–14		
	(32) Doctrine on Divorce		19:1–12	10:1–12			Deut. 24:1–4 Gen. 2:23–25
	(33) Jesus Blesses Children: Objections	Perea	19:13–15	10:13–16	18:15–17		Ps. 131:2
	(34) Rich Young Ruler	Perea	19:16–30	10:17–31	18:18–30		Ex. 20:1–17
	(35) Laborers of the 11th Hour		20:1–16				
	(36) Foretells Death and Resurrection	{Near Jordan	20:17–19	10:32–34	18:31–34		Ps. 22
	(37) Ambition of James and John		20:20–28	10:35–45			
	(38) Blind Bartimaeus Healed	Jericho		10:46–52	18:35–43		
	(39) Interview with Zaccheus	Jericho			19:1–10		
	(40) Parable: the Minas	Jericho			19:11–27		
	(41) Returns to Home of Mary and Martha	Bethany				{11:55— 12:1	
	(42) Plot to Kill Lazarus	Bethany				12:9–11	

Spring A.D. 30	JESUS' FINAL WEEK OF WORK AT JERUSALEM IN 41 EVENTS						
Sunday	(1) Triumphal Entry	Bethany, Jerusalem, Bethany	21:1–9	11:1–11	19:28–44	12:12–19	Zech. 9:9

Date	Event	Location	Matthew	Mark	Luke	John	Related References
Monday	(2) Fig Tree Cursed and Temple Cleansed	Bethany to Jerusalem	21:10–19	11:12–18	19:45–48		Jer. 7:11
	(3) The Attraction of Sacrifice	Jerusalem				12:20–50	Is. 6:10
Tuesday	(4) Withered Fig Tree Testifies	Bethany to Jerusalem	21:20–22	11:19–26			
	(5) Sanhedrin Challenges Jesus. Answered by Parables: Two Sons, Wicked Vinegrowers and Wedding Feast	Jerusalem	21:23–22:14	11:27–12:12	20:1–19		Is. 5:1, 2
	(6) Tribute to Caesar	Jerusalem	22:15–22	12:13–17	20:20–26		
	(7) Sadducees Question the Resurrection	Jerusalem	22:23–33	12:18–27	20:27–40		Ex. 3:6
	(8) Pharisees Question Commandments	Jerusalem	22:34–40	12:28–34			
	(9) Jesus and David	Jerusalem	22:41–46	12:35–37	20:41–44		Ps. 110:1
	(10) Jesus' Last Sermon	Jerusalem	23:1–39	12:38–40	20:45–47		
	(11) Widow's Mite	Jerusalem		12:41–44	21:1–4		Lev. 27:30
	(12) Jesus Tells of the Future	Mt. of Olives	24:1–51	13:1–37	21:5–36		Dan. 12:1
	(13) Parables: Ten Virgins, Talents. The Day of Judgment	Mt. of Olives	25:1–46				Zech. 14:5
	(14) Jesus Tells Date of Crucifixion		26:1–5	14:1, 2	22:1, 2		
	(15) Anointing by Mary at Simon's Feast	Bethany	26:6–13	14:3–9		12:2–8	
	(16) Judas Contracts the Betrayal		26:14–16	14:10, 11	22:3–6		Zech. 11:12
Thursday	(17) Preparation for the Passover	Jerusalem	26:17–19	14:12–16	22:7–13		Ex. 12:14–28
Thursday P.M.	(18) Passover Eaten, Jealousy Rebuked	Jerusalem	26:20	14:17	22:14–16, 24–30		
	(19) Feet Washed	Upper Room				13:1–20	
	(20) Judas Revealed, Defects	Upper Room	26:21–25	14:18–21	22:21–23	13:21–30	Ps. 41:9
	(21) Jesus Warns About Further Desertion; Cries of Loyalty	Upper Room	26:31–35	14:27–31	22:31–38	13:31–38	Zech. 13:7
	(22) Institution of the Lord's Supper	Upper Room	26:26–29	14:22–25	22:17–20		1 Cor. 11:23–34
	(23) Last Speech to the Apostles and Intercessory Prayer	Jerusalem				14:1–17:26	Ps. 35:19
Thursday-Friday	(24) The Grief of Gethsemane	Mt. of Olives	26:30, 36–46	14:26, 32–42	22:39–46	18:1	Ps. 42:6
Friday	(25) Betrayal, Arrest, Desertion	Gethsemane	26:47–56	14:43–52	22:47–53	18:2–12	
	(26) First Examined by Annas	Jerusalem				18:12–14, 19–23	
	(27) Trial by Caiaphas and Council; Following Indignities	Jerusalem	26:57, 59–68	14:53, 55–65	22:54, 63–65	18:24	Lev. 24:16
	(28) Peter's Triple Denial	Jerusalem	26:58, 69–75	14:54, 66–72	22:54–62	18:15–18, 25–27	
	(29) Condemnation by the Council	Jerusalem	27:1	15:1	22:66–71		Ps. 110:1
	(30) Suicide of Judas	Jerusalem	27:3–10				Acts 1:18, 19
	(31) First Appearance Before Pilate	Jerusalem	27:2, 11–14	15:1–5	23:1–7	18:28–38	
	(32) Jesus Before Herod	Jerusalem			23:6–12		
	(33) Second Appearance Before Pilate	Jerusalem	27:15–26	15:6–15	23:13–25	18:39–19:16	Deut. 21:6–9
	(34) Mockery by Roman Soldiers	Jerusalem	27:27–30	15:16–19			
	(35) Led to Golgotha	Jerusalem	27:31–34	15:20–23	23:26–33	19:16, 17	Ps. 69:21
	(36) 6 Events of First 3 Hours on Cross	Calvary	27:35–44	15:24–32	23:33–43	19:18–27	Ps. 22:18
	(37) Last 3 Hours on Cross	Calvary	27:45–50	15:33–37	23:44–46	19:28–30	Ps. 22:1
	(38) Events Attending Jesus' Death		27:51–56	15:38–41	23:45, 47–49		
	(39) Burial of Jesus	Jerusalem	27:57–60	15:42–46	23:50–54	19:31–37	Ex. 12:46
Friday-Saturday	(40) Tomb Sealed	Jerusalem	27:61–66		23:55, 56		Ex. 20:8–11
	(41) Women Watch	Jerusalem		15:47			

Date	Event	Location	Matthew	Mark	Luke	John	Related References
A.D. 30	**THE RESURRECTION THROUGH THE ASCENSION IN 12 EVENTS**						
Dawn of First Day (Sunday, "Lord's Day")	(1) Women Visit the Tomb	Near Jerusalem	28:1–10	16:1–8	24:1–11		
	(2) Peter and John See the Empty Tomb				24:12	20:1–10	
	(3) Jesus' Appearance to Mary Magdalene	Jerusalem		16:9–11		20:11–18	
	(4) Jesus' Appearance to the Other Women	Jerusalem	28:9, 10				
	(5) Guards' Report of the Resurrection		28:11–15				
Sunday Afternoon	(6) Jesus' Appearance to Two Disciples on Way to Emmaus			16:12, 13	24:13–35		1 Cor. 15:5
Late Sunday	(7) Jesus' Appearance to Ten Disciples Without Thomas	Jerusalem		16:14	24:36–43	20:19–25	
One Week Later	(8) Appearance to Disciples with Thomas	Jerusalem				20:26–31	
During 40 Days until Ascension	(9) Jesus' Appearance to Seven Disciples by Sea of Galilee	Galilee				21:1–25	
	(10) Appearance to 500	Mt. in Galilee					1 Cor. 15:6
	(11) Great Commission		28:16–20	16:15–18	24:44–49		
	(12) The Ascension	Mt. Olivet		16:19, 20	24:50–53		Acts 1:4–11

The Jewish Calendar

The Jews used two kinds of calendars:
Civil Calendar—official calendar of kings, childbirth, and contracts.
Sacred Calendar—from which festivals were computed.

NAMES OF MONTHS	CORRESPONDS WITH	NO. OF DAYS	MONTH OF CIVIL YEAR	MONTH OF SACRED YEAR
TISHRI	Sept.–Oct.	30 days	1st	7th
HESHVAN	Oct.–Nov.	29 or 30	2nd	8th
CHISLEV	Nov.–Dec.	29 or 30	3rd	9th
TEBETH	Dec.–Jan.	29	4th	10th
SHEBAT	Jan.–Feb.	30	5th	11th
ADAR	Feb.–Mar.	29 or 30	6th	12th
NISAN	Mar.–Apr.	30	7th	1st
IYAR	Apr.–May	29	8th	2nd
SIVAN	May–June	30	9th	3rd
TAMMUZ	June–July	29	10th	4th
AB	July–Aug.	30	11th	5th
*ELUL	Aug.–Sept.	29	12th	6th

The Jewish day was from sunset to sunset, in 8 equal parts:

FIRST WATCH ..... SUNSET TO 9 P.M.
SECOND WATCH .. 9 P.M. TO MIDNIGHT
THIRD WATCH ..... MIDNIGHT TO 3 A.M.
FOURTH WATCH .. 3 A.M. TO SUNRISE

FIRST WATCH ..... SUNRISE TO 9 A.M.
SECOND WATCH .. 9 A.M. TO NOON
THIRD WATCH ..... NOON TO 3 P.M.
FOURTH WATCH .. 3 P.M. TO SUNSET

*Hebrew months were alternately 30 and 29 days long. Their year, shorter than ours, had 354 days. Therefore, about every 3 years (7 times in 19 years) an extra 29-day-month, VEADAR, was added between ADAR and NISAN.

PROPHECIES OF THE MESSIAH FULFILLED IN JESUS CHRIST

Presented Here in Their Order of Fulfillment

PROPHETIC SCRIPTURE	SUBJECT	FULFILLED
Gen. 3:15, p. 7 "And I will put enmity between you and the woman, and between your seed and her seed; He shall bruise you on the head, and you shall bruise him on the heel."	**seed of a woman**	**Gal. 4:4, p. 1179** But when the fulness of the time came, God sent forth His Son, born of a woman, born under the Law,
Gen. 12:3, p. 14 "And I will bless those who bless you, and the one who curses you I will curse. And in you all the families of the earth shall be blessed."	**descendant of Abraham**	**Matt. 1:1, p. 963** The book of the genealogy of Jesus Christ, the son of David, the son of Abraham.
Gen. 17:19, p. 18 But God said, "No, but Sarah your wife shall bear you a son, and you shall call his name Isaac; and I will establish My covenant with him for an everlasting covenant for his descendants after him."	**descendant of Isaac**	**Luke 3:34, p. 1029** the *son* of Jacob, the *son* of Isaac, the *son* of Abraham, the *son* of Terah, the *son* of Nahor,
Num. 24:17, p. 153 "I see him, but not now; I behold him, but not near; a star shall come forth from Jacob, and a scepter shall rise from Israel, and shall crush through the forehead of Moab, and tear down all the sons of Sheth."	**descendant of Jacob**	**Matt. 1:2, p. 963** To Abraham was born Isaac; and to Isaac, Jacob; and to Jacob, Judah and his brothers;
Gen. 49:10, p. 49 "The scepter shall not depart from Judah, nor the ruler's staff from between his feet, until Shiloh comes, and to him *shall be* the obedience of the peoples."	**from the tribe of Judah**	**Luke 3:33, p. 1029** the *son* of Amminadab, the *son* of Admin, the *son* of Ram, the *son* of Hezron, the *son* of Perez, the *son* of Judah,
Is. 9:7, p. 665 There will be no end to the increase of *His* government or of peace, on the throne of David and over his kingdom, to establish it and to uphold it with justice and righteousness from then on and forevermore. The zeal of the LORD of hosts will accomplish this.	**heir to the throne of David**	**Luke 1:32, 33, p. 1025** "He will be great, and will be called the Son of the Most High; and the Lord God will give Him the throne of His father David; and He will reign over the house of Jacob forever; and His kingdom will have no end."
Ps. 45:6, 7; 102:25–27, p. 551, p. 581 Thy throne, O God, is forever and ever; a scepter of uprightness is the scepter of Thy kingdom. Thou hast loved righteousness, and hated wickedness; therefore God, Thy God, has anointed Thee with the oil of joy above Thy fellows. "Of old Thou didst found the earth; and the heavens are the work of Thy hands. Even they will perish, but Thou dost endure; and all of them will wear out like a garment; like clothing Thou wilt change them, and they will be changed. But Thou art the same, and Thy years will not come to an end."	**anointed and eternal**	**Heb. 1:8–12, p. 1239** But of the Son *He* says, "THY THRONE, O GOD, IS FOREVER AND EVER, AND THE RIGHTEOUS SCEPTER IS THE SCEPTER OF HIS KINGDOM. THOU HAST LOVED RIGHTEOUSNESS AND HATED LAWLESSNESS; THEREFORE GOD, THY GOD, HATH ANOINTED THEE WITH THE OIL OF GLADNESS ABOVE THY COMPANIONS." And, "THOU, LORD, IN THE BEGINNING DIDST LAY THE FOUNDATION OF THE EARTH, AND THE HEAVENS ARE THE WORKS OF THY HANDS; THEY WILL PERISH, BUT THOU REMAINEST; AND THEY ALL WILL BECOME OLD AS A GARMENT, AND AS A MANTLE THOU WILT ROLL THEM UP; AS A GARMENT THEY WILL ALSO BE CHANGED. BUT THOU ART THE SAME, AND THY YEARS WILL NOT COME TO AN END."

PROPHETIC SCRIPTURE	SUBJECT	FULFILLED
Mic. 5:2, p. 893 "But as for you, Bethlehem Ephrathah, *too* little to be among the clans of Judah, from you One will go forth for Me to be ruler in Israel. His goings forth are from long ago, from the days of eternity."	**born in Bethlehem**	**Luke 2:4, 5, 7, p. 1027** And Joseph also went up from Galilee, from the city of Nazareth, to Judea, to the city of David, which is called Bethlehem, because he was of the house and family of David, in order to register, along with Mary, who was engaged to him, and was with child. . . . And she gave birth to her first-born son; and she wrapped Him in cloths, and laid Him in a manger, because there was no room for them in the inn.
Dan. 9:25, p. 847 "So you are to know and discern *that* from the issuing of a decree to restore and rebuild Jerusalem until Messiah the Prince *there will be* seven weeks and sixty-two weeks; it will be built again, with plaza and moat, even in times of distress."	**time for His birth**	**Luke 2:1, 2, p. 1027** Now it came about in those days that a decree went out from Caesar Augustus, that a census be taken of all the inhabited earth. This was the first census taken while Quirinius was governor of Syria.
Is. 7:14, p. 663 "Therefore the Lord Himself will give you a sign: Behold, a virgin will be with child and bear a son, and she will call His name Immanuel."	**to be born of a virgin**	**Luke 1:26, 27, 30, 31, p. 1025** Now in the sixth month the angel Gabriel was sent from God to a city in Galilee, called Nazareth, to a virgin engaged to a man whose name was Joseph, of the descendants of David; and the virgin's name was Mary. . . . And the angel said to her, "Do not be afraid, Mary; for you have found favor with God. And behold, you will conceive in your womb, and bear a son, and you shall name Him Jesus."
Jer. 31:15, p. 748 Thus says the Lord, "A voice is heard in Ramah, lamentation *and* bitter weeping. Rachel is weeping for her children; she refuses to be comforted for her children, because they are no more."	**slaughter of children**	**Matt. 2:16–18, p. 964** Then when Herod saw that he had been tricked by the magi, he became very enraged, and sent and slew all the male children who were in Bethlehem and in all its environs, from two years old and under, according to the time which he had ascertained from the magi. Then that which was spoken through Jeremiah the prophet was fulfilled, saying, "A VOICE WAS HEARD IN RAMAH, WEEPING AND GREAT MOURNING, RACHEL WEEPING FOR HER CHILDREN; AND SHE REFUSED TO BE COMFORTED, BECAUSE THEY WERE NO MORE."
Hos. 11:1, p. 860 When Israel *was* a youth I loved him, and out of Egypt I called My son.	**flight to Egypt**	**Matt. 2:14, 15, p. 964** And he arose and took the Child and His mother by night, and departed for Egypt; and was there until the death of Herod, that what was spoken by the Lord through the prophet might be fulfilled, saying, "OUT OF EGYPT DID I CALL MY SON."
Is. 40:3–5, p. 689 A voice is calling, "Clear the way for the LORD in the wilderness; make smooth in the desert a highway for our God. Let every valley be lifted up, and every mountain and hill be made low; and let the rough ground become a plain, and the rugged terrain a broad valley; then the glory of the LORD will be revealed, and all flesh will see *it* together; for the mouth of the LORD has spoken."	**the way prepared**	**Luke 3:3–6, p. 1028** And he came into all the district around the Jordan, preaching a baptism of repentance for the forgiveness of sins; as it is written in the book of the words of Isaiah the prophet, "THE VOICE OF ONE CRYING IN THE WILDERNESS, 'MAKE READY THE WAY OF THE LORD, MAKE HIS PATHS STRAIGHT. EVERY RAVINE SHALL BE FILLED UP, AND EVERY MOUNTAIN AND HILL SHALL BE BROUGHT LOW; AND THE CROOKED SHALL BECOME STRAIGHT, AND THE ROUGH ROADS SMOOTH; AND ALL FLESH SHALL SEE THE SALVATION OF GOD.'"

PROPHETIC SCRIPTURE	SUBJECT	FULFILLED
Mal. 3:1, p. 930 "Behold, I am going to send My messenger, and he will clear the way before Me. And the Lord, whom you seek, will suddenly come to His temple; and the messenger of the covenant, in whom you delight, behold, He is coming," says the LORD of hosts.	preceded by a forerunner	*Luke 7:24, 27, p. 1034* And when the messengers of John had left, He began to speak to the multitudes about John, "What did you go out into the wilderness to look at? A reed shaken by the wind? . . . This is the one about whom it is written, 'BEHOLD, I SEND MY MESSENGER BEFORE YOUR FACE, WHO WILL PREPARE YOUR WAY BEFORE YOU.'"
Mal. 4:5, 6, p. 931 "Behold, I am going to send you Elijah the prophet before the coming of the great and terrible day of the LORD. And he will restore the hearts of the fathers to *their* children, and the hearts of the children to their fathers, lest I come and smite the land with a curse."	preceded by Elijah	*Matt. 11:13, 14, p. 973* "For all the prophets and the Law prophesied until John. And if you care to accept *it*, he himself is Elijah, who was to come."
Ps. 2:7, p. 529 "I will surely tell of the decree of the LORD: He said to Me, 'Thou art My Son, today I have begotten Thee.'"	declared the Son of God	*Matt. 3:17, p. 965* and behold, a voice out of the heavens, saying, "This is My beloved Son, in whom I am well-pleased."
Is. 9:1, 2, p. 664 But there will be no *more* gloom for her who was in anguish; in earlier times He treated the land of Zebulun and the land of Naphtali with contempt, but later on He shall make *it* glorious, by the way of the sea, on the other side of Jordan, Galilee of the Gentiles. The people who walk in darkness will see a great light; those who live in a dark land, the light will shine on them.	Galilean ministry	*Matt. 4:13–16, p. 966* and leaving Nazareth, He came and settled in Capernaum, which is by the sea, in the region of Zebulun and Naphtali. *This was* to fulfill what was spoken through Isaiah the prophet, saying, "THE LAND OF ZEBULUN AND THE LAND OF NAPHTALI, BY THE WAY OF THE SEA, BEYOND THE JORDAN, GALILEE OF THE GENTILES—THE PEOPLE WHO WERE SITTING IN DARKNESS SAW A GREAT LIGHT, AND TO THOSE WHO WERE SITTING IN THE LAND AND SHADOW OF DEATH, UPON THEM A LIGHT DAWNED."
Ps. 78:2–4, p. 568 I will open my mouth in a parable; I will utter dark sayings of old, which we have heard and known, and our fathers have told us. We will not conceal them from their children, but tell to the generation to come the praises of the LORD, and His strength and His wondrous works that He has done.	speaks in parables	*Matt. 13:34, 35, p. 976* All these things Jesus spoke to the multitudes in parables, and He did not speak to them without a parable, so that what was spoken through the prophet might be fulfilled, saying, "I WILL OPEN MY MOUTH IN PARABLES; I WILL UTTER THINGS HIDDEN SINCE THE FOUNDATION OF THE WORLD."
Deut. 18:15, p. 186 "The LORD your God will raise up for you a prophet like me from among you, from your countrymen, you shall listen to him."	a prophet	*Acts 3:20, 22, p. 1097* and that He may send Jesus, the Christ appointed for you, . . . "Moses said, 'THE LORD GOD SHALL RAISE UP FOR YOU A PROPHET LIKE ME FROM YOUR BRETHREN; TO HIM YOU SHALL GIVE HEED in everything He says to you.'"
Is. 61:1, 2, p. 708 The Spirit of the Lord GOD is upon me, because the LORD has anointed me to bring good news to the afflicted; He has sent me to bind up the brokenhearted, to proclaim liberty to captives, and freedom to prisoners; to proclaim the favorable year of the LORD, and the day of vengeance of our God; to comfort all who mourn,	to bind up the brokenhearted	*Luke 4:18, 19, p. 1030* "THE SPIRIT OF THE LORD IS UPON ME, BECAUSE HE ANOINTED ME TO PREACH THE GOSPEL TO THE POOR. HE HAS SENT ME TO PROCLAIM RELEASE TO THE CAPTIVES, AND RECOVERY OF SIGHT TO THE BLIND, TO SET FREE THOSE WHO ARE DOWNTRODDEN, TO PROCLAIM THE FAVORABLE YEAR OF THE LORD."

PROPHETIC SCRIPTURE	SUBJECT	FULFILLED
Is. 53:3, p. 702 He was despised and forsaken of men, a man of sorrows, and acquainted with grief; and like one from whom men hide their face, He was despised, and we did not esteem Him.	rejected by His own people, the Jews	*John 1:11, p. 1064* He came to His own, and those who were His own did not receive Him. *Luke 23:18, p. 1056* But they cried out all together, saying, "Away with this man, and release for us Barabbas!"
Ps. 110:4, p. 587 The LORD has sworn and will not change His mind, "Thou art a priest forever according to the order of Melchizedek."	priest after order of Melchizedek	*Heb. 5:5, 6, p. 1241* So also Christ did not glorify Himself so as to become a high priest, but He who said to Him, "THOU ART MY SON, TODAY I HAVE BEGOTTEN THEE"; just as He says also in another *passage*, "THOU ART A PRIEST FOREVER ACCORDING TO THE ORDER OF MELCHIZEDEK."
Zech. 9:9, p. 922 Rejoice greatly, O daughter of Zion! Shout *in triumph*, O daughter of Jerusalem! Behold, your king is coming to you; He is just and endowed with salvation, humble, and mounted on a donkey, even on a colt, the foal of a donkey.	triumphal entry	*Mark 11:7, 9, 11, p. 1012* And they brought the colt to Jesus and put their garments on it; and He sat upon it. . . . And those who went before, and those who followed after, were crying out, "Hosanna! BLESSED IS HE WHO COMES IN THE NAME OF THE LORD"; . . . And He entered Jerusalem *and came* into the temple; and after looking all around, He departed for Bethany with the twelve, since it was already late.
Ps. 8:2, p. 531 From the mouth of infants and nursing babes Thou hast established strength, because of Thine adversaries, to make the enemy and the revengeful cease.	adored by infants	*Matt. 21:15, 16, p. 984* But when the chief priests and the scribes saw the wonderful things that He had done, and the children who were crying out in the temple and saying, "Hosanna to the Son of David," they became indignant, and said to Him, "Do You hear what these are saying?" And Jesus said to them, "Yes; have you never read, 'OUT OF THE MOUTH OF INFANTS AND NURSING BABES THOU HAST PREPARED PRAISE FOR THYSELF?'"
Is. 53:1, p. 701 Who has believed our message? And to whom has the arm of the LORD been revealed?	not believed	*John 12:37, 38, p. 1080* But though He had performed so many signs before them, *yet* they were not believing in Him; that the word of Isaiah the prophet might be fulfilled, which he spoke, "LORD, WHO HAS BELIEVED OUR REPORT? AND TO WHOM HAS THE ARM OF THE LORD BEEN REVEALED?"
Ps. 41:9, p. 549 Even my close friend, in whom I trusted, who ate my bread, has lifted up his heel against me.	betrayed by a close friend	*Luke 22:47, 48, p. 1055* While He was still speaking, behold, a multitude *came*, and the one called Judas, one of the twelve, was preceding them; and he approached Jesus to kiss Him. But Jesus said to him, "Judas, are you betraying the Son of Man with a kiss?"
Zech. 11:12, p. 924 And I said to them, "If it is good in your sight, give *me* my wages; but if not, never mind!" So they weighed out thirty *shekels* of silver as my wages.	betrayed for thirty pieces of silver	*Matt. 26:14, 15, p. 991* Then one of the twelve, named Judas Iscariot, went to the chief priests, and said, "What are you willing to give me to deliver Him up to you?" And they weighed out to him thirty pieces of silver.

PROPHETIC SCRIPTURE	SUBJECT	FULFILLED
Ps. 35:11, p. 545 Malicious witnesses rise up; they ask me of things that I do not know.	accused by false witnesses	**Mark 14:57, 58, p. 1018** And some stood up and *began* to give false testimony against Him, saying, "We heard Him say, 'I will destroy this temple made with hands, and in three days I will build another made without hands.'"
Is. 53:7, p. 702 He was oppressed and He was afflicted, yet He did not open His mouth; like a lamb that is led to slaughter, and like a sheep that is silent before its shearers, so He did not open His mouth.	silent to accusations	**Mark 15:4, 5, p. 1018** And Pilate was questioning Him again, saying, "Do You make no answer? See how many charges they bring against You!" But Jesus made no further answer; so that Pilate was amazed.
Is. 50:6, p. 699 I gave My back to those who strike *Me*, and My cheeks to those who pluck out the beard; I did not cover My face from humiliation and spitting.	spat on and struck	**Matt. 26:67, p. 992** Then they spat in His face and beat Him with their fists; and others slapped Him,
Ps. 35:19, p. 545 Do not let those who are wrongfully my enemies rejoice over me; neither let those who hate me without cause wink maliciously.	hated without reason	**John 15:24, 25, p. 1083** "If I had not done among them the works which no one else did, they would not have sin; but now they have both seen and hated Me and My Father as well. But *they have done this* in order that the word may be fulfilled that is written in their Law, 'THEY HATED ME WITHOUT A CAUSE.'"
Is. 53:5, p. 702 But He was pierced through for our transgressions, He was crushed for our iniquities; the chastening for our well-being *fell* upon Him, and by His scourging we are healed.	vicarious sacrifice	**Rom. 5:6, 8, p. 1135** For while we were still helpless, at the right time Christ died for the ungodly. . . . But God demonstrates His own love toward us, in that while we were yet sinners, Christ died for us.
Is. 53:12, p. 702 Therefore, I will allot Him a portion with the great, and He will divide the booty with the strong; because He poured out Himself to death, and was numbered with the transgressors; yet He Himself bore the sin of many, and interceded for the transgressors.	crucified with malefactors	**Mark 15:27, 28, p. 1019** And they crucified two robbers with Him, one on His right and one on His left. [And the Scripture was fulfilled which says, "And He was numbered with transgressors."]
Zech. 12:10, p. 924 "And I will pour out on the house of David and on the inhabitants of Jerusalem, the Spirit of grace and of supplication, so that they will look on Me whom they have pierced; and they will mourn for Him, as one mourns for an only son, and they will weep bitterly over Him, like the bitter weeping over a first-born."	pierced through hands and feet	**John 20:27, p. 1088** Then He said to Thomas, "Reach here your finger, and see My hands; and reach here your hand, and put it into My side; and be not unbelieving, but believing."
Ps. 22:7, 8, p. 538 All who see me sneer at me; they separate with the lip, they wag the head, *saying*, "Commit *yourself* to the LORD; let Him deliver him; let Him rescue him, because He delights in him."	sneered and mocked	**Luke 23:35, p. 1057** And the people stood by, looking on. And even the rulers were sneering at Him, saying, "He saved others; let Him save Himself if this is the Christ of God, His Chosen One."
Ps. 69:9, p. 562 For zeal for Thy house has consumed me, and the reproaches of those who reproach Thee have fallen on me.	was reproached	**Rom. 15:3, p. 1143** For even Christ did not please Himself; but as it is written, "THE REPROACHES OF THOSE WHO REPROACHED THEE FELL UPON ME."

PROPHETIC SCRIPTURE	SUBJECT	FULFILLED
Ps. 109:4, p. 586 In return for my love they act as my accusers; but I am *in* prayer.	**prayer for His enemies**	*Luke 23:34, p. 1057* But Jesus was saying, "Father, forgive them; for they do not know what they are doing." And they cast lots, dividing up His garments among themselves.
Ps. 22:17, 18, p. 538 I can count all my bones. They look, they stare at me; they divide my garments among them, and for my clothing they cast lots.	**soldiers gambled for His clothing**	*Matt. 27:35, 36, p. 994* And when they had crucified Him, they divided up His garments among themselves, casting lots; and sitting down, they *began* to keep watch over Him there.
Ps. 22:1, p. 537 My God, my God, why hast Thou forsaken me? Far from my deliverance are the words of my groaning.	**forsaken by God**	*Matt. 27:46, p. 994* And about the ninth hour Jesus cried out with a loud voice, saying, "Eli, Eli, lama sabachthani?" that is, "My God, My God, why hast Thou forsaken Me?"
Ps. 34:20, p. 544 He keeps all his bones; not one of them is broken.	**no bones broken**	*John 19:32, 33, 36, p. 1087* The soldiers therefore came, and broke the legs of the first man, and of the other man who was crucified with Him; but coming to Jesus, when they saw that He was already dead, they did not break His legs; . . . For these things came to pass, that the Scripture might be fulfilled, "Not a bone of Him shall be broken."
Zech. 12:10, p. 924 "And I will pour out on the house of David and on the inhabitants of Jerusalem, the Spirit of grace and of supplication, so that they will look on Me whom they have pierced; and they will mourn for Him, as one mourns for an only son, and they will weep bitterly over Him, like the bitter weeping over a first-born."	**His side pierced**	*John 19:34, p. 1087* but one of the soldiers pierced His side with a spear, and immediately there came out blood and water.
Is. 53:9, p. 702 His grave was assigned with wicked men, yet He was with a rich man in His death, because He had done no violence, nor was there any deceit in His mouth.	**buried with the rich**	*Matt. 27:57–60, p. 994* And when it was evening, there came a rich man from Arimathea, named Joseph, who himself had also become a disciple of Jesus. This man went to Pilate and asked for the body of Jesus. Then Pilate ordered *it* to be given over *to him*. And Joseph took the body and wrapped it in a clean linen cloth, and laid it in his own new tomb, which he had hewn out in the rock; and he rolled a large stone against the entrance of the tomb and went away.
Ps. 16:10, p. 534 For Thou wilt not abandon my soul to Sheol; neither wilt Thou allow Thy Holy One to undergo decay. *Ps. 49:15, p. 553* But God will redeem my soul from the power of Sheol; for He will receive me. [Selah.	**to be resurrected**	*Mark 16:6, 7, p. 1020* And he said to them, "Do not be amazed; you are looking for Jesus the Nazarene, who has been crucified. He has risen; He is not here; behold, *here is* the place where they laid Him. But go, tell His disciples and Peter, 'He is going before you into Galilee; there you will see Him, just as He said to you.'"

PROPHETIC SCRIPTURE	SUBJECT	FULFILLED
Ps. 68:18, p. 561 Thou hast ascended on high, Thou hast led captive *Thy* captives; Thou hast received gifts among men, even *among* the rebellious also, that the LORD God may dwell *there*.	**His ascension to God's right hand**	*Mark 16:19, p. 1020* So then, when the Lord Jesus had spoken to them, He was received up into heaven, and sat down at the right hand of God. *1 Cor. 15:4, p. 1160* and that He was buried, and that He was raised on the third day according to the Scriptures, *Eph. 4:8, p. 1187* Therefore it says, "WHEN HE ASCENDED ON HIGH, HE LED CAPTIVE A HOST OF CAPTIVES, AND HE GAVE GIFTS TO MEN."

THE PARABLES
OF JESUS CHRIST

Parable	Matthew	Mark	Luke
1. Lamp Under the Peck-measure	5:14–16	4:21, 22	8:16, 17 11:33–36
2. A Wise Man Builds on Rock and A Foolish Man Builds on Sand	7:24–27		6:47–49
3. Unshrunk (New) Cloth on an Old Garment	9:16	2:21	5:36
4. New Wine in Old Wineskins	9:17	2:22	5:37, 38
5. The Sower	13:3–23	4:2–20	8:4–15
6. The Tares (Weeds)	13:24–30		
7. The Mustard Seed	13:31, 32	4:30–32	13:18, 19
8. The Leaven	13:33		13:20, 21
9. The Hidden Treasure	13:44		
10. The Pearl of Great Value	13:45, 46		
11. The Dragnet	13:47–50		
12. The Lost Sheep	18:12–14		15:3–7
13. The Unforgiving Slave	18:23–35		
14. The Laborers in the Vineyard	20:1–16		
15. The Two Sons	21:28–32		
16. The Wicked Vine-growers	21:33–45	12:1–12	20:9–19
17. The Wedding Feast	22:2–14		
18. The Fig Tree	24:32–44	13:28–32	21:29–33
19. The Prudent and Foolish Virgins	25:1–13		
20. The Talents	25:14–30		
21. The Growing Seed		4:26–29	
22. The Absent Householder		13:33–37	
23. The Moneylender and Two Debtors			7:41–43
24. The Good Samaritan			10:30–37
25. A Friend in Need			11:5–13
26. The Rich Fool			12:16–21
27. The Faithful Slave and the Evil Slave			12:35–40
28. The Faithful and Sensible Steward			12:42–48
29. The Barren Fig Tree			13:6–9
30. The Big Dinner			14:16–24
31. Building a Tower and a King Making War			14:25–35
32. The Lost Coin			15:8–10
33. The Lost Son			15:11–32
34. The Unrighteous Steward			16:1–13
35. The Rich Man and Lazarus			16:19–31
36. Unworthy Slaves			17:7–10
37. The Persistent Widow			18:1–8
38. The Pharisee and the Tax-gatherer			18:9–14
39. The Minas (Pounds)			19:11–27

TEACHINGS AND
ILLUSTRATIONS OF CHRIST

Subject	Reference	Subject	Reference	Subject	Reference
Abiding in Christ	John 15:4–10	Character	John 1:47	Drunkenness	Luke 21:34
Ability	Matt. 25:14, 15	Charity	Luke 12:33	Dullness	Matt. 13:13
Ablution	Matt. 6:17, 18	Cheating	Mark 10:19	Duty	Luke 17:10
Abode	John 14:23	Chosen	Matt. 22:14	Dwelling places	John 14:2, 3
Abraham	John 8:37, 56	Church	Matt. 18:17	**Earth**	Matt. 5:18
Abstinence	Luke 21:34	Circumcision	John 7:22, 23	Earthquakes	Mark 13:8
Abundant life	John 10:10	Cleansing	John 15:3	Economy	Matt. 15:37
Access to God	John 10:7, 9	Coin	Matt. 22:19–21		John 6:12
Accountability	Luke 12:47, 48	Coldness	Matt. 24:12	Elect	Matt. 24:24, 31
Accusation,		Communication	Luke 24:17	Election	Matt. 25:34
false	Matt. 5:11	Compassion	Matt. 15:32	Elijah	Matt. 17:11, 12
Adultery	Matt. 5:27, 28		Luke 10:33	Employer	Matt. 20:1–16
Adversity	Luke 24:46	Compromise	Matt. 5:25, 26	Encouragement	Matt. 9:2
Affliction	Matt. 24:7–12	Conceit	Luke 18:10–12	Endowments	Matt. 25:14, 15
Agreement	Matt. 18:19	Conduct,		Endurance	Matt. 10:22
Altar	Matt. 23:18, 19	Christian	Matt. 5:16		Luke 21:19
Ambition	Luke 22:25–30	Confessing		Enemies	Matt. 5:43, 44
Angels	Matt. 13:39, 41	Christ	Matt. 10:32, 33	Eternal life	Matt. 19:29
Anger	Matt. 5:22	Confession		Eternal sin	Mark 3:29
Anxiety	Luke 12:22–31	of sin	Luke 18:13, 14	Etiquette	Luke 10:8
Apostasy	Matt. 13:18–22	Confidence	Mark 10:24	Evil	Matt. 15:19
	Luke 8:13	Conflict	Matt. 10:34–36	Exaltation	Matt. 23:12
Apostles	Luke 11:49	Conscience	John 8:7–9	Example	John 13:15
Appearance	Matt. 6:16	Contention	Matt. 18:15–17	Excuses	Luke 14:18–20
Appearance,		Contentment	John 6:43	Extravagance	Luke 15:11–14
outward	Matt. 23:27, 28	Conversion	Matt. 13:15	**Fainting**	Mark 8:2, 3
Authority	Matt. 21:24	Convict	John 16:8	Faith	Matt. 6:25
	Luke 10:19	Corruption,			Mark 11:22
Avarice	Luke 12:16–21	moral	Luke 11:39		Luke 7:50
Backsliding	Luke 9:62	Courage	Matt. 9:22	Faithfulness	Matt. 25:21
Baptism	Matt. 28:19	Covenant	Mark 14:24	Faithlessness	Matt. 25:24–30
	Acts 1:5	Coveting	Mark 7:21, 22	False prophets	Matt. 24:11
Beatitudes	Matt. 5:3–11	Cross-bearing	Matt. 10:38	False witness	Matt. 19:18
Beelzebul	Matt. 10:25	Crucifixion	Luke 9:22	Farm	Matt. 22:2–6
Begging	Luke 16:3	Cup of water	Matt. 10:42	Fasting	Matt. 6:16–18
Beneficence	Matt. 5:42	**Dancing**	Luke 15:25–27	Faultfinding	Matt. 7:3–5
Betrayal	Matt. 26:21	Daniel	Matt. 24:15	Faults	Matt. 18:15
Bigotry	Luke 18:9–14	Darkness	Luke 11:35	Fear of God	Matt. 10:28
Birds	Matt. 8:20	David	Matt. 12:3	Feast	Luke 14:8
Blasphemy	Matt. 12:31, 32	Day	John 11:9	Feet washing	John 13:12–15
Blessings	Matt. 5:3–11	Deaf	Matt. 13:13–15	Fellowship	Matt. 8:11
Blind guides	Matt. 15:14	Death	Luke 9:22	Flattery	Luke 6:26
Borrowing	Matt. 5:42		John 8:51	Flesh	John 6:53
Bread of life	John 6:32–35	Debts	Matt. 18:24	Flock	Matt. 26:31
Brothers	Matt. 23:8	Deceivers	Matt. 24:4, 5	Following	
Builders	Matt. 7:24	Decision	Matt. 6:24	Christ	Matt. 10:37, 38
	Luke 6:47–49	Defilement	Matt. 15:11,	Food	Matt. 6:11
Burdens	Luke 11:46		18, 19		Matt. 6:25
Burial	Matt. 8:22	Devil	Matt. 13:38, 39		John 6:27
Caesar	Matt. 22:21	Diligence	John 9:4	Fool	Matt. 5:22
Call of God	Matt. 20:16	Disbelief	John 5:38	Formalism	Matt. 23:23–28
Called ones	Matt. 22:14	Discernment	Matt. 16:2, 3	Forsaking all	Luke 14:33
Capital and		Discipleship	Luke 14:33	Foxes	Luke 9:58
labor	Matt. 20:1–15	Disputes	Mark 9:33, 34	Friends	Luke 11:5–8
Capital		Distress	Luke 21:23, 25	Frugality	John 6:12
punishment	Matt. 26:52	Divorce	Matt. 5:31, 32	Fruitfulness	Matt. 13:23
Care of God	Matt. 6:30, 33	Doctrine	Mark 7:7	Fruitlessness	Luke 13:6–9
Caution	Mark 4:24	Doubt	Matt. 21:21	**Generosity**	Matt. 25:34–40
Celibacy	Matt. 19:11, 12	Drunkard	Luke 7:34	Gentiles	Matt. 10:5–7

Subject	Reference	Subject	Reference	Subject	Reference
Gentleness	Matt. 5:5	Integrity	Luke 16:10	Murder	Matt. 15:19
Giving	Luke 6:38	Intercession	John 17:9	Mysteries	
Gladness	Luke 15:32	Investment	Matt. 6:19, 20	of Heaven	Matt. 13:11
Glorifying God	Matt. 5:16	Jealousy	Luke 15:25–30	Narrow way	Matt. 7:13, 14
Gluttony	Luke 21:34	John the Baptist	Luke 7:24–28	Neglect	Luke 12:47
God	Matt. 19:17, 26	Jonah	Matt. 12:39–41	Neighbor	Matt. 19:19
Godlessness	John 5:42, 44	Joy	Matt. 25:21	Neutrality	Matt. 12:30
Golden Rule	Matt. 7:12		Luke 15:7, 10	New birth	John 3:3, 5–8
Gospel	Luke 4:18	Judge not	Matt. 7:1, 2	Noah	Luke 17:26, 27
Grace	2 Cor. 12:9	Judgment	Matt. 11:24	Oath	Matt. 5:33–37
Greatness	Matt. 5:19	Judgment day	Matt. 25:31–46	Obedience	Matt. 12:50
Grumble	John 6:43	Justice	John 5:30	Offering	Matt. 5:23, 24
Guidance	John 16:13	Justification,		Offerings	Luke 21:3, 4
Hairs numbered	Matt. 10:30	self	Luke 16:15	Opportunity	Matt. 5:25
Hand of God	John 10:27–29	Killing	Matt. 5:21, 22	Parables	Mark 4:11, 12
Happiness	Matt. 5:12	Kindness	Luke 10:30–35	Paradise	Luke 23:43
	John 13:16, 17	Kingdom	Luke 7:28	Pardoning	Luke 6:37
Harlots	Matt. 21:31		John 18:36	Parents	Matt. 10:21
Harvest	Matt. 9:37, 38	Kiss	Luke 7:45	Patriotism	Matt. 22:21
Hatred	John 15:18, 19	Knowledge	John 8:31, 32	Peace	Mark 9:50
Healing	Matt. 10:7, 8	Labor	Matt. 20:1–14	Peacemakers	Matt. 5:9
	Mark 2:17	Laughter	Luke 6:21	Penitence	Luke 18:13
Heart	Matt. 13:19	Law	Luke 16:16	Perception	John 8:43
Heaven	Luke 16:17	Lawsuit	Matt. 5:25, 40	Perfection	Matt. 5:48
	John 3:13	Lawyers	Luke 11:46	Persecution	Matt. 24:9
Hell	Matt. 5:22	Leaven	Matt. 16:6	Perseverance	Matt. 10:22
	Matt. 10:28		Luke 13:20, 21	Pharisaism	Matt. 23:2–33
Helper	John 14:16	Lending	Luke 6:34, 35	Pharisee and	
	John 15:26	Lepers	Matt. 10:7, 8	tax-gatherer	Luke 18:10–14
Helpless	John 6:44	Levite	Luke 10:30–32	Pharisees	Matt. 5:20
Hireling	John 10:11–13	Liars	John 8:44, 45	Philanthropy	Luke 11:41
Holy Spirit	John 14:26	Liberality	Luke 6:30, 38	Physician	Matt. 9:12
Home	Mark 5:19	Liberty	Luke 4:18	Piety	John 1:47
Honesty	Mark 10:19	Life	Matt. 6:25	Pleasing God	John 8:29
	Luke 8:15		John 5:40	Pleasures	Luke 8:14
Honor of men	Matt. 6:2	Light	Luke 11:33	Poison	Mark 16:17, 18
Honor			John 8:12	Poll-tax	Matt. 22:19–21
of parents	Matt. 15:3–6	Living water	John 4:10	Polygamy	Matt. 19:8, 9
Hospitality	Luke 14:12–14	Log	Luke 6:41, 42	Poor	Mark 14:7
Humility	Matt. 11:29	Loneliness	John 16:32	Power	Matt. 6:13
	John 13:14	Lord's Supper	Matt. 26:26–29	Prayer	Matt. 6:9–13
Hunger,		Loss of soul	Matt. 16:25, 26		Matt. 7:7–11
spiritual	Matt. 5:6	Lost		Preaching	Mark 16:15, 16
	Luke 6:21	opportunity	Matt. 25:7–12	Procrastination	Matt. 25:3
Hypocrisy	Matt. 6:5	Love	Matt. 22:37–40	Profit and loss	Matt. 16:26
	Luke 6:42	Lukewarmness	Matt. 26:40, 41	Prophets	Matt. 7:15
Ignorance	Matt. 22:29	Lunatic	Matt. 17:14, 15		Matt. 10:41
Immortality	Matt. 25:46	Lust	Mark 4:18, 19	Proselyte	Matt. 23:15
	John 11:25, 26	Magistrates	Luke 12:11, 58	Protection	Luke 18:3
Impartiality		Mammon	Matt. 6:24	Providence	Matt. 6:25–33
of God	Matt. 5:45	Marriage	Matt. 19:4–6	Prudence	Matt. 10:16–20
Inconsistency	Matt. 7:3–5		Mark 12:25	Punishment	Matt. 21:41
	Luke 6:41, 42	Martyrdom	John 16:1–3	Purity	Matt. 5:8
Indecision	Luke 9:62	Mary's choice	Luke 10:41, 42	Ransom	Matt. 20:28
Indifference	Matt. 24:12	Memorial	Matt. 26:13	Reaping	John 4:35–38
Industry	John 4:36	Mercy	Matt. 5:7	Receiving	
Infidelity	John 3:18		Luke 16:24	Christ	Mark 9:37
Influence	Matt. 5:13	Minister	Luke 10:2	Reconciliation	Matt. 5:23, 24
Ingratitude	Luke 17:17, 18	Miracles	Matt. 12:28	Regeneration	Matt. 19:28
Innocence	Matt. 10:16	Money lender,		Rejecting	
Insincerity	Luke 16:15	creditor	Luke 7:41, 42	Christ	John 3:18
Inspiration	Luke 12:12	Moses	Matt. 19:8	Rejoicing	Luke 10:20
Instability	Matt. 7:26, 27	Moses' Law	John 7:19	Release	Luke 4:18
Instruction	John 6:45	Mother	Matt. 10:37	Religion	Matt. 25:34–36
Insufficiency	Mark 10:21	Mourn	Matt. 5:4		Mark 7:6–8

Subject	Reference	Subject	Reference	Subject	Reference
Repentance	Matt. 11:21	Self-sacrifice	Matt. 16:25	Teaching	Matt. 28:19, 20
	Luke 13:28	Serpents	Matt. 23:33		John 13:13–15
Reproof	Matt. 11:21–23		John 3:14	Temperance	Luke 21:34
Resignation	Matt. 26:39	Service	Luke 22:27	Temptations	Matt. 4:1–11
Responsibility	Luke 12:47, 48	Sheep	Luke 15:4–7		Luke 8:13
Rest	Matt. 11:28–30	Shepherd	John 10:1–18	Thieves	Matt. 6:19
	Matt. 26:45	Sickness	Matt. 10:8		John 10:1, 8
Resurrection	John 6:40	Signs	Luke 11:16	Timidness	Mark 4:40
Retaliation	Matt. 5:39–44		John 4:48	Tithes	Luke 18:11, 12
Retribution	Matt. 23:34, 35	Silence	Matt. 17:9	Traditions	Mark 7:9, 13
Reward	Matt. 10:42	Sin	Matt. 26:28	Transgres-	
Riches	Mark 4:19		John 8:34	sions	Matt. 15:2
Righteousness	Matt. 5:6, 20	Sincerity	Matt. 5:13–16	Treasures	Matt. 6:19–21
	John 16:10	Skepticism	John 20:27, 29	Tribulation	Matt. 24:9
Robbers	Luke 10:30	Slaves	Matt. 18:23		John 16:33
	John 10:1		John 15:15	Truth	John 14:6
Robbery	Matt. 23:25	Sleep	Mark 4:26, 27	**Unbelievers**	Luke 12:46
Sabbath	Matt. 12:5–8		Mark 13:35, 36	Uncharitable-	
Sackcloth	Matt. 11:21	Slothfulness	Matt. 25:26–30	ness	John 7:24
Sacrifice	Matt. 12:7	Son of Man	Luke 9:22	Unchastity	Matt. 5:31, 32
Sacrilege	Matt. 21:13	Sorrow	Matt. 19:22	Uncleanness	Matt. 23:27
Sadducees	Matt. 16:6		John 16:6	Unity	John 17:20, 21
Salt	Matt. 5:13	Soul	Matt. 10:28	Unpardonable	
	Mark 9:50		Luke 12:19, 20	sin	Matt. 12:31, 32
Salvation	Luke 19:9	Soul winners	Matt. 4:19	**Vengeance**	Matt. 5:39, 40
	John 4:22	Sowing	Mark 4:14	Vine	John 15:1, 4, 5
Samaritan	Luke 10:30–35	Speech	John 8:43	Visions	Matt. 17:9
Sanctification	John 17:17	Spirit	Matt. 26:41	**Walks of Life**	John 8:12
Satan	Matt. 4:10		Mark 5:8		John 12:35
	Mark 4:15	Statement	Matt. 5:37	War	Matt. 24:6
Scripture	Matt. 21:42	Steadfastness	Matt. 10:22	Watchfulness	Matt. 24:42, 44
	Luke 4:21	Stealing	Matt. 19:18		Luke 12:37–40
Secrecy	Luke 12:2, 3	Steward	Luke 12:42, 43	Wedding	Luke 14:8–10
Security	Luke 6:47, 48		Luke 16:1–8	Widow	Mark 12:43, 44
Seduction	Mark 13:22	Stewardship	Luke 19:13–27	Wine	Luke 5:37–39
Seeking the		Stomach	Matt. 15:17	Wisdom	Luke 21:15
kingdom	Matt. 6:19, 20	Strife	Luke 22:24	Witness	John 8:14
Self-		Stubborn-		Witness, false	Matt. 19:18
condemnation	Matt. 23:29–32	ness	John 5:40	Witnessing	Acts 1:8
	Luke 19:20–24	Stumbling		Wives	Luke 14:20, 26
Self-control	Matt. 5:21	block	Matt. 23:13	Worker	Matt. 10:10
Self-deception	Luke 12:16–21	Submission	Matt. 26:39, 42	Worldliness	Luke 21:34
Self-denial	Matt. 16:24–26	Suffering	Matt. 26:38	Worm	Mark 9:43–48
Self-exaltation	Matt. 23:12	Supper,		Worries	
Self-		The Lord's	Luke 22:14–20	of the world	Matt. 13:22
examination	Matt. 7:3–5	Swearing	Matt. 23:16–22	Worship	Matt. 4:10
Selfishness	Luke 6:32–35	**Talents**	Matt. 18:24	**Yoke**	Matt. 11:28, 29
Self-		Taxes	Matt. 22:19–21	**Zaccheus**	Luke 19:5
righteousness	Matt. 23:23–27	Tax-gatherers	Matt. 5:46, 47	Zeal	John 2:17

THE MIRACLES OF JESUS CHRIST

Miracle	Matthew	Mark	Luke	John
1. Cleansing a Leper	8:2	1:40	5:12	
2. Healing a Centurion's Servant (of paralysis)	8:5		7:1	
3. Healing Peter's Mother-in-law	8:14	1:30	4:38	
4. Healing the Sick at Evening	8:16	1:32	4:40	
5. Stilling the Storm	8:23	4:35	8:22	
6. Demons Entering a Herd of Swine	8:28	5:1	8:26	
7. Healing a Paralytic	9:2	2:3	5:18	
8. Raising the Ruler's Daughter	9:18, 23	5:22, 35	8:40, 49	
9. Healing the Hemorrhaging Woman	9:20	5:25	8:43	
10. Healing Two Blind Men	9:27			
11. Curing a Demon-possessed, Dumb Man	9:32			
12. Healing a Man's Withered Hand	12:9	3:1	6:6	
13. Curing a Demon-possessed, Blind, and Dumb Man	12:22		11:14	
14. Feeding the Five Thousand	14:13	6:30	9:10	6:1
15. Walking on the Sea	14:25	6:48		6:19
16. Healing the Gentile Woman's Daughter	15:21	7:24		
17. Feeding the Four Thousand	15:32	8:1		
18. Healing the Epileptic Boy	17:14	9:17	9:38	
19. Temple Tax in the Fish's Mouth	17:24			
20. Healing Two Blind Men	20:30	10:46	18:35	
21. Withering the Fig Tree	21:18	11:12		
22. Casting Out an Unclean Spirit		1:23	4:33	
23. Healing a Deaf Mute		7:32		
24. Healing a Blind Man at Bethsaida		8:22		
25. Escape from the Hostile Multitude			4:30	
26. Catch of Fish			5:1	
27. Raising of a Widow's Son at Nain			7:11	
28. Healing the Infirm, Bent Woman			13:11	
29. Healing the Man with Dropsy			14:1	
30. Cleansing the Ten Lepers			17:11	
31. Restoring a Servant's Ear			22:51	
32. Turning Water into Wine				2:1
33. Healing the Royal Official's Son (of fever)				4:46
34. Healing an Infirm Man at Bethesda				5:1
35. Healing the Man Born Blind				9:1
36. Raising of Lazarus				11:43
37. Second Catch of Fish				21:1

GOD'S ANSWERS TO MAN'S CONCERNS

Abiding in Christ—John 15:5;
1 John 2:28; 2 John 9
Abundance—Deut. 30:9;
John 10:10; 2 Cor. 9:8
Afflictions—Job 5:17;
2 Cor. 4:17; Heb. 12:11
Anger—Ps. 37:8; Prov. 16:32;
James 1:19
Answered Prayer—
1 Kin. 18:37; Ps. 91:15;
Luke 11:9
Backsliding—Prov. 14:14;
Matt. 24:12; Heb. 10:38
Be Still Before God—
Num. 9:8; Job 37:14;
Ps. 46:10
Believers Preserved—
John 10:28; 17:11;
Phil. 4:6, 7
Benevolence—Prov. 25:21;
Matt. 5:42; Acts 20:35
Chastisement—Deut. 8:5;
Prov. 3:11, 12; Rev. 3:19
Cheerfulness—Prov. 15:13;
John 16:33; Acts 27:25
Christ's Love—John 13:1;
Rom. 8:35; 1 John 3:16
Christ's Majesty—John 18:6;
2 Thess. 2:8; Rev. 1:17
Christian Duty—
Matt. 25:35, 36; Rom. 15:1;
1 Cor. 9:22
Confessing Christ—
Matt. 10:32; Rom. 10:9;
1 John 4:15
Contentment—Prov. 15:16;
Phil. 4:11; Heb. 13:5
Courage—Josh. 1:9;
Dan. 3:16, 17; Phil. 1:28
Divine Comfort—Is. 40:1;
Is. 61:1, 2; John 14:1
Divine Deliverance—
Dan. 6:22; Job 5:19;
2 Tim. 4:18
Divine Enabling—2 Cor. 9:8;
Phil. 4:13; 1 Tim. 1:12
Divine Encouragement—
Is. 41:13; Matt. 9:2;
Acts 23:11
Divine Faithfulness—Ps. 36:5;
1 Cor. 1:9; 1 Pet. 4:19
Divine Fellowship—
Matt. 18:20; Luke 24:15;
Rev. 3:20
Divine Guidance—
Ps. 25:9; 48:14; Is. 42:16

Divine Power—Rom. 4:21;
Eph. 3:20; Jude 24, 25
Divine Providence—Ps. 23:5;
Matt. 14:20; Luke 6:38
Divine Reward—Gen. 15:1;
Ps. 19:9, 11; Matt. 6:4
Divine Sympathy—
Ps. 103:13; John 11:35, 36;
Heb. 4:15
Divisions—Luke 11:17;
1 Cor. 1:10; 3:3
Doubt—Matt. 14:31;
Mark 4:40; Luke 24:25
Dying to Live—Luke 9:24;
John 12:24; Gal. 2:20
Enemies of the Soul—
Luke 22:31; Eph. 6:12;
1 Pet. 5:8
Evil Relationships—Ex. 23:2;
Ps. 1:1; 2 Cor. 6:14
Faith—Rom. 10:17; Gal. 5:16;
Eph. 2:8
Fear of God—Josh. 24:14;
Eccl. 12:13; 1 Pet. 2:17
Fear of Man—Prov. 29:25;
Is. 51:12; John 12:42
Foolishness—Ps. 53:1;
Prov. 15:14; 18:13
Forgiveness—Ps. 130:4;
Matt. 6:14; Acts 5:31
Fruitfulness—Matt. 3:8;
Luke 19:23; John 15:8
Gain Through Loss—
Matt. 19:29; John 12:24;
Phil. 3:8
Gentleness—1 Thess. 2:7;
1 Tim. 2:24; James 3:17
God Our Refuge—Ps. 57:1;
Is. 25:4; 51:16
God's Care for You—
Gen. 28:15; Ps. 121:4;
2 Tim. 1:12
God's Drawing Power—
Jer. 31:3; John 6:44; 12:32
God's Grace—
Rom. 4:16; 9:16; Titus 3:5
God's Love for You—
John 3:16; 1 Pet. 1:18, 19;
Rev. 1:5
Greed—Eccl. 5:10;
Matt. 27:5; 1 Tim. 6:9
Heaven—Matt. 6:20;
Luke 10:20; John 14:2, 3
Hell—Matt. 13:41, 42; 25:41;
Rev. 20:10, 14, 15; 21:8
Hospitality—Rom. 12:13;

Titus 1:8; Heb. 13:2
Humility—Mic. 6:8;
Luke 22:26; Rom. 12:3
Intercession—Is. 53:12;
Luke 22:32; John 17:9
Joy—Neh. 8:10; Ps. 16:11;
John 16:24
Kindness—Rom. 12:10;
1 Cor. 13:14; Eph. 4:32
Liberty—Is. 61:1; Rom. 8:2;
2 Cor. 3:17
Light in Darkness—Is. 60:1;
Mal. 4:2; 2 Pet. 1:19
Living Temples—1 Cor. 3:16;
Eph. 2:20; 1 Pet. 2:5
Living for God—
Rom. 6:11; 14:8; 2 Cor. 5:15
Looking to God—Ps. 34:5;
John 17:1; Acts 7:55
Love to Neighbors—
Mark 12:31; Rom. 13:10;
James 2:8
Man's Unfaithfulness—
Matt. 26:56; John 6:66;
1 John 2:19
Mercy—Prov. 11:17;
Matt. 5:7; Luke 6:36
Obedience—Josh. 11:15;
2 Kin. 18:6; Acts 26:19
Our Eternal Home—
John 14:2; 2 Cor. 5:1;
Rev. 7:9
Patience—Ps. 40:1; Is. 33:2;
Acts 1:4
Popularity—John 12:43;
Acts 24:7; Col. 3:22
Postponed Blessing—Ps. 40:1;
Is. 25:9; Acts 1:4
Power of Prayer—
Matt. 17:21; 21:22;
John 15:7
Praise to God—Ps. 67:3;
Heb. 13:15; 1 Pet. 2:9
Prayerfulness—
Luke 2:37; 6:12;
1 Thess. 3:10
Prayerlessness—Is. 43:22;
Dan. 9:13; Zeph. 1:6
Pride—2 Chr. 32:25;
Prov. 16:18; 1 John 2:16
Promises to the Righteous—
Job 36:7; Ps. 34:15;
Matt. 13:43
Prosperity of the Godly—
Deut. 29:9; Neh. 2:20;
Ps. 1:3

Prudence—Prov. 12:23; 14:15;
Hos. 14:9
Repentance—Luke 13:2, 3;
Acts 3:19; 17:30
Reverence—Ex. 3:5; Ps. 4:4;
Hab. 2:20
Salvation—John 3:16;
Rom. 10:9–13; Eph. 2:8–10
Satisfaction in God—
Ps. 17:15; 107:9; Is. 58:11
Seeking God—Job 23:3;
Jer. 29:13; Acts 17:27
Self-Denial—Matt. 16:24;
Luke 14:26, 27; Rom. 15:1
Simplicity—Ps. 131:2;
1 Cor. 14:20; 1 Pet. 2:2
Sin and Confession—
Prov. 28:13; Jer. 3:13;
1 John 1:9
Spiritual Blindness—
Is. 59:10; Matt. 15:14;
2 Cor. 4:4
Spiritual Carelessness—
Is. 32:9; 47:8; Amos 6:1
Spiritual Cleansing—Is. 1:16;
2 Cor. 7:1; 2 Tim. 2:21
Spiritual Fullness—
John 15:11; Eph. 3:19;
Col. 1:19
Spiritual Growth—Eph. 4:15;
1 Thess. 3:12; 1 Pet. 2:2
Spiritual Hearing—
Prov. 8:34; Luke 8:15;

James 1:19
Spiritual Hindrances—
Gen. 19:26; Matt. 13:58;
Heb. 12:1
Spiritual Hope—Rom. 4:18;
Prov. 14:32; Heb. 16:18, 19
Spiritual Imperatives—
Luke 13:2; John 3:5; 4:24
Spiritual Longing—
Ps. 42:2; 63:1; 143:6
Spiritual Nourishment—
Is. 55:2; John 6:51; Rev. 2:7
Spiritual Power—Zech. 4:6;
Acts 1:8; 6:8
Spiritual Rest—Ex. 33:14;
Ps. 116:7; Matt. 11:29
Spiritual Security—Job 11:18;
Ps. 91:5; 1 Pet. 3:13
Spiritual Stability—
2 Kin. 22:2; Job 23:11;
Acts 20:24
Spiritual Strength—
Is. 40:31; 41:10; Eph. 3:16
Spiritual Thirst—Ps. 63:1;
Is. 1:30; 41:17
Spiritual Treasure—
Matt. 6:29; 19:21; Phil. 3:8
Spiritual Understanding—
1 Kin. 3:9; 1 Cor. 2:14;
Heb. 5:14
Steadfastness—1 Cor. 15:58;
Gal. 5:1; 2 Pet. 3:17
Strength in Weakness—

1 Cor. 1:27; 2 Cor. 12:9;
Heb. 11:33, 34
Suffering for Christ—
Acts 5:41; Rom. 8:17;
1 Pet. 2:20
Teachability—Matt. 18:3;
Luke 11:1; Acts 8:31
Thankfulness—Ps. 100:4;
Col. 1:12; 1 Thess. 5:18
The Primacy of Love—
John 13:35; 1 Cor. 13:1;
1 John 3:14
True Life—Matt. 4:4;
John 6:63; Phil. 2:16
True Religion—Deut. 10:12;
Eccl. 12:13; James 1:27
True Wisdom—Job 28:28;
2 Tim. 3:15; James 3:17
Unworldliness—Rom. 12:2;
1 Cor. 7:31; 2 Tim. 2:4
Value of Godliness—
Deut. 4:40; Is. 3:10;
1 Tim. 6:6
**When You Reach
Desperation**—Ps. 116:6;
Mark 4:38, 40;
Acts 27:20, 22
Worldliness—Matt. 16:26;
Col. 3:2; Titus 2:12
Worship—1 Chr. 16:29;
Ps. 95:6; John 4:24
Zeal—Eccl. 9:10;
1 Cor. 14:12; 2 Tim. 1:6

PRAYERS OF THE BIBLE

Subject	Reference	Subject	Reference
Abijah's army—for victory	2 Chr. 13:14	Jehoahaz—for victory	2 Kin. 13:1–5
Abraham—for a son	Gen. 15:1–6	Jehoshaphat—	
Abraham—for Ishmael	Gen. 17:18–21	for protection	2 Chr. 20:5–12, 27
Abraham—for Sodom	Gen. 18:20–32	Jehoshaphat—for victory	2 Chr. 18:31
Abraham—for Abimelech	Gen. 20:17	Jeremiah—for Judah	Jer. 42:1–6
Abraham's servant—		Jeremiah—for mercy	Jer. 14:7–10
for guidance	Gen. 24:12–52	Jesus—Lord's Prayer	Matt. 6:9–13
Asa—for victory	2 Chr. 14:11	Jesus—praise for revelation	
Cain—for mercy	Gen. 4:13–15	to babes	Matt. 11:25, 26
Centurion—for his servant	Matt. 8:5–13	Jesus—at Lazarus's tomb	John 11:41, 42
Christians—for Peter	Acts 12:5–12	Jesus—for the Father's	
Christians—for kings		glory	John 12:28
in authority	1 Tim. 2:1, 2	Jesus—for the Church	John 17:1–26
Corinthians—for Paul	2 Cor. 1:9–11	Jesus—for deliverance	Matt. 26:39, 42, 44
Cornelius—			Matt. 27:46
for enlightenment	Acts 10:1–33	Jesus—for forgiveness	
Criminal—for salvation	Luke 23:42, 43	for others	Luke 23:34
Daniel—for the Jews	Dan. 9:3–19	Jesus—in submission	Luke 23:46
Daniel—for knowledge	Dan. 2:17–23	Jews—for safe journey	Ezra 8:21, 23
David—for blessing	2 Sam. 7:18–29	Jonah—for deliverance	
David—for help	1 Sam. 23:10–13	from the fish	Jon. 2:1–10
David—for guidance	2 Sam. 2:1	Joshua—for help	
David—for grace	Ps. 25:16	and mercy	Josh. 7:6–9
David—for justice	Ps. 9:17–20	Leper—for healing	Matt. 8:2, 3
Disciples—for boldness	Acts 4:24–31	Manasseh—	
Elijah—for drought		for deliverance	2 Chr. 33:12, 13
and rain	James 5:17, 18	Manoah—for guidance	Judg. 13:8–15
Elijah—for the raising to		Moses—for Pharaoh	Ex. 8:9–13
life of the widow's son	1 Kin. 17:20–23	Moses—for water	Ex. 15:24, 25
Elijah—for triumph		Moses—for Israel	Ex. 32:31–35
over Baal	1 Kin. 18:36–38	Moses—for Miriam	Num. 12:11–14
Elijah—for death	1 Kin. 19:4	Moses—that he might see	Deut. 3:23–25
Elisha—for blindness		the Promised Land	Deut. 34:1–4
and sight	2 Kin. 6:17–23	Moses—for a successor	Num. 27:15–17
Ezekiel—for undefilement	Ezek. 4:12–15	Nehemiah—for the Jews	Neh. 1:4–11
Ezra—for the sins		Paul—for the healing	
of the people	Ezra 9:6–15	of Publius's father	Acts 28:8
Gideon—for proof		Paul—for the Ephesians	Eph. 3:14–21
of his call	Judg. 6:36–40	Paul—for grace	2 Cor. 12:8, 9
Habakkuk—		People of Judah—	
for deliverance	Hab. 3:1–19	for a covenant	2 Chr. 15:12–15
Habakkuk—for justice	Hab. 1:1–4	Peter—for the raising	
Hagar—for consolation	Gen. 21:14–20	of Dorcas	Acts 9:40
Hannah—for a son	1 Sam. 1:10–17	Priests—for blessing	2 Chr. 30:27
Hezekiah—for deliverance	2 Kin. 19:15–19	Rebekah—	
Hezekiah—for health	2 Kin. 20:1–11	for understanding	Gen. 25:22, 23
Holy Spirit—		Reubenites—	
for Christians	Rom. 8:26, 27	for victory	1 Chr. 5:18–20
Isaac—for children	Gen. 25:21, 24–26	Samson—for water	Judg. 15:18, 19
Israelites—for deliverance	Ex. 2:23–25	Samson—for strength	Judg. 16:29, 30
	Ex. 3:7–10	Samuel—for Israel	1 Sam. 7:5–12
Jabez—for prosperity	1 Chr. 4:10	Solomon—for wisdom	1 Kin. 3:6–14
Jacob—all night	Gen. 32:24–30	Tax-gatherer—	
Jacob—for deliverance		for mercy	Luke 18:13
from Esau	Gen. 32:9–12	Zacharias—for a son	Luke 1:13

THE LAWS OF THE BIBLE

BETWEEN THE TESTAMENTS

The four hundred years between the prophecy of Malachi and the advent of Christ are frequently described as "silent," but they were in fact crowded with activity. Although no inspired prophet arose in Israel during those centuries, and the Old Testament was regarded as complete, events took place which gave to later Judaism its distinctive ideology and providentially prepared the way for the coming of Christ and the proclamation of His Gospel.

The Persian Period

The Jews fared well under Persian rule. Cyrus had given them permission to return to Jerusalem and rebuild their Temple and, although they met opposition from the inhabitants of Palestine, it was dedicated during the reign of **Darius the Great.** Ezra, the scribe, and Nehemiah, the layman, sought to strengthen the Palestinian Jewish community and encourage their loyalty to the Law of God. For about a century and a half after Nehemiah's time, the Persian Empire exercised control over Judea, and the Jews were permitted to observe their religious ordinances without interference. Judea was ruled by High Priests who were responsible to the Persian government, a fact which insured the Jews a large measure of autonomy. At the same time, however, it made a political office of the priesthood and sowed the seeds of future trouble. Contests for the office of High Priest were marked by jealousy, intrigue, and even murder. **Johanan, son of Joiada** (Neh. 12:22), is reported to have slain his brother, Joshua, within the Temple precincts.

Johanan was succeeded as High Priest by his brother, **Jaddua,** whose brother Manasseh, according to Josephus, married the daughter of **Sanballat, governor of Samaria.** It was at this time that a Samaritan temple was built on Mount Gerizim which, rather than Zion, was regarded as sacred by the Samaritan community. The sanctuary on Mount Gerizim was destroyed by the Hasmonaean ruler John Hyrcanus (134–104 B.C.), but the mount itself continues to this day to be regarded as sacred by the Samaritans. The woman of Samaria wished to dispute with Jesus concerning the merits of the rival holy places, but the Savior chose to emphasize the spiritual attitude of the worshiper rather than the place of worship (cf. John 4:20). The Sanballat of Josephus cannot have been the same individual as the man of the same name mentioned by Nehemiah (4:1). Josephus does, however, appear to reflect a valid tradition, for a temple seems to have been built on Mount Gerizim about this time. (In 1969 the Samaritans numbered fewer than 300.)

Persia's failure to conquer Greece encouraged subject peoples to seek their independence.

Egypt was constantly attempting to throw off the Persian yoke, and Judea, geographically between the two powers, could not escape involvement. During the reign of **Artaxerxes III (Ochus),** many Jews were implicated in a revolt against Persia. When it failed, the Persians deported them to Babylonia and the southern shores of the Caspian Sea.

Jews had long been in Egypt. Following the murder of Gedaliah, the prophet Jeremiah was forced to join a group of refugees, who sought asylum at Tahpanhes in the eastern Delta (Jer. 43:4–13), and other Judeans doubtless found their way to Egypt to avoid capture by **Nebuchadnezzar.** Migration continued during the Persian Period, and by the fifth century before Christ a Jewish colony of mercenary soldiers was located at **Elephantine Island,** near modern Aswan, at the First Cataract of the Nile. Contrary to the Mosaic Law, these colonists built a temple for themselves, and they combined their devotion to the God of their fathers with pagan elements. The **Elephantine Jews** had correspondence with the Samaritans as well as the Judeans.

Alexander the Great

Persia never succeeded in subduing the Greeks, but an heir of Greek culture, **Alexander of Macedon,** eventually brought to an end the Persian Empire. Alexander was not simply a power-mad despot. A pupil of the philosopher Aristotle, he was thoroughly convinced that Greek culture was the one force that could unify the world. In 333 B.C. he passed from Macedonia into Asia Minor and defeated the Persian armies stationed there. Then he moved southward through Syria and Palestine to Egypt. Tyre and Gaza each offered stubborn resistance, but delays did not discourage Alexander, they simply strengthened his determination to win. There was no need for a campaign against the Jews, and legend makes Alexander a friend of the Jewish people. Jaddua, the High Priest, is said to have come out to meet Alexander, telling him of Daniel's prophecy that the Greek army would be victorious (Dan. 8). Although historians do not take the story seriously, it does illustrate the friendly feelings between the Jews and the Macedonian conqueror. Alexander permitted the Jews to observe their laws, granted them exemption from tribute during Sabbatical Years, and, when he built **Alexandria** in Egypt (331 B.C.), he encouraged Jews to settle there and gave them privileges comparable to those of his Greek subjects.

Alexander was welcomed into Egypt as a deliverer from Persian oppression. His victorious armies retraced their steps through Palestine and

Syria, then moved eastward. The cities of Babylon and Persia fell to Alexander, and he pressed on as far as the Punjab region of India. Although mighty in battle, it was **Hellenistic culture** rather than Macedonian rule that was Alexander's legacy to the Middle East. He determined to found a new city in each country of his empire, which would serve as a model for the reordering of the life of the country as a whole along Greek lines. Materially speaking, this meant the erection of fine public buildings, a gymnasium for games, an open air theatre, and whatever would approximate the life of a Greek city-state. Individuals were encouraged to take Greek names, adopt Greek dress and language—in short, to become Hellenized.

The material aspects of **Hellenism** must have seemed attractive for large segments of the population. Trade and commerce brought wealth to the new merchant class. Libraries and schools were welcomed by the scholar. Better housing and better food brought about a rise in the standard of living. Many in Israel, as elsewhere, were glad to accept this veneer of Greek culture. If idolatry had been the stumbling block to Israel in the pre-exilic period, Hellenism was the great post-exilic temptation. A third-century B.C. writer observed, "In recent times, under the foreign rule of the Persians, and then of the Macedonians, by whom the Persian Empire was overthrown, intermingling with other races has led to many of the traditional Jewish ordinances losing their hold." Many Jews took Greek names, accepted a school of Greek philosophy, and tried to combine the wisdom of Greece with the faith of their fathers. Others resisted Hellenism and became more and more engrossed in the study of their Law.

At the age of thirty-three, Alexander died in Babylon. For a number of years the future of the Near East was uncertain, but the generals succeeded in dividing the Empire among themselves and the tide of Hellenism increased. While the Ptolemies of Egypt and the Seleucids of Syria fought among themselves for land and power, they were in complete agreement concerning their social and cultural mission. The historian W.W. Tarn says that Alexander "so changed the world [that] nothing after him could be as it was before."

The Ptolemies

Following the death of Alexander, Judea was first subject to Antigonus, one of his generals, but it quickly fell to another general, **Ptolemy I, surnamed Soter, "Deliverer,"** who seized Jerusalem on a Sabbath Day in 320 B.C. Ptolemy, whose kingdom centered in Egypt, dealt kindly with the Jews. Many of them settled in Alexandria, which continued to be an important center of Jewish thought for many centuries. Under **Ptolemy II**

(Philadelphus) the Alexandrian Jews translated their Old Testament into Greek. This translation was later known as the Septuagint from the legend of seventy (more correctly seventy-two, six from each of the twelve tribes) who were sent from Judea to produce the Greek translation of the Hebrew Scriptures.

The Jews in Palestine enjoyed a period of prosperity during Ptolemaic times. Tribute tax was paid to the government in Egypt, but local affairs were administered by High Priests who had been responsible for governing their people since Persian times. The greatest figure among the Jews of the Ptolemaic period was **Simon the Just,** the High Priest who is the subject of highest praise in the apocryphal Book of Ecclesiasticus, which calls him, "Great among his brethren and the glory of his people." He is credited with rebuilding the walls of Jerusalem, which had been demolished by Ptolemy I, and is said to have repaired the Temple and directed the excavation of a great reservoir to provide fresh water for Jerusalem in times of drought and siege. In addition to his reputation as High Priest, Simon is also regarded as one of the great teachers of ancient Judaism. His favorite maxim was, "The world rests on three things, on the Law, on Divine Service, and on Charity" (*Pirke Aboth*, i. 2). The identity of Simon the Just poses a historical problem. A High Priest known as Simon I lived during the middle of the third century, and Simon II lived about 200 B.C. One of these is doubtless the Simon the Just of Jewish tradition and legend.

During Ptolemaic times the priestly families of **Onias** and **Tobias** became bitter rivals. The house of Tobias was pro-Egyptian and represented the wealthy class of Jerusalem society. It may have been related to Tobiah the Ammonite (Neh. 2:10; 4:3, 7; 6:1–19), who gave so much trouble to Nehemiah. A papyrus from the time of Ptolemy II speaks of a Jew named Tobias, who was a cavalry commander in the Ptolemaic army stationed at Ammanitis, east of the Jordan. Archaeologists have discovered a mausoleum with the name "Tobiah" from the third century B.C. at Araq el-Emir in central Jordan. The Tobiahs are thought to have been tax collectors, occupying the same function as the New Testament tax-gatherers.

Josephus states that Onias II refused to pay Ptolemy IV twenty talents of silver, which was evidently the tribute tax demanded of the High Priests. By refusing payment, Onias seems to have renounced allegiance to Ptolemy. Joseph, a member of the house of Tobias, then succeeded in having himself appointed tax collector for the whole of Palestine. The tax collector had to go to Alexandria each year to bid for the renewal of the license to gather taxes. Joseph held this influential post for twenty years, under the Ptolemies and, after the victory of Antiochus III, under the Seleucids.

The Seleucids

The Syrian rulers are termed Seleucids because their kingdom, one of the successor states to Alexander's empire, was founded by **Seleucus I (Nicator).** Most of the early rulers bore the names of Seleucus or Antiochus, and they ruled from Antioch on the Orontes River. The energetic ruler Antiochus III, surnamed "the Great," waged a series of battles with Egypt until, in 199 B.C., he wrested Palestine from the Ptolemies after the Battle of Panion, near the sources of the Jordan River. This marked the beginning of a new era of Jewish history for, while the Ptolemies had been tolerant of Jewish institutions, the Seleucids determined to enforce Hellenism on the Jews.

The crisis came during the reign of **Antiochus IV, surnamed Epiphanes,** who found allies in the Hellenistic party in Judea. In the early days of the reign of Antiochus IV, Jerusalem was ruled by the High Priest, Onias III, a descendant of Simon the Just and a strictly orthodox Jew. The Jews, who looked with favor on Greek culture, opposed Onias and espoused the cause of his brother, Jason. By promising large tribute to Antiochus, Jason succeeded in having himself appointed High Priest. Although Antiochus looked upon the high priesthood as a political office which he had a right to fill as he pleased, pious Jews thought of the priesthood as divine in origin and considered its sale to the highest bidder a sin against God.

Jason encouraged the Hellenists who had sought his election. A gymnasium was built in Jerusalem, Greek names became commonplace, and Hebrew orthodoxy was considered obscurantist and obsolete. Yet, Jason argued with his close companion and fellow-Hellenist, **Menelaus,** of the tribe of Benjamin, who offered higher tribute to Antiochus than that paid by Jason, and had himself installed as High Priest.

The orthodox Jews, who had been scandalized when Jason was named High Priest, were more deeply disturbed when Menelaus, a Benjamite with no claim to priestly office, was installed. Jason raised an army to back his claim to the high priesthood, and Menelaus courted the favor of Antiochus. The Syrians, who were campaigning against Egypt, felt it essential to maintain effective control of Palestine. Antiochus staged a sneak attack on Jerusalem one Sabbath Day (when the orthodox would not fight), and slaughtered a large number of the enemies of Menelaus. The city walls were destroyed, and a new fortress, the Akra, was built on the site of the citadel.

Antiochus was determined to remove all traces of orthodox Jewish faith. Israel's God was identified with Jupiter, and a bearded image of the pagan deity (perhaps in the likeness of Antiochus) was erected on the Temple altar, where swine were offered in sacrifice. Jews were forbidden, under penalty of death, to practice circumcision, Sabbath observance, or the celebration of the Feasts of the Jewish calendar. Copies of the Scriptures were ordered destroyed. The laws were enforced with the utmost cruelty. An aged scribe named Fleazar was flogged to death because he would not eat swine's flesh.

By force of arms, Menelaus continued as High Priest and the Hellenizing party gained a victory. Yet, the Hellenizers had gone too far, and their zeal to annihilate the old order proved their own undoing. The orthodox were willing to die for their faith, but not all were convinced that they should die passively.

The Maccabean Revolt

The oppressed Jews were not long in finding a champion. When the emissaries of Antiochus arrived at the village of Modin, about fifteen miles west of Jerusalem, they expected the aged priest, **Mattathias,** to set a good example to his people by coming forward to offer a pagan sacrifice. When Mattathias refused, a timid Jew came forward to perform the sacrifice. The enraged priest approached the altar and killed both the apostate Jew and the emissary of Antiochus. With his five sons, Mattathias destroyed the heathen altar and then fled to the hills to avoid reprisal. Others of orthodox persuasion joined the family of Mattathias in waging guerrilla warfare on the Syrians and the Hellenistic Jews who supported them. The orthodox would not fight on the Sabbath Day, with the result that they were at a distinct military disadvantage. On one Sabbath, a group of the orthodox was surrounded and murdered, for they would not defend themselves. Following this episode, Mattathias suggested the principle that fighting in self-defense was permissible on the Sabbath Day.

Soon after the beginning of the revolt, Mattathias died. He had urged his followers to choose as military leader his third son, **Judas (Hebrew Judah), known as "the Maccabee,"** a word usually interpreted to mean "the hammer." The choice was a good one, for more and more Jews rallied to the cause. The Maccabees, as the followers of Judas were called, were able to hold their own against a series of Syrian armies thrown against them. By a surprise night attack, Judas annihilated an army of Syrians and Hellenistically minded Jews at Emmaus, and then marched toward Jerusalem with the booty he had seized. The Maccabees entered the city and took everything except the Akra. They entered the Temple and removed all the signs of paganism which had been installed there. The altar dedicated to Jupiter was removed and a new altar erected to Israel's God. The statue of Jupiter was ground to dust. Beginning with the twenty-fifth of Kislev (December), they celebrated an eight-day Feast of Dedication, known as Hanukkah, the Festival of Lights. In

this way they marked the end of the three-year period during which the Temple had been desecrated.

Peace was short-lived. The Syrian general, **Lysias,** defeated the Maccabees in a battle near Jerusalem, and besieged the city. During the siege, however, Lysias learned of trouble at home and made an offer of peace to the Jews. The laws against the observance of Judaism would be repealed, and Syria would refrain from interference in the internal affairs of Judea. Menelaus was to be removed from office and the high priesthood given to a mild Hellenizer named **Alcimus.** Lysias promised that Judas and his followers would not be punished. However, the walls of Jerusalem would be destroyed.

A council comprising Maccabean army officers, respected scribes, and elders of the orthodox party was convened at Jerusalem to determine the action to be taken. Against the counsel of Judas, the peace terms were accepted. Alcimus became High Priest; Menelaus was executed, and Judas left the city with a few followers. The fears of Judas proved correct, for Alcimus seized and executed many of the orthodox party. Loyal Jews again turned to Judas and civil war was renewed. Judas, with an ill-equipped army of eight hundred men, met a large Syrian army and died in battle. Thus, the first phase of the Maccabean struggle was ended.

Jonathan, a brother of Judas, fled across the Jordan with several hundred Maccabean soldiers. They were ill-equipped to wage battle, but the next victories were in the field of diplomacy. Two pretenders to the Syrian throne each sought help from the Jews. They saw in Jonathan the man best able to raise and lead a Jewish army. By playing a delaying action, Jonathan was able to support the winning candidate and at the same time make treaties with Sparta and Rome. Before the war was over, Jonathan was High Priest, governor of Judea, and a member of the Syrian nobility. His brother, Simon, became governor of the Philistine coastal area. Jonathan was able to promote the internal prosperity of Judah, and when he died his brother, Simon, succeeded him as ruling High Priest.

Simon was advanced in years when he came to the throne. His major victory was in the field of diplomacy, for by recognizing **Demetrius** as rightful king of Syria he secured for the Jews immunity from taxation which amounted to an acknowledgment of independence. Simon was able also to starve out the Syrian garrison at the Akra and to occupy the cities of Joppa and Bethsura. In recognition of his wise rule, the leaders in Israel named Simon, "leader and High Priest for ever, until there shall arise a faithful prophet." Simon was the last of the sons of Mattathias, and this act legitimized a new dynasty which is termed Hasmonaean, presumably derived from an ancestor of

the Maccabees named Asmonaeus or, in Hebrew, Hashmon. In 134 B.C., Simon and two of his sons were murdered by an ambitious son-in-law. A third son, **John Hyrcanus,** managed to escape and succeed his father as hereditary head of the Jewish state.

The Hasmonaeans

The Syrians recognized the government of John Hyrcanus on condition that he consider himself subject to Syria and promise help in Syrian military campaigns. Certain coastal cities annexed by Jonathan and Simon were also to be relinquished. The efficient rule of Hyrcanus, however, quickly effected the re-conquest of these cities and the addition of **Idumaea** (Old Testament Edom) to Judean territory. These conquests ensured the use of ancient trade routes by the merchant class, but they posed problems to the religiously oriented Jews. Hyrcanus compelled the Idumaeans to become circumcised and accept the Jewish faith, a practice which later Judaism disavows. Hyrcanus also campaigned in Samaria, where he destroyed the temple on Mount Gerizim. The success of Jewish arms might be applauded by the nationalistic element in Judea, but the religious fervor of the earlier Maccabees was no longer evident.

Before John Hyrcanus died in 104 B.C., the borders of the state had been extended on every side. The Maccabean struggle was long past and new rivalries developed. The older Hellenists were discredited, but their ideas were perpetuated in the party of the Sadducees. The orthodox of Maccabean times became the Pharisees of pre-Christian Judaism and the New Testament. Hyrcanus was devout and law-abiding, but his children had little sympathy with traditional Hebrew thought. They numbered themselves among the aristocrats, and they came to look with disdain on the rigidly orthodox Pharisees. Ironically, these heirs of the Maccabees became thoroughly Hellenized.

The death of John Hyrcanus precipitated a dynastic struggle among his children. His eldest son, who preferred his Greek name **Aristobulus** to his Hebrew name, Judah, emerged as victor and threw three of his brothers into prison—two of whom are thought to have starved to death. Another brother was murdered in the palace. In his short reign of but one year, Aristobulus pushed the borders of Judea north to Mount Lebanon and took the title of king. His life was cut short, however, by drink, disease, and the haunting fear of rebellion.

At the time of Aristobulus's death he had but one brother living, and he was in prison. Although his Hebrew name was Jonathan, history knows him by his Greek name **Alexander Jannaeus.** Under Jannaeus the policy of territorial expansion continued. The frontiers of Judea were extended along the Philistine coast toward the

Egyptian frontier and in the Trans-jordan region. The Jewish state approximated the territory controlled by Israel in the days of David and Solomon. It included the whole of Palestine and adjacent areas from the borders of Egypt to Lake Huleh, north of the Sea of Galilee. Perea in Transjordan was subject to Jannaeus, as were the cities of the Coastal Plain except for Ascalon.

The territories incorporated into the Hasmonaean kingdom were, for the most part, quickly Judaised. The Idumaeans came to exercise an important place in Jewish life, and **Galilee** became an important center of Judaism. The Samaritans, however, continued to resist assimilation and cities such as Apollonia and Scythopolis (Old Testament Beth-shean), with only a small Jewish element in their population, kept their non-Jewish character.

Partisan strife marred the reign of Alexander Jannaeus, who showed open contempt for the Pharisees, precipitating civil war. The Pharisees accepted aid from the Syrians in their conflict with Jannaeus, and for a time Jewish independence was in the balance. When the Pharisees felt that they had gained their point, they withdrew their alliance with Syria and hoped for a Jewish state that would be both free of foreign control and tolerant of their viewpoint. Jannaeus sought out the leaders of the rebellion and crucified eight hundred Pharisees. Tradition says that Jannaeus repented on his deathbed, instructing his wife, **Salome Alexandra,** to dismiss his Sadducean advisors and reign with the help of the Pharisees. The tradition may have no historical basis, but Alexandra did turn to the Pharisees for support.

Salome Alexandra had been married successively to Aristobulus and to Alexander Jannaeus. The widow of two Hasmonaean rulers, she reigned in her own right for seven years. She was a woman of seventy when she came to the throne, dividing royal responsibilities between her two sons. **Hyrcanus,** the older son, became High Priest, and his brother, **Aristobulus,** received the military command. Her brother, **Simeon ben Shetah,** was a leader among the Pharisees and this fact may have disposed her to seek peace between the opposing factions of Judaism.

Under Alexandra, the Pharisees had their opportunity to make a constructive contribution to Jewish life. In many areas, particularly education, they were eminently successful. Under the presidency of Simeon ben Shetah, the Sanhedrin (the Jewish Council of State) decreed that every young man should be educated. A comprehensive system of elementary education was inaugurated so that the larger villages, towns, and cities of Judea would produce a literate, informed people. This education was centered in the Hebrew Scriptures.

The wounds of earlier strife were not healed during Alexandra's reign. Although the Pharisees were happy in their new-found recognition, the Sadducees were resentful of the fact that they had lost power. To compound the problem, the Pharisees sought to avenge the massacre of their leaders by Alexander Jannaeus. Sadducean blood was spilt and the makings of another civil war were in the air.

The Sadducees found in Aristobulus, the younger son of Jannaeus and Alexandra, the man they could support as Alexandra's successor. He was a soldier and appealed to the party that dreamed of imperial expansion and worldly power. Hyrcanus, the older brother and rightful heir, was acceptable to the Pharisees. With the death of Alexandra, the partisans of the two sons were ready for a showdown.

When his mother died, **Hyrcanus (II),** who had been serving as High Priest, succeeded to the throne, but his brother, **Aristobulus,** led an army of Sadducees against Jerusalem. Neither Hyrcanus nor the Pharisees were ready for war, and Hyrcanus surrendered his honors to Aristobulus (II), who became king and High Priest. Hyrcanus and Aristobulus thereupon vowed eternal friendship, and Aristobulus's eldest son, Alexander, married Hyrcanus's only daughter, Alexandra. Peace between the brothers was short-lived. Hyrcanus had to flee and Antipater, governor of Idumaea, espoused his cause. With civil war threatening, Pompey appeared with his Roman Legions to ensure the peace of Judea and further the aims of Rome.

The Romans

When **Pompey** suspected Aristobulus of planning to rebel against Rome, he besieged Jerusalem. After three months, he breached the fortifications, entered the city, and reportedly murdered twelve thousand Jews. Pompey and his officers entered the Holy of Holies in the Temple, but he did not touch its costly furnishings and allowed Temple worship to continue. Jerusalem, however, was made tributary to the Romans, and the last vestige of Jewish independence was removed. Judea was incorporated into the Roman province of Syria and it lost the coastal cities, the district of Samaria, and the non-Jewish cities east of the Jordan. **Hyrcanus** was named Ethnarch of Judea, including Galilee, Idumaea, and Perea, and was confirmed again as High Priest. A yearly tribute was due Rome. Aristobulus and a number of other captives were taken to Rome to grace Pompey's triumph. During the voyage, Aristobulus's son Alexander escaped and attempted to organize a revolt against Hyrcanus. With the aid of the Romans, Hyrcanus was able to meet this challenge to his authority.

During the years of strife between **Aristobulus (II)** and **Hyrcanus (II),** the Idumaean governor **Antipater** (or **Antipas**) took a lively interest in the politics of Judea. Antipater was bitterly opposed

to Aristobulus, partly through fear and partly because of his friendship with Hyrcanus. It appears that Hyrcanus relied much on Antipater, and that he was virtually the power behind the throne of Judea. The Jews resented the influence of Antipater almost as much as they smarted under Roman sovereignty. Although the Idumaeans had been incorporated into the Jewish state by John Hyrcanus, they had never been assimilated and ancient rivalries were not forgotten.

In the crisis which followed the murder of **Julius Caesar,** Antipater and his sons showed loyalty to the new regime of **Cassius** by zealously collecting tribute taxes. **Herod,** a son of Antipater, was given the title Procurator of Judea with the promise that he would one day be named king. When **Anthony** defeated Brutus and Cassius at Philippi, Asia again fell into the hands of a new regime. Herod, however, quickly changed loyalties and bribed his way into favor with Anthony.

The eastern part of the once mighty Persian Empire was occupied by a people known as **Parthians,** who had never been subdued by Rome. In 41 B.C. they attacked Jerusalem and made **Antigonus,** son of Aristobulus II, both king and High Priest. Herod, the son of Antipater, who had inherited the throne of Judea at the death of Hyrcanus, was forced to flee to Rome. There he won the favor of Anthony and was officially named "King of the Jews," although the title would have meaning only after the Parthians were driven out. Herod returned to Judea with Roman arms and triumphantly entered Jerusalem as king.

Herod's rule spanned the eventful years from 37 B.C. to 4 B.C. He is best known as the king who feared the birth of a rival "King of the Jews" and decreed the murder of infants in Bethlehem at the time of the birth of Jesus. While that act of Herod cannot be documented from secular records, his other atrocities are well known. He had ten wives in all, and the **Emperor Augustus** is reported to have commented of his family life, "I'd rather be Herod's hog than his son." The hog was an unclean animal and would not be butchered, but Herod's wives and children were violently removed when they interfered with his plans or were suspected of disloyalty.

Although detested by his Jewish subjects, Herod did seek to win their favor. He built and rebuilt cities throughout the land: Samaria became Sebaste in honor of Augustus; Straton's Tower became Caesarea, with a harbor protected by a moat and a wall with ten towers. Fortresses, baths, parks, market places, roads, and other luxuries of Hellenistic culture were part of his building program.

In the eighteenth year of his reign (20–19 B.C.), Herod began the work of rebuilding, on a grand scale, the Jewish Temple in Jerusalem. The main edifice was built by priests in a year and a half, but the work on the entire complex of courts and buildings was not completed until the procuratorship of **Albinus** (A.D. 62–64), less than a decade before it was totally destroyed by the armies of **Titus** (A.D. 70).

The Jewish Sects

The Pharisees, Sadducees, Herodians, and Zealots, who play so important a part in the gospel records, all have their origin during the two centuries before the birth of Christ. They represent different reactions to the continuing clash between Hellenism and Jewish religious life. While the Maccabean struggle had settled the political problem of the relationship between the Syrian Seleucids and Judea, it forced upon Judaism the necessity of determining its own relationship to the outside world.

The Pharisees

A party bearing the name of Pharisee is first mentioned during the reign of John Hyrcanus (134–104 B.C.), and it is evident that even then there was an antagonism between the "orthodox" Pharisee and the more open-minded Sadducee. The word **Pharisee** means "separated one," and the name probably meant, in the first instance, one who had separated himself from the corrupting influence of Hellenism in his zeal for the biblical Law. Josephus says that the Pharisees "appear more religious than others, and seem to interpret the laws more accurately."

Pharisees were punctilious in observing the laws regarding ceremonial purity. For this reason, they could not purchase items of food or drink from a "sinner" for fear of ceremonial defilement. Nor could a Pharisee eat in the house of a sinner, although he might entertain the sinner in his own home. Under such circumstances, the Pharisee would provide the sinner with clothes to wear, for the sinner's clothes might be ceremonially impure.

With a sincere desire to make the Law workable within the changing culture of the Greco-Roman world, the Pharisees developed systems of tradition which sought to apply the Law to a variety of circumstances. During the first century before Christ, two influential Pharisaic teachers gave their names to two schools of legal thought. **Hillel** was the more moderate of the two, ever considerate of the poor and willing to accept Roman rule as compatible with Jewish orthodoxy. **Shammai,** on the other hand, was more strict in his interpretation and bitterly opposed to Rome. His viewpoint ultimately found expression in the sect of **Zealots,** whose resistance to the Romans brought on the destruction of Jerusalem in A.D. 70. **The Talmud** preserves the record of three hundred sixteen controversies between the schools of Hillel and Shammai.

Tradition, in Pharisaic thought, began as a commentary on the Law, but it was ultimately raised to the level of Law itself. To justify this teaching, it was maintained that the "oral law" was given by God to Moses on Mount Sinai along with the "written law" or **Torah** (*Pirke Aboth*, 1.1). The ultimate in this development is reached when the **Mishna** states that oral law must be observed with greater stringency than the written law, because statutory law (that is, oral tradition) affects the life of the ordinary man more intimately than the more remote constitutional law (the written Torah) (*M. Sanhedrin*, 10.3).

In addition to the charge that Pharisaism involved little more than a concern for the minutia of the Law, the New Testament affirms that tradition had largely neglected the real intent of the Law (Matt. 15:3). As in many worthy movements, the early piety of those who had separated themselves from impurity at great cost was exchanged for an attitude of pride in the observance of legal precepts.

Men such as **Nicodemus, Joseph of Arimathea, Gamaliel**, and **Saul of Tarsus** represent some of the nobler souls from the Pharisaic tradition in the New Testament. To Saul, later Paul the apostle, the Pharisee represented the epitome of orthodoxy, "the strictest sect of our religion" (Acts 26:5). Pharisaism began well, and its perversion is a constant reminder that self-complacency and spiritual pride are temptations to which the pious are particularly susceptible.

The Sadducees

Although Pharisees and Sadducees are frequently denounced together in the New Testament, they had little in common except their antagonism to Jesus. The Sadducees were the party of the **Jerusalem aristocracy** and the **high priesthood.** They had made their peace with the political rulers and had attained positions of wealth and influence. Temple administration and ritual were their specific responsibilities. The Sadducees held themselves aloof from the masses and were unpopular with them.

The Pharisaic attempts at applying the Law to new situations were rejected by the Sadducees, who restricted their concept of authority to the Torah, or Mosaic Law. They did not believe in resurrection, spirits, or angels (cf. Mark 12:18; Luke 20:27; Acts 23:8). Their faith was largely a series of negations with the result that they left no positive religious or political system.

While the Pharisees welcomed proselytes (Matt. 23:15), the Sadducean party was closed. None but members of the high priestly and aristocratic families of Jerusalem could become members. With the destruction of the Temple in A.D. 70, the Sadducean party came to an end. Modern Judaism traces its roots to the Pharisees.

The Essenes

Essenes and Pharisees both trace their roots to the orthodox leaders of Maccabean times, who stood their ground against Hellenism. Pharisees maintained a strict orthodoxy within the framework of historical Judaism. They maintained their separation from defilement, but not from the Jewish community itself. Even though the Temple worship was conducted by Sadducees, the Pharisees esteemed it a basic part of their religious inheritance. While the Pharisee might hold himself aloof from "sinners," he lived among them and coveted their esteem.

A more extreme reaction against the influences which tended to corrupt Jewish life was taken by a sect which the ancient writers Philo, Josephus, and Pliny call the Essenes. They seem to have lived for the most part in **monastic communities** such as the one which maintained headquarters at Qumran, near the northwest corner of the Dead Sea.

In seeking to explain Judaism to the Greek speaking world, Josephus spoke of three "philosophies"—those of the Pharisees, Sadducees, and the Essenes. The term "Essene" seems to have had quite an elastic usage, including various groups of monastically minded Jews, who varied among themselves in certain of their practices. Pliny says that the Essenes avoided women and did not marry, but Josephus speaks of an order of marrying Essenes. The excavations at Qumran indicate that women were enrolled in the Qumran community.

Ancient writers speak favorably of the Essenes, who lived a life of rigor and simplicity. Members of the community studied Scripture and other religious books. Each Essene was required to perform manual labor in order to make the community self-supporting. Community of goods was practiced, and strict discipline was enforced by an overseer. Those groups which renounced marriage adopted boys at an early age in order to inculcate and perpetuate the ideals of Essenism. Slavery and war were repudiated.

The Essenes welcomed proselytes, but the novice was required to undergo a period of strict probation before he could become a full-fledged member. Numerically, the Essenes were never large. Philo says that there were four thousand of them, and Pliny speaks of a community north of En Gedi, corresponding to the Qumran area. That there were other settlements is clear, for we are told that all members of the sect were welcome in any of the Essene colonies.

Nothing certain is known of the early history of the sect for, like all reform movements, it traces its origins back to remote times. Philo states that Moses instituted the order, and Josephus says that they existed "ever since the ancient times of the fathers." It is certain that the Essene movement

was at one time an extreme protest against the corruptions which were apparent in pre-Christian Judaism, and that ultimately many members withdrew from the Palestinian community life and sought spiritual purification in places such as the Qumran area.

Regarding themselves as the only true or pure Israel, the Essenes refused to cooperate with what they believed to be the corrupt religious observances at the Jerusalem Temple. The carefully regulated life at the Essene center seems to have served as a substitute for the Temple in the eyes of pious Essenes. The strictness of Essene discipline and the rigidity with which the Law was enforced are stressed by all who write about them. Josephus says that they were stricter than all Jews in abstaining from work on the Sabbath. A passage in the **Damascus Document** (which seems to be Essene in origin) says that it is unlawful to lift an animal from a pit on the Sabbath. Such a view was considered extreme, even by legalistic Pharisees (cf. Matt. 12:11).

The absence of Essenes from the main streams of Jewish life doubtless accounts for the fact that they are not mentioned in the New Testament or in the Jewish Talmud. Although the high morality of the Essenes is indeed commendable, the teaching and practice of Jesus was diametrically opposite to the legalism and asceticism of the Essene teaching. Although the Essenes considered that contact with a member of their own group of a lower order was ceremonially defiling, Jesus did not hesitate to eat and drink with "tax-gatherers and sinners" (Matt. 11:19; Luke 7:34). Although obedient to the Mosaic Law, Jesus had no sympathy with those who made of the Law a burden instead of a blessing. The Sabbath, according to Jesus, was made for man, and it is lawful to do good on the Sabbath Day (Matt. 12:1–12; Mark 2:23–28; Luke 6:6–11; 14:1–6).

Jesus denounced abuses in the Temple and prophesied its destruction, but He did not repudiate the Temple services. He came to Jerusalem for the great Jewish feasts, and after His resurrection, disciples still made their way to the Temple at the hour of prayer (cf. Acts 3). While asceticism and monasticism early gained a foothold in Christian thinking, Christianity in its earliest period was in no sense an ascetic movement. The ministry of Jesus was largely to the "common people," who were rejected by both Pharisee and Essene. Jesus was not ashamed to associate with the people of His generation, so the self-righteous called Him a drunkard, a friend of tax-gatherers and sinners (Matt. 11:19).

Other Sects

The New Testament mentions **Herodians** (Matt. 22:16; Mark 3:6) and **Zealots** (Luke 6:15), groups of Jews at opposite ends of the political spectrum. The Herodians appear to have been Jews of influence and standing who were well disposed to the Herodian rule and, as a result, to the Romans who supported the Herods. The Zealots, on the other hand, were super patriots who determined to resist Rome at all costs. Their fanaticism brought on the war during which the army of Titus destroyed Jerusalem and its Temple (A.D. 70).

Chronology

Date B.C.

612	**Nineveh** destroyed by Medes and Babylonians
587	**Jerusalem** destroyed by Nebuchadnezzar
559	**Cyrus** inherits kingdom of Anshan; beginning of Persian Empire
539	**Babylon** falls to Cyrus; end of Neo-Babylonian Empire
530–522	**Cambyses** suceeds Cyrus; conquest of Egypt
521–486	**Darius I** ruler of Persian Empire
515	**Second Temple** completed by Jews in Jerusalem
486–464	**Xerxes I** attempts the conquest of Greece; time of Esther
480	**Greek naval victory** at Salamis; Xerxes flees
464–423	**Artaxerxes I** rules Persia; age of Nehemiah
334–323	**Alexander of Macedon** conquers the East
311	**Seleucus** conquers Babylon; beginning of the Seleucid dynasty
223–187	**Antiochus (III) the Great,** Seleucid ruler of Syria
198	**Antiochus III** defeats Egypt, gains control of Palestine
175–163	**Antiochus (IV) Epiphanes** rules Syria; Judaism is proscribed
167	**Mattathias** and his sons rebel against Antiochus; beginning of Maccabean revolt
166–160	**Judas** is Maccabees' Leader
160–142	**Jonathan** is High Priest
142–135	**Simon** is High Priest; founds Hasmonaean dynasty
134–104	**John Hyrcanus** expands holdings of independent Jewish state
103	**Aristobulus's** Rule
102–76	**Alexander Jannaeus's** Rule
75–67	**Salome Alexandra** rules; Hyrcanus II High Priest
66–63	**Dynastic battle:** Aristobulus II and Hyrcanus II
63	**Pompey** invades Palestine; Roman rule begins
63–40	**Hyrcanus II** rules, subject to Rome; Antipater exercises increasing power
40–37	**Parthians** conquer Jerusalem; establish Aristobulus II as High Priest and king
37–4	**Herod the Great,** son of Antipater, rules as king; subject to Rome

THE APOCRYPHA

The term Apocrypha is used to designate a collection of ancient Jewish writings which were written between about 250 B.C. and the early Christian centuries. The apocryphal books have come to be regarded as inspired Scripture in the theology of the Roman Catholic Church, but the historic Protestant and Jewish viewpoint ascribes no real inspiration to them.

Why Protestants Reject the Apocrypha

While Protestants study the Apocrypha for the light it throws on the life and thought of pre-Christian Judaism, they reject it as inspired Scripture for the following reasons:

(1) The apocryphal books were not a part of the Old Testament of Jesus and the early Church. The threefold division of the Old Testament—the Law, the Prophets, and the Writings, still used in Hebrew Bibles and Jewish versions of the Old Testament—does not include the apocryphal books and never did. While the Apocrypha was known to Jesus and His disciples, they never quote from it as authoritative Scripture.

(2) Ancient Jewish writers who used the Greek Bible, notably **Philo** and **Josephus,** were acquainted with the Apocrypha but never quote it as Scripture. In fact, Josephus states that nothing had been added to Scripture "from Artaxerxes until our time." The apocryphal book of Second Esdras mentions twenty-four books, corresponding to the Hebrew Bible as it is known today, and seventy other writings which are esoteric in nature (2 Esdras 14:44–48). It is significant that this apocryphal book shows an acquaintance with the acknowledged Old Testament canon as known in the synagogue and in the Protestant churches.

(3) Church Fathers, who were familiar with the Hebrew canon, clearly distinguish between canonical and apocryphal writings. The writings of **Melito of Sardis, Cyril of Jerusalem,** and **St. Jerome** show a recognition of the difference between inspired Scripture and Apocrypha.

(4) The apocryphal books were never declared to be authoritative Scripture until the **Council of Trent** (A.D. 1546). At that time the following apocryphal books were declared canonical: Tobit, Judith, The Wisdom of Solomon, Ecclesiasticus, Baruch (including the Letter of Jeremiah), First and Second Maccabees, the additions to Esther, and the additions to Daniel (viz. Susanna, The Song of the Three Young Men, and Bel and the Dragon). Many Roman Catholic scholars distinguish between proto-canonical books (i.e., our Old Testament) and deuterocanonical books (i.e., the Apocrypha).

(5) Most readers feel that the apocryphal books represent a lower level of writing than that of the canonical Scriptures. They contain numerous historical and geographical inaccuracies and anachronisms and do not breathe the prophetic spirit so evident in canonical writings.

The **Westminster Confession** (1643) states that "the books commonly called Apocrypha, not being of divine inspiration, are no part of the Canon of Scripture, and therefore are of no authority in the Church of God, or to be any otherwise approved or made use of than other human writing." The Reformed Churches have not encouraged the use of the Apocrypha, and as a consequence it is seldom used in contemporary Protestantism. The Anglican Church in its Thirty-nine Articles takes a mediating position, holding that, "the Church doth read [the apocryphal books] for example of life and instruction of manners; but yet doth it not apply them to confess any doctrine."

In addition to the books commonly called Apocrypha, there is a wide variety of other ancient literature, both Jewish and Christian, to which the name **Pseudepigrapha** is often applied. Apocrypha, Pseudepigrapha, sectarian literature from the Qumran Caves, and a wide variety of other ancient writings provide helpful material for understanding the world of the New Testament and the early Church. While not on a par with inspired Scripture, such writings merit close examination.

The Books Commonly Termed Apocrypha Are:

First Esdras (Vulgate, 3 Esdras). The first book of Esdras relates a series of episodes from Old Testament history, beginning with the passover celebrated in Jerusalem by Josiah (c. 621 B.C.) and ending with the public reading of the law by Ezra (c. 444 B.C.). It reproduces the substance of Second Chronicles 33:1—36:23, the whole of Ezra, and Nehemiah 7:73—8:12. An addition to the biblical narrative appears in First Esdras 3:1—5:6, the **Tale of the Three Guardsmen.** Three young men who were acting as bodyguards to King Darius were keeping themselves awake by debating what was the strongest force in the world. One said wine, because of its peculiar power over men; another suggested the king, with unlimited power over his subjects; and the third (**Zerubbabel**) affirmed that woman, who gives birth to man, is strongest, but truth is victor over all things. The king, who was asked to decide the winner, favored Zerubbabel's answer and offered him any reward he might choose. Zerubbabel asked permission to return to Jerusalem to rebuild the Temple. The section ends with a description of the Jews departing from Babylon en route to Jerusalem. Most scholars suggest that First Esdras was composed in Egypt some time after 150 B.C.

Second Esdras (Vulgate, 4 Esdras). The core of Second Esdras (chapters 3—14) purports to describe seven **apocalyptic revelations** granted to Ezra in Babylon. They are concerned with the problem of Israel's suffering and attempt "to justify the ways of God to man." The author was evidently a Jew, who looked forward to the advent of Israel's Messiah and the period of blessedness which He would bring. The introduction (chapters 1 and 2) and the conclusion (chapters 15 and 16) contain additions written from a Christian viewpoint. The core was probably written in Aramaic toward the end of the first century A.D. About the middle of the second century, an introduction was added (in Greek), and a century later the concluding chapters were written. Oriental versions and many of the best Latin manuscripts contain only the core of the book.

Tobit. Tobit is a book of **religious fiction**, probably written in Aramaic during the second century B.C. It tells the story of a pious Jew of the tribe of Naphtali in Galilee who, with his wife Anna and their son Tobias, was taken to Nineveh by **Shalmaneser** (c. 721 B.C., 2 Kin. 18:9-12). In the land of exile they scrupulously obeyed the Jewish Law. When **Tobit** lost his eyesight, he sent his son to Rages in Media to obtain payment of a debt. An angel led him on to Ecbatana, where he fell in love with a beautiful widow whose seven husbands had successively been killed on their marriage day by an evil spirit. Tobias married the virgin-widow and escaped death by burning the inner part of a fish, the smoke of which put the evil spirit to flight. As an added blessing, the gall of the fish was used to cure the blindness of the aged Tobit.

Judith. The story of Judith was probably written in Hebrew by a Palestinian Jew during the years following the Maccabean revolt. It tells how Judith, a Jewish widow, delivered her people from the Assyrian commander, **Holofernes**, who was laying siege to Bethulia. Risking great personal danger, Judith made her way to the tent of Holofernes where she beguiled the Assyrian with her charms. Getting him into a drunken stupor, Judith took the sword of Holofernes, cut off his head, and brought it back to Bethulia as evidence that God had given His people victory over the Assyrians. Judith may be compared with biblical Jael, who killed the Canaanite general Sisera (Judg. 4:17-22).

The Additions to the Book of Esther. During the second or the first century B.C., an Egyptian Jew translated the canonical Book of Esther into Greek, and at the same time interpolated a total of **107 verses** into six places where he felt that a religious note should be added. These pious insertions mention the name of God and prayer, neither of which appear in the canonical Esther. The apocryphal additions add ten verses to Esther 10, and six additional chapters, numbered 11 to 16. In the Greek Septuagint, however, the sup-plementary verses are distributed through the text so as to make one continuous narration.

The Wisdom of Solomon. An Alexandrian Jew, sometime between 150 and 50 B.C., composed an ethical treatise which he named The Wisdom of Solomon in order to gain for it a wider reading. He sought to protect the Jews in Egypt from falling into skepticism, materialism, and idolatry, and to teach his pagan readers the truth of Judaism and the folly of heathenism. The book begins with an exhortation to the rulers of the earth to seek wisdom and follow righteousness. Its theology is based on the Old Testament with modifications derived from Greek philosophical ideas current in Alexandria. Unlike the Old and New Testaments which honor the body, the Wisdom of Solomon (The New American Bible) regards it as something that "weighs down the soul," a mere "earthly tent" which "burdens the thoughtful mind" (9:15). The pre-existence (8:19,20) and immortality (3:1–5) of the soul are maintained, although the Hebrew-Christian doctrine of bodily resurrection is absent.

Ecclesiasticus, or the Wisdom of Jesus the Son of Sirach. Ecclesiasticus, an ethical treatise extolling the virtue of wisdom, was written in Hebrew between 200 and 175 B.C. by a pious scholar from Jerusalem, Jesus the son of Sirach. The author's grandson, an Alexandrian Jew, translated the work into Greek and added a prologue (c. 132 B.C.). It is the longest of the apocryphal books, and the only one with a known author. Like the canonical Proverbs, Ecclesiasticus deals with a wide variety of practical subjects—everything from diet to domestic relationships. The longest continuous section of the book (chapters 44 to 50) is the **Praise of Famous Men**, which briefly describes a long series of Hebrew worthies from **Enoch, Noah,** and **Abraham,** down to **Zerubbabel** and **Nehemiah,** and finally the **High Priest Simon,** a contemporary and friend of the author.

Baruch. The Book of Baruch, ostensibly written by Jeremiah's friend and secretary (Jer. 32:12; 36:4; 51:59), is a composite work which was not completed until the first century B.C. or later. Although the final recension was written in Greek, some sections may be traced to Hebrew originals. The book begins with a **prayer of penitence**, recognizing that the tragedies which befell Jerusalem are the just recompense for her sins (1:1—3:8). A second poetical section explains that **Israel's misfortunes** are due to her neglect of **Wisdom** (3:9—4:4). This Wisdom, whose praises are sung by a philosophically minded writer, is equated with God's law (4:1–3). The third section of the book, also poetic, is a message of **comfort and hope for distressed Israel.** The enemy will be destroyed and the children of Jerusalem will return in triumph! Baruch is the one book of the Apocrypha which breathes something of the fire

of the Old Testament prophets, although it is lacking in originality.

The Letter of Jeremiah. Sometime about 300 B.C., or thereafter, an unknown author wrote an impassioned sermon based on Jeremiah 11:10, in which he showed the utter impotence of gods of wood, silver, and gold. This sermon, known as The Letter of Jeremiah, was originally written in Hebrew (or Aramaic), although it is extant only in Greek and translations derived from the Greek. Since many Greek and Syriac manuscripts, as well as the Latin version, attach The Letter of Jeremiah to the Book of Baruch, it appears as the sixth chapter of Baruch in most English translations of the Apocrypha. The Letter has no relation to Baruch, however, and some ancient codices place it after the biblical Book of Lamentations.

The Prayer of Azariah and the Song of the Three Young Men. (Additions to Daniel, inserted between 3:23 and 3:24.) Sometime during the second or first centuries B.C., the three "additions" to canonical Daniel, which exist as separate books of the Apocrypha, were written by unknown authors. The first of these, The Prayer of Azariah and the Song of the Three Young Men, was probably written in Hebrew by a pious Jew during the period when his people were suffering at the hand of **Antiochus Epiphanes,** or in the period of the **Maccabean revolt** which followed. During the ordeal of the fiery furnace, Azariah is represented as praising God, confessing his people's sins, and praying for national deliverance. The angel of the Lord then came into the furnace and drove out the fiery flame, so that the youths were unharmed. Then from the furnace they sang their praises to God in the Song, which is reminiscent of Psalm 148 in content and Psalm 136 in antiphonal form.

Susanna. It is uncertain whether the original of Susanna was written in Hebrew or Greek. Its unknown author lived sometime during the second or the first century B.C., but we are ignorant of other details concerning his life. Yet, the book itself is recognized as one of the great short stories of world literature. It tells how two immoral elders threatened to testify that they had found Susanna, the beautiful wife of an influential Babylonian Jew, in the arms of a lover, if she would not submit to them. When she repulsed them, they charged her with adultery through the testimony of two witnesses, and she was convicted and sentenced to death. A young man named Daniel, however, interrupted the proceedings and questioned the two witnesses separately. He asked each to identify the tree under which he had seen Susanna and her supposed lover. Betrayed by their own inconsistent answers, the guilty elders were put to death and Susanna was saved. In the Septuagint, the Story of Susanna precedes the canonical Book of Daniel; in the Vulgate it follows it.

Bel and the Dragon. The stories of Bel and the Dragon were probably written in Hebrew toward the middle of the first century B.C. and added to the Book of Daniel by its Greek translator. In the Septuagint it directly follows Daniel, while in the Vulgate it comes after Susanna. The story of Bel is one of the world's oldest detective stories. It tells how **Cyrus,** the Persian king, asked **Daniel** why he did not worship **Bel, the god of Babylon.** Cyrus told Daniel how much flour and oil and how many sheep the god Bel consumed each day. Then, Daniel persuaded Cyrus to deposit the usual provisions in the Temple and then to close and seal the Temple doors. In the meantime, Daniel scattered ashes over the Temple floor. When morning came the food was gone, and the floor was covered with footprints of the priests, their wives and children, who had used a secret entrance under the table to come by night into the Temple and consume the provisions. The king, convinced of the perfidy of Bel's priests, ordered them slain and their Temple destroyed. The Dragon is really a serpent which the king worshiped until Daniel killed it by feeding it lumps of pitch, fat, and hair. The Babylonians, furious at the destruction of their god, demanded that Daniel be put to death. The king reluctantly consented and Daniel was placed in a den of lions (cf. Dan. 6:1–28). The lions did not molest Daniel, who was miraculously fed by the prophet **Habakkuk,** who was caught up by an angel in Judea and taken to the lions' den in **Babylon.** On the seventh day the king took Daniel from the lions' den and cast his enemies into it, whereupon they were immediately devoured. The stories of Bel and the Dragon were intended to ridicule idolatry and discredit heathen priestcraft.

The Prayer of Manasseh. The apocryphal Prayer of Manasseh was probably written sometime during the last two centuries B.C. by a Palestinian Jew. Scholars are uncertain whether it was composed in Hebrew, Aramaic, or Greek. The Prayer is ascribed to Manasseh, the king of Judah who, according to Second Chronicles 33, was taken to Babylon where he repented of the idolatry that had characterized the years of his reign. Mention is made of a prayer offered by Manasseh (2 Chr. 33:19), and a pious Jew appears to have attempted to write such a prayer as Manasseh would have uttered. The Prayer is typical of ancient Jewish liturgical forms. It opens with the ascription of **praise to the Lord,** whose majesty is seen in creation (1–4) and in His mercy toward sinners (5–8). This is followed by **personal confession** (9, 10) and **supplication for pardon** (11–13). The prayer concludes with a **petition for grace** (14) and a doxology (15).

First Maccabees. First Maccabees is a valuable historical record of the forty years beginning with the accession of **Antiochus Epiphanes** to the Syrian throne (175 B.C.) and ending with the death of

Simon the Maccabee (135 B.C.). It was probably written by a Palestinian Jew, in Hebrew, about 100 B.C. The book gives us our best account of the Jewish resistance to Antiochus and the Maccabean wars which ultimately brought independence to the Jewish state. It relates the exploits of three of the sons of Mattathias, the priest who defied Antiochus and sparked the revolt: **Judas** (3:1—9:22), **Jonathan** (9:23—12:53), and **Simon** (13:1—16:24). The annual Jewish festival of Hanukkah, celebrated at the same season as Christmas, commemorates the rededication of the Temple as a result of the bravery of the Maccabees. The festival is mentioned in the New Testament as "the Feast of the Dedication" (John 10:22).

Second Maccabees. Second Maccabees is primarily parallel to the first seven chapters of First Maccabees, covering the period from 175 to 160 B.C. It professes to be an abridgement of a five-volume history written by **Jason of Cyrene** (2:19–23), whose identity is a matter of conjecture. The author of Second Maccabees was evidently an Alexandrian Jew who wrote in Greek. He may have written as early as 120 B.C. or as late as the early first century A.D. Second Maccabees is less historical and more rhetorical than First Maccabees. It is written from the Pharisaic viewpoint and stresses the miraculous and the marvelous in contrast to the more prosaic and objective First Maccabees.

THE ENGLISH BIBLE AND ITS DEVELOPMENT

In increasing numbers English speaking people are turning to the *New American Standard Bible* for their knowledge of the only true God, and of Jesus Christ, whom He has sent, of the divine aspects of Israel's history, of the inspired ideals of the Christian life as revealed to the apostles, and any certain concept of their future, of their own souls and life of glory, and of the earth and of the nations upon it. Bible students have consistently found this translation to be sufficiently up-to-date, to be comprehensible, and at the same time sufficiently literal to carry the underlying sense of the text. Because of the clarity and accuracy with which it communicates the message of God, it is one of the translations most highly valued and widely used by Bible students and Bible study groups.

It is generally agreed that Christianity came to Britain in the second century of our era, possibly soon after the close of the apostolic age. But who brought the Christian faith first to that island, and how extensive its acceptance at that time, we may never know. "Among the many hundreds of religious monuments, civil and military, strewn about Britain from the second to the early fourth century, all are purely pagan." There were some early British martyrs, and Britain was represented at the earlier church councils, but, says the late Professor Charles Oman, "There seems every reason to believe that the main bulk of the population in this remote province of the West remained pagan until a much later date than was the case elsewhere. . . . It is very strange that a religion, which was first publicly tolerated and later encouraged by the government for nearly a hundred years before the fatal year A.D. 410, should have left so few records in stone behind it." What Bibles or parts of Bibles were in Britain in those mysteriously blacked-out decades, we do not know. The oldest book written by a Briton belongs in this period. It was a commentary on the epistles of Paul by the heretic Pelagius. But he left Britain when young, never to return, and wrote the book in Rome.

The Book of Armagh

While for the nearly two hundred years after the departure of the Roman garrison in Britain, A.D. 410, we know almost nothing of the experiences of the Christian church in England, the story is quite different for the church in Ireland, to which mountainous country the Christian faith first came in the fourth century. Within three generations, monasteries sprang up throughout the entire land. By A.D. 600 "the study of sound literature held the foremost place and was pursued with a thoroughness and intensity unknown elsewhere in Europe at that date." It was during this period that *The Book of Armagh* was written, partly in Irish and partly in Latin, containing a non-Vulgate text of the New Testament, the only complete copy of the New Testament that has come down to us produced by the Irish church.

The Latin Bible

It is with the coming of St. Augustine of Canterbury in 597 that any factual history of Christianity in England must begin. We do not know if St. Augustine actually had a Bible with him, though we are sure that there were hundreds of passages of Scripture, especially the Psalter, stored in his mind. Among the gifts of Pope Gregory to the early church at Canterbury, soon thereafter, were a Gregorian Bible, in two volumes, two copies of the Gospels, two Psalters, an exposition of the Epistles and Gospels for several Sundays, all adorned with silver or jewels. Here is the beginning of the history of the Scriptures in Britain. What kind of Bible would Pope Gregory send to Augustine? It would have to be a *Latin* Bible, not a Hebrew Old Testament or a Greek New Testament, and this deserves brief consideration. By the third century of our era, most people in the Western provinces of the Roman Empire knew very little Greek (even in Rome). If they were to have a Bible, it must be a Latin version, the language that was spoken throughout most of the Mediterranean world. When and how Latin Bibles were replaced by English Bibles, which could be read by the laity, is what we now want to consider.

The First English Bibles

Undoubtedly, the first translation of parts of the Bible into Anglo-Saxon were not with pen and ink, on vellum or parchment, but in song and recitation. These Christian songs began with Caedmon, whose discovery of a gift of song is so beautifully set forth by Bede. Bede says that Caedmon "sang first of the creation of the world and the beginning of mankind, and all the story of Genesis, that is the first book of Moses, and again of the Exodus of the people of Israel from the land of Egypt and of the entrance into the promised land, and of many other tales of holy writ . . . and of Christ's incarnation, and of His passion, and of His ascent into Heaven, and of the coming of the Holy Ghost, and the teachings of the apostles; and of the day of future judgment and of the terror of punishment full of torment, and of the sweetness of the heavenly kingdom he wrote many a lay; and also he wrought many others concerning divine

benefits and judgments." Caedmon died about A.D. 680. The second great name in this tradition is Cynewulf, who died a century later in A.D. 783. About this time was composed the famous Christian epic known as *The Christ,* showing a remarkable knowledge of the life of the Savior. The most beautiful gem of all literary compositions of this period is the exquisite *The Dream of the Rood,* the most moving interpretation of the Crucifixion of Christ in the first one thousand years of English literature.

The greatest British scholar in the first half of the eighth century was the Venerable Bede. No one equaled him for the next five hundred years in Britain in knowledge of the Scriptures. His own confession is significant. "I gave all my attention to the study of the Scriptures. . . . From the time that I received the degree of Priest's Orders unto the fifty-ninth year of my age [A.D. 731]." Bede's writings were in Latin, but he did undertake the translation of the Gospels into Anglo-Saxon and on the very day of his death was dictating his translation of John's Gospel. None of these translations have come down to us. St. Aldhelm (d. 709) also translated the Psalms, but these do not exist today.

England's noble King Alfred (849–899), at the beginning of his famous code of laws for his British subjects, used as a preface his own Anglo-Saxon translation of the Ten Commandments. The earliest written translation of the Gospels into Anglo-Saxon that now exists dates from about the tenth century.

The Lindisfarne Gospels

Probably the first extant attempt to bridge this linguistic gap in literary composition is the beautiful *Lindisfarne Gospels* in Latin, originally written about A.D. 700 in an uncial Irish script, containing an interlinear translation written in Anglo-Saxon, added about A.D. 950. About A.D. 1000, appeared the celebrated Aelfric, of whom it has been rightly said, "He is among the first to stand out individually in the records of his contemporaries as one that labored to make the Scriptures available to English scholars in their native tongue." He produced sermons in the West Saxon tongue, wrote commentaries on certain books of the Bible, and composed a condensed version of the first seven books of the Old Testament.

Language changes, however, were rapid then, and by 1300 the Anglo-Saxon language of King Alfred and Aelfric had become almost obsolete. Yet, as a distinguished authority has reminded us, "From the day of Alfred to the time of Chaucer, the language of the English people had a continuous history although it underwent many vicissitudes and suffered great changes. . . . It is this persistence of an English tone and spirit gradually regaining its ascendancy after having been

overlaid for three centuries by the culture of the Normans that gives these Anglo-Saxon manuscripts their chief significance for us. . . . We discern in these ancient versions some permanent core of basic speech that holds over from age to age and constitutes our English idiom, the most English part of our English tongue."

For two hundred years after the Norman conquest (A.D. 1066), French remained the language of ordinary intercourse among the upper class of conquered Britain. In the thirteenth and fourteenth centuries, "its maintenance became increasingly artificial. In the fourteenth century, English won its way back into universal use, and in the fifteenth century French all but disappeared."

The Ormulum Gospels and Acts

At the beginning of the fourteenth century appeared a poetical version of the Gospels and the Acts of the Apostles, accompanied by a commentary known as the *Ormulum,* the work of an Augustinian monk, Orm. Toward the middle of that century, the stories of Genesis and Exodus were translated into rhyming English verse.

The Psalter in Early Middle English

Two prose translations of the Psalter in Early Middle English have survived. One, composed by the famous Richard Rolle, attained great popularity. As an indication of Bible study during the fourteenth century, there are 170 biblical manuscripts of this period still surviving.

The Wycliffe Version

We now come to what may be called the first great effort to place the entire Bible in the hands of the common people in their own language. This is *The Wycliffe Version,* although it is not certain that Wycliffe himself composed any part of it. John Wycliffe (1330–1384) did stir up a desire on the part of many to make available the Holy Scriptures in the language of the people. The first translation was made about 1400 and a second translation, which exercised so much influence, was a revision by John Purvey. Here the idiom is closer to the current language of the day than the earlier version. This is the only Bible in English which existed in Britain until Tyndale more than a century later. *The Wycliffe Bible* is the first complete Bible to appear in England.

The Gutenberg Bible

Between Wycliffe in 1384 and the Tyndale Version 140 years later, some stupendous events changed the whole intellectual and religious atmosphere of Europe. In 1453 Constantinople, the capital of the Eastern Roman Empire, fell. Many Greek scholars migrated to the West with their precious manuscripts. In 1456 there appeared the first book printed with movable type, *The Guten-*

berg Bible, which was to usher in a whole new era for Western man. Universal literacy and universal education were now possible, although not yet realities. Before that century ended, America had been discovered by Christopher Columbus. In 1516 Erasmus published the first Greek New Testament ever to appear in print, which exercised an enormous influence on subsequent biblical translations. In 1517 Luther nailed his ninety-five theses to the church door at Wittenberg. The Reformation may be said to have begun in Switzerland in 1519, and Calvin began his famous work in Geneva in 1541. This is the period of the reign of Henry VIII (1509–1547).

The Tyndale Bible

Tyndale, born in 1494 and educated at Oxford, became obsessed with a desire to produce a new edition of the Bible, in the English of his day, translated from original Greek and Hebrew. Tyndale was expert in seven languages. Failing to secure any encouragement from the Bishop of London, Tyndale crossed the channel to Hamburg (1524), and then to Wittenberg, where he met Luther. It was in Cologne that the first printed English New Testament was issued in 1525. Tyndale, betrayed by a friend, was deceivingly persuaded to come to England, where he was imprisoned and martyred on October 6, 1536, with those famous words upon his lips, "Lord, open the King of England's eyes."

Regarding the Old Testament, it is believed that Tyndale translated the Pentateuch and the book of Jonah. The translation of Isaiah is to be attributed to George Joye. Tyndale continued to work at revising his New Testament, with new editions appearing in 1533, 1534, and 1535. Eighty percent of the text of the *King James Version* is taken from the *The Tyndale Bible*.

So harsh and constant was the denunciation of this version by ecclesiastical authorities, that of the first edition there remains only a fragment now in the British Museum. Of the second edition, only two copies are known today. Of the New Testament, printed at Worms, only two copies have survived to the present time.

The Myles Coverdale Bible

Just before Tyndale died, there appeared *the first complete Bible to be printed in the English tongue,* the work of Myles Coverdale (1485–1568), based on the Latin Vulgate, Tyndale, and the German Bible of Martin Luther. "Next to Tyndale, the man to whom lovers of the English Bible owe the greatest debt is Coverdale." He was the first to separate the Apocrypha from the Old Testament and place it as an appendix. His was the first Bible to introduce chapter summaries as distinct from brief chapter headings found in the Vulgate. So important was Coverdale's version that his translation of the Psalms, revised by himself for

The Great Bible of 1539, is the only one that still appears in the *Book of Common Prayer.*

As an illustration of the opposition of the Church to a Bible appearing in the vernacular tongue, one might consider the proclamation of the King condemning Tyndale's book in the following severe language: "And furthermore, for as much as it is come to the hearing of our said sovereign lord the king, that report is made by divers and many of his subjects, that as it were to all men not only expedient, but also necessary, to have in the English tongue both the New Testament and the Old: and that this highness, his noble men and prelates were bounden to suffer them so to have it; His highness hath therefore semblably there upon consulted with the said primates and virtuous, discrete, and well learned personages in divinity foresaid, and by them all it is thought, that it is not necessary, the said scripture to be in the English tongue, and in the hands of the common people; but that the distribution of the said scripture, and their permitting or denying thereof, dependeth only upon the discretion of the superiors, as they shall think it convenient. And that having respect to the malignity of this present time, with the inclination of the people to erroneous opinions, the translation of the New Testament and the Old into the vulgar tongue of English, should rather be the occasion of continuance or increase of errors among the said people, than any benefit or commodity toward the weal of their souls. And that it shall now be more convenient that the same people have the holy scripture expounded to them, by preachers in their sermons, according as it hath been of old time accustomed before this time."

The Cranmer Bible

In 1537 appeared a folio which in the title affirmed that the translation into English was by Thomas Matthew. The translator's name is now recognized as John Rogers, an associate of Tyndale. This translation was "set forth with the King's most gracious license." Later editions (1540 and 1541) contained a preface by Archbishop Cranmer and are known as *The Cranmer Bible.* Rogers did not know Hebrew and was dependent upon earlier translations. It is said that two-thirds of the Rogers Bible was from Tyndale and one-third from Coverdale. On the title page of the later versions appear for the first time, the words "This is the Bible appointed to the use of churches."

The Great Bible

Coverdale had a major part in a new revision of the Matthew Bible which was called *The Great Bible.* The pages measured 9x15 inches and the text was 8½x13 inches. It was commanded in 1538 that a copy of the English Bible be set up in every parish church, and this Bible was generally

secured for carrying out this order. But because another more accurate version soon appeared *The Great Bible* was not reprinted after 1569. Rogers himself suffered martyrdom in 1555. "It is Rogers' Bible which became the foundation of all later English authorized versions, and it is through Rogers' republication that Tyndale's 1535 version of the New Testament had its great influence upon subsequent versions," notes L.A. Weigle.

In 1546 King Henry VIII issued an order that "no man or woman of what estate, condition, or degree [was] to receive, have, take, or keep Tyndale's or Coverdale's New Testament." And yet *The Great Bible*, for the most part made up of the translations of Tyndale and Coverdale, was given royal approval and commanded to be placed in every church.

The Geneva Bible

The most accurate version until the Authorized Version of 1611 was *The Geneva Bible*. During the reign of Queen Mary (1553–1558), no Bible was printed in England, but a group of scholars in Geneva produced an English version called *The Geneva Bible* in 1560, with a second edition in 1652. The New Testament was edited by William Whittingham, who was married to Calvin's sister. Calvin wrote an introductory epistle. For the first time marginal notations called attention to variations in the Greek manuscripts. This was the first English version to use numbered verses as separate paragraphs. This was the Bible used by Shakespeare, John Bunyan, Oliver Cromwell, and so fervently used by the Puritans. Designated as "the people's book," it held a preeminent place among English versions for seventy-five years. This was the Bible brought over on the Mayflower. From 1560 to 1644, one hundred forty editions of *The Geneva Bible* appeared. The first Bible to be printed in Scotland was a Scottish edition of *The Geneva Bible* in 1579. The verse divisions of Robert Estienne, originally employed in his Greek New Testament in 1551, were used. This was the first Bible to be printed in Roman type instead of the old Black Letter.

The Bishops' Bible

The popularity of *The Geneva Bible* persuaded the Anglican authorities, after the accession of Queen Elizabeth to the throne in 1558, to produce a Bible which could bear the authority of the Church of England. This task was proposed by Archbishop Parker, who appointed a committee to begin the work. They were to use *The Great Bible* as their basis and were to compare it with the Greek and Hebrew texts. The scholarship of these Bishops was not equal to that of the group that had produced *The Geneva Bible*. The finished work was called *The Bishops' Bible*. Nineteen editions were printed from 1568–1606. It was endorsed by Convocation in 1571. In the

1572 edition, Parker published in parallel columns the Psalter of *The Great Bible* and the Psalter of *The Bishops' Bible*. There are fewer differences between *The Bishops' Bible* and the *King James Version* than any other preceding translation.

The Rheims Bible and the Douay Bible

The last two Bibles to be considered, before the *King James Version*, are those known as *The Rheims Bible* and *The Douay Bible*, both Roman Catholic.

The New Testament was published as early as 1582 by the English College, then located at Rheims, and was thus known as *The Rheims New Testament*. The Old Testament, for the most part the work of Gregory Martin, a translation of the Latin Vulgate, was published in 1609, when the English College had returned to Douay and hence the name *The Douay Bible*. The poorest part of this version is acknowledged to be the Psalter, which has been rightly characterized as "a translation of a translation of a translation." There is, of course, a heavy emphasis in this version on ecclesiastical terms. Repentance is here translated *penance*. Here we have such unfamiliar words as *exinaninted*, *donances*, and *commersation*. Instead of *shewbread*, this version reads "proposition of loaves." *Deacon* is translated *minister*, and *elder* is translated *priest*. Ephesians 3:9 is made to read, "the dispensation of the sacrament." (See Eph. 3:9: "to bring to light what is the administration of the mystery.") The New Testament part of this Bible was extensively used by the King James revisers, but the Old Testament was published too late for any such influence.

The King James Version

It is now time to turn to a consideration of the most important English version of the Bible ever to be produced, called sometimes the *Authorized Version* and sometimes the *King James Version* (hereafter we shall refer to it with the initials KJV). In the summer of 1603, when King James was on his way to London to receive the English crown, he was presented with a petition of grievances by the clergy of Puritan convictions, which led the King to call a conference "for hearing and for the determining of things pretended to be amiss in the church." This conference was convened for three days, January 14–16, 1604, and was known as the Hampton Court Conference. During this conference Dr. John Reynolds, the leader of the Puritan party and president of Corpus Christi College, Oxford, made the motion that a new translation of the Bible be undertaken. Although the majority present were against the motion, it appealed to the King, and he ordered that such a translation be undertaken. Fifty-four of the greatest biblical scholars in Great Britain were brought together for this great task and di-

vided into six groups—three to work on a translation of the Old Testament and three on the New Testament. Two groups for the Old and New Testaments were to meet at Oxford, two at Cambridge, and two at Westminster. A recent writer has so well summarized the varied learning of this group that we take the liberty of quoting H. Wheeler Robinson: "The Oxford group was headed by Dr. John Hardinge, Regius Professor of Hebrew, and included Dr. John Reynolds, the originator of the project, whose 'memory and reading were near to a miracle'; Dr. Miles Smith, who 'had Hebrew at his fingers' ends'; Dr. Richard Brett, 'skilled and versed to a criticism in the Latin, Greek, Chaldee, Arabic, and Ethiopic tongues'; Sir Henry Saville, editor of the works of Chrysostom; and Dr. John Harmer, Professor of Greek, 'a most noted Latinist, Grecian, and divine.' The Cambridge committee was at first led by Edward Lively, Regius Professor of Hebrew, who died in 1605 before the work was really begun; and included Dr. Lawrence Chaderton, 'familiar with the Greek and Hebrew tongues and the numerous writings of the Rabbis'; Thomas Harrison, 'noted for his exquisite skill in Hebrew and Greek idioms'; Dr. Robert Spalding, successor to Lively as Professor of Hebrew; Andrew Downes, 'one composed of Greek and industry'; and John Bois, 'a precious Greek and Hebrew scholar.' The Westminster group was headed by Lancelot Andrews, Dean of Westminster, afterwards Bishop of Chichester, of Ely, and finally of Winchester, 'who might have been interpreter general at Babel' . . . ; and included the Hebraist Hadrian Saravia; and William Bedwell, the greatest living Arabic scholar." Since there was a lapse of two or three years between the naming of these committees and the beginning of their labors, the work was begun in 1607 and completed in 1610. The Bible appeared the following year.

Fifteen rules were to bind this large number of revisers. The first reads as follows: "The ordinary Bible read in the Church, commonly called *The Bishops' Bible*, to be followed, and as little altered as the Truth of the original will permit." The fourteenth rule was more comprehensive, reading as follows: "These translations to be used when they agree better with the Text than the Bishops Rule—Tindoll's, Matthews, Coverdales, Whitchurch's, Geneva." In the Preface to the Reader which appeared in this version, the translators stated that they did not hesitate "to consult the Translators or Commentators, *Chaldee, Hebrewe, Syrian, Greeke,* or *Latine,* no nor the *Spanish, French, Italian,* or *Dutch.*"

The new version bore the following title: "The Holy Bible, Conteyning the Old Testament and the New; Newly Translated out of the Originall tongues, with the former Translations diligently compared and revised, by His Majesties speciall commandement. Appointed to be read in Churches. Imprinted at London by Robert Barker, Printer to the Kings most Excellent Majestie. Anno Dom. 1611." The New Testament title was slightly different: "The New Testament of our Lord and Saviour Jesus Christ, Newly translated out of the Originall Greeke; and with the former Translations diligently compared and revised, by His Majesties speciall Commandement. Imprinted at London by Robert Barker, Printer to the Kings most Excellent Majestie. Anno Dom. 1611. cum Privilegio." While this version is called the *Authorized Version,* no act of Parliament was ever passed approving it. King James vigorously promoted such an undertaking, but there was no subsequent official act. The first printing of this Bible was a folio 16x10½ inches. Three editions quickly followed, carrying a considerable number of misprints and variations in spelling. We must ask at this point how much of the KJV was dependent upon earlier versions. It has been said that four percent of the vocabulary goes back to the days of Wycliffe, eighteen percent came from Tyndale, thirteen percent from Coverdale, nineteen percent from the Geneva Bible, four percent from the Bishops' Bible, and three percent from all other preceding versions. Thirty-nine percent of the vocabulary of the KJV is unique. Almost nine-tenths of the New Testament portion of this version can be found word for word in the Tyndale version of 1525. All controversial notes were excluded, but there were over four thousand marginal notes, giving the literal meaning of Hebrew words, and 765 in the New Testament, indicating variant or alternative renderings. The chapter summaries and page headings were new, and some of these chapter headings are indications of current theology and then prevalent principles of biblical interpretation. The Old Testament rested upon the same Masoretic Hebrew text as all subsequent versions, but since no ancient manuscripts of the Greek New Testament arrived in England until 1628, those responsible for this greatest of all versions did not have the advantage of the best Greek text.

During subsequent decades the spelling of the KJV has been modernized, misprints have been corrected, the larger chapter summaries have been abbreviated, and the references in the margin have been examined. Chronological dates were introduced into the margin of the KJV in 1701, based on the chronology of Archbishop Ussher. As early as 1613, the text showed over 300 differences from the original of 1611. Thirty thousand new marginal references were added in versions appearing in the 1760s.

Soon the KJV crowded out all preceding translations except for students interested in specific variations and the development of the English language. For the first time, England was reading one Bible at home and hearing the same Bible read in church. "It thus became bound up with

the life of the nation. Since it stilled all controversy over the best rendering, it gradually came to be accepted as so far absolute that in the minds of myriads there was no distinction between this version and the original texts, and they may almost be said to have believed in the literal inspiration of the very words which composed it," wrote Albert S. Cook. The beauty of the KJV, as well as its enormous influence cannot easily be exaggerated. The translators of the *Revised Version*, nearly three centuries later, declared: "We have had to study this great Version carefully and minutely, line by line; and the longer we have been engaged upon it the more we have learned to admire its simplicity, its dignity, its power, its happy turns of expression, its general accuracy, and, we must not fail to add, the music of its cadences, and the felicities of its rhythm." Even the non-Christian, Thomas Huxley, offered the following glowing tribute to this version of the Scriptures: "Consider the great historical fact that for three centuries this book has been woven into the life of all that is best and noblest in English history; that it has become the national epic of Britain, and is as familiar to noble and simple, from John-o'-Groat's House to Land's End, as Dante and Tasso once were to the Italians; that it is written in the noblest and purest English, and abounds in exquisite beauties of pure literary form; and, finally, that it forbids the veriest hind who never left his village to be ignorant of the existence of other countries and other civilizations, and of a great past stretching back to the furthest limits of the oldest civilizations of the world."

The English Revised Version

It is not necessary to discuss the translations of secondary importance offered during the next three centuries. A number of changes had occurred in the use of the English language, and a great deal of new material was available for ascertaining the Greek text of the New Testament, and much more was known about the Hebrew language. Consequently, on February 10, 1870, Bishop Wilberforce submitted the following resolution to the Upper House of Convocation of the Province of Canterbury: "That a Committee of both Houses to be appointed, with power to confer with any Committee that may be appointed by the Convocation of the Northern Province, to report upon the desirableness of a revision of the Authorized Version of the New Testament, whether by marginal notes or otherwise, in all those passages where plain and clear errors, whether in the Hebrew or Greek text originally adopted by the translators, or in the translation made from the same, shall, on due investigation, be found to exist." In May of the same year, a committee made five suggestions: "1. That it is desirable that a revision of the Authorized Version of the Holy Scriptures be undertaken. 2. That the

revision be so conducted as to comprise both marginal renderings and such emendations as it may be found necessary to insert in the text of the Authorized Version. 3. That in the above resolutions we do not contemplate any new translation of the Bible, or any alteration of the language, except when in the judgment of the most competent scholars such change is necessary. 4. That in such necessary changes, the style of the language employed in the existing version be closely followed. 5. That it is desirable that Convocation should nominate a body of its own members to undertake the work of revision, who shall be at liberty to invite the co-operation of any eminent for scholarship, to whatever nation or religious body they may belong."

Many of the finest biblical scholars in Britain were engaged to translate the Old and New Testaments—fifty-four of them. The first general principle was "to introduce as few alterations as possible into the text of the Authoized Version consistently with faithfulness." The fifth, seventh, and eighth principles were: "5. To make or retain no change in the Text on the second final revision by each Company, except *two-thirds* of those present approve of the same, but on the first revision to decide by simple majorities. 7. To revise the headings of chapters, pages, paragraphs, italics, and punctuation. 8. To refer, on the part of each Company, when considered desirable, to Divines, Scholars, and Literary Men, whether at home or abroad, for their opinions."

The New Testament was issued in May, 1881, and the Old Testament in May, 1885. Two famous Greek scholars, B. F. Westcott and F. J. A. Hort, generally influenced the adoption of what they called the "neutral text." A number of passages were taken out of the text and placed in the margin as not appearing in the earlier Greek texts, for example, John 5:3, 4; First John 5:6, 7; and John 8:1–9. Where parallel passages appeared in two or more books with identical wording in the original, the translations also were made identical. There were many criticisms of the *Revised Version,* and yet many agree with the statement of Professor F. F. Bruce that "the *Revised Version* with these marginal references is still the most useful edition of the Bible for the careful student who knows no language but English." The Old Testament is especially recognized as being a great improvement for accuracy's sake over the KJV.

The American Standard Revised Version

It was hoped that the English and American Committees could be responsible for a single revised version, but so many differences arose that after some years the American Company asked to be released from further cooperation. They would publish their own Revised Version, promising not to do so for fourteen years. In 1897, Thomas

Nelson and Sons entered into an agreement with the American Company to meet the necessary expenses for the preparation of an American revision. Once again they went to work, minutely going over the entire text. Twenty-nine years later, on August 26, 1901, the *American Standard Revised Version* of the Bible was placed on sale and was at once recognized as superior in many ways to the English revision.

Other Versions

One of the more important nineteenth-century translations of the Bible was by the famous compiler of *Young's Concordance*, the British biblical scholar, Robert Young. He published at Edinburgh, as early as 1862, his *Literal Translation of the Bible*, permeated with Young's deep conviction that "every word of the original is God-breathed as the Apostle Paul says in his Second Epistle to Timothy, chapter 3:16." A third edition was issued in 1898.

The outstanding scholar among the Plymouth Brethren in their earlier days was J. N. Darby, who had immense linguistic ability and issued a translation of the Bible, first in French, then in Dutch and German, and then in English. Darby wrote in the preface to his New Testament translation, "Being profoundly convinced of the Divine inspiration of the Scriptures, we have tried in this translation to reproduce as exactly as possible what God has given us in another language. . . ."

Coming into the twentieth century, the first new translation that need be mentioned is *The Twentieth Century New Testament*, the publication of which extended from 1898 to 1901, a careful retranslation based upon the Westcott and Hort text. Great care was taken to weigh every word in the Greek and to translate identical passages verbatim. Dr. E. H. Robertson, in his survey of the more recent versions, says, "There seems to me to be little doubt that this is one of the most careful translations ever undertaken," and reports that the result of a Bible study group which he led for some years was that here appeared "the most faithful rendering of the Greek in nearly every difficult passage we encountered."

The two most widely used translations of the New Testament, until the appearance of the RSV, were those produced by Dr. Weymouth and Dr. Moffatt. Dr. Weymouth's *New Testament in Modern Speech* first appeared in 1902, with brief introductions prefixed to each book and a considerable number of explanatory footnotes. It was frequently revised during his life and for some years after, the later revisions being increasingly liberal in theological tendency.

The New Testament: A New Translation is by Dr. James Moffatt, one of the most distinguished New Testament scholars of the earlier part of our century. This first appeared in 1913. The Old Testament followed in 1924 and the entire Bible, with a final revision, was published in 1935. His work in the Old Testament is generally recognized as being of much less value than his work in the New Testament. Even here Moffatt justly antagonized many Christians by the liberties he took with some texts. For example, the phrase occurring at the opening of John's Gospel, "In the beginning was the Word, and the Word was with God, and the Word was God," Moffatt translates the last phrase "and the Word was divine." So also in translating the genealogy in the first chapter of Matthew in the Moffatt version, it reads: "Jacob the father of Joseph, and Joseph (to whom the virgin Mary was betrothed), the father of Jesus who is called Christ," a translation based on a late and unauthoritative Greek manuscript and contradicted by all the most ancient texts. As an illustration, however, of some of the more revealing passages in Moffatt, we might consider four verses from Second Corinthians: "I live for God as the fragrance of Christ breathed alike on those who are being saved and on those who are perishing, to the one a deadly fragrance that makes for death, to the other a vital fragrance that makes for life" (2 Cor. 2:15, 16); "Hence I never lose heart" (4:16); and "he will increase the crop of your charities—you will be enriched on all hands, so that you can be generous on all occasions, and your generosity, of which I am the agent, will make men give thanks to God" (9:11).

The last four translators we have considered were all from Great Britain. It is time now that an American version should appear, and it did, produced by scholars at the University of Chicago. In 1923 Dr. Edgar J. Goodspeed published his *The New Testament: An American Translation*, based on the Westcott and Hort text. In 1935, assisted by colleagues, a new translation of the entire Bible appeared with the simple title *The Bible: An American Translation*. It was widely used for the first twenty years after its first appearance, although it was never quoted with the same frequency as Moffatt's.

The Revised Standard Version

In 1937, the International Council of Religious Education, in which some forty of the larger denominations in North America were associated, authorized the preparation and publication of a complete new revision, which was carried through by some thirty-two different American scholars. *The New Testament Revised Version* was published in 1946 and the entire Bible in 1952. No version produced in our country has ever aroused so much antagonism, some justified and some unjustified. A number of archaisms have been removed, necessary emendations, due to a better knowledge of the meanings of the original text, have been made. Thus, for example, Deuteronomy 32:8, which in the earlier translations

stated that God had fixed the bounds of the people "according to the number of the children of Israel," now reads "according to the number of the sons of God," which is supported by the Septuagint and the Samaritan Bible and now by a fragment of the Hebrew manuscript found at Qumran.

One most commendable virtue of this version is that it returns to the familiar words of the King James translation of Second Timothy 3:16, from which the Revised Version had departed, the new version reading, "All Scripture is inspired by God and *is* profitable."

A second edition of the *Revised Standard Version* was published in 1971, popularly known as RSV II. This edition includes considerable revision of the New Testament.

The Holy Scripture According to the Masoretic Text: A New Translation, and The Torah

In 1914, the Jewish Publication Society of America published a volume entitled *The Holy Scriptures According to the Masoretic Text: A New Translation* (exclusively of the Old Testament), which has not exercised extensive influence outside Jewish circles. In 1962, the same organization published a new translation of the Pentateuch with the simple title, *The Torah;* in 1978 the second section was published, *The Prophets;* and in 1982 the final portion was published, *The Writings*. This work has been very carefully done, the result of the finest Hebrew scholarship available. But there seems to be a deliberate attempt here to make the Messianic predictions of the Pentateuch void of any Messianic meaning, as for example, Genesis 3:15 which here reads: "I will put enmity between you and the woman and between your offspring and hers; they shall strike at your head and you shall strike at their heel." All other modern translations read "his heel." The modern gentile reader would certainly not get much out of the translation of Exodus 3:14, which here reads: "And God said to Moses, 'Ehyeh-Asher-Ehyeh.'" There are a number of footnotes indicating that the exact meaning of some Hebrew words is not known today, as for example, the twelve stones of Exodus 28:17-20; the creatures mentioned in Deuteronomy 14:5, 6; and the diseases of Deuteronomy 28:22.

The Amplified Bible

The Amplified Bible (1954) is a literal translation with multiple expressions using associated words to convey the original thought. The New Testament uses the Greek text of Westcott and Hort plus 27 translations and revisions. The Old Testament is similarly extensive. The version is intended to supplement other translations authentically, concisely, and in convenient form.

Good News for Modern Man

Good News for Modern Man (Today's English Version) is a translation of the New Testament by Dr. Robert G. Bratcher (and a distinguished review committee) published in 1966. This is a paraphrase which gained enormous popularity in a short period of time. It was intended to communicate the Scriptures to the masses of English-speaking people around the world and has been used as an instrument of evangelism for people outside the church.

The Jersualem Bible

The Jerusalem Bible (1966) is a translation from the Hebrew Masoretic, Greek Septuagint, Dead Sea Scrolls, and accepted Greek and Aramaic New Testament texts—all compared with the French Version. It was produced by 28 principal collaborators in translation and literary revision under Alexander Jones, general editor.

New American Bible

The *New American Bible* (1970) is a Roman Catholic translation that is a highlight of Bible publishing in the present century. All basic texts were consulted, and the work was twenty-six years in the making. Over fifty recognized biblical scholars, the majority of them college professors, labored to produce this outstanding version. Scholars were Catholic, Protestant, and Jewish. The purpose was to produce a more accurate translation from the older manuscripts, and this was made possible by the Pope in 1943. Prior to this version, Catholics had been required to use the Latin Vulgate as the basis for translation.

The Living Bible

A very popular paraphrase, *The Living Bible* (Complete Bible, 1971), is the work of a single translator, Kenneth N. Taylor. The initial source was the *American Standard Version* of 1901, but Dr. Taylor and the Greek and Hebrew specialists he consulted also used the most respected texts available.

New American Standard Bible

The *New American Standard Bible* was translated by an Editorial Board of fifty-four Greek and Hebrew scholars and required nearly eleven years to complete. The producers of this translation believed that interest in the *American Standard Version* of 1901 should be renewed and increased. Recognizing the values of the ASV, the Lockman Foundation, sponsor of the project, felt an urgency to update that version by incorporating recent discoveries of Hebrew and Greek textual sources and by rendering the ASV into more current English. Therefore, in 1959 a new translation project was launched, based on the ASV. The result was the *New American Standard Bible*.

Among the translators, the ASV was highly regarded for its scholarship and accuracy. Furthermore numerous other translations were also consulted along with linguistic tools and literature of biblical scholarship. Decisions about English renderings were made by the consensus of a team composed of educators and pastors.

The translators of the NASB endeavored to keep the original word order whenever possible believing that this was a means the writer used to accent and emphasize what he deemed most important. Words are faithfully reproduced, even to conjunctions such as "and," in the belief that these, too, help to mirror the writer's style and manner of expression. This philosophy is in contrast to the trend toward a freer translation style evident in many of the translations since 1901. The *New American Standard Bible* uses the latest edition of Rudolph Kittel's Hebrew text and the Nestle Greek text, an outgrowth of the Wescott-Hort version. The editorial board has continued to function since publication of the complete Bible in 1971. Minor revisions and refinements have been inserted in more recent editions.

New International Version

The *New International Version* began with work by committees from the Christian Reformed Church and the National Association of Evangelicals. In 1967 the New York Bible Society undertook the financial sponsorship of the translation. The translation is done from the Masoretic Text in the Old Testament and an eclectic Greek text in the New Testament. This modern English version was published as a complete Bible in 1978.

New King James Version

In 1975 Thomas Nelson Publishers began the fifth revision of the *King James Version*. Over one hundred scholars worked on the translation of the *Biblia Hebraica Stuttgartensia* (Old Testament) and the Scrivener Greek Text (New Testament) into modern English using the 1611 and 1769 editions of the *King James Version* as standards.

Other Major Versions Since 1950

The Holy Bible from Ancient Eastern Manuscripts (1957) was intended to convey ancient biblical customs preserved only in the Aramaic texts and to reveal the deeper biblical meanings often hidden in idioms and parables.

The Berkeley Version in Modern English (1959) translates every word using modern terms.

The *New English Bible* (Complete Bible, 1970) required twenty-four years to complete and enlisted the labors of fifty recognized biblical scholars. It is based on the original Greek and Hebrew texts.

J. B. Phillips, an English vicar, translated the New Testament into modern speech, beginning with *Letters to Young Churches* in 1947, followed by *The Gospels* in 1952, *The Young Church in Action* in 1955, the *Book of Revelation* in 1957, and in 1958 the one-volume edition of his completed translation of the New Testament, *The New Testament in Modern Speech. Four Prophets* appeared in 1963.

FIRST MENTIONED THINGS IN THE BIBLE

THE SCARLET THREAD OF REDEMPTION

Introduction

The Bible is a book of redemption. It is that or nothing at all. It is not merely a book of history, or of science, or of anthropology, or of cosmogony. It is a book of salvation and deliverance for lost mankind.

The idea in the word "redemption" is twofold: it refers to a deliverance; and it refers to the price paid for that deliverance, a ransom. We are redeemed from the penalty of sin, from the power of Satan and evil, by the price Jesus paid on the cross for us; and we are redeemed to a new freedom from sin, a new relationship to God, and a new life of love by the appropriation of that atonement for our sins.

The whole of the Bible, whether the Old Testament or the New Testament, looks to the mighty, redemptive atonement of Christ. His blood sacrifice is the ransom paid for our deliverance. He took our sinful nature upon Himself in order that He might satisfy the demands of the law. His sacrifice is accepted as the payment for the debt the sinner owes to God, and His death is accepted as the full payment for man's deliverance.

Our Lord's redemptive work for us is threefold: First, it is closely associated with forgiveness, since we receive forgiveness through the redemptive price of Christ's death. Second, it involves justification, since the deliverance establishes us in a restored position of favor before God. Third, it promises final deliverance from the power of sin at the coming of the Lord. This redemption is "The Scarlet Thread."

The Creation and the Fall

When God made the heavens and the earth, they must have been beautiful, perfect, and pure. In the Garden of Eden, however, through a denial of the Word of God and through a deception of the woman, our first parents fell. Eve was deceived, but Adam chose to die by the side of the woman whom God had created and placed in his arms. When the Lord came to visit the man and his wife in the cool of the day, He could not find them. They were afraid and hid themselves from the Lord because they were naked and ashamed. To hide their guilt, they made for themselves aprons of fig leaves, but when God looked upon the covering, He said, "This will not do." Covering for sin (atonement for sin) cannot be woven by human hands. Therefore, somewhere in the Garden of Eden, the Lord took an innocent animal, and before the eyes of Eve and Adam, God slew that innocent animal as the ground drank up its blood. This is the beginning of "The Scarlet Thread of Redemption." Through the slaughter of an innocent victim, God took coats of skin and covered over the shame and the nakedness of the man and his wife. This is the first sacrifice, and it was offered by the hand of Almighty God. When Adam saw the gasping, spent life of that innocent creature, and when he saw the crimson stain which soiled the ground, it was his first experience of knowing what it meant to die because of sin. So the story of atonement and sacrifice begins and unfolds throughout the Word of God until finally in glory we shall see great throngs of the saints who have washed their robes and made them white in the blood of the Lamb. This is "The Scarlet Thread of Redemption."

From the Seventh Day in Eden to the Call of Abraham

In the Garden of Eden, as the Lord covered over the nakedness of the man and the woman, He turned to Satan and said, "And I will put enmity between you and the woman, and between your seed and her seed; He shall bruise you on the head, and you shall bruise him on the heel" (Gen. 3:15). For centuries the rabbis studied that word of Jehovah God to Satan. "The Seed of the woman." Seed is masculine. The rabbis contemplated the promise of God that the "Seed" of the woman would bruise Satan's head. We now know that the promise is related to the long conflict and struggle betwen the hatred of Lucifer and the love of God in Christ Jesus. It speaks of Jesus at Calvary. Jesus suffered. His heel was bruised. But in that bruising, He defeated once and for all the power of that old serpent, the devil. He bruised his head.

As the man Adam and his wife, Eve, made their first home in earth cursed for their sakes, after a time there were born to them two sons. One was named Cain and the other Abel. In jealousy and insane fury, the older brother killed the younger brother. But the seed of God would be preserved. The Lord, therefore, gave to Eve another son, named Seth. Seth was a man of faith, as Cain was a man of the world. When the children of Seth, the godly remnant, intermarried with the children of Cain, the people of the world, the result was a fallen progeny that filled the earth with violence. Finally, God said it was enough. One hundred twenty years later, He would destroy the world by a flood. But a member of the line of Seth found grace in the sight of the Lord. His name was Noah. To preserve the righteous seed, God told Noah to build an ark; and into that ark of safety, salvation, and hope Noah brought his family. After the passing of the awesome judgment of the flood, the earth once again began its story of redemption through the life of this one man and his three sons.

It was not long, however, until the ravages of sin began to waste the select family of God. Instead of carrying out the great commission of the Lord for mankind to inhabit the whole earth, the people drew together into one plain and announced their purpose to build a tower around which they were to center their civilization and their collective, communal unity. When God looked down and saw their pride, He confused their speech and caused them to "babble." From this "Tower of Babel," therefore, the different parts of the human race, being unable to understand each other, scattered in different directions and so fathered the nations of the earth that grew up from those three great family lines of Noah.

From the Call of Abraham Through the Times of the Judges

We begin the story of Abraham in a dark era. The whole world had been plunged into abysmal idolatry, but God called out this man to leave his home, his place, his country, and his family to go into another country which he would afterward receive for an inheritance. In obedience, Abraham left the Mesopotamian valley and came as a pilgrim, a stranger, and a sojourner into the land of Canaan. There he dwelt, and there God gave him two sons. But the Lord God said to Abraham that Ishmael, the son of a slave woman, would not be the promised seed. When Abraham was a hundred years old and Sarah was ninety years old, God miraculously placed in the arms of the parents the child of promise, whom they named Isaac. Isaac was the father of two sons, Esau and Jacob. The Lord, refusing Esau, chose Jacob whom He renamed, after a deep conversion experience, the "prince of God" or "Israel."

Because of a severe famine in Canaan and because Jacob's son, Joseph, was in Egypt, the entire household of Jacob went down to live in the land of the Nile. Later, there arose a Pharaoh who "did not know" Joseph. The chosen family became slaves to this new ruler of Egypt, and their heavy groaning mounted up to the ears of the Lord God in heaven. The Lord, therefore, raised up the mighty prophet, Moses, to deliver His people from the bondage and slavery of the Egyptians. God worked this deliverance by a miracle called the Passover. "For the LORD will pass through to smite the Egyptians; and when He sees the blood on the lintel and on the two doorposts, the LORD will pass over the door and will not allow the destroyer to come in to your houses to smite *you*" (Ex. 12:23). This way of salvation, through the blood, is once again "The Scarlet Thread of Redemption."

After the Lord God delivered the chosen family from Egypt, He brought them by the leadership of Moses through the parting of the Red Sea into the Sinaitic Peninsula to the base of Mount Horeb. There, for forty days and forty nights, Moses was with God, and there the Lord gave to Moses the pattern of the tabernacle, the ritual instructions of holy worship, and all of the other marvelous things in the Book of Leviticus that portray and prophesy the sacrifice of the Son of God.

After the death of Moses, Joshua went over Jordan and led the wars of conquest. In the first confrontation, at Jericho, an incident happened which gave rise to the title of this summary. The scouts sent out by Joshua to spy out Jericho were saved by the faith and kindness of Rahab. The men of Israel promised life and safety, both for her and her father's house, if she would bind a scarlet thread in her window. This she did, and, when Jericho fell into the hands of Joshua by the intervention of God, Rahab and her family were spared because of that scarlet line, "The Scarlet Thread of Redemption."

After the conquest of Canaan, under Joshua, we have the story of the Judges. The difference between a judge and a king was that a king gave to his son his throne by inheritance, but a judge was raised up in a crisis and endowed with special gifts from God for a period of time. The days of the Judges end with the birth of Samuel.

From the First of the Prophets to the Founding of the Kingdom

During the time of Samuel, the people began to cry for a king. It was the purpose of God in the beginning for the children of Israel to have a king (Deut. 17:14–20), but it hurt the heart of the Lord that the request should come in so vain and rebellious a way as they presented it to Samuel. But according to the word and instruction of God, Samuel anointed Saul to be king over Israel. In his beginning ministry, Saul was a mighty man and carried out the mandates of heaven, but he soon fell away from the instruction of Samuel and fell into gross disobedience to the will of God. The Word of the Lord, therefore, came to Samuel that he must anoint a man after God's own heart. That anointing was directed toward a lad from the shepherd field, a son of Jesse by the name of David.

David and the Kingdoms of Israel and Judah

The first part of David's life as king of Israel was magnificent. Then, in the very prime of his life, at the very height of his glory, he turned aside from the will of God and became self-indulgent and lustful like other Oriental kings. This brought to David an infinite tragedy, one by which the name of God was blasphemed. Nevertheless, God forgave the sin of David and chose him to be the father of that marvelous Son who would sit upon His throne as King forever. A type of that glorious Son of David, was the *immediate* son of David, called Solomon. Solomon also began his reign gloriously and triumphantly, but like his father,

Solomon also fell into tragic decline. Upon his death, the kingdom was divided.

Thereafter, the people of God were divided into two kingdoms: that of the north was called the kingdom of Israel and that of the south was called the kingdom of Judah. The northern kingdom of Israel was taken away into captivity by the cruel and ruthless Assyrians in 722 B.C. The southern kingdom was carried away into Babylonian captivity in 587 B.C. In the days of the Babylonian captivity, Jeremiah prophesied in Jerusalem while Daniel, the prophet-statesman, and Ezekiel, the holy seer, comforted and strengthened the people of God in Mesopotamia.

Out of the Babylonian captivity came three great establishments by which God has blessed our world. First, the Jews were never idolatrous again. Second, the synagogue was born, and from the synagogue came the church. The services of the synagogue are the same type of services we have today. Third, from the captivity came the canon of the Holy Scriptures. Out of tears and suffering came our greatest blessing, "The Scarlet Thread of Redemption."

From the Prophets to the Christ to the Preaching of Paul

Out of the agonies of the days of the kingdoms of Israel and of Judah came the predictions by the prophets of a more glorious Savior and King, whom God would send to His people. When we read a passage like the twenty-second Psalm or the fifty-third chapter of Isaiah, we seem to be standing by the cross of the Son of God. More and more, the great spiritual leaders of Israel and of Judah began to depict the coming of a Redeemer who would save His people from their sins and bring to them the everlasting hope and righteousness of God. This messianic hope became stronger and more gloriously received as the centuries passed.

In 536 B.C. Cyrus the Persian gave the people the right to return from the Babylonian captivity to their homeland in Judah and to build their holy temple in Jerusalem. Thus, the remnant of the captivity returned under Zerubbabel, the political leader; under Joshua, the priestly leader; under Ezra, the scribe; and under Nehemiah, who had been the prime minister at the court of Shushan, the Persian capital. This holy remnant, thus seeking to restore the worship of the true God in Jerusalem and to recreate the political life of Judah, was encouraged by God's messengers, Haggai, Zechariah, and Malachi.

Of the three great restoration prophets, Zechariah is by far the greatest. Zechariah spoke much about Israel, about the end of time, and about the conversion of the people of the Lord. The last prophet is Malachi. He delivered his message from about 450 B.C. to about 425 B.C.

The four-hundred-year period between the Old Testament and the New Testament marks the rise of the Hellenistic empire. God used Alexander the Great to spread abroad throughout the civilized world one culture and one language, which made possible the later preaching of Christ to all men everywhere.

In that inter-biblical period also arose the might of the Roman Empire. When Augustus Caesar was the Roman emperor, and when Rome had the entire world in her hand, the great prophecies of Isaiah, Micah, Nathan to David, Jacob to his son Judah, and the great promise of God Almighty to Eve in the Garden of Eden, came to pass. In the seed progeny of the woman and through the seed of Abraham, all the families of the earth were to be blessed—and our Savior was thus born into the world. "The Scarlet Thread of Redemption" has led us to the birth of Him who has come to redeem the human race from their fallen estate.

In His ministry Jesus early began to teach His disciples that He should suffer and die. When He was transfigured, there appeared Moses and Elijah talking to Him about His death, which He should accomplish in Jerusalem. When He was anointed by Mary of Bethany, He said it was for His burial. When the Greeks came to see Him from afar He said, "And I, if I be lifted up from the earth, will draw all men to Myself" (John 12:32). At the last supper He said, "This is My body, which is for you; do this in remembrance of Me." And again He said, "This cup is the new covenant in My blood; do this, as often as you drink it, in remembrance of Me" (1 Cor. 11:25). Before He went to the cross, He gave Himself in Gethsemane in travail of soul for our redemption (Is. 53:11). And when He bowed His head and died He said, "It is finished!" (John 19:30). When we preach the cross, when we preach the blood, when we preach the sacrificial death of Christ, we are preaching the meaning of His coming into the world. The sacrifice of Christ consummated the great redemptive plan and purpose of God on the earth. This is "The Scarlet Thread of Redemption."

After the resurrection of our Lord, after the giving of the Great Commission to the apostles, and after the ascension of our Savior into heaven, the Lord poured out His Holy Spirit upon His church in Jerusalem on the Day of Pentecost. Then the disciples of Jesus began to make known throughout the earth the Good News of our hope and salvation.

The epistles of Paul are divided into four distinct groups. The first group he wrote on his second missionary journey from Athens and Corinth. They are First and Second Thessalonians. The second group of letters was born on his third missionary journey. While he was in Ephesus, he wrote First Corinthians. Somewhere between Ephesus and Corinth, he wrote Second Corinthians in Macedonia. Then, either in Antioch or

on his way to Antioch, he wrote Galatians and Romans. First and Second Corinthians, Galatians, and Romans, therefore, center around the city of Ephesus. The third group of epistles Paul wrote from the prison in Rome, during his first Roman imprisonment. They are Ephesians, Philippians, Colossians, and Philemon. The fourth and last group of his epistles, written after his first Roman imprisonment were First Timothy, Titus, and Second Timothy, called the pastoral epistles. In all of Paul's letters, there is the constant theme of redemptive love. It is a part of "The Scarlet Thread of Redemption."

The Apocalypse and the Consummation of the Age

We come now to the conclusion of the Bible.

On the Isle of Patmos, a rocky little point in the Mediterranean Sea, several miles southwest of Ephesus, John was exiled to die of exposure and starvation. But there the Lord appears to John in a glorious vision. The vision is called the Revelation, that is, "the unveiling." "The Apocalypse," the unveiling of Jesus Christ in His glory, in His majesty, and in His kingdom, is the reward that God gave to Jesus for saving us, Adam's fallen children, from our sins.

After the vision of the exalted and glorified Christ in chapter one, and after the prophetic words in chapters two and three, John is taken up through an open door into heaven. While John, the translated saint, is with the Savior in heaven, the judgments of Almighty God are poured out on the earth. They are depicted in the opening of the seven seals, the seven trumpets, and the seven bowls. In those dark days John sees a vision in Revelation, chapter seven, concerning the blood-washed redeemed souls in glory. Announcement is made to him through one of the elders that these are they who have come out of the great tribulation and have washed their robes and made them white in the blood of the Lamb. This is "The Scarlet Thread of Redemption" that began with the blood of covering in the Garden of Eden and finds its ultimate and final consummation in the blood-washed throng before the throne of God in glory.

After the seven seals and the judgments, the seven trumpets and the judgments, the seven

bowls and the judgments, and the seven personages and the judgments, we come to the final great Judgment Day of Almighty God. The antiChrist, who professes to be the leader of the nations of the world, is seen gathering the armies of the entire earth together. They are converging from the north, from the east, from the south, from the west, and from the islands of the sea. They are converging for that great day of the Lord. That is the Battle of Armageddon, the last great war the world is going to fight. At Megiddo, the armies of the earth by the millions will converge to face that rendezvous with God. In the midst of this holocaust, Christ will intervene in human history. He comes with His saints. He will deliver His people, shut up in the holy city, and take Satan and bind him for a thousand years in the bottomless pit.

After the binding of Satan for a thousand years, which is called the millenium, Satan is released, and thereafter goes forth once again to lead men in rebellion against God. This is the final conflict which ends forever man's refusal to accept the will of God for their lives. At the end time, in the final resurrection of the wicked dead and the great white throne judgment, the books are opened, and those whose names are not found written in the Lamb's Book of Life are cast out and rewarded according to their deeds. Into the abyss of hell are flung Satan and his angels, along with those who choose Satan and his way of life, plus death and the grave—all are hurled into the fiery flames where the Beast and the False Prophet have already been for a thousand years.

After the purging of the earth of Satan and his minions, and after the judgment upon those who reject Christ and His grace, and after cleansing the earth of the heartache and tears of sickness, sin, death, and the grave, will come the renovation of earth and heaven. It is a new creation with a glorious new heaven and new earth. In it is the holy city, the heavenly Jerusalem, and in it is the dwelling place of God Himself. Tears, death, sorrow, pain, and crying are passed away. There are no graves on the hillsides of glory and no funeral wreaths on the doors of those mansions in the sky.

The book closes with the incomparable message of the hope, salvation, and redemption accomplished in the person and work of the Lord Christ.

LAST THINGS

A basic fundamental of the Christian faith is that God as Creator and Redeemer has been active in time-space events we call human history. And insofar as God has removed Himself from His transcendence to become immanent, thereby touching His creation with His Divine Power, so has human history been transformed and conformed to the Divine Purpose of God. One cannot properly understand human history without previously seeking to understand, if only minutely, the Divine Purposes of God. This is true whether we are speaking of God's creative act, whereby He formed man from the dust of the ground, of His mighty deliverance of Israel from Egypt, of the glorious incarnation of His Only Begotten Son, or of things to come when Jesus Christ, the Righteous Judge and King, comes to bring this present age to its final denouement.

Eschatology, the study of last things, must always keep two facets in focus: (a) the incapability of man's knowledge in foreseeing the future, and (b) the absolute certainty of God's accomplishing perfectly His Divine Will. We must be humble enough to say, with Paul, "For we know in part, and we prophesy in part" (1 Cor. 13:9) and "now we see in a mirror dimly" (1 Cor. 13:12). But we must also hold fast to the hope that "when the perfect comes, the partial will be done away" (1 Cor. 13:10), and wait with assurance that the time is coming when we shall see "face to face" (1 Cor. 13:12) the One who is to be revealed at the end of the ages.

Out of the work of scholars and students of the Scriptures has come varying interpretations of the biblical passages on the last things. The dividing line between liberal and conservative scholars is drawn along the question: Do passages of Scripture which deal with last things, for example, Daniel and Revelation, tell the events of the writer's own day, or do they foretell the events of history future to the writer's own day? Liberal scholars largely endorse the former view, while conservative scholars lean toward the latter. However, neither view by itself is sufficient to explain the kind of biblical literature Daniel and Revelation represent. It is certainly true, for example, that the apostle John, in writing the Revelation, was concerned to address the Christians of his own day. Seven churches and their present situations were addressed; they were commended, exhorted, or reproved. But in an effort to encourage them and clarify for them the purposes of God in the persecutions they were then suffering, John also says he was shown the things which "must take place after these" (Rev. 4:1). There was still to come the vindication of those whom the Lamb did "purchase for God" (Rev. 5:9). Satan and all the powers of evil were yet to be defeated in the coming Judgment of God, and there was still to come a

"new heaven and a new earth" where the saints of God would forever reign with Him who sits upon the throne (Rev. 21:1–5).

Thus in eschatology, there is both a forth-telling and a foretelling. The point is this: While there is certainty of the coming of the last things, they should not be studied in isolation of our present situation. While holding before us the hope of things to come, the last things should also inform us about God's purpose for us now in living righteously and in readiness for the coming of the Lord (see Matt. 24–25; 1 Cor. 15; 1 Thess. 4:13—5:11; 2 Thess. 2; Heb. 10:23–25; 2 Pet. 3).

A central turning point for discussions of the last things among conservative scholars is the millennium, or thousand-year reign of Christ, in Revelation 20:1–10. *Postmillennialism*, popular in the early twentieth century, sees Christ's return after the millennium, which has been brought about by the spread of the church through the power of the Holy Spirit. *Premillennialism* places Christ's second coming before the millennium, which is established by the supernatural intervention of God in Christ. It is interesting that many of the early church Fathers had sympathy for this view. Those who hold to *amillennialism* see the millennium as a figurative expression of the accomplishment of God's Word to Israel, fulfilled in the church. Within any of these three groups, one will find variations of thought concerning particular aspects of the viewpoint under discussion. This should lead us to be cautious about being dogmatic for any single viewpoint of the last things.

But uncertainty in these areas should not be cause for despair, as there are other things about which the Christian can be sure. First could be mentioned the resurrection of the body. The vividness of Ezekiel's vision of the valley of dry bones, while revealing the restoration of Israel, was in itself a vision of a resurrection to life from the grave (Ezek. 37). Daniel 12:2 speaks of a resurrection: "And many of those who sleep in the dust of the ground will awake, these to everlasting life, but the others to disgrace *and* everlasting contempt." Paul says Christ's own resurrection is the assurance of our own resurrection, "But each in his own order: Christ the first fruits, after that those who are Christ's at His coming" (1 Cor. 15:23). Second, we may be sure of Christ's second coming. Daniel 7 is the reference point for the New Testament doctrine of the Son of Man coming "with the clouds of heaven" (Dan. 7:13). As the disciples watched Jesus ascending into heaven, the angels told them that they would also see Him "come in just the same way" (Acts 1:11). Paul told the Thessalonians that His coming would be preceded by the man of lawlessness (2 Thess. 2:1–4). The coming of the Son of Man will be accom-

panied by "great power and glory" (Mark 13:26). Third, there will be judgment. Joel 3 says the Lord will enter into judgment with the nations. Peter speaks of the "judgment and destruction of ungodly men" (2 Pet. 3:7). Paul says that "we must all appear before the judgment seat of Christ, that each one may be recompensed for his deeds in the body, according to what he has done" (2 Cor. 5:10). The final judgment will take place before the very throne of God (Rev. 20:11–15). And after all is said and done, when all tribulations have been suffered, when all of Christ's foes have been defeated, when all things have been made subject to Him, then the new Jerusalem will be "made ready as a bride adorned for her husband" (Rev. 21:2). God shall dwell among men, wiping away every tear, all death, every mourning, and pain. The saints of God will drink from the river of the water of life coming from the throne of God and of the Lamb (Rev. 22:1). The final purpose of God will then have been accomplished when the saints of God join the myriad tongues saying:

"Worthy is the Lamb that was slain to receive power and riches and wisdom and might and honor and glory and blessing.

"To Him who sits on the throne, and to the Lamb, *be* blessing and honor and glory and dominion forever and ever" (Rev. 5:12, 13).

Jewish Feasts

Feast of	Month on Jewish Calendar	Day	Corresponding Month	References
*Passover (Unleavened Bread)	Nisan	14–21	Mar.–Apr.	Ex. 12:43– 13:10; Matt. 26:17–20
*Pentecost (First Fruits or Weeks)	Sivan	6 (50 days after Passover)	May–June	Deut. 16:9–12; Acts 2:1
Trumpets, *Rosh Hashanah*	Tishri	1, 2	Sept.–Oct.	Num. 29:1–6
Day of Atonement, *Yom Kippur*	Tishri	10	Sept.–Oct.	Lev. 23:26–32; Heb. 9:7
*Tabernacles (Booths or Ingathering)	Tishri	15–22	Sept.–Oct.	Neh. 8:13–18; John 7:2
Dedication (Lights), *Hanukkah*	Chislev	25 (8 days)	Nov.–Dec.	John 10:22
Purim (Lots)	Adar	14, 15	Feb.–Mar.	Esth. 9:18–32

*The three major feasts for which all males of Israel were required to travel to the Temple in Jerusalem (Ex. 23:14–19).

A GUIDE
TO CHRISTIAN WORKERS

I. Commission

Give us a watchword for the hour,
A thrilling word, a word of power;
A battle cry, a flaming breath,
A call to conquest or to death;
A word to rouse the church from rest,
To heed the Master's high behest.
The call is given, ye hosts arise,
The watchword is EVANGELIZE!
To fallen men, a dying race,
Make known the gift of gospel grace.
The world that now in darkness lies,
O Church of Christ, EVANGELIZE!

"And Jesus came up and spoke to them, saying, 'All authority has been given to Me in heaven and on earth. Go therefore and make disciples of all the nations, baptizing them in the name of the Father and the Son and the Holy Spirit, teaching them to observe all that I commanded you; and lo, I am with you always, even to the end of the age'" (Matt. 28:18-20).

"But you shall receive power when the Holy Spirit has come upon you; and you shall be My witnesses both in Jerusalem, and in all Judea and Samaria, and even to the remotest part of the earth" (Acts 1:8).

"Now as for you, son of man, I have appointed you a watchman for the house of Israel; so you will hear a message from My mouth, and give them warning from Me. When I say to the wicked, 'O wicked man, you shall surely die,' and you do not speak to warn the wicked from his way, that wicked man shall die in his iniquity, but his blood I will require from your hand" (Ezek. 33:7, 8).

"You are the salt of the earth; but if the salt has become tasteless, how will it be made salty *again?* It is good for nothing anymore, except to be thrown out and trampled under foot by men. You are the light of the world. A city set on a hill cannot be hidden. Nor do *men* light a lamp, and put it under the peck-measure, but on the lamp-stand; and it gives light to all who are in the house. Let your light shine before men in such a way that they may see your good works, and glorify your Father who is in heaven" (Matt. 5:13-16).

II. Compassion

The story is told that Martinelli received $25,000 for singing only twice. Paul and Silas sang one night in a prison. Their song was not rendered with the skill or harmony of that of Martinelli's, but its tenderness touched the heart of the keeper of the prison and echoed through the angel-crowded streets of heaven; and the listening King of kings rewarded those who sang with crowns of glory that will gleam in beauty throughout eternal ages.

An immortal soul is beyond all price. There is no trouble too great, no humiliation too deep, no suffering too severe, no love too strong, no labor too hard, no expense too large, but that it is worth it, if it is spent in the effort to win a soul.

God loves the soul more than all creation. He fashioned it after His own image, and made it like unto Himself. Every soul has departed from God and gone astray, and God has bought the soul back again with a price.

That price was in, and through, and by Jesus Christ. God loves the soul with an everlasting love.

Satan hates the soul. In Satan's enmity toward God he is using all his energy, using every snare, his utmost cunning, employing every means *with the single purpose of ruining the soul of man.*

When a million eternities have each lived their endless ages and have rolled by into the unthinkable past and time is no more, the soul will still be living, *a conscious personality* endowed with perpetual life reunited with the body.

God has said: "And he who is wise wins souls" (Prov. 11:30).

The Bible says: "And those who have insight will shine brightly like the brightness of the expanse of heaven, and those who lead the many to righteousness, like the stars forever and ever" (Dan. 12:3).

Compassion was the heartbeat of our Savior's ministry. "And seeing the multitudes, He felt compassion for them, because they were distressed and downcast like sheep without a shepherd" (Matt. 9:36). "But Thou, O Lord, art a God merciful and gracious, slow to anger and abundant in lovingkindness and truth" (Ps. 86:15).

Heaven is geared to redemption. "I tell you that in the same way, there will be *more* joy in heaven over one sinner who repents, than over ninety-nine righteous persons who need no repentance" (Luke 15:7).

No man who ever had a glimpse of hell would ever want a fellow human being to go there (see Luke 16:28).

"Those who sow in tears shall reap with joyful shouting. He who goes to and fro weeping, carrying *his* bag of seed, shall indeed come again with a shout of joy, bringing his sheaves *with him*" (Ps. 126:5, 6).

III. Concern

One of the first questions raised in recorded history was, "Am I my brother's keeper?" (Gen. 4:9). *Do I have moral obligations toward others?*

"And I searched for a man among them who should build up the wall and stand in the gap before Me for the land, that I should not destroy it; but I found no one" (Ezek. 22:30).

"My flock wandered through all the mountains and on every high hill, and My flock was scattered over all the surface of the earth; and there was no one to search or seek *for them*" (Ezek. 34:6).

"And if you give yourself to the hungry, and satisfy the desire of the afflicted, then your light will rise in darkness, and your gloom *will become like midday*" (Is. 58:10).

"I am telling the truth in Christ, I am not lying, my conscience bearing me witness in the Holy Spirit, that I have great sorrow and unceasing grief in my heart. For I could wish that I myself were accursed, *separated* from Christ for the sake of my brethren, my kinsmen according to the flesh" (Rom. 9:1-3). See also Psalm 106:23, Luke 19:41, Acts 20:31.

Intercession is the way that leads to the winning of souls. No church can prosper without it. No Christian can grow without it. The law of life demands reproduction—that kind should beget kind.

Jesus interceded for each of us. "Therefore, I will allot Him a portion with the great, and He will divide the booty with the strong; because He poured out Himself to death, and was numbered with the transgressors; yet He Himself bore the sin of many, and interceded for the transgressors" (Is. 53:12).

Christ left this command to us: "Therefore beseech the Lord of the harvest to send out workers into His harvest" (Matt. 9:38).

IV. Contact

It began with *personal contact*.

"He found first his own brother Simon, and said to him, 'We have found the Messiah' (which translated means Christ)" (John 1:41).

With Christ came the emphasis of *seeking the lost*. "For the Son of Man has come to seek and to save that which was lost" (Luke 19:10).

The movement of Christianity in this world is scripturally based on personal contact. Anyone who really knows Jesus will want others to know Him.

The secret is in the words of Andrew, "We have *found*." The search for satisfaction in a man's soul is completed in a living knowledge of Jesus Christ. Personal evangelism is sharing this discovery.

"He brought him to Jesus" (John 1:42).

How is this accomplished? Christ gives the answer. "Follow Me, and I will make you fishers of men" (Matt. 4:19). *A love for Christ produces a love for mankind.*

We are to be workmen "who [do] not need to be ashamed" (2 Tim. 2:15). Lives today are complicated by sin. They need more than slogans and formulas. They need personal help. A con-

scientious doctor must deal with each patient separately and so must a conscientious soul-winner.

These guidelines must be kept in mind:

1. I MUST LIVE IT. I can't say to others, "Do as I *say*, but don't do as I *do*." They must see Christ in me (1 Cor. 4:9). My strongest testimony is my daily life.

2. I MUST LOVE PEOPLE. I cannot pretend. The other person knows my motive immediately. The power of evangelism is described in Revelation 22:17, "And the Spirit and the bride say, 'Come.'" When my *concern* for others is in keeping with the concern of the Holy Spirit toward mankind, there is a community of interest in the individual that results in *compulsion*.

3. I MUST MEET THE PUBLIC. Jesus was heaven's artist at this. He never met a stranger. Paul testified, "I have become all things to all men, that I may by all means save some" (1 Cor. 9:22).

Kindness will open doors (Eph. 4:32). It will bring an affirmative response.

4. I MUST LOOK FOR NEED. Jesus said, "*It is* not those who are healthy who need a physician, but those who are sick; I did not come to call the righteous, but sinners" (Mark 2:17).

You will be surprised how many people are ready to talk. They simply need someone in whom they can have confidence. Zaccheus was in trouble. Uninvited, he talked about his sin. *That is my point of contact—human need*.

5. I MUST COMMUNICATE. Keep away from technicalities. Refuse to become involved in debate. The Samaritan woman quibbled: "Our fathers worshiped in this mountain, and you *people* say that in Jerusalem is the place where men ought to worship" (John 4:20). It wasn't her *head* that was troubling her. It was her *heart*. She needed Christ before she needed a church; a Redeemer before she needed a ritual. "'I know that Messiah is coming (He who is called Christ); when that One comes, He will declare all things to us.' Jesus said to her, 'I who speak to you am *He*'" (John 4:25, 26).

6. I MUST CONCENTRATE ON CHRIST. I can get so much "I" into my testimony that spiritual pride will offend the person to whom I am witnessing. The rule of the great Baptist still holds: "He must increase, but I must decrease" (John 3:30). *My business is to present Jesus* (John 12:32). Christ is the attraction.

7. I MUST USE TACT. This suggests a sensitivity to the other man's feelings. It is a spirit of discernment. "But if any of you lacks wisdom, let him ask of God, who gives to all men generously and without reproach, and it will be given to him" (James 1:5). Be natural. Be courteous. Be a good listener. Ask wise questions.

8. I MUST BRING A PERSON TO A DECISION. This can only be accomplished through

1365 GUIDE TO CHRISTIAN WORKERS

the power and presence of the Holy Spirit (John 16:8).

The chance may never come again. *Opportunity is God-given*. Don't gamble with it. Press for a decision. "You do not have because you do not ask" (James 4:2). Don't let people say of you at Judgment Day, "He never asked me to be a Christian!"

9. I MUST TEACH THEM TO LISTEN TO GOD'S VOICE. It is my business to *introduce* them to the Savior. So often the worker only introduces himself. "Yield now and be at peace with Him; thereby good will come to you" (Job 22:21). Let the person with whom you are dealing hear for the first time the voice of God speaking to him or her in reassurance and comfort, and you have built strength.

This is done by teaching the person two or three primary verses of Scripture. Tie the seeker to God's Word. Let your friend know before you leave him that God has spoken these words to him. These words carry a guarantee.

Here is an *example:*

"Truly, truly, I say to you, he who hears My word, and believes Him who sent Me, has eternal life, and does not come into judgment, but has passed out of death into life" (John 5:24).

These are the words of the Son of God. They are spoken to *you*. They are spoken with finality and authority.

10. I MUST MAKE IT CRYSTAL CLEAR THAT THERE IS A DIFFERENCE BETWEEN KNOWING GOD AND KNOWING ABOUT GOD. Hearsay is not enough. *Birth is not something that is second-hand*. "When he puts forth all his own, he goes before them, and the sheep follow him because they know his voice. And a stranger they simply will not follow, but will flee from him, because they do not know the voice of strangers" (John 10:4, 5).

I know God when I get down to business with Him. "Draw near to God and He will draw near to you" (James 4:8). God has expressed His willingness in a covenant, contract, or testament. It bears His signature in the death and resurrection of Jesus Christ. *The moment I exercise faith toward this written word and become personally involved in agreement, that very moment the entire contract, or covenant, is in force toward me.*

If I do not associate the seeker with the Word of God, that person will miss his way. The devil will deceive the inquirer before breakfast. He will lie so cleverly that the inquirer will apologize to worldly associates before the day is over.

Remember! The authority is in the Word of God.

V. A Conversation

Dr. R. G. Lee calls this two-way conversation "convincing confutation." The following are answers to some excuses as Dr. Lee sets them forth.

1. Excuse: "*I want to get established in business first. After that I will be a Christian.*"

Answer: No business should be allowed to cheat one out of heaven's blessings. Property should not kill the privilege of being a child of God. "For what does it profit a man to gain the whole world, and forfeit his soul?" (Mark 8:36). God called one man a fool to his face. "But God said to him, 'You fool! This *very* night your soul is required of you; and *now* who will own what you have prepared?'" (Luke 12:20). He was the man who neglected his soul's welfare by building barns, enlarging crops, and feeding his soul on corn.

Further Scriptures which may be used: Matthew 6:33, Psalm 1:1, 2, Proverbs 29:25, Mark 10:29, 30.

2. Excuse: "*I am not a sinner.*"

Answer: But God says, "THERE IS NONE RIGHTEOUS, NOT EVEN ONE" (Rom. 3:10). "But the Scripture has shut up all men under sin" (Gal. 3:22). If you are not a sinner, are you keeping God's commands? What about Matthew 22:37? "And He said to him, 'YOU SHALL LOVE THE LORD YOUR GOD WITH ALL YOUR HEART, AND WITH ALL YOUR SOUL, AND WITH ALL YOUR MIND.'"

3. Excuse: "*I have no encouragement at home.*"

Answer: Without families we came. Without our families we go. Guilt is personal. Then, too, if you have praying parents, a saintly wife or husband, and godly children, and you continue your selfish resistance to their accepted and your rejected Savior, your guilt is deeper.

4. Excuse: "*I am good enough as I am.*"

Answer: God says you are bad enough—by nature. Man in his natural state does wicked deeds, thinks evil thoughts, goes to bad places, rejects Jesus Christ—because he has an evil heart. No one is naturally good. If you are good, why not become acquainted with Jesus, who is supremely good?

5. Excuse: "*I am as good as others.*"

Answer: Violin players do not take their tones from each other, but from the piano. Builders are constantly using the plumb line, the level, and the square. We need to live by standards—not comparisons. Nobody can claim health because he is better than another diabetic or stronger than another cancer victim. Measure yourself by Jesus if you want to know how good or bad you are. Do not be too sure you are better than many within the Church. They have confessed Jesus before men—as Jesus asked. You have not. Moreover, you are forbidden to judge to justify yourself. You are not saved or lost by the deeds of others.

6. Excuse: "*I have no feeling.*"

Answer: The world isn't run by feeling. Washington did not live at Valley Forge because he felt like it. Most people do most of their worthy acts contrary to feeling. The doctor does not deal with

diseases because of feeling but because of necessity.

Scriptures which may be used: Revelation 3:20, John 3:36, Ephesians 1:13, First Peter 1:8.

7. Excuse: "*I am so weak.*"

Answer: "The steadfast of mind Thou wilt keep in perfect peace, because he trusts in Thee. Trust in the LORD forever, for in GOD the LORD, *we have* an everlasting Rock" (Is. 26:3, 4). Who will keep? The Almighty God. How? "In perfect peace." On what condition? One's mind being "steadfast" on God—not on self, nor circumstances, failures, successes, nor on others. Trust—try not to worry, but trust. In whom? God. How long? All the time. Why? For God is an everlasting Rock.

Further Scriptures which may be used: Jude 24, First Corinthians 10:13, Philippians 1:6, Isaiah 41:10, 13, 14, Second Timothy 1:12.

8. Excuse: "*I am doing the best I can.*"

Answer: How long have you been doing your best? Have you succeeded? How long will it take you to make yourself fit for heaven? Suppose you die now? The best you can do is to acknowledge you cannot do anything to save yourself—except believe.

9. Excuse: "*I am too big a sinner.*"

Answer: Jesus came to save *all* sinners. "It is a trustworthy statement, deserving full acceptance, that Christ Jesus came into the world to save sinners, among whom I am foremost *of all*" (1 Tim. 1:15). Are your sins scarlet? "Come now, and let us reason together," says the LORD, "though your sins are as scarlet, they will be as white as snow; though they are red like crimson, they will be like wool" (Is. 1:18). Are you lost? "For the Son of Man has come to seek and to save that which was lost" (Luke 19:10). Are you without strength? "For while we were still helpless, at the right time Christ died for the ungodly. For one will hardly die for a righteous man; though perhaps for the good man someone would dare even to die. But God demonstrates His own love toward us, in that while we were yet sinners, Christ died for us" (Rom. 5:6-8). "All that the Father gives Me shall come to Me, and the one who comes to Me I will certainly not cast out" (John 6:37).

Further Scriptures which may be used: Matthew 9:13, Hebrews 7:25, Luke 23:39-43.

10. Excuse: "*There are too many hypocrites.*"

Answer: Hypocrites are lost. If you let hypocrites keep you from being saved, you will spend eternity in hell with them. Besides, you have to be smaller than what you hide behind. If you hide behind a hypocrite, you must be smaller than a hypocrite.

Further Scriptures which may be used: Zechariah 13:6, Acts 1:6, Hebrews 12:2, Acts 17:30, 31, Romans 2:1-6; 14:12, Matthew 7:1-5, First Samuel 16:7.

11. Excuse: "*A professing Christian wronged me.*"

Answer: Granted. But is that any reason why you should wrong God and insult Christ, who loved you and gave Himself for you? "He who believes in the Son has eternal life; but he who does not obey the Son shall not see life, but the wrath of God abides on him" (John 3:36).

12. Excuse: "*There is too much to give up.*"

Answer: It is better to give up everything than lose the soul. Put Christ and your soul ahead of all else. Is it too much to give up paste pearls for glittering gems? Dirt for diamonds? Is it too much to give up rags for riches?

Further Scriptures which may be used: Psalms 16:11; 84:11, Proverbs 3:17; 13:15, Matthew 11:30, Isaiah 57:21, Romans 8:32, Mark 8:36, 37, Luke 18:29, 30.

13. Excuse: "*I cannot understand.*"

Answer: Why let mystery cause you to refuse the Master? Do you understand the chemistry of digestion? Does your ignorance of it keep you from eating steak? Can you understand why the same sun and the same soil and the same rain get sweetness into the orange and sourness into the lemon and bitterness into the persimmon?

Lay aside your excuse of mystery and trust God as you trust the telephone to transmit your voice.

Further Scriptures which may be used: Romans 11:33, First Corinthians 1:8; 2:14.

14. Excuse: "*God is unjust.*"

Answer: Who is God? Who are you? Injustice is sin. Do you mean to accuse God of sin? God is so just that He never demands two payments for one debt. Jesus paid your sin debt on the Cross—all of it. Therefore, when you accept Christ, you do not have that sin debt to pay.

15. Excuse: "*Folks would laugh.*"

Answer: It is better to let them laugh than to have God laugh. "I will even laugh at your calamity; I will mock when your dread comes" (Prov. 1:26). Shun evil companions. "Do not enter the path of the wicked, and do not proceed in the way of evil men. The way of the wicked is like darkness; they do not know over what they stumble" (Prov. 4:14, 19). Do not be ashamed of Christ. "Everyone therefore who shall confess Me before men, I will also confess him before My Father who is in heaven. But whoever shall deny Me before men, I will also deny him before My Father who is in heaven" (Matt. 10:32, 33).

16. Excuse: "*Not now.*"

Answer: Every time you say no, it is more difficult to say yes. The time and day is *now*. "For He says, 'AT THE ACCEPTABLE TIME I LISTENED TO YOU, AND ON THE DAY OF SALVATION I HELPED YOU'; behold, now is 'THE ACCEPTABLE TIME,' behold, now is 'THE DAY OF SALVATION'" (2 Cor. 6:2).

Seek the Lord while He may be found. Delay is decision for the wrong way. "Today—if you

would," says the Lord. Tomorrow is the day when the idle man works, the thief becomes honest, the drunkard sober. Tomorrow is a period nowhere to be found except, perhaps, in the fool's calendar. God's call is not a call for tomorrow, but for *today*.

Dr. Lee says of the above, "In this manner do I deal with excuse-makers. With many excuse-makers I have had success. With some, I have not."

Further Scriptures which may be used: Proverbs 27:1; 29:1, Isaiah 55:6, Hebrews 2:3.

Some other common excuses and questions are:

17. Excuse: "*I think you are making too big a fuss about this.*"

Answer: Why is Calvary such a big date in history? "But God demonstrates His own love toward us, in that while we were yet sinners, Christ died for us" (Rom. 5:8).

Isn't your soul important? "For what will a man be profited, if he gains the whole world, and forfeits his soul? Or what will a man give in exchange for his soul?" (Matt. 16:26).

Isn't life uncertain? "But God said to him, 'You fool! This *very* night your soul is required of you; and *now* who will own what you have prepared?'" (Luke 12:20).

Death, judgment, and hell lie ahead (Gal. 6:7, Heb. 9:27).

The Son of God asks for your decision (Rev. 3:20).

18. Excuse: "*I will take my chances.*"

Answer: God always has the last word. "And he said to him, 'Friend, how did you come in here without wedding clothes?' And he was speechless. Then the king said to the servants, 'Bind him hand and foot, and cast him into the outer darkness; in that place there shall be weeping and gnashing of teeth'" (Matt. 22:12, 13).

Nebuchadnezzar gave this testimony, "That the Most High is ruler over the realm of mankind, and bestows it on whom He wishes" (Dan. 4:17). "And all the inhabitants of the earth are accounted as nothing, but He does according to His will in the host of heaven and *among* the inhabitants of earth; and no one can ward off His hand or say to Him, 'What hast Thou done?'" (Dan. 4:35).

God's Word has eternal force (Is. 55:11).

A judgment must be rendered on each life lived (John 5:27-29).

19. Excuse: "*My friends mean so much to me.*"

Answer: Are they your friends or your enemies? "You adulteresses, do you not know that friendship with the world is hostility toward God? Therefore whoever wishes to be a friend of the world makes himself an enemy of God" (James 4:4).

Do your friends care for your soul? "Now when he had spent everything, a severe famine occurred in that country, and be began to be in need. And he went and attached himself to one of the citizens of that country, and he sent him into his fields to feed swine. And he was longing to fill his stomach with the pods that the swine were eating, and no one was giving *anything* to him" (Luke 15:14-16).

You will gain a greater Friend and friends (John 15:15, Matt. 19:29).

Your example can lead your unsaved friends to Christ (John 1:45).

20. Excuse: "*I am going to have a good time in this world and let the next world take care of itself.*"

Answer: Others have followed this course before. "Child, remember that during your life you received your good things, and likewise Lazarus bad things; but now he is being comforted here, and you are in agony" (Luke 16:25).

Your life can prove to be a *charade* (Luke 12:15).

Opportunity brings responsibility (Eccl. 11:9).

21. Excuse: "*Please do not talk to me about it.*"

Answer: I am simply bringing God's message to you. "Now, gird up your loins, and arise, and speak to them all which I command you. Do not be dismayed before them, lest I dismay you before them" (Jer. 1:17). "And go to the exiles, to the sons of your people, and speak to them and tell them, whether they listen or not, 'Thus says the Lord GOD'" (Ezek. 3:11).

My business is to *witness* (2 Cor. 2:15, 16).

22. Excuse: "*I am my own boss.*"

Answer: Wise men and women receive *counsel*. "There is a way *which seems* right to a man, but its end is the way of death" (Prov. 14:12).

The straight way is the best way (Matt. 7:13, 14).

The easiest thing in the world to get is *a wrong answer*.

23. Excuse: "*Frankly, I am skeptical about the whole matter.*"

Answer: Are you honestly looking for *answers*? Will you accept evidence as it would be accepted before a court of law? Are you an *inquirer* or *spiritual subversive*? "For they exchanged the truth of God for a lie, and worshiped and served the creature rather than the Creator" (Rom. 1:25). "And just as they did not see fit to acknowledge God any longer, God gave them over to a depraved mind, to do those things which are not proper" (Rom. 1:28).

Jesus Christ threw out this challenge: "He who is of God hears the words of God; for this reason you do not hear *them*, because you are not of God" (John 8:47).

You can *doubt* to your own peril (2 Thess. 2:10, 12).

The way to find out whether or not a thing is true and worthy of one's acceptance is to put it to *a personal test* (Ps. 34:8).

24. Excuse: "*I want to be absolutely neutral about this matter.*"

Answer: There are some things you can't be

neutral about—food, drink, sleep, light, for instance. That is why Christ likened Himself to the *necessities* of life. "I am the bread of life" (John 6:48). "I am the light of the world; he who follows Me shall not walk in the darkness, but shall have the light of life" (John 8:12).

Jesus said: "He who is not with Me is against Me; and he who does not gather with Me scatters" (Matt. 12:30).

25. Excuse: *"I believe God is too good to damn anyone."*

Answer: That is not what the Bible says. "Therefore the wicked will not stand in the judgment, nor sinners in the assembly of the righteous. For the LORD knows the way of the righteous, but the way of the wicked will perish" (Ps. 1:5, 6).

God bases your salvation or damnation on your acceptance or rejection of Jesus Christ (John 12:48).

It is not God that is hard. It is you! "But because of your stubbornness and unrepentant heart you are storing up wrath for yourself in the day of wrath and revelation of the righteous judgment of God" (Rom. 2:5).

Every agency of God seeks to lead you to repentance (2 Pet. 3:9).

26. Excuse: *"How can I reconcile the doctrine of hell with the Christian's God of salvation?"*

Answer: "Then He will also say to those on His left, 'Depart from Me, accursed ones, into the eternal fire which has been prepared for the devil and his angels'" (Matt. 25:41).

"Judas turned aside to go to his own place" (Acts 1:25).

"The Lord is not slow about His promise, as some count slowness, but is patient toward you, not wishing for any to perish but for all to come to repentance" (2 Pet. 3:9).

"Do I have any pleasure in the death of the wicked," declares the Lord GOD, "rather than that he should turn from his ways and live?" (Ezek. 18:23).

"And these will go away into eternal punishment, but the righteous into eternal life" (Matt. 25:46).

"Child, remember that during your life you received your good things, and likewise Lazarus bad things; but now he is being comforted here, and you are in agony" (Luke 16:25).

"You serpents, you brood of vipers, how shall you escape the sentence of hell?" (Matt. 23:33).

"And do not fear those who kill the body, but are unable to kill the soul; but rather fear Him who is able to destroy both soul and body in hell" (Matt. 10:28).

"Therefore Sheol has enlarged its throat and opened its mouth without measure; and Jerusalem's splendor, her multitude, her din *of revelry*, and the jubilant within her, descend *into it*. So the *common* man will be humbled, and the

man of *importance* abased, the eyes of the proud also will be abased. But the LORD of hosts will be exalted in judgment, and the holy God will show Himself holy in righteousness" (Is. 5:14-16).

27. Excuse: *"I am religious."*

Answer: Religion is often something that is on the outside. "Many will say to Me on that day, 'Lord, Lord, did we not prophesy in Your name, and in Your name cast out demons, and in Your name perform many miracles?' And then I will declare to them, 'I never knew you; DEPART FROM ME, YOU WHO PRACTICE LAWLESSNESS'" (Matt. 7:22, 23).

No man was more religious than Paul (Gal. 1:14, Phil. 3:6, 1 Tim. 1:13, 15).

Cornelius was a religous man who needed to be saved (Acts 11:14).

28. Excuse: *"I am trying to be a Christian."*

Answer: It is not *trying*, it is *trusting* that counts. A drowning man tries with all his might and perishes, but when he trusts in the saving power of another he is rescued. "Behold, God is my salvation, I will trust and not be afraid; for the LORD GOD is my strength and song, and He has become my salvation" (Is. 12:2).

Ishmael was Abraham's fleshly attempt to fulfill the promise of God (he tried). Isaac was God's provision (he trusted) (Rom. 4:3, 5).

No work that you can do for yourself can ever substitute in merit for the work that Jesus has done for you on the Cross (Eph. 2:9).

"For all of us have become like one who is unclean, and all our righteous deeds are like a filthy garment; and all of us wither like a leaf, and our iniquities, like the wind, take us away" (Is. 64:6). To try is to fail! "For whoever keeps the whole law and yet stumbles in one *point*, he has become guilty of all" (James 2:10).

29. Excuse: *"What is sin?"*

Answer: Sin is breaking God's law (1 John 3:10). "All unrighteousness is sin, and there is a sin not *leading* to death" (1 John 5:17).

Unbelief is sin (John 16:8, 9).

Questionable indulgences are sin (Rom. 14:23).

Missing the mark is sin (Rom. 3:23).

Undone duty is sin (James 4:17).

30. Excuse: *"My sins are small, so why worry?"*

Answer: Because any sin torments, "There is no peace for the wicked,' says the LORD" (Is. 48:22).

Because any sin separates you from God (Is. 59:2).

Because any sin enslaves you (John 8:34).

Because any sin excludes from heaven (1 Cor. 6:9).

Because any sin ends in death (Rom. 6:23).

31. Excuse: *"I may be punished but not eternally."*

Answer: If God is eternal and heaven is eternal—hell will be eternal also. "Then He will also

say to those on His left, 'Depart from Me, accursed ones, into the eternal fire which has been prepared for the devil and his angels'" (Matt. 25:41).

There is "a resurrection of judgment" (John 5:28, 29).

Don't forget there is the "second death" (Rev. 20:13-15).

32. Excuse: *"I am too old now to become a Christian."*

Answer: There is no age limit (2 Cor. 6:2).

God has forseen your problem. "But from there you will seek the LORD your God, and you will find *Him* if you search for Him with all your heart and all your soul. When you are in distress and all these things have come upon you, in the latter days, you will return to the LORD your God and listen to His voice. For the LORD your God is a compassionate God; He will not fail you nor destroy you nor forget the covenant with your fathers which He swore to them" (Deut. 4:29-31).

33. Excuse: *"I do not think I am old enough to make a decision."*

Answer: You have reached an age of accountability if you sense Christ's approach to your life. "Remember also your Creator in the days of your youth, before the evil days come and the years draw near when you will say, 'I have no delight in them'" (Eccl. 12:1).

The time to make a decision is when your conscience is tender (2 Sam. 19:35).

The best time is now (Heb. 3:13).

34. Excuse: *"I intend to before I die."*

Answer: Can you determine the hour of your death? *Nothing is so uncertain as life* (Prov. 29:1, Job 34:20).

God warns against *presumption* (James 4:13-17).

There is no time like the present time. "Seek the LORD while He may be found; call upon Him while He is near" (Is. 55:6).

35. Excuse: *"I am afraid I cannot hold out."*

Answer: Jesus not only saves but He keeps. He is the Good Shepherd (John 10:11, 14).

The same One who convicts you is concerned about you. "Faithful is He who calls you, and He also will bring it to pass" (1 Thess. 5:24).

Paul gives his experience. "And He has said to me, 'My grace is sufficient for you, for power is perfected in weakness.' Most gladly, therefore, I will rather boast about my weaknesses, that the power of Christ may dwell in me" (2 Cor. 12:9).

God has made an investment in you and He will work to protect that investment (Phil. 1:6).

To know Him is to have assurance. Commit your entire life to His care. Leave the future in your Master's hands! (2 Tim. 1:12).

36. Excuse: *"I am afraid of persecution."*

Answer: It is a cowardly thing to deny Jesus Christ. "But for the cowardly and unbelieving and abominable and murderers and immoral persons and sorcerers and idolaters and all liars, their part *will be* in the lake that burns with fire and brimstone, which is the second death" (Rev. 21:8).

"For whoever is ashamed of Me and My words in this adulterous and sinful generation, the Son of Man will also be ashamed of him when He comes in the glory of His Father with the holy angels" (Mark 8:38).

So little is asked for so much in return. "For I consider that the sufferings of this present time are not worthy to be compared with the glory that is to be revealed to us" (Rom. 8:18).

It is all or nothing. "If we endure, we shall also reign with Him; if we deny Him, He also will deny us" (2 Tim. 2:12).

You join a select company. It is a chance of a lifetime to do something worthwhile. "Blessed are you when men hate you, and ostracize you, and cast insults at you, and spurn your name as evil, for the sake of the Son of Man. Be glad in that day, and leap *for joy*, for behold, your reward is great in heaven; for in the same way their fathers used to treat the prophets" (Luke 6:22, 23).

He does not ask you to do anything for Him that He did not do for you (Heb. 12:2).

37. Excuse: *"I think that Jesus Christ is only one of the great men in history."*

Answer: He claimed to be God. . . "who, although He existed in the form of God, did not regard equality with God a thing to be grasped" (Phil. 2:6). He was put to death for this claim (Matt. 26:63-65). The resurrection substantiated this claim. "And God raised Him up again, putting an end to the agony of death, since it was impossible for Him to be held in its power" (Acts 2:24).

The moral grandeur of His life surpasses anything on record. "Which one of you convicts Me of sin? If I speak truth, why do you not believe Me?" (John 8:46).

No one has so influenced history (Luke 2:34).

There is the repeated testimony of personal experience. "It is no longer because of what you said that we believe, for we have heard for ourselves and know that this One is indeed the Savior of the world" (John 4:42).

There is the open challenge to prove His divinity for yourself. "If any man is willing to do His will, he shall know of the teaching, whether it is of God, or *whether* I speak from Myself" (John 7:17).

38. Question: *"Why does God allow evil in this world?"*

Answer: Freedom of choice is the Creator's great gift to the human race. "I call heaven and earth to witness against you today, that I have set before you life and death, the blessing and the curse. So choose life in order that you may live, you and your descendants" (Deut. 30:19).

Sin originated in man, not in God. God prevents sin's dominion (Rom. 6:14).

God has, at His own cost, provided a remedy. "I

am the way, and the truth, and the life; no one comes to the Father, but through Me" (John 14:6).

39. Excuse: *"There is so much suffering."*

Answer: This is not the world as God planned it—the world that He said was "very good" (Gen. 1:31). It is the world in which man has spread his sin. "According to what I have seen, those who plow iniquity and those who sow trouble harvest it" (Job 4:8).

God has provided an alternative. "For the wages of sin is death, but the free gift of God is eternal life in Christ Jesus our Lord" (Rom. 6:23).

It is not the world that God intends to establish (Is. 65:20).

40. Question: *"Does this have to be done publicly?"*

Answer: God makes the rules. He has undertaken our salvation completely; therefore He has the right to say how we are to receive it. "Everyone therefore who shall confess Me before men, I will also confess him before My Father who is in heaven. But whoever shall deny Me before men, I will also deny him before My Father who is in heaven" (Matt. 10:32, 33). "For with the heart man believes, resulting in righteousness, and with the mouth he confesses, resulting in salvation" (Rom. 10:10).

Like a true marriage—a miracle of trust happens in the heart first; then an open acknowledgment, through proper ordinances, is made to the public.

"For whoever is ashamed of Me and My words in this adulterous and sinful generation, the Son of Man will also be ashamed of him when He comes in the glory of His Father with the holy angels" (Mark 8:38).

"And I say to you, everyone who confesses Me before men, the Son of Man shall confess him also before the angels of God; but he who denies Me before men shall be denied before the angels of God" (Luke 12:8).

"Nevertheless many even of the rulers believed in Him, but because of the Pharisees they were not confessing *Him*, lest they should be put out of the synagogue; for they loved the approval of men rather than the approval of God" (John 12:42, 43).

41. Question: *"What about baptism?"*

Answer: Baptism like Communion "shows the Lord's death." It is faith you show publicly when you are baptized.

"Or do you not know that all of us who have been baptized into Christ Jesus have been baptized into His death? Therefore we have been buried with Him through baptism into death, in order that as Christ was raised from the dead through the glory of the Father, so we too might walk in newness of life. For if we have become united with *Him* in the likeness of His death, certainly we shall be also *in the likeness* of His resurrection" (Rom. 6:3-5).

Baptism is our open profession before the world

that we are now living a miraculous, supernatural life of Christian grace by the quickening, regenerating power of God in us.

You should be baptized because like your Lord it fulfilleth ". . . all righteousness. . . ." It keeps setting forth the gospel of Jesus before this world. Baptism is one of the first tests of obedience.

42. Excuse: *"I cannot break with my sins."*

Answer: Salvation is a life-and-death choice. "I tell you, no, but, unless you repent, you will all likewise perish" (Luke 13:3).

You cannot live one way and die another way. "For the one who sows to his own flesh shall from the flesh reap corruption, but the one who sows to the Spirit shall from the Spirit reap eternal life" (Gal. 6:8, cf. Rev. 21:8).

You cannot do it in your own strength. "If therefore the Son shall make you free, you shall be free indeed" (John 8:36). "I can do all things through Him who strengthens me" (Phil. 4:13).

Christ can reach you where you are (Heb. 7:25).

43. Excuse: *"I see no harm in worldly amusements."*

Answer: The approach to this question should always be *positive,* and not negative. Instead of asking, "What *harm* is there in it?" I should ask, "What *good* is there in it?"

"And whatever you do in word or deed, *do* all in the name of the Lord Jesus, giving thanks through Him to God the Father" (Col. 3:17).

"Whether, then, you eat or drink or whatever you do, do all to the glory of God" (1 Cor. 10:31).

"All things are lawful for me, but not all things are profitable. All things are lawful for me, but I will not be mastered by anything" (1 Cor. 6:12).

As a Christian, I am responsible to use my body and my mind in trust for God's glory (1 Cor. 6:19, 20).

Sharp warnings appear in the New Testament: "If any man destroys the temple of God, God will destroy him, for the temple of God is holy, and that is what you are" (1 Cor. 3:17). "Therefore, COME OUT FROM THEIR MIDST AND BE SEPARATE,' says the Lord. 'AND DO NOT TOUCH WHAT IS UNCLEAN; and I will welcome you'" (2 Cor. 6:17). "They profess to know God, but by *their* deeds they deny *Him*, being detestable and disobedient, and worthless for any good deed" (Titus 1:16).

My aim should always be to give my utmost for His highest (2 Tim. 2:4).

44. Excuse: *"I am not respectable enough to be a Christian."*

Answer: It is your saving, active faith in Christ that counts. "And he got up and came to his father. But while he was still a long way off, his father saw him, and felt compassion *for him,* and ran and embraced him, and kissed him. And the son said to him, 'Father, I have sinned against heaven and in your sight; I am no longer worthy to be called your son.' But the father said to his slaves,

'Quickly bring out the best robe and put it on him, and put a ring on his hand and sandals on his feet; and bring the fattened calf, kill it, and let us eat and be merry; for this son of mine was dead, and has come to life again; he was lost, and has been found.' And they began to be merry" (Luke 15:20-24). See also Luke 18:10-14.

We can never make ourselves good enough.

"But to the one who does not work, but believes in Him who justifies the ungodly, his faith is reckoned as righteousness" (Rom. 4:5). See also Isaiah 41:13.

45. Excuse: *"I am afraid Jesus will not receive me."*

Answer: You have His word on it. "All that the Father gives Me shall come to Me, and the one who comes to Me I will certainly not cast out" (John 6:37).

God is no respecter of persons (Rom. 10:13, Luke 15:2). See also Revelation 22:17.

46. Excuse: *"I have tried before and failed."*

Answer: One failure need not mean final defeat. *Upon whom did you depend?* Did you make a complete surrender? Did you keep something back? Did you confess Christ publicly? Were you faithful in prayer? Did you seek guidance from the Word? "Now these were more noble-minded than those in Thessalonica, for they received the word with great eagerness, examining the Scriptures daily, *to see* whether these things were so" (Acts 17:11). Did you go to work for Christ? (Luke 11:24-26). See also First Peter 2:2.

Make a full surrender. "I urge you therefore, brethren, by the mercies of God, to present your bodies a living and holy sacrifice, acceptable to God, *which is* your spiritual service of worship" (Rom. 12:1).

Keep in touch! "Keep watching and praying, that you may not enter into temptation; the spirit is willing, but the flesh is weak" (Matt. 26:41).

Be present in church (Heb. 10:25).

47. Excuse: *"I think I have committed the unpardonable sin."*

Answer: You will *know* if you have committed this sin. The desire to be a Christian will be forever past. No spiritual impression will ever again come to your soul. *A hardening process will have taken place.*

"Therefore I say to you, any sin and blasphemy shall be forgiven men, but blasphemy against the Spirit shall not be forgiven. And whoever shall speak a word against the Son of Man, it shall be forgiven him; but whoever shall speak against the Holy Spirit, it shall not be forgiven him, either in this age, or in the *age* to come" (Matt. 12:31, 32).

In another passage we read: "but whoever blasphemes against the Holy Spirit never has forgiveness, but is guilty of an eternal sin" (Mark 3:29).

The tragedy lies in *the eternally unforgiven soul.* Since the Holy Spirit is the agent in convic-

tion and conversion, there can be no rebirth without the Holy Spirit. To sin against the Holy Spirit is to sin against your own soul. To blaspheme against the Holy Spirit is to shut yourself off forever from access to God.

"If anyone sees his brother committing a sin not *leading* to death, he shall ask and *God* will for him give life to those who commit sin not *leading* to death" (1 John 5:16).

You will *know* if you cross this line. Those who have committed this sin are completely given over to Satan and have not the slightest interest in spiritual matters. Paul describes it as "having become callous" (Eph. 4:19).

On the other hand, Satan, *the deceiver,* will lie to you and tell you that you are unpardonable. God makes no exceptions in His offer of salvation.

"And through Him everyone who believes is freed from all things, from which you could not be freed through the Law of Moses" (Acts 13:39).

Murder is not unpardonable. David confessed his sin and was forgiven (Ps. 32:5).

Theft is not unpardonable. The penitent thief on the cross was pardoned (Luke 23:43).

Blasphemy is not unpardonable. Paul was a blasphemer, and he was pardoned (1 Tim. 1:13).

Adultery is not unpardonable. The woman of Samaria was saved (John 4:18).

One of the amazing records of forgiveness is found in First Corinthians 6:9-11.

The person who sincerely asks for pardon will never be refused. "Let the wicked forsake his way, and the unrighteous man his thoughts; and let him return to the LORD, and He will have compassion on him; and to our God, for He will abundantly pardon" (Is. 55:7). "'Come now, and let us reason together,' says the LORD, 'though your sins are as scarlet, they will be as white as snow; though they are red like crimson, they will be like wool'" (Is. 1:18). See also Acts 10:43.

Paul was a great sinner, but he obtained salvation (1 Tim. 1:15, 16).

48. Question: *"Would not suicide be the best way out of my trouble?"*

Answer: There is only one solution for guilt consciousness—forgiveness and cleansing (Job 15:20, 1 John 1:9).

Self-murder only hastens judgment. "So then each one of us shall give account of himself to God" (Rom. 14:12).

A correct relationship with Christ brings a new approach to living. "Therefore if any man is in Christ, *he is* a new creature; the old things passed away; behold, new things have come" (2 Cor. 5:17).

Get the *sin-problem* settled first, and then the *trouble-problem* can be settled (Matt. 6:33).

49. Excuse: *"I am seeking but I cannot find Christ."*

Answer: Christ is not distant. His presence is noticeable, "that they should seek God, if per-

haps they might grope for Him and find Him, though He is not far from each one of us; for in Him we live and move and exist, as even some of your own poets have said, 'For we also are His offspring'" (Acts 17:27, 28).

Paul says that Christ makes Himself real to a person through the exercise of faith (Rom. 10:6-11).

Be sure you are looking in the right direction! "And you will seek Me and find *Me*, when you search for *Me* with all your heart" (Jer. 29:13).

50. Excuse: "*I am ashamed to come to Christ.*"

Answer: "But when He heard this, He said, '*It is* not those who are healthy who need a physician, but those who are sick. But go and learn what *this* means, "I DESIRE COMPASSION, AND NOT SACRIFICE," for I did not come to call the righteous, but sinners'" (Matt. 9:12, 13).

Salvation is for the *lost*. "For while we were still helpless, at the right time Christ died for the ungodly. For one will hardly die for a righteous man; though perhaps for the good man someone would dare even to die. But God demonstrates His own love toward us, in that while we were yet sinners, Christ died for us" (Rom. 5:6-8).

51. Excuse: "*I would like to be a Christian, but I cannot forgive my enemies.*"

Answer: Through God's help you can do what you cannot do otherwise. "With men this is impossible, but with God all things are possible" (Matt. 19:26).

I become a recipient of God's *grace*. "And God is able to make all grace abound to you, that always having all sufficiency in everything, you may have an abundance for every good deed" (2 Cor. 9:8). See also Second Corinthians 12:9.

Tell God only that *you are willing to be made willing* (Matt. 6:14, 15).

52. Excuse: "*I want to be saved, but I cannot believe.*"

Answer: *Whom* does the Bible ask you to believe? "Believe in the Lord Jesus, and you shall be saved, you and your household" (Acts 16:31).

Do you believe that God has saved *others?* Do you believe that He wants to save *you?* Do you believe that He *can* save you? Will you trust Him to save you *now?*

You are saved through the Word which is God's contract with you, and because God wants you to be saved (John 5:24). "But as many as received Him, to them He gave the right to become children of God, *even* to those who believe in His name, who were born not of blood, nor of the will of the flesh, nor of the will of man, but of God" (John 1:12, 13).

Use the faith that God gives you! "For by grace you have been saved through faith; and that not of yourselves, *it is* the gift of God" (Eph. 2:8). See also Romans 5:1.

53. Question: "*Does not the Bible have inconsistencies and contradictions in it?*"

Answer: Where are they? The Bible is *revelation*. "'For My thoughts are not your thoughts, neither are your ways My ways,' declares the LORD. 'For *as* the heavens are higher than the earth, so are My ways higher than your ways, and My thoughts than your thoughts'" (Is. 55:8, 9).

The Bible is a *locked book* to a *locked heart*.

"Many will be purged, purified and refined; but the wicked will act wickedly, the none of the wicked will understand, but those who have insight will understand" (Dan. 12:10). "But a natural man does not accept the things of the Spirit of God; for they are foolishness to him, and he cannot understand them, because they are spiritually appraised" (1 Cor. 2:14).

Certainly there are mysteries presented in God's Word! "As also in all *his* letters, speaking in them of these things, in which are some things hard to understand, which the untaught and unstable distort, as *they do* also the rest of the Scriptures, to their own destruction. You therefore, beloved, knowing this beforehand, be on your guard lest, being carried away by the error of unprincipled men, you fall from your own steadfastness, but grow in the grace and knowledge of our Lord and Savior Jesus Christ. To Him *be* the glory, both now and to the day of eternity. Amen" (2 Pet. 3:16-18).

Know Him and you will know His book!

54. Question: "*How can I know there is a God?*"

Answer: There are *three sources* of material. First, there is the Bible. Second, there is nature. Third, there is man. These point to the Creator. None are possible by happenstance. None could have been produced by accident.

"Because that which is known about God is evident within them; for God made it evident to them" (Rom. 1:19).

"When I consider Thy heavens, the work of Thy fingers, the moon and the stars, which Thou hast ordained" (Ps. 8:3).

"By the word of the LORD the heavens were made, and by the breath of His mouth all their host" (Ps. 33:6).

55. Question: "*Why do I need the blood?*"

Answer: "For the life of the flesh is in the blood, and I have given it to you on the altar to make atonement for your souls; for it is the blood by reason of the life that makes atonement" (Lev. 17:11).

Jesus died for you and me (Matt. 26:28).

"And according to the Law, *one may* almost *say,* all things are cleansed with blood, and without shedding of blood there is no forgiveness" (Heb. 9:22).

He tasted death for me. Thus He bore the supreme penalty of my sins (Rom. 5:9, 10).

It took the greatest price in the universe. "Knowing that you were not redeemed with perishable things like silver or gold from your futile

way of life inherited from your forefathers, but with precious blood, as of a lamb unblemished and spotless, *the blood* of Christ" (1 Pet. 1:18, 19).

56. Question: *"Why should I accept the Bible as the final authority?"*

Answer: *The Bible has survived all unbelievers.* "What then? If some did not believe, their unbelief will not nullify the faithfulness of God, will it? May it never be! Rather, let God be found true, though every man *be found* a liar" (Rom. 3:3, 4).

"All Scripture is inspired by God and profitable for teaching, for reproof, for correction, for training in righteousness" (2 Tim. 3:16).

God's character rests upon the authenticity and authority of the Bible (Mark 13:31).

57. Question: *"What must I do to be saved?"*

Answer: God, through Jesus Christ, His Son, has provided a way for you (Is. 53:5, 6).

Your part is "to receive," God's part is to give you "power to become." "But as many as received Him, to them He gave the right to become children of God, *even* to those who believe in His name" (John 1:12).

Conversion and regeneration go together. When you have turned to God (conversion), He will turn over your life (regeneration). God's part is as essential as your part (John 3:7).

Saving faith reaches out and believes what God's Word says about you. "Truly, truly, I say to you, he who hears My word, and believes Him who sent Me, has eternal life, and does not come into judgment, but has passed out of death into life" (John 5:24).

Your salvation is in your acceptance of what Christ has done for you. Did He, or did He not, die for you? (Acts 16:31).

Outward form is useless until something has happened within your life. Salvation is like marriage. All the ceremony involved can't really marry a couple unless first of all something real toward each other has happened in each of their hearts. When that occurs, they want the whole world to know (Rom. 10:9-19).

God saves sinners only. Are you a sinner? Do you need two things—(1) FORGIVENESS and (2) CLEANSING?

What God has done for others, He will do for you. "For 'WHOEVER WILL CALL UPON THE NAME OF THE LORD WILL BE SAVED'" (Rom. 10:13).

Jesus foretold that excuses and alibis would be given. *Excuses* are never *reasons.*

"But He said to him, 'A certain man was giving a big dinner, and he invited many; and at the dinner hour he sent his slave to say to those who had been invited, "Come; for everything is ready now." But they all alike began to make excuses. The first one said to him, "I have bought a piece of land and I need to go out and look at it; please consider me excused." And another one said, "I have bought five yoke of oxen, and I am going to try them out; please consider me excused." And another one

said, "I have married a wife, and for that reason I cannot come." And the slave came *back* and reported this to his master. Then the head of the household became angry and said to his slave, "Go out at once into the streets and lanes of the city and bring in here the poor and crippled and blind and lame." And the slave said, "Master, what you commanded has been done, and still there is room." And the master said to the slave, "Go out into the highways and along the hedges, and compel *them* to come in, that my house may be filled. For I tell you, none of those men who were invited shall taste of my dinner"'" (Luke 14:16-24).

Let not conscience make you linger,
Nor of fitness fondly dream;
All the fitness he requireth
Is to feel your need of Him.
—Joseph Hart

VI. Conversion

Steps to the Christian Life:

1. REPENT. Turn around. Change your mind. "I tell you, no, but unless you repent, you will all likewise perish" (Luke 13:3).

2. RECEIVE HIM. You need the Savior. Accept Him. "But as many as received Him, to them He gave the right to become children of God, *even* to those who believe in His name" (John 1:12).

3. BE "BORN AGAIN." This is what God does for you. This is the New Birth—a miracle of spiritual life performed by the Holy Spirit. "Who were born not of blood, nor of the will of the flesh, nor of the will of man, but of God" (John 1:13). See also John 11:25.

4. REJOICE PUBLICLY. Make your testimony for Christ, "that if you confess with your mouth Jesus *as* Lord, and believe in your heart that God raised Him from the dead, you shall be saved; for with the heart man believes, resulting in righteousness, and with the mouth he confesses, resulting in salvation" (Rom. 10:9, 10). See also Matthew 10:32, 33.

5. REQUEST WATER BAPTISM. This is an outward testimony to an inward transaction. "He who has believed and has been baptized shall be saved; but he who has disbelieved shall be condemned" (Mark 16:16).

The Bible can never be the private and exclusive property of any one religion. God gave it to the world. It cannot be copyrighted. It is not man's product. Therefore, look for your eternal assurance from the Bible. *It is what God says that counts.*

6. READ THE WORD. The Word is the source of your faith. "These things I have written to you who believe in the name of the Son of God, in order that you may know that you have eternal life" (1 John 5:13). See also Romans 10:17, Psalms 119:105.

7. REACH GOD IN PRAYER. Prayer is con-

versation with God. Life is sustained by union and communion (Eph. 6:18; James 4:2). "And this is the confidence which we have before Him, that, if we ask anything according to His will, He hears us. And if we know that He hears us *in* whatever we ask, we know that we have the requests which we have asked from Him" (1 John 5:14, 15).

8. RELATE YOUR EXPERIENCE TO OTHERS. You maintain strength by exercise. "But if you on your part warn a wicked man to turn from his way, and he does not turn from his way, he will die in his iniquity; but you have delivered your life. Now as for you, son of man, say to the house of Israel, 'Thus you have spoken, saying, "Surely our transgressions and our sins are upon us, and we are rotting away in them; how then can we survive?"'" (Ezek. 33:9, 10).

9. RESIST THE DEVIL. Temptation is not sin. It is yielding to temptation that is sin. "That the proof of your faith, *being* more precious than gold which is perishable, even though tested by fire, may be found to result in praise and glory and honor at the revelation of Jesus Christ" (1 Pet. 1:7).

"For we do not have a high priest who cannot sympathize with our weaknesses, but one who has been tempted in all things as *we are, yet* without sin (Heb. 4:15).

10. RESTITUTION. Your guilt is gone, and you can convert your influence for good. "And Zaccheus stopped and said to the Lord, 'Behold, Lord, half of my possessions I will give to the poor, and if I have defrauded anyone of anything, I will give back four times as much'" (Luke 19:8).

"In view of this, I also do my best to maintain always a blameless conscience *both* before God and before men" (Acts 24:16).

11. "RENDER . . . TO GOD THE THINGS THAT ARE GOD'S." Start tithing your income immediately. "'Will a man rob God? Yet you are robbing Me! But you say, "How have we robbed Thee?" In tithes and offerings. Bring the whole tithe into the storehouse, so that there may be food in My house, and test Me now in this,' says the LORD of hosts, 'if I will not open for you the windows of heaven, and pour out for you a blessing until it overflows'" (Mal. 3:8, 10). See also First Corinthians 16:2.

12. REGULARLY ATTEND CHURCH AND SUNDAY SCHOOL. Associate yourself immediately with God's people. Become a church member (Heb. 10:25).

"And He came to Nazareth, where He had been brought up; and as was His custom, He entered the synagogue on the Sabbath, and stood up to read" (Luke 4:16).

"Seeing that His divine power has granted to us everything pertaining to life and godliness, through the true knowledge of Him who called us by His own glory and excellence" (2 Pet. 1:3).

VII. Convincement

"In Him was life, and the life was the light of men" (John 1:4).

"But in order that you may know that the Son of Man has authority on earth to forgive sins" (Luke 5:24).

It is too late in another world. Forgiveness of sins must be received on this side (1 John 3:2).

What is this assurance? How can I know for certain?

There are second chances in health, money, championships, and education; but when a man passes from this life, he cannot return for a second chance. *Your religion must furnish your proof.* You have a right to demand it.

Calvary is ridiculous if your life can be changed and you do not know it. Something you may have and not know it, is something you can lose and never miss. *The proof of your salvation is not by sensation. It is by Scripture.*

Certain evidences must be manifested in our lives immediately. These evidences are recorded in the Bible.

1. THERE IS AN INFALLIBLE INSIDE WITNESS. "The one who believes in the Son of God has the witness in himself; the one who does not believe God has made Him a liar, because he has not believed in the witness that God has borne concerning His Son" (1 John 5:10). The preacher and the church may tell you that you are all right. But you, *yourself*, are the final judge in that matter.

Christ asked Peter about this. He said, "do you love Me more than these?" (John 21:15). There was no doubt in Peter's mind about his relationship to Jesus.

2. THERE IS A FAMILY RELATIONSHIP. "We know that we have passed out of death into life, because we love the brethren" (1 John 3:14). *You sense a different and vital relationship with God's children.* You are at home with spiritual things. It is a tie stronger than any family background in this world (Gal. 6:10).

3. THERE IS A NEW IMAGE. "Therefore if any man is in Christ, *he is* a new creature; the old things passed away; behold, new things have come" (2 Cor. 5:17). A New Testament Christian is not a patched-up job, a reformed sinner. There is a new will; there are new affections; there is a new purpose because there is a new nature.

The emptiest and unhappiest occupation in the world is trying to act like a Christian when you are not a Christian. You do not gradually stop stealing. You stop stealing. It is miracle, not magic.

4. THERE IS A RESPONSE OF VICTORY. "For whatever is born of God overcomes the world; and this is the victory that has overcome the world—our faith" (1 John 5:4). See also John 17:15, 16. *The born-again man or woman is not motivated by this world-system.*

Fancy yourself on the farm. It is hot midsum-

mer. Nearby is a big mud wallow. Here comes a pig. He grunts with contentment as he wades into the slime. You say, "Mr. Hog, why do you want to submerge in that filth? Why do you not seek a cleaner environment?" That pig has not the slightest interest in your ideas for his betterment. He loves the mud.

Now watch a sheep with long white wool. The moment a sheep notices mud it heads toward safer ground. The sheep has a different nature. So has a New Testament Christian.

These are Bible proofs. "These things I have written to you who believe in the name of the Son of God, in order that you may know that you have eternal life" (1 John 5:13).

Paul testified on two continents (2 Tim. 3:11).

VIII. Camouflage

Today is a day of substitutes. Nylon has been substituted for silk. Oleomargarine has been substituted for butter. There are many substitutes offered for salvation. Beware.

1. SERVICE IS NOT SALVATION. "Woe to you, scribes and Pharisees, hypocrites, because you travel about on sea and land to make one proselyte; and when he becomes one, you make him twice as much a son of hell as yourselves" (Matt. 23:15). How can you lead others to Christ when you do not know Christ yourself?

2. TURNING OVER A NEW LEAF IS NOT SALVATION. Man does not get saved by *reforming,* saying, "I will clean up my life, and begin life anew."

"For all of us have become like one who is unclean, and all our righteous deeds are like a filthy garment; and all of us wither like a leaf, and our iniquities, like the wind, take us away" (Is. 64:6). "How you turned to God from idols to serve a living and true God" (1 Thess. 1:9). *Notice the direction!* They did not turn from idols to God. The new birth is a divine miracle.

3. ASSERTING ONE'S MANHOOD IS NOT SALVATION. Men "dead in your trespasses and sins" (Eph. 2:1) cannot throw back their shoulders and assert their manhood for righteousness. The cross of Christ does not call upon men to assert their manhood. *The cross of Christ exposes men's degradation.* That is part of the "stumbling block of the cross" (Gal. 5:11). It does not appeal to man's pride. It unsparingly shows man that he cannot do anything for himself. He has no righteousness or decency to offer to God.

4. RIGHT THINKING IS NOT SALVATION. It is not cultivating and concentrating on a "divine spark" that is within you. "Behold, I was brought forth in iniquity, and in sin my mother conceived me" (Ps. 51:5). It is not keeping a picture of your mother, sweetheart, or your wife in your billfold, and looking at it frequently. *It is not thinking high thoughts* (Is. 55:8, 9). *How can you think high thoughts with a base nature?*

5. DENYING THE EXISTENCE OF SIN IS

NOT SALVATION. God does not deny sin. *Calvary is God's recognition of sin.* "But the LORD has caused the iniquity of us all to fall on Him" (Is. 53:6). "But the Scripture has shut up all men under sin" (Gal. 3:22). One of the first steps toward salvation is to recognize your sin—not deny it.

6. TO DENY SELF IS NOT SALVATION. The heathen are masters at this. They practice all kinds of asceticism (1 Cor. 13:3). *You are not saved by crucifying yourself.* It is not proving to yourself that you can do hard things.

7. SACRIFICE IS NOT SALVATION. Dying for a great cause—the supreme sacrifice—is not salvation. *Discipline does not cleanse a man from sin.* If that were true, then everybody who entered a penitentiary would become a Christian. Paying for wrongdoing does not make a person a Christian (1 Sam. 15:22).

There is no *side door* into heaven. Jesus said, "I am the door; if anyone enters through Me, he shall be saved" (John 10:9).

"He who does not enter by the door into the fold of the sheep, but climbs up some other way, he is a thief and a robber" (John 10:1). You cannot *steal* your way into heaven.

IX. Christ

The Master has not asked us to do what He did not do constantly during His ministry upon earth. He says, "Follow Me, and I will make you fishers of men" (Matt. 4:19).

His record is one of personal contact from when He said to Andrew, "Come and see" to His assurance to the penitent thief, "Today you shall be with Me in Paradise."

He is clear and concise about God's plan of salvation.

1. He came to meet a human need. "I have not come to call the righteous but sinners . . ." (Luke 5:32). Salvation is for sinners only.

2. He came to be the sinner's substitute. "The good shepherd lays down His life for the sheep" (John 10:11).

3. He came to do what none other can do. "I am the way, and the truth, and the life; no one comes to the Father, but through Me" (John 14:6).

4. He came to provide assurance to the trusting sinner. "Your sins have been forgiven . . . go in peace" (Luke 7:48-50).

James remembers emphatically the passion that his brother manifested toward the lost. He reflects this when he says, "let him know that he who turns a sinner from the error of his way will save his soul from death, and will cover a multitude of sins" (James 5:20).

X. Condensation

The story of salvation can be told in *four words:*

Sin
Calvary
Faith
Life

1. Salvation is needed. "For all have sinned and fall short of the glory of God" (Rom. 3:23).

2. Salvation is provided. "And He Himself bore our sins in His body on the cross, that we might die to sin and live to righteousness; for by His wounds you were healed" (1 Pet. 2:24).

3. Salvation is offered. "For by grace you have been saved through faith; and that not of yourselves, *it is* the gift of God" (Eph. 2:8).

4. Salvation accepted. "He who has the Son has the life; he who does not have the Son of God does not have the life" (1 John 5:12).

There is a time, we know not when,
A place, we know not where;
Which marks the destiny of men
To glory or despair.

There is a line, by us unseen,
Which crosses every path,
Which marks the boundary between
God's mercy and his wrath.

To pass that limit is to die,
To die as if by stealth;
It does not dim the beaming eye,
Nor pale the glow of health.

The conscience may be still at ease,
The spirit light and gay;
And that which pleases still may please,
And care be thrust away.

But on that forehead God hath set
Indelibly a mark;
Unseen by man, for man as yet,
Is blind and in the dark.

He feels perchance that all is well
And every fear is calmed;
He lives, he dies, he walks in hell,
Not only doomed, but damned!

O, Where is that mysterious line
That may by men be crossed,
Beyond which God himself hath sworn,
That he who goes is lost?

An answer from the skies repeats,
"Ye who from God depart."
TODAY, O hear His voice,
TODAY repent and harden not your heart.

—Joseph Addison Alexander

THE GREATEST ARCHAEOLOGICAL DISCOVERIES

and Their Effects on the Bible

I
Introduction

Definition and Importance of Biblical Archaeology

The last 150 years have witnessed the birth, growth, and phenomenal development of the science of biblical archaeology. This new science has performed many wonders in furnishing background material and in illustrating, illuminating, and in many cases authenticating the message and meaning of the Old and New Testament Scriptures.

Biblical archaeology may be defined as a study based on the excavation, decipherment, and critical evaluation of the records of the past as they affect the Bible. While the general field of archaeology is fascinating, much more so is the study of biblical archaeology, since it deals with the Holy Scriptures. This is the reason for the growing enthusiasm for biblical archaeology. The attraction lies in the supreme importance of the message and meaning of the Bible. The Scriptures, by virtue of their character as the inspired revelation of God to man and meeting man's deepest need, today as in the past, have naturally held a paramount place in the interest and affection of mankind. Biblical archaeology, illustrating the Bible in its historical background and contemporary life, attracts a measure of the interest that lies in the Bible itself. Accordingly, this science has a worthy ministry of expanding biblical horizons on the human plane.

No field of research has offered greater challenge and promise than that of biblical archaeology. Until the beginning of the 19th century very little was known of biblical times and biblical backgrounds, except what appeared on the pages of the Old Testament or what happened to be preserved in the writings of classical antiquity. This was considerable for the New Testament era but very little indeed for the Old Testament period. The reason for this is that Greek and Latin historians catalogued very little information before the 5th century B.C. As a result, the Old Testament period was very little known extrabiblically, and what was known was confined to what the Bible gave. This from the viewpoint of contemporary secular history was sparse. The result was that before the beginning of the science of modern archaeology there was practically nothing available to authenticate Old Testament history and literature. One can therefore imagine the fervor aroused among serious Bible students by illuminating discoveries in Bible lands, especially from c. 1800 to the present. In fact, modern archaeology may be said to have had its beginning in 1798, when the rich antiquities of the Nile Valley were opened up to scientific study by Napoleon's Egyptian Expedition.

II
Foundational Discoveries of the Nineteenth Century

Although the most notable discoveries affecting the Bible and particularly the Old Testament were not made until the 20th century, foundational discoveries were made in the 19th century and prepared the way for the modern era.

1. The Rosetta Stone—Key to Egypt's Splendid Past

This very important monument was discovered in 1798 at *Rosetta* (Rashid), near the westernmost mouth of the Nile River, by an officer in Napoleon's Expedition to Egypt. It was a slab of black basalt trilingually inscribed, which may be said to be the key that unlocked the door to knowledge of the language and literature of ancient Egypt and turned out to be the inscription that opened the modern era of scientific biblical archaeology.

The three languages in which this monument was found to be inscribed were the Greek of 200 B.C., two forms of Egyptian writing—the older, more complicated hieroglyphic script and the later simplified and more popular demotic writing, which was the common language of the people. The Greek could at once be read and provided the clue to the decipherment of the other two ancient Egyptian scripts. Sylvester de Sacy of France and J. D. Akerblad of Sweden succeeded in unraveling the demotic Egyptian by identifying the Greek personal names it contained, namely Ptolemy, Arsinoe, and Berenike. Thomas Young of England then proceeded to identify the name of Ptolemy in the hieroglyphic portion, where groups of characters enclosed in oval frames, called cartouches, had already been surmised to be royal names. From this point on, the young Frenchman Jean François Champollion, 1790–1832, was able to decipher the hiero-

glyphics of the monument, show the true nature of this script, make a dictionary, formulate a grammar, and translate numerous Egyptian texts, from the year 1818 to 1832.

Champollion's achievement formally opened up the science of Egyptology. Scholars from henceforth were able to read Egyptian monumental inscriptions and reliefs. From that time forth the literary treasures of the Nile Valley have been opened to scholarly study. Today many universities maintain chairs in the language and culture of ancient Egypt. These studies have opened up vistas of history hitherto unknown so that, from the beginning of Egypt c. 2800 B.C. to 63 B.C. when Rome took over, the entire history of the land of the Nile can fairly well be traced.

All of this has tremendous bearing on the background of the Bible. Egypt figures largely in the patriarchal narratives and the Book of Exodus and all through the Pentateuch. As a result, the background of the story of Joseph and of the sojourn of the Children of Israel in Egypt, their deliverance under Moses, and much of their sojourn in the desert and later history in Canaan can now be set in the general framework of Egyptian history. It can be said that the whole context of Old Testament history, in its broad span from Abraham to Christ, is made immeasurably clearer because of the vast strides in our knowledge of Egypt. That great nation of antiquity interacted with the mighty Assyro-Babylonian empires on the Tigris-Euphrates and with the Hittite power on the Halys across the tiny bridge that was ancient Palestine.

2. The Behistun Inscription—Gateway to Assyrian-Babylonian Antiquity

This famous monument was the key to the languages of Assyria and Babylonia. It consists of a large relief panel containing numerous columns of inscription, which was boldly carved on the face of a mountain about 500 feet above the surrounding plain of Karmanshah on the old caravan route from Babylon to Ecbatana. Unlike the Rosetta Stone written in ancient Egyptian hieroglyphics, and later in popular demotic and in the Greek of the 3rd century B.C., the **Behistun Inscription** was written in the wedge-shaped characters of ancient Assyria-Babylonia. It contained about 1200 lines of inscription. The three languages in which it was inscribed were all written in cuneiform characters, consisting of Old Persian, Elamite, and Akkadian. The third language, the Akkadian, was the wedge-shaped language of ancient Assyria and Babylonia, in which thousands upon thousands of clay tablets discovered in the Tigris-Euphrates region are inscribed.

Early excavations revealed a mass of material on which this curious wedge-shaped Babylonian-Akkadian writing appeared. But it was an unsolved riddle. Practically no progress was made

until a young English officer in the Persian army, Henry C. Rawlinson, in 1835 and the following years made the dangerous climb to the Behistun inscription and made copies and plaster of Paris impressions of it. Rawlinson knew modern Persian and set to work to decipher the old Persian, the cuneiform part of the inscription. After a decade of labor, he finally succeeded in translating the five columns, nearly 400 lines of the old Persian portion of the Behistun Inscription, and sent it to Europe in 1845. The text translation and commentary on it were published in 1847 in the *Journal of the Royal Asiatic Society*.

In conjunction with the literary part of the monument was a life-sized figure with numerous individuals bowing before it. This person turned out to be Darius the Great (522–486 B.C.), the Achemenid prince who saved the Persian Empire from a rebellion. The scene depicts the king, as Rawlinson's translation of the Persian portion of the inscription shows, receiving the submission of the rebels. The emperor is portrayed at the top of the relief accompanied by two attendants. His foot is placed upon the prostrate form of a leading rebel. The king's left hand holds a bow, while his right hand is lifted toward the winged disc symbolizing Ahura-Mazda, the spirit of good, whom Darius, an ardent follower of Zoroaster, worshiped. Behind the rebel stands a procession of rebel leaders, roped together by their necks. Beside and beneath the sculptured panel the numerous columns of the inscription appear, relating in three languages how Darius defended the throne and crushed the revolt.

Working on the supposition that the other inscriptions told the same story, scholars were soon enabled to read the second language, which was the Elamite or Susian. Then last, but most important, they could decipher the Akkadian or Assyro-Babylonian. This was a great discovery, for this wedge-shaped character of writing is recorded on numerous literary remains from the Tigris-Euphrates Valley. It opened up a vast new field of biblical background, so that today, as in the case of the Rosetta Stone opening up the science of Egyptology, the Behistun Inscription has given birth to the science of Assyriology. Moreover, both Egyptology and Assyriology offer great help in understanding biblical backgrounds and biblical history. No Bible dictionary, Bible handbook or commentary that is up to date can ignore the great findings of these sciences.

The task of deciphering cuneiform is increasing with every decade. Numerous cuneiform libraries have been discovered from antiquity. Two at Nineveh were unearthed. These contained thousands of clay tablets. *The library of Ashurbanipal* (669–625 B.C.) contained some 22,000 tablets. Among the tablets unearthed in this collection and sent to the British Museum were Assyrian copies of the Babylonian creation and flood

A gateway into Nebuchadnezzar's Palace in Babylon.
Matson Photo Service

stories. The identification and decipherment of these particular tablets by George Smith in 1872 produced great excitement in the archaeological world.

Not only in Babylonia but in many other places large bodies of cuneiform literature have been uncovered. For example, the famous *Amarna Letters* from Egypt were discovered in 1886 at Tell el-Amarna about 200 miles south of modern Cairo. These Amarna Tablets proved to be diplomatic correspondence of petty princes of Palestine in the 14th century B.C. with the Egyptian court at Amarna. The Amarna Letters give an inside glance into conditions in Palestine just before the conquest by Joshua and the Israelites. Many scholars actually think that they describe aspects of that invasion. One of the documents from the governor of Jerusalem (Urusalim) tells Amenophis IV that the "Habiru" (perhaps the Hebrews) were overrunning many Palestine cities and could not be held back.

Other important bodies of cuneiform literature bearing upon the Bible have been retrieved from Boghaz-Keui and Kanish in Asia Minor. Others come from Susa and Elam, others from the city of Mari on the middle Euphrates, others from Ras Shamra (ancient Ugarit), mentioned in the Amarna Letters and located in North Syria. Others stem from various sites within and without Babylonia. Of first-rate importance then is the Rosetta Stone from Egypt and the Behistun Inscription from Babylonia. These two monuments

may be said to have laid the foundation for the key discoveries of the 20th century.

3. The Moabite Stone—A Sensational Literary Find

This important inscription, found in 1868, offers another example of the discoveries of the 19th century that prepared the way for the great finds of the 20th century. The inscription dates from c. 850 B.C. It was erected by Mesha, king of Moab, and is often styled the *Mesha Stone*. It tells of the wars of Mesha of Moab with Omri, king of Israel, and Omri's successors. It also tells of Mesha's wars with the Edomites. The material recorded on the *Moabite Stone* parallels biblical history recorded in Second Kings, chapters 1 and 3. Numerous places mentioned in the Old Testament occur on the stele (inscribed monument). Among them are Arnon (Num. 21:13; Deut. 2:24), Ataroth (Num. 32:34), Baal-meon or Beth-baal-meon (Josh. 13:17), Beth-bamoth or Bamoth-baal (Josh. 13:17), Beth-diblathaim (Jer. 48:22), Bezer (Josh. 20:8), Dibon (Num. 32:34), Jahaza (Josh. 13:18), Medeba (Josh. 13:9), and Nebo (Num. 32:38).

This inscribed monument or stele measures 3 feet 8½ inches in height, 2 feet 3½ inches in width, and 1 foot 1¾ inches in thickness. Its 34 lines constitute the longest single literary inscription yet recovered extrabiblically dealing with

A replica of the Moabite Stone.   *Matson Photo Service*

Palestine in the period 900–600 B.C. It records that Moab had been conquered by Omri and his son Ahab but was set free from the Israelite yoke by Mesha's god Chemosh. This deity is represented as commanding King Mesha to go to war against Israel, who, according to Second Kings 3:27, offered up his eldest son as a burnt offering upon the wall to propitiate the god Chemosh and to secure his favor.

The Moabite Stone is written in the language of Moab, which was very similar to the Hebrew of the time of Omri and Ahab. This inscription, therefore, has great value in tracing the development of early Hebrew through the centuries. When it was discovered, the Mesha Stone was not only the longest and oldest Phoenician-Hebrew inscription then in existence, it was the only one. Now the **Gezer Calendar** is known and it dates from c. 925 B.C. It is a school boy's exercise written in perfect classical Hebrew. This small limestone tablet, found at ancient Gezer, gives an incidental sidelight on Palestinian agriculture as well as on ancient Hebrew writing. Such discoveries as the Gezer Calendar and the Mesha Stone not only give glimpses into the background of the Bible but form important links in the culture and history of the people outside the pale of Israel.

III
Great Discoveries
of the Twentieth Century

Although such discoveries as the Rosetta Stone, the Behistun Inscription, the Mesha Stone, and the Siloam Inscription are important for their time and laid the foundations of scientific archaeology in the 19th century, it remained for the 20th century to produce the most thrilling and outstanding archaeological finds. During this period biblical archaeology came to be a refined and precise science, adding to the frontiers of biblical knowledge on the human plane and making tremendous contributions to the background, historical and cultural, of the written Word of God.

1. The Code of Hammurabi—Light on Mosaic Laws

A slab of black diorite, over 7 feet tall and some 6 feet wide, was discovered in 1901. This record of the past contains engraved upon it almost 300 paragraphs of legal provision dealing with the commercial, social, domestic, and moral life of the Babylonians of King Hammurabi's time (1728–1676 B.C.). A copy of this code was found by Jacques de Morgan at Susa in Elam, where it had been carried off by the Elamites from Babylon. At the top of the stele the king is shown receiving the laws from the sun god Shamash, patron of law and justice. At some time when Babylon was weak, an Elamite conqueror carried away the monument to Susa. Its finding was one of the most startling legal discoveries in history.

The code is important in furnishing background material for comparison with other ancient bodies of law. It is also natural that it should offer comparative data for the study of the laws of the Pentateuch. The fact that the code is older by over three centuries than the laws of Moses has disposed of some untenable theories of the critics and given rise to others. For instance, the old critical view that detailed codes of law like those recorded in the Pentateuch are anachronistic for such an early period has been exploded by the discovery of Hammurabi's laws and much earlier codes in Mesopotamia.

A discovery of this sort illustrates how archaeology purges out radical critical views, which used to place the origin of many of the laws ascribed to Moses to much later times, such as the 9th, 8th, and 7th centuries B.C., or even later. These erroneous theories had to be drastically revised or entirely rejected. On the other hand, the discovery of the early extrabiblical legal material has led many to adopt an equally faulty view that Hebrew legislation is merely a selection and adaptation of Babylonian law. The only position that is valid as the two bodies of legal material are studied is that the Mosaic code is neither borrowed from, nor dependent upon, the Babylonian. It is divinely given, as it claims to be, and unique in those features that met Israel's peculiar need as an elect, theocratic nation.

The resemblances between the **Mosaic laws** and the **Code of Hammurabi** are clearly due to similarity of antecedents and general intellectual and cultural heritage. It is natural that in codes dealing with peoples in somewhat similar conditions, related racially and culturally, there should be some likeness in the incidents leading to litigation and likewise in the penalties imposed for infringement of common statutes. A striking difference, however, is obtained. These clearly demonstrate that there is no direct borrowing and that the Mosaic law, although later by three centuries, is in no sense dependent upon the Babylonian.

The biblical law of divorce (Deut. 24:1), for instance, permits the man to put away his wife but does not extend the same right to the wife, as does the Babylonian code. Again the so-called **Lex Talionis** is a primitive Semitic law and would be expected to be reflected in various Semitic legal codes. Mosaic injunctions (Ex. 21:23–25; Deut. 19:21) state precisely the same principle of retaliation upon which a number of Hammurabi's laws are based, namely "life for life, eye for eye, tooth for tooth, hand for hand, foot for foot, burn for burn, wound for wound, bruise for bruise."

The Mosaic and Hammurabi codes are **different in content**. The Hebrew code contains many purely religious injunctions and ritual reg-

ulations. The Code of Hammurabi, on the other hand, is civil. However, the priestly laws of Leviticus contain many points of similarity with priestly ritual and practice in western Asia, whether in Canaan or Phoenicia or Mesopotamia. But this in no sense casts doubt on the fact that Israel's religious practices as recorded in the Pentateuch are divinely given and uniquely invested with significance to fit a nation divinely called to serve the one God. In some cases similar cultic practice among surrounding peoples was divinely given to Israel. But at the same time it was invested with a special significance for the worship of the Lord.

The two codes, of course, are *different in their origin*. The Babylonian laws are alleged to have been received by Hammurabi from the sun god Shamash. Moses received his laws directly from the Lord. Hammurabi, despite his reported reception from Shamash, takes credit for them in both the prologue and epilogue of the code. He, not Shamash, established order and equity throughout the land. Moses, in contrast, is only an instrument. The legislation is "Thus says the LORD."

The two codes govern a *different type of society*. Hammurabi's laws are fitted to the irrigation culture and highly commercialized urban society of Mesopotamia. The Mosaic injunctions, on the other hand, suit a simple, agricultural, pastoral people of a dry land like Palestine much less advanced in social and commercial development, but keenly conscious of their divine calling in all phases of their living.

The two codes *differ in their morality*. From the ethical and spiritual standpoint the Mosaic legislation, as would be expected, offers a considerable advance over the Babylonian code. Hammurabi's laws, for example, enumerate at least ten varieties of bodily mutilation prescribed for various offenses. If a doctor performs an operation that is unsuccessful, his hand is to be cut off. In the Mosaic legislation only one instance of mutilation occurs where a wife's hand is to be severed (Deut. 25:11, 12). Also in the Hebrew laws a greater value is set upon human life. A stricter regard for the honor of womanhood is seen and more humane treatment of slaves is enjoined. In addition, the Babylonian code has nothing in it corresponding to that twofold golden thread running through the Mosaic legislation, namely love to God and love to one's neighbor (Matt. 22:37–40).

The Israelite Torah and the Babylonian code may be contrasted as follows: In the Babylonian code there is no control of lust, no limitation of selfishness. The postulate of charity cannot be found. The religious motif is absent, which recognizes sin as the destruction of the people because it is in opposition to the fear of God. In the Hammurabi code every trace of religious thought is absent. Behind the Israelite laws stands the ruling will of a holy God. The laws are stamped throughout with a divine character.

2. The Elephantine Papyri—Light on the Ezra-Nehemiah Era

Discovered in 1903 on the island of Elephantine at the First Cataract of the Nile in Egypt, these important documents give an interesting glimpse of one of the outlying regions of the Persian Empire in the latter part of the 5th century B.C. *The Elephantine Papyri* come from a Jewish military colony which was settled at that place. Inscribed in Aramaic, the language of diplomacy and trade throughout western Asia in the Persian period, and which was gradually replacing Hebrew as the everyday tongue of the Jewish people, the contents are varied, ranging from the copy of the Behistun Inscription of Darius to such a document as a Jewish marriage contract. The letters tell us about the sacking of a Jewish temple at Elephantine in an anti-Jewish persecution about 411 B.C. The Jews at this far-off colony worshiped the Lord whom they referred to by the name of Yahu.

Other letters from Elephantine which have in recent years become known and have been published by the Brooklyn Museum demonstrate that the temple was rebuilt after its destruction. They contain mention of Yahu as "the god who dwells in Yeb, the fortress." Compare Psalm 31:3. These new papyri demonstrate that Egypt was still under the authority of Persia in the first years of Artaxerxes II (404–359 B.C.).

The Elephantine Papyri therefore illuminate the general background of the period of Ezra-Nehemiah and the earlier Persian period. They shed important light on the life of the Jewish dispersion in a remote frontier place such as Elephantine in Egypt. They also are invaluable in giving the scholar a knowledge of the Aramaic language of that period, and many of the customs and names that appear in the Bible are illustrated by these important literary finds.

3. The Hittite Monuments from Boghaz-Keui—Mementos of an Imperial People

In 1906 Professor Hugo Winkler of Berlin began excavations at Boghaz-Keui, a site which lies 90 miles east of Ankara in the great bend of the Halys River in Asia Minor. It was discovered that this was an ancient Hittite capital. Numerous clay tablets were dug up written in texts containing six different languages. A large number of these were inscribed in the cuneiform characters of the Hittite language. Eventually deciphered through the labors of three men and particularly of the Czech scholar Friedrich Hrozny, this language proved to be the key to a great deal of background of interest to the biblical student.

Before the Boghaz-Keui tablets revealed the Hittites to be an ancient people, the biblical refer-

Elephantine Island seen from across the Nile.   *Matson Photo Service*

ences to them used to be regarded in critical circles as historically worthless. In the five books of Moses, references to the Hittites as inhabiting the land of Canaan and as among those whom the Israelites drove out occur in several places (Ex. 33:2; Deut. 7:1, 20:17; Josh. 3:10, 24:11). In the various lists the order varies, and there is not an inkling that one reference might be the name of a powerful imperial people and the other a small local tribe. Less than a century ago the "Hittites" meant little more to the reader of the Bible than the "Hivite" or the "Perizzite" still does.

It was commonly known from the biblical record that when Abraham settled in Hebron he had Hittites as neighbors. It was everyday knowledge that one of David's eminent soldiers was Uriah, a Hittite. But who would have expected that "Hittites" were more prominent than "Gadites" or "Beerothites"?

Now it is known that two great periods of Hittite power are to be noted. The first goes back to c. 1800 B.C., and the second is dated from c. 1400–1200 B.C. In this latter period of Hittite supremacy the powerful rulers reigned at Boghaz-Keui. One of these was named Subbiluliuma. This great conqueror extended his em-

pire to the confines of Syria-Palestine. The great Rameses II of Egypt, in the famous battle of Kadesh, collided with Hittite power. A Hittite treaty of peace with the Pharaoh in the 21st year of the latter's reign was confirmed by a royal marriage.

About 1200 B.C. the great Hittite Empire collapsed, and the Hittite city of Boghaz-Keui fell. However, important centers of Hittite power remained at Carchemish, Sengirli, Hamath, and other places in north Syria. As a result of the excavation and decipherment of various Hittite monuments, the whole context of the ancient biblical world has been illuminated.

Because of this increased background knowledge, such allusions as those to the "kings of the Hittites" (1 Kin. 10:29; 2 Chr. 1:17) are much better understood. Also Ezekiel's reference to unfaithful Jerusalem as having an Amorite for a father and a Hittite for a mother (Ezek. 16:45) are now comprehensible. The manner in which archaeology has brought to light the ancient Hittites furnishes a good example of the way this important science is expanding biblical horizons.

4. The City of Ur—Abraham's Home

An important metropolis of the ancient world,

Ur was located on the Euphrates River in lower Mesopotamia, present-day Iraq. Several centuries before Abraham lived there as a boy and grew up there as a young man, this place was a very important city under the 2nd and 3rd dynasties of Ur, an important line of kings. But the glory of the city was suddenly destroyed in the period from c. 1960–1830 B.C. Foreigners stormed down from the surrounding hills and took the reigning king, Ibi-Sin, a captive and reduced the capital *city of Ur* to ruins. So complete was the eclipse of the city that it lay buried in oblivion for centuries until, like Nineveh, it was resurrected in modern times by the work of archaeologists.

So thoroughly was the ancient city blotted out that when it was referred to in Genesis 11:28–31 and 15:7 as Abraham's ancestral home and the place from which he started on his trek to Palestine, some scribe later had to append the descriptive phrase *"of the Chaldeans"* to the name of the city to give later readers some idea of where it had been located.

The long-lost and buried city was brought to the light of modern study by the work of numerous archaeologists, particularly by the work of Sir Leonard Woolley (1922–1934). Until the year 1854, the site of the ancient city was completely unknown. The Arabs used to call the location *Al-muqayyer, "Mount of bitumen."* It was a forbidding place in a climate of terrific heat and surrounded by intense desolation. In 1854, J. E. Taylor, an English archaeologist, assisted by others, made some preliminary excavations. Some

cylinders turned up inscribed in cuneiform characters declaring that King Nabonidus of Babylon (556–539 B.C.) had restored the famous ziggurat of Ur-Nammu.

Later explorations were made by Campbell Thompson in 1918. H. R. Hall in 1918 continued other excavations, but it was left for the pivotal work of Sir Leonard Woolley, undertaken in 1922 as a joint expedition of the British Museum, the University of Pennsylvania, and the University Museum, to give a complete history and description of the city. The expedition completed twelve very successful archaeological campaigns, and by 1934 the long-lost and buried city of Ur, vanished from the pages of history, had become one of the best-known sites in all the ancient Near East.

Abraham's Native Town. Abraham lived in the city of Ur at the height of its splendor under the 3rd dynasty of kings. This is indicated if we follow the chronology of the Masoretic text of the Hebrew Bible. According to this system of reckoning, Abraham was born c. 2161 B.C. and entered Canaan c. 2086 B.C. Under this time arrangement, the patriarch left the city when it was near the acme of its prosperity. He entered Canaan precisely when Ur reached the pinnacle of its power, for the 3rd dynasty of kings (c. 2070–1969 B.C.) lifted the city to great prominence.

The first king was Ur-Nammu. This monarch had the title of "King of Sumer and Akkad." He built a splendid temple tower or ziggurat at this site. Today this is still preserved as the best monument of its type in all the flat alluvial territory

The city ruins at Ur.   *Matson Photo Service*

The Ziggurat at Ur.   *Matson Photo Service*

of Lower Mesopotamia, the basin of Tigris-Euphrates rivers. It was this structure that Nabonidus, the last of the Babylonian kings, restored in the 6th century B.C.

In the famous *monument of Ur-Nammu* there is extant a contemporary record of the construction of the ziggurat at Ur. This stele is a slab of white limestone measuring 5 feet across and 10 feet in height. At the top of the monument the king is standing in an attitude of prayer. An account of the building of the monument is given, and scenes are inscribed denoting the actual construction. In the days of Ur-Nammu other buildings were built around the ziggurat, and the entire sacred area was dedicated to Nannar, the moon god (patron deity of the city) and his consort, whose name was Nin-Gal.

A king by the name of Dungi succeeded Ur-Nammu, whom Nabonidus declared completed the ziggurat. Dungi was a great ruler who built a magnificent mortuary temple and tomb for himself. His son Bur-Sin succeeded him. He was followed on the throne at Ur by Gimil-Sin and then by Ibi-Sin.

Ur and Abraham. When Abraham lived in the city before he left for Haran and Canaan, Ur was a center of religion and industry. The city was wholly given over to the worship of the moon god cult. The Babylonians were devotees of many deities. But at Ur the moon god Sin was supreme.

Sir Leonard Woolley's lengthy excavations in twelve highly rewarding campaigns have revealed the splendor and the size of the city and also have given details of the *temonos* or the religious section of the city. In other words, Abraham was surrounded on all sides by idolatry. This we have recorded in the Bible in Joshua 24:2. "From ancient times your fathers lived beyond the River, *namely*, Terah, the father of Abraham and the father of Nahor, and they served other gods."

The moon god Sin was given such epithets as "the exalted lord" and "the beautiful lord who shines in the heavens." The immense temple tower, built like a mountain with various stages, contained the holy chamber of Nannar on its uppermost level. Here in this lofty Babylonian temple mystic ritual in honor of the deity was conducted. In front of the immense ziggurat and on the lower level was an open court, a kind of holy market where the people brought their gifts and paid their taxes to the king, who was also their landlord. Accordingly, the city was a kind of theocracy centered in the moon deity.

The sacred area was called the *temenos*. In it were located other sacred buildings and shrines, including houses for the priests and priestesses of Nannar. To the west the river Euphrates flowed near the city walls, and there were canals running around and through the city. In Abraham's day instead of being a hot, forbidding, desert-like region, Ur was a flourishing and beautiful city because of irrigation and civilization. It was surrounded by fertile farms and a busy populace engaged in agriculture and in woolen and textile industries. All of this commerce was centered in religion.

The houses of Ur have been excavated and examined. It is conceivable that Abraham grew up as a lad in one of these residences. There is presumptive evidence that Terah's father worshiped the moon god and was a devotee of Nannar and Nin-Gal. In one of the dwellings, there is a small

domestic chapel with altar niche and family burial vault. It is very likely that Terah worshiped at such an altar.

It is out of this polluted atmosphere of polytheism that God's sovereign grace called Abraham to begin a new line that was to be separated from idolatry and through which Messiah was to come, who would deliver the world from sin and idolatry.

The City Before the Time of Abraham. Ur existed as a brilliant city many hundreds of years before Abraham appeared on the scene. The lower regions of the Tigris-Euphrates basin with its flat land and very fertile soil have been the seat of many ancient empires—Sumer, Babylonia, Assyria, and Chaldea. The first of these civilizations was Sumer, one of the oldest civilized countries in the world. Wrapped in obscurity is the story of the beginnings of Sumer. At least by 3500 B.C. the Sumerians, that is the natives of the flat, alluvial lower courses of the Tigris-Euphrates plain, were advancing in civilization.

In the next thousand years the *Sumerian Empire* diffused culture and civilization over most of western Asia. The extreme southern part of Sumer was called the land of Shinar. It was a flat, mud plain, immensely rich, formed by the sediment of the Tigris-Euphrates River. As these mighty streams flowed into the lower part of the Fertile Crescent, their current slackened, and they deposited huge amounts of a rich, sandy loam and formed a region which today is called Iraq, which is about as large as New Jersey.

With a network of canals running through this rich territory, this region blossomed like a rose. More than 150 years ago, travelers began to wonder about the strange mounds or hillocks of earth which dotted this flat region. What could they possibly be? Now and then antiquarian bits of carved marble or other remnants of bygone civilizations were exposed by the weather. Archaeologists began to dig beneath the truncated hillocks, and it was discovered that they were long-lost and buried cities.

One of these mounds proved to be the city of Ur of biblical fame. From these regions many tablets have been resurrected with cuneiform or wedge-shaped writing on them. These tablets were made of soft mud from the riverbank and carefully inscribed with a flat pen and set out in the sun to dry, or put in the fire to bake in a more firm form. And so, under these truncated mounds were not only buried artifacts and remnants of ancient civilizations but, what is most arresting, there are vast quantities of practically indestructible materials, all inscribed on clay tablets. These have been the basis of resurrecting the history and the civilization of Bible lands in Lower Mesopotamia in the land of Sumer.

The First Dynasty of Ur. In an ancient list of kings called the Sumerian King List in *The Oxford Edition of Cuneiform Texts II*, 1923, by F. Langdon, an interesting story is told of the early rulers of Sumer. Among the line of kings who reigned at Kish, Uruk (biblical Erech, Gen. 10:10), Awan, Adap, Mari, and Akshak are listed several dynasties who ruled at Ur. The first kings at Ur witnessed the culminating phase of the early dynastic period in Mesopotamia (c. 2800–2360 B.C.).

The King List goes on to say, "Uruk was smitten with weapons. Its kingship was carried to Ur. Mes-Anne-pada became king and ruled 80 years. A-Anne-pada, a son of Mes-Anne-pada, reigned . . . years. Meskiag-Nanna, a son of Mes-Anne-pada became king and reigned 36 years. Elulu reigned 25 years. Balulu reigned 36 years. Four kings reigned 177 years. Ur was smitten with weapons."

This line of kings was very powerful and lifted the city-state, since Ur was more than a city, to a high level of culture. This is demonstrated in the discoveries of the royal tombs by Sir Leonard Woolley, dating from c. 2500 B.C. These consisted of rooms and vaults built of brick and stone. Among one of the most interesting finds was the tomb of an important lady named *Shubad of Ur.* Her name is identified by an inscribed cylinder of lapis lazuli. Near her hand was a gold cup. Her lovely artistic headdress contained 9 yards of gold band.

Another exquisite find was the so-called *"Standard of Ur."* This was a wooden panel, 22 inches long by 9 inches wide, skillfully inlaid with mosaic work on both sides depicting scenes of war and peace. In the war panel the king is seen receiving captives. In another the phalanx of the royal army advances. Scenes of fighting with chariots and javelins are depicted. The panel of peace presents a royal family feast. Musicians entertain while servants wait in the banquet hall and bring in spoils captured from the enemy.

The Euphrates River.   *Matson Photo Service*

Certainly the archaeological resurrection of Abraham's ancient city of Ur has greatly illuminated the Bible references to the patriarch and given a much wider view of the historical horizons c. 2000 B.C. The early civilization of the Tigris-Euphrates Valley is becoming better known year after year. Bible dictionaries, encyclopedias, commentaries, and biblical works of every description are highly indebted to the restless and productive spade of the archaeologist. Certainly God has blessed, enabling scholars in our day to study these monuments and other remains of antiquity. The result is greater appreciation of the Bible on the human plane.

It must always be remembered that the Word of God is not only divine but human. It is God's Book for man. On the human side, God has so ordained that the horizons of biblical knowledge may be expanded and increased that we may on the spiritual plane better comprehend the Word of God. How unfortunate it is when the spiritual is divorced from the historical and archaeological, or vice versa, when the historical and archaeological are divorced from the spiritual. The two work hand in hand and help one another. Happy is the student of the Bible who will combine both of these disciplines in a better understanding of the Word of God.

5. The Religious Texts from Ras Shamra (Ugarit)—Canaanite Cults Exposed

One of the most important discoveries of the 20th century was the recovery of hundreds of clay tablets which have been housed in a library situated between two great temples, one dedicated to Baal and another dedicated to Dagon, in the city of *Ugarit*—modern *Ras Shamra* in north Syria. These clay tablets date from the 15th to early 14th centuries B.C. They are inscribed in the earliest-known alphabet written in wedge-shaped signs. Professor H. Bower of the University of Halle recognized this new writing as Semitic. Numbers of scholars such as E. Dhorme and Charles Virolleaud began working on the decipherment of this new Semitic language.

The tablets turned out to be religious and cultic in nature and inscribed in a dialect that was closely akin to biblical Hebrew and Phoenician. Although Semitic in form, this new writing displayed evidences of Akkadian influence, since Mesopotamians wrote on clay tablets with wedge-shaped characters from left to right. First intimations of the archaeological importance of the ancient city of Ugarit, which was unknown until 1928, came in the spring of that year when a Syrian peasant plowing in his field a little north of present-day Minet el-Beida suddenly came across some antiquities. On April 2, 1929, work began at Minet el-Beida under the direction of Claude F. Schaffer. After a month's work he changed to the nearby tell of Ras Shamra. Only a few days' work demonstrated the importance of the new location. On May 20th the first tablets were uncovered. Schaffer continued excavations from 1929 to 1937. Between 1929 and 1933, the bulk of significant religious texts were recovered in the royal library in the area. Many of these were inscribed in an early Canaanite dialect, roughly contemporary with the Mosaic age.

The City of Ugarit. This flourishing second-millennium city, which had been known by scholars from Egyptian inscriptions from the *Tell el Amarna Letters* and *Hittite documents,* was located on the north Syrian coast opposite the island of Cyprus, about 8 miles north of Latakia and 50 miles southwest of Antioch. It was situated on a bay and had a port which could be used by sea-going trade ships. It was a harbor town known in Greek times as Leukos Limen, the white harbor. It is now called *Ras Shamra, "hill of fennel,"* because fennel grows there.

The hill which comprises the ruin of the ancient city has the form of a trapezium with the long side about 670 yards north and south and the longer diagonal about 1,100 yards. The hill is about 22 yards high. The site was located on the important trade route along the coast from Egypt to Asia Minor, which was connected by a road with Aleppo, Mari on the Euphrates, and Babylon. The sea route from Ugarit to Alashiya—that is, Cyprus—was a short one.

Very early, Ugarit struck up a brisk trade with the Aegean Islands. It became an important harbor. One of the main exported articles was copper, which was used in the production of bronze. Copper was imported from Asia Minor and Cyprus. Bronze was produced in Ugarit. Being a Phoenician town, Ugarit, like its sister cities, delivered timber to Egypt. Not only cedars from the interior were exported but other kinds of wood as well. There were also purple dye factories, great heaps of murex shells indicate this. These shells, abundantly found along the east Mediterranean coast, produced a famous dye of antiquity.

Literary Importance of the Texts. After preliminary work by many scholars, Cyrus Gordon worked out a **Ugaritic Grammar** and later put out an edition of the texts called **Ugaritic Literature.** The decipherment of the texts showed the important parallels between Ugaritic and Hebrew literary style and vocabulary. By 1936 H. L. Ginsberg had made some far-reaching observations with regard to common structural elements. Ginsberg's study showed that Canaanite poetry, like Hebrew, was basically accentual, that is, consisted of numbers of feet, each of which was accented. A good example of the survival of Canaanite literary elements in Hebrew religious literature is the following tricolon (unit of three lines) from the *Baal Epic of Ras Shamra:*

"Behold, thine enemies, O Baal;
Behold, thine enemies shalt thou crush;
Behold, thou shalt smite thy foes."

In *Psalm 92:9* there is a striking parallel to this.

"For, behold, Thine enemies, O LORD,
For, behold, Thine enemies will perish;
All who do iniquity will be scattered."

The following tricolon occurs frequently in the
Aqhat Epic:

"Do thou ask for life, O lad Aqhat;
Do thou ask for life, I'll grant it thee,
Eternal life, and I'll accord it thee."

A similar literary device is found in the *Song of
Deborah* (Judg. 5:30).

"To Sisera a spoil of dyed work,
A spoil of dyed work embroidered,
Dyed work of doubled embroidery on the
neck of the spoiler?"

Background material such as this is an invaluable aid in the study of Hebrew poetry and the general literary qualities of style and vocabulary in Old Testament Hebrew. Since the Ugaritic language is very closely connected with biblical Hebrew, much light has been shed upon Hebrew lexicography. Any recent lexicon of Hebrew must take into consideration the vocabulary used at Ugarit. Future Hebrew dictionaries will include many words hitherto misunderstood or only partially known.

For example, the word *beth-heber* (Prov. 21:9; 25:24) hitherto rendered "house" has been shown from Ugaritic and Assyrian to mean specifically "a storehouse." These verses could be rendered: It is better to dwell in a corner of a housetop, than in a storehouse shared with a contentious woman. It is of interest to note that the Egyptian proverbs of Amenemope, which have many parallels to the biblical Book of Proverbs, employs a word for "storehouse" in exactly the same sense.

Religious Significance of the Ugaritic Inscriptions. By far the most important contribution of the religious texts from Ras Shamra (Ugarit) is in giving the Bible student background material for the study of Old Testament religions. The epics set forth very clearly the *Canaanite pantheon.* We now know that this pantheon of the Canaanites was headed up by the god El, the supreme Canaanite deity. This is also a name by which God is known in the Old Testament (cf. Gen. 33:20). This name, El, often occurs in Old Testament poetry (Ps. 18:31, 32; Job 8:3). It occurs frequently also in prose in compound names, for example, El Elyon, the God Most High (Gen. 14:18); El Shaddai, God Almighty (Gen. 17:1); El Hai, the living God (Josh. 3:10). This, however, does not mean any connection, of course, with Canaanite mythology. El is simply the common Semitic word for God. In Ugaritic, El was a bloody, lustful tyrant. The description of him, as well as of other Canaanite gods, fully substantiates the testimony of the Old Testament with regard to the degeneracy and polluting influence of Canaanite religion.

Baal was the son of El. He was the active king of the gods in the Canaanite pantheon and dominated the entire list of gods. He was the deity of the storm and the rain. Thunder was thought to be the reverberation of his voice in the heavens. At Ras Shamra a stele was discovered depicting Baal holding a stylized thunderbolt. Three of the Ugaritic poems concern Baal. Baalism, the worship of this god, was one of the most debilitating and destructive influences which threatened the Hebrews in Palestine and against which they had to be continually on guard.

As the giver of rain and all fertility, Baal figures very prominently in Canaanite mythology. He struggles with Mot, the god of death and the god of drought. In the fight Baal is slain. As a consequence, the seasonal drought occurs from June to late October. Then Anath, sister and lover of Baal, goes out in search of him, discovers his body, and slays his enemy, Mot. Baal is then brought back to life, thus ensuring the revival of vegetation for a seven-year period. The great Baal Epic of Ugarit finds in this representation a central theme.

The Phoenicians at Ugarit not only had gods who were polluted and immoral but also goddesses. Three of these who are prominent are Anath, Astarte, and Asherah. They are patronesses of war and sex. Their character, like that of El and Baal, bears out the pollution and damaging effects of Canaanite religion, since they portray war in its aspect of violence and murder and sex mainly in its lustful connotation of indulgence.

The new knowledge of Canaanite religion aids the Bible student correctly to evaluate the testimony of the Old Testament to the Canaanites. Higher criticism has impugned the morality of the Old Testament writers in such episodes as the divine command to exterminate these cults. Examples are the extermination of the people of Jericho, Saul's extermination of the Amalekites, and the driving out of the Canaanites in general. All of these examples appear in a different view when adjudged in the light of the vileness of Canaanite religion. In Genesis 15:16 the Lord declares, "the iniquity of the Amorite" was not yet "complete" in Abraham's day. But archaeology shows Canaanite religious immorality was complete in Joshua's day, 400 years later, and had to be destroyed.

Now, as a result of the Ras Shamra literature, the nature of Canaanite religion comes before the scholar in its real light. No longer do we have to rely on the witness of early church fathers such as Eusebius, who quotes an earlier authority, or Philo of Byblos, who in turn goes back to a much earlier authority named Sanchuniathon. No longer must we doubt the veracity of this extra-

biblical witness or doubt the authenticity of the Old Testament witness. Now, as a result of archaeology, an independent witness to the effete and degenerate nature of Canaanite cults is available. No longer can critics isolate the Old Testament and accuse it of a low morality in ordering the extermination of the Canaanites. The truth is, archeology points out that the people had become so immoral, so honeycombed with the sins of violence and sexual immorality, that had Joshua and the children of Israel not appeared to take over the land, these people would have perished under the weight of their own iniquity.

"Like priest, like people" is an old adage. Never in all the annals of history was there such a mixture of violence and lust as was combined and made an intricate part of Canaanite cults. So the Scriptures stand as a warning, corroborated by archaeology, of the judgment of God falling upon apostate and sinful religionism. Archaeology helps us to see this in an entirely different light in regard to the Canaanites.

This is especially true when we consider the low moral tone of Canaanite goddesses and gods. El was a brutal and lustful tyrant who was guilty of incest and murder. Baal also was guilty of enormous crimes. How could people worship such deities and not themselves be polluted? No wonder the warning of God was issued again and again for separation from Baalism. No wonder the history of Baal contamination of Israel is a long story of woe and suffering, as God's people were trapped into complicity with Phoenician cults.

The era of Ahab and Jezebel, and the importation of Canaanite fertility cults and intermarriage with the Canaanites, show the devastating effect of such disobedience to the plain warning of God. Exterminating the Canaanite in the time of Joshua was not a question of destroying innocent people. It was a question of destroying or being destroyed, separating or being contaminated, being quarantined from the plague or having the plague destroy everyone.

Later Excavations at Ugarit. During World War II excavations at Ras Shamra were discontinued. They were resumed in 1948 and have been going on regularly. Work under the direction of C. F. Schaffer has been centered upon uncovering the great palace. The most important discoveries in connection with this structure were the royal archives. These archives, discovered in the palace, were of a historical nature in contrast to the mythological ritual texts of the early years, 1929–1937. The archives in the west wing of the building contained administrative documents to a large degree relating to the royal estates. Those in the east wing had documents relating to the capital city. Those in the central archive were mainly legal finds. Almost all documents were inscribed in the common language of these centuries, namely Akkadian. A few were written in Hurrian

and Ugaritic. The names of twelve Ugaritic kings were found in the documents which date from the 18th to the 13th centuries B.C. The seals of the royal acts are remarkable as they all are identical in design at the top, without regard to the name of the reigning king. The motif is well known from Babylonian glyptic art and shows homage being paid to the deified king.

Numbers of fine objects have been recovered from the palace, especially pieces from the king's bedroom. Especially noteworthy was the large ivory foot panel of the royal bedstead, perhaps the largest single piece of ivory carving yet recovered in the Near East. Another remarkable piece found in the campaign of 1952–53 is the ancient Ugaritic alphabet of thirty letters. This piece is now housed in the National Museum at Damascus.

6. The Nuzi Tablets and the Biblical Horites

From this city east of ancient Asshur and a short distance west of Arrapkha, which flourished in the middle centuries of the 2nd millennium B.C., have come several thousand cuneiform texts. These texts have proved of immense value, illustrating the rise of the Hurrians and patriarchal customs. The present site of Nuzi is Yoghlan-Tepe. It is a mound 150 miles north of Baghdad near the foothills of southern Khurdistan. Nuzi was excavated in 1925–1931 by the American School of Oriental Research in Baghdad and Harvard University. The name "Nuzi" was used during its occupation by the Hurrians.

Before the time of the Hurrian settlement the site of Nuzi was occupied by a different ethnic group, called the Subarians. In this older period, the city bore the name of Gasur, and its earliest occupation goes back to prehistoric times. But the vital interest in the town stems from its occupation by the Hurrians and the cuneiform texts which have been excavated from it and from nearby Arrapkha, modern Kirkuk, some 9 miles to the east.

The Nuzi Tablets and the Hurrians. Modern archaeology has not only resurrected the ancient Hittites, who were for centuries practically unknown except for sporadic references on the pages of the Bible, but also the enigmatic Horites. In the books of the Pentateuch there are numbers of references to a perplexing people called Horites. These people were defeated by Chedorlaomer and the invading Mesopotamian army (Gen. 14:6). They were governed by chiefs (Gen. 36:20–30). They are said to have been destroyed by Esau's descendants (Deut. 2:12, 22).

This unknown people used to be thought of as a very local, restricted group of cave dwellers. The name "Horite" was thought to be derived from the Hebrew *hor*, "hole" or "cave." Other than this etymological description the Horites remained completely obscure, not appearing outside the

Pentateuch or in extrabiblical literature. Within the last 35 years, however, archaeology has performed a miracle in resurrecting the ancient Hurrians, the biblical Horites. They are known not to be a local, restricted group but to be a prominent people who took a preeminent place on the stage of ancient history. It is now known that they not only existed but played a far-reaching role in ancient Near Eastern cultural history. As a result of the discovery of the Hurrians, the popular etymology which connects them with "cave dwellers" has had to be abandoned.

The Hurrians or Horites were non-Semitic peoples who, before the beginning of the 2nd millennium B.C., migrated into northeastern Mesopotamia. Their homeland was in the region south of the Caucasus. They appear first upon the horizon of history c. 2400 B.C. in the Zagros Mountains east of the Tigris River. In the period c. 2000–1400 B.C., the Hurrians were very common and widespread in Upper Mesopotamia.

The Nuzi Tablets and the Patriarchs. The main interest of the Nuzi Tablets lies in the illumination of patriarchal times and customs. In the patriarchal narratives, many local practices have been quite obscure to the modern reader. Numerous clay tablets from Nuzi and nearby Arrapkha have in many cases illuminated these customs, so that now we see them as they existed in the general historical background of the time. Although the Nuzi Tablets are to be dated in the 15th and 14th centuries B.C., sometime after the patriarchal period (c. 2000–1800 B.C.), nevertheless, they illustrate the times of the patriarchs. The reason is that when the patriarchs came out of Ur, they sojourned in Haran and mingled in west Hurrian society. But the same customs prevailed by extension among the west Hurrians as among the east Hurrians at Nuzi and Arrapkha. Hence, the results obtained at Nuzi are valid by extension for the west Hurrians, as well as for a period considerably later than the patriarchs.

In Genesis 15:2 Abraham laments his childless condition and the fact that his servant Eliezer was to be his heir. In the light of this situation, God assures the patriarch that he is to have a son of his own to inherit his property. The Nuzi Tablets explain this difficult matter. They tell how a trusted servant, an apparent outsider, could be heir. At ancient Nuzi, it was customary in Hurrian society for a couple who did not have a child to adopt a son to take care of his foster parents as long as they lived, take over when they died, and then in return for his filial duty to become their heir. But it is important to note that if a natural son was born, this agreement was nullified, at least in part, and the natural son became heir. Eliezer was plainly Abraham's adopted son. But the miraculous birth of Isaac, as the promised posterity, altered Eliezer's status as heir.

At Nuzi a marriage contract occasionally included the statement that a given slave girl is presented outright to a new bride, exactly as in the marriage of Leah (Gen. 29:24) and Rachel (29:29). Other marriage provisions specify that a wife of the upper classes who was childless was to furnish her husband with a slave girl as a concubine. In such a case, however, the wife was entitled to treat the concubine's offspring as her own. This last provision illuminates the difficult statement in Genesis 16:2 with its punning: "I shall obtain children through her" which means "I shall be built up through her." It is interesting to note that the related law of Hammurabi, paragraph 144, offers no complete parallel. There the wife is a priestess and is not entitled to claim the children of the concubine for herself.

It is thus seen that in Nuzian law and society in which the patriarchs moved for a time, marriage was regarded primarily for bearing children and not mainly for companionship. In one way or another, it was considered necessary for the family to procreate. After Isaac's birth, Abraham's reluctance to comply with Sarah's demand that Hagar's child be driven out is illustrated by local practice at Nuzi. In the event the slave wife should have a son, that son must not be expelled. In Abraham's case, only a divine dispensation overruled human law and made the patriarch willing to comply.

Cases involving rights of the firstborn occurring in Genesis are also illustrated. In the Bible Esau sells his birthright to Jacob. In the Nuzi Tablets one brother sells a grove which he has inherited for three sheep. Evidently this in value is quite comparable to the savory food for which Esau sold his right.

In Hurrian society birthright was not so much the matter of being the firstborn as of paternal decree. Such decrees were binding above all others when handed down in the form of a deathbed declaration introduced by the following formula: "Behold now, I am old." This situation helps to illuminate Genesis 27, the chapter that tells of Jacob stealing the family blessing.

The obscure *teraphim* are also explained in Nuzian law. We now know that the teraphim were small household deities. Possession of them implied headship of family. In the case of a married daughter, they assured her husband the right to her father's property. Laban had sons of his own when Jacob left for Canaan. They alone had the right to their father's gods. The theft of these important household idols by Rachel was a notorious offense (Gen. 31:19, 30; 35). She aimed at nothing less than to preserve for her husband the chief title to Laban's estate.

The texts from Arrapkha and Nuzi have at last supplied details for explaining these difficult customs. In special circumstances the property could pass to a daughter's husband, but only if the father had handed over his household gods to his

son-in-law as a formal token that the arrangement had proper sanction.

Another custom illuminated is that found in Genesis 12:10–20; 20:2–6; 26:1–11, where the wife of a patriarch is introduced as his sister with no apparent worthy reason. The texts from Nuzi, however, show that among the Hurrians marriage bonds were most solemn, and the wife had legally, although not necessarily through ties of blood, the simultaneous status of sister, so that the term "sister" and "wife" could be interchangeable in an official use under certain circumstances. Thus, in resorting to the wife-sister relationship, both Abraham and Isaac were availing themselves of the strongest safeguards the law, as it existed then, could afford them.

Critical Value. Discoveries such as those at Nuzi and Arrapkha are forcing higher critics to abandon many radical and untenable theories. For example, not long ago it was customary for critics to view the patriarchal stories as retrojections from a much later period and not as authentic stories from the Mosaic age, namely, the 15th century B.C. But now the question rises: How could such authentic local color be retrojected from a later age? The Nuzi Letters have done a great service to students of early Bible history in not only attesting the influence of social customs in the patriarchal age and in the same portion of Mesopotamia from which the patriarchs come,

but also have demonstrated these narratives are authentic to their time. Such discoveries add greatly to our historical background and enable us in our modern day to reveal them in their genuine local color and historical setting.

7. The Mari Letters—Light on the World of the Patriarchs

One of the most historically and archaeologically rewarding sites that has been discovered in Mesopotamia and Bible lands is the city of *Mari,* modern Tell el-Hariri on the Middle Euphrates, about 7 miles northwest of Abu-Kemal, a small town on the Syrian side of the Syro-Iraq frontier. The ancient city owed its importance to being a focal point on caravan routes crossing the Syrian desert and linking the city with Syria and the Mediterranean coast and with the civilizations of Assyria and Babylonia. This site was further identified by William Foxwell Albright in 1932.

Mari began to be excavated in 1933 by Andre Parrot under the auspices of the Musee du Louvre. The results were the digging up of an ancient imperial city of great importance and splendor. World War II interrupted excavations in 1939, after six highly successful campaigns had taken place. In 1951 this work was resumed. After four further campaigns it was broken off in 1956, as a result of the trouble over the Suez Canal.

The excavated ruins of the capital city of Babylon.   *Photo by D. J. Wiseman*

Among the most important discoveries at Mari was the great *temple of Ishtar,* for the Babylonian goddess of propagation, and a temple tower or ziggurat. The temple itself had courts of the Sumerian type, columns, and a cella. The ziggurat or temple tower was similar to that at Ur and other Mesopotamian sites. Statuettes were uncovered to illustrate the popularity of the Ishtar fertility cult. One of the palace murals depicts the fact that the ruling monarch at Mari was believed to have received his staff and ring, the emblems of his authority, from Ishtar.

Another important discovery at Mari was the *royal palace.* A sprawling structure contemporary with the 1st dynasty of Babylon, it was built in the center of the mound and contained almost 300 rooms. The throne room furnished some rare specimens of well-preserved wall paintings. This huge building with its beautifully colored mural paintings, its royal apartments, administrative offices, and scribal school is considered one of the best preserved palaces of the Middle East. The structure was built by later Amorites, who worshiped the deities Adad and Dagon. In the postwar campaign the excavation centered mainly around the older strata going back to buildings of the pre-Sargonic period from the time of the dynasty of Akkad.

The Royal Archives. The most interesting finds, however, were the so-called *Mari Letters,* some 20,000 clay tablets dug up and which have revolutionized knowledge of the ancient biblical world. These documents were written in the dialect of Old Babylonian. They date from the era of Hammurabi, c. 1700 B.C., the same monarch whose code was discovered in 1901 at Susa. These records constitute memoranda of the king and governors of the city-state of Mari, and belong to the time of the kings Yasmah-Adad, under whose reign the construction of the palace was begun, and Zimri-Lim, under whom it was completed. Some of the correspondence is that of King Yasmah-Adad with his father, the powerful empire builder King Shamshi-Adad I of Assyria, as well as with the representatives of the provinces of his realm. King Zimri-Lim's correspondence also figures in exchanges of diplomatic correspondence with King Hammurabi of Babylon, as well as with the king of Aleppo and other vassals. Two letters dispatched from Aleppo to Zimri-Lim deal with prophetic utterances delivered in the name of the god Adad of Aleppo. The subject and tenor of these remind one of biblical prophecies.

Biblical Value of the Mari Texts. These records are of great value to biblical students because they stem from the region which was the home of the Hebrew patriarchs for a number of years before going on to Canaan. However, Abraham's migration from Ur, according to preserved biblical chronology, apparently took place some 400 years before the era of Zimri-Lim and the fall of Mari.

At this time of the 3rd dynasty of Ur, Mari was ruled by the governors of the kings of Ur. Eventually, however, a prince of Mari, Ishbi-Irra, who had brought the city-state of Isin under his dominion c. 2021 B.C., was instrumental in bringing about the downfall of the city of Ur.

Nahor, which figures prominently in the patriarchal narratives (Gen. 24:10), is mentioned quite often in the Mari Letters. One letter from Nahor is sent from a woman of that town to the king and runs as follows:

To my lord say, Thus Inib-Sharrim, thy maid servant. How long must I remain in Nahor. Peace is established and the road is unobstructed. Let my lord write and let me be brought that I may see the face of my lord from whom I am separated. Further, let my lord send me an answer to my tablet.

The term "Habiru," very important since Abraham is the first individual in the Bible to be named a "Hebrew" (Gen. 14:13), is found frequently in the Mari Letters, as is also the case in the Nuzi Letters. In both instances the term apparently means "a wanderer," "one who crosses over," or "one who passes from one place to another." This explanation fits Abraham and the early patriarchs very well since they were nomadic travelers.

When Abraham left Ur in southern Mesopotamia to migrate to Canaan, he no doubt passed through the magnificent city of Mari. There can be little doubt that he and Terah with their families put up in one of the caravansaries there. Perhaps they spent days or weeks in the famous city and went sightseeing in the palace traces of whose grandeur are still visible to the eye of the modern archaeologist.

The city of Mari was idolatrous and in it there was the widespread practice of divination. A diviner was an important official in all phases of daily life at Mari. People went to him for advice in ordinary difficulties of life. Commanders saw him for help in the movement of their troops.

The patriarchs were remarkably free from occult practices and contamination from paganism and divinatory phenomena in general. This fact is true despite the teraphim (household gods) of Rachel and despite the "foreign gods" which Jacob ordered put away and which he hid under a terebinth tree in Shechem (Gen. 35:2–4).

Interestingly, the Mari Letters refer to "sons of the right," that is, "sons of the south," since the directions were taken as one faced the east, and the south would be on one's right hand. These were a fierce tribe of wanderers and called Benjaminites, but they have no connection with the "Benjamites" of the Bible. The name "Benjamin," "son of the south," that is, "southerner," was a term suited to occur in various places, es-

pecially in Mari, where the parallel term "sons of the left," that is, "sons of the north," is found.

The Bible presents Benjamin as being of Palestinian birth after Jacob's return from Mesopotamia. He is set forth as never having been in Mesopotamia at all. Genesis 49:27 describes Benjamin as a "ravenous wolf." This fits the description of the veteran tribe at Mari remarkably well. Any connection, however, is obviously dubious and purely imaginary.

Another interesting sidelight is the fact that the word translated "chieftain," with reference to the plundering Benjaminites, is *dawidum*, meaning "leader." This sheds light on the etymology of the name of Israel's most renowned king, who evidently had a name meaning "the leader."

Historical Value of the Mari Letters. These documents establish that Shamshi-Adad I of Assyria, who ruled c. 1748–1716 B.C., and Hammurabi the Great of Babylon, were contemporaries. With these facts and other details furnished by the Mari documents, the date of Hammurabi can be fixed c. 1728–1676 B.C. This and other evidence have forced scholars to give up identifying Hammurabi of Babylon with Amraphel (Gen. 14:1). The high antiquity of Genesis 14 has been vindicated, but archaeology has not yet succeeded in furnishing the background of the four Mesopotamian kings who invaded the Trans-Jordanic country in the days of Abraham.

Hammurabi was a strong military leader and a great administrator. He was a member of the strong 1st dynasty of Babylon which reigned from 1830 to c. 1550 B.C. The power of this dynasty reached its height under Hammurabi's rule. He was the greatest of all Babylonian rulers. Hammurabi defeated Rim-Sin of Larsa and established himself over all the city-states of Lower Babylonia. His expanding military machine enabled him to destroy Mari. It was his code of laws, as we have seen, that was discovered at Susa in 1901. This famous codification has remained classic in illustrating and illuminating Israelite laws.

It was during the reign of Hammurabi that the Babylonian story of creation was composed. The poem glorified Marduk, the patron god of Babylon, whom Hammurabi established as the national god of Babylonia. In this period, the early Sumerian language became an antiquity and Semitic-Babylonian came into common usage.

The Mari Letters and the Amorites. About 2000 B.C. the Semitic-nomadic peoples, who lived along the desert fringes of the Fertile Crescent, invaded the centers of established civilization. Known as "Westerners," they are preserved in the Old Testament as "Amorites." Amorite states came into existence all over the Mesopotamian area. Nahor, Haran, Mari, Qatna, and Ugarit all appear as Amorite cities with Amorite kings. Babylon itself became the capital of an Amorite state under Hammurabi. This important

historical fact is clearly reflected in the Mari Letters and in the peoples known as "Amorites" or "Westerners." In such a manner archaeology is slowly but surely outlining the historical framework of the patriarchal age. Such discoveries as the Mari Letters prove of incalculable assistance to the historian of the ancient biblical world.

8. The Lachish Ostraca—Jeremiah's Age Lives Again

In the excavations of Lachish, a southwestern Palestinian city, the most astonishing finds were some letters embedded in a layer of burnt charcoal and ashes. They were eighteen in number and were in Hebrew writing done in the ancient Phoenician script. Three more of these letters were discovered in later campaigns in 1938.

Almost all of the letters were written by one named Hoshiah, who was stationed at some military outpost, to Jaosh, who was evidently a high ranking officer in the garrison at Lachish. It was the era of the Babylonian overrunning of Palestine several years before the fall of Jerusalem in 587 B.C. The Babylonians had attacked and partly burned Lachish some ten years before in the reign of Jehoiakim. These particular letters were in the layer of ashes which represent the final destruction of the city. Accordingly, they are to be dated from 588 B.C., when Nebuchadnezzar was making the final siege of Jerusalem and also of Lachish and Azekah.

Identification of Lachish. This large mound, one of the largest occupied in Palestine, is located 30 miles southwest of Jerusalem, 20 miles inland from the Mediterranean and 50 miles west of Hebron. It is mentioned in the Amarna Letters and in earlier Egyptian sources. Its strategic importance is attested by its being on the main route from central Palestine to Egypt. It overlooked the rich Shephelah (terrain which descended to the coastal lowland). The fortress city was an ideal barrier between the Philistine plains and the elevated Judaean country. It was one of the principal fortified cities of Judah and one of the bastions taken by the Israelites in their conquest of Palestine (Josh. 10:31–35). The site of Umm-Lakis was first thought to be Lachish. Then the location was sought at Tell el-Hesy by Sir Flinders Petrie, a pioneer archaeologist. William Foxwell Albright finally identified it correctly with the large mound of Tell el-Duweir.

Nebuchadnezzar captured Lachish in 588–586 B.C. (Jer. 34:7). Marks of a huge conflagration on the road leading up to the gate and on the adjacent wall display that the attackers relied largely upon fire, for which felled olive trees not yet harvested supplied the fuel.

Excavations at Lachish. The Wellcome-Marston Archaeological Expedition in 1933 commenced work there, under the direction of J. L. Starkey. In 1938 Starkey was killed by Arab brig-

ands, and the work was carried on by Lankester Harding and Charles H. Inge.

The Results of the Excavation. Besides evidences of earlier occupation, Lachish disclosed settlement by the Hyksos c. 1720–1550 B.C. These people overran Egypt during this period. A typical Hyksos defense ditch or *fosse*, with a ramp of clay and lime that apparently provided an enclosure for their horses, was brought to light. In the fosse three Canaanite Egyptian temples built between 1450 and 1225 B.C. were excavated. A Persian temple of a much later period was also found. Cemeteries at Lachish yielded a great quantity of pottery, jewelry, scarabs, and skeletal evidence.

A well, 200 feet deep, was located within the city, the remains of a tremendous engineering excavation for water storage, which was not completed. A shaft about 85 feet terminates in a rectangle 80 x 70 feet cut to a depth of 80 feet. The aim was a water system which would have been much larger than that provided by Hezekiah for Jerusalem in the Siloam Tunnel and comparable to similar systems at Gezer and Megiddo.

A good quantity of inscribed material has been removed from the Lachish excavations. A bronze dagger from c. 1700 B.C. contains four pictographic signs, samples of the early script. A bowl and an ewer contain specimens of the same early writing as that found at Serabit el-Khadem. The name "Gedaliah" was found on a jar handle and may be the official whom Nebuchadnezzar set over the land after the fall of Jerusalem (cf. Jer. 40—42).

Contents of the Lachish Letters. But of all the epigraphic discoveries at Lachish, the most important are the Lachish Letters. These letters may be briefly described as follows: Letter 1 lists names, the majority of which are found in the Old Testament. Letters 2 and 5 consist largely of greetings. Letter 3, the longest, contains the most information. This concerns movements of Jewish troops and also makes an interesting note to an unnamed prophet and his word of warning. Letter 4 states that Hoshiah, though observing the signals of Lachish, cannot see those of Azekah. Azekah may well have fallen earlier, for this letter states "We are watching for the signal station at Lachish according to all the signals you are giving, because we cannot see the signals of Azekah." Letter 6 contains the biblical expression, "to weaken the hands of the people." This recalls Jeremiah, who uses a similar expression (Jer. 38:4).

Historical Importance of the Letters. The Lachish Letters give us an independent view of conditions in Judah in the last days before the fall of Jerusalem. As the Neo-Babylonian army advanced, the doom of Jerusalem was sealed, in contrast to its deliverance under the Assyrian, Sennacherib, as Isaiah had predicted (2 Kin.

A clay tablet showing the colophon at the end of a typical Assyrian library tablet. Found at Nineveh.   *British Museum*

19:20, 32–36). Relentlessly, Nebuchadnezzar advanced on the city after a terrible eighteen-month siege, 587 B.C. The walls of the city were broken down, the houses and the temple burned, and the people carried away to exile (2 Kin. 25:1–12).

Jeremiah conducted his difficult ministry in these agonizing times. His reference to Azekah and Lachish is most interesting. "When the army of the king of Babylon was fighting against Jerusalem and against all the remaining cities of Judah, *that is,* Lachish and Azekah, for they *alone* remained as fortified cities among the cities of Judah" (Jer. 34:7).

Tell Zakariya in the Shephelah region has been identified as Azekah. In 1898 it was excavated by Frederick K. Bliss of the Palestine Exploration Fund. It had a strong inner fortress buttressed with eight large towers.

The Lachish Letters concern the time just prior to the fall of the city and present the same conditions of turmoil and confusion that are revealed in the Book of Jeremiah. Numerous place names that occur in the Bible are found in the letters, as well as personal names. Hoshaiah appears in Jeremiah 42:1 and Nehemiah 12:32. God is referred to by the four-letter word YHWH, which are the consonants of the name "Jehovah" or "Yahweh." It is also interesting to note that many of the men's names have Yahweh endings. A prophet like Jeremiah is referred to in the letters. But this is most probably not Jeremiah himself.

So complete was the destruction by the Babylonians that it took many centuries for Judah to recover. The returned remnant was tiny and weak. The small Jewish state stamped its coins with the name "Yehud," that is, Judah, but not until after 300 B.C. do substantial archaeological remains appear, and then they are not abundant. Certainly the Babylonians did a thorough job of destroying Jewish power for many centuries.

The Paleographic Importance of the Letters. Being inscribed in biblical Hebrew, in which the Old Testament Scriptures were written, and with stylistic and vocabulary similarities to the Book of

Jeremiah, these letters are of great paleographic importance. They help the scholar to trace the evolution of the Hebrew alphabet, noting the formation of the letters and their style. They also enable him to see how the Old Testament Scriptures, which were then written, appeared.

Surely research of this type, that makes it possible for the scholar to look back, to resurrect the past, and to see how the language of the Old Testament developed, is fascinating. Great strides are being made in this field of inquiry. It is the one truly bright spot in original biblical studies. This type of study is of immense value in expanding historical backgrounds and illuminating Holy Scripture on the human plane.

9. The Dead Sea Scrolls

The middle of the 20th century saw the greatest manuscript discovery of modern times. In 1947 a young Bedouin shepherd stumbled upon a cave south of Jericho, containing many leather scrolls of Hebrew and Aramaic writing and about 600 fragmentary inscriptions. Great excitement prevailed in the archaeological world. In 1952 new caves containing fragments of later scrolls in Hebrew, Greek, and Aramaic were found. These and other startling manuscript discoveries have been followed by news of additional manuscripts found in other caves in the Dead Sea area.

A. The Date of the Scrolls. After intensive study of the manscripts from the Dead Sea area, scholars define three periods: 1. The Archaic Period c. 200–150 B.C. 2. The Hasmonaean Period c. 150–30 B.C. 3. The Herodian Period c. 30 B.C. to A.D. 70. The great majority originated in the 2nd and 3rd periods, especially the last half of the 2nd period and last half of the 3rd period.

Although attacks have been made against the antiquity and authenticity of these manuscripts, two lines of evidence substantiate their antiquity. **The evidence of radiocarbon count.** This scientific method of dating places the linen in which the scrolls were wrapped in the general era of c. 175 B.C. to A.D. 225. **Paleographic evidence.** Scholars conversant in this science date these documents by the form of the letters and the way they are written in comparison with other eras of writing. They are able to demonstrate that they come in the intermediate period between the script of the 3rd century B.C. and of the middle of the 1st century A.D. W. F. Albright observes, "All competent students of writing conversant with the available material and with paleographic method date the scrolls in the 250 years before A.D. 70."

B. The Contents of the Scrolls. The Dead Sea cave manuscripts contain material partly biblical and partly intertestamental. The biblical includes two scrolls of Isaiah, one complete, and most of the first two chapters of Habakkuk, and fragments of all Old Testament books except Esther. Large numbers of fragmentary manuscripts have been recovered from the Pentateuchal books and Isa-

The area near the Dead Sea where the Qumran scrolls were found.   *Matson Photo Service*

iah. Fragments of Psalms, Jeremiah, and Daniel are numerous.

The scroll of *Isaiah*, in the initial finds from the site of Qumran, has remained the best known of the discoveries. It was the first major biblical manuscript of great antiquity to be recovered. It is earlier by a millennium than the oldest Hebrew text preserved in the Masoretic Hebrew Bible. This Masoretic Hebrew Bible is the basis of all recent translations and does not go back any earlier than A.D. 900.

This fact of the antiquity of the Hebrew text of Isaiah, dating as early as 125–150 B.C., constitutes these discoveries as the greatest of modern times. They are the oldest existing manuscripts of the Bible in any language.

In the original group of manuscripts of 1947 were a commentary on Habakkuk and so-called *Manual of Discipline* of pre-Christian Jewish sect of Essenes. Of unusual interest were manuscripts later purchased by the Hebrew University of Jerusalem, containing a later Isaiah scroll more conformed to the traditional Hebrew, and a document of great interest called *"The War Between the Children of Light and Darkness."* This composition evidently issued from the Maccabaean struggles against Greek paganism in 158–137 B.C.

In winter, 1949, the first manuscript-bearing cave was excavated by two well-known Palestinian archaeologists, Pierre de Vaux and Lankester Harding. Recovered were fragments of Genesis, Deuteronomy, and Judges with a fragment of Leviticus in Old Hebrew script. Nonbiblical finds included a fragment of the *Book of Jubilees*, a work related to the Enoch literature, and some unknown material.

C. Other Manuscript-Yielding Sites. In 1952 a cave was uncovered at Murabbaat in another part of the desert. This yielded manuscripts chiefly from the 2nd century A.D. in Hebrew, Greek, and Aramaic, including a few texts of Genesis, Exodus, Deuteronomy, and Isaiah. Several Hebrew letters were discovered from the period of Simon ben Keseba, that is, Bar Cocheba, who led the revolt in 132–135. A notable exception to the 2nd century A.D. date of this material is an archaic Hebrew papyrus piece, a palimpsest, a list of names and numbers, dated in the 6th century B.C.

In the same general area, other caves have been found, one group in Khirbet Mird, northeast of the monastery of Mar Saba. These contain Arabic papyri, Greek and Christo-Palestinian-Syrian documents, with fragments of biblical codices, all late Byzantine and early Arabic. Another group of manuscripts date from the period of the bulk of the Murabbaat material. Among them is a version of the minor prophets in Greek and a corpus of Nabataean papyri, both of great biblical and historical importance.

D. Excavations at Khirbet Qumran. Khirbet Qumran was excavated between 1951 and 1954. This Essene community, with the nearby caves, proved to be the richest manuscript-yielding center. Members of this Essenic community copied these manuscripts and preserved them by hiding them in the caves. The Essenes at Khirbet Qumran, 7 miles south of Jericho near the shores of the Dead Sea, were next to the Pharisees and Sadducees in importance in sectarian Judaism. This site has become one of the most publicized places in Palestine because of the phenomenal manuscript finds in the cave-dotted cliffs.

Excavations at Khirbet Qumran have fully authenticated this site as the center of Essenic Judaism. As the result of the recovery of coins, pottery, and architectural remains, the story of Qumran's occupation can now be told. Four periods in the later history of the site are traced.

Period 1 extends from its founding c. 110 B.C. under John Hyrcanus. Numerous coins of this ruler were dug up, as well as of other Hasmonaean rulers including Antigonus, 40–37 B.C., the last ruler of this line, to the seventh year of Herod, 31 B.C. At this time an earthquake apparently leveled the site. Indications are that during Herod's reign the place was abandoned because of his antagonism.

Period 2 at Qumran dates from rebuilding and enlargement c. A.D. 1 and Roman destruction in June A.D. 68. During this era in the lifetime of Jesus, John the Baptist, and the early Christian apostles, Qumran flourished, influencing Judaism and the early Christian church. Coins have been found dating from the reign of Archelaus, 4 B.C. to A.D. 6, and from the time of the Roman procurators down to the second year of the first Jewish revolt in A.D. 66–70.

The Roman army, which took Jericho in June, A.D. 68, evidently likewise captured Qumran. One coin, marked with an X, belonged to the Tenth Legion. Iron arrowheads were found in a layer of burned ash in the excavation.

Qumran fell to Roman occupation. Some coins describe *Judaea Capta*. These date in the reign of Titus, A.D. 79–81, and mark **Period 3** as the Roman occupation after Jerusalem's destruction in A.D. 70. Evidence that Qumran structures were converted into army barracks indicates that a Roman garrison was stationed there from A.D. 68–c. A.D. 100. At this time the site apparently was abandoned.

Period 4. Qumran is distinguished by reoccupation of the site during the 2nd Jewish revolt, A.D. 132–135. Coins dating from this era indicate that here the Jews made their last stand to drive the Romans from their country. After that Qumran sank into obscurity.

Architectural Remains at Qumran. The main edifice at Qumran is 100 feet by 120 and formed the communal center and hub of the complex. At

the northwest corner was a massive defense tower with thick walls enforced by stone embankments. Some coins from the time of the 2nd Jewish revolt (A.D. 132–135) attest its use as a fortress against Roman power.

Alongside the general meeting room is the largest hall of the main building. Here was located the scriptorium. Several inkwells of the Roman period, and even some dried ink, indicate that the manuscripts had been copied by the community's scribes.

Also in the complex were two cisterns (artificial reservoirs) carefully plastered. There were installations for ablutions and baptisms. Of the possibly 40 cisterns and reservoirs, the bulk of them must have been used for storage of water in the very hot, dry climate.

Of great interest is the cemetery, containing about 1,000 burial places. De Vaux excavated many of these tombs. They are noted for their lack of jewelry and any evidences of luxury.

E. Khirbet Qumran and the Essenes. Not only do the excavations at Khirbet Qumran demonstrate that it was the headquarters of Essenic Judaism but three authorities, who were contemporary witnesses, attest the same fact, namely, Josephus, Philo, and Pliny. Pliny, for example, locates the Essenes at precisely the spot where Qumran is situated, namely, "on the west side of the Dead Sea." He also designates the town of Engedi as situated "below the Essenes."

Josephus relates their unselfish character, industry, and communal life. He extols their love for common toil, says they dressed in white, and describes their three-year probationary period before admission to the sect, and other phases of discipline. He also mentions their various lustrations and says that they numbered about 4,000. He comments on their celibacy, piety, convictions concerning immortality, and their belief in rewards for righteousness.

Philo gives a similar description of this group in Judaism. The library at Qumran attests their delight in the Bible and literature. This is reflected in information given by Philo and Josephus. The Essenes carefully copied Holy Scripture and took pains to preserve it.

There are difficulties in equating the Essenes at Qumran with the sect described by Philo, Pliny, and Josephus. Nevertheless, the likenesses far outweigh the differences. The evidence would seem to equate Qumran with the Essenes of the 1st century A.D.

F. The Essenes at Qumran and John the Baptist. Concerning John, Luke wrote: "And the child continued to grow, and to become strong in spirit, and he lived in the deserts until the day of his public appearance to Israel" (Luke 1:80). The home of John the Baptist's parents was in the hill country of Judea (Luke 1:39, 40, 65). Although

nothing is known definitely, it is easy to believe that John the Baptist did in some way come in contact with the Essenes. There are many characteristics in his own life that parallel theirs.

Both John and the Qumranites feature Isaiah 40:3 with regard to preparing "the way for the LORD." But John must have early realized that there were some features of the Essenes that were not conducive to preparing the nation for the advent of the Messiah, and so if he ever had a connection with them, he must have broken with them, giving himself to an active ministry of preaching repentance and baptizing in the Jordan Valley.

John's message featured repentance (Matt. 3:2; Mark 1:4; Luke 3:3). Repentance was also a vital note in Qumran theology. They belonged to a "covenant of repentance" and they called themselves "the penitents of Israel." The baptism of repentance, which John administered, was also paralleled by the Essenes who practiced water baptism. John's baptism was an outer indication of inward spiritual renovation, enabling the recipients to recognize the Messiah when He came.

Baptism among the Qumranites, however, was purely ritual, and the recipients were enjoined to separate themselves rigidly from any who did not belong to their community. The severe indictment of the Jewish nation, which was characteristic of John, was also characteristic of the Essenes. They looked upon those not belonging to their sect as "sons of darkness" connected with Belial. They regarded themselves as true Israel, living in accordance with the law. For them alone the baptismal rite could have meaning.

John featured the baptism "with the Holy Spirit and fire" (Matt. 3:11), the baptism with fire being the judgment upon the unrepentant in an eschatological sense. Such judgment of fire is described in a Qumran hymn under the figure of a fiery river overflowing in wrath "on the outcasts" and in "the time of fury for all Belial."

The baptism of the Holy Spirit, on the other hand, is prophesied by John to be the portion of those who would repent and receive the coming Messiah (John 1:33). In Qumran literature not only does God "sprinkle upon him," the Messiah, the spirit of truth as purifying water to cleanse Him from all abominations of falsehood and from the spirit of impurity, but the Messiah sprinkles His people with His Holy Spirit, constituting them His anointed ones.

John the Baptist was intensely missionary and evangelistic in his message. The Qumranites were self-centered, strictly sectarian, and did not spread their convictions. They did adopt children to train in their ways.

John the Baptist was given the honor of preparing the way for the Messiah and being His forerunner. The Qumran community did not recognize the Messiah when He came. Their as-

ceticism led to a deadend. It never conducted them to Him who would take away the sin of the world (John 1:29).

G. The Essenes and Jesus the Messiah. Although the Qumran community had a messianic hope, it was strikingly different from that of the Old Testament. They could not comprehend the combination of King and Priest in *one* Person (Zech. 6:9–15). Neither could they comprehend in the union of the same Person the additional office of a Prophet, although they did feature in their writings the messianic prophecy of "a prophet" (Deut. 18:18, 19).

Their great priest was Messiah of Aaron. Their great military leader, Messiah of Israel; their prophet comprehended in the rule of the community is set down alongside the "messiahs of Aaron and Israel," apparently as a separate messianic figure.

There are other similarities between the organization and teachings of the Qumran group and the teachings of Jesus and the formation of the Christian church. The passage in Matthew 18:15–17 has a striking parallel in Qumran literature.

It is easily seen that with this new material the background of the gospel stories is much more richly illustrated. The Last Supper, the Sermon on the Mount, and numerous other aspects of the earthly life and ministry of Jesus are fitted into a larger framework of historical background material, and to that extent are understood on the human side. However, it is transparently clear that the ministries of John the Baptist and Jesus remain unique. Qumran literature in no sense casts any shadow upon the unique Person and work of Jesus Christ. Christianity stands as authentically growing out of the Old Testament and not connected with later Gnosticism in a post-apostolic era that would jeopardize its historical genuineness.

H. The Dead Sea Scrolls and Literary Criticism of the New Testament. The Dead Sea material has had a stabilizing effect upon New Testament criticism. In the light of the new material, the New Testament appears as a Jewish book with a Christian theology with less Greek influence in its formation than Jewish, and there is reason to date the *synoptic gospels*, beginning with *Mark*, between A.D. 60 and 65.

Especially interesting is the dating of the *Gospel of John*. A radical criticism customarily dated this Gospel about A.D. 150 or later. Thus it was removed from apostolic tradition and treated more as an apocryphal book. Now it is well known that the Fourth Gospel reflects the genuine Jewish background of John the Baptist and Jesus and not a later 2nd century Gnostic milieu. This is clearly attested by the parallels to the conceptual imagery of John's Gospel in the Essenic literature from Qumran.

Jerusalem Temple inscription warning Gentiles against intrusion.   *Matson Photo Service*

There is every evidence to believe in the authenticity of John's Gospel, and there is not the slightest reason critically to date the Gospel after A.D. 90. Indeed, it may be quite a bit earlier. Thus the Dead Sea discoveries and the excavations at Qumran not only give additional background material to the inter-biblical and New Testament period but also help to stabilize higher criticism and purge out radical views that are now shown to be untenable.

The *Book of Hebrews* also is interesting. This is certainly to be definitely dated before the destruction of Jerusalem in 70 A.D. The treatise apparently was planned to offset the Essenic idea of "two anointed ones," one a prince and the other a priest. It was designed to present the Christian and Old Testament doctrine (cf. Zech. 6:9, 15; Ps. 110:1) that Messiah would be *both King and Priest in one Person*. Also the *Book of the Revelation* was doubtless penned toward the end of the 1st century, and, in the light of the Dead Sea Scrolls, may now possibly be dated earlier, that is before A.D. 70. This conclusion is based on its Hebraic background, being illuminated by the evidence from the Dead Sea manuscripts.

10. Jerusalem

Probably no excavation ever carried out has been as important as that carried on by Israeli institutions at the western and southern walls of the temple mountain in Jerusalem. The actual steps and entrances of Herod's temple have been uncovered as have the tiny shops and narrow streets where the merchants must have hawked their wares. The giant stone blocks from the top of the wall, which were thrown down into the streets by Titus's troops in A.D. 70, were found where they fell. In a grave in another part of the city was found the remains of a Jew who had been crucified by the Romans, the first physical evidence of this form of execution ever found. So extensive were these finds that it will be a generation before they are all deciphered and integrated into the historical framework of the Roman Age.

The thrilling story of biblical archaeology is not

yet completed. Other great discoveries as a result of continuous research in Bible lands promise even greater contributions to biblical studies in future years. For example, the recovery of thirteen Coptic codices from Nag Hammadi in Upper Egypt, since 1945, have almost rivaled the Dead Sea Scrolls in actual biblical importance. These even include the apocryphal "Gospel of Thomas" and are of inestimable value, especially from a critical standpoint in dating New Testament literature.

What new and exciting discovery affecting the Bible may we not expect the archaeologist's spade to turn up next? The prospect should engender a love for the Scriptures and a desire to study them employing history, linguistics, and archaeology as the means under the Holy Spirit to a more accurate understanding of the Bible's message to mankind.

11. Ebla

The modern Arabic name for this 140-acre mound in the Northwest corner of Syria is Tell Mardikh. Archaeologists of the University of Rome began digging this mound in 1964 and found an inscription in 1968 that identified this site as ancient Ebla. They uncovered portions of impressive *buildings from the time of the biblical Patriarchs* (1900–1700 B.C.); and beneath these were palaces and temples of the Early Bronze Age (2400–2250 B.C.). This was the discovery of an early but advanced civilization which was previously unknown.

In 1974, 1975, and 1976, three rooms of one palace yielded almost 7000 well-preserved *clay tablets* and about 13,000 fragments of other tablets *with cuneiform writing on them.* This archive of *ancient Sumerian and Canaanite literature* is very important. The tablets contain economic, political, and legal records of Ebla. (Understanding the cultures of Israel's neighbors aids biblical interpretation.) They show that Ebla was a merchant empire. Its rulers controlled trade routes that reached into the Mesopotamian Valley, into

the mountains of modern-day Turkey, and to the edge of the Nile Valley.

But more importantly, some tablets are *dictionaries*—the earliest known—providing the meanings of words used in both the Sumerian and early Canaanite (Eblaite) languages. (Languages help archaeologists understand the cultures.) Many Canaanite words at Ugarit and *Hebrew words in the Old Testament* can be understood more accurately because they also occur on these early tablets.

Many *place names* occur in the Ebla records, including those familiar to readers of the Bible: Haran, Damascus, Hazor, Beth-shan, Shechem, Joppa, Ashkelon, Jerusalem, Dor—and some scholars believe also Sodom and Gomorrah. Since the Bible itself presents these as real places, the Ebla tablets help support its historical reliability.

About 10,000 names of people are found on the tablets. Among them are *biblical names* such as Adam, Eve, Noah, Jubal, Abram, Ishmael, Hagar, Keturah, Bilhah, Israel, Micah, Michael, Saul, David, Jehoram, and Jonah. Although these names do not refer to the biblical personages, they establish that the names in Scripture are authentic.

Sometimes, however, the tablets contain mythic and legendary stories which conflict with the Scriptures (e.g., different creation accounts). Such cases illumine the biblical authors' polemics against pagan worldviews.

The excavation project continues until the present and may be expected to cast more light on the Bible's meaning and reliability.

Acknowledgements: The publisher gratefully acknowledges the cooperation of these sources, whose photographs appear in this article:

British Museum (80–7–19, 277)
G. Eric Matson Collection, The Episcopal House
Professor D. J. Wiseman

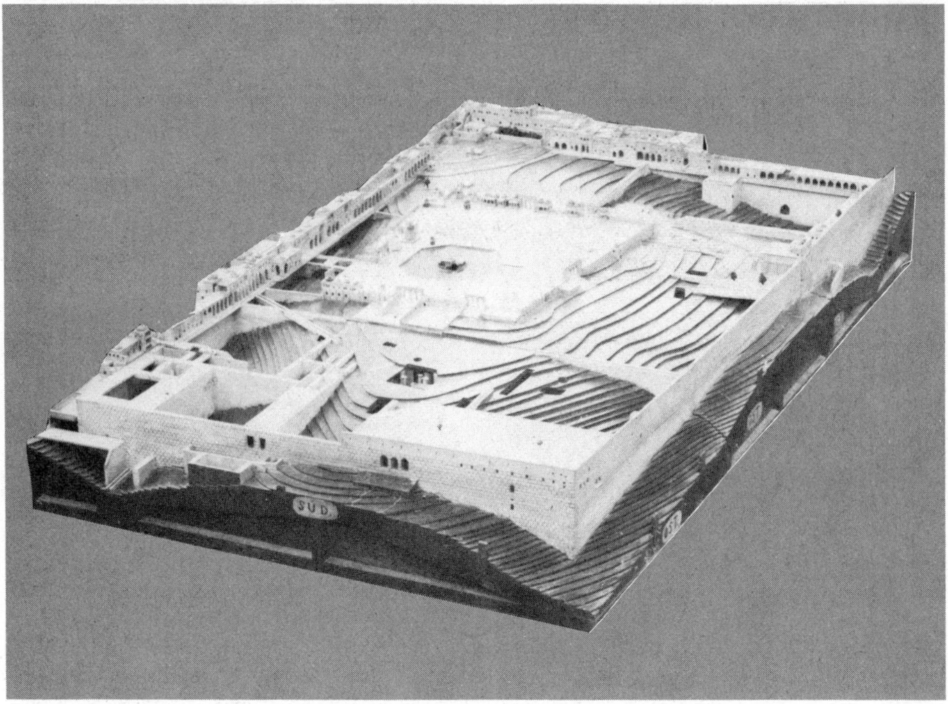

The Temple area in Jerusalem, showing the slope of the hill.   *Matson Photo Service*

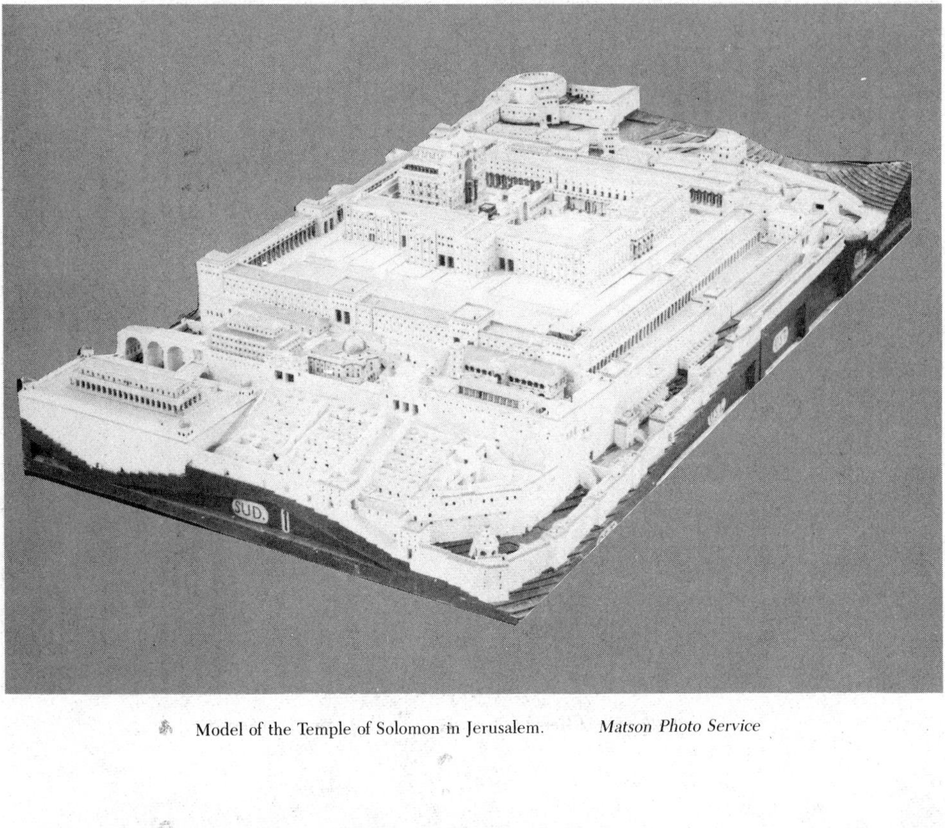

Model of the Temple of Solomon in Jerusalem.   *Matson Photo Service*

Model of the Temple of Zerubbabel in Jerusalem. *Matson Photo Service*

Model of the Temple of Herod in Jerusalem. *Matson Photo Service*

Concordance

The New American Standard

CONCORDANCE

to the

Old and New Testaments

A collection of the principal common words with their most widely used examples in text and lesser usages in reference. Related words, or synonyms follow the key word. The key word is abbreviated in the text to its first letter, e.g., "abide" is "**a**". Variants add suffixes or prefixes, e.g., "abiding" appears as "**a-ing**".

A

ABANDON—*leave* Judg. 6:13, LORD has **a-ed** us
1 Sam. 12:22; Ps. 94:14, LORD . . . a His people
2 Kin. 21:14, I will a the remnant
Ps. 27:9, Do not a me nor forsake me
Jer. 23:33, I shall a you
Acts 2:27, Thou wilt not a my soul to
27:20, hope of our being saved . . . **a-ed**
Ps. 16:10; Prov. 17:14; Is. 2:6; Jer. 12:7; Ezek. 29:5

ABASE—*humble* Ezek. 21:26; Mal. 2:9

ABATE—*decrease* Gen. 8:8,11, water was **a-d**
Deut. 34:7, his vigor **a-d**

ABBA Mark 14:36, saying, A! Father
Rom. 8:15, by which we cry out, A! Father
Gal. 4:6, crying, A! Father

ABHOR—*despise, detest, loathe* Rom. 12:9, A what is evil
Deut. 7:26; Job 19:19; Ps. 78:59; Prov. 24:24; Is. 49:7

ABIDE—*remain, stay* Ps. 9:7, the LORD **a-s** forever
Ps. 15:1, who may a in Thy tent
91:1, Will a in the shadow
102:12, LORD, dost a forever
John 3:36, wrath of God **a-s** on him
5:38, His word **a-ing** in you
8:31, you a in My word
14:25, while **a-ing** with you
15:4, A in Me . . . it **a-s** in the vine . . . you a in Me
15:6, If anyone does not a in Me
15:7, a in Me, and My words a in you
15:9, a in My love
15:10, you will a in My love . . . a in His love
1 Cor. 13:13, But now a faith, hope, love
Heb. 10:34, a better possession and an **a-ing** one
1 Pet. 1:23, living and **a-ing** word of God
1:25, BUT THE WORD OF THE LORD

1 John 3:17, how does the love of God a in him
4:12, God **a-s** in us

ABILITY—*strength* Ezra 2:69, according to . . . a
Dan. 1:4, who had a for serving
Matt. 25:15, according to his own a

ABLE—*adequate* 1 Sam. 6:20, Who is a to stand
Matt. 3:9, God is a from these stones
9:28, believe that I am a to do this
10:28, fear Him who is a to destroy
20:22, Are you a to drink the cup
John 10:29, no one is a to snatch them
Acts 6:10, they were **un-a** to cope with the wisdom
Rom. 8:39, shall be a to separate us
1 Cor. 10:13, tempted beyond what you are a
Eph. 3:18, may be a to comprehend
2 Tim. 2:2, who will be a to teach
James 4:12, the One who is a to save keep
1 Kin. 3:9; 2 Chr. 2:6; Rev. 5:3; 6:17

ABOARD Acts 21:2, went a and set sail

ABODE—*habitation* Jer. 31:23; Jude 6
John 14:23, and make Our a with him

ABOLISH—*destroy* Matt. 5:17, I did not come to a
Eph. 2:15, by **a-ing** in His flesh
2 Tim. 1:10, Christ Jesus, who **a-ed** death

ABOMINABLE—*detestable, rejected*
Jer. 44:4, do not do this a thing
Ezek. 16:25, made your beauty a
1 Pet. 4:3, drinking parties and a idolatries
Ps. 14:1; 53:1; Rev. 21:8

ABOMINATION—*detestable thing*
Ex. 8:26, an a to the Egyptians
Prov. 3:32, an a to the LORD
8:7, an a to my lips
Ezek. 33:29, because of all their **a-s**
Dan. 12:11, the a of desolation
Rev. 17:5, the **a-s** of the earth
Lev. 18:26; Deut. 7:26; 29:17

ABOUND—*excel, multiply*
Ex. 34:6, **a-ing** in lovingkindness and truth
Prov. 28:20, a faithful man will a with blessings
Dan. 4:1, May your peace a
Rom. 15:13, that you may a in hope
1 Cor. 15:58, always **a-ing** in the work of the Lord
1 Cor. 14:12; 2 Cor. 7:15; 9:8

ABOVE—*over* Ex. 20:4, what is in heaven a or on
Ps. 8:1, Thy splendor a the heavens

Matt. 10:24, A disciple is not a his teacher
John 3:31, He who comes from a is a all
8:23, I am from a
Phil. 2:9, the name which is a every name
Col. 3:1; 2 Thess. 2:4; James 1:17

ABSENT Gen. 31:49, we are a one from the other
1 Cor. 5:3, though a in body, but present
2 Cor. 5:6, we are a from the Lord
5:8, a from the body and to be
10:1, but bold toward you when a

ABSTAIN—*depart, separate* Num. 6:3
Acts 15:20, that they a from things
1 Thess. 5:22, a from every form of evil
1 Tim. 4:3, **a-ing** from foods, which
2 Tim. 2:19, who names . . . the Lord a from wickedness
1 Pet. 2:11, strangers to a from fleshly lusts

ABUNDANCE—*surplus, plenty, full, plenteous*
Gen. 41:34, seven years of a
Ps. 52:7, the a of his riches
72:7, And a of peace till
Is. 55:2, delight yourself in a
Matt. 13:12, and he shall have an a
Luke 12:15, when one has an a does his life
Rom. 5:17, receive the a of grace
Phil. 4:18, everything in full, and have an a
Gen. 41:29; Deut. 28:47; Neh. 9:25; Ps. 36:8; 72:16; 73:10; Prov. 24:6; Eccles. 5:10; Phil. 4:12

ABUNDANT—*plenteous* Job 36:28; Ezek. 16:49
Gen. 41:47, land brought forth **a-ly**
Ps. 86:5, a in lovingkindness to all
2 Cor. 1:5, our comfort is a through Christ

ABUSE Judg. 19:25, **a-d** her all night
1 Chr. 10:4, lest these . . . come and a me
Matt. 27:39, passing by were hurling a at Him

ABUSIVE—*filthy* Col. 3:8, a speech from your mouth

ABYSS—*deep, depth* Rom. 10:7, DESCEND INTO THE A
Rev. 20:3, threw him into the a
Luke 8:31; Rev. 11:7; 17:8; 20:1

ACCEPT—*receive* Deut. 33:11, And a the work

ACCEPT (Continued)
Job 2:10, **a** good from God and not **a** adversity
Jer. 2:30, They **a**-ed no chastening
Mark 4:20, hear the word and **a** it
Rom. 15:7, **a** one another
1 Tim. 1:15, statement, deserving full **a**-ance

ACCEPTABLE—favorable, pleasing Ps. 69:13, at an **a** time
Rom. 15:31, may prove **a** to the saints
2 Cor. 6:2, At the **a** time . . . the **a** time
Phil. 4:18, an **a** sacrifice
1 Tim. 2:3, good and **a** in the sight

ACCESS Eph. 2:18, have our **a** in one Spirit
Eph. 3:12, confident **a** through faith in Him

ACCOMPLISH—perform 1 Kin. 5:9, you shall **a** my desire
Ps. 57:2, God who **a**-es all things
John 4:34, and to **a** His work
James 5:16, prayer of a righteous man can **a**

ACCOMPLISHED—realized, wrought
Neh. 6:16, work had been **a** . . . God
Luke 1:1, things **a** among us
John 17:4, having **a** the work
Rom. 15:18, what Christ has **a** through me
James 1:15, when sin is **a**
Luke 12:50; John 19:28; 1 Pet. 5:9

ACCORD—unite Josh. 9:2; Acts 5:12
Acts 4:24, voices to God with one **a**
8:6, the multitudes with one **a**
12:20, one **a** they came to him
18:12, one **a** rose up against Paul
19:29, rushed with one **a** into the
2 Cor. 8:17, gone to you of his own **a**

ACCORDING Gen. 30:34, be **a** to your word
Matt. 16:27; Rom. 2:6, **a** to his deeds
Rom. 8:28, **a** to His purpose
Gal. 3:29, heirs **a** to promise
Rev. 22:12, render to every man **a**
Job 34:11; Jer. 17:10; John 7:24;
  18:31; Rom. 12:6; 16:25; 2 Cor. 8:12

ACCOUNT—declaration, sake, tell
Gen. 2:4, is the **a** of the heavens and the earth
8:21, curse the ground on **a** of man
Esth. 10:2, full **a** of the greatness of Mordecai
1 Sam. 12:22, on **a** of His great name
Matt. 5:11, evil . . . falsely on **a** of Me
Luke 1:1, compile an **a** of the things accomplished
Rom. 3:19, become **a**-able to God
Num. 12:11; Judg. 7:15

ACCUMULATE—heap 2 Tim. 4:3, **a** for themselves teachers

ACCURATE Job 31:6; Acts 18:25

ACCURSED Is. 65:20; Matt. 25:41
Josh. 6:18, make the camp of Israel **a**
Rom. 9:3, wish that I myself were **a**
1 Cor. 12:3, no one . . . says, Jesus is **a**
Gal. 1:8, let him be **a**

ACCUSATION—charge Ezra 4:6, wrote an **a** against

Dan. 6:4, find no ground of **a** or
John 18:29, What **a** do you bring against
Acts 28:19, had any **a** against my nation
1 Tim. 5:19, Do not receive an **a** against

ACCUSE—testify Matt. 27:12, while He was being **a**-d
John 5:45, I will **a** you before the Father
Acts 22:30, why he had been **a**-d by the Jews
Deut. 19:18; Titus 1:6

ACKNOWLEDGE—confess Ps. 32:5, I **a**-d my sin
Prov. 3:6, In all your ways **a** Him
Acts 23:8, Pharisees **a** them all
Rom. 1:28, see fit to **a** God

ACQUAINT Ps. 139:3, **a**-ed with all my ways
Is. 53:3, **a**-ed with grief

ACQUAINTANCE Ps. 88:8, removed my **a**-s far from me
Luke 23:49, all His **a**-s and the women
Job 19:13; Ps. 31:11; 88:18; Luke 2:44

ACQUIRE—get, purchase Ruth 4:10; Prov. 1:5; 18:15
Prov. 4:5, **A** wisdom! **A** understanding
4:7, with all your **a**-ing, get understanding
Matt. 10:9, Do not **a** gold, or silver

ACQUIT—cleanse Job 10:14; Ps. 19:12

ACT—behave Ps. 103:7, made known His . . . **a** to the
1 Cor. 16:13, **a** like men, be strong
John 8:4; 1 Cor. 13:5

A-s of Solomon,	1 Kin.	11:41
Jeroboam,		14:19
Rehoboam,		14:29
Abijam,		15:7
Asa,		15:23
Nadab,		15:31
Baasha,		16:5
Elah,		16:14
Zimri,		16:20
Omri,		16:27
Ahab,		22:39
Jehoshaphat,		22:45
Ahaziah,	2 Kin.	1:18
Joram,		8:23
Jehu,		10:34
Joash,		12:19
Jehoahaz,		13:8
Joash,		13:12
Jehoash,		14:15
Amaziah,		14:18
Jeroboam,		14:28
Azariah,		15:6
Zechariah,		15:11
Shallum,		15:15
Menahem,		15:21
Pekahiah,		15:26
Pekah,		15:31
Jotham,		15:36
Ahaz,		16:19
Hezekiah,		20:20
Manasseh,		21:17
Amon,		21:25
Josiah,		23:28
Jehoiakim,		24:5
David,	1 Chr.	29:29
Uzziah,	2 Chr.	26:22

ACTION—deed, work Acts 5:38, plan or **a** should be of men
1 Sam. 2:3; Dan. 11:28,32; Luke 23:51

ACTIVITY Eccles. 11:5, you do not know the **a** of God
2 Thess. 2:9, accord with the **a** of Satan

ADDER—serpent, viper Is. 59:5, They hatch **a**-s

ADJURE—implore 1 Kin. 22:16, many times must I **a**
Matt. 26:63, I **a** You by the living God
Acts 19:13, I **a** you by Jesus

ADMINISTRATION 1 Cor. 12:28, **a**-s . . . kinds of tongues
2 Cor. 8:20, in our **a** of this
Eph. 1:10, an **a** suitable to the fulness of the times
3:9, **a** of the mystery

ADMONISH—warn Acts 20:31, cease to **a** each one
Acts 27:9, Paul began to **a** them
Rom. 15:14, able also to **a** one another
1 Cor. 4:14, to **a** you as my . . . children
Col. 1:28, **a**-ing every man
3:16, **a**-ing one another with psalms
1 Thess. 5:14, **a** the unruly
2 Thess. 3:15, **a** him as a brother

ADOPTION Rom. 8:15, spirit of **a** as sons
Rom. 8:23, waiting eagerly for our **a** as sons
9:4, to whom belongs the **a**
Gal. 4:5, receive the **a** as sons
Eph. 1:5, predestined us to **a**

ADORN—clothe, array 1 Tim. 2:9, women to **a** themselves
1 Pet. 3:3, let not your **a**-ment
Rev. 21:2, as a bride **a**-ed for her husband
Job 40:10; Is. 61:10; Ezek. 16:11;
  Matt. 23:29; Luke 21:5; Rev. 17:4;
  18:16; 21:19

ADULTERATING 2 Cor. 4:2, not . . . **a** the word of God

ADULTERER Lev. 20:10; Ps. 50:18; Heb. 13:4

ADULTERESS—strange woman Prov. 22:14, mouth of an **a**

ADULTERY Ex. 20:14; Deut. 5:18;
  Matt. 5:27, 28; Luke 18:20; James
  2:11; 2 Pet. 2:14

ADVANCE Gen. 24:1; Luke 1:7

ADVANTAGE—profit Prov. 21:5;
  2 Cor. 2:11
Eccles. 1:3, What **a** does man have in all his work
7:12, the **a** of knowledge
John 16:7, to your **a** that I go away
2 Cor. 12:17, I have not taken **a** of you

ADVERSARY—opponent, foe
1 Cor. 16:9, and there are many **a**-es
Heb. 10:27, which will consume the **a**-es

1 Pet. 5:8, Your **a**, the devil
Ex. 23:22; 1 Kin. 11:14; Ps. 27:2;
89:23

ADVERSITY—*distress, privation*
Deut. 30:15; Job 2:10
Ps. 10:6, I shall not be in a
94:13, relief from the days of **a**
Prov. 17:17, is born for **a**

ADVISE—*inform, counsel* Num.
24:14; Rev. 3:18

ADVOCATE—*witness* Job 16:19,
my **a** is on high
1 John 2:1, we have an **A** with the
Father

AFFAIRS 1 Chr. 26:32, all the **a** of
God and . . . the king
2 Tim. 2:4, entangles himself in the **a**

AFFECTION—*devotion, passion*
2 Cor. 6:12, restrained in your
own **a**-**s**
7:15, his **a** abounds
Deut. 10:15; Phil. 1:8; 2:1;
1 Thess. 2:8

AFFLICT—*oppress, distress,*
trouble
Deut. 26:6, Egyptians . . . **a**-**ed** us
Judg. 16:5, we may bind him to **a**
him
Ps. 82:3, justice to the **a**-**ed** and
destitute
147:6, LORD supports the **a**-**ed**
Is. 61:1, bring good news to the **a**-**ed**
63:9, He was **a**-**ed**
Lam. 3:33, does not **a** willingly
2 Cor. 4:8, *we are* **a**-**ed** in every way
Ex. 1:11,12; 22:22,23; Num. 24:24;
2 Sam. 7:10; 1 Kin. 11:39; 2 Kin.
17:20; Ps. 105:18; Prov. 15:15;
Nah. 1:12

AFFLICTION—*misery, oppression*
Deut. 16:3, the bread of **a**
Job 36:15, delivers the afflicted in
their **a**
Ps. 25:18, Look upon my **a**
Mark 4:17, when **a** or persecution
arises
5:29, she was healed of her **a**
2 Cor. 2:4, out of much **a** and
anguish
8:2, in a great ordeal of **a**
2 Thess. 1:6, **a** those who afflict you
Gen. 29:32; 31:42; 41:52; Job 5:6;
30:16; Eccles. 6:2; Acts 20:23

AFRAID—*dread, fear* Ex. 3:6, **a** to
look at God
Deut. 20:8, Who is the man that is **a**
Ps. 56:4, not be **a**. What can *mere*
man
91:5, **a** of the terror by night
Is. 51:12, are **a** of man who dies
Matt. 14:27, do not be **a**
21:46, they became **a** of the
multitudes
Luke 9:34, they were **a** as they
entered
12:4, **a** of those who kill the body
Gen. 3:10; Ex. 20:20; Josh. 11:6;
Judg. 7:3; Job 9:28; 19:29; Prov.
31:21; Eccles. 9:2; Matt. 1:20;
Mark 4:41; 5:36; 9:32; 11:18; 11:32;
Luke 12:32; 19:21; John 9:22;
2 Cor. 11:3; 12:20; Heb. 13:6

AFTER Acts 13:22, **a** man My heart
Acts 24:17, **a** several years I came

Gal. 2:1, **a** an interval
Gen. 7:4; Judg. 16:22; Dan. 2:39

AFTERWARD—*later, after* Gen.
38:30, And **a** his brother came
Matt. 21:30, he **a** regretted *it*
Mark 16:14, And **a** He appeared

AGAINST Gen. 16:12, hand *will be* **a**
everyone
Lev. 20:3, set My face **a** that man
Matt. 12:30, not with Me is **a** Me
Gal. 5:23, **a** such things there is no
law
Rev. 2:4, have *this* **a** you
Gen. 4:8; Job 16:4; Luke 4:11; Acts
19:38; 1 Pet. 3:12

AGE—*world, generations, elder*
1 Chr. 23:1, Now when David
reached old **a**
Job 12:12, Wisdom is with **a**-**d** men
Matt. 12:32, this **a**, or in the **a** to
come
Luke 16:8, sons of this **a** are more
shrewd
John 9:21, he is of **a**, he shall speak
Eph. 2:7, that in the **a**-**s** to come
Col. 1:26, hidden from the *past* **a**-**s**
Heb. 6:5, powers of the **a** to come
Job 15:10; 32:7; Jer. 6:11; John 9:23;
Philem. 9

AGITATION Ps. 38:8, the **a** of my
heart

AGONY Luke 22:44, being in **a** He
was praying
Acts 2:24, putting an end to the **a** of
death

AGREE—*consent* Matt. 18:19, if two
of you **a** on earth
John 9:22, Jews had already **a**
Acts 5:9, Why is it that you have **a**-**d**
together
15:15, words of the Prophets **a**
28:25, when they did not **a** with one
another
Matt. 20:13; Acts 23:20; 1 Tim. 6:3

AGREEMENT Acts 8:1, Saul was in
hearty **a**
2 Cor. 6:16, what **a** has the temple
1 John 5:8, the three are in **a**

AILMENT—*infirmity* 1 Tim. 5:23,
and your frequent **a**-**s**

AIR 1 Cor. 9:26, not beating the **a**
Eph. 2:2, prince of the power of the
a
1 Thess. 4:17, meet the Lord in the **a**
Job 41:16; 1 Cor. 14:9

ALARM Jer. 4:19, The **a** of war
Num. 10:5,6,7,9; Ps. 31:22; 116:11;
Joel 2:1

ALAS—*woe* 2 Kin. 6:5, A, my
master! For it was
Judg. 6:22; 11:35; Amos 5:16

ALERT—*watch* Matt. 24:42; Acts
20:31, be on the **a**
1 Cor. 16:13, Be on the **a**, stand firm
1 Thess. 5:6, let us be **a** and sober

ALIEN—*stranger, foreigner*
Deut. 10:19, show your love for the **a**
14:21, **a** who is in your town
Acts 7:6, **a**-**s** IN A FOREIGN LAND

Eph. 2:19, no longer strangers
and **a**-**s**
2 Sam. 1:13; Ps. 69:8; Lam. 5:2

ALIENATED Col. 1:21, you were
formerly **a**

ALIVE Num. 16:33; 2 Kin. 5:7; Ps.
55:15
Gen. 43:7; 45:3, Is your father still **a**
Acts 1:3, presented Himself **a**
Rom. 6:13, those **a** from the dead
1 Cor. 15:22, Christ . . . made **a**
Eph. 2:5, made us **a** together with
Christ
1 Pet. 3:18, made **a** in the spirit
Rev. 1:18, I am **a** forevermore

ALL—*whatever* Jer. 1:7, And **a** that I
command you
Matt. 6:32, **a** these things the
Gentiles
Mark 16:15, Go into **a** the world and
preach
Luke 2:10, great joy which shall be
for **a** the people
3:6, A FLESH SHALL SEE THE
SALVATION OF GOD
4:6, I will give you **a** this domain
Acts 2:1, **a** together in one place
1 Cor. 10:26, LORD'S, AND **A** IT
CONTAINS

ALLEGORY Gal. 4:24, This contains
an **a**

ALLIANCE 1 Kin. 3:1, Solomon . . .
marriage **a** with Pharaoh

ALLIED 2 Chr. 18:1; Ps. 94:20

ALLOT Job 7:3, I **a**-**ed** months of
vanity
Rom. 12:3, as God has **a**-**ed** to each a
measure of faith

ALLOW Ex. 12:23, **a** the destroyer to
come
Ps. 16:10, **a** Thy Holy One to see the
pit
Acts 2:27, A THY HOLY ONE TO
UNDERGO
22:22, not be **a**-**ed** to live
1 Cor. 10:13, not **a** you to be tempted
1 Tim. 2:12, do not **a** a woman to
teach

ALLOWANCE 2 Kin. 25:30, for his **a**,
a regular **a** was given
Jer. 52:34, a regular **a** was given him

ALLY Gen. 14:13, these were **a**-**es**
with Abram

ALMIGHTY Gen. 17:1, I am God **A**
Ps. 91:1, shadow of the **A**
Rev. 4:8, *is* THE LORD GOD, THE **A**
11:17, the **A**, who art and who wast
Ex. 6:3; Job 11:7; 29:5; 37:23

ALMS—*charity* Matt. 6:2, therefore
you give **a**
Matt. 6:4, your **a** may be in secret
Acts 10:2; 24:17

ALONE Gen. 2:18, not good for the
man to be **a**
Matt. 4:4, MAN SHALL NOT LIVE ON
BREAD **A**
Luke 9:18, He was praying **a**
John 8:16, I am not **a**
Job 7:16; Mark 14:6

ALREADY—*utterly* Eccles. 1:10, A
it has existed for ages
Matt. 5:28, committed adultery with
her **a**
John 3:18, who does not believe . . .
judged **a**
9:27, He answered them, I told you
a
11:17, had **a** been in the tomb four
days
1 Cor. 5:3, I . . . have **a** judged him
who
6:7, it is **a a** defeat for you
2 Thess. 2:7, mystery of lawlessness
is **a** at work

ALTAR Ps. 43:4, I will go to the **a**
Ezek. 6:4, your **a**-s will become
desolate
Matt. 5:23, your offering at the **a**
Rev. 9:13, four horns of the golden **a**
Gen. 8:20; Ex. 17:15; Lev. 6:9; Judg.
6:24; Matt. 23:19

ALWAYS—*forever, ever* Matt.
28:20, lo, I am with you **a**
Mark 14:7, you do not **a** have Me
Phil. 4:4, Rejoice in the Lord **a**
1 Thess. 4:17, thus we shall **a** be with
the Lord
Deut. 14:23; 2 Tim. 3:7; Heb. 7:25

AM Ex. 3:14, I **A** WHO I **A**
Matt. 18:20, there I **a** in their midst
1 Cor. 15:10, grace of God I **a** what I
a
Gal. 4:12, brethren, become as I **a**

AMASS—*heap* Ps. 39:6, He **a**-es
riches

AMAZE—*astonish, astound*
Matt. 7:28, were **a**-d at His teaching
Luke 9:43, **a**-d at the greatness of
God
Rev. 13:3, the whole earth was **a**-d
Mark 2:12; Luke 24:22; John 9:30

AMAZEMENT—*astonishment* Acts
3:10, with wonder and **a**

AMBITION 1 Thess. 4:11, make it
your **a** to lead
James 3:14,16, bitter jealousy and
selfish **a**

AMBUSH—*wait* Josh. 8:2, Set an **a**
for the city
Josh. 8:4,7,12,14,19,21; Jer. 51:12

AMEN Num. 5:22, the woman shall
say, A. A
Ps. 41:13; 72:19; 89:52, A and A
Matt. 6:13, *the glory, forever.* A
Rev. 3:14, The A, the faithful and
true Witness

ANALYZE—*discern* Luke 12:56, **a**
this present time

ANCIENT—*aged, everlasting, old*
Deut. 33:15, of the **a** mountains
1 Chr. 4:22, the records are **a**
Ps. 24:7, be lifted up, O **a** doors
Dan. 7:9,13,22, A of Days
Matt. 5:21, the **a**-s were told

ANGEL Matt. 4:6, GIVE HIS **A**-S
CHARGE
Luke 20:36, for they are like **a**-s
22:43, an **a** from heaven appeared
John 20:12, beheld two **a**-s in white
2 Cor. 11:14, as an **a** of light

Col. 2:18, worship of the **a**-s
Gen. 24:7; Ps. 78:25; Is. 63:9; Matt.
1:20,24; 2:13; Acts 6:15; 23:8; Heb.
13:2; 2 Pet. 2:4; Rev. 2:1,8,12; 9:11

ANGER—*exasperation, wrath,
indignation*
Ex. 32:19, Moses' **a** burned
Deut. 13:17, from His burning **a**
Job 5:2, And **a** kills the simple
Ps. 30:5, His **a** is but for a moment
Prov. 15:18, the slow to **a**
22:24, a man given to **a**
Eph. 4:26, sun go down on your **a**
James 1:19, slow to speak *and* slow
to **a**
Gen. 39:19; 49:7; Ex. 22:24; Neh.
9:17; Job 9:13; Ps. 37:8; 38:1; Prov.
14:29; Eccles. 5:17; Is. 5:25; 51:17;
54:8; Gal. 5:20

ANGRY—*indignant, enraged*
Prov. 29:22, An **a** man stirs up strife
Is. 64:9, Do not be **a** beyond measure
Eph. 4:26, BE A . . . DO NOT SIN
Gen. 4:6; 18:30; Esth. 1:12; Jon. 4:4;
Matt. 5:22; Heb. 3:10

ANGUISH—*distress, pain* Ps. 55:4;
Is. 30:6; Jer. 6:24

ANIMAL—*beast, creature, cattle*
Gen. 6:7, from man to **a**-s to
creeping things
7:8, Of clean **a**-s and **a**-s that are
not
8:20, took of every clean **a** and
Acts 10:12, four-footed **a**-s and
crawling creatures
2 Pet. 2:12, like unreasoning **a**-s
Ex. 22:19; Ps. 104:25; Jer. 27:6

ANNOUNCE—*proclaim* Is. 52:7, **a**-s
peace . . . **a**-s salvation

ANNUAL 1 Sam. 7:16, used to go **a**-
ly on circuit

ANOINT Matt. 6:17, fast, **a** your head
Mark 14:8, she has **a**-ed My body
16:1, they might come and **a**
Ex. 28:41; Ps. 23:5; 105:15; Luke 7:46;
Acts 10:38; 2 Cor. 1:21; Rev. 3:18

ANSWER—*respond* Ps. 65:5, Thou
dost **a** us
Prov. 15:1, **a** turns away wrath
Eccles. 10:19, money is the **a** to
everything
Mic. 3:7, there is no **a** from God
Luke 2:47, amazed at . . . His **a**-s
Deut. 27:15; Ps. 55:19; Prov. 24:26;
26:4,5; Matt. 26:62; Mark 14:60;
John 19:9; Acts 12:13

ANT Prov. 6:6, Go to the **a**, O
sluggard
Prov. 30:25, The **a**-s are not a strong
folk

ANTICHRIST 1 John 2:18, **a** is
coming
2 John 7, the deceiver and the **a**
1 John 2:22; 4:3

ANXIETY—*sorrow* Ps. 38:18, full of
a because of my sin
Jer. 49:23, There is **a** by the sea

ANXIOUS—*worry, concern,
thought* Jer. 17:8
Matt. 6:25, do not be **a** for your life

6:27; Luke 12:25, being **a** can add a
single
6:31, Do not be **a** then, saying
6:34, be **a** for tomorrow
10:19, **a** about how or what you will
speak
Mark 13:11, do not be **a** beforehand
about what
Luke 12:26, why are you **a** about
other
Phil. 4:6, Be **a** for nothing

APART—*separate, without* Matt.
10:29, **a** from your Father
John 1:3, **a** from Him nothing came
into being
Acts 13:2, Set **a** for Me Barnabas
and
Rom. 3:28, justified by faith **a** from
works

APOSTASY—*backsliding,
faithlessness*
Hos. 14:4, I will heal their **a**
2 Thess. 2:3, *not come* unless the **a**
comes first
Jer. 2:19; 5:6; 8:5; 14:7

APOSTLE Matt. 10:2, names of the
twelve **a**-s
Rom. 1:1, called *as* an **a**
11:13, **a** of the Gentiles
Eph. 4:11, He gave some as **a**-s
Luke 11:49; 1 Cor. 15:9; 2 Cor. 12:11;
Gal. 1:19; 1 Tim. 2:7; 2 Tim. 1:11

APPALL—*astound, amaze,
astonish*
Job 17:8, upright shall be **a**-ed
Ps. 40:15, Let those be **a**-ed because
of their shame
143:4, My heart is **a**-ed within me
Lev. 26:32; Jer. 2:12; Ezek. 4:17;
Dan. 4:19

APPAREL—*garment* 2 Sam. 1:24,
gold on your **a**
Is. 63:1, is majestic in His **a**
Luke 24:4, two men . . . in dazzling **a**
Acts 12:21, put on his royal **a**

APPEAL—*ask, beg, entreat* Acts
25:11, I **a** to Caesar
Acts 28:19, I was forced to **a** to
Caesar
1 Tim. 5:1, **a** to him as a father
Philem. 9, for love's sake I rather **a**
to you
Acts 25:12,21,25; 26:32

APPEAR—*be seen* Gen. 12:7, LORD
a-ed to Abram
Ex. 3:2, **a**-ed to him in a blazing
Mal. 3:2, who can stand when He **a**-s
Acts 2:3, **a**-ed their tongues as of
16:9, a vision **a**-ed to Paul in the
27:20, sun nor stars **a**-ed for many
days
2 Cor. 5:10, we must all **a** before
Heb. 9:24, now to **a** in . . . of God for
us
9:28, shall **a** a second time
1 Pet. 5:4, Chief Shepherd **a**-s
1 John 3:2, it has not **a**-ed . . . if He
should **a**
Gen. 19:14; Num. 14:10; 2 Sam.
22:11; Matt. 1:20; 2:13; 27:53; Mark
16:9

APPEARANCE—*brightness,
radiance, sight*
1 Sam. 16:7, man looks at the
outward **a**

Matt. 6:16, for they neglect their **a**
28:3, his **a** was like lightning
Phil. 2:8, found in **a** as a man
2 Thess. 2:8, **a** of His coming
Num. 11:7; 1 Sam. 16:12; 2 Sam.
11:2; 14:27; Dan. 1:15; Nah. 2:4;
Luke 9:29; Rev. 4:3

APPETITE—*stomach, desire* Prov.
23:2, man of *great* **a**
Phil. 3:19, whose god is *their* **a**
Num. 11:6; Job 38:39; Eccles. 6:7;
Hab. 2:5; Rom. 16:18

APPLE Ps. 17:8, **a** of the eye
Prov. 25:11; Song 2:3,5

APPOINT—*name* Num. 3:10, you
shall **a** Aaron
1 Chr. 17:9, I will **a** a place for My
people
Jon. 1:17, **a-ed** a great fish to
swallow
Mark 3:14, He **a-ed** twelve, that they
Heb. 9:27, **a-ed** for men to die
Gen. 4:15; Job 36:23; Jer. 49:19; John
15:16; 1 Tim. 2:7

APPORTION—*distribute* Josh. 13:7,
a this land for an
Job 21:17, Does God **a** destruction
2 Cor. 10:13, sphere which God **a-ed**
to us

APPRAISE—*discern*
1 Cor. 2:14, they are spiritually **a-d**

APPROACH Matt. 21:34, the harvest
time **a-ed**
Luke 24:15, Jesus Himself **a-ed**
Lev. 18:14,19; Judg. 19:25

APPROPRIATE Eccles. 3:11,
everything **a** in its time
Ezek. 36:5, **a-d** My land for
themselves

APPROVAL Heb. 11:2, men of old
gained **a**
Heb. 11:39, having gained **a** through

APPROVE—*attest* Rom. 14:18, and
a-d by men
Rom. 16:10, **a-d** in Christ
2 Tim. 2:15, present yourself **a-d** to
God

APRON Acts 19:12, handkerchiefs or
a-s

ARCHANGEL 1 Thess. 4:16; Jude 9

ARGUE—*dispute, question* Mark
8:11
Prov. 25:8, out hastily to **a** *your case*
25:9, **A** your case with your
neighbor
Mark 9:14, *some* scribes **a-ing** with
them
Acts 9:29, talking and **a-ing** with
Hellenistic Jews

ARGUMENT Job 23:4, fill my mouth
with **a-s**
Ps. 38:14, whose mouth are no **a-s**

ARISE—*rise, stand* Gen. 31:13, **a**,
leave this land
Job 31:14, do when God **a-s**
Ps. 27:3, war **a** against me
Dan. 11:2, three more kings are
going to **a**
Matt. 11:11, has not **a-n** *anyone*
greater

24:11, false prophets will **a**
Acts 10:13, **A**, Peter, kill and eat
Eph. 5:14, AND A FROM THE DEAD
2 Pet. 1:19, morning star **a-s** in your
hearts
Deut. 9:12; Ps. 3:7; Song 2:13; Matt.
2:13,20; Acts 22:16

ARK Gen. 6:14, an **a** of gopher wood
Heb. 9:4, **a** of the covenant
Ex. 37:1; Matt. 24:38; Rev. 11:19

ARM (n.)—*hand, side* Deut. 33:27,
the everlasting **a-s**
Ps. 37:17, **a-s** of the wicked . . .
broken
Mark 10:16, took them in His **a-s**
Ex. 6:6; Job 26:2; Ps. 98:1; Song 8:6;
Is. 60:4; Zech. 13:6

ARM (v.) Num. 31:3, **A** men from
among you
Luke 11:21, a strong *man* fully **a-ed**
1 Pet. 4:1, **a** yourselves also

ARMOR—*weapon, harness* 1 Kin.
20:11; 22:34; Luke 11:22
Rom. 13:12, put on the **a** of light
Eph. 6:11,13, full **a** of God

ARMY—*host, war* Deut. 24:5; 1 Chr.
12:22; 2 Chr. 26:11

AROMA Gen. 8:21, LORD smelled the
soothing **a**
2 Cor. 2:16, **a** from death . . . **a** from
life

AROUSE—*raise, stir* Is. 42:13, He
will **a** *His* zeal like
Acts 13:50, Jews **a-d** the devout
women
Job 14:12; Is. 41:25; 45:13; Jer. 51:11

ARRAY—*adorn, clothe* Matt. 6:30,
God so **a-s** the grass
Judg. 20:20; Luke 12:28

ARROGANCE—*pride* Prov. 8:13,
Pride and **a** and the evil way
Is. 13:11, **a** of the proud
16:6, *Even* of his **a**, pride, and
Jer. 48:29, his **a** and his self-
exaltation
49:16, **a** of your heart has deceived
you

ARROGANT—*proud* Jer. 48:26,
become **a** toward the LORD
Rom. 1:30, insolent, **a**, boastful
Jude 16, they speak **a-ly**
Rev. 13:5, **a** words and blasphemies
Jer. 50:32; Dan. 5:20; 2 Pet. 2:18

ARROW—*dart, missile* 1 Sam.
20:36, he shot an **a** past him
Job 6:4, **a-s** of the Almighty
Jer. 9:8, Their tongue is a deadly **a**
Job 41:28; Ps. 45:5; Prov. 7:23;
Lam. 3:12

ART 2 Chr. 16:14, blended by the
perfumers' **a**
Acts 17:29, image formed by the **a**

ASCEND Ps. 24:3, may **a** into the hill
of
Ps. 139:8, If I **a** to heaven
John 3:13, no one has **a-ed**
6:62, behold the Son of Man **a-ing**
20:17, I **a** to My Father
Rom. 10:6, WHO WILL A INTO HEAVEN

ASH Gen. 18:27, am *but* dust and **a-
es**
Job 13:12, sayings are proverbs of **a-
es**
42:6, repent in dust and **a-es**
Ps. 102:9, eat **a-es** like bread
Is. 61:3, a garland instead of **a-es**
Matt. 11:21, repented . . . sackcloth
and **a-es**
Luke 10:13, sitting in sackcloth and
a-es
Lev. 6:11; Num. 19:17; 1 Sam. 2:8;
2 Sam. 13:19; 1 Kin. 13:3,5; Esth.
4:1; Job 2:8; 30:19; Ps. 147:16; Is.
44:20; 58:5; Jer. 6:26; Mal. 4:3;
Heb. 9:13

ASHAMED—*confused* Ps. 71:1, me
never be **a**
Mark 8:38, the Son of Man . . . **a** of
him
Rom. 1:16, not **a** of the gospel
Heb. 11:16, not **a** to be called their
God
Gen. 2:25; Ps. 25:2; Is. 24:23; 2 Tim.
1:8; 1 Pet. 4:16

ASHERAH, ASHERIM (pl.)
1 Kin. 15:13, made **a** . . . image as an
A
Ex. 34:13; 2 Kin. 17:10; 2 Chr. 19:3;
33:19; Mic. 5:14

ASIDE 1 Sam. 8:3, turned **a** after
dishonest gain
1 Pet. 2:1, putting **a** all malice

ASK—*appeal, beg, inquire* 1 Kin.
3:5, **A** what *you* wish
Ps. 27:4, One thing I have **a-ed** from
the LORD
Prov. 30:7, Two things I **a-ed** of Thee
Jer. 6:16, **a** for the ancient paths
Matt. 5:42, Give to him who **a-s** of
7:7, **A**, and it shall be given to you
Mark 10:38, not know . . . **a-ing** for
John 4:40, they were **a-ing** Him to
stay
14:16, I will **a** the Father
James 1:5, let him **a** of God
Ruth 3:11; Job 42:4; Ps. 2:8; Is. 7:11;
Zech. 10:1; Matt. 21:22; Mark
10:35; 11:24; Luke 11:11;
1 Cor. 1:22; 10:25; Eph. 3:13;
1 John 5:15

ASLEEP Matt. 9:24, not dead, but **a**
Mark 4:38, was in the stern, **a**
13:36, come suddenly and find you
a
John 11:11, Our friend Lazarus has
fallen **a**
Acts 7:60, having said this, he fell **a**
1 Cor. 15:6, some have fallen **a**
1 Thess. 4:14, those who have fallen
a in Jesus
5:10, whether . . . awake or **a**
Judg. 4:21; 1 Thess. 4:13,15

ASSEMBLE—*gather* 1 Chr. 13:5;
15:3, David **a-d** all Israel
Lev. 8:3; Num. 8:9; 20:8; Deut. 4:10;
31:12; Is. 43:9; Jer. 4:5; 8:14; Ezek.
11:17; Hos. 7:14; Amos 3:9

ASSEMBLY—*band, congregation,
convocation*
Ps. 1:5, in the **a** of the righteous
Joel 2:15, Proclaim a solemn **a**
Heb. 12:23, to the general **a** and
church
Ex. 12:16; Lev. 23:36; Num. 20:10,12;

ASSEMBLY *(Continued)*
Job 11:10; Ps. 26:5; 111:1; Acts 19:39

ASSERT Acts 25:19, whom Paul **a-ed** to be alive
1 Tim. 1:7, they make confident **a-ions**

ASSIGN—*distribute* 1 Cor. 7:17, Lord has **a-ed** to each

ASSOCIATE Rom. 12:16, but **a** with the lowly
Job 19:19; Ps. 50:18; Zech. 13:7; 2 Thess. 3:14

ASSURANCE—*confidence* Job 24:22, no one has **a** of life
Col. 2:2, full **a** of understanding
Heb. 6:11, full **a** of hope
10:22, full **a** of faith
11:1, faith . . . **a** of things hoped for

ASTONISH—*amaze, astound* Matt. 13:54, so that they became **a-ed**
22:33, they were **a-ed** at His teaching
Mark 6:2, many listeners were **a-ed**
7:37, they were utterly **a-ed**
10:26, they were even more **a-ed**
11:18, all the multitude were **a-ed**
Job 21:5; Matt. 19:25; Luke 1:63

ASTOUND—*amaze, astonish* Jer. 4:9, prophets will be **a-ed**
Dan. 8:27, **a-ed** at the vision
Mark 5:42; 10:26

ASTRAY—*err* Ps. 119:176, gone **a** like a lost sheep
Is. 53:6, sheep have gone **a**
1 Tim. 6:21, gone **a** from the faith
Ps. 119:110; Prov. 10:17; Is. 3:12; 9:16; Matt. 18:13; Heb. 3:10

ATE—*eat* Jer. 15:16, words were found and I **a** them
1 Cor. 10:3, all **a** the same spiritual food
Luke 13:26; 24:43; Acts 9:9

ATONEMENT—*reconciliation* Lev. 23:27; 25:9, the day of **a**
Ex. 30:15; 2 Sam. 21:3

ATTAIN—*acquire* Rom. 9:30, **a-ed** righteousness
Phil. 3:11, **a** to the resurrection

ATTENTION—*heed, regard* Prov. 4:1, give **a** . . . gain understanding
16:20, who gives **a** to the word
Is. 5:12, nor pay **a** to the deeds
Heb. 2:1, we must pay closer **a**
Ex. 5:9; Job 33:31; Prov. 29:12; 1 Tim. 1:4; 4:13

ATTEST Acts 2:22, a man **a-ed** to you by God

AUTHOR—*source* Heb. 12:2, the **a** and perfecter of faith

AUTHORITY Eccles. 8:8, **a** over the day of death
Matt. 7:29, teaching them as one having **a**
8:9, For I too am a man under **a**
9:6, **a** on earth to forgive
10:1, **a** over unclean spirits
21:23, By what **a** are You doing these things
28:18, **a** has been given to Me

Luke 5:24, Son of Man has **a** on earth to forgive
9:1, gave them power and **a**
19:17, be in **a** over ten cities
20:8, by what **a** I am doing these things
John 5:27, **a** to execute judgment
10:18, **a** to lay it down . . . **a** to take it up
17:2, Thou gavest Him **a** over all mankind
Acts 8:19, Give this **a** to me as well, so
Rom. 13:1, no **a** except from God
1 Cor. 15:24, all rule and all **a**
1 Tim. 2:12, to teach or exercise **a**
Titus 2:15, reprove with all **a**
2 Pet. 2:10, and despise **a**
Jude 25, majesty, dominion and **a**
Rev. 2:26, GIVE **A** OVER THE NATIONS
Num. 27:20; Is. 22:21; Hab. 1:7; Luke 10:19; 12:5

AVAIL—*profit* Jer. 7:8, deceptive words to no **a**

AVENGE—*vengeance, revenge* 1 Sam. 24:12
Jer. 5:9,29, Shall I not **a** Myself
2 Cor. 7:11, what zeal, what **a-ing** of wrong

AVOID—*refuse* Prov. 4:15, **A** it, do not pass by it
1 Tim. 6:20, **a-ing** worldly *and* empty chatter
2 Tim. 3:5, **a** such men as these

AWAIT—*wait* 1 Cor. 1:7, **a-ing** eagerly the revelation

AWAKE—*watch* Ps. 139:18, when I **a**, I am still with Thee
Eph. 5:14, **A**, SLEEPER
Rev. 16:15, Blessed is the one who stays **a**
Judg. 5:12; Ps. 17:15; Is. 51:9; John 11:11; Rom. 13:11

AWARE Luke 8:46, I was **a** that power had gone

AWE—*fear* Ps. 33:8, inhabitants . . . in **a** of Him
Ps. 119:161, stands in **a** of Thy words
Heb. 12:28, with reverence and **a**

AWESOME—*fearful* Gen. 28:17, How **a** is this place
Ex. 15:11, **A** in praises
Judg. 13:6, angel of God, very **a**
Neh. 1:5, the great and **a** God
Job 37:22, Around God is a majesty **a**
Ps. 89:7, **a** above all those . . . around Him
Song 6:4, **a** as an army with banners
Joel 2:31, great and **a** day of the LORD

AXE—*hatchet* 2 Kin. 6:5, **a** head fell into the water
Matt. 3:10, **a** is already laid at the root
Luke 3:9, the **a** . . . root of the trees
1 Sam. 13:20; 1 Kin. 6:7

B

BABBLER Acts 17:18, this idle **b**

BABE—*immature* Matt. 11:25, reveal . . . to **b-s**
1 Cor. 3:1, to **b-s** in Christ

Heb. 5:13, for he is a **b**
1 Pet. 2:2, like newborn **b-s**
Ps. 8:2; 17:14; Matt. 21:16; Luke 10:21

BABY—*babe, immature* Luke 2:12; 2:16

BACK—*backward* Is. 38:17, sins behind Thy **b**
Num. 24:11; 1 Sam. 10:9; Neh. 9:26; Ezek. 2:10; Mark 13:16

BACKBITING—*slanders* Prov. 25:23, a **b** tongue

BACKSLIDE—*apostasy, faithless* Prov. 14:14, **b-r** in heart will have his fill
Jer. 49:4, O **b-ing** daughter Who trusts

BACKWARD 2 Kin. 20:10, shadow turn **b** ten steps
Gen. 9:23; 49:17; Job 23:8; Jer. 7:24

BAD—*evil, wrong* Gen. 24:50; 31:24,29; Lev. 27:12,14,33; Num. 13:19; 24:13; 2 Sam. 13:22; 2 Cor. 5:10, good or **b**
Lev. 27:10, good for a **b**, or a **b** for a good
Matt. 7:18, good tree cannot produce **b** fruit
Gen. 43:6; Is. 3:11; Jer. 24:2,3; Matt. 13:48

BAG—*purse* Deut. 25:13; 1 Sam. 17:40
Job 14:17, My transgression is sealed up in a **b**
Matt. 10:10, or a **b** for *your* journey
2 Kin. 5:23; Prov. 7:20; 16:11; Mic. 6:11

BAGGAGE 1 Sam. 17:22, David left his **b**

BAKE Gen. 19:3; 40:17; Ex. 12:39; 16:23; Lev. 2:4; 24:5; 26:26; Num. 11:8; 1 Sam. 28:24; Is. 44:15

BAKER Gen. 40:1, **b** of the king of Egypt
Gen. 41:10; 1 Sam. 8:13; Jer. 37:21; Hos. 7:4

BALANCE—*scale* Lev. 19:36, shall have just **b-s**
Prov. 11:1, A false **b** is an abomination to the LORD
16:11, A just **b** and scales belong to the LORD
Job 6:2; Ps. 62:9; Is. 40:12; Ezek. 45:10; Hos. 12:7

BALD—*baldhead* Lev. 13:41, head becomes **b**
Jer. 48:37; Ezek. 29:18

BALDHEAD—*bald* 2 Kin. 2:23, Go up, you **b**

BALDNESS Mic. 1:16, **b** like an eagle
Lev. 21:5; Ezek. 7:18; Amos 8:10

BALM Jer. 8:22, no **b** in Gilead
Gen. 37:25; 43:11; Jer. 46:11; 51:8; Ezek. 27:17

BAND—*bond, chain, fetter* Ex. 27:10; 28:8; 38:10; Judg. 8:26; Ps. 107:14; Is. 58:6

BANISH 2 Sam. 14:13,14; Ezra 7:26

BANK—*mound* Gen. 41:17, **b** of the Nile
Matt. 25:27, put my money in the **b**
Gen. 41:3; Ex. 2:3; 7:15; Ezek. 47:7; Luke 19:23

BANNER—*standard* Ps. 20:5; 60:4
Song 2:4, his **b** over me is love
6:4, awesome as an army with **b-s**

BANQUET—*feast, supper*
Song 2:4; Dan. 5:10; Amos 6:7
Esth. 5:4, the **b** that I have prepared for him
Matt. 23:6; Mark 12:39; Luke 20:46, place of honor at **b-s**
Mark 6:21, Herod on his birthday gave a **b**

BAPTISM—*washing*
Matt. 3:7; Mark 10:38; 1 Pet. 3:21
Matt. 21:25; Mark 11:30; Luke 7:29, **b** of John
Luke 20:4; Acts 1:22; 18:25; 19:3, **b** of John
Mark 1:4; Luke 3:3; Acts 13:24; 19:4, **b** of repentance
Luke 12:50, I have a **b** to undergo
Rom. 6:4, buried with Him through **b**
Col. 2:12, buried with Him in **b**
Eph. 4:5, one Lord, one faith, one **b**

BAPTIZE Matt. 3:11, I **b** you in water
Matt. 3:14, I have need to be **b-d** by You
28:19, **b-ing** them in the name of the Father
Mark 1:8; Luke 3:16, **b** you with the Holy Sp.
John 3:22, He was . . . with them and **b-ing**
Acts 1:5, John **b-d** with water
2:41, those . . . were **b-d**
8:16, **b-d** in the name of the Lord Jesus
9:18, Saul . . . arose and was **b-d**
19:4, John **b-d** with the baptism
Rom. 6:3, **b-d** into Christ Jesus . . . **b-d** into His death
1 Cor. 1:13, were you **b-d** in the name of Paul
12:13, by one Spirit we were all **b-d**
Mark 16:16; Luke 3:7,12,21; 7:29; John 1:25,33; 4:1; Acts 2:38; 8:12,36; 10:47; 16:15,33; 18:8; 22:16; 1 Cor. 10:2; 15:29

BARBARIAN Rom. 1:14; 1 Cor. 14:11

BARBER Ezek. 5:1, use it as a **b-'s** razor

BARE—*naked* Is. 52:10; 1 Cor. 15:37; Heb. 4:13

BARK Ex. 11:7; Is. 56:10

BARLEY Ex. 9:31; Deut. 8:8; Ruth 1:22; John 6:9

BARN Matt. 6:26, nor gather into **b-s**
Luke 12:18, I will tear down my **b-s**
Joel 1:17; Hag. 2:19; Matt. 3:12; 13:30; Luke 12:24

BARRACKS Acts 21:34; 22:24

BARREN—*unfruitful* Gen. 11:30; 29:31; Ex. 23:26; Job 24:21; Is. 54:1; Luke 1:7,36; 23:29

BARS 1 Sam. 23:7; Ps. 107:16; Is. 45:2; Ezek. 38:11

BASE 1 Cor. 1:28, the **b** things of the world

BASIN Ex. 12:22; 1 Chr. 28:17; Jer. 52:19; John 13:5

BASKET Ex. 2:3; 29:23; Judg. 6:19; Jer. 24:2; Amos 8:1; Matt. 14:20; 15:37; 16:9; Mark 6:43; 8:8; 8:19; Luke 9:17; John 6:13

BAT Lev. 11:19; Deut. 14:18; Is. 2:20

BATH—*measure* 1 Kin. 7:26; 2 Chr. 2:10; Ezra 7:22; Is. 5:10

BATHE—*wash* Song 5:12, eyes . . . **b-d** in milk
Lev. 15:5,22; 17:16; Num. 19:7; 2 Sam. 11:2

BATTER—*bruise, crush*
Matt. 12:20, **B-ED REED . . . NOT BREAK**

BATTLE—*war* 1 Sam. 17:47, **b** is the LORD'S
2 Chr. 20:15, the **b** is not yours
1 Sam. 17:20; 1 Chr. 5:20; Job 39:25; 41:8; Ps. 18:39; 55:18; 140:7; 144:1; Eccles. 9:11; Is. 21:15; Jer. 50:22; Luke 14:31

BEACH Matt. 13:2; John 21:4; Acts 21:5

BEAM—*log* 2 Kin. 6:2; Ps. 104:3

BEAR (n.) 1 Sam. 17:34; 2 Sam. 17:8; Prov. 17:12; Is. 11:7; 59:11; Hos. 13:8; Amos 5:19

BEAR (v.)—*carry, sustain* Gen. 43:9; 44:32
Gen. 4:13, punishment is too great to **b**
Ex. 20:16, You shall not **b** false witness
Ps. 91:12, They will **b** you up
Matt. 1:23, VIRGIN . . . SHALL **B** A SON
27:32, to **b** His cross
Mark 15:21, that he might **b** His cross
John 1:7, **b** witness of the light
16:12, you cannot **b** them now
Rom. 8:16, Spirit Himself **b-s** witness
1 Cor. 13:7, **b-s** all things
15:49, **b** the image of the heavenly
Gal. 6:2, **B** one another's burdens
6:5, each one shall **b** his own load
6:17, I **b** on my body
1 John 1:2, we have seen and **b** witness
Ex. 28:12; Lev. 24:15; Deut. 1:9; Prov. 18:14; Lam. 3:27; Ezek. 23:49; Matt. 1:21; Luke 11:46; John 5:31; 8:18; 15:27; Rom. 13:4; 15:1; Heb 9:28

BEARD Lev. 13:29; 1 Sam. 21:13; 2 Sam. 10:4; 20:9; 1 Chr. 19:5; Ps. 133:2; Ezek. 5:1

BEARING—*carrying* Rom. 2:15; Gal. 4:24
John 19:17, **b** His own cross
Col. 3:13, **b** with one another
Heb. 13:13, **b** His reproach

BEAST—*animal, creature* Lev. 26:22; Job 12:7; 18:3

Ps. 50:10, every **b** of the forest is Mine
147:9, He gives to the **b** its food
Eccles. 3:19, no advantage for man over **b**
1 Cor. 15:32, I fought with wild **b-s**
Ps. 49:12; 73:22; Prov. 12:10; James 3:7

BEAT—*flog, hammer* Judg. 6:11; Matt. 26:67
Prov. 23:14, **b** him with the rod
Joel 3:10, **B** your plowshares into swords
Luke 18:13, was **b-ing** his breast
1 Cor. 9:26, as not **b-ing** the air
2 Cor. 11:23, **b-en** times without number

BEAUTIFUL—*appropriate, lovely* Lev. 23:40
Gen. 6:2, daughters of men were **b**
12:11, you are a **b** woman
Is. 4:2, the Branch of the LORD will be **b**
64:11, Our holy and **b** house
Matt. 23:27, tombs which on the outside appear **b**
Acts 3:2, gate of the temple which is called **B**
Rom. 10:15, How **B ARE THE FEET**
Judg. 15:2; Ps. 48:2; Song 1:8; 6:4; Is. 52:1; Jer. 11:16; 13:20

BEAUTY 2 Sam. 1:19; Prov. 31:30; Is. 3:18; Zech. 9:17
Ps. 27:4, To behold the **b** of the LORD
50:2, Out of Zion, the perfection of **b**

BECAME Gen. 26:13, and the man **b** rich
Heb. 11:34, **b** mighty in war

BECOME Ps. 33:1, Praise is **b-ing** to the upright
Luke 2:40, Child . . . to grow and **b** strong

BED—*pallet* Ps. 63:6, remember Thee on my **b**
Matt. 9:6, Rise, take up your **b**
2 Kin. 4:10; Job 7:13; 33:15; Is. 28:20; Ezek. 17:10; Mark 4:21; Luke 8:16

BEES Deut. 1:44; Judg. 14:8; Ps. 118:12; Is. 7:18

BEFALL—*happen* Gen. 42:4; 49:1; Deut. 31:29
Gen. 44:29, harm **b-s** him
Ps. 91:10, No evil will **b** you

BEFIT—*proper, worthy* Ps. 93:5, Holiness **b-s**
1 Tim. 2:10, as **b-s** women making a claim to godliness

BEG—*appeal, ask* Ps. 37:25, his descendants **b-ing** bread
Luke 16:3, I am ashamed to **b**
18:35, blind man by the road, **b-ing**
John 9:8, the one who used to sit and **b**
Ps. 109:10; Prov. 20:4; Luke 9:38

BEGINNING 1 Sam. 3:12; Prov. 8:22,23
Gen. 1:1, In the **b** God created the heavens
Job 8:7, your **b** was insignificant
Ps. 111:10, **b** of wisdom
Prov. 1:7, **b** of knowledge

BEGINNING (Continued)

Eccles. 7:8, end ... better than its **b**
Luke 24:47, **b** from Jerusalem
John 1:1, In the **b** was the Word
Rev. 21:6, the **b** and the end
Matt. 19:8; John 2:11; 2 Cor. 3:1; 8:6;
Col. 1:18; Heb. 3:14; Rev. 22:13

BEGOTTEN—*born* Ps. 2:7, Today I
have **b** Thee
Job 38:28; Acts 13:33; Philem. 10;
Heb. 1:5; 5:5

BEHALF—*place, sake* Job 36:2,
more ... said in God's **b**
2 Cor. 1:11, thanks may be given ...
on our **b**
5:20, we beg you on **b** of Christ

BEHAVE—*act* 1 Sam. 18:30, David
b-d himself more wisely
1 Thess. 2:10, how devoutly ...
we **b-d**

BEHAVIOR—*conduct* James 3:13,
his good **b**
1 Pet. 1:15, holy ... in all *your* **b**
2:12, keep your **b** excellent

BEHEAD Luke 9:9; Rev. 20:4
Matt. 14:10, had John **b-ed** in prison
Mark 6:16, John whom I **b-ed**

BEHOLD—*look* Num. 24:17; Ps.
37:37
Matt. 18:10, angels ... **b** the face of
My Father
John 17:24, that they may **b** My
glory
2 Cor. 3:18, **b-ing** as in a mirror

BEING Gen. 2:7, man became a
living **b**
Matt. 7:11, **b** evil, know how to give
12:34, **b** evil, speak ... good
John 4:9, **b** a Jew, ask me
1 Cor. 8:7, conscience **b** weak
9:21, **b** without the law
Eph. 2:20, **b** the chief cornerstone

BELIEVE—*faith, trust* Ex. 4:5; Matt.
8:13; 9:28
Num. 14:11, how long will they not **b**
in Me
Ps. 78:22, Because they did not **b** in
God
Prov. 14:15, the naive **b-s** everything
Matt. 21:22, everything you ask ...
b-ing you
Mark 5:36, Do not be afraid ...
only **b**
9:23, All things are possible to him
who **b-s**
Luke 8:13, they **b** for a while
24:25, slow of heart to **b**
John 2:22, they **b-d** the Scripture
7:5, not even His brothers were **b-ing** in Him
8:24, unless you **b** that I am He
10:38, though you do not **b** Me, **b**
the works
11:26, everyone who ... **b-s** in Me
shall never die
11:27, Yes, Lord; I have **b-d**
11:48, all men will **b** in Him
17:21, that the world may **b** that
Thou didst send Me
20:25, Unless I shall see ... I will
not **b**
20:29, Blessed *are* they who ... yet
b-d
Rom. 4:11, the father of all who **b**
Heb. 11:6, he who comes to God
must **b** that

James 2:19, You **b** that God is one
... the
1 Pet. 2:6, HE WHO **b-s** IN HIM SHALL
NOT BE
Matt. 21:25; 27:42; Mark 11:24,31;
16:13; Luke 8:50; 24:41; John 1:7;
3:12; 5:44,47; 6:36; 7:48; 10:37;
11:15; 12:36; Acts 4:32; 9:26;
13:39,48; 16:34; Rom. 4:18; 9:33;
10:14; 2 Cor. 4:13; Gal. 3:22;
2 Thess. 1:10

BELLY—*stomach* Gen. 3:14, On
your **b** shall you go

BELONG Luke 23:7, He **b-ed** to
Herod's
1 Cor. 3:21, all things **b** to you
3:23, **b** to Christ ... **b-s** to God

BELOVED—*chosen* Ps. 127:2, He
gives to His **b**
Matt. 3:17; 17:5, This is My **b** Son
Eph. 1:6, bestowed on us in the **B**
5:1, be imitators of God, as **b**
children
Col. 1:13, kingdom of His **b** Son
2 Tim. 1:2, to Timothy, my **b** son
Philem. 16, more than a slave, a **b**
brother
Jude 1, **b** in God the Father
Deut. 33:12; Jer. 12:7; Mark 1:11; 9:7;
Luke 3:22; Rom. 11:28; 12:19; 16:9;
1 Cor. 10:14; 2 Cor. 7:1; 12:19; Phil.
4:1; Col. 4:9; 1 Pet. 2:11; 2 Pet. 1:17

BELOW—*beneath* Gen. 1:9; Deut.
4:39; Prov. 15:24; Jer. 31:37; John
8:23

BELT—*girdle* Mark 1:6, John ... a
leather **b**
Acts 21:11, took Paul's **b** and bound
his own feet
1 Sam. 18:4; 2 Sam. 18:11; 20:8; Ps.
109:19; Prov. 31:24; Is. 3:24; 5:27;
11:5; Ezek. 23:15; Matt. 3:4

BEND—*bow* Ps. 11:2, the wicked **b**
the bow

BENEFACTOR Luke 22:25, those ...
called **B-s**

BENEFIT—*profit, blessing* Ps.
103:2, forget none of His **b-s**
Ps. 116:12, For all His **b-s** toward me
1 Tim. 6:2, those who partake of
the **b**
2 Chr. 32:25; Is. 65:8; Rom. 3:1;
1 Tim. 6:2

BEREAVE—*deprive* Gen. 27:45;
42:36; Lev. 26:22; Jer. 15:7; Ezek.
5:17; 36:12

BESIDE Ps. 23:2, He leads me **b** quiet
waters
Is. 43:11, there is no saviour **b-s** Me
44:6, there is no God **b-s** Me
Matt. 13:4, *seeds* fell **b** the road
2 Cor. 5:13, if we are **b** ourselves, it
is for God
Deut. 11:30; Ruth 2:14; 2 Kin. 21:16;
Is. 32:20

BESIEGE Deut. 20:19; 2 Sam. 11:1;
1 Kin. 16:17; Is. 1:8; Ezek. 4:3; 6:12

BEST Ps. 39:5, man at his **b** is a mere
breath
Luke 15:22, bring out the **b** robe

Gen. 43:11; 1 Sam. 15:9,15; 2 Sam.
18:4

BESTOW—*grant* Ex. 32:29, He may
b a blessing upon you
1 Chr. 29:25, **b-ed** on him royal
majesty
1 Cor. 12:23, we **b** more abundant
honor
1 John 3:1, love the Father has **b-ed**
on us

BETRAY Matt. 27:4, I have sinned by
b-ing
Mark 14:11, he *began* seeking how to
b Him
Luke 22:21, the hand of the one **b-ing** Me
1 Cor. 11:23, the night ... He was
b-ed
Is. 16:3; Matt. 24:10; 26:16; Mark
14:18; Luke 22:22; John 6:64; 21:20

BETROTH Hos. 2:19,20, I will **b** you
to Me
Jer. 2:2; Matt. 1:18; 2 Cor. 11:2

BETTER 1 Sam. 15:22, to obey is **b**
than sacrifice
Ps. 63:3, Thy lovingkindness is **b**
than life
Heb. 11:16, they desire a **b** country
2 Pet. 2:21, **b** for them not to have
known the way
1 Kin. 19:4; Eccles. 2:24; 4:9; 7:10;
Song 1:2; Heb. 1:4

BEWARE Deut. 8:11, **B**, lest you
forget the LORD
Deut. 15:9, **B**, lest there is a base
thought
Matt. 6:1, **B** of practicing your
righteousness
10:17, But **b** of men
16:6, **b** of the leaven of the
Pharisees
Mark 12:38, **B** of the scribes
Luke 12:15, **B**, and be on your guard
against ... greed
Ex. 19:12; Job 36:18; Mark 8:15;
Luke 12:1; 20:46; Phil. 3:2

BEWITCHED Gal. 3:1, You foolish
Galatians, who has **b**

BEYOND 2 Cor. 8:3, **b** their ability
Gal. 1:13, persecute the church of
God **b** measure
Gen. 35:21; Deut. 3:20; John 3:26;
Acts 7:43

BIER 2 Sam. 3:31, David walked
behind the **b**

BILLOWS—*waves* Jon. 2:3, **b** passed
over me

BIND—*wrap* Num. 30:2, an oath to **b**
himself
Prov. 6:21, **B** them continually on
your heart
Is. 61:1, **b** up the brokenhearted
Matt. 16:19, **b** on earth shall be
bound in heaven
Job 38:31; Matt. 12:29; 18:18; Mark
3:27

BIRD—*fowl, swallow* Lev. 20:25,
unclean **b**
Ps. 84:3, **b** also has found a house
124:7, Our soul has escaped as a **b**
Matt. 6:26, Look at the **b-s** of the air
8:20, **b-s** of the air *have* nests

Gen. 1:20; 6:7; 2 Sam. 21:10; Ps. 8:8;
11:1; Prov. 1:17; Eccles. 10:20; Jer.
9:10; 12:9; Hos. 9:8; Luke 9:58;
Rev. 19:17

BIRTH Eccles. 7:1, better than the
day of **b**
Matt. 1:18, **b** of Jesus Christ was
John 9:1, a man blind from **b**
Gen. 38:27; Is. 66:9; Luke 1:14

BIRTHRIGHT Gen. 25:31, First sell
me your **b**
Gen. 27:36, Jacob . . . took away
my **b**
Heb. 12:16, sold his own **b** for a
single meal

BIT (n.) Ps. 32:9; James 3:3

BITE Prov. 23:32; Eccles. 10:8; Amos
5:19; 9:3; Mic. 3:5; Gal. 5:15

BITTER Ex. 1:14, **b** with hard labor
Ex. 12:8, unleavened bread and **b**
herbs
15:23, waters of Marah . . . were **b**
2 Kin. 14:26, affliction of Israel . . .
was very **b**
Is. 24:9, Strong drink is **b** to those
who drink
Matt. 26:75, went out and wept **b-ly**
Job 21:25; Is. 5:20; Luke 22:62

BITTERNESS—*gall* Job 10:1, **b** of
my soul
Prov. 14:10; 17:25, heart knows its
own **b**
Eph. 4:31, Let all **b** and wrath . . . be
put away
Heb. 12:15, no root of **b**
1 Sam. 15:32; Is. 38:15; Lam. 3:19;
Rom. 3:14

BLACK Matt. 5:36, make one hair **b**
or white
Jude 13, for whom the **b** darkness
has been reserved
Rev. 6:5, behold a **b** horse

BLADE Judg. 3:22, fat closed over
the **b**
Mark 4:28, first the **b**, then the head

BLAMELESS Ps. 119:80, May my
heart be **b**
Prov. 11:20, **b** in their walk are His
delight
Acts 24:16, maintain always a **b**
conscience
1 Cor. 1:8, **b** in the day of our Lord
Jesus Christ
Eph. 1:4, holy and **b** before Him
2 Sam. 22:26; Ps. 119:1; Phil. 1:10;
2:15; 3:6; Jude 24; Rev. 14:5

BLASPHEME—*spoke* Is. 52:5, My
name is continually **b-d**
Matt. 9:3, This *fellow* **b-s**
26:65, He has **b-d**
Mark 3:29, **b-s** against the Holy
Spirit
2 Sam. 12:14; Acts 26:11; Rom. 2:24;
1 Tim. 1:20; James 2:7

BLASPHEMY Matt. 12:31, **b** against
the Spirit
Matt. 26:65, you have now heard
the **b**
Mark 3:28, whatever **b-es** they utter
Rev. 2:9, the **b** by those who say
they are Jews

13:5, arrogant words and **b-es**
Mark 14:64; Luke 5:21; John 10:33

BLEMISH—*spot* Heb. 9:14, offered
Himself without **b**
Num. 19:2; Song 4:7; Ezek. 43:22;
45:18; 46:4

BLEND 2 Chr. 16:14, **b-ed** by the
perfumers' art

BLESS—*happy* Josh. 17:14, LORD
has . . . **b-ed**
Ps. 144:15, **b-ed** are the people
whose God is the LORD
Prov. 3:13, **b-ed** is the man who finds
wisdom
10:7, memory of the righteous is **b-ed**
Luke 6:28, **b** those who curse you
Acts 20:35, more **b-ed** to give than to
receive
Titus 2:13, looking for **b-ed** hope
James 3:9, we **b** *our* Lord and Father
Rev. 14:13, Write, **B-ed** are the dead
Gen. 22:17; Deut. 28:3-6; 33:29; Judg.
5:2; 1 Chr. 4:10; Ps. 127:5;
Prov. 28:14; Is. 32:20; 65:16;
Hag. 2:19; Mal. 3:15; John 13:17;
Rom. 12:14; 2 Cor. 11:31;
Titus 2:13; James 5:11; 1 Pet. 3:14;
4:14

BLESSING—*benefit* Gen. 39:5,
LORD's **b** was upon all
Prov. 10:22, **b** of the LORD that
makes rich
28:20, faithful man will abound
with **b-s**
Mal. 3:10, pour out for you a **b**
Rom. 15:29, the fulness of the **b** of
Christ
1 Cor. 10:16, Is not the cup of **b**
Gen. 27:35; Deut. 11:26; 23:5; Neh.
13:2; Job 29:13; Mal. 2:2;
2 Cor. 1:15; James 3:10; Rev. 5:12

BLIND Ex. 23:8, bribe **b-s** the clear-
sighted
Matt. 11:5, *the* B RECEIVE SIGHT
2 Cor. 4:4, **b-ed** the minds of the
unbelieving
1 John 2:11, darkness has **b-ed** his
eyes
Deut. 16:19; 1 Sam. 12:3

BLINDNESS Deut. 28:28; 2 Kin. 6:18;
Zech. 12:4

BLOOD Gen. 9:6, Whoever sheds
man's **b**, By man his **b**
Ps. 72:14, their **b** will be precious in
his sight
Ezek. 9:9, the land is filled with **b**
Matt. 16:17, because flesh and **b** did
not reveal
27:4, by betraying innocent **b**
Luke 22:20, new covenant in My **b**
22:44, His sweat became like drops
of **b**
Acts 20:28, He purchased with His
own **b**
21:25, abstain from meat . . . and
from **b**
Rom. 3:25, a propitiation in His **b**
5:9, justified by His **b**
1 Cor. 10:16, sharing in the **b** of
Christ
11:27, guilty of the body . . . **b** of the
Lord
15:50, flesh and **b** cannot inherit the
kingdom
Eph. 1:7, redemption through His **b**

Heb. 9:22, shedding of **b** there is no
forgiveness
1 Pet. 1:19, the **b** of Christ
Rev. 12:11, the **b** of the Lamb
Gen. 9:4; Ex. 12:22; Lev. 3:17; Josh.
2:19; 1 Kin. 2:32; Is. 9:5;
Ezek. 18:13; Matt. 27:25;
Mark 14:24; John 1:13; 6:54,55,56;
Acts 15:20; 1 Cor. 11:25;
Heb. 10:29; Rev. 7:14

BLOSSOM Gen. 40:10; Eccles. 12:5;
Is. 17:11; 27:6; 35:1; Hos. 14:5;
Hab. 3:17

BLOT—*erase* Ex. 32:32, please **b** me
from Thy book
Deut. 9:14, **b** out their name from
heaven
Ps. 51:1, Thy compassion **b** out my
transgressions
51:9, **b** out all my iniquities
69:28, May they be **b-ed** out of the
book of life
Deut. 25:19; 29:20; 2 Kin. 14:27;
Neh. 4:5; Ps. 109:13,14; Prov. 6:33;
Jer. 18:23

BLOWS Prov. 19:29, **b** for the back of
fools

BOAST—*glory, rejoice, talk* Ps. 34:2,
soul . . . make its **b**
Ps. 49:6, **b** in the abundance of their
riches
Prov. 27:1, do not **b** about tomorrow
Rom. 2:23, You who **b** in the Law
James 4:16, all such **b-ing** is evil
1 Sam. 2:3; 1 Kin. 20:11; 2 Chr. 25:19;
Ps. 5:5; 75:4; Prov. 20:14;
Rom. 2:17; 3:27; 1 Cor. 5:6;
2 Cor. 11:16; Gal. 5:26; Eph. 2:9;
James 3:5; 4:16

BOAT Is. 33:21; John 6:22; Acts
27:16; 27:30

BODILY Luke 3:22, Holy Spirit
descended . . . in **b** form
Col. 2:9, fulness of Deity dwells in **b**
form
1 Tim. 4:8, **b** discipline is only little
profit

BODY—*corpse, flesh* Matt. 6:22,
whole **b** . . . full of light
Mark 5:29, she felt in her **b** that she
was healed
6:29, his **b** and laid it in a tomb
Luke 12:22, do not be anxious . . . for
your **b**
Acts 19:12, carried from his **b** to the
sick
Rom. 6:6, that our **b** of sin might be
done away
12:1, present your **b-es** a living . . .
sacrifice
12:4, many members in one **b**
12:5, we . . . are one **b** in Christ
1 Cor. 9:27, but I buffet my **b**
13:3, if I deliver my **b** to be burned
2 Cor. 5:8, prefer to be absent from
the **b**
Gal. 6:17, I bear on my **b** the brand-
marks of Jesus
1 Pet. 2:24, bore our sins in His **b**
Gen. 47:18; Eccles. 12:12; Matt. 5:29;
6:23; Luke 11:34; 17:37; John 2:21;
Rom. 7:24; 1 Cor. 12:14;
2 Cor. 12:2; Phil. 3:21

BODYGUARD—*guard* Gen. 40:4;
Jer. 39:9

BOISTEROUS—*clamor*
Prov. 9:13, woman of folly is **b**

BOLD Prov. 28:1, righteous are **b** as a
lion
Acts 13:46, Paul and Barnabas spoke
out **b-ly**
Ex. 14:8; Num. 33:3; Rom. 10:20;
2 Cor. 10:2; 10:12

BOLDNESS—*confidence* Acts 4:31,
speak . . . with **b**
Eph. 3:12, we have **b** and confident
access
Phil. 1:20, with all **b**, Christ . . . be
exalted

BOND—*cord* Hos. 11:4, with **b-s** of
love
Eph. 4:3, in the **b** of peace
Col. 3:14, perfect **b** of unity
Ezek. 20:37; Luke 13:16; Jude 6

BOND-SERVANT—*servant* Luke
2:29, let Thy **b** depart
Rom. 1:1, Paul, a **b** of Christ Jesus
Phil. 1:1, Paul and Timothy, **b-s** of
Christ
Titus 1:1; James 1:1; 2 Pet. 1:1

BONE Ezek. 37:7, **b-s** came together,
b to its **b**
Luke 24:39, spirit does not have flesh
and **b-s**
John 19:36, NOT A B OF HIM SHALL BE
BROKEN
Gen. 2:23; Ex. 12:46; Job 20:11;
Ps. 51:8; Prov. 12:4; Matt. 23:27

BOOK Is. 34:16, Seek from the **b** of
the LORD
Mal. 3:16, **b** of remembrance
John 21:25, world itself would not
contain the **b-s**
Phil. 4:3, names are in the **b** of life
Ex. 32:32; Ezra 4:15; Job 19:23; Luke
4:17; Acts 19:19; 1 Tim. 4:13;
Rev. 3:5; 13:8; 17:8; 20:12; 21:27;
22:19

BOOTHS Gen. 33:17; Lev. 23:42,43;
Neh. 8:14

BOOTY—*plunder* Num. 31:32; Is.
53:12; Jer. 38:2; 49:32

BORDER Gen. 47:21, one end of
Egypt's **b** to the other
Ex. 34:24, drive out nations . . . . . .
b-s
Jer. 15:13, . . . within all your **b-s**
50:26, Come to her from the
farthest **b**
Gen. 23:17; Num. 21:13; 34:3; 35:26;
Deut. 3:17; Josh. 12:5; 2 Kin. 3:21;
1 Chr. 4:10; Ps. 147:14; Is. 19:19;
60:18; Ezek. 11:10

BORE—*bear, carry, pierce, yield*
Ex. 19:4, how I **b** you on eagles'
wings
Is. 53:4, our griefs He Himself **b**
53:12, He Himself **b** the sin of many
1 Pet. 2:24, He Himself **b** our sins
Num. 17:8; 2 Kin. 12:9; Jer. 31:19

BORN—*begotten, forth* Job 5:7, man
is **b** for trouble
Job 14:1, Man, who is **b** of woman
Is. 9:6, For a child will be **b** to us
66:8, Can a land be **b** in one day
John 1:13, who were **b** not of blood
3:3, unless one is **b** again

3:6,8, **b** of the Spirit
1 Cor. 15:8, one untimely **b**
1 Pet. 1:3, **b** again to a living hope
1 John 4:7, everyone who loves is **b**
of God
5:4, whatever is **b** of God
overcomes the world
Job 3:3; 15:14; 25:4; Ps. 87:4; 90:2;
Prov. 17:17; Matt. 11:11;
1 Pet. 1:23; 1 John 5:1

BORNE Is. 46:3, been **b** by Me from
birth
Job 34:31; Lam. 5:7; Matt. 20:12

BORROW Deut. 28:12, you shall
not **b**
Prov. 22:7, **b**-er *becomes* the lender's
slave
Ex. 22:14; Deut. 15:6; 2 Kin. 4:3; Ps.
37:21; Matt. 5:42

BOSOM—*breast* Prov. 6:27, fire in
his **b**
Is. 40:11, carry *them* in His **b**
Luke 16:22, carried . . . to Abraham's
b
John 1:18, in the **b** of the Father
Ex. 4:6; Job 31:33; Ps. 35:13

BOTHER—*trouble* Matt. 26:10, do
you **b** the woman

BOTTLE—*jug, wineskin* Judg. 4:19;
Ps. 56:8

BOUGH—*branch* Ps. 80:10, cedars
of God with its **b-s**
Gen. 49:22; Lev. 23:40; Deut. 24:20;
Ps. 80:10; Is. 17:6; Ezek. 31:6

BOUGHT Luke 14:18, I have **b** a
piece of land
1 Cor. 6:20, been **b** with a price
7:23, You were **b** with a price
2 Pet. 2:1, denying the Master who **b**
them

BOUND—*gird, yoke* Prov. 22:15,
Foolishness is **b** up in
Matt. 16:19, **b** in heaven
Acts 20:22, **b** in spirit, I am on my
way to Jerusalem
1 Cor. 7:27, Are you **b** to a wife
2 Cor. 6:14, Do not be **b** together
Gen. 44:30; Mark 5:4

BOUNDARY Prov. 8:29, He set for
the sea its **b**

BOUNTIFUL—*generous*
Ps. 13:6, He has dealt **b-ly** with me
116:7, the LORD has dealt **b-ly** with
you
2 Cor. 9:6, he who sows **b-ly** . . . reap
b-ly
Ps. 119:17; 2 Cor. 9:5

BOUNTY 1 Kin. 10:13, according to
his royal **b**

BOW—*bend, worship* Is. 66:23, to **b**
down
1 Sam. 2:36; Ps. 10:10; Is. 60:14

BOWL—*dish, pitcher* Eccles. 12:6,
golden **b** is crushed
Matt. 26:23, who dipped his hand in
the **b**
Num. 7:25; 1 Kin. 17:12; Amos 6:6;
Zech. 4:2; Mark 14:20

BOY—*child* Is. 11:6, a little **b** will
lead them

Joel 3:3, Traded a **b** for a harlot
Gen. 25:27; Zech. 8:5

BRACELET Gen. 24:22; 24:30; 24:47;
Ex. 35:22; Num. 31:50;
2 Sam. 1:10; Is. 3:19; Ezek. 16:11;
23:42

BRAMBLE—*briar* Judg. 9:14, trees
said to the **b**
Judg. 9:15, fire come out from the **b**

BRANCH—*bough* Jer. 23:5, raise up
for David a righteous **B**
Matt. 13:32, THE BIRDS . . . NEST IN
ITS **B-ES**
21:8, others were cutting **b-es**
John 15:2, every **b** that bears fruit
15:4, **b** cannot bear fruit of itself
15:5, I am the vine, you are the **b-es**
Judg. 9:48; Ezek. 31:3; Mark 11:8;
Luke 13:19; John 12:13; 15:6;
Rom. 11:16

BRAND—*torch* Zech. 3:2; 1 Tim. 4:2

BRAY Job 6:5, wild donkey **b** over
his grass

BREACH Judg. 21:15, LORD had
made a **b** in . . . Israel
Job 16:14, breaks through me with **b**
after **b**
Gen. 38:29; Ex. 22:9; 1 Kin. 11:27;
Neh. 4:7; 6:1; Ps. 60:2; 106:23;
Is. 22:9; 30:13; 58:12;
Amos 4:3; 9:11

BREAD—*food* Ex. 16:4, I will rain **b**
from heaven
Deut. 8:3, man does not live by **b**
alone
Job 22:7, you have withheld **b**
Ps. 132:15, satisfy her needy with **b**
Prov. 31:27, does not eat the **b** of
idleness
Eccles. 11:1, Cast your **b** on the
surface of the waters
Is. 55:2, spend money for what is
not **b**
55:10, seed to the sower and **b** to
the eater
Matt. 4:3, command these stones
become **b**
6:11, Give us this day our daily **b**
Mark 7:27, take the children's **b**
Acts 2:42, the breaking of **b**
20:7, gathered together to break **b**
Ex. 23:25; Josh. 9:5; Judg. 7:13;
1 Kin. 17:6; Job 33:20; Prov. 9:17;
12:11; Matt. 4:4; Luke 4:3,4; 24:35;
Acts 27:35; 2 Thess. 3:8

BREAK—*broke, profane* 2 Chr.
32:1, to **b** into them
Is. 42:3, reed He will not **b**
Luke 5:6, their nets began to **b**
24:30, He took the bread . . . and **b-ing** it
1 Cor. 10:16, bread which we **b** a
sharing in . . . Christ
Job 19:10; Jer. 4:3; Hos. 10:12; Matt.
12:5,20; 14:19; Acts 21:13

BREASTPIECE Ex. 25:7;
28:4,15,22,23; 35:9,27; 39:8;
Lev. 8:8

BREASTPLATE Is. 59:17, put on
righteousness like a **b**
Eph. 6:14, PUT ON THE B OF
RIGHTEOUSNESS

1 Thess. 5:8, put on the **b** of faith and love
Neh. 4:16; Rev. 9:9,17

BREATH—*spirit, wind* Gen. 2:7, **b** of life
Job 7:16, my days are *but* a **b**
12:10, the **b** of all mankind
27:3, **b** of God is in my nostrils
Ps. 150:6, Let everything that has **b** praise the LORD
Acts 17:25, He Himself gives to all life and **b**
Gen. 6:17; 7:15; Eccles. 3:21; Is. 2:22; Ezek. 37:5,10

BREATHE Gen. 2:7, **b-d** into his nostrils the breath
Ezek. 37:9, **b** on these slain
Acts 9:1, **b-ing** threats and murder
Deut. 20:16; Josh. 10:40; 11:11,14; Ps. 27:12; John 20:22

BRETHREN—*brother* Ps. 22:22, tell of Thy name to my **b**
Is. 66:20, all your **b** from all the nations
1 Cor. 14:39, my **b**, desire earnestly to prophesy
2 Cor. 11:26, dangers among false **b**
Gal. 1:2, all the **b** who are with me
2:4, because of false **b**
Eph. 6:23, Peace be to the **b**
Col. 1:2, saints and faithful **b** in Christ
1 Thess. 4:9, love of the **b**
1 Pet. 1:22, sincere love of the **b**
1 John 3:14, because we love the **b**
Mic. 5:3; Rom. 1:13; 7:1; 8:12; Heb. 13:1

BRIAR—*thistle* Luke 6:44, nor . . . pick grapes from a **b**

BRIBE Ex. 23:8, not take a **b**, for a **b** blinds
Is. 1:23, Everyone loves a **b**
5:23, justify the wicked for a **b**
Deut. 10:17; 27:25; 1 Sam. 8:3; 12:3; Ps. 26:10; Is. 33:15; Mic. 7:3

BRICK Gen. 11:3; Ex. 1:14; 5:7; Is. 9:10; 65:3

BRIDE Rev. 21:2, as a **b** adorned for her husband
21:9, the **b**, the wife of the Lamb
22:17, the Spirit and the **b** say, Come
Is. 49:18; 61:10; 62:5; Jer. 2:32; 7:34; 16:9; 25:10; 33:11; Joel 2:16; John 3:29; Rev. 18:23

BRIDEGROOM Jer. 7:34; 16:9; 25:10; 33:11
Matt. 25:1, virgins . . . went out to meet the **b**
John 3:29, He who has the bride is the **b**
Rev. 18:23, voice of the **b**
Ex. 4:25; Ps. 19:5; Is. 61:10; 62:5; Joel 2:16; Matt. 9:15; Mark 2:19; John 2:9

BRIDLE—*guard* James 1:26, not **b** his tongue
2 Kin. 19:28; Prov. 26:3; Is. 37:29

BRIGHT Rev. 22:16, **b** morning star
Lev. 13:2; Job 37:21; Matt. 17:5

BRIGHTNESS—*radiance* Is. 60:3, kings to the **b** of your

Is. 62:1, righteousness goes forth like **b**

BRIMSTONE Gen. 19:24; Is. 30:33; Rev. 9:17; 14:10; 19:20

BRISTLE Job 4:15, hair . . . **b-d** up

BROAD—*wide* Ps. 119:96, commandment is exceedingly **b**
Matt. 7:13, way is **b** that leads to destruction
1 Chr. 4:40; Ps. 104:25; Matt. 23:5

BROILED Luke 24:42, gave Him a piece of **b** fish

BROKE—*break* John 19:32, **b** the legs of the first man
Eph. 2:14, **b** down the barrier
1 Sam. 4:18; 2 Kin. 23:14; 2 Chr. 34:4; Matt. 15:36; 26:26; Mark 6:41

BROKEN—*loose, void* Job 17:1, My spirit is **b**
Ps. 51:17, a **b** spirit; A **b** and a contrite heart
69:20, Reproach has **b** my heart
119:126, have **b** Thy law
Eccles. 12:6, the silver cord is **b**
Jer. 2:13, **B** cisterns
John 10:35, Scripture cannot be **b**
19:36, NOT A BONE OF HIM SHALL BE B

BROKENHEARTED
Ps. 34:18, Lord is near to the **b**

BRONZE Deut. 28:23; 2 Sam. 22:35; Ezra 8:27; Jer. 15:12

BROOD Matt. 3:7, You **b** of vipers, who warned you
Luke 13:34, a hen *gathers* her **b**

BROOK 1 Sam. 17:40; Ps. 110:7
Ps. 42:1, deer pants for the water **b-s**

BROTHER—*brethren* Gen. 4:9, Am I my **b**'s keeper
Prov. 18:24, friend who sticks closer than a **b**
Matt. 10:21, **b** will deliver up **b** to death
23:8, you are all **b-s**
Luke 18:29, no one who has left . . . **b-s**
John 7:5, not even His **b-s** were
1 Cor. 6:6, **b** goes to law with **b**
Gen. 42:8; Prov. 17:17; 18:9,19; 19:7; Eccles. 4:8; Matt. 5:23; Mark 3:35; 10:29; 2 Thess. 3:15

BROTHERHOOD Amos 1:9, covenant of **b**

BROTHERLY Rom. 12:10, in **b** love
2 Pet. 1:7, *your* **b** kindness

BROUGHT—*escape* Matt. 10:18, shall . . . be **b** before governors

BROW Luke 4:29, led Him to the **b** of the hill

BRUISE—*batter, crush* Gen. 3:15, shall **b** you
Is. 1:6, **b-s**, welts, and raw wounds
42:3, A **b-d** reed He will not break

BRUTAL—*senseless, stupid, fierce* Ezek. 21:31; 2 Tim. 3:3

BUCKET Num. 24:7, flow from his **b-s**
Is. 40:15, nations are like a drop from a **b**

BUD—*sprout* Num. 17:8; Is. 18:5

BUFFET—*beat* 2 Cor. 12:7, to **b** me

BUGLE—*trumpet* 1 Cor. 14:8, **b** produces an . . . sound

BUILD 1 Chr. 17:12, He shall **b** for Me a house
Ps. 127:1, Unless the LORD **b-s** the house
Eccles. 3:3, a time to **b** up
1 Cor. 3:12, if any man **b-s** upon the foundation
2 Chr. 6:9; Luke 14:30; Acts 20:32; Rom. 15:20

BUILDER—*maker* Ps. 118:22, the **b-s** rejected
Heb. 11:10, whose architect and **b** is God
1 Pet. 2:7, STONE WHICH THE **B-S** REJECTED
1 Kin. 5:18; Ezra 3:10; Matt. 21:42; Mark 12:10; Luke 20:17; Acts 4:11

BUILDING 1 Cor. 3:9, you are . . . God's **b**
2 Cor. 5:1, we have a **b** from God
Eph. 2:21, **b**, being fitted together

BUILT Eccles. 2:4, I **b** houses for myself
Matt. 7:24, **b** his house upon the rock
Eph. 2:22, **b** together into a dwelling of God

BULL Lev. 4:3, a **b** without defect

BULRUSHES Is. 19:7, **b** by the Nile

BUNDLE Gen. 42:35; Acts 28:3
1 Sam. 25:29, bound in the **b** of living
Matt. 13:30, bind them in **b-s** to burn

BURDEN—*load* Ps. 55:22, Cast your **b** upon the LORD
Matt. 20:12, borne the **b** and . . . heat of the day
Luke 11:46, weigh men down with **b-s** hard to bear
Gal. 6:2, Bear one another's **b-s**
Acts 15:28; 2 Cor. 11:9; 12:16; 1 Thess. 2:9

BURIAL John 19:40, **b** custom of the Jews
Gen. 23:4; Eccles. 6:3; Jer. 22:19; Matt. 26:12

BURN—*kindle* Ex. 3:2, bush was **b-ing** with fire
Ps. 39:3, While I was musing the fire **b-ed**
Prov. 26:23, **b-ing** lips and a wicked heart
Is. 9:18, wickedness **b-s** like a fire
42:3, dimly **b-ing** wick He will not
Luke 3:17, He will **b** up the chaff
24:32, our hearts **b-ing** within us
John 5:35, He was the lamp that was **b-ing**
1 Cor. 13:3, deliver my body to be **b-ed**
Rev. 18:8, she will be **b-ed** up with fire
Gen. 30:2; Ex. 32:12,19; Ps. 11:6;

BURN (Continued)
Is. 33:14; Mal. 4:1; Matt. 13:30;
Rom. 12:20; Heb. 6:8; Rev. 4:5;
19:20

BURNT OFFERING Gen. 22:7; Lev.
1:4; 6:9; Is. 61:8
Ps. 40:6, **B** and sin offering Thou
hast not required
Jer. 6:20, **b-s** are not acceptable
Hos. 6:6, knowledge of God rather
than **b-s**
Mark 12:33, more than all **b-s** and
sacrifices

BURST—break Job 32:19; Matt.
9:17; Mark 2:22; Luke 5:37

BURY Rom. 6:4, **b-ed** with Him
through baptism
1 Cor. 15:4, and that he was **b-ed**
Gen. 23:4; 47:29; Matt. 8:21,22; 14:12;
Luke 9:59,60; Acts 8:2; Col. 2:12

BUSHEL—ephah Amos 8:5, To
make the **b** smaller

BUSINESS—matter Ps. 107:23, Who
do **b** on great waters
1 Thess. 4:11, attend to your own **b**
James 4:13, engage in **b** and make a
profit
Gen. 24:33; Josh. 2:14; Matt. 22:5;
Acts 19:25

BUSYBODIES—meddler 2 Thess.
3:11, acting like **b**
1 Tim. 5:13, also gossips and **b**

BUTTER—curds Job 29:6; Prov.
30:33
Ps. 55:21, His speech was smoother
than **b**

BUY Is. 55:1, **b** and eat . . . **b** wine
and milk
Matt. 13:44, sells all that he has and
b-s that field
Rev. 3:18, **b** from Me gold refined by
fire
13:17, no one should be able to **b** or
to sell
Gen. 42:2; 47:19; Lev. 22:11; Ruth
4:4; Prov. 23:23; Matt. 25:9;
John 4:8; Rev. 18:11

BUYER Is. 24:2; Ezek. 7:12
Prov. 20:14, Bad, bad, says the **b**

BYWORD—taunt Job 30:9
1 Kin. 9:7, Israel will become . . . a **b**
among all peoples
2 Chr. 7:20, a **b** among all peoples
Job 17:6, a **b** of the people
Ps. 44:14, **b** among the nations

C

CAGE Jer. 5:27, a **c** full of birds

CAKE Gen. 18:6; 1 Kin. 17:13;
2 Kin. 20:7

CALAMITY—destruction Job 31:23,
c from God is a terror
Prov. 1:27, **c** comes on like a
whirlwind
2 Sam. 22:19; 24:16; 1 Chr. 21:15; Job
6:30; 21:17; 31:3; Ps. 18:18;
Prov. 24:16; 27:10; Jon. 3:10; 4:2

CALCULATE—count Is. 40:12, **c-d**
the dust of the earth
Luke 14:28, sit down and **c** the cost

CALF Luke 15:23, bring the fattened
c
Heb. 9:12, blood of goats and **c-ves**
Gen. 18:7; Is. 11:6; Rev. 4:7

CALL—address Gen. 4:26, to **c** upon
the name
Ps. 4:1, Answer me when I **c**
Is. 7:14, **c** His name Immanuel
Matt. 9:13, not come to **c** the
righteous
Luke 6:46, why do you **c** Me, Lord,
Lord
John 13:13, **c** Me Teacher, and Lord
1 Cor. 1:26, consider your **c**, brethren
1 Thess. 4:7, God has not **c-ed** us for
. . . impurity
Deut. 4:26; Ruth 1:20; Ps. 18:3;
Prov. 8:1; Is. 5:20; Jer. 3:19

CALLING—summoning Is. 1:13, the
c of assemblies
Rom. 11:29, gifts and the **c** of God
2 Tim. 1:9, called us with a holy **c**
Heb. 3:1, partakers of a heavenly **c**

CALM—still Is. 7:4, be **c**, have no
fear
Jon. 1:11, the sea may become **c**
Matt. 8:26, it became perfectly **c**
Acts 19:36, you ought to keep **c** . . .
do nothing rash

CAMEL Gen. 24:64; Mark 1:6
Matt. 3:4, John . . . a garment of **c-'s**
hair
19:24, easier for a **c** . . . eye of a
needle
23:24, out a gnat and swallow a **c**

CAMP—settle Ex. 14:19, before the **c**
Deut. 23:14, God walks . . . your **c**
Gen. 32:2; Num. 31:19; Ps. 69:25;
Is. 29:3; Zech. 9:8; Rev. 20:9

CANCEL—blot, erase Is. 28:18; Col.
2:14

CAPTIVE Luke 4:18, RELEASE TO THE
C-S
Eph. 4:8, LED C A HOST OF C-S
Ps. 68:18; Jer. 13:17; Col. 2:8

CAPTIVITY Is. 46:2, have
themselves gone into **c**

CAPTURE Job 5:13, **c-s** the wise

CARCASS—corpse Gen. 15:11;
Judg. 14:8

CARE—concern, worry
Gen. 50:24, God . . . take **c** of you
Ps. 142:4, No one **c-s** for my soul
Ezek. 34:12, I will **c** for My sheep
Luke 10:34, to an inn, and took **c** of
him
1 Tim. 3:5, take **c** of the church
1 Pet. 5:7, because He **c-s** for you
Ps. 8:4; Mark 4:38; 1 Cor. 12:25

CAREFUL—guard, diligent Luke
15:8
Prov. 23:1, Consider **c-ly** what is
before you
Eph. 5:15, be **c** how you walk

CARELESS—idle Matt. 12:36, every
c word

CARGO—merchandise Rev. 18:12,
c-es of gold

CAROUSE Rom. 13:13, not in **c-ing**
and drunkenness

CARPENTER—craftsmen 2 Sam.
5:11; 2 Kin. 22:6; Matt. 13:55;
Mark 6:3

CARRIED—wrought Is. 53:4, our
sorrows He **c**
Matt. 8:17, **c** away our diseases
Luke 16:22, was **c** away by the
angels
Heb. 13:9, not be **c** away by . . .
teachings
1 Pet. 4:3, **c** out the desire of the
Gentiles

CARRY—bear, wear Luke 10:4, **c** no
purse, no bag
23:26, placed on him the cross to **c**
2 Cor. 4:10, **c-ing** about in the body
the dying of Jesus
Ex. 23:1; Num. 10:17; 11:14; Deut.
1:31; 1 Sam. 2:28; Ps. 126:6;
Is. 40:11; 52:11; 63:9; Mark 14:13

CART 1 Sam. 6:8, ark of the LORD . . .
on the **c**
1 Sam. 6:7,14; Is. 5:18; 28:28

CASE—matter Job 19:28; 37:19
Deut. 17:8, any **c** is too difficult for
you
Mic. 6:2, the LORD has a **c** against
His people

CASSIA Ex. 30:24; Ps. 45:8; Ezek.
27:19

CAST—drive, throw, thrust
Ps. 51:11, Do not **c** me away
Eccles. 11:1, **C** your bread on the . . .
waters
Luke 4:29, **c** Him out of the city
12:49, **c** fire upon the earth
John 6:37, will certainly not **c** out
1 Pet. 5:7, **c-ing** all your anxiety
upon Him
Josh. 18:10; Job 6:27; Mark 15:32

CATCH—trap Ps. 10:9; Prov. 6:25;
Song 2:15; Luke 5:10

CATTLE—herd Ps. 50:10, **c** on a
thousand hills
Ex. 12:29; 20:10; Lev. 22:19; Num.
31:28; Ps. 104:14; Hab. 3:17

CAUGHT—seized 2 Cor. 12:4, was **c**
up into Paradise
Gal. 6:1, if a man is **c** in any trespass
Gen. 22:13; Ex. 22:7; Judg. 15:4;
John 21:3

CAUSE—purpose Gen. 2:24, For this
c a man shall leave
Ps. 67:1, **c** His face to shine upon us
Prov. 3:30, Do not contend . . .
without **c**
Matt. 19:5, THIS C A MAN SHALL
LEAVE
John 15:25, HATED ME WITHOUT A C
Ps. 112:5; Is. 45:7; Rom. 16:17;
1 Cor. 3:6

CAVE—shelter 1 Kin. 18:4; Zeph.
2:6; John 11:38; Heb. 11:38

CEASE Ex. 23:12, day you shall **c**
from labor
Ps. 46:9, He makes wars to **c**
Luke 7:45, not **c-d** to kiss My feet
1 Cor. 13:8, are tongues, they will **c**

1 Thess. 5:17, pray without **c**-ing
Gen. 8:22; Deut. 15:11; Ps. 37:8;
Prov. 23:4

CEDAR—*fir* 1 Kin. 5:6; 6:15; Job
40:17; Ps. 92:12

CENSER Ezek. 8:11; Rev. 8:3,5

CENSUS—*tax* Luke 2:1, a **c** . . . of all
the inhabited earth
Acts 5:37, rose up in the days of
the **c**

CENT Matt. 5:26, paid up the last **c**
Matt. 10:29, sparrows sold for a **c**
Mark 12:42, two small copper coins
. . . a **c**

CERTAIN—*sure* 2 Pet. 1:10, make **c**
about His calling

CERTIFICATE Matt. 5:31, A **c** OF
DISMISSAL

CHAFF Ps. 1:4; Matt. 3:12

CHAIN—*band* Acts 12:7, **c**-s fell off
his hands
Heb. 11:36, also **c**-s and
imprisonment
Judg. 16:21; 1 Kin. 6:21; Eccles. 7:26;
Mark 5:3; Luke 8:29; Rev. 20:1

CHALCEDONY Rev. 21:19, the
third, **c**

CHAMBER—*room* Gen. 43:30; Judg.
3:20,24; 2 Kin. 4:10; Ps. 19:5;
Joel 2:16

CHAMPION 1 Sam. 17:4,23

CHANCE—*happen* Eccles. 9:11, for
time and **c** overtake
Luke 10:31, by **c** a certain priest

CHANGE—*transform* Ps. 46:2, earth
should **c**
Jer. 13:23, the Ethiopian **c** his skin
Mal. 3:6, I, the LORD, do not **c**
1 Cor. 15:51, we shall all be **c**-d
Gen. 35:2; Job 14:14; Prov. 24:21;
Dan. 2:21

CHANNEL Job 28:10, hews out **c**-s

CHARCOAL—*coal, soot* John 18:18;
21:9

CHARGE—*accusation, crime* Lev.
8:35, **c** of the LORD
2 Chr. 23:6, keep the **c** of the LORD
Ps. 91:11, give His angels **c**
concerning
Matt. 24:45, master put in **c** of his
household
Ex. 23:7; Matt. 4:6; 27:37; Acts 25:27;
1 Cor. 9:18; 1 Tim. 5:21; 1 Pet. 5:3

CHARIOT Ps. 20:7, Some boast in **c**-s
Ps. 104:3, makes the clouds his **c**
Acts 8:28, sitting in his **c** . . . reading
Gen. 46:29; 2 Kin. 2:11; Ps. 46:9

CHARITY—*alms* Luke 12:33, sell . . .
give to **c**

CHARM—*favor* Prov. 31:30, **C** is
deceitful

CHARMER—*babbler* Ps. 58:5;
Eccles. 10:11

CHASE—*drive* Lev. 26:7,8; Deut.
32:30; Job 20:8

CHASTE—*pure* 1 Pet. 3:2, **c** and
respectful behavior

CHASTEN—*discipline* Is. 53:5, **c**-ing
for our well-being
Ps. 38:1; 94:12

CHATTER—*babbling* 1 Tim. 6:20;
2 Tim. 2:16

CHEAT—*deceive, mislead*
Gen. 31:7, father has **c**-ed me

CHEEK Job 16:10; Is. 50:6; Matt. 5:39

CHEER—*merry* Judg. 9:13; 1 Sam.
15:32; Prov. 15:13
Prov. 15:15, **c**-ful heart *has* a
continual feast
2 Cor. 9:7, God loves a **c**-ful giver
James 5:13, Is anyone **c**-ful

CHEESE 1 Sam. 17:18; 2 Sam. 17:29;
Job 10:10

CHICK Matt. 23:37, way a hen
gathers her **c**-s

CHILD Prov. 22:6, Train up a **c** . . .
should go
Prov. 23:13, hold back discipline
from the **c**
Is. 9:6, a **c** will be born to us
Matt. 1:18, Mary . . . with **c** by the
Holy Spirit
2:8, make careful search for the **C**
2:9, stood over where the **C** was
2:13,20, take the **C** and His mother
1 Cor. 13:11, When I was a **c**
Gen. 21:8; Jer. 31:20; Matt. 18:2;
Mark 5:39; Luke 8:54

CHILDBIRTH Ps. 48:6; Rom. 8:22

CHILDHOOD Eccles. 11:9, during
your **c**
2 Tim. 3:15, from **c** you have known

CHILDREN—*babes, immature* Gen.
3:16; 1 Sam. 16:11
Ps. 103:13, father has compassion on
his **c**
Prov. 31:28, **c** rise up and bless her
Jer. 31:15, Rachel is weeping for
her **c**
Ezek. 18:2, **c**-'s teeth are set on edge
Matt. 2:16, slew all the male **c**
2:18, RACHEL WEEPING FOR HER **C**
10:21, **c** WILL RISE UP AGAINST
PARENTS
18:3, and become like **c**
Is. 3:4; 49:21; Matt. 3:9; 11:16; 19:14;
1 John 2:1; Rev. 2:23

CHOICE—*pleasant* 1 Sam. 9:2, **c**
and handsome man
Rom. 9:11, God's purpose according
to His **c**
1 Thess. 1:4, knowing . . . His **c** of
you
Gen. 23:6; 2 Sam. 10:9; Song 4:16;
Acts 15:7; Rom. 11:5,28

CHOKE Matt. 13:22, riches **c** the
word
Mark 4:19, **c** the word
Luke 8:14, **c**-d with worries

CHOOSE—*take* Heb. 11:25, **c**-ing . . .
endure ill treatment
2 Pet. 1:10, calling and **c**-ing you

Ex. 17:9; Deut. 1:13; Josh. 24:15;
Is. 7:15

CHOSEN—*elect, beloved,*
esteemed, loved, choose
Is. 65:9, My **c** ones shall inherit
Luke 9:35, This is My son, My **C** One
Col. 3:12, who have been **c** of God
2 Tim. 2:10, endure all things . . .
who are **c**
1 Pet. 2:9, you are A **C** RACE
Deut. 7:6; Ps. 119:30; Is. 42:1; 45:4;
Matt. 12:18; Rom. 11:7; 1 Tim. 5:21;
1 Pet. 1:1; 2 John 1

CHRIST—*Messiah, Lord* 2 Thess.
3:5; 2 John 9
Matt. 16:16, Thou art the **C**, the Son
Luke 24:46, the **C** should suffer
Acts 2:36, made Him both Lord
and **C**
1 Cor. 1:23, we preach **C** crucified
Phil. 1:21, to live is **C**
Col. 3:4, **C**, who is our life
1 Thess. 4:16, the dead in **C** shall rise

CHRISTIAN Acts 11:26, first called
C-s in Antioch
Acts 26:28, persuade me to become
a **C**
1 Pet. 4:16, if *anyone suffers* as a **C**

CHURCH Matt. 16:18, rock I will
build My **c**
Matt. 18:17, tell it to the **c**; refuses to
listen . . . **c**
Acts 15:4, received by the **c**
1 Cor. 11:18, come together as a **c**
14:35, for a woman to speak in **c**
2 Cor. 11:8, robbed other **c**-es
Eph. 5:23, Christ . . . head of the **c**
1 Tim. 3:5, how will he take care of
the **c**
Heb. 12:23, general assembly and **c**

CIRCULATE 1 Sam. 2:24, LORD's
people **c**-ing

CIRCUMCISE Phil. 3:5, **c**-d the
eighth day
Col. 2:11, in Him you were also **c**-d
Gen. 17:10; Deut. 30:6; Luke 1:59

CIRCUMSTANCE—*degree*
James 1:9, humble **c**-s

CISTERN—*dungeon* Eccles. 12:6,
wheel at the **c** is crushed
Jer. 2:13, hew for themselves **c**-s,
Broken **c**-s
Prov. 5:15; Jer. 38:6

CITIZEN—*free* Eph. 2:19, fellow-**c**-s
with the saints
Luke 15:15; Acts 21:39; 22:28

CITY Num. 35:6; Josh. 15:59, **c** of
refuge
Ps. 46:4, make glad the **c** of God
107:4, an inhabited **c**
127:1, Unless the LORD guards the **c**
Zech. 8:3, the **C** of Truth
Matt. 2:23, resided in a **c** called
Nazareth
4:5, took Him into the holy **c**
5:14, a **c** set on a hill
10:11, whatever **c** or village you
enter
21:10, all the **c** was stirred
Acts 8:8, much rejoicing in that **c**
Heb. 11:10, a **c** which has
foundations
12:22, the **c** of the living God

CITY *(Continued)*
Rev. 21:2, I saw the holy **c**
Gen. 4:17; 11:4; 2 Sam. 19:37; Eccles. 9:14; Is. 1:26; 19:18; 33:20; Matt. 10:14; 21:10; Luke 9:5; 24:49; Acts 7:58

CLAMOR—*boisterous* Eph. 4:31, anger and **c**

CLAN—*thousand* Is. 60:22, become a **c**

CLAP Ps. 47:1, O **c** your hands, all peoples
Is. 55:12, trees of the field will **c**
2 Kin. 11:12; Job 27:23; 34:37; Ps. 98:8; Lam. 2:15; Ezek. 25:6

CLASS—*reckon* Luke 22:37, HE WAS C-ED

CLAW—*hoof* Dan. 4:33, nails like birds' **c**-s

CLAY Job 4:19, who dwell in houses of **c**
Job 33:6, formed out of **c**
Jer. 18:6, **c** in the potter's hand
1 Kin. 7:46; Is. 64:8; Dan. 2:33; John 9:6; Rom. 9:21

CLEAN—*cleanse, acquit, purify*
Ps. 19:9, fear of the LORD is **c**
24:4, who has **c** hands
51:10, Create in me a **c** heart
Matt. 3:12, thoroughly **c** His threshing floor
Matt. 8:2; Mark 1:40; Luke 5:12, Thou canst make me **c**
John 15:3, **c** because of the word
1 Cor. 5:7, **C** out the old leaven
2 Kin. 5:12; Job 14:4; Is. 1:16; 52:11; Matt. 23:26; Luke 11:39,41; John 13:10

CLEANSE—*clean, purify, wash*
Matt. 8:3; 10:8; 11:5, I am willing; be **c-d**
Mark 7:4, not eat unless they **c** themselves
Acts 10:15; 11:9, What God has **c-d**
15:9, **c-ing** their hearts by faith
James 4:8, **C** your hands, you sinners
1 John 1:7, blood . . . **c-s** us from all sin
Prov. 20:9; Luke 4:27; 7:22; 17:17; 2 Cor. 7:1

CLEAR—*pure, plain* Is. 40:3, **C** the way for the LORD
Matt. 7:5, you will see **c-ly** *enough*
Rom. 1:20, have been **c-ly** seen
Rev. 22:1, water of life, **c** as crystal
Gen. 20:16; Num. 14:18; Job 26:13; Is. 32:4

CLEAVE—*cling* Gen. 2:24, shall **c** to his wife
Hab. 3:9, **c** the earth with rivers
Matt. 19:5; Eph. 5:31

CLEFT Song 2:14; Is. 2:21; Jer. 49:16

CLEVER—*skillful, wise* 1 Cor. 1:17, not in **c-ness**
1 Cor. 1:19, **c-ness** of the **c** I will set aside
2 Pet. 1:16, not follow **c-ly** devised tales

CLIMB 1 Sam. 14:13; Jer. 48:44; Luke 19:4; John 10:1

CLING Josh. 23:8, **c** to the LORD your God
Ps. 63:8, My soul **c-s** to Thee
102:5, My bones **c** to my flesh
John 20:17, Stop **c-ing** to Me

CLOAK—*mantle, coat* Ruth 3:15, Give me the **c** . . . on you
Is. 3:7; Matt. 9:20; Acts 12:8; 2 Tim. 4:13

CLOD—*crust* Job 21:33, **c**-s of the valley

CLOSE (adj.)—*intimate, near*
Prov. 18:24, a friend who sticks **c-r** than
Judg. 20:34; Ps. 41:9

CLOSE (v.)—*shut, stop* Gen. 7:16; 8:2, LORD **c-d** it behind
Num. 16:33, the earth **c-d** over them
Acts 28:27, THEY HAVE C-D THEIR EYES
Rom. 3:19, every mouth may be **c-d**
1 John 3:17, **c-s** his heart against him
Rev. 21:25, its gates shall never be **c-d**
Judg. 19:9

CLOTH 1 Sam. 21:9; Matt. 9:16; Luke 2:7; John 11:44

CLOTHE—*array, adorn, wrap* Job 10:11, **C** me with skin
Matt. 6:29, Solomon . . . not **c-d** like
25:36, naked, and you **c-d** Me
1 Pet. 5:5, **c** yourselves with humility
Rev. 7:13, are **c-d** in the white robes
1 Kin. 11:29; Job 40:10; Ps. 65:13; 93:1; Is. 52:1; Luke 24:49; Rev. 3:5

CLOTHES—*dress, garment* Matt. 22:11, not . . . in wedding **c**
James 2:3, one who is wearing the fine **c**
Deut. 29:5; Josh. 9:5; 1 Sam. 19:13; 2 Sam. 12:20; Mark 14:63; James 2:2

CLOTHING—*clothes, dress, raiment*
Matt. 6:25, food, and the body than **c**
7:15, come to you in sheep's **c**
1 Tim. 2:9, with proper **c**
Deut. 8:4; Job 24:10; Jer. 10:9

CLOUD—*darkness* Gen. 9:13, My bow in the **c**
Ex. 13:21, a pillar of **c** by day
20:21, Moses approached the thick **c**
24:15, **c** covered the mountain
Matt. 24:30, SON OF MAN COMING ON THE C-S
Mark 9:7, a **c** formed . . . voice came out of the **c**
Luke 12:54, see a **c** rising in the west
21:27, IN A **c** with power and great glory
Acts 1:9, a **c** received Him out of their sight
1 Thess. 4:17, caught up . . . in the **c**-s
Rev. 1:7, HE IS COMING WITH THE C-S
Ex. 14:24; 33:9; 1 Kin. 8:12; 2 Chr. 6:1; Ps. 99:7; 105:39; Ezek. 30:3; Jude 12

CLUSTER Is. 65:8, new wine is found in the **c**
Num. 13:23; Mic. 7:1; Rev. 14:18

COAL—*soot, charcoal* Prov. 6:28; Is. 6:6
Prov. 25:22, heap burning **c**-s on his head
Rom. 12:20, HEAP . . . C-S UPON HIS HEAD

COAST Acts 27:2, the regions along the **c**

COAT—*cloak* Matt. 5:40, let him have your **c** also

COBRA Job 20:16, He sucks the poison of **c**-s
Ps. 58:4, Like a deaf **c**
91:13, tread upon the lion and **c**

COCK Matt. 26:34,75, before a **c** crows
Mark 13:35, at **c**-crowing, or in the morning

COFFIN—*bier* Gen. 50:26; Luke 7:14

COIN—*money* Matt. 22:19, Show Me the **c** *used* for
Luke 15:8, woman . . . loses **c**

COLD Prov. 25:25, Like **c** water to a weary soul
Matt. 10:42, a cup of **c** water
24:12, love will grow **c**
Rev. 3:15, that you were **c** or hot
Gen. 8:22; Job 24:7; 37:9; Prov. 25:13; John 18:18; 2 Cor. 11:27

COLLAPSED—*fell* Luke 6:49, immediately it **c**

COLLECT—*exact* Luke 3:13, **C** no more
Luke 19:23, would have **c-ed** it with interest

COLLECTION 1 Cor. 16:1, the **c** for the saints

COLOR Ezek. 16:16, high places of various **c**-s

COLT—*foal* Zech. 9:9, a **c**, the foal of a donkey
Matt. 21:2, a donkey tied *there* and a **c** with her
John 12:15, KING COMES . . . ON A DONKEY'S **c**

COMBINE 1 Cor. 2:13, **c-ing** spiritual *thoughts . . . words*

COME—*enter, return* Ps. 95:6, **C**, let us worship
Zech. 9:9, your king is **c-ing** to you
Matt. 6:10, Thy kingdom **c**
11:28, **C** to Me, all who are weary
Mark 10:14, children to **c** to Me
Luke 21:27, SON OF MAN C-ING
John 17:1, Father, the hour has **c**
Rev. 22:20, I am **c-ing** quickly
Mark 14:38; Luke 19:23; 2 Thess. 2:2

COMFORT—*consolation, rest*
Ps. 23:4, Thy rod . . . they **c** me
Is. 61:2, To **c** who mourn
Matt. 5:4, who mourn, for they shall be **c-ed**
Acts 9:31, in the **c** of the Holy Spirit
2 Cor. 1:3, God of all **c**
1:6, for your **c** and salvation
1 Thess. 4:18, **c** one another
2 Thess. 2:17, **c** and strengthen your hearts
Job 29:25; Ps. 77:2; Prov. 29:17;

Eccles. 4:1; Is. 54:11; Lam. 1:21;
Matt. 2:18; Luke 6:24; 16:25; 2 Cor.
7:4,13; 2 Thess. 2:16

COMFORTER—*helper* Job 16:2,
Sorry **c-s** are you all
Ps. 69:20, looked for . . . **c-s**, but I
found none
Nah. 3:7, Where will I seek **c-s** for
you

COMING 2 Sam. 3:25, your going out
and **c** in
Mal. 3:2, endure the day of His **c**
Matt. 11:3, Are You the **C** One
24:30, SON OF MAN **C**
26:64, **C** ON THE CLOUDS OF HEAVEN
John 5:25, an hour is **c** and now is
James 5:8, **c** of the Lord is at hand
2 Pet. 3:4, promise of His **c**

COMMAND—*declare, spoke* Gen.
18:19; Lev. 24:12; Deut. 2:37
Ps. 33:9, He **c-ed**, and it stood fast
Jon. 2:10, LORD **c-ed** the fish
Matt. 1:24, angel of the Lord **c-ed**
him
4:3, Son of God, **c** that these stones
20:21, **C** that . . . these two sons of
mine
Luke 8:25, He **c-s** even the winds
9:54, **c** fire to come down from
heaven
John 15:14, do what I **c** you

COMMANDER—*general* Judg. 5:9;
1 Chr. 27:34; Is. 55:4

COMMANDMENT—*instruction,
duty*
Ex. 20:6, keep My **c-s**
34:28, tablets . . . the Ten **C-s**
Ps. 19:8, **C** of the LORD is pure
Matt. 5:19, one of the least of these
c-s
22:36, which is the great **c**
John 14:15, If you love Me . . . keep
My **c-s**
Prov. 6:20; Eccles. 12:13; Matt. 22:40;
John 15:10

COMMEND—*praise* Eccles. 8:15, So
I **c-ed** pleasure
Acts 20:32, I **c** you to God
1 Cor. 8:8; 2 Cor. 3:1

COMMISSION Acts 26:12, authority
and **c** of . . . priests

COMMIT—*entrust, practice,
wrought*
Ex. 20:14, You shall not **c** adultery
Ps. 31:5, into Thy hand I **c** my spirit
37:5, **C** your way to the LORD
Luke 23:46, into Thy hands I **c** My
spirit
John 8:34, every one who **c-s** sin
Ex. 32:30; Lev. 20:12; Prov. 16:3;
Luke 18:20; 1 Pet. 2:22

COMMON—*prevalent* Lev. 4:27; Jer.
26:23
Acts 2:44, had all things in **c**
Titus 1:4, in a **c** faith
Jude 3, write you about our **c**
salvation

COMMOTION—*disturbance* Jer.
10:22, great **c** out of . . . land

COMPANION—*fellow* Prov. 13:20, **c**
of fools will suffer

Heb. 1:9, OIL OF GLADNESS ABOVE
THY **c-s**
Ex. 2:13; Job 30:29; Eccles. 4:10

COMPANY—*congregation*
Job 15:34, the **c** of the godless

COMPARE Prov. 3:15, nothing . . . **c-
s** with her
Matt. 11:16, to what shall I **c** this
generation
Rom. 8:18, not worthy . . . **c-d** with
the glory

COMPARISON Judg. 8:2; Hag. 2:3

COMPASSION—*lovingkindness,
mercy*
Ex. 33:19, **c** on whom I will show **c**
Ps. 25:6, Remember . . . Thy **c**
72:13, **c** on the poor and needy
103:13, father has **c** on *his* children
111:4, LORD is gracious and **c**-ate
Col. 3:12, put on a heart of **c**
Matt. 9:36; 15:32; Luke 15:20; Rom.
9:15

COMPEL—*force, press* Luke 14:23,
c *them* to come in

COMPETE—*strive* 1 Cor. 9:25,
everyone who **c-s**
2 Tim. 2:5, **c-s** as an athlete

COMPLACENCY Prov. 1:32, **c** of
fools shall destroy them

COMPLAIN James 5:9, Do not **c** . . .
against one another
Job 7:11; Ps. 55:17

COMPLAINING—*babbling*
Prov. 23:29, Who has **c**

COMPLAINT—*grudge* 1 Pet. 4:9
without **c**

COMPLETE—*fulfill, full, utterly*
Is. 2:18, idols will **c-ly** vanish
Col. 2:10, in Him . . . made **c**
James 1:4, that you may be perfect
and **c**
1 John 1:4, our joy may be **c**
Rev. 20:3, thousand years were **c-d**
Gen. 2:1; 29:27; Ex. 5:13; Num. 15:31;
Esth. 1:5; 1 Cor. 1:10; Rev. 20:7

COMPOSE Job 16:4, I could **c** words
against you

COMPOSURE Eccles. 10:4, **c** allays
great offenses

COMPREHEND—*calculate*
Job 37:5, things . . . cannot **c**
John 1:5, darkness did not **c** it

COMPREHENSION— *understanding*
Phil. 4:7, peace . . . surpasses all **c**

COMPULSION—*constrain*
1 Pet. 5:2, not under **c**, but

CONCEAL—*cover, hide* Prov. 12:23;
Is. 3:9; Jer. 50:2
Ps. 40:10, have not **c-ed** thy
lovingkindness
Prov. 27:5, love that is **c-ed**

CONCEIT—*pride*
Phil. 2:3, nothing . . . selfishness or
empty **c**

1 Tim. 6:4, is **c-ed** *and* understands
nothing

CONCEIVE Num. 11:12; Job 15:35;
Ps. 51:5; Matt. 1:20; Acts 5:4;
James 1:15

CONCERN—*care* Col. 4:13, he has a
deep **c** for you
1 Sam. 1:16; Matt. 4:6; John 12:6;
Rom. 1:3; 1 Cor. 7:32; 9:9; 12:1

CONCILIATE—*entreat*
1 Cor. 4:13, slandered, we try to **c**

CONCLUSION
Eccles. 12:13, The **c** when all has
been heard

CONDEMN—*discredit, judge*
Is. 50:9, Who . . . **c-s** Me
Mark 16:16, who has disbelieved
shall be **c-ed**
Gal. 2:11, because he stood **c-ed**
1 John 3:20, in whatever our heart **c-
s** us
Job 9:20; Prov. 12:2; Mark 10:33;
Luke 6:37; Rom. 2:1; 14:23

CONDEMNATION—*judgment*
Rom. 3:8, Their **c** is just
Rom. 8:1, no **c** for those who are in
Matt. 23:14; Mark 12:40; Luke 20:47;
23:40; Rom. 13:2

CONDUCT—*bring, behavior* Job
33:17; Ezek. 7:27; Acts 17:15
Col. 4:5, **C** yourselves with wisdom
2 Pet. 2:7, sensual **c** of unprincipled
men

CONDUIT 2 Kin. 18:17; 20:20; Is. 7:3;
36:2

CONFER—*consult* Acts 4:15; 25:12

CONFESS—*acknowledge* Matt. 3:6,
they **c-ed** their sins
Matt. 10:32, **c** Me before men . . . **c**
him before My Father
Mark 1:5, baptized . . . **c-ing** their
sins
Rom. 10:9, **c** with your mouth
James 5:16, **c** your sins to one
another
1 John 1:9, If we **c** our sins, He is
Ps. 32:5; John 1:20; Rom. 10:10

CONFESSION 2 Cor. 9:13, your **c** of
the gospel of Christ
1 Tim. 6:13; Heb. 10:23

CONFIDENCE—*boldness, trust*
Prov. 3:26; Heb. 3:6
Job 31:24, have put my **c** in gold
Is. 32:17, quietness and **c** forever
2 Cor. 1:12, For our proud **c** is this
Phil. 1:26, your proud **c** in me
3:3, and put no **c** in the flesh
Heb. 4:16, draw near with **c** to the
throne of grace
1 John 4:17, we may have **c** in the
day of judgment

CONFIDENT Eph. 3:12, **c** access
through faith in Him

CONFIRM—*establish* Ps. 90:17, **c**
the work of our hands
Rom. 15:8, to **c** the promises *given* to
the fathers
1 Cor. 1:8, also **c** you to the end
Matt. 18:16; Mark 16:20

CONFIRMATION Phil. 1:7, defense and **c** of the gospel
Heb. 6:16, an oath *given* as **c** is an end

CONFORM Rom. 8:29, *to become c-ed* to the image
Rom. 12:2, do not be **c-ed** to this world
Phil. 3:10, being **c-ed** to His death

CONFOUND Josh. 10:10; Is. 19:3

CONFUSE Gen. 11:7, **c** their language

CONFUSION—*disorder*
1 Sam. 14:20, *was* very great **c**
1 Cor. 14:33, not *a* God of **c**

CONGREGATION—*company, assembly*
Ex. 12:3, Speak to all the **c**
Ps. 82:1, His stand in His own **c**
149:1, **c** of the godly ones

CONQUER Rom. 8:37, **c** through Him
Rev. 6:2, went out **c-ing**, and to **c**

CONSCIENCE Acts 23:1, lived . . . good **c** before God
Rom. 13:5, also for **c** sake
1 Cor. 8:7, their **c** being weak
1 Tim. 3:9, faith with a clear **c**
4:2, **c** as with a branding iron
1 Pet. 3:16, keep a good **c**
Acts 24:16; Rom. 2:15; Heb. 9:14; 10:22

CONSECRATE—*sanctify*
Lev. 11:44, **C** yourselves
1 Sam. 21:4, there is **c-d** bread
Matt. 12:4, They ate **c-d** bread
Ex. 28:38,41; 29:1,21,29,35; 40:9;
Lev. 12:4; 16:19; 25:10; Num. 6:11;
1 Sam. 21:6; 1 Kin. 8:64; 9:3,7;
2 Chr. 7:7

CONSENT—*agree* Prov. 1:10; Is. 1:19; Luke 23:51

CONSIDER—*notice, observe*
Ps. 41:1, blessed is he who **c-s** the helpless
Eccles. 7:14, in the day of adversity **c**
Luke 12:24, **C** the ravens, for they
Heb. 10:24, let us **c** . . . one another
11:26, **c-ing** the reproach of Christ
2 Sam. 19:19; Ps. 44:22; 48:13; 77:5

CONSIDERATION
Acts 27:3, Julius treated Paul with **c**

CONSIST Luke 12:15, his life **c** of his possessions

CONSOLATION—*comfort* Job 15:11, Are the **c-s** of God . . . small
Phil. 2:1, if there is any **c** of love

CONSPIRACY—*plot* 2 Sam. 15:12, the **c** was strong

CONSTRAIN—*persuade, urge* Job 32:18

CONSULT—*confer, counsel* 1 Kin. 12:6,8
Gal. 1:16, I did not . . . **c** with flesh and blood

CONSUME—*eat, devour*
Ex. 3:2, yet the bush was not **c-d**

Ex. 24:17; Is. 29:6; 30:27,30; 33:14, **c-ing** fire
Deut. 4:24, God is a **c-ing** fire
Ezek. 15:7, yet the fire will **c** them
Lev. 10:2; Deut. 5:25; 32:24; Ps. 39:11; 49:14; 69:9; 90:7; Eccles. 4:5; Luke 9:54; John 2:17; Gal. 5:15; James 5:3

CONSUMMATION—*end* Heb. 9:26, at the **c**

CONSUMPTION Lev. 26:16; Deut. 28:22

CONTAIN 1 Kin. 8:27; 1 Pet. 2:6

CONTAINER Luke 8:16, covers it over with a **c**

CONTEMPT Rom. 14:10, regard your brother with **c**
2 Cor. 10:10, his speech **c-ible**
Job 12:21; Prov. 18:3; Dan. 12:2

CONTEND—*strive* Is. 50:8, Who will **c** with Me
Is. 57:16, I will not **c** forever
Jude 3, **c** earnestly for the faith
Judg. 8:1; Job 40:2; Prov. 3:30; Is. 49:25; Jer. 2:9

CONTENT—*satisfy* Luke 3:14, be **c** with your wages
Phil. 4:11, I have learned to be **c**
1 Tim. 6:6, accompanied by **c-ment**
2 Cor. 12:10; Heb. 13:5

CONTENTIOUS Prov. 21:19; 25:24; 1 Cor. 11:16

CONTINUAL—*unceasing, constant*
Num. 4:16; 28:24
Prov. 15:15, cheerful heart *has* a **c** feast

CONTINUALLY—*perpetual*
1 Chr. 16:11, Seek His face **c**
Ps. 34:1, praise shall **c** be in my mouth
Prov. 6:21; Luke 18:5

CONTINUE—*persevere*
Acts 13:43, **c** in the grace of God
Heb. 13:1, Let love of the brethren **c**

CONTRARY—*hostile*
Matt. 14:24, for the wind was **c**
Rom. 11:24, grafted **c** to nature
16:17, **c** to the teaching
2 Cor. 2:7, on the **c** . . . rather forgive
Gal. 2:7, on the **c**, seeing that I
1 Tim. 1:10, **c** to sound teaching

CONTRIBUTE Rom. 12:13, **c-ing** to the needs of the saints

CONTRIBUTION Rom. 15:26, make a **c** for the poor

CONTRITE—*crush* Ps. 51:17, broken and a **c** heart
Is. 66:2, humble and **c** of spirit

CONTROL—*rule* Prov. 25:28, no **c** over his spirit
2 Cor. 5:14, love of Christ **c-s** us

CONTROVERSY—*dispute*
Jer. 25:31, **c** with the nations

CONVERSE—*discuss*
Luke 24:15, while they were **c-ing**

Acts 17:18, philosophers were **c-ing** with him

CONVERSION Acts 15:3, **c** of the Gentiles

CONVERT—*restore*
Matt. 18:3, unless you are **c-ed**

CONVICT—*reprove*
John 8:46, Which one of you **c-s** Me
16:8, **c** the world concerning sin
Heb. 11:1, the **c-ion** of things not seen

CONVINCE—*persuade* Rom. 14:14, am **c-d** in the Lord Jesus
Heb. 6:9, **c-d** of better things

COOK 1 Sam. 8:13; 9:23,24

COOL Gen. 3:8; Luke 16:24

COPE Acts 6:10, unable to **c** with the wisdom

COPPER Deut. 8:9, you can dig **c**
Matt. 10:9, Do not acquire gold . . . or **c**

COPPERSMITH 2 Tim. 4:14, Alexander the **c**

COPY—*transcribe* Deut. 17:18; Josh. 8:32; Heb. 9:24

CORBAN Mark 7:11, have been helped by is **C**

CORD—*band, chain*
Ps. 18:4, **c-s** of death encompassed me
Prov. 5:22, held with the **c-s** of his sin
Eccles. 12:6, the silver **c** is broken
John 2:15, made a scourge of **c-s**
2 Sam. 22:6; Job 36:8; 38:31; 41:1; Is. 5:18

CORNER Prov. 7:12, lurks by every **c**
Matt. 6:5, synagogues and on the street **c-s**
Acts 10:11, lowered by four **c-s** to the ground
Rev. 7:1, at the four **c-s** of the earth

CORNERSTONE—*corner* Ps. 118:22, the chief **c**
Matt. 21:42, BECAME THE CHIEF **C**
Eph. 2:20, Christ . . . being the **c**
Job 38:6; Is. 28:16

CORPSE—*body* Is. 14:19; Nah. 3:3; Matt. 24:28

CORRECT—*reprove*
Prov. 29:17, **C** your son, and he will
Jer. 10:24, **C** me . . . but with justice
2 Tim. 3:16, profitable . . . for **c-ion**

CORRUPT—*depraved, rotten*
Gen. 6:11, the earth was **c**
Ps. 14:1, They are **c**, they have committed
1 Cor. 15:33, Bad company **c-s** good morals
Job 15:16; Is. 1:4; Jer. 6:28; 2 Cor. 7:2; Eph. 4:22

CORRUPTIBLE—*perish*
Rom. 1:23, in the form of **c** man

CORRUPTION—*decay* Lev. 22:25; Rom. 8:21; 2 Pet. 2:19

CORRUPTION (continued)
Gal. 6:8, shall from the flesh reap c
2 Pet. 1:4, the c that is in the world

COST—*wealth, price*
Ps. 49:8, redemption ... soul is c-ly
Is. 55:1, Without money and without c
Matt. 26:7, vial of very c-ly perfume
2 Sam. 24:24; 1 Kin. 5:17; Ezra 6:4,8; John 12:3; 1 Tim. 2:9

COUCH—*pallet* Gen. 49:4,9
Ps. 6:6, dissolve my c with my tears

COUNCIL Mark 15:43; Luke 23:50
Jer. 23:18, stood in the c of the LORD
Acts 5:27, stood them before the c
6:12, brought Stephen before the C

COUNSEL—*advice, opinion*
Ps. 1:1, not walk in the c
33:11, C of the LORD stands
73:24, With Thy c ... guide me
Prov. 13:10, those who receive c
19:20, Listen to c and accept
Is. 28:29, made *His* c wonderful
John 12:10, chief priests took c
Eph. 1:11, after the c of His will
Ex. 18:19; Judg. 19:30; 1 Kin. 12:6; 2 Chr. 10:9; Ezra 4:5; Ps. 32:8; 62:4; Matt. 22:15; Luke 14:31

COUNSELOR
Is. 9:6, will be called Wonderful C
Rom. 11:34, WHO BECAME HIS c
Job 12:17; Prov. 11:14; Mic. 4:9

COUNT—*consider, number* 2 Cor. 5:19; James 5:11
Gen. 15:5, c the stars, if you are able
Prov. 17:28, closes his lips ... c-ed prudent
1 Cor. 4:15, have c-less tutors in Christ
Phil. 3:8, I c all things to be loss
2 Pet. 3:9, as some c slowness

COUNTENANCE Gen. 4:6, why has your c fallen
Num. 6:26, The LORD lift up His c
Ps. 4:6; 89:15, light of Thy c

COUNTRY—*region*
John 4:44, no honor in his own c
Gen. 12:1; Matt. 2:12; Luke 15:13

COURAGE—*cheer* 2 Chr. 15:7, strong and do not lose c
Ps. 27:14, let your heart take c
John 16:33, take c; I have overcome
Matt. 9:2,22; 14:27; Acts 23:11

COURAGEOUS Deut. 31:6; Josh. 1:7

COURSE Ps. 19:5, strong man to run his c
2 Tim. 4:7, have finished the c
James 3:6, sets on fire the c of our life
Judg. 5:20; Acts 20:24

COURT—*council* Ps. 84:10, a day in Thy c-s
Ex. 27:9; Ps. 135:2; Matt. 10:17

COURTEOUS Acts 28:7, entertained us c-ly three days

COVENANT Job 31:1; Acts 3:25; Gal. 4:24
Gen. 6:18, I will establish My c
Num. 10:33, ark of the c of the LORD
2 Kin. 23:2, book of the c

Ps. 25:10; 103:18, To those who keep His c
Matt. 26:28, My blood of the c
Luke 22:20, This cup ... is the new c
2 Cor. 3:6, servants of a new c
3:14, reading of the old c
Heb. 7:22, Jesus ... guarantee of a better c
8:6, mediator of a better c
13:20, blood of the eternal c
Rev. 11:19, the ark of His c

COVER—*hide* Ps. 32:1, Whose sin is c-ed
Ps. 91:4, c you with His pinions
Prov. 10:12, love c-s all transgressions
Matt. 10:26, nothing c-ed that will not be revealed
James 5:20, will c a multitude of sins
1 Pet. 4:8, love c-s a multitude of sins
Gen. 37:26; Ex. 2:3; Job 36:32; Is. 6:2; 50:6; Luke 23:30

COVERING—*raiment*
Ps. 105:39, spread a cloud for a c
1 Cor. 11:15, her hair is given ... for a c
Gen. 3:7; 2 Sam. 17:19; Is. 50:3; 1 Tim. 6:8

COVET—*crave, desire* Mic. 2:2; Rom. 13:9
Ex. 20:17, You shall not c
Mark 7:22, deeds of c-ing *and* wickedness
Acts 20:33, have c-ed no one's silver
Rom. 7:8, produced in me c-ing of every kind

COW—*ox* Is. 11:7, the c and the bear will graze
Lev. 22:28; Job 21:10

COWARDLY—*fearful* Rev. 21:8, for the c and unbelieving

CRAFT—*deceit* Job 15:5, language of the c-y
Ex. 21:14; Is. 2:16; 2 Cor. 12:16

CRAFTINESS—*shrewd* 2 Cor. 4:2, walking in c

CRAFTSMEN 2 Kin. 24:14; Hos. 13:2; Zech. 1:20; Acts 19:24

CRANE—*thrush* Is. 38:14

CRASH Zeph. 1:10, a loud c from the hills

CRAVE—*desire, covet* Mic. 7:1
Prov. 13:4, soul of the sluggard c-s and gets nothing
21:26, All day long he is c-ing

CRAWL—*creep* Acts 10:12, c-ing creatures of the earth

CREATE—*form* Gen. 1:1, c-d the heavens and the earth
Ps. 51:10, C in me a clean heart
Is. 45:12, made the earth, and c-d man
Mal. 2:10, Has not one God c-d us
Eph. 2:10, c-d in Christ Jesus
4:24, God ... c-d in righteousness
Col. 1:16, in Him all things were c-d
Is. 57:19; 65:17; Mark 13:19; Eph. 3:9; 1 Tim. 2:13

CREATION Mark 10:6, beginning of c, *God* MADE THEM
Mark 13:19, c which God created
16:15, preach the gospel to all c
Rom. 1:20, since the c of the world
8:22, whole c groans
2 Pet. 3:4, from the beginning of c

CREATOR Eccles. 12:1, Remember also your C
Is. 40:28, c of the ends of the earth
Rom. 1:25, the creature rather than the C
1 Pet. 4:19, to a faithful C

CREATURE—*animal, beast* Gen. 1:21, every living c
Lev. 11:47, the edible c and the c ... not to be eaten
2 Cor. 5:17, he is a new c; the old things
Rom. 1:23; James 1:18

CREDIT—*thanks* Luke 6:32, what c is *that* to you

CREDITOR Ps. 109:11; Is. 50:1
Deut. 15:2, every c shall release what ... loaned

CREEP Gen. 1:26; Ps. 148:10

CRESCENT Is. 3:18, will take away ... c ornaments

CRIME Job 31:11; Ezek. 7:23

CRIMINAL 2 Tim. 2:9, suffer hardship ... as a c

CRIMSON 2 Chr. 2:7, in purple, c and violet
Is. 1:18, like c, They will be like wool

CRIPPLE Matt. 18:8, better ... to enter life c-d
Luke 14:21, bring in c-d and blind

CRITICIZE Is. 29:24, those who c ... accept instruction

CROCUS Is. 35:1, blossom; Like the c

CROOKED—*perverse* Deut. 32:5; Prov. 21:8; Phil. 2:15
Ps. 125:5, turn aside to their c ways
Eccles. 1:15, c cannot be straightened
Luke 3:5, THE C SHALL BECOME STRAIGHT

CROP Lev. 1:16, take away its c

CROSS—*tree* Matt. 10:38, take his c
Matt. 27:40, come down from the c
John 19:17, went out, bearing His own c
19:25, standing by the c of Jesus
Acts 5:30, hanging Him on a c
1 Cor. 1:17, that the c of Christ should not
Gal. 6:14, except in the c of our Lord
Phil. 2:8, even death on a c
3:18, enemies of the c of Christ
Heb. 12:2, endured the c, despising
1 Kin. 1:6; 1 Cor. 1:18; Eph. 2:16; Col. 1:20

CROUCH—*bow* Job 38:40; Ps. 10:10

CROW Matt. 26:74, immediately a cock c-ed
Mark 14:72; Luke 22:34; 22:60

CROWD—*press*
Mark 2:4, unable to get to Him . . . c
5:27, in the c behind *Him*, and
touched

CROWN—*wreath* Ps. 8:5, c him
with glory
Ps. 103:4, c-s you with
lovingkindness
Prov. 12:4, excellent wife is the c of
14:18, are c-ed with knowledge
14:24, c of the wise is their
16:31, gray head is a c of glory
17:6, grandchildren are the c of old
men
Heb. 2:9, Jesus . . . c-ed with glory
and honor
Gen. 49:26; Ps. 21:3; 65:11

CRUCIFIXION Matt. 26:2, delivered
up for c

CRUCIFY Matt. 27:22, Let Him be c-
ed
Matt. 28:5, Jesus who has been c-ed
Mark 15:13, shouted back, C Him
1 Cor. 1:23, we preach Christ c-ed
Gal. 2:20, I have been c-ed with
Christ
6:14, world has been c-ed to me
Heb. 6:6, c to themselves the Son of
God
Matt. 20:19; 27:35; 1 Cor. 1:13;
2 Cor. 13:4

CRUEL—*fierce* Prov. 11:17; Matt.
15:22

CRUMBS Matt. 15:27; Mark 7:28

CRUSH—*batter* Ps. 34:18, saves
those . . . c-ed in spirit
Is. 53:5, c-ed for our iniquities
53:10, Lord was pleased to c Him
Amos 4:1, who c the needy
Rom. 16:20, c Satan under your feet
2 Cor. 4:8, but not c-ed
Lev. 22:24; 2 Kin. 18:21; Job 39:15;
Jer. 17:18

CRUST Job 7:5, flesh is clothed . . . a
c of dirt

CRY—*outcry*
Gen. 4:10, your brother's blood is c-
ing
Ps. 9:12, the c of the afflicted
130:1, Out of the depths I have c-ed
Matt. 3:3, ONE C-ING IN THE
WILDERNESS
Rev. 21:4, no . . . mourning, or c-ing
Ex. 2:6; 32:18; Lev. 13:45; Ps. 17:1;
27:7; Is. 42:2; Mark 15:37

CRYSTAL Ezek. 1:22; Rev. 4:6; 21:11

CUB 2 Sam. 17:8; Jer. 51:38; Nah.
2:11

CUBIT Gen. 6:15, length of the ark
300 c-s
Esth. 5:14, a gallows fifty c-s high
Matt. 6:27, add a single c to his life's
span
Deut. 3:11; Ezek. 43:13

CUCUMBER Num. 11:5; Is. 1:8

CUD Lev. 11:3; Deut. 14:6

CULTIVATE—*till* Gen. 2:5, no man
to c the ground

Ps. 37:3, Dwell in the land and c
faithfulness
Gen. 2:15; Deut. 28:39; 2 Sam. 9:10;
Ezek. 36:9

CUMMIN Matt. 23:23, and dill and c

CUP Ps. 23:5, My c overflows
Matt. 10:42, a c of cold water
20:22, able to drink the c
23:25, outside of the c
26:27, took a c and gave thanks
26:39, let this c pass from Me
Luke 22:20, c . . . is the new
covenant
John 18:11, the c which the Father
has given
1 Cor. 10:16, the c of blessing
Ps. 116:13; Prov. 23:31; Mark 7:4;
1 Cor. 10:21

CUPBEARER Gen. 40:1; 41:9; 1 Kin.
10:5; 2 Chr. 9:4; Neh. 1:11

CURDLE Job 10:10, and c me like
cheese

CURDS—*butter* Judg. 5:25; Is.
7:15,22

CURE Luke 7:21, At that very time
He c-d many
Luke 13:32, perform c-s today and
tomorrow

CURSE—*oath* Ex. 22:28, You shall
not c God
Mal. 4:6, smite the land with a c
Luke 6:28, bless those who c you
Rom. 3:14, WHOSE MOUTH IS FULL OF
C-ING
Gal. 3:13, redeemed us from the c
Gen. 3:14; 12:3; 27:12; Lev. 19:14;
1 Sam. 3:13; Jer. 42:18; 44:12; Mic.
6:10; Zech. 14:11; Mark 14:71;
Rom. 12:14; James 3:9

CURTAIN Ex. 26:1; Song 1:5; Is.
40:22

CUSHION Mark 4:38, asleep on the c

CUSTODY—*prison* Esth. 2:3,8,14;
Matt. 4:12

CUSTOM—*manner* Luke 4:16, as
was His c
Acts 16:21, c-s which are not lawful
Judg. 11:39; Ezra 4:13; John 18:39;
19:40; Acts 28:17; Rom. 13:7

CUT Matt. 3:10, not bear good fruit is
c down
Matt. 21:8, others were c-ing
branches
26:51, and c off his ear
Acts 7:54, they were c to the quick
Rom. 11:22, you also will be c off
Ex. 9:15; Judg. 1:6; Ps. 12:3; Prov.
10:31; Is. 45:2; Jer. 7:29; Matt. 5:30;
24:51

CYMBAL 2 Sam. 6:5; 1 Chr. 15:16;
16:5; Ps. 150:5; 1 Cor. 13:1

D

DAILY—*continual* Ps. 68:19, who d
bears our burden
Prov. 8:30, I was d His delight
Matt. 6:11; Luke 11:3, Give us . . .
our d bread
Luke 9:23, take up his cross d

Acts 16:5, churches . . . increasing in
number d
17:11, examining the Scriptures d
1 Cor. 15:31, I die d
Dan. 1:5; Acts 6:1; James 2:15

DAINTY Gen. 49:20; Jer. 6:2

DAMAGE—*loss* Ezra 4:13,22; Acts
27:10

DANCE—*skip* 2 Sam. 6:14, David
was d-ing before the Lord
Ps. 30:11, turned . . . mourning into
d-ing
149:3, praise His name with d-ing
150:4, Praise Him with timbrel and
d-ing
Eccles. 3:4, a time to d
Matt. 11:17, We played . . . you did
not d
14:6, daughter of Herodias d-d
Ex. 32:19; Judg. 21:23; 1 Sam. 18:6;
Jer. 31:13; Lam. 5:15; Mark 6:22;
Luke 7:32

DANGER Acts 19:27; 27:9

DARE—*presume*
Acts 5:13, none . . . d-d to associate
Rom. 5:7, someone would d even to
die
1 Cor. 6:1, d to go to law before the
unrighteous
Job 41:10; Jude 9

DARK—*dim, shadow* Num. 12:8,
not in d sayings
Joel 2:10, sun and the moon grow d
Luke 12:3, whatever you have said in
the d
Gen. 15:17; Job 24:16; Is. 9:2; Lam.
4:1

DARKEN—*obscure*
Job 38:2, Who is this that d-s
counsel
Eccles. 12:2, stars are d-ed
Matt. 24:29, THE SUN WILL BE D-ED
Rom. 1:21, their foolish heart was d-
ed
11:10, LET THEIR EYES BE D-ED TO
SEE NOT
Eph. 4:18, being d-ed in their
understanding
Ex. 10:15; Mark 13:24; Rev. 16:10

DARKNESS—*cloud, gloom* Gen.
1:2, d was over the surface
Ex. 10:21, d over the land of Egypt
. . . d which
2 Sam. 22:29, the Lord illumines
my d
Ps. 91:6, pestilence that stalks in d
107:10, those who dwelt in d
112:4, Light arises in the d
Eccles. 2:13, as light excels in d
2:14, the fool walks in d
Matt. 6:23, full of d, how great is
the d
10:27, What I tell you in d, speak
22:13, cast him into the outer d
Luke 1:79, SHINE UPON THOSE WHO
SIT IN D
John 1:5, light shines in the d
3:19, men loved the d rather than
the light
12:35, d may not overtake
Acts 26:18, they may turn from d to
light
Rom. 2:19, a light to those who are
in d

2 Cor. 6:14, what fellowship has light with **d**
Eph. 5:11, unfruitful deeds of **d**
6:12, world forces of this **d**
1 Pet. 2:9, out of **d** into His marvelous light
1 John 1:5, in Him there is no **d** at all
2:9, hates his brother is in the **d**
Deut. 28:29; 1 Sam. 2:9; 2 Sam. 22:10; Job 3:5; 10:22; 12:25; 30:26; Ps. 18:9,28; 88:12; 97:2; 139:12; Prov. 20:20; Is. 58:10; Matt. 25:30; Luke 22:53; 23:44; Rom. 13:12; 1 Cor. 4:5; 2 Cor. 4:6; Col. 1:13; Heb. 12:18; 2 Pet. 2:4; 1 John 1:6

DART—*arrow, missile* Job 41:26, the **d** or the

DASH—*shatter* Is. 13:16, **d-ed** to pieces
Nah. 2:4, **d** to and fro like lightning
2 Kin. 8:12; Ps. 137:9; Jer. 13:14; Hos. 13:16

DATE—*time* Gal. 4:2, the **d** set by the father

DAUGHTER—Gen. 6:1, **d-s** were born to them
Num. 27:8, transfer his inheritance to his **d**
Prov. 31:29, Many **d-s** have done nobly
Eccles. 12:4, **d-s** of song will sing softly
Is. 22:4, destruction of the **d** of my people
Mic. 7:6, **D** rises up against her mother
Heb. 11:24, son of Pharaoh's **d**
Gen. 24:23,47; 27:46; Ex. 21:7; Deut. 28:53; Judg. 11:34; 2 Sam. 1:20; 12:3; Ps. 45:9; 144:12; Prov. 30:15; Jer. 8:21; 9:1; Lam. 2:11; 3:48; Matt. 10:35; Luke 8:42; 12:53; 13:16

DAWN—*light, morning* Deut. 33:2; Josh. 6:15; Judg. 19:26
Ps. 119:147, I rise before **d** and cry for help
139:9, take the wings of the **d**
2 Pet. 1:19, until the day **d-s**
Job 7:4; 38:12; Joel 2:2

DAY—*age, time* Gen. 1:5, God called the light **d**
1 Chr. 29:15, our **d-s** on the earth are like a shadow
Ps. 19:2, **D** to **d** pours forth speech
41:1, deliver him in a **d** of trouble
84:10, a **d** in Thy courts is better
118:24, This is the **d** which the LORD has made
Prov. 3:2, For length of **d-s** and years of life
27:1, you do not know what a **d** may bring
Eccles. 7:1, **d** of *one's* death is better than
12:1, **d-s** of your youth, before the evil **d-s**
Is. 2:12, LORD of hosts will have a **d** of reckoning
13:6, **d** of the LORD is near
58:5, an acceptable **d** to the LORD
Joel 2:11, **d** of the LORD is indeed great
Zech. 4:10, who has despised the **d** of small things
Mal. 3:2, who can endure the **d** of His coming
Matt. 6:11, this **d** our daily bread

24:36, But of that **d** and hour no one knows
John 6:39, raise it up on the last **d**
8:56, Your father Abraham rejoiced to see My **d**
9:4, We must work . . . as long as it is **d**
Rom. 14:5, One man regards one **d** above another
1 Cor. 3:13, the **d** will show it
2 Cor. 6:2, ON THE **D** OF SALVATION
Phil. 1:6, will perfect it until the **d** of Christ
1 Thess. 5:5, all sons of light and sons of **d**
2 Pet. 3:8, one **d** is as a thousand years
Gen. 27:2; Deut. 4:32; 1 Sam. 25:8; 2 Kin. 7:9; Neh. 4:2; Job 1:4; 7:1; 8:9; 14:6; 21:30; Ps. 77:5; Prov. 4:18; Is. 2:2; 10:3; 13:9; 27:3; 65:20; Joel 1:15; 2:1; Mic. 4:1; Zeph. 1:7,14; Zech. 14:1; Mal. 4:5; Matt. 7:22; 24:50; 25:13; Mark 13:32; Luke 12:46; 21:34; John 11:24; 12:48; Acts 2:17,20; 17:31; Rom. 2:5; 1 Thess. 5:2; 2 Tim. 3:1; Heb. 1:2; James 5:3; 2 Pet. 3:3,10; Rev. 6:17; 16:14; 20:10

DAZZLE—*shine* Song 5:10, My beloved is **d-ing**
Luke 24:4, men . . . in **d-ing** apparel

DEAD 1 Sam. 24:14; 2 Sam. 9:8; 16:9, **d** dog
Ps. 31:12, I am forgotten as a **d** man
Eccles. 9:4, a live dog is better than a **d** lion
Is. 26:19, Your **d** will live
Matt. 11:5, and *the* **d** are raised up
22:32, God is not *the* God of *the* **d**
23:27, full of **d** men's bones
John 5:25, **d** shall hear the voice of the Son of God
Acts 10:42, Judge of the living and the **d**
26:23, *His* resurrection from the **d**
Rom. 6:11, consider yourselves to be **d** to sin
14:9, Lord both of the **d** and of the living
1 Cor. 15:15, if in fact the **d** are not raised
2 Cor. 1:9, God who raises the **d**
Eph. 2:1, you were **d** in your trespasses and sins
1 Tim. 5:6, **d** even while she lives
Heb. 6:1, repentance from **d** works
James 2:17, faith, if it has no works, is **d**
2:26, body without the spirit is **d**
Rev. 1:18, I was **d**, and behold, I am alive
3:1, name that you are alive, and you are **d**
14:13, Blessed are the **d** who die in the Lord
Gen. 23:3; Ex. 12:30; Lev. 19:28; Ruth 1:8; Ps. 115:17; Prov. 9:18; Eccles. 4:2; 9:5; 10:1; Jer. 22:10; Matt. 2:19,20; 8:22; 9:24; 10:8; Mark 9:10,26; Luke 7:22; 15:24,32; 16:31; Rom. 7:4; 1 Cor. 15:35; Eph. 5:14; Col. 1:18; 2:13; 1 Thess. 4:16; 2 Tim. 4:1; Heb. 11:4; 13:20; 1 Pet. 4:6; Jude 12; Rev. 1:5; 20:5,12,13

DEADLY 1 Sam. 5:11; Ps. 17:9; Mark 16:18; James 3:8

DEAF Matt. 11:5, lepers are cleansed and *the* **d** hear
Ex. 4:11; Lev. 19:14; Ps. 58:4; Is. 29:18; 42:18; 43:8; Mark 7:37; 9:25; Luke 7:22

DEAL—*allot, treat* Prov. 12:22, those who **d** faithfully are
Ex. 1:10; Lev. 19:11; Ps. 25:3; Is. 21:2; 24:16; 26:10; Jer. 6:13; Hos. 5:7

DEALINGS Judg. 18:7, had no **d** with anyone
John 4:9, Jews have no **d** with Samaritans

DEAR—*beloved* Jer. 31:20, Is Ephraim My **d** son
Acts 20:24, I do not consider my life . . . as **d**
1 Thess. 2:8, you had become very **d** to us

DEATH—*grave* Num. 23:10; Judg. 16:16; 2 Sam. 22:5
Judg. 16:30, whom he killed at his **d** were more
Ruth 1:17, if *anything but* **d** parts you and me
1 Sam. 15:32, Surely the bitterness of **d** is past
2 Sam. 1:23, in their **d** they were not parted
Ps. 23:4, valley of the shadow of **d**
89:48, what man can live and not see **d**
107:10, darkness and in the shadow of **d**
116:15, Precious . . . Is the **d** of His godly ones
Song 8:6, love is as strong as **d**
Is. 25:8, He will swallow up **d** for all time
Ezek. 33:11, no pleasure in the **d** of the wicked
Matt. 2:15, there until the **d** of Herod
16:28; Mark 9:1; Luke 9:27, shall not taste **d**
26:38; Mark 14:34, to the point of **d**
John 5:24, has passed out of **d** into life
8:51, never see **d**
Acts 10:39, **d** by hanging Him on a cross
Rom. 6:23, the wages of sin is **d**
8:2, free from the law of sin and **d**
8:36, WE ARE BEING PUT TO **D** ALL DAY LONG
1 Cor. 11:26, proclaim the Lord's **d** until He comes
15:21, by a man *came* **d**
15:56, the sting of **d** is sin
2 Cor. 4:12, **d** works in us
Phil. 2:8, obedient to the point of **d**, even *d* on
Heb. 2:9, suffering of **d** . . . He might taste **d**
2:15, through fear of **d** were subject to slavery
James 1:15, sin . . . brings forth **d**
5:20, will save his soul from **d**
Rev. 1:18, I have the keys of **d** and of Hades
2:10, Be faithful until **d**
6:8, he who sat on it had the name **D**
9:6, men will seek **d** . . . and **d** flees from them
21:4, there shall no longer be *any* **d**
2 Chr. 25:4; Job 3:21; 7:15; 30:23; Ps. 6:5; 13:3; 18:4; 22:15; 49:14; 68:20;

DEATH *(Continued)*
102:20; 116:3; Prov. 7:27; 8:36;
14:12; 16:25; Is. 38:18; Jer. 8:3;
Ezek. 18:32; Hos. 13:14; Jon. 4:3,8;
Matt. 10:21; 15:4; Mark 7:10; Luke
2:26; 22:33; John 11:4; 12:33;
18:31,32; 21:19; Acts 2:24; Rom.
1:32; 5:10,14,17; 6:5,21; 1 Cor. 3:22;
15:55; 2 Cor. 1:9; 11:23; James 5:6;
1 John 3:14; 5:16; Rev. 2:11; 20:6

DEBATE—*dispute* Acts 15:2,7;
1 Cor. 1:20

DEBT Matt. 6:12, forgive us our **d-s**
1 Sam. 22:2; 2 Kin. 4:7; Neh. 10:31;
Prov. 22:26; Matt. 18:27

DEBTOR—*obligation*
Ezek. 18:7, restores to the **d**
Matt. 6:12, as we also have forgiven
our **d-s**
Luke 7:41, a certain money-lender
had two **d-s**
16:5, summoned each of his
master's **d-s**

DECAY—*corruption* Job 21:20, own
eyes see his **d**
Acts 2:27, HOLY ONE TO UNDERGO D

DECEIT—*falsehood, deception* Ps.
32:2; 36:3; 50:19
Ps. 10:7, mouth full of curses and **d**
and oppression
34:13, your lips from speaking **d**
55:23, Men of bloodshed and **d** will
not live
Prov. 12:5, counsels of the wicked
are **d-ful**
31:30, Charm is **d-ful** and beauty is
vain
Jer. 17:9, heart is more **d-ful** than all
else
2 Cor. 11:13, false apostles, **d-ful**
workers
1 Pet. 2:22, NOR WAS ANY D FOUND
Prov. 27:6; Is. 57:4; Jer. 5:27; 48:10;
Dan. 8:25; Hos. 11:12; Zeph. 1:9;
Mark 7:22; 2 Cor. 12:16; Eph.
4:14,22

DECEITFUL—*false* Ps. 120:3, You **d**
tongue
Ps. 17:1; 26:4

DECEITFULNESS—*deception*
Matt. 13:22; Mark 4:19, **d** of riches

DECEIVE—*cheat, mislead, steal*
Gen. 31:20,27; Num. 25:18
Gen. 29:25, Why then have you **d-d**
me
Jer. 42:20, you have *only* **d-d**
yourselves
Matt. 27:63, we remember that . . .
that **d-r** said
Rom. 3:13, THEY KEEP **D-ING**
2 Cor. 6:8, *regarded* as **d-rs** and yet
true
Eph. 5:6, 1 John 3:7, Let no one **d**
you
1 John 1:8, If we say . . . no sin, we
are **d-ing**
2 John 7, many **d-rs** . . . This is the **d-
r** and the antichrist
Rev. 12:9, Satan, who **d-s** the whole
world
Deut. 11:16; Josh. 7:11; 9:22; 1 Kin.
22:22; 2 Kin. 19:10; Is. 37:10; 44:20;
Jer. 20:7; 37:9; Obad. 3; 1 Cor. 6:9;
15:33; Gal. 6:7; 2 Thess. 2:3;
1 Tim. 2:14; 2 Tim. 3:13; James
1:16; Rev. 19:20

DECEPTION—*deceit*
Jer. 3:10, return to Me . . . in **d**
Matt. 27:64, last **d** will be worse than
the first
Col. 2:8, philosophy and empty **d**

DECEPTIVE Mic. 6:11, a bag of **d**
weights

DECIDE—*determine* 1 Sam. 20:7, he
has **d-d** on evil
2 Chr. 2:1, Solomon **d-d** to build a
house
Ex. 21:22; Acts 3:13; 1 Cor. 7:37

DECISION—*rebuke* Prov. 16:33,
every **d** is from the LORD
Joel 3:14, day . . . is near in the
valley of **d**
Mic. 4:3; Zeph. 3:8

DECK Is. 61:10, As a bridegroom **d-s**
himself

DECLARATION—*account*
Job 13:17, let my **d** *fill* your ears

DECLARE—*explain, relate* Ps. 75:9,
I will **d** it forever
Ps. 92:2, To **d** Thy lovingkindness
145:4, shall **d** Thy mighty acts
Is. 43:21, Will **d** My praise
45:19, **D-ing** things that are upright
46:10, **D-ing** the end from the
beginning
John 4:25, He will **d** all things to us
Acts 20:27, **d-ing** to you the whole
purpose of God
Rom. 1:4, **d-d** with power *to be* the
Son of God
Deut. 30:18; Job 31:37; Ps. 9:11; 30:9;
51:15; Is. 41:26; 45:21; 66:19; Acts
17:30

DECORATE—*deck* Jer. 4:30; 10:4

DECREASE—*abate, subside* Gen.
8:3, the water **d-d**
Ps. 107:38, He does not let their
cattle **d**
John 3:30, He must increase, but I
must **d**

DECREE—*decide, determine* Job
22:28; Ps. 94:20; 148:6
Dan. 11:36, that which is **d-d** will be
done
Prov. 8:15; Dan. 2:9; 9:24; Acts 16:4;
17:7

DEDICATE—*devote*
Ex. 32:29, **D** yourselves today to the
1 Kin. 7:51, Solomon brought things
d-d
8:63, sons of Israel **d-d** the house of
the LORD
Deut. 20:5; Judg. 17:3; 1 Kin. 15:15;
1 Chr. 18:11; 26:27

DEED—*action, practice, work* Gen.
44:15; 2 Sam. 12:14
Ps. 9:1, committed abominable **d-s**
28:4, according to the **d-s** of their
hands
Is. 1:16, Remove the evil of your **d-s**
59:18; Jer. 25:4, according to their
d-s
Luke 24:19, prophet mighty in **d** and
word
John 3:19, their **d-s** were evil
Acts 7:22, man of power in words
and **d-s**
Gal. 5:19, **d-s** of the flesh are evident

Col. 3:17, whatever you do in word
or **d**
Titus 3:1, ready for every good **d**
1 John 3:18, not love with word . . .
but in **d** and truth
Rev. 2:2, I know your **d-s** and your
toil
14:13, for their **d-s** follow with
them
Ezra 9:13; Neh. 13:14; Ps. 66:5; Prov.
20:11; Jer. 32:10,44; Luke 11:48;
23:41; John 8:41; Rom. 2:6

DEEP—*abyss, depth*
Gen. 7:11, fountains of the great **d**
Job 28:14, the **d** says, It is not with
me
Ps. 36:6, Thy judgments are *like* a
great **d**
42:7, **D** calls to **d**
Prov. 19:15, Laziness casts into a **d**
sleep
Matt. 26:38; Mark 14:34, soul is **d-ly**
grieved
Luke 5:4, Put out into **d** water
Rom. 8:26, groanings too **d** for words
Gen. 8:2; Deut. 33:13; Job 4:13;
38:30; Ps. 33:7; 77:16; 106:9;
107:24; Prov. 22:14; 23:27; Is. 7:11;
Luke 6:48; John 4:11

DEER Ps. 42:1, **d** pants for the water
brooks
Is. 35:6, lame will leap like a **d**
Deut. 12:15; 14:5; 1 Kin. 4:23

DEFEAT 1 Chr. 18:1, David **d-ed** the
Philistines
Jer. 37:10, had **d-ed** the entire army
Gen. 14:15; 36:35; Num. 22:6; Josh.
10:33; 12:1,7; 1 Chr. 1:46; 14:11;
18:3; Jer. 46:2

DEFECT—*spot* Lev. 21:17; Deut.
15:21; 2 Sam. 14:25; Job 11:15;
Dan. 1:4

DEFEND—*protect*
Zech. 9:15, LORD of hosts will **d**
them
Acts 7:24; Rom. 2:15; 2 Cor. 12:19

DEFENSE Acts 19:33; 22:1
Phil. 1:7, in the **d** . . . of the gospel

DEFICIENT—*want* Dan. 5:27, and
found **d**

DEFILE—*pollute, profane* Lev.
21:4; Is. 59:3; Jer. 2:7
2 Kin. 23:13, high places . . . the king
d-d
Neh. 13:29, they have **d-d** the
priesthood
Ps. 74:7, **d-d** the dwelling place of
Thy name
79:1, **d-d** Thy holy temple
Matt. 15:11,18,20; Mark 7:15,20,23, **d**
the man
Titus 1:15, to those who are **d-d** . . .
nothing is pure
Heb. 12:15, by it many are **d-d**
James 3:6, that which **d-s** the entire
body
Jude 8, these men also by dreaming
d the flesh
Ezek. 23:38; 36:17; Dan. 1:8; John
18:28; 1 Cor. 8:7

DEFILEMENT—*filth* 2 Cor. 7:1,
from all **d**

DEFRAUD—*deprive, wrong*
1 Cor. 6:7,8; 1 Thess. 4:6, transgress and **d**
1 Sam. 12:3; Lam. 3:36; Mark 10:19

DEGENERATE Jer. 2:21, **d** shoots of a foreign vine

DEGRADE Rom. 1:26, gave them over to **d-ing** passions

DEGREE—*standing* 1 Chr. 17:17; Ps. 62:9

DEITY Col. 2:9, fulness of **D** . . . bodily form

DELAY—*hinder, linger*
Ex. 32:1, the people saw that Moses **d-ed**
Deut. 23:21, shall not **d** to pay it
1 Tim. 3:15, in case I am **d-ed**
Rev. 10:6, there shall be **d** no longer
Gen. 24:56; Ex. 22:29; Acts 9:38; 25:17

DELEGATION—*messenger*
Luke 19:14, sent a **d** after him

DELICACY—*dainty, delicate* Ps. 141:4; Prov. 23:3; Lam. 4:5

DELICATE—*dainty* Deut. 28:54,56; Is. 47:1

DELIGHT (n.)—*affection, luxury, observe, pleasure*
2 Sam. 15:26, I have no **d** in you
Ps. 1:2, his **d** is in the law of the LORD
Prov. 8:31, having my **d** in the sons of men
11:1, a just weight is His **d**
12:22, those who deal faithfully are His **d**
Job 27:10; Ps. 16:3; 119:24,77,92,143,174; Prov. 8:30; 15:8; 16:13; Song 2:3; Is. 58:13; 62:4

DELIGHT (v.)—*desire*
Job 22:26, you will **d** in the Almighty
Ps. 37:4, **D** yourself in the LORD
37:11, **d** themselves in abundant prosperity
51:16, Thou dost not **d** in sacrifice
Eccles. 5:4, He takes no **d** in fools
Is. 42:1, My chosen one *in whom* My soul **d-s**
55:2, **d** yourself in abundance
Mic. 7:18, He **d-s** in unchanging love
1 Sam. 15:22; Neh. 1:11; Ps. 94:19; Prov. 1:22; 2:14; 18:2; 23:26; Is. 11:3; Hos. 6:6; Mal. 3:1

DELIGHTFUL Mal. 3:12, you shall be a **d** land

DELIVER—*rescue, save* Ex. 3:8; Num. 35:25; Deut. 32:39
Job 5:19, From six troubles He will **d** you
Ps. 56:13, **d-ed** my soul from death
Is. 43:13, none who can **d** out of My hand
50:2, have I no power to **d**
Matt. 6:13, **d** us from evil
10:17, they will **d** you up to *the* courts
10:21, brother will **d** up brother
Acts 2:23, **d-ed** up by the predetermined plan

Rom. 4:25, who was **d-ed** up because of our transgressions
2 Cor. 1:10, **d-ed** us from so great a *peril of* death
Gal. 1:4, He might **d** us out of this present evil age
Jude 3, faith which was . . . **d-ed** to the saints
Judg. 7:2; 1 Sam. 10:27; 2 Chr. 20:9; 32:13; Ps. 33:17; Prov. 24:11; Eccles. 9:15; Jer. 1:8; 39:17; Dan. 3:17; 6:14; Joel 2:32; Matt. 26:15; Acts 7:34; 2 Cor. 4:11; 2 Tim. 4:18

DELIVERANCE—*victory, salvation* Gen. 45:7, by a great **d**
Ps. 32:7, surround me with songs of **d**
68:20, God is . . . a God of **d-s**

DELUDE 2 Thess. 2:11, God will send . . . a **d-ing** influence

DEMON—*satyr* Matt. 8:31, **d-s** began to entreat Him
Mark 3:15, authority to cast out the **d-s**
James 2:19, **d-s** also believe and shudder
3:15, is earthly, natural, **d-ic**
Lev. 17:7; Deut. 32:17; Ps. 106:37; Matt. 10:8; 1 Cor. 10:20; Rev. 9:20

DEMONSTRATE—*show* Rom. 5:8, God **d-s** His own love
Rom. 9:22, willing to **d** His wrath

DEMONSTRATION 1 Cor. 2:4, in **d** of the Spirit and of power

DEN Jer. 7:11, Has this house . . . become a **d** of robbers
Dan. 6:7, shall be cast into the lions' **d**
Judg. 6:2; Job 37:8; Is. 11:8; Amos 3:4; Matt. 21:13; Mark 11:17

DENOUNCE—*slander* Jer. 20:10, D him; yes, let us **d** him

DENY—*conceal* Matt. 10:33, whoever shall **d** Me before men
1 Tim. 5:8, he has **d-ed** the faith
2 Tim. 2:13, for He cannot **d** Himself
3:5, they have **d-ed** its power
Titus 2:12, instructing us to **d** ungodliness
Josh. 24:27; Job 6:10; Prov. 30:9; Titus 1:16

DEPART Job 21:14, they say to God, **D** from us
Job 28:28, to **d** from evil is understanding
Ps. 6:8, **D** from me, all you who do iniquity
Prov. 22:6, when he is old he will not **d** from it
27:22, his folly will not **d** from him
Is. 26:14, **d-ed** spirits will not rise
John 13:1, hour had come that He should **d**
2 Cor. 12:8, entreated . . . that it might **d**
Phil. 1:23, desire to **d** and be with Christ
Gen. 49:10; Job 22:17; Ps. 18:21; 34:14; 37:27; 105:38; Matt. 2:13,22; 7:23; 25:41; Luke 2:29; 4:13; 13:27; 21:21; Acts 7:3

DEPARTURE—*death* Luke 9:13, His **d**
2 Tim. 4:6, the time of my **d** has come
2 Pet. 1:15, at any time after my **d**

DEPEND—*hang* Matt. 22:40, two commandments **d** . . . Law

DEPOSE Dan. 5:20, he was **d-d** from his royal throne

DEPRAVE Rom. 1:28, gave them over to a **d-d** mind
2 Tim. 3:8, men of **d-d** mind

DEPRIVE Is. 38:10, **d-d** of the rest of my years
1 Cor. 7:5, Stop **d-ing** one another
1 Tim. 6:5, **d-d** of the truth

DEPTH—*abyss, deep*
Ps. 95:4, In whose hand are the **d-s** of the earth
107:26, they went down to the **d-s**
Prov. 25:3, heavens for height . . . for **d**
Mic. 7:19, cast all their sins Into the **d-s** of the sea
Matt. 13:5, they had no **d** of soil
18:6, better . . . be drowned in the **d** of the sea
Mark 4:5, it sprang up because it had no **d** of soil
Rom. 8:39, nor height, nor **d** . . . separate us
11:33, **d** of the riches
1 Cor. 2:10, searches all things, even the **d-s** of God
Job 41:31, Ps. 86:13; Prov. 8:24; Is. 63:13

DEPUTY—*proconsul* 1 Kin. 22:47, a **d** was king

DERIDE—*mock, scoff, sneer* Ps. 119:51, utterly **d** me

DERISION—*laughingstock, shame* Ex. 32:25; Ps. 79:4
Ps. 44:13, a **d** to those around us
Jer. 20:8; Ezek. 23:32; 36:4; Hos. 7:16

DESCEND Gen. 28:12, angels of God . . . **d-ing**
Matt. 7:25,27, rain **d-ed**, and the floods came
Mark 1:10, Spirit like a dove **d-ing** upon Him
Rom. 10:7, WHO WILL D INTO THE ABYSS
Ps. 49:17; Prov. 30:4; Matt. 11:23; John 1:32,33; Eph. 4:10

DESCENDANT—*seed* Ps. 37:28, **d-s** of the wicked will be
Rom. 4:18, So SHALL YOUR D-S BE

DESCENT Luke 19:37, near the **d** of the Mount

DESCRIPTION Josh. 18:4, write a **d** of it according to

DESERT—*wild* Ps. 78:40, grieved Him in the **d**
Is. 35:1, the **d** will be glad
40:3, in the **d** a highway for our God
43:19, Rivers in the **d**
51:3, her **d** like the garden of the LORD

DESERT *(Continued)*
Prov. 21:19; Jer. 17:6; 25:24; 50:39;
Luke 1:80

DESERT—*leave, forsake* 2 Kin.
25:11, the **d-ers** who had
2 Tim. 4:16, but all **d-ed** me
Heb. 13:5, I WILL NEVER D YOU

DESERVE—*due, worthy*
Matt. 26:66, He is **d-ing** of death
Luke 23:41, receiving what we **d** for
our deeds
1 Tim. 1:15, statement, **d-ing** full
acceptance
Judg. 9:16; Ezra 9:13

DESIGN—*device, devise* Ex. 31:4;
35:32,35; 2 Chr. 2:14

DESIRABLE Ps. 19:10, more **d** than
gold
Prov. 19:22, What is **d** in a man is
his kindness
Ezek. 23:6,12,23, **d** young men
Gen. 3:6; Prov. 8:11

DESIRE (n.)—*appetite* Job 31:16;
Ps. 10:3; 140:8; Prov. 13:12
Gen. 3:16, your **d** shall be for your
husband
Ps. 21:2, given him his heart's **d**
37:4, He will give you the **d-s** of
your heart
112:10, **d** of the wicked will perish
145:16, satisfy the **d** of every living
thing
Prov. 10:24; 11:23, the **d** of the
righteous
Mic. 7:3, great man speaks the **d** of
his soul
Rom. 10:1, my heart's **d** . . . is for
their salvation
Eph. 2:3, **d-s** of the flesh and of the
mind
Phil. 1:23, having the **d** to depart
Prov. 21:25; Ezek. 24:16,21,25; Mark
4:19; Col. 3:5

DESIRE (v.)—*want, wish, crave*
Deut. 14:26; 1 Sam. 2:16
Ps. 34:12, Who is the man who **d-s**
life
51:6, Thou dost **d** truth
73:25, besides Thee, I **d** nothing on
earth
Luke 22:15, earnestly **d-d** to eat this
Passover
1 Cor. 12:31, earnestly **d** the greater
gifts
14:1, yet **d** earnestly spiritual *gifts*
Gal. 6:12, who **d** to make a good
showing in the flesh
Heb. 11:16, they **d** a better *country*
Job 13:3; Ps. 40:6; 45:11; 107:30;
Prov. 3:15, 23:3; Eccles. 2:10;
Matt. 13:17; Gal. 4:9; 1 Tim. 3:1

DESOLATE—*lonely, waste* Lev.
26:31; Is. 54:1; 62:4
Matt. 23:38, your house is being left
to you **d**
Jer. 2:12; 12:10; Ezek. 6:6; Joel 2:3;
Zech. 7:14; Luke 13:35; Acts 1:20;
Gal. 4:27

DESOLATION—*ruins, waste*
Jer. 25:9; Ezek. 35:9, an everlasting **d**
32:43, a **d** without man or beast
Dan. 9:26, there will be war; **d-s** are
determined
11:31; 12:11, abomination of **d**
Zeph. 1:15, day of destruction and **d**

2 Kin. 22:19; Josh. 8:28; Ps. 46:8;
Is. 61:4; Luke 21:20

DESPAIR—*faint, sorrow* 1 Sam.
27:1; Job 6:26; Eccles. 2:20
Deut. 28:65, failing of eyes, and **d** of
soul
2 Cor. 4:8, perplexed, but not **d-ing**

DESPERATE Jer. 17:9, The heart . . .
is **d-ly** sick

DESPISE—*reject, scorn, spurn* Gen.
16:4; Num. 15:31
Gen. 25:34, Esau **d-d** his birthright
Job 5:17, do not **d** the discipline of
the Almighty
36:5, God is mighty but does not **d**
any
Ps. 51:17, a contrite heart . . . Thou
wilt not **d**
Prov. 1:7, Fools **d** wisdom and
instruction
15:32, He who neglects discipline **d-**
s himself
Eccles. 9:16, wisdom of the poor
man is **d-d**
Zech. 4:10, who has **d-d** the day of
small things
Matt. 6:24; Luke 16:13, hold to one
and **d** the other
18:10, do not **d** one of these little
ones
1 Cor. 1:28, base things . . . and the
d-d
Heb. 12:2, endured the cross, **d-ing**
the shame
1 Sam. 2:30; 2 Sam. 6:16; Neh. 4:4;
Job 19:18; Ps. 73:20; 102:17;
119:163; Prov. 6:30; 13:13; 15:20;
Is. 5:24; 49:7; Jer. 49:15;
Ezek. 21:10; 22:8; Mal. 1:6;
1 Cor. 11:22; 16:11; 1 Thess. 5:20

DESPONDENCY—*anguish,
distress*
Ex. 6:9, on account of *their* **d**

DESTINE—*appoint, name*
1 Thess. 5:9, God has not **d-d** us for
wrath

DESTITUTE—*deprive* Ezek. 32:15
Ps. 102:17, regarded the prayer of
the **d**
Heb. 11:37, being, **d**, afflicted, ill-
treated

DESTROY—*defile, pollute, abolish,
ruin, waste*
2 Sam. 1:14, **d** the LORD'S anointed
Ps. 40:14, seek my life to **d** it
Prov. 1:32, complacency of fools
shall **d** them
Is. 23:14, your stronghold is **d-ed**
Matt. 2:13, search . . . to **d** Him
6:19, where moth and rust **d**
10:28, fear Him who is able to **d**
12:14; Mark 3:6, they might **d** Him
Mark 14:58, I will **d** this temple
Luke 6:9, is it lawful . . . to save a
life or **d** it
17:27, flood came and **d-ed** them all
1 Cor. 3:17, If any man **d-s** the
temple
Gal. 1:13, church of God . . . tried to
d it
1:23, the faith which he once tried
to **d**
2:18, if I rebuild what I once **d-ed**
2 Pet. 3:12, heavens will be **d-ed** by
burning
1 John 3:8, **d** the works of the devil

Gen. 6:17; Ex. 22:20; Deut. 9:14;
1 Sam. 15:6; Job 10:8; Ps. 63:9;
145:20; Prov. 28:24; 31:3;
Eccles. 9:18; Is. 10:7; 11:9;
Jer. 13:14; 23:1; Ezek. 9:1; 22:27;
Dan. 8:24; Matt. 22:7; Mark 1:24;
11:18; 12:9; 15:29; Luke 4:34; 20:16;
John 2:19; Rom. 14:15; James 4:12;
2 Pet. 2:12; 3:11; Jude 5

DESTROYER—*robber* Judg. 16:24,
Even the **d** of our country
Job 12:6; 15:21; Is. 49:17; Jer. 22:7

DESTRUCTION—*calamity, ruin*
Ps. 35:8, Let **d** come upon him
Ps. 52:2, Your tongue devises **d**
91:6, **d** that lays waste at noon
Prov. 16:18, Pride goes before **d**
Is. 19:18, called the City of **D**
59:7, Devastation and **d** are in their
highways
Lam. 2:11; 3:48; 4:10, **d** of the
daughter of my people
Matt. 7:13, way is broad that leads
to **d**
Rom. 9:22, vessels of wrath prepared
for **d**
Phil. 3:19, whose end is **d**
1 Thess. 5:3, **d** will come upon them
suddenly
1 Tim. 6:9, desires plunge to ruin
and **d**
2 Chr. 22:4; Esth. 8:6; Job 21:17;
Ps. 5:9; 57:1; 73:18; Prov. 17:19;
19:13; Is. 10:22; 14:23; 28:2;
Jer. 17:18; 50:22; Hos. 13:9;
Rom. 3:16; 2 Thess. 1:9; 2 Pet. 2:1,3;
3:16; Rev. 17:8

DESTRUCTIVE—*false* Prov. 17:4, a
d tongue
2 Pet. 2:1, secretly introduce **d**
heresies

DETAIN Judg. 13:15,16; 1 Sam. 21:7

DETERMINE—*decide* Job 14:5, his
days are **d-d**
Luke 22:22, Son . . . as it has been
d-d
Acts 17:26, having **d-d** *their*
appointed times
1 Cor. 2:2, I **d-d** to know nothing

DETEST—*despise, loathe* Deut.
7:26; Jer. 4:1; Amos 6:8

DETESTABLE—*abominable*
Deut. 14:3, eat any **d** thing
Is. 66:17, swine's flesh, **d** things
Luke 16:15, is **d** in the sight of God
Job 15:16; Jer. 16:18; Ezek. 5:11;
7:20; 11:18; 37:23

DEVASTATE—*waste* Nah. 2:2; 3:7

DEVASTATION—*oppression*
Ps. 12:5, the **d** of the afflicted

DEVICE—*design, plan, scheme*
Prov. 1:31, satiated . . . own **d-s**

DEVIOUS—*perverse* Prov. 4:24, put
d lips far from you

DEVISE—*design, plan, scheme,
fashion*
Prov. 3:29, Do not **d** harm against
your neighbor
6:14, **d-s** evil continually
14:22, will they not go astray who **d**
evil

2 Pet. 1:16, cleverly **d-d** tales
Esth. 9:25; Ps. 2:1; 10:2; 21:11; 35:4;
  41:7; 94:20; Prov. 6:18; 12:2;
  Is. 32:7,8; Zech. 7:10; Acts 4:25

DEVOTE—*dedicate* Rom. 12:10, Be
  d-d to one another
Col. 4:2, **D** yourselves to prayer
Num. 18:14; Ezek. 44:29

DEVOTION Eccles. 12:12, excessive
  d *to books is wearying*

DEVOUR—*consume, swallow*
2 Sam. 2:26, Shall the sword **d**
  forever
11:25, the sword **d-s** one as well as
  another
Zeph. 1:18; 3:8, all the earth will be
  d-ed
Matt. 13:4, birds came and **d-ed**
  them
23:14, you **d** widows' houses
Luke 15:30, son of yours . . . has **d-ed**
  your wealth
Gal. 5:15, if you bite and **d** one
  another
Gen. 37:20; 2 Sam. 18:8; 22:9; Job
  18:13; Ps. 18:8; 50:3; 52:4; Prov.
  30:14; Is. 1:7,20; Jer. 2:30; 30:16;
  Amos 4:9; Mal. 3:11; Mark 12:40;
  Luke 8:5; 2 Cor. 11:20

DEVOUT—*God-fearing*
Luke 2:25, Simeon . . . righteous
  and **d**
Acts 2:5; 8:2, **d** men
Acts 10:2; 13:50; 22:12

DEW Gen. 27:28, God give you of the
  d of heaven
Judg. 6:37, If there is **d** on the fleece
  only
2 Sam. 17:12, we will fall on him as
  the **d** falls
Prov. 3:20, the skies drip with **d**
Is. 18:4, Like a cloud of **d** in the heat
  of harvest
Dan. 4:15,23,25,33, drenched with
  the **d** of heaven
Ex. 16:13; Num. 11:9; Deut. 32:2;
  33:13; 2 Sam. 1:21; 1 Kin. 17:1;
  Job 29:19; 38:28; Ps. 110:3; 133:3;
  Prov. 19:12; Is. 26:19; Hos. 6:4;
  13:3; 14:5; Hag. 1:10

DIADEM—*turban* Is. 28:5; 62:3

DIAMOND Ex. 28:18; 39:11; Jer. 17:1;
  Ezek. 28:13

DID—*put* Gen. 6:22; Job 1:5
2 Chr. 18:23, How **d** the Spirit . . .
  pass
Matt. 13:58, He **d** not do many
  miracles
John 9:26, What **d** He do to you
15:24, works which no one else **d**
1 Cor. 13:11, **d** away with childish
  things

DIE—*depart* Gen. 2:17; 20:7; 1 Sam.
  14:44; 22:16; 1 Kin. 2:37,42; Ezek.
  3:18; 33:8, you shall surely **d**
Deut. 14:21, not eat anything which
  d-s of itself
Ruth 1:17, Where you **d**, I will **d**
1 Sam. 26:16, *all* of you must
  surely **d**
Job 2:9, his wife said . . . Curse God
  and **d**
3:11, Why did I not **d** at birth

14:14, If a man **d-s**, will he live
  again
21:23, One **d-s** in his full strength
Ps. 49:10, *even* wise men **d**
49:17, when he **d-s** he will carry
  nothing away
Prov. 10:21, fools **d** for lack of
  understanding
Eccles. 2:16, wise man and fool
  alike **d**
Ezek. 18:4, soul who sins will **d**
18:32, no pleasure in . . . who **d-s**
Matt. 26:35, Even if I must **d** with
  you
Luke 8:52, she has not **d-d**, but is
  asleep
16:22, poor man **d-d** . . . rich man
  also **d-d**
John 6:49, ate the manna . . . and
  they **d-d**
11:25, who believes . . . live even if
  he **d-s**
11:51, that Jesus was going to **d** for
  the nation
12:24, a grain of wheat falls . . . and
  d-s
Rom. 5:6, Christ **d-d** for the ungodly
5:7, one will hardly **d** for a
  righteous man
6:2, How shall we who **d-d** to sin
14:9, Christ **d-d** and lived *again*
14:15, him for whom Christ **d-d**
1 Cor. 15:31, I **d** daily
2 Cor. 5:14, one **d-d** for all, therefore
  all **d-d**
Phil. 1:21, to **d** is gain
Col. 2:20, If you have **d-d** with Christ
1 Thess. 4:14, we believe that Jesus
  d-d and rose
5:10, who **d-d** for us, that . . . we
  may live
Heb. 9:27, appointed for men to **d**
  once
11:13, All these **d-d** in faith
Gen. 3:3; 25:8; 27:4; 45:28; Lev. 10:6;
  Num. 18:32; Prov. 14:32; 30:7;
  Jer. 26:8; 27:13; Ezek. 18:20,31;
  33:11,14; Matt. 22:25; Mark 5:39;
  John 11:44; 19:7; Acts 9:37; 21:13;
  Rom. 6:10; 7:9; 8:34; 14:7;
  1 Cor. 8:11; 15:3,22; Gal. 2:19;
  2 Tim. 2:11; 1 Pet. 2:24; Rev. 9:6;
  14:13

DIFFER Rom. 12:6, we have gifts
  that **d**
1 Cor. 15:41, star **d-s** from star in
  glory
Deut. 25:13; Gal. 4:1

DIFFERENCE—*distinction* Ezek.
  44:23

DIFFICULT—*hard* Jer. 32:27; Ezek.
  3:5
Gen. 18:14, Is anything too **d** for the
  LORD
1 Kin. 10:1; 2 Chr. 9:1, test Solomon
  with **d** questions
Jer. 32:17, Nothing is too **d** for Thee
John 6:60, This is a **d** statement

DIG Ex. 21:33; Deut. 6:11; 8:9; Job
  3:21; 24:16; Ezek. 12:5; Luke 13:8;
  16:3

DIGNITY—*majesty* Gen. 49:3; Esth.
  6:3; 1 Tim. 2:2

DILIGENCE—*effort, speed* Ezra
  6:12, carried out with all **d**

Prov. 4:23, Watch over your heart
  with all **d**
Rom. 12:11, not lagging behind in **d**

DILIGENT—*careful, eager,*
  thorough Prov. 1:28; Heb. 4:11
Prov. 11:27, **d-ly** seeks good seeks
  favor
Eph. 4:3, **d** to preserve the unity
2 Tim. 2:15, Be **d** to present yourself
  approved
2 Pet. 1:15, I will also be **d**

DILL Is. 28:25,27

DILUTE—*mix* Is. 1:22, drink **d-d**
  with water

DIM—*dark* Job 17:7, My eye has
  also grown **d**
1 Cor. 13:12, see in a mirror **d-ly**
Gen. 27:1; 48:10; Deut. 34:7;
  1 Sam. 3:2; Ps. 69:23; Eccles. 12:3

DIMINISH—*dwindle, reduce* Lev.
  25:16; Ezek. 16:27

DINE—*eat* Gen. 43:16; Prov. 23:1

DINNER—*lunch, supper* Matt. 22:4;
  Luke 14:12
Luke 14:16, certain man was giving a
  big **d**

DIP 2 Kin. 5:14 *himself* seven
  times in the Jordan
Matt. 26:23, **d-ed** his hand with Me
  in the bowl
Luke 16:24, **d** the tip of his finger in
  water and
Rev. 19:13, clothed with a robe **d-ed**
  in blood
Gen. 37:31; Lev. 4:6; 9:9; Josh. 3:15;
  Ruth 2:14; 1 Sam. 14:27;
  Mark 14:20; John 13:26

DIRECT—*arrange, order* Is. 40:13;
  Jer. 10:23; 1 Thess. 3:11
Prov. 16:9, the LORD **d-s** his steps
23:19, **d** your heart in the way
2 Thess. 3:5, **d** your hearts into the
  love of God

DIRGE Matt. 11:17, we sang a **d**

DIRTY James 2:2, a poor man in **d**
  clothes

DISAPPOINT—*frustrate* Ps. 22:5,
  they trusted . . . not **d-ed**
1 Pet. 2:6, SHALL NOT BE **D-ED**

DISASTER—*evil* Jer. 17:17; Ezek.
  7:5

DISCERN—*appraise, analyze,*
  recognize
1 Kin. 3:9, **d** between good and evil
Matt. 16:3, **d** the appearance of the
  sky
Heb. 5:14, senses trained to **d** good
  and evil
Gen. 41:33; Deut. 32:29;
  2 Sam. 14:17; Job 4:16; 6:30;
  Prov. 7:7; 8:5

DISCERNING—*understanding*
Deut. 1:13, Choose wise and **d**
1 Kin. 3:12, a wise and **d** heart
Prov. 16:21, wise in heart will be
  called **d**

DISCERNMENT—*judgment*
Ps. 119:66, Teach me good **d**

DISCERNMENT *(Continued)*
Is. 27:11, not a people of **d**
1 Sam. 25:33; 1 Kin. 3:11

DISCIPLE—*pupil* Matt. 10:24, A **d** is
not above his teacher
Matt. 12:2, Your **d-s** do what is not
lawful
26:56, all the **d-s** left Him and fled
28:7, tell His **d-s** that He has risen
28:19, make **d-s** of all nations
Mark 14:14; Luke 22:11, Passover
with My **d-s**
Luke 6:13, He called His **d-s** to Him
11:1, just as John also taught his
d-s
14:26,27, cannot be My **d**
19:37, **d-s** began to praise God
joyfully
19:39, Teacher, rebuke Your **d-s**
John 2:11, His **d-s** believed in Him
6:66, many of His **d-s** withdrew
13:5, began to wash the **d-s'** feet
13:35, all men will know you are
My **d-s**
19:26, **d** whom He loved standing
nearby
Acts 9:26, associate with the **d-s**
11:26, **d-s** were first called
Christians
Is. 8:16; Matt. 10:1,42; 11:1; 15:2;
17:16; 19:13; 20:17; 22:16; 26:18,35;
28:13; Mark 2:18; 4:34; 7:2,5; 10:13;
Luke 5:30,33; 6:20; 14:33; John 4:2;
6:22; 7:3; 8:31; 9:27,28; 15:8;
18:1,15,16,17,25; 19:38; 20:2,18,26;
21:7,20,23,24; Acts 9:1; 20:30; 21:16

DISCIPLINE—*chasten, exercise*
Job 5:17; Prov. 3:11, not despise **d** of
the Almighty
Prov. 16:22, **d** of fools is folly
19:18, **D** your son while there is
hope
1 Cor. 11:32, we are **d-d** by the Lord
1 Tim. 4:7, **d** yourself for the purpose
of godliness
Heb. 12:6, THE LORD LOVES HE **D-S**
Deut. 4:36; 8:5; 1 Kin. 12:11;
Heb. 12:8

DISCONTENTED 1 Sam. 22:2,
everyone . . . **d**

DISCOURAGE—*dishearten* Num.
32:7,9

DISCOVER—*reveal, find* Job 11:7, **d**
the depths of God

DISCREDIT—*condemn*
2 Cor. 6:3, the ministry be not **d-ed**
8:20, no one should **d** us

DISCRETION—*understanding,
wisdom*
1 Chr. 22:12, LORD give you **d**
Prov. 11:22, beautiful woman who
lacks **d**

DISCUSS—*converse, reason* Matt.
16:7; Mark 9:33; Luke 6:11; 24:15

DISDAIN 1 Sam. 17:42, he **d-ed** him
(David)
Job 30:1, whose fathers I **d-ed**

DISEASE—*affliction* Ps. 103:3, heals
all your **d-s**
Matt. 4:23, healing every kind of **d**
Luke 9:1, gave them power . . . to
heal **d-s**
Ex. 15:26; Deut. 7:15; 28:60;

2 Chr. 16:12; Ezek. 34:4; Matt. 4:24;
Acts 28:9

DISGRACE—*shame, reproach* Gen.
34:7; Lev. 20:17; Job 10:15;
Prov. 6:33; 14:34; Jer. 14:21;
1 Cor. 11:4,5,6

DISGUISE—*pretend* 1 Sam. 21:13,
David **d-d** his sanity
1 Sam. 28:8, Saul **d-d** himself
1 Kin. 22:30; 2 Chr. 18:29, king of
Israel **d-d** himself
1 Kin. 14:2; 20:38; 2 Chr. 35:22;
Job 24:15

DISGUST—*exclude, alienate* Ezek.
23:17, became **d-ed** with

DISH—*bowl* Gen. 27:4; 2 Kin. 21:13

DISHEARTEN Is. 42:4, will not be **d-
ed** or crushed

DISHONEST Amos 8:5, cheat with **d**
scales

DISHONOR—*disgrace, shame* Ezra
4:14; Ps. 35:26; 71:13
John 8:49, I honor My Father, and
you **d** Me
1 Cor. 15:43, it is sown in **d**
2 Cor. 6:8, by glory and **d**
2 Tim. 2:20, some to honor and some
to **d**
Ps. 83:16; Prov. 12:16; Rom. 1:24;
2:23; James 2:6

DISLOCATE—*joint*
Gen. 32:25, Jacob's thigh was **d-d**

DISMAY—*astound, discourage*
Deut. 1:21, Do not fear or be **d-ed**
Deut. 31:8; Josh. 1:9; 8:1; 10:25;
1 Sam. 17:11; 1 Chr. 22:13; 28:20;
2 Chr. 20:15,17; 32:7; Job 41:22;
Jer. 1:17; 8:9,21; 17:18; 30:10;
46:27; Ezek. 2:6; 3:9; Obad. 9

DISMISS 2 Chr. 23:8; Acts 19:41

DISOBEDIENCE Rom. 5:19, one
man's **d**
Eph. 2:2, spirit . . . working in the
sons of **d**
5:6 wrath of God comes upon the
sons of **d**
Heb. 2:2, **d** received a just
recompense

DISOBEDIENT—*rebellious* Neh.
9:26; Luke 1:17; Titus 3:3
Acts 26:19, did not prove **d** to the
heavenly vision
Rom. 1:30; 2 Tim. 3:2, **d** to parents
10:21, A **D** AND OBSTINATE PEOPLE
1 Pet. 3:20, spirits who once were **d**

DISOBEY 1 Kin. 13:26, **d-ed** the
command of the LORD

DISORDER—*confusion* James 3:16,
d and every evil thing

DISPERSE—*spread* Esth. 3:8; Is.
11:12; Ezek. 20:23; 36:19;
Zeph. 3:10

DISPERSION Jer. 25:34; John 7:35

DISPLAY—*declare* Esth. 1:11; Ps.
60:4; Is. 3:9
Ps. 8:1, Who hast **d-ed** Thy splendor
above

John 9:3, works of God might
be **d-ed**

DISPLEASE Gen. 48:17; Num. 22:34;
1 Sam. 8:6; 18:8; Prov. 24:18;
Is. 59:15; Jon. 4:1

DISPLEASURE—*anger, fury*
Deut. 9:19, anger and hot **d**

DISPOSSESS Num. 14:12; Deut. 7:17

DISPUTE—*contend, controversy,
debate* Deut. 25:1; Heb. 7:7
Phil. 2:14, Do all things without . . .
d-ing
Jude 9, when he **d-d** with the devil

DISREGARD—*despise* Titus 2:15,
Let no one **d** you

DISSENSION—*division* Acts 23:7
Acts 15:2, Paul and Barnabas had
great **d**
Rom. 16:17, keep your eye on those
who cause **d-s**
1 Tim. 2:8, without wrath and **d**

DISSIPATION Eph. 5:18, wine, for
that is **d**
Titus 1:6, accused of **d** or rebellion

DISSOLVE—*melt* Ps. 6:6, I **d** my
couch with my tears
Job 30:22; Nah. 2:6

DISTAFF Prov. 31:19, her hands to
the **d**

DISTANCE Gen. 22:4; Matt. 26:58

DISTANT—*far* Luke 15:13, into a **d**
country

DISTILL—*drip* Deut. 32:2, My
speech **d** as the dew

DISTINCTION—*difference* Ex. 11:7;
Lev. 11:47; 20:25
Lev. 10:10, **d** between the holy and
the profane
Rom. 3:22; 10:12; for there is no **d**
Ezek. 22:26; Acts 15:9; 1 Cor. 14:7

DISTINCTLY—*plain*
Deut. 27:8, all the words . . . **d**

DISTINGUISH—*discern* Ezra 3:13;
1 Cor. 12:10
2 Sam. 19:35, Can I **d** between good
and bad
Mal. 3:18, **d** between the righteous
and the wicked

DISTORT—*pervert* Gal. 1:7, **d** the
gospel of Christ

DISTRACTED Luke 10:40, Martha
was **d** with

DISTRESS—*adversity, privation*
Gen. 35:3; Deut. 4:30
2 Chr. 20:9, cry to Thee in our **d**
Ps. 25:17, Bring me out of my **d-es**
Prov. 1:27, when **d** *and* anguish
come on you
Mark 14:33, began to be very **d-ed**
1 Thess. 3:7, in all our **d** and
affliction
James 1:27, orphans and widows in
their **d**
Deut. 28:53; 1 Sam. 26:24; 2 Sam. 4:9;
24:14; 2 Kin. 19:3; 2 Chr. 33:12;
Prov. 24:10; Is. 25:4; 29:2; 33:2;

Jer. 16:19; Lam. 1:20; Zeph. 1:17;
Luke 21:23; Rom. 2:9; 1 Cor. 7:26;
Phil. 1:17; 1 Tim. 5:10

DISTRIBUTE—*apportion*
Luke 18:22, **d** it to the poor
John 6:11, He **d-d** to those who were
seated

DISTURBANCES
Luke 21:9, when you hear of war
and **d**

DISTURBED 1 Sam. 28:15, Why
have you **d** me by bringing
Ps. 42:5; 43:5, Why have you become
d within me

DIVIDE—*apportion* 1 Kin. 3:25, **D**
the living child in two
Ps. 22:18, **d** my garments among
them
Prov. 16:19, **d** the spoil with the
proud
Luke 11:17, Any kingdom **d-d**
against itself
Eph. 2:14, broke down the barrier of
the **d-ing** wall
Is. 53:12; Dan. 2:41; Matt. 27:35;
Luke 15:12

DIVINATION Acts 16:16, having a
spirit of **d**
Num. 22:7; Jer. 14:14; Ezek. 13:6,9

DIVINE Heb. 9:1, regulations of **d**
worship
2 Pet. 1:4, partakers of *the* **d** nature
Gen. 30:27; Mic. 3:11; Zech. 10:2

DIVISION—*dissension* Ex. 8:23, put
a **d** between My people
1 Chr. 23:6, divided them into **d-s**
John 7:43, arose a **d** in the multitude
1 Cor. 1:10, and there be no **d-s**
among you

DIVORCE Lev. 21:14, widow, or a **d-**
d woman
Deut. 24:1,3, a certificate of **d**
Jer. 3:8, given her a writ of **d**
Matt. 5:31, WHOEVER D-S HIS WIFE

DO—*practice, work* Gen. 11:6;
30:31; 1 Kin. 2:6
Ex. 20:9, Six days . . . labor and **d** all
your work
Ps. 1:3, in whatever he **d-es**, he
prospers
34:14, Depart from evil and **d** good
Eccles. 3:14, everything God **d-es**
will remain forever
Matt. 12:50, whoever shall **d** the will
of My Father
John 7:17, If any man is willing to **d**
His will
15:5, apart from Me you can **d**
nothing
Acts 16:30, what must I **d** to be
saved
Rom. 13:3, **D** what is good
1 Cor. 9:23, I **d** all things for the sake
of the gospel
11:24, **d** this in remembrance of Me
Gal. 6:10, let us **d** good to all men
2 Tim. 4:5, **d** the work of an
evangelist
Heb. 10:7, BEHOLD, I HAVE COME . . .
TO D THY WILL
1 Pet. 3:11, TURN AWAY FROM EVIL
AND D GOOD
Prov. 2:14; 24:29; Matt. 23:3;
John 2:5; 5:30

DOCTRINE—*teaching*
Eph. 4:14, every wind of **d**
1 Tim. 4:6, of the faith and of the
sound **d**
Titus 1:9, able both to exhort in
sound **d**

DOER—*workmen* Rom. 2:13, the **d-s**
of the Law will be justified
James 1:22, prove yourselves **d-s** of
the word
4:11, you are not a **d** of the law

DOG Eccles. 9:4, a live **d** is better
than a dead lion
1 Sam. 17:43; 2 Sam. 3:8; Ps. 22:16;
59:6; Is. 56:10; Luke 16:21;
Phil. 3:2; Rev. 22:15

DOING—*deeds*
Acts 10:38, He went about **d** good
Rom. 2:7, perseverance in **d** good
Gal. 6:9, let us not lose heart in **d**
good
Eph. 6:6, **d** the will of God from the
heart
2 Thess. 3:13, do not grow weary of
d good
2 Cor. 8:11; 1 Pet. 2:15; 3:17

DOMAIN—*estate* Jude 6, angels
who did not keep their own **d**
Luke 4:6; Col. 1:13

DOMINION—*kingdom, rule*
Ps. 103:22, in all places of His **d**
Zech. 9:10, His **d** will be from sea to
sea
Col. 1:16, thrones or **d-s** or rulers
1 Pet. 4:11, belongs the glory and **d**
forever
1 Chr. 29:11; Job 25:2; Eph. 1:21;
Rev. 1:6

DONE—*wrought* Matt. 6:10, Thy
will be **d**
Matt. 18:19, shall be **d** for them by
My Father
Mark 14:6, has **d** a good deed to Me
Gen. 20:9; Ex. 31:15; Eccles. 2:11

DONKEY Zech. 9:9, mounted on a **d**
Matt. 21:2, you will find a **d** tied
there
Num. 22:30; Prov. 26:3; Jer. 22:19;
Matt. 21:5; 2 Pet. 2:16

DOOMED—*silenced* Ps. 79:11, those
who are **d** to die
Jer. 8:14, God has **d** us

DOOR—*entrance*
Gen. 4:7, sin is crouching at the **d**
Ex. 12:7, put it on the two **d-posts**
Ps. 141:3, Keep watch over the **d** of
my lips
Matt. 6:6, WHEN YOU HAVE SHUT
YOUR D, pray
John 10:9, I am the **d**
1 Cor. 16:9, a wide **d** for effective
service
James 5:9, Judge is standing right at
the **d**
Rev. 3:8, put before you an open **d**
Gen. 6:16; 18:1; Judg. 4:20;
2 Sam. 11:9; 2 Chr. 12:10; Job 31:9;
Prov. 26:14; Ezek. 40:38;
Matt. 25:10; John 18:16; Rev. 4:1

DOUBLE—*twice* Gen. 43:12; Ps.
12:2; 1 Tim. 5:17
2 Kin. 2:9, **d** portion of your spirit be
upon me

Is. 40:2, **D** for all her sins
James 1:8, *being* a **d-minded** man
Jude 12, without fruit, **d-ly** dead

DOUBT—*misgiving* Matt. 14:31, you
of little faith, why did you **d**
Matt. 21:21, if you have faith and do
not **d**
28:17, but some were **d-ful**
Luke 24:38, why do **d-s** arise in your
hearts
Rom. 14:23, he who **d-s** is
condemned if he eats

DOUGH—*flour* 2 Sam. 13:8, Tamar
took **d**, kneaded *it*

DOVE Ps. 55:6, O that I had wings
like a **d**
Matt. 3:16, Spirit of God descending
as a **d**
10:16, shrewd as serpents . . .
innocent as **d-s**
Gen. 8:8; Song 1:15; Is. 38:14;
John 1:32

DOWN Ps. 23:2, makes me lie **d** in
green pastures
Matt. 4:6, Son of God throw Yourself
d
8:32, whole herd rushed **d** the steep
bank
Gen. 12:10; 2 Sam. 3:35; Eccles. 3:21;
John 8:6

DRAG—*draw* James 2:6, the rich
who . . . **d** you into court
Jer. 12:3; 15:3; Acts 8:3

DRAGON Is. 51:9; Rev. 20:2

DRANK—*drink* 1 Cor. 10:4, all **d** the
same spiritual drink
Gen. 9:21; Dan. 1:5; Mark 14:23;
John 4:12

DRAW Ps. 69:18, **d** near to my soul
Is. 12:3, **d** water from the springs of
salvation
Jer. 31:3, I have **d-n** you with
lovingkindness
Luke 21:28, your redemption is **d-ing**
near
John 4:11, You have nothing to **d**
with
12:32, if I be lifted up . . . will **d** all
men to Myself
Heb. 10:22, let us **d** near with a
sincere heart
James 4:8, **D** near to God . . . He will
d near to you
Gen. 24:13; Judg. 3:22; 19:9; Prov.
20:5; Zeph. 3:2; Acts 11:10

DREAD—*fear* Ps. 27:1, Whom shall
I **d**
Prov. 1:27, **d** comes like a storm
Deut. 28:66; Job 3:25; Ps. 14:5;
Is. 7:16; 8:13

DREAM Gen. 28:12, he had a **d**, and
behold, a ladder
Gen. 37:19, Here comes this **d-er**
Dan. 1:17, Daniel understood all . . .
d-s
Joel 2:28, Your old men will **d**
dreams
Matt. 2:12, warned *by* God in a **d**
2:13, appeared to Joseph in a **d**
Jude 8, these men also by **d-ing**
defile the flesh
Gen. 20:3; Judg. 7:13; Job 20:8;

DREAM (Continued)
Ps. 73:20; 126:1; Is. 29:7;
Matt. 1:20; 2:19; 27:19; Acts 2:17

DRENCHED—wet Dan. 4:15, d with
the dew of heaven

DRESS—array, clothe Mark 15:17;
Luke 7:25; 1 Pet. 3:3
Matt. 11:8, A man d-ed in soft
clothing

DREW Gen. 47:29; Matt. 26:51; Acts
5:37
Ex. 2:10, I d him out of the water
Acts 1:26, they d lots for them

DRIED—parched, withered Job
18:16; Jer. 23:10
Gen. 8:7, water was d up from the
earth
Ps. 22:15, My strength is d up

DRIES Joel 1:12, rejoicing d up

DRINK—libation Lev. 10:9, Do not
d wine or strong d
Job 21:20, d the wrath of the
Almighty
Ps. 80:5, made them to d tears
Prov. 20:1, strong d a brawler
Is. 22:13, Let us eat and d, for
tomorrow
Matt. 11:18, neither eating nor d-ing
25:35, I was thirsty and you gave
Me d
26:27, D from it, all of you
26:29, day when I d it new with you
27:34, GAVE HIM WINE TO D MINGLED
WITH GALL
1 Cor. 10:4, all drank the same
spiritual d
10:21, You cannot d the cup of the
Lord
11:25, as often as you d it
Num. 6:3; 1 Kin. 17:6; Prov. 5:15;
7:18; Eccles. 9:7; Is. 24:9; Joel 1:5;
Luke 5:39; 17:27; John 6:55; 18:11;
Rom. 12:20; Heb. 6:7

DRIP Prov. 27:15, constant d-ing on a
day of steady rain
Job 36:28; Ps. 65:11; Song 4:11; Is.
45:8

DRIVE—chase Ps. 1:4, chaff which
the wind d-s away
Gen. 4:14; 21:10; Judg. 11:7;
2 Kin. 9:20; Ps. 35:5; Is. 58:3

DROP—leak, drip Deut. 32:2; Job
36:27
Is. 40:15, nations are like a d from a
bucket
Luke 22:44, His sweat became like d-
s of blood

DROUGHT—famine Jer. 14:1, in
regard to the d

DROVE John 2:15; Acts 13:50

DROWNED Ex. 15:4, his officers are
d in the Red Sea
Matt. 18:6, d in the depth of the sea

DROWSY Matt. 25:5, got d and
began to sleep

DRUNK—drink Eph. 5:18, do not
get d with wine
Lev. 11:34; Deut. 32:42; Is. 29:9; 63:6;
John 2:10; 1 Thess. 5:7

DRUNKARD Deut. 21:20; Ps. 69:12;
Joel 1:5; 1 Cor. 5:11

DRUNKENNESS
Luke 21:34, weighted down
with . . . d
Rom. 13:13, not in carousing and d
Gal. 5:21, envyings, d, carousings
and things

DRY—parch, scorch, wither
Ezek. 37:4, O d bones, hear the word
Gen. 1:9; Ps. 63:1; Prov. 17:1; Ezek.
17:24; Luke 23:31

DUE—deserve, owe Gal. 6:9, in d
time we shall reap
Lev. 10:13; Ps. 104:27

DUG Ps. 7:15; 57:6; Is. 51:1; Ezek. 8:8;
Matt. 21:33; 25:18; Luke 6:48

DULL—red Gen. 49:12, eyes are d
from wine

DUMB—silent Mark 7:37, deaf to
hear, and d to speak
Ps. 31:18, Let the lying lips be d
Ex. 4:11; Ps. 39:2; Matt. 9:32;
1 Cor. 12:2; 2 Pet. 2:16

DUNGEON—pit Gen. 41:14, out of
the d

DUST Gen. 2:7, LORD God formed
man of d
Gen. 3:19, you are d, And to d you
shall return
Ps. 103:14, He is mindful we are
but d
Matt. 10:14, shake off the d of your
feet
Gen. 3:14; 13:16; 1 Sam. 2:8;
2 Sam. 22:43; Job 30:19; 34:15;
42:6; Ps. 18:42; 30:9; 72:9; Is. 26:19;
40:15; 65:25; Dan. 12:2; Luke 10:11;
Acts 22:23; Rev. 18:19

DWELL—abide, remain, live
Ps. 5:4, No evil d-s with Thee
15:1, Who may d on Thy holy hill
23:6, will d in the house of the LORD
24:1, world, and those who d in it
91:1, d-s in the shelter of the Most
High
Prov. 3:33, He blesses the d-ing of
the righteous
Luke 16:9, receive you into the
eternal d-ings
2 Cor. 5:2, our d-ing from heaven
Eph. 2:22, d-ing of God in the Spirit
3:17, Christ may d in your hearts
Phil. 4:8, mind d on these things
Col. 1:19, for all the fulness to d in
Him
1 Tim. 6:16, d-s in unapproachable
light
2 Pet. 1:14, laying aside . . . earthly
d-ing
Gen. 4:20; Deut. 12:11; 1 Chr. 17:1;
Ezra 7:15; Ps. 33:14; Prov. 15:31;
Is. 57:15; Luke 21:35

DWELT—sat Ps. 107:10, those who
d in darkness

DWINDLE—diminish
Prov. 13:11, wealth . . . by fraud d-s

E

EACH Acts 17:27, not far from e one
of us

Rom. 14:12, e one of us shall give
account
Phil. 2:3, let e of you regard one
another
2 Thess. 1:3, the love of e one of you
Ex. 18:7; Ps. 85:10; Is. 57:2; Ezek. 4:6;
Acts 2:3

EAGER—hasty Ps. 17:12; Eccles. 7:9

EAGERLY—fervently
Rom. 8:19, creation waits e for
Gal. 4:17, They e seek you
2 Tim. 1:17, in Rome, he e searched
for me

EAGLE Ps. 103:5, youth is renewed
like the e
Is. 40:31, with wings like e-s
Ex. 19:4; Deut. 28:49; 2 Sam. 1:23;
Job 9:26; 39:27; Ezek. 1:10; 17:3;
Dan. 4:33; Obad. 4; Rev. 4:7; 12:14

EAR Prov. 20:12, The hearing e and
the seeing eye
Prov. 25:12, a wise reprover to a
listening e
Is. 55:3, Incline your e and come to
Me
1 Cor. 2:9, EYE HAS NOT SEEN AND E
HAS NOT HEARD
Rev. 2:7, He who has an e, let him
hear
Neh. 1:6; Job 12:11; 29:11; 42:5;
Ps. 45:10; 58:4; 78:1; 94:9;
Prov. 15:31; 18:15; 22:17;
Eccles. 1:8; Is. 48:8; 50:4; 59:1;
Jer. 9:20; Amos 3:12; Matt. 11:15;
1 Cor. 12:16

EARLY Gen. 26:31; Song 7:12; Hos.
6:4; Mark 16:2; Luke 24:22;
John 20:1; James 5:7

EARNEST—pledge 2 Cor. 8:8; Phil.
1:20

EARNESTLY—diligently, fervently
Ps. 63:1, seek Thee e
1 Cor. 12:31, But e desire the greater
gifts
Col. 4:12, always laboring e for you
James 5:17, he prayed e that it might
not rain
Jude 3, contend e for the faith

EARNS Hag. 1:6, he who e, e wages
to put into a purse

EARS—hearing 2 Sam. 7:22, heard
with our e
Job 15:21, Sounds of terror are in
his e
28:22, With our e we have heard
Ps. 34:15, His e are open to their cry
115:6, They have e, but they cannot
hear
Prov. 21:13, shuts his e to the cry of
the poor
26:17, Like one who takes a dog by
the e
Mark 8:18, HAVING E, DO YOU NOT
HEAR
2 Tim. 4:3, wanting to have their e
tickled
James 5:4, reached the e of the Lord
1 Pet. 3:12, HIS E ATTEND TO THEIR
PRAYER
Ps. 135:17; Is. 6:10; Matt. 10:27;
11:15; 13:15,16; 26:51; 28:14;
Mark 4:9; 7:33; 14:47; Acts 7:51;
17:20

EARTH—*ground, land, soil*
Gen. 18:25, Shall not the judge of all the **e** deal
Ex. 9:29, the **e** is the LORD's
Num. 14:21, all the **e** will be filled with the glory
Josh. 3:11; Zech. 6:5, Lord of all the **e**
Job 26:7, hangs the **e** on nothing
Ps. 8:1, Thy name in all **e**
24:1, The **e** is the LORD's
33:5, **e** is full of the lovingkindness of the LORD
46:6, raised His voice, the **e** melted
97:1, LORD reigns; let the **e** rejoice
104:5, He established the **e**
104:24, The **e** is full of Thy possessions
Eccles. 1:4, the **e** remains forever
Is. 11:9, **e** will be full of the knowledge
51:6, the **e** will wear out like a garment
66:1, the **e** is My footstool
Jer. 51:15, made the **e** by His power
Mic. 1:2, Listen, O **e** and all it contains
Hab. 2:14, **e** will be filled with the knowledge
3:3, the **e** is full of His praise
Zech. 4:10, eyes of the LORD ... the **e**
Matt. 5:5, gentle, for they shall inherit the **e**
6:10, on **e** as it is in heaven
6:19, treasures upon **e**
16:19; 18:18, shall bind on **e**
Luke 2:14, on **e** peace
John 12:32, lifted up from the **e**
17:4, I glorified Thee on the **e**
1 Cor. 15:47, first man is from the **e**, **e-y**
15:48, As is the **e-y**, so also ... who are **e-y**
Col. 3:2, not on the things that are on **e**
2 Pet. 3:13, new heavens and a new **e**
Rev. 20:11, from whose presence **e** and heaven fled
21:1, a new **e**
Gen. 1:1,11; 7:10; 8:22; 10:25; Deut. 32:1; Josh. 23:14; 1 Kin. 8:27; 2 Kin. 5:17; 2 Chr. 6:18; Job 9:24; 12:8; 19:25; 38:4; 41:33; Ps. 2:8; 16:3; 34:16; 41:2; 46:2,8,10; 47:9; 50:4; 57:5; 58:11; 63:9; 65:8,9; 67:6; 68:8; 71:20; 72:6,16; 73:25; 75:3; 83:18; 90:2; 97:9; 99:1; 102:25; 104:13; 108:5; 112:2; 115:16; 119:19,64,90; 146:4; 147:8; 148:13; Prov. 3:19; 8:23,26; 11:31; 25:3; 30:14,16,21,24; Eccles. 3:21; 12:7; Is. 4:2; 13:13; 14:16; 24:1,19; 26:9,21; 34:1; 40:22,28; 44:24; 45:22; 48:13; 49:13; 65:16; Jer. 31:22; Ezek. 34:27; 43:2; Hos. 2:22; Amos 8:9; Jon. 2:6; Mic. 6:2; 7:17; Nah. 1:5; Zeph. 3:8; Hag. 1:10; Matt. 5:35; 10:34; 23:9; Mark 4:28; 9:3; John 3:31; Acts 8:33; 22:22; Rom. 10:18; 1 Cor. 15:49; Heb. 8:4; 11:13; 12:25,26; James 3:15; 5:5,18; 2 Pet. 3:7,10; Rev. 5:10; 7:3; 18:1; 20:9

EARTHEN Jer. 19:1; Lam. 4:2
2 Cor. 4:7, have this treasure in **e** vessels

EARTHLY John 3:12, If I told you **e** things
2 Cor. 5:1, **e** tent which is our house
Phil. 3:19, set their minds on **e** things
James 3:15, wisdom ... is **e**, natural, demonic

EARTHQUAKE 1 Kin. 19:11; Is. 29:6; Amos 1:1; Zech. 14:5; Matt. 24:7; 27:54; Acts 16:26; Rev. 6:12; 8:5; 11:13; 16:18

EASE—*rest, prosperity* Job 12:5, He who is at **e**
Amos 6:1, Woe to those who are at **e**
Zech. 1:15, nations who are at **e**
Matt. 19:24; Mark 10:25; Luke 18:25, **e-ier** for a camel
Luke 12:19, take your **e**
Heb. 12:1, sin which so **e-ily** entangles us
Ex. 18:22; Job 21:23; Is. 32:9,11

EAST Judg. 6:3; 7:12, 1 Kin. 4:30, sons of the **e**
Ps. 103:12, As far as the **e**
Matt. 2:1, magi from the **e**
2:2, His star in the **e**
Gen. 28:14; Ex. 10:13; Job 1:3; Ps. 48:7; 75:6; Is. 27:8; 43:5; Ezek. 8:16; 17:10; Hos. 12:1; Joel 2:20; Jon. 4:5; Zech. 8:7; 14:4; Matt. 8:11; 24:27; Luke 13:29; Rev. 16:12; 21:13

EASY Prov. 14:6, knowledge is **e** to him
Matt. 11:30, My yoke is **e**

EAT—*consume, dine, feast* Prov. 31:27, not **e** the bread
Is. 55:1, come, buy and **e**
Ezek. 3:1, **e** this scroll
Dan. 4:33, began **e-ing** grass like cattle
Matt. 6:25; Luke 12:22, what you shall **e**
11:19, Son of Man came **e-ing** and drinking
15:20, **e** with unwashed hands
26:26, Take, **e**; this is My body
Mark 2:16, He was **e-ing** with the sinners
Luke 12:19, **e**, drink *and* be merry
15:2, receives sinners and **e-s** with them
22:30, may **e** and drink at My table
John 4:32, food to **e** that you do not know about
Acts 12:23, **e-en** by worms and died
Rom. 14:17, kingdom of God is not **e-ing**
1 Cor. 11:29, **e-s** and drinks judgment to himself
2 Thess. 3:10, not work, neither let him **e**
Heb. 13:10, have no right to **e**
Rev. 2:7, **e** of the tree of life
Gen. 2:16; 3:17; 9:4; Lev. 19:26; Deut. 6:11; 8:10; 12:16; Josh. 5:12; 1 Kin. 19:5; 2 Kin. 6:28; Neh. 5:2; 8:10; Ps. 22:26; 80:13; Prov. 1:31; 24:13; 25:27; Eccles. 5:12; Is. 1:19; 3:10; 4:1; 7:15; 11:7; 65:13, 25; Jer. 24:2; 29:17; 31:29; Ezek. 18:2; Hos. 4:10; 10:13; Mic. 6:14; Hag. 1:6; Matt. 9:11; 12:1; 14:16; Mark 6:31,37; 11:14; Luke 9:13; 10:8; 15:23; John 6:53; Acts 10:13; Rom. 14:2; 1 Cor. 8:13; 9:4; 10:27,31; Rev. 10:10; 19:18

EDGE—*bank* Josh. 3:8; Eccles. 10:10; Jer. 31:30
Prov. 5:4, sharp as a **two-e-d** sword

EDICT—*word* Ezra 6:11, violates this **e**

EDIFICATION Rom. 15:2, please his neighbor ... to his **e**
1 Cor. 14:3, speaks to men for **e**
14:26, all things be done for **e**

EDIFY—*encourage* 1 Cor. 8:1, but love **e-es**
1 Cor. 10:23, lawful, but not all things **e**
14:5, church may receive **e-ing**

EDUCATE Acts 22:3, **e-d** under Gamaliel

EFFECT—*wise* Acts 7:6, God spoke to this **e**

EFFECTIVE 1 Cor. 16:9, door for **e** *service*
James 5:16, The **e** prayer

EFFEMINATE 1 Cor. 6:9, Do not be deceived ... nor **e**

EFFORT—*diligence* 2 Tim. 4:9; Jude 3

EGG Job 6:6; 39:14; Is. 59:5; Jer. 17:11
Luke 11:12, asked for an **e** ... give him a scorpion

ELDERS—*older, aged* 1 Sam. 15:30; Job 12:20; 32:9
Matt. 15:2; Mark 7:3, tradition of the **e**
Acts 14:23, appointed **e** for them in every church
1 Tim. 5:17, Let the **e** who rule
James 5:14, call for the **e**
Prov. 31:23; Titus 1:5; 1 Pet. 5:1; Rev. 4:4; 7:13

ELECT—*chosen* Matt. 24:22; Mark 13:20, sake of the **e**
Matt. 24:24, mislead, if possible, even the **e**
Mark 13:22, to lead the **e** astray
Luke 18:7, God bring about justice for His **e**
Rom. 8:33, charge against God's **e**

ELEMENT Gal. 4:3, **e-al** things
2 Pet. 3:10, **e-s** will be destroyed

ELOQUENT—*skillful* Ex. 4:10, never been **e**
Acts 18:24, Jew named Apollos ... an **e** man

ELUDE—*escape* John 10:39, He **e-d** their grasp

EMBITTERED Acts 14:2, **e** them against

EMBRACE 2 Kin. 4:16, Prov. 5:20; Song 2:6
Gen. 33:4, Esau ran ... and **e-d** him
48:10, Joseph ... and **e-d**
Eccles. 3:5, a time to **e** ... to shun **e-ing**
Luke 15:20, ran and **e-d** him

EMBROIDER—*weave* Ex. 35:35; Ezek. 16:10,13; 27:7,16,24

EMERALD Ex. 28:17; Ezek. 28:13; Rev. 4:3; 21:19

EMINENT—*foremost* 2 Cor. 11:5, inferior . . . **e** apostles

EMPTINESS—*vanity* Is. 34:11, plumb line of **e**
Jer. 2:5, And walked after **e**

EMPTY—*vain, void* 2 Kin. 18:20, *they are* only **e** words
Is. 55:11, not return to Me **e**
Eph. 5:6, deceive you with **e** words
1 Tim. 6:20, worldly and **e** chatter
Gen. 31:42; Is. 3:21; 23:15;
Deut. 15:13; Judg. 7:16; Ruth 1:21;
2 Sam. 1:22; 2 Kin. 4:3; Job 22:9;
26:7; Mark 12:3; Luke 1:53; 20:10

ENCAMP Ps. 27:3; 34:7; 53:5; Jer. 50:29

ENCIRCLE Ps. 22:12, bulls of Bashan have **e-d** me

ENCLOSE Job 38:8; Ps. 139:5

ENCOUNTER James 1:2, when you **e** various trials

ENCOURAGE—*strengthen* 2 Chr. 35:2; Is. 41:7
Deut. 1:38; 3:28; 2 Sam. 11:25, **e** him
1 Sam. 23:16, **e-d** him in God
Ezra 6:22, to **e** them in the work
1 Thess. 5:11, Therefore **e** one another
Heb. 3:13, **e** one another
10:25, but **e-ing** *one another*

ENCOURAGEMENT—*consolation* Acts 4:36, Son of **E**
Rom. 15:5, God who gives perseverance and **e**
Phil. 2:1, if . . . any **e** in Christ
Heb. 6:18, may have strong **e**

ENCUMBRANCE—*weight* Heb. 12:1, also lay aside every **e**

END—*goal, outcome* Gen. 6:13, **e** of all flesh
Job 6:11, what is my **e**
Ps. 2:8, *very* **e-s** of the earth
7:9, wicked come to an **e**
39:4, LORD, make me to know my **e**
Prov. 14:12, **e** is the way of death
Eccles. 4:8, no **e** to all his labor
Is. 9:7, no **e** to the increase of *His* government
Jer. 8:20, Harvest is past, summer is **e-ed**
Ezek. 21:25; 35:5, punishment of the **e**
Matt. 10:22; Mark 13:13, endured to the **e**
13:39, harvest is the **e** of the age
28:20, with you always, even to the **e**
Luke 1:33, His kingdom will have no **e**
21:9, the **e** *does* not *follow* immediately
John 13:1, He loved them to the **e**
Rom. 10:4, Christ is the **e** of the law
Heb. 7:3, beginning of days, nor **e** of life
Rev. 21:6; 22:13, the beginning and the **e**
Num. 23:10; Ps. 9:6; 19:6; 73:17;
102:27; 107:27; Eccles. 7:8;
Jer. 5:31; Lam 4:18; Ezek. 7:2;

Dan. 11:45; 12:13; Matt. 24:6,13; Mark 13:7; Heb. 6:8

ENDLESS Eccles. 12:12, writing . . . books is **e**
1 Tim. 1:4, attention to myths and **e** genealogies

ENDOW—*clothe* Gen. 30:20; 2 Chr. 2:13

ENDURANCE—*patience* James 1:4, let **e** have *its* perfect
5:11, **e** of Job

ENDURE—*persevere* Ps. 104:31, LORD **e** forever
Ps. 111:3; 112:3, His righteousness **e-s** forever
Mal. 3:2, who can **e** the day of His coming
Matt. 10:22, one who has **e-d** to the end
24:13, **e-s** to the end
1 Cor. 9:12, but we **e** all things
13:7, **e-s** all things
2 Tim. 2:12, if we **e**, we shall also reign
4:3, not **e** sound doctrine
James 5:11, count those blessed who **e-d**
Ex. 18:23; Esth. 8:6; Job 6:11; Ps. 72:5,17; Prov. 27:24; Is. 66:22; Ezek. 22:14; Joel 2:11; Mark 13:13; Heb. 12:7

ENEMY—*foe* Ps. 23:5, in the presence of my **e-es**
Ps. 61:3, tower of strength against the **e**
72:9, his **e-es** lick the dust
Prov. 24:17, Do not rejoice when your **e** falls
25:21, **e** is hungry, give him food to eat
Matt. 5:44; Luke 6:27,35, love your **e-es**
10:36, A MAN'S **E-ES** . . . HIS HOUSEHOLD
Acts 2:35, I MAKE THINE **E-ES** A FOOTSTOOL
Rom. 5:10, while we were **e-es**, we were reconciled
James 4:4, friend of the world . . . **e** of God
Ex. 23:22; Deut. 32:31; Judg. 5:31;
1 Kin. 21:20; Job 13:24; Ps. 8:2;
119:98; 127:5; Prov. 16:7; 27:6;
Is. 63:10; Mic. 7:6; Rom. 12:20;
Gal. 4:16

ENGAGE 1 Chr. 9:33; Luke 1:27

ENGINE 2 Chr. 26:15, he made **e-s** of *war*

ENGRAVE—*graven* Ex. 28:11; 32:16; 35:35; 38:23; 39:14; Zech. 3:9; 2 Cor. 3:7

ENGULF Ps. 78:53, the sea **e-ed** their enemies

ENJOY Lev. 26:34, land will **e** its sabbaths
2 Chr. 36:21, land had **e-ed** its sabbaths
Eccles. 2:1, **e** yourself
5:18, **e** oneself in all one's labor
1 Tim. 6:17, supplies us with all things to **e**
Heb. 11:25, **e** the passing pleasures of sin

ENLARGE—*extend* Gen. 9:27; Is. 5:14
Ps. 25:17, troubles of my heart are **e-d**
119:32, Thou wilt **e** my heart

ENLIGHTEN—*illumine* Ps. 19:8, pure, **e-ing** the eyes
Eph. 1:18, eyes of your heart may be **e-ed**
Heb. 6:4, those who have once been **e-ed**

ENMITY—*hostile* Gen. 3:15; Luke 23:12; Eph. 2:15,16

ENOUGH—*plenty, much* Num. 16:9, **e** . . . that the God of Israel
Matt. 6:34, *Each* day has **e** trouble
Mark 14:41, It is **e**; the hour has come
Luke 15:17, hired men have more than **e** bread
Gen. 45:28; Ex. 36:5; Num. 16:3;
2 Sam. 24:16; 1 Kin. 19:4;
1 Chr. 21:15; Prov. 30:15; Hos. 4:10;
Hag. 1:6; Matt. 10:25; 25:9;
Luke 22:38

ENRAGE—*angry* Prov. 6:34, jealousy **e-s** man
Matt. 2:16, Herod . . . became very **e-d**

ENRICH 1 Sam. 17:25; Ps. 65:9; Ezek. 27:33
1 Cor. 1:5, in everything you were **e-ed**
2 Cor. 9:11, be **e-ed** in everything

ENSLAVED Titus 3:3, **e** to various lusts and pleasures

ENTANGLE—*trap* 2 Tim. 2:4, No soldier . . . **e-s** himself
Heb. 12:1, sin which so easily **e-s** us

ENTER—*come* Ps. 100:4, **E** His gates with thanksgiving
Ps. 118:20, righteous will **e** through it
Is. 57:2, He **e-s** into peace
Ezek. 44:16, They shall **e** My sanctuary
Matt. 5:20, you shall not **e** the kingdom
7:13, **E** by the narrow gate
10:5; do not **e** . . . city of the Samaritans
10:11, village you **e**, inquire
10:12, **e** the house, give it your greeting
18:8; Mark 9:43, better . . . **e** life crippled
19:17, if you wish to **e** into life, keep
25:21, **e** into the joy of your master
Luke 9:34, afraid as they **e-ed** the cloud
22:46, that you may not **e** into temptation
John 10:1, does not **e** by the door
10:9, if anyone **e-s** through Me
Rom. 5:12, sin **e-ed** into the world
1 Cor. 2:9, *which* HAVE NOT **E-ED** THE HEART
Gen. 6:18; Job 22:4; 38:16; Is. 2:10;
26:2,20; Ezek. 2:2; Hab. 3:16;
Luke 13:24; John 3:5; 2 Tim. 3:6;
Heb. 3:11,18; 4:10; 6:20

ENTICE—*deceive, seduce* Judg. 14:15; 16:5; 2 Chr. 18:19
Prov. 1:10, if sinners **e** you

James 1:14, **e-d** by his own lust
2 Pet. 2:14, **e-ing** unstable souls
2:18, they **e** by fleshly desires

ENTRANCE—*door* Ezek. 8:5,
jealousy at the **e**
Matt. 27:60, rolled a large stone
against the **e**
2 Pet. 1:11, **e** into the eternal
kingdom

ENTREAT—*appeal, ask, beg* Ex.
8:8; 32:11; 2 Sam. 24:25
Matt. 8:34, they **e-ed** Him to depart
from their region
Mark 5:10, he *began* to **e** Him
earnestly
2 Cor. 5:20, as though God were **e-
ing** through us
Eph. 4:1, I therefore . . . **e** you to
walk
1 Tim. 2:1, I urge that **e-es** *and*
prayers
1 Kin. 13:6; 2 Chr. 33:12; Job 21:15;
Prov. 19:6; Jer. 26:19; Matt. 8:5,31;
Luke 8:31; 15:28; 2 Cor. 12:8

ENTRUST—*commit*
Luke 12:48, whom they **e-ed** much

ENVIOUS Ps. 37:1; 73:3
Prov. 24:1, Do not be **e** of evil men
24:19, Or be **e** of the wicked

ENVY (n.)—*jealousy* Matt. 27:18;
Mark 15:10
Rom. 1:29, full of **e**, murder
Phil. 1:15, preaching Christ even
from **e**
1 Tim. 6:4, out of which arise **e**
Titus 3:3, spending life in malice
and **e**
1 Pet. 2:1, putting aside all malice . . .
and **e**

ENVY (v.) Gen. 26:14, Philistines **e-
ed** him
Prov. 3:31, Do not **e** a man of
violence
23:17, Do not let your heart **e**
sinners
Gal. 5:26, **e-ing** one another

EPHAH—*bushel* Ex. 16:36; 29:40;
Lev. 19:36; Ezek. 45:10; Zech. 5:8

EPHOD Ex. 28:4; 39:2; Judg. 8:27;
17:5; 1 Sam. 2:18; 23:9; Hos. 3:4

EPOCH—*season*
Dan. 2:21, changes times and **e-s**
Acts 1:7, to know times or **e-s**

EQUAL—*equity, right* John 5:18,
Himself **e** with God
2 Cor. 8:14, that there may be **e-ity**
Phil. 2:6, not regard **e-ity** with God
Job 28:17,19; Ps. 55:13; Is. 40:25;
46:5; Matt. 20:12

EQUIP—*furnish*
2 Tim. 3:17, **e-ed** for every good
work
Heb. 13:21, **e** you in every good
thing

EQUITY—*equal, uprightness,
straight* Ps. 17:2; 98:9
Prov. 1:3, Righteousness, justice,
and **e**
2:9, discern righteousness . . . and **e**

ERASE—*blot* Rev. 3:5, I will not **e**
his name

ERECT—*upright*
Gen. 33:20, Then he **e-ed** there an
altar
37:7, sheaf rose . . . stood **e**

ERR—*stray, mistake* Ps. 95:10,
people who **e**

ERROR—*mistake, sin* Is. 32:6; 2
Pet. 3:17; Jude 11
Ps. 19:12, Who can discern *his* **e-s**
Eccles. 10:5, evil I have seen . . . like
an **e**
James 5:20, from the **e** of his way
1 John 4:6, we know . . . the spirit
of **e**

ESCAPE—*deliverance, refuge,
elude*
Prov. 19:5, he who tells lies wll not **e**
Eccles. 7:26, who is pleasing to God
will **e**
Is. 20:6; Heb. 2:3, how shall we **e**
1 Cor. 10:13, provide the way of **e**
Heb. 11:34, **e-d** the edge of the
sword
2 Pet. 1:4, **e-d** the corruption that is
in the world
Gen. 19:17; Deut. 23:15; 1 Kin. 18:40;
2 Kin. 9:15; Esth. 4:13; Job 11:20;
19:20; Ps. 124:7; Obad. 17;
Matt. 23:33; Mark 14:52;
Luke 21:36; Heb. 11:34

ESSENTIAL—*excellent*
Rom. 2:18, approve . . . that are **e**

ESTABLISH—*confirm, direct,
plant, strengthen*
Ps. 119:5, that my ways may be **e-ed**
119:38, **E** Thy word to Thy servant
Prov. 16:12, throne is **e-ed** on
righteousness
Is. 16:5, A throne . . . **e-ed** in
lovingkindness
Rom. 16:25, able to **e** you according
to
1 Thess. 3:13, He may **e** your hearts
2 Pet. 1:12, been **e-ed** in the truth
Gen. 17:19; Job 37:15; Ps. 65:6; Prov.
3:19; Is. 51:16; Jer. 10:12; 51:15;
Rom. 3:31; 10:3

ESTATE—*domain, standard* Ps.
136:23, low **e**
Luke 15:13, squandered his **e** with
loose living

ESTEEM—*regard, consider*
Ps. 119:128, I **e** right . . . precepts
1 Thess. 5:13, you **e** them very highly
in love

ESTEEMED—*beloved, chosen,
loved* 1 Sam. 18:23; Dan. 9:23
1 Sam. 2:30, despise Me will be **e-ed**
lightly
Is. 53:4, we ourselves **e** Him stricken
Luke 16:15, highly **e** among men

ESTIMATION—*imagination*
Rom. 11:25, wise in your own **e**

ESTRANGE Job 19:13; Ps. 58:3;
Ezek. 14:5

ETERNAL—*everlasting* Deut. 33:27;
Matt. 18:8 Is. 9:6, name will be
called . . . **E** Father
Matt. 19:16, I may obtain **e** life

19:29, shall inherit **e** life
25:46, righteous into **e** life
Mark 10:17; Luke 10:25, what . . . to
inherit **e** life
10:30, in the world to come, **e** life
John 3:15, may in Him have **e** life
3:16, whoever believes . . . have **e**
life
3:36, who believes in the Son has **e**
life
5:39, search the Scriptures . . . have
e life
6:68, You have words of **e** life
10:28, I give **e** life to them
12:25, hates his life . . . keep it to
life **e**
17:3, **e** life, that they may know
Thee
Rom. 2:7, seek for glory and honor
. . . **e** life
5:21, righteousness to **e**
6:23, free gift of God is **e** life
2 Cor. 4:17, an **e** weight of glory
4:18, things which are not seen
are **e**
5:1, house . . . **e** in the heavens
Gal. 6:8, from the Spirit reap **e** life
Eph. 3:11, in accordance with the **e**
purpose
1 Tim. 1:17, Now to the King **e**,
immortal
6:12, take hold of the **e** life
Titus 1:2, in the hope of **e** life
Heb. 5:9, source of **e** salvation
9:14, through the **e** Spirit
1 Pet. 5:10, called you to His **e** glory
in Christ
1 John 2:25, promise . . . made to us,
e life
5:11, God has given us **e** life
Rev. 14:6, having an **e** gospel to
preach
Matt. 25:41,46; Mark 3:29; Luke 16:9;
18:18; John 4:14,36; 6:54; 12:50;
17:2; Acts 13:46,48; Rom. 6:22;
16:26; 2 Thess. 1:9; 2:16; Heb. 6:2;
9:12,15; 1 John 1:2; 3:15; 5:20;
Jude 6,7

ETERNITY—*world*
Eccles. 3:11, set **e** in their heart
Mic. 5:2, goings forth . . . from the
days of **e**

EUNUCH—*chamberlain, official*
Esth. 1:10; Is. 56:3; Matt. 19:12;
Acts 8:27

EVANGELIST Acts 21:8, Philip the **e**
Eph. 4:11, He gave some . . . *as* **e-s**
2 Tim. 4:5, do the work of an **e**

EVAPORATE—*fail, gone* Ex. 16:14;
Job 14:11

EVENING—*close* Ps. 104:23, to his
labor until **e**
Jer. 6:4, shadows of the **e** lengthen
Zech. 14:7, at **e** time there will be
light
Luke 24:29, for it is *getting* toward **e**
Judg. 20:23; 1 Sam. 14:24;
1 Kin. 17:6; Ps. 55:17; 90:6; 141:2;
Eccles. 11:6; Matt. 8:16; 14:23;
Mark 1:32

EVER—*forever* Ps. 52:8; Matt. 21:19;
Mark 11:14; Rev. 14:11
Ps. 48:14, Our God forever and **e**
51:3, my sin is **e** before me
Rev. 11:15, He will reign forever
and **e**
22:5, they shall reign forever and **e**

EVERLASTING—*endure, eternal, ancient, perpetual*
Gen. 21:33; Is. 40:28, the E God
Deut. 33:27, underneath are the e arms
Ps. 90:2, from e to e, Thou art God
106:1; 107:1; 136:1, lovingkindness is e
139:24, lead me in the e way
Is. 26:4, in GOD ... *have* an e Rock
35:10; 51:11; 61:7, e joy
Jer. 31:3, loved you with an e love
Gen. 9:16; Ps. 103:17; 119:142; 138:8; Prov. 8:23; 10:25; Is. 45:17; 54:8; 55:13; 56:5; 60:19,20; 63:12; Dan. 4:34; 7:14

EVERMORE—*ever, forever* Ps. 92:7; John 6:34

EVERY Gen. 6:5, e intent ... of his heart was only evil
Ps. 119:101, restrained my feet from e evil way
119:104, I hate e false way
Prov. 30:5, E word of God is tested
Eccles. 3:1, a time for e event under heaven
Is. 45:23, e knee will bow
55:1, Ho! E one who thirsts
Jer. 25:5, Turn now e one from his evil way
Matt. 4:4, ON E WORD THAT PROCEEDS
7:8, For e one who asks receives
John 3:8, so is e one who is born of the Spirit
2 Cor. 10:5, taking e thought captive
Eph. 1:21, far above all rule ... e name
2 Tim. 2:21, prepared for e good work
Heb. 12:1, lay aside e encumbrance
James 1:17, E good thing ... e perfect gift
1 John 4:1, do not believe e spirit
Rev. 20:13, e one of them according to their deeds
22:12, e man according to what he has done
Deut. 4:4; Prov. 2:9; 7:12; John 18:37; Rom. 14:11; 1 Tim. 2:8; 2 Tim. 2:19

EVERYONE Ps. 32:6, e who is godly pray
Eccles. 10:3, demonstrates to e *that* he is a fool
Luke 11:10, For e who asks receives
19:26, to e who has shall *more* be given

EVERYTHING Prov. 14:15, The naive believes e
1 Tim. 4:4, e created by God is good

EVERYWHERE Mark 1:45; 16:20; Acts 17:30

EVIDENCE—*mouth* Deut. 17:6, the e of two witnesses

EVIDENT—*see* Gal. 3:11; Heb. 7:14

EVIL—*bad, wicked, reproach*
Gen. 38:7, e in the sight of the LORD
Deut. 23:9, keep yourself from every e
1 Kin. 21:25, sold himself to do e
Ps. 15:3, Nor does e to his neighbor
23:4, I fear no e
34:14; 37:27, Depart from e, and do good
91:10, No e will befall you

97:10, Hate e, you who love the LORD
Jer. 7:26, did e more than their fathers
Matt. 5:11, all kinds of e against you falsely
6:13, deliver us from e
7:11; Luke 11:13, If you then, being e
12:45, this e generation
27:23; Mark 15:14, what e has He done
Mark 9:39, speak e of Me
Luke 6:45, e *man* out of the e treasure
John 3:20, does e hates the light
Rom. 12:17, Never pay back e for e to anyone
12:21, overcome e with good
Eph. 5:16, because the days are e
1 Thess. 5:22, abstain from every form of e
1 Tim. 6:10, love of money is a root of all e
James 3:8, tongue; *it is* a restless e
1 John 2:13, overcome the e one
5:19, world lies ... power of the e one
Gen. 6:5; 8:21; 50:20; Deut. 31:29; 2 Sam. 14:17; 1 Kin. 3:9; Ezra 4:12; Job 30:26; Ps. 35:12; 40:12; 109:5; Prov. 3:7; 6:18; 14:19; 15:3; 17:13; Is. 5:20; 7:15,16; 57:1; Jer. 2:13,19; Hab. 1:13; Matt. 9:4; 22:10; Luke 6:22,35; Acts 23:5; Rom. 7:19; 1 Thess. 5:15; 3 John 11

EVILDOERS Ps. 37:1, Fret not ... because of e
Ps. 37:9, e will be cut off
Ps. 119:115; Is. 1:4; 9:17; Luke 13:27; 1 Pet. 4:15

EWE Num. 6:14; 2 Sam. 12:3; Ps. 78:71

EXACT—*lend, collect* Deut. 15:2, he shall not e it
Heb. 1:3, e representation of His nature

EXALT—*extol, lift, raise* Ps. 34:3, let us e His name
Ps. 46:10, I will be e-ed in the earth
108:5, Be e-ed, O God, above the heavens
Prov. 4:8, Prize her, and she will e you
14:34, Righteousness e-s a nation
Matt. 11:23; Luke 10:15, e-ed to heaven
23:12; Luke 14:11; 18:14, e-s himself
Luke 1:46, My soul e-s the Lord
Acts 5:31, He is the one whom God e-ed
Phil. 1:20, Christ shall ... be e-ed in my body
2:9, God highly e-ed Him
Ex. 15:1; 1 Sam. 2:10; 1 Chr. 29:11; Job 37:23; Ps. 89:16; 92:10; 97:9; Prov. 11:11; Is. 52:13; Ezek. 21:26; Dan. 4:37; 2 Cor. 12:7; 2 Thess. 2:4; James 4:10; 1 Pet. 5:6

EXAMINE—*investigate, search* Job 7:18; Acts 22:24
Ps. 26:2, E me, O LORD
Acts 17:11, e-ing the Scriptures daily
1 Cor. 11:28, let a man e himself
2 Cor. 13:5, e yourselves

EXAMPLE—*model, pattern* James 5:10; 2 Pet. 2:6; Jude 7

John 13:15; I gave you an e
1 Cor. 10:6, these things happened as e-s
10:11, to them as an e
1 Tim. 4:12, an e of those who believe
Heb. 4:11, same e of disobedience
1 Pet. 2:21, Christ also ... leaving you an e
5:3, proving to be e-s to the flock

EXASPERATE—*anger*
Col. 3:21, do not e your children

EXCEED—*great, surpass, utterly*
Ps. 43:4, God my e-ing joy
119:96, Thy commandment is e-ingly broad
Prov. 30:24, Four things ... are e-ingly wise
Jon. 3:3, Nineveh was an e-ingly great city
Mark 9:3, His garments became ... e-ingly white
Eph. 3:20, able to do e-ing abundantly
Gen. 27:34; Num. 14:7; 1 Kin. 10:7; Matt. 2:10

EXCEL Prov. 31:29, you e them all
Eccles. 2:13, wisdom e-s folly
1 Thess. 4:1, that you may e still more

EXCELLENCE—*great, preeminent*
Ex. 15:7, of Thine e
Ruth 3:11, are a woman of e
Phil. 4:8, if there is any e
2 Pet. 1:5, supply moral e ... knowledge

EXCELLENT—*noble* Prov. 12:4, e wife is the crown
1 Cor. 12:31, a still more e way
Phil. 1:10, approve the things that are e
Heb. 1:4, a more e name
Prov. 17:7; 22:20; Is. 12:5

EXCEPT—*save* Gen. 14:24; Ps. 18:31
Matt. 11:27, knows the Son, e the Father
Luke 18:19, No one is good e God alone
Acts 26:29, e for these chains
Rom. 9:29, E THE LORD ... HAD LEFT TO US A POSTERITY

EXCESS Is. 16:6; 1 Pet. 4:4

EXCHANGE Matt. 16:26; Mark 8:37, give in e for his soul
Luke 24:17, these words that you are e-ing
Rom. 1:25, they e-d the truth of God

EXCLUDE—*alienated*
Eph. 4:18, e-d from the life of God

EXCUSE Luke 14:18, began to make e-s
Rom. 1:20, they are without e

EXECUTE—*perform* Deut. 33:21; Ps. 149:7
Ps. 9:16, He has e-d judgment
John 5:27, Him authority to e judgment
Rom. 9:28, LORD WILL E HIS WORD
Jude 15, to e judgment

EXEMPT Matt. 17:26, the sons are e

EXERCISE Jer. 9:24, the LORD who
  e-s lovingkindness
  Matt. 20:25; Mark 10:42, **e** authority
  over them

EXHAUST Judg. 4:21; 1 Kin. 17:14

EXHORT Acts 2:40, many other
  words ... **e-ing** them
  2 Tim. 4:2, **e**, with great patience
  Titus 1:9, able both to **e** in sound
  doctrine
  2:15, **e** and reprove
  1 Pet. 5:12, **e-ing** and testifying

EXHORTATION Luke 3:18; Acts
  20:2; Rom. 12:8; Heb. 13:22

EXILE 2 Sam. 15:19; Is. 51:14

EXORCISTS Acts 19:13, some of the
  Jewish **e**

EXPANSE—*firmament* Gen. 1:6;
  Ezek. 1:25

EXPECT Gen. 48:11; Job 30:26; Luke
  6:35; Acts 3:5

EXPECTATION Prov. 10:28; 11:7,23
  Phil. 1:20, my earnest **e** and hope
  Heb. 10:27, terrifying **e** of judgment

EXPEDIENT—*advantageous*
  John 11:50, **e** for you that one

EXPERT Jer. 50:9; Acts 26:3

EXPLAIN Luke 24:27, **e-ed** to them
  Luke 24:32, He was **e-ing** the
  Scriptures
  John 1:18, He has **e-ed** Him
  Acts 18:26, **e-ed** to him the way of
  God
  28:23, **e-ing** to them ... about the
  kingdom of God

EXPLICIT 1 Tim. 4:1, Spirit **e-ly** says

EXPLORE Eccles. 2:3, I **e-ed** with my
  mind

EXPOSE—*reprove*
  Eph. 5:11, instead even **e** them

EXPRESS
  Ezek. 1:3, word of the LORD came **e-
  ly**

EXTEND Is. 44:13, he **e-s** a
  measuring line
  Deut. 12:20; Ezra 7:28; Ps. 109:12;
  Is. 66:12

EXTOL—*exalt* Ex. 15:2, will **e** Him
  Ps. 30:1; 145:1, I will **e** Thee

EXTORTIONER Is. 16:4, **e** has come
  to an end

EXTRAORDINARY Dan. 5:12; 6:3

EXULT—*rejoicing*
  1 Thess. 2:19, or joy or crown of **e-
  ation**

EYE—*look* Gen. 3:7; 27:1; 49:12;
  Num. 10:31; 24:3,15
  Ex. 21:24; Lev. 24:20; Deut. 19:21;
  Matt. 5:38, **e** for **e**
  Deut. 12:8; Judg. 17:6; 21:25, right in
  his **e-s**
  16:19, bribe blinds the **e-s** of the
  wise

32:10, as the pupil of His **e**
2 Chr. 16:9, **e-s** of the LORD move
Job 19:27, whom my **e-s** shall see
Ps. 11:4, **e-s** ... test the sons of men
  19:8, enlightening the **e-s**
  34:15, **e-s** of the LORD are toward
  the righteous
  36:1, no fear of God before his **e-s**
  69:3; 119:82; Lam. 2:11, My **e-s** fail
Prov. 6:17, Haughty **e-s**, a lying
  tongue
  27:20, Nor are the **e-s** of man ever
  satisfied
Is. 33:17, **e-s** will see the King
  40:26; Jer. 13:20, Lift up your **e-s**
Jer. 5:21, Who have **e-s**, but see not
  16:17, My **e-s** are on all their ways
Zech. 4:10, **e-s** of the LORD which
  range
Matt. 6:22, lamp of the body is the **e**
  13:16, blessed are your **e-s**
  18:9, **e** causes you to stumble, pluck
  it out
Mark 8:18, HAVING **e-s**, DO YOU NOT
  SEE
Luke 4:20, **e-s** ... were fixed upon
  Him
  24:16, their **e-s** were prevented
  from recognizing
John 9:6, applied clay to his **e-s**
Heb. 4:13, laid bare to the **e-s** of Him
1 John 2:16, the lust of the **e-s**
Deut. 3:27; 4:19; 34:7; 1 Kin. 1:20;
  8:29,52; 20:6; 2 Kin. 6:17;
  2 Chr. 6:20,40; 34:28; Job 10:18;
  29:11,15; Ps. 15:4; 33:18; 94:9;
  119:18; 132:4; 145:15; Prov. 10:26;
  20:12; 23:29; 30:17; Eccles. 1:8;
  2:14; 6:9; 11:7; Is. 1:15; 22:4; 29:10;
  32:3; 42:7; 52:8; 64:4; Jer. 9:1;
  13:17; 14:17; 24:6; Ezek. 12:2;
  24:16,25; Hab. 1:13; Matt. 5:29;
  Luke 11:34; John 11:37; 1 Cor. 2:9;
  Gal. 3:1; 4:15; Eph. 1:18; 1 Pet. 3:12;
  2 Pet. 2:14

EYESALVE Rev. 3:18, **e** to anoint
  your eyes

EYESERVICE Eph. 6:6, not by way
  of **e**

EYEWITNESSES Luke 1:2, **e** and
  servants of the Word
2 Pet. 1:16, we were **e** of His majesty

F

FABLES—*myths* 1 Tim. 4:7, worldly
  f fit only for old women

FACE—*countenance*
  Gen. 3:19, By the sweat of your **f**
  Num. 6:25, Lord make His **f** shine on
  you
  Ps. 34:16, the **f** of the Lord is against
  evildoers
  67:1, cause His **f** to shine upon us
  84:9, look upon the **f** of Thine
  anointed
  Is. 25:8, wipe tears away from all **f-s**
  Matt. 6:17, when you fast ... wash
  your **f**
  Luke 24:5, bowed their **f-s** to the
  ground
  John 11:44, his **f** was wrapped
  around with a cloth
  2 Cor. 3:18, with unveiled **f**
  beholding
  1 Pet. 3:12, THE **f** OF THE LORD IS
  AGAINST

Rev. 1:16, His **f** was like the sun
  shining
Gen. 17:3; Ex. 33:11; 33:23;
  2 Kin. 14:8; Ezra 9:6; Job 33:26;
  Ps. 13:1; 24:6; 83:16; Prov. 15:13;
  27:19; Eccles. 8:1; Is. 50:6; Jer. 5:3;
  Matt. 6:16; 26:67

FADE—*wither*
  James 1:11, rich man ... will **f** away
  1 Pet. 1:4, an inheritance ... will not
  f away
  Ps. 90:6; Is. 28:1

FAIL—*spent, lack* Deut. 31:6, He
  will not **f** you or
  Luke 22:32, that your faith may not **f**
  1 Cor. 13:8, Love never **f-s**
  Deut. 4:31; 1 Sam. 3:19; 17:32; Neh.
  4:10; Job 11:20; 19:14; Ps. 38:10;
  Is. 44:12,25; Hab. 3:17

FAILURE Rom. 11:12, their **f** be
  riches for the Gentiles

FAINT—*languish* Job 23:16, has
  made my heart **f**
  Ps. 61:2, when my heart is **f**
  Luke 21:26, men **f-ing** from fear
  Is. 1:5; Jon. 2:7; Matt. 15:32

FAIR Ps. 45:2; Is. 11:4; Matt. 16:2;
  Acts 27:8; Col. 4:1

FAITH—*believe, trust* Matt. 9:2;
  15:28; Mark 4:40
  Hab. 2:4, the righteous will live by
  his **f**
  Matt. 6:30, O men of little **f**
  17:20, **f** as a mustard seed
  Mark 11:22, Have **f** in God
  Luke 7:50, Your **f** has saved you
  17:5, Increase our **f**
  18:8, will He find **f** on earth
  22:32, that your **f** may not fail
  Acts 14:27, door of **f** to the Gentiles
  15:9, cleansing their hearts by **f**
  Rom. 5:1, having been justified by **f**
  10:17, **f** comes from hearing
  1 Cor. 15:14, your **f** also is vain
  16:13, stand firm in the **f**
  2 Cor. 13:5, if you are in the **f**
  Gal. 2:16, through **f** in Christ Jesus
  Eph. 2:8, by grace ... through **f**
  4:5, one Lord, one **f**, one baptism
  6:16, taking up the shield of **f**
  Col. 2:5, stability of your **f** in Christ
  1 Thess. 5:8, breastplate of **f** and
  love
  2 Thess. 1:3, your **f** is greatly
  enlarged
  1 Tim. 4:1, some will fall away from
  the **f**
  2 Tim. 4:7, I have kept the **f**
  Heb. 10:22, in full assurance of **f**
  12:2, author and perfecter of **f**
  James 1:3, testing of your **f** produces
  endurance
  1 Pet. 1:5, power of God through **f**
  Jude 20, building ... on your most
  holy **f**
  Rev. 2:13, did not deny My **f**
  Luke 8:25; Acts 6:5; 20:21; Rom.
  4:14; 1 Cor. 13:2; Gal. 5:5;
  Phil. 1:25; 1 Thess. 1:3; 1 Tim. 1:2;
  3:9; Titus 1:13; 2:2,10; Heb. 10:39;
  11:1; James 2:1; 2 Pet. 1:5

FAITHFUL—*trustworthy*
  Ps. 31:23, The Lord preserves the **f**
  Prov. 12:22, who deal **f-ly** are His
  27:6, **F** are the wounds of a friend

FAITHFUL *(Continued)*
1 Cor. 1:9, God is **f**, through whom you were
Eph. 1:1, who are **f** in Christ Jesus
1 Thess. 5:24, **F** is He who calls you
1 Tim. 1:12, He considered me **f**
2 Tim. 2:2, these entrust to **f** men
Heb. 10:23, He who promised is **f**
Rev. 2:10, Be **f** until death
Num. 12:7; Deut. 7:9; 1 Sam. 2:35;
2 Kin. 12:15; Neh. 9:8; Ps. 101:6;
119:86; Prov. 13:17; 14:5; Is. 1:21;
Matt. 24:45; 25:23; 1 Pet. 4:19;
Rev. 1:5; 19:11

FAITHFULNESS—*truth* Deut. 32:4,
A God of **f** and without
Ps. 143:1, Answer me in Thy **f**
Rom. 3:3, nullify the **f** of God
Gal. 5:22, Kindness, goodness, **f**
Deut. 32:20; Ps. 89:1; Is. 11:5; Matt.
23:23

FAITHLESS Jer. 3:6,8,11,12,22; 31:22

FALL Ps. 16:6, The lines have **f-en** . . . in pleasant places
Matt. 7:25, house; and *yet* it did not **f**
7:27, and great was its **f**
10:29, not one . . . will **f** to the ground
15:14, both will **f** into a pit
Mark 14:27, You will all **f** away
Luke 8:13, in time of temptation **f** away
1 Cor. 10:12, take heed lest he **f**
15:6,18, have **f-en** asleep
Gal. 5:4, you have **f-en** from grace
1 Tim. 3:6, **f** into the condemnation
6:9, rich **f** into temptation
Heb. 6:6, and then have **f-en** away
10:31, **f** into the hands of the living God
Judg. 18:25; Job 4:13; Ps. 5:10; 37:24;
38:17; Prov. 24:16; Eccles. 4:10;
11:3; Dan. 3:5; 11:26; Mic. 7:8;
Matt. 12:11; Luke 2:34; Rom. 14:4;
Heb. 4:11; 2 Pet. 3:17

FALSE—*deceitful, vain*
Ex. 5:9, pay no attention to **f** words
20:16, you shall not bear **f** witness
23:1, shall not carry a **f** rumor
Ps. 33:17, horse is a **f** hope for victory
119:104,128, I hate every **f** way
Prov. 6:19; 12:17; 14:5; 19:5, **f** witness
Matt. 24:24, **f** Christs and **f** prophets
Ex. 23:7; Lam. 2:14; Zech. 10:2;
Matt. 19:18; Mark 13:22;
2 Thess. 2:9

FALSEHOOD—*deceitfulness* Ps.
144:8; Jer. 13:25; Mic. 2:11
Ps. 24:4, lifted up his soul to **f**
119:163, I hate and despise **f**
Prov. 20:17, Bread obtained by **f** is sweet
Jer. 14:14, prophesying **f** in My name
Eph. 4:25, laying aside **f**

FALSELY Jer. 5:31, The prophets prophesy **f**
Matt. 5:11, say . . . evil against you **f**
Luke 3:14, accuse *anyone* **f**
1 Tim. 6:20, what is **f** called knowledge
Gen. 21:23; Lev. 6:3; Deut. 19:18;
Hos. 7:1

FAME 1 Kin. 10:1, the **f** of Solomon
Is. 66:19, heard My **f**

2 Cor. 8:18, whose **f** *in the* things of
Num. 14:15; Josh. 6:27

FAMILY Gen. 12:3, all the **f-es** of the earth
Eph. 3:15, every **f** in heaven
Gen. 10:5; Deut. 29:18; Judg. 6:15;
Job 31:34; Ps. 107:41; Jer. 3:14;
31:1

FAMINE—*drought* Gen. 12:10;
41:27,54; 42:19
Matt. 24:7, there will be **f-s** and earthquakes
Mark 13:8, will *also* be **f-s**
Luke 15:14, a severe **f** occurred in that country
Rom. 8:35, or **f**, or nakedness, or peril
2 Kin. 4:38; 1 Chr. 21:12; 2 Chr. 6:28;
Neh. 5:3; Job 5:20; Ps. 33:19;
Is. 14:30; Jer. 14:12; Amos 8:11;
Acts 7:11; 11:28

FAMISH—*hunger* Gen. 41:55, Egypt was **f-ed**

FAMOUS 1 Chr. 5:24, men of valor, **f** men

FANG Joel 1:6, the **f-s** of a lioness

FAR—*distant* Ps. 22:11, Be not **f** from me
Ps. 103:12, As **f** as the east is from the west
119:155, Salvation is **f** from the wicked
Prov. 15:29, LORD is **f** from the wicked
Jer. 23:23, a God **f** off
Matt. 15:8, THEIR HEART IS **F** AWAY FROM ME
Mark 12:34, are not **f** from the kingdom
Acts 17:27, though He is not **f** from
2 Cor. 4:17, glory **f** beyond all comparison
Eph. 1:21, **f** above all rule
Gen. 18:25; Ex. 23:7; Deut. 13:7;
Josh. 9:6; 2 Sam. 20:20; Ps. 97:9;
Prov. 4:24; 27:10; Is. 60:4;
Ezek. 11:15; John 21:8; Eph. 2:17

FARE Jon. 1:3, Tarshish, paid the **f**

FAREWELL Acts 15:29, you will do well. **F**

FARTHEST—*utmost* Mark 13:27, **F** END of the earth

FASHION—*appearance* Job 10:8, Thy hands **f-ed**
Ps. 33:15, He who **f-s** the hearts
1 Kin. 7:15; Job 31:15; Is. 44:12;
Jer. 18:11

FAST Matt. 4:2, after He had **f-ed** forty days
Matt. 6:16, whenever you **f**, do not . . . as the
6:17, when you **f**, anoint your head
Acts 13:3, when they had **f-ed** and prayed
Is. 58:3,4,5,6; Joel 1:14; Zech. 7:5;
Mark 2:18,19; Luke 18:12

FASTING—*hungry* Ps. 109:24, weak from **f**
Matt. 6:16,18, seen **f** by men
Luke 2:37, serving . . . with **f-s** and prayers

Acts 14:23, having prayed with **f**
Esth. 4:3; Ps. 35:13; Joel 2:12; Mark 2:18

FAT Prov. 13:4, soul of the diligent is made **f**
Prov. 15:30, Good news puts **f** on the bones
Luke 15:23, bring the **f-ned** calf
James 5:5, you have **f-ned** your hearts
Gen. 45:18; Judg. 3:17; Neh. 8:10;
9:25; Ps. 73:4; 119:70

FATE Eccles. 2:14; 9:2,3

FATHER Gen. 2:24, leave his **f** and his mother
Gen. 9:23, covered the nakedness of their **f**
17:4, **f** of a multitude of nations
Ex. 20:12, Honor your **f** and your mother
Job 29:16, I was a **f** to the needy
Ps. 22:4, In Thee our **f-s** trusted
103:13, as a **f** has compassion on his
Prov. 10:1, A wise son makes a **f** glad
17:6, glory of sons is their **f-s**
Is. 9:6, Eternal **F**, Prince of Peace
63:16, Thou art our **F**
Matt. 3:9, We have Abraham for our **f**
5:16, glorify your **F** who is in heaven
6:1, your **F** who is in heaven
6:4,6,18, your **F** who sees in secret
6:9, Our **F** who art in heaven
7:21, he who does the will of My **F**
10:35, SET A MAN AGAINST HIS **F**
11:25, I praise Thee O **F**, Lord of
11:27, knows the Son, except the **F**
28:19, baptizing . . . name of the **F**
Mark 8:38, comes in the glory of His **F**
Luke 2:49, be in My **F-'s** *house*
11:2, **F**, hallowed be Thy Name
23:34, Jesus was saying, **F** forgive them
23:46, **F** . . . HANDS I COMMIT
John 2:16, stop making My **F-'s** house a
5:17, My **F** is working until now and
10:15, **F** knows me and I know the **F**
14:2, In My **F-'s** house are many
17:1, **F**, the hour has come; glorify
2 Cor. 1:3, **F** of mercies and God of all
Eph. 3:14, I bow my knees before the **F**
6:4, **f-s**, do not provoke your children
Phil. 2:11, to the glory of God the **F**
Heb. 1:5, I will be a **F** to Him
1 Pet. 1:3, Blessed be the God and **F**
2 Pet. 1:17, honor . . . from God the **F**
Jude 1, are the called, beloved in God the **F**
Rev. 1:6, priests to His God and **F**
Gen. 4:20; 43:7; 48:17; Ex. 21:15;
Deut. 5:9; 1 Sam. 17:34;
2 Sam. 7:12; Job 17:14; 38:28;
Ps. 68:5; 89:26; Prov. 1:8; 6:20;
Jer. 3:19; Mal. 2:10; Matt. 11:26;
26:29; Mark 14:36; Luke 10:21;
15:18; 24:49; 1 Cor. 4:15; Heb. 3:9;
1 John 2:13; 2 John 4

FATHERLESS—*orphan*
Prov. 23:10, the fields of the **f**

FATNESS—*abundance*
Ps. 65:11, Thy paths drip *with* **f**
Gen. 27:28; Judg. 9:9; Ps. 63:5; 73:7

FAULT—*offense* 1 Sam. 29:3; Ps.
19:12; Rom. 9:19

FAULTLESS—*blameless*
Heb. 8:7, *covenant* had been **f**

FAVOR—*beauty, charm, grace,
pleasure, supplication*
Ps. 90:17, let the **f** of the Lord our
God
Prov. 8:35; 12:2; 18:22, obtains **f** from
the Lord
13:15, Good understanding
produces **f**
Luke 2:52, increasing . . . in **f** with
God and men
Acts 2:47, having **f** with all the
people
Gen. 6:8; 39:21; Ex. 3:21; 33:12; Deut.
33:23; 1 Sam. 13:12; Esth. 2:17;
Ps. 5:12; 30:5; 51:18; 85:1;
Prov. 14:35; 19:12; Eccles. 9:11;
Dan. 1:9; Zech. 11:7

FAVORABLE—*acceptable*
Ps. 77:7, will He never be **f** again
Is. 61:2, proclaim the **f** year of the
Lord

FEAR (n.)—*dread, awe, terror* Gen.
9:2; 20:11; Deut. 2:25
Ps. 19:9, the **f** of the Lord is clean
53:5, in great *where* no **f** had been
111:10; Prov. 9:10, **f** . . . is the
beginning of wisdom
Prov. 1:7, **f** . . . is the beginning of
knowledge
10:27, **f** of the Lord prolongs life
14:26, **f** of the Lord there is strong
confidence
14:27, **f** of the Lord is a fountain of
life
15:16, better is a little with the **f** of
the Lord
19:23, the **f** of the Lord *leads* to life
29:25, the **f** of man brings a snare
Luke 21:26, men fainting from **f**
John 7:13; 19:38; 20:19, for **f** of the
Jews
Rom. 13:3, not a cause of **f** for good
behavior
1 Cor. 2:3, in weakness and in **f**
2 Cor. 5:11, knowing the **f** of the
Lord
7:5, conflicts without, **f**-s within
7:11, what **f**, what longing, what
zeal
Eph. 6:5; Phil. 2:12, with **f** and
trembling
Deut. 11:25; 1 Chr. 14:17; Job 4:6;
39:22; Ps. 34:11; 36:1; Prov. 3:25;
Is. 8:12; Jer. 32:40; Matt. 14:26;
Rom. 3:18; Heb. 2:15; Jude 12,23

FEAR (v.)—*be afraid, revere* Gen.
22:12; 42:18
1 Kin. 18:12, I . . . have **f-ed** the Lord
from my youth
Job 1:9, Job **f** God for nothing
Ps. 27:1, Whom shall I **f**
118:6, will not **f**; what can man do
Prov. 31:30, woman who **f-s** the
Lord, she shall be praised
Eccles. 12:13, **f** God and keep His
commandments
Matt. 10:26, Therefore do not **f** them

10:28, do not **f** those who kill the
body
10:31, do not **f**; you are of . . . value
Luke 23:40, Do you not even **f** God
Ex. 1:21; 14:13; 18:21; Deut. 4:10;
5:29; 28:58; Neh. 7:2; Job 11:15;
Ps. 27:3; 31:19; 34:9; 66:16; 76:7;
86:11; 112:7; 115:11; 119:74;
Prov. 3:7; 24:21; 28:14; Eccles. 3:14;
5:7; Is. 8:12; 35:4; 41:10; 43:5;
Jer. 5:24; 10:7; 33:9; Dan. 6:26;
Mal. 3:16; Matt. 14:5; 21:26;
Mark 5:33; Luke 12:5; 18:2; 20:19;
Acts 10:35; 13:26; Rom. 8:15; 11:20;
Gal. 4:11; Col. 3:22; Heb. 4:1;
1 John 4:18

FEARFUL Ps. 139:14, I am **f-ly** and
wonderfully made
1 Tim. 5:20, that the rest also may
be **f**

FEAST—*banquet* Judg. 14:10; Esth.
9:17
Prov. 15:15, heart *has* a continual **f**
John 7:37, the great *day* of the **f**
Job 1:4; Ps. 35:16; Eccles. 7:2; 10:16;
Is. 1:14; Jer. 16:8; Mal. 2:3; Luke
2:42; John 7:8,14; 13:29; 1 Cor. 5:8;
Jude 12

FEATHERS—*plumage, wings*
Dan. 4:33, hair . . . like eagles' **f**

FED Deut. 8:3, humbled you and **f**
you with manna
Ezek. 34:8, shepherds **f** themselves
and did not feed
Luke 16:21, longing to be **f** with the
crumbs

FEEBLE Job 4:4, you have
strengthened **f** knees
Is. 35:3, strengthen the **f**
Heb. 12:12, strengthen . . . the knees
that are **f**
Gen. 30:42; Neh. 4:2

FEED—*tend* 1 Kin. 22:27; Ps. 81:16;
Prov. 30:8
Prov. 15:14, the mouth of fools **f-s** on
folly
Matt. 6:26, your heavenly Father **f-s**
them
25:37, see You hungry and **f** you
Luke 12:24, *yet* God **f-s** them
Rom. 12:20, ENEMY IS HUNGRY, **F** HIM
Is. 44:20; Jer. 3:15; Hos. 12:1; Matt.
15:27; Mark 7:28

FEEL Gen. 27:12, Perhaps my father
will **f** me
Judge. 16:26, Let me **f** the pillars
Ps. 115:7, have hands, but they
cannot **f**
1 Tim. 5:11, **f** sensual desires in
disregard of

FEET—*footstool* Ps. 8:6, all things
under his **f**
Ps. 22:16, pierced my hands and
my **f**
31:8, set my **f** in a large place
40:2, set my **f** upon a rock
56:13; 116:8, my **f** from stumbling
66:9, does not allow our **f** to slip
119:105, word is a lamp to my **f**
122:2, **f** are standing within your
gates
Prov. 1:16; 6:18; Is. 59:7, their **f** run
to evil
5:5, Her **f** go down to death

Is. 49:23; Matt. 10:14; Mark 6:11;
Luke 9:5, dust of your **f**
52:7, lovely on the mountains Are
the **f**
Dan. 2:33, **f** partly of iron and partly
of clay
10:6, **f** . . . of polished bronze
Nah. 1:3, clouds are the dust beneath
His **f**
1:15, the **f** of him who brings good
news
Zech. 14:4, His **f** will stand on the
Mount of Olives
Luke 1:79, guide our **f** into the way
of peace
8:35, sitting down at the **f** of Jesus
24:39, See My hands and My **f**
John 12:3, anointed the **f** of Jesus
13:5, began to wash the disciples' **f**
Acts 4:35,37; 5:2, laid . . . at the
apostles' **f**
Rom. 3:15, THEIR **F** ARE SWIFT TO
SHED BLOOD
10:15, How BEAUTIFUL ARE THE **F** OF
THOSE WHO
16:20, crush Satan under your **f**
Eph. 6:15, shod your **f** with the
preparation
Rev. 1:15, 2:18, **f** like burnished
bronze
1:17, I fell at his **f** as a dead man
19:10, I fell at his **f** to worship
22:8, I fell down to worship at the **f**
of
Gen. 49:10; Josh. 3:15; Ruth 3:14;
1 Sam. 2:9; 2 Sam. 4:4; 22:37;
2 Kin. 6:32; 9:35; 13:21; Neh. 9:21;
Job 29:15; Ps. 73:2; 115:7;
Prov. 4:26; 6:13,28; 7:11; 19:2; Song
5:3; 7:1; Is. 3:16; 6:2; 23:7; 26:6;
60:13; Lam. 3:34; Ezek. 2:1,2; 3:24;
24:17,23; 25:6; 32:2; 34:18,19;
Matt. 7:6; 18:8; 28:9; Mark 12:36;
Luke 7:38; 10:39; John 11:2; 12:3;
20:12; Acts 3:7; 21:11; 1 Cor. 12:21;
1 Tim. 5:10; Rev. 13:2

FELL—*came, collapsed* Gen. 4:5;
Josh. 6:20; 1 Kin. 18:38
Matt. 13:4, some seeds **f** beside the
road
Luke 8:23, Jesus **f** asleep
10:30, he **f** among robbers
13:4, on whom the tower in
Siloam **f**
Acts 1:26, the lot **f** to Matthias
10:44, the Holy Spirit **f** upon all
those
19:35, *image* which **f** down from
heaven
20:9, Eutychus . . . **f** down from the
third floor
2 Kin. 6:5; Jon. 1:7; Luke 10:36; Acts
13:36; 2 Pet. 3:4; Rev. 16:19

FELLOW Ps. 45:7, oil of joy above
Thy **f-s**
Acts 24:5, pest and a **f** who stirs up
Rom. 8:17, and **f-heirs** with Christ
Eph. 2:19, **f-citizens** with the saints
3:6, Gentiles are **f-heirs**
2 Kin. 9:11; Matt. 24:49; Acts 22:22;
Heb. 8:11

FELLOWSHIP—*share* Ps. 55:14, had
sweet **f** together
2 Cor. 6:14, What **f** has light with
darkness
13:14, **f** of the Holy Spirit
Gal. 2:9, right hand of **f**
1 John 1:3, our **f** is with the Father
1:7, **f** with one another

FELLOW-WORKER—*helper*
Rom. 16:3, Prisca and Aquila my **f-s**
Phil. 2:25, my brother and **f**
 4:3, **f-s**, whose names are in the book
1 Thess. 3:2, **f** in the gospel of Christ
Philem. 24, *as do . . .* my **f-s**
3 John 8, **f-s** with the truth

FELT Gen. 27:22, he **f** him and said, The voice
Matt. 9:36, He **f** compassion for them
Ex. 10:21; Mark 5:29

FEMALE Gen. 1:27, male and **f** He created them
Gen. 6:19; Lev. 3:1; 5:6; Num. 5:3;
 Deut. 4:16; Matt. 19:4; Mark 10:6;
 Gal. 3:28

FERTILE—*fruit* Is. 5:1, vineyard on a **f** hill

FERTILIZER Luke 13:8, dig around it and . . . **f**

FERVENT Acts 18:25, being **f** in spirit
Rom. 12:11, **f** in spirit, serving
1 Pet. 4:8, keep **f** in your love

FERVENTLY Luke 22:44, in agony He was praying very **f**

FESTIVAL—*feast* Amos 5:21; 8:10;
 Matt. 26:5; Mark 14:2

FETTER—*band, chain* 2 Sam. 3:34;
 Job 36:8; Ps. 2:3; 105:18;
 Prov. 7:22; Luke 8:29

FEVER Matt. 8:14, mother-in-law . . . sick in bed with a **f**
Luke 4:38, suffering from a high **f**
John 4:52, seventh hour the **f** left him
Deut. 28:22; Matt. 8:15; Acts 28:8

FEW Gen. 47:9, **f** and unpleasant . . . years
Matt. 9:37, but the workers are **f**
 22:14, many are called, but **f** *are* chosen
 25:21, faithful with a **f** things
Mark 8:7, had a **f** small fish
1 Pet. 3:20, a **f**, that is, eight persons
Rev. 2:14, I have a **f** things against you
Gen. 24:55; 29:20; 34:30; Lev. 25:52;
 Num. 13:18; Deut. 4:27; 33:6;
 Josh. 7:3; 1 Sam. 14:6; 1 Chr. 16:19;
 2 Chr. 29:34; Neh. 2:12; Job 10:20;
 Ps. 105:12; 109:8; Eccles. 5:2; 9:14;
 Ezek. 12:16; Luke 12:48; 13:23

FIELD—*garden* Prov. 31:16, She considers a **f**
Matt. 6:28, how the lilies of the **f** grow
 13:38, the **f** is the world
 27:10, GAVE THEM FOR THE POTTER'S **F**
Luke 2:8, shepherds staying out in the **f-s**
 15:15, sent him into his **f-s**
 17:36, Two men will be in the **f**
John 4:35, **f-s** . . . white for harvest
Acts 1:18, acquired a **f** with the price
 1:19, that is, **F** of Blood
Gen. 2:5,20; 23:20; 25:29; Ex. 9:19,22;
 10:15; 23:11; Lev. 19:9,19;
 Num. 23:14; Deut. 11:15; 20:19;

Judg. 9:43; Ruth 2:3,8;
 1 Sam. 20:24; 30:11; 2 Sam. 14:6;
 1 Kin. 11:29; Job 5:23; Ps. 96:12;
 Prov. 24:30; Is. 1:8; 5:8; Jer. 4:17;
 26:18; 32:44; Lam. 4:9; Dan. 4:15;
 Hos. 2:12; Joel 1:20; James 5:4

FIERCE Rev. 19:15, **f** wrath of God the Almighty
Gen. 49:7; Num. 25:4; Job 41:10;
 Prov. 27:4; Is. 33:19

FIERY Num. 21:6; Deut. 28:22; Ps. 21:9; 1 Pet. 4:12

FIFTEEN Gen. 5:10; Judg. 8:10; Hos. 3:2; Gal. 1:18

FIFTH Gen. 1:23; Lev. 5:16; Neh. 6:5;
 Jer. 1:3; Rev. 6:9

FIFTY Lev. 25:10, consecrate the **f-eth** year
Gen. 6:15; Ex. 18:21; 26:5; Lev. 23:16;
 Esth. 5:14; Luke 9:14; John 8:57;
 Acts 13:19

FIG Gen. 3:7, they sewed **f** leaves together
Matt. 21:19, the **f** tree withered
Mark 13:28, the parable from the **f** tree
Luke 6:44, men do not gather **f-s** from thorns
James 3:12, Can a **f** tree . . . produce olives
Rev. 6:13, as a **f** tree casts its unripe **f-s**
Deut. 8:8; Judg. 9:11; Jer. 29:17;
 Matt. 7:16; Mark 11:13; John 1:48

FIGHT Ex. 14:14, The LORD will **f** for you
1 Tim. 1:18, you may **f** the good **f**
 6:12, **F** the good **f** of faith
James 4:2, *so* you **f** and quarrel
Josh. 9:2; 1 Sam. 8:20; Neh. 4:20; Ps. 35:1

FIGURATIVE 1 Cor. 4:6, I have **f-ly** applied to myself

FIGURE—*graven* Lev. 26:1; Deut. 4:16

FILL Gen. 42:25, gave orders to **f** their bags
Jer. 23:24, **f** the heavens and the earth
Gen. 1:22; Job 41:7; Ps. 83:16; Prov. 7:18; Is. 8:8; 65:11; Mic. 3:8; Matt. 22:10

FILTH—*uncleanness*
Is. 4:4, LORD has washed away the **f**
 64:6, deeds are like a **f-y** garment
James 1:21, putting aside all **f-iness**
Is. 28:8; Nah. 3:6

FIND—*discover* Gen. 18:26, If I **f** in Sodom fifty
Num. 32:23, be sure your sin will **f** you out
Deut. 4:29, you will **f** Him if you search
Prov. 8:35, he who **f-s** Me **f-s** life
 18:22, he who **f-s** a wife **f-s** a good thing
Is. 35:10, They will **f** gladness and joy
Matt. 7:7, Seek, and you shall **f**
 10:39, lost his life . . . shall **f** it

11:29, YOU SHALL **F** REST FOR YOUR SOULS
Mark 13:36, **f** you asleep
Luke 2:12, you will **f** a baby wrapped
 15:8, search . . . until she **f-s** it
 23:4, I **f** no guilt in this man
John 10:9, go in and out, and **f** pasture
Acts 7:46, **f** a dwelling place for the God of
Gen. 32:5; Ruth 1:9; 2 Sam. 15:25;
 20:6; Prov. 1:13; 3:4; Song 3:1; 5:8;
 Matt. 21:2; Mark 11:2; Luke 11:9;
 John 18:38; Acts 23:9; 2 Cor. 9:4;
 Rev. 18:14

FINE—*good* Ps. 19:10, than much **f** gold; Sweeter
Matt. 13:45, merchant seeking **f** pearls
Luke 16:19, in purple and **f** linen
Rev. 19:14, clothed in **f** linen, white
Gen. 41:42; Ex. 16:14; 25:4; Ps. 81:16

FINGER John 8:6, Jesus . . . with His **f** wrote on the ground
John 20:25, put my **f** into the place of the nails
 20:27, Reach here your **f**
Ex. 8:19; Lev. 4:6; Deut. 9:10;
 2 Sam. 21:20; 1 Kin. 12:10;
 1 Chr. 20:6; Prov. 6:13; Jer. 52:21;
 Mark 7:33; Luke 11:20; 16:24

FINISH—*end, spend* 2 Chr. 7:11, Solomon **f-ed** the house
John 19:30, said, It is **f-ed**
Acts 20:24, that I may **f** my course
Ex. 40:33; Ps. 90:9; Mark 3:26;
 2 Cor. 8:11

FIR—*cedar* 2 Sam. 6:5; Ps. 104:17;
 Ezek. 27:5

FIRE—*flame, burn* Ex. 13:21, pillar of **f** by night
Num. 3:4, offered strange **f** before the LORD
1 Kin. 18:38, Then **f** of the LORD fell
Neh. 9:12, with a pillar of **f** by night
Ps. 105:39, to illumine by night
Is. 66:15, the LORD will come in **f**
Dan. 3:25, walking *about* in the midst of the **f**
Matt. 3:11, baptize you . . . Holy Spirit and **f**
Mark 9:43, into the unquenchable **f**
Acts 2:3, tongues as of **f**
1 Cor. 3:13, *to be* revealed with **f**
Rev. 3:18, gold refined by **f**
 21:8, lake that burns with **f** and brimstone
Gen. 19:24; 22:6; Ex. 3:2; 9:24; Lev.
 6:13; Deut. 9:3; Job 18:5; Ps. 46:9;
 Jer. 23:29; Matt. 3:10,12; Luke 3:17;
 12:49; Jude 7

FIREPAN Lev. 16:12, take a **f** full of coals

FIRM—*hard, steadfast* Josh. 3:17, LORD stood **f** on dry
Is. 22:23, *like* a peg in a **f** place
1 Cor. 7:37, stands **f** in his heart
2 Tim. 2:19, the **f** foundation of God stands
Heb. 3:6, hope **f** until the end
1 Pet. 5:9, resist him, **f** in *your* faith

FIRMAMENT—*expanse* Ps. 19:1, **f** is declaring the work of

FIRST—*leader, eminent, foremost*
Gen. 38:28
Matt. 6:33, seek f His kingdom
7:5, f take the log out of
19:30, many *who are* f will be last
20:27, be f among you
28:1, the f *day* of the week
1 John 4:19, because He f loved us
Rev. 1:17, I am the f and the last
2:4, you have left your f love
21:4, the f things have passed away
22:13, Omega, the f and the last
Deut. 26:10; Prov. 3:9; 18:17; Hos. 2:7; Mark 3:27; 10:44; Acts 1:1

FIRST-BORN Luke 2:7, she gave birth to her f son
Heb. 12:23, church of the f
Gen. 10:15; 19:37; 27:19; Ex. 11:5

FIRST FRUITS Ex. 23:16, the f of your labors
Rom. 8:23, the f of the Spirit
James 1:18, the f among His creatures
Rev. 14:4, f to God and to the Lamb

FISH Matt. 14:17, five loaves and two f
Luke 5:6, a great quantity of f
11:11, asked by his son for a f
Gen. 1:26; Num. 11:5; 2 Chr. 33:14; Is. 50:2; Jon. 1:17; John 21:10

FISHERMEN Is. 19:8; Jer. 16:16

FISHERS—*fishermen* Matt. 4:19, I will make you f of men
Mark 1:17, I will make you become f of men

FIT—*ready, prepare, worthy*
Matt. 3:11, not . . . f to remove His sandals
Luke 9:62, f for the kingdom of God
Eph. 2:21, whole building, being **f-ed** together
4:16, whole body, being **f-ed** and held together

FITTING—*opportune* Matt. 3:15, it is f for us to fulfill
Eph. 5:4, jesting, which are not f
Col. 3:18, as is f in the Lord

FIVE 1 Sam. 17:40, f smooth stones from the brook
Matt. 14:17, f loaves and two fish
25:2, f of them were foolish . . . f
25:20, who had received the f talents
Gen. 5:6; Ex. 22:1; Lev. 26:8; 2 Chr. 4:2; 2 Cor. 11:24; Rev. 17:10

FIXED Luke 16:26, there is a great chasm f

FLAG Is. 30:17, a f on a mountain top

FLAME—*fire* Is. 4:5, of a **f-ing** fire by night
Rev. 19:12, eyes *are* a f of fire
Gen. 3:24; Judg. 13:20; Ps. 106:18; Song 8:6; Is. 5:24; 10:17; Ezek. 20:47; Dan. 7:9; 10:6; Joel 2:5; Acts 7:30; 2 Thess. 1:7

FLASH Job 15:12, why do your eyes f
Acts 22:6, bright light suddenly **f-ed** from heaven
Deut. 32:41; Ezek. 1:13; 21:10; Nah. 3:3

FLASK—*vessel* Matt. 25:4, took oil in **f-s**

FLAT Josh. 6:5,20, wall fell down f

FLATTER Job 32:21, Nor f *any* man
Ps. 5:9, They f with their tongue
Prov. 7:21, **f-ing** lips she seduces him
1 Thess. 2:5, we never came with **f-ing** speech

FLAX Ex. 9:31; Judg. 15:14; Ezek. 40:3

FLEA 1 Sam. 24:14; 26:20

FLED—*escape* Matt. 26:56, left Him and f
Mark 16:8, f from the tomb
Rev. 20:11, whose presence earth and heaven f
Gen. 14:10; 31:21; 39:18; Is. 22:3

FLEE—*wander* Lev. 26:17, f when no one is pursuing
Ps. 11:1, F *as* a bird to your mountain
139:7, I f from Thy presence
Prov. 28:1, wicked f when no one
Is. 16:2, like **f-ing** birds
Matt. 3:7, f from the wrath to come
1 Tim. 6:11, But f from these things, you man
2 Tim. 2:22, f from youthful lusts
Gen. 16:8; Is. 30:16; Matt. 2:13; Rev. 9:6

FLEECE—*shear* Judg. 6:37; Job 31:20

FLESH—*body, meat, life*
Gen. 2:24, they shall become one f
Ps. 84:2, f sing for joy to the living God
136:25, Who gives food to all f
Is. 40:6, All f is grass
Matt. 16:17, because f and blood did not reveal
26:41, but the f is weak
Luke 24:39, spirit does not have f and bones
John 1:14, the Word became f
3:6, which is born of the f is f
Rom. 8:6, mind set on the f is death
2 Cor. 1:17, according to the f . . . should be
10:4, weapons . . . not of the f
Gal. 6:8, f shall from the f reap
Eph. 2:3, indulging the desires of the f
5:31, TWO SHALL BECOME ONE F
6:12, struggle is not against f
1 Pet. 2:11, abstain from **f-ly** lusts
Gen. 2:23; 7:21; 37:27; Num. 16:22; Job 19:26; 41:23; Ps. 16:9; Rom. 9:8; Jude 23; Rev. 19:21

FLIES—*fly* Job 20:8; Ps. 78:45; Prov. 23:5; Eccles. 10:1

FLIGHT Amos 2:14, F will perish from the swift
Matt. 24:20, your f may not be in the winter
Heb. 11:34, put foreign armies to f

FLINT—*stone* Zech. 7:12, hearts like f so
Ex. 4:25; Deut. 8:15; 32:13; Ps. 114:8; Is. 5:28; Ezek. 3:9

FLOCK—*fold, sheep* Gen. 4:2,4; 29:2; 30:31,38

Is. 40:11, Like a shepherd He will tend His f
Jer. 23:2, scattered My f and driven
Matt. 26:31, SHEEP OF THE F SHALL BE SCATTERED
Luke 2:8, keeping watch over their f by night
12:32, Do not be afraid, little f
John 10:16, become one f *with* one Shepherd
1 Pet. 5:2, the f of God among you
Ex. 2:16; 10:9; Judg. 5:16; 1 Sam. 16:19; 17:34; 2 Chr. 32:28; Ps. 77:20; Prov. 27:23; Is. 13:20; Ezek. 45:15; Amos 6:4; Hab. 3:17

FLOG Mark 13:9, you will be **f-ed**

FLOOD Gen. 7:17, f came upon the earth
Gen. 9:15, never . . . the water become a f
Matt. 7:25, **f-s** came, and the winds blew
Luke 17:27, f came and destroyed them all
Gen. 6:17; Dan. 9:26

FLOODGATES Gen. 7:11, f of the sky were opened

FLOOR Gen. 50:11; Ruth 3:3; 1 Kin. 6:30; 7:7; Joel 2:24; Matt. 3:12

FLOUR—*dough* Ex. 29:2; Lev. 2:1; Ezek. 16:13; Rev. 18:13

FLOURISH—*blossom, green*
Ps. 72:7, may the righteous f
92:7, all who did iniquity **f-ed**
103:15, a flower . . . so he **f-es**
Prov. 11:28, will f like the *green* leaf
Ezek. 17:24, make the dry tree f

FLOW—*gush* Ex. 3:8, land **f-ing** with milk and honey
John 7:38, shall f rivers of living water
Job 20:28; Ps. 147:18; Jer. 9:18; Joel 3:18; Mark 5:29

FLOWER Ps. 103:15, As a f of the field, so he
1 Pet. 1:24, AND THE F FALLS OFF
Job 14:2; Song 2:12; Is. 28:1

FLUENTLY—*well* Ex. 4:14, he speaks f

FLUSH Job 16:16, My face is **f-ed** from weeping

FLUTE 1 Sam. 10:5; 1 Kin. 1:40; 1 Cor. 14:7; Rev. 18:22

FLY Job 5:7, As sparks f upward
Gen. 1:20; Is. 14:29; Rev. 8:13; 12:14; 19:17

FOAL—*colt* Job 11:12; Zech. 9:9

FOE—*enemy*
1 Chr. 21:12, swept away before your **f-s**

FOLD—*flock* Eccles. 4:5, The fool **f-s** his hands
John 10:16, sheep, which are not of this f
Num. 32:24; Ps. 50:9; Prov. 6:10

FOLLOW—*cling, imitate, pursue*
Gen. 24:5; 44:4; Ex. 11:8

FOLLOW (Continued)
Ruth 1:16, turn back from **f-ing** you
Ps. 23:6, goodness and
  lovingkindness will **f** me
Matt. 4:19, He said to them, **F** Me
  4:20, left the nets, and **f-ed** Him
  8:19, **f** You wherever You go
  12:15, And many **f-ed** Him
  16:24, take up his cross, and **f** Me
  19:21, and come, **f** Me
Luke 22:39, disciples also **f-ed** Him
John 10:27, I know them, and they **f**
  Me
Jude 16, **f-ing** after their own lusts
Rev. 14:4, the ones who **f** the Lamb
Num. 15:39; 1 Sam. 12:14; Ps.
  119:150; Jer. 48:2; Mark 5:37;
  14:54; Luke 22:10; John 18:15;
  Acts 5:36; Rev. 14:13

FOLLY—foolishness
Prov. 14:18, The naive inherit **f**
  15:2, mouth of fools spouts **f**
  24:9, devising of **f** is sin
Judg. 19:23; Prov. 15:21

FOND—greedy 1 Tim. 3:8, or **f** of
  sordid gain

FONDLE Is. 66:12, **f-d** on the knees

FOOD—bread, meat Ps. 69:21, gall
  for my **f**
Ps. 136:25, Who gives **f** to all flesh
Matt. 6:25, Is not life more than **f**
John 4:34, My **f** is to do the will of
  Him
  6:55, My flesh is true **f**
1 Cor. 6:13, **F** is for the stomach
James 2:15, in need of daily **f**
Gen. 1:29; 2:9; 3:6; 43:2; Lev. 3:11;
  Deut. 10:18; Ruth 1:6; Job 38:41;
  Ps. 78:25; 145:15; Prov. 6:8; 20:13;
  23:3; 28:19; 30:8; Is. 65:25;
  Matt. 3:4; 1 Tim. 6:8

FOOL—foolish, unwise Ps. 14:1, The
  f has said in his
Prov. 1:7, **F-s** despise wisdom and
  instruction
  15:5, A **f** rejects his father's
  discipline
  26:3, a rod for the back of **f-s**
  29:11, A **f** always loses his temper
Eccles. 10:14, the **f** multiplies words
Rom. 1:22, wise, they became **f-s**
1 Cor. 4:10, We are **f-s** for Christ's
  sake
1 Sam. 26:21; 2 Sam. 3:33; Prov.
  24:7; Hos. 9:7; Matt. 5:22; 23:17

FOOLISH—fool, boastful, folly,
  unwise
Prov. 14:17, quick-tempered man
  acts **f-ly**
Luke 24:25, O **f** men and slow of
  heart
Rom. 1:14, the wise and to the **f**
1 Cor. 3:18, let him become **f**
Eph. 5:17, then do not be **f**
Gen. 31:28; Deut. 32:6; Job 5:3; Lam.
  2:14; Matt. 25:8; 1 Pet. 2:15

FOOLISHNESS—folly Prov. 14:24;
  Is. 9:17; 2 Cor. 11:21

FOOT Prov. 25:17, **f** rarely be in your
  neighbor's house
Matt. 4:6, LEST YOU STRIKE YOUR **F**
Luke 4:11, STRIKE YOUR **F** AGAINST A
  STONE
Rev. 10:2, placed his right **f** on the
  sea
Gen. 8:9; 41:44; Deut. 2:28; 33:24;

Num. 11:21; Josh. 14:9; 2 Sam. 8:4;
  21:20; 1 Chr. 20:6; Ps. 26:12; 91:12;
  121:3; Prov. 3:23; 25:19; Jer. 12:5;
  Matt. 22:13

FOOTSTOOL—feet 1 Chr. 28:2, for
  the **f** of our God
Ps. 99:5, And worship at His **f**
  110:1, Thine enemies a **f**
  132:7, Let us worship at His **f**
Is. 66:1, the earth is My **f**
James 2:3, or sit down by my **f**

FORBEARANCE Eph. 4:2, showing **f**
  to one another
Prov. 25:15; Rom. 3:25

FORBID—hinder 1 Cor. 14:39, do
  not **f** to speak in tongues
1 Tim. 4:3, men who **f** marriage and
Num. 30:5,8,11; Luke 23:2

FORCE—compel Matt. 5:41, **f** you to
  go one mile
Luke 3:14, Do not take money . . .
  by **f**
Gen. 31:31; 1 Sam. 2:16; Job 30:18;
  36:19; Dan. 11:10; Matt. 11:12;
  Heb. 9:17

FOREHEAD 1 Sam. 17:49, stone
  sank into his **f**
Rev. 9:4, seal of God on their **f-s**
  17:5, upon her **f** a name was written
Ex. 28:38; Lev. 13:42; Is. 48:4; Jer.
  3:3; Ezek. 3:8; 9:4

FOREIGN—strange Gen. 35:2, Put
  away the **f** gods
Ex. 2:22, a sojourner in a **f** land
1 Kin. 11:1, Solomon loved many **f**
  women
Ezra 10:2, have married **f** women
Ps. 137:4, LORD's song in a **f** land
Heb. 11:34, put **f** armies to flight

FOREIGNER—alien, sojourner
Ruth 2:10, since I am a **f**
Prov. 5:20, embrace the bosom of a **f**
Deut. 14:21; 15:3; Job 19:15; Obad.
  11

FOREMOST—first
Matt. 22:38, great and **f**
  commandment
Mark 12:28, commandment is the **f**
  of all
1 Tim. 1:15, among whom I am **f** of
  all

FOREST—wood Ps. 50:10, every
  beast of the **f** is Mine
James 3:5, how great a **f** is set
  aflame
1 Sam. 22:5; 2 Sam. 18:8; 1 Kin. 7:2;
  1 Chr. 16:33; Ps. 83:14; Is. 10:18;
  44:14; 56:9; Jer. 5:6; 21:14;
  Ezek. 15:2; Amos 3:4

FOREVER—always, evermore,
  utmost Gen. 3:22; 6:3
1 Chr. 17:14, throne shall be
  established **f**
Ps. 9:7, the LORD abides **f**
  16:11, there are pleasures **f**
  23:6, in the house of the LORD **f**
  29:10, the LORD sits as King **f**
  33:11, counsel of the LORD stands **f**
  86:12, will glorify Thy name **f**
  89:52, Blessed be the LORD **f**
  92:8, O LORD, art on high **f**
  102:12, Thou, O LORD, dost abide **f**

  119:89, **F**, O LORD, Thy word is
  settled
  121:8, LORD will guard your going
  out . . . **f**
  133:3, the blessing . . . life **f**
Prov. 27:24, riches are not **f**
Eccles. 3:14, everything God
  does . . . **f**
Is. 40:8, word of our God stands **f**
  57:15, exalted One Who lives **f**
  57:16, For I will not contend **f**
John 6:51, eats of this bread, he shall
  live **f**
  12:34, the Christ is to remain **f**
  14:16, Helper, that he may be with
  you **f**
Rom. 9:5, God blessed **f**
2 Cor. 11:31, Lord Jesus, He who is
  blessed **f**
Eph. 3:21, all generations **f** and ever
Heb. 7:25, He is able to save **f**
  7:28, a Son, made perfect **f**
  13:8, today, yes and **f**
Ex. 14:13; Deut. 5:29; 12:28; 32:40;
  Ps. 12:7; 23:6; 61:4; 73:26; 77:8;
  113:2; 115:18; 132:14; 146:6;
  Prov. 21:28; Is. 26:4; 34:10;
  Lam. 3:31

FOREVERMORE Rev. 1:18, I am
  alive **f**

FORFEIT Dan 1:10, make me **f** my
  head to the king

FORGAVE Ps. 78:38, **f** their iniquity,
  and
Matt. 18:27, and **f** him the debt
Luke 7:42, he graciously **f** them both
  7:43, the one whom he **f** more

FORGET—neglect, forsake
Deut. 6:12, lest you **f** the LORD
Ps. 9:17, all the nations who **f** God
  13:1, Wilt Thou **f** me forever
  74:23, Do not **f** the voice of Thine
  88:12, in the land of **f-fulness**
  119:176, I do not **f** Thy
  commandments
Prov. 3:1, My son, do not **f** my
  teaching
Heb. 6:10, **f** your work and the love
Gen. 27:45; 41:51; Deut. 4:9; Prov.
  4:5; 31:5; Is. 54:4; Jer. 2:32; 23:27

FORGIVE—forgave, pardon
Ps. 86:5, good, and ready to **f**
  99:8, a **f-ing** God to them
Matt. 6:12, **f** us our debts, as we
  6:14, if you **f** men for
  6:15, if you do not **f** men
  9:5, Your sins are **f-n**
  9:6, on earth to **f** sins
Mark 2:7, who can **f** sins but God
  alone
  11:26, your **f** you do not
Luke 7:47, sins . . . many, have been
  f-n
  23:34, Father **f** them
2 Cor. 2:10, whom you **f** anything, I **f**
  also
Eph. 4:32, **f-ing** each other
Col. 2:13, **f-n** us all our
  transgressions
1 John 1:9, righteous to **f** us our sins
Gen. 50:17; Ex. 32:32; Num. 30:5; Ps.
  25:18; 79:9; Jer. 18:23

FORGIVENESS—pardon
Neh. 9:17, art a God of **f**
Ps. 130:4, there is **f** with Thee
Matt. 26:28, for **f** of sins

Mark 1:4; Luke 24:47, repentance for the f of sins
3:29, Holy Spirit never has f
Acts 10:43, has received f of sins
13:38, through Him f of sins is proclaimed
26:18, they may receive f of sins
Eph. 1:7, the f of our trespasses
Col. 1:14, redemption, the f of sins
Heb. 9:22, shedding of blood . . . no f

FORGOT Deut. 32:18, f the God who gave you birth

FORGOTTEN—*neglect* Job 19:14, friends have f me
Ps. 9:18, needy will not always be f
Ezek. 23:35, Because you have f Me
Matt. 16:5, had f to take bread
Luke 12:6, is f before God
James 1:24, f what kind of person
Gen. 41:30; Job 28:4; Ps. 31:12; 77:9; Jer. 2:32; Lam. 2:6

FORK 1 Sam. 2:13; Matt. 3:12

FORM—*fashion* Ps. 95:5, His hands f-ed the dry land
Is. 53:2, no *stately* f or majesty
Mark 4:32, f-s large branches
16:12, He appeared in a different f
1 Cor. 7:31, the f of this world is passing
Gal. 4:19, until Christ is f-ed in you
2 Pet. 3:5, earth was f-ed out of water
Gen. 1:2; 2:7; Job 4:16; 33:6; Song 2:14; Is. 43:1; 44:13; 45:7; Amos 4:13; 7:1; Acts 17:29

FORMER—*past* 1 Pet. 1:14, conformed to the f lusts
Gen. 40:13; Deut. 4:32; 24:4; Ruth 4:7; Is. 42:9; 46:9; 65:16; Ezek. 16:55

FORNICATION—*immorality* Matt. 15:19; John 8:41

FORSAKE—*fail, leave, reject* Job 6:14; Ps. 27:9; 38:21
Josh. 1:5, not fail you or f you
2 Chr. 15:2, f Him, He will f you
Ezra 9:9, our God has not f-n us
Ps. 22:1, God, why hast Thou f-n me
27:10, father and my mother have f-n me
Prov. 1:8, do not f your mother's teaching
9:6, F *your* folly and live
Is. 53:3, despised and f-n of men
55:7, Let the wicked f his way
Matt. 27:46, GOD, WHY HAST THOU F-N ME
2 Cor. 4:9, persecuted, but not f
Heb. 13:5, NOR WILL I EVER F YOU
Jer. 5:7; Ezek. 9:9; 20:8; Mark 15:34; 2 Pet. 2:15

FORSOOK—*left, deserted* Deut. 32:15; 1 Kin. 12:8; 2 Chr. 12:1

FORTIFICATION—*stronghold* Is. 25:12, unassailable f-s of

FORTIFY—*strengthen* Num. 32:17; Deut. 3:5; Josh. 10:20; 1 Sam. 6:18; 2 Kin. 3:19; Is. 34:13; Jer. 5:17; 51:53

FORTRESS—*stronghold, power* 2 Sam. 22:2, my rock and my f

Ps. 91:2, My refuge and my f
2 Sam. 22:33; Ps. 18:2; Dan. 11:19

FORTY Gen. 7:4, the earth f days and f nights
Ex. 16:35, Israel ate the manna f years
Matt. 4:2, fasted f days and f nights
Gen. 7:17; Ex. 34:28; Num. 33:38; Ps. 95:10; Mark 1:13

FORWARD—*further*
2 Kin. 20:9, shadow go f ten steps
Job 23:8; Is. 41:21; Jer. 7:24; Ezek. 1:9; Acts 19:33

FOUGHT—*waged war* Num. 21:1, then he f against Israel
Judg. 5:20, stars f from heaven
2 Chr. 20:29, the LORD had f against
1 Cor. 15:32, I f with wild beasts
2 Tim. 4:7, I have f the good fight

FOUL Ezek. 32:2; 34:19

FOUND—*caught, proved*
Judg. 14:18, not have f out my riddle
Jer. 15:16, Thy words were f and I
Dan. 5:27, weighed on the scales and f deficient
Matt. 8:10, not f such great faith
10:39, He who has f his life shall
Mark 14:37, f them sleeping
Luke 2:46, they f Him in the temple
15:6, I have f my sheep
24:2, f the stone rolled away
John 1:41, We have f the Messiah
Acts 13:22, I have f David the son of
1 Cor. 15:15, we are even f *to be* false witnesses
Phil. 2:8, being f in appearance
Gen. 2:20; 6:8; Lev. 6:3; Deut. 17:2; Ruth 2:10,13; Job 28:12; Ps. 84:3; Prov. 25:16; Eccles. 7:29; Is. 51:3; Dan. 6:11; Mal. 2:6; Matt. 27:32; Mark 11:4; 14:40; Rev. 18:24

FOUNDATION—*habitation, founded* 2 Sam. 22:8; Job 4:19
Ps. 89:14; 97:2, Right and justice are the f
Matt. 13:35, SINCE THE F OF THE WORLD
Luke 6:48, laid a f upon the rock
Rom. 15:20, upon another man's f
2 Tim. 2:19, the firm f of God stands
Heb. 1:10, DIDST LAY THE F OF THE EARTH
6:1, a f of repentance
Ps. 87:1; 104:5; Prov. 10:25; Is. 28:16

FOUNDED Ps. 24:2, He has f it upon the seas
Prov. 3:19, by wisdom f the earth
Matt. 7:25, f upon the rock
Ex. 9:18; Amos 9:6

FOUNTAIN—*spring, well* Gen. 7:11, f-s of the great deep
Ps. 36:9, with Thee is the f of life
Prov. 14:27, fear of the LORD is a f of life

FOUR Mark 13:27, FROM THE F WINDS
Luke 19:8, give back f times as much
Gen. 2:10; Ex. 25:12; 2 Kin. 7:3; Is. 11:12; Matt. 15:38; John 11:39

FOURTEEN Gen. 31:41; 2 Chr. 13:21; 30:15; Is. 36:1; Matt. 1:17; Acts 27:27; 2 Cor. 12:2

FOURTH Gen. 1:19; Ex. 20:5; Judg. 19:5; Matt. 14:25; Rev. 6:7

FOWL—*bird* 1 Kin. 4:23; Ps. 148:10

FOX Judg. 15:4; Neh. 4:3; Song 2:15; Ezek. 13:4; Matt. 8:20; Luke 13:32

FRAGMENT—*piece*
John 6:12, Gather up the left-over f-s

FRAGRANCE 2 Cor. 2:15, we are a f of Christ
Song 1:3; 2:13

FRANKINCENSE Ex. 30:34; 1 Chr. 9:29; Song 4:6; Matt. 2:11

FRAUD—*mischief*
Acts 13:10, full of all deceit and f

FREE Matt. 10:8, f-ly you received, f-ly give
John 8:32, the truth shall make you f
Rom. 6:7, he who has died is f-d
6:22, now having been f-d from sin
8:2, f from the law
Gal. 5:1, that Christ set us f
Gen. 2:16; Deut. 15:8; Josh. 2:20; Ps. 110:3; Is. 58:6; Eph. 6:8; Rev. 19:18

FREEDOM—*liberty* 1 Pet. 2:16, use your f as a
Rom. 8:21; Gal. 5:13

FREEWILL Lev. 22:18; Ezra 7:16; Ps. 119:108

FREQUENT 1 Tim. 5:23, your f ailments

FRESH Prov. 5:15, f water from your own well
James 3:11, *both* f and bitter water
Job 33:25; Ps. 92:10; James 3:12

FRET Prov. 24:19, Do not f yourself because of

FRICTION—*dispute*
1 Tim. 6:5, constant f between men

FRIEND Prov. 17:17, A f loves at all times
Prov. 18:24, a f who sticks closer
Matt. 11:19, a f of tax-gatherers and sinners
John 15:13, lay down his life for his f-s
Gen. 38:12; Ex. 33:11; Judg. 14:20; Job 16:20; Ps. 38:11; Mic. 7:5; Matt. 20:13

FRIENDSHIP James 4:4, do you not know that f

FROGS Ex. 8:2; Ps. 78:45; 105:30; Rev. 16:13

FRONT Ex. 28:27, ephod, on the f of it

FROST—*ice* Gen. 31:40; Ex. 16:14; Ps. 78:47; Jer. 36:30

FRUIT—*labor, produce* Ps. 1:3, yields its f in its season
Prov. 11:30, f of the righteous
Matt. 3:8, Therefore bring forth f
7:16, know them by their f-s
John 4:36, f for life eternal
Rom. 7:4, bear f for God
Col. 1:10, bearing f in every good work

FRUIT *(Continued)*
James 3:17, full of mercy and good **f-s**
Gen. 1:11; 3:6; Lev. 27:30; Ps. 92:14; 128:2; Song 4:16; Jer. 2:7; 6:19

FRUSTRATE
Ezra 4:5; Job 5:12; Prov. 15:22; Is. 14:27

FUEL
Is. 9:5,19; Ezek. 15:4; 21:32

FUGITIVE
Judg. 12:4; Is. 15:5; 52:12

FULFILL—*complete*
Matt. 2:15, prophet might be **f-ed**
2:17, prophet was **f-ed** saying
3:15, fitting for us to **f** all righteousness
5:17, not come to abolish, but to **f**
Luke 22:16, it is **f-ed** in the kingdom
1 Cor. 7:3, husband **f** his duty to his wife
Gal. 6:2, **f** the law of Christ
2 Tim. 4:5, **f** your ministry
1 Chr. 17:11; 2 Chr. 36:21; Ps. 20:5; 148:8; Matt. 1:22

FULL—*complete, whole*
1 Chr. 21:24; Ps. 92:14; Prov. 4:18
Ps. 33:5, earth is **f** of the lovingkindness
Is. 11:9, will be **f** of knowledge
Matt. 6:2,5,16, have their reward in **f**
14:20, twelve **f** baskets
23:27, **f** of dead men's bones
Luke 4:1, **f** of the Holy Spirit
11:34, body also is **f** of light
John 1:14, **f** of grace and truth
Eph. 6:11, the **f** armor of God
James 5:11, the Lord is **f** of compassion
Acts 2:13; 1 Cor. 7:36; Col. 1:25

FULLER—*launderer*
2 Kin. 18:17; Mal. 3:2

FUNCTION
Rom. 12:4, members do not have the same **f**

FURIOUS
2 Kin. 9:20; Dan. 2:12

FURNACE—*oven*
Ps. 12:6; Is. 31:9; Dan. 3:6,15; Matt. 13:42; Rev. 1:15

FURNISH
Deut. 15:14; Mark 14:15

FURNITURE
Ex. 31:7, all the **f** of the tent

FURROWS
Job 31:38; Ps. 65:10; 129:3

FURTHER
Ex. 21:22; Num. 22:26; 1 Sam. 10:3; Matt. 26:65; Acts 24:4; Heb. 12:9

FURY—*displeasure*
Gen. 27:44; Ps. 2:5; Ezek. 19:12; Heb. 10:27

FUTILE—*vain*
1 Sam. 12:21, **f** things . . . because they are **f**
Acts 4:25, PEOPLES DEVISE **F** THINGS
Rom. 1:21, **f** in their speculations

FUTILITY—*vanity*
Rom. 8:20, creation was subjected to **f**
Eph. 4:17, walk, in the **f** of their mind

FUTURE—*end, reward*
Prov. 24:20, no **f** for the evil man
Deut. 32:29; Jer. 31:17

G

GAIN—*price, profit*
Prov. 10:2, Ill-gotten **g-s** do not
Matt. 16:26; Luke 9:25, if he **g-s** the whole world
Phil. 3:8, that I may **g** Christ
1 Tim. 6:5, godliness . . . means of **g**
1 Pet. 5:2, not for sordid **g**
1 Sam. 8:3; Prov. 3:14; Is. 33:15; Ezek. 22:12,27

GALE
Mark 4:37, arose a fierce **g** of wind

GALL
Ps. 69:21, Matt. 27:34; Acts 8:23

GALLERY
Ezek. 41:15; 42:3

GALLOWS
Esth. 5:14; 7:10; 9:25

GANGRENE
2 Tim. 2:17, will spread like **g**

GARDEN—*field*
Gen. 3:8, God walking in the **g**
John 18:1, where there was a **g**
19:41, in the **g** a new tomb
Gen. 2:8; 3:10; Deut. 11:10; Lam. 2:6; Joel 2:3; John 18:26; 20:15

GARMENT—*clothing, dress*
Gen. 41:42, in **g-s** . . . linen
Ex. 28:2, make holy **g-s** for Aaron
Ps. 22:18, divide my **g-s** among them
102:26, wear out like a **g**
Matt. 27:35, DIVIDED UP HIS **G-S** . . . CASTING
28:3, his **g** as white as snow
Luke 23:34, DIVIDING UP HIS **G-S**
Heb. 1:11, BECOME OLD AS A **G**
Gen. 3:21; 25:25; 38:14; 39:12; Ex. 19:10; Esth. 8:15; Is. 59:17; 63:1; Ezek. 27:24; Joel 2:13; Matt. 3:4; Mark 5:28; John 21:7; Acts 10:30

GARNER—*barn*
Ps. 144:13, Let our **g-s** be full

GARRISON—*pillars*
1 Sam. 10:5; 14:12; 1 Chr. 18:13

GASH—*cut*
Mark 5:5, **g-ing** himself

GATE
Gen. 28:17, this is the **g** of heaven
Ps. 24:7, Lift your heads, O **g-s**
100:4, Enter His **g-s** with
Matt. 7:13, Enter by the narrow **g**
16:18, **g-s** of Hades shall not
Gen. 22:17; Judg. 16:3; Is. 38:10; Acts 12:14

GATHER—*assemble*
Is. 40:11, His arm . . . **g** the lambs
John 4:36, **g-ing** fruit for life
6:12, **G** up the . . . fragments
Gen. 1:10; 31:46; 37:7; 41:35; Ps. 33:7; Is. 66:18; Matt. 26:3; Acts 19:40; Rev. 14:19

GAVE—*provide*
Gen. 2:20, Adam **g** names to all
Gen. 3:12, Thou **g-st** to be with me
Ps. 69:21, they **g** me vinegar to drink
Eccles. 12:7, return to God who **g** it
Mark 8:6, He **g** thanks and broke them
John 3:16, He **g** His only begotten Son
13:26, morsel . . . He : . . **g** it to Judas

19:30, bowed . . . **g** up His spirit
Rom. 1:28, **g** them over to a depraved mind
1 Tim. 2:6, who **g** Himself as a ransom
Is. 50:6; Matt. 10:1; 26:48; Luke 7:44; Eph. 1:22

GAZE
Ex. 19:21; Job 31:1

GENEALOGY—*descent*
Heb. 7:3,6

GENERAL
Heb. 12:23, to the **g** assembly and church

GENERATION—*ages*
Deut. 1:35; Luke 21:32; Eph. 3:5
Ps. 90:1, dwelling place in all **g-s**
100:5, His faithfulness to all **g-s**
Matt. 1:17, to David are fourteen **g-s**
24:34, this **g** will not pass away
Luke 1:48, all **g-s** will count me blessed
Eph. 3:21, all **g-s** forever and ever
Phil. 2:15, a crooked and perverse **g**

GENEROUS—*bountiful*
Prov. 22:9; Is. 32:5

GENTILE—*nations*
Matt. 6:7, as the **G-s** do
Luke 2:32, LIGHT OF REVELATION TO THE **G-s**
Acts 4:25, WHY DID THE **G-s** RAGE
14:2, stirred the minds of the **G-s**
Rom. 11:11, salvation *has come to* the **G-s**
Gal. 1:16, I might preach Him among the **G-s**

GENTLE—*compassionate*
1 Kin. 19:12, sound of a **g** blowing
Prov. 15:1, **g** answer turns away wrath
Matt. 5:5, Blessed are the **g**
1 Cor. 4:21, with love and a spirit of **g-ness**
2 Cor. 10:1, **g-ness** of Christ
Gal. 5:23, **g-ness**, self-control
Eph. 4:2, with all humility and **g-ness**
1 Thess. 2:7, we proved to be **g** among you
1 Tim. 6:11, love, perseverance *and* **g-ness**
Titus 3:2, to be uncontentious, **g**
1 Pet. 3:4, a **g** and quiet spirit
Ps. 18:35; Matt. 21:5; 1 Tim. 3:3; Heb. 5:2; 1 Pet. 2:18

GESTURE—*motion*
John 13:24, Simon Peter therefore **g-d**

GET—*acquire, take*
Gen. 34:4; Judg. 11:5; 14:2
Prov. 4:7, with all your acquiring, **g** understanding
Matt. 16:23, **G** behind Me, Satan
Luke 18:12, tithes of all that I **g**
1 Kin. 17:10; Job 9:18; Is. 30:11; 56:12; Jer. 36:21

GIANT—*Rephaim*
1 Chr. 20:6, he . . . was descended from **g-s**

GIFT
Gen. 25:6, Abraham gave **g-s** while he was
Ps. 68:18, hast received **g-s** among men
127:3, children are a **g** of the LORD
Prov. 18:16, A man's **g** makes room for him
21:14, A **g** in secret subdues anger

GIFT
Matt. 2:11, presented to Him **g-s**
John 4:10, you knew the **g** of God
Acts 2:38, the **g** of the Holy Spirit
Rom. 6:23, **g** of God is eternal life
James 1:17, every perfect **g** is from above

GIRD—*bound* Ex. 29:5; Job 38:3; Ps. 45:3; John 13:5
John 21:18, when you were younger . . . **g** . . . will **g** you
Eph. 6:14, **G-ED YOUR LOINS WITH TRUTH**
Rev. 1:13, **g-ed** across His breast with a golden

GIRDLE—*belt, waistband* 2 Kin. 1:8; Rev. 1:13; 15:6, golden **g**
Job 12:18, binds their loins with a **g**

GIRL—*maiden, woman* Gen. 24:55; 34:4; Joel 3:3; Matt. 14:11; 26:69; Mark 6:28; John 18:17; Acts 12:13; 16:16

GIVE Num. 6:26, on you, And **g** you peace
Ps. 21:4, He asked life . . . Thou didst **g** it
Prov. 26:16, seven men . . . **g** a . . . answer
Is. 9:6, a son will be **g-n** to us
Matt. 6:11, **G** us this day our daily
10:8, freely **g**
15:36, **g-ing** thanks, He broke them
16:19, **g** you the keys
26:9, **g-n** to the poor
28:18, All authority has been **g-n** to Me
Luke 6:38, **G**, and it will be **g-n** to you
11:9, ask, and it shall be **g-n** to you
22:19, My body which is **g-n** for you
John 5:22, has **g-n** all judgment
6:11, and having **g-n** thanks
14:27, My peace I **g** to you
Acts 3:6, what I do have I **g** to you
12:23, he did not **g** God the glory
20:35, more blessed to **g** than to
Rom. 12:20, IF HE IS THIRSTY, **G** HIM A DRINK
14:6, he **g-s** thanks to God
1 Cor. 3:10, grace of God which was **g-n**
2 Cor. 12:7, was **g-n** me a thorn in
Eph. 4:27, do not **g** the devil an opportunity
5:20, always **g-ing** thanks
James 4:6, But He **g-s** a greater grace . . . **G-S GRACE**
1 John 5:11, has **g-n** us eternal life
Gen. 1:29; Ex. 20:12; Ps. 29:11; 68:11; 80:1; 145:15; Luke 1:77; 19:8; Rev. 19:8

GLAD Ps. 32:11, Be **g** in the LORD
Ps. 100:2, Serve the LORD with **g-ness**
122:1, I was **g** when they said to me
Prov. 10:1, wise son makes a father **g**
Matt. 5:12, Rejoice and be **g**
Luke 1:14, you will have joy and **g-ness**
6:23, Be **g** in that day, and leap
12:32, Father has chosen **g-ly** to give
Acts 2:46, **g-ness** and sincerity of heart
2 Cor. 11:19, bear with the foolish **g-ly**

Ex. 4:14; Num. 10:10; Deut. 28:47; 1 Chr. 16:31; Ps. 16:9; Is. 16:10

GLASS—*crystal* Job 28:17; Rev. 4:6

GLEAMING—*glitter*
Nah. 3:3, Swords flashing, spears **g**

GLEAN Lev. 19:10; Ruth 2:8,15,17; Is. 17:6; Jer. 49:9

GLISTEN Ps. 104:15, make his face **g** with oil

GLOOM Deut. 5:22; Job 3:5
Matt. 6:16, **g-y** face as the hypocrites do
Heb. 12:18, darkness and **g** and whirlwind

GLORIFY—*honor* Ps. 86:12, will **g** Thy name forever
Is. 66:5, Let the LORD be **g-ed**
Matt. 5:16, **g** your Father who is in heaven
John 12:28, Father **g** Thy name
13:31, is the Son of Man **g-ed**
16:14, He shall **g** Me
17:1, **g** Thy Son . . . **g** Thee
Acts 13:48, **g-ing** the word of the Lord
1 Cor. 6:20, **g** God in your body
Heb. 5:5, Christ did not **g** Himself

GLORIOUS—*exalt, glory, honor*
Neh. 9:5, Thy **g** name
Ps. 87:3, **G** things are spoken of you
1 Tim. 1:11, the **g** gospel of the blessed God

GLORY—*honor, splendor* Ex. 16:7, see . . . **g** of the Lord
Ps. 24:7, the King of **g** may come in
Prov. 16:31, gray head is a crown of **g**
Is. 6:3, earth is full of His **g**
66:19, heard . . . nor seen My **g** . . . **g** among the nations
Matt. 6:13, power, and the **g**
6:29, Solomon in all his **g** did not clothe
Luke 2:9, **g** of the Lord shone around
2:14, **G** to God in the highest
17:18, turned back to give **g** to God
John 5:44, you receive **g** from one another
9:24, Give **g** to God
Rom. 2:7, in doing good seek for **g** and honor
3:23, fall short of the **g** of God
2 Cor. 4:4, gospel of the **g** of Christ
Phil. 3:21, with the body of His **g**
Heb. 2:7, THOU HAST CROWNED HIM WITH **G** AND HONOR
Jude 25, through Jesus Christ . . . be **g**
Ex. 33:18; 1 Chr. 16:24; 29:11; Job 29:20; Ps. 105:3; Is. 35:2; Jer. 13:16; Ezek. 10:4; Hos. 4:7; John 8:50; James 1:9

GLUTTON Prov. 23:20; Matt. 11:19

GNASH—*grind* Ps. 35:16; 37:12; 112:10; Lam. 2:16; Matt. 8:12

GNAT Matt. 23:24, who strain out a **g**

GNAWED Rev. 16:10, they **g** their tongues

GO Ex. 14:15, Tell the sons of Israel to **g** forward

Ex. 23:23, My angel will **g** before you
33:14, My presence shall **g** with you
Ruth 1:16, where you **g**, I will **g**
Ps. 139:7, Where can I **g** from
Matt. 5:41, force you to **g** one mile; . . . two
6:6, when you pray, **G** INTO YOUR INNER ROOM
Luke 10:37, **G** and do the same
John 14:12, I **g** to the Father
Gen. 12:1; 32:26; Deut. 17:8; 23:23; Job 23:8; Ps. 42:4; Prov. 22:6; Hos. 2:7; Mic. 2:10; Matt. 21:29

GOAD Judg. 3:31; 1 Sam. 13:20,21
Eccles. 12:11, words of wise men are like **g-s**

GOAL Phil. 3:14, press on toward the **g**
1 Tim. 1:5, **g** of our instruction is love

GOAT Ex. 26:7; Lev. 3:12; Num. 15:27; 1 Sam. 19:13; Dan. 8:5; Matt. 25:32; Heb. 9:13

GODDESS 1 Kin. 11:5; Acts 19:27,37

GOD-FEARING Acts 10:22, Cornelius . . . a righteous and **G** man
Acts 17:17, reasoning . . . with the Jews and **G** *Gentiles*

GODLESS Job 8:13, hope of the **g** will perish
Job 15:34, company of the **g** is barren
Is. 9:17, every one is **g**
Acts 2:23, hands of **g** men and put Him to death

GODLINESS 1 Tim. 2:2, in all **g** and dignity
1 Tim. 3:16, great is the mystery of **g**
4:8, but **g** is profitable
6:6, **g** *actually* is a means . . . contentment
2 Tim. 3:5, holding to a form of **g**
2 Pet. 1:7, **g**, brotherly kindness

GODLY 1 Sam. 2:9, keeps the feet of His **g** ones
Ps. 12:1, for the **g** man ceaseth
37:28, not forsake His **g** ones
2 Cor. 1:12, in holiness and **g** sincerity
2 Pet. 2:9, rescue the **g** from temptation

GODS Ex. 20:3, have no other **g** before Me
Judg. 5:8, New **g** were chosen
Is. 37:12, **g** of those nations . . . deliver
Jer. 22:9, bowed down to other **g**
Dan. 2:47, your God is a God of **g**
Gal. 4:8, by nature are no **g**

GOING Ps. 121:8, guard your **g** out
Is. 20:2, **g** naked and barefoot
Matt. 25:8, our lamps are **g** out
Mark 1:16, He was **g** along by the sea of Galilee
10:32, road, **g** up to Jerusalem
John 14:5, not know where You are **g**
Gen. 15:12; Mic. 5:2; Matt. 26:46

GOLD Job 22:25, The Almighty will be your **g**

GOLD (Continued)
Ps. 19:10, more desirable than g . . . much fine g
Prov. 8:19, g, even pure g
Matt. 2:11, to Him gifts of g
Acts 3:6, Peter said . . . not possess silver and g
20:33, coveted no one's silver or g
1 Pet. 1:7, more precious than g
Rev. 3:18, buy from Me g refined
Gen. 2:12; 24:22; Ex. 3:22; Job 31:24; Ps. 72:15; Prov. 16:16; 25:11; Lam. 4:1; Zech. 9:3; Matt. 10:9; James 2:2; Rev. 21:15

GOLDEN Job 37:22, Out of the north comes g splendor
Lev. 8:9; 1 Sam. 6:18; Dan. 3:5; Rev. 1:12

GOLDSMITH Neh. 3:31,32; Is. 40:19; 46:6

GONE Judg. 19:11, the day was almost g
Ps. 19:4, line has g out through
Prov. 7:19, g on a long journey
Hos. 4:18, Their liquor g
Mark 5:30, power . . . had g forth
Rom. 13:12, The night is almost g
2 Pet. 2:15, they have g astray
Gen. 31:30; Song 2:11; Lam. 1:3

GOOD Gen. 1:4, that the light was g
Gen. 50:20, God meant it for g
2 Chr. 6:41, godly ones rejoice in what is g
Esth. 10:3, sought the g of his people
Ps. 106:1; 136:1, give thanks . . . for He is g
Prov. 22:1, A g name . . . more desired
Is. 1:17, Learn to do g
Jer. 33:11, For the LORD is g, For His lovingkindness
Jon. 4:4, Do you have g reason
Matt. 3:10, does not bear g fruit
19:16, what g thing shall I do
Mark 9:50, Salt is g, but if the salt
Luke 1:19, to bring you this g news
6:27, do g to those who hate you
10:42; Mary has chosen the g part
John 10:14, I am the g shepherd
Acts 23:1, lived my life . . . g conscience
Rom. 2:7, perseverance in doing g
2:10, every man who does g
12:21, overcome evil with g
Gal. 6:10, do g to all men
Phil. 4:8, whatever is of g repute
1 Tim. 6:12, Fight the g fight of faith
1 Pet. 3:11, TURN . . . FROM EVIL AND DO G
Gen. 15:15; Lev. 27:10; Job 7:7; Prov. 25:25; Is. 39:8; Jer. 24:3; Amos 5:14; Matt. 25:23; Luke 18:19; Acts 6:3; Gal. 6:12; 2 Thess. 2:16; James 1:17

GOODNESS Ex. 33:19; 2 Sam. 2:6; Ps. 25:7
Ps. 23:6, Surely g and lovingkindness will follow
31:19, How great is Thy g
Gal. 5:22, kindness, g, faithfulness
2 Thess. 1:11, fulfill every desire for g

GOODS—possessions Gen. 14:21; Ezek. 38:12; Luke 12:19

GORGEOUS Luke 23:11, dressed Him in a g robe

GOSPEL Matt. 4:23, the g of the kingdom
Matt. 11:5, HAVE THE G PREACHED
Mark 16:15, preach the g to all
Luke 4:18, PREACH THE G TO THE POOR
Rom. 1:16, I am not ashamed of the g
2 Cor. 10:14, in the g of Christ
11:4, or a different g
Gal. 1:7, distort the g of Christ
Eph. 1:13, g of your salvation
6:15, G OF PEACE
Phil. 1:5, participation in the g
Col. 1:23, from the hope of the g
Rev. 14:6, an eternal g

GOSSIP Rom. 1:29, malice; they are g-s
2 Cor. 12:20, g, arrogance, disturbances

GOVERN—rule Gen. 1:16, to g the day . . . g the night

GOVERNMENT—authority Is. 9:6, g will rest on His

GOVERNOR—commander Matt. 27:11; Acts 7:10

GRACE—favor Ps. 45:2; 2 Thess. 2:16
Luke 2:40, the g of God was upon Him
John 1:16, received, and g upon g
Rom. 1:5, through whom we have received g
5:2, this g in which we stand
16:20, The g of our Lord Jesus be with you
2 Cor. 9:8, make all g abound
12:9, My g is sufficient
1 Thess. 1:1, G to you and peace
Philem. 25, g of the Lord Jesus Christ
Heb. 4:16, the throne of g . . . may find g
James 4:6, GIVES G TO THE HUMBLE
2 Pet. 3:18, grow in the g

GRACIOUS—kind Neh. 9:31, art a g and compassionate God
Ps. 6:2, Be g to me, O LORD
111:4, LORD is g and compassionate
Luke 4:22, wondering at the g words
Gen. 43:29; Ex. 33:19; Ps. 77:9; 112:4; 119:29; Prov. 19:17, 26:25; Amos 5:15

GRAFT Rom. 11:23, God is able to g them in
Rom. 11:24, g-ed contrary to nature . . . branches are g-ed

GRAIN—kernel John 12:24, unless a g of wheat falls
1 Cor. 15:37, a bare g, perhaps of wheat
Gen. 41:5; Lev. 2:14; 2 Sam. 17:19; 2 Kin. 4:42; Jer. 23:28; Amos 9:9; Matt. 12:1; Mark 4:28

GRANDCHILDREN Prov. 17:6, G . . . crown of old men

GRANDMOTHER 2 Tim. 1:5, in your g Lois

GRANT—give, provide
Job 10:12, Thou hast g-ed me life
Ps. 85:7, g us Thy salvation

Prov. 10:24, of the righteous will be g-ed
Mark 10:37, G that we may sit
Rev. 3:21, He who overcomes, I will g . . . to sit
Is. 63:7; Luke 22:29

GRAPE Num. 6:3; Deut. 32:14; Jer. 49:9; Matt. 7:16; Luke 6:44

GRASS—vegetation
Ps. 103:15, man, his days are like g
Is. 40:6, All flesh is g
40:7, the g withers, the flower
Matt. 6:30, if God so arrays the g of the field
1 Pet. 1:24, ALL FLESH IS LIKE G
Num. 22:4; 2 Sam. 23:4; 2 Kin. 19:26; Ps. 102:11; Prov. 27:25; Is. 5:24; 15:6; 37:27; Dan. 5:21

GRASSHOPPER—caterpillar
Num. 13:33, we became like g-s
Lev. 11:22; 2 Chr. 6:28; Is. 40:22

GRATITUDE 1 Tim. 4:4, is received with g

GRAVE—tomb Gen. 35:20; 2 Sam. 3:32; Ps. 5:9; Ezek. 37:12; Nah. 1:14

GRAY Gen. 42:38, bring my g hair down . . . in sorrow
1 Sam. 12:2, I am old and g
Deut. 32:25; Job 15:10; Ps. 71:18; Hos. 7:9

GRAZE—feed Is. 5:17; 11:7; 27:10; 65:25

GREAT—excellent, big Gen. 12:2; 15:1; Ex. 18:11; 32:30
Gen. 1:16, two lights; the g-er light
Ps. 48:1, G is the LORD
Mal. 4:5, the g and terrible day
Matt. 2:10, rejoiced exceedingly, with g joy
4:16, DARKNESS SAW A G LIGHT
5:12, your reward in heaven is g
7:27, g was its fall
11:11, he who is least . . . is g-er than he
Luke 2:10, good news of a g joy
6:23, your reward is g in heaven
John 5:20, g-er works than these
15:13, G-er love has no one
1 Cor. 13:13, g-est of these is love
1 Tim. 6:6, godliness . . . a means of g gain
Jude 24, stand in the presence . . . g joy
Rev. 8:10, a g star fell from heaven
15:3, G AND MARVELOUS ARE THY WORKS
Deut. 1:17; 2 Sam. 5:10; 19:32; 1 Chr. 16:25; Neh. 9:27; Job 31:25; Ps. 57:10; Prov. 15:16; Jer. 9:19; Dan. 4:22; Zeph. 1:14; Matt. 15:28; Luke 5:6; Acts 11:5; 2 Cor. 3:12

GREATLY—utterly
Gen. 20:8, men were g frightened
John 3:29, rejoices g because of the
Phil. 4:10, I rejoiced in the Lord g
Gen. 3:16; Num. 14:39; 1 Sam. 28:5; Ps. 89:7; Zech. 9:9; Mark 12:27

GREATNESS—magnitude Ps. 51:1, g of Thy compassion
Luke 9:43, the g of God
2 Cor. 4:7, the surpassing g of the power

Eph. 1:19, surpassing **g** of His power toward us
1 Chr. 29:11; Neh. 13:22; Ps. 150:2; Is. 63:1

GREED Is. 56:11, the dogs are **g-y**
Luke 12:15, Beware . . . every form of **g**
1 Thess. 2:5, a pretext for **g**

GREEK Acts 16:1; 21:37; Rom. 2:9; 1 Cor. 12:13; Gal. 3:28; Rev. 9:11

GREEN—*luxuriant*
Ps. 23:2, lie down in **g** pastures
Gen. 1:30; Ps. 92:14; Jer. 17:2; Ezek. 17:24; Luke 23:31

GREET Matt. 10:12, house, give it your **g-ing**
1 Cor. 16:20, All the brethren **g** you. **G** one another
1 Pet. 5:14, **G** one another with a kiss
Matt. 23:7; 2 Tim. 4:21

GREW Gen. 21:8; 1 Sam. 2:21
Ex. 16:21, when the sun **g** hot
Mark 4:7, thorns **g** up and choked it

GRIEF—*sorrow* Ps. 77:10, It is my **g**
Prov. 17:25, A foolish son is a **g** to his
Is. 53:4, our **g-s** He Himself bore
Heb. 13:17, with joy and not with **g**

GRIEVE Is. 63:10, And **g-d** His Holy Spirit
Matt. 26:38, My soul is deeply **g-d**
Mark 3:5, **g-d** at their hardness of heart
John 21:17, Peter was **g-d** because He
Eph. 4:30, do not **g** the Holy Spirit of God
Gen. 6:6; 45:5; Neh. 8:10; Ps. 78:40; Amos 6:6; Nah. 3:7

GRIND Is. 3:15, **g-ing** the face of the poor
Matt. 24:41, women . . . **g-ing** at the mill
Judg. 16:21; Eccles. 12:3,4; Is. 47:2; Mark 9:18

GROAN Ex. 2:24, God heard their **g-ing**
Acts 7:34, HAVE HEARD THEIR G-S
Rom. 8:22, whole creation **g-s** and suffers
8:26, **g-ings** too deep for words
2 Cor. 5:2, in this *house* we **g**
Job 24:12; Is. 42:14; Ezek. 30:24; Joel 1:18

GROPE Deut. 28:29; Job 12:25; Is. 59:10; Acts 17:27

GROUND—*earth, land, soil*
Gen. 3:17, Cursed is the **g**
4:2, a tiller of the **g**
Matt. 25:25, hid your talent in the **g**
Luke 19:44, will level you to the **g**
John 8:6, His finger wrote on the **g**
9:6, He spat on the **g**
Acts 7:33, ARE STANDING IS HOLY G
9:8, Saul got up from the **g**
Eph. 3:17, rooted and **g-ed** in love
Gen. 2:5,7,9; 8:21; Num. 16:30; Deut. 28:56; Josh. 3:17; 2 Sam. 14:22; Job 5:6; Ps. 89:44; Is. 3:26; 29:4; Jer. 4:3; 14:4; Lam. 2:21; Hos. 10:12; Amos 3:5; 9:9;

Matt. 25:18; Mark 4:31; Acts 9:4; 26:14; Heb. 6:7

GROUP Mark 6:39, recline by **g-s** . . . grass

GROVE Judg. 15:5, with the vineyards and **g-s**

GROW 1 Sam. 3:2, eyesight had begun to **g** dim
Matt. 6:28, lilies of the field **g**
24:12, people's love will **g** cold
Luke 2:40, And the Child continued to **g**
Acts 12:24, word of the Lord continued to **g**
19:20, word of the Lord was **g-ing** mightily
1 Cor. 3:6, but God was causing the **g-th**
2 Cor. 10:15, as your faith **g-s**
Eph. 4:15, we are to **g** up . . . into Him
1 Pet. 2:2, you may **g** in respect
2 Pet. 3:18, **g** in the grace and knowledge
Gen. 26:13; 48:16; Judg. 16:22; 2 Sam. 10:5; 2 Kin. 19:29; Ps. 147:8

GROWL Is. 59:11, All of us **g** like bears

GROWN Ezek. 7:11, Violence has **g** into a rod
Ex. 2:11; Lev. 13:37; Deut. 32:15; 2 Kin. 4:18; Prov. 24:31

GRUDGE Lev. 19:18; 2 Cor. 9:7

GRUMBLE Phil. 2:14, Do all things without **g-ing**
Ex. 17:3; Luke 15:2; John 6:43

GUARANTOR Job 17:3, Who . . . will be my **g**

GUARD—*keep, watch* Ps. 39:1, I will **g** my ways
Mark 14:44, lead Him away under **g**
Phil. 4:7, **g** your hearts and minds
1 Tim. 6:20, **g** what has been entrusted to you
1 John 5:21, children, **g** yourselves from idols
Ex. 23:13; 1 Chr. 11:25; Job 7:12; Prov. 2:11; Ezek. 38:7; Acts 5:23; 28:16

GUARDIAN—*overseer*
1 Pet. 2:25, Shepherd and **G** . . . souls

GUEST 1 Kin. 1:41; Prov. 9:18; Matt. 22:10

GUIDANCE—*counsel*
Prov. 11:14, Where there is no **g**
20:18, war by wise **g**

GUIDE—*direct, lead* Ps. 48:14, He will **g** us until death
Prov. 12:26, righteous is a **g** to his neighbor
Is. 58:11, And the LORD will . . . **g** you
Matt. 15:14, if a blind man **g-s** a blind man
Luke 1:79, **g** our feet . . . way of peace
Rom. 2:19, are a **g** to the blind
Deut. 32:12; Job 38:32; Matt. 23:16; Acts 8:31

GUILE—*deceit* John 1:47, in whom is no **g**
1 Pet. 2:1, all malice and all **g**
3:10, LIPS FROM SPEAKING G

GUILT Luke 23:22, found in Him no **g** demanding death
1 Cor. 11:27, **g-y** of the body and the blood
James 2:10, one *point*, he has become **g-y** of all
Gen. 42:21; Lev. 6:4; Num. 5:31; 35:31; Deut. 25:2; 2 Sam. 3:8; 14:13; Ezra 9:6; Jer. 51:5; Ezek. 22:4; Hos. 10:2; Hab. 1:11; Luke 23:4; John 18:38; 19:4,6

GUSH—*flow* Ps. 78:20; Is. 48:21; Acts 1:18

H

HABITATION—*abode, camp* Is. 32:18; 33:20; Acts 17:26
Ps. 26:8, I love the **h** of Thy house
71:3, Be Thou to me a rock of **h**
132:13, He has desired it for His **h**
Is. 63:15, Thy holy and glorious **h**

HADES Matt. 16:18; Luke 16:23; Acts 2:31; Rev. 1:18

HAIL Matt. 26:49, **H**, Rabbi
Matt. 27:29, **H**, King of the Jews
Rev. 16:21, **h-stones** . . . came down from heaven upon men
Ex. 9:23; Job 38:22; Ps. 148:8; Is. 28:17; 32:19; Mark 15:18; Luke 1:28; John 19:3

HAIR 1 Kin. 1:52, not one of his **h-s** will fall
Matt. 3:4, garment of camel's **h**
5:36, cannot make one **h** white
10:30; Luke 12:7, **h-s** of your head . . . numbered
Luke 7:38, wiping them with the **h** of her head
John 11:2, Mary . . . wiped His feet with her **h**
1 Cor. 11:14, if a man has long **h**
1 Tim. 2:9, not with braided **h**
Rev. 1:14, His **h** were white like white wool
Gen. 42:38; 44:29; Judg. 20:16; Neh. 13:25; Job 4:15; Mark 1:6; 1 Pet. 3:3

HAIRY—*rough* Zech. 13:4, **h** robe in order to deceive
Gen. 25:25; 27:11; 2 Kin. 1:8; Ps. 68:21

HALLELUJAH Rev. 19:1,3,4,6, saying **h**

HALLOWED—*consecrated, sanctified*
Matt. 6:9; Luke 11:2, **H** be Thy name

HAMMER—*beat* Is. 2:4, **h** their swords into plowshares
Judg. 4:21; 1 Kin. 6:7; Is. 41:7; Jer. 23:29; Mic. 4:3

HAND—*power* Ps. 16:11, In Thy right **h** there are pleasures
Ps. 24:4, has clean **h-s** and a pure heart
31:5; Luke 23:46, Into Thy **h** I commit my spirit
90:17, confirm the work of our **h-s**
137:5, my right **h** forget her *skill*

HAND (Continued)
Eccles. 9:10, Whatever your **h** finds to do
Is. 28:4, it is in his **h**
40:12, in the hollow of His **h**
Jer. 18:6, like the clay in the potter's **h**
Lam. 2:4, His right **h** like an adversary
Matt. 3:2; 4:17; 10:7, kingdom ... is at **h**
4:6, ON THEIR H-S THEY WILL BEAR
11:27, **h-ed** over to Me by My Father
26:18, My time is at **h**
Mark 14:62, SITTING AT THE RIGHT H OF POWER
16:19, SAT DOWN AT THE RIGHT H OF GOD
John 10:28, snatch them out of My **h**
2 Cor. 5:1, a house not made with **h-s**
Heb. 10:31, fall into the **h-s** of the living God
James 4:8, Cleanse your **h-s**
1 Pet. 4:7, end of all things is at **h**
1 John 1:1, our **h-s** handled
Gen. 3:22; 16:12; 24:2; 47:29; Ex. 21:24; 33:22; Deut. 8:17; 19:21; 33:3; 1 Sam. 5:11; 12:3; 26:18; 2 Sam. 24:14; 1 Kin. 18:44; 2 Kin. 5:11; 1 Chr. 21:13; 29:14; Ezra 7:9; Neh. 2:8,18; Job 12:10; 19:21; 40:14; Ps. 68:31; 80:17; 139:10; Prov. 3:16; 10:4; 12:24; 19:24; 26:15; Eccles. 2:24; Is. 5:25; 9:12; 10:4; 14:27; 53:10; 56:2; Ezek. 7:17; 21:7; Dan. 4:35; Mic. 7:3; Hab. 2:9; Zeph. 3:16; Matt. 3:12; 6:3; 18:8; Mark 9:43; 14:41; Luke 3:17; 9:44; John 20:27; 1 Cor. 12:15; Col. 2:11; 1 Thess. 4:11; 1 Tim. 2:8

HANDBREADTH Ex. 25:25; 1 Kin. 7:26; 2 Chr. 4:5; Ezek. 40:5
Ps. 39:5, Thou hast made my days as **h-s**

HANDFUL—hand Lev. 2:2; 5:12; 1 Kin. 20:10
1 Kin. 17:12, only a **h** of flour in the bowl

HANDKERCHIEF Acts 19:12, **h-s** ... carried from his body

HANDLE—touch Song 5:5; Jer. 2:8; Ezek. 27:29
2 Tim. 2:15, **h-ing** accurately the word of truth
1 John 1:1, our hands **h-d**, concerning the Word of Life

HANDMAID—servant, slave Ps. 86:16; 116:16

HANDSOME—becoming 1 Sam. 16:18, and a **h** man

HANG Deut. 21:23, who is **h-ed** is accursed of God
Job 26:7, He ... **h-s** the earth on nothing
Matt. 27:5, Judas went away and **h-ed** himself
Gal. 3:13, CURSED IS EVERY ONE WHO **H-S**

HAPPEN—befall Lev. 10:19; Deut. 22:6; Judg. 6:13; Dan. 10:14

HAPPINESS—joy Deut. 24:5, shall give **h** to his wife
Eccles. 9:7, eat your bread in **h**

HAPPY—bless Job 5:17, **h** is the man whom God reproves
Prov. 14:21, **h** is he who is gracious to the poor
Rom. 14:22, H is he who does not condemn himself

HARASS Deut. 2:9, Do not **h** Moab

HARBOR—haven Acts 27:12, **h** was not suitable

HARD—difficult, firm Ex. 1:14; Num. 11:11; Deut. 1:17
Matt. 19:23, is **h** for a rich man to enter ... heaven
25:24, I knew you to be a **h** man
Mark 10:24, **h** it is to enter the Kingdom of God
Acts 26:14, **h** for you to kick against the goads
2 Tim. 2:3, Suffer **h-ship** ... as a good soldier
Deut. 15:18; 2 Kin. 2:10; Job 38:30; 41:24; Prov. 13:15; 18:19; Is. 8:21; Mark 10:23; Luke 18:24

HARDEN—hardness Job 38:38; Prov. 29:1
John 12:40, HE **H-ED** THEIR HEART
Rom. 9:18, He **h-s** whom He desires
Heb. 3:13, **h-ed** by deceitfulness of sin
3:15; 4:7, DO NOT **H** YOUR HEARTS

HARDNESS—stubborn Matt. 19:8; Mark 10:5, **h** of heart
Mark 3:5, grieved at their **h** of heart
16:14, He reproached ... **h** of heart

HARLOT Matt. 21:31, **h-s** will get into the kingdom
Luke 15:30, devoured your wealth with **h-s**
Josh. 6:17; Prov. 7:10; 29:3; Is. 1:21; 23:17; Jer. 2:20; Ezek. 16:15; Joel 3:3; Rev. 17:5

HARM—evil, hurt Lev. 19:27; Judg. 15:3; 2 Kin. 4:41
1 Chr. 16:22; Ps. 105:15, do my prophets no **h**
Prov. 12:21, No **h** befalls the righteous
1 Pet. 3:13, who is there to **h** you
Prov. 3:30; Jer. 25:6; Acts 16:28; 28:5; Rev. 6:6

HARMONY 2 Cor. 6:15, what **h** has Christ with

HARNESS—armor Jer. 46:4, H the horses

HARP—lyre, instrument 1 Sam. 16:16; Ps. 33:2; 49:4; 57:8
Job 30:31, my **h** is turned to mourning
Ps. 137:2, Upon the willows ... hung our **h-s**
Is. 5:12; 24:8; Amos 6:5; 1 Cor. 14:7; Rev. 5:8; 14:2

HARROW—instrument Job 39:10, will he **h** the valleys

HARRY Job 18:11, terrors ... **h** him at every step

HARSH 1 Sam. 20:10, father answers you **h-ly**
Gen. 16:6; 1 Sam. 25:3; Prov. 15:1

HARVEST—reap, ripe
Gen. 8:22, Seedtime and **h** ... cease
Job 4:8, who sow trouble **h** it
Jer. 8:20, **h** is past, summer is ended
Joel 3:13, the **h** is ripe
Matt. 9:37, **h** is plentiful
9:38; Luke 10:2, the Lord of the **h**
13:30, both to grow together until the **h**
13:39, **h** is the end of the age
Mark 4:29, puts in the sickle ... **h** has come
John 4:35, fields, that they are white for **h**
Rev. 14:15, the **h** of the earth is ripe
Ex. 22:29; 23:16; 34:22; Lev. 19:9; Deut. 24:19; 1 Sam. 12:17; Job 5:5; Prov. 6:8; 10:5; 25:13; 26:1; Is. 9:3; 16:9; 18:4; Jer. 5:17; 51:33

HASTE—hurry, urgent
Prov. 7:23, she goes ... snare
28:22, evil eye **h-ns** after wealth
2 Pet. 3:12, **h-ning** the coming of the day of God
Ex. 12:11; Ps. 22:19; Eccles. 1:5; Is. 52:12; Mark 6:25

HASTILY—hurried Prov. 25:8, Do not go out **h** to argue
1 Tim. 5:22, lay hands upon any one too **h**

HASTY—impetuous Prov. 29:20, a man who is **h**
Eccles. 5:2, Do not be **h** in word

HATCH Jer. 17:11, As a partridge that **h-es** eggs

HATCHET—axe, war-club Ps. 74:6, smash with **h** and hammers

HATE Ps. 81:15, Those who **h** the LORD
Ps. 97:10, H evil, you who love the LORD
Prov. 6:16, six things which the LORD **h-s**
8:13, fear of the LORD is to **h** evil
13:24, who spares his rod **h-s** his son
15:10, He who **h-s** reproof will die
Eccles. 3:8, A time to love, and a time to **h**
Matt. 6:24, he will **h** the one and love the other
10:22, Mark 13:13; Luke 21:17, will be **h-d**
Luke 6:22, Blessed are you when men **h** you
6:27, do good to those who **h** you
14:26, not **h** his own father and mother
John 3:20, does evil **h-s** the light
12:25, he who **h-s** his life
15:18; 1 John 3:13, If the world **h-s** you
15:23, He who **h-s** Me **h-s** My Father also
Rom. 1:30, slanderers, **h-rs** of God
7:15; I am doing the very thing I **h**
Eph. 5:29, no one ever **h-d** his own flesh
Titus 3:3, hateful, **h-ing** one another
1 John 2:9; 3:15; 4:20, **h-s** his brother
Gen. 24:60; Lev. 19:17; 26:17; 1 Kin. 22:8; 2 Chr. 18:7; 19:2; Ps.

34:21; 36:2; 139:21; Prov. 1:22;
Is. 1:14; 61:8; Ezek. 23:29;
Amos 5:15; Mic. 3:2; Zech. 8:17;
Mal. 1:3; John 7:7; Rom. 9:13

HAUGHTY—*proud, lofty, high*
Ps. 131:1, nor my eyes **h**
Prov. 16:18, **h** spirit before stumbling
Rom. 12:16, do not be **h** in mind
2 Sam. 22:28; Prov. 6:17; 21:24;
Zeph. 3:11

HAUNT—*habitation* Is. 34:13, also
be a **h** of jackals

HAVEN—*harbor* Gen. 49:13; Ps.
107:30

HAWK Lev. 11:16; Deut. 14:15; Job
39:26

HEAD—*chief* 2 Kin. 6:5, axe **h** fell
into the water
Ps. 24:7, Lift up your **h-s**, O gates
Prov. 25:22, burning coals on his **h**
Eccles. 2:14, wise man's eyes are in
his **h**
Matt. 14:8, Give me . . . **h** of John the
Baptist
27:39, WAGGING THEIR **H-S**
Luke 21:18, not a hair of your **h** will
perish
21:28, straighten up and lift up your
h-s
John 13:9, also my hands and my **h**
1 Cor. 11:3, Christ is the **h** of every
man
Eph. 1:22, Him as **h** over all things
5:23, Christ also is the **h** of the
church
Col. 2:19, not holding fast to the **H**
Rev. 1:14, His **h** and His hair were
white
Gen. 3:15; 1 Sam. 1:11; 9:22;
2 Kin. 4:19; Ps. 66:12; Is. 3:16;
59:17; Jer. 18:16; Dan. 2:38; 7:6;
Matt. 5:36; 6:17; Acts 21:24

HEAL 2 Chr. 7:14, and will **h** their
land
Ps. 147:3, He **h-s** the broken-hearted
Prov. 3:8, will be **h-ing** to your body
Is. 53:5, by His scourging we are **h-**
ed
Jer. 3:22, I will **h** your faithlessness
Hos. 14:4, I will **h** their apostasy
Matt. 10:8, **H** the sick, raise the dead
Mark 3:2, He would **h** him on the
Sabbath
Luke 4:23, Physician, **h** yourself
9:2, kingdom of God, and to
perform **h-ing**
9:11, those who had need of **h-ing**
Acts 9:34, Jesus Christ **h-s** you
1 Cor. 12:9, gifts of **h-ing** by the one
Spirit
James 5:16, pray . . . that you may be
h-ed
Rev. 22:2, the **h-ing** of the nations
Ex. 15:26; Num. 12:13; Deut. 32:39;
Job 5:18; Ps. 6:2; Prov. 13:17;
Jer. 17:14; 30:13; Matt. 4:23

HEALTH Jer. 30:17, will restore you
to **h**
3 John 2, prosper and be in good **h**

HEAP—*store* Prov. 25:22, **h** burning
coals on his head
Is. 25:2, made a city into a **h**
Gen. 31:46; Ex. 15:8; Deut. 32:23;
Josh. 3:13; Ps. 33:7; Ezek. 24:10;
Hab. 1:10

HEAR Job 27:9, Will God **h** his cry
Ps. 4:1, O God . . . **h** my prayer
135:17, have ears, but they do not **h**
Is. 28:14, **h** the word of the LORD
Ezek. 37:4, dry bones, **h** the word of
the LORD
Matt. 11:15, ears to **h**, let him **h**
13:13, while **h-ing** they do not **h**
15:10, **H** and understand
17:5, I am well pleased; **h** Him
Mark 7:37, He makes even the deaf
to **h**
John 5:24, he who **h-s** My word
10:3, the sheep **h** his voice
12:47, if any one **h-s** My sayings
Acts 17:32, We shall **h** you again
James 1:19, let every one be quick
to **h**
Rev. 3:20, if any one **h-s** My voice
Lev. 5:1; Deut. 6:4; 1 Sam. 15:14;
1 Kin. 8:30; Job 15:8; 26:14;
Ps. 38:13; 65:2; Is. 1:2; Matt. 10:27;
Rom. 11:8

HEARD Matt. 2:18, A VOICE WAS **H** IN
RAMAH
Acts 4:4, who had **h** the message
believed
19:10, lived in Asia **h** the word
1 Cor. 2:9, EYE HAS NOT SEEN AND
EAR HAS NOT **H**
2 Cor. 12:4, **h** inexpressible words
Phil. 4:9, learned and received and **h**
Rev. 10:4, I **h** a voice from heaven
Gen. 3:10; Ps. 10:17; Eccles. 12:13;
Song 2:12; Is. 65:19; Jer. 31:15;
Ezek. 1:24; Matt. 6:7; Luke 1:13

HEARING—*ears* Prov. 20:12, The **h**
ear
Prov. 23:9, Do not speak in the **h** of
a fool
Matt. 24:6, you will be **h** of wars
Rom. 10:17, So faith *comes* from **h**
Heb. 5:11, since you have become
dull of **h**

HEART—*desire, mind*
Gen. 8:21, intent of man's **h** is evil
1 Sam. 16:7, LORD looks at the **h**
1 Kin. 3:9, an understanding **h**
15:3, his **h** was not wholly devoted
1 Chr. 28:9, serve Him with a
whole **h**
Ps. 19:14, the meditation of my **h**
44:21, He knows the secrets of
the **h**
51:10, Create in me a clean **h**
51:17, broken and contrite **h**
119:11, Thy word I have treasured
in my **h**
Prov. 4:23, Watch . . . **h** with all
diligence
17:22, joyful **h** is good medicine
25:20, sings songs to a troubled **h**
Jer. 17:9, **h** is more deceitful than all
else
17:10, I, the LORD search the **h**
Matt. 5:8, Blessed are the pure in **h**
5:28, committed adultery . . . in
his **h**
6:21, treasure is, there will your **h**
be
11:29, I am gentle and humble in **h**
15:8, THEIR **H** IS FAR AWAY FROM ME
19:8, Because of your hardness of **h**
Mark 12:30, LOVE THE LORD . . .
YOUR **H**
Luke 2:19, pondering them in her **h**
2:51, treasured all *these* things in
her **h**
24:25, slow of **h** to believe

John 14:1, Let not your **h** be troubled
Acts 2:37, they were pierced to the **h**
Rom. 8:27, He who searches the **h-s**
knows
10:10, for with the **h** man believes
Eph. 3:17, Christ may dwell in your
h-s
5:19, making melody with your **h**
6:5, in the sincerity of your **h**
Phil. 4:7, guard your **h-s** and your
minds
Col. 3:22, but with sincerity of **h**
2 Thess. 3:5, Lord direct your **h-s**
into
Heb. 4:12, thoughts and intentions of
the **h**
10:22, draw near with a sincere **h**
James 1:26, deceives his *own* **h**
2 Pet. 1:19, morning star arises in
your **h-s**
Ex. 4:21; 31:6; Num. 15:39; Deut.
28:65; Josh. 5:1; Judg. 5:16;
1 Sam. 10:9; 13:14; 2 Sam. 6:16;
2 Chr. 15:15; Job 23:16; 29:13;
41:24; Ps. 4:7; 9:1; 12:2; 15:2; 17:3;
22:14; 27:3; 38:10; 111:1;
Prov. 12:20; 16:5; 23:7,26;
Eccles. 8:5; 11:9; Song 8:6; Is. 35:4;
47:10; Jer. 11:20; 24:7; Ezek. 11:19;
18:31; 21:7; 44:7,9; Joel 2:13;
Mal. 4:6; Matt. 12:34; 2 Cor. 3:3;
6:11; 9:7

HEAT—*outburst* Gen. 8:22; 18:1; Job
24:19; Is. 25:4
2 Pet. 3:10, be destroyed with
intense **h**
Rev. 16:9, men were scorched with
fierce **h**
Jer. 2:24; Hos. 7:4; Matt. 20:12

HEAVEN—*sky* Gen. 1:1, God
created the **h-s**
Gen. 1:8, God called the expanse **h**
28:17, this is the gate of **h**
Ps. 19:1, **h-s** are telling . . . glory of
God
103:11, high as the **h-s** are above
the earth
Is. 65:17, new **h-s** and a new earth
Mal. 3:10, open for you the windows
of **h**
Matt. 3:2, Repent . . . kingdom of **h** is
3:17, behold, a voice out of the **h-s**
5:3, Blessed . . . theirs is the
kingdom of **h**
5:12, your reward in **h** is great
6:9, Our Father who art in **h**
6:10, On earth as it is in **h**
6:14, your **h-ly** Father will also
forgive
10:7, kingdom of **h** is at hand
16:19, keys of the kingdom of **h**
Mark 13:31, **H** and earth will pass
away
Luke 10:20, your names are recorded
in **h**
15:18, have sinned against **h**
John 3:13, from **h**, *even* the Son of
Man
1 Cor. 15:40, are also **h-ly** bodies
15:47, second man is from **h**
2 Cor. 5:1, eternal in the **h-s**
12:2, was caught up to the third **h**
Gal. 1:8, or an angel from **h**, should
preach
Eph. 6:9, their Master and yours is
in **h**
Phil. 3:20, our citizenship is in **h**
Heb. 11:12, AS THE STARS OF **H**
12:23, who are enrolled in **h**

HEAVEN *(Continued)*
James 5:12, do not swear, either by **h**
Rev. 4:1, a door *standing* open in **h**
21:1, I saw a new **h**
Ex. 20:22; Deut. 33:13; 1 Sam. 2:10; 1 Kin. 8:27; 2 Kin. 7:2; Job 11:8; 22:12,14; Eccles. 5:2; Is. 14:12; Jer. 7:18; 23:24; Ezek. 32:8; John 3:12; 1 Cor. 15:48

HEAVY Matt. 11:28, who are weary and **h** laden
Matt. 26:43, their eyes were **h**
Ex. 17:12; 2 Chr. 10:10,11; Ps. 38:4; Prov. 27:3; Zech. 12:3; Matt. 23:4

HEDGE Luke 14:23, highways and along the **h**-s
Job 1:10; Prov. 15:19; Mic. 7:4

HEED Ps. 17:1; 55:2; Jer. 2:31

HEEL Gen. 3:15; 25:26; 49:17; Ps. 41:9

HEIGHT Rom. 8:39, nor **h**, nor depth
Job 22:12; Prov. 25:3; Rev. 21:16

HEIR Rom. 8:17, **h**-s also, **h**-s of God
Gal. 4:7, an **h** through God
James 2:5, **h**-s of the kingdom
Gen. 15:3; Jer. 49:1; Matt. 21:38

HELD Ezek. 31:15, and **h** back its rivers

HELL Mark 9:47, to be cast into **h**
James 3:6, tongue . . . is set on fire by **h**
2 Pet. 2:4, angels . . . cast them into **h**
Matt. 5:22; 10:28; 23:15

HELMET 1 Sam. 17:5, had a bronze **h** on his head
Is. 59:17, **h** of salvation on His head
Eph. 6:17, take the **h** of salvation

HELP 1 Sam. 7:12, the LORD has **h**-ed us
Ps. 33:20, He is our **h** and our shield
42:11, The **h** of my countenance
46:1, very present **h** in trouble
121:1, whence shall my **h** come
Matt. 15:25, Lord, **h** me
Mark 9:24, **h** *me* in my unbelief
2 Cor. 1:11, **h**-ing us through your prayers
Heb. 4:16, grace to **h** in time of need
Job 5:16; 6:13; Is. 41:6,13; Mark 7:11

HELPER—*comforter*
Gen. 2:18, I will make him a **h**
Ps. 10:14, **h** of the orphan
30:10, O LORD, be Thou my **h**
54:4, Behold, God is my **h**
John 14:16, will give you another **H**
Heb. 13:6, THE LORD IS MY **H**

HEMORRHAGE—*blood* Matt. 9:20; Mark 5:25; Luke 8:43

HEMORRHOIDS Deut. 28:27; 1 Sam. 5:6; 6:4

HERB Luke 11:42, tithe . . . every garden **h**
2 Kin. 4:39; 19:26; Ps. 37:2; Prov. 27:25; Is. 37:27

HERD—*cattle* Gen. 13:5; Jon. 3:7; Matt. 8:30

HERITAGE—*gift, possession* Ps. 16:6, my **h** is beautiful

Job 20:29; Ps. 135:12; 136:21,22; Is. 49:8

HESITATE 1 Kin. 18:21, How long *will* you **h**

HID—*cover, secret* Gen. 3:8, man and his wife **h** themselves
Matt. 10:26, and **h**-en that will not be known
13:44, treasure **h**-en in the field
25:25, **h** your talent in the ground
Mark 4:22, For nothing is **h**-en
1 Cor. 2:7, **h**-en wisdom, which God predestined
Col. 3:3, your life is **h**-en with Christ
Deut. 33:19; Josh. 2:4; 1 Sam. 20:24; 2 Sam. 17:9; Job 40:13; Ps. 19:6,12; 69:5; Is. 45:3; Dan. 2:22; Luke 8:17; John 8:59; Heb. 11:23

HIDE—*conceal, cover* Gen. 18:17; Job 14:13; 20:12; Ps. 27:5,9; Is. 2:10; Jer. 38:14

HIGH—*rank* Ps. 103:11, **h** as the heavens are above . . . earth
Matt. 4:8, devil took Him to a very **h** mountain
Mark 5:7, Jesus, Son of the Most **H** God
11:10, HOSANNA in the **h**-est
Luke 2:14, Glory to God in the **h**-est
John 19:31, for that Sabbath was a **h** day
Heb. 3:1, Jesus, the Apostle and **H** Priest
Gen. 29:7; Job 11:8; 22:12; Ps. 49:2; 91:14; Prov. 24:7; Is. 32:15; Luke 1:78

HIGHWAY—*way*
Num. 20:17, go along the king's **h**
Is. 35:8, **h** . . . called the **h** of holiness
40:3, a **h** for our God
59:7, Devastation and . . . in their **h**-s
Deut. 2:27; Prov. 15:19; Is. 11:16; 19:23; 49:11; 62:10; Matt. 22:9; Luke 14:23

HILL—*mountains*
Ps. 24:3, Who may ascend into the **h**
50:10, cattle on a thousand **h**-s
Matt. 5:14, city set on a **h** cannot be hidden
Luke 4:29, led Him to the brow of the **h**
Gen. 49:26; Deut. 11:11; Ps. 15:1; Is. 5:1; Luke 23:30

HINDER—*delay, forbid, restrain*
Matt. 19:14, do not **h** them from coming to Me
Mark 9:39, But Jesus said, Do not **h** him
Gal. 5:7, who **h**-ed you from obeying
1 Pet. 3:7, your prayers may not be **h**-ed
Mark 9:38; Luke 11:52; 18:16

HINDRANCE 1 Cor. 9:12, cause no **h** to the gospel

HIRE Is. 7:20, shave with a razor, **h**-d
Matt. 20:1, went out early . . . to **h** laborers
20:7, Because no one **h**-d us
Luke 15:19, as one of your **h**-d men

HIT 2 Cor. 11:20, if he **h**-s you in the face

HOARD—*store* Amos 3:10, **h** up violence and devastation

HOLD—*keep, retain*
Prov. 4:13, Take **h** of instruction
Is. 4:1, seven women . . . **h** of one man
Matt. 6:24, he will **h** to one
Mark 7:8, **h** to the tradition of men
Luke 8:15, heard the word, and **h** it fast
Phil. 2:16, **h**-ing fast the word of life
1 Thess. 5:21, **h** fast to that which is good
Titus 1:9, **h**-ing fast the faithful word
Job 2:9; 27:6; Ps. 64:5; Prov. 4:4; Is. 33:15; Jer. 20:9; Acts 7:60; Phil. 2:29

HOLE—*opening* Matt. 8:20, foxes have **h**-s
2 Kin. 12:9; Is. 11:8; Ezek. 8:7; Hag. 1:6

HOLINESS—*holy, sanctity* Ex. 15:11
Ps. 93:5, H befits Thy house
Is. 35:8, be called the highway of **h**
2 Cor. 7:1, perfecting **h** in the fear of God
1 Thess. 3:13, hearts unblameable in **h**
Heb. 12:10, we may share His **h**

HOLY—*holiness, sacred, sanctify* Ex. 3:5; 28:36
Ex. 20:8, sabbath day, to keep it **h**
Deut. 5:12, Observe the sabbath . . . keep it **h**
7:6, you are a **h** people
1 Chr. 16:10, Glory in His **h** name
Ps. 11:4, LORD is in His **h** temple
16:10, allow Thy **H** One to see the pit
145:21, bless His **h** name forever
Is. 6:3, **H**, **H**, **H**, is the LORD of hosts
Hab. 2:20, LORD is in His **h** temple
Matt. 7:6, not give what is **h** to dogs
Luke 1:49, **h** is His name
4:34, the **H** One of God
John 17:11, **H** Father, keep them in Thy name
Acts 2:27, THY **H** ONE
Rom. 12:1, your bodies a living and **h** sacrifice
1 Cor. 3:17, the temple of God is **h**
7:34, **h** both in body and spirit
Eph. 1:4, be **h** and blameless before Him
Col. 1:22, **h** and blameless
1 Tim. 2:8, lifting up **h** hands
2 Tim. 1:9, called us with a **h** calling
Lev. 20:7; Deut. 33:2; 1 Sam. 2:2; 2 Kin. 4:9; 1 Chr. 16:29; Job 15:15; Ps. 47:8; 89:5; 99:9; Jer. 17:22,24,27; 31:23; Mark 6:20; Rom. 16:16

HOLY SPIRIT—*spirit*
Matt. 1:20, in her is of the **H**
Matt. 3:11, baptize you with the **H**
Luke 3:22, **H** descended upon Him in bodily
4:1, Jesus, full of the **H**
11:13, give the **H** to those
12:12, **H** will teach you
John 14:26, Helper, the **H**
20:22, Receive the **H**
Acts 2:4, all filled with the **H**
2:38, receive the gift of the **H**
7:51, always resisting the **H**
10:38, the **H** and with power

19:2, Did you receive the **H**
Rom. 9:1, witness in the **H**
Eph. 1:13, with the **H** of promise
4:30, do not grieve the **H** of God
1 Thess. 4:8, God who gives His **H** to you

HOME Eccles. 12:5, man goes to his eternal **h**
2 Cor. 5:6, are at **h** in the body
Titus 2:5, sensible, pure, workers at **h**
Lev. 18:9; Deut. 24:5; 1 Kin. 13:15;
  2 Chr. 25:19; Prov. 7:19; Mark 5:19;
  1 Cor. 11:34; 14:35

HOMESTEAD—*habitation* Luke 11:21; Acts 1:20

HONEST—*good, true* Gen. 42:11, we are **h** men
Luke 8:15, an **h** and good heart

HONOR—*splendor* Ex. 20:12, **H** your father and your mother
Lev. 19:32, **h** the aged
Prov. 15:33, before **h** comes humility
Matt. 6:2, that they may be **h-ed** by men
13:57, A prophet is not without **h**
15:8, **H-S ME WITH THEIR LIPS**
John 5:23, all may **h** the Son
Rom. 2:10, glory and **h** and peace
1 Tim. 6:16, To Him *be* **h** and eternal dominion
Heb. 13:4, *Let* marriage *be held* in **h**
1 Pet. 2:17, **H** all men . . . **h** the king
3:7, grant her **h** as a fellow-heir
Rev. 5:13, *be* blessing and **h** and glory
1 Sam. 2:30; 9:6; 1 Kin. 3:13;
  1 Chr. 29:28; Job 19:9; Ps. 50:23;
  Eccles. 6:2; Is. 49:5; Matt. 15:4;
  Rom. 12:10; 13:7; 1 Tim. 5:17

HONORABLE—*noble* Is. 9:15; Nah. 3:10
Rom. 9:21, one vessel for **h** use . . . another for common
Phil. 4:8, brethren . . . whatever is **h**
Heb. 13:18, conduct ourselves **h-y** in all things

HOOF—*claw* Lev. 11:3,4,5,6,7,26, whatever divides a **h**
Deut. 14:6,7,8; Ps. 69:31; Is. 5:28; Jer. 47:3; Ezek. 32:13; Zech. 11:16

HOOK 2 Kin. 19:28; Is. 37:29, put My **h** in your nose
Job 41:2, pierce his jaw with a **h**
Ezek. 29:4; 38:4; Amos 4:2

HOPE—*comfort, expectation, confidence, trust*
Job 13:15, I will **h** in Him
Ps. 39:7, My **h** is in Thee
62:5, my **h** is from Him
Prov. 13:12, **H** deferred *makes* the heart sick
19:18, Discipline your son while there is **h**
Acts 2:26, **MY FLESH ALSO WILL ABIDE IN H**
23:6, **h** and resurrection of the dead
28:20, for the sake of the **h** of Israel
Rom. 4:18, **h** against **h** he believed
5:5, **h** does not disappoint
8:24, **h** that is seen is not **h**
12:12, rejoicing in **h**
15:4, Scriptures we might have **h**
1 Cor. 13:7, **h-s** all things
13:13, now abide faith, **h**, love

2 Cor. 3:12, Having therefore such a **h**
Gal. 5:5, waiting for the **h** of righteousness
Eph. 4:4, you were called in one **h**
Col. 1:23, away from the **h** of the gospel
1:27, Christ in you, the **h** of glory
1 Thess. 5:8, as a helmet, the **h** of salvation
1 Tim. 4:10, our **h** on the living God
Titus 3:7, *the* **h** of eternal life
Heb. 6:19, **h** we have as an anchor
11:1, assurance of *things* **h-d** for
1 Pet. 1:3, born again to a living **h**
Ruth 1:12; Job 7:6; Ps. 9:18; 71:5;
  Prov. 26:12; Eccles. 9:4; Is. 20:5;
  57:10; Jer. 29:11; 1 Cor. 9:10;
  2 Cor. 1:7; 2 Thess. 2:16

HORN—*trumpet* Gen. 22:13; Lev. 25:9; Josh. 6:5; 2 Sam. 22:3;
  1 Chr. 15:28; Dan. 3:5; 7:7; Rev. 5:6

HORRIBLE Jer. 5:30; 23:14; Hos. 6:10

HORROR Ps. 55:5; Jer. 25:18

HORSE Ps. 33:17, A **h** is a false hope
Gen. 49:17; 1 Kin. 10:29; Job 39:19;
  Ps. 32:9; Prov. 26:3; Jer. 4:13; 46:4;
  Hos. 14:3

HOSPITABLE 1 Tim. 3:2, must be above reproach . . . **h**
Titus 1:8, but **h**, loving what is good
1 Pet. 4:9, Be **h** to one another

HOSPITALITY Rom. 12:13, practicing **h**

HOST—*army, camp, innkeeper*
Ps. 24:10, LORD of **h-s**, He is the King
Luke 2:13, multitude of the heavenly **h**
Deut. 4:19; Josh. 5:15; Ps. 27:3; Is. 48:2; Rom. 16:23

HOSTILE—*enmity, contrary* Lev. 26:21, you act with **h-ity**
Rom. 8:7, mind set on the flesh is **h**
1 Thess. 2:15, but **h** to all men
Heb. 12:3, endured such **h-ity** by sinners
James 4:4, friendship with the world is **h-ity**

HOT—*branding* Ps. 39:3, My heart was **h** within me
Rev. 3:15, are neither cold nor **h**
Ex. 16:21; Deut. 9:19; Job 6:17; Prov. 6:28

HOT-TEMPERED Prov. 29:22, a **h** man abounds

HOUR—*time* Matt. 20:12, men have worked *only* one **h**
Matt. 24:36, day and **h** no one knows
26:40, watch with Me for one **h**
Mark 15:34, ninth **h** Jesus cried out
Luke 22:59, about an **h** had passed
John 5:25, an **h** is coming and now is
12:27, Father, save Me from this **h**
17:1, Father, the **h** has come
Matt. 8:13; Mark 13:32; Luke 12:39;
  John 11:9; Acts 3:1; Rom. 13:11;
  Rev. 3:10

HOUSE—*temple* Ps. 23:6, dwell in the **h** of the LORD

Ps. 127:1, Unless the LORD builds the **h**
Prov. 9:1, Wisdom has built her **h**
Matt. 2:11, they came into the **h** and saw
7:25, winds blew, and burst against that **h**
10:12, enter the **h**, give it your greeting
12:25, city or **h** divided against itself
21:13, **MY H SHALL BE CALLED A H**
Luke 11:17, a **h** divided against itself falls
John 14:2, Father's **h** are many dwelling places
Acts 2:46, breaking bread from **h** to **h**
7:48, does not dwell in **h-s** . . . human hands
7:49, **WHAT KIND OF H WILL YOU BUILD**
Rom. 16:5, church that is in their **h**
2 Cor. 5:1, **h** not made with hands
1 Tim. 5:13, go around from **h** to **h**
1 Pet. 2:5, built up as a spiritual **h**
Gen. 15:3; Ex. 20:2,17; Deut. 8:12;
  22:8; 2 Kin. 20:1; Neh. 13:11;
  Job 27:18; 30:23; Ps. 55:14; 84:3;
  93:5; 102:7; Prov. 24:3; Eccles. 7:2;
  Is. 5:8; Matt. 23:38; Mark 12:40;
  Luke 10:7

HOUSEHOLD—*home* Prov. 31:27, ways of her **h**
Gal. 6:10, who are of the **h** of the faith
Eph. 2:19, and are of God's **h**
1 Tim. 3:4, manages his own **h** well
3:15, conduct himself in the **h** of God
Gen. 18:19; 26:14; Ex. 1:1; Matt. 10:36; 13:52; John 19:27; 2 Tim. 3:6

HUMBLE—*abase, gentle* Mic. 6:8, walk **h-ly** with your God
Matt. 11:29, I am gentle and **h** in heart
23:12, exalts . . . shall be **h-d**; and . . . **h-s** himself
Phil. 3:21, body of our **h** state
4:12, get along with **h** means
James 4:6, **BUT GIVES GRACE TO THE H**
1 Pet. 5:6, **H** yourselves under the mighty hand
Ex. 10:3; Num. 12:3; Deut. 8:2;
  2 Chr. 34:27; Job 40:12; Ps. 35:13;
  37:11; Prov. 6:3; 11:2; Dan. 4:37;
  Zech. 9:9

HUMILIATE 2 Cor. 12:21, my God may **h** me before you

HUMILIATION—*confusion* Is. 45:16; Jer. 3:25
Acts 8:33, in **h** His judgment was taken

HUMILITY—*humble, self-abasement*
Prov. 15:33, before honor comes **h**
18:12, **h** *goes* before honor
22:4, The reward of **h**
Phil. 2:3, with **h** of mind
Col. 3:12, put on a heart of . . . **h**
1 Pet. 5:5, clothe yourselves with **h**

HUNG Ps. 137:2, Upon the willows . . . we **h** our harps
Matt. 18:6; Mark 9:4; Luke 17:2, better . . . millstone be **h** around his neck

HUNGER

HUNGER Ps. 34:10, lions do lack and suffer **h**
Prov. 10:3, not allow the righteous to **h**
19:15, an idle man will suffer **h**
Is. 49:10, They will not **h** or thirst
Matt. 5:6; Luke 6:21, Blessed are those who **h**
John 6:35, comes to Me shall not **h**
Deut. 28:48; Luke 6:25; 15:17

HUNGRY Ps. 146:7, Who gives food to the **h**
Prov. 25:21, If your enemy is **h**
Matt. 4:2, He then became **h**
12:1, His disciples became **h**
12:3, David did, when he became **h**
15:32, do not wish to send them away **h**
25:35, For I was **h**
Rom. 12:20, BUT IF YOUR ENEMY IS **H**
1 Cor. 11:34, If anyone is **h**
Deut. 8:3; 2 Sam. 17:29; Job 22:7; Ps. 50:12; Is. 29:8; Ezek. 18:7; 1 Cor. 11:21; Phil. 4:12

HUNT Gen. 10:9, a mighty **h-er** before the LORD
Gen. 27:5; 1 Sam. 26:20; Ps. 140:11; Ezek. 13:18; Mic. 7:2

HURRIED Prov. 20:21, inheritance gained **h-ly**

HURRY—*speed* 1 Sam. 20:38, **H**, be quick, do not stay

HURT—*harm* Ps. 15:4, He swears to his own **h**
Is. 11:9; Mark 16:18

HUSBAND—*bridegroom*
Prov. 12:4, wife is a crown of her **h**
John 4:16, Go, call your **h**
Rom. 7:2,3, if her **h** dies
1 Cor. 7:3, **h** fulfill his duty to his wife
Eph. 5:23, **h** is the head of the wife
5:25, **H-s**, love your wives
Rev. 21:2, bride adorned for her **h**
Gen. 3:16; 29:32; 30:20; Is. 54:5; Hos. 3:1; Mark 10:12; 1 Cor. 7:2; 2 Cor. 11:2

HUSH—*silence* Acts 21:40, there was a great **h**

HYMN Matt. 26:30, singing a **h**, they went out
Eph. 5:19, in psalms and **h-s** and spiritual songs

HYPOCRISY Matt. 23:28, you are full of **h**
Rom. 12:9, Let love be without **h**
1 Tim. 4:2, means of the **h** of liars
James 3:17, wisdom from above ... without **h**

HYPOCRITE—*godless* Matt. 6:2, as the **h-s** do ... synagogues
Matt. 6:5, not to be as the **h-s**
6:16, gloomy face as the **h-s** *do*
7:5, You **h**, first take the log
22:18, Why are you testing Me, you **h-s**
23:13, scribes and Pharisees, **h-s**
Luke 12:56, You **h-s**! You know how to analyze

I

ICE—*frost* Job 37:10, breath of God **i** is made

IDLE Prov. 19:15, an **i** man will suffer hunger
Prov. 31:27, not eat the bread of **i-ness**
Matt. 20:6, Why have you been standing ... **i**
1 Tim. 5:13, not merely **i**, but also gossips

IDOL—*image* Ex. 20:4, make for yourself an **i**
Acts 15:20, abstain from ... **i-s**
1 Cor. 10:7, do not be **i-aters**
1 John 5:21, guard yourselves from **i-s**
Lev. 19:4; 26:1; Is. 66:3; Jer. 50:38

IGNORANCE—*unintentionally*
Acts 17:23, What ... worship in **i**
17:30, overlooked the times of **i**
Eph. 4:18, because of the **i** that is in them
1 Pet. 2:15, silence the **i** of foolish men

IGNORANT 2 Cor. 2:11, not **i** of his schemes
2 Tim. 2:23, refuse foolish and **i** speculations

ILLEGITIMATE Deut. 23:2; Heb. 12:8

ILLNESS—*infirmity* Gal. 4:13, a bodily **i**

ILLUMINE Ps. 18:28, God **i-s** my darkness

IMAGE—*likeness* Gen. 1:26, make man in Our **i**
Gen. 9:6, **i** of God He made man
1 Cor. 11:7, **i** and glory of God
Col. 1:15, **i** of the invisible God

IMAGINATION—*estimation*
Prov. 18:11, wall in his own **i**

IMITATE—*follow* 3 John 11, do not **i** what is evil

IMITATORS—*followers* Eph. 5:1, be **i** of God
1 Thess. 2:14, become **i** of the churches of God

IMMATURE—*babes, children*
Rom. 2:20, teacher of the **i**

IMMEDIATELY Matt. 3:16, went up **i** from the water
Matt. 4:20, **i** left the nets
21:2, **i** you will find a donkey tied
26:74, And **i** a cock crowed
Mark 4:15, **i** Satan comes
Luke 12:54, **i** you say, A shower is coming
14:5, **i** pull him out ... Sabbath
21:9, the end does not *follow* **i**
John 5:9, **i** the man became well
19:34, **i** there came out blood and water
Acts 9:18, **i** there fell from his eyes
9:20, **i** he began to proclaim Jesus
21:30, the doors were shut
Rev. 4:2, **i** I was in the Spirit
Matt. 13:21; 26:49; Mark 6:25; Luke 17:7; Acts 13:11

IMMORALITY—*fornication* Matt. 19:9, except for **i**
1 Cor. 6:18, Flee **i**
1 Thess. 4:3, abstain from sexual **i**
Rev. 2:20, they commit *acts of* **i**
17:2, the wine of her **i**

IMMORTALITY 1 Cor. 15:53, mortal ... put on **i**
1 Tim. 6:16, who alone possesses **i**
2 Tim. 1:10, brought life and **i**

IMPATIENT Num. 21:4, people became **i**

IMPEL—*drive* Mark 1:12, the Spirit **i-ed** Him

IMPERISHABLE 1 Cor. 9:25, perishable ... an **i**
1 Cor. 15:52, the dead will be raised **i**
1 Pet. 1:4, *obtain* an inheritance *which is* **i**

IMPETUOUS Hab. 1:6, Chaldeans, That fierce and **i** people

IMPLORE—*adjure* Job 8:5, **i** the compassion of the Almighty
Mark 5:7, I **i** you by God

IMPOSSIBLE Matt. 19:26, With men this is **i**
Luke 1:37, nothing will be **i** with God
Heb. 6:18, it is **i** for God to lie
11:6, without faith it is **i** to

IMPROPER 1 Cor. 14:35, **i** for a woman to speak

IMPROVISE Amos 6:5, Who **i** to the sound of the harp

IMPUTE—*reckon* Rom. 5:13, sin is not **i-d** when there is

INAUGURATED—*dedicated*
Heb. 9:18, first covenant ... not **i**
10:20, way which He **i** for us

INCITE Luke 23:14, one who **i-s** the people

INCLINE Josh. 24:23, **i** your hearts to the LORD
Ps. 119:36, **i** my heart to Thy
Is. 37:17, **I** Thine ear, O LORD

INCREASE—*multiply, produce* Job 31:12; Prov. 28:8
Ps. 62:10, riches **i**, do not set *your* heart
Eccles. 1:18, **i-ing** knowledge results in **i-ing** pain
Luke 2:52, **i-ing** in wisdom and stature
11:29, the crowds were **i-ing**
Col. 1:10, **i-ing** in the knowledge of God

INDEBTED Rom. 15:27, they are **i**

INDEED—*surely, truly* Gen. 3:1, **I**, has God said, You shall
Ex. 4:25, **i** a bridegroom of blood
Num. 14:21, but **i**, as I live
1 Kin. 8:27, God **i** dwell on the earth
2 Chr. 6:18, will God **i** dwell with mankind
John 8:36, you shall be free **i**
Rom. 14:20, All things **i** are clean
1 Tim. 5:5, she who is a widow, **i**

INDEPENDENT 1 Cor. 11:11, woman i of man . . . man i . . . woman

INDESTRUCTIBLE—*endless* Heb. 7:16, power of an i life

INDIGNANT Matt. 20:24; Luke 13:14

INDIGNATION—*anger* Jer. 15:17; Nah. 1:6
Ps. 7:11, God who has i every day
69:24, Pour out Thine i on them
Is. 30:27, lips are filled with i

INEXPERIENCED—*tender* 1 Chr. 22:5, My son . . . young and i

INFECTION—*plague* Lev. 13:2, becomes an i of leprosy

INFERIOR—*base* Is. 3:5, And the i against the honorable

INFIRMITIES—*sickness, weakness* Matt. 8:17, HIMSELF TOOK OUR I

INFLICT Job 5:18, He i-s pain, and gives relief

INFORM—*speak* Ruth 4:4; 2 Sam. 15:28; Ezra 4:16
Job 17:5, who i-s against friends

INHABITANTS Gen. 34:30; Num. 13:32; Ps. 49:1; Joel 2:1

INHABITED—*habitation* Ps. 107:7,36, an i city

INHERIT—*possess, possession* Ex. 32:13, they shall i it
Ps. 37:11, humble will i the land
Prov. 3:35, The wise will i honor
14:18, The naive i folly
Matt. 5:5, gentle . . . i the earth
19:29, shall i eternal life
25:34, i the kingdom prepared
Luke 10:25, do to i eternal life
1 Cor. 6:9, shall not i the kingdom
15:50, perishable i the imperishable
Rev. 21:7, who overcomes shall i these things

INHERITANCE—*possession* Judg. 11:2; Ps. 28:9
Ps. 2:8, give the nations as Thine i
94:14, Nor will He forsake His i
Jer. 3:19, most beautiful i of the nations
Mark 12:7, the i will be ours
Acts 7:5, He gave him no i
Eph. 1:11, also we have obtained an i
1 Pet. 1:4, an i which is imperishable
Prov. 13:22; Eccles. 7:11; Jer. 12:7,8,9,15; Joel 2:17; Mic. 2:2; Mal. 1:3

INIQUITY—*injustice* Lev. 16:22; Job 4:8; 13:26
Deut. 5:9, visiting the i of the fathers
Ps. 25:11, Pardon my i, for it is great
51:9, blot out all my i-es
Is. 53:5, He was crushed for our i-es
James 3:6, tongue is . . . world of i
Ps. 32:5; 51:5; 79:8; Prov. 22:8; Is. 1:4; 31:2; Jer. 31:30; Ezek. 18:30; 33:8

INJUNCTION—*decree* Dan. 6:7,8

INJURE—*wrong* Acts 7:26, why do you i one

INJUSTICE—*iniquity* Lev. 19:15, do no i
Deut. 32:4, A God of faithfulness without i

INNER—*inward* Matt. 6:6, GO INTO YOUR I ROOM
2 Cor. 4:16, i man is being renewed day by day

INNERMOST—*inward* Job 38:36, wisdom in the i being

INNKEEPER—*host* Luke 10:35, denarii . . . gave them to the i

INNOCENT—*blameless, righteous* Ex. 23:7
Is. 59:7, hasten to shed i blood
Matt. 27:4, have sinned by betraying i blood
27:24, I am i of this Man's blood
Luke 23:47, this man was i
Phil. 2:15, blameless and i, children of God
Heb. 7:26, holy, i, undefiled
2 Sam. 3:28; Job 4:7; 22:19; Prov. 6:17; Matt. 10:16; 12:5,7

INQUIRE—*ask* Judg. 18:5, I of God
Matt. 2:4, i of them where the Christ

INSANE—*mad* 1 Sam. 21:13, acted i-ly in their hands
John 10:20, has a demon, and is i

INSCRIBE Hab. 2:2, And i it on tablets

INSCRIPTION Dan. 5:8, could not read the i

INSECTS Ex. 8:21, I will send swarms of i on you

INSENSITIVE Is. 6:10, Render . . . this people i

INSIDE—*within* Gen. 9:21, uncovered himself i his tent
Matt. 23:26, Pharisee . . . clean the i of the cup
Acts 5:23, we found no one i
Rev. 5:1, throne a book written i

INSIGNIFICANT—*mean, small* 2 Sam. 7:19, i in Thine eyes
Job 8:7, your beginning was i
40:4, Behold, I am i; what can
Acts 21:39, citizen of no i city

INSOLENCE—*pride* 1 Sam. 17:28, I know your i

INSPIRE—*spiritual* Hos. 9:7, i-d man is demented

INSTANT—*moment* Num. 16:21, consume i-ly

INSTITUTION 1 Pet. 2:13, Submit . . . to every human i

INSTRUCT—*discipline* Neh. 9:20, Thy good Spirit to i
Ps. 32:8, I will i you and teach you
Matt. 10:5, twelve Jesus sent . . . i-ing them
Rom. 2:18, being i-ed out of the Law

INSTRUCTION—*admonition* Job 36:10, He opens . . . ear to i
Matt. 11:1, i-s to His twelve disciples
Rom. 15:4, was written for our i

1 Cor. 7:10, i-s, not I, but the Lord
10:11, written for our i
Eph. 6:4, discipline and of the Lord
1 Tim. 1:5, goal of our i is love
Heb. 6:2, of i about washing and laying on of hands

INSTRUMENT—*object, vessel* Acts 9:15, he is a chosen i
Rom. 6:13, as i-s of unrighteousness
2 Sam. 12:31; 1 Chr. 20:3; Ps. 150:4; Ezek. 33:32

INSULT—*reproach* Job 19:3, ten times you have i-ed me
Luke 6:22, heap i-s upon you

INTEGRITY—*upright* Gen. 20:5; Job 2:3; Prov. 19:1
Ps. 15:2, He who walks with i
26:1, have walked in my i
Prov. 10:9, who walks in i walks securely
20:7, righteous man who walks in his i

INTELLIGENT—*prudent* Matt. 11:25, hide . . . wise and i
Mark 12:34, Jesus saw that he had . . . i-ly

INTENSE 2 Pet. 3:10, destroyed with i heat

INTENT Gen. 8:21, i of man's heart is evil
Deut. 31:21, for I know their i
Acts 1:10, gazing i-ly into the sky

INTERCEDE 1 Sam. 2:25, who can i
Is. 53:12, i-d for the transgressors
Rom. 8:26, the Spirit Himself i-s for us

INTERCESSION—*petition* Heb. 7:25, always lives to make i

INTEREST—*usury* Ex. 22:25, not charge him i
Deut. 23:20, You may charge i to a foreigner
Ps. 15:5, not put out his money at i
Matt. 25:27, my money back with i
Luke 19:23, collected it with i

INTERMARRY Ezra 9:14, and i with the peoples

INTERPRET—*understand* Gen. 41:8, dreams . . . no one who could i them
1 Cor. 12:10, the i-ation of tongues
14:27, and let one i
2 Pet. 1:20, a matter of one's own i-ation

INTIMATE—*close* Job 19:14, my i friends have forgotten
Prov. 17:9, matter separates i friends

INTRODUCTION Rom. 5:2, obtained our i by faith

INVALIDATE Matt. 15:6, you i-d the word of God
Mark 7:13, thus i-ing the word of God

INVESTIGATE—*examine* Ezra 10:16, convened . . . to i

INVESTIGATION Acts 25:26, after the i has taken place

INVOLVE—*exercise* Ps. 131:1, Nor do I i myself

INWARD—*within* Matt. 7:15, **i-ly** are wolves

IRON 2 Kin. 6:6, and made the i float
Job 19:24, with an i stylus and lead
Ps. 2:9, break them with a rod of i
1 Tim. 4:2, seared . . . as with a branding i
Gen. 4:22; Deut. 3:11; 8:9; 33:25; Judg. 1:19; Job 40:18; Prov. 27:17; Jer. 11:4

IRREVERENCE
2 Sam. 6:7, struck him down . . . for his i

IRRITATE—*fret* 1 Sam. 1:6, provoke . . . to i her

IVORY 1 Kin. 10:18; Song 7:4; Amos 6:4

J

JACKAL Job 30:29, a brother to **j-s**
Jer. 9:11, Jerusalem . . . haunt of **j-s**

JAR—*jug, pitcher, vessel* 1 Kin. 17:10, water in j
John 19:29, A j full of sour wine
Gen. 24:14; 1 Kin. 14:3; 19:6; 2 Kin. 2:20

JAVELIN—*spear* Josh. 8:18, Stretch out the j
Job 41:29, at the rattling of the j

JEALOUS—*envy, zealous*
Ex. 20:5, LORD your God, am a j God
1 Cor. 13:4, love is kind, *and* is not j
Gen. 30:1; 37:11; Ex. 34:14; Num. 11:29; 25:11; Josh. 24:19; Is. 11:13; Ezek. 31:9; Nah. 1:2; Acts 7:9; 17:5; Rom. 10:19; 2 Cor. 11:2

JEALOUSY—*envy, jealous* Num. 5:14; Prov. 6:34
Rom. 13:13, not in strife and j
1 Cor. 3:3, since there is j . . . among you
2 Cor. 12:20, *there may be* strife, j
James 3:14, if you have bitter j
3:16, where j and selfish ambition exist
Prov. 27:4; Song 8:6; Acts 13:45; Rom. 11:14; Gal. 5:20

JEOPARDIZE Ruth 4:6, j my own inheritance

JEWEL—*pearl* Prov. 3:15, more precious than **j-s**
Prov. 31:10, her worth is far above **j-s**

JOIN—*couple* Ex. 23:1; 26:6; Is. 5:8
Matt. 19:6, What . . . God has **j-ed** together
1 Cor. 6:17, one who **j-s** himself to the Lord

JOINT—*dislocate* Ps. 22:14, bones are out of j

JOURNEY—*walk, way*
Ezra 8:21, seek from Him a safe j
Mark 13:34, like a man, away on a j
Luke 9:3, Take nothing for your j
13:33, must j on today and tomorrow

15:13, a j into a distant country
Acts 9:3, **j-ed**, he was approaching Damascus
2 Cor. 11:26, I have been on frequent **j-s**
Gen. 33:12; Josh. 9:11; Neh. 2:6; Matt. 10:10; Acts 1:12

JOY Prov. 17:21, father of a fool has no j
Matt. 2:10, with great j
25:21, enter into the j of your master
Luke 15:7, j in heaven over one sinner
John 15:11, My j may be in you
Rom. 14:17, and j in the Holy Spirit
Gal. 5:22, fruit of the Spirit is love, j
Phil. 2:2, make my j complete
James 1:2, Consider it all j . . . encounter . . .
1 John 1:4, our j may be made complete
1 Chr. 15:16; Ezra 3:12; Job 29:13; 33:26

JOYFUL—*merry* Ps. 21:6; 66:1; Is. 52:9
Ps. 126:5, sow in tears . . . reap with j shouting
Prov. 17:22, j heart is good medicine

JUDGE Gen. 18:25, the J of all the earth
Matt. 7:1, not j lest you be **j-d**
John 3:17, God did not send the Son . . . to j
7:24, but j with righteous judgment
7:51, Our Law does not j a man
12:47, not come to j the world
Acts 10:42, J of the living and the dead
2 Thess. 2:12, all may be **j-d** who did not believe
Heb. 4:12, word of God . . . able to j the thoughts
12:23, God the J of all
13:4, adulterers God will j
Gen. 16:5; Matt. 7:2

JUDGMENT—*justice, sentence*
Ps. 1:5, wicked will not stand in the j
19:9, **j-s** of the LORD are true
Matt. 10:15, Gomorrah in the day of j
11:24, Sodom in *the* day of j
27:19, he was sitting on the **j**-seat
John 3:19, this is the j, that the light is
5:29, resurrection of j
5:30, judge; and My j is just
1 Cor. 11:29, eats and drinks j to himself
Heb. 9:27, after this *comes* j
10:27, terrifying expectation of j
James 3:1, shall incur a stricter j
5:12, may not fall under j
2 Pet. 3:7, kept for the day of j
1 John 4:17, confidence in the day of j
Jude 15, to execute j upon all
Rev. 18:20, God has pronounced j for you
19:2, HIS **J-S** ARE TRUE AND RIGHTEOUS
Ex. 12:12; Lev. 18:4; Deut. 1:17; Ezra 7:26; Ps. 112:5; 2 Pet. 2:11; Jude 9

JUG—*bottle, wineskin* 1 Sam. 1:24; 10:3; 16:20; 25:18; 26:16; 2 Sam. 16:1

JUST—*right* Job 25:4, can a man be j with God
John 5:30, My judgment is j
Heb. 2:2, received a j recompense
1 Pet. 3:18, Christ also died . . . *the* j for *the* **un-j**
Lev. 19:36; Ps. 17:1; Luke 23:41

JUSTICE—*right, righteousness*
Job 8:3, Does God pervert j
Ps. 89:14, Righteousness and j are the
Prov. 28:5, Evil men do not understand j
Amos 5:24, let j roll down like waters
Mic. 6:8, to do j, to love kindness
Gen. 18:19; Deut. 16:19; Job 8:3; 36:6; Prov. 21:3; Is. 59:14; Jer. 10:24

JUSTIFY—*clear, vindicate* Gen. 44:16; Ps. 51:4
Luke 10:29, wishing to j himself
Rom. 8:33, God is the one who **j-es**

K

KEEP—*hold, guide, preserve* Gen. 18:19
Ex. 20:6, love Me and k My commandments
20:8, sabbath day, to k it holy
Num. 6:24, Lord bless you, and k you
Ps. 17:8, **K** me as the apple of the eye
34:13, **K** your tongue from evil
Matt. 19:17, enter into life, k the commandments
Luke 3:8, fruits in **k**-ing with your repentance
John 8:51, if anyone **k-s** My word
12:25, shall k it to life eternal
14:23, If anyone loves Me, he will k My word
17:15, k them from the evil *one*
1 Tim. 1:19, **k-ing** faith and a good conscience
5:14, bear children, k house
5:22, k yourself free from sin
James 1:27, k oneself unstained by the world
Jude 21, k yourselves in the love of God
Lev. 23:32; Prov. 1:15; Eccles. 3:6; Matt. 26:18; 1 Cor. 14:28; 1 Tim. 6:12

KEEPER—*guard* Gen. 4:9, Am I my brother's k
Ps. 121:5, The LORD is your k

KEPT—*observed* Gen. 37:11, his father k the saying
Mark 10:20, Teacher I have k all these things
Jude 6, He has k in eternal bonds

KERNEL—*grain* Amos 9:9, not a k will fall to the ground

KEY Matt. 16:19, **k-s** of the kingdom of heaven
Luke 11:52, taken away the k of knowledge
Rev. 1:18, I have the **k-s** of death and of Hades
9:1, k of the bottomless pit

KIDNAP—*steal* Deut. 24:7, man is caught **k-ing**

KIDNEY Job 16:13, splits my **k**-s open

KILL 1 Sam. 17:50, Philistine and **k-ed** him
Matt. 10:28, **k** the body . . . unable to **k** the soul
Luke 9:22, **k-ed**, and be raised up . . . third day
15:23, bring the fattened calf, **k** it
John 5:18, Jews were seeking . . . to **k** Him
7:19, Why do you seek to **k** Me
10:10, comes only to steal, and **k**
Acts 11:7, Arise, Peter; **k** and eat
2 Cor. 3:6, the letter **k**-s . . . Spirit gives life
Gen. 4:8,14,23; Ex. 13:15; 21:14; Num. 31:8; 2 Kin. 5:7; Job 5:2; Ps. 10:8; Acts 10:13; 1 Tim. 1:9

KIND—*gentle, gracious* Matt. 5:11, say all **k**-s of evil
1 Cor. 13:4, Love is patient, love is **k**
Eph. 4:32, be **k** to one another
2 Tim. 2:24, but be **k** to all
Gen. 1:11; 6:19; 2 Chr. 10:7

KINDLE—*burn* Ex. 35:3; Prov. 26:21; Is. 50:11

KINDNESS—*goodness, loyalty* Ruth 3:10, your last **k** to be
Prov. 31:26, teaching of **k** is on her tongue
Acts 24:4, grant us, by your **k**
Rom. 11:22, **k** and severity of God
2 Cor. 6:6, in patience, in **k**, in the Holy Spirit
Col. 3:12, put on a heart of compassion, **k**
1 Pet. 2:3, tasted the **k** of the Lord
2 Pet. 1:7, *your* godliness, brotherly **k**

KING 1 Sam. 8:5, appoint a **k** for us to judge us
1 Sam. 10:24, Long live the **k**
Ps. 5:2, my **K** and my God
24:8, Who is the **K** of glory
Jer. 10:7, fear Thee, O **K** of the nations
Matt. 2:2, who has been born **K** of the Jews
2:9, having heard the **k**
10:18, brought before governors and **k**-s for My sake
21:5, BEHOLD YOUR **K** IS COMING TO YOU
27:11, Are You the **K** of the Jews
Luke 23:2, that He Himself is Christ, a **K**
John 12:15, YOUR **K** COMES SITTING ON A . . . COLT
1 Tim. 6:15, **K** of kings and Lord of lords
1 Pet. 2:17, fear God, honor the **k**
Judg. 9:8; 17:6; Job 18:14; Prov. 8:15; 22:29; Eccles. 10:20; Is. 43:15

KINGDOM—*dominion* Ps. 22:28, For the **k** is the LORD's
Ps. 145:13, Thy **k** is an everlasting **k**
Matt. 3:2, the **k** of heaven is at hand
4:23, the gospel of the **k**
6:10, Thy **k** come, Thy will be done
13:38, these are the sons of the **k**
16:19, give you the keys of the **k**
19:14, **k** of heaven belongs to such as these
26:29, in My Father's **k**
Mark 10:24, hard it is to enter the **k** of God

12:34, not far from the **k** of God
Luke 6:20, for yours is the **k** of God
12:32, to give you the **k**
22:29, as My Father has granted me a **k**
John 3:3, he cannot see the **k** of God
18:36, My **k** is not of this world
Rom. 14:17, the **k** of God is not eating and drinking
Col. 1:13, to the **k** of His beloved Son
2 Tim. 4:18, bring me safely to His heavenly **k**
James 2:5, heirs of the **k** which He promised
Ex. 19:6; Esth. 1:20; Obad. 21

KISS Matt. 26:48, Whomever I shall **k**
Luke 7:45, has not ceased to **k** My feet
15:20, embraced him and **k**-ed him
22:48, betraying the Son of Man with a **k**
Rom. 16:16, Greet one another with a holy **k**
1 Pet. 5:14, Greet one another with a **k** of love
Gen. 29:11; 2 Sam. 20:9; Song 1:2

KNEE Gen. 41:43, Bow the **k**
Rom. 14:11, EVERY **K** SHALL BOW TO ME
Phil. 2:10, at the name of Jesus every **k** should bow
Heb. 12:12, strengthen . . . the **k**-s that are feeble

KNEEL Gen. 24:11, made the camels **k** down
Ps. 95:6, Let us **k** before the LORD
Matt. 27:29, they **k**-ed down before Him
Luke 22:41, He **k**-t down and *began* to pray

KNEW Jer. 1:5, Before I formed you . . . I **k** you
Matt. 7:23, I will declare . . . I never **k** you
Luke 6:8, But He **k** what they were thinking
John 4:10, If you **k** the gift of God
2 Cor. 5:21, made Him who **k** no sin *to be* sin

KNIFE—*sword* Prov. 30:14, jaw teeth *like* **k**-s

KNOCK—*smite* Nah. 2:10, knees **k-ing**
Matt. 7:7, **k** and it shall be opened
Luke 13:25, stand outside and **k** on the door
Acts 12:13, when he **k**-ed at the door
Rev. 3:20, I stand at the door and **k**

KNOW—*discern, recognize, understand*
Ex. 1:8, new king . . . who did not **k** Joseph
Deut. 4:9, **k-n** to your sons and your grandsons
Job 19:25, I **k** that my Redeemer lives
Ps. 1:6, the LORD **k**-s the way of the righteous
46:10, **k** that I am God
56:9, This I **k**, that God is for me
Prov. 27:1, do not **k** what a day may bring
Eccles. 8:5, wise heart **k**-s the proper time

Is. 59:8, They do not **k** the way of peace
Matt. 6:3, left hand **k** what your right hand
7:11, **k** how to give good gifts
7:20, you will **k** them by their fruits
25:12, I do not **k** you
Luke 10:22, no one **k**-s who the Son is
19:42, If you had **k-n** in this day
22:57, Woman, I do not **k** Him
John 8:32, you shall **k** the truth
10:14, I **k** My own, and My own **k** Me
14:7, If you had **k-n** Me . . . **k-n** My Father
21:17, You **k** all things; You **k** that I love You
Acts 1:7, not for you to **k** the times
1 Cor. 1:21, did not *come to* **k** God
13:2, and **k** all mysteries
13:9, we **k** in part and we prophesy
13:12, **k** in part, but then I shall **k** fully
2 Cor. 12:2, **k** a man in Christ . . . caught up
Eph. 3:19, to **k** the love of Christ
2 Tim. 3:15, **k-n** the sacred writings
1 John 3:2, We **k** that, if He should appear
3 John 12, you **k** that our witness is true
Rev. 2:2, I **k** your deeds
19:12, name written . . . no one **k**-s except Himself
Gen. 3:22; 28:16; Deut. 29:4; 1 Sam. 3:7; Job 13:18; Ps. 81:5; Eccles. 9:5; Is. 7:15; Hos. 6:3; Jon. 4:11; Matt. 9:30; 12:33; Mark 1:24; 13:33; Acts 19:15

KNOWLEDGE Gen. 2:9, tree of the **k** of good and evil
Ps. 19:2, night to night reveals **k**
139:6, *Such* **k** is too wonderful for me
Prov. 1:7, fear of the LORD the beginning of **k**
10:14, Wise men store up **k**
17:27, who restrains his words has **k**
Is. 11:9, full of the **k** of the LORD
Acts 24:22, more exact **k** about the Way
Rom. 10:2, but not in accordance with **k**
11:33, wisdom and **k** of God
1 Cor. 8:1, **K** makes arrogant, but love edifies
13:8, if *there is* **k**, it will be done away
15:34, some have no **k** of God
Eph. 3:19, love of Christ which surpasses **k**
Col. 2:3, treasures of wisdom and **k**
1 Tim. 2:4, come to the **k** of the truth
2 Pet. 1:5, in *your* moral excellence, **k** 1:6, in *your* **k**, self-control
3:18, grow in the grace and **k** of our LORD
Deut. 1:39; 1 Sam. 2:3; 2 Chr. 1:10; Job 10:7; 21:22; Eccles. 1:18; Is. 28:9; Hos. 4:6; Luke 11:52

L

LABOR—*fruit, toil, tribute, weary*
Ex. 20:9, Six days you shall **l**
Ps. 127:1, They **l** in vain who build it
Prov. 14:23, In all **l** there is profit
Eccles. 2:22, what does a man get in all his **l**

LABOR (Continued)
Is. 42:14, like a woman in l I will groan
1 Cor. 15:10, I l-ed even more than all of them
Gal. 4:11, perhaps I have l-ed over you in vain
4:19, again in l until Christ
Eph. 4:28, rather let him l, performing
Phil. 1:22, this will mean fruitful l
1 Thess. 1:3, work of faith and l of love
2 Thess. 3:8, with l and hardship we kept
Rev. 12:2, cried out, being in l and in pain
Gen. 49:15; Job 7:1; Ps. 78:46; Prov. 12:24; Eccles. 4:9; 2 Cor. 11:27

LABORER 1 Kin. 9:21, Solomon . . . forced l-s

LACK—need, void, want Deut. 28:48, in the l of all things
Deut. 32:28, a nation l-ing in counsel
Judg. 18:10, place where there is no l
Prov. 7:7, young man l-ing sense
10:21, fools die for l of understanding
Is. 34:16, None will l its mate
Matt. 19:20, what am I still l-ing
Mark 10:21, One thing you l
James 1:4, l-ing in nothing
1:5, if any of you l-s wisdom
Deut. 8:9; 1 Kin. 8:25; Prov. 6:32; Eccles. 10:3

LADY 2 John 1, to the chosen l

LAGGING Rom. 12:11, not l behind in diligence

LAID Mark 6:5, He l His hands upon a few sick
Luke 12:19, many goods l up for many years
John 11:34, Where have you l him
2 Tim. 4:8, l up for me the crown of righteousness
1 John 3:16, He l down His life for us
1 Kin. 17:19; Job 6:2; 38:6

LAIR Job 38:40, lie in wait in their l

LAMB Gen. 22:8, God will provide . . . the l
Is. 40:11, In His arm He will gather the l-s
53:7, Like a l that is led to slaughter
65:25, wolf and the l shall graze together
Hos. 4:16, Like a l in a large field
Luke 10:3, send you out as l-s
John 1:29, Behold the L of God
21:15, Tend My l-s
Acts 8:32, AS A L BEFORE ITS SHEARER IS SILENT
1 Pet. 1:19, a l unblemished and spotless

LAME Job 29:15, feet to the l
Matt. 11:5, and the l walk
Mark 9:45, better for you to enter life l
2 Sam. 9:13; Zeph. 3:19; Matt. 15:31; Acts 14:8

LAMENT—mourn Luke 8:52; 23:27; Rev. 18:9

LAMP—light Ps. 18:28, Thou dost light my l

Ps. 119:105, Thy word is a l to my feet
Matt. 5:15, light a l, and put it under
6:22, l of the body is the eye
25:8, our l-s are going out
Rev. 22:5, light of l nor . . . of sun
1 Sam. 3:3; 2 Sam. 22:29; Job 18:6; Prov. 20:27; Zeph. 1:12; Rev. 4:5

LAMPSTAND Ex. 25:31; 1 Kin. 7:49; 2 Kin. 4:10; Luke 8:16

LAND—country, earth, ground Gen. 1:9, let the dry l appear
Deut. 6:3, l flowing with milk and honey
Ps. 37:29, righteous will inherit the l
88:12, in the l of forgetfulness
Is. 66:8, Can a l be born in one day
Jer. 22:29, O l, l, l, Hear the word of the LORD
Matt. 2:6, AND YOU, BETHLEHEM, L OF JUDAH
27:45, darkness fell upon all the l
Luke 14:18, have bought a piece of l
23:44, darkness fell over the whole l
Heb. 11:29, Red Sea as . . . through dry l
Gen. 15:18; Ex. 1:7; Deut. 8:8; 1 Sam. 6:5; Job 28:13; Ps. 25:13; 37:9,11,22; 60:2; Prov. 25:25; Eccles. 5:9; Is. 2:7; Jer. 15:10; Ezek. 9:9; Mic. 7:2; Mal. 4:6; Acts 4:37

LANGUAGE—word, voice Gen. 10:5, one according to his l
11:1, whole earth used the same l
Ezek. 3:5,6, unintelligible speech or difficult l
Acts 2:6, hearing them speak in his own l
1 Cor. 14:10, many kinds of l-s

LANGUISH—faint Ps. 119:81, My soul l-es for Thy salvation

LAPIS LAZULI—sapphire Ezek. 28:13, The l, the turquoise

LARGE—vast Ps. 31:8; Matt. 28:12; Luke 22:12; Gal. 6:11

LASHES Luke 12:47, shall receive many l

LAST—utmost Ps. 30:5, weeping may l for the night
Is. 44:6, I am the first and I am the l
Matt. 5:26, have paid up the l cent
12:45, the l state of that man
19:30, first will be l; and the l, first
John 6:39, raise it up on the l day
1 Cor. 15:45, The l Adam became a life-giving spirit
15:52, at the l trumpet
1 Pet. 1:5, revealed in the l time
Rev. 1:17, I am the first and the l
Is. 7:9; Luke 11:26

LATER—afterward John 13:36, you shall follow l

LATTICE—window Is. 60:8, like the doves to their l-s

LAUGH—mock Gen. 18:13, Why did Sarah l
Job 8:21, fill your mouth with l-ter
Prov. 14:13, Even in l-ter the heart . . . in pain
Eccles. 3:4, time to weep, and a time to l

Matt. 9:24, they were l-ing at Him
Luke 6:25, Woe to you who l now
James 4:9, let your l-ter be turned

LAUGHINGSTOCK—derision Jer. 20:7, a l all day long

LAUNDERER—fuller Mark 9:3, no l . . . can whiten them

LAW—teaching Ps. 19:7, l of the LORD is perfect
Prov. 29:18, happy is he who keeps the l
Matt. 5:17, came to abolish the L
7:12, this is the L and the Prophets
12:2, disciples do what is not l-ful
12:4, bread . . . not l-ful for him to eat
John 7:51, Our L does not judge a man
Rom. 13:10, love . . . fulfillment of the l
Gal. 3:24, L has become our tutor
5:23, against such things there is no l
6:2, thus fulfill the l of Christ
Heb. 7:19, L made nothing perfect
James 1:25, the perfect l, the l of liberty
Ex. 12:49; Josh. 1:8; 2 Kin. 22:8; Prov. 28:7; John 19:7; Rom. 2:14; 4:15; 1 Cor. 6:2,7; Titus 3:9

LAWLESS—wicked 2 Thess. 2:8, l one will be revealed

LAWLESSNESS—iniquity Matt. 24:12, because l is increased
2 Cor. 6:14, righteousness and l
1 John 3:4, and sin is l

LAY Ps. 3:5, I l down and slept
Matt. 6:19, Do not l up for yourselves treasures
John 10:11, good shepherd l-s down His life
10:15, I l down My life for the sheep
Rom. 13:12, l aside the deeds of darkness

LAZY—idle, slothful Ex. 5:8,17
Matt. 25:26, You wicked, l slave
Titus 1:12, evil beasts, l gluttons

LEAD—guide 2 Chr. 23:13; Ps. 25:9; 27:11; Is. 40:11
Ex. 13:21, cloud by day to l them on the way
Ps. 23:2, He l-s me beside quiet waters
25:5, L me in Thy truth
Is. 11:6, a little boy will l them
Matt. 6:13, do not l us into temptation
John 10:3, calls his own sheep . . . l-s them out
1 Tim. 2:2, may l a tranquil and quiet life

LEADER—first, head Num. 16:2; Luke 22:26
Matt. 2:6, AMONG THE L-S OF JUDAH

LEAK—drop Eccles. 10:18, the house l-s

LEARN—instruction Deut. 31:13; Is. 1:17
Prov. 1:5, wise man will . . . increase in l-ing
Is. 2:4, never again will they l war

Matt. 11:29, l from Me
Acts 26:24, great l-ing is driving you
mad
Eph. 4:20, you did not l Christ
2 Tim. 3:7, always l-ing
Heb. 5:8, He l-ed obedience

LEAST—*young* 2 Kin. 18:24, l of my
master's servants
Matt. 2:6, NO MEANS L AMONG THE
LEADERS
5:19, called l in the kingdom of
heaven
11:11, he who is l . . . is greater
1 Cor. 15:9, I am the l of the apostles
Eph. 3:8, To me, the very l of all
saints

LEATHER—*skin* Matt. 3:4, John . . .
l belt about his waist
Mark 1:6, *wore* a l belt around his
waist

LEAVE—*abandon, desert, forsake*
Ex. 20:7; Job 9:27
Gen. 2:24, man shall l his father . . .
mother
Ruth 1:16, Do not urge me to l you
Ps. 49:10, l their wealth to others
Matt. 18:12, does he not l the ninety-
nine
19:5, MAN SHALL L HIS FATHER AND
MOTHER
John 14:27, Peace I l with you
16:28, I am l-ing the world again
Prov. 2:17; 3:3

LEAVEN Ex. 12:19; Lev. 6:17
Matt. 13:33, kingdom of heaven is
like l
16:6, beware of the l of the
Pharisees
Luke 13:21, It is like l
1 Cor. 5:6, a little l l-s the whole
lump
5:7, Clean out the old l

LEFT—*remain* Matt. 19:27, l
everything and followed You
Matt. 26:56, disciples l Him and fled
Mark 1:18, l the nets and followed
Him
Luke 5:11, l everything and followed
Him
Heb. 11:27, By faith he l Egypt
Gen. 7:23; Matt. 14:20

LEND—*loan* Deut. 15:6; Neh. 5:10;
Luke 11:5
Prov. 22:7, borrower *becomes* the l-
er's slave
Luke 6:34, Even sinners l to sinners

LENGTH—*long* Prov. 3:2; Ezek.
31:7; Eph. 3:18

LENGTHEN Matt. 23:5, l the tassels
of *their* garments

LEOPARD Jer. 13:23, Or the l his
spots
Rev. 13:2, beast . . . was like a l
Is. 11:6; Hos. 13:7

LEPER Matt. 10:8, cleanse *the* l-s
Matt. 11:5, *the* l-s are cleansed
Lev. 13:51; 2 Chr. 26:21; Matt. 8:2;
Mark 14:3

LEPROUS Lev. 13:51, the mark is a l
malignancy

LESS Gen. 1:16, l-er light to govern
the night
Is. 40:17, regarded by Him as l than
nothing
2 Cor. 12:15, am I to be loved the l

LET—*suffer* Matt. 19:14, L the
children alone, and

LETTER 2 Cor. 3:2, You are our l
2 Cor. 3:3, you are a l of Christ
2 Pet. 3:16, as also in all *his* l-s
2 Chr. 2:11; Acts 15:30; Rom. 16:22;
2 Cor. 7:8; Col. 4:16; 2 Thess. 2:15;
3:14

LEVEL—*plain* Ps. 27:11, lead me in
a l path
Luke 19:44, will l you to the ground

LEVY—*collection* 2 Chr. 24:6, the l
fixed by Moses

LIAR Job 24:25; John 8:55
Rom. 3:4, every man . . . a l
1 Tim. 4:2, by means of the
hypocrisy of l-s
1 John 5:10, God has made Him a l

LIBATION—*drink* Gen. 35:14,
poured out a l

LIBERTY Ps. 119:45, I will walk at l
Is. 61:1, proclaim l to the captives
2 Cor. 3:17, where the Spirit . . . is,
there is l
Gal. 2:4, to spy out our l
James 1:25, perfect law, the *law* of l

LICK 1 Kin. 21:19; Ps. 72:9; Luke
16:21

LIE—*guile, lay, sleep, vain* Deut.
19:11; 31:16
Ps. 4:8, In peace I will both l down
23:2, makes me l down in green
pastures
Rom. 1:25, exchanged the truth of
God for a l
Col. 3:9, Do not l to one another
Heb. 6:18, impossible for God to l
Rev. 14:5, no l was found in their
mouth
Job 7:21; 34:6; 40:21; Ps. 119:69;
Eccles. 4:11; Song 1:7; Jer. 8:8;
Acts 5:3

LIFE—*flesh, living, soul* Ex. 21:23;
Deut. 30:19
Gen. 2:7, into his nostrils the breath
of l
Ps. 16:11, make known to me the
path of l
36:9, with Thee is the fountain of l
89:47, Remember what my span of l
is
133:3, LORD commanded . . . l
forever
Prov. 3:16, Long l is in her right
hand
8:35, he who finds me finds l
Matt. 6:25, do not be anxious for
your l
6:27, cubit to his l-'s span
10:39, who has lost his l for My
sake
16:25, whoever wishes to save his l
19:16, that I may obtain eternal l
20:28, give His l a ransom for many
Mark 8:35, wishes to save his l shall
lose it
10:17, shall I do to inherit eternal l
13:20, no l would have been saved

Luke 12:23, l is more than food
18:30, in the age to come, eternal l
John 4:36, gathering fruit for l
eternal
5:21, Son also gives l to whom He
wishes
5:24, passed out of death into l
6:35, I am the bread of l
10:11, shepherd lays down His l
11:25, I am the resurrection and
the l
12:25, who loves his l loses it
14:6, the way, the truth, and the l
15:13, lay down his l for his friends
17:3, this is eternal l
20:31, you may have l in His name
Acts 3:15, put to death the Prince
of l
Rom. 6:4, walk in newness of l
6:23, gift of God is eternal l
8:11, give l to your mortal bodies
2 Cor. 3:6, but the Spirit gives l
Gal. 6:8, from the Spirit reap
eternal l
Phil. 2:16, holding fast the word of l
4:3, names are in the book of l
Col. 3:4, Christ, who is our l
1 Tim. 2:2, a tranquil and quiet l
Titus 3:7, hope of eternal l
James 1:12, receive the crown of l
1 John 1:1, concerning the Word
of l
5:12, who has the Son has l
Rev. 2:10, give you the crown of l
13:8, not been written . . . book of l
of the Lamb
Deut. 32:39; Josh. 2:14; 1 Sam. 25:29;
Job 10:1; Ps. 22:20; 35:17;
Prov. 4:13,23; Jer. 21:8; 31:12;
38:16; Ezek. 18:27; Dan. 12:2;
Luke 12:15; 15:24; Titus 3:3;
Rev. 7:17

LIFT—*exalt, set, take* Num. 6:26,
LORD l up . . . countenance
Ps. 3:3, the One who l-s my head
24:7, L up your heads, O gates
116:13, l up the cup of salvation
121:1, l up my eyes to the
mountains
Is. 2:4, Nation will not l up sword
John 3:14, Moses l-ed up the serpent
Acts 1:9, He was l-ed up
Gen. 13:14; Ex. 14:16; Job 38:34; Ps.
134:2; Is. 5:26; 11:12; 13:2; 40:4;
Luke 18:13

LIGHT—*dawn, lamp* Ex. 10:23; Job
18:5; 38:19
Gen. 1:3, Let there be l; and there
was l
Ps. 4:6, l of Thy countenance upon
us
27:1, my l and my salvation
119:105, a l to my path
Is. 2:5, let us walk in the l of the
LORD
60:1, Arise, shine; for your l has
come
Matt. 5:14, You are the l of the
world
5:15, Nor do men l a lamp
6:22, whole body will be full of l
11:30, My load is l
Luke 2:32, l OF REVELATION TO THE
GENTILES
16:8, more shrewd . . . than the sons
of l
John 1:7, bear witness of the l
1:9, There was the true l
8:12, I am the l of the world
12:35, Walk while you have the l

LIGHT (Continued)
1 Cor. 4:5, bring to l the things hidden
2 Cor. 4:4, l of the gospel of glory
Eph. 5:8, walk as the children of l
1 John 1:7, if we walk in the l as He
Prov. 4:18; Eccles. 11:7; Is. 5:20; Jer. 31:35; Mic. 7:9; Matt. 10:27

LIKE—desire Luke 20:36,46

LIKENESS—image Ex. 20:4; Deut. 4:16; Matt. 22:20
Gen. 1:26, in Our image, according to Our l
Rom. 8:3, in the l of sinful flesh
Phil. 2:7, made in the l of men

LILY Song 2:1, l of the valleys
Hos. 14:5, He will blossom like the l
Matt. 6:28, Observe how the l-es of the field

LIMIT—short Num. 11:23, LORD's power l-ed
Job 15:8, l wisdom to yourself

LINE Joel 2:7, they each march in l

LINEN Gen. 41:42; Prov. 31:24; Jer. 13:1; Mark 15:46; John 20:5; Rev. 19:14

LINGER 2 Sam. 1:9; Prov. 23:30

LINTEL Ex. 12:7, on the l of the houses

LION 1 Pet. 5:8, devil, prowls about like a roaring l
Gen. 49:9; 1 Sam. 17:34; 1 Chr. 11:22; Job 10:16; Ps. 7:2; 57:4; Prov. 28:1; Eccles. 9:4; Rev. 9:8

LISTEN—hear Mark 4:3, L to this . . . sower
Mark 4:24, Take care what you l to
John 6:60, who can l to it
Eph. 1:13, l-ing to the message of truth
Gen. 4:23; Ex. 18:19; 20:19; Deut. 4:30; 11:27; Job 13:17; 35:13; 37:14; Prov. 23:22; 25:12; Eccles. 5:1; Dan. 9:19; Amos 5:23

LIT—enlighten Ps. 97:4, His lightnings l up the world

LITTLE—small Ps. 8:5, a l lower than God
Ps. 37:16, Better is the l of the righteous
Prov. 6:10, l sleep, a l slumber, A l folding
15:16, a l with the fear of the LORD
16:8, Better is a l with righteousness
Is. 11:6, a l boy will lead them
Matt. 6:30, O men of l faith
Luke 7:47, he who is forgiven l, loves l
12:32, Do not be afraid, l flock
John 7:33, For a l while longer I am with you
1 Cor. 5:6, a l leaven leavens the whole lump
Heb. 2:7, FOR A L WHILE LOWER THAN THE
Gen. 18:4; Judg. 4:19; 1 Sam. 2:19; Eccles. 5:12; Song 2:15; Is. 28:10

LIVE—abide, reside, stay Gen. 3:22; 42:18; Deut. 4:26

Deut. 8:3, man does not l by bread alone
Job 19:25, my Redeemer l-s
Prov. 21:9, better to l in a corner of a roof
Hab. 2:4, righteous will l by his faith
Matt. 4:4, MAN SHALL NOT L ON BREAD ALONE
Mark 12:44, put in . . . all she had to l on
Luke 10:28, DO THIS, AND YOU WILL L
20:38, for all l to Him
John 11:25, who believes in Me shall l even if he dies
Rom. 1:17, RIGHTEOUS man SHALL L BY FAITH
8:12, to l according to the flesh
14:8, if we l, we l for the Lord
14:9, Christ died and l-d again
2 Cor. 5:15, no longer l for themselves
Gal. 2:20, no longer l who l, but Christ l-s in me
Phil. 1:21, to me, to l is Christ
James 4:15, If the Lord wills, we shall l
Job 7:16; Ps. 119:175; Is. 55:3; Jer. 49:18; Ezek. 5:11; Matt. 12:45

LIVING Gen. 2:7, man became a l being
1 Kin. 3:25, Divide the l child in two
Matt. 16:16, Son of the l God
John 4:10, He would have given you l water
6:51, I am the l bread
7:38, rivers of l water
Acts 10:42, Judge of the l and the dead
Rom. 12:1, your bodies a l . . . sacrifice
1 Cor. 15:45, Adam, BECAME A L SOUL
2 Cor. 6:16, temple of the l God
Heb. 4:12, word of God is l
Num. 16:48; Deut. 5:26; Job 28:13; Eccles. 7:2; Dan. 6:26; 2 Pet. 2:8

LOAD—burden Matt. 11:30, My l is light
Matt. 23:4, they tie up heavy l-s

LOAN—lend
Deut. 23:19, or anything that may be l-ed

LOATHE Ps. 95:10; Amos 6:8

LOATHSOME Gen. 46:34, every shepherd is l to . . . Egyptians
Job 6:7, are like l food to me

LOAVES 1 Sam. 10:3, carrying three l of bread
Matt. 14:17, five l and two fish
Mark 6:52, the incident of the l

LOBE Ex. 29:13; Lev. 3:4,10,15

LOCK—shut Deut. 33:25; Judg. 16:13; Ezek. 44:20
Acts 5:23, prison-house l-ed quite securely

LOCUST—grasshopper Ex. 10:13; Lev. 11:22; Judg. 6:5; 1 Kin. 8:37; Job 39:20; Prov. 30:27; Joel 2:25; Nah. 3:17; Matt. 3:4

LODGE Job 19:4; 41:22
Ruth 1:16, where you l, I will l

LOFTY Is. 10:33, l will be abased

LOG—beam Eccles. 10:9; Luke 6:42
Matt. 7:5, first take the l out of your own eye

LOINS—waist Ex. 12:11; 2 Kin. 4:29
Eph. 6:14, GIRDED YOUR L WITH TRUTH

LONELY Ps. 25:16, be gracious . . . For I am l

LONG—length Ex. 2:3; 2 Sam. 3:1; Prov. 3:16
Matt. 23:14, for a pretense you make l prayers
1 Cor. 11:14, if a man has l hair
Eph. 6:3, LIVE L ON THE EARTH
Rev. 6:10, How l, O Lord

LONG (v.)—desire Job 3:21; Ps. 84:2
Luke 16:21, l-ing to be fed with the crumbs
Rom. 8:19, anxious l-ing of the creation
2 Cor. 5:2, l-ing to be clothed with our dwelling
1 Tim. 6:10, by l-ing for it have wandered away
1 Pet. 1:12, things into which angels l to look
2:2, like newborn babes, l for the pure milk

LOOK—see Ex. 3:6, he was afraid to l at God
Ps. 84:9, l upon the face of Thine anointed
Matt. 11:3, shall we l for someone else
14:19, and l-ing up toward heaven
Luke 2:38, l-ing for the redemption of Jerusalem
2:44, began l-ing for Him among their
9:62, hand to the plow and l-ing back
John 4:35, l on the fields
Acts 3:4, Peter . . . said, L at us
10:21, I am the one you are l-ing for
Gal. 6:1, l-ing to yourself, lest you
Phil. 2:4, do not . . . l out for your . . . interests
2 Pet. 3:13, l-ing for new heavens
Rev. 14:1, l l-ed, and behold, the Lamb
Gen. 19:17; Ex. 3:2; Job 35:5; Ps. 91:8; 114:3; Prov. 23:31; Eccles. 12:3; Is. 17:7; Luke 17:23

LOOM Judg. 16:14, pulled out the pin of the l

LOOSE—release Job 38:31, l the cords of Orion
Ps. 116:16, Thou hast l-d my bonds
Matt. 16:19, l on earth . . . l-d in heaven
Luke 15:13, his estate with l living

LORD 2 Cor. 1:24, Not that we l it over your faith
2 Thess. 2:2, day of the L has come

LOSE Joel 2:10, stars l their brightness
Matt. 10:39, who has found his life shall l it
16:25, save his life shall l it
Mark 9:41, he shall not l his reward

LOSS—damage Dan. 6:2; Acts 27:10
2 Cor. 7:9, you might not suffer l

LOST

LOST—*perish* Lev. 6:3; Ps. 119:176
Matt. 10:6, go to the l sheep of . . . Israel
18:11, come to save that which was l
Luke 15:24, he was l and has been found
John 6:12, fragments that nothing may be l

LOT—*portion* Lev. 16:8; Num. 26:55
Ps. 22:18, for my clothing they cast l-s
Prov. 1:14, Throw in your l with us
Jon. 1:7, cast l-s and the l fell on Jonah
John 19:24, Let us not tear it, but cast l-s for it
Acts 1:26, the l fell to Matthias

LOUD—*great* Rev. 21:3, I heard a l voice from the throne

LOVE (v.) Ex. 20:6; Neh. 13:26; Ps. 31:23; Zech. 8:17
Lev. 19:18, you shall l your neighbor as yourself
Deut. 6:5, l the LORD your God with all
Prov. 3:12, whom the LORD l-s He reproves
8:17, I l those who l me
12:1, whoever l-s discipline l-s knowledge
17:17, friend l-s at all times
20:13, Do not l sleep
Eccles. 3:8, time to l, and a time to hate
Amos 5:15, Hate evil, l good
Matt. 5:44, l your enemies
6:5, for they l to stand
6:24, hate the one and l the other
22:39, L YOUR NEIGHBOR AS YOURSELF
Luke 6:27, l your enemies
John 3:16, God so l-d the world
2 Cor. 9:7, God l-s a cheerful giver
Eph. 5:2, walk in l, just as Christ l-d you
Col. 3:19, Husbands, l your wives
Titus 2:4, l their husbands, to l their children
James 2:8, L YOUR NEIGHBOR AS YOURSELF
1 John 4:7, let us l one another . . . every one who l-s

LOVE (n.) Prov. 10:12, l covers all transgressions
Matt. 24:12, most people's l will grow cold
John 13:35, if you have l for one another
15:13, Greater l has no one than this
Rom. 12:9, Let l be without hypocrisy
1 Cor. 13:1, do not have l
14:1, Pursue l
Gal. 5:13, through l serve one another
Col. 3:14, beyond . . . *put on* l
1 Tim. 1:5, our instruction is l
6:10, l of money is a root of . . . evil
2 Tim. 2:22, righteousness, faith, l
Heb. 13:1, Let l of the brethren continue
1 Pet. 4:8, l covers a multitude of sins
2 Pet. 1:7, brotherly kindness, Christian l
1 John 4:7, l is from God

3 John 6, your l before the church
Jude 21, keep yourselves in the l of God
Rev. 2:4, you have left your first l
Gen. 29:20; 2 Sam. 1:26

LOVELY—*beautiful* Song 1:5, I am black but l
Is. 52:7, How l on the mountains

LOVINGKINDNESS—*compassion, mercy*
Ezra 3:11, His l is upon Israel forever
Ps. 86:15, a God . . . abundant in l
89:1, I will sing of the l of the LORD
117:2, His l is great toward us

LOW 1 Sam. 2:7, He brings l, He also exalts
Ps. 8:5, hast made him a little l-er than God
Jer. 9:10, l-ing of the cattle

LOWLIEST Dan. 4:17, And sets it over the l of men

LOWLY Job 5:11; Ps. 138:6
Rom. 12:16, associate with the l

LOYALTY 2 Sam. 16:17; Prov. 20:6

LUMP—*cake* Rom. 11:16, *dough* be holy, the l is also
1 Cor. 5:6, leavens the whole l of *dough*
5:7, that you may be a new l

LUNCH—*dinner* Luke 11:37, Pharisee asked Him to have l

LURK Prov. 7:12, And l-s by every corner

LUST—*desire* Matt. 5:28, looks on a woman to l for her
Rom. 13:14, no provision . . . regard to *its* l-s
James 4:2, You l and do not have
1 John 2:16, l of the flesh . . . l of the eyes
Jude 16, following after their own l-s

LUXURIANT Ps. 37:35; Hos. 10:1

LUXURIOUS James 5:5, lived l-ly on the earth

LUXURY Prov. 19:10, L is not fitting for a fool
Luke 7:25, live in l are *found* in royal palaces

LYING Prov. 6:17, Haughty eyes, a l tongue
Prov. 12:22, L lips are an abomination

LYRE—*harp* Gen. 4:21; Ps. 57:8; Is. 5:12

M

MAD—*insane* Eccles. 2:2, It is m-ness
Acts 26:24, learning is driving you m

MADE Gen. 1:7, God m the expanse
Ps. 8:5, m him a little lower than God
119:73, Thy hands m me
Eccles. 7:29, that God m men upright
Matt. 9:22, your faith has m you well
2 Cor. 5:21, m Him who knew no sin *to be* sin

Eph. 3:7, of which I was m a minister
Heb. 6:4, m partakers of the Holy Spirit
Ex. 4:11; Job 4:14; 17:6

MAGI—*wise* Matt. 2:1, m from the east arrived
Matt. 2:7, Herod secretly called the m
2:16, been tricked by the m

MAGIC Acts 19:19, those who practiced m

MAGNIFICENT—*gorgeous* Ezek. 23:12, m-ly dressed, horsemen

MAGNIFY Ps. 34:3, O m the LORD with me
Acts 19:17, name . . . Jesus was being m-ed
Rom. 11:13, I m my ministry
2 Sam. 7:26; Job 7:17; Eccles. 1:16

MAGNITUDE—*greatness* Jer. 13:22, the m of your iniquity

MAID Prov. 30:19, way of a man with a m
Gen. 16:6; Ruth 2:8; 3:9

MAIDEN Judg. 5:30; Job 41:5; Ps. 68:25

MAINTAIN Rom. 3:28, we m that a man is justified

MAJESTIC—*excellent* Ps. 8:1, Lord, How m is Thy name
Ps. 16:3; 2 Pet. 1:17

MAJESTY—*dignity, excellence*
Ps. 93:1, He is clothed with m
Is. 53:2, no *stately* form or m
Heb. 1:3, right hand of the M on high
Jude 25, glory, m, dominion and authority
Job 37:22; Is. 35:2; 2 Pet. 2:10; Jude 8

MAKE Gen. 1:26, Let Us m man in Our image
Gen. 2:18, m him a helper suitable for him
Ps. 25:4, M me know Thy ways, O LORD
Jer. 18:3, he was, m-ing something on the wheel
Matt. 3:3, M READY THE WAY OF THE LORD
4:19, I will m you fishers of men
5:34, m no oath at all
John 1:23, M STRAIGHT THE WAY OF THE LORD
James 4:13, engage in business and m a profit
2 Pet. 1:10, m certain about His calling and
Ex. 20:4,25; Deut. 8:18; Job 17:12; Luke 12:33; Rom. 10:19

MAKER Job 4:17; 35:10; Is. 17:7; 54:5; Jer. 10:16

MALE Gen. 5:2, He created them m and female
Matt. 2:16, slew all the m children
19:4, MADE THEM M AND FEMALE
Gen. 34:25; Deut. 4:16; Gal. 3:28

MALICE—*wickedness*
Matt. 22:18, Jesus perceived their m
1 Pet. 2:1, putting aside all m
1 Cor. 5:8; Eph. 4:31; Col. 3:8

MALICIOUS—*false* Ex. 23:1, to be a
m witness
2 Tim. 3:3, **m** gossips, without

MALIGN—*speak* Titus 3:2, to **m** no
one

MAN—*fellow, person, self* Gen.
1:26; 4:23
Gen. 3:22, the **m** has become like
one of Us
Job 5:7, For **m** is born for trouble
Ps. 1:1, blessed is the **m** who does
not walk in the
Matt. 4:4, M SHALL NOT LIVE ON
BREAD ALONE
8:20, Son of M has nowhere to lay
26:61, This **m** stated, I am able to
destroy
26:71, This **m** was with Jesus
Mark 2:27, not **m** for the Sabbath
10:25, for a rich **m** to enter
Luke 6:45, The good **m** . . . the evil **m**
9:22, The Son of M must suffer
22:59, this **m** also was with Him
23:2, found this **m** misleading our
nation
John 1:6, a **m**, sent from God
3:4, How can a **m** be born when
19:5, Behold, the M
1 Cor. 13:11, when I became a **m**
15:21, by a **m** *came* death
Eph. 4:13, to a mature **m**
James 1:8, a double-minded **m**,
unstable in
Lev. 16:21; Num. 12:3; 1 Sam. 16:17;
1 Kin. 2:2; 2 Kin. 5:8; Job 14:1;
25:6; 33:12; Ps. 19:5; 37:37; Prov.
3:4; Eccles. 4:8; Is. 2:22; Matt. 26:2;
John 7:12; 9:29; 2 Cor. 12:2

MANAGE—*rule* 1 Tim. 3:5, how to
m his own household

MANGER Job 39:9; Prov. 14:4; Is. 1:3

MANIFEST—*reveal* John 17:6; Rom.
10:20; Col. 1:26

MANIFOLD—*various* Eph. 3:10, the
m wisdom of God
1 Pet. 4:10, the **m** grace of God

MANKIND 2 Chr. 6:18; Job 4:17

MANNER Gen. 31:35, **m** of women is
upon me

MANTLE—*garment* Heb. 1:12, AS A
M THOU WILT ROLL THEM UP
1 Kin. 19:19; Is. 59:17

MANURE—*refuse*
Luke 14:35, for the soil or for the **m**
pile

MANY—*multitude* Ps. 104:24, how
m are Thy works
Song 8:7, M waters cannot quench
love
Jer. 14:7, our apostasies have been **m**
Matt. 7:22, M will say to Me on that
day
22:14, **m** are called, but few
Luke 7:47, her sins, which are **m**
21:8, **m** will come in My name
John 14:2, house are **m** dwelling
places
Acts 2:43, **m** wonders and signs
Rom. 12:4, **m** members in one body
1 Cor. 11:30, **m** . . . are weak . . . a
number sleep

James 3:1, **m** *of you* become
teachers
Jude 14, **m** thousands of His holy
ones
Rev. 1:15, sound of **m** waters
Gen. 16:10; 1 Kin. 11:1; Job 13:23; Ps.
71:7; Prov. 14:20

MARCH—*walk* Joel 2:8, **m** every
one in his path
Nah. 2:5, stumble in their **m**

MARK Ps. 37:37, M the blameless
2 Thess. 3:17, a distinguishing **m** in
every letter
Rev. 14:9, receives a **m** on his
forehead
19:20, **m** of the beast

MARKET PLACES
Matt. 11:16, like children sitting in
the **m**
Mark 6:56, laying the sick in the **m**

MARRIAGE Matt. 22:30, marry, are
given in **m**
Heb. 13:4, Let **m** *be held* in honor
Rev. 19:7, **m** of the Lamb has come

MARRY Matt. 5:32, whoever **m-es** a
divorced woman
Matt. 19:9, **m-es** another commits
adultery
19:10, it is better not to **m**
Mark 12:25, they neither **m**, nor
Luke 20:34, sons of this age **m**
1 Cor. 7:9, better to **m** than to burn
1 Tim. 5:11, widows . . . want to get
m-ed

MARVEL—*wonder* Ps. 71:7, I have
become a **m** to many
Matt. 8:10, when Jesus heard *this*,
He **m-ed**
15:31, the multitude **m-ed**
Mark 5:20, and everyone **m-ed**
John 3:7, Do not **m** that I said to you
1 Pet. 2:9, out of darkness into His
m-ous light
Rev. 15:3, GREAT AND M-OUS ARE THY
WORKS

MASSAH—*temptation* Ps. 95:8, in
the day of M

MASTER—*dominion, teacher* Job
3:19; Eph. 6:5
Matt. 6:24, No one can serve
two **m-s**
10:24, nor a slave above his **m**
Rom. 6:9, death no longer is **m** over
Him
1 Cor. 3:10, as a wise **m-builder** I laid

MATERIAL Deut. 22:11, not wear a
m mixed . . . together
1 Cor. 9:11, we should reap **m** things

MATTER Gen. 21:17; 30:15; 1 Sam.
11:5; 21:8

MEAN—*thought* Gen. 50:20, **m-t** evil
against me
Ex. 34:7, by no **m-s** leave *the guilty*
unpunished
Matt. 9:13, go and learn what
this **m-s**
Acts 17:20, know . . . what these
things **m**
1 Cor. 14:11, do not know the **m-ing**
of the language
Gal. 5:6, neither circumcision . . . **m-s**
anything

MEANINGLESS—*vain*
Matt. 6:7, do not use **m** repetition

MEASURE Eph. 4:7, according to the
m of Christ's gift
Rev. 21:16, **m-d** the city with the rod
Gen. 18:6; Deut. 25:15; 2 Kin. 7:1; Ps.
80:5; Matt. 7:2

MEAT—*flesh* Ex. 16:3; Deut. 12:20

MEDDLER—*busybody*
1 Pet. 4:15, troublesome **m**

MEDIATOR Gal. 3:19, by the agency
of a **m**
Gal. 3:20, a **m** is not for one *party*
1 Tim. 2:5, one **m** also between God
and men
Heb. 8:6, **m** of a better covenant
12:24, to Jesus the **m** of a new
covenant

MEDITATE Gen. 24:63, Isaac went
out to **m**
Ps. 1:2, in His law he **m-s** day and
night
19:14, **m-ion** of my heart

MEDIUM Lev. 19:31; 1 Sam. 28:7

MEETING—*congregation* Acts
13:43, **m** of the synagogue had

MELODY Is. 51:3, sound of a **m**
Eph. 5:19, making **m** with your heart

MELT—*dissolve* Josh. 2:11; Ps. 46:6;
75:3; 97:5; Is. 14:31

MEMBER Matt. 10:25, how much
more the **m-s** . . . household
1 Cor. 6:15, your bodies are **m-s** of
Christ
12:12, the body . . . has many **m-s**
12:14, body is not one **m**, but many

MEMORIAL Ex. 3:15; 17:14; Josh.
4:7; Acts 10:4

MEMORY Prov. 10:7, **m** of the
righteous is blessed
Matt. 26:13, spoken of in **m** of her
Job 18:17; Ps. 9:6; 109:15

MEN Ps. 116:11, All **m** are liars
Mark 1:17, I will make you . . .
fishers of **m**
Luke 20:4, from heaven or from **m**
1 Thess. 2:4, not as pleasing **m** but
God
Gen. 6:1; 1 Sam 4:9; Job 11:3; Ps.
26:4; 82:7; Matt. 10:17; Mark 6:21;
Acts 17:5

MENTION Ps. 71:16; Is. 63:7; Rom.
1:9,10

MERCHANDISE John 2:16, My
Father's house a house of **m**

MERCHANT 1 Kin. 10:28; Hos. 12:7;
Rev. 18:3

MERCY—*compassion*
2 Sam. 24:14, for His **m-es** are great
Matt. 5:7, for they shall receive **m**
18:33, I had **m** on you
Rom. 9:15, M ON WHOM I HAVE M
12:1, by the **m-es** of God
1 Cor. 7:25, as one who by the **m** of
the LORD
Eph. 2:4, God, being rich in **m**

James 5:11, full of compassion and *is* **m-ful**

MERRY—*joyful* Eccles. 8:15, drink and be **m**
Luke 12:19, eat, drink *and* be **m**
15:29, might be **m** with my friends

MESSAGE—*tidings, word, report, speech*
Luke 4:32, His **m** was with authority
Acts 20:7, his **m** until midnight
Judg. 3:19,20; Jer. 49:14; Is. 53:1; Luke 4:36

MESSENGER Matt. 11:10, MY **M** BEFORE YOUR FACE
2 Cor. 12:7, a **m** of Satan
2 Kin. 6:32; Hag. 1:13

MESSIAH—*Lord, Christ* John 1:41, found the **M**

MIDDLE Josh. 12:2; Ruth 3:8; Prov. 30:19

MIDNIGHT Ps. 119:6; Matt. 25:6; Acts 16:25; 20:7

MIDST—*middle, within*
Matt. 10:16, sheep in the **m** of
18:20, there I am in their **m**
Luke 17:21, kingdom of God is in your **m**
24:36, He Himself stood in their **m**
John 20:26, Jesus ... stood in their **m**

MIGHT Job 39:19, give the horse *his* **m**
Zech. 4:6, Not by **m** or by power
Acts 19:20, word ... was growing **m-ily**
Eph. 1:19, working of the strength of His **m**
Col. 1:29, which **m-ily** works within me
Gen. 49:3; Deut. 6:5; Judg. 5:31; 2 Sam. 6:14; Eccles. 9:10; Jer. 9:23

MIGHTY 2 Sam. 1:19, How have the **m** fallen
Ps. 24:8, strong and **m** ... **m** in battle
89:13, Thy hand is **m**
Jer. 48:17, How has the **m** scepter been broken
Joel 3:10, weak say, I am a **m** man
Mic. 4:3, decisions for **m**, distant nations
Luke 24:19, prophet **m** in deed and word
Acts 2:11, the **m** deeds of God
18:24, **m** in the Scriptures
2 Cor. 13:3, but **m** in you
1 Pet. 5:6, the **m** hand of God
Gen. 6:4; 10:9; Deut. 10:17; Is. 19:4; 63:1; Jer. 32:18

MILE Luke 24:13; John 11:18; Rev. 14:20

MILK Ex. 3:8, land flowing with **m** and honey
1 Cor. 3:2, I gave you **m** to drink
Heb. 5:12, you have come to need **m**
1 Pet. 2:2, pure **m** of the word
Gen. 49:12; Judg. 4:19; Job 10:10; Prov. 30:33

MIND—*heart* Ps. 7:9, tries the hearts and **m-s**
Mark 5:15, and in his right **m**
Acts 28:6, changed their **m-s**

Rom. 1:28, over to a depraved **m**
8:7, **m** set on the flesh is hostile
1 Cor. 1:10, complete in the same **m**
2 Cor. 13:11, be **like-m-ed**, live in peace
Phil. 2:2, being of the same **m**
2:3, with humility of **m** let each
Col. 3:2, Set your **m** on
James 1:8, a **double-m-ed** man
1 Pet. 1:13, gird your **m-s** for action
Gen. 40:14; Ps. 31:12; Is. 46:8; Jer. 17:10; Dan. 4:16; Rom. 14:5; 1 Tim. 6:5; 2 Pet. 1:15

MINISTER Is. 61:6; Eph. 3:7

MINISTRY—*service* 1 Cor. 12:5; 2 Cor. 9:12
Acts 6:4, to the **m** of the word
2 Cor. 5:18, **m** of reconciliation
Col. 4:17, Take heed to the **m**
2 Tim. 4:5, fulfill your **m**
Heb. 8:6, obtained a more excellent **m**

MIRACLE—*marvel, sign, mighty*
Matt. 11:21, if the **m-s** had occurred in Tyre
Ex. 34:10; Mark 6:5; 1 Cor. 12:10

MIRROR 1 Cor. 13:12, we see in a **m** dimly
James 1:23, his natural face in a **m**
Ex. 38:8; Job 37:18; Is. 3:23

MISCARRIAGE Ex. 21:22, so that she has a **m**

MISCARRY—*young* Ex. 23:26, no one **m-ing**

MISCHIEF Job 15:35, They conceive **m**

MISERY Job 10:15; Rom. 3:16

MISGIVING Acts 10:20, accompany them without **m-s**

MISGUIDE Heb. 5:2, deal gently with the ignorant and **m-d**

MISLEAD Deut. 27:18, **m-s** a blind person
Job 12:16, misled and the **m-er** belong to Him
Matt. 24:24, so as to **m** ... even the elect

MISSILE Eph. 6:16, flaming **m-s** of the evil one

MISTAKE Eccles. 5:6; Matt. 22:29; Mark 12:24

MISTREAT—*wrong* Jer. 22:3, do not **m** or do violence
Matt. 22:6; Luke 18:32; Acts 7:19

MIX Deut. 22:11; Prov. 23:30; Dan. 2:41; Rev. 18:6

MOCK Prov. 14:9, Fools **m** at sin
Prov. 20:1, Wine is a **m-er**
Gal. 6:7, God is not **m-ed**
2 Kin. 2:23; Job 21:3; 30:1; Hab. 1:10; Matt. 27:29

MODE Judg. 13:12, shall be the boy's **m** of life

MODEL 2 Thess. 3:9, offer ourselves as a **m**

MOMENT—*instant* Ps. 30:5, His anger is for a **m**
Job 34:20, In a **m** they die
1 Cor. 15:52, in a **m**, in the twinkling of an

MONEY—*gain* Gen. 43:12; Deut. 21:14
Eccles. 5:10, who loves **m** will not be satisfied
10:19, **m** is the answer to everything
Matt. 21:12, tables of the **m-changers**
Mark 6:8, no **m** in their belt
Luke 19:23, why ... not put the **m** ... bank
1 Tim. 3:3, free from the love of **m**
6:10, love of **m** is a root ... of evil
2 Kin. 5:26; Eccles. 7:12; Jer. 32:25; Amos 2:6

MONEYLENDER—*creditor*
Luke 7:41, certain **m** had two

MONGREL Zech. 9:6, a **m** race

MONSTER Gen. 1:21, created the great sea **m-s**
Job 7:12, sea, or the sea **m**
Ezek. 32:2, **m** in the seas

MOON—*crescent* Matt. 24:29, **M** WILL NOT GIVE ITS LIGHT
Luke 21:25, signs in the sun and **m**
Gen. 37:9; Josh. 10:12; 1 Sam. 20:5; Job 31:26; Ps. 136:9; Song 6:10; Is. 1:13; Joel 2:31; Acts 2:20

MORALS 1 Cor. 15:33, Bad company corrupts good **m**

MORNING—*early* Job 38:7, **m** stars sang together
2 Pet. 1:19, the **m** star arises in your hearts
Rev. 22:16, the bright **m** star
Gen. 19:15; Ex. 8:20; Deut. 28:67; Ps. 55:17; Eccles. 11:6

MORSEL—*piece* Job 31:17; Prov 17:1

MORTAL Rom. 6:12, sin reign in your **m** body
Rom. 8:11, give life to your **m** bodies
1 Cor. 15:53, **m** ... put on immortality
2 Cor. 4:11, manifested in our **m** flesh

MOST—*many, very* Matt. 24:12, **m** people's love will grow
2 Cor. 11:5, least inferior to the **m** eminent

MOTHER Gen. 2:24, leave his father ... **m**
Ex. 20:12, Honor your father and your **m**
Matt. 1:18, When His **m** Mary ... betrothed
2:11, Child with Mary His **m**
2:13, **m** and flee to Egypt
19:19, HONOR YOUR FATHER AND **M**
John 19:27, the disciple, Behold, your **m**
Heb. 7:3, Without father, without **m**
Gen. 3:20; Ex. 22:30; Lev. 22:27; Deut. 22:6; Job 17:14; Ezek. 16:44; Hos. 2:2; Matt. 12:48

MOTION Ex. 15:16; Acts 12:17

MOTIVES—*thought* 1 Cor. 4:5, m of men's hearts
James 2:4, judges with evil m

MOUND—*bank* 2 Sam. 20:15, a m against the city

MOUNTAINS Ps. 121:1, will lift up my eyes to the m
Is. 5:25; Mic. 1:4

MOUNTED Zech. 9:9, m on a donkey
Matt. 21:5, GENTLE, AND M UPON A DONKEY

MOURN—*weep, wail*
Is. 61:2, To comfort all who m
Matt. 2:18, WEEPING AND GREAT M-ING
5:4, Blessed are those who m
Luke 6:25, for you shall m and weep
James 4:9, laughter be turned into m-ing
Rev. 1:7, TRIBES . . . M OVER HIM
Gen. 37:35; Deut. 21:13; Jer. 9:17; 15:5; 2 Cor. 12:21

MOUTH—*speech* Ps. 19:14, the words of my m
Ps. 39:1, guard my m as with a muzzle
Prov. 13:3, who guards his m preserves
Song 4:3, your m is lovely
Matt. 4:4, PROCEEDS OUT OF THE M OF GOD
13:35, OPEN MY M IN PARABLES
Acts 3:21, m of His holy prophets
James 3:3, put the bits . . . horses' m-s
Ex. 4:11; Judg. 7:6; Job 8:21; 15:6; Ps. 8:2; 71:15; Prov. 4:24

MOVE 2 Chr. 16:9, eyes of the LORD m
Mark 1:41, m-d with compassion, He stretched
Acts 17:28, in Him we live and m
2 Pet. 1:21, m-d by the Holy Spirit
Gen. 1:2; Deut. 19:14; 1 Sam. 1:13; Jer. 4:24

MUCH Prov. 25:27, not good to eat m honey
Prov. 29:1, hardens his neck after m reproof
Eccles. 1:18, in m wisdom there is m grief
Luke 7:47, for she loved m
16:10, faithful also in m

MULTIPLY Gen. 1:22; Ex. 32:13; Deut. 6:3

MULTITUDE Matt. 14:15, send the m-s away
Luke 23:27, following Him a great m
James 5:20, cover a m of sins
1 Pet. 4:8, love covers a m of sins
Gen. 17:4; Ex. 23:2; Deut. 1:10

MURDER Ex. 20:13, You shall not m
Rom. 1:29, full of envy, m, strife
Matt. 5:21; 19:18

MURDERER Num. 35:16; John 8:44; Acts 28:4; 1 John 3:15

MURMUR Ps. 55:17, I will complain and m

MUSIC 1 Sam. 18:6; Luke 15:25

MUST—*ought* Acts 5:29, We m obey God

MUZZLE Deut. 25:4, not m the ox while
1 Cor. 9:9, 1 Tim. 5:18, NOT M THE OX WHILE

MYRRH Matt. 2:11, frankincense and m
John 19:39, mixture of m and aloes
Gen. 43:11; Ps. 45:8; Song 5:13

MYSTERY—*secret* Dan. 4:9, no m baffles you
Matt. 13:11, m-es of the kingdom
1 Cor. 2:7, God's wisdom in a m
4:1, stewards of the m-es
13:2, know all m-es . . . knowledge
Eph. 3:9, administration of the m
6:19, the m of the gospel
1 Tim. 3:9, the m of the faith

MYTHS—*fables* 1 Tim. 1:4, pay attention to m
Titus 1:14, paying attention to Jewish m

N

NAILS John 20:25, in His hands the imprint of n
Deut. 21:12; Dan. 4:33

NAIVE—*simple* Prov. 14:15, n believes everything

NAKED—*bare* Gen. 2:25; Job 1:21; 26:6; Matt. 25:36

NAME—*appoint* Job 1:21, Blessed be the n of the LORD
Ps. 8:1, How majestic is Thy n
18:49, sing praises to Thy n
72:17, his n endure forever . . . n increase
102:15, nations will fear the n of the LORD
111:9, Holy and awesome is His n
Prov. 22:1, good n is to be more desired
Matt. 6:9, Hallowed be Thy n
10:2, n-s of the twelve apostles are
18:5, one such child in My n
Mark 5:9, My n is Legion; for we are many
Luke 21:8, many will come in My n
John 15:16, you ask of the Father in My n
Acts 3:16, on the basis of faith in His n
4:12, no other n under heaven
Phil. 2:9, n which is above every n
4:3, whose n-s are in the book of life
Gen. 3:20; 30:28; Ex. 20:7; Deut. 29:20; Neh. 9:10; Prov. 30:9; Is. 42:8; 48:2; 57:15; Matt. 10:22; Eph. 1:21; 3 John 14

NARROW—*strait* Matt. 7:13, Enter by the n gate

NATION—*generation, Gentile*
Ps. 33:12, Blessed is the n whose God
Prov. 14:34, Righteousness exalts a n
Is. 2:4, N will not lift up sword against n
Matt. 24:7, n will rise against n
28:19, Go . . . make disciples of all the n-s
Acts 2:5, devout men, from every n

Gal. 3:8, ALL THE N-S SHALL BE BLESSED
Rev. 5:9, and tongue and people and n
Gen. 12:2; 20:4; Ex. 19:6; Lev. 26:33; Ps. 2:1; 102:15; Is. 18:2; 52:15; 66:19; Jer. 51:58; John 11:50; Rev. 11:2

NATIVE Acts 28:2,4

NATURAL Rom. 1:26, exchanged the n function
1 Cor. 15:44, it is sown a n body

NATURE 1 Cor. 11:14, Does not even n itself teach
2 Pet. 1:4, partakers of the divine n

NEAR—*close* Ps. 34:18, n to the brokenhearted
Ps. 145:18, n to all who call upon Him
Mark 13:28, you know that the summer is n
Eph. 2:13, brought n by the blood of Christ
Phil. 4:5, The Lord is n
Heb. 10:22, draw n with a sincere heart
James 4:8, Draw n to God and He will draw n
Ex. 19:22; Deut. 4:7; Ps. 22:11; Prov. 27:10; Joel 3:14

NECESSARY—*need*
Luke 10:42, *only* a few things are n
24:26, Was it not n for the Christ to suffer

NECK Gen. 27:16; Ex. 13:13; Deut. 28:48; Prov. 3:3; Matt. 18:6

NEED—*want* Prov. 25:16, Eat *only* what you n
Matt. 6:8, your Father knows what you n
9:12, not . . . healthy who n a physician
21:3, The Lord has n of them
Luke 15:14, he began to be in n
Phil. 4:19, God shall supply all your n-s
Heb. 4:16, help in time of n
1 John 3:17, beholds his brother in n
Rev. 3:17, have n of nothing
1 Cor. 12:21; 1 Thess. 4:12

NEEDLESS Gal. 2:21, then Christ died n-ly

NEEDY Ps. 9:18, n will not always be forgotten
Ps. 72:13, compassion on the poor and n
Is. 14:30, n will lie down in security
Ex. 23:6; Deut. 15:11; Job 29:16; Ps. 40:17; 69:33

NEGLECT—*forget*
Matt. 6:16, they n their appearance
Luke 15:29, I have never n-ed a command
Heb. 13:2,16

NEGLIGENCE—*error* Dan. 6:4, no n or corruption was *to be*

NEGLIGENT Prov. 10:4, works with a n hand

NEIGHBOR—*fellow-citizen*
Lev. 19:18, you shall love your n

Prov. 3:29, Do not devise harm against your **n**
27:10, Better is a **n** who is near
Hab. 2:15, who make your **n-s** drink
Matt. 5:43, YOU SHALL LOVE YOUR **N**
Luke 10:29, who is my **n**

NEST—*lodge* Matt. 8:20, birds have **n-s**
Luke 13:19, birds ... **n-ed** in its branches
Num. 24:21; Deut. 32:11; Jer. 49:16; Obad. 4

NET Job 19:6; Ps. 57:6; Is. 51:20; Matt. 13:47

NEVER Matt. 7:23, I **n** knew you
John 4:14, of the water ... shall **n** thirst
7:46, **N** did a man speak the way
8:51, he shall **n** see death
Heb. 13:5, I WILL **N** DESERT YOU
Deut. 15:11; Job 3:16; Ps. 31:1

NEW Lev. 23:14, roasted grain nor **n** growth
Ps. 33:3, Sing to Him a **n** song
Eccles. 1:9, nothing **n** under the sun
Is. 65:17, create **n** heavens and a **n** earth
Ezek. 11:19, put a **n** spirit within them
John 13:34, A **n** commandment I give to you
2 Cor. 5:17, a **n** creature ... **n** things have come
Eph. 4:24, put on the **n** self
Rev. 21:1, a **n** heaven and a **n** earth

NEWS—*tidings* Gen. 29:13, heard the **n** of Jacob
2 Kin. 7:9, day is a day of good **n**
Is. 52:7, feet of him who brings good **n**
Luke 2:10, good **n** of a great joy
1 Thess. 3:6, good **n** of your faith
Prov. 15:30; Matt. 14:1; Mark 1:28,45

NIGHT Ex. 13:21, a pillar of fire by **n**
Ps. 19:2, **n** to **n** reveals knowledge
91:5, not be afraid of the terror by **n**
Is. 21:11, Watchman, how far gone is the **n**
Luke 2:8, watch over their flock by **n**
John 9:4, **n** is coming, when no man can work
Rom. 13:12, **n** is almost gone
2 Cor. 11:27, through many sleepless **n-s**
1 Thess. 5:2, like a thief in the **n**
Gen. 1:5; Josh. 1:8; Job 17:12

NOBLE Ps. 45:9; Prov. 8:6

NOISE—*sound* Is. 22:2, You who were full of **n**
Jer. 50:22, **n** of the battle is in the land
Acts 2:2, came from heaven a **n**
1 Cor. 13:1, have become a **n-y** gong

NONSENSE Luke 24:11, words appeared ... as **n**

NOSTRIL Ezek. 16:12, put a ring in your **n**

NOTHING Job 26:7, hangs the earth on **n**
Ps. 49:17, he will carry **n** away
Prov. 13:7, pretends to be rich, but has **n**

John 15:5, apart from Me you can do **n**
1 Cor. 4:4, conscious of **n** against myself
Gal. 6:3, thinks he is something when he is **n**
Phil. 4:6, Be anxious for **n**
1 Tim. 4:7, have **n** to do with worldly fables
James 1:4, perfect and complete, lacking in **n**
Ex. 21:11; Lam. 1:12; Luke 6:35

NOTICE—*visit* Jer. 15:15, Remember me, take **n** of me
Matt. 6:1, righteousness ... to be **n-d** by them
Matt. 7:3; Luke 6:41

NOURISH 1 Tim. 4:6, **n-ed** on the words of the faith

NULLIFY Rom. 3:3; 4:14; Gal. 2:21; 3:17

NUMBER—*measure, count* Num. 1:3; Job 14:16; Ps. 139:18; Matt. 10:30; 2 Cor. 11:23

NURSE Gen. 35:8; Ex. 2:7; Num. 11:12; 1 Thess. 2:7

O

OAK 2 Sam. 18:10; Is. 1:30; Amos 2:9

OATH—*vow* Gen. 26:3; Josh. 2:20; Acts 23:12

OBEDIENCE Rom. 16:26, to **o** of faith
2 Cor. 10:5, to the **o** of Christ
Heb. 5:8, He learned **o** from the things

OBEDIENT 2 Cor. 2:9, whether you are **o** in all things
Phil. 2:8, **o** to the point of death
1 Pet. 1:14, As **o** children

OBEY—*follow* Ps. 103:20, **O-ing** voice of His word
Matt. 8:27, the winds and the sea **o** Him
Acts 5:29, **o** God rather than men
Eph. 6:1, Children, **o** your parents
Heb. 11:8, By faith Abraham ... **o-ed**
13:17, **O** your leaders
1 Pet. 1:2, that you may **o** Jesus Christ
Ex. 19:5; Josh. 1:17; 1 Sam. 15:22; Is. 1:19

OBLIGATE Matt. 23:16, whoever swears by the gold ... **o-d**

OBLIGATION Num. 32:22, be free of **o** toward the LORD
Rom. 1:14, I am under **o** both to Greeks
8:12, we are under **o**, not to the flesh
Gal. 5:3, he is under **o** to keep the whole Law

OBSCURE Prov. 22:29; Luke 23:45

OBSERVE—*keep* Deut. 5:15, to **o** the sabbath day
Prov. 6:6, **O** her ways and be wise
Matt. 6:28, **O** how the lilies of the field

28:20, teaching them to **o** all that I commanded
Luke 11:28, hear the word of God, and **o** it
Rom. 14:6, He who **o-s** the day, **o-s** it for the Lord
Prov. 5:2; 6:20; Jer. 2:10; Gal. 4:10

OBSOLETE Heb. 8:13, He has made the first **o**

OBSTACLE Rom. 14:13, not to put an **o** ... in a brother's

OBTAIN—*purchase* Prov. 8:35, **o-s** favor from the LORD
1 Thess. 5:9, for **o-ing** salvation through our Lord
Heb. 11:35, that they might **o** a better resurrection
Gen. 16:2; Acts 8:20

OCCASION 1 Tim. 5:14, give the enemy no **o** for reproach

ODIOUS Ex. 5:21; 1 Sam. 13:4

OFFEND Ex. 2:13, he said to the **o-er**
Job 34:31, I will not **o** *any more*

OFFENSE—*strange* Job 19:17, breath is **o-ive** to my wife
1 Cor. 10:32, Give no **o**
1 Pet. 2:8, AND A ROCK OF **O**
Gen. 41:9; Eccles. 10:4; Jer. 23:13

OFFER—*present* Ps. 50:14, **O** to God a sacrifice
Mal. 1:8, Why not **o** it to your governor
Matt. 5:23, presenting your **o-ing** at the altar
5:24, come and present your **o-ing**
Luke 6:29, **o** him the other also
Heb. 9:14, **o-ed** Himself without blemish

OFFICE Judg. 5:14; Ps. 109:8; 1 Tim. 3:1; Heb. 7:5

OFFICER—*governor* Jer. 20:1, chief **o** in the house ... LORD

OFFICIAL 2 Kin. 20:18; 23:11; Is. 39:7; Dan. 1:9; Matt. 9:18

OFFSPRING Deut. 28:53; Is. 65:9

OFTEN Luke 13:34, How **o** I wanted to gather
1 Cor. 11:26, as **o** as you eat this bread

OIL Matt. 25:8, Give us some of your **o**
Luke 10:34, pouring **o** and wine on them
Rev. 6:6, harm the **o** and the wine
Ex. 29:6; Job 29:6; Ps. 23:5; 45:7; 55:21; 104:15; 133:2; Prov. 5:3; Luke 7:46

OINTMENT Job 41:31; John 12:5

OLD Matt. 9:17, new wine into **o** wineskins
John 3:4, man be born when he is **o**
Rom. 6:6, our **o** self was crucified
1 Cor. 5:7, Clean out the **o** leaven
2 Cor. 3:14, reading of the **o** covenant
5:17, the **o** things passed away
Col. 3:9, laid aside the **o** self

OLD (Continued)
Rev. 12:9, serpent of o who is called the devil
Gen. 15:15; 44:20; Ruth 1:12; 1 Sam. 12:2; Job 42:17; Prov. 20:29; Matt. 9:16; Heb. 11:2

OLDER—aged
Job 32:4, waited ... because they were ... o
Titus 2:2,3, O men are to be temperate

ONCE—soon 1 Sam. 9:13, you will find him at o
Matt. 15:28, daughter was healed at o
21:20, did the fig tree wither at o
Rom. 6:10, died to sin, o for all
Heb. 9:28, offered o to bear the sins
Gen. 18:32; Is. 66:8

ONE Matt. 6:24, No o can serve two masters
Matt. 19:5, TWO SHALL BECOME O FLESH
John 10:30, I and the Father are o
17:21, that they may all be o
Gal. 6:4, let each o examine his own work
Eph. 4:4, o body and o Spirit ... o hope
1 Tim. 2:5, o God, and o mediator
James 4:12, only o Lawgiver and Judge
Gen. 1:5; Deut. 6:4; 1 Sam. 21:15; 2 Sam. 6:20; Job 33:23; Mark 8:30; John 19:41

ONLY Gen. 6:5, thoughts of his heart ... o evil
Ps. 62:2, He o is my rock ... salvation
Luke 24:18, You the o one visiting
Rom. 16:27, o wise God ... glory forever
Heb. 11:17, his o begotten son
Jude 25, o God ... our Lord, be glory

OPEN—explain, wide
Matt. 7:7, knock and it shall be o-ed
20:33, we want our eyes to be o-ed
John 1:51, you shall see the heavens o-ed
Rev. 4:1, a door standing o in heaven
5:2, Who is worthy to o the book
Gen. 3:5; Job 29:23; Ps. 5:9; 51:15; Prov. 27:5; Is. 26:2; 42:7; Ezek. 16:63; Luke 13:25

OPENING Prov. 8:3; Song 5:4

OPINION—counsel 2 Cor. 8:10, give my o in this matter

OPPONENT—adversary Matt. 5:25; Luke 18:3; Phil. 1:28

OPPORTUNE Mark 14:11, betray Him at an o time

OPPORTUNITY—occasion
Gal. 5:13, turn your freedom ... o
Eph. 4:27, do not give the devil an o

OPPOSE—resist Ezra 10:15, Jahzeiah ... o-d this
Rom. 13:2, he who resists authority has o-d
James 4:6, GOD IS O-D TO THE PROUD

OPPOSITION Num. 14:34; Gal. 5:17

OPPRESS—afflict
Acts 10:38, healing all who were o-ed
James 2:6, Is it not the rich who o you
Gen. 15:13; Lev. 19:13; 1 Sam. 1:15; Job 5:4; Hos. 12:7

OPPRESSION—affliction
Ps. 62:10, Do not trust in o
Eccles. 7:7, o makes a wise man mad
Is. 30:20; Ezek. 22:12

ORCHARD—garden Song 6:11, down to the o of nut trees

ORDAIN Ex. 29:29,35; Ps. 8:3; Acts 7:53

ORDER 2 Kin. 20:1; Ps. 5:3; Mark 5:43; Luke 5:14; Titus 1:5; Philem. 8; Heb. 5:6

ORDINANCE—statute Job 38:33; Rom. 13:2; Eph. 2:15

ORPHAN—fatherless
Ex. 22:22, not afflict any widow or o
James 1:27, visit o-s and widows
Deut. 10:18; 14:29; 24:17; Job 31:17; Ps. 10:14; Is. 1:23; 10:2; Jer. 49:11; Hos. 14:3; Mal. 3:5

OTHER Ex. 22:20; Mark 16:13

OUGHT John 4:20, place where men o to worship
Heb. 5:12, you o to be teachers
James 3:10, these things o not to be

OUT Ex. 3:10, bring My people ... o of Egypt
Ex. 7:5, when I stretch o My hand
Num. 32:23, your sin will find you o
Prov. 31:20, she stretches o her hands to
Matt. 12:13, Stretch o your hand
12:34, o of that which fills the heart
13:3, the sower went o to sow
Mark 1:41, He stretched o His hand and touched
7:26, cast the demon o of her daughter
2 Tim. 4:2, in season and o of season
Gen. 8:7,8,18; 19:10; 24:45; Ex. 3:11; Judg. 20:25; 1 Sam. 30:21; 2 Sam. 19:7; Is. 37:36; Jer. 32:21

OUTBURST—heat
Deut. 29:24, Why this great o of anger

OUTCOME—end Rom. 6:21, the o of those things is death
Rom. 6:22, the o, eternal life
Heb. 13:7, the o of their way of life
James 5:11, seen the o of the Lord's dealings
1 Pet. 1:9, obtaining as the o of your faith
4:17, what will be the o

OUTCRY Gen. 18:21; Ps. 144:14

OUTER—outward
2 Cor. 4:16, o man is decaying

OUTSIDE—without Deut. 32:25, O the sword
Rev. 22:15, O are the dogs

OUTWARD Rom. 2:28, o in the flesh

OVEN Gen. 15:17, smoking o and a flaming torch

OVER—spent Luke 24:29, day is now nearly o
Eph. 4:6, who is o all

OVERCOME Luke 9:32, companions had been o with sleep
John 16:33, I have o the world
Rom. 12:21, Do not be o by evil
1 John 2:13, you have o the evil one
Jer. 20:7; 23:9

OVEREXTENDING—stretching
2 Cor. 10:14, we are not o

OVERFLOW 2 Cor. 7:4, I am o-ing with joy
Ps. 23:5; Prov. 3:10; Song 8:7

OVERLAID 2 Chr. 3:5, he o the main room with cypress

OVERPOWER—prevail
Matt. 16:18, gates of Hades shall not o it

OVERSEER Phil. 1:1, including the o-s and deacons
1 Tim. 3:1, aspires to the office of o
Titus 1:7, o must be above reproach

OVERTAKE Amos 9:10; 1 Thess. 5:4

OVERTHROW Ex. 23:24; Acts 5:39

OVERWHELM Ex. 17:13, Joshua o-ed Amalek

OWE—due Matt. 18:28, Pay back what you o
18:34, repay all that was o-d him
Rom. 13:8, O nothing to anyone
Philem. 19, you o to me even your own self

OWN Prov. 14:10, heart knows its o bitterness
John 1:11, came to His o ... o did not receive
10:3, calls his o sheep by name
Acts 2:6, speak in his o language
1 Tim. 5:8, does not provide for his o
2 Pet. 3:3, following after their o lusts

OX—cow Prov. 7:22, as an o goes to the slaughter
1 Tim. 5:18, MUZZLE THE O WHILE HE IS THRESHING
Lev. 22:28; Job 6:5; Prov. 15:17

P

PACT Is. 28:15, we have made a p

PAIN—sorrow, torment, grief Gen. 3:16, multiply Your p
1 Chr. 4:9, Because I bore him with p
Job 6:10, I rejoice in unsparing p
Ps. 127:2, eat the bread of p-ful labors
Eccles. 1:18, knowledge results in increasing p
Is. 14:3, gives you rest from your p
Jer. 30:15, Your p is incurable
Lam. 1:12, any p like my p
Matt. 8:6, home, suffering great p
Job 2:13; 15:20; Ps. 73:4; Lam. 3:51; Rev. 21:4

PAIR Judg. 19:3; Is. 21:7

PALATE—*mouth*
Job 29:10, their tongue stuck to their **p**

PALLET Mark 2:9, take up your **p** and walk
John 5:11; Acts 5:15

PALPITATING Is. 35:4, to those with **p** heart fear not

PANEL Jer. 22:14; Hag. 1:4

PANGS—*sorrow* Mark 13:8, beginning birth **p**

PANIC—*trouble* Is. 22:5, has a day of **p**

PANT Job 7:2, a slave who **p-s** for the shade

PAPYRUS Is. 18:2, in **p** vessels

PARAPET Deut. 22:8, a **p** for your roof

PARCH—*dried* Ps. 69:3; Is. 53:2

PARDON Is. 55:7 He will abundantly **p**
Luke 6:37, **p**, and you will be **p-ed**
Ex. 23:21; 2 Chr. 30:18; Ps. 25:11

PARENTS Matt. 10:21, CHILDREN WILL RISE UP AGAINST **P**
Luke 2:41, His **p** used to go to Jerusalem
18:29, left house . . . or **p**
John 9:2, who sinned, this man, or his **p**
Rom. 1:30, disobedient to **p**
2 Cor. 12:14, for *their* **p**, but **p** for *their* children
Eph. 6:1, Children obey your **p**
2 Tim. 3:2, disobedient to **p**, ungrateful

PART Num. 18:20, nor own any **p** among them
Matt. 5:29, one of the **p-s** of your body perish
Luke 10:42, Mary has chosen the good **p**
John 13:8, you have no **p** with Me
Acts 8:21, You have no **p** or portion
1 Cor. 13:9, we know in **p**

PARTAKERS—*partners* Eph. 5:7, do not be **p** with them
Heb. 3:1, **p** of a heavenly calling
3:14, **p** of Christ
6:4, **p** of the Holy Spirit
2 Pet. 1:4, **p** of *the* divine nature

PARTIAL Prov. 28:21, To show **p-ity** is not good
Matt. 22:16, for You are not **p** to any
Acts 10:34, God is not one to show **p-ity**
Rom. 2:11, no **p-ity** with God
Lev. 19:15; Deut. 1:17

PARTICIPATE Eph. 5:11, do not **p** in the unfruitful deeds

PARTNERS Matt. 23:30, not have been **p** with them

PASS Matt. 26:39, let this cup **p** from Me
John 5:24, **p-ed** out of death into life
2 Cor. 5:17, old things **p-ed** away

Heb. 11:25, enjoy the **p-ing** pleasures of sin
Rev. 21:1, first earth **p-ed** away
Gen. 15:17; Ps. 109:23; Prov. 4:15; Is. 16:8; Acts 7:30

PASSION Prov. 14:30, But **p** is rottenness to the bone
Rom. 1:26, gave them over to degrading **p-s**
Col. 3:5, as dead to . . . **p**
1 Thess. 4:5, not in lustful **p**

PASSOVER Ex. 12:11, it is the LORD'S **P**
Matt. 26:17, prepare for You to eat the **P**
Luke 22:15, desired to eat this **P**
John 18:39, release someone for you at the **P**
Acts 12:4, intending after the **P**
1 Cor. 5:7, Christ our **P** also has been sacrificed

PAST Song 2:11, the winter is **p**, The rain
Jer. 8:20, Harvest is **p**, summer is ended

PASTOR—*shepherd* Eph. 4:11, some as **p-s** and teachers

PASTURE—*feed* Song 1:7; Is. 61:5; Jer. 6:3; Zech. 11:4

PATCH—*piece* Matt. 9:16, puts a **p** of unshrunk cloth

PATH—*way* Job 12:24, makes them wander in a **p-less** waste
Ps. 16:11, make known to me the **p** of life
119:105, a light to my **p**
Prov. 4:18, **p** of the righteous is like the light
Eccles. 11:5, the **p** of the wind
Matt. 3:3, MAKE HIS **P-S** STRAIGHT
Rom. 3:17, **P** OF PEACE . . . NOT KNOWN
Gen. 49:17; Job 28:7; Ps. 27:11

PATIENCE Matt. 18:26, Have **p** with me
2 Cor. 6:6, in **p**, in kindness
Col. 1:11, steadfastness and **p**
2 Tim. 4:2, with great **p** and instruction

PATIENT—*gentle* 1 Cor. 13:4, Love is **p**, love is kind
James 5:8, You too be **p**
2 Pet. 3:9, is **p** toward you

PATTERN—*example* Phil. 3:17, according to **p**

PAY Matt. 18:28, **P** back what you owe
Gen. 50:15; Ex. 22:7; Deut. 23:21; Job 22:27; Mark 12:15

PEACE Num. 6:26, give you **p**
Ps. 34:14, Seek **p**, and pursue it
37:37, man of **p** will have a posterity
119:165, who love Thy law have great **p**
Eccles. 3:8, time for war, and a time for **p**
Is. 9:6, Eternal Father, Prince of **P**
Matt. 10:13, let your *greeting of* **p**
10:34, I did not come to bring **p**
Mark 9:50, be at **p** with one another

Luke 1:79, guide our feet . . . way of **p**
2:14, on earth **p** among men
John 14:27, **P** I leave you; My **p**
20:19, **P** be with you
Acts 24:2, we have through you attained **p**
Rom. 15:33, the God of **p** be with you
1 Cor. 7:15, God has called us to **p**
Gal. 5:22, fruit of the Spirit is . . . **p**
Eph. 2:14, He Himself is our **p**
Phil. 4:7, **p** of God, which surpasses all
1 Thess. 5:13, Live in **p** with one another
5:23, may the God of **P** . . . sanctify
2 Thess. 3:16, Lord of **p** . . . grant you **p**
Heb. 12:14, Pursue **p** with all men
James 2:16, Go in **p**
1 Pet. 5:14, **P** be to you all
Gen. 15:15; Lev. 26:6; 2 Kin. 9:17; Job 15:21; Ps. 4:8; 147:14; Prov. 3:17; 16:7; Is. 36:16; 52:7; 57:19; Jer. 6:14

PEARLS—*jewel*
Job 28:18, acquisition of wisdom . . . **P**

PECK Matt. 13:33, hid in three **p-s** of meal

PECK-MEASURE Matt. 5:15; Mark 4:21

PEG—*nail* Judg. 4:21; Is. 22:23

PENALTY 2 Thess. 1:9, pay the **p** of eternal destruction

PEOPLE Ps. 100:3, *We are* His **p** and the sheep
Prov. 11:14, no guidance, the **p** fall
29:18, no vision, the **p** are unrestrained
Matt. 1:21, save His **p** from their sins
Mark 7:6, **p** HONORS ME WITH THEIR LIPS
John 11:50, man should die for the **p**
Jude 16, flattering **p** for . . . advantage
Ex. 6:7; Ruth 1:16; Ps. 2:1; Mark 6:5; Acts 5:16

PERCEIVING Mark 2:8, Jesus, **p** in His spirit

PERDITION John 17:12, the son of **p**

PERFECT Deut. 32:4, The Rock! His work is **p**
Ps. 19:7, law of the LORD is **p**
Matt. 5:48, Therefore you are to be **p**
1 Cor. 13:10, but when the **p** comes
2 Cor. 12:9, power is **p-ed** in weakness
Phil. 1:6, **p** it until the day of Christ Jesus
James 1:4, endurance have *its* **p** result
1:25, **p** law, the *law* of liberty
1 John 4:17, love is **p-ed** with us

PERFECTER Heb. 12:2, author and **p** of faith

PERFORM—*wrought* Is. 26:12, **p-ed** for us all our works
Ps. 103:6; Luke 1:8; Rom. 4:21

PERFUME Is. 3:24, instead of
sweet **p**
Matt. 26:7; Luke 7:46

PERFUMERS 1 Sam. 8:13, daughters
for **p**

PERHAPS Mark 11:13; Acts 17:27;
1 Cor. 15:37

PERISH—*fail* Ps. 1:6, way of the
wicked will **p**
Matt. 8:25, Save us, Lord; we are **p-
ing**
18:14, one of these little ones **p**
John 6:27, work for the food which
p-s
1 Cor. 9:25, *do it* to receive a **p-able**
wreath
15:42, It is sown a **p-able** body
15:53, this **p-able** must put on
2 Cor. 4:3, veiled to those who are **p-
ing**
1 Pet. 1:23, not of seed which is **p-
able**
2 Pet. 3:9, not wishing for any to **p**
Num. 17:12; 2 Sam. 1:27; Job 34:15;
Prov. 22:8; Ezek. 37:11

PERJURY Zech. 8:17, do not love **p**

PERMISSION Mark 5:13, And He
gave them **p**

PERMIT—*suffer* Matt. 3:15, **P** *it* at
this time

PERPETUAL Ex. 40:15; Num. 25:13,
a **p** priesthood
Heb. 7:3, abides a priest **p-ly**
Ex. 31:16; Ps. 9:6; Jer. 15:18; 51:39;
Hab. 3:6

PERSECUTE Matt. 5:11, when *men*
revile you, and **p** you
5:44, pray for those who **p** you
10:23, they **p** you in this city, flee
John 15:20, If they **p-d** Me, they will
also **p**
Acts 9:4, Saul, why are you **p-ing** Me
1 Cor. 4:12, when we are **p-d**, we
endure
2 Cor. 4:9, **p-d**, but not forsaken
Job 19:22; Ps. 143:3

PERSEVERANCE Luke 21:19, By
your **p** you will win
Rom. 2:7, by **p** in doing good
5:3, tribulation brings about **p**
15:4, **p** and the encouragement of
the Scriptures
2 Thess. 1:4, for your **p** and faith

PERSEVERE Rom. 12:12, hope, **p-
ing** in tribulation
James 1:12, Blessed is a man who **p-
s** under trial

PERSON—*soul* Lev. 4:2, If a **p** sins
unintentionally
Eccles. 12:13, this *applies to* every **p**
Is. 32:6, keep the hungry **p**
unsatisfied
Rom. 13:1, Let every **p** be in
subjection
Jude 4, certain **p-s** have crept in
unnoticed

PERSUADE 2 Kin. 4:8, she **p-d** him
to eat food
Prov. 25:15, a ruler may be **p-d**
Acts 26:28, you will **p** me

PERSUASIVE 1 Cor. 2:4, were not in
p words
Col. 2:4, delude you with **p** argument

PERVERSE Acts 20:30, speaking **p**
things
Phil. 2:15, a crooked and **p**
generation
Deut. 32:5,20; Ps. 101:4; Prov. 23:33

PERVERSION Lev. 18:23, it is a **p**

PERVERT Deut. 16:19; 2 Sam. 22:27;
Job 8:3; Prov. 10:31

PETITION Ps. 20:5, the LORD fulfill
all your **p-s**
1 Tim. 2:1, prayers, **p-s** and
thanksgivings
1 Sam. 1:17; Dan. 6:7,13

PHYSICIAN Jer. 8:22, Is there no **p**
there
Matt. 9:12, not . . . healthy who need
a **p**
Luke 4:23, **P**, heal yourself
Col. 4:14, Luke, the beloved **p**

PICK Mark 16:18, they will **p** up
serpents
Gen. 8:11; Mark 2:23

PIECE Matt. 14:20, left over of the
broken **p-s**
Mark 6:43, twelve full baskets of
broken **p-s**
Gen. 18:5; Ruth 2:14; 1 Sam. 2:36;
Luke 24:42

PIERCE—*wound* Judg. 5:26,
shattered and **p-d** his temple
Ps. 22:16, They **p-d** my hands . . .
feet
Is. 53:5, **p-d** through for our
transgressions
Zech. 12:10, on Me whom they have
p-d
Luke 2:35, **p** even your own soul
John 19:34, soldiers **p-d** His side

PIETY 1 Tim. 5:4, practice **p** in
regard

PILES Job 27:16, he **p** up silver like
dust

PILLAGE Nah. 3:1, city, . . . full of
lies *and* **p**

PILLAR Gen. 19:26, she became a **p**
of salt
Job 26:11, The **p-s** of heaven tremble
Gal. 2:9, John, who were reputed to
be **p-s**
1 Tim. 3:15, **p** and support of the
truth
Prov. 9:1; Ezek. 26:11

PILOT James 3:4, inclination of the **p**
desires

PIT—*destruction, dungeon*
Gen. 14:10, Siddim . . . tar **p-s**
37:20, throw him into one of the **p-s**
Ex. 21:33, a man opens a **p**, or digs
a **p**
Job 17:14, I call to the **p**, You are my
father
33:18, his soul from the **p**
Ps. 16:10, Holy One to see the **p**
103:4, redeems your life from the **p**
Prov. 23:27, a harlot is a deep **p**

PLAY Gen. 4:21; Ex. 32:6; 1 Sam.
16:17; 1 Kin. 1:40; Job 41:5;

Lam. 3:53, they have silenced me in
the **p**
Matt. 15:14, both will fall into a **p**

PITCH Gen. 6:14, cover it . . . with **p**
Gen. 33:19, where he had **p-ed** his
tent
Ex. 2:3, covered it over with tar
and **p**

PITCHER—*bowl, jar*
Judg. 7:16, put trumpets and empty
p-s
1 Kin. 18:33, fill four **p-s**
Eccles. 12:6, the **p** by the well is
shattered
Mark 14:13, man . . . carrying a **p** of
water

PITY—*compassion* Ex. 2:6; Deut.
7:16; Job 19:21

PLACE—*room* Deut. 33:27, eternal
God is a dwelling **p**
Ps. 31:8, set my feet in a large **p**
Prov. 15:3, eyes . . . LORD . . . in
every **p**
Matt. 23:6, love the **p** of honor at
banquets
24:51, **p** with the hypocrites
26:36, a **p** called Gethsemane
27:33, a **p** called Golgotha . . . **P** of a
Skull
28:6, **p** where He was lying
Luke 4:17, **p** where it was written
14:8, do not take the **p** of honor
John 14:2, go to prepare a **p** for you
Acts 13:47, I HAVE **P-D** YOU AS A
LIGHT FOR
1 Cor. 14:16, fills the **p** of the
ungifted
2 Pet. 1:19, lamp shining in a dark **p**
Rev. 20:11, no **p** was found for them
Gen. 1:9; 30:2; Ex. 3:5; 21:13; Num.
32:14; Deut. 2:23; 34:6; Judg. 18:10;
Job 9:6; 16:4; Ps. 24:3; Is. 49:20;
Jer. 51:51; Dan. 8:14; Hab. 3:11;
Luke 14:9; John 18:2

PLAGUE Gen. 12:17; Rev. 16:21; 21:9

PLAIN—*distinct, clear* Is. 40:4;
Mark 7:35; John 16:25

PLAN—*devise* Ps. 36:4, He **p-s**
wickedness upon his bed
Prov. 16:9, mind of a man **p-s** his
way
19:21, Many are the **p-s** in a man's
heart
2 Sam. 14:14; Prov. 15:22; Jer. 18:12

PLANT Gen. 3:18, you shall eat the
p-s of the field
Ps. 1:3, tree . . . **p-ed** by streams
Eccles. 3:2, A time to **p**, and a time
to
Matt. 13:32; Mark 4:32, larger than
. . . the garden **p-s**
15:13, **p** . . . Father did not **p**
Mark 12:1, A man **P-ED** A VINEYARD
Luke 17:6, be **p-ed** in the sea
1 Cor. 3:6, I **p-ed**, Apollos watered
Gen. 1:29,30; 2:5,8; 9:3; Ex. 9:22,25;
10:12,15; Deut. 6:11; 2 Kin. 19:29;
Job 14:9; Ps. 92:13

PLASTER Ezek. 13:10, **p** it over with
whitewash

Ps. 33:3; Is. 11:8; Matt. 11:17;
1 Cor. 14:7

PLEAD Gen. 42:21; Deut. 3:23; 1
Sam. 12:7; Ps. 43:1; Is. 1:17

PLEASANT—*smooth, sweet*
Ps. 16:6, lines have fallen . . . **p**
133:1, how good and how **p** it is
Eccles. 5:12, sleep of the working
man is **p**
2 Sam. 1:23; Prov. 9:17; 16:24; Is.
30:10

PLEASE Matt. 3:17, Son, in whom I
am well **p-d**
Rom. 15:1, not *just* **p** ourselves
15:3, Christ did not **p** Himself
1 Cor. 7:33, how he may **p** his wife
7:34, how she may **p** her husband
10:5, God was not well **p-d**
Heb. 13:16, sacrifices God is **p-d**

PLEASING—*acceptable*
Prov. 16:7, man's ways . . . **p** . . .
Lᴏʀᴅ
Matt. 11:26, it was **well-p** in Thy
sight
John 8:29, things that are **p** to Him
2 Cor. 5:9, to be **p** to Him
Eph. 5:10, what is **p** to the Lord
Gen. 2:9; 1 Kin. 3:10

PLEASURE Ps. 16:11, there are **p-s**
forever
Ps. 149:4, Lᴏʀᴅ takes **p** in His people
Luke 8:14, worries and riches and
p-s
Phil. 2:13, to work for *His* good **p**
Heb. 11:25, the passing **p-s** of sin
Gen. 18:12; Job 36:11; Prov. 21:17;
Is. 53:10

PLEDGE Prov. 22:26, among those
who give **p-s**
2 Cor. 1:22, the Spirit in our hearts
as a **p**
5:5, gave to us the Spirit as a **p**
Eph. 1:14, given as a **p** of our
inheritance
1 Tim. 5:12, set aside their
previous **p**

PLENTEOUS Is. 30:23, it will be rich
and **p**

PLENTIFUL Ps. 68:9, didst shed
abroad a **p** rain
Matt. 9:37, harvest is **p**

PLENTY Gen. 33:9; Prov. 3:10; 12:11;
Joel 2:26

PLOT Prov. 30:32, if you have **p-ed**
evil
Matt. 26:4; Acts 9:23; 23:13

PLOW Is. 2:4, their swords into **p-shares**
Joel 3:10, **p-shares** into swords
Luke 9:62, putting his hand to the **p**
1 Cor. 9:10, to **p** in hope
Deut. 22:10; Job 4:8; Prov. 20:4

PLUCK Ps. 25:15; Ezek. 17:22

PLUMAGE Job 39:13, pinion and **p**
of love

PLUNDER (n.)—*booty* Judg. 5:19;
Hab. 2:7; Zeph. 1:13

PLUNDER (v.)—*spoil* Matt. 12:29,
he will **p** his house
Ex. 3:22; Ps. 76:5; Is. 42:22

PLUNGE 1 Tim. 6:9, desires which **p**
men into ruin

POINT Jer. 17:1; Mark 5:23; James
2:10

POISON Ps. 140:3; Jer. 8:14; Amos
6:12; Mark 16:18

POLE—*staff* Num. 13:23, carried it
on a **p** between two

POLLUTE—*spot* Num. 35:33; Jer.
16:18; Jude 23

POMP Is. 14:11, Your **p** *and* the
music

PONDER Prov. 5:6, **p** the path of life
Luke 2:19, **p-ing** them in her heart

POOR Prov. 13:7, *Another* pretends
to be **p**
Prov. 20:13, lest you become **p**
Amos 5:11, impose heavy rent upon
the **p**
Matt. 5:3, Blessed are the **p** in
11:5, the **ᴘ ʜᴀᴠᴇ ᴛʜᴇ ɢᴏsᴘᴇʟ
ᴘʀᴇᴀᴄʜᴇᴅ**
26:11, **p** you have with you always
Mark 10:21, and give *it* to the **p**
12:42, And a **p** widow came
Luke 4:18, **ᴘʀᴇᴀᴄʜ ᴛʜᴇ ɢᴏsᴘᴇʟ ᴛᴏ
ᴛʜᴇ ᴘ**
19:8, my possessions I will give to
the **p**
2 Cor. 8:9, for your sake He became
p
James 2:5, God choose the **p** of this
1 Sam. 2:8; 2 Sam. 12:4; Prov. 22:22;
Is. 3:15; 1 Cor. 13:3

PORPOISE SKINS Ex. 25:5; 26:14

PORTION Deut. 32:9, Lᴏʀᴅ's **p** is His
people
2 Kin. 2:9, double **p** of your spirit
Ps. 119:57, The Lᴏʀᴅ is my **p**
Gen. 31:14; Eccles. 11:2; Acts 8:21

POSSESS Gen. 15:7; 24:60; Ps. 44:3;
Is. 54:3; 2 Cor. 6:10

POSSESSION—*property, treasure*
Gen. 17:8
Matt. 24:47, in charge of all his **p-s**
Luke 19:8, half of my **p-s** I will give
to the
Ex. 6:8; 19:5; 21:16; 34:9; Deut. 4:20;
Ps. 104:24; Acts 2:45

POSSIBLE Matt. 19:26, with God all
things **p**
Matt. 26:39, **p**, let this cup pass
Luke 18:27, are **p** with God
Rom. 12:18, If **p**, so far as it depends

POT Ex. 16:3; 2 Kin. 4:40; Job 41:31;
Jer. 1:13

POUR Eccles. 11:3, clouds are full,
they **p** out rain
Joel 2:28, **p** out My Spirit on all
mankind
Matt. 26:7, **p-ed** it upon His head
Luke 22:20, cup which is **p-ed** . . .
covenant in My blood
John 2:15, **p-ed** out the coins

Acts 10:45, gift of the Holy Spirit . . .
p-ed out
Rom. 5:5, love of God **p-ed** out
within our hearts
Phil. 2:17, if I am being **p-ed** out as
Rev. 16:2, **p-ed** out his bowl
1 Sam. 1:15; Job 10:10; 29:6; Is. 44:3;
Matt. 9:17

POVERTY Prov. 23:21, glutton will
come to **p**
Prov. 30:8, neither **p** nor riches
2 Cor. 8:9, through His **p**

POWER—*authority, strength*
Deut. 8:18, you to make wealth
1 Chr. 29:11, the **p** and the glory
Is. 40:29, *who* lacks might He
increases **p**
Matt. 6:13, kingdom, and the **p**, and
Mark 5:30, **p** . . . from Him had gone
forth
9:1, kingdom of God . . . come with
p
13:26, ɪɴ ᴄʟᴏᴜᴅs with great **p**
14:62, ᴀᴛ ᴛʜᴇ ʀɪɢʜᴛ ʜᴀɴᴅ ᴏF **P**
Luke 1:35, **p** of the Most High will
overshadow
4:14, in the **p** of the Spirit
22:69, ʀɪɢʜᴛ ʜᴀɴᴅ of the **p** ᴏF ɢᴏᴅ
Acts 1:8, you shall receive **p** when
8:10, called the Great **P** of God
Rom. 1:4, with **p** to be the Son of
God
1:16, the **p** of God for salvation
1 Cor. 1:24, Christ the **p** of God
15:56, the **p** of sin is the law
2 Cor. 12:9, **p** is perfected in
weakness
Eph. 1:21, authority and **p** and
dominion
2:2, prince of the **p** of the air
Phil. 3:21, exertion of the **p**
Heb. 1:3, by the word of His **p**
11:34, quenched the **p** of fire
Ex. 15:6; Judg. 7:2; Job 40:16; Ps.
49:15; Prov. 3:27; Jer. 18:21;
1 Cor. 5:4; 1 Pet. 3:22

PRACTICE Ps. 28:4, evil of their **p-s**
Matt. 6:1, Beware of **p-ing** your
righteousness
Acts 19:18, disclosing their **p-s**
1 Cor. 11:16, we have no other **p**
Col. 3:9, laid aside the old self with
its *evil* **p-s**
1 Tim. 5:4, **p** piety in regard to their
own family
1 John 1:6, we lie and do not **p** the
truth
3:8, the one who **p-s** sin is of the

PRAETORIUM Matt. 27:27, soldiers
. . . took Jesus into the **P**
Mark 15:16, took Him . . . into the
palace (that is, the **P**)
John 18:28, led Jesus . . . into the **P**
18:33, Pilate . . . entered . . . into
the **P**

PRAISE—*bless, commend*
Ex. 15:11, Awesome in **p-s**
Ps. 89:5, heavens will **p** Thy wonders
Prov. 27:21, man *is tested* by the **p**
Matt. 11:25, I **p** Thee, O Father
Luke 16:8, his master **p-d** the
unrighteous steward
Rom. 2:29, his **p** is not from men
Phil. 4:8, if anything worthy of **p**
James 5:13, Let him sing **p-s**
Deut. 10:21; 1 Chr. 16:9; Neh. 12:46;
Ps. 22:25; Prov. 12:8; Is. 38:18

PRAY—*ask* Is. 45:20, And **p** to a god who cannot save
Matt. 5:44, **p** for those who persecute
6:5, And when you **p**
6:6, **p** to your Father . . . in secret
6:7, **p-ing**, do not use meaningless
14:23, mountain by Himself to **p**
26:41, Keep watching and **p-ing**, that
Mark 11:24, you **p** and ask, believe
Luke 11:1, Lord, teach us to **p** just
18:1, they ought to **p** and not
22:40, **P** that you may not . . . temptation
1 Cor. 11:13, for a woman to **p** to God
14:14, if I **p** in a tongue
Col. 1:9, not ceased to **p** for you
1 Thess. 5:17, **p** without ceasing
James 5:13, suffering? Let him **p**
5:16, and **p** for one another
Gen. 20:7; Ex. 33:18; 1 Sam. 7:5; 12:23; Jon. 1:14

PRAYER Ps. 55:1, Give ear to my **p**, O God
Is. 56:7, called a house of **p**
Matt. 17:21, out except by **p** and fasting
21:22, everything . . . in **p**, believing
Luke 6:12, whole night in **p**
19:46, A HOUSE OF P
Acts 3:1, the hour of **p**
Rom. 1:10, in my **p-s** making request
12:12, devoted to **p**
1 Cor. 7:5; Col. 4:2, devote yourselves to **p**
1 Pet. 3:7, your **p-s** may not be hindered
1 Kin. 8:45; Neh. 11:17; Ps. 4:1

PREACH—*declare, exhort, proclaim*
Matt. 4:17, that time Jesus began to **p**
10:7, go, **p**, saying . . . kingdom . . . is at hand
11:1, and **p** in their cities
11:5, POOR . . . GOSPEL P-ED to them
Mark 13:10, gospel . . . **p-ed** to all the nations
16:15, **p** the gospel to all
Luke 4:43, **p** the kingdom of God
Acts 13:32, we **p** to you the good news of the promise
1 Cor. 1:17, not . . . to baptize, but to **p**
1:23, we **p** Christ crucified
2 Cor. 4:5, we do not **p** ourselves
1 Tim. 6:2, Teach and **p** these *principles*
2 Tim. 4:2, **p** the word, be ready

PREACHER Eccles. 1:1, words of the **P**
Rom. 10:14, how shall they hear without a **p**
1 Tim. 2:7, I was appointed a **p**
2 Pet. 2:5, Noah, a **p** of righteousness

PREACHING—*talk, word* Matt. 3:1, John . . . **p**
Mark 1:4, **p** a baptism of repentance
1:39, **p** and casting out the demons
Acts 5:42, teaching and **p** Jesus
8:4, scattered went about **p** the word
Rom. 16:25, **p** of Jesus Christ
1 Cor. 15:14, then our **p** is vain

PRECEDE 1 Thess. 4:15, **p** those who have fallen asleep

PRECEPT—*statute* Ps. 19:8, **p-s** of the LORD are right

PRECIOUS—*excellent* Ps. 36:7, How **p** is Thy lovingkindness
Ps. 116:15, **P** in the sight of the LORD
Prov. 3:15, more **p** than jewels
Is. 44:9, their **p** things are of no profit
1 Pet. 1:7, more **p** than gold which
1:19, but with **p** blood . . . of Christ

PREDETERMINE Acts 2:23, **p-d** plan and foreknowledge of God

PREEMINENT—*excellence* Gen. 49:3, **P** in dignity and **p** in

PREPARATION—*serve* Luke 10:40, distracted with all her **p-s**

PREPARE—*fashion, furnish, ready* Gen. 18:6
Ps. 23:5, dost **p** a table before me
78:19, God **p** a table in the
Matt. 11:10, WHO WILL P YOUR WAY
25:34, the kingdom **p-d** for you
John 14:2, I go to **p** a place for you
1 Cor. 2:9, P-D FOR THOSE WHO LOVE HIM
Heb. 11:3, worlds were **p-d** by the word
Lev. 7:9; Job 12:5; Ps. 57:6; Rom. 9:22

PRESCRIBE—*command* 1 Tim. 4:11, **P** and teach these things

PRESENCE Ex. 33:14, My **p** shall go *with you*
Ps. 23:5, **p** of my enemies
44:3, light of Thy **p**
95:2, before His **p** with thanksgiving
Is. 64:2, nations may tremble at Thy **p**
Luke 13:26, ate and drank in Your **p**
Jude 24, **p** of His glory blameless
Rev. 14:10, in the **p** of the Lamb

PRESENT—*offer, yield*
Gen. 43:11, to the man as a **p**
Ps. 46:1, A very **p** help in trouble
Mal. 1:8, **p** the blind . . . **p** the lame and
Luke 2:22, to **p** Him to the Lord
Rom. 6:13, **p-ing** the members of your body to sin
12:1, **p** your bodies a living sacrifice
1 Cor. 5:3, but **p** in spirit
Col. 1:22, **p** you before Him holy and blameless
2 Tim. 2:15, **p** yourself approved to God
4:10, loved this **p** world

PRESERVATION—*health* Acts 27:34, food . . . for your **p**

PRESERVE—*guard, keep*
2 Sam. 18:18, no son to **p** my name
Ps. 16:1, **P** me, O God, for I take refuge
86:2, **p** my soul, for I am a godly man
Prov. 14:3, lips of the wise will **p** them
Luke 17:33, loses *his* life shall **p** it

Eph. 4:3, diligent to **p** the unity of the Spirit
1 Thess. 5:23, soul and body be **p-d** complete

PRESS Matt. 27:32, they **p-ed** . . . to bear His cross
Luke 6:38, good measure **p-ed** down
Phil. 3:14, I **p** on toward the goal

PRESUME—*dare* Rom. 15:18, I will not **p** to speak

PRESUMPTION Prov. 13:10, Through **p** comes nothing

PRETEND—*disguise* 2 Sam. 14:2, **p** to be a mourner
1 Kin. 14:5,6, **p** to be another woman
Luke 20:20, sent spies who **p-ed** to be righteous

PRETTY Jer. 46:20, Egypt is a **p** heifer

PREVAIL Gen. 7:20, water **p-ed** fifteen cubits higher
1 Sam. 2:9, not by might shall a man **p**
Ps. 65:3; Jer. 20:7

PREVALENT Eccles. 6:1, an evil . . . it is **p**

PREVENT Matt. 3:14, John tried to **p** Him,

PREY Ps. 76:4; Ezek. 22:25

PRICE Acts 1:18, field with the **p** of his wickedness
5:2, kept back *some* of the **p**
1 Cor. 6:20, you have been bought with a **p**
Lev. 25:16; Dan. 11:39; Mic. 3:11

PRIDE Prov. 16:18, **P** goes before destruction
Mark 7:22, slander, **p** *and* foolishness
1 John 2:16, the boastful **p** of life
Prov. 8:13; Is. 13:19; 60:15; Ezek. 32:12

PRIEST Gen. 14:18, **p** of God Most High
Ex. 19:6, shall be to Me a kingdom of **p-s**
1 Sam. 2:35, raise up for Myself a faithful **p**
Ps. 110:4, **p** forever . . . order of Melchizedek
Ezek. 44:21, Nor shall any of the **p-s** drink wine
Matt. 2:4, together all the chief **p-s**
8:4, SHOW YOURSELF TO THE P
Heb. 2:17, faithful high **p**
3:1, High **P** of our confession
5:6, P FOREVER . . . ORDER OF MELCHIZEDEK
2 Chr. 15:3; Is. 24:2

PRIME—*flower* 1 Sam. 2:33, will die in the **p** of life

PRINCE—*ruler* Ex. 2:14, Who made you a **p** or a judge
2 Sam. 3:38, **p** and a great man has fallen
Is. 9:6, **P** of Peace
Acts 3:15, put to death the **P** of life
5:31, as a **P** and a Saviour
Eph. 2:2, **p** of the power of the air

PRINCESS—*lady* Judg. 5:29, Her wise **p-es** would answer

PRINCIPALITY Rom. 8:38, nor **p-es** . . . nor powers

PRISON Judg. 16:21, he was a grinder in the **p**
Ps. 142:7, Bring my soul out of **p**
Matt. 14:10, had John beheaded in the **p**
Acts 5:19, Lord . . . opened the gates of the **p**
16:27, jailer . . . had seen the **p** doors opened
1 Kin. 22:27; Rev. 18:2

PRISONER Ps. 102:20, groaning of the **p**
Ps. 146:7, the LORD sets the **p-s** free
Matt. 27:15, release for the multitude *any* one **p**
Rom. 7:23, making me a **p** of the law
Eph. 3:1, Paul, the **p** of Christ Jesus
2 Tim. 1:8, ashamed . . . or of me His **p**

PRIVATION—*adversity, distress*
Is. 30:20, given you bread of **p**

PRIZE Col. 2:18, defrauding you of your **p**

PROCEED Deut. 8:3, everything that **p-s** out of the mouth
Jer. 9:3, **p** from evil to evil
Matt. 4:4, WORD THAT **P-S** OUT OF THE MOUTH
Mark 7:21, heart of men, **p** the evil thoughts
John 15:26, who **p-s** from the Father
2 Tim. 3:13, imposters will **p** . . . to worse

PROCLAIM—*declare, tell*
Ex. 33:19; Deut. 32:3, **p** the name of the LORD
Is. 61:1, **p** liberty to the captives
61:2, **p** the favorable year of the LORD
Jer. 34:15, **p-ing** release to his neighbor
Matt. 10:27; Luke 12:3, **p-ed** upon the housetops
Acts 17:3, Jesus whom I am **p-ing** to you
17:23, you worship in ignorance, this I **p** to
26:23, **p** light both to the *Jewish* and
1 Pet. 3:19, made **p-ation** to the spirits
1 John 1:3, what we have seen and heard we **p**

PROCONSUL—*deputy* Acts 13:7; 18:12; 19:38

PRODUCE—*yield* Deut. 14:22, tithe all the **p**
Ps. 67:6, the earth has yielded its **p**
2 Tim. 2:23, knowing that they **p** quarrels
James 3:12, Neither can salt water **p** fresh
Lev. 25:19; Hos. 10:1

PRODUCTIVE Luke 12:16, land . . . was **p**

PROFANE—*defile, pollute* Lev. 21:7,23; Ezek. 22:8

Ex. 31:14, Everyone who **p-s** it . . . put to death
Lev. 20:3, to **p** My holy name
Ezek. 23:38, have **p-d** My sabbaths
1 Tim. 1:9, law . . . for the unholy and **p**

PROFESS—*confession* Rom. 1:22, **P-ing** to be wise
Titus 1:16, They **p** to know God

PROFIT Job 15:3, words which are not **p-able**
Prov. 14:23, In all labor there is **p**
15:27, who **p-s** illicitly troubles his own
Matt. 16:26; Luke 9:25, will a man be **p-ed**
John 6:63, the flesh **p-s** nothing
Acts 16:19; hope of **p** was gone
1 Cor. 6:12; 10:23, not all things are **p-able**
13:3, not have love, it **p-s** me nothing
1 Tim. 4:8, bodily discipline is only of little **p**
2 Tim. 3:16, Scripture . . . **p-able** for teaching
James 4:13, engage in business and make a **p**
Gen. 37:26; Prov. 3:14; Is. 48:17; Jer. 16:19

PROGRESS Phil. 1:12, greater **p** of the gospel

PROLONG Prov. 10:27, fear of the Lord **p-s** life

PROMINENCE Acts 13:50, devout women of **p**

PROMINENT Mark 15:43, Joseph . . . **p** member

PROMISCUITY Rom. 13:13, not in sexual **p** and sensuality

PROMISE Acts 2:33, **p** of the Holy Spirit
Acts 26:6, hope of the **p** made by God
Rom. 4:14, **p** is nullified
9:8, children of the **p**
Gal. 3:14, might receive the **p** of the Spirit
Eph. 6:2, first commandment with a **p**
2 Tim. 1:1, **p** of life in Christ Jesus
Titus 1:2, **p-d** long ages ago
Heb. 10:23, for He who **p-d** is faithful
2 Pet. 1:4, His precious and magnificent **p-s**

PROMOTE Esth. 5:11; Ps. 140:8

PRONOUNCE—*utter* Jer. 1:16, I will **p** My judgments
Luke 23:24, Pilate **p-d** sentence

PROOF Acts 17:31, furnished **p** to all men
2 Cor. 8:24, show them the **p** of your love
13:3, **p** of the Christ who speaks in me

PROPER Rom. 13:13, Let us behave **p-ly** as in the day
1 Cor. 11:13, is it **p** for a woman to pray
14:40, let all things be done **p-ly**

Eph. 5:3, as is **p** among saints
1 Thess. 4:12, you may behave **p-ly** toward outsiders
1 Tim. 2:6, testimony *borne* at the **p** time

PROPERTY—*goods*
Gen. 34:10, and acquire **p** in it
Matt. 12:29, carry off his **p**
19:22, one who owned much **p**
Acts 2:45, selling their **p** and possessions

PROPHECY Dan. 9:24, seal up vision and **p**
1 Cor. 13:2, if I have the gift of **p**
2 Pet. 1:21, no **p** was ever made by . . . human will
Rev. 19:10, testimony . . . is the spirit of **p**

PROPHESY 1 Sam. 10:11, he **p-ed** now with the prophets
Is. 30:10, not **p** to us what is right
Matt. 7:22, did we not **p** in Your name
26:68, **P** to us, You Christ
1 Cor. 13:9, know in part, and we **p** in part
1 Chr. 25:3; Jer. 14:14; Ezek. 37:4; Joel 2:28

PROPHET Matt. 1:22, spoken . . . through the **p**
Matt. 2:5, it had been written by the **p**
2:15, through the **p** might be fulfilled
2:17, Jeremiah the **p**
5:12, so they persecuted the **p-s**
10:41, **p** shall receive a **p-'s** reward
11:9, one who is more than a **p**
11:13, all the **p-s** and the Law
13:57, **p** is not without honor
21:11, the **p** Jesus, from Nazareth
Luke 4:24, no **p** is welcome in his home town
6:23, their fathers used to treat the **p-s**
John 1:21, Are you the **P**
4:19, perceive that You are a **p**
7:52, see that no **p** arises out of Galilee
Acts 13:15, reading of the Law and the **P-s**
1 Cor. 14:37, If anyone thinks he is a **p**
Eph. 4:11, some *as* apostles, and some *as* **p-s**
Heb. 1:1, to the fathers in the **p-s**
Gen. 20:7; Deut. 13:1; 18:18; Judg. 4:4; 1 Sam. 9:9; 1 Kin. 20:35; Is. 9:15; Jer. 23:11; Ezek. 13:3; Hos. 12:10; Amos 7:14; Acts 13:6

PROPHETIC 1 Thess. 5:20, do not despise **p** utterances
2 Pet. 1:19, the **p** word made more sure

PROSELYTE Matt. 23:15, make one **p**
Acts 2:10, both Jews and **p-s**
13:43, God-fearing **p-s** followed Paul

PROSPER 1 Sam. 18:14, David was **p-ing**
Ps. 10:5, His ways **p** at all times
Prov. 28:13, his transgressions will not **p**
1 Cor. 16:2, save, as he may **p**
Gen. 39:3; 1 Sam. 18:5

PROSPERITY—*wealth*
Ezra 9:12, never seek . . . their **p**
Job 21:13, spend their days in **p**
Ps. 25:13, His soul will abide in **p**
73:3, saw the **p** of the wicked
Acts 19:25, our **p** depends upon this business

PROSPEROUS Prov. 11:25, generous man will be **p**

PROSTITUTES Hos. 4:14, offer sacrifices with temple **p**

PROSTRATE 2 Sam. 9:6, fell on his face and **p-d** himself
Job 14:10, man dies and lies **p**

PROTECT Is. 31:5, He will **p** and deliver it

PROTECTION Num. 14:9, Their **p** has been removed
Eccles. 7:12, wisdom is **p** *just as* money is **p**

PROUD—*arrogant, conceited*
Ps. 94:2, recompense to the **p**
Luke 1:51, **p** in the thoughts of their heart
James 4:6, GOD IS OPPOSED TO THE **P**
Is. 3:16; 13:11

PROVE—*test* Prov. 30:6; 2 Cor. 8:8
Acts 9:22, **p-ing** that this *Jesus* is the Christ
Rom. 12:2, **p** what the will of God is

PROVERB 1 Kin. 4:32, He also spoke 3,000 **p-s**
1 Kin. 9:7, Israel will become a **p** and a byword
Deut. 28:37; Jer. 24:9; 2 Pet. 2:22

PROVIDE—*gave* Gen. 22:8, God will **p** for Himself the Lamb
Neh. 9:15, didst **p** bread from heaven
1 Tim. 5:8, if any one does not **p** for his own
Lev. 25:24; 1 Sam. 16:17

PROVISION Josh. 9:5, bread of their **p** was dry
Ps. 132:15, abundantly bless her **p**
Rom. 13:14, make no **p** for the flesh

PROVOKE Prov. 20:2, who **p-s** him to anger
1 Cor. 13:5, is not **p-d**
Eph. 6:4, do not **p** your children to anger
2 Chr. 25:19; Job 12:6

PROW Acts 27:41, the **p** stuck fast and remained

PROWL—*walk* Ps. 104:20, beast of the forest
1 Pet. 5:8, devil, **p-s** about like a roaring lion

PRUDENT Prov. 12:16, **p** man conceals dishonor
Prov. 19:14, a **p** wife is from the LORD
Jer. 49:7, good counsel been lost to the **p**

PSALMS Ps. 95:2, shout joyfully to Him with **p**
Luke 20:42, David . . . says in the book of **P**
24:44, the **P** must be fulfilled

Eph. 5:19, speaking to one another in **p**

PUGNACIOUS 1 Tim. 3:3, addicted to wine or **p**

PULL Ps. 31:4, **p** me out of the net
Luke 14:5, **p** him out on a Sabbath day

PULVERIZE Mic. 4:13, That you may **p** many peoples

PUNISH—*visit* Lev. 26:18,28, will **p** you seven times
Is. 13:11, **p** the world for its evil
Lam. 4:22, He will **p** your iniquity
2 Cor. 10:6, to **p** all disobedience
Prov. 22:3; Luke 23:16; Acts 26:11

PUNISHMENT Gen. 4:13, **p** is too great to bear
Job 19:29, the **p** of the sword
Matt. 25:46, go away into eternal **p**
2 Cor. 2:6, Sufficient . . . is this **p**
1 John 4:18, because fear involves **p**
Jude 7, the **p** of eternal fire

PUPIL Deut. 32:10, **p** of His eye
Luke 6:40, a **p** is not above his teacher

PURCHASE Gen. 49:32, field . . . **p-d** from
Acts 20:28, He **p-d** with His own blood
Rev. 5:9, **p** for God with Thy blood

PURE Ps. 12:6, words of the LORD are **p** words
Ps. 19:8, commandment of the LORD is **p**
24:4, clean hands and a **p** heart
Matt. 5:8, Blessed are the **p** in heart
2 Cor. 11:2, present you *as* a **p** virgin
Phil. 4:8, whatever is **p**
1 Tim. 1:5, love from a **p** heart
Titus 1:15, To the **p**, all things are **p**
2:5, *be* sensible, **p**
James 1:27, **p** and undefiled religion
2 Sam. 22:27; Job 4:17; 11:4; 15:15; Song 6:10; Dan. 7:9

PURGE Dan. 12:10, Many will be **p-d**, purified, refined

PURIFY Ps. 51:7, **P** me with hyssop
1 Pet. 1:22, obedience . . . **p-ed** your souls
2 Pet. 1:9, **p-cation** from his former sins
2 Kin. 2:21; Dan. 12:10

PURPOSE—*cause, devise, reason*
Jer. 49:20, **p-s** which He has **p-d**
Lam. 2:17, The LORD has done what He **p-d**
Ezek. 22:9, **p** of shedding blood
Luke 7:30, rejected God's **p**
Acts 26:16, for this **p** I have appeared to you
Rom. 8:28, called according to His **p**
Eph. 3:11, in accordance with the eternal **p**
6:22, for this very **p**
Heb. 6:17, unchangeableness of His **p**
1 Pet. 4:6, has for this **p** been preached

PURSE Is. 46:6; Hag. 1:6; Luke 12:33

PURSUE—*follow, persecute, sought* Gen. 31:36
Ps. 34:14, Seek peace, and **p** it
Prov. 21:21, who **p-s** righteousness and loyalty
Heb. 12:14, **P** peace with all men
1 Pet. 3:11, SEEK PEACE AND **P** IT
Lev. 26:17; Judg. 3:28; 2 Sam. 1:6; Job 30:15; Ps. 7:1; Is. 5:11

PUSH—*thrust* Ps. 118:13, **p-ed** me violently

PUT Gen. 3:15, I will **p** enmity Between you and
Ex. 9:15, now I had **p** forth My hand
Ps. 40:3, **p** a new song in my mouth
Matt. 1:19, desired to **p** her away secretly
12:18, I WILL **P** MY SPIRIT UPON HIM
26:52, **P** your sword back into its place
Mark 12:42, widow came . . . **p** in two
Luke 9:62, **p-ing** his hand to the plow
John 19:2, crown of thorns . . . **p** it on His head
20:27, hand, and **p** it into My side
Rom. 13:14, **p** on the Lord Jesus Christ
1 Cor. 15:53, **p** on the imperishable, **p** on immortality
Eph. 4:24, **p** on the new self
6:11, **P** on the full armor of God
1 Pet. 2:1, **p-ing** aside all malice
Rev. 14:15, **P** in your sickle
Josh. 1:18; 2 Chr. 18:22; Job 31:24; 38:36; Song 8:6; Mark 4:21; John 21:7

Q

QUAKE—*tremble, shake*
Judg. 5:4, The earth **q-d**, the heavens
Judg. 5:5; Ps. 68:8

QUARREL—*contend, war*
Ex. 21:18, if men have a **q**
James 4:1, source of **q-s** and conflicts
Ex. 17:2; Prov. 20:3; 1 Cor. 1:11

QUEEN 1 Kin. 10:1, the **q** of Sheba
Is. 47:5, the **q** of kingdoms
Matt. 12:42, **Q** of *the* South shall rise
Esth. 1:9; Is. 47:7; Jer. 7:18; Acts 8:27

QUENCH 1 Thess. 5:19, Do not **q** the Spirit
Ps. 104:11; Song 8:7

QUESTION 1 Kin. 10:1, test with difficult **q-s**
Mark 11:29, I will ask you one **q**
22:35, a lawyer, asked Him a **q**
Acts 18:15, **q-s** about words and names
1 Cor. 10:25, without asking **q-s** for conscience' sake
1 Tim. 6:4, **q-s** and disputes about words

QUICK—*swift, soon* Acts 7:54, cut to the **q**
Titus 1:7, not **q-tempered**, not addicted to
James 1:19, every one be **q** to hear
Judg. 2:23; John 11:31

QUICKLY—*shortly, suddenly*
Matt. 5:25, Make friends **q** with your opponent

QUICKLY John 13:27, what you do, do **q**
Rom. 9:28, EXECUTE HIS WORD ... Q
Rev. 3:11; 22:20, I am coming **q**
Gen. 18:6; Deut. 7:4; Ps. 31:2; Eccles.
4:12; 2 Thess. 2:2

QUICK-TEMPERED Prov. 14:17;
14:29; Titus 1:7

QUIET Job 20:20, he knew no **q**
within him
Ps. 23:2, beside **q** waters
1 Thess. 4:11, your ambition to lead
a **q** life
1 Tim. 2:2, lead a tranquil and **q** life
Prov. 17:1; Eccles. 9:17; Amos 6:10

QUILT 1 Sam. 19:13, put a **q** of goats'
hair

QUOTA Ex. 5:18, deliver the **q** of
bricks

R

RABBI Matt. 26:25; Mark 9:5

RABBIT Lev. 11:6; Deut. 14:7

RACE Eccles. 9:11, r is not to the
swift
Nah. 2:4, chariots r madly in the
streets
1 Cor. 9:24, those who run in a r all
run
1 Pet. 2:9, A CHOSEN R, A ROYAL

RADIANCE Heb. 1:3, r of His glory

RADIANT Jer. 31:12, r over the
bounty of the LORD

RAFTER Hab. 2:11, the r will answer
it

RAGES—frets Prov. 19:3, his heart r
against

RAID Gen. 49:19, raiders shall r him
... r at their heels

RAIMENT—clothing Is. 63:3, I
stained all My r

RAIN Gen. 7:12, r fell upon the earth
for forty days
Ex. 16:4, will r bread from heaven
for you
Matt. 5:45, r on the righteous ...
unrighteous
7:25, and the r descended
Heb. 6:7, ground that drinks the r
Lev. 26:4; Deut. 32:2; Job 24:8; Prov.
25:14; 25:23; Song 2:11

RAISE Matt. 20:19, third day He ...
r-d up
John 2:19, in three days I will r it up
6:39, r it up on the last day
1 Cor. 15:13, not even Christ ... r-d
15:35, How are the dead r-d
15:42, it is r-d
15:44, r-d a spiritual body
Eph. 2:6, r-d us up with Him
Col. 3:1, If ... been r-d up with
Christ
Heb. 11:19, God is able to r men
from
Deut. 18:18; Judg. 2:16; Is. 2:2; Dan.
12:7; Hos. 6:2; Mic. 4:1; Luke 3:8

RAISIN 2 Sam. 6:19; Song 2:5; Hos.
3:1

RAMPARTS—siege works Ps. 48:13;
Is. 26:1

RAN—fled Luke 8:34, they r away
and reported

RANK—high Ps. 62:9, men of r are a
lie

RANSOM Matt. 20:28, give His life a
r for many
1 Tim. 2:6, gave Himself as a r for all
Ex. 30:12; Prov. 6:35

RAPID—swift Prov. 6:18, Feet that
run r-ly to evil

RARE—precious
1 Sam. 3:1, word from the LORD
was r

RASH Job 6:3, my words have been r

RATION—provision Dan. 1:5; Luke
12:42

RAVAGE Gen. 41:30; 1 Sam. 6:5;
Acts 8:3

RAVINE—valley Luke 3:5, EVERY R
SHALL BE

RAYS Hab. 3:4, He has r flashing
from His hand

READ Hab. 2:2, one who r-s it may
run
Luke 4:16, stood up to r
Acts 8:28, was r-ing the prophet
Isaiah
2 Cor. 3:14, at the r-ing of the old
covenant
1 Tim. 4:13, give attention to the
public r-ing
Rev. 1:3, Blessed is he who r-s
Ex. 24:7; Is. 34:16; Dan. 5:8

READINESS 2 Cor. 8:12, if the r is
present

READY 1 Chr. 7:11; Ps. 86:5; Prov.
24:27

REALIZED Prov. 13:19, Desire r is
sweet

REALLY—indeed Luke 24:34, The
Lord has r risen

REAP—harvest Hos. 8:7, they r the
whirlwind
Matt. 6:26, neither do they r, nor
25:26, r where I did not sow
Luke 12:24, ravens ... neither sow
nor r
2 Cor. 9:6, shall also r sparingly
Gal. 6:7, this he will also r
6:8, flesh r corruption
6:9, in due time we shall r
Lev. 19:9; Ps. 126:5; Prov. 22:8;
Rev. 14:16

REASON—thought
Job 23:7, the upright would r with
Him
Is. 1:18, let us r together
Luke 5:22, Why are you r-ing in your
hearts
Acts 17:17, he was r-ing in the
synagogue
1 Cor. 3:20, KNOWS THE R-INGS of the
wise
1 Tim. 1:16, for this r I found mercy

**James 3:17, gentle, r-able, full of
mercy**

REBEL Ps. 107:11, r-ed against the
words of God
Is. 63:10, r-ed ... grieved His Holy
Spirit
Num. 14:9; 1 Sam. 12:15; Ezek. 20:21

REBELLION—transgression 1 Sam.
24:11; Job 13:23

REBELLIOUS—disobedient
1 Tim. 1:9, those who are lawless
and r
Ex. 23:21; Deut. 9:7; Ps. 66:7; 78:8;
Jer. 5:23

REBUILD Is. 58:12, r the ancient
ruins

REBUKE—reprove, reproof
Matt. 8:26, r-d the winds and
17:18, Jesus r-d him, and the
demon
Mark 9:25, r-d the unclean spirit
Luke 4:39, He r-d the fever, and it
left
1 Tim. 5:1, not sharply r an older
man
Job 26:11; Ps. 38:1; Prov. 27:5;
Zech. 3:2

RECEIVE—accept Prov. 1:3, r
instruction in wise
Matt. 10:8, freely you r-d, freely give
10:14, whoever does not r you
10:40, who r-s you r-s Me
10:41, who r-s a prophet in the
name of
11:5, BLIND R SIGHT
18:5, r-s one such child
25:27, r-d my money back with
interest
Mark 16:19, r-d up into heaven
Luke 15:2, This man r-s sinners
20:47, r greater condemnation
John 1:11, His own did not r Him
5:44, r glory from one another
14:3, r you to Myself
20:22, R the Holy Spirit
Acts 20:35, blessed to give than to r
Rom. 5:17, r the abundance of grace
8:15, r-d a spirit of adoption
1 Cor. 3:8, will r his own reward
9:24, one r-s the prize
Gal. 4:5, r the adoption as sons
1 Thess. 1:6, r-d the word in much
2 Thess. 2:10, did not r the love of
the
Heb. 2:2, r-d a just recompense
James 1:12, r the crown of life
Job 3:12; Is. 40:2

RECEPTION—feast Luke 14:13, you
give a r

RECKLESS 2 Tim. 3:4, treacherous, r
... lovers of pleasure

RECKON—impute Rom. 4:4, his
wage is not r-ed
Rom. 4:6, God r-s righteousness

RECLINE—sat Matt. 9:10; 26:20, He
was r-ing

RECOGNIZE—know Acts 19:15, I r
Jesus
Gen. 27:23; 1 Cor. 14:38

RECOMPENSE—reward
Ps. 94:2, Render r to the proud

RECOMPENSE *(Continued)*
Heb. 2:2, received a just **r**
Ps. 28:4; Jer. 51:6

RECONCILE Matt. 5:24, be **r-d** to
your brother
1 Cor. 7:11, be **r-d** to her husband
2 Cor. 5:20, be **r-d** to God
Col. 1:20, **r** all things to Himself

RECONCILIATION
Rom. 5:11, we have now received
the **r**

RECORD—*write* Hab. 2:2, **R** the
vision

RECOVERY—*health* Is. 58:8, your **r**
will speedily spring

RED—*dull* Gen. 25:25, first came
forth **r**, all over
Ex. 10:19, drove them into the **R** Sea
Prov. 23:31, on the wine when it is **r**
Is. 1:18, they are **r** like crimson
Zech. 1:8, man was riding on a **r**
horse
Matt. 16:2, fair weather . . . sky is **r**
Rev. 6:4, another, a **r** horse, went out

REDEEM—*purchase*
Ex. 6:6, **r** you with an outstretched
arm
Ps. 26:11, **R** me, and be gracious
49:15, God will **r** my soul
Gal. 3:13, **r-ed** us from the curse
Titus 2:14, **R US FROM EVERY . . . DEED**
Ruth 4:4; 2 Sam. 4:9

REDEEMER Job 19:25, know that
my **R** lives
Ps. 19:14, my rock and my **r**
Is. 63:16, our Father, Our **R**
Jer. 50:34, Their **R** is strong

REDEMPTION Ps. 130:7, with Him
is abundant **r**
Luke 21:28, your **r** is drawing near
Rom. 3:24, **r** which is in Christ Jesus
Eph. 1:7, **r** through His blood
4:30, sealed for the day of **r**

REDUCE—*diminish* Ex. 5:8, you are
not to **r** any of it

REED—*bulrushes, rod*
Ex. 2:3, set it among the **r-s** by
Is. 42:3, bruised **r** He will not break
Matt. 27:30, **r** and *began* to beat Him
27:48, wine, and put it on a **r**
Is. 36:6; Matt. 11:7

REEF Jude 12, hidden **r-s** in your
love-feasts

REEL Is. 28:7, these also **r** with wine

REFINE—*purify, try* Ps. 12:6, silver
. . . **r-d** seven times
Rev. 3:18, gold **r-d** by fire

REFORM Acts 24:2, **r-s** are being
carried out

REFRAIN 1 Pet. 3:10, **R HIS TONGUE
FROM EVIL**
Ex. 23:5; Job 30:10; 1 Cor. 9:6;
2 Cor. 12:6

REFRESH—*comfort* 1 Cor. 16:18, **r-
ed** my spirit and yours
Gen. 18:5; Ex. 23:12; 31:17; Song 2:5

REFUGE—*defense, strength, trust*
2 Sam. 22:3, God, my rock, in whom
I take **r**
Ps. 46:1, God is our **r** and strength
Is. 17:10, remembered the rock of
your **r**
33:16, His **r** will be the impregnable
rock
Judg. 9:15; Ps. 55:8; Is. 28:17;
Jer. 16:19

REFUSE (n.) Ex. 29:14; Judg. 3:22;
Is. 57:20

REFUSE (v.) Gen. 23:6, none . . . will
r you his grave
Prov. 21:25, his hands **r** to work
Matt. 2:18, **SHE R-D TO BE COMFORTED**
Acts 10:47, no one can **r** the water
for these
2 Tim. 2:23, **r** foolish and ignorant
speculations
Jer. 13:10; Heb. 12:25

REFUTE Job 32:12; Titus 1:9

REGARD Rom. 14:5, **r-s** one day
above another
Phil. 2:3, you **r** one another as more
important
Gen. 4:4; Job 18:3; 41:27; Prov. 15:5;
Is. 17:7; Lam. 4:2; Luke 7:2

REGION Matt. 2:22, he departed for
the **r-s** of Galilee
Mark 5:17; Luke 2:8; Acts 27:2

REGISTER—*number, written* Num.
11:26; 2 Sam. 24:4

REGRET 1 Sam. 15:35, the LORD **r-ed**
that
2 Cor. 7:10, produces a repentance
without **r**

REGULAR Dan. 8:11; 11:31; 12:11, **r**
sacrifice

REIGN—*rule* Ex. 15:18, LORD shall **r**
forever and
Luke 19:14, not want this man to **r**
over
1 Cor. 15:25, must **r** until He has put
2 Tim. 2:12, we shall also **r** with Him
Rev. 20:6, **r** with Him for a thousand
years
Gen. 37:8; Judg. 9:8; Prov. 8:15;
Is. 32:1

REJECT Prov. 3:11, do not **r** the
discipline of the LORD
Prov. 15:5, A fool **r-s** his father's
discipline
Matt. 21:42, **STONE . . . BUILDERS R-ED**
Luke 10:16, the one who **r-s** you **r-s**
Me
17:25, **r-ed** by this generation
John 12:48, He who **r-s** Me
1 Thess. 4:8, who **r-s** *this* is not **r-ing**
man but God
2 Tim. 3:8, **r-ed** as regards the faith
1 Pet. 2:4, **r-ed** by men
2:7; Ps. 118:22, **STONE . . . BUILDERS
R-ED**
Num. 11:20; Ps. 53:5; Is. 14:19; 30:12;
33:15; Jer. 6:30; Ezek. 20:13,16;
Hos. 4:6; Amos 2:4

REJOICE Prov. 5:18, **r** in the wife of
your youth
Matt. 2:10, they **r-d** exceedingly
5:12, **R**, and be glad

John 14:28, loved Me, you would
have **r-d**
Rom. 12:15, **R** with those who **r**
1 Cor. 13:6, not **r** in unrighteousness
Phil. 3:1, brethren, **r** in the Lord
4:4, **R** in the Lord always
1 Thess. 5:16, **R** always
1 Pet. 1:8, **r** with joy inexpressible
Job 21:12; Eccles. 11:9; Is. 60:5; Luke
10:21; 1 Thess. 3:9

REJOICING Ps. 19:8, LORD are right,
r the heart
Ps. 65:12, hills gird themselves
with **r**
Joel 1:12, **r** dries up
Acts 5:41, **r** . . . been considered
worthy
8:39, went on his way **r**
Rom. 12:12, **r** in hope, persevering
2 Cor. 6:10, sorrowful yet always **r**

RELATE Acts 8:33, **WHO SHALL R HIS
GENERATION**

RELATIONSHIP
Matt. 19:10, **r** of the man with his
wife

RELATIVE Luke 1:36,58

RELEASE—*deliverance, liberty*
Lev. 25:10, proclaim a **r** through the
land
Matt. 27:26, Then he **r-d** Barabbas
Mark 15:9, **r** for you the King . . .
Jews
Luke 4:18, **PROCLAIM R TO THE
CAPTIVES**
23:20, Pilate, wanting to **r** Jesus
John 19:12, Pilate made efforts to **r**
Him
Rom. 7:6, we have been **r-d** from the
Law
1 Cor. 7:27, Are you **r-d** from a wife
Heb. 11:35, not accepting their **r**
Rev. 1:5, **r-d** us from our sins

RELIEF Job 32:20, speak that I may
get **r**

RELIEVED Ps. 4:1, Thou hast **r** me
in my distress

REMAIN—*abide, live, reside*
Gen. 8:22, While the earth **r-s**
Eccles. 1:4, But the earth **r-s** forever
Matt. 2:13, **r** there until I tell
11:23, **r-ed** to this day
26:38, **r** here and keep watch
John 1:32, He **r-ed** upon Him
19:31, not **r** on the cross
21:22, want him to **r** until I come
1 Cor. 3:14, If any man's work . . . **r-s**
7:8, they **r** as I am
7:11, let her **r** unmarried
Gal. 2:5, gospel might **r** with you
1 Thess. 4:15, **r** until the coming of
Titus 1:5, set in order what **r-s**
Rev. 3:2, strengthen the things that **r**
Ex. 16:29; Deut. 9:9; 1 Sam. 5:7;
16:11; Job 14:2; 21:34; John 8:35

REMARKABLE—*strange*
Luke 5:26, seen **r** things today

REMEMBER Gen. 9:15, I will **r** My
covenant
Ex. 20:8, **R** the sabbath day
Job 7:7, **R** that my life is *but* breath
11:16, As waters . . . passed by . . . **r**
it
Ps. 25:7, not **r** the sins of my youth

Eccles. 12:1, **R** also your Creator
Jer. 31:34, their sin I will **r** no more
Matt. 26:75, Peter **r-ed** the word
which Jesus
27:63, **r** . . . that deceiver said
Luke 17:32, **R** Lot's wife
23:42, **r** me when You come in
John 15:20, **R** the word that I said
Acts 20:35, **r** the words of the Lord
Gal. 2:10, us to **r** the poor
Heb. 13:7, **R** those who led you
Rev. 2:5, **R** . . . from where you have
fallen
Deut. 5:15; 32:7; 1 Chr. 16:12;
Ps. 63:6; 105:42; Is. 46:8; Jer. 15:15;
Lam. 3:20; Ezek. 21:32; Acts 10:31;
Heb. 13:3

REMEMBRANCE Mal. 3:16, a book
of **r** was written
Luke 22:19, do this in **r** of Me
1 Cor. 11:25, drink *it*, in **r** of Me
Eccles. 1:11; Is. 26:14; 43:26

REMNANT Rom. 11:5, **r** according
to *God's* gracious choice
Deut. 3:11; Jer. 6:9; 23:3; Mal. 2:15

REMOTE—*utmost* Neh. 1:9, most **r**
part of the heavens

REMOVE Gen. 8:13, Noah **r-d** the
covering of the ark
Ex. 3:5, **r** your sandals from your
feet
1 Kin. 15:12, **r-d** all the idols
2 Kin. 17:23, LORD **r-d** Israel from
His sight
Ps. 103:12, **r-d** our transgressions
Is. 29:13, **r** their hearts far from
Ezek. 36:26, **r** the heart of stone
Matt. 3:11, not *even* fit to **r** His
sandals
Luke 22:42, **r** this cup from Me
John 11:39, **R** the stone
1 Cor. 13:2, so as to **r** mountains
Ruth 4:8; 2 Kin. 18:4; Job 24:2

REND 1 Kin. 19:11; Is. 64:1; Joel 2:13

RENDER—*repay* Matt. 22:21, **r** to
Caesar the things that
Rom. 13:7, **R** to all . . . due them
Deut. 32:41; Ps. 94:2; Prov. 24:12

RENEW Ps. 51:10, **r** a steadfast spirit
within
Ps. 103:5, youth is **r-ed** like the
Lam. 5:21, **R** our days as of old
Rom. 12:2, **r-ing** of your mind
2 Cor. 4:16, inner man is being **r-ed**
day by day
Col. 3:10, **r-ed** to a true knowledge
Titus 3:5, **r-ing** by the Holy Spirit

REPAY—*recompense* Gen. 44:4, **r-d**
evil for good
Matt. 6:4,6,18, in secret will **r** you
Luke 10:35, return, I will **r** you
Rom. 12:19, I WILL **R**, SAYS THE LORD
1 Thess. 5:15, no one **r-s** . . . evil for
evil
Philem. 19, own hand, I will **r** it
Heb. 10:30, VENGEANCE IS MINE, I
WILL **R**
Deut. 7:10; 32:6; 2 Sam. 3:39;
Jer. 18:20; 51:56; Luke 14:14

REPENT Job 42:6, **r** in dust and
ashes
Matt. 3:2, **R**, for the kingdom of
11:21, **r-ed** long ago in sackcloth

Mark 1:15, **r** and believe in the
gospel
6:12, preached that *men* should **r**
Luke 13:3, unless you **r**, you will all
15:7, one sinner who **r-s**
Acts 2:38, **R**, and . . . be baptized
3:19, **R** therefore and return
26:20, **r** and turn to God
Num. 23:19; Ezek. 18:30

REPENTANCE Matt. 3:8, fruit . . .
with *your* **r**
Matt. 3:11, in water for **r**
Mark 1:4, a baptism of **r**
Luke 24:47, **r** for forgiveness of sins
Acts 26:20, performing deeds . . . to **r**
2 Cor. 7:10, God produces a **r**
without regret
Heb. 6:1, laying . . . foundation of **r**
2 Pet. 3:9, all to come to **r**

REPHAIM—*giant*
Deut. 3:13, it is called the land of **R**

REPORT Matt. 2:8, have found *Him*,
r to me
Matt. 11:4, Go and **r** to John the
things
Luke 7:17, this **r** concerning Him
John 12:38, WHO HAS BELIEVED OUR **R**

REPROACH Jer. 29:18, a hissing and
a **r**
Ezek. 5:14, a **r** among the nations
Matt. 11:20, He began to **r** the cities
1 Tim. 3:7, fall into **r** and the snare
of
Titus 2:8, speech which is beyond **r**
Heb. 11:26, considering the **r** of
Christ
Gen. 30:23; Job 27:6; Ps. 4:2; 44:13;
119:39; Is. 51:7; Jer. 24:9; Hos.
12:14; Rom. 15:3

REPROBATE Ps. 15:4, a **r** is
despised

REPROOF Prov. 15:10, who hates **r**
will die
2 Tim. 3:16, for teaching, for **r**, for
correction
Prov. 1:30; 10:17; 15:5; 29:1,15

REPROVE—*correct*
Job 5:17, the man whom God **r-s**
Prov. 3:12, whom the LORD loves He
r-s
Matt. 18:15, **r** him in private
2 Tim. 4:2, **r**, rebuke, exhort, with . . .
patience
Rev. 3:19, I love, I **r** and discipline
Lev. 19:17; Job 13:10; 40:2; Prov. 9:8;
Jer. 2:19

REPUTATION—*report*
Acts 6:3, seven men of good **r**
1 Tim. 5:10, having a **r** for good
works

REPUTE—*report* Phil. 4:8, whatever
is of good **r**

REQUEST—*desire*
Rom. 1:10, in my prayers making **r**
Phil. 4:6, let your **r-s** be made known
Judg. 8:24; 1 Kin. 2:16; Neh. 2:4; Job
6:8; Mark 15:6

REQUIRE Mic. 6:8, what does the
Lord **r** of you
Luke 12:20, night your soul is **r-d** of
you
1 Cor. 4:2, it is **r-d** of stewards

Gen. 9:5; Deut. 10:12; Ezra 3:4; Ps.
10:13; Is. 1:12

RESCUE Ps. 144:10; 2 Pet. 2:7

RESERVED 1 Pet. 1:4, **r** in heaven
for you
2 Pet. 3:7, are being **r** for fire
Gen. 27:36; Job 21:30

RESIDE Matt. 2:23, **r-d** in a city
called Nazareth
Lev. 19:34; Eccles. 7:9; Jer. 49:18

RESIST Matt. 5:39, do not **r** him who
is evil
Luke 21:15, opponents will be able to
r or
Acts 7:51, are always **r-ing** the Holy
Spirit
Rom. 13:2, he who **r-s** authority has
opposed
Heb. 12:4, not yet **r-ed** to the point
of shedding
James 4:7, **R** the devil, and he

RESOLUTELY—*steadfastly*
1 Chr. 28:7, **r** performs My
Luke 9:51, He **r** set His face to go

RESPECT Matt. 21:37, They will **r**
my son
Luke 18:2, and did not **r** man
Eph. 5:33, let the wife . . . **r** her
husband
1 Pet. 3:2, chaste and **r-ful** behavior
Gen. 34:19; Mal. 1:6; 1 Pet. 2:18

RESPOND Is. 19:22, LORD, and He
will **r** to them
Col. 4:6, how you should **r** to each
person

RESPONSE 2 Kin. 4:31, was neither
sound nor **r**

REST—*stand* Josh. 1:13, God gives
you **r**
Josh. 14:15, the land had **r** from war
Ps. 37:7, **R** in the LORD and wait
116:7, Return to your **r**, O my soul
Prov. 14:33, Wisdom **r-s** in the heart
Is. 11:2, Spirit of the LORD will **r**
upon Him
11:10, His **r-ing** place will be
glorious
Jer. 6:16, find **r** for your souls
Matt. 11:28, and I will give you **r**
11:29, R FOR YOUR SOULS
Luke 11:24, waterless places seeking
r
1 Cor. 2:5, **r** on the wisdom of men
2 Cor. 2:13, I had no **r** for my spirit
Heb. 3:11, THEY SHALL NOT ENTER
MY **r**
1 Pet. 4:2, live the **r** of the time in
Gen. 5:29; 8:9; 49:15; Ex. 10:5;
Deut. 28:65; Ruth 1:9; 2 Sam. 4:5;
Job 3:17; 11:18; Prov. 19:20;
Eccles. 4:6; Is. 14:3; 38:10; 57:2;
Lam. 5:5; Matt. 22:6; Rev. 19:21

RESTED Gen. 2:2, and He **r** on the
seventh day
Ex. 24:16, glory of the LORD **r**
Acts 2:3, tongues of fire . . . **r** on
each one

RESTITUTION Lev. 6:5; 2 Sam. 12:6

RESTORE—*turn* Ps. 19:7, perfect **r-**
ing the soul
Ps. 23:3, He **r-s** my soul; He guides

RESTORE *(Continued)*
Matt. 17:11, is coming, and will r all things
Mark 3:5, his hand was r-d
James 5:15, prayer . . . will r the one who is sick
Gen. 20:7; Neh. 3:8; 4:2; Ps. 80:3; Jer. 30:17

RESTRAIN Prov. 10:19, who r-s his lips is wise
Acts 14:18, they with difficulty r-ed the crowds
2 Cor. 6:12, You are not r-ed by us, but
Gen. 8:2; Job 7:11; 11:10; Jer. 31:16; 2 Pet. 2:16

RESTRICT Jer. 36:5, I am r-ed; I cannot go

RESULT—*work* Eph. 4:14, As a r . . . no longer
James 1:4, endurance have *its* perfect r

RESURRECTION Matt. 22:23, say there is no r
Matt. 22:30, r they neither marry, nor
Luke 14:14, at the r of the righteous
20:27, who say that there is no r
20:36, being sons of the r
John 5:29, r of life . . . r of judgment
11:25, the r, and the life
Acts 24:15, r of both the righteous and the
24:21, For the r of the dead
1 Cor. 15:13, if there is no r
Phil. 3:11, attain to the r
Heb. 11:35, might obtain a better r
1 Pet. 1:3, living hope through the r
Rev. 20:5, This is the first r

RETAIN John 20:23, r the sins of any . . . r-ed

RETIRE Ps. 127:2, To r late

RETRIBUTION Hos. 9:7, days of r have come
Rom. 11:9, STUMBLING BLOCK . . . A R

RETURN—*turn back*
Gen. 43:18, money . . . r-ed in our sacks
Deut. 30:2, r to the LORD your God
Eccles. 4:9, a good r for their labor
Mal. 3:7, R to Me, and I will r to you
Matt. 10:13, let your . . . peace r to you
Luke 2:39, they r-ed to Galilee
4:14, r-ed . . . in the power of the Spirit
10:17, the seventy r-ed with joy
24:9, r-ed from the tomb
Acts 3:19, Repent therefore and r
1 Tim. 5:4, make some r to their parents
1 Pet. 2:25, now you have r-ed to the
3:9, not r-ing evil for evil
Gen. 3:19; 32:9; Ex. 14:28; Ruth 1:12; 1 Sam. 7:3; 25:21; 2 Sam. 1:22; 1 Kin. 22:17; Job 1:21; 10:21; 33:25; Eccles. 12:2,7; Is. 10:22; 55:11; Jer. 3:22; 4:1; Ezek. 16:55; Dan. 4:36; Matt. 12:44; Acts 13:34

REVEAL—*manifest* Job 20:27, will r his iniquity
Is. 40:5, glory of the LORD will be r-ed
53:1, arm of the LORD been r-ed
Matt. 11:25, didst r them to babes

16:17, blood did not r *this* to you
Luke 17:30, the Son of Man is r-ed
Rom. 8:18, glory that is to be r-ed to us
8:19, r-ing of the sons of God
1 Cor. 3:13, it is *to be* r-ed with fire
Gal. 1:16, to r His Son in me
Eph. 3:5, r-ed to His holy apostles
2 Thess. 2:3, man of lawlessness is r-ed
2:8, lawless one will be r-ed
1 Pet. 1:5, be r-ed in the last time
1 Sam. 14:8,11; Job 12:22; Prov. 11:13; 25:9; Is. 26:21; Dan. 2:47

REVEL 2 Pet. 2:13, to r in the daytime

REVELATION Rom. 16:25, the r of the mystery
1 Cor. 1:7, awaiting eagerly the r
14:6, speak . . . by way of r
Gal. 1:12, through a r of Jesus Christ
2:2, because of a r that I went up
Eph. 1:17, spirit of wisdom and r
Rev. 1:1, The R of Jesus Christ

REVENGE Jer. 20:10, take our r on him
Rom. 12:19, Never take your own r

REVERE Lev. 19:30; Zeph. 3:7

REVERENCE—*fear*
Ps. 2:11, Worship the LORD with r
5:7, bow in r for Thee
Heb. 11:7, in r prepared an ark
12:28, service with r and awe
Job 15:4; Is. 29:13

REVILE Ps. 74:10, long, will the adversary r
Matt. 5:11, when *men* r you
Acts 23:4, Do you r God's high priest
1 Cor. 4:12, when we are r-d, we bless
1 Pet. 2:23, being r-d, He did not r
4:14, r-d for the name of Christ

REVIVE Ps. 119:88, R me . . . Thy lovingkindness

REWARD—*recompense*
Job 15:31, emptiness will be his r
Ps. 58:11, a r for the righteous
Prov. 11:18, righteousness *gets* a true r
Is. 62:11, His r is with Him
Matt. 5:12, your r in heaven is great
6:1, no r with your Father who
6:2,5,16, have their r in full
10:42, shall not lose his r
1 Cor. 3:8, will receive his own r
Heb. 11:26, he was looking to the r
2 John 8, that you may receive a full r
Rev. 22:12, My r is with Me
Gen. 15:1; Ruth 2:12; Prov. 11:31; Is. 1:23; 45:13

RICH Gen. 13:2, Abram was very r in livestock
Jer. 9:23, r man boast of his riches
Matt. 19:23, hard for a r man to enter
Luke 1:53, sent away the r empty-handed
6:24, woe to you who are r
16:1, There was a certain r man
16:21, *crumbs* . . . falling from the r man's table
18:23, for he was extremely r

1 Cor. 4:8, filled, you have already become r
Eph. 2:4, God, being r in mercy
Col. 3:16, word of Christ r-ly dwell within
1 Tim. 6:18, to be r in good works
James 1:11, r man . . . will fade away
2:6, Is it not the r who oppress you
Rev. 13:16, r and the poor, and the free
Gen. 49:20; Ex. 30:15; 1 Sam. 2:7; Ps. 49:2; Prov. 10:4; 18:23; Eccles. 10:20

RICHES—*possessions* Prov. 11:4, R do not profit in the day
Prov. 22:1, more desired than great r
30:8, neither poverty nor r
Matt. 13:22, deceitfulness of r
Luke 8:14, choked with worries and r
Rom. 10:12, abounding in r for all who call
Eph. 1:7, r of His grace
3:8, unfathomable r of Christ
1 Tim. 6:17, hope on the uncertainty of r
James 5:2, Your r are rotted
1 Kin. 3:11; Job 20:15; 36:19; Ps. 62:10; Prov. 3:16; Jer. 9:23

RIDE 1 Kin. 1:33; Is. 19:1; Ezek. 23:12

RIGHT—*justice, just*
Judg. 17:6, man did what was r
Ps. 19:8, precepts of the LORD are r
Prov. 14:12, a way *which seems* r
Hos. 14:9, ways of the LORD are r
Matt. 5:29, r eye makes you stumble
22:44, SIT AT MY R HAND
26:64, AT THE R HAND OF POWER
Mark 5:15, and in his r mind
16:19, SAT DOWN AT THE R HAND OF GOD
Luke 22:50, cut off his r ear
John 1:12, the r to become children of God
Acts 8:21, your heart is not r
Rom. 9:21, potter have a r over the clay
12:17, r in the sight of all men
1 Cor. 9:18, full use of my r in the
2 Cor. 13:7, you may do what is r
Gal. 2:9, r hand of fellowship
Phil. 4:8, whatever is r
2 Pet. 2:15, forsaking the r way
Rev. 22:14, r to the tree of life
Gen. 24:48; Ex. 21:10; Deut. 12:25; 21:17; 2 Kin. 10:15; Job 9:2; 34:6; Prov. 24:26; Is. 41:13; Jer. 40:4; Ezek. 18:25,29; 33:17,20

RIGHTEOUS Gen. 6:9, Noah was a r man
Ps. 7:9, establish the r
Prov. 10:30, r will never be shaken
11:28, r will flourish
Jer. 23:5, David a r Branch
Hab. 2:4, the r will live by his faith
Matt. 5:45, rain on *the* r and *the* unrighteous
9:13, not come to call *the* r
10:41, a r man's reward
13:43, R WILL SHINE FORTH
25:46, r into eternal life
Luke 15:7, ninety-nine r persons
23:50, Joseph . . . a good and r man
John 7:24, with r judgment
Acts 7:52, the coming of the R One
Rom. 1:17, THE R *man* SHALL LIVE BY FAITH
3:10, NONE R, NOT EVEN

1 Tim. 1:9, Law ... for a r man
James 5:16, prayer of a r man can
1 Pet. 4:18, THAT THE R IS SAVED
1 John 1:9, r to forgive us our sins
2:1, Jesus Christ the r
Gen. 18:23; Ex. 9:27; 23:7; 1 Sam.
  24:17; Job 9:20; Ps. 1:5; 11:5; 33:1;
  37:16; 55:22; 119:75,137; Prov. 2:20;
  3:33; 4:18; 13:5; 16:13; 24:16; 28:1;
  Eccles. 3:17; 7:16; Is. 26:7; 32:1;
  53:11; Jer. 33:15; Ezek. 13:22; Dan.
  9:14; Amos 2:6

RIGHTEOUSNESS—*judgment,*
  justice
Ps. 23:3, in the paths of r
  96:13, judge the world in r
  97:6, heavens declare His r
  111:3, His r endures forever
Prov. 14:34, R exalts a nation
  16:8, Better is a little with r
Jer. 22:13, builds his house without r
  23:6, The LORD our r
Dan. 12:3, lead the many to r
Matt. 3:15, fitting for us to fulfill all r
  5:6, hunger and thirst for r
  5:10, persecuted ... sake of r
  5:20, your r surpasses *that*
  6:1, your r before men
  6:33, seek first ... and His r
Luke 1:75, holiness and r before Him
Rom. 4:3,22; Gal. 3:6, RECKONED TO
  HIM AS R
  5:18, through one act of r
  8:10, spirit is alive ... r
2 Cor. 6:14, what partnership have r
  and
Gal. 2:21, if *comes* through Law
Eph. 4:24, created in r
  6:14, BREASTPLATE OF R
1 Tim. 6:11, pursue r
2 Tim. 4:8, the crown of r
Heb. 7:2, king of r
  12:11, peaceful fruit of r
James 1:20, anger ... not achieve
  the r
1 Pet. 3:14, for the sake of r
1 John 3:10, does not practice r is
  not
Gen. 15:6; 18:19; 1 Sam. 26:23; Job
  27:6; 29:14; 36:3; Ps. 17:15; 48:10;
  Prov. 10:2; 11:19; Is. 45:8; 48:18;
  51:5; 59:17; 60:17; Jer. 31:23;
  Ezek. 18:5; 33:13; Hos. 10:12; Mal.
  4:2; Acts 13:10

RIPE Gen. 40:10; Jer. 24:2; Joel 3:13;
  Rev. 14:15,18

RISE Prov. 31:15, She r-s also while
Matt. 24:7, nation ... r against
  nation
  27:63, I *am* to r again
Mark 12:25, when they r from the
  dead
  13:12, children will r up against
  parents
  16:6, He has r-n, He is not here
Luke 5:23, R and walk
  11:31, Queen of the South shall r
  12:54, cloud r-ing in the west
  22:46, R and pray that
  24:34, Lord has really r-n
1 Thess. 4:16, dead in Christ shall r
Gen. 19:2; Lev. 19:32; Num. 24:17;
  Josh. 12:1; Ps. 35:11; 86:14; 113:3;
  Is. 32:9; 60:1; Jer. 47:2; Matt. 14:2;
  Luke 16:31

RIVER—*water* Ps. 46:4, a r whose
  streams make glad

Eccles. 1:7, All the r-s flow into the
  sea
Mark 1:5, baptized by him in the
  Jordan R
John 7:38, shall flow r-s of living
  water
2 Cor. 11:26, in dangers from r-s
Rev. 22:1, a r of the water of life
Gen. 2:10; Josh. 1:4; 24:2; Job 40:23;
  Ps. 24:2; 66:6; 137:1; Is. 11:15;
  Lam. 2:18; Ezek. 47:5

ROAD—*way* Luke 19:36, garments
  in the r
Acts 9:27, seen the Lord on the r

ROAM Job 1:7, From r-ing about on
  the earth

ROAR 1 Pet. 5:8, devil prowls about
  like a r-ing lion
2 Pet. 3:10, heavens pass away with
  a r
1 Chr. 16:32; Job 4:10; 37:4; Ps.
  96:11; Jer. 25:30

ROAST Lev. 2:14, grain r-ed in the
  fire

ROB Prov. 22:22, Do not r the poor
Mal. 3:8, Will a man r God
2 Cor. 11:8, I r-ed other churches
Judg. 9:25; Prov. 17:12; 28:24; Is.
  10:2

ROBBER Jer. 7:11, become a den of
  r-s
Matt. 21:13, making it a r-s' den
Mark 15:27, crucified two r-s with
  Him
Luke 10:30, he fell among r-s
  22:52, come out ... as against a r
John 10:1, he is a thief and a r
  18:40, Now Barabbas was a r
Acts 19:37, neither r-s of temples

ROBBERY Ps. 62:10, do not vainly
  hope in r
Matt. 23:25, full of r and self-
  indulgence
Luke 11:39, full of r and wickedness

ROBE—*garment* Is. 61:10, with a r
  of righteousness
Matt. 27:28, put a scarlet r on Him
Mark 12:38, walk around in long r-s
  16:5, young man ... wearing a
  white r
Luke 15:22, bring out the best r
  20:46, like to walk around in
  long r-s
John 19:2, arrayed Him in a purple r
Rev. 1:13, a r reaching to the feet
  7:14, have washed their r-s
  19:16, on His r and on His thigh
1 Sam. 24:4; Job 1:20; 29:14

ROCK—*stone, strength* Num. 20:11,
  struck the r twice
Ps. 19:14, LORD, my r and my
  redeemer
  31:3, Thou art my r and my fortress
Matt. 7:24, built his house upon the r
  13:5, fell upon the r-y places
  16:18, upon this r I will build My
  church
Mark 15:46, tomb ... hewn out in
  the r
Luke 8:6, other seed fell on r-y *soil*
Rom. 9:33, A R OF OFFENSE
1 Cor. 10:4, were drinking from a
  spiritual r
Ex. 17:6; 33:22; Deut. 32:4,13; 1 Sam.

2:2; 2 Sam. 22:2; Job 19:24; 28:2;
  29:6; Ps. 18:2; 27:5; Prov. 30:19; Is.
  8:14; 26:4; 51:1; Jer. 5:3

ROD Ps. 2:9, break them with a r of
  iron
Ps. 23:4, Thy r and Thy staff, they
  comfort
Prov. 13:24, spares his r hates his
  son
2 Cor. 11:25, Three times ... beaten
  with r-s
Heb. 9:4, Aaron's r which budded
Rev. 19:15, rule them with a r of iron
Gen. 30:37; Num. 17:8; 2 Sam. 7:14;
  Prov. 26:3; Is. 10:5; Ezek. 20:37;
  40:5; 41:8

ROGUE Is. 32:5, r be spoken of *as*
  generous

ROLL Is. 34:4, sky will be r-ed up
Matt. 27:60, he r-ed a large stone
  against
  28:2, came and r-ed away the stone
Is. 22:18; Mark 16:3; Heb. 1:12

ROOF Gen. 19:8; Josh. 2:6; 2 Sam.
  11:2; Matt. 8:8; Mark 2:4

ROOM Jer. 22:14, build myself a r-y
  house
Matt. 6:6, GO INTO YOUR INNER R
Mark 14:15, large upper r furnished
Luke 2:7, no r for them in the inn
Acts 1:13, went up to the upper r
Gen. 6:14; Judg. 3:24; Prov. 18:16;
  Matt. 24:26; Rom. 12:19

ROOT Matt. 3:10, axe ... laid at the r
  of the trees
Mark 4:6, it had no r, it withered
Rom. 11:16, if the r be holy
Eph. 3:17, being r-ed and grounded
  in love
1 Tim. 6:10, money is a r of all sorts
  of evil
Deut. 29:18; Job 5:3; Ps. 80:9; Is.
  5:24; 53:2; Jer. 12:2

ROPE Is. 3:24, Instead of a belt, a r

ROSE (n.) Song 2:1, I am the r of
  Sharon

ROSE (v.) Josh. 3:16, waters ... r up
  in one heap

ROT—*wither* Is. 19:6, reeds and
  rushes will r
Zech. 14:12, tongue will r in their
  mouth
James 5:2, Your riches have r-ed

ROTTEN Matt. 7:17, r tree bears bad
  fruit

ROUND Lev. 19:27, not r off the side-
  growth

ROUGH Prov. 18:23; Is. 40:4

ROUT Judg. 4:15; 8:12; 2 Sam. 22:15;
  Ps. 18:14

RUBBISH Phil. 3:8, count them but r

RUIN—*destruction*
Ex. 9:31, flax ... barley were r-ed
Prov. 10:15, r of the poor is their
  poverty
  18:7, fool's mouth is his r
  26:28, flattering mouth works r

RUIN *(Continued)*
Song 2:15, foxes that are **r-ing** the vineyards
Luke 6:49, **r** of that house was great
Acts 15:16, WILL REBUILD ITS R-S
Job 2:3; Ps. 74:3; Prov. 10:14,29; 14:28; Is. 23:13; 61:4; Lam. 2:13

RULE Judg. 8:22, **R** over us
Job 34:30, godless men should not **r**
Rom. 15:12, TO R OVER THE GENTILES
Gal. 6:16, will walk by this **r**
Eph. 1:21, far above all **r** and authority
Col. 3:15, peace of Christ **r** in your hearts
Rev. 2:27, R THEM WITH A ROD OF IRON
Gen. 1:26; Ps. 8:6; 49:14; Prov. 8:16; 16:32; Is. 3:12; 26:13

RULER Ex. 22:28, nor curse a **r** of your people
Matt. 2:6, SHALL COME FORTH A R, WHO WILL SHEPHERD
9:34, **r** of the demons
Mark 10:42, **r-s** of the Gentiles
John 3:1, Nicodemus, a **r** of the Jews
12:31, **r** of this world shall be cast out
Acts 7:27, WHO MADE YOU A R AND JUDGE
Eph. 6:12, struggle is . . . against the **r-s**
Titus 3:1, Remind them to be subject to **r-s**
Gen. 42:6; Ps. 2:2; Prov. 6:7; 29:12; Is. 22:3

RUMOR Matt. 24:6, wars and **r-s** of wars
Ex. 23:1; Ezek. 7:26

RUN Prov. 1:16, their feet **r** to evil
Is. 40:31, **r** and not get tired
1 Cor. 9:24, those who **r** in a race all **r**
Gal. 5:7, You were **r-ing** well
Heb. 12:1, let us **r** with endurance the race
Gen. 49:22; Lev. 15:13; 2 Kin. 4:22; Ps. 18:29; 19:5; Prov. 6:18; Ezek. 32:14; Gal. 2:2

RUSH Matt. 8:32, herd **r-ed** down the steep
Rev. 9:9, many horses **r-ing** to battle

RUSHES—*reeds* Job 8:11; Is. 19:6

RUST Matt. 6:19, moth and **r** destroy
James 5:3, Your gold and your silver have **r-ed**

RUTHLESS—*terrible*
Ezek. 28:7, most **r** of the nations

S

SABBATH Ex. 20:8, Remember the **s** day
Lev. 25:8, count off seven **s-s** of years
Matt. 12:8, is Lord of the **S**
28:1, Now late on the **S**
Mark 2:27, **S** was made for man
3:4, on the **S** to do good
John 19:31, that **S** was a high day
Acts 1:12, a **S** day's journey away
Ex. 16:26; 20:11; 31:15; 35:3; Lev. 26:2; Num. 15:32; Deut. 5:12; 2 Kin. 4:23

SACKCLOTH Matt. 11:21, repented . . . in **s**
Rev. 6:12, sun became black as **s** *made* of hair
Esth. 4:1; Job 16:15; Dan. 9:3

SACRED 2 Kin. 12:18, Joash . . . took all the **s** things
2 Tim. 3:15, have known the **s** writings

SACRIFICE Ps. 51:17, **s-s** of God are a broken
Matt. 9:13, COMPASSION, AND NOT S
Rom. 12:1, bodies a living and holy **s**
1 Cor. 8:1, things **s-d** to idols
10:20, they **s** to demons
Phil. 4:18, an acceptable **s**, well pleasing
Heb. 9:26, put away sin by the **s** of
11:4, a better **s** than Cain
13:16, such **s-s** God is pleased
Gen. 31:54; Ex. 12:27; Prov. 15:8; Is. 43:23; Dan. 11:31; Hos. 6:6; Acts 7:41

SAD—*sore* Prov. 15:13, when the heart is **s**
Is. 59:11, And moan **s-ly** like doves
Neh. 2:2; Luke 24:17

SADDLE Gen. 31:34, the camel's **s**

SAFE Job 21:9, houses are **s** from fear
Luke 15:27, received him back **s** and sound
Acts 27:43, centurion . . . bring Paul **s-ly**
Phil. 3:1, it is a **s-guard** for you

SAFETY Ezek. 39:6, inhabit the coastlands in **s**

SAIL Acts 28:13, from there we **s-ed** around

SAINT Matt. 27:52, bodies of the **s-s** . . . were raised
Acts 26:10, lock up . . . **s-s** in prisons
Rom. 1:7, called *as* **s-s**
8:27, He intercedes for the **s-s**
1 Cor. 6:2, **s-s** will judge the world
Eph. 2:19, fellow-citizens with the **s-s**
Phil. 1:1, all the **s-s** in Christ Jesus
1 Thess. 3:13, Lord Jesus with all His **s-s**
Rev. 14:12, perseverance of the **s-s**
20:9, the camp of the **s-s**

SAKE Ps. 23:3, For His name's **s**
Ps. 44:22, for Thy **s** we are killed
Is. 42:21, for His righteousness' **s**
Matt. 16:25, loses his life for My **s**
Mark 13:20, for the **s** of the elect
Luke 6:22, the **s** of the Son of Man
18:29, for the **s** of the kingdom of God
Rom. 8:36, THY S WE ARE . . . PUT TO DEATH
13:5, for conscience' **s**
1 Cor. 9:23, for the **s** of the gospel
2 Cor. 8:9, for your **s** He became poor
Phil. 1:29, for Christ's **s** . . . suffer for his **s**
1 Tim. 5:23, wine for the **s** of your stomach
Titus 1:11, for the **s** of sordid gain
2 John 2, for the **s** of the truth

SALT Gen. 19:26, became a pillar of **s**
Matt. 5:13, You are the **s** of the earth
Mark 9:50, **S** is good
Col. 4:6, seasoned, *as it were*, with **s**
James 3:12, *can* **s** water produce fresh
Judg. 9:45; Job 6:6

SALVATION Ps. 3:8, **S** belongs to the LORD
Ps. 27:1, LORD is my light and my **s**
62:1, From Him is my **s**
85:9, **s** is near to those who fear Him
98:3, seen the **s** of our God
Is. 59:17, helmet of **s** on His head
Luke 1:71, **S** FROM OUR ENEMIES
2:30, mine eyes have seen Thy **s**
3:6, FLESH SHALL SEE THE S OF GOD
19:9, **s** has come to this house
Acts 4:12, is **s** in no one else
13:26, word of this **s** is sent out
16:17, proclaiming to you the way of **s**
Rom. 1:16, power of God for **s**
11:11, **s** has come to the Gentiles
2 Cor. 6:2, ON THE DAY OF S
7:10, repentance . . . *leading* to **s**
Eph. 6:17, take the helmet of **s**
Phil. 2:12, work out your **s** with fear
1 Thess. 5:9, obtaining **s** through our Lord
2 Tim. 3:15, wisdom that leads to **s**
Titus 2:11, grace of God . . . bringing **s**
Heb. 1:14, who will inherit **s**
2:3, if we neglect so great a **s**
9:28, not to bear sin . . . for **s**
1 Pet. 1:5, through faith for a **s**
2 Pet. 3:15, patience of our Lord *to be* **s**
Rev. 7:10, **S** to our God who sits
12:10, Now the **s**, and the power
Gen. 49:18; Ex. 15:2; Deut. 32:15; Job 13:16; Ps. 116:13; 119:155; Is. 12:3; 33:2; 49:6; 51:6; 52:7; 56:1; Jon. 2:9; Zech. 9:9

SAME Ps. 102:27, But Thou art the **s**
Matt. 5:46, even the tax gatherers do the **s**
Luke 2:8, in the **s** region . . . shepherds
23:40, under the **s** sentence of
Rom. 10:12, **s** Lord is Lord of all
1 Cor. 12:4, **s** of gifts, but the **s** Spirit
Heb. 13:8, Christ . . . **s** yesterday and today

SANCTIFY Lev. 22:32, I am the LORD who **s-es**
John 10:36, whom the Father **s-ed**
17:17, **S** them in the truth
Rom. 15:16, **s-ed** by the Holy Spirit
1 Cor. 6:11, washed, but you were **s-ed**
7:14, wife is **s-ed** . . . believing husband
1 Thess. 5:23, God of peace . . . **s** you entirely
Heb. 2:11, who **s-es** and those who are **s-ed**
Gen. 2:3; Ex. 13:2; Is. 29:23; Ezek. 20:20; 44:24

SANCTITY 1 Tim. 2:15, faith and love and **s**

SANCTUARY Ps. 150:1, Praise God in His **s**
Is. 60:13, beautify the place of My **s**
Heb. 8:2, a minister in the **s**

Ex. 25:8; Lev. 19:30; Ps. 73:17;
Amos 7:13

SAND Gen. 32:12, descendants as the
s of the sea
Matt. 7:26, built his house upon the s
Heb. 11:12, s . . . BY THE SEASHORE
Deut. 33:19; Job 29:18; Prov. 27:3

SANDAL Matt. 3:11, fit to remove
His **s-s**
Matt. 10:10, tunics, or **s-s**, or
Ex. 12:11; Deut. 29:5; Amos 2:6;
Mark 1:7; Acts 7:33

SANK Gen. 42:28, their hearts s

SAPPHIRE—*lapis lazuli* Ex. 28:18;
Song 5:14; Rev. 21:19

SASH Ex. 28:40; 29:9

SAT Mark 16:19, s DOWN AT THE
RIGHT HAND OF GOD
Luke 7:15, the dead man s up
Ex. 2:15; 16:3; Jon. 4:5; Mark 11:2

SATAN Matt. 4:10, Begone, S
Matt. 12:26, S casts out S
16:23, Get behind Me, S
Mark 1:13, forty days being tempted
by S
Luke 10:18, watching S fall from
heaven
22:3, S entered into Judas
Acts 5:3, why has S filled your heart
Rom. 16:20, crush S under your feet
2 Cor. 2:11, no advantage . . . of us
by S
1 Thess. 2:18, *yet* S thwarted us
1 Tim. 1:20, I have delivered over
to S
Rev. 3:9, *those* of the synagogue of S
12:9, called the Devil and S
20:7, S . . . released from his prison
Job 1:6; Zech. 3:2

SATIATE Is. 34:5, My sword is **s-d**

SATISFY Ps. 22:26, afflicted shall eat
and be **s-ed**
Ps. 91:16, with long life I will s him
Mark 8:4, s these men with bread
Gen. 25:8; Lev. 26:26; Esth. 5:13; Job
21:23; 27:14; 38:27; Ps. 78:30; Prov.
6:30; 27:20; Is. 29:8; Joel 2:26;
Mark 15:15

SATYR—*demon* 2 Chr. 11:15, he set
up priests . . . for the **s-s**

SAVE—*deliver, escape, except*
Ps. 6:4, S me because of Thy
lovingkindness
86:2, s Thy servant who trusts in
Thee
Is. 35:4, God will come . . . He will s
you
45:22, Turn to Me, and be **s-d**
63:1, mighty to s
Jer. 8:20, summer is ended . . . we
are not **s-d**
Matt. 1:21, s His people from their
sins
10:22, who has endured . . . will be
s-d
16:25, s his life shall lose it
18:11, come to s that which is lost
19:25, Then who can be **s-d**
Mark 3:4, to s a life or to kill
13:13, one who has endured . . . will
be **s-d**
16:16, been baptized shall be **s-d**

Luke 7:50, Your faith has **s-d** you; go
in peace
23:35, let Him s Himself if . . . the
Christ
John 3:17, world should be **s-d**
through Him
10:9, enters through Me, he shall be
s-d
12:27, Father, s Me from this hour
Acts 4:12, by which we must be **s-d**
16:30, what must I do to be **s-d**
Rom. 5:10, we shall be **s-d** by His life
8:24, in hope we have been **s-d**
1 Cor. 7:16, s your husband . . . s
your wife
16:2, each . . . put aside and s
Eph. 2:5, by grace you have been **s-d**
1 Tim. 1:15, into the world to s
sinners
2 Tim. 1:9, who has **s-d** us, and
called us
James 1:21, able to s your souls
4:12, able to s and to destroy
1 Pet. 4:18, WITH DIFFICULTY . . .
RIGHTEOUS **S-D**
Deut. 28:29; 33:29; 1 Sam. 14:6; Job
22:29; Ps. 28:9; 44:7; 60:5;
Prov. 20:22; Jer. 30:10; 42:11; Ezek.
18:27; Amos 2:14; Acts 28:4

SAVIOR 2 Sam. 22:3, My s, Thou
dost save me
Ps. 106:21, forgot God their S
Is. 19:20, He will send them a S
43:11, there is no s besides Me
45:21, a righteous God and a S
49:26, know that I, the LORD, am
your S
Luke 2:11, a S, who is Christ the
Lord
John 4:42, One is indeed the S of the
world
Acts 5:31, as a Prince and a S
Eph. 5:23, He Himself *being* the S of
the body
1 Tim. 4:10, God, who is the S of all
men
2 Tim. 1:10, appearing of our S
Christ Jesus
Titus 2:13, God and S, Christ Jesus
2 Pet. 1:11, our Lord and S Jesus
Christ
1 John 4:14, sent the Son *to be* the S

SAW Gen. 1:4, God s that the light
was good
Matt. 2:2, s His star in the east
2:11, s the Child with Mary
Mark 1:10, s the heavens opening
John 1:48, under the fig tree, I s you
Num. 22:23; Job 29:11; Eccles. 2:13;
Is. 59:16; Dan. 4:5

SAY—*speak* Ps. 106:48, let all the
people s,
Matt. 7:22, Many will s to Me on
that day
16:13, Who do people s . . . Son of
Man is
Luke 7:40, Simon, I have something
to s to you
17:21, nor will they s, Look, here *it
is*
1 John 1:8, If we s that we have no
sin
Rev. 22:17, Spirit and the bride s,
Come
Gen. 20:13; Ex. 3:13; Deut. 9:4; Job
33:32; 37:19; Prov. 3:28; 30:15;
Is.58:9

SAYING Gen. 37:11; Ps. 78:2; Luke
18:34

SCALE Prov. 20:23, a false s is not
good
Is. 40:15, as a speck of dust on the **s-
s**
Amos 8:5, to cheat with dishonest **s-
s**
Mic. 6:11, Can I justify wicked **s-s**
Rev. 6:5, a pair of **s-s** in his hand
Job 31:6; Is. 40:12; 46:6; Jer. 32:10

SCALE-ARMOR Jer. 46:4; 51:3

SCARCE—*want*
Ezek. 4:17, bread and water will be s
Is. 13:12; Luke 9:39

SCARLET Is. 1:18, Though your sins
are as s
Matt. 27:28, put a s robe on Him
Rev. 17:3, woman sitting on a s
beast
Gen. 38:28; Ex. 25:4; Josh. 2:18; Song
4:3; Jer. 4:30; Nah. 2:3

SCATTER Ps. 92:9, All who do
iniquity will be **s-ed**
Matt. 21:44, it will s him like dust
26:31, the flock shall be **s-ed**
Lev. 26:33; Job 18:15; 38:24; Ps.
141:7; Prov. 11:24; Is. 41:16; Jer.
23:1

SCENT Job 39:25, he **s-s** the battle
from afar

SCHEME Esth. 8:3; Job 5:5; Ps. 37:7;
Dan. 11:24,25; Mic. 2:1; 2 Cor. 2:11

SCOFF Ps. 2:4, The Lord **s-s** at them
Luke 16:14, the Pharisees . . . were **s-
ing** at Him

SCOFFER Acts 13:41, BEHOLD, YOU **S-
S**, AND MARVEL

SCORCH Jer. 4:11, A **s-ing** wind
from the bare heights

SCORN Deut. 32:15; Prov. 30:17;
Ezek. 25:6,15; 36:5

SCOURGE Job 5:21, hidden from the
s of the tongue
Matt. 10:17, s you in their
synagogues
20:19, mock and s and crucify Him
27:26, but Jesus he **s-d**
John 2:15, He made a s of cords
Heb. 12:6, **s-s** EVERY SON WHOM HE
RECEIVES

SCRIBE Matt. 2:4, chief priests and
s-s of the people
Matt. 23:13, Woe to you, **s-s** and
Pharisees
Mark 1:22, authority, and not as **s-s**
12:38, Beware of the **s-s**
1 Cor. 1:20, Where is the s
Neh. 8:4; Jer. 8:8

SCRIPTURE(S), *writing*
Matt. 21:42, Did you never read in
the **S-s**
22:29, not understanding the **S-s**
Mark 14:49, that the **S-s** might be
fulfilled
Luke 4:21, Today this **S** has been
fulfilled

SCRIPTURE(S) *(Continued)*
24:32, He was explaining the S-s to us
John 5:39, You search the S-s
10:35, the S cannot be broken
20:9, they did not understand the S
Acts 18:24, he was mighty in the S-s
Rom. 4:3, For what does the S say
15:4, encouragement of the S-s
2 Tim. 3:16, All S is inspired by God

SCROLL—*roll* Jer. 36:2, Take a s and write
Ezek. 3:1, eat this s, and go
Zech. 5:1, behold, *there was a* flying s

SEA Gen. 1:10, He called s-s
Gen. 1:26, rule over the fish of the s
Ex. 10:19, drove them into the Red S
Ps. 24:2, founded it upon the s-s
107:23, down to the s in ships
146:6, The s and all that is in them
Is. 57:20, wicked are like the tossing s
Matt. 8:26, rebuked the winds and the s
14:26, saw Him walking on the s
Rev. 4:6, s of glass like crystal
21:1, There is no longer *any* s
2 Sam. 17:11; Job 7:12; 38:8; Ps. 65:5; Is. 11:9; Jer. 25:22; Nah. 1:4; 2 Cor. 11:26

SEAL—*shut* Dan. 12:4, s up the book . . . end of time
Rom. 4:11, s of the righteous of the faith
2 Cor. 1:22, who also s-ed us
Eph. 1:13, s-ed in Him with the Holy Spirit
Rev. 5:1, s-ed up with seven s-s
9:4, s of God on their foreheads
1 Kin. 21:8; Job 14:17; Song 4:12; 8:6; Is. 29:11; Jer. 32:10; Dan. 9:24; 12:4

SEA MONSTER Ps. 148:7; Matt. 12:40

SEARCH 1 Chr. 28:9, LORD s-es all hearts
Job 28:3, to the farthest limit he s-es out
Ps. 139:23, S me . . . know my heart
Prov. 20:27, S-ing all the innermost parts
Jer. 17:10, I, the LORD, s the heart
Matt. 2:8, make careful s for the Child
2:13, Herod is going to s
John 5:39, You s the Scriptures, because
7:52, S, and see that no prophet arises
2 Tim. 1:17, he eagerly s-ed for me
Judg. 5:16; 1 Sam. 26:20; 1 Kin. 1:3

SEASON—*times* Ps. 1:3, yields its fruit in its s
Ps. 104:27, their food in due s
Luke 14:34, with what will it be s-ed
Gal. 4:10, observe days . . . s-s and years
Col. 4:6, with grace, s-ed, *as it were,* with salt
2 Tim. 4:2, ready in s *and* out of s
Gen. 1:14; Lev. 26:4; Job 5:26

SEAT—*sat* Ps. 1:1, Nor sit in the s of the scoffers
Matt. 23:6, chief s-s in the synagogues
27:19, sitting on the judgment s
Luke 10:39, Mary . . . s-ed at His feet

Rom. 14:10, the judgment s of God
Ex. 25:17; 1 Sam. 4:18; Ezek. 28:2

SECOND Matt. 22:39, And a s is like it
1 Cor. 15:47, the s man is from heaven
Rev. 2:11, not be hurt by the s death
Gen. 1:8; Ezek. 10:14

SECRET Ps. 44:21, knows the s-s of the heart
Prov. 9:17, bread *eaten* in s is pleasant
21:14, gift in s subdues anger
Matt. 6:4, your alms may be in s
6:6,18, your Father who is in s
Rom. 2:16, God will judge the s-s
16:25, kept s for long ages past
Deut. 27:15; Job 11:6; 15:8; Song 2:14; Is. 45:3,19; Hab. 3:14

SECRETLY Josh. 2:1, two men as spies s
Judg. 4:21, went s to him
Matt. 1:19, Joseph . . . put her away s
2:7, Then Herod s called the
John 11:28, called Mary her sister, saying s
Deut. 13:6; Job 13:10; 31:27

SECURE—*sure* Prov. 3:23, walk in your way s-ly
Matt. 27:66, made the grave s
Acts 16:23, the jailer to guard them s-ly
Lev. 26:5; Ezek. 34:27

SECURITY Judg. 18:7, living in s

SEDUCES—*entice* Ex. 22:16, if a man s a virgin

SEE—*perceive* Ex. 33:20, no man can s Me and live
Job 19:26, without my flesh I shall s God
Ps. 16:10, allow Thy Holy One to s the pit
34:8, s that the LORD is good
66:5, Come and s the works of God
115:5, eyes, but they cannot s
Is. 35:2, s the glory of the LORD
62:2, nations will s your righteousness
Joel 2:28, young men will s visions
Matt. 5:16, may s your good works
11:8, what did you go out to s
16:28, s the Son of Man coming
Luke 2:26, would not s death before
8:10, s-ING THEY MAY NOT S
John 4:29, s a man who told me
7:52, Search, and s that no prophet
12:19, s that you are not doing any good
16:16, little while, and you will s Me
1 Cor. 13:12, now we s in a mirror dimly
Heb. 12:14, no one will s the Lord
1 John 3:2, we shall s Him just as He is
Ex. 10:23; Num 14:23; 24:17; Job 6:28; 9:11; 24:15; 34:32; Ps. 36:9; 49:19; Eccles. 6:9; Song 7:12; Is. 29:18; Ezek. 12:2

SEED—*descendant, offspring*
Gen. 8:22, S-time and harvest
Matt. 13:22, s was sown among the thorns
13:31, heaven is like a mustard s

Luke 8:5, sower went out to sow his s
8:11, the s is the word of God
1 Pet. 1:23, not of s which is perishable
Gen. 1:11; Lev. 19:19; 26:16; Eccles. 11:6; Is. 55:10; Hag. 2:19

SEEK—*desire, search* 2 Chr. 7:14, pray, and s My face
Ps. 24:6, generation of those who s Him
34:14, S peace and pursue it
63:1, I shall s Thee earnestly
119:2, s Him with all *their* heart
Prov. 8:17, who diligently s me will find me
Is. 55:6, S the LORD while He may be found
Jer. 29:13, you will s Me and find *Me*
Amos 5:4, S Me that you may live
Matt. 6:33, s first His kingdom
7:7, s, and you shall find
12:46, His brothers were . . . s-ing to speak
Mark 8:12, this generation s for a sign
Luke 11:10, he who s-s finds
John 1:38, What do you s
5:30, I do not s My own will
8:50, One who s-s and judges
1 Cor. 10:24, Let no one s his own good
13:5, it does not s its own
Phil. 4:17, Not that I s the gift . . . I s for the profit
Col. 3:1, keep s-ing the things above
Deut. 4:29; 2 Chr. 16:12; Job 7:21; Eccles. 7:25; Is. 34:16; Ezek. 7:25; 34:16; Dan. 9:3; Hos. 10:12; Amos 5:14; Gal. 1:10

SEEM—*appear* Gen. 29:20; Prov. 14:12

SEEN—*appeared* Gen. 9:14, bow shall be s in the cloud
Is. 6:5, my eyes have s the King
Luke 2:30, eyes have s Thy salvation
John 1:18, no man has s God at any time
Rom. 8:24, hope that is not s is not hope
1 Cor. 2:9, EYE HAS NOT S
Heb. 11:1, conviction of things not s
Gen. 32:30; Job 5:3; 38:22

SEIZE—*take* John 7:30, seeking . . . to s Him
Jer. 50:24; Mic. 2:2

SELECT Acts 6:3, s from among you . . . seven men

SELF Rom. 6:6, our old s was crucified
Col. 3:9, laid aside the old s

SELF-ABASEMENT Col. 2:18, delighting in s
Col. 2:23, wisdom in self-made religion and s

SELF-CONTROL Acts 24:25, righteousness, s, and the judgment
Gal. 5:23, gentleness, s

SELFISH Phil. 2:3, do nothing from s-ness
James 3:14,16, jealousy and s ambition

SELL Prov. 23:23, Buy truth, and do
not **s** *it*
Matt. 19:21, go *and* **s** your
possessions
Gen. 25:31; Lev. 25:29; Deut. 2:28;
2 Kin. 4:7

SEND—*cast* Is. 6:8, Whom shall I **s**
. . . Here
Matt. 5:45, **s-s** rain on *the* righteous
9:38, **s** out workers into His harvest
1 Cor. 7:13, let her not **s** her husband
away
16:11, **s** him on his way in peace
2 Thess. 2:11, **s** . . . a deluding
influence
Gen. 7:4; 24:7; Num. 13:2; Job 5:10;
38:35

SENSELESS—*stupid* Ps. 49:10,
stupid and the **s** alike perish
Ps. 92:6, **s** man has no knowledge

SENSIBLE Tit. 2:5, *to be* **s**, pure,
workers at home

SENSUAL Ezek. 33:32, like a **s** song

SENSUALITY Eph. 4:19, given . . .
over to **s**
Rev. 18:3, rich by the wealth of her **s**

SENSUOUS Rev. 18:7, she . . . lived
s-ly

SENT Is. 61:1, He has **s** me to bind
up the broken-hearted
Matt. 10:5, These twelve Jesus **s** out
after
Luke 4:18, He has **s** Me to proclaim
release
Acts 13:4, So, being **s** out by the
Holy Spirit
Gal. 4:4, God **s** forth His Son
1 Pet. 1:12, Holy Spirit **s** from
heaven
1 John 4:9, that God has **s** His only
begotten
Gen. 8:7,8; Is. 48:16

SENTENCE—*condemnation*
Matt. 23:33, escape the **s** of hell

SEPARATE—*divide* Gen. 1:4, God
s-d the light
Prov. 16:28, a slanderer **s-s** intimate
friends
Matt. 19:6, let no man **s**
25:32, He will **s** them from one
another
Rom. 8:35, Who shall **s** us from the
love
Gen. 13:9; Lev. 20:24; Job 41:17;
Ps. 22:7

SERIOUS Acts 25:7, **s** charges
against him

SERPENT Gen. 3:1, Now the **s** was
more crafty
Num. 21:9, Moses made a bronze **s**
Ps. 58:4, venom of a **s**
Matt. 10:16, be shrewd as **s-s**
Mark 16:18, they will pick up **s-s**
John 3:14, Moses lifted up the **s** in
the wilderness
2 Cor. 11:3, lest as the **s** deceived
Eve
Rev. 12:9, the **s** of old who is called
the devil
Gen. 49:17; Ex. 7:12; Deut. 32:33;
Ps. 91:13; Prov. 23:32; Is. 30:6; Jer.
8:17

SERVANT—*minister* Job 1:8, have
you considered My **s** Job
Ps. 31:16, face to shine upon Thy **s**
Matt. 20:26, shall be your **s**
Luke 1:2, and **s-s** of the Word
2 Cor. 3:6, **s-s** of a new covenant
11:23, Are they **s-s** of Christ
1 Tim. 4:6, be a good **s** of Christ
Jesus
Gen. 9:25; Ex. 14:31; Ruth 2:9;
1 Sam. 3:9; Ezra 7:24; Job 4:18;
Prov. 11:29; Joel 2:29

SERVE—*worship, minister*
Ps. 100:2, S the Lord with gladness
Matt. 4:10, GOD, AND **s** HIM ONLY
6:24, No one can **s** two masters
20:28, not come to be **s-d**, but to **s**
John 12:26, If any one **s-s** Me, let
him
Acts 24:14, I do **s** the God of our
fathers
Rom. 7:6, so that we **s** in newness of
the Spirit
12:11, fervent in spirit, **s-ing** the
Lord
Gal. 5:13, through love **s** one another
1 Tim. 3:10, let them **s** as deacons
Josh. 22:5; 1 Chr. 6:10; 24:2; Jer. 5:19

SERVICE—*ministry*
Rom. 12:1, *which* is your spiritual **s**
Eph. 4:12, for the work of **s**
Phil. 2:30, was deficient in your **s** to
me
Heb. 12:28, offer to God an
acceptable **s**
Is. 32:17; Jer. 22:13

SET Gen. 9:13, I **s** my bow in the
cloud
Ex. 2:3, she . . . **s** it among the reeds
Deut. 30:19, I have **s** before you life
and death
Ps. 40:2, He **s** my feet upon a rock
Matt. 5:14, A city **s** on a hill cannot
Col. 3:2, S your mind on the things
above
James 3:6, and is **s** on fire by hell
Lev. 17:10; Prov. 9:2; Eccles. 10:6; Is.
3:24; 38:1; Jer. 5:26; Ezek. 2:2

SETTING Prov. 25:11, apples of gold
in **s-s** of silver

SETTLE—*reckon* Matt. 25:19, came
and **s-d** accounts with them
Deut. 21:5; Nah. 3:17

SEVEN Gen. 29:20, Jacob served **s**
years for Rachel
Ps. 119:164, S times a day I praise
Thee
Is. 4:1, For **s** women will take hold
of one man
Matt. 12:45, along with it **s** other
spirits
18:21, forgive him? Up to **s** times
Acts 6:3, **s** men of good reputation
Rev. 1:4, John to the **s** churches
1:12, I saw **s** golden lampstands
3:1, He who has the **s** Spirits of
God
15:1, **s** angels who had **s** plagues
Gen. 21:29; Prov. 9:1; Eccles. 11:2;
Dan. 9:25; Zech. 4:2

SEVERE—*great* Matt. 28:2, a **s**
earthquake
Song 8:6; Ezek. 34:4

SHACK Is. 24:20, it totters like a **s**

SHACKLES Mark 5:4, the **s** broken
in pieces

SHADOW 2 Kin. 20:11, **s** on the
stairway back ten steps
Ps. 17:8, Hide me in the **s** of Thy
wings
23:4, valley of the **s** of death
91:1, abide in the **s** of the Almighty
Col. 2:17, a *mere* **s** of what is to
come
Heb. 8:5, copy and **s** of the heavenly
things
James 1:17, no variation, or shifting
s
1 Chr. 29:15; Song 2:17

SHAKE—*tremble*
Prov. 10:30, righteous . . . never be **s-
n**
Is. 13:13, earth . . . **s-n** from its place
Matt. 10:14, **s** off the dust of your
feet
11:7, A reed **s-n** by the wind
Luke 6:38, pressed down, **s-n**
together
Job 4:14; 16:4; Ps. 109:23

SHAME Acts 5:41, worthy to suffer **s**
2 Cor. 4:2, things hidden because of **s**
Phil. 3:19, glory is in their **s**
1 John 2:28, not shrink . . . Him in **s**
Prov. 19:26; Is. 54:4; Zeph. 3:5

SHARE—*portion* Luke 15:12, **s** of
the estate
1 Cor. 10:16, a **s-ing** in the blood of
Christ
10:20, to become **s-rs** in demons
Gal. 6:6, **s** . . . with him who teaches
1 Tim. 6:18, ready to **s**
Heb. 13:16, doing good and **s-ing**

SHARP Deut. 32:41, **s-en** My flashing
sword
Ps. 57:4, tongue a **s** sword
64:3, **s-ened** their tongue
Prov. 5:4, S as a two-edged sword
27:17, Iron **s-ens** iron
Eccles. 10:10, does not **s-en** *its* edge
Heb. 4:12, **s-er** than any two-edged
sword

SHATTER Ex. 15:6; Ps. 2:9

SHAVE Gen. 41:14; Judg. 16:19;
2 Sam. 10:4; Is. 7:20; 1 Cor. 11:6

SHEAR Deut. 18:4, first **s-ing** of your
sheep

SHED—*pour* Matt. 26:28, My blood
. . . **s** on behalf of many
Rom. 3:15, feet are swift to **s** blood
Gen. 9:6; Prov. 1:16

SHEEP—*flock* Ps. 44:22, a **s** to be
slaughtered
Ps. 100:3, the **s** of his pasture
119:176, astray like a lost **s**
Is. 53:6, All of us like **s** have gone
astray
53:7, **s** . . . silent before its shearers
Matt. 9:36, **s** without a shepherd
10:16, I send you out as **s**
15:24, lost **s** of the house of Israel
25:32, separates the **s** from the
goats
26:31, **s** of the flock . . . scattered
Luke 15:6, found my **s** which was
lost
John 10:3, calls his own **s** by name
10:7, I am the door of the **s**

SHEEP *(Continued)*
10:27, My **s** hear My voice
21:16, Shepherd My **s**
Heb. 13:20, great Shepherd of the **s**
1 Pet. 2:25, straying like **s**
Gen. 29:9; Num. 27:17; 1 Sam. 15:14;
Job 31:20; Jer. 12:3; 50:6

SHEKELS—*piece* Gen. 23:16; Zech.
11:12

SHELTER Ps. 5:11, mayest Thou **s**
them
Ps. 61:4, refuge in the **s** of Thy wings
Gen. 19:8; Is. 1:8; 4:6; 32:2; Jon. 4:5

SHEOL Deut. 32:22, burns to the
lowest . . . of **S**
Job 17:13, look for **S** as my home
26:6, Naked is **S** before Him
Ps. 16:10, not abandon my soul to **S**
30:3, brought up my soul from **S**
49:15, redeem . . . from the power
of **S**
86:13, my soul from the depths of **S**
139:8, If I make my bed in **S**
Prov. 5:5, Her steps lay hold of **S**
Ezek. 32:21, speak . . . from the
midst of **S**
Amos 9:2, Though they dig into **S**
Jon. 2:2, help from the depth of **S**
2 Sam. 22:6; Prov. 27:20; Song 8:6;
Hab. 2:5

SHEPHERD (n.)—*pastor*
Ps. 23:1, The LORD is my **s**
28:9, Be their **s** also
Is. 40:11, Like a **s** He will tend His
flock
Jer. 3:15, I will give you **s-s**
23:1, **s-s** who are destroying . . . the
sheep
Zech. 11:16, I am going to raise up
a **s**
Matt. 9:36, like sheep without a **s**
26:31, I will strike down the **s**
Luke 2:8, **s-s** staying out in the fields
John 10:11, I am the good **s**
Heb. 13:20, the great **S** of the sheep
1 Pet. 2:25, returned to the **S** and
Guardian
5:4, when the Chief **S** appears
Rev. 7:17, the Lamb . . . shall be
their **s**
Gen. 46:34; 48:15; Num. 27:17;
1 Sam. 17:40; Jer. 10:21; Ezek.
34:5; 37:24; Zeph. 2:6

SHEPHERD (v.)—*fed* Ps. 78:72,
David **s-ed**
Matt. 2:6, WHO WILL **s** MY PEOPLE
John 21:16, **S** My sheep
Acts 20:28, to **s** the church of God
1 Pet. 5:2, **s** the flock of God

SHIELD Ps. 18:2, My **s** and the horn
of my salvation
Ps. 28:7, my strength and my **s**
91:4, His faithfulness is a **s**
Eph. 6:16, taking up the **s** of faith
Gen. 15:1; 2 Sam. 22:3,31; Ps. 7:10;
89:18; Prov. 2:7

SHINE Num. 6:25, make His face **s**
on you
Job 9:7, sun not to **s**
41:32, Behind him . . . a wake to **s**
Prov. 4:18, **s-s** brighter and brighter
Is. 60:1, Arise, **s**; for your light has
come
Matt. 5:16, Let your light **s** before
men
13:43, RIGHTEOUS WILL **s** FORTH
John 1:5, light **s-s** in the darkness

2 Pet. 1:19, a lamp **s-ing** in a dark
place
1 John 2:8, true light is already **s-ing**

SHOCK Deut. 1:29, Do not be **s-ed**,
nor fear them

SHONE Luke 2:9, glory of the Lord **s**
around
Ex. 34:29; 2 Kin. 3:22

SHOOK Neh. 5:13, also **s** out . . . my
garment
Acts 28:5, he **s** the creature off
Heb. 12:26, His voice **s** the earth

SHOOT Is. 11:1, a **s** will spring from
. . . Jesse
Is. 53:2, grew up . . . like a tender **s**
1 Sam. 20:20; Ps. 11:2; 64:4

SHORT Rom. 3:23, fall **s** of the glory
of God
1 Cor. 7:29, time has been **s-ened**

SHOT 1 Sam. 20:20, as though I **s** at a
target

SHOULD Matt. 23:23, these . . .
things you **s** have done

SHOUT Josh. 6:16, Joshua said . . . **S**
Ps. 47:5, God has ascended with a **s**
66:1, **S** joyfully to God
Matt. 25:6, at midnight . . . a **s**
1 Thess. 4:16, descend from heaven
with a **s**

SHOW—*demonstrate*
Matt. 22:19, **S** Me the coin
John 14:8, Lord, **s** us the Father
1 Cor. 3:13, for the day will **s** it
Gal. 6:12, make a good **s-ing** in the
flesh
Gen. 12:1; Ex. 33:18; Deut. 5:10;
2 Sam. 10:12; 1 Chr. 19:13; Job 11:6

SHOWER 1 Kin. 18:41; Ps. 65:10; Jer.
14:22; Luke 12:54

SHREWD—*wise*
Job 5:13, wise by their own **s-ness**
Matt. 10:16, be **s** as serpents

SHRINE Ezek. 16:24,31,39

SHRINK—*draw* Heb. 10:38, IF HE **S-S**
BACK, MY SOUL HAS NO PLEASURE

SHUDDER Jer. 2:12, and **s**, be very
desolate
James 2:19, demons also believe,
and **s**

SHUN—*refrain* Eccles. 3:5, time to **s**
embracing

SHUT—*close* Matt. 6:6, WHEN YOU
HAVE **s** YOUR DOOR
Matt. 23:13, **s** off the kingdom of
heaven
Gal. 3:23, being **s** up to the faith
Job 5:16; Prov. 21:13; Dan. 6:22

SICK Prov. 13:12, Hope . . . *makes* the
heart **s**
Matt. 10:8, Heal the **s**, raise
25:36, I was **s**, and you visited Me
Mark 1:30, Simon's mother-in-law
. . . lying **s**
2:17, physician, but those who are **s**
Luke 7:2, and **s** and about to die
John 11:2, brother Lazarus was **s**
James 5:14, Is anyone among you **s**

5:15, prayer . . . restore the one who
is **s**
Ps. 41:3; Song 2:5

SICKLE Deut. 16:9, put the **s** to the
standing grain
Joel 3:13, Put in the **s** . . . harvest is
ripe
Rev. 14:15, Put in your **s** and reap

SICKLINESS Is. 17:11, a day of **s**
and incurable pain

SICKNESS Matt. 4:23, healing every
kind of **s**
Matt. 10:1, authority . . . to heal . . . **s**
Luke 13:12, are freed from your **s**
John 5:5, thirty-eight years in his **s**
11:4, This **s** is not unto death
Deut. 7:15; 2 Kin. 1:2; 8:8,9

SIDE Ezek. 36:3, crushed you from
every **s**
John 19:34, pierced His **s** with a
spear
20:20, showed . . . His hands and
His **s**

SIEGEWORKS Deut. 20:20; Eccles.
9:14

SIGHT Ps. 19:14, acceptable in Thy **s**
Ps. 90:4, thousand years in Thy **s**
Matt. 11:5, BLIND RECEIVE **s**
20:34, they received their **s**
Luke 4:18, RECOVERY OF **s** TO THE
BLIND
Acts 9:9, three days without **s**
22:13, Saul, receive your **s**
2 Cor. 5:7, walk by faith, not by **s**
Gen. 2:9; 18:3; Ruth 2:13; Job 19:15

SIGN—*signal, witness, wonder*
Gen. 9:12, the **s** of the covenant
Ex. 3:12, this shall be a **s** to you
12:13, blood shall be a **s** . . . on the
houses
Ps. 86:17, Show me a **s** for good
Matt. 12:38, we want a **s** from You
16:3, cannot *discern* the **s-s** of the
times
24:3, *will be* the **s** of Your coming
Mark 13:22, show **s-s** and wonders
16:20, confirmed the word by
the **s-s**
Luke 1:22, he kept making **s-s** to
them
21:25, will be **s-s** in sun
23:8, hoping to see some **s**
performed
John 2:11, beginning of *His* **s-s** Jesus
did
10:41, John performed no **s**
11:47, this man is performing many
s-s
Acts 5:12, many **s-s** and wonders
were taking place
1 Cor. 1:22, Jews ask for **s-s**
Phil. 1:28, a **s** of destruction
2 Thess. 2:9, all power and **s-s**
Rev. 12:1, a great **s** appeared in
heaven
15:1, saw another **s** in heaven
Gen. 4:15; Ex. 31:13; Is. 7:11,14;
55:13; Ezek. 14:8

SIGNAL Mark 14:44, had given them
a **s**
Is. 11:10; 30:17

SILENCE Ps. 62:1, My soul *waits* in **s**
for God

Titus 1:11, who must be **s-d**
Rev. 8:1, there was **s** in heaven

SILENT Eccles. 3:7, A time to be **s**
Matt. 26:63, But Jesus kept **s**
Luke 1:20, you shall be **s** and unable
to speak
9:36, they kept **s**, and reported to
no one
Acts 18:9, go on speaking . . . not
be **s**
1 Cor. 14:28, keep **s** in the church
14:34, Let the women keep **s**
Judg. 18:19; Esth. 7:4; Job 6:24; 13:13

SILVER Matt. 10:9, Do not acquire
gold, or **s**
Matt. 26:15, thirty pieces of **s**
Acts 3:6, I do not possess **s** and gold
8:20, May your **s** perish with you
20:33, coveted no one's **s**
James 5:3, gold and **s** have rusted
Gen. 13:2; Job 27:16; Prov. 16:16;
25:11; Is. 1:22; 39:2; Jer. 6:30;
Zech. 11:12

SIMPLE—*naive* Ps. 19:7, making
wise the **s**
Ps. 116:6, LORD preserves the **s**

SIN—*transgression* Ps. 25:7,
remember the **s-s**
Ps. 51:3, my **s** is ever before me
Prov. 14:9, Fools mock at **s**
Is. 1:18, your **s-s** are as scarlet
Matt. 1:21, save His people from
their **s-s**
3:6, as they confessed their **s-s**
12:31, **s** and blasphemy . . . forgiven
men
18:15, if your brother **s-s**
18:21, brother **s** against me
26:28, for forgiveness of **s-s**
Mark 2:7, forgive **s-s** but God alone
Luke 11:4, forgive us our **s-s**
John 1:29, Lamb . . . takes away **s** of
the world
8:7, He who is without **s**
8:11, go your way . . . **s** no more
15:22, they have no excuse for
their **s**
16:8, convict the world concerning **s**
Acts 22:16, wash away your **s-s**
26:18, receive forgiveness of **s-s**
Rom. 5:12, **s** entered into the world
6:23, wages of **s** is death
14:23, whatever is not from faith
is **s**
1 Cor. 15:3, Christ died for our **s-s**
15:56, sting of death is **s**
2 Cor. 5:21, who knew no **s** *to
be* **s** on our behalf
Heb. 9:7, for the **s-s** of the people
11:25, enjoy the . . . pleasures of **s**
James 5:16, confess your **s-s** to one
another
5:20, cover a multitude of **s-s**
1 Pet. 2:22, WHO COMMITTED NO **S**
1 John 1:8, If we say we have no **s**
1:9, If we confess our **s-s**
2:1, If anyone **s-s**, we have an
Advocate
3:4, **s** is lawlessness
5:16, there is a **s** leading to death
5:17, All unrighteousness is **s**
Rev. 1:5, released us from our **s-s**
Gen. 4:7; 18:20; Ex. 10:17; 32:30; Job
1:22; 2:10; Ps. 51:2; 79:9; Is. 30:1;
Mic. 6:7

SINCE Matt. 18:25, **s** he did not have
the means to repay

1 Cor. 11:7, **s** he is the image and
glory
Heb. 2:14, **S** then the children share
Gen. 41:39; Deut. 12:12

SINFUL Mark 8:38, **s** generation
Luke 5:8, I am a **s** man, O Lord
Rom. 8:3, the likeness of **s** flesh
Num. 32:14; Is. 1:4

SING—*shout, utter* Ps. 5:11, Let
them ever **s** for joy
Ps. 33:3, **S** to Him a new song
100:2, Come before Him with joyful
s-ing
1 Cor. 14:15, I shall **s** with the spirit
Col. 3:16, **s-ing** with thankfulness
James 5:13, cheerful? Let him **s**
praises
Ex. 15:1; Judg. 5:12; 2 Sam. 22:50;
1 Chr. 16:23; 2 Chr. 23:13; Job
29:13; Prov. 29:6; Is. 5:1; Rev. 5:9

SINK Prov. 2:18, her house **s-s** down
to death

SINNED Ps. 41:4, I have **s** against
Thee
Ps. 51:4, Thee only, I have **s**
Luke 15:18, **s** against heaven
Rom. 3:23, **s**, and fall short of the
glory
5:12, spread to all men, because
all **s**
1 John 1:10, If we say that we have
not **s**
Lev. 5:16; Deut. 1:41; Dan. 9:15

SINNER Ps. 1:1, stand in the path of
s-s
Matt. 9:10, tax-gatherers and **s-s**
9:13, call *the* righteous, but **s-s**
11:19, a friend of . . . **s-s**
Mark 2:17, to call *the* righteous, but
s-s
14:41, into the hands of **s-s**
Luke 6:34, Even **s-s** lend to **s-s**
15:7, *more* joy in heaven over one **s**
18:13, be merciful to me, the **s**
John 9:31, God does not hear **s-s**
Rom. 5:8, while we were yet **s-s**
1 Tim. 1:15, Jesus came . . . to save **s-
s**
James 4:8, Cleanse your hands, you
s-s
Prov. 1:10; 13:21; 23:17; Eccles. 9:18

SISTER Job 17:14, my mother, and
my **s**
Matt. 12:50, is My brother and **s**
Luke 10:39, had a **s** called Mary
Gen. 12:13; Prov. 7:4; Song 8:8; Rom.
16:1

SIT Ps. 1:1, **S** in the seat of scoffers
Ps. 26:4, not **s** with deceitful men
110:1, **S** at My right hand
Matt. 4:16, WERE **S-ING IN DARKNESS**
9:9, Matthew, **s-ing** in the tax office
26:36, **S** here while I go
27:61, Mary, **s-ing** opposite the
grave
Luke 2:46, temple, **s-ing** . . . midst of
the teachers
8:35, **s-ing** down at the feet of Jesus
John 12:15, **S-ING ON A DONKEY'S COLT**
Acts 8:28, **s-ing** in his chariot
Gen. 18:1; 1 Kin. 22:19; Job 2:8;
Ezek. 28:2

SITUATE Ps. 144:15, people who are
so **s-d**

SIZE—*stature* Num. 13:32, are men
of great **s**

SKILL Ps. 137:5, my right hand
forget her **s**

SKILLFUL Gen. 25:27; Ex. 28:8;
1 Sam. 16:16; Ps. 139:15; Is. 3:3

SKIN Ex. 34:29, the **s** of his face
shone
Job 2:4, **S** for **s**
10:11, Clothe me with **s** and flesh
Jer. 13:23, Ethiopian change his **s**
Job 19:20; 30:30

SKIP Job 21:11, children **s** about

SKULL Judg. 9:53, Abimelech's head,
crushing his **s**
Matt. 27:33, which means Place of
a **S**

SKY Ps. 36:5, faithfulness *reaches* to
the **s-s**
Matt. 16:2,3, for the **s** is red
Luke 12:56, analyze the appearance
. . . the **s**
Gen. 1:26,28; Deut. 4:17; 2 Sam.
21:10; Job 37:18; Prov. 30:19;
James 5:18

SLACK Prov. 18:9, who is **s** in his
work

SLAIN 1 Sam. 18:7; 29:5, Saul has **s**
his thousands
Rev. 5:12, Worthy . . . Lamb that
was **s**

SLANDER Ps. 15:3, He does not **s**
Prov. 30:10, Do not **s** a slave to his
master
1 Cor. 4:13, when we are **s-ed**, we try
to conciliate
2 Cor. 12:20, disputes, **s-s**, gossip
Eph. 4:31, and **s** be put away from
you

SLANDERER—*whisperer*
Prov. 16:28, **s** separates . . . friends
Rom. 1:30, **s-s**, haters of God

SLAP Job 16:10, **s-ed** me on the
cheek
Matt. 5:39, **s-s** you on your right
cheek

SLAUGHTER—*sacrifice*
Ps. 44:22, as sheep to be **s-ed**
Is. 53:7, lamb that is led to **s**
Rom. 8:36, AS SHEEP TO BE **S-ED**
James 5:5, in a day of **s**
Prov. 7:22; Jer. 46:10

SLAVE Prov. 22:7, borrower becomes
the lender's **s**
Matt. 25:21, Well done . . . faithful **s**
1 Cor. 7:21, Were you called while
a **s**
9:27, body and make it my **s**
Gal. 4:7, no longer a **s**, but a son
Ex. 23:12; Lev. 19:20; 25:39,44; Deut.
15:15; 16:12; 24:18; Col. 3:22

SLAVERY—*bondage* Rom. 8:15, a
spirit of **s**
Gal. 5:1, subject again to a yoke of **s**
Heb. 2:15, subject to **s** all their lives

SLAY—*destroy* Job 5:2, vexation **s-s**
the foolish man
Job 13:15, Though He **s** me, I will
hope

SLAY (Continued)
Ps. 34:21, Evil shall **s** the wicked
2 Thess. 2:8, the Lord will **s** with the breath of

SLEDGE Is. 41:15, a new, sharp threshing **s**

SLEEP Gen. 2:21, deep **s** to fall upon the man
Ps. 13:3, **s** the *sleep of* death
Prov. 6:10, A little **s**, a little slumber
Eccles. 5:12, **s** of the working man
Matt. 1:24, Joseph arose from his **s**
26:40,43, found them **s-ing**
26:45, Are you still **s-ing** and taking
Acts 20:9, sinking into a deep **s**
1 Cor. 15:51, we shall not all **s**
1 Thess. 5:7, those who **s** do their **s-ing** at night
Ps. 76:6; Prov. 3:24; 20:13; Jer. 31:26; Mark 14:40

SLEW Matt. 2:16, **s** all the male children

SLING 1 Sam. 17:40, his **s** was in his hand
Judg. 20:16; 1 Sam. 25:29

SLOTHFUL Prov. 12:27, **s** man does not roast

SLOW Ex. 4:10, **s** of speech and **s** of tongue
Ps. 103:8, **S** to anger and abounding
Prov. 16:32, He who is **s** to anger
Luke 24:25, foolish men and **s** of heart
James 1:19, **s** to speak *and* **s** to anger
2 Pet. 3:9, The Lord is not **s**

SLUGGISH Heb. 6:12, that you may not be **s**

SLUMBER Ps. 121:3, who keeps you will not **s**
Prov. 6:10, A little sleep, a little **s**
Job 33:15; Ps. 132:4; Is. 5:27; 56:10

SMALL—*little* Prov. 30:24, Four things are **s** on the earth
Mark 8:7, They also had a few **s** fish
James 3:4, directed by a very **s** rudder
3:5, tongue is a **s** part of the body
Num. 26:56; 35:8; Deut. 25:13; Is. 10:19

SMEAR Ezek. 22:28, prophets have **s-ed** whitewash

SMELL Gen. 27:27; Deut. 4:28; Ps. 115:6

SMELT Is. 1:25, **s** away your dross with lye

SMOKE Gen. 15:17; Job 41:20; Ps. 102:3; Prov. 10:26; Is. 6:4

SMOLDERING Matt. 12:20, **s** WICK HE WILL

SMOOTH Ps. 55:21, speech was **s-er** than butter
Prov. 5:3, **s-er** than oil is her speech
Is. 45:13, I will make all his ways **s**
Luke 3:5, THE ROUGH ROADS **s**
Gen. 27:11,16; 1 Sam. 17:40; Prov. 6:24; 11:5; Is. 40:3

SNAKE Matt. 7:10, he will not . . . a **s**, will he

SNARE—*web* Prov. 7:23, bird hastens to the **s**
Rom. 11:9, THEIR TABLE BECOME A **S**
2 Tim. 2:26, *escape* from the **s** of the devil
Ex. 10:7; Job 34:30; Ps. 91:3; Eccles. 7:26

SNATCH—*pluck* John 10:12, the wolf **s-es** them
John 10:28, **s** them out of My hand
Jude 23, **s-ing** them out of the fire

SNEER—*scoff* Luke 23:35, the rulers were **s-ing**

SNOW Ps. 51:7, I shall be whiter than **s**
Prov. 26:1, Like **s** in summer
Is. 1:18, scarlet . . . be as white as **s**
Matt. 28:3, his garment as white as **s**
Rev. 1:14, white like white wool, like **s**
Num. 12:10; Job 9:30; 38:22; Prov. 25:13

SOBER—*watch* Acts 26:25, utter words of **s** truth
1 Thess. 5:6, let us be alert and **s**
2 Tim. 4:5, be **s** in all things
1 Pet. 4:7, **s** spirit . . . purpose of prayer
5:8, Be of **s** spirit

SOFT Matt. 11:8, who wear **s** *clothing* are in
Ps. 65:10; Prov. 25:15

SOIL—*earth, ground* Ezek. 17:5, planted it in fertile **s**
Matt. 13:5; Mark 4:5, did not have much **s**
13:8, others fell on the good **s**
James 5:7, the precious produce of the **s**
Rev. 3:4, few . . . who have not **s-ed** their garments

SOJOURN Gen. 26:3; Ex. 12:48

SOJOURNER—*foreigner, alien* Ex. 2:22; 12:45; 18:3; 20:10

SOLD Gen. 25:33, **s** his birthright
Gen. 45:4, brother Joseph, whom you **s** into
Matt. 10:29, two sparrows **s** for a cent
13:46, went and **s** all that he had
Acts 5:1, his wife Sapphira, **s** a piece of
Rom. 7:14, of flesh, **s** into bondage to sin
Lev. 25:23; 1 Kin. 21:20; Joel 3:3

SOLDIER Mark 15:16, the **s-s** took Him away
Luke 23:36, the **s-s** also mocked Him
John 19:23, four parts, a part to every **s**
Acts 28:16, with the **s** who was guarding
2 Tim. 2:3, as a good **s** of Christ Jesus

SOLVE—*dissolve* Dan. 5:12, **s-ing** of difficult problems
5:16, give interpretations and **s** difficult

SOMEBODY Acts 5:36, Theudas rose up, claiming to be **s**

SOMEONE Luke 8:46, **S** did touch Me

SOMETHING—*this* 1 Kin. 2:14, have **s** *to say* to you
Hab. 1:5, *I* am doing **s** in your days
Luke 7:40, I have **s** to say to you
Acts 25:26, I may have **s** to write

SON 2 Sam. 13:37, *David* mourned for his **s**
Ps. 2:7, Thou art My **S**
8:4, **s** of man, that Thou dost care
Prov. 10:1, A wise **s** makes a father glad
17:25, A foolish **s** is a grief
Is. 7:14, a virgin will . . . bear a **s**
14:12, O star of the morning . . . **s** of
60:4, Your **s-s** will come from afar
Dan. 7:13, One like a **S** of Man
Hos. 11:1, out of Egypt I called My **s**
Matt. 1:25, virgin until she gave birth to a **S**
2:15, OUT OF EGYPT . . . CALL MY **S**
3:17, This is My beloved **S**
11:27, No one knows the **S**
13:55, Is not this the carpenter's **s**
16:16, the **S** of the living God
22:42, Christ, whose **s** is He
26:63, are the Christ, the **S** of God
27:43, I am the **S** of God
Mark 5:7, Jesus, the **S** of the Most High God
12:6, one more *to send,* a **S**
14:61, the **S** of the Blessed *One*
Luke 1:31, bear a **s**, and you shall name
2:7, birth to her first-born **s**
4:22, Is this not Joseph's **s**
15:11, A certain man had two **s-s**
15:24, this **s** of mine was dead
John 4:50, Go your way, your **s** lives
5:21, the **S** also gives life
6:42, this Jesus, the **s** of Joseph
12:36, may become **s-s** of light
14:13, may be glorified in the **S**
19:26, Woman, behold, your **s**
Acts 4:36, translated . . . **S** of Encouragement
Rom. 8:32, did not spare His own **S**
Gal. 4:7, but a **s**; and if a **s**
2 Thess. 2:3, revealed, the **s** of destruction
Heb. 6:6, again crucify . . . the **S** of God
1 John 2:22, denies the Father and the **S**
Rev. 21:7, be his God . . . will be My **s**
Gen. 6:2; 22:2; 37:33; Ex. 20:10; Deut. 8:5; 2 Kin. 2:3; Job 5:4; Eccles. 4:8; Is. 30:9; Ezek. 2:1; Mal. 3:17

SONG—*music, taunt* Ex. 15:2, LORD is my strength and **s**
Judg. 5:12, Awake, awake, sing a **s**
Job 35:10, gives **s-s** in the night
Ps. 33:3, Sing to Him a new **s**
137:4, How . . . sing the LORD's **s**
Prov. 25:20, Sings **s-s** to a troubled heart
Eccles. 12:4, the daughters of **s**
Song 1:1, The **S** of **S-s**
Eph. 5:19, hymns and spiritual **s-s**
Is. 5:1; 23:16; 24:9; Ezek. 33:32

SOON—*shortly* Ex. 2:18, you come back so **s**
Job 32:22, Maker would **s** take me away
Heb. 13:23, if he comes **s**

SOOT Lam. 4:8, appearance is blacker than s

SOOTHE Gen. 8:21, LORD smelled a **s-ing** aroma

SORDID Titus 1:11, for the sake of s gain

SORE Luke 16:21, dogs ... licking his **s-s**

SORROW Gen. 42:38, bring ... down ... in s
Ps. 31:10, my life is spent with s
Eccles. 7:3, S is better than laughter
Is. 35:10, s and sighing will flee away
53:3, A man of **s-s**
Jer. 8:18, My s is beyond healing
John 16:20, be **s-ful**, but your s
2 Cor. 2:2, For if I cause you s
2:5, he has caused s not to me
2:7, overwhelmed by excessive s
7:9, made **s-ful** according to the will of God
7:10, s ... produces a repentance
Jer. 45:3; Luke 22:45

SORRY Gen. 6:6, the LORD was s ... made man
Jer. 13:14, I will not show pity nor be s

SOUGHT—seek, visit Is. 26:16, they s Thee in distress
Matt. 2:20, who s the Child's life
21:46, they s to seize Him
Gal. 4:18, to be eagerly s
Ex. 33:7; Eccles. 7:29

SOUL—life, person
Deut. 4:29, with all your heart ... s
1 Sam. 1:26, As your s lives
Job 33:30, bring back his s from the pit
Ps. 16:10, not abandon my s to Sheol
19:7, LORD is perfect, restoring the s
23:3, He restores my s
24:4, not lifted up his s to falsehood
42:1, So my s pants for Thee
62:1, My s waits in silence for God
63:1, My s thirsts for Thee
103:1, Bless the LORD, O my s
107:9, satisfied the thirsty s
Prov. 24:12, who keeps your s
25:25, cold water to a weary s
Ezek. 18:4, s who sins will die
Matt. 10:28, unable to kill the s
11:29, FIND REST FOR YOUR **S-S**
16:26, world, and forfeits his s
26:38, My s is deeply grieved
Luke 1:46, My s exalts the Lord
12:19, say to my s, S you have many
John 12:27, My s has become troubled
Acts 4:32, were of one heart and s
1 Thess. 5:23, your spirit and s and body
Heb. 4:12, division of s and spirit
6:19, as an anchor of the s
10:39, to the preserving of the s
James 1:21, is able to save your **s-s**
5:20, save his s from death
1 Pet. 2:11, which wage war against the s
2 Pet. 2:14, enticing unstable **s-s**
Deut. 4:9; Judg. 16:16; 1 Sam. 18:1; Job 3:20; 10:1

SOUND—roar, shout, voice Ex. 32:17; Lev. 26:36

Gen. 3:8, heard the s of the LORD God
Prov. 3:21, Keep s wisdom
Luke 15:27, received him back safe and s
1 Tim. 1:10, contrary to s teaching
2 Tim. 1:13, Retain ... standard of s words
Titus 1:13, may be s in the faith
Rev. 1:15, s of many waters
8:7, And the first **s-ed**
Judg. 4:21; 1 Kin. 18:41; 19:12; Job 15:21; 33:15; Prov. 2:7; Eccles. 12:4; Jer. 25:10; Joel 2:1

SOUR Jer. 31:29, fathers have eaten s grapes

SOURCE Heb. 5:9, the s of eternal salvation

SOUTH Matt. 12:42, Queen of the S
Luke 12:55, see a s wind blowing
Acts 27:13, when a moderate s wind came up
Job 37:9,17; Eccles. 11:3

SOW Job 4:8, those who s trouble harvest it
Ps. 126:5, s in tears shall reap
Prov. 22:8, who **s-s** iniquity ... reap vanity
Is. 55:10, furnishing seed to the **s-er**
Matt. 6:26, birds ... they do not s
13:3, **s-er** went out to s
Luke 12:24, neither s nor reap
19:21, reap what you did not s
John 4:36, he who **s-s** and he who reaps
1 Cor. 9:11, **s-ed** spiritual things in you
15:42, **s-n** a perishable body
15:44, **s-n** a natural body
2 Cor. 9:6, he who **s-s** sparingly
Gal. 6:7, whatever a man **s-s**
James 3:18, is **s-n** in peace
Gen. 47:23; Lev. 26:16; Deut. 22:9; Job 31:8; Eccles. 11:4,6; Is. 32:20; Jer. 4:3; Hos. 8:7

SPACE—time Lev. 25:30, the s of a full year

SPACIOUS—large Ex. 3:8, to a good and s land

SPARE Ps. 78:50, s their soul from death
Prov. 13:24, **s-s** his rod hates his son
Acts 20:29, not **s-ing** the flock
Rom. 8:32, did not s His own Son
11:21, not s the natural branches
2 Cor. 9:6, who sows **s-ingly**
13:2, I come again, I will not s
2 Pet. 2:4, God did not s angels
Is. 9:19; Jer. 50:14; Mal. 3:17

SPARKLE Prov. 23:31, When it **s-s** in the cup

SPEAK—tell, utter Ps. 135:16, but they do not s
Prov. 23:9, Do not s ... hearing of a fool
Eccles. 3:7, silent, and a time to s
Is. 32:4, stammerers will hasten to s clearly
Matt. 10:19, how or what you will s
10:20, Spirit of your Father who **s-s**
Mark 16:17, will s with new tongues
Luke 1:20, silent and unable to s
6:26, all men s well of you
John 3:11, we s that which we know

7:46, Never did a man s ... this man **s-s**
8:45, because I s the truth
16:13, not s on His own initiative
Acts 2:4, began to s with other tongues
18:9, not be afraid ... but go on **s-ing**
19:6, they began **s-ing** with tongues
Rom. 3:5, I am **s-ing** in human terms
1 Cor. 2:7, we s God's wisdom
13:1, I s with the tongues of men
13:11, I used to s as a child
2 Cor. 12:4, a man is not permitted to s
Eph. 5:19, **s-ing** to one another
6:20, s boldly, as I ought to s
Titus 3:8, I want you to s confidently
James 1:19, slow to s and slow to anger
2:12, so s and so act
4:11, not s against one another
1 Pet. 4:11, Whoever **s-s**, let him s
2 Pet. 2:18, **s-ing** out arrogant words
Gen. 18:32; Ex. 4:14; Lev. 1:2; Num. 22:35; Deut. 5:24; 1 Kin. 12:7; Job 2:13; 11:5; 33:14; 41:3; Ps. 28:3; 41:5; 101:7; Is. 29:4; 40:2; Mark 13:11; John 12:49; 2 Cor. 12:6

SPEAR 1 Sam. 26:7, his s stuck in the ground
2 Sam. 1:6, Saul was leaning on his s
Ps. 46:9, cuts the s in two
Is. 2:4, their **s-s** into pruning hooks
Joel 3:10, pruning hooks into **s-s**
John 19:34, pierced His side with a s

SPECIFICALLY 1 Sam. 20:21, If I s say to the lad

SPECULATIONS—question
Rom. 1:21, futile in their s
2 Cor. 10:5, We are destroying s
2 Tim. 2:23, foolish and ignorant s

SPED—fly Ps. 18:10, He s upon the wings of the wind

SPEECH—message, word Ex. 4:10, slow of s
Rom. 16:18, by their smooth and flattering s
1 Cor. 1:17, not in cleverness of s
2 Cor. 11:6, even if I am unskilled in s
Col. 4:6, s always be with grace
Deut. 32:2; Job 13:17; Prov. 17:7; Is. 33:19; Ezek. 3:5

SPEED—quickly Is. 5:19, Let Him make s
Luke 18:8, bring about justice ... **s-ily**

SPELT Ezek. 4:9, beans, lentils, millet and s

SPEND Is. 55:2, Why do you s money
2 Cor. 12:15, I will most gladly s and
Gen. 19:2; Num. 22:8; Job 21:13

SPENT Gen. 47:15, money was all s
Ps. 31:10, my life is s with sorrow
Mark 5:26, s all that she had

SPICE Ex. 35:28; Song 8:2; Ezek. 24:10; John 19:40

SPIES Gen. 42:9, You are s
Josh. 6:23, young men who were s
Luke 20:20, sent s who pretended
Heb. 11:31, she had welcomed the s

SPIRIT Gen. 1:2, the **S** of God was moving
Ps. 31:5, Into Thy hand I commit my **s**
51:10, renew a steadfast **s** within me
Eccles. 12:7, the **s** will return to God
Is. 11:2, **s** of wisdom . . . understanding
32:15, Until the **S** is poured
61:1, **S** of the Lord GOD is upon
Joel 2:28, pour out My **S** on all mankind
Matt. 1:18, with child by the Holy **S**
3:16, **S** of God descending
5:3, Blessed are the poor in **s**
10:1, authority over unclean **s-s**
10:20, **S** of your Father who speaks
12:18, PUT MY **S** UPON HIM
12:31, blasphemy against the **S**
12:45, seven other **s-s** more
27:50, cried . . . yielded up His **s**
28:19, Son and the Holy **S**
Mark 1:8, baptize you with the Holy **S**
1:10, **S** like a dove descending
14:38, **s** is willing, but
Luke 1:15, be filled with the Holy **S**
4:18, **S** OF THE LORD IS UPON ME
11:13, give the Holy **S** to those
24:37, thought . . . seeing a **s**
24:39, **s** does not have flesh
John 3:5, is born of water . . . **s**
4:24, God is **s**
14:17, that is the **S** of truth
Acts 2:4, all filled with the Holy **S**
18:25, being fervent in **s**
Rom. 2:29, by the **S**, not by
8:6, mind set on the **S** is life
15:19, in the power of the **S**
1 Cor. 2:10, the **S** searches all things
2:13, taught by the **S**
3:16, **S** of God dwells in you
5:3, absent . . . present in **s**
12:4, gifts, but the same **S**
14:15, I shall pray with the **s**
2 Cor. 3:6, of the letter, but of the **S**
13:14, fellowship of the Holy **S**
Gal. 4:6, sent forth the **S** of His Son
5:16, walk by the **S**
5:22, fruit of the **S** is love
Eph. 1:13, with the Holy **S** of promise
2:18, access in one **S** to
4:4, body and one **S**
4:30, not grieve the Holy **S** of
Phil. 1:27, standing firm in one **s**
1 Thess. 5:19, Do not quench the **S**
Heb. 4:12, division of soul and **s**
James 2:26, body without the **s** is dead
1 Pet. 4:6, in the **s** according . . . will of God
1 John 4:1, not believe every **s**
5:7, **S** who bears witness
5:8, the **S** and the water . . . blood
Rev. 1:10, in the **S** on the Lord's
14:13, Yes, says the **S**
22:17, **S** and the bride say
Ex. 31:3; Judg. 9:23; 2 Kin. 2:9; Eccles. 7:8; Is. 42:1; 57:15; Ezek. 11:19; Acts 2:17

SPIRITIST Lev. 20:27; 2 Kin. 23:24

SPIRITUAL Rom. 15:27, shared in their **s** things
1 Cor. 10:3, ate the same **s** food
14:1, desire . . . **s** gifts
15:44, raised a **s** body
Eph. 1:3, blessed us . . . every **s** blessing

5:19, hymns and **s** songs
1 Pet. 2:5, built up as a **s** house

SPIT Job 30:10, refrain from **s-ing** . . . face
Matt. 26:67, they **s** in His face
27:30, they **s** on Him
Mark 8:23, after **s-ing** on his eyes
14:65, some began to **s** at Him
John 9:6, made clay of the **s-tle**

SPLENDID—gorgeous Luke 7:25, who are **s-ly** clothed

SPLENDOR—glory, honor
Ps. 8:1, hast displayed Thy **s**
96:6, **S** and majesty are before Him

SPLIT Lev. 11:3,7,26

SPOIL—plunder Gen. 49:27; Prov. 16:19; Is. 10:2; Ezek. 25:7

SPOKE—declared, told Gen. 8:15, God **s** to Noah
Ps. 33:9, He **s**, and it was done
40:10, I have **s-n** of Thy faithfulness
62:11, Once God has **s-n**
78:19, they **s** against God
87:3, Glorious things are **s-n** of you
Prov. 25:11, word **s-n** in right circumstances
Matt. 13:34, Jesus **s** . . . in parables
Mark 14:9, be **s-n** of in memory
Rom. 14:16, thing be **s-n** of as evil
1 Cor. 14:5, that you all **s** in tongues
Heb. 1:2, last days has **s-n** to us
2 Pet. 1:21, men . . . **s** from God
Mal. 3:16; Mark 7:32

SPOT—blemish, defect
Gen. 30:32, speckled and **s-ed** sheep
Jer. 13:23, Or the leopard his **s-s**
Eph. 5:27, having no **s** or wrinkle
1 Pet. 1:19, lamb unblemished and **s-less**

SPREAD—disperse
Prov. 15:7, lips . . . wise **s** knowledge
Matt. 21:8, multitude **s** their garments
Ex. 1:12; 9:29; Job 29:19; 37:18; Prov. 7:16; 29:5; Is. 19:8; 33:23; Ezek. 12:15; 16:8; Joel 2:2; Luke 19:36

SPRING—well Ps. 85:11, Truth **s-s** from the earth
Is. 45:8, righteousness **s** up with it
58:11, like a **s** of water
John 4:14, well of water **s-ing** up
Heb. 12:15, root of bitterness **s-ing**
Rev. 7:17, **s-s** of the water of life
21:6, thirsts from the **s** of the water
Gen. 16:7; 2 Kin. 3:19; Prov. 5:16; 25:26; Song 4:12; Is. 11:1

SPROUT—grow Gen. 1:11; Ex. 10:5; Ps. 90:5; 92:7; Is. 61:11

SPURNED—despised Ps. 10:13; 107:11; Prov. 1:30; 5:12

SPY Judg. 1:23, house of Joseph **s-ed** out Bethel

SQUANDERED—wasted Luke 15:13, **s** his estate

SQUARE Gen. 19:2; Ex. 27:1; Judg. 19:20; Rev. 21:16

STABILITY Col. 2:5, **s** of your faith

STAFF Gen. 38:18, your **s** that is in your hand
Ex. 7:12, Aaron's **s** swallowed up
Ps. 23:4, Thy rod and Thy **s**
Matt. 10:10, sandals, or a **s**
Ex. 4:4; Judg. 6:21; 2 Kin. 4:29; Is. 14:5; Ezek. 4:16; Zech. 11:10; Mark 6:8

STAIN 1 Tim. 6:14, commandment without **s**
2 Pet. 2:13, They are **s-s** and blemishes

STAIRWAY 2 Kin. 20:11, brought the shadow on the **s** back
Is. 38:8, shadow on the **s** . . . sun on the **s** of

STAND—arise, form, rest, stood Gen. 18:2
Ps. 1:5, will not **s** in the judgment
130:3, O Lord, who could **s**
Is. 40:8, word of our God **s-s** forever
Matt. 6:5, love to **s** and pray
12:25, house divided . . . shall not **s**
20:3, **s-ing** idle in the market place
Mark 11:25, whenever you **s** praying forgive
John 1:26, among you **s-s** One
19:25, were **s-ing** by the cross
20:11, Mary was **s-ing** outside
Acts 1:11, why do you **s** looking into
7:33, PLACE ON WHICH YOU ARE **S-ING** IS HOLY
21:40, Paul, **s-ing** on the stairs
Rom. 5:2, this grace in which we **s**
14:4, Lord is able to make him **s**
1 Cor. 16:13, **s** firm in the faith
2 Cor. 1:24, in your faith you are **s-ing** firm
Eph. 6:14, **S** firm . . . HAVING GIRDED YOUR LOINS
1 Tim. 3:13, obtain . . . a high **s-ing**
2 Tim. 2:19, foundation of God **s-s**
Rev. 3:20, Behold I **s** at the door
5:6, Lamb **s-ing**, as if slain
20:12, dead **s-ing** before the throne
Ex. 14:13; Num. 22:22; Josh. 10:12; Job 8:15; Prov. 22:29; 27:4; Is. 50:8; Jer. 6:16; 35:19; Ezek. 2:1; 13:5; Amos 7:7; Nah. 1:6

STANDARD—banner
Ps. 74:4, set up their own **s-s** for signs
Is. 13:2, Lift up a **s**
1 Chr. 17:17; Is. 5:26; 18:3; 31:9

STAR Gen. 1:16, He made the **s-s** also
Num. 24:17, A **s** shall come forth . . . Jacob
Job 38:7, morning **s-s** sang together
Ps. 147:4, counts the number of the **s-s**
Matt. 2:2, saw His **s** in the east
2:7, ascertained . . . time the **s** appeared
2:10, when they saw the **s**
24:29, **s-s** WILL FALL from the sky
1 Cor. 15:41, for **s** differs from **s**
2 Pet. 1:19, **s** arises in your hearts
Jude 13, wandering **s-s**, for whom **s-s**
Rev. 1:16, right hand He held seven **s-s**
8:10, great **s** fell from heaven
8:11, **s** is called Wormwood
22:16, the bright morning **s**
Job 22:12; Ps. 136:9; Jer. 31:35

STARE Song 1:6, Do not **s** at me

STARVE Zeph. 2:11, He will **s** all the gods

STATE—*declare* Josh. 20:4; Luke 1:48

STATEMENT Matt. 5:37, your **s** be, Yes, yes
John 6:60, This is a difficult **s**
1 Tim. 1:15, It is a trustworthy **s**

STATURE—*size* 1 Sam. 16:7, the height of his **s**
Luke 2:52, increasing in wisdom and **s**
19:3, he was small in **s**

STATUTE—*precept*
Ps. 119:12, Teach me Thy **s-s**
Mal. 3:7, turned aside from My **s-s**
Gen. 26:5; Ex. 29:9; Lev. 18:5; Num. 35:29; Is. 10:1; Ezek. 5:7

STAY—*lodge, remain* Luke 2:8, shepherds **s-ing**
Luke 19:5, today I must **s** at your house
24:29, **S** with us . . . over. And . . . **s** with them
John 1:38, Rabbi . . . where are you **s-ing**
2:12, there they **s-ed** a few days
Acts 10:6, **s-ing** with a . . . tanner named Simon
1 Pet. 1:17, time of your **s** *upon earth*
Gen. 19:17; Ruth 2:8; 1 Sam. 20:38; 22:23; Ps. 18:18; Hos. 3:3; Luke 1:56; John 1:39; Acts 18:3

STEADFAST—*resolute*
Job 11:15, you would be **s**
Ps. 51:10, renew a **s** spirit within me
57:7, My heart is **s**, O God, my
112:7, His heart is **s**, trusting
1 Cor. 15:58, brethren, be **s**
Col. 1:11, all **s-ness** and patience
2 Thess. 3:5, into the **s-ness** of Christ

STEAL—*deceive* Matt. 6:19, break in and **s**
Matt. 19:18, YOU SHALL NOT **S**
Ex. 20:15; Lev. 19:11; Deut. 5:19; 2 Sam. 19:3; Prov. 30:9; Mark 10:19; Eph. 4:28

STEALTH—*craft* Mark 14:1, to seize Him by **s**

STEED 1 Kin. 4:28; Esth. 8:10

STEP Job 18:8, he **s-s** on the webbing
Rom. 4:12, follow in the **s-s** of the faith
1 Pet. 2:21, you to follow in His **s-s**
1 Kin. 10:19; Job 14:16; 29:6; Prov. 5:5

STERN Eccles. 8:1, causes his **s** face to beam

STEWARD Gen. 43:19, near to Joseph's house
Luke 12:42, faithful and sensible **s**
1 Cor. 4:1, **s-s** of the mysteries of God
4:2, it is required of **s-s**

STEWARDSHIP Luke 16:2, an account of your **s**
1 Cor. 9:17, I have a **s** entrusted to me
Eph. 3:2, the **s** of God's grace

STICK Prov. 18:24, friend who **s-s**
Num. 22:27; 2 Kin. 6:6; Job 33:21; 38:38; Ezek. 37:16,19

STILL Lev. 5:17, **s** he is guilty
Judg. 7:4, people are **s** too many
Dan. 11:35, **s** *to come* . . . appointed time
Matt. 19:20, what am I **s** lacking
Luke 24:44, while I was **s** with you
Rom. 5:6, while we were **s** helpless
Josh. 10:12; Ps. 65:7; 107:29; Jer. 8:14; Mark 4:39

STING 1 Cor. 15:55, O DEATH . . . YOUR **S**
1 Cor. 15:56, **s** of death is sin
Prov. 23:32; Rev. 9:10

STINKWEED Job 31:40, And **s** instead of barley

STIR Deut. 32:11, eagle that **s-s** up its nest
Ps. 35:23, **S** up Thyself, and awake
Prov. 10:12, Hatred **s-s** up strife
15:1, harsh word **s-s** up anger
28:25, arrogant man **s-s** up strife
29:22, angry man **s-s** up strife
Acts 14:2, Jews who disbelieved **s-ed** up
2 Pet. 3:1, I am **s-ing** up your

STOCKS Job 13:27; Acts 16:24

STOLE Gen. 31:19; 2 Sam. 15:6; Prov. 9:17

STOMACH Mark 7:19, but into his **s**

STONE Ex. 34:1, Cut out . . . two **s** tablets
Deut. 9:9, the tablets of **s**
1 Sam. 17:49, from it a **s** and slung
Ps. 118:22, **s** which the builders rejected
Ezek. 20:32, serving wood and **s**
Dan. 2:34, a **s** was cut out without
Matt. 3:9, God is able from these **s-s**
4:3, command . . . **s-s** become bread
4:6, YOUR FOOT AGAINST A **S**
7:9, will give him a **s**
21:42, **s** WHICH THE BUILDERS REJECTED
27:60, large **s** against the entrance
28:2, rolled away the **s** and sat
Luke 19:44, one **s** upon another
John 2:6, six **s** waterpots
8:7, first to throw a **s** at her
11:39, Jesus said, Remove the **s**
Acts 7:59, went on **s-ing** Stephen
2 Cor. 3:3, not on tablets of **s**
1 Pet. 2:5, also, as living **s-s**
2:8, **s** OF STUMBLING
Gen. 11:3; 29:3; Ex. 15:16; 20:25; Lev. 20:2; Num. 15:35; Deut. 8:9; 2 Sam. 17:13; 1 Kin. 6:18; 2 Kin. 12:12; 2 Chr. 34:11; Job 14:19; 41:24; Ps. 18:12; 91:12; Prov. 26:27; 27:3; Is. 28:16; 54:11; 57:6; Ezek. 11:19; Amos 5:11; Hab. 2:11; Luke 22:41; Rev. 2:17

STOOD Deut. 31:15, pillar of cloud **s** at
Josh. 10:13, So the sun **s** still
Matt. 2:9, came and **s** over where
4:5, devil . . . **s** Him on the pinnacle
Luke 4:16, and **s** up to read
24:36, He Himself **s** in their midst

Col. 1:25, according to the **s** from God

John 21:4, Jesus **s** on the beach
Rev. 13:1, he **s** on the sand

STOP 1 Kin. 18:44; Ps. 63:11; 2 Cor. 11:10

STORE Prov. 10:14, Wise men **s** up knowledge
Luke 12:17, I have no place to **s** my crops
1 Tim. 6:19, **s-ing** up treasure
James 5:3, have **s-d** up your treasure

STOREHOUSE—*treasure* Deut. 28:12; Job 38:22

STORM—*tempest, whirlwind* Jon. 1:4, a great **s**
Jon. 1:12, this great **s** *has come* upon you
Matt. 16:3, *There will be* a **s** today
Acts 27:18, we were being violently **s-tossed**
2 Pet. 2:17, mists driven by a **s**
Job 21:18; 37:9; Ps. 55:8; 107:25; Is. 25:4; Ezek. 38:9

STRAIGHT—*equity* Matt. 3:3, MAKE PATHS **S**
Luke 3:5, CROOKED SHALL BECOME **S**
John 1:23, MAKE **S** THE WAY OF THE LORD
Acts 9:11, street called **S**
Heb. 12:13, make **s** paths for your feet
1 Sam. 6:12, Ps. 5:8; Eccles. 1:15; Mic. 3:9

STRAIGHTFORWARD Gal. 2:14, not **s** about the truth

STRAIT—*narrow* 1 Sam. 13:6, they were in a **s**

STRANGE Heb. 13:9, varied and **s** teachings
1 Pet. 4:12, some **s** thing was happening
Jude 7, went after **s** flesh

STRANGER—*alien, sojourner* Gen. 23:4, I am a **s** and
Matt. 25:35, I was a **s**, and you invited
27:7, Potter's Field . . . for **s-s**
John 10:5, do not know the voice of **s-s**
Eph. 2:19, you are no longer **s-s** and aliens
Heb. 13:2, show hospitality to **s-s**
Gen. 15:13; Ex. 22:21; Is. 1:7; Jer. 22:3

STRATEGIC Mark 6:21, a **s** day came when Herod

STRAW Gen. 24:25; Ex. 5:7; 1 Kin. 4:28; Job 41:27; Is. 11:7

STRAY Prov. 7:25, not **s** into her paths
James 5:19, any among you **s-s** from the truth
1 Pet. 2:25, **s-ing** like sheep

STREAM—*river* Ps. 1:3, planted by the **s-s** of water
Is. 32:2, **s-s** of water in a dry country

STREET—*square*
Prov. 1:20, Wisdom shouts in the **s**
Is. 59:14, truth has stumbled in the **s**
Matt. 6:2, **s-s**, that they may be honored

STREET *(Continued)*
6:5, pray . . . on the s corners
Acts 9:11, s called Straight
Rev. 21:21, s of the city was pure
gold
2 Sam. 1:20; 22:43; Jer. 37:21;
Nah. 2:4

STRENGTH Ex. 15:2, the LORD is my
s and song
Ps. 28:7, LORD is my s and my shield
46:1, God is our refuge and s
Prov. 20:29, glory of young men . . . s
Is. 40:29, He gives s to the weary
Mark 12:30, MIND, AND WITH ALL
YOUR S
1 Pet. 4:11, by the s which God
supplies
Rev. 1:16, sun shining in its s
Gen. 4:12; Judg. 6:14; 8:21; 16:6;
1 Sam. 28:20; Job 6:12; 21:23; Ps.
84:7; Prov. 31:3; Eccles. 9:16; Is.
41:1; Hab. 3:19

STRENGTHEN—*fortify* 1 Sam.
30:6, David s-ed
Is. 35:3, s the feeble
Luke 22:32, s your brothers
Col. 1:11, s-ed with all power
2 Thess. 2:17, s your hearts in every
1 Tim. 1:12, who has s-ed me
Heb. 13:9, heart to be s-ed by grace
James 5:8, s your hearts, for the
coming
1 Pet. 5:10, confirm, s *and* establish
you
Deut. 3:28; Judg. 16:28; 2 Chr. 11:11;
Job 4:3; Is. 35:3; Ezek. 34:16; Nah.
3:14

STRETCH Ps. 68:31, s out her hands
to God
Ps. 104:2, s-ing out heaven like
Is. 28:20, too short . . . to s out
Job 30:24; 38:5; Jer. 10:12

STRETCHER Luke 5:19, let him
down . . . with his s

STRICKEN Is. 53:4, we . . . esteemed
Him s
Is. 1:5; Jer. 14:19

STRICT Acts 26:5, the s-est sect of
our religion

STRIFE—*quarrel*
Prov. 16:28, perverse man spreads s
18:6, fool's lips bring s
Rom. 13:13, not in s and jealousy
1 Cor. 3:3, jealousy and s among you
Gal. 5:20, enmities, s, jealousy
Titus 3:9, foolish controversies . . .
and s
Gen. 13:7; Prov. 6:14,19; 10:12; 13:10;
20:3; Is. 58:4

STRIKE Ex. 7:17, I will s the water
Ex. 12:12, s down all the first-born
Ps. 91:12; Matt. 4:6; Luke 4:11, s
your foot
Matt. 26:31, I WILL S DOWN THE
SHEPHERD
Acts 23:3, God is going to s you
Gen. 4:23; Prov. 17:26; 19:25; Is.
49:10; Jer. 18:18

STRING Ps. 11:2; 33:2; Hab. 3:19

STRIP Ps. 29:9, s-s the forests bare

STRIPES Deut. 25:3, beat him with s

STRIVE Gen. 6:3, Spirit shall not s
with man
Ps. 103:9, not always s *with us*
Luke 13:24, S to enter by the narrow
door

STRONG—*courage* 2 Sam. 22:33,
God is my s fortress
Ps. 24:8, the LORD s and mighty
Prov. 20:1, s drink a brawler
Jer. 50:34, Their Redeemer is s
Luke 2:40, Child . . . grow and
become s
1 Cor. 4:10, we are weak, but you
are s
2 Cor. 12:10, when I am weak, then I
am s
Eph. 6:10, be s in the Lord
Heb. 11:34, from weakness were
made s
James 3:4, ships . . . driven by s
winds
Gen. 49:14; Ex. 10:19; 14:21; Lev.
10:9; Deut. 31:6; Judg. 14:18; Job
17:9; Ps. 19:5; Prov. 31:6; Song 8:6;
Is. 5:11; 41:6; Ezek. 30:21; Luke
14:31

STRONGHOLD—*fortress, refuge*
Ps. 9:9, s in times of trouble
59:9,17, For God is my s
94:22, the LORD has been my s
2 Sam. 5:9; 22:3; 1 Chr. 11:5,7; Ps.
62:2; Prov. 10:29; Ezek. 33:27

STRUCK—*touched*
Job 19:21, hand of God has s me
Ex. 7:20; Num. 20:11; 22:23; Acts
12:23

STRUGGLE Col. 2:1, how great a s I
have

STUBBORN Rom. 2:5, s-ness and
unrepentant heart
Jer. 3:17; Hos. 4:16

STUMBLE—*fall*
Matt. 5:29, right eye makes you s
11:6, blessed . . . keeps from s-ing
over
Luke 17:2, cause one of these . . . to s
James 3:2, For we all s in many
ways
1 Pet. 2:8, s because they are
disobedient
2 Pet. 1:10, you will never s
Prov. 3:23; Is. 8:14; 40:30; Jer. 50:32;
Dan. 11:19

STUMBLING BLOCK—*ruin*
Ezek. 18:30, not become a s
Matt. 16:23, Satan! You are a s to
Me
18:7, Woe . . . because of its s-s
Gal. 5:11, the s of the cross

STUPID—*senseless* Ps. 49:10; Prov.
30:2; Jer. 10:8,21

STUPOR Rom. 11:8, gave them a
spirit of s

SUBJECT Luke 2:51, He continued in
s-ion to them
Rom. 8:20, was s-ed to futility
Eph. 5:24, church is s to Christ
Titus 2:5, s to their own husbands
Heb. 2:8, PUT ALL THINGS IN S-ION
UNDER
12:9, s to the Father

1 Pet. 3:22, and powers had been s-
ed to Him
5:5, be s to your elders

SUBMISSIVE 1 Tim. 2:11, instruction
with . . . s-ness
1 Pet. 2:18, be s to your masters
3:1, be s to your own husbands

SUBSIDED Judg. 8:3, their anger . . .
s

SUBSTANCE Deut. 33:11, O LORD,
bless his s

SUCCESS Gen. 24:12, grant me s
today

SUDDENLY Mark 13:36, come s and
find
Luke 21:34, come on you s like a
trap
Acts 2:2, s there came from heaven
Job 21:13; Is. 29:5

SUFFER Job 3:20, light given to him
who s-s
Ps. 34:10, lions do lack and s hunger
Mark 8:31, Son of Man must s many
Luke 24:46, Christ should s and rise
again
Acts 28:5, into the fire and s-ed no
harm
2 Tim. 2:3, S hardship with *me*
James 5:13, Is anyone among you s-
ing
1 Pet. 2:21, Christ also s-ed for you
4:13, you share the s-ings of Christ

SUFFICIENT Ex. 36:7, material they
had was s
Lev. 25:47, means of a stranger . . .
becomes s
John 6:7, denarii worth of bread is
not s
2 Cor. 12:9, My grace is s for you

SUIT Gen. 2:18; 2 Sam. 15:2

SULLEN 1 Kin. 21:5, your spirit is
so s

SUM 1 Pet. 3:8, To s up, let all be
harmonious

SUMMER Jer. 8:20, past, s is ended
Matt. 24:32, you know that s is near
Gen. 8:22; Ps. 74:17; Prov. 26:1;
Zech. 14:8

SUMMON—*call* Num. 10:2, use
them for s-ing
Job 9:19, who can s Him

SUN Eccles. 1:9, nothing new under
the s
Is. 38:8 s-'s shadow went back ten
steps
Matt. 5:45, causes His s to rise
13:43, RIGHTEOUS . . . SHINE FORTH
AS THE S
Luke 21:25, will be signs in s
1 Cor. 15:41, There is one glory of
the s
Eph. 4:26, s go down on your anger
Rev. 12:1, woman clothed with the s
22:5, nor the light of the s
Gen. 15:12; Ex. 16:21; Lev. 22:7;
Josh. 10:12; Ps. 72:5; 84:11; 104:19;
121:6; Song. 6:10; Is. 60:19; Ezek.
32:7; Amos 8:9

SUNK Ps. 38:2, Thine arrows have s
deep

SUNRISE Luke 1:78, the **S** from on high shall visit us

SUNSHINE 2 Sam. 23:4, Through s after rain

SUPERIORITY 1 Cor. 2:1, not come with s of speech

SUPPER John 13:4, rose from s and laid aside
1 Cor. 11:20, not to eat the Lord's **S**
Rev. 19:9, marriage s of the Lamb

SUPPLANTS Prov. 30:23, maidservant . . . s her mistress

SUPPLICATION Ex. 9:28, Make s to the LORD
Ps. 28:2, Hear the voice of my s-s
Dan. 9:3, seek *Him* by prayer and s-s

SUPPLY Is. 3:1, s of bread . . . s of water

SUPPORT Matt. 10:10, worker is worthy of his s
Ex. 17:12; 2 Tim. 4:16

SURE—*trust* Num. 32:23, be s your sin will find you out
Ps. 19:7, testimony of the LORD is s
Heb. 13:18, s that we have a good conscience
2 Pet. 1:19, prophetic word made more s

SURELY Gen. 2:17, eat from it you shall s die
Gen. 28:16, S the LORD is in this place
Deut. 14:22, s tithe all the produce
Ps. 23:6, S goodness and lovingkindness
Is. 53:4, S our griefs He . . . bore
Mark 14:70 S you are *one* of them
Heb. 6:14, s BLESS YOU . . . s MULTIPLY YOU
Ex. 31:13; 2 Sam. 17:11; Job 35:13; Jer. 23:39

SURFACE Gen. 1:2; 7:18; Job 38:30

SURMISE Acts 27:27, sailors *began* to s

SURPASS 2 Chr. 9:6, You s the report I heard
Eph. 1:19, the s-ing greatness of His power
2:7, the s-ing riches of His grace

SURPLUS Mark 12:44, put in out of their s

SURPRISE 1 Pet. 4:12, do not be s-d . . . fiery ordeal

SURROUND Ps. 18:5, cords of Sheol s-ed me
Luke 19:43, your enemies . . . and s you

SUSTAIN Gen. 13:6; 36:7; Song 2:5

SWALLOW Matt. 23:24, gnat and s a camel
1 Cor. 15:54, DEATH IS S-ED UP IN VICTORY
Gen. 41:7,24; Num. 16:34; Job 20:15; Is. 25:8; Jon. 1:17; Hab. 1:13

SWEAR Gen. 50:5; Lev. 19:12; Is. 45:23; Zech. 5:3; Matt. 23:18; 26:74; Mark 14:71; James 5:12

SWEET 2 Sam. 23:1, the s psalmist of Israel
Ps. 55:14, had s fellowship together
Prov. 3:24, your sleep will be s
9:17, Stolen water is s
Is. 5:20; 43:24; Jer. 6:20

SWELL—*bulge* Num. 5:21,22; Deut. 8:4

SWIFT Job 7:6, My days are s-er than
Eccles. 9:11, race is not to the s
Rom. 3:15, FEET ARE S TO SHED BLOOD

SWINDLER Luke 18:11, 1 Cor. 5:11, 6:10

SWINE Prov. 11:22, ring of gold in a s-'s snout
Matt. 7:6, throw your pearls before s
Mark 5:11, big herd of s feeding there
Luke 15:15, into his fields to feed s

SWOOP Job 9:26, eagle that s-s on its prey

SWORD Gen. 3:24, flaming s which turned
Gen. 27:40, by your s you shall live
Ps. 57:4, their tongue a sharp s
64:3, sharpened their tongue like a s
Prov. 5:4, Sharp as a two-edged s
Is. 2:4; Mic. 4:3, hammer their s-s into plowshares
Hos. 2:18, abolish the bow, the s, and war
Matt. 10:34, not . . . peace, but a s
26:51, drew out his s and struck the slave
26:52, take up the s shall perish by the s
Eph. 6:17, s of the Spirit
Rev. 1:16, mouth became a sharp . . . s
Ex. 5:3; Deut. 32:25; Judg. 3:16,21,22; 2 Sam. 2:26; Is. 2:4; Jer. 15:2; Hos. 1:7

SYNAGOGUE Matt. 6:2, the s-s and in the streets
Matt. 6:5, pray in the s-s and on
12:9, He went into their s
13:54, teaching them in their s
John 16:2, make you outcasts from the s
18:20, I always taught in s-s
Acts 9:20, proclaim Jesus in the s-s
Rev. 2:9, but are a s of Satan

T

TABERNACLE Ex. 26:1, t with ten curtains
Matt. 17:4, make three t-s here
Rev. 21:3, t of God is among men

TABLE Is. 21:5, They set the t
Matt. 21:12, t-s of the money-changers
Mark 7:28, dogs under the t feed
John 2:15, overturned their t-s
Acts 6:2, word of God . . . to serve t-s
1 Cor. 10:21, partake of the t of the Lord

Lev. 24:6; Judg. 1:7; 2 Kin. 4:10; Ps. 23:5

TABLET Ex. 24:12, give you the stone t-s
Ex. 31:18, two t-s of the testimony
Luke 1:63, asked for a t
2 Cor. 3:3, on t-s of human hearts
Is. 8:1; Jer. 17:1

TAKE Ex. 20:7, not t the name of the LORD
Ex. 34:9, t us as Thine own possession
Prov. 4:13, T hold of instruction
Is. 4:1, seven women will t hold of
Matt. 5:40, t your shirt
7:5, first t the log out . . . eye
11:29, T My yoke upon you
26:26, T, eat; this is My body
Mark 2:9, Arise, and t up your pallet
13:33, T heed, keep on the alert
Luke 9:3, T nothing for your journey
John 1:29, t-s away the sin of the world
20:2, have t-n away the Lord
Acts 1:20, HIS OFFICE LET ANOTHER MAN T
Eph. 6:16, t-ing up the shield of faith
Rev. 10:9, T it, and eat it
Gen. 3:22; 12:19; 22:2; Num. 30:2; Judg. 21:22; 1 Sam. 4:3; Ezek. 18:17; 37:19; Hos. 1:2; Mic. 2:4; Matt. 21:21; 1 Cor. 13:5

TALE 2 Pet. 1:16, cleverly devised t-s

TALK Acts 20:9, as Paul kept on t-ing
Eph. 5:4, *no* filthiness and silly t
Titus 1:10, empty t-ers and deceivers
Job 11:2; 15:3; Prov. 24:2; Luke 1:65

TARGET—*mark* 1 Sam. 20:20; Lam. 3:12

TASK Eccles. 2:26, sinner He has given the t

TASTE Ex. 16:31, t was like wafers
Ps. 34:8, t and see that the LORD is good
Matt. 16:28, shall not t death
Acts 23:14, t nothing until we have killed Paul
Heb. 2:9, t death for every one
6:4, t-d of the heavenly gift
Job 6:6; 34:3; Prov. 24:13; Dan. 10:3

TAUGHT Ps. 71:17, hast t me from my youth
Is. 54:13, sons will be t of the LORD
John 8:28, I speak . . . as the Father t Me
Gal. 1:12, nor was I t it
1 Thess. 4:9, t by God to love one another

TAUNT Deut. 28:37; Job 30:9

TAX—*tribute* Num. 31:28, levy a t for the LORD
Matt. 17:24, teacher not pay the . . . t
22:19, coin *used* for the **poll-t**
Luke 20:22, pay t-es to Caesar
Rom. 13:7, t to whom is *due*
2 Kin. 23:35; Matt. 9:9

TAX-GATHERER Matt. 5:46, even the t-s do the same
Matt. 10:3, Matthew the t
Luke 18:13, t, standing some distance away

TEACH Ps. 25:4, T me Thy paths
Ps. 27:11, T me Thy way, O LORD
143:10, T me to do Thy will
Prov. 1:8, do not forsake your
mother's **t-ing**
Matt. 7:29, **t-ing** them as *one* having
authority
11:1, t and preach in their cities
15:9, T-ing AS THEIR DOCTRINES
Mark 1:22, they were amazed at His
t-ing
4:2, **t-ing** them . . . in parables
Luke 11:1, Lord, t us to pray
19:47, **t-ing** daily in the temple
John 7:16, My **t-ing** is not Mine, but
His
14:26, He will t you all things
Acts 1:1, Jesus began to do and t
2:42, devoting . . . to the apostles' **t-
ing**
15:35, **t-ing** and preaching
Rom. 2:21, t another, do you not t
yourself
16:17, contrary to the **t-ing** which
you learned
1 Cor. 11:14, nature itself t you
Col. 2:22, commandments and **t-ings**
of men
3:16, **t-ing** and admonishing
1 Tim. 1:3, not to t strange doctrines
2:12, do not allow a woman to t
2 Tim. 3:10, you followed my **t-ing**
Titus 2:3, **t-ing** what is good
Heb. 8:11, NOT T EVERY ONE HIS
FELLOW
Rev. 2:20, **t-es** and leads my bond-
servants
2:24, the rest . . . who do not hold
this **t-ing**
Ex. 4:12; Deut. 32:2; 1 Kin. 8:36; Job
11:4; 15:5; 21:22; 37:19; Prov. 4:2;
Is. 28:9

TEACHER Matt. 8:19, T, I will follow
You
Matt. 10:24, disciple is not above
his t
17:24, Does your t not pay
23:8, for One is your T
Mark 5:35, why trouble the T any
more
Luke 2:46, in the midst of the **t-s**
5:17, Pharisees and **t-s** of the law
John 3:2, come from God *as* a t
3:10, Are you the t of Israel
13:13, You call Me T and Lord
Acts 5:34, Gamaliel, a t of the Law
Rom. 2:20, a t of the immature
1 Cor. 12:29, All are not **t-s**
Eph. 4:11, some *as* pastors and **t-s**
1 Tim. 2:7, t of the Gentiles in faith
2 Tim. 4:3, accumulate for
themselves **t-s**
James 3:1, Let not many *of you*
become **t-s**
2 Pet. 2:1, be false **t-s** among you
1 Chr. 25:8; Prov. 5:13

TEAR—*rend* Eccles. 3:7, time to t
apart
Matt. 5:29, makes you stumble, t it
out
7:6, turn and t you to pieces
Luke 12:18, I will t down my barns
John 19:24, Let us not t it, but cast
Lev. 10:6; Job 18:4; Ps. 7:2; Prov.
14:1; Ezek. 13:20

TEAR—*weep* Ps. 80:5, fed them . . .
bread of **t-s**
Ps. 126:5, sow in **t-s** shall reap with
joyful shouting

Is. 25:8, God will wipe **t-s** away
Luke 7:38, wet His feet with her **t-s**
2 Tim. 1:4, even as I recall your **t-s**
Rev. 7:17, God shall wipe away
every t
21:4, He shall wipe away every t
2 Kin. 20:5; Ps. 56:8; Eccles. 4:1; Is.
16:9; Jer. 9:1; Lam. 1:2; 2:18

TEETH Gen. 49:12; Job 13:14; 19:20;
41:14; Ps. 57:4; Prov. 10:26; Jer.
31:29; Amos 4:6; Matt. 8:12

TELL 1 Chr. 16:24; Ps. 96:3, T of His
glory among
Ps. 19:1, heavens are **t-ing** of the
glory of God
66:16, I will t of what He has done
for my soul
118:17, t of the works of the LORD
Matt. 8:4, See that you t no one
26:63, t us whether You are the
Christ
Luke 13:32, Go and t that fox
John 18:34, did others t you about
Me
Ex. 19:3; Lev. 5:1; Judg. 14:14; Ps.
2:7; Eccles. 10:14; Dan. 2:2,36; Joel
1:3; Zeph. 3:13

TEMPER Prov. 29:11, A fool . . . loses
his t

TEMPERATE Titus 2:2, Older men
are to be t

TEMPEST Job 9:17; Ps. 55:8; Is. 28:2;
Amos 1:14

TEMPLE—*house* 2 Sam. 22:7, from
His t He heard my voice
Ps. 11:4, LORD is in His holy t
Is. 6:4, t was filling with smoke
Jer. 7:4, t of the LORD, the t of the
LORD
Matt. 4:5, pinnacle of the t
12:6, something greater than the t
Mark 14:58, destroy this t made with
hands
Luke 23:45, veil of the t was torn
John 2:19, Destroy this t . . . I will
raise it
2:21, speaking of the t of His body
1 Cor. 3:17, t of God is holy . . . what
you are
2 Cor. 6:16, we are the t of the living
God
2 Thess. 2:4, takes his seat in the t of
God
Rev. 21:22, God . . . and the Lamb
are its t
1 Sam. 1:9; 1 Chr. 29:1; Neh. 6:11

TEMPT—*test* Matt. 4:1, Jesus . . . t-
ed by the devil
Matt. 4:3, **t-er** came and said to Him
Luke 4:2, forty days while **t-ed** by
the devil
1 Cor. 10:13, not allow you to be **t-ed**
1 Thess. 3:5, tempter might have **t-ed**
you
Heb. 4:15, **t-ed** in all things as *we are*
James 1:13, God cannot be **t-ed** by
evil

TEMPTATION—*trial*
Matt. 6:13, do not lead us into t
26:41, you may not enter into t
Luke 8:13, time of t fall away
1 Cor. 10:13, No t has overtaken you
2 Pet. 2:9, rescue the godly from t

TEN Deut. 10:4, the T
Commandments
Ps. 91:7, t thousand at your right
hand
Matt. 25:1, comparable to t virgins
Luke 15:8, if she has t silver coins
17:17, Were there not t cleansed
Gen. 31:7; Num. 14:22; Job 19:3; Ps.
33:2; Song 5:10; Is. 38:8; Ezek.
45:14; Dan. 1:14; 7:7

TEND John 21:15,17

TENDER Is. 53:2, He grew up . . . like
a t shoot
Matt. 24:32, branch has already
become t
Luke 1:78, t mercy of our God
Eph. 4:32, **t-hearted**, forgiving each
other
Gen. 18:7; 2 Sam. 23:4; 2 Kin. 22:19

TENT—*tabernacle* 1 Kin. 12:16, To
your **t-s**, O Israel
Ps. 15:1, who may abide in Thy t
61:4, dwell in Thy t forever
84:10, in the **t-s** of wickedness
Is. 38:12, Like a shepherd's t
Gen. 4:20; 18:1; 24:67; 25:27; Num.
24:5; Job 12:6; Song 1:8; Jer. 10:20

TENTH—*tithe* Gen. 14:20, he gave
him a t of all
Heb. 7:2, Abraham apportioned a t
part
7:5, to collect a t from the people
Rev. 11:13, a t of the city fell

TERMS Gal. 3:15, Speak in t of
human relations

TERRIBLE—*dread*
Deut. 8:15, great and t wilderness
Mal. 4:5, the great and t day of the
LORD
Mark 9:26, throwing him into t
convulsions

TERRIFYING Is. 21:1, wilderness,
from a t land
Heb. 10:27, t expectation of
judgment
10:31, t thing to fall into the hands
of

TERROR—*fear, dread* Ps. 91:5,
afraid of the t by night
Luke 21:11, **t-s** and great signs
Lev. 26:16; Deut. 32:25; Job 15:21;
24:17; 41:14; Ps. 116:3; Eccles.
12:5; Is. 33:18

TEST—*try* Gen. 22:1, God **t-ed**
Abraham
Ex. 17:2, Why do you t the LORD
Deut. 6:16, shall not put the LORD . . .
to the t
2 Sam. 22:31, word of the LORD
is **t-ed**
Job 12:11, Does not the ear t words
Ps. 26:2, T my mind and my heart
Prov. 30:5, Every word of God
is **t-ed**
Is. 28:16, a **t-ed** stone . . . costly
Matt. 22:18, Why are you **t-ing** Me
Acts 5:9, put the Spirit . . . to the t
1 Cor. 3:13, fire itself will t . . . man's
work
2 Cor. 13:5, T yourselves *to see* if
you are
James 1:3, **t-ing** of your faith
1 Pet. 1:7, even though **t-ed** by fire
4:12, fiery ordeal . . . for your **t-ing**

1 John 4:1, t the spirits to see
Ex. 20:20; 1 Kin. 10:1

TESTIFY Acts 2:40, many other
words he . . . **t-ed**
20:24, to t solemnly of the gospel
26:22, **t-ing** both to small and great
Gal. 5:3, t again to every man
1 Pet. 5:12, **t-ing** that this is the true
Ex. 23:2; 2 Sam. 1:16; 1 Kin. 21:10;
Job 15:6; Is. 59:12

TESTIMONY—*witness* Ps. 19:7, t of
the LORD is sure
Ps. 119:46, speak of Thy **t-s** before
kings
Matt. 8:4, the offering . . . for a t
Luke 22:71, need do we have of t
John 8:17, the t of two men is true
1 Cor. 1:6, t concerning Christ was
confirmed
2 Tim. 1:8, ashamed of the t of our
Lord
Titus 1:13, This t is true
Rev. 19:10, t of Jesus is the spirit
Ex. 16:34; 25:16; 31:18; Lev. 16:13;
Num. 35:30; Is. 8:16

THANK 1 Chr. 16:7, to give **t-s** to the
LORD
1 Chr. 16:34, O give **t-s** to the LORD
Ps. 92:1, good to give **t-s** to the LORD
100:4, Give **t-s** to Him
Matt. 15:36, giving **t-s**, He broke
them
26:27, took a cup and gave **t-s**
Luke 18:11, God, I t Thee that I am
not
22:19, when He had given **t-s**, He
broke
Rom. 6:17, But **t-s** be to God
14:6, he gives **t-s** to God
1 Cor. 14:16, Amen at your giving of
t-s
15:57, but **t-s** be to God
Eph. 1:16, do not cease giving **t-s** for
you
5:20, always giving **t-s** for all things
1 Thess. 3:9, what **t-s** can we render
to God
5:18, in everything give **t-s**
2 Thess. 1:3, always to give **t-s** to
God

THANKSGIVING—*gratitude*
Ps. 26:7, with the voice of t
95:2, before His presence with t
100:4, Enter His gates with t
Phil. 4:6, supplication with t
Rev. 7:12, and t and honor and
power
Lev. 7:12; Neh. 11:17

THEIR Gen. 15:13, a land that is not
t-s
Matt. 5:3, **t-s** is the kingdom of
heaven
1 Cor. 1:2, Christ, t Lord and ours

THEN—*therefore* Gen. 4:26, **T** *men*
began to call
Ex. 15:1, **T** Moses . . . sang this song
Matt. 6:9, Pray, t, in this way
24:14, t the end shall come
Mark 4:28, first the blade, t the head
13:26, T THEY SHALL SEE THE SON
Luke 20:25, T render to Caesar
Rom. 3:9, What t? Are we better
1 Cor. 13:12, but t face to face
2 Cor. 12:10, t I am strong

THERE Gen. 1:3, Let t be light; and t
was
Lev. 7:7, t is one law for them
Matt. 2:13, remain t until I tell you
24:23, Behold, here is Christ or t *He
is*
Luke 8:32, t was a herd of many
swine
Rev. 21:25, t shall be no night t

THEREFORE 1 Pet. 4:1, **T**, since
Christ has suffered
1 Pet. 4:7, t, be of sound judgment

THICK Ex. 10:22; Deut. 32:15; Joel
2:2

THIEF Matt. 6:19, **t-s** break in and
steal
John 10:10, t comes only to steal
1 Cor. 6:10, nor **t-s**, nor covetous
1 Thess. 5:2, just like a t in the night
Deut. 24:7; Job 24:14; Ps. 50:18;
Prov. 29:24; Is. 1:23; Joel 2:9

THINE Luke 22:42, not My will, but
T be done
John 17:10, Mine are **T**, and **T** are
Mine

THING Ps. 8:6, put all **t-s** under his
feet
Eccles. 3:1, appointed time for
every-t
Matt. 19:20, All these **t-s** I have kept
19:26, with God all **t-s** are possible
21:24, I will ask you one t
Mark 9:23, All **t-s** are possible to
him
10:21, One t you lack
Luke 2:19, Mary treasured . . . these
t-s
10:42, *only* a few **t-s** are necessary
John 14:14, ask Me **any-t** in My
name
Acts 2:44, had all **t-s** in common
Phil. 3:13, but one I *do*
4:8, let your mind dwell on these **t-s**
1 Tim. 4:15, Take pains with
these **t-s**
James 3:10, **t-s** ought not to be this
way
Rev. 16:3, every living t in the sea
died
Gen. 7:23; 15:1; Ex. 20:17; Job 42:2;
Ps. 2:1; Eccles. 9:5; Is. 7:13; 12:5;
Ezek. 8:17

THINK—*esteem, thought* Prov. 23:7,
as he **t-s**
Matt. 5:17, not t that I came to
abolish
22:42, do you t about the Christ
John 5:39, you t that in them . . . life
Rom. 12:3, but to t so as . . . sound
14:14, to him who **t-s** anything to
be unclean
1 Cor. 13:11, child, t as a child
14:20, do not be children in your **t-
ing**
2 Cor. 11:16, no one t me foolish
Gal. 6:3, anyone **t-s** he is something
James 1:26, **t-s** himself to be
religious

THIRD Ex. 20:5, t and fourth
generations
Matt. 16:21, raised up on the t day
Luke 24:21, is the t day since
John 21:17, said to him the t time
1 Cor. 15:4, raised on the t day
2 Cor. 12:2, caught up to the t
heaven

THIRST Ps. 42:2, My soul **t-s** for God
Matt. 5:6, t for righteousness
25:35, I was **t-y**, and you gave
John 4:13, drinks of this water
shall t
6:35, believes . . . shall never t
19:28, said, I am **t-y**
Rom. 12:20, IF HE IS **T-Y**, GIVE HIM
2 Cor. 11:27, in hunger and t
Ex. 17:3; Judg. 15:18; Job 24:11; Ps.
69:21; 104:11; Is. 29:8; 41:17; 49:10;
65:13; Lam. 4:4

THIRTY Matt. 26:15, to him t pieces
of silver
Ex. 21:32; Num. 20:29; Judg. 10:4;
12:9; 14:12; Zech. 11:12; Luke 3:23

THIRTY-NINE
2 Cor. 11:24, received . . . t lashes

THIS—*something* Rev. 2:4, I have t
against you

THISTLE Is. 34:13, Nettles and **t-s** in
its fortified cities

THORN—*hook* Prov. 15:19, as a
hedge of **t-s**
Prov. 26:9, *Like* a t . . . into the hand
of
Is. 55:13, Instead of the t bush the
cypress
Jer. 4:3, not sow among **t-s**
12:13, sown wheat . . . reaped **t-s**
Matt. 7:16, Grapes . . . from t bushes
13:7, others fell among the **t-s**
27:29, weaving a crown of **t-s**
John 19:5, wearing the crown of **t-s**
2 Cor. 12:7, a t in the flesh
Gen. 3:18; Num. 33:55; Judg. 8:7;
Eccles. 7:6; Song 2:2

THOROUGH—*diligent*
Deut. 19:18, judges shall investigate
t-ly

THOUGHT—*reason, motive, plot*
Gen. 6:5, **t-s** of his heart
1 Chr. 28:9, every intent of the **t-s**
Job 21:27, I know your **t-s**
Ps. 94:11, know the **t-s** of man
Is. 55:8, My **t-s** are not your **t-s**
Matt. 9:4, Jesus knowing their **t-s**
15:19, heart come evil **t-s**

THOUSAND—*countless, clan*
1 Sam. 18:7, slain his **t-s** . . . David
his ten **t-s**
Job 9:3, answer Him . . . a t *times*
Ps. 84:10, a day in Thy . . . better
than . . . t
91:7, t may fall . . . ten t at your
right
Eccles. 7:28, found one man among
a t
Mark 6:44, five t men who ate
8:9, about four t were *there*
1 Cor. 14:19, ten t words in a tongue
2 Pet. 3:8, t years as one day
Jude 14, came with many **t-s** of His
Lev. 26:8; Eccles. 6:6
Song 4:4; Is. 30:17; Jer. 32:18; Dan.
7:10; Rev. 5:11

THRASH Judg. 8:7, t your bodies
with the thorns

THREE Job 2:11, Job's t friends
heard
Prov. 30:15, t things . . . not be
satisfied
30:18, t things . . . too wonderful

THREE *(Continued)*
30:21, t things ... earth quakes
30:29, t things ... are stately
Dan. 6:10, knees t times a day
Jon. 1:17, fish t days and t nights
Matt. 12:40, JONAH WAS T DAYS AND
  T NIGHTS
17:4, make t tabernacles here
18:20, two or t have gathered
26:34, deny Me t times
27:63, After t days I *am*
Luke 2:46, after t days they found
  Him
10:36, Which of these t ... a
  neighbor
John 2:19, in t days I will raise it
Acts 2:41, about t thousand souls
9:9, t days without sight
1 Cor. 13:13, faith, hope, love, these t
Gen. 6:10; Ex. 34:23; Eccles. 4:12;
  Luke 12:52; 2 Cor. 11:25; 12:8

THRESH—*tread, beat, trample*
Deut. 25:4; 2 Sam. 24:21; 1 Chr.
  21:20; Is. 21:10; 1 Tim. 5:18

THRESHING FLOOR
Matt. 3:12, thoroughly clean His t

THRESHOLD—*door* Ps. 84:10, stand
  at the t of the house

THREW—*toss, put*
2 Sam. 16:13, cast stones and t dust
2 Kin. 9:33, So they t her down
Luke 9:42, t him ... convulsion
19:35, they t their garments on the
  colt

THRIVE Job 8:16, He t-s before the
  sun

THROAT Ps. 69:3, crying; my t is
  parched
Rom. 3:13, T IS AN OPEN GRAVE
Ps. 5:9; 115:7; Prov. 23:2

THRONE Ps. 11:4, LORD'S t is in
  heaven
Ps. 93:2, t is established from of old
Is. 66:1, Heaven is My t
Matt. 5:34, for it is THE T OF GOD
19:28, sit upon twelve t-s
Acts 7:49, HEAVEN IS MY T
Heb. 1:8, THY T ... IS FOREVER AND
  EVER
4:16, with confidence to the t of
  grace
Rev. 4:2, t was standing in heaven
20:11, I saw a great white t
Gen. 41:40; Ex. 11:5; 1 Kin. 22:19

THRONG Ps. 55:14, in the house of
  God in the t

THROUGH Is. 43:2, t the waters ... t
  the fire
Matt. 19:24, camel ... t the eye of a
  needle
Luke 6:1, passing t *some* grainfields
John 3:17, world should be saved t
  Him
Acts 10:43, bear witness that t His
  name
Rom. 1:8, thank my God t Jesus
  Christ
Gal. 4:7, then an heir t God
Eph. 2:8, you have been saved t faith
Phil. 4:13, do all things t Him
1 John 4:9, we might live t Him
Gen. 12:6; Ex. 14:16; Eccles. 10:18;
  Is. 62:10

THROW Gen. 37:20, t him into one of
  the pits
Eccles. 3:6, time to keep ... time to t
  away
Luke 9:39, t-s him into a convulsion

THRUSH Jer. 8:7, the swift and the t

THRUST—*cast, push* Josh. 23:5;
  Prov. 12:18; 18:5

THUNDER Mark 3:17, Boanerges ...
  Sons of T
John 12:29, multitude ... saying that
  it had t-ed
Rev. 14:2, voice ... like the sound of
  loud t
Ex. 9:23; 1 Sam. 2:10; 2 Sam. 22:14;
  Job 26:14; Ps. 81:7; Is. 29:6

THWART 2 Sam. 15:34; 17:14;
  1 Thess. 2:18

TIDINGS—*message, news*
Ps. 112:7, He will not fear evil t
Rom. 10:15, BRING GLAD T OF GOOD
  THINGS

TILL—*cultivate* Jer. 27:11; Heb. 6:7

TIMBER—*wood*
2 Chr. 2:16, cut whatever t you need

TIME—*season, day, hour* Gen. 4:3;
  Judg. 15:1; Prov. 25:13
Job 22:16, snatched away before
  their t
Eccles. 3:1-8, appointed t for
  everything
9:12, man does not know his t
Is. 25:8, will swallow up death for
  all t
Dan. 12:7, for a t, t-s, and half a t
Hos. 10:12, it is t to seek the LORD
Matt. 2:7, ascertained from them
  the t
24:45, give them their food ...
  proper t
26:18, My t is at hand
John 7:6, My t is not yet at hand
1 Cor. 7:29, the t has been shortened
Gal. 6:9, in due t we shall reap
1 Tim. 2:6, testimony *borne* at the
  proper t
Jude 18, In the last t there shall be
  mockers
Rev. 1:3, for the t is near
2:21, I gave her t to repent
Eccles. 7:17; Song 2:12; Amos 5:13;
  Hag. 1:2; Zech. 14:7; Matt. 13:30;
  24:43; Acts 5:34

TIMELY Prov. 15:23, how delightful
  is a t word

TIMES—*season*
1 Chr. 12:32, men who understood
  the t
Job 24:1, t not stored up by the
  Almighty
Ps. 9:9, stronghold in t of trouble
31:15, My t are in Thy hand
Dan. 2:21, changes the t and epochs
Matt. 16:3, *discern* the signs of the t
Acts 1:7, not for you to know t
Rev. 12:14, time and t and half a
  time

TIMID—*fearful* Matt. 8:26; Mark
  4:40

TINGLE 1 Sam. 3:11; 2 Kin. 21:12;
  Jer. 19:3

TIP Job 38:37, Or t the water jars of
  the heavens

TIRED Gen. 27:46, I am t of living

TITHE—*tenth* Lev. 27:30, all the t of
  the land
Num. 18:26, take from ... Israel
  the t
18:28, offering to the LORD from
  your t-s
Deut. 12:17, the t of your grain
14:22, t all the produce
Matt. 23:23, you t mint and dill
Luke 18:12, pay t-s of all that I get
Heb. 7:8, mortal men receive t-s

TODAY—*age, day, life* Gen. 41:9,
  mention t of my own offenses
Ps. 2:7, T I have begotten Thee
Luke 23:43, t you shall be with Me in
  Paradise
Acts 13:33; Heb. 1:5, T I HAVE
  BEGOTTEN Thee
Heb. 13:8, Jesus Christ *is* the same
  ... t

TOIL—*labor, work, trouble*
Gen. 5:29, the t of our hands
31:42, and the t of my hands
Job 9:29, Why then should I t in vain
Matt. 6:28, do not t nor do they spin
1 Cor. 15:58, knowing that your t is
  not *in* vain

TOLD Matt. 24:25, I have t you in
  advance
Mark 3:9, He t His disciples
Luke 2:18, t them by the shepherds
John 4:39, t me all the things that I
  have done
14:2, not so, I would have t you

TOMB—*grave, place*
Is. 22:16, you have hewn a t for
Matt. 23:27, like whitewashed t-s
27:52, the t-s were opened
John 11:17, been in the t four days
12:17, Lazarus out of the t
19:41, in the garden a new t, in
  which
20:11, standing outside the t
  weeping
Rev. 11:9, bodies to be laid in a t

TOMORROW Prov. 27:1, Do not
  boast about t
Is. 22:13, drink, for t we may die
Matt. 6:34, do not be anxious for t
James 4:14, not know ... life will be
  like t

TONE—*voice* Gal. 4:20, and to
  change my t

TONGUE—*language*
Ex. 4:10, speech and slow of t
Job 5:21, hidden from the scourge of
  the t
Ps. 5:9, They flatter with their t
34:13, keep your t from evil
57:4, their t a sharp sword
64:3, sharpened their t like a sword
140:3, sharpen their t-s as a serpent
Prov. 12:18, t of the wise brings
  healing
15:4, soothing t is a tree of life
25:15, soft t breaks the bone
Is. 30:27, His t is like a consuming
  fire
Mark 7:35, impediment of his t was
  removed
16:17, they will speak with new t-s

TONGUE

Luke 16:24, in water and cool off my **t**
Acts 2:4, began to speak with other **t-s**
Rom. 14:11, EVERY T SHALL GIVE PRAISE
1 Cor. 13:1, with the **t-s** of men and of
14:4, who speaks in a **t** edifies himself
14:5, that you all spoke in **t-s**
14:14, if I pray in a **t**
14:39, do not forbid to speak in **t-s**
Phil. 2:11, every **t** should confess . . . Jesus
James 3:5, **t** is a small part
3:8, no one can tame the **t**
1 Pet. 3:10, REFRAIN HIS T FROM EVIL
Rev. 5:9, *men* from every tribe and **t**
Job 6:30; 20:12; 29:10; Prov. 6:17; Is. 50:4; Jer. 9:8

TOOK Gen. 8:9, **t** her, and brought her into the ark
Ex. 4:7, **t** it out of his bosom

TOOTH Ex. 21:24; Lev. 24:20
Deut. 19:21, eye, **t** for **t**
Prov. 25:19, like a bad **t**
Matt. 5:38, EYE FOR AN EYE, AND A T FOR A T

TOP Gen. 28:12, **t** reaching to heaven
Ex. 19:20, to the **t** of the mountain
2 Kin. 19:26, as grass on the house **t-s**
Matt. 27:51, veil . . . torn . . . from **t** to bottom
Heb. 11:21, leaning on the **t** of his staff

TORCH Gen. 15:17, a flaming **t** which passed
Judg. 15:5, set fire to the **t-es**
Dan. 10:6, his eyes were like flaming **t-es**

TORE Matt. 26:65, high priest **t** his robes
2 Sam. 13:19; 1 Kin. 11:30; Job 1:20

TORMENT Job 19:2, How long will you **t** me
Luke 8:28, do not **t** me
16:23, Hades . . . being in **t**
16:28, to this place of **t**
2 Pet. 2:8, felt *his* righteous soul **t-ed**
Rev. 9:5, **t** was like the **t** of a scorpion

TORN Gen. 37:33, Joseph . . . been **t** to pieces
Josh. 9:4, wineskins, worn-out and **t**
Job 18:14, is **t** from the security
Matt. 27:51, veil of the temple was **t**

TOSS—*shake* Job 7:4, I am continually **t-ing**
Is. 54:11, **storm-t-ed,** and not comforted
Acts 22:23, **t-ing** dust into the air
Eph. 4:14, **t-ed** here and there by waves
James 1:6, driven and **t-ed** by the wind

TOTTER Is. 24:20; 28:7

TOUCH—*handle* Gen. 3:3, not eat from it or **t** it
Ps. 105:15, Do not **t** My anointed ones
Matt. 9:21, If I only **t** His garment

Mark 5:30, Who **t-ed** My garments
Luke 24:39, it is I Myself; **t** Me and see
1 Cor. 7:1, not to **t** a woman
Col. 2:21, do not taste, do not **t**
Ex. 19:12; Lev. 5:2; Job 5:19

TOWARD—*against* Rom. 8:7, is hostile **t** God

TOWER—*stronghold*
Prov. 18:10, name . . . is a strong **t**
Matt. 21:33, AND BUILT A T
Gen. 11:4; Ps. 48:12; Mic. 4:8

TRADE—*craft* Acts 18:3, he was of the same **t**
Acts 19:25, with the workmen of similar **t-s**

TRADER 2 Chr. 9:14, the **t-s** and merchants

TRAIN—*fit, instruct* 1 Chr. 12:8, men **t-ed** for war
2 Tim. 3:16, for **t-ing** in righteousness
Heb. 5:14, senses **t-ed** to discern good and evil
12:11, to those who have been **t-ed**

TRAMPLE Job 9:8, **t-s** down the waves
Prov. 25:26, *Like* a **t-d** spring
Hab. 3:12, didst **t** the nations

TRANSCRIBE
Prov. 25:1, proverbs . . . king of Judah, **t-d**

TRANSFORM—*change*
Rom. 12:2, **t-ed** by the renewing of
Phil. 3:21, who will **t** the body

TRANSGRESS Num. 14:41; Josh. 7:11; Jer. 2:8

TRANSGRESSION—*trespass, sin*
Job 14:17, My **t** is sealed up
33:9, pure without **t**
Ps. 32:1, he whose **t** is forgiven
39:8, Deliver me from all my **t-s**
51:3, I know my **t-s**
103:12, removed our **t-s** from us
Matt. 6:14, forgive men for their **t-s**
Col. 2:13, forgiven us all our **t-s**
Gen. 31:36; Ex. 34:7; Num. 14:18; Josh. 24:19; Prov. 10:12; 29:6; Is. 53:5; Ezek. 18:30; Matt. 6:15

TRANSGRESSOR
Ps. 37:38, **t-s** will be . . . destroyed
51:13, I will teach **t-s** Thy ways
Is. 53:12, numbered with the **t-s**
Mark 15:28, reckoned with **t-s**
James 2:11, become a **t** of the law

TRANSLATE Ezra 4:18, has been **t-d** and read
John 1:42, which **t-d** means Peter

TRAP—*entangle*
Matt. 22:15, how they might **t**
Mark 12:13, to **t** Him in a statement

TREACHEROUS
Prov. 2:22, the **t** will be uprooted
13:15, way of the **t** is hard
2 Sam. 18:13; Prov. 22:12; Is. 21:2; 24:16; Jer. 3:20; Lam. 1:2; Hos. 5:7; Mal. 2:10

TREAD—*trample* Luke 10:19, **t** upon serpents

Rev. 19:15, **t-s** the wine press
Job 24:11; Is. 16:10; 41:25; Jer. 25:30

TREASURE—*possession, gain*
Gen. 43:23, given you **t** in your
Is. 33:6, fear of the LORD is his **t**
Matt. 2:11, opening their **t-s** they presented
6:21, where your **t** is, there will
12:35, out of his good **t** brings
13:44, **t** hidden in the field
19:21, you shall have **t** in heaven
Col. 2:3, hidden all the **t-s** of wisdom
James 5:3, stored up your **t**
Deut. 33:19; Job 3:21; 23:12; Prov. 21:20

TREAT Mark 12:4, **t-ed** him shamefully
Luke 2:48, why have You **t-ed** us this way

TREE—*grove, cross* Gen. 1:11, fruit **t-s** bearing
Gen. 2:9, **t** of life . . . knowledge
3:8, God among the **t-s**
Ps. 1:3, **t** firmly planted by streams
37:35, like a luxuriant **t**
104:16, **t-s** of the LORD drink their fill
Prov. 3:18, She is a **t** of life
Is. 55:12, **t-s** . . . will clap *their* hands
Matt. 3:10, every **t** . . . not bear good fruit
7:17, good **t** bears good fruit
12:33, **t** is known by its fruit
Mark 8:24, see men . . . like **t-s**
Luke 19:4, climbed up into a sycamore **t**
John 1:50, saw you under the fig **t**
Jude 12, autumn **t-s** without fruit
Rev. 2:7, eat of the **t** of life
Gen. 18:4; 21:33; Deut. 20:19; 21:22; Judg. 9:8; Prov. 27:18; Song 8:5; Is. 40:20; Mic. 4:4

TREMBLE—*fear*
1 Chr. 16:30; Ps. 96:9, T before Him . . . earth
Job 26:11, pillars of heaven **t**
Ps. 4:4, T, and do not sin
Is. 13:13, make the heavens **t,** and the earth
Mark 5:33, woman fearing and **t-ing**
Phil. 2:12, with fear and **t-ing**
2 Pet. 2:10, do not **t** when they revile
Lev. 26:6; Deut. 20:3; Ps. 2:11

TRENCH 2 Kin. 3:16, valley full of **t-es**

TRESPASS—*fault*
Gal. 6:1, if a man is caught in any **t**
Eph. 2:1, dead in your **t-s** and sins

TRIAL Deut. 7:19, great **t-s** which your eyes saw
Acts 4:9, if we are on **t** today
Gal. 4:14, a **t** to you in my bodily condition
James 1:12, a man who perseveres under **t**

TRIBE Gen. 49:28, these are the twelve **t-s**
Num. 1:4, a man of each **t**
Ps. 122:4, even the **t-s** of the LORD
Matt. 24:30, all the **t-s** of the earth
Luke 22:30, judging the twelve **t-s**

TRIBULATION—*affliction*
Matt. 24:21, will be a great **t**
John 16:33, world you have **t**

TRIBULATION *(Continued)*
Rom. 5:3, t brings about
  perseverance
12:12, persevering in t
Eph. 3:13, not to lose heart at my **t-s**

TRIBUNAL—*judgment*
Acts 25:10, standing before Caesar's
  t

TRIBUTE—*tax* Ezra 7:24, impose
  tax, t or toll

TRICK—*craftiness* Matt. 2:16,
  Herod . . . **t-ed** by the magi
Luke 20:23, He detected their **t-ery**

TRIED Ex. 2:15, Pharaoh . . . t to kill
  Moses
Ps. 12:6, As silver t in a furnace

TRIM Ex. 30:7, when he **t-s** the lamps

TRIUMPH Ex. 32:18, sound of the
  cry of t

TROUBLE—*distress, affliction,*
  pain
1 Kin. 20:7, see how this man is
  looking for t
Job 4:8, plow iniquity . . . who sow t
  harvest it
5:6, does t sprout from the ground
5:7, man is born for t
Ps. 9:9, A stronghold in times of t
25:18, my affliction and my t
27:5, day of t He will conceal
41:1, deliver him in a day of t
Prov. 10:10, who winks the eye
  causes t
25:20, sings songs to a **t-d** heart
31:7, remember his t no more
Eccles. 8:6, a man's t is heavy
Matt. 2:3, Herod . . . heard it, he was
  t-d
Luke 6:18, **t-d** with unclean spirits
24:38, Why are you **t-d**
John 12:27, My soul has become **t-d**
Acts 20:10, Do not be **t-d**
1 Pet. 3:14, DO NOT BE **T-D**
Gen. 41:51; Ps. 77:4; 138:7; Is. 65:16;
  Ezek. 32:9

TRUE—*sure*
Prov. 11:18, sows righteousness . . . t
  reward
Luke 16:11, entrust the t *riches*
John 1:9, There was the t light
6:32, gives you the t bread
6:55, My flesh is t food . . . is t drink
7:28, He who sent Me is t
8:17, testimony of two men is t
Rom. 3:4, let God be found t
Phil. 4:8, whatever is t
Titus 1:13, This testimony is t
1 Pet. 5:12, the t grace of God
Rev. 3:14, faithful and t Witness

TRULY—*indeed* Josh. 7:20, T, I have
  sinned
Is. 45:15, T, Thou art a God who
Matt. 5:18, For t I say to you
John 1:51, T, t, I say to you
Gen. 24:49; 2 Sam. 14:5

TRUMPET—*horn* Is. 27:13, great t
  will be blown
Matt. 6:2, alms, do not sound a t
Ex. 19:16; Judg. 7:16

TRUST—*faith, confidence*
2 Chr. 20:20, t in the LORD . . . t
Job 8:14, whose t a spider's web
Ps. 4:5, And t in the LORD

118:8, Than to t in man
Prov. 11:28, **t-s** in his riches will fall
31:11, husband **t-s** in her
Is. 26:4, T in the LORD forever
Jer. 7:4, Do not t in deceptive words
20:10, All my **t-ed** friends
Mic. 7:5, Do not t in a neighbor
2 Cor. 1:9, should not t in ourselves
Heb. 2:13, I WILL PUT MY T IN HIM

TRUSTWORTHY—*true*
Prov. 20:6, who can find a t man
1 Tim. 3:1; 4:9, It is a t statement

TRUTH 1 Kin. 2:4, walk before Me
  in t
Ps. 15:2, speaks t in his heart
119:160, Thy word is t
Prov. 3:3, not let kindness and t
  leave you
23:23, Buy t, and do not sell *it*
Matt. 22:16, we know that You are **t-**
  ful
Luke 4:25, But I say to you in t
John 1:14, full of grace and t
8:32, t shall make you free
14:6, way, and the t, and the life
Rom. 1:25, t of God for a lie
Gal. 2:5, t of the gospel might
  remain
Phil. 1:18, in pretense or in t
1 Tim. 3:15, pillar and support of
  the t
2 Tim. 2:15, handling . . . the word
  of t
1 John 1:8, the t is not in us
Gen. 42:16; 1 Kin. 22:16; Is. 39:8;
  Zech. 8:16

TRY—*prove* Luke 14:19, oxen . . .
  going to t them
Luke 19:3, **t-ing** to see who Jesus
  was
Deut. 4:34; Is. 22:4; Acts 9:26

TUNIC—*garment, coat* Gen. 37:3;
  Lev. 16:4; Matt. 10:10; Luke 9:3

TURBAN—*diadem* Job 29:14; Ezek.
  21:26

TURMOIL—*trouble* Prov. 15:16; Jer.
  50:34

TURN 2 Kin. 20:10, shadow t
  backward ten steps
2 Chr. 34:2, did not t aside to the
  right or to the left
Job 23:11, kept His way and not **t-ed**
  aside
Ps. 119:157, I do not t aside from
  Thy
Prov. 7:25, Do not let your heart t
  aside
Is. 45:22, T to Me, and be saved
53:6, Each . . . has **t-ed** to his own
  way
Jer. 26:3, everyone will t from his
  evil way
Hos. 11:7, My people are bent on **t-**
  ing from Me
Joel 2:31, sun will be **t-ed** into
  darkness
Matt. 5:39, cheek, t to him the other
Acts 1:25, from which Judas **t-ed**
  aside
1 Tim. 5:15, **t-ed** aside to follow
  Satan
James 5:20, who **t-s** a sinner from
  the error
1 Pet. 3:11, T AWAY FROM EVIL
Ex. 23:2; Deut. 17:11; Ruth 1:16;
  1 Kin. 20:26; 2 Kin. 17:13; Job 1:1;

2:3; 23:13; 36:21; Ps. 80:14; 119:51;
  Prov. 4:5; Is. 1:4; Jer. 23:20; Joel
  2:14

TUTOR—*instruct* 1 Cor. 4:15, have
  countless **t-s** in Christ

TWELVE Gen. 17:20, become the
  father of t princes
Gen. 35:22, there were t sons of
  Jacob
Matt. 10:1, summoned His t disciples
Mark 3:14, He appointed t
Luke 2:42, when He became t
John 11:9, t hours in the day
Rev. 12:1, a crown of t stars

TWICE—*doubly*
Gen. 41:32, repeating . . . dream to
  Pharaoh t
Num. 20:11, struck the rock t
1 Sam. 18:11, David escaped . . . t
Mark 14:30, before a cock crows t
Luke 18:12, I fast t a week

TWITTER Is. 38:14, *like* a crane, so
  I t

TWO—*both* Gen. 1:16, God made the
  t great lights
Ex. 31:18, t tablets of the testimony
Matt. 2:16, children . . . t years old
5:41, one mile, go with him t
6:24, No one can serve t masters
18:19, t of you agree on earth
19:5, T SHALL BECOME ONE FLESH
Luke 17:35, t women grinding
1 Cor. 6:16, T WILL BECOME ONE
  FLESH
Gal. 4:24, these *women* are t
  covenants
Eph. 2:15, make the t into one new
  man
Lev. 8:2; Eccles. 4:9

U

UGLY—*bad* Gen. 41:3, u and gaunt

UMPIRE Job 9:33, There is no u
  between us

UNAPPROACHABLE
1 Tim. 6:16, dwells in u light

UNAPPROVED
2 Cor. 13:7, though we . . . appear u

UNAWARE Rom. 1:13, do not want
  you to be u

UNBELIEF Mark 9:24, help *me* in
  my u
Rom. 11:23, continue in their u
Heb. 3:12, an evil, **u-ing** heart

UNBELIEVERS Luke 12:46, a place
  with the u
1 Cor. 14:23, ungifted men or u
2 Cor. 6:14, bound together with u

UNBLEMISHED 1 Pet. 1:19, u and
  spotless

UNCEASING Rom. 9:2, sorrow and
  u grief

UNCLEAN Lev. 5:2, person touches
  any u thing
2 Chr. 29:5, **u-ness** out from the holy
  place
Job 14:4, make the clean out of
  the u

Ps. 106:39, became **u** in their practices
Is. 6:5, man of **u** lips
Ezek. 4:13, eat their bread **u**
Matt. 10:1, authority over **u** spirits
Mark 5:13, **u** spirits entered the swine
9:25, He rebuked the **u** spirit
Luke 9:42, Jesus rebuked the **u** spirit
Acts 10:14, eaten anything unholy and **u**
Rom. 14:14, nothing is **u** in itself
Rev. 16:13, three **u** spirits like frogs
18:2, prison of every **u** spirit
21:27, nothing **u** . . . shall ever come into it

UNCOVER Ezek. 21:24; Hos. 7:1

UNDEFILED Heb. 7:26, holy, innocent, **u**
Heb. 13:4, *marriage* bed *be* **u**
James 1:27, pure and **u** religion

UNDER Ex. 23:5, lying *helpless* **u** its load
Matt. 5:15, put it **u** the peck-measure
John 1:50, saw you **u** the fig tree
Rom. 3:9, Jews and Greeks are all **u** sin
Eph. 1:22, all things . . . **u** His feet
1 Pet. 5:6, **u** the mighty hand of God

UNDERGARMENTS Lev. 6:10; 16:4; Ezek. 44:18

UNDERSTAND—*know, perceive*
1 Chr. 28:19
Gen. 11:7, not **u** one another's speech
Jer. 17:9, the heart . . . Who can **u** it
Matt. 15:17, Do you not **u**
Luke 24:45, opened . . . to **u** the Scriptures
John 8:43, Why do you not **u** what I am saying
Acts 10:34, **u** *now* that God is not one
2 Pet. 3:16, some things hard to **u**
Prov. 1:6; Is. 6:9; Dan. 8:17; Matt. 15:10

UNDERSTANDING—*comprehending*
Prov. 2:2, Incline your heart to **u**
Jer. 10:12, by His **u** He has stretched
Matt. 15:16, Are you also still without **u**
Eph. 4:18, being darkened in their **u**
2 Tim. 2:7, Lord will give you **u**
Ex. 36:1; Job 17:4; Ps. 32:9

UNDISCIPLINED 2 Thess. 3:7, not act in an **u** manner
2 Thess. 3:11, leading an **u** life

UNDISTURBED Judg. 8:28, land was **u** for forty years
2 Chr. 14:1, land was **u** for ten years

UNEDUCATED Acts 4:13, that they were **u** and untrained

UNFAITHFUL Ezra 10:2, **u** to our God

UNFATHOMABLE Rom. 11:33, How . . . **u** His ways

UNFEELING Ps. 17:10, closed their **u** heart

UNFOLDING Ps. 119:130, **u** of Thy words gives light

UNFRUITFUL—*barren*
2 Kin. 2:19, water is bad, and the land is **u**
Matt. 13:22; Mark 4:19, and it becomes **u**
1 Cor. 14:14, my mind is **u**
Eph. 5:11, **u** deeds of darkness
2 Pet. 1:8, neither useless nor **u** in the true knowledge

UNGIFTED—*uneducated*
1 Cor. 14:16, the **u** say the Amen

UNGODLY—*wicked, worthless*
Rom. 5:6, Christ died for the **u**
Titus 2:12, to deny **u-ness**
Jude 18, after their own **u** lusts

UNHOLY—*common*
Acts 10:15, no *longer* consider **u**

UNIMPRESSIVE—*weak*
2 Cor. 10:10, personal presence is **u**

UNINTENTIONALLY Lev. 4:2; 5:15; Num. 15:27

UNITE Phil. 2:2, same love, **u-d** in spirit
Heb. 4:2, not **u-d** by faith

UNJUST—*unrighteous*
Prov. 29:27, **u** man is abominable
Jer. 17:11, makes a fortune, but **u-ly**
Heb. 6:10, God is not **u** so as to forget
1 Pet. 3:18, *the* just for *the* **u**

UNKNOWN Acts 17:23, TO AN **U** GOD
2 Cor. 6:9, as **u** yet well-known
Gal. 1:22, I was still **u** by sight

UNLESS—*except* Gen. 32:26, **u** you bless me
Ps. 127:1, U the LORD builds the house
Matt. 5:20, **u** your righteousness surpasses
18:3, **u** you are converted
24:22, **u** those days had been cut short
Mark 13:20, **u** the Lord had shortened *those* days
Luke 13:3, **u** you repent, you will . . . perish
John 3:2, **u** God is with him
3:3, **u** one is born again
4:48, U *you people* see signs
6:53, **u** you eat the flesh
20:25, U I shall see . . . imprint of the nails
Rom. 10:15, shall they preach **u** they are sent
1 Cor. 15:36, does not come to life **u** it dies
2 Tim. 2:5, **u** he competes according to the rules
Deut. 32:30; Is. 1:9; Amos 3:3

UNLOVING Rom. 1:31, untrustworthy, **u**
2 Tim. 3:3, **u**, irreconcilable

UNOCCUPIED Matt. 12:44, finds it **u**

UNPLEASANT—*evil*
Gen. 47:9, few and **u** have been the years

UNPROFITABLE Titus 3:9, they are **u** and worthless
Heb. 13:17, this would be **u** for you

UNPUNISHED Ex. 21:19; 1 Kin. 2:9
Ex. 20:7, LORD will not leave him **u**

UNQUENCHABLE
Matt. 3:12, burn . . . chaff with **u** fire
Mark 9:43, into the **u** fire

UNREASONING 2 Pet. 2:12, like **u** animals

UNRESTRAIN
Prov. 29:18, no vision, people are **u-ed**

UNRIGHTEOUS—*unjust*
Is. 55:7, **u** man his thoughts
Matt. 5:45, rain on *the* righteous and *the* **u**
Luke 16:10, **u** in . . . little thing is **u** also in much
16:11, faithful in the *use of* **u** Mammon
Rom. 3:5, God who inflicts wrath is not **u**
1 Cor. 6:9, **u** shall not inherit the kingdom
2 Pet. 2:9, keep the **u** under punishment

UNRIGHTEOUSNESS
1 Cor. 13:6, not rejoice in **u**
1 John 5:17, All **u** is sin

UNRULY 1 Thess. 5:14, admonish the **u**
2 Thess. 3:6, who leads an **u** life

UNSETTLING Acts 15:24, **u** your souls

UNSTEADY Prov. 25:19, and an **u** foot

UNSUSPECTING Rom. 16:18, hearts of the **u**

UNTAUGHT—*uneducated*
2 Pet. 3:16, **u** and unstable distort

UNTIE Luke 19:30, a colt . . . **u** it and bring it

UNTIL John 5:17, My Father is working **u** now

UNTIMELY 1 Cor. 15:8, to one **u** born

UNTRAINED Acts 4:13, uneducated and **u** men

UNWISE Deut. 32:6, O foolish and **u** people
Eph. 5:15, walk, not as **u** men

UNWORTHY Gen. 32:10, **u** of all the lovingkindness
Luke 17:10, We are **u** slaves

UP Ex. 15:8, flowing waters stood **u** like a heap

UPHOLD Ps. 119:117, U me that I may be safe
Is. 41:13, God, who **u-s** your right hand

UPPER 2 Sam. 11:21, woman throw an **u** millstone

UPPER *(Continued)*
Luke 22:12, large, furnished, **u** room
Acts 1:13, they went up to the **u** room
19:1, Paul ... passed through the **u** country

UPRIGHT Deut. 32:4, Righteous and **u** is He
Prov. 4:11, led you in **u** paths
Eccles. 7:29, God made men **u**
Mic. 7:2, is no **u** person among men
Acts 14:10, Stand **u** on your feet
1 Thess. 2:10, devoutly and **u-ly** and blamelessly
Num. 23:10; Job 1:8; 4:7

UPRIGHTNESS Prov. 17:26; Is. 59:14; Mal. 2:6

UPROAR 1 Kin. 1:41, city making such an **u**
Ps. 2:1, Why are the nations in an **u**

UPROOT Job 19:10, has **u-ed** my hope
Luke 17:6, Be **u-ed** and be planted

UPSET—*turn* 2 Sam. 6:6, oxen nearly **u** it
Acts 17:6, men ... **u** the world have come here
2 Tim. 2:18, **u** the faith of some
Titus 1:11, **u-ing** whole families

UPWARD Phil. 3:14, prize of the **u** call

URGE—*constrain* Ruth 1:16, Do not **u** me to leave you
Prov. 16:26, his hunger **u-s** him *on*
Luke 24:29, And they **u-d** Him, saying
Rom. 12:1, I **u** you therefore, brethren

URGENT 1 Sam. 21:8, king's matter was **u**

USE Gen. 21:15; Deut. 32:23
1 Chr. 12:2, **u-ing** both the right hand and
2 Cor. 3:12, **u** great boldness in *our* speech
1 Tim. 5:23, **u** a little wine for the sake

USELESS Lev. 26:16, sow your seed **u-ly**
Rom. 3:12, TOGETHER THEY HAVE BECOME U

USURIOUS Lev. 25:36, not take **u** interest from him

USURY—*interest* Neh. 5:10, leave off this **u**
Prov. 28:8, increases his wealth by ... **u**

UTENSILS Ex. 31:8, the table also and its **u**

UTMOST—*remote*
1 Thess. 2:16, wrath has come ... to the **u**

UTTER—*speak* Ps. 119:171, Let my lips **u** praise
Acts 26:25, I **u** words of sober truth
1 Cor. 14:9, **u** by the tongue speech

UTTERANCE Luke 21:15, give you **u** and wisdom
Acts 2:4, Spirit was giving them **u**

2 Cor. 8:7, in faith and **u** and knowledge
Eph. 6:19, **u** may be given to me

UTTERLY—*greatly* Is. 42:17, be **u** put to shame
Rom. 7:13, sin might become **u** sinful

V

VAGRANT Gen. 4:12, a **v** and a wanderer

VAIN—*empty, futile* Ps. 2:1, peoples devising a **v** thing
Prov. 12:11, he who pursues **v** *things*
1 Cor. 15:14, then our preaching is **v**

VALLEY—*ravine*
Ps. 23:4, through the **v** of the shadow
Song 2:1, The lily of the **v-s**
Jer. 31:40, the whole **v** of the dead bodies
Ezek. 37:1, **v**; and it was full of bones
Joel 3:14, the **v** of decision
Gen. 14:17; 19:17; Josh. 10:12;
2 Sam. 18:18; 1 Kin. 20:28; 2 Kin. 3:16

VALUATION Lev. 5:15, according to your **v** in silver
Lev. 27:25, Every **v** of yours
Num. 18:16, redeem them, by your **v**

VALUE—*price* Matt. 10:31, you are of more **v** than
Matt. 12:12, how much more **v** is a man than a sheep
13:46, one pearl of great **v**

VANITY—*breath, emptiness, futility*
Prov. 22:8, sows iniquity will reap **v**
Eccles. 1:2, V of **v-es**! All is **v**
2 Pet. 2:18, arrogant *words* of **v**

VARICOLORED—*colored*
Gen. 37:3, made him a **v** tunic
Gen. 37:23,32

VARIETY 1 Cor. 12:4, there are **v-es** of gifts

VARIOUS—*manifold*
Matt. 4:24, taken with **v** diseases
24:7, in **v** places there will be famines
2 Tim. 3:6, led on by **v** impulses
James 1:2, when you encounter **v** trials
1 Pet. 1:6, distressed by **v** trials

VAST—*large* Is. 22:18, To be cast into a **v**

VAULT Job 22:14, walks on the **v** of heaven

VEGETABLES Deut. 11:10; 1 Kin. 21:2
Prov. 15:17, better is a dish of **v** where love is
Rom. 14:2, he who is weak eats **v** *only*

VEGETATION—*grass* Gen. 1:11, earth sprout **v**
Ps. 104:14, **v** for the labor of man
Gen. 1:12; Ps. 105:35; Is. 42:15;
Jer. 12:4

VEIL Is. 25:7, **v** ... stretched over all nations
Matt. 27:51, **v** of the temple was torn
2 Cor. 3:13, put a **v** over his face
Heb. 6:19, which enters within the **v**
9:3, behind the second **v**
Gen. 24:65; Ex. 34:33; Lev. 4:6; Song 4:1; Is. 47:2

VENGEANCE—*revenge*
Lev. 19:18, You shall not take **v**
Deut. 32:35, V is Mine
Ps. 94:1, O LORD, God of **v**
Is. 34:8, the LORD has a day of **v**
Heb. 10:30, V IS MINE
Gen. 4:15; 2 Sam. 22:48; Ps. 18:47;
Jer. 15:15; Nah. 1:2

VENOM—*poison*
Deut. 32:24, **v** of crawling things
32:33, wine is the **v** of serpents
Job 20:14, the **v** of cobras

VENTURE Job 4:2, one **v-s** a word with you

VERY Gen. 1:31, behold, it was **v** good
Num. 12:3, Moses was **v** humble
Judg. 3:17, Eglon was a **v** fat man
1 Sam. 5:11, hand of God was **v** heavy
Ps. 46:1, A **v** present help in trouble
Matt. 17:15, an epileptic, and is **v** ill
Mark 16:2, **v** early on the first day
Luke 12:7, the **v** hairs of your head
Ex. 14:10; Mark 6:26

VESSEL Num. 5:17, holy water in ... **v**
Ps. 31:12, I am like a broken **v**
Rom. 9:22, **v-s** of wrath
2 Cor. 4:7, treasure in earthen **v-s**
2 Tim. 2:21, will be a **v** for honor
1 Pet. 3:7, as with a weaker **v**
Rev. 2:27, AS THE V-S OF THE POTTER
Ex. 7:19; 2 Kin. 4:3; Is. 22:24;
Jer. 48:11

VEXATION—*wrath* Prov. 12:16, fool's **v** is known

VICTORIOUS Rev. 15:2, come off **v** from the beast

VICTORY—*deliverance*
2 Sam. 23:10, LORD brought ... great **v**
2 Kin. 5:1, had given **v** to Syria
1 Chr. 11:14, the LORD saved them by a great **v**
29:11, the glory and the **v**
Ps. 98:1, holy arm have gained the **v**
Matt. 12:20, HE LEADS JUSTICE TO V
1 Cor. 15:54, DEATH IS SWALLOWED UP IN V
15:55, DEATH, WHERE IS YOUR V
1 John 5:4, **v** that has overcome the world

VIGOR Deut. 34:7, Moses ... nor his **v** abated

VINDICATE Ps. 82:3, V the weak and fatherless
Matt. 11:19, wisdom is **v-d** by her deeds

VINE Matt. 26:29, drink ... fruit of the **v**
John 15:1, I am the true **v**
Gen. 40:9; Judg. 9:12; 1 Kin. 4:25;
Ps. 128:3; Song 2:13; Is. 36:16; Jer.

VINE
2:21; Ezek. 19:10; Joel 1:12;
Mal. 3:11

VINEGAR Ruth 2:14; Ps. 69:21; Prov.
10:26

VINEYARD 1 Cor. 9:7, Who plants a
v, and does not eat
Gen. 9:20; Lev. 19:10; 1 Kin. 21:1;
Song 1:6; 2:15; Is. 1:8; Jer. 12:10;
Matt. 20:4

VIOLATE 2 Sam. 13:12, do not v me
Rom. 4:15, law, neither is there v-ion

VIOLENCE Gen. 6:11, earth was
filled with v
Ps. 55:9, v and strife in the city
Prov. 4:17, drink the wine of v
16:29, man of v entices his neighbor
Is. 53:9, He had done no v
Matt. 11:12, kingdom of heaven
suffers v
Gen. 49:5; Job 5:21; Ps. 27:12; Prov.
26:6; Is. 60:18; Jer. 22:3

VIOLENT Ps. 18:48, rescue me from
the v man
Ps. 37:35, seen a v, wicked man
Prov. 11:16, v men attain riches
Matt. 8:28, so exceedingly v that no
one

VIPER—adder, serpent Job 20:16, v-
's tongue
Matt. 3:7, You brood of v-s
Acts 28:3, a v came out because of
the heat
Is. 11:8; 14:29; 30:6

VIRGIN—maid, maiden
Matt. 1:23, v SHALL BE WITH CHILD
1:25, kept her a v
25:1, comparable to ten v-s
Luke 1:27, v-'s name was Mary
1 Cor. 7:28, if a v should marry
2 Cor. 11:2, to Christ . . . a pure v
Gen. 24:16; Ex. 22:16,17; Judg. 19:24;
Job 31:1; Ps. 148:12; Jer. 2:32;
31:13

VISIBLE Eph. 5:13, v when . . .
exposed by the light

VISION Prov. 29:18, Where there is
no v
Is. 22:1, concerning the valley of v
Joel 2:28, young men will see v-s
Hab. 2:2, Record the v And inscribe
it
Matt. 17:9, Tell the v to no one
Acts 2:17, YOUNG MEN SHALL SEE V-S
2 Cor. 12:1, to v-s and revelations
Gen. 15:1; 1 Sam. 3:1; Job 20:8; Lam.
2:9; Dan. 2:19

VISIT Ex. 20:5, v-ing the iniquity of
Matt. 25:36, sick, and you v-ed Me
Luke 1:68, v-ed us . . . redemption
for His people
James 1:27, v orphans and widows

VOICE—sound Ps. 19:3, Their v is
not heard
Prov. 5:13, the v of my teachers
Eccles. 5:3, the v of a fool
Song 2:12, v of the turtledove
Is. 28:23, Give ear and hear my v
Matt. 2:18, v WAS HEARD IN RAMAH
3:3, v OF ONE CRYING
3:17, behold, a v out of the heavens
Mark 9:7, v came out of the cloud

Luke 3:4, v of one crying . . .
wilderness
John 5:25, v of the Son of God
Acts 10:13, v came to him, Arise,
Peter
Rom. 10:18, V HAS GONE OUT INTO
ALL
1 Thess. 4:16, v of the archangel
Heb. 12:26, His v shook the earth
2 Pet. 2:16, dumb donkey . . . v of a
man
Rev. 3:20, if any one hears My v
5:11, heard the v of many angels
Deut. 4:30; Josh. 6:10; 2 Sam. 19:35;
Job 4:10; Is. 40:3; Jer. 7:34; Dan.
4:31; Rev. 6:1

VOID—empty
Gen. 1:2, earth was formless and v
Jer. 19:7, make v the counsel
Rom. 4:14, faith is made v

VOLUNTARILY—willing 1 Cor.
9:17, I do this v

VOLUNTEER Judg. 5:2, That the
people v-ed

VOMIT Job 20:15, will v them up
Prov. 26:11, dog that returns to its v
Is. 19:14, staggers in his v
Jon. 2:10, fish . . . v-ed Jonah up
2 Pet. 2:22, DOG RETURNS TO ITS
OWN V

VOTIVE—vow Lev. 7:16, his offering
is a v

VOW—oath, votive Gen. 28:20,
Jacob made a v
Deut. 23:22, if you refrain from v-ing
Judg. 11:30, Jephthah made a v
2 Sam. 15:7, let me go and pay my v
Ps. 22:25, I shall pay my v-s
Eccles. 5:5, not v . . . v and not pay
Matt. 5:33, MAKE FALSE V-S . . .
FULFILL YOUR V-S
Acts 18:18, he was keeping a v

VULTURES Matt. 24:28, the v will
gather
Luke 17:37, will the v be gathered

W

WAGED—fought
Rev. 12:7, dragon and his angels w
war

WAGES—hire Gen. 30:18, God has
given me w
Deut. 23:18, the w of a dog
Job 7:2, hired man . . . waits for
his w
Luke 3:14, be content with your w
10:7; 1 Tim. 5:18, laborer is worthy
. . . w
John 4:36, who reaps is receiving w
2 Pet. 2:13, w of doing wrong
2:15, w of unrighteousness
Gen. 29:15; Ex. 2:9; Lev. 19:13;
Deut. 24:15; Prov. 11:18; Jer. 22:13;
Hag. 1:6; Zech. 8:10; 11:12;
Mal. 3:5

WAIL—mourn, weep Jer. 9:19,
voice of w-ing is heard
Mark 5:38, loudly weeping and w-ing
Esth. 4:3; Mic. 1:8

WAIST Matt. 3:4, leather belt about
his w

WAISTBAND Jer. 13:1, Go and buy
. . . a linen w

WAIT Gen. 49:18, For Thy salvation
I w
Ps. 25:5, For Thee I w all day
27:14; 37:34, W for the LORD
119:81, I w for Thy word
Prov. 1:18, w for their own blood
Is. 26:8, have w-ed for Thee eagerly
30:18, He w-s on high
Mark 15:43, w-ing for the kingdom
Luke 12:36, men who are w-ing
Rom. 8:23, w-ing eagerly for our
adoption
Gal. 5:5, w-ing for the hope of
Phil. 3:20, we . . . w for a Savior
Ruth 3:18; 2 Kin. 5:2; Job 14:14;
Lam. 3:10; Dan. 12:12; Hos. 6:9;
Mic. 7:2; Hab. 2:3; 3:16

WALK—follow, journey Gen. 3:8,
God w-ing in the garden
Gen. 5:24, Enoch w-ed with God
Ex. 14:29, Israel w-ed on dry land
Lev. 26:3, If you w in My statutes
Josh. 18:8, Go and w through the
land
1 Sam. 2:30, w before Me forever
Job 22:14, w-s on the vault of
Ps. 1:1, not w in the counsel of
15:2, He who w-s with integrity
23:4, w through the valley of
26:3, have w-ed in Thy truth
39:6, man w-s about as a phantom
Prov. 10:9, w-s in integrity w-s
securely
Eccles. 2:14, fool w-s in darkness
Is. 2:3, we may w in His paths
2:5, w in the light of the LORD
3:16, w with heads held high
9:2, people who w in darkness
Amos 3:3, Do two men w together
unless
Mic. 6:8, w humbly with your God
Matt. 9:5, Rise, and w
14:29, Peter . . . w-ed on the water
John 6:19, Jesus w-ing on the sea
Acts 3:6, name of Jesus . . . w
14:8, lame . . . who had never w-ed
Rom. 6:4, w in newness of life
1 Cor. 3:3, fleshly . . . not w-ing like
mere men
2 Cor. 4:2, not w-ing in craftiness
5:7, w by faith, not by sight
Gal. 5:16, w by the Spirit
6:16, w by this rule
Eph. 4:1, w in a manner worthy of
5:2, w in love, just as Christ also
5:8, w as children of light
Col. 2:6, so w in Him
1 Thess. 2:12, w in a manner worthy
1 John 2:6, w in the same manner as
He w-ed
Rev. 3:4, will w with Me in white
21:24, nations shall w by its light
Deut. 33:25; 1 Kin. 2:4; Job 1:7;
Eccles. 10:7; Jer. 2:5; 9:14; Ezek.
36:12; Hos. 11:10; Zeph. 1:17; Mal.
2:6; John 7:1

WALL Ex. 14:22, waters were like
a w
Josh. 2:15, she was living on the w
2 Kin. 20:2, turned his face to the w
Neh. 4:6, So we built the w
Acts 9:25, w, lowering him in a
basket
23:3, strike you, you white-washed
w
Eph. 2:14, barrier of the dividing w
Heb. 11:30, w-s of Jericho fell

WALL (Continued)

Rev. 21:12, had a great and high **w**
Gen. 49:22; 1 Kin. 20:30; Job 24:11;
　Ps. 18:29; Prov. 18:11; Is. 25:4; Jer.
　52:4; Ezek. 4:2; 8:7; 12:5; Joel 2:9;
　Amos 7:7; Hab. 2:11

WANDER—flee Gen. 21:14, **w-ed**

about in the wilderness
Ps. 55:7, I would **w** far away
　119:21, Who **w** from Thy
　commandments
Prov. 27:8, bird . . . **w-s** from her nest
1 Tim. 6:10, **w-ed** away from the
　faith
Jude 13, **w-ing** stars, for whom
Job 15:23; Is. 35:8; Lam. 4:14;
　Hos. 9:17

WANT—lack, need

Job 30:3, From **w** and famine they
　are
Ps. 23:1, shepherd, I shall not **w**
Prov. 28:27, who gives to the poor
　never **w**
Mark 9:35, If any one **w-s** to be first
Luke 23:8, Herod . . . had **w-ed** to see
　Him
Gal. 4:21, you who **w** to be under
　law

WAR—fight, quarrel, battle Gen.

14:2; Ex. 13:17
Josh. 11:23, the land had rest from **w**
Ps. 46:9, makes **w-s** to cease
　55:21, his heart was **w**
　76:3, weapons of **w**
Eccles. 3:8, A time for **w**
Is. 2:4, never . . . will they learn **w**
Dan. 9:26, to the end there will be **w**
Matt. 24:6, hearing of **w-s** and
　rumors of **w-s**
Rom. 7:23, waging **w** against the law
　of my
2 Cor. 10:3, do not **w** according to
　the flesh
James 4:1, wage **w** in your members
1 Pet. 2:11, which wage **w** against
　the soul
Rev. 12:7, there was **w** in heaven
　19:11, He judges and wages **w**
Num. 21:14; Prov. 20:18; Mic. 2:8;
　Rev. 2:16

WAR-CLUB Jer. 51:20, You are

My **w**

WARD Dan. 4:35, no one can **w** off

His hand

WARFARE 2 Sam. 17:8, father is an

expert in **w**
2 Cor. 10:4, weapons of our **w** are
　not

WARM Eccles. 4:11, two lie down . . .

keep **w**
Mark 14:54, **w-ing** himself at the fire
John 18:25, Peter was standing and
　w-ing himself
James 2:16, be **w-ed** and be filled
1 Kin. 1:1; 2 Kin. 4:34; Job 31:20;
　Is. 47:14; Hag. 1:6

WARN Ezek. 33:8, speak to **w** the

wicked
Matt. 2:12, having been **w-ed** by God
　2:22, **w-ed** by God in a dream
　3:7, vipers, who **w-ed** you to flee
Titus 3:10, after a first and second
　w-ing
Heb. 8:5, Moses was **w-ed** by God
　11:7, being **w-ed** by God
2 Kin. 6:10; Eccles. 12:12

WARRIOR Job 16:14; Eccles. 9:11

WASH—bathe, cleanse 2 Kin. 5:10,

Go . . . **w** in the Jordan
Ps. 26:6, **w** my hands in innocence
　51:2, **W** me . . . from my iniquity
Is. 1:16, **W** yourselves, make
　yourselves clean
Matt. 6:17, **w** your face
　15:2, not **w** their hands when
Luke 11:38, first . . . **w-ed** before the
　meal
John 9:7, Go, **w** in the pool of Siloam
Acts 22:16, **w** away your sins
1 Cor. 6:11, you were **w-ed** . . .
　sanctified
1 Tim. 5:10, she has **w-ed** the saints'
　feet
Heb. 6:2, instruction about **w-ings**
　9:10, drink and various **w-ings**
　10:22; bodies **w-ed** with pure water
Gen. 18:4; Ex. 19:10; 1 Kin. 22:38;
　Job 9:30; Jer. 4:14; Ezek. 16:9

WASTE Prov. 23:8, And **w** your

compliments
Matt. 12:25; Luke 11:17, kingdom
　. . . laid **w**
　26:8, What is the point of this **w**
Rev. 18:19, in one hour she has been
　laid **w**
Lev. 26:31; Ps. 79:7; Is. 5:6; 45:18;
　Jer. 33:12; Ezek. 6:6; Joel 1:7

WATCH—observe, guard Gen.

31:49, Lord **w**
Ps. 63:6, in the night **w-es**
Prov. 4:23, **W** over your heart with
　all diligence
　8:34, **W-ing** daily at my gates
Eccles. 11:4, He who **w-es** the wind
　will not sow
Matt. 26:40, could not keep **w** with
　Me
Luke 2:8, keeping **w** over their flock
Heb. 13:17, they keep **w** over your
　souls
Ex. 14:24; 2 Kin. 11:5; Job 7:20;
　Prov. 4:26; Zech. 11:11

WATCHMAN Is. 21:11, **W**, how far

gone is the night
2 Kin. 9:17; Song 3:3; Hos. 9:8

WATER Gen. 1:2, over the surface of

the **w-s**
Ex. 2:10, drew him out of the **w**
　15:8, The flowing **w-s** stood up
2 Sam. 14:14, like **w** spilled on the
　ground
Job 14:19, **W** wears away stones
Ps. 1:3, planted by streams of **w**
　23:2, beside quiet **w-s**
　106:32, wrath at the **w-s** of Meribah
Prov. 9:17, Stolen **w** is sweet
Eccles. 11:1, your bread on the . . .
　w-s
Is. 1:30, garden that has no **w**
　11:9, As the **w-s** cover the sea
Jer. 2:13, fountain of living **w-s**
Matt. 3:11, baptize you in **w**
　10:42, little ones even a cup of
　cold **w**
Mark 14:13, man . . . carrying a
　pitcher of **w**
Luke 7:44, gave Me no **w** for My feet
John 3:5, unless one is born of **w**
　4:10, given you living **w**
Acts 1:5, John baptized with **w**
　8:36, Look! **W**! What prevents
1 Cor. 3:6, I planted, Apollos **w-ed**

Eph. 5:26, washing of **w** with the
　word
1 Tim. 5:23, No longer drink **w**
　exclusively
James 3:11, fresh and bitter **w**
1 Pet. 3:20, eight persons . . . through
　the **w**
1 John 5:6, who came by **w** and
　blood
Rev. 22:17, take the **w** of life without
　cost
Gen. 24:43; Ex. 20:4; Deut. 8:7; Josh.
　7:5; Judg. 5:4; 6:38; 1 Kin. 13:22;
　2 Kin. 3:11; Neh. 9:11; Job 8:11;
　11:16; Ps. 22:14; 46:3; Prov. 5:15;
　20:5; Song 5:12; Is. 19:5; 32:2; Jer.
　8:14; Lam. 1:16; Ezek. 4:11; 7:17;
　Dan. 1:12; 2 Pet. 3:5

WATERLESS Matt. 12:43, unclean

spirit . . . passes through **w**

WAVE Ps. 42:7, Thy **w-s** have rolled

over me
Is. 48:18, righteousness like the **w-s**
Matt. 8:24, covered with the **w-s**
Mark 4:37, **w-s** were breaking over
　the boat
Jude 13, wild **w-s** of the sea
2 Sam. 22:5; Job 9:8; Zech. 2:9

WAX Ps. 22:14, My heart is like **w**

WAY—journey, manner, path,

road
Gen. 3:24, **w** to the tree of life
Josh. 23:14, the **w** of all the earth
Job 3:23, a man whose **w** is hidden
Ps. 1:6, the **w** of the righteous
　18:30, His **w** is blameless
　25:8, instructs sinners in the **w**
Is. 30:21, This is the **w**, walk in it
Jer. 12:1, **w** of the wicked prospered
Ezek. 3:18, wicked from his wicked
　w
Matt. 2:12, departed . . . by another
　w
　3:3, READY THE **W** OF THE LORD
　6:9, Pray, then, in this **w**
　7:13, the **w** is broad
　15:32, lest they faint on the **w**
Mark 1:3, MAKE READY THE **W** OF THE
　LORD
　9:33, What were you discussing on
　the **w**
Luke 1:79, into the **w** of peace
John 1:23, STRAIGHT THE **W** OF THE
　LORD
　14:6, I am the **w**, and the truth, and
Acts 9:2, found any belonging to
　the **W**
1 Cor. 12:31, a still more excellent **w**
2 Cor. 4:8, afflicted in every **w**
Heb. 10:20, by a new and living **w**
James 5:20, from the error of his **w**
2 Pet. 2:2, **w** of the truth will be
　maligned
　2:15, forsaking the right **w**
Jude 11, gone the **w** of Cain
1 Sam. 12:23; 2 Sam. 22:33; Neh.
　9:19; Ps. 50:23; Prov. 7:27; 12:15;
　Is. 26:7; 40:3; Jer. 2:36; 6:16;
　Nah. 1:3; Mal. 3:1

WAYS Deut. 8:6, to walk in His **w**

2 Kin. 17:13, Turn from your evil **w**
Prov. 6:6, ant . . . Observe her **w**
Is. 2:3, teach us concerning His **w**
Hab. 3:6, His **w** are everlasting
Rom. 11:33, unfathomable His **w**
1 Cor. 4:17, **w** which are in Christ
James 1:8, unstable in all his **w**

Judg. 5:6; Prov. 3:17; Lam. 3:40;
Ezek. 7:3

WEAK—*unimpressive*
Matt. 26:41; Mark 14:38, but the
flesh is **w**
Acts 20:35, you must help the **w**
Rom. 4:19, without becoming **w** in
faith
1 Cor. 1:27, **w** things of the world
4:10, we are **w** , but you are strong
1 Thess. 5:14, help the **w**
Num. 13:18; Judg. 16:17; Is. 14:10;
Joel 3:10

WEAKNESS—*infirmity*
Rom. 15:1, bear the **w-es** of those
1 Cor. 1:25, **w** of God is stronger
than
2:3, with you in **w** and in fear
15:43, it is sown in **w**
2 Cor. 12:9, power is perfected in **w**
13:4, crucified because of **w**
Heb. 4:15, sympathize with our **w-es**
11:34, from **w** were made strong

WEALTH—*substance, prosperity*
Gen. 31:1
Deut. 8:18, giving you power to
make **w**
2 Chr. 1:11, not ask for riches, **w**
Job 5:5, schemer is eager for their **w**
Ps. 49:6, those who trust in their **w**
Prov. 3:9, Honor the LORD from
your **w**
13:7, poor, but has great **w**
13:11, **W** *obtained* by fraud
Eccles. 5:19, given riches and **w**
Is. 45:3, hidden **w** of secret places
Hag. 2:7, come with the **w** of all
nations
2 Cor. 8:2, **w** of their liberality
Rev. 3:17, rich, and have become
w-y
18:19, became rich by her **w**
Ruth 2:1; Job 20:10; Prov. 23:4, Is.
5:17

WEAPONS—*armor*
Eccles. 9:18, Wisdom is better than
w
Jer. 21:4, turn back the **w** of war
Ezek. 32:27, down to Sheol with
their **w**
2 Cor. 6:7, **w** of righteousness
10:4, **w** of our warfare
Deut. 1:41; 1 Sam. 31:9; 2 Chr. 23:10;
Neh. 4:17; Job 20:24

WEAR Deut. 22:5, woman shall not
w man's clothing
Job 14:19, Water **w-s** away stones
John 19:5, Jesus . . . **w-ing** the crown
of
James 2:3, who is **w-ing** the fine
clothes
1 Pet. 3:3, and **w-ing** gold jewelry
Ex. 18:18; Deut. 8:4; Is. 50:9; Dan.
7:25; Matt. 11:8

WEARY—*faint, exhaust*
Job 3:17, there the **w** are at rest
Prov. 23:4, Do not **w** yourself to gain
riches
25:25, cold water to a **w** soul
Eccles. 12:12, **w-ing** to the body
Is. 5:27, No one in it is **w** or
stumbles
40:29, strength to the **w**
40:31, They will walk and not
become **w**
50:4, sustain the **w** one with a word

Hab. 2:13, nations grow **w** for
nothing
Matt. 11:28, Come to Me, all who
are **w**
John 4:6, **w-ed** from His journey
Gal. 6:9, if we do not grow **w**
2 Sam. 17:2; Ps. 69:3; Prov. 25:17;
Jer. 6:11

WEATHER—*day* Matt. 16:2, *will be
fair* **w**

WEAVE—*embroider* Ex. 28:39;
38:23

WEB Job 18:8, he steps on the **w-ing**

WEDDING—*marriage* Song 3:11,
day of his **w**
John 2:1, there was a **w** in Cana

WEEK Gen. 29:27, Complete the
bridal **w**
Ex. 34:22, celebrate the Feast of **W-s**
Dan. 9:24, Seventy **w-s** have been
decreed
Matt. 28:1, first *day* of the **w**
Luke 18:12, I fast twice a **w**

WEEP 1 Sam. 1:8, Hannah, why do
you **w**
Neh. 8:9, do not mourn or **w**
Job 16:16, face is flushed from **w-ing**
16:20, My eye **w-s** to God
Eccles. 3:4, A time to **w**, and a time
to laugh
Matt. 2:18, RACHEL **W-ING** FOR HER
13:42, **w-ing** and gnashing of
Mark 5:39, Why make a commotion
and **w**
Luke 6:21, Blessed *are* you who **w**
now
7:32, you did not **w**
John 11:31, to the tomb to **w** there
Acts 9:39, widows stood beside him
w-ing
Rom. 12:15, who rejoice, and **w** with
James 4:9, miserable and mourn
and **w**
Rev. 5:4, I *began* to **w** greatly
5:5, Stop **w-ing**; behold, the Lion
Gen. 43:30; Num. 11:13; Deut. 34:8;
Judg. 11:37; Ps. 6:8; Is. 22:4; Jer.
9:1; Joel 1:5

WEIGH Prov. 16:2, the LORD **w-s** the
motives
Dan. 5:27, you have been **w-ed** on
the scales
Gen. 23:16; 24:22; 1 Sam. 2:3; Job
6:2; Ps. 58:2

WEIGHT Lev. 19:36, just balances,
just **w-s**
Prov. 11:1, a just **w** is His delight
Ezek. 4:16, will eat bread by **w**
2 Cor. 4:17, eternal **w** of glory
Deut. 25:15; Job 28:25; Mic. 6:11

WELFARE 1 Sam. 17:18, the **w** of
your brothers

WELL—*health, whole* Gen. 43:28,
father is **w**
Deut. 4:40, that it may go **w** with
you
1 Sam. 9:10, **W** said; come
2 Sam. 18:29, Is it **w** with the young
man
Eccles. 12:6, pitcher by the **w** is
shattered
Matt. 3:17, whom I am **w** pleased
Mark 7:37, has done all things **w**

Luke 5:31, not . . . **w** who need a
physician
6:26, men speak **w** of you
John 4:6, Jacob's **w** was there
5:6, Do you wish to get **w**
Gal. 5:7, You were running **w**
1 Tim. 3:4, his own household **w**
Gen. 4:7; Lev. 24:16; 2 Sam. 17:21;
20:9; 1 Chr. 11:17; Prov. 5:15;
Eccles. 8:13; Song 4:15; Acts 15:29

WENT Is. 38:8, sun's *shadow* **w** back
ten steps
Mark 1:28, news about Him **w** out
Jude 7, **w** after strange flesh

WEPT—*weep* Gen. 50:17, Joseph **w**
when they
Matt. 26:75, went out and **w** bitterly
Luke 19:41, city and **w** over it
John 11:35, Jesus **w**

WEST Gen. 12:8, with Bethel on
the **w**
Ex. 10:19, a very strong **w** wind
Ps. 107:3, east and from the **w**
Dan. 8:4, saw the ram butting **w-
ward**

WET—*drench* Job 24:8, **w** with the
mountain rains
Luke 7:44, **w** My feet with her tears

WHATEVER—*all* Ps. 1:3, in **w** he
does, he prospers
Eccles. 9:10, **W** your hand finds to
do
Matt. 7:12, **w** you want others to do
for you
Luke 12:3, **w** you have said in the
dark
John 11:22, **w** You ask of God
Rom. 14:23, **w** is not from faith is sin
1 Cor. 10:31, eat or drink or **w** you
do
Gal. 6:7, for **w** a man sows
Eph. 6:8, **w** good things each one
does
Phil. 4:8, **w** is true, **w** is honorable
Col. 3:17, **w** you do in word or deed
Gen. 31:16; Job 37:12

WHEAT—*kernel* Matt. 3:12, gather
His **w** into the barn
Luke 22:31, to sift you like **w**
John 12:24, unless a grain of **w** falls
Rev. 6:6, quart of **w** for a denarius
Gen. 30:14; Ex. 34:22; Deut. 8:8;
Judg. 6:11; 1 Sam. 12:17; Job 31:40

WHEEL—*whirl* Eccles. 12:6, **w** at
the cistern is crushed
Is. 5:28, **w-s** like a whirlwind
Ezek. 1:16, one **w** were within
another
1 Kin. 7:33; Prov. 20:26; Dan. 7:9;
Nah. 3:2

WHELP Gen. 49:9; Deut. 33:22

WHERE Gen. 3:9, **W** are you
Ruth 1:17, **W** you die, I will die
Job 28:12, **w** can wisdom be found
Ps. 42:3, **W** is your God
139:7, **W** can I go from Thy Spirit
Prov. 29:18, **W** there is no vision
Is. 19:12, **w** are your wise men
Matt. 2:2, **W** is He who has been
born
Luke 8:25, **W** is your faith
John 8:19, **W** is Your Father
8:21, **w** I am going, you cannot
come

WHERE (*Continued*)
11:34, W have you laid him
Rom. 4:15, w there is no law
Gen. 28:15; 1 Sam. 27:10; 1 Cor. 1:20

WHILE—*moment* Is. 26:20, Hide for
a little w
John 5:35, willing to rejoice for a w

WHIP 1 Kin. 12:11, disciplined you
with w-s
Prov. 26:3, A w is for the horse
Nah. 3:2, The noise of the w

WHIRL Ps. 83:13, God, make them
... w-ing dust

WHIRLWIND—*storm, wind*
2 Kin. 2:1, Elijah by a w to
Ps. 58:9, sweep them away with a w
Prov. 1:27, calamity comes on ... w
Jer. 4:13; Hos. 8:7

WHISPER Ps. 41:7, hate me w
together

WHITE Gen. 49:12, teeth w from
milk
Ps. 51:7, I shall be w-r than snow
Is. 1:18, They will be as w as snow
Matt. 5:36, make one hair w or black
Luke 9:29, clothing *became* w *and*
gleaming
John 4:35, they are w for harvest
Acts 23:3, you w-washed wall
Rev. 6:2, and behold, a w horse
Num. 12:10; Job 6:6; Dan. 7:9

WHOLE Gen. 2:6, water the w
surface
Matt. 6:22, w body will be full of
light
1 Cor. 5:6, leavens the w lump
1 John 2:2, *those of* the w world

WICK—*flax* Matt. 12:20,
SMOLDERING W HE WILL NOT PUT
OUT

WICKED—*evil, lawless, ungodly*
Ex. 23:1
Ps. 1:1, not walk in the counsel of
the w
Prov. 4:19, way of the w is like
darkness
10:30, w will not dwell in the land
11:7, When a w man dies
13:9, lamp of the w goes out
Is. 53:9, His grave ... with w men
Acts 17:5, taking along some w men
from the
24:15, both the righteous and the w
Job 8:22; 10:15; 11:20; Ps. 10:13; 12:8;
17:13; Eccles. 7:17; Ezek. 3:18;
Dan. 12:10

WICKEDNESS—*evil* Gen. 6:5, the w
of man was great
Ps. 10:7, Under his tongue is ... w
Prov. 4:17, they eat the bread of w
Is. 9:18, w burns like a fire
32:6, his heart inclines toward w
Acts 8:22, repent of this w of yours
Eph. 6:12, spiritual *forces* of w in the
heavenly
Judg. 20:3; Jer. 14:20; Ezek. 3:19;
Hos. 10:13

WIDE Nah. 3:13, gates of your land
are opened w
Matt. 7:13, for the gate is w
28:15, story was w-ly spread

WIDOW Matt. 23:14, you devour w-s
houses

Mark 12:43, w put in more than all
Luke 18:5, this w bothers me
1 Tim. 5:3, Honor w-s who are w-s
indeed
Gen. 38:11; Ex. 22:22; Lev. 21:14;
2 Sam. 14:5; Job 22:9; Ps. 68:5; Is.
1:17

WIELD Judg. 5:14, those who w the
staff of office

WIFE Gen. 2:24, shall cleave to his w
Ex. 20:17, not covet your neighbor's
w
Prov. 12:4, excellent w ... crown of
her husband
18:22, finds a w finds a good thing
Matt. 5:31, WHOEVER DIVORCES HIS w
Luke 17:32, Remember Lot's w
1 Cor. 7:2, each man have his own w
Eph. 5:23, husband ... head of the w
1 Tim. 3:2, husband of one w
Lev. 18:15; Job 31:10; Ps. 128:3

WILD Gen. 37:20,33, w beast
devoured him
Mark 1:6, John ... diet was locusts
and w honey
Gen. 16:12; Job 11:12; Ps. 104:11

WILDERNESS—*desert*
Deut. 29:5, forty years in the w
Is. 35:6, waters will break forth in
the w
40:3, Clear the way ... LORD in
the w
43:19, make a roadway in the w
Matt. 3:1, preaching ... w of Judea
3:3, VOICE ... CRYING IN THE w
4:1, led ... into the w to be tempted
24:26, Behold, He is in the w
Mark 1:13, He was in the w forty
days
John 6:31, Our fathers ate manna in
the w
1 Cor. 10:5, laid low in the w
Heb. 3:8, DAY OF TRIAL IN THE w
Rev. 12:6, woman fled into the w
Gen. 16:7; Ex. 5:3; 14:11; 19:2;
Lev. 7:38; Ps. 65:12; 102:6; Is. 51:3;
Jer. 2:6; 17:6

WILL Ps. 40:8, delight to do Thy w
Matt. 6:10, Thy w be done
7:21, who does the w of My Father
Mark 3:35, whoever does the w of
God
Luke 22:42, not My w, but Thine be
done
John 1:13, w of the flesh ... w of
man
4:34, w of Him who sent Me
Acts 21:14, w of the Lord be done
Rom. 12:2, may prove what the w of
God is
1 Cor. 4:19, if the Lord w-s
Eph. 5:17, what the w of the Lord is
Phil. 2:13, both to w and to work
Heb. 10:9, HAVE COME TO DO THY w
James 4:15, If the Lord w-s, we shall
live

WILLING Ps. 51:12, with a w spirit
Matt. 26:41, spirit is w ... flesh is
weak
Luke 22:42, Father, if Thou art w
Gen. 24:5; Ex. 35:5; 1 Chr. 28:9

WIN—*gain* Prov. 11:30, he who is
wise w-s souls
Matt. 28:14, we will w him over and
keep

Luke 21:19, perseverance you will w
... souls
1 Cor. 9:20, that I might w the Jews
9:24, Run in such a way that you
may w

WIND—*breath, whirlwind*
Job 16:3, no limit to w-y words
Ps. 1:4, chaff which the w drives
Is. 17:13, like the chaff ... before
the w
Matt. 7:25, floods came, and the w-s
blew
11:7, reed shaken by the w
Mark 4:41, w and the sea obey Him
Luke 8:24, He rebuked the w
John 3:8, w blows where it wishes
Acts 2:2, noise like a violent, rushing
w
Eph. 4:14, every w of doctrine
Heb. 1:7, MAKES HIS ANGELS w-s
James 3:4, are driven by strong w-s
Jude 12, carried along by w-s
Gen. 8:1; 1 Kin. 19:11; 2 Kin. 3:17;
Prov. 11:29; Eccles. 5:16; Song
4:16; Is. 7:2; Jer. 22:22; Ezek. 37:9;
Hos. 8:7; Rev. 6:13

WINDOW Josh. 2:15, by a rope
through the w
Acts 20:9, sitting on the w-sill
2 Cor. 11:33, through a w in the wall
Judg. 5:28; 2 Kin. 7:2; Jer. 9:21;
Joel 2:9

WINE—*vinegar* Lev. 10:9, Do not
drink w
Ps. 60:3, Thou hast given us w to
drink
Jer. 35:6, We will not drink w
Matt. 9:17, new w into old wineskins
27:48, sponge, he filled it with sour
w
Mark 15:23, give Him w mixed with
myrrh
Luke 10:34, pouring oil and w on
them
John 2:3, when the w gave out
2:9, water which had become w
19:29, A jar full of sour w
Acts 2:13, are full of sweet w
Eph. 5:18, do not get drunk with w
1 Tim. 3:3, not addicted to w
Rev. 6:6, not harm the oil and the w
Gen. 9:24; 1 Sam. 1:14; 2 Sam. 13:28;
Prov. 3:10; Eccles. 9:7; Song 1:2;
Is. 5:22

WINESKIN—*jug* Job 32:19, Like
new w-s it is
Ps. 119:83, like a w in the smoke
Matt. 9:17; Mark 2:22, new wine ...
fresh w-s
Josh. 9:13; Luke 5:37

WINGS—*feathers* Job 39:13,
ostriches' w flap
Ps. 17:8, in the shadow of Thy w
91:4, under His w you may seek
refuge
Prov. 23:5, *wealth* certainly makes
itself w
Mal. 4:2, with healing in its w
Matt. 23:37, chicks under her w
Luke 13:34, her brood under her w
Ex. 19:4; Lev. 1:17; Deut. 32:11;
Ruth 2:12; 2 Sam. 22:11; Is. 6:2;
Jer. 48:9; Ezek. 1:6; Zech. 5:9

WINK Ps. 35:19; Prov. 6:13

WINNOW Is. 30:24; 41:16; Matt. 3:12

WINTER Gen. 8:22; Song 2:11; 1 Cor. 16:6

WIPE—*blot, erase* Is. 25:8, God will w tears
Is. 44:22, **w-d** out your transgressions
John 11:2, **w-d** His feet with her hair
Acts 3:19, Repent . . . sins may be **w-ed** away
Rev. 21:4, He shall w away every tear

WISDOM Ex. 28:3, endowed with the spirit of w
1 Kin. 2:6, act according to your w
2 Chr. 1:10, Give me now w
Job 12:2, with you w will die
Ps. 51:6, make me know w
Prov. 1:7, Fools despise w and instruction
4:5, Acquire w! Acquire understanding
24:3, By w a house is built
Eccles. 1:18, in much w there is much grief
7:12, w preserves the lives
Jer. 9:23, wise man boast of his w
Mic. 6:9, it is sound w to fear Thy name
Matt. 11:19, w is vindicated by her deeds
Luke 2:52, Jesus kept increasing in w and stature
21:15, give you utterance and w
2 Cor. 1:12, not in fleshly w
2 Tim. 3:15, w that leads to salvation
James 1:5, if any of you lacks w
Rev. 13:18, Here is w

WISE—*shrewd* Gen. 3:6, tree . . . to make one w
Job 17:10, I do not find a w man
Ps. 19:7, making w the simple
Prov. 3:7, not be w in your own eyes
Luke 10:21, hide these things from *the* w
Rom. 1:14, the w and to the foolish
1 Cor. 1:19, DESTROY THE WISDOM OF THE W
3:18, that he may become w
Eph. 5:15, not as unwise men, but as w
James 3:13, Who . . . is w and understanding
Is. 19:12; Hos. 13:13

WISH—*desire* Luke 5:39, drinking old *wine* **w-es** for new
8:20, brothers are . . . **w-ing**
10:24, prophets and kings **w-ed** to see
John 16:19, Jesus knew they **w-ed** to question
1 Cor. 10:27, If one . . . invites you, and you w
2 Pet. 3:9, not **w-ing** for any to perish

WITHDRAW Josh. 8:26; 1 Sam. 14:19

WITHER Ps. 1:3, leaf does not w
Ps. 37:2, w quickly like the grass
102:11, I w away like grass
Is. 34:4, As a leaf **w-s** from the vine
64:6, w like a leaf
Jer. 8:13, the leaf shall w
Zech. 11:17, His arm will be totally **w-ed**
Matt. 13:6, had no root, they **w-ed**
Mark 3:1, man . . . with a **w-ed** hand

11:20, fig tree **w-ed** from the roots up
James 1:11, **w-s** the grass

WITHHELD Job 22:7, from the hungry you . . . w bread
Hag. 1:10, sky has w its dew

WITHHOLD Prov. 11:24,26

WITHIN Ps. 51:10, renew a steadfast spirit w me
Jer. 31:33, put My law w them
Mark 7:23, evil things proceed from w
1 Cor. 5:12, not judge those who are w *the church*
2 Cor. 7:5, conflicts without, fears w
Prov. 22:18; Ezek. 11:19

WITHOUT 2 Chr. 15:3, Israel was w the true God
Is. 52:3, redeemed w money
Matt. 13:57, prophet is not w honor
Mark 14:58, made w hands
John 8:7, He who is w sin
Rom. 12:9, love be w hypocrisy
2 Cor. 7:5, conflicts w, fears within
Eph. 2:12, no hope and w God in the world
1 Thess. 5:17, pray w ceasing
1 Tim. 6:14, commandment w stain
Heb. 7:3, W father, w mother, w genealogy
13:2, entertained angels w knowing it
James 2:20, faith w works is useless
2 Pet. 2:17, are springs w water
Jude 12, w fear . . . w water . . . w fruit
Job 5:9; 8:11; Hos. 7:11; Col. 2:11

WITNESS—*advocate, testimony* Ex. 4:8, w of the last sign
20:16, shall not bear false w
Judg. 11:10, LORD is w between us
Job 21:29, do you not recognize their w
Ps. 89:37, w in the sky is faithful
Matt. 19:18; Mark 10:19, NOT BEAR FALSE W
John 1:7, he might bear w of the light
1:32, John bore w saying, I have
3:11, bear w . . . do not receive our w
5:39, these that bear w of Me
8:14, w of Myself, My w is true
21:24, we know his w is true
1 Cor. 15:15, found *to be* false **w-es** of God
2 Cor. 1:23, God as w to my soul
Phil. 1:8, For God is my w
Heb. 10:15, Holy Spirit also bears w
1 John 5:8, three that bear w
5:9, If we receive the w of men
Rev. 1:5, Christ, the faithful w
Gen. 31:48; Deut. 4:26; Job 16:19; Prov. 6:19; Is. 19:20

WIVES Deut. 17:17, Neither shall he multiply w
Eph. 5:22, W *be subject to* . . . husbands
1 Pet. 3:1, you w, be submissive
3:7, husbands, live with your w

WOE Prov. 23:29, Who has w?
Mark 14:21, w to that man by whom
Rev. 8:13, W, w, w . . . who dwell on the earth
18:10,16,19, W, w, the great city

Num. 21:29; Job 10:15; Ps. 120:5; Is. 6:5; Jer. 4:13; 44:11; Matt. 11:21

WOLF Is. 65:25, w and the lamb shall graze
Matt. 7:15, inwardly are ravenous **w-s**
10:16, sheep in the midst of **w-s**
Gen. 49:27; Jer. 5:6

WOMAN Gen. 2:23, She shall be called W
Ex. 2:9, w took the child
Deut. 22:5, w shall not wear man's clothing
Ruth 2:5, Whose young w is this
3:11, you are a w of excellence
Job 14:1, Man, who is born of a w
Prov. 11:16, gracious w attains honor
Is. 49:15, w forget her nursing child
Matt. 5:28, looks on a w to lust for her
15:28, O w, your faith is great
Luke 7:44, said to Simon, Do you see this w
10:38, a w named Martha
John 4:7, w of Samaria to draw water
8:4, w has been caught in adultery
Acts 9:36, w abounding with deeds of kindness
1 Cor. 7:1, a man not to touch a w
7:2, each w have her own husband
14:35, a w to speak in church
Gal. 4:4, His Son, born of a w
1 Tim. 2:11, Let a w quietly receive instruction
Rev. 12:1, w clothed with the sun
Judg. 11:2; 1 Sam. 1:15; Eccles. 9:9

WOMB Gen. 25:23, Two nations are in your w
Ex. 13:2, first offspring of every w
Job 1:21, Naked . . . from my mother's w
Luke 1:41, baby leaped in her w
John 3:4, enter . . . into his mother's w
Acts 3:2, lame from his mother's w
Num. 12:12; Deut. 7:13; Ruth 1:11; Ps. 110:3; Prov. 30:16; Is. 44:2

WOMEN 2 Sam. 1:26, Than the love of w
1 Kin. 11:1, loved many foreign w
Ezra 10:2, have married foreign w
Prov. 31:3, not your strength to w
Is. 4:1, seven w will take hold of one man
Matt. 24:41, Two w *will be* grinding
Mark 15:40, *some* w looking on from afar
Acts 17:4, and a number of the leading w
1 Tim. 2:9, w to adorn themselves in proper
4:7, fables fit only for old w
2 Tim. 3:6, weak w weighed down with sins
Titus 2:4, young w to love their husbands
1 Pet. 3:5, the holy w also
Gen. 31:35; Judg. 5:24; Song 1:8; Jer. 50:37

WON Matt. 18:15, you have w your brother

WONDER—*marvel, sign* 1 Chr. 16:9, Speak of all His **w-s**
Job 37:14, consider the **w-s** of God
Ps. 9:1, I will tell of all Thy **w-s**
72:18, Who alone works **w-s**

WONDER *(Continued)*
78:12, He wrought **w-s** before their fathers
Is. 9:6, name will be called **W-ful** Counselor
Joel 2:30, display **w-s** in the sky
Rom. 15:19, power of signs and **w-s**
2 Thess. 2:9, signs and false **w-s**
Deut. 4:34; Dan. 6:27

WONDROUS—*marvelous* Job 9:10, w works
Job 37:5, God thunders . . . **w-ly**
Ps. 17:7, **W-ly** show Thy lovingkindness
71:17, I still declare Thy **w** deeds
Joel 2:26, dealt **w-ly** with you

WOOD Gen. 6:14, an ark of gopher **w**
1 Cor. 3:12, stones, **w**, hay, straw
Rev. 18:12, *made* from very costly **w**
Deut. 19:5; 2 Kin. 2:24; 2 Chr. 27:4; Neh. 8:4; Job 41:27; Prov. 26:20; Jer. 7:18; Lam. 5:4; Ezek. 24:10

WOOL Ps. 147:16, He gives snow like **w**
Is. 1:18, They will be like **w**
Heb. 9:19, scarlet **w** and hyssop
Rev. 1:14, His hair . . . white like white **w**
Deut. 22:11; Judg. 6:37; Ezek. 44:17; Dan. 7:9

WORD—*edict, message, speech* Gen. 15:1
Gen. 11:1, same language . . . same **w-s**
Ps. 12:6, **w-s** of the Lord are pure **w-s**
19:3, There is no speech, nor are there **w-s**
19:14, Let the **w-s** of my mouth
Prov. 15:1, a harsh **w** stirs up anger
15:23, how delightful is a timely **w**
Is. 5:24, despised the **w** of the Holy One
29:11, **w-s** of a sealed book
Matt. 4:4, on every **w** that proceeds
6:7, for their many **w-s**
7:24, every one who hears these **w-s**
8:8, but just say the **w**
10:14, nor heed your **w-s**
12:36, every careless **w** that men . . . speak
Mark 4:14, The sower sows the **w**
4:18, ones who have heard the **w**
7:13, invalidating the **w** of God
Luke 1:2, eyewitnesses and servants of the **W**
John 1:1, the beginning was the **W**
1:14, the **W** became flesh
6:68, **w-s** of eternal life
8:51, if anyone keeps My **w**
Acts 2:41, received his **w** were baptized
6:7, **w** of God kept on spreading
Rom. 10:8, **w** IS NEAR YOU . . . **w** of faith
1 Cor. 1:17, kingdom of God . . . in **w-s**
1:18, the **w** of the cross is to those
2 Cor. 4:2, not . . . adulterating the **w** of God
Gal. 5:14, Law is fulfilled in one **w**
Eph. 4:29, Let no unwholesome **w** proceed . . . mouth
5:6, deceive you with empty **w-s**
Phil. 2:16, holding fast the **w** of life
Col. 3:16, Let the **w** of Christ . . . dwell within you
4:3, open up to us a door for the **w**

1 Thess. 1:5, gospel did not come . . . in **w** only
2 Thess. 2:17, in every good work and **w**
1 Tim. 4:5, sanctified by the **w** of God
2 Tim. 2:15, handling accurately the **w** of truth
Titus 1:9, holding fast the faithful **w**
Heb. 2:2, **w** spoken through angels
4:12, **w** of God is living
James 1:21, receive the **w** implanted
1:22, prove yourselves doers of the **w**
1 Pet. 1:23, living and abiding **w** of God
2 Pet. 1:19, prophetic **w** *made* more sure
1 John 1:1, concerning the **W** of life
Rev. 19:13, name is called The **W** of God
Gen. 30:34; Ex. 20:1; Lev. 10:7; Num. 30:2; Deut. 5:5; Josh. 24:26; Judg. 13:12; 1 Sam. 3:1; 2 Kin. 9:5; 18:36; 1 Chr. 21:19; 2 Chr. 6:17; Job 2:13; 6:25; 12:11; Ps. 49:13; 55:21; Eccles. 5:2; Jer. 5:13; Mal. 1:1

WORK—*deed, labor, toil* Gen. 2:2, God completed His **w**
Ex. 20:9, Six days . . . do all your **w**
30:25, the **w** of a perfumer
Lev. 23:3, For six days **w** may be done
1 Sam. 14:45, he has **w-ed** with God this day
Neh. 4:6, the people had a mind to **w**
Ps. 19:1, declaring the **w** of His hands
62:12, a man according to his **w**
Prov. 16:3, Commit your **w-s** to the LORD
Eccles. 5:12, sleep of the **w-ing** man
7:13, Consider the **w** of God
10:12, LORD has completed all His **w**
Matt. 5:16, may see your good **w-s**
11:2, John . . . heard of the **w-s** of Christ
20:12, last men have **w-ed** *only* one hour
Mark 16:20, the Lord **w-ed** with them
Luke 5:5, we **w-ed** hard all night
13:14, six days in which **w** should be
John 5:17, **w-ing** until now, and I
6:27, Do not **w** for the food which
6:28, may **w** the **w-s** of God
9:4, **w** the **w-s** of Him who sent Me
Acts 18:3, they were **w-ing**
Rom. 2:15, show the **w** of the Law
3:20, by the **w-s** of the Law no flesh
3:28, justified by faith apart from **w-s** of the Law
8:28, all things to **w** together for good
16:12, who has **w-ed** hard in the Lord
1 Cor. 3:13, man's **w** will become evident
3:14, If any man's **w** . . . remains
4:12, **w-ing** with our own hands
2 Cor. 6:1, **w-ing** together *with Him*
Gal. 2:8, effectually **w-ed** for Peter
Eph. 2:9, not as a result of **w-s**
4:12, saints for the **w** of service
Phil. 2:12, **w** out your salvation
2:13, both to will and to **w**
Col. 1:10, bearing fruit in every good **w**

2 Thess. 3:8, labor and hardship we kept **w-ing**
3:10, If anyone will not **w**
1 Tim. 6:18, be rich in good **w-s**
2 Tim. 4:5, do the **w** of an evangelist
Heb. 6:1, repentance from dead **w-s**
James 2:18, show you my faith by my **w-s**
1 John 3:8, destroy the **w-s** of the devil
Deut. 4:28; 1 Sam. 14:6; 1 Chr. 23:4; 2 Chr. 15:7; Is. 5:19; Ezek. 46:1

WORKER Ps. 52:2, O **w** of deceit
Prov. 10:29, **w-s** of iniquity
Matt. 10:10, **w** is worthy of his support
1 Cor. 12:29, are not **w-s** of miracles
Phil. 3:2, beware of the evil **w-s**
Titus 2:5, sensible, pure, **w-s** at home

WORKMAN Eph. 2:10, For we are His **w-ship**
Ex. 38:23; 2 Kin. 22:5

WORLD—*age* 2 Sam. 22:16, foundations of the **w**
2 Chr. 16:30, **w** is firmly established
Job 34:13, laid *on Him* the whole **w**
Ps. 17:14, From men of the **w**
Prov. 8:26, first dust of the **w**
Is. 14:21, fill . . . the **w** with cities
Matt. 5:14, You are the light of the **w**
13:38, the field is the **w**
Mark 10:30, **w** to come, eternal life
John 1:10, **w** was made through Him
3:16, God so loved the **w**
4:42, Savior of the **w**
6:33, gives light to the **w**
7:7, **w** cannot hate you
8:12, I am the light of the **w**
Acts 17:6, men who have upset the **w**
Rom. 5:12, sin entered into the **w**
1 Cor. 1:28, base things of the **w**
2:12, not the spirit of the **w**
2 Cor. 7:10, sorrow of the **w** produces death
1 Tim. 6:17, rich in this present **w**
James 1:27, unstained by the **w**
2 Pet. 2:5, did not spare the ancient **w**
1 John 2:15, Do not love the **w**
2:17, the **w** is passing away

WORLDLY—*profane* 1 Tim. 4:7, **w** fables fit only for old
2 Tim. 2:16, avoid **w** *and* empty chatter

WORM Ex. 16:20, it bred **w-s** and became foul
Job 7:5, My flesh is clothed with **w-s**
Ps. 22:6, But I am a **w**
Is. 14:11, And **w-s** are your covering
Mark 9:48, where THEIR **W** DOES NOT DIE
Acts 12:23, he was eaten by **w-s**
Job 24:20; Jon. 4:7

WORMWOOD
Deut. 29:18, poisonous fruit and **w**
Prov. 5:4, she is bitter as **w**
Jer. 23:15, feed them **w**
Amos 5:7, turn justice into **w**
Rev. 8:11, star is called **W**

WORN—*old* Deut. 29:5, sandal has not **w** out

WORRY Luke 8:14, choked with **w-es** and riches

WORRY

Luke 10:41, you are **w-ed** and bothered
12:29, do not keep **w-ing**

WORSE Matt. 9:16, a **w** tear results
John 5:14, nothing **w** may befall you
1 Cor. 11:17, better but for the **w**
2 Tim. 3:13, proceed *from bad* to **w**

WORSHIP—*bow, serve*
Ex. 34:14, shall not **w** any other
Ps. 2:11, **W** the LORD with reverence
29:2, **W** the LORD in holy array
Matt. 2:2, and have come to **w** Him
2:8, come and **w** Him
2:11, fell down and **w-ed** Him
4:10, SHALL **W** THE LORD YOUR GOD
John 4:20, place where men ought to **w**
4:22, we **w** that which we know
Phil. 3:3, **w** in the Spirit of God
Heb. 9:6, performing the divine **w**
Rev. 4:10, **w** Him who lives forever
Gen. 22:5; Deut. 6:13; 2 Chr. 29:28

WORTH—*price* Prov. 31:10, her **w** is far above jewels

WORTHLESS—*ungodly* Prov. 16:27, A **w** man
Matt. 25:30, cast out the **w** slave
Gal. 4:9, **w** elemental things
Titus 1:16, **w** for any good deed
James 1:26, this man's religion is **w**
Judg. 9:4; Is. 5:2

WORTHY—*befit, deserving, fit*
1 Kin. 1:52, If he will be a **w** man
Matt. 10:10, worker is **w** of his support
10:11, enter, inquire who is **w** in it
10:13, if the house is **w**
10:37, who loves father more . . . not **w** of Me
Luke 10:7, laborer is **w** of his wages
Rom. 16:2, a manner **w** of the saints
Phil. 1:27, a manner **w** of the gospel
Eph. 4:1, manner **w** of the calling
1 Thess. 2:12, walk in a manner **w** of God
Heb. 11:38, the world was not **w**
Rev. 5:2, Who is **w** to open the book

WOUND—*bruise, pierce*
Luke 10:34, bandaged up his **w-s**
Acts 19:16, fled . . . naked and **w-ed**
1 Pet. 2:24, by His **w-s** you were healed
Gen. 4:23; Ex. 21:25; Deut. 32:39; Job 34:6; Ps. 147:3; Prov. 23:29; Jer. 30:12,17; Nah. 3:19; Mark 12:4

WRANGLE 2 Tim. 2:14, not to **w** about words

WRAPPED Matt. 27:59, **w** it in a clean linen
Mark 15:46, **w** Him in the linen sheet
Luke 2:7, she **w** Him in cloths
Gen. 38:14; 1 Kin. 19:13; Job 26:8; Is. 59:17; Ezek. 16:10; 21:15

WRAPPINGS—*cloth* John 11:44; 20:7

WRATH—*anger, indignation* Deut. 29:28
Ps. 6:1, Nor chasten me in Thy **w**
Matt. 3:7, flee from the **w** to come
John 3:36, **w** of God abides on him
Rom. 2:5, **w** for yourself in the day of **w**

3:5, God who inflicts **w** is not unrighteous
Eph. 2:3, by nature children of **w**
Col. 3:6, **w** of God will come
1 Thess. 5:9, has not destined us for **w**
Heb. 3:11, I swore in My **w**
Rev. 6:16, from the **w** of the Lamb
Ps. 37:8; 89:38; Is. 27:4; Jer. 4:4; 6:11; 30:23; Ezek. 5:13; 23:25; Mic. 5:15; Nah. 1:2

WREATH—*crown*
1 Cor. 9:25, to receive a perishable **w**

WRITE—*record* Ex. 17:14; Is. 8:1
Prov. 3:3, **w** them on the tablet of your heart
Mark 10:4, **w** a certificate of divorce
John 19:21, Do not **w**, The King of the Jews
Rom. 16:22, I, Tertius, who **w** this letter
Heb. 10:16, UPON THEIR MIND I WILL **W** THEM
2 John 12, **w** . . . not . . . with paper and ink
Rev. 14:13, **W**, Blessed are the dead

WRITING—*inscription, letter*
Eccles. 12:12, the **w** of many books is endless
John 5:47, if you do not believe his **w-s**
1 Tim. 3:14, I am **w** these things to you
2 Tim. 3:15, you have known the sacred **w-s**
Philem. 19, **w** this with my own hand
1 John 2:8, **w** a new commandment
2 John 5, **w** . . . a new commandment
Ex. 32:16; 1 Chr. 28:19; Dan. 10:21

WRITTEN Ex. 31:18, **w** by the finger of God
Job 19:23, that my words were **w**
Mal. 3:16, book of remembrance was **w**
Matt. 2:5, been **w** by the prophet
4:4, It is **w**, MAN SHALL NOT LIVE
4:6, for it is **w**, HE WILL GIVE
11:10, one about whom it was **w**
John 19:22, What I have **w** I have **w**
Acts 1:20, **w** in the book of Psalms
Rom. 2:15, Law **w** in their hearts
Rev. 13:8, not been **w** . . . in the book of life
17:5, forehead a name *was* **w**

WRONG—*defraud, wicked* Ex. 22:21, not **w** a stranger
Lev. 25:14, you shall not **w** one another
2 Sam. 24:17, I who have done **w**
Matt. 20:13, Friend, I am doing you no **w**
John 18:23, If I have spoken **w-ly**
Rom. 13:10, Love does no **w**
1 Cor. 6:7, Why not rather be **w-ed**
2 Cor. 7:2, we **w-ed** no one
Rev. 22:11, Let the one who does **w**, still do **w**
Gen. 16:5; 1 Chr. 12:17; Esth. 1:16

WRONGDOER—*unrighteous* Ps. 71:4, the **w** and

WROTE Ex. 24:4, Moses **w** down all the words
Jer. 36:18, **w** them with ink on the
Mark 12:19, Teacher, Moses **w**

Luke 1:63, he asked for a tablet and **w**
John 8:6, finger **w** on the ground
3 John 9, I **w** something to the church

WROUGHT—*accomplished* John 3:21, been **w** in

X, Y, Z

YEAR—*annual* Gen. 1:14, for seasons . . . **y-s**
Ps. 90:4, thousand **y-s** in Thy sight
90:9, finished our **y-s** like a sigh
Prov. 4:10, **y-s** of your life will be many
Is. 61:2, favorable **y** of the LORD
Luke 3:23, was about thirty **y-s** of age
Gal. 4:10, months and season and **y-s**
Rev. 9:15, day and month and **y**
Gen. 7:11; Ex. 13:10; Lev. 16:34; Num. 14:34; 2 Sam. 14:26; 1 Kin. 17:1; 2 Chr. 14:6; Job 10:5; Jer. 11:23; Joel 2:25; Matt. 2:16

YEARN—*faint* Ps. 84:2, longed and even **y-ed**

YESTERDAY Ex. 5:14, **y** or today in making brick
Job 8:9, For we are *only* of **y**
Ps. 90:4, in Thy sight Are like **y**
Acts 7:28, KILLED THE EGYPTIAN **Y**
Heb. 13:8, the same **y** and today

YET—*still* Ps. 37:10, **Y** a little while
John 2:4, My hour has not **y** come
Heb. 11:7, things not **y** seen
1 John 3:2, appeared as **y** what we shall be
Deut. 9:29; Jon. 3:4

YIELD—*bear, produce* Ps. 1:3, Which **y-s** its fruit in
Ps. 67:6, earth has **y-ed** its produce
Heb. 12:11, **y-s** the peaceful fruit

YIELDING—*bearing* Gen. 1:11,29; Mark 4:8

YOKE Matt. 11:29, Take My **y** upon you
Matt. 11:30, For My **y** is easy
Gal. 5:1, to a **y** of slavery
1 Tim. 6:1, under the **y** as slaves
Gen. 27:40; Lev. 26:13; Deut. 28:48; 1 Kin. 12:4; Is. 9:4; Jer. 27:2; Lam. 1:14

YOUNG Ps. 37:25, been **y**, and now I am old
Prov. 20:29, glory of **y** men is their
Eccles. 11:9, Rejoice, **y** man, during your
Is. 11:7, Their **y** will lie down together
Acts 2:17, **Y** MEN SHALL SEE VISIONS
Titus 2:4, **y** women to love . . . husbands
1 John 2:13, I am writing . . . **y** men
Deut. 32:11; Judg. 6:15; 1 Sam. 8:16; Job 19:18; Ezek. 17:4

YOUNGER Luke 15:13, **y** son gathered
John 21:18, when you were **y**
1 Tim. 5:11, refuse *to put* **y** widows
1 Pet. 5:5, You **y** men, likewise
Gen. 25:23; Judg. 15:2

YOUR—*Thine* Gen. 22:2, y son, y
  only son
Ex. 4:4, Stretch out y hand and
  grasp *it*
2 Chr. 20:15, battle is not y-s but
  God's
Luke 6:20, y-s is the kingdom of God
  15:31, all that is mine is y-s
John 15:20, they will keep y-s also
2 Cor. 12:14, I do not seek what is
  y-s
Gen. 45:20; Josh. 2:14; 1 Kin. 20:4;
  Jer. 5:19

YOURSELVES
Matt. 6:19, Do not lay . . . y treasures
Mark 9:50, Have salt in y

Luke 12:33, make y purses
Rom. 6:13, present y to God
2 Cor. 13:5, recognize . . . y
1 John 5:21, guard y from idols
Jude 21, keep y in the love of God
Gen. 18:4; Lev. 11:44; Deut. 4:16;
  Josh. 24:22; 2 Chr. 29:31; Jer. 37:9

YOUTH—*childhood* Acts 26:4, life
  from my y up
1 Tim. 4:12, look down on your y-
  fulness
2 Tim. 2:22, flee from y-ful lusts
Gen. 8:21; Num. 30:16; Judg. 8:20;
  Job 33:25; Ps. 25:7; Prov. 5:18; Is.
  40:30; Jer. 3:4; 31:19

ZEAL—*concern* 2 Kin. 10:16, see my
  z for the LORD
Ps. 119:139, My z has consumed me
John 2:17, Z FOR THY HOUSE WILL
Rom. 10:2, have a z for God
2 Cor. 7:7, your z for me
  7:11, what longing, what z
Phil. 3:6, as to z
2 Sam. 21:2; Eccles. 9:6; Is. 26:11;
  59:17

ZEALOUS—*eager* 1 Kin. 19:10, very
  z for the LORD
Acts 21:20, all z for the law
1 Cor. 14:12, z of spiritual *gifts*
Titus 2:14, z for good deeds
Rev. 3:19, be z therefore, and repent

Index to Maps

The following index is divided into two parts, one for Map 5, Jerusalem, and the other for all the other maps. Place names are usually given as shown on the maps; sometimes they are followed by alternate names and spellings, which are set in parentheses. If a place name is not given as shown on the map, it is followed, in parentheses, by the alternate name or spelling that does appear on the map (example: *Melita* (*Malta* on map)). Where a place name refers to a large area, the index gives the location of the name. Where a name refers to a river, the index gives the source and mouth of the river.

In the index to Maps 1 through 4 and 6 through 9, major political divisions, such as countries and regions, are shown in capital letters (examples: EGYPT, PALESTINE). Cities are shown in upper and lower case as usual (example: Hebron). Geographical features are shown in italics (example: *Jordan River*).

INDEX TO MAPS

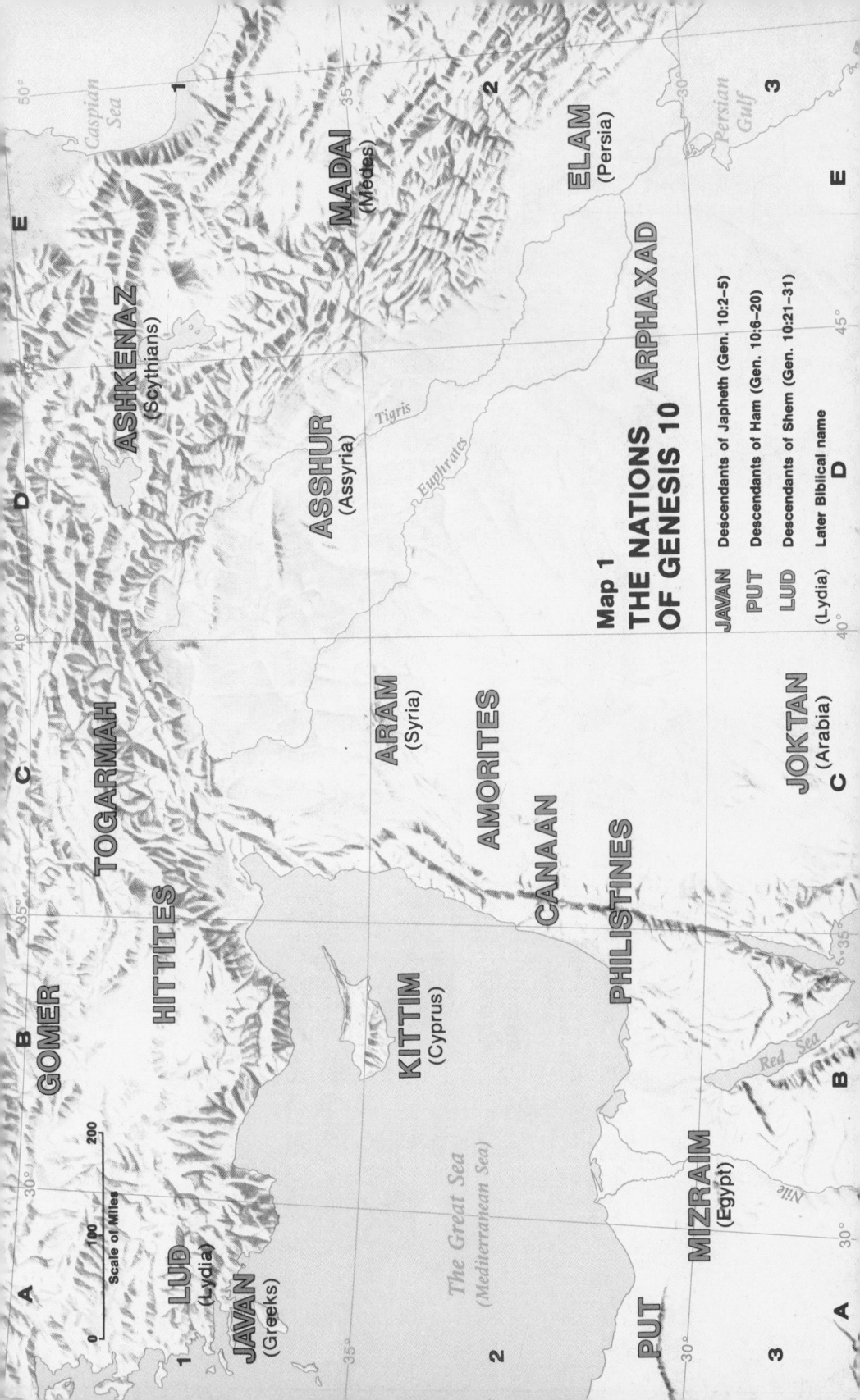

Map 1
THE NATIONS
OF GENESIS 10

JAVAN   Descendants of Japheth (Gen. 10:2–5)
PUT   Descendants of Ham (Gen. 10:6–20)
LUD   Descendants of Shem (Gen. 10:21–31)
(Lydia) Later Biblical name

GOMER

TOGARMAH

HITTITES

ASHKENAZ
(Scythians)

MADAI
(Medes)

ASSHUR
(Assyria)

ELAM
(Persia)

ARPHAXAD

ARAM
(Syria)

AMORITES

CANAAN

PHILISTINES

KITTIM
(Cyprus)

JOKTAN
(Arabia)

LUD
(Lydia)

JAVAN
(Greeks)

PUT

MIZRAIM
(Egypt)

Caspian Sea

Tigris

Euphrates

Persian Gulf

The Great Sea
(Mediterranean Sea)

Red Sea

Nile

Scale of Miles
0   100   200

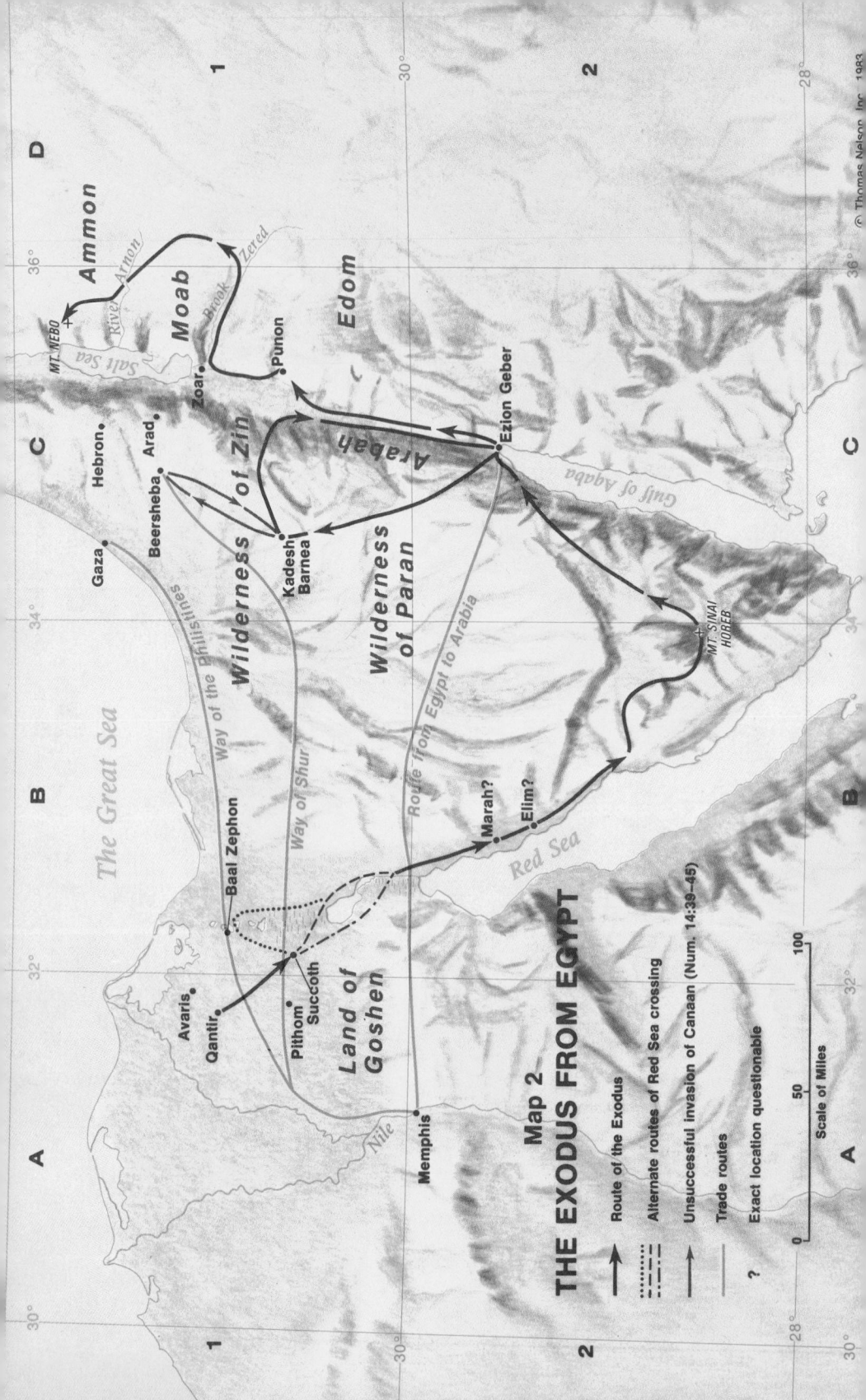

THE EXODUS FROM EGYPT

Map 2

Route of the Exodus

Alternate routes of Red Sea crossing

Unsuccessful invasion of Canaan (Num. 14:39–45)

Trade routes

? Exact location questionable

Scale of Miles

0   50   100

© Thomas Nelson, Inc. 1983

The Great Sea

Avaris
Qantir
Memphis
Nile
Land of Goshen
Pithom
Succoth
Baal Zephon
Way of the Philistines
Way of Shur
Route from Egypt to Arabia
Gaza
Hebron
Beersheba
Arad
Kadesh Barnea
Wilderness of Zin
Wilderness of Paran
Zoar
Punon
Salt Sea
MT. NEBO
Ammon
Moab
River Arnon
Brook Zered
Edom
Arabah
Ezion Geber
Gulf of Aqaba
MT. SINAI HOREB
Red Sea
Marah?
Elim?

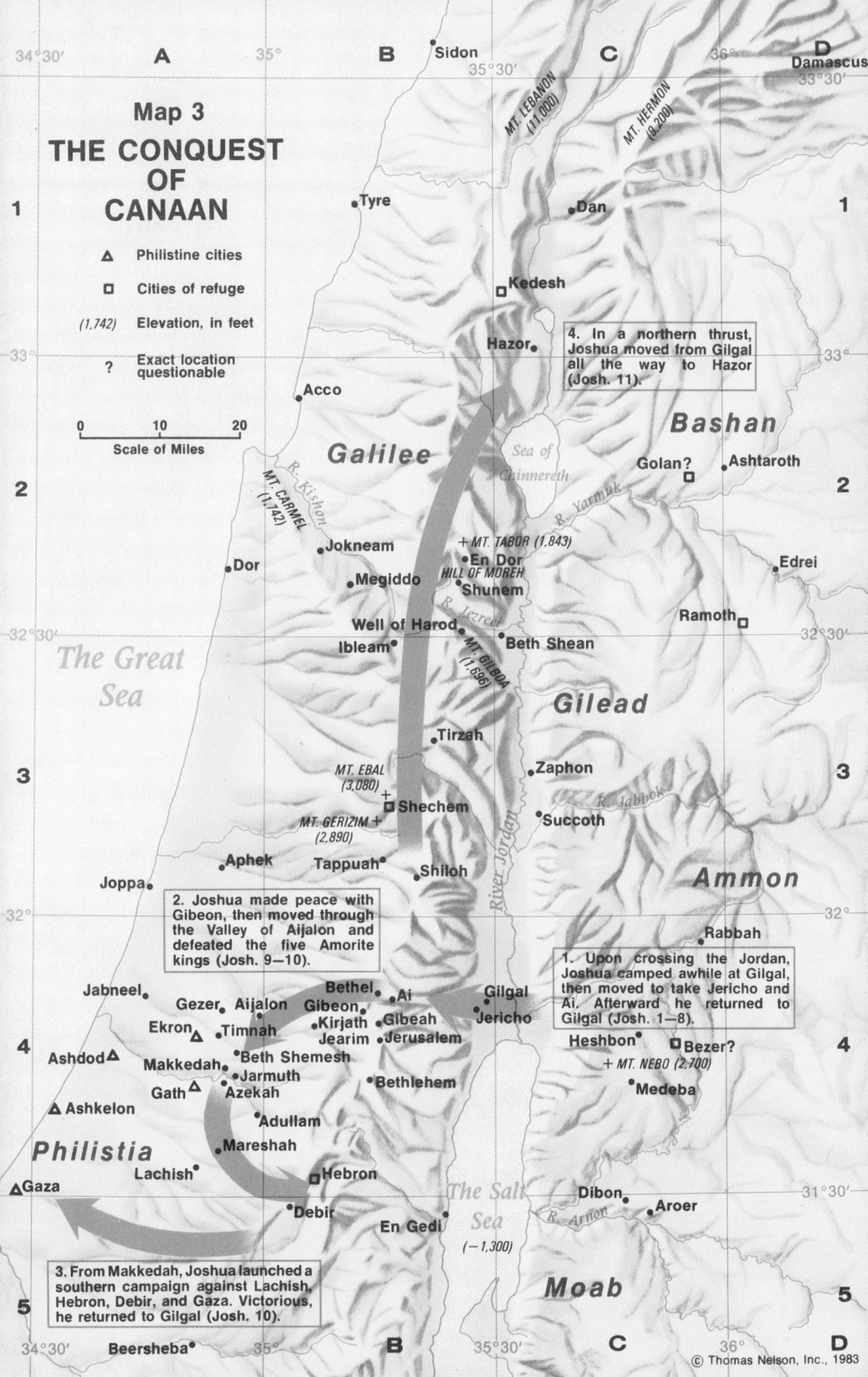

Map 3
THE CONQUEST OF CANAAN

△ Philistine cities

☐ Cities of refuge

(1,742) Elevation, in feet

? Exact location questionable

Scale of Miles
0   10   20

4. In a northern thrust, Joshua moved from Gilgal all the way to Hazor (Josh. 11).

2. Joshua made peace with Gibeon, then moved through the Valley of Aijalon and defeated the five Amorite kings (Josh. 9—10).

1. Upon crossing the Jordan, Joshua camped awhile at Gilgal, then moved to take Jericho and Ai. Afterward he returned to Gilgal (Josh. 1—8).

3. From Makkedah, Joshua launched a southern campaign against Lachish, Hebron, Debir, and Gaza. Victorious, he returned to Gilgal (Josh. 10).

Sidon

Damascus

MT. LEBANON (11,000)

MT. HERMON (9,200)

Tyre

Dan

Kedesh

Hazor

Bashan

Acco

Golan?

Ashtaroth

Galilee

Sea of Chinnereth

R. Kishon

MT. CARMEL (1,742)

R. Yarmuk

Jokneam

+MT. TABOR (1,843)

En Dor

HILL OF MOREH

Edrei

Megiddo

Shunem

Dor

Well of Harod

Ramoth

Ibleam

Beth Shean

R. Jezreel

MT. GILBOA (1,696)

Gilead

The Great Sea

Tirzah

Zaphon

MT. EBAL (3,080) +

Shechem

R. Jabbok

Succoth

MT. GERIZIM (2,890) +

Aphek

Tappuah

Shiloh

Ammon

Joppa

River Jordan

Rabbah

Jabneel

Bethel

Ai

Gilgal

Gezer

Aijalon

Gibeon

Jericho

Ekron

Timnah

Kirjath Jearim

Gibeah

Jerusalem

Heshbon

Bezer?

Ashdod

Makkedah

Beth Shemesh

+ MT. NEBO (2,700)

Gath

Jarmuth

Bethlehem

Medeba

Ashkelon

Azekah

Adullam

Philistia

Mareshah

Lachish

Hebron

Dibon

Gaza

Debir

Aroer

En Gedi

The Salt Sea (−1,300)

R. Arnon

Moab

Beersheba

© Thomas Nelson, Inc., 1983

34°30' A 35° B 35°30' C 36° D

33°30'

1

33°

2

32°30'

3

32°

4

31°30'

5

Map 4
THE KINGDOM YEARS

Probable extent of Israelite control during the Kingdom of Solomon, c. 950 B.C.

The Kingdoms of Israel and Judah, c. 860 B.C.

Boundary between Israel and Judah

? Exact location questionable

0   25   50
Scale of Miles

1

Riblah

Zobah

Byblos

Phoenicia

MT. LEBANON

MT. HERMON

Sidon
Zarephath

Damascus

Tyre

Dan

Syria

Kedesh

Hazor

The Great Sea

Acco

Sea of Chinnereth

Ashtaroth

R. Yarmuk

Golan?

MT. CARMEL

Dor
Jokneam
Megiddo
Taanach
Jezreel
Ramoth Gilead

Dothan

MT. GILBOA

Jabesh Gilead

Tirzah
Samaria
Shechem

Zaphon
Succoth

Jordan R.

R. Jabbok

Aphek
Shiloh

Joppa

ISRAEL

Rabbah

Ammon

Mizpah
Bethel

Jabneh
Gezer
Ramah

Heshbon

Philistia

Jerusalem
Bethlehem

Medeba

Beth Shemesh

Ashkelon
Eglon?
Adullam
Tekoa

Dibon

Gaza

Hebron

Aroer

Ziklag?
Debir

The Salt Sea

R. Arnon

Arad

Beersheba

Moab

Kir Hareseth

Zoar

R. Zered

JUDAH

Bozrah

Kadesh Barnea

Edom

Teman

Brook of Egypt

Note: Other place names significant during the time of the Kingdoms are found on Map 3.

Ezion Geber
Elath

© Thomas Nelson, Inc., 1983

Map 5
JERUSALEM—
FROM DAVID TO CHRIST

Bethesda Place names of Christ's time

Ophel Suggested locations of place names
        from earlier kingdom period

? Exact location questionable

Suggested extent of the City of David

Suggested extent of Solomon's expansion

Suggested extent of Hezekiah's expansion

Probable extent of Nehemiah's reconstruction

Possible location of walls during Christ's time

0   250   500 Yards
Scale

Calvary?

Bethesda

Sheep Gate

Gate of Benjamin

Temple

Horse Gate

Royal Palace

KIDRON VALLEY

Gethsemane?

Spring of Gihon

Ophel

Hezekiah's Tunnel

City of David

Fountain Gate

Praetorium

Gate of Ephraim

Mishneh

Pool of Siloam

Refuse Gate

Christ's Tomb?
Calvary?

Herod's Palace

Caiaphas' House?

Caiaphas' House?

Essene Gate

VALLEY OF HINNOM

© Thomas Nelson, Inc., 1983

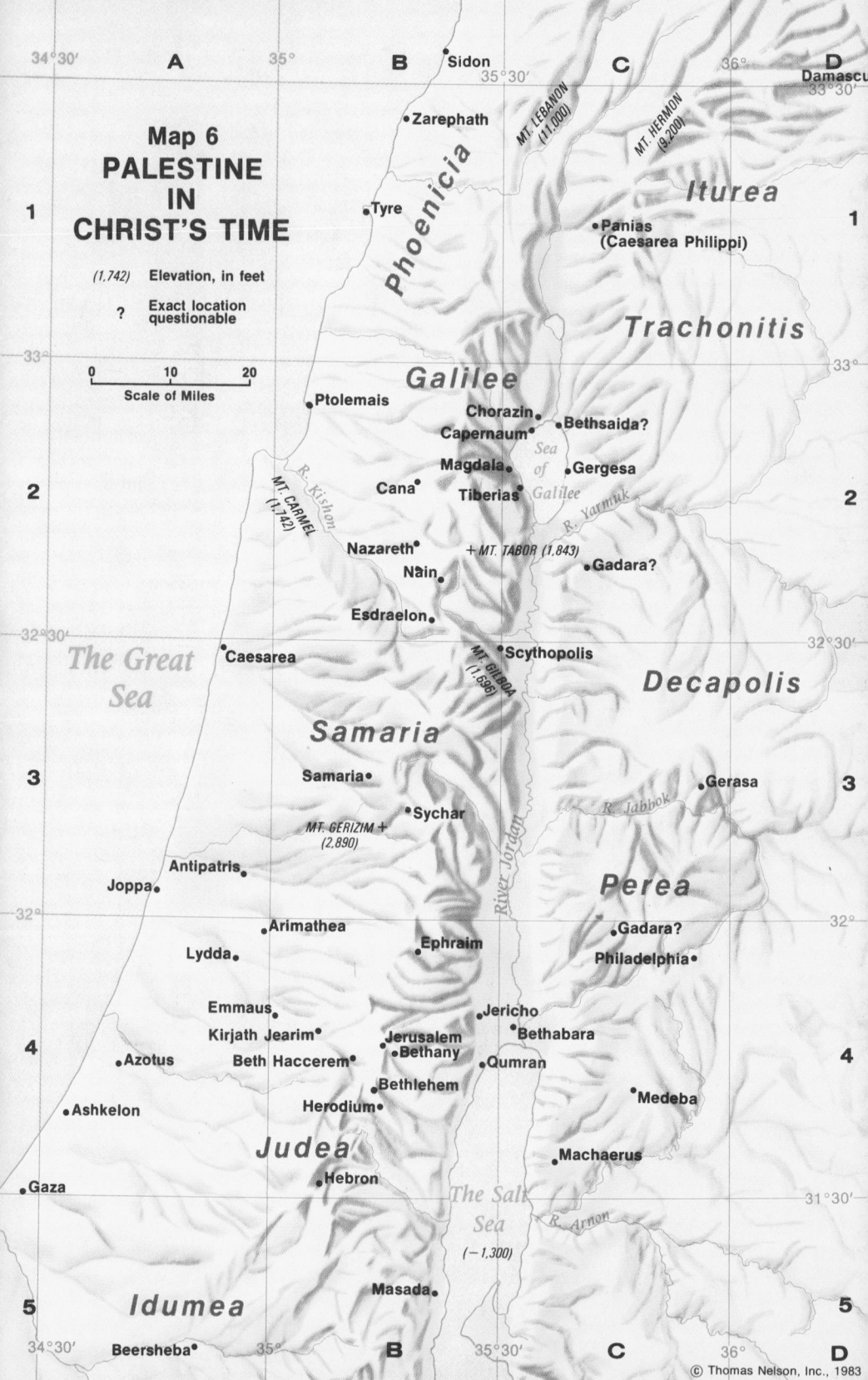

Map 6
PALESTINE IN CHRIST'S TIME

(1,742) Elevation, in feet

? Exact location questionable

Scale of Miles
0   10   20

34°30'   A   35°   B   35°30'   C   36°   D

Sidon

Zarephath

Phoenicia

MT. LEBANON (11,000)

MT. HERMON (9,200)

Damascu

33°30'

Iturea

Tyre

Panias
(Caesarea Philippi)

1

Trachonitis

33°

Galilee

Ptolemais

Chorazin
Capernaum   **Bethsaida?**

Magdala   Sea   **Gergesa**
of

Cana   **Tiberias**   **Galilee**

R. Kishon

MT. CARMEL (1,742)

R. Yarmuk

2

Nazareth   + MT. TABOR (1,843)

Nain   **Gadara?**

Esdraelon

32°30'   **Scythopolis**   32°30'

Caesarea   MT. GILBOA (1,696)

The Great Sea   **Decapolis**

Samaria

Samaria   **Gerasa**   3

Sychar   R. Jabbok

MT. GERIZIM + (2,890)

Antipatris   River Jordan   **Perea**

32°   **Gadara?**   32°

Joppa

Arimathea   **Ephraim**   **Philadelphia**

Lydda

Emmaus   **Jericho**

Kirjath Jearim   **Jerusalem**   **Bethabara**

Bethany

Azotus   **Beth Haccerem**   **Qumran**

4   **Bethlehem**   **Medeba**   4

Ashkelon   **Herodium**

Judea

Gaza   **Machaerus**

Hebron   31°30'

The Salt Sea   R. Arnon

(−1,300)

5   **Idumea**   **Masada**   5

Beersheba

34°30'   35°   B   35°30'   C   36°   D

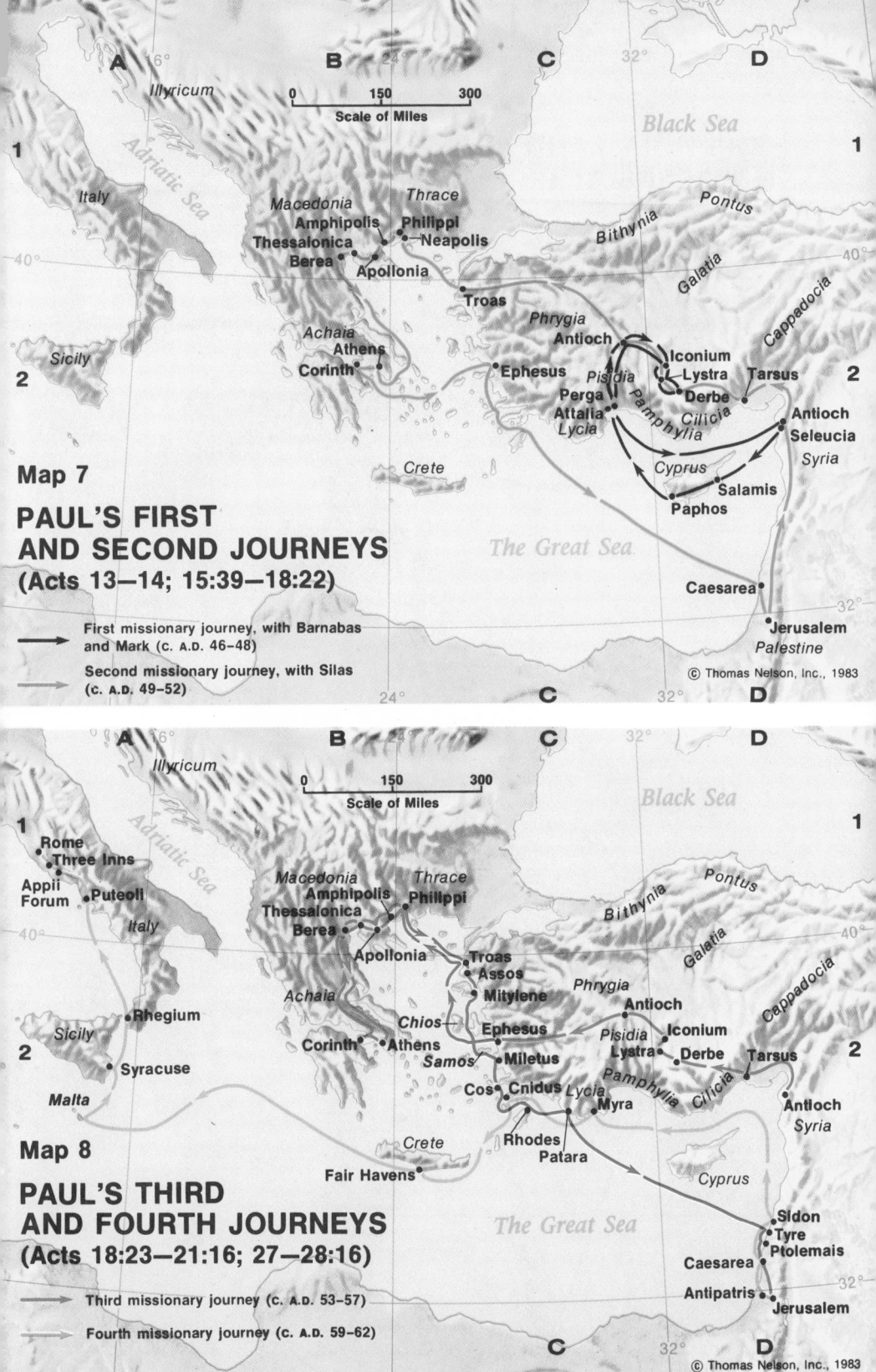

Map 9
THE HOLY LAND
IN MODERN TIMES

Area occupied by Israel since June, 1967

Scale of Miles
0   25   50

LEBANON

SYRIA

ISRAEL

JORDAN

EGYPT

Mediterranean Sea

Tripoli

Beirut

Sidon

Damascus

LEBANON MTS.
ANTI-LEBANON MTS.
BEKAA VALLEY

Tyre
Dan
U.N. Buffer Zone
1973 Line

Qiryat
Shemona

Quneitra
1967 Cease-Fire Line

Nahariyya
Safad
Sea of Galilee
Golan Heights

Akko
Haifa
Tiberias

Nazareth
Dera

Afula
Ramtha

Beth Shean

Hadera
Netanya
Tulkarm
Jarash

Herzliyya
Nablus
West Bank
Jordan River

Tel Aviv
Yafo
Petah
Tiqwa

Rishon le Zion
Lod
Amman

Ramla
Ramalah

Ashdod
Jericho

Jerusalem
Bethlehem
Madaba

Ashqelon
Gaza
Qiryat Gat
Hebron
Dead Sea

En Gedi
Dhiban

Beersheba

Al-Arish
Karak

Negev

Arabah

Sinai

Elat
Aqaba

© Thomas Nelson, Inc., 1983